BROADCASTING, CABLE

YEARBOOK 2010

BROADCASTING & CABLE YEARBOOK 2010

was prepared by ProQuest's Serials Editorial Department in collaboration
with R.R. Bowker's Production and Information Technology Departments

Product Development
Yvette Diven, Director, Product Management, Serials

Editorial
Laurie Kaplan, Director Serials
Nancy Bucenec, Managing Editor
Valerie Mahon, Managing Editor
Joseph A. Esser and Jennifer Williams, Associate Editors
Carolyn Hamilton, Assistant Editor

Bowker Production
Doreen Gravesande, Senior Director, Production
Andy Haramasz, Manager, Raw Data and Data Distribution
Myriam Nunez, Project Manager, Content Integrity
Lorena Soriano, Project Manager, Production
Gunther Stegmann II, Project Manager, Production

Information Technology Group
Steve Gorski, Programmer Analyst

Computer Operations Group
John Nesselt, UNIX Administrator

BROADCASTING CABLE
YEARBOOK 2010

Published by
ProQuest LLC
630 Central Avenue
New Providence, NJ 07974 USA

Marty Kahn, CEO

For sales inquiries Telephone: 908-286-1090, Toll-free: 1-888-BOWKER2 (1-888-269-5372); FAX: 908-219-0182
Editorial Development and Production by R.R. Bowker LLC, New Providence, NJ

International Standard Book Number
ISBN 13: 978-1-60030-122-3

International Standard Serial Number
0000-1511

Library of Congress Control Number
71-649524

Printed and Bound in the United States of America

ISBN 13: 978-1-60030-122-3

9 781600 301223

Table of Contents

Index to Sections

Index to Advertisers

Glossary of Terms Used in *Broadcasting & Cable Yearbook*

AM—Amplitude modulation. Also referring to audio service broadcast over 535 khz-1705 khz.

Analog—A continuous electrical signal that carries information in the form of variable physical values, such as amplitude or frequency modulation.

Basic cable service—Package of programming on cable systems eligible for regulation by local franchising authorities under 1992 Cable Act, including all local broadcast signals and PEG (public, educational and government) access channels.

Cable television—System that transmits original programming, and programming of broadcast television stations, to consumers over wired network.

CC—Closed captioning. Method of transmitting textual information over television channel's vertical blanking interval; transmissions are deciphered with decoders; decoded transmissions appear as text superimposed over television image.

Clear channel—AM radio station allowed to dominate its frequency with up to 50 kw of power; their signals are generally protected for distance of up to 750 miles at night.

Closed circuit—The method of transmission of programs or other material that limits its target audience to a specific group rather than the general public.

Coaxial cable—Cable with several common axis lines under protective sheath used for television signal transmissions.

Common carrier—Telecommunication company that provides communications transmission services to the public.

DAB—Digital audio broadcasting. Modulations for sending digital rather than analog audio signals by either terrestrial or satellite transmitter with audio response up to compact disc quality (20 khz).

DBS—Direct broadcast satellite. High powered satellite authorized to broadcast direct to homes.

Digital—A discontinuous electrical signal that carries information in binary fashion. Data is represented by a specific sequence of off-on electrical pulses.

Directional antenna—An antenna that directs most of its signal strength in a specific direction rather than at equal strength in all directions. Used chiefly in AM radio operation.

Downlink—Earth station used to receive signals from satellites.

Earth station—Equipment used for transmitting or receiving satellite communications.

EDTV—Enhanced-definition television. Proposed intermediate systems for evolution to full HDTV, usually including slightly improved resolution and sound, with a wider (16:9) aspect ratio.

Effective competition—Market status under which cable TV systems are exempt from regulation of basic tier rates by local franchising authorities, as defined in 1992 Cable Act. To claim effective competition, a cable system must compete with at least one other multichannel provider that is available to at least 50% of an area's households and is subscribed to by more than 15% of the households.

Encryption—System for scrambling signals to prevent unauthorized reception.

ENG—Electronic news gathering.

ETV—Educational television.

Fiber-optic cable—Wires made of glass fiber used to transmit video, audio, voice or data providing vastly wider bandwidth than standard coaxial cable.

Field—Half of the video information in the frame of a video picture. The NTSC system displays 59.94 fields per second.

FM—Frequency modulation. Also referring to audio service broadcast over 88 mhz-108 mhz.

Footprint—Area on earth within which a satellite's signal can be received.

Frame—A full video picture. The NTSC system displays 29.97 525-line frames per second.

Frequency—The number of cycles a signal is transmitted per second, measured in hertz.

Geostationary orbit—Orbit 22,300 miles above earth's equator where satellites circle earth at same rate earth rotates.

ghz—Gigahertz. One billion hertz (cycles) per second.

HDTV—High-definition television.

Headend—Facility in cable system from which all signals originate. (Local and distant television stations, and satellite programming, are picked up and amplified for retransmission through system.)

Hertz—A measurement of frequency. One cycle per second equals one hertz (hz).

Independent television—Television stations that are not affiliated with networks and that do not use the networks as a primary source of their programming.

Information services—Broad term used to describe full range of audio, video and data transmission services that can be transmitted over the air or by cable.

Interactive—Allowing two-way data flow.

Interlaced scanning—Television transmission technique in which each frame is divided into two fields. NTSC system interleaves odd-numbered lines with even-numbered lines at a transmission rate of 59.94 fields per second.

ITFS—Instructional Television Fixed Service.

khz—Kilohertz. One thousand hertz (cycles) per second.

LED—Light emitting diode. Type of semiconductor that lights up when activated by voltage.

LO—Local origination channel.

MDS—Multipoint distribution service.

mhz—Megahertz. One million hertz (cycles) per second.

Microwave—Frequencies above 1,000 mhz.

MSO—Multiple cable systems operator.

Must carry—Legal requirement that cable operators carry local broadcast signals. Cable systems with 12 or fewer channels must carry at least three broadcast signals; systems with 12 or more channels must carry up to one-third of their capacity; systems with 300 or

fewer subscribers are exempt. The 1992 Cable Act requires broadcast station to waive must-carry rights if it chooses to negotiate retransmission compensation (see "Retransmission consent").

NTSC—National Television System Committee. Committee that recommended current American standard color television.

PCM—Pulse code modulation. Conversion of voice signals into digital code.

PPV—Pay-per-view.

Progressive scanning—TV system where video frames are transmitted sequentially, unlike interlaced scanning in which frames are divided into two fields.

PSA—Public service announcement.

PTV—Public television.

Public radio—Radio stations and networks that are operated on a noncommercial basis.

Public television—Television stations and networks that operate as noncommercial ventures.

RCC—Radio common carrier. Common carriers whose major businesses include radio paging and mobile telephone services.

Retransmission consent—Local TV broadcasters' right to negotiate a carriage fee with local cable operators, as provided in 1992 Cable Act.

SCA—Subsidiary communications authorizations. Authorizations granted to FM broadcasters for using subcarriers on their channels for other communications services.

Shortwave—Transmissions on frequencies of 6-25 mhz.

SHF—Super high frequency.

Signal-to-noise ratio—The ratio between the strength of an electronically produced signal to interfering noises in the same bandwidth.

SMATV—Satellite master antenna television.

STV—Subscription television.

Superstation—Local television station whose signal is retransmitted via satellite to cable systems beyond reach of over-the-air signal.

Teletext—A one-way electronic publishing service that can be transmitted over the vertical blanking interval of a standard television signal or the full channel of a television station or cable television system. The major use today is for closed-captioning.

Translator—Broadcast station that rebroadcasts signals of other stations without originating its own programming.

Transponder—Satellite transmitter/receiver that picks up signals transmitted from earth, translates them into new frequencies and amplifies them before retransmitting them back to ground.

UHF—Ultra high frequency band (300 mhz-3,000 mhz), which includes TV channels 14-83.

Uplink—Earth station used for transmitting to satellite.

VHF—Very high frequencies (30 mhz-300 mhz), which include TV channels 2-13 and FM radio.

Videotext—Two-way interactive service that uses either two-way cable or telephone lines to connect a central computer to a television screen.

List of Abbreviations Used in *Broadcasting & Cable Yearbook*

*	noncommercial
a	annual
A&E	Arts & Entertainment
actg	acting
admin	administrative
adv	advertising
affil	affiliate
affrs	affairs
AFRTS	Armed Forces Radio and TV Service
alt	alternate
ant	antenna
AOR	album-oriented rock
AP	Associated Press
assn	association
assoc	associate
asst	assistant
atty	attorney
aur	aural
aux	auxiliary
bcst	broadcast
bcstg	broadcasting
bcstr	broadcaster
bd	board
BET	Black Entertainment Television
bi-m	every two months
bk rev	book reviews
bldg	building
bor	borough
btfl	beautiful
C-SPAN	Cable Satellite Public Affairs Network
CATV	community antenna television
CBC	Canadian Broadcasting Corp.
CEO	chief executive officer
ch	channel
CH	critical hours
chg	charge
CHR	contemporary hit radio
chmn	chairman
circ	circulation
coml	commercial
contemp	contemporary
COO	chief operating officer
coord	coordinator
CP	construction permit
CRTC	Canadian Radio-television and Telecommunications Commission
C&W	country & western
D	day
d	daily
DA	directional antenna
dance rev	dance reviews
DBS	direct broadcast satellite
dev	development
dir	director
div	diverse
DMA	Designated Market Area
dups	duplicates
Eds	editors
Ed Bd	Editorial Board
educ	educational
engr	engineer
engrg	engineering
EPG	Electronic Program Guide
ERP	effective radiated power
ESPN	Entertainment & Sports Programming Network
ETV	educational television
exec	executive
FCC	Federal Communications Commission
film rev	film reviews
fortn	fortnightly
Fr	French
g	ground
gen	general
Ger	German
govt	government
HAAT	height above average terrain
HBO	Home Box Office
horiz	horizontal polarization
hqtrs	headquarters
ind	independent
info	information
instal	installation
ISBN	International Standard Book Number
ISSN	International Standard Serial Number
illus	illustrations
irreg	irregular
It	Italian
khz	kilohertz
kw	kilowatts
loc	local
LPTV	low power television
LS	local sunset
lstng	listening
lw	long wave
m	meters
MDS	Multipoint Distribution Service
mdse	merchandising
mfg	manufacturing
mgng	managing
mgr	manager
mgmt	management
mhz	megahertz
mi	miles
mktg	marketing
MMDS	Multichannel Multipoint Distribution Service
mo	month
mod	modification
MOR	middle of the road
MSO	multiple system operator
mthy	monthly
MTV	Music Television
mus	music
music rev	music reviews
mw	medium wave
N	night
na	not available
NAB	National Association of Broadcasters
natl	national
net	network
NPR	National Public Radio
nwspr	newspaper
off	officer
opns	operations
per	personnel
play rev	play reviews (theatre reviews)
Pol	Polish
pop	population
PR	public relations
pres	president
PRI	Public Radio International
progmg	programming
progsv	progressive
prom	promotion
PSA	presunrise authority, public service announcement
ptnr	partner
pub affrs	public affairs
publ	publicity
q	quarterly
quad	quadraphonic
record rev	record reviews
rel	relations
relg	religion
rep	representative
RFE	Radio Free Europe
rgn	region
rgnl	regional
RL	Radio Liberty
rsch	research
s-a	twice annually
s-m	twice monthly
s-w	twice weekly
sec	secretary
sep	separate
sh	shares
SH	specified hours
sls	sales
SMATV	satellite master antenna television
Sp	Spanish
sr	senior
ST	shares time
stn	station
sub	subscriber

List of Abbreviations

supt	superintendent	**TNN**	The Nashville Network	**UPN**	United Paramount Network
supvr	supervisor	**traf**	traffic	**var**	variety
svcs	services	**trans**	translators	**vert**	vertical polarization
sw	short wave	**treas**	treasurer	**VHF**	very high frequency
t	terrain	**twp**	township	**video rev**	video reviews
tech	technical	**TWX**	Teletypewriter Exchange	**vis**	visual
tele rev	television reviews	**U**	unlimited	**VOA**	Voice of America
3/m	three times a month	**UHF**	ultra high frequency	**vp**	vice president
3/y	three times a year	**UPI**	United Press International	**w**	watts
				wkly	weekly

Section A
Industry Overview

Television Markets Ranked by Number of TV Homes

Listed below are the Nielsen Media Research Designated Market Areas (DMAs) ranked by the number of television households. The estimates are from September 2008.

DMA Rank	Designated Market Area	TV Households
1	New York	7,433,820
2	Los Angeles	5,654,260
3	Chicago	3,492,850
4	Philadelphia	2,950,220
5	Dallas-Fort Worth	2,489,970
6	San Francisco-Oakland-San Jose	2,476,450
7	Boston (Manchester)	2,409,080
8	Atlanta	2,369,780
9	Washington, DC (Hagerstown)	2,321,610
10	Houston	2,106,210
11	Detroit	1,926,970
12	Phoenix	1,855,930
13	Tampa-St. Petersburg, Sarasota	1,822,160
14	Seattle-Tacoma	1,819,970
15	Minneapolis-St. Paul	1,730,530
16	Miami-Fort Lauderdale	1,546,920
17	Cleveland	1,524,930
18	Denver	1,524,210
19	Orlando-Daytona Beach-Melbourne	1,466,420
20	Sacramento-Stockton-Modesto	1,399,520
21	St. Louis	1,249,820
22	Portland, OR	1,175,100
23	Pittsburgh	1,156,460
24	Charlotte	1,122,860
25	Indianapolis	1,114,970
26	Baltimore	1,102,080
27	Raleigh-Durham (Fayetteville)	1,080,680
28	San Diego	1,066,680
29	Nashville	1,016,290
30	Hartford & New Haven	1,014,990
31	Kansas City	937,970
32	Columbus, OH	925,840
33	Salt Lake City	919,390
34	Cincinnati	915,570
35	Milwaukee	905,350
36	Greenville-Spartanburg-Asheville-Anderson	858,050
37	San Antonio	818,560
38	West Palm Beach-Fort Pierce	779,430
39	Grand Rapids-Kalamazoo-Battle Creek	741,420
40	Birmingham (Anniston, Tuscaloosa)	739,750
41	Harrisburg-Lancaster-Lebanon-York	738,880
42	Las Vegas	728,410
43	Norfolk-Portsmouth-Newport News	718,020
44	Albuquerque-Santa Fe	689,120
45	Oklahoma City	687,300
46	Greensboro-High Point-Winston Salem	685,110
47	Jacksonville, Brunswick	674,860
48	Memphis	673,770
49	Austin	667,670
50	Louisville	667,230
51	Buffalo	631,120
52	Providence-New Bedford	622,580
53	New Orleans	602,740

DMA Rank	Designated Market Area	TV Households
54	Wilkes Barre-Scranton	594,570
55	Fresno-Visalia	574,900
56	Little Rock-Pine Bluff	567,060
57	Albany-Schenectady-Troy	556,750
58	Richmond-Petersburg	550,240
59	Knoxville	547,930
60	Mobile-Pensacola (Fort Walton Beach)	537,810
61	Tulsa	529,540
62	Fort Myers-Naples	509,530
63	Lexington	503,260
64	Dayton	483,790
65	Charleston-Huntington	479,750
66	Flint-Saginaw-Bay City	465,790
67	Roanoke-Lynchburg	461,420
68	Tucson (Sierra Vista)	456,030
69	Wichita-Hutchinson Plus	450,930
70	Green Bay-Appleton	444,210
71	Des Moines-Ames	432,410
72	Honolulu	429,940
73	Toledo	425,890
74	Springfield, MO	421,960
75	Spokane	416,630
76	Omaha	411,520
77	Portland-Auburn	410,890
78	Paducah-Cape Girardeau-Harrisburg-Mt. Vernon	393,260
79	Columbia, SC	393,170
80	Rochester, NY	390,590
81	Syracuse	388,000
82	Huntsville-Decatur, Florence	386,520
83	Champaign & Springfield-Decatur	386,000
84	Shreveport	385,770
85	Madison	378,740
86	Chattanooga	366,780
87	Harlingen-Weslaco-Brownsville-McAllen	349,910
88	Cedar Rapids-Waterloo & Dubuque	346,330
89	South Bend-Elkhart	334,720
90	Jackson, MS	334,650
91	Colorado Springs-Pueblo	334,390
92	Tri-Cities, TN-VA	332,840
93	Burlington-Plattsburgh	331,320
94	Waco-Temple-Bryan	329,690
95	Baton Rouge	326,390
96	Savannah	319,160
97	Davenport-Rock Island-Moline	309,600
98	El Paso	308,080
99	Charleston, SC	307,610
100	Fort Smith-Fayetteville-Springdale-Rogers	297,920
101	Johnstown-Altoona	293,860
102	Evansville	292,220
103	Greenville-New Bern-Washington	289,050
104	Myrtle Beach-Florence	285,010
105	Tallahassee-Thomasville	282,390
106	Lincoln & Hastings-Kearney	281,290
107	Fort Wayne	275,350
108	Reno	271,080
109	Youngstown	268,930
110	Tyler-Longview (Lufkin & Nacogdoches)	265,200
111	Springfield-Holyoke	262,850

DMA Rank	Designated Market Area	TV Households
112	Boise	262,290
113	Sioux Falls (Mitchell)	260,190
114	Lansing	258,650
115	Augusta	253,950
116	Peoria-Bloomington	248,510
117	Traverse City-Cadillac	247,650
118	Montgomery (Selma)	247,230
119	Eugene	242,790
120	Fargo-Valley City	241,120
121	Santa Barbara-Santa Maria-San Luis Obispo	240,190
122	Macon	239,820
123	Lafayette, LA	230,670
124	Monterey-Salinas	225,350
125	Bakersfield	220,730
126	Yakima-Pasco-Richland-Kennewick	216,780
127	La Crosse-Eau Claire	215,610
128	Columbus, GA	213,980
129	Corpus Christi	197,290
130	Chico-Redding	197,280
131	Amarillo	192,090
132	Rockford	188,860
133	Columbus-Tupelo-West Point	188,740
134	Wilmington	187,480
135	Wausau-Rhinelander	184,220
136	Monroe-El Dorado	179,190
137	Columbia-Jefferson City	179,010
138	Topeka	175,940
139	Duluth-Superior	173,180
140	Medford-Klamath Falls	171,830
141	Beaumont-Port Arthur	165,440
142	Palm Springs	159,240
143	Lubbock	158,070
144	Salisbury	157,940
145	Wichita Falls & Lawton	157,820
146	Erie	157,610
147	Albany, GA	156,800
148	Joplin-Pittsburg	156,560
149	Sioux City	154,900
150	Anchorage	150,620
151	Panama City	147,520
152	Terre Haute	145,450
153	Bangor	145,100
154	Rochester-Mason City-Austin	144,700
155	Bluefield-Beckley-Oak Hill	142,570
156	Odessa-Midland	141,560
157	Binghamton	138,930
158	Minot-Bismarck-Dickinson	136,730
159	Wheeling-Steubenville	133,700
160	Gainesville	129,960
161	Sherman, TX-Ada, OK	128,100
162	Idaho Falls-Pocatello	124,220
163	Biloxi-Gulfport	121,750
164	Yuma-El Centro	115,650
165	Abilene-Sweetwater	115,310
166	Missoula	111,340
167	Hattiesburg-Laurel	110,330
168	Clarksburg-Weston	109,150
169	Utica	106,280

DMA Rank	Designated Market Area	TV Households
170	Billings	106,030
171	Quincy-Hannibal-Keokuk	103,910
172	Dothan	100,950
173	Jackson, TN	98,050
174	Rapid City	96,450
175	Elmira	96,090
176	Lake Charles	95,410
177	Watertown	94,960
178	Harrisonburg	92,900
179	Alexandria, LA	89,630
180	Marquette	89,290
181	Jonesboro	80,900
182	Bowling Green	80,260
183	Charlottesville	76,600
184	Grand Junction-Montrose	73,360
185	Meridian	72,280
186	Lima	70,690
187	Greenwood-Greenville	70,050
188	Laredo	68,110
189	Lafayette, IN	67,070
190	Butte-Bozeman	65,480
191	Great Falls	64,910
192	Bend, OR	64,830
193	Parkersburg	63,760
194	Twin Falls	63,540
195	Eureka	60,900
196	San Angelo	54,980
197	Casper-Riverton	54,340
198	Cheyenne-Scottsbluff	54,120
199	Mankato	52,230
200	Ottumwa-Kirksville	51,270
201	St. Joseph	46,840
202	Fairbanks	37,110
203	Zanesville	32,550
204	Presque Isle	31,270
205	Victoria	31,260
206	Helena	27,040
207	Juneau	25,250
208	Alpena	17,520
209	North Platte	15,250
210	Glendive	3,940

Top 25 Cable System Operators

Ranked by Basic Subscribers*

Rank	Company	Subscribers
1	Comcast	24,182.0
2	Time Warner	13,069.0
3	Cox	5,328.3
4	Charter	5,045.7
5	Cablevision Systems	3,108.0
6	Bright House (e)	2,307.8
7	Mediacom	1,318.0
8	Suddenlink Communications	1,268.7
9	Insight Communications	707.6
10	Cable One	669.5
11	RCN	366.0
12	WideOpenWest (e)	363.8
13	Bresnan	309.4
14	Service Electric (e)	290.7
15	Atlantic Broadband	285.5
16	Armstrong	247.3
17	Knology	232.8
18	Midcontinent Communications (&)	206.2
19	MetroCast Cablevision **	188.9
20	Blue Ridge (e)	177.4
21	Broadstripe (e)	158.4
22	Buckeye CableSystem (e)	147.8
23	General Communication	147.7
24	Wave (e)	141.2
25	MidOcean Partners (e)	139.8

* As of December 2008.
** Includes Vista III Media.
(e) Estimate.
(&) Counts include recent sale or acquisition.
Subs in mil. Data actual.
Note: Unless otherwise noted, counts include owned and managed subscribers.

U.S. Sales of Television Receivers 1983-2009

Data compiled by Consumer Electronics Association

Year	Analog Color TV Units	Analog Color TV Dollars	Digital TV Units	Digital TV Dollars	LCD TV Units	LCD TV Dollars	TV/VCR/DVD Combinations Units	TV/VCR/DVD Combinations Dollars	Projection TV Units	Projection TV Dollars
1983	11,179	3,443	n/a	n/a	n/a	n/a	n/a	n/a	n/a	n/a
1984	13,092	3,875	n/a	n/a	n/a	n/a	n/a	n/a	n/a	n/a
1985	13,993	4,114	n/a	n/a	n/a	n/a	n/a	n/a	266	488
1986	15,399	4,481	n/a	n/a	n/a	n/a	n/a	n/a	304	530
1987	16,805	4,890	n/a	n/a	n/a	n/a	n/a	n/a	293	527
1988	17,768	4,691	n/a	n/a	n/a	n/a	n/a	n/a	302	529
1989	19,557	5,359	n/a	n/a	n/a	n/a	n/a	n/a	265	478
1990	18,453	5,148	n/a	n/a	n/a	n/a	424	178	351	626
1991	17,951	5,134	n/a	n/a	n/a	n/a	662	265	380	683
1992	21,056	6,591	n/a	n/a	n/a	n/a	936	375	404	714
1993	23,005	7,316	n/a	n/a	n/a	n/a	1,629	599	465	841
1994	24,715	7,225	n/a	n/a	n/a	n/a	2,017	710	636	1,117
1995	23,231	6,798	n/a	n/a	n/a	n/a	2,205	723	820	1,417
1996	22,384	6,492	n/a	n/a	n/a	n/a	2,199	697	887	1,426
1997	21,293	6,036	n/a	n/a	n/a	n/a	2,311	684	917	1,361
1998	22,204	6,122	14	43	n/a	n/a	3,147	832	1,070	1,577
1999	23,218	6,199	121	295	n/a	n/a	4,148	1,014	1,232	1,632
2000	24,175	6,503	648	1,426	832	107	4,964	968	1,216	1,481
2001	21,167	5,130	1,460	2,648	845	101	4,630	790	933	1,060
2002	22,469	5,782	4,145	6,383	935	246	4,870	733	681	733
2003	20,791	4,756	5,532	8,692	1,253	664	4,373	778	276	293
2004	19,934	3,526	8.002	12,300	1,842	1,579	3,643	867	97	85
2005	16,934	2,790	11,369	15,563	4,077	3,258	3,348	650	20	15
2006	8,761	1,000	23,504	23,380	10,325	8,430	2,028	340	5	3
2007	1,166	115	26,904	25,184	16,843	14,520	184	26	-	-
2008 (e)	-	-	32,743	26,936	23,764	18,117	-	-	-	-
2009 (p)	-	-	34,639	26,344	26,790	18,737	-	-	-	-

Dollar figure in millions and represent factory sales price multiplied by unit sales to dealers.

Unit figures include distributor sales and factory direct sales to dealers. All unit figures are in thousands (add 000).

n/a=not available

(e)=estimate

(p)=projection

Television Sets in Use

	In Home (000)	Avg. Sets Per HH
1970	81,040	1.39
1971	85,290	1.42
1972	89,770	1.45
1973	95,330	1.47
1974	100,020	1.51
1975	105,460	1.54
1976	108,890	1.56
1977	113,440	1.59
1978	118,630	1.63
1979	124,570	1.67
1980	128,190	1.68
1981	132,260	1.70
1982	142,460	1.75
1983	148,910	1.79
1984	149,180	1.78
1985	155,410	1.83
1986	157,500	1.83
1987	162,750	1.86
1988	168,260	1.90
1989	175,580	1.94
1990	193,320	2.10
1991	193,200	2.08
1992*	192,480	2.09
1993	200,565	2.15
1994	211,443	2.24
1995	217,067	2.28
1996	222,753	2.32
1997	228,740	2.36
1998	235,010	2.40
1999	240,320	2.42
2000	244,990	2.43
2001	248,160	2.43
2002	254,360	2.41
2003	260,230	2.44
2004	268,260	2.47
2005	287,000	2.62
2006	301,380	2.73
2007	310,840	2.79
2008	310,470	2.83

1970-79, as of September of prior year; 1980 to date as of January of calendar year; excludes Alaska and Hawaii prior to 1989.
* Reflects adjustments to conform to the 1990 census.

55 Years of Station Transactions

Dollar volume of transactions (number of stations changing hands)

YEAR	RADIO ONLY*	GROUPS*	TV ONLY	TOTAL
1954	$10,224,047 (187)	$26,213,323 (18)	$23,906,760 (27)	$60,344,130
1955	27,333,104 (242)	22,351,602 (11)	23,394,660 (29)	$73,079,366
1956	32,563,378 (316)	65,212,055 (24)	17,830,395 (21)	$115,605,828
1957	48,207,470 (357)	47,490,884 (28)	28,489,206 (38)	$124,187,560
1958	49,868,123 (407)	60,872,618 (17)	16,796,285 (23)	$127,537,026
1959	65,544,653 (436)	42,724,727 (15)	15,227,201 (21)	$123,496,581
1960	51,763,285 (345)	24,648,400 (10)	22,930,225 (21)	$99,341,910
1961	55,532,516 (282)	42,103,708 (13)	31,167,943 (24)	$128,804,167
1962	59,912,520 (306)	18,822,745 (8)	23,007,638 (16)	$101,742,903
1963	43,457,584 (305)	25,045,726 (3)	36,799,768 (16)	$105,303,078
1964	52,296,480 (430)	67,185,762 (20)	86,274,494 (36)	$205,756,736
1965	55,933,300 (389)	49,756,993 (15)	29,433,473 (32)	$135,123,766
1966	76,633,762 (367)	28,510,500 (11)	30,574,054 (31)	$135,718,316
1967	59,670,053 (316)	32,086,297 (9)	80,316,223 (30)	$172,072,573
1968	71,310,709 (316)	47,556,634 (9)	33,588,069 (20)	$152,455,412
1969	108,866,538 (343)	35,037,000 (5)	87,794,032 (32)	$231,697,570
1970	86,292,899 (268)	1,038,465 (3)	87,454,078 (19)	$174,785,442
1971	125,501,514 (270)	750,000 (2)	267,296,410 (27)	$393,547,924
1972	114,424,673 (239)	0 (0)	156,905,864 (37)	$271,330,537
1973	160,933,557 (352)	2,812,444 (4)	66,635,144 (25)	$230,381,145
1974	168,998,012 (369)	19,800,000 (5)	118,983,462 (24)	$307,781,474
1975	131,065,860 (363)	0 (0)	128,420,101 (22)	$259,485,961
1976	180,663,820 (413)	1,800,000 (3)	108,459,657 (32)	$290,923,477
1977	161,236,169 (344)	0 (0)	128,635,435 (25)	$289,871,604
1978	331,557,239 (586)	30,450,000 (5)	289,721,159 (51)	$651,728,398
1979	335,597,000 (546)	463,500,000 (52)	317,581,000 (47)	$1,116,678,000
1980	339,634,000 (424)	27,000,000 (3)	534,150,000 (35)	$900,784,000
1981	447,838,060 (625)	78,400,000 (6)	227,950,000 (24)	$754,188,060
1982	470,722,833 (597)	0 (0)	527,675,411 (30)	$998,398,244
1983	621,077,876 (669)	332,000,000 (10)	1,902,701,830 (61)	$2,855,779,706
1984	977,024,266 (782)	234,500,000 (2)	1,252,023,787 (82)	$2,463,548,053
1985	1,414,816,073 (1,558)	962,450,000 (218)	3,290,995,000 (99)	$5,668,261,073
1986	1,490,131,426 (959)	1,993,021,955 (192)	2,709,516,490 (128)	$6,192,669,871
1987	1,236,355,748 (775)	4,610,965,000 (132)	1,661,832,724 (59)	$7,509,153,472
1988	1,841,630,156 (845)	1,326,250,000 (106)	1,779,958,042 (70)	$4,947,838,198
1989	1,148,524,765 (663)	533,599,078 (40)	1,541,055,033 (84)	$3,223,178,876
1990	868,636,700 (1,045)	411,037,150 (60)	696,952,350 (75)	$1,976,626,200
1991	534,694,500 (793)	206,995,500 (61)	273,365,000 (38)	$1,015,055,000
1992	603,192,980 (667)	318,176,050 (24)	124,004,000 (41)	$1,045,373,030
1993	815,450,000 (633)	756,722,000 (NA)	1,728,711,000 (101)	$3,300,883,000
1994	970,400,000 (494)	1,800,000,000 (154)	2,200,000,000 (89)	$4,970,400,000
1995	792,440,000 (524)	2,790,000,000 (213)	4,740,000,000 (112)	$8,322,440,000
1996	2,840,820,000 (671)	12,034,000,000 (345)	10,488,000,000 (99)	$25,362,820,000
1997	2,461,570,000 (630)	14,580,000,000 (329)	6,400,000,000 (108)	$23,441,570,000
1998	1,596,210,000 (589)	14,080,000,000 (271)	7,120,000,000 (90)	$22,796,210,000
1999	1,718,000,000 (382)	26,880,000,000 (196)	4,720,000,000 (86)	$33,318,000,000
2000**	24,900,000,000 (1,794)	0 (0)	8,800,000,000 (154)	$33,700,000,000
2001**	3,800,000,000 (1,000)	0 (0)	4,900,000,000 (108)	$8,700,000,000
2002**	5,594,141,000 (836)	0 (0)	2,529,039,000 (249)	$8,123,180,000
2003**	2,400,000,000 (950)	0 (0)	520,000,000 (97)	$2,920,000,000
2004**	1,897,422,000 (901)	0 (0)	871,923,000 (66)	$2,769,345,000
2005**	2,791,531,000 (895)	0 (0)	2,842,439,000 (86)	$5,633,970,000
2006**	22,871,247,000 (2101)	0 (0)	18,127,686,000 (180)	$40,998,933,000
2007**	1,488,628,000 (1,187)	0 (0)	4,616,018,000 (295)	$6,104,646,000
2008**	642,344,000 (749)	0 (0)	745,511,000 (48)	$1,387,855,000
TOTAL	$92,239,870,648	$85,110,886,616	$100,129,129,403	$277,479,886,667

Note: Dollar volume figures represent total considerations reported for all transactions with exception of minority interest transfers in which control of stations did not change hands and stations sold as part of larger company transactions. Although all states have been approved by the FCC, they may not necessarily have reached final closing. Prior to 1978, combined AM-FM facilities were counted as one station in computing total number of stations traded. Now AM-FM combinations are counted as two stations.
*Starting in 1993, the Radio only column includes only stand alone AM and FM deals and the Groups column contains AM-FM combos and all other multiple station deals. In previous years the AM-FM combos were included under Radio only.
**Figures for 2000 to 2008 courtesy of BIA Financial Network.

Record of Television Station Growth Since Television Began

	TV Authorized	On Air
Jan. 1, 1946*	9	6
Jan. 1, 1947*	52	
Jan. 1, 1948*	73	17
Jan. 1, 1949	124	50
Jan. 1, 1950	111	97
Jan. 1, 1951	109	107
Jan. 1, 1952	108	108
Jan. 1, 1953*	273	129
Jan. 1, 1954	567	356
Jan. 1, 1955	576	439 [1]
Jan. 1, 1956	590	482 [2]
Jan. 1, 1957	631	511
Jan. 1, 1958	657	544 [3]
Jan. 1, 1959	666	562 [4]
Jan. 1, 1960	673	573 [5]
Jan. 1, 1961	634	583
Jan. 1, 1962	654	563
Jan. 1, 1963	662	579
Jan. 1, 1964	661	582
Jan. 1, 1965	676	586
Jan. 1, 1966	702	596
Jan. 1, 1967	769	623
Jan. 1, 1968	818	644
Jan. 1, 1969	834	672
Jan. 1, 1970	1,038	872
Jan. 1, 1971	1,025	892
Jan. 1, 1972	1,004	905
Jan. 1, 1973	1,001	922
Jan. 1, 1974	1,002	938
Jan. 1, 1975	1,010	952
Jan. 1, 1976	1,030	962
Jan. 1, 1977	1,029	984
Jan. 1, 1978	1,045	986
Jan. 1, 1979	1,059	992
Jan. 1, 1980	1,094	1,013
Jan. 1, 1981	1,143	1,019
Jan. 1, 1982	1,168	1,020
Jan. 1, 1983	1,276	1,090
Jan. 1, 1984	1,318	1,149
Jan. 1, 1985	1,505	1,194
Oct. 30, 1986	1,493	1,220
Oct. 31, 1987	1,558	1,285
Jan. 1, 1988	1,615	1,342
Jan. 1, 1989	1,683	1,395
Jan. 1, 1990	1,684	1,436
Jan. 1, 1991	1,690	1,469
Jan. 1, 1992	1,688	1,488
Jan. 1, 1993	1,688	1,505
Jan. 1, 1994		1,518
Jan. 1, 1995		1,520
Jan. 1, 1996		1,544
Jan. 1, 1997		1,554
Jan. 1, 1998		1,564
Jan. 1, 1999		1,589
Jan. 1, 2000		1,616
Jan. 1, 2001		1,663
Jan. 1, 2002		1,686
Jan. 1, 2003		1,719
Jan. 1, 2004		1,733
Jan. 1, 2005		1,748
Jan. 1, 2006		1,750
Jan. 1, 2007		1,756
Jan. 1, 2008		1,759
Jan. 1, 2009		1,759

*Comparable figures for all services not available at this date.

[1] Includes stations with Special Temporary Authorizations (STAs), which either had not started operations as of this date, had started but had gone dark, or had received authorizations but turned them back with or without operating.

[2] Includes 2 licenses that had suspended operation and 37 stations with STAs in same category as footnote 1.

[3] Includes 7 licenses that had suspended operation and 40 stations with STAs in same category as footnote 1.

[4] Includes 6 licenses that had suspended operation and 38 stations with STAs in same category as footnote 1.

[5] Includes 10 licenses that had suspended operation and 38 stations with STAs in same category as footnote 1.

Top 20 Cable Networks

Primetime Mon-Sun 8PM to 11PM

	Rating	Total Homes (000)
USA	2.0	2290
FOXNC	1.5	1745
DSNY	1.5	1676
TNT	1.3	1490
NAN (1)	1.2	1365
TBSC	1.2	1349
ESPN	1.0	1180
AEN	1.0	1112
TOON (1)	0.9	1055
HIST	0.9	986
FX	0.9	975
HALL	0.8	969
LIF	0.8	966
FAM	0.8	935
HGTV	0.8	915
DISC	0.8	907
CNN	0.8	876
SPIKE	0.7	855
SCIFI	0.7	853
AMC	0.7	824

Total Programming Day

	Rating	Total Homes (000)
NICK	1.5	1693
NAN	1.1	1314
USA	1.1	1215
DSNY	1.0	1169
FOXNC	0.9	1005
TNT	0.8	957
ADSM	0.8	885
TOON	0.7	842
TBSC	0.7	803
ESPN	0.6	706
LIF	0.6	685
AEN	0.6	666
HIST	0.6	636
CNN	0.5	609
TRU	0.5	598
SPIKE	0.5	575
DISC	0.5	571
FX	0.5	563
HGTV	0.5	544
HALL	0.5	537

2009 Year-To-Date 12/29/2008-04/19/2009.
Total Programming Day=M - Sun 6AM - 6AM or Individual Network's Total Programming Day and Sun 6AM - 3AM for Most Current Week
(1) Cable Network did not telecast during the entire daypart.
Coverage area ratings are within each cable network's universe.
Total U.S. ratings and household projections are based on 114.5 million TV homes.
This report includes only those cable networks who supply program names to the industry.

Top 100 Television Programs

Full Season: 9/22/08-5/20/09

RANK	PROGRAM	NETWORK	US AA% LIVE + SD
1	SUPER BOWL XLIII (6:32P)	NBC	42.1
2	AFC CHAMPIONSHIP ON CBS (6:44P)	CBS	22
3	ACADEMY AWARDS	ABC	20.8
4	NBC NFL PLAYOFF GAME 2	NBC	16.1
5	FEDEX BCS NATL CHAMP	FOX	15.9
6	AMERICAN IDOL-WEDNESDAY	FOX	15
7	OSCAR'S RED CARPET 2009	ABC	14.6
8	AMERICAN IDOL THU SP-1/29	FOX	14.6
9	AMERICAN IDOL-TUESDAY	FOX	14.5
10	FOX NFC PLAYOFF-SAT	FOX	13.8
11	AMER IDL THU RSLT SP-3/26	FOX	13.7
12	AMERICAN IDOL THU SP-3/5	FOX	13
13	DANCING WITH THE STARS	ABC	12.8
14	AMERICAN IDOL THU SP-2/26	FOX	12.6
15	OFFICE 2/1	NBC	12.5
16	DANCING W/STARS SP-9/23	ABC	12.2
17	FOX WRLD SERIES GM5 CONCL	FOX	11.9
18	BACHELOR:AFTER FINAL ROSE	ABC	11.7
19	CSI	CBS	11.6
20	GRAMMY AWARDS	CBS	11.4
21	NCIS	CBS	10.9
22	CBS NCAA BSKBL CHAMPSHIPS	CBS	10.8
23	MENTALIST, THE	CBS	10.8
24	DANCING W/STARS RESULTS	ABC	10.7
25	DANCING W/STARS RESULT SP	ABC	10.5
26	TOSTITOS FIESTA BOWL	FOX	10.4
27	MENTALIST, THE - SUN SPCL	CBS	10.4
28	NBC SUNDAY NIGHT FOOTBALL	NBC	10
29	CRIMINAL MINDS 10PM-SP	CBS	9.9
30	CBS SUNDAY MOVIE-SPECIAL	CBS	9.8
31	CSI - 8PM SPECIAL	CBS	9.8
32	CMA AWARDS	ABC	9.8
33	DESPERATE HOUSEWIVES	ABC	9.8
34	GREY'S ANATOMY-THU 9PM	ABC	9.5
35	GOLDEN GLOBE AWARDS	NBC	9.5
36	FOX WORLD SERIES GAME 4	FOX	9.3
37	CRIMINAL MINDS	CBS	9.3
38	FOX WORLD SERIES GAME 1	FOX	9.2
39	BARBARA WALTERS PRESENTS	ABC	9.1
40	CSI: MIAMI	CBS	9.1
41	TWO AND A HALF MEN	CBS	9.1
42	SNL PRESIDENTIAL BASH '08	NBC	9
43	60 MINUTES	CBS	9
44	ACM AWARDS	CBS	8.9
45	BARBARA WALTERS SP-1/7	ABC	8.7
46	CSI: NY	CBS	8.6
47	CBS NCAA BSKBL CHAMP SA-2	CBS	8.5
48	VOTE 2008-9:00PM	ABC	8.5
49	WITHOUT A TRACE	CBS	8.3
50	CSI: NY THURSDAY 10PM SP	CBS	8.3
51	SURVIVOR: GABON FINALE	CBS	8.2
52	FOX WORLD SERIES GAME 5	FOX	8.2
53	FOX WORLD SERIES GAME 2	FOX	8.1
54	SURVIVOR: GABON	CBS	8.1

RANK	PROGRAM	NETWORK	US AA% LIVE + SD
55	HOUSE	FOX	8
56	NEIGHBORHOOD BALL-1/20	ABC	7.9
57	CBS NCAA BSKBL-BRIDGE	CBS	7.8
58	ALLSTATE SUGAR BOWL	FOX	7.8
59	DATELINE NBC 2/10	NBC	7.8
60	DANCING W/STARS RECAP #5	ABC	7.8
61	ELEVENTH HOUR	CBS	7.8
62	BACHELOR:AFTR FINAL ROSE2	ABC	7.8
63	BONES SP-4/15 8P	FOX	7.7
64	60 MINUTES SPECIAL	CBS	7.7
65	MENTALIST, THE-10PM SP	CBS	7.7
66	E.R. RETROSPECTIVE	NBC	7.7
67	COLD CASE	CBS	7.6
68	MENTALIST, THE-FRIDAY-SP	CBS	7.6
69	BARBARA WALTERS SP-11/26	ABC	7.6
70	24: REDEMPTION PREQUEL	FOX	7.6
71	NCIS 9P-SPECIAL	CBS	7.6
72	AMERICA'S GOT TALENT-WED	NBC	7.5
73	BACHELOR, THE	ABC	7.5
74	SURVIVOR: TOCANTINS	CBS	7.5
75	HALLMARK HALL OF FAME	CBS	7.4
76	NCIS FRIDAY 9PM SPECIAL	CBS	7.4
77	BARBARA WALTERS SP-2/22	ABC	7.4
78	AMERICAN MUSIC AWARDS	ABC	7.4
79	DECISION '08 PRIME	NBC	7.4
80	NFL REGULAR SEASON L	ESPN	7.4
81	SURVIVOR: GABON REUNION	CBS	7.4
82	NCIS FRIDAY 9PM-SPECIAL	CBS	7.3
83	24	FOX	7.2
84	BROTHERS & SISTERS	ABC	7.2
85	OT, THE	FOX	7.1
86	DANCING W/STARS RECAP #4	ABC	7.1
87	RULES OF ENGAGEMENT	CBS	7
88	CSI - THANKSGIVING SP	CBS	7
89	SURVIVOR:TOCANTINS FINALE	CBS	7
90	VOTE 2008-8:00PM	ABC	6.9
91	CBS NCAA BSKBL CHMP FR 2	CBS	6.9
92	MICHAEL J FOX SP-5/7	ABC	6.8
93	COLD CASE - SPECIAL	CBS	6.8
94	MENTALIST, THE-10PM SPCL	CBS	6.8
95	CASTLE	ABC	6.8
96	SNL:WKND UPDT 10/9	NBC	6.8
97	LAW AND ORDER:SVU	NBC	6.7
98	CBS NCAA BSKBL CHMP TH 2	CBS	6.7
99	GHOST WHISPERER	CBS	6.7
100	KENNEDY CENTER HONORS	CBS	6.7

Source: Television Bureau of Advertising, based on data from Nielsen Galaxy Lightning. Ranked by average audience percentage of the total number of homes in the U.S. with TV sets. Ad-supported subscription television only.

Top 10 Cable Programs

RANK	PROGRAM	NETWORK	US AA% LIVE + SD
80	NFL REGULAR SEASON L	ESPN	7.4
103	ELECTION NIGHT 08	CNN	6.7
195	AMERICAS ELECTION HQ	FXNC	5.2
203	PRESIDENTIAL DEBATE	FXNC	5.1
213	NBA PLAYOFFS-CONF FNLS L	ESPN	5
221	MLB ALCS	TBSC	4.9
251	2009 NBA ALL STAR GAME	TNT	4.5
295	S KIDS CHOICE 09	NICK	4.1
304	BURN NOTICE	USA	4.1
317	NBA ALLSTAR SAT NIGHT	TNT	4

Source: Television Bureau of Advertising, based on data from Nielsen Galaxy Lightning. Ranked by average audience percentage of the total number of homes in the U.S. with TV sets.

Television Advertising Shares

	Network*	Spot	Local	Synd.*	Cable	Total
1970	$1,658	$1,234	$704	-	-	$3,596
1971	1,593	1,145	796	-	-	3,534
1972	1,804	1,318	969	-	-	4,091
1973	1,968	1,377	1,115	-	-	4,460
1974	2,145	1,497	1,212	-	-	4,854
1975	2,306	1,623	1,334	-	-	5,263
1976	2,857	2,154	1,710	-	-	6,721
1977	3,460	2,204	1,948	-	-	7,612
1978	3,975	2,607	2,373	-	-	8,955
1979	4,599	2,873	2,682	-	-	10,154
1980	5,130	3,269	2,967	50	72	11,488
1981	5,540	3,746	3,368	75	160	12,889
1982	6,144	4,364	3,765	150	290	14,713
1983	6,955	4,827	4,345	300	452	16,879
1984	8,318	5,488	5,084	420	733	20,043
1985	8,060	6,004	5,714	520	989	21,287
1986	8,342	6,570	6,514	600	1,173	23,199
1987	8,500	6,846	6,833	762	1,321	24,262
1988	9,172	7,147	7,270	901	1,641	26,131
1989	9,110	7,354	7,612	1,288	2,095	27,459
1990	9,863	7,788	7,856	1,109	2,631	29,247
1991	9,533	7,110	7,565	1,253	3,145	28,606
1992	10,249	7,551	8,079	1,370	3,830	31,079
1993	10,209	7,800	8,435	1,576	4,451	32,471
1994	10,942	8,993	9,464	1,734	5,209	36,342
1995	11,600	9,119	9,985	2,016	6,166	38,886
1996	13,081	9,803	10,944	2,218	7,778	43,824
1997	13,020	9,999	11,436	2,438	8,750	45,643
1998	13,736	10,659	12,169	2,609	10,340	49,513
1999	13,961	10,500	12,680	2,870	12,570	52,581
2000	15,888	12,264	13,542	3,108	15,455	60,257
2001	14,300	9,223	12,256	3,102	15,736	54,617
2002	15,000	10,920	13,114	3,034	16,297	58,365
2003	15,030	9,948	13,520	3,434	18,814	60,746
2004	16,713	11,370	14,507	3,674	21,527	67,791
2005	16,128	10,040	14,260	3,865	23,654	67,947
2006	16,676	11,626	14,887	3,691	25,025	71,905
2007	16,643	10,138	14,411	3,329	20,614	70,840
2008	17,226	9,834	13,114	3,560	21,440	65,174

all figures in millions
*Fox is included in syndication prior to 1990; it is included in network starting in 1990. PAX, UPN and WB/ION, CW & MyNetwork currently in syndication.

© 2009 Television Bureau of Advertising, Nielsen Media Research. Reprinted with permission.

Top 25 TV Advertisers

Jan. 1, 2008-Dec. 31, 2008

Rank	Parent Company	Jan - Dec $
1	PROCTER & GAMBLE CO	$2,040,698,253
2	AT&T INC	$1,364,232,649
3	GENERAL MOTORS CORP	$1,299,269,143
4	VERIZON COMMUNICATIONS INC	$1,168,612,835
5	TOYOTA MOTOR CORP	$881,918,763
6	JOHNSON & JOHNSON	$857,517,819
7	YUM! BRANDS INC	$830,325,041
8	FORD MOTOR CO	$795,110,244
9	CERBERUS CAPITAL MANAGEMENT LP	$780,850,602
10	HONDA MOTOR CO LTD	$707,532,051
11	GENERAL ELECTRIC CO	$704,533,572
12	NISSAN MOTOR CO LTD	$680,035,656
13	MCDONALDS CORP	$675,340,961
14	GENERAL MILLS INC	$662,383,166
15	WALT DISNEY CO	$655,689,503
16	TIME WARNER INC	$648,303,951
17	GLAXOSMITHKLINE PLC	$594,937,288
18	PFIZER INC	$575,806,798
19	SPRINT NEXTEL CORP	$572,955,066
20	BERKSHIRE HATHAWAY INC	$570,596,273
21	NATL AMUSEMENTS INC	$528,502,718
22	PEPSICO INC	$510,867,974
23	SONY CORP	$485,998,124
24	STICHTING INBEV	$484,214,853
25	US GOVERNMENT	$455,635,408
	Total	**$19,531,868,711**

Source: Nielsen Monitor-Plus.

Top 25 TV Advertising Categories

Jan. 1, 2008-Dec. 31, 2008

Product Category	Jan - Dec $
Automotive	$8,151,125,167
RESTAURANT-QUICK SVC	$3,668,794,995
Pharmaceuticals	$2,966,523,756
TELEPH SVCS-WIRELESS	$28,820,053
MOTION PICTURE	$2,680,080,041
STORE-DEPT	$206,896,382
DIR RESP PROD	$1,474,987,005
POLITICAL CAMPAIGN	$1,270,256,249
RESTAURANT	$1,223,561,164
INSURANCE-AUTO	$1,163,615,293
Automotive-Dealerships	$1,137,634,457
STORE-FURNITURE	$985,355,598
CREDIT CARD SVCS	$89,894,177
BEER	$867,766,802
RECORDINGS-VIDEO	$730,437,037
LEGAL SVCS	$674,388,454
SATELLITE COMM SVCS	$58,918,559
CABLE TV SVCS	$584,487,716
PROFESSIONAL ORGN	$560,885,834
BANK SVCS	$544,845,122
CEREAL	$540,072,596
FINANCIAL-INVESTMENT SVCS	$517,402,383
STORE-HOME IMPROVEMENT	$516,620,895
ENTERTAINMENT SFTWRE	$398,876,074
INSURANCE	$371,959,348
Total	**$31,414,205,157**

Source: Nielsen Monitor-Plus.

A Brief History of Broadcasting and Cable

By Mark K. Miller, freelance writer and former managing editor, *Broadcasting & Cable* magazine

We could start our history of the electronic media in many places. We chose November 2, 1920. On that day, in Pittsburgh, Westinghouse Electric and Manufacturing Co.'s KDKA, generally acknowledged as the first licensed commercial radio station in the United States, broadcast the results of the Harding-Cox presidential elections. The broadcast demonstrated that radio was more than a novelty, that it could have real impact on our culture and our politics. The broadcast touched off a revolution that continues to this day. To give you a clear sense of the history, our history takes it decade by decade, assigning a theme to each.

1920s: Radio Begins Finding Its Way

Although we begin with that KDKA broadcast in 1920, there had been a lot of radio activity prior to that. Inventors and hobbyists had been filling the airwaves with signals, often on a very haphazard basis, for years. And government experiments during World War I contributed much to the growing volume of radio knowledge.

On August 20, 1920, WWJ(AM) Detroit, owned by the Detroit News, began what it claimed to be the first regular broadcasting schedule when it inaugurated daily broadcasts.

In 1922 the superheterodyne circuit as a broadcast receiver is demonstrated by its inventor, Edwin H. Armstrong, and will prove to become the industry standard. By May, there are 80 licensed radio stations in the United States; by year's end the number has grown to 569.

The rest of the decade is filled with examples of radio's surging growth and the unfettered vision of inventors around the world. In 1923 Dr. Vladimir K. Zworykin files for a U.S. patent for an all-electronic television system.

Stations begin to link themselves into "chains" or networks via telephone lines and numerous experiments test the feasibility of transmitting short-wave signals across the oceans, from airplanes and ships.

The 1924 Republican convention in Cleveland and the Democratic convention in New York are broadcast over networks, and in 1925 President Calvin Coolidge's inaugural ceremony is broadcast by 24 stations in a transcontinental network. The government was taking notice of the burgeoning industry, and in 1926 the Federal Radio Commission is created in response to the chaos caused by the explosive growth of broadcasting.

But it was the launch of the National Broadcasting Co. on November 15, 1926, that marked the beginning of the network system of broadcasting that exists to this day. NBC was a joint venture of radio equipment manufacturers RCA (30 percent), General Electric (50 percent), and Westinghouse (20 percent). The initial broadcast was carried by 25 stations ranging from the East Coast to St. Louis and Kansas City, Missouri, and was estimated to have been heard by almost half of the nation's five million homes equipped with radios. In 1928 NBC would establish a permanent coast-to-coast radio network.

NBC's entry was followed in 1927 by that of the Columbia Broadcasting System, which debuted with a basic network of 16 stations. Two years later, William S. Paley, 27, purchases a controlling interest and is elected president.

There is also continuing activity on the television front. In 1927 Philo T. Farnsworth applies for a patent on his image dissector television camera tube and in 1929 Russian inventor Vladimir Zworykin demonstrates his kinescope, or cathode ray television receiver, before a meeting of the Institute of Radio Engineers.

1930s: The Rise of Radio Entertainment

It was in the 1930s that the "American Plan" of advertising-supported radio flourished, making it extremely unlikely that proponents (and there were many) of the "European Plan" of a government-operated medium would prevail. The attractiveness of free, high-quality entertainment during the Great Depression resulted in larger and larger audiences for the networks, exactly what companies needed to advertise their products.

As listening skyrocketed (about 12 million U.S. homes had a radio in 1930, by 1940 the figure was 28.5 million and car radios were becoming standard equipment), so too did the fortunes of the major networks: NBC's Red and Blue, CBS and Mutual (plus numerous regional nets). With radio personalities such as Jack Benny, Charles Correll, and Freeman Gosden (Amos 'n' Andy), Eddie Cantor, Burns and Allen, and Major Bowes attracting larger and larger audiences, advertisers wanted more precise listening figures. So in 1936 A.C. Nielsen Co. proposed its Audimeter, which would be attached to a sampling of radio sets and measure audience size.

Work continued on television. By 1937 there were 17 experimental TV stations operating and President Franklin D. Roosevelt was seen on TV when he opened the 1939 New York World's Fair.

1940s: The Rise of Radio News

As Europe was engulfed in war and the United States appeared headed toward the conflict, Americans turned to their radios to stay informed. During 1940, the networks' typical weekly schedules contained 56 quarter hours during the day as opposed to only 33 in evening programming in 1939 and none during daytime hours. CBS had Edward R. Murrow in London and his team of correspondents across Europe, while NBC had Fred Bate, Max Jordan, William Kierker, and many others. When the United States was attacked by Japan on December 7, 1941, network news reporting preempted regular programming. And the audience for President Roosevelt's broadcast to the nation on December 9, the day after war was declared, attracted the largest audience to that time, about 90 million. By the end of the week, all the networks and most stations were operating around the clock. For the first time, a war was heard by the people back home.

In addition to war reporting, coverage of domestic news was on the rise. With a tremendous amount of public interest in the 1944 presidential campaign, the networks canceled all commercial programs that would have interfered with their coverage of the Republican and Democratic conventions and used more than 300 reporters, technicians, and officials at each.

When the war ended and the era of the atomic bomb and the cold war began, the networks put their news departments to work on radio documentaries. CBS established a documentary unit that later resulted in a separate series, Ed Murrow and Fred Friendly's Hear It Now.

1950s: The Rise of Television Entertainment

While television had been in development since the 1920s and there had been experimental broadcasts since the 1930s, it wasn't until after World War II that the networks were able to concentrate on developing programming, manufacturers were able to return to making sets, and the public was able to afford them. (At the beginning of 1952 about 19 million U.S. homes had a TV set, and by the end of the decade that number was about 46.5 million.) The post-war economy was booming and the country's optimism was reflected in many of those early TV shows. Some of radio's stars made the transition to TV, as did many of the radio show formats. Soap operas (*The Guiding Light* on CBS), comedies (*Life of Riley* on NBC), westerns (*Gunsmoke* on CBS), dramas (*Kraft Television Theater* on NBC and ABC), variety (*Toast of the Town with Ed Sullivan* on CBS), and quiz shows (*Twenty One* on NBC) emerged as early favorites. And the TV syndication business was born when Frederic W. Ziv began selling shows such as 1951's *Bold Venture* with Humphrey Bogart and Lauren Bacall to local and regional advertisers and stations.

At the beginning of the decade RCA and CBS were in a battle: the companies each wanted FCC approval of a system for color TV. RCA eventually prevailed in 1953 because programs broadcast in its "compatible color" could still be watched on existing black and white sets. Another innovation that was to change television programming dramatically was unveiled in 1956 when Ampex Corp. demonstrated its videotape recorder at the National Association of Radio and Television Broadcasters convention and received $4 million in orders.

1960s: The Rise of Television News

Television journalism came of age in the 1960s. As the decade began, the FCC suspended its equal-time requirement for presidential and vice presidential candidates (following the suggestion of CBS President Frank Stanton), paving the way for the four "Great Debates" between Vice President Richard Nixon and Senator John F. Kennedy. The first debate, broadcast from Chicago on September 26, was seen by 75 million viewers, a record at that time. It changed the course of political campaigning and, quite probably, the course of the election. In 1961, the newly elected President Kennedy, recognizing the influence of the medium, allowed television to cover his press conferences. In 1963 the networks expanded their evening newscasts from 15 minutes to a half-hour. The nation was stunned when President Kennedy was assassinated in November 1963 and it's been said that television news came of age with its coverage. For four days following, the networks suspended normal programming and commercials with NBC-TV on the air for more than 71 hours, CBS-TV for 55, and ABC-TV for 60. The network coverage cost an unprecedented $32 million and CBS research showed that 93 percent of U.S. homes watched coverage of JFK's burial and that the average set was in use for more than 13 consecutive hours.

Americans were transfixed by coverage of the space race, beginning with Alan Shepard's suborbital flight in 1961 and culminating in live pictures of the moon landing in 1969. Americans were also presented with almost nightly images not so uplifting, with coverage of the civil rights movement and the Vietnam war (the networks established news bureaus in Saigon in 1965) becoming almost nightly subjects. The decade ended on two disappointing notes for broadcasters. Shortly after the election of Richard Nixon in 1968, Vice President Spiro Agnew began a series of speeches attacking the media and accusing the press of bias against the administration. And in 1969 the Supreme Court's decision in the Red Lion case upheld the FCC's fairness doctrine and personal attack rules, saying they "enhance rather than abridge the freedoms of speech and press protected by the First Amendment."

1970s: The Rise of FM and Satellites

While the technique of broadcasting using frequency modulation was patented by Edwin Armstrong in 1933, the first station built in 1939, and an FM band allocated by the FCC in 1940, growth of the new radio service was very slow. Delayed by World War II and a suspicion by many AM station owners that the new service would offer unwanted competition, it wasn't until the late 1960s that large numbers of consumers began buying FM receivers. Another handicap was beginning to be resolved in 1971 when car manufacturers began to include FM-equipped radios as standard equipment in about 20 percent of the new models (that number would rise to 50 percent within five years).

To differentiate FM stations from those on the AM band, and to take advantage of FM's higher fidelity, programmers developed new formats. One of the most innovative was the "underground" or "progressive" sound introduced by Tom Donahue at KMPX(FM) San Francisco in the late 1960s that played album tracks not heard on the tightly formatted top 40 AM stations. But "underground" wasn't the only sound to be heard on FM or even the predominant one. There was also the very aboveground sound of carefully researched syndicated formats. Coupled with the increased use of

automation equipment, services like Drake-Chenault's "Solid Gold" and Bonneville's easy listening formats turned many money-losing FM stations into profit centers. This success was translated into value as multimillion-dollar prices for FM stations became common. And for the first time industry observers began predicting that FM would overtake AM as the band for music, with AM becoming primarily a news and information medium.

The phenomenon of the 1970s was the development of international broadcasting live via satellites. RCA inaugurated the nation's first domestic satellite communications service in 1974, using a Canadian satellite, later launching its Satcom series of birds. But the breakthrough came in 1975 when Home Box Office, Time Inc.'s pay cable subsidiary, announced plans to extend its service from the Northeast to nationwide via satellite.

The next year, 1976, Ted Turner, owner of two TV stations, begins using the satellite to distribute the signal of his Atlanta UHF station, WTCG, to cable systems across the country, dubbing it the "superstation." Buoyed by his success, in 1978 Turner announced plans to sell his other station, WRET-TV Charlotte, North Carolina, and use the money to start CNN, a 24-hour cable news service to be distributed by satellite.

Later in 1978, the FCC moved to enhance the competitive environment of satellite-distributed TV superstations by endorsing an "open entry" policy for the resale carriers that wished to feed local stations to cable television systems. Then in April 1979, a former Nixon administration staffer and cable trade reporter, Brian Lamb, persuaded a critical mass of the cable industry to support the Cable Satellite Public Affairs Network (C-SPAN). The new service provided satellite gavel-to-gavel television coverage of the House of Representatives proceedings.

1980s: The Rise of Cable Television

Building on the innovation of satellite delivery pioneered by HBO, the cable industry began to be viewed as more than just a relay service for TV stations. Now it could offer alternative channels. (The strategy paid off in increased demand: in 1980 cable had 20 percent penetration of U.S. TV households and by the end of the decade it was seen in 60 percent.) Ted Turner launched his Cable News Network on June 1, 1980, sending 24-hour-a-day news to 172 cable systems from its Atlanta studios.

Innovations and new cable channels appeared in almost every year of the decade. Most pay cable channels begin to scramble their satellite signals and in 1998 AT&T demonstrates laser-modulated fiber optics offering wider bandwidth and greater signal quality than coaxial cable.

1990s: The Rise of Mega-Media Companies

The modern media era really began in 1989 with the announcement that Time Inc. and Warner Communications Inc. had agreed to swap stock and merge into what would be the largest media and entertainment company in the world. The media landscape would only continue to change, and at an accelerating pace. A deregulatory wind was blowing through Washington in the 1990s.

In 1992 the FCC raised the cap on the number of radio stations a company could own from 12 AM and 12 FM to 18 of each and also permitted two of each service to be co-located in the same large market. A flurry of duopoly deals followed. The next year, the commission gave the big three TV networks a conditional OK to enter the lucrative network rerun business, when it lifts its financial interest and syndication rules (full repeal comes in 1995).

The year 1994 sees the radio caps raised again, to 20 AM and 20 FM. The FCC also said that it was time to acknowledge the dramatic changes in the video marketplace with equally dramatic deregulation of its TV ownership policies. The commission proposed new rules that would allow broadcasters to own as many stations as they want as long as they remain within the cap on total national audience reach. At the same time, the commission proposed raising that cap of 25 percent of the nation's TV households by 5 percent every three years to a maximum of 50 percent.

In another mega-merger, Viacom buys Paramount Communications. This is quickly followed in 1995 by announcements of Disney's $18.5 billion purchase of ABC, Time Warner's purchase of Turner Broadcasting System in an $8 billion stock swap, Westinghouse's $5.4 billion purchase of CBS, and Comcast's $1.6 billion purchase of the Scripps cable holdings. The big four TV networks get more competition in 1995 as The WB and United Paramount Network debut.

More deregulation appears with the Telecommunications Act of 1996, which eliminated cable rate regulation and the bar to telephone company-cable competition, resulting in AT&T and other phone companies offering packages that included cable, telephone, and Internet services and cable companies offering phone service. (This resulted in AT&T becoming the country's largest cable operator in 1999 when it bought TCI for $50 billion.) The 1996 act also eliminated the cap on radio station ownership and companies wasted no time in expanding their portfolios both through acquisitions and mergers (including Westinghouse/CBS-Infinity, which merged in 1996 in a $4.9 billion deal).

In 1997, TV group owner Bud Paxson began the seventh broadcast TV network with his PAX TV. Radio deals continued to proliferate, with a huge upsurge in station sales in 1998 and the mega-merger of Clear Channel's $6.35 billion purchase of Jacor.

The decade ends in a flurry of activity in 1999 with the FCC allowing ownership of two TV and up to six radio stations in top markets. AT&T bought Media One, Viacom spent $36 billion for CBS and the two largest radio groups, Clear Channel and AMFM, combined, leaving the merged Clear Channel owning 830 stations.

2000s: The Rise of Digital

Digital technology began to make a major impact. Cable used it to increase significantly the number of channels it offered to justify higher monthly fees and to meet the competition from channel-rich satellite technology. In contrast to cable, TV broadcasting has been slow to put digital technology to work. With digital, TV broadcasters could offer multiple channels of conventional TV, HDTV, or a little bit of both. But digital TV broadcasting has been mired in standards disputes and the resulting chicken-and-egg problem of receivers and programming: consumers are slow to replace their analog sets if there is little digital programming to watch and producers are hesitant to invest in new production equipment if few viewers are watching. But the transition continues.

The first digital TV station, WRAL-DT Raleigh, North Carolina, went on the air in 1996 and the FCC made digital channel assignments to all analog stations in 1997. On September 8, 2008 commercial broadcasters serving the Wilmington, NC TV market made the transition from analog to digital television. Then some stations decided to make an early change to digital TV for various reasons. On January 15, 2009 Hawaii's full-power TV stations made the switch to digital TV. The date all stations were to switch to digital TV, February 17, 2009, was changed to June 12, 2009 give everybody more time to get ready for the digital transition. Finally, on June 12, 2009, the historic switch to digital television occurred. On the June 12, 2009 date the FCC reported 971 full-power TV stations made the switch to digital television.

The Internet became a TV medium, with the quality and quantity of video available over the Web rapidly increasing throughout the first half of the decade. A major milestone was reached in October 2005 when Disney announced it would make some of its most popular ABC primetime shows available to users of the new Apple Video iPods. The price of each video download: $1.99. The announcement prompted the other big media companies to begin repurposing primetime programming on the net. By the summer of 2006, all recognized that the Web would eventually become a TV medium at least the equal of broadcasting, cable, and satellite.

The first push for digital audio (other than that delivered by DBS or digital cable) is satellite-delivered radio. Sirius XM Radio Inc. offers nationwide subscription service to receivers in cars and homes. Terrestrial radio is just beginning to make the digital transition. In-band, on-channel (IBOC) technology developed by iBiquity Digital Corp. allows radio stations to overlay their analog service with a digital one. As of August 2009, approximately 1,922 radio stations were on the air with digital radio technology. Over 900 radio stations offer new FM multicast channels (HD2/HD3). There are more than 1,070 multicast channels. HD Radio is the brand name iBiquity uses for its digital AM and FM radio technology. HD is part of the brand name and does not stand for either high definition or hybrid digital. (HD Radio is a proprietary trademark of iBiquity Digital Corp.) Much of the HD Radio information is available on the www.hdradio.com web site. The HD Digital Radio Alliance at www.hdradioalliance.com was actively promoting the digital radio technology.

A Chronology of the Electronic Media

From Isaac Newton to Janet Jackson: A Chronology of the Electronic Media

By Mark K. Miller, freelance writer and former managing editor, *Broadcasting & Cable* magazine

1666

Sir Isaac Newton performs basic experiments on the spectrum.

1794

Allessandro Volta of Italy invents the voltaic cell, a primitive battery.

1827

George Ohm of Germany shows the relationship between resistance, amperage and voltage. Sir Charles Wheatstone of England invents an acoustic device to amplify sounds that he calls a "microphone."

1844

Samuel F.B. Morse tests the first telegraph with "What hath God wrought?" message sent on link between Washington and Baltimore.

1858

First trans-Atlantic cable completed. President James Buchanan and Queen Victoria exchange greetings.

1867

James Clerk Maxwell of Scotland develops the electromagnetic theory.

1875

George R. Carey of Boston proposes a system that would transmit and receive moving visual images electrically.

1876

Alexander Graham Bell invents the telephone.

1877

Thomas A. Edison applies for a patent on a "phonograph or talking machine."

1878

Sir William Cooke of England passes high voltage through a wire in a sealed glass tube, causing a pinkish glow—evidence of cathode rays. It's the first step toward the development of the vacuum tubes.

1884

Paul Nipkow of Germany patents a mechanical, rotating facsimile scanning disk.

1886

Heinrich Hertz of Germany proves that electromagnetic waves can be transmitted through space at the speed of light and can be reflected and refracted.

1895

Wilheim Conrad Roentgen of Germany discovers X-rays.

Guglielmo Marconi sends and receives his first wireless signals across his father's estate at Bologna, Italy.

1896

Marconi applies for British patent for wireless telegraphy. He receives an American patent a year later.

1899

Marconi flashes the first wireless signals across the English Channel.

1900

Constantin Perskyi (France) coins the word television at the International Electricity Congress, part of the 1900 Paris Exhibition.

1901

Marconi at Newfoundland, Canada, receives the first trans-Atlantic signal, the letter "S," transmitted from Poldhu, England.

1906

Dr. Lee de Forest invents the audion, a three-element vacuum tube, having a filament, plate and grid, which leads to the amplification of radio signals.

1910

Enrico Caruso and Emmy Destinn, singing backstage at the Metropolitan Opera House in New York, broadcast through the De Forest radiophone and are heard by an operator on the SS Avon at sea and by wireless amateurs in Connecticut.

United States approves an act requiring certain passenger ships to carry wireless equipment and operators.

1912

The *Titanic* disaster proves the value of wireless at sea; 705 lives saved. Jack Phillips and Harold Bride are the ship's wireless operators.

1920

On August 20, 8MK (later, WWJ) in Detroit, owned by the Detroit News, starts what is later claimed to be regular broadcasting.

The Westinghouse Co.'s KDKA(AM) Pittsburgh broadcasts the Harding-Cox election on returns November 2 as the country's first licensed commercial radio station.

1921

The Dempsey-Carpentier fight is broadcast from Boyle's Thirty Acres in Jersey City through a temporarily installed transmitter at Hoboken, New Jersey. Major J. Andrew White was the announcer. This event gave radio a tremendous boost.

1922

The superheterodyne circuit is demonstrated by its inventor, Edwin H. Armstrong. It dramatically improves AM radio reception.

WEAF(AM) New York broadcasts what is claimed to be the first commercially sponsored program on September 7. The advertiser is the Queensborough Corp., a real estate organization.

WOI(AM) Ames, Iowa, goes on air as the country's first licensed educational station.

1923

Dr. Vladimir K. Zworykin files for a U.S. patent for an all-electronic television system.

A "chain" broadcast features a telephone tie-up between WEAF(AM) New York and WNAC(AM) Boston.

1924

The Republican convention in Cleveland and the Democratic convention in New York are broadcast over networks.

1925

President Calvin Coolidge's inaugural ceremony is broadcast by 24 stations in a transcontinental network.

1926

President Coolidge signs the Dill-White Radio Bill creating the Federal Radio Commission and ending the chaos on the radio dial caused by the wild growth of broadcasting.

National Broadcasting Co. is organized on November 1 with WEAF(AM) and WJZ(AM) in New York as key stations and Merlin Hall Aylesworth as president. Headquarters are at 711 Fifth Ave., New York.

1927

The Columbia Broadcasting System goes on the air with a basic network of 16 stations. Major J. Andrew White is president.

Philo T. Farnsworth applies for a patent on his image dissector television camera tube.

1928

NBC establishes a permanent coast-to-coast radio network.

1929

William S. Paley, 27, is elected president of the Columbia Broadcasting System.

Vladimir Zworykin demonstrates his kinescope or cathode ray television receiver before a meeting of the Institute of Radio Engineers on November 19.

1930

Experimental TV station W2XBS is opened by National Broadcasting Co. in New York.

1931

Experimental television station W2XAB is opened by Columbia Broadcasting System in New York.

The first issue of *Broadcasting* magazine appears on October 15.

The National Association of Broadcasters reports that more than half of the nation's radio stations are operating without a profit.

1932

CBS, NBC, and New York area stations, notably WOR(AM), go into round-the-clock operations to cover the Lindbergh kidnapping, radio's biggest spot-news reporting job to date.

NBC lifts its ban on recorded programs for its owned-and-operated stations, but continues to bar them from network use.

NBC withdraws prohibitions against price mentions

on the air during daytime hours; two months later, both NBC and CBS allow price mentions at nighttime as well.

1933

Associated Press members vote to ban network broadcasts of AP news and to restrict local broadcasts to bulletins to stipulated times with air credit to member newspapers.

The American Newspaper Publishers Association declares radio program schedules are advertising and should be published only if paid for.

CBS assigns publicity director Paul White to organize a nationwide staff to collect news for network broadcast. General Mills agrees to sponsor twice-daily newscasts.

1934

Congress passes the Communication Act, which, among other things, replaces the Federal Radio Commission with the Federal Communications Commission.

1935

RCA announces that it is taking television out of the laboratory for a $1 million field-test program.

1936

A year of TV demonstrations begins in June with the Don Lee Broadcasting System's first public exhibition of cathode ray television in the U.S., using a system developed by Don Lee TV director Harry Lubcke. One month later, RCA demonstrates its system of TV with transmissions from the Empire State Building, and Philco follows with a seven-mile transmission in August.

FM (frequency modulation) broadcasting, a new radio system invented by Major Edwin H. Armstrong, is described at an FCC hearing as static-free, free from fading and cross-talk, having uniformity day and night in all seasons and greater fidelity of reproduction.

A.C. Nielsen, revealing his firm's acquisition of the MIT-developed "Audimeter," proposes a metered tuning method of measuring radio audience size.

1937

WLS(AM) Chicago recording team of Herb Morrison, announcer, and Charles Nehlsen, engineer, on a routine assignment at Lakehurst, New Jersey, records an on-the-spot account of the explosion of the German dirigible Hindenburg. NBC breaks its rigid rule against recordings to put it on the network.

1938

Broadcasting publishes the first facsimile newspaper in a demonstration at the National Association of Broadcasters convention.

1939

After 15 years of litigation, the patent for iconoscope-kinescope tubes, the basis for electronic television, is granted to Dr. Vladimir Zworykin.

A telecast of the opening ceremonies of the New York World's Fair marks the start of a regular daily television schedule by RCA-NBC in New York.

The first baseball game ever televised—Princeton vs. Columbia—appears on NBC.

1940

The FCC authorizes commercial operation of FM, but puts TV back into the laboratory until the industry reaches an agreement on technical standards.

CBS demonstrates a system of color TV developed by its chief TV engineer, Dr. Peter Goldmark.

1941

Bulova Watch Co., Sun Oil Co., Lever Bros. and Procter & Gamble sign as sponsors of the first commercial telecasts on July 1 over NBC's WNBT(TV) New York (until then W2XBS).

President Roosevelt's broadcast to the nation on December 9, the day after war is declared, has the largest audience in radio history—about 90 million listeners.

1942

The Advertising Council is organized by advertisers, agencies, and media to put the talents and techniques of advertising at the disposal of the government to inspire and instruct the public concerning the war effort.

1943

Edward J. Noble buys the Blue Network from RCA for $8 million in cash. RCA had two networks, NBC Red and NBC Blue.

1944

With the FCC approval of the transfer of owned stations, the Blue Network assumes the name of its holding company, the American Broadcasting Co.

1945

Pooled coverage of the Nazi surrender in May brings the American people full details of the end of the war in Europe. Peace heralds a communications boom: Not only will programming restrictions end, but new station construction, frozen for the duration, will proceed at an explosive pace soon after V-J Day in August.

1946

A telecast of the Louis-Conn heavyweight title fight, sponsored by Gillette Safety Razor Co. on a four-city hookup, reaches an estimated 100,000 viewers and convinces skeptics that television is here to stay.

RCA demonstrates its all-electronic system of color TV.

Bristol-Myers is the first advertiser to sponsor a television network program—Geographically Speaking—which debuted October 27 on NBC TV's two-station network.

1947

Radio comedian Fred Allen uses a gag, which NBC had ruled out, about network vice presidents, and is cut off the air while he tells it. The story is front-page news across the country as the sponsor's ad agency demands a rebate for 35 seconds of dead air.

1948

Texaco puts an old-style vaudeville show on NBC TV; the hour-long series stars Milton Berle.

1949

The Academy of Television Arts & Sciences presents the first Emmy Awards at ceremonies televised by KTSL(TV) Los Angeles.

1950

General Foods drops actress Jean Muir, who denies any communist affiliations or sympathies, from the cast of The Aldrich Family (NBC TV) after protests against her appearance by "a number of groups." The Joint Committee Against Communism claims credit for her removal, announcing a drive to "cleanse" radio and television of pro-communist actors, directors, and writers.

The FCC approves CBS's color TV system, effective November 20. The network promises 20 hours of color programming a week within two months. TV set manufacturers are divided, however, over whether to make sets, since the CBS system is incompatible with black-and-white broadcasts. In the meantime, RCA continues work on its color system.

1951

Witness Frank Costello's hands provide TV's picture of the week as he refuses to expose his face to cameras covering New York hearings on organized crime of the Senate Crime Investigation Committee, chaired by Senator Estes Kefauver (D-Tenn.)

Sixteen advertisers sponsor the first commercial color telecast, an hour-long program on a five-station East Coast CBS TV hook-up.

Bing Crosby Enterprises announces the development of a system for recording video and audio programs on magnetic tape. The pictures shown at demonstrations are described as "hazy" but "viewable." A year later the images are described as improved "more than 20-fold."

1952

By rushing equipment across the country, from Bridgeport, Connecticut, to Portland, Oregon, KPTV(TV) Portland goes on the air as the first commercial UHF TV station.

1953

With the end of daylight-saving time, CBS TV and NBC TV inaugurate "hot kinescope" systems to put programs on the air on the West Coast at the same clock hour as in the East.

RCA demonstrates black-and-white and color TV programs recorded on magnetic tape. RCA-NBC Board Chairman David Sarnoff says two years of finishing touches are needed before the system is ready for market.

The FCC approves RCA's compatible (with black-and-white transmission) color TV standards. System supplants the incompatible CBS system.

1954

CBS President Frank Stanton broadcasts the first network editorial, urging that radio and TV be allowed to cover congressional hearings.

1955

A contract between the DuMont TV network and Jackie Gleason Enterprises calls for Gleason's The Honeymooners to be done as a filmed program for CBS TV on Saturday nights.

1956

Ampex Corp. unveils the first practical videotape recorder at the National Association of Radio and Television Broadcasters convention in Chicago. The company takes in $4 million in orders.

1957

Videotape recorders are seen as the solution to the TV networks' daylight-saving time problems.

1958

Subliminal TV messages are put under the spotlight at hearings in Los Angeles and Washington.

The BBDO ad agency converts live commercials to videotape.

1959

Sixty-eight TV stations defy the broadcasters' code of conduct by refusing to drop Preparation H commercials.

The quiz show scandal climaxes when famed Twenty-One prizewinner Charles Van Doren admits to a House committee that he had been provided with answers and strategies in advance. The sad ending to the quiz show era prompts cancellation of big-prize shows and vows by NBC and CBS to end deceptive practices.

1960

A satellite sends weather reports back from a 400-mile-high orbit.

RKO-Zenith plans a $10 million test of an on-air pay TV system in Hartford, Connecticut.

Sam Goldwyn offers a package of movies to television.

The last daytime serial on network radio ends.

The opening Kennedy-Nixon debate attracts the largest TV audience to date.

1961

FCC Chairman Newton Minnow shakes up the National Association of Broadcasters convention with his assessment of TV programming: Although it occasionally shines with programs like *Twilight Zone* and *CBS Reports*, it is, more than anything, from sign-on to sign-off "a vast wasteland."

Off-network shows become popular as syndicated fare.

The Ampex "electronic editor" permits inserts and additions to be made in videotape without physical splices.

ABC TV engineers develop a process for the immediate playback of videotape recordings in slow motion.

1962

John Glenn's orbital space flight is seen by 135 million TV viewers.

Telstar, AT&T's orbiting satellite, provides a glamorous debut for global television.

1963

Astronaut Gordon Cooper sends back the first TV pictures from space.

All radio and TV network commercials and entertainment programming are canceled following the assassination of President Kennedy. In the same week, the first trans-Pacific broadcast via satellite previews live TV coverage of the 1964 Olympics in Tokyo.

1964

The government and the tobacco companies each ponder their next move after the surgeon general's report links cigarette smoking and lung cancer. Within weeks, American Tobacco drops sports broadcasts, radio stations begin to ban cigarette ads and CBS TV orders a de-emphasis of cigarette use on programs.

1965

Early Bird, the first commercial communications satellite, goes into stationary orbit, opening trans-Atlantic circuits for TV use.

1966

Fred W. Friendly quits as president of CBS News when his new boss, John Schneider, CBS group vice president for broadcasting, cancels coverage of a Senate hearing on the Vietnam War and runs a rerun of *I Love Lucy* instead.

Network TV viewers see live close-up pictures of the moon—sent back by Surveyor I—as they come into the Jet Propulsion Laboratory.

1967

ABC Radio introduces a radical plan: four networks instead of one, each tailored to suit different station formats.

President Johnson signs the Public Broadcasting Act into law, establishing the Corporation for Public Broadcasting, federal funding mechanism.

1968

The Children's Television Workshop is created by the Ford Foundation, the Carnegie Corp., and the Office of Education to develop a 26-week series of hour-long color programs for preschool children. *Sesame Street* is the result.

The U.S. Supreme Court gives the FCC jurisdiction over all cable TV systems.

Pictures taken inside Apollo 7 in flight and sent back to Earth revive public interest in the space program.

NBC TV earns the life-long ire of sports fans when it cuts off the end of a Jets-Raiders game to air its made-for-TV movie *Heidi*. Viewers miss the Raiders' two-touchdowns-in-nine-seconds defeat of the Jets.

1969

The Corporation for Public Broadcasting plans the creation of the Public Broadcasting Service to distribute programming to noncommercial TV stations.

In the same week that ABC-TV announces its $8 million *Monday Night Football* deal (games to begin in 1970), Apollo 10 sends back the first color TV pictures of the moon and of Earth from the moon.

The world watches live coverage of Neil Armstrong's walk on the moon.

1970

House and Senate conferees agree on legislation to outlaw cigarette advertising on radio and TV, but change the bill's effective date from January 1, 1971, to January 2, so commercials can appear on New Year's Day football telecasts.

The FCC rules that TV stations in the top 50 markets cannot accept more than three hours of network programming between 7 and 11 p.m., and bars them from domestic syndication and from acquiring subsidiary rights in independently produced programs.

1971

National Public Radio debuts with a 90-station interconnected lineup.

1972

Judge Benjamin Hooks of Memphis, Tennessee, is nominated to the FCC. He becomes the first black to serve on a federal regulatory agency.

Home Box Office Inc., New York, is formed as a subsidiary of Sterling Communications to provide pay-cable TV systems with live and film programming.

1973

Western Union becomes the first company to receive federal permission to launch a commercial communications satellite in the U.S.

Broadcast media around the world open their coverage of the Senate select committee's investigation of the Watergate scandal.

1974

RCA inaugurates the nation's first domestic satellite communications service, using a Canadian satellite.

More than 110 million viewers watch President Nixon announce his resignation.

1975

Home Box Office, Time Inc.'s pay cable subsidiary, announces that it will inaugurate a satellite delivery network in the fall.

1976

Ampex Corp. and CBS develop the electronic still-store system, which uses a digital recording technique to store 1,500 frames in random mode, each accessible in 100 milliseconds.

Cable network launches include Showtime and Univision.

1977

ABC's eight-day telecast of the miniseries *Roots* becomes the most watched program in television history, with ratings in the mid-40s and shares in the mid-60s. Eighty million people watch at least some part of the final episode.

Sony unveils its Betamax videocassette in August and later the same month RCA introduces its SelectaVision home videotape recorder.

1978

The U.S. Supreme Court upholds the FCC in the "seven dirty words" case involving Pacifica's WBAI(FM) New York. The ruling says the FCC may regulate and punish for the broadcasting of "indecent material."

1979

Ampex demonstrates its digital videotape recorder at the Society of Motion Picture and Television Engineers conference in San Francisco in February. Sony unveils its version two months later.

Cable network launches include C-SPAN, ESPN, The Movie Channel, and Nickelodeon.

1980

"Who Shot J.R.?" episode of *Dallas* garners the highest rating for any program in modern TV history, with a 53.3 rating and a 76 share.

Cable network launches include Cable News Network, Black Entertainment Television, the Learning Channel, Bravo, and USA Network.

1981

With five ENG cameras rolling, the shooting of President Reagan becomes history's most heavily covered assassination attempt.

The first U.S. demonstration of high-definition television (HDTV) takes place at the annual convention of the Society of Motion Picture and Television Engineers. The Japanese Broadcasting Corp.'s (NHK) 1,125-line analog system draws raves from engineers and filmmakers.

Cable network launches include MTV: Music Television and the Eternal Word Television Network.

1982

Having reached a settlement with the Justice Department to divest itself of its 23 local telephone companies, communications giant AT&T hopes to lead the country into the "information age." The National Cable Television Association, Congress, and the FCC wonder what the agreement has wrought.

Cable network launches include the Weather Channel and the Playboy Channel.

1983

Reagan appointee Mark Fowler, chairman of the FCC, tells a common carrier conference that the U.S. is heading toward a regulation-free telecommunications marketplace.

In February, the two-and-a-half-hour final episode of CBS's *M*A*S*H* is the most watched program in TV history, garnering a 60.3 rating and a 77 share.

Cable network launches include the Disney Channel and Country Music Television.

1984

The U.S. Supreme Court rules that home videotaping is legal.

Congress passes the Cable Telecommunications Act of 1984, landmark legislation deregulating cable. Law accelerates the growth of cable.

Cable network launches include the Arts & Entertainment Network (A&E), American Movie Classics, and Lifetime.

1985

Ted Turner makes inquiries at the FCC about a possible takeover of CBS. Later, in March, media company Capital Cities Communications purchases ABC for $3.5 billion. Turner's efforts to acquire CBS fail by the end of July, when a federal judge approves the network's stock buyback plan.

The Advanced Television Services Committee (ATSC) votes in favor of the NHK HDTV standard: 1,125 lines, 60 fields, 2:1 interlace, 5.33:3 ratio. This standard is put forward by the U.S. to the International Radio Consultative Committee (CCIR) for consideration as the international standard. The CCIR adopts the recommendation later in the year.

Having lost his bid to buy CBS, Ted Turner makes a $1.5 billion offer for MGM/UA.

Cable network launches include The Discovery Channel, Home Shopping Network, and VH-1.

1986

MGM and Color Systems Technology sign an agreement for the conversion of 100 of the studio's black-and-white films to color.

Cable network launches include C-SPAN2 and QVC.

1987

Fox Broadcasting Co. introduces its primetime lineup with 108 affiliates in its bid to become the fourth major U.S. commercial television network.

The National Association of Broadcasters and the Association for Maximum Service Television broadcast HDTV over standard TV channels during public demonstrations in Washington.

President Reagan vetoes legislation to write the fairness doctrine into law. The doctrine required broadcast stations to allow opposing views of issues, but critics claimed that it discouraged open debate.

Cable network launches include Movietime (renamed E! Entertainment Television in 1990), The Travel Channel, and Telemundo.

1988

The FCC adopts preliminary ground rules for HDTV. It tentatively decides to require HDTV broadcasts to be compatible with NTSC sets and says it will not make additional spectrum available outside the VHF and UHF bands for HDTV because there is enough already available to accommodate the service.

Cable network launches include Turner Network Television.

1989

Time Inc. and Warner Communications agree to swap stock and merge into what will be world's largest media and entertainment company.

1990

Digital audio broadcasting is demonstrated at the National Association of Broadcasters convention and is heralded as the HDTV of radio.

General Instrument revolutionizes the development of high-definition television by proposing an all-digital system. The video compression system also has implications for satellite transmissions.

Cable network launches include CNBC and The Inspiration Network (INSP).

1991

The U.S. air attack on Iraq begins January 16 with dramatic live coverage from network reporters in Baghdad. CNN is the lone network to maintain contact with its Baghdad reporters through the night.

Free to move around Moscow and ready to commit resources to coverage, television and radio provide gripping details of the short-lived Soviet coup and the collapse of communism in the Soviet Union. During his detention in the Crimea, Soviet President Mikhail Gorbachev keeps track of events by listening to the BBC, Voice of America, and Radio Liberty.

Cable network launches include Court TV, Comedy Central, and Encore.

1992

In March, the Supreme Court let stand an appeals court ruling that struck down the FCC's around-the-clock ban on broadcast indecency as unconstitutional and requiring the commission to establish a safe harbor—a part of the day when few children are tuning in and during which radio and TV stations may broadcast without fear of FCC sanctions for indecency.

General Instrument and MIT show the first over-the-air digital HDTV transmission to Washington lawmakers and regulators. The 12-minute transmission of 1,050-line

video was broadcast by noncommercial WETA-TV Washington.

The FCC raises the limit on radio stations a single company may own from 12 AM and 12 FM to 30 of each, then backpedals and lowers the caps to 18 each, with no more than two AMs and two FMs in large markets and three stations—only two in the same service—in small markets.

Fox expands its programming lineup to seven nights a week, ending its status as a "weblet" and becoming the fourth full-fledged commercial TV network in the U.S.

The FCC unanimously approves allowing broadcast TV networks to purchase cable systems that serve no more than 10 percent of U.S. homes and up to 50 percent of a particular market's homes.

The FCC tells TV broadcasters they will have five years to begin broadcasting in HDTV once the agency adopts a standard and makes channels available.

Cable network launches include The Cartoon Network and the Sci Fi Channel.

1993

Warner Bros. announces it will launch a fifth broadcast TV network in 1994.

The FCC expands the AM band's upper limit from 1605 kHz to 1705 kHz.

General Instrument, Zenith, AT&T, and the ATRC join forces as the "Grand Alliance" to develop a single HDTV system. Later in the year, the Grand Alliance announces its support of the emerging MPEG-2 digital compression HD system: six-channel, CD-quality Dolby AC-3 music system; 1,920-pixel by 1,080-line interlaced scanning picture; and progressive scanning.

Paramount Communications begins talks with TV stations about forming a fifth broadcast TV network.

Southwestern Bell and Cox Cable form a $4.9-billion partnership.

Cable network launches include ESPN2 and the Television Food Network.

1994

Two companies, Hubbard's United States Satellite Broadcasting and Hughes's DirecTV, begin direct broadcast satellite transmissions to 18-inch home dish antennas from a shared satellite.

Paramount and Viacom merge in a deal worth $9.2 billion, forming the world's most powerful entertainment company. Viacom's Sumner Redstone becomes the new company's chairman. Later in the year, Viacom adds Blockbuster Entertainment to its portfolio.

Cable network launches include FX, Home & Garden TV, the International Film Channel, Starz!, Trio, the Game Show Network, and Turner Classic Movies.

1995

Seagram pays $7 billion for the 80 percent of Hollywood studio MCA Inc. owned by Matsushita Electric Industrial Co. Seagram is controlled by the Bronfman family and is headed by President/CEO Edgar Bronfman Jr.

The Megamedia Age begins when, in the same week, Walt Disney Co. announces it is buying Capital Cities/ABC for $18.5 billion and then Westinghouse Electric Co. releases word of its purchase of CBS Inc. for $5.4 billion.

Time Warner and Turner Broadcasting System agree to merge in an $8 billion stock swap deal.

Live television coverage of the verdict in the O.J. Simpson murder trial sets viewing records when 150 million people watch the jury return a "not guilty" verdict.

Microsoft buys 50 percent stake in NBC's cable channel America's Talking for $250 million. AT's talk format will be dropped and the network will become a news operation after being rechristened MSNBC.

The FCC repeals its Prime Time Access and Fin-Syn rules. These rules restricted the major broadcast networks from owning interest in their own primetime programming.

Cable network launches include CNN/fn, The Golf Channel, Great American Country, the History Channel, and the Outdoor Life Network.

1996

Congress passes—and President Clinton signs—the Telecommunications Act of 1996, the first major overhaul of telecommunication legislation since 1934. Its key provisions include: replacing the 12-station TV ownership limit with a national home coverage cap of 35 percent; eliminating the national ownership limits on radio stations and allowing one company to own different numbers of stations locally, depending on the market size; requiring TV sets sold in the U.S. to be equipped with a V-chip to enable blocking of channels based on encoded ratings; deregulating cable rates.

Westinghouse/CBS buys Infinity Broadcasting for $4.9 billion, creating the country's largest radio station group in terms of earnings. The deal results in Westinghouse/CBS owning 83 radio stations in 15 markets.

The FCC releases its first list of proposed digital TV channel assignments for all U.S. analog television stations.

In July, WRAL-HD Raleigh, North Carolina, begins HDTV transmission on channel 32 under an experimental FCC license, making it the first HDTV station to broadcast in the U.S.

The Washington-based Model HDTV Station Project demonstrates live, over-the-air digital TV transmission and reception. A few months later, it bounces digital signals off a satellite and displays them on a receiver.

Cable network launches include Animal Planet, Fox News Channel, MSNBC, the Sundance Channel, and TVLand.

1997

After several starts and stops, the TV industry unveils content-based V-chip ratings to mixed reviews. Recalcitrant NBC maintains it will not implement the new ratings.

Paxson Communications chief Bud Paxson announces plans to launch a new television network, Pax Net, using his 73 owned UHF stations as a base and airing family friendly off-network programming.

ABC Television Network President Preston Padden and Sinclair Broadcasting President David Smith say broadcasters ought to consider using DTV channels for broadcasting multiple channels of conventional TV rather than a single channel of HDTV.

Hearst Corp. (8 TVs) and Argyle Television (6 TVs) join their TV stations and create a new company, Hearst-Argyle Television Inc., that is valued at $1.8 billion.

The FCC gives TV broadcasters a second channel for the delivery of HDTV and other digital services and said that all network affiliates in the top 10 markets have 24 months to start broadcasting a digital signal; those in markets 11-30 have 30 months; all other commercial stations have five years. Noncommercial broadcasters have six.

DTV service provider EchoStar plans to launch two satellites that will give it the ability to provide local broadcast TV signals to about 43 percent of the U.S.

Cable network launches include WE.

1998

The National Association of Broadcasters agrees to support plans by satellite TV providers to retransmit local TV station signals into their markets as long as the satellite services carry all a market's signals.

At 2:17 p.m. on February 27, WFAA-TV Dallas broadcast what it claims is the first non-experimental HDTV signal (in 1080i, 16:9 format). The broadcast began with a half-hour of taped HD programming, followed by a live simulcast of the station's NTSC programming that was upconverted to HDTV. The next month, Sinclair Broadcasting becomes the first TV group owner to broadcast multiple digital channels.

AT&T pays $50 billion for cable system giant Tele-Communications Inc.

Paxson Communications launches its broadcast television network, now called Pax TV, with a lineup of 90 stations covering about 75 percent of U.S. TV homes.

Radio group owner Clear Channel Communications purchases competitor Jacor Communications for $4.4 billion. The deal gives Clear Channel 453 stations in 101 markets. The year's other big deals include: Chancellor Media's purchase of Capstar Broadcasting for $3.9 billion; Hearst-Argyle Television's purchase of Pulitzer Broadcasting for $1.85 billion; Chancellor's

purchase of LIN Television for $1.5 billion; and Sinclair Broadcast Group's purchase of Sullivan Broadcasting for $1 billion.

CBS is the first broadcast TV network to air a live HDTV sports event with its Nov. 8 telecast of the New York Jets-Buffalo Bills NFL game. It is carried by CBS stations in New York; Philadelphia; Washington; Cincinnati; Charlotte, North Carolina; Raleigh, North Carolina; and Columbus, Ohio.

Hughes Electronics Corp., parent of DBS provider DirecTV, announces deal to buy rival U.S. Satellite Broadcasting from Hubbard Broadcasting for $1.3 billion. The DBS business now has three providers: DirecTV, EchoStar, and Primestar.

Cable network launches include BBC America, the Biography Channel, Cinemax, Tech TV, and Toon Disney.

1999

Hughes Electronics Corp., parent of DBS provider DirecTV, buys rival Primestar for $1.1 billion plus stock. The DBS business now has two providers: DirecTV and EchoStar.

Paxson Broadcasting sells its 30 percent interest in The Travel Channel to the cable channel's 70 percent owner, Discovery Channel.

MSO Comcast offers $58 billion for MediaOne Group's cable systems. AT&T then comes in with a $69 billion offer that has AT&T swapping and selling Comcast systems with 2 million subscribers for roughly $9 billion. In return, Comcast agrees to withdraw its $58 billion offer.

CBS pays $2.5 billion for syndication giant King World Productions, whose properties include the hit shows *Oprah, Wheel of Fortune,* and *Jeopardy!*

FCC votes to allow a broadcaster to own two TV stations in a market under certain conditions and liberalizes its radio/TV cross-ownership restrictions. A flood of station deals follow.

Viacom Inc. buys CBS Corp. for $36 billion, merging Viacom's Paramount Station Group, UPN network, cable networks, and other properties, with those of CBS.

Clear Channel Communications pays $23.5 billion in stock and assumption of debt for the 443 radio stations of AMFM Inc., the country's largest radio broadcaster. Clear Channel will have to divest about 100 stations to comply with FCC and Justice Department regulations. Those spinoffs will bring Clear Channel $4.3 billion.

Legislation takes affect allowing satellite delivery of local television stations in their markets, increasing DBS providers' ability to compete with cable.

2000

America Online Inc. and Time Warner merge in a deal worth $181 billion. The merged company, AOL Time Warner, combines the company that serves the largest number of Internet users with the largest producer of TV shows and movies and cable programming, plus cable systems passing 20 percent of U.S. homes.

Tribune Co. buys Times Mirror Co. for $6.5 billion, acquiring seven daily newspapers and various magazines. The deal will give Tribune co-ownership of TV stations and major daily newspapers in the top three markets and the assets to sell packages of multimedia advertising to clients on national, regional, and local levels.

Harry Pappas, head of Pappas Television, the country's largest privately held TV station group, announces plans to launch Azteca America, the third U.S. Hispanic television network (Univision and Telemundo are the others) in 2001.

Cable network launches include Oxygen.

2001

FCC approves the $5.4-billion sale of Chris-Craft Broadcasting's ten TV stations to Fox Television.

DBS operator EchoStar Communications engineers a $26-billion bid for competitor DirecTV, owned by GM's Hughes Corp. The move follows attempts by Rupert Murdoch's News Corp. to acquire DirecTV. But regulatory reviews keep the deal in limbo.

XM Satellite Radio begins broadcasting a nationwide radio service of 200 channels from two satellites—"Rock" and "Roll"—in orbit above the equator. The Washington-based company charges subscribers $9.95 a month for the service. A rival, New York-based Sirius Satellite Radio, plans to launch a similar service later in the year.

The September 11 terrorist attacks on New York and Washington result in around-the-clock news coverage, dropping commercials. It's estimated that the networks lost $200 million-$300 million in the first four days of coverage. Four FM and nine New York TV stations whose antennas were on top of the World Trade Center are knocked off the air and several stations lost employees who had been manning the transmitters in Tower 1. Across the country, broadcasters raised money and arranged blood drives. The fall TV season is delayed, late-night talk/comedy shows are put on hiatus, the Emmy Awards are postponed, and several industry gatherings are canceled.

NBC buys Telemundo, the No. 2 U.S. Spanish-language TV network, for $2.7 billion.

Comcast negotiates $72 billion merger with rival cable operator AT&T Broadband, topping bids by AOL Time Warner and Cox Communications.

Cable network launches include ABC Family, Hallmark Channel, and National Geographic Television.

2002

Sirius Satellite Radio launches its satellite-delivered subscription radio service in four markets in February, then rolls out nationally in July. Sirius follows XM Satellite Radio to become the second U.S. satellite radio programmer.

Prompted by lawsuits from Fox, Viacom, NBC, and Time Warner, a three-judge panel of the federal appeals court in Washington refuses to uphold an FCC rule limiting a TV station group owner's audience reach to 35 percent of U.S. TV households and strikes down a rule barring a cable system from owning TV stations in its market. The court orders the FCC to rewrite or justify the ownership limit rule.

Tom Brokaw of NBC News announces he will step down as evening news anchor after the 2004 presidential election, to be succeeded by NBC's Brian Williams. Brokaw will then focus on in-depth reporting projects.

The Securities and Exchange Commission begins a formal investigation into the accounting practices of cable MSO Adelphia Communications. Five of Adelphia's top executives—including founder John Rigas and his two sons, Michael and Tim—are arrested on fraud charges, alleging that the family used the company as a "personal piggy bank," financing various personal transactions, including $3.1 billion in loans for stock and family businesses.

The FCC mandates that all TV sets must be equipped with digital tuners by 2007 and proposes strong copy-protection measures intended to prevent widespread copying and streaming of content over the Internet.

Lifestyle diva Martha Stewart, whose media empire included TV, magazines, and books, is investigated by the Justice Department for allegedly lying to federal authorities looking into insider trading involving Stewart's sale of ImClone Systems stock the day before it became public that the Food and Drug Administration had denied the company's application to market a new cancer drug.

In October, both the FCC and the Department of Justice reject DBS operator EchoStar Communications' proposed $26-billion purchase of competitor DirecTV, and a revised agreement fails to sway either agency. In December, EchoStar withdrew its merger request from the FCC. Rupert Murdoch's News Corp., whose previous bid for DirecTV had been rebuffed, puts together a new deal.

2003

Rupert Murdoch's News Corp. receives FCC and Justice Department approval of its deal to acquire 34 percent of DBS operator DirecTV's parent company Hughes Electronics for $6.6 billion in cash and stock.

New York City's Metropolitan Television Alliance agrees to place a new broadcast tower for New York-area television stations on top of the Freedom Tower, a 1,776-foot office tower that will be built on the site of the World Trade Center, where the stations' towers were located prior to 9/11. The MTVA comprises all the city's major TV broadcasters. After the terrorist attacks, most of the stations operated from backup facilities atop the Empire State Building. Ground is expected to be broken on the Freedom Tower in the summer of 2004, and broadcasters should begin operating from the tower by 2008.

The FCC releases new media ownership rules in response to a federal appeals court ruling in 2002. Among the changes: raising the national coverage cap for TV groups from 35 percent to 45 percent; allowing ownership of two TV stations (duopoly) in markets with five or more commercial stations; allowing ownership of three TV stations (triopoly) in markets with at least 18 stations; newspaper-TV cross-ownership is permitted in markets with at least four TV stations; radio-TV cross-ownership now include newspapers in the formula—owners in markets with nine or more TV stations face no cross-ownership restrictions per se but are limited by individual radio and TV limits applicable to specific markets. TV-duopoly owners would not be permitted to own newspapers in markets with fewer than nine TV stations. In markets with three or fewer TV stations, no cross-ownership of TV, radio, or newspapers is permitted. In markets with four to eight TV stations, an owner may form one of the following combos: (1) A daily newspaper, one TV station, up to one-half the number of radio stations permitted to one owner in that market. (2) A daily newspaper, the total number of radio stations permitted to one owner there, no TV stations. (3) Two TV stations and the total number of radio stations permitted there. Congress quickly reacts with legislation introduced by Rep. John Dingell (D-Mich.), which would restore the 35 percent cap. Other critics of the new rules challenge them in federal court.

Liberty Media pays $7.9 billion for Comcast's 56 percent stake in home shopping giant QVC. With 2002 sales of $4.4 billion, QVC is not just the largest shopping network, it's the second-largest television network of any kind.

A panel of federal appeals court judges in Philadelphia agrees with public advocacy groups and imposes a stay of the FCC's new broadcast-ownership rules scheduled to take effect on September 4. The stay will remain in effect until lawsuits to overturn the new rules are settled. The Philadelphia court then decides to retain the case attacking the new FCC broadcast-ownership limits rather than granting broadcast networks' pleas to transfer it to a court in Washington.

The Bush White House brokered a surprise compromise over media deregulation by agreeing to permanently set the national TV station ownership cap at 39 percent of U.S. television households. That percentage allows Fox and Viacom to retain all their stations. Wielding a threat to veto a catch-all spending bill over a provision that would roll the limit back to 35 percent, aides to President Bush persuaded Senate Appropriations Committee Chairman Ted Stevens (R-Alaska) to back down from the tighter limit. Stevens's action came less than a week after he had persuaded reluctant House leadership to go along with the old level. The compromise splits the difference between the 45 percent limit set by the FCC in June and the previous 35 percent level that rank-and-file lawmakers on both sides of Capitol Hill had been pushing to reinstate. The agreement is part of a spending bill that funds the FCC and many other agencies in fiscal 2004.

After a 36-year run, the California Cable Telecommunications Association's annual Western Cable Show makes its curtain call in December, citing consolidation in the cable industry and economic pressure.

Cable network launches include Spike TV.

2004

NBC gets Federal Trade Commission approval for its $14 billion purchase of Vivendi Universal Entertainment, its last regulatory hurdle. The FCC was not required to review the deal because it involved no station licenses. Among other things, NBC acquires USA Network and the Sci Fi Network. The new entity will be called NBC Universal.

Congress and the FCC react swiftly to the "wardrobe malfunction" that bared Janet Jackson's breast during the MTV-produced half-time entertainment in CBS TV's Super Bowl broadcast. Congress passes legislation that dramatically increases the limits on FCC fines for indecency violations.

Congress and the FCC take the first steps toward punishing stations that air "excessively" violent shows. Under orders from leaders of the House Commerce Committee, FCC Chairman Michael Powell by the end of the year will start investigating whether the commission should restrict onscreen violence. Cable can't count on immunity either. Growing ranks of lawmakers say cable must do more to make sure that children aren't exposed to potentially traumatizing content.

A panel of federal appeals court judges in Philadelphia concludes that the FCC wasn't justified in its June

2003 decision relaxing ownership restrictions in the newspaper, television, and radio industries. The rules, which were blocked from taking effect in September 2003, have been sent back to the FCC for a rewrite. A frustrated FCC Chairman Michael Powell criticized the decision, claiming that it created a "clouded and confused state of media law" and makes it nearly impossible for his agency to design standards for ownership limits.

Cable network launches include TV One.

2005

George W. Bush, on January 20, becomes the first president to have his inauguration covered in HDTV. ABC News deploys 36 HD cameras and four HD production vehicles throughout the parade route to give viewers an unparalleled view of American history.

President Bush chooses FCC commissioner Kevin Martin to be chairman of the agency.

In a King Solomon-like answer to critics that Viacom has become too big to grow, Chairman Sumner Redstone proposes cleaving it in half. The resulting companies would be Viacom and CBS Corp.

Longtime ABC World News Tonight anchor Peter Jennings, 67, died August 7 at his home in Manhattan, four months after being diagnosed with lung cancer.

Following Hurricane Katrina, local TV broadcasters and cable operators in the Gulf Coast area say rebuilding their stations and plants could take several months.

The Disney-ABC Television Group announces that three ABC shows, Desperate Housewives, Lost, and Night Stalker will be available for purchase from the Apple iTunes store for $1.99 an episode. The announcement prompts the other big media companies to begin repurposing primetime programming on the Internet. It's soon clear that the Web is the next big TV medium.

2006

In January, PBS dips into the ranks of its member stations and selects Paula Kerger of WNET New York to succeed Pat Mitchell as president of the noncommercial network.

After battling to be the broadcasting fifth network for 11 years and mostly lackluster years, WB and UPN stun the broadcasting industry in January by deciding to merger into The CW. To fill the vacuum created by the loss of one network, Fox creates My Network Television, a mini network built around telenovelas, a popular Spanish TV format. Both CW and MNT debut in September.

Two years after the Janet Jackson wardrobe malfunction at the Super Bowl, broadcasters are still feeling the fallout. In March, the FCC issues another round of fines topped by $3.6 million against CBS affiliates for airing an episode of Without a Trace. A few months later, Congress increases ten-fold the base indecency fine to $325,000 per incident.

Ending a year of speculation, CBS announces in March the hiring of Katie Couric, the popular co-host of NBC's Today Show, to anchor the CBS Evening News. With new set and features, she begins her reign as anchor on September 5. Longtime anchor Dan Rather resigned from the job in March 2005 after botching a 60 Minutes story critical of President Bush's military record. CBS News's Washington Bureau Chief Bob Schieffer anchored the news during the Rather-Couric interregnum.

2007

On January 29 ION Media Networks Inc. changed the name of its TV network to ION Television.

In 2007 The Sopranos ended an eight-year run on HBO. There was much speculation about the final moments of the finale when the show faded to black.

After years of acquiring stations, on April 20 Clear Channel Communications Inc. entered into an agreement to sell its Television Group. And, as of June 30, the company had entered into definitive agreements to sell 389 radio stations in 77 markets.

2008

On July 25 the FCC approved the merger of Sirius Satellite Radio Inc. and XM Satellite Holdings Inc. On July 29 the two companies announced they had completed their merger, and that the new company would change its name to Sirius XM Radio Inc.

The FCC announced that Wilmington, NC, would be the first market to test the transition to digital television before the nationwide transition to DTV on February 17, 2009. The commercial broadcasters serving the Wilmington market agreed to turn off their analog signals at noon on September 8, 2008. Beginning at noon on September 8 WWAY (ABC), WECT (NBC), WSFX-TV (Fox), WILM-LP (CBS) and W51CW (Trinity Broadcasting) planned to broadcast only digital signals to their viewers in the five North Carolina counties that comprise the Wilmington, NC, market.

2009

The nationwide transition from analog to digital television, scheduled for February 17, 2009, was delayed until June 12, 2009 to allow more time to get ready for the digital transition. The National Telecommunications and Information Administration (NTIA) provided consumers with a TV converter box coupon program to help the consumers make the switch to digital TV. Both the FCC and TV stations across the U.S. made a mighty effort to inform consumers about the coming switch and to help the consumers make the switch. Some TV stations made the switch to digital television early. Notably Hawaii's full-power TV stations made the switch to digital TV on January 15, 2009. Finally on June 12, 2009 full-power TV stations all over the U.S. became all-digital. The FCC reported 971 full-power TV stations made the switch on June 12.

Later in June 2009 the FCC adopted an order allowing AM radio stations to use FM radio translators to increase their reach within a local community. The FCC action gave AM stations an opportunity to overcome technical problems in their coverage areas.

Walter Cronkite, anchor and managing editor of the CBS Evening News from 1962 to 1981, died on July 17, 2009. A memorial service was scheduled for September 9 at Lincoln Center in New York.

The FCC and the Rules of Broadcasting

The following manual is a reproduced copy of "The Public and Broadcasting: How to Get the Most Service from your Local Station," the FCC's overview of the laws, policies and regulations that govern broadcast TV and radio stations. It is reprinted here with the permission of the FCC. The agency invites those with questions about the manual to visit its web site (www.fcc.gov) or to call 1-888-CALLFCC (1-888-225-5322).

INTRODUCTION

This Manual is published by the Federal Communications Commission (the "FCC" or the "Commission"), the federal agency directed by Congress to regulate broadcasting. It provides a brief overview of the FCC's regulation of broadcast radio and television licensees, describing how the FCC authorizes broadcast stations, the various rules relating to broadcast programming and operations with which stations must comply, and the essential obligation of licensees that their stations serve their local communities. The Manual also outlines how you can become involved in assessing whether your local stations are complying with the FCC's rules and meeting these service obligations, and what you can do if you believe that they are not.

In exchange for obtaining a valuable license to operate a broadcast station using the public airwaves, each radio and television licensee is required by law to operate its station in the "public interest, convenience and necessity." This means that it must air programming that is responsive to the needs and problems of its local community of license.

To do so, each station licensee must affirmatively identify those needs and problems and then specifically treat those local matters that it deems to be significant in the news, public affairs, political and other programming that it airs. As discussed in this Manual, each station must provide the public with information about how it has met this obligation by means of quarterly reports, which contain a listing of the programming that it has aired that the licensee believes provided significant treatment of issues facing the community. As discussed in detail in this Manual, each station also must maintain and make available to any member of the public for inspection, generally at its studio, a local public inspection file which contains these reports, as well as other materials that pertain to the station's operations and dealings with the FCC and with the community that it is licensed to serve. The public file is an excellent resource to gauge a station's performance of its obligations as a Commission licensee. In the future, television stations with websites will be required to post most of the content of their public files on their websites, or on the website of their state local broadcasters association, if permitted.

The purpose of this Manual is to provide you with the basic tools necessary to ensure that the stations that are licensed to serve you meet their obligations and provide high quality broadcast service. Station licensees, as the trustees of the public's airwaves, must use the broadcast medium to serve the public interest. We at the FCC want you to become involved, if you have any concerns about a local station - including its general operation, programming or other matters - by making your opinion known to the licensee and, if necessary, by advising us of those concerns so that we can take appropriate action. An informed and actively engaged public plays a vital role in helping each station to operate appropriately and serve the needs of its local community.

This Manual provides only a general overview of our broadcast regulation. It is not intended to be a comprehensive or controlling statement of the broadcast rules and policies. Our Internet home page (www.fcc.gov) contains additional information about the Commission, our rules, current FCC proceedings, and other issues. At the close of each section of this Manual, we provide links to those places on the FCC website that provide additional information about the subject matter discussed in the section. Although we will periodically update this Manual and maintain the current version on the FCC website at www.fcc.gov/mb/audio/decdoc /public_and_broadcasting.html, we urge you to also make use of the resources contained in these links, which may outline any more recent developments in the law not discussed in the current version of the

Manual. If you have any specific questions, you may also contact our Broadcast Information Specialist for radio or television, depending on the nature of your inquiry, by calling toll-free, by facsimile, or by sending an e-mail in the manner noted at the end of this Manual.

THE FCC AND ITS REGULATORY AUTHORITY

The Communications Act.

The FCC was created by Congress in the Communications Act for the purpose of "regulating interstate and foreign commerce in communication by wire and radio so as to make available, so far as possible, to all the people of the United States, without discrimination on the basis of race, color, religion, national origin, or sex, a rapid, efficient, Nation wide, and world wide wire and radio communications service . . . ." (In this context, the word "radio" covers both broadcast radio and television.) The Communications Act authorizes the FCC to "make such regulations not inconsistent with law as it may deem necessary to prevent interference between stations and to carry out the provisions of [the] Act." It directs us to base our broadcast licensing decisions on the determination of whether those actions will serve the public interest, convenience, and necessity.

How the FCC Adopts Rules.

As is the case with most other federal agencies, the FCC generally cannot adopt or change rules without first describing or publishing the proposed rules and seeking comment on them from the public. We release a document called a Notice of Proposed Rule Making, in which we explain the new rules or rule changes that we are proposing and establish a filing deadline for public comment on them. (All such FCC Notices are included in the Commission's Daily Digest and are posted on our website at http://www.fcc.gov /Daily_Releases/Daily_Digest). After we have had a chance to hear from the public and have considered all comments received, we generally have several options. We can: (1) adopt some or all of the proposed rules, (2) adopt a modified version of some or all of the proposed rules, (3) ask for public comment on additional issues relating to the proposals, or (4) end the rulemaking proceeding without adopting any rules at all. You can find information about how to file comments in our rulemaking proceedings on our Internet website at www.fcc.gov/cgb/consumerfacts /howtocomment.html. The site also provides instructions on how you can file comments electronically. In addition to adopting rules, we also establish broadcast regulatory policies through the individual cases that we decide, such as those involving license renewals, station sales, and complaints about violations of FCC rules.

The FCC and the Media Bureau.

The FCC has five Commissioners, each of whom is appointed by the President and confirmed by the Senate. Serving under the Commissioners are a number of Offices and operating Bureaus. One of those is the Media Bureau, which has day-to-day responsibility for developing, recommending, and administering the rules governing the media, including radio and television stations. The FCC's broadcast rules are contained in Title 47 of the Code of Federal Regulations ("CFR"), Parts 73 (broadcast) and 74 (auxiliary broadcast, including low power TV, and translator stations). Our rules of practice and procedure can be found in Title 47 CFR, Part 1. A link to those rules can be found on our website at http://wireless.fcc.gov /index.htm?job=rules_and_regulations. Additional information about the Commission's Offices and Bureaus, including their respective functions, can be found at

http://www.fcc.gov/aboutus.html.

FCC Regulation of Broadcast Radio and Television.

The FCC allocates (that is, designates a portion of the broadcast spectrum to) new broadcast stations based upon both the relative needs of various communities for additional broadcast outlets and specified engineering standards designed to prevent interference among stations and to other communications users. As noted above, whenever we review an application - whether to build a new station, modify or renew a license or sell a station - we must determine if its grant would serve the public interest. As discussed earlier, we expect station licensees to be aware of the important problems and issues facing their local communities and to foster public understanding by presenting programming that relates to those local issues. As discussed in this Manual, however, broadcasters - not the FCC or any other government agency - are responsible for selecting the material that they air. By operation of the First Amendment to the U.S. Constitution, and because the Communications Act expressly prohibits the Commission from censoring broadcast matter, our role in overseeing program content is very limited.

We license only individual broadcast stations. We do not license TV or radio networks (such as CBS, NBC, ABC or Fox) or other organizations with which stations have relationships (such as PBS or NPR), except to the extent that those entities may also be station licensees. We also do not regulate information provided over the Internet, nor do we intervene in private disputes involving broadcast stations or their licensees. Instead, we usually defer to the parties, courts, or other agencies to resolve such disputes.

THE LICENSING OF TV AND RADIO STATIONS

Commercial and Noncommercial Educational Stations.

The FCC licenses FM radio and TV stations as either commercial or noncommercial educational ("NCE"). (All AM radio stations are licensed as commercial facilities.) Commercial stations generally support themselves through the sale of advertising. In contrast, NCE stations generally meet their operating expenses with contributions received from listeners and viewers, and also may receive government funding. In addition, NCE stations may receive contributions from for profit entities, and are permitted to acknowledge such contributions or underwriting donations with announcements naming and generally describing the contributing party or donor. However, NCE stations may not broadcast commercials or other promotional announcements on behalf of for-profit entities. These limitations on NCE stations are discussed further at page 21 of this Manual.

Applications to Build New Stations; Length of the License Period.

Before a party can build a new TV or radio station, it first must apply to the FCC for a construction permit. The applicant must demonstrate in its application that it is qualified to construct and operate the station as specified in its application and that its proposed facility will not cause objectionable interference to any other station. Once its application has been granted, the applicant is issued a construction permit, which authorizes it to build the station within a specified period of time, usually three years. After the applicant (now considered a "permittee") builds the station, it must file a license application, in which it certifies that it has constructed the station consistent with the technical and other terms specified in its construction permit. Upon grant

of that license application, the FCC issues the new license to operate to the permittee (now considered a "licensee"), which authorizes the new licensee to operate for a stated period of time, up to eight years. At the close of this period, the licensee must seek renewal of its station license.

Applications for License Renewal.

Licenses expire and renewal applications are due on a staggered basis, based upon the state in which the station is licensed. Before we can renew a station's license, we must first determine whether, during the preceding license term, the licensee has served the public interest; has not committed any serious violations of the Communications Act or the FCC's rules; and has not committed other violations which, taken together, would constitute a pattern of abuse. To assist us in this evaluative process, a station licensee must file a renewal application (FCC Form 303-S), in which it must respond concerning whether:

• it has sent us certain required reports;

• neither it nor its owners have or have had any interest in a broadcast application involved in an FCC proceeding in which character issues were resolved adversely to the applicant or were left unresolved, or were raised in connection with a pending application;

• its ownership is consistent with the Communications Act's restrictions on licensee interests held by foreign governments, foreign corporations, and non-U.S. citizens;

• there has not been an adverse finding or adverse final action against it or its owners by a court or administrative body in a civil or criminal proceeding involving a felony, mass media-related antitrust or unfair competition law, the making of fraudulent statements to a governmental unit, or discrimination;

• there were no adjudicated violations of the Communications Act or the Commission's rules during the current license term;

• neither the licensee nor its owners have been denied federal benefits due to drug law violations;

• its station operation complies with the Commission's radiofrequency ("RF") radiation exposure standards;

• it has, in a timely manner, placed and maintained certain specified materials in its public inspection file (as discussed at pages 25-31 of this Manual);

• it has not discontinued station operations for more than 12 consecutive months during the preceding license term and is currently broadcasting programming;

• it has filed FCC Form 396, the Broadcast Equal Employment Opportunity Program Report; and

• if the application is for renewal of a television license, it has complied with the limitations on commercial matter aired during children's programming and filed the necessary Children's Television Programming Reports (FCC Form 398) (as discussed at page 17 of this Manual).

Digital Television.

After February 17, 2009, all full-power TV stations are required to stop broadcasting in analog and continue broadcasting only in digital. This is known as the "DTV transition." Because digital is much more efficient than analog, part of the scarce and valuable spectrum that is currently used for analog broadcasting will be used for important new services such as enhanced public safety communications for police, fire departments, and emergency rescue workers. Part of the spectrum will also be made available for advanced wireless services such as wireless broadband.

Digital broadcasting also enables television stations to offer viewers several benefits. For example, stations broadcasting in digital can offer viewers improved picture and sound quality as well as more programming options (referred to as "multicasting") because digital technology gives each television station the ability to broadcast multiple channels at the same time.

Consumers who receive television signals via over-the-air antennas (as opposed to subscribers to pay services like cable and satellite TV) will be able to receive digital signals on their analog sets if they purchase a digital-to-analog converter box that converts the digital signals to analog. Alternatively, if consumers purchase a digital television (a TV with built in digital tuner), they will be able to receive digital broadcast programming. If your TV set receives local broadcast stations through a paid provider such as cable or satellite TV, it is already prepared for the DTV transition.

Regarding consumers who are shopping for new televisions, the Commission's digital tuner rule prohibits the importation or interstate shipment of any device containing an analog tuner unless it also contains a digital tuner. Retailers may continue to sell analog-only devices from existing inventory. However, at the point of sale, retailers must post notices advising consumers that TV sets and equipment such as VCRs that contain only an analog tuner will not be able to receive over-the-air-television signals from full-power broadcast stations after February 17, 2009, without the use of a digital-to-analog converter box.

Television broadcasters must promote public awareness of the DTV transition with an on-air education campaign, providing consumers with information about the transition. They must report their efforts on a quarterly basis by filing FCC Form 388 with the Commission, posting each such Form on their website and placing them in their station public inspection files.

While the February 17, 2009, deadline for ending analog broadcasts does not apply to low-power, Class A, and TV translator stations, these stations will eventually transition to all-digital service. In the meantime, some consumers may continue to receive programming from these stations in analog format after the transition date.

Additional information concerning the DTV transition can be found on the FCC's website, at http://www.dtv.gov, or by calling toll free 1-888-CALL-FCC (Voice) or 1-888-TELL-FCC (TTY).

Digital Radio.

The FCC has also approved digital operation for AM and FM radio broadcast stations (often referred to as "HD Radio"). As with DTV, digital radio substantially improves the quality of the radio signal and allows a station to offer multicasting over several programming streams, as well as certain enhanced services. Unlike the mandatory digital transition deadline for television stations however, radio stations will be able to continue to operate in analog and will have discretion whether also to transmit in digital and, if so, when to begin such operation. In order to receive the digital signals of those stations that choose to so operate, consumers will have to purchase new receivers.

Because digital radio technology allows a radio station to transmit simultaneously in both analog and digital, however, listeners will be able to continue to use their current radios to receive the analog signals of radio stations that transmit both analog and digital signals. Receivers are being marketed that incorporate both modes of reception, with the ability to automatically switch to the analog signal if the digital signal cannot be detected or is lost by the receiver. For additional information about digital radio, see http://www.fcc.gov/mb/audio/digital/index.html.

Public Participation in the Licensing Process

Renewal Applications. You can submit a protest against a station's license renewal application by filing a formal petition to deny its application, or by sending us an informal objection to the application. Before its license expires, each station licensee must broadcast a series of announcements providing the date its license will expire, the filing date for the renewal application, the date by which formal petitions against it must be filed, and the location of the station's public inspection file that contains the application. Petitions to deny the application must be filed by the end of the first day of the last full calendar month of the expiring license term. (For example, if the license expires on December 31, we must receive any petition at our Washington, D.C. headquarters by the end of the day on December 1.)

Broadcast licenses generally expire on a staggered basis, by state, with most radio licenses next expiring between October 1, 2011 and August 1, 2014, and most television licenses expiring between October 1, 2012 and August 1, 2015, one year after the radio licenses in the same state. A listing of the next expiration dates for radio and television licenses, by state, can be found on the Commission's website at http://www.fcc.gov/localism/renewals.html. Before you file a petition to deny an application, you should check our rules and policies to make sure that your petition complies with our procedural requirements. A more complete description of these procedures and requirements can be found on the Commission's website at http://www.fcc.gov/localism/renew_process_handout.pdf. You can also file an informal objection at any time before we either grant or deny the application. Instructions for filing informal objections can be found on the Commission's website at http://www.fcc.gov/localism/renew_process_handout.pdf. If you have any specific questions, you may also contact our Broadcast Information Specialist for radio or television, depending on the nature of your inquiry, by calling toll-free, by facsimile, or by sending an e-mail in the manner noted at pages 32-33 of this Manual.

Other Types of Applications. You can also participate in the application process by filing a petition to deny when someone applies for a new station, and when a station is to be sold (technically called an "assignment" of the license), its licensee is to undergo a major transfer of stock or other ownership, or control (technically called a "transfer of control"), or the station proposes major facility changes. The applicant is required to publish a series of notices in the closest local newspaper, containing information similar to that noted above regarding renewal applications, when it files these types of applications. Upon receipt of the application, the FCC will issue a Public Notice and begin a 30-day period during which petitions to deny these applications may be filed. (All FCC Public Notices are included in the Commission's Daily Digest and are posted on our website at http://www.fcc.gov/Daily_Releases/Daily_Digest). As with renewal applications, you can also file an informal objection to these types of applications, or any other applications, at any time before we either grant or deny the application. Again, if you have any specific questions about our processes or the status of a particular application involving a station, you may contact our Broadcast Information Specialist for radio or television, depending on the nature of your inquiry, by calling toll-free, by facsimile, or by sending an e-mail in the manner noted at pages 32-33 of this Manual.

BROADCAST PROGRAMMING: BASIC LAW AND POLICY

The FCC and Freedom of Speech

The First Amendment, as well as Section 326 of the Communications Act, prohibits the Commission from censoring broadcast material and from interfering with freedom of expression in broadcasting. The Constitution's protection of free speech includes that of programming that may be objectionable to many viewer or listeners. Thus, the FCC cannot prevent the broadcast of any particular point of view. In this regard, the Commission has observed that "the public interest is best served by permitting free expression of views." However, the right to broadcast material is not absolute. There are some restrictions on the material that a licensee can broadcast. We discuss these restrictions below.

Licensee Discretion

Because the Commission cannot dictate to licensees what programming they may air, each individual radio and TV station licensee generally has discretion to select what its station broadcasts and to otherwise determine how it can best serve its community of license. Licensees are responsible for selecting their entertainment programming, as well as programs concerning local issues, news, public affairs, religion, sports events, and other subjects. As discussed at page 29 of this Manual, broadcast licensees must periodically make available detailed information about the programming that they air to meet the needs and problems of their communities, which can be found in each station public file. They also decide how their programs will be structured and whether to edit or reschedule material for broadcasting. In light of the First Amendment and Section 326 of the Communications Act, we do not substitute our judgment for that of the licensee, nor do we advise stations on artistic standards, format, grammar, or the quality of their programming. Licensees also have broad discretion regarding commercials, with the exception of those for political candidates during an election and the limitations on advertisements aired during children's programming (we discuss these respective requirements at pages 13-14, and 17 of this Manual).

Criticism, Ridicule, and Humor Concerning Individuals, Groups, and Institutions

The First Amendment's guarantee of freedom of speech similarly protects programming that stereotypes or may otherwise offend people with regard to their religion, race, national background, gender, or other characteristics. It also protects broadcasts that criticize or ridicule established customs and institutions, including the government and its officials. The Commission recognizes that, under our Constitution, people must be free to say things that the majority may abhor, not only what most people may find tolerable or congenial. However, if you are offended by a station's programming, we urge you to make your concerns known to the station licensee, in writing.

Programming Access

In light of their discretion to formulate their programming, station licensees are not required to broadcast everything that is offered or otherwise suggested to them. Except as required by the Communications Act, including the use of stations by candidates for public office (discussed at pages 13-14 of this Manual), licensees have no obligation to allow any particular person or group to participate in a broadcast or to present that person or group's remarks.

BROADCAST PROGRAMMING: LAW AND POLICY ON SPECIFIC KINDS OF PROGRAMMING

Broadcast Journalism

Introduction. As noted above, in light of the fundamental importance of the free flow of information to our democracy, the First Amendment and the Communications Act bar the FCC from telling station licensees how to select material for news programs, or prohibiting the broadcast of an opinion on any subject. We also do not review anyone's qualifications to gather, edit, announce, or comment on the news; these decisions are the station licensee's responsibility. Nevertheless, there are two issues related to broadcast journalism that are subject to Commission regulation: hoaxes and news distortion.

Hoaxes. The broadcast by a station of false information concerning a crime or catastrophe violates the FCC's rules if:

• the station licensee knew that the information was false, broadcasting the false information directly causes substantial public harm, and

• it was foreseeable that broadcasting the false information would cause such harm.

In this context, a "crime" is an act or omission that makes the offender subject to criminal punishment by law, and a "catastrophe" is a disaster or an imminent disaster involving violent or sudden events affecting the public. The broadcast must cause direct and actual damage to property or to the health or safety of the general public, or diversion of law enforcement or other public health and safety authorities from their duties, and the public harm must begin immediately. If a station airs a disclaimer before the broadcast that clearly characterizes the program as fiction and the disclaimer is presented in a reasonable manner under the circumstances, the program is presumed not to pose foreseeable public harm. Additional information about the hoax rule can be found on the FCC's website at http://www.fcc.gov/cgb/consumerfacts/falsebroadcast.html.

News Distortion. The Commission often receives complaints concerning broadcast journalism, such as allegations that stations have aired inaccurate or one-sided news reports or comments, covered stories inadequately, or overly dramatized the events that they cover. For the reasons noted above, the Commission generally will not intervene in such cases because it would be inconsistent with the First Amendment to replace the journalistic judgment of licensees with our own. However, as public trustees, broadcast licensees may not intentionally distort the news: the FCC has stated that "rigging or slanting the news is a most heinous act against the public interest." The Commission will investigate a station for news distortion if it receives documented evidence of such rigging or slanting, such as testimony or other documentation, from individuals with direct personal knowledge that a licensee or its management engaged in the intentional falsification of the news. Of particular concern would be evidence of the direction to employees from station management to falsify the news. However, absent such a compelling showing, the Commission will not intervene. For additional information about news distortion, see http://www.fcc.gov/cgb/consumerfacts/journalism.html.

Political Broadcasting: Candidates for Public Office. In recognition of the particular importance of the free flow of information to the public during the electoral process, the Communications Act and the Commission's rules impose specific obligations on broadcasters regarding political speech.

• Reasonable Access. The Communications Act requires that broadcast stations provide "reasonable access" to candidates for federal elective office. Such access must be made available during all of a station's normal broadcast schedule, including television prime time and radio drive time. In addition, federal candidates are entitled to purchase all classes of time offered by stations to commercial advertisers, such as preemptible and non-preemptible time. The only exception to the access requirement is for bona fide news programming (as defined below), during which broadcasters may choose not to sell airtime to federal candidates. Broadcast stations have discretion as to whether to sell time to candidates in state and local elections.

• Equal Opportunities. The Communications Act requires that, when a station provides airtime to a legally qualified candidate for any public office (federal, state, or local), the station must "afford equal opportunities to all other such candidates for that office." The equal opportunities provision of the Communications Act also provides that the station "shall have no power of censorship over the material broadcast" by the candidate. The law exempts from the equal opportunities requirement appearances by candidates during bona fide news programming, defined as an appearance by a legally qualified candidate on a bona fide newscast, interview, or documentary (if the appearance of the candidate is incidental to the presentation of the subject covered by the documentary) or on-the-spot coverage of a bona fide news event (including debates, political conventions and related incidental activities).

In addition, a station must sell political advertising time to certain candidates during specified periods before a primary or general election at the lowest rate charged for the station's most favored commercial advertiser. Stations must maintain and make available for public inspection, in their public inspection files, a political file containing certain documents and information, discussed in this Manual. For additional information about the political rules, see http://www.fcc.gov/mb/policy/political/.

Objectionable Programming

Programming Inciting "Imminent Lawless Action." The Supreme Court has held that the government may curtail speech if it is both: (1) intended to incite or produce "imminent lawless action;" and (2) likely to "incite or produce such action." Even when this legal test is met, any review that might lead to a curtailment of speech is generally performed by the appropriate criminal law enforcement authorities, not by the FCC.

Obscene, Indecent, or Profane Programming. Although, for the reasons discussed earlier, the Commission is generally prohibited from regulating broadcast content, the courts have held that the FCC's regulation of obscene and indecent programming is constitutional, because of the compelling societal interests in protecting children from potentially harmful programming and supporting parents' ability to determine the programming to which their children will be exposed at home.

Obscene material is not protected by the First Amendment and cannot be broadcast at any time. To be obscene, the material must have all of the following three characteristics:

• an average person, applying contemporary community standards, must find that the material, as a whole, appeals to the prurient interest;

• the material must depict or describe, in a patently offensive way, sexual conduct specifically defined by applicable law; and

• the material, taken as a whole, must lack serious literary, artistic, political, or scientific value.

Indecent material is protected by the First Amendment, so its broadcast cannot constitutionally be prohibited at all times. However, the courts have upheld Congress' prohibition of the broadcast of indecent material during times of the day in which there is a reasonable risk that children may be in the audience, which the Commission has determined to be between the hours of 6 a.m. and 10 p.m. Indecent programming is defined as "language or material that, in context, depicts or describes, in terms patently offensive as measured by contemporary community standards for the broadcast medium, sexual or excretory organs or activities." Broadcasts that fall within this definition and are aired between 6 a.m. and 10 p.m. may be subject to enforcement action by the FCC.

Profane material also is protected by the First Amendment, so its broadcast cannot be outlawed entirely. The Commission has defined such program matter to include language that is both "so grossly offensive to members of the public who actually hear it as to amount to a nuisance" and is sexual or excretory in nature or derived from such terms. Such material may be the subject of possible Commission enforcement action if it is broadcast within the same time period applicable to indecent programming: between 6 a.m. and 10 p.m.

How to File an Obscenity, Indecency, or Profanity Complaint:

In order to allow its staff to make a determination of whether complained-of material is actionable, the Commission requires that complainants provide certain information: (1) the date and time of the alleged broadcast; (2) the call sign, channel or frequency of the station involved; and (3) the details of what was actually said (or depicted) during the alleged indecent, profane, or obscene broadcast. Submission of an audio or video tape, CD, DVD or other recording or transcript of the complained-of material is not required but is helpful, as is specification of the name of the program, the on-air personality, song, or film, and the city and state in which the complainant saw or heard the broadcast.

The fastest and easiest way to file a complaint containing this information is to use the FCC's electronic complaint form, Form 475B, which is available on the FCC's website at http://fjallfoss.fcc.gov/cgb/fcc475B.cfm.

You also may file a complaint about objectionable programming by mailing it to:

Federal Communications Commission
Consumer & Governmental Affairs Bureau
Consumer Inquiries and Complaints Division
445 12th Street, S.W.
Washington, D.C. 20554.

If you are submitting an audio or video tape, DVD, CD or other type of media with your complaint, you should send it to the following address to avoid mail processing damage:

Federal Communications Commission
Consumer & Governmental Affairs Bureau
Consumer Inquiries and Complaints Division
9300 East Hampton Drive
Capitol Heights, Maryland 20743.

You can also electronically file your complaint at fccinfo@fcc.gov.

You may also complain by calling the Commission, toll-free, at 1-(888)-CALL-FCC (1-(888)-225-5322) (Voice) or 1-(888)-TELL-FCC (1-(888)-835-5322) (TTY).

For additional information on the complaint process for obscene, indecent or profane material, visit http://www.fcc.gov/eb/oip.

Violent Programming. Many members of the public have expressed concern about violent television programming and the negative impact such broadcast material may have upon children. In response to these concerns, and at the request of 39 members of the U.S. House of Representatives, the FCC conducted a proceeding seeking public comment on violent programming. In April 2007, the Commission delivered to Congress a Report recommending that the industry voluntarily commit to reducing the amount of such programming viewed by children. The Commission also suggested that Congress consider enacting legislation that would better support parents' efforts to safeguard their children from such objectionable programming. The Commission's Report can be accessed at

http://fjallfoss.fcc.gov/edocs_public/attachmatch/FCC-07-50A1.pdf .

The V-Chip and TV Program Ratings. In light of the widespread concern about obscene, indecent, profane, violent, or otherwise objectionable programming, in 1996, Congress passed a law to require TV sets with screens 13 inches or larger to be equipped with a "V-Chip" - a device that allows parents to program their sets to block TV programming that carries a certain rating. Since 2000, all such sets manufactured with screens 13 inches or larger must contain the V-Chip technology. This technology, which must be activated by parents, works in conjunction with a voluntary television rating system created and administered by the television industry and others, which enables parents to identify programming containing sexual, violent, or other content that they believe may be harmful to their children. All of the major broadcast networks and most of the major cable networks are encoding their programming with this ratings information to work with the V Chip. However, some programming, such as news and sporting events, and unedited movies aired on premium cable channels, are not rated. In 2004, the FCC expanded the V-Chip requirement to apply also to devices that do not have a display screen but are used with a TV set, such as a VCR or a digital-to-analog converter box.

For more information about this ratings program, including a description of each ratings category, please see the FCC's V Chip website at http://www.fcc.gov/cgb/consumerfacts/vchip.html.

Other Broadcast Content Regulation

Station Identification. Stations must air identification announcements when they sign on and off for the day. They also must broadcast these announcements every hour, as close to the start of the hour as possible, at a natural programming break. TV stations may make these announcements on-screen or by voice only. Official station identification includes the station's call letters, followed by the community specified in its license as the station's location. Between the call letters and its community, the station may insert the name of the licensee, the station's channel number, and/or its frequency. It may also include any additional community or communities, as long as it first names the community to which it is licensed by the FCC. DTV stations also may identify their digital multicast programming streams separately if they wish, and, if so, must follow the format described in the FCC's rules.

Commencing as of a date to be determined, for television stations, twice daily, the station identification will also have to include a notice of the existence, location and accessibility of the station's public file The notice will have to state that the station's public file is available for inspection and that members of the public can view it at the station's main studio and on its station website. Broadcast of at least one of these announcements will be required between the hours of 6 p.m. and midnight.

Children's Television Programming. Throughout its license term, every TV station must serve the educational and informational needs of children both by means of its overall programming and through programming that is specifically designed to serve those needs. Licensees are eligible for routine staff-level approval of the Children's Television Act portion of their renewal applications if they air at least three hours of "core" children's television programming, per week, or proportionally more if they provide additional free digital programming streams. Core programming is defined as follows:

• Educational and Informational. The programming must further the educational and informational needs of children 16 years old and under (this includes their intellectual/cognitive or social/emotional needs).

• Specifically Designed to Serve These Needs. A program is considered "specifically designed to serve the educational and information needs of children" if: (1) that is its significant purpose; (2) it is aired between the hours of 7 a.m. and 10 p.m.; (3) it is a regularly scheduled weekly program; and (4) it is at least 30 minutes in duration.

To ensure that parents and other interested parties are informed of the educational and informational children's programming that their area stations offer, television

licensees must identify each program specifically designed to "educate and inform" children by displaying the icon "E/I" throughout the program. In addition, commercial stations must provide information identifying such programs to the publishers of program guides.

During the broadcast of TV programs aimed at children 12 and under, advertising may not exceed 10.5 minutes an hour on weekends and 12 minutes an hour on weekdays.

These rules apply to analog and digital broadcasting. As discussed at page 9 of this Manual, television stations have traditionally operated with analog technology. Television stations, however, are in the process of switching to digital broadcasting, which greatly enhances their capability to serve their communities. Among other things, digital technology permits stations to engage in multicasting, that is, to air more than one stream of programming at the same time. Digital stations that choose to air more than one stream of free, over-the-air video programming must air proportionately more children's educational programming than stations that air only one stream of free, over-the-air video programming.

Each television licensee is required to prepare and place in the public inspection file at the station a quarterly Children's Television Programming Report (FCC Form 398) identifying its core programming. These reports must also be filed electronically with the FCC each quarter and can be viewed on the FCC's website, at http://www.fcc.gov/mb/engineering/kidvid. This requirement of the station's public file is discussed at page 29 of this Manual.

The FCC has created a children's educational television website to inform parents and other members of the public about the obligation of every television broadcast station to provide educational and informational programming for children. This website provides access to background information about these obligations, as well as information about children's educational programs that are aired on television stations in your area and throughout the country. This website also can help TV stations comply with the children's television requirements. You can access the children's educational television website by going to the FCC's main website at http://www.fcc.gov and double-clicking on the "Parents' Place" listing under "Consumer Center" on the FCC home page. Alternatively, you can go directly to the children's television website at http://www.fcc.gov/parents/childrenstv.html.

Station-Conducted Contests. A station that broadcasts or advertises information about a contest that it conducts must fully and accurately disclose the material terms of the contest, and must conduct the contest substantially as announced or advertised. Contest descriptions may not be false, misleading, or deceptive with respect to any material term, including the factors that define the operation of the contest and affect participation, such as entry deadlines, the prizes that can be won, and how winners will be selected. Additional information about the contest rule can be found at http://www.fcc.gov/cgb/consumerfacts/contests.html.

Lotteries. Federal law prohibits the broadcast of advertisements for a lottery or information concerning a lottery. A lottery is any game, contest, or promotion that contains the elements of prize, chance, and "consideration" (a legal term that means an act or promise that is made to induce someone into an agreement). For example, casino gambling is generally considered to be a "lottery" subject to the terms of the advertising restriction although, as discussed below, the prohibition is not applied to truthful advertisements for lawful casino gambling. Many types of contests, depending on their particulars, also are covered under this definition.

The statute and FCC rules list a number of exceptions to this prohibition, principally advertisements for: (1) lotteries conducted by a state acting under the authority of state law, when the advertisement or information is broadcast by a radio or TV station licensed to a location in that state or in any other state that conducts such a lottery; (2) gambling conducted by an Indian Tribe under the Indian Gaming Regulatory Act; (3) lotteries authorized or not otherwise prohibited by the state in which they are conducted, and which are conducted by a not for profit organization or a governmental organization; and (4) lotteries conducted as a promotional activity by commercial organizations

that are clearly occasional and ancillary to the primary business of that organization, as long as the lotteries are authorized or not otherwise prohibited by the state in which they are conducted.

In 1999, the Supreme Court held that the prohibition on broadcasting advertisements for lawful casino gambling could not constitutionally be applied to truthful advertisements broadcast by radio or television stations licensed in states in which such gambling is legal. Relying upon the reasoning in that decision, the FCC and the United States Department of Justice later concluded that the lottery advertising prohibition may not constitutionally be applied to the broadcast of any truthful advertisements for lawful casino gambling, whether or not the state in which the broadcasting station is located permits casino gambling. Additional information about the rule concerning lotteries can be found at http://www.fcc.gov/cgb/consumerfacts/contests.html.

Soliciting Funds. No federal law prohibits the broadcast by stations of requests for funds for legal purposes (including appeals by stations for contributions to meet their operating expenses), if the money or other contributions are used for the announced purposes. However, federal law prohibits fraud by wire, radio or television - including situations in which money solicited for one purpose is used for another - and doing so may lead to FCC sanctions, as well as to criminal prosecution by the U.S. Department of Justice. Additional information about fund solicitation can be found at http://www.fcc.gov/cgb/consumerfacts/contests.html.

Broadcast of Telephone Conversations.

Before broadcasting a telephone conversation live or recording a telephone conversation for later broadcast, a station must inform any party to the call of its intention to broadcast the conversation. However, that notification is not necessary when the other party knows that the conversation will be broadcast or such knowledge can be reasonably presumed, such as when the party is associated with the station (for example, as an employee or part-time reporter) or originates the call during a program during which the station customarily broadcasts the calls. For additional information on the rule concerning the broadcast of telephone conversations, see http://www.fcc.gov/eb/broadcast/telphon.html.

ACCESS TO BROADCAST MATERIAL BY PEOPLE WITH DISABILITIES

The Communications Act and the Commission's rules require television station licensees to broadcast certain information that makes viewing more accessible to people with disabilities.

Closed Captioning

Closed captioning is a technology designed to provide access to television programming by persons with hearing disabilities by displaying, in text form, the audio portion of a broadcast, as well as descriptions of background noise and sound effects. Closed captioning is hidden as encoded data transmitted within the television signal. A viewer wishing to see the captions must use a set-top decoder or a television with built-in decoder circuitry. All television sets with screens 13 inches or larger manufactured since mid-1993, including digital sets, have built-in decoder circuitry.

As directed by Congress in the Telecommunications Act of 1996, the FCC has adopted rules requiring closed captioning of most, but not all, television programming. The rules require those that distribute television programs directly to home viewers, including broadcast stations, to comply with these rules. The rules also provide certain exemptions from the captioning requirements. Additional information on the closed captioning requirements may be found on the FCC website at http://www.fcc.gov/cgb/dro/caption.html.

Access to Emergency Information

The FCC also requires television stations to make the local emergency information that they provide to viewers accessible to persons with disabilities. Thus, if emergency information is provided aurally, such information also must be provided in a visual format for persons who are deaf or hard of hearing. The emergency information may be closed captioned or presented through an

alternative method of visual presentation. Such methods include open captioning, crawls, or scrolls that appear on the screen. The information provided visually must include critical details regarding the emergency and how to respond. Critical details could include, among other things, specific information regarding the areas that will be affected by the emergency, evacuation orders, detailed descriptions of areas to be evacuated, specific evacuation routes, approved shelters or the way to take shelter in one's home, instructions on how to secure personal property, road closures, and how to obtain relief assistance. Similarly, if the emergency information is presented visually, it must be made accessible. If the emergency information interrupts programming, such as through a crawl, such information must be accompanied with an aural tone to alert persons with visual disabilities that the station is providing this information so that such persons may be alerted to turn to another source, such as a radio, for more information. Additional information concerning this requirement can be found on the FCC website at http://ftp.fcc.gov/cgb/consumerfacts /emergencyvideo.html.

BUSINESS PRACTICES AND ADVERTISING

Business Practices, Advertising Rates, and Profits

Except for the requirements concerning political advertisements (discussed at pages 13-14 of this Manual), the limits on the number of commercials that can be aired during children's programming (see page 17), and the prohibition of advertisements over noncommercial educational stations (see pages 21-22), the Commission does not regulate a licensee's business practices, such as its advertising rates or its profits. Rates charged for broadcast time are matters for private negotiation between sponsors and stations. Further, except for certain classes of political advertisements (see pages 13-14), station licensees have full discretion to accept or reject any advertising.

Employment Discrimination and Equal Employment Opportunity ("EEO")

The FCC requires that all licensees of radio and TV stations afford equal opportunity in employment. We also prohibit employment discrimination on the basis of race, color, religion, national origin, or sex. However, religious stations are permitted to require that some or all of their employees meet a religious qualification.

Our EEO recruitment rules have three prongs. They require all stations that employ five or more full-time employees (defined as those regularly working 30 hours a week or more) to:

• widely distribute information concerning each full-time job vacancy, except for vacancies that need to be filled under demanding or other special circumstances;

• send notices of openings to organizations in the community that are involved in employment if the organization requests such notices; and

• engage in general outreach activities every two years, such as job fairs, internships, and other community events.

Each licensee with five or more full-time employees must maintain records of its recruitment efforts, and create and place in its public file an annual public file report listing specified information about its recruitment efforts. (The requirements for the EEO portion of the public file are discussed at page 28 of this Manual.) The annual EEO public file report must also be posted on a station's website, if one exists. In addition, television licensees with five or more full-time employees and radio licensees with 11 or more full-time employees must file an FCC Form 397 Broadcast Mid-Term Report. Each licensee, regardless of size, must file an FCC Form 396 EEO Program Report with its license renewal application. Finally, a prospective station licensee must file an FCC Form 396-A Broadcast Model Program Report with its new station or assignment or transfer application. The FCC reviews EEO compliance at the time that it considers the station renewal application, when it reviews Broadcast Mid-Term Reports, when it receives EEO complaints, and during random station audits. A full range of enforcement actions is available for EEO violations, including the imposition of reporting conditions, forfeitures, short-term license renewal, and license revocation.

All EEO forms are electronically filed and are available for public review in CDBS, the FCC's access database (to access these reports, see http://fjallfoss.fcc.gov /prod/cdbs/pubacc/prod/eeo_search.htm). As discussed at page 27 of this Manual, in addition, copies of all FCC EEO audit letters, licensee responses, and FCC rulings must be included in the audited station's public file and are available for public review at the FCC Public Reference Center in Washington, D.C. Additional information concerning the EEO rules is available at http://www.fcc.gov/mb/policy/eeo/.

Sponsorship Identification

The sponsorship identification requirements contained in the Communications Act and the Commission's rules generally require that, when money or other consideration for the airing of program material has been received by or promised to a station, its employees or others, the station must broadcast full disclosure of that fact at the time of the airing of the material, and identify who provided or promised to provide the consideration. This requirement is grounded in the principle that members of the public should know who is trying to persuade them with the programming being aired. This disclosure requirement also applies to the broadcast of musical selections for consideration (so-called "payola") and the airing of certain video news releases. In the case of advertisements for commercial products or services, it is sufficient for a station to announce the sponsor's corporate or trade name, or the name of the sponsor's product (where it is clear that the mention of the product constitutes a sponsorship identification). For additional information about the sponsorship identification and payola rules, see http://www.fcc.gov /cgb/consumerfacts/PayolaRules.html.

Underwriting Announcements on Noncommercial Educational Stations

Noncommercial educational stations may acknowledge contributions over the air, but they may not broadcast commercials or otherwise promote the goods and services of for profit donors or underwriters. Acceptable "enhanced underwriting" acknowledgements of for profit donors or underwriters may include: (1) logograms and slogans that identify but do not promote; (2) location information; (3) value-neutral descriptions of a product line or service; and (4) brand names, trade names, and product service listings. However, such acknowledgements may not interrupt the station's regular programming. For additional information about the underwriting rules, see http://www.fcc.gov/eb /broadcast/enhund.html.

Loud Commercials

The FCC does not regulate the volume of broadcast programming, including commercials. Surveys and technical studies reveal that the perceived loudness of particular broadcast matter is a subjective judgment that varies with each viewer and listener and is influenced by many factors, such as the material's content and style and the voice and tone of the person speaking. The FCC has found no evidence that stations deliberately raise audio and modulation levels to emphasize commercial messages.

Manually controlling the set's volume level or using the "mute" button with a remote control constitutes the simplest approach to reducing volume levels deemed to be excessive. Many television receivers are equipped with circuits that are designed to stabilize the loudness between programs and commercials. These functions usually must be activated through the receiver's "set up/audio" menu. Should these techniques fail to resolve the problem, you may consider addressing any complaint about broadcast volume levels to the licensee of the station involved. Additional information about loud commercials can be found at http://www.fcc.gov/cgb /consumerfacts/backgroundnoise.html.

False or Misleading Advertising.

The Federal Trade Commission has primary responsibility for determining whether an advertisement is false or deceptive and for taking action against the sponsor. The Food and Drug Administration has primary responsibility for the safety of food and drug products. Depending on the nature of the advertisement, you should contact these agencies regarding advertisements that you believe may be false or misleading. Additional information about false or misleading advertising can be found at http://www.fcc.gov/cgb/consumerfacts /advertising.html.

Offensive Advertising

Unless a broadcast advertisement is found to be in violation of a specific law or rule, the government cannot take action against it. However, if you believe that an advertisement is offensive because of the nature of the item advertised, the scheduling of the announcement, or the manner in which the message is presented, you should consider addressing your complaint directly to the station or network involved, providing the date and time of the broadcast and the product or advertiser in question. This will help those involved in the selection of advertising material to become better informed about audience opinion.

Tobacco and Alcohol Advertising

Federal law prohibits the airing of advertising for cigarettes, little cigars, smokeless tobacco, and chewing tobacco on radio, TV, or any other medium of electronic communication under the FCC's jurisdiction. However, the advertising of smoking accessories, cigars, pipes, pipe tobacco, or cigarette making machines is not prohibited. Congress has not enacted any law prohibiting broadcast advertising of any kind of alcoholic beverage, and the FCC does not have a rule or policy regulating such advertisements.

Subliminal Programming

The Commission sometimes receives complaints regarding the alleged use of subliminal perception techniques in broadcast programming. Subliminal programming is designed to be perceived on a subconscious level only. Regardless of whether it is effective, the broadcast of subliminal material is inconsistent with a station's obligation to serve the public interest because it is designed to be deceptive.

BLANKETING INTERFERENCE

Rules

Some members of the public situated close to a radio station's transmitting antenna may experience impaired reception of other stations. This is called "blanketing" interference. The Commission's rules impose certain obligations on licensees to resolve such interference complaints. Complaints about such interference involving radio stations are handled by the Media Bureau's Audio Division. Blanketing interference is a less common occurrence with television stations than with radio stations due to the location and height of TV transmitting antennas. If this phenomenon does occur with a television station, the Media Bureau's Video Division will handle complaints on a case-by case-basis, subject to the radio guidelines noted below.

At the outset, the policy is designed to provide protection from interference for individuals within a certain distance from a station (in an area known as the station's "blanketing contour") and only involving electronic devices that pick up an over-the-air signal from a broadcast radio or television station. Thus, stations are not required to resolve interference complaints involving the following:

• A complaint from a party located outside of the station's blanketing contour (115 dBu contour for FM stations, 1 V/m contour for AM stations).

• Improperly installed antenna systems.

• Use of high gain antennas or antenna booster amplifiers.

• Mobile receivers, including but not limited to car radios, portable stereos or cellular phones.

• Non radio frequency ("RF") devices, including but not limited to, tape recorders, CD players, MP3 players or "land-line" telephones.

• Cordless telephones.

For complaints from parties located within the station's blanketing contour involving non-mobile television or radio receivers, a station must resolve the interference complaint at no cost to the complaining party if the party notifies the station of the problem during the first year that the station operates its new or modified facilities. For similar complaints received after the first year of such operation has passed, although the station is not financially responsible for resolving the complaint, it must provide effective technical assistance to the complaining party. These efforts must include the provision of information and assistance sufficiently

specific to enable the complaining party to eliminate all blanketing interference and not simply an attempt by the station to correct the problems. Such assistance entails providing specific details about proper corrective measures to resolve the blanketing interference. For example, stations should provide the complaining party with diagrams and descriptions which explain how and where to use radiofrequency chokes, ferrite cores, filters, and/or shielded cable. In addition, effective technical assistance also includes recommending replacement equipment that would work better in high radiofrequency fields. Effective technical assistance does not mean referring the complainant to the equipment manufacturer.

How to Resolve Blanketing Interference Problems.

If you believe that you are receiving blanketing or any other type of interference to broadcast reception, we encourage you to first communicate directly, in writing, with the licensee of the station that you believe is causing the interference. If the licensee does not satisfactorily resolve the problem, you can mail, fax, or e-mail a complaint to us as follows:

• For radio stations:

> Federal Communications Commission
> Audio Division, Media Bureau
> Washington, D.C. 20554
> Fax number: (202) 418-1411
> E-mail address: radioinfo@fcc.gov

• For TV stations:

> Federal Communications Commission
> Video Division, Media Bureau
> 445 12th St., S.W.
> Washington, D.C. 20554
> Fax number: (202) 418-2827
> E-mail address: tvinfo@fcc.gov

Your complaint should include: (1) your name, address, and phone number; (2) the call letters of each station involved; (3) each location at which the interference occurs; and (4) each specific device receiving the interference. The more specific your complaint is, the easier it is for us and any station involved to identify and resolve the interference problem.

OTHER INTERFERENCE ISSUES

In many cases in which you receive interference on your television set or radio, the source of the problem could be with your equipment, which may not be adequately designed with circuitry or filtering to reject the unwanted signals of nearby transmitters. We recommend that you contact the equipment manufacturer or the store at which the equipment was purchased to attempt to resolve the interference problem. You can find more information about broadcast interference on the Commission's website, at http://www.fcc.gov/cgb/consumerfacts/interference.html.

THE LOCAL PUBLIC INSPECTION FILE

Requirement to Maintain a Public Inspection File

Our rules require that all licensees and permittees of TV and radio stations and applicants for new broadcast stations maintain a file available for public inspection. This file must contain documents relevant to the station's operation and dealings with the community and the FCC. The public inspection file generally must be maintained at the station's main studio. To obtain the location and phone number of a station's main studio, consult your local telephone directory, or call the station's business office. You may also be able to find this information on the station's Internet website, if one exists.

Purpose of the File

Because we do not routinely monitor each station's programming and operations, viewers and listeners are an important source of information about the nature of their area stations' programming, operations, and compliance with their FCC obligations. The documents contained in each station's public inspection file have information about the station that can assist the public in this important monitoring role.

As discussed in this Manual, every station has an obligation to provide news, public affairs, and other programming that specifically treats the important issues facing its community, and to comply with the Communications Act, the Commission's rules, and the terms of its station license. We encourage a continuing dialogue between broadcasters and members of the public to ensure that stations meet their obligations and remain responsive to the needs of the local community. Because you watch and listen to the stations that we license, you can be a valuable and effective advocate to ensure that your area's stations comply with their localism obligation and other FCC requirements.

Viewing the Public Inspection File

Each broadcast licensee, permittee, and applicant must make its station public inspection file available to members of the public at any time during regular business hours. Although you do not need to make an appointment to view the file, making one may be helpful both to the station and to you.

A station that chooses to maintain all or part of its public file on a computer database must provide you a computer terminal if you wish to review the file. As of a date to be determined, television stations will also be required to post most of the content of their public files on their Internet websites, if they have them, or on their state broadcasters association's website, if permitted. Radio stations have not yet been required to post their files on their websites, but may do so if they wish. If you want to view a station's public file over the Internet, you should check its website or contact the station to determine if the file is posted.

You may request copies of materials in the file, which the station must provide to you at a reasonable charge, by visiting the station in person. In addition, if the station's public file is located outside of its community of license (and you live within the station's service area and your request does not involve the station's political file), you may request copies of materials in the file over the telephone. To facilitate telephone requests, we require stations to provide you a copy of the current version of this Manual free of charge if you so request. The Manual can help you identify other documents you may ask to have mailed to you. Stations should assist callers in this process and answer questions you may have about the actual contents of the public file. This information may include, for example, the number of pages and time periods covered by a particular ownership report or children's television programming report, or the types of applications actually maintained in the station's public file and the dates on which they were filed with the FCC. Finally, if you ask a broadcast station for photocopies of material in its public inspection file, the station may require you to pay for those photocopies. Therefore, the station may require a guarantee of payment in advance (such as with a deposit or a credit card). The station must pay the postage for copies requested by telephone. Stations must fulfill requests for copies within a reasonable period of time, which generally should not exceed seven calendar days after the request is made. For additional information on these public file requirements, see http://www.fcc.gov/eb/broadcast/pif.html.

Contents of the File.

The following materials must be maintained in each station public inspection file:

The License. Stations must keep a copy of their current FCC construction permit or license in the public file, together with any material documenting Commission-approved modifications to the authorization. The license or permit reflects the station's authorized technical parameters (such as its frequency, call letters, operating power and transmitter location), as well as any special conditions imposed by the FCC on the station's operation. It also indicates when it was issued and when it will expire.

Applications and Related Materials. The public file must contain copies of all applications involving the station filed with the Commission that are still pending before either the FCC or the courts. These include applications to sell the station or to modify its facilities (for example, to increase power, change the antenna system, or change the transmitter location). If a petition to deny any application was filed, the file must contain a statement to that effect, and the name and address of the petitioning party.

Applications must be maintained until "final" FCC action on them, when the action can no longer be appealed or reversed.

The station must also keep copies of any granted construction permit or assignment or transfer application if its grant required us to waive our rules. Applications that required a waiver, together with any related material, will reflect each particular rule that we waived, and must be maintained as long as any such waiver remains in effect.

Also, if the FCC renewed the station license for less than a full term, the station must keep that renewal application (FCC Form 303-S) in the file until grant of its next renewal application by final FCC action. We may grant such a short-term renewal when we are concerned about the station's performance over the previous term. These concerns will be reflected in the renewal-related materials in the public file.

Citizen Agreements. Commercial stations must keep copies of any written agreements that they make with local viewers or listeners. These "citizen agreements" may deal with programming, employment, or other issues of community concern. The station must keep these agreements in the public file for as long as they are in effect.

Contour Maps. The public file must contain copies of any station service contour maps or other information submitted with any application filed with the FCC that reflects the station's service contours and/or its main studio and transmitter locations. The Commission's application forms require submission of contour maps only from stations that do not certify that their signals cover their city of license. These documents must stay in the file for as long as they remain current and accurate regarding the station.

Material Relating to an FCC Investigation or Complaint. Stations must keep material relating to any matter that is the subject of an FCC investigation (including EEO audits) or a complaint that the station has violated the Communications Act or FCC rules. The station must keep this material in its file until the FCC notifies it that the material may be discarded. Since the FCC is not involved in disputes regarding matters unrelated to the Communications Act or FCC rules, such as private contractual disputes, stations do not have to retain material relating to such disputes in the public file.

Ownership Reports and Related Material. The public file must contain a copy of the most recent, complete ownership report (FCC Form 323 for commercial stations, FCC Form 323-E for noncommercial educational stations) filed for the station. Among other things, these reports disclose the names of the owners of the station licensee and their ownership interests, list any contracts related to the station that are required to be filed with the FCC, and identify any interests in other broadcast stations held by the station licensee or its owners.

List of Contracts Required to be Filed with the FCC. Stations must keep in the public file either copies of all the contracts that they have to file with the FCC, or an up-to-date list identifying all such contracts. If the station keeps a list and a member of the public asks to see copies of the actual contracts, the station must provide the copies to the requester within seven calendar days. Contracts required to be maintained or listed in the public inspection file include:

• contracts relating to network service (network affiliation contracts);

• contracts relating to ownership or control of the licensee or permittee or its stock. Examples include articles of incorporation, bylaws, agreements providing for the assignment of a license or permit or affecting stock ownership or voting rights (stock options, pledges, or proxies), and mortgage or loan agreements that restrict the licensee or permittee's freedom of operation; and

• management consultant agreements with independent contractors, and contracts relating to the utilization in a management capacity of any person other than an officer, director, or regular employee of the licensee.

Political File. Stations must keep a file which contains "a complete record of a request to purchase broadcast time that: (A) is made by or on behalf of a legally qualified candidate for public

office; or (B) communicates a message relating to any political matter of national importance, including: (i) a legally qualified candidate; (ii) any election to federal office; or (iii) a national legislative issue of public importance." The file must identify how the station responded to such requests and, if the request was granted, the charges made, a schedule of time purchased, the times the spots actually aired, the rates charged, and the classes of time purchased. The file also must reflect any free time provided to a candidate. The station must keep the political records in the file for two years after the spot airs. (You can find more information regarding the political broadcasting laws at pages 13-14 of this Manual.)

EEO Materials. As noted earlier, licensees must submit certain forms containing EEO information and include copies in their station public files. Thus, all stations employing five or more full-time employees must put an EEO public file report in their station public file each year. We also require each radio and TV station licensee to file a Form 396 EEO Program Report with its license renewal application and to include the Report in its public file. Those licensees that file a Form 397 Broadcast Mid-Term Report must also include a copy in the public file. These materials must be retained in the file until final action on the station's next license renewal application. A new station applicant or prospective station buyer, if it intends to employ five or more full-time employees, must file a Form 396-A Broadcast EEO Model Program Report with its new station assignment or transfer application and the Report must be included in the public file as a part of the underlying application and retained in the file until the grant of the underlying application becomes final. (You can find more information regarding the EEO rules at pages 20-21 of this Manual.)

"The Public and Broadcasting." Stations must keep a copy of the current version of this Manual in the public file and provide a copy, upon request, to any member of the public. As noted above, you can also request a copy from the FCC or access it on our Internet website at http://www.fcc.gov/mb/audio/decdoc/public_and_broadcasting.html.

Letters and E-Mails from the Public. Commercial stations must keep in their files, for at least three years, written comments, suggestions, and e-mails received from the public regarding their operation. (Noncommercial educational stations are not subject to this requirement.) This obligation is limited to comments, suggestions, and e-mails sent to station management or a publicized station address. Letters need not be placed in the public inspection file when the author has requested that the letter not be made public or when the licensee feels that it should be excluded from public inspection because of the nature of its content (such as defamatory or obscene letters). Moreover, although television stations that post their public file materials on their websites must include e-mails received from the public, they need not post letters from the public, as long as they include hard copies of such letters in their public files, and a notice on their website that the letters can be located in the file. As noted above, all or a part of a station public file may be maintained on a computer database, as long as a computer terminal is made available, at the location of the file, for members of the public who wish to review the file. Accordingly, as an alternative to maintaining hard copies of e-mails in the public file, a station may place the e-mails on a computer database, as long as a terminal is made available at the location of the public file to members of the public who wish to review the file.

Quarterly Programming Reports. Every three months, each broadcast radio and television station licensee must prepare and place in its station public file a list of programs containing its most significant treatment of community issues during the preceding three months ("issues/programs lists"). The list must briefly describe both the issue and the programming during which the issue was discussed, including the date and time that each such program was aired and its title and duration. The licensee must keep these lists in the file until the next grant of the station renewal application has become final. Television stations will be required to file a Standardized Television Disclosure Form instead of these lists once that form is approved and made available. The form, which will also be filed quarterly, will require commercial and noncommercial educational television broadcasters to provide detailed information on the efforts of their station to

provide programming responsive to issues facing their communities in a standardized format.

Children's Television Programming Reports. As discussed at pages 17-18 of this Manual, the Children's Television Act of 1990 and our rules require each TV station to serve the educational and informational needs of children by means of its overall programming and through programming that is specifically designed to serve such needs. Commercial TV stations must make and retain in their files Children's Television Programming Reports (FCC Form 398) identifying the educational and informational programming for children aired by the station. (Noncommercial educational stations are not required to prepare these reports.) The report must include the name of the person at the station responsible for collecting comments on the station's compliance with the Children's Television Act. The station has to prepare these reports each calendar quarter, and it must place them in the public file separate from the file's other material. The licensee must keep these lists in the file until the next grant of the station renewal application has become final. You can also view each station's reports on our website at http://www.fcc.gov/parents/localprograms.html.

Records Regarding Children's Programming Commercial Limits. As also discussed at page 17 of this Manual, the Children's Television Act of 1990 and our rules limit the type and amount of advertising that may be aired during TV programming directed to children 12 and under. Stations must keep records that substantiate compliance with this limitation in their public files and retain them until the next grant of the station renewal application has become final.

Time Brokerage Agreements. A time brokerage agreement is a type of contract that generally involves a station's sale of blocks of airtime to a third-party broker, who then supplies the programming to fill that time and sells the commercial spot announcements to support the programming. Commercial radio and television stations must keep in their public files a copy of every agreement involving: (1) time brokerage of that station, or (2) time brokerage by any other station owned by the same licensee. These agreements must be maintained in the file for as long as they are in force.

Lists of Donors. Noncommercial educational television and radio stations must keep in their public files a list of donors supporting each specific program. These lists must be retained for two years after the program at issue airs.

Local Public Notice Announcements. As discussed at pages 10-11 of this Manual, when someone files an application to build a new station or to renew, sell, or modify an existing station, we generally require the applicant to make a series of local announcements to inform the public of the application's existence and nature. These announcements are either published in a local newspaper or made over the air on the station, and are intended to give the public an opportunity to comment on the application. A statement certifying compliance with this requirement, including the dates and times that notice was given, must be placed in the public file. The only exception to this public notice requirement is when the proposed station sale is "pro forma" and will not result in a change of ultimate control, or the modification application does not contemplate a "major change" of the station facilities.

Must-Carry or Retransmission Consent Election. The public file for all commercial television stations must also contain documentation of the station's election for carriage over cable and satellite systems. In this regard, there are two ways that a broadcast TV station can choose to be carried over a cable or satellite system: "must-carry" or "retransmission consent." Each is discussed below.

Must-Carry. TV stations are generally entitled to be carried on cable television systems in their local markets. A station that chooses to exercise this right receives no compensation from the cable system. Satellite carriers may decide to offer local stations in a designated market area. If they choose to offer one station, then they must carry all the stations in that market that request carriage.

Retransmission Consent. Instead of exercising their "must-carry" rights, commercial TV stations may choose to receive compensation from a cable system or satellite carrier in return for granting permission to the cable system or satellite carrier to carry the station. This option is available only to commercial TV stations. Because it is possible that a station that elects this option may not reach an agreement with the cable system, it may ultimately not be carried by the system.

Every three years, commercial TV stations must decide whether their relationship with each local cable system and satellite carrier that offers local service will be governed by must-carry or by retransmission consent agreements. Each commercial station must keep a copy of its decision in the public file for the three-year period to which it pertains.

Noncommercial stations are not entitled to compensation in return for carriage on a cable or satellite system, but they may request mandatory carriage on the system. A noncommercial station making such a request must keep a copy of the request in the public file for the duration of the period to which it applies.

DTV Transition Consumer Education Activity Reports. Each broadcast television station must place in its station public file on a quarterly basis an FCC Form 388 DTV Consumer Education Quarterly Activity Report outlining its efforts during the previous quarter to educate consumers on the transition to digital television. These reports must be maintained in the file for one year. Additional information about the DTV transition can be found at page 9 of this Manual.

COMMENTS OR COMPLAINTS ABOUT A STATION

Comments to Stations and Networks.

If you feel the need to do so, we encourage you to write directly to station management or to network officials to comment on their broadcast service. These are the people responsible for creating and selecting the station's programs and announcements and determining station operation. Letters to station and network officials keep them informed about audience needs and interests, as well as on public opinion on specific material and practices. Individuals and groups can often resolve problems with stations at the local level.

Comments/Complaints to the FCC.

We give full consideration to the broadcast complaints, comments, and other inquiries that we receive. As stated above, we encourage you to first contact the station or network directly about programming and operating issues. If your concerns are not resolved in this manner, with the exception of complaints about obscene, indecent, or profane programming, which should be submitted in the manner described at page 15 of this Manual, and complaints about blanketing interference discussed at page 24, the best way to provide all the information the FCC needs to process your complaint about other broadcast matters is to complete fully the on-line complaint Form 2000E, which can be found at http://www.fcc.gov/cgb/complaints.html. You can also call in, e-mail or file your complaint in hard copy with the FCC's Consumer Center in the following manner:

Federal Communications Commission
Consumer & Governmental Affairs Bureau
Consumer Inquiries and Complaints Division
445 12th St., S.W.
Washington, D.C. 20554

Fax number: (202) 418-0232
Telephone number: (888) 225-5322 (voice); (888)835-5322 (TTY)
E-mail address:fccinfo@fcc.gov

If you are submitting an audio or video tape, DVD, CD or other type of media with your complaint, you should send it to the following address to avoid mail processing damage:

Federal Communications Commission
Consumer & Governmental Affairs Bureau
Consumer Inquiries and Complaints Division
9300 East Hampton Drive
Capitol Heights, Maryland 20743

If you do not use the on-line complaint Form 2000E, your complaint, at a minimum, should indicate: (1) the call letters of the station; (2) the city and state in which the station is located; (3) the name, time, and date of the specific program or advertisement in question, if applicable; (4) the name of anyone contacted at the station, if applicable; and (5) a statement of the problem, as specific as possible, together with an audio or video tape, CD, DVD or other recording or transcript of the program or advertisement that is the subject of your complaint (if possible). Please include your name and address if you would like information on the final disposition of your complaint; you may request confidentiality. We prefer that you submit complaints in writing, although you may submit complaints that are time-sensitive by telephone, especially if they involve safety concerns. Please be aware that we can only act on allegations that a station has violated a provision of the Communications Act or the FCC's rules or policies.

In addition to (or instead of) filing a complaint, you can file a petition to deny or an informal objection to an application that a station licensee has filed, such as a license renewal application. This procedure is discussed at pages 10-11 of this Manual. You may obtain further information on the petition to deny process on the Commission's website, at http://www.fcc.gov/localism /renew_process_handout.pdf . You may also wish to consider reviewing our rules or contacting an attorney. You can find links to our rules on the Commission website, at http://wireless.fcc.gov /index.htm?job=rules_and_regulations. As noted earlier, the rules governing broadcast stations are generally found in Part 73 of Title 47 of the Code of Federal Regulations.

BROADCAST INFORMATION SPECIALISTS

We have created contact points at the Commission, accessible via toll-free telephone numbers, by fax, or over the Internet, dedicated to providing information to members of the public regarding how they can become involved in the Commission's processes. Should you have questions about how do so, including inquiries about our complaint or petitioning procedures or the filing and status of the license renewal, modification or assignment or transfer application for a particular station, you may contact one of our Broadcast Information Specialists, by calling, by facsimile, or by sending an e-mail, as noted below:

- If your question relates to a radio station:

  Toll-Free: (866) 267-7202 (Voice) or (877) 479-1433 (TTY)
  Fax: (202) 418-1411
  E-Mail: radioinfo@fcc.gov

- If your question relates to a television station:

  Toll-Free: (866) 918-5777 (Voice) or (866) 787-6222 (TTY)
  Fax: (202) 418-2827
  E-Mail: tvinfo@fcc.gov

If your question relates to both a radio and a television station or is general in nature, you may contact either specialist.

Section B

Television

Section B

Broadcast Television

TV Group Ownership

A

ABC Inc., 2300 Riverside Dr., Burbank, CA, 91521. Phone: (818) 249-9999. Web Site:www.abc.go.com Ownership: ABC Enterprises Inc., 100%. Note: ABC Enterprises Inc. is 100% owned by Disney Enterprises Inc. Disney Enterprises Inc. is 100% owned by The Walt Disney Co.

Stns: 10 TV. WLS, Chicago; WJRT-TV, Flint-Saginaw-Bay City, MI; KFSN-TV, Fresno-Visalia, CA; KTRK, Houston; KABC, Los Angeles; WABC-TV, New York; WPVI, Philadelphia; WTVD, Raleigh-Durham (Fayetteville), NC; KGO, San Francisco-Oakland-San Jose; WTVG, Toledo, OH.

Stns: 43 AM. 3 FM. KDIS-FM Little Rock, AR; KMIK Tempe, AZ; KSPN(AM) Los Angeles, CA; KMKY Oakland, CA; KDIS(AM) Pasadena, CA; KIID(AM) Sacramento, CA; KDDZ Arvada, CO; WDZK Bloomfield, CT; WBWL Jacksonville, FL; WMYM(AM) Miami, FL; WDYZ(AM) Orlando, FL; WMNE(AM) Riviera Beach, FL; WWMI Saint Petersburg, FL; WDWD Atlanta, GA; WSDZ Belleville, IL; WMVP Chicago, IL; WRDZ La Grange, IL; WRDZ-FM Plainfield, IN; KQAM Wichita, KS; WDRD(AM) Newburg, KY; WBYU New Orleans, LA; WMKI(AM) Boston, MA; WFDF(AM) Farmington Hills, MI; KDIZ Golden Valley, MN; KPHN Kansas City, MO; WGFY Charlotte, NC; WCOG Greensboro, NC; WWJZ Mount Holly, NJ; KALY Los Ranchos de Albuquerque, NM; WDDY(AM) Albany, NY; WEPN(AM) New York, NY; WQEW New York, NY; WWMK Cleveland, OH; KDZR(AM) Lake Oswego, OR; WEAE Pittsburgh, PA; WDDZ(AM) Pawtucket, RI; KESN(FM) Allen, TX; KMIC(AM) Houston, TX; KMKI Plano, TX; KRDY(AM) San Antonio, TX; KWDZ(AM) Salt Lake City, UT; WDZY Colonial Heights, VA; WRJR(AM) Portsmouth, VA; WHKT Portsmouth, VA; KKDZ Seattle, WA; WKSH(AM) Sussex, WI.

Robert A. Iger, pres; Phillip J. Meek, pres; Lawrence J. Pollock, chmn owned TV stns.

ACME Communications Inc., 2101 E. Fourth St., Suite 202A, Santa Ana, CA, 92705. Phone: (714) 245-9499. Fax: (714) 245-9494.E-mail: t.allen@acmecomm.com Web Site:www.acmecommunications.com Ownership: Alta Cpmmunications; Seaport Capital.

Stns: 8 TV. KASY, Albuquerque-Santa Fe, NM; KWBQ, Albuquerque-Santa Fe, NM; KRWB-TV, Albuquerque-Santa Fe, NM; WBUI, Champaign & Springfield-Decatur, IL; WBDT, Dayton, OH; WIWB, Green Bay-Appleton, WI; WBXX, Knoxville, TN; WBUW, Madison, WI.

Jamie Kellner, chmn/CEO; Doug Gealy, pres/COO; Tom Allen, exec VP & CFO.

Access.1 Communications Corp., 11 Penn Plaza, 16th Fl., New York, NY, 10001. Phone: (212) 714-1000. Fax: (212) 714-1563. Ownership: Sydney L. Small, 54.12%; Black Enterprise/Greenwich Street Capital Partners, 19.47%; MESBIC Ventures Inc., 5.54%; Chesley Maddox-Dorsey, 2.84%; and Adriane Gaines, 1.85%.

Stns: 1 TV. WMGM-TV, Philadelphia.

Stns: 5 AM. 10 FM. KSYR(FM) Benton, LA; KDKS-FM Blanchard, LA; KBTT(FM) Haughton, LA; KLKL(FM) Minden, LA; KOKA Shreveport, LA; WGYM(AM) Hammonton, NJ; WWRL(AM) New York, NY; KOYE(FM) Frankston, TX; KOOI-FM Jacksonville, TX; KFRO Longview, TX; KYKX-FM Longview, TX; KCUL Marshall, TX; KCUL-FM Marshall, TX; KTAL-FM Texarkana, TX; KKUS(FM) Tyler, TX.

Sydney L. Small, chmn/CEO.

Allbritton Communications Co., 1000 Wilson Blvd., Suite 2700, Arlington, VA, 22209. Phone: (703) 647-8700. Fax: (703) 647-8707.

Stns: 8 TV. WCFT, Birmingham (Anniston, Tuscaloosa), AL; WJSU, Birmingham (Anniston, Tuscaloosa), AL; WCIV, Charleston, SC; WHTM, Harrisburg-Lancaster-Lebanon-York, PA; KATV, Little Rock-Pine Bluff, AR; WSET-TV, Roanoke-Lynchburg, VA; KTUL, Tulsa, OK; WJLA-TV, Washington, DC (Hagerstown, MD).

Allbritton Communications, through affiliated company, publishes the *Enfield* (CT) *Press*, *The Longmeadow* (MA) *News*, *Westfield* (MA) *Evening News* & *The Penny Saver*, Westfield, MA.

Also owns Cable-NewsChannel 8, Arlington, VA. All 100% owned.

Frederick Ryan Jr., pres; Robert L. Allbritton, CEO.

AsianMedia Group LLP, 1990 S. Bundy Dr., c/o KSCI, Suite 850, Los Angeles, CA, 90025. Phone: (310) 478-1818. Fax: (310) 479-8118.E-mail: info@la18.tv Web Site:www.la18.tv Ownership: Leonard Green & Partners, LLP. LPTV: KUAN-LP Poway, CA.

Stns: 2 TV. KIKU, Honolulu, HI; KSCI, Los Angeles.

Peter Mathes, chmn/CEO; John Chang, CFO.

Astral Media Inc., 2100 rue Sainte-Catherine Ouest, Bureau 1000, Montreal, PQ, H3H 2T3. Canada. Phone: (514) 939-5000. Fax: (514) 939-1515. Web Site:www.astralmedia.com Ownership: Abgreen Holdings Ltd., 55.71% vote; 654625 Ontario Inc., 13.63% vote.

Stns: 2 TV. CJDC, Dawson Creek, BC; CFTK, Terrace, BC.

Stns: 24 AM. 62 FM. CJAY-FM Calgary, AB; CKMX Calgary, AB; CIBK-FM Calgary, AB; CFBR-FM Edmonton, AB; CFRN Edmonton, AB; CFMG-FM Saint Albert, AB; CFKC Creston, BC; CJDC Dawson Creek, BC; CKRX-FM Fort Nelson, BC; CHRX-FM Fort St. John, BC; CKNL-FM Fort St. John, BC; CKGR Golden, BC; CKIR Invermere, BC; CKFR(AM) Kelowna, BC; CHSU-FM Kelowna, BC; CILK-FM Kelowna, BC; CKTK-FM Kitimat, BC; CKKC-FM Nelson, BC; CKZX-FM New Denver, BC; CJOR Osoyoos, BC; CJMG-FM Penticton, BC; CKOR Penticton, BC; CHTK Prince Rupert, BC; CIOR Princeton, BC; CKCR Revelstoke, BC; CISL Richmond, BC; CKXR-FM Salmon Arm, BC; CHOR Summerland, BC; CFTK Terrace, BC; CJFW-FM Terrace, BC; CJAT-FM Trail, BC; CKZZ-FM Vancouver, BC; CICF-FM Vernon, BC; CKX-FM Brandon, MB; CKXA-FM Brandon, MB; CFQX-FM Selkirk, MB; CKMM-FM Winnipeg, MB; CKBC-FM Bathurst, NB; CIBX-FM Fredericton, NB; CKHJ(AM) Fredericton, NB; CFXY-FM Fredericton, NB; CIKX-FM Grand Falls, NB; CJCJ-FM Woodstock, NB; CKTO-FM Truro, NS; CKTY-FM Truro, NS; CHAM Hamilton, ON; CKOC Hamilton, ON; CKLH-FM Hamilton, ON; CKSL London, ON; CJBK(AM) London, ON; CJBX-FM London, ON; CIQM-FM London, ON; CKQB-FM Ottawa, ON; CHVR-FM Pembroke, ON; CHRE-FM Saint Catharines, ON; CHTZ-FM Saint Catharines, ON; CKTB Saint Catharines, ON; CJEZ-FM Toronto, ON; CKFM-FM Toronto, ON; CFRB Toronto, ON; CFVM-FM Amqui, PQ; CFIX-FM Chicoutimi, PQ; CHRD-FM Drummondville, PQ; CJDM-FM Drummondville, PQ; CKTF-FM Gatineau, PQ; CIMF-FM Gatineau, PQ; CIMO-FM Magog, PQ; CITE-FM Montreal, PQ; CHOM-FM Montreal, PQ; CKMF-FM Montreal, PQ; CJFM-FM Montreal, PQ; CJAD Montreal, PQ; CHIK-FM Quebec, PQ; CITF-FM Quebec, PQ; CIKI-FM Rimouski, PQ; CJOI-FM Rimouski, PQ; CJMM-FM Rouyn-Noranda, PQ; CJAB-FM Saguenay, PQ; CFEI-FM Saint Hyacinthe, PQ; CFZZ-FM Saint Jean-Iberville, PQ; CKSM Shawinigan, PQ; CITE-FM-1 Sherbrooke, PQ; CIGB-FM Trois Rivieres, PQ; CHEY-FM Trois Rivieres, PQ; CJMV-FM Val d'Or, PQ; CHBD-FM Regina, SK.

Ian Greenberg, pres/CEO.

B

Bahakel Communications, Box 32488, Charlotte, NC, 28232. Phone: (704) 372-4434. Fax: (704) 335-9904. Ownership: 2000 Bahakel Descendents Trust, 100%.

Stns: 8 TV. WCCU, Champaign & Springfield-Decatur, IL; WRSP-TV, Champaign & Springfield-Decatur, IL; WCCB, Charlotte, NC; WOLO, Columbia, SC; WABG-TV, Greenwood-Greenville, MS; WBBJ, Jackson, TN; WAKA, Montgomery-Selma, AL; WFXB, Myrtle Beach-Florence, SC.

Stns: 4 AM. 5 FM. KILO-FM Colorado Springs, CO; KRXP(FM) Pueblo West, CO; KOKZ-FM Waterloo, IA; KWLO(AM) Waterloo, IA; KXEL Waterloo, IA; KFMW-FM Waterloo, IA; WDEF Chattanooga, TN; WDEF-FM Chattanooga, TN; WDOD Chattanooga, TN.

Beverly B. Poston, pres; Stephen Bahakel, Sr VP radio div; Russell Schwartz, Sr VP business affrs/gen counsel; Bill Napier, VP eng/tech; Anna Rufty, VP Hum Res.

Barrington Broadcasting Group, LLC., 2500 W. Higgins Rd., Suite 155, Hoffman Estates, IL, 60169-7275. Phone: (847) 884-1877. Fax: (847) 755-3045.E-mail: info@barringtontv.com Web Site:www.barringtontv.com Ownership: Pilot Group LP, 100% of votes.

Stns: 18 TV. WFXL, Albany, GA; KVIH, Amarillo, TX; KVII-TV, Amarillo, TX; KXRM, Colorado Springs-Pueblo, CO; WACH, Columbia, SC; KRCG, Columbia-Jefferson City, MO; WEYI-TV, Flint-Saginaw-Bay City, MI; WBSF, Flint-Saginaw-Bay City, MI; KGBT-TV, Harlingen-Weslaco -Brownsville-McAllen, TX; WLUC, Marquette, MI; WPDE, Myrtle Beach-Florence, SC; KTVO, Ottumwa, IA-Kirksville, MO; WHOI, Peoria-Bloomington, IL; KHQA-TV, Quincy, IL-Hannibal, MO-Keokuk, IA; WSTM, Syracuse, NY; WNWO, Toledo, OH; WPBN, Traverse City-Cadillac, MI; WTOM, Traverse City-Cadillac, MI.

Paul M. McNicol, sr VP; K. James Yager, CEO; Chris Cornelius, pres/COO; Warren Spector, CFO; Paul McNicol, sec; Mary Flodin, sr VP; Keith Bland, sr VP.

Beach TV Properties Inc., Box 9556, Panama City Beach, FL, 32407.

Stns: 2 TV. WAWD, Mobile, AL-Pensacola (Ft. Walton Beach), FL; WPCT, Panama City, FL.

Byron J. Colley, pres.

Belo Corp, (Television Group). 400 S. Record St., Dallas, TX, 75202. Phone: (214) 977-6600. Fax: (214) 977-6603. Web Site:www.belo.com Ownership: Belo Corp.

Stns: 19 TV. KVUE, Austin, TX; KTVB, Boise, ID; WCNC, Charlotte, NC; WFAA, Dallas-Ft. Worth; KHOU, Houston; WHAS, Louisville, KY; WWL, New Orleans, LA; WVEC, Norfolk-Portsmouth-Newport News, VA; KTVK, Phoenix (Prescott), AZ; KASW, Phoenix (Prescott), AZ; KGW, Portland, OR; KENS, San Antonio, TX; KING, Seattle-Tacoma, WA; KONG, Seattle-Tacoma, WA; KREM, Spokane, WA; KSKN, Spokane, WA; KMOV, St. Louis, MO; KMSB, Tucson (Sierra Vista), AZ; KTTU, Tucson (Sierra Vista), AZ.

The publishing division of Belo Corp., publishes the following dailies: *The Dallas* (TX) *Morning News* and *The Press-Enterprise*, Riverside, CA; *Denton Record Chronicle*, Denton, TX; *The Providence Journal*, Providence, RI; *Arlington Morning News*, Arlington, VA. Other interests: News cable channels (100% owned): Northwest Cable News, Texas Cable News, 24/7 Newschannel (distribution in ID from Boise, ID). News cable channel partnerships in the following DMAs: Phoenix, AZ; New Orleans; and Norfolk-Portsmouth-Newport News, VA.

Robert W. Decherd, chmn; Dunia A. Shive, pres/COO.

Block Communications Inc., 6450 Monroe St., Sylvania, OH, 43560. Phone: (419) 724-6448. Fax: (419) 724-6167. Web Site:www.blockcommunications.com Ownership: Estate of William Block, Allan Block, John R. Block.

Stns: 4 TV. KTRV-TV, Boise, ID; WLIO, Lima, OH; WDRB, Louisville, KY; WMYO, Louisville, KY.

Block Communications Inc. publishes the *Toledo* OH *Blade* & *Pittsburgh* (PA) *Post-Gazette*.

Allan Block, chmn; Gary J. Blair, exec VP; Jodi Miehls, treas; David Huey, pres.

Bonneville International Corporation, Broadcast House, Box 1160, Salt Lake City, UT, 84110-1160. Phone: (801) 575-7500. Fax: (801) 575-7521. Web Site:www.bonnint.com Ownership: Deseret Management Corp. Deseret Management Corp. owns *The Deseret Morning News*, a Salt Lake City, UT, daily.

Stns: 1 TV. KSL, Salt Lake City, UT.

Stns: 8 AM. 21 FM. KTAR-FM Glendale, AZ; KPKX(FM) Phoenix, AZ; KMVP Phoenix, AZ; KTAR(AM) Phoenix, AZ; KSWD(FM) Los Angeles, CA; WTOP-FM Washington, DC; WFED(AM) Washington, DC; WDRV(FM) Chicago, IL; WILV(FM) Chicago, IL; WXOS(FM) East St. Louis, IL; WARH(FM) Granite City, IL; WTMX-FM Skokie, IL; WWDV(FM) Zion, IL; WYGY(FM) Fort Thomas, KY; WIL-FM Saint Louis, MO; WKRQ-FM Cincinnati, OH; WUBE-FM Cincinnati, OH; WREW(FM) Fairfield, OH; KSL-FM Midvale, UT; KRSP-FM Salt Lake City, UT; KSFI-FM Salt Lake City, UT; KSL Salt Lake City, UT; WWWT-FM Manassas, VA; KTTH(AM) Seattle, WA; KIRO Seattle, WA; KIRO-FM Tacoma, WA; WTLP(FM) Braddock Heights, MD; WWFD(AM) Frederick, MD; WZAA(AM) Silver Spring, MD.

Bruce T. Reese, pres/CEO; Robert A. Johnson, exec VP & COO.

Bonten Media Group LLC, 675 Third Ave., Suite 2521, New York, NY, 10017. Phone: (212) 710-7771. Fax: (212) 949-0909. Ownership: Diamond Castle Partners IV LP, 100% votes.

Stns: 7 TV. KTXS-TV, Abilene-Sweetwater, TX; KTVM, Butte-Bozeman, MT; KRCR, Chico-Redding, CA; KAEF-TV, Eureka, CA; KCFW, Missoula, MT; KECI-TV, Missoula, MT; WCYB-TV, Tri-Cities, TN-VA.

Randall D. Bongarten, pres/CEO.

C

CBS Television Stations Group, 524 W. 57th St., 3rd Fl., New York, NY, 10019. Phone: (212) 975-4321. Web Site:cbslocal.com Ownership: Viacom Inc., 100%.

Stns: 30 TV. WUPA, Atlanta; WJZ, Baltimore, MD; WSBK, Boston (Manchester, NH); WBZ, Boston (Manchester, NH); WBBM, Chicago; KTVT, Dallas-Ft. Worth; KTXA, Dallas-Ft. Worth; KCNC, Denver, CO; WKBD-TV, Detroit;

WWJ-TV, Detroit; KCAL-TV, Los Angeles; KCBS, Los Angeles; WBFS, Miami-Ft. Lauderdale, FL; WFOR-TV, Miami-Ft. Lauderdale, FL; WCCO, Minneapolis-St. Paul, MN; KCCO, Minneapolis-St. Paul, MN; KCCW, Minneapolis-St. Paul, MN; WUPL, New Orleans, LA; WCBS-TV, New York; WGNT, Norfolk-Portsmouth-Newport News, VA; WPSG, Philadelphia; KYW, Philadelphia; KDKA, Pittsburgh, PA; WPCW, Pittsburgh, PA; KMAX, Sacramento -Stockton-Modesto, CA; KOVR, Sacramento -Stockton-Modesto, CA; KPIX, San Francisco-Oakland-San Jose; KBCW, San Francisco-Oakland-San Jose; KSTW, Seattle-Tacoma, WA; WTOG, Tampa-St. Petersburg (Sarasota), FL.

Tom Kane, pres/CEO; Anton Guitano, exec VP.

CP Media LLC, 1181 Hwy. 315, Wilkes-Barre, PA, 18702. Phone: (570) 970-5600. Ownership: Sedgwick Media LLC, 65%; and Dallas Media LLC, 33.64%.

Stns: 4 TV. WGFL, Gainesville, FL; WTLH, Tallahassee, FL-Thomasville, GA; WQMY, Wilkes Barre-Scranton, PA; WOLF, Wilkes Barre-Scranton, PA.

John Parente, pres.

CTVglobemedia, 9 Channel Nine Ct., Scarborough, ON, M1S 4B5. Canada. Phone: (416) 332-5000. Fax: (416) 332-5283.E-mail: ctvglobemediacommunications @ctvglobemedia.com Web Site:www.ctvglobemedia.com Ownership: Ontario Teachers' Plan Board, 25%; The Woodbridge Co. Ltd., 23.59%; Torstar Corp., 20%; 1565117 Ontario Ltd., 16.41%; and BCE Inc., 15%.

Stns: 10 TV. CKVR, Barrie, ON; CKX, Brandon, MB; CJAL, Edmonton, AB; CKX-1, Foxwarren, MB; CFPL-TV, London, ON; CHRO-TV-43, Ottawa, ON; CHRO, Pembroke, ON; CIVI-TV, Victoria, BC; CHWI-TV, Windsor, ON; CKNX, Wingham, ON.

Stns: 10 AM. 23 FM. CKCE-FM Calgary, AB; CHBN-FM Edmonton, AB; CFBT-FM Vancouver, BC; CKST Vancouver, BC; CFUN Vancouver, BC; CHQM-FM Vancouver, BC; CFAX Victoria, BC; CHBE-FM Victoria, BC; CFWM-FM Winnipeg, MB; CHIQ-FM Winnipeg, MB; CFRW(AM) Winnipeg, MB; CIOO-FM Halifax, NS; CJCH-FM Halifax, NS; CJPT-FM Brockville, ON; CFLY-FM Kingston, ON; CKLC-FM Kingston, ON; CKKW-FM Kitchener, ON; CFCA-FM Kitchener, ON; CKLY-FM Lindsay (city of Kawartha Lakes), ON; CHST-FM London, ON; CFGO Ottawa, ON; CFRA Ottawa, ON; CJMJ-FM Ottawa, ON; CKKL-FM Ottawa, ON; CKQM-FM Peterborough, ON; CKPT-FM Peterborough, ON; CHUM Toronto, ON; CHUM-FM Toronto, ON; CKLW Windsor, ON; CIDR-FM Windsor, ON; CIMX-FM Windsor, ON; CKWW Windsor, ON; CKGM Montreal, PQ.

John R. Gossling, CFO; Ivan Fecan, pres/CEO; Paul Sparkes, sr VP; Bonnie Brownlee, sr VP; Chris Gordon, pres, radio division.

CTV Inc., Box 9, Station O, Scarborough, ON, M4A 2M9. Canada. Phone: (416) 332-5000. Fax: (416) 332-5283. Web Site:www.ctv.ca Ownership: CTVglobemedia Inc., 100% (see listing).

Stns: 40 TV. CKYB, Brandon, MB; CJCH-6, Caledonia, NS; CFCN, Calgary, AB; CKCD, Campbellton, NB; CJCH-1, Canning, NS; CKCW-1, Charlottetown, PE; CKCK-1, Colgate, SK; CJOH-8, Cornwall, ON; CJOH-6, Deseronto, ON; CFRN, Edmonton, AB; CICI-1, Elliot Lake, ON; CKMC-1, Golden Prairie, SK; CJCH, Halifax, NS; CITO-2, Kearns, ON; CKCO, Kitchener, ON; CFCN-5, Lethbridge, AB; CKBQ, Melfort, SK; CKCW, Moncton, NB; CFCF, Montreal, PQ; CKNY-TV, North Bay, ON; CJOH-TV, Ottawa, ON; CIPA, Prince Albert, SK; CKCK, Regina, SK; CKCW-TV-2, Saint Edward, PE; CKLT, Saint John, NB; CKCO-3, Sarnia, ON; CFQC, Saskatoon, SK; CHBX, Sault Ste. Marie, ON; CICI, Sudbury, ON; CKMC, Swift Current, SK; CJCB, Sydney, NS; CITO, Timmins, ON; CFTO, Toronto, ON; CKAM, Upsalquitch Lake, NB; CIVT, Vancouver, BC; CIEW, Warmley, SK; CKCO-2, Wiarton, ON; CKCK-2, Willow Bunch, SK; CKY, Winnipeg, MB; CICC, Yorkton, SK.

Stns: 1 FM. CFJR-FM Brockville, ON.

Ivan Fecan, CEO; Rick Brace, pres, revenue, business planning & sports; Susanne Boyce, pres, creative & content & channels.

Cadillac Telecasting Co., 7669 S. 45 Rd., Cadillac, MI, 49601. Phone: (231) 775-9813. Fax: (231) 775-1898.E-mail: info@fox33.com Web Site:www.fox33.com Ownership: Alexander Bolea, 100%.

Stns: 2 TV. WFQX-TV, Traverse City-Cadillac, MI; WFUP, Traverse City-Cadillac, MI.

Alexander Bolea, pres.

California Oregon Broadcasting Inc., Box 1489, Medford, OR, 97501. Phone: (541) 779-5555. Fax: (541) 779-1151.E-mail: cobiadmin@kobi5.com Ownership: Patricia C. Smullin and Carol Anne Smullin Brown. Other interests: Cable TV: Crestview Cable TV (systems in Oregon).

Stns: 3 TV. KLSR, Eugene, OR; KOBI, Medford-Klamath Falls, OR; KOTI, Medford-Klamath Falls, OR.

Patricia C. Smullin, owner.

CanWest Global Communications Corp., 201 Portage Ave., 31st Fl., Winnipeg, MB, R3B 3L7. Canada. Phone: (204) 956-2025. Fax: (204) 947-9841.E-mail: bleslie@canwest.com Web Site:www.canwestglobal.com Ownership: Asper Family 85% voting shares, 45% of equity.

Stns: 16 TV. CICT, Calgary, AB; CHEK-5, Campbell River, BC; CHCA-TV-1, Coronation, AB; CITV, Edmonton, AB; CIHF, Halifax, NS; CHCH, Hamilton, ON; CHBC-TV, Kelowna, BC; CISA-TV, Lethbridge, AB; CJNT, Montreal, PQ; CKMI, Quebec City, PQ; CHCA-TV, Red Deer, AB; CFRE, Regina, SK; CFSK, Saskatoon, SK; CHAN, Vancouver, BC; CHEK, Victoria, BC; CKND-TV, Winnipeg, MB.

Leonard Asper, pres/CEO; David Asper, exec VP.

Capital Community Broadcasting Inc., 360 Egan Dr., Juneau, AK, 99801-1748. Phone: (907) 586-1670. Fax: (907) 586-3612.

Stns: 1 TV. KTOO-TV, Juneau, AK.

Stns: 3 FM. KRNN(FM) Juneau, AK; KXLL(FM) Juneau, AK; KTOO-FM Juneau, AK.

Capitol Broadcasting Co. Inc., Box 12000, Raleigh, NC, 27605. Phone: (919) 821-8555. Fax: (919) 821-8733. Web Site:www.cbc-raleigh.com Ownership: Capitol Holding Co. Inc.

Stns: 4 TV. WMYT-TV, Charlotte, NC; WJZY, Charlotte, NC; WRAL-TV, Raleigh-Durham (Fayetteville), NC; WRAZ, Raleigh-Durham (Fayetteville), NC.

Stns: 1 AM. 8 FM. WKXB-FM Burgaw, NC; WCMC-FM Creedmoor, NC; WLGD(FM) Jacksonville, NC; WSFM(FM) Oak Island, NC; WRAL(FM) Raleigh, NC; WNCM(FM) Sharpsburg, NC; WAZO(FM) Southport, NC; WILT(FM) Wilmington, NC; WMFD Wilmington, NC.

James F. Goodmon, pres/CEO; Vicke S. Murray, sec; Daniel P. McGrath, VO/CFO; Michael D. Hill, VP/gen counsel; James R. Hefner, III, VP, tv.

CaribeVision Station Group LLC, 1401 Brickell Ave., Suite 500, Miami, FL, 33131. Phone: (305) 381-8500. Fax: (305) 381-6225. Ownership: CaribeVision Holdings Inc., 100%.

Stns: 4 TV. WKPV, Ponce, PR; WJPX, San Juan, PR; WJWN, San Sebastian, PR; WIRS, Yauco, PR.

Carlos Barba, CEO.

Chambers Communications Corp., Box 7009, Eugene, OR, 97401. Phone: (541) 485-5611. Fax: (541) 342-1568. Web Site:www.cmc.net/chambers E-mail: kezi@kezi.com Ownership: Carolyn S. Chambers. Other interests: Oregon cable TV.

Stns: 4 TV. KOHD, Bend, OR; KEZI, Eugene, OR; KDKF, Medford-Klamath Falls, OR; KDRV, Medford-Klamath Falls, OR.

Scott Chambers, pres; Carolyn Chambers, CEO.

Christian Faith Broadcasting Inc., 3809 Maple Ave., Castalia, OH, 44824. Phone: (419) 684-5311. Fax: (419) 684-5378.E-mail: wggn@lrbcg.com

Stns: 2 TV. WGGN, Cleveland-Akron (Canton), OH; WLLA, Grand Rapids-Kalamazoo-Battle Creek, MI.

Stns: 3 FM. WJKW-FM Athens, OH; WGGN-FM Castalia, OH; WLRD(FM) Willard, OH.

Shelby Gillam, pres; Rusty Yost, VP.

Christian Television Corporation Inc., 6922 142nd Ave. N., Largo, FL, 33771. Phone: (727) 535-5622. Fax: (727) 531-2497. Web Site:www.ctnonline.com Ownership: Robert D'Andrea, 25% of votes; Virginia Oliver, 25% of votes; Jimmy Smith, 25% of votes; and Wayne Wetzel, 25% of votes.

Stns: 2 TV. KFXB-TV, Cedar Rapids-Waterloo-Iowa City & Dubuque, IA; WCLF, Tampa-St. Petersburg (Sarasota), FL.

Robert D'Andrea, pres.

Citadel Communications Co. LTD., (Coronet Communications, Capital Communications, Citadel Comm. LLC.). 44 Pondfield Rd., Suite 12, Bronxville, NY, 10708. Phone: (914) 793-3400. Fax: (914) 793-3693.E-mail: citnyltd@aol.com Ownership: (Coronet Communications, Capital Communications, Citadel Comm. LLC.)

Stns: 4 TV. WHBF-TV, Davenport, IA-Rock Island-Moline, IL; WOI-DT, Des Moines-Ames, IA; KLKN, Lincoln & Hastings-Kearney, NE; KCAU, Sioux City, IA.

Philip J. Lombardo, CEO. WTSO Madison, WI; WIBA Madison, WI; WIBA-FM Madison, WI; WMEQ(AM) Menomonie, WI; WMEQ-FM Menomonie, WI; WQBW(FM) Milwaukee, WI; WISN Milwaukee, WI; WRIT-FM Milwaukee, WI; WOKY Milwaukee, WI; WKKV-FM Racine, WI; WMAD(FM) Sauk City, WI; WXXM(FM) Sun Prairie, WI; WMIL-FM Waukesha, WI; WMRE Charles Town, WV; WVHU(AM) Huntington, WV; WKEE-FM Huntington, WV; WTCR-FM Huntington, WV; WTCR Kenova, WV; WAMX-FM Milton, WV; WHNK(AM) Parkersburg, WV; WDMX-FM Vienna, WV; WEGW-FM Wheeling, WV; WKWK-FM Wheeling, WV; WBBD Wheeling, WV; WWVA(AM) Wheeling, WV; KXBG(FM) Cheyenne, WY; KOLZ-FM Cheyenne, WY; WCAO Baltimore, MD; WQSR(FM) Baltimore, MD; WCHH(FM) Baltimore, MD; WPOC-FM Baltimore, MD; WWFG-FM Ocean City, MD; WTGM Salisbury, MD; WSBY-FM Salisbury, MD; WJDY(AM) Salisbury, MD; WOSC-FM Bethany Beach, DE; WDSD(FM) Dover, DE; WDOV Dover, DE; WRDX(FM) Smyrna, DE; WWTX(AM) Wilmington, DE; WILM Wilmington, DE

L. Lowry Mays Sr., chmn; Mark P. Mays Sr., CEO; Randall T. Mays Sr., pres; Kenneth E. Wyker Sr., sr VP; Herbert W. Hill Sr., sr VP; Craig Millar, sr VP.

Cocola Broadcasting Companies LLC, 706 W. Herndon Ave., Fresno, CA, 93650. Phone: (559) 435-7000. Fax: (559) 435-3201.E-mail: info@cocolatv.com Web Site:www.cocolatv.com Ownership: Gary M. Cocola, owner

Stns: 3 TV. KKJB, Boise, ID; KGMC, Fresno-Visalia, CA; KBBC-TV, Los Angeles.

Gary M. Cocola, pres/CEO.

Communications Corp. of America, Box 53708, Lafayette, LA, 70505-3708. Phone: (337) 237-1142. Fax: (337) 237-1373. Ownership: SP ComCorp LLC, approximately 75%.

Stns: 10 TV. WGMB-TV, Baton Rouge, LA; KTSM-TV, El Paso (Las Cruces, NM), TX; WEVV-TV, Evansville, IN; KVEO-TV, Harlingen-Weslaco-Brownsville-McAllen, TX; KADN-TV, Lafayette, LA; KPEJ-TV, Odessa-Midland, TX; KMSS, Shreveport, LA; KETK, Tyler-Longview (Lufkin & Nacogdoches), TX; KWKT-TV, Waco-Temple-Bryan, TX; KYLE-TV, Waco-Temple-Bryan, TX.

Thomas R. Galloway, chmn; Wayne Elmore, pres/CEO.

Cordillera Communications Inc., 600 E. Superior St., Suite 203, Duluth, MN, 55802. Phone: (218) 625-3045. Fax: (218) 625-3047. Web Site:www.cordillera.tv Ownership: Evening Post Publishing Co., 100%.

Stns: 11 TV. KTVQ, Billings, MT; KXLF-TV, Butte-Bozeman, MT; KBZK, Butte-Bozeman, MT; KOAA, Colorado Springs-Pueblo, CO; KRIS-TV, Corpus Christi, TX; KRTV, Great Falls, MT; KATC, Lafayette, LA; WLEX, Lexington, KY; KPAX-TV, Missoula, MT; KSBY, Santa Barbara-Santa Maria-San Luis Obispo, CA; KVOA, Tucson (Sierra Vista), AZ.

Terrance Hurley, pres; Lamont Wallis, VP; Andrew Suk, VP tech & engrg.

Cornerstone TeleVision Inc., 1 Signal Hill Dr., Wall, PA, 15148-1499. Phone: (412) 824-3930. Fax: (412) 824-5442.E-mail: info@ctvn.org Web Site:www.ctvn.org Ownership: Nonprofit.

Stns: 2 TV. WKBS, Johnstown-Altoona, PA; WPCB, Pittsburgh, PA.

Ron Hembree, pres.

Corus Entertainment Inc., 630 3rd Ave. S.W., Suite 105, Calgary, AB, T2P 4L4. Canada. Phone: (403) 444-4244. Fax: (403) 444-4242. Web Site:www.corusent.com Ownership: J.R. Shaw controls an aggregate of 80% of the voting rights.

Stns: 3 TV. CKWS, Kingston, ON; CHEX-TV-2, Oshawa, ON; CHEX, Peterborough, ON.

Stns: 15 AM. 37 FM. CHQR Calgary, AB; CFGQ-FM Calgary, AB; CKRY-FM Calgary, AB; CKNG-FM Edmonton, AB; CISN-FM Edmonton, AB; CHQT Edmonton, AB; CHED Edmonton, AB; CFMI-FM New Westminster, BC; CKNW New Westminster, BC; CFOX-FM Vancouver, BC; CHMJ(AM) Vancouver, BC; CJKR-FM Winnipeg, MB; CJOB Winnipeg, MB; CJGV-FM Winnipeg, MB; CIQB-FM Barrie, ON; CHAY-FM Barrie, ON; CJXY-FM Burlington, ON; CJDV-FM Cambridge, ON; CKCB-FM Collingwood, ON; CJSS-FM Cornwall, ON; CFLG-FM Cornwall, ON; CJUL(AM) Cornwall, ON; CJOY Guelph, ON; CIMJ-FM Guelph, ON; CING-FM Hamilton, ON; CHML Hamilton, ON; CFMK-FM Kingston, ON; CFFX-FM Kingston, ON; CKBT-FM Kitchener-Waterloo, ON; CFPL London, ON; CFPL-FM London, ON; CILQ-FM North York, ON; CKRU Peterborough, ON; CKWF-FM Peterborough, ON; CFHK-FM St. Thomas, ON; CFMJ(AM) Toronto, ON; CFNY-FM Toronto, ON; CKDK-FM Woodstock, ON; CJRC-FM Gatineau, PQ; CFOM-FM Levis, PQ; CHMP-FM Longueuil, PQ; CFEL-FM Montmagny, PQ; CFQR-FM Montreal, PQ; CKAC Montreal, PQ; CINW(AM) Montreal, PQ; CKRS-FM Saguenay, PQ; CIME-FM Saint Jerome, PQ; CHLT-FM Sherbrooke, PQ; CKOY-FM Sherbrooke, PQ; CHLN-FM Trois Rivieres, PQ; CKOI-FM Verdun, PQ; CINF(AM) Verdun, PQ.

John M. Cassaday, pres.

Cowles California Media Co., W. 999 Riverside Ave., Spokane, WA, 99201. Phone: (509) 459-5520. Fax: (509) 459-3815. Ownership: Cowles Company, 100%. Note:

Cowles Company also owns 100% of KHQ Inc. (see listing).

Stns: 2 TV. KION-TV, Monterey-Salinas, CA; KCOY, Santa Barbara-Santa Maria-San Luis Obispo, CA.

Elizabeth Allison Cowles, pres.

Cox Television, Box 105357, Atlanta, GA, 30348-5357. Phone: (678) 645-0000. Fax: (678) 645-5250. Web Site:www.coxenterprises.com Ownership: Cox Enterprises Inc., 100%. Note: Cox Enterprises Inc. also owns 100% of Cox Radio Inc. (see listing in section D under Radio Group Ownership).

Stns: 14 TV. WSB-TV, Atlanta; WSOC-TV, Charlotte, NC; WAXN-TV, Charlotte, NC; WHIO, Dayton, OH; KFOX, El Paso (Las Cruces, NM), TX; WJAC, Johnstown-Altoona, PA; WFTV, Orlando-Daytona Beach-Melbourne, FL; WRDQ, Orlando-Daytona Beach-Melbourne, FL; WPXI, Pittsburgh, PA; KRXI-TV, Reno, NV; KTVU, San Francisco-Oakland-San Jose; KICU, San Francisco-Oakland-San Jose; KIRO, Seattle-Tacoma, WA; WTOV-TV, Wheeling, WV-Steubenville, OH.

Bruce Baker, exec VP.

Crossroads Television System, 1295 N. Service Rd., Burlington, ON, L7R 4X5. Canada. Phone: (905) 331-7333. Fax: (905) 332-6005.E-mail: cts@ctstv.com Web Site:www.ctstv.com

Stns: 3 TV. CKCS-TV, Calgary, AB; CKES-TV, Edmonton, AB; CITS-TV, Hamilton, ON.

Fred Vanstone, chmn; Dick Gray, pres.

Cunningham Broadcasting Corporation, 2000 W. 41st St., Baltimore, MD, 21211. Phone: (410) 662-9688. Fax: (410) 662-0816.

Stns: 5 TV. WNUV, Baltimore, MD; WTAT, Charleston, SC; WTTE, Columbus, OH; WRGT-TV, Dayton, OH; WMYA-TV, Greenville-Spartanburg, SC-Asheville, NC-Anderson, SC.

Robert Simmons, CEO.

The Curators of the University of Missouri, (Business Services Division). University of Missouri, 316 University Hall, Columbia, MO, 65211. Phone: (573) 882-2388. Fax: (573) 882-0010. Web Site:www.umsystem.edu Ownership: (Business Services Division).

Stns: 1 TV. KOMU, Columbia-Jefferson City, MO.

Stns: 6 FM. KBIA(FM) Columbia, MO; KCUR-FM Kansas City, MO; KAUD-FM Mexico, MO; KMNR-FM Rolla, MO; KMST(FM) Rolla, MO; KWMU-FM Saint Louis, MO.

Michael Dunn, gen mgr; Martin Siddall, gen mgr .

D

Dispatch Broadcast Group, 770 Twin Rivers Dr., Columbus, OH, 43215. Phone: (614) 460-3700. Fax: (614) 460-2809. Web Site:www.10tv.com Ownership: Dispatch Printing Company

Stns: 2 TV. WBNS, Columbus, OH; WTHR, Indianapolis, IN.

Stns: 1 AM. 1 FM. WBNS Columbus, OH; WBNS-FM Columbus, OH.

Owns *The Columbus* (OH) *Dispatch, This Week* & *Ohio Magazine.*

Tamara J. Clapsaddle, controller; Michael J. Fiorile, pres.

Diversified Communications, 121 Free St., Box 7437, Portland, ME, 04112-7437. Phone: (207) 842-5400. Fax: (207) 842-5405. Web Site:www.divbusiness.com Ownership: Horace A. Hildreth Jr., Josephine H. Detmer. See Cross-Ownership, Sect. A. Cable TV: New England Cablevision Inc.

Stns: 2 TV. WABI-TV, Bangor, ME; WCJB-TV, Gainesville, FL.

David H. Lowell, pres.

R.H. Drewry Group, Box 708, Lawton, OK, 73502. Phone: (580) 353-0820. Phone: (580) 355-7000. Fax: (580) 357-3811. Ownership: R.H. Drewry owns 69% of KSWO-TV. KFDA-TV is a joint venture owned by Lawton Cablevision (50%), KSWD-TV (45%), KSWO(AM) (2 1/2%) and KRHD-AM-FM (2 1/2%). KWAB(TV) and KWES-TV are owned by KSWO Television Inc. and Lawton Cablevision Inc. (50%). KXXV(TV) is owned by Centrex Television L.P. Cable TV.

Stns: 5 TV. KFDA, Amarillo, TX; KWAB, Odessa-Midland, TX; KWES, Odessa-Midland, TX; KXXV, Waco-Temple-Bryan, TX; KSWO, Wichita Falls, TX & Lawton, OK.

Robert H. Drewry, pres; Larry Patton, VP.

Duhamel Broadcasting Enterprises, Box 1760, Rapid City, SD, 57709. Phone: (605) 342-2000. Fax: (605) 342-7305. Web Site:www.kotatv.com Ownership: William F. Duhamel, 63%; Peter A. and Lois G. Duhamel, 37%.

Stns: 4 TV. KDUH, Cheyenne, WY-Scottsbluff, NE; KHSD-TV, Rapid City, SD; KOTA-TV, Rapid City, SD; KSGW-TV, Rapid City, SD.

Stns: 1 AM. 1 FM. KOTA Rapid City, SD; KDDX(FM) Spearfish, SD.

William F. Duhamel, pres.

E

Eagle Creek Broadcasting LLC, 2111 University Park Dr., Suite 650, Okemos, MI, 48864. Phone: (517) 347-4141. Phone: (517) 347-4675.E-mail: bradybw1@comcast.net Ownership: Alta Communications VIII L.P., 86.21% votes, 21.29% total assets; Brian W. Brady, 7.36% votes, 4.89% total assets.

Stns: 2 TV. KZTV, Corpus Christi, TX; KVTV, Laredo, TX.

Brian Brady, pres/CEO.

Entravision Communications Corp., 2425 Olympic Blvd., Suite 6000W, Santa Monica, CA, 90404. Phone: (310) 447-3872. Fax: (310) 447-3899.E-mail: kthompson@entravision.com Web Site:www.entravision.com Ownership: Walter F. Ulloa, Philip W. Wilkinson, Paul Zevnik.

Stns: 20 TV. KLUZ, Albuquerque-Santa Fe, NM; WUNI, Boston (Manchester, NH); KVSN-DT, Colorado Springs-Pueblo, CO; KORO, Corpus Christi, TX; KCEC, Denver, CO; KINT, El Paso (Las Cruces, NM), TX; KTFN, El Paso (Las Cruces, NM), TX; KNVO, Harlingen-Weslaco -Brownsville-McAllen, TX; WUVN, Hartford & New Haven, CT; KLDO, Laredo, TX; KINC, Las Vegas, NV; KSMS, Monterey-Salinas, CA; KUPB, Odessa-Midland, TX; WVEN-TV, Orlando-Daytona Beach-Melbourne, FL; KREN, Reno, NV; KPMR, Santa Barbara-Santa Maria-San Luis Obispo, CA; WVEA-TV, Tampa-St. Petersburg (Sarasota), FL; WJAL, Washington, DC (Hagerstown, MD); KDCU-DT, Wichita-Hutchinson Plus, KS; KVYE, Yuma, AZ-El Centro, CA.

Stns: 12 AM. 37 FM. KVVA-FM Apache Junction, AZ; KMIA(AM) Black Canyon City, AZ; KDVA(FM) Buckeye, AZ; KLNZ-FM Glendale, AZ; KRRN(FM) Kingman, AZ; KSSE(FM) Arcadia, CA; KSEH(FM) Brawley, CA; KCVR-FM Columbia, CA; KXSE(FM) Davis, CA; KWST(AM) El Centro, CA; KSSD(FM) Fallbrook, CA; KLOK-FM Greenfield, CA; KMXX-FM Imperial, CA; KCVR Lodi, CA; KRCX-FM Marysville, CA; KDLE(FM) Newport Beach, CA; KTSE-FM Patterson, CA; KLYY(FM) Riverside, CA; KBMB(FM) Sacramento, CA; KDLD(FM) Santa Monica, CA; KSES-FM Seaside, CA; KNTY(FM) Shingle Springs, CA; KMBX(AM) Soledad, CA; KLOB-FM Thousand Palms, CA; KMIX-FM Tracy, CA; KSSC(FM) Ventura, CA; KPVW(FM) Aspen, CO; KMXA Aurora, CO; KJMN-FM Castle Rock, CO; KXPK-FM Evergreen, CO; WLQY Hollywood, FL; WNUE-FM Titusville, FL; KRZY Albuquerque, NM; KRZY-FM Santa Fe, NM; KQRT(FM) Las Vegas, NV; KRNV-FM Reno, NV; KKPS-FM Brownsville, TX; KVLY-FM Edinburg, TX; KHRO(AM) El Paso, TX; KOFX-FM El Paso, TX; KINT-FM El Paso, TX; KSVE(AM) El Paso, TX; KYSE(FM) El Paso, TX; KFRQ-FM Harlingen, TX; KGOL Humble, TX; KBZO Lubbock, TX; KNVO-FM Port Isabel, TX; KAIQ(FM) Wolfforth, TX; WACA Wheaton, MD.

Walter F. Ulloa, chmn/CEO; Philip Wilkinson, pres/COO; Larry Safir, exec VP.

Equity Media Holdings Corp., 1 Shackleford Dr., Suite 400, Little Rock, AR, 72211. Phone: (501) 219-2400. Fax: (501) 221-1101. Web Site:www.emdaholdings.com

Stns: 15 TV. KEYU, Amarillo, TX; KBTZ, Butte-Bozeman, MT; KWWF, Cedar Rapids-Waterloo-Iowa City & Dubuque, IA; KTUW, Cheyenne, WY-Scottsbluff, NE; KQCK, Cheyenne, WY-Scottsbluff, NE; KTVC, Eugene, OR; KLMN, Great Falls, MT; KKYK-DT, Little Rock-Pine Bluff, AR; KMMF, Missoula, MT; KUOK, Oklahoma City, OK; KEGS, Reno, NV; KBNY, Salt Lake City, UT; KBCJ, Salt Lake City, UT; KWBM, Springfield, MO; WPXS, St. Louis, MO.

Larry Morton, pres; Greg Fess, VP; Max Hooper, VP; James Heamsberger, VP; Lori Withrow, sec; Emilia Chastain, treas; John Oxendine, CEO.

Esteem Broadcasting, 13865 E. Elliott Dr., Marshall, IL, 62441. Phone: (217) 826-6095. Ownership: David Bailey, 100%.

Stns: 3 TV. WFXI, Greenville-New Bern-Washington, NC; WYDO, Greenville-New Bern-Washington, NC; WEMT, Tri-Cities, TN-VA.

David L. Bailey, pres.

F

Family Stations Inc., 290 Hegenberger Rd., Oakland, CA, 94621. Phone: (510) 568-6200. Fax: (510) 568-6190. Ownership: Nonprofit corporation.

Stns: 1 TV. WFME, New York.

Stns: 12 AM. 55 FM. WBFR-FM Birmingham, AL; KEAF(FM) Fort Smith, AR; KPHF-FM Phoenix, AZ; KFRB-FM Bakersfield, CA; KHAP(FM) Chico, CA; KFRJ(FM) China Lake, CA; KFRP(FM) Coalinga, CA; KECR El Cajon, CA; KFNO-FM Fresno, CA; KXBC(FM) Garberville, CA; KEFR-FM Le Grand, CA; KFRN Long Beach, CA; KEBR Rocklin, CA; KEAR-FM Sacramento, CA; KEAR(AM) San Francisco, CA; KHFR(FM) Santa Maria, CA; KFRS-FM Soledad, CA; KPRA-FM Ukiah, CA; KFRY(FM) Pueblo, CO; WCTF Vernon, CT; WMFL-FM Florida City, FL; WFTI-FM Saint Petersburg, FL; WWFR(FM) Stuart, FL; WFRP(FM) Americus, GA; WFRC-FM Columbus, GA; KDFR(FM) Des Moines, IA; KEGR(FM) Fort Dodge, IA; KYFR Shenandoah, IA; WJCH-FM Joliet, IL; KPOR-FM Emporia, KS; WOFR(FM) Schoolcraft, MI; KFRD(FM) Butte, MT; KFRT(FM) Butte, MT; KFRW(FM) Great Falls, MT; KBFR(FM) Bismarck, ND; WKDN-FM Camden, NJ; WFME-FM Newark, NJ; KXFR(FM) Socorro, NM; WFBF-FM Buffalo, NY; WFRH-FM Kingston, NY; WFRS-FM Smithtown, NY; WFRW-FM Webster, NY; WCUE Cuyahoga Falls, OH; WOTL-FM Toledo, OH; WYTN-FM Youngstown, OH; KYOR(FM) Newport, OR; KPFR(FM) Pine Grove, OR; KQFE-FM Springfield, OR; WUFR(FM) Bedford, PA; WEFR-FM Erie, PA; WFRJ-FM Johnstown, PA; WXFR(FM) State College, PA; WFCH-FM Charleston, SC; KKAA(AM) Aberdeen, SD; KQFR(FM) Rapid City, SD; KQKD(AM) Redfield, SD; KIFR(FM) Alice, TX; KEDR(FM) Bay City, TX; KTXB-FM Beaumont, TX; KUFR-FM Salt Lake City, UT; KARR Kirkland, WA; KJVH-FM Longview, WA; WWJA(FM) Janesville, WI; WMWK-FM Milwaukee, WI; WFSI-FM Annapolis, MD; WBGR Baltimore, MD; WBMD Baltimore, MD.

Harold Camping, pres.

Fisher Communications Inc., 100 4th Ave. N., Suite 440, Suite 1525, Seattle, WA, 98109. Phone: (206) 404-7000. Fax: (206) 404-7050. Web Site:www.fsci.com

Stns: 13 TV. KBAK-TV, Bakersfield, CA; KBCI-TV, Boise, ID; KCBY, Eugene, OR; KPIC, Eugene, OR; KVAL, Eugene, OR; KIDK-TV, Idaho Falls-Pocatello, ID; KATU, Portland, OR; KUNP, Portland, OR; KUNS-TV, Seattle-Tacoma, WA; KOMO, Seattle-Tacoma, WA; KLEW-TV, Spokane, WA; KIMA-TV, Yakima-Pasco-Richland-Kennewick, WA; KEPR, Yakima-Pasco-Richland-Kennewick, WA.

Stns: 4 AM. 4 FM. KIKF(FM) Cascade, MT; KXGF Great Falls, MT; KINX(FM) Great Falls, MT; KQDI Great Falls, MT; KQDI-FM Great Falls, MT; KVI(AM) Seattle, WA; KOMO(AM) Seattle, WA; KPLZ(FM) Seattle, WA.

Collen Brown, pres/CEO; Sheri Leonard, asst.

Fort Myers Broadcasting Co., 2824 Palm Beach Blvd., Fort Myers, FL, 33916. Phone: (239) 334-1111. Fax: (239) 334-0744.E-mail: manaager@winktv.com Web Site:winktv.com Ownership: Brian A. McBride.

Stns: 1 TV. WINK-TV, Ft. Myers-Naples, FL.

Stns: 2 AM. 2 FM. WINK-FM Fort Myers, FL; WNPL(AM) Golden Gate, FL; WPTK(AM) Pine Island Center, FL; WTLQ-FM Punta Rassa, FL.

Brian McBride, pres/CEO; Gary Gardner, VP/gen mgr.

Forum Communications Co., Box 2020, Fargo, ND, 58107. Phone: (701) 235-7311. Fax: (701) 241-5406. Web Site:www.in-forum.com

Stns: 4 TV. WDAY-TV, Fargo-Valley City, ND; WDAZ-TV, Fargo-Valley City, ND; KBMY, Minot-Bismarck-Dickinson, ND; KMCY, Minot-Bismarck-Dickinson, ND.

Stns: 1 AM. 1 FM. WZUU-FM Allegan, MI; WDAY Fargo, ND.

Forum Communications Co. owns the *Alexandria* (MN) *Echo Press; The Pioneer,* Bemidj, MN; *Detroit Lakes* (MN) *Tribune; The Becker County Record,* Detroit Lakes, MN; *Park Rapids* (MN) *Enterprise; The Wadena* (MN) *Pioneer Journal; West Central Daily Tribune,* Willmar, MN; *The Daily Globe;* Worthington, MN; *The Daily Republic,* Mitchell SD; *The Dickinson Press,* Dickinson, ND & *The* (ND) *Forum.*

William C. Marcil, pres.

Four Points Media Group, 299 S. Main St., Suite 150, Salt Lake City, UT, 84111. Phone: (801) 973-3000. Fax: (801) 973-3387. Ownership: TV Stations Holding LLC, 100%.

Stns: 5 TV. KEYE, Austin, TX; WLWC, Providence, RI-New Bedford, MA; KUSG, Salt Lake City, UT; KUTV, Salt Lake City, UT; WTVX, West Palm Beach-Ft. Pierce, FL.

Mark Ploof, COO.

Fox Television Stations Inc., 1999 S. Bundy Dr., Los Angeles, CA, 90025-5235. Phone: (310) 584-2000. Web Site:www.newscorp.com Ownership: Fox Entertainment Group Inc., 85.2% voting interest. Note: Fox Entertainment Group Inc. is a wholly-owned subsidiary of News Corp.

Stns: 29 TV. WAGA-TV, Atlanta; KTBC, Austin, TX;

WUTB, Baltimore, MD; WFXT, Boston (Manchester, NH); WFLD, Chicago; WPWR-TV, Chicago; KDFI, Dallas-Ft. Worth; KDFW, Dallas-Ft. Worth; WJBK, Detroit; WOGX, Gainesville, FL; KRIV, Houston; KTXH, Houston; WDAF-TV, Kansas City, MO; KTTV, Los Angeles; KCOP, Los Angeles; WHBQ, Memphis, TN; WFTC, Minneapolis-St. Paul, MN; KFTC, Minneapolis-St. Paul, MN; KMSP, Minneapolis-St. Paul, MN; WNYW, New York; WWOR, New York; WOFL, Orlando-Daytona Beach-Melbourne, FL; WRBW, Orlando-Daytona Beach-Melbourne, FL; WTXF, Philadelphia; KSAZ-TV, Phoenix (Prescott), AZ; KUTP, Phoenix (Prescott), AZ; WTVT, Tampa-St. Petersburg (Sarasota), FL; WTTG, Washington, DC (Hagerstown, MD); WDCA, Washington, DC (Hagerstown, MD).

Kevin Hale, gen mgr; Jack Abernethy, CEO; Roger Ailes, chmn; Dennis Swanson, pres.

Freedom Communications Inc., Broadcast Division, Box 19549, Irvine, CA, 92623-9549. Phone: (949) 253-2315. Fax: (949) 798-3527. Web Site:www.freedom.com Ownership: Freedom Communications Holdings Inc., 100%.

Stns: 8 TV. WCWN, Albany-Schenectady-Troy, NY; WRGB, Albany-Schenectady-Troy, NY; KFDM-TV, Beaumont-Port Arthur, TX; WTVC, Chattanooga, TN; WWMT, Grand Rapids-Kalamazoo-Battle Creek, MI; WLAJ, Lansing, MI; KTVL, Medford-Klamath Falls, OR; WPEC, West Palm Beach-Ft. Pierce, FL.

Freedom Communications Inc., publishes 28 daily & 37 wkly nwsprs in 12 states.

Doreen Wade, pres.

G

Gannett Broadcasting, (Division of Gannett Co. Inc.). 7950 Jones Branch Dr., Mclean, VA, 22107. Phone: (703) 854-6760. Fax: (703) 854-2005. Web Site:www.gannett.com Ownership: (Division of Gannett Co. Inc.)

Stns: 23 TV. WATL, Atlanta; WXIA, Atlanta; WLBZ, Bangor, ME; WGRZ, Buffalo, NY; WKYC, Cleveland-Akron (Canton), OH; WLTX, Columbia, SC; KTVD, Denver, CO; KUSA, Denver, CO; WZZM, Grand Rapids-Kalamazoo-Battle Creek, MI; WFMY-TV, Greensboro-High Point-Winston Salem, NC; WJXX, Jacksonville, FL; WTLV, Jacksonville, FL; WBIR, Knoxville, TN; KTHV, Little Rock-Pine Bluff, AR; WMAZ-TV, Macon, GA; KARE, Minneapolis-St. Paul, MN; KNAZ, Phoenix (Prescott), AZ; KPNX, Phoenix (Prescott), AZ; WCSH, Portland-Auburn, ME; KXTV, Sacramento -Stockton-Modesto, CA; KSDK, St. Louis, MO; WTSP, Tampa-St. Petersburg (Sarasota), FL; WUSA, Washington, DC (Hagerstown, MD).

Gannett owns 101 daily newspapers, including the national newspaper *USA Today*, and non-daily newspapers throughout the country.

Dave Lougee, pres.

Glenwood Communications Corp., 222 Commerce St., Kingsport, TN, 37660. Phone: (423) 246-9578. Fax: (423) 246-6261.E-mail: golz@wkpttv.com Web Site:www.wkpttv.com Ownership: William M. Boyd; Hugh N. Boyd Trust.

Stns: 1 TV. WKPT-TV, Tri-Cities, TN-VA.

Stns: 4 AM. 4 FM. WOPI Bristol, TN; WRZK-FM Colonial Heights, TN; WKTP Jonesborough, TN; WKPT Kingsport, TN; WTFM-FM Kingsport, TN; WMEV Marion, VA; WMEV-FM Marion, VA; WVEK-FM Weber City, VA.

George E. DeVault Jr., pres.

Global BC, (A Division of Global Communications Ltd.). 7850 Enterprise St., Burnaby, BC, V5A 1V7. Canada. Phone: (604) 420-2288. Fax: (604) 422-6427. Web Site:www.canada.com Ownership: CanWest Global Communications Corp., 100% (see listing).

Stns: 6 TV. CHAN-2, Bowen Island, BC; CHAN-5, Brackendale, BC; CHAN-1, Chilliwack, BC; CHKM-TV, Kamloops, BC; CHAN-3, Squamish, BC; CHAN-7, Whistler, BC.

Brett Manlove, VP sls; Roy Gardner, gen mgr; Fatbir Nijjar, VP finance; John O'Connor, VP.

Global Television, (a division of CanWest MediaWorks Inc.). 81 Barber Greene Rd., Don Mills, ON, M3C 2A2. Canada. Phone: (416) 446-5311. Fax: (416) 446-5447. Web Site:www.globaltv.com Ownership: CanWest Global Communications Corp., 100% (see listing).

Stns: 9 TV. CIII-2, Bancroft, ON; CIII-7, Midland, ON; CIII-29, Oil Springs, ON; CIII-6, Ottawa, ON; CIII-4, Owen Sound, ON; CIII, Paris, ON; CIII-27, Peterborough, ON; CIII-22, Stevenson, ON; CIII-41, Toronto, ON.

W.K. Hunt, VP/gen mgr; Kathleen Dore, pres.

Granite Broadcasting Corp., 767 Third Ave., 34th Fl., New York, NY, 10017. Phone: (212) 826-2530. Fax: (212) 826-2858. Web Site:www.granitetv.com

Stns: 10 TV. WBNG, Binghamton, NY; WKBW, Buffalo, NY; WMYD, Detroit; KBJR-TV, Duluth, MN-Superior, WI; KRII, Duluth, MN-Superior, WI; KSEE, Fresno-Visalia, CA; WISE-TV, Ft. Wayne, IN; WEEK, Peoria-Bloomington, IL; KOFY-TV, San Francisco-Oakland-San Jose; WTVH, Syracuse, NY.

W. Don Cornwell, chmn/CEO; Larry Willis, CFO; Stuart Beck, pres; Ellen McClain, CEO; John Deushane, COO.

Grant Communications Inc., 915 Middle River Dr., Suite 409, Fort Lauderdale, FL, 33304. Phone: (954) 568-2000. Fax: (954) 568-2015. Ownership: The Milton Grant Living Trust, Jack L. Lewis, business trustee.

Stns: 7 TV. KGCW, Davenport, IA-Rock Island-Moline, IL; KLJB, Davenport, IA-Rock Island-Moline, IL; WZDX, Huntsville-Decatur (Florence), AL; WLAX, La Crosse-Eau Claire, WI; WEUX, La Crosse-Eau Claire, WI; WFXR, Roanoke-Lynchburg, VA; WWCW, Roanoke-Lynchburg, VA.

Mark Ryan, CFO.

Gray Television Inc., Box 1867, Albany, GA, 31702-1867. Phone: (229) 888-9390. Fax: (229) 888-9374. Web Site:www.graytvinc.com E-mail: cindy.holden@gcslink.com Ownership: Bull Run Corp., Datasouth Computer Corp. and affiliated companies. Other interests: Porta Phone Paging Inc. and Lynqx.

Stns: 34 TV. WRDW-TV, Augusta, GA; WBKO, Bowling Green, KY; WSAZ-TV, Charleston-Huntington, WV; WCAV, Charlottesville, VA; KKTV, Colorado Springs-Pueblo, CO; WTVY, Dothan, AL; KKCO, Grand Junction-Montrose, CO; WITN-TV, Greenville-New Bern-Washington, NC; WHSV-TV, Harrisonburg, VA; WVLT-TV, Knoxville, TN; WEAU-TV, La Crosse-Eau Claire, WI; WILX, Lansing, MI; WKYT-TV, Lexington, KY; WYMT-TV, Lexington, KY; KGIN, Lincoln & Hastings-Kearney, NE; KOLN, Lincoln & Hastings-Kearney, NE; WMTV, Madison, WI; WTOK-TV, Meridian, MS; WOWT-TV, Omaha, NE; WJHG-TV, Panama City, FL; WTAP-TV, Parkersburg, WV; KOLO, Reno, NV; WIFR, Rockford, IL; KXII, Sherman, TX-Ada, OK; WNDU, South Bend-Elkhart, IN; WCTV, Tallahassee, FL-Thomasville, GA; WSWG, Tallahassee, FL-Thomasville, GA; WIBW-TV, Topeka, KS; KWTX-TV, Waco-Temple-Bryan, TX; KBTX-TV, Waco-Temple-Bryan, TX; WSAW-TV, Wausau-Rhinelander, WI; KAKE, Wichita-Hutchinson Plus, KS; KUPK-TV, Wichita-Hutchinson Plus, KS; KLBY, Wichita-Hutchinson Plus, KS.

Gray Communiations publishes, through Albany Herald Publishing Co., *The Albany* (GA) *Herald* & publishes, through The Rockdale Citizen Publishing Co., *The Rockdale Citizen*, Conyers, GA & *The Gwinnett Daily Post*, Lawrenceville, GA. Gray Communications also publishes *The Goshen News*, Goshen, IN.

James Ryan, VP/CFO; J. Mack Robinson, chmn/CEO; Robert A. Beizer, VP law & dev; Wayne Martin, rgnl VP TV; Robert S. Prather Jr., pres/COO.

Griffin Communications L.L.C., 7401 N. Kelley Ave., Oklahoma City, OK, 73111. Phone: (405) 843-6641. Fax: (405) 841-9135. Web Site:www.griffincommunications.net

Stns: 3 TV. KWTV, Oklahoma City, OK; KOTV, Tulsa, OK; KQCW, Tulsa, OK.

David Griffin, pres; Steve Foerster, VP; Dick Dutton, VP; Joyce Reed, VP; Kathy Haney, VP; Ted Strickland, CFO.

Groupe TVA Inc., Tele-4/CFCM-TV, 1000 Myrand Ave., Ste.-Foy, PQ, G1V 2W3. Canada. Phone: (418) 688-9330. Fax: (418) 681-4239. Ownership: Quebecor Media Inc., 99.92%; and others, 0.08%.

Stns: 8 TV. CJPM, Chicoutimi, PQ; CFTM, Montreal, PQ; CFCM, Quebec City, PQ; CFER, Rimouski, PQ; CFER-TV-2, Sept-Iles, PQ; CHLT, Sherbrooke, PQ; CKXT-TV, Toronto, ON; CHEM, Trois-Rivieres, PQ.

Serge Gouin, pres.

H

HITV License Subsidiary Inc., 1100 Wilson Blvd., Suite 3000, Arlington, VA, 22209. Phone: (703) 247-7500. Fax: (703) 247-7505. Web Site:www.mcgcapital.com Ownership: HITV Operating Co. Inc., 100% of votes.

Stns: 3 TV. KGMD, Hilo, HI; KGMB, Honolulu, HI; KGMV, Wailuku, HI.

Michael McHugh, pres.

Hearst Television Inc., 300 W. 57th St., 39th Fl., New York, NY, 10019. Phone: (212) 887-6800. Fax: (212) 887-6855. Web Site:www.hearsttelevision.com Ownership: The Hearst Corp., 100%.

Stns: 35 TV. KOAT, Albuquerque-Santa Fe, NM; KOCT, Albuquerque-Santa Fe, NM; KOVT, Albuquerque-Santa Fe, NM; WBAL, Baltimore, MD; WCVB-TV, Boston (Manchester, NH); WMUR, Boston (Manchester, NH); WNNE, Burlington, VT-Plattsburgh, NY; WPTZ, Burlington, VT-Plattsburgh, NY; WLWT, Cincinnati, OH; KCCI, Des Moines-Ames, IA; KHBS, Ft. Smith-Fayetteville -Springdale-Rogers, AR; KHOG-TV, Ft. Smith-Fayetteville -Springdale-Rogers, AR; WXII, Greensboro-High Point-Winston Salem, NC; WYFF, Greenville-Spartanburg, SC-Asheville, NC-Anderson, SC; WGAL, Harrisburg -Lancaster-Lebanon-York, PA; KHVO, Hilo, HI; KITV, Honolulu, HI; WAPT, Jackson, MS; KMBC-TV, Kansas City, MO; KCWE, Kansas City, MO; WLKY-TV, Louisville, KY; WISN, Milwaukee, WI; KSBW, Monterey-Salinas, CA; WDSU, New Orleans, LA; KOCO-TV, Oklahoma City, OK; KETV, Omaha, NE; WESH, Orlando-Daytona Beach-Melbourne, FL; WKCF, Orlando-Daytona Beach-Melbourne, FL; WTAE-TV, Pittsburgh, PA; WMTW, Portland-Auburn, ME; KQCA, Sacramento-Stockton-Modesto, CA; KCRA, Sacramento -Stockton-Modesto, CA; WMOR, Tampa-St. Petersburg (Sarasota), FL; KMAU, Wailuku, HI; WPBF, West Palm Beach-Ft. Pierce, FL.

, pres/CEO.

Heritage Broadcasting Co of MI, Box 627, Cadillac, MI, 49601. Phone: (231) 775-3478. Fax: (231) 775-3671. Web Site:www.9and10news.com Ownership: Heritage Broadcasting Group Inc., 100%.

Stns: 2 TV. WWTV, Traverse City-Cadillac, MI; WWUP, Traverse City-Cadillac, MI.

Mario F. Lacobelli, pres; William E. Kring, VP/gen mgr.

Hero Broadcasting LLC, 14450 Commerce Way, Miami Lakes, FL, 33016. Phone: (305) 863-5727.E-mail: linette.rodriguez@herobroadcasting.com Web Site:www.herobroadcasting.com Ownership: Hero Broadcasting Holding Inc., 100%.

Stns: 2 TV. KBEH, Los Angeles; KMOH, Phoenix (Prescott), AZ.

Robert Behar, pres/CEO; Linette Rodriguez, mktg dir.

High Plains Broadcasting Inc., Box 288, Kaw City, OK, 74641. Phone: (580) 269-2215. Web Site:www.newporttv.com Ownership: James H. Martin, 100%.

Stns: 6 TV. KGET-TV, Bakersfield, CA; KGPE, Fresno-Visalia, CA; WTEV-TV, Jacksonville, FL; KUCW, Salt Lake City, UT; WOAI-TV, San Antonio, TX; KFTY, San Francisco-Oakland-San Jose.

James H. Martin, pres.

Hoak Media Corporation, 500 Crescent Ct., Suite 220, Dallas, TX, 75201. Phone: (972) 960-4848. Fax: (972) 960-4899. Web Site:www.hoakmedia.com

Stns: 17 TV. KALB-TV, Alexandria, LA; KREG, Denver, CO; KVLY, Fargo-Valley City, ND; KREX, Grand Junction-Montrose, CO; KREY, Grand Junction-Montrose, CO; KHAS, Lincoln & Hastings-Kearney, NE; KMOT, Minot-Bismarck-Dickinson, ND; KFYR, Minot-Bismarck-Dickinson, ND; KQCD, Minot-Bismarck-Dickinson, ND; KUMV, Minot-Bismarck-Dickinson, ND; KNOE-TV, Monroe, LA-El Dorado, AR; KNOP-TV, North Platte, NE; WMBB, Panama City, FL; KSFY-TV, Sioux Falls (Mitchell), SD; KPRY, Sioux Falls (Mitchell), SD; KABY, Sioux Falls (Mitchell), SD; KAUZ, Wichita Falls, TX & Lawton, OK.

Eric Van den Branden, pres.

Hubbard Broadcasting Inc., 3415 University Ave., St. Paul, MN, 55114. Phone: (651) 646-5555. Fax: (651) 642-4103.E-mail: jmahoney@hbi.com

Stns: 13 TV. WNYT, Albany-Schenectady-Troy, NY; KOBG-TV, Albuquerque-Santa Fe, NM; KOB, Albuquerque-Santa Fe, NM; KOBF, Albuquerque-Santa Fe, NM; KOBR, Albuquerque-Santa Fe, NM; WDIO-DT, Duluth, MN-Superior, WI; WIRT-DT, Duluth, MN-Superior, WI; KRWF, Minneapolis-St. Paul, MN; KSAX, Minneapolis-St. Paul, MN; KSTP, Minneapolis-St. Paul, MN; KSTC-TV, Minneapolis-St. Paul, MN; KAAL, Rochester, MN-Mason City, IA-Austin, MN; WHEC, Rochester, NY.

Stns: 2 AM. 2 FM. WFMP(FM) Coon Rapids, MN; KSTP(AM) Saint Paul, MN; KSTP-FM Saint Paul, MN; WIXK(AM) New Richmond, WI.

Stanley S. Hubbard, chmn/pres/CEO; Stanley E. Hubbard II, VP; Virginia H. Morris, VP; Robert W. Hubbard, VP; Julia D. Coyte, VP; Gerald D. Deeney, sr VP/treas/CFO; Harold C. Crump, VP; C. Thomas Newberry, VP; Linda S. Tremere, VP; Sue J. Cook, VP; Edward J. Aiken, VP; Kari Rominski, sec; Gary R. Macomber, asst sec.

I

ION Media Networks Inc., 601 Clearwater Park Rd., West Palm Beach, FL, 33401-6233. Phone: (561) 659-4122. Fax: (561) 655-7246. Fax: (561) 659-4252.E-mail: sethgrossman@paxson.com Web Site:www.ionmedianetworks.com Ownership: Publicly traded company on the Amex ticker (ION). Note: ION Media Networks also owns Infomall TV Network, three state radio networks (Alabama Radio Network, Florida Radio Network, Tennessee Radio Network), three rgnl sports networks (University of Florida Sports Network, University of Miami

Sports Network, Penn State Sports Network), outdoor adv.

Stns: 58 TV. WYPX, Albany-Schenectady-Troy, NY; WPXA-TV, Atlanta; WPXH-TV, Birmingham (Anniston, Tuscaloosa), AL; WPXG-TV, Boston (Manchester, NH); WBPX-TV, Boston (Manchester, NH); WDPX-TV, Boston (Manchester, NH); WPXJ, Buffalo, NY; KPXR-TV, Cedar Rapids-Waterloo-Iowa City & Dubuque, IA; WLPX, Charleston-Huntington, WV; WCPX-TV, Chicago; WVPX-TV, Cleveland-Akron (Canton), OH; KPXD-TV, Dallas-Ft. Worth; KPXC, Denver, CO; KFPX-TV, Des Moines-Ames, IA; WPXD-TV, Detroit; WZPX-TV, Grand Rapids-Kalamazoo-Battle Creek, MI; WGPX-TV, Greensboro-High Point-Winston Salem, NC; WEPX-TV, Greenville-New Bern-Washington, NC; WPXU-TV, Greenville-New Bern-Washington, NC; WHPX-TV, Hartford & New Haven, CT; KPXO-TV, Honolulu, HI; KPXB-TV, Houston; WIPX-TV, Indianapolis, IN; WPXC-TV, Jacksonville, FL; KPXE-TV, Kansas City, MO; WPXK-TV, Knoxville, TN; WUPX-TV, Lexington, KY; KPXN-TV, Los Angeles; WPXM-TV, Miami-Ft. Lauderdale, FL; WPXE-TV, Milwaukee, WI; KPXM-TV, Minneapolis-St. Paul, MN; WNPX-TV, Nashville, TN; WPXL-TV, New Orleans, LA; WPXN, New York; WPXV-TV, Norfolk-Portsmouth-Newport News, VA; KWWT, Odessa-Midland, TX; KOPX-TV, Oklahoma City, OK; WOPX-TV, Orlando-Daytona Beach-Melbourne, FL; WPPX-TV, Philadelphia; KPPX-TV, Phoenix (Prescott), AZ; KPXG-TV, Portland, OR; WPXQ-TV, Providence, RI-New Bedford, MA; WRPX-TV, Raleigh-Durham (Fayetteville), NC; WFPX-TV, Raleigh-Durham (Fayetteville), NC; WPXR-TV, Roanoke-Lynchburg, VA; KSPX-TV, Sacramento -Stockton-Modesto, CA; KUPX-TV, Salt Lake City, UT; KPXL-TV, San Antonio, TX; KKPX-TV, San Francisco-Oakland-San Jose; KWPX-TV, Seattle-Tacoma, WA; KGPX-TV, Spokane, WA; WXPX-TV, Tampa-St. Petersburg (Sarasota), FL; KTPX-TV, Tulsa, OK; WPXW-TV, Washington, DC (Hagerstown, MD); WWPX-TV, Washington, DC (Hagerstown, MD); WTPX-TV, Wausau-Rhinelander, WI; WPXP-TV, West Palm Beach-Ft. Pierce, FL; WQPX-TV, Wilkes Barre-Scranton, PA.

R. Brandon Burgess, CEO.

Independent Communications Inc., 2817 W. 11th St., Sioux Falls, SD, 57104. Phone: (605) 338-0017. Fax: (605) 338-7173.E-mail: fox17@kttw.com Ownership: Independent Communications Inc.

Stns: 2 TV. KTTM, Sioux Falls (Mitchell), SD; KTTW, Sioux Falls (Mitchell), SD.

Ed Hoffman, gen mgr .

International Broadcasting Corp., 1554 Bori St., San Juan, PR, 00927-6113. Phone: (787) 274-1800. Fax: (787) 281-9758. Ownership: Pedro Roman Collazo, 100%. Note: Pedro Roman Collazo, as an individual, owns WVOZ(AM) San Juan, PR.

Stns: 3 TV. WVEO, Aguadilla, PR; WVOZ, Ponce, PR; WTCV, San Juan, PR.

Stns: 7 AM. 1 FM. WRSJ(AM) Bayamon, PR; WGIT(AM) Canovanas, PR; WVOZ-FM Carolina, PR; WIBS Guayama, PR; WXRF Guayama, PR; WTIL Mayaguez, PR; WEKO(AM) Morovis, PR; WCHQ(AM) Quebradillas, PR.

Pedro Roman Callazo, pres; Margarita Nazario, gen mgr .

J

Journal Communications Inc., 333 W. State St., Milwaukee, WI, 53203. Phone: (414) 224-2616. Fax: (414) 224-2469. Web Site:www.jc.com

Stns: 11 TV. KIVI-TV, Boise, ID; KNIN, Boise, ID; WFTX-TV, Ft. Myers-Naples, FL; WGBA-TV, Green Bay-Appleton, WI; WSYM, Lansing, MI; KTNV-TV, Las Vegas, NV; WTMJ, Milwaukee, WI; KMTV-TV, Omaha, NE; KMIR-TV, Palm Springs, CA; KGUN-TV, Tucson (Sierra Vista), AZ; KWBA-TV, Tucson (Sierra Vista), AZ.

Stns: 9 AM. 26 FM. KGMG-FM Oracle, AZ; KFFN Tucson, AZ; KMXZ-FM Tucson, AZ; KQTH(FM) Tucson, AZ; KJOT(FM) Boise, ID; KGEM(AM) Boise, ID; KCID(AM) Caldwell, ID; KTHI(FM) Caldwell, ID; KRVB(FM) Nampa, ID; KQXR-FM Payette, ID; KYQQ(FM) Arkansas City, KS; KFXJ(FM) Augusta, KS; KFTI-FM Newton, KS; KICT-FM Wichita, KS; KFTI(AM) Wichita, KS; KFDI-FM Wichita, KS; KSGF-FM Ash Grove, MO; KZRQ-FM Mount Vernon, MO; KSPW(FM) Sparta, MO; KSGF(AM) Springfield, MO; KTTS-FM Springfield, MO; KKCD-FM Omaha, NE; KSRZ-FM Omaha, NE; KEZO-FM Omaha, NE; KXSP(AM) Omaha, NE; KQCH(FM) Omaha, NE; KXBL(FM) Henryetta, OK; KFAQ(AM) Tulsa, OK; KVOO-FM Tulsa, OK; WCYQ(FM) Karns, TN; WKHT(FM) Knoxville, TN; WKTI(AM) Powell, TN; WWST(FM) Sevierville, TN; WTMJ Milwaukee, WI; WLWK-FM Milwaukee, WI.

Journal Communications Inc., publisher of the morning *Milwaukee* (WI) *Journal Sentinel*, owns 100% of Journal Broadcast Corp.

Douglas G. Kiel, pres.

K

KEVN Inc., Box 677, Rapid City, SD, 57709. Phone: (605) 394-7777. Fax: (605) 348-9128.E-mail: news@blackhillsfox.com Web Site:www.blackhillsfox.com

Stns: 2 TV. KEVN-TV, Rapid City, SD; KIVV-TV, Rapid City, SD.

Cindy McNeill, VP/gen mgr; Robert Slocum, CFO; Bill Reyner, pres; Kathy Silk, rgnl sls mgr.

KHQ Inc., Box 600, Spokane, WA, 99210-4102. Phone: (509) 448-6000. Fax: (509) 448-3231. Ownership: Cowles Publishing Company, 100%.

Stns: 3 TV. KHQ, Spokane, WA; KNDO, Yakima-Pasco -Richland-Kennewick, WA; KNDU, Yakima-Pasco -Richland-Kennewick, WA.

Cowles Publishing owns *Spokesman-Review*, Spokane, WA.

Lon C. Lee, pres.

KM Communications Inc., 3654 Jarvis Ave., Skokie, IL, 60076. Phone: (847) 674-0864. Fax: (847) 674-9188. Web Site:www.kmcommunications.com

Stns: 3 TV. KWKB, Cedar Rapids-Waterloo-Iowa City & Dubuque, IA; KPIF, Idaho Falls-Pocatello, ID; KEJB, Monroe, LA-El Dorado, AR.

Stns: 3 AM. 9 FM. WPNG(FM) Pearson, GA; KTKB-FM Hagatna, GU; KTKB(AM) Tamuning, GU; KEWA(AM) Ewa Beach, HI; KQMG Independence, IA; KQMG-FM Independence, IA; WLCN(FM) Atlanta, IL; WMKB(FM) Earlville, IL; KBWM(FM) Breckenridge, TX; KKEV(FM) Centerville, TX; KBDK(FM) Leakey, TX; KHMR(FM) Lovelady, TX.

Myoung Hwa Bae, pres; Kevin J. Bae, VP/gen mgr.

L

LIN Television Corporation, 4 Richmond Sq., Providence, RI, 02906. Phone: (401) 454-2880. Fax: (401) 454-2817.E-mail: deborah.jacobson@lintv.com Web Site:www.lintv.com Ownership: Hicks, Muse, Tate & Furst 47%.

Stns: 30 TV. KBIM, Albuquerque-Santa Fe, NM; KREZ, Albuquerque-Santa Fe, NM; KRQE, Albuquerque-Santa Fe, NM; KXAM, Austin, TX; KXAN-TV, Austin, TX; WIVB-TV, Buffalo, NY; WNLO, Buffalo, NY; WAND, Champaign & Springfield-Decatur, IL; WWHO, Columbus, OH; WDTN, Dayton, OH; WANE-TV, Ft. Wayne, IN; WOOD-TV, Grand Rapids-Kalamazoo-Battle Creek, MI; WOTV, Grand Rapids-Kalamazoo-Battle Creek, MI; WLUK-TV, Green Bay-Appleton, WI; WCTX, Hartford & New Haven, CT; WTNH, Hartford & New Haven, CT; WNDY, Indianapolis, IN; WISH-TV, Indianapolis, IN; WLFI, Lafayette, IN; WNJX, Mayaguez, PR; WALA-TV, Mobile, AL-Pensacola (Ft. Walton Beach), FL; WBPG, Mobile, AL-Pensacola (Ft. Walton Beach), FL; WVBT, Norfolk-Portsmouth-Newport News, VA; WAVY-TV, Norfolk-Portsmouth-Newport News, VA; WTIN-TV, Ponce, PR; WPRI, Providence, RI-New Bedford, MA; WAPA, San Juan, PR; WWLP, Springfield-Holyoke, MA; WTHI, Terre Haute, IN; WUPW, Toledo, OH.

Vincent L. Sadusky, CEO; Richard Schmaeling, CFO.

Lake Superior Community Broadcasting Corp., 1390 Bagley St., Alpena, MI, 49707. Phone: (989) 356-3434. Ownership: Stephen A. Marks, 100%.

Stns: 2 TV. WBKP, Marquette, MI; WBUP, Marquette, MI.

Landmark Communications Inc., (Landmark Broadcast Division.). 150 W. Brambleton Ave., Norfolk, VA, 23510. Phone: (757) 446-2000. Fax: (757) 446-2179. Web Site:www.landmarkcommunications.com Ownership: (Landmark Broadcast Division.)

Stns: 2 TV. KLAS, Las Vegas, NV; WTVF, Nashville, TN.

Landmark Communications Inc. publishes the following daily newspapers: *Citrus County Crhonicle*, Crystal River, FL; *News-Enterprise*, Elizabethtown, KY; *The Carroll County Times*, Westminster, MD; *Los Alamos Monitor*, Los Alamos, NM; *News & Record*, Greensboro, NC; *The Virginian-Pilot*, Norfolk, VA; *Roanoke Times*, Roanoke, VA. Landmark Community Newspapers, Shelbyville, KY, publishes four community dailies, four tri-wklys, nine semi-wklys, 29 wklys, 39 shoppers & free newspapers, & 38 special-interest publications. Landmark Communications owns 49.9% of Capital-Gazette Communications Inc., publisher of *The Capital* (a daily newspaper in Annapolis, MD), *The Maryland Gazette* (a twice-weekly newspaper in Glen Burnie, MD), *Washingtonian Magazine* & weekly newspapers in Bowie & Crofton, MD.

Frank Batten Jr., chmn; Decker Anstrom, pres.

Le Sea Broadcasting, Box 12, South Bend, IN, 46624. Phone: (574) 291-8200. Fax: (574) 291-9043.E-mail: leseabroadcasting@lesea.com Web Site:www.lesea.com

Stns: 8 TV. KWHD, Denver, CO; KWHH, Hilo, HI; KWHE, Honolulu, HI; WHMB-TV, Indianapolis, IN; WHNO, New Orleans, LA; WHME, South Bend-Elkhart, IN; KWHB, Tulsa, OK; KWHM, Wailuku, HI.

Stns: 3 FM. WHPZ-FM Bremen, IN; WHME-FM South Bend, IN; WHPD(FM) Dowagiac, MI.

Peter Sumrall, pres/CEO.

Liberman Broadcasting Inc., 1845 Empire Ave., Burbank, CA, 91504. Phone: (818) 729-5300. Fax: (818) 729-5678.E-mail: LBIinfo@lbimedia.com Web Site:www.lbimedia.com Ownership: Lenard D. Liberman, 47.5-49% votes, 40-42.5% equity; Jose Liberman 2003 Annuity Trust, 23.75-24.5% votes, 20-21.25% equity; Esther Liberman 2003 Annuity Trust, 23.75-24.5% votes, 20-21.25% equity; public shareholders of Liberman Broadcasting Inc., 2-5% votes, 15-20% equity.

Stns: 4 TV. KMPX, Dallas-Ft. Worth; KZJL, Houston; KRCA, Los Angeles; KPNZ, Salt Lake City, UT.

Stns: 7 AM. 15 FM. KEBN(FM) Garden Grove, CA; KBUE(FM) Long Beach, CA; KHJ(AM) Los Angeles, CA; KBUA(FM) San Fernando, CA; KRQB(FM) San Jacinto, CA; KVNR Santa Ana, CA; KWIZ-FM Santa Ana, CA; KTCY(FM) Azle, TX; KXGJ-FM Bay City, TX; KQQK(FM) Beaumont, TX; KBOC(FM) Bridgeport, TX; KJOJ Conroe, TX; KNTE-FM El Campo, TX; KJOJ-FM Freeport, TX; KEYH Houston, TX; KQUE Houston, TX; KNOR(FM) Krum, TX; KZZA(FM) Muenster, TX; KZMP-FM Pilot Point, TX; KTJM-FM Port Arthur, TX; KSEV(AM) Tomball, TX; KZMP(AM) University Park, TX.

Lenard Liberman, pres; Brett Zane, CEO.

Liberty Media Corp., 12300 Liberty Blvd., Englewood, CO, 80112. Phone: (720) 875-5400. Web Site:www.libertymedia.com Ownership: John C. Malone, 29.97% votes, 3.32% of total assets.

Stns: 2 TV. WFRV, Green Bay-Appleton, WI; WJMN, Marquette, MI.

John C. Malone, chmn; Gregory B. Maffei, pres/CEO.

Lincoln Financial Media, 100 N. Greene St., Greensboro, NC, 27420. Phone: (336) 691-3000. Fax: (336) 691-3222. Web Site:www.lincolnfinancialmedia.com Ownership: Lincoln National Corp., 100%.

Stns: 5 AM. 10 FM. KSOQ-FM Escondido, CA; KIFM-FM San Diego, CA; KBZT(FM) San Diego, CA; KNSN(AM) San Diego, CA; KSON(FM) San Diego, CA; KYGO-FM Denver, CO; KRWZ(AM) Denver, CO; KQKS-FM Lakewood, CO; KEPN(AM) Lakewood, CO; KKFN(FM) Longmont, CO; WLYF(FM) Miami, FL; WMXJ-FM Pompano Beach, FL; WAXY South Miami, FL; WQXI Atlanta, GA; WSTR-FM Smyrna, GA.

Ed Hull, pres, Lincoln Financial Sports; John Shreves, pres & Lincoln Financial TV; Don Benson, pres, Lincoln Financial Radio.

Local TV LLC, 1717 Dixie Hwy., Suite 650, Ft. Wright, KY, 41011. Phone: (859) 448-2700. Fax: (859) 331-6014. Web Site:www.localtvllc.com Ownership: Local TV Holdings LLC, 100%.

Stns: 17 TV. WJW, Cleveland-Akron (Canton), OH; WQAD, Davenport, IA-Rock Island-Moline, IL; KDVR, Denver, CO; KFCT, Denver, CO; WHO-DT, Des Moines-Ames, IA; KFSM-TV, Ft. Smith-Fayetteville-Springdale-Rogers, AR; WGHP, Greensboro-High Point-Winston Salem, NC; WHNT, Huntsville-Decatur (Florence), AL; WREG, Memphis, TN; WITI, Milwaukee, WI; WTKR, Norfolk-Portsmouth-Newport News, VA; KAUT-TV, Oklahoma City, OK; KFOR, Oklahoma City, OK; WTVR, Richmond-Petersburg, VA; KSTU, Salt Lake City, UT; KTVI, St. Louis, MO; WNEP, Wilkes Barre-Scranton, PA.

Bobby Lawrence, CEO; Pam Taylor, CFO.

London Broadcasting Co. Inc., 5052 Addison Circle, Addison, TX, 75001. Phone: (214) 812-9600. Web Site:londonbroadcastingcompany.com Ownership: SunTx LBC Holdings L.P., 67.21%; SunTx Fulcrum Fund II—SBIC L.P., 30.37%; Terry E. London, .76%; Philip Hurley, .45%.

Stns: 3 TV. KBMT, Beaumont-Port Arthur, TX; KYTX, Tyler-Longview (Lufkin & Nacogdoches), TX; KCEN-TV, Waco-Temple-Bryan, TX.

Terry E. London, pres; Philip H. Hurley, COO; Carl W. Kornmeyer, CFO.

M

MAX Media L.L.C., 900 Laskin Rd., Virginia Beach, VA, 23451. Phone: (757) 437-9800. Fax: (757) 437-0034. Web Site:www.maxmediallc.com Ownership: MBG-GG LLC, 42.0345%; MBG Quad-C Investors I Inc., 41.4124%;

Aardvarks Also LLC, 6.1967%; Colonnade Max Investors Inc., 4.8671%; Quad-C Max Investors Inc., 4.6799%; MBG Quad-C Investors II Inc., 0.6221%; and Quad-C Max Investors II Inc., 0.1872%.

Stns: 7 TV. WMEI, Arecibo, PR; KULR-TV, Billings, MT; WNKY, Bowling Green, KY; KWYB, Butte-Bozeman, MT; WVIF, Christiansted, VI; KTMF, Missoula, MT; WPFO, Portland-Auburn, ME.

Stns: 12 AM. 24 FM. KVLD(FM) Atkins, AR; KCJC(FM) Dardanelle, AR; KCAB Dardanelle, AR; KVOM Morrilton, AR; KVOM-FM Morrilton, AR; KWKK-FM Russellville, AR; WCIL Carbondale, IL; WUEZ(FM) Carterville, IL; WXLT(FM) Christopher, IL; WOOZ-FM Harrisburg, IL; WJPF Herrin, IL; KZIM Cape Girardeau, MO; KEZS-FM Cape Girardeau, MO; KGIR Cape Girardeau, MO; KCGQ-FM Gordonville, MO; KMAL(AM) Malden, MO; KLSC(FM) Malden, MO; KWOC Poplar Bluff, MO; KJEZ-FM Poplar Bluff, MO; KKLR-FM Poplar Bluff, MO; KGKS-FM Scott City, MO; KSIM(AM) Sikeston, MO; WQDK-FM Ahoskie, NC; WGAI(AM) Elizabeth City, NC; WCMS-FM Hatteras, NC; WCXL(FM) Kill Devil Hills, NC; WFYY(FM) Bloomsburg, PA; WYGL-FM Elizabethville, PA; WWBE-FM Mifflinburg, PA; WLGL-FM Riverside, PA; WYGL Selinsgrove, PA; WCMS(AM) Newport News, VA; WGH-FM Newport News, VA; WVHT(FM) Norfolk, VA; WVBW(FM) Suffolk, VA; WXEZ-FM Yorktown, VA.

John A. Trinder, pres.

Malara Broadcast Group Inc., 9257 Bailey Ln., Fairfax, VA, 22031. Phone: (703) 253-2020. Ownership: TCM Media Associates LLC, 100%.

Stns: 2 TV. KDLH, Duluth, MN-Superior, WI; WPTA, Ft. Wayne, IN.

Manship Stations, Box 2906, Baton Rouge, LA, 70821. Phone: (225) 387-2222. Fax: (225) 336-2246. Web Site:www.2theadvocate.com

Stns: 2 TV. WBRZ-TV, Baton Rouge, LA; KRGV, Harlingen-Weslaco-Brownsville-McAllen, TX.

Also owns Baton Rouge *Morning Advocate* & Saturday & Sunday *Advocate*.

Richard F. Manship, pres.

Mark III Media Inc., 2312 Sagewood, Casper, WY, 82601. Phone: (307) 235-3962. Ownership: Julie Jaffe, 35%; Jennifer Lechter, 35%; and Mark R. Nalbone, 30%.

Stns: 3 TV. KGWC, Casper-Riverton, WY; KGWL, Casper-Riverton, WY; KGWR, Salt Lake City, UT.

Julie Jaffe, pres.

McGraw-Hill Broadcasting Co., c/o KGTV(TV), 4600 Air Way, San Diego, CA, 92102. Phone: (619) 237-6212. Fax: (619) 262-2275. E-mail: equinn@kgtv.com Web Site:www.mcgraw-hill.com Ownership: The McGraw-Hill Companies, 100%.

Stns: 4 TV. KERO, Bakersfield, CA; KMGH, Denver, CO; WRTV, Indianapolis, IN; KGTV, San Diego, CA.

McGraw-Hill Inc., owner of the McGraw-Hill Broadcasting Co., publishes *Business Week* magazine & various trade publications.

Darrell K. Brown, pres; Tim Boling, engrg dir.

McKinnon Broadcasting Co., 5002 S. Padre Island Dr., Corpus Christi, TX, 78411. Phone: (361) 986-8300. Fax: (361) 986-8411. Ownership: Michael McKinnon.

Stns: 2 TV. KIII, Corpus Christi, TX; KUSI, San Diego, CA.

Michael McKinnon, pres/CEO.

Media General Broadcast Group, 111 N. 4th St., Richmond, VA, 23219. Phone: (804) 775-4600. Fax: (804) 775-4601. Web Site:www.mgbg.com Ownership: Media General Inc.

Stns: 18 TV. WJBF, Augusta, GA; WVTM, Birmingham (Anniston, Tuscaloosa), AL; WCBD-TV, Charleston, SC; WRBL, Columbus, GA; WCMH, Columbus, OH; WNCT-TV, Greenville-New Bern-Washington, NC; WSPA-TV, Greenville-Spartanburg, SC-Asheville, NC-Anderson, SC; WYCW, Greenville-Spartanburg, SC-Asheville, NC-Anderson, SC; WHLT, Hattiesburg-Laurel, MS; WJTV, Jackson, MS; WKRG, Mobile, AL-Pensacola (Ft. Walton Beach), FL; WBTW, Myrtle Beach-Florence, SC; WJAR, Providence, RI-New Bedford, MA; WNCN, Raleigh-Durham (Fayetteville), NC; WSLS, Roanoke-Lynchburg, VA; WSAV-TV, Savannah, GA; WFLA-TV, Tampa-St. Petersburg (Sarasota), FL; WJHL, Tri-Cities, TN-VA.

The Dothan Eagle, Opelika-Auburn News, The Enterprise Ledger, all AL; *The Denver Post* (20% ownership), CO; *The Tampa Tribune,* (Sebring) *Highlands Today,* (Brooksville) *Hernando Today, Jackson County Floridan,* FL; *Winston-Salem Journal,* (Concord & Kannapolis) *Independent Tribune, Hickory Daily Record, Statesville Record & Landmark, The* (Morganton) *News Herald, The Reidsville Review, The* (Eden) *Daily News, The* (Marion) *McDowell News,* NC; *The* (Florence) *Morning News,* SC; *Richmond Times-Dispatch, Bristol Herald Courier, The* (Lynchburg) *News & Advance,*

The (Charlottesville) *Daily Progress, Potomac* (Woodbridge) *News, Danville Register & Bee, The* (Waynesboro) *News Virginian, Manassas Journal Messenger, Culpeper Star-Exponent, Virginia Business* (monthly magazine), VA. Media General also owns nearly 100 weeklies and other periodicals and Media General News Service, DC.

James A. Zimmerman Jr., pres; Edward H. Deichman Jr., VP finance; Richard W. Roberts Jr., VP; Ardell Hill, VP; Peter McCampbell Jr., VP/dir sls; Daniel Bradley, VP; Steve Gleason Jr., progmg VP; Catherine Gugerty, dir mktg; James Conschafter Jr., VP; Tom Conway Jr., VP; Paul Gaulke Jr., mktg VP.

Meredith Broadcasting Group, Meredith Corp., 1716 Locust St., Des Moines, IA, 50309-3023. Phone: (515) 284-2159. Fax: (515) 284-2514. Web Site:www.meredith.com Ownership: Meredith Broadcasting is an operating group of Meredith Corp., Des Moines, IA.

Stns: 11 TV. WGCL-TV, Atlanta; WNEM-TV, Flint-Saginaw-Bay City, MI; WHNS, Greenville-Spartanburg, SC-Asheville, NC-Anderson, SC; WFSB, Hartford & New Haven, CT; KSMO-TV, Kansas City, MO; KCTV, Kansas City, MO; KVVU, Las Vegas, NV; WSMV, Nashville, TN; KPHO-TV, Phoenix (Prescott), AZ; KPTV, Portland, OR; KPDX, Portland, OR.

Stns: 1 AM. WNEM(AM) Bridgeport, MI.

The publishing group includes:

Magazines: *American Baby, American Patchwork & Quilting, Better Homes & Gardens, Country Home, Country Home Country Gardens, Creative Home, Decorating, Do It Yourself, Garden, Deck, and Landscape, Garden Shed, Ladies' Home Journal, Midwest Living, MORE, Renovation Style, Successful Farming, Traditional Home,* and *Wood,* along with more than 170 special interest titles.

Paul Karpowic, pres; Douglas Lowe, exec VP.

Mission Broadcasting Inc., 7650 Chippewa Rd., Suite 305, Brecksville, OH, 44141. Phone: (440) 526-2227. Fax: (330) 336-8454. Fax: (440) 546-1903. E-mail: dpthatcher@sbcglobal.net

Stns: 14 TV. KRBC, Abilene-Sweetwater, TX; KCIT, Amarillo, TX; KHMT, Billings, MT; WFXP, Erie, PA; KODE, Joplin, MO-Pittsburg, KS; KAMC, Lubbock, TX; KTVE, Monroe, LA-El Dorado, AR; WTVO, Rockford, IL; KSAN-TV, San Angelo, TX; KOLR, Springfield, MO; WFXW-TV, Terre Haute, IN; WUTR, Utica, NY; KJTL, Wichita Falls, TX & Lawton, OK; WYOU, Wilkes Barre-Scranton, PA.

David Smith, pres; Nancie Smith, VP; Dennis Thatcher, COO.

Morris Multimedia Inc., 27 Abercorn St., Savannah, GA, 31401. Phone: (912) 233-1281. Fax: (912) 238-2059. Web Site:www.morrismultimedia.com Ownership: Charles H. Morris.

Stns: 5 TV. WXXV, Biloxi-Gulfport, MS; WDEF-TV, Chattanooga, TN; WCBI-TV, Columbus-Tupelo-West Point, MS; WTVQ-DT, Lexington, KY; WMGT-TV, Macon, GA.

Daily newspapers, weekly newspapers.

Charles H. Morris, pres.

Mountain Broadcasting Corp., 99 Clinton Rd., West Caldwell, NJ, 07006. Phone: (973) 852-0300. Fax: (973) 808-5516. Ownership: Sun Young Joo, 66% votes, 35.2% total assets; John H. Joo, 14% votes, 6.3% total assets; Victor C. Joo, 14% votes, 5.6% total assets; Sun Hoo Joo, 6% votes, 2.9% total assets; and Hansen Lau, 5.7% total assets.

Stns: 1 TV. WMBC-TV, New York.

Stns: 3 AM. WPWA Chester, PA; WBTK(AM) Richmond, VA; WWGB Indian Head, MD.

Sun Young Joo, pres.

Multicultural Capital Trust, c/o 11077 Swansfield Rd., Columbia, MD, 21044-2724. Phone: (202) 350-9658. Fax: (703) 991-7120. Ownership: Lee W. Shubert, trustee, 100% votes.

Stns: 3 TV. WMFP, Boston (Manchester, NH); WRAY, Raleigh-Durham (Fayetteville), NC; KCNS, San Francisco-Oakland-San Jose.

Morgan Murphy Media, 7025 W. Raymond Rd., Madison, WI, 53719. Phone: (608) 271-4321. Fax: (608) 271-0800. E-mail: tbier@wisctv.com Web Site:www.morganmurphymedia.com Ownership: Evening Telegram Co. owns 100% of KVEW(TV), KXLY-AM-FM-TV, KXLY-DT and KAPP(TV). Evening Telegram Co. owns 84.4% of Television Wisconsin Inc., with an additional 15.2% of the stn held by Evening Telegram stockholders.

Stns: 5 TV. WKBT, La Crosse-Eau Claire, WI; WISC-TV, Madison, WI; KXLY-TV, Spokane, WA; KAPP, Yakima-Pasco-Richland-Kennewick, WA; KVEW, Yakima-Pasco-Richland-Kennewick, WA.

Stns: 4 AM. 4 FM. KXLX(AM) Airway Heights, WA; KXLY Spokane, WA; KZZU-FM Spokane, WA; KEZE-FM Spokane, WA; WGLR Lancaster, WI; WGLR-FM Lancaster, WI; WPVL Platteville, WI; WPVL-FM Platteville, WI.

The Evening Telegram principals own *Madison Magazine,* Madison, WI.

Elizabeth Murphy Burns, pres; George Nelson, exec VP; David Sanks, exec VP; Steve Herling, exec VP; Brian Lubarski, gen mgr; Scott Chorski, VP/gen mgr.

N

NBC Universal Television Stations, 30 Rockefeller Plaza, New York, NY, 10112. Phone: (212) 664-4444. Fax: (212) 664-5830. Web Site:www.nbcuni.com Ownership: General Electric Co. owns 100% of NBC Telemundo Holding Co., which is the single controlling shareholder of NBC Telemundo Inc. NBC Telemundo Inc. in turn owns 100% of NBC Telemundo License Co. and NBC License Co.

Stns: 10 TV. WMAQ, Chicago; KXTX, Dallas-Ft. Worth; WVIT, Hartford & New Haven, CT; KNBC, Los Angeles; WTVJ, Miami-Ft. Lauderdale, FL; WNBC, New York; WCAU, Philadelphia; KNSD, San Diego, CA; KNTV, San Francisco-Oakland-San Jose; WRC, Washington, DC (Hagerstown, MD).

John Wallace, pres.

Neuhoff Family L.P., 1501 N. Washington Ave., Danville, IL, 61832. Phone: (217) 442-1700. Phone: (217) 787-9200. Fax: (217) 431-1489. E-mail: mhulvey@cooketech.net Web Site:neuhoffmedia.com Ownership: Neuhoff Corp., North Palm Beach, FL, 100% of votes.

Stns: 1 TV. KMVT, Twin Falls, ID.

Stns: 4 AM. 8 FM. WRHK-FM Danville, IL; WDAN(AM) Danville, IL; WDNL(FM) Danville, IL; WDZ(AM) Decatur, IL; WDZQ(FM) Decatur, IL; WSOY(AM) Decatur, IL; WSOY-FM Decatur, IL; WXAJ(FM) Hillsboro, IL; WCZQ-FM Monticello, IL; WFMB(AM) Springfield, IL; WFMB-FM Springfield, IL; WCVS-FM Virden, IL.

Mike Hulvey, gen mgr; Geoff Neuhoff, pres.

New Vision Television LLC, 3500 Lenox Rd., Suite 640, Atlanta, GA, 30326. Phone: (404) 995-4711. Fax: (404) 995-4712. Web Site:www.newvisiontv.com Ownership: HBK NV LLC, 97.5%; Jason Elkin, 2%; and John Heinen, 0.5%.

Stns: 13 TV. WIAT, Birmingham (Anniston, Tuscaloosa), AL; KHAW-TV, Hilo, HI; KHON-TV, Honolulu, HI; KOIN, Portland, OR; KIMT, Rochester, MN-Mason City, IA-Austin, MN; WJCL, Savannah, GA; KSNT, Topeka, KS; KAII-TV, Wailuku, HI; KSNW, Wichita-Hutchinson Plus, KS; KSNC, Wichita-Hutchinson Plus, KS; KSNG, Wichita-Hutchinson Plus, KS; KSNK, Wichita-Hutchinson Plus, KS; WKBN, Youngstown, OH.

Jason Elkin, chmn/CEO; John Heinen, pres/COO.

NewCap Inc., 745 Windmill Rd., Dartmouth, NS, B3B1C2. Canada. Phone: (902) 468-7557. Fax: (902) 468-7558. Web Site:www.ncc.ca Ownership: H.R. Steele, Blavin & Company.

Stns: 2 TV. CITL, Lloydminster, AB; CKSA, Lloydminster, AB.

Stns: 22 AM. 42 FM. CKBA-FM Athabasca, AB; CJPR-FM Blairmore, AB; CJEG-FM Bonnyville, AB; CIXF-FM Brooks, AB; CIBQ Brooks, AB; CFXL-FM Calgary, AB; CFUL-FM Calgary, AB; CFCW-FM Camrose, AB; CFCW Camrose, AB; CJXK-FM Cold Lake, AB; CKDQ Drumheller, AB; CKRA-FM Edmonton, AB; CIRK-FM Edmonton, AB; CFXE-FM Edson, AB; CHFT-FM Fort McMurray, AB; CKVH High Prairie, AB; CFXH-FM Hinton, AB; CKSA-FM Lloydminster, AB; CKGY-FM Red Deer, AB; CIZZ-FM Red Deer, AB; CHLW(AM) Saint Paul, AB; CHSL-FM Slave Lake, AB; CKSQ(AM) Stettler, AB; CKKY Wainwright, AB; CKWY-FM Wainwright, AB; CFOK(AM) Westlock, AB; CKJR Wetaskiwin, AB; CFXW-FM Whitecourt, AB; CHNK-FM Winnipeg, MB; CKJS Winnipeg, MB; CFRK-FM Fredericton, NB; CJXL-FM Moncton, NB; CJMO-FM Moncton, NB; CKIM Baie Verte, NF; CHVO-FM Carbonear, NF; CFLC-FM Churchill Falls, NF; CKVO Clarenville, NF; CKXX-FM Corner Brook, NF; CFCB Corner Brook, NF; CKGA Gander, NF; CKXD-FM Gander, NF; CFLN Goose Bay, NF; CKCM Grand Falls, NF; CKXG-FM Grand Falls-Windsor, NF; CHCM Marystown, NF; CFNW Port au Choix, NF; CFCV-FM Saint Andrews, NF; VOCM(AM) Saint John's, NF; CJYQ Saint John's, NF; CKIX-FM Saint John's, NF; CFSX Stephenville, NF; CFLW Wabush, NF; CFRQ-FM Dartmouth, NS; CKUL-FM Halifax, NS; CIJK-FM Kentville, NS; CHRK-FM Sydney, NS; CIHT-FM Ottawa, ON; CILV-FM Ottawa, ON; CHNO-FM Sudbury, ON; CIGM-FM Sudbury, ON; CJUK-FM Thunder Bay, ON; CKTG-FM Thunder Bay, ON; CHTN-FM Charlottetown, PE; CKQK-FM Charlottetown, PE.

H.R. Steele, chmn; Scott Weatherby, CEO; R.G. Steele, pres/CEO.

Newfoundland Broadcasting Co., (NTV & OZ Networks). Box 2020, St. John's, NF, A1C 5S2. Canada. Phone: (709) 722-5015. Fax: (709) 726-5107. E-mail: ozfm@ozfm.com Web Site:www.ntv.ca Ownership: Geoffrey W. Stirling,

89.95%; G. Scott Stirling, 10%; and others, 0.05%.

Stns: 6 TV. CJOM, Argentia, NF; CJWB, Bonavista, NF; CJWN, Corner Brook, NF; CJOX-1, Grand Bank, NF; CJCN, Grand Falls, NF; CJSV, Stephenville, NF.

Stns: 8 FM. CJOZ-FM Bonavista Bay, NF; CJKK-FM Clarenville, NF; CKOZ-FM Corner Brook, NF; CIOZ-FM Marystown, NF; CHOS-FM Rattling Brook, NF; CKSS-FM Red Rocks, NF; CHOZ-FM Saint John's, NF; CIOS-FM Stephenville, NF.

Scott G. Stirling, pres/CEO; Doug Neal, engrg dir.

Newport Television LLC, 460 Nichols Rd., Suite 250, Kansas City, MO, 64112. Phone: (816) 751-0200. Fax: (816) 751-0250.E-mail: info@newporttv.com Web Site:www.newporttv.com

Stns: 27 TV. WXXA-TV, Albany-Schenectady-Troy, NY; WIVT, Binghamton, NY; WKRC-TV, Cincinnati, OH; WETM, Elmira (Corning), NY; KMTR, Eugene, OR; KTCW, Eugene, OR; KMCB, Eugene, OR; KTVF, Fairbanks, AK; WHP-TV, Harrisburg-Lancaster-Lebanon-York, PA; WJKT, Jackson, TN; WAWS, Jacksonville, FL; KASN, Little Rock-Pine Bluff, AR; KLRT-TV, Little Rock-Pine Bluff, AR; WLMT, Memphis, TN; WPTY, Memphis, TN; WJTC, Mobile, AL-Pensacola (Ft. Walton Beach), FL; WPMI-TV, Mobile, AL-Pensacola (Ft. Walton Beach), FL; WHAM-TV, Rochester, NY; KTVX, Salt Lake City, UT; KVOS, Seattle-Tacoma, WA; WSYR-TV, Syracuse, NY; KMYT-TV, Tulsa, OK; KOKI, Tulsa, OK; WWTI, Watertown, NY; KSAS-TV, Wichita-Hutchinson Plus, KS; KAAS, Wichita-Hutchinson Plus, KS; KOCW, Wichita-Hutchinson Plus, KS.

Sandy DiPasquale, pres/CEO; Craig Millar, sr VP; Jim Martin, sr VP.

News-Press & Gazette Co., Box 29, St. Joseph, MO, 64502. Phone: (816) 271-8500. Fax: (816) 271-8695. Ownership: David R. Bradley Jr., Henry H. Bradley, Lyle E. Leimkuhler. Cable TV: NPG Cable of Arizona.

Stns: 7 TV. KTVZ, Bend, OR; KRDO-TV, Colorado Springs-Pueblo, CO; KVIA-TV, El Paso (Las Cruces, NM), TX; KJCT, Grand Junction-Montrose, CO; KIFI, Idaho Falls-Pocatello, ID; KESQ-TV, Palm Springs, CA; KECY-TV, Yuma, AZ-El Centro, CA.

Stns: 2 AM. 1 FM. KESQ Indio, CA; KUNA-FM La Quinta, CA; KRDO(AM) Colorado Springs, CO.

News-Press & Gazette Co. publishes the *St. Joseph News-Press*, St. Joseph, MO.

John Kueneke, pres.

Newsweb Corp., 1645 W. Fullerton Ave., Chicago, IL, 60614. Phone: (773) 975-0401. Fax: (773) 975-1301. Ownership: Fred Eychaner, 100%.

Stns: 1 TV. KCDO-TV, Denver, CO.

Stns: 5 AM. 4 FM. WCPT-FM Arlington Heights, IL; WSBC(AM) Chicago, IL; WCFJ Chicago Heights, IL; WAIT(AM) Crystal Lake, IL; WCPY(FM) De Kalb, IL; WKIF-FM Kankakee, IL; WCPQ(FM) Park Forest, IL; WCPT(AM) Willow Springs, IL; WNDZ Portage, IN.

Fred Eychaner, CEO; Charley Gross, COO.

Nexstar Broadcasting Group Inc., 909 Lake Carolyn Pkwy., Suite 1450, Irving, TX, 75039. Phone: (972) 373-8800. Fax: (972) 373-8888. Web Site:www.nexstar.tv

Stns: 33 TV. KTAB, Abilene-Sweetwater, TX; KAMR, Amarillo, TX; KBTV, Beaumont-Port Arthur, TX; KSVI, Billings, MT; WCFN, Champaign & Springfield-Decatur, IL; WCIA, Champaign & Springfield-Decatur, IL; WDHN, Dothan, AL; WJET-TV, Erie, PA; WTVW, Evansville, IN; KFTA-TV, Ft. Smith-Fayetteville-Springdale-Rogers, AR; KNWA-TV, Ft. Smith-Fayetteville-Springdale-Rogers, AR; WFFT-TV, Ft. Wayne, IN; WLYH-TV, Harrisburg-Lancaster-Lebanon-York, PA; WCWJ, Jacksonville, FL; WTAJ-TV, Johnstown-Altoona, PA; KSNF, Joplin, MO-Pittsburg, KS; KARK, Little Rock-Pine Bluff, AR; KARZ-TV, Little Rock-Pine Bluff, AR; KLBK, Lubbock, TX; KARD, Monroe, LA-El Dorado, AR; KMID, Odessa-Midland, TX; WMBD, Peoria-Bloomington, IL; WROC-TV, Rochester, NY; WQRF, Rockford, IL; KLST, San Angelo, TX; KTAL, Shreveport, LA; KSFX-TV, Springfield, MO; KQTV, St. Joseph, MO; WTWO-TV, Terre Haute, IN; WFXV, Utica, NY; WHAG-TV, Washington, DC (Hagerstown, MD); KFDX, Wichita Falls, TX & Lawton, OK; WBRE, Wilkes Barre-Scranton, PA.

Perry Sook, chmn/pres/CEO; Matt Devine, CFO; Timothy Busch, COO; Brian Jones, COO.

Northwest Broadcasting Inc., 2111 University Park Dr., Suite 650, Okemos, MI, 48864. Phone: (517) 347-4141. Fax: (517) 347-4675.E-mail: bradybw1@comcast.net Ownership: LPTV: WBPN-LP Morris, NY; and KCYU-LP Yakima, WA.

Stns: 4 TV. WICZ, Binghamton, NY; KMVU-DT, Medford-Klamath Falls, OR; KAYU-TV, Spokane, WA; KFFX-TV, Yakima-Pasco-Richland-Kennewick, WA.

Brian Brady, pres/CEO.

P

Pacific Christian Church, Box 15667, Honolulu, HI, 96830. Phone: (808) 440-1350.E-mail: info@oceaniachurch.org Ownership: James W. Gustafson, 33% votes; Diane Sandlin, 33% votes; and Heather M. Vaikona, 33% votes.

Stns: 2 TV. KLEI, ; KUPU, Honolulu, HI

James W. Gustafson, pres.

Pappas Telecasting Companies, 500 S. Chinowth Rd., Visalia, CA, 93277. Phone: (559) 733-7800. Fax: (559) 733-7878. Web Site:www.pappastv.com Ownership: Harry J. Pappas.

Stns: 17 TV. WLGA, Columbus, GA; KDMI, Des Moines-Ames, IA; KCWI-TV, Des Moines-Ames, IA; KDBC-TV, El Paso (Las Cruces, NM), TX; KMPH-TV, Fresno-Visalia, CA; KFRE-TV, Fresno-Visalia, CA; WWAZ-TV, Green Bay-Appleton, WI; WCWG, Greensboro-High Point-Winston Salem, NC; KAZH, Houston; KWNB, Lincoln & Hastings-Kearney, NE; KHGI, Lincoln & Hastings-Kearney, NE; KAZA-TV, Los Angeles; KPTM, Omaha, NE; KTNC, San Francisco-Oakland-San Jose; KUNO-TV, San Francisco-Oakland-San Jose; KPTH, Sioux City, IA; KSWT, Yuma, AZ-El Centro, CA.

Stns: 2 AM. KMPH(AM) Modesto, CA; KTRB(AM) San Francisco, CA.

Harry J. Pappas, chmn/CEO; Dennis J. Davis, pres/COO; Bruce M. Yeager, exec VP/CFO.

Parker Broadcasting Inc., 5341 Tate Ave., Plano, TX, 75093. Phone: (214) 704-7559. Ownership: Barry J.C. Parker, 100%.

Stns: 2 TV. KXJB, Fargo-Valley City, ND; KFQX, Grand Junction-Montrose, CO.

Parkin Broadcasting LLC, 11766 Wilshire Blvd., Suite 405, Los Angeles, CA, 90025-6573. Phone: (310) 478-3213. Ownership: Todd Parkin, 100%.

Stns: 2 TV. WTGS, Savannah, GA; WYTV, Youngstown, OH.

Todd Parkin, CEO.

The Jim Pattison Broadcast Group, 460 Pemberton Terrace, Kamloops, BC, V2C 1T5. Canada. Phone: (250) 372-3322. Fax: (250) 374-0445. Web Site:www.jpbroadcast.com Ownership: Jim Pattison Group.

Stns: 4 TV. CFJC-TV, Kamloops, BC; CHAT, Medicine Hat, AB; CHAT-1, Pivot, AB; CKPG, Prince George, BC.

Stns: 29 FM. CIBW-FM Drayton Valley, AB; CJXX-FM Grande Prairie, AB; CHLB-FM Lethbridge, AB; CFMY-FM Medicine Hat, AB; CHAT-FM Medicine Hat, AB; CFDV-FM Red Deer, AB; CHUB-FM Red Deer, AB; CHBW-FM Rocky Mountain House, AB; CJBZ-FM Taber, AB; CKLR-FM Courtenay, BC; CHBZ-FM Cranbrook, BC; CHDR-FM Cranbrook, BC; CJDR-FM Fernie, BC; CKBZ-FM Kamloops, BC; CIFM-FM Kamloops, BC; CKLZ-FM Kelowna, BC; CKOV-FM Kelowna, BC; CKWV-FM Nanaimo, BC; CHWF-FM Nanaimo, BC; CIBH-FM Parksville, BC; CHPQ-FM Parksville, BC; CJAV-FM Port Alberni, BC; CKDV-FM Prince George, BC; CKKN-FM Prince George, BC; CJJR-FM Vancouver, BC; CKPK-FM Vancouver, BC; CKIZ-FM Vernon, BC; CJZN-FM Victoria, BC; CKKQ-FM Victoria, BC.

Rick Arnish, pres; Bill Dinicol, VP Finance; Bruce Davis, VP sls; Loretta Lewis, admin asst.

Pollack Broadcasting Co., 5500 Poplar Ave. #1, Memphis, TN, 38119. Phone: (901) 685-3993. Fax: (901) 685-3995.E-mail: wpollack@midsouth.rr.com Ownership: William H. Pollack, 100%. Note: Group also owns KWCE-LP Alexandria, LA.

Stns: 2 TV. KLAX, Alexandria, LA; KIEM, Eureka, CA.

Stns: 3 AM. 3 FM. KBOA-FM Piggott, AR; KCRV Caruthersville, MO; KCRV-FM Caruthersville, MO; KBOA Kennett, MO; KTMO(FM) New Madrid, MO; KMIS Portageville, MO.

William H. Pollack, pres.

Post-Newsweek Stations Inc., 550 W. Lafayette Blvd., Detroit, MI, 48226. Phone: (313) 223-2260. Fax: (313) 223-2263. Ownership: Post-Newsweek Stations is a subsidiary of the publicly traded Washington Post Co.

Stns: 6 TV. WDIV-TV, Detroit; KPRC-TV, Houston; WJXT, Jacksonville, FL; WPLG, Miami-Ft. Lauderdale, FL; WKMG, Orlando-Daytona Beach-Melbourne, FL; KSAT, San Antonio, TX.

The Washington Post Co. publishes the *Washington DC Post*, the *Everett* (WA) *Herald*, *Newsweek* magazine, *Newsweek International* (New York, NY), *Newsweek Japan* & *Newsweek Korea*.

Prime Cities Broadcasting Inc., Box 4026, 3130 E. Broadway Ave, Bismarck, ND, 58502-4026. Phone: (701) 355-0026. Fax: (701) 250-7244.E-mail: kndx@fox26.tv

Web Site:www.myfoxbis.com Ownership: John Tupper, Bruce Fox.

Stns: 2 TV. KNDX, Minot-Bismarck-Dickinson, ND; KXND, Minot-Bismarck-Dickinson, ND.

John B. Tupper, pres/CEO; Gary O'Halloran, gen mgr .

Q

Quincy Newspapers Inc., 130 S. Fifth St., Quincy, IL, 62301. Phone: (217) 223-5100. Fax: (217) 223-5019. Web Site:www.qni.biz

Stns: 12 TV. WVVA, Bluefield-Beckley-Oak Hill, WV; KWWL, Cedar Rapids-Waterloo-Iowa City & Dubuque, IA; WQOW-TV, La Crosse-Eau Claire, WI; WXOW-TV, La Crosse-Eau Claire, WI; WKOW, Madison, WI; WGEM-TV, Quincy, IL-Hannibal, MO-Keokuk, IA; KTTC, Rochester, MN-Mason City, IA-Austin, MN; WREX-TV, Rockford, IL; KTIV, Sioux City, IA; WSJV, South Bend-Elkhart, IN; WAOW-TV, Wausau-Rhinelander, WI; WYOW, Wausau-Rhinelander, WI.

Stns: 1 AM. 1 FM. WGEM Quincy, IL; WGEM-FM Quincy, IL.

Quincy Newspapers Inc. owns the *Quincy* (IL) *Herald-Whig*, and the *New Jersey Herald*, Newton, NJ.

Thomas A. Oakley, pres.

R

RNC MEDIA Inc., 380 av Murdoch, Rouyn-Noranda, PQ, J9X 1G5. Canada. Phone: (819) 762-0741. Fax: (819) 762-6331.

Stns: 5 TV. CKRN-3, Bearn-Fabre, PQ; CFGS-TV, Gatineau, PQ; CHOT-TV, Gatineau, PQ; CKRN-TV, Rouyn-Noranda, PQ; CFVS, Val d'Or, PQ.

Stns: 9 FM. CHPR-FM Hawkesbury, ON; CHXX-FM Donnacona, PQ; CHLX-FM Gatineau, PQ; CFTX-FM Gatineau, PQ; CJLA-FM Lachute, PQ; CKLX-FM Montreal, PQ; CHOI-FM Quebec, PQ; CHOA-FM Rouyn-Noranda, PQ; CHGO-FM Val d'Or, PQ.

Pierre R. Brosseau, pres.

Ramar Communications II Ltd., Box 3757, Lubbock, TX, 79452. Phone: (806) 745-3434. Fax: (806) 748-1949. Web Site:www.ramarcom.com E-mail: bmoran@ramarcom.com Ownership: Ray Moran, 51%; Brad Moran, 49%.

LubbockTX , 9800 University Ave.

Stns: 4 TV. KTLL-TV, Albuquerque-Santa Fe, NM; KUPT, Albuquerque-Santa Fe, NM; KTEL-TV, Albuquerque-Santa Fe, NM; KJTV-TV, Lubbock, TX.

Stns: 1 AM. 3 FM. KTTU-FM Brownfield, TX; KJTV(AM) Lubbock, TX; KXTQ-FM Lubbock, TX; KLZK(FM) New Deal, TX.

Ray Moran, chmn; Brad Moran, pres.

Raycom Media Inc., 201 Monroe St., RSA Tower, 20th Fl, Montgomery, AL, 36104. Phone: (334) 206-1400. Fax: (334) 206-1555. Web Site:www.raycommedia.com Ownership: Raycom Media Inc. Other interests: Raycom Sports, New York, NY; Charlotte, NC; Ft. Lauderdale, FL; Nashville, TN; and Chicago, IL.

Stns: 41 TV. WALB, Albany, GA; KASA-TV, Albuquerque-Santa Fe, NM; WAFB, Baton Rouge, LA; WLOX, Biloxi-Gulfport, MS; WBRC, Birmingham (Anniston, Tuscaloosa), AL; WCSC, Charleston, SC; WBTV, Charlotte, NC; WXIX, Cincinnati, OH; WUAB, Cleveland-Akron (Canton), OH; WOIO, Cleveland-Akron (Canton), OH; WIS, Columbia, SC; WTVM, Columbus, GA; WDFX, Dothan, AL; WFIE, Evansville, IN; WDAM-TV, Hattiesburg-Laurel, MS; KHBC, Hilo, HI; KHNL, Honolulu, HI; KFVE, Honolulu, HI; WAFF, Huntsville-Decatur (Florence), AL; WLBT, Jackson, MS; KAIT, Jonesboro, AR; WTNZ, Knoxville, TN; KPLC, Lake Charles, LA; WAVE, Louisville, KY; KCBD, Lubbock, TX; WMC, Memphis, TN; WSFA, Montgomery-Selma, AL; WMBF-TV, Myrtle Beach-Florence, SC; KFVS-TV, Paducah, KY-Cape Girardeau, MO-Harrisburg-Mount Vernon, IL; WPGX, Panama City, FL; WWBT, Richmond-Petersburg, VA; WTOC, Savannah, GA; KSLA, Shreveport, LA; WTOL, Toledo, OH; KOLD, Tucson (Sierra Vista), AZ; KTRE, Tyler-Longview (Lufkin & Nacogdoches), TX; KLTV, Tyler-Longview (Lufkin & Nacogdoches), TX; KOGG, Wailuku, HI; WFLX, West Palm Beach-Ft. Pierce, FL; WECT, Wilmington, NC; WWAY, Wilmington, NC.

Paul McTear, pres/CEO.

Red River Broadcast Co. L.L.C., Box 9115, Fargo, ND, 58106. Phone: (701) 277-1515. Fax: (701) 277-1830. Ownership: Curtis Squire Inc., 100%. Myron Kunin owns 100% of Curtis Squire Inc.

Stns: 7 TV. KQDS-TV, Duluth, MN-Superior, WI; KVRR, Fargo-Valley City, ND; KBRR, Fargo-Valley City, ND; KJRR, Fargo-Valley City, ND; KNRR, Fargo-Valley City, ND; KDLT-TV, Sioux Falls (Mitchell), SD; KDLV-TV, Sioux Falls

(Mitchell), SD.

Ro Grignon, pres; Kathy M. Lau, VP/gen mgr.

Reiten Television Inc., Box 1686, Minot, ND, 58702-1686. Phone: (701) 852-2104. Fax: (701) 838-9360.E-mail: dreiten@kxnet.com Web Site:www.kxmc.com

Stns: 4 TV. KXMA, Minot-Bismarck-Dickinson, ND; KXMB, Minot-Bismarck-Dickinson, ND; KXMC, Minot-Bismarck-Dickinson, ND; KXMD, Minot-Bismarck-Dickinson, ND.

David Reiten, chmn.

Remstar Broadcasting Inc., 85 rue Saint-Paul Ouest, Bureau 300, Montreal, PQ, H2Y 3V4. Canada. Phone: (514) 847-1136. Fax: (514) 847-0019.E-mail: remstar@remstarcorp.com Web Site:www.remstarcorp.com Ownership: Julien Remillard, 50%; and Maxime Remillard, 50%.

Stns: 5 TV. CFRS, Jonquiere, PQ; CFJP, Montreal, PQ; CFAP, Quebec City, PQ; CFKS, Sherbrooke, PQ; CFKM, Trois-Rivieres, PQ.

Roberts Broadcasting Co., 1408 N. Kingshighway Blvd., St. Louis, MO, 63113. Phone: (314) 367-4600. Fax: (314) 367-0174. Web Site:www.upn46stl.com Ownership: St. Louis/Denver LLC.

Stns: 5 TV. WZRB, Columbia, SC; KTFD-DT, Denver, CO; WAZE-TV, Evansville, IN; WRBJ, Jackson, MS; WRBU, St. Louis, MO.

Michael Roberts, CEO; Steven C. Roberts, pres.

Rockfleet Broadcasting Inc., 575 Madison Ave., 10th Fl., New York, NY, 10022. Phone: (212) 605-0401. Phone: (631) 204-0830. Fax: (212) 605-0402. Fax: (631) 204-0832. Ownership: Rockfleet Holdings, 100%.

Stns: 2 TV. WVII, Bangor, ME; WJFW-TV, Wausau-Rhinelander, WI.

R. Joseph Fuchs, pres/CEO.

Rogers Broadcasting Ltd., 777 Jarvis St., Toronto, ON, M4Y 3B7. Canada. Phone: (416) 935-8200. Web Site:www.rogers.com Ownership: Rogers Media Inc., 100%. Note: Rogers Media Inc. is 100% owned by Rogers Communications Inc.

Stns: 10 TV. CKAL, Calgary, AB; CJCO-TV, Calgary, AB; CKEM, Edmonton, AB; CJEO-TV, Edmonton, AB; CHMI-TV, Portage la Prarie, MB; CITY-TV, Toronto, ON; CFMT, Toronto, ON; CJMT-TV, Toronto, ON; CHNM-TV, Vancouver, BC; CKVU, Vancouver, BC.

Stns: 6 AM. 43 FM. CFFR Calgary, AB; CJAQ-FM Calgary, AB; CHMN-FM Canmore, AB; CKER-FM Edmonton, AB; CHDI-FM Edmonton, AB; CKYX-FM Fort McMurray, AB; CJOK-FM Fort McMurray, AB; CFGP-FM Grande Prairie, AB; CFRV-FM Lethbridge, AB; CJRX-FM Lethbridge, AB; CKMH-FM Medicine Hat, AB; CKQC-FM Abbotsford, BC; CKGO-FM-1 Boston Bar, BC; CKCL-FM Chilliwack, BC; CKSR-FM Chilliwack, BC; CFSR-FM Hope, BC; CISP-FM Pemberton, BC; CKKS-FM Sechelt, BC; CKWX Vancouver, BC; CKLG-FM Vancouver, BC; CHTT-FM Victoria, BC; CIOC-FM Victoria, BC; CISW-FM Whistler, BC; CITI-FM Winnipeg, MB; CKY-FM Winnipeg, MB; CKNI-FM Moncton, NB; CHNI-FM Saint John, NB; CFLT-FM Dartmouth, NS; CJNI-FM Halifax, NS; CKXC-FM Kingston, ON; CIKR-FM Kingston, ON; CKGL Kitchener, ON; CHYM-FM Kitchener, ON; CIKZ-FM Kitchener-Waterloo, ON; CHUR-FM North Bay, ON; CKAT(AM) North Bay, ON; CKFX-FM North Bay, ON; CHEZ-FM Ottawa, ON; CHAS-FM Sault Ste. Marie, ON; CJQM-FM Sault Ste. Marie, ON; CKBY-FM Smiths Falls, ON; CJMX-FM Sudbury, ON; CJRQ-FM Sudbury, ON; CJQQ-FM Timmins, ON; CKGB-FM Timmins, ON; CJCL Toronto, ON; CKIS-FM Toronto, ON; CFTR Toronto, ON; CHFI-FM Toronto, ON.

Rael Merson, pres.

S

Saga Communications Inc., 73 Kercheval Ave., Suite 201, Grosse Pointe Farms, MI, 48236. Phone: (313) 886-7070. Fax: (313) 886-7150.E-mail: chapsburg@sagacom.com Web Site:www.sagacommunications.com Ownership: Edward K. Christian, 56.5% of the voting stock. Other Interests: Illinois Radio Network, Michigan Radio Network, Michigan Farm Radio Network.

Stns: 3 TV. WXVT, Greenwood-Greenville, MS; KOAM, Joplin, MO-Pittsburg, KS; KAVU-TV, Victoria, TX.

Stns: 28 AM. 59 FM. KEGI(FM) Jonesboro, AR; KDXY(FM) Lake City, AR; KJBX(FM) Trumann, AR; KLTI-FM Ames, IA; KRNT Des Moines, IA; KSTZ(FM) Des Moines, IA; KPSZ(AM) Des Moines, IA; KIOA(FM) Des Moines, IA; KAZR(FM) Pella, IA; KICD Spencer, IA; KICD-FM Spencer, IA; KLLT(FM) Spencer, IA; WIXY-FM Champaign, IL; WLRW-FM Champaign, IL; WXTT(FM) Danville, IL; WYMG(FM) Jacksonville, IL; WABZ(FM) Sherman, IL; WTAX(AM) Springfield, IL; WQQL(FM) Springfield, IL; WDBR(FM) Springfield, IL; WCFF(FM) Urbana, IL; WEGI(AM) Fort Campbell, KY; WCVQ-FM Fort Campbell, KY; WVVR(FM) Hopkinsville, KY; WZZP(FM) Hopkinsville, KY; WEGI-FM Oak Grove, KY; WHNP(AM) East Longmeadow, MA; WPVQ(FM) Greenfield, MA; WHMQ(AM) Greenfield, MA; WHAI(FM) Greenfield, MA; WHMP Northampton, MA; WLZX(FM) Northampton, MA; WAQY-FM Springfield, MA; WRSI(FM) Turners Falls, MA; WVAE(AM) Biddeford, ME; WCLZ(FM) Brunswick, ME; WBAE Portland, ME; WGAN(AM) Portland, ME; WPOR(FM) Portland, ME; WZAN Portland, ME; WMGX(FM) Portland, ME; WYNZ-FM Westbrook, ME; WOXL-FM Biltmore Forest, NC; WYSE(AM) Canton, NC; WTMT(FM) Weaverville, NC; WMLL(FM) Bedford, NH; WZBK(AM) Keene, NH; WKBK(AM) Keene, NH; WKNE(FM) Keene, NH; WZID(FM) Manchester, NH; WFEA Manchester, NH; WSNI(FM) Swanzey, NH; WINQ(FM) Winchester, NH; WIII(FM) Cortland, NY; WHCU Ithaca, NY; WYXL-FM Ithaca, NY; WNYY(AM) Ithaca, NY; WQNY-FM Ithaca, NY; WQEL-FM Bucyrus, OH; WBCO(AM) Bucyrus, OH; WSNY(FM) Columbus, OH; WVMX(FM) Delaware, OH; WJZA(FM) Pickerington, OH; WODB(FM) Richwood, OH; KMIT-FM Mitchell, SD; KUQL(FM) Wessington Springs, SD; WKFN(AM) Clarksville, TN; WINA Charlottesville, VA; WWWV-FM Charlottesville, VA; WQMZ(FM) Charlottesville, VA; WVAX(AM) Charlottesville, VA; WCNR(FM) Keswick, VA; WNOR(FM) Norfolk, VA; WJOI Norfolk, VA; WAFX-FM Suffolk, VA; WKVT Brattleboro, VT; WKVT-FM Brattleboro, VT; WRSY(FM) Marlboro, VT; KGMI Bellingham, WA; KISM-FM Bellingham, WA; KBAI(AM) Bellingham, WA; KPUG Bellingham, WA; WJZX(FM) Brookfield, WI; WJMR-FM Menomonee Falls, WI; WJYI Milwaukee, WI; WKLH-FM Milwaukee, WI; WHQG(FM) Milwaukee, WI

Edward K. Christian, pres/CEO; Marcia Lobaito, VP business affrs; Sam Bush, CFO; Warren Lada Sr., VP opns.

SagamoreHill Broadcasting LLC, 3825 Inverness Way, Augusta, GA, 30901. Phone: (706) 855-8506. Ownership: Duff Ackerman & Goodrich QP Fund II L.P., 74.777%; Broadcast Media Group LLC, 12.35%; Duff Ackerman & Goodrich II L.P., 7.0635%; DAG GP Fund II LLC, 4.2514%; and Louis Wall, 0.77%.

Stns: 6 TV. KGWN, Cheyenne, WY-Scottsbluff, NE; KSTF, Cheyenne, WY-Scottsbluff, NE; WLTZ, Columbus, GA; KGNS, Laredo, TX; WBMM, Montgomery-Selma, AL; WNCF, Montgomery-Selma, AL.

Louis Wall, pres.

SagamoreHill Midwest LLC, 3825 Inverness Way, Augusta, GA, 30907. Phone: (706) 855-8506. Ownership: Louis Wall, 100%.

Stns: 2 TV. WWMB, Myrtle Beach-Florence, SC; KXLT, Rochester, MN-Mason City, IA-Austin, MN.

Sage Broadcasting Corp., 406 S. Irving, San Angelo, TX, 76903. Phone: (325) 655-6006. Fax: (325) 655-8461. Ownership: Suzanne S. Brown, 32%; Sherry S. Hawk, 32%; Paris R. Schindler, 32%; Anne Marie Carter, 3%; and Timothy R. Brown, 0.33%.

Stns: 2 TV. KXVA, Abilene-Sweetwater, TX; KIDY, San Angelo, TX.

Sainte Partners II L.P., Box 4159, Modesto, CA, 95352-4159. Phone: (209) 523-0777. Fax: (209) 523-0839.E-mail: csmith@sainte.tv Ownership: Chester Smith, gen ptnr, & Naomi Smith, gen ptnr; & other limited ptnrs.

Stns: 2 TV. KCVU, Chico-Redding, CA; KBVU, Eureka, CA.

Schurz Communications Inc., 225 W. Colfax Ave., South Bend, IN, 46626. Phone: (574) 287-1001. Fax: (574) 287-2257.E-mail: mburdick@schurz.com Web Site:www.schurz.com Ownership: Franklin D. Schurz Jr., James M. Schurz, Scott C. Schurz and Mary Schurz, trustees.

Stns: 9 TV. WAGT, Augusta, GA; WDBJ, Roanoke-Lynchburg, VA; WSBT, South Bend-Elkhart, IN; KYTV, Springfield, MO; KBSD-DT, Wichita-Hutchinson Plus, KS; KBSH-DT, Wichita-Hutchinson Plus, KS; KBSL-DT, Wichita-Hutchinson Plus, KS; KWCH-DT, Wichita-Hutchinson Plus, KS; KSCW-DT, Wichita-Hutchinson Plus, KS.

Stns: 4 AM. 8 FM. WASK-FM Battle Ground, IN; WXXB(FM) Delphi, IN; WASK Lafayette, IN; WKOA-FM Lafayette, IN; WSBT South Bend, IN; WNSN-FM South Bend, IN; KFXS-FM Rapid City, SD; KKLS Rapid City, SD; KKMK-FM Rapid City, SD; KOUT-FM Rapid City, SD; KRCS-FM Sturgis, SD; KBHB Sturgis, SD.

Schurz Communications publishes the following nwsprs: *Imperial Valley Press, Southside Times-Beech, Times; Bedford Times-Mail, Bloomington Herald-Times*, & *South Bend Tribune, Martinsville Reporter, Danville Advocate-Messenger, The Herald Mail Co.; Daily American,* Somerset, PA.

Marcia K. Burdick, sr VP bcstg; Franklin D. Schurz Jr., chmn; Todd F. Schurz, pres.

Scripps Howard Broadcasting Co., Box 5380, 312 Walnut St., 28th Fl., Cincinnati, OH, 45201. Phone: (513) 977-3000. Fax: (513) 977-3728. Web Site:www.scripps.com Ownership: The E.W. Scripps Co.

Stns: 10 TV. WMAR, Baltimore, MD; WCPO, Cincinnati, OH; WEWS-TV, Cleveland-Akron (Canton), OH; WXYZ, Detroit; KMCI, Kansas City, MO; KSHB-TV, Kansas City, MO; KNXV, Phoenix (Prescott), AZ; WFTS-TV, Tampa-St. Petersburg (Sarasota), FL; KJRH, Tulsa, OK; WPTV, West Palm Beach-Ft. Pierce, FL.

Newspapers include: *Abilene Reporter-News; The Albuquerque Tribune; Anderson Independent-Mail; Birmingham Post-Herald; The Cincinnati Post; The Commercial Appeal* (Memphis); *Corpus Christi Caller-Times; Daily Camera* (Boulder); *Evansville Courier & Press; The Gleaner* (Henderson); *The Knoxville News-Sentinel; Naples Daily News; Redding Record Searchlight; Rocky Mountain News* (Denver); *San Angelo Standard-Times; The Stuart News; The Sun* (Bremerton); *The Tribune* (Ft. Pierce); *Ventura County Star; Vero Beach Press Journal; Wichita Falls Times Record News.*

William B. Peterson, sr VP, TV station group & The E.W. Scripps Co.

Sinclair Broadcast Group Inc., 10706 Beaver Dam Rd., Hunt Valley, MD, 21030. Phone: (410) 568-1500. Fax: (410) 568-1533.E-mail: ir@sbgnet.com Web Site:www.sbgi.net Ownership: Smith brothers (major shareholders).

Stns: 47 TV. WBFF, Baltimore, MD; WABM, Birmingham (Anniston, Tuscaloosa), AL; WNYO-TV, Buffalo, NY; WUTV, Buffalo, NY; KGAN, Cedar Rapids-Waterloo-Iowa City & Dubuque, IA; WICD, Champaign & Springfield-Decatur, IL; WICS, Champaign & Springfield-Decatur, IL; WMMP, Charleston, SC; WCHS, Charleston-Huntington, WV; WVAH, Charleston-Huntington, WV; WSTR-TV, Cincinnati, OH; WSYX, Columbus, OH; WKEF, Dayton, OH; KDSM-TV, Des Moines-Ames, IA; WSMH, Flint-Saginaw-Bay City, MI; WXLV, Greensboro-High Point-Winston Salem, NC; WMYV, Greensboro-High Point-Winston Salem, NC; WLOS, Greenville-Spartanburg, SC-Asheville, NC-Anderson, SC; KVCW, Las Vegas, NV; KVMY, Las Vegas, NV; WDKY-TV, Lexington, KY; WMSN, Madison, WI; WCGV, Milwaukee, WI; WVTV, Milwaukee, WI; WUCW, Minneapolis-St. Paul, MN; WEAR, Mobile, AL-Pensacola (Ft. Walton Beach), FL; WFGX, Mobile, AL-Pensacola (Ft. Walton Beach), FL; WZTV, Nashville, TN; WUXP-TV, Nashville, TN; WTVZ-TV, Norfolk-Portsmouth-Newport News, VA; KOCB, Oklahoma City, OK; KOKH, Oklahoma City, OK; KBSI, Paducah, KY-Cape Girardeau, MO-Harrisburg-Mount Vernon, IL; WYZZ, Peoria-Bloomington, IL; WPGH, Pittsburgh, PA; WPMY, Pittsburgh, PA; WGME, Portland-Auburn, ME; WLFL, Raleigh-Durham (Fayetteville), NC; WRDC, Raleigh-Durham (Fayetteville), NC; WRLH-TV, Richmond-Petersburg, VA; WUHF, Rochester, NY; KABB, San Antonio, TX; KMYS, San Antonio, TX; KDNL, St. Louis, MO; WSYT, Syracuse, NY; WTWC-TV, Tallahassee, FL-Thomasville, GA; WTTA, Tampa-St. Petersburg (Sarasota), FL.

David D. Smith, pres/CEO; J.Duncan Smith, sec; Frederick Smith, treas; David B. Amy, exec VP, CFO.

Smith Media License Holdings LLC, 1215 Cole St., St. Louis, MO, 63106. Phone: (314) 853-7736. Ownership: Smith Media LLC, 100%.

Stns: 6 TV. KIMO, Anchorage, AK; WFFF, Burlington, VT-Plattsburgh, NY; KATN, Fairbanks, AK; KJUD, Juneau, AK; KEYT, Santa Barbara-Santa Maria-San Luis Obispo, CA; WKTV, Utica, NY.

Southeastern Media Holdings Inc., 3500 Colonnade Pkwy., Suite 600, Birmingham, AL, 35243. Phone: (205) 298-7100. Fax: (205) 298-7104. Ownership: Community Newspaper Holdings Inc., 100%. Web site: www.cnhi.com

Stns: 4 TV. WFXG, Augusta, GA; WXTX, Columbus, GA; WUPV, Richmond-Petersburg, VA; WSFX-TV, Wilmington, NC.

Community Newspaper Holdings Inc. is the parent company for daily, wkly and semiweekly newspapers published in more than 200 communities throughout the U.S.

Michael E. Reed, pres/CEO.

Southern Broadcast Corp. of Sarasota, 1477 10th St., Sarasota, FL, 34236. Phone: (941) 923-8840. Fax: (941) 924-3971. Ownership: Calkins Media Inc., 100% of total assets.

Stns: 3 TV. WAAY-TV, Huntsville-Decatur (Florence), AL; WTXL, Tallahassee, FL-Thomasville, GA; WWSB, Tampa-St. Petersburg (Sarasota), FL.

Spanish Broadcasting System Inc., 2601 South Bayshore Dr., PH 2, Coconut Grove, FL, 33133. Phone: (305) 441-6901. Fax: (305) 446-5148. Web

Site:www.spanishbroadcasting.com Ownership: Raul Alarcon Jr., Jose Grimalt.

Stns: 1 TV. WSBS-TV, Miami-Ft. Lauderdale, FL.

Stns: 20 FM. KLAX-FM East Los Angeles, CA; KXOL-FM Los Angeles, CA; KRZZ(FM) San Francisco, CA; WRMA-FM Fort Lauderdale, FL; WCMQ-FM Hialeah, FL; WXDJ-FM North Miami Beach, FL; WLEY-FM Aurora, IL; WPAT-FM Paterson, NJ; WSKQ-FM New York, NY; WODA(FM) Bayamon, PR; WRXD(FM) Fajardo, PR; WMEG-FM Guayama, PR; WZET(FM) Hormigueros, PR; WNOD(FM) Mayaguez, PR; WIOB-FM Mayaguez, PR; WIOC-FM Ponce, PR; WZMT-FM Ponce, PR; WEGM(FM) San German, PR; WZNT-FM San Juan, PR; WIOA(FM) San Juan, PR.

Raul Alarcon Jr., pres/CEO; Jose Grimalt, exec VP.

Sunbeam Television Corp., 1401 79th St. Causeway, Miami, FL, 33141. Phone: (305) 751-6692. Fax: (305) 757-2266.E-mail:7news@wsvn.com Web Site:www.wsvn.com Ownership: Edmund N. Ansin, 83.09% votes, 80.15% assets; James L. Ansin, 6.3% votes, 7.06% assets; Andrew L. Ansin, 6.3% votes, 7.06% assets; and Andrew L. Ansin, James L. Ansin and Stephanie L. Ansin (as trustees for Stephanie L. Ansin), 4.31% votes, 5.73% assets.

Stns: 3 TV. WHDH, Boston (Manchester, NH); WLVI, Boston (Manchester, NH); WSVN, Miami-Ft. Lauderdale, FL.

Edmund N. Ansin, pres; Deisy Bermudez, progmg dir.

Sunbelt Communications Co., c/o KVBC(TV), 1500 Foremaster Ln., Las Vegas, NV, 89101. Phone: (702) 642-3333. Fax: (702) 657-3423.E-mail: ch3@kvbc.com Web Site:www.kvbc.com Ownership: James E. Rogers.

Stns: 10 TV. KCWY-DT, Casper-Riverton, WY; KBAO, Great Falls, MT; KBBJ, Great Falls, MT; KTVH-DT, Helena, MT; KJWY, Idaho Falls-Pocatello, ID; KPVI-DT, Idaho Falls-Pocatello, ID; KRNV-DT, Reno, NV; KENV-DT, Salt Lake City, UT; KXTF, Twin Falls, ID; KYMA-DT, Yuma, AZ-El Centro, CA.

Ralph Toddre, pres.

Surtsey Media LLC, 73 Kercheval Ave., Suite 100, Grosse Pointe Farms, MI, 48236. Phone: (313) 884-7878. Ownership: Dana C. Raymant, 100%.

Stns: 2 TV. KFJX-TV, Joplin, MO-Pittsburg, KS; KVCT, Victoria, TX.

S-VOX, 171 E. Liberty St., Suite 230, Toronto, ON, M6K 3P6. Canada. Phone: (416) 368-3194. Fax: (416) 368-9774. Web Site:www.s-vox.com

Stns: 2 TV. CHNU-TV, Fraser Valley, BC; CIIT-TV, Winnipeg, MB.

Bill Roberts, pres/CEO; Peter Miller, COO.

T

Sarkes Tarzian Inc., Box 62, Bloomington, IN, 47402. Phone: (812) 332-7251. Fax: (812) 331-4575. Ownership: Tom Tarzian; Gray Television Inc.

Stns: 2 TV. WRCB, Chattanooga, TN; KTVN, Reno, NV.

Stns: 1 AM. 3 FM. WTTS-FM Bloomington, IN; WGCL Bloomington, IN; WLDE-FM Fort Wayne, IN; WAJI(FM) Fort Wayne, IN.

Tom Tolar, pres, TV; Tom Tarzian, chmn; Geoff Vargo, pres, radio; Bob Davis, CFO; Valerie Carney, gen counsel.

Tele Inter-Rives Ltee., 298 Boulevard Theriault, Riviere-du-Loup, PQ, G5R 4C2. Canada. Phone: (418) 867-1341. Fax: (418) 867-4710. Web Site:www.cimt.ca Ownership: 101885 Canada Ltee., 54.37%; Groupe TVA Inc., 44.66% (see listing); and Marc Simard, 0.97%.

Stns: 4 TV. CHAU, Carleton, PQ; CIMT, Riviere-du-Loup, PQ; CKRT, Riviere-du-Loup, PQ; CFTF-TV, Riviere-du-Loup, PQ.

Marc Simard, pres.

Telemundo Television Stations, 2290 W. 8th Ave., Hialeah, FL, 33010. Phone: (305) 884-8200. Fax: (305) 889-7950. Web Site:www.telemundo.com Ownership: General Electric Co., 100%. See also NBC Universal Television Stations (see listing).

Stns: 14 TV. WNEU, Boston (Manchester, NH); WSNS, Chicago; KDEN, Denver, CO; KNSO, Fresno-Visalia, CA; KTMD, Houston; KVEA, Los Angeles; KWHY, Los Angeles; WSCV, Miami-Ft. Lauderdale, FL; WNJU, New York; KTAZ, Phoenix (Prescott), AZ; KVDA, San Antonio, TX; KSTS, San Francisco-Oakland-San Jose; WKAQ-TV, San Juan, PR; KHRR, Tucson (Sierra Vista), AZ.

Vincent Sadusky, CFO/treas; Juan Antunez, VP gen counsel/sec. VP/finance; Ibra Morales, pres.

Tele-Quebec, 1000 rue Fullum, Montreal, PQ, H2K 3L7. Canada. Phone: (514) 521-2424. Fax: (514) 873-4413.E-mail: info@telequebec.qc.ca Web Site:www.telequebec.tv

Ownership: La Societe de radio-television du Quebec is a para-governmental organization. Its mandate is to manage an educ TV net throughout the province of Quebec.

Stns: 11 TV. CIVF, Baie-Trinite, PQ; CIVP, Chapeau, PQ; CIVV, Chicoutimi, PQ; CIVO-TV, Gatineau, PQ; CIVM, Montreal, PQ; CIVQ, Quebec City, PQ; CIVB, Rimouski, PQ; CIVA, Rouyn, PQ; CIVG, Sept-Iles, PQ; CIVS, Sherbrooke, PQ; CIVC, Trois-Rivieres, PQ.

Paul Beaugrand Champagne, pres/dir gen; Mario Clement, dir mgr programming; Line Simoneau, dir mgr admin/fianances /human resources; Denis Belisle, dir sec gen; Cecile Bellemare, dir dev projects; Jacques Legace, dir dev institutional; Danielle Beaudry, dir production.

Tri-State Christian Television, Box 1010, Marion, IL, 62959. Phone: (618) 997-9333. Fax: (618) 997-1859. Web Site:www.tct.tv Ownership: Nonprofit corporation. LPTV: WDWO-CA Detroit, MI; and WDYR-CA Dyersburg, TN.

Stns: 7 TV. WNYB, Buffalo, NY; WRLM, Cleveland-Akron (Canton), OH; WAQP, Flint-Saginaw-Bay City, MI; WINM, Ft. Wayne, IN; WTLJ, Grand Rapids-Kalamazoo-Battle Creek, MI; WLXI, Greensboro-High Point-Winston Salem, NC; WTCT, Paducah, KY-Cape Girardeau, MO-Harrisburg-Mount Vernon, IL.

Garth W. Coonce, pres; Shane Chaney, CFO.

Tribune Broadcasting Co., 435 N. Michigan Ave., Suite 1800, Chicago, IL, 60611. Phone: (312) 222-3333. Fax: (312) 329-0611. Web Site:www.tribune.com Ownership: The Tribune Employee Stock Ownership Plan as implemented through the Tribune Employee Stock Ownership Trust, Oak Brook, IL, 100%.

Stns: 24 TV. WGN-TV, Chicago; KDAF, Dallas-Ft. Worth; KWGN, Denver, CO; WXMI, Grand Rapids-Kalamazoo-Battle Creek, MI; WPMT, Harrisburg -Lancaster-Lebanon-York, PA; WTIC, Hartford & New Haven, CT; WTXX, Hartford & New Haven, CT; KIAH, Houston; WTTK, Indianapolis, IN; WTTV, Indianapolis, IN; WXIN, Indianapolis, IN; KTLA, Los Angeles; WSFL-TV, Miami-Ft. Lauderdale, FL; WGNO, New Orleans, LA; WNOL, New Orleans, LA; WPIX, New York; WPHL, Philadelphia; KRCW-TV, Portland, OR; KTXL, Sacramento -Stockton-Modesto, CA; KSWB, San Diego, CA; KCPQ, Seattle-Tacoma, WA; KMYQ, Seattle-Tacoma, WA; KPLR, St. Louis, MO; WDCW, Washington, DC (Hagerstown, MD).

Stns: 1 AM. WGN(AM) Chicago, IL.

John Vitanovec, exec VP; Ed Wilson, pres.

Trinity Broadcasting Network, 2442 Michelle Dr., Tustin, CA, 92780. Phone: (714) 832-2950. Fax: (714) 730-0657.E-mail: comments@tbn.org Web Site:www.tbn.org Ownership: Nonprofit corporation.

Stns: 25 TV. KNAT-TV, Albuquerque-Santa Fe, NM; WHSG-TV, Atlanta; WTJP-TV, Birmingham (Anniston, Tuscaloosa), AL; WELF-TV, Chattanooga, TN; WWTO, Chicago; WDLI-TV, Cleveland-Akron (Canton), OH; KDTX, Dallas-Ft. Worth; WKOI-TV, Dayton, OH; KPJR-DT, Denver, CO; KAAH-TV, Honolulu, HI; WCLJ-TV, Indianapolis, IN; KTBN, Los Angeles; WBUY-TV, Memphis, TN; WHFT-TV, Miami-Ft. Lauderdale, FL; WMPV, Mobile, AL-Pensacola (Ft. Walton Beach), FL; WMCF, Montgomery-Selma, AL; WPGD-TV, Nashville, TN; WTBY-TV, New York; KTBO Oklahoma City, OK; WHLV-TV, Orlando-Daytona Beach-Melbourne, FL; WGTW-TV, Philadelphia; KPAZ, Phoenix (Prescott), AZ; KTBW, Seattle-Tacoma, WA; KTAJ-TV, St. Joseph, MO; KDOR-TV, Tulsa, OK.

Paul F. Crouch, pres; Rod Henke, VP sls; Ben Miller, VP engrg; Janice Crouch, VP progmg.

Tucker Broadcasting of Traverse City Inc., 9434 N. Sunset Ridge, Fountain Hills, AZ, 85268. Phone: (480) 836-2181.E-mail: bentucker13@cox.net Ownership: Tucker Media and Management Consulting L.L.C., 100%.

Stns: 2 TV. WGTQ, Traverse City-Cadillac, MI; WGTU, Traverse City-Cadillac, MI.

Tyler Media Broadcasting Corp., 5101 S. Shields Blvd., Oklahoma City, OK, 73129. Phone: (405) 616-5500. Fax: (405) 616-5505. Web Site:www.kkng.com Ownership: Ty A. Tyler, Tony J. Tyler and Tony J. Tyler 2000 Irrevocable Trust, Tony J. Tyler, trustee.

Stns: 1 TV. KTUZ-TV, Oklahoma City, OK.

Stns: 2 AM. 3 FM. KOJK(FM) Blanchard, OK; KOCY(AM) Del City, OK; KKNG-FM Newcastle, OK; KTUZ-FM Okarche, OK; KTLR(AM) Oklahoma City, OK.

Skip Stow, market mgr; Robert De Negri, CFO.

U

United Communications Corp., 5800 7th Ave., Kenosha, WI, 53140. Phone: (262) 657-1000. Fax: (262) 657-6226.E-mail: hbrown@kenoshanews.com Web Site:www.kenoshanews.com Ownership: Howard J. Brown,

Lucy Brown Minn, Sarah Brown Russ, Amy Brown Tuchler. Note: Group also owns LPTV stn WNYF-CA Watertown, NY.

Stns: 2 TV. KEYC-TV, Mankato, MN; WWNY, Watertown, NY.

Other media: Dailies: *Kenosha News*, Kenosha, WI; *Sun Chronicle*, Attleboro, MA; *Public Opinion*, Watertown, SD. Weeklies: *Zion-Benton News*, Zion, IL; *Foxboro Reporter*, Foxboro, MA; *Lake Geneva Regional News*, Lake Geneva, WI. Shoppers: *Bulletin*, Kenosha, WI; *News-Bargaineer*, Zion, IL; *Coteau Shopper*, Watertown, SD.

Howard J. Brown, pres; Kenneth Dowdell, VP; Ronald Montemurro, VP.

Univision Communications Inc., 5999 Center Dr., Los Angeles, CA, 90045. Phone: (310) 216-3434. Fax: (310) 556-3568. Web Site:www.univision.net/corp/en/overview.jsp Ownership: Broadcasting Media Partners Inc.

Stns: 40 TV. KTFQ-DT, Albuquerque-Santa Fe, NM; WUVG-DT, Atlanta; KUVI-DT, Bakersfield, CA; WUTF-DT, Boston (Manchester, NH); WLII-DT, Caguas, PR; WXFT-DT, Chicago; WGBO-DT, Chicago; WQHS-DT, Cleveland-Akron (Canton), OH; KUVN-DT, Dallas-Ft. Worth; KSTR-DT, Dallas-Ft. Worth; KFTV-DT, Fresno-Visalia, CA; KTFF-DT, Fresno-Visalia, CA; KXLN-DT, Houston; KFTH-DT, Houston; KMEX-DT, Los Angeles; KFTR-DT, Los Angeles; WAMI-DT, Miami-Ft. Lauderdale, FL; WLTV-DT, Miami-Ft. Lauderdale, FL; WXTV-DT, New York; WFUT-DT, New York; WFTY-DT, New York; WOTF-DT, Orlando-Daytona Beach-Melbourne, FL; WUVP-DT, Philadelphia; KFPH-DT, Phoenix (Prescott), AZ; KTVW-DT, Phoenix (Prescott), AZ; WSTE-DT, Ponce, PR; WSUR-DT, Ponce, PR; WUVC-DT, Raleigh-Durham (Fayetteville), NC; KUVS-DT, Sacramento-Stockton-Modesto, CA; KTFK-DT, Sacramento-Stockton-Modesto, CA; KUTH-DT, Salt Lake City, UT; KNIC-DT, San Antonio, TX; KWEX-DT, San Antonio, TX; KFSF-DT, San Francisco-Oakland-San Jose; KDTV-DT, San Francisco-Oakland-San Jose; WFTT-DT, Tampa-St. Petersburg (Sarasota), FL; KFTU-DT, Tucson (Sierra Vista), AZ; KUVE-DT, Tucson (Sierra Vista), AZ; KAKW-DT, Waco-Temple-Bryan, TX; WFDC-DT, Washington, DC (Hagerstown, MD).

Joe Uva, CEO.

V

VCY America Inc., 3434 W. Kilbourn Ave., Milwaukee, WI, 53208. Phone: (414) 935-3000. Fax: (414) 935-3015.E-mail: vcy@vcyamerica.org Web Site:www.vcyamerica.org

Stns: 1 TV. WVCY, Milwaukee, WI.

Stns: 1 AM. 19 FM. KVCY-FM Fort Scott, KS; KCVS(FM) Salina, KS; WVCN(FM) Baraga, MI; WVCM(FM) Iron Mountain, MI; WQRN(FM) Cook, MN; KVCS(FM) Spring Valley, MN; WJIC-FM Zanesville, OH; KVCF(FM) Freeman, SD; KVCX-FM Gregory, SD; KVCH(FM) Huron, SD; KVFL(FM) Pierre, SD; KVSD(FM) Wasta, SD; WVCF-FM Eau Claire, WI; WVFL(FM) Fond du Lac, WI; WVCY-FM Milwaukee, WI; WVCY Oshkosh, WI; WVCS(FM) Owen, WI; WVCX(FM) Tomah, WI; WEGZ(FM) Washburn, WI; WVRN(FM) Wittenberg, WI.

Vic Eliason, VP/gen mgr; Jim Schneider, progmg dir.

The Victory Television Network, Box 22007, Little Rock, AR, 72221-2007. Phone: (501) 223-2525. Fax: (501) 221-3837.E-mail: jim.grant@vtntv.com Web Site:www.vtntv.com Ownership: Agape Church Inc.

Stns: 3 TV. KVTJ-DT, Jonesboro, AR; KVTN-DT, Little Rock-Pine Bluff, AR; KVTH-DT, Little Rock-Pine Bluff, AR.

Jim Grant, gen mgr; Pastor Happy Caldwell, pres.

W

Waterman Broadcasting Corp., Box 7578, Fort Myers, FL, 33911-7578. Phone: (239) 939-2020. Fax: (239) 939-7903. Web Site:www.water.net Ownership: Bernard Waterman, Edith Waterman.

Stns: 2 TV. WVIR-TV, Charlottesville, VA; WBBH, Ft. Myers-Naples, FL.

Bernard Waterman, pres; Steve Pontius, exec VP; Joe Ernest, VP.

Weigel Broadcasting Co., 26 N. Halsted St., Chicago, IL, 60661. Phone: (312) 705-2600. Fax: (312) 705-2656. Web Site:www.wciu.com Ownership: Weigel Broadcasting Co., limited ptnr; Madison Halsted LLC, gen ptnr.

Stns: 3 TV. WCIU-TV, Chicago; WDJT, Milwaukee, WI; WBME-TV, Milwaukee, WI.

Norman Shapiro, pres; Howard Shapiro, chmn; Neal Savin, exec VP.

West Virginia Media Holdings LLC, Box 11848, Charleston, WV, 25339-1848. Phone: (304) 720-6527. Fax: (304) 345-7280. Web Site:www.wvmh.com Ownership: West Virginia Medio Partners, LP.

Stns: 4 TV. WVNS-TV, Bluefield-Beckley-Oak Hill, WV; WOWK, Charleston-Huntington, WV; WBOY, Clarksburg-Weston, WV; WTRF-TV, Wheeling, WV-Steubenville, OH.

Bray Cary, pres/CEO; Marty Becker, chmn.

Mel Wheeler Inc., 5009 S. Hulen, Suite 101, Fort Worth, TX, 76132-1989. Phone: (817) 294-7644. Fax: (817) 294-8519. Ownership: Leonard E. Wheeler, 34.73%; Stephen J. Wheeler, 33.63% votes, 33.31% assets; and Clark V. Wheeler, 31.64%.

Stns: 2 TV. KPOB, Paducah, KY-Cape Girardeau, MO-Harrisburg-Mount Vernon, IL; WSIL-TV, Paducah, KY-Cape Girardeau, MO-Harrisburg-Mount Vernon, IL.

Stns: 2 AM. 4 FM. WVBE-FM Lynchburg, VA; WXLK-FM Roanoke, VA; WVBE(AM) Roanoke, VA; WSLQ-FM Roanoke, VA; WSLC-FM Roanoke, VA; WFIR(AM) Roanoke, VA.

Leonard Wheeler, pres; Clark Wheeler, VP; Gretchen Cummings, sec/treas.

White Knight Holdings Inc., 9257 Bailey Ln., Fairfax, VA, 22031-1903. Phone: (703) 253-2027. Ownership: Malara Enterprises LLC, 100%.

Stns: 3 TV. WVLA-TV, Baton Rouge, LA; KSHV-TV, Shreveport, LA; KFXK-TV, Tyler-Longview (Lufkin & Nacogdoches), TX.

Anthony J. Malara III, pres.

Wilderness Communications LLC, 3501 Northwest Evangeline Thruway, Carencro, LA, 70520. Phone: (337) 896-1600. Fax: (337) 896-2695. Ownership: Chatelain Group.

Stns: 2 TV. KBCA, Alexandria, LA; KLWB, Lafayette, LA.

Withers Broadcasting Co., Box 1508, Mount Vernon, IL, 62864. Phone: (618) 242-3500. Fax: (618) 242-4444. Ownership: W. Russell Withers Jr., 100%.

Stns: 3 TV. WDTV, Clarksburg-Weston, WV; WVFX, Clarksburg-Weston, WV; WDHS, Marquette, MI.

Stns: 11 AM. 20 FM. KOKX Keokuk, IA; KRNQ(FM) Keokuk, IA; WKIB(FM) Anna, IL; WRUL-FM Carmi, IL; WROY Carmi, IL; WCEZ(FM) Carthage, IL; WILY Centralia, IL; WRXX-FM Centralia, IL; WEBQ-FM Eldorado, IL; WISH-FM Galatia, IL; WEBQ Harrisburg, IL; WTAO-FM Herrin, IL; WDDD-FM Johnston City, IL; WMOK Metropolis, IL; WREZ-FM Metropolis, IL; WZZT-FM Morrison, IL; WYNG(FM) Mount Carmel, IL; WMIX Mount Vernon, IL; WMIX-FM Mount Vernon, IL; WVZA(FM) Murphysboro, IL; WSSQ-FM Sterling, IL; WSDR Sterling, IL; WHET(FM) West Frankfort, IL; WFRX West Frankfort, IL; WZZL-FM Reidland, KY; WGKY-FM Wickliffe, KY; KGMO(FM) Cape Girardeau, MO; KAPE Cape Girardeau, MO; KJXX(AM) Jackson, MO; KRHW Sikeston, MO; KBXB(FM) Sikeston, MO.

W. Russell Withers Jr., pres.

Woods Communications Corp., One WCOV Ave., Montgomery, AL, 36111. Phone: (334) 288-7020. Fax: (334) 288-5414. Web Site:www.wcov.com Ownership: David D. Woods, 100%.

Stns: 2 TV. KLCW-TV, Lubbock, TX; WCOV, Montgomery-Selma, AL.

David Woods, pres/CEO.

Wooster Republican Printing Co., (dba Dix Communications). 212 E. Liberty St., Wooster, OH, 44691. Phone: (330) 264-3511. Fax: (330) 263-5013. Web Site:www.dixcom.com Ownership: (dba Dix Communications).

Stns: 1 TV. KFBB, Great Falls, MT.

Stns: 3 AM. 6 FM. WNDT(FM) Alachua, FL; WOGK(FM) Ocala, FL; WNDD-FM Silver Springs, FL; WKVX Wooster, OH; WQKT(FM) Wooster, OH; WTBO Cumberland, MD; WKGO-FM Cumberland, MD; WFRB Frostburg, MD; WFRB-FM Frostburg, MD.

Wooster Republican Printing Co. publishes *The Daily Record,* Wooster, OH.

Robert C. Dix, TV div chmn; G. Charles Dix, VP; Dale E. Gerber, CFO.

Word Broadcasting Network Inc., Box 19229, Louisville, KY, 40259. Phone: (502) 964-3304. Fax: (502) 966-9692. Web Site:www.wbna21.com Ownership: Robert W. Rodgers, 20%; Gregory A. Holt, 20%; Melissa Fraser, 20%; Cleddie Kieth, 20%; and Margaret A. Rodgers, 20%.

Stns: 1 TV. WBNA, Louisville, KY.

Stns: 3 AM. WYMM(AM) Jacksonville, FL; WVHI Evansville, IN; WYRM(AM) Norfolk, VA.

Bob Rogers, pres; Greg Holt, VP.

Word of God Fellowship Inc., 3901 Hwy. 121 S., Bedford, TX, 76021. Phone: (817) 571-1229. Fax: (817) 571-7458. Web Site:www.daystar.com Ownership: Marcus D. Lamb, 20%; Joni T. Lamb, 20%; Corrine Lamb, 20%; Jimmie K. Lamb, 20%; John Calender, 20%.

Stns: 10 TV. WNGS, Buffalo, NY; KRMT, Denver, CO; KWOG, Ft. Smith-Fayetteville-Springdale-Rogers, AR; WMAK, Knoxville, TN; KOCM, Oklahoma City, OK; WBIF, Panama City, FL; KUTF, Salt Lake City, UT; KCBU, Salt Lake City, UT; KQUP, Spokane, WA; WNYI, Syracuse, NY.

Marcus D. Lamb, pres.

Wyomedia Corp., 1856 Skyview Dr., Casper, WY, 82601. Phone: (307) 577-5923. Fax: (307) 234-4005. Ownership: Marvin Gussman, 100%.

Stns: 4 TV. KFNB, Casper-Riverton, WY; KFNE, Casper-Riverton, WY; KLWY, Cheyenne, WY-Scottsbluff, NE; KFNR, Denver, CO.

Marvin Gussman, chmn/pres.

Y

Young Broadcasting Inc., 599 Lexington Ave., 47th Fl., New York, NY, 10022. Phone: (212) 754-7070. Fax: (212) 758-1229. Web Site:www.youngbroadcasting.com Ownership: Vincent J. Young, Gabelli Asset Management Inc., New South Capital Management Inc.

Stns: 14 TV. WCDC, Albany-Schenectady-Troy, NY; WTEN, Albany-Schenectady-Troy, NY; KWQC, Davenport, IA-Rock Island-Moline, IL; WBAY, Green Bay-Appleton, WI; WATE, Knoxville, TN; KLFY, Lafayette, LA; WLNS, Lansing, MI; WKRN, Nashville, TN; KCLO, Rapid City, SD; WRIC-TV, Richmond-Petersburg, VA; KRON-TV, San Francisco-Oakland-San Jose; KDLO, Sioux Falls (Mitchell), SD; KELO-TV, Sioux Falls (Mitchell), SD; KPLO, Sioux Falls (Mitchell), SD.

Vincent Young, chmn; James Morgan, exec VP, CFO; Deborah McDermott, pres.

Key to Television Listings

Television listings include TV stations in the United States, its territories and Canada. All collected data for these listings include information current to summer 2008. To use the television key, see boldface numbers and corresponding explanations.

(1) WOF-TV—(2) Analog channel: 17. Digital Channel: 53. Analog hrs: 24 2,200 kw vis, 20 kw aur, ant 500t/300g. TL: N36 49 21 W108 47 32 (CP: Ant 750t/550g) **(3)**On air date: Apr 13, 1952. **(4)** Box 100, Dothan, AL 36301. Phone: (909) 555-1000. FAX: (909) 999-9999. Web Site: www.wof.tv. **(5)** Licensee: WOF Broadcasting Co. **(6)** Group owner: Acme Stations (acq 7-20-69; $2 million; **(6a)** FTR 7-29-69). **(7)** Population served: 230,000 **(8)** Natl. Network: CBS. **(9)** Natl. Rep: Jones, Tri-State. Washington Atty: Goltz & Stick. **(10)** News staff: 3; News: 10 hrs wkly. **(11) Key Personnel:**

Jud Jones . . . . .pres & gen mgr
D. Spark . . . . .chief engr

(1) Station call letters as assigned by the Federal Communications Commission (FCC) or Canadian Radio-television and Telecommunications Commission (CRTC).

(2) Analog channel and digital channels, hours of operation (analog and digital), power, antenna, location and construction permit. WOF-TV operates with 2,200 kilowatts (effective radiated power) visual and 20 kilowatts aural. Its antenna is 500 feet above average terrain and 300 feet above ground. N36 49 21 W108 47 32 refers to the geographical coordinates (latitude and longitude) of the transmitter location. WOF-TV holds a construction permit for an antenna height change to 750 feet above average terrain, 550 feet above ground.

(3) Date station first went on the air (regardless of subsequent ownership changes).

(4) Address and zip code, telephone and fax number, web site and e-mail address.

(5) Licensee name.

(6) Ownership and date of acquisition (if not original owner). If a station has been sold, any available sale information is listed following the acquisition date. WOF-TV is owned by Acme Stations.

(6a) FTR date refers to Broadcasting & Cable magazine's weekly "For the Record" column that appeared in the magazine until June 8, 1998, where station sales were recorded as received from the FCC.

(7) Population served refers to the station's potential market.

(8) Network programming. WOF-TV's national network is CBS.

(9) Representatives and Washington attorney. Sales representatives are listed with the national rep first, then regional.

(10) Number of staff providing local news and number of local news aired weekly.

(11) Key personnel.

An asterisk (*) preceding station call letters indicates noncommercial stations.

Directory of TV Stations in the United States

Alabama

Anniston

see Birmingham (Anniston, Tuscaloosa), AL market

Birmingham (Anniston, Tuscaloosa), AL

(DMA 40)

WABM— Digital Channel: 36. Digital Hrs: 24 1,442 kw vis, 144 kw aur. ant 1,029t TL: N33 27 57 W86 47 45 On air date: January 1986. 651 Beacon Pkwy. W., Suite 105, Birmingham, AL, 35209. Phone: (205) 943-2168. Fax: (205) 250-6788. Web Site: www.wabm68.com. Licensee: Birmingham (WABM-TV) Licensee Inc. **Group Owner:** Glencairn Ltd. (acq 2-1-2002). Population Served: 522,420 Natl. Network: MyNetworkTV,

Key Personnel:
Steve Marks . . . . CFO
Scott Campbell . . . . gen mgr
Charlie Slaight . . . . gen sls mgr & adv dir
Lucrecia Rubio . . . . progmg dir & engrg dir
Peggy Johnson . . . . news dir
John Batspm . . . . chief of engrg
Mary Ann Huie . . . . traf mgr

*WBIQ— Digital Channel: 10. Digital Hrs: 24 316 kw vis, 31.6 kw aur. 1,325t/1,042g TL: N33 29 19 W86 47 58 On air date: Apr 28, 1955. 2112 11th Ave. S., Suite 400, Birmingham, AL, 35205. Phone: (205) 328-8756. Fax: (205) 251-2192. Web Site: www.aptv.org. Licensee: Alabama ETV Commission. Population Served: 1,400,000 Natl. Network: PBS, . Alabama Public Television Washington Atty: Dow, Lohnes & Albertson, PLLC.
Key Personnel:
Allan Pizzato . . . . CEO
Charles Grantham . . . . COO
Pauline Howland . . . . CFO
John Brady . . . . dev VP & dev dir

WBRC— Digital Channel: 50. Digital Hrs: 24 100 kw vis, 10 kw aur. ant 1,377t/1,010g TL: N33 29 19 W86 47 58 On air date: July 1, 1949. Box 6, Birmingham, AL, 35201. 1720 Valley View Dr., Mooresville, AL 35209. Phone: (205) 322-6666. Fax: (205) 583-4386. Web Site: www.wbrc.com. Licensee: WBRC License Subsidiary LLC. **Group Owner:** (group owner; (acq 3-31-2009; exchange for WTVR-TV Richmond, VA). Population Served: 1,000,000 Natl. Network: Fox, . Natl. Rep: TeleRep,. News staff: 53; News: 21 hrs wkly.
Key Personnel:
Mike McClain . . . . VP
Lou Kirchen . . . . gen mgr
Roy Gardner. . . . . opns mgr
Jay Abbattista . . . . sls VP
Mike Lewis . . . . gen sls mgr
Sonya Ridderhoff . . . . natl sls mgr
Wayne Farr . . . . progmg dir
Jerry Thorn . . . . chief of engrg

WCFT-TV— Digital Channel: 33.1,225 kw vis, 203 kw aur. 540t/442g TL: N33 10 27 W87 29 09 On air date: Oct 27, 1965. 800 Concourse Pkwy., Suite 200, Birmingham, AL, 35244. 4000 37th St. E., Tuscaloosa, AL 35405. Phone: (205) 403-3340. Fax: (205) 403-3329. Web Site: www.abc3340.com. Licensee: TV Alabama Inc. Group Owner: Allbritton Communications Co. (acq 1996; $20 million). Population Served: 84,000 Natl. Network: ABC, . Washington Atty: Hogan & Hartson.
Key Personnel:
Mike Murphy . . . . gen mgr
Gary Watkins . . . . opns dir

*WCIQ— Digital Channel: 7. Digital Hrs: 24 316 kw vis, 31.6 kw aur. 2,000t/537g TL: N33 29 07 W85 48 33 On air date: Jan 7, 1955. 2112 11th Ave. S., Suite 400, Birmingham, AL, 35205. Phone: (205) 328-8756. Fax: (205) 251-2192. Web Site: www.aptv.org. Licensee: Alabama ETV Commission. Natl. Network: PBS, . Alabama Public Television Washington Atty: Dow, Lohnes & Albertson, PLLC.

Key Personnel:
Allan Pizzato . . . . CEO
Charles Grantham . . . . COO
Pauline Howland . . . . CFO & gen mgr
Polly Anderson. . . . . dev VP

WDBB— Digital Channel: 18. Digital Hrs: 24 2,240 kw vis. ant 2,214t/1,966g TL: N33 28 51 W87 24 03 On air date: Oct 1, 1984. 651 Beacon Pkwy. W., Suite 105, Birmingham, AL, 35209. Phone: (205) 943-2168. Fax: (205) 250-6788. Web Site: www.wtto21.com. Licensee: WDBB-TV Inc. Ownership: Cecil Heftel; H. Carl Parmer; D&C L.L.C. (acq 1-19-95; $1.5 million). Population Served: 250,000 Natl. Rep: Adam Young,. Washington Atty: Fletcher, Heald & Hildreth. Wire Svc: NOAA Weather Wire Svc: Weather Wire News staff: 20; News: 15 hrs wkly.
Key Personnel:
Scott Campbell . . . . gen mgr
Steve Marks . . . . CEO & opns mgr
Amy Hughes . . . . sls dir & rgnl sls mgr
Lucrecia Rubio. . . . . mktg dir & progmg dir
Mary Ann Huie . . . . adv dir & traf mgr
Peggy Johnson . . . . progmg dir & news dir
John Batson . . . . engrg mgr & chief of engrg

WIAT— Digital Channel: 30. Digital Hrs: 24 2,163 kw vis, 216 kw aur. ant 1,382t/1,134g TL: N33 29 02 W86 48 21 On air date: Oct 17, 1965. 2075 Goldencrest Dr., Birmingham, AL, 35209. P.O. Box 59496, Birmingham, AL 35259. Phone: (205) 322-4200. Fax: (205) 320-2710. Web Site: www.cbs42.com. Licensee: NVT Birmingham Licensee LLC. Group Owner: Media General Broadcast Group (acq 10-6-2006; $35 million with KIMT(TV) Mason City, IA). Population Served: 700,000 Natl. Network: CBS, . Natl. Rep: TeleRep,. Washington Atty: Dow, Lohnes & Albertson. News: 6 hrs wkly.
Key Personnel:
Bill Ballard . . . . pres & VP gen mgr
Greg Butler. . . . . opns dir & opns mgr
Jim Ottolin . . . . gen sls mgr
Bill Payer . . . . news dir

WJSU-TV— Digital Channel: 9. Digital Hrs: 24 5,000 kw vis. ant 1,299t/538g TL: N33 36 24 W86 25 03 On air date: Oct 26, 1969. Alabama's ABC 33/40, Box 360039, Birmingham, AL, 35236. Phone: (205) 403-3340. Fax: (205) 403-3329. Web Site: www.abc3340.com. Licensee: TV Alabama Inc. Group Owner: Allbritton Communications Co. (acq 1-24-2000). Population Served: 91,000 Natl. Network: ABC, . Washington Atty: Haley, Bader & Potts. News staff: 16; News: 9 hrs wkly.
Key Personnel:
Mike Murphy . . . . gen mgr
Gary Watkins . . . . opns mgr

WPXH-TV— Digital Channel: 45. Digital Hrs: 24 225 kw vis. ant 1,014t/918g TL: N33 53 27 W86 28 13 On air date: Apr 26, 1986. 2085 Goldencrest Dr., Birmingham, AL, 35209. Phone: (205) 870-4404. Fax: (205) 870-0744. Licensee: ION Media License Co. LLC, debtor-in-possession. Group Owner: Paxson Communications Corp. Population Served: 1,000,000 Natl. Network: ION Television, . Washington Atty: Fletcher, Heald & Hildreth. News: 8 hrs wkly.
Key Personnel:
Debra Perry . . . . gen mgr & gen mgr

WTJP-TV— Digital Channel: 26. Digital Hrs: 24 1,000 kw vis. ant 1,079t/702g TL: N33 48 53 W86 26 55 On air date: July 22, 1986. 313 Rosedale Ave., Gadsden, AL, 35901-5361. Phone: (256) 546-8860. Fax: (256) 543-8623. Web Site: www.tbn.org. Licensee: Trinity Christian Center of Santa Ana Inc. dba Trinity Broadcasting Network. Group Owner: Trinity Broadcasting Network (acq 5-8-2000). Population Served: 1,600,000
Key Personnel:
Paul F. Crouch. . . . . CEO & pres
Terry Hickey . . . . exec VP
Gary Hodges . . . . gen mgr & gen sls mgr
Curtiss Kemp . . . . chief of engrg

WTTO— Digital Channel: 28.765 kw vis. ant 1,402t/1,075g TL: N33 29 04 W86 48 25 On air date: Apr 21, 1982. 651 Beacon Pkwy. W., Suite 105, Huntsville, AL, 35209. Phone: (205) 943-2168. Fax: (205) 290-2114 / (205) 250-6788. Web Site: www.wtto21.com. Licensee: WTTO Licensee LLC (acq 12-21-90). Natl. Network: CW, . Natl. Rep: Millennium Sales & Marketing,. Washington Atty: Arter & Hadden.

Key Personnel:
Chris Hummel . . . . CEO & CFO
Scott Campbell . . . . gen mgr
Amy Hughes . . . . rgnl sls mgr & prom dir
Lucrecia Rubio . . . . adv dir & progmg dir
Peggy Johnson . . . . news dir
John Batson . . . . engrg dir & chief of engrg
Mary Ann Huie . . . . traf mgr

WUOA— Digital Channel: 6.26 kw vis. ant 1,296t/1,007g TL: N33 29 02 W86 48 21 On air date: 2000. Box 870172, Tuscaloosa, AL, 35487. Phone: (205) 348-7000. Fax: (205) 348-7002. Web Site: www.tuscaloosanews.com/section/WVUA. Licensee: The Board of Trustees of the University of Alabama. (acq 11-30-2004; donation).
Key Personnel:
Roy Clem . . . . gen mgr

WVTM-TV— Digital Channel: 13.316 kw vis, 47.4 kw aur. ant 1,340t/1,073g TL: N33 29 26 W86 47 48 On air date: May 1949. 1732 Valley View Dr., Birmingham, AL, 35209. Phone: (205) 558-7300 (news) / (205) 933-1313. Fax: (205) 933-7516 (sales).E-mail: newscomments@nbc13.com Web Site: www.nbc13.com. Licensee: Media General Communications Inc. Group Owner: NBC TV Stations Division (acq 6-26-2006; grpsl). Population Served: 2,500,000 Natl. Network: NBC, . Natl. Rep: Harrington, Righter & Parsons,. News staff: 70; News: 24 hrs wkly.
Key Personnel:
Clark Dumornay . . . . opns mgr
Joe Tracy . . . . sls VP
Ed Moran . . . . natl sls mgr
Mike Sherry . . . . mktg mgr & prom dir
Yvette Miley . . . . progmg dir
Yvette M. Miley . . . . news dir
Terese Messick . . . . pub affrs dir
Chuck Blackwood . . . . engrg dir
Michele Brown . . . . traf mgr
Jim Dunaway. . . . . sports cmtr
Jerry Tracey . . . . weather dir

Decatur

see Huntsville-Decatur (Florence), AL market

Dothan, AL
(DMA 172)

WDFX-TV— Digital Channel: 33. Digital Hrs: 21 1,120 kw vis. ant 466t TL: N31 12 30 W85 36 51 On air date: Feb 23, 1991. 2221 Ross Clark Cir., Dothan, AL, 36301. Phone: (334) 794-3434. Fax: (334) 794-0034. Web Site: www.wdfxfox34.com. Licensee: Raycom America License Subsidiary LLC. Group Owner: Raycom Media Inc. (acq 10-14-2003; grpsl). Population Served: 104,000 Natl. Network: Fox, . Washington Atty: Borsari & Paxson.
Key Personnel:
Eric Steffens . . . . gen mgr
Jennifer Otto . . . . mktg mgr & prom dir
Wes Roten . . . . chief of engrg
Brandi Johnson . . . . traf mgr

WDHN— Digital Channel: 21. Digital Hrs: 24 1,000 kw vis, 100 kw aur. ant 625t/640g TL: N31 14 25 W85 18 43 On air date: Aug 7, 1970. Box 6237, Dothan, AL, 36302. 5274 E. Hwy. 52, Webb, AL 36302. Phone: (334) 793-1818. Fax: (334) 793-2623. Web Site: www.wdhn.com. Licensee: Nexstar Broadcasting Inc. Group Owner: Nexstar Broadcasting Group Inc. (acq 8-1-2003; $40 million with KARK-TV Little Rock, AR). Population Served: 277,000 Natl. Network: ABC, . Washington Atty: Fletcher, Heald & Hildreth. News staff: 8; News: 7 hrs wkly.
Key Personnel:
Mike Smith . . . . VP & gen mgr progmg dir
Janie Hinson . . . . gen sls mgr
Yolanda Everett . . . . prom dir
Mike Quinn. . . . . news dir
Edna Darrow . . . . pub affrs dir
Neal Riddle . . . . chief of engrg

*WGIQ— Digital Channel: 44. Digital Hrs: 24 5,000 kw vis. ant 902t/715g TL: N31 43 05 W85 26 03 On air date: Sept 9, 1968. 2112 11th Ave. S., Suite 400, Birmingham, AL, 35205. Phone: (205) 328-8756. Fax: (205) 251-2192. Web Site: www.aptv.org. Licensee: Alabama ETV Commission. Natl. Network: PBS, . Alabama Public Television Washington Atty: Dow, Lohnes & Albertson, PLLC.

Key Personnel:

Allan Pizzato	CEO
Pauline Howland	CFO
John Brady	dev VP

WTVY— Digital Channel: 36. Digital Hrs: 24 100 kw vis, 20 kw aur. ant 1,670t/1,909g TL: N30 55 10 W85 44 28 On air date: Feb 12, 1955. Box 1089, Dothan, AL, 36302. 285 N. Foster St., Dothan, AL 36303. Phone: (334) 792-3195. Fax: (334) 793-3947. Web Site: www.wtvynews4.com. Licensee: Gray Television Licensee Inc. Group Owner: Gray Television Inc. (acq 8-29-2002; grpsl). Population Served: 230,000 Natl. Network: CBS, CW, MyNetworkTV, . Natl. Rep: Continental Television Sales,. Wire Svc: AP News staff: 20; News: 16 hrs wkly.

Key Personnel:

Roger Buckett	gen mgr
Richard Morgan	gen sls mgr
Millicent Smith	natl sls mgr & prom dir
Judy Calhoun	rgnl sls mgr
Katie McManus Faye	news dir
Tom Johnson	chief of engrg
Cynthia Crawford	traf mgr

Florence

see Huntsville-Decatur (Florence), AL market

Huntsville-Decatur (Florence), AL
(DMA 82)

WAAY-TV— Digital Channel: 32.1,255 kw vis, 125 kw aur. ant 1,790t/999g TL: N34 44 15 W86 32 02 On air date: Aug 1, 1959. 1000 Monte Sano Blvd., Huntsville, AL, 35801. Phone: (256) 533-3131. Fax: (256) 533-6616. Web Site: www.waaytv.com. Licensee: WAAY-TV License LLC. Group Owner: Piedmont Television Holdings LLC (acq 1-31-2007; $41.645 million). Population Served: 866,000 Natl. Network: ABC, . Washington Atty: Cohn & Marks.

Key Personnel:

Ray Depa	VP
Manny Valbo	gen mgr
Ben Boles,	opns mgr & prom mgr
Chris Kidd	gen sls mgr
Dave Keller	progmg dir
Al Carl	news dir
Jim Bowman	chief of engrg
Robin Dorning	traf mgr & film dir
Chris Ganoe	pub svc dir
Shane Butler	weather dir

WAFF— Digital Channel: 48. Digital Hrs: 24 1,170 kw vis, 234 kw aur. 1,900t/1,526g TL: N34 42 39 W86 32 07 On air date: July 4, 1954. 1414 N. Memorial Pkwy., Huntsville, AL, 35801. Phone: (256) 533-4848. Fax: (256) 533-1337.E-mail: webmaster@waff.com Web Site: www.waff.com. Licensee: Raycom America License Subsidiary LLC. Group Owner: Raycom Media Inc. (acq 3-16-97; grpsl). Population Served: 879,000 Natl. Network: NBC, . Natl. Rep: Harrington, Righter & Parsons,. Washington Atty: Covington & Burling. Wire Svc: AP News staff: 43; News: 26 hrs wkly.

Key Personnel:

Vanessa Oubre	VP & gen mgr
Dale Stafford	gen sls mgr
Becky Shores	mktg mgr
Leigh Michal	progmg mgr
Adam Henning	news dir
J.T. Harriman	engrg dir
Catherine Young	traf mgr

*WFIQ— Digital Channel: 22. Digital Hrs: 24 851 kw vis. ant 725t/515g TL: N34 34 40 W87 46 54 On air date: Aug 16, 1967. 2112 11th Ave. S., Suite 400, Birmingham, AL, 35205. Phone: (205) 328-8756. Fax: (205) 251-2192. Web Site: www.aptv.org. Licensee: Alabama ETV Commission. Natl. Network: PBS, . Alabama Public Television Washington Atty: Dow, Lohnes & Albertson, PLLC.

Key Personnel:

Allan Pizzato	CEO
Pauline Howland	CFO
John Brady	dev VP

WHDF— Digital Channel: 14. Digital Hrs: 24 2,510 kw vis. ant 1,414t/1,315g TL: N35 00 09 W87 08 09 On air date: Oct 29, 1957. 200 Andrew Jackson Way, Huntsville, AL, 35801. 840 Cypress Mill Rd., Florence, AL 35630. Phone: (256) 767-1515 /1550. Fax: (256) 764-7750. Web Site: www.thevalleyscw.tv. Licensee: Huntsville TV L.L.C. Ownership: James L. Lockwood Jr., 100% Population Served: 500,000 Natl. Network: CW, . Natl. Rep: Blair Television,.

Key Personnel:

Shanda Love	CEO & gen sls mgr
Louann Thomson	gen mgr
Brian Capaldo	stn mgr
Tim Rovere	chief of engrg
Kim Loveless	traf mgr

*WHIQ— Digital Channel: 24. Digital Hrs: 24 1,230 kw vis. ant 1,155t/312g TL: N34 44 14 W86 31 46 On air date: November 1965. 2112 11th Ave. S., Suite 400, Birmingham, AL, 35205. Phone: (205) 328-8756. Fax: (205) 251-2192. Web Site: www.aptv.org. Licensee: Alabama ETV Commission. Population Served: 259,550 Natl. Network: PBS, . Alabama Public Television Washington Atty: Dow, Lohnes & Albertson, PLLC.

Key Personnel:

Allan Pizzato	CEO
Charles Grantham	COO
Pauline Howland	CFO
John Brady	dev VP

WHNT-TV— Digital Channel: 46. Digital Hrs: 24 1,279 kw vis, 254 kw aur. ant 1,750t/944g TL: N34 44 19 W86 31 56 On air date: Nov 28, 1963. 200 Holmes Ave., Huntsville, AL, 35801. Box 19, Huntsville, AL 35801. Phone: (256) 533-1919. Fax: (256) 533-4503. Fax: (256) 536-9468 (news).E-mail: feedback@whnt19.com Web Site: www.whnt.com. Licensee: Local TV Alabama License LLC. Group Owner: The New York Times Co. (acq 5-7-2007; grpsl). Population Served: 251,100 Natl. Network: CBS, . Washington Atty: Koteen & Naftalin.

Key Personnel:

Stan Pylant	gen mgr & sls VP
Robert Alverson	opns mgr & progmg dir
Heather Carlton	rgnl sls mgr
Holy Griggs	mktg dir
Kevin Osgood	news dir
Steve King	engrg dir

WZDX— Digital Channel: 41. Digital Hrs: 24 Note: Fox is on WZDX(TV) ch 54, MyNetworkTV is on WZDX-DT ch 41. 2,400 kw vis, 240 kw aur. ant 1,699t/906g TL: N34 44 12 W86 31 59 On air date: Apr 14, 1985. Box 3889, Huntsville, AL, 35810. 1309 N. Memorial Pkwy., Huntsville, AL 35801. Phone: (256) 533-5454. Fax: (256) 533-5315. Web Site: www.fox54.com. Licensee: Huntsville Television Acquisition Licensing LLC. Group Owner: Grant Communications (acq 4-90; $6.1 million). Natl. Network: Fox, MyNetworkTV, Natl. Rep: TeleRep,.

Key Personnel:

Everett Lawrence	natl sls mgr
Bob Boyer	prom mgr
Elizabeth Zaideman	progmg dir & progmg mgr
Wes Hall	chief of engrg
Emily Parsons	traf mgr

Mobile, AL-Pensacola (Ft. Walton Beach), FL
(DMA 60)

WALA-TV— Digital Channel: 9. Digital Hrs: 24 316 kw vis, 47 kw aur. ant 1,246t/1,200g TL: N30 41 17 W87 47 54 On air date: Jan 14, 1953. 1501 Satchel Paige Dr., Mobile, AL, 36606. Phone: (251) 434-1010. Fax: (251) 434-1073 / 1061.E-mail: info@fox10tv.com Web Site: www.fox10tv.com. Licensee: LIN of Alabama LLC. Group Owner: Emmis Communications Corp. (acq 11-30-2005; grpsl). Population Served: 1,509,000 Natl. Network: Fox, . Natl. Rep: TeleRep,. Washington Atty: Fisher, Wayland, Cooper, Leader & Zaragoza. News staff: 45; News: 23 hrs.

Key Personnel:

Matt Pumo	gen sls mgr
Mike Kelly	natl sls mgr
Kristen Mosley	mktg mgr & prom mgr
Bob Cashen	news dir
Roland Fields	chief of engrg

WAWD— Digital Channel: 49.490 kw vis. ant 161t TL: N30 23 35 W86 29 41 On air date: Aug 1, 1998. 8317 Front Beach Rd., Suite 23, Panama City, FL, 32407. Phone: (850) 234-2773. Fax: (850) 234-1179. Web Site: www.tripsmarter.com. Licensee: Beach TV Properties Inc. Group Owner: Beach TV Properties Inc. (acq 10-29-99; $175,000). Washington Atty: Baraff, Koerner, Olender & Hochberg.

Key Personnel:

Robin Quinlan	gen mgr
Mike Hartzog	stn mgr

WBPG— Digital Channel: 25.1510 kw vis, 1,010t TL: N30 36 37 W87 36 26 On air date: Sept 1, 2001. 1501 Satchel Paige Dr., Mobile, AL, 36606. Phone: (251) 434-1010. Fax: (251) 434-1073 / 1061. Licensee: LIN of Alabama LLC. Group Owner: Emmis Communications Corp. (acq 7-7-2006; grpsl). Population Served: 1,200,000 Natl. Network: CW, . Natl. Rep: TeleRep,.

Key Personnel:

Carey Golden	gen sls mgr
Mike Kelly	natl sls mgr
Kristen Mosley	mktg mgr
Roland Fields	chief of engrg

WDPM-DT— Digital Channel: 23.435 kw vis. ant 1,750t/3g TL: N30 36 40 W87 36 27 Not on air, target date: unknown: 3901 Hwy. 121 S., Bedford, TX, 76021-3009. Phone: (817) 571-1229. Fax: (817) 571-7458.E-mail: contactus@daystar.com Web Site: www.daystar.com. Permittee: Word of God Fellowship Inc. Ownership: Marcus D. Lamb, 20%; Joni T. Lamb, 20%; Corinne Lamb, 20%; Jimmie K. Lamb, 20%; and John Calender, 20% (acq 8-1-2008; $1,425,000 for CP).

Key Personnel:

Marcus D. Lamb	pres

WEAR-TV—(Pensacola, FL) Digital Channel: 17. Digital Hrs: 24 1,000 kw vis. ant 1,899t/1,860g TL: N30 36 45 W87 38 43 On air date: Jan 13, 1954. Box 12278, Pensacola, FL, 32581. 4990 Mobile Hwgy, Pensacola, FL 32506. Phone: (850) 456-3333. Fax: (850) 455-0159.E-mail: comments@wear.sbjnet.com Web Site: www.weartv.com. Licensee: WEAR Licensee L.L.C. Group Owner: Sinclair Broadcast Group Inc. (acq 10-8-97). Population Served: 440,800 Natl. Network: ABC, . Natl. Rep: Millennium Sales & Marketing,. Washington Atty: Shaw Pittman LLP. News staff: 30; News: 14 hrs wkly.

Key Personnel:

Terry Cole	gen mgr
Kyle Brinkman	news dir
David Brown	chief of engrg

*WEIQ— Digital Channel: 41. Digital Hrs: 24 1,170 kw vis, 117 kw aur. 600t/545g TL: N30 39 33 W87 53 33 On air date: Nov 6, 1964. 2112 11th Ave. S., Suite 400, Birmingham, AL, 35205. Phone: (205) 328-8756. Fax: (205) 251-2192. Web Site: www.aptv.org. Licensee: Alabama ETV Commission. Natl. Network: PBS, . Alabama Public Television Washington Atty: Dow, Lohnes & Albertson, PLLC.

Key Personnel:

Allan Pizzato	CEO
Pauline Howland	CFO
Kathie Martin	dev VP

WFBD— Digital Channel: 48.5,000 kw vis. ant 454t/452g TL: N30 52 W86 13 12 Not on air, target date: unknown: 118 S. Bellevue, Suite 222, Memphis, TN, 38104. Phone: (901) 516-8970. Permittee: George S. Flinn Jr. Ownership: George S. Flinn Jr., 100%.

Key Personnel:

George S. Flinn Jr.	gen mgr

WFGX— Digital Channel: 50. Digital Hrs: 24 635 kw vis, 63.6 kw aur. ant 280t/250g TL: N30 26 36 W86 35 56 On air date: Apr 7, 1987. Box 12278, Pensacola, FL, 32581. 4990 Mobile Hgwy., Fort Walton Beach, FL 32506. Phone: (850) 456-3333. Fax: (850) 453-4335.E-mail: wfgx@wfgxtv.com Web Site: www.wfgxtv.com. Licensee: WFGX Licensee LLC. Group Owner: Sinclair Broadcast Group Inc. (acq 3-31-2004; $520,000). Population Served: 216,300 Natl. Network: MyNetworkTV, . Washington Atty: Shaw Pittman LLP.

Key Personnel:

David D. Smith	pres
Terry Cole	gen mgr
Joe Smith	opns mgr

WHBR— Digital Channel: 34. Digital Hrs: 24 5,000 kw vis, 500 kw aur. 1,365t/1,330g TL: N30 37 35 W87 38 50 (CP: 3,500 kw vis) On air date: Jan 27, 1986. Box 2633, Pensacola, FL, 32513. 6500 Pensacola Blvd., Pensacola, FL 32505. Phone: (850) 473-8633. Fax: (850) 473-8671.E-mail: dmayo@whbr.org Web Site: www.whbr.org. Licensee: Christian Television of Pensacola/Mobile Inc. Ownership: David C. Gibbs III, Wayne Wetzel , Bill Anderson and Ginny Oliver. (acq 12-16-97). Washington Atty: Gammon & Grange.

Key Personnel:

Bob D'Andrea	pres
Wayne Wetzel	VP
David Mayo	gen mgr

WJTC— Digital Channel: 45. Digital Hrs: 24 3,289 kw vis, 328.9 kw aur. 1,493t TL: N30 35 18 W87 33 16 On air date: December 1984. 661 Azalea Rd., Mobile, AL, 36609. Phone: (251) 602-1544. Fax: (251) 602-1547.E-mail: utv44@online.com Web Site: www.utv44.com. Licensee: Newport Television License LLC. Group Owner: Clear Channel Communications Inc. (acq 3-14-2008; grpsl). Population Served: 1,229,000 Natl. Rep: Millennium Sales & Marketing,. Washington Atty: Covington & Burling.

Key Personnel:

Donita Todd	gen mgr
Tim Woodard	opns mgr
Shea Grandquest	gen sls mgr
Nona Simmons	prom mgr & prom

WKRG-TV— Digital Channel: 27.100 kw vis, 20 kw aur. ant 1,906t/1,879g TL: N30 41 20 W87 49 49 On air date: Sept 5, 1955. 555 Broadcast

Dr., Mobile, AL, 36606. Phone: (251) 479-5555. Fax: (251) 473-8130. Fax: TWX: 810-741-4263. Web Site: www.krg.com. Licensee: Media General Communications Inc. Group Owner: Media General Broadcast Group (acq 3-27-2000; grpsl). Population Served: 425,700 Natl. Network: CBS, . Washington Atty: Wiley, Rein & Fielding.
Key Personnel:
Joe Goleniowski . . . . . pres & VP gen mgr
Warren Fiihr . . . . . gen sls mgr
Robin Delaney . . . . . mktg dir
Darrel Taylor. . . . . progmg mgr
Dan Cates . . . . . news dir
Jim Richard . . . . . chief of engrg
Beverly Hartman. . . . . traf mgr

WMPV-TV— Digital Channel: 20. Digital Hrs: 24 700 kw vis. ant 1,735t/1,765g TL: N30 36 40 W87 36 26 On air date: Dec 19, 1985. W. I65. Station Rd. South, Mobile, AL, 36693. Phone: (251) 661-2101. Fax: (251) 661-7121. Web Site: www.tbn.org. Licensee: Trinity Broadcasting Network. Group Owner: (group owner; (acq 5-8-2000; grpsl). Washington Atty: Fisher, Wayland, Cooper, Leader & Zaragoza.
Key Personnel:
Linda Dixon . . . . . gen mgr & stn mgr
Heather McCollum. . . . . progmg dir
LaTroynnda Cunningham. . . . . pub affrs dir
Alvin Goins . . . . . chief of engrg
Jason Purifoy . . . . . traf mgr

WPAN— Digital Channel: 40.3088 kw vis, 309 kw aur. 720t/749g TL: N30 24 09 W86 59 35 On air date: Feb 14, 1984. 3300 N. Pace, Blv. Suite 172, Pensacola, FL, 32505. 2105 W. Gregory St., Pensacola, FL 32523. Phone: (850) 433-1766. Fax: (850) 433-1641. Licensee: Franklin Media Inc. Ownership: John L. Franklin, 20%; Delores A. Franklin, 20%; Joseph C. Denison, 20%; Robert Gatlin, 20%; Glyn Lowery, 20% (acq 5-23-88). Washington Atty: Pepper & Corazzini.
Key Personnel:
John Franklin . . . . . gen mgr & stn mgr

WPMI-TV— Digital Channel: 15. Digital Hrs: 24 5,000 kw vis, 500 kw aur. ant 1,847t/1,847g TL: N30 36 40 W87 36 27 On air date: Mar 12, 1982. 661 Azalea Rd., Mobile, AL, 36609-1515. Phone: (251) 602-1500. Fax: (251) 602-1547.E-mail: nbc15@online.com Web Site: www.wpmi.com. Licensee: Newport Television License LLC. Group Owner: Clear Channel Communications Inc. (acq 3-14-2008; grpsl). Population Served: 1,229,000 Natl. Network: NBC, . Natl. Rep: Millennium Sales & Marketing,. Washington Atty: Covington & Burling. News staff: 50; News: 5 hrs wkly.
Key Personnel:
Shea Grandquest . . . . . gen mgr & gen sls mgr
Tim Woodward. . . . . opns mgr
Robert Herron . . . . . natl sls mgr
Ric Phillips . . . . . rgnl sls mgr
Jean Stanley . . . . . prom mgr
Kelly Barher . . . . . progmg dir
Joe Raia. . . . . news dir
Tim Reid . . . . . chief of engrg

***WSRE—** Digital Channel: 31.1,000 kw vis. ant 1,801t/1,830g TL: N30 36 40.3 W87 36 26.9 On air date: Sept 11, 1967. Bldg. 23, 1000 College Blvd., Pensacola, FL, 32504-8998. Phone: (850) 484-1200. Fax: (850) 484-1255.E-mail: rolandphillips@wsre.pbs.org Web Site: www.wsre.org. Licensee: District Board of Trustees of Pensacola Junior College. (acq 8-31-71). Population Served: 251,000 Natl. Network: PBS, .
Key Personnel:
Sandy Cesartiray . . . . . gen mgr & stn mgr

Montgomery-Selma, AL (DMA 118)

***WAIQ—** Digital Channel: 27. Digital Hrs: 24 1,420 kw vis, 142 kw aur. 600t/525g TL: N32 22 52 W86 17 30 On air date: Dec 18, 1962. 2112 11th Ave. S., Suite 400, Birmingham, AL, 35205. Phone: (205) 328-8756. Fax: (205) 251-2192. Web Site: www.aptv.org. Licensee: Alabama ETV Commission. Natl. Network: PBS, . Alabama Public Television Washington Atty: Dow, Lohnes & Albertson, PLLC.
Key Personnel:
Allan Pizzato . . . . . CEO
Charles Grantham . . . . . COO
Pauline Howland . . . . . pres & CFO
John Brady . . . . . gen mgr & dev VP

WAKA— Digital Channel: 42. Digital Hrs: 24 316 kw vis, 63.5 kw aur. ant 1,760t/1,757g TL: N32 08 58 W86 46 48 On air date: Mar 17, 1960. Box 230667, Montgomery, AL, 36123. 3020 East Blvd., Montgomery, AL 36123. Phone: (334) 271-8888. Fax: (334) 272-6444. Web Site: www.waka.com. Licensee: Alabama Broadcasting Partners. Group Owner: Bahakel Communications (acq 8-85). Population Served: 600,000 Natl. Network: CBS, . Wire Svc: U.S. Weather Service News staff: 22; News: 9 hrs wkly.
Key Personnel:
Jim Caruthers. . . . . gen mgr
Steffanie Patterson . . . . . gen sls mgr & rgnl sls mgr
Mark Smith. . . . . progmg dir
Rob Martin. . . . . news dir
Thomas Mayberry. . . . . chief of engrg
Richard Baker. . . . . traf mgr

WBIH— Digital Channel: 29.3,900 kw vis. ant 1,338t/1,171g TL: N32 32 27 W86 50 33 On air date: 2002. 225 N. Memorial, Suite 222, Prattville, AL, 36067. Phone: (334) 491-2900. Fax: (334) 491-2929. Licensee: Flinn Broadcasting Corp.
Key Personnel:
Derrick Freeman . . . . . gen mgr

WBMM— Digital Channel: 22. Digital Hrs: 24 65 kw vis. ant 1,118t/941g TL: N32 04 05 W85 56 41 On air date: June 1, 2002. 3251 Harrison Rd., Montgomery, AL, 36109. Phone: (334) 270-3200. Fax: (334) 271-6348. Web Site: www.cwmontgomery.com. Licensee: SagamoreHill Broadcasting of Alabama LLC. Group Owner: Equity Broadcasting Corp. (acq 7-26-2006; $2 million). Natl. Network: CW, . Natl. Rep: Blair Television,. Washington Atty: Wiley Rein LLP.
Key Personnel:
Jesse Grear . . . . . gen mgr

WCOV-TV— Digital Channel: 20. Digital Hrs: 24 2,667 kw vis, 266.7 kw aur. 2,043t TL: N31 58 32 W86 09 46 On air date: Apr 23, 1953. c/o WCOV-TV, One WCOV Ave., Montgomery, AL, 36111. Box 250045, Montgomery, AL 36125. Phone: (334) 288-7020. Fax: (334) 288-5414.E-mail: mail@wcov.com Web Site: www.wcov.com. Licensee: Woods Communications Corp. Group Owner: (group owner; (acq 12-1-85; $4 million;6-10-85). Population Served: 484,987 Natl. Network: Fox, . Natl. Rep: Millennium Sales & Marketing,. Washington Atty: Kenkel, Barnard & Edmundson.
Key Personnel:
David Woods. . . . . pres & gen mgr

***WDIQ—** Digital Channel: 10. Digital Hrs: 24 100 kw vis, 10 kw aur. 695t/566g TL: N31 33 16 W86 23 32 On air date: Aug 8, 1956. 2112 11th Ave. S., Suite 400, Birmingham, AL, 35205. Phone: (205) 328-8756. Fax: (205) 251-2192. Web Site: www.aptv.org. Licensee: Alabama ETV Commission. Population Served: 400,000 Natl. Network: PBS, . Alabama Public Television Washington Atty: Dow, Lohnes & Albertson, PLLC.
Key Personnel:
Allan Pizzato . . . . . CEO
Pauline Howland . . . . . CFO
John Brady . . . . . dev VP

***WIIQ—** Digital Channel: 19. Digital Hrs: 24 447 kw vis, 44.7 kw aur. 1,082t/999g TL: N32 22 01 W87 52 03 On air date: Sept 13, 1971. 2112 11th Ave. S., Suite 400, Birmingham, AL, 35205-2884. Phone: (205) 328-8756. Fax: (205) 251-2192. Web Site: www.aptv.org. Licensee: Alabama ETV Commission. Natl. Network: PBS, . Washington Atty: Dow, Lohnes & Albertson, PLLC.
Key Personnel:
Allan Pizzato . . . . . CEO
Charles Grantham . . . . . COO
Pauline Howland . . . . . CFO
John Brady . . . . . dev VP

WMCF-TV— Digital Channel: 46. Digital Hrs: 24 851 kw vis. ant 426t/459g TL: N32 24 13 W86 11 49 On air date: Oct 12, 1985. 300 Mendel Pkwy. W., Montgomery, AL, 36117. Phone: (334) 272-0045. Fax: (334) 277-6635. Licensee: Trinity Broadcasting Network. Group Owner: (group owner; (acq 5-8-2000; grpsl). Washington Atty: Baraff, Keorner, Olender & Hochberg.
Key Personnel:
P. Crouch . . . . . pres
Aaron Motley . . . . gen mgr & stn mgr opns mgr & progmg mgr
Linda Bell. . . . . pub affrs dir
Larry Dean . . . . . chief of engrg

WNCF— Digital Channel: 32. Digital Hrs: 24 83 kw vis. ant 1,788t/1,771g TL: N32 08 30 W86 44 42 On air date: Mar 12, 1964. 3251 Harrison Rd., Montgomery, AL, 36109. Phone: (334) 270-3200. Fax: (334) 271-6348.E-mail: gsingleton@wncftv.com Web Site: www.wncftv.com. Licensee: Channel 32 Montgomery L.L.C. (acq 1999; $8 million). Population Served: 667,000 Natl. Network: ABC, . Natl. Rep: Blair Television,. Washington Atty: Wiley, Rein & Fielding. News staff: 2; News: one hr wkly.
Key Personnel:
Jesse Grear . . . . . gen mgr
Lanier Harris. . . . . gen sls mgr
Clie Waller . . . . . rgnl sls mgr & prom mgr
Lois Crenshaw . . . . . progmg dir
Ed Cole. . . . . chief of engrg
Linda Babers . . . . . traf mgr

WRJM-TV— Digital Channel: 48. Digital Hrs: 24 2,820 kw vis. ant 1066t/913g TL: N32 03 37 W85 57 02 On air date: Dec. 5, 2000. Josie Park Broadcasting Inc., 285 E. Broad St., Ozark, AL, 36360. 315 S. Three Notch St., Troy, AL 36081. Phone: (334) 670-6766. Fax: (334) 670-6717.E-mail: wrjm67@troycable.net Web Site: www.wrjm.com. Licensee: Josie Park Broadcasting Inc.. Ownership: H. Jack Misell, 67%; Walter P. Lunsford, 33% Population Served: 611,750 Natl. Network: MyNetworkTV, . Washington Atty: Borsari and Assoc, PLC.
Key Personnel:
Jack Misell . . . . . CEO & gen mgr
Walter P. Lunsford . . . . . VP
Nicky Vull. . . . . stn mgr
Boyd Mizell . . . . . opns mgr
Buddy Johnson. . . . . natl sls mgr
Sonny Strassburger . . . . . rgnl sls mgr
Vincent Hodges . . . . . prom mgr
Don Hess . . . . . progmg dir
Jenny Dykes . . . . . pub affrs dir
Dan Mizell . . . . . engrg VP
Crystal Blair . . . . . traf mgr
Nicky Bull . . . . . film dir

WSFA— Digital Channel: 12. Digital Hrs: 24 316 kw vis, 63.2 kw aur. ant 2,000t/1,935g TL: N31 58 32 W86 09 46 On air date: Dec 25, 1954. 12 E. Delano Ave., Montgomery, AL, 36105. Phone: (334) 288-1212. Fax: (334) 613-8301. Fax: (334) 613-8303. Web Site: www.wsfa.com. Licensee: WSFA License Subsidiary LLC. Group Owner: Liberty Corp. (acq 1-31-2006; grpsl). Population Served: 210,600 Natl. Network: NBC, . Natl. Rep: Harrington, Righter & Parsons,. Washington Atty: Dow, Lohnes & Albertson.
Key Personnel:
Hoyt Andres . . . . . gen mgr & stn mgr
Mark Wilder . . . . . opns dir
James Belton . . . . . natl sls mgr
Lewis Fryer . . . . . rgnl sls mgr
Edith Parten . . . . . mktg dir
Denise Vickers . . . . . news dir
Craig Young . . . . . engrg mgr
Ken Thayer . . . . . chief of engrg

Opelika

see Columbus, GA market

Selma

see Montgomery-Selma, AL market

Tuscaloosa

see Birmingham (Anniston, Tuscaloosa), AL market

Alaska

Anchorage, AK (DMA 150)

***KAKM—** Digital Channel: 8. Digital Hrs: 24 162 kw vis, 16.2 kw aur. 780t/808g TL: N61 25 22 W149 52 20 On air date: May 7, 1975. 3877 University Dr., Anchorage, AK, 99508. Phone: (907) 563-7070. Fax: (907) 273-9192.E-mail: questions@kakm.org Web Site: www.kakm.org. Licensee: Alaska Public Telecommunications Inc. Population Served: 250,000 Natl. Network: PBS, . Washington Atty: Dow, Lohnes & Albertson.
Key Personnel:
Steve Lindbeck . . . . . gen mgr
Will Peterson. . . . . dev dir & dev mgr

KDMD— Digital Channel: 32. Digital Hrs: 24 5,000 kw vis, 500 kw aur. 98t TL: N61 09 57 W149 54 01 On air date: February 1990. 1310 E. 66th Ave., Anchorage, AK, 99518-1915. Phone: (907) 562-5363. Fax: (907) 562-5346.E-mail: stationmail@kdmd.tv Web Site: www.kdmd.tv. Licensee: Ketchikan TV LLC. (acq 6-19-2002). Population Served: 300,000
Key Personnel:
David Drucker . . . . . CEO
Bill Vanderpoel . . . . . pres
Andy Tierney. . . . . gen mgr & stn mgr sls VP
Don Nelson . . . . . chief of engrg

KIMO— Digital Channel: 12. Digital Hrs: 24 316 kw vis, 31.6 kw aur. ant 781t TL: N61 25 22 W149 52 20 On air date: Oct 31, 1967. 2700 E. Tudor Rd., Anchorage, AK, 99507. Phone: (907) 561-1313. Fax: (907) 561-1377.E-mail: info@aksuperstation.com Web Site:

www.aksuperstation.com. Licensee: Smith Media License Holdings LLC. Group Owner: Smith Broadcasting Group Inc. (acq 11-8-2004; grpsl). Population Served: 250,000 Natl. Network: ABC, CW, . Natl. Rep: Continental Television Sales,.

Key Personnel:

Sean Bradley . . . . VP & gen mgr sls dir & gen sls mgr
Nate Kimmell . . . . prom mgr
Terri Bradley . . . . progmg mgr & traf mgr
Ty Hardt. news dir
George Heacock . . . . chief of engrg

KTBY— Analog Channel: 4. Digital Channel: 20. Digital Hrs: 24 234.4 kw vis. ant 148t/230g TL: N61 13 11 W149 53 24 On air date: Dec 2, 1983. 440 E. Benson Blvd., Anchorage, AK, 99503. Phone: (907) 274-0404. Fax: (907) 264-5180. Web Site: www.ktbytv.com. Licensee: Coastal Television Broadcasting Co. LLC.. Ownership: William A. Fielder III, 100% Group Owner: Piedmont Television Holdings LLC (acq 5-7-2008; $3.243 million). Population Served: 290,000 Natl. Network: Fox, .

Key Personnel:

Kirsten Bolton . . . . gen mgr & gen sls mgr
Kyle Keller . . . . opns mgr

KTUU-TV— Digital Channel: 10. Digital Hrs: 24 100 kw vis, 10 kw aur. ant 721t/715g TL: N61 25 22 W149 52 20 On air date: December 1953. Tudor Park, 701 E. Tudor Rd., Suite 220, Delta, AK, 99503. Phone: (907) 762-9202. Fax: (907) 561-0882. Fax: (907) 563-3318.E-mail: ktuu@ktuu.com Web Site: www.ktuu.com. Licensee: Channel 2 Broadcasting Co. Ownership: Residential and Z&L Trust. (acq 3-9-2001). Population Served: 208,100 Natl. Network: NBC, . News staff: 40; News: 12 hrs wkly.

Key Personnel:

Greg D. Zaser . . . . pres
Susan Lucas . . . . gen mgr
Trent McNelly . . . . opns mgr
Andy MacLeod. . . . . gen sls mgr
Nancy Johnson. natl sls mgr & mktg dir prom mgr & progmg mgr film buyer
Dianna Rowedder. . . . . adv dir & adv mgr rsch dir
John Tracy. news dir
Barry Sowinski. . . . . pub affrs dir
Leland Verschueren . . . . chief of engrg
Doris Tronstad. . . . . traf mgr
Bauy Sowinski . . . . pub svc dir
John Carpenter . . . . sports cmtr
Jackie Purcell . . . . weather dir

KTVA— Digital Channel: 28. Digital Hrs: 24 45 kw vis, 5 kw aur. 300t/392g TL: N61 11 33 W149 54 01 On air date: Dec 11, 1953. 1007 W. 32nd Ave., Anchorage, AK, 99503. Phone: (907) 273-3192. Fax: (907) 273-3189.E-mail: 11news@ktva.com Web Site: www.ktva.com. Licensee: Alaska Broadcasting Company Inc. Ownership: MediaNews Group Inc. (acq 5-25-2000; grpsl). Population Served: 306,000 Natl. Network: CBS, . Rgnl. Rep: Rgnl rep: Art Moore Washington Atty: Wilkinson, Barker, Knauer & Quinn. News staff: 16; News: 7 hrs wkly.

Key Personnel:

Jerry Bever . . . . gen mgr & stn mgr
Bush Houston . . . . opns mgr
Laurie Bruce. . . . . gen sls mgr
Cyd Terhune . . . . progmg dir
Staci Chil . . . . news dir
Tom Lambert. . . . . chief of engrg
Monica Bouvier . . . . traf mgr & weather dir

KYES-TV— Digital Channel: 5. Digital Hrs: 24 5.9 kw vis, 50 kw aur. ant 820t/160g TL: N61 20 10 W149 30 49 On air date: November 1989. 3700 Woodland Dr., Suite 800, Anchorage, AK, 99517. Phone: (907) 248-5937. Fax: (907) 339-3889. Web Site: www.yes.com. Licensee: Fireweed Communications LLC. Ownership: Jeremy Lansman, 51%; Carol Schatz, 49% (acq 12-11-91; $100 & assumption of debt; 1-6-92). Population Served: 254,479 Natl. Network: MyNetworkTV, . Washington Atty: Benjamin Perez. News: one hr wkly.

Key Personnel:

Jeremy Lansman . . . . pres & chief of engrg
Carol Schatz. . . . . gen mgr & progmg mgr
Lori Erickson . . stn mgr & gen sls mgr natl sls mgr & rgnl sls mgr
Roy Nederbrock. . . . . chief of opns
Maryann Spinella. . . . . prom mgr
Amy Simonson . . . . traf mgr

***KYUK-TV—** Analog Channel: 4.4.68 kw vis, 933 w aur. ant 206t/253g TL: N60 47 33 W161 46 22 On air date: August 1973. Pouch 468, Bethel, AK, 99559. Phone: (907) 543-3131. Fax: (907) 543-3130. Web Site: www.kyuk.org. Licensee: Bethel Broadcasting Inc. Population Served: 12,000 Natl. Network: PBS, ABC, CBS, . Washington Atty: Wilkinson, Barker, Knauer & Quinn. Wire Svc: DAC News staff: 5; News: 3 hrs wkly.

Key Personnel:

Joan Hamilton. chmn
Ron Daugherty . . . . gen mgr
Jose Seibert . . . . progmg dir & engrg dir
Alexie Isaac . . . . film dir

Rebroadcasts KUAC-TV Fairbanks 100%.

Fairbanks, AK

(DMA 202)

KATN— Digital Channel: 18.28.2 kw vis, 5.5 kw aur. ant 200t/151g TL: N64 50 42 W147 42 52 On air date: Mar 1, 1955. 516 2nd Ave., Suite 400, Fairbanks, AK, 99701. Phone: (907) 452-2125. Fax: (907) 456-8225.E-mail: info@aksuperstation.com Web Site: www.aksuperstation.com. Licensee: Smith Media License Holdings LLC. Group Owner: Smith Broadcasting Group Inc. (acq 11-8-2004; grpsl). Population Served: 84,800 Natl. Network: ABC, . News: 6p - 11p wkly.

Key Personnel:

Sean Bradley . . . . VP & gen mgr
Mike Hammer . . . . opns VP
Jeff Glaser. . . . . sls VP
Rita Corwin . . . . mktg dir & prom dir pub svc dir
Terri Bradley . . . . progmg dir
Ty Hardt. . . . . news dir
Gerilynne Buonocore . . . . pub affrs dir
George Heacock . . . . engrg dir
Mary Hicks . . . . traf mgr
John Seibol . . . . sports cmtr
Cary Carrigan . . . . weather dir

Rebroadcasts KIMO-TV Anchorage 99%.

KFXF— Digital Channel: 7. Digital Hrs: 20 6.1 kw vis. ant 879t/298g TL: N64 55 20 W147 42 55 On air date: Feb 27, 1995. 3650 Bradock St., Fairbanks, AK, 99701. Phone: (907) 452-3697. Fax: (907) 456-3428. Web Site: www.TVTV.com. Licensee: Tanana Valley Television Co. Ownership: Bill St. Pierre 60%, Mike Young, Dave Wike. Population Served: 80,000 Natl. Network: Fox, . Washington Atty: Baker & Hostetler. News staff: 4; News: 10 hr wkly.

Key Personnel:

John Hoff . . . . gen mgr & gen sls mgr
Christine Fry . . . . stn mgr & opns mgr progmg dir
Darryl Lewis . . . . news dir
Dave Sala. . . . . chief of engrg
Trent Heineken . . . . traf mgr

KJNP-TV— Digital Channel: 20. Digital Hrs: 24 18.66 kw vis, 2.8 kw aur. ant 1,619t/191g TL: N64 52 44 W148 03 10 On air date: Dec 7, 1981. Box 56359, 2501 Mission Rd., North Pole, AK, 99705-1359. Phone: (907) 488-2216. Fax: (907) 488-5246.E-mail: kjnp@mosquitonet.com Web Site: www.mosquitonet.com/~kjnp. Licensee: Evangelistic Alaska Missionary Fellowship. Population Served: 8,100 Washington Atty: Fletcher, Heald & Hildreth.

Key Personnel:

Genevieve Nelson . . . . CEO
Yvonne Carriker . . . . pres
Richard T. Olson. VP
Julie Beaver . . . . stn mgr

KTVF— Digital Channel: 26.50 kw vis, 5 kw aur. ant 50t/168g TL: N64 50 36 W147 42 48 On air date: Feb 17, 1955. 3528 International Way, Fairbanks, AK, 99701. Phone: (907) 458-1800. Fax: (907) 458-1820. Web Site: www.webcenter11.com. Licensee: Newport Television License LLC. Group Owner: Clear Channel Communications Inc. (acq 3-14-2008; grpsl). Population Served: 85,000 Natl. Network: NBC, . Natl. Rep: Blair Television,. Washington Atty: Covington & Burling. News staff: 6; News: 9 hrs wkly.

Key Personnel:

DeeDee Caciari. . . . . gen mgr
David Castor . . . . stn mgr & opns mgr chief of engrg
Deedee Caciari. . . . . gen sls mgr
Celia Vissers . . . . progmg dir
Billie Sundgren . . . . news dir & sports cmtr
Richard Port. . . . . traf mgr & weather dir

***KUAC-TV—** Digital Channel: 9.30 kw vis. ant 554t/117g TL: N64 54 42 W147 46 38 On air date: Dec 22, 1971. Box 755620, Univ. of Alaska-Fairbanks, 312 Tanana Dr., Fairbanks, AK, 99775-5620. Phone: (907) 474-7491. Fax: (907) 474-5064.E-mail: comments@kuac.org Web Site: www.kuac.org. Licensee: University of Alaska. Population Served: 70,000 Natl. Network: PBS, .

Key Personnel:

Greg Petrowich. . . . . CEO & sls dir
Claudia Clark . . . . gen mgr & progmg dir
Jeremy Cate. opns mgr
Gretchen Gordon . . . . dev dir
Tammy Tragis-McCook. . . . . mktg mgr
Joseph Forgue . . . . chief of engrg
Anne Biberman . . . . sls
Keith Martin . . . . engr

Juneau, AK

(DMA 207)

KJUD— Digital Channel: 11. Digital Hrs: 24 Note: ABC is on KJUD(TV) ch 8, CW is on KJUD-DT ch 11. 239 w vis, 47 w aur. ant 1,160t/69g TL: N58 18 06 W134 26 29 On air date: Feb 19, 1956. 175 S. Franklin St., Senate Bldg., Juneau, AK, 99801. Phone: (907) 561-1313 / (907) 586-3145. Fax: (907) 561-1377 / (907) 463-3041.E-mail: info@aksuperstation.com Web Site: www.aksuperstation.com. Licensee: Smith Media License Holdings LLC. Group Owner: Smith Broadcasting Group Inc. (acq 11-8-2004; grpsl). Population Served: 59,825 Natl. Network: ABC, CW, Washington Atty: Kaye, Scholer, Fierman, Hays & Handler. News staff: 9; News: 5 hrs wkly.

Key Personnel:

John Bradley . . . . gen mgr
Jeff Glaser . . . . gen sls mgr
Terri Bradley . . . . progmg dir
Ty Hardt. . . . . news dir
Gerilynne Buonocore. . . . . pub affrs dir & traf mgr
George Heacock . . . . chief of engrg

KTNL-TV— Digital Channel: 7. Digital Hrs: 24 350 w vis, 30 w aur. ant -708t/112g TL: N57 03 01 W135 20 04 On air date: Sept 1, 1966. 520 Lake St., Sitka, AK, 99835. Phone: (907) 747-5749. Fax: (907) 747-8440.E-mail: stationmail@ktnl.tv Web Site: www.ktnl.tv. Licensee: Ketchikan TV LLC. (acq 6-19-2002). Population Served: 52,000 Natl. Network: CBS, . Washington Atty: Wilkinson, Barker, Knauer L.L.P.

Key Personnel:

David Drucker . . . . CEO
Bill Vanderpoel . . . . VP
Charlene Nelson . . . . gen mgr
Garrett Leighton . . . . opns mgr
Amanda McMellon. . . . . sls dir

***KTOO-TV—** Digital Channel: 10. Digital Hrs: 24 1 kw vis. ant -1,191t/72g TL: N58 17 56 W134 24 07 On air date: Oct 1, 1978. 360 Egan Dr., Juneau, AK, 99801. Phone: (907) 586-1670. Fax: (907) 586-3612.E-mail: ktoo@ktoo.org Web Site: www.ktoo.org. Licensee: Capital Community Broadcasting Inc. Population Served: 60,000 Natl. Network: PBS, . Washington Atty: Schwartz, Woods & Miller. News staff: one; News: one hr wkly.

Key Personnel:

Bill Legere . . . . pres & gen mgr
Jim Mahan . . . . stn mgr
Cheryl Levitt. dev dir
William Judy . . . . engrg dir

Rebroadcasts KUAC-TV Fairbanks 95%.

KUBD— Digital Channel: 13.1.5 kw vis. ant -226t/62g TL: N55 20 59 W131 40 12 On air date: Feb 11, 2000. 516 Stedman St., Ketchikan, AK, 99901. Phone: (907) 225-4613. Fax: (907) 247-5365. Licensee: Ketchikan TV LLC. Ownership: David M. Drucker, 100% (acq 6-19-2002).

Arizona

Phoenix (Prescott), AZ

(DMA 12)

***KAET—** Digital Channel: 8. Digital Hrs: 24 40 kw vis. ant 1,801t/308g TL: N33 20 00 W112 03 49 On air date: Jan 30, 1961. Box 871405, Tempe, AZ, 85287. Stauffer Hall B-Wing, Arizona State Univ., Tempe, AZ 85287. Phone: (480) 965-8888. Fax: (480) 965-1000. Web Site: www.kaet.asu.edu. Licensee: Arizona Board of Regents. Population Served: 3,300,000 Natl. Network: PBS, . Washington Atty: Covington & Burling. Foreign lang progmg: SpanishS 1 News staff: 7; News: 3 hrs wkly.

Key Personnel:
Greg Giczi . . . gen mgr
Beth Vershure . . . stn mgr
John Martinez . . . opns mgr
Kelly McCullough . . . dev dir & dev mgr mktg dir & mktg mgr
John Menzies . . . prom mgr
Michael Philipsen . . . news dir
Joseph Manning . . . engrg mgr

KASW— Digital Channel: 49.2,510 kw vis. ant 1,774t TL: N33 20 01 W112 03 44 On air date: September 1995. c/o TV Stn KTVK, 5555 N. 7th Ave., Phoenix, AZ, 85013. Phone: (602) 207-3333. Fax: (602) 207-3477. Web Site: www.azfamily.com. Licensee: KASW-TV Inc. Group Owner: Belo Corp., Broadcast Division (acq 1-24-2000). Natl. Network: CW, .
Key Personnel:
Dean Apostalides . . . gen mgr
Skip Cass . . . stn mgr
Rick Soltesz . . . gen sls mgr
Brock Kruzie . . . natl sls mgr
Scott Rein. . . . rgnl sls mgr
Mark Demopoulos . . . progmg dir
Mike Stone . . . chief of engrg
Shana Crane . . . traf mgr

KAZT-TV— Digital Channel: 7. Digital Hrs: 24 3.2 kw vis. ant 2,598t/98g TL: N34 41 15 W112 07 01 On air date: Sept 5, 1982. 4343 E. Camelback Rd., Suite 130, Phoenix, AZ, 85018. Phone: (602) 977-7700. Fax: (602) 224-2214.E-mail: jburnton@aztv.com Web Site: www.aztv.com. Licensee: KAZT L.L.C. Ownership: Londen Media Group L.L.C., 96%; and Ron Bergamo, 4% (acq 4-1-2002; $7.336 million). Population Served: 1,800,000 Natl. Rep: Petry Television Inc.,. Washington Atty: Shaw Pittman. Wire Svc: AP News staff: 6; News: 11 hrs/week.
Key Personnel:
John Ryan . . . CFO
Jeff Burnton . . . gen mgr
Richard Howe . . . stn mgr
Eric Cohen . . . progmg dir & progmg mgr
Cheryl Strong . . . traf mgr

KCFG— Digital Channel: 32. Digital Hrs: 24 1 kw vis. ant 1,948t TL: N35 14 26 W111 35 48 On air date: 2001. 2616 North Steves Blvd., Flagstaff, AZ, 86004. Phone: (928) 526-5234. Fax: (928) 526-1172. Web Site: www.kcfg.net. Licensee: KM Television of Flagstaff L.L.C.
Key Personnel:
John Banker . . . gen mgr

***KDTP—** Digital Channel: 11. Digital Hrs: 24 Note: affiliated with the Daystar Television Network. 160 kw vis. ant 997t/525g TL: N34 23 19 W110 59 36 On air date: 2001. Box 612066, Dallas, TX, 75261. Phone: (602) 207-3939. Web Site: www.daystar.com. Licensee: Community Television Educators Inc. Foreign lang progmg: SpanishS 4
Key Personnel:
Mike Woodworth . . . chief of engrg

KFPH-DT— Digital Channel: 13. Digital Hrs: 24 316 kw vis. ant 1,555t/239g TL: N34 58 05 W111 30 29 On air date: 1991. 2158 N. 4th St., Flagstaff, AZ, 86004. Phone: (928) 527-1300. Fax: (928) 527-1394. Web Site: www.univision.com. Licensee: TeleFutura Partnership of Flagstaff. Group Owner: Univision Communications Inc. (acq 10-2-2001; $19.113 million plus assumption of liabilities with KFTU-TV Douglas). Natl. Network: TeleFutura (Spanish), . Foreign lang progmg: SpanishS 168
Key Personnel:
Jose Luis Padilla . . . gen mgr

KMOH-TV— Digital Channel: 19.25.2 kw vis. ant 1,896t/57g TL: N35 01 57 W114 21 56 On air date: Feb 22, 1988. 2332 Kingman Ave., Kingman, AZ, 86401. Phone: (928) 753-2724. Fax: (305) 863-5709. Web Site: www.mtvtr3sphx.com. Licensee: Hero Licenseco LLC. Group Owner: (group owner; (acq 4-11-2008; $100 million with KBEH(TV) Oxnard, CA). Population Served: 138,000
Key Personnel:
Mara Rankin . . . gen mgr
Jerry Albers . . . opns mgr
Charlie Trice . . . engrg dir

KNAZ-TV— Digital Channel: 2. Digital Hrs: 24 100 kw vis, 5 kw aur. ant 1,597t/284g TL: N34 58 06 W111 30 28 On air date: May 2, 1970. 2201 N. Vickey St., Flagstaff, AZ, 86004. Box 3360, Flagstaff, AZ 86004. Phone: (928) 526-2232. Fax: (928) 526-8110.E-mail: 2news@knaztv2.com Licensee: Multimedia Holdings Corp. Group Owner: Gannett Broadcasting (acq 1997; $6.25 million with KMOH-TV Kingman). Population Served: 150,000 Natl. Network: NBC, . Washington Atty: Dow, Lohnes & Albertson.

Key Personnel:
Jerome Parra . . . gen mgr
Scott Jones . . . opns mgr & sls dir
Stan Pierce . . . gen sls mgr
Marge Divine . . . progmg dir & traf mgr
Mark Casey . . . news dir
Jon Koger . . . chief of engrg

KNXV-TV— Digital Channel: 15. Digital Hrs: 24 631 kw vis, 63.1 kw aur. ant 1,710t/282g TL: N33 20 00 W112 03 46 On air date: Sept 9, 1979. 515 N. 44th St., Phoenix, AZ, 85008. Phone: (602) 273-1500. Fax: (602) 685-3000.E-mail: news15@abc15.com Web Site: www.abc15.com. Licensee: Scripps Howard Broadcasting Co. Group Owner: (group owner, see Cross-Ownership; (acq 1-9-85; $26.6 million). Population Served: 2,877,000 Natl. Network: ABC, . Natl. Rep: Eagle Television Sales,. Washington Atty: Baker & Hostetler.
Key Personnel:
Janice Todd . . . gen mgr & stn mgr
Ryan Steward. . . . opns mgr & engrg mgr chief of engrg
Kimberly Steele . . . natl sls mgr
Jim Hart . . . prom mgr
Amy Wilson . . . progmg mgr
Bob Sullivan . . . news dir
Colleen Reid. . . . pub affrs dir & pub svc dir
Will Bruner . . . chief of engrg
Janet Romero. . . . traf mgr
Craig Fouhy . . . sports cmtr
Bill Bellis . . . weather dir
Tracy Kornet . . . women's int ed

***KPAZ-TV—** Digital Channel: 20. Digital Hrs: 24 1,000 kw vis. ant 1,604t/148g TL: N33 20 02.5 W112 03 42 On air date: Sept 16, 1967. 3551 E. McDowell Rd., Phoenix, AZ, 85008. Phone: (602) 273-1477. Fax: (602) 267-9427. Licensee: Trinity Broadcasting of Arizona Inc. Group Owner: Trinity Broadcasting Network (acq 1977). Washington Atty: Joseph E. Dunne III.
Key Personnel:
Oralena Valero . . . stn mgr
Gary Nichols . . . chief of engrg

KPHO-TV— Digital Channel: 17. Digital Hrs: 24 100 kw vis, 10 kw aur. 1,768t/387g TL: N33 20 02 W112 03 40 On air date: Dec 4, 1949. 4016 N. Black Canyon Hwy., Phoenix, AZ, 85017. Phone: (602) 264-1000. Fax: (602) 650-5510. Fax: (602) 650-5545.E-mail: cbs5news@kpho.com Web Site: www.kpho.com. Licensee: Meredith Corp. Group Owner: Meredith Broadcasting Group, Meredith Corp., see Cross-Ownership (acq 6-25-52; grpsl; 6-30-52). Population Served: 1,600,000 Natl. Network: CBS, . Natl. Rep: Harrington, Righter & Parsons,. Washington Atty: Dow Lohnes. Wire Svc: Weather Wire News staff: 60; News: 30.5 hrs wkly.
Key Personnel:
Mitch Nye. . . . gen sls mgr
Seth Parker. . . . progmg VP & progmg dir
Tom Bell. . . . news dir & engrg dir

KPNX—(Mesa, Digital Channel: 12. Digital Hrs: 24 316 kw vis, 46.8 kw aur. 1,780t/350g TL: N33 20 00 W112 03 48 On air date: Apr 23, 1953. Box 711, Phoenix, AZ, 85004. 1101 N. Central Ave., Phoenix, AZ 85001. Phone: (602) 257-1212. Fax: (602) 261-6135. Fax: (602) 257-6619 (news).E-mail: webmaster@12news.com Licensee: Multimedia Holdings Corp. Group Owner: Gannett Broadcasting (acq 6-7-79; grpsl;6-11-79). Population Served: 2,989,000 Natl. Network: NBC, . News staff: 70.
Key Personnel:
John Misner . . . gen mgr
Dan Mayasich . . . gen sls mgr

KPPX-TV— Digital Channel: 51.4,875 kw vis, 487 kw aur. 1,749t/354g TL: N33 20 03 W112 03 38 On air date: Feb 15, 1999. 1101 N. Central Ave., Phoenix, AZ, 85004. Phone: (602) 808-0729. Fax: (602) 808-8864. Web Site: www.ionline.tv. Licensee: America 51 L.P., debtor-in-possession. Group Owner: Paxson Communications Corp. (acq 1-2-2001; $6.6 million for 51%). Natl. Network: ION Television, . Washington Atty: Skadden, Arps, Slate, Meagher & Flom.
Key Personnel:
Kathy Lawrence . . . gen mgr & stn mgr gen sls mgr
Maureen Rowe . . . traf mgr

KSAZ-TV— Digital Channel: 10. Digital Hrs: 24 316 kw vis, 47 kw aur. 1,700t/264g TL: N33 20 03 W112 03 43 (CP: Ant 1,829t) On air date: Oct 24, 1953. 511 W. Adams St., Phoenix, AZ, 85003. Phone: (602) 257-1234. Fax: (602) 262-0177 (602) 262-0181. Fax: (602) 262-0456 (sales). Licensee: KSAZ License Inc. Group Owner: Fox Television Stations Inc. (acq 11-96; grpsl). Population Served: 4,000,000 Natl. Network: Fox, . Natl. Rep: Fox Stations Sales,. Washington Atty: Koteen & Naftalin. News staff: 96; News: 38 hrs wkly.

Key Personnel:
Patrick Nevin . . . gen mgr
Paul Austill . . . opns mgr
Ron Parodi . . . natl sls mgr
David Saline . . . progmg dir
Doug Bannard . . . news dir
Jim Kauffman . . . chief of engrg
Jamie Fischer . . . traf mgr

KTAZ— Digital Channel: 39. Digital Hrs: 24 550 kw vis. ant 1,763t/323g TL: N33 20 03 W112 03 38 On air date: July 4, 2000. 4625 S. 33rd Pl., Phoenix, AZ, 85040. Phone: (602) 648-3900. Licensee: NBC Telemundo License Co. Group Owner: Telemundo Group Inc. (acq 9-26-2002; $7.5 million with KPHZ-LP Phoenix and KPSW-LP Phoenix). Natl. Network: Telemundo (Spanish), . Washington Atty: Wiley, Rein, Fielding. Foreign lang progmg: SpanishS 168

KTVK— Digital Channel: 24. Digital Hrs: 24 100 kw vis, 15.1 kw aur. ant 1,670t/231g TL: N33 20 01 W112 03 45 (CP: Ant 1,778t) On air date: Feb 28, 1955. 5555 N. 7th Ave., Phoenix, AZ, 85013. Phone: (602) 207-3333.E-mail: feedback@azfamily.com Web Site: www.azfamily.com. Licensee: KTVK Inc. Group Owner: Belo Corp., Broadcast Division (acq 9-3-99; $315 million cash including 50% of Arizona News Channel). Population Served: 1,720,000 Natl. Rep: TeleRep,. Wire Svc: AP News staff: 100+; News: 48 hrs wkly.
Key Personnel:
Mark Higgins . . . pres & gen mgr weather dir
Jamie Aitken . . . stn mgr
Marie McGlynn . . . sls VP
Teri Lane. . . . mktg dir
Sandy Breland . . . news dir
Jim Cole . . . engrg dir

KTVW-DT— Digital Channel: 33.2,290 kw vis, 229 kw aur. 1,710t/282g TL: N33 20 00 W112 03 46 (CP: Ant 1,673t) On air date: Sept 2, 1979. 6006 South 30th St., Phoenix, AZ, 85042. Phone: (602) 243-3333. Fax: (602) 276-8658. Licensee: KTVW License Partnership G.P. Group Owner: Univision Communications Inc. (acq 5-17-89; $23 million;6-5-89). Population Served: 500,000 Natl. Network: Univision (Spanish), . Foreign lang progmg: SpanishS 168
Key Personnel:
Jose Luis Padilla . . . gen mgr
Carlos Flys. . . . opns VP
Andrew Deschapelles . . . rgnl sls mgr
Javier Ramis . . . mktg dir & prom dir
Virginia Luna . . . progmg dir
Marco Flores . . . news dir
Tom Foy . . . chief of engrg
Nelda Chavarria . . . traf mgr

KUTP— Digital Channel: 26. Digital Hrs: 24 2,750 kw vis, 275 kw aur. 1,792t/381g TL: N33 20 01 W112 03 32 On air date: Dec 23, 1985. 511 W. Adam St., Phoenix, AZ, 85003. Phone: (602) 257-1234. Fax: (602) 262-0177/ 5123. Web Site: www.kutp.com. Licensee: Fox Television Stations Inc. Group Owner: (group owner; (acq 7-31-2001; grpsl). Population Served: 1,122,800 Natl. Network: MyNetworkTV, . Washington Atty: Wilmer, Cutler & Pickering.
Key Personnel:
Patrick Nevin . . . gen mgr
Jim Kauffman. . . . opns dir & opns mgr chief of engrg
David Saline . . . gen sls mgr & progmg dir
Doug Bannard. . . . progmg dir & news dir
Jamie Fischer . . . rsch dir & traf mgr

Prescott

see Phoenix (Prescott), AZ market

Sierra Vista

see Tucson (Sierra Vista), AZ market

Tucson (Sierra Vista), AZ (DMA 68)

KFTU-DT— Digital Channel: 36. Digital Hrs: 24 100 kw vis. ant 30t/180g TL: N31 22 08 W109 31 45 On air date: 2001. 1111 G Ave., Douglas, AZ, 85607. Phone: (520) 805-1773. Fax: (520) 805-1768. Licensee: TeleFutura Partnership of Douglas. Group Owner: Univision Communications Inc. (acq 10-2-2001; $19.113 million plus assumption of liabilities with KFPH-TV Flagstaff). Foreign lang progmg: SpanishS 168

Key Personnel:
Jose Luis Padilla . . . . . gen mgr
Carlos Flys . . . . . opns mgr
Alfonso Romero . . . . . rgnl sls mgr
Javier Ramis . . . . . prom dir & adv dir
Salvador Ocano . . . . . progmg dir
Marco Flores . . . . . news dir
Tom Foy . . . . . chief of engrg
Nelda Chavarria . . . . . traf mgr

KGUN-TV— Digital Channel: 9. Digital Hrs: 24 110 kw vis, 21.94 kw aur. ant 3,739t/220g TL: N32 24 53 W110 42 58 On air date: June 3, 1956. 7280 E. Rosewood St., Tucson, AZ, 85710. Phone: (520) 722-5486. Fax: (520) 733-7099. Fax: (520) 733-7070. Web Site: www.kgun9.com. Licensee: Journal Broadcast Corp. Group Owner: Emmis Communications Corp. (acq 12-5-2005; grpsl). Population Served: 1,050,000 Natl. Network: ABC, . Natl. Rep: MMT,. Washington Atty: Reed Smith LLP. Wire Svc: NOAA Weather News staff: 47; News: 22 hrs wkly.
Key Personnel:
Julie Brinks. . . . . gen mgr
Kelly Donnell. . . . . opns dir & opns mgr prom mgr
Adam Johnston . . . . . gen sls mgr
Kara Quintela . . . . . natl sls mgr
Thor Wasbotten . . . . . news dir
Stephen Somerville . . . . . chief of engrg
Sue Bock . . . . . traf mgr

KHRR— Digital Channel: 40. Digital Hrs: 24 1,550 kw vis, 155 kw aur. ant 2,030t/184g TL: N32 14 55 W111 06 57 On air date: Jan 1, 1985. 5151 E. Broadway, Suite 600, Tucson, AZ, 85711. Phone: (520) 322-6888. Fax: (520) 319-9148. Web Site: www.telemundo.com. Licensee: NBC Telemundo License Co. Group Owner: Telemundo Group Inc. (acq 1-1-2003; $20 million with KDRX-CA Phoenix). Population Served: 333,650 Natl. Network: Telemundo (Spanish), . Foreign lang progmg: SpanishS 168 News staff: 7; News: 5 hrs wkly.
Key Personnel:
Araceli De Leon. . . . . gen mgr
Lupita Celaya . . . . . opns dir & progmg dir
Martha Muniz . . . . . prom dir & prom mgr
Sergio Pedroza. . . . . news dir & pub affrs dir
Pablo Sierra. . . . . film dir
Abelardo Oquita . . . . . news cmtr

KMSB— Digital Channel: 25. Digital Hrs: 8:30 AM-5:30 PM 480 kw vis. ant 3,683t/174g TL: N32 24 56 W110 42 50 On air date: Feb 1, 1967. 1855 N. 6th Ave., Tucson, AZ, 85705-5061. Phone: (520) 770-1123. Fax: (520) 629-7185. Web Site: www.kmsb.com. Licensee: Belo TV Inc. Group Owner: Belo Corp., Broadcast Division (acq 2-28-97; grpsl). Natl. Network: Fox, . Natl. Rep: TeleRep,. Washington Atty: Wiley, Rein & Fielding.
Key Personnel:
Lou Medran . . . . . opns dir
John Stringer. . . . . sls dir & gen sls mgr
Jim Watson . . . . . rgnl sls mgr
Brian Gee . . . . . mktg dir
Brian Baltosewicz . . . . . prom dir
Lynn Bernadett . . . . . progmg dir
Bob Lee . . . . . pub affrs dir
Walcott Denison III . . . . . chief of engrg
Tricia Terrell. . . . . rsch dir
Dale Warshaw . . . . . pub svc dir

KOLD-TV— Digital Channel: 32. Digital Hrs: 24 302 kw vis, 3 kw aur. ant 2,040t/187g TL: N32 14 56 W110 06 58 On air date: Jan 13, 1953. 7831 N. Business Park Dr., Tucson, AZ, 85743. Phone: (520) 744-1313. Fax: (520) 744-5233. Web Site: www.kold.com. Licensee: KOLD License Subsidiary LLC. Group Owner: Raycom Media Inc. (acq 9-12-96). Population Served: 1,100,000 Natl. Network: CBS, . Natl. Rep: Harrington, Righter & Parsons,. Washington Atty: Covington & Burling. Wire Svc: NWS (National Weather Service) Wire Svc: AP News: 27 hrs wkly.
Key Personnel:
Jim Arnold . . . . . VP & gen mgr stn mgr
Bob Gaff . . . . . opns mgr
Adam Weyne . . . . . gen sls mgr
Bob Duffy. . . . . rgnl sls mgr
Lec Coble . . . . . mktg dir
Michelle Germano . . . . . news dir
Stewart Roman. . . . . chief of engrg

KTTU— Digital Channel: 19. Digital Hrs: 8:30 AM-5:30 PM 2510 kw vis, 251 kw aur. ant 1,970t/200g TL: N32 14 55 W111 06 57 On air date: Dec 31, 1984. 1855 N. 6th Ave., Tucson, AZ, 85705. Phone: (520) 624-0180. Fax: (520) 629-7185. Web Site: www.kttu.com. Licensee: KTTU-TV Inc. Group Owner: Belo Corp., Broadcast Division (acq 2-28-2002; $18 million). Population Served: 750,000 Natl. Network: MyNetworkTV, . Natl. Rep: TeleRep,. Washington Atty: Hogan & Hartson. Foreign lang progmg: SpanishS 1
Key Personnel:
Lou Medran . . . . . pres & opns mgr
John Stringer . . . . . gen mgr & sls dir
Jim Watson . . . . . rgnl sls mgr
Brian Baltosewicz . . . . . prom dir
Brian Gee . . . . . progmg dir
Walcott Denison III . . . . . chief of engrg

***KUAS-TV—** Digital Channel: 28.151 kw vis, 15.1 kw aur. 570t/15g TL: N32 12 53 W111 00 21 (CP: 30.2 kw vis) On air date: January 1986. Box 210067, University of Arizona, Carthage, AZ, 85721-0067. Phone: (520) 621-5828. Fax: (520) 621-4122 (news). Web Site: www.kuat.org. Licensee: Arizona Board of Regents, University of Arizona. Natl. Network: PBS, . Washington Atty: Dow, Lohnes & Albertson. Foreign lang progmg: SpanishS 1
Key Personnel:
Jack Parris. . . . . gen mgr
Rudy Casillas . . . . . progmg dir & progmg mgr
Rebecca Kunsberg . . . . . film buyer & traf mgr
Hector Gonzalez . . . . . news dir
John Anderson . . . . . chief of engrg

***KUAT-TV—** Digital Channel: 30. Digital Hrs: 24 667.5 kw vis. ant 3,582t/163g TL: N32 24 55 W110 42 51 On air date: Mar 8, 1959. Box 210067, University of Arizona, Tucson, AZ, 85721-0067. 1423 E. University Blvd., Tucson, AZ 85721-0067. Phone: (520) 621-5828. Fax: (520) 621-4122 (news). Web Site: www.kuat.org. Licensee: Arizona Board of Regents, University of Arizona. Population Served: 800,000 Natl. Network: PBS, . Washington Atty: Dow, Lohnes & Albertson. Foreign lang progmg: SpanishS 7
Key Personnel:
Jack Gibson . . . . . gen mgr
Michael Serres. . . . . prom mgr
Rudy Casillas . . . . . progmg dir & film buyer
Peter Michaels . . . . . news dir
David Ross . . . . . chief of engrg

KUVE-DT— Digital Channel: 46.1,679 kw vis. ant 3,592t/174g TL: N32 24 54 W110 42 56 On air date: 2002. 2301 N. Forbes Blvd., Suite 103, Tucson, AZ, 85745. Phone: (520) 204-1245. Fax: (520) 204-1247. Licensee: Univision Television Group Inc. Group Owner: Univision Communications Inc. (acq 9-24-2003; $12.3 million). Natl. Network: Univision (Spanish), .
Key Personnel:
Ramon J. Pineda . . . . . gen mgr

KVOA— Digital Channel: 23. Digital Hrs: 24 35 kw vis, 18 kw aur. 3,610t/223g TL: N32 12 53 W111 00 20 On air date: Sept 15, 1953. Box 5188, Tucson, AZ, 85703-0188. 209 W. Elm St., Tucson, AZ 85705-6538. Phone: (520) 792-2270. Fax: (520) 620-1309. Web Site: www.kvoa.com. Licensee: KVOA Communications Inc. Group Owner: Cordillera Communications Inc. (acq 12-31-93; $13.25 million; 11-15-93). Population Served: 1,061,000 Natl. Network: NBC, . Natl. Rep: Millennium Sales & Marketing,. Washington Atty: Dow, Lohnes & Albertson. News: 27 hrs wkly.
Key Personnel:
Gary R. Nielsen. . . . . pres & gen mgr
Dave Kerrigan . . . . . opns mgr
Yvette Perez . . . . . mktg dir
Kathleen Choal . . . . . news dir

KWBA-TV— Digital Channel: 44.1,000 kw vis, 100 kw aur. ant 1,046t/125g TL: N31 45 32 W110 48 03 On air date: Jan 1, 1999. 7280 E. Rosewood St., Tucson, AZ, 85710. Phone: (520) 722-5486. Fax: (520) 733-7050.E-mail: soundoff@kwba.com Web Site: www.kwba.com. Licensee: Journal Broadcast Corp. Group Owner: Cascade Broadcasting Group L.L.C. (acq 7-22-2008; $11.885 million). Natl. Network: CW, . Washington Atty: Leventhal Senter & Lerman PLLC.
Key Personnel:
Julie Brinks. . . . . gen mgr

Yuma, AZ-El Centro, CA (DMA 164)

KAJB— Digital Channel: 36.5,000 kw vis. ant 1,404t/308g TL: N33 03 02 W114 49 38 On air date: 2002. 1803 N. Imperial Ave., El Centro, CA, 92243. Phone: (760) 482-7777. Fax: (760) 482-0099. Licensee: Calipatria Broadcasting Com. L.L.C. Ownership: Kenneth D. Pollin. (acq 12-16-97; $30,000). Foreign lang progmg: SpanishS 168
Key Personnel:
Eric Chavez . . . . . gen mgr
Albert Valdez . . . . . stn mgr

KECY-TV— Digital Channel: 9. Digital Hrs: 24 Note: Fox is on KECY-TV ch 9, ABC is on KECY-DT ch 48. 316 kw vis, 31.6 kw aur. ant 1,720t/460g TL: N33 03 19 W114 49 39 On air date: Dec 11, 1968. 1965 S. 4th Ave., Suite B, Yuma, AZ, 85364. Phone: (928) 539-9990. Fax: (928) 343-0218. Licensee: Gulf-California Broadcast Co. (acq 5-5-2008; $2 million). Population Served: 250,000 Natl. Network: Fox, ABC, Natl. Rep: Millennium Sales & Marketing,. Washington Atty: Smithwick & Belendiuk.
Key Personnel:
Deborah Weekes . . . . . gen mgr
Darin Coragata. . . . . gen sls mgr
Deborah Weeks . . . . . natl sls mgr
Jesus Corona . . . . . prom mgr
Adriana Sanchez. . . . . progmg mgr
Linda Young . . . . . traf mgr

KSWT— Digital Channel: 13. Digital Hrs: 5:45 AM-3 AM Note: CBS is on KSWT(TV) ch 13, CW is on KSWT-DT ch 16. 20 kw vis. ant 1,574t TL: N33 03 17 W114 49 34 On air date: Dec 1, 1963. 1301 S. 3rd Ave., Yuma, AZ, 85364. Phone: (928) 782-5113. Fax: (928) 783-0866.E-mail: kswt@adelphia.net Web Site: www.kswt.com. Licensee: Pappas Arizona License LLC. Group Owner: Pappas Telecasting Companies (acq 9-8-2000; $5.375 million). Population Served: 303,000 Natl. Network: CBS, CW, Washington Atty: Paul, Hastings, Janofsky & Walker. News staff: 8; News: 5 hrs wkly.

KVYE— Digital Channel: 22. Digital Hrs: 24 316 kw vis. 895t TL: N33 03 21 W115 49 44 On air date: July 1996. 1803 N. Imperial Ave., El Centro, CA, 92243. Phone: (760) 482-7777. Fax: (760) 482-0099.E-mail: avaldez@entravision.com Web Site: www.entravision.com. Licensee: Entravision Holdings L.L.C. Group Owner: Entravision Communications Co. L.L.C. (acq 2-19-98; $500,000 for CP). Population Served: 147,000 Natl. Network: Univision (Spanish), . Washington Atty: Thompson, Hine & Flory L. Foreign lang progmg: SpanishS 24 News staff: 8; News: 5 hrs wkly.
Key Personnel:
Walter Ulloa. . . . . CEO
Philip Wilkinson . . . . . CFO
Albert Valdez. . . . . gen mgr & opns mgr

KYMA-DT— Digital Channel: 11. Digital Hrs: 24 316 kw vis, 31.6 kw aur. ant 518t/1,617g TL: N33 03 10 W114 49 40 On air date: January 1988. 1385 S. Pacific Ave., Yuma, AZ, 85365-1725. Phone: (928) 782-1111. Fax: (928) 782-5401. Web Site: www.kyma.com. Licensee: Yuma Broadcasting Co. Group Owner: Sunbelt Communications Co. (acq 6-6-89; $60,000;6-26-89). Population Served: 86,900 Natl. Network: NBC, . Washington Atty: Dow, Lohnes & Albertson. News staff: 24; News: 12 hrs wkly.
Key Personnel:
Paul Heebink. . . . . gen mgr
Barbara Monroy . . . . . progmg dir & traf mgr
Luis Cruz . . . . . news dir
Robbie Decorse . . . . . chief of engrg & farm dir

Arkansas

El Dorado

see Monroe, LA-El Dorado, AR market

Fayetteville

see Ft. Smith-Fayetteville-Springdale-Rogers, AR market

Ft. Smith-Fayetteville -Springdale-Rogers, AR (DMA 100)

***KAFT—** Digital Channel: 9.37.9 kw vis. ant 1,650t/1,064g TL: N35 48 53 W94 01 41 On air date: Sept 18, 1976. Box 1250, Conway, AR, 72033. 350 S. Donaghey, Conway, AR 72034. Phone: (501) 682-2386. Phone: (800) 662-2386. Fax: (501) 682-4122.E-mail: info@aetn.org Web Site: www.aetn.org. Licensee: Arkansas Educational Television Commission. Population Served: 657,000 Natl. Network: PBS, . Rgnl. Network: SECA. Washington Atty: Dow, Lohnes & Albertson.
Key Personnel:
Allen Weatherly . . . . . gen mgr
Tony Brooks . . . . . stn mgr
Robert Bland . . . . . opns dir
Mona Dixon . . . . . dev dir

KFSM-TV— Digital Channel: 18. Digital Hrs: 24 100 kw vis, 12.7 kw aur. ant 1,086t/1,173g TL: N35 30 43 W94 21 38 On air date: Dec 3, 1956. Box 369, 318 N. 13th St. (72901), Calgary, AR, 72901. Phone: (479) 783-3131. Fax: (479) 783-3295. Web Site: www.5newsonline.com. Licensee: Local TV Arkansas License LLC. Group Owner: The New

York Times Co. (acq 5-7-2007; grpsl). Population Served: 883,500 Natl. Network: CBS, . Washington Atty: DowLohnes, PLLC. News staff: 36; News: 28 hrs wkly.
Key Personnel:
Debby Etzkorn . . . . pres & progmg dir
Van Comer. . . . . gen mgr
Mark LaCrue . . . . gen sls mgr
Rose Smith . . . . prom mgr & traf mgr
Jimmy Poole . . . . chief of engrg

KFTA-TV— Digital Channel: 27. Digital Hrs: 24 2,510 kw vis, 251 kw aur. ant 1,040t/499g TL: N35 42 37 W94 08 15 On air date: Nov 12, 1978. 15 South Block Ave., Suite 101, Fayetteville, AR, 72701. Phone: (479) 571-5100. Fax: (479) 571-8914.E-mail: news@knwa.com Web Site: nwahomepage.com. Licensee: Nexstar Broadcasting Inc. (acq 1-7-2005; $10 million with KNWA-TV Rogers). Population Served: 690,000 Natl. Network: Fox, . Natl. Rep: TeleRep,. Washington Atty: Holland & Knight. News staff: 45; News: 20.5 hrs wkly.
Key Personnel:
Mike Vaughn . . . . VP & gen mgr
Cheryl Gwym . . . . opns mgr

KHBS— Digital Channel: 21.Note: ABC is on KHBS(TV) ch 40, CW is on KHBS-DT ch 21. 3,160 kw vis, 316 kw aur. ant 2,000t/500g TL: N35 04 16 W94 40 46 On air date: July 28, 1971. 2415 N. Albert Pike, Fort Smith, AR, 72904-5698. Phone: (479) 783-4040. Fax: (479) 785-5375.E-mail: news@4029tv.com Web Site: www.thehometownchannel.com. Licensee: KHBS Hearst-Argyle Television Inc. Group Owner: Hearst-Argyle Television Inc. (acq 7-16-97; grpsl). Population Served: 153,700 Natl. Network: ABC, CW, Washington Atty: Wiley, Rein & Fielding. News staff: 30; News: 15 hrs wkly.
Key Personnel:
Jim Prestwood . . . . gen mgr

KHOG-TV— Digital Channel: 15. Digital Hrs: 24 (Su-F) 1410 kw vis, 150 kw aur. ant 890t/556g TL: N36 00 57 W94 04 59 On air date: December 1977. 2415 N. Albert Pike, Fort Smith, AR, 72904. Phone: (479) 783-4040 / (479) 521-1010. Fax: (479) 785-5375 / (479) 479-9124.E-mail: news@4029tv.com Web Site: www.thehometownchannel.com. Licensee: KHBS Hearst-Argyle Television Inc. Group Owner: Hearst-Argyle Television Inc. (acq 7-16-97; grpsl). Population Served: 250,000 Natl. Network: ABC, CW, . Washington Atty: Wiley, Rein & Fielding.
Key Personnel:
Jim Prestwood . . . . gen mgr

KNWA-TV— Digital Channel: 50. Digital Hrs: 22 1,000 kw vis. ant 876t/480g TL: N36 24 47.8 W93 57 16.8 On air date: Aug 23, 1989. 15 South Block St., Suite 101, Fayetteville, AR, 72701. Phone: (479) 571-5100. Fax: (479) 571-8914. Web Site: www.nwahomepage.com. Licensee: Nexstar Broadcasting Inc. (acq 1-7-2005; $10 million with KFTA-TV Fort Smith). Population Served: 107,830 Natl. Network: NBC, . Natl. Rep: Blair Television,. Washington Atty: Drinker, Biddle & Reath. News staff: 27; News: 17 hrs wkly.
Key Personnel:
Mike Vaughn . . . . VP & gen mgr
Eric Dunivan. . . . . natl sls mgr
Brook Thomas . . . . news dir
Lisa Kelsey. . . . . sls
Satellite of KFTA-TV Fort Smith.

KPBI— Digital Channel: 34. Digital Hrs: 24 1,000 kw vis. ant 736t/322g TL: N36 24 41 W93 57 12 On air date: 2000. Stn currently dark Two Greenwich Plaza, Greenwich, CT, 06830. Phone: (203) 542-4200. Licensee: SP NW Arkansas LLC.. Ownership: SP Television LLC, 100% Group Owner: Equity Broadcasting Corp. (acq 8-4-2009; $500,000).
Key Personnel:
Duane Lammers . . . . pres
Ed Mule . . . . gen mgr

KWOG— Digital Channel: 39. Digital Hrs: 24 35 kw vis. ant 374t/315g TL: N36 11 07 W94 17 49 On air date: Dec 11, 1995. Box 612066, Dallas, TX, 75261-2066. Phone: (817) 571-1229. Fax: (817) 571-8962. Web Site: ww2.daystar.com. Licensee: Word of God Fellowship Inc. (acq 7-7-2006; $1.5 million).
Key Personnel:
Harvey Rogers . . . . chief of engrg

Harrison

see Springfield, MO market

Jonesboro, AR (DMA 181)

KAIT— Digital Channel: 8. Digital Hrs: 24 316 kw vis, 47.9 kw aur. ant 1,750t/1,799g TL: N35 53 17 W90 56 09 On air date: July 15, 1963. Box 790, Jonesboro, AR, 72403-0790. 472 Country Rd. 766, Jonesboro, AZ 72401. Phone: (870) 931-8888. Fax: (870) 933-8058 (news). Fax: (870) 931-1371(sales). Web Site: www.kait8.com. Licensee: KAIT License Subsidiary LLC. Group Owner: Liberty Corp. (acq 1-31-2006; grpsl). Population Served: 704,000 Natl. Network: ABC, . Natl. Rep: Harrington, Righter & Parsons,. Washington Atty: Covington & Burling. Wire Svc: Weather Wire Wire Svc: AP News staff: 32; News: 17 hrs wkly.
Key Personnel:
Tim Ingram . . . . VP & gen mgr
Ronnie Weston . . . . opns dir
Stephanie Duckworth . . . . sls dir & gen sls mgr
Ralph Caudill . . . . natl sls mgr
Jeremy Shirley . . . . mktg dir & pub affrs dir
Randy Parrott. news dir
Gerald Erickson. . . . . chief of engrg
Tory Shirley . . . . rsch dir
Debi Gann . . . . traf mgr
Glenn Marini . . . . sports cmtr

***KTEJ—** Digital Channel: 20.1,230 kw vis, 123 kw aur. 1,020t/969g TL: N35 54 14 W90 46 14 On air date: May 1, 1976. Box 1250, Conway, AR, 72033. 350 S. Donaghey, Conway, AR 72034. Phone: (501) 682-2386. Phone: (800) 662-2386. Fax: (501) 682-4122. Web Site: www.aetn.org. Licensee: Arkansas Educational Television Commission. Population Served: 505,000 Natl. Network: PBS, . Rgnl. Network: SECA. Washington Atty: Dow, Lohnes & Albertson.
Key Personnel:
Allen Weatherly . . . . gen mgr
Tony Brooks . . . . stn mgr
Robert Bland . . . . opns dir
Mona Dixon . . . . dev dir

KVTJ-DT— Digital Channel: 48. Digital Hrs: 24 1,000 kw vis. 1,023t/1,791g TL: N35 53 17 W90 56 09 On air date: June 6, 1998. 701 Napa Valley Dr., Little Rock, AR, 72211. Phone: (501) 223-2525. Fax: (501) 221-3837.E-mail: jim.grant@vtntv.com Web Site: www.vtntv.com. Licensee: Agape Church Inc. Group Owner: The Victory Television Network (acq 1995).
Key Personnel:
Jim Grant . . . . gen mgr

Little Rock-Pine Bluff, AR (DMA 56)

KARK-TV— Digital Channel: 32. Digital Hrs: 24 100 kw vis, 20 kw aur. 1,650t/1,175g TL: N34 47 57 W92 29 59 On air date: Apr 15, 1954. 1401 W. Capitol Ave., Suite 104, Little Rock, AR, 72201. Phone: (501) 340-4444. Fax: (501) 376-1852. Web Site: www.kark.com. Licensee: Nexstar Broadcasting Inc. Group Owner: Nexstar Broadcasting Group Inc. (acq 8-1-2003; $40 million with WDHN(TV) Dothan, AL). Population Served: 1,177,000 Natl. Network: NBC, . Natl. Rep: Petry Television Inc.,. Wire Svc: Photofax News staff: 40; News: 22 hrs wkly.
Key Personnel:
Rick Rogala . . . . gen mgr
Craig Castrellon . . . . gen sls mgr
Cindy Rochelle. . . . . natl sls mgr
Ed Tudor . . . . prom dir
Mary Mobbs. . . . . progmg dir & traf mgr
Bill Addington . . . . chief of engrg

KARZ-TV— Digital Channel: 44. Digital Hrs: 24 1,000 kw vis. ant 1,471t/860g TL: N34 47 57 W92 29 59 On air date: Dec 1, 1997. 1401 W. Capitol Ave., Suite 104, Little Rock, AR, 72201. Phone: (501) 340-4444. Fax: (501) 376-1852. Web Site: www.arkansasmatters.com. Licensee: Nexstar Broadcasting Inc. Group Owner: Equity Broadcasting Corp. (acq 3-12-2009; $4 million). Natl. Network: MyNetworkTV, .
Key Personnel:
Rick Rogala . . . . gen mgr

KASN— Digital Channel: 39.5,000 kw vis, 500 kw aur. ant 2,008t/1,910g TL: N34 26 31 W92 13 03 On air date: June 17, 1986. 10800 Colonel Glenn, Little Rock, AR, 72204. Phone: (501) 225-0038 / 0016. Fax: (501) 225-0428. Web Site: www.fox16.com. Licensee: Newport Television License LLC. Group Owner: (group owner; (acq 3-14-2008; grpsl). Population Served: 481,000 Natl. Network: CW, .
Key Personnel:
Chuck Spohn. . . . . gen mgr
Vickie McRae . . . . gen sls mgr
Holly Rose . . . . rgnl sls mgr
Jim Hays. . . . . mktg dir
Miranda Morris . . . . progmg dir
Michael Fabac . . . . news dir & rsch dir
Alan Finne. . . . . chief of engrg
Joan Hall. . . . . traf mgr
Jonothan Nettles . . . . pub svc dir
John Foster . . . . film dir

KATV— Digital Channel: 22.316 kw vis, 36.5 kw aur. 2,272t/2,000g TL: N34 28 23 W92 12 11 On air date: Dec 18, 1953. Box 77, Little Rock, AR, 72203. Phone: (501) 324-7777. Fax: (501) 324-7899. Web Site: www.katv.com. Licensee: KATV L.L.C. Group Owner: Allbritton Communications Co. (acq 2-14-83; grpsl). Population Served: 169,700 Natl. Network: ABC, . Washington Atty: Hogan & Hartson.
Key Personnel:
Dale Nicholson . . . . pres & gen mgr
Mark Rose . . . . gen sls mgr
Richard Farrester . . . . progmg dir
Randy Dixon . . . . news dir
Fred Anderson . . . . chief of engrg
Laura Story . . . . traf mgr & pub svc dir

***KEMV—** Digital Channel: 13.100 kw vis, 10 kw aur. 1,390t/995g TL: N35 48 47 W92 17 24 On air date: Nov 11, 1980. Box 1250, Conway, AR, 72033. 350 S. Donaghey, Conway, AR 72034. Phone: (501) 450-1727. Phone: (501) 682-2386. Fax: (501) 682-4122. Web Site: www.aetn.org. Licensee: Arkansas Educational Television Commission. Population Served: 655,000 Natl. Network: PBS, . Rgnl. Network: SECA. Washington Atty: Dow, Lohnes & Albertson.
Key Personnel:
Allen Weatherly . . . . gen mgr
Tony Brooks . . . . stn mgr
Robert Bland . . . . opns dir
Mona Dixon . . . . dev dir & dev mgr

***KETG—** Digital Channel: 13.316 kw vis, 31.6 kw aur. 1,070t/1,110g TL: N33 54 26 W93 06 46 On air date: Oct 2, 1976. Box 1250, Conway, AR, 72033. 350 S. Donaghey St., Conway, AR 72034. Phone: (501) 682-2386. Phone: (800) 662-2386. Fax: (501) 682-4122.E-mail: info@aetn.org Web Site: www.aetn.org. Licensee: Arkansas Educational Television Commission. Population Served: 379,000 Natl. Network: PBS, . Rgnl. Network: SECA. Washington Atty: Dow, Lohnes & Albertson.
Key Personnel:
Allen Weatherly . . . . gen mgr
Tony Brooks . . . . stn mgr
Robert Bland . . . . opns dir
Mona Dixon . . . . dev dir

***KETS—** Digital Channel: 7.100 kw vis, 10 kw aur. 1,780t/2,000g TL: N34 28 23 W92 12 11 On air date: Dec 4, 1966. Box 1250, Conway, AR, 72033. 350 S. Donaghey, Conway, AR 72034. Phone: (501) 682-2386. Phone: (800) 662-2386. Fax: (501) 682-4122. Web Site: www.aetn.org. Licensee: Arkansas Eucational Television Commission. Population Served: 1,523,000 Natl. Network: PBS, . Rgnl. Network: SECA. Washington Atty: Dow, Lohnes & Albertson.
Key Personnel:
Allen Weatherly . . . . gen mgr
Tony Brooks . . . . stn mgr
Robert Bland . . . . opns dir
Mona Dixon . . . . dev dir

***KKAP—** Digital Channel: 36. Digital Hrs: 24 1,000 kw vis. ant 1,296t/656g TL: N34 47 56 W92 29 45 On air date: 2001. 3901 Hwy 121, Bedford, TX, 76034. Phone: (817) 571-1229. Fax: (817) 571-7458. Web Site: www.daystart.com. Licensee: Educational Broadcasting Corp. Ownership: Dr. Tracy Harris, 14%; Eric S. Erickson, 14%; Gregory Fess, 14%; Joni T. Lamb, 14%; Larry Morton, 14%; Marcus Lamb, 14%; and Max Hooper, 14% (acq 7-6-2001; $1 million).

KKYK-DT— Digital Channel: 49.1,000 kw vis. ant 600t/571g TL: N33 16 15 W92 42 14 On air date: 1997. 1 Shackelford Dr., Little Rock, AR, 72211. Phone: (501) 219-2400. Fax: (501) 604-8004. Licensee: Arkansas 49 Inc., debtor in possession. Group Owner: Equity Broadcasting Corp. (acq 9-15-99).
Key Personnel:
Neal Ardman . . . . gen mgr
Tammy Graham . . . . opns mgr
Aaron Rothberg . . . . gen sls mgr
Chuck Stanely . . . . chief of engrg

KLRT-TV— Digital Channel: 30. Digital Hrs: 24 5,000 kw vis, 500 kw aur. ant 1,772t/1,266g TL: N34 47 57 W92 29 52 On air date: June 26, 1983. 10800 Colonel Glenn, Little Rock, AR, 72204. Phone: (501) 225-0016. Fax: (501) 225-0428. Web Site: www.fox16.com. Licensee: Newport Television License LLC. Group Owner: Clear Channel Communications Inc. (acq 3-14-2008; grpsl). Natl. Network: Fox, . Washington Atty: Covington & Burling.
Key Personnel:
Chuck Spohn. . . . . gen mgr
Vicki McRae. . . . . gen sls mgr
Jim Hays. . . . . mktg dir
Logan Wilcoxson . . . . prom dir
Miranda Morris . . . . progmg dir
Michael Fabac . . . . news dir & pub affrs dir
Alan Finne. . . . . chief of engrg
Joan Hall. . . . . traf mgr

KTHV— Digital Channel: 12. Analog Hrs: 00 Digital Hrs: 24 316 kw vis, 38 kw aur. 1,709t TL: N34 47 57 W92 29 59 On air date: Nov 27,

1955. Box 269, Little Rock, AR, 72203. 720 Izard St., Little Rock, AR 72201. Phone: (501) 376-1111. Fax: (501) 376-3324.E-mail: 11listens@todaysthu.com Web Site: www.todaysthv.com. Licensee: Arkansas Television Co. Group Owner: Gannett Broadcasting (acq 11-30-94; $27 million;1-16-95). Population Served: 152,483 Natl. Network: CBS, . Natl. Rep: Blair Television,. Washington Atty: Wiley, Rein & Fielding. News staff: 55; News: 20 hrs wkly.

Key Personnel:

Larry Audas	chmn & pres gen mgr
Alison Fletcher	opns mgr & chief of opns chief of engrg
Leslie Heizman	gen sls mgr
Chad Kelley	natl sls mgr
Joanne Canelli	rgnl sls mgr
David Craft	mktg VP & mktg dir prom VP & prom dir
Bobbie Rawlins	progmg dir
Mark Raines	news dir
Sharon Addington	traf mgr
Theba Lolley	pub affrs dir & pub svc dir

KVTH-DT— Digital Channel: 26. Digital Hrs: 24 245 kw vis, 24.5 kw aur. 941t TL: N32 22 20 W93 02 47 (CP: 5,000 kw vis, ant 902t. TL: N34 22 17 W93 02 16) On air date: 1991. 701 Napa Valley Dr., Little Rock, AR, 72211. Phone: (501) 223-2525. Fax: (501) 221-3837.E-mail: jim.grant@vtntv.com Web Site: www.vtntv.com. Licensee: Agape Church. Group Owner: The Victory Television Network (acq 1994).

Key Personnel:

Jim Grant	gen mgr

Satellite of KVTN(TV) Pine Bluff.

KVTN-DT— Digital Channel: 24. Digital Hrs: 24 4,370 kw vis, 43.7 kw aur. ant 594t/594g TL: N34 31 55 W92 02 41 On air date: Dec 1, 1988. 701 Napa Valley Dr., Little Rock, AR, 72211. Phone: (501) 223-2525. Fax: (501) 221-3837.E-mail: jim.grant@vtntv.com Web Site: www.vtntv.com. Licensee: Agape Church Inc. Group Owner: The Victory Television Network (acq 6-87); $41,000;5-1-87). Washington Atty: John Fiorini.

Key Personnel:

Jim Grant	gen mgr
Andrea Qualls	prom dir
Kim Worden	progmg dir
Ron Brown	engrg dir
Sharon Case	traf mgr

Pine Bluff

see Little Rock-Pine Bluff, AR market

Rogers

see Ft. Smith-Fayetteville-Springdale-Rogers, AR market

Springdale

see Ft. Smith-Fayetteville-Springdale-Rogers, AR market

California

Bakersfield, CA
(DMA 125)

KBAK-TV— Digital Channel: 33. Digital Hrs: 24 1,700 kw vis, 340 kw aur. 3,730t/230g TL: N35 27 11 W118 35 25 On air date: Aug 23, 1953. Box 2929, Bakersfield, CA, 93303. 1901 Westwind Dr., Bakersfield, CA 93301. Phone: (661) 327-7955. Fax: (661) 327-5603. Web Site: eyeoutforyou.com. Licensee: Fisher Broadcasting - California TV L.L.C. (acq 1-1-2008; $55 million). Population Served: 566,000 Natl. Network: CBS, . Natl. Rep: Continental Television Sales,. Washington Atty: Pillsbury Winthrop Shaw Pittman LLP. Wire Svc: AP News staff: 40; News: 30.5 hrs wkly.

Key Personnel:

Troy McGuire	gen mgr
Pete Capra	opns mgr & chief of engrg
Cindi Dias	gen sls mgr
Tracy Peoples	prom dir & engrg dir
Nancy Clarke	progmg dir & progmg mgr
Meaghan St.Pierre	news dir
Janice Curliss	traf mgr

KERO-TV— Digital Channel: 10. Digital Hrs: 24 1,760 kw vis, 64.6 kw aur. 3,700t/183g TL: N35 27 14 W118 35 37 On air date: Sept 26, 1953. 321 21st St., Bakersfield, CA, 93301. Phone: (661) 637-2323. Fax: (661) 322-1701. Web Site: www.thebakersfieldchannel.com.

Licensee: McGraw-Hill Broadcasting Co. Group Owner: (group owner; (acq 3-8-72); grpsl;3-13-72). Population Served: 2,034,000 Natl. Network: ABC, . Natl. Rep: Harrington, Righter & Parsons,. Washington Atty: Holland & Knight.

Key Personnel:

Steve McEvoy	gen mgr
Steve Taylor	prom mgr
Craig Jahelka	progmg VP & progmg dir
Todd Karli	news dir
Tom Wimberly	engrg mgr & chief of engrg
Maxcine Cole	traf mgr
Lesley Kirk	edit dir

KGET-TV— Analog Channel: 17. Digital Channel: 25.5,000 kw vis, 500 kw aur. ant 1,400t/288g TL: N35 26 20 W118 44 23 On air date: Nov 8, 1959. 2120 L St., Bakersfield, CA, 93301. Phone: (661) 283-1700. Fax: (661) 283-1794. Web Site: www.kget.com. Licensee: High Plains Broadcasting License Co. LLC. Group Owner: Clear Channel Communications Inc. (acq 9-15-2008; grpsl). Population Served: 523,000 Natl. Network: NBC, . News staff: 33; News: 27 hrs wkly.

Key Personnel:

Teri Riley	VP & gen mgr
Kristi Spitzer	sls dir
Jim Tripeny	prom mgr
Shirley Sanford	progmg dir
John Pilios	news dir
Kathleen McNeil	pub affrs dir
Tom Ballew	chief of engrg

KUVI-DT— Digital Channel: 45. Digital Hrs: 24 5,000 kw vis, 500 kw aur. ant 1,325t/144g TL: N36 26 20 W118 44 24 On air date: Dec 18, 1988. 5801 Truxtun Ave., Bakersfield, CA, 93309. Phone: (661) 324-0045. Fax: (661) 334-2693. Web Site: www.kuvi45.com. Licensee: KUVI License Partnership G.P. Group Owner: Univision Communications Inc. (acq 2-4-98; $14,010,800). Population Served: 508,000 Natl. Network: MyNetworkTV, . Washington Atty: Shaw Pittman.

Key Personnel:

Denise Snanoudt	natl sls mgr
Maritere Alvarez-Jackson	rgnl sls mgr
Teresa Ford	gen mgr & opns mgr progmg dir & film buyer
Maria Herrandez	pub affrs dir
Ken Richter	chief of engrg
Clerinda Briones	traf mgr
Maria Hernandez	pub svc dir
Joe Gaiski	film dir

Calipatria

see Yuma, AZ-El Centro, CA market

Chico-Redding, CA
(DMA 130)

KCVU— Digital Channel: 20. Digital Hrs: 24 2,510 kw vis, 252 kw aur. ant 2,447t/250g TL: N39 57 45 W121 42 40 On air date: November 1990. 300 Main St., Chico, CA, 95928-5438. Phone: (530) 893-1234. Fax: (530) 899-5475.E-mail: info@fox30.com Web Site: www.fox30.com. Licensee: Sainte Partners II L.P. Group Owner: (group owner) Population Served: 445,000 Natl. Network: Fox, . Natl. Rep: Millennium Sales & Marketing,. Washington Atty: Fletcher, Heald & Hildreth. News: 0 hrs wkly.

Key Personnel:

Doug Holroyd	gen mgr
Bert Westhoff	natl sls mgr
Glenn Taylor	rgnl sls mgr
Paula Murphy	progmg mgr
Ken Rice	chief of engrg
Betsy Brewer	prom

KHSL-TV— Digital Channel: 43. Digital Hrs: 24 Note: CBS is on KHSL-TV ch 12, CW is on KHSL-DT ch 43. 316 kw vis, 38 kw aur. ant 1,300t/287g TL: N39 57 30 W121 42 48 On air date: Aug 29, 1953. 3460 Silverbell Rd., Chico, CA, 95973. Phone: (530) 342-0141. Fax: (530) 342-4905.E-mail: khsltv@khsltv.com Web Site: www.khsltv.com. Licensee: Catamount Broadcasting of Chico-Redding Inc.. Ownership: Catamount Holdings LLC, 100% votes Group Owner: Catamount Broadcast Group (acq 7-30-98; $10 million). Population Served: 480,000 Natl. Network: CBS, CW, Natl. Rep: Continental Television Sales,. Washington Atty: Haley, Bader & Potts. News staff: 34; News: 20 hrs wkly.

Key Personnel:

John Stall	gen mgr
Marnie McDonald	gen sls mgr
Morgan Schmidt	prom dir & prom mgr
Shannon Bomar	progmg dir
Trisha Coder	news dir
Dave Sien	chief of engrg

*KIXE-TV— Digital Channel: 9. Digital Hrs: 18 15 kw vis. ant 3,578t/86g TL: N40 36 09 W122 39 01 On air date: Oct 5, 1964. 603

N Market St., Redding, CA, 96003-3609. Phone: (530) 243-5493. Fax: (530) 243-7443.E-mail: channel9@kixe.org Web Site: www.kixe.org. Licensee: Northern California Educational TV Association Inc. Population Served: 500,000 Natl. Network: PBS, . Washington Atty: Schwartz, Woods & Miller. News: one hr wkly.

Key Personnel:

Myron A. Tisdel	pres & gen mgr
Renee Cooper	CFO
Myron Tisdel	stn mgr
Mike Lampella	opns dir
Anne Kerns	dev dir
Fred Gaines	rgnl sls mgr
Rob Keenan	progmg dir & progmg mgr
Sue Maxey	chief of engrg
Ken Simmon	traf mgr

KNVN— Digital Channel: 24. Digital Hrs: 24 321 kw vis. ant 1,771t/10g TL: N40 15 31 W122 05 24 On air date: Sept 24, 1985. 3460 Silverbell Rd., Chico, CA, 95973. Phone: (530) 894-6397. Fax: (530) 342-2405.E-mail: news@knvn.com Web Site: www.knvn.com. Licensee: Chico License L.L.C. Ownership: William Guy Evans, 51%; Janice Atkinson Evans, 49% (acq 6-2000; $9.2 million). Natl. Network: NBC, . Washington Atty: Leventhal, Senter & Lerman.

Key Personnel:

John Stall	gen mgr
Steve Sorenson	stn mgr
Scott Howard	news dir

KRCR-TV— Digital Channel: 7.115 kw vis, 22.4 kw aur. ant 3,620t/126g TL: N40 36 10 W122 39 00 On air date: Aug 1, 1956. Box 992217, 755 Auditorium Dr., Redding, CA, 96001. Phone: (530) 243-7777. Fax: (530) 243-0217.E-mail: info@krcrtv.com Web Site: www.krcrtv.com. Licensee: BlueStone License Holdings Inc. Group Owner: Lamco Communications Inc. (acq 5-31-2007; grpsl). Population Served: 180,000 Natl. Network: ABC, . Natl. Rep: Petry Television Inc.,. News staff: 21; News: 16 hrs wkly.

Key Personnel:

Penny Loll	progmg dir
Jennifer Scarbrough	news dir
Lance Cratty	chief of engrg
Jeremy Alexander	traf mgr

El Centro

see Yuma, AZ-El Centro, CA market

Eureka, CA
(DMA 195)

KAEF-TV— Digital Channel: 22.45 kw vis. ant 1,804t/419g TL: N40 43 39 W123 58 17 On air date: Aug 1, 1987. 540 E St., Eureka, CA, 95501. Phone: (707) 444-2323. Fax: (707) 445-9451.E-mail: kaeftv@kadf.com Licensee: BlueStone License Holdings Inc. Group Owner: Lamco Communications Inc. (acq 5-31-2007; grpsl). Natl. Network: ABC, . Washington Atty: Covington & Burling LLP. News staff: 2; News: 2 hrs wkly.

Key Personnel:

Leslie Lollich	gen mgr

KBVU— Digital Channel: 28. Digital Hrs: 24 50 kw vis. ant 1,683t/0g TL: N40 43 39 W123 58 17 On air date: July 20, 1994. 730 7th St., Suite 201, Eureka, CA, 95501. Phone: (707) 442-2999. Fax: (707) 441-0111. Web Site: www.eurekatelevision.tv. Licensee: Sainte Partners II L.P. Group Owner: (group owner; acq 7-24-97). Natl. Network: Fox, . Natl. Rep: Millennium Sales & Marketing,. Washington Atty: Womble, Carlyle, Sandrige & Rice.

Key Personnel:

Chester Smith	CEO
Don Smullin	gen mgr & stn mgr

*KEET— Digital Channel: 11. Digital Hrs: 24 182 kw vis. ant 1,804t/420g TL: N40 43 38 W123 58 16 On air date: Apr 14, 1969. Box 13, Eureka, CA, 95502. 7246 Humboldt Hill Rd., Eureka, CA 95503. Phone: (707) 445-0813. Fax: (707) 445-8977.E-mail: letters@keet.pbs.org Web Site: www.keet.com. Licensee: Redwood Empire Pub TV Inc. Population Served: 130,000 Natl. Network: PBS, .

Key Personnel:

Ronald L. Schoenherr	CEO & pres
Seth Frankel	opns dir
Karen Barnes	dev dir & progmg dir
Claire Reynolds	prom dir & pub svc dir
Joel Householter	chief of engrg
Therese Buck	traf mgr & pub svc dir

KIEM-TV— Digital Channel: 3. Digital Hrs: 24 100 kw vis, 10 kw aur. ant 1,650t/249g TL: N40 43 52 W123 57 06 On air date: Oct 25, 1953. 5650 S. Broadway, Eureka, CA, 95503. Phone: (707) 443-3123. Fax: (707) 442-6084. Web Site: www.kiem-tv.com. Licensee: Pollack/Belz

Broadcasting Co. L.L.C. Group Owner: Pollack Broadcasting Co. (acq 5-1-96; $3 million). Population Served: 139,400 Natl. Network: NBC, . Natl. Rep: Continental Television Sales,.
Key Personnel:
Robert Browning . . . gen mgr
Phil Wright . . . opns mgr & prom mgr
Hank Ingham . . . gen sls mgr
Shawna Brisco . . . progmg dir
Bob Brown . . . news dir
Bob Mottaz . . . chief of engrg
Marsha Kane . . . traf mgr

KVIQ— Digital Channel: 17.100 kw vis, 10.5 kw aur. ant 1,740t/377g TL: N40 43 36 W123 28 18 On air date: Apr 1, 1958. 730 7th St., Suite 201, Eureka, CA, 95501. Phone: (707) 443-3061. Fax: (707) 443-4435. Web Site: www.kviq.com. Licensee: Raul Broadcasting Co. of Eureka Inc.. Ownership: Raul Palazuelos, 100% Group Owner: Clear Channel Communications Inc. (acq 4-25-2005; $2 million). Population Served: 24,337 Natl. Network: CBS, .
Key Personnel:
John Burgess . . . gen mgr
Penny King . . . stn mgr & gen sls mgr
Rick St. Charles . . . prom dir
Lauren Faucett . . . progmg dir
Deve Silurrbrand . . . news dir
Jim Mixou . . . chief of engrg

Fresno-Visalia, CA (DMA 55)

KAIL— Digital Channel: 7. Digital Hrs: 24 2,510 kw vis, 251 kw aur. ant 1,906t/140g TL: N37 04 23 W119 15 52 On air date: Dec 18, 1961. 1590 Alluvial Ave., Clovis, CA, 93611. Phone: (559) 299-9753. Fax: (559) 299-1523. Web Site: www.kail.tv. Licensee: Trans-America Broadcasting Corp.. Ownership: Albert J. Williams, 79.9%; Jack M. Reeder, 20.1%. (acq 12-23-66; $236,500;12-26-66). Population Served: 1,700,000 Natl. Network: MyNetworkTV, . Washington Atty: Miller & Fields. News staff: 3; News: 5 hrs wkly.
Key Personnel:
G. Borrego . . . pres
Charles Williams . . . gen mgr
Mike Nicassio . . . opns mgr & chief of opns
Dave Hetrick . . . gen sls mgr
Robert Jenkins . . . progmg dir
Angela Bartley . . . traf mgr
Terrence Kendrials . . . prom VP & prom

KFRE-TV—(Sanger, Digital Channel: 36. Digital Hrs: 24 4,287 kw vis. ant 2,102t/246g TL: N37 04 37 W119 26 01 On air date: July 17, 1985. 5111 E. McKinley Ave., Fresno, CA, 93727. Phone: (559) 435-5900/(559) 252-5900. Fax: (559) 255-0275. Web Site: www.kfre.com. Licensee: KFRE(TV) License LLC. Group Owner: Pappas Telecasting Companies (acq 12-22-2003; $25 million). Population Served: 1,583,500 Natl. Network: CW, . Washington Atty: Cohn & Marks. News staff: 5; News: 2 hrs wkly.
Key Personnel:
Jack Peck . . . gen mgr
Ken Felder . . . stn mgr & gen sls mgr
Mark Hodorowski . . . mktg dir & progmg dir & progmg mgr

KFSN-TV— Digital Channel: 30. Digital Hrs: 24 260 kw vis, 26 kw aur. ant 2,050t/238g TL: N37 04 38 W119 26 00 On air date: May 10, 1956. 1777 G St., Fresno, CA, 93706-1688. Phone: (559) 442-1170. Fax: (559) 233-5844 (sls). Fax: (559) 266-5024 (news). Web Site: www.abc30.com. Licensee: KFSN Television LLC. Group Owner: (group owner). Population Served: 527,770 Natl. Network: ABC, . Natl. Rep: ABC National Television Sales,. Washington Atty: ABC Legal. News staff: 50; News: 30 hrs wkly.
Key Personnel:
Bob A. Hall . . . pres & gen mgr
Ron Neil . . . rgnl sls mgr & engrg dir
Charlene Ciavaglia . . . progmg mgr
Tracey Watkowski . . . news dir
Beth Marney . . . pub affrs dir

KFTV-DT— Digital Channel: 20. Digital Hrs: 24 5,000 kw vis, 605 kw aur. ant 1,984t/216g TL: N37 04 22 W119 25 50 On air date: July 1972. 3239 W. Ashlan Ave., Fresno, CA, 93722. Phone: (559) 222-2121. Fax: (559) 222-2890. Fax: (559) 222-0917. Web Site: www.univision.net. Licensee: KFTV L.P., G.P. Group Owner: Univision Communications Inc. (acq 8-87). Population Served: 637,000 Natl. Network: Univision (Spanish), . Washington Atty: Shaw Pittman LLP. Foreign lang progmg: SpanishS 168 News staff: 58; News: 8 hrs wkly.
Key Personnel:
Maria L. Gutierrez . . . gen mgr
Maria Gutierrez . . . stn mgr
Brett Covish . . . opns mgr & gen sls mgr
Ken Holden . . . chief of engrg

KGMC—(Clovis, Digital Channel: 43. Digital Hrs: 24 335 kw vis. ant 1,778t/102g TL: N37 04 26 W119 25 52 On air date: Sept 11, 1992. 706 W. Herndon Ave., Fresno, CA, 93650. Phone: (559) 432-4300. Phone: (559) 435-7000. Fax: (559) 435-3201.E-mail: info@cocolatv.com Web Site: www.cocolatv.com. Licensee: Gary M. Cocola. Group Owner: Cocola Broadcasting Companies (acq 11-19-92). Population Served: 1,400,000 Washington Atty: Dow, Lohnes & Albertson.
Key Personnel:
Gary M. Cocola . . . CEO & pres
Nick Giotto . . . opns dir
Kevin Mosesian . . . natl sls mgr
Nick Giotto . . . rgnl sls mgr
Joe Verdugo . . . adv dir
Nori Zahari . . . progmg VP
Al Kinney . . . engrg mgr

KGPE— Digital Channel: 34. Digital Hrs: 24 2,500 kw vis. ant 1,958t/226g TL: N37 04 14 W119 25 31 On air date: Oct 1, 1953. 4880 N. First St., Fresno, CA, 93720. Phone: (559) 222-2411. Fax: (559) 222-5593.E-mail: programming@cbs47.tv Web Site: www.cbs47.tv. Licensee: High Plains Broadcasting License Co. LLC. Group Owner: Clear Channel Communications Inc. (acq 9-15-2008; grpsl). Population Served: 1,453,000 Natl. Network: CBS, . Natl. Rep: Millennium Sales & Marketing,. Washington Atty: Pillsbury Winthrop Shaw Pittman LLP. News staff: 50; News: 28hrs wkly.
Key Personnel:
Steve Stendlove . . . exec VP
TB A . . . chief of opns & gen sls mgr
David King . . . natl sls mgr
Jim Holland . . . news dir
Tom Long . . . sls dir & rgnl sls mgr & sports cmtr

KMPH-TV—(Visalia, Digital Channel: 28.2,950 kw vis, 442 kw aur. ant 2,730t/252g TL: N36 17 12 W118 50 20 On air date: Oct 11, 1971. 5111 E. McKinley Ave., Fresno, CA, 93727-2033. Phone: (559) 255-2600. Fax: (559) 255-0275.E-mail: viewercomments@kmph.com Web Site: www.kmph.com. Licensee: KMPH(TV) License LLC. Group Owner: Pappas Telecasting Companies (acq 6-1-78; $3,105,550). Population Served: 1,432,000 Natl. Network: Fox, . Natl. Rep: TeleRep,. Washington Atty: Fletcher, Heald & Hildreth. News staff: 21; News: 7 hrs wkly.
Key Personnel:
Harry J. Pappas . . . pres
LeBon Abercrombie . . . exec VP
John Carpenter . . . VP
Jack Peck . . . gen mgr
Ken Felder . . . gen sls mgr
Mark Hodorowski . . . prom mgr
Debbie Sweeney . . . progmg dir
Roger Gadley . . . news dir
Jim Boston . . . chief of engrg
Jonet Williams . . . traf mgr

KNSO— Digital Channel: 11.5,000 kw vis. ant 1,830t/174g TL: N37 04 19 W119 25 49 On air date: Mar 22, 1996. 30 River Park Pl. W., Suite 200, Fresno, CA, 93720. Phone: (559) 252-5101. Fax: (559) 252-2747. Web Site: www.telemundofresno.com. Licensee: NBC Telemundo License Co. Group Owner: Telemundo Group Inc. (acq 4-30-2003; $33 million). Natl. Network: Telemundo (Spanish), . Foreign lang progmg: SpanishS 110
Key Personnel:
Manuel Cervantes . . . gen mgr & sls VP

***KNXT—** Digital Channel: 50. Digital Hrs: 50 2,140 kw vis, 214 kw aur. ant 2,739t TL: N36 17 14 W118 50 17 On air date: Nov 2, 1986. 1550 N. Fresno St., Fresno, CA, 93703. Phone: (559) 488-7440. Fax: (559) 488-7444.E-mail: knxt49@hotmail.com Web Site: www.dioceseoffresno.org. Licensee: Board of Directors Diocese of Fresno Education Corp. Population Served: 1,600,000 Foreign lang progmg: SpanishS 7
Key Personnel:
Bishop John T. Steinback . . . pres
Colin Dougherty . . . gen mgr

KSEE— Digital Channel: 38. Digital Hrs: 24 1,600 kw vis, 320 kw aur. ant 2,350t/321g TL: N36 44 45 W119 16 53 On air date: June 1, 1953. 5035 E. McKinley Ave., Fresno, CA, 93727-1964. Phone: (559) 454-2424. Fax: (559) 454-2487. Web Site: www.ksee24.com. Licensee: Ksee License, Inc. Group Owner: (group owner; (acq 12-93; $32 million with WTVH(TV) Syracuse, NY;8-30-93). Population Served: 165,972 Natl. Network: NBC, . Natl. Rep: Harrington, Righter & Parsons,. Washington Atty: Akin, Gump, Strauss, Hauer & Feld.
Key Personnel:
Todd McWilliams . . . pres & gen mgr
George Hillis . . . chief of opns & progmg mgr chief of engrg
Jan Katzenberger . . . gen sls mgr & prom dir
Kathleen Goble . . . natl sls mgr
Chris Zanghi . . . rgnl sls mgr
Julie Akins . . . news dir

KTFF-DT— Digital Channel: 48. Digital Hrs: 24 2,510 kw vis, 251 kw aur. ant 1,443t TL: N36 17 14 W118 50 17 On air date: May 6, 1992. 3239 W. Ashlan Ave., Fresno, CA, 93722-4402. Phone: (559) 439-6100. Fax: (559) 439-5950. Web Site: www.telefutura.com. Licensee: TeleFutura Fresno LLC. Group Owner: Univision Communications Inc. (acq 2-7-2003; $35 million). Natl. Network: TeleFutura (Spanish), .
Key Personnel:
Maria L. Gutierrez . . . gen mgr
Brett Covish . . . opns mgr
Jose Elgorriga . . . gen sls mgr
Darrell Jennings . . . rgnl sls mgr
Samuel Belilty . . . progmg dir & news dir
Ken Holden . . . chief of engrg
Azucena Gomez . . . traf mgr

***KVPT—** Digital Channel: 40. Digital Hrs: 6 AM-11:59 PM 562 kw vis, 112 kw aur. ant 2,220t/245g TL: N36 44 45 W119 16 52 On air date: Apr 10, 1977. 1544 Van Ness Ave., Fresno, CA, 93721. Phone: (559) 266-1800. Fax: (559) 650-1880.E-mail: web@kvpt.org Web Site: www.kvpt.org. Licensee: Valley Public Television Inc. (acq 11-1-87). Population Served: 2,500,000 Natl. Network: PBS, . Washington Atty: Fletcher, Heald & Hildreth. Foreign lang progmg: SpanishS 6 News staff: 35.
Key Personnel:
Paula Castadio . . . CEO & mktg dir
Douglas E. Noll . . . chmn
Phyllis Brotherton . . . CFO
Jim Page . . . opns mgr & mktg dir
Eva Torres . . . dev dir & sls dir
Jerry Lee . . . progmg VP & progmg dir
Rodger Hixon . . . chief of engrg

Los Angeles (DMA 2)

KABC-TV— Digital Channel: 7. Digital Hrs: 24 25 kw vis. ant 3,208t/451g TL: N34 13 37 W118 03 58 On air date: Sept 16, 1949. 500 Circle Seven Dr., Glendale, CA, 91201. Phone: (818) 863-7777. Fax: (818) 863-7080.E-mail: abc7@abc.com Web Site: www.abc7.com. Licensee: ABC Inc. Group Owner: (group owner; (acq 1-6-86; grpsl;7-15-85). Population Served: 15,077,000 Natl. Network: ABC, . Wire Svc: UPI
Key Personnel:
Arnold J. Kleiner . . . gen mgr

KAZA-TV— Digital Channel: 47. Digital Hrs: 24 5,000 kw vis. ant 1,220t TL: N33 21 00 W118 21 05 On air date: July 28, 2001. 500 S. Chinowth Rd., Visalia, CA, 93277. Phone: (559) 733-7800. Phone: (818) 241-5400. Fax: (559) 733-7878. Web Site: pappastv.com. Licensee: Pappas Southern California License LLC. Group Owner: Pappas Telecasting Companies. Foreign lang progmg: SpanishS 168
Key Personnel:
Harry J. Pappas . . . CEO
Eduardo Urbiola . . . gen mgr
Alberto Ezquerro . . . gen sls mgr
Ramon Delgado . . . progmg dir
Oscar Salcedo . . . news dir
Joe Berardi . . . chief of engrg
Yolanda Williamson . . . traf mgr

KBBC-TV— Digital Channel: 20.4.2 kw vis. ant 3,031t/30g TL: N37 24 43 W118 11 06 On air date: 2007. Cocola Broadcasting Companies, 706 W. Herndon Ave., Fresno, CA, 93650-1033. Phone: (559) 435-7000. Fax: (559) 435-3201. Web Site: www.cocolatv.com. Licensee: Bellagio Broadcasting LLC.
Key Personnel:
Lawrence H. Rogow . . . gen mgr

KBEH— Digital Channel: 24. Digital Hrs: 24 1,000 kw vis. ant 2,867t/52g TL: N34 12 48 W118 03 41 On air date: Aug 17, 1985. 950 Flynn Rd., Suite C, Camarillo, CA, 93012. Phone: (805) 388-0081. Fax: (305) 863-5701. Web Site: www.mtvtr3sla.com. Licensee: Hero Licenseco LLC. Group Owner: Bela LLC (acq 4-11-2008; $100 million with KMOH-TV Kingman, AZ). Washington Atty: Fletcher, Heald & Hildreth.
Key Personnel:
Mara M. Rankin . . . gen mgr

KCAL-TV— Digital Channel: 9. Digital Hrs: 24 25 kw vis. ant 3,205t/423g TL: N34 13 38 W118 04 00 On air date: Oct 6, 1948. 6121 Sunset Blvd., Hollywood, CA, 90028. Phone: (323) 467-9999/(323) 460-3000. Fax: (323) 464-2526.E-mail: kcalnews@cbs.com Web Site: www.kcal.com. Licensee: Los Angeles Television Station KCAL LLC. Group Owner: Viacom Television Stations Group (acq 5-3-2002; $650 million). Population Served: 5,006,380 Natl. Network: CBS, . Natl. Rep: Adam Young,. Wire Svc: Conus Wire Svc: World Television News Service

Key Personnel:
Patrick McClenahan . . . . gen mgr

KCBS-TV— Digital Channel: 43. Digital Hrs: 24 36.3 kw vis, 7.26 kw aur. ant 3,632t/974g TL: N34 13 57 W118 04 18 On air date: May 6, 1948. 6121 Sunset Blvd., Los Angeles, CA, 90028. Phone: (323) 460-3000. Fax: (323) 460-3733. Web Site: www.cbs2.com. Licensee: CBS Inc. Group Owner: CBS (acq 12-27-50; $3.6 million; 1-1-51). Population Served: 14,400,000 Natl. Network: CBS, . News staff: 104; News: 26 hrs wkly.
Key Personnel:
Patrick McClenahan . . . . pres & gen mgr
Paul Latham. . . . . CFO
Melanie Steensland . . . . opns dir
Garen Vandebeek . . . . prom dir
Virginia Hunt . . . . progmg dir
Nancy Bauer Gonzalez . . . . news dir
Craig Harrison . . . . engrg dir
Tim McGowan. . . . . rsch dir
Cheryl Marlowe . . . . traf mgr
Stephanie Rodriguez. . . . . pub svc dir

***KCET—** Digital Channel: 28. Digital Hrs: 19 2,455 kw vis, 245.5 kw aur. ant 3,038t/330g TL: N34 13 26 W118 03 44 On air date: Sept 28, 1964. 4401 Sunset Blvd., Los Angeles, CA, 90027. Phone: (323) 666-6500. Fax: (323) 953-5523. Web Site: www.kcet.org. Licensee: Community TV of Southern California. Population Served: 4,600,000 Natl. Network: PBS, . Rgnl. Network: Eastern Educ., Pacific Mtn. Washington Atty: Arent, Fox, Kintner, Plotkin & Kahn.
Key Personnel:
Al Jerome. . . . . CEO & pres gen mgr
Debbie Hinton . . . . CFO
Roger Terracina . . . . opns mgr & dev VP

KCOP— Digital Channel: 13.161 kw vis, 32.4 kw aur. ant 2,972t/187g TL: N34 13 29 W118 03 48 On air date: Sept 17, 1948. 1999 S. Bundy Dr., Los Angeles, CA, 90025. Phone: (310) 584-2000. Fax: (310) 584-2024. Web Site: www.myfoxla.com. Licensee: Fox Television Stations Inc. Group Owner: (group owner; (acq 7-31-2001; grpsl). Population Served: 149,000 Natl. Network: MyNetworkTV, . Washington Atty: Wilmer, Cutler & Pickering.
Key Personnel:
Kevin Hale . . . . gen mgr

KDOC-TV— Digital Channel: 32. Digital Hrs: 24 2,390 kw vis. ant 3,024t/249g TL: N34 13 36 W118 03 58 On air date: Oct 1, 1982. 18021 Cowan, Irvine, CA, 92614-6023. Phone: (949) 442-9800. Fax: (949) 261-5956/(949) 221-4171.E-mail: mmerker@kdoctv.net Web Site: www.kdoctv.net. Licensee: Ellis Communications KDOC Licensee LLC. (acq 2006; $149.5 million). Washington Atty: Cohn & Marks.
Key Personnel:
Pat Boone. . . . . pres
Calvin Brack . . . . VP
John Davis. . . . . gen mgr
Tom Jimenez . . . . gen sls mgr
Dale Foshee. . . . . rgnl sls mgr
Michelle Merker . . . . mktg dir & prom VP pub affrs dir
John Atkinson . . . . progmg mgr & pub svc dir
Roger Knipp . . . . chief of engrg
Paula Corso . . . . traf mgr

KFTR-DT—(Ontario, Digital Channel: 29. Digital Hrs: 24 2,450 kw vis, 372 kw aur. ant 3,040t/323g TL: N34 13 37 W118 03 58 On air date: Apr 21, 1984. 5999 Center Dr., Los Angeles, CA, 90045. Phone: (310) 348-3411. Fax: (310) 348-4849. Licensee: Univision Partnership of Southern California. Group Owner: Univision Communications Inc. (acq 5-21-2001; grpsl). Natl. Network: TeleFutura (Spanish), . Washington Atty: Wiley, Rein & Fielding. Foreign lang progmg: SpanishS 168
Key Personnel:
Maelia Macin . . . . gen mgr
Mark Dante . . . . gen sls mgr
Luis De La Parra. . . . . mktg dir & prom dir
Amy Rico . . . . progmg mgr & traf mgr
Chris Homer . . . . chief of engrg

KHIZ— Digital Channel: 44. Digital Hrs: 24 3,160 kw vis, 627 kw aur. ant 1,699t/203g TL: N34 36 34 W117 17 11 On air date: 1987. Box 1468, Victorville, CA, 92393-1468. 15605 Village Dr., Victorville, CA 92394. Phone: (760) 241-6464. Fax: (760) 241-0056. Web Site: www.khiztv.com. Licensee: KAZN-TV Licensee LLC.. Ownership: TVPlus LLC, 100% (acq 11-1-2007; $7.95 million). Population Served: 5,000,000 Washington Atty: Wilkinson, Barker & Knauer. News staff: 10; News: 5 hrs wkly.
Key Personnel:
Arthur Liu . . . . pres
Garrett Law . . . . gen mgr
Stella Montoya. . . . . progmg dir & traf mgr

KJLA— Digital Channel: 49. Digital Hrs: 24 5,000 kw vis. ant 1,738t/397g TL: N34 18 10 W119 13 41 On air date: October 1990. 2323 Corinth Ave., West Los Angeles, CA, 90064. Phone: (310) 943-5288. Fax: (310) 943-5299.E-mail: kjlainfo@kjla.com Web Site: www.kjla.com. Licensee: KJLA LLC. Ownership: LATV LLC (acq 11-14-94;1-2-95). Population Served: 13,000,000 Washington Atty: Thompson Hine & Flory. Foreign lang progmg: SpanishS 20
Key Personnel:
Walter Ulloa . . . . pres
Ed Safa . . . . CFO
Daniel Crowe. . . . . exec VP
Mike Seros. . . . . opns dir
Richard Deanda . . . . dev dir & rgnl sls mgr

***KLCS—** Analog Channel: 58. Analog Hrs: 6 AM-midnight 550 kw vis, 110 kw aur. 3,050t/180g TL: N34 13 26 W118 03 45 On air date: Nov 5, 1973. 1061 W. Temple St., Los Angeles, CA, 90012. Phone: (213) 625-6958/(213) 241-4000. Fax: (213) 481-1019.E-mail: info@klcs.org Web Site: www.klcs.org. Licensee: Los Angeles Unified School District. Ownership: Los Angeles Unified School Dist. Population Served: 15,000,000 Natl. Network: PBS, . Washington Atty: Cohn & Marks. News: 5 hrs wkly.
Key Personnel:
Dr. Janalyn W. Glymph . . . . gen mgr & stn mgr
Myles Jang . . . . dev dir
Sabrina Thomas . . . . . . opns dir & progmg dir & progmg mgr

KMEX-DT— Digital Channel: 34. Digital Hrs: 24 1,950 kw vis, 195 kw aur. ant 2,940t/170g TL: N34 13 35 W118 03 56 On air date: Sept 30, 1962. 5999 Center Dr., Los Angeles, CA, 90045. Phone: (310) 216-3434. Fax: (310) 348-3459. Web Site: www.univision.com (keyword: Los Angeles). Licensee: KMEX License Partnership G.P. Group Owner: Univision Communications Inc. Population Served: 281,606 Natl. Network: Univision (Spanish), . Wire Svc: UPI Foreign lang progmg: SpanishS 168 News: 17 hrs wkly.
Key Personnel:
A. Jerrold Perenchio . . . . CEO & chmn
Jose Delgado . . . . pres
George Blank . . . . CFO
Maelia Macin . . . . gen mgr
Mark Dante . . . . gen sls mgr
Luis De la Parra. . . . . mktg dir
Antoinette Gill . . . . progmg dir & traf mgr
Jorge Mattey . . . . news dir
Christina Sanchez-Camino . . . . . . pub affrs dir & pub svc dir
Chris Homer . . . . engrg mgr & chief of engrg
Harry Whitman. . . . . rsch dir
Alejandro Luna . . . . sports cmtr

KNBC— Digital Channel: 36.44.7 kw vis, 7.76 kw aur. ant 3,200t/496g TL: N34 13 32 W118 03 52 On air date: 1998. 3000 W. Alameda Ave., Burbank, CA, 91523. Phone: (818) 840-4444. Fax: (818) 840-3003. Web Site: www.nbclosangeles.com. Licensee: NBC Telemundo License Co. Group Owner: NBC TV Stations Division (acq 6-5-86). Natl. Network: NBC, . Natl. Rep: NBC TV Stations Sales,. Wire Svc: Reuters Wire Svc: UPI
Key Personnel:
Robert Long . . . . VP
Craig Robinson . . . . gen mgr
Robert L. Long . . . . news dir
Christa Morris. . . . . traf mgr

***KOCE-TV—** Digital Channel: 48. Digital Hrs: 24 2,354 kw vis. ant 3,113t/321g TL: N34 13 35 W118 03 57 On air date: November 1972. 17011 Beach Blvd., Suite 1550, Huntington Beach, CA, 92647. Phone: (714) 842-5797. Fax: (714) 895-0852.E-mail: kmische@koce.org Web Site: www.koce.org. Licensee: KOCE-TV Foundation. (acq 11-1-2004; $25.5 million). Population Served: 1,560,000 Natl. Network: PBS, . Washington Atty: Vorys, Sater, Seymour & Pease. News: 12.5 hrs wkly.
Key Personnel:
JoEllen Allen . . . . chmn
Mike Taylor . . . . VP & news dir
Mel Rogers. . . . . gen mgr
Ed Miskevich . . . . stn mgr
Kurt Mische . . . . dev dir
Pat Petrick . . . . prom dir & progmg dir
Susan Truesdale . . . . CFO & progmg dir
Gordon Smith . . . . chief of engrg

KPXN-TV— Digital Channel: 38.1,000 kw vis. ant 2,983t/173g TL: N34 12 46 W118 03 41 On air date: Jan 7, 1994. 3000 W. Alameda Ave., Suite 32622, Burbank, CA, 91523. Phone: (818) 840-4444. Fax: (818) 840-2129. Web Site: www.ionline.tv. Licensee: ION Media Los Angeles License Inc., debtor-in-possession. Group Owner: Paxson Communications Corp. (acq 3-22-95; $18 million;6-19-95). Population Served: 13,000,000 Natl. Network: ION Television, .
Key Personnel:
Alisha Wofford . . . . VP & traf mgr
Paula Madison . . . . gen mgr & chief of engrg
Rob Word. . . . . stn mgr & progmg dir
Mark Douglas . . . . gen sls mgr
Steve Vinke . . . . chief of engrg

KRCA— Digital Channel: 45.2,630 kw vis. ant 2,936t/138g TL: N34 12 50 W118 03 40 On air date: Dec 17, 1988. 1813 Victory Pl., Burbank, CA, 91504. Phone: (818) 563-5722. Fax: (818) 972-2694.E-mail: info@lbimedia.com Licensee: KRCA License LLC. Group Owner: Liberman Broadcasting Inc. (acq 6-18-90). Foreign lang progmg: SpanishS 52
Key Personnel:
Michael Sheron . . . . gen sls mgr
Winter Horton . . . . gen mgr & progmg dir
Chris Buchanan. . . . . chief of engrg

KSCI— Digital Channel: 18. Digital Hrs: 24 2,583 kw vis. ant 2,949t/164g TL: N34 12 47.8 W118 03 41 On air date: June 30, 1977. 1990 S. Bundy Dr., Suite 850, Los Angeles, CA, 90025. Phone: (310) 478-1818. Fax: (310) 479-8118.E-mail: info@kscitv.com Web Site: www.la18.tv. Licensee: KSLS Inc. Group Owner: Asian Media Group (acq 1-18-01; $165 million cash for 69.4%). Population Served: 6,000,000 Washington Atty: Wilkinson, Barker, Knauer LLP. News staff: 12; News: 12 hrs wkly.
Key Personnel:
Peter Mathes . . . . chmn
Brian Reed. . . . . gen mgr

KTBN-TV—(Santa Ana, Digital Channel: 33.631 kw vis, 126 kw aur. ant 2,890t/202g TL: N34 13 32 W118 03 44 On air date: Jan 5, 1967. Box A, Santa Ana, CA, 92711. 2442 Michelle Dr., Tustin, CA 92780. Phone: (714) 832-2950. Fax: (714) 665-2191. Web Site: www.tbn.org. Licensee: Trinity Broadcasting Network. Group Owner: (group owner; (acq 8-2-74; $1,266,400;8-19-74). Washington Atty: Joseph E. Dunne III.
Key Personnel:
Phyllis Smith . . . . gen mgr

KTLA— Digital Channel: 31. Digital Hrs: 24 44.7 kw vis, 6.7 kw aur. ant 6,176t/473g TL: N34 13 36 W118 03 56 On air date: Jan 22, 1947. 5800 Sunset Blvd., Los Angeles, CA, 90028. Phone: (323) 460-5500. Fax: (323) 460-5405. Web Site: www.ktla.com. Licensee: KTLA Inc. Group Owner: Tribune Broadcasting Co. (acq 12-20-2007; grpsl). Population Served: 14,443,000 Natl. Network: CW, . Natl. Rep: TeleRep,. Washington Atty: Dow Lohnes PLLC. Wire Svc: Reuters Wire Svc: NWS (National Weather Service) Foreign lang progmg: SpanishS 22 News: 22 hrs wkly.
Key Personnel:
Don Corsini . . . . gen mgr
John Moczulski . . . . stn mgr
Patricia Tang. gen sls mgr
Jymm Adams. . . . . prom dir
Jeff Wald . . . . news dir
Chris Neuman . . . . engrg dir
Dave Cox . . . . chief of engrg
Gretchen Dible. . . . . rsch dir
Lupe Ramirez . . . . traf mgr
Ray Gonzales . . . . pub affrs dir & pub svc dir

KTTV— Digital Channel: 11. Digital Hrs: 24 166 kw vis, 20 kw aur. ant 2,940t/237g TL: N34 13 29 W118 03 47 On air date: Jan 1, 1949. 1999 S. Bundy Dr., Los Angeles, CA, 90025. Phone: (310) 584-2000. Fax: (310) 584-2024. Web Site: www.myfoxla.com. Licensee: Fox Television Stations Inc. Group Owner: (group owner; (acq 11-14-86; grpsl). Population Served: 14,254,000 Natl. Network: Fox, . News: 25 hrs wkly.
Key Personnel:
Kevin Hale. . . . . gen mgr

***KVCR-DT—** Digital Channel: 26.1,318 kw vis, 131.8 kw aur. ant 3,166t/215g TL: N30 57 57 W117 17 05 On air date: Sept 11, 1962. 701 S. Mt. Vernon Ave., San Bernardino, CA, 92410. Phone: (909) 384-4444. Fax: (909) 885-2116.E-mail: info@kvcr.org Web Site: www.kvcr.org. Licensee: San Bernardino Community College District. Population Served: 17,000,000 Natl. Network: PBS, . Rgnl. Network: Pacific.
Key Personnel:
Larry R. Ciecalone. gen mgr
Kenn Couch . . . . stn mgr & dev dir
Al Gondos . . . . opns dir
Lillian Vasquez . . . . prom dir
Don Leiffer. . . . . progmg dir
Thomas Guptill . . . . chief of engrg
Patty Littlejohn . . . . traf mgr

KVEA—(Corona, Digital Channel: 39.2,630 kw vis, 263 kw aur. ant 2,890t/200g TL: N34 13 27 W118 03 45 On air date: June 29, 1966. 3000 W. Alameda, Burbank, CA, 91523. Phone: (818) 260-5700. Fax: (818) 260-5222.E-mail: angelnews@ibsys.com Web Site: www.telemundo52.com. Licensee: NBC Telemundo License Co. Group Owner: Telemundo Group Inc. (acq 4-12-2002; grpsl). Population Served: 711,000 Natl. Network: Telemundo (Spanish), . Foreign lang progmg: SpanishS 168
Key Personnel:
Jose Valle . . . . pres & gen mgr

KVMD— Digital Channel: 23.12 kw vis. ant 295t TL: N34 09 15 W116 11 50 6448 Hallee Rd., Suite 3, Joshua Tree, CA, 92252. Phone: (760)

366-9881. Fax: (760) 366-1342. Web Site: www.kumd-tv.com. Licensee: KVMD Licensee Co. LLC. Ownership: Ronald L. Ulloa, 100% (acq 4-5-2001; $900,000).
Key Personnel:
Larry Peterson. gen mgr & stn mgr stn mgr & opns mgr gen sls mgr
Ken Brown . . . . chief of engrg
Sherrie Karr . . . . pub svc dir

KWHY-TV— Digital Channel: 42. Digital Hrs: 20 2,630 kw vis, 257 kw aur. ant 2,916t/182g TL: N34 13 36 W118 03 59 On air date: Mar 25, 1963. 3400 W. Olive Ave., Suite 600, Burbank, CA, 91505-5539. Phone: (818) 260-5822. Fax: (818) 260-5805. Web Site: www.kwhy.com. Licensee: NBC Telemundo License Co. Group Owner: Telemundo Group Inc. (acq 4-12-2002; grpsl). Population Served: 5,000,000 Washington Atty: Cohn & Marks. Wire Svc: Reuters Foreign lang progmg: SpanishS 87 News staff: 6; News: 12 hrs wkly.
Key Personnel:
Raul Rodriguez . . . . VP & gen mgr

KXLA— Digital Channel: 51.2,340 kw vis. ant 3,113t/325g TL: N34 13 35 W118 03 58 On air date: 2001. 2323 Corinth Ave., Los Angeles, CA, 90064. Phone: (310) 478-0055. Fax: (310) 478-8070. Web Site: www.kxlatv.com. Licensee: Rancho Palos Verdes Broadcasters Inc. Ownership: RPVB Lender Inc. (acq 8-27-01; up to $40 million for stock with KXLA-DT Rancho Palos Verdes).
Key Personnel:
Ron Ulloa . . . . pres & gen mgr & progmg dir
Ken Brown . . . . chief of engrg

Modesto

see Sacramento-Stockton-Modesto, CA market

Monterey-Salinas, CA
(DMA 124)

KCBA— Digital Channel: 13. Digital Hrs: 24 2,328 kw vis, 283 kw aur. 2,414t/355g TL: N36 45 19 W121 30 05 On air date: Nov 1, 1981. 1550 Moffett St., Salinas, CA, 93905. Phone: (831) 422-3500. Fax: (831) 754-1120. Web Site: www.kcba.com. Licensee: Seal Rock Broadcasters LLC. Ownership: George V. Kristie and Lance W. Anderson, mgng members (acq 1-5-00; $11 million). Natl. Network: Fox, . Washington Atty: Rubin, Winston, Diercks, Harris & Cooke. News: 10 hrs wkly.
Key Personnel:
Paul Dughie . . . . gen mgr
Greta Richards . . . . gen sls mgr & prom mgr
Raymond Ochs . . . . prom mgr
Monica Escobedo . . . . film buyer & traf mgr
Traciann Zeravica . . . . news dir
Adam Perez . . . . engrg dir & chief of engrg

KION-TV—(Monterey, Digital Channel: 32.1,350 kw vis, 135 kw aur. ant 2,530t/222g TL: N36 32 05 W121 37 14 On air date: Feb 2, 1969. 1550 Moffett St., Salinas, CA, 93905. Phone: (831) 784-1702/(831) 422-3500. Fax: (831) 784-6395. Web Site: www.kion46.com. Licensee: Cowles California Media Co. Group Owner: Clear Channel Communications Inc. (acq 5-7-2008; $41 million with KCOY-TV Santa Maria). Population Served: 516,000 Natl. Network: CBS, . Washington Atty: Skadden, Arps, Slate, Meagher & Flom LLP. Wire Svc: UPI News staff: 25; News: 8 hrs wkly.
Key Personnel:
Mark Faylor . . . . VP & gen mgr
Lonlee . . . . stn mgr

***KQET—** Digital Channel: 25.81.1 kw vis. ant 2,291t/153g TL: N36 45 22.9 W121 30 04.9 On air date: November 1989. c/o KTEH, 1585 Schallenburger Rd., San Jose, CA, 95110-1301. Phone: (408) 795-5400. Fax: (408) 995-5446. Web Site: www.kteh.org. Licensee: Northern California Public Broadcasting Inc. (acq 10-1-2006). Natl. Network: PBS, .
Key Personnel:
Tom Fanella. CEO

KSBW— Digital Channel: 8. Digital Hrs: 24 158 kw vis, 15.8 kw aur. 2,940t/1,552g TL: N37 03 30 W121 46 33 On air date: Sept 11, 1953. 238 John St., Salinas, CA, 93901. Phone: (831) 758-8888. Fax: (831) 424-3750. Web Site: www.theksbwchannel.com. Licensee: Hearst-Argyle Stations Inc. Group Owner: Hearst-Argyle Television Inc. (acq 6-1-98). Population Served: 740,000 Natl. Network: NBC, . Natl. Rep: Eagle Television Sales,. Washington Atty: Brooks, Pierce, McLendon, Humphrey & Leonard. News staff: 31; News: 31 hrs wkly.
Key Personnel:
Joseph W. Heston. . . . . pres & gen mgr
Jose Camacho . . . . opns mgr & mktg mgr engrg mgr
Wendy Hillan . . . . gen sls mgr & natl sls mgr
Bill Mushrush . . . . mktg dir & prom dir adv dir
Britt Govea . . . . mktg mgr
Karen Pren . . . . progmg mgr
Lawton Dodd . . . . news dir
Theresa Wright. pub affrs dir & traf mgr pub svc dir & consumer affrs dir edit dir
Don Engelhardt. . . . . engrg dir
Dennis Lehnen . . . . sports cmtr
Jim Vanderzwaan . . . . weather dir

KSMS-TV—(Monterey, Digital Channel: 31.1,260 kw vis. 2,299t TL: N36 45 23 W121 30 05 On air date: Sept 1, 1986. 67 Garden Ct., Monterey, CA, 93940. Phone: (831) 373-6767. Fax: (831) 373-6700. Web Site: www.entravision.com. Licensee: Entravision Holdings L.L.C. Group Owner: Entravision Communications Co. L.L.C. (acq 4-25-97). Natl. Network: Univision (Spanish), . Foreign lang progmg: SpanishS 168
Key Personnel:
Philip Wilkinson . . . . pres & VP
Aaron Scoby . . . . gen mgr
Jeanie Harrison . . . . gen sls mgr

Oakland

see San Francisco-Oakland-San Jose market

Palm Springs, CA
(DMA 142)

KESQ-TV— Digital Channel: 42. Digital Hrs: 24 Note: ABC is on KESQ-TV ch 42, CW is on KESQ-DT ch 52. 316 kw vis. ant 745t/72g TL: N33 51 58 W116 26 02 On air date: Oct 5, 1968. 42-650 Melanie Pl., Palm Desert, CA, 92211. Phone: (760) 773-0342. Fax: (760) 773-5107. Web Site: www.kesq.com. Licensee: Gulf-California Broadcast Co. (acq 4-24-96; $19.4 million). Population Served: 329,000 Natl. Network: ABC, CW, Natl. Rep: Continental Television Sales,. Washington Atty: Smithwick & Belendiuk. Wire Svc: News 1 Wire Svc: AP News staff: 40; News: 17 hrs wkly.
Key Personnel:
Bob Allen. . . . . pres & exec VP gen mgr
Todd Graham . . . . opns mgr
Bob Ruderman . . . . sls dir & gen sls mgr
Ken Spalding. . . . . progmg dir & progmg mgr
Bob Smith . . . . news dir
Rich Brockman . . . . engrg dir & chief of engrg

KMIR-TV— Digital Channel: 46. Digital Hrs: 24 490 kw vis. 679t/123g TL: N33 52 00 W116 25 56 On air date: Oct 26, 1968. 72-920 Parkview Dr., Palm Desert, CA, 92260. Phone: (760) 568-3636/(760) 340-1623. Fax: (760) 568-1176.E-mail: news@kmir6.com Web Site: www.kmir6.com. Licensee: Journal Broadcast Corp. Group Owner: Journal Broadcast Group Inc. (acq 6-11-99; $28.1 million). Population Served: 318,000 Natl. Network: NBC, . Washington Atty: Koteen & Naftalin. News staff: 30; News: 27 hrs wkly.
Key Personnel:
Lyle Schulze. . . . . VP & gen mgr
Frank Keller . . . . opns mgr
Tony Billett . . . . gen sls mgr
Scott Johnson . . . . rgnl sls mgr & adv dir
Mayra Mancilla . . . . progmg mgr & traf mgr
Russ Kilgore . . . . news dir
Tim Balint . . . . chief of engrg
Karen Devine . . . . news cmtr

Redding

see Chico-Redding, CA market

Sacramento-Stockton-Modesto, CA
(DMA 20)

***KBSV—** Digital Channel: 15.421 w vis. ant 1,888t/36g TL: N37 30 28 W121 22 20.2 On air date: Apr 14, 1996. Box 4116, Modesto, CA, 95352. Phone: (209) 538-9801. Fax: (209) 538-2795.E-mail: kssv@aol.com Web Site: www.betnahrain.org/kbsv. Licensee: Bet-Nahrain Inc.
Key Personnel:
Dr. Sargon Dadesho. . . . . pres
Shemiran Daniel . . . . VP & gen mgr

KCRA-TV— Digital Channel: 35. Digital Hrs: 24 100 kw vis, 10 kw aur. ant 1,938t/2,000g TL: N38 15 52 W121 29 22 On air date: Sept 3, 1955. 3 Television Cir., Sacramento, CA, 95814-0794. Phone: (916) 446-3333. Fax: (916) 441-4050 (news). Web Site: www.thekcrachannel.com. Licensee: Hearst-Argyle Stations Inc. Group Owner: Hearst-Argyle Television Inc. (acq 2-18-99). Natl. Network: NBC, . Natl. Rep: Petry Television Inc.,. Washington Atty: Koteen & Naftalin. News: 55 hrs wkly.
Key Personnel:
Elliott Troshinsky . . . . gen mgr

KMAX-TV— Digital Channel: 21.5,000 kw vis, 500 kw aur. ant 1,830t/2,000g TL: N38 15 52 W121 29 22 On air date: Oct 5, 1974. 2713 Kovr Dr., West Sacramento, CA, 95605-1600. Phone: (916) 374-1313. Fax: (916) 374-1304. Web Site: www.cw31.com. Licensee: Sacramento Television Stations Inc. Group Owner: Viacom Television Stations Group (acq 3-24-98; $100 million). Population Served: 254,413 Natl. Network: CW, . Foreign lang progmg: SpanishS 33
Key Personnel:
Kevin Walsh. . . . . VP & gen mgr
Gavin Joe. natl sls mgr
Drew Fowler. . . . . prom mgr
Rita Gazitano . . . . progmg mgr
Brent Baader . . . . news dir
Bob Hess . . . . chief of engrg
Diane Mielenz. traf mgr

KOVR—(Stockton, Digital Channel: 25. Digital Hrs: 24 316 kw vis, 47.4 kw aur. ant 2,001t/2,011g TL: N38 14 24 W121 30 03 On air date: Sept 5, 1954. 2713 KOVR Dr., West Sacramento, CA, 95605. Phone: (916) 374-1313. Fax: (916) 374-1459. Fax: (916) 374-1304. Web Site: www.cbs13.com. Licensee: Sacramento Television Stations Inc. Group Owner: Sinclair Broadcast Group Inc. (acq 4-29-2005; $285 million). Population Served: 2,250,000 Natl. Network: CBS, . News staff: 120; News: 21 hrs wkly.
Key Personnel:
Kevin Walsh . . . . gen mgr
Rita Gazitano . . . . progmg dir & progmg mgr
Denise Dituri . . . . pub affrs dir & traf mgr
Bob Hess . . . . engrg dir & chief of engrg

KQCA—(Stockton, Digital Channel: 46.5,000 kw vis, 500 kw aur. ant 1,761t/1,769g TL: N38 15 54 W121 29 24 On air date: Apr 13, 1986. 58 Television Cir., Sacramento, CA, 95814-0794. Phone: (916) 446-3333. Fax: (916) 554-4658. Web Site: www.my58.com. Licensee: Hearst-Argyle Stations Inc. Group Owner: Hearst-Argyle Television Inc. (acq 1-24-2000; less than $1 million). Population Served: 2,100,000 Natl. Network: MyNetworkTV, . Washington Atty: Skadden, Arps, Slate, Meagher & Flom.
Key Personnel:
Elliot Troshinsky. . . . . gen mgr
Jerry Brehm . . . . sls dir & natl sls mgr
Patrick Donnelly . . . . gen sls mgr
Jim Caselli . . . . mktg dir & progmg dir
Gene Robinson . . . . prom mgr
Dan Weiser . . . . news dir
Stefan Hadl . . . . pub affrs dir & engrg dir
Lori Kesler . . . . traf mgr & pub svc dir

KSPX-TV— Digital Channel: 48. Digital Hrs: 24 1,000 kw vis, 100 kw aur. ant 1,604t/1,609g TL: N38 15 54 W121 29 24 On air date: Aug 27, 1990. 3352 Mather Field Rd., Rancho Cordova, CA, 95670. Phone: (916) 368-2929. Fax: (916) 368-0225. Licensee: ION Media Sacramento License Inc., debtor-in-possession. Group Owner: Paxson Communications Corp. (acq 5-25-2000; $17.725 million). Natl. Network: ION Television, . Washington Atty: Wiley, Rein & Fielding. News staff: 75; News: 7 hrs wkly.
Key Personnel:
Jim Eaton. . . . . gen sls mgr
Lee Roberts . . . . gen mgr & pub affrs dir
Frank Ernandes. . . . . engrg dir & chief of engrg

KTFK-DT— Digital Channel: 26. Digital Hrs: 24 1,950 kw vis, 195 kw aur. ant 2,980t/90g TL: N37 53 35 W121 53 58 On air date: July 11, 1988. 1710 Arden Way, Sacramento, CA, 95815. Phone: (916) 927-1900. Licensee: TeleFutura Sacramento LLC. Group Owner: Univision Communications Inc. (acq 12-1-2003; $65 million). Population Served: 8,941,512 Natl. Network: TeleFutura (Spanish), . Foreign lang progmg: SpanishS 168
Key Personnel:
Diego Ruiz . . . . gen mgr & stn mgr stn mgr
Steve Stuck . . . . gen sls mgr

KTXL— Digital Channel: 40. Digital Hrs: 24 950 kw vis. ant 1,971t/1,971g TL: N38 16 18 W121 30 18 On air date: Oct 26, 1968. 4655 Fruitridge Rd., Sacramento, CA, 95820-5299. Phone: (916) 454-4422. Fax: (916) 739-1079. Web Site: www.fox40.com. Licensee: Channel 40 Inc. Group Owner: Tribune Broadcasting Co. (acq 12-20-2007; grpsl). Population Served: 8,245,000 Natl. Network: Fox, . Natl. Rep: TeleRep,. News: 17 hrs wkly.

Key Personnel:

Bob Ramsey	VP & gen mgr
Bill Gee	opns mgr
Mike Armstrong	gen sls mgr
Lori Misika	natl sls mgr
Natalie Grant	progmg dir & progmg mgr
Tom Burke	news dir
Aileen Falkenstein	pub affrs dir & pub svc dir
Jack Davis	chief of engrg
Candace Shropshire	rsch dir
Misty DeVoll	traf mgr
Greg Saunders	pub svc dir
Jim Crandell	sports cmtr
Kristina Wagner	weather dir

KUVS-DT—(Modesto, Digital Channel: 18.5,000 kw vis, 560 kw aur. ant 1,877t/250g TL: N38 14 20 W121 28 52 On air date: Aug 26, 1966. 1710 Arden Way, Sacramento, CA, 95815. 1150 9th St., Suite 1505, Modesto, CA 95354. Phone: (916) 927-1900. Fax: (916) 614-1902. Web Site: www.univision.com. Licensee: KUVS License Partnership G.P. Group Owner: Univision Communications Inc. (acq 3-6-97; $40 million). Population Served: 3,480,000 Natl. Network: Univision (Spanish), . Washington Atty: Shaw Pittman. Foreign lang progmg: SpanishS 168 News staff: 30; News: 12 hrs wkly.

Key Personnel:

Steve Stuck	gen mgr

*KVIE— Digital Channel: 9. Digital Hrs: 24 100 kw vis, 10 kw aur. ant 1,804t/1,811g TL: N38 16 18 W121 30 22 On air date: Feb 23, 1959. 2595 Capitol Oaks Dr., Sacramento, CA, 95833. Phone: (916) 929-5843. Fax: (916) 929-7215.E-mail: publicinfo@kvie.org Web Site: www.kvie.org. Licensee: KVIE Inc. Population Served: 4,200,000 Natl. Network: PBS, . Washington Atty: Dow, Lohnes & Albertson.

Key Personnel:

David Hosley	pres
David Lowe	gen mgr & mktg VP
Jan Tilmon	progmg VP
Michael Wall	chief of engrg

KXTV— Digital Channel: 10. Digital Hrs: 24 316 kw vis, 5.13 kw aur. ant 1,953t/1,960g TL: N38 14 24 W121 30 03 On air date: Mar 20, 1955. 400 Broadway, Sacramento, CA, 95818-2041. Phone: (916) 441-2345. Fax: (916) 321-3384. Web Site: www.news10.net. Licensee: KXTV Inc. Group Owner: Gannett Broadcasting (acq 1999; swap with KVUE(TV) Austin, TX). Population Served: 2,200,000 Natl. Network: ABC, . Natl. Rep: Blair Television,. Washington Atty: Wiley, Rein & Fielding.

Key Personnel:

Russell Postell	pres & gen mgr
Kelly Bradley	gen sls mgr
Dustin Snyder	natl sls mgr & rgnl sls mgr
Ron Comings	news dir
Rod Robinson	chief of engrg

Salinas

see Monterey-Salinas, CA market

San Diego, CA
(DMA 28)

KFMB-TV— Analog Channel: 8. Digital Channel: 55. Analog Hrs: 7 AM-1 AM 316 kw vis, 63.2 kw aur. ant 745t/249g TL: N32 50 17 W117 14 57 On air date: May 16, 1949. 7677 Engineer Rd., San Diego, CA, 92111. Box 85888, San Diego, CA 92186. Phone: (858) 571-8888. Fax: (858) 495-9363. Web Site: www.kfmb.com. Licensee: Midwest Television Inc. Ownership: Elisabeth Meyer Kimmel, 51% of class B voting stock; August C. Meyer Jr., 49% of class B voting stock Group Owner: (group owner; (acq 4-17-2007; with KFMB-AM-FM San Diego). Population Served: 710,000 Natl. Network: CBS, . Natl. Rep: TeleRep,. Washington Atty: Covington & Burling. Wire Svc: UPI

Key Personnel:

Ed Trimble	pres & gen mgr
Rich Lochmann	opns mgr & engrg mgr
John Marquiss	sls dir
Sheri Kowalke	rgnl sls mgr
Thelma Presichi	traf mgr

KGTV— Digital Channel: 10. Digital Hrs: 24 20.7 kw vis. ant 745t/223g TL: N32 50 20 W117 14 56 On air date: Sept 13, 1953. 4600 Air Way, San Diego, CA, 92102. Phone: (619) 237-1010. Fax: (619) 262-1302. Web Site: www.10news.com. Licensee: McGraw-Hill Broadcasting Co. Group Owner: (group owner; (acq 6-1-72; grpsl;3-13-72). Population Served: 735,000 Natl. Network: ABC, . Natl. Rep: Harrington, Righter & Parsons,. Washington Atty: DowLohnes, PLLC. News staff: 65; News: 35 hrs wkly.

Key Personnel:

Jeffrey Block	gen mgr
Mike Biltucci	opns dir & opns mgr
Ken Rycyzn	gen sls mgr
Sean Kennedy	news dir
Pam Smith	engrg mgr & traf mgr
Andrew Lombard	chief of engrg

KNSD— Analog Channel: 39. Digital Channel: 40.2,510 kw vis. and 1,893t/154g TL: N32 41 48 W116 56 06 On air date: Nov 14, 1965. 225 Broadway, San Diego, CA, 92101. Phone: (619) 231-3939. Fax: (619) 578-0225.E-mail: feedback@nbcsandiego.com Web Site: www.nbcsandiego.com. Licensee: Station Venture Operations LP. Group Owner: NBC TV Stations Division (acq 3-2-98; with KXAS-TV Fort Worth, TX). Natl. Network: NBC, . Washington Atty: Pepper & Corazzini. Foreign lang progmg: SpanishS 3

Key Personnel:

Jackie Bradford	pres & gen mgr
Randy Mickler	opns mgr

*KPBS— Analog Channel: 15. Digital Channel: 30. Analog Hrs: 24 Digital Hrs: 24 3,310 kw vis, 302 kw aur. ant 1,876t/182g TL: N32 41 53 W116 56 03 On air date: June 25, 1967. 5200 Campanile Dr., San Diego, CA, 92182-5400. Phone: (619) 594-1515. Fax: (619) 594-3812.E-mail: letters@kpbs.org. Licensee: Board of Trustees, California State University for San Diego State University. Population Served: 2,000,000 Natl. Network: PBS, . Wire Svc: AP

Key Personnel:

Doug Myrland	gen mgr
Keith York	progmg dir
John Decker	news dir
Anna Bunge	traf mgr

KSWB-TV— Analog Channel: 69. Digital Channel: 19. Analog Hrs: 24 (W-S) 4,790 kw vis, 479 kw aur. 1,950t/151g TL: N32 41 47 W116 56 07 On air date: Oct 1, 1984. 7191 Engineer Rd., San Diego, CA, 92111. Phone: (858) 492-9269. Fax: (858) 268-0401. Web Site: www.fox5sandiego.com. Licensee: KSWB Inc. Group Owner: Tribune Broadcasting Co. (acq 12-20-2007; grpsl). Population Served: 943,500 Natl. Network: Fox, . Natl. Rep: TeleRep,. Washington Atty: Dow Lohnes PLLC. News: 14 hrs wkly.

Key Personnel:

Ray Schonbak	VP & gen mgr

KUSI-TV— Analog Channel: 51. Digital Channel: 18. Analog Hrs: 24 2,820 kw vis, 288 kw aur. ant 1,916t/177g TL: N32 41 49 W116 56 05 On air date: Sept 13, 1982. Box 719051, San Diego, CA, 92171. 4575 Viewridge Ave., Houston, CA 92123. Phone: (858) 571-5151. Fax: (858) 505-5050. Web Site: www.kusi.com. Licensee: Channel 51 of San Diego Inc. Group Owner: McKinnon Broadcasting Co. (acq 6-29-90;4-30-90). Washington Atty: Cohn & Marks. News staff: 70; News: 51 hrs wkly.

Key Personnel:

Michael Dean McKinnon	gen mgr & opns VP
Craig Hume	news dir
Richard Large	engrg dir & chief of engrg

XETV—(Tijuana, MEX) Analog Channel: 6. Analog Hrs: 24 100 kw vis, 50 kw aur. 1,000t/550g On air date: Jan 29, 1953. 8253 Ronson Rd., San Diego, CA, 92111. Phone: (858) 279-6666. Fax: (858) 268-9388. Web Site: www.sandiego6.com. Licensee: Radio-Television SA. Ownership: Grupo Televisa, 100%. Population Served: 920,570 Natl. Network: CW, . Washington Atty: Leventhal, Senter & Lerman. News: 20 hrs wkly.

Key Personnel:

Rodrigo Salazar	CFO
Richard Doutre Jones	VP & gen mgr
Richard Jones	stn mgr
Bob Anderson	opns dir & opns mgr
Chuck Dunning	gen sls mgr
Harry Melkerson	natl sls mgr
Lynda DiLorenzo	rgnl sls mgr
Judy Albrecht	prom dir & prom mgr
Deirdre Bianchi	progmg dir & progmg mgr
Raphael Ahlgren	pub affrs dir
Gary Stigall	chief of engrg
Kendall McMahon	rsch dir
Nieves Garcia	traf mgr
Raff Ahlgren	pub svc dir

XEWT-TV—(Tijuana, MEX) Analog Channel: 12. Analog Hrs: 20 325 kw vis, 32.5 kw aur. 1,000t/200g TL: N32 30 06 W117 02 23 On air date: July 12, 1960. Box 434537, San Diego, CA, 92143. 637 Third Ave., Suite B, Chulavista, CA 91910. Phone: (800) TELEV 12. Phone: (619) 585-9398. Fax: (619) 585-9463. Web Site: www.televisa.com. Licensee: Televisora de Calimex, SA. Ownership: Televisa, S.A. Population Served: 2,200,000 Washington Atty: Leventhal, Senter & Lerman. Foreign lang progmg: SpanishS 168 News staff: 50; News: 11 hrs wkly.

Key Personnel:

Ricardo Azcarraga	gen mgr
Lourdes Numez	opns mgr

San Francisco-Oakland-San Jose
(DMA 6)

KBCW— Digital Channel: 45. Digital Hrs: 24 5,000 kw vis, 500 kw aur. ant 1,610t/977g TL: N37 45 19 W122 27 06 On air date: Jan 2, 1968. 855 Battery St., San Francisco, CA, 94111-1509. Phone: (415) 765-8144. Fax: (415) 765-8844.E-mail: feedback@kbcwtv.com Web Site: www.kbcwtv.com / www.cwbayarea.com. Licensee: San Francisco Television Station KBCW Inc. Group Owner: Viacom Television Stations Group (acq 11-6-2001; swap with WDCA(TV) Washington, DC; and KTXH(TV) Houston, TX). Population Served: 6,373,000 Natl. Network: CW, . Washington Atty: Hogan & Hartson.

Key Personnel:

Ron Longinotti	pres & gen mgr
Steve Poitres	VP & stn mgr
Arturo Riera	sls dir

KCNS— Digital Channel: 39. Digital Hrs: 24 5,000 kw vis, 500 kw aur. ant 1,443t/726g TL: N37 45 20 W122 27 05 On air date: Jan 3, 1986. 1550 Bryant St., Suite 740, San Francisco, CA, 94103. Phone: (415) 863-3800. Fax: (415) 863-3998.E-mail: kcnstv@pacbell.net Web Site: www.kcnstv.com. Licensee: MTB San Francisco Licensee LLC. Group Owner: Scripps Howard Broadcasting Co. (acq 2-2-2009). Population Served: 7,150,000

Key Personnel:

Andrea Yamazaki	gen mgr & stn mgr
Douglas Benson	pub affrs dir

*KCSM-TV— Digital Channel: 43. Digital Hrs: 24 536 kw vis. ant 1,404t/672g TL: N37 45 19 W122 27 06 On air date: Oct 12, 1964. 1700 W. Hillsdale Blvd., San Mateo, CA, 94402. Phone: (650) 574-6586. Fax: (650) 524-6975. Web Site: www.kcsm.org. Licensee: San Mateo County Community College District. Population Served: 487,000 Natl. Network: PBS, . Washington Atty: Tierney & Swift. Foreign lang progmg: SpanishS 8

Key Personnel:

Marilyn Lawrence	gen mgr
Alisa Clancy	opns mgr
Shelly Rogers	dev dir
Michelle Muller	engrg dir

KDTV-DT— Digital Channel: 51.3,980 kw vis, 398 kw aur. ant 2,509t/439g TL: N37 29 57 W121 52 16 On air date: Aug 13, 1975. 50 Fremont St., 41st Fl., San Francisco, CA, 94105. Phone: (415) 538-8000. Fax: (415) 538-8053. Web Site: www.univison.com. Licensee: KDTV License Partnership G.P. Group Owner: Univision Communications Inc. Population Served: 1,023,300 Natl. Network: Univision (Spanish), . Washington Atty: Fisher, Wayland, Cooper, Leader & Zaragoza. Foreign lang progmg: SpanishS 168 News staff: 15; News: 5 hrs wkly.

Key Personnel:

Jim VanTassell	VP & opns mgr
Marcela Medina	gen mgr
Ernie Rizzuti	gen sls mgr
Maria Rodriguez	progmg dir
Sandra Thomas	news dir
Mike Roberts	chief of engrg
Maria Rodriguez	traf mgr

KFSF-DT— Digital Channel: 34. Digital Hrs: 24 3,470 kw vis, 346 kw aur. ant 1,528t/797g TL: N37 45 19 W122 27 16 On air date: Nov 25, 1986. 50 Fremont St., 4th Fl., San Francisco, CA, 94105. Phone: (415) 538-6466. Fax: (415) 538-8053. Licensee: TeleFutura San Francisco LLC. Group Owner: Univision Communications Inc. (acq 12-18-2001; $39 million). Population Served: 5,500,000 Natl. Network: TeleFutura (Spanish), . Foreign lang progmg: SpanishS 168

Key Personnel:

Jim VanTassell	CFO & opns mgr
Marcela Medina	gen mgr
Ernie Rizzuto	stn mgr & gen sls mgr
Maria S. Rodriguez	dev VP & progmg dir
Sandra Thomas	news dir
Mike Roberts	chief of engrg
Maria Rodriguez	traf mgr

KFTY— Digital Channel: 32. Digital Hrs: 24 302 kw vis, 60.4 kw aur. ant 3,080t/172g TL: N38 40 10 W122 37 52 On air date: May 1, 1981. 533 Mendocino Ave., Santa Rosa, CA, 95401. Phone: (707) 526-5050. Fax: (707) 526-7429. Web Site: www.kfty.com. Licensee: High Plains Broadcasting License Co. LLC. Group Owner: Clear Channel Communications Inc. (acq 2-20-2009; $1 million). Population Served: 1,500,000 Washington Atty: Pillsbury Winthrop Shaw Pittman LLP. Wire Svc: NWS (National Weather Service) Wire Svc: Bay City News Service News staff: 14; News: 7 hrs wkly.

Key Personnel:
John Burgess. VP & gen mgr rgnl sls mgr & mktg VP mktg dir & prom VP prom dir & progmg VP progmg dir & news dir
Richard Starkey . . . . opns mgr & chief of opns
Rob Rector . . . . gen sls mgr
Eric Casella. . . . . progmg dir & news dir
Brad Thompson . . . . chief of engrg & weather dir

KGO-TV— Digital Channel: 7.23.8 kw vis. ant 1,702t/951g TL: N37 45 19 W122 27 06 On air date: May 5, 1949. 900 Front St., San Francisco, CA, 94111-1450. Phone: (415) 954-7777. Fax: (415) 956-6402. Web Site: www.abc7news.com. Licensee: KGO-TV Inc. Group Owner: ABC Inc. (acq 6-27-86; grpsl;7-15-85). Population Served: 5,094,700 Natl. Network: ABC, .
Key Personnel:
Valari Staab . . . . gen mgr
Kevin Keeshan . . . . news dir

KICU-TV— Digital Channel: 36. Digital Hrs: 24 4,098 kw vis, 409.8 kw aur. ant 2,250t/600g TL: N37 29 17 W121 51 59 On air date: Oct 3, 1967. 2102 Commerce Dr., San Jose, CA, 95131-1804. Phone: (408) 953-3636. Web Site: www.kicu.com. Licensee: KTVU Partnership. Group Owner: Cox Broadcasting (acq 2-18-00; $130 million). Population Served: 5,824,520 Washington Atty: Leventhal, Senter & Lerman. News staff: 3; News: .5 hr wkly.
Key Personnel:
Tom Raponi . . . . gen mgr
Robert Martinez . . . . sls VP & gen sls mgr
Carolyn Chang . . . . progmg dir & progmg mgr
Chuck Pracna . . . . chief of engrg

KKPX-TV— Digital Channel: 41. Digital Hrs: 24 1,000 kw vis. ant 1,371t/290g TL: N37 41 15 W122 26 01 On air date: Nov 12, 1986. 848 Battery St., San Francisco, CA, 94111. Phone: (415) 276-1400. Fax: (415) 276-1401. Web Site: www.pax.tv. Licensee: Paxson San Jose License Inc. Group Owner: Paxson Communications Corp. (acq 3-22-95; $5 million;6-19-95). Natl. Network: ION Television, . Washington Atty: Joseph E. Dunne III.
Key Personnel:
Carol Denham . . . . gen mgr
Bob Getsla . . . . chief of engrg
Mark Faris . . . . traf mgr

***KMTP-TV—** Digital Channel: 33. Digital Hrs: 24 1,334 kw vis, 267 kw aur. ant 1,610t/885g TL: N37 45 20 W122 27 05 On air date: Aug 31, 1991. 1010 Cooperation Way, Palo Alto, CA, 94303. Phone: (415) 777-3232. Fax: (415) 552-3209.E-mail: kmtpgm@pacbell.net Web Site: www.kmtp.org. Licensee: Minority Television Project. Population Served: 2,000,000 Natl. Network: PBS, .
Key Personnel:
Arlene Stevens . . . . opns dir & progmg dir news dir
Booker T. Wade Jr. . . . . gen mgr & dev dir

KNTV— Analog Channel: 11. Digital Channel: 12. Analog Hrs: 24 80 kw vis, 8 kw aur. 2,770t/291g TL: N37 06 40 W121 50 34 On air date: Sept 12, 1955. 2450 N. 1st St., San Jose, CA, 95131. Phone: (408) 286-1111. Fax: (408) 422-4425. Web Site: www.nbc11.com. Licensee: NBC Telemundo License Co. Group Owner: NBC TV Stations Division (acq 4-30-2002; $230 million). Population Served: 700,000 Natl. Network: NBC, . Natl. Rep: Harrington, Righter & Parsons,. Washington Atty: Akin, Gump, Strauss, Hauer & Feld. News: 20 hrs wkly.
Key Personnel:
Rich Cerussi . . . . gen mgr
Caroline Chang . . . . progmg dir
Jim Sanders . . . . news dir

KOFY-TV— Digital Channel: 19.Note: Azteca America is on KOFY-DT ch 19. 3,470 kw vis, 347 kw aur. ant 1,548t/820g TL: N37 45 19 W122 27 06 On air date: Apr 1, 1968. 2500 Marin St., San Francisco, CA, 94124. Phone: (415) 821-2020. Fax: (415) 821-1518. Web Site: www.yourtv20.com. Licensee: KBWB License Inc. Group Owner: Granite Broadcasting Corp. (acq 7-20-98; $173.75 million). Population Served: 1,200,000 Natl. Rep: MMT,.
Key Personnel:
Craig Coane . . . . pres & CFO gen mgr
Dennis McNamara . . . . stn mgr & sls VP
Dave Figura . . . . opns mgr & mktg dir
Chris Flynn . . . . gen sls mgr
Steve Jones. . . . . gen sls mgr & natl sls mgr
Jennifer King . . . . prom mgr
Michele Ball . . . . progmg dir
Frank Brucks . . . . chief of engrg & rsch dir

KPIX-TV— Digital Channel: 29.100 kw vis, 10 kw aur. ant 1,660t/980g TL: N37 45 20 W122 27 05 On air date: Dec 22, 1948. 855 Battery St., San Francisco, CA, 94111-1597. Phone: (415) 362-5550. Fax: (415) 765-8844. Web Site: www.cbs5.com. Licensee: CBS Broadcasting Inc. Group Owner: Viacom Television Stations Group (acq 5—4-2000; grpsl). Population Served: 2,253,220 Natl. Network: CBS, . Natl. Rep: CBS TV Stations National Sales,. Washington Atty: Wilkes, Artis, Hedrick & Lane. Wire Svc: Reuters News staff: 87; News: 20 hrs wkly.
Key Personnel:
Ron Longinotti . . . . pres & VP gen mgr
Dee Joyce . . . . mktg dir
Tom Spitz . . . . progmg dir
Dan Rosenheim. . . . . news dir
Rosemary Roach. . . . . pub affrs dir
Mike Englehaupt . . . . chief of engrg

***KQED—** Digital Channel: 30. Digital Hrs: 24 316 kw vis, 37 kw aur. ant 1,670t/980g TL: N37 45 17 W122 27 06 On air date: June 10, 1954. 2601 Mariposa St., San Francisco, CA, 94110-1426. Phone: (415) 864-2000. Fax: (415) 553-2241.E-mail: (name)@kqed.org Web Site: www.kqed.org. Licensee: Northern California Public Broadcasting Inc. Population Served: 6,200,000 Natl. Network: PBS, . Washington Atty: Arnold & Porter LLP. News staff: 8; News: 1/2 hr wkly.
Key Personnel:
Jeff Clarke . . . . CEO & pres
Jo-Anne Wallace . . . . gen mgr & stn mgr
Michael Isip. stn mgr
Traci Eckels. . . . . dev VP
Donald Derheim . . . . sls VP

***KRCB—** Digital Channel: 23. Digital Hrs: 6 AM-noon 68.823 kw vis, 6.882 kw aur. ant 2,034t TL: N38 25 07 W122 40 33 On air date: Dec 2, 1984. 5850 Labath Ave., Rohnert Park, CA, 94928. Phone: (707) 584-2000. Fax: (707) 585-1363.E-mail: viewer@krcb.org Web Site: www.krcb.org. Licensee: Rural California Broadcasting Corp. Population Served: 2,300,000 Natl. Network: PBS, . Foreign lang progmg: SpanishS 3 News staff: one.
Key Personnel:
Larry Stratton . . . . COO & progmg dir
Nancy Dobbs . . . . CEO & pres & gen mgr

KRON-TV— Digital Channel: 38. Digital Hrs: 24 1,000 kw vis. ant 1,678t/946g TL: N37 45 19 W122 27 06 On air date: Nov 15, 1949. 1001 Van Ness Ave., San Francisco, CA, 94109. Phone: (415) 441-4444. Fax: (415) 561-8142. Web Site: www.kron.com. Licensee: Young Broadcasting of San Francisco Inc. Group Owner: Young Broadcasting Inc. (acq 6-26-2000; $823 million). Population Served: 6,700,000 Natl. Network: MyNetworkTV, . Natl. Rep: Adam Young,. Washington Atty: Brooks, Pierce. Wire Svc: Conus News: 42 hrs wkly.
Key Personnel:
Mark Antonitis . . . . pres & gen mgr
Mary Kennedy . . . . stn mgr & traf mgr
Mark Mano. . . . . opns dir & opns mgr
Sarah Squiers . . . . dev dir & rgnl sls mgr
Karen Orofino . . . . sls VP & gen sls mgr
Ben Holland . . . . natl sls mgr
Jeffrey Weinstock . . . . mktg dir & prom dir adv dir
Pat Patton. progmg VP
Stacy Owen . . . . news dir
Javier Valeucia. . . . . pub affrs dir
Craig Porter . . . . chief of engrg
Leslie Smith. . . . . rsch dir
Sandy Lee . . . . consumer affrs dir

KSTS— Digital Channel: 49.2,510 kw vis. ant 2,257t/420g TL: N37 29 57 W121 52 16 On air date: May 31, 1981. 2450 N 1st St., San Jose, CA, 95131-1002. Phone: (408) 435-8848 / (408) 944-4848. Fax: (408) 433-5921. Web Site: www.ksts.com. Licensee: NBC Telemundo License Co. Group Owner: Telemundo Group Inc. (acq 4-12-2002; grpsl). Population Served: 1,700,000 Natl. Network: Telemundo (Spanish), . Washington Atty: Hogan & Hartson. Wire Svc: Reuters Wire Svc: UPI Foreign lang progmg: SpanishS 100 News staff: 10; News: 3 hrs wkly.
Key Personnel:
Eduardo Dominuez . . . . gen mgr

***KTEH—** Digital Channel: 50.661 kw vis, 132 kw aur. ant 1,922t/137g TL: N37 29 07 W121 51 57 On air date: October 1964. 1585 Schallenbuger Rd., San Jose, CA, 95110-1301. Phone: (408) 795-5400. Fax: (408) 995-5446. Web Site: www.kteh.org. Licensee: Northern California Public Broadcasting Inc. (acq 10-1-2006). Population Served: 453,000 Natl. Network: PBS, . Rgnl. Network: Pacific. Washington Atty: Schwartz, Woods & Miller. Foreign lang progmg: SpanishS 3
Key Personnel:
Thomas Fanella . . . . CEO

KTLN-TV— Digital Channel: 47. Digital Hrs: 24 1,100 kw vis, 110 kw aur. ant 1,319t/59g TL: N38 09 00 W122 35 31 On air date: Aug 31, 1998. 100 Pelicanway, Sute -E, San Rafael, CA, 914901. Phone: (415) 924-7500. Fax: (415) 924-0264.E-mail: ktln@tln.com Web Site: www.ktln.tv. Licensee: Christian Communications of Chicagoland Inc. (acq 12-10-98; $500,000). Population Served: 7,000,000
Key Personnel:
Jerry K. Rose . . . . CEO & pres
James Nichols . . . . CFO
Debra Fraser . . . . gen mgr
Brian Avery . . . . stn mgr

KTNC-TV— Digital Channel: 14. Digital Hrs: 24 40 kw vis. ant 3,155t/290g TL: N37 52 54 W121 55 05 On air date: June 19, 1983. 1700 Montgomery St., Suite 400, San Francisco, CA, 94111. Phone: (415) 398-4242. Fax: (415) 352-1800.E-mail: rpineda@ktnc.com Web Site: www.ktnc.com. Licensee: KTNC License LLC. Group Owner: Pappas Telecasting Companies (acq 10-29-97). Population Served: 10,000,000 Washington Atty: Fletcher, Heald & Hildreth. Foreign lang progmg: SpanishS 168
Key Personnel:
Dennis Davis . . . . CEO
Harry Pappas . . . . chmn & pres
Fernando Acosta . . . . gen mgr
LeBon Abercrombie . . . . dev dir
Roberto Pineda . . . . gen sls mgr

KTSF— Digital Channel: 27. Digital Hrs: 24 2,510 kw vis, 500 kw aur. ant 1,380t/259g TL: N37 41 12 W122 26 03 On air date: Sept 4, 1976. 100 Valley Dr., Brisbane, CA, 94005-1350. Phone: (415) 468-2626. Fax: (415) 467-7559.E-mail: admin@ktsftv.com Web Site: www.ktsf.com. Licensee: Lincoln Broadcasting Co., a California L.P. Population Served: 6,000,000 Washington Atty: Law Office of Michael D. Berg. Wire Svc: Bay City News Service Wire Svc: AP Wire Svc: CNN News staff: 40; News: 24 hrs wkly.
Key Personnel:
Lillian L. Howell . . . . chmn
Lincoln C. Howell . . . . pres
Michael Sherman . . . . gen mgr
Mike Fusaro . . . . chief of opns & engrg dir
Lisa Yokota. . . . . mktg dir
Victor Marino . . . . progmg dir
Rose Shirinian . . . . news dir

KTVU—(Oakland, Digital Channel: 44. Digital Hrs: 24 400 kw vis. ant 1,679t/945g TL: N37 45 19 W122 27 06 On air date: Mar 3, 1958. Box 22222, Oakland, CA, 94623. Phone: (510) 834-1212. Fax: (510) 272-9957. Web Site: www.ktvu.com. Licensee: KTVU Partnership. Group Owner: Cox Enterprises (acq 10-16-63; $12.36 million;10-21-63). Population Served: 2,253,000 Natl. Network: Fox, . Natl. Rep: TeleRep,. Washington Atty: Dow, Lohnes & Albertson. Wire Svc: Reuters Wire Svc: NWS (National Weather Service)
Key Personnel:
Jeff Block . . . . VP
Tim McVay . . . . gen mgr & stn mgr
Greg Bilte. gen sls mgr
Dan Haass . . . . natl sls mgr
Caroline Chang . . . . progmg mgr
Ed Chapuis . . . . news dir
Rosy Chu . . . . pub affrs dir & pub svc dir
Don Thompson . . . . engrg mgr
Ken Manley . . . . chief of engrg
Pat Macholl. . . . . rsch dir
Tom Vacar . . . . consumer affrs dir

KUNO-TV— Digital Channel: 8.225 kw vis, 22.5 kw aur. ant 2,446t/186g TL: N39 41 38 W123 34 43 On air date: Feb 1, 1990. 500 S. Chinowth Rd., Visalia, CA, 93277. Phone: (707) 964-8888. Fax: (707) 964-8150. Licensee: Concord License LLC. Group Owner: Pappas Telecasting Companies (acq 6-12-97; $1.75 million). Natl. Rep: Blair Television,.
Key Personnel:
Ricardo Pineda . . . . gen mgr

San Jose

see San Francisco-Oakland-San Jose market

San Luis Obispo

see Santa Barbara-Santa Maria-San Luis Obispo, CA market

Santa Barbara-Santa Maria-San Luis Obispo, CA

(DMA 121)

KCOY-TV— Analog Channel: 12. Digital Channel: 19.115 kw vis, 22.9 kw aur. 1,940t/140g TL: N34 54 37 W120 11 08 On air date: Mar 16, 1964. 1211 W. McCoy Ln., Santa Maria, CA, 93455. Phone: (805) 925-1200. Fax: (805) 349-2740.E-mail: Kevinharlan@kcoy.com Web Site: www.kcoy.com. Licensee: Cowles California Media Co. Group Owner: Clear Channel Communications Inc. (acq 5-7-2008; $41 million iwith KION-TV Monterey). Population Served: 462,000 Natl. Network: CBS, . Natl. Rep: Continental Television Sales,. Washington Atty: Skadden, Arps, Slate, Meagher & Flom LLP. News staff: 42; News: 28 hrs wkly.

Key Personnel:

Kevin Harlan . . . . VP & gen mgr

Cathy Gunther. . sls dir & gen sls mgr rgnl sls mgr

Laurie Pipan. . . . . prom mgr

Monica Esconbido . . . . progmg mgr

Jimmy Sprague . . . . chief of engrg

KEYT-TV— Analog Channel: 3. Digital Channel: 27. Analog Hrs: 24 hrs 50 kw vis, 5.9 kw aur. ant 3,010t/210g TL: N34 31 32 W119 57 28 On air date: July 24, 1953. 730 Miramonte Dr., Santa Barbara, CA, 93109. Phone: (805) 882-3933. Fax: (805) 882-3934.E-mail: keyt@aol.com Web Site: www.keyt.com. Licensee: Smith Media License Holdings LLC. Group Owner: Smith Broadcasting Group Inc. (acq 11-8-2004; grpsl). Population Served: 900,000 Natl. Network: ABC, . Natl. Rep: Continental Television Sales,. Washington Atty: Hogan & Hartson. Wire Svc: AP Wire Svc: CNN News staff: 25; News: 21 hrs wkly.

Key Personnel:

Michael Granados . . . . gen mgr

Pio Rongavilla. . . . . gen sls mgr

Jeff Martin. . . . . prom mgr & pub affrs dir

Renee Foley . . . . progmg dir

Jim Bunner . . . . news dir

Dave Williams. . . . . chief of engrg

Caryn Meager . . . . traf mgr

Gerry Fall . . . . sports cmtr

Allen Rose . . . . weather dir

KPMR— Analog Channel: 38. Digital Channel: 21.2,690 kw vis. ant 2,877t TL: N34 31 32 W119 57 28 On air date: April 1, 2001. Entravision Communications Corp., 2425 Olympic Blvd., Suite 6000W, Santa Monica, CA, 90404. Phone: (805) 685-3800 / (310) 447-3870. Fax: (805) 685-6892. Web Site: www.entravision.com. Licensee: Entravision Holdings LLC. Group Owner: Entravision Communications Corp. (acq 11-2-2000; $4.75 million). Natl. Network: Univision (Spanish), . Foreign lang progmg: SpanishS 168

Key Personnel:

Gabe Quiroz . . . . gen mgr

Michael Scanlon . . . . gen sls mgr

Andres Angulo . . . . news dir

Angelique Caabrera . . . . traf mgr

KSBY— Analog Channel: 6. Digital Channel: 15. Analog Hrs: 24 Note: NBC is on KSBY(TV) ch 6, CW is on KSBY-DT ch 15. 100 kw vis, 12 kw aur. ant 2,250t/452g TL: N35 21 37 W120 39 17 On air date: May 1953. 1772 Calle Joaquin, San Luis Obispo, CA, 93405. Phone: (805) 541-6666. Fax: (805) 541-5142.E-mail: ksby@ksby.com Web Site: www.ksby.com. Licensee: KSBY Communications Inc. Group Owner: New Vision Group LLC (acq 2-18-2005; $67.75 million). Population Served: 494,800 Natl. Network: NBC, CW, Natl. Rep: TeleRep,. Washington Atty: Latham & Watkins.

Key Personnel:

Wade O'Hagen . . . . CFO

Evan Pappas . . . . gen mgr

Carl Edge . . . opns dir & progmg dir progmg mgr

Madeline Palaszeuski . . . . . prom dir & prom mgr

Madeline Palaszewski . . . . pub affrs dir

Aaron Klohs. . . . . chief of engrg

Elizabeth Friedmann . . . . traf mgr

Tony Cipolla . . . . news cmtr

Dave Alles . . . . sports cmtr

Teresa Garcia . . . . weather dir

KTAS— Analog Channel: 33. Digital Channel: 34. Analog Hrs: 24 Digital Hrs: 24 60.3 kw vis. ant 1,443t/75g TL: N35 21 38 W120 39 21 On air date: 1990. Box 172, Santa Maria, CA, 93456. 330 W. Carmen Ln., Santa Maria, CA 93458. Phone: (805) 928-7700. Fax: (805) 928-8606.E-mail: ktastv@fix.net Licensee: Raul and Consuelo Palazuelos. (acq 7-3-97). Natl. Network: Telemundo (Spanish), . Washington Atty: Wiley, Rein & Fielding, LLC. Foreign lang progmg: SpanishS 168 News staff: 6; News: 3 hrs wkly.

Key Personnel:

Sandy Keefer. gen mgr & opns mgr chief of opns & gen sls mgr

Roger Hernandez. . . . . news dir

Telemundo.

Santa Maria
see Santa Barbara-Santa Maria-San Luis Obispo, CA market

Stockton
see Sacramento-Stockton-Modesto, CA market

Visalia
see Fresno-Visalia, CA market

Yreka City
see Medford-Klamath Falls, OR market

Colorado

Colorado Springs-Pueblo, CO
(DMA 91)

KKTV— Digital Channel: 10. Digital Hrs: 24 234 kw vis, 46.8 kw aur. ant 2,380t/351g TL: N38 44 41 W104 51 41 On air date: Dec 7, 1952. Box 2110, Colorado Springs, CO, 80901. 3100 N. Nevada Ave., Colorado Springs, CO 80901. Phone: (719) 634-2844. Fax: (719) 632-0808. Fax: (719) 442-6981. Web Site: www.kktv.com. Licensee: WEAU Licensee Corp. Group Owner: Gray Television Inc. (acq 10-25-02; grpsl). Population Served: 700,000 Natl. Network: CBS, MyNetworkTV, . Natl. Rep: Continental Television Sales,. News staff: 42; News: 27 hrs wkly.

Key Personnel:

Robert Prather . . . . pres

Charles Peterson. . . . . VP

Tim Merritt . . . . gen mgr

Emily Edwards. . . . . opns mgr

Marion Houghton . . . . gen sls mgr

Michelle Hughes. . . . . . . mktg dir & prom mgr

Becky Tomek. . . . . . . progmg dir & progmg mgr

Nick Matesi . . . . news dir

John Burrell . . . . chief of engrg

Deborah Bullock. . . . . traf mgr

KOAA-TV—(Pueblo, Digital Channel: 42.100 kw vis, 10 kw aur. ant 1,310t/977g TL: N38 22 25 W104 33 27 On air date: June 13, 1953. Box 195, 2200 7th Ave., Pueblo, CO, 81002-0195. 530 Communications Cir., Colorado Springs, CO 81003. Phone: (719) 544-5781. Phone: (719) 632-5030. Fax: (719) 228-6277. Fax: (719) 228-6265. Web Site: www.koaa.com. Licensee: Sangre De Cristo Communications Inc. Group Owner: Evening Post Publishing Co. (acq 8-6-76; $4.5 million;8-30-76). Population Served: 500,000 Natl. Network: NBC, . Natl. Rep: Harrington, Righter & Parsons,. Washington Atty: Dow, Lohnes & Albertson. News staff: 23; News: 7 hrs wkly.

Key Personnel:

David Whitaker . . . . pres & gen mgr

Tom Wright . . . . . . gen sls mgr & natl sls mgr

Ron Eccher. . . . . progmg dir & film buyer

Cindy Aubrey . . . . news dir

Patricia Cone . . . . pub affrs dir

Quentin Henry . . . . chief of engrg

Pauline Quintana . . . . traf mgr

Lisa Lyden . . . . news cmtr

Lee Douglas . . . . sports cmtr

Mike Daniels . . . . weather dir

KRDO-TV— Digital Channel: 24. Digital Hrs: 24 282 kw vis, 29 kw aur. ant 2,080t/100g TL: N38 44 41 W104 51 38 On air date: Sept 21,

1953. 399 S. 8th St., Colorado Springs, CO, 80905. Phone: (719) 632-1515. Fax: (719) 475-0815. Web Site: www.krdo.com. Licensee: Pikes Peak Television Inc. Group Owner: (group owner) (acq 6-26-2006; $45 million with KJCT(TV) Grand Junction). Population Served: 761,000 Natl. Network: ABC, . Natl. Rep: Airtime TV,. Rgnl. Rep: Rgnl rep: Blair Television

Key Personnel:

David Bradley Jr. . . . . pres

Neil Klockziem . . . . gen mgr

*KTSC— Digital Channel: 8. Digital Hrs: 24 22.4 kw vis. ant 2,362t/321g TL: N38 44 43 W104 51 39 On air date: Feb 3, 1971. 2200 Bonforte Blvd., Pueblo, CO, 81001-4901. Phone: (719) 543-8800. Fax: (719) 549-2208.E-mail: ktsc@rmpbs.org Web Site: www.rmpbs.org. Licensee: Rocky Mountain Public Broadcasting Network Inc. (acq 1999; $2.375 million). Population Served: 219,930 Natl. Network: PBS, .

Key Personnel:

Tom Scheel . . . . chmn & dev dir

James Morgese. . . . . pres & gen mgr

Wynona Sullivan. . . . . stn mgr

Tiffany Q. Tyson . . . . mktg dir

Donna Sanford. . . . . progmg dir

Ian Hartley . . . . chief of engrg

KVSN-DT— Digital Channel: 48.350 kw vis. ant 2,280t/271g TL: N38 44 42 W104 51 37 On air date: 2009. 777 Grant St., Suite 500, Denver, CO, 80203. Phone: (303) 832-0050. Fax: (303) 832-3410. Web Site: www.entravision.com. Licensee: Entravision Holdings LLC. Natl. Network: Univision (Spanish), .

Key Personnel:

Walter F. Ulloa . . . . CEO

Mario Carrera. . . . . gen mgr

KXRM-TV— Digital Channel: 22. Digital Hrs: 24 1,054 kw vis, 105.4 kw aur. ant 2,085t/125g TL: N38 44 40 W104 51 37 On air date: Dec 24, 1984. 560 Wooten Rd., Colorado Springs, CO, 80915. Phone: (719) 596-2100. Fax: (719) 591-4180.E-mail: info@kxrm.com Web Site: www.coloradoconnection.com. Licensee: Barrington Colorado Springs License LLC. Group Owner: Raycom Media Inc. (acq 8-11-2006; grpsl). Natl. Network: Fox, . Natl. Rep: TeleRep,. Washington Atty: Covington & Durling. Wire Svc: CNN News: 3.5 hrs wkly.

Key Personnel:

K. James Yager . . . . CEO

Steve Dant . . . . pres & gen mgr

Dan Corken. . . . . gen sls mgr

Leanne Franke . . . . rgnl sls mgr

Patti Clements . . . . progmg dir

Matt Gerstner . . . . chief of engrg

Joe Cole . . . . sports cmtr

Denver, CO
(DMA 18)

*KBDI-TV—(Broomfield, Digital Channel: 13. Digital Hrs: 24 33.6 kw vis. ant 2,421t/75g TL: N39 40 55 W105 29 49 On air date: Feb 22, 1980. 2900 Welton St., Denver, CO, 80205. Phone: (303) 296-1212.

Fax: (303) 296-6650. Web Site: www.kbdi.org. Licensee: Colorado Public Television Inc. Population Served: 500,000 Natl. Network: PBS, . Washington Atty: Mintz, Levin, Cohn, Ferris, Glovsky & Popeo.
Key Personnel:
Dr. Willard Rowland Jr. . . . . CEO & chmn
Dr. Willard Rowland . . . . pres
Kim Johnson . . . . opns VP
Darrow Hodges . . . . dev VP & adv VP
Kirby McClure. . . . . progmg dir

KCDO-TV— Digital Channel: 23. Digital Hrs: 21 599 kw vis. ant 669t/459g TL: N40 34 57 W103 01 56 On air date: Jan 1, 1964. c/o KTVD(TV), 11203 E. Peakview Ave., Centennial, CO, 80111. Phone: (303) 792-2020. Fax: (303) 790-4633. Licensee: Channel 20 TV Co. Group Owner: Newsweb Corp. (acq 8-31-99; $240,000). Washington Atty: Covington & Burling. News: 17 hrs wkly.
Key Personnel:
Greg Armstrong . . . . gen mgr
Hilary Castine . . . . prom mgr
Rita McCoy . . . . pub affrs dir
Michael Dant. . . . . chief of engrg
Diana Farrens. . . . . traf mgr
Rebroadcasts KTVD(TV) Denver 100%.

KCEC— Digital Channel: 51.2,498 kw vis. ant 764t TL: N39 43 47 W105 07 16 On air date: Oct 19, 1990. 777 Grant St., 5th Fl., Monroe, CO, 80203. Phone: (303) 832-0050. Fax: (303) 832-3410. Licensee: Entravision Holdings L.L.C. Group Owner: Entravision Communications Co. L.L.C. (acq 4-25-97). Population Served: 624,000 Natl. Network: Univision (Spanish), . Foreign lang progmg: SpanishS 168
Key Personnel:
Walter Ulloa . . . . pres
Mario M. Carrera . . . . gen mgr
Don Daboub. . . . . gen sls mgr
Mark Goodrich . . . . natl sls mgr
Kathy Berumen . . . . prom dir & pub svc dir
Erma Atencio. . . . . progmg mgr & traf mgr
Rodolfo Cardenas . . . . news dir
Jamie Moreno. . . . . pub affrs dir & rsch dir
Carl Cutforth . . . . engrg mgr
Luis Canela . . . . sports cmtr
Sergio Schwartz . . . . weather dir

KCNC-TV— Digital Channel: 35. Digital Hrs: 24 100 kw vis, 35.1 kw aur. ant 1,480t/833g TL: N39 43 48 W105 14 02 On air date: Dec 24, 1953. 1044 Lincoln St., Denver, CO, 80203. Phone: (303) 861-4444. Web Site: www.cbs4denver.com. Licensee: CBS Television Stations Inc. Group Owner: Viacom Television Stations Group (acq 9-10-95; grpsl). Population Served: 2,642,000 Natl. Network: CBS, . Natl. Rep: CBS TV Stations National Sales,. Wire Svc: Conus Wire Svc: PR Newswire Wire Svc: Medialink News staff: 90; News: 28.5 hrs wkly.
Key Personnel:
Walt DeHaven . . . . gen mgr
David Layne. . . . . opns mgr
Aaron Inman . . . . sls dir & natl sls mgr
David Rash . . . . gen sls mgr
Cathy Considine . . . . rgnl sls mgr
Wendy Holmes . . . . progmg dir

KDEN— Digital Channel: 29.5,000 kw vis. ant 1,066t/964g TL: N40 05 47 W104 54 04 On air date: 1999. 1120 Lincoln St., Suite 800, Denver, CO, 80203-2137. Phone: (303) 832-0402 (Denver). Fax: (303) 832-0777. Licensee: NBC Telemundo License Co. (acq 7-13-2006; $42 million). Natl. Network: Telemundo (Spanish), . Washington Atty: NBC Legal. Foreign lang progmg: SpanishS 168 News staff: one; News: one hr wkly.
Key Personnel:
Don Brown . . . . CEO
Clara Rivas . . . . VP & gen mgr

KDVR— Digital Channel: 32. Digital Hrs: 24 5,000 kw vis, 500 kw aur. ant 1,038t/440g TL: N39 43 45 W105 14 12 On air date: Aug 10, 1983. 100 E. Speer Blvd., Denver, CO, 80203. Phone: (303) 595-3131. Phone: (888) 595-3131. Fax: (303) 566-2931. Fax: (303) 566-7631. Web Site: www.myfoxcolorado.com. Licensee: Community Television of Colorado License LLC. Group Owner: (group owner; (acq 7-14-2008; grpsl). Natl. Network: Fox, .
Key Personnel:
Dennis Leonard . . . . VP & gen mgr
Ray Dowdle . . . . gen sls mgr
John Hirsch . . . . progmg dir & film buyer
Patti Brady . . . . traf mgr

KFCT— Digital Channel: 21. Digital Hrs: 24 1,860 kw vis. ant 840t/705g TL: N40 38 23 W104 49 05 On air date: October 1994. c/o TV Stn KDVR, 100 E. Speer Blvd., Denver, CO, 80203. Phone: (303) 595-3131. Fax: (303) 566-2931. Web Site: www.myfoxcolorado.com. Licensee: Community Television of Colorado License LLC. Group Owner: (group owner; (acq 7-14-2008; grpsl). Natl. Network: Fox, .
Key Personnel:
Ray Dowdle . . . . sr VP & gen sls mgr
William Schneider . . . . gen mgr
Catherine Andrey . . . . natl sls mgr
Sheryl Personett . . . . rgnl sls mgr
Clyde Becker . . . . prom VP & prom mgr
John Hirsch . . . . progmg mgr
Bill Dallman . . . . news dir
Jon Takayama . . . . pub affrs dir
Skip Erickson . . . . engrg VP & engrg mgr
Satellite of KDVR(TV) Denver.

KFNR— Digital Channel: 9. Digital Hrs: 24 1.66 kw vis, 166 w aur. ant 230t/449g TL: N41 46 15 W107 14 25 On air date: Apr 16, 1986. 1856 Skyview Dr., Casper, WY, 82601. Phone: (307) 577-5923. Fax: (307) 234-4005.E-mail: klwy@coffey.com Licensee: Wyomedia Corp. (acq 2-28-2009; with KFNE(TV) Riverton). Natl. Network: Fox, . Washington Atty: Drinker Biddle & Reath LLP.
Key Personnel:
Mark Nalbone. . . . . gen mgr
Terry Lane . . . . opns mgr & progmg dir
Judie Lewis . . . . gen sls mgr & rgnl sls mgr
Joe Lownden . . . . prom dir
Dave Ericson. . . . . chief of engrg
Tony Lattea. . . . . traf mgr

KMGH-TV— Digital Channel: 7.48 kw vis. ant 1,178t/653g TL: N39 43 51 W105 13 54 On air date: Nov 1, 1953. 123 Speer Blvd., Denver, CO, 80203. Phone: (303) 832-7777. Fax: (303) 832-0119. Web Site: www.thedenverchannel.com. Licensee: McGraw-Hill Broadcasting Co. Inc. Group Owner: McGraw-Hill Broadcasting Co. (acq 6-1-72; grpsl; 3-13-72). Population Served: 4,662,800 Natl. Network: ABC, . Natl. Rep: Harrington, Righter & Parsons,.
Key Personnel:
Byron F. Grandy . . . . VP & gen mgr
Barry Edmond . . . . opns mgr
John Curry . . . . gen sls mgr
Laura Horgis. . . . . natl sls mgr

KPJR-DT— Digital Channel: 38.1,000 kw vis. ant 1,187t/23g TL: N40 05 59 W104 54 02 Not on air, target date: unknown: Box C-11949, Santa Ana, CA, 92711. Phone: (714) 832-2950. Fax: (714) 730-0657. Web Site: www.tbn.org. Permittee: Trinity Christian Center of Santa Ana Inc. (acq 9-16-2008; $37.5 million for CP).
Key Personnel:
Paul F. Crouch . . . . pres

KPXC-TV— Digital Channel: 43. Digital Hrs: 24 5,000 kw vis, 500 kw aur. ant 1,168t/85g TL: N39 40 24 W105 13 03 On air date: Sept 10, 1987. 3001 S. Jamaica Ct., Suite 200, Aurora, CO, 80014. Phone: (303) 751-5959. Fax: (303) 751-5993. Web Site: www.ionline.tv /stations/list.cfm. Licensee: Paxson Denver License Inc. Group Owner: Paxson Communications Corp. (acq 7-1-96; grpsl). Natl. Network: ION Television, . Washington Atty: Cole, Raywid & Braverman. News: 24 hrs wkly.
Key Personnel:
Bud Paxson . . . . pres
Christy Bradford . . . . rgnl sls mgr
Mark Cornetta . . . . gen sls mgr & progmg mgr
Brian Schauer . . . . chief of engrg
Geri Crawley . . . . traf mgr

KREG-TV— Digital Channel: 23.67.6 kw vis, 6.76 kw aur. ant 2,530t/256g TL: N39 25 05 W107 22 01 On air date: Dec 15, 1983. Box 789, Grand Junction, CO, 81502. 345 Hillcrest Dr., Grand Junction, CO 81501. Phone: (970) 963-3333. Fax: (970) 242-0886.E-mail: rtillery@krextv.com Web Site: www.krextv.com. Licensee: Hoak Media of Colorado LLC. Group Owner: Hoak Media Corporation (acq 10-10-2003; grpsl). Population Served: 135,450 Natl. Network: CBS, . Natl. Rep: Petry Television Inc.,. Washington Atty: Gardner, Carton & Douglas.
Key Personnel:
Ron Tillery . . . . gen mgr

***KRMA-TV—** Digital Channel: 18. Digital Hrs: 24 100 kw vis, 15.1 kw aur. ant 880t/213g TL: N39 43 48 W105 15 00 On air date: Jan 30, 1956. 1089 Bannock St., Denver, CO, 80204. Phone: (303) 892-6666. Fax: (303) 620-5600. Web Site: www.rmpbs.org. Licensee: Rocky Mountain Public Broadcasting Network Inc. Population Served: 2,000,000 Natl. Network: PBS, . Washington Atty: Dow & Lohnes. News: one hr wkly.
Key Personnel:
James N. Morgese . . . . pres & gen mgr
Bill Wengert . . . . CFO & dev mgr
Donna Sanford . . . . progmg dir
John Anderson . . . . chief of engrg

***KRMT—** Digital Channel: 40. Digital Hrs: 24 1,000 kw vis. ant 1,128t/151g TL: N39 35 59 W105 12 35 On air date: Jan 4, 1994. 12014 W. 64th Ave., Arvada, CO, 80004. Phone: (303) 423-4141. Fax: (303) 424-0571. Web Site: www.daystar.com. Licensee: Word of God Fellowship Inc. (acq 5-29-97; $1.95 million). Population Served: 2,000,000 Washington Atty: Hogan & Hartson. Foreign lang progmg: SpanishS 3
Key Personnel:
Marcus D. Lamb . . . . CEO & pres
Joni Lamb . . . . exec VP
Janice Smith. . . . . natl sls mgr

***KRMZ—** Digital Channel: 10. Digital Hrs: 24 5,500 kw vis, 500 kw aur. ant 515t/98g TL: N40 27 43 W106 51 02 On air date: May 1988. 1089 Bannock St., Denver, CO, 80204. Phone: (303) 892-6666. Fax: (303) 620-5600. Web Site: www.krma.org. Licensee: Rocky Mountain Public Broadcasting Network Inc. Group Owner: Telemundo Group Inc. (acq 2-2-2007). Population Served: 15,000 Natl. Network: PBS, . Rocky Mountain PBS
Key Personnel:
Bill Wengert . . . . CFO
James N. Morgese . . . . pres & gen mgr
Donna Sanford . . . . progmg dir
Rebroadcasts KRMA-TV Denver 100%.

***KRNE-TV—** Digital Channel: 12. Digital Hrs: 18 75 kw vis. ant 1,056t/26g TL: N42 40 37 W101 42 39 On air date: Dec 9, 1968. 1800 N. 33rd St., Lincoln, NE, 68503. Phone: (402) 472-3611. Fax: (402) 472-1785.E-mail: net1@unl.edu Web Site: www.netnebraska.org. Licensee: Nebraska Educational Telecommunications Commission. Natl. Network: PBS, . National Educational Telecommunications Association Washington Atty: Dow, Lohnes & Albertson.
Key Personnel:
Rod Bates . . . . gen mgr
Satellite of KUON-TV Lincoln.

KTFD-DT— Digital Channel: 15.2,400 kw vis. ant 1,151t/138g TL: N39 40 18 W105 13 12 On air date: March 1986. 777 Grant St., 5th Fl., Denver, CO, 80203. Phone: (303) 832-1414. Fax: (303) 832-3410. Licensee: Spanish Television of Denver Inc. Group Owner: Roberts Broadcasting Co. (acq 2-27-2003). Natl. Network: TeleFutura (Spanish), . Foreign lang progmg: SpanishS 168
Key Personnel:
Mario Carrera. . . . . gen mgr
Chris Matthews . . . . opns mgr & natl sls mgr
Luis Caneda . . . . prom dir & progmg dir

KTVD— Digital Channel: 19. Digital Hrs: 24 1,000 kw vis, 100 kw aur. ant 1,227t/16g TL: N39 43 51 W105 13 54 On air date: Dec 1, 1988. 500 Speer Blvd., Denver, CO, 80231. Phone: (303) 871-9999. Fax: (303) 790-4633.E-mail: feedback@ktvd.com Web Site: www.ktvd.com. Licensee: Multimedia Holdings Corp. Group Owner: Newsweb Corp. (acq 6-26-2006; $155 million). Natl. Network: MyNetworkTV, .
Key Personnel:
Mark Cornetta . . . . gen mgr
Patricia Wilson. . . . . gen sls mgr

KUSA— Digital Channel: 9.45 kw vis. ant 1,156t/630g TL: N39 43 50.6 W105 13 53.6 On air date: Oct 12, 1952. 500 Speer Blvd., Denver, CO, 80203. Phone: (303) 871-9999. Fax: (303) 698-4719 (sales).E-mail: kusa@9news.com Web Site: www.9news.com. Licensee: Multimedia Holdings Corp. Group Owner: Gannett Broadcasting (Division of Gannett Co. Inc.) (acq 6-7-79; grpsl;6-11-79). Population Served: 3,535,000 Natl. Network: NBC, . Washington Atty: Wiley, Rein & Fielding.
Key Personnel:
Mark Cornetta . . . . pres & gen mgr
Patricia Wilson. . . . . gen sls mgr
Patti Dennis . . . . news dir
Don Perez. . . . . engrg dir

KWGN-TV— Digital Channel: 34. Digital Hrs: 24 100 kw vis, 20 kw aur. ant 1,050t/449g TL: N39 43 58 W105 14 08 On air date: July 18, 1952. 6160 S. Wabash Way, Greenwood Village, CO, 80111. Phone: (303) 740-2222. Fax: (303) 740-2847. Web Site: www.cw2.com. Licensee: KWGN Inc. Group Owner: Tribune Broadcasting Co., see Cross-Ownership (acq 12-20-2007; grpsl). Population Served: 2,600,000 Natl. Network: CW, . Natl. Rep: TeleRep,. Washington Atty: Dow Lohnes PLLC. News: 29.5 hrs wkly.
Key Personnel:
Dennis O'Brien. . . . . CFO
Dennis Leonard . . . . gen mgr
John Strassner . . . . sls dir & gen sls mgr
Natalie Grant. . . . . progmg dir
Carl Bilek . . . . news dir
Beverly Martinez . . . . pub affrs dir
Donna Laboy . . . . traf mgr

KWHD— Digital Channel: 45. Digital Hrs: 24 5,000 kw vis, 1,000 kw aur. ant 713t TL: N39 25 58 W104 39 18 On air date: July 1, 1990. 12999 E. Adam Aircraft, Englewood, CO, 80112. Phone: (303)

799-8853. Fax: (303) 792-5303. Web Site: www.mykwhd.com. Licensee: LeSea Broadcasting. Group Owner: (group owner) Population Served: 1,578,660, Foreign lang progmg: SpanishS 1

Key Personnel:
Pete Sumrall . . . . . CEO
Dan Smith . . . . . gen mgr
Ron Vincent . . . . . chief of engrg

***KWYP-TV—** Digital Channel: 8. Digital Hrs: 24 37 kw vis. ant 1,043t/144g TL: N41 17 17 W105 26 42 On air date: December 2004. Wyoming Public Television, 2660 Peck Ave., Riverton, WY, 82501. Phone: (307) 856-6944. Fax: (307) 856-3893. Web Site: wyoptv.org. Licensee: Central Wyoming College. Natl. Network: PBS, .

Key Personnel:
JoAnne McFarland . . . . . pres
Dan Schiedel . . . . . gen mgr
Michael Dietz . . . . . progmg dir
Bob Spain . . . . . chief of engrg

Durango

see Albuquerque-Santa Fe, NM market

Grand Junction-Montrose, CO (DMA 184)

KFQX— Digital Channel: 15.10.7 kw vis. ant 1,384t TL: N39 03 56 W108 44 52 On air date: 2000. 345 Hillcrest Dr., Grand Junction, CO, 81501. Phone: (970) 242-5285. Fax: (970) 242-0886.E-mail: rtillery@krextv.com Web Site: www.krextv.com. Licensee: Parker Broadcasting of Colorado LLC. (acq 12-27-2004). Natl. Network: Fox, .

Key Personnel:
Ron Tillery . . . . . gen mgr
Shawna Greiger. . . . . sls VP & mktg VP
Maranda Wolter. . . . . prom VP
Shelley Nelson . . . . . progmg VP
Keira Bresnalhan . . . . . news dir
Maranda Wolter . . . . . pub affrs dir
Don May . . . . . engrg VP

KJCT— Digital Channel: 7. Digital Hrs: 24 120.2 kw vis, 12 kw aur. ant 2,720t/141g TL: N39 02 55 W108 15 06 On air date: Oct 22, 1979. 8 Foresight Cir., Grand Junction, CO, 81505. Phone: (970) 245-8880. Fax: (970) 245-8249. Web Site: www.kjct8.com. Licensee: Pikes Peak Television Inc. Group Owner: (group owner) (acq 6-26-2006; $45 million with KRDO-TV Colorado Springs). Population Served: 175,000 Natl. Network: ABC, . Natl. Rep: Blair Television,. Rgnl. Rep: Rgnl rep: Blair Television Washington Atty: Smithwick & Belendiuk, P.C. News staff: 21; News: 19.5 wkly.

Key Personnel:
David Bradley Jr. . . . . . pres
Kristy Santiago . . . . . gen mgr

KKCO— Digital Channel: 12. Digital Hrs: 24 155 kw vis. ant 1,407t TL: N39 04 00 W108 44 41 On air date: July 19, 1996. 2325 Interstate Ave., Grand Junction, CO, 81505. Phone: (970) 243-1111. Fax: (970) 243-1770. Web Site: www.nbc11news.com.E-mail: billv@nbc11news.com Licensee: Gray Television Licensee Inc. (acq 1-31-2005; $13.5 million with translator K50EZ Montrose). Population Served: 200,000 Natl. Network: NBC, CW, . Natl. Rep: Millennium Sales & Marketing,. Washington Atty: Wood, Maines & Brown, Chartered. News staff: 35; News: 28 hrs wkly.

Key Personnel:
J. Mack Robinson. . . . . pres
Debbie Varecha . . . . CFO & min affrs dir pub svc dir & farm dir
Paul Varecha . . . . . opns VP & prom dir
Sandy Moore . . . . . progmg dir & traf mgr
Peter Franklin . . . . . mus dir & cultural affrs dir
Jean Reynolds. . . . . news dir & feature ed
William Varecha. gen mgr & dev VP sls VP & mktg VP film buyer & engrg dir
Roger LaFrance . . . . . chief of engrg
Jean Reynolds . . . . . financial ed
Scott Sarra. . . . . sports cmtr
R. McCain . . . . . weather dir
Jessica Peterson. . . . . women's int ed & women's cmtr

KREX-TV— Digital Channel: 2. Digital Hrs: 20 12.9 kw vis, 2.5 kw aur. ant 10t/343g TL: N39 05 15 W108 33 56 On air date: May 22, 1954. Box 789, 345 Hillcrest Dr., Grand Junction, CO, 81501. Phone: (970) 242-5000. Fax: (970) 242-0886.E-mail: rtillery@krextv.com Web Site: www.krextv.com. Licensee: Hoak Media of Colorado LLC. Group Owner: Hoak Media Corporation (acq 11-12-2003; grpsl). Population Served: 139,000 Natl. Network: CBS, . Natl. Rep: Petry Television Inc.,. News staff: 15; News: 30 hrs wkly.

Key Personnel:
Ron Tillery . . . . . gen mgr
Dave Colvin . . . . . opns mgr

KREY-TV— Digital Channel: 13.6.17 kw vis, 1.36 kw aur. ant 79t/113g TL: N38 31 02 W107 51 12 On air date: Aug 26, 1956. 614 N. First, Montrose, CO, 81401. Phone: (970) 249-9601. Fax: (970) 249-9610.E-mail: kreytv@gwe.net Licensee: Hoak Media of Colorado LLC. Group Owner: Hoak Media Corporation (acq 10-10-2003; grpsl). Population Served: 17,000 Natl. Network: CBS, NBC, .

Key Personnel:
Chris Larum. . . . . stn mgr

***KRMJ—** Digital Channel: 18. Digital Hrs: 24 186 kw vis. ant 2,896t TL: N39 03 14 W108 15 13 On air date: January 1997. c/o KRMA-TV, 1089 Bannock St., Denver, CO, 80204. Phone: (970) 245-1818. Fax: (970) 255-2700. Web Site: www.rmpbs.org. Licensee: Rocky Mountain Public Broadcasting Network Inc. Natl. Network: PBS, . Washington Atty: Dow, Lohnes & Albertson.

Key Personnel:
James Morgese . . . . . pres & gen mgr
Angie Salazar . . . . . stn mgr
Suzanne Banning. . . . . dev dir
Donna Sanford . . . . . progmg dir
John Anderson . . . . . engrg dir & chief of engrg

Rebroadcasts KRMA-TV Denver 99.9%.

Montrose

see Grand Junction-Montrose, CO market

Pueblo

see Colorado Springs-Pueblo, CO market

Connecticut

Bridgeport

see New York market

Hartford & New Haven, CT (DMA 30)

WCTX— Digital Channel: 39. Digital Hrs: 24 5,000 kw vis, 500 kw aur. ant 1,029t TL: N41 25 23 W72 57 06 On air date: Apr 3, 1995. 8 Elm St., New Haven, CT, 06510. Phone: (203) 782-5900. Fax: (203) 782-5995. Licensee: WTNH Broadcasting Inc. Group Owner: LIN Television Corporation (acq 3-2002). Population Served: 1 m,ill,ion Natl. Network: MyNetworkTV, . Natl. Rep: Petry Television Inc.,. News: 8.5 hrs wkly.

Key Personnel:
Roger Hess . . . . . sls dir
Karen Rorke. . . . . natl sls mgr & rgnl sls mgr
Sem Dietrich . . . . . natl sls mgr & rgnl sls mgr
Mary Lee Weber. . . . . mktg dir
Deanna Banas-Kluk . . . . . progmg dir
Kirk Varner. . . . . news dir
Francine DuVerger . . . . . engrg dir & chief of engrg

***WEDH—** Digital Channel: 45. Digital Hrs: 6 AM-midnight (M-S); 7:30 692 kw vis, 69 kw aur. 860t/455g TL: N41 46 27 W72 48 20 On air date: Oct 1, 1962. 1049 Asylum Ave., Hartford, CT, 06105. Phone: (860) 278-5310. Fax: (860) 275-7500. Web Site: www.cptv.org. Licensee: Connecticut Public Broadcasting Inc. Population Served: 837,990 Natl. Network: PBS, . Rgnl. Network: Eastern Educ. Washington Atty: Schwartz, Woods & Miller.

Key Personnel:
Jerry Franklin . . . . . CEO & pres gen mgr
Meg Sakellarides. . . . . CFO
Larry Rifkin. . . . . exec VP & progmg VP
Haig Papasian . . . . . opns VP
Joseph Zareski . . . . . opns dir
Dean Orton . . . . . dev dir & progmg dir

***WEDN—** Digital Channel: 9. Digital Hrs: 6 AM-midnight (M-S); 7:30 AM-midnight (S 801.64 kw vis, 80.16 kw aur. 480t/476g TL: N41 31 11 W72 10 04 On air date: Mar 5, 1967. 1049 Asylum Ave., Hartford, CT, 06105. Phone: (860) 278-5310. Fax: (860) 275-7403. Web Site: www.cptv.org. Licensee: Connecticut Public Broadcasting. Population Served: 400,000 Natl. Network: PBS, . Rgnl. Network: Eastern Educ.

Key Personnel:
Jerry Franklin . . . . . CEO & pres gen mgr
Meg Sakellarides . . . . . CFO
Larry Rifkin. . . . . exec VP
Haig Papasian. . . . . opns VP & opns dir
Christopher Flynn . . . . . dev VP

***WEDY—** Digital Channel: 6. Digital Hrs: 24 4.47 kw vis, 500 w aur. ant 270t/102g TL: N41 19 42 W72 54 25 On air date: November 1974. 1049 Asylum Ave., Hartford, CT, 06105. Phone: (860) 278-5310. Fax: (860) 275-7500. Web Site: www.cptv.org. Licensee: Connecticut Public Broadcasting Inc. Population Served: 1,300,000 Natl. Network: PBS, .

Key Personnel:
Jerry Franklin . . . . . CEO & pres gen mgr
Meg Sakellarides . . . . . CFO
Larry Rifkin. . . . . exec VP & progmg VP
Haig Papasian . . . . . opns VP
Joseph Zareski . . . . . opns dir
Dean Orton . . . . . dev VP & dev dir

Rebroadcasts WEDH(TV) Hartford 100%.

WFSB— Digital Channel: 33. Digital Hrs: 24 100 kw vis, 20 kw aur. 904t/518g TL: N41 46 30 W72 48 20 On air date: Sept 23, 1957. 3 Constitution Plaza, Hartford, CT, 06103-1821. Phone: (860) 728-3333. Fax: (860) 247-8940. Fax: (860) 728-0263 (News Room). Web Site: www.wfsb.com. Licensee: Meredith Corp. dba WFSB. Group Owner: Meredith Broadcasting Group, Meredith Corp. (acq 9-4-97; $159 million). Population Served: 3,888,000 Natl. Network: CBS, . Natl. Rep: Harrington, Righter & Parsons,. Washington Atty: Garvey, Schubert & Barer. News: 36 hrs wkly.

Key Personnel:
Klarn DePalma . . . . . gen mgr
John Ahearn. . . . . opns mgr
Bill Whittle . . . . . gen sls mgr
Stephanie Turner . . . . . mktg dir
Shelly Smith. . . . . prom mgr
Gary Brown . . . . . news dir
Victor Zarrillio . . . . . engrg dir
Rob Luciano . . . . . rsch dir

WHPX-TV— Digital Channel: 26.2,792 kw vis, 279 kw aur. 1,251t TL: N41 25 05 W72 11 55 On air date: Sept 15, 1986. 3 Shaws Cove, Suite 226, New London, CT, 06320. Phone: (860) 444-2626. Fax: (860) 440-2601. Web Site: www.ionline.tv. Licensee: ION Media Hartford License Inc., debtor-in-possession. Group Owner: Paxson Communications Corp. (acq 2-25-2000; grpsl). Natl. Network: ION Television, .

WTIC-TV— Digital Channel: 31.5,000 kw vis, 1,000 kw aur. 1,692t/1,339g TL: N41 42 13 W72 49 57 On air date: Sept 17, 1984. One Corporate Ctr., Hartford, CT, 06103. Phone: (860) 527-6161. Fax: (860) 727-0158.E-mail: newsteam@fox61.com Web Site: www.fox61.com. Licensee: Tribune Television Co. Group Owner: Tribune Broadcasting Co. (acq 12-20-2007; grpsl). Natl. Network: Fox, . Natl. Rep: TeleRep,. News staff: 31; News: 6 hrs wkly.

WTNH— Digital Channel: 10.166 kw vis, 16.6 kw aur. 1,210t/909g TL: N41 25 23 W72 57 06 (CP: 175 kw vis, ant 863t) On air date: June 15, 1948. Box 1859, 8 Elm St., New Haven, CT, 06510. Phone: (203) 784-8888. Fax: (203) 789-2010.E-mail: wtnh@wtnh.com Web Site: www.wtnh.com. Licensee: LIN Television Inc. Group Owner: LIN Television Corporation (acq 12-94; $120.17 million; 1-2-95). Population Served: 1,000,000 Natl. Network: ABC, . Natl. Rep: Petry Television Inc.,. Washington Atty: Lin Legal. News staff: 77; News: 32 hrs wkly.

Key Personnel:
Jamie Holowaty . . . . . opns dir
Roger Hess. . . . . sls dir & sls dir
Roger Megroz . . . . . natl sls mgr
Phil Jermain . . . . . rgnl sls mgr
Mary Lee Weber . . . . . mktg dir & pub affrs dir
Deanna Barns-Kluk . . . . . progmg mgr
Kirk Varner. . . . . news dir
Francine DuVerger . . . . . engrg dir
Tony Marnaio . . . . . rsch dir
Connie Fitch . . . . . pub svc dir

WTXX— Digital Channel: 20.2,239 kw vis, 223.9 kw aur. ant 1,200t/1,013g TL: N41 31 04 W73 01 07 On air date: Sept 4, 1953. One Corporate Ctr., Hartford, CT, 06103. Phone: (860) 520-6573. Phone: (203) 758-3900. Fax: (860) 727-0158.E-mail: newsteam@foxx61.com Web Site: www.fox61.com. Licensee: WTXX Inc. (acq 12-20-2007; grpsl). Population Served: 1,000,000 Natl. Network: CW, . Natl. Rep: MMT,.

Key Personnel:
Richard Graziano . . . . . gen mgr & opns mgr

WUVN— Digital Channel: 46. Digital Hrs: 24 3,272 kw vis, 327.2 kw aur. 980t TL: N41 46 30 W72 48 04 On air date: Sept 25, 1954. 1 Constitution Plaza, Suite 7, Hartford, CT, 06103. Phone: (860)

278-1818. Fax: (860) 278-1811. Web Site: www.wuvntv.com. Licensee: Entravision Holdings LLC. Group Owner: Entravision Communications Corp. (acq 1-4-01; $18 million). Natl. Network: Univision (Spanish), . Washington Atty: Wiley, Rein & Fielding. News: 5 hrs wkly.
Key Personnel:
Robert Smith . . . . opns mgr
Ulysses Arrigoitia . . . . gen mgr & gen sls mgr
Rob Donner . . . . natl sls mgr
Meg Godin . . . . . . mktg mgr & prom mgr adv mgr & rsch dir
Renee Barbour . . . . progmg mgr & traf mgr
Dania Alexandrino . . . . mus dir
Sara Suarez . . . . news dir
Fran Vaccain . . . . chief of engrg
Omar Cabrara . . . . sports cmtr
Miguel Montoya . . . . weather dir

WVIT—(New Britain, Digital Channel: 35. Digital Hrs: 24 5,000 kw vis, 500 kw aur. 1,479t/1,051g TL: N41 42 00 W72 49 59 On air date: Feb 13, 1953. 1422 New Britain Ave., West Hartford, CT, 06110. Phone: (860) 521-3030. Fax: (860) 521-4860. Fax: (860) 521-3110. Licensee: NBC Telemundo License Co. Group Owner: NBC TV Stations Division (acq 12-07-97; trade). Population Served: 912,970 Natl. Network: NBC, . Natl. Rep: NBC TV Stations Sales,.
Key Personnel:
Dave Doebler . . . . pres & gen mgr
David Bondanza . . . . opns dir & engrg dir
Bill Nandi . . . . opns mgr & chief of opns
Steve Smith . . . . sls VP
Eric Bloom . . . . natl sls mgr
Marcie Miller . . . . mktg mgr & rsch dir
Maria Famicielli . . . . prom dir & adv dir
Ronni Attenello . . . . progmg dir
B.J. Finnell . . . . news dir
LaVerne Jefferys . . . . . pub affrs dir & min affrs dir pub svc dir
Colleen Green . . . . traf mgr
Kevin Nathan . . . . sports cmtr
Brad Field . . . . weather dir

New Haven

see Hartford & New Haven, CT market

Delaware

Seaford

see Salisbury, MD market

Wilmington

see Philadelphia market

District of Columbia

Washington, DC (Hagerstown, MD) (DMA 9)

WDCA— Digital Channel: 35. Digital Hrs: 24 4,000 kw vis, 400 kw aur. ant 770t/809g TL: N38 57 49 W77 06 18 On air date: Apr 20, 1966. 5151 Wisconsin Ave. N.W., Truro, DC, 20016-4124. Phone: (202) 895-3050. Fax: (202) 895-3340.E-mail: upn20wdca@paramount.com Web Site: www.upn20wdca.com. Licensee: Fox Television Stations Inc. Group Owner: (group owner; (acq 11-6-2001; with KTXH(TV) Houston, TX in swap for KBHK-TV San Francisco, CA). Population Served: 5,000,000 Natl. Network: MyNetworkTV, . Natl. Rep: Fox Stations Sales,. Washington Atty: Leventhal, Senter & Lerman.
Key Personnel:
Duffy Dyer . . . . stn mgr
Mike Lewis . . . . gen mgr & gen sls mgr

WDCW— Digital Channel: 50. Digital Hrs: 24 4,168 kw vis. ant 828t/735g TL: N38 57 44 W77 01 36 On air date: November 1981. 2121 Wisconsin Ave. N.W., Suite 350, Washington, DC, 20007. Phone: (202) 965-5050. Fax: (202) 965-0050. Web Site: thecwdc.trb.com. Licensee: WDCW Broadcasting Inc. Group Owner: Tribune Broadcasting Co. (acq 12-20-2007; grpsl). Population Served: 3,000,000 Natl. Network: CW, . Natl. Rep: Harrington, Righter & Parsons,.

Key Personnel:
Dennis Fitzsimons . . . . CEO
Eric Meyrowitz . . . . VP & gen mgr
Chip Shenkan . . . . gen sls mgr
Brett Burke . . . . natl sls mgr
Jim Byrne . . . . mktg dir & prom mgr
John Handley . . . . chief of engrg

*WETA-TV— Digital Channel: 27. Digital Hrs: 6:30 AM-2:30 AM 2,254 kw vis. 756t TL: N38 57 49 W77 06 18 (CP: Ant 764t) On air date: Oct 2, 1961. 2775 S. Quincy St., Arlington, VA, 22206. Phone: (703) 998-2600. Fax: (703) 998-3401. Web Site: www.weta.org. Licensee: Greater Washington Educational Telecommunications Association Inc. Population Served: 3,000,000 Natl. Network: PBS, . Rgnl. Network: Eastern Educ. Washington Atty: Dow, Lohnes & Albertson.
Key Personnel:
Sharon Rockefeller . . . . pres
Joe Bruns . . . . CFO & exec VP chief of opns
Karen Fritz . . . . gen mgr
Chad Davis . . . . progmg dir

WFDC-DT— Digital Channel: 15.2,680 kw. vis. ant 567t/407g TL: N38 56 24 W77 04 54 On air date: Aug 3, 1993. 101 Constitution Ave. N.W., # LL, Washington, DC, 20001. Phone: (301) 589-0030. Fax: (301) 495-9556.E-mail: rguernica@entravisiondc.com Web Site: www.entravision.com. Licensee: TeleFutura D.C. LLC. Group Owner: Univision Communications Inc. (acq 6-1-2001; $30 million). Natl. Network: Univision (Spanish), . Foreign lang progmg: SpanishS 168
Key Personnel:
Rudy Guernica . . . . gen mgr & stn mgr
Ernesto Clavijo . . . . news dir
Fred Willard . . . . chief of engrg

*WFPT— Digital Channel: 28.41.2 kw vis. ant 518t/485g TL: N39 15 37 W77 18 44 On air date: 1986. 11767 Owings Mills Blvd., Owings Mills, MD, 21117-1499. Phone: (410) 356-5600. Fax: (410) 581-6579.E-mail: comments@mpt.org Web Site: www.mpt.org. Licensee: Maryland Public Broadcasting Commission. Population Served: 600,000 Natl. Network: PBS, . Washington Atty: Schwartz, Woods & Miller.
Key Personnel:
Robert Shuman . . . . CEO & pres
Larry Unger . . . . CFO
Kirby Storms . . . . chief of engrg
Rebroadcasts WMPB(TV) Baltimore 100%.

WHAG-TV— Digital Channel: 26. Digital Hrs: 24 1,352 kw vis, 135.2 kw aur. 1,230t/453g TL: N39 39 35 W77 57 57 On air date: Jan 3, 1970. 13 E. Washington St., Hagerstown, MD, 21740. Phone: (301) 797-4400. Fax: (301) 733-1735. Fax: (301) 745-4093.E-mail: hbreslin@nbc25.com Web Site: www.your4state.com. Licensee: Nexstar Broadcasting Inc. Group Owner: Nexstar Broadcasting Group Inc. (acq 12-31-2003; grpsl). Population Served: 1,334,320 Natl. Network: NBC, . Natl. Rep: Continental Television Sales,. Washington Atty: Drinker Biddle & Reath L.L.P. News: 20 hrs wkly.
Key Personnel:
Hugh J. Breslin . . . . VP & gen mgr
Hugh Breslin . . . . gen sls mgr & progmg dir
Melissa Fountain . . . . prom mgr
Mark Kraham . . . . news dir
Michael Doty . . . . chief of engrg
Daniel McCarty . . . . traf mgr

*WHUT-TV— Digital Channel: 33. Digital Hrs: 18 500 kw vis, 158 kw aur. 700t/809g TL: N38 57 49 W77 06 18 On air date: Nov 17, 1980. 2222 4th St. N.W., Washington, DC, 20059. Phone: (202) 806-3200. Fax:(202) 806-3300.E-mail: j-lawson@howard.edu Web Site: www.whut.org. Licensee: Howard University. Population Served: 2,200,000 Natl. Network: PBS, . Washington Atty: Arnold & Porter. Wire Svc: Bloomberg Financial
Key Personnel:
Jennifer Lawson . . . . gen mgr
Samuel Hyder . . . . opns dir
Elizabeth Ventura . . . . dev dir

WJAL— Digital Channel: 39. Digital Hrs: 24 4,000 kw vis, 400 kw aur. ant 1,335t/275g TL: N39 53 31 W77 58 02 On air date: May 5, 1987. Box 190, Chambersburg, PA, 17201-0190. 262 Swamp Fox Rd., Chambersburg, PA 17201. Phone: (717) 375-4000. Fax: (717) 375-4052.E-mail: adsales@wjal.com Web Site: www.wjal.com. Licensee: Entravision Holdings LLC. Group Owner: Entravision Communications Corp. (acq 6-20-2001; $10.7 million including $400,000 bridge loan). Population Served: 1,361,190 Washington Atty: Leventhal, Senter & Lerman. News: 5 hrs local news wkly.
Key Personnel:
Steve Ullom . . . . stn mgr
C. Griffen . . . . engr

WJLA-TV— Digital Channel: 7. Digital Hrs: 24 30 kw vis. ant 771t/604g TL: N38 57 01 W77 04 47 On air date: Oct 3, 1947. 1100

Wilson Blvd., 6th Fl., Arlington, VA, 22209. Phone: (703) 236-9552. Fax: (703) 236-2345. Web Site: www.wjla.com. Licensee: ACC Licensee Inc. Group Owner: Allbritton Communications Co. (acq 1-76; grpsl). Population Served: 5,517,000 Natl. Network: ABC, . Washington Atty: Dow, Lohnes & Albertson, PLLC. News: 24 hrs wkly.
Key Personnel:
Frederick Ryan Jr. . . . . stn mgr & gen mgr

*WNVC— Digital Channel: 24. Digital Hrs: 24 1,230 kw vis, 123 kw aur. ant 1,049t/689g TL: N38 52 28 W77 13 24 (CP: 1,260 kw vis, 126 kw aur, ant 705t/345g) On air date: June 1, 1983. 8101A Lee Hwy., Falls Church, VA, 22042. Phone: (703) 770-7100. Web Site: WWW.mhznetworks.org. Licensee: Commonwealth Public Broadcasting Corp. (acq 6-4-2004). Population Served: 4,000,000 Washington Atty: Wiley, Rein & Fielding.
Key Personnel:
Fred Thomas . . . . gen mgr

*WNVT— Digital Channel: 30. Digital Hrs: 24 2,290 kw vis, 229 kw aur. ant 751t/651g TL: N38 37 42 W77 26 20 On air date: Mar 1, 1972. 8101A Lee Hwy., Falls Church, VA, 22042. Phone: (703) 770-7100. Web Site: www.mhznetworks.org. Licensee: Commonweath Public Broadcasting Corp. (acq 6-4-2004). Population Served: 1,500,000 Washington Atty: Wiley, Rein & Fielding.
Key Personnel:
Fred Thomas . . . . gen mgr

WPXW-TV— Digital Channel: 34. Digital Hrs: 24 1,000 kw vis, 100 kw aur. ant 846t/663g TL: N38 57 01 W77 04 47 On air date: Mar 26, 1978. 6199 Old Arrington Ln., Fairfax Stn., VA, 22039. Phone: (703) 503-7966. Fax: (703) 503-1225. Web Site: www.ionline.tv. Licensee: ION Media Washington License Inc., debtor-in-possession. Group Owner: Paxson Communications Corp. (acq 4-16-97; $30 million). Natl. Network: ION Television, . Washington Atty: Wilmer, Cutler & Pickering.
Key Personnel:
Bud Paxton . . . . pres & gen mgr

WRC-TV— Digital Channel: 48. Digital Hrs: 24 100 kw vis, 15.1 kw aur. 778t/662g TL: N38 56 24 W77 04 54 On air date: June 27, 1947. 4001 Nebraska Ave. N.W., Washington, DC, 20016. Phone: (202) 885-4000. Fax: (202) 885-4104. Web Site: www.nbc4.com. Licensee: NBC Telemundo License Co. Group Owner: NBC TV Stations Division. Population Served: 4,000,000 Natl. Network: NBC, . Natl. Rep: NBC TV Stations Sales,. Wire Svc: UPI
Key Personnel:
Michael Jack . . . . pres & gen mgr

WTTG— Digital Channel: 36.100 kw vis, 15 kw aur. 770t/705g TL: N38 57 21 W77 04 57 On air date: Jan 1, 1947. 5151 Wisconsin Ave. N.W., Washington, DC, 20016. Phone: (202) 244-5151. Fax: (202) 244-1745. Web Site: www.fox5dc.com. Licensee: Fox Television Stations Inc. Group Owner: (group owner; (acq 3-86; grpsl). Population Served: 4,000,000 Natl. Network: Fox, . Natl. Rep: TeleRep,. Washington Atty: Hogan & Hartson.
Key Personnel:
Duffy Dyer . . . . VP & gen mgr

WUSA— Digital Channel: 9. Digital Hrs: 24 12.6 kw vis. ant 771t/604g TL: N38 57 01 W77 04 47 On air date: Jan 16, 1949. 4100 Wisconsin Ave. N.W., Washington, DC, 20016. Phone: (202) 895-5999. Fax: (202) 364-6163.E-mail: 9news@wusatv9.com Web Site: www.wusatv9.com. Licensee: The Detroit News Inc. Group Owner: Gannett Broadcasting (Division of Gannett Co. Inc.) (acq 2-18-86). Population Served: 756,510 Natl. Network: CBS, . Natl. Rep: Blair Television,. Washington Atty: Reed Smith LLP. News: 39 hrs wkly.
Key Personnel:
Allans Horlick . . . . stn mgr
Darryll Green . . . . pres & gen mgr & engrg dir

*WVPY— Digital Channel: 21. Digital Hrs: 24 141 kw vis. ant 1,309t/89g TL: N38 57 36 W78 19 52 On air date: Aug 22, 1996. c/o WVPT, 298 Port Republic Rd., Harrisonburg, VA, 22801. Phone: (540) 434-5391. Fax: (540) 434-7084. Web Site: www.wvpt.net. Licensee: Shenandoah Valley Educational TV Corp. Population Served: 345,000 Natl. Network: PBS, . Washington Atty: Covington & Burling.
Key Personnel:
Tony Mancari . . . . COO
David Mullins . . . . gen mgr
Wanda Zimmerman . . . . progmg dir
Rebroadcasts WVPT Staunton 100%.

*WWPB— Digital Channel: 44. Digital Hrs: 24 4,070 kw vis. ant 1,223t/390g TL: N39 39 04 W77 58 15 On air date: 1986. 11767 Owings Mills Blvd., Owings Mills, MD, 21117-1499. Phone: (410) 356-5600. Fax: (410) 581-6579.E-mail: comments@mpt.org Web Site:

www.mpt.org. Licensee: Maryland Public Broadcasting Commission. Population Served: 600,000 Natl. Network: PBS, . Washington Atty: Schwartz, Woods & Miller.
Key Personnel:
Robert Shuman . . . . CEO & pres
Larry Unger . . . . CFO
Kirby Storms . . . . chief of engrg
Rebroadcasts WMPB(TV) Baltimore 100%.

WWPX-TV— Digital Channel: 12. Digital Hrs: 19 23 kw vis. ant 1,030t/243g TL: N39 27 27 W78 03 52 On air date: Oct 1, 1991. 74 Swinging Bridge Rd., Martinsburg, WV, 25401. Phone: (304) 267-4950. Web Site: www.ionline.tv. Licensee: ION Media Martinsburg License Inc., debtor-in-possession. Group Owner: Paxson Communications Corp. (acq 6-1-2000). Natl. Network: ION Television, . Washington Atty: Cohn & Marks.
Key Personnel:
Randy McCann . . . . gen mgr & sls dir

Florida

Daytona Beach

see Orlando-Daytona Beach-Melbourne, FL market

Destin

see Mobile, AL-Pensacola (Ft. Walton Beach), FL market

Fort Walton Beach

see Mobile, AL-Pensacola (Ft. Walton Beach), FL market

Ft. Lauderdale

see Miami-Ft. Lauderdale, FL market

Ft. Myers-Naples, FL
(DMA 62)

WBBH-TV— Digital Channel: 15.5,000 kw vis, 500 kw aur. ant 1,482t/1,500g TL: N26 49 27 W81 45 51 On air date: Dec 19, 1968. 3719 Central Ave., Fort Myers, FL 33901. Phone: (239) 939-2020. Fax: (239) 939-3244.E-mail: comments@nbc-2.com Web Site: www.nbc-2.com. Licensee: Waterman Broadcasting Corp. of Fla. Group Owner: Waterman Broadcasting Corp. Natl. Network: NBC, . Natl. Rep: Continental Television Sales,. Washington Atty: Cohn & Marks. News staff: 80; News: 32 hrs wkly.
Key Personnel:
Bernard Waterman . . . . pres
Gerry Poppe. CFO
Steven Pontius . . . . exec VP & gen mgr
Bob Beville. . . . . sls dir

WFTX-TV—(Cape Coral, Digital Channel: 35. Digital Hrs: 24 930 kw vis. ant 1,325t/1,322g TL: N26 47 42 W81 48 05 On air date: Oct 14, 1985. 621 S.W. Pine Island Rd., Cape Coral, FL, 33991. Phone: (239) 574-3636. Fax: (239) 574-2025. Web Site: www.fox4florida.com. Licensee: Journal Broadcast Corp. (acq 12-5-2005; grpsl). Population Served: 413,000 Natl. Network: Fox, . Washington Atty: Dow, Lohnes & Albertson.
Key Personnel:
Judy Kenney . . . . VP & gen mgr
Brent Struense . . . . mktg dir
Forrest Carr . . . . news dir

*WGCU— Digital Channel: 31.1,321 kw vis, 158 kw aur. ant 963t/992g TL: N26 48 54 W81 45 44 On air date: Aug 15, 1983. 10501 FGCU Blvd. S., West Palm Beach, FL, 33965. Phone: (239) 590-2300 / 7072. Fax: (239) 590-2310. Web Site: www.wgcu.org. Licensee: Board of Trustees, Florida Gulf Coast University. (acq 11-16-01). Natl. Network: PBS, . Washington Atty: Cohn & Marks.

Key Personnel:
Kathleen Davey . . . . gen mgr & stn mgr stn mgr
Michael Stepp . . . . opns mgr
Joseph Maggio . . . . chief of opns & progmg mgr
Amy Tardiff . . . . rgnl sls mgr & news dir

WINK-TV— Digital Channel: 9. Digital Hrs: 24 316 kw vis, 31.6 kw aur. ant 1,478t/1,519g TL: N26 48 01 W81 45 48 On air date: Mar 18, 1954. 2824 Palm Beach Blvd., Fort Myers, FL, 33916. Phone: (239) 334-1111. Fax: (239) 334-0744.E-mail: webmaster@winktv.com Web Site: www.winktv.com. Licensee: Fort Myers Broadcasting Co. Group Owner: (group owner) Population Served: 1,061,000 Natl. Network: CBS, . Natl. Rep: Eagle Television Sales,. Washington Atty: Leibowitz & Associates. News staff: 55; News: 32 hrs wkly.
Key Personnel:
Brian A. McBride . . . . CEO & pres
Wayne Simons . . . . VP & gen mgr & sls dir
Jesse Daniels . . . . natl sls mgr & rgnl sls mgr

WRXY-TV— Digital Channel: 33. Digital Hrs: 24 5,000 kw vis, 500 kw aur. ant 800t/790.5g TL: N26 47 08 W81 47 41 On air date: Jan 29, 1995. Box 50490, Ft. Myers, FL, 33994-0490. 40000 Horseshoe Rd., Punta Gorda, FL 33982. Phone: (239) 543-7200. Fax (239) 543-6800.E-mail: wrxy@wrxytv.com Licensee: West Coast Christian Television Inc. Ownership: David C. Gibbs III, Wayne Wetzel and Bill Anderson. (acq 12-16-97).
Key Personnel:
Paul Lodato . . . . gen mgr
Steven Speheger . . . chief of opns & engrg dir & chief of engrg

WXCW— Digital Channel: 45. Digital Hrs: 24 5,000 kw vis, 500 kw aur. ant 1,496t/1,496g TL: N26 47 08 W81 47 40 On air date: Oct 22, 1990. 2824 Palm Beach Blvd., Fort Myers, FL, 33916. Phone: (239) 338-1111. Fax: (239) 479-5592. Web Site: www.wb6tv.com. Licensee: Sun Broadcasting Inc.. Ownership: Joseph C. Schwartzel, 100% Group Owner: Acme Communications Inc. (acq 2-16-2007; $45 million). Natl. Network: CW, . Natl. Rep: Millennium Sales & Marketing,. Washington Atty: Dickstein Shapiro Morin & Oshinsky L.L.P. News: 13.5 hrs wkly.
Key Personnel:
Joe Schwartzel . . . . gen mgr
Jack Spiess . . . . chief of opns
Jim Schwartzel . . . . sls dir

WZVN-TV— Digital Channel: 41. Digital Hrs: 24 5,000 kw vis, 500 kw aur. ant 1,206t/1,224g TL: N26 25 22 W81 37 49 On air date: Aug 21, 1974. 3719 Central Ave., Fort Myers, FL, 33901. Phone: (239) 939-2020. Fax: (239) 939-3244 (news). Fax: (239) 939-4801.E-mail: comments@nbc-2.com Web Site: abc-7.com. Licensee: Montclair Communications Inc. Ownership: Lara Kunkler. (acq 10-10-1996; $21.3 million). Population Served: 451,700 Natl. Network: ABC, . Natl. Rep: Continental Television Sales,. Washington Atty: Irwin, Campbell & Tannenwald. News staff: 85; News: 19.5 hrs wkly.
Key Personnel:
Lara Kunkler . . . . pres
Laura Kunkler. . . . . gen mgr
Chris Rhodes . . . . opns mgr & mktg dir

Ft. Pierce

see West Palm Beach-Ft. Pierce, FL market

Ft. Walton Beach

see Mobile, AL-Pensacola (Ft. Walton Beach), FL market

Gainesville, FL
(DMA 160)

WCJB-TV— Digital Channel: 16. Digital Hrs: 24 2,818 kw vis, 282 kw aur. ant 1,049t/985g TL: N29 32 11 W82 24 00 On air date: Apr 7, 1971. 6220 N.W. 43rd St., Gainesville, FL, 32653. Phone: (352) 377-2020. Fax: (352) 373-6516.E-mail: tv20news@wcjb.com Web Site: www.wcjb.com. Licensee: Diversified Broadcasting Inc. Group Owner: Diversified Communications (acq 12-1-76; 11-1-76). Population Served: 370,710 Natl. Network: ABC, CW, . Washington Atty: Irwin, Campbell & Tannenwald. News staff: 35; News: 17 hrs wkly.
Key Personnel:
Carolyn Barrett . . . . pres & gen mgr & stn mgr

WGFL— Digital Channel: 28. Digital Hrs: 24 5,000 kw vis, 53 kw aur. ant 911t TL: N29 37 47 W82 34 24 On air date: Sept 20, 1997. 1703 N.W. 80th Blvd., Gainesville, FL, 32606. Phone: (352) 332-1128. Fax: (352) 332-1506. Web Site: www.mygainesville.tv. Licensee: New Age

Media of Gainesville License LLC. (acq 3-31-2007; grpsl). Population Served: 400,000 Natl. Network: CBS, MyNetworkTV, .
Key Personnel:
Todd Senter . . . . gen mgr
Sue Edwards . . . . opns dir

WNBW-DT— Digital Channel: 9. Digital Hrs: 24 4.9 kw vis. ant 918t/918g TL: N29 37 47 W82 34 25 On air date: Jan 1, 2009. 1703 N.W. 80th Blvd., Gainesville, FL, 32606. Phone: (352) 332-1128. Fax: (352) 332-1506. Web Site: www.mygainesville.tv. Licensee: MPS Media of Gainesville License LLC.. Ownership: Eugene J. Brown, 100% votes (acq 7-25-2008; $864,937 for CP). Natl. Network: NBC, .
Key Personnel:
Todd Senter . . . . gen mgr

WOGX— Digital Channel: 31. Digital Hrs: 6 AM-2 AM 2,750 kw vis, 275 kw aur. ant 918t/855g TL: N29 21 32 W82 19 53 On air date: Nov 1, 1983. 1551 S.W. 37th Ave., Ocala, FL, 34474. 35 Skyline Dr., Lake Mary, FL 32746. Phone: (352) 873-6951. Phone: (407) 644-3535. Fax: (352) 237-5423. Web Site: www.wofl.com. Licensee: Fox Television Stations Inc. Group Owner: (group owner; acq 6-17-2002; with WOFL(TV) Orlando). Natl. Network: Fox, . Natl. Rep: TeleRep,. Washington Atty: Skadden, Arps, Slate, Meagher & Flom. News staff: 35; News: 7 hrs wkly.
Key Personnel:
Stan Knott . . . . gen mgr
Satan Knott. . . . . stn mgr

*WUFT— Digital Channel: 36. Digital Hrs: 21 100 kw vis, 20 kw aur. ant 860t/869g TL: N29 42 34 W82 23 40 On air date: Nov 10, 1958. 2200 Weimer Hall, Univ. of Florida, Gainesville, FL, 32611. Phone: (352) 392-5551. Fax: (352) 392-5731.E-mail: info@wuft.org Web Site: www.wuft.org. Licensee: Board of Trustees, University of Florida. Population Served: 250,000 Natl. Network: PBS, . Washington Atty: Schwartz, Woods & Miller. News: 3 hrs wkly.
Key Personnel:
Richard Lehner . . . . gen mgr
Titus Rush . . . . stn mgr
Brent Williams . . . . dev dir
Rob Carr . . . . chief of engrg

Jacksonville, FL
(DMA 47)

WAWS— Digital Channel: 32.Note: Fox is on WAWS(TV) ch 30, MyNetworkTV is on WAWS-DT ch 32. 2,789 kw vis, 278.9 kw aur. ant 991t/1,030g TL: N30 16 53 W81 36 15 (CP: 5,000 kw vis, 508 kw aur, ant 991t/997g) On air date: Feb 15, 1981. 11700 Central Pkwy., Unit 2, Jacksonville, FL, 32224. Phone: (904) 642-3030. Fax: (904) 642-5665.E-mail: info@fox30online.com Web Site: www.fox30jax.com. Licensee: Newport Television License LLC. Group Owner: Clear Channel Communications Inc. (acq 3-14-2008; grpsl). Population Served: 1,100,000 Natl. Network: Fox, MyNetworkTV, Natl. Rep: Continental Television Sales,. Washington Atty: Covington & Burling.
Key Personnel:
Jack Potter . . . . sls dir & gen sls mgr

WCWJ— Digital Channel: 34. Digital Hrs: 24 4,680 kw vis, 500 kw aur. ant 1,049t TL: N30 16 36 W81 33 47 On air date: Feb 19, 1966. 9117 Hogan Road, Jacksonville, FL, 32216. 9117 Hogan Rd., Jacksonville, FL 32216. Phone: (904) 641-1700. Fax: (904) 642-7201. Web Site: www.yourjax.com. Licensee: Nexstar Broadcasting Inc. Group Owner: Media General Broadcast Group (acq 5-1-2009). Population Served: 1,000,000 Natl. Network: CW, . Washington Atty: Drinker Biddle & Reath LLP.
Key Personnel:
Marc Hefner . . . . gen sls mgr
Mark Marshman . . . . opns mgr & chief of engrg

*WJCT— Digital Channel: 7. Digital Hrs: 18 18 kw vis. ant 991t/16g TL: N30 16 51 W81 34 12 On air date: Sept 10, 1958. 100 Festival Park Ave., Jacksonville, FL, 32202. Phone: (904) 353-7770. Fax: (904) 358-6331.E-mail: wjct@wjct.org Web Site: www.wjct.org. Licensee: WJCT Inc. Population Served: 650,000 Natl. Network: PBS, . Washington Atty: Schwartz, Woods & Miller.
Key Personnel:
Michael T. Boylan. . . . . CEO & pres gen mgr
Steven Wallace . . . . chmn
Jocelyn Enriquez . . . . CFO
Rick Johnson . . . . sr VP & opns VP
Jeri Cirillo. . . . . dev VP

*WJEB-TV— Digital Channel: 44.1,000 kw vis. ant 945t/932g TL: N30 16 34 W81 33 52 On air date: May 29, 1991. 3101 Emerson Expwy., Jacksonville, FL, 32277. Phone: (904) 399-8413. Fax: (904) 399-8423.E-mail: prayer@wjeb.org Web Site: www.wjeb.org. Licensee: Jacksonville Educators Broadcasting Inc. Natl. Network: PBS, .

Key Personnel:
Collette D. Snowden . . . . gen mgr & stn mgr
Clayton Roney . . . . engrg mgr

WJXT— Digital Channel: 42. Digital Hrs: 24 100 kw vis, 20 kw aur. 930t/996g TL: N30 16 23 W81 33 13 (CP: Ant 436t) On air date: Sept 15, 1949. Box 5270, Jacksonville, FL, 32247. 4 Broadcast Pl. , Jacksonville, FL 32207. Phone: (904) 399-4000. Fax: (904) 399-1828.E-mail: jaxnews@news4jax.com Web Site: www.news4jax.com. Licensee: Post-Newsweek Stations, Fla. Inc. Group Owner: Post-Newsweek Stations Inc. (acq 1-28-53; grpsl;2-2-53). Population Served: 671,400 Natl. Rep: MMT,. Washington Atty: Covington & Burling. News staff: 75; News: 51 hrs wkly.
Key Personnel:
Ann Sutton . . . . VP & stn mgr natl sls mgr
Tina Schultz . . . . opns mgr
Wayne Reid . . . . gen sls mgr
Mike Guerrieri . . . . mktg dir & pub svc dir
Mo Ruddy . . . . news dir

WJXX— Digital Channel: 10. Digital Hrs: 24 5,000 kw vis. 659t/725g TL: N30 04 27 W81 48 23 On air date: Feb 9, 1997. 1070 East Adam St., Jacksonville, FL, 32202. Phone: (904) 354-1212. Fax: (904) 353-3455.E-mail: news@firstcoastnews.com Web Site: www.firstcoastnews.com. Licensee: Gannett River States Publishing Corp. Group Owner: Gannett Broadcasting (acq 3-15-00; $81 million). Natl. Network: ABC, .
Key Personnel:
Ken Tonning . . . . pres & gen mgr opns dir
Glenn Sebold . . . . progmg dir
Mike McCormick . . . . news dir

WPXC-TV— Digital Channel: 24. Digital Hrs: 24 5,000 kw vis. ant 1,371t TL: N31 08 22 W81 56 15 On air date: Apr 2, 1990. 7434 Blythe Island Hwy., Brunswick, GA, 31523. Phone: (912) 267-0021. Fax: (912) 261-9582. Web Site: www.ionline.tv. Licensee: Paxson Jax License Inc. Group Owner: Paxson Communications Corp. (acq 12-6-2000; $3.07 million). Natl. Network: ION Television, . Washington Atty: Fleischman & Walsh.
Key Personnel:
Joseph Koker . . . . VP

WTEV-TV— Digital Channel: 19. Digital Hrs: 24 5,000 kw vis, 500 kw aur. ant 980t/990g TL: N30 16 34 W81 33 58 On air date: Aug 1, 1980. 11700 Central Pkwy., Unit 2, Jacksonville, FL, 32224. Phone: (904) 642-3030. Fax: (904) 642-5665.E-mail: info@cbs47.com Web Site: ActionNewsJax.com. Licensee: High Plains Broadcasting License Co. LLC. Group Owner: Clear Channel Communications Inc. (acq 9-15-2008; grpsl). Population Served: 1,100,000 Natl. Network: CBS, . Natl. Rep: Millennium Sales & Marketing,. Washington Atty: Pillsbury Winthrop Shaw Pittman LLP. News staff: 72; News: 22 hrs wkly.
Key Personnel:
Adrian West . . . . gen sls mgr & progmg dir

WTLV— Digital Channel: 13. Digital Hrs: 24 316 kw vis, 31.6 kw aur. 1,049t/999g TL: N30 16 23 W81 33 13 On air date: Sept 1, 1957. 1070 E. Adams St., Jacksonville, FL, 32202. Phone: (904) 354-1212. Fax: (904) 633-8899.E-mail: news@firstcoastnews.com Web Site: www.firstcoastnews.com. Licensee: Multimedia Cablevision Inc. Group Owner: Gannett Broadcasting (Division of Gannett Co. Inc.) (acq 5-12-75; $11,401,217;4-14-75). Population Served: 1,265,000 Natl. Network: NBC, . Natl. Rep: Blair Television,. Washington Atty: Reed, Smith, Shaw & McClay. News staff: 54; News: 17 hrs wkly.
Key Personnel:
Ken Tonning . . . . pres & gen mgr
Sam Folley . . . . natl sls mgr

***WXGA-TV—** Digital Channel: 8.316 kw vis, 47.9 kw aur. ant 1,030t/1,089g TL: N31 13 17 W82 34 24 On air date: Dec 4, 1961. 6433 TV-Tower Rd., Milwood, GA, 31552. Phone: (912) 338-5200. Web Site: www.gpb.org. Licensee: Georgia Public Telecommunications Commission. Natl. Network: PBS, .
Key Personnel:
Chris Allen . . . . stn mgr

Melbourne

see Orlando-Daytona Beach-Melbourne, FL market

Miami-Ft. Lauderdale, FL (DMA 16)

WAMI-DT— Digital Channel: 47. Digital Hrs: 24 5,000 kw vis, 500 kw aur. ant 866t/869g TL: N25 57 59 W80 12 33 On air date: Aug 10, 1988. 8550 N.W. 33rd St., Miami, FL, 33122. Phone: (305) 421-1900. Fax: (305) 463-9154. Web Site: www.univision.com. Licensee: TeleFutura Miami LLC. Group Owner: Univision Communications Inc. (acq 6-6-2001; grpsl). Natl. Network: TeleFutura (Spanish), . Washington Atty: Hogan & Hartson. News staff: 35; News: 3 hrs wkly.
Key Personnel:
Luis Fernandez Rocha . . . . VP
Luis Fernandez Rocha . . . . gen mgr
Marilyn Hansen . . . . gen sls mgr

***WBEC-TV—** Digital Channel: 40. Digital Hrs: 24 5,000 kw vis. ant 1,000t/1,000g TL: N25 59 10 W80 11 36 On air date: 2001. Broward Education Communications Network, 6600 S.W. Nova Dr., Fort Lauderdale, FL, 33317. Phone: (754) 321-1000. Fax: (754) 321-1180.E-mail: feedback@becon.tv Web Site: www.becon.tv. Licensee: The School Board of Broward County, Florida. (acq 3-31-2000). Population Served: 1,600,000
Key Personnel:
Ognian Dimov . . . . gen mgr
Tom Forte . . . . traf mgr

WBFS-TV— Digital Channel: 32.5,000 kw vis, 500 kw aur. ant 924g TL: N25 57 59 W80 12 33 On air date: Dec 9, 1984. 8900 N.W. 18th Terr., Doral, FL, 33172. Phone: (305) 621-3333. Fax: (305) 628-3900.E-mail: upn33@wbfs.com Web Site: www.upn33.com. Licensee: Viacom Stations Group of Miami Inc. Group Owner: Viacom Television Stations Group. Natl. Network: MyNetworkTV, .
Key Personnel:
Shaun McDonald . . . . gen mgr
Tom Doerr . . . . stn mgr

WFOR-TV— Digital Channel: 22. Digital Hrs: 24 100 kw vis, 10 kw aur. ant 997t/997g TL: N25 58 07 W80 13 20 On air date: Mar 21, 1949. 8900 N.W. 18th Terr., Doral, FL, 33172. Phone: (305) 591-4444. Fax: (305) 639-4444. Web Site: www.cbs4news.com. Licensee: CBS Television Stations Inc. Group Owner: Viacom Television Stations Group. Population Served: 3,909,276 Natl. Network: CBS, . Natl. Rep: CBS TV Stations National Sales,. Wire Svc: NWS (National Weather Service) News staff: 90; News: 30 hrs wkly.
Key Personnel:
Shaun McDonald . . . . pres & gen mgr
Michael Applebaum . . . . gen mgr & gen sls mgr
Tom Cury . . . . sls dir
Tracy Letize . . . . progmg dir
Adrienne Roark . . . . news dir
Juan Andrea . . . . engrg dir
Franklin Anderson . . . . chief of engrg

WGEN-TV— Digital Channel: 8. Digital Hrs: 24 2.65 kw vis. ant 179t/168g TL: N24 33 18 W81 48 05 On air date: Jan 1, 1995. 527 Southard St. W., Key West, FL, 33040-6871. Phone: (305) 293-4333. Fax: (305) 293-4007.E-mail: amonge@wegentv.com Web Site: www.wgent.tv.com. Licensee: Sonia Licensed Subsidiary LLC. Ownership: Community Property Trust under the De La Pena Family Trust of 11/26/01, 50%; and Husband's Separate Trust under the De La Pena Family Trust of 11/26/01, 50% (acq 4-16-2004; $2.75 million).
Key Personnel:
Alberto Monge . . . . gen mgr & stn mgr

***WHFT-TV—** Digital Channel: 46. Digital Hrs: 24 1,000 kw vis. ant 1,010t/1,010g TL: N25 59 34 W80 10 27 On air date: Mar 17, 1975. 3324 Pembroke Rd., Pembroke Park, FL, 33021. Phone: (954) 962-1700. Fax: (954) 962-2817. Web Site: www.tbn.org. Licensee: Trinity Broadcasting of Florida Inc. Group Owner: Trinity Broadcasting Network (acq 5-14-80; $10 million). Population Served: 1,000,000 Washington Atty: Colby M. May. Foreign lang progmg: SpanishS 0
Key Personnel:
Paul F. Crouch . . . . pres
T. Hines . . . . gen mgr

***WLRN-TV—** Digital Channel: 20. Digital Hrs: 24 2,820 kw vis, 283 kw aur. ant 1,014t/1,010g TL: N25 57 30 W80 12 44 On air date: June 26, 1962. 172 N.E. 15th St., Calgary, FL, 33132. Phone: (305) 995-1717. Fax: (305) 995-2299.E-mail: info@wlrn.org Web Site: www.wlrn.org. Licensee: The School Board of Miami-Dade County, FL. Population Served: 4,200,000 Natl. Network: PBS, . Rgnl. Network: SECA. Washington Atty: Leibowitz & Associates.
Key Personnel:
John LaBonia . . . . gen mgr
Ginette Grey . . . . dev mgr

WLTV-DT— Digital Channel: 23.4,470 kw vis. ant 974t TL: N25 58 07 W80 13 20 On air date: Nov 15, 1967. 9405 N.W. 41st St., Miami, FL, 33178. Phone: (305) 470-2323. Fax: (305) 471-3959. Web Site: www.univision.net. Licensee: WLTV L.P. Group Owner: Univision Communications Inc. (acq 8-7-88). Population Served: 4,600,000 Natl. Network: Univision (Spanish), . Washington Atty: Wiley, Rein & Fielding. Foreign lang progmg: SpanishS 168 News staff: 70; News: 24 hrs/week.
Key Personnel:
Luis Fernandez-Rocha . . . . gen mgr
Bert Delgado . . . . opns dir
Teri Vila Caballero . . . . gen sls mgr
Evi Fabrega . . . . prom mgr
Emilio Marrero . . . . news dir
Douglas Petersen . . . . chief of engrg
Mary Fuentes . . . . traf mgr

***WPBT—** Digital Channel: 18. Digital Hrs: 24 100 kw vis, 20 kw aur. 932t/923g TL: N25 57 30 W80 12 44 On air date: Aug 12, 1955. Box 610002, Miami, FL, 33261-0002. 14901 N.E. 20th Ave., Miami, FL 33261-0002. Phone: (305) 949-8321. Fax: (305) 944-4211.E-mail: channel2@channel2.org Web Site: www.channel2.org. Licensee: Community Television Foundation of South Florida Inc. Population Served: 1,300,000 Natl. Network: PBS, . Washington Atty: Wilmer, Cutler & Pickering.
Key Personnel:
Rick Schneider . . . . CEO & pres & gen mgr
Dave Mullins . . . . mktg VP
Jody Rafkind . . . . prom mgr

WPLG— Digital Channel: 10. Digital Hrs: 24 316 kw vis, 47.9 kw aur. 1,042t/1,046g TL: N25 57 59 W80 12 44 On air date: Nov 20, 1961. 3900 Biscayne Blvd., Miami, FL, 33137. Phone: (305) 576-1010. Fax: (305) 325-2381. Web Site: www.local10.com. Licensee: Post-Newsweek Stations, Fla. Inc. Group Owner: Post-Newsweek Stations Inc. (acq 9-27-69; grpsl;10-6-69). Population Served: 3,274,000 Natl. Network: ABC, . Natl. Rep: MMT,. Washington Atty: Covington & Burling.
Key Personnel:
David Boylan . . . . VP & gen mgr
Sharon Harrison . . . . opns mgr
Mimi Del Ca. progmg mgr

WPXM-TV— Digital Channel: 35. Digital Hrs: 24 323 kw vis. ant 925t/922g TL: N25 59 09 W80 11 37 On air date: Oct 15, 1992. 9100 S. Dadeland Blvd., Suite 1804, Miami, FL, 33156. Phone: (954) 622-6835. Fax: (954) 622-6843. Web Site: www.ionline.tv. Licensee: ION Media License Co., debtor-in-possession. Group Owner: Paxson Communications Corp. (acq 12-12-97). Natl. Network: ION Television, .
Key Personnel:
Doug Barker . . . . pres & gen mgr

WSBS-TV— Digital Channel: 3. Digital Hrs: 24 11.2 kw vis, 1.1 kw aur. ant 203t TL: N24 33 18 W81 48 07 On air date: June 1, 1993. 2601 S. Bayshore Dr., Suite 2020, Coconut Grove, FL, 33133. Phone: (305) 644-4800. Fax: (786) 470-1667.E-mail: info@mega.tv Web Site: www.mega.tv. Licensee: WDLP Licensing Inc. (acq 2-28-2006; $37.25 million with WSBS-CA Miami). Population Served: 35,000 Foreign lang progmg: SpanishS 168
Key Personnel:
Alex Aleman . . . . gen mgr & stn mgr

WSCV— Digital Channel: 30. Digital Hrs: 24 5,000 kw vis. 827t TL: N25 57 59 W80 12 33 On air date: Dec 6, 1968. 15000 S.W. 27th St., Miramar, FL, 33027. Phone: (954) 622-6000. Fax: (954) 622-6107.E-mail: wtvjdesk@nbc.com Web Site: www.telemundo51.com. Licensee: NBC Telemundo License Co. Group Owner: Telemundo Group Inc. (acq 4-12-2002; grpsl). Population Served: 2,000,000 Natl. Network: Telemundo (Spanish), . Foreign lang progmg: SpanishS 168 News staff: 70; News: 16 hrs wkly.
Key Personnel:
Don Browne . . . . CEO
Manuel Martinez. gen mgr
Jorge Carballo . . . . gen sls mgr
Migdalia Figueroa. . . . . mktg mgr
Maria Christina Barros . . . . progmg dir

WSFL-TV— Digital Channel: 19. Digital Hrs: 24 5,000 kw vis, 500 kw aur. ant 905t/905g TL: N25 58 07 W80 13 20 On air date: Oct 16, 1982. 200 E. Las Olas Blvd., 11th Fl., Fort Lauderdale, FL, 33301. Phone: (954) 627-7300. Fax: (954) 355-5200. Web Site: wsfltv.sun -sentinel.com. Licensee: Channel 39 Inc. Group Owner: Tribune Broadcasting Co. (acq 12-20-2007; grpsl). Population Served: 3,247,000 Natl. Network: CW, . Natl. Rep: TeleRep,. News: 3.5 hrs wkly.
Key Personnel:
Ed Wilson . . . . pres
Cam Trinh . . . . CFO
Howard Greenberg. . . . . gen mgr
Allyson Meyers . . . . stn mgr
Mark Drury . . . . prom dir & prom mgr
Natalie Grant. . . . . progmg dir & progmg mgr
Rudy Morris . . . . chief of engrg
Terry Ferber . . . . traf mgr

WSVN— Digital Channel: 7. Digital Hrs: 24 316 kw vis, 30.2 kw aur. 950t/1,002g TL: N25 57 49 W80 12 44 On air date: July 29, 1956. 1401 79th St. Causeway, Miami, FL, 33141. Phone: (305) 751-6692.

Fax: (305) 757-2266. Fax: TWX: (810) 848-6151. Web Site: www.wsvn.com. Licensee: Sunbeam Television Corp. (acq 10-4-67; 10-16-67). Population Served: 333,859 Natl. Network: Fox, . Natl. Rep: Harrington, Righter & Parsons,. Washington Atty: Koteen & Naftalin.
Key Personnel:
Edmund N. Ansin . . . . . pres
Steven Cejas . . . . . exec VP
Robert W. Leider . . . . . gen mgr

WTVJ— Digital Channel: 31. Digital Hrs: 24 100 kw vis, 15.9 kw aur. ant 1,842t/1,841.5g TL: N25 32 24 W80 28 07 On air date: Sept 20, 1967. NBC 6 WTVD, 15000 S.W. 27th St., Miramar, FL, 33027. Phone: (954) 622-6000.E-mail: wtvjdesk@nbc.com Web Site: www.nbcmiami.com. Licensee: NBC Telemundo License Co. Group Owner: NBC TV Stations Division (acq 1995). Population Served: 3,594,000 Natl. Network: NBC, . Natl. Rep: NBC TV Stations Sales,. Wire Svc: NWS (National Weather Service)
Key Personnel:
Amanda Calpin . . . . . gen mgr
Ardyth R. Diercks . . . . . gen mgr & sls VP

Naples

see Ft. Myers-Naples, FL market

Orlando-Daytona Beach-Melbourne, FL

(DMA 19)

WACX—(Leesburg, Digital Channel: 40. Digital Hrs: 24 1,000 kw vis. ant 1,619t/1,591g TL: N28 35 11.6 W81 04 58.2 On air date: Mar 6, 1982. Box 608040, Orlando, FL, 32860. 285 W. Central Pkwy., Altamonte Springs, FL 32714. Phone: (407) 263-4040.E-mail: superchannel @superchannel.com Web Site: www.wacxtv.com. Licensee: Associated Christian Television System Inc. (acq 6-8-83;7-4-83). Population Served: 3,500,000 Washington Atty: Koerner & Olender. Foreign lang progmg: SpanishS 0
Key Personnel:
Claud Bowers . . . . . CEO & pres pres & gen mgr
Carol Gentry. . . . . gen sls mgr
Linda Jerrold . . . . . traf mgr

***WBCC—** Digital Channel: 30. Digital Hrs: 24 182 kw vis. ant 1,610t/1,588g TL: N28 36 35 W81 03 35 On air date: Jan 12, 1988. 1519 Clearlake Rd., Cocoa, FL, 32922. Phone: (321) 433-7110. Fax: (321) 433-7154.E-mail: wbcc@brevardcc.edu Web Site: www.wbcctv.org. Licensee: Brevard Community College. Population Served: 1.5 m,ill,ion Natl. Network: PBS, .
Key Personnel:
Dr. James Drake . . . . . pres
Philip T. Wallace . . . . . gen mgr & stn mgr

***WDSC-TV—** Digital Channel: 33. Digital Hrs: 20 708 kw vis, 201.4 kw aur. ant 577t/567g TL: N29 10 24 W81 09 24 On air date: Feb 1, 1988. Box 9245, Daytona Beach, FL, 32120-2811. 1200 W. International Speedway Blvd., Daytona Beach, FL 32114. Phone: (386) 506-4415. Fax: (386) 506-4427.E-mail: channel15@dbc.edu Web Site: www.wceu.org. Licensee: Daytona State College Inc. (acq 6-30-2002). Population Served: 3,500,000 Natl. Network: PBS, . Washington Atty: Fletcher, Heald & Hildreth.
Key Personnel:
Bruce E. Dunn . . . . . gen mgr & gen sls mgr
Bill Schwartz . . . . . engrg dir & chief of engrg

WESH—(Daytona Beach, Digital Channel: 11.100 kw vis, 10 kw aur. 1,650t/1,670g TL: N28 56 17 W81 18 58 On air date: June 11, 1956. 1021 N. Wymore Rd., Winter Park, FL, 32789. Phone: (407) 645-2222. Fax: (407) 539-7812.E-mail: desk@wesh.com Web Site: www.wesh.com. Licensee: WESH-TV Broadcasting. Group Owner: Hearst-Argyle Television Inc. (acq 1999; grpsl). Population Served: 1,735,900 Natl. Network: NBC, . Washington Atty: Brooks, Pierce, McLendon, Humphrey & Leonard.
Key Personnel:
James J. Carter . . . . . pres & VP gen mgr
Rick Scharf . . . . . opns mgr
Rob Halpern. . . . . gen sls mgr
Justin Jones. . . . . natl sls mgr
Lenora Boutte . . . . . progmg dir & progmg mgr
Bob Long . . . . . news dir
Richard Monn . . . . . chief of engrg
Penni Ward Rojas . . . . . traf mgr

WFTV— Digital Channel: 39. Digital Hrs: 24 316 kw vis, 31.6 kw aur. ant 1,570t/1,543g TL: N28 36 08 W81 05 37 On air date: Feb 1, 1958. Box 999, Orlando, FL, 32802. 490 E. South St., Orlando, FL 32801-2841. Phone: (407) 841-9000. Fax: (407) 422-1887. Fax: (407) 481-2891 (news). Web Site: www.wftv.com. Licensee: WFTV-TV Holdings Inc. Group Owner: Cox Communications Inc. (acq 8-85; $185 million). Population Served: 2,400,000 Natl. Network: ABC, . News staff: 80; News: 25 hrs wkly.
Key Personnel:
Shawn Bartelt . . . . . VP & gen mgr
Chip Reif . . . . . opns mgr
Lisa Hines . . . . . gen sls mgr
Bob St. Charles . . . . . mktg mgr
Bob Jordan . . . . . news dir

WHLV-TV— Digital Channel: 51. Digital Hrs: 24 4,680 kw vis, 468 kw aur. ant 934t/1,005g TL: N28 18 26 W80 54 48 On air date: Aug 16, 1982. 31 Skyland Dr., Lake Mary, FL, 32746. Phone: (407) 423-5200. Fax: (407) 423-8153.E-mail: ed@tv52.org Web Site: www.tv52.org. Licensee: Trinity Christian Center of Santa Ana Inc. Group Owner: (group owner; (acq 9-19-2006; $50 million). Population Served: 3,068,000 Washington Atty: Gammon & Grange.
Key Personnel:
Mark Reynolds . . . . . gen mgr
Ed Griffis . . . . . opns VP
Eileen Kelly . . . . . progmg dir & progmg
Marshall Royalty . . . . . chief of engrg

WKCF—(Clermont, Digital Channel: 17. Digital Hrs: 24 5,000 kw vis. ant 1,683t TL: N28 35 12 W81 04 58 On air date: December 1988. 1021 North Wymore Rd., Winter Park, FL, 32789. Phone: (407) 645-1818. Fax: (407) 647-4163.E-mail: wb18wkcf@wb18.com Web Site: www.wb18.com. Licensee: Orlando Hearst-Argyle Television Inc. Group Owner: Emmis Communications Corp. (acq 7-7-2006; $217.5 million). Population Served: 1,345,700 Natl. Network: CW, . Natl. Rep: Harrington, Righter & Parsons,.
Key Personnel:
James Carter . . . . . pres
James J. Carter. . . . . gen mgr & gen sls mgr
Steve Rifkin . . . . . opns dir & mktg dir
Tom Post . . . . . natl sls mgr
Lenora Boutte . . . . . progmg mgr
Richard Monn . . . . . chief of engrg
Penni Ward Rojas . . . . . traf mgr

WKMG-TV— Digital Channel: 26. Digital Hrs: 24 74.1 kw vis, 14.8 kw aur. ant 1,460t/1,484g TL: N28 36 08 W81 05 37 (CP: 100 kw vis, 20 kw aur, ant 1,840t) On air date: July 1, 1954. 4466 N. John Young Pkwy., Orlando, FL, 32804. Phone: (407) 291-6000. Fax: (407) 521-1204. Fax: (407) 298-2122 (news). Web Site: www.local6.com. Licensee: Post-Newsweek Stations Orlando Inc. Group Owner: Post-Newsweek Stations Inc. (acq 9-4-97). Population Served: 3,600,000 Natl. Network: CBS, . Natl. Rep: MMT,. Washington Atty: Covington & Burling. News staff: 80; News: 24 hrs wkly.
Key Personnel:
Alan Frank . . . . . pres & gen sls mgr
Skip Valet . . . . . gen mgr

***WMFE-TV—** Digital Channel: 23. Digital Hrs: 18 1,350 kw vis. ant 1,246t/1,220g TL: N28 36 08 W81 05 37 On air date: Mar 25, 1965. 11510 E. Colonial Dr., Orlando, FL, 32817-4699. Phone: (407) 273-2300. Fax: (407) 206-2791. Web Site: wmfe.org. Licensee: Community Communications Inc. Ownership: Community Licensee, 100%. Population Served: 1,301,000 Natl. Network: PBS, . Washington Atty: Schwartz, Woods & Miller.
Key Personnel:
Jose Fajardo . . . . . CEO
Bill Sublette. . . . . chmn
Jack Church . . . . . pres & mktg VP
Dale Spear. . . . . sr VP & progmg VP

WOFL— Digital Channel: 22. Digital Hrs: 24 2,570 kw vis, 513 kw aur. 1,479t/1,486g TL: N28 36 17 W81 05 13 On air date: Oct 15, 1979. 35 Skyline Dr., Lake Mary, FL, 32746. Phone: (407) 644-3535. Fax: (407) 333-3535. Web Site: www.wofl.com. Licensee: Fox Television Stations Inc. Group Owner: (group owner; (acq 6-17-2002; with WOGX(TV) Ocala). Population Served: 1,500,000 Natl. Network: Fox,
Key Personnel:
Stan Knott. . . . . gen mgr & stn mgr
Terry Walden . . . . . progmg mgr

WOPX-TV— Digital Channel: 48. Digital Hrs: 24 1,000 kw vis. ant 1,496t/1,469g TL: N28 05 37 W81 07 28 On air date: June 1986. 7091 Grand Natl Dr., Suite 100, Orlando, FL, 32819. Phone: (407) 370-5600. Fax: (407) 363-1757. Web Site: www.iontelevision.com. Licensee: ION Media Orlando License Inc., debtor-in-possession. Group Owner: Paxson Communications Corp. (acq 12-12-97; $13,161,274). Population Served: 685,000 Natl. Network: ION Television, . Washington Atty: Dow, Lohnes & Albertson.
Key Personnel:
Connie Fiala . . . . . gen mgr

WOTF-DT— Digital Channel: 43. Digital Hrs: 24 4,170 kw vis, 854 kw aur. ant 1,049t/1,005g TL: N28 18 26 W80 54 48 On air date: July 5, 1982. 1021 North Wymore Rd., Winter Park, FL, 32789. Phone: (321) 254-4343. Fax: (321) 254-9343. Web Site: www.univision.com. Licensee: Univision of Melbourne Inc. Group Owner: Univision Communications Inc. (acq 5-21-2001; grpsl). Washington Atty: Dow, Lohnes & Albertson. Foreign lang progmg: SpanishS 168
Key Personnel:
Sylvia Willis. . . . . VP
Bill Bauman . . . . . gen mgr & stn mgr

WRBW— Digital Channel: 41. Digital Hrs: 24 5,000 kw vis. 1,525t TL: N28 34 51 W81 04 32 On air date: June 6, 1994. 35 Skyline Dr., Lake Mary, FL, 32746. Phone: (407) 644-3535. Fax: (407) 741-5048.E-mail: wrbw@wrbw.com Web Site: www.wrbw.com. Licensee: Fox Television Stations Inc. Group Owner: (group owner; (acq 7-31-2001; grpsl). Natl. Network: MyNetworkTV, .
Key Personnel:
Stan Knott . . . . . gen mgr
Terry Walden. . . . . opns dir & progmg mgr

WRDQ— Digital Channel: 27. Digital Hrs: 24 5,000 kw vis, 500 kw aur. ant 1,866t/1,840g TL: N28 16 44 W81 01 25 On air date: 2000. 490 E. South St., Orlando, FL, 32801. Phone: (407) 841-9000. Fax: (407) 422-1414. Web Site: www.wrdq.com. Licensee: WFTV-TV Holdings Inc. Group Owner: Cox Communications Inc. (acq 2-1-2001).
Key Personnel:
Shawn Bartelt. . . . . gen mgr
Mario Mendosa. . . . . gen sls mgr
Bob Jordan . . . . . news dir

WTGL— Digital Channel: 46. Digital Hrs: 24 1,200 kw vis. ant 462t/377g TL: N28 40 48 W81 49 16 On air date: December 2000. 31 Skyline Dr., Lake Mary, FL, 32746. Phone: (407) 215-6745. Fax: (407) 215-6777.E-mail: receptionist@tv45.org Web Site: www.tv45.org. Licensee: Good Life Broadcasting Inc. Group Owner: (group owner; (acq 11-19-2001; with WTGL-TV Cocoa). Population Served: 2,000,000 Washington Atty: Leventhal, Senter & Lerman.
Key Personnel:
Gene Polino . . . . . chmn

WVEN-TV—(Daytona Beach, Digital Channel: 49. Digital Hrs: 24 2,750 kw vis, 2,750 kw aur. 1,063t TL: N29 17 10 W81 29 37 On air date: October 1988. 523 Douglas Ave., Suite 100, Altamonte Springs, FL, 32714. Phone: (407) 774-2626. Fax: (407) 774-3384. Licensee: Entravision Holdings L.L.C. Group Owner: Entravision Communications Corp. (acq 9-15-00; $22.55 million). Natl. Network: Univision (Spanish), . Foreign lang progmg: SpanishS 168
Key Personnel:
Antonio Guernica . . . . . CEO & gen mgr

Panama City, FL

(DMA 151)

WBIF— Digital Channel: 51.50 kw vis. ant 833t/856g TL: N30 30 42 W85 29 17 On air date: 2002. Stn currently dark 3901 Hwy. 121 S., Bedford, TX, 76021. Phone: (817) 571-1229. Fax: (817) 571-7458. Web Site: www.daystar.com. Licensee: Word of God Fellowship Inc. Group Owner: Equity Broadcasting Corp. (acq 7-31-2009; grpsl).
Key Personnel:
Marcus D. Lamb . . . . . pres

***WFSG—** Digital Channel: 38. Digital Hrs: 5 AM-11:30 PM 1,147 kw vis, 48.6 kw aur. 509t/499g TL: N30 22 02 W85 55 29 On air date: July 11, 1988. Public TV Ctr., 1600 Red Barber Plaza, Tallahassee, FL, 32310. Phone: (850) 487-3170. Fax: (850) 487-3093.E-mail: mail@wfsu.org Web Site: www.wfsu.org. Licensee: Board of Regents of Florida. (acq 2-28-86). Population Served: 100,000 Natl. Network: PBS, . Washington Atty: Cohn & Marks.
Key Personnel:
Patrick Keating . . . . . gen mgr
Charles Allen . . . . . dev dir
Jannie Whitt . . . . . prom dir & prom mgr
Mike Dunn . . . . . progmg dir
David Lauther . . . . . chief of engrg
Rebroadcasts WFSU-TV Tallahassee.

WJHG-TV— Digital Channel: 7. Digital Hrs: 24 316 kw vis, 34 kw aur. ant 870t/887g TL: N30 26 00 W85 24 51 On air date: Dec 1, 1953. 8195 Front Beach Rd., Panama City Beach, FL, 32407. Phone: (850) 234-7777. Fax: (850) 233-6647. Web Site: www.wjhg.com. Licensee: WEAU Licensee Corp. Group Owner: Gray Television Inc. (acq 6-29-60; $340,000;7-4-60). Population Served: 79,000 Natl. Network: NBC, CW, MyNetworkTV, . Natl. Rep: Continental Television Sales,. Washington Atty: Venable, Baetjer, Howard & Civiletti.

Key Personnel:
Jon McKee . . . . opns mgr
Tracy Connors . . . . gen mgr & gen sls mgr

WMBB— Digital Channel: 13. Digital Hrs: 24 316 kw vis, 63 kw aur. ant 1,549t/1,464g TL: N30 21 09 W85 23 26 On air date: Oct 3, 1973. 613 Harrison Ave., Panama City, FL, 32401-2623. Phone: (850) 769-2313. Fax: (850) 769-8231.E-mail: dstrong@wmbb.com Web Site: www.wmbb.com. Licensee: Hoak Media of Panama City License LLC. Group Owner: Media General Broadcast Group (acq 7-15-2008; $60 million with KALB-TV Alexandria, LA). Population Served: 192,200 Natl. Network: ABC, . Natl. Rep: Blair Television,. Washington Atty: Akin Gump Strauss Hauer & Feld LLP. News staff: 24; News: 143 hrs wkly.
Key Personnel:
Bill Byrd . . . . gen mgr
Marc Morriston . . . . prom dir

WPCT— Digital Channel: 47.126 kw vis. ant 194t/180g TL: N30 10 59 W85 46 42 On air date: 1997. Box 9556, Panama City Beach, FL, 32407. Phone: (850) 234-2773. Fax: (850) 234-1179. Web Site: www.tripsmarter.com. Licensee: Beach TV Properties Inc. Group Owner: (group owner)
Key Personnel:
Jud Colley. . . . . pres
Mike Hartzog . . . . gen mgr

WPGX— Digital Channel: 9. Digital Hrs: 24 1,260 kw vis, 126 kw aur. ant 748t TL: N30 23 42 W85 32 02 On air date: May 21, 1988. Fox TV Ctr., 637 Luverne Ave., Panama City, FL, 32401. Phone: (850) 784-0028. Fax: (850) 784-1773. Licensee: WPGX License Subsidiary LLC. Group Owner: Raycom Media Inc. (acq 12-15-2003; grpsl). Population Served: 250,000 Natl. Network: Fox, . Natl. Rep: Millennium Sales & Marketing,. Washington Atty: Leventhal, Senter & Lerman.
Key Personnel:
David Cavileer . . . . VP & gen mgr chief of engrg
Sue Stewart. . . . . opns mgr & prom mgr

Pensacola

see Mobile, AL-Pensacola (Ft. Walton Beach), FL market

Sarasota

see Tampa-St. Petersburg (Sarasota), FL market

St. Petersburg

see Tampa-St. Petersburg (Sarasota), FL market

Tallahassee, FL-Thomasville, GA (DMA 105)

WCTV—(Thomasville, GA) Digital Channel: 46. Digital Hrs: 24 97.5 kw vis, 19.5 kw aur. ant 2,031t/2,000g TL: N30 40 13 W83 56 26 On air date: Sept 15, 1955. 1801 Halstead Blvd., Tallahassee, FL, 32309. Phone: (850) 893-6666. Fax: (850) 893-5193. Web Site: www.wctv6.com. Licensee: Gray Television Licensee Inc. Group Owner: Gray Television Inc. (acq 1996; $165 million with WVLT-TV Knoxville, TN). Natl. Network: CBS, MyNetworkTV, . Natl. Rep: Continental Television Sales,. Washington Atty: Wiley-Rein, LLC. Wire Svc: AP
Key Personnel:
Nick Waller. . . . . pres & gen mgr
Heather Pryor . . . . gen sls mgr
Ella Paris . . . . natl sls mgr
Mike Smith. news dir
Joan Palos . . . . traf mgr

***WFSU-TV—** Digital Channel: 32.316 kw vis, 31.6 kw aur. 777t/774g TL: N30 21 29 W84 36 39 On air date: Sept 20, 1960. 1600 Red Barber Plaza, Tallahassee, FL, 32310. Phone: (850) 487-3170. Fax: (850) 487-3093.E-mail: mail@wfsu.org Web Site: www.wfsu.org. Licensee: Florida Board of Regents & Florida State University. Population Served: 170,000 Natl. Network: PBS, .
Key Personnel:
Patrick Keating . . . . gen mgr
Charles Allen . . . . dev dir
Beckie Hamilton. . . . . progmg dir

WFXU— Digital Channel: 48. Digital Hrs: 24 2,500 kw vis. ant 443t TL: N30 33 00 W83 00 46 On air date: July 1998. 4190 N.W. 93rd Ave., Gainesville, FL, 32653. Phone: (352) 371-7772. Licensee: Budd Broadcasting Co. Inc.. Ownership: Harvey Budd, 50%; Ilene Budd, 50%. (acq 1-19-2007; $100,000).
Key Personnel:
Harvey Budd . . . . CEO

WSWG— Digital Channel: 43. Analog Hrs: 24 Digital Hrs: 24 1,700 kw vis, 257 kw aur. ant 920t/950g TL: N31 10 18 W83 21 57 (CP: 1,365 kw vis, ant 922t) On air date: Sept 1, 1995. Box 1987, Moultrie, GA, 31776. 107 2nd Ave. S.W., Moultrie, GA 31768. Phone: (229) 985-1340. Fax: (229) 985-7549. Web Site: wswgtv.com. Licensee: Gray Television Licensee Inc. (acq 11-10-2005; $3.75 million). Natl. Network: CBS, MyNetworkTV, . Washington Atty: Robert Bizer.
Key Personnel:
Chris Mossman . . . . pres & gen sls mgr
Nick Waller. . . . . gen mgr
Jared Yost . . . . rgnl sls mgr
Jim Killinger . . . . chief of engrg

WTLF— Digital Channel: 24.24 kw vis. ant 128t/171g TL: N30 29 40 W84 25 03 On air date: 2004. Box 949, Midway, FL, 32343. 950 Commerce Blvd., Midway, FL 32343. Phone: (850) 576-4990. Fax: (850) 576-0200. Licensee: MPS Media of Tallahassee License LLC.. Ownership: Eugene J. Brown, 100% votes Group Owner: (group owner). (acq 3-31-2007; $3.044 million with WSWB(TV) Scranton, PA). Natl. Network: CW, .
Key Personnel:
David Hinterschied. . . . . gen mgr

WTLH—(Bainbridge, GA) Digital Channel: 50. Digital Hrs: 24 5,000 kw vis. ant 1,958t/1,961g TL: N30 40 51 W83 58 21 On air date: 1989. 950 Commerce Blvd., Box 949, Midway, FL, 32343. Phone: (850) 576-4990. Fax: (850) 576-0200.E-mail: fox49@fox49.com Web Site: www.myfoxtallahassee.com. Licensee: New Age Media of Tallahassee License LLC. Group Owner: Pegasus Broadcast Television Inc. (acq 3-31-2007; grpsl). Population Served: 569,000 Natl. Network: Fox, CW, . Natl. Rep: Petry Television Inc.,.
Key Personnel:
John Parente . . . . CEO
Mike Yanuzzi . . . . exec VP & sr VP
David Hinterschied. . . . . gen mgr
Tana Kenny . . . . gen sls mgr
Don Abel . . . . progmg dir
Mike Brown . . . . chief of engrg
Tyrone Hayes . . . . chief of opns & opns

WTWC-TV— Digital Channel: 40. Digital Hrs: 24 3,160 kw vis, 316 kw aur. 880t/821g TL: N30 35 11 W84 14 11 On air date: Apr 21, 1983. 8440 Deerlake Rd. S., Tallahassee, FL, 32312. Phone: (850) 893-4140. Fax: (850) 893-6974. Web Site: www.wtwe40.com. Licensee: WTWC Licensee L.L.C. Group Owner: Sinclair Broadcast Group Inc. (acq 1999; grpsl). Natl. Network: NBC, . Natl. Rep: Millennium Sales & Marketing,. Washington Atty: Dow, Lohnes & Albertson. News staff: 30; News: 14 hrs wkly.
Key Personnel:
Bob W. Franklin. . . . . gen mgr
Mike Plumber . . . . stn mgr

WTXL-TV— Digital Channel: 27. Digital Hrs: 24 3,000,000 watts. 1,700 TL: N30 34 27 W84 12 09 On air date: Sept 16, 1976. 8440 Deer Lake Rd., Tallahassee, FL, 32312. Phone: (850) 893-4140. Fax: (850) 668-1460. Web Site: www.wtxl.com. Licensee: Southern Broadcast Corp. of Sarasota. (acq 11-30-2005; $12 million). Population Served: 268,000 Natl. Network: ABC, . Washington Atty: Keck, Mahin & Cate. News staff: 26; News: 24 hrs wkly.
Key Personnel:
Gary Shorts . . . . CEO
Mike Plummer . . . . stn mgr
Steve Rollison. . . . . gen mgr & news dir

Tampa-St. Petersburg (Sarasota), FL (DMA 13)

WCLF— Digital Channel: 21. Digital Hrs: 24 5000 kw vis, 500 kw aur. ant 1,410t/1,538g TL: N28 11 04 W82 45 39 On air date: October 1979. Box 6922, Clearwater, FL, 33758. 6922 142nd Ave., Largo, FL 33771. Phone: (727) 535-5622. Fax: (727) 531-2497. Web Site: www.ctnonline.com. Licensee: Christian Television Corporation Inc. Group Owner: (group owner; (acq 12-16-97). Population Served: 10,000,000 Natl. Network: CTV, . Washington Atty: Gammon & Grange. Foreign lang progmg: SpanishS 2
Key Personnel:
Robert DeAndrea . . . . pres & gen mgr & stn mgr

***WEDU—**(Tampa, Digital Channel: 13. Digital Hrs: 24 100 kw vis, 20 kw aur. 1,551t TL: N27 49 48 W82 15 59 On air date: Oct 27, 1958. Box 4033, Tampa, FL, 33677-4033. 1300 North Blvd., Tampa, FL 33607. Phone: (813) 254-9338. Fax: (813) 253-0826. Web Site: www.wedu.org. Licensee: Florida West Coast Pub Broadcasting Inc. Population Served: 3,200,000 Natl. Network: PBS, . Washington Atty: Schwartz, Woods & Miller.
Key Personnel:
Richard M. Lobo . . . . CEO & pres
Patrick Perkins. . . . . CFO
Frank Wolynski . . . . opns VP
Susanna Grady . . . . dev VP
Ellyne Lonergan . . . . progmg VP
Mike Seymour. . . . . progmg

WFLA-TV—(Tampa, Digital Channel: 7.316 kw vis, 31.6 kw aur. ant 1,545t/1,535g TL: N27 50 32 W82 15 46 On air date: Feb 14, 1955. Box 1410, Tampa, FL, 33601. 200 South Parker St., Tampa, FL 33608. Phone: (813) 228-8888. Fax: (813) 221-5787. Web Site: www.wfla.com. Licensee: Media General Communications Inc. Group Owner: Media General Broadcast Group, see Cross-Ownership (acq 1965; $17.5 million). Population Served: 3,332,000 Natl. Network: NBC, . Natl. Rep: Harrington, Righter & Parsons,. Washington Atty: Dow, Lohnes & Albertson. Wire Svc: UPI
Key Personnel:
Michael Pumo . . . . pres & gen mgr
Rick McEwen. . . . . opns dir

WFTS-TV—(Tampa, Digital Channel: 29. Digital Hrs: 24 2.63 kw vis, 260 w aur. 1,546t/1,649g TL: N27 50 32 W82 15 46 On air date: Dec 14, 1981. 4045 N. Himes Ave., Tampa, FL, 33607. Phone: (813) 354-2828. Fax: (813) 878-2828. Web Site: www.abcactionnews.com. Licensee: Tampa Bay Television Inc. Group Owner: Scripps Howard Broadcasting Co., see Cross-Ownership (acq 1-2-86; grpsl). Natl. Network: ABC, . Natl. Rep: Eagle Television Sales,. Washington Atty: Baker & Hostetler.
Key Personnel:
Bill Carey . . . . VP & gen mgr
Jack Winter . . . . opns mgr
Chris Raynor . . . . prom mgr

WFTT-DT—(Tampa, Digital Channel: 47. Digital Hrs: 24 4,200 kw vis, 420 kw aur. ant 1,600t/1,580g TL: N27 50 32 W82 15 46 On air date: Feb 1, 1988. 2610 W. Hillsborough Ave., Tampa, FL, 33614. Phone: (813) 872-6262. Fax: (813) 998-3600.E-mail: info@univision.com Web Site: univision.com. Licensee: TeleFutura Tampa LLC. Group Owner: Univision Communications Inc. (acq 5-21-2001; grpsl). Population Served: 1,600,000 Natl. Network: TeleFutura (Spanish), . Washington Atty: Wiley, Rein & Fielding. Foreign lang progmg: SpanishS 168
Key Personnel:
Lilly Gonzalez. gen mgr
Nelson Castillo. . . . . gen sls mgr
Steve Hess . . . . chief of engrg
Carol Davis. . . . . traf mgr

WMOR-TV— Digital Channel: 19. Digital Hrs: 24 5,000 kw vis, 500 kw aur. ant 1086t/1087g TL: N27 50 15 W81 56 53 On air date: Apr 24, 1986. 7201 E. Hillsborough Ave., Tampa, FL, 33610-4126. Phone: (813) 626-3232. Fax: (813) 622-7732. Web Site: www.moretv32.com. Licensee: WMOR-TV Company. Group Owner: Hearst-Argyle Television Inc. (acq 1996; $25.5 million). Population Served: 3,177,000 Natl. Rep: MMT,. Washington Atty: Brooks, Pierce, McLendon, Humphrey & Leonard.
Key Personnel:
Ken Lucas . . . . VP & gen mgr
Roy Tym . . . . natl sls mgr
Bonita Elias . . . . rgnl sls mgr
Pete George . . . . prom mgr
Joseph Pauly . . . . progmg mgr

WTOG—(Saint Petersburg, Digital Channel: 44. Digital Hrs: 24 5,000 kw vis, 285 kw aur. ant 1,649t/1,507g TL: N27 49 48 W82 15 59 On air date: Nov 4, 1968. 365 105th Terr. N.E., Saint Petersburg, FL, 33716. Phone: (727) 576-4444. Fax: (727) 570-4458. Web Site: cw44.com. Licensee: CBS Operations Inc. Group Owner: Viacom Television Stations Group (acq 9-19-96). Population Served: 1,710,400 Natl. Network: CW, . Natl. Rep: TeleRep,. Wire Svc: NWS (National Weather Service)
Key Personnel:
Laura Caruso . . . . VP & gen mgr stn mgr & sls dir
Steve Soldinger . . . . gen mgr

WTSP—(Saint Petersburg, Digital Channel: 10.316 kw vis, 31.6 kw aur. 1,549t/1,538g TL: N28 11 04 W82 45 39 On air date: July 17, 1965. 11450 Gandy Blvd., Saint Petersburg, FL, 33702. Phone: (727) 577-1010. Fax: (727) 578-7637. Web Site: www.wtsp.com. Licensee: Pacific and Southern Co. Group Owner: Gannett Broadcasting (acq 12-31-96). Population Served: 4,583,600 Natl. Network: CBS, . Natl. Rep: Blair Television,. Washington Atty: Wiley, Rein & Fielding.
Key Personnel:
Sam Rosenwasser . . . . gen mgr & stn mgr
Lee Griffin. . . . . opns mgr
Pete Nikiel . . . . mktg mgr

WTTA—(Saint Petersburg, Digital Channel: 38. Digital Hrs: 24 5,000 kw vis, 500 kw aur. ant 1,867t/1,500g TL: N27 50 32 W82 15 46 On

air date: June 21, 1991. 7622 Bald Cypress Pl., Tampa, FL, 33614. Phone: (813) 886-9882. Fax: (813) 880-8100 / 8154.E-mail: comments@wtta38.com Web Site: www.wtta38.com. Licensee: Bay Television Inc. Population Served: 3,617,000 Natl. Network: MyNetworkTV, . Washington Atty: Shaw Pittman.
Key Personnel:
Julie Nelson . . . . pres & gen mgr

WTVT—(Tampa, Digital Channel: 12. Digital Hrs: 24 316 kw vis, 47.4 kw aur. 1,416t/1,549g TL: N27 49 09 W82 14 26 On air date: April 1955. Box 31113, Tampa, FL, 33631-3113. 3213 W. Kennedy Blvd., Tampa, FL 33609. Phone: (813) 876-1313. Fax: (813) 871-3135.E-mail: news@wtvt.com Web Site: www.wtvt.com. Licensee: TVT License Inc. Group Owner: Fox Television Stations Inc. (acq 11-96; grpsl). Population Served: 2,935,000 Natl. Network: Fox, . Washington Atty: Hogan & Hartson. Wire Svc: Conus News staff: 100; News: 46 hrs wkly.
Key Personnel:
Bill Schneider. . . . . pres & gen mgr
Jim Benedict . . . . opns dir

***WUSF-TV**—(Tampa, Digital Channel: 34. Digital Hrs: 24 475 kw vis. ant 1,486t/1,479g TL: N27 50 52 W82 15 48 On air date: Sept 12, 1966. Univ. of South Florida, 4202 Fowler Ave., Tampa, FL, 33620. Phone: (813) 974-4000. Fax: (813) 974-4806.E-mail: pholley@wusf.org Web Site: www.wusf.org. Licensee: University of South Florida. Population Served: 3,000,000 Natl. Network: PBS, . Washington Atty: Cohn & Marks.
Key Personnel:
Jo Ann Urofsky . . . . gen mgr
Pat Holly . . . . stn mgr
Jeff Hammel. opns mgr
Cathy Coccia . . . . dev dir
Susan Geiger. . . . . progmg dir

WVEA-TV— Digital Channel: 25. Digital Hrs: 24 5,000 kw vis, 500 kw aur. 572t/570g TL: N27 06 01 W82 22 18 On air date: May 3, 1991. 2610 W. Hillsborough Ave., Tampa, FL, 33614-6132. Phone: (813) 872-6262. Fax: (813) 998-3600.E-mail: info@wvea.entravision.com Web Site: www.wvea.entravision.com. Licensee: Entravision Holdings L.L.C. Group Owner: Entravision Communications Corp. (acq 1999; $17 million). Population Served: 1,600,000 Natl. Network: Univision (Spanish), . Washington Atty: Thompson Hine, LLP. Wire Svc: AP Foreign lang progmg: SpanishS 168 News staff: 14; News: 3.5 hrs wkly.
Key Personnel:
Lilly Gonzalez. . . . . gen mgr
Nelson Castillo . . . . gen sls mgr
Pilar Ortiz . . . . news dir
Bill Mierisch . . . . chief of engrg
Margaret Stanfield . . . . traf mgr

WWSB— Digital Channel: 24. Digital Hrs: 24 2,871 kw vis, 431 kw aur. ant 771t/814g TL: N27 33 27 W82 21 59 On air date: Oct 23, 1971. 1477 10th St., Sarasota, FL, 34236. Phone: (941) 923-8840. Fax: (941) 924-3971/ (941) 923-8709.E-mail: generalmanager@wwsb.tv Web Site: www.wwsb.tv. Licensee: Southern Broadcast Corp. of Sarasota. (acq 3-26-86; $40,500). Population Served: 157,310 Natl. Network: ABC, . Washington Atty: Leibowitz & Associates. News staff: 45; News: 21 hrs wkly.
Key Personnel:
Gary Shorts . . . . CEO
J. Manuel Calvo. . . . . pres & gen mgr
Jason Wildanstein . . . . opns dir

WXPX-TV— Digital Channel: 42.257 kw vis. ant 1,555t/1,548g TL: N27 49 10 W82 15 39 On air date: Aug 1, 1994. 4444 66th St N., Clearwater, FL, 33764-7204. Phone: (813) 314-5462. Fax: (813) 314-5464. Web Site: www.ionline.tv. Licensee: ION Media License Co. LLC, debtor-in-possession. Group Owner: Paxson Communications Corp. (acq 12-15-97). Natl. Network: ION Television, .

West Palm Beach-Ft. Pierce, FL (DMA 38)

WFGC— Digital Channel: 49. Digital Hrs: 24 5,000 kw vis, 500 kw aur. ant 410t TL: N26 45 47 W80 12 19 On air date: May 21, 1993. 1900 S. Congress Ave., Suite A, West Palm Beach, FL, 33406. Phone: (561) 642-3361. Fax: (561) 967-5961.E-mail: comments@wfgc.com Web Site: www.wfgc.com. Licensee: Christian TV of Palm Beach County Inc.. Ownership: David C. Gibbs III, Wayne Wetzel and Bill Anderson. (acq 12-16-97). Washington Atty: Gammon & Grange.
Key Personnel:
Wayne Wetzel . . . . pres
Neville Chankersingh . . . . CFO
Mike Gonzalez . . . . gen mgr
Chris Mavros. . . . . chief of engrg

WFLX— Digital Channel: 28. Digital Hrs: 24 5,000 kw vis, 500 kw aur. ant 1,540t/1,533g TL: N26 34 37 W80 14 32 On air date: Aug 14, 1982. 4119 W. Blue Heron Blvd., West Palm Beach, FL, 33404. Phone: (561) 845-2929. Fax: (561) 863-1238. Web Site: www.wflx.com. Licensee: Raycom National Inc. Group Owner: Raycom Media Inc. (acq 1998). Natl. Network: Fox, . Natl. Rep: Harrington, Righter & Parsons,.
Key Personnel:
John Spinola . . . . VP & gen mgr
John Heislman. . . . . gen sls mgr & natl sls mgr

WPBF— Digital Channel: 16. Digital Hrs: 24 5,000 kw vis, 500 kw aur. ant 1,529t/1,549g TL: N26 50 09 W80 05 44 On air date: Jan 1, 1989. 3970 RCA Blvd., Suite 7007, Palm Beach Gardens, FL, 33410. Phone: (561) 694-2525. Fax: (561) 624-1089. Web Site: www.wpbfnews.com. Licensee: WPBF-TV Co. Group Owner: Hearst-Argyle Television Inc. (acq 8-1-97). Population Served: 772,000 Natl. Network: ABC, . Natl. Rep: Continental Television Sales,. News staff: 48; News: 25 hrs wkly.
Key Personnel:
Caroline Scollard-Taplett. . . . . VP
Russ Larish. . . . . gen mgr & progmg dir

WPEC— Digital Channel: 13. Digital Hrs: 24 90 kw vis. ant 1,014t/1,004g TL: N26 35 18 W80 12 30 On air date: Jan 1, 1955. Box 198512, West Palm Beach, FL, 33419-8512. 1100 Fairfield Dr., West Palm Beach, FL 33419-8512. Phone: (561) 844-1212. Fax: (561) 842-1212. Web Site: www.wpecnews12.com. Licensee: Freedom Broadcasting of Florida Licensee L.L.C. Group Owner: Freedom Broadcasting Inc. (acq 2-1-96; $150 million). Population Served: 1,400,000 Natl. Network: CBS, . Natl. Rep: TeleRep,. Washington Atty: Latham & Watkins. News: 24 hrs wkly.
Key Personnel:
Doreen Wade . . . . pres & VP
Diana Wilkin. . . . . VP & gen mgr
Donn Colee . . . . stn mgr & progmg mgr
Doug Wolfmueller. . . . . gen sls mgr
Mary Gregg . . . . natl sls mgr
Jim Posey. . . . . rgnl sls mgr
Steve Hunsicker. news dir
Keith Betts. . . . . engrg dir & chief of engrg

WPTV— Digital Channel: 12. Digital Hrs: 24 100 kw vis, 20 kw aur. 990t/1,031g TL: N26 35 20 W80 12 43 On air date: Aug 22, 1954. 1100 Banyan Blvd., West Palm Beach, FL, 33401. Phone: (561) 655-5455. Fax: (561) 653-5719.E-mail: newstips@wptv.com Web Site: www.wptv.com. Licensee: Scripps Howard Broadcasting Co. Group Owner: (group owner; (acq 12-27-61; $2 million; 12-25-61). Population Served: 1,200,000 Natl. Network: NBC, . Natl. Rep: Harrington, Righter & Parsons,. Washington Atty: Baker & Hostetler. Wire Svc: Reuters News staff: 75; News: 27 hrs wkly.
Key Personnel:
Kenneth W. Lowe . . . . CEO
Joseph G. Ne Castro . . . . CFO
Steve Wasserman. . . . . sr VP & VP & gen mgr

WPXP-TV— Digital Channel: 36. Digital Hrs: 24 1,000 kw vis, 200 kw aur. ant 1,263t/1,261g TL: N26 35 20 W80 12 44 On air date: 1998. 500 Australian Ave., Suite 200, 601 Clearwater Park Rd., West Palm Beach, FL, 33401. Phone: (561) 686-6767. Fax: (561) 682-3475. Web Site: www.ionline.tv. Licensee: ION Media West Palm Beach License Inc., debtor-in-possession. Group Owner: Paxson Communications Corp. (acq acq 6-5-2009). Natl. Network: ION Television, .
Key Personnel:
Doug Barker . . . . gen mgr

***WTCE-TV**— Digital Channel: 38.1,000 kw vis. ant 974t/968g TL: N27 01 31 W80 10 43 On air date: May 1990. 3601 N. 25th St., Fort Pierce, FL, 34946. Phone: (772) 489-2701. Fax: (772) 489-6833. Web Site: www.wtcebellsouth.net. Licensee: Jacksonville Educators Broadcasting Inc. (acq 7-6-90; $630,089). Population Served: 151,000
Key Personnel:
Charles Massi . . . . gen mgr & stn mgr & pub affrs dir

WTVX— Digital Channel: 34.5,000 kw vis, 500 kw aur. ant 1,492t/1,520g TL: N27 07 20 W80 23 21 On air date: Apr 5, 1966. 1700 Palm Beach Lakes Blvd. Ste 150, 4411 Beacon Cir., West Palm Beach, FL, 33401-2017. Phone: (561) 841-3434. Fax: (561) 848-9150. Web Site: www.wtvx.com. Licensee: WPB TV Licensee Corp. Group Owner: Viacom Television Stations Group (acq 11-21-2007; grpsl). Population Served: 898,000 Natl. Network: CW, . Natl. Rep: TeleRep,. Washington Atty: Wiley Rein LLP.
Key Personnel:
Arika Zink . . . . gen mgr

***WXEL-TV**— Digital Channel: 27. Digital Hrs: 24 400 kw vis. ant 1,443t/1,440g TL: N26 34 37 W80 14 32 On air date: July 7, 1982. Box 6607, West Palm Beach, FL, 33405-6607. 3401 South Congress Ave., Boynton Beach, FL 33426. Phone: (561) 737-8000. Fax: (561) 369-3067.E-mail: jcarr@wxel.org Web Site: www.wxel.org. Licensee: Barry Telecommunications Inc. Ownership: Barry University (acq 4-16-97). Population Served: 2,000,000 Natl. Network: PBS, . Washington Atty: Schwartz, Woods & Miller.
Key Personnel:
Jerry Carr. . . . . CEO
Bernard Henneberg . . . . CFO
Jerry Carr . . . . gen mgr
Fred Flaxman . . . . dev VP
Ross Cooper . . . . sls dir & mktg dir & mktg mgr
Lee Rowand . . . . prom dir

Georgia

Albany, GA (DMA 147)

***WABW-TV**— Digital Channel: 6.5,000 kw vis, 500 kw aur. ant 1,240t/1,224g TL: N31 08 05 W84 06 16 On air date: Jan 1, 1967. 260 14th St. N.W., Atlanta, GA, 30318. Phone: (404) 685-2400. Fax: (404) 685-2591.E-mail: ask@gpb.org Web Site: www.gpb.org. Licensee: Georgia Public Telecommunications Commission. Natl. Network: PBS, .
Key Personnel:
Bonnie Bean . . . . CFO
Bob Houghton . . . . gen mgr

***WACS-TV**— Digital Channel: 8. Digital Hrs: 19 4.7 kw vis. ant 1,092t/1,056g TL: N31 56 15 W84 33 15 On air date: Mar 6, 1967. 260 14th St. N.W., Atlanta, GA, 30318. Phone: (404) 685-2400. Fax: (404) 685-2591.E-mail: ask@gpb.org Web Site: www.gpb.org. Licensee: Georgia Public Telecommunications Commission. Natl. Network: PBS, . Washington Atty: Arent, Fox, Kintner, Plotkin & Kahn.
Key Personnel:
Bob Houghton . . . . gen mgr

WALB— Digital Channel: 10.316 kw vis, 43.6 kw aur. ant 974t/951g TL: N31 19 52 W83 51 43 On air date: Apr 7, 1954. Box 3130, 1709 Stuart Ave., Albany, GA, 31706. Phone: (229) 446-1010. Fax: (229) 446-4000.E-mail: walb@walb.com Web Site: www.walb.com. Licensee: WALB License Subsidiary LLC. Group Owner: Liberty Corp. (acq 1-31-2006; grpsl). Population Served: 424,000 Natl. Network: NBC, . Natl. Rep: Continental Television Sales,. News staff: 5; News: 15 hrs wkly.
Key Personnel:
James Wilcox . . . . pres & gen mgr & stn mgr
Dawn Hobby . . . . news dir

WFXL— Digital Channel: 12. Digital Hrs: 24 1,580 kw vis, 150 kw aur. ant 991t/968g TL: N31 19 52 W83 51 43 On air date: Feb 14, 1982. Box 4050, Albany, GA, 31706. 1201 Stuart Ave., Albany, GA 31707. Phone: (229) 435-3100. Fax: (229) 903-8240. Web Site: www.wfxl.com. Licensee: Barrington Albany License LLC. Group Owner: Raycom Media Inc. (acq 8-11-2006; grpsl). Population Served: 385,000 Natl. Network: Fox, . Natl. Rep: MMT,. Washington Atty: Covington & Burling. News staff: 7; News: 4 hrs wkly.
Key Personnel:
Jenny Collins . . . . gen mgr
Deborah Owens . . . . stn mgr
Pat Coffman. . . . . opns mgr
Teri Underwood . . . . gen sls mgr
Terry Graham. . . . . news dir
Ken Clubb. chief of engrg
Brandi Fickel . . . . mktg

WSST-TV— Analog Channel: 55. Digital Channel: 51. Digital Hrs: 24 91 kw vis. ant 361t/374g TL: N31 53 35 W83 48 18 On air date: May 22, 1989. Box 917, 112 S. 7th St., Detroit, GA, 31015. Phone: (229) 273-0001. Fax: (229) 273-8894.E-mail: wsst@sowega.net Web Site: www.wsst.com. Licensee: Sunbelt-South Telecommunications Ltd. Ownership: William B. Goodson, 65%; Phillip A. Streetman, 35%. Population Served: 600,000 Washington Atty: Law Offices of Scott Cinnamon.
Key Personnel:
Phillip Streetman . . . . sr VP & VP stn mgr & news dir
Sara J. Howell . . . . gen sls mgr
Lee W. Wright . . . . progmg dir
Shelby Goodson. traf mgr

Atlanta (DMA 8)

WAGA-TV— Digital Channel: 27. Digital Hrs: 24 100 kw vis, 20 kw aur. 1,076t/1,103g TL: N33 47 51 W84 20 02 On air date: April 1949. 1551 Briarcliff Rd. N.E., Atlanta, GA, 30306. Phone: (404) 875-5555. Fax: (404) 898-0238. Web Site: www.fox5atlanta.com. Licensee: New

World Communications of Atlanta Inc. Group Owner: (group owner; (acq 11-96; grpsl). Population Served: 4,000,000 Natl. Network: Fox, . News: 38 hrs wkly.
Key Personnel:
Gene McHugh . . . . gen mgr
Neil Mazur . . . . opns VP & opns dir

*WATC-DT— Digital Channel: 41. Digital Hrs: 24 398 kw vis, 39.8 kw aur. 423t TL: N33 48 40 W84 21 51 On air date: Apr 14, 1996. 1862 Enterprise Dr., Norcross, GA, 30093. Phone: (770) 300-9828. Fax: (770) 300-9838. Web Site: www.watc.tv. Licensee: Community Television Inc. (acq 6-3-93; $79,866;6-28-93).
Key Personnel:
James Thompson . . . . pres & gen mgr
Joanne Thompson . . . . VP
Greg West . . . . prom dir & progmg dir

WATL— Digital Channel: 25.2,682 kw vis, 402 kw aur. 1,170t/1,174g TL: N33 48 27 W84 20 26 On air date: July 5, 1976. One Monroe Pl., Atlanta, GA, 30324. Phone: (404) 881-3600. Fax: (404) 881-3749. Web Site: www.myatltv.com. Licensee: Gannett Georgia L.P. Group Owner: Tribune Broadcasting Co. (acq 8-7-2006; $180 million). Population Served: 4,112,000 Natl. Network: MyNetworkTV, . Natl. Rep: Blair Television,. Washington Atty: Wiley, Rein & Fielding.
Key Personnel:
Bob Walker. . . . . gen mgr
Jack Walsh . . . . gen sls mgr
Steven Fredericks. . . . . natl sls mgr

WGCL-TV— Digital Channel: 19. Digital Hrs: 24 2,333 kw vis, 233 kw aur. 1,089t/1,145g TL: N33 48 27 W84 20 26 On air date: June 6, 1971. Box 93524, Atlanta, GA, 30377. 425 14th St. NW, Atlanta, GA 30318. Phone: (404) 325-4646. Fax: (404) 327-3004. Fax: (404) 327-3003.E-mail: cbs46news@cbs46.com Web Site: www.cbs46.com. Licensee: Meredith Corp. Group Owner: Meredith Broadcasting Group, Meredith Corp. (acq 2-22-99; $370 million swap with KCPQ(TV) Tacoma, WA). Population Served: 5,725,787 Natl. Network: CBS, . Natl. Rep: Harrington, Righter & Parsons,. Washington Atty: Dow, Lohnes & Albertson, PLLC. News staff: 80; News: 14.5 hrs wkly.
Key Personnel:
Andy Alford . . . . VP & gen mgr
Joanna Hemleb . . . . gen sls mgr
Steve Schwaid . . . . news dir

*WGTV— Digital Channel: 8. Digital Hrs: 6 AM-midnight 316 kw vis, 56.2 kw aur. ant 1,132t/420g TL: N33 48 18 W84 08 40 On air date: May 23, 1960. 260 14th St. N.W., Atlanta, GA, 30318. Phone: (404) 685-2400. Fax: (404) 685-2431.E-mail: info@gpb.org Web Site: www.gpb.org. Licensee: Georgia Public Telecommunications Commission. Ownership: Ga. Public TV Net. Population Served: 1,500,000 Natl. Network: PBS, . Washington Atty: Arent, Fox, Kintner, Plotkin & Kahn.
Key Personnel:
Nancy Hall . . . . pres

*WHSG-TV— Analog Channel: 63. Digital Channel: 44. Digital Hrs: 24 1,000 kw vis. ant 994t/941g TL: N33 44 41 W84 21 36 On air date: Feb 22, 1991. 1550 Agape Way, Decatur, GA, 30035. Phone: (404) 288-1156. Fax: (404) 288-5613. Web Site: www.tbn.org. Licensee: Trinity Broadcasting Network Inc. Group Owner: (group owner; (acq 11-21-89). Population Served: 90,000
Key Personnel:
Dorothy Casoria. . . . . gen mgr

*WPBA— Digital Channel: 21. Digital Hrs: 24 1,380 kw vis. 1,096t TL: N33 45 35 W84 20 07 On air date: Feb 17, 1958. 740 Bismark Rd. N.E., Atlanta, GA, 30324-4102. Phone: (678) 686-0321. Fax: (678) 686-0356. Web Site: www.WPBA.org. Licensee: Board of Education of the City of Atlanta. Population Served: 2,500,000 Natl. Network: PBS, . Washington Atty: Schwartz, Woods & Miller. News: 1.5 hrs wkly.
Key Personnel:
Milton Clipper. . . . . gen mgr & stn mgr & progmg dir

WPCH-TV— Digital Channel: 20.2,224 kw vis, 224 kw aur. ant 1,093t/1,042g TL: N33 46 57 W84 23 20 On air date: Sept 1, 1967. 1050 Techwood Dr. N.W., Atlanta, GA, 30318. Phone: (404) 827-1717. Fax: (404) 885-2148. Web Site: www.tbssuperstation.com. Licensee: Superstation Inc., div of Turner Broadcasting System. Ownership: R.E. Turner III, 32.03%; TCI, 24.43%; Time-Warner, 20.34%. (acq 1-70). Population Served: 60,714,000 Natl. Rep: TBS,.

WPXA-TV— Digital Channel: 51. Digital Hrs: 24 1,000 kw vis. ant 2,040t/809g TL: N34 18 48 W84 38 55 On air date: Jan 15, 1988. 601 Clearwater Park Dr., West Palm Beach, FL, 33401. Phone: (404) 885-7646. Fax: (404) 881-9553. Web Site: www.ionline.tv. Licensee: ION Media Atlanta License Inc., debtor-in-possession. Group Owner: Paxson Communications Corp. (acq 7-13-94; $9.5 million). Population Served: 3,900,000 Natl. Network: ION Television, . Washington Atty: Dow, Lohnes & Albertson.

Key Personnel:
Lowell Paxson . . . . CEO
James Bocock . . . . pres
Scott Jolles. . . . . gen mgr

WSB-TV— Digital Channel: 39. Digital Hrs: 24 100 kw vis, 20 kw aur. ant 1,037t/1,076g TL: N33 45 51 W84 21 42 On air date: Sept 29, 1948. 1601 W. Peachtree St. N.E., Atlanta, GA, 30309. Phone: (404) 897-7000. Fax: (404) 897-6246 (gen mgr).E-mail: talk2us@wsbtv.com Web Site: www.wsbtv.com. Licensee: Georgia Television Company. Group Owner: Cox Broadcasting Natl. Network: ABC, . Natl. Rep: TeleRep,. Washington Atty: Dow, Lohnes & Albertson.
Key Personnel:
Bill Hoffman . . . . VP & gen mgr
David Lamothe . . . . opns dir
Deborah Denechaud . . . . sls dir
Steve Riley . . . . mktg dir
Art Rogers . . . . progmg dir
Marian Pittman . . . . news dir
Jocelyn Dorsey . . . . pub affrs dir
Gary Alexander . . . . engrg dir

WUPA— Digital Channel: 43. Digital Hrs: 24 1,000 kw vis. ant 1,102t/1,056g TL: N33 44 40 W84 21 36 On air date: Aug 22, 1981. Phoenix Business Park, 2700 Northeast Expwy., Atlanta, GA, 30345. Phone: (404) 325-6969. Fax: (404) 633-4567. Web Site: www.cwatlantatv.com. Licensee: Viacom Stations Group of Atlanta Inc. Group Owner: Viacom Television Stations Group (acq 5-4-2000; grpsl). Population Served: 5,422,000 Natl. Network: CW, . Washington Atty: Wiley, Rein & Fielding.
Key Personnel:
Meg LaVigne . . . . gen mgr

WUVG-DT— Digital Channel: 48.1,258 kw vis, 125.8 kw aur. 1,351t/1,236g TL: N34 12 27 W83 47 38 On air date: April 1989. 3350 Peach Tree Rd., Suite 1250, Atlanta, GA, 33026. Phone: (404) 926-2300. Fax: (404) 926-2320. Web Site: www.univision.com. Licensee: Univision Partnership of Atlanta. Group Owner: Univision Communications Inc. (acq 6-6-2001; grpsl). Population Served: 750,000 Natl. Network: Univision (Spanish), . Washington Atty: William M. Barnard. Foreign lang progmg: SpanishS 168
Key Personnel:
Tammy Heinen . . . . gen mgr

WXIA-TV— Digital Channel: 10.316 kw vis, 63.2 kw aur. 1,048t/1,040g TL: N33 45 24 W84 19 55 On air date: Sept 30, 1951. 1611 W. Peachtree St. N.E., Atlanta, GA, 30309. Phone: (404) 892-1611. Fax: (404) 881-0675. Web Site: www.11alive.com. Licensee: Gannett Georgia L.P. Group Owner: Gannett Broadcasting, division of Gannett Co. Inc. (acq 6-7-79; grpsl;6-11-79). Population Served: 1,592,000 Natl. Network: NBC, . Washington Atty: Reed Smith LLP.
Key Personnel:
Robert Walker . . . . pres & VP & gen mgr

Augusta, GA
(DMA 115)

WAGT— Digital Channel: 30. Digital Hrs: 24 65 kw vis, 6.5 kw aur. ant 1,590t/1,478g TL: N33 25 15 W81 50 19 On air date: Dec 24, 1968. 905 Broad St, Augusta, GA, 30901. Phone: (706) 826-0026. Fax: (706) 724-4028. Fax: (706) 724-7491. Web Site: www.nbcaugusta.com. Licensee: WAGT Television Inc. Group Owner: Schurz Communications Inc. (acq 7-1-80; $5 million). Population Served: 267,730 Natl. Network: NBC, CW, . Natl. Rep: Petry Television Inc.,. Washington Atty: Hogan & Hartson. News staff: 28; News: 8 hrs wkly.
Key Personnel:
Marilyn Brock . . . . stn mgr
Ed Everest . . . . prom mgr
Scott Brady . . . . news dir
Dave DeFrehn . . . . chief of engrg

*WCES-TV— Digital Channel: 6. Digital Hrs: 24 5,000 kw vis, 500 kw aur. ant 1,480t/1,465g TL: N33 15 33 W82 17 09 On air date: Sept 12, 1966. Box 525, Wrens, GA, 30833. Phone: (706) 547-0293. Fax: (800) 222-4788.E-mail: viewerservices@gpb.org Web Site: www.gpb.org. Licensee: Georgia Public Telecommunications Commission. Natl. Network: PBS, .
Key Personnel:
Juanita Rachel . . . . chief of engrg

*WEBA-TV— Digital Channel: 33. Digital Hrs: 24 661 kw vis. ant 800t/809g TL: N33 11 13 W81 23 54 On air date: Sept 5, 1967. 1101 George Rogers Blvd., Columbia, SC, 29201. Phone: (803) 737-3545. Fax: (803) 737-3495.E-mail: mail@myetv.org Web Site: www.myetv.org. Licensee: South Carolina ETV Commission. Natl. Network: PBS, .

Key Personnel:
Maurice "Moss" Bresnahan . . . . CEO & pres & sr VP
L.W. Griffin Jr. engrg VP

WFXG— Digital Channel: 31. Digital Hrs: 24 Note: virtual channel 54.1 4,517 kw vis, 451 kw aur. 1,120t/1,506g TL: N33 25 00 W81 50 60 On air date: May 23, 1991. 3933 Washington Rd., Augusta, GA, 30907. Box 204540 , Augusta, GA 30917-4540. Phone: (706) 650-5400. Fax: (706) 650-8411.E-mail: gtomlinson@wfxg.com Web Site: www.wfxg.com. Licensee: Southeastern Media Holdings Inc. Group Owner: (group owner; (acq 12-1-2003; $40 million with WXTX(TV) Columbus). Natl. Network: Fox, Washington Atty: Miller & Fields.
Key Personnel:
Barry Barth. . . . . gen mgr
Paul Brewer . . . . gen sls mgr

WJBF— Digital Channel: 42.100 kw vis, 20 kw aur. ant 1,624t/1,472g TL: N33 24 20 W81 50 01 On air date: Nov 23, 1953. Box 1404, Augusta, GA, 30903. 1001 Reynolds St., Augusta, GA 30901. Phone: (706) 722-6664. Fax: (706) 722-0022. Web Site: www.wjbf.com. Licensee: Media General Broadcasting of South Carolina Holdings Inc. Group Owner: Media General Broadcast Group (acq 3-27-2000; grpsl). Population Served: 613,000 Natl. Network: ABC, . Washington Atty: Dow, Lohnes & Albertson, PLLC. News: 22 hrs wky.
Key Personnel:
Gene Kirkconnell . . . . gen mgr
Bill Stewart . . . . gen sls mgr
Charles Coleman . . . . natl sls mgr
Scot Seabolt. . . . . rgnl sls mgr
Cil Frazier . . . . mktg dir
Mary Jones . . . . progmg dir & progmg
Mark Rosen . . . . news dir
Cary Hale . . . . chief of engrg
Roberto Vasquez. . . . . reporter

WRDW-TV— Digital Channel: 12. Digital Hrs: 24 316 kw vis, 30.2 kw aur. ant 1,590t/1,506g TL: N33 24 29 W81 50 36 On air date: Feb 14, 1954. Box 1212, Augusta, GA, 30903-1212. 1301 Georgia Ave., North Augusta, SC 29841. Phone: (803) 278-1212. Fax: (803) 279-8316.E-mail: wrdw@wrdw.com Web Site: www.wrdw.com. Licensee: Gray Television Licensee Inc. Group Owner: Gray Television Inc. (acq 1-4-96; $34 million). Population Served: 604,000 Natl. Network: CBS, MyNetworkTV, . Natl. Rep: Continental Television Sales,. News staff: 35; News: 20 hrs wkly.
Key Personnel:
John Ray . . . . pres & gen mgr
Estelle Parsley. . . . . opns dir & news dir
Michael Oates . . . . gen sls mgr & natl sls mgr
Edward Elser. . . . . chief of engrg

Bainbridge
see Tallahassee, FL-Thomasville, GA market

Brunswick
see Jacksonville, FL market

Chatsworth
see Chattanooga, TN market

Columbus, GA
(DMA 128)

*WJSP-TV— Digital Channel: 23. Digital Hrs: 24 5,000 kw vis, 500 kw aur. ant 1,512t/1,102g TL: N32 51 08 W84 42 04 On air date: Aug 10, 1964. 609 Whitehouse Pkwy, Warm Springs, GA, 31830. 260 14th St, N.W., Atlanta, GA 30318. Phone: (706) 655-2145. Fax: (404) 685-2431.E-mail: ask@gpb.org Web Site: www.gpb.org. Licensee: Georgia Public Telecommunications Commission. Natl. Network: PBS,

Key Personnel:
Alfons Pynenburg . . . . chief of engrg

WLGA— Digital Channel: 47. Digital Hrs: 24 302 kw vis. ant 1,059t/984g TL: N32 19 25 W84 46 46 On air date: May 16, 1982. 1800 Pepperell Pkwy., Opelika, AL, 36801. Phone: (334) 745-0066. Fax: (334) 749-5768.E-mail: mbrooks@pappastv.com Web Site: www.wlgatv.com. Licensee: Pappas Telecasting of Opelika L.P. (a Delaware limited partnership). Group Owner: (group owner; (acq 1996; $1.6 million). Natl. Network: CW, . Washington Atty: Paul, Hastings, Janofsky & Walker.

Key Personnel:
Harry J. Pappas . . . . pres
Mike Brooks . . . . gen mgr
Walter Dix. . . . . opns mgr

WLTZ— Digital Channel: 35. Digital Hrs: 24 1,070 kw vis, 209 kw aur. ant 1,310t/1,319g TL: N32 27 29 W84 53 08 On air date: Oct 29, 1970. 6140 Buena Vista Rd., Columbus, GA, 31907. Box 12289, Columbus, GA 31917. Phone: (706) 561-3838. Fax: (706) 563-8467. Fax: (706) 561-3880 (sales).E-mail: wltz@wltz.com Web Site: www.wltz.com. Licensee: SagamoreHill Broadcasting of Georgia LLC. (acq 8-10-2007; $10.6 million). Population Served: 189,600 Natl. Network: NBC, . Natl. Rep: Blair Television,. Washington Atty: Wiley, Rein & Fielding.
Key Personnel:
Louis Wall . . . . pres
Charles Izlar . . . . CFO
Tom Breazeale . . . . VP & gen mgr
Drew Rhodes . . . . stn mgr
Charles Collins . . . . opns dir

WRBL— Digital Channel: 15. Digital Hrs: 24 100 kw vis, 12 kw aur. ant 1,780t/1,749g TL: N30 19 25 W84 46 46 On air date: Nov 15, 1953. Box 270, Columbus, GA, 31902-0270. 1350 13th Ave., Columbus, GA 31902-0270. Phone: (706) 323-3333. Fax: (706) 327-6655. Fax: (706) 323-0841. Web Site: www.wrbl.com. Licensee: Media General Broadcasting of South Carolina Holdings Inc. Group Owner: Media General Broadcast Group (acq 3-27-2000; grpsl). Population Served: 769,000 Natl. Network: CBS, . Natl. Rep: MMT,. Washington Atty: Dow, Lohnes & Albertson.
Key Personnel:
Otis Pickett . . . . VP & gen mgr

WTVM— Digital Channel: 11.284 kw vis, 52.5 kw aur. ant 1,650t/1,749g TL: N32 19 25 W84 46 46 On air date: Oct 6, 1953. Box 1848, Harrisonburg, GA, 31902. Phone: (706) 324-6471. Fax: (706) 322-7527.E-mail: newsleader@wtvm.com Web Site: www.wtvm.com. Licensee: WTVM License Subsidiary Inc. Group Owner: Raycom Media Inc. (acq 1996; grpsl). Population Served: 496,000 Natl. Network: ABC, . Natl. Rep: Harrington, Righter & Parsons,. Washington Atty: Powell, Goldstein, Frazer & Murphy.
Key Personnel:
Lee Brantley . . . . VP & gen mgr
Rick Moll . . . . news dir

WXTX— Digital Channel: 49. Digital Hrs: 24 1,000 kw vis, 100 kw aur. ant 1,140t/1,121g TL: N32 27 49 W84 52 37 On air date: June 17, 1983. Box 1848, Columbus, GA, 31902. Phone: (706) 324-6471. Fax: (706) 322-7527.E-mail: programming@wxtx.com Web Site: www.wxtx.com. Licensee: Southeastern Media Holdings Inc. Group Owner: (group owner; acq 12-1-2003; $40 million with WFXG(TV) Augusta). Natl. Network: Fox, . Washington Atty: Fisher, Wayland, Cooper, Leader & Zaragoza.
Key Personnel:
Lee Brantley . . . . gen mgr
Rick Moll . . . . news dir

Dalton

see Chattanooga, TN market

Macon, GA
(DMA 122)

WGNM— Digital Channel: 45. Digital Hrs: 24 52 kw vis, 5.2 kw aur. ant 608t/685g TL: N32 44 58 W83 33 35 On air date: Nov 30, 1990. 178 Steven Dr., Macon, GA, 31210. Phone: (478) 474-8400. Fax: (478) 474-4777.E-mail: recet@wgnm.com Web Site: www.wgnm.com. Licensee: Christian Television Network Inc. Ownership: Jimmy Smith, 25%; Robert T. D'Andrea, 25%; Virginia Oliver, 25%; and Wayne Wetzel, 25% (acq 12-31-2003; $3 million). Population Served: 210,000 Washington Atty: Allen & Harold. News: one hr wkly.
Key Personnel:
Robert D'Andrea . . . . pres
Rip Kenley . . . . gen mgr
Edie Spradley . . . . traf mgr

WGXA— Digital Channel: 16.1,290 kw vis, 252 kw aur. ant 800t/898g TL: N32 45 08 W83 33 38 On air date: Apr 21, 1982. Box 340, 599 Martin Luther King Blvd., Macon, GA, 31201. Phone: (478) 745-2424. Fax: (478) 745-6057 (news). Web Site: www.fox24.com. Licensee: Fox24 of Macon LLC. Ownership: Frontier Television Investors L.L.C., 100% Group Owner: GOCOM Communications (acq 11-20-2007; $18.8 million). Natl. Network: Fox, MyNetworkTV, . Washington Atty: Leibowitz & Spencer.

Key Personnel:
Keith True . . . . exec VP & gen mgr & stn mgr

WMAZ-TV— Digital Channel: 13. Digital Hrs: 24 316 kw vis, 62 kw aur. 780t/1,209g TL: N32 45 10 W83 33 32 On air date: Sept 27, 1953. Box 5008, Macon, GA, 31208. 1314 Gray Hwy., Macon, GA 31211. Phone: (478) 752-1313. Fax: (478) 752-1331. Web Site: www.13wmaz.com. Licensee: Gannett Georgia L.P. Group Owner: Gannett Broadcasting (acq 12-4-95). Population Served: 563,000 Natl. Network: CBS, . Washington Atty: Wiley, Rein & Fielding. News staff: 39; News: 27 hrs wkly.
Key Personnel:
Dodie Cantrell . . . . VP & gen mgr consumer affrs dir
Frank Shurling . . . . gen sls mgr
Jeff Dudley . . . . mktg dir & prom dir
Irene Ray . . . . traf mgr

WMGT-TV— Digital Channel: 40. Digital Hrs: 24 760 kw vis, 154 kw aur. ant 893t/837g TL: N32 45 12 W83 33 46 On air date: Aug 26, 1968. Box 4328, Macon, GA, 31208-4328. 301 Poplar St., Macon, GA 31201. Phone: (478) 745-4141. Fax: (478) 742-2626.E-mail: info@wmgt.com Web Site: www.wmgt.com. Licensee: Morris Network Inc. Group Owner: Morris Multi-Media (acq 11-30-78; $2.8 million;12-18-78). Population Served: 531,000 Natl. Network: NBC, . Natl. Rep: Millennium Sales & Marketing,. Washington Atty: McFadden, Evans & Sill.
Key Personnel:
Dean Hinson . . . . pres
Derek Brown . . . . gen mgr
Debbie Wright . . . . progmg dir
Mike Roberts . . . . news dir

*WMUM-TV— Digital Channel: 7.5,000 kw vis, 50 kw aur. ant 1,087t/1,168g TL: N32 28 11 W83 15 17 On air date: Jan 1, 1968. 243 Cary Salem Rd., Cochran, GA, 31014. Phone: (478) 934-3095. Licensee: Georgia Public Telecommunications Commission. Natl. Network: PBS, .
Key Personnel:
Randy Cranford. . . . . chief of engrg

WPGA-TV— Digital Channel: 32. Digital Hrs: 24 1,170 kw vis, 117 kw aur. 810t TL: N32 33 20 W83 44 14 On air date: March 1995. 1691 Forsyth St., Macon, GA, 31201. Phone: (478) 745-5858. Fax: (478) 745-5800. Web Site: www.wpga.tv. Licensee: Radio Perry Inc. Population Served: 473,000 Natl. Network: ABC, . Washington Atty: Brown, Nietert & Kaufman. News: 3 hrs wkly.
Key Personnel:
Lowell Register. . . . . pres
Debbie Hart . . . . gen mgr
Len Register . . . . opns mgr
Julie Register . . . . prom mgr

Savannah, GA
(DMA 96)

WGSA— Digital Channel: 35. Digital Hrs: 24 316 kw vis. ant 482t TL: N31 45 53 W82 13 38 On air date: May 1, 1992. 401 Mall Blvd., Suite 202A, Savannah, GA, 31406. Phone: (912) 692-8000. Fax: (912) 692-0400. Licensee: Southern TV Corp. Ownership: Dan L. and Betty Jo Johnson, 42.5%. (acq 6-3-98; $3.2 million). Natl. Network: CW, . Washington Atty: Irwin, Campbell & Tannenwald.
Key Personnel:
Dan L. Johnson . . . . CEO & chmn pres
Charles E. Robb . . . . CFO
Jo Johnson . . . . exec VP
Fred Pierce . . . . gen mgr

WJCL— Digital Channel: 22. Digital Hrs: 24 3,830 kw vis, 383 kw aur. 1,430t/1,478g TL: N32 03 30 W81 20 20 On air date: July 18, 1970. 10001 Abercorn St., Savannah, GA, 31406. Phone: (912) 925-0022. Fax: (912) 921-2235.E-mail: comments@wjcl.com Web Site: www.abc22tv.com. Licensee: NVT Savannah Licensee LLC. Group Owner: Piedmont Television Holdings LLC (acq 9-19-2007; $17.5 million). Population Served: 721,000 Natl. Network: ABC, . Natl. Rep: Petry Television Inc.,. Washington Atty: Wiley Rein LLP. News staff: 14; News: 5 hrs wkly.
Key Personnel:
Jason Elkin . . . . CEO
Lynn Fairbanks . . . . gen mgr
Dave German . . . . opns mgr

*WJWJ-TV— Digital Channel: 44. Digital Hrs: 6 AM-3 AM 851 kw vis, 169 kw aur. 1,279t/1,320g TL: N32 42 44 W80 40 49 On air date: Sept 19, 1976. Box 1165, Beaufort, SC, 29901. 925 Ribaut Rd., Beaufort, SC 29902. Phone: (843) 524-0808. Fax: (843) 524-1016.E-mail: wjwj@hargray.com Web Site: www.wjwj.org. Licensee: South Carolina ETV Commission. Population Served: 245,000 Natl. Network: PBS, .

Key Personnel:
Scott Johnson . . . . opns mgr
Juan Singleton . . . . news dir
Mike Milburn . . . . chief of engrg

WSAV-TV— Digital Channel: 39.100 kw vis, 20 kw aur. ant 1,476t/1,532g TL: N32 03 32 W81 17 57 On air date: Feb 1, 1956. 1430 E. Victory Dr., Savannah, GA, 31404. Phone: (912) 651-0300. Fax: (912) 651-0304. Web Site: www.wsav.com. Licensee: Media General Broadcasting Inc. Group Owner: Media General Broadcast Group (acq 7-25-97; grpsl). Population Served: 230,000 Natl. Network: NBC, MyNetworkTV, . Washington Atty: Dow, Lohnes & Albertson.
Key Personnel:
Jim Berman. . . . . VP
Brad Moses . . . . gen mgr
Dave Stagnitto . . . . progmg dir
Kevin Brennan . . . . news dir

WTGS— Digital Channel: 28. Digital Hrs: 24 5,000 kw vis, 500 kw aur. ant 1,484t/1,496g TL: N32 02 45 W81 20 27 On air date: Sept 1, 1985. 10001 Abercorn St., Savannah, GA, 31406. Phone: (912) 925-2287. Fax: (912) 925-7026.E-mail: comments@wjcl.com Web Site: www.fox28tv.com. Licensee: Parkin Broadcasting of Savannah License LLC. (acq 9-19-2007; $17.5 million). Natl. Network: Fox, . Washington Atty: Drinker Biddle & Reath LLP. News: 5 hrs wkly.
Key Personnel:
Todd Parkin . . . . CEO
Dave Tillery . . . . gen mgr
Dave German . . . . opns mgr
Jennifer Burns . . . . natl sls mgr
Kurt Hetager . . . . prom mgr & pub affrs dir
Erik Schrader . . . . news dir
Ed Youmans . . . . chief of engrg
Karon Johnson . . . . traf mgr
Frank Sulkowski . . . . sports cmtr
Jeff Kirk . . . . weather dir

WTOC-TV— Digital Channel: 11.316 kw vis, 31.6 kw aur. 1,470t/1,531g TL: N32 03 14 W81 21 01 On air date: Feb 14, 1954. Box 8086, Savannah, GA, 31412. 11 The News Place-Chatham Center, Savannah, GA 31405. Phone: (912) 234-1111. Fax: (912) 238-5133. Web Site: www.wtoc.com. Licensee: Raycom America License Subsidiary LLC. Group Owner: Raycom Media Inc. (acq 4-15-97; grpsl). Population Served: 558,300 Natl. Network: CBS, . Natl. Rep: Harrington, Righter & Parsons,. Washington Atty: Covington & Burling.
Key Personnel:
William Cathcart . . . . VP & gen mgr
Craig Harney . . . . opns mgr

*WVAN-TV— Digital Channel: 9. Digital Hrs: 18 316 kw vis, 34.7 kw aur. ant 1,050t/1,086g TL: N32 08 48 W81 37 05 On air date: Sept 16, 1963. 260 14th St. N.W., 86 Vandiver St., Atlanta, GA, 30318. Phone: (912) 653-4996. Fax: (404) 685-2591.E-mail: ask@gpb.org Web Site: www.gpb.org. Licensee: Georgia Public Telecommunications Commission. Population Served: 205,900 Natl. Network: PBS, .
Key Personnel:
Bob Houghton . . . . gen mgr

Thomasville

see Tallahassee, FL-Thomasville, GA market

Toccoa

see Greenville-Spartanburg, SC-Asheville, NC-Anderson, SC market

Valdosta

see Tallahassee, FL-Thomasville, GA market

Waycross

see Jacksonville, FL market

Hawaii

KLEI— Digital Channel: 25. Digital Hrs: 24 2.5 kw vis. ant 2,857t/195g TL: N19 43 16 W155 55 15 On air date: 1988. Box 235770, Honolulu, HI, 96823. Phone: (808) 329-8120. Fax: (808) 443-0424.E-mail: info@klei.tv Web Site: www.klei.tv. Licensee: Pacific Christian Church. (acq 9-5-2008; donation). Washington Atty: Fletcher, Heald & Hildreth.

Key Personnel:
James W. Gustafson . . . . pres

KGMD-TV— Digital Channel: 9.2 kw vis. ant 102t/239g TL: N19 43 00 W155 08 13 On air date: May 15, 1955. c/o KGMB, 1534 Kapiolani Blvd., Honolulu, HI, 96814. Phone: (808) 973-5462. Fax: (808) 941-8153.E-mail: kgmbnews@kgmb9.com Web Site: www.kgmb.com. Licensee: HITV License Subsidiary Inc. Group Owner: Emmis Communications Corp. (acq 6-4-2007; grpsl). Natl. Network: CBS, . Natl. Rep: Harrington, Righter & Parsons,.
Key Personnel:
Rick Blangiardi . . . . pres
Rick Brangiarei . . . . gen mgr

KHAW-TV— Digital Channel: 11. Analog Hrs: 24/7 Digital Hrs: 24/7 3.35 kw vis. ant 100t/240g TL: N19 43 00 W155 08 13 On air date: Nov 27, 1961. c/o KHON-TV, 88 Piikoi St., Honolulu, HI, 96814. Phone: (808) 591-2222. Fax: (808) 591-9085.E-mail: khan@khon.emmis.com Web Site: www.khon.com. Licensee: NVT Hawaii Licensee LLC. Group Owner: Emmis Communications Corp. (acq 11-1-2007; grpsl). Natl. Network: Fox, . Natl. Rep: Harrington, Righter & Parsons,. Washington Atty: Wiley Rein LLP. News staff: 45; News: 25 hrs wkly.
Key Personnel:
Joseph McNamara. . . . . gen mgr
Gelene Welch . . . . gen sls mgr
Lori Silva . . . . news dir
Alexander Rogers . . . . sports cmtr
Satellite of KHON-TV Honolulu.

KHBC-TV— Digital Channel: 22. Digital Hrs: 24 8 kw vis. ant -558t/145g TL: N19 43 51 W155 04 11 On air date: Aug 22, 1983. c/o KHNL, 150-B Puuhale Rd., Honolulu, HI, 96819. Phone: (808) 847-3246. Fax: (808) 845-3616.E-mail: news8@khnl.com Web Site: www.khnl.com. Licensee: KHNL/KFVE License Subsidiary LLC. Group Owner: Raycom Media Inc. (acq 9-2-99; grpsl). Natl. Network: NBC, . Washington Atty: Covington & Burling.
Key Personnel:
John Fink. . . . . pres & VP & gen mgr
Rebroadcasts KHNL(TV) Honolulu 100%.

KHVO— Digital Channel: 13. Digital Hrs: 24 2 kw vis. ant -302t/239g TL: N19 43 00 W155 08 13 On air date: May 15, 1960. 801 S. King St., Honolulu, HI, 96813. Phone: (808) 535-0400. Licensee: Hearst-Argyle Stations Inc. Group Owner: Hearst-Argyle Stations Inc. (acq 7-16-97; grpsl). Natl. Network: ABC, .
Key Personnel:
Michael Rosenberg . . . . gen mgr
Satellite of KITV Honolulu.

KWHH— Digital Channel: 23. Digital Hrs: 24 14.9 kw vis. ant 108t/151g TL: N19 43 00 W155 08 13 On air date: Oct 1, 1989. Century Square, 1188 Bishop St., Suite 502, Honolulu, HI, 96813. Phone: (808) 538-1414. Fax: (808) 526-0326.E-mail: kwhe@lesea.com Web Site: www.lesea.com. Licensee: Le Sea Broadcasting Corp. Group Owner: (group owner; (acq 10-1-89; $8,277;12-26-89). Washington Atty: Gardner, Carton & Douglas.
Key Personnel:
Peter Sumrall . . . . pres
Anthony Hale . . . . CFO
Tony Boquer . . . . gen mgr
Rebroadcasts KWHE Honolulu 100%.

Honolulu, HI
(DMA 72)

***KAAH-TV—** Digital Channel: 27. Digital Hrs: 24 1,000 kw vis. ant 1,893t/40g TL: N21 23 45 W158 05 58 On air date: Dec 23, 1982. 1152 Smith St., Honolulu, HI, 96817. Phone: (808) 521-5826. Fax: (808) 599-6238.E-mail: tbnkaahtv26@hotmail.com Web Site: www.tbn.org. Licensee: Trinity Christian Center of Santa Ana Inc. dba Trinity Broadcasting Network. Group Owner: Trinity Broadcasting Network (acq 7-1-2000; grpsl). Population Served: 1,250,000 Washington Atty: Colby May.
Key Personnel:
Paul F. Crouch . . . . pres
Paul Crouch Jr. . . . . exec VP
Jan Crouch. . . . . VP
Cheryl Witbeck . . . . gen mgr
Satellite of KTBN-TV Los Angeles (Santa Ana), CA 95%.

***KALO—** Digital Channel: 38. Digital Hrs: 24 155 kw vis. ant 1,893t/40g TL: N21 23 45 W158 05 58 On air date: 2000. Box 8969, Honolulu, HI, 96830. Phone: (808) 591-8282. Fax: (808) 591-1250. Web Site: www.kalo-tv.com. Licensee: Pacifica Broadcasting Co. Population Served: 1,400,000 Washington Atty: Fletcher, Heald & Hildreth, P.L.C., Harry F. Cole, Esq.

Key Personnel:
Donald Laidlaw . . . . gen mgr

KBFD-DT— Digital Channel: 33. Digital Hrs: 24 49.6 kw vis. ant -118t/400g TL: N21 18 49 W157 51 43 On air date: Mar 7, 1986. Century Sq., 1188 Bishop St., Honolulu, HI, 96813. Phone: (808) 521-8066. Fax: (808) 521-5233.E-mail: jeffchung@kbfd.com Web Site: www.kbfd.com. Licensee: Allen Broadcasting Corp. Ownership: June Ho Chung, 52%; Yun Hee Chung, 30%; Kea Sung Chung, 10%; Ok Soon Chung, 8%. Population Served: 1,200,000 Washington Atty: Wilkinson, Barker, Knauer L.L.P. News staff: 4; News: 6 hrs wkly.
Key Personnel:
Kea Sung Chung. . . . . CEO & pres
June Ho Chung . . . . exec VP
Jeff Chung . . . . gen mgr

KFVE— Digital Channel: 23. Digital Hrs: 24 5.4 kw vis. ant 1,463t/40g TL: N21 22 55 W158 06 19 On air date: Feb 7, 1988. 150 B Puuhale Rd., Honolulu, HI, 96819. Phone: (808) 847-3246. Fax: (808) 845-3616. Web Site: www.ksthehometeam.com. Licensee: KHNL/KFVE License Subsidiary LLC. Group Owner: Raycom Media Inc. (acq 12-28-99). Natl. Network: MyNetworkTV, . Washington Atty: Brown, Nietert & Kaufman. News: 7 hrs wkly.
Key Personnel:
John Fink. . . . . VP & gen mgr

KGMB— Digital Channel: 22.40 kw vis. ant 2,063t/161g TL: N21 24 03 W158 06 10 On air date: Dec 1, 1962. 1534 Kapiolani Blvd., Honolulu, HI, 96814. Phone: (808) 973-5462. Fax: (808) 973-9354.E-mail: kgmb9news@kgmb9.com Web Site: www.kgmb9.com. Licensee: HITV License Subsidiary Inc. Group Owner: Emmis Communications Corp. (acq 6-4-2007; grpsl). Population Served: 1,150,000 Natl. Network: CBS, . Natl. Rep: Harrington, Righter & Parsons,.
Key Personnel:
Rick Blangiardi . . . . pres & gen mgr

***KHET—** Digital Channel: 11. Digital Hrs: 17 15.7 kw vis. ant 2,050t/150g TL: N21 24 03 W158 06 10 On air date: Apr 15, 1966. Box 11599, Harrisonburg, HI, 96822. 2350 Dole St., Harrisonburg, HI 96822. Phone: (808) 973-1000. Fax: (808) 973-1090.E-mail: email@pbshawaii.org Web Site: www.pbshawaii.org. Licensee: Hawaii Public Broadcasting Authority. Population Served: 1,100,000 Natl. Network: PBS, . Washington Atty: Wilkes, Artis, Hedrick & Lane.
Key Personnel:
Mike McCartney . . . . CEO & gen mgr

KHNL— Digital Channel: 35. Digital Hrs: 24 5.9 kw vis. ant 1,486t/40g TL: N21 22 55 W158 06 19 On air date: July 4, 1962. 150 B. Puuhale Rd., Honolulu, HI, 96819. Phone: (808) 847-3246. Fax: (808) 845-3616.E-mail: news8@khnl.com Web Site: www.khnl.com. Licensee: KHNL/KFVE License Subsidiary LLC. Group Owner: Raycom Media Inc. (acq 9-2-99; grpsl). Population Served: 412,000 Natl. Network: NBC, . Natl. Rep: TeleRep,. Washington Atty: Covington & Burling. Wire Svc: CNN Wire Svc: AP Wire Svc: NBC News: 23 hrs wkly.
Key Personnel:
John Fink. . . . . VP & gen mgr

KHON-TV— Digital Channel: 8. Analog Hrs: 24/7 Digital Hrs: 24/7 7.2 kw vis. ant -39t/415g TL: N21 17 46 W157 50 36 On air date: Dec 15, 1952. 88 Piikoi St., Honolulu, HI, 96814. Phone: (808) 591-2222. Fax: (808) 591-9085.E-mail: news@khon.com Web Site: www.khon.com. Licensee: NVT Hawaii Licensee LLC. Group Owner: Emmis Communications Corp. (acq 11-1-2007; grpsl). Population Served: 1,150,000 Natl. Network: Fox, CW, . Natl. Rep: Harrington, Righter & Parsons,. News staff: 45; News: 25 hrs wkly.
Key Personnel:
Susii Hearst . . . . gen sls mgr
Gelene Welch . . . . progmg mgr
Lori Silva . . . . news dir

KIKU— Digital Channel: 19. Digital Hrs: 24 215.9 kw vis. ant 1,988t/223g TL: N21 23 51.4 W158 06 00.9 On air date: Dec 30, 1983. 737 Bishop St., Suite 1430, Honolulu, HI, 96813. Phone: (808) 847-2021. Fax: (808) 841-3326. Web Site: www.kikutv.com. Licensee: KHLS Inc. Group Owner: Asian Media Group (acq 1-18-2001; $165 million cash for 69.4%). Natl. Rep: Petry Television Inc.,. Washington Atty: Skadden, Arps, Slate, Meagher & Flom.
Key Personnel:
Phyllis Kihara . . . . gen mgr & progmg mgr

KITV— Digital Channel: 40. Digital Hrs: 24 85 kw vis. 3t/415g TL: N21 17 37 W157 50 34 On air date: Apr 16, 1954. 801 S. King St., Honolulu, HI, 96813. Phone: (808) 535-0400. Fax: (808) 536-8777.E-mail: news@kitv.com Web Site: www.kitv.com. Licensee: Hearst-Argyle Stations Inc. Group Owner: Hearst-Argyle Television Inc. (acq 7-16-97; grpsl). Population Served: 324,871 Natl. Network: ABC, . Natl. Rep: Eagle Television Sales,. Washington Atty: Brooks, Pierce, McLendon, Humphrey & Leonard. News staff: 40; News: 20 hrs wkly.

Key Personnel:
Michael Rosenberg . . . . gen mgr

KKAI— Digital Channel: 50. Digital Hrs: 24 12 kw vis. ant 1,223t/107g TL: N21 19 23 W157 40 53 On air date: 2005. 875 Waimanu St., Suite 638, Honolulu, HI, 96813. Phone: (808) 922-5300. Fax: (808) 441-0092.E-mail: info@kkai.tv Web Site: www.kkai.tv. Licensee: Kailua Television LLC. Ownership: Kailua Television Partners. Washington Atty: Fletcher, Heald & Hildreth.
Key Personnel:
William Alatini. . . . . gen mgr

KPXO-TV— Digital Channel: 41. Digital Hrs: 24 34 kw vis. ant 2,073t/45g TL: N21 19 49 W157 45 24 On air date: 1998. 875 Waimanu St., Suite 630, Honolulu, HI, 96813. Phone: (808) 591-1275. Fax: (808) 591-1409. Web Site: www.ionmedia.tv. Licensee: Paxson Hawaii License Inc. Group Owner: Paxson Communications Corp. (acq 8-12-98; $6.9 million). Natl. Network: ION Television, .
Key Personnel:
Jeff Maguire . . . . gen mgr

KUPU— Digital Channel: 15. Digital Hrs: 24 12 kw vis. ant 1,223t/107g TL: N21 19 23 W157 40 53 On air date: 2004. Box 235770, Honolulu, HI, 96823. Phone: (808) 943-0007. Fax: (808) 440-1375.E-mail: info@oceaniachurch.org Web Site: www.kupu.tv. Licensee: Pacific Christian Church. (acq 9-28-2006). News staff: 12; News: 14 hrs wkly.
Key Personnel:
James W. Gustafson . . . . pres

***KWBN—** Digital Channel: 43.22 kw vis. ant 1,893t/69g TL: N21 23 45 W158 05 58 On air date: 2000. 3901 Hwy. 121, Bedford, TX, 76021. Phone: (817) 571-1229. Fax: (817) 571-7458. Web Site: www.daystar.com. Licensee: Ho'ona'auao Community Television Inc.
Key Personnel:
Marcus D. Lamb . . . . pres

KWHE— Digital Channel: 31.20.1 kw vis. ant 16t/436g TL: N21 18 49 W157 51 43 On air date: Mar 7, 1988. Century Square, 1188 Bishop St., Suite 502, Honolulu, HI, 96813. Phone: (808) 538-1414. Fax: (808) 526-0326.E-mail: kwhe@lesea.com Web Site: kwhe.com. Licensee: LeSea Broadcasting Corp. Group Owner: (group owner; (acq 8-15-86; $825,000; 6-16-86). Washington Atty: Gardner, Carton & Douglas.
Key Personnel:
Peter Sumrall . . . . pres
Anthony Hale . . . . CFO
Tony Boquer . . . . gen mgr
Mauro Pena . . . . chief of engrg

KAII-TV— Digital Channel: 7. Analog Hrs: 24/7 Digital Hrs: 24/7 3.69 kw vis. ant 2,470t/161g TL: N20 39 37 W156 21 46 On air date: Nov 17, 1958. 88 Piikoi St., Honolulu, HI, 96814. Phone: (808) 591-2222. Fax: (808) 593-8479.E-mail: news@khon.com Web Site: www.khon.com. Licensee: NVT Hawaii Licensee LLC. Group Owner: Emmis Communications Corp. (acq 11-1-2007; grpsl). Natl. Network: Fox, . Natl. Rep: Harrington, Righter & Parsons,. Washington Atty: Wiley Rein LLP.
Key Personnel:
Joseph McNamara. . . . . gen mgr
Susii Hearst . . . . gen sls mgr
Gelene Welch . . . . progmg mgr
Lori Silva . . . . news dir
Alexander Rogers . . . . news cmtr
Satellite of KHON(TV) Honolulu 100%.

KGMV— Digital Channel: 24.77 kw vis. ant 2,476t/187g TL: N20 39 37 W156 21 46 On air date: Apr 24, 1955. c/o KGMB, 1534 Kapiolani Blvd., Honolulu, HI, 96814. Phone: (808) 973-5462. Fax: (808) 973-9354.E-mail: kmb9news@kgmb9.com Web Site: www.kgmb9.com. Licensee: HITV License Subsidiary Inc. Group Owner: Emmis Communications Corp. (acq 6-4-2007; grpsl). Population Served: 8,280 Natl. Network: CBS, . Natl. Rep: Harrington, Righter & Parsons,.
Key Personnel:
Rick Blangiardi . . . . pres & gen mgr

KMAU— Digital Channel: 12. Digital Hrs: 24 9 kw vis. ant 2,450t/161g TL: N20 39 37 W156 21 46 On air date: Nov 28, 1955. 801 S. King St., Honolulu, HI, 96813. Phone: (808) 535-0400. Licensee: Hearst-Argyle Stations Inc. Group Owner: Hearst-Argyle Television Inc. (acq 7-16-97; grpsl). Population Served: 324,871 Natl. Network: ABC, .
Key Personnel:
Michael Rosenberg . . . . gen mgr
Satellite of KITV Honolulu.

***KMEB—** Digital Channel: 10.21.2 kw vis. ant 2,450t/161g TL: N20 39 37 W156 21 46 On air date: Sept 22, 1966. Box 11599, Honolulu, HI, 96822. 2350 Dole St., Honolulu, HI 96822. Phone: (808) 973-1000. Fax: (808) 973-1090.E-mail: email@pbshawaii.org Web Site: www.pbshawaii.org. Licensee: Hawaii Public Broadcasting Authority. Natl. Network: PBS, .

Key Personnel:
Mike McCartney . . . . CEO & gen mgr & gen mgr
Satellite of *KHET Honolulu.

KOGG— Digital Channel: 16. Digital Hrs: 24 50 kw vis. ant 2,683t/183g TL: N20 39 37 W156 21 46 On air date: Aug 22, 1989. c/o KHNL, 150-B Puuhale Rd., Honolulu, HI, 96819. Phone: (808) 847-3246. Fax: (808) 845-3616.E-mail: news@khnl.com Web Site: www.khnl.com. Licensee: KHNL/KFVE License Subsidiary LLC. Group Owner: Raycom Media Inc. (acq 9-2-99; grpsl). Natl. Network: NBC, .
Key Personnel:
John Fink . . . . pres & VP & gen mgr
100% rebroadcast satellite of KHNL(TV) Honolulu.

KWHM— Digital Channel: 21.23.5 kw vis. ant 2,476t/187g TL: N20 39 37 W156 21 46 On air date: 1993. Century Square, 1188 Bishop St., Suite 502, Honolulu, HI, 96813. Phone: (808) 538-1414. Fax: (808) 526-0326. Web Site: www.lesea.com. Licensee: Le Sea Broadcasting Corp. Group Owner: (group owner) Washington Atty: Gardner, Carton & Douglas.
Key Personnel:
Peter Sumrall . . . . pres
Anthony Hale . . . . CFO
Tony Boquer . . . . gen mgr
Mauro Pena . . . . chief of engrg
Satellite of KWHE Honolulu.

Idaho

Boise, ID

(DMA 112)

*KAID— Digital Channel: 21. Digital Hrs: 24 57.2 kw vis, 5.7 kw aur. ant 2,474t/142g TL: N43 45 16 W116 05 56 On air date: Dec 31, 1971. 1455 N. Orchard St., Boise, ID, 83706. Phone: (208) 373-7220. Fax: (208) 373-7245.E-mail: idptv@idahoptv.org Web Site: www.idahoptv.org. Licensee: Idaho State Board of Education. Population Served: 157,000 Natl. Network: PBS, . Washington Atty: Fletcher, Heald & Hildreth. News staff: 5; News: 3 hrs wkly.
Key Personnel:
Peter Morrill . . . . gen mgr
Kim Philipps . . . . dev dir

KBCI-TV— Digital Channel: 28. Digital Hrs: 24 65 kw vis, 7.0l kw aur. ant 2,550t/100g TL: N43 45 17 W116 05 53 On air date: Nov 26, 1953. 140 N. 16th St., Boise, ID, 83702. Phone: (208) 472-2222. Fax: (208) 472-2212.E-mail: comments@kbcitv.com Web Site: www.2news.tv.com. Licensee: Fisher Broadcasting - Idaho TV L.L.C. Group Owner: Fisher Broadcasting Company (acq 7-1-99; grpsl). Population Served: 604,000 Natl. Network: CBS, . Natl. Rep: Continental Television Sales,. Washington Atty: Shaw Pittman. News staff: 37; News: 19 hrs wkly.
Key Personnel:
Colleen Brown . . . . CEO
Larry Roberts . . . . VP & gen mgr
Eric Jordan . . . . gen sls mgr & pub affrs dir
Sean McBride . . . . prom dir
Yvonne Simons . . . . news dir

KIVI-TV—(Nampa, Digital Channel: 24.589 kw vis. ant 2,815t/307g TL: N43 45 21 W116 05 54 On air date: Feb 1, 1974. 1866 E. Chisholm Dr., Nampa, ID, 83687. Phone: (208) 336-0500. Fax: (208) 381-6682. Web Site: www.kivitv.com. Licensee: Journal Broadcast Corp. Group Owner: Journal Communications Inc. (acq 11-15-2001). Population Served: 580,000 Natl. Network: ABC, . News staff: 45; News: 19.5 hrs wkly.
Key Personnel:
Bob Rosenthal . . . . VP & gen mgr
Ken Richie . . . . gen sls mgr
Norma Petty . . . . rgnl sls mgr
Jason Knose . . . . mktg dir
Scott Picken . . . . news dir
Jeff Hoffert . . . . chief of engrg
Brian Perkins . . . . traf mgr

KKJB— Digital Channel: 39. Digital Hrs: 24 1,295 kw vis. ant 1,752t/164g TL: N43 44 23 W116 08 15 On air date: 2005. Cocola Broadcasting Companies, 706 W. Herndon Ave., Fresno, CA, 93650. Phone: (208) 331-3900. Fax: (559) 435-3201.E-mail: info@cocolatv.com Web Site: www.cocolatv.com. Licensee: Boise Telecasters L.P. Group Owner: Cocola Broadcasting Companies (acq 5-7-2004; $3 million for CP). Washington Atty: Dow, Lohnes & Albertson, LLPC.

Key Personnel:
Gary Cocola . . . . CEO
John Her . . . . opns mgr
Seth Diviney . . . . gen sls mgr
Ralph Malerich . . . . engr

KNIN-TV— Digital Channel: 10. Digital Hrs: 24 162 kw vis. ant 2,690t/210g TL: N43 45 18 W116 05 52 On air date: 1993. 816 W. Bannock St., Suite 402, Boise, ID, 83702. Phone: (208) 331-0909. Fax: (208) 344-0119. Web Site: www.knin.com. Licensee: Journal Broadcast Corp. Group Owner: Banks Broadcasting Inc. (acq 4-23-2009; $6.6 million). Natl. Network: CW, . Natl. Rep: Blair Television,. Washington Atty: Leventhal Senter & Lerman PLLC.
Key Personnel:
James P. Prather . . . . pres
Larry Newton . . . . gen mgr & gen sls mgr

KTRV-TV— Digital Channel: 13. Digital Hrs: 24 178 kw vis, 18.2 kw aur. ant 2,760t/220g TL: N43 45 18 W116 05 52 On air date: Oct 18, 1981. One 6th St. N., Nampa, ID, 83687. Phone: (208) 466-1200. Fax: (208) 467-6958.E-mail: comments@ktrv.com Web Site: www.fox12idaho.com. Licensee: Idaho Independent Television Inc. Group Owner: Block Communications Inc. (acq 4-23-85; $4.9 million;3-25-85). Population Served: 500,000 Natl. Network: Fox, . Washington Atty: Dow, Lohnes & Albertson. News staff: 12; News: 7 hrs wkly.
Key Personnel:
Rick Joseph . . . . pres & gen mgr
Ed Crampton . . . . opns mgr
Ken Hunter . . . . sls dir
C.J. Gish . . . . progmg mgr
Kelly Cross . . . . news dir
Daniel Paixao . . . . chief of engrg

KTVB— Digital Channel: 7. Analog Hrs: 24 Digital Hrs: 24 27 kw vis. ant 2,644t/189g TL: N43 45 16 W116 05 56 On air date: July 12, 1953. PO Box 7, Boise, ID, 83707. 5407 Fairview Ave, Boise, ID. Phone: (208) 375-7277. Fax: (208) 378-1762.E-mail: info@ktvb.com Web Site: www.ktvb.com. Licensee: KTVB-TV Inc. Group Owner: Belo Corp., Broadcast Division (acq 1997; grpsl). Population Served: 677,000 Natl. Network: NBC, . Natl. Rep: TeleRep,. Washington Atty: Wiley, Rein & Fielding. News: 27 hrs wkly.
Key Personnel:
Douglas L. Armstrong . . . . pres
Douglas Armstrong . . . . gen mgr
Paul Budell . . . . opns mgr
Kristi Edmunds . . . . sls dir
Tom Zito . . . . natl sls mgr
Jim Gilchriest . . . . news dir
Brad Bond . . . . sls

Coeur d'Alene

see Spokane, WA market

Idaho Falls-Pocatello, ID

(DMA 162)

KBEO— Digital Channel: 11.30 kw vis. ant 1,978t/180g TL: N43 38 14 W110 38 03 On air date: 2002. KM Communications Inc., 3654 W. Jarvis Ave., Skokie, IL, 60076. Phone: (847) 674-0864. Fax: (847) 674-9188. Licensee: Pocatello Channel 15 LLC. Ownership: Myoung Hwa Bae, 100%.

KFXP— Digital Channel: 31.68.5 kw vis. ant 1,466t/512g TL: N42 55 15 W112 20 44 On air date: July 17, 1998. 902 E. Sherman St., Pocatello, ID, 83201. Phone: (208) 232-6666. Fax: (208) 232-6678. Web Site: www.kpvi.com. Licensee: Compass Communications of Idaho Inc. Natl. Network: Fox, .
Key Personnel:
Bill Fouch . . . . gen mgr
Patrick Anderson . . . . gen sls mgr
Rockky Hansen . . . . prom dir
Brenda Baumgartner . . . . news dir
Robin Estopinal . . . . chief of engrg

KIDK-TV— Digital Channel: 36. Digital Hrs: 24 100 kw vis, 14.4 kw aur. ant 1,600t/200g TL: N43 29 51 W112 39 50 On air date: Dec 20, 1953. Box 1255 E. 17th St., Idaho Falls, ID, 83404. 145 S. Arthur, Pocatello, ID 83204. Phone: (208) 522-5100. Fax: (208) 535-0946.E-mail: comments@kidk.com Web Site: www.kidk.com. Licensee: Fisher Broadcasting - S.E. Idaho TV L.L.C. Group Owner: Fisher Broadcasting Company (acq 12-4-01 grpsl). Population Served: 102,130 Natl. Network: CBS, . Washington Atty: Shaw, Pittman. News staff: 20; News: 15 hrs wkly.

Key Personnel:
Gina Berger . . . . gen mgr

KIFI-TV— Digital Channel: 8. Digital Hrs: 24 63 kw vis. ant 1,522t/141g TL: N43 30 04 W112 39 43 On air date: Jan 21, 1961. Box 2148, Idaho Falls, ID, 83403. Phone: (208) 525-2520. Fax: (208) 522-1930. Fax: (208) 529-2443 (news). Web Site: www.localnews8.com. Licensee: NPG of Idaho Inc. Group Owner: (group owner) (acq 8-1-2005; $12.5 million). Population Served: 300,000 Natl. Network: ABC, CW, Telemundo (Spanish), . Washington Atty: Smithwick & Belendiuk P.C. News staff: 35; News: 30 hrs wkly.
Key Personnel:
John Kueneke . . . . pres
Mark Danielson . . . . gen mgr
Monte Young . . . . gen sls mgr

*KISU-TV— Digital Channel: 17. Digital Hrs: 24 122 kw vis, 12.2 kw aur. ant 1,527t/144g TL: N43 30 02 W112 39 36 On air date: July 7, 1971. Campus Box 8111, Pocatello, ID, 83209. 1455 N. Orchard St., Boise, ID 83706. Phone: (208) 282-2857. Fax: (208) 282-2848.E-mail: idptv@idahoptv.org Web Site: www.idahoptv.org. Licensee: Idaho State Board of Education. Natl. Network: PBS, .
Key Personnel:
Peter Morrill . . . . gen mgr
Kim Neilsen . . . . stn mgr
Dave Turnmire . . . . chief of engrg

KJWY— Digital Channel: 2. Digital Hrs: 24 178 w vis, 17.8 w aur. ant 997t TL: N43 27 42 W110 45 10 On air date: 1991. Box 7454, Jackson, WY, 83002. Phone: (307) 733-2066. Fax: (307) 733-4834. Web Site: www.kjwy2.com. Licensee: Two Ocean Broadcasting Co. Group Owner: Sunbelt Communications Co. (acq 11-95; grpsl). Population Served: 25,000 Natl. Network: NBC, . News staff: one; News: 5 hrs wkly.
Key Personnel:
James Rogers . . . . CEO
Ralph Toddre . . . . exec VP
Christel Rahme. stn mgr & sls dir adv dir & progmg dir news dir & edit dir
Robin Estopinal . . . . engrg dir
Carl Shuptrine . . . . news cmtr

KPIF— Digital Channel: 15. Digital Hrs: 24 5,000 kw vis. ant 1,073t/262g TL: N42 51 50 W112 31 10 On air date: 2006. 5023 Rainbow Ln., Chubbuck, ID, 83202-7607. Phone: (208) 237-5743. Web Site: www.kpif.net. Licensee: Pocatello Channel 15 L.L.C.. Ownership: Myoung Hwa Bae, 100% (acq 12-1-2003). Natl. Network: CW, .
Key Personnel:
Brian Nugent . . . . gen mgr
Lu Contreras . . . . traf mgr

KPVI-DT—(Pocatello, Digital Channel: 23. Digital Hrs: 24 505 kw vis. ant 1,307t/338g TL: N42 55 12.8 W112 20 44.6 On air date: Apr 26, 1974. Box 667, Pocatello, ID, 83204. Phone: (208) 232-6666. Fax: (208) 233-6678. Web Site: www.kpvi.com. Licensee: Oregon Trail Broadcasting Co. Group Owner: Sunbelt Communications Co. (acq 11-15-95). Population Served: 309,000 Natl. Network: NBC, . Natl. Rep: Blair Television,. Wire Svc: AP News staff: 23; News: 17 hrs wkly.
Key Personnel:
Bill Fouch . . . . gen mgr
Rebroadcasts: KJWY Jackson Hole, WY.

Lewiston

see Spokane, WA market

Moscow

see Spokane, WA market

Pocatello

see Idaho Falls-Pocatello, ID market

Twin Falls, ID

(DMA 194)

KIDA— Digital Channel: 5.10.25 kw vis. ant 1,830t/59g TL: N43 38 36 W114 23 49 On air date: 2003. Blue Lakes Blvd. N., Suite 101, Twins Falls, ID, 83301. Phone: (954) 732-9539.E-mail: mturnerco@aol.com Licensee: Marcia T. Turner dba Turner Enterprises.

Key Personnel:
Marcia Turner . . . gen mgr

***KIPT-TV—** Digital Channel: 22. Digital Hrs: 24 22.4 kw vis. 528t/69g TL: N42 43 47 W114 24 52 On air date: Jan 18, 1992. c/o KAID, 1455 N. Orchard St., Boise, ID, 83706. Phone: (208) 373-7220. Fax: (208) 373-7245.E-mail: idptv@idahoptv.org Web Site: www.idahoptv.org. Licensee: State Board of Education, State of Idaho. Natl. Network: PBS, . Washington Atty: Fletcher, Heald & Hildreth.
Key Personnel:
Peter Morrill . . . gen mgr
Kim Philipps . . . dev dir
Rebroadcasts KAID Boise 100%.

KMVT— Digital Channel: 11. Digital Hrs: 24 132 kw vis. ant 1,059t/607g TL: N42 43 47 W114 24 52 On air date: May 30, 1955. 1100 Blue Lakes Blvd. N., Twin Falls, ID, 83301. Phone: (208) 733-1100. Fax: (208) 733-4649. Web Site: www.kmvt.com. Licensee: Neuhoff Family L.P. Group Owner: (group owner; (acq 8-3-2004; $17.3 million). Population Served: 160,100 Natl. Network: CBS, . Natl. Rep: Continental Television Sales,. Washington Atty: Schwartz, Woods & Miller. Wire Svc: AP News staff: 14; News: 10 hrs wkly.
Key Personnel:
Lee Wagner . . . gen mgr & progmg dir
Lisa Collins . . . gen sls mgr
Paul Johnson . . . mktg mgr & prom mgr
Joe Martin . . . news dir
Rodger Martin . . . chief of engrg
Deborah Flores . . . traf mgr

KXTF— Digital Channel: 34. Digital Hrs: 24 100 kw vis. 538t TL: N42 43 42 W114 24 43 On air date: Jan 31, 1989. 1061 Blue Lakes Blvd. N., Twin Falls, ID, 83301. Phone: (208) 733-0035. Fax: (208) 733-0160. Web Site: www.kxtf.com. Licensee: Sunbelt Broadcasting Co. Group Owner: Sunbelt Communications Co. Population Served: 163,300 Natl. Network: Fox, . Washington Atty: Hamel & Park. News: 2 hrs wkly.
Key Personnel:
Bill Fouch . . . gen mgr
Joe Nielsen . . . stn mgr
Patrick Anderson . . . gen sls mgr
Rocky Hanson . . . prom mgr
Brenda Baumgartner . . . news dir
Robin Estopinal . . . chief of engrg

Illinois

Bloomington

see Peoria-Bloomington, IL market

Carbondale

see Paducah, KY-Cape Girardeau, MO-Harrisburg-Mount Vernon, IL market

Champaign & Springfield-Decatur, IL (DMA 83)

WAND— Digital Channel: 18. Digital Hrs: 24 5,000 kw vis, 1,000 kw aur. ant 1,290t/1,314g TL: N39 37 07 W88 49 55 On air date: Aug 16, 1953. 904 Southside Dr., Decatur, IL, 62521. Phone: (217) 424-2500. Fax: (217) 424-2583. Web Site: www.wandtv.com. Licensee: WAND Television Inc. Group Owner: LIN Television Corporation (acq 2-27-95;5-22-95). Population Served: 1,205,000 Natl. Network: NBC, . Washington Atty: Schwartz, Woods & Miller.
Key Personnel:
Ron Pulera . . . gen mgr
Denise Daniels . . . gen sls mgr
Tracey Cole . . . stn mgr & progmg mgr
Jim Platzer . . . news dir
Hal Campbell . . . chief of engrg

WBUI— Digital Channel: 22. Digital Hrs: 24 1,951 kw vis, 195.1 kw aur. ant 1,030t/1,351g TL: N39 56 56 W88 50 12 On air date: May 14, 1984. 2510 Pkwy Ct., Decatur, IL, 62526. Phone: (217) 428-2323. Fax: (217) 428-6455.E-mail: promotions@centralillinoiscw.com Web Site: www.centralillinoiscw.com. Licensee: Acme TV Licenses of Illinois L.L.C. Group Owner: Acme Communications Inc. (acq 6-14-99; $13.3 million). Population Served: 382,460 Natl. Network: CW, . Natl. Rep: MMT,.

Key Personnel:
Bill Snider . . . gen mgr
Chad Happersett . . . stn mgr
Allen White . . . gen sls mgr
Scott Washburn . . . opns mgr & chief of engrg

WCCU— Digital Channel: 26. Digital Hrs: 24 3,360 kw vis, 218 kw aur. ant 442t/829 TL: N40 18 42 W87 54 48 On air date: 1987. 119 W. Church St., Champaign, IL, 61820. Phone: (217) 403-9927. Fax: (217) 403-1007. Web Site: www.myfoxchampaign.com. Licensee: Springfield Broadcasting Partners. Group Owner: Bahakel Communications (acq 7-20-92). Natl. Network: Fox, .
Key Personnel:
Peter O'Brien . . . gen mgr
Randy Stone . . . gen sls mgr
Jeff Kaufmann . . . prom dir
Jack Richardson . . . chief of engrg
Rebroadcasts WRSP-TV Springfield 100%.

WCFN— Digital Channel: 13. Digital Hrs: 24 5 kw vis. ant 576t/585g TL: N39 47 27 W89 30 53 On air date: 1987. Box 20, 509 S. Neil St., Champaign, IL, 61820. Phone: (217) 356-8333. Fax: (217) 373-3680.E-mail: program@wcia.com Web Site: www.wcfn.tv. Licensee: Nexstar Finance Inc. Group Owner: Nexstar Broadcasting Group Inc. (acq 5-19-2000; grpsl). Natl. Network: MyNetworkTV, . Natl. Rep: Blair Television,. Washington Atty: Drinker-Biddle-Reath.
Key Personnel:
Russ Hamilton . . . gen mgr
Don Osika . . . sls dir
Linda Voorhees . . . rgnl sls mgr
Peter Carlson . . . prom mgr
Holly Kennedy . . . progmg dir
Darren Martin . . . chief of engrg

WCIA— Digital Channel: 48.100 kw vis, 20 kw aur. ant 940t/981g TL: N40 06 23 W88 26 59 On air date: Nov 14, 1953. Box 20, 509 S. Neil, Champaign, IL, 61824-0020. Phone: (217) 356-8333. Fax: (217) 373-3680.E-mail: webmaster@wcia.com Web Site: www.wcia.com. Licensee: Nexstar Finance Inc. Group Owner: Nexstar Broadcasting Group Inc. (acq 5-19-2000; grpsl). Natl. Network: CBS, . Washington Atty: Covington & Burling.
Key Personnel:
Russ Hamilton . . . gen mgr
Don Osika . . . sls dir
Linda Voorhees . . . rgnl sls mgr
Peter Carlson . . . prom mgr
Holly Kennedy . . . progmg dir
Darren Martin . . . chief of engrg

***WEIU-TV—** Digital Channel: 50. Digital Hrs: 24 48.5 kw vis, 4.85 kw aur. ant 234t/213g TL: N39 28 43 W88 10 21 On air date: July 1, 1986. 1521 Buzzard Hall, 600 Lincoln Ave., Charleston, IL, 61920. Radio & TV Ctr., Eastern Illinois Univ. , Charleston, IL 61920. Phone: (217) 581-5956. Phone: (877) 727-9348. Fax: (217) 581-6650.E-mail: weiu@weiu.net Web Site: www.weiu.net. Licensee: Eastern Illinois University. Population Served: 500,000 Natl. Network: PBS, . Washington Atty: Cohn & Marks. News staff: 25; News: 3 hrs wkly.
Key Personnel:
Denis Roche . . . gen mgr
Jeff Owens . . . sls dir
Ke'an Rogers . . . prom mgr
Linda Kingery . . . progmg mgr
Kelly Runyon . . . news dir
Kevin Armstrong . . . chief of engrg

WICD— Digital Channel: 41. Digital Hrs: 24 358 kw vis, 35 kw aur. ant 1,300t/1,338g TL: N40 04 11 W87 54 45 On air date: Apr 24, 1959. 250 S. Country Fair Dr., Champaign, IL, 61821-2920. Phone: (217) 351-8500. Fax: (217) 351-6056. Web Site: www.wicd15.com. Licensee: WICD License L.L.C. Group Owner: Sinclair Broadcast Group Inc. (acq 7-2-99; $81 million with WICS(TV) Springfield). Population Served: 332,000 Natl. Network: ABC, . Washington Atty: Wiley, Rein & Fielding. News staff: 20; News: 17 hrs wkly.
Key Personnel:
David Smith . . . CEO
Tim Mathis . . . pres & gen mgr
Erik Snell . . . prom mgr
Deana Reece . . . news dir
Jim Wnek . . . chief of engrg

WICS— Digital Channel: 42. Digital Hrs: 24 676 kw vis, 67.6 kw aur. ant 1,430t/1,458g TL: N39 48 15 W89 27 40 On air date: Oct 30, 1953. Box 3920, Springfield, IL, 62703-1999. 2680 E. Cook St., Springfield, IL 62703-1999. Phone: (217) 753-5620. Fax: (217) 753-8177.E-mail: comments@wics.com Web Site: www.wics.com. Licensee: WICS Licensee L.L.C. Group Owner: Sinclair Broadcast Group Inc. (acq 7-1-99). Population Served: 336,000 Natl. Network: ABC, . Natl. Rep: Millennium Sales & Marketing,. Washington Atty: Dow, Lohnes PLLC. News staff: 32; News: 22 hrs wkly.

Key Personnel:
Tim Mathis . . . gen mgr
Jim Waldeck . . . opns dir & engrg dir

***WILL-TV—** Digital Channel: 9. Digital Hrs: 24 30 kw vis. ant 991t/987g TL: N40 02 18 W88 40 10 On air date: Aug 1, 1955. Campbell Hall for Public Telecommunications, 300 N. Goodwin Ave., Urbana, IL, 61801-2316. Phone: (217) 333-1070. Fax: (217) 244-6386.E-mail: will-tv@uiuc.edu Web Site: www.will.illinois.edu. Licensee: University of Illinois Board of Trustees. Population Served: 2,000,000 Natl. Network: PBS, . Washington Atty: Dow, Lohnes & Albertson.
Key Personnel:
Carl Caldwell . . . stn mgr
David Thiel . . . progmg dir & chief of engrg
Rick Finnie . . . chief of engrg

WRSP-TV— Digital Channel: 44. Digital Hrs: 24 2,000 kw vis, 200 kw aur. ant 1,442t/1,449g TL: N39 47 57 W89 26 46 On air date: June 1, 1979. 3003 Old Rochester Rd., Springfield, IL, 62703. Phone: (217) 523-8855. Fax: (217) 523-4410. Web Site: www.myfoxspringfield.com. Licensee: Springfield Independent Television Inc. Group Owner: Bahakel Communications (acq 7-20-92). Population Served: 384,100 Natl. Network: Fox, .
Key Personnel:
Jeff Kaufmann . . . pres & prom mgr
Peter O'Brien . . . gen mgr
Randy Stone . . . gen sls mgr
Jack Richardson . . . chief of engrg

***WSEC—** Digital Channel: 15. Digital Hrs: 6 AM-midnight 28.25 kw vis, 2.83 kw aur. ant 313t/339g TL: N39 44 08 W90 10 32 On air date: Aug 21, 1984. Box 6248, Springfield, IL, 62708. Phone: (217) 483-7887. Fax: (217) 483-1112. Web Site: www.wsec.tv. Licensee: West Central Illinois Educational Telecommunication Corp. Population Served: 915,000 Natl. Network: PBS, . Washington Atty: Dow, Lohnes & Albertson.
Key Personnel:
Jerold Gruebel . . . CEO & pres gen mgr
Richard Plotkin . . . opns VP
Ed Strong . . . adv dir

Chicago (DMA 3)

WBBM-TV— Digital Channel: 12. Digital Hrs: 24 8 kw vis. ant 1,630t/1,635g TL: N41 52 44 W87 38 08 On air date: August 1940. 630 N. McClurg Ct., Chicago, IL, 60611. Phone: (312) 202-2222. Fax: (312) 943-7193. Web Site: www.cbs2chicago.com. Licensee: CBS Broadcasting Inc. Group Owner: Viacom Television Stations Group (acq 2-9-53; $6 million;2-16-53). Population Served: 8,000,000 Natl. Network: CBS, . Natl. Rep: CBS TV Stations National Sales,. Wire Svc: Reuters
Key Personnel:
Bruno Cohen . . . gen mgr
Al Connor . . . gen sls mgr
Will Sliger . . . prom dir
Fran Preston . . . progmg dir
Jeff Kiernan . . . news dir
Tom Schnecke . . . chief of engrg

WCIU-TV— Digital Channel: 27. Digital Hrs: 24 5,000 kw vis, 500 kw aur. ant 1,555t/1,552g TL: N41 52 44 W87 38 10 On air date: Feb 6, 1964. 26 N. Halsted St., Chicago, IL, 60661. Phone: (312) 705-2600. Fax: (312) 705-2656. Web Site: www.wciu.com. Licensee: WCIU-TV L.P. Group Owner: Weigel Broadcasting Co. Population Served: 9,194,000 Natl. Rep: Harrington, Righter & Parsons,. Washington Atty: Cohn & Marks.
Key Personnel:
Neal Sabin . . . gen mgr
Molly Kelly . . . stn mgr
Brad Lesak . . . gen sls mgr
Sean Long . . . progmg dir
Kyle Walker . . . chief of engrg

WCPX-TV— Digital Channel: 43.200 kw vis. ant 1,673t/1,667g TL: N41 52 44 W87 38 08 On air date: May 31, 1976. 333 S. Desplains St., Suite 101, Chicago, IL, 60661-8735. Phone: (312) 376-8520. Fax: (312) 575-8735. Web Site: www.ionline.tv. Licensee: ION Media Chicago License Inc., debtor-in-possession. Group Owner: Paxson Communications Corp. (acq 8-11-98; $120 million including all interest in KWOK(TV) Novato, CA and other telecasting progmg rights). Population Served: 10,000,000 Natl. Network: ION Television, . Washington Atty: Dow, Lohnes & Albertson.
Key Personnel:
Allen Dagger . . . gen mgr & chief of engrg
Rich Lindsey . . . traf mgr

WFLD— Digital Channel: 31.5,000 kw vis, 500 kw aur. ant 1,415t/1,456g TL: N41 53 55 W87 37 23 On air date: Jan 6, 1966. 205 N. Michigan

Ave., Chicago, IL, 60601. Phone: (312) 565-5532. Fax: (312) 565-5517. Web Site: www.myfoxchicago.com. Licensee: Fox Television Stations Inc. Group Owner: (group owner; (acq 11-14-86; grpsl). Population Served: 825,300 Natl. Network: Fox, . Natl. Rep: Fox Stations Sales,. News: 35.5 hrs wkly.

Key Personnel:
John Baich . . . . chief of engrg

WGBO-DT— Digital Channel: 38.5,000 kw vis, 500 kw aur. ant 1,296t/1,456g TL: N41 53 56 W87 37 23 On air date: Sept 17, 1981. 541 N. Fairbanks Ct., Suite 1100, Chicago, IL, 60611. Phone: (312) 670-1000. Fax: (312) 494-6492. Web Site: www.univision.com. Licensee: WGBO License Partnership G.P. Group Owner: Univision Communications Inc. (acq 2-27-95;5-22-95). Population Served: 200,000 Natl. Network: Univision (Spanish), . Washington Atty: Shaw Pittman LLP. Foreign lang progmg: SpanishS 168 News staff: 18.

Key Personnel:
Vincent Cordero . . . . sr VP & gen mgr
Sean Delahuanty . . . . gen sls mgr
Francisco Garcia . . . . prom dir
Yolanda Lopez De Otero . . . . news dir
George Molnar . . . . chief of engrg

WGN-TV— Digital Channel: 19. Digital Hrs: 24 600 kw vis. ant 1,568t/1,568g TL: N41 52 44 W87 38 10 On air date: Apr 5, 1948. 2501 W. Bradley Pl., Chicago, IL, 60618-4718. Phone: (773) 528-2311. Fax: (773) 528-6857. Web Site: wgntv.com. Licensee: WGN Continental Broadcasting Co., debtor-in-possession. Group Owner: Tribune Broadcasting Co., see Cross-Ownership (acq 12-20-2007; grpsl). Population Served: 3,469,110 Natl. Network: CW, . Natl. Rep: TeleRep,. Washington Atty: Dow Lohnes PLLC. Wire Svc: AP Wire Svc: City News Bureau News: 32 hrs wkly.

Key Personnel:
Marty Wilke . . . . gen mgr
Errol Gerber . . . . stn mgr & sls dir
Joanne Stern . . . . prom dir
Greg Caputo . . . . news dir
Marc Drazin . . . . engrg dir

WJYS— Digital Channel: 36. Digital Hrs: 24 145 kw vis. ant 1,673t/1,667g TL: N41 52 44 W87 38 08 On air date: Mar 2, 1991. 18600 S. Oak Park Ave., Tinley Park, IL, 60477. Phone: (708) 633-0001. Fax: (708) 633-0040.E-mail: cs@wjystv62.net Licensee: Jovon Broadcasting Corp. Population Served: 7,100,000

Key Personnel:
Joseph Stroud . . . . gen mgr
Eric Ferguson . . . . stn mgr & chief of engrg

WLS-TV— Digital Channel: 7.4.75 kw vis. ant 1,689t/1,686g TL: N41 52 44 W87 38 08 On air date: Sept 17, 1948. 190 N. State St., Chicago, IL, 60601. Phone: (312) 750-7777. Fax: (312) 750-7015. Web Site: www.abc7chicago.com. Licensee: WLS Television Inc. Group Owner: ABC Inc. (acq 6-27-86; grpsl; 7-15-85). Population Served: 3,200,000 Natl. Network: ABC, . Wire Svc: PR Newswire Wire Svc: Dow Jones Financial News Services Wire Svc: Sports Wire News staff: 151; News: 8 hrs wkly.

Key Personnel:
Emily L. Barr . . . . pres & gen mgr
Joseph Trimarco . . . . opns mgr
Ed Pearson . . . . gen sls mgr
Tom Hebel . . . . prom dir
Ellen Crawley . . . . progmg dir & rsch dir
Jennifer Graves . . . . news dir
Kal Hassan . . . . engrg dir
Mike Ozog . . . . traf mgr

WMAQ-TV— Digital Channel: 29.40.1 kw vis, 8.0 kw aur. ant 1,320t/1,456g TL: N41 53 56 W87 37 23 On air date: January 1948. 454 N. Columbus Dr., Chicago, IL, 60654-5555. Phone: (312) 836-5555. Web Site: www.nbc5.com. Licensee: NBC Telemundo License Co. Group Owner: NBC TV Stations Division (acq 6-5-86). Population Served: 3,204,710 Natl. Network: NBC, . Natl. Rep: NBC TV Stations Sales,.

Key Personnel:
Larry Wert . . . . pres & gen mgr
Patrica Golden . . . . sls VP
Jan Jaros . . . . engrg dir
Toni Falvo . . . . mktg dir & progmg dir & rsch dir

WPWR-TV—(Gary, IN) Digital Channel: 51. Digital Hrs: 24 5,000 kw vis, 600 kw aur. ant 1,620t/1,624g

TL: N41 52 44 W87 38 10 On air date: Jan 18, 1987. 205 N. Michigan Ave., Chicago, IL, 60614. Phone: (312) 565-5533. Fax: (312) 565-5517. Web Site: www.my50chicago.com. Licensee: Fox Television Stations Inc. Group Owner: (group owner; (acq 8-21-2002; $425 million). Population Served: 6,000,000 Natl. Network: MyNetworkTV, . Natl. Rep: Fox Stations Sales,.

Key Personnel:
Patrick Mullen. . . . . gen mgr
John Baich . . . . chief of engrg

WSNS— Digital Channel: 45.4,260 kw vis, 500 kw aur. ant 1,420t/1,456g TL: N41 53 56 W87 37 23 On air date: Apr 5, 1970. 454 N. Columbus Dr., Chicago, IL, 60611. Phone: (312) 836-3000. Fax: (312) 836-3034. Web Site: www.telemundochicago.com. Licensee: NBC Telemundo License Co. Group Owner: Telemundo Group Inc. (acq 4-12-2002; grpsl). Population Served: 1,800,000 Natl. Network: Telemundo (Spanish), . Washington Atty: Cohn & Marks. Foreign lang progmg: SpanishS 138 News staff: 12; News: 5 hrs wkly.

Key Personnel:
Ed Fernandez . . . . VP & gen mgr

***WTTW—** Digital Channel: 47.60.3 kw vis, 12 kw aur. ant 1,630t/1,710g TL: N41 52 44 W87 38 10 On air date: Sept 6, 1955. 5400 N. St. Louis Ave., Chicago, IL, 60625. Phone: (773) 583-5000. Fax: (773) 583-3046. Web Site: www.networkchicago.com. Licensee: Window to the World Communications Inc. Population Served: 10,000,000 Natl. Network: PBS, . Washington Atty: Schwartz, Woods & Miller. News staff: 15; News: 5 hrs wkly.

Key Personnel:
Daniel Schmidt. . . . . CEO & pres
Farrell Frentress. . . . . exec VP
Reese Marcusson . . . . CFO & opns VP
Donna Davies . . . . dev VP
Dan Soles . . . . progmg VP & progmg dir

WWTO-TV— Digital Channel: 10. Digital Hrs: 24 80 kw vis. ant 1,361t/26g TL: N41 16 51 W88 56 13 On air date: Dec 1, 1986. 420 E. Stevenson Rd., Ottawa, IL, 61350. Phone: (815) 434-2700. Fax: (815) 434-2458. Web Site: www.tbn.org. Licensee: Trinity Broadcasting Network. Group Owner: (group owner; (acq 7-1-2000; grpsl). Washington Atty: Joseph E. Dunne III.

Key Personnel:
Charlie Boyd . . . . pres & chief of engrg
Marlene Zepeda . . . . gen mgr & stn mgr

WXFT-DT— Digital Channel: 50.5,000 kw vis, 500 kw aur. ant 1,600t/1,621g TL: N41 52 44 W87 38 10 On air date: Apr 20, 1982. 541 N. Fairbanks Ct., Suite 1100, Chicago, IL, 60611. Phone: (312) 670-1000. Fax: (312) 467-5821. Web Site: www.univision.com. Licensee: TeleFutura Chicago LLC. Group Owner: Univision Communications Inc. (acq 5-21-2001; grpsl). Natl. Network: TeleFutura (Spanish), . Washington Atty: Wiley, Rein & Fielding. Wire Svc: City News Bureau

Key Personnel:
Vincent Cordero . . . . gen mgr
Sean Delahunty . . . . gen sls mgr
Francisco Garcia . . . . prom dir
Yolanda Lopez De Otero . . . . news dir
George Molnar . . . . chief of engrg

***WYCC—** Digital Channel: 21.98.9 kw vis. ant 1,240t/23g TL: N41 53 56 W87 37 23 On air date: Sept 20, 1965. 7500 S. Pulaski Rd., Chicago, IL, 60652. Phone: (773) 838-7878. Fax: (773) 581-2071.E-mail: comments@wycc.org Web Site: www.wycc.org. Licensee: College Dist. #508, County of Cook. (acq 11-3-81). Natl. Network: PBS, . Washington Atty: Dow, Lohnes & Albertson. Foreign lang progmg: SpanishS 5

Key Personnel:
Maria Moore . . . . gen mgr
Arthur Wood . . . . stn mgr
Larry Eskridge . . . . prom mgr & engrg mgr
Cynthia Syperek . . . . progmg dir & progmg mgr

***WYIN—** Analog Channel: 56. Digital Channel: 17. Analog Hrs: 24 Digital Hrs: 24 1,353 kw vis, 1.3 kw aur. 1,003t/998g TL: N41 20 56 W87 24 02 (CP: Ch

17, N41 52 44 W87 38 10, 300 Kw) On air date: Nov 15, 1987. 8625 Indiana Pl., Merrillville, IN, 46410. Phone: (219) 756-5656. Fax: (219) 755-4312.E-mail: mail@lakeshoreptv.com Web Site: www.lakeshoreptv.com. Licensee: Northwest Indiana Public Broadcasting Inc. Population Served: 8,737,442 Natl. Network: PBS, . Washington Atty: Schwartz, Woods & Miller.

Key Personnel:
Thomas Carroll . . . . CEO & pres

Decatur
see Champaign & Springfield-Decatur, IL market

East St. Louis
see St. Louis, MO market

Harrisburg
see Paducah, KY-Cape Girardeau, MO-Harrisburg-Mount Vernon, IL market

Marion
see Paducah, KY-Cape Girardeau, MO-Harrisburg-Mount Vernon, IL market

Moline
see Davenport, IA-Rock Island-Moline, IL market

Mount Vernon
see Paducah, KY-Cape Girardeau, MO-Harrisburg-Mount Vernon, IL market

Olney
see Terre Haute, IN market

Peoria-Bloomington, IL
(DMA 116)

WAOE— Digital Channel: 39.331 kw vis. ant 584t TL: N40 43 26 W89 29 04 On air date: 2000. 2907 Springfield Rd., East Peoria, IL, 61611. Phone: (309) 674-5900. Fax: (309) 674-5959. Web Site: my59.tv. Licensee: Four Seasons Peoria LLC. Ownership: Venture Technologies Group LLC, 48.5%; Malibu Broadcasting LLC, 48.5%; and Paul H. Koplin, 3% (acq 9-15-99). Natl. Network: MyNetworkTV, .

Key Personnel:
Mark DeSantis . . . . VP & gen mgr
Sara Horn . . . . stn mgr
Pete Russell . . . . gen sls mgr
Tim Campbell . . . . prom mgr
Jim Garrott. . . . . news dir

WEEK-TV— Digital Channel: 25. Digital Hrs: 24 2,400 kw vis, 239 kw aur. 680t/604 TL: N40 37 48 W89 32 51 On air date: Feb 1, 1953. 2907 Springfield Rd., East Peoria, IL, 61611. Phone: (309) 698-2525. Fax: (309) 698-9663 (sales). Fax: (309) 698-3737 (news).E-mail: news25@week.com Web Site: www.week.com. Licensee: WEEK-TV License Inc. Group Owner: Granite Broadcasting Corp. (acq 10-31-88; $33 million). Population Served: 467,800 Natl. Network: NBC, . Washington Atty: Akin, Gump, Strauss, Hauer & Feld. News staff: 26; News: 16 hrs wkly.

Key Personnel:
Mark DeSantis . . . . gen mgr
Dennis Riley . . . . chief of engrg

WHOI— Digital Channel: 19. Digital Hrs: 24 2,240 kw vis, 224 kw aur. ant 636t/632g TL: N40 39 11 W89 35 14 On air date: Oct 20, 1953. 500 N. Stewart St., Creve Coeur, IL, 61610. Phone: (309) 698-1919. Fax: (309) 698-1910. Web Site: www.hoinews.com. Licensee: Barrington

Broadcasting Peoria Corp. Group Owner: Barrington Broadcasting Corp. (acq 4-30-2004; $23.5 million with KHQA-TV Hannibal, MO). Population Served: 532,000 Natl. Network: ABC, CW, . Natl. Rep: Harrington, Righter & Parsons,. Washington Atty: Covington & Burling. News: 7 hrs wkly.
Key Personnel:
Leo T Henning . . . gen mgr
Jon Skorburg . . . stn mgr
Tom Stemmler . . . opns mgr & prom mgr
Valerie Bricka . . . rgnl sls mgr
Donna Thompson . . . progmg dir
Jolie Alois . . . news dir
Jim Malone . . . chief of engrg

WMBD-TV— Digital Channel: 30. Digital Hrs: 24 2,050 kw vis, 406 kw aur. ant 635t/548g TL: N40 38 07 W89 32 19 On air date: Jan 1, 1958. 3131 N. University, Peoria, IL, 61604. Phone: (309) 688-3131. Fax: (309) 686-8650. Web Site: www.wmbd.com. Licensee: Nexstar Finance Inc. Group Owner: Nexstar Broadcasting Group Inc. (acq 1999). Population Served: 547,760 Natl. Network: CBS, . Washington Atty: Covington & Burling.
Key Personnel:
Coby Cooper . . . VP & gen mgr
Barry Allentuck . . . sls dir
Nancy Linebaugh . . . natl sls mgr
Travis Herriford . . . rgnl sls mgr
David Tomlianovich . . . prom dir
Herman Marvel . . . news dir

***WTVP—** Digital Channel: 46. Digital Hrs: 24 1,410 kw vis, 251 kw aur. 710t/599g TL: N40 37 44 W89 34 12 On air date: June 23, 1971. 101 State St, Peoria, IL, 61602. Phone: (309) 677-4747. Fax: (309) 677-4730.E-mail: wtvpmail@wtvp.pbs.org Web Site: www.wtvp.org. Licensee: Illinois Valley Public Telecommunication Corp. Population Served: 750,000 Natl. Network: PBS, . Washington Atty: Dow, Lohnes PLLC.
Key Personnel:
Chet Tomczyk . . . CEO & pres gen mgr
Jackie Luebcke . . . opns mgr
Linda Miller . . . progmg VP

WYZZ-TV— Digital Channel: 28.1,200 kw vis, 112 kw aur. 979t/1,006g TL: N40 38 45 W89 10 45 (CP: 5,000 kw vis, ant 965t) On air date: Oct 18, 1982. 3131 N. University, Peoria, IL, 61604. Phone: (309) 688-3131. Fax: (309) 686-8650. Web Site: www.22fox.com. Licensee: WYZZ Licensee Inc. Group Owner: Sinclair Broadcast Group Inc. (acq 1996; $23 million). Natl. Network: Fox, . Natl. Rep: Harrington, Righter & Parsons,. Washington Atty: Shaw Pittman LLP.
Key Personnel:
Kevin Harlan . . . gen mgr
Barry Allantuck . . . sls dir
Nancy Linebaugh . . . natl sls mgr
Curt Bolak . . . rgnl sls mgr
Kirby Matthews . . . prom dir
Chris Manson . . . news dir
Herman Marvel . . . chief of engrg

Quincy, IL-Hannibal, MO-Keokuk, IA (DMA 171)

KHQA-TV—(Hannibal, MO) Digital Channel: 7. Digital Hrs: 24 316 kw vis. ant 889t/805g TL: N39 58 22 W91 19 54 On air date: Sept 23, 1953. 301 S. 36th St., Quincy, IL, 62301. Phone: (217) 222-6200. Fax: (217) 228-3164/(217) 222-5078.E-mail: khqa@khqa.com Web Site: www.khqa.com. Licensee: Barrington Broadcasting Quincy Corp. Group Owner: Barrington Broadcasting Corp. (acq 4-30-2004; $23.5 million with WHOI(TV) Peoria, IL). Population Served: 41,100 Natl. Network: CBS, ABC, . Natl. Rep: Continental Television Sales,. Washington Atty: Covington & Burling. News staff: 12; News: 13 hrs wkly.
Key Personnel:
Robert B. Sherman . . . CEO
Jon Van Ness . . . gen mgr & stn mgr
Mava Clingingsmith . . . gen sls mgr & natl sls mgr
Cindy Johnson . . . rgnl sls mgr & traf mgr
Jim Malone . . . chief of engrg

WGEM-TV— Digital Channel: 10. Digital Hrs: 24 316 kw vis, 31.6 kw aur. 780t/673g TL: N39 57 03 W91 19 54 On air date: Sept 4, 1953. Box 80, 513 Hampshire, Quincy, IL, 62306. Phone: (217) 228-6600. Fax: (217) 228-6670. Web Site: wgem.com. Licensee: Quincy Broadcasting Co. Group Owner: Quincy Newspapers Inc. Population Served: 350,000 Natl. Network: NBC, CW, Fox, . Natl. Rep: Blair Television,. Washington Atty: Wilkinson, Barker, Knauer & Quinn. Wire Svc: AP News staff: 25; News: 20 hrs wkly.
Key Personnel:
Thomas A. Oakley . . . CEO
Ralph M. Oakley . . . VP
Tom Allen . . . gen mgr
Carlos Fernandez . . . stn mgr

***WMEC—** Digital Channel: 21. Digital Hrs: 6 AM-midnight 24.15 kw vis, 2.42 kw aur. 519t/535g TL: N40 25 40 W90 40 58 On air date: Oct 1, 1984. Box 6248, Springfield, IL, 62708. Phone: (217) 483-7887. Phone: (800) 232-3605. Fax: (217) 483-1112. Web Site: www.wmec.tv. Licensee: West Central Illinois Educational Telecommunications Corp. Population Served: 915,000 Natl. Network: PBS, . Washington Atty: Dow, Lohnes & Albertson.
Key Personnel:
Jerold Gruebel . . . CEO & pres gen mgr
Richard Plotkin . . . opns VP & opns dir
Ed Strong . . . adv dir

***WQEC—** Digital Channel: 34. Digital Hrs: 6 AM-midnight 14.8 kw vis, 1.48 kw aur. 567t/495g TL: N39 58 44 W91 18 33 On air date: Mar 11, 1985. Box 6248, Springfield, IL, 62708. Phone: (217) 483-7887. Phone: (800) 232-3605. Fax: (217) 483-1112. Web Site: www.wqec.tv. Licensee: West Central Illinois Educational Telecommunications Corp. Population Served: 915,000 Natl. Network: PBS, . Washington Atty: Dow, Lohnes & Albertson.
Key Personnel:
Jerold Gruebel . . . CEO & pres gen mgr
Richard Plotkin . . . opns VP & opns dir
Ed Strong . . . adv dir

WTJR— Digital Channel: 32. Digital Hrs: 24 179.2 kw vis, 31.5 kw aur. ant 1,025t/948g TL: N39 58 18 W91 19 42 On air date: Jan 1, 1986. 222 North 6th St., Quincy, IL, 62301. Phone: (217) 228-1616.E-mail: tv16@wtjr.org Web Site: www.wtjr.org. Licensee: Christian Television Network Inc. Ownership: Robert D'Andrea, 20% votes; Virginia Oliver, 20% votes; Jimmy Smith, 20% votes; Wayne Wetzel, 20% votes; Robert S. Young, 20% votes (acq 5-23-2006; $2.1 million). Population Served: 350,000
Key Personnel:
Donette Douglas . . . gen mgr & stn mgr
Jim Wilson . . . engr

Rock Island

see Davenport, IA-Rock Island-Moline, IL market

Rockford, IL (DMA 132)

WIFR—(Freeport, Digital Channel: 41. Digital Hrs: 24 676 kw vis, 85.2 kw aur. 720t/731g TL: N42 17 48 W89 10 15 On air date: Sept 12, 1965. Box 123, Rockford, IL, 61105. 2523 N. Meridian Rd., Rockford, IL 61101. Phone: (815) 987-5300. Fax: (815) 987-0981.E-mail: talkto23@wifr.com Web Site: www.wifr.com. Licensee: WEAU Licensee Corp. Group Owner: Gray Television Inc. (acq 8-29-2002; grpsl). Population Served: 187,500 Natl. Network: CBS, . Natl. Rep: Continental Television Sales,. Washington Atty: Covington & Burling. News staff: 19; News: 19 hrs wkly.
Key Personnel:
Greg Graber . . . VP & gen mgr stn mgr
Dave Smith . . . opns mgr & news dir
Tim Myers . . . gen sls mgr

WQRF-TV— Digital Channel: 42.525 kw vis, 5.25 kw aur. 700 TL: N42 17 26 W89 09 51 On air date: Nov 27, 1978. 1917 N. Meridian Rd., Rockford, IL 61101. Phone: (815) 963-5413. Fax: (815) 963-6113. Licensee: Nexstar Finance Inc. Group Owner: Nexstar Broadcasting Group Inc. (acq 12-31-03; grpsl). Natl. Network: Fox, . Washington Atty: Arter & Hadden.
Key Personnel:
Joseph Denk . . . VP & gen mgr
Eileen Boucek . . . stn mgr
Tina Mickelson . . . sls dir
Sean Anderson . . . prom mgr
Jose Cabezas . . . progmg mgr
Kent Harrell . . . news dir
Mike Real . . . chief of engrg

WREX-TV— Digital Channel: 13. Digital Hrs: 24 316 kw vis, 39.8 kw aur. 710t/652g TL: N42 17 50 W89 14 24 On air date: Oct 1, 1953. Box 530, Rockford, IL, 61105. 10322 W. Auburn Rd., Rockford, IL 61103. Phone: (815) 335-2213. Fax: (815) 335-2055.E-mail: wrex@wrex.com Web Site: www.wrex.com. Licensee: WREX Television LLC. Group Owner: Quincy Newspapers Inc., see Cross-Ownership (acq 7-31-95; $18 million). Population Served: 452,000 Natl. Network: NBC, CW, . Natl. Rep: Blair Television,. Washington Atty: Wilkinson, Barker & Knauer.
Key Personnel:
John Chadwick . . . VP & gen mgr
Gerry Meinders . . . prom dir & chief of engrg
Kim Arney . . . progmg mgr
Maggie Hradecky . . . news dir

WTVO— Digital Channel: 16.646 kw vis. ant 666t/676g TL: N42 17 14 W89 10 15 On air date: May 3, 1953. Box 470, Rockford, IL, 61105. 1917 N. Meridian Rd., Rockford, IL 61101. Phone: (815) 963-5413. Fax: (815) 963-6113. Web Site: www.mystateline.com. Licensee: Mission Broadcasting Inc. Group Owner: (group owner; (acq 1-4-2005; $20,750,000). Population Served: 350,000 Natl. Network: ABC, MyNetworkTV, . Washington Atty: Wiley, Rein & Fielding. News staff: 16; News: 7 hrs wkly.
Key Personnel:
Joseph Denk . . . VP & gen mgr
Eileen Boucek . . . stn mgr
Tina Mickelson . . . sls dir
Sean Anderson . . . prom mgr
Jose Cabezas . . . progmg mgr
Kent Harrell . . . news dir
Mike Real . . . chief of engrg

Springfield

see Champaign & Springfield-Decatur, IL market

Indiana

Elkhart

see South Bend-Elkhart, IN market

Evansville, IN (DMA 102)

WAZE-TV— Digital Channel: 20. Digital Hrs: 24 1,143 kw vis, 114.3 kw aur. ant 1,194t/1,053g TL: N37 24 46 W87 31 32 On air date: September 1997. 1277 N. St. Joseph Ave., Evansville, IN, 47720. Phone: (812) 425-1900. Fax: (812) 423-3405.E-mail: cw19@roberts-companies.com Web Site: www.cwaze.com. Licensee: Roberts Broadcasting Co. of Evansville, IN LLC. Group Owner: (group owner; (acq 12-14-2006; $1 million). Population Served: 689,000 Natl. Network: CW, . Washington Atty: Fletcher, Healld & Hildreth.
Key Personnel:
Greg Pittman . . . gen mgr & opns dir gen sls mgr
Stan Marinoff . . . progmg dir
Jim McFarland . . . chief of engrg

WEHT— Digital Channel: 7.60 kw vis, 6.2 kw aur. ant 1,030t/988g TL: N37 51 56 W87 34 04 On air date: Sept 11, 1953. Box 25, Evansville, IN, 47701. 800 Marywood Dr. , Henderson, KY 42420. Phone: (800) 879-8542. Fax: (270) 827-0561.E-mail: contactus@news25.us Web Site: www.news25.us. Licensee: Gilmore Broadcasting Corp. Ownership: National City Bank of Michigan/Illinois, directed by G. Lennon & M. Lemieux (acq 1-15-2003). Population Served: 185,000 Natl. Network: ABC, . Washington Atty: Wiley, Rein & Fielding.
Key Personnel:
Doug Padgett . . . gen mgr
Mike Riley . . . stn mgr & gen sls mgr
Melisse Marks . . . prom mgr
Ginny Powers . . . progmg mgr
Mark Glover . . . news dir
Darren Gibson . . . chief of engrg

WEVV-TV— Digital Channel: 45. Digital Hrs: 24 1,250 kw vis, 125 kw aur. ant 1,000t/1,000g TL: N37 53 17 W87 32 37 On air date: Nov 17, 1983. 44 Main St., Evansville, IN, 47708-1450. Phone: (812) 464-4444. Fax: (812) 465-4559. Web Site: www.wevv.com. Licensee: Comcorp of Indiana License Corp. Group Owner: Communications Corp. of America (acq 1999; $27.5 million). Natl. Network: CBS, . Washington Atty: Leventhal, Senter & Lerman. News staff: 30; News: 9 hrs wkly.
Key Personnel:
Jim Barondt . . . gen mgr
Tim Black . . . stn mgr
John Bennett . . . opns mgr & chief of engrg
Sandy Eickhoff . . . gen sls mgr
Joanne Provenzano . . . progmg dir

WFIE— Digital Channel: 46. Digital Hrs: 24 2,510 kw vis. ant 1,017t/905g TL: N37 53 14 W87 31 07 On air date: Nov 9, 1953. Box 1414, Evansville, IN, 47701. 1115 Mt. Auburn Rd., Evansville, IN 47720. Phone: (812) 426-1414. Fax: (812) 426-1945.E-mail: wfie@14wfie.com Web Site: www.14wfie.com. Licensee: WFIE License Subsidiary LLC. Group Owner: Liberty Corp. (acq 1-31-2006; grpsl). Population Served: 290,000 Natl. Network: NBC, . Washington Atty: Dow, Lohnes & Albertson. News staff: 35.

Key Personnel:

Debbie Bush	gen mgr
Laura Lovejoy	gen sls mgr
Adam Frary	mktg dir
C.J. Hoyt	news dir
Bobby Barnett	chief of engrg
Kirk Williams	progmg

*WKMA-TV— Digital Channel: 42.55.1 kw vis. ant 977t/30g TL: N37 11 21 W87 30 49 On air date: Sept 23, 1968. 600 Cooper Dr., Lexington, KY, 40502. Phone: (606) 258-7000. Fax: (606) 258-7399.E-mail: info@ket.org Web Site: www.ket.org. Licensee: Kentucky Authority for Educational TV. Natl. Network: PBS, . Kentucky Educational Television

Key Personnel:

Malcolm Wall	chmn
Craig Cornwell	opns mgr & progmg dir
Tim Bischoff	dev VP & mktg dir
Robert Ball	engrg dir

*WKOH— Digital Channel: 30.63.3 kw vis. ant 407t/26g TL: N37 51 07 W87 19 44 On air date: Mar 1, 1979. 600 Cooper Dr., Lexington, KY, 40502. Phone: (606) 258-7000. Fax: (606) 258-7399.E-mail: dbritton@cket.org Web Site: www.ket.org. Licensee: Kentucky Authority for Educational TV. Natl. Network: PBS, . Rgnl. Network: SECA. Kentucky Educational Television Washington Atty: Kenkel, Barnard & Edmundson.

Key Personnel:

Malcolm Wall	chmn
Craig Cornwell	opns mgr & progmg mgr
Tim Bischoff	mktg dir

*WNIN— Digital Channel: 9. Digital Hrs: 18 19 kw vis. ant 997t/899g TL: N37 59 01 W87 16 13 On air date: Mar 16, 1970. 405 Carpenter St., Evansville, IN, 47708. Phone: (812) 423-2973. Fax: (812) 428-7548.E-mail: wnin@wnin.org Web Site: www.wnin.org. Licensee: Tri-State Public Teleplex Inc. (acq 9-12-73). Population Served: 138,764 Natl. Network: PBS, . Washington Atty: Dow, Lohnes PLLC.

Key Personnel:

David Dial	pres & gen mgr
Bonnie Rheinhardt	opns VP & prom mgr progmg VP
Tonya Wolf	gen sls mgr
Don Hollingsworth	mktg VP & chief of engrg

WTVW— Digital Channel: 28. Digital Hrs: 24 316 kw vis, 63.2 kw aur. ant 1,013t/880g TL: N38 01 27 W87 21 43 On air date: Aug 26, 1956. 477 Carpenter St., Evansville, IN, 47708. Phone: (812) 424-7777. Fax: (812) 421-4040. Web Site: www.tristatehomepage.com. Licensee: Nexstar Broadcasting Inc. Group Owner: Nexstar Broadcasting Group Inc. (acq 10-30-2003; grpsl). Population Served: 686,500 Natl. Network: Fox, . Natl. Rep: Blair Television,. Washington Atty: Arter & Hadden. News: 22.5 hrs wkly.

Key Personnel:

Jeff Fischer	gen sls mgr
Jay Hiett	rgnl sls mgr
Mike Smith	gen mgr & stn mgr & progmg mgr
Bob Walters	news dir
Dan Jordan	chief of engrg

Ft. Wayne, IN
(DMA 107)

WANE-TV— Digital Channel: 31. Digital Hrs: 24 2,450 kw vis. ant 827t/804g TL: N41 05 38 W85 10 48 On air date: Sept 26, 1954. Box 1515, Fort Wayne, IN, 46801. 2915 W. State Blvd., Fort Wayne, IN 46808. Phone: (260) 424-1515. Fax: (260) 407-1607. Web Site: www.wane.com. Licensee: Indiana Broadcasting L.L.C. Group Owner: LIN Television Corporation (acq 11-14-94;12-12-94). Population Served: 268,610 Natl. Network: CBS, . News staff: 35; News: 22 hrs wkly.

Key Personnel:

Alan Riebe	gen mgr & natl sls mgr
Jim Riecken	opns mgr
Mike Luckett	natl sls mgr
Tom Antisdel	rgnl sls mgr
Jerry Grider	prom dir
Nancy Applegate	progmg mgr
Ted Linn	news dir
April McCampbell	pub affrs dir
Mark Johnson	chief of engrg

WFFT-TV— Digital Channel: 36. Digital Hrs: 24 600 kw vis, 38 kw aur. ant 780t/805g TL: N41 06 33 W85 11 44 On air date: Dec 21, 1977. 3707 Hillegas Rd., Fort Wayne, IN 46808. Box 8655, Fort Wayne, IN 46808. Phone: (260) 471-5555. Fax: (260) 484-4331.E-mail: fox55@wfft.com Web Site: www.wfft.com. Licensee: Nexstar Finance Inc. Group Owner: Nexstar Broadcasting Group Inc. (acq 12-31-2003; grpsl). Population Served: 1,855,000 Natl. Network: Fox, . Natl. Rep: Blair Television,. Washington Atty: Drinker, Biddle & Reath.

Key Personnel:

Perry A. Sook	CEO & pres
Matt Devine	CFO
Tim Busch	sr VP
Bill Ritchhart	VP
William Richhart	gen mgr

*WFWA— Digital Channel: 40. Digital Hrs: 24 1,380 kw vis, 138 kw aur. ant 730t/744g TL: N41 06 13 W85 11 28 On air date: Dec 1, 1989. 2501 E. Coliseum Blvd., Fort Wayne, IN, 46805-1562. Phone: (260) 484-8839. Fax: (260) 482-3632.E-mail: info@wfwa.org Web Site: www.wfwa.org. Licensee: Fort Wayne Public Television. Population Served: 274,300 Natl. Network: PBS, . Washington Atty: Wiley Rein LLP.

Key Personnel:

Bruce Haines	pres & gen mgr
Rich Bienz	gen mgr
Matt Kyle	opns VP
Kris Hensler	progmg mgr & chief of engrg

WINM— Digital Channel: 12. Digital Hrs: 24 16.5 kw vis. ant 433t/436g TL: N41 27 15 W84 48 10 On air date: Mar 10, 1983. Box 159, Butler, IN, 46721. 02966 Rd. 1, Edgerton, IN 43517. Phone: (419) 298-3703. Fax: (419) 298-3707.E-mail: winm@tct.tv Web Site: www.tct.tv Licensee: Tri-State Christian TV. Group Owner: (group owner; (acq 1-24-91; $400,000; 2-11-91).

Key Personnel:

Leo Vogt	gen mgr
Mike Reynolds	chief of engrg

WISE-TV— Digital Channel: 18. Digital Hrs: 24 320 kw vis. ant 735t TL: N41 06 07.9 W85 11 04.9 On air date: Nov 21, 1953. 3401 Butler Rd., Fort Wayne, IN, 46808. Box 2121, Fort Wayne, IN 46801-2121. Phone: (260) 422-7474. Fax: (260) 483-2568.E-mail: indianasnewscenter @indianasnewscenter.com Web Site: www.indianasnewscenter.com. Licensee: WISE-TV License LLC. Group Owner: New Vision Group LLC (acq 3-8-2005; $44.2 million). Population Served: 222,480 Natl. Network: NBC, MyNetworkTV, . Washington Atty: Drinker, Biddle & Reath, LLP. News staff: 32; News: 14 hrs wkly.

Key Personnel:

Dan Hoffman	sls dir
Tad Frank	prom mgr
Peter Neumann	news dir
Bret Angel	engrg dir

WPTA— Digital Channel: 24. Digital Hrs: 24 562 kw vis, 55 kw aur. ant 735t/745g TL: N41 06 07.9 W85 11 04.9 On air date: Sept 28, 1957. 3401 Butler Rd., Fort Wayne, IN, 46808. Phone: (260) 483-0584. Fax: (260) 483-2568.E-mail: news@indianasnewscenter.com Web Site: www.indianasnewscenter.com. Licensee: Malara Broadcast Group of Fort Wayne License LLC. Group Owner: (group owner; (acq 12-8-2004; $45.9 million). Population Served: 562,700 Natl. Network: ABC, CW, . Washington Atty: Akin, Gump, Strauss, Hauer & Feld. News staff: 31; News: 31 hrs wkly.

Key Personnel:

Anthony Malara	pres
Dan Hoffman	gen mgr & sls dir
Doug Barrow	stn mgr
Tad Frank	prom dir
Peter Neumann	news dir

Gary

see Chicago market

Hammond

see Chicago market

Indianapolis, IN
(DMA 25)

WCLJ-TV— Digital Channel: 42.850 kw vis. ant 1,030t/968g TL: N39 24 12 W86 08 50 On air date: August 1987. 2528 U.S. 31 S., Greenwood, IN, 46143. Phone: (317) 535-5542. Fax: (317) 535-8584. Licensee: Trinity Broadcasting of Indiana Inc. Group Owner: Trinity Broadcasting Network.

Key Personnel:

Mark Crouch	gen mgr
Ken Harl	chief of engrg

*WDTI— Digital Channel: 44.9.77 kw vis. ant 548t/636g TL: N39 50 25 W86 10 34 On air date: April 1992. Indianapolis Community Television Inc., 3901 Hwy. 121 S., Bedford, TX, 76021. Phone: (817) 571-1229. Phone: (817) 571-7458. Web Site: www.daystar.com/schedules.htm. Licensee: Indianapolis Community Television Inc. Ownership: Dr. Alan Bullock, 14.3%; Joni T. Lamb, 14.3%; Marcus D. Lamb, 14.3%; Peter Keenan, 14.3%; Rob Price, 14.3%; and Vernon Piercey, 14.3% (acq 8-2-2004; $4 million). Population Served: 750,000 Washington Atty: Koerner & Olender.

Key Personnel:

Marcus D. Lamb	pres & gen mgr

*WFYI— Digital Channel: 21. Digital Hrs: 24 1,135 kw vis, 114 kw aur. ant 847t/867g TL: N39 53 59 W86 12 01 On air date: Oct 4, 1970. 1401 N. Meridian St., Indianapolis, IN, 46202. Phone: (317) 636-2020. Fax: (317) 633-7418.E-mail: sjensen@wfyi.org Web Site: www.wfyi.org. Licensee: Metropolitan Indianapolis Public Broadcasting. Population Served: 792,500 Natl. Network: PBS, .

Key Personnel:

Lloyd Wright	pres
Anthony Lorenz	CFO
Alan Cloe	exec VP & sr VP

WHMB-TV— Digital Channel: 20. Digital Hrs: 24 530 kw vis. ant 974t/974g TL: N39 53 40 W86 12 21 On air date: Jan 25, 1971. Box 50450, Indianapolis, IN, 46250. 10511 Greenfield Ave., Noblesville, IN 46060. Phone: (317) 773-5050. Fax: (317) 776-4051.E-mail: kpasson@lesea.com Web Site: www.whmbtv.com. Licensee: LeSea Broadcasting of Indianapolis Inc. Group Owner: (group owner; (acq 8-15-72; $354,618;9-4-72). Population Served: 2,700,000 Washington Atty: Gardner, Carton & Douglas. News: one hr wkly.

Key Personnel:

Pete Sumrall	CEO & VP
Tony Hale	pres & CFO
Keith Passon	gen mgr & gen sls mgr

*WIPB— Digital Channel: 23. Analog Hrs: 24 676 kw vis, 67.6 kw aur. ant 510t/548g TL: N40 09 38 W85 22 42 On air date: May 8, 1953. Edmund F. Ball Bldg., Ball State Univ., Muncie, IN, 47306. Phone: (765) 285-1249. Fax: (765) 285-5548.E-mail: wipb@bsu.edu Web Site: www.bsu.edu/wipb. Licensee: Ball State University. (acq 10-31-71; $125,000;12-6-71). Population Served: 450,000 Natl. Network: PBS, . Rgnl. Network: CEN. Washington Atty: Schwartz, Woods & Miller.

Key Personnel:

Alice Cheney	gen mgr
Bob Fairchild	chief of engrg

WIPX-TV— Digital Channel: 27. Digital Hrs: 24 165 kw vis. ant 1,017t/915g TL: N39 24 16 W86 08 37 On air date: Dec 27, 1988. 601 Clearwater Park Rd., West Palm Beach, FL, 33401. Phone: (317) 486-0633. Web Site: www.ionline.tv. Licensee: ION Media Indianapolis License Inc., debtor-in-possession. Group Owner: Paxson Communications Corp. (acq 2-18-2000; grpsl). Population Served: 825,000 Natl. Network: ION Television, . Washington Atty: Fisher, Wayland, Cooper, Leader & Zaragoza.

WISH-TV— Digital Channel: 9.316 kw vis, 42.7 kw aur. ant 990t/997g TL: N39 45 39 W86 00 21 On air date: July 1, 1954. 1950 N. Meridian St., Indianapolis, IN, 46202. Phone: (317) 923-8888. Fax: (317) 926-1144 (sales).E-mail: newsdesk@wishtv.com Web Site: www.wishtv.com. Licensee: Indiana Broadcasting L.L.C. Group Owner: LIN Television Corporation (acq 11-14-94;12-12-94). Population Served: 1,339,500 Natl. Network: CBS, . Natl. Rep: Petry Television Inc.,. Washington Atty: Covington & Burling. Wire Svc: AP

Key Personnel:

Julie Zoumbaris	sls dir
Lance Carwile	progmg dir & progmg mgr
Kevin Finch	news dir
Terry Van Bibber	edit dir

WNDY-TV— Digital Channel: 32. Digital Hrs: 24 5,000 kw vis, 600 kw aur. ant 1,082t TL: N40 08 57 W85 56 15 On air date: Nov 1, 1987. 1950 N. Meridian St., Indianapolis, IN, 46202. Phone: (317) 923-8888. Fax: (317) 926-1144 (sales).E-mail: newsdesk@MyINDYtv.com Web Site: www.indytv.com. Licensee: Indiana Broadcasting LLC. Group Owner: Viacom Television Stations Group (acq 3-31-2005; $85 million with WWHO(TV) Chillicothe, OH). Natl. Network: MyNetworkTV, . Natl. Rep: Blair Television,. Washington Atty: Covington & Burling.

Key Personnel:

Julie Zoumbaris	sls dir
Lance Carwile	progmg dir
Patti McGettigan	news dir
Terry VanBibber	engrg dir

WRTV— Digital Channel: 25. Digital Hrs: 24 100 kw vis, 20 kw aur. ant 990t/1,019g TL: N39 53 59 W86 12 02 On air date: May 30, 1949. 1330 N. Meridian St., Indianapolis, IN, 46202. Phone: (317) 269-1440 (news). Fax: (317) 269-1400.E-mail: newstips@theindychannel.com Web Site: www.theindychannel.com. Licensee: McGraw-Hill Broadcasting Co. Inc. Group Owner: McGraw-Hill Broadcasting Co. (acq 6-1-72). Population Served: 1,100,000 Natl. Network: ABC, . Natl. Rep: Harrington, Righter & Parsons,. Washington Atty: Holland & Knight.

Key Personnel:
Don Lundy . . . . gen mgr
Sally Kohn . . . . gen sls mgr
Paul Montgomery . . . . prom mgr & progmg mgr
Jason Heath . . . . news dir
Brian Vetor . . . . chief of engrg

WTHR— Digital Channel: 13. Digital Hrs: 24 316 kw vis, 63.2 kw aur. ant 980t/1,039g TL: N39 55 43 W86 10 55 On air date: Oct 30, 1957. Box 1313, Indianapolis, IN, 46206. 1000 N. Meridian St., Indianapolis, IN 46204. Phone: (317) 636-1313. Fax: (317) 636-3717. Fax: (317) 632-6720 (news). Web Site: www.wthr.com. Licensee: VideoIndiana Inc. Group Owner: Dispatch Broadcast Group (acq 10-1-75; $17.65 million;9-1-75). Population Served: 1,077,400 Natl. Network: NBC, . Washington Atty: Sidley & Austin.
Key Personnel:
Rich Pegram . . . . pres & gen mgr
Jim Tellus . . . . stn mgr
Tim Warner . . . . gen sls mgr
Jeff Dutton . . . . prom dir
Rod Porter . . . . progmg dir
Roger Bishop . . . . chief of engrg

***WTIU—** Digital Channel: 14. Digital Hrs: 24 200 kw vis, 39.8 kw aur. ant 710t/647g TL: N39 08 32 W86 29 43 On air date: March 1969. Radio-TV Bldg., Indiana Univ., 1229 E. 7th St., Bloomington, IN, 47405. Phone: (812) 855-5900. Phone: (812) 855-8000. Fax: (812) 855-0729.E-mail: wtiu@indiana.edu Web Site: www.wtiu.indiana.edu. Licensee: Trustees of Indiana University. Population Served: 500,000 Natl. Network: PBS, . Washington Atty: Crowell & Moring. News staff: 2; News: 3 hrs wkly.
Key Personnel:
Perry Metz. . . . . CEO & gen mgr
Phil Meyer . . . . stn mgr
Brad Howard . . . . opns mgr

WTTK— Digital Channel: 29. Digital Hrs: 24 550 kw vis. ant 984t/1,004g TL: N39 53 20 W86 12 07 On air date: May 1988. 6910 Network Place, Indianapolis, IN, 46278. Phone: (800) 968-4434. Fax: (317) 687-6531, (317) 687-6534. Web Site: www.thecw4.com. Licensee: Tribune Broadcast Holdings Inc. Group Owner: Tribune Broadcasting Co. (acq 12-20-2007; grpsl). Population Served: 900,000 Natl. Network: CW, . Natl. Rep: TeleRep,.
Key Personnel:
Jerry Martin . . . . gen mgr
Tim McNamara. . . . . gen sls mgr
Kurt Tovey . . . . prom dir
Harry Ford . . . . progmg dir
Rich Kittlestved . . . . engrg dir
Satellite of WTTV(TV) Bloomington.

WTTV—(Bloomington, Digital Channel: 48. Digital Hrs: 24 55 kw vis, 11 kw aur. ant 1,200t/1,170g TL: N39 24 26 W86 08 52 On air date: Nov 11, 1949. 6910 Network Pl., Indianapolis, IN, 46278. Phone: (317) 632-5900. Fax: (317) 687-6532.E-mail: info@thecw4.com Web Site: www.thecw4.com. Licensee: Tribune Broadcast Holdings Inc. Group Owner: Tribune Broadcasting Co. (acq 12-20-2007; grpsl). Population Served: 744,624 Natl. Network: CW, . Natl. Rep: TeleRep,. Washington Atty: Dow Lohnes PLLC.
Key Personnel:
Jerry Martin . . . . VP & gen mgr
Tim McNamara. . . . . gen sls mgr
Kurt Tovey . . . . prom dir
Harry Ford . . . . progmg dir
Rich Kttilstved . . . . engrg dir

WXIN— Digital Channel: 45. Digital Hrs: 24 2,090 kw vis, 209 kw aur. ant 990t/1,030g TL: N39 53 20 W86 12 07 On air date: Feb 1, 1984. 6910 Network Pl., Indianapolis, IN, 46278. Phone: (317) 632-5900. Fax: (317) 687-6532.E-mail: info@fox59.com Web Site: www.fox59.com. Licensee: Tribune Television Co. Group Owner: Tribune Broadcasting Co. (acq 12-20-2007; grpsl). Population Served: 963,320 Natl. Network: Fox, . Natl. Rep: TeleRep,. Washington Atty: Dow Lohnes PLLC. News: 19 hrs wkly.
Key Personnel:
Jerry Martin . . . . VP & gen mgr
Tim McNamara . . . . sls dir
Kurt Tovey . . . . prom dir
Harry Ford . . . . progmg dir
Rich Kittilstved . . . . engrg dir

Lafayette, IN
(DMA 189)

WLFI-TV— Digital Channel: 11. Digital Hrs: 24 1,490 kw vis, 298 kw aur. 778t/755 TL: N40 23 20 W86 36 46 On air date: June 15, 1953. 2605 Yeager Rd., West Lafayette, IN, 47906. Phone: (765) 463-1800. Fax: (765) 463-7979. Web Site: www.wlfi.com. Licensee: Primeland Television Inc. Group Owner: LIN Television Corporation (acq 4-1-2000; in exchange for 67% of WAND(TV) Decatur, IL). Population Served: 342,100 Natl. Network: CBS, . Natl. Rep: Petry Television Inc.,. Wire Svc: UPI News staff: 30; News: 22 hrs wkly.
Key Personnel:
Tom Combs. stn mgr
Chris Hilgendorf . . . . opns mgr
Jenny Olszewski . . . . sls dir
Deb McMahan. . . . . prom mgr
Rick Thedwall . . . . progmg mgr
Chris Morisse. . . . . news dir
Mark Brooks . . . . chief of engrg

Richmond

see Dayton, OH market

Salem

see Louisville, KY market

South Bend-Elkhart, IN
(DMA 89)

WHME-TV— Digital Channel: 46. Digital Hrs: 24 933 kw vis. ant 1,000t/953g TL: N41 35 43 W86 09 38 On air date: July 27, 1974. 61300 S. Ironwood Rd., South Bend, IN, 46614. Phone: (574) 291-8200. Fax: (574) 291-9043. Web Site: www.whme.com. Licensee: Lester Sumrall Evangelistic Association. Group Owner: Le Sea Broadcasting (acq 6-10-77; $496,000;7-27-77). Population Served: 477,400 Washington Atty: Gardner, Carton & Douglas.
Key Personnel:
Peter Sumrall . . . . gen mgr & stn mgr
Mike Swinehart. . . . . opns mgr
Anna Riblet . . . . rgnl sls mgr
Wes Hylton . . . . VP & chief of engrg

WNDU-TV— Digital Channel: 42. Digital Hrs: 24 800 kw vis. ant 1,016t/969g TL: N41 36 20 W86 12 46 On air date: July 15, 1955. Box1616, South Bend, IN, 46634. 54516 State Rd. 933, SouthBend, IN 46634. Phone: (574) 284-3000. Fax: (574) 284-3009.E-mail: newscenter16@wndu.com Web Site: www.wndu.com. Licensee: Michiana Telecasting Corp. (acq 3-6-2006; $85 million). Population Served: 294,530 Natl. Network: NBC, .
Key Personnel:
CJ Beutein. . . . . pres & news dir
John O'Brien . . . . gen mgr
Howard Voss . . . . gen sls mgr
Michael Fowler . . . . prom dir & progmg dir
George Molnar . . . . chief of engrg

***WNIT—** Digital Channel: 35. Digital Hrs: 24 708 kw vis, 77 kw aur. ant 530t/500g TL: N41 36 59 W86 11 43 On air date: Feb 14, 1974. Box 3434, Elkhart, IN, 46515. 2300 Charger Blvd., Elkhart, IN 46514. Phone: (574) 675-9648. Fax: (574) 262-8497.E-mail: wnit@wnit.org Web Site: www.wnit.org. Licensee: Michiana Public Broadcasting Corp. Population Served: 478,000 Natl. Network: PBS, . Washington Atty: Dow, Lohnes & Albertson.
Key Personnel:
Amy Cassidy . . . . CFO
Mary Pruess . . . . pres & gen mgr
Brian Hoover . . . . opns dir
Diane Marlow . . . . traf mgr

WSBT-TV— Digital Channel: 22. Digital Hrs: 24 4,790 kw vis, 479 kw aur. ant 1,070t/1,047g TL: N41 37 00 W86 13 01 On air date: Dec 21, 1952. 1301 E. Douglas Rd., Mishawaia, IN, 46545. Phone: (574) 233-3141. Fax: (574) 288-6630.E-mail: wsbtnews@wsbt.com Web Site: www.wsbt.com. Licensee: WSBT Inc. Group Owner: Schurz Communications Inc., see Cross-Ownership Population Served: 771,300 Natl. Network: CBS, . Natl. Rep: Harrington, Righter & Parsons,. Washington Atty: Wilmer Hale. News staff: 40; News: 22 hrs wkly.
Key Personnel:
John Mann. . . . . pres & gen mgr
Bob Johnson . . . . opns dir & progmg dir
Beth Young . . . . sls dir
Ted Smucker. . . . . natl sls mgr
Scott Leiter . . . . prom mgr
Gene Hail . . . . chief of engrg

WSJV—(Elkhart, Digital Channel: 28. Digital Hrs: 24 5,000 kw vis, 500 kw aur. ant 1,086t/1,045g TL: N41 36 58 W86 11 38 On air date: Mar 15, 1954. Box 28, South Bend, IN, 46624. Phone: (574) 679-9758. Fax: (574) 294-1267.E-mail: fox28@fox28.com Web Site: www.fox28.com. Licensee: WSJV Television Inc. Group Owner: Quincy Newspapers Inc., see Cross-Ownership (acq 3-31-75; $3.2 million;4-14-75). Population Served: 774,000 Natl. Network: Fox, . Washington Atty: Wilkinson, Barker, Knauer & Quinn. News staff: 22; News: 16 hrs wkly.
Key Personnel:
Heather Stewart. . . . . pres & progmg dir
Stephen Morris . . . . gen mgr

Terre Haute, IN
(DMA 152)

WFXW-TV— Digital Channel: 39. Digital Hrs: 24 2,140 kw vis, 214 kw aur. ant 976t/1,004g TL: N39 13 58 W87 23 49 On air date: Apr 3, 1973. Box 299, Terre Haute, IN, 47808. 10849 US Hwy. 41, Terre Haute, IN 47850. Phone: (812) 696-2121. Fax: (812) 696-2755.E-mail: info@mywabashvalley.com Web Site: www.mywabashvalley.com. Licensee: Mission Broadcasting Inc. Group Owner: (group owner). Population Served: 70,286 Natl. Network: Fox, . News: 2 hrs wkly.
Key Personnel:
Timothy Sturgess . . . . gen mgr
Lois Mathis . . . . stn mgr
Chris Collins. . . . . gen sls mgr
Chris O'Nea; . . . . prom mgr
Tom McClanahan . . . . gen mgr & news dir
Bruce Yowell. . . . . chief of engrg

WTHI-TV— Digital Channel: 10. Digital Hrs: 24 316 kw vis, 31.6 kw aur. ant 960t/993g TL: N39 14 36 W87 23 07 On air date: July 22, 1954. PO Box 1486, Terre Haute, IN, 47808. 918 Ohio St., Terre Haute, IN 47807. Phone: (812) 232-9481. Fax: (812) 232-8953. Web Site: www.wthitv.com. Licensee: Indiana Broadcasting LLC. Group Owner: Emmis Communications Corp. (acq 11-30-2005; grpsl). Population Served: 164,800 Natl. Network: CBS, . Natl. Rep: Petry Television Inc.,.
Key Personnel:
Todd Weber . . . . VP & gen mgr stn mgr & gen sls mgr

WTWO-TV— Digital Channel: 36. Digital Hrs: 24 100 kw vis, 19.5 kw aur. 950t/999g TL: N39 14 33 W87 23 29 On air date: Sept 1, 1965. Box 299, Terre Haute, IN, 47808. 10849 N. U.S. Hwy. 41, Farmersburg, IN 47850. Phone: (812) 696-2121. Fax: (812) 696-2755.E-mail: station@wtwo.com Web Site: www.mywabashvalley.com. Licensee: Nexstar Broadcasting Inc. Group Owner: Nexstar Broadcasting Inc. (acq 2-14-97; with KQTV(TV) Saint Joseph, MO). Population Served: 162,320 Natl. Network: NBC, . Washington Atty: Drinker, Biddle & Reath LLP. News staff: 25; News: 20 hrs wkly.
Key Personnel:
Timothy Sturgess . . . . gen mgr
Richard Haddox . . . . stn mgr
Derek Brown . . . . gen sls mgr
Chris Collins. . . . . rgnl sls mgr
Chris O'Neal. prom mgr
Tom McClanahan . . . . news dir
Bruce Yowell. . . . . chief of engrg

***WUSI-TV—** Digital Channel: 19. Digital Hrs: 24 977 kw vis, 195 kw aur. ant 930t/976g TL: N38 50 18 W88 07 46 On air date: Aug 19, 1968. 1100 Lincoln Dr., Suite 1003, SUI Mailcode 6602, Carbondale, IL, 62901. 1003 Communications Bldg. , Caarbondale, IL 62901-6602. Phone: (618) 453-4343. Fax: (618) 453-6186. Web Site: www.wsiu.org. Licensee: Board of Trustees, Southern Illinois University. Population Served: 151,180 Natl. Network: PBS, . Washington Atty: Cohn & Marks. Wire Svc: AP
Key Personnel:
Delores Kerstein. . . . . CFO & stn mgr
Terry Harvey . . . . engrg dir
Trina Thomas . . . . progmg
Rebroadcasts WSIU-TV Carbondale 100%.

***WVUT—** Digital Channel: 22. Digital Hrs: 7am-11:30 pm 1,150 kw vis, 115 kw aur. 570t/560g TL: N38 39 06 W87 28 37 On air date: Feb 15, 1968. Davis Hall, 1200 N. 2nd St., Vincennes, IN, 47591. Phone: (812) 888-4345. Fax: (812) 882-2237.E-mail: wvut@vinu.edu Web Site: www.vubroadcastinng.org. Licensee: Board of Trustees for the Vincennes Univ. (acq 9-16-76;10-11-76). Population Served: 250,000 Natl. Network: PBS, . Washington Atty: Fletcher, Heald & Hildreth. Wire Svc: UPI News staff: 4; News: 5 hrs wkly.
Key Personnel:
Al Rerko. . . . . gen mgr
Jill Ballinger . . . . opns mgr
Sharon Keifer. . . . . progmg dir

Iowa

Ames

see Des Moines-Ames, IA market

Cedar Rapids-Waterloo-Iowa City & Dubuque, IA
(DMA 88)

KCRG-TV— Digital Channel: 9.316 kw vis, 63.2 kw aur. ant 1,988t/1,926g TL: N42 18 59 W91 51 31 On air date: Oct 15, 1953. Box 816, Cedar Rapids, IA, 52406-0816. 501 2nd Ave. S.E., Cedar Rapids, IA 52401.

Phone: (319) 395-9999. Fax: (319) 398-8378. Web Site: www.kcrg.com. Licensee: Cedar Rapids TV Co.. Ownership: The Gazette Co., 100% Group Owner: The Gazette Co. (acq 8-12-54; $101,500;8-23-54). Population Served: 323,380 Natl. Network: ABC, . Washington Atty: Wiley, Rein & Fielding.

Key Personnel:
Joseph F. Hladky III. . . . . CEO & pres
John Phelan III . . . . gen mgr
John Phelan . . . . stn mgr

KFXA— Digital Channel: 27. Digital Hrs: 24 4,470 kw vis. ant 1,473t/1,486g TL: N42 05 25 W92 05 13 On air date: August 1995. Box 3131, Cedar Rapids, IA, 52406-3131. Phone: (319) 393-2800. Fax: (319) 395-7028.E-mail: kfxa@kfxa.tv Web Site: www.kfxa.tv. Licensee: Second Generation of Iowa Ltd. Ownership: Tom Embrescia, Larry Blum. Natl. Network: Fox, . News staff: 6; News: 13.5 hrs wkly.

Key Personnel:
Larry Blum . . . . pres
Greg Stuart . . . . opns mgr

KFXB-TV— Digital Channel: 43. Digital Hrs: 24 646 kw vis, 64.6 kw aur. ant 841t TL: N42 31 05 W90 37 16 On air date: Sept 12, 1976. 744 Main St., Dubuque, IA, 52001. Phone: (563) 690-1704. Fax: (563) 557-9383. Web Site: www.kfxb.net. Licensee: Christian Television Network of Iowa Inc. Group Owner: (group owner; (acq 8-2-2004). Population Served: 90,000

Key Personnel:
Tom Bond . . . . gen mgr & gen sls mgr

KGAN— Digital Channel: 51. Digital Hrs: 24 100 kw vis, 20 kw aur. ant 1,450t/1,355g TL: N42 17 39 W91 53 10 On air date: Sept 30, 1953. Box 3131, Cedar Rapids, IA, 52406. 600 Old Marion Rd. N.E., Cedar Rapids, IA 52406. Phone: (319) 395-9060. Fax: (319) 395-0987.E-mail: kgan@kgan.com Web Site: www.kgan.com. Licensee: KGAN Licensee L.L.C. Group Owner: Sinclair Broadcast Group Inc. (acq 1999; grpsl). Population Served: 117,040 Natl. Network: CBS, . Natl. Rep: Millennium Sales & Marketing,. Washington Atty: Shaw Pittman. Wire Svc: AP Wire Svc: CBS News staff: 35; News: 12 hrs wkly.

Key Personnel:
Michael Sullivan . . . . gen mgr & stn mgr
Ruth Barnett . . . . opns dir

***KIIN—** Digital Channel: 12.316 kw vis, 31.6 kw aur. 1,440t/1,449g TL: N41 43 14 W91 20 29 On air date: Feb 8, 1970. Box 6450, Iowa Public TV, Johnston, IA, 50131-6450. 6450 Corporate Dr., Johnston, IA 50131. Phone: (515) 242-3100.E-mail: public_information@iptv.org Web Site: www.iptv.org. Licensee: Iowa Public Broadcasting Board. Natl. Network: PBS, . Washington Atty: Dow, Lohnes PLLC.

Key Personnel:
Daniel K. Miller . . . . gen mgr

KPXR-TV— Analog Channel: 48. Digital Channel: 47. Analog Hrs: 24 500 kw vis. ant 1,014t/910g TL: N42 17 17 W91 52 54 On air date: May 3, 1997. 1957 Blairs Ferry Rd. N.E., Cedar Rapids, IA, 52402-5819. Phone: (319) 378-1260. Fax: (319) 378-0076. Web Site: www.ionline.tv. Licensee: ION Media License Co. LLC, debtor-in-possession. Group Owner: Paxson Communications Corp. (acq 7-15-97; $5 million). Population Served: 442,400 Natl. Network: ION Television, .

Key Personnel:
Vikki Steele . . . . stn mgr

***KRIN—** Digital Channel: 35.5,000 kw vis, 500 kw aur. ant 1,851t/1,795g TL: N42 18 59 W91 51 31 On air date: Dec 15, 1974. Box 6450, Iowa PublicTV, Johnston, IA, 50131-6450. 6450 Corporate Dr., Johnston, IA 50131-6450. Phone: (515) 242-3100.E-mail: public_information@iptv.org Web Site: www.iptv.org. Licensee: Iowa Public Broadcasting Board. Natl. Network: PBS, . Washington Atty: Dow, Lohnes PLLC.

Key Personnel:
Daniel K. Miller . . . . gen mgr

KWKB— Digital Channel: 25. Digital Hrs: 24 5,000 kw vis. ant 1,446t/1,460g TL: N41 43 28 W91 21 07 On air date: 1999. 1547 Baker Ave., West Branch, IA, 52358. Phone: (319) 643-5952. Fax: (319) 643-3124.E-mail: wb20@kwkb.com Web Site: www.kwkb.com. Licensee: KM Television of Iowa L.L.C. Natl. Network: CW, MyNetworkTV, .

Key Personnel:
Donald Bae . . . . gen mgr
Jeff Hoffman. . . . . opns mgr & chief of engrg
Jim Walker . . . . rgnl sls mgr
Trish Wethington . . . . . . progmg dir & progmg dir & traf mgr

KWWF— Digital Channel: 22. Digital Hrs: 24 70 kw vis. ant 647t/672g TL: N42 24 35 W92 05 10 On air date: April 4, 2003. 1 Shackleford Dr., Little Rock, AR, 72211. 501 Sycamore St., Suite 710, Waterloo, IA 50703. Phone: (319) 287-5841. Licensee: EBC Waterloo Inc., debtor in possession. Group Owner: Equity Broadcasting Corp. (acq 8-6-2004; $5 million with WNYI(TV) Ithaca, NY).

KWWL—(Waterloo, Digital Channel: 7. Digital Hrs: 24 316 kw vis, 27 kw aur. ant 1,980t/2,000g TL: N42 24 04 W91 50 43 On air date: November 1953. 500 E. 4th St., Huntsville, IA, 50703. Phone: (319) 291-1200. Fax: (319) 274-0466.E-mail: kwwl@kwwl.com Web Site: www.kwwl.com. Licensee: KWWL Television Inc. Group Owner: Raycom Media Inc. (acq 7-1-2006; $63 million). Population Served: 322,400 Natl. Network: NBC, . Natl. Rep: Blair Television,. Washington Atty: Covington & Burling. Wire Svc: AP News staff: 40; News: 22 hrs wkly.

Key Personnel:
Chris Hussey . . . . mktg mgr
Don Morehead. mus dir
Jon Okerstrom . . . . news dir
Kim Leer. . . . . stn mgr & opns

Council Bluffs

see Omaha, NE market

Davenport, IA-Rock Island-Moline, IL (DMA 97)

KGCW— Digital Channel: 41. Digital Hrs: 24 54.3 kw vis, 5.43 kw aur. ant 315t TL: N40 49 25 W91 08 22 On air date: Jan 6, 1988. 937 E. 53rd St., Davenport, IA, 52807. Phone: (563) 386-1818. Fax: (563) 386-8543.E-mail: qandc@kgcwtv.com Web Site: www.kgcwtv.com. Licensee: Burlington Television Acquisition Licensing LLC. (acq 1995; $400,000). Population Served: 590,000 Natl. Network: CW, . Natl. Rep: TeleRep,. Washington Atty: Wilkinson, Barker, Knauer & Quinn.

Key Personnel:
Jaime Horowitz . . . . stn mgr & gen sls mgr
Tony Wilkins. . . . . natl sls mgr & rgnl sls mgr
Tim Emmerson. prom mgr
John Bain. progmg mgr

KLJB— Digital Channel: 49. Digital Hrs: 24 3,000 kw vis, 300 kw aur. ant 1,010t/993g TL: N41 19 17 W90 22 47 On air date: July 28, 1985. 937 E. 53rd St., Suite D, Davenport, IA, 52807. Phone: (563) 386-1818. Fax: (563) 386-8543. Web Site: www.kljb.com. Licensee: Quad Cities Television Acquisition Licensing LLC. Population Served: 737,000 Natl. Network: Fox, . Natl. Rep: TeleRep,. Washington Atty: Wilkinson, Barker, Knauer & Quinn. News: 3 hrs wkly.

Key Personnel:
Kathy DeBoeuf . . . . stn mgr & opns mgr
Jaime Horowitz. . . . . gen sls mgr
Tony Wilkins. . . . . natl sls mgr & rgnl sls mgr
Tim Emmerson. prom mgr
John Bain. progmg mgr

***KQIN—** Digital Channel: 34.6.76 kw vis, 676 w aur. ant 213t TL: N41 31 58 W90 34 40 On air date: December 1991. 6600 34th Ave., Moline, IA, 61265. Phone: (309) 796-2424. Fax: (309) 796-2484.E-mail: wqpt@bhc.edu Web Site: www.wqpt.org. Licensee: Iowa Public Broadcasting Board. (acq 5-22-2003; $200,000).

Key Personnel:
Rick Best . . . . gen mgr
Lora Adams . . . . dev dir
Lora Adams . . . . mktg dir
Jerry Myers . . . . progmg mgr
Steve Ellis. . . . . chief of engrg

Satellite of *WQPT-TV Moline IL 100%.

KWQC-TV— Digital Channel: 36. Digital Hrs: 24 100 kw vis, 15.1 kw aur. ant 940t/978g TL: N41 32 49 W90 28 35 On air date: Oct 31, 1949. 805 Brady St., Davenport, IA, 52803. Phone: (563) 383-7000. Fax: (563) 383-7129. Web Site: www.kwqc.com. Licensee: Young Broadcasting of Davenport Inc. Group Owner: Young Broadcasting Inc. (acq 4-15-96; $55 million). Population Served: 98,469 Natl. Network: NBC,. Natl. Rep: Adam Young,. Washington Atty: Wiley, rein & Fielding.

Key Personnel:
Cathie Whiteside. . . . . stn mgr
John Hegeman. . . . . opns mgr
Jeff Glass. . . . . rgnl sls mgr
Trish Tague. mktg dir
Jeff Bilyeu . . . . prom mgr
Doug Bierman . . . . chief of engrg
Mary Ann Zack . . . . traf mgr

WHBF-TV— Digital Channel: 4. Digital Hrs: 5 AM-2 AM 100 kw vis, 10 kw aur. ant 1,342t/1,383g TL: N41 32 49 W90 28 35 On air date: July 1, 1950. 231 18th St., Rock Island, IL, 61201. Phone: (309) 786-5441. Fax: (309) 788-4975.E-mail: sales@cbs4qc.com Web Site: www.cbs4qc.com. Licensee: Coronet Communications Co. Group Owner: Citadel Communications Co. Ltd. (acq 3-16-87; grpsl;11-17-86). Population Served: 312,000 Natl. Network: CBS, . Natl. Rep: Continental Television Sales,. Washington Atty: Latham & Watkins. News staff: 22; News: 7 hrs wkly.

Key Personnel:
J.D. Walls . . . . pres & opns dir progmg
Martha Huggins . . . . CFO & VP gen mgr
Todd Grady . . . . natl sls mgr
Patty Gilbert. prom mgr
Arthur Steadman . . . . news dir
Ron Schmidt . . . . chief of engrg
Steve Garman. . . . . sls

WQAD-TV— Digital Channel: 38. Digital Hrs: 24 282 kw vis, 23.2 kw aur. ant 1,010t/1,066g TL: N41 18 44 W90 22 47 On air date: Aug 1, 1963. 3003 Park 16th St., Moline, IL, 61265. Phone: (309) 764-8888. Fax: (309) 764-5763.E-mail: wqad@wqad.com Web Site: www.wqad.com. Licensee: Local TV Illinois License LLC. Group Owner: The New York Times Co. (see Cross-Ownership). (acq 5-7-2007; grpsl). Population Served: 322,200 Natl. Network: ABC, . News staff: 75; News: 22.5 hrs wkly.

Key Personnel:
Larry Rosmilso . . . . pres
Lisa Short. . . . . mktg mgr
Rick Serre. . . . . chief of engrg

***WQPT-TV—** Digital Channel: 23. Digital Hrs: 18 148 kw vis, 14.8 kw aur. ant 320t/355g TL: N41 28 31 W90 26 50 On air date: Nov 3, 1983. 6600 34th Ave., Moline, IL, 61265. Phone: (309) 796-2424. Fax: (309) 796-2484.E-mail: wqpt@bhc.edu Web Site: www.wqpt.org. Licensee: Black Hawk College. Population Served: 500,000 Natl. Network: PBS, . Washington Atty: Drinker, Biddle & Reath.

Key Personnel:
Rick Best . . . . gen mgr
Lora Adams . . . . dev dir & mktg dir
Jerry Myers . . . . progmg mgr
Steve Ellis. . . . . chief of engrg

Des Moines-Ames, IA (DMA 71)

KCCI— Digital Channel: 8. Digital Hrs: 24 28.3 kw vis. ant 1,958t/1,942g TL: N41 48 35 W93 37 16 On air date: July 31, 1955. 888 9th St., Des Moines, IA, 50309-1288. Phone: (515) 247-8888. Fax: (515) 244-0202. Fax: (515) 471-8910.E-mail: Web Site: www.kcci.com. Licensee: KCCI Television Inc. Group Owner: Hearst-Argyle Television Inc. (acq 1999; grpsl). Natl. Network: CBS, . Natl. Rep: Eagle Television Sales,. Washington Atty: Brooks, Pierce, McLendon, Humprey & Leonard, LLP. News staff: 50; News: 30 hrs wkly.

Key Personnel:
Paul Fredericksen . . . . pres & gen mgr
Bob Day. . . . . opns dir
Dave Porepp . . . . gen sls mgr
Anne Marie Caudron . . . . natl sls mgr
Nanci Elder. . . . . mktg dir
Dave Busiek . . . . news dir
Steve Houg . . . . chief of engrg

KCWI-TV— Digital Channel: 23. Digital Hrs: 24 5,000 kw vis. ant 2,011t TL: N41 49 47 W93 36 56 On air date: Jan 20, 2001. 2701 S.E. Convenience Blvd., Suite 1, Ankeny, IA, 50021. Phone: (515) 964-2323. Fax: (515) 965-6900.E-mail: yourstation@kcwi23.com Web Site: www.kcwi23.com. Licensee: KPWB License LLC. Group Owner: Pappas Telecasting Companies. Natl. Network: CW, .

Key Personnel:
Ted Stephens. . . . . gen mgr
Jim Cordero . . . . opns mgr

***KDIN-TV—** Digital Channel: 11.22.5 kw vis. ant 1,968t/1,942g TL: N41 48 33 W93 36 53 On air date: Apr 27, 1959. Box 6450, Iowa Public TV, Johnston, IA, 50131-6450. 6450 Corporate Dr., Johnston, IA 50131. Phone: (515) 242-3100.E-mail: public_information@iptv.org Web Site: www.iptv.org. Licensee: Iowa Public Broadcasting Board. Population Served: 360,000 Natl. Network: PBS, . Washington Atty: Dow, Lohnes PLLC. Wire Svc: NWS (National Weather Service)

Key Personnel:
Daniel K. Miller . . . . gen mgr

KDMI— Digital Channel: 19.1,000 kw vis. ant 1,942t/2,893g TL: N41 49 47 W93 36 56 On air date: 2006. 2701 S.E. Convenience Blvd., Suite 1, Ankeny, IA, 50021. Phone: (515) 964-2323. Fax: (515) 965-6900.E-mail: yourstation@kcwi23.com Licensee: KDMI License LLC. (acq 12-15-2005; $1 million for CP). Natl. Network: CW, MyNetworkTV, .

Key Personnel:
Ted Stephens. . . . . gen mgr

KDSM-TV— Digital Channel: 16. Digital Hrs: 24 500 kw vis. ant 2,007t/1,965g TL: N41 49 47 W93 36 56 On air date: 1983. 4023 Fleur Dr., Des Moines, IA, 50321. Phone: (515) 287-1717. Fax: (515) 287-0064.E-mail: programming@kdsm17.com Web Site: www.kdsm.com. Licensee: KDSM Licensee L.L.C. Group Owner: Sinclair Broadcast

Group Inc. Population Served: 249,413 Natl. Network: Fox, . Natl. Rep: Millennium Sales & Marketing,. Washington Atty: Dow, Lohnes & Albertson. News staff: 7; News: 4 hrs wkly.
Key Personnel:
Mike Wilson . . . . VP & gen mgr
Beth Grant. . . . . opns VP
Carolyn Lawrence . . . . gen sls mgr
Julie Quick-Alcorn . . . . progmg dir
Doug Hammond . . . . chief of engrg

***KEFB—** Digital Channel: 34.37.23 kw vis. ant 505t/472g TL: N41 58 49 W93 44 23 On air date: 2005. Box 201, Huxley, IA, 50124-0201. Phone: (515) 597-3138. Licensee: Family Educational Broadcasting Inc.
Key Personnel:
Doug Sheldahl . . . . pres

KFPX-TV— Digital Channel: 39. Digital Hrs: 24 1,000 kw vis. ant 2,001t/1,965g TL: N41 49 48 W93 36 54 On air date: 1998. 4570 114th St., Urbandale, IA, 50322. Phone: (515) 331-3939. Fax: (515) 331-1312. Web Site: www.ionline.tv. Licensee: Paxson Des Moines License Inc. Group Owner: Paxson Communications Corp. Natl. Network: ION Television, .
Key Personnel:
Doug Bognar . . . . rgnl sls mgr
Dave Ohmstede . . . . chief of engrg
Marsha Theis. . . . . traf mgr & progmg

***KTIN—** Analog Channel: 21. Digital Channel: 25.1,580 kw vis, 158 kw aur. 1,160t/1,206g TL: N42 49 02 W94 24 40 On air date: Apr 8, 1977. Box 6450, Iowa Public TV, Johnston, IA, 50131-6450. 6450 Corporate Dr., Johnston, IA 50131. Phone: (515) 242-3100.E-mail: public_information@iptv.org Web Site: www.iptv.org. Licensee: Iowa Public Broadcasting Board. Natl. Network: PBS, . Washington Atty: Dow, Lohnes PLLC.
Key Personnel:
Daniel K. Miller . . . . gen mgr

WHO-DT— Digital Channel: 13. Digital Hrs: 24 36.5 kw vis. ant 1,968t/1,942g TL: N41 48 33 W93 36 53 On air date: Apr 15, 1954. 1801 Grand Ave., Des Moines, IA, 50309. Phone: (515) 242-3500. Fax: (515) 242-3743. Fax: (515) 242-3796 (news). Web Site: www.whotv.com. Licensee: Local TV Iowa License LLC. Group Owner: The New York Times Co. (acq 5-7-2007; grpsl). Population Served: 500,000 Natl. Network: NBC, . Natl. Rep: Millennium Sales & Marketing,. Washington Atty: Covington & Burling. News staff: 50; News: 30 hrs wkly.
Key Personnel:
Robert L. Lawrence . . . . pres
Rebecca Jess. . . . . VP
Dale R. Wood . . . . gen mgr
Mark McGeary . . . . gen sls mgr
Tim Gardner. . . . . prom mgr
Rod Petersen. . . . . news dir
Brad Olk . . . . chief of engrg

WOI-DT—(Ames, Digital Channel: 5. Digital Hrs: 5 AM-2 AM 100 kw vis, 20 kw aur. ant 1,850t/2,000g TL: N41 48 33 W93 36 53 On air date: Feb 21, 1950. 3903 Westown Pkwy., West Des Moines, IA, 50266. Phone: (515) 457-9645. Fax: (515) 457-1034.E-mail: info@myabc5.com Web Site: www.myabc5.com. Licensee: Capital Communications Co. Inc. Group Owner: Citadel Communications Company Ltd., Coronet Communications Co. (acq 3-1-94; $12.7 million). Population Served: 559,700 Natl. Network: ABC, . Natl. Rep: Continental Television Sales,. Washington Atty: Latham & Watkins. Wire Svc: AP News staff: 25; News: 15 hrs wkly.
Key Personnel:
Philip J. Lombardo. . . . . CEO & chmn
Ray Cole . . . . pres & gen mgr
Randy Shelton . . . . opns dir

Dubuque

see Cedar Rapids-Waterloo-Iowa City & Dubuque, IA market

Iowa City

see Cedar Rapids-Waterloo-Iowa City & Dubuque, IA market

Keokuk

see Quincy, IL-Hannibal, MO-Keokuk, IA market

Mason City

see Rochester, MN-Mason City, IA-Austin, MN market

Ottumwa, IA-Kirksville, MO (DMA 200)

KTVO—(Kirksville, MO) Digital Channel: 33. Digital Hrs: 24 100 kw vis, 14.3 kw aur. ant 1,112t/1,050g TL: N40 31 47 W92 26 29 On air date: Nov 21, 1955. Box 949, Hwy. 63 N., Kirksville, MO, 63501. 15518 Hwy. 63 N., Kirksville, MO 63501. Phone: (660) 627-3333. Phone: (641) 682-3333. Fax: (660) 627-1885. Fax: (641) 682-1572. Web Site: www.ktvo.com. Licensee: Barrington Kirksville License LLC. Group Owner: Raycom Media Inc. (acq 8-11-2006; grpsl). Population Served: 44,500 Natl. Network: ABC, . Natl. Rep: Harrington, Righter & Parsons,. Washington Atty: Covington & Burling. News staff: 16; News: 14 hr wkly.
Key Personnel:
Crystal Amini-Rad . . . . gen mgr
Merle Snyder . . . . natl sls mgr
Melissa Billington. . . . . progmg mgr
Marlene Speas . . . . news dir & pub svc dir
John Wise. chief of engrg

KYOU-TV— Digital Channel: 15. Digital Hrs: 24 2090 kw vis, 209 kw aur. 1,200t TL: N41 11 42 W91 57 15 On air date: June 29, 1987. 820 W. 2nd St., Ottumwa, IA, 52501. Phone: (641) 684-5415. Fax: (641) 682-5173.E-mail: reception@kyoutv.com Web Site: www.kyoutv.com. Licensee: Ottumwa Media Holdings LLC. Ownership: Thomas B. Henson, 90%; and Macon B. Moye, 10% (acq 12-15-2003; $4 million). Natl. Network: Fox, . Natl. Rep: MMT,. Washington Atty: Covington & Burling.
Key Personnel:
Dianne Little . . . . gen mgr & gen sls mgr
Dave Cecil . . . . opns mgr
Phil Benjamin . . . . chief of engrg

Red Oak

see Omaha, NE market

Sioux City, IA (DMA 149)

KCAU-TV— Digital Channel: 9. Digital Hrs: 20-21 245 kw vis, 49 kw aur. 2,020t/2,000g TL: N42 35 12 W96 13 57 On air date: Mar 28, 1953. 625 Douglas St., Sioux City, IA, 51101. Phone: (712) 277-2345. Fax: (712) 277-3733. Web Site: www.kcautv.com. Licensee: Citadel Communications Co. Ltd. Group Owner: Citadel Communications Co. Ltd., Coronet Communications Co. (acq 10-1-85; $15 million). Population Served: 166,000 Natl. Network: ABC, . Washington Atty: Latham & Watkins.
Key Personnel:
Mary Ann Johnson . . . . VP & gen mgr
David Jones . . . . opns dir
Dan Ackerman . . . . chief of engrg
Karen Arndt. . . . . traf mgr

KMEG— Digital Channel: 39. Digital Hrs: 20 280 kw vis, 75.9 kw aur. ant 1,152t/1,000g TL: N42 30 53 W96 18 13 On air date: Sept 5, 1967. 100 Gold Cir., Dakota Dunes, SD, 57049. Phone: (712) 277-3554. Fax: (712) 277-4732.E-mail: kmegtv@kmeg.com Web Site: www.kmegtv.com. Licensee: Waitt Broadcasting Inc.. Ownership: Waitt Media Inc., 100% of total assets Group Owner: (group owner; (acq 6-23-98; $12.25 million). Population Served: 289,800 Natl. Network: CBS, . Natl. Rep: Harrington, Righter & Parsons,. Washington Atty: Wilkinson, Barker, Knauer & Quinn.
Key Personnel:
Harry Pappas . . . . CEO & pres
Steve Seline . . . . chmn
Mike Delich . . . . pres
John Schuele . . . . CFO
Scott Eymer . . . . gen mgr
Paul Miller . . . . stn mgr
Mary Ann Johnson . . . . opns mgr & gen sls mgr

KPTH— Digital Channel: 49. Digital Hrs: 24 5,000 kw vis. ant 1,948t TL: N42 35 16 W96 13 22 On air date: May 9, 1999. 100 Gold Cir., North Sioux City, SD, 57049. Phone: (402) 241-4400. Fax: (402) 241-4444/(402) 241-4046.E-mail: yourstation@kpth.com Web Site: www.kpth.com. Licensee: Pappas Telecasting of Sioux City L.P. (a DE limited partnership). Group Owner: Pappas Telecasting Companies Population Served: 280,000 Natl. Network: Fox, MyNetworkTV, . Natl. Rep: Harrington, Righter & Parsons,.
Key Personnel:
Howard Shrier . . . . CEO
Harry Pappas . . . . chmn
Scott Eymer . . . . gen mgr
Mary Johnson . . . . gen sls mgr
Mary Ann Johnson . . . . rgnl sls mgr & mktg mgr
Ed Bok . . . . chief of engrg

***KSIN-TV—** Digital Channel: 28.400 kw vis. ant 1,142t/943g TL: N42 30 53 W96 18 15 On air date: Jan 4, 1975. Box 6450, Iowa Public TV, Johnston, IA, 50131-6450. 6450 Corporate Dr., Joohnston, IA 50131. Phone: (515) 242-3100.E-mail: public_information@iptv.org Web Site: www.iptv.org. Licensee: Iowa Public Broadcasting Board. Natl. Network: PBS, . Washington Atty: Dow, Lohnes PLLC.
Key Personnel:
Daniel K. Miller . . . . gen mgr

KTIV— Digital Channel: 41. Digital Hrs: 24 100 kw vis, 20 kw aur. 1,920t/2,000g TL: N42 35 12 W96 13 57 On air date: Oct 9, 1954. 3135 Floyd Blvd., Sioux City, IA, 51108. Phone: (712) 239-4100. Fax: (712) 239-2621.E-mail: ktiv4@ktiv.com Web Site: www.ktiv.com. Licensee: KTIV Television Inc. Group Owner: Quincy Newspapers Inc., see Cross-Ownership (acq 11-20-89). Population Served: 156,950 Natl. Network: NBC, CW, . Natl. Rep: Blair Television,. Washington Atty: Wilkinson, Barker, Knauer & Quinn. News: 19.5 hrs wkly.
Key Personnel:
Jerry Watson . . . . VP
Adrian Wisner . . . . gen mgr & gen sls mgr
David Madsen. . . . . stn mgr
Bridget Breen. . . . . news dir
Richard Herr . . . . chief of engrg

***KXNE-TV—** Digital Channel: 19. Digital Hrs: 18 1,682.67 kw vis. 1,141t/1093g TL: N42 14 15 W97 16 41 (CP: 776 kw vis, ant 1,122t/1,149g) On air date: Nov 10, 1967. 1800 N. 33rd St., Lincoln, NE, 68503. Phone: (402) 472-3611. Fax: (402) 472-1785.E-mail: net1@unl.edu Web Site: www.netnebraska.org. Licensee: Nebraska Educational Telecommunications Commission. Natl. Network: PBS, . National Educational Telecommunications Association Washington Atty: Dow, Lohnes & Albertson. News staff: 3; News: 30 min.wkly.
Key Personnel:
Rod Bates . . . . gen mgr
Satellite of *KUON-TV Lincoln.

Waterloo

see Cedar Rapids-Waterloo-Iowa City & Dubuque, IA market

Kansas

Hutchinson Plus

see Wichita-Hutchinson Plus, KS market

Lawrence

see Kansas City, MO market

Pittsburg

see Joplin, MO-Pittsburg, KS market

Topeka, KS (DMA 138)

KSNT— Digital Channel: 27. Digital Hrs: 24 912 kw vis, 138 kw aur. 1,050t/1,149g TL: N39 05 34 W95 47 04 On air date: Dec 28, 1967. Box 2700, Topeka, KS, 66601. 6835 N.W. Hwy. 24, Topeka, KS 66618. Phone: (785) 582-4000. Fax: (785) 582-5283. Fax: (785) 582-4783.E-mail: 27news@ksnt.com Web Site: www.ksnt.com. Licensee: NVT Topeka Licensee LLC. Group Owner: Emmis Communications Corp. (acq 11-1-2007; grpsl). Population Served: 294,000 Natl. Network: NBC, CW, . Natl. Rep: Harrington, Righter & Parsons,. Wire Svc: AP News staff: 30; News: 25 hrs wkly.
Key Personnel:
Matt Broxterman. . . . . VP & rgnl sls mgr
Jean Turnbough . . . . gen mgr & gen sls mgr natl sls mgr
Nate Hill . . . . prom dir & news dir
Charlie Good. . . . . chief of engrg

KSQA— Analog Channel: 22.5,000 kw vis. ant 738t/26g TL: N39 03 50 W95 45 49 Not on air, target date: unknown: 1155 Connecticut Ave. N.W., Suite 600, Washington, DC, 20036. Phone: (202) 861-0870. Fax: (202) 429-0657. Permittee: Cooper Fowler Media Co. Ownership: Sheila J. Talley Robertson, 51%; and Gregory M. Talley, 49%.
Key Personnel:
James L. Winston . . . . gen mgr

KTKA-TV— Digital Channel: 49. Digital Hrs: 24 2,690 kw vis. ant 1,486t/1,415g TL: N39 01 34 W95 55 01 On air date: June 19, 1983. Box 4949, Topeka, KS, 66604. 2121 S.W. Chelsea Dr., Topeka, KS 66614. Phone: (785) 273-4949. Fax: (785) 273-7811.E-mail: 49email@ktka.tv Web Site: www.ktka.tv. Licensee: Free State Communications LLC.. Ownership: Orbiter LLC, 100% (acq 8-29-2005; $6.2 million). Natl.

Network: ABC, . Natl. Rep: Millennium Sales & Marketing,. Washington Atty: Cohn & Marks. News staff: 21; News: 15 hrs wkly.
Key Personnel:
Ann Niccum . . . . prom mgr
Angie Cox . . . . progmg dir
Ike Walker . . . . news dir & traf mgr
Kathy Mohn . . . . gen mgr & engrg mgr

***KTWU—** Digital Channel: 11. Digital Hrs: 24 316 kw vis, 31.6 kw aur. ant 991t/903g TL: N39 03 50 W95 45 49 On air date: Oct 21, 1965. 1700 SW College Ave., Topeka, KS, 66621. Phone: (785) 670-1111. Fax: (785) 670-1112.E-mail: ktwu-press@lists.washburn.edu Web Site: ktwu.washburn.edu. Licensee: Washburn University of Topeka. Population Served: 151,000 Natl. Network: PBS, .
Key Personnel:
Eugene Williams . . . . gen mgr
Cindy Barry . . . . dev dir
Kevin Goodman . . . . mktg dir
Val VanDerSluis . . . . progmg dir
Duane Loyd . . . . chief of engrg
Mary Livingston . . . . traf mgr

WIBW-TV— Digital Channel: 13. Digital Hrs: 24 23 kw vis. ant 1,355t/1,194g TL: N39 00 22 W96 02 57 On air date: Nov 15, 1953. 631 S.W. Commerce Pl., Topeka, KS, 66615. Phone: (785) 272-6397. Fax: (785) 272-0117.E-mail: 13news@wibw.com Web Site: www.wibw.com. Licensee: WEAU Licensee Corp. Group Owner: Gray Television Inc. (acq 8-29-2002; grpsl). Population Served: 850,000 Natl. Network: CBS, MyNetworkTV, . Natl. Rep: Continental Television Sales,. Washington Atty: Covington & Burling. News staff: 26; News: 30.5 hrs wkly.
Key Personnel:
Jim Ogle . . . . gen mgr
Mark Doan . . . . opns dir & chief of engrg
Lisa Chapman . . . . rgnl sls mgr
Sharon Cole . . . . progmg mgr
Jon Janes . . . . news dir

Wichita-Hutchinson Plus, KS (DMA 69)

KAAS-TV— Digital Channel: 17. Digital Hrs: 24 238.3 kw vis, 23.83 kw aur. ant 663t/466g TL: N39 06 16 W97 36 30 On air date: April 1988. 316 N. West St., Wichita, KS, 67203. Phone: (316) 942-2424. Fax: (316) 942-8927.E-mail: programming@foxkansas.com Web Site: www.foxkansas.com. Licensee: Newport Television License LLC. Group Owner: Clear Channel Communications Inc. (acq 3-14-2008; grpsl). Natl. Network: Fox, . Washington Atty: Covington & Burling.
Key Personnel:
Kent Cornish . . . . gen mgr
Jon Deeble . . . . chief of opns
Jeff McClausland . . . . sls dir & rgnl sls mgr
Jim Hanning . . . . natl sls mgr
Shawn Wheat . . . . prom mgr
Fatma Al-Tamim . . . . progmg dir
Dave Caruso . . . . chief of engrg
Satellite of KSAS-TV Wichita.

KAKE-TV— Digital Channel: 10. Digital Hrs: 24 316 kw vis, 44.7 kw aur. 1,030t/1,079g TL: N37 46 54 W97 31 10 On air date: Oct 19, 1954. 1500 North West St., Wichita, KS, 67203. Phone: (316) 943-4221. Fax: (316) 943-5493. Web Site: www.kake.com. Licensee: Gray Television Licensee, Inc. Group Owner: Gray Television Inc. (acq 8-29-2002; grpsl). Population Served: 300,000 Natl. Network: ABC, . Natl. Rep: Continental Television Sales,. Washington Atty: Covington & Burling. News staff: 40; News: 16 hrs wkly.
Key Personnel:
Terry Cole . . . . pres & gen mgr
Dave Grant . . . . stn mgr & news dir
Patrick Myers . . . . opns dir
Dan Wall . . . . gen sls mgr
Bryan Frye . . . . mktg dir & prom mgr

KBSD-DT— Digital Channel: 6.100 kw vis, 10 kw aur. 720t/600g TL: N37 38 28 W100 20 40 On air date: July 24, 1957. 100 Airport Rd., Dodge City, KS, 67801. Phone: (620) 227-3121. Fax: (620) 225-1675. Web Site: www.kbsd6.com. Licensee: Sunflower Broadcasting Inc. Group Owner: Media General Broadcast Group (acq 9-25-2006; grpsl). Population Served: 80,000 Natl. Network: CBS, .
Key Personnel:
Joan Barnett . . . . gen mgr
Les Bach . . . . stn mgr & chief of engrg
Tony Thompson . . . . gen sls mgr
David Bell . . . . prom dir
Laverne Goering . . . . progmg dir
Michelle Gors . . . . news dir
Rebroadcasts KWCH-(TV) Wichita 95%.

KBSH-DT— Digital Channel: 7. Digital Hrs: 24 316 kw vis, 33.6 kw aur. 710t/812g TL: N38 53 01 W99 20 15 On air date: Sept 1, 1958. 2300 Hall St., Hays, KS, 67601. Phone: (785) 625-5277. Fax: (785) 625-1161. Web Site: www.kbsh7.com. Licensee: Sunflower Broadcasting Inc. Group Owner: Media General Broadcast Group (acq 9-25-2006; grpsl). Population Served: 60,000 Natl. Network: CBS, . Natl. Rep: Harrington, Righter & Parsons,. Washington Atty: Dow, Lohnes & Albertson. News staff: 1; News: 24 hrs wkly.
Key Personnel:
Todd F. Schurz . . . . pres
Joan Barrett . . . . gen mgr
Brian McDonough . . . . gen sls mgr
Ken Clifford . . . . rgnl sls mgr
David Bell . . . . mktg mgr
Laverne Goering . . . . prom dir
Michelle Gors . . . . progmg VP & news dir
Les Bach . . . . chief of engrg
Rebroadcasts KWCH-TV Wichita 90%.

KBSL-DT— Digital Channel: 10. Digital Hrs: 24 316 kw vis, 56.2 kw aur. ant 990t/975 TL: N39 28 09 W101 33 20 On air date: Apr 28, 1959. Box 629, Goodland, KS, 67735. 3023 W. 31 St., Goodland, KS 67735. Phone: (785) 899-2321. Fax: (785) 899-3138.E-mail: kbsltv@eaglecom.net Web Site: www.kwch.com. Licensee: Sunflower Broadcasting Inc. Group Owner: Media General Broadcast Group (acq 9-25-2006; grpsl). Natl. Network: CBS, .
Key Personnel:
Joan Barrett . . . . gen mgr
Brian McDonough . . . . rgnl sls mgr
Dennis Massier . . . . chief of engrg
Brenda Libal . . . . traf mgr
Satellite of KWCH-TV Hutchinson.

***KDCK—** Digital Channel: 21. Digital Hrs: 17 190 kw vis. ant 250t TL: N37 49 30 W100 10 36 On air date: March 1998. Box 9, 604 Elm St., Bunker Hill, KS, 67626. Phone: (785) 483-6990. Fax: (785) 483-4605.E-mail: shptv@shptv.org Web Site: www.shptv.org. Licensee: Smoky Hills Public Television. Natl. Network: PBS, . Washington Atty: Dow, Lohnes PLLC.
Key Personnel:
Lawrence Holden . . . . CEO & gen mgr
Terry Cutler . . . . chief of opns & news dir

KDCU-DT— Digital Channel: 31.570 kw vis. ant 905t/909g TL: N37 48 01 W97 31 29 Not on air, target date: unknown: 2425 Olympic Blvd., Suite 6000 West, Santa Monica, CA, 90404. Phone: (310) 447-3870. Fax: (310) 447-3899. Web Site: www.entravision.com. Permittee: Entravision Holdings LLC.
Key Personnel:
Walter F. Ulloa . . . . CEO

KLBY— Digital Channel: 17. Digital Hrs: 24 100 kw vis, 21 kw aur. ant 770t/3,420g TL: N39 15 09 W101 21 09 On air date: July 4, 1984. 2900 E. Schulman Ave., Garden City, KS, 67846. Phone: (620) 275-1560. Web Site: www.kake.com. Licensee: Gray Television Licensee Inc. Group Owner: Gray Television Inc. (acq 8-29-2002; grpsl). Population Served: 165,000 Natl. Network: ABC, . Washington Atty: Covington & Burling. News staff: 2.
Key Personnel:
Bryce Baker . . . . gen mgr
Satellite of KAKE-TV Wichita.

KMTW— Digital Channel: 35. Digital Hrs: 24 3,467 kw vis. ant 1,063t TL: N37 56 23 W97 30 42 On air date: Jan 6, 2001. 316 N. West St., Wichita, KS, 67203. Phone: (316) 942-2424. Fax: (316) 942-8927. Web Site: www.mytvwichita.com. Licensee: Mercury Broadcasting Co. Inc.. Ownership: Van H. Archer III, 100% Group Owner: (group owner; (acq 7-1-2001). Population Served: 718,125 Natl. Network: MyNetworkTV, . Natl. Rep: Millennium Sales & Marketing,. Washington Atty: Fletcher, Heald & Hildreth.
Key Personnel:
Kent Cornish . . . . gen mgr
Jeff Causland . . . . sls dir
Jim Hanning . . . . natl sls mgr
Fatma Al-Tamim . . . . progmg dir
David Caruso . . . . chief of engrg

KOCW— Digital Channel: 14. Digital Hrs: 24 150 kw vis. ant 525t TL: N38 37 54 W98 50 52 On air date: 2001. 316 N. West St., Wichita, KS, 67203. Phone: (316) 942-2424. Fax: (316) 942-8927.E-mail: programming@foxkansas.com Web Site: www.foxkansas.com. Licensee: Newport Television License LLC. Group Owner: Clear Channel Communications Inc. (acq 3-14-2008; grpsl). Natl. Network: Fox, . Washington Atty: Covington & Burling.
Key Personnel:
Kent Cornish . . . . gen mgr
Jon Deeble . . . . opns dir
Jeff McCousland . . . . sls dir
Jim Hanning . . . . natl sls mgr
Shawn Wheat . . . . prom dir
Fatma Al-Tamim . . . . progmg dir
David Caruso . . . . engrg dir
Satellite of KSAS-TV Wichita 100%.

***KOOD—** Digital Channel: 16. Digital Hrs: 17 496 kw vis. ant 997t/961g TL: N38 46 16 W98 44 16 On air date: Nov 10, 1982. Box 9, 604 Elm St., Bunker Hill, KS, 67626. Phone: (785) 483-6990. Fax: (785) 483-4605. Web Site: www.shptv.org. Licensee: Smoky Hills Public Television Corp. Natl. Network: PBS, . Washington Atty: Dow, Lohnes & Albertson. Foreign lang progmg: SpanishS 1
Key Personnel:
Jayne Heller . . . . CEO & dev dir
Lawrence Holden . . . . gen mgr
Jane Habiger . . . . mktg dir
Mary-Pat Waymaster . . . . progmg dir
Terry Cutler . . . . chief of engrg
Glenna Letsch . . . . traf mgr

***KPTS—** Digital Channel: 8. Digital Hrs: 24 32 kw vis. ant 800t/742g TL: N38 03 21 W97 46 35 On air date: Jan 7, 1970. 320 W. 21st St. N., Wichita, KS, 67203. Phone: (316) 838-3090. Fax: (316) 838-8586.E-mail: tv8@kpts.org Web Site: www.kpts.org. Licensee: Kansas Public Telecommunications Service Inc. (acq 1979). Population Served: 120,250 Natl. Network: PBS, . Washington Atty: Dow, Lohnes PLLC.
Key Personnel:
Dave McClintock . . . . gen mgr & engrg dir
Jesse Huxman . . . . progmg mgr
David Brewer . . . . traf mgr

KSAS-TV— Digital Channel: 26. Digital Hrs: 24 3,300 kw vis, 331 kw aur. ant 1,120t/1,165g TL: N37 46 40 W97 30 37 On air date: Aug 24, 1985. 316 N. West St., Wichita, KS, 67203. Phone: (316) 942-2424. Fax: (316) 942-8927.E-mail: programming@foxkansas.com Web Site: www.foxkansas.com. Licensee: Newport Television License LLC. Group Owner: Clear Channel Communications Inc. (acq 3-14-2008; grpsl). Population Served: 548,050 Natl. Network: Fox, . Natl. Rep: Millennium Sales & Marketing,. Washington Atty: Covington & Burling.
Key Personnel:
Kent Cornish . . . . gen mgr
Jon Deeble . . . . chief of opns
Jeff McClausland . . . . sls dir
Jim Hanning . . . . natl sls mgr
Shawn Wheat . . . . prom dir
Fatma Al-Tamim . . . . progmg dir
Dave Caruso . . . . chief of engrg

KSCW-DT— Digital Channel: 19. Digital Hrs: 24 1,000 kw vis. ant 1,381t/1,320g TL: N38 03 38 W97 45 49 On air date: 2000. 2815 E. 37th N, Wichita, KS, 67219. Phone: (316) 303-0700. Fax: (316) 303-0160 (sales; traffic). Fax: (316) 303-9807.E-mail: programming@kansascw.com Web Site: www.kansascw.com. Licensee: Sunflower Broadcasting Inc. Group Owner: Banks Broadcasting Inc. (acq 7-20-2007; $6.8 million). Population Served: 443,690 Natl. Network: CW, .
Key Personnel:
Joan M. Barrett . . . . pres & gen mgr
Marty Heffner . . . . opns mgr & chief of opns engrg VP
Marcus Wilkerson . . . . gen sls mgr
Lisa Bryce . . . . progmg mgr & traf mgr
Shawn Hilferty . . . . mktg dir & prom dir & pub affrs dir

KSNC— Digital Channel: 22.100 kw vis, 17.8 kw aur. 970t/1,005g TL: N38 25 54 W98 46 18 On air date: Nov 28, 1954. 833 N. Main St., Wichita, KS, 67203. Phone: (316) 265-3333. Fax: (316) 292-1197.E-mail: ksnc@ksn.com Web Site: www.ksn.com. Licensee: NVT Wichita Licensee LLC. Group Owner: Emmis Communications Corp. (acq 11-1-2007; grpsl). Population Served: 25,000 Natl. Network: NBC, . Natl. Rep: TeleRep,.
Key Personnel:
Al Buck . . . . gen mgr
Dan Shurtz . . . . gen sls mgr
Gregg Cox . . . . prom mgr
Betty Erickson . . . . progmg mgr
Jason Kravarik . . . . news dir
Warren Kunkle . . . . chief of engrg

KSNG— Digital Channel: 11.200 kw vis, 24.5 kw aur. 800t/837g TL: N37 46 40 W100 52 08 On air date: Nov 5, 1958. 833 N. Main St., Wichita, KS, 67203. Phone: (316) 265-3333. Fax: (316) 292-1197. Web Site: www.ksn.com. Licensee: NVT Wichita Licensee LLC. Group Owner: Emmis Communications Corp. (acq 11-1-2007; grpsl). Population Served: 165,000 Natl. Network: NBC, . Natl. Rep: TeleRep,. Washington Atty: Wiley Rein LLP.
Key Personnel:
Al Buck . . . . gen mgr
Dan Shurtz . . . . gen sls mgr & pub svc dir
Gregg Cox . . . . prom mgr & pub affrs dir
Betty Erickson . . . . progmg mgr & news cmtr
Jason Kravarik . . . . news dir
Warren Kunkle . . . . chief of engrg

KSNK— Digital Channel: 12. Digital Hrs: 24 295 kw vis, 60 kw aur. ant 709t/676g TL: N39 49 48 W100 42 04 On air date: Nov 28, 1959. 833 N. Main St., Wichita, KS, 67203. Phone: (316) 265-3333. Fax: (316) 292-1197. Web Site: www.ksn.com. Licensee: NVT Wichita Licensee LLC. Group Owner: Emmis Communications Corp. (acq 11-1-2007;

grpsl). Population Served: 682,080 Natl. Network: NBC, . Natl. Rep: TeleRep,. Washington Atty: Wiley Rein LLP.
Key Personnel:
Al Buch . . . . . gen mgr
Dan Shurtz . . . . . gen sls mgr
Gregg Cox . . . . . prom mgr
Betty Erickson . . . . . progmg dir & progmg mgr
Jason Kravarik . . . . . news dir
Warren Kunkle . . . . . chief of engrg

KSNW— Digital Channel: 45.100 kw vis, 20 kw aur. 1,000t/1,071g TL: N37 46 37 W97 31 01 On air date: Sept 1, 1955. 833 N. Main St., Wichita, KS, 67203. Phone: (316) 265-3333. Fax: (316) 292-1197.E-mail: news@ksn.com Web Site: www.ksn.com. Licensee: NVT Wichita Licensee LLC. Group Owner: Emmis Communications Corp. (acq 11-1-2007; grpsl). Population Served: 1,307,352 Natl. Network: NBC, . Natl. Rep: TeleRep,. Washington Atty: Wiley Rein LLP.
Key Personnel:
Al Buch . . . . . gen mgr
Dan Shurtz . . . . . gen sls mgr
Greg Cox . . . . . prom mgr
Betty Erickson . . . . . progmg dir & progmg mgr
Jason Kravarik . . . . . news dir
Warren Kunkle . . . . . chief of engrg

***KSWK—** Digital Channel: 8. Digital Hrs: 18 100 kw vis, 20 kw aur. 561t/586g TL: N37 49 38 W101 06 35 On air date: Mar 15, 1989. Box 9, 604 Elm St., Bunker Hill, KS, 67626. Phone: (785) 483-6990. Fax: (785) 483-4605. Web Site: www.shptv.org. Licensee: Smoky Hills Public Television Corp. Natl. Network: PBS, . Washington Atty: Dow, Lohnes PLLC.
Key Personnel:
Lawrence Holden . . . . . CEO & gen mgr
Jayne Heller . . . . . dev dir
Mary-Pat Waymaster . . . . . progmg dir
Terry Cutler . . . . . chief of engrg

KUPK-TV— Digital Channel: 13. Digital Hrs: 24 225 kw vis, 45 kw aur. ant 870t/881g TL: N37 39 01 W100 40 06 On air date: Nov 8, 1964. 2900 E. Schulman Ave., Garden City, KS, 67846-9064. Phone: (620) 275-1560. Web Site: www.kake.com. Licensee: Gray Television Licensee Inc. Group Owner: Gray Television Inc. (acq 8-29-2002; grpsl). Population Served: 435,000 Natl. Network: ABC, . Washington Atty: Covington & Burling. News staff: 2; News: 7 hrs wkly.
Key Personnel:
Bryce Baker . . . . . gen mgr
Satellite of KAKE-TV Wichita.

KWCH-DT—(Hutchinson, Digital Channel: 12. Digital Hrs: 24 316 kw vis, 63.1 kw aur. ant 1,522t/1,504g TL: N38 03 40 W97 45 49 On air date: July 1, 1953. 2815 E. 37th St. N., Wichita, KS, 67219. Box 12, Wichita, KS 67201. Phone: (316) 838-1212. Fax: (316) 831-6198. Web Site: www.kwch.com. Licensee: Sunflower Broadcasting Inc. Group Owner: Media General Broadcast Group (acq 9-25-2006; grpsl). Population Served: 425,000 Natl. Network: CBS, . Rgnl. Network: Kansas Net. Natl. Rep: Harrington, Righter & Parsons,. Washington Atty: Dow, Lohnes & Albertson. Wire Svc: NWS (National Weather Service) Wire Svc: AP News staff: 42; News: 24 hrs wkly.
Key Personnel:
Todd F. Schurz . . . . . pres
Marshall Morton . . . . . CFO
Gary Hoipemer . . . . . sr VP & VP
Joan Barrett . . . . . gen mgr
Brian McDonough . . . . . gen sls mgr
Tim Vanderzwaag . . . . . natl sls mgr
David Bell . . . . . prom mgr & pub affrs dir
Laverne Goering . . . . . progmg dir & film buyer
Michele Gors . . . . . news dir
Les Bach . . . . . chief of engrg
Lynn Kingsley . . . . . traf mgr
Cindy Klose . . . . . news cmtr
Bruce Haertl . . . . . sports cmtr
Merril Teller . . . . . weather dir

***KWKS—** Digital Channel: 19.464 kw vis. ant 1,256t/1,224g TL: N39 14 31 W101 21 38 On air date: 2007. Box 9, Bunker Hill, KS, 67626-0009. Phone: (785) 483-6990. Fax: (785) 483-4605. Web Site: www.shptv.org. Licensee: Smoky Hills Public Television Corp. Natl. Network: PBS, . Washington Atty: Dow, Lohnes, LLC.
Key Personnel:
Lawrence Holden . . . . . CEO & gen mgr
Terry Cutler . . . . . chief of engrg

Kentucky

Ashland

see Charleston-Huntington, WV market

Bowling Green, KY (DMA 182)

WBKO— Digital Channel: 13. Digital Hrs: 24 22 kw vis. ant 723t/543g TL: N37 03 49 W86 26 07 On air date: June 3, 1962. Box 13000, Bowling Green, KY, 42102-9800. 2727 Russellville Rd., Bowling Green, KY 42102-9800. Phone: (270) 781-1313. Fax: (270) 781-1814. Web Site: www.wbko.com. Licensee: WEAU Licensee Corp. Group Owner: Gray Television Inc. (acq 8-29-2002; grpsl). Population Served: 67,300 Natl. Network: ABC, CW, Fox, . Natl. Rep: Continental Television Sales,. Washington Atty: Covington & Burling. News staff: 22; News: 17 hrs wkly.
Key Personnel:
Brad Odil . . . . . sr VP & stn mgr sls VP & gen sls mgr
Rick McCue . . . . . VP & gen mgr stn mgr
Tammy Martin . . . . . prom dir & prom dir prom mgr & engrg dir
Barbara Powell . . . . . progmg mgr
Henry Chu . . . . . news dir
Wilbum England . . . . . chief of engrg

***WKGB-TV—** Digital Channel: 48.54.8 kw vis. ant 768t/548g TL: N37 05 22 W86 38 05 On air date: Sept 23, 1968. 600 Cooper Dr., Lexington, KY, 40502. Phone: (859) 258-7000. Fax: (859) 258-7399. Web Site: www.ket.org. Licensee: Kentucky Authority for Educational TV. Natl. Network: PBS, .
Key Personnel:
Malcolm Wall . . . . . opns dir
Tim Bischoff . . . . . mktg dir
Craig Cornwell . . . . . progmg dir

***WKYU-TV—** Digital Channel: 18. Digital Hrs: 8 AM-midnight 400 kw vis, 20 kw aur. ant 648t/603g TL: N37 03 52 W86 26 07 On air date: Jan 17, 1989. Academic Complex 153, Western Kentucky Univ., Bowling Green, KY, 42101-1034. Phone: (270) 745-2400. Fax: (270) 745-2084.E-mail: wkyupbs@wkyu.edu Web Site: www.wkyu.org. Licensee: Western Kentucky University. Natl. Network: PBS, . Washington Atty: Leventhal, Senter & Lerman. News staff: one; News: one hr wkly.
Key Personnel:
Gary Ransdell . . . . . pres
Jack Hanes . . . . . gen mgr
Linda Gerossky . . . . . stn mgr

WNKY— Digital Channel: 16. Digital Hrs: 24 631 kw vis, 63.1 kw aur. ant 561t TL: N37 02 10 W86 10 20 On air date: Dec 15, 1991. 325 Emmett Ave., Bowling Green, KY, 42101. Phone: (270) 781-2140. Fax: (270) 842-7140.E-mail: wnky@nbc40.tv Web Site: whky.net. Licensee: MMK License LLC. Group Owner: MAX Media L.L.C. (acq 3-1-2003; $7 million). Natl. Network: NBC, CBS, . Natl. Rep: Millennium Sales & Marketing,. Washington Atty: Williams & Mullen, P.C.
Key Personnel:
Ed Groves . . . . . pres & gen mgr
Greg Fotos . . . . . gen sls mgr
Gerald Keith . . . . . prom dir
Susan E. Jackson . . . . . progmg dir
Heather Davison . . . . . pub affrs dir
Andrew Miladin . . . . . rsch dir
Kathy Werner . . . . . traf mgr

Covington

see Cincinnati, OH market

Harlan

see Knoxville, TN market

Lexington, KY (DMA 63)

WDKY-TV— Digital Channel: 31. Digital Hrs: 24 5,000 kw vis, 500 kw aur. ant 1,154t/1,126g TL: N37 52 51 W84 19 16 On air date: Feb 10, 1986. Chevy Chase Plaza, 836 Euclid Ave., Suite 201, Lexington, KY, 40502. Phone: (859) 269-5656. Fax: (859) 269-3774. Web Site: www.wdky56.com. Licensee: WDKY Licensee L.L.C. Group Owner: Sinclair Broadcast Group Inc. (acq 1996; $63 million with KOCB(TV) Oklahoma City, OK). Population Served: 487,900 Natl. Network: Fox, . Natl. Rep: Millennium Sales & Marketing,. Washington Atty: Fisher, Wayland, Cooper, Leader & Zaragoza. News: 7 hrs wkly.
Key Personnel:
Marvin Bartlett . . . . . CEO & news dir
Michael Brickey . . . . . gen mgr & stn mgr
Kevin Neumann . . . . . gen sls mgr & natl sls mgr
Jeff Sleete . . . . . mktg VP & mktg dir
Rick White . . . . . natl sls mgr & progmg dir
Dave Koller . . . . . chief of engrg

***WKHA—** Digital Channel: 16.53.2 kw vis. ant 1,210t/528g TL: N37 11 35 W83 11 17 On air date: June 6, 1968. 600 Cooper Dr., Lexington, KY, 40502. Phone: (859) 258-7000. Fax: (859) 258-7399. Web Site: www.ket.org. Licensee: Kentucky Authority for Educational TV. Natl. Network: PBS, . Kentucky Educational Television
Key Personnel:
Mike Brower . . . . . opns mgr
Robert Ball . . . . . dev VP
Tim Bischoff . . . . . mktg dir
Craig Cornwell . . . . . progmg dir & engrg dir

***WKLE—** Digital Channel: 42.45.8 kw vis. ant 845t/788g TL: N37 52 45 W84 19 33 On air date: Sept 23, 1968. 600 Cooper Dr., Lexington, KY, 40502. Phone: (859) 258-7000. Fax: (859) 258-7399. Web Site: www.ket.org. Licensee: Kentucky Authority for Educational TV. Population Served: 3,500,000 Natl. Network: PBS, . Rgnl. Network: SECA. Kentucky Educational Television Washington Atty: Kenkel, Barnard & Edmundson.
Key Personnel:
Craig Cornwell . . . . . opns mgr & progmg dir
Robert Ball . . . . . progmg dir

***WKMR—** Digital Channel: 15.51.4 kw vis. ant 948t/538g TL: N38 10 38 W83 24 17 On air date: Sept 23, 1968. 600 Cooper Dr., Lexington, KY, 40502. Phone: (859) 258-7000. Fax: (606) 258-7399. Web Site: www.ket.org. Licensee: Kentucky Authority for Educational TV. Natl. Network: PBS, . Kentucky Educational Television
Key Personnel:
Craig Cornwell . . . . . opns mgr & progmg mgr
Tim Bischoff . . . . . mktg dir
Robert Ball . . . . . engrg dir

***WKSO-TV—** Digital Channel: 14.53.3 kw vis. ant 1,407t/905g TL: N37 10 03 W84 49 30 On air date: Sept 23, 1968. 600 Cooper Dr., Lexington, KY, 40502. Phone: (606) 258-7000. Fax: (606) 258-7399.E-mail: info@ket.org Web Site: www.ket.org. Licensee: Kentucky Authority for Educational TV. Natl. Network: PBS, . Kentucky Educational Television
Key Personnel:
Craig Cornwell . . . . . opns mgr & progmg mgr
Tim Bischoff . . . . . mktg dir
Robert Ball . . . . . engrg dir

WKYT-TV— Digital Channel: 13. Digital Hrs: 24 30 kw vis. ant 926t/900g TL: N38 02 23 W84 24 10 On air date: Sept 30, 1957. Box 55037, Lexington, KY, 40555-5037. 2851 Winchester Rd., Lexington, KY 40509. Phone: (859) 299-0411. Fax: (859) 299-5531.E-mail: wmartin@wkyt.com Web Site: www.wkyt.com. Licensee: Gray Television Licensee, Inc. Group Owner: Gray Television Inc. (acq 1-21-76;2-9-76). Population Served: 871,000 Natl. Network: CBS, . Natl. Rep: Harrington, Righter & Parsons,. Washington Atty: Venable, Baetjer, Howard & Civiletti. News staff: 50; News: 43 hrs wkly.
Key Personnel:
Wayne Martin . . . . . pres & gen mgr
Michael D. Kanarek . . . . . opns VP
Chris Martin . . . . . sls VP
Barbara Howard . . . . . progmg dir
Robert Thomas . . . . . news dir

WLEX-TV— Digital Channel: 39. Digital Hrs: 24 1,104 kw max vis, 110 kw aur. 640t/670g TL: N37 55 23 W84 09 14 On air date: Mar 15, 1955. Box 1457, Lexington, KY, 40588-1457. 1065 Russell Cave Rd., Lexington, KY 40505. Phone: (859) 259-1818. Fax: (859) 255-2418. Fax: TWX: 859-254-1272.E-mail: wlextv@wlextv.com Web Site: www.wlextv.com. Licensee: WLEX Communications L.L.C. Group Owner: Cordillera Communications Inc. (acq 7-8-99; $99.1 million). Population Served: 720,300 Natl. Network: NBC, . Washington Atty: Dow, Lohnes PLLC.
Key Personnel:
Tim Gilbert . . . . . chmn & pres gen mgr
Sandra Byron . . . . . CFO
Sean Franklin . . . . . opns mgr
Chris Fedele . . . . . sls dir
Mary West . . . . . gen sls mgr
Sandy Stevenson . . . . . natl sls mgr
Chip Alfred . . . . . prom dir & pub affrs dir
Teresa Cassidy . . . . . progmg dir & progmg
Bruce Carter . . . . . news dir
Tony Michalski . . . . . chief of engrg
Randy Green . . . . . traf mgr

WLJC-TV— Digital Channel: 7. Digital Hrs: 24 92.75 kw vis, 9.275 kw aur. 665 TL: N37 36 23 W83 41 16 (CP: 73.45 kw vis, 7.345 kw aur, ant 646.2t) On air date: Oct 16, 1982. PO Box Y, 219 Radio Station Loop, Beattyville, KY, 41311. Phone: (606) 464-3600. Fax: (606) 464-5021.E-mail: wljc@wljc.com Web Site: www.wljc.com. Licensee: Hour of Harvest Inc. Natl. Rep: Rgnl Reps,. Washington Atty: Fletcher, Heald & Hildreth.
Key Personnel:
Margaret Drake . . . . . pres
Jonathan Drake . . . . . gen mgr
Rachel Bogale . . . . . opns mgr
Kim Mitchell . . . . . gen sls mgr & progmg dir
Allan Mulford . . . . . chief of engrg

WTVQ-DT— Digital Channel: 40. Analog Hrs: 24 Digital Hrs: 24 Note: digital ch 36.2 (part of digital ch 40) broadcasts weather 24 hrs each

day. 1,580 kw vis, 158 kw aur. 994t/1,000g TL: N38 02 03 W84 23 39 On air date: June 2, 1968. 6940 Man-O-War Blvd., Lexington, KY, 40509-8412. Phone: (859) 294-3636. Fax: (859) 293-5002.E-mail: programming@wtvq.com Web Site: www.wtvq.com. Licensee: WTVQ-TV Inc. Group Owner: Media General Broadcast Group (acq 5-13-2008; $16.5 million). Population Served: 1,981,200 Natl. Network: ABC, Natl. Rep: MMT,. Washington Atty: Fletcher, Heald & Hildreth. Wire Svc: UPI News staff: 40; News: 27 hrs wkly.

Key Personnel:
Mark Pimentel . . . . . VP & gen mgr
Mitch Bukata . . . . . mktg dir
Tai Takahashi . . . . . news dir

WUPX-TV— Digital Channel: 21.5,000 kw vis. ant 1,463t/1,310g TL: N37 54 26 W83 38 01 On air date: June 1998. 2166 McCausey Ridge Rd., Frenchburg, KY, 40322. Phone: (606) 784-7932. Fax: (606) 768-9278. Web Site: www.ionline.tv. Licensee: Paxson Lexington License Inc. Group Owner: Paxson Communications Corp. (acq 4-27-2001; $8 million).

Key Personnel:
Merv Lawson . . . . . stn mgr & chief of engrg

WYMT-TV— Digital Channel: 12. Digital Hrs: 24 2,630 kw vis, 263 kw aur. 1,560t/1,029g TL: N37 11 38 W83 10 52 On air date: Oct 20, 1969. Box 1299, 199 Black Gold Blvd., Hazard, KY, 41702. Phone: (606) 436-5757. Fax: (606) 439-3760. Web Site: www.wymtnews.com. Licensee: Gray Television Licensee Inc. Group Owner: Gray Television Inc. (acq 9-2-94). Population Served: 216,670 Natl. Network: CBS, . Natl. Rep: Harrington, Righter & Parsons,. News staff: 15.

Key Personnel:
Ernestine Cornett . . . . . gen mgr
James Boggs . . . . . gen sls mgr
Edna Eldridge. . . . . prom dir & prom mgr progmg dir
Neil Middleton . . . . . news dir
Phillip Hayes . . . . . adv mgr & chief of engrg

Louisville, KY (DMA 50)

WAVE— Digital Channel: 47.100 kw vis, 10 kw aur. ant 1,820t/1,690g TL: N38 27 23 W85 25 28 On air date: Nov 24, 1948. Box 32970, Louisville, KY, 40232. 725 S. Floyd St. , Louisville, KY 40203. Phone: (502) 585-2201. Fax: (502) 561-4115. Web Site: www.wave3.com. Licensee: WAVE License Subsidiary LLC. Group Owner: Liberty Corp. (acq 1-31-2006; grpsl). Population Served: 1,500,000 Natl. Network: NBC, . Natl. Rep: Harrington, Righter & Parsons,. Washington Atty: Covington & Burling.

Key Personnel:
Steve Langford . . . . . gen mgr
Nick Ulmer . . . . . stn mgr & gen sls mgr
Bob Mack . . . . . mktg dir
Dan Foos . . . . . progmg dir
Jim Sears . . . . . chief of engrg

WBKI-TV— Digital Channel: 19. Digital Hrs: 24 5,000 kw vis, 595.74 kw aur. ant 1,269t/1,086g TL: N37 31 51 W85 26 45 On air date: Apr 6, 1983. 1601 Alliant Ave., Louisville, KY, 40299. Phone: (502) 809-3400. Fax: (502) 266-6262.E-mail: hr@wb34.com Web Site: www.cwlouisville.com. Licensee: Louisville TV Group LLC. Ownership: Fusion Communications Inc., 50%; PLLW-LLC, 50% Group Owner: Cascade Broadcasting Group L.L.C. (acq 8-10-2009; $1.6 million). Natl. Network: CW, . Natl. Rep: Harrington, Righter & Parsons,. Washington Atty: Rini Coran PC.

Key Personnel:
Craig Hoffman . . . . . opns mgr
Terry Glaser . . . . . gen sls mgr
Myra Jane Jaspan . . . . . progmg mgr

WBNA— Digital Channel: 8. Analog Hrs: 00 Digital Hrs: 24 2,000 kw vis, 200 kw aur. 696t TL: N38 01 59 W85 45 16 On air date: Apr 2, 1986. 3701 Fern Valley Rd., Louisville, KY, 40219. Phone: (502) 964-2121. Fax: (502) 966-9692. Web Site: www.wbna-21.com. Licensee: Word Broadcasting Network Inc. Group Owner: (group owner) Natl. Network: ION Television, . Washington Atty: Pepper & Corazzini.

Key Personnel:
Tom Fawbush. . . . . pres & gen mgr
Harry Monroe . . . . . chief of engrg

WDRB— Digital Channel: 49. Digital Hrs: 24 5,000 kw vis, 500 kw aur. 1,283t/1,003g TL: N38 21 00 W85 50 57 On air date: Feb 28, 1971. 624 W. Muhammad Ali Blvd., Louisville, KY, 40203. Phone: (502) 585-0700. Fax: (502) 589-5559. Web Site: www.fox41.com. Licensee: Independence Television Co. Group Owner: Block Communications Inc. (acq 3-84; $10 million; 1-2-84). Population Served: 298,451 Natl. Network: Fox, . Natl. Rep: TeleRep,. Washington Atty: Dow, Lohnes & Albertson. News staff: 45; News: 35 hrs wkly.

Key Personnel:
Bill Lamb . . . . . pres & gen mgr
Harry Beam . . . . . opns mgr
Marti Hazel . . . . . gen sls mgr
Rick Burrice . . . . . natl sls mgr
Barry Fulmer . . . . . news dir
Gary Schroder . . . . . chief of engrg

WHAS-TV— Digital Channel: 11.135 kw vis, 13.5 kw aur. 1,290t/973g TL: N38 21 23 W85 50 52 On air date: Mar 27, 1950. 520 W. Chestnut St., Louisville, KY, 40201. Phone: (502) 582-7711. Fax: (502) 582-7279.E-mail: whasprogramming@whas11.com Web Site: www.whas11.com. Licensee: Belo Kentucky Inc. Group Owner: Belo Corp., Broadcast Division (acq 2-97; grpsl). Population Served: 550,500 Natl. Network: ABC, . Washington Atty: Covington & Burling.

Key Personnel:
Allan Cohen . . . . . gen mgr
Mark Pimentel. . . . . stn mgr
Lori Morgan . . . . . gen sls mgr
Kirk Szesny . . . . . mktg dir
Joy Pritchett . . . . . progmg dir
Aaron Ramey. . . . . news dir
Neal Metersky . . . . . chief of engrg

WKMJ-TV— Digital Channel: 38.61.6 kw vis. ant 715t/367g TL: N38 22 01 W85 49 54 On air date: Aug 31, 1970. 600 Cooper Dr., Lexington, KY, 40502. Phone: (859) 258-7000. Fax: (859) 258-7399. Web Site: www.ket.org. Licensee: Kentucky Authority for Educational TV. Natl. Network: PBS, . Kentucky Educational Television

Key Personnel:
Craig Cornwell. . . . . opns mgr & progmg mgr
Mike Brower . . . . . dev mgr
Tim Bischoff . . . . . mktg dir & pub affrs dir
Robert Ball . . . . . engrg dir

***WKPC-TV—** Digital Channel: 17.60.3 kw vis. ant 777t/423g TL: N38 22 01 W85 49 54 On air date: Sept 5, 1958. 600 Cooper Dr., Lexington, KY, 40502. Phone: (859) 258-7000. Fax: (859) 258-7399. Web Site: www.ket.org. Licensee: Kentucky Authority for Educational Television. Population Served: 519,000 Natl. Network: PBS, . Kentucky Educational Television Washington Atty: Schwartz, Woods & Miller.

Key Personnel:
Craig Cornwell. . . . . opns mgr & progmg mgr
Mike Brower. . . . . dev VP
Tim Bischoff . . . . . mktg dir & progmg VP
Robert Ball . . . . . chief of engrg

***WKZT-TV—** Digital Channel: 43. Digital Hrs: 24 61 kw vis. ant 584t/571g TL: N37 40 55 W85 50 31 On air date: Sept 23, 1968. 600 Cooper Dr., Lexington, KY, 40502. Phone: (859) 258-7000. Fax: (859) 258-7399. Web Site: www.ket.org. Licensee: Kentucky Authority for Educational TV. Natl. Network: PBS, . Kentucky Educational Television

Key Personnel:
Mike Brower . . . . . dev mgr
Tim Bischoff . . . . . opns mgr & mktg dir
Craig Cornwell . . . . . progmg mgr & engrg dir

WLKY-TV— Digital Channel: 26. Digital Hrs: 24 4,300 kw vis, 430 kw aur. 1,260t/989g TL: N38 22 10 W85 50 02 On air date: Sept 18, 1961. Box 6205, 1918 Mellwood Ave., Louisville, KY, 40206. Phone: (502) 893-3671. Fax: (502) 897-2384. Web Site: www.wlky.com. Licensee: Hearst-Argyle Properties Inc. Group Owner: Hearst-Argyle Television Inc. (acq 3-18-99; grpsl). Natl. Network: CBS, . Washington Atty: Brooks, Pierce, McLendon, Humphrey & Leonard. Wire Svc: UPI News: 37.5 hrs wkly.

Key Personnel:
Greg Baird . . . . . gen sls mgr
Michael Neelly . . . . . news dir

WMYO— Digital Channel: 51. Digital Hrs: 24 5,000 kw vis. ant 1,305t TL: N38 42 29 W86 05 57 On air date: Mar 15, 1994. 624 W. Muhammed Ali Blvd., Louisville, KY, 40203. Phone: (502) 585-0700. Fax: (502) 589-5559. Web Site: www.wmyo.com. Licensee: Independence Television Co. Group Owner: Block Communications Inc. (acq 3-30-2001). Natl. Network: MyNetworkTV, . Natl. Rep: TeleRep,. Washington Atty: Dow, Lohnes & Albertson.

Key Personnel:
Bill Lamb . . . . . pres & gen mgr
Steve Ballard . . . . . CFO
Harry Beam . . . . . opns mgr
Marti Hazel . . . . . gen sls mgr
Rick Burrice . . . . . natl sls mgr
Gary Schroder . . . . . chief of engrg

Madisonville

see Evansville, IN market

Newport

see Cincinnati, OH market

Owensboro

see Evansville, IN market

Owenton

see Cincinnati, OH market

Paducah, KY-Cape Girardeau, MO-Harrisburg-Mount Vernon, IL (DMA 78)

KBSI— Digital Channel: 22. Digital Hrs: 24 1,860 kw vis, 186 kw aur. 1,768t/1,524g TL: N37 24 23 W89 33 44 On air date: Sept 10, 1983. 806 Enterprise, Cape Girardeau, MO, 63703. Phone: (573) 334-1223. Fax: (573) 334-1208. Web Site: www.kbsi23.com. Licensee: KBSI Licensee L.P. Group Owner: Sinclair Broadcast Group Inc. (acq 1998; grpsl). Population Served: 850,000 Natl. Network: Fox, . Natl. Rep: Millennium Sales & Marketing,.

Key Personnel:
Tom Tipton. . . . . gen mgr
Rob Chronister . . . . . opns dir
Jennifer Chronister . . . . . gen sls mgr
Glenn Ralston . . . . . natl sls mgr
Chuck Moffitt . . . . . prom mgr
Alan Muster . . . . . progmg dir
Chris Girard . . . . . chief of engrg
John Schreiner . . . . . traf mgr
Mary Robbins . . . . . pub svc dir

KFVS-TV— Digital Channel: 12. Digital Hrs: 24 316 kw vis, 63.2 kw aur. 2,001t/1,678g TL: N37 25 46 W89 30 14 On air date: Oct 3, 1954. PO Box 100, Cape Girardeau, MT, 63702. 310 Broadway, Cape Girardeau, MT 63702. Phone: (573) 335-1212. Fax: (573) 335-6303.E-mail: manager@kfvs12.com Web Site: www.kfvs12.com. Licensee: Raycom America License Subsidiary LLC. Group Owner: Raycom Media Inc. (acq 4-97; grpsl). Population Served: 910,000 Natl. Network: CBS, . Natl. Rep: Harrington, Righter & Parsons,. Washington Atty: Covington & Burling. News staff: 45; News: 28 hrs wkly.

Key Personnel:
Mike Smythe . . . . . gen mgr
Mike Wunderlich. . . . . opns dir
Joe Trepasso . . . . . gen sls mgr
Brad Zaruba. . . . . natl sls mgr
Karen Wade. . . . . rgnl sls mgr
Paul Keener . . . . . mktg dir
Dan Timpe. . . . . prom dir
Kathy Cowan. . . . . progmg dir & pub affrs dir
Mark Little . . . . . news dir
Arnold Killian. . . . . chief of engrg
Sherry Westbrook . . . . . rsch dir
Linda Seabaugh . . . . . traf mgr
Todd Richards . . . . . sports cmtr
Bob Reeves . . . . . weather dir

KPOB-TV— Digital Channel: 15. Digital Hrs: 24 389 kw vis, 38.9 kw aur. 600t/526g TL: N36 48 02 W90 27 03 On air date: Sept 15, 1967. 1416 Country Air Dr., Carterville, IL, 62918. Phone: (618) 985-2333. Fax: (618) 985-3709. Web Site: www.wsiltv.com. Licensee: Mel Wheeler Inc. Group Owner: (group owner; (acq 5-12-83; $6.6 million;6-6-83). Natl. Network: ABC, . Washington Atty: Brooks, Pierce, McLendon, Humphrey & Leonard.

Key Personnel:
Steve Wheeler . . . . gen mgr
Harold McDaniel . . . . opns mgr
Pat Victoria . . . . chief of engrg
Satellite of WSIL-TV Harrisburg IL.

WDKA— Digital Channel: 49. Digital Hrs: 24 2,610 kw vis, 275 kw aur. ant 1,079t/1,848g TL: N37 23 42 W88 56 23 On air date: June 1997. 806 Enterprise St., Cape Girardeau, MO, 63703. Phone: (573) 334-1223. Fax: (573) 334-1208. Web Site: www.wdka49.com. Licensee: WDKA Acquisition Corp. Natl. Network: MyNetworkTV, .
Key Personnel:
Tom Tipton . . . . gen mgr
Rob Chronister . . . . opns dir
Jennifer Chronister . . . . gen sls mgr
Glenn Ralston . . . . natl sls mgr
Chuck Moffitt . . . . prom dir
Alan Muster . . . . progmg dir
Chris Girard . . . . chief of engrg

***WKMU—** Digital Channel: 36.56.9 kw vis. ant 613t/581g TL: N36 41 34 W88 32 11 On air date: Oct 9, 1968. 600 Cooper Dr., Lexington, KY, 40502. Phone: (859) 258-7000. Fax: (859) 258-7399. Web Site: www.ket.org. Licensee: Kentucky Authority for Educational TV. Natl. Network: PBS, . Kentucky Educational Television
Key Personnel:
Craig Cornwell . . . . opns dir & progmg mgr
Tim Bischoff . . . . mktg dir
Robert Ball . . . . engrg dir

***WKPD—** Digital Channel: 41.55.7 kw vis. ant 469t/472g TL: N37 05 39 W88 40 20 On air date: May 31, 1971. 600 Cooper Dr., Lexington, KY, 40502. Phone: (859) 258-7000. Fax: (859) 258-7399. Web Site: www.ket.org. Licensee: Kentucky Authority for Educational TV. (acq 2-28-78). Natl. Network: PBS, . Rgnl. Network: SECA. Kentucky Educational Television Washington Atty: Kenkel, Barnard & Edmundson.
Key Personnel:
Mike Brower . . . . opns mgr
Tim Bischoff . . . . mktg dir
Craig Cornwell . . . . progmg mgr
Robert Ball . . . . engrg dir

WPSD-TV— Digital Channel: 32. Digital Hrs: 24 100 kw vis, 13.8 kw aur. ant 1,581t/1,593g TL: N37 11 31 W88 58 53 On air date: May 28, 1957. Box 1197, Paducah, KY, 42002-1197. 100 Television Ln., Paducah, KY 42003. Phone: (270) 415-1900. Fax: (270) 415-2020.E-mail: bevans@wpsdlocal16.com Web Site: www.wpsdtv.com. Licensee: WPSD-TV LLC. Ownership: Paxton Media Group Inc., see Cross-Ownership. (acq 12-3-01). Population Served: 333,000 Natl. Network: NBC, . Natl. Rep: Continental Television Sales,. Washington Atty: Covington & Burling. News staff: 49; News: 23 hrs wkly.
Key Personnel:
Richard Paxton . . . . pres & gen mgr
Bill Evans . . . . opns VP
Mark Hall . . . . opns mgr
David Jernigan . . . . sls VP & progmg VP
Bob Crosno . . . . rgnl sls mgr
Cathy Crecelius . . . . prom mgr
Griff Potter . . . . news dir
Joey Gill . . . . chief of engrg & traf mgr

WSIL-TV— Digital Channel: 34. Digital Hrs: 24 100 kw vis, 20 kw aur. 1,120t/1,000g TL: N37 36 46 W88 52 20 On air date: December 1953. 1416 Country Aire Dr, Carterville, IL, 62918. Phone: (618) 985-2333. Fax: (618) 985-3709. Web Site: www.wsiltv.com. Licensee: WSIL TV Inc. Group Owner: Mel Wheeler Inc. (acq 5-12-83; grpsl;6-6-83). Population Served: 927,000 Natl. Network: ABC, . Natl. Rep: Continental Television Sales,. Washington Atty: Brooks, Pierce, McLendon, Humprey & Leonard.
Key Personnel:
Steve Wheeler . . . . pres & gen mgr

***WSIU-TV—** Digital Channel: 8. Digital Hrs: 24 53 kw vis. ant 890t/861g TL: N38 06 11 W89 14 40 On air date: November 1961. 1003 Communications Bldg., 1100 Lincoln Dr., Carbondale, IL, 62901. Phone: (618) 453-4343. Fax: (618) 453-6186. Web Site: www.wsiu.org. Licensee: Board of Trustees of Southern Illinois University. Population Served: 326,000 Natl. Network: PBS, . Washington Atty: Cohn & Marks. Wire Svc: AP News staff: one; News: 2 hrs wkly.
Key Personnel:
Delores Kerstein . . . . CFO
Renee Dillard . . . . mktg dir
Terry Harvey . . . . engrg dir
Monica Tichenor . . . . prom
Trina Thomas . . . . progmg
Rebroadcasts WUSI-TV Olney 99%.

WTCT— Digital Channel: 17. Digital Hrs: 24 2,600 kw vis, 260 kw aur. 775t/500g TL: N37 33 26 W89 01 24 On air date: Aug 16, 1981. Box 698, 11717 Rt. 37 N., Marion, IL, 62959. Phone: (618) 997-4700. Fax: (618) 993-9778. Web Site: www.tct.tv. Licensee: Tri-State Christian TV. Group Owner: (group owner; (acq 5-29-84; $1.2 million).
Key Personnel:
Fortune Brayfield . . . . gen mgr & stn mgr
Todd Creamer . . . . chief of engrg

Pikeville

see Charleston-Huntington, WV market

Louisiana

Alexandria, LA (DMA 179)

KALB-TV— Digital Channel: 35. Digital Hrs: 24 100 kw vis, 20 kw aur. 1,590t/1,586g TL: N31 02 15 W92 29 45 On air date: Sept 29, 1954. Box 951, Alexandria, LA, 71309. 605 Washington St., Alexandria, LA 70301. Phone: (318) 445-2456. Fax: (318) 442-7427.E-mail: news@kalb.com Web Site: www.kalb.com. Licensee: Hoak Media of Alexandria License LLC. Group Owner: Media General Broadcast Group (acq 7-15-2008; $60 million with WMBB(TV) Panama City, FL). Population Served: 504,400 Natl. Network: NBC, CBS, . Washington Atty: Akin Gump Strauss Hauer & Feld LLP.
Key Personnel:
Eric Van den Branden . . . . pres
Les Golmon . . . . gen mgr
Les Golman . . . . stn mgr

KBCA— Digital Channel: 41. Digital Hrs: 24 5,000 kw vis. ant 993t/975g TL: N30 54 17 W92 37 28 On air date: June 1, 2005. Delta Media Corp., 3501 Northwest Evangeline Thruway, Carencro, LA, 70520. Phone: (337) 896-1600. Fax: (337) 896-2695.E-mail: info@cwtv41.com Web Site: www.cwtv41.com. Licensee: Wilderness Communications LLC. (acq 4-1-2006). Natl. Network: CW, . Natl. Rep: Roslin Television Sales,. Washington Atty: Fletcher, Heald & Hildreth.
Key Personnel:
Charles Chatelain . . . . pres
Eddie Blanchard . . . . gen mgr
Leila Dablan . . . . gen sls mgr

KLAX-TV— Digital Channel: 31. Digital Hrs: 24 1,309 kw vis, 131 kw aur. 1,092t/1,028g TL: N31 33 54 W92 32 59 On air date: Mar 3, 1983. Box 8818, 1811 England Dr., Alexandria, LA, 71303. Phone: (318) 473-0031. Fax: (318) 442-9984. Web Site: www.klax-tv.com. Licensee: Pollack-Belz Communication Co. Inc. (acq 6-3-88; $1.1 million). Natl. Network: ABC, . Washington Atty: Wood, Maines & Brown. News staff: 4; News: 5.5 hrs wkly.
Key Personnel:
William H. Pollack . . . . pres
David Carlson . . . . CFO
Ken Nolan . . . . gen mgr
Lisa Ballance . . . . gen sls mgr
Frances Yeager . . . . prom dir
D. Herbert . . . . chief of engrg
Vernilla Brooks . . . . traf mgr

***KLPA-TV—** Digital Channel: 26. Digital Hrs: 24 2,040 kw vis, 204 kw aur. 1,360t/1,329g TL: N31 33 56 W92 32 50 On air date: July 1, 1983. 7733 Perkins Rd., Baton Rouge, LA, 70810. Phone: (225) 767-5660. Phone: (800) 272-8161. Fax: (225) 767-4299. Web Site: www.lpb.org. Licensee: Louisiana Educational Television Authority. Population Served: 1,000,000 Natl. Network: PBS, . Washington Atty: Schwartz, Woods & Miller.
Key Personnel:
Beth Courtney . . . . CEO & pres
Bob Neese . . . . prom mgr
Jennifer Howze . . . . progmg dir
Randy Ward . . . . opns mgr & engrg dir

Baton Rouge, LA (DMA 95)

WAFB— Digital Channel: 9. Digital Hrs: 24 316 kw vis, 63 kw aur. 1,670t/1,729g TL: N30 21 58 W91 12 47 On air date: Apr 19, 1953. 844 Government St., Baton Rouge, LA, 70802. Phone: (225) 383-9999. Fax: (225) 379-7891. Fax: TWX: 510-993-3406.E-mail: news@wafb.com Web Site: www.wafb.com. Licensee: WAFB License Subsidiary LLC. Group Owner: Raycom Media Inc. (acq 12-31-96; grpsl). Population Served: 266,640 Natl. Network: CBS, . Natl. Rep: Harrington, Righter & Parsons,. Washington Atty: Covington & Burling.
Key Personnel:
Sandy Breland . . . . gen mgr
Vicki Kellum . . . . gen sls mgr
Ellen Salmon . . . . rgnl sls mgr
Brent Ledet . . . . prom mgr
Vicki Zimmerman . . . . news dir
Dale Russell . . . . chief of engrg

WBRZ-TV— Digital Channel: 13. Digital Hrs: 24 DTV 2.2 news, DTV 2.3 weather 30 kw vis. ant 1,689t/1,681g TL: N30 17 49 W91 11 40 On air date: Apr 14, 1955. Box 2906, Baton Rouge, LA, 70821. 1650 Highland Rd., Dalton, LA 70802. Phone: (225) 387-2222. Fax: (225) 336-2246.E-mail: news@wbrz.com Web Site: www.2theadvocate.com. Licensee: Louisiana Television Broadcasting LLC. Group Owner: Manship Stations (acq 1958; $548,000). Population Served: 723,000 Natl. Network: ABC, Natl. Rep: Blair Television,. Washington Atty: Pillsbury Winthrop Shaw Pittman LLP. News staff: 47; News: 22 hrs wkly.
Key Personnel:
James "Rocky" Daboval . . . . gen mgr
Steve Storey . . . . gen sls mgr
Denise Murrell . . . . natl sls mgr
Denise Akers . . . . mktg dir
Michelle Martone . . . . progmg dir & progmg mgr
Chuck Bark . . . . news dir
Clyde Pierce . . . . engrg dir & chief of engrg
Bobby Bernard . . . . traf mgr

WGMB-TV— Digital Channel: 45. Digital Hrs: 24 3,871 kw vis. ant 1,164t TL: N30 19 35 W91 16 36 On air date: Aug 11, 1991. 10000 Perkins Rd, Baton Rouge, LA, 70810. Phone: (225) 769-0044. Fax: (225) 769-9462. Web Site: www.fox44.com. Licensee: Comcorp of Baton Rouge. Group Owner: Communications Corp. of America (acq 2-13-95; 5-8-95). Population Served: 710,500 Natl. Network: Fox, . Washington Atty: Fletcher, Heald & Hildreth.
Key Personnel:
Phil Waterman . . . . CFO & gen mgr stn mgr
Tom Poehler . . . . natl sls mgr
Lee Stolf . . . . rgnl sls mgr & adv dir
Meisie Pacris . . . . prom mgr
Destiny Kelley . . . . progmg dir
Karen Mire . . . . pub affrs dir
Cecil Connella . . . . chief of engrg

***WLPB-TV—** Digital Channel: 25. Digital Hrs: 24 2,570 kw vis, 257 kw aur. 994t/1,030g TL: N30 22 22 W91 12 16 On air date: Sept 6, 1975. 7733 Perkins Rd., Baton Rouge, LA, 70810. Phone: (225) 767-5660. Phone: (800) 272-8161. Fax: (225) 767-4299. Web Site: www.lpb.org. Licensee: Louisiana Educational Television Authority. Population Served: 1,000,000 Natl. Network: PBS, . Washington Atty: Schwartz, Woods & Miller. News staff: 3; News: one hr wkly.
Key Personnel:
Beth Courtney . . . . CEO & pres
Bob Graziano . . . . stn mgr
Jennifer Howze . . . . opns mgr & progmg dir
Randy Ward . . . . engrg dir

WVLA-TV— Digital Channel: 34. Digital Hrs: 22 5,000 kw vis, 1,000 kw aur. ant 1,750t TL: N30 19 35 W91 16 36 On air date: Oct 16, 1971. 10000 Perkins Rd., Baton Rouge, LA, 70810. Phone: (225) 766-3233. Fax: (225) 768-9200. Web Site: www.nbc33tv.com. Licensee: Knight Broadcasting of Baton Rouge. Group Owner: White Knight Holdings Inc. (acq 1996; $23.975 million). Population Served: 773,400 Natl. Network: NBC, . Washington Atty: Pillsbury, Winthrop, Shaw & Pittman LLP. News staff: 3; News: 6 hrs wkly.
Key Personnel:
Phil Waterman . . . . gen mgr & stn mgr
Brooks Hogg . . . . sls dir
Tom Poehler . . . . natl sls mgr
Doreen Morgan . . . . mktg mgr
Scott Thomson . . . . prom mgr
Suzanne Marva . . . . progmg dir
Jeff Hamburger . . . . news dir
Elaine Harrison . . . . pub affrs dir & pub svc dir
Terry Freeman . . . . engrg VP
Cecil Connella . . . . chief of engrg
Carla Hatfield . . . . rsch dir
Shannon Guidry . . . . traf mgr
Leo Honeycutt . . . . news cmtr

Lafayette, LA (DMA 123)

KADN-TV— Digital Channel: 16.2,630 kw vis, 231 kw aur. ant 1,181t/1,282g TL: N30 21 44 W92 12 53 On air date: Feb 28, 1980. 123 N. Easy St., Lafayette, LA, 70506. Phone: (337) 237-1500. Fax: (337) 237-2526. Web Site: www.kadn.com. Licensee: Comcorp of Louisiana License Corp. (acq 12-9-2004; $13,125,000). Population Served: 650,000 Natl. Network: Fox, . Washington Atty: Fletcher, Heald & Hildreth.

Key Personnel:
Tom Poehler . . . . pres & gen mgr natl sls mgr
Morgan Polito . . . . rgnl sls mgr
Katie Flash . . . . prom mgr
Vikki Chapman. . . . . progmg mgr
Tony Guillory. . . . . chief of engrg

KATC— Digital Channel: 28.100 kw vis, 20 kw aur. 1,740t/1,793g TL: N30 02 19 W92 22 15 On air date: Sept 19, 1962. Box 63333, Lafayette, LA, 70596-3333. 1103 Eraste Landry Rd., Lafayette, LA 70596-3333. Phone: (337) 235-3333. Fax: (337) 235-9363.E-mail: webmaster@katctv.com Web Site: www.katc.com. Licensee: KATC Communications Inc. Group Owner: Cordillera Communications Inc. (acq 1995; $24.5 million). Population Served: 618,500 Natl. Network: ABC, . Natl. Rep: Continental Television Sales,. Washington Atty: Dow, Lohnes. Wire Svc: AP Wire Svc: CNN News staff: 45; News: 19.5 hrs wkly.
Key Personnel:
Andrew Shenkan . . . . gen mgr
Bonnie R. Will . . . . gen sls mgr
Arte Richard . . . . mktg dir & mktg mgr
Letitia Walker. . . . . news dir
Don Mouton . . . . chief of engrg
Joy Bernard . . . . traf mgr

KLFY-TV— Digital Channel: 10. Digital Hrs: 24 20.3 kw vis. ant 1,729t/1,735g TL: N30 19 19 W92 16 59 On air date: June 3, 1955. Box 90665, Lafayette, LA, 70509. Phone: (337) 981-4823. Fax: (337) 984-8323. Web Site: www.klfy.com. Licensee: Young Broadcasting of Louisiana Inc. Group Owner: Young Broadcasting Inc. (acq 5-28-88; $51 million;12-14-87). Population Served: 205,190 Natl. Network: CBS, . Natl. Rep: Adam Young,. Washington Atty: Wiley, Rein & Fielding. News staff: 24; News: 14 hrs wkly.
Key Personnel:
Mike Barras . . . . gen mgr
Spencer Bienvenu . . . . gen sls mgr
Carolyn Chretien . . . . progmg dir & traf mgr
Dwight Dugas. . . . . news dir
Rodney Evans . . . . chief of engrg

***KLPB-TV—** Digital Channel: 23. Digital Hrs: 24 2,140 kw vis, 214 kw aur. 1,190t/1,225g TL: N30 02 38 W92 22 14 On air date: May 2, 1981. 7733 Perkins Rd., Baton Rouge, LA, 70810. Phone: (225) 767-5660. Phone: (800) 272-8161. Fax: (225) 767-4299. Web Site: www.lpb.org. Licensee: Louisiana Educational Television Authority. Population Served: 1,000,000 Natl. Network: PBS, . Washington Atty: Schwartz, Woods & Miller.
Key Personnel:
Beth Courtney. . . . . CEO & pres
Randy Ward . . . . chmn & chief of engrg
Steve Graziano . . . . stn mgr
Jennifer Howze . . . . progmg dir

KLWB— Digital Channel: 50. Digital Hrs: 24 5,000 kw vis. ant 994t/998g TL: N30 20 32 W91 58 32 On air date: June 1, 2006. 3501 Northwest Evangeline Thruway, Carencro, LA, 70520. Phone: (337) 896-1600. Fax: (337) 896-2695.E-mail: info@cwtv50.com Web Site: www.cwtv50.com. Licensee: Wilderness Communications LLC. (acq 8-1-2006). Natl. Network: CW, . Natl. Rep: Roslin Television Sales,. Washington Atty: Fletcher, Heald & Hildreth.
Key Personnel:
Eddie Blanchard. . . . . gen mgr
Dave Pierce . . . . gen sls mgr
Connie Hanks. . . . . progmg dir

Lake Charles, LA
(DMA 176)

***KLTL-TV—** Digital Channel: 20. Digital Hrs: 24 1,260 kw vis, 126 kw aur. ant 1,030t/1,058g TL: N30 23 59 W93 00 10 On air date: May 5, 1981. 7733 Perkins Rd., Baton Rouge, LA, 70810. Phone: (225) 767-5660. Phone: (800) 272-8161. Fax: (225) 767-4299. Web Site: www.lpb.org. Licensee: Louisiana Educational Television Authority. Population Served: 1,000,000 Natl. Network: PBS, . Rgnl. Network: SECA. Washington Atty: Schwartz, Woods & Miller.
Key Personnel:
Beth Courtney. . . . . CEO & pres
Steve Graziano . . . . chmn & stn mgr
Jennifer Howze . . . . progmg dir
Randy Ward . . . . engrg dir

KPLC— Digital Channel: 7. Digital Hrs: 24 31 kw vis. ant 1,479t/1,476g TL: N30 23 46 W93 00 03 On air date: September 1954. Box 1490, Lake Charles, LA, 70602. 320 Division St., Lake Charles, LA 70602. Phone: (337) 439-9071. Fax: (337) 437-7600.E-mail: vbilbo@kplctv.com Web Site: www.kplctv.com. Licensee: KPLC License Subsidiary LLC. Group Owner: Liberty Corp. (acq 1-31-2006; grpsl). Population Served: 1,450,100 Natl. Network: NBC, . Natl. Rep: Harrington, Righter & Parsons,. Washington Atty: Covington & Burling LP. News staff: 31.
Key Personnel:
Jim Serra . . . . gen mgr
Dianna Mayo . . . . opns mgr
John Ware . . . . gen sls mgr
Stephanie Cormeaux . . . . rgnl sls mgr
Robin Daugereau . . . . progmg dir
Scott Flannagan. . . . . news dir
John Scott. . . . . chief of engrg
Mari Wilson . . . . pub svc dir

KVHP— Digital Channel: 30. Digital Hrs: 24 700 kw vis, 131 kw aur. 453t/404g TL: N30 11 50 W93 13 12 (CP: 2,507 kw vis, ant 1,292t) On air date: Dec 12, 1982. 129 W. Prien Lake Rd., Lake Charles, LA, 70601. Phone: (337) 474-1316. Fax: (337) 477-0715.E-mail: info@watchfox.com Web Site: www.watchfox.com. Licensee: National Communications Inc. (acq 10-3-96). Population Served: 236,000 Natl. Network: Fox, . Washington Atty: Baraff, Koerner, Olender & Hochberg. News staff: 20; News: 9 hrs wkly.
Key Personnel:
Madelyn Bonnot. . . . . gen mgr
Gary Mutchler . . . . gen sls mgr
Mary Stevens . . . . natl sls mgr
Crystal Miller. . . . . prom dir & prom mgr
Kim Anderson. . . . . progmg dir
Mark Ewing . . . . chief of engrg
Robin Killmer . . . . traf mgr

Monroe, LA-El Dorado, AR
(DMA 136)

KAQY— Digital Channel: 11.316 kw vis. ant 1,771t/1,929g TL: N32 05 41 W92 10 39 On air date: Dec 10, 1998. Box 4309, Monroe, LA, 71211. 3100 Sterlington Rd., Monroe, LA 71203. Phone: (318) 325-3011. Fax: (318) 327-7519. Web Site: www.abc-11.com. Licensee: Monroe Broadcasting Inc. Ownership: Charles H. Chatelain, 100% (acq 11-98). Natl. Network: ABC, .
Key Personnel:
Joe Currie . . . . gen mgr
Carolyn Clampit . . . . stn mgr & gen sls mgr
Mike Halbrook . . . . prom mgr
Doug Ginn . . . . progmg mgr
Pat O'Brien . . . . chief of engrg

KARD— Digital Channel: 36.1,000 kw vis, 100 kw aur. ant 1,708t/1,720g TL: N32 05 42 W92 10 34 On air date: Oct 6, 1974. 200 Pavilion Rd., West Monroe, LA, 71292. Phone: (318) 323-1972. Fax: (318) 322-0926. Web Site: www.kard.com. Licensee: Nexstar Broadcasting Inc. Group Owner: Nexstar Broadcasting Group Inc. (acq 12-31-2003; grpsl). Natl. Network: Fox, . Washington Atty: Arter & Hadden.
Key Personnel:
Mark Cummings . . . . gen mgr & pub svc dir
Chris Tingle . . . . gen sls mgr
Esther Phillips . . . . prom mgr
Irma Campbell . . . . progmg mgr
Randall Kamma. . . . . news dir
Joey Guy . . . . chief of engrg

KEJB— Digital Channel: 43.5,000 kw vis. ant 1,738t/1,706g TL: N33 04 41 W92 13 41 On air date: October 2003. 1001 N. 11th St., Monroe, LA, 71201. Phone: (318) 322-4394. Fax: (318) 322-8732. Web Site: www.kejb.com. Licensee: KM Television of El Dorado L.L.C. Group Owner: KM Communications Inc. Natl. Network: MyNetworkTV, .
Key Personnel:
Terri Egloff . . . . gen mgr & stn mgr rgnl sls mgr
Jeremy Tucker . . . . opns dir
Vince Anderson . . . . sls

***KETZ—** Digital Channel: 12.4,000 kw vis. ant 1,765t/1,738g TL: N33 04 41 W92 13 41 On air date: 2006. Box 1250, Conway, AR, 72033. Phone: (501) 682-2386. Fax: (501) 682-4122. Web Site: www.aetn.org. Licensee: Arkansas Educational Television Commission. Natl. Network: PBS, .
Key Personnel:
Allen Weatherly . . . . gen mgr

***KLTM-TV—** Digital Channel: 13. Digital Hrs: 24 316 kw vis, 31.6 kw aur. 1,777t/1,989g TL: N32 11 45 W92 04 10 On air date: Sept 8, 1976. 7733 Perkins Rd., Baton Rouge, LA, 70810. Phone: (225) 767-5660. Phone: (800) 272-8161. Fax: (225) 767-4299. Web Site: www.lpb.org. Licensee: Louisiana Educational Television Authority. Population Served: 1,000,000 Natl. Network: PBS, . Washington Atty: Schwartz, Woods & Miller.
Key Personnel:
Beth Courtney. . . . . CEO & pres
Steve Graziano . . . . stn mgr
Randy Ward. . . . . prom mgr & engrg dir
Jennifer Howze . . . . progmg dir

KMCT-TV— Digital Channel: 38. Digital Hrs: 24 560 kw vis, 56 kw aur. 498t/500g TL: N32 30 21 W92 08 54 On air date: Apr 7, 1986. 701 Parkwood Dr., West Monroe, LA, 71291-5435. Phone: (318) 322-1399. Fax: (318) 323-3783.E-mail: lamb@lambbroadcasting.org Web Site: www.lambbroadcasting.org. Licensee: Louisiana Christian Broadcasting Inc.. Ownership: Lamb Broadcasting Inc., 100% Group Owner: (group owner; (acq 7-13-2004). Washington Atty: Hardy, Chautin & Balkin. News: 6 hrs wkly.
Key Personnel:
Mike Reed . . . . pres & gen mgr & stn mgr
David Thompson . . . . chief of engrg

KNOE-TV— Digital Channel: 8. Digital Hrs: 24 316 kw vis, 31.6 kw aur. ant 1,930t/1,985g TL: N32 11 50 W92 04 14 On air date: Sept 27, 1953. Box 4067, Monroe, LA, 71211. 1400 Oliver Rd., Monroe, LA 71201. Phone: (318) 388-8888. Fax: (318) 388-0070. Fax: (318) 322-8774.E-mail: knoetv@knoe.com Web Site: www.knoe.com. Licensee: Hoak Media of Louisiana License LLC. (acq 10-3-2007; $47 million). Population Served: 428,000 Natl. Network: CBS, CW, . Natl. Rep: Blair Television,. Washington Atty: Cohn & Marks. Wire Svc: CBS Wire Svc: AP Wire Svc: CNN News staff: 28; News: 22 hrs wkly.
Key Personnel:
Eric Van den Branden . . . . pres
Roy Frostenson . . . . gen mgr
Tom Peas . . . . stn mgr
Tom Cole . . . . opns mgr
John Matherne. . . . . gen sls mgr
Taylor Henry . . . . news dir
Jerry Harkins. . . . . chief of engrg

KTVE— Digital Channel: 27.822.8 kw vis. ant 1,909t/1,883g TL: N33 04 41 W92 13 41 On air date: Dec 3, 1955. 200 Pavillion Rd., West Monroe, LA, 71292. Phone: (318) 323-1972. Fax: (318) 322-9718. Web Site: www.nbc10news.net. Licensee: Mission Broadcasting Inc. Group Owner: Piedmont Television Holdings LLC. (acq 1-16-2008; $7.7 million). Population Served: 171,600 Natl. Network: NBC, . Washington Atty: Drinker Biddle & Reath. News staff: 26; News: 13 hrs wkly.
Key Personnel:
Mark Cummings. . . . . gen mgr
Chris Tingle . . . . gen sls mgr
Esther Phillips . . . . prom mgr
Sharon Jones . . . . progmg mgr
Randall Kamma. . . . . news dir
Joe Holland . . . . chief of engrg

New Orleans, LA
(DMA 53)

KGLA-DT— Digital Channel: 42.1,000 kw vis. ant 964t/964g TL: N29 58 41 W89 56 26 On air date: June 1, 2007. Box 50790, New Orleans, LA, 70150. Phone: (504) 913-1540. Fax: (504) 340-4737. Web Site: www.mayavision.tv. Licensee: Mayavision Inc.. Ownership: Ernesto Schweikert III, 100% (acq 9-15-2006; $950,000). Natl. Network: Telemundo (Spanish), . Foreign lang progmg: SpanishS 168
Key Personnel:
Ernesto Schweikert III . . . . pres

WDSU— Digital Channel: 43. Digital Hrs: 24 100 kw vis, 20 kw aur. 928t/928g TL: N29 56 59 W89 57 28 On air date: Dec 18, 1948. 846 Howard Ave., New Orleans, LA, 70113. Phone: (504) 679-0600. Fax: (504) 679-0745.E-mail: feedback6@wdsu.com Web Site: www.wdsu.com. Licensee: New Orleans Hearst-Argyle Television Inc. Group Owner: Hearst-Argyle Television Inc. (acq 1999; grpsl). Population Served: 675,076 Natl. Network: NBC, . Natl. Rep: Eagle Television Sales,. Washington Atty: Brooks, Pierce, McLendon, Humphrey & Leonard. Wire Svc: AP News staff: 60; News: 32 hrs. wkly.
Key Personnel:
Joel Vilmenay. . . . . pres & gen mgr
Wendy Walters . . . . dev dir
Frank Raterman . . . . gen sls mgr
Joseph Schiltz . . . . prom dir
Johnathan Shelley . . . . progmg dir & news dir
Chet Guillot . . . . chief of engrg
Greg Turner. . . . . rsch dir
Joe Rosemeyer . . . . edit mgr

WGNO— Digital Channel: 26. Digital Hrs: 24 3,140 kw vis. ant 1,014t/1,015g TL: N29 58 57 W89 56 58 On air date: Oct 16, 1967. One Gallaria Blvd, Suite 850, Metairce, LA, 70001. Phone: (504) 525-3838. Fax: (504) 569-0908.E-mail: abc26news@tribune.com Web Site: www.abc26.com. Licensee: Tribune Television New Orleans Inc. Group Owner: Tribune Broadcasting Co. (acq 12-20-2007; grpsl).

Population Served: 1,231,000 Natl. Network: ABC, . Natl. Rep: TeleRep,. Washington Atty: Dow Lohnes PLLC.
Key Personnel:
Phil Waterman . . . gen mgr
John Cruse . . . gen sls mgr
Bob Noonan . . . news dir
Steve Zanolini . . . chief of engrg

WHNO— Digital Channel: 21. Digital Hrs: 24 5,000 kw vis, 500 kw aur. 905t TL: N29 55 11 W90 01 29 On air date: October 1994. 839 Saint Charles Ave. Suite 309, New Orleans, LA, 70130-3744. Phone: (504) 681-0210. Fax: (504) 681-0180.E-mail: whno@lesea.com Web Site: www.whno.com. Licensee: Le Sea Broadcasting Corp. Group Owner: Le Sea Broadcasting News: 10 hrs wkly.
Key Personnel:
Steve Warnecke . . . progmg mgr
Bob Lawrence . . . chief of engrg
Sue Bosio . . . traf mgr
David Vasquez . . . sls

***WLAE-TV—** Digital Channel: 31.55 kw vis, 11 kw aur. 1,020t/1,045g TL: N29 58 57 W89 57 09 (CP: 2,290 kw vis, 229 kw aur) On air date: July 8, 1984. 3330 N. Causeway Blvd., Suite 345, Metairie, LA, 70002-3573. Phone: (504) 866-7411. Fax: (504) 840-9838. Web Site: www.pbs.org/wlae. Licensee: Educational Broadcasting Foundation Inc. Population Served: 270,000 Natl. Network: PBS, . Washington Atty: Marmet & McCombs. Foreign lang progmg: SpanishS 3
Key Personnel:
Ron Yager . . . gen mgr
Barbara Wick . . . progmg dir

WNOL-TV— Digital Channel: 15.5,000 kw vis, 500 kw aur. 1,049t/1,049g TL: N29 58 41 W89 56 26 On air date: Mar 25, 1984. 1400 Poydras St., Suite 745, New Orleans, LA, 70112-5100. Phone: (504) 525-3838. Fax: (504) 569-0908.E-mail: abc26news@tribune.com Web Site: www.neworleanscw38.com. Licensee: Tribune Television New Orleans Inc. Group Owner: Tribune Broadcasting Co. (acq 12-20-2007; grpsl). Population Served: 1,000,000 Natl. Network: CW, . Natl. Rep: MMT,.
Key Personnel:
Phil Waterman . . . pres & gen mgr
Bob Noonan . . . gen mgr & news dir
John Cruse . . . gen sls mgr
Steve Zanolini . . . chief of engrg

WPXL-TV— Digital Channel: 50. Digital Hrs: 24 1,000 kw vis, 100 kw aur. ant 892t/895g TL: N29 55 11 W90 01 29 On air date: Mar 19, 1989. 3900 Veterans Memorial Blvd., Suite 202, Metairie, LA, 70002. Phone: (504) 887-9795. Fax: (504) 887-1518. Web Site: www.ionline.tv. Licensee: ION Media New Orleans License Inc., debtor-in-possession. (acq 6-5-2009).
Key Personnel:
Ami Jenkins . . . gen mgr & opns mgr progmg dir
Matt Pate . . . gen mgr & rgnl sls mgr
Ernie Harvey . . . chief of engrg

WUPL— Digital Channel: 24. Digital Hrs: 24 4,376 kw vis, 437.6 kw aur. ant 658t On air date: June 1, 1995. 1024 N Rampart St, New Orleans, LA, 70116. Phone: (504) 529-4444. Web Site: wupltv.com. Licensee: CBS Radio Stations Inc. Group Owner: Viacom Television Stations Group. Natl. Network: MyNetworkTV, .
Key Personnel:
Bud Brown . . . gen mgr
Mike Zikmund . . . gen sls mgr
Christopher Merrifield . . . prom dir
Carol St.Martin . . . progmg mgr
Robert Gass . . . chief of engrg

WVUE-DT— Digital Channel: 8. Digital Hrs: 24 316 kw vis, 31.6 kw aur. ant 990t/1,046g TL: N29 57 14 W89 56 58 On air date: Feb 1, 1959. 1025 S. Jefferson Davis Pkwy., New Orleans, LA, 70125. Phone: (504) 486-6161. Fax: (504) 483-1101.E-mail: fox8programming@fox8tv.net Web Site: www.fox8live.com. Licensee: Louisiana Media Co. LLC.. Ownership: Benson Football L.L.C. Group Owner: Emmis Communications Corp. (acq 7-18-2008; $41 million). Population Served: 1,648,000 Natl. Network: Fox, . Natl. Rep: Harrington, Righter & Parsons,. News staff: 54; News: 21 hrs wkly.
Key Personnel:
Joe Cook . . . gen mgr
Michelle Kehoe Ogden . . . natl sls mgr
Heidi Hoffmeister . . . progmg dir
Mikel Schaefer . . . news dir

WWL-TV— Digital Channel: 36. Digital Hrs: 24 100 kw vis, 10 kw aur. 1,000t/1,049g TL: N29 54 23 W90 02 23 On air date: Sept 7, 1957. 1024 N. Rampart St., New Orleans, LA, 70116. Phone: (504) 529-4444. Fax: (504) 529-6483. Web Site: www.wwltv.com. Licensee: WWL-TV Inc. Group Owner: Belo Corp. (acq 1994). Population Served: 609,000 Natl. Network: CBS, . Natl. Rep: TeleRep,. Washington Atty: Holland & Knight.

Key Personnel:
Bud Brown . . . gen mgr
Mike Zikmund . . . gen sls mgr
Christopher Merrifield . . . prom dir & pub affrs dir
Carol St. Martin . . . progmg mgr
Robert Gass . . . chief of engrg

***WYES-TV—** Digital Channel: 11. Digital Hrs: 24 316 kw vis, 31.6 kw aur. 1,010t/1,046g TL: N89 56 58 W29 57 14 On air date: Apr 1, 1957. Box 24026, New Orleans, LA, 70184. Phone: (504) 486-5511.E-mail: info@wyes.org Web Site: www.wyes.org. Licensee: Greater New Orleans Educational TV Foundation. Population Served: 675,000 Natl. Network: PBS, . Washington Atty: Schwartz, Woods & Miller.
Key Personnel:
Randall Feldman . . . CEO

Shreveport, LA
(DMA 84)

***KLTS-TV—** Digital Channel: 24. Digital Hrs: 24 1,620 kw vis, 162 kw aur. 1,070t/1,080g TL: N32 40 41 W93 55 35 On air date: Aug 9, 1978. 7733 Perkins Rd., Baton Rouge, LA, 70810. Phone: (225) 767-5660. Fax: (225) 767-4299. Web Site: www.lpb.org. Licensee: Louisiana Education Television Authority. Population Served: 1,000,000 Natl. Network: PBS, . Washington Atty: Schwartz, Woods & Miller.
Key Personnel:
Beth Courtney . . . CEO & pres
Steve Graziano . . . stn mgr
Jennifer Howze . . . progmg dir
Randy Ward . . . engrg dir

KMSS-TV— Digital Channel: 34. Digital Hrs: 24 4,570 kw vis, 457 kw aur. 1,813t/1,781g TL: N32 36 51 W93 48 59 On air date: Oct 6, 1985. 3519 Jewella Ave., Shreveport, LA, 71109. Phone: (318) 631-5677. Fax: (318) 631-4194. Web Site: www.kmsstv.com. Licensee: Comcorp of Texas License Corp. Group Owner: Communications Corp. of America (acq 10-94). Natl. Network: Fox, . Washington Atty: Fletcher, Heald & Hildreth, PLC.
Key Personnel:
Paula Hayward . . . gen mgr & stn mgr
Susan Newman . . . gen sls mgr
Mike Halbrook . . . prom mgr & pub affrs dir
Doug Ginn . . . progmg dir
Pat O'Brien . . . chief of engrg

KPXJ— Digital Channel: 21.3,020 kw vis. ant 469t TL: N32 44 40 W93 22 54 On air date: 1999. Box 4066, Shreveport, LA, 71104. 312 E. Kings Hwy, Shreveport, LA 71104. Phone: (318) 861-5800. Fax: (318) 219-4600. Web Site: www.kpxj21.com. Licensee: Minden Television Co. LLC. Ownership: Lauren Wray Ostendorff, 100% (acq 5-7-2004; $10 million). Natl. Network: CW, . Washington Atty: Garvey, Schubert & Barer.
Key Personnel:
Lauren Wray Ostendorff . . . pres
George Sirven . . . gen mgr

KSHV-TV— Digital Channel: 44.500 kw vis. ant 1,657t/1,600g TL: N32 39 57 W93 55 58 On air date: Apr 15, 1994. 3519 Jewella Ave., Shreveport, LA, 71109. Phone: (318) 631-4545. Fax: (318) 621-9688. Web Site: www.kshv.com. Licensee: White Knight Broadcasting of Shreveport License Corp. Group Owner: White Knight Holdings Inc. (acq 1995; $3.8 million). Population Served: 410,000 Natl. Network: MyNetworkTV, . Washington Atty: Pillsbury, Winthrop, Shaw Pittman, LLC.
Key Personnel:
Paula Hayward . . . gen mgr
Issac Turner . . . sls dir & progmg
Susan Newman . . . gen sls mgr & rgnl sls mgr
Jim Dull . . . mktg dir & prom mgr
Steve Henry . . . chief of engrg

KSLA— Digital Channel: 17.316 kw vis, 40.7 kw aur. 1,800t/1,800g TL: N32 40 29 W93 55 59 On air date: Jan 1, 1954. 1812 Fairfield Ave., Shreveport, LA, 71101. Phone: (318) 222-1212. Fax: (318) 677-6703.E-mail: ksla@ksla.com Web Site: ksla.com. Licensee: KSLA License Subsidiary LLC. Group Owner: Raycom Media Inc. (acq 9-1-96; grpsl). Population Served: 461,600 Natl. Network: CBS, . Natl. Rep: TeleRep,. Wire Svc: UPI
Key Personnel:
James Smith . . . VP & gen mgr
Cindy Delaney . . . sls dir
Barbara Bennett . . . prom dir
Jayne Ruben . . . news dir
Ted Small . . . chief of engrg
Delena Leary . . . pub svc dir

KTAL-TV—(Texarkana, TX) Digital Channel: 15.1,000 kw vis, 100 kw aur. ant 1,490t/1,430g TL: N32 54 11 W94 00 20 On air date: Aug 16, 1953. 3150 N. Market St., Shreveport, LA, 71107. Box 7428, Shreveport, LA 71107. Phone: (318) 629-6000. Fax: (318) 629-6001. Web Site: www.arklatexhomepage.com. Licensee: Nexstar Broadcasting Inc. Group Owner: Nexstar Broadcasting Group Inc. (acq 9-11-2000; $35.25 million). Natl. Network: NBC, . Washington Atty: Covington & Burling.
Key Personnel:
Scott Thomas . . . gen mgr
Chaunte Robinson . . . progmg dir
Andrew Pontz . . . news dir
Kevin Southernland . . . chief of engrg

KTBS-TV— Digital Channel: 28. Digital Hrs: 24 100 kw vis, 20 kw aur. 1,780t/1,800g TL: N32 41 08 W93 46 00 On air date: Sept 3, 1955. Box 44227, Shreveport, LA, 71134-4227. 312 E. Kings Hwy., Shreveport, LA 71104-3554. Phone: (318) 861-5800. Fax: (318) 219-4680.E-mail: ktbsnews@ktbs.com Web Site: www.ktbs.com. Licensee: KTBS Inc. Ownership: Helen H. Wray, Florence H. Wray, George D. Wray Jr. Population Served: 750,000 Natl. Network: ABC, . Washington Atty: Fletcher, Heald & Hildreth. Wire Svc: AP
Key Personnel:
Lauren Wray Ostendorff . . . pres
George Sirven . . . gen mgr
Linda Howard . . . rgnl sls mgr
Cheryl May . . . prom mgr
Randy Bain . . . news dir
Dale Cassidy . . . chief of engrg
Bernadette Collier . . . progmg

Maine

Auburn

see Portland-Auburn, ME market

Bangor, ME
(DMA 153)

WABI-TV— Digital Channel: 19. Digital Hrs: 24 40 kw vis, 6 kw aur. ant 1,316t/490g TL: N44 42 13 W69 04 47 On air date: Jan 25, 1953. 35 Hildreth St., Bangor, ME, 04401. Phone: (207) 947-8321. Fax: (207) 941-9378.E-mail: wabi@wabi.tv Web Site: www.wabi.tv. Licensee: Community Broadcasting Service. Group Owner: Diversified Communications (acq 10-7-53; $125,000;10-12-53). Population Served: 200,000 Natl. Network: CBS, CW, . Natl. Rep: Continental Television Sales,. Washington Atty: Irwin, Campbell & Tannenwald. Wire Svc: AP News staff: 30; News: 25 hrs wkly.
Key Personnel:
Michael Young . . . VP & gen mgr
Tom Gass . . . sls dir
Steve Hiltz . . . progmg dir
Jim Morris . . . news dir
Dale Carter . . . chief of engrg
Keith Allen . . . opns

WLBZ— Digital Channel: 2. Digital Hrs: 24 51.3 kw vis, 10.2 kw aur. 630t/99g TL: N44 44 10 W68 40 17 On air date: Sept 12, 1954. 329 Mt. Hope Ave., Bangor, ME, 04401. Phone: (207) 942-4821. Fax: (207) 945-6816. Fax: (207) 942-2109 (news). Web Site: www.wlbz2.com. Licensee: Pacific and Southern Co. Inc. Group Owner: Gannett Broadcasting (acq 1998; $110 million with WCSH(TV) Portland). Population Served: 214,800 Natl. Network: NBC, . Washington Atty: Wiley, Rein & Fielding. News staff: 22; News: 33 hrs wkly.
Key Personnel:
Judy Haran . . . gen mgr
Mark Parent . . . prom dir
Mike Marshall . . . progmg dir
Heather Seavey . . . news dir & edit mgr
Dave Mundee . . . engrg dir & chief of engrg
Debbie Briggs . . . traf mgr
Charlene Belanger . . . pub svc dir
John Smist . . . sports cmtr
Steve McKay . . . weather dir

***WMEB-TV—** Digital Channel: 9.299 kw vis, 30 kw aur. 990t/369g TL: N44 45 36 W68 33 59 On air date: Sept 23, 1963. 1450 Lisbon St., Lewiston, ME, 04240. Phone: (800) 884-1717. Phone: (207) 783-9101. Fax: (207) 783-5193. Fax: (207) 942-2857.E-mail: comments@mpbn.org Web Site: www.mpbn.org. Licensee: Maine Public Broadcasting Corp. (acq 6-23-92;7-13-92). Population Served: 151,000 Natl. Network: PBS, . Rgnl. Network: Eastern Educ. Washington Atty: Dow, Lohnes PLLC. Foreign lang progmg: SpanishS 1

Key Personnel:
Jim Dowe . . . . . gen mgr
Lou Morin . . . . . mktg mgr
Jeff Pierce . . . . . prom dir & prom mgr
Charles Beck . . . . . progmg mgr
Keith Shortall . . . . . news dir

***WMED-TV—** Digital Channel: 10.31.6 kw vis, 6.2 kw aur. 430t/190g TL: N45 01 44 W67 19 24 On air date: September 1965. 1450 Lisbon St., Lewiston, ME, 04240. 65 Texas Ave, Bangor, ME 04401. Phone: (800) 884-1717. Phone: (207) 783-9101. Fax: (207) 783-5193. Fax: (207) 942-2857.E-mail: comments@mpbn.net Web Site: www.mpbn.org. Licensee: Maine Public Broadcasting Corp. (acq 6-23-92;7-13-92). Natl. Network: PBS, . Washington Atty: Dow, Lohnes PLLC. Foreign lang progmg: SpanishS 1
Key Personnel:
Jim Dowe . . . . . gen mgr
Lou Morin . . . . . mktg mgr
Jeff Pierce . . . . . prom mgr
Charles Beck . . . . . progmg mgr
Keith Shortall . . . . . news dir

WVII-TV— Digital Channel: 7.316 kw vis, 31.6 kw aur. ant 819t/137g TL: N44 45 35 W68 34 01 On air date: Oct 15, 1965. 371 Target Industrial Cir., Bangor, ME, 04401. Phone: (207) 945-6457. Fax: (207) 942-0511.E-mail: tv7news@wvii.com Web Site: www.wvii.com. Licensee: Bangor Communications LLC. Group Owner: Rockfleet Broadcasting Inc. Population Served: 429,000 Natl. Network: ABC, Fox, . Natl. Rep: Continental Television Sales,. Washington Atty: Mullin, Rhyne, Emmons & Topel. News staff: 15; News: 6 hrs wkly.
Key Personnel:
Mike Palmer . . . . . VP
Mike Palmer . . . . . gen mgr
Keryn Smith . . . . . gen sls mgr & natl sls mgr
Sue Lovell . . . . . rgnl sls mgr
Gene Hardin . . . . . prom mgr & pub affrs dir
George Thomas . . . . . news dir
Mike Staples . . . . . chief of engrg & engr

Portland-Auburn, ME
(DMA 77)

***WCBB—** Analog Channel: 10. Digital Channel: 17.309 kw vis, 30.9 kw aur. 1,000t/641g TL: N44 09 16 W70 00 37 On air date: Nov 13, 1961. 1450 Lisbon St., Lewiston, ME, 04240. Phone: (800) 884-1717. Phone: (207) 783-9101. Fax: (207) 783-5193. Fax: (207) 942-2857.E-mail: comments@mpbn.net Web Site: www.mpbn.net. Licensee: Maine Public Broadcasting Corp. (acq 6-23-92;7-13-92). Population Served: 600,000 Natl. Network: PBS, . Rgnl. Network: Eastern Educ. Washington Atty: Dow, Lohnes PLLC. Foreign lang progmg: SpanishS 2
Key Personnel:
Jim Dowe . . . . . gen mgr
Lou Morin . . . . . mktg mgr
Jeff Pierce . . . . . prom mgr
Charles Becks . . . . . progmg mgr
Keith Shortall . . . . . news dir

WCSH— Analog Channel: 6. Digital Channel: 44.100 kw vis, 20 kw aur. ant 2,000t/1,292g TL: N43 51 32 W70 42 40 On air date: Dec 1, 1953. One Congress Sq., Portland, ME, 04101. Phone: (207) 828-6666. Fax: (207) 828-6620.E-mail: wcsh6@wcsh6.com Web Site: www.wcsh6.com. Licensee: Pacific and Southern Co. Inc. Group Owner: Gannett Broadcasting (acq 1-98). Population Served: 948,000 Natl. Network: NBC, . Washington Atty: Wiley, Rein & Fielding.
Key Personnel:
Steve Thaxton . . . . . pres & gen mgr
Mike Marshall . . prom VP & prom mgr progmg VP & progmg mgr
Mike Curry . . . . . news dir
Dave Mundee . . . . . chief of engrg

WGME-TV— Analog Channel: 13. Digital Channel: 38.295 kw vis, 29.5 kw aur. ant 1,609t/1,665g TL: N43 55 28 W70 29 28 On air date: May 16, 1954. 81 Northport Dr., Portland, ME, 04103. Phone: (207) 797-1313. Fax: (207) 878-3505.E-mail: tvmail@wgme.com Web Site: www.wgme.com. Licensee: WGME Licensee L.L.C. Group Owner: Sinclair Broadcast Group Inc. (acq 5-3-99; grpsl). Population Served: 340,000 Natl. Network: CBS, . Washington Atty: Dow, Lohnes PLLC. News staff: 55; News: 25 hrs wkly.
Key Personnel:
Alisa Burris . . . . . pres & prom
Don Barr . . . . . gen sls mgr
Kate Reilly . . . . . progmg dir
Robb Atkinson . . . . . stn mgr & rgnl sls mgr & news dir
Craig Clark . . . . . engrg dir
Gary Legters . . . . . opns

***WLED-TV—** Digital Channel: 48. Digital Hrs: 24 93.3 kw vis, 9.33 kw aur. ant 1,280t/400g TL: N44 21 14 W71 44 23 On air date: Feb 7, 1968. 268 Mast Rd., Durham, NH, 03824-4601. Phone: (603) 868-1100. Fax: (603) 868-7552.E-mail: themailbox@nhptv.org Web Site: www.nhptv.org. Licensee: University of New Hampshire. Natl. Network: PBS, . New Hampshire Public Television Washington Atty: Schwartz, Woods & Miller.
Key Personnel:
Peter A. Frid . . . . . gen mgr
Dennis Malloy . . . . . dev dir & sls dir
Jeff Moris . . . . . prom mgr
Brian Shepperd . . . . . engrg dir & chief of engrg
Rebroadcasts *WENH Durham 100%.

***WMEA-TV—** Analog Channel: 26. Digital Channel: 45.589 kw vis, 117 kw aur. 800t/550g TL: N43 25 00 W70 48 09 On air date: March 1975. 1450 Lisbon St, Lewiston, ME, 04240. 65 Texas Ave., Bangor, ME 04401. Phone: (207) 783-9101. Fax: (207) 942-2857. Fax: (207) 783-5193.E-mail: comments@mpbn.net Web Site: www.mpbn.net. Licensee: Maine Public Broadcastig Corp. (acq 6-23-92;7-13-92). Population Served: 500,000 Natl. Network: PBS, . Washington Atty: Dow, Lohnes PLLC.
Key Personnel:
Christopher Amann . . . . . CFO
P. James Dowe . . . . . pres & gen mgr

WMTW—(Poland Spring, Analog Channel: 8. Digital Channel: 46. Analog Hrs: 24 Digital Hrs: 24 316 kw vis. ant 1,994t/1,630g TL: N43 50 44 W70 45 43 On air date: Aug 31, 1954. Box 8, Auburn, ME, 04210. 99 Danville Corner Rd, Auburn, ME 04210. Phone: (207) 782-1800. Phone: (207) 775-1800. Fax: (207) 783-7371. Fax: (207) 782-2165.E-mail: wmtw@wmtw.com Web Site: www.wmtw.com. Licensee: Hearst-Argyle Properties Inc. Group Owner: Hearst-Argyle Television Inc. (acq 5-11-2004; $37.5 million). Natl. Network: ABC, . Natl. Rep: Eagle Television Sales,. Washington Atty: Brooks & Pierce. Wire Svc: AP News: 13.5 hrs wkly.
Key Personnel:
David Abel . . . . . gen mgr
Gary Jensen . . . . . gen sls mgr
Gloria Shallcross . . . . . progmg mgr
George Matz . . . . . news dir

WPFO— Digital Channel: 23. Analog Hrs: 24 5,000 kw vis. 1,086t TL: N44 09 15 W70 00 37 On air date: Apr 24, 2003. 233 Oxford St., Suite 35, Portland, ME, 04101. Phone: (207) 828-0023. Fax: (207) 347-7330. Web Site: www.myfoxmaine.com. Licensee: CMCG Portland License LLC. Group Owner: MAX Media L.L.C. (acq 4-7-2003; $10 million with WVIF(TV) Christiansted, VI). Population Served: 400,000 Natl. Network: Fox, . Natl. Rep: TeleRep,. Washington Atty: Williams Mullen & Garvey, Schubert & Barer. News staff: one; News: 18.5 hrs wkly.
Key Personnel:
Tom MacArthur . . . . . gen mgr
Rob Barry . . . . . natl sls mgr
Teresa Pinney . . . . . prom mgr
Dave Cox . . . . . chief of engrg
Cathy Robbins . . . . . traf mgr

WPME— Analog Channel: 35. Digital Channel: 28. Analog Hrs: 24 1,100 kw vis, 110 kw aur. ant 840t TL: N43 51 06 W70 19 40 (CP: 5,000 kw vis, ant 912t) On air date: Aug 1, 1997. 4 Ledgeview Dr., Westbrook, ME, 04092. Phone: (207) 774-0051. Fax: (207) 774-6849.E-mail: comments@ourmaine.com Web Site: www.ourmaine.com. Licensee: MPS Media of Portland License LLC.. Ownership: Eugene J. Brown, 100% votes Group Owner: (group owner; (acq 3-31-2007; $4 million). Population Served: 865,000 Natl. Network: MyNetworkTV, . Washington Atty: Fletcher, Heald & Hildreth. News: 3.5 hrs wkly.
Key Personnel:
Douglas Finck . . . . . gen mgr & stn mgr
Doouglas Finck . . . . . gen sls mgr
Cory Culleton . . . . . rgnl sls mgr
Matt Maloney . . . . . progmg mgr
Roy Ouellette . . . . . chief of engrg

WPXT— Analog Channel: 51. Digital Channel: 43. Analog Hrs: 24 3,035 kw vis, 303 kw aur. ant 1,000t/720g TL: N43 51 06 W70 19 40 On air date: 1986. 4 Ledgeview Dr., Westbrook, ME, 04092. Phone: (207) 774-0051. Fax: (207) 774-6849.E-mail: comments@ourmaine.com Web Site: www.ourmaine.com. Licensee: New Age Media of Maine License LLC.. Ownership: Sedgwick Media LLC, 65%; Frank M. Henry, 33.64%; Michael Yanuzzi, 1.36% Group Owner: Pegasus Broadcast Television Inc. (acq 3-31-2007; grpsl). Population Served: 865,000 Natl. Network: CW, . Washington Atty: Leventhal Senter & Lerman PLLC. News staff: 25; News: 3.5 hrs wkly.
Key Personnel:
Douglas Finck . . . . . gen mgr & gen sls mgr
Cory Culleton . . . . . rgnl sls mgr
Matt Maloney . . . . . progmg mgr
Roy Ouellette . . . . . chief of engrg

Presque Isle, ME
(DMA 204)

WAGM-TV— Digital Channel: 8.120.0 kw vis, 12.0 kw aur. 1,148t/142g TL: N46 43 04 W67 48 34 On air date: Oct 13, 1956. 12 Brewer Rd., Presque Isle, ME, 04769. Phone: (207) 764-4461. Fax: (207) 764-5329.E-mail: wagmtv@wagmtv.com Web Site: www.wagmtv.com. Licensee: NEPSK Inc. Ownership: Peter P. Kozloski, 100%. (acq 3-8-91; grpsl;4-1-91). Population Served: 89,000 Natl. Network: CBS, Fox, . Washington Atty: Koteen & Naftalin. News staff: 12; News: 14 hrs wkly.
Key Personnel:
Gordon Wark . . . . . gen mgr
Linda Connolly . gen sls mgr & natl sls mgr rgnl sls mgr & prom dir prom mgr & progmg mgr
Jon Gulliver . . . . . news dir
Brett Lovley . . . . . chief of engrg

***WMEM-TV—** Digital Channel: 10.299 kw vis, 30 kw aur. 1,090t/158g TL: N46 33 05 W67 48 37 On air date: Feb 17, 1964. 1450 Lisbon St., Lewiston, ME, 04240-3514. 65 Texas Ave., Bangor, ME 04401. Phone: (800) 884-1717. Phone: (207) 783-9101. Fax: (207) 783-5193. Fax: (207) 942-2857.E-mail: comments@mpbn.net Web Site: www.mpbc.net. Licensee: Maine Public Broadcasting Network. (acq 6-23-92;7-13-92). Population Served: 151,000 Natl. Network: PBS, . Washington Atty: Dow, Lohnes PLLC. Foreign lang progmg: SpanishS 2
Key Personnel:
P. James Dowe . . . . . CEO & pres

Maryland

Baltimore, MD
(DMA 26)

WBAL-TV— Digital Channel: 11. Digital Hrs: 24 316 kw vis, 31.6 kw aur. 1,000t/998g TL: N39 20 05 W76 39 03 On air date: Mar 11, 1948. 3800 Hooper Ave., Baltimore, MD, 21211. Phone: (410) 467-3000. Fax: (410) 338-6238. Web Site: www.wbaltv.com. Licensee: WBAL Hearst-Argyle Television Inc. Group Owner: (group owner) Population Served: 905,759 Natl. Network: NBC, . Natl. Rep: Eagle Television Sales,. Washington Atty: Brooks, Pierce, McLendon, Humphrey & Leonard. Wire Svc: UPI News staff: 63; News: 24 hrs wkly.
Key Personnel:
Jordan Wertlieb . . . . . gen mgr
Michelle Butt . . . . . news dir
Wanda Draper . . . . . progmg dir & pub affrs dir

WBFF— Digital Channel: 46.1,292 kw vis, 258 kw aur. 1,266t TL: N39 20 10 W76 38 59 On air date: Apr 11, 1971. 2000 W. 41st St., Baltimore, MD, 21211. Phone: (410) 467-4545. Fax: (410) 467-5090. Web Site: www.foxbaltimore.com. Licensee: Chesapeake Television Licensee L.L.C. Group Owner: Sinclair Broadcast Group Inc. (acq 9-10-90; grpsl; 10-15-90). Population Served: 905,759 Natl. Network: Fox, . Natl. Rep: TeleRep,. Washington Atty: Shaw Pittman.
Key Personnel:
William Fanshawe . . . . . gen mgr
Russell Lucas . . . . . opns dir & opns mgr
Peter Paisley . . . . . sls dir & gen sls mgr
Sharon Wylie . . . . . mktg dir & mktg mgr
Peter Ferraro . . . . . prom mgr
Mary Press . . . . . progmg dir
Scott Livingston . . . . . news dir
David Hackney . . . . . engrg mgr

WJZ-TV— Digital Channel: 13.316 kw vis, 31.6 kw aur. 990t TL: N39 20 05 W76 39 03 On air date: Nov 2, 1948. 3725 Malden Ave., Baltimore, MD, 21211. Phone: (410) 466-0013. Fax: (410) 578-7502.E-mail: ness@wjz.com Web Site: www.wjz.com. Licensee: Viacom Inc. Group Owner: Viacom Television Stations Group (acq 6-28-57; $4.4 million;7-1-57). Population Served: 935,759 Natl. Network: CBS, . Washington Atty: Wilkes, Artis, Hedrick & Lane. Wire Svc: UPI
Key Personnel:
Jay B. Newman . . . . . VP & gen mgr
Vee Bennedetto . . . . . opns dir
Sara Scott . . . . . sls dir
Gail Bending . . . . . news dir
Susan Otradovec . . . . . pub affrs dir
Rick Seaby . . . . . engrg dir
Michelle Dowd-Wood . . . . . progmg

WMAR-TV— Digital Channel: 38. Digital Hrs: 24 100 kw vis, 11 kw aur. 1,000t/999g TL: N39 20 05 W76 39 03 On air date: Oct 27, 1947. 6400 York Rd., Baltimore, MD, 21212. Phone: (410) 377-2222. Fax: (410) 377-0493.E-mail: hooper@wmar.com Web Site: www.abc2news.com. Licensee: Scripps-Howard Broadcasting Co. Group Owner: (group owner; (acq 1991; $125 million;9-3-90). Population Served: 905,759 Natl. Network: ABC, . Natl. Rep: Harrington, Righter & Parsons,. Washington Atty: Baker & Hostetler. Wire Svc: AP

Key Personnel:
Bill Hooper . . . . VP & gen mgr
Peggy Phille. . . . . stn mgr & news dir
Shirley Pridgeon. sls dir
Darlene Dorman. . . . . progmg dir
David Silverstein . . . . news dir
Paul Garnet . . . . chief of engrg

***WMPB—** Digital Channel: 29. Digital Hrs: 24 646 kw vis, 76.38 kw aur. ant 820t/672g TL: N39 27 01 W76 46 37 On air date: 1986. 11767 Owings Mills Blvd., Owings Mills, MD, 21117-1499. Phone: (410) 356-5600. Fax: (410) 581-6579.E-mail: comments@mpt.org Web Site: www.mpt.org. Licensee: Maryland Public Broadcasting Commission. Population Served: 600,000 Natl. Network: PBS, . Washington Atty: Schwartz, Woods & Miller.
Key Personnel:
Robert J. Shuman . . . . CEO & pres
Larry D. Unger. . . . . CFO
George Beneman . . . . opns VP
Kirby Storms . . . . chief of engrg

***WMPT—** Digital Channel: 42. Digital Hrs: 24 5,000 kw vis. ant 895t/827g TL: N39 00 36 W76 36 33 On air date: 1986. 11767 Owings Mills Blvd., Owings Mills, MD, 21117-1499. Phone: (410) 356-5600. Fax: (410) 581-6579.E-mail: comments@mpt.org Web Site: www.mpt.org. Licensee: Maryland Public Broadcasting Commission. Population Served: 3000000 Natl. Network: PBS, . Washington Atty: Schwartz, Woods & Miller.
Key Personnel:
Robert Shuman . . . . CEO & pres
Larry Unger . . . . CFO
Kirby Storms . . . . chief of engrg
Rebroadcasts WMPB(TV) Baltimore 100%.

WNUV— Digital Channel: 40. Digital Hrs: 24 5,000 kw vis, 500 kw aur. 1,148t/998g TL: N39 17 15 W76 45 38 On air date: July 1, 1982. 2000 W. 41st St., Baltimore, MD, 21211. Phone: (410) 467-8854. Fax: (410) 467-5093. Web Site: www.wbbaltimore.com. Licensee: Baltimore (WNUV-TV) Licensee Inc. Group Owner: Cunningham Broadcasting Corporation (acq 1-9-2002). Natl. Network: CW, . Washington Atty: Arter & Hadden.
Key Personnel:
William Fanshawe . . . . gen mgr
Russell Lucas . . . . opns mgr & opns mgr
Billy Robbins . . . . gen sls mgr & rgnl sls mgr
Sharon Wylie . . . . mktg mgr
Peter Ferraro . . . . prom mgr
Mary Press. . . . . progmg dir
David Hackney . . . . chief of engrg

WUTB— Digital Channel: 41. Digital Hrs: 24 1,170 kw vis, 117 kw aur. 1,069t/996g TL: N39 17 15 W76 45 38 On air date: December 1985. 4820 Seton Dr., Suite M-N, Baltimore, MD, 21215. Phone: (410) 358-2400. Fax: (410) 764-7232.E-mail: wttg-hr@foxtv.com Web Site: www.my24wutb.com. Licensee: Fox Television Stations Inc. Group Owner: (group owner; (acq 7-31-2001; grpsl). Natl. Network: MyNetworkTV, . Natl. Rep: Fox Stations Sales,. Washington Atty: Law Offices of Hogan & Hartson.
Key Personnel:
Alan J. Sawyer. . . . . VP & gen mgr
Brock Abernathy . . . . natl sls mgr
Shirley Pridgeon . . . . rgnl sls mgr
Dan Carlin. . . . . progmg VP
Duane Myers. . . . . chief of engrg
Eduardo Zuniga . . . . traf mgr

Frederick

see Washington, DC (Hagerstown, MD) market

Hagerstown

see Washington, DC (Hagerstown, MD) market

Oakland

see Pittsburgh, PA market

Salisbury, MD (DMA 144)

WBOC-TV— Analog Channel: 16. Digital Channel: 21. Analog Hrs: 24 4,070 kw vis, 407 kw aur. 980t/1,003g TL: N38 30 16 W75 38 35 On air date: July 15, 1954. Box 2057, Salisbury, MD, 21802-2057. 1729 N. Salisbury Blvd., Salisbury, MD 21801. Phone: (410) 749-1111. Fax: (410) 749-2361.E-mail: wboc@wboc.com Web Site: www.wboc.com. Licensee: WBOC Inc. Ownership: Draper Holdings Business Trust. (acq 9-80; $8 million). Population Served: 85,500 Natl. Network: CBS, Fox, . Washington Atty: Covington & Burling. News staff: 40; News: 31 hrs wkly.
Key Personnel:
Craig Jahelka . . . . VP & gen mgr
K. Jahelka . . . . stn mgr
David Speicher. . . . . natl sls mgr
Bob Bachman . . . . rgnl sls mgr
Mary Borger. . . . . mktg mgr & prom mgr pub svc dir
John Dearing . . . . news dir
Danny Panicella . . . . chief of engrg

***WCPB—** Analog Channel: 28. Digital Channel: 56. Analog Hrs: 24 2,190 kw vis. ant 515t/515g TL: N38 23 09 W75 35 33 On air date: 1986. 11767 Owings Mills Blvd., Owings Mills, MD, 21117-1499. Phone: (410) 356-5600. Fax: (410) 581-6579.E-mail: comments@mpt-org Web Site: www.mpt.org. Licensee: Maryland Public Broadcasting Commission. Population Served: 600,000 Natl. Network: PBS, . Washington Atty: Schwartz, Woods & Miller.
Key Personnel:
Robert Shuman . . . . CEO & pres
Larry Unger . . . . CFO
George Benaman II . . . . VP
Kirby Storms . . . . chief of engrg
Rebroadcasts WMPB(TV) Baltimore 100%.

***WDPB—** Digital Channel: 44. Digital Hrs: 24 191 kw vis, 19.1 kw aur. ant 640t/657g TL: N38 39 15 W75 36 42 On air date: December 1982. The Linden Bldg., 625 Orange St., Wilmington, DE, 19801. Phone: (302) 888-1200. Fax: (302) 575-0346.E-mail: whyydbc@whyy.org Web Site: www.whyy.org. Licensee: WHYY Inc. (acq 2-28-86). Natl. Network: PBS, . Washington Atty: Schwartz, Woods & Miller. News staff: 10; News: 3 hrs wkly.
Key Personnel:
Molly Dickinson Shephard. . . . . CEO & chmn
David A. Othmer. . . . . VP
William Marrazzo . . . . gen mgr
William J. Marrazzo . . . . pres & stn mgr

WMDT— Analog Channel: 47. Digital Channel: 53. Analog Hrs: 20 2,190 kw vis, 219 kw aur. ant 997t/1,024g TL: N38 30 06 W75 44 09 On air date: Apr 11, 1980. Box 4009, Salisbury, MD, 21803-4009. 202 Downtown Plaza, Salisbury, MD 21801. Phone: (410) 742-4747. Fax: (410) 742-5767.E-mail: wmdt@wmdt.com Web Site: www.wmdt.com. Licensee: Delmarva Broadcast Service LLC.. Ownership: Marion B. Brechner, 51%; Berl M. Brechner, 49%. (acq 1982). Population Served: 248,969 Natl. Network: ABC, CW, . Washington Atty: Cohn & Marks. News staff: 23; News: 12 hrs wkly.
Key Personnel:
Kathleen McLain . . . . gen mgr
Phil Bankert . . . . gen sls mgr
Michael Polk. progmg mgr
Dawn Mitchell. . . . . news dir
Bill Hoctor . . . . chief of engrg

Massachusetts

Adams

see Albany-Schenectady-Troy, NY market

Boston (Manchester, NH) (DMA 7)

WBPX-TV— Analog Channel: 68. Digital Channel: 32. Digital Hrs: 24 1,000 kw vis. ant 1,184t/1,175g TL: N42 18 10 W71 13 07 On air date: January 1979. 1120 Soldiers Field Rd., Boston, MA, 02134. Phone: (617) 787-6868. Fax: (617) 787-4114. Web Site: www.ionline.tv. Licensee: ION Media Boston License Inc., debtor-in-possession. Group Owner: Paxson Communications Corp. (acq 5-2-2000; grpsl). Population Served: 6,366,400 Natl. Network: ION Television, . Wire Svc: Reuters News: 20 hrs wkly.
Key Personnel:
Robert Gilbert. . . . . gen mgr & sls VP
Dianne McLaughlin . . . . opns mgr
William Spitzer. . . . . dev VP

WBZ-TV— Digital Channel: 30. Digital Hrs: 24 60.3 kw vis, 9.75 kw aur. ant 1,160t/1,199g TL: N42 18 37 W71 14 14 On air date: June 9, 1948. 1170 Soldiers Field Rd., Boston, MA, 02134. Phone: (617) 787-7000. Fax: (617) 787-5969.E-mail: webmaster@wbztv.com Web Site: www.wbztv.com. Licensee: Viacom Inc. Group Owner: Viacom Television Stations Group. Population Served: 641,071 Natl. Network: CBS, . Natl. Rep: CBS TV Stations National Sales,. Washington Atty: Wilkes, Artis, Hedrick & Lane. Foreign lang progmg: SpanishS 1 News staff: 81; News: 20 hrs wkly.
Key Personnel:
Ed Piette . . . . pres & gen mgr
Jack Barry . . . . opns dir & engrg dir
Helen Wynyard. . . . . gen sls mgr
Wendy McMahon . . . . mktg dir
Christine Ferrara . . . . progmg mgr

WCVB-TV— Digital Channel: 20. Digital Hrs: 24 61.7 kw vis. ant 1,158t TL: N42 18 37 W71 14 14 On air date: Mar 19, 1972. 5 TV Pl., Needham, MA, 02494. Phone: (781) 449-0400. Fax: (781) 433-4490/(781) 433-4022. Web Site: www.thebostonchannel.com. Licensee: WCVB Hearst-Argyle Television Inc. Group Owner: Hearst-Argyle Television Inc. (acq 7-16-97; grpsl). Population Served: 5,874,000 Natl. Network: ABC, . Natl. Rep: Eagle Television Sales,. Washington Atty: Brooks, Pierce, McLendon, Humphrey & Leonard. Wire Svc: PR Newswire Foreign lang progmg: SpanishS 1 News: 30 hrs wkly.
Key Personnel:
Bill Fine . . . . pres & gen mgr
Gloria Spence . . . . CFO
Elizabeth Cheng . . . . VP
Joseph Rebelo. opns mgr
Peter Hennessey . . . . gen sls mgr
Andrew Vrees . . . . news dir

WDPX-TV— Digital Channel: 40.500 kw vis. ant 502t/404g TL: N41 41 20 W70 20 49 On air date: July 19, 1985. 1120 Soldiers Field Rd., Boston, MA, 02134. Phone: (617) 787-6868. Fax: (617) 787-4114. Web Site: www.ionline.net. Licensee: ION Media Boston License Inc., debtor-in-possession. Group Owner: Paxson Communications Corp. (acq 5-2-2000; grpsl). Washington Atty: Arter & Hadden.
Key Personnel:
Robert Gilbert. . . . . gen mgr
Satellite of WBPX-TV Boston.

***WEKW-TV—** Digital Channel: 49. Digital Hrs: 24 95.5 kw vis, 9.55 kw aur. ant 1,080t/455g TL: N43 02 00 W72 22 04 On air date: May 21, 1968. 268 Mast Rd., Durham, NH, 03824-4601. Phone: (603) 868-1100. Fax: (603) 868-7552.E-mail: themailbox@nhptv.org Web Site: www.nhptv.org. Licensee: University of New Hampshire. Population Served: 631,000 Natl. Network: PBS, . Washington Atty: Schwartz, Woods & Miller.
Key Personnel:
Peter A. Frid . . . . gen mgr
Dennis Malloy . . . . sls dir
Jeff Morris . . . . adv mgr
Mercedes Sabio. . . . . progmg dir
Brian Shepperd. . . . . chief of engrg

***WENH-TV—** Digital Channel: 11. Digital Hrs: 24 316 kw vis, 31.6 kw aur. ant 970t/390g TL: N43 10 33 W71 12 29 On air date: July 6, 1959. 268 Mast Rd., Durham, NH, 03824-4601. Phone: (603) 868-1100. Fax: (603) 868-7552.E-mail: themailbox@nhptv.org Web Site: www.nhptv.org. Licensee: University of New Hampshire. Population Served: 631,000 Natl. Network: PBS, . Rgnl. Network: Eastern Educ. Washington Atty: Schwartz, Woods & Miller. News: 2 hrs wkly.
Key Personnel:
Peter Frid . . . . gen mgr

WFXT— Digital Channel: 31. Digital Hrs: 21 1,380 kw vis, 106 kw aur. ant 1,170t/1,101g TL: N42 18 12 W71 13 08 On air date: Oct 10, 1977. WFXT-TV 25 Fox Dr., Dedham, MA, 02026. Phone: (781) 467-2525. Fax: (781) 467-7213. Web Site: www.myfoxboston.com. Licensee: Fox Television Stations Inc. Group Owner: (group owner; (acq 7-95;3-6-95). Population Served: 2,126,300 Natl. Network: Fox, . News staff: 70; News: 7 hrs wkly.
Key Personnel:
Gregg Kelley . . . . VP & gen mgr
Chris Tzianabos . . . . gen sls mgr
Lisa Graham . . . . news dir
Steve Harrington . . . . engrg VP
Tricia Maloney . . . . rsch dir & progmg

***WGBH-TV—** Digital Channel: 19. Digital Hrs: 24 87.1 kw vis, 8.71 kw aur. 1,040t/1,199g TL: N42 13 37 W71 14 14 On air date: May 2, 1955. One Guest Ave, Boston, MA, 02135. Phone: (617) 300-5400. Fax: (617) 300-1026.E-mail: feedback@wgbh.org Web Site: www.wgbh.org. Licensee: WGBH Educational Foundation. Population Served: 1,550,000 Natl. Network: PBS, . Rgnl. Network: Eastern Educ. Washington Atty: Covington & Burling.
Key Personnel:
Jonathan C. Abbott . . . . COO & exec VP
Henry Becton Jr. . . . . pres
Marita Rivero . . . . VP & gen mgr

***WGBX-TV—** Analog Channel: 44. Digital Channel: 43.500 kw vis. ant 1,282t/1,269g TL: N42 18 37 W71 14 14 On air date: Sept 25, 1967.

One Guest St, Boston, MA, 02135. Phone: (617) 300-5400. Fax: (617) 300-1013.E-mail: feedback@wgbh.org Web Site: www.wgbh.org. Licensee: WGBH Educational Foundation. Population Served: 2,100,000 Natl. Network: PBS, . Washington Atty: Covington & Burling.
Key Personnel:
Jonathan C. Abbott . . . . COO & exec VP progmg dir
Henry P. Becton Jr. pres
Marita Rivero . . . . VP & gen mgr gen mgr & prom VP

WHDH-TV— Digital Channel: 7.316 kw vis, 63.2 kw aur. 1,000t/1,069g TL: N42 18 40 W71 13 00 On air date: June 21, 1948. 7 Bulfinch Pl., Boston, MA, 02114. Phone: (617) 725-0777. Fax: (617) 723-6117. Web Site: www.whdh.com. Licensee: WHDH-TV Co. (acq 6-3-93; $204 million; 6-21-93). Population Served: 5,330,400 Natl. Network: NBC, . Natl. Rep: TeleRep,. Washington Atty: Holland & Knight.
Key Personnel:
Mike Carson. . . . . VP & gen mgr
Chris Wayland . . . . gen sls mgr
J.T. Smith . . . . natl sls mgr
Marc Lehner . . . . rgnl sls mgr & pub svc dir
Joan McCready . . . . progmg mgr
Linda Miele . . . . news dir
Jim Shultis. . . . . engrg dir

WLVI-TV—(Cambridge, Digital Channel: 41. Digital Hrs: 24 2,240 kw vis, 166 kw aur. ant 1,186t/1,201g TL: N42 18 12 W71 13 08 On air date: Aug 31, 1953. 7 Bulfinch Pl., Boston, MA, 02114. Phone: (617) 725-0777. Fax: (617) 723-6117. Web Site: www.cw56.com. Licensee: WHDH-TV. Group Owner: Tribune Broadcasting Co. (acq 12-19-2006; $113.7 million). Population Served: 641,071 Natl. Network: CW, . Natl. Rep: TeleRep,. Washington Atty: Holland & Knight. News staff: 44; News: 7 hrs wkly.
Key Personnel:
Mike Carson . . . . gen mgr
Robert P. Burns . . . . gen sls mgr
Heather Hazelton. . . . . natl sls mgr
Joan McCready . . . . progmg dir
Linda Miele . . . . news dir
Jim Shultis. . . . . engrg dir & chief of engrg

WMFP— Digital Channel: 18. Digital Hrs: 24 5,000 kw vis. 610t/669g TL: N42 21 29 W71 03 40 On air date: Oct 16, 1987. 1 Beacon St. 35th Fl, Boston, MA, 02108. Phone: (617) 720-1062. Licensee: MTB Boston Licensee LLC. Group Owner: Scripps Howard Broadcasting Co. (acq 2-2-2009). Washington Atty: Sciarrino & Shubert PLLC.
Key Personnel:
Bill Desmond . . . . stn mgr & chief of engrg

WMUR-TV— Digital Channel: 9. Digital Hrs: 24 282 kw vis, 33.5 kw aur. ant 1,030t/227g TL: N42 58 59 W71 35 19 On air date: Mar 9, 1954. 100 S. Commercial St., Manchester, NH, 03101. Phone: (603) 641-9000. Fax: (603) 641-9005 (admin).E-mail: storyideas@wmur.com Web Site: www.wmur.com. Licensee: Hearst-Argyle Properties Inc. Group Owner: Hearst-Argyle Properties Inc. (acq 3-28-01; $185 million). Population Served: 100,000 Natl. Network: ABC, . Natl. Rep: Eagle Television Sales,. Washington Atty: Brooks, Pierce, McLendon, Humphrey & Leonard. Wire Svc: AP News staff: 54; News: 29 hrs wkly.
Key Personnel:
Jeff Bartlett . . . . gen mgr & stn mgr

WNEU— Digital Channel: 34. Digital Hrs: 24 1,410 kw vis, 141 kw aur. ant 1,010t/138g TL: N42 59 02 W71 35 20 On air date: 1987. One Sundial Ave., Suite 501, Manchester, NH, 03103. Phone: (603) 647-6060.E-mail: wneu@comcast.net Licensee: NBC Telemundo License Co. Group Owner: Telemundo Group Inc. (acq 10-22-2002; $26 million). Population Served: 1,500,000 Natl. Network: NBC, Telemundo (Spanish), . Washington Atty: Davis Wright Tremaine L.L.P. Foreign lang progmg: SpanishS 168
Key Personnel:
Donna Sill . . . . stn mgr
David Raymond. . . . . chief of engrg

WPXG-TV— Analog Channel: 21. Digital Channel: 33. Analog Hrs: 24 190 kw vis. ant 1,128t/259g TL: N43 11 04 W71 19 12 (CP: Ant 1,050t) On air date: Apr 16, 1984. 1120 Soldiers Field Rd., Boston, MA, 02134. Phone: (617) 787-6868. Fax: (617) 787-4114. Web Site: www.ionline.tv. Licensee: ION Media Boston License Inc., debtor-in-possession. Group Owner: Paxson Communications Inc. (acq 5-2-2000; grpsl).
Key Personnel:
Robert Gilbert . . . . gen mgr & sls VP mktg mgr & progmg mgr
Paul Strieby . . . . chief of engrg
Satellite of WBPX Boston.

WSBK-TV— Digital Channel: 39. Digital Hrs: 24 3,160 kw vis, 316 kw aur. ant 1,161t/1,013g TL: N42 18 12 W71 13 08 On air date: Oct 12, 1964. 1170 Soldiers Field Rd., Boston, MA, 02134. Phone: (617) 787-7000. Fax: (617) 787-5969.E-mail: webmaster@tv38.com Web Site: tv38.com. Licensee: Viacom Inc. Group Owner: Viacom Television Stations Group (acq 2-27-95;5-22-95). Population Served: 2,140,000 News: 4 hrs wkly.
Key Personnel:
Ed Piette . . . . pres & gen mgr opns dir
Helen Wynyard. . . . . gen sls mgr
Wendy McMahon . . . . mktg dir
Christine Ferrara . . . . progmg mgr
Jack Barry. chief of engrg

WUNI— Digital Channel: 29. Digital Hrs: 24 1,150 kw vis, 245 kw aur. ant 1,528t/1,349g TL: N42 20 09 W71 42 57 On air date: Jan 2, 1970. 33 Fourth Ave., Needham, MA, 02494. Phone: (781) 433-2727. Fax: (781) 433-2750. Fax: (781) 433-2701.E-mail: feedback@wunitv.com Web Site: www.wunitv.com. Licensee: Entravision 27 L.L.C. Group Owner: Entravision Communications Corp. (acq 1-4-01; $47.5 million). Population Served: 3,500,000 Natl. Network: Univision (Spanish), . Washington Atty: Thompson Hine LLP. Wire Svc: AP Foreign lang progmg: SpanishS 168 News staff: 13; News: 3 hrs wkly.
Key Personnel:
Alexander von Lichtenberg . . . . gen mgr
Bob Kerrigan . . . . opns mgr
Scott McGavick . . . . gen sls mgr
Rob Donner . . . . natl sls mgr
Meg Godin . . . . mktg mgr & prom mgr
Sara Suarez . . . . news dir
Fran Vaccari . . . . chief of engrg
Renee Barbour . . . . traf mgr

WUTF-DT— Digital Channel: 27. Digital Hrs: 24 3,311 kw vis. ant 1,168t/1,227g TL: N42 23 02 W71 29 37 On air date: Feb 12, 1985. 71 Parmenter Rd., Hudson, MA, 01749. Phone: (978) 562-0660. Fax: (978) 562-1166. Web Site: univision.com. Licensee: Univision Partnership of Massachusetts. Group Owner: Univision Communications Inc. (acq 5-21-2001; grpsl). Population Served: 2,200,000 Natl. Network: TeleFutura (Spanish), . Washington Atty: Shaw Pittman. Foreign lang progmg: SpanishS 168
Key Personnel:
Rolo Duartas. . . . . gen mgr & stn mgr
Richard A. Peper . . . . chief of engrg
Renee Barbour . . . . traf mgr

WWDP— Digital Channel: 10. Digital Hrs: 24 11.9 kw vis. ant 466t/489g TL: N42 00 38 W71 02 42 On air date: Sept 15, 1996. 6740 Shady Oak Rd., Eden Prairie, MN, 55344. Phone: (952) 943-6000. Fax: (952) 943-6566. Web Site: www.shopnbc.com. Licensee: Norwell Television LLC. Ownership: ValueVision Media Acquisition Inc. (acq 4-1-2003).
Key Personnel:
Jon Stoltz . . . . gen mgr

***WYDN—** Digital Channel: 47.1,000 kw vis. ant 1,046t/20g TL: N42 18 37 W71 14 14 On air date: 2000. Box 612066, Dallas, TX, 75261-2066. 99Asnebumskit Rd., Paxton, MA 01612. Phone: (817) 571-1229. Fax: (817) 571-7458.E-mail: comments@daystar.com Web Site: www.daystar.com. Licensee: Educational Public TV Corp.
Key Personnel:
Arnold Toraz . . . . gen mgr

WZMY-TV— Digital Channel: 35. Digital Hrs: 24 4,790 kw vis, 479 kw aur. ant 699t TL: N42 44 07 W71 23 36 On air date: Sept 5, 1983. 11 A Street, Derry, NH, 03038. Phone: (603) 845-1000. Fax: (603) 434-8627. Web Site: www.mytvstation.tv. Licensee: ShootingStar Broadcasting of New England LLC. Ownership: ShootingStar Inc., 100% of votes; Alta ShootingStar Corp., approximately 98% of the nonvoting preferred membership units (acq 9-16-2004; $31 million). Population Served: 5,200,000 Natl. Network: MyNetworkTV, . Natl. Rep: Blair Television,. Washington Atty: Leventhal, Senter & Lerman. Wire Svc: AP News: 5 hrs wkly.
Key Personnel:
Diane Sutter. CEO & pres
Gene Steinberg . . . . progmg mgr
Jane Senk . . . . traf mgr

Holyoke

see Springfield-Holyoke, MA market

New Bedford

see Providence, RI-New Bedford, MA market

Pittsfield

see Albany-Schenectady-Troy, NY market

Springfield-Holyoke, MA (DMA 111)

***WGBY-TV—** Digital Channel: 22. Digital Hrs: 6:45 AM-3 AM 50 kw vis. ant 1,004t/124g TL: N42 14 29 W72 38 56 On air date: Sept 26, 1971. 44 Hampden St., Springfield, MA, 01103. Phone: (413) 781-2801. Fax: (413) 731-5093.E-mail: feedback@wgby.org Web Site: www.wgby.org. Licensee: WGBH Educational Foundation. Population Served: 203,000 Natl. Network: PBS, . Washington Atty: Covington & Burling.
Key Personnel:
Russell Peotter . . . . VP
Russell J. Peotter . . . . gen mgr
Charley Rose . . . . mktg dir
Lynn Roginski . . . . progmg dir & opns
Ray Miller . . . . chief of engrg

WGGB-TV— Digital Channel: 40. Digital Hrs: 24 4,250 kw vis, 425 kw aur. 1,056t/167g TL: N42 14 30 W72 38 56 On air date: Apr 14, 1953. 1300 Liberty St., Springfield, MA, 01104. Phone: (413) 733-4040. Fax: (413) 781-5733. Web Site: www.wggb.com. Licensee: Gormally Broadcasting Licenses LLC. Ownership: Gormally Broadcasting LLC, 100% Group Owner: Sinclair Broadcast Group Inc. (acq 11-1-2007; $21.15 million). Population Served: 345,000 Natl. Network: ABC, Fox, . Natl. Rep: Millennium Sales & Marketing,. Rgnl. Rep: Rgnl rep: Millennium
Key Personnel:
Dave Kaufman . . . . gen mgr
Dean Davidson . . . . opns dir & engrg dir chief of engrg
Carol Moran. . . . . progmg mgr
David Baer. . . . . news dir

WWLP— Digital Channel: 11. Digital Hrs: 24 4,170 kw vis, 417 kw aur. 877t/530g TL: N42 05 05 W72 42 14 On air date: Mar 17, 1953. Box 2210, Springfield, MA, 01102-2210. One Broadcast Ctr., Chieopee, MA 01013. Phone: (413) 377-2200. Fax: (413) 377-2261. Web Site: www.wwlp.com. Licensee: WWLP Broadcasting L.L.C. Group Owner: LIN Television Corporation (acq 10-20-2000; about $128 million). Natl. Network: NBC, . Natl. Rep: Blair Television,. Washington Atty: Covington & Burling. Wire Svc: AP
Key Personnel:
William Pepin. . . . . gen mgr
John Baran . . . . stn mgr
Carl Miller . . . . sls dir
Lowell McLane . . . . natl sls mgr
Anna Giza . . . . prom dir
Michael Garreffi . . . . news dir
Dave Cote. . . . . chief of engrg

Michigan

Alpena, MI (DMA 208)

WBKB-TV— Digital Channel: 11. Digital Hrs: 24 316 kw vis, 32.4 kw aur. 665t/500g TL: N44 42 25 W83 31 23 On air date: Sept 22, 1975. 1390 Bagley St., Alpena, MI, 49707. Phone: (989) 356-3434. Fax: (989) 356-4188.E-mail: wbkbtv@speednetllc.com Web Site: www.wbkbtv.com. Licensee: Thunder Bay Broadcasting Corp. Ownership: Stephen A. Marks, 88.56%. Population Served: 76,000 Natl. Network: CBS, . Natl. Rep: Millennium Sales & Marketing,. Washington Atty: Cohn & Marks. Wire Svc: UPI News staff: 6; News: 5.5 hrs wkly.
Key Personnel:
Stephen A. Marks. . . . . pres
Mary Compton . . . . gen sls mgr & prom dir
Barb Bowen . . . . rgnl sls mgr
Mark Nowak . . . . chief of engrg

***WCML—** Digital Channel: 24. Digital Hrs: 6:45 AM-midnight 106 kw vis, 15.1 kw aur. ant 1,289t/1,148g TL: N45 08 18 W84 09 45 On air date: 1975. Central Michigan Univ., 1999 E. Campus Dr., Mt. Pleasant, MI, 48859. Phone: (989) 774-3105. Fax: (989) 774-4427.E-mail: schud1ra@cmich.edu Web Site: www.wcmu.org. Licensee: Central Michigan University. Natl. Network: PBS, . Washington Atty: Dow, Lohnes & Albertson.
Key Personnel:
Ed Grant . . . . stn mgr
Rich Schudiske . . . . progmg dir & progmg mgr
Randy Kapenga. . . . . engrg dir & chief of engrg
Satellite of WCMU-TV Mt. Pleasant.

Battle Creek

see Grand Rapids-Kalamazoo-Battle Creek, MI market

Bay City

see Flint-Saginaw-Bay City, MI market

Cadillac

see Traverse City-Cadillac, MI market

Detroit (DMA 11)

WADL— Digital Channel: 39. Digital Hrs: 24 1,243 kw vis, 248 kw aur. ant 630t TL: N42 33 15 W82 53 15 On air date: May 20, 1989. 22590 15 Mile Rd., Clinton Twp, MI, 48035-2814. Phone: (586) 790-3838.

Fax: (586) 790-3841. Web Site: www.wadldetroit.com. Licensee: Adell Broadcasting Corp. Ownership: Adell Broadcasting Corp. (acq 9-3-03). Population Served: 1,800,000 Natl. Rep: Blair Television,.
Key Personnel:
Kevin Adell . . . . CEO & gen sls mgr
Lewis Gibbs . . . . pres
Fredrica Crowe. . . . . gen sls mgr
Jamie Harrington . . . . progmg mgr
Tom Ponsart . . . . chief of engrg
Evelyn Brown . . . . traf mgr

WDIV-TV— Digital Channel: 45. Digital Hrs: 24 100 kw vis, 10 kw aur. ant 1,004t TL: N42 28 58 W83 12 19 On air date: Mar 4, 1947. 550 W. Lafayette Blvd., Detroit, MI, 48226. Phone: (313) 222-0444. Phone: (313) 222-0454. Fax: (313) 222-0592. Web Site: www.clickondetroit.com. Licensee: Post-Newsweek Stations, Michigan Inc. Group Owner: Post-Newsweek Stations Inc. (acq 6-24-78). Population Served: 1,753,000 Natl. Network: NBC, . Natl. Rep: MMT,. Washington Atty: Covington & Burling.
Key Personnel:
Alan Frank . . . . gen mgr
Ted Pearse . . . . sls VP
Neil Goldstein. . . . . news dir
Marcus Williams . . . . chief of engrg

WJBK— Digital Channel: 7. Digital Hrs: 24 100 kw vis, 10 kw aur. ant 1,000t/1,057g TL: N42 27 38 W83 12 47 On air date: Oct 24, 1948. Box 2000, Southfield, MI, 48037. 16550 W. Nine Mile Rd., Southfield, MI 48075. Phone: (248) 557-2000. Fax: (248) 557-6343.E-mail: contact@myfoxdetroit.com Web Site: www.myfoxdetroit.com. Licensee: WJBK License Inc. Group Owner: Fox Television Stations Inc. (acq 1-22-97; grpsl). Population Served: 1,800,000 Natl. Network: Fox, . Wire Svc: Reuters News staff: 140; News: 36 hrs wkly.
Key Personnel:
Jeff Murri . . . . VP & gen mgr
Sheila Bruce. . . . . opns mgr & sls VP
Ann Marie Carlton . . . . natl sls mgr
Terry D'Esposito . . . . mktg dir
Keith Stironek. . . . . prom dir
Connie Davis. . . . . progmg dir & progmg mgr film dir
Dana Hahn. . . . . news dir
Katie Fehr . . . . . pub affrs dir & pub svc dir consumer affrs dir
Tim Redmond . . . . chief of engrg
Kelly Collins. rsch dir
Sue Ayala . . . . traf mgr

WKBD-TV— Digital Channel: 14. Digital Hrs: 24 2,340 kw vis, 209 kw aur. ant 960t/1,053g TL: N42 29 01 W83 18 44 On air date: Jan 10, 1965. 26905 W. 11 Mile Rd., Southfield, MI, 48034. Phone: (248) 355-7000. Fax: (248) 359-7494.E-mail: shows@wkbdtv.com Web Site: www.cw50detroit.com. Licensee: Detroit Television Station WKBD Inc. Group Owner: Viacom Television Stations Group (acq 9-1-93; $105 million;9-13-93). Population Served: 5,521,787 Natl. Network: CW, . Natl. Rep: TeleRep,.
Key Personnel:
Trey Fabacher . . . . VP & gen mgr
Michael Michell . . . . stn mgr
Patrick Donnelly . . . . gen sls mgr
Mike Shippey . . . . natl sls mgr
Pam Shecter . . . . prom mgr
Paul A. Prange . . . . progmg dir
Edward Foxworth. . . . . pub affrs dir
Chuck Davis . . . . engrg dir & chief of engrg

WMYD— Digital Channel: 21.500 kw vis. ant 1,063t/1,055g TL: N42 26 53 W83 10 23 On air date: Sept 15, 1968. 27777 Franklin Rd., Suite 1220, Southfield, MI, 48034. Phone: (248) 355-2020. Fax: (248) 355-0368. Web Site: www.tv20detroit.com. Licensee: WXON License Inc. Group Owner: Granite Broadcasting Corp. (acq 1-31-97; $175 million). Population Served: 4,000,000 Natl. Network: MyNetworkTV, . Washington Atty: Akin, Gump, Strauss, Hauer & Feld.
Key Personnel:
Sarah Norat-Phillips . . . . gen mgr
David Bangura . . . . stn mgr & gen sls mgr
Carolyn Worford . . . . opns dir & opns mgr progmg dir
Ken Frierson. . . . . natl sls mgr
Dan Riley . . . . chief of engrg

WPXD-TV— Digital Channel: 31. Digital Hrs: 24 184 kw vis. ant 1,076t/1,010g TL: N42 22 25 W84 04 10 On air date: Jan 12, 1981. 3975 Varsity Dr., Ann Arbor, MI, 48108. Phone: (734) 973-7900. Fax: (734) 973-7906.E-mail: helenskinner@ionmedia.tv Web Site: www.ionline.tv. Licensee: Paxson Communications License Co. L.L.C. Group Owner: Paxson Communications Corp. (acq 12-11-97; $35 million including LPTV ch). Natl. Network: ION Television, . Washington Atty: Verner, Liipfert, Bernhard, McPherson & Hand.
Key Personnel:
Helen Skinner . . . . opns mgr
Robert Thompson. . . . . pres & chief of engrg

***WTVS—** Analog Channel: 56. Digital Channel: 43. Digital Hrs: 24 600 kw vis. ant 1,043t/1,033g TL: N42 26 52 W83 10 23 On air date: Oct 3, 1955. Riley Broadcast Ctr, 1 Clover Ct, Wixom, MI, 48393. Phone: (313) 873-7200. Fax: (313) 876-8118.E-mail: email@dptv.org Web Site: www.detroitpublictv.org. Licensee: Detroit Educational Television Foundation. Population Served: 4,500,000 Natl. Network: PBS, . Rgnl. Network: CEN. Rgnl. Rep: Rgnl rep: Karole White Washington Atty: Schwartz, Woods & Miller.
Key Personnel:
Daniel Alpert . . . . COO & gen mgr stn mgr
John Wenzel . . . . CFO
Tim Wilson . . . . mktg dir
Dave Devereaux . . . . prom VP
Daniel Gaitens . . . . progmg dir
John O'Donnell . . . . pub affrs dir
Helge Blucher . . . . engrg VP & chief of engrg

WWJ-TV— Digital Channel: 44. Digital Hrs: 24 5000 kw vis, 500 kw aur. ant 1073t/1,059g TL: N42 26 52 W83 10 23 On air date: September 1975. 26905 W. 11-Mile Rd., Southfield, MI, 48034. Phone: (248) 355-7000. Fax: (248) 359-7499.E-mail: shows@wwjtv.com Web Site: www.wwjtv.com. Licensee: CBS Broadcasting Inc. Group Owner: Viacom Television Stations Group (acq 1995; $24 million). Population Served: 4,854,707 Natl. Network: CBS, . Natl. Rep: CBS TV Stations National Sales,. Washington Atty: Hogan & Hartson.
Key Personnel:
Jennifer Purtan. . . . . VP & gen sls mgr sls
Trey Fabacher . . . . VP & gen mgr
Mike Montano . . . . natl sls mgr
Pam Shecter. . . . . prom dir
Paul Prange . . . . progmg dir
Chuck Davis . . . . engrg dir & chief of engrg

WXYZ-TV— Digital Channel: 41. Digital Hrs: 24 316 kw vis, 31.6 kw aur. ant 1,000t/1,073g TL: N42 28 15 W83 15 00 On air date: Oct 9, 1948. 20777 W.10 Mile Rd., Southfield, MI, 48037. Phone: (248) 827-7777. Fax: (248) 827-9444.E-mail: talkback@wxyz.com Web Site: www.detnow.com. Licensee: Channel 7 Detroit Inc. Group Owner: Scripps Howard Broadcasting Co., see Cross-Ownership (acq 1-2-86; grpsl). Population Served: 4,500,000 Natl. Network: ABC, . Natl. Rep: Eagle Television Sales,. Washington Atty: Baker & Hostetler. Wire Svc: Reuters
Key Personnel:
Grace Gilchrist . . . . VP
Robert Silva . . . . gen mgr
Mike Murri . . . . gen sls mgr
Steve Kopicki . . . . natl sls mgr
Mike MacLean . . . . rgnl sls mgr
Marla Drutz. . . . . progmg dir
Andrea Parquet-Taylor. . . . . news dir & traf mgr
Ray Thurber . . . . engrg dir & chief of engrg
Gary Schlaff. . . . . rsch dir

Flint-Saginaw-Bay City, MI (DMA 66)

WAQP— Digital Channel: 48. Digital Hrs: 24 1,000 kw vis, 100 kw aur. ant 1,023t/1,049g TL: N43 13 18 W84 03 14 On air date: Mar 26, 1985. 2865 Trautner Dr., Saginaw, MI, 48604-9483. Phone: (989) 249-5969.E-mail: waqp@tct.tv Licensee: TCT of Michigan Inc. Group Owner: Tri-State Christian Television.
Key Personnel:
Garth W. Coonce . . . . pres
Shane Chaney. . . . . CFO
Tina Coonce . . . . sr VP
Chris Gabriel . . . . gen mgr
John W. Dady . . . . chief of engrg

WBSF— Digital Channel: 46. Digital Hrs: 24 1,600 kw vis. ant 1,004t/1,023g TL: N43 28 26.75 W83 50 44.65 On air date: Sept. 15, 2006. 2225 W. Willard Rd., Clio, MI, 48420-8847. Phone: (810) 687-1000. Phone: (989) 755-0525. Fax: (810) 687-4925.E-mail: mail@nbc25.net Web Site: www.cw46online.com. Licensee: Barrington Bay City License LLC. (acq 4-14-2005; $4.5 million for CP). Population Served: 104,868 Natl. Network: CW, . Natl. Rep: Harrington, Righter & Parsons,. Washington Atty: Covington & Burling LLP. Wire Svc: AP
Key Personnel:
Matt Kreiner . . . . gen mgr
Jon Bengston . . . . opns dir & progmg dir
Becky Butcher . . . . gen sls mgr
Jeff Reinarz . . . . prom mgr
Don Shafer. . . . . news dir
TB D . . . . chief of engrg

***WCMU-TV—** Digital Channel: 26. Digital Hrs: 6 AM-midnight 450 kw vis. ant 981t/941g TL: N43 45 11 W85 12 40 On air date: Mar 29, 1967. Central Michigan Univ., 1999 E. Campus Dr., Mount Pleasant, MI, 48859. Phone: (989) 774-3105. Fax: (989) 774-4427.E-mail: schud1ra@cmich.edu Web Site: www.wcmu.org. Licensee: Central Michigan University. Population Served: 151,000 Natl. Network: PBS, . Washington Atty: Dow, Lohnes & Albertson.
Key Personnel:
Ed Grant . . . . gen mgr & stn mgr
Rick Schudiske . . . . progmg dir

***WDCP-TV—** Analog Channel: 19. Digital Channel: 18. Analog Hrs: 24 1,290 kw vis, 129 kw aur. 459t/493g TL: N43 33 43 W83 58 54 On air date: Oct 12, 1964. Frank N. Andersen Broadcast Center, 1961 Delta Rd., University Center, MI, 48710. Phone: (877) 472-7677. Phone: (989) 686-9362. Fax: (989) 686-0155.E-mail: wdcq@delta.edu Web Site: www.delta.edu/broadcasting. Licensee: Delta College. Population Served: 1,200,000 Natl. Network: PBS, . Washington Atty: Cohn & Marks.
Key Personnel:
Jean Goodnow. . . . . pres
Barry Baker . . . . gen mgr
Tom Bennett . . . . stn mgr
Tom Garnett . . . . chief of engrg

***WDCQ-TV—** Digital Channel: 15. Digital Hrs: 24 85.1 kw vis, 8.51 kw aur. ant 508t/469g TL: N43 41 26 W82 56 29 On air date: Dec 12, 1986. University Ctr., 1961 Delta Rd., University Center, MI, 48710. Phone: (877) 472-7677. Fax: (989) 686-0155.E-mail: wdcq@delta.edu Web Site: www.delta.edu/broadcasting. Licensee: Delta College. Population Served: 1,200,000 Natl. Network: PBS, . Washington Atty: Cohn & Marks.
Key Personnel:
Jean Goodnow. . . . . pres
Barry Baker . . . . gen mgr
Pam Clark . . . . stn mgr
Tom Garnett . . . . chief of engrg

WEYI-TV—(Saginaw, Digital Channel: 30. Digital Hrs: 24 2,040 kw vis, 203 kw aur. ant 1,296t/1,292g TL: N43 13 01 W83 43 17 On air date: Apr 5, 1953. 2225 W. Willard Rd., Clio, MI, 48420. Phone: (810) 687-1000. Phone: (989) 755-0525. Fax: (810) 687-4925.E-mail: mail@nbc25.net Web Site: www.nbc25online.com. Licensee: Barrington Broadcasting Flint Corp. Group Owner: Barrington Broadcasting Corp. (acq 5-14-2004; $24 million). Population Served: 104,868 Natl. Network: NBC, . Natl. Rep: Harrington, Righter & Parsons,. Washington Atty: Covington & Burling LLP. Wire Svc: AP News: 19.5 hrs wkly.
Key Personnel:
Matt Kreiner . . . . gen mgr & opns mgr
Becky Butcher . . . . gen sls mgr
Jeff Reinarz . . . . prom mgr
Jon Bengston . . . . progmg dir & opns
Don Shafer. . . . . news dir
TB D . . . . chief of engrg

***WFUM—** Digital Channel: 28.500 kw vis. ant 846t/30g TL: N42 53 56 W83 27 41 On air date: Aug 23, 1980. Michigan-Television, Univ. of Michigan-Flint, 303 E. Kearsley St., Flint, MI, 48502. Phone: (810) 762-3028. Fax: (810) 233-6017.E-mail: information@michigantelevision.org Web Site: www.michigantelevision.org. Licensee: Board of Regents, University of Michigan. Population Served: 3,485,000 Natl. Network: PBS, . Washington Atty: Dow, Lohnes PLLC.
Key Personnel:
Steve Schram . . . . gen mgr
Jennifer White. . . . . stn mgr
Wayne Henderson. . . . . chief of engrg

WJRT-TV— Digital Channel: 12. Digital Hrs: 24 18.2 kw vis. ant 938t/962g TL: N43 13 49 W84 03 32 On air date: Oct 12, 1958. 2302 Lapeer Rd., Flint, MI, 48503. Phone: (810) 233-3130. Fax: (810) 257-2834.E-mail: wjrt@abc.com Web Site: www.abc12.com. Licensee: Flint License Subsidiary Corp., a wholly owned subsidiary of WJRT Inc. Group Owner: ABC Inc. (acq 1995; $155 million with WTVG(TV) Toledo, OH). Population Served: 828,350 Natl. Network: ABC, . Natl. Rep: ABC National Television Sales,. Wire Svc: ESSA Weather Service Wire Svc: AP News staff: 49; News: 34 hrs wkly.
Key Personnel:
Thomas Bryson . . . . pres & gen mgr
Daniel C. Aube. . . . . gen sls mgr
Cheri Foss . . . . natl sls mgr & rgnl sls mgr
Brock Rice . . . . rgnl sls mgr
Sara Jo Gallock . . . . mktg dir & progmg dir
James Bleicher . . . . news dir

WNEM-TV—(Bay City, Digital Channel: 22.100 kw vis, 20 kw aur. ant 1,029t/1,049g TL: N43 28 13 W83 50 35 On air date: Feb 16, 1954. Box 531, Saginaw, MI, 48606. 107 N. Franklin St., Saginaw, MI 48607. Phone: (989) 755-8191. Fax: (989) 758-2111. Fax: (989) 758-2112.E-mail: wnem@wnem.com Web Site: www.wnem.com. Licensee: Meredith Corp. Group Owner: Meredith Broadcasting Group, Meredith Corp. (acq 4-16-69; $11.5 million;4-21-69). Population Served: 1,251,000 Natl. Network: CBS, MyNetworkTV, . Natl. Rep: TeleRep,. Washington Atty: Haley, Bader & Potts.
Key Personnel:
Al Blinke . . . . VP & gen mgr
Jeff Guilbert . . . . gen sls mgr
Karen Frey . . . . prom dir & progmg dir news dir
Ian Rubin . . . . news dir
Mike Tamme . . . . chief of engrg

WSMH— Digital Channel: 16. Digital Hrs: 24 245 kw vis. ant 1,199t/1,219g TL: N43 13 31 W84 04 33 On air date: Dec 15,1984.

G-3463 W. Pierson Rd., Flint, MI, 48504. Phone: (810) 785-8866. Fax: (810) 785-8963. Web Site: www.wsmh66.com. Licensee: WSMH Licensee L.L.C. Group Owner: Sinclair Broadcast Group Inc. (acq 2-28-96; $33 million). Population Served: 473,700 Natl. Network: Fox, . Natl. Rep: Millennium Sales & Marketing,. News: 7 hrs wkly.

Key Personnel:

John Hummel.	gen mgr
Chad Conklin	gen sls mgr
Pete Glass	chief of engrg

Grand Rapids-Kalamazoo-Battle Creek, MI

(DMA 39)

*WGVK— Digital Channel: 5. Digital Hrs: 18 44.7 kw vis, 4.47 kw aur. ant 410t/295g TL: N42 18 24 W85 39 26 On air date: Oct 1, 1984. 301 W. Fulton St., Grand Rapids, MI, 49504-6492. Phone: (616) 331-6666. Fax: (616) 331-6625.E-mail: wgvu@gvsu.edu Web Site: www.wgvu.org. Licensee: Grand Valley State University. Population Served: 180,000 Natl. Network: PBS, . Washington Atty: Mark Van Bergh. News staff: 15; News: one hr wkly.

Key Personnel:

Michael T. Walenta.	gen mgr
Pamela Holtz	dev mgr & prom mgr
Gary Hunt	sls dir
Carrie Corbin	progmg dir
Fred Martino	news dir
Robert Lumbert.	engrg dir
Ed Spier	traf mgr & sports cmtr
Scott vander Werf	mus critic

Rebroadcasts WGVU-TV Grand Rapids 100%.

*WGVU-TV— Digital Channel: 11. Digital Hrs: 20 1,000 kw vis, 100 kw aur. ant 857t/859g TL: N42 57 35 W85 53 45 On air date: Dec 17, 1972. 301 W. Fulton St., Grand Rapids, MI, 49504-6492. Phone: (616) 331-6666. Fax: (616) 331-6625.E-mail: wgvu@gvsu.edu Web Site: www.wgvu.org. Licensee: Board of Control, Grand Valley State University. Population Served: 638,940 Natl. Network: PBS, . Washington Atty: Mark Van Bergh.

Key Personnel:

Michael Walenta.	gen mgr
Pamela Holtz.	dev mgr & prom mgr
Gary Hunt	sls dir
Carrie Corbin	progmg dir
Bob Lumbert.	engrg dir
Ed Spier	traf mgr
Scott VanderWerf.	mus critic

Rebroadcasts WGVK (TV) Kalamazoo 100%.

WLLA— Digital Channel: 45. Digital Hrs: 24 2,510 kw vis, 65 kw aur. ant 1,046t/339g TL: N42 33 52 W85 27 31 On air date: June 30, 1987. Box 3157, Kalamazoo, MI, 49003. 7048 E. Kilgore Rd., Kalamazoo MI 49003. Phone: (269) 345-6421. Fax: (269) 345-5665.E-mail: deloris@wlla.com Web Site: www.wlla.com. Licensee: Christian Faith Broadcasting Inc. Group Owner: (group owner; (acq 1-13-86; $35,000;12-9-85). Population Served: 2,400,000

Key Personnel:

Richard Hawkins. gen mgr & mktg mgr progmg dir & chief of engrg	

WOOD-TV— Digital Channel: 7. Digital Hrs: 24 316 kw vis, 31.6 kw aur. ant 991t TL: N42 41 13 W85 30 35 On air date: Aug 15, 1949. Box B, Grand Rapids, MI, 49501. 120 College Ave. S.E., Grand Rapids, MI 49503. Phone: (616) 456-8888. Fax: (616) 771-9676.E-mail: woodtv@woodtv.com Web Site: www.woodtv.com. Licensee: Wood License Co. LLC. Group Owner: LIN Television Corporation (acq 6-30-99). Population Served: 1,871,000 Natl. Network: NBC, . Washington Atty: Covington & Burling.

Key Personnel:

Diane Kniowski.	pres & gen mgr stn mgr
Craig Cole.	opns mgr & progmg dir
Brent Denny	gen sls mgr & natl sls mgr
Molly Kelly	mktg mgr & prom mgr
Ethan Beute	adv mgr & rsch dir
Patti McGethgain	news dir
Eva Cooper.	pub affrs dir
Ken Selvig.	engrg dir & chief of engrg

WOTV— Digital Channel: 20. Digital Hrs: 24 5,000 kw vis, 200 kw aur. ant 1,079t/938g TL: N42 34 15 W85 28 07 On air date: July 24, 1971. Box B, Grand Rapids, MI, 49501. 120 College Ave. S.E., Grand Rapids, MI 49503. Phone: (269) 968-9341. Fax: (269) 660-1222.E-mail: wotv@wotv.com Web Site: www.wotv.com. Licensee: Wood License Co. LLC. Group Owner: LIN Television Corporation (acq 12-6-2001; $2.25 million). Population Served: 1,871,000 Natl. Network: ABC, . Washington Atty: Covington & Burling. News staff: 25; News: 13 hrs wkly.

Key Personnel:

Diane Kniowski	pres & gen mgr gen mgr & gen sls mgr
Ann Marie Young	sls dir
Swaina Noble	natl sls mgr
Molly Kelly	mktg mgr
Ethan Beute	prom mgr
Craig Cole	progmg dir
Patti McGethgain	news dir
Dave Morse	chief of engrg

WTLJ— Digital Channel: 24. Digital Hrs: 24 4,395 kw vis, 440 kw aur. ant 1,000t/989g TL: N42 57 25 W85 54 07 On air date: Nov 1, 1986. 10290 48th Ave., Allendale, MI, 49401. Phone: (616) 895-4154. Fax: (616) 892-4401.E-mail: wtlj@tct.tv Web Site: www.tct.tv. Licensee: TCT of Michigan Inc. Group Owner: Tri-State Christian Television (acq 1-15-92; $1.5 million;2-10-92). Population Served: 2,000,000

Key Personnel:

Vic Van Deventer	gen mgr & stn mgr
Vic VanDeventer	mktg mgr & progmg dir
Frank Ayre.	chief of engrg

WWMT— Digital Channel: 8. Digital Hrs: 24 100 kw vis, 20 kw aur. ant 1,000t/1,130g TL: N42 37 56 W85 32 16 On air date: June 1, 1950. 590 W. Maple St., Kalamazoo, MI, 49008. Phone: (269) 388-3333. Fax: (269) 388-8228.E-mail: newschannel3@wwmt.com Web Site: www.wwmt.com. Licensee: Freedom Broadcasting of Michigan Licensee L.L.C. Group Owner: Freedom Communications Inc., Broadcast Division (acq 7-18-98; $170 million with WLAJ(TV) Lansing). Population Served: 1,861,000 Natl. Network: CBS, CW, . Natl. Rep: TeleRep,. Washington Atty: Akin, Gump, Strauss, Hauer & Feld. News: 25 hrs wkly.

Key Personnel:

James Lutton	VP & gen mgr
James Wagner	gen sls mgr
Mark Bishop	mktg dir
Kathy Younkin	news dir
Jim Steffey	chief of engrg

WXMI— Digital Channel: 19. Digital Hrs: 21 1,300 kw vis, 130 kw aur. ant 802t/1,081g TL: N42 41 15 W85 31 57 On air date: March 1982. 3117 Plaza Dr. N.E., Grand Rapids, MI, 49525. Phone: (616) 364-8722. Fax: (616) 364-8506.E-mail: feedback@wxmi.com Web Site: www.wxmi.com. Licensee: Tribune Television Holdings Inc. Group Owner: Tribune Broadcasting Co. (acq 12-20-2007; grpsl). Population Served: 722,900 Natl. Network: Fox, . Natl. Rep: Harrington, Righter & Parsons,. News staff: 30; News: 4 hrs wkly.

Key Personnel:

Patricia Hamilton	VP & gen mgr
Patty Kolb	stn mgr
Jeff Cartwright.	sls dir & progmg dir
Pennie Westers	rgnl sls mgr
Travis Henkaline	prom dir
Mark Krause	progmg dir
Dale Scholten	chief of engrg

WZPX-TV— Digital Channel: 44. Digital Hrs: 24 212 kw vis. ant 1,000t/971g TL: N42 40 45 W85 03 57 On air date: 1996. 2610 Horizon Dr. S.E., Suite E, Grand Rapids, MI, 49546. Phone: (616) 222-4343. Fax: (616) 493-2677. Web Site: www.ionline.tv. Licensee: ION Media Battle Creek License Inc., debtor-in-possession. Group Owner: Paxson Communications Corp. (acq 3-13-00; grpsl). Population Served: 4,500,000 Natl. Network: ION Television, .

Key Personnel:

Tina Hill	stn mgr

WZZM— Digital Channel: 13. Digital Hrs: 24 16.5 kw vis. ant 1,064t/1,025g TL: N43 18 35 W85 54 45 On air date: Nov 1, 1962. Box Z, Grand Rapids, MI, 49501. 645 Three Mile Rd., N.W., Grand Rapids MI 49544. Phone: (616) 785-1313. Fax: (616) 785-1301.E-mail: management@wzzm13.com Web Site: www.wzzm13.com. Licensee: Combined Communications Corp. of Oklahoma Inc. Group Owner: Gannett Broadcasting (acq 1-27-97; grpsl). Population Served: 635,000 Natl. Network: ABC, . Natl. Rep: Blair Television,. News: 26 hrs wkly.

Key Personnel:

Janet Mason.	pres & gen mgr stn mgr
Chuck Mikowski	VP & prom dir
Kim Krause	gen sls mgr
Pam Rankin	mktg mgr & prom mgr
Tim Geraghty	news dir
Catherine Behrendt	progmg

Kalamazoo

see Grand Rapids-Kalamazoo-Battle Creek, MI market

Lansing, MI
(DMA 114)

WHTV— Digital Channel: 34. Digital Hrs: 24 8.91 kw vis. ant 239t TL: N42 14 08 W84 24 00 On air date: 1999. 2820 E. Saginaw St., Lansing, MI, 48912-4240. Phone: (517) 372-9497. Fax: (517) 372-9499.E-mail: info@my18.tv Web Site: www.my18.tv. Licensee: Spartan-TV LLC. Population Served: 250,000 Natl. Network: MyNetworkTV,

Key Personnel:

Lori Harper.	stn mgr & progmg mgr
Corey Cummings	chief of engrg

WILX-TV— Digital Channel: 10. Digital Hrs: 24 309 kw vis, 61.7 kw aur. 970t/983g TL: N42 26 33 W84 34 21 On air date: Mar 15, 1959. 500 American Rd., Lansing, MI, 48911. Phone: (517) 393-0110. Fax: (517) 393-8555.E-mail: news@wilx.com Web Site: www.wilx.com. Licensee: Gray Television Licensee Inc. Group Owner: Gray Television Inc. (acq 8-29-2002; grpsl). Population Served: 592,400 Natl. Network: NBC, . Natl. Rep: Continental Television Sales,. News staff: 45.

Key Personnel:

Mike King	gen mgr
John O'Brien	gen sls mgr
Paul Crockett	rgnl sls mgr
Craig Tucker.	prom mgr
Kevin Ragan	news dir
Gary King	chief of engrg
Lisa Dyck	traf mgr

*WKAR-TV— Analog Channel: 23. Digital Channel: 55.1,100 kw vis, 219 kw aur. 975t/1,038g TL: N42 42 08 W84 24 51 On air date: Jan 15, 1954. 283 Communication Arts Bldg., Michigan State Univ., East Lansing, MI, 48824-1212. Phone: (517) 432-9527. Fax: (517) 353-7124.E-mail: mail@wkar.org Web Site: www.wkar.org. Licensee: Michigan State University. Population Served: 3,000,000 Natl. Network: PBS, . Washington Atty: Schwartz, Woods & Miller.

Key Personnel:

De Anne Hamilton	gen mgr
Cindy Herfindahl	dev dir & film buyer
Jeanie Croope	prom dir & prom mgr
Kent Wieland	stn mgr & progmg dir
Gary Blievernicht	engrg dir

WLAJ— Digital Channel: 51. Digital Hrs: 24 1,660 kw vis, 166 kw aur. ant 976t/1,009g TL: N42 25 31 W84 31 26 (CP: 3,320 kw vis, 332 kw aur, ant 981t/1,014g) On air date: Oct 13, 1990. 5815 S. Pennsylvania Ave., Lansing, MI, 48911-5230. Phone: (517) 394-5300. Fax: (517) 887-0077. Web Site: www.wlaj.com. Licensee: WLAJ License Inc. Group Owner: Freedom Communications Inc., Broadcast Division (acq 6-22-98; $170 million with WWMT(TV) Kalamazoo). Natl. Network: ABC, CW, . News staff: 10; News: 5 hrs wkly.

Key Personnel:

Jim Lutttan	VP
Ross Reardon	pres & gen mgr & rgnl sls mgr
Cathy Younkin	news dir
Gary Williams	chief of engrg

WLNS-TV— Digital Channel: 36.100 kw vis, 20 kw aur. 1,000t/1,023g TL: N42 41 14 W84 22 35 On air date: May 1, 1950. Box 40226, Lansing, MI, 48901. 2820 E. Saginaw St., Lansing, MI 48912. Phone: (517) 372-8282. Fax: (517) 374-7610.E-mail: wlns@wlns.com Web Site: www.wlns.com. Licensee: Young Broadcasting of Lansing Inc. Group Owner: Young Broadcasting Inc. (acq 9-15-86; $72 million; 4-14-86). Population Served: 1,000,000 Natl. Network: CBS, . Washington Atty: Wiley, Rein & Fielding.

Key Personnel:

Clay Koenig	gen mgr & gen sls mgr
Doug Powers	stn mgr
Gene Shanahan	opns mgr
Teresa Morton	progmg dir
Phil Hendrix	news dir
Cory Cumming	chief of engrg

WSYM-TV— Analog Channel: 47. Digital Channel: 38. Analog Hrs: 24 Digital Hrs: 24 1,350 kw vis, 135 kw aur. 1,000t/1,036g TL: N42 28 03 W84 39 06 On air date: Dec 1, 1982. 600 W. St. Joseph St., Suite 47, Lansing, MI, 48933. Phone: (517) 484-7747. Fax: (517) 484-3144.E-mail: fox47news@fox47news.com Web Site: www.fox47news.com. Licensee: Journal Broadcast Corp. Group Owner: Journal Broadcast Group Inc. (acq 11-9-85; 12-3-84). Natl. Network: Fox, . Natl. Rep: Harrington, Righter & Parsons,. Washington Atty: Crowell & Moring. News staff: 22; News: 10 hrs wkly.

Key Personnel:

Gary Baxter	VP & gen mgr
Jami Anderson	natl sls mgr
Kip Bohne	mktg mgr & prom mgr

Marquette, MI
(DMA 180)

WBKP— Digital Channel: 5. Digital Hrs: 24 100 kw vis. ant 968t TL: N47 02 11 W88 41 43 On air date: Oct 30, 1996. 2025 U.S. 41 W., Marquette, MI, 49855. Phone: (906) 225-5700. Fax: (906) 225-5598.E-mail: 510@lscbc.com Licensee: Lake Superior Community Broadcasting

Corp. Group Owner: (group owner; (acq 1-15-2004; $500,000 with WBUP(TV) Ishpeming). Natl. Network: CW, . News staff: 7; News: 10 hrs wkly.
Key Personnel:
Ken Lindeman . . . chmn & stn mgr
Bob McDonald . . . gen sls mgr
Randy Carlisle . . . prom mgr
Steve Marks . . . progmg mgr
Gerry Heyn . . . chief of engrg

WBUP— Digital Channel: 10.133 kw vis. ant 344t/310g TL: N46 21 10 W87 51 15 On air date: Jan 30, 2003. 2025 US 41 W., Marquette, MI, 49855. Phone: (906) 225-5700. Fax: (906) 225-5598.E-mail: 510@lscbc.com Web Site: www.wbuptv.com. Licensee: Lake Superior Community Broadcasting Corp. Group Owner: (group owner; (acq 1-15-2004; $500,000 with WBKP(TV) Calumet). Natl. Network: ABC, . Washington Atty: Latham and Watkins.
Key Personnel:
Ken Lindeman . . . stn mgr
Bob McDonald . . . gen sls mgr
Randy Carlisle . . . prom mgr
Gerry Heyn . . . chief of engrg

WDHS— Digital Channel: 8. Digital Hrs: 24 2 kw vis, 200 w aur. 508t TL: N45 49 14 W88 02 39 (CP: 30.2 kw, ant 623t) On air date: September 1986. 1500 W. B St., Iron Mountain, MI, 49801-8888. Phone: (906) 776-8888. Fax: (906) 776-8888. Licensee: W. Russell Withers Jr. Group Owner: Withers Broadcasting Co. Population Served: 200,000
Key Personnel:
Sue Quadrani . . . gen mgr

WJMN-TV— Digital Channel: 48. Digital Hrs: 24 100 kw vis, 20 kw aur. 1,192t/1,048g TL: N48 06 04 W86 56 52 On air date: Oct 7, 1969. Box 19055, Green Bay, WI, 54307. Phone: (920) 437-5411. Phone: (906) 226-3023 (sales). Fax: (920) 437-5769 (news). Licensee: WFRV and WJMN Television Station Inc. Group Owner: Viacom Television Stations Group. (acq 4-16-2007; with WFRV-TV Green Bay, WI). Population Served: 300,000 Natl. Network: CBS, . Natl. Rep: TeleRep,.
Key Personnel:
R. Perry Kidder . . . pres & VP gen mgr
Dale Mitchell . . . opns dir & engrg dir
Jackie Stewart . . . sls dir
Mike Smith . . . natl sls mgr
Kit Overlock . . . rgnl sls mgr
Kristen Kent . . . mktg mgr & pub affrs dir pub svc dir
Monica Zegers . . . prom dir & adv mgr
Jay Schabow . . . progmg mgr
H. Lee Hitter . . . news dir
Jill Harkoff . . . traf mgr
Erin Davisson . . . news cmtr
Mike Austin . . . farm dir
Larry McCarren . . . sports cmtr
Tom Mahoney . . . weather dir
Satellite of WFRV-TV Green Bay, WI.

WLUC-TV— Digital Channel: 35. Digital Hrs: 21 100 kw vis, 20 kw aur. ant 978t/1,018g TL: N46 20 11 W87 50 55 On air date: Apr 29, 1956. 177 U.S. Hwy. 41 East, Negaunee, MI, 49866. Phone: (906) 475-4161. Fax: (906) 475-4824.E-mail: tv6@wluctv6.com Web Site: www.uppermichiganssource.com. Licensee: Barrington Marquette License LLC. Group Owner: Raycom Media Inc. (acq 8-11-2006; grpsl). Population Served: 292,600 Natl. Network: NBC, Fox, . Natl. Rep: Harrington, Righter & Parsons,. Washington Atty: Covington & Burling. Wire Svc: AP News staff: 22; News: 16 hrs wkly.
Key Personnel:
Dan DiLoreto . . . natl sls mgr
Loraine Koski . . . progmg dir
Brian Cabell . . . news dir
Sonny Reschka . . . opns mgr & chief of engrg

***WNMU—** Digital Channel: 13. Digital Hrs: 18 15.4 kw vis. ant 1,060t/1,026g TL: N46 21 10.2 W87 51 14.5 On air date: Dec 28, 1972. Northern Michigan Univ., 1401 Presque Isle Ave., Marquette, MI, 49855-5301. Phone: (906) 227-9668. Fax: (906) 227-2905.E-mail: tv13@nmu.edu Web Site: www.nmu.edu/wnmutv. Licensee: Board of Control of Northern Michigan University. Population Served: 250,000 Natl. Network: PBS, . Washington Atty: Cohn & Marks. Wire Svc: UPI News: one hr wkly.
Key Personnel:
Eric Smith . . . gen mgr
Bruce Turner . . . stn mgr

WZMQ— Digital Channel: 19.41.6 kw vis. ant 813t/499g TL: N46 36 14 W87 37 15 On air date: 2003. 3148 Mid Valley Dr., De Pere, WI, 54115. Phone: (920) 532-9483.E-mail: gm@wzmqtv.com Web Site: www.wzmqtv.com. Licensee: MMMRC LLC.. Ownership: Paul B. Belschner, 33.3%; Scott R. Smet, 33.3%; and Chad L. Smet, 33.3% Group Owner: Equity Broadcasting Corp. (acq 6-22-2009; $100,000 and assumption of assumed liabilities). Natl. Network: MyNetworkTV, .

Saginaw

see Flint-Saginaw-Bay City, MI market

Traverse City-Cadillac, MI (DMA 117)

***WCMV—** Digital Channel: 17.274.2 kw vis, 27.42 kw aur. 587t/303g TL: N44 08 22 W85 20 28 On air date: Sept 7, 1984. Central Michigan Univ., 1999 E. Campus Dr., Mt. Pleasant, MI, 48859. Phone: (989) 774-3105. Fax: (989) 774-4427.E-mail: schud1r@cmich.edu Web Site: www.wcmu.org. Licensee: Central Michigan University. Natl. Network: PBS, . Washington Atty: Dow, Lohnes & Albertson.
Key Personnel:
Edwards Grant . . . gen mgr & stn mgr
Rick Schudiske . . . progmg dir
Rebroadcasts WCMU(TV) Mt. Pleasant 100%.

***WCMW—** Digital Channel: 21.50 kw vis. ant 305t/277g TL: N44 03 57 W86 19 58 On air date: Sept 7, 1984. Central Michigan Univ., 1999 E. Campus Dr., Mt. Pleasant, MI, 48859. Phone: (989) 774-3105. Fax: (989) 774-4427.E-mail: schud1ra@cmich.edu Web Site: www.wcmu.org. Licensee: Central Michigan University. Natl. Network: PBS, . Washington Atty: Dow, Lohnes & Albertson.
Key Personnel:
Ed Grant . . . stn mgr
Rick Schudiske . . . progmg dir
Satellite of WCMU-TV Mt. Pleasant.

WFQX-TV— Digital Channel: 32. Digital Hrs: 24 776 kw vis, 77.6 kw aur. ant 1,023t/650g TL: N44 08 53 W85 20 45 On air date: Oct 12, 1989. 7669 S. 45 Rd., Cadillac, MI, 49601. Phone: (231) 775-9813. Fax: (231) 775-1898.E-mail: info@fox33.com Web Site: www.fox33.com. Licensee: Cadillac Telecasting Co. Group Owner: Rockfleet Broadcasting Inc. (acq 10-31-2007; $11 million with WFUP(TV) Vanderbilt). Population Served: 188,120 Natl. Network: Fox, . Washington Atty: Womble, Carlyle, Sandridge & Rice PLLC. News: 3 hrs wkly.
Key Personnel:
Bruce Pfeiffer . . . gen mgr & sls VP
Ginny Buzzell . . . prom VP & prom mgr
Greg Buzzell . . . opns VP & engrg VP & chief of engrg

WFUP— Digital Channel: 45. Digital Hrs: 24 851 kw vis, 85.1 kw aur. ant 1,063t/2,168g TL: N45 10 12 W84 45 04 On air date: Sept 24, 1992. 7669 S. 45 Rd., Cadillac, MI, 49601. Phone: (231) 775-9813. Fax: (231) 775-1898.E-mail: info@fox33.com Web Site: www.fox33.com. Licensee: Cadillac Telecasting Co. Group Owner: Rockfleet Broadcasting Inc. (acq 10-31-2007; $11 million with WFQX-TV Cadillac). Population Served: 142,291 Natl. Network: Fox, . Washington Atty: Womble, Carlyle, Sandridge & Rice PLLC. News staff: 5; News: 3 hrs wkly.
Key Personnel:
Bruce Pfeiffer . . . gen mgr & sls VP natl sls mgr
Greg Buzzell . . . opns VP & opns mgr engrg VP
Julia Horchner . . . opns mgr & progmg dir
Ginny Buzzell . . . prom VP & prom mgr
Quentin Parker . . . news dir & chief of engrg
Satellite of WFQX-TV Cadillac.

WGTQ— Digital Channel: 8.316 kw vis, 163.6 kw aur. 978t/864g TL: N46 03 06 W84 06 40 On air date: Nov 3, 1976. 8513 M-72 West, Traverse City, MI, 49684-5562. Phone: (231) 946-2900. Fax: (231) 946-0945.E-mail: wgtu@wgtu.com Web Site: www.wgtu.com. Licensee: Tucker Broadcasting of Traverse City Inc. Group Owner: MAX Media L.L.C. (acq 4-1-2008; $10 million with WGTU(TV) Traverse City). Natl. Network: ABC, . Washington Atty: Pillsbury Winthrop Shaw Pittman LLP.
Key Personnel:
Jill Saarela . . . gen mgr
Betsy Bard . . . gen sls mgr
Craig Toomey . . . rgnl sls mgr
Greg Johnson . . . prom mgr
Lynne Bennett . . . progmg mgr & traf mgr
Mike Miller . . . chief of engrg
Satellite of WGTU(TV) Traverse City, rebroadcast 100%.

WGTU— Digital Channel: 29. Digital Hrs: 24 1,303 kw vis. ant 1,289t/1,216g TL: N44 44 53 W85 04 08 On air date: Aug 23, 1971. 8513 M-72 West, Traverse City, MI, 49684-5562. Phone: (231) 946-2900. Fax: (231) 946-0945.E-mail: wgtu@wgtu.com Web Site: www.wgtu.com. Licensee: Tucker Broadcasting of Traverse City Inc. Group Owner: MAX Media L.L.C. (acq 4-1-2008; $10 million with WGTQ(TV) Sault Ste. Marie). Population Served: 400,000 Natl. Network: ABC, . Washington Atty: Pillsbury Winthrop Shaw Pittman LLP.
Key Personnel:
Jill Saarela . . . gen mgr
Betsy Bard . . . gen sls mgr
Craig Toomey . . . rgnl sls mgr
Greg Johnson . . . prom mgr
Lynne Bennett . . . progmg mgr & traf mgr
Mike Miller . . . opns mgr & chief of engrg

WPBN-TV— Digital Channel: 7. Digital Hrs: 24 316 kw vis, 63.2 kw aur. ant 1,348t/1,130g TL: N44 16 33 W85 42 49 On air date: Sept 13, 1954. 8513 M-72 West, Traverse City, MI 49684-5562. Phone: (231) 947-7770. Fax: (231) 947-0354. Fax: (231) 947-1229.E-mail: tv7-4@tv7-4.com Web Site: www.tv7-4.com. Licensee: Barringtron Traverse City License LLC. Group Owner: Raycom Media Inc. (acq 8-11-2006; grpsl). Population Served: 300,000 Natl. Network: NBC, . Natl. Rep: Harrington, Righter & Parsons,. Washington Atty: Covington & Burling.
Key Personnel:
Jill Saarela . . . gen mgr
Kim St. Mary . . . mktg mgr
Mary Speck . . . progmg mgr
Doug DeYoung . . . news dir
Mike Miller . . . chief of engrg

WTOM-TV— Digital Channel: 35. Digital Hrs: 24 100 kw vis, 20 kw aur. ant 620t/590g TL: N45 39 01 W84 20 37 On air date: May 16, 1959. 8513 M-72 West, Traverse City, MI, 49684-5562. Phone: (231) 947-7770. Fax: (231) 947-1229. Fax: (231) 947-0354.E-mail: tv7-4@tv7-4.com Web Site: www.tv7-4.com. Licensee: Barrington Traverse City License LLC. Group Owner: Raycom Media Inc. (acq 8-11-2006; grpsl). Natl. Network: NBC, . Washington Atty: Covington & Burling.
Key Personnel:
Jill Saarela . . . gen mgr
Kim St. Mary . . . mktg mgr
Mary Speck . . . progmg mgr
Doug DeYoung . . . news dir
Mike Miller . . . chief of engrg
Satellite of WPBN-TV Traverse City.

WWTV— Digital Channel: 9. Digital Hrs: 24 316 kw vis, 63.1 kw aur. 1,635t/1,295g TL: N44 08 12 W85 20 33 On air date: Dec 11, 1953. Box 627, Cadillac, MI, 49601. Phone: (231) 775-3478. Fax: (231) 775-3671.E-mail: info@9and10news.com Web Site: www.9and10news.com. Licensee: Heritage Broadcasting Co. of Michigan.. Ownership: . (acq 3-3-89; grpsl;3-20-89). Population Served: 300,000 Natl. Network: CBS, . Washington Atty: Wamble Carlyle. Wire Svc: UPI
Key Personnel:
William Kring . . . CFO & gen mgr
John DeMarsh . . . sls VP & gen sls mgr
Tessia Klix . . . prom mgr
Sherri Magiera . . . progmg dir
Kevin Dunaway . . . news dir
Lowell Shore . . . chief of engrg
Satellite of WWUP-TV Sault Ste. Marie.

WWUP-TV— Digital Channel: 10.316 kw vis, 31.6 kw aur. ant 1,214t/1,092g TL: N46 03 36 W84 05 57 On air date: June 15, 1962. Box 627, Cadillac, MI, 49601. Phone: (231) 775-3478. Fax: (231) 775-3671.E-mail: info@9and10news.com Web Site: www.9and10news.com. Licensee: Heritage Broadcasting Co. of Michigan. (acq 3-3-89; grpsl;3-20-89). Natl. Network: CBS, . Washington Atty: Wamble Carlyle.
Key Personnel:
William Kring . . . gen mgr
John DeMarsh . . . gen sls mgr
Tessia Klix . . . prom mgr
Sherri Magiera . . . progmg dir
Kevin Dunaway . . . news dir
Lowell Shore . . . chief of engrg

Minnesota

Austin

see Rochester, MN-Mason City, IA-Austin, MN market

Crookston

see Fargo-Valley City, ND market

Duluth, MN-Superior, WI (DMA 139)

KBJR-TV—(Superior, WI) Digital Channel: 19.100 kw vis, 20 kw aur. ant 1,010t/804g TL: N46 47 21 W92 06 51 On air date: Mar 11, 1954. 246 S. Lake Ave., Duluth, MN, 55802-2304. Phone: (218) 720-9600.

Fax: (218) 720-9699.E-mail: news6@kbjr.com Web Site: www.northlandnewscenter.com. Licensee: KBJR License Inc. Group Owner: Granite Broadcasting Corp. (acq 11-1-88; $12.8 million; 9-23-74). Population Served: 325,000 Natl. Network: NBC, MyNetworkTV, . Washington Atty: Akin, Gump, Strauss, Hauer & Feld. News staff: 80; News: 10 hrs wkly.

Key Personnel:

Robert Wilmers	gen mgr
David Jensch	stn mgr

KCWV— Digital Channel: 27.63 kw vis. ant 751t/520g TL: N46 47 30 W92 07 21 Not on air, target date: unknown: 275 Goodwyn, Memphis, TN, 38111. Phone: (901) 375-9324. Permittee: George S. Flinn III.

Key Personnel:

George S. Flinn III	gen mgr

KDLH— Digital Channel: 33. Digital Hrs: 5:30 AM-2 AM 100 kw vis, 20 kw aur. ant 990t/816g TL: N46 47 07 W92 07 15 On air date: Mar 14, 1954. 246 S. Lake Ave., Duluth, MN, 55802. Phone: (218) 733-0303. Fax: (218) 727-7515. Web Site: www.kdlh.com. Licensee: Malara Broadcast Group of Duluth Licensee LLC. Group Owner: New Vision Group LLC (acq 3-14-2005; $10.8 million). Population Served: 203,100 Natl. Network: CBS, CW, . Natl. Rep: Harrington, Righter & Parsons,. Washington Atty: Wolf Bloch. News staff: 17; News: 12 hrs wkly.

Key Personnel:

Anthony J Malara	pres
Kelli Latuska	gen mgr & pub svc dir
Carl Keller	sls dir & natl sls mgr
Nate Stoltman	mktg dir & mktg mgr prom mgr
Jeff Reinarz	adv dir
Barb Wentworth	progmg dir
Derrick Hinds	news dir
Larry Erickson	engrg dir
Mary Rhodes	traf mgr
Jason Kuss	sports cmtr
Phil Johnson	weather dir

KQDS-TV— Digital Channel: 17. Digital Hrs: 18 955 kw vis. ant 590t TL: N46 47 41 W92 07 05 On air date: November 1994. 2001 London Rd., Duluth, MN, 55812. Phone: (218) 728-1622. Fax: (218) 728-1557.E-mail: dhileman@kqdsfox21.tv Licensee: KQDS Acquisition Corp. Group Owner: Red River Broadcast Co. LLC (acq 10-21-98; grpsl). Population Served: 172,000 HH Natl. Network: Fox, . Natl. Rep: Harrington, Righter & Parsons,. News staff: 20; News: 2.5 hrs wkly.

Key Personnel:

Ro Grignon	pres
Kathy Lau	VP & opns dir
Dave Hileman	gen mgr & gen sls mgr natl sls mgr
Julie Moravchik	news dir

KRII— Digital Channel: 11.63 kw vis. ant 657t/607g TL: N47 51 39 W92 56 46 On air date: Nov 27, 2002. 246 South Lake Ave., Duluth, MN, 55802-2304. Phone: (218) 720-9600. Fax: (218) 720-9660.E-mail: news6@kbjr.com Web Site: www.news6.tv. Licensee: Channel 11 License Inc. Group Owner: Granite Broadcasting Corp. (acq 5-9-2001; grpsl). Population Served: 70,000 Natl. Network: NBC, .

Key Personnel:

David Jensch	stn mgr
Vincent Nelson	sls dir
Chris Hussey	prom mgr
Barb Wentworth	progmg mgr
Derrick Hinds	news dir
Larry Erickson	engrg dir

Satellite of KBJR-TV Superior, WI.

WDIO-DT— Digital Channel: 10. Digital Hrs: 24 316 kw vis, 105 kw aur. ant 987t/836g TL: N46 47 13 W92 07 17 On air date: Jan 24, 1966. Box 16897, Duluth, MN, 55816-0897. 10 Observation Rd., Duluth, MN 55811-3506. Phone: (218) 727-6864. Fax: (218) 727-4415.E-mail: news@wdio.com Web Site: www.wdio.com. Licensee: WDIO-TV L.L.C. Group Owner: Hubbard Broadcasting Inc. (acq 12-87; grpsl). Population Served: 176,000 Natl. Network: ABC, . Washington Atty: Fletcher, Heald & Hildreth. News staff: 18; News: 9 hrs wkly.

Key Personnel:

George Couture	gen mgr
Deb Messer	sls dir
Jeff Laumdergan	natl sls mgr
Jeff Laumdergan	prom dir
Dave Poirer	progmg dir
Steve Goodspeed	news dir
Mike Hatlestad	chief of engrg

*WDSE— Digital Channel: 8.316 kw vis, 31.6 kw aur. ant 950t/788g TL: N46 47 31 W92 07 21 On air date: Sept 1, 1964. 632 Niagara Ct., Duluth, MN, 55811-3098. Phone: (218) 724-8567. Fax: (218) 724-4269.E-mail: email@wdse.org Web Site: www.wdse.org. Licensee: Duluth-Superior Area Educ TV Corp. Population Served: 151,000 Natl. Network: PBS, . Washington Atty: Arnold & Porter.

Key Personnel:

Allen Harmon	gen mgr
Cheryl Leeper	gen sls mgr
Beth Lyden	prom mgr
Ron Anderson	progmg mgr
Rex Greenwell	chief of engrg

WIRT-DT— Digital Channel: 13.125 kw vis, 21.6 kw aur. ant 670t/476g TL: N47 22 52 W92 57 18 On air date: Sept 1, 1967. Box 16897, Duluth, MN, 55816-0897. 10 Observation Rd., Duluth, MN 55811-3506. Phone: (218) 727-6864. Fax: (218) 727-4415.E-mail: news@wdio.com Web Site: www.wdio.com. Licensee: WDIO-TV L.L.C. Group Owner: Hubbard Broadcasting Inc. (acq 12-87; grpsl). Natl. Network: ABC, .

Key Personnel:

George Couture	VP & gen mgr
Deb Messer	sls dir
Jeff Laumdergan	natl sls mgr & prom dir
Dave Poirer	progmg dir
Steve Goodspeed	news dir
Mike Hatlestad	chief of engrg

Satellite of WDIO-TV Duluth.

Mankato, MN
(DMA 199)

KEYC-TV— Digital Channel: 12. Digital Hrs: 5 AM-1 AM 15.2 kw vis. ant 1,040t/1,055g TL: N43 56 14 W94 24 41 On air date: Oct 5, 1960. Box 128, Mankato, MN, 56002. 1570 Lookout Dr., N. Mankato, MN 56003. Phone: (507) 625-7905. Fax: (507) 625-5745.E-mail: keyc@keyc.com Web Site: www.keyc.tv. Licensee: United Communications Corp. Group Owner: (group owner; acq 10-14-77; $5 million). Population Served: 352,000 Natl. Network: CBS, Fox, . Natl. Rep: Continental Television Sales,. Washington Atty: Wood, Maines & Nolan. Wire Svc: AP Wire Svc: CBS Wire Svc: NWS (National Weather Service) News staff: 19; News: 13 hrs wkly.

Key Personnel:

Dennis M. Wahlstrom	VP & gen mgr natl sls mgr
Sharon Freitag	opns mgr
John Ginther	rgnl sls mgr
Jan Ellanson	prom mgr & progmg dir progmg mgr
Terry Rudenick	chief of engrg
Sue Briggs	traf mgr
Jane Kolars	pub svc dir
Dan Ruiter	news cmtr
Lynn Ketelsen	farm dir
Perry Dyke	sports cmtr
Mark Tarello	weather dir

Minneapolis-St. Paul, MN
(DMA 15)

KARE—(Minneapolis, Digital Channel: 11.316 kw vis, 31.6 kw aur. 1,440t/1,375g TL: N45 03 44 W93 08 21 On air date: Sept 1, 1953. 8811 Olson Memorial Hwy., Minneapolis, MN, 55427. Phone: (763) 546-1111. Fax: (763) 546-8590. Web Site: www.kare11.com. Licensee: Multimedia Holdings Corp. Group Owner: Gannett Broadcasting (division of Gannett Co. Inc.) (acq 4-13-83; $75 million;5-7-83). Population Served: 2,500,000 Natl. Network: NBC, ,

Key Personnel:

John Remes	pres & gen mgr
Tom Lindner	news dir
Jeff Phillips	chief of engrg

*KAWB— Digital Channel: 28. Digital Hrs: 24 214 kw vis. 745t/677g TL: N46 25 21 W94 27 41 On air date: Mar 1, 1988. 1500 Birchmont Dr. NE #9, Bemidji, MN, 56601-2600. Phone: (218) 751-3407. Fax: (218) 751-3142.E-mail: viewerservices@lakelandptv.org Web Site: www.lakelandptv.org. Licensee: Northern Minnesota Public TV Inc. Ownership: Community Population Served: 160,000 Natl. Network: PBS, . Washington Atty: Dow, Lohnes PLLC. News: 2.5 hrs wkly.

Key Personnel:

Rollin Buck	pres
Bill Sanford	gen mgr
Dan Hegstad	stn mgr
Jess Skala	opns mgr
Sharon Pugh	dev dir & dev mgr

*KAWE— Digital Channel: 9. Digital Hrs: 24 316 kw vis, 31.6 kw aur. 1,080t/1,000g TL: N47 42 03 W94 29 15 On air date: June 1, 1980. 1500 Birchmont Dr. NE #9, Bemidji, MN, 56601-2699. Phone: (218) 751-3407. Fax: (218) 751-3142.E-mail: viewerservices@lakelandptv.org Web Site: www.lakelandptv.org. Licensee: Northern Minnesota Public TV Inc. Ownership: Community Population Served: 165,000 Natl. Network: PBS, . Washington Atty: Dow, Lohnes PLLC. News staff: 7; News: 2.5 hrs wkly.

Key Personnel:

Rollin Buck	pres
Bill Sanford	gen mgr
Jess Skala	opns mgr
Sharon Pugh	dev dir & dev mgr

KCCO-TV— Digital Channel: 7.316 kw vis, 63.1 kw aur. 1,120t/1,133g TL: N45 41 03 W95 08 14 On air date: Oct 8, 1958. 90 S. 11th St., Minneapolis, MN, 55403. Phone: (612) 339-4444. Fax: (612) 330-2627.E-mail: wcconewstips@wcco.com Web Site: www.wcco.com. Licensee: CBS Broadcasting Inc. Group Owner: Viacom Television Stations Group. Population Served: 150,000 Natl. Network: CBS, . Natl. Rep: TeleRep,. Washington Atty: Rosenman & Colin. Wire Svc: NOAA Weather

Key Personnel:

Susan Adams Loyd	progmg dir & VP gen mgr & stn mgr
Kevin Argall	gen sls mgr
Scott Libin	news dir
Gary Kroger	engrg dir

KCCW-TV— Digital Channel: 12.316 kw vis, 63.1 kw aur. 930t/999g TL: N46 56 03 W94 27 25 On air date: Jan 1, 1964. 90 S. 11th St., Minneapolis, MN, 55403. Phone: (612) 339-4444. Fax: (612) 330-2627. Web Site: www.wcco.com. Licensee: CBS Broadcasting Inc. Group Owner: Viacom Television Stations Group. Population Served: 150,000 Natl. Network: CBS, . Washington Atty: Rosenman & Colin.

Key Personnel:

Susan Adams Loyd	progmg dir & VP gen mgr & stn mgr
Kevin Argall	gen sls mgr
Scott Libin	news dir
Gary Kroger	engrg dir

KFTC— Digital Channel: 26. Digital Hrs: 24 5,000 kw vis. 354t TL: N47 22 18 W94 52 56 Not on air, target date: 2000: 11358 Viking Dr., Eden Prairie, MN, 55344. Phone: (952) 944-9999. Fax: (952) 942-0286.E-mail: fox9news@foxtv.com Web Site: www.my29tv.com. Licensee: Fox Television Stations Inc. Group Owner: (group owner; (acq 9-21-2001; grpsl). Natl. Network: MyNetworkTV, .

Key Personnel:

Carol Rueppel	gen mgr
Bill Dallman	news dir
Marc Majeres	chief of engrg

Satellite of WFTC Minneapolis.

KMSP-TV—(Minneapolis, Digital Channel: 9. Digital Hrs: 24 316 kw vis, 31.6 kw aur. 1,427t/1,430g TL: N44 51 32 W93 25 09 On air date: Jan 9, 1955. 11358 Viking Dr., Eden Prairie, MN, 55344-7258. Phone: (952) 944-9999. Fax: (952) 942-0286.E-mail: fox9news@foxtv.com Web Site: www.myfox9.com. Licensee: Fox Television Stations Inc. Group Owner: (group owner; (acq 7-31-2001; grpsl). Population Served: 1,100,000 Natl. Network: Fox, . Wire Svc: AP News staff: 64; News: 19.5 hrs wkly.

Key Personnel:

Carol Rueppel	gen mgr
Bill Dallman	news dir
Marc Majeres	chief of engrg

KPXM-TV— Digital Channel: 40. Digital Hrs: 24 1,000 kw vis. ant 1,420t/1,335g TL: N45 03 44 W93 08 21 On air date: Nov 24, 1982. 22601 176th St. NW, Big Lake, MN, 55309. Phone: (763) 263-8666. Fax: (763) 263-6600. Web Site: www.ionline.tv. Licensee: ION Media Minneapolis License Inc., debtor in possession. Group Owner: Paxson Communications Corp. (acq 10-1-96; $12 million). Population Served: 1,100,000 Natl. Network: ION Television, . Washington Atty: Mullin, Rhyne, Emmons & Topel.

Key Personnel:

Robert Getze	rgnl sls mgr
Joe Brunke	chief of engrg
Corey Ziegler	traf mgr

KRWF— Digital Channel: 27. Digital Hrs: 24 1,230 kw vis, 123 kw aur. 548t/536g TL: N44 29 03 W95 29 27 On air date: Apr 14, 1987. Box 189, Alexandria, MN, 56308. 415 Fillmore St. , Alexandria MN 56308. Phone: (320) 763-5729. Fax: (320) 763-4627.E-mail: ksax@ksax.com Web Site: ksax.com. Licensee: KSAX-TV Inc. Group Owner: Hubbard Broadcasting Inc. Natl. Network: ABC, . Washington Atty: Holland & Knight.

Key Personnel:

Robert Hubbard	gen mgr
Edward Smith	stn mgr & gen sls mgr
Larry Eckblad	chief of engrg

KSAX— Digital Channel: 42. Digital Hrs: 24 2,770 kw vis, 277 kw aur. 1,176t/1,164g TL: N45 41 59 W95 10 36 On air date: Sept 15, 1987. Box 189, Worcester, MN, 56308. 415 Fillmore St. , Alexandria, MN 56308. Phone: (320) 763-5729. Fax: (320) 763-4627.E-mail: ksax@ksax.com Web Site: www.ksax.com. Licensee: KSAX-TV Inc. Group Owner: Hubbard Broadcasting Inc. Natl. Network: ABC, . Natl. Rep: Petry Television Inc.,. Washington Atty: Holland & Knight. Wire Svc: AP

Key Personnel:
Robert Hubbard . . . . . gen mgr
Edward Smith . . . . . stn mgr & gen sls mgr
Larry Eckblad . . . . . chief of engrg

KSTC-TV—(Minneapolis, Digital Channel: 45. Digital Hrs: 24 1,000 kw vis. ant 1,404t/1,316g TL: N45 03 45 W93 08 21 On air date: 1995. 3415 University Ave., St. Paul, MN, 55114-2099. Phone: (651) 645-4500. Fax: (651) 523-7320. Web Site: www.kstc45.com. Licensee: KSTC.TV LLC. Group Owner: Hubbard Broadcasting Inc. (acq 4-24-2000). Population Served: 3,100,000 Washington Atty: Holland & Knight LLP.
Key Personnel:
Susan Wenz . . . . . gen mgr
Andy Stavast . . . . . gen sls mgr
Joe Johnston . . . . . mktg mgr
Michael E. Smith . . . . . progmg dir & progmg mgr
Christopher Berg . . . . . news dir
Dick Rice . . . . . chief of engrg

KSTP-TV—(Saint Paul, Digital Channel: 35. Digital Hrs: 24 100 kw vis, 15.1 kw aur. 1,430t/1,375g TL: N45 03 45 W93 08 22 On air date: Apr 23, 1948. 3415 University Ave., Saint Paul, MN, 55114. Phone: (651) 646-5555. Fax: (651) 642-4172. Web Site: www.kstp.com. Licensee: KSTP-TV LLC. Group Owner: Hubbard Broadcasting Inc. Natl. Network: ABC, . Natl. Rep: Petry Television Inc.,. Washington Atty: Holland and Knight. Wire Svc: AP News: 27.5 hrs wkly.
Key Personnel:
Robert Hubbard . . . . . pres & gen mgr & stn mgr
Monica Doyle . . . . . opns mgr
John McCormick . . . . . gen sls mgr
Andrea Creech . . . . . mktg mgr
Michael Smith . . . . . progmg dir & progmg mgr
Lindsay Radford . . . . . news dir
Dick Rice . . . . . chief of engrg

***KTCA-TV—**(Saint Paul, Digital Channel: 34. Digital Hrs: 24 100 kw vis, 20 kw aur. 1,336t/1,372g TL: N45 03 30 W93 07 27 On air date: Sept 3, 1957. 172 E. 4th St., St. Paul, MN, 55101. Phone: (651) 222-1717. Fax: (651) 229-1282.E-mail: viewerservices@tpt.org Web Site: www.tpt.org. Licensee: Twin Cities Public TV Inc. Population Served: 1,400,000 Natl. Network: PBS, .
Key Personnel:
Jim Pagliarini . . . . . CEO
Dan Thomas . . . . . COO & progmg dir
Jim Paliarini . . . . . pres & exec VP
Stephen Usery . . . . . mktg VP & news dir
Bruce Jacobs . . . . . chief of engrg

***KTCI-TV—**(Saint Paul, Digital Channel: 26. Digital Hrs: 24 331 kw vis, 33.1 kw aur. ant 1,298t/1,471g TL: N45 03 29 W93 07 27 On air date: May 3, 1965. 172 E. 4th St., Saint Paul, MN, 55101. Phone: (651) 222-1717. Fax: (651) 229-1282.E-mail: viewerservices@tpt.org Web Site: www.tpt.org. Licensee: Twin Cities Public Television Inc. Population Served: 1,400,000 Natl. Network: PBS, .
Key Personnel:
Jim Pagliarini . . . . . CEO & pres
Dan Thomas . . . . . COO
Stephen Usery . . . . . mktg VP
Bruce Jacobs . . . . . chief of engrg

***KWCM-TV—** Digital Channel: 10. Digital Hrs: 24 316 kw vis, 37.1 kw aur. 1,250t/1,274g TL: N45 10 03 W96 00 02 On air date: Feb 7, 1966. 120 W. Schlieman Ave., Appleton, MN, 56208-1351. Phone: (800) 726-3178. Fax: (320) 289-2634.E-mail: yourtv@pioneer.org Web Site: www.pioneer.org. Licensee: West Central Minnesota Educational TV Co. Population Served: 750,000 Natl. Network: PBS, . Washington Atty: Fletcher, Heald & Hildreth.
Key Personnel:
Les Heen . . . . . pres & gen mgr
Jon Panzer . . . . . stn mgr & engrg VP chief of engrg
Shirley Schwarz . . . . . progmg dir

WCCO-TV—(Minneapolis, Digital Channel: 32.100 kw vis, 10 kw aur. 1,430t/1,375g TL: N45 03 45 W93 08 21 On air date: July 1, 1949. 90 S. 11th St., Minneapolis, MN, 55403. Phone: (612) 339-4444. Fax: (612) 330-2627. Web Site: wcco.com. Licensee: CBS Broadcasting Inc. Group Owner: Viacom Television Stations Group (acq 2-92; grpsl; 7-26-76). Population Served: 434,400 Natl. Network: CBS, . Natl. Rep: CBS TV Stations National Sales,. Wire Svc: WU Wire Svc: Reuters News staff: 75; News: 23 hrs wkly.
Key Personnel:
Susan Adams Loyd . . . . . progmg dir & VP & gen mgr
Kevin Argall . . . . . gen sls mgr
Scott Libin . . . . . news dir
Gary Kroger . . . . . engrg dir

WFTC—(Minneapolis, Digital Channel: 29. Digital Hrs: 24 5,000 kw vis, 500 kw aur. 1,223t/1,205g TL: N45 03 30 W93 07 27 On air date: October 1982. 11358 Viking Dr., Eden Prairie, MN, 55344. Phone: (952) 944-9999. Fax: (952) 942-0286.E-mail: fox9news@foxtv.com Web Site: www.my29tv.com. Licensee: Fox Television Stations Inc. Group Owner: (group owner; (acq 10-1-2001; grpsl). Natl. Network: MyNetworkTV, . Wire Svc: AP News: 3.5 hrs wkly.
Key Personnel:
Carol Rueppel . . . . . gen mgr
Bill Dallman . . . . . news dir
Marc Majeres . . . . . chief of engrg

***WHWC-TV—** Digital Channel: 27. Digital Hrs: 24 291 kw vis. ant 1,148t/1,169g TL: N45 02 49 W91 51 47 On air date: Nov 18, 1973. 821 University Ave., Madison, WI, 53706. Phone: (608) 263-2121. Fax: (608) 263-9363.E-mail: comments@wpt.org Web Site: www.wpt.org. Licensee: State of Wisconsin-Educational Communications Board. Natl. Network: PBS, . Washington Atty: Dow, Lohnes & Albertson.
Key Personnel:
Mike Edgette . . . . . opns dir
Jon Miskowski . . . . . dev dir & chief of engrg
Michael Bridgeman . . . . . prom mgr
Mary Clare Sorenson . . . . . adv dir & progmg mgr
Kathy Bissen . . . . . news dir
Dick Taugher . . . . . chief of engrg

WUCW—(Minneapolis, Digital Channel: 22. Digital Hrs: 24 4,570 kw vis, 457 kw aur. 1,150t/1,450g TL: N45 03 30 W93 07 27 On air date: Sept 22, 1982. 1640 Como Ave., St. Paul, MN, 55108. Phone: (651) 646-2300. Fax: (651) 646-1220. Web Site: www.thecwtc.com. Licensee: KLGT Licensee L.L.C. Group Owner: Sinclair Broadcast Group Inc. (acq 3-16-98; $52.5 million). Population Served: 1,700,000 Natl. Network: CW, .
Key Personnel:
Joe Tracy . . . . . gen mgr & stn mgr
Eric Lazar . . . . . natl sls mgr
Tom Burke . . . . . rgnl sls mgr
Cece Smith . . . . . progmg mgr
Steve Lunde . . . . . chief of engrg

Rochester, MN-Mason City, IA-Austin, MN
(DMA 154)

KAAL— Digital Channel: 36.100 kw vis, 10 kw aur. 1,049t/1,000g TL: N43 37 42 W93 09 12 On air date: Aug 17, 1953. Box 577, Austin, MN, 55912. 1701 10th Pl. N.E., Austin, MN 55912. Phone: (507) 437-6666. Fax: (507) 433-9560. Web Site: www.kaaltv.com. Licensee: KAAL-TV LLC. Group Owner: Hubbard Broadcasting Inc. (acq 12-13-00; $9.5 million). Natl. Network: ABC, . Washington Atty: Schwartz, Woods & Miller. News staff: 18; News: 11 hrs wkly.
Key Personnel:
David Harbert . . . . . gen mgr & news dir
Ila Teskey . . . . . gen sls mgr & rgnl sls mgr
Sheryl Barlon . . . . . mktg dir & progmg dir
Dan Collado . . . . . prom mgr
Wendell Nelson . . . . . chief of engrg
Harlan Carlson . . . . . traf mgr
Jan Thompson . . . . . progmg

KIMT— Digital Channel: 42. Digital Hrs: 21 100 kw vis, 10 kw aur. 1,510t/1,525g TL: N43 22 20 W92 49 59 (CP: 5 kw aur, 97.7 kw vis, ant 1,550t/1,569g) On air date: May 15, 1954. 112 N. Pennsylvania Ave., Mason City, IA, 50401. Phone: (641) 423-2540. Fax: (641) 423-9309.E-mail: mail@kimt.com Web Site: www.kimt.com. Licensee: NVT Mason City Licensee LLC. Group Owner: Media General Broadcast Group (acq 10-6-2006; $35 million with WIAT-TV Birmingham, AL). Population Served: 343,000 Natl. Network: CBS, . Natl. Rep: Harrington, Righter & Parsons,. Washington Atty: Covington & Burling. News staff: 21; News: 19 hrs wkly.
Key Personnel:
Steve Martinson . . . . . VP & gen mgr
Michael Fitzgerald . . . . . gen sls mgr
Jerome Risting . . . . . prom mgr & progmg dir
John Murray . . . . . news dir
Larry Eckblad . . . . . chief of engrg
Wayne Kohlhaas . . . . . rgnl sls mgr & sls

***KSMQ-TV—** Digital Channel: 20.319.2 kw vis. ant 993t/1,000g TL: N43 38 34 W92 31 35 On air date: Oct 17, 1972. 2000 8th Ave. N.W., Austin, MN, 55912. Phone: (507) 433-0678. Fax: (507) 433-0670.E-mail: ksmq@ksmq.org Web Site: www.ksmq.org. Licensee: KSMQ Public Service Media Inc. (acq 5-27-2005). Population Served: 650,000 Natl. Network: PBS, . Rgnl. Network: CEN. Washington Atty: Schwartz, Woods & Miller.
Key Personnel:
Sandra Session-Robertson . . . . . CEO & pres
Suzi Stone . . . . . progmg dir
Shawn Weitzel . . . . . chief of engrg

KTTC— Digital Channel: 10. Digital Hrs: 24 316 kw vis, 46.8 kw aur. ant 1,260t/1,314g TL: N43 34 15 W92 25 37 On air date: July 16, 1953. 6301 Bandel Rd. N.W., Rochester, MN, 55901. Phone: (507) 288-4444. Fax: (507) 288-6324. Fax: (507) 288-6278 (news).E-mail: kttc@kttc.com Web Site: www.kttc.com. Licensee: KTTC TV Inc. Group Owner: Quincy Newspapers Inc. (acq 7-1-76; $4.25 million;5-24-76). Population Served: 500,000 Natl. Network: NBC, CW, . Natl. Rep: Blair Television,. Washington Atty: Wilkinson, Barker, Knauer & Quinn. Wire Svc: AP Wire Svc: CNN Wire Svc: NBC News staff: 15; News: 11 hrs wkly.
Key Personnel:
Jerry Watson . . . . . gen mgr
Elizabeth Dahlen . . . . . stn mgr & mktg dir
Dave Ferber . . . . . natl sls mgr
Rita Duda . . . . . prom mgr
Vickie Broughton . . . . . progmg dir & progmg mgr
Tim Morgan . . . . . engrg dir & chief of engrg

KXLT-TV— Digital Channel: 46. Digital Hrs: 24 1510 kw vis. ant 1,125 t TL: N43 38 34 W92 31 35 On air date: Aug 1, 1987. 6301 Bandel Rd. N.W., Rochester, MN, 55901. Phone: (507) 252-4747. Fax: (507) 252-5050.E-mail: comments@fox47kxlt.com Web Site: www.fox47kxlt.com. Licensee: SagamoreHill of Minnesota Licenses LLC. (acq 3-31-2005; $2.05 million). Natl. Network: Fox, . Washington Atty: Rosenman & colin. News: 7 hrs wkly.
Key Personnel:
Louis Wall . . . . . gen mgr
Liz Dahlen . . . . . stn mgr
Kristopher Lake . . . . . gen sls mgr
Rita Duda . . . . . prom dir & prom mgr
Samantha Bishop . . . . . progmg mgr
Tim Morgan . . . . . engrg dir & chief of engrg

***KYIN—** Digital Channel: 18.1,740 kw vis, 174 kw aur. 1,430t/1,565g TL: N43 22 25 W92 51 00 On air date: May 14, 1977. Box 6450, Iowa Public TV, Johnston, IA, 50131-6450. 6450 Corporate Dr., Johnston, IA 50131. Phone: (515) 242-3100.E-mail: public_information@iptv.org Web Site: www.iptv.org. Licensee: Iowa Public Broadcasting Board. Natl. Network: PBS, . Washington Atty: Dow, Lohnes PLLC.
Key Personnel:
Daniel K. Miller . . . . . gen mgr

St. Paul
see Minneapolis-St. Paul, MN market

Thief River Falls
see Fargo-Valley City, ND market

Worthington
see Sioux Falls (Mitchell), SD market

Mississippi

Biloxi-Gulfport, MS
(DMA 163)

WLOX— Digital Channel: 13. Digital Hrs: 24 10.9 kw vis. ant 1,338t/1,259g TL: N30 43 22 W89 05 28 On air date: Sept 15, 1962. 208 De Buys Rd., Biloxi, MS, 39531. Phone: (228) 896-1313. Fax: (228) 896-0749.E-mail: wlox@wlox.com Web Site: www.wlox.com. Licensee: WLOX License Subsidiary LLC. Group Owner: Liberty Corp. (acq 1-31-2006; grpsl). Population Served: 120,700 Natl. Network: ABC, . Washington Atty: Covington & Burling. Wire Svc: AP News staff: 44; News: 18 hrs wkly.
Key Personnel:
Leon Long . . . . . VP & gen mgr
Dave Vincent . . . . . stn mgr
Roger Garrett . . . . . opns mgr
Linda Sherman . . . . . gen sls mgr
Don Moore . . . . . rgnl sls mgr
Darlene Duffano . . . . . progmg dir
David Vincent . . . . . news dir
John Armstrong . . . . . chief of engrg

***WMAH-TV—** Digital Channel: 16. Digital Hrs: 24 150 kw vis. ant 1,565t/1,512g TL: N30 45 18 W88 56 44 On air date: Jan 14, 1972. 3825 Ridgewood Rd., Jackson, MS, 39211. Phone: (601) 432-6565. Fax: (601) 432-6654 / (601) 432-6311. Web Site: www.mpbonline.org. Licensee: Mississippi Authority for Educational TV. Natl. Network: PBS, . Mississippi Educational Broadcasting Washington Atty: Schwartz, Woods & Miller.

Key Personnel:
Judy Lewis . . . . . exec VP & gen mgr
Bob Buie. . . . . opns dir
teresa Collier . . . . . news dir

WXXV-TV— Digital Channel: 48. Digital Hrs: 24 300 kw vis. ant 1,496t/1,414g TL: N30 44 48 W89 03 30 On air date: Feb 14, 1987. P.O. Box 2500, Gulfport, MS, 39505. 14351 Hwy. 49 N., Gulfport, MS 39503. Phone: (228) 832-2525. Fax: (228) 832-4442.E-mail: info@wxxv25.com Web Site: www.wxxv25.com. Licensee: Morris Network of Mississippi Inc. Group Owner: Morris Network Inc. (acq 5-22-97; $17.475 million). Natl. Network: Fox, . Natl. Rep: Millennium Sales & Marketing,. Washington Atty: Fletcher, Heald & Hildroth.
Key Personnel:
Dean Hinson. . . . . pres
Bobby Edwards . . . . . gen mgr
Leah Mays . . . . . prom dir
Ray Luke . . . . . opns dir & gen sls mgr & chief of engrg
Jimmy Spears. . . . . traf mgr

Columbus-Tupelo-West Point, MS (DMA 133)

WCBI-TV— Digital Channel: 35. Digital Hrs: 24 100 kw vis, 10 kw aur. ant 1,996t/1,800g TL: N33 45 06 W88 52 40 On air date: July 13, 1956. 201 5th St. S., Columbus, MS, 39701. Phone: (662) 327-4444. Fax: (662) 329-1004.E-mail: comments@wcbi.com Web Site: www.wcbi.com. Licensee: WCBI-TV LLC. Group Owner: Morris Multi-Media (acq 1-14-2004; $20 million). Population Served: 165,000 Natl. Network: CBS, CW, MyNetworkTV, . Washington Atty: Fletcher, Heald & Hildreth. Wire Svc: Weather Wire
Key Personnel:
Bobby Berry . . . . . gen mgr & progmg dir progmg mgr
Derek Rogers . . . . . sls dir & gen sls mgr
Susan Bell . . . . . prom mgr
Russ Geller . . . . . news dir
Gary Savage . . . . . pub affrs dir & chief of engrg
Donna Hitchcock. . . . . traf mgr
Rob Smith . . . . . weather dir

WKDH— Digital Channel: 45. Digital Hrs: 20 537 kw vis. ant 1,610t/1,368g TL: N33 47 39.6 W89 05 15.8 On air date: June 2002. Box 1645, Tupelo, MS, 38802-1645. Phone: (662) 842-7620. Fax: (662) 842-6342. Fax: (662) 844-7061. Web Site: www.wkdh.com. Licensee: Southern Broadcasting Inc. Natl. Network: ABC, . Washington Atty: Garvey, Schubert & Barer.
Key Personnel:
Walter Spain. . . . . pres
Gerald Stanford. . . . . chief of engrg

WLOV-TV— Digital Channel: 16. Digital Hrs: 5:30 AM-1:30 AM 390 kw vis. ant 1.669t/1,426g TL: N33 47 39.6 W89 05 15.8 On air date: May 29, 1983. Box 1732, Tupelo, MS, 38802. Phone: (662) 842-2227. Fax: (662) 844-7061.E-mail: manager@wlov.com Web Site: www.wlov.com. Licensee: Lingard Broadcasting Corp. Ownership: Jack Lingard, 100%. (acq 4-12-94). Natl. Network: Fox, . Natl. Rep: Continental Television Sales,. Washington Atty: Robert E. Levine, Esq. Wire Svc: AP News: 5 hrs wkly.
Key Personnel:
Jennifer Dennington . . . . . gen mgr
Marty Davis . . . . . chief of engrg

***WMAA—** Digital Channel: 43.81 kw vis. ant 668t/658g TL: N33 50 31 W88 41 48 Not on air, target date: unknown: 3825 Ridgewood Rd., Jackson, MS, 39211. Phone: (601) 432-6565. Fax: (601) 432-6392. Web Site: www.mpbonline.org. Licensee: Mississippi Authority for Educational Television. Natl. Network: PBS, . Mississippi Educational Broadcasting
Key Personnel:
Judy Lewis. . . . . gen mgr
Ron Evans. . . . . news dir
Lee Tapley . . . . . pub affrs dir

***WMAB-TV—** Digital Channel: 10. Digital Hrs: 24 100 kw vis, 10 kw aur. ant 1,250t/1,091g TL: N33 21 07 W89 08 56 On air date: July 4, 1971. 3825 Ridgewood Rd., Jackson, MS, 39211. Phone: (601) 432-6565. Fax: (601) 432-6654. Fax: (601) 432-6311. Web Site: www.mpbonline.org. Licensee: Mississippi Authority for Educational TV. Population Served: 734,380 Natl. Network: PBS, . Washington Atty: Schwartz, Woods & Miller. News staff: 4.
Key Personnel:
Judy Lewis. . . . . gen mgr
Bob Buie. . . . . opns dir
Mari Irby. . . . . prom dir
Teresa Collier. . . . . news dir

***WMAE-TV—** Digital Channel: 12. Digital Hrs: 24 100 kw vis, 8.91 kw aur. ant 741t/538g TL: N34 40 00 W88 45 05 On air date: Aug 11, 1974. 3825 Ridgewood Rd., Jackson, MS, 39211. Phone: (601) 432-6565. Fax: (601) 432-6654. Fax: (601) 432-6311. Web Site: www.mpbonline.org. Licensee: Mississippi Authority for Educational TV. Natl. Network: PBS, . Mississippi Educational Broadcasting Washington Atty: Schwartz, Woods & Miller.
Key Personnel:
Judy Lewis. . . . . gen mgr
Teresa Collier. . . . . news dir

WTVA— Digital Channel: 8. Digital Hrs: 24 316 kw vis, 31.6 kw aur. ant 1,781t/1,585g TL: N33 47 40 W89 05 16 On air date: Mar 18, 1957. Box 350, Tupelo, MS, 38802-0350. 1359 Rd. 681, Tupelo, MS 38802. Phone: (662) 842-7620. Fax: (662) 844-7061.E-mail: manager@wtva.com Web Site: www.wtva.com. Licensee: WTVA Inc.. Ownership: Mary Jane Spain, 51%; Margaret Spain, 40%; and estate of Frank K. Spain, 9%. Group Owner: (group owner). Natl. Network: NBC, . Natl. Rep: Continental Television Sales,. Washington Atty: Garvey, Schubert & Barer. News staff: 22; News: 17 hrs wkly.
Key Personnel:
Mary Jane Spain . . . . . pres
Phil Sullivan . . . . . gen mgr & stn mgr
Jon Hall . . . . . opns dir
Larry Harris . . . . . gen sls mgr
Robert Davidson . . . . . news dir
Wendell Robinson. . . . . chief of engrg

Greenville

see Greenwood-Greenville, MS market

Greenwood-Greenville, MS (DMA 187)

WABG-TV— Digital Channel: 32. Digital Hrs: 24 100 kw vis, 10 kw aur. ant 2,000t/2,136g TL: N33 22 23 W90 32 31 On air date: Oct 20, 1959. Box 1243, 849 Washington Ave., Greenville, MS, 38701. Box 720, 2001 Garrard Ave., Greenwood, MS 38930. Phone: (662) 332-0949. Fax: (662) 344-1814. Web Site: www.wabg.com. Licensee: Mississippi Broadcasting Partners. Group Owner: Bahakel Communications Natl. Network: ABC, Fox, . Natl. Rep: Continental Television Sales,. News staff: 16; News: 13 hrs wkly.
Key Personnel:
Sherry Nelson . . . . . gen mgr & stn mgr
Jonas Oswalt . . . . . rgnl sls mgr
Donnie Reid . . . . . progmg dir & progmg mgr
Pam Chatman . . . . . news dir
Larry Nixon . . . . . chief of engrg

***WMAO-TV—**(Greenwood, Digital Channel: 25. Digital Hrs: 24 537 kw vis, 53.7 kw aur. ant 1,040t/1,061g TL: N33 22 34 W90 32 31 On air date: Sept 15, 1972. 3825 Ridgewood Rd., Jackson, MS, 39211. Phone: (601) 432-6565. Fax: (601) 432-6654. Fax: (601) 432-6311. Web Site: www.mpbonline.org. Licensee: Mississippi Authority for Educational TV. Mississippi Educational Broadcasting Washington Atty: Schwartz, Woods & Miller.
Key Personnel:
Judy Lewis . . . . . exec VP & gen mgr
Bob Buie. . . . . opns dir
Teresa Collier. . . . . dev dir & news dir

WXVT— Digital Channel: 15. Digital Hrs: 24 2,746 kw vis, 549 kw aur. ant 887t/919g TL: N33 39 26 W90 42 18 On air date: Nov 7, 1980. 3015 E. Reed Rd., Greenville, MS, 38703. Phone: (662) 334-1500. Fax: (662) 378-8122. Web Site: www.wxvt.com. Licensee: Saga Broadcasting LLC. Group Owner: Saga Communications Inc. (acq 7-1-99; $5.2 million). Population Served: 137,000 Natl. Network: CBS,
Key Personnel:
Darren Lehrmann . . . . . gen mgr
Larry Cazavan. . . . . gen sls mgr
Carolyn Byars. . . . . progmg dir
Earl Phelps . . . . . news dir
Paul Serio. . . . . chief of engrg

Gulfport

see Biloxi-Gulfport, MS market

Hattiesburg-Laurel, MS (DMA 167)

WDAM-TV—(Laurel, Digital Channel: 28. Digital Hrs: 21 316 kw vis, 47 kw aur. ant 510t/575g TL: N31 27 12 W89 17 05 On air date: June 8, 1956. Box 16269, Hattiesburg, MS, 39404-6269. 2362 Hwy. 11 N., Moselle, MS 39459. Phone: (601) 544-4730. Fax: (601) 584-9302.E-mail: info@wdam.com Web Site: www.wdam.com. Licensee: WDAM License Subsidiary Inc. Group Owner: Raycom Media Inc. (acq 9-24-96; grpsl). Population Served: 244,500 Natl. Network: NBC, . Natl. Rep: Harrington, Righter & Parsons,. Washington Atty: Covington & Burling. News staff: 26; News: 20 hrs wkly.
Key Personnel:
Jim Cameron . . . . . VP & gen mgr
Ted Palmer . . . . . gen sls mgr
Wanda Morrison . . . . . natl sls mgr
Pam McGovern. . . . . mktg mgr & prom dir
Betty Young . . . . . progmg dir
Randy Swan . . . . . news dir
Jim Wilkinson . . . . . engrg mgr & chief of engrg
Steve Taylor . . . . . weather dir

WHLT— Digital Channel: 22. Digital Hrs: 24 1,000 kw vis, 100 kw aur. ant 797t/707g TL: N31 24 20 W89 14 13 On air date: Jan 12, 1987. 5912 Hwy. 49, The Cloverleaf Center, Suite A, Hattiesburg, MS, 39401. Phone: (601) 545-2077. Fax: (601) 545-3589.E-mail: wbabbidge@whlt.com Web Site: www.cbs22thehub.com. Licensee: Media General Broadcasting Inc. Group Owner: Media General Broadcast Group (acq 7-25-97; grpsl). Natl. Network: CBS, . Natl. Rep: MMT,.
Key Personnel:
Robert Romine . . . . . gen mgr
Wally Babbidge . . . . . stn mgr & gen sls mgr
Gary Wolverton . . . . . prom mgr
Jackie McDonald . . . . . progmg dir
Gary Wright. . . . . engrg mgr & chief of engrg

Holly Springs

see Memphis, TN market

Jackson, MS (DMA 90)

WAPT— Digital Channel: 21. Digital Hrs: 24 4,780 kw vis, 478 kw aur. ant 1,178t/1,072g TL: N32 16 39 W90 17 41 On air date: Oct 3, 1970. 7616 Channel 16 Way, Jackson, MS, 39209. Phone: (601) 922-1607. Fax: (601) 922-1663. Web Site: www.wapt.com. Licensee: WAPT Hearst-Argyle Television Inc. Group Owner: Hearst-Argyle Televison Inc. (acq 7-16-97; grpsl). Population Served: 280,000 Natl. Network: ABC, . News staff: 26; News: 14 hrs wkly.
Key Personnel:
Stuart Kellogg . . . . . gen mgr
Jeff Wolfe. . . . . gen sls mgr & rgnl sls mgr
Carl Gustafson . . . . . natl sls mgr
Bruce Barkley. . . . . news dir
Tom Bondurant . . . . . chief of engrg
Linda Bozone . . . . . traf mgr
David Hartman . . . . . weather dir
Nichole Davis . . . . . progmg

WDBD— Digital Channel: 40. Digital Hrs: 24 981.2 kw vis. ant 1,961t/1,853g TL: N32 12 49.4 W90 22 56.2 On air date: Nov 30, 1984. One FOXNEWS 40 Pl., Jackson, MS, 39209. Phone: (601) 922-1234. Fax: (601) 922-0268. Web Site: www.fox40first.com. Licensee: Jackson Television L.L.C. Ownership: Sheldon H. Galloway, 100% voting control (acq 9-30-2003; $13.4 million with WXMS-LP Jackson). Natl. Network: Fox, . Natl. Rep: Millennium Sales & Marketing,. Washington Atty: Fisher, Wayland, Cooper, Leader & Zaragoza.
Key Personnel:
Leigh White . . . . . gen mgr
Lizzy Ingalls. . . . . prom mgr
Mike Ingalls . . . . . news dir
Robert Flanagan . . . . . chief of engrg
Regina James. . . . . traf mgr

WJTV— Digital Channel: 12. Digital Hrs: 24 49.2 kw vis. ant 1,610t/1,571g TL: N32 14 26 W90 24 15 On air date: Mar 15, 1954. 1820 TV Rd., Jackson, MS, 39204-4148. Phone: (601) 372-6311. Fax: (601) 969-4601. Web Site: www.wjtv.com. Licensee: Media General Broadcasting Inc. Group Owner: Media General Broadcast Group (acq 7-25-97; grpsl). Population Served: 477,300 Natl. Network: CBS, . Natl. Rep: MMT,. Washington Atty: Dow Lohnes LLC. News staff: 34; News: 21 hrs wkly.
Key Personnel:
Bob Romine . . . . . gen mgr
William Cromwell . . . . . sls dir
Rick Russell. . . . . mktg dir & news dir
Stephen Patton . . . . . prom dir
Jackie McDonald . . . . . progmg mgr
Steve Schrader. . . . . chief of engrg

WLBT— Digital Channel: 7. Digital Hrs: 24 10.3 kw vis. ant 1,276t/1,174g TL: N32 12 49 W90 22 56 On air date: Dec 28, 1953. 715 S. Jefferson St., Jackson, MS, 39201. Phone: (601) 948-3333. Fax: (601) 960-4412.E-mail: news@wlbt.com Web Site: www.wlbt.com. Licensee: WLBT License Subsidiary LLC. Group Owner: Liberty Corp.

(acq 1-13-2006; grpsl). Population Served: 320,000 Natl. Network: NBC, . Natl. Rep: Continental Television Sales,. Washington Atty: Dow, Lohnes & Albertson. Wire Svc: AP
Key Personnel:
Dan Modisett . . . . gen mgr
Frankie Thomas . . . . gen sls mgr
Dennis Smith . . . . news dir
Curtis McKnight . . . . chief of engrg
Teresa White . . . . traf mgr

*WMAU-TV— Digital Channel: 18. Digital Hrs: 24 550 kw vis, 55 kw aur. ant 1,121t/1,066g TL: N31 22 19 W90 45 05 On air date: Jan 14, 1972. 3825 Ridgewood Rd., Jackson, MS, 39211. Phone: (601) 432-6565. Fax: (610) 432-6654 / (601) 432-6311. Web Site: www.mpbonline.org. Licensee: Mississippi Authority for Educational TV. Natl. Network: PBS, . Mississippi Educational Broadcasting Washington Atty: Schwartz, Woods & Miller.
Key Personnel:
Judy Lewis . . . . gen mgr
Teresa Collier . . . . news dir & engrg dir

*WMPN-TV— Digital Channel: 20. Digital Hrs: 24 912 kw vis, 91.2 kw aur. ant 1,958t/1,997g TL: N32 12 46 W90 22 54 On air date: Feb 1, 1970. 3825 Ridgewood Rd., Jackson, MS, 39211. Phone: (601) 432-6565. Fax: (601) 432-6654. Fax: (601) 432-6311. Web Site: www.mpbonline.org. Licensee: Mississippi Authority for Educational TV. Population Served: 1,100,000 Natl. Network: PBS, . Washington Atty: Schwartz, Woods & Miller.
Key Personnel:
Judy Lewis . . . . gen mgr
Bob Buie . . . . opns dir
Teresa Collier . . . . news dir

WNTZ-TV— Digital Channel: 49. Digital Hrs: 24 1,170 kw vis, 117 kw aur. ant 843t/848g TL: N31 30 33 W91 24 19 On air date: Nov 16, 1985. 4615 Parliament Dr., Suite 103, Alexandria, LA, 71303. Phone: (318) 443-4700. Fax: (318) 443-4899. Web Site: www.fox48tv.com. Licensee: ComCorp of Alexandria License Corp.. Ownership: ComCorp Broadcasting Inc. Group Owner: White Knight Holdings Inc. (acq 6-22-98). Natl. Network: Fox, MyNetworkTV, . Natl. Rep: Millennium Sales & Marketing,. Washington Atty: Shaw Pittman L.L.P.
Key Personnel:
Sharon Rachal . . . . gen mgr & gen mgr gen sls mgr
Vikki Chapman . . . . progmg mgr
Ron Taylor . . . . chief of engrg

WRBJ— Digital Channel: 34.1,400 kw vis. ant 1,229t/1,242g TL: N32 07 18 W89 32 52 On air date: January 2006. 745 N. State St., Jackson, MS, 39202. Phone: (601) 974-5700. Fax: (601) 974-5711. Web Site: cw34jackson.com. Licensee: Roberts Broadcasting of Jackson, MS, LLC. Group Owner: Roberts Broadcasting Co. Natl. Network: CW, . Natl. Rep: Harrington, Righter & Parsons,. Washington Atty: Fletcher, Heald & Hildreth.
Key Personnel:
Robin Jackson . . . . natl sls mgr
Charles Flowers . . . . chief of engrg
Tracy Mallett . . . . traf mgr

WUFX— Digital Channel: 41. Digital Hrs: 24 981.2 kw vis. ant 1,961t/1,853g TL: N32 12 49.4 W90 22 56.2 On air date: 2004. One Great Place, Jackson, MS, 39209. Phone: (601) 922-1234. Fax: (601) 922-0268. Web Site: www.gomiss.com. Licensee: Mississippi Television LLC.. Ownership: JW Mississippi LLC (acq 9-5-2007). Natl. Network: MyNetworkTV,
Key Personnel:
Will Hammond . . . . rgnl sls mgr
Lizzy Ingalls . . . . prom mgr
Mike Ingalls . . . . news dir
Robert Flanagan . . . . chief of engrg
Regina James . . . . traf mgr

WWJX— Digital Channel: 51.5,000 kw vis. ant 1,260t/1,200g TL: N32 14 26 W90 24 15 Not on air, target date: unknown: 188 S. Bellevue, Suite 222, Memphis, TN, 38104. Phone: (901) 516-8970. Permittee: George S. Flinn Jr. Ownership: George S. Flinn Jr., 100%
Key Personnel:
George S. Flinn Jr. . . . . gen mgr

Laurel
see Hattiesburg-Laurel, MS market

Meridian, MS
(DMA 185)

*WGBC— Digital Channel: 31. Digital Hrs: 24 89.1 kw vis, 8.91 kw aur. 610t/405g TL: N32 19 34 W88 41 12 (CP: 1,600 kw vis, ant 613t/408g) On air date: Sept 15, 1991. Box 2424, Meridian, MS,

39302. 1151 Crestview Cir., Meridian, MS 39301. Phone: (601) 485-3030. Fax: (601) 693-9889. Web Site: www.wgbctv.com. Licensee: Robert M. Ledbetter Enterprises LLC.. Ownership: Robert M. Ledbetter Jr., 100% (acq 6-20-2006; $750,000). Population Served: 64,700 Natl. Network: NBC, . Natl. Rep: Millennium Sales & Marketing,. Washington Atty: Wiley, Rein & Fielding.
Key Personnel:
Jet Scarbrough . . . . opns mgr & chief of engrg

*WMAW-TV— Analog Channel: 14. Digital Channel: 44. Analog Hrs: 24 Digital Hrs: 24 550 kw vis, 55 kw aur. ant 1,210t/1,069g TL: N32 08 18 W89 05 36 On air date: Jan 14, 1972. 3825 Ridgewood Rd., Jackson, MS, 39211. Phone: (601) 432-6565. Fax: (601) 432-6654. Fax:(601) 432-6311. Web Site: www.mpbonline.org. Licensee: Mississippi Authority for Educational TV. Population Served: 499,869 Natl. Network: PBS, . Mississippi Educational Broadcasting Washington Atty: Schwartz, Woods & Miller. News staff: 4.
Key Personnel:
Judy Lewis . . . . gen mgr
Teresa Collier . . . . news dir

WMDN— Digital Channel: 24. Digital Hrs: 24 724 kw vis, 72.4 kw aur. 662t/388g TL: N32 19 40 W88 41 31 (CP: 724 kw vis, ant 581t. TL: N32 18 43 W88 41 33) On air date: June 10, 1986. Box 2424, Meridian, MS, 39302. 1151Crestview Cir., Meridian, MS 39301. Phone: (601) 693-2424. Fax: (601) 693-7126.E-mail: administration@wmdn.net Web Site: www.wmdntv.com. Licensee: Meridian Media LLC.. Ownership: Sharlyn Threadgill, 50%; and Wade Threadgill, 50% (acq 1-23-2008; $5.8 million). Population Served: 45,083 Natl. Network: CBS, . Natl. Rep: Millennium Sales & Marketing,. Washington Atty: Fletcher, Heald & Hildreth.
Key Personnel:
Mike Reed . . . . stn mgr
Susan Ross . . . . gen mgr & gen sls mgr

WTOK-TV— Digital Channel: 11.. 316 kw vis, 47.9 kw aur. ant 536t/315g TL: N32 19 38 W88 41 28 On air date: Sept 27, 1953. Box 2988, Meridian, MS, 39302. 815 23rd Ave., Meridian, MS 39301. Phone: (601) 693-1441. Fax: (601) 483-3266. Web Site: www.wtok.com. Licensee: Gray Television Licensee Corp. Group Owner: Gray Television Inc. (acq 8-29-2002; grpsl). Population Served: 635,000 Natl. Network: ABC, CW, Fox, Natl. Rep: Continental Television Sales,. Washington Atty: Wiley, Rein & Fielding, LLP. Wire Svc: AP News staff: 15; News: 15 hrs wkly.
Key Personnel:
Tim Walker . . . . gen mgr & opns mgr
Julie Walker . . . . prom mgr
Matt Willis . . . . progmg dir
John Johnson . . . . news dir & pub affrs dir
Brad LeBrun . . . . chief of engrg
Lindsey Hall . . . . sports cmtr

Oxford
see Memphis, TN market

Tupelo
see Columbus-Tupelo-West Point, MS market

West Point
see Columbus-Tupelo-West Point, MS market

Missouri

Cape Girardeau
see Paducah, KY-Cape Girardeau, MO-Harrisburg-Mount Vernon, IL market

Columbia-Jefferson City, MO
(DMA 137)

KMIZ— Digital Channel: 17. Digital Hrs: 24 1,000 kw vis. ant 1,141t/1,069g TL: N38 46 29 W92 33 22.3 On air date: Dec 5, 1971. 501 Business Loop 70 E., Columbia, MO, 65201. Phone: (573) 449-0917. Fax: (573) 875-7078.E-mail: info@kmiz.com Web Site: www.kmiz.com. Licensee: JW Broadcasting LLC. Ownership: Alta/JW Broadcasting Investor Corp., 52.38%; and DJ Broadcasting LLC, 47.62% (acq 11-12-2003). Population Served: 379,700 Natl. Network:

ABC, MyNetworkTV, Fox, . Natl. Rep: Petry Television Inc.,. Washington Atty: Covington & Burling. Wire Svc: AP News staff: 12; News: 19 hrs wkly.
Key Personnel:
Randy Wright . . . . VP & gen mgr
Mark Hotchkiss . . . . sls dir & gen sls mgr
Sean Stone . . . . prom mgr
Cynthia Clark . . . . film buyer & traf mgr
Curtis Varns . . . . news dir
Rick Hartford . . . . chief of engrg

*KMOS-TV— Digital Channel: 15. Digital Hrs: 18 322 kw vis. ant 1,978t/1,965g TL: N38 42 16 W92 52 03 On air date: Dec 22, 1979. University of Central Missouri, Wood 11, Warrensburg, MO, 64093. Phone: (660) 543-4155. Fax: (660) 543-8863.E-mail: kmos@kmos.org Web Site: www.kmos.org. Licensee: Central Missouri State University. (acq 6-6-78; $1,000). Population Served: 1,500,000 Natl. Network: PBS, . Washington Atty: Shaw Pittman.
Key Personnel:
Donald W. Peterson . . . . gen mgr
Fred Hunt . . . . opns mgr
Michael O'Keefe . . . . progmg mgr
Dorothy McGrath . . . . pub affrs dir
John Long . . . . chief of engrg

KNLJ— Digital Channel: 20. Digital Hrs: 24 2,040 kw vis, 204 kw aur. ant 1,028t/945g TL: N38 44 16 W92 05 20 On air date: Mar 30, 1986. Box 2525, New Bloomfield, MO, 65603-2525. 9810 State Rd. AE, New Bloomfield, MO 65603. Phone: (573) 896-5105. Fax: (573) 896-4376.E-mail: traffic@knlj.tv Web Site: www.knlj.tv. Licensee: New Life Evangelistic Center Inc. Population Served: 149,000 Washington Atty: John H. Midlen Jr.
Key Personnel:
Larry Rice . . . . gen mgr
Charles Hale . . . . gen sls mgr
James Shackleford . . . . progmg dir
Shawn Baker . . . . chief of engrg

KOMU-TV— Digital Channel: 8. Digital Hrs: 24 13.6 kw vis. ant 794t/738g TL: N38 53 17 W92 15 48 On air date: Dec 21, 1953. 5550 Hwy. 63 S., Columbia, MO, 65201. Phone: (573) 882-8888. Fax: (573) 884-8888. Web Site: www.komu.com. Licensee: The Curators of the University of Missouri. Group Owner: (group owner) Population Served: 157,510 Natl. Network: NBC, CW, . Natl. Rep: Millennium Sales & Marketing,. Washington Atty: Shaw Pittman. News staff: 23; News: 20 hrs wkly.
Key Personnel:
Martin Siddall . . . . gen mgr
Tom Dugan . . . . gen sls mgr
John Parker . . . . natl sls mgr
Matt Garrett . . . . prom dir
Stacey Woelfel . . . . news dir
Chris Swisher . . . . chief of engrg

KRCG— Digital Channel: 12. Digital Hrs: 5 AM-2 AM 316 kw vis, 47.4 kw aur. ant 1,010t/929g TL: N38 41 28 W92 05 43 On air date: Feb 13, 1955. Box 659, Jefferson City, MO, 65102. 10188 Old Hwy. 54 N., New Bloomfield, MO 65063. Phone: (573) 896-5144. Fax: (573) 896-5193.E-mail: info@krcg.com Web Site: www.krcg.com. Licensee: Barrington Broadcasting Missouri Corp. Group Owner: (group owner) (acq 12-27-2004; $38 million). Population Served: 960,700 Natl. Network: CBS, . Washington Atty: Pepper & Corazzini. News staff: 14; News: 14 hrs wkly.
Key Personnel:
Betsy Farris . . . . gen mgr
Lee Gordon . . . . stn mgr & progmg dir progmg dir
Wendy Gustofson . . . . natl sls mgr
Roger Hulett . . . . rgnl sls mgr
Gregg Palermo . . . . prom mgr & news dir
Jim Malone . . . . chief of engrg

Hannibal
see Quincy, IL-Hannibal, MO-Keokuk, IA market

Jefferson City
see Columbia-Jefferson City, MO market

Joplin, MO-Pittsburg, KS
(DMA 148)

KFJX-TV— Digital Channel: 13. Digital Hrs: 24 hrs. 5,000 kw vis. ant 1,112t/1,069g TL: N37 18 46 W94 48 59 On air date: 2003. Box 659, Pittsburg, KS, 66762-0659. Phone: (417) 782-1414. Fax: (417) 206-4081.E-mail: ddishman@fox14tv.com Web Site: www.fox14tv.com.

Licensee: Surtsey Media LLC. Group Owner: (group owner; (acq 3-7-2003). Population Served: 350,000 Natl. Network: Fox, . News staff: 4; News: 3 hrs wkly.
Key Personnel:
Darren Dishman . . . . gen mgr & stn mgr

KOAM-TV— Digital Channel: 7. Digital Hrs: 24 316 kw vis, 63.1 kw aur. 1,090t/1,159g TL: N37 13 15 W94 42 25 On air date: Dec 13, 1953. Box 659, Pittsburg, KS, 66762-0659. 2950 N.E. Hwy. 69, Pittsburg, KS 66762-0659. Phone: (417) 624-0233. Fax: (417) 624-3115, sls & admin.E-mail: email@koamtv.com Web Site: www.koamtv.com. Licensee: Saga Quad States Communications LLC. Group Owner: Saga Communications Inc. (acq 10-12-94; $8.55 million). Population Served: 343,000 Natl. Network: CBS, . Natl. Rep: Continental Television Sales,. News: 19 hrs wkly.
Key Personnel:
Danny Thomas . . . . pres & gen mgr film buyer
Vance Lewis . . . . prom dir
Kristi Spencer . . . . news dir
Larry White . . . . chief of engrg

KODE-TV— Digital Channel: 43. Digital Hrs: 24 316 kw vis, 63.2 kw aur. 1,020t/999g TL: N37 04 36 W94 32 10 On air date: Sept 26, 1954. Box 46, Joplin, MO, 64802. 1928 W. 13th St., Joplin, MO 64802. Phone: (417) 623-7260. Fax: (417) 623-3736. Web Site: www.kode-tv.com. Licensee: Mission Broadcasting of Joplin Inc. Group Owner: Mission Broadcasting Inc. (acq 2-27-2002; $6 million). Natl. Network: ABC, . Washington Atty: Cohn. News staff: 18; News: 16 hrs wkly.
Key Personnel:
Shirley Morton . . . . gen mgr & stn mgr
Gary Hood . . . . gen sls mgr
Janice Rohman . . . . progmg dir & traf mgr sports cmtr
Larry Young . . . . news dir
Jeff Hadley . . . . chief of engrg

***KOZJ—** Digital Channel: 25.55 kw vis. ant 922t/850g TL: N37 04 37 W94 32 15 On air date: June 1, 1986. Box 1226, Joplin, MO, 64802. 403 S. Main St., Joplin, MO 64801. Phone: (417) 782-2226. Fax: (417) 782-7222.E-mail: mail@optv.org Web Site: www.optv.org. Licensee: Board of Governors of Southwest Missouri State University. (acq 4-25-2001; $1.3 million assumption of debt with KOZK(TV) Springfield). Natl. Network: PBS, . Washington Atty: Dow, Lohns PLLC.
Key Personnel:
Brent Moore . . . . pres & chief of engrg
Tammy Wiley . . . . gen mgr
Norma Scott . . . . dev dir
Tom Carter . . . . progmg dir
Rebecca Scott . . . . spec ev coord
Satellite of *KOZK Springfield.

KSNF— Digital Channel: 46.175 kw vis. ant 1,057t/979g TL: N37 04 33 W94 33 16 On air date: Sept 2, 1967. Box 1393, Joplin, MO, 64802. 1502 Cleveland, Joplin, MO 64801. Phone: (417) 781-2345. Fax: (417) 782-2417. Web Site: www.ksntv.com. Licensee: Nexstar Finance Inc. Group Owner: Nexstar Broadcasting Group Inc. (acq 11-6-97; grpsl). Population Served: 343,000 Natl. Network: NBC, . Washington Atty: Arter & Hadden.
Key Personnel:
John Hoffman . . . . gen mgr
Debra Palmer . . . . sls dir & gen sls mgr
Larry Young . . . . news dir
Jeff Hadley . . . . chief of engrg
Robin Richey . . . . progmg

Kansas City, MO

(DMA 31)

***KCPT—** Digital Channel: 18. Digital Hrs: 24 1,150 kw vis, 115 kw aur. ant 1,171t TL: N39 04 59 W94 28 49 On air date: Mar 29, 1961. 125 E. 31st St., Kansas City, MO, 64108. Phone: (816) 756-3580. Fax: (816) 931-2500.E-mail: kcpt@kcpt.org Web Site: www.kcpt.org. Licensee: Public TV 19 Inc. (acq 1-1-72; $22,226;2-14-72). Population Served: 1,300,000 Natl. Network: PBS, . Washington Atty: Arter & Hadden.
Key Personnel:
Victor Hogstrom . . . . CEO & pres

KCTV— Digital Channel: 24.100 kw vis, 15.1 kw aur. ant 1,130t/1,042g TL: N39 04 15 W94 34 57 On air date: Sept 27, 1953. Box 5555, Kansas City, MO, 64109-0155. 4500 Shawnee Mission Pkwy., Fairway, KS 66205. Phone: (913) 677-5555. Fax: (913) 677-7109.E-mail: kctv5@kctv5.com Web Site: www.kctv5.com. Licensee: Meredith Corp. Group Owner: Meredith Broadcasting Group, Meredith Corp., see Cross-Ownership (acq 10-1-53; $2 million). Natl. Network: CBS, . Natl. Rep: TeleRep,.
Key Personnel:
Kirk Black . . . . VP & gen mgr stn mgr
Dave Duncan . . . . gen sls mgr
Michael Cornette . . . . natl sls mgr
Jason Mullenix . . . . rgnl sls mgr
Beth Green . . . . progmg dir
Tracy Brogden-Miller . . . . news dir
Tom Casey . . . . engrg dir & chief of engrg
Erin Mahoney . . . . traf mgr

KCWE— Digital Channel: 31. Digital Hrs: 24 5,000 kw vis. ant 1,174t/1,089g TL: N39 05 01 W94 30 57 On air date: Sept 14, 1996. 1049 Central, Kansas City, MO, 64105. Phone: (816) 221-9999. Fax: (816) 760-9149. Web Site: www.thekansascitychannel.com. Licensee: KCWE-TV Company. (acq 10-3-2006; $10.96 million). Population Served: 875,090 Natl. Network: CW, . Natl. Rep: Harrington, Righter & Parsons,.
Key Personnel:
Robert Liepold . . . . pres & gen mgr
Peggy Madigan . . . . sls dir
Jerry Agresti . . . . engrg dir

KMBC-TV— Digital Channel: 29. Digital Hrs: 24 1,000 kw vis, 100 kw aur. ant 1,174t/1,089g TL: N39 05 01 W94 30 57 On air date: Aug 1, 1952. 6455 Windchester Ave, Kansas City, MO, 64105. Phone: (816) 221-9999. Fax: (816) 760-9245. Web Site: www.thekansascitychannel.com. Licensee: KMBC Hearst-Argyle Television Inc. Group Owner: Hearst-Argyle Television Inc. (acq 7-16-97; grpsl). Population Served: 875,090 Natl. Network: ABC, . Natl. Rep: Eagle Television Sales,. Washington Atty: Brooks, Pierce, McLendon, Humphrey & Leonard. Wire Svc: AP Wire Svc: CNN Wire Svc: ABC News staff: 55; News: 28 hrs wkly.
Key Personnel:
Wayne Godsey . . . . VP & gen mgr
Peggy Madigan . . . . sls dir & gen sls mgr
Michael Sipes . . . . news dir
Jerry Agresti . . . . engrg dir & chief of engrg

KMCI— Digital Channel: 41. Digital Hrs: 24 1,000 kw vis. ant 1,062t/1,122g TL: N38 58 42 W94 32 01 On air date: February 1988. 4720 Oak St., Kansas City, MO, 64112. Phone: (816) 753-4141. Fax: (816) 932-4122.E-mail: comments@38thespot.com Web Site: www.38thespot.com. Licensee: Scripps Howard Broadcasting Co. Group Owner: (group owner; (acq 2-3-2000). Population Served: 2,182,000 Natl. Rep: Harrington, Righter & Parsons,.
Key Personnel:
Craig Allison . . . . VP & gen mgr
Alan Fuchsman . . . . gen sls mgr
Dana Boyd . . . . progmg dir
Peggy Phillip . . . . news dir
Jay Nix . . . . chief of engrg

KPXE-TV— Digital Channel: 51. Digital Hrs: 6 AM-1 AM 1,000 kw vis. ant 1,112t/1,136g TL: N39 01 20 W94 30 49 On air date: Dec 1, 1978. 4720 Oak St., Kansas City, MO, 64112. Phone: (816) 924-5050. Fax: (816) 931-1818. Web Site: www.ionline.tv. Licensee: ION Media Kansas City License Inc., debtor-in-possession. Group Owner: Paxson Communications Corp. (acq 3-3-97; $16.4 million). Population Served: 750,000 Natl. Network: ION Television, . Washington Atty: Wiley, Rein & Fielding. Foreign lang progmg: SpanishS 1
Key Personnel:
Frank Barajas . . . . gen mgr
Alan Fuchsman . . . . adv dir
Dave Campbell . . . . chief of engrg

KSHB-TV— Digital Channel: 42. Digital Hrs: 24 3,450 kw vis. ant 1,036t/1,097g TL: N38 58 42 W94 32 01 On air date: Sept 28, 1970. 4720 Oak St., Kansas City, MO, 64112. Phone: (816) 753-4141. Fax: (816) 932-4122.E-mail: programming@nbcactionnews.com Web Site: www.nbcactionnews.com. Licensee: Scripps Howard Broadcasting Co. Group Owner: (group owner; (acq 10-28-77;10-3-77). Population Served: 2,182,000 Natl. Network: NBC, . Natl. Rep: Harrington, Righter & Parsons,. News staff: 75; News: 32 hrs wkly.
Key Personnel:
Craig Allison . . . . VP & gen mgr prom dir
John McKenna . . . . gen sls mgr
Dana Boyd . . . . progmg dir
Debbie Bush . . . . news dir
Jay Nix . . . . chief of engrg

KSMO-TV— Digital Channel: 47.1,795 kw vis, 179 kw aur. ant 1,119t/1,167g TL: N39 05 26 W94 28 18 On air date: Dec 7, 1983. 4500 Shawnee Mission Pkwy, Fairway, KS, 66205. Phone: (913) 621-6262. Fax: (913) 621-4703.E-mail: ksmo@myKSMOtv.com Web Site: www.myksmotv.com. Licensee: Meredith Corp. Group Owner: Sinclair Broadcast Group Inc. (acq 9-29-2005; $26.8 million). Population Served: 1,681,165 Natl. Network: MyNetworkTV, . Natl. Rep: Millennium Sales & Marketing,.
Key Personnel:
Kirk Black . . . . VP & gen mgr
Darrin McDonald . . . . gen sls mgr
Beth Green . . . . progmg dir & progmg
Tom Casey . . . . chief of engrg

WDAF-TV— Digital Channel: 34. Digital Hrs: 24 100 kw vis, 10 kw aur. ant 1,130t/1,163g TL: N39 04 20 W94 35 45 On air date: Oct 16, 1949. 3030 Summit, Kansas City, MO, 64108. Phone: (816) 753-4567. Fax: (816) 931-3984. Web Site: www.myfoxkc.com. Licensee: WDAF License Inc. Group Owner: Fox Television Stations Inc. (acq 1-23-97; grpsl). Population Served: 1,562,000 Natl. Network: Fox, . Natl. Rep: Fox Stations Sales,. News staff: 115; News: 49 hrs wkly.
Key Personnel:
Cheryl McDonald . . . . VP & gen mgr
Kelly Satalowich . . . . sls VP
Matt Rankin . . . . progmg dir
Jim Moore . . . . engrg VP

Kirksville

see Ottumwa, IA-Kirksville, MO market

Poplar Bluff

see Paducah, KY-Cape Girardeau, MO-Harrisburg-Mount Vernon, IL market

Springfield, MO

(DMA 74)

KOLR— Digital Channel: 10. Digital Hrs: 24 30 kw vis. ant 2,070t/1,945g TL: N37 13 08 W92 56 56 On air date: Mar 14, 1953. 2650 E. Division, Springfield, MO, 65803. Phone: (417) 862-1010. Fax: (417) 862-6439.E-mail: dwasson@kolr10.com Web Site: www.ozarksfirst.com. Licensee: Mission Broadcasting Inc. Group Owner: (group owner; (acq 12-30-2003). Population Served: 1,472,000 Natl. Network: CBS, . News staff: 30; News: 22 hrs wkly.
Key Personnel:
Mark Gordon . . . . gen mgr & natl sls mgr
Dean Wasson . . . . stn mgr & progmg mgr
Dave Thomason . . . . gen sls mgr & prom mgr
Dave Bowen . . . . prom mgr & chief of engrg
Polly Van Doren-Orr . . . . news dir
David Smith . . . . pub affrs dir & engrg dir

***KOZK—** Digital Channel: 23. Digital Hrs: 24 100 kw vis. ant 2,024t/1,925g TL: N37 10 11 W92 56 30 On air date: Jan 21, 1975. 901 S. National, Springfield, MO, 65897. Phone: (417) 836-3500. Fax: (417) 863-3569.E-mail: mail@optv.org Web Site: www.optv.org. Licensee: Board of Governors of Missouri State University. Population Served: 650,000 Natl. Network: PBS, . Washington Atty: Dow, Lohnes PLLC.
Key Personnel:
Brent Moore . . . . gen mgr & chief of engrg
Norma Scott . . . . stn mgr
Tom Carter . . . . progmg dir
Rebecca Scott . . . . spec ev coord

KRBK— Digital Channel: 49.10 kw vis. ant 327t/190g TL: N37 49 10 W92 44 52 Not on air, target date: unknown: 1 S. Memorial Dr., 20th Fl., St. Louis, MO, 63102. Phone: (314) 345-1000. Permittee: Koplar Communications International Inc. Ownership: Edward J. Koplar, 100%
Key Personnel:
Edward J. Koplar . . . . pres

KSFX-TV— Digital Channel: 28. Digital Hrs: 24 1,000 kw vis, 100 kw aur. ant 1,617t/1,486g TL: N37 13 08 W92 56 56 On air date: Sept 22, 1968. 2650 E. Division St., Springfield, MO, 65803. Phone: (417) 862-2727. Fax: (417) 831-4209. Web Site: www.ozarksfirst.com. Licensee: Nexstar Broadcasting Inc. Group Owner: Nexstar Broadcasting Group Inc. (acq 12-31-2003; grpsl). Population Served: 890,000 Natl. Network: Fox, . News: 12 hrs wkly.
Key Personnel:
Dave Thomason . . . . VP & gen sls mgr
Mark Gordon . . . . gen mgr
Dave Bowen . . . . prom mgr
Nancy Bingaman . . . . progmg mgr
Polly Van Doren-Orr . . . . news dir
David Smith . . . . engrg dir

KSPR— Digital Channel: 19. Digital Hrs: 24 5,010 kw vis, 112 kw aur. 1,995t/1,816g TL: N37 13 08 W92 56 56 (CP: 1,000 kw aur) On air date: Mar 17, 1983. Box 6030, Springfield, MO, 65801-6030. 1359 St. Louis St., Springfield, MO 65802. Phone: (417) 831-1333. Fax: (417) 831-4125. Web Site: www.springfield33.com. Licensee: Perkin Media LLC.. Ownership: William N. Perkin, 100% Group Owner: Piedmont Television Holdings LLC (acq 2007; $20.629 million). Natl. Network: ABC, . Washington Atty: Sciarrino and Associates PLLC. News staff: 21; News: 9 hrs wkly.

Key Personnel:
Brad Belote . . . . news dir
Neal Evans . . . . chief of engrg

KWBM— Digital Channel: 31. Digital Hrs: 24 191 kw vis. ant 1,112t/1,063g TL: N36 42 18 W93 03 45 On air date: 2002. 1736 E. Sunshine St., Suite 831, Springfield, MO, 65804. Phone: (417) 877-9231. Fax: (417) 877-9015. Web Site: www.my31tv.com. Licensee: EBC Harrison Inc., debtor in possession. (acq 9-21-2004; $8,666,670). Natl. Network: MyNetworkTV, . Natl. Rep: Roslin Television Sales,. Rgnl. Rep: Rgnl rep: Susan Cochran
Key Personnel:
S. Lanken . . . . pres & gen mgr

KYTV— Digital Channel: 44. Digital Hrs: 24 100 kw vis, 20 kw aur. ant 2,040t/2,000g TL: N37 10 11 W92 56 30 On air date: Oct 1, 1953. 999 W. Sunshine, P.O. Box 3500, Springfield, MO, 65807. Phone: (417) 268-3000. Fax: (417) 268-3100.E-mail: ky3@ky3.com Web Site: www.ky3.com. Licensee: KY-3 Inc. Group Owner: Schurz Communications Inc. (acq 2-19-87; $50.8 million; 1-19-87). Natl. Network: NBC, CW, . Natl. Rep: Harrington, Righter & Parsons,. News staff: 40; News: 24 hrs wkly.
Key Personnel:
Mike Scott . . . . gen mgr
Mary Chalender. . . . . sls dir & gen sls mgr
Dan McGrane . . . . mktg dir & prom mgr
Trenna Underhill . . . . progmg dir & progmg mgr
Kirk Lemons . . . . chief of engrg

St. Joseph, MO
(DMA 201)

KQTV— Digital Channel: 7. Digital Hrs: 20 40 kw vis. ant 587t/481g TL: N39 46 12 W94 47 53 On air date: Sept 27, 1953. Box 8369, Saint Joseph, MO, 64508. 4000 & Faraon St., Saint Joseph, MO 64506. Phone: (816) 364-2222. Fax: (816) 364-3787. Fax: TWX: 910-777-7872.E-mail: kq2@kq2.com Web Site: www.kq2.com. Licensee: Nexstar Broadcasting Inc. Group Owner: Nexstar Broadcasting Group Inc. (acq 2-14-97; with WTWO(TV) Terre Haute, IN). Population Served: 256,000 Natl. Network: ABC, . Natl. Rep: Blair Television, Petry Television Inc.,. Washington Atty: Drinker, Biddle & Reath. News staff: 18; News: 16 hrs wkly.
Key Personnel:
Heather Shearin . . . . VP & gen mgr
Steve Cline . . . . opns mgr
Jim Conlon . . . . prom mgr
Bridget Blevins . . . . news dir
Bill Smith . . . . chief of engrg

KTAJ-TV— Digital Channel: 21. Digital Hrs: 24 1,000 kw vis, 100 kw aur. ant 1,036t/1,053g TL: N39 01 20 W94 30 49 On air date: Oct 6, 1986. 4402 A S. 40th St., Saint Joseph, MO, 64503. Phone: (816) 364-1616. Fax: (816) 364-6729.E-mail: ktaj@tbn.org Web Site: www.tbn.org. Licensee: Trinity Christian Center of Santa Ana Inc. dba Trinity Broadcasting Network. Group Owner: Trinity Broadcasting Network (acq 5-8-2000; grpsl).
Key Personnel:
Paul Crouch . . . . pres
Jan Crouch. . . . . VP
Julie A. Cluck. stn mgr & mktg mgr prom mgr & adv mgr progmg mgr
Andrae Hannon . . . . pub affrs dir
Jeff Landers . . . . engrg dir & chief of engrg
Andrea McKinley. . . . . traf mgr

St. Louis, MO
(DMA 21)

KDNL-TV— Digital Channel: 31. Digital Hrs: 24 2,190 kw vis, 219 kw aur. ant 1,099t/1,123g TL: N38 34 50 W90 19 45 On air date: June 8, 1969. 1215 Cole St., Saint Louis, MO, 63106. Promotions/Tape Delivery, 1261 Dublin Rd., Columbus, OH 43215. Phone: (314) 436-3030. Web Site: www.abcstlouis.com. Licensee: KDNL Licensee L.L.C. Group Owner: Sinclair Broadcast Group Inc. (acq 5-30-96). Population Served: 1,088,550 Natl. Network: ABC, . Natl. Rep: Millennium Sales & Marketing,. Washington Atty: Shaw, Pittman.
Key Personnel:
Tom Tipton. . . . . gen mgr
Jim Wright . . . . opns dir & engrg dir
Andrea Schaffer . . . . natl sls mgr
Sandra Habeck. . . . . progmg mgr & pub svc dir
Martha Perry . . . . rsch dir
Frankie Horan. . . . . traf mgr

***KETC**— Digital Channel: 39. Digital Hrs: 24 295 kw vis, 29.5 kw aur. 1,070t/1,073g TL: N38 28 56 W90 23 53 On air date: Sept 20, 1954. 3655 Olive St., Saint Louis, MO, 63108. Phone: (314) 512-9000. Fax: (314) 512-9005. Web Site: www.ketc.org. Licensee: St. Louis Regional Educational and Public Television Commission. Population Served: 2,900,000 Natl. Network: PBS, . Washington Atty: Dow, Lohnes & Albertson.
Key Personnel:
Jack Galmiche. . . . . CEO & pres
Dick Skalski . . . . COO & sr VP
Richard Skalski . . . . CFO
Chrys Marlow . . . opns VP & opns dir engrg VP & chief of engrg
Patrick Murphy . . . . prom VP
Patti Kistler. . . . . progmg VP & progmg dir

KMOV— Digital Channel: 24. Digital Hrs: 24 100 kw vis, 15 kw aur. 1,097t/1,201g TL: N38 31 47 W90 17 58 On air date: July 8, 1954. One Memorial Dr., Saint Louis, MO, 63102. Phone: (314) 621-4444. Fax: (314) 444-3367. Fax: (314) 621-4755.E-mail: channel4@kmov.com Web Site: www.kmov.com. Licensee: KMOV-TV Inc. Group Owner: Belo Corp., Broadcast Division (acq 6-02-97; grpsl). Population Served: 3,500,000 Natl. Network: CBS, . Natl. Rep: TeleRep,. Washington Atty: Wiley, Rein & Fielding. News staff: 70; News: 29 hrs wkly.
Key Personnel:
Allan Cohen . . . . pres & gen mgr
Jim Rothschild . . . . opns dir & prom mgr
Robert Totsch . . . . gen sls mgr
Paul Conaty . . . . natl sls mgr
Liz Mullen. . . . . progmg mgr
Jenie Garner . . . . news dir
Walt Nichol . . . . engrg dir & chief of engrg
Laura Larrabee . . . . traf mgr

KNLC— Digital Channel: 14.1,148 kw vis. ant 1,300t/1,009g TL: N38 21 40 W90 32 55 On air date: Sept 12, 1982. Box 924, Saint Louis, MO, 63188. 1411 Locust St., St. Louis, MO 63188. Phone: (314) 436-2424. Fax: (314) 436-2434.E-mail: judy@knlc.tv Web Site: www.knlc.tv. Licensee: New Life Evangelistic Center Inc. Population Served: 1,200,000 Washington Atty: Midlen & Guillot.
Key Personnel:
Larry Rice. . . . . pres & gen mgr stn mgr
Ray Redlich . . . . VP
Judy Redlich . . . . sls dir
Victor Anderson . . . . progmg dir
Jim Barnes . . . . chief of engrg

KPLR-TV— Digital Channel: 26. Digital Hrs: 24 316 kw vis, 32 kw aur. ant 1,010t/1,033g TL: N38 31 47 W90 17 58 On air date: Apr 28, 1959. 2250 Ball Dr., Saint Louis, MO, 63146. Phone: (314) 447-1111. Fax: (314) 447-6404.E-mail: administration4@tribune.com Web Site: www.cb11tv.com. Licensee: KPLR Inc. Group Owner: Tribune Broadcasting Co. (acq 12-20-2007; grpsl). Population Served: 1,906,000 Natl. Network: CW, . Natl. Rep: TeleRep,. News: 4 hrs wkly.
Key Personnel:
Sheldon Ripson . . . . sr VP & news dir
Glen P. Callanan . . . . gen sls mgr
Suzi Schrappen . . . . prom dir
Gwen Moore . . . . progmg dir
Greg Boling . . . . chief of engrg

KSDK— Digital Channel: 35. Digital Hrs: 24 100 kw vis, 20 kw aur. 1,090t/1,148g TL: N38 34 05 W90 19 55 On air date: Feb 8, 1947. 1000 Market St., Saint Louis, MO, 63101. Phone: (314) 421-5055. Fax: (314) 444-5164.E-mail: comments@ksdk.com Web Site: www.ksdk.com. Licensee: Multimedia KSDK Inc. Group Owner: Gannett Broadcasting (acq 11-30-95; grpsl). Population Served: 2,500,000 Natl. Network: NBC, . Natl. Rep: Blair Television,. Washington Atty: Wiley, Rein & Fielding.
Key Personnel:
Lynn Beall . . . . pres & gen mgr
Julie Heskett . . . . VP
Mike Meara . . . . gen sls mgr
Mike Shipley . . . . mktg mgr & news dir
Jeff Winget . . . . prom dir & news dir
Rebecca Rahm. . . . . progmg dir & progmg mgr
Dave Hummert . . . . chief of engrg

KTVI— Digital Channel: 43. Digital Hrs: 24 100 kw vis, 20 kw aur. ant 1,089t/1,014g TL: N38 32 07 W90 22 23 On air date: Aug 10, 1953. 5915 Berthold Ave., Saint Louis, MO, 63110. Phone: (314) 647-2222. Fax: (314) 644-7419. Web Site: www.myfoxstl.com. Licensee: Community Television of Missouri License LLC. Group Owner: Fox Television Stations Inc. (acq 7-14-2008; grpsl). Population Served: 622,236 Natl. Network: Fox, . Washington Atty: Dow Lohnes PLLC. News: 37.5 hrs wkly.
Key Personnel:
Spencer Koch . . . . VP & gen mgr
Kurt Krueger. . . . . gen sls mgr
Cindy Solomon . . . . natl sls mgr
Steve Mills . . . . rgnl sls mgr
Kathryn Collett . . . . prom dir
Elaine Claspill. . . . . progmg dir
Ernie Dachel . . . . chief of engrg

WPXS— Digital Channel: 21. Digital Hrs: 24 1,000 kw vis. ant 298t/279g TL: N38 41 19 W89 33 38 On air date: Mar 1, 1983. 4751 Cartter Rd., Kell, IL, 62853. Phone: (618) 822-6900. Fax: (618) 822-6526.E-mail: wpxs@mvn.net Licensee: EBC St. Louis Inc. Group Owner: Equity Broadcasting Corp. (acq 4-26-2001; $17.75 million with KDUO(TV) Flagstaff, AZ). Population Served: 506,000
Key Personnel:
Dee Rose . . . . stn mgr & gen sls mgr

WRBU— Digital Channel: 47. Digital Hrs: 24 5,000 kw vis, 500 kw aur. 1,749t/849g TL: N38 23 18 W90 29 16 On air date: September 1989. 1408 N. Kingshighway Blvd., Suite 300, St. Louis, MO, 63113. Phone: (314) 256-4600. Fax: (314) 256-4655.E-mail: contest@my46stl.com Web Site: www.my46stl.com. Licensee: Roberts Broadcasting Co. Group Owner: (group owner). Population Served: 2,200,000 Natl. Network: MyNetworkTV, . Natl. Rep: Harrington, Righter & Parsons,. Washington Atty: Dow, Lohnes & Albertson. News staff: 4.
Key Personnel:
Bonni Burns . . . . gen mgr
Aliah Baker . . . . mktg mgr
Stan Marinoff. . . . . prom dir
Monica Nettles-Johnson. . . . . progmg dir
Chris Meisch. . . . . chief of engrg

Montana

Billings, MT
(DMA 170)

KHMT— Analog Channel: 4. Digital Channel: 22. Digital Hrs: 24 1,000 kw vis. ant 812t/368g TL: N45 44 24 W108 08 18 On air date: Aug 16, 1995. 445 S. 24th St. W., Billings, MT, 59102. Phone: (406) 652-4743. Fax: (406) 652-6963.E-mail: steves@khmt.com Web Site: www.yourbigsky.com. Licensee: Mission Broadcasting Inc. Group Owner: (group owner; (acq 12-30-2003). Population Served: 150,000 Natl. Network: Fox, . Washington Atty: Drinker, Biddle & Reath L.L.P.
Key Personnel:
Sandra Zoldowski . . . . gen mgr & opns mgr
Patricia King . . . . progmg dir
Ron Walden . . . . chief of engrg

KSVI— Analog Channel: 6. Digital Channel: 18. Digital Hrs: 24 1,000 kw vis. ant 746t/290g TL: N45 48 26 W108 20 25 On air date: 1993. 445 S. 24th St. W., Billings, MT, 59102. Phone: (406) 652-4743. Fax: (406) 652-6963.E-mail: steves@khmt.com Web Site: www.yourbigsky.com. Licensee: Nexstar Broadcasting Inc. Group Owner: Nexstar Broadcasting Group Inc. (acq 12-31-2003; grpsl). Population Served: 150,000 Natl. Network: ABC, . Washington Atty: Drinker, Biddle & Reath L.L.P.
Key Personnel:
Sandra Zoldowski . . . . gen mgr
Patricia King . . . . progmg dir
Ron Walden . . . . chief of engrg

KTVQ— Digital Channel: 10. Digital Hrs: 24 26.1 kw vis. ant 590t/369g TL: N45 46 01 W108 27 26 On air date: Nov 9, 1953. 3203 3rd Ave. N., Billings, MT, 59101. Phone: (406) 252-5611. Fax: (406) 252-9938.E-mail: news@ktvq.com Web Site: www.ktvq.com. Licensee: Evening Post Publishing Co. Group Owner: Cordillera Communications Inc. (acq 1994; $8.5 million). Population Served: 250,000 Natl. Network: CBS, CW, . Natl. Rep: Harrington, Righter & Parsons,. Washington Atty: Dow, Lohnes & Albertson. Wire Svc: AP News staff: 21; News: 17 hrs wkly.
Key Personnel:
Monty Wallis . . . . pres & gen mgr
John Webber . . . . progmg dir & chief of engrg
Jon Stepanek. . . . . news dir

KULR-TV— Digital Channel: 11. Digital Hrs: 24 16 kw vis. ant 626t/361g TL: N45 45 35 W108 27 14 On air date: Mar 15, 1958. 2045 Overland Ave., Billings, MT, 59102. Phone: (406) 656-8000. Fax: (406) 652-8207.E-mail: generalmanager@kulr.com Web Site: www.kulr8.com. Licensee: MMM License II LLC. Group Owner: MAX Media L.L.C. (acq 6-16-2004; $11 million). Population Served: 242,000 Natl. Network: NBC, . Wire Svc: AP News staff: 24; News: 20 hrs wkly.
Key Personnel:
John A. Trinder. . . . . pres
Bruce Cummings . . . . gen mgr
Rafael Archille . . . . gen sls mgr
Blaire Martin . . . . news dir
Kris Aschim . . . . pub svc dir
Rebroadcasts KYUS(TV) Miles City.

KYUS-TV— Digital Channel: 3. Digital Hrs: 24 1.03 kw vis. ant 99t/75g TL: N46 25 34 W105 51 38 On air date: 2003. Not on air, target date: unknown: Stn currently dark c/o KXGN-TV, 210 S. Douglas, Glendive, MT, 59330. Phone: (406) 377-3377. Fax: (406) 365-2181.E-mail: kxgnkdzn@midrivers.com Licensee: KYUS-TV Broadcasting Corp.

Ownership: Stephen A. Marks Population Served: 14,321 Natl. Network: NBC, . Natl. Rep: Adam Young,.
Key Personnel:
Stephen A. Marks . . . . pres
Paul Sturlaugson . . . . gen mgr

Bozeman

see Butte-Bozeman, MT market

Butte-Bozeman, MT
(DMA 190)

KBTZ— Digital Channel: 24.50 kw vis. ant 1,870t/171g TL: N46 00 24 W112 26 30 On air date: Aug 1, 2002. Stn currently dark Equity Broadcasting Corp., 1 Shackleford Dr., Suite 400, Little Rock, AR, 72211. 5115 US Hwy. 93 S., Missoula, MT 59804. Phone: (406) 542-8900. Fax: (501) 604-8004. Licensee: Montana License Sub, Inc., debtor in possession. Group Owner: Equity Broadcasting Corp.
Key Personnel:
Greg Fess. . . . . pres
Neal Ardman . . . . gen mgr
Sid Weathorford . . . . chief of engrg

KBZK— Digital Channel: 13. Digital Hrs: 20 18.9 kw vis. ant 889t/314g TL: N45 40 24 W110 52 02 On air date: September 1987. 90 TVWAY, Bozeman, MT, 59718. 1128 E. Main, Bozeman, MT 59715. Phone: (406) 586-3280. Fax: (406) 586-4135.E-mail: receptionist@kbzk.com Web Site: kbzk.com. Licensee: KCTZ Communications Inc. Group Owner: Cordillera Communications Inc. (acq 12-93). Population Served: 75,000 Natl. Network: CBS, CW, . Washington Atty: Dow, Lohnes & Albertson. Wire Svc: AP News staff: 3.
Key Personnel:
Terry Hurley . . . . pres
Pat Cooney . . . . gen mgr
Tim Gazy . . . . stn mgr & gen sls mgr & mktg mgr
John Sherer . . . . news dir
Andy Suk . . . . engrg dir
Ron Schlosser . . . . chief of engrg

KTVM— Digital Channel: 6. Digital Hrs: 24 11.2 kw vis. ant 1,939t/175g TL: N46 00 27 W112 26 30 On air date: May 12, 1970. 201 S. Wallace, Suite A5, Bozeman, MT, 59715. Phone: (406) 586-0296. Fax: (406) 586-0554.E-mail: news@ktvm.com Web Site: www.ktvm.com. Licensee: BlueStone License Holdings Inc. Group Owner: Lamco Communications Inc. (acq 5-31-2007; grpsl). Population Served: 59,300 Natl. Network: NBC, . Natl. Rep: Continental Television Sales,. Washington Atty: Covington & Burling LLP.
Key Personnel:
Charlie Henrich . . . . gen mgr
Swan Beck . . . . stn mgr
Scott Bruce . . . . rgnl sls mgr
Jean Zosel . . . . prom dir & progmg dir
Charlie Cannaliato. . . . . chief of engrg

***KUSM—** Digital Channel: 8. Digital Hrs: 24 44 kw vis. ant 817t/305g TL: N45 40 24 W110 52 02 On air date: Oct 1, 1984. Box 173340, Visual Communications, Bldg. 183, Montana State Univ., Bozeman, MT, 59717-3340. Phone: (406) 994-3437. Fax: (406) 994-6545.E-mail: kusm@montanapbs.org Web Site: www.montanapbs.org. Licensee: Montana State University. Population Served: 46,000 Natl. Network: PBS, .
Key Personnel:
Eric Hyyppa . . . . gen mgr & stn mgr
Lisa Titus . . . . dev dir
Amy Colson . . . . prom dir
Aaron Pruitt . . . . progmg dir
Dean Lawver. . . . . engrg dir & chief of engrg
Paul Heitt-Rennie . . . . traf mgr

KWYB— Digital Channel: 19. Digital Hrs: 24 2,684 kw vis. ant 1,955t TL: N46 00 29 W112 26 30 On air date: September 1996. 505 W. Park, Butte, MT, 59701. Phone: (406) 782-7185. Fax: (406) 723-9269. Web Site: www.kwyb.com. Licensee: MMM License LLC. Group Owner: MAX Media LLC (acq 2-5-2001; grpsl). Natl. Network: ABC, Fox, . Washington Atty: Reddy, Begley & McCormick.
Key Personnel:
Linda Gray. . . . . pres & pres gen mgr
Leslie Stoll . . . . natl sls mgr
Linda Julius . . . . prom VP & progmg mgr
Mike Warner . . . . chief of engrg

KXLF-TV— Digital Channel: 5. Digital Hrs: 24 10 kw vis. ant 1,929t/158g TL: N46 00 27 W112 26 30 On air date: Aug 14, 1953. 1003 S. Montana, Butte, MT, 59701. Box 3500, Butte, MT 59702. Phone: (406) 496-8400. Fax: (406) 782-8906. Web Site: www.montanasnewsstation.com. Licensee: KXLF Communications Inc. Group Owner: Cordillera Communications Inc. (acq 12-15-86; grpsl; 9-29-86). Population Served: 134,400 Natl. Network: CBS, CW, . Natl. Rep: Harrington, Righter & Parsons,. Washington Atty: Dow, Lohnes & Albertson. Wire Svc: AP News staff: 12; News: 16 hrs wkly.
Key Personnel:
Lynn Hopewell . . . . opns mgr
Pat Cooney . . . . gen mgr & stn mgr & gen sls mgr
John Sherer . . . . news dir
Mike Warner . . . . chief of engrg

Glendive, MT
(DMA 210)

KXGN-TV— Digital Channel: 5. Digital Hrs: 24 14.8 kw vis, 2.9 kw aur. ant 500t/146g TL: N47 03 15 W104 40 45 On air date: Nov 1, 1957. 210 S. Douglas, Glendive, MT, 59330. Phone: (406) 377-3377. Fax: (406) 365-2181.E-mail: kxgnkdzn@midrivers.com Web Site: www.glendivebroadcasting.com. Licensee: Glendive Broadcasting Corp.. Ownership: Stephen A. Marks. Group Owner: Glendive Broadcasting Corp. Population Served: 6,305 Natl. Network: CBS, NBC, . Washington Atty: Davis Wright Tremaine LLP. Wire Svc: UPI
Key Personnel:
Stephen A. Marks. . . . . pres
Paul Sturlaugson . . . gen mgr & gen sls mgr adv mgr & news dir
Lauri Harbig . . . . progmg dir
Mike Huseby. . . . . chief of engrg
Nikki Mannim . . . . traf mgr & sports cmtr

Great Falls, MT
(DMA 191)

KBAO— Digital Channel: 13. Digital Hrs: 24 5 kw vis. ant 1,929t TL: N47 10 46 W109 32 05 On air date: Dec 5, 2001. 620 N.E. Main Street, Lewistown, MT, 59457. Phone: (406) 457-1212. Fax: (406) 442-5106.E-mail: kernst@ktvh.com Web Site: www.beartoothnbc.com. Licensee: Beartooth Communications Co. Group Owner: (group owner). Natl. Network: NBC, .
Key Personnel:
Kathy Ernst . . . . gen mgr
Curtis Grevenitz. . . . . news dir
Mike Anderson . . . . chief of engrg

KBBJ— Digital Channel: 9. Digital Hrs: 24 316 kw vis. ant 482t TL: N48 29 39 W109 42 48 On air date: Dec 5, 2001. #2 Cowan Drive, Room 213B, Havre, MT, 59501. Phone: (406) 457-1212. Fax: (406) 442-5106.E-mail: kernst@ktvh.com Web Site: www.beartoothnbc.com. Licensee: Beartooth Communications Co. Group Owner: (group owner). Natl. Network: NBC, .
Key Personnel:
Kathy Ernst . . . . gen mgr
Curtis Grevenitz. . . . . news dir
Mike Anderson . . . . chief of engrg

KFBB-TV— Digital Channel: 8. Digital Hrs: 18 100 kw vis, 20 kw aur. ant 590t/540g TL: N47 32 08 W111 17 02 On air date: Mar 21, 1954. Box 1139, Great Falls, MT, 59403-1139. 3200 Old Havre Hwy., Black Eagle, MT 59414. Phone: (406) 453-4377. Fax: (406) 727-9703.E-mail: kfbb@kfbb.com Web Site: www.kfbb.com. Licensee: KFBB L.L.C. Group Owner: Dix Communications (acq 7-1-82; $5.2 million;5-17-82). Population Served: 161,800 Natl. Network: ABC, . Washington Atty: Baker & Hostetler. Wire Svc: Direct Line Weather Wire News staff: 6; News: 6 hrs wkly.
Key Personnel:
Danette Sukut . . . . gen mgr & stn mgr gen sls mgr
Julie Klesh . . . . news dir
Roy Davis . . . . chief of engrg
Linda Julius . . . . progmg

KLMN— Digital Channel: 26.50 kw vis. ant 213t/164g TL: N47 32 23 W111 17 06 On air date: 2003. Stn currently dark 118 6th St. S., Great Falls, MT, 59401. 5115 US Hwy. 93 S., Missoula, MT 59804. Phone: (406) 251-1360. Fax: (406) 251-1364. Licensee: Montana License Sub, Inc., debtor in possession. Group Owner: Equity Broadcasting Corp.
Key Personnel:
Tom Shannon . . . . opns VP

KRTV— Digital Channel: 7. Digital Hrs: 20 100 kw vis, 10 kw aur. ant 590t/550g TL: N47 32 09 W111 17 02 On air date: Oct 5, 1958. Box 2989, Great Falls, MT, 59403. 3300 Old Havre Hwy., Black Eagle, MT 59414. Phone: (406) 791-5400. Fax: (406) 791-5479.E-mail: krtv@krtv.com Web Site: www.montanasnewsstation.com. Licensee: KRTV Communications Inc. Group Owner: Cordillera Communications Inc. (6-86). Population Served: 80,000 Natl. Network: CBS, CW, . Natl. Rep: Harrington, Righter & Parsons,. Washington Atty: Dow, Lohnes & Albertson. Wire Svc: AP Wire Svc: CNN News staff: 15; News: 15 hrs wkly.
Key Personnel:
Jon Saunders. gen mgr
Art Taft . . . . prom mgr
Jerry Howard . . . . news dir
Marlowe Rames . . . . engrg dir
Roxie Rattray . . . . progmg

KTGF— Digital Channel: 45. Digital Hrs: 24 2,040 kw vis, 204 kw aur. ant 1,046t/830g TL: N47 36 26 W111 21 27 On air date: Sept 21, 1986. 118 6th St. S., Box 169, Great Falls, MT, 59403. Phone: (406) 761-8816. Fax: (406) 454-3484.E-mail: ktgf@ktgf.com Web Site: www.ktgf.com. Licensee: Destiny Licenses LLC.. Ownership: Destiny Communications LLC, 100% Group Owner: MAX Media LLC (acq 11-24-2004; $3 million with translator K47DP Lewistown). Washington Atty: Garvey, Schubert & Barer.
Key Personnel:
Darnell Washington. . . . . CEO & pres natl sls mgr
Andrea Dean . . . . stn mgr
Jennifer Rimmel . . . . progmg mgr

Helena, MT
(DMA 206)

KMTF— Digital Channel: 29. Digital Hrs: 24 316 kw vis. ant 1,899t TL: N46 35 47 W112 17 47 On air date: 1998. 100 W. Lyndale Ave., Helena, MT, 59601. Phone: (406) 457-1010. Fax: (406) 457-2758.E-mail: cw10@surewest.net Web Site: www.cwhelena.com. Licensee: Rocky Mountain Broadcasting Co. Natl. Network: CW, .
Key Personnel:
Jon Gibson. . . . . gen mgr
Paul Albertson. stn mgr

KTVH-DT— Digital Channel: 12. Digital Hrs: 24 17.5 kw vis. ant 2,339t/144g TL: N46 49 35 W111 42 33 On air date: Jan 1, 1958. 100 W. Lyndale Ave., Suite A, Fort Myers, MT, 59601. Phone: (406) 457-1212. Fax: (406) 442-5106.E-mail: kernst@ktvh.com Web Site: www.beartoothnbc.com. Licensee: Beartooth Communications Co. Group Owner: Sunbelt Communications Co. (acq 7-9-97). Population Served: 140,000 Natl. Network: NBC, . Washington Atty: Gerald S. Rourke. News staff: 8; News: 7 hrs wkly.
Key Personnel:
Kathy Ernst . . . . gen mgr
Curtus Grevenitz . . . . news dir
Mike Anderson . . . . chief of engrg

Missoula, MT
(DMA 166)

KCFW-TV— Digital Channel: 9. Digital Hrs: 24 17 kw vis. ant 2,788t/220g TL: N48 00 48 W114 21 55 On air date: June 10, 1968. Box 857, Kalispell, MT, 59901. 401 First Ave. E., Kalispell, MT 59901. Phone: (406) 755-5239. Fax: (406) 752-8002.E-mail: news@kcfw.com Web Site: www.nbcmontana.com. Licensee: BlueStone License Holdings Inc. Group Owner: Lamco Communications Inc. (acq 5-31-2007; grpsl). Population Served: 79,600 Natl. Network: NBC, . Washington Atty: Covington & Burling LLP. News staff: 5; News: 6 hrs wkly.
Key Personnel:
Rebecca Swan . . . . gen mgr
Jacque Walawander. . . . . gen sls mgr
Jean Zosel . . . . prom dir & progmg dir
Wade Muehlhof . . . . stn mgr & news dir
Chris Neuhausen . . . . chief of engrg

KECI-TV— Digital Channel: 13. Digital Hrs: 24 302 kw vis, 30.2 kw aur. 2,001t/290g TL: N47 01 04 W114 00 47 On air date: July 1, 1954. 340 W. Main, Missoula, MT, 59802. Box 5268, Missoula, MT 59806-5268. Phone: (406) 721-2063. Fax: (406) 721-2083/(406) 549-6507.E-mail: news@keci.tv Web Site: www.nbcmontana.com. Licensee: BlueStone License Holdings Inc. Group Owner: Lamco Communications Inc. (acq 5-31-2007; grpsl). Population Served: 104,700 Natl. Network: NBC, . Natl. Rep: Continental Television Sales,. Washington Atty: Covington & Burling LLP. News: 14 hrs wkly.
Key Personnel:
Charlie Henrich . . . . gen mgr & natl sls mgr
Jacque Walawander. . . . . rgnl sls mgr
Jean Zosel . . . . . . mktg dir & prom dir progmg dir & rsch dir
Jim Harmon . . . . news dir & sports cmtr
Charlie Cannaliato. . . . . chief of engrg
Sharikay Austin . . . . traf mgr
Kathie Bowers . . . . film dir

KMMF— Digital Channel: 17. Digital Hrs: 24 50 kw vis. ant 2,060t/85g TL: N46 48 08 W113 58 19 On air date: May 1, 2001. Stn currently dark 5115 US Hwy. 93 S., Missoula, MT, 59804. Phone: (406) 542-8900. Fax: (406) 728-4800. Web Site: www.ktmf.com. Licensee: Montana License Sub, Inc., debtor in possession. Group Owner: Equity Broadcasting Corp. Washington Atty: Irwin, Caampbell & Tannenwald.

Key Personnel:
Linda Gray . . . . pres & gen mgr
Mike Warner . . . . chief of engrg

KPAX-TV— Digital Channel: 7. Digital Hrs: 24 275 kw vis, 49 kw aur. 2,150t/284g TL: N47 01 06 W114 00 41 On air date: June 5, 1970. 1049 W. Central, Missoula, MT, 59801. Phone: (406) 542-4400. Fax: (406) 543-7111.E-mail: office@kpax.com Web Site: www.kpax.com. Licensee: KPAX-TV Communications Inc. Group Owner: Cordillera Communications Inc. Population Served: 207,200 Natl. Network: CBS, CW, . Washington Atty: Dow, Lohnes & Albertson. News: 15 hrs wkly.
Key Personnel:
Bob Hermes . . . . gen mgr & stn mgr
Jim McLean . . . . sls dir & gen sls mgr
James Rafferty . . . . prom mgr & pub svc dir
Tammy Engle . . . . progmg dir
Joel Lundstad . . . . news dir & news cmtr
Larry Arbaugh . . . . chief of engrg

KTMF— Digital Channel: 23. Digital Hrs: 24 1,820 kw vis. 2,054t TL: N47 01 10 W114 00 46 On air date: Nov 16, 1990. 2200 Stephens Ave., Missoula, MT, 59801. Phone: (406) 542-8900. Fax: (406) 728-4800.E-mail: ktmf@ktmf.com Web Site: www.abcmontana.com. Licensee: MMM License LLC. Group Owner: MAX Media LLC (acq 2-5-2001; grpsl). Natl. Network: ABC, Fox, . Washington Atty: Reddy, Begley & McCormick.
Key Personnel:
Linda Gray . . . . pres & gen mgr
Leslie Stoll . . . . gen sls mgr & natl sls mgr
Linda Julius . . . . progmg dir & progmg mgr
Mike Warner . . . . chief of engrg
Rebroadcasts KTMF (LP) Kalispell 90%.

***KUFM-TV—** Digital Channel: 11. Digital Hrs: 24 125 kw vis. 2,116t/259g (CP: 3 kw vis, ant 2,070t) On air date: Jan 18, 1997. PARTV 180, 32 Campus Dr., Univ. of Montana, Missoula, MT, 59812. Phone: (406) 243-4101. Fax: (406) 243-3299.E-mail: kufm@montanapbs.org Web Site: www.montanapbs.org. Licensee: The University of Montana. Natl. Network: PBS, .
Key Personnel:
William Marcus . . . . gen mgr & stn mgr
Daniel Dauterive . . . . opns dir
Rebroadcasts KUSM(TV) Bozeman 85%.

Nebraska

Alliance

see Cheyenne, WY-Scottsbluff, NE market

Hastings

see Lincoln & Hastings-Kearney, NE market

Kearney

see Lincoln & Hastings-Kearney, NE market

Lincoln & Hastings-Kearney, NE (DMA 106)

KFXL-TV— Digital Channel: 51. Digital Hrs: 24 14 kw vis. ant 410t/490g TL: N40 51 10 W96 40 36 On air date: June 26, 2006. 707 N. 48th St., Suite B, Lincoln, NE, 68504. Phone: (402) 464-5694. Fax: (402) 466-1311. Licensee: Lincoln Broadcasting LLC. Ownership: World Investments Inc. Natl. Network: Fox, . Washington Atty: Hogan & Hartson.
Key Personnel:
Steve Harry. . . . . stn mgr

KGIN— Digital Channel: 11. Digital Hrs: 24 25 kw vis. ant 1,032t/1,014g TL: N40 35 14 W98 48 10 On air date: Oct 1, 1961. Box 1069, Grand Island, NE, 68801. 123 N. Locust St., Grand Island, NE 68802. Phone: (308) 382-6100. Fax: (308) 382-3216.E-mail: kgin1011@hotmail.com Web Site: www.kolnkgin.com. Licensee: WEAU Licensee Corp. Group Owner: Gray Television Inc. (acq 7-30-98; grpsl). Population Served: 240,800 Natl. Network: CBS, MyNetworkTV, . Natl. Rep: Continental Television Sales,. Washington Atty: Pepper & Corazzini.
Key Personnel:
Clint Simmons. gen sls mgr & rgnl sls mgr mktg mgr & adv mgr news dir & pub affrs dir
Satellite of KOLN Lincoln.

KHAS-TV— Digital Channel: 5. Digital Hrs: 6AM-12:35AM 100 kw vis, 20 kw aur. ant 731t/768g TL: N40 39 06 W98 23 04 On air date: Jan 1, 1956. 6475 Osborne Dr. W., Hastings, NE, 68901. Phone: (402) 463-1321. Fax: (402) 463-6551.E-mail: khas@khastv.com Web Site: www.khastv.com. Licensee: Hoak Media of Nebraska License LLC. Group Owner: (group owner; (acq 12-21-2005; with KNOP-TV North Platte). Population Served: 600,000 Natl. Network: NBC, . Washington Atty: Fletcher, Heald & Hildreth. Wire Svc: Skycom
Key Personnel:
Ulysses Carlini . . . . gen mgr
Alan Uerling . . . . opns mgr
Connie Caldwell . . . . gen sls mgr
Connie Cardwell . . . . rgnl sls mgr
Jackie Ackerman . . . . prom mgr
Jackie Arkerman. . . . . progmg dir
Dennis Kellogg . . . . news dir

KHGI-TV— Digital Channel: 13. Digital Hrs: 24 316 kw vis, 31.6 kw aur. ant 1,110t/1,163g TL: N40 39 28 W98 52 04 On air date: Dec 24, 1953. Box 220, Kearney, NE, 68848-0220. 1078 25th Rd., Axtell, NE 68924. Phone: (308) 743-2494. Fax: (308) 743-2644.E-mail: comments@nebraska.tv Web Site: www.nebraska.tv. Licensee: Pappas Telecasting of Central Nebraska L.P. (DE limited partnership). Group Owner: Pappas Telecasting Companies (acq 7-1-96; grpsl). Population Served: 257,910 Natl. Network: ABC, . Natl. Rep: Harrington, Righter & Parsons,. News staff: 26; News: 17.5 hrs wkly.
Key Personnel:
Mark Baumert . . . . CEO & news dir
Scott Swenson. . . . . pres & progmg mgr
Jerry Fuehrer . . . . exec VP & chief of engrg
Vincent Barresi . . . . gen mgr
Susan Christensen . . . . gen sls mgr
Anita Wragge . . . . prom mgr

***KHNE-TV—** Digital Channel: 28. Digital Hrs: 18 605 kw vis, 60.5 kw aur. ant 1,220t/1,238g TL: N40 46 20 W98 05 21 On air date: Nov 17, 1968. 1800 N. 33rd St., Lincoln, NE, 68503. Phone: (402) 472-3611. Fax: (402) 472-1785.E-mail: net1@unl.edu Web Site: www.netnebraska.org. Licensee: Nebraska Educational Telecommunications Commission. Natl. Network: PBS, . National Educational Telecommunications Association Washington Atty: Dow, Lohnes & Albertson. News staff: 3; News: 30 min. wkly.
Key Personnel:
Rod Bates . . . . gen mgr
Satellite of *KUON-TV Lincoln.

KLKN— Digital Channel: 8. Digital Hrs: 20 25.9 kw vis. ant 1,433t/1,406g TL: N40 52 59 W97 18 19 On air date: Dec 3, 1964. 3240 S. 10th St., Lincoln, NE, 68502. Phone: (402) 434-8000. Fax: (402) 436-2236.E-mail: 8@klkntv.com Web Site: www.klkntv.com. Licensee: Citadel Communications Co. L.L.C. Group Owner: Citadel Communications Co. Ltd. (acq 11-15-86;7-28-86). Population Served: 655,000 Natl. Network: ABC, . Natl. Rep: Millennium Sales & Marketing,. Washington Atty: Latham & Watkins. Wire Svc: AP News staff: 21; News: 22 hrs wkly.
Key Personnel:
Roger Moody . . . . gen mgr
Jeff Swanson . . . . opns dir
Kay Wonderlich . . . . natl sls mgr
Phil Maddern . . . . rgnl sls mgr
Mark Haggar . . . . news dir
Dan Ackerman . . . . chief of engrg

***KLNE-TV—** Digital Channel: 26. Digital Hrs: 18 100 kw vis, 10 kw aur. ant 1,062t/1,065g TL: N40 23 05 W99 27 30 On air date: Sept 6, 1965. 1800 N. 33rd St., Lincoln, NE, 68503. Phone: (402) 472-3611. Fax: (402) 472-1785.E-mail: net1@unl.edu Web Site: www.netnebraska.org. Licensee: Nebraska Educational Telecommunications Commission. Natl. Network: PBS, . National Educational Telecommunications Association Washington Atty: Dow, Lohnes & Albertson.
Key Personnel:
Rod Bates . . . . gen mgr
Satellite of *KUON-TV Lincoln.

***KMNE-TV—** Digital Channel: 7. Digital Hrs: 18 316 kw vis, 31.6 kw aur. ant 1,484t/1,524g TL: N42 20 05 W99 29 01 On air date: Sept 1, 1967. 1800 N. 33rd St., Lincoln, NE, 68503. Phone: (402) 472-3611. Fax: (402) 472-1785.E-mail: net1@unl.edu Web Site: www.netnebraska.org. Licensee: Nebraska Educational Telecommunications Commission. Natl. Network: PBS, . National Educational Telecommunications Association Washington Atty: Dow, Lohnes & Albertson.
Key Personnel:
Rod Bates . . . . gen mgr
Satellite of *KUON-TV Lincoln.

KOLN— Digital Channel: 10. Digital Hrs: 24 28 kw vis. ant 1,489t/1,465g TL: N40 48 11 W97 10 52 On air date: Feb 18, 1953. 840 North 40th Street, Lincoln, NE, 68503. Phone: (402) 467-4321. Fax: (402) 467-9210.E-mail: info@1011now.com Web Site: www.1011now.com. Licensee: Gray Television Licensee Inc. Group Owner: Gray Television Inc. (acq 7-30-98; grpsl). Population Served: 604,530 Natl. Network: CBS, MyNetworkTV, . Natl. Rep: Continental Television Sales,. Washington Atty: Holland & Knight, LLP. Wire Svc: AP
Key Personnel:
Jason Effinger . . . . pres
Heath Miller . . . . gen mgr
Stephanie McGowen . . . . opns mgr
Kris Ryan . . . . gen sls mgr
Marty Winters . . . . natl sls mgr
Nikki Bates . . . . prom dir & progmg mgr
Troy Frankforter. . . . . opns dir & prom mgr
Jerry Howard . . . . news dir
Clint Simmons . . . . pub affrs dir
Brent Haun . . . . chief of engrg

KSNB-TV— Digital Channel: 4. Digital Hrs: 24 100 kw vis, 12.6 kw aur. ant 1,131t/1,086g TL: N40 05 13 W97 55 13 On air date: Oct 1, 1965. Box 220, Kearney, NE, 68848-0220. 1078 25 Rd., Axell, NE 68924. Phone: (308) 743-2494. Fax: (308) 743-2644.E-mail: comments@nebraska.tv Web Site: www.nebraska.tv. Licensee: Colins Broadcasting Co. (acq 2-17-99; $333,333). Population Served: 257,910 Natl. Network: Fox, . Natl. Rep: Harrington, Righter & Parsons,. News: 13 hrs wkly.
Key Personnel:
Vince Barresi . . . . gen mgr
Susan Christensen . . . . gen sls mgr
Anita Wragge . . . . prom mgr
Scott Swenson. progmg mgr
Mark Baumert . . . . news dir
Jerry Fuehrer. . . . . chief of engrg
Satellite of KTVG Grand Island.

KTVG-TV— Digital Channel: 16. Digital Hrs: 24 1,000 kw vis. ant 610t/571g TL: N40 43 44 W98 34 13 On air date: December 1992. Box 220, Kearney, NE, 68848. 1078 25 Rd., Axtell, NE 68924. Phone: (308) 734-2794. Fax: (308) 743-2644.E-mail: comments@nebraska.tv Web Site: www.nebraska.tv. Licensee: Hill Broadcasting Inc. Natl. Network: Fox, . Natl. Rep: Harrington, Righter & Parsons,.
Key Personnel:
Vince Barresi . . . . gen mgr
Susan Christensen . . . . gen sls mgr
Anita Wragge . . . . prom mgr
Scott Swenson. progmg mgr
Mark Baumert . . . . news dir
Jerry Fuehrer. . . . . chief of engrg

***KUON-TV—** Digital Channel: 12. Digital Hrs: 18 316 kw vis, 31.6 kw aur. ant 830t/879g TL: N41 08 18 W96 27 19 On air date: Nov 1, 1954. 1800 N. 33rd St., Lincoln, NE, 68503. Phone: (402) 472-3611. Fax: (402) 472-1785.E-mail: net1@unl.edu Web Site: www.netnebraska.org. Licensee: University of Nebraska. (acq 7-28-54;8-2-54). Population Served: 670,000 Natl. Network: PBS, . National Educational Telecommunications Association Washington Atty: Dow, Lohnes & Albertson. News staff: 3; News: 30 min. wkly.
Key Personnel:
Rod Bates . . . . gen mgr

KWNB-TV— Digital Channel: 6. Digital Hrs: 24 100 kw vis, 21.6 kw aur. ant 737t/586g TL: N40 37 29 W101 01 58 On air date: Feb 9, 1956. Box 220, Kearney, NE, 68848. 1078 25 Rd., Axtell, NE 68924. Phone: (308) 743-2794. Fax: (308) 743-2644. Web Site: www.nebraska.tv. Licensee: Pappas Telecasting of Central Nebraska L.P. (DE limited partnership). Group Owner: Pappas Telecasting Companies (acq 7-1-96; grpsl). Population Served: 257,910 Natl. Network: ABC, . Natl. Rep: Harrington, Righter & Parsons,. News staff: 26; News: 17.5 hrs wkly.
Key Personnel:
Vince Barresi . . . . gen mgr
Susan Christensen . . . . gen sls mgr
Anita Wragge . . . . prom mgr
Scott Swensen . . . . progmg dir
Mark Baumert . . . . news dir
Jerry Fuehrer. . . . . chief of engrg
Rebroadcasts KHGI-TV, Kearney, 100%.

McCook

see Wichita-Hutchinson Plus, KS market

Merriman

see Denver, CO market

Norfolk

see Sioux City, IA market

North Platte, NE (DMA 209)

KNOP-TV— Digital Channel: 2. Digital Hrs: 18 100 kw vis, 15 kw aur. 630t/608g TL: N41 12 13 W100 43 58 On air date: Dec 2, 1958. Box

749, North Platte, NE, 69103. N. Hwy. 83, North Platte, NE 69101. Phone: (308) 532-2222. Fax: (308) 532-9579.E-mail: lewysknop@knoptv.com. Web Site: www.knopnews2.com. Licensee: Hoak Media of Nebraska License LLC. Group Owner: (group owner; (acq 12-21-2005; with KHAS-TV Hastings). Population Served: 14,500 Natl. Network: NBC, . Natl. Rep: Blair Television,. Washington Atty: Fletcher, Heald & Hildreth. Wire Svc: AP News staff: 10; News: 15 hrs wkly.

Key Personnel:
Lewys Carlini	gen mgr
Darlene Lyman	gen sls mgr
Gregg Hoover	prom dir
Jacques Harms	news dir
Mike McNeil	chief of engrg

*KPNE-TV— Digital Channel: 9. Digital Hrs: 18 316 kw vis, 31.6 kw aur. 1,020t/1,006g TL: N41 01 16 W101 09 10 On air date: Sept 12, 1966. 1800 N. 33rd St., Lincoln, NE, 68503. Phone: (402) 472-3611. Fax: (402) 472-1785.E-mail: net1@unl.edu Web Site: www.netnebraska.org. Licensee: Nebraska Educational Telecommunications Commission. Natl. Network: PBS, . National Educational Telecommunications Association Washington Atty: Dow, Lohnes & Albertson.

Key Personnel:
Rod Bates	gen mgr

Satellite of *KUON-TV Lincoln.

Omaha, NE
(DMA 76)

*KBIN-TV— Digital Channel: 33.575 kw vis, 57.5 kw aur. ant 317t/163g TL: N41 15 14 W95 50 07 On air date: Sept 7, 1975. Box 6450, Iowa Public TV, Johnston, IA, 50131-6450. 6450 Corporate Dr., Johnston , IA 50131. Phone: (515) 242-3100.E-mail: public_information@iptv.org Web Site: www.iptv.org. Licensee: Iowa Public Broadcasting Board. Natl. Network: PBS, . Washington Atty: Dow, Lohnes PLLC.

Key Personnel:
Daniel K. Miller	gen mgr

KETV— Digital Channel: 20. Digital Hrs: 24 316 kw vis, 31.6 kw aur. ant 1,373t/1,330g TL: N41 18 32 W96 01 33 On air date: Sept 17, 1957. 2665 Douglas St., Omaha, NE, 68131-2699. Phone: (402) 345-7777. Fax: (402) 522-7755. Fax: (402) 522-7761. Web Site: www.ketv.com. Licensee: KETV Hearst-Argyle Television Inc. Group Owner: Hearst-Argyle Television Inc. (acq 3-18-99; grpsl). Population Served: 1,504,300 Natl. Network: ABC, . Natl. Rep: Eagle Television Sales,. News: 28 hrs wkly.

Key Personnel:
Sarah Smith	pres & gen mgr
Brian Sather	gen sls mgr
Rose Ann Shannon	news dir
Warren Behrens	chief of engrg
Linda Hood	progmg

*KHIN— Digital Channel: 35.2,040 kw vis, 204 kw aur. ant 1,560t/1,503g TL: N41 20 40 W95 15 21 On air date: Sept 7, 1975. Box 6450, Iowa Public TV, Johnston, IA, 50131-6450. 6450 Corporate Dr., Johnston, IA 50131. Phone: (515) 242-3100.E-mail: public_information@iptv.org Web Site: www.iptv.org. Licensee: Iowa Public Broadcasting Board. Natl. Network: PBS, . Washington Atty: Dow, Lohnes PLLC.

Key Personnel:
Daniel K. Miller	gen mgr

KMTV-TV— Digital Channel: 45. Digital Hrs: 24 1,000 kw vis. ant 1,290t/1,213g TL: N41 18 22 W96 01 37 On air date: Sept 1, 1949. 10714 Mockingbird Dr., Omaha, NE, 68127. Phone: (402) 592-3333.E-mail: feedback@action3news.com Web Site: www.action3news.com. Licensee: Journal Broadcast Corp. Group Owner: Emmis Communications Corp. (acq 3-27-2007). Population Served: 357,800 Natl. Network: CBS, . News: 23 hrs wkly.

Key Personnel:
Rob Burton	gen mgr
Eric Hanneman	gen sls mgr
Willie Garrett	mktg dir
Renee Rich	progmg dir
Ken Dudzik	news dir
Scott Krayenhagen	chief of engrg

KPTM— Digital Channel: 43. Digital Hrs: 24 5,000 kw vis, 500 kw aur. ant 1,558t/1,479g TL: N41 04 15 W96 13 30 On air date: Apr 6, 1986. 4625 Farnam St., Omaha, NE, 68132. Phone: (402) 558-4200. Fax: (402) 554-4290.E-mail: contact42@kptm.com Web Site: www.kptm.com. Licensee: KPTM (TV) License LLC. Group Owner: Pappas Telecasting Companies (acq 3-14-86). Natl. Network: Fox, MyNetworkTV, . Natl. Rep: TeleRep,. Washington Atty: Paul, Hastings, Janofsky & Walker. Wire Svc: FNS News staff: 20; News: 7 hrs wkly.

Key Personnel:
Randy Oswald	exec VP & gen mgr
Chris McDade	opns mgr
Jeff Miller	gen sls mgr
Tim Moan	rgnl sls mgr
Sam Lawson	prom mgr
Darlene Goldsberry	progmg mgr

KXVO— Digital Channel: 38. Digital Hrs: 24 5,000 kw vis, 500 kw aur. ant 1,558t/1,464g TL: N41 04 15 W96 13 30 On air date: June 10, 1995. 4625 Farnam St., Omaha, NE, 68132. Phone: (402) 554-1500. Fax: (402) 554-4290.E-mail: contact42@kptm.com Web Site: www.kxvo.com. Licensee: Mitts Telecasting Co. Ownership: (LMA to Pappas Telecasting Companies) (acq 6-13-2000; $972,000). Natl. Network: CW, . Natl. Rep: TeleRep,. Washington Atty: Bryan Cave.

Key Personnel:
Randy Oswald	exec VP & gen mgr
Jeff Miller	gen sls mgr
Tim Moan	rgnl sls mgr
Sam Lawson	prom mgr
Darlene Goldsberry	progmg mgr
Chris McDade	opns

*KYNE-TV— Digital Channel: 17. Digital Hrs: 18 525 kw vis, 52.5 kw aur. ant 426t/396g TL: N41 15 28 W96 00 32 On air date: Oct 19, 1965. 1800 N. 33rd St., Lincoln, NE, 68503. Phone: (402) 472-3611. Fax: (402) 472-1785.E-mail: net1@unl.edu Web Site: www.netnebraska.org. Licensee: Nebraska Educational Telecommunications Commission. Population Served: 500,000 Natl. Network: PBS, . National Educational Telecommunications Association Washington Atty: Dow, Lohnes & Albertson. News staff: 3; News: 30 min. wkly.

Key Personnel:
Rod Bates	gen mgr

Satellite of *KUON-TV Lincoln.

WOWT-TV— Digital Channel: 22. Digital Hrs: 24 100 kw vis, 20 kw aur. ant 1,371t/1,344g TL: N41 18 40 W96 01 37 On air date: Aug 29, 1949. 3501 Farnam St., Omaha, NE, 68131-3356. Phone: (402) 346-6666. Fax: (402) 233-7880.E-mail: sixonline@wowt.com Web Site: www.wowt.com. Licensee: Gray Television Licensee LLC. Group Owner: Gray Television Inc. (acq 10-2002; grpsl). Population Served: 347,328 Natl. Network: NBC, . Natl. Rep: Continental Television Sales,. Washington Atty: Fletcher, Heald & Hildreth. News staff: 52; News: 37 hrs wkly.

Key Personnel:
Frank Jonas	gen mgr
Don Felton	gen sls mgr
Vic Richards	prom dir
Gail Backer	progmg mgr
John Clark	news dir
Rick Klutts	chief of engrg

Scottsbluff
see Cheyenne, WY-Scottsbluff, NE market

Nevada

Elko
see Salt Lake City, UT market

Ely
see Salt Lake City, UT market

Las Vegas, NV
(DMA 42)

KBLR— Analog Channel: 39. Digital Channel: 40. Analog Hrs: 24 Digital Hrs: 24 1,320 kw vis, 132 kw aur. ant 1,204t/223g TL: N36 00 31 W115 00 22 (CP: 2,800 kw vis) On air date: Apr 20, 1989. 73 Spectrum Blvd., Las Vegas, NV, 89101. Phone: (702) 258-0039. Fax: (702) 258-0556. Web Site: http://telemundo.yahoo.com. Licensee: Summit Media Limited Partnership. Ownership: Scott Gentry, Bruce F. Becker, William O'Connell, et al. (acq 1993; $1.5 million;9-20-93). Population Served: 1,300,000 Natl. Network: Telemundo (Spanish), . Washington Atty: KMZ Rosenman. Foreign lang progmg: SpanishS 168 News staff: 8; News: 2 hrs wkly.

Key Personnel:
Carlos Sanchez	VP & gen mgr
Julie Sanchez	stn mgr
Bill George	natl sls mgr
Brenda Macias	news dir

KINC— Digital Channel: 16. Digital Hrs: 24 1,000 kw. ant 1,871t/125g TL: N35 56 46 W115 02 34 On air date: October 1995. 500 Pilot Rd., Suite D, Las Vegas, NV, 89119. Phone: (702) 434-0015. Fax: (702) 434-0527. Web Site: www.kinc.entravision.com. Licensee: Entravision Holdings L.L.C. Group Owner: Entravision Communications Co. L.L.C. Population Served: 1,625,000 Natl. Network: Univision (Spanish), . Washington Atty: Thompson Hine L.L.P. Foreign lang progmg: SpanishS 168 News: 5 hrs wkly.

Key Personnel:
Chris Roman	gen mgr
J.R. Des Amours	natl sls mgr
Karina Barcena	prom dir & prom mgr
Erin Thomas	traf mgr

KLAS-TV— Digital Channel: 7. Digital Hrs: 24 316 kw vis, 57.5 kw. ant 2,001t/272g TL: N35 56 44 W115 02 33 On air date: July 22, 1953. 3228 Channel 8 Dr., Las Vegas, NV, 89109. Phone: (702) 792-8888. Fax: (702) 792-9034. Web Site: www.lasvegasnow.com. Licensee: KLAS Inc., a Nevada Corp. Group Owner: Landmark Communications Inc. (acq 7-1-78; $8 million). Population Served: 315,000 Natl. Network: CBS, . Natl. Rep: Continental Television Sales,. Washington Atty: Wiley, Rein Fielding, LLP.

Key Personnel:
Emily Neilson	pres & gen mgr
Linda Bonnici	sls VP
Doug Kramer	chief of engrg

*KLVX— Digital Channel: 11. Digital Hrs: 24 295 kw vis, 29.5 kw aur. ant 1,220t/176g TL: N36 00 27 W115 00 24 On air date: Mar 25, 1968. 4210 Channel 10 Dr., Las Vegas, NV. Phone: (702) 799-1010. Fax: (702) 799-5586. Web Site: www.klvx.org. Licensee: Clark County School District Board of Trustees. Population Served: 986,152 Natl. Network: PBS, . Washington Atty: Wiley, Rein & Fielding. Wire Svc: Accu-Weather

Key Personnel:
Tom Axtell	gen mgr & stn mgr
TB D	dev mgr
Cyndy Robbins	progmg dir

KMCC— Digital Channel: 32. Digital Hrs: 24 416 kw vis. ant -207t/270g TL: N35 10 08 W114 38 09 On air date: 2005. 3100 S. Needles Hwy., Suite 1700, Laughlin, NV, 89029. Phone: (702) 298-2222. Fax: (702) 298-3495. Licensee: Mojave Broadcasting Co. Ownership: Suzanne E. Rogers, 48% of votes; Perry C. Rogers, 28% of votes; and Kimberly Rogers Cell, 24% of votes. Population Served: 64,051 Natl. Rep: Blair Television,. Washington Atty: Wiley, Rein & Fielding.

Key Personnel:
Bruce Clark	gen mgr & chief of engrg

KTNV-TV— Digital Channel: 13. Digital Hrs: 24 30.5 kw vis. ant 1,988t/222g TL: N35 56 43 W115 02 32 On air date: May 4, 1956. 3355 S. Valley View Blvd., Las Vegas, NV, 89102. Phone: (702) 876-1313. Fax: (702) 871-1961.E-mail: desk@ktnv.com Web Site: www.ktnv.com. Licensee: Journal Broadcast Corp. Group Owner: Journal Broadcast Group Inc. (acq 6-29-79). Population Served: 1,564,000 Natl. Network: ABC, . Natl. Rep: Petry Television Inc.,. Washington Atty: Crowell & Moring. News staff: 60; News: 22 hrs wkly.

Key Personnel:
Jim Prather	exec VP & VP gen mgr & stn mgr
Thom Poterfield	gen sls mgr
Jim Koonce	mktg dir
Karin Movesian	prom mgr & news dir
Marie Shea	progmg dir
Loretta Seitz	traf mgr

KVBC-DT— Digital Channel: 2. Digital Hrs: 24 100 kw vis, 10 kw aur. ant 1,263t/226g TL: N36 00 32 W115 00 19 On air date: Oct 1, 1979. 1500 Foremaster Ln., Las Vegas, NV, 89101. Phone: (702) 642-3333. Fax: (702) 657-3152 (news).E-mail: news3@kvbc.com Web Site: www.kvbc.com. Licensee: Valley Broadcasting Co. Ownership: James Rogers, 49.97%; Louis Wiener Jr. Estate, 30%; Janet Rogers, 12.53%. Population Served: 1,101,000 Natl. Network: NBC, . Washington Atty: Dow, Lohnes & Albertson. News staff: 55; News: 29 hrs wkly.

Key Personnel:
James E. Rogers	CEO
Ralph Toddre	pres
Lisa Howfield	gen mgr
Joanne Nasby	gen sls mgr & natl sls mgr
Dale Wyman	prom dir
Dick Tuiniga	news dir
Mark Guranik	engrg dir & chief of engrg
Pam Sewell	traf mgr

KVCW— Digital Channel: 29. Digital Hrs: 24 1,350 kw vis, 500 kw aur. ant 1,906t/80g TL: N35 56 44 W115 02 31 On air date: Aug 1, 1989.

3830 S. Jones Blvd., Las Vegas, NV, 89103. Phone: (702) 952-4600. Fax: (702) 873-1233. Web Site: www.thecwlasvegas.tv. Licensee: Channel 33 Inc. Group Owner: Sinclair Broadcast Group Inc. (acq 2-23-2000; $33 million for stock). Population Served: 1,566,000 Natl. Network: CW, . Washington Atty: Fletcher, Heald & Hildreth.

Key Personnel:

Rob Weisbord	gen mgr
Tom Anderson	sls dir
Tommie Gonzalez	progmg dir
Mike Brown	chief of engrg

KVMY— Digital Channel: 22. Digital Hrs: 24 400 kw vis, 40 kw aur. ant 1,160t/115g TL: N36 00 26 W115 00 24 On air date: July 31, 1984. 3830 S. Jones Blvd., Las Vegas, NV, 89103. Phone: (702) 382-2121. Fax: (702) 382-1351. Web Site: www.mylvtv.com. Licensee: KUPN Licensee L.L.C. Group Owner: Sinclair Broadcast Group Inc. (acq 5-30-97; $87 million). Population Served: 864,000 Natl. Network: MyNetworkTV, . Washington Atty: Dow, Lohnes & Albertson.

Key Personnel:

David Smith	CEO & pres opns mgr
Rob Weisbord	gen mgr
Chris Cohen	sls dir
Mike Brown	chief of engrg

KVVU-TV—(Henderson, Digital Channel: 9. Digital Hrs: 24 86 kw vis. ant 1,262t/170g TL: N36 00 26 W115 00 22 On air date: October 1967. 25 TV-5 Dr., Henderson, NV, 89014. Phone: (702) 435-5555. Fax: (702) 436-2507. Web Site: www.fox5vegas.com. Licensee: KVVU Broadcasting Corp. Group Owner: Meredith Broadcasting Group, Meredith Corp., see Cross-Ownership (acq 5-85; $36 million). Population Served: 1,246,200 Natl. Network: Fox, . Natl. Rep: TeleRep,. Washington Atty: Haley, Bader & Potts.

Key Personnel:

Darrin McDonald	gen mgr

Reno, NV
(DMA 108)

KAME-TV— Digital Channel: 20. Digital Hrs: 24 631 kw vis, 63.1 kw aur. ant 620t/152g TL: N39 19 07 W119 47 51 On air date: Oct 1, 1983. 4920 Brookside Ct., Reno, NV, 89502. Phone: (775) 856-2121. Fax: (775) 856-2100. Web Site: www.foxreno.com. Licensee: Broadcast Development Corp. (acq 2-28-94). Population Served: 500,000 Natl. Network: MyNetworkTV, . Natl. Rep: TeleRep,. Washington Atty: Bryan Cave.

Key Personnel:

Steve Cummings	VP & gen mgr
Ray Stofer	chief of opns & chief of engrg
Amy Chapman	rgnl sls mgr

KEGS— Digital Channel: 50.30 kw vis. ant 1,446t/35g TL: N38 03 05 W117 13 30 On air date: 2002. Equity Broadcasting Corp., 1 Shackleford Dr., Suite 400, Little Rock, AR, 72211. Phone: (501)

219-2400. Fax: (501) 604-8004. Licensee: Nevada Channel 3 Inc., debtor in possession.

Key Personnel:

Neal Ardman	pres & gen mgr
Jeff Timpa	progmg dir
Mike Brown	chief of engrg

*KNPB— Digital Channel: 15. Digital Hrs: 24 5.01 kw vis, 1 kw aur. 459t/93g TL: N39 35 01 W119 47 52 On air date: October 1983. 1670 N. Virginia St., Reno, NV, 89503. Phone: (775) 784-4555. Fax: (775) 784-1438.E-mail: info@knpb.org Web Site: www.knpb.org. Licensee: Channel 5 Public Broadcasting Inc. Natl. Network: PBS, . Washington Atty: Schwartz, Woods & Miller.

Key Personnel:

Pat Miller	gen mgr
Barbara Harmon	progmg mgr

KOLO-TV— Digital Channel: 8. Digital Hrs: 24 166 kw vis, 30.2 aur. 2,929t/119g TL: N39 18 49 W119 53 00 On air date: Sept 27, 1953. 4850 Ampere Dr., Reno, NV, 89502. Phone: (775) 858-8888. Fax: (775) 858-8855. Web Site: www.kolotv.com. Licensee: Gray Television Licensee Corp. Group Owner: Gray Television Inc. (acq 12-10-2002; $41.5 million with K12IX Austin, K58AO Crystal Bay, K03DN Ely/McGill and K49CK Stead/Lawton, all NV). Population Served: 432,400 Natl. Network: ABC, . Natl. Rep: Millennium Sales & Marketing,. Washington Atty: Haley, Bader & Potts. News: 22 hrs wkly.

Key Personnel:

Matt James	gen mgr
Bruce Lekband	prom mgr

KREN-TV— Digital Channel: 26. Digital Hrs: 24 1,820 kw vis, 182 kw aur. ant 2,923t/139g TL: N39 18 47 W119 52 59 On air date: Nov 1, 1985. 5166 Meadowood Mall Cir., Reno, NV, 89502-6502. Phone: (775) 333-2727. Fax: (775) 327-6868.E-mail: renofrontdesk@kren.com Web Site: www.kren.com. Licensee: Entravision Holdings LLC. Group Owner: Pappas Telecasting Companies (acq 4-1-2009; $4 million). Natl. Network: CW, . Natl. Rep: Harrington, Righter & Parsons,. Washington Atty: Thompson Hine LLP.

Key Personnel:

Harry Pappas	CEO
Easter Dominquez	gen mgr
Leslie Sadley	prom dir
Alan Plotkin	adv mgr
Debbie Sweeney	progmg VP
Leslie SAdley	pub affrs dir
James Ocon	chief of engrg
Bill May	rsch dir
Miriam Carbajal	traf mgr

KRNV-DT— Digital Channel: 7. Digital Hrs: 24 17.4 kw vis, 3.4 kw aur. ant 420t/92g TL: N39 35

03 W119 48 06 On air date: Sept 30, 1962. Box 7160, Reno, NV, 89510. 1790 Vassar St., Reno, NV 89502. Phone: (775) 322-4444. Fax: (775) 785-1208. Fax: (775) 785-1206.E-mail: comments@krnv.com Web Site: www.krnv.com. Licensee: Sierra Broadcasting Co.. Ownership: James E. Rogers. Group Owner: Sunbelt Communications Co. (acq 9-13-89). Population Served: 172,863 Natl. Network: NBC, . Washington Atty: Gerald S. Rourke. News staff: 26; News: 14 hrs wkly.

Key Personnel:

Mary Beth Farrell	gen mgr & stn mgr
John Finkbohner	opns mgr
Mark Murakami	rgnl sls mgr
Jon Killoran	news dir
Barbara Monroy	traf mgr

KRXI-TV— Digital Channel: 44. Digital Hrs: 24 178 kw vis, 17.8 kw aur. 2,808t/207g TL: N39 35 25 W119 55 40 On air date: Dec 3, 1995. 4920 Brookside Ct., Reno, NV, 89502. Phone: (775) 856-1100. Fax: (775) 856-1101. Web Site: www.foxreno.com. Licensee: KTVU Partnership. Natl. Network: Fox, . Natl. Rep: TeleRep,. Washington Atty: Dow, Lohnes & Albertson.

Key Personnel:

Steve Cmmings	gen mgr
Steve Cummings	gen sls mgr
Mandy Anderson	rgnl sls mgr
Mike Arnold	chief of engrg

KTVN— Digital Channel: 13. Digital Hrs: 24 89.1 kw vis, 8.9 kw aur. 2,152t/187g TL: N39 15 29 W119 42 37 On air date: June 4, 1967. Box 7220, Reno, NV, 89510. 4925 Energy Way, Reno, NV 89502. Phone: (775) 858-2222. Fax: (775) 861-4298.E-mail: ktvn@ktvn.com Web Site: www.ktvn.com. Licensee: Sarkes Tarzian Inc. Group Owner: (group owner; (acq 8-13-80; $12.5 million). Population Served: 669,000 Natl. Network: CBS, . Washington Atty: Leventhal, Senter & Lerman. News staff: 35; News: 22.5 hrs wkly.

Key Personnel:

Tom Tarzian	chmn
Tom Tolar	pres
Bob Davis	CFO
Lawson Fox	gen mgr
John Richardson	gen sls mgr
Sharon Facque	natl sls mgr
Ann Burns	prom mgr & pub affrs dir
Pat Hall	progmg dir
Jason Pasco	news dir
Jack Antonio	chief of engrg
Mike Alger	weather dir

KWNV— Digital Channel: 7. Digital Hrs: 24 890 w vis. ant 2,132t TL: N41 00 41 W117 45 59 On air date: 1998. c/o KRNV, 1790 Vassar St., Reno, NV, 89502. Phone: (775) 322-4444. Fax: (775) 785-1208.E-mail: comments@krnv.com Licensee: Sierra Broadcasting Co. Natl. Network: NBC, .

Key Personnel:
John Finkbohner . . . . opns mgr
Barbara Monroy . . . . traf mgr
Rebroadcasts KRNV-DT Reno 100%.

New Hampshire

Concord

see Boston (Manchester, NH) market

Derry

see Boston (Manchester, NH) market

Durham

see Boston (Manchester, NH) market

Keene

see Boston (Manchester, NH) market

Littleton

see Portland-Auburn, ME market

Manchester

see Boston (Manchester, NH) market

Merrimack

see Boston (Manchester, NH) market

New Jersey

Atlantic City

see Philadelphia market

Burlington

see Philadelphia market

Camden

see Philadelphia market

Linden

see New York market

Montclair

see New York market

New Brunswick

see New York market

Newark

see New York market

Newton

see New York market

Paterson

see New York market

Secaucus

see New York market

Trenton

see Philadelphia market

Vineland

see Philadelphia market

West Milford

see New York market

Wildwood

see Philadelphia market

New Mexico

Albuquerque-Santa Fe, NM
(DMA 44)

KASA-TV— Digital Channel: 27. Digital Hrs: 24 28.2 kw vis, 2.82 kw aur. 1,968t/178g TL: N35 46 50 W106 31 35 On air date: May 8, 1981. 13 Broadcast Plaza S.W., Albuquerque, NM, 87104. Phone: (505) 243-2285. Fax: (505) 248-1464.E-mail: kasa@kasa.com Web Site: www.kasa.com. Licensee: KASALicense Subsidiary, LLC. Group Owner: Raycom Media Inc. (acq 9-2-99; grpsl). Population Served: 1,664,000 Natl. Network: Fox, . Natl. Rep: TeleRep,. Washington Atty: Covington & Burling. News: 7 hrs wkly.
Key Personnel:
Bill Anderson . . . . gen mgr
Jim Giudecess . . . . natl sls mgr
Frank Montoya . . . . rgnl sls mgr
Michelle Donaldson . . . . news dir
Pat Gonzales . . . . traf mgr

KASY-TV— Digital Channel: 45. Digital Hrs: 24 1,450 kw vis. ant 4,153t TL: N35 12 45 W106 26 56 On air date: Oct 6, 1995. 8341 Washington St. N.E., Albuquerque, NM, 87113. Phone: (505) 797-1919. Fax: (505) 938-4401. Web Site: www.my50.tv. Licensee: Acme Television Licenses of New Mexico L.L.C. Group Owner: Acme Communications Inc. (acq 6-18-99; $25.4 million). Natl. Network: MyNetworkTV, . Washington Atty: Leventhal, Senter & Lerman.
Key Personnel:
Stan Gill . . . . gen mgr
Dan Marchese . . . . gen sls mgr
Chris Iller . . . . prom mgr
Larry Oliver . . . . chief of engrg

*KAZQ— Digital Channel: 17. Digital Hrs: 24 263 kw vis. ant 4,090t/110g TL: N35 12 51 W106 27 01 On air date: Oct 12, 1987. 4501 Montgomery Blvd. N.E., Albuquerque, NM, 87109. Phone: (505) 884-8355. Fax: (505) 883-1229.E-mail: kazq32@kazq32.org Web Site: www.kazq32.org. Licensee: Alpha-Omega Broadcasting of Albuquerque Inc. Ownership: Non-profit corporation. Population Served: 800,000 Washington Atty: Donald E. Martin. Foreign lang progmg: SpanishS 2
Key Personnel:
Raymond Franks . . . . pres
Brenton Franks. VP & gen mgr
Jeffrey Helmers . . . . gen mgr & dev dir
Howard Holley . . . . progmg dir

KBIM-TV— Digital Channel: 10. Digital Hrs: 24 316 kw vis, 40.7 kw aur. ant 1,999t/1,839g TL: N33 03 20 W103 49 12 On air date: Feb 26, 1966. Box 910, Roswell, NM, 88202. 214 N. Main St., Roswell, NM 88202. Phone: (575) 622-2120. Fax: (505) 623-6606. Web Site: www.kbimtv.com. Licensee: LIN of New Mexico LLC. Group Owner: Emmis Communications Corp. (acq 11-30-2005; grpsl). Population Served: 300,000 Natl. Network: CBS, . Washington Atty: Reed, Smith, Shaw & McClay. News staff: 11; News: 6 hrs wkly.

Key Personnel:
Gene Munsey . . . . VP & gen mgr gen sls mgr
Marcus Damberger . . . . opns mgr
Pat Gonzales . . . . traf mgr
Rebroadcasts KRQE(TV) Albuquerque 90%.

KCHF— Digital Channel: 10. Digital Hrs: 24 263 kw vis, 26.3 kw aur. 2,027t/272g TL: N35 47 15 W106 31 35 On air date: Jan 21, 1984. Box 4338, Albuquerque, NM, 87196. 27556 I 25 &. Frontage Rd., Santa Fe, NM 87508. Phone: (505) 345-1991 (radio). Phone: (505) 473-1111. Fax: (505) 345-5669. Web Site: www.kchf.com. Licensee: Son Broadcasting Inc. Population Served: 660,000 Washington Atty: Gammon & Grange. Foreign lang progmg: SpanishS 4
Key Personnel:
Belarmino R. Gonzalez . . . . CEO & chmn pres
Annette Garcia . . . . gen mgr
Mary Kay Gonzales . . . . progmg dir
Rob Ramseyer . . . . chief of engrg

KLUZ-TV— Digital Channel: 42. Digital Hrs: 24 1,200 kw vis. ant 4,120t/118g TL: N35 12 41 W106 26 56 On air date: September 1987. 2725 Broadbent Pkwy. N.E., Suite E, Albuquerque, NM, 87107. Phone: (505) 342-4141. Phone: (505) 344-5589. Fax: (505) 344-8714. Web Site: www.univision.com. Licensee: Entravision Holdings L.L.C. Group Owner: Entravision Communications Co. L.L.C. (acq 3-21-99). Population Served: 819,330 Natl. Network: Univision (Spanish), . Foreign lang progmg: SpanishS 168 News staff: 10; News: 1/2 hr wkly.
Key Personnel:
Walter Ulloa . . . . CEO
Phillip Wilkinson . . . . pres
John DiLorenzo . . . . CFO
Margarita Wilder . . . . gen mgr & gen sls mgr
Kambiz Victory . . . . chief of engrg

KNAT-TV— Analog Channel: 23. Digital Channel: 24. Digital Hrs: 24 360 kw vis. ant 4,130t/108g TL: N35 12 54 W106 27 02 On air date: Oct 17, 1975. 1510 Coors Rd. N.W., Albuquerque, NM, 87121. Phone: (505) 836-6585. Fax: (505) 831-0025.E-mail: cmansfield@tbn.org Web Site: www.tbn.org. Licensee: Trinity Broadcasting Network. Group Owner: (group owner; acq 5-8-2000; grpsl). Population Served: 800,000 Natl. Network: NBC, . Washington Atty: Joseph E. Dunne III. Foreign lang progmg: SpanishS 3
Key Personnel:
Cynthia Mansfield . . . . gen mgr & dev dir

*KNMD-TV— Digital Channel: 9. Digital Hrs: 24 200 w vis. ant 4,070t/46g TL: N35 12 45 W106 26 58 On air date: Sept 12, 2004. 1130 University Blvd. N.E., Albuquerque, NM, 87102. Phone: (505) 277-2121. Fax: (505) 277-2191.E-mail: viewer@knme.org Web Site: www.knmetv.org. Licensee: The Regents of the University of New Mexico. Population Served: 857,000 Natl. Network: PBS, . Washington Atty: Dow, Lohnes & Albertson, LLC.
Key Personnel:
Ted A. Garcia . . . . CEO & gen mgr
Jim Gale . . . . engrg dir

*KNME-TV— Digital Channel: 35. Digital Hrs: 24 26.9 kw vis, 5.6 kw aur. ant 4,228t/172g TL: N35 12 44 W106 26 57 On air date: May 5, 1958. 1130 University Blvd. N.E., Albuquerque, NM, 87102. Phone: (505) 277-2121. Web Site: www.knmetv.org. Licensee: Regents of University of New Mexico and Board of Education, Albuquerque. Population Served: 945,000 Natl. Network: PBS, . Washington Atty: Dow, Lohnes & Albertson.
Key Personnel:
Chad Davis . . . . gen mgr
Joanne Bachmann . . . . dev dir
Jim Gale . . . . engrg dir

KOAT-TV— Digital Channel: 7. Digital Hrs: 24 26.5 kw vis. ant 4,238t/233g TL: N35 12 53 W106 27 01 On air date: Sept 28, 1953. Box 25982, Albuquerque, NM, 87125. 3801 Carlisle N.E., Albuquerque, NM 87107. Phone: (505) 884-7777. Fax: (505) 884-6282.E-mail: koatdesk@hearst.com Web Site: www.koat.com. Licensee: KOAT Hearst Television Inc. Group Owner: Hearst-Argyle Television Inc. (acq 3-18-99; grpsl). Population Served: 543,751 Natl. Network: ABC, . Washington Atty: Brooks, Pierce, McLendon, Humphrey & Leonard. Wire Svc: UPI
Key Personnel:
Mary Lynn Roper . . . . pres & gen mgr

KOB— Digital Channel: 26. Digital Hrs: 24 270 kw vis. ant 4,189t/170g TL: N35 12 42 W106 26 58 On air date: Nov 29, 1948. Box 1351, Albuquerque, NM, 87103. 4 Broadcast Plaza S.W., Albuquerque, NM 87104. Phone: (505) 243-4411. Fax: (505) 764-2522.E-mail: kobtv@kob.com Web Site: www.kob.com. Licensee: KOB-TV L.L.C. Group Owner: Hubbard Broadcasting Inc. (acq 3-15-57; grpsl;3-18-57). Population Served: 568,700 Natl. Network: NBC, . Washington Atty: Fletcher, Heald & Hildreth. Wire Svc: UPI News: 12 hrs wkly.

Key Personnel:
Mike Burgess . . . . VP
Susan Raybon . . . . gen mgr
Susan Connor. . . . . stn mgr & opns mgr
Jeff Finkel. . . . . gen sls mgr & natl sls mgr
Vince Gasparich. . . . . prom dir
Juanita Garay . . . . progmg mgr
Rhonda Aubrey . . . . news dir
Joan Lucas . . . . pub affrs dir
Sean Anker . . . . engrg dir & chief of engrg
Elena Hernandez. . . . . rsch dir
Jackie Gregory . . . . traf mgr
J.P. Murrieta . . . . sports cmtr
Larry Rice . . . . weather dir

KOBF— Digital Channel: 12. Digital Hrs: 24 316 kw vis, 31.6 kw aur. 410t/209g TL: N36 41 43 W108 13 14 On air date: 1972. Box 1620, Farmington, NM, 87499. 825 W. Broadway, Farmington, NM 87401. Phone: (505) 326-1141. Fax: (505) 327-5196. Web Site: www.kob.com. Licensee: KOB-TV L.L.C. Group Owner: Hubbard Broadcasting Inc. (acq 9-19-83; $2.35 million;8-15-83). Population Served: 109,000 Natl. Network: NBC, . Washington Atty: Fletcher, Heald & Hildreth. News staff: 6; News: 4 hrs wkly.
Key Personnel:
Don Baughan . . . . opns mgr
Satelite of KOB-TV Albuquerque.

KOBG-TV— Digital Channel: 12. Digital Hrs: 24 6 kw vis. ant 1,647t/190g TL: N32 51 49 W108 14 27 On air date: 2001. Box 1351, Albuquerque, NM, 87103. Phone: (505) 243-4411. Fax: (505) 764-2522.E-mail: kobtv@kob.com Web Site: www.kob.com. Licensee: KOB-TV LLC. Natl. Network: NBC, .
Key Personnel:
Mike Burgess. . . . . gen mgr
Satellite of KOB-TV Albuquerque.

KOBR— Digital Channel: 8. Digital Hrs: 24 316 kw vis, 52.5 kw aur. ant 1,748t/1,542g TL: N33 22 31 W103 46 12 On air date: June 24, 1953. 124 E. 4th St., Roswell, NM, 88201. Phone: (505) 625-8888. Fax: (505) 625-8866.E-mail: kobtv@kob.com Web Site: www.kob.com. Licensee: Stanley S. Hubbard Revocable Trust. Group Owner: Hubbard Broadcasting Inc. (acq 8-10-2001). Population Served: 307,000 Natl. Network: NBC, . Washington Atty: Fletcher, Heald & Hildreth. News staff: 4.
Key Personnel:
Stanley S. Hubbard . . . . pres
Charlie Blanco . . . . gen mgr & stn mgr
Dusty Deane . . . . prom mgr
Wayne Koontz . . . . chief of engrg
Nora Nieto . . . . traf mgr
Rebroadcasts KOB-TV Albuquerque 90%.

KOCT— Digital Channel: 19. Digital Hrs: 24 15 kw vis. ant 1,092t/905g TL: N32 47 38 W104 12 29 On air date: August 1959. Box 25982, Albuquerque, NM, 87125. 3801 Carlisle N.E., Albuquerque, NM 87107. Phone: (505) 884-7777. Fax: (505) 884-6282.E-mail: koatdesk@hearst.com Web Site: www.koat.com. Licensee: KOAT Hearst Television Inc. Group Owner: Hearst-Argyle Television Inc. (acq 3-18-99; grpsl). Natl. Network: ABC, . Washington Atty: Brooks, Pierce, McLendon, Humphrey & Leonard.
Key Personnel:
Mary Lynn Roper . . . . gen mgr
Satellite of KOAT-TV Albuquerque.

KOFT— Analog Channel: 3. Digital Channel: 8. Analog Hrs: 24 Digital Hrs: 24 100 kw vis. ant 413t/269g TL: N36 41 48 W108 10 39 Not on air, target date: unknown: Box 25982, Albuquerque, NM, 87125. 3801 Carlisle N.E., Albuquerque, NM 87107. Phone: (505) 884-7777. Fax: (505) 884-6282.E-mail: koatdesk@hearst.com Web Site: www.koat.com. Permittee: KOAT Hearst-Argyle Television Inc. Natl. Network: ABC, . Washington Atty: Verner, Liipfert, Bernhard, McPherson & Hand.
Key Personnel:
Mary Lynn Roper . . . . pres & gen mgr

KOVT— Digital Channel: 10. Digital Hrs: 24 3.2 kw vis. ant 1,591t/112g TL: N32 51 46 W108 14 28 On air date: Sept 9, 1987. Box 25982, c/o KOAT-TV, Albuquerque, NM, 87125. 3801 Carlisle N.E., Albuquerque, NM 87107. Phone: (505) 884-7777. Fax: (505) 884-6282.E-mail: koatdesk@hearst.com Web Site: www.koat.com. Licensee: KOAT Hearst Television Inc. Group Owner: Hearst-Argyle Television Inc. (acq 3-18-99; grpsl). Population Served: 550,000 Natl. Network: ABC, . Washington Atty: Brooks, Pierce, McLendon, Humphrey & Leonard.
Key Personnel:
Mary Lynn Roper . . . . pres & gen mgr
Satellite of KOAT-TV Albuquerque.

KREZ-TV— Digital Channel: 15.6.17 kw vis. ant 361t/141g TL: N37 15 46 W107 53 58 On air date: Sept 4, 1965. 158 Bodo Dr., Durango, CO 81303. Phone: (970) 259-6666. Fax: (970) 247-8472. Licensee: LIN of Colorado LLC. Group Owner: Emmis Communications Corp. (acq 11-30-2005; grpsl). Population Served: 66,000 Natl. Network: CBS, NBC, .
Key Personnel:
Bill Anderson. . . . . gen mgr & stn mgr
Christopher Bartsh . . . . gen mgr & stn mgr
Satellite of KRQE(TV) Albuquerque, NM.

***KRMU—** Digital Channel: 20. Digital Hrs: 24 8.51 kw vis. ant 308t/46g TL: N37 15 45 W107 54 07 On air date: Jan 2005. 1089 Bannock St., Denver, CO, 80204. Phone: (303) 892-6666. Fax: (303) 620-5600. Web Site: www.rmpbs.org. Licensee: Rocky Mountain Public Broadcasting Network, Inc. Permittee: Rocky Mountain Public Broadcasting Network Inc. Natl. Network: PBS, . Washington Atty: Dow, Lohnes & Albertson.
Key Personnel:
Bill Wengert . . . . CFO
James N. Morgese . . . . pres & gen mgr
Donna Sanford . . . . progmg dir
Rebroadcasts KRMJ-TV Grand Junction 100%.

KRPV— Digital Channel: 27. Digital Hrs: 24 50 kw vis. ant 399t/269g TL: N33 23 50 W104 22 34 On air date: Sept 15, 1986. Box 61000, Midland, TX, 79711. Box 967, 2606 S. Main, Roswell, NM 88203-0967. Phone: (800) 707-0420. Fax: (505) 622-3424.E-mail: info@ptcbglc.com Web Site: www.godslearningchannel.com. Licensee: Prime Time Christian Broadcasting. Population Served: 272,826 Foreign lang progmg: SpanishS 4
Key Personnel:
Al Cooper. . . . . . . CEO & pres gen mgr & gen sls mgr engr
Tommy Cooper . . . . VP

KRQE— Digital Channel: 13. Digital Hrs: 24 89.1 kw vis, 9 kw aur. ant 4,178t/141g TL: N35 12 40 W106 26 57 On air date: Oct 3, 1953. 13 Broadcast Plaza S.W., Albuquerque, NM, 87104. Phone: (505) 243-2285. Fax: (505) 248-1464.E-mail: Bill.Anderson@krqe.com Web Site: www.krqe.com. Licensee: LIN of New Mexico LLC. Group Owner: Emmis Communications Corp. (acq 11-30-2005; grpsl). Population Served: 1,710,000 Natl. Network: CBS, . Natl. Rep: Harrington, Righter & Parsons,. Washington Atty: Reed, Smith, Shaw & McClay. Wire Svc: CBS News staff: 65; News: 24 hrs wkly.
Key Personnel:
Bill Anderson . . . . gen mgr
Gina Galindo . . . . opns dir
Mary Lou Davis . . . . natl sls mgr
Frank Montoya. . . . . rgnl sls mgr
Parker Harms. mktg dir
Don Pierce . . . . progmg dir & progmg mgr
Michelle Donaldson . . . . news dir
Frank Lilley . . . . engrg dir
Marilyn Painter. . . . . rsch dir
Pat Gonzales . . . . traf mgr

KRWB-TV— Digital Channel: 21.5,000 kw vis. ant 420t/449g TL: N33 06 01 W104 15 15 On air date: 2004. 8341 Washington St. N.E., Albuquerque, NM, 87113. Phone: (505) 797-1919. Fax: (505) 938-4401. Licensee: Acme Television Licenses of New Mexico LLC. Group Owner: ACME Communications Inc. (acq 1-7-2004).
Key Personnel:
Stan Gill. . . . . gen mgr
Larry Oliver . . . . chief of engrg

KTEL-TV— Digital Channel: 25. Digital Hrs: 24 113 kw vis. ant 440t/400g TL: N32 26 09 W104 11 14 On air date: 2001. Box 30068, Albuquerque, NM, 87190. 2400 Monroe St. N. E., Albuquerque, NM 87110. Phone: (505) 884-5353. Fax: (505) 889-8390.E-mail: gzavala@kteltv.com Licensee: Ramar Communications II Ltd. Group Owner: (group owner; (acq 8-10-99; $10,000). Natl. Network: Telemundo (Spanish), . Foreign lang progmg: SpanishS 168
Key Personnel:
Ray Moran . . . . CEO
Brad Moran . . . . pres
Gabriel Zavala . . . . gen mgr

KTFQ-DT— Digital Channel: 22. Digital Hrs: 24 5,000 kw vis. ant 1,233t/1,046g TL: N35 24 44 W106 43 32 On air date: Apr 28, 1999. 2725 Broadbent Pkwy. N.E., Suite E, Albuquerque, NM, 87107. Phone: (505) 342-4141. Fax: (505) 344-8714. Web Site: www.univision.com. Licensee: TeleFutura Albuquerque LLC. Group Owner: Univision Communications Inc. (acq 5-30-2003; $20 million). Natl. Network: TeleFutura (Spanish), . Foreign lang progmg: SpanishS 168

KTLL-TV— Digital Channel: 33. Digital Hrs: 24 50 kw vis. ant 400t/66g TL: N37 15 46 W107 53 45 On air date: 2002. Box 3757, Ramar Communications, Lubbock, TX, 79452. Phone: (806) 745-3434. Fax: (806) 748-1949. Web Site: www.fox34.com. Licensee: Ramar Communications II Ltd. Group Owner: (group owner; (acq 1-24-2001). Natl. Network: Telemundo (Spanish), . Foreign lang progmg: SpanishS 168
Key Personnel:
Brad Moran . . . . pres & gen mgr
Gabriel Zavala . . . . gen mgr

KUPT— Digital Channel: 29. Digital Hrs: 24 50 kw vis. ant 515t/499g TL: N32 43 28 W103 05 46 On air date: 1989. Box 3757, Lubbock, TX, 79452. 9800 University Ave., Lubbock, TX 77551-5556. Phone: (806) 745-3434. Fax: (806) 748-1949. Licensee: Ramar Communications II Ltd. Group Owner: (group owner; (acq 6-4-97; $200,000). Population Served: 30,000 Washington Atty: Leventhal, Senter & Lerman.
Key Personnel:
Brad Moran . . . . pres
Chuck Hinez . . . . gen mgr
Scott Cawthron. . . . . opns mgr
Terri Holt. progmg dir

KWBQ— Digital Channel: 29. Digital Hrs: 24 5,000 kw vis. ant 1,971t TL: N35 46 50 W106 31 35 On air date: December 1998. 8341 Washington St. N.E., Albuquerque, NM, 87113. Phone: (505) 797-1919. Fax: (505) 344-1145. Web Site: www.newmexicoscw.tv. Licensee: Acme TV Licenses of New Mexico L.L.C. Group Owner: ACME Communications Inc. Natl. Network: CW, .
Key Personnel:
Stan Gill . . . . gen mgr & stn mgr
Dan Marchese . . . . gen sls mgr
Chris Iller . . . . prom mgr
Larry Oliver . . . . chief of engrg

Clovis

see Amarillo, TX market

Las Cruces

see El Paso (Las Cruces, NM), TX market

Portales

see Amarillo, TX market

Santa Fe

see Albuquerque-Santa Fe, NM market

New York

Albany-Schenectady-Troy, NY (DMA 57)

WCDC— Digital Channel: 36. Digital Hrs: 24 538 kw vis, 53 kw aur. 3,688t/248g TL: N42 38 14 W73 10 07 On air date: Feb 5, 1954. 341 Northern Blvd., Albany, NY, 12204. Phone: (518) 436-4822. Fax: (518) 462-6065.E-mail: news@wten.com Web Site: www.wten.com. Licensee: Young Broadcasting of Albany Inc. Group Owner: Young Broadcasting Inc. (acq 10-11-89; grpsl; 9-11-89). Natl. Network: ABC, . Washington Atty: Wiley, Rein & Fielding. News staff: 37; News: 15 hrs wkly.
Key Personnel:
Renee LeSpina . . . . gen mgr
Satellite of WTEN-TV Albany.

WCWN— Digital Channel: 43. Digital Hrs: 24 2,950 kw vis. ant 1,109t TL: N42 37 37 W74 00 40 On air date: Sept 27, 1993. 1400 Balltown Rd., Schenectady, NY, 12309. Phone: (518) 346-6666. Fax: (518) 381-3770. Web Site: www.capitalregionscw.com. Licensee: Freedom Broadcasting of New York Licensee L.L.C. Group Owner: Tribune Broadcasting Co. (acq 12-5-2006; $17 million). Natl. Network: CW, .
Key Personnel:
Robert Furlong. . . . . VP & gen mgr
Fred Lass . . . . chief of engrg
Nicole Parianos . . . . mktg

***WMHT—** Analog Channel: 17. Digital Channel: 34. Digital Hrs: 24 325 kw vis. ant 1,397t/456g TL: N42 37 31 W74 00 38 On air date: May 2, 1962. 4 Global View, Troy, NY, 12180. Phone: (518) 880-3400. Fax: (518) 880-3409.E-mail: email@wmht.org Web Site: www.wmht.org. Licensee: WMHT Educational Telecommunications. Population Served: 600,000 Natl. Network: PBS, . Rgnl. Network: Eastern Educ. Washington Atty: Schwartz, Woods & Miller.

Key Personnel:
Robert Altman . . . . pres

WNYA— Digital Channel: 13. Digital Hrs: 24 1,580 kw vis. ant 1,000t/141g TL: N42 30 09 W73 18 58 On air date: September 2003. 17 Fern Ave., Schenectady, NY, 12306. Phone: (518) 381-3751. Fax: (518) 381-3740. Web Site: www.mytv4albany.com. Licensee: Venture Technologies Group LLC.. Ownership: Lawrence H. Rogow (acq 7-30-2003). Natl. Network: MyNetworkTV, . Natl. Rep: TeleRep,. Washington Atty: Wiley, Rein LLP.
Key Personnel:
Alisha Siligato. . . . . traf mgr

WNYT— Digital Channel: 12.178 kw vis, 19.9 kw aur. 1,171t/737g TL: N42 47 08 W73 37 44 On air date: June 15, 1956. Box 4035, 715 N. Pearl St., Albany, NY, 12204. Phone: (518) 436-4791. Phone: (518) 207-4700. Web Site: www.wnyt.com. Licensee: WNYT-TV LLC. Group Owner: Hubbard Broadcasting Inc. (acq 9-19-96). Population Served: 1,245,000 Natl. Network: NBC, . Natl. Rep: Petry Television Inc.,. News: 27 hrs wkly.
Key Personnel:
Stephen Baboulis . . . . gen mgr
Tony McManus. . . . . gen sls mgr
Paul Lewis. . . . . news dir
Richard Klein. . . . . engrg dir
Maryann Ryan. . . . . progmg

WRGB—(Schenectady, Digital Channel: 6. Digital Hrs: 24 4.64 kw vis. ant 1,299t/362g TL: N42 37 31 W74 00 38 On air date: Jan 13, 1928. 1400 Balltown Rd., Schenectady, NY, 12309. Phone: (518) 346-6666. Fax: (518) 381-3707 (progm). Fax: (518) 381-3736 (gen mgr). Web Site: www.wrgb.com. Licensee: Freedom Broadcasting of New York Licensee L.L.C. Group Owner: Freedom Communications Inc. (acq 3-4-86; 11-25-85). Population Served: 1,280,600 Natl. Network: CBS, . Natl. Rep: TeleRep,. Washington Atty: Latham & Watkins. Wire Svc: AP News: 26.5 hrs wkly.
Key Personnel:
Scott Flanders . . . . CEO
Doreen Wade . . . . pres
Robert J. Furlong . . . . VP & gen mgr progmg mgr
Robert Epstein. . . . . gen sls mgr
Robert Hewitt . . . . natl sls mgr
Tim Pennings . . . . prom mgr
Lisa Jackson . . . . news dir
Fred Lass . . . . engrg dir & chief of engrg
Karen Olmstead . . . . traf mgr

WTEN— Digital Channel: 26. Digital Hrs: 24 316 kw vis, 31.6 kw aur. ant 1,000t/276g TL: N42 38 15 W73 59 54 On air date: Oct 14, 1953. 341 Northern Blvd., Albany, NY, 12204. Phone: (518) 436-4822. Fax: (518) 462-6065.E-mail: news@news10.com Web Site: www.wten.com. Licensee: Young Broadcasting of Albany Inc. Group Owner: Young Broadcasting Inc. (acq 10-11-89; grpsl). Population Served: 1,258,000 Natl. Network: ABC, . Washington Atty: Wiley, Rein & Fielding. News staff: 50; News: 22 hrs wkly.
Key Personnel:
Rene LaSpina . . . . pres & gen mgr

WXXA-TV— Digital Channel: 7. Digital Hrs: 23 3,020 kw vis, 302 kw aur. ant 1,200t/465g TL: N42 37 01 W74 00 46 On air date: July 30, 1982. 28 Corporate Cir., Albany, NY, 12203. Phone: (518) 862-2323. Phone: (518) 862-0995. Fax: (518) 862-0865. Fax: (518) 862-0930.E-mail: news@fox23news.com Web Site: www.fox23news.com. Licensee: Newport Television License LLC. Group Owner: Clear Channel Communications Inc. (acq 3-14-2008; grpsl). Population Served: 1,288,000 Natl. Network: Fox, . Natl. Rep: Millennium Sales & Marketing,. Washington Atty: Covington & Burling. News staff: 70; News: 23.5 hrs wkly.
Key Personnel:
Sandy DiPasquale . . . . CEO & pres exec VP
Steve Kimatian . . . . exec VP
Bill Sally. . . . . gen mgr
Chuck Hunt . . . . sls dir
Ardelle Hirsch . . . . natl sls mgr & mktg
Paul Pelliccia . . . . progmg dir
Gene Ross. . . . . news dir
Sargent Cathrall . . . . chief of engrg

WYPX— Digital Channel: 50. Analog Hrs: 24 Digital Hrs: 24 450 kw vis. ant 679t/675g TL: N42 59 04 W74 10 56 On air date: Dec 14, 1987. 1 Charles Blvd, Guilderland, NY, 12084. Phone: (518) 464-0143. Fax: (518) 464-0633. Web Site: www.ionline.tv. Licensee: Channel 55 of Albany Inc. Group Owner: Paxson Communications Corp. (acq 6-1-96; $2.5 million). Natl. Network: ION Television, . Natl. Rep: NBC TV Stations Sales,. News: 5 hrs wkly.

Key Personnel:
Dean Goodman . . . . CEO
Lowell "Bud" Paxson . . . . chmn
Renee Osterlitz. . . . . stn mgr & traf mgr
Steve Appel . . . . gen sls mgr
Claude Pine . . . . pub affrs dir & chief of engrg
Chris Iorio . . . . pub svc dir

Binghamton, NY
(DMA 157)

WBNG-TV— Digital Channel: 7. Digital Hrs: 23 20.4 kw vis. ant 1,122t/660g TL: N42 03 31 W75 57 06 On air date: Dec 1, 1949. 560 Columbia Dr., Johnson City, NY, 13790. Phone: (607) 729-8812. Fax: (607) 797-6211.E-mail: wbng@wbngtv.com Web Site: www.wbng.com. Licensee: WBNG License Inc. Group Owner: Television Station Group LLC (acq 7-26-2006; $45 million). Population Served: 154,400 Natl. Network: CBS, CW, . Natl. Rep: Continental Television Sales,. Washington Atty: Latham & Watkins. Wire Svc: AP News: 24.5 hrs wkly.
Key Personnel:
Matt Rosenfeld . . . . pres & gen mgr
Kate Garger . . . . progmg dir
Greg Catlin. . . . . news dir
Chris Ball . . . . chief of engrg
Janet Heatherman . . . . traf mgr

WICZ-TV— Digital Channel: 8.7.9 kw vis. ant 1,217t TL: N42 03 22 W75 56 39 On air date: Nov 1, 1957. 4600 Vestal Pkwy. E., Vestal, NY, 13850. Phone: (607) 770-4040. Fax: (607) 798-7950.E-mail: fox40@wicz.com Web Site: www.wicz.com. Licensee: Stainless Broadcasting L.P. Group Owner: Northwest Broadcasting Inc. (acq 7-15-97; $16 million cash-out merger with KTVZ(TV) Bend, OR). Population Served: 337,000 Natl. Network: Fox, . Washington Atty: Leventhal, Senter & Lerman. News staff: 13; News: 2 hrs wkly.
Key Personnel:
Brian Brady . . . . CEO
Bill Quarles . . . . CFO
John Leet . . . . gen mgr

WIVT— Digital Channel: 34. Digital Hrs: 22 2,820 kw vis. ant 928t/528g TL: N42 03 39 W75 56 36 On air date: Nov 25, 1962. 203 Ingraham Hill Rd., Binghamton, NY, 13903. Phone: (607) 771-3434. Fax: (607) 723-1034. Web Site: www.NewsChannel34.com. Licensee: Newport Television License LLC. Group Owner: Clear Channel Communications Inc. (acq 3-14-2008; grpsl). Population Served: 400,000 Natl. Network: ABC, . Natl. Rep: Millennium Sales & Marketing,.
Key Personnel:
Sandy DiPasquale . . . . pres
John Birchall . . . . VP & gen mgr stn mgr
John King . . . . opns VP & engrg VP chief of engrg
Abiodun Sadik . . . . chief of opns
Maura Burtis. . . . . natl sls mgr & rgnl sls mgr
Jim La Vasser. prom mgr
Vince Spacolia . . . . progmg dir
Jim Ehmke. . . . . news dir
Boyd Chapman . . . . traf mgr
Jim LaVasser. pub svc dir
Steve Princivalli. . . . . weather dir

***WSKG-TV—** Digital Channel: 42. Digital Hrs: 24 603 kw vis, 60.3 kw aur. ant 1,230t/927g TL: N42 03 22 W75 56 39 On air date: May 12, 1968. Box 3000, Binghamton, NY, 13902. 601 Gates Rd., Vestal, NY 13850. Phone: (607) 729-0100. Fax: (607) 729-7328.E-mail: mail@wskg.org Web Site: www.wskg.org. Licensee: WSKG Public Telecommunications Council. Natl. Network: PBS, . Rgnl. Network: Eastern Educ. Washington Atty: Dow, Lohnes & Albertson.
Key Personnel:
Brian Sicora . . . . CEO & pres gen mgr
Nancy Christensen. . . . . opns dir & gen sls mgr

Buffalo, NY
(DMA 51)

WGRZ— Digital Channel: 33.480 kw vis. ant 968t/874g TL: N42 43 07 W78 33 47 On air date: Aug 14, 1954. 259 Delaware Ave., Buffalo, NY, 14202. Phone: (716) 849-2222. Fax: (716) 849-7602. Web Site: www.wgrz.com. Licensee: Multimedia Entertainment Inc. Group Owner: Gannett Broadcasting (acq 1-27-97; grpsl). Population Served: 1,325,500 Natl. Network: NBC, . Wire Svc: Newsweek Wire Svc: CNBC Wire Svc: NBC Wire Svc: UPI
Key Personnel:
Jim Toellner . . . . pres & gen mgr

WIVB-TV— Digital Channel: 39. Digital Hrs: 24 100 kw vis, 20 kw aur. ant 1,201t/1,060g TL: N42 39 33 W78 37 33 On air date: May 14, 1948. 2077 Elmwood Ave., Buffalo, NY, 14207. Phone: (716) 874-4410. Fax: (716) 879-4896. Web Site: www.wivb.com. Licensee: WIVB Broadcasting L.L.C. Group Owner: LIN Television Corporation (acq 12-16-97). Population Served: 1,200,00 Natl. Network: CBS, . Washington Atty: Covington & Burling.
Key Personnel:
Dan Meyers . . . . gen mgr & mktg mgr adv mgr
Diane Breen . . . . progmg dir
Dennis Majewicz . . . . chief of engrg

WKBW-TV— Digital Channel: 38. Digital Hrs: 24 358 kw vis. ant 1,420t/1,037g TL: N42 38 14.8 W78 37 11.9 On air date: Nov 30, 1958. 7 Broadcast Plaza, Buffalo, NY, 14202. Phone: (716) 845-6100. Fax: (716) 842-1855. Fax: TWX: 710-522-1846. Web Site: www.wkbw.com. Licensee: Granite Broadcasting Corp. Group Owner: (group owner; (acq 1995; $13.42 million). Population Served: 1,720,000 Natl. Network: ABC, . Natl. Rep: TeleRep,. Washington Atty: Akin, Gump, Strauss, Haver & Feld.
Key Personnel:
William Ransom. gen mgr
Mike Anger . . . . chief of engrg

***WNED-TV—** Digital Channel: 43. Digital Hrs: 24 156 kw vis. ant 1,076t/1,086g TL: N43 01 48 W78 55 15 On air date: Mar 30, 1959. Box 1263, Buffalo, NY, 14240. Horizons Plaza, 140 Lower Terr., Buffalo, NY 14202. Phone: (716) 845-7000. Fax: (716) 845-7036. Web Site: www.wned.org. Licensee: Western New York Public Broadcasting Association. Population Served: 8,000,000 Natl. Network: PBS, . Rgnl. Network: Eastern Educ. Washington Atty: Schwartz, Woods & Miller.
Key Personnel:
Donald Boswell . . . . CEO & pres
Michael Trapper . . . . CFO & gen sls mgr mktg mgr & adv mgr
Richard Daly . . . . sr VP
Ron Santora . . . . progmg dir
Rich Borosky . . . . traf mgr

WNGS— Digital Channel: 7. Digital Hrs: 24 15.5 kw vis. ant 1,348t/963g TL: N42 38 15 W78 37 12 On air date: 1997. Stn currently dark 3901 Hwy. 121 S., Bedford, TX, 76021. Phone: (817) 571-1229. Fax: (817) 571-7458. Web Site: www.daystar.com. Licensee: Word of God Fellowship Inc. Group Owner: Equity Broadcasting Corp. (acq 7-31-2009; grpsl). Population Served: 500,000
Key Personnel:
Marcus D. Lamb . . . . pres

WNLO— Digital Channel: 32. Digital Hrs: 24 955 kw vis, 95.5 kw aur. ant 1,030t/1,039g TL: N43 01 48 W78 55 15 On air date: May 13, 1987. 2077 Elmwood Ave., Buffalo, NY, 14207. Phone: (716) 874-4410. Fax: (716) 879-4896. Web Site: www.cw23.com. Licensee: WIVB Broadcasting L.L.C. Group Owner: LIN Television Corporation (acq 6-6-2001; $26.2 million). Population Served: 1,200,000 Natl. Network: CW, . Washington Atty: Covington & Burling.
Key Personnel:
Dan Meyers . . . . mktg mgr & adv mgr
Diane Breen . . . . progmg dir
Dennis Majewicz . . . . chief of engrg

WNYB— Digital Channel: 26. Digital Hrs: 24 1,000 kw vis. ant 1,519t/1,059g TL: N42 23 36 W79 13 44 On air date: Sept 24, 1988. 5775 Big Tree Rd., Orchard Park, NY, 14127. Phone: (716) 662-2659. Fax: (716) 667-2499.E-mail: wnyb@tct.tv Licensee: Faith Broadcasting Network Inc. Group Owner: Tri-State Christian Television (acq 5-7-2002).
Key Personnel:
Loren Speery . . . . gen mgr & sls dir

WNYO-TV— Digital Channel: 49. Digital Hrs: 24 198 kw vis. ant 1,233t/1,021g TL: N42 46 58 W78 27 28 On air date: Sept 2, 1987. 699 Hertel Ave., Suite 100, Buffalo, NY, 14207. Phone: (716) 447-3200. Fax: (716) 875-4919.E-mail: wnyo@spgnet.com Web Site: www.mytvbuffalo.com. Licensee: New York Television Inc. Group Owner: Sinclair Broadcast Group Inc. (acq 1-25-2002; $51.5 million for stock). Population Served: 645,000 Natl. Network: MyNetworkTV, .
Key Personnel:
Nick Maginni . . . . gen mgr
Donald Stewart . . . . opns dir & engrg dir
Jose Chapa . . . . gen sls mgr
Mike Bice. . . . . prom mgr

WPXJ-TV— Digital Channel: 23.708 kw vis. ant 1,456t TL: N42 53 42 W78 00 56 On air date: 2000. 601 Clearwater Park Rd., West Palm Beach, NY, 33401. 726 Exchange St., Suite 605, Buffalo, NY 14210. Phone: (716) 852-1818. Fax: (716) 852-8288. Web Site: www.ionline.tv. Licensee: Paxson Buffalo License Inc. (acq 7-15-97; $3 million).
Key Personnel:
Barb Lipka . . . . opns mgr

WUTV— Digital Channel: 14. Digital Hrs: 24 1,050 kw vis, 105 kw aur. ant 920t/959g TL: N43 01 32 W78 55 43 On air date: Dec 21, 1970. 699 Hertel Ave., Suite 100, Buffalo, NY, 14207. Phone: (716)

477-3200. Fax: (716) 875-4919.E-mail: wutv@spgnet.com Web Site: www.wutv.com. Licensee: WUTV Licensee LLC. Group Owner: Sinclair Broadcast Group Inc. (acq 12-10-01; grpsl). Population Served: 645,000 Natl. Network: Fox, . Natl. Rep: Harrington, Righter & Parsons,. Washington Atty: Arter & Hadden.
Key Personnel:

Nick Magnini	gen mgr
Donald Stewart	opns dir & engrg dir
Jose Chapa	gen sls mgr
Mike Bice	prom mgr

Corning

see Elmira (Corning), NY market

Elmira (Corning), NY
(DMA 175)

WENY-TV— Digital Channel: 36. Digital Hrs: 24 Note: ABC is on WENY-TV ch 36, CW is on WENY-DT ch 55. 75 kw vis. ant 1,122t/20g TL: N42 08 31 W77 04 40 On air date: Nov 19, 1969. 474 Old Ithaca Rd., Horseheads, NY, 14845. Phone: (607) 739-3636. Fax: (607) 739-1418.E-mail: info@weny.com Web Site: www.weny.com. Licensee: Lilly Broadcasting L.L.C. Ownership: Lilly Broadcasting, LLC (acq 10-17-99; $4.8 million). Population Served: 250,000 Natl. Network: ABC, CW, Washington Atty: Cordon & Kelly. News: 10 hrs wkly.
Key Personnel:

Kevin Lilly	CEO & pres
Brian Lilly	exec VP & VP
Nick White	VP
Peter Veto	gen mgr & stn mgr opns mgr
Bridgid Allinger	gen sls mgr
Patrick Reilly	prom dir
Scott Cook	news dir
Dan Beach	traf mgr

WETM-TV— Digital Channel: 18. Digital Hrs: 24 603 kw vis. ant 1,233t/817g TL: N42 06 22 W76 52 17 On air date: Sept 10, 1956. Box 1207, Elmira, NY, 14901. 101 E. Water St., Elmira, NY 14901. Phone: (607) 733-5518. Fax: (607) 734-1176.E-mail: info@wetmtv.com Web Site: www.wetmtv.com. Licensee: Newport Television License LLC. Group Owner: Smith Broadcasting Group Inc. (acq 3-14-2008; grpsl). Population Served: 91,000 Natl. Network: NBC, . Washington Atty: Covington & Burling. News staff: 21; News: 14 hrs wkly.
Key Personnel:

Randy Reid	gen mgr
Bob Cibulsky	gen sls mgr & rgnl sls mgr

WFBT— Digital Channel: 14.676 w vis. Ant 643t/241g TL: N42 18 33 W77 13 17 Not on air, target date: unknown: 1153 Route 44-55, Clintondale, NY, 12515. Phone: (845) 883-7457. Permittee: William H. Walker III.
Key Personnel:

William H. Walker III	gen mgr

*WSKA— Digital Channel: 30. Digital Hrs: 24 25 kw vis. ant 1,096t/774g TL: N42 08 29.73 W77 04 39.11 On air date: July 2006. Box 3000, Binghamton, NY, 13902-3000. Phone: (607) 729-0100. Fax: (607) 729-7328.E-mail: wskg-mail@pbs.org Web Site: www.wskg.org. Licensee: WSKG Public Telecommunications Council. Natl. Network: PBS, .
Key Personnel:

Brian Sicora	gen mgr

Rebroadcast of WSKG-TV Binghamton.

WYDC— Digital Channel: 48. Digital Hrs: 24 136 kw vis. ant 423t TL: N42 02 29 W77 15 18 On air date: September 1994. 33 E. Market St., Corning, NY, 14830. Phone: (607) 937-5000. Fax: (607) 937-4019.E-mail: jmattison@wydctv.com Web Site: www.wydctv.com. Licensee: WYDC Inc. Ownership: Bill Christian, CEO (acq 11-19-97; $1.75 million). Population Served: 94,000 Natl. Network: Fox, . Washington Atty: Drinker Biddle & Reath LLP.
Key Personnel:

Bill Christian	CEO & gen mgr
Robin Pickering	traf mgr

New York
(DMA 1)

WABC-TV— Digital Channel: 7. Digital Hrs: 24 11.69 kw vis. ant 1,328t/1,322g TL: N40 44 54 W73 59 10 On air date: Aug 10, 1948. 7 Lincoln Sq., New York, NY, 10023. Phone: (212) 456-7777. Fax: (212) 456-2290. Web Site: www.7online.com. Licensee: ABC Inc. Group Owner: (group owner). Natl. Network: ABC, . Natl. Rep: ABC National Television Sales,.

Key Personnel:

Rebecca Campbell	pres & gen mgr
Evelyn del Cerro	opns mgr
Scott Simensky	sls VP & gen sls mgr
Alyson Roznee	mktg VP & mktg mgr
Art Moore	progmg VP & progmg dir
Kenny Plotnik	news dir
Saundra Thomas	pub affrs dir
Bill Beam	engrg VP & engrg dir
Kurt Hanson	chief of engrg

WCBS-TV— Digital Channel: 33. Digital Hrs: 24 284 kw. ant 1,302t/1,296g TL: N40 44 54 W73 59 10 On air date: July 1, 1941. 524 W. 57 St., New York, NY, 10019. Phone: (212) 975-4321. Fax: (212) 975-4677.E-mail: cbsnewyork@cbs.com Web Site: www.wcbstv.com. Licensee: CBS Broadcasting Inc. Group Owner: Viacom Television Stations Group. Natl. Network: CBS, . Natl. Rep: CBS TV Stations National Sales,.
Key Personnel:

Peter Dunn	pres & gen mgr
Vincent McCarthy	natl sls mgr
David M. Friend	news dir

*WEDW— Digital Channel: 49. Digital Hrs: 24 91 kw vis. ant 728t/476g TL: N41 16 44 W73 11 08 On air date: Dec 17, 1967. 1049 Asylum Ave., Hartford, CT, 06105. Phone: (860) 278-5310. Fax: (860) 275-7500. Web Site: www.cptv.org. Licensee: Connecticut Public Broadcasting. Population Served: 2,500,000 Natl. Network: PBS, .
Key Personnel:

Jerry Franklin	pres & gen mgr engrg VP
Meg Sakellarides	CFO
Haig Papasian	opns VP
Joseph Zareski	opns dir & chief of engrg
Dean Orton	dev dir & news dir
Larry Rifkin	progmg VP

*WFME-TV— Digital Channel: 29. Digital Hrs: 24 200 kw vis. ant 548t/141g TL: N40 47 18 W74 15 19 On air date: 1997. 289 Mt. Pleasant Ave., West Orange, NJ, 07052. Phone: (973) 736-3600. Fax: (973) 736-4832. Fax: (510) 562-1023.E-mail: wfme@wfme.net Web Site: www.familyradio.com. Licensee: Family Stations of New Jersey Inc. Group Owner: (group owner).
Key Personnel:

Harold Camping	gen mgr
Charles Menut	stn mgr & rgnl sls mgr
Charles H. Menut	chief of engrg

WFTY-DT— Digital Channel: 23. Digital Hrs: 24 655 kw vis. ant 718t/656g TL: N40 53 23 W72 57 13 On air date: November 1973. 3200 Expressway Dr. S., Islandia, NY, 11749. Phone: (631) 582-6700. Fax: (631) 582-8337. Web Site: www.univision.com. Licensee: Univision New York LLC. Group Owner: Univision Communications Inc. (acq 5-21-2001; grpsl). Population Served: 3,000,000 Washington Atty: Wiley, Rein & Fielding. Foreign lang progmg: SpanishS News: 4 hrs wkly.
Key Personnel:

Cristina Schwarz	VP & gen mgr
David Marinace	chief of engrg

WFUT-DT— Digital Channel: 30. Digital Hrs: 24 200 kw vis. ant 1,407t/1,398g TL: N40 44 54 W73 59 10 On air date: Sept 29, 1974. Univison 41, 500 Frank W. Burr Blvd., 6th Fl., Teaneck, NJ, 07666. Phone: (201) 287-4042. Fax: (201) 287-9422. Licensee: Univision New York LLC. Group Owner: Univision Communications Inc. (acq 5-21-2001; grpsl). Washington Atty: Shaw, Pittman. Foreign lang progmg: SpanishS 168
Key Personnel:

Ramon Pineda	VP
Morris Marotta	stn mgr
John De Simon	sls VP
Norma Morato	news dir

Rebroadcasts WFTY-DT Smithtown, NY 100%.

*WLIW— Digital Channel: 21. Digital Hrs: 24 89.9 kw vis. ant 364t/254g TL: N40 47 19 W73 27 09 On air date: Jan 6, 1969. Box 21, Plainview, NY, 11803. Phone: (516) 367-2100. Fax: (516) 692-7629. Web Site: www.wliw.org. Licensee: Educational Broadcasting Corp. (acq 1-31-2003). Population Served: 2,000,000 Natl. Network: PBS, . Washington Atty: Schwartz, Woods & Miller. Wire Svc: UPI
Key Personnel:

Neal Shapiro	pres
Terrel Cass	gen mgr

WLNY-TV— Digital Channel: 47. Digital Hrs: 24 1,000 kw vis. ant 633t/620g TL: N40 53 50 W72 54 56 On air date: Apr 28, 1985. 270 S. Service Rd., Suite 55, Melville, NY, 11747. Phone: (631) 777-8855. Fax: (631) 777-8180.E-mail: ny55@aol.com Web Site: www.wlnytv.com. Licensee: WLNY LP. Ownership: WLNY GP Inc., gen ptnr; WLNY LP

Inc., limited ptnr. WLNY Holdings Inc. owns 100% of the voting stock. Population Served: 4,200,000 Washington Atty: Cohn & Marks. News: 2 hrs wkly.
Key Personnel:

Marvin R. Chauvin	CEO
David Feinblatt	pres & gen mgr
Gerald Diorio	opns VP
Elliot Simmons	sls VP & rgnl sls mgr
Andy Starr	natl sls mgr
Richard Rose	news dir & news cmtr
Richard Mulliner	engrg mgr
Rosie Miranda	traf mgr
C.J. Papa	sports cmtr

WMBC-TV— Digital Channel: 18. Digital Hrs: 24 1,000 kw vis. ant 820t/633g TL: N40 51 53 W74 12 03 On air date: Apr 26, 1993. 99 Clinton Rd., West Caldwell, NJ, 07006. Phone: (973) 852-0300. Fax: (973) 808-5516.E-mail: info@wmbctv.com Web Site: www.wmbctv.com. Licensee: Mountain Broadcasting Corp. Population Served: 13,000,000 Washington Atty: Fleischman & Walsh. News staff: 8; News: 5 hrs wkly.
Key Personnel:

Hansen Lau	pres & news dir
Victor C. Joo	gen mgr
Joon S. Joo	chief of engrg

WNBC— Digital Channel: 28. Digital Hrs: 24 200.2 kw vis. ant 1,302t/1,296g TL: N40 44 54 W73 59 10 On air date: July 1, 1941. 30 Rockefeller Plaza, New York, NY, 10112. Phone: (212) 664-4444. Fax: (212) 664-2994 (news). Web Site: www.wnbc.com. Licensee: NBC Telemundo License Co. Group Owner: NBC TV Station Division (acq 6-5-86; grpsl). Natl. Network: NBC, .
Key Personnel:

Karen Seminara	CFO
Thomas M. O'Brien	pres & gen mgr
Mathew Braatz	opns dir
Mark Lund	sls VP
David Hyman	prom VP
Adele Rifkin	progmg dir
Evan Kutner	rsch dir
Laurie Wiseman	traf mgr
Len Berman	sports cmtr

*WNET—(Newark, NJ) Digital Channel: 13. Digital Hrs: 24 9.3 kw vis. ant 1,328t/1,322g TL: N40 44 54 W73 59 10 On air date: Jan 2, 1948. 450 W. 33rd St., New York, NY, 10001-2605. Phone: (212) 560-1313. Fax: (212) 560-1314. Web Site: www.thirteen.org. Licensee: Educational Broadcasting Corp. (acq 1970). Natl. Network: PBS, . Rgnl. Network: Eastern Educ. Washington Atty: Leventhal, Senter & Lerman. News: 5 hrs wkly.
Key Personnel:

Neal Shapiro	CEO & pres & pres

*WNJB— Digital Channel: 8. Digital Hrs: 24 17.9 kw vis. ant 705t/374g TL: N40 37 17 W74 30 15 On air date: June 5, 1973. Box 777, Trenton, NJ, 08625-0777. 25 S. Stockton St., Trenton, NJ 08608-1832. Phone: (609) 777-5000. Fax: (609) 633-2920.E-mail: audience@njn.org Web Site: www.njn.net. Licensee: New Jersey Public Broadcasting Authority. Population Served: 9,800,000 Natl. Network: PBS, . New Jersey Network Washington Atty: Schwartz, Woods & Miller. News: 2 hrs wkly.
Key Personnel:

Janice Selinger	engrg dir

Satellite of *WNJT(TV) Trenton.

*WNJN— Digital Channel: 51. Digital Hrs: 24 1,225 kw vis. ant 764t/590g TL: N40 51 53 W74 12 03 On air date: June 5, 1973. Box 777, Trenton, NJ, 08625-0777. 25 S. Stockton St., Trenton, NJ 08608-1832. Phone: (609) 777-5000. Fax: (609) 633-2920.E-mail: audience@njn.org Web Site: www.njn.net. Licensee: New Jersey Public Broadcasting Authority. Population Served: 3,000,000 Natl. Network: PBS, . New Jersey Network Washington Atty: Schwartz, Woods & Miller. News: 3 hrs wkly.

Satellite of *WNJT Trenton.

WNJU—(Linden, NJ) Digital Channel: 36. Digital Hrs: 24 4,570 kw vis, 977 kw aur. ant 1,508t/1,730g TL: N40 42 43 W74 00 49 On air date: May 16, 1965. 2200 Fletcher Ave., 6th Floor, Fort Lee, NJ, 07024. Phone: (201) 969-4247. Fax: (201) 969-4120. Web Site: www.telemundo47.com. Licensee: NBC Telemundo License Co. Group Owner: Telemundo Group Inc. (acq 4-12-2002; grpsl). Natl. Network: Telemundo (Spanish), . Washington Atty: Hogan & Hartson. Foreign lang progmg: SpanishS 168
Key Personnel:

Manuel Martinez	gen mgr
Lenny Stole	chief of engrg
Sylvia Santiago	traf mgr

*WNYE-TV— Digital Channel: 24. Digital Hrs: 24 2,450 kw vis, 245 kw aur. ant 1,296t/1,289g TL: N40 44 54 W73 59 10 On air date: Apr 3,

1967. One Centre St., 27th Fl, New York, NY, 10007. Phone: (212) 669-7400. Fax: (212) 669-8448.E-mail: tv@tv.nyc.gov Web Site: www.nyc.gov/tv. Licensee: New York City Dept. of Info Technology & Telecommunications. Population Served: 18,000,000 Washington Atty: Arnold & Porter.
Key Personnel:
Arick Wierson . . . . . gen mgr
Trevor Scotland . . . . . progmg mgr
Chang Kim . . . . . chief of engrg

WNYW— Digital Channel: 44. Digital Hrs: 24 500 kw vis. ant 1,391t/1,384g TL: N40 44 54 W73 59 10 On air date: May 2, 1944. 205 E. 67th St., New York, NY, 10068. Phone: (212) 452-5555. Fax: (212) 452-5750. Web Site: www.myfoxny.com. Licensee: Fox Television Stations Inc. Group Owner: (group owner; (acq 11-14-86; grpsl). Population Served: 7,900,000 Natl. Network: Fox, .
Key Personnel:
Lew Leone . . . . . gen mgr
Al Shjarback . . . . . opns VP
Dianne Doctor . . . . . news dir
Audrey Pass . . . . . pub affrs dir
Al Shjarback . . . . . engrg VP
Edward Harris . . . . . engrg dir

WPIX— Digital Channel: 11. Digital Hrs: 24 7.5 kw vis. ant 1,328t/1,322g TL: N40 44 54 W73 59 10 On air date: June 15, 1948. 220 E. 42nd St., New York, NY, 10017. Phone: (212) 949-1100. Fax: (212) 210-2591. Web Site: www.cw11.com. Licensee: WPIX Inc. Group Owner: Tribune Broadcasting Co. (acq 12-20-2007; grpsl). Population Served: 12,000,000 Natl. Network: CW, . Natl. Rep: TeleRep,. Washington Atty: Dow Lohnes PLLC. Wire Svc: UPI News: 19.5 hrs wkly.
Key Personnel:
Betty Ellen Berlamino . . . . . pres & gen mgr
Bob Marra . . . . . gen sls mgr
Karen Scott . . . . . news dir
Michael Gano . . . . . chief of engrg

WPXN-TV— Digital Channel: 31. Digital Hrs: 24 55 kw vis, 5.5 kw aur. ant 1,543t/1,569g TL: N40 42 43 W74 00 49 On air date: Nov 1, 1962. 1330 Avenue of the Americas, 32nd Fl, New York, NY, 10019. Phone: (212) 757-3100. Fax: (212) 956-2661. Web Site: www.ionline.tv. Licensee: Paxson Communications License Co. L.L.C. Group Owner: Paxson Communications Corp. (acq 3-4-98; $257.5 million). Population Served: 1,025,000 Natl. Network: ION Television, .
Key Personnel:
Mildred Diaz . . . . . opns mgr
Jack Davidson . . . . . chief of engrg

WRNN-TV— Digital Channel: 48. Digital Hrs: 24 5,000 kw vis, 500 kw aur. ant 1,939t/276g TL: N42 05 06 W74 06 00 On air date: Dec 15, 1985. 800 Westchester Ave., Suite S-640, Rye Brook, NY, 10573. Phone: (914) 417-2700. Fax: (914) 696-0279.E-mail: comments@rnntv.com Web Site: www.rnntv.com. Licensee: WRNN License Co. LLC. (acq 7-31-2001). Washington Atty: Baker & Hostetler. News staff: 9; News: 82 hrs wkly.
Key Personnel:
Christian French . . . . . COO
Richard French . . . . . gen mgr
Danny Kischel . . . . . opns dir
Sal Martirano . . . . . gen sls mgr
Carl Peters . . . . . chief of engrg

WSAH— Digital Channel: 42.2.5 kw vis, 2 kw aur. ant 620t/300g TL: N41 21 43 W73 06 48 On air date: Sept 28, 1987. 7 Wakely St., Seymour, CT, 06483. Phone: (203) 881-1153. Fax: (203) 881-1302. Licensee: MTB Bridgeport-NY Licensee LLC.. Ownership: Multicultural Television Broadcasting LLC, 100% Group Owner: Scripps Howard Broadcasting Co. (acq 11-15-2006; grpsl). Washington Atty: Crowell & Moring.
Key Personnel:
Ronald Barnes . . . . . gen mgr

WTBY-TV— Digital Channel: 27. Digital Hrs: 24 5,000 kw vis, 500 kw aur. 852t/894g TL: N41 43 09 W73 59 47 On air date: Apr 19, 1981. 451 Fishkill Ave. #4, Beacon, NY, 12508-1247. Phone: (845) 896-4610. Fax: (845) 896-4614.E-mail: wtby@tbn.org Web Site: www.tbn.org. Licensee: Trinity Broadcasting of N.Y. Inc. Group Owner: Trinity Broadcasting Network (acq 7-13-82; $2.97 million;6-21-82). Washington Atty: Joseph E. Dunne III.
Key Personnel:
Paul Crouch . . . . . pres
Chris Elia . . . . . gen mgr
Maria Idoni . . . . . pub affrs dir
Paul Swartzendruber . . . . . chief of engrg

WWOR-TV—(Secaucus, NJ) Digital Channel: 38. Digital Hrs: 24 170 kw vis. ant 1,302t/1,296g TL: N40 44 54 W73 59 10 On air date: Oct 11, 1949. 9 Broadcast Plaza, Secaucus, NJ, 07096. Phone: (201) 348-0009. Web Site: www.my9newyork.com. Licensee: Fox Television Stations Inc. Group Owner: (group owner; a(cq 7-31-2001; grpsl). Population Served: 13,000,000 Natl. Network: MyNetworkTV, . Wire Svc: Conus News staff: 70; News: 7 hrs wkly.
Key Personnel:
Lew Leone . . . . . VP & gen mgr
Debbie von Ahrens . . . . . sls dir & prom mgr
Scott Matthews . . . . . news dir

WXTV-DT— Digital Channel: 40. Digital Hrs: 24 2,340 kw vis, 234 kw aur. ant 1,381t TL: N40 44 54 W73 59 10 On air date: Aug 4, 1968. 500 Frank W. Burr Blvd., 6th Fl., Teaneck, NJ, 07666-6802. Phone: (201) 287-4042. Fax: (201) 287-9423. Fax: (201) 287-9427 (news). Licensee: WXTV License Partnership G.P. Group Owner: Univision Communications Inc. (acq 1986; grpsl). Population Served: 3,600,000 Natl. Network: Univision (Spanish), . Washington Atty: Shaw, Pittman. Foreign lang progmg: SpanishS 168 News: 17 hrs wkly.
Key Personnel:
Morris Marotta . . . . . stn mgr & chief of engrg
John De Simon . . . . . sls VP
Ramon Pineda . . . . . VP & prom mgr
Norma Morato . . . . . news dir

North Pole

see Burlington, VT-Plattsburgh, NY market

Plattsburgh

see Burlington, VT-Plattsburgh, NY market

Rochester, NY (DMA 80)

WHAM-TV— Digital Channel: 13. Digital Hrs: 24 Note: ABC is on WHAM-TV ch 13 and WHAM-DT ch 59, CW is on WHAM-DT ch 59. 316 kw vis, 47.9 kw aur. ant 500t/363.5g TL: N43 08 07 W77 35 03 On air date: Sept 15, 1962. Box 20555, Rochester, NY, 14602-0555. 4225 West Henrietta Rd., Rochester, NY 14623. Phone: (585) 334-8700. Fax: (585) 359-1570. Web Site: 13wham.com. Licensee: Newport Television License LLC. Group Owner: Clear Channel Communications Inc. (acq 3-14-2008; grpsl). Population Served: 393,630 Natl. Network: ABC, Natl. Rep: Millennium Sales & Marketing,. Washington Atty: Covington & Burling. Wire Svc: AP Wire Svc: CNN Wire Svc: Bloomberg News News staff: 64; News: 24 hrs wkly.
Key Personnel:
Chuck Samuels . . . . . gen mgr
David DiProsa . . . . . gen sls mgr
Mark Zeger . . . . . natl sls mgr
Amanda DeVito . . . . . rgnl sls mgr
Kevin Kalvitis . . . . . prom dir
Stan Manson . . . . . engrg mgr

WHEC-TV— Digital Channel: 10. Digital Hrs: 24 316 kw vis, 39.8 kw aur. 499t/352g TL: N43 08 07 W77 35 02 On air date: Nov 1, 1953. 191 East Ave., Rochester, NY, 14604. Phone: (585) 546-5670. Fax: (585) 454-7433. Fax: (585) 546-5688. Web Site: www.10nbc.com. Licensee: WHEC-TV LLC. Group Owner: Hubbard Broadcasting Inc. (acq 9-19-96). Population Served: 296,233 Natl. Network: NBC, . Natl. Rep: Petry Television Inc.,. Washington Atty: Arent, Fox, Kintner, Plotkin & Kahn. News: 22 hrs wkly.
Key Personnel:
Arnold Klinsky . . . . . gen mgr & stn mgr
Sherron Sheridan . . . . . opns mgr
Joe Fazio . . . . . gen sls mgr
Lynette Baker . . . . . progmg dir

WROC-TV— Digital Channel: 45. Digital Hrs: 24 316 kw vis, 48.5 kw aur. ant 499t/345g TL: N43 08 07 W77 35 02 On air date: June 14, 1949. 201 Humboldt St., Rochester, NY, 14610-1093. Phone: (585) 288-8400. Fax: (585) 288-7679. Web Site: www.wroctv.com. Licensee: Nexstar Broadcasting Inc. Group Owner: Nexstar Broadcasting Group Inc. (acq 12-9-99; $46 million). Population Served: 957,000 Natl. Network: CBS, . News staff: 40; News: 14 hrs wkly.
Key Personnel:
Tim Busch . . . . . VP
Don Loy . . . . . stn mgr

WUHF— Digital Channel: 28. Digital Hrs: 24 1,200 kw vis, 200 kw aur. ant 499t/345g TL: N43 08 07 W77 35 03 On air date: January 1980. 201 Humboldt St., Rochester, NY, 14610. Phone: (585) 232-3700. Fax: (585) 546-4774. Web Site: rochesterhomepage.net. Licensee: WUHF Licensee LLC. Group Owner: Sinclair Broadcast Group Inc. (acq 4-12-2002; for assumption liabilities). Population Served: 957,000 Natl. Network: Fox, . Washington Atty: Pillsbury, Winthrop & Shaw Pittman. News: 3.5 hrs wkly.
Key Personnel:
Don Roberts . . . . . stn mgr

***WXXI-TV—** Digital Channel: 16. Digital Hrs: 24 906 kw vis, 90.6 kw aur. 500t/343g TL: N43 08 07 W77 35 03 On air date: September 1966. Box 30021, Rochester, NY, 14603-3021. 280 State St., Rochester, NY 14614. Phone: (585) 325-7500. Fax: (585) 258-0335. Web Site: www.wxxi.org. Licensee: WXXI Public Broadcasting Council. Natl. Network: PBS, . Rgnl. Network: CEN. Washington Atty: Schwartz, Woods & Miller. News staff: 4; News: 2 hrs wkly.
Key Personnel:
Norm Silverstein . . . . . CEO & pres
Susan Rogers . . . . . COO & exec VP
Robert Owens . . . . . progmg dir
Kent Hatfield . . . . . engrg VP

Saranac Lake

see Burlington, VT-Plattsburgh, NY market

Schenectady

see Albany-Schenectady-Troy, NY market

Syracuse, NY (DMA 81)

***WCNY-TV—** Digital Channel: 25. Digital Hrs: 18 2,312 kw vis, 231 kw aur. 1,380t/964g TL: N42 56 42 W76 01 28 On air date: Dec 20, 1965. Box 2400, Syracuse, NY, 13220-2400. 506 Old Liverpool Rd., Liverpool, NY 13088. Phone: (315) 453-2424. Fax: (315) 451-8824.E-mail: wcny-online@wcny.org Web Site: www.wcny.org. Licensee: Public Broadcasting Council of Central New York. Population Served: 600,000 Natl. Network: PBS, . Washington Atty: Dow, Lohnes & Albertson.
Key Personnel:
Robert Daino . . . . . CEO & pres
Colleen Edwards . . . . . CFO
Brian Damm . . . . . mktg VP
Larry Goodsight . . . . . mktg dir
John Duffy . . . . . chief of engrg

WNYI— Digital Channel: 20. Digital Hrs: 24 15 w vis. ant 3t/69g TL: N42 25 46 W76 29 48 On air date: 2004. Stn currently dark 3901 Hwy. 121 S., Bedford, TX, 76021. Phone: (817) 571-1229. Fax: (817) 571-7458. Web Site: www.daystar.com. Licensee: Word of God Fellowship Inc. Group Owner: Equity Broadcasting Corp. (acq 7-31-2009;. grpsl).
Key Personnel:
Marcus D. Lamb . . . . . pres

WNYS-TV— Digital Channel: 44. Digital Hrs: 24 794 kw vis, 79.4 kw aur. ant 1,471t/1019g TL: N42 52 50 W76 11 59 On air date: Oct 7, 1989. 1000 James St., Syracuse, NY, 13203. Phone: (315) 472-6800. Fax: (315) 471-8889.E-mail: info@wb43.com Web Site: www.wb43.com. Licensee: RKM Media Inc. Ownership: Ron Philips. (acq 7-2-96). Natl. Network: MyNetworkTV, . Washington Atty: Fletcher, Heald & Hildreth.
Key Personnel:
Aaron Olander . . . . . gen mgr
Peter Spartano . . . . . opns dir
Donald O'Connor . . . . . gen sls mgr
Krysten Bellen . . . . . natl sls mgr
Ed Kampf . . . . . rgnl sls mgr
Ed Sautter . . . . . prom mgr
Linda Deeb . . . . . progmg mgr
Roy Taylor . . . . . engrg dir & chief of engrg
Joan Lescenski . . . . . traf mgr

WSPX-TV— Digital Channel: 15. Digital Hrs: 24 46.77 kw vis. 686t TL: N42 56 54 W76 01 21 On air date: Nov 24, 1998. 6508-B Basile Row, East Syracuse, NY, 13057. Phone: (315) 414-0178. Fax: (315) 414-0482. Web Site: www.ionline.tv. Licensee: Paxson Syracuse License Inc. Ownership: Paxson Communications of Syracuse-56 Inc., 100% (acq 4-29-99).
Key Personnel:
Margo McCaffery . . . . . stn mgr
Al Szablak . . . . . chief of engrg
Melissa Dragicevich . . . . . traf mgr

WSTM-TV— Digital Channel: 24. Digital Hrs: 24 100 kw vis, 20 kw aur. ant 1,000t/594g TL: N42 56 40 W76 07 08 On air date: Feb 15, 1950. 1030 James St., Syracuse, NY, 13203. Phone: (315) 477-9400. Fax: (315) 474-5082. Web Site: www.wstm.com. Licensee: Barrington Syracuse License LLC. Group Owner: Raycom Media (acq 8-11-2006; grpsl). Population Served: 385,100 Natl. Network: NBC, . Natl. Rep: TeleRep,. Washington Atty: Covington & Burling. News staff: 45; News: 27.5 hrs wkly.

Key Personnel:

Chris Geiger	VP & gen mgr gen sls mgr
Dave Rhea	gen sls mgr
Judy Fitzgerald	natl sls mgr
Peggy Phillip	news dir

WSYR-TV— Digital Channel: 17. Digital Hrs: 24 79.4 kw vis, 11.8 kw aur. ant 1,515t/959g TL: N42 56 42 W76 01 28 On air date: Sept 9, 1962. Box 699, 5904 Bridge St., East Syracuse, NY, 13057. Phone: (315) 446-9999. Fax: (315) 446-9283.E-mail: newschannel9@9wsyr.com Web Site: www.9wsyr.com. Licensee: Newport Television License LLC. Group Owner: Clear Channel Communications Inc. (acq 3-14-2008; grpsl). Population Served: 389,700 Natl. Network: ABC, . Natl. Rep: Millennium Sales & Marketing,. News staff: 55; News: 22.5 hrs wkly.

Key Personnel:

Sandy DiPasquale	pres
Theresa E. Underwood	VP & gen mgr stn mgr
John King	opns dir & engrg VP
Sally Stamp	sls dir
Todd Guard	rgnl sls mgr & sls
Vince Spicola	progmg dir
Jim Tortora	news dir
Francis Fasuyi	engrg mgr
Craig Riker	chief of engrg
Boyd Chapman	traf mgr
Rod Wood	financial ed
Dave Eichorn	weather dir
Carrie Lazarus	women's int ed
Bill Evans	sls

WSYT— Digital Channel: 19. Digital Hrs: 24 1,000 kw vis, 100 kw aur. ant 1,471t/1019g TL: N42 52 50 W76 11 59 On air date: Feb 15, 1986. 1000 James St., Syracuse, NY, 13203. Phone: (315) 472-6800. Fax: (315) 471-8889.E-mail: info@wsyt68.com Web Site: www.wsyt68.com. Licensee: WSYT Licensee L.P. Group Owner: Sinclair Broadcast Group Inc. (acq 7-7-98; grpsl). Natl. Network: Fox, . News: 3.5 hrs wkly.

Key Personnel:

Aaron Olander	gen mgr
Peter Spartano	opns dir
Donald O'Connor	gen sls mgr
Krysten Bellen	natl sls mgr
Ed Kampf	rgnl sls mgr
Leslie Baycura	prom mgr
Linda Deeb	progmg dir & progmg mgr
Vinnie Lopez	engrg dir
Joan Lescenski	traf mgr

WTVH— Digital Channel: 47. Digital Hrs: 24 100 kw vis, 20 kw aur. 950t/556g TL: N42 57 19 W76 06 34 On air date: Dec 1, 1948. 980 James St., Syracuse, NY, 13203. Phone: (315) 425-5555. Fax: (315) 425-5513.E-mail: wtvh@wtvh.com Web Site: www.wtvh.com. Licensee: WTVH License Inc. Group Owner: Granite Broadcasting Corp. Population Served: 197,208 Natl. Network: CBS, . Natl. Rep: Harrington, Righter & Parsons,. Washington Atty: Akin, Gump, Strauss, Hauer & Feld. News staff: 42; News: 24 hrs wkly.

Key Personnel:

Matt Rosenfeld	pres & gen mgr
Amy Collins	natl sls mgr
Bob Wickwire	rgnl sls mgr
Nicole Pooler	progmg mgr
Frank Kracher	news dir
Kevin Wright	chief of engrg
Laura Cherchio	traf mgr

Troy

see Albany-Schenectady-Troy, NY market

Utica, NY
(DMA 169)

WFXV— Digital Channel: 27. Digital Hrs: 24 42.7 kw vis, 4.27 kw aur. 646t/189g TL: N43 02 14 W75 26 40 (CP: 854 kw vis.) On air date: Dec 9, 1986. 5956 Smith Hill Rd., Utica, NY, 13502. Phone: (315) 797-5220. Fax: (315) 797-5409.E-mail: info@utica.tv Web Site: www.utica.tv. Licensee: Nexstar Finance Inc. Group Owner: Nexstar Broadcasting Group Inc. (acq 12-31-03; grpsl). Population Served: 1,000,000 Natl. Network: Fox, . Washington Atty: Arter & Hadden.

Key Personnel:

Steve Merren	gen mgr
Bob Hajec	chief of engrg

WKTV— Digital Channel: 29.34.7 kw vis, 6.9 kw aur. 1,380t/1,065g TL: N43 06 09 W74 56 27 On air date: Dec 1, 1949. Box 2, Utica, NY, 13503. 5936 Smith Hill Rd., Utica, NY 13502. Phone: (315) 733-0404. Fax: (315) 793-3498. Web Site: www.wktv.com. Licensee: Smith Media License Holdings LLC. Group Owner: Smith Broadcasting Group Inc. (acq 11-8-2004; grpsl). Natl. Network: NBC, CW, . Natl.

Rep: Continental Television Sales,. Washington Atty: Dow, Lohnes & Albertson, PLLC. News: 31.5 hrs wkly.

Key Personnel:

Vic Vetters	VP & gen mgr
Ken McCoy	stn mgr
Frank Abbadessa	rgnl sls mgr
Dave Streeter	prom mgr
Steve McMurray	news dir
Tom McNicholl	chief of engrg

WUTR— Digital Channel: 30. Digital Hrs: 24 1,150 kw vis, 173 kw aur. ant 800t/400g TL: N43 08 43 W75 10 35 On air date: Feb 28, 1970. 5956 Smith Hill Rd., Utica, NY, 13502. Phone: (315) 797-5220. Fax: (315) 797-5409.E-mail: info@wutr.com Web Site: www.wutr.com. Licensee: Mission Broadcasting Inc. Group Owner: (group owner) (acq 4-1-2004; $3.725 million). Population Served: 104,100 Natl. Network: ABC, .

Key Personnel:

Diane Siembab	stn mgr
Steve Merren	sls dir & gen sls mgr
Steve Ventura	opns mgr & rgnl sls mgr
Allen Williams	prom mgr
Domenick Cecconi	progmg dir & news dir
Michael Moran	chief of engrg

Watertown, NY
(DMA 177)

*WNPI-DT— Digital Channel: 23.60.5 kw vis. ant 794t/725g TL: N44 29 29 W74 51 27 On air date: Aug 30, 1971. 1056 Arsenal St., Watertown, NY, 13601. Phone: (315) 782-3142. Fax: (315) 782-2491. Web Site: www.wpbstv.org. Licensee: St. Lawrence Valley ETV Council, Inc. Population Served: 220,000 Natl. Network: PBS, . Rgnl. Network: Eastern Educ. Washington Atty: Schwartz, Woods & Miller.

Key Personnel:

Thomas F. Hanley	pres & gen mgr
Lynn Brown	dev dir & progmg dir
Joline Furgison	mktg dir & progmg mgr

*WPBS-DT— Digital Channel: 41.59 kw vis. ant 1,212t/914g TL: N43 51 46 W75 43 39 On air date: Aug 5, 1971. 1056 Arsenal St., Watertown, NY, 13601. Phone: (315) 782-3142. Fax: (315) 782-2491. Web Site: www.wpbstv.org. Licensee: St. Lawrence Valley ETV Council, Inc. Population Served: 151,000 Natl. Network: PBS, . Rgnl. Network: Eastern Educ. Washington Atty: Schwartz, Woods & Miller.

Key Personnel:

Thomas F. Hanley	pres & gen mgr
Lynn Brown	dev dir & progmg dir

WWNY-TV—(Carthage, Digital Channel: 7. Digital Hrs: 6am - 2am 316 kw vis, 47 kw aur. ant 718t/572g TL: N43 57 16 W75 43 45 (CP: Ant 725t/579g) On air date: Oct 22, 1954. 120 Arcade St., Watertown, NY, 13601. Phone: (315) 788-3800. Fax: (315) 782-7468. Fax: (315) 788-3787.E-mail: wwny@wwnytv.net Web Site: wwnytv.net. Licensee: United Communications Corp. Group Owner: (group owner) (acq 12-5-81; $8.1 million;6-1-81). Population Served: 107,406 Natl. Network: CBS, . Washington Atty: Wood, Maines & Brown, Chartered. News staff: 16; News: 19 hrs wkly.

Key Personnel:

Cathy Pircsuk	gen mgr
Patrick Powers	gen sls mgr

WWTI— Digital Channel: 21. Digital Hrs: 24 Note: ABC is on WWTI(TV) ch 50, CW is on WWTI-DT ch 21. 1,000 kw vis, 100 kw aur. ant 1,268t/1,000g TL: N43 52 47 W75 43 11 On air date: January 1988. 1222 Arsenal St., Watertown, NY, 13601. Phone: (315) 785-8850. Fax: (315) 785-0127. Web Site: www.newswatch50.com. Licensee: Newport Television License LLC. Group Owner: Clear Channel Communications Inc. (acq 3-14-2008; grpsl). Natl. Network: ABC, CW, Natl. Rep: Millennium Sales & Marketing,. Wire Svc: AP News staff: 10; News: 5 hrs wkly.

Key Personnel:

David Males	gen mgr & gen sls mgr natl sls mgr
Keith Rudes	chief of engrg

North Carolina

Asheville
see Greenville-Spartanburg, SC-Asheville, NC-Anderson, SC market

Canton
see Greenville-Spartanburg, SC-Asheville, NC-Anderson, SC market

Charlotte, NC
(DMA 24)

WAXN-TV— Digital Channel: 50. Digital Hrs: 24 1,100 kw vis. ant 1,155t/1,010g TL: N35 15 41 W80 43 38 On air date: Oct 15, 1994. 1901 North Tryon St., Charlotte, NC, 28206. Phone: (704) 338-9999.

Fax: (704) 371-3131. Web Site: www.action64.com. Licensee: WSOC-TV Holdings Inc. Group Owner: Cox Communications Inc. (acq 1-31-2000). Population Served: 2,490,000 Natl. Rep: TeleRep,. Washington Atty: Dow, Lohnes & Albertson.

Key Personnel:

Dave Siegler	opns mgr
Sally Ganz	mktg dir
Kay Hall	progmg dir
Robin Whitmeyer	news dir
Ted Hand	engrg dir
Patricia Marsden	rsch dir
Kierstin Boujlil	traf mgr

WBTV— Analog Channel: 3. Digital Channel: 23. Analog Hrs: 24 Digital Hrs: 24 100 kw vis, 10 kw aur. ant 1,860t/1,987g TL: N35 21 51 W81 11 13 On air date: July 15, 1949. One Julian Price Pl., Charlotte, NC, 28208. Phone: (704) 374-3500. Fax: (704) 374-3614. Web Site: www.wbtv.com. Licensee: WBTV License Subsidiary LLC. Group Owner: Jefferson-Pilot Communications Co. (acq 3-31-2008; grpsl). Population Served: 1,300,000 Natl. Network: CBS, . Natl. Rep: Petry Television Inc.,. Washington Atty: Wiley, Rein & Fielding. Wire Svc: UPI

Key Personnel:

Nick Simonette	gen mgr
Don Shaw	opns dir
Shelly Hill	prom dir & progmg dir
Ron Yoslov	chief of engrg

WCCB— Digital Channel: 27. Digital Hrs: 24 2,090 kw vis, 230 kw aur. 1,276t/1,143g TL: N35 15 56 W80 44 06 On air date: Dec 7, 1953. One Television Pl., Charlotte, NC, 28205. Phone: (704) 372-1800. Fax: (704) 376-3415. Fax: (704) 332-7941.E-mail: wccb@foxcharlotte.tv Web Site: www.foxcharlotte.tv. Licensee: North Carolina Broadcasting Partners. Group Owner: Bahakel Communications Population Served: 2,121,000 Natl. Network: Fox, . News staff: one.

Key Personnel:

John Hutchinson	VP & gen mgr
Jim White	stn mgr
Gaston Bates	gen sls mgr
Ken White	news dir
Rick Aydlett	chief of engrg

WCNC-TV— Digital Channel: 22. Digital Hrs: 24 5,000 kw vis, 250 kw aur. ant 1,964t/1,954g TL: N35 20 49 W81 10 15 On air date: July 9, 1967. 1001 Wood Ridge Center Dr., Charlotte, NC, 28217-1901. Phone: (704) 329-3636. Fax: (704) 357-4980. Web Site: www.wcnc.com. Licensee: WCNC-TV Inc. Group Owner: Belo Corp., Broadcast Division (acq 1997; grpsl). Population Served: 663,800 Natl. Network: NBC, . Natl. Rep: Harrington, Righter & Parsons,. Washington Atty: Wiley, Rein & Fielding.

Key Personnel:

Timothy J. Morrissey	pres
Stuart B. Powell	gen mgr
Ann Marie Young	sls dir

WHKY-TV— Digital Channel: 40. Digital Hrs: 24 950 kw vis. ant 823t/164g TL: N35 39 28 W81 24 24 On air date: Feb 14, 1968. Box 1059, Hickory, NC, 28603. 526 Main Ave. S.E., Hickory, NC 28603. Phone: (828) 322-1290. Fax: (828) 322-8256.E-mail: whky@whky.com Web Site: www.whky.com. Licensee: Long Communications LLC. Ownership: Thomas E. Long, 49%; Roberta S. Long, 41%; Jeffrey Long, 10% (acq 12-31-2001; with WHKY(AM) Hickory). Population Served: 2,200,000 Washington Atty: Hardy & Carey. News staff: 4; News: 5 hrs wkly.

Key Personnel:

Thomas Long	gen mgr
Jeff Long	stn mgr
Patty Guthrie	gen sls mgr & prom mgr
Jim Karas	news dir
Heather Isenhour	traf mgr

WJZY— Digital Channel: 47.500 kw vis, 50 kw aur. ant 1,948t/1,949g TL: N35 21 44 W81 09 19 On air date: Mar 9, 1987. 3501 Performance Rd., Charlotte, NC, 28214. Phone: (704) 398-0046. Fax: (704) 393-8407.E-mail: info@wjzy.com Web Site: www.wjzy.com. Licensee: WJZY-TV Inc. Group Owner: Capitol Broadcasting Co. Inc. (acq 11-87; $1.581 million). Natl. Network: CW, . Natl. Rep: Millennium Sales & Marketing,. Washington Atty: Fletcher, Heald & Hildreth.

Key Personnel:

Will Davis	gen mgr
Shawn Harris	stn mgr
Matt Livoti	gen sls mgr
Brian Corrigan	natl sls mgr
Andre Boyd	prom mgr
Joe Heaton	progmg dir & pub affrs dir pub svc dir
John Bishop	chief of engrg
Robin Symos	rsch dir
Mary Sellars	traf mgr

WMYT-TV— Digital Channel: 39.5,000 kw vis. ant 1,870t TL: N35 21 44 W81 09 19 On air date: October 1994. 3501 Performance Rd.,

Charlotte, NC, 28214. Phone: (704) 398-0046. Fax: (704) 393-8407.E-mail: info@wmyt12.com Web Site: www.wmyt12.com. Licensee: WMYT-TV Inc. Group Owner: Capitol Broadcasting Co. Inc. (acq 2—2000; $4.5 million). Natl. Network: MyNetworkTV, . Natl. Rep: Millennium Sales & Marketing,.

Key Personnel:

Will Davis . . . gen mgr
Shawn Harris . . . sls dir
Brian Corrigan . . . natl sls mgr
Robin Symes . . . mktg dir & rsch dir
Andre Boyd . . . prom mgr
Joe Heaton . . . progmg dir & pub affrs dir
John Bishop . . . chief of engrg
Mary Sellars . . . traf mgr

***WNSC-TV—** Digital Channel: 15.676 kw vis, 136 kw aur. ant 688t TL: N34 50 24 W81 01 07 On air date: Jan 3, 1978. Box 11766, Rock Hill, SC, 29731. 454 S. Anderson Rd., Rock Hill, SC 29731. Phone: (803) 324-3184. Fax: (803) 324-0580. Web Site: www.muetv.org. Licensee: S.C. Educ TV Commission. Population Served: 870,000 Natl. Network: PBS, .

Key Personnel:

Maurice Bresnahan . . . pres
Bruce Bauman . . . sls dir
Tim Coughill . . . stn mgr & progmg dir
David Taylor . . . chief of engrg

WSOC-TV— Digital Channel: 34. Digital Hrs: 24 316 kw vis, 31.6 kw aur. ant 1,194t/1,050g TL: N35 15 41 W80 43 38 On air date: Apr 28, 1957. Box 34665, Charlotte, NC, 28234. 1901 N. Tryon St., Charlotte, NC 28206. Phone: (704) 338-9999. Web Site: www.wsoctv.com. Licensee: WSOC-TV Holdings Inc. Group Owner: Cox Broadcasting Inc. (acq 4-13-59; grpsl; 4-13-59). Population Served: 2,490,000 Natl. Network: ABC, . Natl. Rep: TeleRep,. Washington Atty: Dow, Lohnes & Albertson.

Key Personnel:

Joe Pomilla . . . gen mgr
Dave Siegler . . . opns mgr
Sally Ganz . . . mktg dir
Kay Hall . . . progmg dir

***WTVI—** Digital Channel: 11. Digital Hrs: 24 2,750 kw vis, 550 kw aur. ant 1,247t/1,221g TL: N35 12 25 W80 47 30 On air date: Aug 27, 1965. 3242 Commonwealth Ave., Charlotte, NC, 28205. Phone: (704) 372-2442. Fax: (704) 335-1358. Web Site: www.wtvi.org. Licensee: Charlotte-Mecklenburg Public Broadcasting Authority. Population Served: 1,600,000 Natl. Network: PBS, . Washington Atty: Schwartz, Woods & Miller.

Key Personnel:

Elsie Garner . . . CEO & pres gen mgr
Tom Green . . . chief of engrg

***WUNE-TV—** Digital Channel: 17. Digital Hrs: 24 1,550 kw vis, 154 kw aur. ant 1,791t/420g TL: N36 03 47 W81 50 33 On air date: Sept 11, 1967. Box 14900, Research Triangle Park, NC, 27709-4900. 10 TW Alexander Dr., Research Triangle Park, NC 27709. Phone: (919) 549-7000. Fax: (919) 549-7201.E-mail: viewer@unctv.org Web Site: www.unctv.org. Licensee: University of North Carolina. Population Served: 9,000,000 Natl. Network: PBS, . Washington Atty: Schwartz, Woods & Miller.

Key Personnel:

Tom Howe . . . gen mgr

***WUNG-TV—** Digital Channel: 44. Digital Hrs: 24 5,000 kw vis, 500 kw aur. ant 1,384t TL: N35 21 30 W80 36 37 On air date: Sept 11, 1967. Box 14900, Research Triangle Park, NC, 27709-4900. Phone: (919) 549-7000. Fax: (919) 549-7201.E-mail: viewer@unctv.org Web Site: www.unctv.org. Licensee: University of North Carolina. Population Served: 9,000,000 Natl. Network: PBS, . Washington Atty: Schwartz, Woods & Miller.

Key Personnel:

Tom Howe . . . gen mgr

Durham

see Raleigh-Durham (Fayetteville), NC market

Edenton

see Norfolk-Portsmouth-Newport News, VA market

Fayetteville

see Raleigh-Durham (Fayetteville), NC market

Greensboro-High Point-Winston Salem, NC (DMA 46)

WCWG— Digital Channel: 19. Digital Hrs: 24 5,000 kw vis. ant 1,814t/1,797g TL: N35 52 02 W79 49 26 On air date: Oct 30, 1985. 622 Guilford College Rd., Suite G, Greensboro, NC, 27409. Phone: (336) 510-2020. Fax: (336) 517-2020.E-mail: info@wcwg20.com Web Site: www.wcwg20.com. Licensee: WTWB License LLC. Group Owner: Pappas Telecasting Companies (acq 1995; $4 million). Population Served: 1,543,000 Natl. Network: CW, . Natl. Rep: TeleRep,. Washington Atty: Paul, Hastings, Janofsky & Walker LLP.

Key Personnel:

Rosalie Drake . . . gen mgr
Joe Sigman . . . sls dir & prom mgr
Eric Jordan . . . gen sls mgr
David Edrington . . . progmg mgr
Don Moore . . . chief of engrg

WFMY-TV— Digital Channel: 51. Digital Hrs: 24 100 kw vis, 19.5 kw aur. ant 1,842t/1,914g TL: N35 52 13 W79 50 25 On air date: Sept 22, 1949. PO Box TV 2, Greensboro, NC, 27420. 1615 Phillips Ave., Greensboro, NC 27405. Phone: (336) 379-9369. Fax: (336) 273-3444.E-mail: news2@wfmy.com Web Site: www.wfmynews2.com. Licensee: WFMY Television Corp. Group Owner: Gannett Broadcasting (division of Gannett Co. Inc.) (acq 2-1-88). Population Served: 634,130 Natl. Network: CBS, . Wire Svc: CBS Wire Svc: AP News: 32 hrs wkly.

Key Personnel:

Deborah Hooper . . . pres & gen mgr
Deana Coble . . . opns dir
Bill Lancaster . . . gen sls mgr
Chris Delaporte . . . rgnl sls mgr
David Reeve . . . mktg mgr & prom mgr
David Briscoe . . . progmg mgr
Gina Katzmark . . . news dir
Jim Walton . . . chief of engrg
Sharon Blandin . . . traf mgr
Greg Kerr . . . sports cmtr

WGHP— Digital Channel: 8. Digital Hrs: 24 300 kw vis. ant 1,305t/1,217g TL: N35 48 46 W79 50 29 On air date: Oct 14, 1963. HP-8, High Point, NC, 27261. 2005 Francis St., High Point, NC 27263. Phone: (336) 841-8888. Fax: (336) 841-8051. Web Site: www.myfox8wghp.com. Licensee: Community Television of North Carolina License LLC. Group Owner: (group owner; (acq 7-14-2008; grpsl). Population Served: 533,300 Natl. Network: Fox, . Natl. Rep: Fox Stations Sales,. Wire Svc: AP News staff: 75; News: 39 hrs wkly.

Key Personnel:

Karen Adams . . . VP & gen mgr progmg dir
Ramona Alexander . . . sls VP
Ross Mason . . . chief of engrg

WGPX-TV— Digital Channel: 14. Digital Hrs: 24 1,000 kw vis, 100 kw aur. ant 784t/773g TL: N36 14 54 W79 39 21 On air date: Aug 7, 1984. 1114 N. O'Henry Blvd., Greensboro, NC, 27405. Phone: (336) 272-9227. Fax: (336) 272-9298. Web Site: www.ionline.tv. Licensee: ION Media Greensboro License Inc., debtor-in-possession. Group Owner: Paxson Communications Corp. (acq 1996; $5.5 million). Natl. Network: ION Television, . Natl. Rep: Roslin,. Washington Atty: Baraff, Koerner, Olender & Hochberg.

Key Personnel:

Dana Lambert . . . stn mgr
Steve Hall . . . chief of engrg
Stephanie Black . . . traf mgr

WLXI— Digital Channel: 43. Digital Hrs: 24 130 kw vis. ant 1,729t/1,719g TL: N35 52 02 W79 49 26 On air date: Mar 1, 1984. 2109 Patterson St., Greensboro, NC, 27407. Phone: (336) 855-5610. Fax: (336) 855-3645.E-mail: wlxi@tct.tv Licensee: Radiant Life Ministries Inc. Group Owner: Tri-State Christian Television (acq 10-7-91; $1.9 million;10-28-91). Population Served: 2,500,000 Washington Atty: Joseph E. Dunne III.

Key Personnel:

Larry Patton . . . gen mgr
Gil Couch . . . chief of engrg

WMYV— Digital Channel: 33. Digital Hrs: 24 1,100 kw vis, 110 kw aur. ant 1,696t/1,726g TL: N35 52 13 W79 50 25 On air date: May 9, 1981. 3500 Myer Lee Dr., Winston Salem, NC, 27101. Phone: (336) 722-4545. Fax: (336) 723-8217.E-mail: info@my48.tv Web Site: www.my48.tv. Licensee: WUPN Licensee LLC. Group Owner: Sinclair Broadcast Group Inc. (acq 1-9-2002; $50,000 and cancellation of debt). Natl. Network: MyNetworkTV, . Natl. Rep: Millennium Sales & Marketing,. Washington Atty: Arter & Hadden. News: 7 hrs wkly.

Key Personnel:

Ron Inman . . . gen mgr
Fran McRae . . . gen sls mgr
Eric Gabriel . . . prom mgr
Jeanette Pruitt . . . progmg dir
Zane Parnell . . . chief of engrg

***WUNL-TV—** Digital Channel: 32. Digital Hrs: 24 5,000 kw vis, 500 kw aur. ant 1,653t/328g TL: N36 22 34 W80 22 14 On air date: Feb 22, 1973. Box 14900, Research Triangle Park, NC, 27709-4900. 10 TW Alexander Dr., Research Triangle Park, NC 27709-4900. Phone: (919) 549-7000. Fax: (919) 549-7201.E-mail: viewer@unctv.org Web Site: www.unctv.org. Licensee: University of North Carolina. Natl. Network: PBS, . Washington Atty: Schwartz, Woods & Miller.

Key Personnel:

Tom Howe . . . gen mgr

WXII-TV— Digital Channel: 31. Digital Hrs: 24 316 kw vis, 63.5 kw aur. ant 1,980t/680g TL: N36 22 31 W78 08 50 On air date: Sept 30, 1953. 700 Coliseum Dr., Winston-Salem, NC, 27106. Phone: (336) 721-9944. Fax: (336) 703-6300. Web Site: www.wxii12.com. Licensee: WXII Hearst-Argyle Television Inc. Group Owner: Hearst-Argyle Television Inc. (acq 3-18-99; grpsl). Population Served: 2,183,000 Natl. Network: NBC, . Washington Atty: Brooks, Pierce, McLendon, Humphrey & Leonard.

Key Personnel:

Mark Strand . . . pres & prom mgr
Barry Klaus . . . CFO & news dir
John Norvell . . . sr VP & chief of engrg
Henry E. Price . . . gen mgr
Michael Pulitzer . . . stn mgr & progmg mgr

WXLV-TV— Digital Channel: 29. Digital Hrs: 24 5,000 kw vis, 500 kw aur. ant 2,000t/768g TL: N36 22 37 W80 22 10 On air date: Sept 24, 1979. 3500 Myer Lee Dr., Winston-Salem, NC, 27101. Phone: (336) 722-4545. Fax: (336) 723-8217.E-mail: info@abc45.com Web Site: www.abc45.com. Licensee: WXLV Licensee LLC. Group Owner: Sinclair Broadcast Group Inc. (acq 12-10-01; grpsl). Population Served: 548,000 Natl. Network: ABC, . Washington Atty: Arter & Hadden. News: 2.5 hrs wkly.

Key Personnel:

Ron Inman . . . gen mgr
Fran McRae . . . gen sls mgr
Eric Gabriel . . . prom mgr
Jeanette Pruitt . . . progmg dir
Zane Parnell . . . chief of engrg

Greenville-New Bern-Washington, NC (DMA 103)

WCTI-TV—(New Bern, Digital Channel: 12. Digital Hrs: 24 32.8 kw vis. ant 1,932t/1,929g TL: N35 06 15 W77 20 12 On air date: Sept 1, 1963. Box 12325, 225 Glenburnie Dr., New Bern, NC, 28561. Phone: (252) 638-1212. Fax: (252) 637-4141. Fax: (252) 636-6816. Web Site: www.wtci12.com. Licensee: Newport License Holdings Inc.. Ownership: Bonten Media Group, LLC (acq 6-15-2004; $4 million). Population Served: 233,000 Natl. Network: ABC, . Natl. Rep: Continental Television Sales,. Washington Atty: Koteen & Naftalin.

Key Personnel:

James Ottolin . . . gen mgr
Ingrid Johansen . . . news dir
Ken Hughes . . . VP & chief of engrg

WEPX-TV— Digital Channel: 51. Digital Hrs: 24 143 kw vis. ant 505t/473g TL: N35 24 09 W77 25 10 On air date: Dec 9, 1998. 1301 S. Glenburnie Rd., New Bern, NC, 28562. Phone: (252) 636-2550. Fax: (252) 633-7851. Licensee: ION Media Greenville License Inc., debtor-in-possession. Group Owner: Paxson Communications Corp. (acq 4-13-99; $3.55 million). Natl. Network: MyNetworkTV, .

Key Personnel:

Gary Griffey . . . engrg dir
Tammy Mason . . . traf mgr

WFXI— Digital Channel: 8. Digital Hrs: 24 Note: Fox is on WFXI(TV) ch 4, MyNetworkTV is on WFXI-DT ch 24. 316 kw vis, 31.6 kw aur. ant 817t/810g TL: N34 53 01.017 W76 30 22.27 On air date: Nov 1, 1989. 5441 Hwy. 70 E., Morehead City, NC, 28557. Phone: (252) 240-0888. Fax: (252) 240-2028.E-mail: email@fox8fox14.com Web Site: www.fox8fox14.com. Licensee: Esteem Broadcasting of North Carolina LLC. Group Owner: Piedmont Television Holdings LLC (acq 12-31-2007; $5.885 million wtih WYDO(TV) Greenville). Natl. Network: Fox, MyNetworkTV, Washington Atty: Cohn & Marks. News: 4 hrs wkly.

Key Personnel:

David L. Bailey . . . pres
Bill Fielder . . . exec VP
Don Fisher . . . VP & gen mgr natl sls mgr
Scott Foley . . . opns dir
Lisa Leonard . . . gen sls mgr & rgnl sls mgr
Billy Poplin . . . rgnl sls mgr
Walt Young . . . prom mgr
Linda Murphy . . . progmg dir & pub svc dir
Andrea Griffith . . . news dir
Andy Kozik . . . chief of engrg
Lisa Reed . . . traf mgr

Rebroadcasts WYDO(TV) Greenville 100%.

WITN-TV—(Washington, Digital Channel: 32. Digital Hrs: 24 795 kw vis. ant 1,948t/1,958g TL: N35 21 55 W77 23 38 On air date: Sept 28, 1955. Box 468, 3057 Hwy. 17 S., Washington, NC, 27889. Phone: (252) 946-3131. Fax: (252) 946-0279.E-mail: witn@witntv.com Web Site: www.witntv.com. Licensee: Gray Television Licensee LLC. Group

Owner: Gray Television Inc. (acq 8-1-97; $39.4 million). Population Served: 1,388,000 Natl. Network: NBC, . Natl. Rep: Blair Television,. Wire Svc: AP News staff: 28; News: 27.5 hrs wkly.
Key Personnel:
Chris Mossman . . . . . gen mgr
Michael Riddle . . . . . opns mgr & prom mgr progmg mgr
Mark Gentner . . . . . gen sls mgr
Stephanie Shoop . . . . . news dir
Jeff Pearce . . . . . chief of engrg

WNCT-TV— Digital Channel: 10. Digital Hrs: 24 316 kw vis, 31.6 kw aur. ant 1,879t/2,000g TL: N35 21 55 W77 23 38 On air date: Dec 22, 1953. 3221 South Evans St., Greenville, NC, 27834. Phone: (252) 355-8500. Fax: (252) 355-8568.E-mail: newsdesk@wnct.com Web Site: www.wnct.com. Licensee: Media General Broadcasting Inc. Group Owner: Media General Broadcast Group (acq 3-21-97; grpsl). Population Served: 457,340 Natl. Network: CBS, CW, . Natl. Rep: MMT,. Washington Atty: Dow, Lohnes & Albertson.
Key Personnel:
Vickie Jones . . . . . gen mgr
Jerry Hogan . . . . . gen sls mgr
Melissa Preas . . . . . news dir
Bertie Cartwright . . . . . chief of engrg

WPXU-TV— Digital Channel: 34. Digital Hrs: 24 2,000 kw vis. ant 987t TL: N34 29 38 W77 29 18 On air date: 2004. c/o WEPX, 1301 S. Glenbernie Rd., New Bern, NC, 28562. Phone: (252) 636-2550. Fax: (252) 633-7851. Licensee: Paxson Jacksonville License Inc. Group Owner: Paxson Communications Corp. (acq 10-1-99; $200,000). Natl. Network: MyNetworkTV, .
Key Personnel:
Gary Griffey . . . . . engrg dir
Tammy Mason. . . . . traf mgr

***WUNK-TV—** Digital Channel: 23. Digital Hrs: 24 1,260 kw vis, 126 kw aur. ant 1,151t/1,138g TL: N35 33 10 W77 36 06 On air date: 1972. Box 14900, Research Triangle Park, NC, 27709-4900. 10 TW Alexander Dr., Research Triangle Park, NC 27709. Phone: (919) 549-7000. Fax: (919) 549-7201.E-mail: viewer@unctv.org Web Site: www.unctv.org. Licensee: University of North Carolina. Population Served: 9,000,000 Natl. Network: PBS, . Washington Atty: Schwartz, Woods & Miller. News staff: 15; News: 3 hrs wkly.
Key Personnel:
Tom Howe . . . . . gen mgr

***WUNM-TV—** Digital Channel: 19. Digital Hrs: 24 3,020 kw vis, 302 kw aur. ant 1,840t/1,761g TL: N35 06 18 W77 20 15 On air date: March 1982. Box 14900, Research Triangle Park, NC, 27709-4900. Phone: (919) 549-7000. Fax: (919) 549-7201.E-mail: viewer@unctv.org Web Site: www.unctv.org. Licensee: University of North Carolina. Population Served: 9,000,000 Natl. Network: PBS, . Washington Atty: Schwartz, Woods & Miller.
Key Personnel:
Tom Howe . . . . . gen mgr

WYDO— Digital Channel: 47. Digital Hrs: 24 1,104 kw vis. ant 686t TL: N35 26 44 W77 22 08 On air date: June 30, 1992. 5441 Hwy. 70 E., Morehead City, NC, 28557. Phone: (252) 240-0888. Fax: (252) 756-9250.E-mail: email@fox8fox14.com Web Site: www.fox8fox14.com. Licensee: Esteem Broadcasting of North Carolina LLC. Group Owner: GOCOM Communications (acq 12-31-2007; $5.885 million with WFXXI(TV) Morehead City). Population Served: 228,000 Natl. Network: Fox, . Washington Atty: Wilkinson, Barker, Knauer & Quinn.
Key Personnel:
Don Fisher. . . . . gen mgr
Andrea Griffith . . . . . news dir
Andy Kozik . . . . . chief of engrg
Satellite of WFXI Morehead City 100%.

High Point

see Greensboro-High Point-Winston Salem, NC market

Lumberton

see Myrtle Beach-Florence, SC market

Manteo

see Norfolk-Portsmouth-Newport News, VA market

New Bern

see Greenville-New Bern-Washington, NC market

Raleigh-Durham (Fayetteville), NC (DMA 27)

WFPX-TV— Digital Channel: 36. Digital Hrs: 24 1,000 kw vis, 100 kw aur. ant 794t/794g TL: N34 53 05 W79 04 29 On air date: Mar 14, 1985. Drawer 62, Lumber Bridge, NC, 28357. 19234 NC 71 Hwy N., Lumber Bridge, NC 28357. Phone: (910) 843-3884. Phone: (910) 843-3885. Fax: (910) 843-2873. Web Site: www.ionmedia.tv. Licensee: ION Media License Co. LLC, debtor-in-possession. Group Owner: Paxson Communications Corp. (acq 10-20-97; $4.5 million). Population Served: 275,000 Natl. Network: ION Television, . Natl. Rep: Adam Young,. Washington Atty: Baraff, Koerner, Olender & Hochberg.
Key Personnel:
Rhonda Schulik . . . . . rgnl sls mgr
Robbie Brock. . . . . progmg dir & pub affrs dir & chief of engrg
Deborah Howard. . . . . traf mgr

WLFL— Digital Channel: 27. Digital Hrs: 24 5,000 kw vis, 232 kw aur. 1,675t/1,150g TL: N35 42 52 W78 49 01 On air date: Dec 18, 1981. 3012 Highwoods Blvd., Suite 101, Raleigh, NC, 27604. Phone: (919) 872-9535. Fax: (919) 878-3758.E-mail: info@wlfl22.com Web Site: www.wlfl22.com. Licensee: WLFL Licensee L.L.C. Group Owner: Sinclair Broadcast Group Inc. Population Served: 755,300 Natl. Network: CW, . Natl. Rep: Millennium Sales & Marketing,. Washington Atty: Shaw, Pittman. News staff: 36; News: 7 hrs wkly.
Key Personnel:
Neal Davis . . . . . gen mgr
Kim Rivenbark . . . . . prom mgr
Gary Todd . . . . . engrg dir

WNCN— Digital Channel: 17. Digital Hrs: 24 5,000 kw vis, 500 kw aur. ant 2,001t/1,902g TL: N35 40 29 W78 31 40 On air date: Apr 11, 1988. 1205 Front St., Raleigh, NC, 27609. Phone: (919) 836-1717. Fax: (919) 836-1687. Web Site: www.nbc17.com. Licensee: Media General Communications Inc. Group Owner: NBC TV Stations Division. (acq 6-26-2006; grpsl). Natl. Network: NBC, . Natl. Rep: MMT,. News: 30 hrs wkly.
Key Personnel:
Barry Leffler . . . . . gen mgr & stn mgr
Carol Ward . . . . . gen sls mgr
Teresa Doring . . . . . progmg dir & progmg mgr
Russell Mizelle . . . . . chief of engrg

WRAL-TV— Digital Channel: 48. Digital Hrs: 24 100 kw vis, 10 kw aur. 2,005t/2,000g TL: N35 40 35 W78 32 09 On air date: Dec 15, 1956. Box 12000, Raleigh, NC, 27605. 2619 Western Blvd., Raleigh, NC 27606. Phone: (919) 821-8555. Fax: (919) 821-8517. Fax: TWX: 510-928-1833. Web Site: www.wral.com. Licensee: Capitol Broadcasting Co. Inc. Group Owner: (group owner) Population Served: 2,120,000 Natl. Network: CBS, . Natl. Rep: TeleRep,. Washington Atty: Holland & Knight. Wire Svc: NWS (National Weather Service) Wire Svc: AP News staff: 100; News: 30 hrs wkly.
Key Personnel:
TBA . . . . . gen mgr
Quinn Koontz. . . . . sls dir
Laura Stillman . . . . . natl sls mgr & natl sls mgr
John Harris. . . . . progmg dir
Rick Gall . . . . . news dir
Peter Sockett. . . . . chief of engrg

WRAY-TV— Digital Channel: 42. Digital Hrs: 24 1,800 kw vis. ant 1,768t/1,738g TL: N35 49 53 W78 08 50 On air date: 1995. 4909 Suite E. Expressway Dr., Wilson, NC, 27895-3583. Phone: (252) 243-0584. Fax: (252) 237-6290. Licensee: MTB Raleigh Licensee LLC. Group Owner: Scripps Howard Broadcasting Co. (acq 2-2-2009).
Key Personnel:
Harold Rabinowitz . . . . . gen mgr & chief of engrg
Harold Rabionowitz . . . . . stn mgr

WRAZ— Digital Channel: 49. Digital Hrs: 24 5,000 kw vis, 500 kw aur. 1,088t/967g TL: N35 42 55 W78 49 04 (CP: Ant 1,965t) On air date: 1995. Box 30050, Durham, NC, 27702. 512 S. Mangum St., 1st Floor, Durham, NC 27701. Phone: (919) 595-5050. Fax: (919) 595-5028. Web Site: www.fox50.com. Licensee: WRAZ-TV Inc. Group Owner: Capitol Broadcasting Co. Inc. (acq 2000; $1 million). Natl. Network: Fox, . Natl. Rep: TeleRep,. Washington Atty: Holland & Knight.
Key Personnel:
Thomas Schenck . . . . . gen mgr
Chris Downey. . . . . chief of opns
Evelyn Booker . . . . . gen sls mgr
Kevin Kolbe . . . . . mktg dir & prom dir
Joanne Stanley . . . . . progmg mgr
Jim Gamble . . . . . chief of engrg

WRDC— Digital Channel: 28. Digital Hrs: 24 5,000 kw vis, 250 kw aur. ant 2,000t/1,976g TL: N35 40 35 W78 32 09 On air date: Nov 4, 1968. 3012 Highwoods Blvd., Suite 101, Raleigh, NC, 27604. Phone: (919) 872-2854. Fax: (919) 878-3758.E-mail: info@myrdctv.com Web Site: www.myrdctv.com. Licensee: Raleigh (WRDC-TV) Licensee Inc. Group Owner: Sinclair Broadcast Group Inc. (acq 11-15-01; $2.3 million in stock). Population Served: 493,000 Natl. Network: MyNetworkTV, . Natl. Rep: Millennium Sales & Marketing,. Washington Atty: Fisher, Wayland, Cooper, Leader & Zaragoza.
Key Personnel:
Neal Davis . . . . . gen mgr
Lon Goldman . . . . . natl sls mgr & rgnl sls mgr
Kim Rivenbark . . . . . prom mgr
Donna Russell . . . . . news dir
Gary Todd . . . . . engrg dir & chief of engrg

WRPX-TV— Digital Channel: 15. Digital Hrs: 24 180 kw vis. ant 1,161t/1,135g TL: N36 06 11 W78 11 29 On air date: Aug 31, 1987. 3209 Gresham Lake Rd., Suite 151, Raleigh, NC, 27615. Phone: (919) 827-4800. Fax: (919) 876-1415. Web Site: www.ionmedia.tv. Licensee: ION Media Raleigh License Inc., debtor-in-possession. Group Owner: Paxson Communications Corp. (acq 4-5-2000; grpsl). Population Served: 352,154 Natl. Network: ION Television, . Natl. Rep: Roslin,. Washington Atty: Mitchell, Fielstra & Assoc.
Key Personnel:
Michelle Barnhill . . . . . opns mgr
Rhonda Schulik . . . . . rgnl sls mgr
Deborah Howard. . . . . traf mgr

WTVD— Digital Channel: 11. Digital Hrs: 24 316 kw vis, 47.4 kw aur. 1,990t/2,000g TL: N35 40 05 W78 31 58 On air date: Sept 2, 1954. 411 Liberty, Durham, NC, 27701. Phone: (919) 683-1111. Fax: (919) 682-7476 (sales). Fax: (919) 682-7225 (admin). Web Site: www.abc11tv.com. Licensee: WTVD Television LLC. Group Owner: (group owner; a(cq 5-24-57; $1,417,800; 5-3-57). Population Served: 804,000 Natl. Network: ABC, . Washington Atty: Wilmer, Cutler & Pickering.
Key Personnel:
John H. Idler . . . . . pres & gen mgr

***WUNC-TV—** Digital Channel: 25. Digital Hrs: 24 100 kw vis, 20 kw aur. ant 1,538t/1,269g TL: N35 51 59 W79 10 00 On air date: Jan 8, 1955. Box 14900, Research Triangle Park, NC, 27709-4900. 10 TW Alexander Dr., Research Triangle Park, NC 27709. Phone: (919) 549-7000. Fax: (919) 549-7201.E-mail: viewer@unctv.org Web Site: www.unctv.org. Licensee: University of North Carolina. Population Served: 9,000,000 Natl. Network: PBS, . Washington Atty: Schwartz, Woods & Miller.
Key Personnel:
Tom Howe . . . . . gen mgr

***WUNP-TV—** Digital Channel: 36. Digital Hrs: 24 125 kw vis. ant 1,207t/1,135g TL: N36 17 27 W77 50 11 On air date: 1985. Box 14900, Research Triangle Park, NC, 27709-4900. 10 T W Alexander Dr., Research Triangle Park, NC 27709. Phone: (919) 549-7000. Fax: (919) 549-7201.E-mail: viewer@unctv.org Web Site: www.unctv.org. Licensee: University of North Carolina. Natl. Network: PBS, . Washington Atty: Schwartz, Woods & Miller.
Key Personnel:
Tom Howe . . . . . gen mgr

WUVC-DT— Digital Channel: 38. Digital Hrs: 24 5,000 kw vis, 500 kw aur. ant 1,842t/1,749g TL: N35 30 45 W75 58 40 On air date: June 1, 1981. 230 Donaldson St., 3rd Fl., ., Fayetteville, NC, 28301. Lake Plaza East, 900 Ridgefield Dr., Ste. 100, Raleigh, NC 27609. Phone: (910) 323-4040. Fax: (910) 323-3924. Web Site: www.univision.com. Licensee: Capital Broadcasting Partners. Group Owner: Univisiion Communications Inc. (acq 3-31-2003). Population Served: 947,750 Natl. Network: Univision (Spanish), . Washington Atty: Brooks, Pierce, McLendon, Humphrey & Leonard. Foreign lang progmg: SpanishS 168
Key Personnel:
Mike Munoz . . . . . gen mgr
Todd Schlachter . . . . . natl sls mgr
Maria Tajman . . . . . progmg dir & traf mgr
Armando Trull . . . . . news dir
William Acevedo . . . . . chief of engrg
Yvonne Cerna. . . . . prom mgr & rsch dir

Washington

see Greenville-New Bern-Washington, NC market

Wilmington, NC (DMA 134)

WECT— Digital Channel: 44. Digital Hrs: 24 710 kw vis. ant 1,935t/23g TL: N34 07 53 W78 11 17 On air date: Apr 9, 1954. 322 Shipyard Blvd., Wilmington, NC, 28412. Phone: (910) 791-8070. Fax: (910) 392-1509.E-mail: wect@wect.com Web Site: www.wect.com. Licensee: Raycom America License Subsidiary LLC. Group Owner: Raycom Media Inc. (acq 9-12-96; grpsl). Population Served: 369,000 Natl. Network: NBC, . Natl. Rep: Harrington, Righter & Parsons,. Rgnl. Rep: Rgnl rep: Covington & Burling

Key Personnel:
Gary McNair . . . . . gen mgr
Mark Mendenhall . . . . . gen sls mgr
Dave Toma . . . . . mktg dir
Herschel Howie . . . . . prom mgr
Raeford Brown . . . . . news dir
Dan Ullmer . . . . . chief of engrg
Donna Lanier . . . . . traf mgr

WSFX-TV— Digital Channel: 30. Digital Hrs: 24 80 kw vis. ant 1,935t/23g TL: N34 07 53 W78 11 17 On air date: Sept 24, 1984. 322 Shipyard Blvd., Wilmington, NC, 28412. Phone: (910) 791-8070. Fax: (910) 202-0493.E-mail: tpostema@wsfx.com Web Site: www.wsfx.com. Licensee: Southeastern Media Holdings Inc. (acq 9-22-2003; $14 million). Population Served: 542,000 Natl. Network: Fox, . Natl. Rep: MMT,. Washington Atty: Baraff, Koerner, Olender & Hochberg. News staff: 6; News: 3 hrs wkly.
Key Personnel:
Tom Postema . . . . . gen mgr & gen sls mgr & natl sls mgr
Herschel Howie . . . . . prom mgr
Raeford Brown . . . . . news dir
Dan Ullner . . . . . chief of engrg
Kim Herring . . . . . traf mgr
Bob Bonner . . . . . sports cmtr
George Elliott . . . . . weather dir

***WUNJ-TV—** Digital Channel: 29. Digital Hrs: 24 4,470 kw vis, 447 kw aur. 1,813t TL: N34 07 51 W78 11 16 On air date: 1971. Box 14900, Research Triangle Park, NC, 27709-4900. 10 TW Alexander Dr., Research Triangle Park, NC 27709-4900. Phone: (919) 549-7000. Fax: (919) 549-7201.E-mail: viewer@unctv.org Web Site: www.unctv.org. Licensee: University of North Carolina. Population Served: 9,000,000 Natl. Network: PBS, . Washington Atty: Schwartz, Woods & Miller.
Key Personnel:
Tom Howe . . . . . gen mgr

WWAY— Digital Channel: 46. Digital Hrs: 24 1,000 kw vis. and 1,935t/23g TL: N34 07 53 W78 11 17 On air date: Oct 1, 1964. 615 N. Front St., Wilmington, NC, 28401. Phone: (910) 762-8581. Fax: (910) 762-8367.E-mail: acombs@wwaytv3.com Web Site: www.wwaytv3.com. Licensee: WWAY-TV LLC. Group Owner: Liberty Corp. (acq 1-31-2006; grpsl). Population Served: 120,284 Natl. Network: ABC, .
Key Personnel:
Andy Combs . . . . . gen mgr
Billy Stratton . . . . . chief of engrg

North Dakota

Bismarck

see Minot-Bismarck-Dickinson, ND market

Dickinson

see Minot-Bismarck-Dickinson, ND market

Fargo-Valley City, ND

(DMA 120)

KBRR— Digital Channel: 10. Digital Hrs: 18 590 w vis. ant 630t/640g TL: N47 58 38 W96 36 18 On air date: July 1985. Box 9115, Fargo, ND, 58106. Phone: (701) 277-1515. Fax: (701) 277-1830. Licensee: Red River Broadcast Co. L.L.C. Group Owner: (group owner) Natl. Network: Fox, . Washington Atty: Crowell & Moring.
Key Personnel:
Jim Shaw . . . . . pres & news dir
Ed Beiswenger . . . . . gen sls mgr
Kathy Lau . . . . CEO & VP gen mgr & prom mgr & progmg mgr
Dave Hoffman . . . . . chief of engrg
Satellite of KVRR(TV) Fargo, ND.

***KCGE-DT—** Digital Channel: 16. Digital Hrs: 24 105 kw vis. ant 720t/720g TL: N47 58 38 W96 36 18 On air date: October 2003. Box 3240, Fargo, ND, 58108. Phone: (701) 241-6900. Fax: (701) 239-7650.E-mail: info@prairiepublic.org Web Site: www.prairiepublic.org. Licensee: Prairie Public Broadcasting Inc. Natl. Network: PBS, .
Key Personnel:
John E. Harris III . . . . . CEO & pres
Steve Wennblom . . . . . progmg mgr
Satellite of KFME(TV) Fargo, ND.

KCPM— Digital Channel: 27. Digital Hrs: 24 5,000 kw vis. ant 1,991t/1,955g TL: N47 16 45 W97 20 26 On air date: Jan 1, 2003. Box 9292, Fargo, ND, 58106. Phone: (701) 364-9900. Fax: (605) 334-5575.E-mail: mail@kcpm.tv Licensee: G.I.G. of North Dakota LLC. (acq 8-7-2001). Natl. Network: MyNetworkTV, .
Key Personnel:
Charles D. Poppen . . . . . gen mgr

***KFME—** Digital Channel: 13. Digital Hrs: 20 56.2 kw vis. ant 1,122t/1,128g TL: N47 00 45 W97 11 41 On air date: Jan 19, 1964. Box 3240, Fargo, ND, 58108-3240. 207 N. 5th St., Fargo, ND 58102. Phone: (701) 241-6900. Fax: (701) 239-7650.E-mail: info@prairiepublic.org Web Site: www.prairiepublic.org. Licensee: Prairie Public Broadcasting Inc. Population Served: 362,400 Natl. Network: PBS, . Prairie Public Television Washington Atty: Dow, Lohnes & Albertson.
Key Personnel:
John E. Harris III . . . . . CEO & pres
Ann Clark . . . . . dev dir
Steve Wennblom . . . . . progmg mgr

***KGFE—** Digital Channel: 15. Digital Hrs: 24 100 kw vis, 10 kw aur. ant 1,382t/1,255g TL: N48 08 24 W97 59 38 On air date: Sept 9, 1974. Box 3240, Fargo, ND, 58108-3240. 207 N. 5th St., Fargo, ND 58102. Phone: (701) 241-6900. Fax: (701) 239-7650.E-mail: info@prairiepublic.org Web Site: www.prairiepublic.org. Licensee: Prairie Public Broadcasting Inc. Population Served: 362,400 Natl. Network: PBS, . Washington Atty: Dow, Lohnes & Albertson.
Key Personnel:
John E. Harris III . . . . . CEO & pres
Steve Wennblom . . . . . progmg mgr
Satellite of *KFME Fargo.

***KJRE—** Digital Channel: 20. Digital Hrs: 24 407 kw vis, 40.7 kw aur. ant 587t TL: N46 17 55 W98 51 58 On air date: May 12, 1992. Box 3240, Fargo, ND, 58108-3240. 207 N. 5th St., Fargo, ND 58102. Phone: (701) 241-6900. Fax: (701) 239-7650.E-mail: info@prairiepublic.org Web Site: www.prairiepublic.org. Licensee: Prairie Public Broadcasting Inc. Natl. Network: PBS, . Washington Atty: Dow, Lohnes & Albertson.
Key Personnel:
John E. Harris III . . . . . CEO & pres
Steve Wennblom . . . . . progmg mgr
Satellite of *KFME(TV) Fargo.

KJRR— Digital Channel: 7. Digital Hrs: 18 10.6 kw vis. ant 443t/449g TL: N46 55 27 W98 46 19 On air date: Sept 1, 1988. Box 9115, Fargo, ND, 58106. Phone: (701) 277-1515. Fax: (701) 277-1830. Licensee: Red River Broadcast Co. L.L.C. Group Owner: (group owner). Natl. Network: Fox, . Washington Atty: Crowell & Moring.
Key Personnel:
Jim Shaw . . . . . CEO & news dir
Ed Beiswenger . . . . . pres & gen sls mgr
Kathy Lau . . . . . VP & gen mgr prom mgr & progmg dir
Dave Hoffman . . . . . chief of engrg
Satellite of KVRR(TV) Fargo.

***KMDE—** Digital Channel: 25.134 kw vis. ant 802t/729g TL: N48 03 47.8 W99 20 08.7 On air date: 2006. Box 3240, Fargo, ND, 58108-3240. Phone: (701) 241-6900. Fax: (701) 239-7650.E-mail: info@prairiepublic.org Web Site: www.prairiepublic.org. Licensee: Prairie Public Broadcasting Inc. Natl. Network: PBS, . Prairie Public Television
Key Personnel:
John E. Harris III . . . . . CEO & pres
Steve Wennblom . . . . . progmg mgr
Satellite of KFME Fargo.

KNRR— Analog Channel: 12. Digital Channel: 15. Analog Hrs: 18 Digital Hrs: 18 316 kw vis, 31.6 kw aur. 1,394t TL: N48 59 42 W97 24 26 (CP: 158 kw vis, 15.8 kw aur) On air date: 1985. Box 9115, Fargo, ND, 58106. Phone: (701) 277-1515. Fax: (701) 277-1830. Licensee: Red River Broadcast Co. L.L.C. Group Owner: (group owner) Natl. Network: Fox, . Washington Atty: Crowell & Moring.
Key Personnel:
Dave Hoffman . . . . . CEO & chief of engrg
Jim Shaw . . . . . pres & news dir
Ed Beiswenger . . . . . gen sls mgr
Kathy Lau . . . . . VP & gen mgr prom mgr & progmg mgr
Satellite of KVRR(TV) Fargo.

KVLY-TV— Digital Channel: 44. Digital Hrs: 24 304 kw vis, 45.7 kw aur. ant 2,000t/2,063g TL: N47 20 36 W97 17 17 On air date: Oct 11, 1959. 1350 21st Ave. S., Fargo, ND, 58103. Phone: (701) 237-5211. Fax: (701) 237-5396.E-mail: mail@kvlytv11.com Web Site: www.kvlytv11.com. Licensee: Hoak Media of Dakota License LLC. Group Owner: Wicks Television L.L.C. (acq 1-3-2007; grpsl). Population Served: 577,000 Natl. Network: NBC, . Natl. Rep: Blair Television,. Washington Atty: Wyrick, Robbins, Yates & Pontin. Wire Svc: AP News staff: 36; News: 16 hrs wkly.
Key Personnel:
Charlie Johnson . . . . . gen mgr & stn mgr news dir
Jeff Petrik . . . . . opns mgr & progmg mgr
Ron Westrick . . . . . gen sls mgr
Roger Johnson . . . . . chief of engrg

KVRR— Digital Channel: 19. Digital Hrs: 18 4,150 kw vis, 415 kw aur. ant 1,095t TL: N46 40 26 W96 13 40 On air date: Feb 14, 1983. Box 9115, Fargo, ND, 58106. Phone: (701) 277-1515. Fax: (701) 277-1830. Licensee: Red River Broadcast Co L.L.C. Group Owner: (group owner) Natl. Network: Fox, . Washington Atty: Crowell & Moring.
Key Personnel:
Dave Hoffman . . . . . chmn & chief of engrg
Jim Shaw . . . . . pres & news dir
Ed Beiswinger . . . . . gen sls mgr
Kathy Lau . . . . . VP & gen mgr prom mgr & progmg mgr

KXJB-TV—(Valley City, Digital Channel: 38. Digital Hrs: 20 97.7 kw vis, 10 kw aur. ant 2,030t/2,060g TL: N47 16 45 W97 20 18 On air date: Sept 11, 1954. 1350 21st Ave. S., Fargo, ND, 58103-3313. Phone: (701) 282-0444. Fax: (701) 232-0493.E-mail: news@kvoytv11.com Web Site: www.kx4.com. Licensee: Parker Broadcasting of Dakota LLC. Group Owner: Catamount Broadcast Group (acq 1-3-2007). Population Served: 150,000 Natl. Network: CBS, . Natl. Rep: Continental Television Sales,. Washington Atty: Cohn & Marks. News staff: 20; News: 10 hrs wkly.
Key Personnel:
Charlie Johnson . . . . . gen mgr & stn mgr
Mark Von Bank . . . . . gen sls mgr
Jeff Petrik . . . . . progmg mgr
Mike Morken . . . . . news dir
Ron Barr . . . . . chief of engrg
Wendy Bernier . . . . . prom

WDAY-TV— Digital Channel: 21. Digital Hrs: 5 AM-2 AM 100 kw vis, 11.4 kw aur. ant 1,150t/1,206g TL: N47 00 43 W97 11 58 On air date: June 1, 1953. Box 2466, Fargo, ND, 58108. 301 S. 8th St., Fargo, ND 58103. Phone: (701) 237-6500. Fax: (701) 241-5368. Web Site: www.wday.com/tv. Licensee: Forum Communications Co. Group Owner: (group owner; (acq 7-20-60; $900,000;7-25-60). Population Served: 214,200 Natl. Network: ABC, CW, .
Key Personnel:
Mark Prather . . . . . gen mgr
Carol Anhorn . . . . . gen sls mgr
Susan Eider . . . . . prom mgr & progmg mgr
Jeff Nelson . . . . . news dir
Tom Thompson . . . . . chief of engrg

WDAZ-TV— Digital Channel: 8. Digital Hrs: 19 316 kw vis, 50 kw aur. ant 1,480t/1,461g TL: N48 08 24 W97 59 38 On air date: Jan 29, 1967. Box 12639, Grand Forks, ND, 58208-2639. 2220 S. Washington, Grand Forks, ND 58201. Phone: (701) 775-2511. Fax: (701) 746-8565.E-mail: bkerr@wdaz.com Web Site: www.wdaz.com. Licensee: Forum Communications Co. Group Owner: (group owner) Population Served: 214,000 Natl. Network: ABC, . Washington Atty: Holland & Knight.
Key Personnel:
Robert Kerr . . . . . gen mgr
Rob Horken . . . . . gen sls mgr & adv dir
Cassie Walder . . . . . news dir
Jeff Awes . . . . . engrg dir & chief of engrg
Satellite of WDAY-TV Fargo.

Minot-Bismarck-Dickinson, ND

(DMA 158)

***KBME-TV—** Digital Channel: 22. Digital Hrs: 20 79.4 kw vis, 7.9 kw aur. ant 1,394t/1,044g TL: N46 35 17 W100 48 30 On air date: June 18, 1979. Box 3240, Fargo, ND, 58108-3240. 207 N. 5th St., Fargo, ND 58102. Phone: (701) 241-6900. Fax: (701) 239-7650.E-mail: info@prariepublic.org Web Site: www.prariepublic.org. Licensee: Prairie Public Broadcasting Inc. Natl. Network: PBS, . Washington Atty: Dow, Lohnes & Albertson.
Key Personnel:
John E. Harris III . . . . . CEO & pres
Ann Clark . . . . . dev dir
Steve Wennblom . . . . . progmg mgr
Satellite of KFME-TV Fargo, ND.

KBMY— Digital Channel: 16. Digital Hrs: 18 75 kw vis. ant 935t TL: N46 35 15 W100 48 20 On air date: Mar 31, 1985. 3128 East Broadway Ave., Fort Myers, ND, 58501. Phone: (701) 223-1700. Fax: (701) 258-0886.E-mail: kndx@westdakotafox.com Web Site: www.abc17.tv. Licensee: KBMY-KMCY LLC. Group Owner: Forum Communications Co. Natl. Network: ABC, . Washington Atty: Marmet & McCombs.

Key Personnel:
Mark Prather . . . . gen mgr & gen sls mgr
Tony Kruckenberg. . . . . chief of engrg
Rebroadcasts KMCY Minot 100%.

***KDSE—** Digital Channel: 9. Digital Hrs: 20 214 kw vis, 21.4 kw aur. ant 806t/538g TL: N46 43 34 W102 54 56 On air date: Aug 4, 1982. Box 3240, 207 N. 5th St., Fargo, ND, 58108-3240. Phone: (701) 241-6900. Fax: (701) 239-7650.E-mail: info@prairiepublic.org Web Site: www.prairiepublic.com. Licensee: Prairie Public Broadcasting Inc. Natl. Network: PBS, . Washington Atty: Dow, Lohnes & Albertson.
Key Personnel:
John E. Harris III. . . . . CEO & pres
Steve Wennblom . . . . progmg mgr
Satellite of KFME(TV) Fargo.

KFYR-TV— Digital Channel: 31. Digital Hrs: 24 100 kw vis, 13.5 kw aur. ant 1,400t/1,101g TL: N46 36 17 W100 48 30 On air date: Dec 19, 1953. Box 1738, Bismarck, ND, 58502. 200 N. 4th St., Bismarck, ND 58501. Phone: (701) 255-5757. Fax: (701) 255-8220. Web Site: www.kfyrtv.com. Licensee: Hoak Media of Dakota License LLC. Group Owner: Wicks Television L.L.C. (acq 1-3-2007; grpsl). Population Served: 330,000 Natl. Network: NBC, . Washington Atty: Hogan & Hartson. News staff: 29; News: 24 hrs wkly.
Key Personnel:
Dick Heidt . . . . gen mgr
Barry Schumaier . . . . gen sls mgr
Jim Sande . . . . progmg dir

KMCY— Digital Channel: 14. Digital Hrs: 18 513 kw vis, 89.1 kw aur. 2,720t/649g TL: N48 03 13 W101 23 05 On air date: June 22, 1985. 3128 E. Broadway, Bismarck, ND, 58501. Phone: (701) 223-1700. Fax: (701) 258-0886.E-mail: kndx@westdakotafox.com Web Site: www.abc14.tv. Licensee: KBMY-KMCY LLC. Group Owner: Forum Communications Co. Natl. Network: ABC, . Washington Atty: Marmet & McCombs.
Key Personnel:
Mark Prather . . . . gen mgr
Tony Kruckenberg . . . . chief of engrg

KMOT— Digital Channel: 10. Digital Hrs: 24 214 kw vis, 42.7 kw aur. 680t/690g TL: N48 12 56 W101 19 05 On air date: Jan 21, 1958. Box 1120, Minot, ND, 58702. 1800 S.W. 16th, Minot, ND 58701. Phone: (701) 852-4101. Fax: (701) 838-8195. Web Site: www.kmot.com. Licensee: Hoak Media of Dakota License LLC. Group Owner: Wicks Television L.L.C. (acq 1-3-2007; grpsl). Natl. Network: NBC, . Washington Atty: Hogan & Hartson.
Key Personnel:
Tom Ross . . . . gen mgr & gen sls mgr
Nick Dreyer . . . . news dir
Mike Robinson . . . . chief of engrg
Satellite of KFYR-TV Bismarck.

KNDX— Digital Channel: 26. Digital Hrs: 18 1,797 kw vis. ant 1,112t TL: N46 35 23 W100 48 02 On air date: 2001. Box 4026, Bismarck, ND, 58502. Phone: (701) 355-0026. Fax: (701) 250-7244. Web Site: www.fox26.tv. Licensee: Prime Cities Broadcasting Inc. Natl. Network: Fox, .
Key Personnel:
Gary O'Halloran. . . . . gen mgr
Richard Farley . . . . chief of engrg

***KPSD-TV—** Digital Channel: 13. Digital Hrs: 24 316 kw vis, 31.6 kw aur. ant 1,700t/1,696g TL: N45 03 20 W102 15 40 On air date: September 1973. Box 5000, Vermillion, SD, 57069-5000. 555 N. Dakota St., Vermillion, SD 57069. Phone: (605) 677-5861. Phone: (800) 456-0766. Fax: (605) 677-5010.E-mail: programming@sdpb.org Web Site: www.sdpd.org. Licensee: South Dakota Board of Directors for Educational Telecommunications. Population Served: 40,000 Natl. Network: PBS, . Washington Atty: Cohn & Marks.
Key Personnel:
Julie Andersen . . . . pres
Terry Spencer. . . . . dev dir & dev mgr
Bob Bosse . . . . progmg dir

KQCD-TV— Digital Channel: 7. Digital Hrs: 24 316 kw vis, 31.6 kw aur. 731t/645g TL: N46 56 48 W102 59 17 On air date: July 28, 1980. 373 21 St. E., Dickinson, ND, 58601. Phone: (701) 483-7777. Fax: (701) 483-8231.E-mail: kqcd@kqcd.com Web Site: www.kqcd.com. Licensee: Hoak Media of Dakota License LLC. Group Owner: Wicks Television L.L.C. (acq 1-3-2007; grpsl). Population Served: 16,000 Natl. Network: NBC, . Washington Atty: Hogan & Hartson.
Key Personnel:
Dick Heidt. . . . . gen mgr & stn mgr
Barry Schumaier . . . . gen sls mgr
LuWanna Lawrence. . . . . prom mgr
Jim Sande . . . . progmg mgr
Monica Hannan . . . . news dir
Brian Funk. . . . . chief of engrg
Satellite of KFYR-TV Bismarck.

***KSRE—** Digital Channel: 40. Digital Hrs: 20 100 kw vis, 10 kw aur. ant 1,059t/983g TL: N48 03 03 W101 23 24 On air date: January 1980. Box 3240, Fargo, ND, 58108-3240. Phone: (701) 241-6900. Fax: (701) 239-7650.E-mail: info@prairiepublic.org Web Site: www.prairiepublic.org. Licensee: Prairie Public Broadcasting. Population Served: 750,000 Natl. Network: PBS, . Washington Atty: Dow, Lohnes & Albertson.
Key Personnel:
John E. Harris III. . . . . CEO & pres
Steve Wennblom . . . . progmg mgr
Satellite of KFME Fargo.

KUMV-TV— Digital Channel: 8. Digital Hrs: 24 166 kw vis, 33.1 kw aur. 1,060t/874g TL: N48 08 02 W103 51 36 On air date: Feb 11, 1957. Box 1287, Williston, ND, 58802-1287. 602 Main St., Willinston, ND 58801. Phone: (701) 572-4676. Fax: (701) 572-0118.E-mail: kumv@kumv.com Web Site: www.kumv.com. Licensee: Hoak Media of Dakota License LLC. Group Owner: Wicks Television L.L.C. (acq 1-3-2007; grpsl). Population Served: 35,000 Natl. Network: NBC, . News staff: 2; News: 6 hrs wkly.
Key Personnel:
Deborah Burton. . . . . gen mgr & gen sls mgr
Jim Sande . . . . progmg mgr
Hawlie Ohe . . . . news dir
Scott Aune. . . . . chief of engrg
Satellite of KFYR-TV Bismarck.

***KWSE—** Digital Channel: 11. Digital Hrs: 20 9.48 kw vis. ant 905t TL: N48 08 30 W103 53 34 On air date: March 1983. Box 3240, Fargo, ND, 58108-3240. Phone: (701) 241-6900. Fax: (701) 239-7650.E-mail: info@prairiepublic.org Web Site: www.prairiepublic.org. Licensee: Prairie Public Broadcasting Inc. Natl. Network: PBS, . Washington Atty: Dow, Lohnes & Albertson.
Key Personnel:
John E. Harris III. . . . . CEO & pres
Steve Wennblom . . . . progmg mgr
Satellite of KFME(TV) Fargo.

KXMA-TV— Digital Channel: 19. Digital Hrs: 20 100 kw vis, 10 kw aur. 840t/621g TL: N46 43 30 W102 54 58 On air date: October 1956. 1625 W. Villard, Dickinson, ND, 58601. Phone: (701) 483-1400. Fax: (701) 483-1401.E-mail: webmasterb@kxnet.com Web Site: www.kxnet.com. Licensee: Reiten Television Inc. Group Owner: (group owner; (acq 12-4-84; $362,500). Population Served: 16,000 Natl. Network: CBS, . Washington Atty: Fisher, Wayland, Cooper, Leader & Zaragoza.
Key Personnel:
Tim Reiten . . . . gen mgr
Bruce Dintelman . . . . gen sls mgr
Julie Bernhardt. . . . . natl sls mgr
Tom Gerhardt. . . . . news dir
Rocky Hefty . . . . chief of engrg

KXMB-TV— Digital Channel: 12. Digital Hrs: 20 19.1 kw vis. ant 1,457t/1,151g TL: N46 35 23 W100 48 20 On air date: Nov 19, 1955. 1811 N. 15th St., Bismarck, ND, 58501. Phone: (701) 223-9197. Fax: (701) 223-3320.E-mail: webmasterb@kxnet.com Web Site: www.kxnet.com. Licensee: Reiten Television Inc. Group Owner: (group owner; (acq 1-27-71; $1.2 million;2-8-71). Population Served: 60,000 Natl. Network: CBS, . Washington Atty: Fisher, Wayland, Cooper, Leader & Zaragoza. News staff: 11; News: 9 hrs wkly.
Key Personnel:
Tim Reiten . . . . gen mgr & stn mgr
Bruce Dintelman . . . . gen sls mgr
Julie Bernhardt. . . . . natl sls mgr
Tom Gerhardt. . . . . news dir
Rocky Hefty . . . . chief of engrg

KXMC-TV— Digital Channel: 13. Digital Hrs: 20 316 kw vis, 31.6 kw aur. 1,128t/1,061g TL: N48 03 02 W101 20 29 On air date: Apr 1, 1953. Box 1686, Minot, ND, 58702. 2121 2nd St. SE, Minot, ND 58701. Phone: (701) 852-2104. Fax: (701) 838-9360.E-mail: webmasterb@kxnet.com Web Site: www.kxnet.com. Licensee: Reiten Television Inc. Group Owner: (group owner; (acq 7-31-74;8-19-74). Population Served: 75,000 Natl. Network: CBS, . Natl. Rep: Continental Television Sales,. Washington Atty: Fisher, Wayland, Cooper, Leader & Zaragoza. News staff: 10; News: 9 hrs wkly.
Key Personnel:
David Reiten . . . . pres & gen mgr
Darren Lenertz. . . . . gen sls mgr
Jim Olson . . . . news dir
Rocky Hefty . . . . chief of engrg

KXMD-TV— Digital Channel: 14. Digital Hrs: 20 174 kw vis, 17.4 kw aur. 980t/840g TL: N48 08 22 W103 53 24 On air date: Oct 25, 1969. Box 790, Williston, ND, 58801. 1802 13th Ave. W., Williston, NC 58801. Phone: (701) 572-2345. Fax: (701) 572-0658. Licensee: Reiten Television Inc. Group Owner: (group owner). Population Served: 34,000 Natl. Network: CBS, . Washington Atty: Fisher, Wayland, Cooper, Leader & Zaragoza.
Key Personnel:
Darren Lenertz. . . . . gen mgr & stn mgr
Amanda Luchsinger. . . . . gen sls mgr
Jim Olson . . . . news dir
Bob Turneau . . . . chief of engrg

KXND— Digital Channel: 24. Digital Hrs: 18 740.4 kw vis. ant 784t/663g TL: N48 03 14 W101 26 03 On air date: 2001. Prime Cities Broadcasting Inc., 3130 E Broadway, Bismarck, ND, 58502. Phone: (203) 431-3366. Phone: (701) 355-0026. Fax: (203) 431-3864. Web Site: www.westdakotafox.com. Licensee: Prime Cities Broadcasting Inc. Population Served: 353,000 Natl. Network: Fox, .
Key Personnel:
Gary O'Halloran. . . . . gen mgr
Richard Farley . . . . chief of engrg

Valley City

see Fargo-Valley City, ND market

Ohio

Akron

see Cleveland-Akron (Canton), OH market

Canton

see Cleveland-Akron (Canton), OH market

Cincinnati, OH (DMA 34)

***WCET—** Digital Channel: 34. Digital Hrs: 24 400 kw vis. ant 1,069t/899g TL: N39 07 27 W84 31 18 On air date: July 26, 1954. 1223 Central Pkwy., Cincinnati, OH, 45214-2890. Phone: (513) 381-4033. Fax: (513) 381-7520.E-mail: comments@cetconnect.org Web Site: www.cetconnect.org. Licensee: Greater Cincinnati TV Educational Foundation. Population Served: 1,500,000 Natl. Network: PBS, . Washington Atty: Dow, Lohnes & Albertson.
Key Personnel:
Jack Dominic . . . . COO
Susan Howarth. . . . . CEO & pres & gen mgr
Ricardo O. Ang II . . . . opns mgr & traf mgr
Brian Snape. prom mgr
Neal Schmidt. . . . . chief of engrg
Sherry Sargeant . . . . sls

WCPO-TV— Digital Channel: 10. Digital Hrs: 24 316 kw vis, 28.2 kw aur. ant 1,000t/890g TL: N39 07 31 W84 29 57 On air date: July 26, 1949. 1720 Gilbert Ave., Cincinnati, OH, 45202. Phone: (513) 721-9900. Fax: (513) 721-7717.E-mail: bfee@wcpo.com Web Site: www.wcpo.com. Licensee: Scripps Howard Broadcasting Co. Group Owner: (group owner) Population Served: 452,524 Natl. Network: ABC, . Washington Atty: Baker & Hostetler. Wire Svc: UPI News staff: 70; News: 24 hrs wkly.
Key Personnel:
Bill Fee . . . . gen mgr
Bill Fee . . . . progmg dir
Joe Martinelli. engrg dir

***WCVN-TV—** Digital Channel: 24.53.5 kw vis. ant 384t/269g TL: N39 01 50 W84 30 23 On air date: Sept 9, 1969. 600 Cooper Dr., Lexington, KY, 40502. Phone: (859) 258-7000. Fax: (859) 258-7399. Web Site: www.ket.org. Licensee: Kentucky Authority for Educational TV. Natl. Network: PBS, . Kentucky Educational Television
Key Personnel:
Mike Brower. opns mgr
Craig Cornwell . . . . progmg dir
Tim Bischoff . . . . mktg dir & pub affrs dir
Robert Ball . . . . engrg dir

***WKON—** Digital Channel: 44.49.7 kw vis. ant 702t/7g TL: N38 31 31 W84 48 39 On air date: Sept 23, 1968. 600 Cooper Dr., Lexington, KY, 40502. Phone: (859) 258-7000. Fax: (859) 258-7390.E-mail: dbritton@ket.org Web Site: www.ket.org. Licensee: Kentucky Authority for Educational TV. Natl. Network: PBS, . Kentucky Educational Television
Key Personnel:
Craig Cornwell. . . . . progmg mgr
Tim Bischoff . . . . mktg dir & pub affrs dir
Robert Ball . . . . engrg dir

WKRC-TV— Digital Channel: 12. Digital Hrs: 24 316 kw vis, 31.6 kw aur. ant 1,000t/974g TL: N39 06 58 W84 30 05 On air date: April 1949. 1906 Highland Ave., Cincinnati, OH, 45219. Phone: (513) 763-5500. Fax: (513) 763-5554. Web Site: www.wkrc.com. Licensee: Newport Television License LLC. Group Owner: Clear Channel Communications Inc. (acq 3-14-2008; grpsl). Population Served: 759,000 Natl. Network: CBS, CW, . Natl. Rep: TeleRep,. Washington Atty: Covington & Burling.

Key Personnel:
Les Vann . . . . . gen mgr & sls VP
Kurt Thelen . . . . . engrg dir

WLWT— Digital Channel: 35. Digital Hrs: 24 100 kw vis, 10 kw aur. ant 1,000t/849g TL: N39 07 17 W84 31 18 On air date: Feb 9, 1948. 1700 Young St., Cincinnati, OH, 45202. Phone: (513) 412-5000. Fax: (513) 412-6121.E-mail: newsdesk@wlwt.com Web Site: www.wlwt.com. Licensee: Hearst-Argyle Stations Inc. Group Owner: Hearst-Argyle Television Inc. (acq 7-16-97; grpsl). Population Served: 792,000 Natl. Network: NBC, . Natl. Rep: Eagle Television Sales,. Washington Atty: Brooks, Pierce, McLendon, Humphrey & Leonard.
Key Personnel:
Richard J. Dyer . . . . . pres & gen mgr
Mark Diangela . . . . . gen sls mgr
Brennan Donnellan . . . . . news dir
Paul Nowakowski . . . . . chief of engrg

***WPTO—** Digital Channel: 28. Digital Hrs: 19 400 kw vis. ant 880t/900g TL: N39 07 19 W84 32 52 On air date: Oct 14, 1959. 110 S. Jefferson St., Dayton, OH, 45402. Phone: (937) 220-1600. Fax: (937) 220-1642. Web Site: www.thinktv.org. Licensee: Greater Dayton Public Television Inc. (acq 1975). Population Served: 2,900,000 Natl. Network: PBS, . Rgnl. Network: CEN, Ohio Educ Bcstg, Eastern Educ. Ohio Educ. Telecommunications Washington Atty: Dow, Lohnes & Albertson. News staff: one; News: one hr wkly.
Key Personnel:
David Fogarty. . . . . pres & gen mgr
Suzanne O'Brien . . . . . CFO
Ed Valles . . . . . dev dir
Kitty Lensman. . . . . mktg dir
Sue Brinson. . . . . prom mgr
Gloria Skurski. . . . . progmg dir
Jim Wiener . . . . . progmg mgr
H. Fred Stone . . . . . engrg dir
George Hopstetter . . . . . engrg mgr & chief of engrg

WSTR-TV— Digital Channel: 33. Digital Hrs: 24 5,000 kw vis, 500 kw aur. ant 1,105t/925g TL: N39 12 01 W84 31 22 On air date: January 1980. 5177 Fishwick Dr., Cincinnati, OH, 45216. Phone: (513) 641-4400. Fax: (513) 242-2633. Web Site: www.my64.tv. Licensee: Sinclair Communications Group. Group Owner: Sinclair Broadcast Group Inc. (acq 1996; $11 million). Population Served: 820,000 Natl. Network: MyNetworkTV, . Washington Atty: Cole, Raywid & Braverman.
Key Personnel:
Jon Lawhead . . . . . gen mgr
Eric Lazar. . . . . natl sls mgr
Pete Ferraro. . . . . prom mgr
Rick White . . . . . progmg dir
Terry Roberts . . . . . engrg mgr
Wendy Fodel . . . . . rsch dir
Laurel Adams . . . . . traf mgr

WXIX-TV—(Newport, KY) Digital Channel: 29. Digital Hrs: 24 227 kw vis. ant 951t/932g TL: N39 07 19 W84 32 52 On air date: Aug 1, 1968. 19 Broadcast Plaza, 635 W. 7th St., Cincinnati, OH, 45203. Phone: (513) 421-1919. Fax: (513) 421-2829.E-mail: fox19@fox19.com Web Site: www.fox19.com. Licensee: wxix License Subsidiary, LLC. Group Owner: Raycom Media Inc. (acq 1998; $45 million; grpsl). Population Served: 1,946,000 Natl. Network: Fox, . Natl. Rep: TeleRep,. Washington Atty: Covington & Burling. News staff: 57; News: 23 hrs wkly.
Key Personnel:
Paul McTear. . . . . CEO
Bill Lanesey . . . . . gen mgr
Rick Oliver . . . . . opns mgr & progmg dir progmg dir
Branden Frantz. . . . . gen sls mgr
Matt Kidwell. . . . . natl sls mgr & rgnl sls mgr
Ron Stricker. . . . . rgnl sls mgr

Cleveland-Akron (Canton), OH (DMA 17)

WBNX-TV—(Akron, Digital Channel: 30. Digital Hrs: 24 1,000 kw vis, 100 kw aur. ant 1,168t/1,099g TL: N41 23 02 W81 41 44 On air date: Dec 1, 1985. 2690 State Rd., Cuyahoga Falls, OH, 44223. Phone: (330) 922-5500.E-mail: clevelandswb@wbnx.com Web Site: www.wbnx.com. Licensee: Winston Broadcasting Network Inc. (acq 5-20-87;1-19-87). Population Served: 2,230,000 Natl. Network: CW, . Natl. Rep: Adam Young,. Washington Atty: Irwin, Campbell & Tannenwald.
Key Personnel:
Lou Spangler. . . . . pres & gen mgr
Annie Keith . . . . . stn mgr & progmg dir
Colleen Metheney . . . . . opns mgr & traf mgr
Eddie Brown. . . . . gen sls mgr
Patty Armstrong . . . . . prom dir
Don Richardson . . . . . chief of engrg

WDLI-TV— Digital Channel: 39. Digital Hrs: 24 900 kw vis. ant 958t/16g TL: N41 03 20 W81 35 38 On air date: Jan 3, 1967. 1764 Wadsworth Rd., Akron, OH, 44320-3142. Phone: (330) 753-5542. Fax: (330) 753-4563.E-mail: wdli@tbn.org Licensee: Trinity Broadcasting Network. Group Owner: (group owner; (acq 4-15-86; $4.5 million;9-23-85). Population Served: 1,500,000 Washington Atty: Joseph E. Dunne III.
Key Personnel:
Joanne L. Mann . . . . . stn mgr

***WEAO—** Digital Channel: 50. Digital Hrs: 24 685 kw vis, 68.56 kw aur. ant 1,047t/923g TL: N40 04 58 W81 38 00 On air date: September 1975. Box 5191, 1750 Campus Center Dr., Kent, OH, 44240-5191. Phone: (330) 677-4549. Fax: (330) 678-0688.E-mail: questions@wneo.pbs.org Web Site: www.pbs4549.org. Licensee: Northeastern Educational TV of Ohio Inc. Population Served: 3,920,000 Natl. Network: PBS, . Washington Atty: Dow, Lohnes & Albertson. News: one hr wkly.
Key Personnel:
Trina Cutter . . . . . pres
Bill O'Neil. . . . . stn mgr
Don Freeman. . . . . dev dir & progmg dir
Rebroadcasts WNEO(TV) Alliance 100%.

WEWS-TV— Digital Channel: 15. Digital Hrs: 24 93.3 kw vis, 10 kw aur. ant 1,020t/851g TL: N41 22 27 W81 43 06 On air date: Dec 17, 1947. 3001 Euclid Ave., Cleveland, OH, 44115. Phone: (216) 431-5555. Fax: (216) 431-3666. Web Site: www.newsnet5.com. Licensee: Scripps Howard Broadcasting Co. Group Owner: (group owner, see Cross-Ownership) Population Served: 1,463,900 Natl. Network: ABC, . Natl. Rep: Eagle Television Sales,. Washington Atty: Baker & Hostetler. Wire Svc: Reuters News: 22 hrs wkly.
Key Personnel:
Victoria Regan . . . . . gen mgr

WGGN-TV— Digital Channel: 42. Digital Hrs: 24 1,480 kw vis, 148 kw aur. ant 774t/730g TL: N41 23 48 W82 47 31 On air date: Dec 5, 1982. Box 247, Castalia, OH, 44824. Phone: (419) 684-5311. Fax: (419) 684-5378.E-mail: wggn@lrbcg.com Web Site: www.cfbroadcast.com. Licensee: Christian Faith Broadcasting Inc. Group Owner: (group owner) Population Served: 750,000 Washington Atty: Joseph E. Dunne III.
Key Personnel:
Shelby Gillam . . . . . pres
Rusty Yost . . . . . gen mgr & chief of engrg
Roy Bilman . . . . . traf mgr & pub svc dir

WJW— Digital Channel: 8. Digital Hrs: 24 30 kw vis. ant 1,122t/836g TL: N41 21 48 W81 42 58 On air date: Dec 19, 1949. 5800 S. Marginal Rd., Cleveland, OH, 44103. Phone: (216) 431-8888. Fax: (216) 432-4282. Web Site: www.myfoxcleveland.com. Licensee: Community Television of Ohio License LLC. Group Owner: Fox Television Stations Inc. (acq 7-14-2008; grpsl). Population Served: 1,431,000 Natl. Network: Fox, .
Key Personnel:
Susan Pace . . . . . VP
Greg Easterly. . . . . gen mgr
Paul Perozeni . . . . . gen sls mgr
Paul Bodamer . . . . . natl sls mgr
Barb Toth . . . . . rgnl sls mgr
Kevin Salyer . . . . . prom VP & progmg VP
Sonya Thompson . . . . . news dir
Janice Nemergut. . . . . traf mgr

WKYC— Digital Channel: 17. Digital Hrs: 24 868 kw vis. ant 1,007t/861g TL: N41 23 10 W81 41 21 On air date: October 1948. 1333 Lakeside Ave., Cleveland, OH, 44114. Phone: (216) 344-3333. Fax: (216) 344-3326.E-mail: news@wkyc.com Web Site: www.wkyc.com. Licensee: WKYC-TV Inc. Group Owner: Gannett Broadcasting (acq 12-4-95; grpsl). Population Served: 2,800,000 Natl. Network: NBC, .
Key Personnel:
Tom Humpage . . . . . gen sls mgr

WMFD-TV— Digital Channel: 12. Digital Hrs: 24 294 kw vis, 29.4 kw aur. ant 591t/472g TL: N40 45 50 W82 37 04 On air date: Mar 3, 1988. 2900 Park Ave. W., Mansfield, OH, 44906. Phone: (419) 529-5900. Fax: (419) 529-2319.E-mail: comments@wmfd.com Web Site: www.wmfd.com. Licensee: Mid-State Television Inc. (acq 5-31-92;6-15-92). Population Served: 1,000,000 Washington Atty: Fletcher, Heald & Hildreth. Wire Svc: AP Wire Svc: CNN News staff: 12; News: 36 hrs wkly.
Key Personnel:
Gunther Meisse . . . . . pres & gen mgr
Robert Meisse. . . . . stn mgr & opns mgr

WOIO— Digital Channel: 10. Digital Hrs: 24 3,720 kw vis, 372 kw aur. ant 1,151t/1,113g TL: N41 23 15 W81 41 43 On air date: May 19, 1985. 1717 E. 12th St., Cleveland, OH, 44114. Phone: (216) 771-1943. Fax: (216) 515-7152. Web Site: www.woio.com. Licensee: Raycom National Inc. Group Owner: Raycom Media Inc. (acq 8-13-98). Population Served: 2,000,000 Natl. Network: CBS, . Natl. Rep: TeleRep,. Washington Atty: Covington & Burling.
Key Personnel:
Bill Applegate . . . . . gen mgr
Lisa McManus . . . . . stn mgr & progmg mgr
Jim Stunek . . . . . opns dir
Lynda King . . . . . gen sls mgr
Rob Boenau. . . . . mktg dir & prom dir
Dan Salamone . . . . . news dir
Emily Davis . . . . . pub affrs dir & pub svc dir
Bob Maupin . . . . . engrg dir & chief of engrg
Jean Niznik. . . . . traf mgr
Todd Galloway . . . . . rsch dir & sports cmtr

WQHS-DT— Digital Channel: 34. Digital Hrs: 24 525 kw vis, 200 kw aur. ant 1,160t/1,029g TL: N41 23 02 W81 42 06 On air date: Mar 3, 1981. 2861 W. Ridgewood Dr., Parma, OH, 44134. Phone: (440) 888-0061. Fax: (440) 888-7023. Web Site: www.univision.com. Licensee: Univision Partnership of Ohio. Group Owner: Univision Communications Inc. (acq 5-21-2001; grpsl). Population Served: 3,500,000 Natl. Network: Univision (Spanish), . Washington Atty: Wiley, Rein & Fielding. Wire Svc: UPI Foreign lang progmg: SpanishS 168
Key Personnel:
Rolo Duartes . . . . . gen mgr
Jose Godur . . . . . gen sls mgr
Dave Smith . . . . . chief of engrg
Bud Bush . . . . . traf mgr

WRLM— Digital Channel: 47. Digital Hrs: 24 1000 kw vis, 100 kw aur. ant 440t/423g TL: N41 06 33 W81 20 10 On air date: March 1982. 4385 Sherman Rd., Kent, OH, 44240-6847. Phone: (330) 677-6760. Licensee: Radiant Life Ministries Inc. Group Owner: Scripps Howard Broadcasting Co. (acq 6-25-2009; $7 million). Population Served: 1,500,000 Washington Atty: Colby M. May.
Key Personnel:
Glenn Foldessy. . . . . gen mgr & stn mgr & chief of engrg

WUAB— Digital Channel: 28. Digital Hrs: 24 4,680 kw vis, 468 kw aur. ant 1,102t/947g TL: N41 22 45 W81 43 12 On air date: Sept 15, 1968. 1717 E. 12th St., Cleveland, OH, 44114. Phone: (216) 771-1943. Fax: (216) 515-7152. Web Site: www.wuab.com. Licensee: Raycom National Inc. Group Owner: Raycom Media Inc. (acq 3-2-00). Population Served: 3,700,000 Natl. Network: MyNetworkTV, . Washington Atty: Covington & Burling. Wire Svc: Reuters
Key Personnel:
Bill Applegate. . . . . gen mgr
Jim Stunek . . . . . opns dir
Lynda King . . . . . gen sls mgr
Rob Boenau. . . . . mktg dir & prom dir
Lisa McManus . . . . . progmg mgr
Dan Salamone . . . . . news dir
Emily Davis . . . . . pub affrs dir & pub svc dir
Bob Maupin . . . . . chief of engrg
Todd Galloway. . . . . chief of engrg & rsch dir
Jean Niznik. . . . . traf mgr

***WVIZ—** Digital Channel: 26. Digital Hrs: 24 2,140 kw vis, 214 kw aur. ant 997t/809g TL: N41 20 28 W81 44 24 On air date: Feb 7, 1965. 1375 Euclid Ave., Cleveland, OH, 44115-1826. Phone: (216) 916-6100. Fax: (216) 916-6123. Web Site: www.wviz.org. Licensee: Ideastream. (acq 2-27-2001). Population Served: 1,700,000 Natl. Network: PBS, .
Key Personnel:
Jerry Wareham . . . . . CEO & pres
Kit Jensen . . . . . COO
Bob Calsin . . . . . CFO
Bob Stern . . . . . stn mgr & gen sls mgr
Kent A. Geist . . . . . dev dir
Maureen Paschke . . . . . mktg dir
Jane Temple . . . . . prom dir & adv dir
David Kanzeg. . . . . progmg dir
Thomas Furnas. . . . . chief of engrg
Kimberlee Bimuller . . . . . traf mgr

WVPX-TV— Digital Channel: 23. Digital Hrs: 24 1,000 kw vis. ant 987t/925g TL: N41 03 53 W81 34 59 On air date: July 19, 1953. 1333 Lakeside Ave., East, Cleveland, OH, 44114. Phone: (216) 344-3333. Fax: (216) 344-7430. Web Site: www.ionline.tv. Licensee: ION Media Akron License Inc., debtor-in-possession. Group Owner: Paxson Communications Corp. (acq 2-29-96; $40 million; with WBPT(TV) Bridgeport, CT). Population Served: 1,500,000 Natl. Network: ION Television, . Washington Atty: Dow, Lohnes & Albertson.
Key Personnel:
Robert Getze . . . . . gen sls mgr
Amy Sheridan. . . . . pub affrs dir & traf mgr pub svc dir
James Thomas . . . . . chief of engrg

Columbus, OH (DMA 32)

WBNS-TV— Digital Channel: 21. Digital Hrs: 24 316 kw vis, 31.6 kw aur. ant 890t/1,029g TL: N39 58 16 W83 01 40 On air date: Oct 5, 1949. 770 Twin Rivers Dr., Columbus, OH, 43215. Phone: (614)

460-3700. Fax: (614) 460-2826. Web Site: www.10tv.com. Licensee: WBNS TV Inc. Group Owner: Dispatch Broadcast Group Population Served: 690,000 Natl. Network: CBS, . Washington Atty: Sidley & Austin. News staff: 80; News: 31 hrs wkly.

Key Personnel:

Tom Griesdorn	gen mgr
Frank Wilson	opns dir & mktg dir progmg dir
Mike Berry	opns mgr
Chuck Devendra	gen sls mgr
Pat Wise	natl sls mgr
Doug Jones	prom mgr
John Cardenas	news dir
Angela Pace	pub affrs dir
Pat Ingram	chief of engrg
Tim Londergan	rsch dir
Mollie Ducey	traf mgr

WCMH-TV— Digital Channel: 14. Digital Hrs: 24 100 kw vis, 15 kw aur. ant 903t/1,029g TL: N39 58 15 W83 01 39 On air date: Apr 3, 1949. 3165 Olentangy River Rd., Columbus, OH, 43202. Box 4, Columbus, OH 43216. Phone: (614) 263-4444. Fax: (614) 447-9107. Web Site: www.nbc4i.com. Licensee: Media General Communications Inc. Group Owner: NBC TV Stations Division (acq 6-26-2006; grpsl). Population Served: 1,782,500 Natl. Network: NBC, . Natl. Rep: MMT,. News staff: 60; News: 31.5 hrs wkly.

Key Personnel:

Marshall N. Morton	pres
Dan Bradley	gen mgr
Debra Grivois	opns dir
Mike Cash	sls VP
Juilee Clark	natl sls mgr
Ken Lubker	rgnl sls mgr
Janna Buckey	mktg VP
Stan Sanders	news dir

*WOSU-TV— Digital Channel: 38. Digital Hrs: 24 250 kw vis. ant 954t/971g TL: N40 09 33 W82 55 23 On air date: Feb 20, 1956. 2400 Olentangy River Rd., Columbus, OH, 43210. Phone: (614) 292-9678. Fax: (614) 688-3399. Fax: (614) 688-3343.E-mail: wosu@wosu.org Web Site: wosu.org. Licensee: Ohio State University. Population Served: 1,800,000 Natl. Network: PBS, . Rgnl. Network: CEN. Washington Atty: Dow, Lohnes & Albertson.

Key Personnel:

Thomas Rieland	gen mgr
Edwin Clay	stn mgr
Janice "Sheri" Walker	opns mgr
Doug Partusch	dev dir
Tom Lahr	chief of engrg

*WOUB-TV— Digital Channel: 27. Digital Hrs: 24 1,000 kw vis, 100 kw aur. ant 800t/856g TL: N39 18 50 W82 08 54 On air date: Jan 3, 1963. 9 S. College St., Athens, OH, 45701. Phone: (740) 593-4555. Fax: (740) 593-0240.E-mail: woub@woub.org Web Site: www.woub.org. Licensee: Ohio University. Population Served: 151,000 Natl. Network: PBS, . Rgnl. Network: Ohio Educ Bcstg. Ohio Educ. Telecommunications Washington Atty: Dow, Lohnes & Albertson. News staff: 3; News: 3 hrs wkly.

Key Personnel:

Carolyn Bailey-Lewis	gen mgr
David Wiseman	opns VP
Steve Skidmore	opns dir
Scott Martin	opns mgr
Loring Lovett	rgnl sls mgr
Mark Brewer	progmg dir & film buyer
Joan Butcher	progmg mgr & traf mgr
Tim Sharp	news dir
Dave Wiseman	engrg VP

*WOUC-TV— Digital Channel: 35. Digital Hrs: 24 759 kw vis. ant 1,263t/1,174g TL: N40 05 32 W81 17 19 On air date: July 23, 1973. 9 S. College St., Athens, OH, 45701. Phone: (740) 593-4555. Fax: (740) 593-0240.E-mail: woub@woub.org Web Site: www.wouc.org. Licensee: Ohio University. (acq 12-10-75;12-22-75). Natl. Network: PBS, . Rgnl. Network: Ohio Educ Bcstg. Ohio Educ. Telecommunications Washington Atty: Cohn & Marks.

Key Personnel:

Carolyn Bailey-Lewis	gen mgr
David Wiseman	opns VP & engrg VP
Steve Skidmore	opns dir
Scott Martin	opns mgr
Loring Lovett	rgnl sls mgr
Mark Brewer	progmg dir
Joan Butcher	progmg mgr & traf mgr

Rebroadcasts WOUB-TV Athens 100%.

WSFJ-TV— Digital Channel: 24. Digital Hrs: 24 1,000 kw vis. ant 436t/279g TL: N40 04 44 W82 41 42 On air date: Mar 9, 1980. 3948 Townsfair Way, Suite 220, Columbus, OH, 43219. Phone: (614) 416-6080. Fax: (614) 416-6345.E-mail: comments@gtn51.com Web Site: www.gtn51.com. Licensee: Guardian Enterprise Group Inc. Ownership: Guardian Vision International Inc., 92.61%; Richard

Schilg, 1.39%; and others, 6% Population Served: 1,935,300 Washington Atty: Koerner & Olender P.C. News staff: one.

Key Personnel:

Dale Remy	gen mgr
Rob Kasper	opns dir
Elaine Kistler	gen sls mgr
Dave Wilson	progmg dir & traf mgr
Jason Knapp	chief of engrg & chief of engrg
Erin Merten	prom

WSYX— Digital Channel: 13. Digital Hrs: 24 100 kw vis, 10 kw aur. ant 938t/1,035g TL: N39 56 16 W83 01 16 On air date: Aug 30, 1949. 1261 Dublin Rd., Columbus, OH, 43215. Phone: (614) 481-6666. Fax: (614) 481-6828. Web Site: www.wsyx6.com. Licensee: WSYX Licensee Inc. Group Owner: Sinclair Broadcast Group Inc. (acq 1998; $228 million). Population Served: 500,000 Natl. Network: ABC, MyNetworkTV, . Natl. Rep: Millennium Sales & Marketing,.

Key Personnel:

Dan Mellon	gen mgr
Lyn Tolan	stn mgr & news dir
Tony D'Angelo	sls dir
Lorie Luthman	gen sls mgr
Mike Hansen	mktg dir
Rick White	progmg dir
Dan Carpenter	chief of engrg
Linda Siler	traf mgr

WTTE— Digital Channel: 36. Digital Hrs: 24 1,440 kw vis, 141 kw aur. ant 876t/938g TL: N39 56 14 W83 01 16 On air date: June 1, 1984. 1261 Dublin Rd., Columbus, OH, 43215. Phone: (614) 481-6666. Fax: (614) 485-1458. Web Site: www.wtte28.com. Licensee: Columbus (WTTE-TV) Licensee Inc. Group Owner: Cunningham Broadcasting Corporation (acq 1-9-2002). Population Served: 1,500,000 Natl. Network: Fox, . Natl. Rep: Millennium Sales & Marketing,.

Key Personnel:

Dan Mellon	gen mgr
Tony D'Angelo	sls dir
Mike Hansen	mktg dir
Rick White	progmg dir & progmg dir
Lyn Tolan	news dir
Zoe Anne Del Borrell	pub affrs dir
Dan Carpenter	engrg dir & chief of engrg

WWHO— Digital Channel: 46. Digital Hrs: 24 5,000 kw vis, 500 kw aur. ant 1,145t/1,115g TL: N39 35 20 W83 06 44 On air date: Aug 31, 1987. 1160 Dublin Rd., Suite 400, Columbus, OH, 43215. Phone: (614) 485-5300. Fax: (614) 485-5339. Web Site: www.wwhotv.com. Licensee: WWHO Broadcasting LLC. Group Owner: Viacom Television Stations Group. (acq 3-31-2005; $85 million with WNDY-TV Marion, IN). Natl. Network: CW, . Washington Atty: Wiley, Rein & Fielding.

Key Personnel:

Ellen Daly	stn mgr & rgnl sls mgr

Dayton, OH
(DMA 64)

WBDT— Digital Channel: 26. Digital Hrs: 24 770 kw vis. ant 1,145t/1,118g TL: N39 43 28 W84 15 18 On air date: September 1980. 2589 Corporate Pl., Miamisburg, OH, 45342. Phone: (937) 384-9226. Fax: (937) 384-7392. Web Site: daytonscw.com. Licensee: Acme Television Licenses of Ohio L.L.C. Group Owner: Acme Communications Inc. (acq 6-14-99; grpsl). Natl. Network: CW, . Natl. Rep: MMT,.

Key Personnel:

John Hannon	VP
Melanie Simon	gen sls mgr
Billie Sue Adkins	natl sls mgr
Al Schmidt	chief of engrg

WDTN— Digital Channel: 50. Digital Hrs: 24 100 kw vis, 10 kw aur. ant 1,010t/960g TL: N39 43 07 W84 15 22 On air date: Mar 15, 1949. 4595 S. Dixie Ave., Dayton, OH, 45439. Phone: (937) 293-2101. Fax: (937) 294-6542.E-mail: newstips@wdtn.com Web Site: www.wdtn.com. Licensee: WDTN Broadcasting LLC. Group Owner: LIN Television Corporation (acq 11-8-2002; grpsl). Population Served: 1,277,000 Natl. Network: NBC, . Natl. Rep: Blair Television,.

Key Personnel:

Lisa Barhorst	gen mgr
Steve Diorio	stn mgr
Jim Atkinson	chief of opns & chief of engrg
Alison Wilkerson	sls VP & gen sls mgr
Sheryl Brownlee	gen sls mgr
Joe Mulligan	natl sls mgr
Jason Doyle	prom VP
Lisa barhorst	progmg VP
Sharon Howard	pub affrs dir & pub svc dir
Janice Barney	traf mgr
Jack Pohl	sports cmtr
Carl Nichols	weather dir

WHIO-TV— Digital Channel: 41. Digital Hrs: 24 200 kw vis, 38 kw aur. ant 1,141t/1,059g TL: N39 44 02 W84 14 53 On air date: Feb 26,

1949. 1414 Wilmington Ave., Dayton, OH, 45420. Box 1206, Dayton, OH 45420. Phone: (937) 259-2111. Fax: (937) 259-2005.E-mail: 7online@whiotv.com Web Site: www.whiotv.com. Licensee: Miami Valley Broadcasting Corp. Group Owner: Cox Broadcasting Population Served: 1,276,400 Natl. Network: CBS, . Natl. Rep: TeleRep,. Washington Atty: Dow, Lohnes & Albertson.

Key Personnel:

Harry Delaney	VP & gen mgr
Chuck Eastman	opns dir & opns mgr engrg dir
James Cosby	gen sls mgr
Tony Getts	prom dir
Fantine Kerckaert	progmg dir
David Bennallack	news dir

WKEF— Digital Channel: 51. Digital Hrs: 24 2,340 kw vis, 234 kw aur. ant 1,152t/1,094g TL: N39 43 15 W84 15 39 On air date: Sept 27, 1964. 45 Broadcast Plaza, Dayton, OH, 45408. Phone: (937) 263-2662. Fax: (937) 268-2332. Web Site: www.daytonsnewsource.com. Licensee: WKEF Licensee L.P. Group Owner: Sinclair Broadcast Group Inc. (acq 7-7-98; grpsl). Population Served: 1,773,600 Natl. Network: ABC, . News: 17 hrs wkly.

Key Personnel:

Dean Ditman	gen mgr
Jason Matlock	prom dir
Roland Martel	engrg dir

WKOI-TV— Digital Channel: 39. Digital Hrs: 24 600 kw vis. ant 971t/948g TL: N39 30 44 W84 38 09 On air date: May 11, 1982. Box 1057, Richmond, IN, 47375. 1702 S. 9th St., Richmond, IN 47374-7203. Phone: (765) 935-2390. Web Site: na org. Licensee: Trinity Broadcasting of Indiana. Group Owner: Trinity Broadcasting Network (acq 9-81). Washington Atty: Gammon & Grange.

Key Personnel:

Mark Crouch	gen mgr

*WPTD— Digital Channel: 16. Digital Hrs: 24 155 kw vis. ant 1,148t/1,132g TL: N39 43 16 W84 15 00 On air date: Mar 20, 1967. 110 S. Jefferson St., Dayton, OH, 45402-2415. Phone: (937) 220-1600. Fax: (937) 220-1642. Web Site: www.thinktv.org. Licensee: Greater Dayton Public TV Inc. Population Served: 243,601 Natl. Network: PBS, . Rgnl. Network: Eastern Educ, CEN, Ohio Educ Bcstg. Ohio Educ. Telecommunications Washington Atty: Dow, Lohnes & Albertson. News staff: one; News: 1 hr wkly.

Key Personnel:

David Fogarty	pres & gen mgr
George Hopstetter	opns mgr & engrg mgr
Ed Valles	dev dir & dev mgr
Kitty Lensman	mktg mgr
Sue Brinson	prom mgr
Gloria Skurski	progmg dir
Jim Wiener	progmg mgr
H. Fred Stone	engrg dir

WRGT-TV— Digital Channel: 30. Digital Hrs: 24 5,000 kw vis, 501 kw aur. ant 1,171t/1,158g TL: N39 43 28 W84 15 18 On air date: Sept 23, 1984. 45 Broadcast Plaza, Dayton, OH, 45408. Phone: (937) 263-4500. Fax: (937) 268-5265. Web Site: www.daytonsnewsource.com. Licensee: WRGT Licensee LLC. Group Owner: Cunningham Broadcasting Corporation (acq 11-15-2001; grpsl). Population Served: 1,773,600 Natl. Network: Fox, MyNetworkTV, . News: 16 hrs wkly.

Key Personnel:

Dean Ditmen	gen mgr
Julie Gossard	natl sls mgr
Jason Matlock	prom dir
Roland Martel	engrg dir

Lima, OH
(DMA 186)

WLIO— Digital Channel: 8. Digital Hrs: 24 661 kw vis, 132 kw aur. ant 540t/549g TL: N40 44 54 W84 07 55 On air date: March 1953. Box 1689, Lima, OH, 45802. 1424 Rice Ave., Lima, OH 45805. Phone: (419) 228-8835. Fax: (419) 229-7091. Fax: (419) 225-6109. Web Site: www.wlio.com. Licensee: Lima Communications Corp. Group Owner: BlockCommunications Inc. (acq 2-1-72; $1.5 million). Population Served: 460,000 Natl. Network: NBC, CW, . Washington Atty: Dow, Lohnes & Albertson. News staff: 17; News: 24 hrs wkly.

Key Personnel:

Bruce A. Opperman	pres & gen mgr
Dave Plaugher	CFO
Dave Plaugher	stn mgr
Kevin Creamer	sls VP & rsch dir
Kylie Fortman	prom mgr & progmg dir film buyer & pub svc dir
Lon Tegels	news dir
Tom Hendrixson	pub affrs dir
Fred Vobbe	engrg VP & chief of engrg
Mary Griffin	traf mgr

WTLW— Digital Channel: 44. Digital Hrs: 24 912 kw vis, 91.2 kw aur. 679t/706g TL: N40 45 47 W84 10 59 On air date: June 13, 1982. 1844

Baty Rd., Lima, OH, 45807. Phone: (419) 339-4444. Fax: (419) 339-1736.E-mail: kbowers@wtlw.com Web Site: www.wtlw.com. Licensee: American Christian Television Services Inc. Population Served: 200,000 Washington Atty: Wiley, Rein & Fielding.

Key Personnel:

Kevin Bowers . . . . CEO & stn mgr
Rick Corcoran . . . . chief of engrg

Portsmouth

see Charleston-Huntington, WV market

Steubenville

see Wheeling, WV-Steubenville, OH market

Toledo, OH
(DMA 73)

***WBGU-TV—** Digital Channel: 27. Digital Hrs: 24 1,000 kw vis, 100 kw aur. 1,060t/1,035g TL: N41 08 13 W83 54 23 On air date: Feb 10, 1964. 245 Troup St., Bowling Green, OH, 43403. Phone: (419) 372-2700. Fax: (419) 372-7048.E-mail: www@wbgu.bqsu.edu Web Site: www.wbgu.org. Licensee: Bowling Green State University. (acq 11-17-76;12-13-76). Population Served: 1.2 m,ill,ion Natl. Network: PBS, . Rgnl. Network: Ohio Educ Bcstg. Ohio Educ. Telecommunications Washington Atty: Cohn & Marks.

Key Personnel:

Patrick Fitzgerald . . . . gen mgr & stn mgr
Deb Boyce . . . . prom dir
Ron Gargasz . . . . progmg mgr
Al Bowe . . . . chief of engrg

***WGTE-TV—** Digital Channel: 29. Digital Hrs: 24 1,000 kw vis, 135 kw aur. 1,017t/1,034g TL: N41 39 27 W83 25 55 On air date: Oct 10, 1960. 1270 S. Detroit Ave., Toledo, OH, 43614. Box 30, Toledo, OH 43614. Phone: (419) 380-4600. Fax: (419) 380-4710. Web Site: www.wgte.org. Licensee: Public Broadcasting Foundation of N.W. Ohio. Population Served: 409,500 Natl. Network: PBS, . Rgnl. Network: Ohio Educ Bcstg. Ohio Educ. Telecommunications Washington Atty: Schwartz, Woods & Miller.

Key Personnel:

Marlon P. Kiser . . . . CEO & pres gen mgr
Marlon Kiser . . . . CFO & stn mgr
Barbara Heslop . . . . opns mgr
Ross Pfeiffer . . . . dev dir
Lindsey Eberly . . . . sls dir
Jen Homier . . . . mktg dir
Darren LaShelle . . . . progmg dir & progmg mgr
Dan Niedzwiecki . . . . engrg dir

WLMB— Digital Channel: 5. Digital Hrs: 24 4,747 kw vis. 571t TL: N41 44 41 W84 01 06 On air date: Oct 19, 1998. Box 908, Dominion Broadcasting Inc., 26693 Eckel Rd., Perrysburg, OH, 43552. Phone: (419) 874-8862. Fax: (419) 874-8867.E-mail: info@wlmb.com Web Site: www.wlmb.com. Licensee: Dominion Broadcasting Inc. Ownership: Larry Whatley, 33.3%; Ron Mighell, 33.3%; Jamey Schmitz, 33.3%. Population Served: 1,500,000 Washington Atty: Wiley, Rein & Fielding.

Key Personnel:

Jamey Schmitz . . . . gen mgr
Curt Miller . . . . gen sls mgr
Brooke Myerholtz . . . . progmg dir
Eric Jingst . . . . chief of engrg

WNWO-TV— Digital Channel: 49. Digital Hrs: 24 4,370 kw vis, 437 kw aur. TL: N41 40 03 W83 21 22 On air date: May 3, 1966. 300 S. Byrne Rd., Toledo, OH, 43615. Phone: (419) 535-0024. Fax: (419) 535-0202. Web Site: www.nbc24.com. Licensee: Barrington Toledo License LLC. Group Owner: Raycom Media Inc. (acq 8-11-2006; grpsl). Population Served: 1,097,400 Natl. Network: NBC, . Natl. Rep: TeleRep,. News: 22 hrs wkly.

Key Personnel:

Rick Lipps . . . . gen mgr
Jon Skonburg . . . . stn mgr
Hank Thompson . . . . chief of engrg

WTOL— Digital Channel: 11. Digital Hrs: 23 316 kw vis, 38 kw aur. 1,000t/1,046g TL: N41 40 22 W80 22 47 On air date: Dec 5, 1958. 730 N. Summit St., Toledo, OH, 43604. Phone: (419) 248-1111. Fax: (419) 248-1177.E-mail: news@wtol.com Web Site: www.wtol.com. Licensee: WTOL License Subsidiary LLC. Group Owner: Liberty Corp. (acq 1-31-2006; grpsl). Population Served: 2,414,100 Natl. Network: CBS, . Natl. Rep: Harrington, Righter & Parsons,. Washington Atty: Dow, Lohnes & Albertson. News staff: 50; News: 25 hrs wkly.

Key Personnel:

Bob Chirdon . . . . gen mgr
Linda Blackburn . . . . gen sls mgr
Nancy Bright . . . . natl sls mgr
Steve Israel . . . . progmg dir
Mitch Jacob . . . . news dir & pub affrs dir
Eric Bergman . . . . chief of engrg

WTVG— Digital Channel: 13. Digital Hrs: 24 316 kw vis, 18.2 kw aur. 1,000t/1,049g TL: N41 41 00 W83 24 49 On air date: July 21, 1948. 4247 Dorr St., Toledo, OH, 43607. Phone: (419) 531-1313. Fax: (419) 531-1399. Web Site: www.13abc.com. Licensee: WTVG Inc. Group Owner: Capital Cities/ABC Video Enterprises International (acq 1995; $155 million with WJRT-TV Flint, MI). Population Served: 450,000 Natl. Network: ABC, . Washington Atty: Koteen & Naftalin. News staff: 30; News: 10 hrs wkly.

Key Personnel:

David Zamichow . . . . pres & gen mgr
Mary Gerken . . . . sls dir
Tamara Rost . . . . progmg dir
Brian Trauring . . . . news dir
Ernestine Weathers . . . . pub affrs dir
Barry Gries . . . . engrg dir

WUPW— Digital Channel: 46. Digital Hrs: 24 1,950 kw vis, 195 kw aur. 1,220t/1,250g TL: N41 39 21 W83 26 40 On air date: Sept 22, 1985. Four SeaGate, Toledo, OH, 43604. Phone: (419) 244-3600. Fax: (419) 244-8842.E-mail: wupw@wupw.com Web Site: www.foxtoledo.com. Licensee: WUPW Broadcasting LLC. Group Owner: LIN Television Corporation (acq 11-8-2002; grpsl). Natl. Network: Fox, . Natl. Rep: Blair Television,. Washington Atty: Shrinsky, Weitzman & Eisen. News staff: 5; News: 5 hrs wkly.

Key Personnel:

Ray Maselli . . . . gen mgr
Gary Yoder . . . . gen sls mgr & natl sls mgr
Brian Lorenzen . . . . rgnl sls mgr
Betsy Russell . . . . mktg dir & prom dir
Cathy Stoner . . . . progmg dir
Steve France . . . . news dir
Steve Crum . . . . engrg dir

Youngstown, OH
(DMA 109)

WFMJ-TV— Digital Channel: 20.3,720 kw vis, 372 kw aur. ant 990t/1,085g TL: N41 04 46 W80 38 25 On air date: Mar 8, 1953. 21 WFMJ, 101 W. Boardman St., Youngstown, OH, 44503. Phone: (330) 744-8611. Fax: (330) 744-3402.E-mail: information@wfmj.com Web Site: www.wfmj.com. Licensee: WFMJ Television Inc. Ownership: Mark A. Brown and Betty H. Brown Jagnow. (acq 7-14-93;8-2-93). Population Served: 721,200 Natl. Network: NBC, CW, . Natl. Rep: Blair Television,. Rgnl. Rep: Rgnl rep: OAB Washington Atty: Fisher, Wayland, Cooper, Leader & Zaragoza. News staff: 20; News: 10 hrs wkly.

Key Personnel:

John A. Grdic . . . . VP
John A. Grdic . . . . gen mgr
Jack Grdic . . . . gen sls mgr & progmg dir opns
Kathie Brickman . . . . natl sls mgr
Jack Stevenson . . . . mktg dir
Mona Alexander . . . . news dir
Bob Flis . . . . chief of engrg

WKBN-TV— Digital Channel: 41. Digital Hrs: 24 871 kw vis, 87.1 kw aur. ant 1,430t/1,432g TL: N41 03 28 W80 38 42 On air date: Jan 6, 1953. 3930 Sunset Blvd., Youngstown, OH, 44512. Phone: (330) 782-1144. Fax: (330) 782-3504. Fax: (330) 783-1834. Web Site: www.wkbn.com. Licensee: NVT Youngstown Licensee LLC. Group Owner: Piedmont Television Holdings LLC (acq 3-2-2007; $47 million). Population Served: 274,700 Natl. Network: CBS, . Natl. Rep: Continental Television Sales,. Washington Atty: Wiley Rein LLP. News staff: 50; News: 25 hrs wkly.

Key Personnel:

David Coy . . . . gen mgr
John Amann . . . . opns mgr & prom mgr
Jill Duffy . . . . natl sls mgr
Nikki Manuel . . . . rgnl sls mgr
Phyllis Rappach . . . . progmg dir
Gary Coursen . . . . news dir
Thomas Zocolo . . . . chief of engrg
Don Guthrie . . . . weather dir

***WNEO—** Digital Channel: 45. Digital Hrs: 24 1260 kw vis, 126 kw aur. 830t/770g TL: N40 54 23 W80 54 40 On air date: May 1973. Box 5191, Kent, OH, 44240-5191. Phone: (330) 677-4549. Fax: (330) 678-0688.E-mail: questions@wneo.org Web Site: www.pbs4549.org. Licensee: Northeastern Educational TV of Ohio Inc. Population Served: 450,000 Natl. Network: PBS, . Washington Atty: Dow, Lohnes & Albertson. News: one hr wkly.

Key Personnel:

Trina Cutter . . . . pres
Bill O'Neal . . . . gen mgr & stn mgr
Don Freeman . . . . progmg dir

WYTV— Digital Channel: 36. Digital Hrs: 24 912 kw vis, 110 kw aur. ant 580t/637g TL: N41 03 43 W80 38 07 On air date: Oct 30, 1957. 3939 Sunset Blvd., Youngstown, OH, 44512. Phone: (330) 783-2930. Fax: (330) 782-8154. Web Site: www.wytv.com. Licensee: Parkin Broadcasting of Youngstown License LLC. Group Owner: Chelsey Broadcasting Co. (acq 8-15-2007). Population Served: 693,000 Natl. Network: ABC, MyNetworkTV, . Washington Atty: Drinker Biddle & Reath LLP. News staff: 26; News: 20 hrs wkly.

Key Personnel:

Dave Coy . . . . gen mgr
Dan Messersmith . . . . gen sls mgr
Karen Brown . . . . prom mgr
Bill Lough . . . . chief of engrg
Sue Fedelia . . . . traf mgr
Bob Hannon . . . . sports cmtr
Stan Boney . . . . weather dir

Zanesville, OH
(DMA 203)

WHIZ-TV— Digital Channel: 40. Digital Hrs: 24 588 kw vis, 58.8 kw aur. 540t/508g TL: N39 55 42 W81 59 06 On air date: May 23, 1953. 629 Downard Rd., Zanesville, OH, 43701. Phone: (740) 452-5431. Fax: (740) 452-6553.E-mail: slauka@whiznews.com Web Site: www.whiznews.com. Licensee: Southeastern Ohio TV System. Ownership: Norma Littick Revocable Trust. Population Served: 450,000 Natl. Network: NBC, . Washington Atty: Leventhal, Senter & Lerman. News staff: 14; News: 10 hrs wkly.

Key Personnel:

N.J. Littick . . . . chmn
H.C. Littick . . . . pres
Doug Pickrell . . . . sls dir
Brian Wagner . . . . progmg VP
George Hiotis . . . . news dir
Dan Slentz . . . . chief of engrg
Carolyn Rider . . . . traf mgr
Aaron Spragg . . . . sports cmtr
Wesley Sass . . . . weather dir

Oklahoma

Ada

see Sherman, TX-Ada, OK market

Lawton

see Wichita Falls, TX & Lawton, OK market

Oklahoma City, OK
(DMA 45)

KAUT-TV— Digital Channel: 40. Digital Hrs: 24 ant 1,560t/1,596g TL: N35 35 22 W97 29 03 On air date: Nov 3, 1980. 11901 N. Eastern Ave., Oklahoma City, OK, 73131. Phone: (405) 516-4300. Fax: (405) 516-4329. Web Site: www.ok43.com. Licensee: Local TV Oklahoma License LLC. Group Owner: Viacom Television Stations Group (acq 5-7-2007; grpsl). Population Served: 500,000 Natl. Network: MyNetworkTV, .

Key Personnel:

Wes Milbourn . . . . stn mgr & gen sls mgr
Peter Grignon . . . . natl sls mgr
Stacy Johnson . . . . progmg dir
William Nichols . . . . chief of engrg
Elisa Parr . . . . rsch dir

***KETA-TV—** Digital Channel: 13. Digital Hrs: 24 316 kw vis, 31.6 kw aur. ant 1,525t/1,578g TL: N35 32 58 W97 29 50 On air date: Apr 13, 1956. Box 14190, Waynesboro, OK, 73113. Phone: (405) 848-8501. Fax: (405) 841-9216. Web Site: www.oeta.tv. Licensee: Oklahoma Educational TV Authority. Population Served: 300,000 Natl. Network: PBS, . Washington Atty: Dow Lohnes PLLC. News staff: 8; News: 3 hrs wkly.

Key Personnel:
John McCarroll . . . gen mgr
Bill Thrash . . . stn mgr
Mike Palmer . . . opns dir & opns mgr
Bob Sands . . . news dir
Earle Conners . . . engrg dir
Richard Ladd . . . chief of engrg

KFOR-TV— Digital Channel: 27. Digital Hrs: 24 97.7 kw vis, 19.5 kw aur. ant 1,540t/1,602g TL: N35 34 07 W97 29 20 On air date: June 6, 1949. 444 E. Britton Rd., Oklahoma City, OK, 73114. Phone: (405) 424-4444. Fax: (405) 478-6206. Web Site: www.kfor.com. Licensee: Local TV Oklahoma License LLC. Group Owner: The New York Times Co. (acq 5-7-2007; grpsl). Population Served: 2,177,200 Natl. Network: NBC, . Natl. Rep: Millennium Sales & Marketing,. Washington Atty: Koteen & Naftalin. Wire Svc: UPI News staff: 73; News: 29 hrs wkly.
Key Personnel:
Wes Milbourn . . . stn mgr & gen sls mgr
Peter Grignon . . . natl sls mgr
Luanne Stuart . . . prom dir
Belinda Lane . . . progmg dir
Bob Ablah . . . chief of engrg
Sandy Moyers . . . traf mgr

KOCB— Digital Channel: 33. Digital Hrs: 24 1,170 kw vis, 117 kw aur. ant 1,210t/1,258g TL: N35 33 36 W97 29 07 On air date: Oct 28, 1979. 1228 .E. Wilshire Blvd., Oklahoma City, OK, 73111. Phone: (405) 843-2525. Fax: (405) 478-1027 (405) 475-9163(Sales). Web Site: www.kocb.com. Licensee: KOCB License L.L.C. Group Owner: Sinclair Broadcast Group Inc. (acq 1996; $63 million with WDKY-TV Danville, KY). Population Served: 1,666,000 Natl. Network: CW, . Natl. Rep: Harrington, Righter & Parsons,.
Key Personnel:
John Rossi . . . gen mgr
Dan Loving . . . sls dir
Joe Spadea . . . news dir
Steve Bottkol . . . engrg dir

KOCM— Digital Channel: 46.50 kw vis. ant 1,364t/1,401g TL: N35 35 52 W97 29 22 On air date: 2004. Daystar Television Network, Box 612066, Dallas, TX, 75261-2066. Phone: (817) 571-1229. Phone: (405) 292-4600. Fax: (817) 571-7458.E-mail: cpmments@daystar.com Web Site: www.daystartv.net. Licensee: Word of God Fellowship Inc. (acq 8-19-2002; $3.6 million).
Key Personnel:
Joni Show . . . gen mgr

KOCO-TV— Digital Channel: 7. Digital Hrs: 24 100 kw vis, 14.5 kw aur. 1,519t/1,562g TL: N35 33 45 W97 29 24 (CP: Ant 1,515t/1,558g) On air date: July 15, 1954. 1300 E. Britton Rd., Oklahoma City, OK, 73131. Phone: (405) 478-3000. Fax: (405) 475-5242. Web Site: www.koco.com. Licensee: Ohio/Oklahoma Hearst-Argyle Television Inc. Group Owner: Hearst-Argyle Television Inc. (acq 7-16-97; grpsl). Population Served: 663,200 Natl. Network: ABC, . Natl. Rep: Eagle Television Sales,. Washington Atty: Brooks, Pierce, McLendon. Wire Svc: NWS (National Weather Service) Wire Svc: AP News staff: 55; News: 30 hrs news progrg wkly.
Key Personnel:
Brent Hensley . . . pres & gen mgr
Christine Toldt . . . opns dir
Tom Comerford . . . gen sls mgr
Stephanie Croswait . . . news dir
David Evans . . . engrg dir & chief of engrg

KOKH-TV— Digital Channel: 24. Digital Hrs: 24 3,470 kw vis, 347 kw aur. ant 1,560t/1,586g TL: N35 32 58 W97 29 18 On air date: Jan 26, 1979. 1228 E. Wilshire Blvd., Oklahoma City, OK, 73111. Box 14925, Oklahoma City, OK 73111. Phone: (405) 843-2525. Fax: (405) 478-1027 (405) 475-9163(Sales). Web Site: www.okcfox.com. Licensee: Sullivan Broadcasting Co. IV Inc. Group Owner: Sinclair Broadcast Group Inc. (acq 1998; grpsl). Population Served: 796,000 Natl. Network: Fox, . Natl. Rep: Harrington, Righter & Parsons,.
Key Personnel:
John Rossi . . . gen mgr
Dan Loving . . . sls dir
Joe Spadea . . . news dir
Steve Bottkol . . . engrg dir

KOPX-TV— Digital Channel: 50. Digital Hrs: 24 200 kw vis. ant 1,584t/1,617g TL: N35 35 52 W97 29 22 On air date: February 1997. 13424 Railway Dr., Oklahoma City, OK, 73114. Phone: (405) 478-9562. Fax: (405) 751- 6867. Web Site: www.ionline.tv. Licensee: Paxson Oklahoma City License Inc. Group Owner: Paxson Communications Corp. (acq 9-27-96; $6.395 million). Natl. Network: ION Television, . Washington Atty: Dow, Lohnes and Albertson PLLC.
Key Personnel:
Brandon Burgess . . . pres
Carol Wright-Holzhaver . . . sr VP
Steve Brooks . . . gen mgr & stn mgr
David A. Glenn . . . engrg VP
Rod Roberts . . . chief of engrg
Les Moorman . . . traf mgr

KSBI— Digital Channel: 51. Digital Hrs: 24 1,000 kw vis. ant 1,502t/1,540g TL: N35 35 52 W97 29 22 On air date: Sept 19, 1988. 1350 S.E. 82nd St., Oklahoma City, OK, 73149. Phone: (405) 631-7335. Fax: (405) 631-7367.E-mail: info@ksbitv.com Web Site: www.ksbitv.com. Licensee: Family Broadcasting Group Inc. Ownership: Angela Brus, 38.4%; Brady M. Brus, 22.8%; Brenda Deimund, 22.8%; and Seekfirst Media Partners LLC, 16%. Population Served: 567,200 Washington Atty: Booth, Freret, Imlay & Tepper.
Key Personnel:
Brady Brus . . . CEO & pres gen mgr
Cody Blount . . . chief of engrg

KTBO-TV— Digital Channel: 15. Digital Hrs: 24 700 kw vis. ant 1,174t/1,151g TL: N35 34 35 W97 29 09 On air date: Mar 6, 1981. 1600 E. Heffner Rd., Oklahoma City, OK, 73131. Phone: (405) 848-1414.E-mail: comments@tbn.org Web Site: www.tbn.org. Licensee: Trinity Broadcasting of Oklahoma City Inc. Group Owner: Trinity Broadcasting Network. Population Served: 1,544,000 Washington Atty: Joseph E. Dunne III.
Key Personnel:
Paul Crouch . . . pres
Linda Cook . . . gen mgr
Jan Crouch . . . prom dir & pub affrs dir
Ken Howerton . . . chief of engrg

KTUZ-TV— Digital Channel: 29. Digital Hrs: 24 5,000 kw vis. ant 836t TL: N35 16 50 W97 20 14 On air date: 2000. 5101 S. Shields Blvd., Oklahoma City, OK, 73129. Phone: (405) 616-9900. Fax: (405) 616-5511. Web Site: http://telemundo.yahoo.com. Licensee: Oklahoma Land Company LLC. Group Owner: Tyler Media Broadcasting Corp. (acq 9-30-2004; $12,375,000). Natl. Network: Telemundo (Spanish), . Foreign lang progmg: SpanishS 168
Key Personnel:
Amando Rubio . . . gen mgr

KUOK— Analog Channel: 35.320 kw vis. ant 1,112t/1,059g TL: N36 16 06 W99 26 56 On air date: 2004. Equity Media Holdings Corp., 1 Shackleford Dr., Suite 400, Little Rock, AR, 72211. Phone: (501) 219-2400. Fax: (501) 716-3502. Licensee: Woodward Broadcasting Inc., debtor in possession. Group Owner: Equity Broadcasting Corp. Natl. Network: Univision (Spanish), . Foreign lang progmg: SpanishS 168
Key Personnel:
Larry Morton . . . pres
Gordon Hodges . . . gen mgr

***KWET—** Digital Channel: 8. Digital Hrs: 24 30 kw vis. ant 994t/958g TL: N35 35 36 W99 40 01 On air date: Aug 6, 1978. Box 14190, Oklahoma City, OK, 73113. 7403 N. Kelley Ave., Oklahoma City, OK 73111. Phone: (405) 848-8501. Phone: (580) 497-2594. Fax: (405) 841-9216. Web Site: www.oeta.tv. Licensee: Oklahoma Educational TV Authority. Population Served: 647,390 Natl. Network: PBS, . Washington Atty: Cohn & Marks. News staff: 20; News: 4 hrs wkly.
Key Personnel:
John McCarroll . . . gen mgr
Bill Thrash . . . stn mgr
Mike Palmer . . . opns mgr
Bob Sands . . . news dir
Earle Connors . . . engrg dir
Richard Ladd . . . chief of engrg

KWTV— Digital Channel: 9. Digital Hrs: 24 62.2 kw vis. ant 1,525t/1,530g TL: N35 32 58 W97 29 49 On air date: Dec 20, 1953. 7401 N. Kelley Ave., Oklahoma City, OK, 73113. Phone: (405) 843-6641. Fax: (405) 841-9926. Web Site: www.newsok.com. Licensee: Griffin OKC Licensing L.L.C. (acq 7-1-98). Population Served: 582,000 Natl. Network: CBS, . Natl. Rep: TeleRep,. Washington Atty: Holland & Knight. Wire Svc: CBS Wire Svc: NWS (National Weather Service) News staff: 80; News: 36 hrs wkly.
Key Personnel:
Rob Krier . . . VP & gen mgr
Wade Deaver . . . sls dir
Kim Eubank . . . progmg dir
Blaise Labbe . . . news dir
Julie Cameron . . . engrg dir & chief of engrg
Jeanetta Jackson . . . traf mgr

Tulsa, OK (DMA 61)

KDOR-TV— Digital Channel: 17. Digital Hrs: 24 3,980 kw vis, 398 kw aur. 1,040t/1,089g TL: N36 30 59 W95 46 10 On air date: Jan 11, 1987. 2120 N. Yellowood, Broken Arrow, OK, 74012. Phone: (918) 250-0777. Fax: (918) 461-8817.E-mail: kdor@tbn.org Web Site: www.tbn.org. Licensee: Trinity Broadcasting Network. Group Owner: (group owner; (acq 5-8-2000; grpsl).
Key Personnel:
Paul Crouch Sr. . . . CEO & pres
Craig Nelson . . . gen mgr & stn mgr

KGEB— Digital Channel: 49. Digital Hrs: 24 1,770 kw vis, 177 kw aur. 597t/672g TL: N36 02 39 W95 57 11 On air date: Jan 24, 1996. 7777 S. Lewis Ave., Tulsa, OK, 74171. Phone: (918) 488-5300. Fax: (918) 495-7388.E-mail: kgeb@oru.edu Web Site: www.kgeb.net. Licensee: University Broadcasting Inc.
Key Personnel:
Walter Richardson . . . gen mgr
Christi Vanover . . . progmg mgr & traf mgr
William P. Lee . . . chief of engrg
Amy Calvert . . . sls & mktg

KJRH— Digital Channel: 8. Digital Hrs: 24 100 kw vis, 10 kw aur. ant 1,828t TL: N36 01 15 W95 40 32 On air date: Dec 5, 1954. 3701 S. Peoria Ave., Tulsa, OK, 74105-3269. Phone: (918) 743-2222. Fax: (918) 748-1460.E-mail: news@kjrh.com Web Site: www.kjrh.com. Licensee: Scripps Howard Broadcasting Co. Group Owner: Scripps Howard Stations, see Cross-Ownership (acq 1-1-71; $7.8 million). Population Served: 1,143,000 Natl. Network: NBC, . Natl. Rep: Eagle Television Sales,. Washington Atty: Baker & Hostetler. News staff: 50; News: 26.5 hrs wkly.
Key Personnel:
Ken Lowe . . . CEO
Michael Vrabac . . . VP & gen mgr
Nick R. Clark . . . gen sls mgr
Peter Noll . . . prom mgr
Steve Weinstein . . . news dir
Samantha Knowlton . . . pub affrs dir
Dale Vennes . . . chief of engrg
Karen Framel . . . rsch dir
Lisa Langford . . . traf mgr
Al Jerkens . . . sports cmtr
Dan Threlkeld . . . weather dir

KMYT-TV— Digital Channel: 42. Digital Hrs: 24 1,350 kw vis, 270 kw aur. ant 1,510t/1,368g TL: N36 01 10 W95 39 24 On air date: May 17, 1981. 2625 S. Memorial Dr., Tulsa, OK, 74129-2600. Phone: (918) 388-5100. Fax: (918) 493-5739. Web Site: www.my41tulsa.com. Licensee: Newport Television License LLC. Group Owner: Clear Channel Communications Inc. (acq 3-14-2008; grpsl). Population Served: 511,000 Natl. Network: MyNetworkTV, . Natl. Rep: Millennium Sales & Marketing,. Washington Atty: Covington & Burling.
Key Personnel:
Sandy DiPasquale . . . pres
Jim Hanning . . . sls dir
Kari Barrett . . . natl sls mgr
Amber Musselman . . . mktg dir
Chooi Ning . . . progmg dir
Brian Egan . . . chief of engrg
Joan King . . . traf mgr

***KOED-TV—** Digital Channel: 11. Digital Hrs: 24 35 kw vis. ant 1,709t/1,640g TL: N36 01 15 W95 40 32 On air date: Jan 12, 1959. 811 N. Sheridan, Tulsa, OK, 74115. Phone: (918) 838-7611 (800) 580-7614. Fax: (918) 838-1807. Web Site: www.oeta.onenet.net. Licensee: Oklahoma Educational TV Authority. Population Served: 500,000 Natl. Network: PBS, . Washington Atty: Dow Lohnes PLLC. Foreign lang progmg: SpanishS 8
Key Personnel:
Bill Thrash . . . stn mgr
Liz Exon . . . news dir
Roger Newton . . . chief of engrg

***KOET—** Digital Channel: 31. Digital Hrs: 24 1,000 kw vis. ant 1,194t/541g TL: N35 11 01 W95 20 19 On air date: Aug 22, 1978. Box 14190, Oklahoma City, OK, 73113. Phone: (405) 848-8501. Phone: (918) 469-3430. Fax: (405) 841-9216. Web Site: www.oeta.onenet.net. Licensee: Oklahoma Educational Television Authority. Natl. Network: PBS, . Washington Atty: Dow Lohnes PLLC.
Key Personnel:
John McCarroll . . . gen mgr
Bill Thrash . . . stn mgr
Mike Palmer . . . opns dir & opns mgr
Bob Sands . . . news dir
Earle Connors . . . engrg dir
Richard Ladd . . . chief of engrg

KOKI-TV— Digital Channel: 22. Digital Hrs: 24 3,310 kw vis, 331 kw aur. ant 1,313t/1,274g TL: N36 01 36 W95 40 44 On air date: Oct 26, 1980. 2625 S. Memorial Dr., Tulsa, OK, 74129-2600. Phone: (918) 491-0023. Fax: (918) 491-6650. Web Site: www.fox23.com. Licensee: Newport Television License LLC. Group Owner: Clear Channel Communications Inc. (acq 3-14-2008; grpsl). Population Served: 450,000 Natl. Network: Fox, . Washington Atty: Covington & Burling. News staff: 38; News: 7 hrs wkly.

Key Personnel:

Sandy DiPasquale	pres
Craig Millar	VP
Holly Allen	gen mgr & sls dir
David Brace	natl sls mgr
Deedra Determan	mktg dir & mktg mgr prom mgr
Chooi Ning	progmg dir
Melanie Henry	news dir
Brian Egan	chief of engrg
Kristi Littledave	rsch dir
Joan King	traf mgr
Jon Slater	weather dir

KOTV— Digital Channel: 45. Digital Hrs: 24 100 kw vis, 50 kw aur. ant 1,885t/1,849g TL: N36 01 15 W95 40 32 On air date: Nov 30, 1949. Box 6, Tulsa, OK, 74101. 302 S. Frankfort, Tulsa, OK 74120. Phone: (918) 732-6000. Fax: (918) 732-6016. Web Site: www.kotv.com. Licensee: Griffin Licensing L.L.C. (acq 12-6-2000; $82 million). Population Served: 1,893,300 Natl. Network: CBS, . Natl. Rep: TeleRep,. Washington Atty: Dow, Lohnes & Albertson. News staff: 40.

Key Personnel:

Ted Strickland	CFO
Regina Moon	gen mgr
John Quesnel	opns dir
Ron Harig	news dir
Don Root	chief of engrg
Vickie Gilmartin	rsch dir
Donita Quesnel	pub svc dir
Travis Meyer	weather dir

KQCW— Digital Channel: 20. Digital Hrs: 24 5,000 kw vis. ant 823t/777g TL: N35 45 08 W95 48 15 On air date: Sept 12, 1999. 233 South Detroit Ave., Suite 100, Tulsa, OK, 74120. Phone: (918) 270-1919. Fax: (918) 732-6016. Web Site: www.wb19.com. Licensee: Griffin Licensing L.L.C. Group Owner: Cascade Broadcasting Group L.L.C. (acq 12-9-2005; $14.5 million). Natl. Network: CW.

Key Personnel:

Regina Moon	gen mgr
John Quesnel	opns mgr
Donita Quesnel	pub affrs dir
Don Root	chief of engrg

*KRSC-TV— Digital Channel: 36. Analog Hrs: NA Digital Hrs: 24 2,750 kw vis. 840t TL: N36 24 05 W95 36 33 On air date: July 1, 1987. RSU Public Television, 1701 W. Will Rogers Blvd., Claremore, OK, 74017-3252. Phone: (800) 823-7210. Fax: (918) 343-7952.E-mail: krsc-tv@rsu.edu Web Site: www.rsupublictv.org. Licensee: Board of Regents of Oklahoma Colleges. Washington Atty: Schwartz, Woods & Miller. Foreign lang progmg: SpanishS 2

Key Personnel:

Dan Schiedel	gen mgr
OPEN	progmg dir
Jim Mertins	chief of engrg

KTPX-TV— Digital Channel: 28. Digital Hrs: 24 1,000 kw vis, 100 kw aur. ant 718t/551g TL: N35 50 02 W96 07 28 On air date: July 1997. 5800 E. Skelly Dr., Suite 101, Tulsa, OK, 74135. Phone: (918) 664-1044 (817) 633-6843(Sales). Fax: (918) 664-4913. Web Site: www.ionline.tv. Licensee: ION Media Tulsa License Inc., debtor-in-possession. Group Owner: Paxson Communications Corp. (acq 8-21-98; $404,000 for 51% of stock). Population Served: 887,000 Natl. Network: ION Television, .

Key Personnel:

Matthew Pate	rgnl sls mgr
Peter A. De Les Dernier	stn mgr & pub affrs dir
Janeen Rode	traf mgr & pub svc dir

KTUL— Digital Channel: 10. Digital Hrs: 24 316 kw vis, 31.6 kw aur. 1,900t/1,809g TL: N35 58 08 W95 36 55 On air date: Sept 18, 1954. Box 8, Tulsa, OK, 74101-0008. 3333 S. 29th West Ave., Tulsa, OK 74107. Phone: (918) 445-8888. Fax: (918) 445-9316. Web Site: www.ktul.com. Licensee: KTUL L.L.C. Group Owner: Allbritton Communications Co. (acq 4-83; grpsl). Population Served: 355,500 Natl. Network: ABC, . Washington Atty: Hogan & Hartson. Wire Svc: AP News staff: 50; News: 17 hrs wkly.

Key Personnel:

Pat Baldwin	pres & gen mgr
Roger Herring	opns dir & chief of engrg
Carol Jones	natl sls mgr
Marcia Baker	rgnl sls mgr
Deborah Kurin	mktg dir & rsch dir
Larry Nitz	prom mgr & pub svc dir
Amy Miller	progmg dir
Sean McLaughlin	news dir
Randi Carson	pub affrs dir
David Shaffer	engrg mgr & chief of engrg
Teri Adcock	traf mgr
Cindy Morrison	consumer affrs dir
Chris Lincoln	sports cmtr
Frank Mitchell	weather dir

KWHB— Digital Channel: 47. Digital Hrs: 24 835 kw vis. ant 1,509t/1,424g TL: N36 01 15 W95 40 32 On air date: Apr 1, 1985.

8835 S. Memorial, Tulsa, OK, 74133. Phone: (918) 254-4701. Fax: (918) 254-5614. Web Site: www.lesea.com. Licensee: LeSea Broadcasting. Group Owner: (group owner; (acq 5-14-86; $3.4 million;4-14-86). Washington Atty: John Fiorini.

Key Personnel:

Peter Sumrall	CEO & VP
Royal Aills	gen mgr
Keith Krebbs	stn mgr

Oregon

Bend, OR
(DMA 192)

*KOAB-TV— Digital Channel: 11.90 kw vis. ant 804t/325g TL: N44 04 41 W121 19 57 On air date: Feb 24, 1970. 7140 S.W. Macadam Ave., Portland, OR, 97709. Phone: (503) 244-9900. Fax: (503) 293-1919. Web Site: www.opb.org. Licensee: Oregon Public Broadcasting. Ownership: Charles J. Swindells. (acq 9-20-93; grpsl;10-11-93). Natl. Network: PBS, . Washington Atty: Schwartz, Woods & Miller.

Key Personnel:

Steve Bass	CEO & pres
Dan Metziga	dev dir

KOHD— Digital Channel: 51.84.1 kw vis. ant 675t/200g TL: N44 04 40.6 W121 19 56.9 On air date: 2006. Box 7009, Eugene, OR, 97401. Phone: (541) 485-5611. Fax: (541) 342-1568.E-mail: genmgr@kohd.com Web Site: www.kohd.com. Licensee: Three Sisters Broadcasting LLC. Natl. Network: ABC, .

Key Personnel:

Jerry Upham	gen mgr

KTVZ— Digital Channel: 21. Digital Hrs: 24 250 kw vis. ant 646t/167g TL: N44 04 40 W121 19 49 On air date: Nov 6, 1977. Box 6038, Bend, OR, 97708. Phone: (541) 383-2121. Fax: (541) 382-1616.E-mail: ktvz@ktvz.com Web Site: www.ktvz.com. Licensee: NPG of Oregon Inc. Group Owner: News-Press & Gazette Co. (acq 4-17-2002; $18.9 million). Population Served: 131,600 Natl. Network: NBC, CW, Fox, Telemundo (Spanish), . Natl. Rep: Continental Television Sales,. News staff: 19; News: 20 hrs wkly.

Key Personnel:

Chris Gallu	gen mgr & opns mgr
Eric Bradley	stn mgr
Bob Singer	sls dir
Mike Bothwell	news dir
Amdaor Velasquez	chief of engrg

Eugene, OR
(DMA 119)

KCBY-TV— Digital Channel: 11. Digital Hrs: 8 AM-5 PM 11.5 kw vis, 1.1 kw aur. ant 680t/200g TL: N43 23 26 W124 07 47 On air date: Oct 1, 1960. 3451 Broadway, North Bend, OR, 97459. Phone: (541) 269-1111. Fax: (541) 269-7464.E-mail: webmaster@kcby.com Web Site: www.kcby.com. Licensee: Fisher Broadcasting - Oregon TV L.L.C. Group Owner: Fisher Broadcasting Company (acq 12-4-2001; grpsl). Natl. Network: CBS, . Washington Atty: Dow, Lohnes & Albertson. News staff: 4.

Key Personnel:

Dino Francois	prom dir & news dir
Paul Greene	progmg dir & chief of engrg

*KEPB-TV— Digital Channel: 29. Digital Hrs: 17 389 kw vis, 38.9 kw aur. ant 905t TL: N44 00 06 W123 06 48 On air date: Sept 27, 1990. 7140 S.W. Macadam Ave., Portland, OR, 97219. Phone: (503) 244-9900. Fax: (503) 293-1919.E-mail: info@opb.org Web Site: www.opb.org. Licensee: Oregon Public Broadcasting.. Ownership: Board of directors. (acq 9-20-93; grpsl;10-11-93). Natl. Network: PBS, .

Key Personnel:

Don McKay	engrg VP

KEZI— Digital Channel: 9. Digital Hrs: 24 316 kw vis, 47.4 kw aur. ant 1,768t/495g TL: N44 06 57 W122 59 57 On air date: Dec 19, 1960. Box 7009, Eugene, OR, 97401. 2975 Chad Dr., Eugene, OR 97408. Phone: (541) 485-5611. Fax: (541) 342-1568.E-mail: kezi@kezi.com Web Site: kezi.com. Licensee: KEZI Inc. Group Owner: Chambers Communications Corp. (acq 8-30-83; $18 million). Population Served: 279,240 Natl. Network: ABC, . News staff: 28; News: news program 22 hrs wkly.

Key Personnel:

Carolyn S. Chambers	CEO & chmn
Scott Chambers	pres
Mark J. Hatfield	gen mgr

KLSR-TV— Digital Channel: 31. Digital Hrs: 5:30 AM-2:30 AM 3,090 kw vis, 309 kw aur. ant 850t/200g TL: N44 00 04 W123 06 22 On air date: Oct 31, 1991. 2940 Chad Dr., Eugene, OR, 97408. Phone: (541) 683-2525. Phone: (541) 683-3434. Fax: (541) 683-8016. Web Site: klsrtv.com. Licensee: California Oregon Broadcasting Inc. Group Owner: (group owner; (acq 9-1-94; $2.65 million;9-19-94). Population Served: 505,000 Natl. Network: Fox, . Washington Atty: Fletcher, Heald & Hildreth.

Key Personnel:

Patricia Smullin	pres
Mark Metzger	gen mgr & gen sls mgr
Johnathon Johnson	opns dir
Scott Bonnell	natl sls mgr & rgnl sls mgr
Sandra Dornon-Belmont	progmg dir
Steve Woodward	pub affrs dir
Tim Hershiser	engrg dir & chief of engrg
Jeannie Crane	traf mgr

KMCB— Digital Channel: 22. Digital Hrs: 24 12.3 kw vis. ant 623t TL: N43 23 39 W124 07 56 On air date: July 8, 1991. 3825 International Ct., Springfield, OR, 97477. Phone: (541) 746-1600. Fax: (541) 747-0866. Web Site: www.kmtr.com. Licensee: Newport Television License LLC. Group Owner: Clear Channel Communications Inc. (acq 3-14-2008; grpsl). Natl. Network: NBC, . Natl. Rep: Millennium Sales & Marketing,. Rgnl. Rep: Rgnl rep: Blair. Washington Atty: Covington & Burling. Wire Svc: AP News: 22 hrs wkly.

Key Personnel:

Cambra Ward	VP
Cambra Ward	gen mgr
Kurt Thelen	opns mgr
Satellite of KMTR(TV) Eugene.	

KMTR— Digital Channel: 17. Digital Hrs: 24 1,919 kw vis, 370.99 kw aur. ant 1,685t/478g TL: N44 06 58 W122 59 55 On air date: Oct 4, 1982. 3825 International Ct., Springfield, OR, 97477. Phone: (541) 746-1600. Fax: (503) 747-0866. Web Site: www.kmtr.com. Licensee: Newport Television License LLC. Group Owner: Clear Channel Communications Inc. (acq 3-14-2008; grpsl). Population Served: 518,000 Natl. Network: NBC, . Natl. Rep: Millennium Sales & Marketing,. Rgnl. Rep: Rgnl rep: Blair. Washington Atty: Covington & Burling. Wire Svc: AP News staff: 22; News: 15 hrs wkly.

Key Personnel:

Kurt Thelen	opns mgr

*KOAC-TV— Digital Channel: 7. Digital Hrs: 20 245 kw vis. ant 1,500t/279g TL: N44 38 25 W123 16 25 On air date: Oct 7, 1957. 7140 S.W. Macadam Ave., Portland, OR, 97219. Phone: (503) 244-9900. Fax: (503) 293-1919. Web Site: www.opb.org. Licensee: Oregon Public Broadcasting. Ownership: Board of directors. (acq 1993; grpsl;9-20-93). Population Served: 1,000,000 Natl. Network: PBS, . Washington Atty: Schwartz, Woods & Miller. Wire Svc: UPI

Key Personnel:

Steve Boss	CEO & pres
Tom Doggett	progmg VP & progmg dir
Morgan Holm	news dir & pub affrs dir
Don McKay	engrg VP & chief of engrg

KPIC— Digital Channel: 19. Digital Hrs: 24 5.37 kw vis, 550 w aur. ant 1,000t/173g TL: N43 14 20 W123 18 42 On air date: Apr 1, 1956. Box 1345, 655 W. Umpqua, Roseburg, OR, 97471. Phone: (541) 672-4481. Fax: (541) 672-4482.E-mail: sales@kpic.com Web Site: www.kpic.com. Licensee: South West Oregon TV Broadcasting Corp. Group Owner: Fisher Broadcasting Company (acq 1999; grpsl). Population Served: 90,000 Natl. Network: CBS, . Washington Atty: Dow, Lohnes & Albertson. News staff: 4; News: 14 hrs wkly.

Key Personnel:

Connie Williamson	stn mgr
Dino Francois	prom mgr
Paul Greene	progmg dir
Mike Hill	chief of engrg
Satellite of KVAL-TV Eugene.	

KTCW— Digital Channel: 45. Digital Hrs: 24 13.63 kw vis. ant 728t TL: N43 14 08 W123 19 17 On air date: Apr 8, 1992. 3825 International Ct., Springfield, OR, 97477-1090. Phone: (541) 746-1600. Fax: (541) 747-0866. Web Site: www.kmtr.com. Licensee: Newport Television License LLC. Group Owner: Clear Channel Communications Inc. (acq 3-14-2008; grpsl). Natl. Network: NBC, . Washington Atty: Covington & Burling. Wire Svc: AP News: 22 hrs wkly.

Key Personnel:

Cambra Ward	VP & gen mgr stn mgr & progmg dir
Kurt Thelen	opns mgr & chief of engrg
Mike Chisholm	gen sls mgr
Robert McMichaels	news dir
Satellite of KMTR Eugene.	

KTVC— Digital Channel: 18. Digital Hrs: 24 42.7 kw vis. ant 692t TL: N43 14 09 W123 19 16 On air date: 1988. Equity Media Holdings

Corporation, 1 Shackleford Dr., Suite 400, Little Rock, AR, 72211. Phone: (501) 219-2400. Fax: (501) 221-1101. Licensee: Roseburg Broadcasting Inc., debtor in possession. Group Owner: Equity Broadcasting Corp. (acq 11-30-2001; $800,000). Washington Atty: Irwin, Campbell & Tannenwald.
Key Personnel:
Greg Fess . . . . CEO & gen mgr
Pat Doran. . . . . CFO
James Hearnsberger . . . . VP

KVAL-TV— Digital Channel: 13. Digital Hrs: 24 316 kw vis, 63.1 kw aur. ant 1,480t/851g TL: N44 00 07 W123 06 53 On air date: Apr 16, 1954. Box 1313, Eugene, OR, 97440-1313. 4575 Blanton Rd., Eugene, OR 97405. Phone: (541) 342-4961. Fax: (541) 342-7252 (sales). Fax: (541) 342-2635 (admin).E-mail: kval@kval.com Web Site: www.kval.com. Licensee: Fisher Broadcasting - Oregon TV L.L.C. Group Owner: Fisher Broadcasting Company (acq 12-4-01; grpsl). Population Served: 920,000 Natl. Network: CBS, . Rgnl. Rep: Rgnl rep: Petry Washington Atty: Pillsbury, Winthrop & Pittman. News: 17 hrs wkly.
Key Personnel:
Colleen Brown . . . . CEO
Coleen Brown . . . . pres
Greg Raschio . . . . VP & gen mgr stn mgr
Paul Greene. opns mgr

Klamath Falls

see Medford-Klamath Falls, OR market

Medford-Klamath Falls, OR (DMA 140)

***KBDM—** Analog Channel: 20.100 kw vis. ant 3,231t/46g TL: N42 04 55 W122 43 07 Not on air, target date: unknown: 301 Olive Ave., Suite 104, West Palm Beach, FL, 33401. Phone: (561) 355-4573. Permittee: Northern California Public TV.
Key Personnel:
Lester Williams. . . . . gen mgr & stn mgr

KBLN— Digital Channel: 30. Digital Hrs: 24 9.77 kw vis. ant 2,145t/121g TL: N42 22 56 W123 16 29 On air date: 2002. Better Life Television, Box 766, Grants Pass, OR, 97528. Phone: (541) 474-3089. Fax: (541) 474-9409.E-mail: kbln@betterlifetv.tv Web Site: www.betterlifetv.tv. Licensee: Better Life Television Inc. (acq 2-20-01).
Key Personnel:
Marta Davis . . . . gen mgr & stn mgr
Ron Davis . . . . stn mgr

KDKF— Digital Channel: 29. Digital Hrs: 5:30 AM-2 AM 6.03 kw vis, 603 w aur. 2,267t/164g TL: N42 05 50 W121 37 59 On air date: Oct 17, 1989. 231 E. Main St., Klamath Falls, OR, 97601. Phone: (541) 883-3131. Fax: (541) 883-8931. Web Site: www.kdrv.com. Licensee: Soda Mountain Broadcasting Inc. Group Owner: Chambers Communications Corp. (acq 12-5-2001). Population Served: 42,000 Natl. Network: ABC, . Washington Atty: Fletcher, Heald & Hildreth. News staff: 20; News: 12 hrs wkly.
Key Personnel:
Maiwi Renard. gen mgr
Satellite of KDRV(TV) Medford, OR.

KDRV— Digital Channel: 12. Digital Hrs: 24 191 kw vis, 38.1 kw aur. 2,701t/168g TL: N42 41 32 W123 13 46 On air date: Feb 26, 1984. 1090 Knutson Ave., Medford, OR, 97504. Phone: (541) 773-1212. Fax: (541) 779-9261. Web Site: www.kdrv.com. Licensee: Soda Mountain Broadcasting Inc. Group Owner: Chambers Communications Corp. (acq 12-5-2001). Natl. Network: ABC, . Natl. Rep: Millennium Sales & Marketing,. Washington Atty: Fisher, Wayland, Cooper, Leader & Zaragoza. Wire Svc: AP News staff: 12; News: 20 hrs wkly.
Key Personnel:
Renard N. Maiuri . . . . gen mgr
Rick Carrrara. . . . . chief of engrg

***KFTS—** Digital Channel: 33. Digital Hrs: 24 9.23 kw vis, 923 w aur. 2,152t/103g TL: N42 05 50 W121 37 59 On air date: March 1977. 28 South Fir St. Suite 200, Medford, OR, 97501. Phone: (541) 779-0808. Fax: (541) 779-2178. Web Site: www.soptv.org. Licensee: Southern Oregon Public Television Inc. Population Served: 30,000 Natl. Network: PBS, .
Key Personnel:
Mark Stanislawski. . . . . CEO & pres gen mgr
Tom Werner . . . . chief of engrg
Satellite of KSYS(TV) Medford 100%.

KMVU-DT— Digital Channel: 26. Digital Hrs: 24 110 kw vis. ant 1,444t/113g TL: N42 17 54 W122 44 53 On air date: Aug 8, 1994. 820 Crater Lake Ave., Suite 105, Medford, OR, 97504. Phone: (541) 772-2600. Fax: (541) 772-7364.E-mail: reception@kmvu-tv.com Web Site: www.fox26medford.com. Licensee: Broadcasting Licenses L.P. Group Owner: Northwest Broadcasting Inc. Population Served: 390,000 Natl. Network: Fox, . Natl. Rep: Continental Television Sales,. Washington Atty: Leventhal, Senter & Lerman.
Key Personnel:
Brian Brady . . . . pres
Cary Jones . . . . gen mgr & stn mgr
Michael Garry . . . . engr

KOBI— Digital Channel: 5. Digital Hrs: 24 60.3 kw vis, 8.13 kw aur. 2,700t/155g TL: N42 41 49 W123 13 39 On air date: Aug 1, 1953. Box 1489, Medford, OR, 97501. 125 S.Fir, Medford, OR 97501. Phone: (541) 779-5555. Fax: (541) 779-5564.E-mail: kobi@kobi5.com Web Site: www.localnewscomesfirst.com. Licensee: California Oregon Broadcasting Inc. Group Owner: (group owner). Population Served: 475,000 Natl. Network: NBC, . Natl. Rep: Blair Television,. Washington Atty: Wiley, Rein & Fielding.
Key Personnel:
Patricia C. Smullin . . . . pres
Dan Acklen. news dir

KOTI— Digital Channel: 13. Digital Hrs: 24 9 kw vis. ant 2,162t/115g TL: N42 05 48 W121 37 57 On air date: Apr 5, 1956. Box 2K, 222 S. 7th, Klamath Falls, OR, 97601. Phone: (541) 882-2222. Phone: (541) 779-5555. Fax: (541) 883-7664.E-mail: news@koti2.com Web Site: www.localnewscomesfirst.com. Licensee: California Oregon Broadcasting Inc. Group Owner: (group owner). Population Served: 102,000 Natl. Network: NBC, . Washington Atty: Wiley Rein LLP. News staff: 2.
Key Personnel:
Patricia Smallin. pres
Bob Wise . . . . gen mgr
Dennis Siewert. . . . . gen sls mgr & natl sls mgr
Donna Rodriquez . . . . progmg dir
Dan Acklen. news dir
Scott McMahon . . . . chief of engrg
Donna Rodriguez . . . . traf mgr
Rebroadcasts KOBI Medford 90%.

***KSYS—** Digital Channel: 8. Digital Hrs: 24 30 kw vis, 3 kw aur. 2,683t TL: N42 41 31 W123 13 46 On air date: Jan 17, 1977. 34 S. Fir St., Medford, OR, 97501. Phone: (541) 779-0808. Fax: (541) 779-2178. Web Site: www.soptv.org. Licensee: Southern Oregon Public Television Inc. Population Served: 137,140 Natl. Network: PBS, . Rgnl. Network: Pacific.
Key Personnel:
Mark Stanislawski. . . . . CEO & pres gen mgr
Tom Werner . . . . chief of engrg

KTVL— Digital Channel: 10. Digital Hrs: 24 132 kw vis, 26.3 aur. 3,310t/151g TL: N42 04 55 W122 43 07 On air date: Oct 3, 1961. Box 10, Medford, OR, 97501. 1440 Rossanley Dr., Medford, OR 97501. Phone: (541) 773-7373. Fax: (541) 779-0451.E-mail: ktvl@ktvl.com Web Site: www.ktvl.com. Licensee: Freedom Broadcasting of Oregon Licensee L.L.C. Group Owner: Freedom Broadcasting Inc. (acq 8-28-81; $12.5 million). Population Served: 402,000 Natl. Network: CBS, CW, . Natl. Rep: TeleRep,. Washington Atty: Latham & Watkins. News: 16 hrs wkly.
Key Personnel:
Kingsley Kelley. . . . . VP & gen mgr
Dan Casey . . . . gen sls mgr
Lila Hampton . . . . natl sls mgr & traf mgr
Mike Gantenbein . . . . prom mgr
Sheila Giorgetti . . . . progmg dir
Manny Fantis. news dir
Carl Randall . . . . chief of engrg

Pendleton

see Yakima-Pasco-Richland-Kennewick, WA market

Portland, OR (DMA 22)

KATU— Digital Channel: 43. Digital Hrs: 24 100 kw vis, 20 kw aur. ant 1,560t/918g TL: N45 31 14 W122 44 37 On air date: Mar 15, 1962. 2153 N.E. Sandy Blvd., Portland, OR, 97232. Box 2, Portland, OR 97207. Phone: (503) 231-4222. Fax: (503) 231-4233.E-mail: custserv@katu.com Web Site: www.katu.com. Licensee: Fisher Broadcasting - Portland TV L.L.C. Group Owner: Fisher Broadcasting Company (acq 12-4-01; grpsl). Population Served: 784,400 Natl. Network: ABC, . Natl. Rep: TeleRep,. Washington Atty: Fisher, Wayland, Cooper, Leader & Zaragoza. News: varies hrs wkly.
Key Personnel:
John Tamerlano . . . . gen mgr
Jo Anne James . . . . stn mgr & gen sls mgr
Steve Linde . . . . natl sls mgr
Steve Denari. . . . . prom dir & pub affrs dir
Dan Pratt . . . . news dir
Alan Batdorf . . . . chief of engrg
Ellen Johanson . . . . rsch dir
Trish McCarthy . . . . traf mgr
Steve Arena . . . . sports cmtr

KGW— Digital Channel: 8. Digital Hrs: 24 316 kw vis, 60.3 kw aur. ant 1,768t/924g TL: N45 31 21 W122 44 46 On air date: Dec 15, 1956. 1501 S.W. Jefferson St., Portland, OR, 97201. Phone: (503) 226-5000. Fax: (503) 226-4448. Web Site: www.kgw.com. Licensee: KGW-TV Inc. Group Owner: Belo Corp., Broadcast Division (acq 1997; grpsl). Population Served: 1,086,100 Natl. Network: NBC, . Natl. Rep: Blair Television,. Washington Atty: Wiley, Rein & Fielding. Wire Svc: UPI News: 35 hrs wkly.
Key Personnel:
Paul Fry . . . . pres
DJ Wilson. . . . . gen mgr & stn mgr
Brenda Buratti . . . . progmg dir
Rod Gramer . . . . news dir

***KNMT—** Digital Channel: 45. Digital Hrs: 24 1,000 kw vis. ant 1,492t/731g TL: N45 30 58 W122 43 59 On air date: Nov 17, 1989. 432 N.E. 74th Ave., Portland, OR, 97213. Phone: (503) 252-0792. Fax: (503) 256-4205. Web Site: www.nmtv.org . Licensee: National Minority TV Inc.. Ownership: Paul F. Crouch; Jane Duff; Jan Crouch.
Key Personnel:
Jane P. Duff . . . . pres
Dr. Paul F. Crouch. VP
Adolfo Carbajal . . . . stn mgr & progmg mgr
Bonnie Gaulding . . . . pub affrs dir
Steven Hendrix . . . . chief of engrg

KOIN— Digital Channel: 40.100 kw vis, 15.1 kw aur. ant 1,760t/989g TL: N45 30 58 W122 43 59 On air date: Oct 15, 1953. 222 S.W. Columbia St., Portland, OR, 97201. Phone: (503) 464-0600. Fax: (503) 464-0655.E-mail: koin@koin.com Web Site: www.koin.com. Licensee: NVT Portland Licensee LLC. Group Owner: Emmis Communications Corp. (acq 11-1-2007; grpsl). Population Served: 2,700,000 Natl. Network: CBS, . News: 27 hrs wkly.
Key Personnel:
Tim . Perry. . . . . gen mgr
Rodger O'Connor . . . . mktg dir
Nicole Meyers . . . . progmg dir & rsch dir
Lynn Heider . . . . news dir
David Bird . . . . engrg dir
Carl Gonzales. traf mgr

***KOPB-TV—** Digital Channel: 10. Digital Hrs: 24 316 kw vis, 31.6 kw aur. ant 1,740t/1,081g TL: N45 31 22 W122 45 07 On air date: Feb 6, 1961. 7140 S.W. Macadam Ave., Portland, OR, 97219-3099. Phone: (503) 244-9900. Fax: (503) 293-1919. Web Site: www.opb.org. Licensee: Oregon Public Broadcasting. Ownership: Board of directors. (acq 9-20-93; grpsl;10-11-93). Population Served: 2,000,000 Natl. Network: PBS, . Washington Atty: Schwartz, Woods & Miller.
Key Personnel:
Steve Bass . . . . CEO & pres
Dan Metziga. . . . . dev dir

KPDX—(Vancouver, WA) Digital Channel: 30. Digital Hrs: 24 3,200 kw vis, 319 kw aur. ant 1,785t/1,081g TL: N45 31 22 W122 45 07 On air date: October 1983. 14975 N.W. Greenbrier Pkwy., Beaverton, OR, 97006-5731. Phone: (503) 906-1249. Fax: (503) 548-6910.E-mail: webstaff@kptv.com Web Site: www.kpdx.com. Licensee: Meredith Corp. Group Owner: Meredith Broadcasting Group, Meredith Corp. (acq 7-1-97; grpsl). Natl. Network: MyNetworkTV, . Natl. Rep: TeleRep,. Washington Atty: Dow, Lohnes & Albertson. Wire Svc: AP
Key Personnel:
Patrick McCreery . . . . gen mgr
Andy Delaporte. . . . . gen sls mgr
Lee Petrik . . . . progmg dir

KPTV— Digital Channel: 12. Digital Hrs: 24 316 kw vis, 31.6 kw aur. ant 1,780t/1,049g TL: N45 31 19 W122 44 53 On air date: Sept 20, 1952. 14975 N.W. Greenbrier Pkwy., Beaverton, OR, 97006. Phone: (503) 906-1249. Fax: (503) 548-6910.E-mail: webstaff@kptv.com Web Site: kptv.com. Licensee: Meredith Corp. Group Owner: Meredith Broadcasting Group, Meredith Corp. (acq 6-17-2002; swap). Population Served: 2,901,900 Natl. Network: Fox, . Natl. Rep: TeleRep,. Washington Atty: Dow, Lohnes & Albertson. Wire Svc: AP News: 42.5 hrs wkly.
Key Personnel:
Patrick McCreery . . . . gen mgr
Andy Delaporte. . . . . gen sls mgr
Matt Hyatt . . . . prom mgr
Lee Petrik . . . . progmg dir & progmg mgr

KPXG-TV— Digital Channel: 22. Digital Hrs: 24 1,702 kw vis, 170 kw aur. ant 1,187t/945g TL: N45 00 00 W122 41 37 On air date: Nov 21,

1981. 811 SW Naito Pkwy, Suite 100, Portland, OR, 97204. Phone: (503) 222-2221. Fax: (503) 222-4613. Web Site: www.ionline.tv. Licensee: ION Media Portland License Inc., debtor-in-possession. Group Owner: Paxson Communications Corp. (acq 5-14-98; $30 million).
Key Personnel:
Linda Massana . . . opns mgr
Tim mance . . . chief of engrg

KRCW-TV— Digital Channel: 33. Digital Hrs: 24 5,000 kw vis, 500 kw aur. ant 4,707t TL: N45 00 35 W122 20 17 On air date: May 1989. 10255 S.W. Arctic Dr., Beaverton, OR, 97005. Phone: (503) 644-3232. Fax: (971) 223-0457.E-mail: questions@wb32tv.com Web Site: portlandscw.trb.com. Licensee: Tribune Broadcast Holdings Inc. Group Owner: Tribune Broadcasting Co. (acq 12-20-2007; grpsl). Population Served: 2.826 m,ill,ion Natl. Network: CW, . Natl. Rep: TeleRep,. Washington Atty: Dow Lohnes PLLC. News: 3.5 hrs wkly.
Key Personnel:
Pam Pearson. . . . gen mgr & gen sls mgr
Jeremy Berk. . . . gen sls mgr
Pat Shearer . . . chief of engrg

***KTVR—** Digital Channel: 13. Digital Hrs: 17 65 kw vis. ant 2,542t/161g TL: N45 18 33 W117 43 54 On air date: Dec 6, 1964. 7140 S.W. Macadam Ave., Portland, OR, 97219-3099. Phone: (503) 244-9900. Fax: (503) 293-1919. Web Site: www.opb.org. Licensee: Oregon Public Broadcasting. Ownership: Board of directors. (acq 1993; grpsl; 9-20-93). Natl. Network: PBS, . Washington Atty: Schwartz, Woods & Miller.
Key Personnel:
Steve Bass . . . CEO & pres
Tom Doggett . . . progmg dir
Morgan Holm . . . news dir & pub affrs dir
Don McKay . . . chief of engrg

KUNP— Digital Channel: 16.60.3 kw vis. ant 2,535t/56g TL: N45 18 35 W117 43 57 On air date: 2004. 2153 N.E. Sandy Blvd., Portland, OR, 97232. Phone: (503) 231-4222. Fax: (503) 231-4233. Web Site: www.kunptv.com. Licensee: Fisher Radio Regional Group. Group Owner: Equity Broadcasting Corp. (acq 11-1-2006; $19.3 million with KUNP-LP Portland). Natl. Network: Univision (Spanish), . Foreign lang progmg: SpanishS 168
Key Personnel:
John Tamerlano . . . gen mgr
Davis Smith . . . gen sls mgr

Pennsylvania

Altoona

see Johnstown-Altoona, PA market

Erie, PA
(DMA 146)

WFXP— Digital Channel: 22. Digital Hrs: 24 850 kw vis, 85 kw aur. ant 938t/717g TL: N42 02 25 W80 04 09 On air date: Sept 2, 1986. 8455 Peach St., Erie, PA, 16509. Phone: (814) 864-2400. Fax: (814) 864-5393.E-mail: webmaster@fox66.tv Web Site: www.yourerie.com. Licensee: Mission Broadcasting of Wichita Falls Inc. Group Owner: Mission Broadcasting Inc. (acq 10-22-98). Population Served: 412,700 Natl. Network: Fox, . Washington Atty: Arter & Hadden. News: 3.5 hrs wkly.
Key Personnel:
Beverly Joyce . . . stn mgr
Tim Dunst . . . sls dir

WICU-TV— Digital Channel: 12. Digital Hrs: 24 5.4 kw vis. ant 1,006t/757g TL: N42 03 50 W80 00 21 On air date: Mar 15, 1949. 3514 State St., Erie, PA, 16508. Phone: (814) 454-5201. Fax: (814) 455-0703.E-mail: info@wicu12.com Web Site: www.wicu12.com. Licensee: SJL of Pennsylvania License Subsidiary LLC. (acq 8-96; $11 million). Population Served: 129,231 Natl. Network: NBC, . Washington Atty: Latham & Watkins. News staff: 20; News: 22 hrs wkly.
Key Personnel:
Brian Lilly . . . pres & gen mgr
Matt Filippi. . . . sls dir & gen sls mgr
Paula Randolph . . . progmg dir
Phil Hayes . . . news dir
John Wilkosz. . . . engrg dir & chief of engrg

WJET-TV— Digital Channel: 24. Digital Hrs: 24 523 kw vis. ant 997t/777g TL: N42 02 25 W80 04 09 On air date: Apr 2, 1966. 8455 Peach St., Erie, PA, 16509. Phone: (814) 864-2400. Fax: (814) 868-3041.E-mail: lbaxter@wjettv.com Web Site: www.yourerie.com. Licensee: Nexstar Finance Inc. Group Owner: Nexstar Broadcasting Group Inc. (acq 12-16-97; $18.5 million). Population Served: 412,000 Natl. Network: ABC, . Washington Atty: Drinker, Riddle & Reath. News: 3.5 hrs wkly.
Key Personnel:
Bob Bach . . . rgnl sls mgr
Barbara Behr . . . progmg mgr
Lou Baxter. . . . news dir
Mary Scheuer . . . pub affrs dir
Lorne Earle . . . chief of engrg

***WQLN—** Digital Channel: 50. Digital Hrs: 24 1,000 kw vis, 100 kw aur. ant 879t/679g TL: N42 02 31 W80 03 57 On air date: Aug 13, 1967. 8425 Peach St., Erie, PA, 16509. Phone: (814) 864-3001. Fax: (814) 864-4077.E-mail: wqln@wqln.org Web Site: www.wqln.org. Licensee: Public Broadcasting of Northwest Pa. Inc. Population Served: 151,000 Natl. Network: PBS, . Rgnl. Network: Pa. Pub Net. Pennsylvania Public Television Network Washington Atty: Dow, Lohnes & Albertson.
Key Personnel:
Dwight Miller . . . pres & gen mgr
Tracey B. Ferrier. . . . VP
Ed Upton . . . engrg dir

WSEE-TV— Digital Channel: 16. Digital Hrs: 24 1,170 kw vis, 117 kw aur. ant 941t/741g TL: N42 02 20 W80 03 45 On air date: Apr 24, 1954. 1220 Peach St., Erie, PA, 16501. Phone: (814) 455-7575. Fax: (814) 454-5541.E-mail: wsee@wsee.tv Web Site: www.wsee.tv. Licensee: Lilly Broadcasting of Pennslvania License Subsidiary LLC. Ownership: Kevin T. Lilly, 100% (acq 11-28-2002;. $10 million). Population Served: 500,000 Natl. Network: CBS, CW, . Washington Atty: Lathan & Watkins. News staff: 25; News: 14 hrs wkly.
Key Personnel:
Kevin T. Lilly. . . . pres
John Christenson . . . gen mgr
Tracy Stufft . . . stn mgr & progmg dir
Scott Bremner . . . news dir
Dan Nungesser. . . . chief of engrg

Harrisburg-Lancaster-Lebanon-York, PA
(DMA 41)

WGAL— Digital Channel: 8.112 kw vis, 21.4 kw aur. ant 1,361t/824g TL: N40 02 04 W76 37 08 On air date: Mar 18, 1949. Box 7127, Lancaster, PA, 17604. 1300 Columbia Ave., Lancaster, PA 17603. Phone: (717) 393-5851. Fax: (717) 393-9484. Web Site: www.wgal.com. Licensee: WGAL Hearst-Argyle Television Inc. Group Owner: Hearst-Argyle Television Inc. (acq 1999; grpsl). Population Served: 1,620,000 Natl. Network: NBC, . Natl. Rep: Eagle Television Sales,. Washington Atty: Brooks, Pierce. News staff: 53; News: 29 hrs wkly.
Key Personnel:
Paul Quinn. . . . pres & gen mgr
Bob Good. . . . opns mgr
Nancy Tulli . . . gen sls mgr
Andy Scheid. . . . natl sls mgr
John Baldwin . . mktg mgr & prom mgr pub affrs dir & pub svc dir
Heather Bruce . . . progmg dir & progmg mgr
Dan O'Donnell . . . news dir
Robert Good. . . . chief of engrg
Cindy Stone. . . . rsch dir
Kim Groff. . . . traf mgr
Brian Roche . . . consumer affrs dir
Pat Pringpe . . . sports cmtr

WGCB-TV— Digital Channel: 30. Digital Hrs: 24 500 kw vis. ant 571t/299g TL: N39 54 18 W76 35 00 On air date: Apr 28, 1979. Box 88, Red Lion, PA, 17356-0088. Phone: (717) 246-1681. Fax: (717) 244-9316.E-mail: businessoffice@wgcbtv.com Web Site: www.wgcbtv.com. Licensee: Red Lion Broadcasting Co. Ownership: Estate of John H. Norris, Anna L. Plourde-Norris, executrix, 60%; Anna L. Plourde-Norris, 40% Population Served: 600,000 Washington Atty: Booth, Freret, Imlay and Tepper.
Key Personnel:
John H. Norris. . . . CEO
John Peeling . . . gen mgr & stn mgr progmg dir
Anna L. Plourde-Norris . . . dev VP
Gordon Moul. . . . natl sls mgr
Jerry Jacobs . . . mktg dir
Donald Horst. . . . chief of engrg

WHP-TV— Digital Channel: 21. Digital Hrs: 24 450 kw vis. ant 1,210t/462g TL: N40 20 43 W76 52 09 On air date: Apr 15, 1953. 3300 N. Sixth St., Harrisburg, PA, 17110. Phone: (717) 238-2100. Fax: (717) 238-8744. Fax: (717) 236-0198. Web Site: www.whptv.com. Licensee: Newport Television License LLC. Group Owner: Clear Channel Communications Inc. (acq 3-14-2008; grpsl). Population Served: 713,070 Natl. Network: CBS, . News staff: 23; News: 24 hrs wkly.
Key Personnel:
Lou Castriota Sr.. . . . opns dir & progmg dir
Stu Brenner . . . natl sls mgr
Sherry Taylor . . . prom dir
Greg Zoerb . . . news dir
Rob Hershey. . . . engrg dir
Danielle Deritis . . . traf mgr

WHTM-TV— Digital Channel: 10. Digital Hrs: 24 2,400 kw vis, 240 kw aur. ant 1,119t/608g TL: N40 18 57 W76 57 02 On air date: June 19, 1953. Box 5860, 3235 Hoffman St., Harrisburg, PA, 17110-5860. Phone: (717) 236-2727. Fax: (717) 232-5272. Web Site: www.abc27.com. Licensee: Harrisburg Television Inc. Group Owner: Allbritton Communication Co. (acq 1996; $113 million). Population Served: 535,310 Natl. Network: ABC, . News staff: 46; News: 27 hrs wkly.
Key Personnel:
Joe Lewin . . . pres & gen mgr
Rob Saylor . . . gen sls mgr
Paul Roda. . . . natl sls mgr
Betty Bryan Fish . . . prom dir
Trishia Falk. . . . progmg dir
Dennis Fisher. . . . news dir
Jan Strock. . . . chief of engrg

***WITF-TV—** Digital Channel: 36. Digital Hrs: 24 1,100 kw vis, 110 kw aur. ant 1,396t/724g TL: N40 20 45 W76 52 06 On air date: Nov 22, 1964. Box 2954, Harrisburg, PA, 17105. 4801 Lindle Rd., Harrisburg, PA 17111. Phone: (717) 704-3000. Fax: (717) 704-3659.E-mail: info@witf.org Web Site: www.witf.org. Licensee: WITF Inc. Population Served: 550,000 Natl. Network: PBS, . Rgnl. Network: Eastern Educ. Washington Atty: Dow, Lohnes & Albertson.
Key Personnel:
Kathleen A. Pavelko . . . CEO & pres
Gregory Poland . . . CFO
Michael Greenwald . . . dev VP
Charles Lichty . . . sls VP
Craig Cohen . . . progmg dir
Ron Kain . . . engrg dir

WLYH-TV— Digital Channel: 23. Digital Hrs: 24 1,050 kw vis, 210 kw aur. ant 1,361t/1,059g TL: N40 15 45 W76 27 53 On air date: Oct 15, 1953. 3300 N. Sixth St., Harrisburg, PA, 17011. Phone: (717) 238-2100. Fax: (717) 238-8744. Web Site: www.cw15.com. Licensee: Nexstar Broadcasting Inc. Group Owner: Television Station Group LLC (acq 12-29-2006; $56 million with WTAJ-TV Altoona). Population Served: 713,000 Natl. Network: CW, .
Key Personnel:
Perry Sook . . . pres
Lou Castriota Sr.. . . . opns dir & progmg dir
Scott Beaver . . . sls dir
Stuart Brenner . . . natl sls mgr
Sherry Taylor . . . prom dir
Greg Zoerb . . . news dir
Rob Hershey. . . . chief of engrg

WPMT— Digital Channel: 47. Digital Hrs: 24 2,140 kw vis, 214 kw aur. ant 1,361t/948g TL: N40 01 38 W76 36 00 On air date: Dec 22, 1952. 2005 S. Queen St., York, PA, 17403. Phone: (717) 843-0043. Fax: (717) 843-9741.E-mail: fox43@mail.fox43.com Web Site: www.fox43.com. Licensee: Tribune Television Co. Group Owner: Tribune Broadcasting Co. (acq 12-20-2007; grpsl). Natl. Network: Fox, . Natl. Rep: TeleRep,. News staff: 45; News: 17 hrs wkly.
Key Personnel:
Larry Delia. . . . gen mgr
Keith McFarland. . . . opns dir
Matthew Uhl. . . . gen sls mgr
Dave Farish. . . . prom mgr
Sandy Hawk. . . . progmg dir & progmg mgr pub affrs dir
Jim DePury . . . news dir
Jim Myers . . . engrg dir
Melissa Slatky. . . . rsch dir
Cindy Jansky . . . traf mgr
Evan Forrester . . . news cmtr
Todd Sadowski . . . sports cmtr
Jim Buchanan . . . weather dir

Johnstown-Altoona, PA
(DMA 101)

WATM-TV— Digital Channel: 24. Digital Hrs: 20 182 kw vis, 18.2 kw aur. ant 1,062t/276g TL: N40 34 05 W78 26 40 On air date: November 1974. 1450 Scalp Ave., Johnstown, PA, 15904. Phone: (814) 266-8088. Phone: (814) 949-8823. Fax: (814) 266-7749. Fax: (814) 949-4780. Web Site: www.abc23.com. Licensee: Palm Television LP. Ownership: Gregory P. Filandrinos. (acq 8-17-99; $12.5 million). Natl. Network: ABC, . Washington Atty: Dow, Lohnes & Albertson. Wire Svc: AP

Key Personnel:
Frank Quitoni . . . . pres & gen mgr
Jim Penna . . . . news dir

WJAC-TV— Digital Channel: 34. Digital Hrs: 24 70.8 kw vis, 10.6 kw aur. ant 1,120t/175g TL: N40 22 17 W78 58 58 On air date: Sept 15, 1949. 49 Old Hickory Ln., Johnstown, PA, 15905. Phone: (814) 255-7600. Fax: (814) 255-7675. Web Site: www.wjactv.com. Licensee: WPXI-TV Holdings Inc. Group Owner: Cox Broadcasting (acq 9-22-2000). Population Served: 287,760 Natl. Network: NBC, . Washington Atty: Dow, Lohnes & Albertson. News staff: 38; News: 25 hrs news wkly.
Key Personnel:
Richard D. Schrott . . . . VP
Richard B. Schrott . . . . gen mgr

WKBS-TV— Digital Channel: 46. Digital Hrs: 24 200 kw vis. ant 1,014t/175g TL: N40 34 12 W78 26 26 On air date: 1985. One Signal Hill Dr., Wall, PA, 15148-1499. Phone: (877) 437-4446. Fax: (412) 824-5442.E-mail: info@ctvn.org Web Site: www.ctvn.org. Licensee: Cornerstone Television Inc. Group Owner: (group owner) Washington Atty: Pillsbury, Winthrop & Shaw Pittman.
Key Personnel:
Ron Hembree . . . . pres
Steve Johnson . . . . opns dir
Tom McGough . . . . gen sls mgr
Tom Hollis . . . . progmg

***WPSU-TV—** Digital Channel: 15. Digital Hrs: 24 810 kw vis. ant 1,354t/948g TL: N41 07 20 W78 26 29.8 On air date: Mar 1, 1965. 238 Outreach Bldg., University Park, PA, 16802-3899. Phone: (814) 865-3333. Fax: (814) 863-9786.E-mail: wpsu@psu.edu Web Site: www.wpsu.org. Licensee: The Pennsylvania State University. Population Served: 1,200,000 Natl. Network: PBS, . Rgnl. Network: Eastern Educ, CEN, Pa. Pub Net. Pennsylvania Public Television Network Washington Atty: Paul, Hastings, Janofsky & Walker. Wire Svc: AP
Key Personnel:
Ted Krichels . . . . gen mgr
Kate Domico . . . . opns dir
Tom Yourchak . . . . dev dir
Greg Petersen . . . . mktg dir & progmg dir
Melanie Doebler . . . . prom mgr
Ashear Barr . . . . adv dir
Russ Rockwell . . . . chief of engrg
Amy Kelley . . . . traf mgr

WTAJ-TV— Digital Channel: 32. Digital Hrs: 24 214 kw vis, 21.9 kw aur. 1,110t/277g TL: N40 34 01 W78 26 31 On air date: Mar 1, 1953. 5000 6th Ave., Altoona, PA, 16602. Phone: (814) 942-1010. Fax: (814) 946-8746. Web Site: www.wtajtv.com. Licensee: Nexstar Broadcasting Inc. Group Owner: Television Station Group LLC (acq 12-29-2006; $56 million with WLYH-TV Lancaster). Population Served: 700,000 Natl. Network: CBS, . Washington Atty: Latham & Watkins. Wire Svc: AP News staff: 39; News: 29 hrs wkly.
Key Personnel:
Phil Dubrow . . . . VP & gen mgr sls dir
Dave Beeney . . . . mktg dir
Tony DeGol . . . . news dir
Randy Chamberlin . . . . chief of engrg

WWCP-TV— Digital Channel: 8. Digital Hrs: 24 166 kw vis, 16.6 kw aur. 1,208t TL: N40 10 53 W79 09 05 On air date: Oct 13, 1986. 1450 Scalp Ave., Johnstown, PA, 15904. Phone: (814) 266-8088. Fax: (814) 266-7749. Web Site: www.fox8tv.com. Licensee: Peak Media of Pennsylvania Licensee LLC. Ownership: Peak Media of Pennsylvania LLC. Natl. Network: Fox, . Washington Atty: Dow, Lohnes & Albertson. Wire Svc: AP
Key Personnel:
Frank Quitoni . . . . pres & gen mgr
Jim Penna . . . . news dir

Lancaster

see Harrisburg-Lancaster-Lebanon-York, PA market

Lebanon

see Harrisburg-Lancaster-Lebanon-York, PA market

Philadelphia (DMA 4)

KYW-TV— Digital Channel: 26. Digital Hrs: 24 100 kw vis, 10 kw aur. 1,000t/1,116g TL: N40 02 39 W75 14 26 On air date: Sept 3, 1941. 1555 Hamilton St., Philadelphia, PA, 19130. Phone: (215) 977-5300. Fax: (215) 977-5644. Web Site: www.cbs3.com. Licensee: CBS Broadcasting Inc. Group Owner: Viacom Television Stations Group (acq 5-4-2000; grpsl). Population Served: 1,688,210 Natl. Network: CBS, . Natl. Rep: CBS TV Stations National Sales,. Washington Atty: Wilkes, Artis, Hedrick & Lane.
Key Personnel:
Jon Hitchcock. . . . . pres & gen mgr
Robin Magyar . . . . stn mgr
Robert Fein . . . . sls dir
Roy Coddington . . . . natl sls mgr
Perry Casciato . . . . progmg dir
Susan Schiller . . . . news dir
Rich Paleski . . . . chief of engrg

WBPH-TV— Digital Channel: 9. Digital Hrs: 24 2,950 kw vis. ant 936t/482g TL: N40 33 52 W75 26 24 On air date: 1991. 813 N. Fenwick St., Allentown, PA, 18109. Phone: (610) 433-4400. Fax: (610) 433-8251.E-mail: info@wbph.org Web Site: www.wbph.org. Licensee: Sonshine Family TV Inc. Ownership: Patricia Huber, 100%. Population Served: 1,600,000
Key Personnel:
Pat Huber . . . . CEO & pres

WCAU— Digital Channel: 34. Digital Hrs: 24 191 kw vis, 19.1 kw aur. 1,160t/1,139g TL: N40 02 36 W75 14 12 On air date: Mar 15, 1948. 10 Monument Rd., Bala Cynwyd, PA, 19004. Phone: (610) 668-5510. Fax: (610) 668-3700.E-mail: nbc10@nbc.com Web Site: www.nbc10.com. Licensee: NBC Telemundo License Co. Group Owner: NBC TV Stations Division (acq 9-10-95). Population Served: 2,640,400 Natl. Network: NBC, . Natl. Rep: NBC TV Stations Sales,. Wire Svc: UPI Wire Svc: AP News staff: 110; News: 21 hrs wkly.
Key Personnel:
Dennis Bianchi . . . . pres & gen mgr
Joe Marsini . . . . CFO
Jim Barger . . . . opns dir & engrg dir
Joe Collins . . . . sls VP
Lauren Bacigalupi . . . . prom VP & adv VP
Lawana Scales . . . . progmg dir
Chris Blackman . . . . news dir
JoAnne Wilder . . . . pub affrs dir & pub svc dir
Joan Erle . . . . rsch dir
Christa Morris . . . . traf mgr
Tracy Davidson . . . . consumer affrs dir
Howard Eskin . . . . sports cmtr
Amy Freeze . . . . weather dir

WFMZ-TV— Digital Channel: 46. Digital Hrs: 24 5,000 kw vis. ant 1,027t/590g TL: N40 33 52 W75 26 24 On air date: Nov 25, 1976. 300 E. Rock Rd., Allentown, PA, 18103. Phone: (610) 797-4530. Fax: (610) 791-2288 (sales).E-mail: release@wfmz.com Web Site: www.WFMZ.com. Licensee: Maranatha Broadcasting Co. Ownership: Richard C. Dean, 54%; others, 46%. Population Served: 7,000,000 Washington Atty: Bentley Law Offices. Wire Svc: AP Wire Svc: Accu-Weather Wire Svc: PR Newswire News staff: 120; News: 32 hrs wkly.
Key Personnel:
Barry Fisher . . . . gen mgr
Kevin Arndt . . . . gen sls mgr
Brad Rinehart. . . . . news dir
Richard Dean . . . . chmn & weather dir

WGTW-TV— Digital Channel: 27. Digital Hrs: 24 160 kw vis. ant 1,161t/1,082g TL: N40 02 30 W75 14 11 On air date: August 1992. 960 Ashland Ave., Folcraft, PA, 19032. Phone: (610) 583-1370. Fax: (610) 583-1476. Web Site: www.tbn.org. Licensee: Trinity Christian Center of Santa Ana Inc. (acq 10-1-2004; $7 million plus assumption of $41 million in debt).
Key Personnel:
Al Box. . . . . gen mgr

***WHYY-TV—** Digital Channel: 12. Digital Hrs: 24 309 kw vis, 30.9 kw aur. 960t/1,148g TL: N40 02 30 W75 14 24 On air date: Sept 12, 1963. Independence Mall W., 150 N. 6th St., Philadelphia, PA, 19106. 625 Orange St., Wilmington, DE 19801. Phone: (215) 351-1200. Phone: (302) 888-1200. Fax: (215) 351-0398. Fax: (302) 575-0346.E-mail: talkback@whyy.org Web Site: www.whyy.org. Licensee: WHYY Inc. Ownership: WHYY Inc. Population Served: 7,000,000 Natl. Network: PBS, . Washington Atty: Schwartz, Woods & Miller. News staff: 10; News: 5 hrs wkly.
Key Personnel:
William J. Marrazzo. . . . . CEO & pres
Bruce Flamm . . . . CFO
Paul Gluck. . . . . VP & stn mgr

***WLVT-TV—** Digital Channel: 39. Digital Hrs: 24 490 kw vis, 97.7 kw aur. 990t/516g TL: N40 33 58 W75 26 06 On air date: September 1965. 123 Sesame St., Bethlehem, PA, 18015. Phone: (610) 867-4677. Fax: (610) 867-3544. Web Site: www.wlvt.org. Licensee: Lehigh Valley Public Telecommunications Corp. Population Served: 2,500,000 Natl. Network: PBS, . Rgnl. Network: Eastern Educ, Pa. Pub Net. Pennsylvania Public Television Network Washington Atty: Dow, Lohnes. Foreign lang progmg: SpanishS 1
Key Personnel:
Patricia Simon . . . . CEO
David E. Smith . . . . chief of engrg

WMCN-TV— Digital Channel: 44. Digital Hrs: 24 200 kw vis. ant 931t/905g TL: N39 43 41 W74 50 39 On air date: Oct 1, 1986. 19 S. New York Ave., Atlantic City, NJ, 08401. Phone: (609) 441-1120. Fax: (609) 441-9559.E-mail: contact@wmcn.tv Web Site: www.wmcn.tv. Licensee: Lenfest Broadcasting L.L.C. Ownership: H. Chase Lenfest, member/owner (acq 7-19-2000; $9 million). Population Served: 750,000 Washington Atty: Wiley, Rein & Fielding.
Key Personnel:
H. Chase Lenfest. . . . . pres & CEO
Robert M. Lund . . . . VP & gen mgr
Steve Cass . . . . sls dir & progmg
Mark Chesterton . . . . progmg mgr
Vojislav Radosavljevic . . . . chief of engrg

WMGM-TV— Digital Channel: 36. Digital Hrs: 24 741 kw vis, 74.1 kw aur. ant 420t/416g TL: N39 07 28 W74 45 56 On air date: Jan 25, 1966. 1601 New Rd., Linwood, NJ, 08221. Phone: (609) 927-4440. Fax: (609) 926-8875.E-mail: news@nbc40.net Web Site: www.nbc40.net. Licensee: Access.1 New Jersey License Co. Group Owner: Access.1 Communications Corp. (acq 2004; grpsl). Population Served: 400,000 Natl. Network: NBC, . Wire Svc: AP News: 8 hrs wkly.
Key Personnel:
Chesley Maddox-Dorsey . . . . pres
Arthur Benjamin Jr. . . . . CFO & VP
Ron Smith . . . . gen mgr
Roger Powe . . . . gen sls mgr

***WNJS—** Digital Channel: 22. Digital Hrs: 24 2,323 kw vis, 348 kw aur. 890t/937g TL: N39 43 41 W74 50 39 On air date: Oct 23, 1972. Box 777, Trenton, NJ, 08625-0777. 25 S. Stockton St., Trenton, NJ 08608-1832. Phone: (609) 777-5000. Fax: (609) 633-2920.E-mail: audience@njn.org Web Site: www.njn.net. Licensee: New Jersey Public Broadcasting Authority. Population Served: 3,000,000 Natl. Network: PBS, . New Jersey Network Washington Atty: Schwartz, Woods & Miller. News: 2 hrs wkly.
Satellite of *WNJT Trenton.

***WNJT—** Digital Channel: 43. Digital Hrs: 24 hrs. 1,950 kw vis, 285 kw aur. 1,049t/989g TL: N40 16 58 W74 41 11 On air date: Apr 5, 1971. Box 777, Trenton, NJ, 08625-0777. 25 S. Stockton St., Trenton, NJ 08608-1832. Phone: (609) 777-5000. Fax: (609) 633-2920.E-mail: audience@njn.org Web Site: www.njn.net; showcase.njn.net. Licensee: New Jersey Public Broadcasting Authority. Population Served: 3,500,000 Natl. Network: PBS, . Rgnl. Network: Eastern Educ. New Jersey Network Washington Atty: Schwartz, Woods & Miller. News: 10 hrs wkly.
Key Personnel:
Joann Ruscio . . . . mktg dir
Andre Butts . . . . progmg dir
William Jobes. . . . . news dir
William Schnorbus . . . . chief of engrg

WPHL-TV— Digital Channel: 17. Digital Hrs: 8:30am - 5:30pm 2,340 kw vis, 300 kw aur. ant 1,313t/1,092g TL: N40 02 30 W75 14 24 On air date: Sept 17, 1965. 5001 Wynnefield Ave., Philadelphia, PA, 19131. Phone: (215) 878-1700. Fax: (215) 879-3665.E-mail: wphltv@aol.com Web Site: myph17.trb.com. Licensee: Tribune Broadcasting Co. Group Owner: (group owner, see Cross-Ownership; (acq 12-20-2007; grpsl). Population Served: 2,700,000 Natl. Network: MyNetworkTV, . Natl. Rep: TeleRep,. Washington Atty: Dow Lohnes PLLC.
Key Personnel:
Vince Giannini . . . . VP & gen mgr
Patrick Loftus . . . . gen sls mgr

WPPX-TV— Digital Channel: 31. Digital Hrs: 24 200 kw vis. ant 1,227t/1,147g TL: N40 02 30 W75 14 11 On air date: July 9, 1986. 3901 B. Main St., Suite 301, Philadelphia, PA, 19127. Phone: (215) 482-4770. Fax: (215) 482-4777. Web Site: www.ionline.tv. Licensee: ION Media Philadelphia License Inc., debtor-in-possession. Group Owner: (group owner; (acq 1-20-95; $9.635 million;3-20-95). Population Served: 2,700,000 Natl. Network: ION Television, .
Key Personnel:
Robert Marc Backman . . . . gen mgr
Joe Collins . . . . gen sls mgr
Shawn Edwards . . . . rgnl sls mgr
Daniel Borowicz . . . . chief of engrg
Liz Dunleary . . . . traf mgr

WPSG— Digital Channel: 32. Digital Hrs: 24 5,000 kw vis, 500 kw aur. ant 1,160t/1,179g TL: N40 02 21 W75 14 13 On air date: June 15, 1981. 101 S. Independence Mall E., Kansas City, PA, 19106. Phone: (215) 977- 5700. Fax: (215) 977- 5220.E-mail: cwphilly@wpsg.com

Web Site: cwphilly.com. Licensee: Viacom Stations Group of Philadelphia Inc. Group Owner: Viacom Television Stations Group (acq 1995). Natl. Network: CW, . Washington Atty: Fisher, Wayland, Cooper, Leader & Zaragoza.
Key Personnel:
Jon Hitchcock. . . . . pres & gen mgr
Robin Magyar . . . . . stn mgr
John Brown . . . . . sls dir
Susan Schiller . . . . . news dir
Rich Paleski . . . . . chief of engrg

WPVI-TV— Digital Channel: 6. Digital Hrs: 24 30.2 kw vis. ant 1,089t/1,073g TL: N40 02 39 W75 14 26 On air date: Sept 13, 1947. 4100 City Ave., Philadelphia, PA, 19131. Phone: (215) 878-9700. Fax: (215) 581-4515. Fax: (215) 581-4530 (news). Web Site: www.6abc.com. Licensee: ABC Inc. Group Owner: (group owner; (acq 4-27-71; grpsl). Population Served: 2,600,000 Natl. Network: ABC, . Washington Atty: Wilmer, Cutler & Pickering.
Key Personnel:
Bernie Prazenica . . . . . pres & gen mgr
James Aronow . . . . . sls VP
Dirk Ohley. . . . . natl sls mgr
Bob Liga . . . . . rgnl sls mgr
Paula McDermott. . . . . mktg mgr
Caroline Welch . . . . . progmg dir
Carla Carpenter. . . . . news dir
Linda Munich . . . . . pub affrs dir
Hank Volpe . . . . . engrg VP
Elliott Cohen . . . . . rsch dir
Stacy Silver. . . . . traf mgr
Terry Belford. . . . . film dir
Jim Gardner . . . . . news cmtr
Gary Papa. . . . . sports cmtr
Cecily Tynan . . . . . weather dir
Lisa Thomas Laury . . . . . women's cmtr

WTVE— Digital Channel: 25. Digital Hrs: 24 1,450 kw vis, 290 kw aur. ant 751t/125g TL: N40 21 15 W75 53 56 (CP: 5,000 kw vis, 500 kw aur, ant 1,260t. TL: N40 19 35 W75 42 14) On air date: February 1980. 1729 N. 11th St., Reading, PA, 19604. Phone: (610) 921-9181. Fax: (610) 921-9139. Web Site: www.wtve.com. Licensee: WRNN-TV Associates LP.. Ownership: New Mass Media Inc., gen ptnr, 1.5%; and Hudson Valley Holdings L.P., 98.5% (acq 5-12-2008; $13.5 million). Washington Atty: Covington & Burling.
Key Personnel:
George Mattmiller . . . . . gen mgr
Sal Martirano . . . . . gen sls mgr

WTXF-TV— Digital Channel: 42. Digital Hrs: 24 260 kw vis. ant 1,125t/1,109g TL: N40 02 26 W75 14 19 On air date: May 18, 1965. 330 Market St., Philadelphia, PA, 19106. Phone: (215) 925-2929. Fax: (215) 982-5499(sls). Web Site: www.myfoxphilly.com. Licensee: Fox Television Stations Inc. Group Owner: Fox Television Stations Inc. (acq 1995; $200 million). Natl. Network: Fox, . News: 36.5 hrs wkly.
Key Personnel:
Michael Renda. . . . . VP & gen mgr
Vincent M. Manzi. . . . . gen sls mgr

WUVP-DT— Digital Channel: 29. Digital Hrs: 24 4,070 kw vis, 407 kw aur. ant 1,299t/1,220g TL: N40 02 30 W75 14 11 On air date: July 13, 1981. 4449 N. Delsea Dr., Newfield, NJ, 08344. 1700 Market St., Suite 1550, Philadelphia, PA 19103. Phone: (856) 691-6565. Fax: (856) 691-2483.E-mail: notibreve_65@univision.net Web Site: www.univision.com. Licensee: Univision Philadelphia LLC. Group Owner: Univision Communications Inc. (acq 8-21-2001; grpsl). Natl. Network: Univision (Spanish), . Foreign lang progmg: SpanishS 168
Key Personnel:
Diana Bald. . . . . gen mgr
John Duffin . . . . . natl sls mgr
Raul de la Rosa . . . . . rgnl sls mgr
Josue Duarte . . . . . prom mgr
John Skelnik. . . . . chief of engrg

WWSI— Digital Channel: 49. Digital Hrs: 24 322 kw vis. ant 971t/968g TL: N39 37 53 W74 21 12 On air date: 1990. 1341 N. Delaware Ave., Suite 408, Philadelphia, PA, 19125. One S. New York Ave., Atlantic City, NJ 08401. Phone: (215) 634-8862. Phone: (609) 449-0094. Fax: (215) 425-2683. Fax: (609) 441-9559.E-mail: jrivera@wwsi-tv.com Web Site: www.wwsi-tv.com. Licensee: Hispanic Broadcasters of Philadelphia L.L.C. Ownership: Council Tree Hispanic Broadcasters L.L.C. (acq 5-14-2002). Natl. Network: Telemundo (Spanish), . Foreign lang progmg: SpanishS 168 News staff: 4; News: 3 hrs wkly.
Key Personnel:
Jimmy Rivers. . . . . gen mgr
Michael Brendzel. . . . . dev VP

***WYBE—** Digital Channel: 35. Digital Hrs: 24 1,000 kw vis. ant 1,125t/1,046g TL: N40 02 30 W75 14 11 On air date: June 10, 1990. 8200 Ridge Ave., Philadelphia, PA, 19128-1604. Phone: (215) 483-3900. Fax: (215) 483-6908. Web Site: www.wybe.org. Licensee: Independence Public Media of Philadelphia Inc. Ownership: Independence Media. Population Served: 3,800,000 Washington Atty: Drinker, Biddle & Reath L.L.P. Foreign lang progmg: SpanishS 15
Key Personnel:
Howard Blumenthal . . . . . CEO

Pittsburgh, PA
(DMA 23)

KDKA-TV— Analog Channel: 2. Digital Channel: 25.100 kw vis, 10 kw aur. 995t/683g TL: N40 29 38 W80 01 09 On air date: January 1949. One Gateway Ctr., Pittsburgh, PA, 15222. Phone: (412) 575-2200. Fax: (412) 575-3207. Web Site: kdka.com. Licensee: CBS Broadcasting Inc. Group Owner: Viacom Television Stations Group (acq 5-4-2000; grpsl). Population Served: 1,494,264 Natl. Network: CBS, . Natl. Rep: CBS TV Stations National Sales,. Washington Atty: Wilkes, Artis, Hedrick & Lane.
Key Personnel:
Chris Pike . . . . . gen mgr

***WGPT—** Analog Channel: 36. Digital Channel: 54. Analog Hrs: 24 245 kw vis. ant 3,225t/199g TL: N39 24 14 W79 17 37 On air date: 1986. 11767 Owings Mills Blvd., Owings Mills, MD, 21117-1499. Phone: (410) 356-5600. Fax: (410) 581-6579.E-mail: comments@mpt.org Web Site: www.mpt.org. Licensee: Maryland Public Broadcasting Commission. Population Served: 600,000 Natl. Network: PBS, . Washington Atty: Schwartz, Woods & Miller.
Key Personnel:
Robert Shuman . . . . . CEO & pres
Larry Unger . . . . . CFO
Kirby Storms . . . . . chief of engrg
Rebroadcasts WMPB(TV) Baltimore 100%.

***WNPB-TV—** Digital Channel: 33. Digital Hrs: 24 3,000 kw vis, 347 kw aur. ant 1,499t/515g TL: N39 41 45 W79 45 45 On air date: Feb 23, 1969. 191 Scott Ave., Morgantown, WV, 26508. Phone: (304) 284-1440. Fax: (304) 284-1454.E-mail: audienceservices@wvpubcast.org Web Site: www.wvpubcast.org. Licensee: West Virginia Educational Broadcasting Authority. (acq 7-1-83). Population Served: 109,450 Natl. Network: PBS, . Rgnl. Network: SECA. Washington Atty: Wilkinson, Barker, Knauer & Quinn. News staff: 2; News: one hr wkly.
Key Personnel:
Bill Acker . . . . . gen mgr
Marilyn Divita . . . . . dev dir
Jack Wells. . . . . engrg dir

WPCB-TV— Analog Channel: 40. Digital Channel: 50. Digital Hrs: 24 362 kw vis. ant 866t/705g TL: N40 23 34 W79 46 54 On air date: Apr 15, 1979. Signal Hill Dr., Wall, PA, 15148-1499. Phone: (412) 824-3930. Fax: (412) 824-5442.E-mail: info@ctvn.org Web Site: www.ctvn.org. Licensee: Cornerstone Television Inc. (acq 7-78). Washington Atty: Shaw Pittman. Foreign lang progmg: SpanishS 1
Key Personnel:
Ron Hembree . . . . . pres
Chuck Alexander . . . . . CFO
Steve Johnson . . . . . engrg dir
Martha Helmstadter . . . . . traf mgr
Tom Hollis. . . . . progmg dir & progmg

WPCW— Analog Channel: 19. Analog Hrs: 24 3,020 kw vis. ant 1,115t/371g TL: N40 10 52 W79 07 46 On air date: Oct 15, 1953. 1 Gateway Center, Pittsburgh, PA, 15222. Phone: (412) 575-2200. Fax: (412) 575-2500. Web Site: pittsburghscw.com. Licensee: Pittsburgh Television Station WNPA Inc. Group Owner: Viacom Television Stations Group (acq 12-9-98; $39 million). Population Served: 42,476 Natl. Network: CW, .
Key Personnel:
Chris Pike . . . . . gen mgr

WPGH-TV— Analog Channel: 53. Digital Channel: 43. Analog Hrs: 24 Digital Hrs: 24 2,340 kw vis, 117 kw aur. ant 1,023t/702g TL: N40 29 43 W80 00 17 On air date: July 14, 1953. 750 Ivory Ave., Pittsburgh, PA, 15214. Phone: (412) 931-5300. Fax: (412) 931-8135. Web Site: www.wpgh53.com. Licensee: WPGH Licensee L.L.C. Group Owner: Sinclair Broadcast Group Inc. (acq 8-30-91; $55 million;7-15-91). Population Served: 2,828,400 Natl. Network: Fox, . Natl. Rep: Millennium Sales & Marketing,. Washington Atty: Pillsbury, Winthrop & Pittman.
Key Personnel:
Alan Frank. . . . . gen mgr
Jim Lapiana . . . . . sls dir
Kerry Check . . . . . engrg dir

WPMY— Analog Channel: 22. Digital Channel: 42. Analog Hrs: 24 Digital Hrs: 24 3,800 kw vis, 190 kw aur. ant 918t/797g TL: N40 26 23 W79 43 11 On air date: Sept 26, 1978. 750 Ivory Ave., Pittsburgh, PA, 15214. Phone: (412) 931-5300. Fax: (412) 931-8135. Web Site: www.wcwb22.com. Licensee: WCWB Licensee LLC. Group Owner: Sinclair Broadcast Group Inc. (acq 12-10-2001; $17.808 million). Population Served: 2,800,000 Natl. Network: MyNetworkTV, . Natl. Rep: Millennium Sales & Marketing,. Washington Atty: Pillsbury, Winthrop & Pittman.
Key Personnel:
Alan Frank . . . . . gen mgr
Jim Lapiana . . . . . sls dir
Kerry Check . . . . . pub affrs dir & engrg dir

WPXI— Analog Channel: 11. Digital Channel: 48. Analog Hrs: 24 316 kw vis, 58.9 kw aur. 991t/849g TL: N40 27 48 W80 00 18 On air date: Sept 1, 1957. 4145 Evergreen Rd., Pittsburg, PA, 15214. Phone: (412) 237-1100. Fax: (412) 323-8097.E-mail: comments@wpxi.com Web Site: www.wpxi.com. Licensee: WPXI-TV Holdings Inc. Group Owner: Cox Broadcasting (acq 1-1-65; $20.5 million; 11-30-64). Population Served: 1,500,000 Natl. Network: NBC, . Natl. Rep: TeleRep,. Washington Atty: Dow, Lohnes & Albertson.
Key Personnel:
Ray Carter. . . . . gen mgr
Gary Bogart. . . . . gen sls mgr
Darryl Griffin. . . . . natl sls mgr
Mark Barash . . . . . progmg dir
Carrie Harding . . . . . news dir
Annette Parks . . . . . engrg dir

***WQED—** Digital Channel: 13.25 kw vis. ant 689t/528g TL: N40 26 46 W79 57 51 On air date: Apr 1, 1954. 4802 Fifth Ave., Pittsburgh, PA, 15213. Phone: (412) 622-1300. Fax: (412) 622-6413.E-mail: viewers@wqed.org Web Site: www.wqed.org. Licensee: WQED Multimedia. Population Served: 1,130,000 Natl. Network: PBS, . Washington Atty: Schwartz, Woods & Miller. Wire Svc: Reuters
Key Personnel:
George L. Miles Jr. . . . . . CEO & pres & pres
Debbie Aabert . . . . . gen mgr & stn mgr

WQEX— Analog Channel: 16. Analog Hrs: 24 667 kw vis, 66.1 kw aur. ant 705t/601g TL: N40 26 46 W79 57 51 On air date: Sept 14, 1959. 4802 Fifth Ave., Pittsburgh, PA, 15213. Phone: (412) 622-1300. Fax: (412) 622-1488.E-mail: wqexviewers@wqed.org Web Site: www.wqed.org/wqex. Licensee: WQED Multimedia. Natl. Network: NBC, . Washington Atty: Schwartz, Woods & Miller.
Key Personnel:
George Miles . . . . . pres
Dorothy Frank . . . . . sls dir
Jill Lykins. . . . . prom mgr
Paul Byers. . . . . engrg dir

WTAE-TV— Analog Channel: 4. Digital Channel: 51. Analog Hrs: 24 100 kw vis, 10 kw aur. ant 961t/1,017g TL: N40 16 49 W79 48 11 On air date: Sept 14, 1958. 400 Ardmore Blvd., Pittsburgh, PA, 15221-3090. Phone: (412) 242-4300. Fax: (412) 244-4595. Web Site: www.thepittsburghchannel.com. Licensee: WTAE Hearst-Argyle Television Inc. Group Owner: Hearst-Argyle Television Inc. (acq 7-16-97; grpsl). Population Served: 2,700,000 Natl. Network: ABC, . Natl. Rep: Eagle Television Sales,. Washington Atty: Brooks, Pierce, McLendon, Humphrey & Leonard. News staff: 70; News: 32 hrs wkly.
Key Personnel:
Bob Bee . . . . . gen sls mgr & natl sls mgr
Leslie Wojdowski . . . . . mktg mgr
Luanne Russell . . . . . traf mgr

Scranton

see Wilkes Barre-Scranton, PA market

Wilkes Barre-Scranton, PA
(DMA 54)

WBRE-TV—(Wilkes-Barre, Digital Channel: 11. Digital Hrs: 24 3,020 kw vis, 604 kw aur. 1,670t/870g TL: N41 11 01 W75 52 02 On air date: Jan 1, 1953. 62 S. Franklin St., Wilkes-Barre, PA, 18701-1201. Phone: (570) 823-2828. Fax: (570) 823-4523.E-mail: wbrenews@nbga.net Web Site: www.pahomepage.com. Licensee: Nexstar Broadcasting Inc. Group Owner: Nexstar Broadcasting Group Inc. (acq 11-14-97; $47 million). Population Served: 1,413,000 Natl. Network: NBC, . Natl. Rep: Continental Television Sales,. Washington Atty: Drinker, Biddle & Reath, LLP. News staff: 68; News: 24 hrs wkly.
Key Personnel:
Louis J. Abitabilo . . . . . VP
Randy Williams . . . . . stn mgr & opns dir opns dir
Cheryl Olive . . . . . sls dir
Ron Krisulevicz . . . . . news dir

WNEP-TV— Digital Channel: 50. Digital Hrs: 24 1,150 kw vis, 115 kw aur. ant 1,660t/781g TL: N41 10 58 W75 52 21 On air date: Feb 9, 1954. 16 Montage Mountain Rd., Moosic, PA, 18507. Phone: (570) 346-7474. Fax: (570) 347-0359.E-mail: email@wnep.com Web Site: www.wnep.com. Licensee: Local TV Pennsylvania License LLC.

Group Owner: The New York Times Co. (acq 5-7-2007; grpsl). Population Served: 1,884,000 Natl. Network: ABC, . Natl. Rep: Millennium Sales & Marketing,. Washington Atty: Covington & Burling. Wire Svc: AP Wire Svc: PR Newswire News staff: 64; News: 36 hrs wkly.
Key Personnel:
Chuck Morgan . . . gen mgr
David Lewandoski . . . opns mgr
Mike Last . . . gen sls mgr
Diane Frain . . . mktg dir
Laurie LaMaster . . . prom dir & prom mgr
Debbie Drechin . . . progmg mgr
Frank Gerardi . . . pub affrs dir & pub svc dir
Mike Morkavage . . . chief of engrg

WOLF-TV— Digital Channel: 45. Digital Hrs: 24 1,000 kw vis, 100 kw aur. 1,079t/381g TL: N41 02 13 W76 05 07 (CP: 1,600 kw vis, ant 1,656t. TL: N41 10 58 W75 52 26) On air date: June 3, 1985. 1181 Hwy. 315, Plains, PA, 18702. Phone: (570) 970-5600. Fax: (570) 970-5601.E-mail: fox56@fox56.com Web Site: www.nepatoday.com. Licensee: New Age Media of Pennsylvania License LLC. Group Owner: Pegasus Broadcast Television Inc. (acq 3-31-2007; grpsl). Population Served: 1,700,000 Natl. Network: Fox, . Rgnl. Rep: Rgnl rep: Petry Washington Atty: Leventhal Senter & Lerman PLLC. News: 6.5 hrs wkly.
Key Personnel:
Michael Yanuzzi . . . pres
Jon Cadman . . . gen mgr
Dan Mecca . . . natl sls mgr
Bob Spager . . . rgnl sls mgr

WQMY— Digital Channel: 29. Digital Hrs: 24 1,320 kw vis. ant 800t/177g TL: N41 11 57 W77 07 38 On air date: Jan 22, 1993. 1181 Hwy. 315, Plains, PA, 18702. Phone: (570) 970-5600. Fax: (570) 970-5601.E-mail: nepatoday@fox56.com Web Site: www.nepatoday.com. Licensee: New Age Media of Pennsylvania License LLC. Group Owner: Pegasus Broadcast Television Inc. (acq 3-31-2007; grpsl). Natl. Network: MyNetworkTV, . Washington Atty: Leventhal Senter & Lerman PLLC.
Key Personnel:
Jon Cadmon . . . gen mgr & gen sls mgr
Dan Mecca . . . natl sls mgr
Bob Spager . . . rgnl sls mgr

WQPX-TV— Digital Channel: 32.528 kw vis. ant 1,161t/248g TL: N41 26 06 W75 43 35 On air date: 1998. 409 Lackawanna Ave., Suite 700, Scranton, PA, 18503. Phone: (570) 344-6400. Fax: (570) 344-3303.E-mail: reginalanzo@ionmedia.tv Web Site: www.ionmedia.tv. Licensee: ION Media Scranton License Inc., debtor-in-possession. Group Owner: Paxson Communications Corp. (acq 7-31-98; $6 million). Natl. Network: ION Television, . Washington Atty: Schwartz, Woods & Miller.
Key Personnel:
Regina Lanzo . . . opns mgr
Robert Andrade . . . chief of engrg
Jean Biondollo . . . traf mgr

WSWB— Digital Channel: 31. Digital Hrs: 24 100 kw vis. ant 1,155t/259g TL: N41 26 09 W75 43 46 On air date: Nov 26, 1998. 1181 Hwy. 315, Plains, PA, 18702. Phone: (570) 970-5600. Fax: (570) 970-5601.E-mail: myfoxnepa@fox56.com Web Site: www.myfoxnepa.com. Licensee: MPS Media of Scranton License LLC.. Ownership: Eugene J. Brown, 100% votes Group Owner: (group owner; (acq 3-31-2007; $3.044 million with WTLF(TV) Tallahassee, FL). Population Served: 1,700,000 Natl. Network: CW, .
Key Personnel:
Michael Yanuzzi . . . pres & gen mgr
Jon Cadman . . . gen mgr
Aldo Cardoni . . . opns mgr
Maria Hayduk . . . natl sls mgr
Bob Spager . . . rgnl sls mgr
Linda Greenwald . . . progmg dir
Steve Phillips . . . pub affrs dir
Rich Chofey . . . chief of engrg
Lisa Miller . . . traf mgr

***WVIA-TV—** Digital Channel: 41. Digital Hrs: 24 1,000 kw vis, 100 kw aur. 1,670t/845g TL: N41 10 55 W75 752 17 On air date: Sept 26, 1966. 100 WVIA Way, Pittston, PA, 18640-6197. Phone: (570) 826-6144. Phone: (570) 344-1244. Fax: (570) 655-1180. Web Site: www.wvia.org. Licensee: Northeastern Pennsylvania Educational TV Association. Population Served: 1,500,000 Natl. Network: PBS, . Rgnl. Network: Eastern Educ. Pennsylvania Public Television Network Washington Atty: Dow, Lohnes & Albertson.
Key Personnel:
A. William Kelly . . . pres
Thomas P. Curra . . . sr VP
Joseph Glynn . . . engrg VP

WYOU— Digital Channel: 13. Digital Hrs: 24 2,945 kw vis, 294 kw aur. ant 842g TL: N41 10 58 W75 52 26 On air date: June 7, 1953. 62 S. Franklin St., Wilkes-Barre, PA, 18701. Phone: (570) 961-2222. Fax: (570) 344-4484. Web Site: www.wyou.com. Licensee: Mission Broadcasting Inc. Group Owner: (group owner; (acq 1-5-98; $21 million). Population Served: 580,290 Natl. Network: CBS, . Natl. Rep: Blair Television,. Washington Atty: Drinker, Biddle & Reath LLP. News: 19.5 hrs wkly.
Key Personnel:
Louis J. Abitabilo . . . gen mgr
Randy Williams . . . opns dir & natl sls mgr
Cheryl Olive . . . sls dir
Steve Genett . . . natl sls mgr
Bob Spager . . . rgnl sls mgr
Susan Kalinowski . . . progmg dir & progmg mgr
Frank Andrews . . . news dir

York

see Harrisburg-Lancaster-Lebanon-York, PA market

Rhode Island

Providence, RI-New Bedford, MA (DMA 52)

WJAR— Digital Channel: 51.316 kw vis, 50 kw aur. ant 1,000t/940g TL: N41 51 54 W71 17 15 On air date: July 10, 1949. 23 Kenney Dr., Cranston, RI, 02920. Phone: (401) 455-9100. Fax: (401) 455-9168. Fax: (401) 455-9140. Web Site: www.turnto10.com. Licensee: Media General Communications Inc. Group Owner: NBC TV Stations Division (acq 6-26-2006; grpsl). Population Served: 846,000 Natl. Network: NBC, . Natl. Rep: Harrington, Righter & Parsons,. Foreign lang progmg: SpanishS 1
Key Personnel:
Lisa Churchville . . . gen mgr & stn mgr
Clark Smith . . . opns dir & chief of engrg
Jeff Walkes . . . gen sls mgr
Valerie McCain . . . natl sls mgr
Barbara Beresford . . . mktg dir
Betty Jo Cugini . . . news dir
Elaine Moy-Gederman . . . progmg

WLNE-TV—(New Bedford, MA) Digital Channel: 49. Digital Hrs: 24 100 kw vis, 22.4 kw aur. ant 940t/996g TL: N41 46 39 W70 55 41 On air date: Jan 1, 1963. 10 Orms St., Providence, RI, 02904. Phone: (401) 453-8000. Fax: (401) 331-4399. Web Site: www.abc6.com. Licensee: Global Broadcasting of Southern New England LLC.. Ownership: Global Broadcasting LLC, 100% Group Owner: Freedom Broadcasting Inc. (acq 10-9-2007; $14 million). Population Served: 1,437,000 Natl. Network: ABC, . Natl. Rep: TeleRep,. Washington Atty: Latham & Watkins.
Key Personnel:
Stephen Doerr . . . VP & gen mgr
Jim Brown . . . opns mgr & engrg dir chief of engrg
Michael Brostek . . . rgnl sls mgr
Bill Mushrush . . . prom dir
BJ Finnell . . . news dir

WLWC—(New Bedford, MA) Digital Channel: 22. Digital Hrs: 24 5,000 kw vis, 250 kw aur. ant 808t/833g TL: N41 38 13 W70 55 41 On air date: Apr 17, 1997. One State St., Providence, RI, 02908. Phone: (401) 351-8828. Fax: (401) 351-0222. Web Site: cw28tv.com. Licensee: Providence TV Licensee Corp. Group Owner: Viacom Television Stations Group (acq 11-21-2007; grpsl). Natl. Network: CW, . Natl. Rep: TeleRep,. Washington Atty: Wiley Rein LLP.
Key Personnel:
Pam Bergeron . . . sls dir
Lisa Pesanello . . . natl sls mgr
Tina Castano . . . rgnl sls mgr

WNAC-TV— Digital Channel: 12. Digital Hrs: 24 3,720 kw vis, 372 kw aur. ant 1,033t/900g TL: N41 52 14 W71 17 45 On air date: December 1981. 25 Catamore Blvd., East Providence, RI, 02914. Phone: (401) 438-7200. Fax: (401) 434-3761.E-mail: info@wpri.com Web Site: www.wpri.com. Licensee: WNAC LLC. Ownership: Super Towers Inc., 100% (acq 4-22-2002). Natl. Network: Fox, MyNetworkTV, . Natl. Rep: Blair Television,.
Key Personnel:
Jay Howell . . . pres & VP gen mgr
Steve Carro . . . opns mgr
Patrick Wholey . . . gen sls mgr
Nancy Mayers . . . natl sls mgr
John Macek . . . rgnl sls mgr
Andy Bernstein . . . mktg dir
Susan Tracy-Durant . . . prom mgr
Pam Brennan . . . progmg mgr
Joe Abouzeid . . . news dir
Christine Peabody . . . pub affrs dir
William Hague . . . engrg dir & chief of engrg

WPRI-TV— Digital Channel: 13. Digital Hrs: 24 316 kw vis, 31.6 kw aur. 910t/1,099g TL: N41 52 37 W71 16 56 On air date: Mar 27, 1955. 25 Catamore Blvd., East Providence, RI, 02914-1203. Phone: (401) 438-7200. Fax: (401) 434-3761. Web Site: www.wpri.com. Licensee: TVL Broadcasting of Rhode Island LLC. Group Owner: LIN Television Corporation (acq 11-8-2002; grpsl). Population Served: 550,000 Natl. Network: CBS, . Natl. Rep: Blair Television,.
Key Personnel:
Jay Howell . . . pres & VP gen mgr
Gregg Monte . . . opns mgr
Patrick Wholey . . . gen sls mgr
Patti St. Pierre . . . natl sls mgr
Andrew Bernstein . . . mktg dir
Susan Tracy-Durant . . . prom mgr
Pam Brennan . . . progmg mgr
Glenn Laxton . . . pub affrs dir
William Hague . . . chief of engrg
Kathy Douglas . . . traf mgr
Susan Durant . . . pub svc dir
Michael Marinelli . . . sports cmtr
Tony Petrarca . . . weather dir

WPXQ-TV— Digital Channel: 17. Digital Hrs: 24 1,000 kw vis. ant 748t/589g TL: N41 29 41 W71 47 06 On air date: Apr 2, 1992. 3 Shaws CV, Ste 226, New London, CT, 06320-4943. Phone: (401) 455-9263. Fax: (401) 455-9156.E-mail: Robert.melfi@nbc.com Web Site: www.ionline.tv. Licensee: Ocean State Television LLC, debtor-in-possession.. Ownership: A joint venture of Paxson Communications Corp. and Offshore Broadcasting Corp. (Raymond Yorke, 100%). Group Owner: Paxson Communications Corp. (acq 8-2-96). Natl. Network: ION Television, . Washington Atty: Cohn & Marks. News: 5 hrs wkly.
Key Personnel:
Robert J. Melfi . . . gen sls mgr

***WSBE-TV—** Digital Channel: 21. Digital Hrs: 24 1,230 kw vis, 123 kw aur. ant 597t/508g TL: N41 48 18 W71 28 24 On air date: June 5, 1967. 50 Park Ln., Providence, RI, 02907. Phone: (401) 222-3636. Fax: (401) 222-3407.E-mail: info@rlpbs.org Web Site: www.rlpbs.org. Licensee: Rhode Island Public Telecommunications Authority. Population Served: 1,000,000 Natl. Network: PBS, . Washington Atty: Schwartz, Woods & Miller.
Key Personnel:
David Piccerelli . . . CFO
Kathryn Larsen . . . stn mgr & progmg dir
Dexter B. Merry . . . chief of opns
Tracey Cugno . . . dev dir
Michael Bert . . . chief of engrg

South Carolina

Allendale

see Augusta, GA market

Anderson

see Greenville-Spartanburg, SC-Asheville, NC-Anderson, SC market

Beaufort

see Savannah, GA market

Charleston, SC (DMA 99)

WCBD-TV— Digital Channel: 50. Digital Hrs: 24 100 kw vis, 10 kw aur. ant 1,950t TL: N32 56 24 W79 41 45 On air date: Sept 25, 1954. 210 W. Coleman Blvd., Mt. Pleasant, SC, 29464. Phone: (843) 884-2222. Fax: (843) 881-3410. Web Site: www.wcbd.com. Licensee: Media General Broadcasting Inc. Group Owner: Media General Broadcast Group (acq 3-1-83; $8 million;1-24-83). Population Served: 295,039 Natl. Network: NBC, CW, . Natl. Rep: Harrington, Righter & Parsons,. Washington Atty: Cohn & Marks. News staff: 29; News: 17 hrs wkly.
Key Personnel:
Rick Lipps . . . gen mgr
Patric J. Ryal . . . gen sls mgr & natl sls mgr
Mark Bradley . . . mktg mgr
Sam Barclay . . . chief of engrg

WCIV— Digital Channel: 34. Digital Hrs: 24 100 kw vis, 20 kw aur. ant 1,958t/1,958g TL: N32 55 28 W79 41 58 On air date: Oct 23, 1962. Box 22165, Charleston, SC, 29413-2165. 888 Allbritton Blvd., Mt.

Pleasant, SC 29464. Phone: (843) 881-4444. Fax: (843) 849-2507 (admin). Fax: (843) 849-2515 (sales). Web Site: www.abcnews4.com. Licensee: WCIV Inc. Group Owner: Allbritton Communications Co. (acq 1-26-76; grpsl). Population Served: 1,500,000 Natl. Network: ABC, . Washington Atty: Hogan & Hartson. Wire Svc: Conus News staff: 32; News: 12 hrs wkly.
Key Personnel:
Suzanne Teagle . . . gen mgr
Terry Wright . . . opns mgr & chief of engrg
Octavia Walker . . . natl sls mgr
Chuck Groome . . . rgnl sls mgr
Tim Greeney . . . prom mgr
Deborah Jackson . . . progmg mgr
Perry Boxx . . . news dir
Sybil Blanton . . . traf mgr

WCSC-TV— Digital Channel: 47. Digital Hrs: 24 100 kw vis, 20 kw aur. ant 1,958t TL: N32 55 28 W79 41 58 On air date: June 19, 1953. 2126 Charlie Hall Blvd., Charleston, SC, 29414. Phone: (843) 402-5555. Fax: (843) 402-5744. Web Site: www.wcsc.com. Licensee: WCSC License Subsidiary LLC. (acq 3-31-2008; grpsl). Population Served: 617,800 Natl. Network: CBS, . News staff: 44; News: 21 hrs wkly.
Key Personnel:
Rita O'Neill . . . gen mgr
Riten Scotte . . . stn mgr
Brian Stephenson . . . dev mgr
Amy Spencer . . . gen sls mgr
Amanda Childs . . . prom mgr
Riten O'Neil . . . progmg mgr
Mary Rigby . . . news dir
Mike Gurthie . . . engrg dir
Lowell Knoff . . . chief of engrg

***WITV—** Digital Channel: 7. Digital Hrs: 24 316 kw vis. ant 1,850t/1,837g TL: N32 55 28 W79 41 58 On air date: Jan 19, 1964. 1101 George Rogers Blvd., Columbia, SC, 29201. Phone: (803) 737-3545. Web Site: www.myetv.org. Licensee: South Carolina ETV Commission. Natl. Network: PBS, . Washington Atty: Dow, Lohnes & Albertson.
Key Personnel:
Maurice "Moss" Bresnahan . . . CEO & pres & engrg VP

WMMP— Digital Channel: 36. Digital Hrs: 24 3,251 kw vis, 50 kw aur. ant 994t TL: N32 47 15 W79 51 00 On air date: November 1992. 4301 Arco Ln., Charleston, SC, 29418. Phone: (843) 744-2424. Fax: (843) 554-9649.E-mail: comments@wmmp36.com Web Site: www.wmmp36.com. Licensee: WMMP Licensee L.P. Group Owner: Sinclair Broadcast Group Inc. (acq 1998; grpsl). Natl. Network: MyNetworkTV, .
Key Personnel:
David Tynan . . . VP & gen mgr
Mary Margaret Johnson . . . gen mgr & gen sls mgr
Jason Lewis . . . mktg mgr & prom mgr
Bill Littleton . . . progmg dir & progmg mgr
Sallie Moultrie . . . traf mgr

WTAT-TV— Digital Channel: 24. Digital Hrs: 24 5,000 kw vis, 497.5 kw aur. ant 1,800t/1,800g TL: N32 56 24 W79 41 45 On air date: Sept 7, 1985. 4301 Arco Ln., Charleston, SC, 29418. Phone: (843) 744-2424. Fax: (843) 554-9649.E-mail: comments@wmmp36.com Web Site: www.wtat24.com. Licensee: WTAT Licensee LLC. Group Owner: Cunningham Broadcasting Corporation (acq 11-15-2001; grpsl). Natl. Network: Fox, . Washington Atty: Arter & Hadden. News: 3.5 hrs wkly.
Key Personnel:
David Tynan . . . gen mgr
Mary Margaret Johnson . . . gen sls mgr
Jason Lewis . . . prom VP & prom mgr
Bill Littleton . . . progmg dir
Sallie Moultrie . . . traf mgr

Columbia, SC (DMA 79)

WACH— Digital Channel: 48. Digital Hrs: 24 5,000 kw vis, 500 kw aur. ant 633t/623g TL: N34 02 39 W80 59 52 On air date: 1988. 1400 Pickens St., Columbia, SC, 29201. Phone: (803) 252-5757. Fax: (803) 212-7270.E-mail: webmaster@wach.com Web Site: www.wach.com. Licensee: Barrington Columbia License LLC. Group Owner: Raycom Media Inc. (acq 8-11-2006; grpsl). Natl. Network: Fox, . Natl. Rep: TeleRep,. Washington Atty: Covington & Burling.
Key Personnel:
Scott McBride . . . VP & gen mgr
Phil Shreves . . . opns mgr & chief of engrg
Cheri Spets . . . gen sls mgr
Barbara Bethea . . . rgnl sls mgr & mktg dir prom dir & news dir
Reese Barkley . . . pub affrs dir & rsch dir pub svc dir
Nina Gibson . . . traf mgr
Ernest Robinson . . . sports cmtr
Tim Miller . . . weather dir

WIS— Digital Channel: 10. Digital Hrs: 24 57 kw vis. ant 1,578t/1,489g TL: N34 07 29 W80 45 23 On air date: Nov 7, 1953. 1111 Bull St., Columbia, SC, 29201. Box 367, Columbia, SC 29202. Phone: (803) 799-1010. Fax: (803) 758-1171.E-mail: dtodd@wistv.com Web Site: www.wistv.com. Licensee: WIS License Subsidiary LLC. Group Owner: Liberty Corp. (acq 1-31-2006; grpsl). Population Served: 314,000 Natl. Network: NBC, . Natl. Rep: Harrington, Righter & Parsons,. Washington Atty: Covington & Burling LLP. News: 26.5 hrs wkly.
Key Personnel:
Donita Todd . . . VP & gen mgr
Quentin Kenney . . . gen sls mgr
Barry Ahrendt . . . mktg dir & progmg dir
Brad Neuhoff . . . news dir
Emir Hadziahmetovic . . . chief of engrg

WKTC— Digital Channel: 39. Digital Hrs: 24 12.9 kw vis. ant 541t TL: N33 54 52 W80 17 39 On air date: 1997. 120-A Pontiac Business Center Dr., Elgin, SC, 29045. Phone: (803) 419-6363. Fax: (803) 419-6399.E-mail: mail@wktctv.com Web Site: www.wktctv.com. Licensee: WBHQ Columbia LLC.. Ownership: Stefanie Rein and David Canfield (as Joint Tenants), 100% votes, 8.18% total assets (acq 10-17-2005; $2.2 million). Natl. Network: MyNetworkTV, . Natl. Rep: MMT,. Washington Atty: Pillsbury, Withrop, Shaw Pittman.
Key Personnel:
Stefanie Rein . . . gen mgr

WLTX— Digital Channel: 17. Digital Hrs: 24 5,000 kw vis, 500 kw aur. ant 1,749t/1,706g TL: N34 05 49 W80 45 51 On air date: Sept 1, 1953. 6027 Garners Ferry Rd., Columbia, SC, 29209. Phone: (803) 776-3600. Fax: (803) 695-3714. Web Site: www.wltx.com. Licensee: Pacific and Southern Co. Inc. Group Owner: Gannett Broadcasting (acq 4-29-98; $87.5 million). Population Served: 1,013,410 Natl. Network: CBS, . Natl. Rep: TeleRep,. Wire Svc: AP News: 27 hrs wkly.
Key Personnel:
Rich O'Dell . . . gen mgr
Lou Schottelkotte . . . gen sls mgr
Jim Hays . . . mktg mgr
Marybeth Jacoby . . . news dir
Terry Wright . . . chief of engrg

WOLO-TV— Digital Channel: 8. Digital Hrs: 24 3,550 kw vis, 355 kw aur. ant 830t TL: N34 03 23 W80 58 49 On air date: Oct 1, 1961. Box 4217, Columbia, SC, 29240. 5807 Shakespeare Rd., Columbia, SC 29223. Phone: (803) 754-7525. Fax: (803) 754-6147. Web Site: www.wolo.com. Licensee: South Carolina Broadcasting Partners. (acq 7-20-92). Population Served: 480,000 Natl. Network: ABC, . Wire Svc: AP
Key Personnel:
Chris Bailey . . . gen mgr & stn mgr

***WRJA-TV—** Digital Channel: 28. Digital Hrs: 24 647 kw vis. ant 1,161t/1,161g TL: N33 52 51 W80 16 15 On air date: Sept 7, 1975. 18 N. Harvin St., Sumter, SC, 29150. Phone: (803) 773-5546. Fax: (803) 775-1059.E-mail: wrjatv@ftc-i.net Web Site: www.wrja.org. Licensee: South Carolina ETV Commission. Population Served: 87,000 Natl. Network: PBS, .
Key Personnel:
Victor Miller . . . gen mgr
Kevin Jordan . . . engrg mgr

***WRLK-TV—** Digital Channel: 32. Digital Hrs: 24 570 kw vis. ant 1,030t/971g TL: N34 07 06 W80 56 13 On air date: Sept 5, 1966. Box 11000, Columbia, SC, 29211. 1101 George Rogers Blvd., Columbia, SC 29211. Phone: (803) 737-3200. Phone: (803) 737-3212. Fax: (803) 737-3417.E-mail: mail@myetv.org Web Site: www.myetv.org. Licensee: South Carolina ETV Commission. Population Served: 3,200,000 Natl. Network: PBS, . Washington Atty: Dow, Lohnes & Albertson.
Key Personnel:
Maurice "Moss" Bresnahan . . . CEO & pres
Maurice Bresnahan . . . gen mgr & stn mgr
L.W. Griffin Jr. . . . engrg VP & engrg dir

WZRB— Digital Channel: 47.750 kw vis. ant 630t/518g TL: N34 02 38 W80 59 51 On air date: Jan 1, 2005. 1747 Cushman Dr., Columbia, SC, 29204. Phone: (803) 714-2347. Fax: (803) 691-3848. Web Site: www.cw47columbia.com. Licensee: Roberts Broadcasting Co. of Columbia, SC LLC. Group Owner: Roberts Broadcasting Co. Population Served: 915,000 Natl. Network: CW, . Washington Atty: Dow, Lohnes & Albertson.
Key Personnel:
Dody Yarborough . . . gen mgr

Florence

see Myrtle Beach-Florence, SC market

Greenville-Spartanburg, SC-Asheville, NC-Anderson, SC (DMA 36)

WGGS-TV— Digital Channel: 16. Digital Hrs: 24 2,240 kw vis. ant 1,145t/167g TL: N34 56 26 W82 24 41 On air date: October 1972. Box 1616, Greenville, SC, 29602. 3409 Rutherford Rd., Taylors, SC 29687. Phone: (864) 244-1616. Fax: (864) 292-8481.E-mail: ccbtv16@aol.com Web Site: www.dovebroadcasting.com. Licensee: Carolina Christian Broadcasting Inc. Ownership: James H. Thompson, 100%. Population Served: 750,000 Washington Atty: Hardy & Chautin.
Key Personnel:
James W. Thompson . . . pres & gen mgr
Joanne Thompson . . . VP
Billy Rainey . . . sls dir
Dante Thompson . . . natl sls mgr
Pete Littlefield . . . chief of engrg
Derek Myers . . . edit dir
Kym MacKinnon . . . progmg

WHNS— Digital Channel: 21. Digital Hrs: 24 3,390 kw vis, 398 kw aur. ant 2,509t/1,604g TL: N35 10 56 W82 40 56 On air date: Apr 1, 1984. 21 Interstate Ct., Greenville, SC, 29615. Phone: (864) 288-2100. Fax: (864) 297-0728.E-mail: whns@foxcarolina.com Web Site: www.foxcarolina.com. Licensee: Meredith Corp. Group Owner: Meredith Broadcasting Group, Meredith Corp. (acq 7-1-97; grpsl). Population Served: 1,700,000 Natl. Network: Fox, . Natl. Rep: TeleRep,. Washington Atty: Dow, Lohnes & Albertson. News staff: 45; News: 27 hrs wkly.
Key Personnel:
Steve Lacy . . . CEO
William Kerr . . . chmn
Paul Karpowicz . . . pres
Dalton Lee . . . CFO
Douglas Lowe . . . exec VP
Guy W. Hempel . . . VP & gen mgr
Jeff Guilbert . . . gen sls mgr
Alan DeFlorio . . . natl sls mgr
April White . . . mktg mgr
Kelly Boan . . . news dir
Jim Barnes . . . chief of engrg
Susan Hodgins . . . rsch dir
Rhonda Ross . . . traf mgr

WLOS—(Asheville, NC) Digital Channel: 13. Digital Hrs: 24 170 kw vis, 19.6 kw aur. ant 2,804t/339g TL: N35 25 32 W82 45 25 On air date: Sept 18, 1954. 110 Technology Dr., Asheville, NC, 28803. Phone: (828) 684-1340. Fax: (828) 651-4618.E-mail: news@wlos.com Web Site: www.wlos.com. Licensee: WLOS Licensee L.L.C. Group Owner: Sinclair Broadcast Group Inc. (acq 6-96). Population Served: 815,000 Natl. Network: ABC, . Natl. Rep: Harrington, Righter & Parsons,. Washington Atty: Dow, Lohnes & Albertson. News staff: 57; News: 24 hrs wkly.
Key Personnel:
Jack Connors . . . gen mgr
Audra Swain . . . chief of opns & sls dir
Guy Chancey . . . mktg dir
Scott Bradsher . . . progmg mgr
Julie Fries . . . news dir
Rollin Thompkins . . . chief of engrg

WMYA-TV— Digital Channel: 14. Digital Hrs: 8 AM-5 PM 2,570 kw vis, 257 kw aur. ant 1,050t/1,020g TL: N34 38 51 W82 16 13 On air date: Dec 1, 1953. 24 Verdae Blvd., Suite 203, Greenville, SC, 29607. 110 Technology Dr., (Tapes & Traffic), Asheville, NC 28803. Phone: (864) 297-1313. Fax: (864) 297-8085. Web Site: www.my40.tv. Licensee: Anderson (WFBC-TV) Licensee Inc. Group Owner: Cunningham Broadcasting Corporation (acq 1-7-2002). Population Served: 815,000 Natl. Network: MyNetworkTV, .
Key Personnel:
David D. Smith . . . pres
J. Duncan Smith . . . exec VP
Frederick G. Smith . . . VP
Steven M. Marks . . . chief of opns
Darren Shapiro . . . sls VP
Gregg Sigel . . . natl sls mgr
Jeff Sleete . . . mktg VP & mktg dir
M. William Butler . . . progmg VP
Joe DeFeo . . . news dir & pub affrs dir

WNEG-TV— Digital Channel: 24. Digital Hrs: 24 647 kw vis, 129 kw aur. ant 835t/600g TL: N34 36 44 W83 22 05 On air date: Sept 9, 1984. 802 E. Dyle Street, Toccoa, GA, 30577. Phone: (706) 886-0032. Fax: (706) 886-7033. Web Site: www.wneg32.com. Licensee: UGARF Media Holdings LLC.. Ownership: University of Georgia Research Foundation Inc., 100% equity owner Group Owner: Media General Broadcast Group (acq 8-18-2008; $1,437,500). Natl. Network: CBS, . Natl. Rep: MMT,. Washington Atty: Fletcher, Heald & Hildreth. News staff: 6; News: 13 hrs wkly.
Key Personnel:
Jim Sanders . . . gen mgr & stn mgr stn mgr
David Austin . . . gen sls mgr
Tony Garrison . . . prom mgr
Stephanie Harrison . . . progmg mgr
J. Walker . . . chief of engrg
Stephanie Cauthen . . . rsch dir

***WNEH—** Digital Channel: 18.1,780 kw vis. ant 771t/656g TL: N34 22 21 W82 10 03 On air date: Sept 10, 1984. 1101 George Rogers Blvd.,

Columbia, SC, 29201. Phone: (803) 737-3545.E-mail: mail@myetv.org Web site: www.myetv.org. Licensee: South Carolina Educational TV Commission. Natl. Network: PBS, .
Key Personnel:
Maurice Bresnahan . . . . CEO & pres & stn mgr

*WNTV— Digital Channel: 9. Digital Hrs: 24 5,000 kw vis. ant 1,286t/262g TL: N34 56 26 W82 24 38 On air date: Sept 15, 1963. 1101 George Rogers Blvd., Columbia, SC, 29201. Phone: (803) 737-3545. Phone: (803) 737-9959. Fax: (803) 737-3495.E-mail: mail@myetv.org Web site: www.myetv.org. Licensee: South Carolina ETV Commission. Population Served: 550,000 Natl. Network: PBS, .
Key Personnel:
Maurice "Moss" Bresnahan . . . . . . CEO & pres & stn mgr
L.W. Griffin Jr. . . . . engrg VP

*WRET-TV— Digital Channel: 43. Digital Hrs: 24 1,740 kw vis, 174 kw aur. ant 970t/859g TL: N34 52 09 W81 49 15 On air date: Sept 4, 1980. Box 4069, Spartanburg, SC, 29305-4069. Phone: (864) 503-9371. Fax: (864) 503-3615. Web site: www.wret.org. Licensee: South Carolina Educational TV Commission. Population Served: 1,000,000 Natl. Network: PBS, . Washington Atty: Dow, Lohnes & Albertson.
Key Personnel:
William Richardson . . . . opns mgr
Gary Stevens . . . . chief of engrg
Satellite of WNTV Greenville.

WSPA-TV—(Spartanburg, Digital Channel: 7. Digital Hrs: 24 316 kw vis, 31.6 kw aur. ant 2,001t/258g TL: N35 10 12 W82 17 27 On air date: Apr 29, 1956. Box 1717, Spartanburg, SC, 29304. 250 International Dr., Spartanburg, SC 29303. Phone: (864) 576-7777. Fax: (864) 587-4480. Web site: www.wspa.com. Licensee: Media General Broadcasting of So. Carolina Holding Inc. Group Owner: Media General Broadcasting of So. Carolina Holding (acq 3-27-2000; grpsl). Population Served: 784,300 Natl. Network: CBS, . Washington Atty: Dow, Lohnes. Wire Svc: UPI News staff: 51; News: 26.5 hrs wkly.
Key Personnel:
Jim Zimmerman . . . . pres
Phil Lane . . . . VP & gen mgr
Jimmy Lizer . . . . opns mgr
Mike Krejci . . . . gen sls mgr
Megan Hanningan . . . . mktg dir

*WUNF-TV— Digital Channel: 25. Digital Hrs: 24 2,690 kw vis, 269 kw aur. ant 2,676t/339g TL: N35 25 32 W82 45 25 On air date: Sept 11, 1967. Box 14900, Research Triangle Park, NC, 27709-4900. 10 TW Alexander Dr., Research Triangle Park, NC 27709. Phone: (919) 549-7000. Fax: (919) 549-7201.E-mail: viewer@unctv.org Web site: www.unctv.org. Licensee: University of North Carolina. Population Served: 9,000,000 Natl. Network: PBS, . Washington Atty: Schwartz, Woods & Miller.
Key Personnel:
Tom Howe . . . . gen mgr

*WUNW— Analog Channel: 27.10.7 kw vis. ant 1,555t/68g TL: N35 34 06 W82 54 25 Not on air, target date: unknown: Box 14900, Research Triangle Park, NC, 27709-4900. Phone: (919) 549-7000. Fax: (919) 549-7201. Web site: www.unctv.org. Permittee: University of North Carolina.
Key Personnel:
Tom Howe . . . . gen mgr

WYCW— Digital Channel: 45.5,000 kw vis, 250 kw aur. ant 1,823t TL: N35 13 20 W82 32 58 On air date: June 1986. Box 1717, Spartanburg, SC, 29304. 250 International Dr., Spartanburg, NC 29303. Phone: (864) 576-7777. Fax: (864) 595-4615. Web site: www.carolinascw.com. Licensee: Media General Broadcasting of South Carolina Holdings Inc. Group Owner: Media General Broadcast Group (acq 1-15-2002; $4.5 million). Population Served: 1.950 m,ill,ion Natl. Network: CW, . Washington Atty: Dow, Lohnes & Albertson.
Key Personnel:
Jim Zimmerman . . . . pres
Jim Conschafter . . . . sr VP
Phil Lane . . . . gen mgr
Randy Ingram . . . . stn mgr
Jimmy Lizer . . . . opns mgr

WYFF— Digital Channel: 36. Digital Hrs: 24 1,000 kw vis. ant 1,955t/833g TL: N35 06 43 W82 36 24 On air date: Dec 31, 1953. Box 788, Greenville, SC, 29602. 505 Rutherford St., Greenville, SC 29609. Phone: (864) 242-4404. Fax: (864) 240-5329.E-mail: news4@wyff.com Web site: www.wyff4.com. Licensee: WYFF Hearst-Argyle Television Inc. Group Owner: Hearst-Argyle Television Inc. (acq 3-18-99; grpsl). Population Served: 1,601,700 Natl. Network: NBC, . Natl. Rep: Eagle Television Sales,. Washington Atty: Brooks, Pierce, McLendon, Humphrey & Leonard. Wire Svc: AP News staff: 55; News: 28 hrs wkly.

Key Personnel:
Michael J. Hayes . . . . pres & gen mgr
Doug Durkee . . . . opns dir & opns mgr chief of engrg
John Humphrey . . . . gen sls mgr
Blake Bridges . . . . natl sls mgr
Steve Eaton . . . . rgnl sls mgr
Cathy Petropoulos . . . . mktg dir
Marsa Jarrett . . . . prom mgr & pub affrs dir
Danny Ross . . . . progmg dir
Justin Antoniotte. . . . . news dir
Melanie Richey . . . . traf mgr

Hardeeville

see Savannah, GA market

Myrtle Beach-Florence, SC
(DMA 104)

WBTW— Digital Channel: 13. Digital Hrs: 24 316 kw vis, 31.6 kw aur. ant 1,950t/2,000g TL: N34 22 02 W79 19 22 On air date: Oct 18, 1954. 3430 N. TV Rd., Florence, SC, 29501-0013. 101 McDonald Ct., Myrtle Beach, SC 29588. Phone: (843) 317-1313. Fax: (843) 317-1410. Web Site: www.scnow.com. Licensee: Media General Communications Inc. Group Owner: Media General Broadcast Group (acq 3-27-2000; grpsl). Population Served: 221,280 Natl. Network: CBS, . Natl. Rep: Harrington, Righter & Parsons,. News staff: 38:; News: 78 hrs wkly.
Key Personnel:
Michael Caplan . . . . VP & gen mgr gen mgr
Brian Lang . . . . gen sls mgr
Chuck Spruill . . . . mktg mgr
David Halt . . . . news dir
Scott Johnson . . . . chief of engrg
Sandra Sellers . . . . traf mgr

WFXB— Digital Channel: 18. Digital Hrs: 24 5,000 kw vis. ant 1,519t/1,506g TL: N34 11 19 W79 11 00 On air date: July 5, 1984. 3364 Huger St., Calgary, SC, 29577. Phone: (843) 828-4300. Fax: (843) 828-4343. Web Site: www.wfxb.com. Licensee: Springfield Broadcasting Partners. (acq 8-18-2006; $19.5 million). Population Served: 1,200,000 Natl. Network: Fox, . Natl. Rep: Millennium Sales & Marketing,. Washington Atty: Fisher, Wayland, Cooper, Leader & Zaragoza. News staff: 50+; News: 2.5 hrs wkly.
Key Personnel:
Dave Milligan . . . . COO & gen mgr

*WHMC— Digital Channel: 9. Digital Hrs: 24 1,740 kw vis. ant 820t/839g TL: N33 57 05 W79 06 31 On air date: Sept 2, 1980. 1101 George Rogers Blvd., Columbia, SC, 29201. Phone: (803) 737-3545. Phone: (803) 737-9959. Fax: (803) 737-3495.E-mail: mail@myetv.org Web site: www.myetv.org. Licensee: South Carolina Educational TV Commission. Natl. Network: PBS, .
Key Personnel:
Maurice "Moss" Bresnahan . . . . . . CEO & pres & stn mgr
L.W. Griffin Jr. . . . . engrg VP

*WJPM-TV— Digital Channel: 45. Digital Hrs: 24 646 kw vis. ant 795t/778g TL: N34 16 48 W79 44 35 On air date: Sept 3, 1967. 1101 George Rogers Blvd., Columbia, SC, 29201. Phone: (803) 737-3545. Phone: (803) 737-9959. Fax: (803) 737-3495.E-mail: mail@myetv.org Web site: www.myetv.org. Licensee: South Carolina ETV Commission. Natl. Network: PBS, .
Key Personnel:
Maurice "Moss" Bresnahan . . . . CEO & pres

WMBF-TV— Digital Channel: 32. Digital Hrs: 24 165 kw vis. ant 610t/607g TL: N33 43 50 W79 04 32 On air date: Aug 8, 2008. Box 3579, 918 Frontage Rd. E., Myrtle Beach, SC, 29578. Phone: (843) 839-9623. Fax: (843) 839-9625. Web Site: www.wmbfnews.com. Licensee: Raycom TV Broadcasting (acq 1-31-2006; grpsl). Natl. Network: NBC, . Natl. Rep: TeleRep,. Washington Atty: Covington & Burling. Wire Svc: AP News staff: 33; News: 27 hrs wkly.
Key Personnel:
Ted Fortenberry . . . . VP & gen mgr
Eileen Russo . . . . gen sls mgr
Matt Miller . . . . news dir

WPDE-TV— Digital Channel: 16. Digital Hrs: 24 1,290 kw vis, 129 kw aur. ant 1,948t/2,008g TL: N34 21 53 W79 19 49 On air date: Nov 22, 1980. 1194 Atlantic Ave., Conway, SC, 29526. Phone: (843) 234-9733. Fax: (843) 234-9739.E-mail: feedback@wpde.com. Web site: www.wpdetv.com. Licensee: Barrington Broadcasting of South Carolina Corp. Group Owner: Diversified Communications (acq 2-6-2006; $24.1 million). Population Served: 162,200 Natl. Network: ABC, . Washington Atty: Irwin, Campbell & Tannenwald.

Key Personnel:
William Huggins . . . . VP & gen mgr

*WUNU— Digital Channel: 31. Digital Hrs: 24 3,160 kw vis. 1,046t TL: N34 47 51 W79 02 41 On air date: Sept 23, 1996. Box 14900, Research Triangle Park, NC, 27709-4900. 10 TW Alexander Dr., Research Triangle Park, NC 27709. Phone: (919) 549-7000. Fax: (919) 549-7201.E-mail: viewer@unetv.org Web Site: www.unctv.org. Licensee: University of North Carolina. Natl. Network: PBS, . Washington Atty: Schwartz, Woods & Miller.
Key Personnel:
Tom Howe . . . . gen mgr

WWMB— Digital Channel: 21. Digital Hrs: 24 2,090 kw vis, 209 kw aur. ant 1,989t TL: N33 55 14 W79 32 08 On air date: Nov 1, 1994. Box 51150, Myrtle Beach, SC, 29579. Phone: (843) 234-9733. Fax: (843) 234-9739. Web Site: www.cwtv21.com. Licensee: SagamoreHill of Carolina Licenses LLC. (acq 2-6-2006; $2.4 million). Natl. Network: CW, .
Key Personnel:
Louis Wall . . . . CEO & gen mgr
Laura Walls . . . . stn mgr & chief of engrg
Leigh Vaters . . . . gen sls mgr
Marty Shelley . . . . prom mgr
Billy Huggins . . . . progmg mgr
Mike Gathrie . . . . engrg mgr
Robert Blair . . . . chief of engrg
Debbie Yost . . . . traf mgr & traf mgr

Rock Hill
see Charlotte, NC market

Spartanburg
see Greenville-Spartanburg, SC-Asheville, NC-Anderson, SC market

South Dakota

Eagle Butte
see Minot-Bismarck-Dickinson, ND market

Mitchell
see Sioux Falls (Mitchell), SD market

Rapid City, SD
(DMA 174)

*KBHE-TV— Digital Channel: 26. Digital Hrs: 24 39.8 kw vis, 7.2 kw aur. 649t/469g TL: N44 03 09 W103 14 38 (CP: 45.62 kw vis, ant 662t. TL: N44 03 07 W103 14 36) On air date: July 1967. 3650 Skyline Dr., Rapid City, SD, 57701. Phone: (605) 394-2551. Fax: (605) 394-6895.E-mail: admin@sdpb.org Web Site: www.sdpb.org. Licensee: South Dakota Board of Directors for Educational Telecommunications. Population Served: 151,000 Natl. Network: PBS, .
Key Personnel:
Julie Anderson. . . . . stn mgr
Terry Spencer . . . . dev dir

KCLO-TV— Digital Channel: 16. Digital Hrs: 24 690 kw vis, 69 kw aur. 520t/4,201g TL: N44 04 14 W103 15 01 On air date: November 1988. 501 S. Philips Ave., Sioux Falls, SD, 57104. Phone: (605) 336-1100. Fax: (605) 334-3447.E-mail: kelotv@keloland.com Web Site: www.keloland.com. Licensee: Young Broadcasting of Rapid City Inc. Group Owner: (group owner; (acq 1996; grpsl). Natl. Network: CBS, . Natl. Rep: Adam Young,. Washington Atty: Brooks, Pierce, McLendon, Humphrey & Leonard.
Key Personnel:
Paul Farmer . . . . opns mgr & mktg dir
Karen Floyd . . . . progmg dir
Mark Millage . . . . news dir
John Hertz . . . . chief of engrg

KEVN-TV— Digital Channel: 7. Digital Hrs: 5 AM-2 AM 263 kw vis, 26.3 kw aur. ant 669t/623g TL: N44 04 00 W103 15 01 On air date: July 4, 1976. Box 677, Rapid City, SD, 57709. 2000 Skyline Dr., Rapid City, SD 57701. Phone: (605) 394-7777. Fax: (605) 348-9128. Fax: (605) 394-3652.E-mail: news@blackhillsfox.com Web Site:

www.blackhillsfox.com. Licensee: KEVN Inc. Group Owner: Mission TV LLC (acq 8-26-98; $5.5 million with KIVV-TV Lead). Population Served: 160,000 Natl. Network: Fox, . Natl. Rep: Millennium Sales & Marketing,. Washington Atty: Law Offices of Hogan & Hartson. Wire Svc: AP News staff: 14; News: 9 hrs wkly.

Key Personnel:

Bob Slocum . . . CFO
Cindy McNeil . . . VP & gen mgr
Nancy Reber . . . rgnl sls mgr
Jack Caudill . . . news dir
Lance Cratty . . . chief of engrg

KHSD-TV— Digital Channel: 10. Digital Hrs: 24 34.8 kw vis. ant 1,889t/564g TL: N44 19 36 W103 50 12 On air date: Nov 2, 1966. Box 1760, Rapid City, SD, 57709-1760. 518 Saint Joseph St., Rapid City, SD 57701. Phone: (605) 342-2000. Fax: (605) 342-7305. Web Site: www.kotatv.com. Licensee: Duhamel Broadcasting Enterprises. Group Owner: (group owner) Population Served: 241,224 Natl. Network: ABC, . Washington Atty: Shaw Pittman.

Key Personnel:

William F. Duhamel . . . pres & gen mgr
Monte Loos. . . . opns dir & progmg dir film buyer & engrg dir
Steve Duffy . . . gen sls mgr
Gerry Fenske . . . rgnl sls mgr
John Petersen . . . news dir
Satellite of KOTA-TV Rapid City.

KIVV-TV— Digital Channel: 5. Digital Hrs: 5 AM-2 AM 100 kw vis, 10 kw aur. ant 1,851t/638g TL: N44 19 30 W103 50 14 On air date: July 4, 1976. Box 677, Rapid City, SD, 57709. 2000 Skyline Dr., Rapid City, SD 57709. Phone: (605) 394-7777. Fax: (605) 348-9128.E-mail: news@blackhillsfox.com Web Site: www.blackhillsfox.com. Licensee: KEVN Inc. Group Owner: Mission TV LLC (acq 8-26-98; $5.5 million with KEVN-TV Rapid City). Population Served: 160,000 Natl. Network: Fox, . Natl. Rep: Millennium Sales & Marketing,. Washington Atty: Law Offices of Hogan & Hartson. Wire Svc: AP News staff: 14; News: 9 hrs wkly.

Key Personnel:

Bob Slocum . . . CFO
Cindy McNeil . . . VP & gen mgr
Nancy Reber . . . rgnl sls mgr
Jack Caudill . . . news dir
Lance Cratty . . . chief of engrg
Satellite of KEVN-TV Rapid City.

KNBN— Digital Channel: 21. Digital Hrs: 20 1,500 kw vis. ant 440t TL: N44 01 19 W103 15 33 On air date: May 14, 2000. Box 9549, Rapid City, SD, 57709. 2424 S. Plaza Dr., Rapid City, SD 57709. Phone: (605) 355-0024. Fax: (605) 355-9274.E-mail: webmaster@newscenter1.com Web Site: www.newscenter1.com. Licensee: Rapid Broadcasting Co.James F. Simpson, 10.5%; Scott Barbour, 9.1%; Leeann Rieman, 9.1%; Frank Simpson, 8.3%; Clark D. Moyle, 8.1%;; Gilbert D. Moyle III, 8.1%; W.R. Barbour, 6.1%; William F. Turner, 3.2%; Suzanne M. Gabrielson, 2.4%; Charles H. Lien, 2.4%; and David M. Simpson, 1.3% Group Owner: (group owner). Natl. Network: NBC, . News: 11 hrs wkly.

Key Personnel:

Jim Simpson. . . . VP & gen mgr
Mark Walter . . . opns mgr
Darren Koehne. . . . gen sls mgr
Steve Weaver . . . rgnl sls mgr

KOTA-TV— Digital Channel: 2. Digital Hrs: 24 18.2 kw vis. ant 672t/551g TL: N44 04 08 W103 15 03 On air date: July 1, 1955. Box 1760, Rapid City, SD, 57709-1760. 518 St. Joseph St., Rapid City, SD 57701-1760. Phone: (605) 342-2000. Fax: (605) 342-7305. Web Site: www.kotatv.com. Licensee: Duhamel Broadcasting Enterprises. Group Owner: (group owner) Population Served: 241,224 Natl. Network: ABC, . Washington Atty: Shaw Pittman. Wire Svc: AP News: 9 hrs wkly.

Key Personnel:

William F. Duhamel . . . pres & gen mgr
Monte Loos. opns mgr & progmg dir film buyer & engrg mgr chief of engrg
Steve Duffy . . . natl sls mgr
Gerry Fenske . . . rgnl sls mgr
John Peterson . . . news dir

KSGW-TV— Digital Channel: 13.316 kw vis, 63.2 kw aur. ant 1,220t TL: N44 37 20 W107 06 57 On air date: Oct 28, 1977. Box 1760, Rapid City, SD, 57709-1760. Phone: (605) 342-2000. Fax: (605) 342-7305. Web Site: www.kotatv.com. Licensee: Duhamel Broadcasting Enterprises. Group Owner: (group owner) Population Served: 241,224 Natl. Network: ABC, . Washington Atty: Shaw Pittman. News: 8 hrs wkly.

Key Personnel:

William Duhamel . . . pres & gen mgr
Steve Duffy . . . gen sls mgr
Gerry Fenske . . . rgnl sls mgr
Fred Whitley . . . prom dir
Monte Loos . . . progmg dir & film buyer
John Petersen . . . news dir

KSWY— Digital Channel: 7.3.2 kw vis. ant 1,181t/79g TL: N44 37 20 W107 06 57 On air date: 2002. Stn currently dark Box 4218, Helena, MT, 59604-4218. Phone: (406) 442-2655.E-mail: tvinvestor@gmail.com Web Site: www.jctvonline.com. Licensee: Western Family Television Inc.. Ownership: Roger Lonnquist, 34%; Verdell Lonnquist, 33%; Janice Lonnquist, 33% Group Owner: (group owner). (acq 5-9-2009; swap for WJCW-LP Sheridan).

Key Personnel:

Roger Lonnquist . . . pres

***KZSD-TV—** Digital Channel: 8.275 kw vis, 27.5 kw aur. ant 869t/571g TL: N43 26 06 W101 33 14 On air date: Feb 8, 1978. Box 5000, Vermillion, SD, 57069-5000. 555 N. Dakota St., Vermillion, SD 57069-5000. Phone: (605) 677-5861. Fax: (605) 677-5010.E-mail: programming@sdpb.org Web Site: www.sdpb.org. Licensee: South Dakota Board of Directors for Educational Telecommunications. Natl. Network: PBS, . Washington Atty: Cohn & Marks.

Key Personnel:

Julie Andersen . . . pres
Craig Jensen . . . opns mgr
Terry Spencer . . . dev dir
Carol Robertson. . . . prom dir
Bob Bosse . . . progmg dir
Stacey Decker. . . . engrg mgr
Steve Thum. . . . traf mgr

Sioux Falls (Mitchell), SD (DMA 113)

KABY-TV— Digital Channel: 9.316 kw vis, 31.6 kw aur. ant 1,401t TL: N45 06 32 W97 53 30 On air date: Nov 28, 1958. 717 Hwy. 281 N., Aberdeen, SD, 57401. Phone: (605) 225-9200. Phone: (605) 336-1300. Fax: (605) 225-9226. Licensee: Hoak Media of Dakota License LLC. Group Owner: Wicks Television L.L.C. (acq 1-3-2007; grpsl). Natl. Network: ABC, .

Key Personnel:

Jack Hansen . . . gen mgr
Eugene Schultz. . . . chief of engrg
Satellite of KSFY-TV Sioux Falls.

***KCSD-TV—** Digital Channel: 24. Digital Hrs: 24 13.3 kw vis, 1.3 kw aur. 177t/135g TL: N43 32 07 W96 44 34 On air date: June 13, 1995. Box 5000, Vermillion, SD, 57069-5000. 555 N. Dakota St., Vermillion, SD 57069-5000. Phone: (605) 677-5861. Fax: (605) 677-5010.E-mail: programming@sdpb.org Web Site: www.sdpb.org. Licensee: South Dakota Board of Directors for Educational Telecommunications. Population Served: 150,000 Natl. Network: PBS, . Washington Atty: Cohn & Marks.

Key Personnel:

Julie Andersen . . . pres
Craig Jensen . . . opns mgr
Terry Spencer. . . . dev mgr
Fritz Miller. . . . mktg mgr
Bob Bosse. . . . progmg dir & progmg mgr

KDLO-TV— Digital Channel: 3. Digital Hrs: 24 100 kw vis, 20 kw aur. 1,690t/1,710g TL: N44 57 57 W97 35 22 On air date: September 1955. 501 S. Phillips, Sioux Falls, SD, 57104. Phone: (605) 336-1100. Fax: (605) 334-3447.E-mail: kelotv@keloland.com Web Site: www.keloland.com. Licensee: Young Broadcasting of Sioux Falls Inc. Group Owner: Young Broadcasting Inc. (acq 6-1-96; grpsl). Natl. Network: CBS, . Natl. Rep: Adam Young,. Washington Atty: Brooks, Pierce, McLendon, Humphrey & Leonard.

Key Personnel:

Mark Millage . . . gen mgr
Paul Farmer . . . prom dir
John Hertz. . . . chief of engrg
Karen Floyd. . . . progmg
Satellite of KELO-TV Sioux Falls 100%.

KDLT-TV— Digital Channel: 47. Digital Hrs: 24 4,000 kw vis. ant 1,991t TL: N43 30 17 W96 33 22 On air date: November 1998. c/o KDLT(TV), 3600 S. Westport Ave., Sioux Falls, SD, 57106-6325. Phone: (605) 361-5555. Fax: (605) 361-7017. Fax: (605) 361-3982.E-mail: info@kdlt.com Web Site: www.kdlt.com. Licensee: Red River Broadcast Co. L.L.C. Group Owner: (group owner) Population Served: 582,000 Natl. Network: NBC, . Natl. Rep: Harrington, Righter & Parsons,. Washington Atty: Holland and Knight. Wire Svc: AP News staff: 25; News: 19 hrs wkly.

Key Personnel:

Myron Kunin. . . . CEO
Ro Grignon . . . pres
Kathy Lau . . . VP
Mari Ossenfort . . . gen mgr
Susan Endres . . . opns mgr
Amanda Sievert. . . . prom VP & pub svc dir
Jen Wahle . . . news dir
Donald Sturzenbecher . . . chief of engrg
Stacey Torvik . . . traf mgr
Rusty Lord. . . . weather dir

KDLV-TV— Digital Channel: 26. Digital Hrs: 24 100 kw vis, 10 kw aur. ant 981t/998g TL: N43 45 33 W98 24 44 On air date: June 12, 1960. 3600 S. Westport Ave., Sioux Falls, SD, 57106-6325. Phone: (605) 361-5555. Fax: (605) 361-3982/(605) 361-7017. Web Site: www.kdlt.com. Licensee: Red River Broadcast Co. L.L.C. Group Owner: (group owner; (acq 8-26-94; $4 million; 9-12-94). Population Served: 582,000 Natl. Network: NBC, . Natl. Rep: Harrington, Righter & Parsons,. Washington Atty: Holland & Knight. Foreign lang progmg: SpanishS 4 News staff: 25; News: 20 hrs wkly.

Key Personnel:

Ro Grignon . . . pres
Mari Ossenfort . . . gen mgr & gen sls mgr adv mgr
Emily Dimock . . . prom mgr & pub affrs dir pub svc dir
Susan Endres . . . opns mgr & progmg mgr
Bobbi Lauer . . . news dir
Don Sturzenbecher . . . chief of engrg
Mark Ovenden . . . sports cmtr
Jerrid Sebesta . . . weather dir
Satellite of KDLT-TV Sioux Falls.

***KDSD-TV—** Digital Channel: 17. Digital Hrs: 24 1,350 kw vis, 135 kw aur. 1,171t/1,062g TL: N45 29 55 W97 40 35 On air date: Jan 1, 1972. Box 5000, Vermillion, SD, 57069-5000. 555 N. Dakota St., Vermillion, SD 57069-5000. Phone: (605) 677-5861. Fax: (605) 677-5010.E-mail: programming@sdpb.org Web Site: www.sdpb.org. Licensee: South Dakota Board of Directors for Educational Telecommunications. Natl. Network: PBS, . Washington Atty: Cohn & Marks.

Key Personnel:

Julie Andersen . . . pres
Craig Jensen . . . opns mgr
Terry Spencer . . . dev dir
Fritz Miller. . . . mktg mgr
Bob Bosse . . . progmg dir

KELO-TV— Digital Channel: 11. Digital Hrs: 24 316 kw vis, 28.8 kw aur. ant 2,001t/1,952g TL: N43 31 07 W96 32 05 On air date: May 1953. 501 S. Phillips, Sioux Falls, SD, 57104. Phone: (605) 336-1100. Fax: (605) 334-3447. Fax: (605) 357-5530. Web Site: www.keloland.com. Licensee: Young Broadcasting of Sioux Falls Inc. Group Owner: Young Broadcasting Inc. (acq 6-1-96; grpsl). Population Served: 306,000 Natl. Network: CBS, MyNetworkTV, . Natl. Rep: Adam Young,. Washington Atty: Brooks, Pierce, McLendon, Humphrey & Leonard.

Key Personnel:

Jay Huizenga. . . . pres & gen mgr
Paul Farmer. . . . mktg dir & prom dir
Karen Floyd . . . progmg dir
Mark Millage . . . news dir
John Hertz. . . . chief of engrg

***KESD-TV—** Digital Channel: 8. Digital Hrs: 24 245 kw vis, 51.3 kw aur. ant 751t/801g TL: N44 20 10 W97 13 41 On air date: Feb 6, 1968. Box 5000, Vermillion, SD, 57069. Phone: (605) 677-5861. Fax: (605) 677-5010.E-mail: admin@sdpb.org Web Site: www.sdpb.org. Licensee: South Dakota Board of Directors for Educational Telecommunications. Population Served: 151,000 Natl. Network: PBS, . Rgnl. Network: CEN. Washington Atty: Cohn & Marks.

Key Personnel:

Terry Spencer . . . dev dir

KPLO-TV— Digital Channel: 13. Digital Hrs: 24 100 kw vis, 15 kw aur. 1,110t/711g TL: N43 57 55 W99 36 11 On air date: July 1957. 501 S. Phillips, Sioux Falls, SD, 57104. Phone: (605) 336-1100. Fax: (605) 334-3447.E-mail: kelotv@keloland.com Web Site: www.keloland.com. Licensee: Young Broadcasting of Sioux Falls Inc. Group Owner: Young Broadcasting Inc. (acq 6-1-96; grpsl). Natl. Network: CBS, . Natl. Rep: Adam Young,. Washington Atty: Brooks, Pierce, McLendon, Humphrey & Leonard.

Key Personnel:

Mark Millage . . . gen mgr & news dir
Paul Farmer . . . mktg dir
Karen Floyd . . . progmg dir
John Hertz. . . . chief of engrg
Satellite of KELO-TV Sioux Falls 100%.

KPRY-TV— Digital Channel: 19.100 kw vis, 20 kw aur. ant 1,240t/1,089g TL: N44 03 07 W100 05 03 On air date: February 1976. 300 N. Dakota Ave., Sioux Falls, SD, 57104. Phone: (605) 336-1300. Fax: (605) 336-7936. Licensee: Hoak Media of Dakota License LLC. Group Owner: Wicks Television L.L.C. (acq 1-3-2007; grpsl). Natl. Network: ABC, . Washington Atty: Arent, Fox, Kintner, Plotkin & Kahn. News staff: 45; News: 15 hrs wkly.

Key Personnel:

Jack Hanson . . . gen mgr
Kelly Manning . . . stn mgr
Eugene Schultz. . . . chief of engrg

***KQSD-TV—** Digital Channel: 11. Digital Hrs: 24 234 kw vis, 28 kw aur. 1,040t/826g TL: N45 16 34 W99 59 03 On air date: Jan 1, 1976. Box 5000, Vermillion, SD, 57069-5000. 555 N. Dakota St., Vermillion, SD 57069. Phone: (605) 677-5861. Phone: (800) 456-0766. Fax: (605) 677-5010.E-mail: programming@sdpb.org Web Site: www.sdpb.org.

Licensee: South Dakota Board of Directors for Educational Telecommunications. Natl. Network: PBS, . Washington Atty: Cohn & Marks.
Key Personnel:
Julie Andersen . . . . . pres
Craig Jensen . . . . . opns mgr
Terry Spencer . . . . . dev dir
Fritz Miller. . . . . mktg mgr
Bob Bosse. . . . . progmg dir & progmg mgr

KSFY-TV— Digital Channel: 13. Digital Hrs: 24 316 kw vis, 39.8 kw aur. ant 2,000t/1,985g TL: N43 31 07 W96 32 05 On air date: July 31, 1960. 300 N. Dakota Ave., Suite 100, Sioux Falls, SD, 57104. Phone: (605) 336-7936. Fax: (605) 336-3468. Web Site: www.ksfy.com. Licensee: Hoak Media of Dakota License LLC. Group Owner: Wicks Television L.L.C. (acq 1-3-2007; grpsl). Population Served: 500,000 Natl. Network: ABC, . Natl. Rep: TeleRep,. News staff: 30; News: 15 hrs wkly.
Key Personnel:
Kelly Manning . . . . . gen mgr
Ryan Welsh . . . . . gen sls mgr
Darrel Nelson . . . . . chief of engrg

***KSMN—** Digital Channel: 15. Digital Hrs: 24 1,260 kw vis. 1,089t TL: N43 53 52 W95 56 50 On air date: 1997. 120 W. Schlieman Ave., Appleton, MN, 56208-1351. Phone: (800) 726-3178. Fax: (320) 289-2634.E-mail: yourtv@pioneer.org Web Site: www.pioneer.org. Licensee: West Central Minnesota Educational TV Co. Natl. Network: PBS, .
Key Personnel:
Les Heen . . . . . pres & gen mgr
Shirley Schwarz. . . . . progmg dir
Jon Panzer . . . . . chief of engrg
KWCM, Appleton.

***KTSD-TV—** Digital Channel: 10. Digital Hrs: 24 316 kw vis, 31.6 kw aur. 1,601t/1,327g TL: N43 57 55 W99 35 56 On air date: Aug 1, 1970. Box 5000, Vermillion, SD, 57069-5000. 555 N. Dakota St., Vermillion, SD 57069-5000. Phone: (605) 677-5861. Phone: (800) 456-0766. Fax: (605) 677-5010.E-mail: programming@sdpb.org Web Site: www.sdpb.org. Licensee: South Dakota Board of Directors for Educational Telecommunications. Natl. Network: PBS, . Washington Atty: Cohn & Marks.
Key Personnel:
Julie Andersen . . . . . pres
Craig Jensen . . . . . opns mgr
Terry Spencer . . . . . dev dir
Bob Bosse . . . . . progmg dir

KTTM— Digital Channel: 12. Digital Hrs: 20 316 kw vis, 31.6 kw aur. ant 860t TL: N44 11 39 W98 19 05 On air date: Sept 7, 1991. c/o KTTW, 2817 W. 11th St., Sioux Falls, SD, 57104. Phone: (605) 338-0017. Fax: (605) 338-7173.E-mail: yourcomments@foxnews.com Web Site: www.kttw.com. Licensee: Independent Communications Inc. Natl. Network: Fox, . Natl. Rep: Continental Television Sales,.
Key Personnel:
Ed Hoffman . . . . . gen mgr
Stacey Sieverding . . . . . gen sls mgr
Judy Buie . . . . . progmg dir
Satellite of KTTW(TV) Sioux Falls 100%.

KTTW— Digital Channel: 7. Digital Hrs: 20 195 kw vis, 19.5 kw aur. ant 495t/499g TL: N43 29 20 W96 45 40 On air date: Nov 1, 1986. Box 5103, Sioux Falls, SD, 57117-5103. 2817 W. 11th St., Sioux Falls, SD 57104. Phone: (605) 338-0017. Fax: (605) 338-7173.E-mail: yourcomments@foxnews.com Web Site: www.kttw.com. Licensee: Independent Communications Inc. (acq 3-9-88). Population Served: 216,000 Natl. Network: Fox, . Washington Atty: Reddy, Begley & McCormick.
Key Personnel:
Ed Hoffman . . . . . gen mgr & stn mgr
Stacey Sieverding . . . . . gen sls mgr
Judy Buie . . . . . progmg dir

***KUSD-TV—** Digital Channel: 34. Digital Hrs: 24 100 kw vis, 20 kw aur. ant 760t/656g TL: N43 03 00 W96 47 12 On air date: July 5, 1961. Box 5000, Vermillion, SD, 57069. 555 N. Dakota St., Vermillion, SD 57069. Phone: (605) 677-5861. Fax: (605) 677-5010.E-mail: programming@sdpb.org Web Site: www.sdpb.org. Licensee: South Dakota Board of Directors for Educational Telecommunications. Population Served: 304,000 Natl. Network: PBS, . Rgnl. Network: CEN. Washington Atty: Cohn & Marks.
Key Personnel:
Julie Andersen . . . . . pres
Craig Jensen . . . . . opns mgr
Terry Spencer . . . . . dev dir
Fritz Miller . . . . . mktg mgr & prom dir
Bob Bosse . . . . . progmg dir

KWSD— Digital Channel: 36. Digital Hrs: 24 3,020 kw vis. ant 1,168t TL: N43 30 19 W96 34 20 On air date: 2001. Box 9609, Rapid City, SD, 57709-9609. 3220 W. 57th St., Suite 111, Sioux Falls, SD 57108. Phone: (605) 355-0024. Fax: (605) 338-5484.E-mail: jsimpson@newscenter1.com Web Site: www.siouxfallscw.com. Licensee: J.F. Broadcasting LLC. Ownership: James F. Simpson, 100% Group Owner: (group owner); (acq 3-2-2007; $300,000). Natl. Network: CW, .
Key Personnel:
Jim Simpson . . . . . gen mgr
Mark Walter . . . . . opns mgr
Mike Smith . . . . . gen sls mgr

Tennessee

Chattanooga, TN
(DMA 86)

WDEF-TV— Digital Channel: 12. Digital Hrs: 24 26 kw vis. ant 1,260t/16g TL: N35 08 06 W85 19 25 On air date: Apr 25, 1954. 3300 Broad St., Chattanooga, TN, 37408. Phone: (423) 785-1200. Fax: (423) 785-1271.E-mail: news@wdef.com Web Site: www.wdef.com. Licensee: WDEF-TV Inc. Group Owner: Media General Broadcast Group (acq 10-13-2006; $23 million). Population Served: 856,000 Natl. Network: CBS, . Natl. Rep: Harrington, Righter & Parsons,. Washington Atty: Fletcher, Heald & Hildreth, P.L.C. News staff: 29; News: 19.5 hrs wkly.
Key Personnel:
Phillip D. Cox. . . . . gen mgr

WDSI-TV— Digital Channel: 40. Digital Hrs: 24 5,000 kw vis, 500 kw aur. 1,214t TL: N35 12 34 W85 16 39 On air date: Jan 24, 1972. 1101 E. Main St., Chattanooga, TN, 37408. Phone: (423) 265-0061. Fax: (423) 265-3636.E-mail: info@myfoxchattanooga.com Web Site: www.myfoxchattanooga.com. Licensee: New Age Media of Tennessee License LLC.. Ownership: Sedgwick Media LLC, 65%; Dallas Media LLC, 33.64%; Michael Yanuzzi, 1.36% Group Owner: Pegasus Broadcast Television Inc. (acq 3-31-2007; Natl. Network: Fox, MyNetworkTV, . Washington Atty: Leventhal Senter & Lerman PLLC. News: 3.5 hrs/week.
Key Personnel:
Patrick Notley. . . . . chief of opns
Tracye McCarthy . . . . . gen mgr & gen sls mgr
Nathan Mears . . . . . natl sls mgr
Jenny Giddens . . . . . progmg dir
Latricia Thomas. . . . . news dir
Patrick Motley . . . . . chief of engrg
Tonetta Jones . . . . . traf mgr

WELF-TV— Digital Channel: 16. Digital Hrs: 24 640 kw vis. ant 1,492t/466g TL: N34 57 07 W85 22 58 On air date: 1994. 384 S. Campus Rd., Lookout Mountain, GA, 30750. Phone: (706) 820-1663. Fax: (706) 820-1735.E-mail: welf@tbn.org Web Site: www.tbn.org. Licensee: Trinity Broadcasting Network. Group Owner: (group owner; (acq 5-8-2000; grpsl). Population Served: 586,000
Key Personnel:
Onya Richter . . . . . stn mgr

WFLI-TV— Digital Channel: 42. Digital Hrs: 24 1,306 kw vis, 131 kw aur. ant 1,065t/1,016g TL: N34 55 57 W84 58 32 On air date: May 25, 1987. 1101 E. Main St., Chattanooga, TN, 37408. Phone: (423) 265-0061. Fax: (423) 265-3636. Web Site: www.thecwchattanooga.com. Licensee: MPS Media of Tennessee License LLC. Ownership: Eugene J. Brown, 100% Group Owner: Meredith Broadcasting Group, Meredith Corp. (acq 4-1-2008; $6.8 million). Natl. Network: CW, . Natl. Rep: MMT,. Washington Atty: Fletcher, Heald & Hildreth.
Key Personnel:
Tracye McCarthy . . . . . gen mgr

***WNGH-TV—** Digital Channel: 33. Digital Hrs: 24 5,000 kw vis. ant 1,851t TL: N34 45 06 W84 42 54 On air date: Feb 1, 1967. 2765 Ft. Mountain State Park Rd., Chatsworth, GA, 30705. Phone: (706) 422-1947. Web Site: www.gpb.org. Licensee: Georgia Public Telecommunications Commission. Natl. Network: PBS, . Washington Atty: Arent, Fox, Kintner, Plotkin & Kahn.
Key Personnel:
Hugh Pearson . . . . . chief of engrg

WRCB— Digital Channel: 13. Digital Hrs: 24 111 kw vis. ant 1,214t/380g TL: N35 09 40 W85 18 51 On air date: May 6, 1956. 900 Whitehall Rd., Chattanooga, TN, 37405. Phone: (423) 267-5412. Fax: (423) 267-6840. Fax: (423) 756-3148 (news).E-mail: ttolar@wrcbtv.com Web Site: www.wrcbtv.com. Licensee: Sarkes Tarzian Inc. Group Owner: (group owner); (acq 10-82; $16 million;10-18-82). Population Served: 863,000 Natl. Network: NBC, . Natl. Rep: Continental Television Sales,. Washington Atty: Leventhal, Senter & Lerman. Wire Svc: AP News: 22 hrs wkly.
Key Personnel:
Tom Tarzian. . . . . chmn
Bob Davis. . . . . CFO
Tom Tolar . . . . . pres & gen mgr
Doug Loveridge . . . . . opns mgr
Ralph Flynn . . . . . gen sls mgr
Ronnie Minton . . . . . prom dir
Pam Teague . . . . . progmg dir
Derrall Stalvey . . . . . news dir
Dan Sommers . . . . . chief of engrg

***WTCI—** Digital Channel: 29. Digital Hrs: 24 1,480 kw vis, 148 kw aur. ant 1,200t TL: N35 12 26 W85 16 52 On air date: Mar 8, 1970. 4411 Amnicola Hwy., Chattanooga, TN, 37406. Phone: (423) 629-0045. Fax: (423) 698-8557. Web Site: www.wtcitv.org. Licensee: The Greater Chattanooga PTV Corp. (acq 7-84). Population Served: 310,000 Natl. Network: PBS, . Washington Atty: Dow, Lohnes & Albertson.
Key Personnel:
Paul Grove . . . . . pres
Susan Cates . . . . . progmg VP
Kevin Lusk . . . . . pub affrs dir
Pam Carpenter . . . . . traf mgr

WTVC— Digital Channel: 9. Digital Hrs: 24 316 kw vis, 31.6 kw aur. ant 1,056t/246g TL: N35 09 38 W85 19 06 On air date: Feb 11, 1958. 4279 Benton Dr., Chattanooga, TN, 37406. Phone: (423) 756-5500. Fax: (423) 757-7400. Fax: (423) 757-7401.E-mail: news@newschannel9.com Web Site: www.newschannel9.com. Licensee: Freedom Broadcasting of Tennessee Licensee L.L.C. Group Owner: Freedom Broadcasting Inc. (acq 12-13-83; grpsl; 1-2-84). Population Served: 350,000 Natl. Network: ABC, . Natl. Rep: TeleRep,. Washington Atty: Latham & Watkins. News staff: 55; News: 32 hrs wkly.
Key Personnel:
Dennis W. Brown. . . . . opns mgr
Michael Costa . . . . . VP & gen mgr & natl sls mgr

Jackson, TN
(DMA 173)

WBBJ-TV— Digital Channel: 43.316 kw vis, 31.6 kw aur. ant 1,060t/1,065g TL: N35 38 15 W88 41 32 On air date: Mar 5, 1955. 346 Muse St., Jackson, TN, 38301. Phone: (731) 424-4515. Fax: (731) 424-9299. Web Site: www.wbbjtv.com. Licensee: Tennessee Broadcasting Partners. (acq 7-20-92). Population Served: 198,150 Natl. Network: ABC, .
Key Personnel:
Jerry Moore . . . . . gen mgr
Robert Fay . . . . . gen sls mgr
Anthony Matrisciano . . . . . progmg dir
Ken Galey . . . . . news dir
Randy McCaskill . . . . . chief of engrg

WJKT— Digital Channel: 39.4,680 kw vis, 468 kw aur. ant 1,056t/1,004g TL: N35 47 22 W89 06 14 On air date: Apr 16, 1985. 2701 Union Ave. Ext., Memphis, TN, 38112. Phone: (901) 323-2430. Fax: (901) 323-9503. Web Site: www.myeyewitnessnews.com. Licensee: Newport Television License LLC. Group Owner: Clear Channel Communications Inc. (acq 3-14-2008;. grpsl). Natl. Network: Fox, .
Key Personnel:
Jack Peck . . . . . gen mgr

***WLJT—** Digital Channel: 47. Digital Hrs: 17 316 kw vis, 63.1 kw aur. 640t/496g TL: N35 45 12 W88 36 10 On air date: Feb 1, 1968. Box 966, Martin, TN, 38237-0966. Clement Hall, U.T.-Martin, Martin, TN 38238. Phone: (731) 881-7561. Fax: (731) 881-7566.E-mail: wljt@wljt.org Web Site: www.wljt.org. Licensee: West Tennessee Public Television Council Inc. Population Served: 211,000 Natl. Network: PBS, .
Key Personnel:
Dave Hinman . . . . . CEO & gen mgr opns dir
Bud Grimes . . . . . pres
Monica Shumake. . . . . CFO
Emily Elliston . . . . . VP
Katrina Cobb . . . . . opns dir & prom dir
Shorri Puckett . . . . . dev dir
Robbie Green . . . . . mktg mgr

Knoxville, TN
(DMA 59)

WAGV— Digital Channel: 51.1,000 kw vis. ant 1,971t/460g TL: N36 48 00 W83 22 36 On air date: 2000. Box 1867, Abingdon, VA, 24212-1867. 8594 Hidden Valley Rd., Abingdon, VA 24210. Phone: (276) 676-3806. Fax: (276) 676-3572.E-mail: lisa@livingfaithtv.com Web Site: www.livingfaithtv.com. Licensee: Living Faith Ministries Inc. Ownership: Non-stock corporation.

Key Personnel:
Lisa Smith . . . . CFO & sls VP
Lisa C. Smith. . . . . sls dir
Michael D. Smith . . . . CEO & pres & mktg dir
Satellite of WLFG(TV) Grundy, VA.

WATE-TV— Digital Channel: 26. Digital Hrs: 24 930 kw vis. ant 1,736t/1,363g TL: N36 00 13 W83 56 34 On air date: Oct 1, 1953. Box 2349, Knoxville, TN, 37901. 1306 N.E. Broadway, Cave City, TN 37917. Phone: (865) 637-6666. Fax: (865) 525-4091. Web Site: www.wate.com. Licensee: WATE G.P. Group Owner: Young Broadcasting Inc. (acq 11-14-94; grpsl;9-12-94). Population Served: 174,587 Natl. Network: ABC, . Natl. Rep: Adam Young,. News staff: 50; News: 24 hrs wkly.
Key Personnel:
Tony Kahl . . . . stn mgr & gen sls mgr
Jan Wade . . . . progmg dir
Robb Atkinson . . . . news dir
Bill Evans. . . . . pub affrs dir
Bob Williams. chief of engrg

WBIR-TV— Digital Channel: 10. Digital Hrs: 24 316 kw vis, 38 kw aur. ant 1,791t/1,505g TL: N36 00 19 W83 56 23 On air date: Aug 13, 1956. 1513 Hutchison Ave., Knoxville, TN, 37917. Phone: (865) 637-1010. Fax: (865) 637-6280. Fax: (865) 637-6908.E-mail: wbir@wbir.gannett.com Web Site: www.wbir.com. Licensee: Gannett Pacific Corp. Group Owner: Gannett Broadcasting (acq 12-4-95; grpsl). Population Served: 1,252,000 Natl. Network: NBC, . Washington Atty: Wiley, Rein & Fielding. News staff: 50; News: 24 hrs wkly.
Key Personnel:
Jeff Lee . . . . pres & gen mgr progmg dir
Debbie Brizendine . . . . gen sls mgr
Julie Morris. . . . . prom dir
Bill Shory . . . . news dir
Gary Davis . . . . chief of engrg
Joy Davidson . . . . traf mgr

WBXX-TV— Digital Channel: 20. Digital Hrs: 24 652 kw vis. ant 2,411t/754g TL: N36 06 33 W84 20 17 On air date: Oct 4, 1997. 10427 Cogdill Rd., Suite 100, Knoxville, TN, 37932. Phone: (865) 777-9220. Fax: (865) 777-9221.E-mail: promotions@easttennesseecw.com Web Site: www.easttennesseecw.com. Licensee: Acme Television Licenses of Tennessee L.L.C. Group Owner: Acme Communications Inc. (acq 8-28-97; $13.2 million). Population Served: 5,381 Natl. Network: CW, . Natl. Rep: MMT,. Washington Atty: Dickstein Shapiro Morin & Oshinsky L.L.P.
Key Personnel:
Dan Phillippi. . . . . VP & gen mgr
Joanne Marcenkus . . . . gen sls mgr
Lisa Faulkner. . . . . progmg dir
Ferdy Guidry. chief of engrg
Anna Robins . . . . prom

***WETP-TV—** Digital Channel: 41. Digital Hrs: 17.5 100 kw vis, 20 kw aur. ant 1,760t/499g TL: N36 22 52 W83 10 48 On air date: Mar 15, 1967. 1611 E. Magnolia Ave., Knoxville, TN, 37917. Phone: (865) 595-0220. Fax: (865) 595-0300.E-mail: etptv.mail@etptv.org Web Site: www.etptv.org. Licensee: East Tennessee Public Communications Corp. (acq 10-1-83). Population Served: 1,800,000 Natl. Network: PBS, . Rgnl. Network: SECA.
Key Personnel:
Teresa James. . . . . pres & gen mgr
Frank Miller . . . . opns VP
Kelly Hodges . . . . dev dir & mktg dir
Evelyn Clarke . . . . prom mgr
Bob Hutchinson . . . . progmg dir
Chris Smith . . . . pub affrs dir & pub svc dir
Curtis Allin. . . . . chief of engrg

***WKOP-TV—** Digital Channel: 17. Digital Hrs: 17.5 2,240 kw vis, 224 kw aur. ant 1,683t/1,360g TL: N36 00 19 W83 56 23 On air date: Aug 15, 1990. 1611 E. Magnolia Ave., Knoxville, TN, 37917. Phone: (865) 595-0220. Fax: (865) 595-0300.E-mail: etptvmail@etptv.org Web Site: www.etptv.org. Licensee: East Tennessee Public Communications Corp. Natl. Network: PBS, . Rgnl. Network: SECA.
Key Personnel:
Teresa James . . . . pres
Jim Tindell . . . . gen mgr
Frank Miller . . . . opns VP
Kelly Hodges . . . . dev dir & mktg dir
Evelyn Clarke . . . . prom mgr
Bob Hutchinson . . . . progmg dir
Chris Smith . . . . pub affrs dir & pub svc dir
Curtis Allin. . . . . chief of engrg

WMAK— Digital Channel: 7.55 kw vis. ant 1,253t/1,017g TL: N36 00 36 W83 55 57 On air date: July 31, 2004. Box 612066, Dallas, TX, 75261. Phone: (817) 571-1229. Fax: (817) 571-7458. Web Site: www.daystar.com. Licensee: Word of God Fellowship Inc. Group Owner: (group owner). (acq 7-13-2009; $2 million). Washington Atty: Koerner & Olender.
Key Personnel:
Marcus D. Lamb . . . . pres

WPXK-TV— Digital Channel: 23. Digital Hrs: 24 1,000 kw vis. ant 1,735t/1,363g TL: N36 00 13 W83 56 34 On air date: Mar 12, 1991. Bldg. D, 9000 Executive Park Dr., Suite 300, Knoxville, TN, 37923. Phone: (865) 693-4343. Fax: (865) 251-4305. Web Site: www.ionline.tv. Licensee: ION Media Knoxville Licensee Inc., debtor-in-possession. Group Owner: Paxson Communications Corp. (acq 9-23-98). Population Served: 490,000 Natl. Network: ION Television, .
Key Personnel:
Carol Wright-Holzhauer . . . . VP
Holly Jones . . . . opns mgr

WTNZ— Digital Channel: 34. Digital Hrs: 24 930 kw vis. ant 1,729t/1,356g TL: N36 00 13 W83 56 34 On air date: Dec 31, 1983. Bldg. D, 9000 Executive Park Dr., Suite 300, Knoxville, TN, 37923. Phone: (865) 693-4343. Fax: (865) 691-6904. Fax: (865) 691-6770. Web Site: wtnzfox43.com. Licensee: Raycom America License Subsidiary LLC. Group Owner: Raycom Media Inc. (acq 1996; grpsl). Population Served: 534,410 Natl. Network: Fox, . Natl. Rep: TeleRep,. Washington Atty: Covington & Burling. News: 7 hrs wkly.
Key Personnel:
Paul McTear . . . . CEO & CFO
John Hayes . . . . gen mgr

WVLR— Digital Channel: 48.5,000 kw vis. ant 1,414t/280g TL: N36 15 30 W83 37 43 On air date: 2003. 306 Kyker Ferry Rd., Koduk, FL, 37764. Phone: (865) 932-4803. Fax: (865) 932-4102. Web Site: www.tv48.org. Licensee: Volunteer Christian Television Inc. (acq 4-22-2002).
Key Personnel:
Theron Woodward . . . . gen mgr
Scott Dunkel . . . . chief of engrg

WVLT-TV— Digital Channel: 30. Digital Hrs: 24 316 kw vis, 31.6 kw aur. ant 1,290t/1,073g TL: N36 00 36 W83 55 57 On air date: Dec 8, 1988. Box 59088, Knoxville, TN, 37950. 6450 Papermill Rd., Knoxville, TN 37919. Phone: (865) 450-8888. Fax: (865) 450-8869. Web Site: www.volunteertv.com. Licensee: Gray Television Licensee Inc. Group Owner: Gray Television Inc. (acq 1996; $165 million with WCTV(TV) Thomasville, GA). Population Served: 1,000,000 Natl. Network: CBS, MyNetworkTV, . Natl. Rep: Continental Television Sales,. News staff: 35; News: 24.5 hrs wkly.
Key Personnel:
Chris Baker . . . . CFO & exec VP gen mgr
Richard Torbett. gen sls mgr
Marty Parham . . . . progmg VP

Memphis, TN
(DMA 48)

WBUY-TV— Digital Channel: 41. Digital Hrs: 24 675 kw vis. ant 459t/469g TL: N34 59 20 W89 41 13 On air date: Sept 13, 1991. 3447 Cazassa Rd., Memphis, TN, 38116-3609. Phone: (901) 396-9541. Fax: (901) 396-9585.E-mail: wbuy@tbn.org Web Site: www.tbn.org. Licensee: Trinity Broadcasting Network. Group Owner: (group owner); (acq 5-8-2000; grpsl).
Key Personnel:
Tamela Calvin . . . . stn mgr
Cliff Pickell . . . . opns dir & progmg dir
Douglas Puryear . . . . chief of engrg

WHBQ-TV— Digital Channel: 13. Digital Hrs: 24 316 kw vis, 63.2 kw aur. ant 1,000t/1,076g TL: N35 10 28 W89 50 41 On air date: Sept 27, 1953. 485 S. Highland St., Memphis, TN, 38111. Phone: (901) 320-1313. Fax: (901) 323-0092. Fax: (901) 320-1366 (News). Web Site: www.myfoxmemphis.com. Licensee: Fox Television Stations Inc. Group Owner: (group owner; (acq 7-5-95; $80 million). Population Served: 1,135,000 Natl. Network: Fox, . Natl. Rep: Fox Stations Sales,. News staff: 55; News: 27 hrs wkly.
Key Personnel:
Rupert Murdoch . . . . chmn
Betsy Swanson . . . . CFO
John Koski . . . . gen mgr & progmg dir
Bill Lane . . . . gen sls mgr
Kim Moore . . . . natl sls mgr
Paul Sloan. . . . . prom dir & pub affrs dir
Ken Jobe . . . . news dir
David Brant . . . . chief of engrg

***WKNO—** Digital Channel: 29. Digital Hrs: 24 835 kw vis. ant 1,050t/1,020g TL: N35 09 16 W89 49 20 On air date: June 25, 1956. Box 241880, Memphis, TN, 38124-1880. 900 Getwell Rd., Memphis, TN 38111. Phone: (901) 458-2521. Fax: (901) 325-6505.E-mail: wknopi@wkno.org Web Site: www.wkno.org. Licensee: Mid-South Public Communications Foundation. Population Served: 1,600,000 Natl. Network: PBS, . Washington Atty: Schwartz, Woods & Miller.
Key Personnel:
Michael LaBonia . . . . CEO & pres
Russ A. Abernathy . . . . stn mgr
Charles McLarty . . . . dev dir

WLMT— Digital Channel: 31.5,000 kw vis, 500 kw aur. ant 1,000t/1,000g TL: N35 09 17 W89 49 20 On air date: April 1983. Clear Channel Television Ctr, 2701 Union Ext., Memphis, TN, 38112. Phone: (901) 323-2430. Fax: (901) 323-9503.E-mail: eyewitnessnews @upn30memphis.com Web Site: www.myeyewitnessnews.com. Licensee: Newport Television License LLC. Group Owner: Clear Channel Communications Inc. (acq 3-14-2008; grpsl). Population Served: 961,000 Natl. Network: CW, . Washington Atty: Covington & Burling.
Key Personnel:
Jim Doty . . . . gen sls mgr
Robyn Callaway. . . . . opns dir & rgnl sls mgr
Jim Turpin . . . . news dir

***WMAV-TV—** Digital Channel: 36. Digital Hrs: 24 225 kw vis,. ant 1,381t/1,276g TL: N34 17 28 W89 42 21 On air date: May 19, 1972. 3825 Ridgewood Rd., Jackson, MS, 39211. Phone: (601) 432-6565. Fax: (601) 432-6654. Fax: (601) 432-6311. Web Site: www.mpbonline.org. Licensee: Mississippi Authority for Educational TV. Population Served: 1,220,000 Natl. Network: PBS, . News staff: 4.
Key Personnel:
Marie Antoon . . . . gen mgr
Bob Buie. . . . . opns dir
Teresa Collier. . . . . news dir

WMC-TV— Digital Channel: 5. Digital Hrs: 24 100 kw vis, 20 kw aur. ant 1,010t/1,088g TL: N35 10 09 W89 53 12 On air date: Dec 11, 1948. 1960 Union Ave., Memphis, TN, 38104. Phone: (901) 726-0555. Fax: (901) 278-7633. Web Site: www.wmctvstations.com. Licensee: Raycom America License Subsidiary LLC. Group Owner: Raycom Media Inc. (acq 1997; grpsl). Population Served: 600,200 Natl. Network: NBC, . Natl. Rep: TeleRep,. Washington Atty: Goldberg, Godles, Wiener & Wright.
Key Personnel:
Howard Meagle . . . . VP
Lee Meridith . . . . gen mgr
Lee Meredith . . . . stn mgr
Gary Macko . . . . natl sls mgr
Jim Himes. . . . . rgnl sls mgr & mktg VP
Lori Beth Pickle . . . . mktg dir
Richard Enderwood . . . . prom dir
Peggy Phillip . . . . news dir

WPTY-TV— Digital Channel: 25.3,020 kw vis, 600.6 kw aur. ant 1,011t/1,043g TL: N35 12 11 W89 48 16 On air date: Sept 10, 1978. 2701 Union Ave. Ext., Memphis, TN, 38112. Phone: (901) 323-2430. Fax: (901) 323-9503. Web Site: www.myeyewitnessnews.com. Licensee: Newport Television License LLC. Group Owner: Clear Channel Communications Inc. (acq 3-14-2008; grpsl). Population Served: 961,000 Natl. Network: ABC, . Washington Atty: Covington & Burling. News staff: 50; News: 7 hrs wkly.

WPXX-TV— Digital Channel: 51. Digital Hrs: 24 5,000 kw vis, 500 kw aur. 800t/768g TL: N35 09 17 W89 49 20 On air date: October 1994. 7200 Goodlett Farm Pky, Ste 102, Cordova, TN, 38016. Phone: (901) 384-6650. Fax: (901) 388-8128. Web Site: www.my50memphis.com. Licensee: Flinn Broadcasting Corp. (acq 8-27-90; $220,000;11-19-90). Natl. Network: MyNetworkTV, .
Key Personnel:
Mitchell Maund . . . . gen mgr

WREG-TV— Digital Channel: 28.100 kw vis, 20 kw aur. 1,000t/1,077g TL: N35 10 52 W89 49 56 On air date: Jan 1, 1956. 803 Channel 3 Dr., Memphis, TN, 38103. Phone: (901) 543-2333. Fax: (901) 543-2198. Fax: (901) 543-2167 (news). Licensee: Local TV Tennessee License LLC. Group Owner: The New York Times Co. (acq 5-7-2007; grpsl). Population Served: 1,000,000 Natl. Network: CBS, . Natl. Rep: Eagle Television Sales,. Washington Atty: Koteen & Naftalin. Wire Svc: New York Times News Service News staff: 50.
Key Personnel:
Robert L. Lawrence . . . . pres
Ronald A. Walter . . . . gen mgr
Wes Pollard . . . . prom VP & prom dir
Bruce Moore . . . . news dir
Christine Di Stadio . . . . rsch dir
Laura Thompson. . . . . traf mgr
Maureen O'Connor . . . . pub svc dir
Norm Brewer . . . . news cmtr
Jim Jaggers. . . . . reporter
Austen Onek . . . . weather dir

***WTWV—** Digital Channel: 23.1,000 kw vis. ant 856t/869g TL: N35 12 34 W89 49 01 On air date: 2009. 6080 Mt. Moriah, Memphis, TN,

38115. Phone: (901) 485-3027. Web Site: www.goodnewstv23.com. Licensee: Christian Worldview Broadcasting Corp.. Ownership: Fred R. Flinn, 14.32%; Barbara A. Duncan-Cody, 14.28%; Benjamin Hooks, 14.28%; Arthur M. Townsend, 14.28%; George S. Flinn Jr., 14.28%; and Heidi Shafer, 14.28%.

Key Personnel:
Don Lawler. gen mgr

Nashville, TN (DMA 29)

***WCTE—** Digital Channel: 22. Digital Hrs: 24 1,320 kw vis, 77.6 kw aur. 1,394t/804g TL: N36 10 26 W85 20 37 On air date: Aug 21, 1978. Box 2040, Cookeville, TN, 38502. 1151 Stadium Dr.,Ste 104, Cookeville, TN 38501. Phone: (931) 528-2222. Fax: (931) 372-6284.E-mail: info@wcte.org Web Site: www.wcte.org. Licensee: Upper Cumberland Broadcast Council. (acq 12-20-85;11-18-85). Population Served: 385,000 Natl. Network: PBS, .

Key Personnel:
Becky Magura . . . . pres & gen mgr
Donna Castle. . . . . dev dir & progmg dir

WHTN— Digital Channel: 38.5,000 kw vis, 500 kw aur. ant 820t/391g TL: N36 04 54 W86 25 57 On air date: Dec 30, 1983. 9582 Lebanon Rd., Mt. Juliet, TN, 37122. Phone: (615) 754-0039. Fax: (615) 754-0047.E-mail: info@nashville39.com Web Site: www.ctnonline.com. Licensee: Christian Television Network Inc. Ownership: David C. Gibbs III, 20%; Jimmy Smith, 20%; Robert D'Andrea, 20%; Virginia Oliver, 20%; and Wayne Wetzel, 20%. Washington Atty: Gammon & Grange. Foreign lang progmg: SpanishS 0 News staff: one; News: 2 hrs wkly.

Key Personnel:
Monica Schmelter. . . . . gen mgr & stn mgr

WJFB— Digital Channel: 44. Digital Hrs: 24 2,240 kw vis. ant 528t/259g TL: N36 09 13 W86 22 46 On air date: 1989. 200 E. Spring St., Lebanon, TN, 37087. Phone: (615) 444-8206. Fax: (615) 444-7592.E-mail: bclinic@bellsouth.net Licensee: Bryant Broadcasting Inc. Ownership: Joe Bryant, 100%. Population Served: l,500,000 News staff: 2; News: 4 hrs wkly.

Key Personnel:
Dr. Joe Bryant . . . . pres
Pat Bryant . . . . gen mgr

WKRN-TV— Digital Channel: 27. Digital Hrs: 24 100 kw vis, 10 kw aur. 1,350t/942g TL: N36 02 49 W86 49 49 On air date: Nov 29, 1953. 441 Murfreesboro Rd., Nashville, TN, 37210. Phone: (615) 369-7222. Fax: (615) 369-7388. Web Site: www.wkrn.com. Licensee: WKRN G.P. Group Owner: Young Broadcasting Inc. (acq 4-17-89; $42 million; 5-8-89). Population Served: 1,844,000 Natl. Network: ABC, . Natl. Rep: Adam Young,. Washington Atty: Wiley, Rein & Fielding. News staff: 45; News: 25 hrs wkly.

Key Personnel:
Gwen Kinsey . . . . pres & gen mgr
Steve Watt . . . . gen sls mgr
Mike Tarrolley . . . . mktg dir & pub svc dir
Michele Dube . . . . progmg dir
Matthew Zelkind. . . . . news dir
Dave Parker . . . . chief of engrg

WNAB— Digital Channel: 23. Digital Hrs: 24 3,250 kw vis. ant 1,393t/1,193g TL: N36 15 50 W86 47 39 On air date: Nov 29, 1995. 2994 Sidco Dr., Nashville, TN, 37204. Phone: (615) 650-5858. Fax: (615) 650-5859. Web Site: www.cw58.net. Licensee: Nashville License Holdings LLC. Ownership: Michael Lambert, mgng member. (acq 10-14-98; $30 million). Natl. Network: CW, .

Key Personnel:
Michael Lambert . . . . pres
Michael Jones . . . . CFO
Mark Dillion. . . . . stn mgr
DeJuan Buford . . . . gen sls mgr
Dale Bukowski. . . . . natl sls mgr & rgnl sls mgr
Lee Scott. . . . . prom mgr
Michael Hook . . . . progmg mgr
Patty Daugherty . . . . traf mgr

***WNPT—** Digital Channel: 8.295 kw vis, 29.5 kw aur. 1,280t/832 TL: N36 02 49 W86 49 49 On air date: Sept 10, 1962. 161 Rains Ave., Nashville, TN, 37203. Phone: (615) 259-9325. Fax: (615) 248-6120.E-mail: tv8@wnpt.net Web Site: www.wnpt.net. Licensee: Nashville Public Television Inc. Population Served: 1500000 Natl. Network: PBS, . Washington Atty: Schwartz, Woods & Miller.

Key Personnel:
Steven M. Bass . . . . CEO
Beth Curley . . . . pres & sr VP chief of opns
Charles Brimbelow . . . . VP
Justin Harvey. . . . . progmg dir

WNPX-TV— Digital Channel: 36. Digital Hrs: 24 733 kw vis, 73.3 kw aur. ant 1,406t/1,250g TL: N36 16 04 W86 47 44 On air date: Sept 3, 1993. 1281 N. Mt. Juliet Rd., Suite K, Mt. Juliet, TN, 37122. Phone: (615) 773-6100. Fax: (615) 726-2854. Fax: (615) 773-6106. Web Site: www.ionline.tv. Licensee: ION Media License Co. LLC, debtor-in-possession. Group Owner: Paxson Communications Corp. (acq 9-4-97; $4.3 million). Population Served: 2,474,000 Natl. Network: ION Television, .

Key Personnel:
Lowell "Bud" Paxson . . . . CEO
Tim Cooke . . . . engr

WPGD-TV— Digital Channel: 33. Digital Hrs: 24 1,000 kw vis. ant 1,351t/1,194g TL: N36 16 05 W86 47 45 On air date: Sept 23, 1992. 36 Music Village Blvd., Hendersonville, TN, 37075. Phone: (615) 822-1243. Fax: (615) 822-1642. Web Site: www.tbn.org. Licensee: Trinity Broadcasting Network. Group Owner: (group owner; (acq 7-2000; grpsl). Population Served: 700,000

Key Personnel:
Russell Hall . . . . gen mgr
Allen Partlow. . . . . chief of engrg

WSMV-TV— Digital Channel: 10.100 kw vis, 10 kw aur. 1,424t/1,382g TL: N36 08 27 W86 51 56 On air date: Sept 30, 1950. 5700 Knob Rd., Nashville, TN, 37209. Phone: (615) 353-2231. Fax: (615) 353-2375. Web Site: www.wsmv.com. Licensee: Meredith Corp. Group Owner: Meredith Broadcasting Group, Meredith Corp. (acq 11-1-94; $159 million;12-5-94). Population Served: 823,540 Natl. Network: NBC, . Natl. Rep: TeleRep,. Washington Atty: Wilmer, Cutler & Pickering.

Key Personnel:
Elden Hale. . . . . gen mgr

WTVF— Digital Channel: 5. Digital Hrs: 24 100 kw vis, 10 kw aur. 1,394t/1,138g TL: N36 16 05 W86 47 16 On air date: Aug 6, 1954. 474 James Robertson Pkwy., Nashville, TN, 37219. Phone: (615) 244-5000. Fax: (615) 248-5353. Fax: TWX: 810-371-1168.E-mail: news@newschannel5.com Web Site: www.newschannel5.com. Licensee: NewsChannel 5 Network LP. Group Owner: Landmark Communications Inc. (acq 9-12-91; $46 million;9-30-91). Population Served: 2,268,000 Natl. Network: CBS, . Washington Atty: Hogan & Hartson. News: 24 hrs wkly.

Key Personnel:
Debbie Turner . . . . gen mgr
Mark Binda. progmg dir
Mike Cutler. . . . . news dir

WUXP-TV— Digital Channel: 21. Digital Hrs: 24 5,000 kw vis, 500 kw aur. ant 1,417t/1,217g TL: N36 15 50 W86 47 39 On air date: Feb 18, 1984. 631 Mainstream Dr., Nashville, TN, 37228. Phone: (615) 259-5630. Fax: (615) 259-3962. Web Site: www.mytv30web.com. Licensee: WUXP Licensee LLC. Group Owner: Sinclair Broadcast Group Inc. (acq 12-10-2001; $2.829 million). Natl. Network: MyNetworkTV, . Washington Atty: Arter & Hadden.

Key Personnel:
Stephen A. Mann . . . . gen mgr
Mark Dillon . . . . stn mgr
Pam Combest . . . . sls dir
Dejuan Buford . . . . gen sls mgr
Dale Bukowski . . . . natl sls mgr
Greg Carr. rgnl sls mgr
Lee R. Scott. . . . . . mktg dir & prom dir adv dir & progmg dir
Deborah Williams . . . . prom mgr & adv mgr
Iman Tate. . . . . progmg mgr
Lee Peterson . . . . pub affrs dir
Gibson Prichard . . . . engrg mgr
David Birdsong . . . . chief of engrg

WZTV— Digital Channel: 15. Digital Hrs: 24 3,240 kw vis, 324 kw aur. ant 1,161t/1,063g TL: N36 08 27 W86 51 56 (CP: ant 1,407t/1,207g. TL: N36 15 50 W86 47 39) On air date: March 1976. 631 Mainstream Dr., Nashville, TN, 37228. Phone: (615) 259-5617. Fax: (615) 259-3962.E-mail: comments@wztv.com Web Site: www.wztv.com. Licensee: WZTV Licensee LLC. Group Owner: Sinclair Broadcast Group Inc. (acq 12-10-01; grpsl). Population Served: 2,167,000 Natl. Network: Fox, . Washington Atty: Arter & Hadden. News staff: 9; News: 7 hrs wkly.

Key Personnel:
Steve Mann . . . . gen mgr & stn mgr
Pamela Minnicks . . . . gen sls mgr
Beckey Dan . . . . prom dir
David Birdsong . . . . chief of engrg
Kelly Shields . . . . traf mgr
Randy Keys . . . . film dir
Laura Faber . . . . news cmtr
Tim Ross . . . . weather dir

Tri-Cities, TN-VA (DMA 92)

WCYB-TV— Digital Channel: 5. Digital Hrs: 24 83.2 kw vis, 10.6 kw aur. ant 2,230t/90g TL: N36 26 57 W82 06 31 On air date: Aug 13, 1956. 101 Lee St., Bristol, VA, 24201. Phone: (276)-645-1555. Fax: (276) 645-1513.E-mail: news@wcyb.tv Web Site: www.wcyb.tv. Licensee: BlueStone License Holdings Inc. Group Owner: Lamco Communications Inc. (acq 5-31-2007; grpsl). Population Served: 725,000 Natl. Network: NBC, CW, Fox, . Washington Atty: Covington & Burling LLP.

Key Personnel:
Jim McKerman . . . . VP
Jim Martin . . . . gen mgr

WEMT— Digital Channel: 38. Digital Hrs: 24 3,020 kw vis, 302 kw aur. ant 2,609t/143g TL: N36 01 24 W82 42 56 On air date: Nov 8, 1985. Box 3489 CRS, Johnson City, TN, 37602-3489. 3206 Hanover Rd., Johnson City, TN 37602-3489. Phone: (423) 283-3900. Fax: (423) 283-4938. Web Site: www.wemt39.com. Licensee: Esteem License Holdings Inc. Group Owner: Sinclair Broadcast Group Inc. (acq 5-31-2007; for stock). Natl. Network: Fox, . Washington Atty: Shaw, Pittman.

Key Personnel:
Leesa Wilcher . . . . gen mgr & gen sls mgr
Amy McClary . . . . rgnl sls mgr
Jim Hartline . . . . chief of engrg
Rebecca Berry . . . . traf mgr

WJHL-TV— Digital Channel: 11. Digital Hrs: 24 245 kw vis, 30 kw aur. 2,320t/228g TL: N36 25 55 W82 08 15 On air date: Oct 26, 1953. Box 1130, Johnson City, TN, 37605. 338 E. Main St., Johnson City, TN 37601. Phone: (423) 926-2151. Fax: (423) 434-4537.E-mail: jdempsey@wjhl.com Web Site: www.wjhl.com. Licensee: Media General Broadcasting Inc. Group Owner: Media General Broadcast Group (acq 3-21-97; grpsl). Population Served: 267,200 Natl. Network: CBS, . Natl. Rep: Harrington, Righter & Parsons,. Washington Atty: Dow, Lohnes and Albertson.

Key Personnel:
Jack Dempsey . . . . gen mgr & film buyer
Lisa Wilcher . . . . gen sls mgr
Ed Oliver. . . . . mktg dir
Christine Riser . . . . news dir
Mike Moore . . . . chief of engrg
Kenny Hawkins . . . . sports cmtr
Mark Reynolds . . . . weather dir

WKPT-TV— Digital Channel: 27. Digital Hrs: 24 1,260 kw vis, 42 kw aur. ant 2,320t/225g TL: N36 25 54 W82 08 15 On air date: Aug 20, 1969. 222 Commerce St., Kingsport, TN, 37660. Phone: (423) 246-9578. Fax: (423) 246-6261/(423) 246-1863.E-mail: gdevault@hvbc.com Web Site: www.wkpttv.com. Licensee: Holston Valley Broadcasting Corp.. Ownership: Glenwood Communications Corp, 100%. Group Owner: Glenwood Communications Corp. Population Served: 322,000 Natl. Network: ABC, . Natl. Rep: Harrington, Righter & Parsons,. Washington Atty: Dennis J. Kelly.

Key Personnel:
George E. DeVault Jr. . . . . pres & gen mgr
Bette Lawson . . . . CFO
Lamar Reid . . . . gen sls mgr
Fred Falin . . . . progmg dir

WLFG— Digital Channel: 49. Digital Hrs: 24 1,150 kw vis, 115 kw aur. ant 2,503t TL: N36 49 47 W82 04 45 On air date: 1995. Box 1867, Abingdon, VA, 24212. Phone: (276) 676-3806. Fax: (276) 676-3572.E-mail: mike@livingfaithtelevision.com Web Site: www.lstv.com. Licensee: Living Faith Ministries Inc. (acq 12-21-2005).

Key Personnel:
Michael D. Smith . . . . CEO & chmn
Michael D. Smith . . . . pres
Lisa Smith . . . . VP & progmg VP pub svc dir & local news ed
Michael D. Smith . . . . gen mgr
Wade McGeorge . . . . sls dir
Wayne Price . . . . engrg mgr
Sue Howington . . . . traf mgr

***WMSY-TV—** Digital Channel: 42. Digital Hrs: 24 755 kw vis, 115 kw aur. 1,360t/247g TL: N36 54 01 W81 32 35 On air date: Aug 1, 1981. Blue Ridge PBS, 1215 McNeil Dr. S.W., Roanoke, VA, 24015. Phone: (540) 344-0991. Fax: (540) 344-2148.E-mail: info@blueridgepbs.org Web Site: www.brptv.com. Licensee: Blue Ridge Public Television Inc. Natl. Network: PBS, .

Key Personnel:
Edwin Whitmore . . . . chmn
Anita Sims . . . . CFO
Beverly Fitzpatrick Jr. . . . . exec VP
Jack K. Neal. . . . . CEO & pres & gen mgr

***WSBN-TV—** Digital Channel: 32. Digital Hrs: 24 690 kw vis, 61.7 kw aur. 1,940t/242g TL: N36 53 52 W82 37 22 On air date: Mar 29, 1971. Blue Ridge PBS, 1215 McNeil Dr. S.W., Roanoke, VA, 24032. Phone: (540) 344-0991. Fax: (540) 344-2148.E-mail: info@blueridgepbs.org Web Site: www.brptv.com. Licensee: Blue Ridge Public Television Inc. Natl. Network: PBS, .

Key Personnel:
Beverly Fitzpatrick . . . . . chmn & exec VP
Jack Neal . . . . . gen mgr
Barbara Spencer . . . . . pub affrs dir
Erwin Roman . . . . . engrg VP & chief of engrg

Texas

Abilene-Sweetwater, TX
(DMA 165)

KPCB— Digital Channel: 17.464 kw vis. ant 443t TL: N32 46 52 W100 53 52 On air date: 1997. Box 61000, Midland, TX, 79711-1000. 88 E. County Rd. 112, Snyder, TX 79549. Phone: (800) 707-0420. Fax: (325) 573-9417.E-mail: info@ptcbglc.com Web Site: www.godslearningchannel.com. Licensee: Prime Time Christian Broadcasting Inc.
Key Personnel:
Jeff Tveit. . . . . gen mgr

KRBC-TV— Analog Channel: 9. Digital Channel: 29.1,000 kw vis. ant 846t/30g TL: N32 16 38 W99 35 51 On air date: Aug 31, 1953. Box 5309, Abilene, TX, 79608. Phone: (325) 692-4242. Fax: (325) 695-9922.E-mail: ksbcnews@krbc.tv Web Site: www.krbc.tv. Licensee: Mission Broadcasting Inc. Group Owner: (group owner; (acq 6-13-2003; $10 million with KSAN-TV San Angelo). Population Served: 1,000,000 Natl. Network: NBC, . Washington Atty: Hogan & Hartson.
Key Personnel:
David Smith. . . . . CEO & CFO
Eric Thomas . . . . . gen mgr
Justin Riggar . . . . . gen sls mgr
Tom Vodak. . . . . news dir

KTAB-TV— Analog Channel: 32. Digital Channel: 24. Analog Hrs: 24 1,000 kw vis. ant 846t/620g TL: N32 16 38 W99 35 51 On air date: Oct 6, 1979. Box 5309, Abilene, TX, 79608. 4510 S. 14th St., Abilene, TX 79605. Phone: (915) 695-2777. Fax: (915) 691-5822.E-mail: news@ktab.tv Web Site: bigcountryhomepage.com. Licensee: Nexstar Finance Inc. Group Owner: Nexstar Broadcasting Group Inc. (acq 8-15-99; $16.7 million). Population Served: 106,900 Natl. Network: CBS, . News staff: 12; News: 8 hrs wkly.
Key Personnel:
Eric Thomas . . . . . gen mgr

KTXS-TV—(Sweetwater, Digital Channel: 20. Digital Hrs: 24 316 kw vis, 31.6 kw aur. ant 1,400t/1,069g TL: N32 24 48 W100 06 25 On air date: Jan 30, 1956. Box 2997, Abilene, TX, 79604. 4420 N. Clack, Abilene, TX 79601. Phone: (325) 677-2281. Fax: (325) 676-9231. Web Site: www.ktxs.com. Licensee: BlueStone License Holdings Inc. Group Owner: Lamco Communications Inc. (acq 5-31-2007; grpsl). Population Served: 230,100 Natl. Network: ABC, CW, .
Key Personnel:
Jackie Rutledge . . . . . VP & gen mgr
Jorge Montoya . . . . . gen sls mgr & film buyer
David Caldwell. . . . . prom mgr
Sylvia Holmes . . . . . progmg dir
Iain Munro . . . . . news dir
Leland Ohlhausen. . . . . chief of engrg

KXVA— Digital Channel: 15. Digital Hrs: 24 165 kw vis. ant 978t/769g TL: N32 16 31 W99 35 23 On air date: Jan 17, 2001. 500 Chestnut, Ste. 804, Abilene, TX, 79602. Phone: (325) 672-5606. Fax: (325) 676-2437. Web Site: www.kxvafox.com. Licensee: Sage Broadcasting Corp. (acq 1-26-2005). Population Served: 364,000 Natl. Network: Fox, . Natl. Rep: Millennium Sales & Marketing,. Washington Atty: Fletcher, Heard and Hildreth0.
Key Personnel:
Bill Carter . . . . . pres
Bujuan McCoy . . . . . gen mgr
Rebroadcasts KIDY(TV) San Angelo 98%.

Amarillo, TX
(DMA 131)

***KACV-TV—** Digital Channel: 8. Digital Hrs: 24 5 kw vis. ant 1,702t/1,580g TL: N35 22 30 W101 52 56 On air date: Aug 29, 1988. Box 447, Amarillo, TX, 79178. 2408 S. Jackson, Amarillo, TX 79178. Phone: (806) 371-5222. Fax: (806) 371-5258.E-mail: kacvtv@actx.edu Web Site: www.kacvtv.org. Licensee: Amarillo Junior College District. Population Served: 400,000 Natl. Network: PBS, . Washington Atty: Cohn & Marks LLP.
Key Personnel:
Jackie Smith. . . . . opns mgr
Joli Lindseth. . . . . dev dir
Michelle Macon . . . . . dev mgr
Ellen Robertson Neal . . . . . pub affrs dir

KAMR-TV— Digital Channel: 19.100 kw vis, 10 kw aur. ant 1,420t/1,440g TL: N35 18 52 W101 50 47 On air date: Mar 18, 1953. Box 751, 1015 S. Fillmore St., Amarillo, TX, 79101. Phone: (806) 383-3321. Fax: (806) 381-2943.E-mail: nbc4@kamr.com Web Site: www.kamr.com. Licensee: Nexstar Finance Inc. Group Owner: Nexstar Broadcasting Group Inc. (acq 12-31-03; grpsl). Population Served: 432,300 Natl. Network: NBC, . Washington Atty: Arter & Hadden.
Key Personnel:
Mark McKay . . . . . gen mgr & progmg dir
Sherry Avara. . . . . gen sls mgr
Heather Brunson . . . . . rgnl sls mgr
Amanda Bustamane . . . . . prom mgr
NyLynn Nichols . . . . . news dir
Ken High . . . . . chief of engrg
Lori Kimber. . . . . traf mgr
Cindy Perez . . . . . pub svc dir
Dennis de la Pena . . . . . sports cmtr
Steve McCauley . . . . . weather dir

KCIT— Digital Channel: 15. Digital Hrs: 24 1,280 kw vis, 128 kw aur. 1,521t/1,463g TL: N35 20 33 W101 49 20 On air date: Oct 1, 1982. Box 1414, Amarillo, TX, 79105. 1015 S. Fillmore, Amarillo, TX 79101. Phone: (806) 374-1414. Fax: (806) 349-9083. Web Site: fox14.tv. Licensee: Mission Broadcasting Inc. Group Owner: (group owner; (acq 1999; $28.5 million with KJTL(TV) Wichita Falls). Population Served: 473,000 Natl. Network: Fox, . Natl. Rep: Blair Television,. Washington Atty: Drinker Biddle & Reath L.L.P. News: 3 hrs wkly.
Key Personnel:
Amanda Bustamante . . . . . gen mgr & stn mgr
Deb York . . . . . rgnl sls mgr
Mike Crowell . . . . . mktg dir
Jim O'Malley . . . . . progmg dir
Wesley Willson . . . . . chief of engrg

***KENW—** Digital Channel: 32. Digital Hrs: 24 100 kw vis, 20 kw aur. ant 1,150t/1,085g TL: N33 33 19 W103 39 03 On air date: Sept 1, 1974. Eastern New Mexico Univ., 52 Broadcast Ctr., Portales, NM, 88130. Phone: (505) 562-2112. Fax: (505) 562-2590.E-mail: kenwtv@enmu.edu Web Site: www.kenw.org. Licensee: Regents of Eastern New Mexico University. Population Served: 400,000 Natl. Network: PBS, . Washington Atty: Dow, Lohnes & Albertson, PLLC. Wire Svc: AP Foreign lang progmg: SpanishS 1 News staff: 2; News: 3 hrs wkly.
Key Personnel:
Steven Gamble. . . . . pres
Ronnie Birdsong. . . . . VP
Duane Ryan . . . . . gen mgr
Rena Garrett . . . . . mktg dir & mktg mgr
Linda Stefanovic. . . . . progmg dir
John Kirby . . . . . news dir
Don Criss. . . . . pub affrs dir
Jeff Burmeister . . . . . chief of engrg

KEYU— Digital Channel: 31.700 kw vis. ant 1,002t/965g TL: N35 20 33 W101 49 20 On air date: 2004. 1616 S. Kentucky, Suite D-130, Amarillo, TX, 79102. Phone: (806) 359-8900. Fax: (806) 352-8912. Web Site: www.univision-amarillo.com. Licensee: Borger Broadcasting Inc., debtor in possession. Group Owner: Equity Broadcasting Corp. Natl. Network: Univision (Spanish), . Foreign lang progmg: SpanishS 168
Key Personnel:
Jim MacDonald . . . . . gen mgr

KFDA-TV— Digital Channel: 10. Digital Hrs: 24 316 kw vis, 31.6 kw aur. 1,572t/1,493g TL: N35 17 34 W101 50 42 On air date: Apr 4, 1953. Box 10, Amarillo, TX, 79105-0010. 7900 Broadway, Amarillo, TX 79108. Phone: (806) 383-1010. Phone: (806) 383-6397. Fax: (806) 381-9859. Web Site: www.newschannel10.com. Licensee: Panhandle Telecasting Co. Group Owner: R.H. Drewry Group (acq 10-4-76; $3 million;9-13-76). Population Served: 548,000 Natl. Network: CBS, . Washington Atty: Shaw Pittman. Wire Svc: AP News staff: 32; News: 19.5 hrs wkly.
Key Personnel:
Bill Drewry . . . . . pres
Larry Patton . . . . . sr VP
Brent McClure . . . . . VP & gen mgr
Richard Fulkerson . . . . . opns mgr
Joyce Austin . . . . . gen sls mgr & natl sls mgr rgnl sls mgr
Tony Smitherman . . . . . mktg dir
Tim Cato . . . . . prom mgr
Shawn Venhaus. . . . . news dir
Tim Winn . . . . . chief of engrg
Tonya Triveno. . . . . traf mgr
Jake Riddell . . . . . sports cmtr
Dave Oliver . . . . . weather dir

KPTF— Digital Channel: 18.5,000 kw vis. ant 331t TL: N34 21 48 W103 13 05 On air date: 2002. Box 61000, Midland, TX, 79711-1000. Phone: (800) 707-0420. Fax: (432) 563-1736.E-mail: info@ptcbglc.com Web Site: www.GLC.US.com. Licensee: Prime Time Christian Broadcasting Inc. (acq 12-23-99).
Key Personnel:
Al Cooper . . . . . gen mgr

KVIH-TV— Analog Channel: 12. Digital Channel: 20. Analog Hrs: 4-9:37 PM (M-F); 6 AM-9:37 PM (S, Su) 178 kw vis, 35.3 kw aur. ant 670t/719g TL: N34 11 34 W103 16 44 On air date: December 1957. One Broadcast Ctr., Amarillo, TX, 79101. Phone: (806) 373-1787. Fax: (806) 371-7329.E-mail: info@kvii.com Web Site: www.kvii.com. Licensee: Barrington Broadcasting Texas Corp. Group Owner: New Vision Group LLC (acq 8-2-2005; $22.5 million with KVII-TV Amarillo, TX). Natl. Network: ABC, . Washington Atty: Wiley, Rein & Fielding.
Key Personnel:
K. James Yager . . . . . pres
Mac Douglas . . . . . VP
Lynn Fairbanks . . . . . gen mgr & gen sls mgr
Keith Workman. . . . . rgnl sls mgr
Curtis Weaver . . . . . prom mgr
Paula Harris . . . . . progmg dir
Bill Canady . . . . . chief of engrg
Margaret Burris . . . . . traf mgr
Audra Yeager. . . . . pub svc dir
Bryan White . . . . . film dir
Lee Baker . . . . . sports cmtr
Steve Kersh . . . . . weather dir
Satellite of KVII-TV Amarillo, TX.

KVII-TV— Digital Channel: 7. Digital Hrs: 24 316 kw vis, 31.6 kw aur. ant 1,703t/1,626g TL: N35 22 29 W101 52 58 On air date: Nov 1, 1957. One Broadcast Ctr., Amarillo, TX, 79101. Phone: (806) 373-1787. Fax: (806) 371-7329.E-mail: info@kvii.com Web Site: www.kvii.com. Licensee: Barrington Broadcasting Texas Corp. Group Owner: New Vision Group LLC (acq 8-2-2005; $22.5 million with KVIH-TV Clovis, NM). Population Served: 262,200 Natl. Network: ABC, CW, . Washington Atty: Wiley, Rein & Fielding. Foreign lang progmg: SpanishS 2 News: 36 hrs wkly.
Key Personnel:
K. James Yager . . . . . pres
Lyn Fairbanks. . . . . gen mgr
Dusty Green . . . . . opns dir & opns mgr news dir
Connie Mosley. . . . . gen sls mgr & rgnl sls mgr
Bill Canady . . . . . chief of engrg

Austin, TX
(DMA 49)

KEYE-TV— Digital Channel: 43. Digital Hrs: 24 2,510 kw vis, 251 kw aur. ant 1,290t/1,299g TL: N30 19 10 W97 48 06 On air date: Dec 4, 1983. 10700 Metric Blvd., Austin, TX, 78758. Phone: (512) 835-0042. Fax: (512) 837-6753. Web Site: www.keyetv.com. Licensee: Austin TV Licensee Corp. Group Owner: Viacom Television Stations Group (acq 11-21-2007; grpsl). Natl. Network: CBS, . Natl. Rep: TeleRep,. Washington Atty: Wiley Rein LLP. News staff: 50; News: 20 hrs wkly.
Key Personnel:
Amy Villarreal. . . . . VP & gen mgr stn mgr
Dusty Granberry . . . . . opns mgr
Jeff Stern . . . . . sls dir
Fred Undstrom . . . . . natl sls mgr
Lee Maaz. . . . . rgnl sls mgr
Stan Teater . . . . . prom mgr
Gary Vinson. . . . . progmg mgr
Suzanne Black . . . . . news dir
Art Smith . . . . . chief of engrg
Mike Smith . . . . . traf mgr
Rush Evans . . . . . film dir
Andy Liscano. . . . . sports cmtr
Cliff Morrison . . . . . weather dir

***KLRU—** Digital Channel: 22.700 kw vis. ant 1,173t/1,124g TL: N30 19 19 W97 48 12 On air date: May 4, 1979. 2504 B Whitis St., Austin, TX, 78712. Phone: (512) 471-4811. Fax: (512) 475-9090. Web Site: www.klru.org. Licensee: Capital of Texas Public Telecomm. Natl. Network: PBS, . Washington Atty: Cohn & Marks.
Key Personnel:
Bill Stotesbery. . . . . CEO & CEO pres
Pat Wertz. . . . . CFO
Dick Peterson. . . . . exec VP & opns VP
Karin Morrison . . . . . VP
Bill Statesbury . . . . . gen mgr
Lori Holliday. . . . . dev VP
Ed Bailey . . . . . sls VP
Maury Sullivan . . . . . mktg VP & adv VP
Cheryl Sawyer . . . . . prom VP
Maria Rodriguez . . . . . progmg VP
David Kuipers . . . . . engrg VP

KNVA— Digital Channel: 49.5,000 kw vis. ant 1,227t/1,109g TL: N30 19 33 W97 47 58 On air date: Aug 1, 1994. 908 W. MLK Jr. Blvd,

Calgary, TX, 78701. 908 W. Martin Luther King Blvd., Austin, TX 78701. Phone: (512) 478-5400. Fax: (512) 476-1520. Web Site: www.thecwaustin.com. Licensee: 54 Broadcasting Inc. Ownership: Diane Levy, 25%; Frank Goldberg, 25%; Mark Goldberg, 25%; and Richard Goldberg, 25% (acq 6-10-2004). Natl. Network: CW, .

Key Personnel:

Eric Lassberg	gen mgr
Denise Daniels	gen sls mgr
Bryan Hastings	natl sls mgr
Amy Coplen	rgnl sls mgr
Tish Saliani	prom dir
Jamie Aragon	progmg dir & traf mgr
Michael Fabac	news dir
Mark Dunham	engrg dir

KTBC— Digital Channel: 7. Digital Hrs: 24 316 kw vis, 31.6 kw aur. ant 1,261t/1,114g TL: N30 18 36 W97 47 33 On air date: Nov 27, 1952. 119 E. 10th St., Austin, TX, 78701. Phone: (512) 476-7777. Fax: (512) 495-7060.E-mail: management@fox7.com Web Site: www.myfoxaustin.com. Licensee: KTBC License Inc. Group Owner: Fox Television Stations Inc. (acq 1-97). Population Served: 1,152,000 Natl. Network: Fox, . News staff: 54; News: 24 hrs wkly.

Key Personnel:

Mark Rodman	VP & gen mgr
Scott Moore	gen sls mgr
Kathie Smith	mktg VP & prom VP prom dir
Holly Morrison-Breaux	progmg dir
Pam Vaught	news dir
Rob Cunningham	pub affrs dir
Ken Smith	chief of engrg
Karen McCarty	rsch dir
Gloria Frazier	traf mgr
Dave Cody	sports cmtr
Scott Fisher	weather dir

KVUE— Digital Channel: 33. Digital Hrs: 24 1,950 kw vis, 327 kw aur. 1,270t/1,184g TL: N30 19 20 W97 48 10 On air date: Sept 12, 1971. Box 9927, Austin, TX, 78766. 3201 Steck Ave., Austin, TX 78757. Phone: (512) 459-6521. Fax: (512) 533-2215.E-mail: listens@kvue.com Web Site: www.kvue.com. Licensee: KVUE Television Inc. Group Owner: Belo Corp., Broadcast Division (acq 6-1-99; swap with KXTV(TV) Sacramento, CA). Population Served: 1,152,300 Natl. Network: ABC, . Natl. Rep: Harrington, Righter & Parsons,. News: 29.5.

Key Personnel:

Patti C. Smith	pres & VP & gen mgr

KXAM-TV— Digital Channel: 27.3,236 kw vis, 324 kw aur. 883t/459g TL: N30 40 36 W98 33 59 On air date: Sept 6, 1991. 908 W. Martin Luther King Jr. Blvd., Austin, TX, 78701. 908 W. Martin Luther King Jr. Blvd., Austin, TX 78701. Phone: (512) 476-3636. Fax: (512) 476-1520. Fax: (512) 469-0630. Web Site: www.kxam.com. Licensee: KXAN Inc. Group Owner: LIN Television Corp. Natl. Network: NBC, .

Key Personnel:

Eric Lassberg	gen mgr
Todd Krauss	opns dir
Denise Daniels	gen sls mgr
Amy Coplen	natl sls mgr
Tish Saliani	prom dir
Michael Fabac	news dir
Mark Dunham	engrg dir

KXAN-TV— Digital Channel: 21. Digital Hrs: 24 2,000 kw vis, 200 kw aur. ant 1,268t/1,168g TL: N30 19 33 W97 47 58 On air date: Feb 12, 1965. 908 W. Martin Luther King Blvd., Calgary, TX, 78701. 908 W. Martin Luther King Blvd., Austin, TX, 78701. Phone: (512) 476-3636. Fax: (512) 476-1520. Fax: (512) 469-0630. Web Site: www.kxan.com. Licensee: KXAN Inc. Group Owner: LIN Television Corporation (acq 11-14-94;12-12-94). Natl. Network: NBC, . Washington Atty: Covington & Burling. News staff: 60; News: 22 hrs wkly.

Key Personnel:

Eric Lassberg	gen mgr
Denise Daniels	gen sls mgr
Amy Coplen	rgnl sls mgr
Tish Saliani	prom dir
Michael Fabac	news dir
Mark Dunham	engrg dir
Laura Franklin	rsch dir & news cmtr
Jamie Aragon	traf mgr
Jim Spencer	weather dir

Beaumont-Port Arthur, TX
(DMA 141)

KBMT— Digital Channel: 12.18.2 kw vis. ant 1,000t/994g TL: N30 11 26 W93 53 08 On air date: June 18, 1961. Box 1550, 525 I-10 S., Dover, TX, 77704. Phone: (409) 838-1212. Phone: (409) 833-7512. Fax: (409) 835-1617. Web Site: www.kbmt12.com. Licensee: KBMT License Co. LLC. Group Owner: McKinnon Broadcasting Co. (acq

7-31-2009; $25 million). Population Served: 463,900 Natl. Network: ABC, NBC, . Washington Atty: Wiley Rein LLP. News staff: 26; News: 13 hrs wkly.

Key Personnel:

Terry E. London	pres
Dan Robbins	VP & gen mgr
Mike Elord	stn mgr
Don Williams	opns dir
David King	natl sls mgr
Elda Gaudet	rgnl sls mgr
Don Haener	prom mgr
Elizabeth West	progmg dir
Miles Resnick	news dir
Mark Cormier	chief of engrg
Jan Kirk	traf mgr
Gary Smith	film dir

KBTV-TV—(Port Arthur, Digital Channel: 40. Digital Hrs: 24 1,000 kw vis. ant 829t/826g TL: N30 09 20 W93 59 10 On air date: Oct 22, 1957. 6155 Eastex Fwy., Ste 300, Beaumont, TX, 77706-6707. Phone: (409) 840-4444. Fax: (409) 985-4927. Fax: (409) 899-4639 (news). Web Site: www.kbtv4.tv. Licensee: Nexstar Broadcasting Inc. Group Owner: Nexstar Broadcasting Group Inc. (acq 11-6-97; grpsl). Population Served: 573,710 Natl. Network: NBC, . Natl. Rep: Blair Television,. Washington Atty: Drinker, Biddle & Roth. Wire Svc: AP

Key Personnel:

Duane Lammers	COO
Perry Sook	CEO & pres
Chris Puritt	gen mgr
Ed Stowell	chief of opns
Paul Bergen	news dir
Dawn Stout	pub affrs dir
Charlie Ravell	chief of engrg
Margie Redkey	traf mgr
James Ware	sports cmtr
Dana Melancon	weather dir

KFDM-TV— Digital Channel: 21. Digital Hrs: 24 350 kw vis. ant 899t/895g TL: N30 08 24 W93 58 44 On air date: Apr 24, 1955. Box 7128, 2955 I-10 E., Beaumont, TX, 77726-7128. Phone: (409) 892-6622. Fax: (409) 892-6665. Web Site: www.kfdm.com. Licensee: Freedom Broadcasting of Texas Licensee L.L.C. Group Owner: Freedom Broadcasting Inc. (acq 1-4-84; grpsl; 1-2-84). Population Served: 163,500 Natl. Network: CBS, CW, . Natl. Rep: TeleRep,. Washington Atty: Latham & Watkins.

Key Personnel:

Larry Beaulieu	VP & gen mgr stn mgr & mktg mgr

*KITU-TV— Analog Channel: 34. Digital Channel: 33.1,000 kw vis. ant 1,023t/1,027g TL: N30 10 41 W93 54 26 On air date: June 21, 1986. 11221 IH 10, Orange, TX, 77630. Phone: (409) 745-3434. Fax: (409) 745-4752. Web Site: www.communityedtv.org. Licensee: Community Educational Television Inc.

Key Personnel:

Dr. Reginald Cherry	pres
Wayne Ozio	gen mgr & stn mgr
Carol Tallent	pub svc dir

Brownsville
see Harlingen-Weslaco-Brownsville-McAllen, TX market

Bryan
see Waco-Temple-Bryan, TX market

Corpus Christi, TX
(DMA 129)

*KEDT— Digital Channel: 23.1,480 kw vis, 148 kw aur. ant 970t/996g TL: N27 39 12 W97 33 55 On air date: Oct 15, 1972. 4455 S. Padre Island Dr., Suite 38, Corpus Christi, TX, 78411. Phone: (361) 855-2213. Fax: (361) 855-3877. Web Site: www.kedt.org. Licensee: South Texas Public Broadcasting System. Population Served: 450,000 Natl. Network: PBS, . Washington Atty: Schwartz, Woods & Miller.

Key Personnel:

Trey McCampbell	chmn
Don Dunlap	pres & gen mgr
Norma Camarillo	CFO
Myra Lombardo	VP
Cody Blount	opns dir & engrg dir chief of engrg
Molly Goodwin	sls dir
Robert Chabot	prom VP & mus dir
Sylvia Coronado	progmg dir & progmg mgr
Johanna Zwernemann	asst music dir

KIII— Digital Channel: 8. Digital Hrs: 24 100 kw vis, 10 kw aur. ant 958t/948g TL: N27 39 30 W97 36 04 On air date: May 4, 1964. 5002

S. Padre Island Dr., Corpus Christi, TX, 78411. Box 6669, Corpus Christi, TX 78466. Phone: (361) 986-8300. Fax: (361) 986-8311.E-mail: news@kiiitv.com Web Site: www.kiiitv.com. Licensee: Channel 3 of Corpus Christi Inc. Group Owner: McKinnon Broadcasting Co. (acq 7-79; $171,720). Population Served: 505,900 Natl. Network: ABC, . Natl. Rep: Continental Television Sales,. Washington Atty: Cohn & Marks. Foreign lang progmg: SpanishS 3 News staff: 30; News: 17.5 hrs wkly.

Key Personnel:

Michael D. McKinnon	pres
Dick Drilling	VP & gen mgr progmg dir
Scott Jones	opns dir
Bill Beck	gen sls mgr
Larry Hogue	natl sls mgr
Richard Longoria	news dir
Ralph Quiroz	chief of engrg
Paula (Spears) Tilton	traf mgr

KORO— Digital Channel: 27.1,450 kw vis, 146 kw aur. ant 762t/750g TL: N27 45 11 W97 38 14 On air date: Apr 15, 1977. Box 2667, Corpus Christi, TX, 78403. 102 N. Mesquite, Corpus Christi, TX 78403. Phone: (361) 883-2823. Fax: (361) 883-2931. Licensee: Entravision Holdings L.L.C. Group Owner: Entravision Communications Co. L.L.C. (acq 3-17-98; $1.336 million). Population Served: 364,500 Natl. Network: Univision (Spanish), . Washington Atty: Mullin, Rhyne, Emmons & Topel. Foreign lang progmg: SpanishS 168 News staff: 5; News: 5 hrs wkly.

Key Personnel:

Anita Saenz-Carvalho	gen mgr

KRIS-TV— Digital Channel: 13.100 kw vis, 10 kw aur. ant 987t TL: N27 44 28 W97 36 08 On air date: May 22, 1956. Box 840, Corpus Christi, TX, 78403. 409 S. Staples, Corpus Christi, TX 78403. Phone: (361) 886-6100. Fax: (361) 886-6175. Fax: TWX: 910-876-1442. Web Site: www.kristv.com. Licensee: KVOA Communications Inc. Group Owner: Cordillera Communications Inc. Population Served: 493,000 Natl. Network: NBC, CW, . Washington Atty: Nixon, Hargrave, Devans & Doyle. News staff: 31; News: 14 hrs wkly.

Key Personnel:

Tim Noble	pres & gen mgr & gen mgr
Bob Webb	chief of opns
Don Grubaugh	gen sls mgr & natl sls mgr
Jay Sanchez	prom mgr
James H. Smith	progmg dir
Sandra Richards	news dir
Steve West	chief of engrg
Heidi Garcia	pub svc dir
Janell Webb	film dir
Dale Nelson	weather dir

KUQI— Digital Channel: 38.50 kw vis. ant 810t/794g TL: N27 45 31.8 W97 36 26.3 On air date: 2008. 600 Leopard St., Suite 1924, Corpus Christi, TX, 78473. Phone: (361) 882-1414. Web Site: www.kuqitv.com. Licensee: High Maintenance Broadcasting LLC.. Ownership: Lauryn Hoffmann, 47%; Deidre Gillis, 47%; and Vanisha Mallory, 6% (acq 2-15-2008;. $6.6 million for CP). Natl. Network: Fox, .

Key Personnel:

Don Gillis	gen mgr

KZTV— Digital Channel: 10.316 kw vis, 47.9 kw aur. ant 940t/984g TL: N27 46 50 W97 38 03 On air date: Sept 30, 1956. 301 Artesian St., Corpus Christi, TX, 78401. Phone: (361) 883-7070. Fax: (361) 882-8553.E-mail: contactus@kztv10.com Web Site: www.kztv10.com. Licensee: Eagle Creek of Corpus Christi LLC. Group Owner: Eagle Creek Broadcasting LLC (acq 6-13-2002; grpsl). Population Served: 350,000 Natl. Network: CBS, . News staff: 18.

Key Personnel:

Billy Brotherton	gen mgr & progmg dir
Norman Barron	rgnl sls mgr
Hollis Grizzard	news dir
Russell Vaughan	chief of engrg

Dallas-Ft. Worth
(DMA 5)

KDAF— Digital Channel: 32. Digital Hrs: 24 5,000 kw vis, 500 kw aur. ant 1,696t/1,529g TL: N32 35 58 10 On air date: July 29, 1984. 8001 Carpenter Fwy., Dallas, TX, 75247. Phone: (214) 252-9233. Fax: (214) 252-3379.E-mail: cw33news@tribune.com Web Site: cw33.trb.com. Licensee: Tribune Broadcasting Co. Group Owner: (group owner). (acq 12-20-2007; grpsl). Population Served: 4,000,000 Natl. Network: CW, . Natl. Rep: TeleRep,. Washington Atty: Dow Lohnes PLLC. News staff: 40; News: 6 hrs wkly.

Key Personnel:

Joe Young	VP & gen mgr
Steve McDonald	gen sls mgr
David Duitch	news dir
Rick Anderson	chief of engrg

KDFI— Digital Channel: 36.5,000 kw vis, 500 kw aur. ant 1,690t/1,529g TL: N32 35 22 W96 58 10 On air date: Jan 26, 1981. 400 N. Griffin

St., Dallas, TX, 75202. Phone: (214) 720-4444. Fax: (214) 720-3207.E-mail: kdfi27@foxinc.com Web Site: www.myfoxdfw.com. Licensee: New DMIC Inc. Group Owner: Fox Television Stations Inc. (acq 2-18-00; $6.2 million). Population Served: 4,000,000 Natl. Network: MyNetworkTV, . Natl. Rep: Fox Stations Sales,.
Key Personnel:
Mark LeValley . . . . engrg VP

KDFW— Digital Channel: 35. Digital Hrs: 24 100 kw vis, 20 kw aur. ant 1,676t/1,517g TL: N32 35 06 W96 58 41 On air date: Dec 3, 1949. 400 N. Griffin St., Dallas, TX, 75202. Phone: (214) 720-4444. Fax: (214) 720-3177 (gen.mgr.). Fax: (214) 720-3263 (news).E-mail: kdfw@foxtv.com Web Site: www.myfoxdfw.com. Licensee: KDFW License Inc. Group Owner: Fox Television Stations Inc. (acq 1-97; grpsl). Population Served: 4,000,000 Natl. Network: Fox, . News: 50 hrs wkly.
Key Personnel:
Kathy Saunders . . . . VP & gen mgr
Dennis Welsh . . . . sls VP
Jeff Gurley . . . . gen sls mgr
Jennifer Owen . . . . natl sls mgr
John Kukla . . . . prom VP
TBA . . . . prom mgr
Andy Alexander. . . . . progmg dir & rsch dir
Maria Barrs . . . . news dir
Rochelle Brown . . . . . pub affrs dir & min affrs dir pub svc dir
Mark LeValley . . . . engrg VP
Kay Shera . . . . traf mgr

***KDTN—** Digital Channel: 43.1,000 kw vis. ant 1,621t/1,473g TL: N32 32 35 W96 57 32 On air date: Feb 2, 1988. Box 612066, Dallas, TX, 75261. Phone: (817) 571-1229. Fax: (817) 571-7458. Web Site: www.daystar.com. Licensee: Community Television Educators of DFW Inc. Ownership: Dr. Alan Bullock, 20%; Jack Howard, 20%; Joni Lamb, 20%; Kory Ford, 20%; and Marcus D. Lamb, 20% (acq 10-24-2003; $20 million). Population Served: 1,800,000
Key Personnel:
Arnold Torres . . . . gen mgr
Jennette Hawkins. . . . . progmg mgr

***KDTX-TV—** Digital Channel: 45. Digital Hrs: 24 1,000 kw vis, 100 kw aur. ant 1,620t/1,473g TL: N32 32 36 W96 57 32 On air date: June 1986. 2823 W. Irving Blvd., Irving, TX, 75061. Phone: (972) 313-1333. Fax: (972) 790-5853. Web Site: www.tbn.org. Licensee: Trinity Broadcasting of Texas Inc. Group Owner: Trinity Broadcasting Network (acq 7-86; $1.6 million;5-6-86).
Key Personnel:
Paul F. Crouch . . . . pres
Steve Fjordbak . . . . gen mgr & progmg dir
Jennye Gardner . . . . pub affrs dir
Jim Forman . . . . chief of engrg

***KERA-TV—** Digital Channel: 14.316 kw vis, 31.6 kw aur. ant 1,540t/1,347g TL: N32 34 43 W96 57 12 On air date: Sept 14, 1960. 3000 Harry Hines Blvd., Dallas, TX, 75201. Phone: (214) 871-1390. Fax: (214) 754-0635. Web Site: www.kera.org. Licensee: North Texas Public Broadcasting Inc. Population Served: 4,950,000 Natl. Network: PBS, . Washington Atty: Schwartz, Woods & Miller.
Key Personnel:
Mary Anne Alhadeff . . . . gen mgr & stn mgr

KFWD— Digital Channel: 9. Digital Hrs: 5 AM-2 AM 55 kw vis. ant 1,791t/1,617g TL: N32 35 19 W96 58 05 On air date: Sept 1, 1988. 606 Young St., Dallas, TX, 75202. Phone: (214) 977-6780. Fax: (214) 977-6544. Web Site: www.kfwd.tv. Licensee: HIC Broadcast Inc. Population Served: 5,000,000 Washington Atty: Dow, Lohnes & Albertson.
Key Personnel:
Roland Hernandez . . . . CEO
Steve Brooks . . . . gen sls mgr
Tony J. Montes. . . . . stn mgr & progmg dir
Don Guemmer . . . . chief of engrg
Sandra Ventura . . . . traf mgr

KLDT— Digital Channel: 39.1,000 kw vis. ant 1,673t/1,489g TL: N32 35 07 W96 58 06 On air date: 1999. 2450 Rockbrook, Louisville, TX, 75067. Phone: (972) 316-2115. Fax: (972) 316-1112. Licensee: Johnson Broadcasting of Dallas Inc.
Key Personnel:
Jason Clegg. . . . . pub affrs dir & chief of engrg

KMPX— Analog Channel: 29. Digital Channel: 30. Analog Hrs: 24 5,000 kw vis, 1,000 kw aur. ant 1,758t/1,610g TL: N32 35 19 W96 58 05 On air date: Sept 15, 1993. Box 612066, Dallas, TX, 75261-2066. 4201 Pool Rd., Colleyville, TX 76034-5017. Phone: (817) 868-7776. Fax: (817) 571-7458.E-mail: comments@daystar.com Web Site: www.daystar.tv. Licensee: Liberman Television of Dallas License LLC. Group Owner: Liberman Broadcasting Inc. (acq 1-12-2004; $37 million). Population Served: 4,000,000
Key Personnel:
Joni Snow . . . . gen mgr

KPXD-TV— Digital Channel: 42.1,000 kw vis. ant 1,624t/1,476g TL: N32 32 36 W96 57 32 On air date: December 1996. 600 Six Flags Dr. Ste 652, Arlington, TX, 76011-6353. Phone: (817) 654-6467. Web Site: www.ionline.tv. Licensee: ION Media Dallas License Inc., debtor-in-possession. Group Owner: Paxson Communications Corp. (acq 4-4-97; $2.5 million for 51%). Natl. Network: ION Television, .
Key Personnel:
Rick Fetter . . . . gen mgr & stn mgr

KSTR-DT— Digital Channel: 48.5,000 kw vis, 500 kw aur. ant 1,200t/1,032g TL: N32 35 24 W96 58 21 On air date: Apr 17, 1984. 2323 Bryan St., Ste. 1900, Dallas, TX, 75201. Phone: (214) 954-4900. Phone: (214) 758-2300. Fax: (214) 954-4920. Fax: (214) 758-2395. Web Site: www.univision.com. Licensee: Telefutura Dallas LLC. Group Owner: Univision Communications Inc. (acq 6-6-2001; grpsl). Natl. Network: TeleFutura (Spanish), . Washington Atty: Wiley, Rein & Fielding.
Key Personnel:
Rebecca Munoz-Diaz. . . . . gen mgr

KTAQ— Digital Channel: 46.4,680 kw vis. ant 663t/646g TL: N33 09 32 W96 08 34 On air date: April 1, 1994. Box 8547, Greenville, TX, 75404. 1058 Country Rd., Greenville, TX 75404. Phone: (903) 455-8847. Fax: (903) 455-8891. Licensee: Simons Broadcasting LP. Ownership: Mike Simons, 99%; and Simons Asset Management L.L.C., 1% (acq 4-1-92; $50,000 for CP;4-13-92).
Key Personnel:
Mike Simons . . . . gen mgr

KTVT— Digital Channel: 11. Digital Hrs: 24 23 kw vis. ant 1,707t/1,545g TL: N32 34 43 W96 57 12 On air date: Sept 11, 1955. Box 2495, Fort Worth, TX, 76113. 5233 Bridge St., Fort Worth, TX 76103. Phone: (817) 451-1111/654-1100. Fax: (817) 457-1897.E-mail: news@ktvt.com Web Site: www.cbs11tv.com. Licensee: CBS Stations Group of Texas L.P. Group Owner: Viacom Television Stations Group (acq 8-3-99; $485 million in stock). Population Served: 6,100,000 Natl. Network: CBS, . Washington Atty: Leventhal, Senter & Lerman. News staff: 100; News: 27 hrs wkly.
Key Personnel:
Steve Mauldin . . . . pres & gen mgr
Gary Schneider . . . . sr VP & VP stn mgr
Steve Williams . . . . opns mgr
Adam Levy. . . . . sls dir
David Hershey. . . . . mktg dir & prom dir
Ken Foote . . . . progmg dir
Scott Diener . . . . news dir
Bill Schully . . . . engrg mgr
Carla Alexander . . . . traf mgr

KTXA— Digital Channel: 19. Digital Hrs: 24 750 kw vis. ant 1,640t/1,479g TL: N32 34 43 W96 57 12 On air date: Jan 4, 1981. 10111 N. Central Expwy., Dallas, TX, 75231. 5233 Bridge St., Fort Worth, TX 76103. Phone: (214) 743-2100. Fax: (214) 743-2121. Fax: (214) 743-2150.E-mail: news@ktvt.com Web Site: ktxa.com. Licensee: Television Station KTXA L.P. Group Owner: Viacom Television Stations Group (acq 2-28-91). Population Served: 6,100,000 Washington Atty: Leventhal, Senter & Lerman.
Key Personnel:
Steve Mauldin . . . . pres & gen mgr
Gary Schneider. . . . . sr VP & stn mgr
Steve Williams . . . . opns mgr
Julia O'Hickey . . . . sls dir
Kyle Brawner . . . . natl sls mgr
David Hershey. . . . . mktg dir & prom dir
Ken Foote . . . . progmg dir
Scott Diener . . . . news dir
Bill Schully . . . . engrg mgr
Carla Alexander . . . . traf mgr

KUVN-DT—(Garland, Digital Channel: 23.5,000 kw vis, 1,000 kw aur. ant 1,142t TL: N32 54 04 W96 41 14 On air date: Sept 25, 1986. 2323 Bryan St., Suite 1900, Dallas, TX, 75201-2646. Phone: (214) 758-2300. Fax: (214) 758-2324. Web Site: www.univision.com. Licensee: KUVN License Partnership L.P. Group Owner: Univision Communications Inc. (acq 5-88; $5.2 million). Natl. Network: Univision (Spanish), . Foreign lang progmg: SpanishS 168 News staff: 22; News: 10 hrs wkly.
Key Personnel:
Becky Munoz-Diaz. . . . . gen mgr

KXAS-TV— Digital Channel: 41. Digital Hrs: 24 100 kw vis, 20 kw aur. ant 1,686t/1,527g TL: N32 35 15 W96 57 59 On air date: Sept 29, 1948. 3900 Barnett, Fort Worth, TX 76103. Phone: (817) 429-5555. Phone: (214) 745-5555. Fax: (817) 654-6362.E-mail: nbc5i@nbc.com Web Site: www.nbc5i.com. Licensee: Station Venture Operations LP. Ownership: NBC Telemundo License Co., 79.62% of the equity; Hicks Muse, 20.38% of the equity (acq 3-2-98). Population Served: 4,500,000 Natl. Network: NBC, . Natl. Rep: NBC TV Stations Sales,. News: 37 hrs wkly.
Key Personnel:
Jim Borden . . . . opns mgr

KXTX-TV— Digital Channel: 40.4,470 kw vis, 447 kw aur. ant 1,679t/1,521g TL: N32 35 07 W96 58 06 On air date: Feb 5, 1968. 3900 Barrett St., Fort Worth, TX, 76103. Phone: (214) 521-3900. Fax: (214) 303-5156. Web Site: www.telemundodallas.com. Licensee: NBC Telemundo License Co. Group Owner: NBC TV Stations Division (acq 4-12-2002; grpsl). Population Served: 4,351,700 Natl. Rep: Harrington, Righter & Parsons,. Washington Atty: Fisher, Wayland, Cooper, Leader & Zaragoza. Foreign lang progmg: SpanishS 168
Key Personnel:
Jose Valle . . . . gen mgr
Brian McCall. opns mgr

WFAA— Digital Channel: 8. Digital Hrs: 24 45 kw vis. ant 1,679t/1,499g TL: N32 35 06 W96 58 41 On air date: Sept 17, 1949. Communications Ctr., 606 Young St., Dallas, TX, 75202-4870. Phone: (214) 748-9631. Fax: (214) 977-6268. Fax: TWX: 910-861-4139. Web Site: wfaa.com. Licensee: WFAA-TV Inc. Group Owner: Belo Corp., Broadcast Division (acq 2-1950). Population Served: 3,591,600 Natl. Network: ABC, . Natl. Rep: TeleRep,. Washington Atty: Wiley, Rein & Fielding. Wire Svc: Reuters Wire Svc: NWS (National Weather Service) News staff: 85; News: 28 hrs wkly.
Key Personnel:
Robert W. Iecherd . . . . CEO
Mike Devlin . . . . pres & gen mgr
Angela E. Betasso . . . . sls VP
Eric Nelson . . . . natl sls mgr
Nick Nicholson . . . . mktg VP
Jim Glass . . . . prom dir
Cathy Helean . . . . prom mgr
David Walther. . . . . progmg dir
David Johnson . . . . engrg dir

El Paso (Las Cruces, NM), TX (DMA 98)

***KCOS—** Digital Channel: 13. Digital Hrs: 18 224 kw vis, 22.4 kw aur. ant 869t/342g TL: N31 47 15 W106 28 47 On air date: Aug 18, 1978. Box 26668, El Paso, TX, 79926. Phone: (915) 590-1313. Fax: (915) 594-5394.E-mail: cbrush@kcostv.org Web Site: www.kcostv.org. Licensee: El Paso Public Television Foundation. Population Served: 262,000 Natl. Network: PBS, . Washington Atty: Cohn & Marks.
Key Personnel:
Craig Brush . . . . CEO & pres & gen mgr

KDBC-TV— Digital Channel: 18. Digital Hrs: 24 100 kw vis, 10 kw aur. ant 1,558t/377g TL: N31 47 46 W106 28 57 On air date: Dec 14, 1952. Box 1799, El Paso, TX, 79999. 2201 Wyoming Ave., El Paso, TX 79999. Phone: (915) 496-4444. Fax: (915) 496-4591 (sls). Fax: (915) 496-4593 (news).E-mail: news@kdbc4.com Web Site: www.kdbc4.com. Licensee: KDBC License LLC. Group Owner: Pappas Telecasting Companies (acq 3-29-2004; $20 million). Population Served: 940,800 Natl. Network: CBS, MyNetworkTV, . Natl. Rep: Harrington, Righter & Parsons,. Washington Atty: Fletcher, Heald & Hildreth, P.L.C. Wire Svc: AP News staff: 25; News: 15 hrs wkly.
Key Personnel:
Bram Watkins. . . . . gen mgr
John Burton . . . . gen sls mgr & natl sls mgr
Cheri Dorsey . . . . rgnl sls mgr
Dan Somes . . . . chief of engrg
Yolonda Garcia . . . . traf mgr
Robert Bettes. . . . . weather dir

KFOX-TV— Digital Channel: 15. Digital Hrs: 24 398 kw vis, 39.8 kw aur. ant 1,981t/367g TL: N31 48 55 W106 29 20 On air date: August 1979. 6004 N. Mesa, El Paso, TX, 79912. Phone: (915) 833-8585. Fax: (915) 833-1358. Web Site: www.kfoxtv.com. Licensee: KTVU Partnership. Group Owner: Cox Broadcasting (acq 1996; $20.855 million). Population Served: 231,400 Natl. Network: Fox, . Natl. Rep: TeleRep,. Washington Atty: Dow, Lohnes & Albertson. News staff: 23; News: 6 hrs wkly.
Key Personnel:
John Witte . . . . gen mgr

KINT-TV— Digital Channel: 25.2,240 kw vis, 224 kw aur. ant 1,499t/350g TL: N31 47 46 W106 28 57 On air date: May 5, 1984. 5426 N. Mesa, El Paso, TX, 79912. Phone: (915) 581-1126. Fax: (915) 581-1393.E-mail: info@univision26.com Web Site: univision26.com. Licensee: Entravision Communications Co. L.L.C. Group Owner: (group owner; (acq 6-4-97; grpsl). Natl. Network: Univision (Spanish), . Washington Atty: Thompson, Hine & Flory L. Foreign lang progmg: SpanishS 168 News staff: 14; News: 10 hrs wkly.

Key Personnel:
David Candelaria . . . gen mgr
Diana De Lara . . . gen sls mgr
Dan Kempner . . . natl sls mgr
Abel Rodriguez . . . prom dir & pub affrs dir
Gustavo Barraza . . . news dir
Alfredo Durand . . . chief of engrg
Nidia Holguin . . . rsch dir
Sylvia Martinez . . . progmg dir & traf mgr
Luis Zuniga . . . sports cmtr
Aldo Acosta . . . weather dir

***KRWG-TV—** Digital Channel: 23. Digital Hrs: 6 AM-midnight 1,000 kw vis, 100 kw aur. ant 672t/171g TL: N32 17 33 W106 41 51 On air date: June 29, 1973. Box 30001, MSC TV22, NMSU, Las Cruces, NM, 88003. 2915 McFie Cir., Rm. 100, Las Cruces, NM 88003. Phone: (575) 646-2222. Fax: (575) 646-1924.E-mail: krwgtv@nmsu.edu Web Site: www.krwg-tv.org. Licensee: Regents of New Mexico State University. Population Served: 500,000 Natl. Network: PBS, . Washington Atty: Dow, Lohnes & Albertson. Wire Svc: AP Foreign lang progmg: SpanishS 2 News: 3 hrs wkly.
Key Personnel:
Glen Cerny . . . gen mgr
J.D. Jarvis . . . opns mgr
Anthony Casaus . . . dev dir
William Saggerson . . . chief of engrg

***KSCE—** Digital Channel: 39. Digital Hrs: 24 50.1 kw vis, 5 kw aur. ant 1,827t/172g TL: N31 48 55 W106 29 17 On air date: Apr 15, 1989. 6400 Escondido Dr., El Paso, TX, 79912. Phone: (915) 585-8838. Fax: (915) 585-8841.E-mail: ksce@aol.com Web Site: www.kscetv.com. Licensee: Channel 38 Christian Television. Ownership: Non-profit corporation. Population Served: 950,000 Washington Atty: James L. Oyster. Foreign lang progmg: SpanishS 28
Key Personnel:
Grace Rendall . . . VP & gen mgr & opns dir

KTDO— Digital Channel: 47. Digital Hrs: 24 79.4 kw vis, 7.9 kw aur. ant 113t TL: N32 02 30 W106 27 41 On air date: Nov 11, 1984. 10033 Carnegie, El Paso, TX, 79925. Phone: (915) 591-9595. Fax: (915) 591-9896. Web Site: www.telemundo.com. Licensee: ZGS El Paso Televison LP. Ownership: ZGS Broadcast Holdings Inc., 100% (acq 9-13-2004; $11.8 million). Population Served: 850,000 Natl. Network: Telemundo (Spanish), . Washington Atty: Reed, Smith, Shaw & McClay. Foreign lang progmg: SpanishS 168
Key Personnel:
Lorena Caltamon . . . gen mgr
Phillip Cortez . . . gen sls mgr & mktg mgr & adv mgr
Monic Diaz . . . progmg dir
Elios Ventanilla . . . chief of engrg

KTFN— Digital Channel: 51.1,000 kw vis, 50 kw aur. ant 1,827t/199g TL: N31 48 55 W106 29 17 On air date: 1991. 5426 N. Mesa, El Paso, TX, 79912. Phone: (915) 581-1126. Fax: (915) 581-1393.E-mail: info@univision26.com Web Site: univision26.com. Licensee: Entravision Holdings LLC. Group Owner: Entravision Communications Corp. (acq 12-10-01; $18 million). Foreign lang progmg: SpanishS 168
Key Personnel:
Dan Kempner . . . pres & natl sls mgr
David Candelaria . . . gen mgr
Diana DeLara . . . gen sls mgr
Abel Rodriguez . . . prom dir
Alfredo Durand . . . progmg dir & chief of engrg

KTSM-TV— Analog Channel: 9. Digital Channel: 16. Analog Hrs: 24 Digital Hrs: 24 316 kw vis, 42.7 kw aur. ant 1,910t/370g TL: N31 48 18 W106 28 57 On air date: Jan 4, 1953. 801 N. Oregon St., El Paso, TX, 79902. Phone: (915) 532-5421. Fax: (915) 532-6793.E-mail: ktsmtv@whc.net Web Site: www.ktsm.com. Licensee: ComCorp of El Paso License Corp. Group Owner: Communications Corp. of America (acq 7-25-97; $30.5 million for stock with KTSM-AM-FM). Population Served: 333,110 Natl. Network: NBC, . Natl. Rep: Millennium Sales & Marketing,. Washington Atty: Fletcher, Heald & Hildreth. Wire Svc: AP News staff: 33; News: 19.5 hrs wkly.
Key Personnel:
Gary Sotir . . . gen mgr
Danny Aguilar . . . sls VP & gen sls mgr
Debra Hastings . . . natl sls mgr
Victor Veuegus . . . news dir
Courtney Elam . . . pub affrs dir
Ernie Hartt . . . engrg dir

KVIA-TV— Analog Channel: 7. Digital Channel: 17. Analog Hrs: 24 316 kw vis, 31.6 kw aur. ant 820t/296g TL: N31 47 15 W106 28 47 On air date: Sept 1, 1956. 4140 Rio Bravo, El Paso, TX, 79902. Phone: (915) 496-7777. Fax: (915) 532-0070.E-mail: kvia@kvia.com Web Site: www.kvia.com. Licensee: NPG of Texas L.P. (acq 12-9-94; $19.9 million;1-23-95). Population Served: 800,000 Natl. Network: ABC, CW, . Washington Atty: Robert Thompson. News staff: 30; News: 31.5 hrs wkly.

Key Personnel:
David Bradley . . . CEO
John Kueneke . . . pres
Kevin Lovell . . . gen mgr
Chris Swann . . . opns mgr
Nathan Price . . . sls dir
Dan Overstreet . . . natl sls mgr
David Gonzalez . . . prom dir
Karla Huelga . . . progmg dir & pub affrs dir
Eric Huseby . . . news dir
Elias Ventanilla . . . chief of engrg

XHIJ—(Ciudad Juarez, MEX) Analog Channel: 44. Analog Hrs: 20 240 kw vis, 60 kw aur. 1,200t/150g On air date: Oct 16, 1980. 5925 Cromo Dr., El Paso, TX, 79912. Phone: (915) 585-6344. Fax: (915) 585-6333. Web Site: www.canal44.com. Licensee: Arnoldo Cabada de la O. Ownership: Arnoldo Cabada De la O, 52%; Luis Cabada Alvidrez, Sergio Cabada Alvidrez & Jesus Cabada Alvidrez, each 16%. Natl. Network: Telemundo (Spanish), . Foreign lang progmg: SpanishS 126 News staff: 20; News: 15 hrs wkly.
Key Personnel:
Sergio Cavada . . . gen mgr

Ft. Worth

see Dallas-Ft. Worth market

Harlingen-Weslaco -Brownsville-McAllen, TX (DMA 87)

KGBT-TV— Digital Channel: 31. Digital Hrs: 24 100 kw vis, 18.7 kw aur. ant 1,299t/1,293g TL: N26 08 55 W97 49 17 On air date: October 1953. 9201 W. Expwy. 83, Harlingen, TX, 78552. Phone: (956) 366-4444. Fax: (956) 366-4494.E-mail: listens@kgbt4.com Web Site: www.kgbt4.com. Licensee: Barrington Harlingen License LLC. Group Owner: Liberty Corp. (acq 8-11-2006; grpsl). Population Served: 944,772 Natl. Network: CBS, . Washington Atty: Dow, Lohnes & Albertson. Foreign lang progmg: SpanishS 10 News staff: 29; News: 22 hrs wkly.
Key Personnel:
Teresa Burgess . . . gen mgr
Phil Rich . . . opns mgr
Randy Roberts . . . gen sls mgr
Beau Pillet . . . mktg dir & prom mgr
Kimberly Wyatt . . . news dir
Monica Ortiz . . . progmg

***KLUJ-TV—** Digital Channel: 34.45 kw vis. ant 928t/928g TL: N26 13 00 W97 46 48 On air date: June 25, 1984. Box 1647, 1920LOOP Coneway Dr., Suite 117, Harlingen, TX, 78551. Phone: (956) 425-4225. Fax: (956) 412-1740.E-mail: klujtv@asbglobal.net Licensee: Community Educational TV Inc. (acq 4-84). Natl. Network: PBS, . Washington Atty: Joseph E. Dunne III. Foreign lang progmg: SpanishS 7
Key Personnel:
Margie Gonzales . . . gen mgr
Mar Campos . . . stn mgr

***KMBH—** Digital Channel: 38. Digital Hrs: 24 2,240 kw vis, 22.4 kw aur. ant 1,220t/1,169g TL: N26 07 14 W97 49 18 On air date: Oct 8, 1985. Box 2147, Harlingen, TX, 78551. 1701 Tennessee St., Harlingen, TX 78551. Phone: (956) 421-4111. Fax: (956) 421-4150.E-mail: rgveduca@aol.com Web Site: www.kmbh.org. Licensee: RGV Educational Broadcasting Inc. Population Served: 975,000 Natl. Network: PBS, . Washington Atty: Thelen Reid & Priest LLP. Foreign lang progmg: SpanishS 2
Key Personnel:
Father Pedro Briseno . . . CEO & pres gen mgr
John Ross . . . chief of engrg

KNVO— Digital Channel: 49.3,162 kw vis, 316.2 kw aur. ant 524t/548g TL: N26 05 20 W98 03 44 On air date: Oct 12, 1992. 801 N. Jackson Rd., McAllen, TX, 78501. Phone: (956) 687-4848. Fax: (956) 687-7784. Licensee: Entravision Holdings L.L.C. Group Owner: Entravision Communications Co. L.L.C (acq 4-25-97). Natl. Network: Univision (Spanish), . Washington Atty: Schwartz, Woods & Miller. Foreign lang progmg: SpanishS 168
Key Personnel:
Larry Safir . . . gen mgr
Joe Medrano . . . news dir

KRGV-TV— Digital Channel: 13. Digital Hrs: 24 100 kw vis, 19.1 kw aur. ant 950t/995g TL: N26 09 54 W97 48 45 On air date: Apr 10, 1954. Box 5, Weslaco, TX, 78599. 900 E. Expwy. 83, Weslaco, TX 78596. Phone: (956) 631-5555. Fax: (956) 973-5016. Web Site: www.krgv.com. Licensee: Mobile Video Tapes Inc. Group Owner: Manship Stns (acq 1-28-64; grpsl;2-3-64). Population Served: 215,500 Natl. Network: ABC, . Washington Atty: Cohn & Marks. Foreign lang progmg: SpanishS 1 News staff: 28; News: 12 hrs wkly.
Key Personnel:
Richard Manship . . . chmn & pres
John Kittleman . . . gen mgr
Michelle Martone . . . opns mgr & progmg dir
Robert Ledesma . . . sls dir & natl sls mgr
Jerry Berg . . . prom mgr
Jenny Martinez . . . news dir
Jerry Lee Berg . . . pub affrs dir & pub svc dir
Chuck Salge . . . chief of engrg
Ginger Walker . . . traf mgr
Chris Manzo . . . film dir
Marianne Manko . . . consumer affrs dir
Dave Brown . . . sports cmtr
Tim Smith . . . weather dir

***KTLM—** Digital Channel: 40. Digital Hrs: 24 355 kw vis. ant 1,893t/1,886g TL: N26 31 01 W98 39 07 On air date: Oct 8, 1999. 7th Fl., 3900 N. 10th St., McAllen, TX, 78501. Phone: (956) 686-0040. Fax: (956) 686-0770. Web Site: www.telemundo40.com. Licensee: Sunbelt Multimedia Co. Ownership: Sam F. Vale, 99.5% (acq 8-12-2005; $3.15 million). Population Served: 1,000,000 Natl. Network: Telemundo (Spanish), . Foreign lang progmg: SpanishS 168 News staff: 12; News: 8 hrs wkly.
Key Personnel:
Emmett Wells . . . gen mgr

KVEO-TV— Digital Channel: 24. Digital Hrs: 24 2,570 kw vis, 1,000 kw aur. ant 1,460t/1,454g TL: N26 05 59 W97 50 16 On air date: Dec 19, 1981. 394 N. Expressway, Brownsville, TX, 78521. Box 4314, Brownsville, TX 78521. Phone: (956) 544-2323. Fax: (956) 544-4636. Web Site: www.kveo.com. Licensee: Communications Corp. of America. Group Owner: (group owner; (acq 2-13-95;5-8-95). Population Served: 700,000 Natl. Network: NBC, . Washington Atty: Dow, Lohnes. Wire Svc: AP
Key Personnel:
Steve Pruett . . . pres
Bill Jorn . . . gen mgr
Sheldon Galloway . . . dev VP & progmg dir
Greg Boulanger . . . prom dir

Houston (DMA 10)

KAZH— Digital Channel: 41. Digital Hrs: 24 1,000 kw vis, 100 kw aur. ant 1,902t/1,887g TL: N29 34 15 W95 30 37 On air date: 1987. 2620 Fountain View, Ste.322, Houston, TX, 77057. Phone: (713) 467-5757. Fax: (713) 783-4157. Web Site: www.kazh57.com. Licensee: KAZH License LLC. Group Owner: Pappas Telecasting Companies (acq 7-7-99; $28 million). Foreign lang progmg: SpanishS 168
Key Personnel:
Harry J. Pappas . . . CEO & pres
Emilio Nicolas Jr. . . . gen mgr
Emilio Nicolas Jr.. . . . stn mgr

***KETH-TV—** Digital Channel: 24. Digital Hrs: 24 1,000 kw vis. ant 1,902t TL: N29 34 15 W95 30 37 On air date: July 1987. 10902 S. Wilcrest Dr., Houston, TX, 77099. Phone: (281) 561-5828. Fax: (281) 561-9793. Web Site: www.communityedtv.org. Licensee: Community Educational Television Inc. Population Served: 231,128 News: 3 hrs wkly.
Key Personnel:
Laura Hanks . . . opns mgr
Rod Harty . . . chief of engrg

KFTH-DT— Digital Channel: 36. Digital Hrs: 24 5,000 kw vis, 500 kw aur. ant 1,781t/1,155g TL: N29 34 06 W95 29 57 On air date: Jan 27, 1986. 5100 SW Freeway, Houston, TX, 77056. Phone: (713) 662-4545. Fax: (713) 965-2610.E-mail: info@univision.net Web Site: www.univision.net. Licensee: TeleFutura Houston LLC. Group Owner: Univision Communications Inc. (acq 5-21-2001; grpsl). Natl. Network: TeleFutura (Spanish), . Foreign lang progmg: SpanishS 168
Key Personnel:
Jerold Perenchio . . . CEO
Mike Wortsman . . . pres
George Blank . . . CFO
Craig H. Bland . . . VP & gen mgr
Jose Oti . . . gen sls mgr
Chas Witson . . . natl sls mgr
Michael Thomas . . . rgnl sls mgr
Arlene Kelsch . . . mktg mgr & rsch dir
Charlie Lozano . . . prom VP
Sanjuio Salazar . . . progmg mgr
Grace Olivares-Hernandez . . . pub affrs dir
Tom Daniels . . . chief of engrg
Sanjui Salazan . . . traf mgr

KHOU— Digital Channel: 11. Digital Hrs: 24 25 kw vis. ant 1,945t/1,935g TL: N29 33 40 W95 30 04 On air date: Mar 22, 1953. 1945 Allen

Pkwy., Houston, TX, 77019. Phone: (713) 526-1111. Fax: (713) 521-4326.E-mail: 11listens@khou.com Web Site: www.khou.com. Licensee: KHOU-TV Inc. Group Owner: Belo Corp., Broadcast Division (acq 1984; grpsl; 11-17-83). Population Served: 5,000,000 Natl. Network: CBS, . Natl. Rep: TeleRep,. Wire Svc: Reuters
Key Personnel:
Susan McEldoon . . . . . pres & gen mgr
Dan Lyons . . . . . sls dir
Keith Connors . . . . . news dir

KIAH— Digital Channel: 38. Digital Hrs: 25 5,000 kw vis, 500 kw aur. ant 1,950t/1,970g TL: N29 34 06 W95 29 57 On air date: Jan 6, 1967. 7700 Westpark Dr., Houston, TX, 77063. Phone: (713) 781-3939. Fax: (713) 781-3441. Web Site: khcw.trb.com. Licensee: KHCW Inc. Group Owner: Tribune Broadcasting Co. (acq 12-20-2007; grpsl). Population Served: 5,000,000 Natl. Network: CW, . Natl. Rep: Harrington, Righter & Parsons,. Washington Atty: Dow Lohnes PLLC. News staff: 34; News: 4 hrs wkly.
Key Personnel:
Roger Bare . . . . . VP & gen mgr

***KLTJ—** Digital Channel: 23. Digital Hrs: 24 5,000 kw vis, 500 kw aur. ant 1,856t/1,847g TL: N29 17 56 W95 14 11 On air date: July 22, 1989. 1050 Gemini, Houston, TX, 77058. Phone: (281) 212-1022. Fax: (281) 212-1031.E-mail: comments@daystar.com Web Site: www.daystar.com. Licensee: Word of God Fellowship Inc. aka Community TV Educators. (acq 10-18-99; $9.5 million). Population Served: 1,452,000 Foreign lang progmg: SpanishS 10
Key Personnel:
Nathan Williams . . . . . gen mgr

KNWS-TV— Digital Channel: 47. Digital Hrs: 24 2,290 kw vis. ant 1,640t/1,624g TL: N29 33 40 W95 30 04 On air date: Nov 3, 1993. 8440 Westpark, Houston, TX, 77063. Phone: (713) 974-5151. Fax: (713) 974-5188. Web Site: www.knws51.com. Licensee: Johnson Broadcasting Inc. Ownership: Douglas R. Johnson, 100%. Washington Atty: Smithwick & Belendiuk.
Key Personnel:
Douglas R. Johnson . . . . . pres
Jack Dabbah. . . . . gen mgr & stn mgr
Chris Bourne . . . . . opns dir & chief of opns

KPRC-TV— Digital Channel: 35. Digital Hrs: 24 100 kw vis, 10 kw aur. ant 1,929t/1,969g TL: N29 34 06 W95 29 57 On air date: Jan 1, 1949. Box 2222, Houston, TX, 77252. 8181 Southwest Fwy., Houston, TX 77074. Phone: (713) 222-2222. Fax: (713) 270-9334. Web Site: www.click2houston.com. Licensee: Post-Newsweek Stations Inc. Group Owner: (group owner; (acq 4-22-94;5-2-94). Population Served: 1,938,670 Natl. Network: NBC, . Natl. Rep: MMT,. Washington Atty: Covington & Burling. Wire Svc: AP News staff: 80; News: 34 hrs wkly.
Key Personnel:
Larry Blackerby . . . . . gen mgr
Tammy Dean . . . . . opns dir
Ben Oldham . . . . . gen sls mgr
Mr. Skip Valet. . . . . news dir
Dale Werner . . . . . chief of engrg

KPXB-TV— Digital Channel: 32. Digital Hrs: 18 1,000 kw vis. ant 1,899t/1,884g TL: N29 34 15 W95 30 37 On air date: June 16, 1989. 256 N. Sam Houston Pkwy. E., Suite 49, Houston, TX, 77060. Phone: (281) 820-4900. Fax: (281) 820-3916. Web Site: www.ionline.tv. Licensee: Paxson Houston License Inc. Group Owner: Paxson Communications Corp. (acq 1995; $7.9 million). Population Served: 3,050,000 Natl. Network: ION Television, . Washington Atty: Pepper & Corazzini.
Key Personnel:
Alex Stroot . . . . . stn mgr
Wendy Wiesinger . . . . . engr

KRIV— Digital Channel: 26. Digital Hrs: 24 1,000 kw vis, 100 kw aur. ant 1,961t/1,945g TL: N29 34 28 W95 29 37 On air date: Aug 15, 1971. Box 22810, Houston, TX, 77227. 4261 Southwest Fwy., Houston, TX 77027. Phone: (713) 479-2600. Fax: (713) 479-2604. Web Site: www.myfoxhouston.com. Licensee: Fox Television Stations Inc. Group Owner: (group owner) Population Served: 1697900 Natl. Network: Fox, . Natl. Rep: Fox Stations Sales,. Washington Atty: Molly Pauker. Wire Svc: AP
Key Personnel:
D'Artagnan Bebel . . . . . gen mgr
Charles Hughes . . . . . opns VP & engrg VP
Sheila Birenbaun . . . . . opns dir
Du Juan McCoy . . . . . sls VP
Larry Parker . . . . . prom VP
Stan Wasilik . . . . . progmg dir
Kathy Williams . . . . . news dir
Lisa Whitlock . . . . . pub affrs dir
Geri Fieler . . . . . traf mgr
Mark Berman. . . . . sports cmtr

KTBU— Digital Channel: 42. Digital Hrs: 24 5,000 kw vis, 500 kw aur. ant 1,817t/1,801g TL: N30 13 53 W95 07 26 On air date: July 15, 1998. 7026 Old Katy Rd., Suite 201, Houston, TX, 77024. Phone: (713) 864-1999. Fax: (713) 864-1993. Web Site: www.thetube.net. Licensee: Humanity Interested Media L.P. Ownership: HIM GP LLC, gen ptnr, owned 100% by US Farm & Ranch Supply Co. Inc. dba USFR Media Group (acq 3-20-2006; $30 million).
Key Personnel:
Matt Reiss Jr.. . . . . gen mgr
Bruce Dinehart . . . . . stn mgr
Phil Lonsway . . . . . gen sls mgr
Lara Bell . . . . . pub affrs dir
Eric Peterson. . . . . chief of engrg

KTMD— Digital Channel: 48. Digital Hrs: 21 5,000 kw vis, 500 kw aur. ant 1,958t/1,944g TL: N29 34 15 W95 30 37 On air date: Dec 12, 1987. 1235 N. Loop W., Suite 125, Houston, TX, 77008. Phone: (713) 974-4848. Fax: (713) 243-7850. Fax: (713) 782-5575. Web Site: www.ktmd.com. Licensee: NBC Telemundo License Co. Group Owner: Telemundo Group Inc. (acq 4-12-2002; grpsl). Natl. Network: Telemundo (Spanish), . Washington Atty: Hogan & Hartson. Foreign lang progmg: SpanishS 160 News staff: 14; News: 7 hrs wkly.
Key Personnel:
Roel Medina . . . . . gen mgr
Dominic Fails . . . . . gen sls mgr
Gregorio Cervantes . . . . . natl sls mgr

KTRK-TV— Digital Channel: 13.32.4 kw vis. ant 1,929t/1,912g TL: N29 34 27 W95 29 37 On air date: Nov 20, 1954. Box 13, Houston, TX, 77001. 3310 Bissonnet St., Houston, TX 77005. Phone: (713) 666-0713. Fax: (713) 663-0013. Web Site: www.ABC13.com. Licensee: ABC Inc. Group Owner: (group owner; (acq 7-17-67). Population Served: 1,466,500 Natl. Network: ABC, . Wire Svc: TWX
Key Personnel:
Henry Florsheim . . . . . pres & gen mgr & stn mgr

KTXH— Digital Channel: 19.5,000 kw vis, 500 kw aur. ant 1,811t/2,008g TL: N29 34 34 W95 30 36 On air date: Nov 7, 1982. 4261 Southwest Frwy., Houston, TX, 77027. Phone: (713) 479-2600. Fax: (713) 479-2859. Licensee: Fox Television Stations Inc. Group Owner: (group owner; (acq 11-6-2001; with WDCA(TV) Washington, DC in swap for KBHK-TV San Francisco, CA). Population Served: 1,510,580 Natl. Network: MyNetworkTV, .
Key Personnel:
D'Artagnan Bebel . . . . . gen mgr
Charles Hughes. . . . . opns VP

***KUHT—** Digital Channel: 8. Digital Hrs: 24 316 kw vis, 63.2 kw aur. ant 1,970t/2,049g TL: N29 34 28 W95 29 37 On air date: May 12, 1953. 4343 Elgin ., Houston, TX, 77204-0008. Phone: (713) 748-8888. Phone: (800) 364-8300. Fax: (713) 743-8867. Web Site: www.houstonpbs.org. Licensee: University of Houston System, Board of Regents. Population Served: 3,770,000 Natl. Network: PBS, . Washington Atty: Dow, Lohnes & Albertson. Foreign lang progmg: SpanishS 12
Key Personnel:
John Hesse . . . . . gen mgr & stn mgr
Jack K. Neal . . . . . stn mgr
Steve Pyndus. . . . . opns dir

KXLN-DT— Digital Channel: 45. Digital Hrs: 24 5,000 kw vis, 500 kw aur. ant 1,948t/1,929g TL: N29 33 44 W95 30 35 On air date: Sept 18, 1987. 5100 SW Freeway, Houston, TX, 77056. Phone: (713) 662-4545. Fax: (713) 965-2610.E-mail: info@univision.net Web Site: www.univision.net. Licensee: KXLN License Partnership G.P. Group Owner: Univision Communications Inc. (acq 2-24-95;5-22-95). Natl. Network: Univision (Spanish), . Washington Atty: Fisher, Wayland, Cooper, Leader & Zaragoza. Foreign lang progmg: SpanishS 165 News staff: 23; News: 7 hrs wkly.
Key Personnel:
Craig Bland. . . . . VP & gen mgr stn mgr
Jeff Hoffman . . . . . stn mgr
Jose Oti . . . . . gen sls mgr
Charles Wilson. . . . . natl sls mgr
Charlie Lozano . . . . . prom dir
Cindy Chisum . . . . . progmg dir & traf mgr
Juan Garcia . . . . . news dir
Grace C. Olivares . . . . . pub affrs dir
Chuck Promrose . . . . . chief of engrg
Stacey Nasser Miller . . . . . rsch dir
Grace Olivares . . . . . pub svc dir
Edmundo Sanchez . . . . . sports cmtr
Hector Villarreal. . . . . weather dir

KZJL— Digital Channel: 44.1,700 kw vis. ant 1,898t/1,885g TL: N29 33 44 W95 30 35 On air date: 1995. 1845 Emppire Ave., Burbank, CA, 91504. Phone: (818) 563-5722. Licensee: KZJL License LLC. Group Owner: Liberman Broadcasting Inc. (acq 1-10-2001; $57 million).
Key Personnel:
Winter Horton. . . . . gen mgr

Laredo, TX (DMA 188)

KGNS-TV— Digital Channel: 8. Digital Hrs: 20 316 kw vis, 42.2 kw aur. ant 1,021t/1,049g TL: N27 40 22 W99 39 23 On air date: Jan 6, 1956. 120 W. Del Mar Blvd., Laredo, TX, 78041-2203. Phone: (956) 727-8888. Fax: (956) 727-5336.E-mail: email8@pro8news.com Web Site: pro8news.com. Licensee: SagamoreHill Broadcasting of Texas LLC. (acq 9-28-2004; $14.4 million). Population Served: 30,000 Natl. Network: CW, NBC, Telemundo (Spanish), . Natl. Rep: Continental Television Sales,. Washington Atty: Wiley, Rein & Fielding, LLP. Foreign lang progmg: SpanishS 8 News staff: 26; News: 17 hrs wkly.
Key Personnel:
Louis Wall. . . . . pres
Carlos Salinas . . . . . gen mgr & natl sls mgr rgnl sls mgr
Ramiro Saucedo . . . . . prom mgr
Jose Luis Salinas . . . . . adv mgr & pub affrs dir
Olga Ramirez. . . . . progmg dir
Ray Gomez . . . . . news dir
David York. . . . . chief of engrg

KLDO-TV— Digital Channel: 19. Digital Hrs: 18 3,720 kw vis, 372 kw aur. 220t TL: N27 30 03 W99 30 37 On air date: Dec 17, 1984. 222 Bob Bullock Loop, Laredo, TX, 78043. Phone: (956) 727-0027. Fax: (956) 727-2673. Web Site: www.entravision.com. Licensee: Entravision Holdings L.L.C. Group Owner: Entravision Communications Co. L.L.C. (acq 7-30-97; $6.2 million). Natl. Network: Univision (Spanish), . Washington Atty: Martin E. Firestone. Foreign lang progmg: SpanishS 126
Key Personnel:
Terry Elena Ordaz . . . . . gen mgr
Elia Solis. . . . . gen sls mgr & film buyer
Jose Gomez. . . . . rgnl sls mgr
Jose Salinas . . . . . prom mgr & progmg dir
Marisa Limon . . . . . news dir
Merlin Miller . . . . . chief of engrg

KVTV— Digital Channel: 13.85.1 kw vis, 17.4 kw aur. ant 918t/1,033g TL: N27 31 14 W99 31 19 On air date: Dec 29, 1973. 2600 Shea & Anna St., Laredo, TX, 78041. Phone: (956) 727-1300. Fax: (956) 712-0185. Web Site: www.cbs13kvtv.com. Licensee: Eagle Creek of Laredo LLC. Group Owner: Eagle Creek Broadcasting LLC (acq 6-13-2002; grpsl). Population Served: 450,000 Natl. Network: CBS, .
Key Personnel:
Dale Remy . . . . . gen mgr & stn mgr
Joe Herrera . . . . . gen sls mgr
Carol Rostohar . . . . . prom dir & pub affrs dir
Kent Harrell . . . . . news dir
George Sanders . . . . . chief of engrg

Longview

see Tyler-Longview (Lufkin & Nacogdoches), TX market

Lubbock, TX (DMA 143)

KAMC— Digital Channel: 27. Digital Hrs: 24 2,000 kw vis, 374 kw aur. ant 840t/871g TL: N33 30 57 W101 50 54 On air date: Nov 12, 1968. 7403 S. University, Lubbock, TX, 79423. Phone: (806) 745-2828. Fax: (806) 748-2214.E-mail: jsherwood@klbk13.tv Web Site: www.everythinglubbock.com. Licensee: Mission Broadcasting Inc. Group Owner: (group owner; (acq 12-17-2003). Population Served: 357,000 Natl. Network: ABC, . Washington Atty: Bryan Cave. News staff: 26; News: 39 hrs wkly.
Key Personnel:
Greg McAlister . . . . . gen mgr & stn mgr
Chuck Spaugh . . . . . opns dir
Gary Melton . . . . . sls dir & gen sls mgr
Jeff Pitner . . . . . prom dir & pub affrs dir
Shanna Smith. . . . . progmg dir
Russ Protect . . . . . news dir
Eric Hosch. . . . . chief of engrg
Rosie Duran . . . . . traf mgr
Ron Roberts . . . . . weather dir

KCBD— Digital Channel: 11.316 kw vis, 60 kw aur. ant 804t/702g TL: N33 32 32 W101 50 14 On air date: May 10, 1953. 5600 Avenue A, Lubbock, TX, 79404. Phone: (806) 744-1414. Fax: (806) 744-0449.E-mail: kcbd@kcbd.com Web Site: www.kcbd.com. Licensee: KCBD License Subsidiary LLC. Group Owner: Liberty Corp. (acq 1-31-2006; grpsl). Population Served: 254,000 Natl. Network: NBC, . Washington Atty: Dow, Lohnes & Albertson.
Key Personnel:
Dan Jackson . . . . . gen mgr & gen sls mgr
Brent McClure . . . . . opns mgr & mktg dir prom mgr
Beverly McBeth . . . . . gen sls mgr
Peggy Sullivan. . . . . progmg mgr
Benji Snead . . . . . news dir
Ricky Price . . . . . chief of engrg
Michele Doggett . . . . . traf mgr
Josh Young . . . . . pub svc dir

KJTV-TV— Digital Channel: 35. Digital Hrs: 24 3,720 kw vis, 372 kw aur. ant 840t/893g TL: N33 30 08 W101 52 20 On air date: Dec 10,

1981. Box 3757, Lubbock, TX, 79452. 9800 University Ave., Lubbock, TX 79452. Phone: (806) 745-3434. Fax: (806) 748-1949. Web Site: www.fox34.com. Licensee: Ramar Communications II Ltd. Group Owner: (group owner) Population Served: 378,200 Natl. Network: Fox, . Natl. Rep: Millennium Sales & Marketing,. Washington Atty: Leventhal, Senter & Lerman. News staff: 20; News: 7 hrs wkly.
Key Personnel:
Brad Moran . . . . gen mgr
Scott Cawthron. . . . . opns mgr
Marc Gilmour . . . . gen sls mgr
Jana Hill . . . . prom mgr
Terri Holt . . . . progmg mgr
Amy Goin . . . . traf mgr

KLBK-TV— Digital Channel: 40.316 kw vis, 25.1 kw aur. 880t/836g TL: N33 31 33 W101 52 07 On air date: Nov 13, 1952. 7403 S. University Ave., Lubbock, TX, 79423. Phone: (806) 745-2345. Fax: (806) 748-2214. Web Site: www.everythinglubbock.com. Licensee: Nexstar Finance Inc. Group Owner: Nexstar Broadcasting Group Inc. (acq 12-31-03; grpsl). Population Served: 376,000 Natl. Network: CBS, . Washington Atty: Arter & Hadden. News staff: 47; News: 27 hrs wkly.
Key Personnel:
Greg McAlister . . . . gen mgr
Chuck Spaugh . . . . opns mgr
Gary Melton . . . . sls dir
Shanna Smith . . . . progmg mgr
Russ Poteet . . . . news dir
Eric Hosch. . . . . chief of engrg

KLCW-TV— Digital Channel: 43.70.8 kw vis. ant 748t TL: N33 30 08 W101 52 20 On air date: 2002. 9800 University Ave., Lubbock, TX, 79423. Phone: (806) 745-3434. Fax: (806) 748-9387.E-mail: bmoran@ramarcom.com Web Site: www.fox34.com. Licensee: Woods Communications Corp. Group Owner: (group owner) Natl. Network: CW, .
Key Personnel:
Brad Moran . . . . gen mgr

KPTB— Digital Channel: 16.214 kw vis. 272t TL: N33 33 12 W101 49 13 On air date: 1999. Box 61000, Midland, TX, 79711. 5604 Martin Luther King Blvd., Lubbock, TX 79404. Phone: (800) 707-0420 (806) 846-5200. Fax: (806) 749-7732.E-mail: info@ptcbglc.com Web Site: www.godslearningchannel.com. Licensee: Prime Time Christian Broadcasting Inc.
Key Personnel:
Jeff Tveit. . . . . gen mgr
Jeff Cooper . . . . stn mgr

***KTXT-TV—** Digital Channel: 39. Digital Hrs: 24 100 kw vis, 25 kw aur. 440t/817g TL: N33 34 55 W101 53 25 On air date: Oct 16, 1962. Box 42161, Lubbock, TX, 79409-2161. 17th St. & Indiana Ave. , Lubbock, TX 79409-2161. Phone: (806) 742-2209. Fax: (806) 742-1274. Web Site: www.ktxt.org. Licensee: Texas Tech University. Population Served: 375,000 Natl. Network: PBS, . Washington Atty: Cohn & Marks.
Key Personnel:
Pat Cates . . . . gen mgr

Lufkin

see Tyler-Longview (Lufkin & Nacogdoches), TX market

McAllen

see Harlingen-Weslaco-Brownsville-McAllen, TX market

Midland

see Odessa-Midland, TX market

Nacogdoches

see Tyler-Longview (Lufkin & Nacogdoches), TX market

Odessa-Midland, TX
(DMA 156)

KMID— Digital Channel: 26. Digital Hrs: 24 100 kw vis, 10 kw aur. 1,050t/1,147g TL: N32 05 14 W102 17 12 On air date: Dec 18, 1953. Box 60230, 3200 Laforce Blvd., Midland, TX, 79711. Phone: (432) 563-2222. Fax: (432) 563-5819.E-mail: news@kmid.tv Web Site: www.kmid.tv. Licensee: Nexstar Finance Inc. Group Owner: Nexstar Broadcasting Group Inc. (acq 7-31-2000; $10 million). Population Served: 794,000 Natl. Network: ABC, . Alabama Public Television Natl. Rep: Blair Television,. Washington Atty: Cohn & Marks. News staff: 23; News: 17 hrs wkly.
Key Personnel:
Chris Pruitt. . . . . gen mgr
Kirk Keller . . . . stn mgr

KMLM— Digital Channel: 42.1,120 kw vis, 112 kw aur. ant 479t/473g TL: N32 02 53 W102 17 44 On air date: Oct 18, 1988. Box 61000, Midland, TX, 79711-1000. 12706 W. Highway 80 E., Odessa, TX 79765. Phone: (800) 707-0420 (432) 563-0420. Fax: (432) 563-1736.E-mail: info@ptcbglc.com Web Site: www.GLC.US.com. Licensee: Prime Time Christian Broadcasting Inc. Population Served: 245,000
Key Personnel:
Al Cooper . . . . gen mgr & stn mgr
Matt Montgomery . . . . chief of engrg

KOSA-TV— Digital Channel: 7. Digital Hrs: 24 316 kw vis, 39.8 kw aur. ant 741t/715g TL: N31 51 50 W102 34 41 On air date: Jan 1, 1956. Box 107, 4101 E. 42nd St., J-7, Odessa, TX, 79762. Phone: (432) 580-5672. Fax: (432) 580-8010.E-mail: news@cbs7.com Web Site: www.cbs7.com. Licensee: ICA Broadcasting I Ltd. (acq 3-10-00; $8 million). Population Served: 350,000 Natl. Network: CBS, MyNetworkTV, . Natl. Rep: Continental Television Sales,. Washington Atty: Covington & Burling LLP. Foreign lang progmg: SpanishS 1 News staff: 22; News: 16 hrs wkly.
Key Personnel:
John Bushman . . . . chmn
Barry Marks . . . . pres & gen mgr
John Nichols . . . . CFO
Dale Palmer . . . . stn mgr
Rick McGee . . . . opns mgr

***KPBT-TV—** Digital Channel: 38. Digital Hrs: 15 513 kw vis, 51.3 kw aur. ant 289t/306g TL: N31 51 59 W102 22 50 On air date: Mar 24, 1986. Box 8940, Midland, TX, 79708-8940. 201 West University, Odessa, TX 79764. Phone: (432) 563-5728. Fax: (432) 563-5731.E-mail: kpbt@kpbt.org Web Site: www.kpbt.org. Licensee: Permian Basin Public Telecommunications Inc. (acq 2-2-2006; $1). Population Served: 350,000 Natl. Network: PBS, .
Key Personnel:
John H. James . . . . chmn
Daphne Dowdy. . . . . gen mgr & stn mgr
Domingo Machuca . . . . chief of engrg
Amy Lynch. . . . . traf mgr & progmg

KPEJ-TV— Digital Channel: 23. Digital Hrs: 24 2,880 kw vis. ant 1,099t/1,102g TL: N32 05 51 W102 17 21 On air date: June 16, 1986. Box 11009, 1550 W. I-20, Odessa, TX, 79763. Phone: (432) 580-0024. Fax: (432) 337-3707.E-mail: jfaltus@kpejtv.com Web Site: www.kpejtv.com. Licensee: Comcorp of Texas License Corp. Group Owner: Communications Corp. of America (acq 10-31-90; grpsl;11-19-90). Population Served: 133,600 Natl. Network: Fox, . Washington Atty: Fletcher, Heald & Hildreth.
Key Personnel:
Laura Wolf . . . . gen mgr
Jayne Faltus. . . . . progmg mgr

KUPB— Digital Channel: 18.5,000 kw vis. ant 930t/948g TL: N31 50 19 W102 31 59 (CP: ant 922t/951g) On air date: 2001. Box 61907, Midland, TX, 79711. 10313 West County Road 117, Midland, TX 79706. Phone: (432) 563-1826. Fax: (432) 563-0215. Web Site: www.entravision.com. Licensee: Entravision Holdings LLC. Group Owner: Entravision Communications Corp. Natl. Network: Univision (Spanish), . Washington Atty: Thompson, Hine & Flory L. Foreign lang progmg: SpanishS 168
Key Personnel:
Walter Ulloa . . . . CEO
Philip C. Wilkinson . . . . pres
John DeLorenzo . . . . CFO
Larry Safir . . . . exec VP
Leticia Martinez . . . . gen mgr & stn mgr

KWAB-TV— Digital Channel: 33.12.9 kw vis, 1.5 kw aur. 380t/497g TL: N32 15 14 W101 26 44 On air date: Jan 15, 1956. Box 60150, Midland, TX, 79711. Phone: (432) 567-9999. Fax: (432) 567-9994. Web Site: www.kwes.com. Licensee: Midessa Television Co. (acq 9-9-91; $4.85 million with KWES-TV Odessa; 9-23-91). Natl. Network: NBC, .
Key Personnel:
Mac Douglas . . . . gen mgr

KWES-TV— Digital Channel: 9.316 kw vis, 45.7 kw aur. ant 1,282t/1,039g TL: N31 59 17 W102 52 41 On air date: Dec 1, 1958. Box 60150, Midland, TX, 79711-0150. 11320 County Rd. 127 W., Midland, TX 79711. Phone: (432) 567-9999. Fax: (432) 567-9992.E-mail: info@kwestv.com Web Site: www.kwes.com. Licensee: Midessa Television Co. Group Owner: R.H. Drewry Group (acq 10-31-91; $4.85 million with KWAB(TV) Big Spring;9-23-91). Natl. Network: NBC, .
Key Personnel:
Mac Douglas. . . . . gen mgr & stn mgr
Carlos Fernandez . . . . news dir

KWWT— Digital Channel: 30. Digital Hrs: 24 50 kw vis. ant 482t/485g TL: N32 02 52.5 W102 17 44 On air date: 2001. Paxson Communications Corp., 601 Clearwater Park Rd., West Palm Beach, FL, 33401. Phone: (432) 563-5795. Web Site: www.cwtv.com. Licensee: WinStar Odessa Inc. Group Owner: Paxson Communications Corp. (acq 9-4-98). Natl. Network: CW, .
Key Personnel:
William L. Watson . . . . gen mgr

Port Arthur

see Beaumont-Port Arthur, TX market

San Angelo, TX
(DMA 1976)

KIDY— Analog Channel: 6. Digital Channel: 19. Analog Hrs: 24 Digital Hrs: 24 100 kw vis, 10 kw aur. 946t/1,000g TL: N31 35 21 W100 31 00 On air date: May 12, 1984. 406 S. Irving, San Angelo, TX, 76903. Phone: (325) 655-6006. Fax: (325) 655-8461.E-mail: kidy@foxsanangelo.com Web Site: foxsanangelo.com. Licensee: Sage Broadcasting Corp. Population Served: 172,800 Natl. Network: Fox, . Natl. Rep: Millennium Sales & Marketing,. Washington Atty: Fletcher, Heald & Hildreth. News staff: 2.
Key Personnel:
Paris Schindler. . . . . CEO
Bill Carter . . . . pres & stn mgr
Teddye Read . . . . natl sls mgr

KLST— Analog Channel: 8. Analog Hrs: 24 316 kw vis, 31.6 kw aur. 1,450t/1,500g TL: N31 22 01 W100 02 48 On air date: June 23, 1953. 2800 Armstrong St., San Angelo, TX, 76903-2799. Phone: (325) 949-8800. Fax: (325) 658-1118.E-mail: klst@klst.net Web Site: www.klst.tv. Licensee: Nexstar Broadcasting Inc. (acq 9-2-2004; $12 million). Population Served: 100,000 Natl. Network: CBS, . Washington Atty: Skadden, Arps, Slate, Meagher & Flom. News staff: 12; News: 17 hrs wkly.
Key Personnel:
Perry Sook . . . . pres
Joy Kimbell . . . . exec VP
Tom Stovall . . . . gen mgr
Mark McCain . . . . opns mgr
Lanny Kiest . . . . gen sls mgr
Don Plachno. . . . . prom mgr & pub svc dir
Gordon Hay . . . . progmg dir
Kathy Munoz . . . . news dir & edit dir
Roland Bigley . . . . chief of engrg
Teresa Gill . . . . traf mgr
Kathy Owens . . . . film dir
Ray Green. . . . . weather dir
Pat Attebery. . . . . women's int ed & women's cmtr

KSAN-TV— Analog Channel: 3.17.8 kw vis, 3.5 kw aur. 600t/469g TL: N31 37 22 W100 26 14 On air date: Feb 8, 1962. 2800 Armstrong St., San Angelo, TX, 76903. Phone: (325) 949-8800. Fax: (325) 655-1118.E-mail: nbc3@wcc.com Web Site: www.ksan.tv. Licensee: Mission Broadcasting Inc. Group Owner: (group owner; (acq 6-13-2003; $10 million with KRBC-TV Abilene). Natl. Network: NBC, . Natl. Rep: Blair Television,. Washington Atty: Kenkel, Barnard & Edmundson.
Key Personnel:
Tom Stovall . . . . stn mgr
Albert Gutierrez . . . . rgnl sls mgr
Kathy Munoz . . . . news dir
Len Martinez. . . . . chief of engrg

San Antonio, TX
(DMA 37)

KABB— Digital Channel: 30. Digital Hrs: 24 5,000 kw vis, 500 kw aur. ant 1,503t/1,503g TL: N29 17 27 W98 16 12 On air date: Dec 17, 1987. 4335 N.W. Loop 410, San Antonio, TX, 78229-5168. Phone: (210) 366-1129. Fax: (210) 377-4758.E-mail: kabbtv@kabb.com Web Site: www.kabb.com. Licensee: KABB Licensee L.L.C. Group Owner: Sinclair Broadcast Group Inc. Population Served: 1,500,000 Natl. Network: Fox, . Natl. Rep: Millennium Sales & Marketing,. Washington Atty: Shaw, Pittman. News staff: 35; News: 7 hrs wkly.

Key Personnel:
Dean Radla . . . . sls dir
Robert Canales. . . . . natl sls mgr

KCWX— Digital Channel: 5.23.7 kw vis. ant 1,351t/1,102g TL: N30 08 13 W98 36 35 5400 Fredericksburg Rd., San Antonio, TX, 78229. Phone: (210) 366-5000. Fax: (210) 348-9142. Fax: (210) 377-8779. Web Site: www.mysanantonio.com. Licensee: Corridor Television L.L.P. Natl. Network: CW, .
Key Personnel:
Robert G. McGann. . . . . gen mgr
Boots Walker . . . . sls dir
Rich Barton . . . . engrg dir

KENS— Digital Channel: 39.1,000 kw vis, 100 kw aur. ant 1,446t/1,450g TL: N29 16 11 W98 15 55 On air date: Feb 15, 1950. Box TV5, San Antonio, TX, 78299. 5400 Fredericksburg Rd., San Antonio, TX 78229. Phone: (210) 366-5000. Fax: (210) 377-0740. Web Site: www.mysanantonio.com. Licensee: KENS-TV Inc. Group Owner: Belo Corp., Broadcast Division (acq 1997; $75 million with co-located AM plus interest in Television Food Network). Population Served: 700,000 Natl. Network: CBS, . Natl. Rep: TeleRep,. Washington Atty: Wiley, Rein & Fielding. Wire Svc: NWS (National Weather Service) News staff: 55; News: 24 hrs wkly.
Key Personnel:
Bob McGann . . . . gen mgr
Boots Walker . . . . sls dir
Allen Lansing . . . . prom dir
Kurt Davis . . . . news dir
Frank Peterman . . . . engrg dir
Mandy Liles . . . . rsch dir

***KHCE-TV—** Digital Channel: 16. Digital Hrs: 16 360 kw vis. ant 1,076t/1,066g TL: N29 17 24 W98 15 20 On air date: July 1989. 15533 Capital Port Dr., San Antonio, TX, 78249. Box 691246, San Antonio, TX 78249. Phone: (210) 479-0123. Fax: (210) 492-5679. Web Site: www.khce.org. Licensee: San Antonio Community Educational TV Inc. Ownership: Dr. Reginald Cherry, 20%; Dr. Paul F. Crouch Sr., 20%; Richard Clayton Trotter, 20%; Cynthia Diaz, 20%; and Suzanna Shuler Harkley, 20% (acq 9-4-97; $3.125 million gift). Population Served: 1,000,000
Key Personnel:
Paul Crouch . . . . pres
Dr. Cherry . . . . VP
Laura Hanks . . . . gen mgr
Dorcas Rogers . . . . stn mgr
Jessica Mathews . . . . progmg dir
Sharon Denney . . . . pub affrs dir
Mike Bundrant . . . . engrg VP

***KLRN—** Digital Channel: 9.302 kw vis, 30.2 kw aur. ant 960t/1,051g TL: N29 19 33 W98 21 25 On air date: Sept 10, 1962. 501 Broadway, San Antonio, TX, 78215-1820. Phone: (210) 270-9000. Fax: (210) 270-9078.E-mail: info@klrn.org Web Site: www.klrn.org. Licensee: Alamo Public Telecommunications Council. (acq 8-11-89). Population Served: 3,000,000 Natl. Network: PBS, . Washington Atty: Cohn & Marks.
Key Personnel:
Mike Novak. . . . . chmn
Charles Vaughn . . . . sr VP
Joanne Winik. . . . . gen mgr
Cynthia Shields . . . . dev VP

KMYS— Digital Channel: 32. Digital Hrs: 24 5,000 kw vis, 500 kw aur. ant 1,758t TL: N29 36 37 W98 53 35 On air date: Nov 6, 1985. 4335 N.W. Loop 410, San Antonio, TX, 78229-5168. Phone: (210) 366-1129. Fax: (210) 377-4758.E-mail: kmys@kmys.tv Web Site: www.kmys.tv. Licensee: San Antonio (KRRT-TV) Licensee Inc. Group Owner: Sinclair Broadcast Group Inc. (acq 12-10-01; grpsl). Population Served: 1,500,000 Natl. Network: MyNetworkTV, . Washington Atty: Shaw, Pittman.
Key Personnel:
Dean Radla . . . . sls dir
Stephanie Shumway. . . . . natl sls mgr
Yvette Reyna . . . . prom dir

KNIC-DT— Digital Channel: 18.400 kw vis. ant 656t/551g TL: N29 41 48 W98 30 45 On air date: 2006. 411 E. Durango Blvd., San Antonio, TX, 78204-1309. Phone: (210) 227-4141. Fax: (210) 227-0469. Web Site: www.univision.com. Licensee: TeleFutura Partnership of San Antonio. Natl. Network: TeleFutura (Spanish), . Foreign lang progmg: SpanishS 168
Key Personnel:
David Loving. . . . . gen mgr & stn mgr

KPXL-TV— Digital Channel: 26. Digital Hrs: 24 228 kw vis. ant 1,709t/1,469g TL: N29 37 11 W99 02 55 On air date: Feb 19, 1999. 6100 Bandera Rd., Suite 304, San Antonio, TX, 78238. Phone: (210) 682-2626. Fax: (210) 682-3155. Web Site: www.ionline.tv. Licensee: ION Media San Antonio License Inc., debtor-in-possession. Group Owner: Paxson Communications Corp. (acq 6-24-99; $5 million for remaining 51%). Natl. Network: ION Television, .
Key Personnel:
Kathy Williams . . . . gen mgr & stn mgr & opns mgr

KSAT-TV— Digital Channel: 12. Digital Hrs: 22 316 kw vis, 63.2 kw aur. ant 1,483t/1,505g TL: N29 16 11 W98 15 31 On air date: Jan 21, 1957. 1408 N. St. Mary's St., San Antonio, TX, 78215. Phone: (210) 351-1200. Fax: (210) 351-1310. Web Site: www.ksat.com. Licensee: Post-Newsweek Stations Inc. Group Owner: (group owner; (acq 2-28-94;5-2-94). Population Served: 1,000,000 Natl. Network: ABC, . Natl. Rep: MMT,. Washington Atty: Covington & Burling. News: 21 hrs wkly.
Key Personnel:
James Joslyn . . . . VP & gen mgr

KTRG— Digital Channel: 28. Digital Hrs: 24 316 kw vis. ant 328t/285g TL: N29 20 39 W100 51 39 On air date: September 1996. Box 530391, Harlingen, TX, 78553. Phone: (956) 421-2635. Fax: (956) 428-7556. Licensee: SATV 10 LLC.. Ownership: SLN Management Group LLC (acq 4-30-2007; $550,000). Population Served: 500,000 Foreign lang progmg: SpanishS 24

KVAW— Digital Channel: 24.12.6 kw vis, 1.26 kw aur. ant 279t TL: N28 43 32 W100 28 35 On air date: 1991. 2524 Veterans Blvd., Eagle Pass, TX, 78852. Phone: (830) 773-3668. Phone: (830) 752-0312. Fax: (830) 773-3668. Web Site: www.kvaw16.com. Licensee: Dr. Joseph A. Zavaletta. Ownership: Dr. Joseph A. Zavaletta, 100% (acq 8-23-2004; $300,000). Population Served: 150,000
Key Personnel:
Dr. Joseph Zavaretta . . . . gen mgr

KVDA— Digital Channel: 38. Digital Hrs: 5:30 AM-2:05 PM (N-F); 5:30 AM-2 PM (S, Su) 5,000 kw vis, 500 kw aur. ant 1,495t/1,025g TL: N29 29 87 W98 29 53 On air date: Sept 10, 1989. 6234 San Pedro, San Antonio, TX, 78216. Phone: (210) 340-8860/8661. Fax: (210) 341-3962/(210)341-2051(news). Web Site: www.kvda.com. Licensee: NBC Telemundo License Co. Group Owner: Telemundo Group Inc. (acq 4-12-2002; grpsl). Population Served: 817,000 Natl. Network: Telemundo (Spanish), . Washington Atty: Hogan & Hartson. Wire Svc: Reuters Foreign lang progmg: SpanishS 112 News staff: 11; News: 10 hrs wkly.
Key Personnel:
Arturo Fux . . . . gen sls mgr
Maricela Arce. . . . . prom dir
Maricela Arce . . . . pub affrs dir

KWEX-DT— Digital Channel: 41. Digital Hrs: 24 580 kw vis. ant 1,417t/1,420g TL: N29 17 38 W98 15 31 On air date: June 10, 1955. 411 E. Durango Blvd., San Antonio, TX, 78204. Phone: (210) 227-4141/(210) 242-7451 (news). Fax: (210) 227-0469/(210) 226-0131 (news). Web Site: www.univision.com. Licensee: KWEX License Partnership L.P. Group Owner: Univision Communications Inc. (acq 7-86; grpsl). Population Served: 2,478,680 Natl. Network: Univision (Spanish), . Washington Atty: Fisher, Wayland, Cooper, Leader & Zaragoza. Foreign lang progmg: SpanishS 168 News: 5 hrs wkly.
Key Personnel:
David Loving . . . . VP & gen mgr

WOAI-TV— Digital Channel: 48. Digital Hrs: 24 100 kw vis, 18 kw aur. ant 1,476t/1,531g TL: N29 16 10 W98 15 55 On air date: Dec 11, 1949. Box 2641, San Antonio, TX, 78299. 1031 Navarro St., San Antonio, TX 78205. Phone: (210) 226-4444. Fax: (210) 224-9898. Web Site: www.woai.com. Licensee: High Plains Broadcasting License Co. LLC. Group Owner: Clear Channel Communications Inc. (acq 9-15-2008; grpsl). Population Served: 960,500 Natl. Network: NBC, . Washington Atty: Pillsbury Winthrop Shaw Pittman LLP. News staff: 68; News: 19.5 hrs wkly.
Key Personnel:
Donita Todd . . . . VP & gen mgr
Greg Derkowski . . . . prom mgr & adv
Carolyn Mastin. . . . . progmg mgr
Mark Pipitone. . . . . news dir
Liz Quinones . . . . pub affrs dir
Harold Friesenhahn . . . . chief of engrg

Sherman, TX-Ada, OK (DMA 161)

KTEN— Digital Channel: 10. Digital Hrs: 0 316 kw vis, 47.5 kw aur. 1,458t/1,500g TL: N34 21 34 W96 33 34 On air date: June 1, 1954. 10 High Point Cir., Denison, TX, 75020. Phone: (903) 337-4000. Fax: (908) 465-1207. Fax: (903) 465-1368.E-mail: 10news@kten.com Web Site: www.kten.com. Licensee: Channel 49 Acquisition Corp. Ownership: Lockwood Corp. Population Served: 238,000 Natl. Network: NBC, CW, . Natl. Rep: Continental Television Sales,. Washington Atty: Brooks, Pierce, McLendon, Humprey & Leonard. Wire Svc: AP News staff: 25; News: 36 hrs wkly.
Key Personnel:
Asa Jessee . . . . gen mgr
Brian Capaldo . . . . stn mgr
Ken Braswell . . . . gen sls mgr
TBD . . . . news dir
Kris Anderson . . . . chief of engrg

KXII— Digital Channel: 12. Digital Hrs: 24 hrs. 224 kw vis, 22.4 kw aur. ant 1,781t/1,698g TL: N34 01 58 W96 48 00 On air date: July 1956. Box 1175, 4201 Texoma Pkwy., Sherman, TX, 75091-1175. Phone: (903) 892-8123. Fax: (903) 893-7858.E-mail: comments @kxii.com Web Site: www.kxii.com. Licensee: Gray Television Licensee Inc. Group Owner: Gray Television Inc. (acq 6-29-99; $41.5 million). Population Served: 301,000 Natl. Network: CBS, Fox, MyNetworkTV, . Natl. Rep: Millennium Sales & Marketing,. Washington Atty: Womble, Carlyle, Sandridge & Rice, PLLC. News: 30 hrs wkly.
Key Personnel:
Rick Dean. . . . . VP & gen mgr progmg dir
Todd Bates . . . . sls dir & gen sls mgr & rgnl sls mgr
Rachel Shockey. prom dir
Matt Brown. . . . . news dir
Randy Wells . . . . chief of engrg
Nancy Alley. . . . . traf mgr
Richard Flaker . . . . pub svc dir
David Reed . . . . sports cmtr
Alan Crone . . . . weather dir

Sweetwater

see Abilene-Sweetwater, TX market

Temple

see Waco-Temple-Bryan, TX market

Texarkana

see Shreveport, LA market

Tyler-Longview (Lufkin & Nacogdoches), TX (DMA 110)

KCEB— Digital Channel: 51.5,000 kw vis. ant 829t/716g TL: N32 35 36 W94 49 10 On air date: July 20, 2003. 701 N. Access Rd., Longview, TX, 75602. Phone: (903) 236-0051. Fax: (903) 753-6637. Licensee: Estes Broadcasting Inc. Ownership: Dimension Enterprises Ltd. (acq 11-24-2003). Natl. Network: CW, . Washington Atty: Fletcher, Heald & Hildreth.
Key Personnel:
Tony Cruz . . . . gen mgr
Tyrene Carl . . . . gen sls mgr

KETK-TV— Digital Channel: 22. Digital Hrs: 24 hrs 5,000 kw vis, 500 kw aur. ant 1,583t/1,437g TL: N32 03 40 W95 18 50 On air date: March 1987. 4300 Richmond Rd., Tyler, TX, 75703. Phone: (903) 581-5656. Fax: (903) 561-1648. Web Site: www.ketknbc.com. Licensee: Comcorp of Tyler License Corp. Group Owner: Communications Corp. of America (acq 11-12-2004; $38 million). Natl. Network: NBC, . Natl. Rep: Millennium Sales & Marketing,. Washington Atty: Dow, Lohnes. News staff: 37; News: 27 hrs wkly.
Key Personnel:
Dave Tillery . . . . gen mgr
Chris Dudley. opns mgr
Eric Jontra . . . . sls dir
K.J. Lambein . . . . prom dir & pub svc dir
Yolanda Clater . . . . progmg dir
Neal Barton . . . . news dir
John Cummings . . . . chief of engrg
Connie Jobe . . . . traf mgr

KFXK-TV— Digital Channel: 31. Digital Hrs: 20 4,680 kw vis, 36.70 kw aur. ant 1,249t/1,199g TL: N32 15 35 W94 57 02 On air date: Sept 9, 1984. 701 N. Access Rd., Longview, TX, 75602. Phone: (903) 236-0051. Fax: (903) 753-6637. Web Site: www.fox51.com. Licensee: Warwick Communications Inc. Group Owner: White Knight Holdings Inc. (acq 9-1-99; $11.5 million for stock plus 3 low-power stns). Natl. Network: Fox, .

Key Personnel:
Sheldon Galloway. . . . . pres
Dave Tillery . . . . gen mgr
Suzanne Calhoun. . . . . natl sls mgr
Drew Balch . . . . progmg dir & progmg mgr opns
Neal Barton . . . . news dir
Connie Jobt. . . . . traf mgr

KLTV— Digital Channel: 7. Digital Hrs: 24 316 kw vis, 31.6 kw aur. 991t/1,079g TL: N32 32 21 W95 13 16 On air date: Oct 15, 1954. Box 957, 105 W. Ferguson, Tyler, TX, 75702. Phone: (903) 597-5588. Fax: (903) 510-7847. Web Site: www.kltv.com. Licensee: Civco Inc. Group Owner: Liberty Corp. (acq 1-13-2006; grpsl). Population Served: 82,000 Natl. Network: ABC, . Washington Atty: Covington & Burling.
Key Personnel:
Brad Streit . . . . gen mgr
Mary Ryan . . . . opns dir & natl sls mgr
Pat Stacey . . . . gen sls mgr
Mark Scirto . . . . rgnl sls mgr & weather dir
Cathy Carmichael . . . . progmg dir
Kenny Boles . . . . news dir
Butch Adair . . . . chief of engrg
Hazel Kennedy . . . . rsch dir & traf mgr

KTRE— Digital Channel: 9. Digital Hrs: 24 158 kw vis, 31.7 kw aur. 670t TL: N31 25 09 W94 48 02 On air date: Aug 31, 1955. Box 729, Lufkin, TX, 75902-0792. 358 TV Rd., Pollok, TX 75969. Phone: (936) 853-5873. Fax: (936) 853-3084.E-mail: dlorenz@ktre.com Web Site: www.ktre.com. Licensee: Raycom Media, Inc. Group Owner: Liberty Corp. (acq 1-13-2006; grpsl). Population Served: 260,000 Natl. Network: ABC, . Washington Atty: Covington & Burling. Foreign lang progmg: SpanishS 1 News staff: 15; News: 20 hrs wkly.
Key Personnel:
Paul H. McTear Jr. CEO
Melissa Thurber . . . . chmn & CFO
Paul H. McTear. . . . . pres
Wayne Dougherty . . . . exec VP
Artie Bedard . . . . sr VP & VP gen mgr

KYTX— Digital Channel: 18. Digital Hrs: 24 Note: CBS is on KYTX(TV) ch 19, MyNetworkTV is on KYTX-DT ch 18. 4,270 kw vis. ant 1,499t/1,545g TL: N31 54 20 W95 05 05 On air date: Sept 1, 1991. 2211 ESE Loop 323, Tyler, TX, 75701. 911 W Loop 281, Suite 112, Longview, TX 75604. Phone: (903) 581-2211. Fax: (903) 581-5769. Web Site: www.cbs19.tv. Licensee: KYTX License Co. LLC. Group Owner: MAX Media L.L.C. (acq 2-18-2008; $25 million). Natl. Network: CBS, Natl. Rep: Blair Television,. Washington Atty: Wiley Rein LLP. Wire Svc: AP News staff: 25; News: 19.5 hrs wkly.
Key Personnel:
John Gaston . . . . gen mgr
Chesley Bryan . . . . natl sls mgr
Margaret Strout . . . . progmg mgr & traf mgr
Dan Delgado . . . . news dir
Moe Strout . . . . chief of engrg

Victoria, TX
(DMA 205)

KAVU-TV— Digital Channel: 15. Digital Hrs: 5 AM-1 AM 2140 kw vis, 2.14 kw aur. 1,020t/1,067g TL: N28 48 06 W96 33 09 On air date: July 4, 1982. 3808 N. Navarro, Victoria, TX, 77901. Phone: (361) 575-2500. Fax: (361) 575-2255. Web Site: www.myvictoriaonline.com. Licensee: Saga Broadcasting LLC. Group Owner: Saga Communications Inc. (acq 10-20-98; $11.875 million; with KNAL(AM) Victoria). Population Served: 288,845 Natl. Network: ABC, . Natl. Rep: Continental Television Sales,. Rgnl. Rep: Rgnl rep: Katz Continental Washington Atty: Smithwick & Belendiuk, P.C. Wire Svc: AP News staff: 17; News: 29 hrs wkly.
Key Personnel:
Jeff Pryor . . . . gen mgr & gen sls mgr
John Garcia . . . . opns mgr
Rebecca Sarlls . . . . progmg dir
Doug Tisdale . . . . news dir
Sean McBride . . . . prom mgr & pub affrs dir
Kevin John . . . . engrg mgr
Jennifer Rosales. traf mgr

KVCT— Digital Channel: 11. Digital Hrs: Midnight-5 AM 155 kw vis, 15.5 kw aur. ant 489t/494g TL: N28 46 41 W96 57 38 On air date: Nov 21, 1969. 3808 N. Navarro St., Houston, TX, 77901. Phone: (361) 575-2500. Fax: (361) 575-2255. Web Site: www.myvictoriaonline.com. Licensee: Surtsey Media LLC. Group Owner: (group owner; (acq 4-26-99). Population Served: 288,845 Natl. Network: Fox, . Natl. Rep: Continental Television Sales,. Washington Atty: Fletcher, Heald & Hildreth, P.L.C. Wire Svc: AP News: 2.5 hrs wkly.

Key Personnel:
Jeff Pryor . . . . gen mgr
John Garcia . . . . opns mgr
Darren Lehrmann. . . . . gen sls mgr
Rebecca Sarlls . . . . progmg dir
Doug Tisdale . . . . news dir
Sean McBride . . . . pub affrs dir
Kevin John . . . . chief of engrg
Jennifer Rosales. traf mgr

Waco-Temple-Bryan, TX
(DMA 94)

KAKW-DT— Digital Channel: 13.1,660 kw vis. ant 1,814t/1,791g TL: N30 43 33 W97 59 24 On air date: 1996. 2233 W. Northloop Blvd., Austin, TX, 78731. Phone: (512) 453-8899. Fax: (512) 533-2874. Licensee: Univision Communications Inc. Group Owner: (group owner; (acq 12-10-2001; $12 million). Natl. Network: Univision (Spanish), . Foreign lang progmg: SpanishS 168

***KAMU-TV—** Digital Channel: 12.22.9 kw vis, 2.29 kw aur. ant 390t/379g TL: N30 37 48 W96 20 33 On air date: Feb 15, 1970. Texas A&M Univ., College Station, TX, 77843-4244. Phone: (979) 845-5611. Fax: (979) 845-1643. Web Site: www.kamu.tamu.edu. Licensee: Texas A&M University. Population Served: 151,000 Natl. Network: PBS, .
Key Personnel:
Rodney Zent . . . . gen mgr
Jon Bennett . . . . stn mgr & progmg dir
John Prihoda . . . . opns mgr
Elaine Hoyak . . . . dev dir
Wayne Pecena . . . . engrg dir
Ken Nelson . . . . chief of engrg
Sherill Simpson . . . . traf mgr

KBTX-TV— Digital Channel: 50.69.2 kw vis, 6.9 kw aur. ant 1,689t/1,544g TL: N30 33 10 W96 01 50 On air date: May 22, 1957. 4141 E. 29th Street, Bryan, TX, 77802. Phone: (979) 846-7777. Fax: (979) 846-1490 (sls). Fax: (979) 846-1888 (news). Web Site: www.kbtx.com. Licensee: Gray Television Licensee Inc. Group Owner: Gray Television Inc. (acq 6-29-99; $97.5 million cash and shares with KWTX-TV Waco). Population Served: 2,000,000 Natl. Network: CBS, CW, . Natl. Rep: Millennium Sales & Marketing,. Wire Svc: AP News staff: 30; News: 19 hrs. wkly.
Key Personnel:
Jon Boaz . . . . gen sls mgr
Mike Wright . . . . VP & gen mgr & natl sls mgr
Mike George . . . . news dir
Mandy Riske . . . . opns

KCEN-TV— Digital Channel: 9. Digital Hrs: 24 100 kw vis, 10 kw aur. ant 830t/833g TL: N31 16 24 W97 13 14 On air date: Nov 1, 1953. 111 West Central Ave., Temple, TX, 76501. Phone: (254) 859-5481. Fax: (254) 859-4004.E-mail: news@kcentv.com Web Site: www.kcentv.com. Licensee: KCEN License Co. LLC. (acq 5-1-2009; $26 million Population Served: 315,700 tvhh Natl. Network: NBC, . Natl. Rep: Blair Television,. Washington Atty: Wiley Rein LLP. Wire Svc: AP News staff: 33; News: 17 hrs wkly.
Key Personnel:
Terry E. London . . . . pres
Gayle Kiger . . . . VP & gen mgr

***KNCT—** Digital Channel: 46. Digital Hrs: 24 500 kw vis. ant 1,286t/1,117g TL: N30 59 08.4 W97 37 50.1 On air date: Nov 23, 1970. Box 1800, Killeen, TX, 76540-9990. Telecommunications Bldg., 6200 W. Centex Expwy., Killeen, TX 76540-9990. Phone: (254) 526-1176. Fax: (254) 526-1850.E-mail: knct@knct.org Web Site: www.knct.org. Licensee: Central Texas College. Natl. Network: PBS, . News staff: one; News: one hr wkly.
Key Personnel:
Max Rudolph . . . . gen mgr
Fred McNeilly . . . . prom mgr
Ruth Wedergren . . . . progmg dir & film buyer
Steve Sulzer . . . . engrg mgr

***KWBU-TV—** Digital Channel: 20. Digital Hrs: 24 79.4 kw vis, 7.9 kw aur. ant 508t/446g TL: N31 30 31 W97 10 03 On air date: May 22, 1989. One Bear Pl., # 97296, Waco, TX, 76798-7296. Phone: (254) 710-3472. Phone: (254) 710-7888. Fax: (254) 710-3874.E-mail: clare@kwbu.org Web Site: www.kwbu.org. Licensee: Brazos Valley Public Broadcasting Foundation. Ownership: Baylor University. (acq 12-6-93; $80,000;12-20-93). Population Served: 100000 Natl. Network: PBS, . Washington Atty: Cohn & Marks.
Key Personnel:
Polly Anderson . . . . CEO & gen mgr
Larry Brumley. chmn & pres
Nab Holmes . . . . dev dir
Clare Paul . . . . prom mgr & progmg mgr
Michael Hagerty . . . . news dir & pub affrs dir
Tony Poole. . . . . engrg dir & chief of engrg

KWKT-TV— Digital Channel: 44. Digital Hrs: 24 4,170 kw vis, 417 kw aur. ant 1,811t/1,673g TL: N31 18 52 W97 19 37 (CP: ant 1,829t/1,672g. TL: N31 18 53.4 W97 19 36) On air date: March 1988. Box 2544, Waco, TX, 76702-2544. 8803 Woodway Dr., Waco, TX 76712. Phone: (254) 776-3844. Fax: (254) 388-5958.E-mail: info@kwkt.com Web Site: kwkt.com. Licensee: Comcorp of Texas License Corp. Group Owner: Communications Corp. of America (acq 10-31-90; grpsl;11-19-90). Natl. Network: Fox, MyNetworkTV, . Natl. Rep: Millennium Sales & Marketing,. Washington Atty: Fletcher, Heald & Hildreth.
Key Personnel:
Duane Sartor. gen mgr & stn mgr opns mgr & mktg mgr prom mgr & progmg dir
Bill Knobler . . . . gen sls mgr
Robin Rice . . . . natl sls mgr
Amy Bishop . . . . pub affrs dir & pub svc dir
Lou Strowger. . . . . chief of engrg

KWTX-TV— Digital Channel: 10. Digital Hrs: 24 39 kw vis. ant 1,820t/1,630g TL: N31 19 19 W97 19 02 On air date: April 1955. Box 2636, Waco, TX, 76702-2636. 6700 American Plaza, Waco, TX 76712. Phone: (254) 776-1330. Fax: (254) 751-1088.E-mail: mail@kwtx.com Web Site: www.kwtx.com. Licensee: Gray Television Licensee Inc. Group Owner: Gray Television Inc. (acq 6-29-99; $97.5 million cash and shares with KBTX-TV Bryan). Population Served: 763,000 Natl. Network: CBS, CW, . Natl. Rep: Millennium Sales & Marketing,. Washington Atty: Venable Attorneys at Law. News staff: 36; News: 20 hrs wkly.
Key Personnel:
Jason Effinger . . . . gen mgr
Ken Musgrave . . . . opns mgr
Bob Bunch . . . . gen sls mgr

KXXV— Digital Channel: 26. Digital Hrs: 24/7 5,000 kw vis, 500 kw aur. ant 1,841t/1,706g TL: N31 20 16 W97 18 36 On air date: Jan 1, 1985. Box 2522, Waco, TX, 76702. 1909 S. New Rd., Waco, TX 76711. Phone: (254) 754-2525. Fax: (254) 752-1002.E-mail: news25@kxxv.com Web Site: www.kxxv.com. Licensee: Centex Television L.P. Group Owner: R.H. Drewry Group (acq 1994). Natl. Network: ABC, Telemundo (Spanish), . News staff: 18; News: 14.5 hrs wkly.
Key Personnel:
Mike Lee. . . . . VP & gen mgr stn mgr
Jeff Armstrong . . . . gen sls mgr
Darlene Mahler . . . . natl sls mgr & rgnl sls mgr
Dennis Kinney . . . . news dir
Randy Lee. chief of engrg
ABC, Telemundo, Weather Now(Local Weather).

KYLE-TV— Digital Channel: 28.50 kw vis. ant 722t/640g TL: N30 41 18 W96 25 35 On air date: Oct 31, 1994. 2402 Broadmoor Dr., Suite B-101, Bryan, TX, 77805. Phone: (979) 774-1800. Fax: (979) 774-1901. Web Site: www.kyle28.com. Licensee: Comcorp of Bryan License Corp. Group Owner: Communications Corp. of America (acq 1996; $1.1 million). Population Served: 200,000 Natl. Network: Fox, MyNetworkTV, . Washington Atty: Gardner, Carton & Douglas.
Key Personnel:
Duane Sartor . . . . stn mgr & gen sls mgr
Mark Kremer. gen sls mgr
Lou Strauger. . . . . chief of engrg
Satellite of KWKT(TV) Waco.

Weslaco

see Harlingen-Weslaco-Brownsville-McAllen, TX market

Wichita Falls, TX & Lawton, OK
(DMA 145)

KAUZ-TV— Digital Channel: 22.200 kw vis. ant 1,020t/994g TL: N33 54 04 W98 32 21 On air date: Mar 1, 1953. Box 2130, Wichita Falls, TX, 76307. Phone: (940) 322-6957. Fax: (940) 761-3331. Fax: TWX: 910-890-5836.E-mail: email@kauz.com Web Site: www.kauz.com. Licensee: Hoak Media of Wichita Falls L.P. Group Owner: Hoak Media Corporation (acq 11-5-2003; $8.2 million). Population Served: 385,000 Natl. Network: CBS, CW, . Natl. Rep: Harrington, Righter & Parsons,. Washington Atty: Covington & Burling. Wire Svc: CBS News staff: 20; News: 15 hrs wkly.
Key Personnel:
Mike DeLier . . . . gen mgr
Gary Lucus . . . . opns mgr
Randy Blake. gen sls mgr
Kyle Williams . . . . natl sls mgr
Mark Walker. rgnl sls mgr
Jackie McCartney . . . . prom mgr
Elayne Thompson . . . . progmg dir
Drew Hadwall. . . . . news dir
Tony Guess . . . . chief of engrg

KFDX-TV— Digital Channel: 28. Digital Hrs: 24 100 kw vis, 20 kw aur. ant 1,000t/1,045g TL: N33 53 23 W98 33 20 On air date: Apr 12, 1953.

4500 Seymour Hwy., Wichita Falls, TX, 76309. Box 4888, Wichita Falls, TX 76309. Phone: (940) 691-0003. Fax: (940) 691-0330.E-mail: kfdx@kfdx.com Web Site: www.kfdx.com. Licensee: Nexstar Broadcasting Inc. Group Owner: Nexstar Broadcasting Group Inc. (acq 11-6-97; grpsl). Population Served: 162,800 Natl. Network: NBC, . Washington Atty: Arter & Hadden. News staff: 24; News: 19.5 hrs wkly.

Key Personnel:

Troy Short . . . VP & prom mgr
Julie Pruett . . . gen mgr
Greg Collier . . . opns mgr
Wayne Reed . . . sls dir & rgnl sls mgr
Terry Porter . . . chief of engrg

KJTL— Digital Channel: 15. Digital Hrs: 20 2,820 kw vis, 282 kw aur. 1,079t/1,000g TL: N34 12 06 W98 43 44 On air date: May 18, 1985. Box 4888, 4500 Seymour Hwy., Wichita Falls, TX, 76309. Phone: (940) 691-1808. Fax: (940) 691-4856.E-mail: kjtl@fox18.com Web Site: www.texomashomepage.com. Licensee: Mission Broadcasting of Wichita Falls License Inc. Group Owner: Mission Broadcasting Inc. (acq 1999; $28.5 million with KCIT(TV) Amarillo). Natl. Network: Fox, . Washington Atty: Spector & Goldberg.

Key Personnel:

Stephanie Reed . . . gen mgr & stn mgr

KSWO-TV— Digital Channel: 11. Digital Hrs: 24 316 kw vis, 63.1 kw aur. 1,050t/1,059g TL: N34 12 55 W98 43 13 On air date: Mar 8, 1953. Box 708, Hwy. 7, Lawton, OK, 73502. Phone: (580) 355-7000. Fax: (580) 357-3811. Web Site: www.kswo.com. Licensee: KSWO TV Inc. Group Owner: R.H. Drewry Group Population Served: 300,000 Natl. Network: ABC, .

Key Personnel:

Larry Patton . . . gen mgr & stn mgr
Joe Bartnik . . . chief of engrg

Utah

Salt Lake City, UT (DMA 33)

KBCJ— Analog Channel: 6. Digital Channel: 16.1,000 kw vis. ant 2,217t/128g TL: N40 21 22 W109 08 41 Not on air, target date: unknown: Equity Media Holdings Corp., 1 Shackleford Dr., Suite 400, Little Rock, AR, 72211. Phone: (501) 219-2400. Fax: (501) 716-3502. Permittee: Vernal Broadcasting Inc., debtor in possession. Group Owner: Equity Broadcasting Corp. (acq 5-11-2001).

Key Personnel:

Doug Cryle . . . opns mgr

KBNY— Analog Channel: 6. Digital Channel: 27.300 kw vis. ant 1,073t/92g TL: N39 15 58 W114 54 05 Not on air, target date: unknown: Equity Broadcasting Corp., 1 Shackelford Dr., Suite 400, Little Rock, AR, 72211. Phone: (501) 219-2400. Fax: (501) 604-8404. Licensee: Nevada Channel 6 Inc., debtor in possession. Population Served: 498,000.

***KBYU-TV—** Digital Channel: 44. Digital Hrs: 24 162 kw vis, 35 kw aur. ant 2,941t/100g TL: N40 36 28 W112 09 33 On air date: Nov 15, 1965. 2000 Ironton Blvd., Provo, UT, 84606. Phone: (801) 422-8450. Fax: (801) 422-8478.E-mail: kbyu@byu.edu Web Site: www.kbyu.org. Licensee: Brigham Young University. Population Served: 629,850 Natl. Network: PBS, . Washington Atty: Wilkinson, Barker, Knauer & Quinn. Foreign lang progmg: SpanishS 3 News staff: 3; News: 3 hrs wkly.

Key Personnel:

Derek Marquis . . . gen mgr
Jim Bell . . . mktg mgr
Wendy Thomas . . . progmg mgr
Wesley Sims . . . news dir
Brian Leifson . . . chief of engrg

KCBU— Digital Channel: 11.51.1 kw vis. ant 2,158t/167g TL: N39 45 22 W110 59 22 On air date: 2003. Stn currently dark 3901 Hwy. 121 S., Bedford, TX, 76021. Phone: (817) 571-1229. Fax: (817) 571-7458. Web Site: www.daystar.com. Licensee: Word of God Fellowship Inc. (acq 7-31-2009; grpsl).

Key Personnel:

Marcus D. Lamb . . . pres

KCSG— Digital Channel: 14. Digital Hrs: 24 25 w vis. ant 1,263t/56g TL: N37 38 22 W113 02 00 On air date: September 1985. 158 W. 1600 S., Suite 200, St. George, UT, 84770. Phone: (435) 634-7500. Fax: (435) 674-2774.E-mail: info@kcsg.com Web Site: www.kcsg.com. Licensee: Southwest Media LLC. Ownership: Stephen W. Wade, 100% votes (acq 10-18-2005). Natl. Network: MyNetworkTV, . Washington Atty: Garvey, Schubert & Barer.

Key Personnel:

Ray Hardy . . . gen mgr
Patrick Donahoo . . . gen sls mgr
E. Morgan Skinner Jr. . . . prom mgr & pub affrs dir
Carl Arky . . . news dir
Ben VanBenthem . . . chief of engrg

KENV-DT— Digital Channel: 10. Digital Hrs: 24 3.09 kw vis. ant 1,850t TL: N40 41 52 On air date: March 1997. 1025 Chilton Cir., Elko, NV, 89801. Phone: (775) 777-8500. Fax: (775) 777-7758. Web Site: www.kenvtv.com. Licensee: Ruby Mountain Broadcasting Co. Group Owner: Sunbelt Communications Co. (acq 11-8-96). Population Served: 37,000 Natl. Network: NBC, .

Key Personnel:

John Finkbohner . . . opns mgr
Terry Hritz . . . gen mgr & stn mgr & adv mgr

Rebroadcasts KRNV-DT Reno.

KGWR-TV— Digital Channel: 13. Digital Hrs: 24 209 kw vis, 10 kw aur. ant 1,624t/148g TL: N41 26 21 W109 06 42 On air date: Oct 21, 1977. 1856 Skyview Dr., Casper, WY, 82601. Phone: (307) 234-1111. Fax: (307) 234-4005. Licensee: Mark III Media Inc. Group Owner: Chelsey Broadcasting Co. (acq 5-31-2006; grpsl). Population Served: 19,000 Natl. Network: CBS, . Washington Atty: Covington & Burling.

Key Personnel:

Mark Nalbone . . . gen mgr
Terry Lane . . . opns mgr

Satellite of KGWC-TV Casper.

KJZZ-TV— Digital Channel: 46. Digital Hrs: 24 1,637 kw vis, 163.7 kw aur. ant 3,847t/241g TL: N40 39 12 W112 12 06 On air date: Feb 14, 1989. 301 West South Temple, Calgary, UT, 84101. Phone: (801) 537-1414. Fax: (801) 238-6414. Web Site: www.kjzz.com. Licensee: Larry H. Miller Communications Corp. Ownership: Larry H. Miller, 100%. (acq 2-12-93;3-15-93). Population Served: 616,720 Natl. Rep: Blair Television,. Washington Atty: Fleischman & Walsh.

Key Personnel:

Chris Baum . . . gen mgr
Randy Wright . . . opns VP & opns dir
Bob Gauld . . . sls VP & natl sls mgr
Marc Lowry . . . gen sls mgr
Eric Schulz . . . mktg dir
Dean Paynter . . . prom mgr
Robert Quigley . . . progmg dir & pub affrs dir
Mike Grover . . . chief of engrg
Charla Hastings . . . traf mgr

KPNZ— Digital Channel: 24. Digital Hrs: 24 1,514 kw vis. ant 4,031t/197g TL: N40 39 33 W112 12 07 On air date: 1999. 150 N. Wright Brothers Dr., Suite 520, Salt Lake City, UT, 84116. Phone: (801) 519-2424. Fax: (801) 359-1272.E-mail: info@utahs24tv.com Web Site: www.utahs24tv.com. Licensee: KRCA License LLC. (acq 11-30-2007; $10 million).

Key Personnel:

Wayne Casa . . . gen mgr

KSL-TV— Digital Channel: 38. Digital Hrs: 24 33.4 kw vis, 6.8 kw aur. ant 3,831t/249g TL: N40 39 35 W112 12 04 On air date: June 1, 1949. 55 N. Third W., Salt Lake City, UT, 84110-1160. Phone: (801) 575-5555. Fax: (801) 575-5830 (sales). Fax: (801) 575-5560 (news). Web Site: www.ksl.com. Licensee: Bonneville International Corp. Group Owner: (group owner) Population Served: 1,873,000 Natl. Network: NBC, . Natl. Rep: Eagle Television Sales,. Washington Atty: Wilkinson, Barker, Knauer & Quinn. Wire Svc: UPI Foreign lang progmg: SpanishS 5 News staff: 65; News: 21 hrs wkly.

Key Personnel:

Bruce Christensen . . . gen mgr

KSTU— Digital Channel: 28. Digital Hrs: 24 112 kw vis, 11.2 kw aur. ant 3,660t/144 TL: N40 39 33 W112 12 08 On air date: Oct 9, 1978. 5020 W. Amelia Earhart Dr., Salt Lake City, UT, 84116. Phone: (801) 532-1300. Fax: (801) 537-5335.E-mail: news@fox13.com Web Site: www.myfoxutah.com. Licensee: Community Television of Utah License LLC. Group Owner: (group owner; (acq 7-14-2008; grpsl). Population Served: 1,900,000 Natl. Network: Fox, . Natl. Rep: Fox Stations Sales,. News: 34 hrs wkly.

Key Personnel:

Tim Ermish . . . VP & gen mgr
Ken Freedman . . . gen sls mgr
Kent Carlton . . . natl sls mgr
Kirt Burton . . . rgnl sls mgr
Melanie Say . . . prom VP & progmg VP
Renai Bodley . . . news dir
Al Schultz . . . engrg VP

KTMW— Digital Channel: 20.1,660 kw vis. ant 3,841t TL: N40 39 12 W112 12 06 On air date: 2002. 314 S. Redwood Rd., Salt Lake City, UT, 84104-3536. Phone: (801) 973-8820. Fax: (801) 973-7145. Web Site: www.tv20.org. Licensee: Alpha & Omega Communications LLC. Ownership: Connie Whitney, 33.33%; Isaac Max Jaramillo, 33.33%; and Patricia Openshaw, 33.33% (acq 7-31-2003; $1.5 million). Population Served: 1.5 m,ill,ion Natl. Rep: Apex Media Sales Inc.,. Washington Atty: Wood, Maines & Nolan, Chartered.

Key Personnel:

Pat Openhaw . . . pres
Dennis Ermel . . . gen mgr & progmg mgr
Anthon Jeppesan . . . opns mgr
Michelle Ermel . . . prom mgr
Dennis Silver . . . chief of engrg

KTVX— Digital Channel: 40.32.4 kw vis, 4.9 kw aur. ant 3,870t TL: N40 36 50 W112 11 05 On air date: Apr 15, 1948. 2175 W. 1700 S., Salt Lake City, UT, 84104. Phone: (801) 975-4444. Fax: (801) 975-4442.E-mail: news@abc4.com Web Site: www.abc4.com. Licensee: Newport Television License LLC. Group Owner: Clear Channel Communications Inc. (acq 3-14-2008; grpsl). Population Served: 2,082,000 Natl. Network: ABC, . News staff: 50; News: 14 hrs wkly.

Key Personnel:

David D'Antuono . . . VP & gen mgr
Dennis Elsbury . . . mktg dir
Scott Terrill . . . prom dir
Karen Zabriskie . . . progmg mgr
David Bird . . . news dir & engrg dir
Bob Lyon . . . chief of engrg
John Cronan . . . rsch dir
Shara Meredith . . . traf mgr
Sharr Lewis . . . pub svc dir
Marti Skold . . . weather dir

KUCW— Digital Channel: 48.5,000 kw vis, 500 kw aur. ant 777t/347g TL: N41 15 17 W112 14 13 On air date: October 1985. 2175 West 1700 South, Salt Lake City, UT, 84104. Phone: (801) 975-4444. Fax: (801) 975-4442.E-mail: info@cw30.com Web Site: www.cw30.com. Licensee: High Plains Broadcasting License Co. LLC. Group Owner: Acme Communications Inc. (acq 9-15-2008; grpsl). Population Served: 150,000 Natl. Network: CW, . Natl. Rep: MMT,.

Key Personnel:

David D' Antuono . . . gen mgr

***KUED—** Digital Channel: 42.155 kw vis, 15.5 kw aur. ant 3,030t/204g TL: N40 36 29 W112 09 36 On air date: Jan 20, 1958. 101 S. Wasatch Dr., Room 215, Salt Lake City, UT, 84112. Phone: (801) 581-7777. Fax: (801) 585-5096. Web Site: www.kued.org. Licensee: University of Utah. Population Served: 2,000,000 Natl. Network: PBS, .

Key Personnel:

Larry Smith . . . gen mgr

***KUEN—** Digital Channel: 36. Digital Hrs: 15 166 kw vis, 16.6 kw aur. ant 2,882t/78g TL: N40 36 30 W112 09 34 On air date: Dec 1, 1986. 101 Wasatch Dr., Suite 215, Salt Lake City, UT, 84112. Phone: (801) 581-2999. Fax: (801) 585-6105.E-mail: resources@uen.org Web Site: www.uen.org. Licensee: Utah State Board of Regents. Population Served: 1,500,000 Foreign lang progmg: SpanishS 0

Key Personnel:

Mike Peterson . . . gen mgr & progmg dir

***KUES—** Digital Channel: 19.1.21 kw vis. ant 1,446t TL: N38 38 04 W112 03 33 On air date: 2001. 101 Wasatch Dr., Salt Lake City, UT, 84112. Phone: (801) 581-2999. Fax: (801) 581-3576. Licensee: University of Utah.

Key Personnel:

Philip Titus . . . engrg dir

***KUEW—** Digital Channel: 18.6.35 kw vis. ant -180t TL: N37 03 49 W113 34 20 On air date: 2003. 101 Wasatch Dr., Salt Lake City, UT, 84112. Phone: (801) 581-2999. Fax: (801) 585-6105. Web Site: www.kued.com. Licensee: University of Utah.

Key Personnel:

Steven Hess . . . gen mgr

KUPX-TV— Digital Channel: 29. Digital Hrs: 24 530 kw vis. ant 3,841t/194g TL: N40 39 12 W112 12 06 On air date: November 1997. 466 C Lawndale Dr., Salt Lake City, UT, 84115. Phone: (801) 474-0016. Fax: (801) 463-9667. Web Site: www.ionline.tv. Licensee: ION Media Salt Lake City License Inc., debtor-in-possession. Group Owner: Paxson Communications Corp. Population Served: 800,000 Natl. Network: ION Television, .

Key Personnel:

Jim Powell . . . gen sls mgr

KUSG— Digital Channel: 9.9.8 kw vis. ant 138t TL: N37 03 49 W113 34 20 On air date: Aug 12, 1999. 299 S. Main, Ste 156, Salt Lake City, UT, 84111. Phone: (801) 973-3000. Fax: (801) 973-3002. Web Site: www.kutv.com. Licensee: SLC TV Licensee Corp. Group Owner: Viacom Television Stations Group. (acq 11-21-2007; grpsl). Natl. Network: CBS, . Natl. Rep: TeleRep,.

Key Personnel:
David W. Phillips . . . . VP
David Phillips . . . . gen mgr
Scott Jones . . . . opns dir
Kipp Greene . . . . engrg dir & chief of engrg
Rebroadcasts KUTV Salt Lake City 100%.

KUTF— Digital Channel: 12.22.3 kw vis. ant 2,263t/279g TL: N41 47 03 W112 13 55 On air date: Dec. 1, 2001. Stn currently dark 3901 Hwy. 121 S., Bedford, TX, 76021. Phone: (817) 571-1229. Fax: (817) 571-7458. Web Site: www.daystar.com. Licensee: Word of God Fellowship Inc. Group Owner: Equity Broadcasting Corp. (acq 7-31-2009; grpsl).
Key Personnel:
Marcus D. Lamb . . . . pres

KUTH-DT— Digital Channel: 32.3,072 kw vis. ant 2,663t/125g TL: N40 16 45 W111 56 00 On air date: 2003. 215 S. State ST., Ste. 100-A, Salt Lake City, UT, 84111-2348. Phone: (801) 519-9784. Fax: (801) 519-9785.E-mail: aurias@ebcorp.net Web Site: www.univision-utah.com. Licensee: Univision Salt Lake City LLC. Group Owner: Cocola Broadcasting Companies (acq 10-20-2004; $9.5 million). Natl. Network: Univision (Spanish), . Foreign lang progmg: SpanishS 168 News: 5 hrs wkly.
Key Personnel:
Arlene Urias . . . . . . gen mgr & gen sls mgr & natl sls mgr

KUTV— Digital Channel: 34. Digital Hrs: 24 45.7 kw vis, 9.1 kw aur. ant 3,060t/233g TL: N40 36 23 W112 09 47 On air date: Sept 26, 1954. 299 S. Main St., Suite 150, Salt Lake City, UT, 84111. Phone: (801) 973-3000. Fax: (801) 973-3387. Web Site: www.kutv2.com. Licensee: SLC TV Licensee Corp. Group Owner: Viacom Television Stations Group (acq 11-21-2007; grpsl). Population Served: 2,131,000 Natl. Network: CBS, . Natl. Rep: TeleRep,. Washington Atty: Wiley Rein LLP. News staff: 73; News: 34.5 hrs wkly.
Key Personnel:
Dave Phillips . . . . gen mgr
Scott Jones . . . . opns mgr

KVNV— Digital Channel: 3. Digital Hrs: 24 1.08 kw vis. ant 913t/49g TL: N39 14 46 W114 55 36 On air date: 2001. 1500 Foremaster Lane, Las Vegas, NV, 89101. Phone: (702) 642-3333. Fax: (702) 657-3256. Web Site: www.kvbc.com. Licensee: PMCM TV LLC. Ownership: Richard T. Morena, 25%; Robert E. McAllan, 25%; Alfred D. Colantoni, 25%; Jules L. Plangere Jr., 25% Group Owner: Sunbelt Communications Co. (acq 11-12-2008; $200,000). Natl. Network: NBC, .
Key Personnel:
Lisa Howfield . . . . gen mgr
Joanne Nasby . . . . gen sls mgr
Mark Guranik . . . . chief of engrg
Rebroadcasts KVBC(TV) Las Vegas.

Vermont

Burlington, VT-Plattsburgh, NY

(DMA 93)

WCAX-TV— Digital Channel: 22. Digital Hrs: 24 443 kw vis. ant 2,772t/151g TL: N44 31 32 W72 48 58 On air date: Sept 26, 1954. Box 4508, Burlington, VT, 05406-4508. Phone: (802) 652-6300. Fax: (802) 652-6319. Web Site: www.wcax.com. Licensee: Mount Mansfield TV Inc. Ownership: Peter R. Martin, James S. Martin, Marcia H. Martin Boyer and Donald P. Martin. Population Served: 550,000 Natl. Rep: Harrington, Righter & Parsons,. Washington Atty: Wilmer Cutler Pickering Hale and Dorr LLP. News staff: 35; News: 15 hrs wkly.
Key Personnel:
Peter Martin . . . . pres & progmg dir
Phil Scharf . . . . opns dir
Bruce Grindle . . . . gen sls mgr & natl sls mgr
Jim Strader . . . . prom dir & pub svc dir
Marselis Parsons . . . . news dir
Joe Tymecki . . . . engrg VP & chief of engrg
Brenda Bouvier . . . . traf mgr
Alex Martin . . . . feature ed
J.J. Chioffi . . . . sports cmtr
Sharon Myer . . . . weather dir

*WCFE-TV— Digital Channel: 38. Digital Hrs: 6:30 AM-1:30 AM 462 kw vis, 46.2 kw aur. ant 2,417t/410g TL: N44 41 43 W73 53 00 On air date: Mar 6, 1977. One Sesame St., Plattsburgh, NY, 12901. Phone: (518) 563-9770. Fax: (518) 561-1928.E-mail: mlpbs@mountainlake.org. Web Site: www.mountainlake.org. Licensee: Mountain Lake Public Telecommunications Council. Population Served: 4,000,000 Natl. Network: PBS, . Washington Atty: Dow, Lohnes & Albertson.

Key Personnel:
Alice Recore . . . . CEO & pres gen mgr
Charlie Zarbo . . . . engrg dir

*WETK— Digital Channel: 32. Digital Hrs: 24 1,350 kw vis, 135 kw aur. ant 2,673t/87g TL: N44 31 32 W72 48 54 On air date: Oct 16, 1967. 204 Ethan Allen Ave., Colchester, VT, 05446-3129. Phone: (802) 655-4800.E-mail: view@vpt.org Web Site: www.vpt.org. Licensee: Vermont ETV Inc. (acq 11-6-89). Natl. Network: PBS, . Rgnl. Network: Eastern Educ. Vermont Public Television Washington Atty: Covington & Burling.
Key Personnel:
John King . . . . CEO & pres
Lee Ann Lee . . . . dev VP & mktg VP

WFFF-TV— Digital Channel: 43. Digital Hrs: 24 5,000 kw vis. ant 1,738t TL: N44 31 32 W72 48 54 On air date: 1997. 298 Mountain View Dr., Colchester, VT, 05446. Phone: (802) 660-9333. Fax: (802) 660-8673. Web Site: www.fox44.net. Licensee: Smith Media License Holdings LLC. (acq 11-15-2004; grpsl). Natl. Network: Fox, CW, . Vermont Public Television Natl. Rep: Continental Television Sales,. Wire Svc: AP News staff: 30; News: 24.5 hrs/week.
Key Personnel:
Vacant . . . . news dir
Matt Servis . . . . chief of engrg

WNMN— Digital Channel: 40.50 kw vis. ant 1,443t/46g TL: N44 09 35 W74 28 34 On air date: September 2007. 732 Prospect St., Champlain, NY, 12919. Phone: (518) 297-2727. Fax: (518) 298-3210. Licensee: Channel 61 Associates LLC.
Key Personnel:
Gary Clarke . . . . gen mgr

WNNE— Digital Channel: 25. Digital Hrs: 24 2,240 kw vis, 2.24 kw aur. ant 2,220t/149g TL: N43 26 38 W72 27 17 On air date: Sept 27, 1978. Box 1310, White River Junction, VT, 05001. Phone: (802) 295-3100. Fax: (802) 295-9056. Fax: (802) 295-3983. Web Site: wnne.com. Licensee: Hearst-Argyle Stations Inc. Group Owner: Hearst-Argyle Television Inc. Population Served: 133,000 Natl. Network: NBC, .
Key Personnel:
Paul SAnds . . . . gen mgr

WPTZ—(North Pole, NY) Digital Channel: 14. Digital Hrs: 24 25.1 kw vis, 4.3 kw aur. ant 1,991t/978g TL: N44 34 26 W73 40 29 On air date: Dec 8, 1954. 5 Television Dr., Plattsburgh, NY, 12901. 533 Roosevelt Highway, Colchester, VT 05446. Phone: (518) 561-5555. Fax: (518) 561-5940. Web Site: www.wptz.com. Licensee: Hearst-Argyle Stations Inc. Group Owner: Hearst-Argyle Television Inc. (acq 6-1-98). Natl. Network: NBC, . News staff: 31; News: 23 hrs wkly.
Key Personnel:
Paul Sands . . . . gen mgr
Bruce Lawson . . . . sls dir
Chris Duley . . . . natl sls mgr
Susan Acklen . . . . prom mgr
Jim Gratton . . . . progmg dir
Kyle Grines . . . . news dir
Andrew Lombard . . . . chief of engrg
Laura Lareau . . . . traf mgr

*WVER— Digital Channel: 9. Digital Hrs: 24 15 kw vis. ant 1,263t/130g TL: N43 39 31 W73 06 25 On air date: Mar 18, 1968. 204 Ethan Allen Ave., Colchester, VT, 05446. Phone: (802) 655-4800.E-mail: veiw@vpt.org Web Site: www.vpt.org. Licensee: Vermont ETV Inc. Natl. Network: PBS, . Vermont Public Television Washington Atty: Covington & Burling.
Key Personnel:
John E. King . . . . CEO & pres
Shahid Khan . . . . chmn
Andrea Bergeon . . . . CFO
Lee Ann Lee . . . . dev VP
Peter Shea . . . . sls dir
Jeff Vande Griek . . . . prom dir
Kelly Luoma . . . . progmg mgr & film buyer
Joe Merone . . . . pub affrs dir
Rob Belle-Isle . . . . engrg VP & engrg dir
Satellite of WETK(TV) Burlington.

WVNY— Digital Channel: 13. Digital Hrs: 24 1,000 kw vis, 100 kw aur. ant 2,739t/310g TL: N44 31 40 W72 48 58 On air date: Aug 19, 1968. 298 Mountain View Dr., Colchester, VT, 05446. Phone: (802) 660-9333. Fax: (802) 660-8673.E-mail: abc22@abc22.com Web Site: www.abc22.com. Licensee: Lambert Broadcasting of Burlington LLC. Ownership: Michael Lambert, 100% (acq 5-21-2005; $10.2 million plus assumption of liabilities). Natl. Network: ABC, . Natl. Rep: Continental Television Sales,.

Key Personnel:
Vic Vetters . . . . gen mgr
Ken Kaszubowski . . . . opns dir
Gena Boyden . . . . gen sls mgr
Leigh Gross . . . . natl sls mgr & progmg dir
Matthew Servis . . . . chief of engrg

*WVTA— Digital Channel: 24. Digital Hrs: 24 1,050 kw vis, 105 kw aur. ant 2,245t/414g TL: N43 26 15 W72 27 09 On air date: Mar 18, 1968. 204 Ethan Allen Ave., Colchester, VT, 05446. Phone: (802) 655-4800.E-mail: view@vpt.org Web Site: www.vpt.org. Licensee: Vermont ETV Inc. Natl. Network: PBS, . Vermont Public Television Washington Atty: Covington & Burling.
Key Personnel:
John E. King . . . . CEO & pres
Lee Ann Lee . . . . dev VP
Peter Shea . . . . sls dir
Jeff Vande Griek . . . . prom dir
Kelly Luoma . . . . progmg mgr & film buyer
Joseph Merone . . . . pub affrs dir
Rob Belle-Isle . . . . . . engrg VP & engrg dir & chief of engrg
Satellite of *WETK Burlington.

*WVTB— Digital Channel: 18. Digital Hrs: 24 589 kw vis, 58.9 kw aur. ant 1,940t/139g TL: N44 34 15 W71 53 36 On air date: Feb 26, 1968. 204 Ethan Allen Ave., Colchester, VT, 05446. Phone: (802) 655-4800.E-mail: view@vpt.org Web Site: www.vpt.org. Licensee: Vermont ETV Inc. Natl. Network: PBS, . Vermont Public Television Washington Atty: Covington & Burling.
Key Personnel:
John King . . . . CEO & pres
Lee Ann Lee . . . . dev VP
Satellite of WETK(TV) Burlington.

Virginia

Arlington

see Washington, DC (Hagerstown, MD) market

Bristol

see Tri-Cities, TN-VA market

Charlottesville, VA

(DMA 183)

WCAV— Digital Channel: 19. Digital Hrs: 24 2,380 kw vis. ant 1,180t/332g TL: N37 59 05 W78 28 49 On air date: Aug 15, 2004. 999 2nd St. S.E., Charlottesville, VA, 22902. Phone: (434) 242-1919. Fax: (434) 220-0398. Web Site: www.charlottesvillenewsplex.tv. Licensee: Gray Television Licensee Inc. Group Owner: Gray Television Inc. (acq 5-28-2004; $1 million for CP). Natl. Network: CBS, .
Key Personnel:
Roger Burchett . . . . gen mgr
Jim McCabe . . . . gen sls mgr
Jeremy Settle . . . . news dir

*WHTJ— Digital Channel: 46. Digital Hrs: 8:30 AM - 5 PM 340 kw vis. ant 1,089t/236g TL: N37 58 59 W78 29 02 On air date: May 19, 1989. Box 40, Charlottesville, VA, 22902. 528 E. Main St., Charlottesville, VA 22902. Phone: (434) 295-7671. Fax: (434) 295-2813. Web Site: www.ideastations.org. Licensee: Commonwealth Public Broadcasting Corp. Natl. Network: PBS, . Washington Atty: Wiley, Rein & Fielding.
Key Personnel:
Conni Lombardo . . . . VP & stn mgr
D.J. Crotteau . . . . gen mgr & stn mgr
Lisa Tait . . . . dev VP & dev dir
John Felton . . . . progmg VP & progmg dir
Rebroadcasts WCVE-TV Richmond.

WVIR-TV— Digital Channel: 32. Digital Hrs: 24 5,000 kw vis, 500 kw aur. 1,187t/289g TL: N37 59 00 W78 28 54 On air date: Mar 11, 1973. Box 769, Charlottesville, VA, 22902. Phone: (434) 220-2900. Fax: (434) 220-2904.E-mail: newsdesk@nbc29.com Web Site: www.nbc29.com. Licensee: Virginia Broadcasting Corp. Group Owner: Waterman Broadcasting Corp. Population Served: 250,000 Natl. Network: NBC, . Natl. Rep: Continental Television Sales,. Washington Atty: Cohn & Marks. Wire Svc: AP News staff: 50; News: 32 hrs wkly.

Key Personnel:
Harold Wright . . . . VP & gen mgr mktg dir
Jim Fernald . . . . gen sls mgr
Ralph Tobias . . . . prom dir & progmg dir
Neal Bennett . . . . news dir
Bob Jenkins . . . . chief of engrg

Fairfax

see Washington, DC (Hagerstown, MD) market

Front Royal

see Washington, DC (Hagerstown, MD) market

Goldvein

see Washington, DC (Hagerstown, MD) market

Grundy

see Tri-Cities, TN-VA market

Harrisonburg, VA
(DMA 178)

WHSV-TV— Digital Channel: 49. Digital Hrs: 20 832 kw vis, 432 kw aur. ant 2,130t/337g TL: N38 36 05 W78 37 57 On air date: Oct 19, 1953. 50 N. Main St., Harrisonburg, VA, 22802. Phone: (540) 433-9191. Fax: (540) 433-4028; (540)433-2700 (news).E-mail: whsv@whsv.com Web Site: www.whsv.com. Licensee: WEAU Licensee Corp. Group Owner: Gray Television Inc. (acq 8-29-2002; grpsl). Population Served: 350,000 Natl. Network: ABC, Fox, MyNetworkTV, . Washington Atty: Wiley, Rein LLP. News staff: 18; News: 16 hrs wkly.
Key Personnel:
Tim Merritt . . . . gen sls mgr & mktg mgr
Tina Wood . . . . natl sls mgr & rgnl sls mgr
Jeremy Harman . . . . prom mgr
Tracey Jones. . . . . gen mgr & progmg mgr
Ed Reams . . . . news dir
Sean Harper . . . . chief of engrg

*WVPT— Digital Channel: 11. Digital Hrs: 24 525 kw vis, 67.6 kw aur. 2,230t/46g TL: N38 09 54 W79 18 51 On air date: Sept 9, 1968. 298 Port Republic Rd., Harrisonburg, VA, 22801. Phone: (540) 434-5391. Fax: (540) 434-7084.E-mail: wvptcomments@wvpt.net Web Site: www.wvpt.net. Licensee: Shenandoah Valley ETV Corp. Population Served: 500,000 Natl. Network: PBS, . Washington Atty: Covington & Burling.
Key Personnel:
Richard Parker . . . . gen mgr
Tony Mancari. . . . . opns VP

Lynchburg

see Roanoke-Lynchburg, VA market

Manassas

see Washington, DC (Hagerstown, MD) market

Marion

see Tri-Cities, TN-VA market

Newport News

see Norfolk-Portsmouth-Newport News, VA market

Norfolk-Portsmouth-Newport News, VA
(DMA 43)

WAVY-TV—(Portsmouth, Digital Channel: 31. Digital Hrs: 24 316 kw vis, 38.9 kw aur. 990t/1,026g TL: N36 49 14 W76 30 41 On air date: Sept 1, 1957. 300 Wavy St., Portsmouth, VA, 23704. Phone: (757) 393-1010. Fax: (757) 399-7628.E-mail: doug.davis@wavy.com Web Site: www.wavy.com. Licensee: WAVY Broadcasting L.L.C. Group Owner: LIN Television Corporation (acq 12-16-97; grpsl). Population

Served: 694,000 Natl. Network: NBC, . Natl. Rep: Petry Television Inc.,. Washington Atty: Covington & Burling. Wire Svc: AP News staff: 80; News: 31 hrs wkly.
Key Personnel:
Doug Davis . . . . pres & gen mgr
John Cochran . . . . gen sls mgr
Judy Triska. . . . . prom dir
Mark Johnson . . . . engrg dir
Eather White . . . . traf mgr

WGNT— Digital Channel: 50. Digital Hrs: 24 2,340 kw vis, 234 kw aur. ant 971t/1,026g TL: N36 48 43 W76 27 45 On air date: Oct 1, 1961. 1318 Spratley St., Portsmouth, VA, 23704-1829. Phone: (757) 393-2501. Fax: (757) 399-3303.E-mail: cw27@wgnttv.com Web Site: www.cw.27.com. Licensee: CBS Television Stations Inc. Group Owner: Viacom Television Stations Group (acq 10-31-97; $42.5 million). Population Served: 1,500,000 Natl. Network: CW, . Natl. Rep: Harrington, Righter & Parsons,.
Key Personnel:
Steven Soldinger . . . . VP & gen mgr
Jon Erkenbrack . . . . gen sls mgr
Chuck Martin . . . . natl sls mgr
Chris Wolf . . . . prom dir & progmg dir
Kafi Rouse . . . . pub affrs dir & pub svc dir
George Randell. . . . . chief of engrg
Diane Hall . . . . traf mgr

WHRE— Digital Channel: 7.5,000 kw vis. ant 1,017t/1,014g TL: N36 48 31 W76 30 12 On air date: Mar 27, 2006. 168 Business Park Dr., Suite 200, Virginia Beach, VA, 23462. Phone: (757) 473-3702. Web Site: www.hon.org. Licensee: Copeland Channel 21 LLC.
Key Personnel:
Robert O. Copeland . . . . gen mgr

*WHRO-TV—(Hampton-Norfolk, Digital Channel: 16. Digital Hrs: 24 2,630 kw vis, 263 kw aur. ant 964t/964g TL: N36 48 32 W76 30 13 On air date: Oct 2, 1961. Not on air, target date: DTV on Air 2/5/2001: 5200 Hampton Blvd., Norfolk, VA, 23508. Phone: (757) 889-9400. Fax: (757) 489-0007.E-mail: info@whro.org Web Site: www.whro.org. Licensee: Hampton Roads Educ. Telecommunications Association Inc. Population Served: 707,750 Natl. Network: PBS, . Washington Atty: Dow-Lohnes. News staff: 2; News: 1 hr wkly.
Key Personnel:
Bert Schmidt . . . . CEO
Colleen Ingraham. . . . . CFO
Virginia Thumm . . . . sr VP

WPXV-TV— Digital Channel: 46. Digital Hrs: 24 1,000 kw vis. ant 1,181t/1,168g TL: N36 48 31 W76 30 13 On air date: 1994. 230 Clearfield Ave. #104, Virginia Beach, VA, 23462. Phone: (757) 499-1261. Fax: (757) 499-1679. Web Site: www.ionline.tv/stations/list.cfm. Licensee: ION Media License Co. LLC, debtor-in-possession. Group Owner: Paxson Communications Corp. (acq 12-18-97; $14.75 million). Natl. Network: ION Television, .
Key Personnel:
Rhonda Nelson. opns mgr
Cindy Arthur . . . . progmg mgr

WSKY-TV— Digital Channel: 9. Digital Hrs: 24 100 kw vis. ant 1,030t/1,023g TL: N36 08 08 W75 49 28 On air date: Oct 1, 2001. 920 Corporate Ln., Chesapeake, VA, 23320. Phone: (757) 382-0004. Fax: (757) 382-0365.E-mail: programming@wsky4.com Web Site: www.4hamptonroads.com. Licensee: Sky Television LLC. Ownership: Danbeth Communications Inc., 51% (acq 8-19-2002). Population Served: 1,278,000 Washington Atty: Leventhal, Senter and Lerman.
Key Personnel:
Glenn Holterhaus . . . . CEO & pres gen mgr & stn mgr
Jacquelyn Smullen . . . . CFO & VP gen sls mgr
Tom Powers. . . . . opns VP & opns dir
Ed Marlowe. . . . . prom mgr & progmg mgr
Jeff Mercer . . . . pub affrs dir & pub svc dir
Molly Scullin . . . . traf mgr

WTKR— Digital Channel: 40. Digital Hrs: 24 100 kw vis, 20 kw aur. ant 980t/1,029g TL: N36 48 56 W76 28 00 On air date: Apr 2, 1950. 720 Boush St., Norfolk, VA, 23501-0300. Phone: (757) 446-1000. Fax: (757) 446-1376. Web Site: www.wtkr.com. Licensee: Local TV Virginia License LLC. Group Owner: The New York Times Co. (acq 5-7-2007; grpsl). Population Served: 1,700,000 Natl. Network: CBS, . Washington Atty: Reed, Smith, Shaw & McClay.
Key Personnel:
Jeff Hoffman . . . . gen mgr
Jeff McCallister . . . . stn mgr & gen sls mgr
Tina Luque Blacklocke . . . . news dir

WTVZ-TV— Digital Channel: 33. Digital Hrs: 24 5,000 kw vis, 500 kw aur. ant 909t/1,026g TL: N36 48 32 W76 30 13 On air date: Sept 24, 1979. 900 Granby St., Norfolk, VA, 23510. Phone: (757) 622-3333. Fax: (757) 623-1541.E-mail: comments@wtv233.com Web Site:

www.mytvz.com. Licensee: WTVZ Licensee L.L.C. Group Owner: Sinclair Broadcast Group Inc. (acq 2-9-95; $47 million;5-8-95). Population Served: 1,300,000 Natl. Network: MyNetworkTV, . Washington Atty: Gardner, Carton & Douglas.
Key Personnel:
Bill Scasfide . . . . gen mgr
Bill Barber . . . . chief of engrg

*WUND-TV— Digital Channel: 20. Digital Hrs: 24 543 kw vis. ant 1,604t/1,604g TL: N35 54 00 W76 20 45 On air date: Sept 10, 1965. Box 14900, Research Triangle Park, NC, 27709-4900. 10 TW Alexander Dr., Research Triangle Park, NC 27709. Phone: (919) 549-7000. Fax: (919) 549-7201.E-mail: viewer@unctv.org Web Site: www.unctv.org. Licensee: University of North Carolina. Population Served: 9,000,000 Natl. Network: PBS, .
Key Personnel:
Tom Howe . . . . gen mgr

WVBT— Digital Channel: 29. Analog Hrs: 0 Digital Hrs: 24 240 kw vis. ant 856t TL: N36 49 14 W76 30 41 On air date: March 1993. 243 Wythe St., Portsmouth, VA, 23704. Phone: (757) 393-4343. Fax: (757) 763-5447.E-mail: doug.davis@wavy.com Web Site: www.fox43tv.com. Licensee: WAVY Broadcasting LLC. Group Owner: LIN Television Corporation (acq 1-9-2002; $4.25 million). Natl. Network: Fox, . Washington Atty: Covington & Burling.
Key Personnel:
Mark Gentner . . . . stn dir
Andy Hilton . . . . natl sls mgr
John Lipscomb . . . . rgnl sls mgr

WVEC—(Hampton, Digital Channel: 13. Digital Hrs: 24 35 kw vis. ant 1,191t/1,184g TL: N36 48 59 W76 28 06 On air date: Sept 19, 1953. 613 Woodis Ave., Norfolk, VA, 23510. Phone: (757) 625-1313. Fax: (757) 628-6220. Fax: (757) 628-5855 (news). Web Site: www.wvec.com. Licensee: WVEC Television Inc. Group Owner: Belo Corp., Broadcast Division (acq 11-28-83; grpsl; 12-29-83). Population Served: 1,253,200 Natl. Network: ABC, . Natl. Rep: TeleRep,. Wire Svc: Reuters News staff: 65; News: 24 hrs wkly.
Key Personnel:
Tod A. Smith . . . . pres & gen mgr
Amy Warren . . . . sls dir & traf mgr
T.J. Dula . . . . natl sls mgr
Deborah Shollenberger . . . . progmg dir
Rich Lebenson . . . . news dir
Wendy Juren . . . . pub affrs dir
John Dolive . . . . chief of engrg
Jeff Lawson . . . . weather dir

Norton

see Tri-Cities, TN-VA market

Petersburg

see Richmond-Petersburg, VA market

Portsmouth

see Norfolk-Portsmouth-Newport News, VA market

Richmond-Petersburg, VA
(DMA 58)

*WCVE-TV— Digital Channel: 42. Digital Hrs: 24 436 kw vis. ant 1,135t/994g TL: N37 30 45 W77 36 05 On air date: Sept 14, 1964. 23 Sesame St., Richmond, VA, 23235. Phone: (804) 320-1301. Fax: (804) 320-8729. Web Site: www.ideastations.org.E-mail: info@ideastations.org Licensee: Commonwealth Public Broadcasting Corp. Population Served: 462,000 Natl. Network: PBS, . Washington Atty: Wiley, Rein & Fielding.
Key Personnel:
Curtis Monk . . . . pres
Lisa Tait . . . . dev VP
John Felton . . . . progmg VP

*WCVW— Digital Channel: 44. Digital Hrs: 24 112 kw vis. ant 1,076t/935g TL: N37 30 45 W77 36 05 On air date: Dec 22, 1966. 23 Sesame St., Richmond, VA, 23235. Phone: (804) 320-1301. Fax: (804) 320-8729. Web Site: www.ideastations.org E-mail: info@ideastations.org Licensee: Commonwealth Public Broadcasting Corporation. Population Served: 450,000 Natl. Network: PBS, . Washington Atty: Wiley, Rein & Fielding.

Key Personnel:
Curtis Monk . . . . pres
Lisa Tait . . . . dev VP
John Felton . . . . progmg VP

WRIC-TV—(Petersburg, Digital Channel: 22. Digital Hrs: 24 269 kw vis, 34.4 kw aur. ant 1,050t/999g TL: N37 30 46 W77 36 06 On air date: Aug 15, 1955. 301 Arboretum Pl., Richmond, VA, 23236-3464. Phone: (804) 330-8888. Fax: (804) 330-8882.E-mail: news@wric.com Web Site: www.wric.com. Licensee: Young Broadcasting of Richmond Inc. Group Owner: (group owner; (acq 11-14-94; grpsl; 9-12-94). Population Served: 1,255,000 Natl. Network: ABC, . Natl. Rep: Adam Young,. Washington Atty: Brooks, Pierce, McLendon, Humphrey & Leonard.
Key Personnel:
Robert Peterson. . . . . gen mgr
Matthew Zelkird . . . . stn mgr

WRLH-TV— Digital Channel: 26. Digital Hrs: 24 2,588 kw vis, 259 kw aur. ant 1,259 TL: N37 30 21 W77 41 58 On air date: Feb 20, 1982. 1925 Westmoreland St., Richmond, VA, 23230. Phone: (804) 358-3535. Phone: (804) 359-3510. Fax: (804) 358-1495. Web Site: www.foxrichmond.com. Licensee: WRLH Licensee LLC. Group Owner: Sinclair Broadcast Group Inc. (acq 12-10-01; grpsl). Population Served: 484,000 Natl. Network: Fox, MyNetworkTV, . Washington Atty: Arter & Hadden. News staff: 15; News: 3 hrs wkly.
Key Personnel:
Darren Shapiro . . . . sls VP
Steve Genett . . . . gen sls mgr
Bill Norris . . . . rgnl sls mgr
Mark Bartholmew . . . . prom dir
Charles Rouse . . . . chief of engrg

WTVR-TV— Digital Channel: 25. Digital Hrs: 24 100 kw vis, 15.1 kw aur. 1,049t/840g TL: N37 34 00 W77 28 36 On air date: Apr 22, 1948. 3301 W. Broad St., Richmond, VA, 23230. Phone: (804) 254-3600. Fax: (804) 254-3699. Web Site: www.wtvr.com. Licensee: Community Television of Alabama License LLC. Group Owner: Raycom Media Inc. (acq 3-31-2009; exchange for WBRC(TV) Birmingham, AL). Population Served: 1,148,000 Natl. Network: CBS, . Natl. Rep: TeleRep,. Washington Atty: Dow Lohnes PLLC. Wire Svc: AP
Key Personnel:
Peter Maroney . . . . VP & gen mgr
Don Cox . . . . opns dir & engrg dir
Tina Woody . . . . opns mgr
Stephen Hayes. . . . . gen sls mgr
James Taguchi . . . . natl sls mgr
Steve Young . . . . rgnl sls mgr & sls
Bill Anderson . . . . mktg dir & news dir
Blake Peddicore . . . . prom mgr & progmg

WUPV— Digital Channel: 47. Digital Hrs: 24 1,581 kw vis, 158 kw aur. 859t/850g TL: N37 44 32 W77 15 18 On air date: Mar 9, 1990. 3301 West Broad St., Richmond, VA, 23230. Phone: (804) 254-3600. Fax: (804) 342-5746. Web Site: www.cwrichmond.tv. Licensee: Southeastern Media Holdings Inc. (acq 11-3-2006; $47 million). Population Served: 1,237,000 Natl. Network: CW, . Natl. Rep: Harrington, Righter & Parsons,.
Key Personnel:
John Rezabeck . . . . gen mgr
Blake Peddicord. . . . . progmg dir
Don Cox . . . . engrg dir
Gene Todd. chief of engrg
Shayne Rogers . . . . traf mgr

WWBT— Digital Channel: 12. Digital Hrs: 24 316 kw vis, 63.1 kw aur. ant 790t/1,000g TL: N37 30 23 W77 30 12 On air date: Apr 29, 1956. Box 12, Richmond, VA, 23218. 5710 Midlothian Tpke., Richmond, VA 23225. Phone: (804) 230-1212. Fax: (804) 230-2793.E-mail: newsroom@nbc12.com Web Site: www.nbc12.com. Licensee: WWBT License Subsidiary LLC. Group Owner: Jefferson-Pilot Communications Co. (acq 3-31-2008; grpsl). Population Served: 771,400 Natl. Network: NBC, . Washington Atty: Wiley, Rein.
Key Personnel:
Donald S. Richards . . . . gen mgr
Michael Park. . . . . opns mgr
M. Kym Grinnage. . . . . gen sls mgr
Nancy Kent . . . . news dir

Roanoke-Lynchburg, VA (DMA 67)

***WBRA-TV—** Digital Channel: 3. Digital Hrs: 24 1,820 kw vis, 182 kw aur. 2,089t/265g TL: N37 11 45 W80 09 18 On air date: Aug 1, 1967. Box 13246, Roanoke, VA, 24032. Blue Ridge PBS, 1215 McNeil Dr. S.W., Roanoke, VA 24015. Phone: (540) 344-0991. Fax: (540) 344-2148.E-mail: info@blueridgepbs.org Web Site: www.blueridgepbs.org. Licensee: Blue Ridge Public Television Inc. Population Served: 445,000 Natl. Network: PBS, .

Key Personnel:
Steve Blanks . . . . chmn
Anita Simms. . . . . CFO
Will Anderson. . . . . opns VP
Sherry Spradlin . . . . progmg dir
Erwin Roman. . . . . chief of engrg

WDBJ— Digital Channel: 18. Digital Hrs: 24 316 kw vis, 62.5 kw aur. 2,000t/78g TL: N37 11 42 W80 09 22 On air date: Oct 3, 1955. Box 7, Roanoke, VA, 24022-0007. 2807 Hershberger Rd, Roanoke, VA 24017-1941. Phone: (540) 344-7000. Fax: (540) 344-5097.E-mail: firstinitiallastname@wdbj7.com Web Site: www.wdbj7.com. Licensee: WDBJ Television Inc. Group Owner: Schurz Communications Inc. (acq 11-1-69; $8.2 million; 11-10-69). Population Served: 1,013,000 Natl. Network: CBS, MyNetworkTV, . Natl. Rep: Harrington, Righter & Parsons,. Washington Atty: Wilmer Cutler Pickering Hale and Dorr. Wire Svc: UPI Wire Svc: AP News staff: 54; News: 18 hrs wkly.
Key Personnel:
Jeffrey A. Marks. . . . . pres & gen mgr
Angela McCaskill . . . . CFO
Ray Sullivan. . . . . gen sls mgr & natl sls mgr
Kelly Zuber . . . . prom mgr & pub svc dir
Mike Bell . . . . progmg dir
Amy Morris. . . . . news dir
Carl Guffey . . . . engrg dir

WDRL-TV— Digital Channel: 24.5,000 kw vis, 1,000 kw aur. ant 522t On air date: August 1994. 5002 Airport Rd., Roanoke, VA, 24012. Phone: (540) 366-2424. Fax: (540) 366-7530.E-mail: manager@wdrl-tv.com Web Site: www.wdrl-tv.com. Licensee: MNE Broadcasting L.L.C.. Ownership: Melvin N. Eleazer, 100%. (acq 8-31-2006).
Key Personnel:
Mel Eleazer . . . . gen mgr & stn mgr
Amy Ragsdale . . . . opns mgr
Dave Ross . . . . rgnl sls mgr
Rob Ruthenberg . . . . progmg mgr
Nel Kirt. . . . . pub affrs dir
Rebroadcasts W54BT(TV) Roanoke 100%.

WFXR— Digital Channel: 17. Digital Hrs: 24 2,690 kw vis, 269 kw aur. ant 1,991t/200g TL: N37 11 46 W80 09 16 On air date: March 1986. Box 2127, Roanoke, VA, 24009-2127. 2618 Colonial Ave. S.W., Roanoke, VA 24015. Phone: (540) 344-2127. Fax: (540) 345-1912. Fax: (540) 342-2753.E-mail: info@fox2127.com Web Site: www.fox2127.com. Licensee: Grant Broadcasting System II Inc. Group Owner: (group owner; (acq 9-93; $5.5 million with WWCW(TV) Lynchburg; 6-14-93). Population Served: 206,000 Natl. Network: Fox, CW, . Washington Atty: Birch, Horton, Bittner & Cherot. News staff: 2; News: 2 hrs wkly.
Key Personnel:
Dave Bunnell. . . . . gen mgr
Ralph C . . . . stn mgr

WPXR-TV— Digital Channel: 36. Digital Hrs: 24 700 kw vis. ant 2,043t/180g TL: N37 11 37 W80 09 25 On air date: Jan 3, 1986. 401 3rd St. S.W., Roanoke, VA, 24011. Phone: (540) 857-0038. Fax: (540) 345-8568.E-mail: shirleybundy@1onmedia.tv Web Site: www.ionline.tv. Licensee: ION Media License Co. LLC, debtor-in-possession. Group Owner: Paxson Communications Corp. (acq 10-28-97). Population Served: 369,000 Natl. Network: ION Television, .
Key Personnel:
George Stein. . . . . chief of engrg
Genia Wright . . . . traf mgr

WSET-TV— Digital Channel: 13. Digital Hrs: 24 302 kw vis, 50 kw aur. 2,050t/1,240g TL: N37 18 54 W79 38 06 On air date: Feb 8, 1953. Box 11588, Lynchburg, VA, 24506-1588. 2320 Langhorne Rd., Lynchburg, VA 24501. Phone: (434) 528-1313. Fax: (434) 847-0458.E-mail: wset@wset.com Web Site: www.wset.com. Licensee: WSET, Incorporated. Group Owner: Allbritton Communications Co. (acq 10-76; grpsl). Population Served: 1,023,000 Natl. Network: ABC, . Natl. Rep: Continental Television Sales,. Washington Atty: Sidley, Austin, LLP. Wire Svc: AP Wire Svc: ABC News staff: 41; News: 12 hrs wkly.
Key Personnel:
Randall J. Smith . . . . pres & gen mgr
K.C. Spiron. . . . . opns dir & opns mgr
Paul Glover . . . . sls dir
John Crumpler . . . . prom dir
Bill Foy . . . . news dir

WSLS-TV— Digital Channel: 30. Digital Hrs: 24 316 kw vis, 47 kw aur. 2,001t/242g TL: N37 12 02 W80 08 55 On air date: Dec 11, 1952. Box 10, Roanoke, VA, 24022-0010. 401 3rd St. S.W., Roanoke, VA 24011. Phone: (540) 981-9110. Phone: 540-981-9126. Fax: (540) 343-3157/(540)343-2059.E-mail: news@wsls.com Web Site: www.wsls.com. Licensee: Media General Broadcasting Inc. Group Owner: Media General Broadcast Group (acq 3-21-97; grpsl). Population Served: 392,000 Natl. Network: NBC, . Washington Atty: Wiley, Rein & Fielding. News staff: 33; News: 15 hrs wkly.

Key Personnel:
Kathy Mohn . . . . VP & gen mgr
Robert Kerry . . . . opns VP
Candy Crigger . . . . gen sls mgr
Scott Martin . . . . natl sls mgr
Daniel Coyle . . . . mktg VP

WWCW— Digital Channel: 20. Digital Hrs: 24 4,207 kw vis, 421 kw aur. ant 1,640t/966g TL: N37 19 14 W79 37 58 On air date: February 1986. Box 2127, Roanoke, VA, 24009-2127. 2618 Colonial Ave. S.W., Roanoke, VA 24015. Phone: (540) 344-2127. Fax: (540) 345-1912/(540) 342-2753.E-mail: info@fox2127.com Web Site: www.fox2127.com. Licensee: GB Lynchburg Licensing LLC. (acq 9-15-93; $5.5 million with satellite stn WFXR-TV Roanoke;6-14-93) Natl. Network: Fox, CW, . Washington Atty: Birch, Horton, Bittner & Cherot. News staff: 2; News: one hr wkly.

Tri-Cities

see Tri-Cities, TN-VA market

Washington

Kennewick

see Yakima-Pasco-Richland-Kennewick, WA market

Pasco

see Yakima-Pasco-Richland-Kennewick, WA market

Richland

see Yakima-Pasco-Richland-Kennewick, WA market

Seattle-Tacoma, WA (DMA 14)

KBCB— Digital Channel: 19. Digital Hrs: 24 Note: shopping television network: ShopNBC 165 kw vis. ant 2,483t/487g TL: N48 40 46 W122 50 31 On air date: December 1994. 4164 Meridian St., Suite 102, Bellingham, WA, 98226. 800 5th Ave., Suite 4100, Seattle, WA 98104. Phone: (360) 647-8842. Phone: (206) 447-1430. Fax: (360) 647-9204. Fax: (206) 447-1431.E-mail: kbcb@kbcbtv.com Web Site: www.kbcbtv.com. Licensee: World Television of Washington LLC. Ownership: Venture Technologies Group LLC, 68.67%; and Frank Washington, 31.33%. Population Served: 1,690,000 Washington Atty: Wiley, Rein & Fielding. News: 4 hrs wkly.
Key Personnel:
Garry Spire . . . . CEO
Larry Rogow . . . . chmn
Paul Koplin . . . . pres
Dewi Cashion . . . . CFO & gen mgr
Brian Holton . . . . VP
Shelli Jones. . . . . stn mgr
Karen Bean . . . . opns mgr

***KBTC-TV—** Digital Channel: 27.676 kw vis, 67.6 kw aur. ant 761t/326g TL: N47 16 41 W122 30 42 On air date: Sept 25, 1961. 2320 S. 19th St., Tacoma, WA, 98405. Phone: (253) 680-7700. Fax: (253) 680-7725. Web Site: www.kbtc.org. Licensee: Bates Technical College. (acq 11-29-91; with KXOT(FM) Tacoma;12-16-91). Population Served: 800,000 Natl. Network: PBS, .
Key Personnel:
Debbie Emond . . . . gen mgr
Darin Gerchak. . . . . chief of opns & chief of engrg
Lamont Walton . . . . news dir

***KCKA—** Digital Channel: 19.661 kw vis, 66.1 kw aur. ant 1,138t TL: N46 33 16 W123 03 26 On air date: October 1982. 2320 S. 19th St., Tacoma, WA, 98405. Phone: (253) 680-7700. Fax: (253) 680-7725. Web Site: www.kbtc.org. Licensee: Bates Technical College. (acq 11-29-91;12-16-91). Population Served: 800,000 Natl. Network: PBS, . Washington Atty: Akin, Gump, Strauss, Hauer & Feld.

Key Personnel:
Debbie Emond . . . . gen mgr
Mary Thompson . . . . prom dir
Lamont Walton . . . . news dir & pub affrs dir
Darin Gerchak . . . . chief of engrg
Tim Howe . . . . traf mgr
Rebroadcasts KBTC(TV) Tacoma.

KCPQ—(Tacoma, Digital Channel: 13. Digital Hrs: 24 316 kw vis, 31.6 kw aur. 2,000t/708g TL: N47 32 53 W122 48 22 (CP: Ant 1,191t. TL: N47 36 59 W122 18 23) On air date: 1954. 1813 Westlake Ave. N., Seattle, WA, 98109-2706. Phone: (206) 674-1313. Fax: (206) 674-1777.E-mail: askus@kcpq.com Web Site: q13.trb.com. Licensee: Tribune Television Northwest Inc. Group Owner: Tribune Broadcasting Co. (acq 12-20-2007; grpsl). Population Served: 1,225,000 Natl. Network: Fox, . Natl. Rep: TeleRep,. Washington Atty: Dow Lohnes PLLC. Wire Svc: SportsTicker News staff: 44; News: 21 hrs wkly.
Key Personnel:
Pamela Pearson. . . . . gen mgr
Mark Boe. stn mgr
Paul Rennie . . . . sls dir
Houman Aliabadi . . . . natl sls mgr
Natalie Grant . . . . progmg dir
Steve Kraycik. . . . . news dir
Marty Gustafson . . . . pub affrs dir
Michael Goodman. . . . . engrg dir
Jeremy Dietz . . . . rsch dir
Wendy Anderson. . . . . traf mgr
Walter Kelley. . . . . weather dir

***KCTS-TV—** Digital Channel: 9. Digital Hrs: 24 316 kw vis, 50 kw aur. ant 830t/590g TL: N47 36 58 W122 18 28 On air date: Dec 7, 1954. 401 Mercer, Seattle, WA, 98109. Phone: (206) 728-6463. Fax: (206) 443-6691.E-mail: viewer@kcts.org Web Site: www.kcts.org. Licensee: KCTS Television. Ownership: KCTS Television board of directors (acq 7-15-87). Population Served: 3,359,300 Natl. Network: PBS, . Washington Atty: Dow, Lohnes & Albertson.
Key Personnel:
William Mohler. CEO
Bob Flowers . . . . chmn
Randy Brinson . . . . gen mgr
Cliff Anderson . . . . engrg dir & chief of engrg

KHCV— Digital Channel: 44. Digital Hrs: 24 2,000 kw vis. ant 2,283t TL: N47 30 17 W121 58 06 On air date: 2001. 19825 Willows Rd. NE., Suite 140, Redmond, WA, 98052. Phone: (425) 497-1515. Fax: (425) 497-8629.E-mail: khcvtv@khcvtv.com Web Site: www.khcvtv.com. Licensee: North Pacific International Television Inc. Ownership: Dr. Kenneth & Charlene Casey (acq 12-24-92;11-23-92). Population Served: 3,000,000 Natl. Network: Azteca America (Spanish), . Foreign lang progmg: SpanishS 168
Key Personnel:
Dr. Kenneth Casey . . . . pres
Charlene Casey . . . . CFO
Emoree Martin . . . . gen mgr & stn mgr
Stephanie Ogle . . . . progmg dir
Chris Casey. engrg VP

KING-TV— Digital Channel: 48. Digital Hrs: 24 100 kw vis, 15.1 kw aur. 820t/570g TL: N47 37 55 W122 20 59 (CP: Ant 1,168t/918g) On air date: Nov 25, 1948. 333 Dexter Ave. N., Seattle, WA, 98109. Phone: (206) 448-5555. Fax: (206) 448-3195. Web Site: www.king5.com. Licensee: KING-TV Inc. Group Owner: Belo Corp., Broadcast Division (acq 1997; grpsl). Population Served: 3,848,400 Natl. Network: NBC, . Natl. Rep: TeleRep,. Washington Atty: Fletcher, Heald & Hildreth.
Key Personnel:
Pat Costello . . . . gen mgr

KIRO-TV— Digital Channel: 39.316 kw vis, 63.2 kw aur. 820t/599g TL: N47 38 01 W122 21 20 On air date: Feb 8, 1958. 2807 3rd Ave., Seattle, WA, 98121. Phone: (206) 728-7777. Fax: (206) 728-8230. Web Site: www.kirotv.com. Licensee: KIRO-TV Inc. Group Owner: Cox Broadcasting (acq 4-16-97). Population Served: 1,047,300 Natl. Network: CBS, . Natl. Rep: Harrington, Righter & Parsons,. Washington Atty: Dow, Lohnes & Albertson, PLLC. News staff: 115; News: 46 hrs wkly.
Key Personnel:
Eric Lerner. gen mgr
Holly Grambihler . . . . dev mgr & rgnl sls mgr
Pat Norris. . . . . gen sls mgr & rgnl sls mgr
Dave Blakely. . . . . natl sls mgr
Therese Weiler . . . . progmg dir
Todd Mokhtari . . . . news dir
John Walters. engrg dir
Pat Otis. . . . . chief of engrg

KMYQ— Digital Channel: 25. Digital Hrs: 24 5,000 kw vis, 501 kw aur. ant 890t/639g TL: N47 36 57 W122 18 26 On air date: June 22, 1985. 1813 Westlake Ave., Seattle, WA, 98109. Phone: (206) 674-1313. Fax: (206) 674-1777.E-mail: askus@ktwbtv.com Web Site: ktwbtv.trb.com. Licensee: Tribune Television Holdings Inc. Group Owner: Tribune Broadcasting Co. (acq 12-20-2007; grpsl). Population Served: 3,516,000 Natl. Network: MyNetworkTV, . Natl. Rep: TeleRep,. Washington Atty: Dow Lohnes PLLC.
Key Personnel:
Pamela Pearson. . . . . gen mgr
Mark Boe. stn mgr
Paul Rennie . . . . sls dir
Adam Bischoff . . . . natl sls mgr
Natalie Grant . . . . progmg dir
Michael Goodman. . . . . engrg dir & chief of engrg
Jeremy Dietz . . . . rsch dir
Wendy Anderson. . . . . traf mgr
Marty Gustafson . . . . pub svc dir

KOMO-TV— Digital Channel: 38. Digital Hrs: 24 100 kw vis, 15 kw aur. 810t/550g TL: N47 37 55 W122 21 09 (CP: Ant 1,151t. TL: N47 37 56 W122 21 11) On air date: Dec 10, 1953. 140 4th Ave. N., Seattle, WA, 98109. Phone: (206) 404-4000. Fax: (206) 404-4034. Web Site: www.komotv.com. Licensee: Fisher Broadcasting - Seattle TV L.L.C. Group Owner: Fisher Broadcasting Company (acq 12-4-01; grpsl). Population Served: 3,700,000 Natl. Network: ABC, . Natl. Rep: Blair Television,. Washington Atty: Shaw Pittman.
Key Personnel:
James Clayton . . . . gen mgr
Lloyd Low. . . . . natl sls mgr
Doreen Kaylor . . . . progmg dir
Holly Gauntt . . . . news dir

KONG— Digital Channel: 31. Digital Hrs: 24 700 kw vis. ant 715t/417g TL: N47 37 55 W122 20 59 On air date: 1997. 333 Dexter Ave. N., Seattle, WA, 98109. Phone: (206) 448-3166. Phone: (206) 448-5555. Fax: (206) 448-3167. Web Site: www.kongtv.com. Licensee: KONG-TV Inc. Group Owner: Belo Corp., Broadcast Division (acq 2-18-2000). Washington Atty: Thompson, Hine & Flory L.
Key Personnel:
Ray Heacox . . . . gen mgr & stn mgr

KSTW—(Tacoma, Digital Channel: 11. Digital Hrs: 24 316 kw vis, 47.8 kw aur. ant 891t/637g TL: N47 36 56 W122 18 29 On air date: Mar 1, 1953. 602 Oakesdale Ave. S.W., Renton, WA, 98057. Phone: (206) 441-1111. Fax: (206) 861-8915. Web Site: kstw.com. Licensee: CW Television Stations Inc. Group Owner: Viacom Television Stations Group (acq 4-16-97). Population Served: 1,400,000 Natl. Network: CW, .
Key Personnel:
Steve Gahler . . . . VP & gen sls mgr
Amber Stelzer . . . . natl sls mgr
Megan Temple . . . . mktg dir
D. Poor. . . . . prom mgr
Tom Spitz . . . . progmg dir
Ron Diotte. . . . . engrg dir
Florence Higa. traf mgr

KTBW-TV— Digital Channel: 14. Digital Hrs: 24 575 kw vis. ant 1,551t/236g TL: N47 32 50 W122 47 40 On air date: Mar 30, 1984. 1909 S. 341st Pl., Federal Way, WA, 98003. Phone: (253) 927-7720. Phone: (253) 874-7420. Fax: (253) 874-7432.E-mail: ktbw@tbn.org Licensee: Trinity Broadcasting of Washington. Group Owner: Trinity Broadcasting Network
Key Personnel:
Paul F. Crouch . . . . pres
Mary Jane Allen . . . . stn mgr

KUNS-TV— Digital Channel: 50.3,800 kw vis, 500 kw aur. ant 2,358t/279g TL: N47 30 17 W121 58 04 On air date: 2000. 140 4th Ave. N., Suite 440, Seattle, WA, 98109. Phone: (206) 404-5867. Fax: (206) 248-6818.E-mail: info@kunstv.com Web Site: www.kunstv.com. Licensee: Fisher Broadcasting - Bellevue TV L.L.C. (acq 9-26-2006; $16 million). Natl. Network: Univision (Spanish), . Foreign lang progmg: SpanishS 168

KVOS-TV— Digital Channel: 35. Digital Hrs: 24 234 kw vis, 45.7 kw aur. ant 2,368t/139g TL: N48 40 40 W122 49 48 On air date: June 3, 1953. 1151 Ellis St., Bellingham, WA, 98225. Phone: (360) 671-1212. Phone: (604) 681-1212 (sales). Fax: (360) 647-0824. Fax: (604) 736-4510. Web Site: www.kvos.com. Licensee: Newport Television LLC. Group Owner: Clear Channel Communications Inc. (acq 3-14-2008; grpsl). Population Served: 2,000,000 Natl. Rep: Airtime TV,. Washington Atty: Covington & Burling. News staff: 10; News: one hr wkly.

***KWDK—** Digital Channel: 42. Digital Hrs: 24 144 kw vis. ant 2,280t/197g TL: N47 30 17 W121 58 06 On air date: 2000. 18000 International Blvd., Ste 1007, Seatac, WA, 98188. Phone: (425) 251-4313. Web Site: www.daystar.com. Licensee: Puget Sound Educational TV Inc.

KWPX-TV— Digital Channel: 33. Digital Hrs: 24 14.8 kw vis, 1.5 kw aur. 938t TL: N47 36 17 W122 19 46 On air date: May 17, 1989. Box 426, Preston, WA, 98050. 8112-C 304th Ave. SE, Preston, WA 98050. Phone: (425) 222-6010. Fax: (425 222-6032. Web Site: www.ionline.tv. Licensee: ION Media License Co. LLC, debtor-in-possession. Group Owner: Paxson Communications Corp. (acq 2-2-98; $35 million). Natl. Network: ION Television, .

Spokane, WA
(DMA 75)

KAYU-TV— Digital Channel: 28. Digital Hrs: 24 2,400 kw vis, 120 kw aur. ant 1,971t/794g TL: N47 34 44 W117 17 46 On air date: Oct 31, 1982. 4600 S. Regal St., Spokane, WA, 99223. Phone: (509) 448-2828. Fax: (509) 448-0926. Web Site: www.myfoxspokane.com. Licensee: Mountain Licenses L.P. Group Owner: Northwest Broadcasting Inc. (acq 1996; $6.44 million). Population Served: 999,000 Natl. Network: Fox, . Natl. Rep: Millennium Sales & Marketing,. Washington Atty: Leventhal, Senter and Lerman. Wire Svc: AP News: 8 hrs wkly.
Key Personnel:
Brian Brady . . . . CEO
Bill Quarles . . . . CFO
Jon Rand . . . . gen mgr
Rick Andrycha . . . . opns mgr
David Lockhert. . . . . gen sls mgr
Becky Martin. . . . . natl sls mgr
Kim Rogge. prom dir
Ron Sweatte. . . . . chief of engrg

***KCDT-TV—** Digital Channel: 45. Digital Hrs: 24 12.3 kw vis, 1.2 kw aur. 1,525t TL: N47 43 54 W116 43 47 On air date: October 1991. c/o KAID, 1455 N. Orchard St., Boise, ID, 83706. Box 443101, University of Idaho, Moscow, ID 83844-3101. Phone: (208) 885-1226.E-mail: idptv@idahoptv.org Web Site: www.idahoptv.org. Licensee: State Board of Education, State of Idaho. Natl. Network: PBS, . Washington Atty: Fletcher, Heald & Hildreth.
Key Personnel:
Peter Morrill . . . . gen mgr
Kris Freeland . . . . stn mgr
Kim Philipps . . . . dev dir
Rebroadcasts KUID Moscow 100%.

KGPX-TV— Digital Channel: 34. Digital Hrs: 24 104 kw vis. ant 1,476t/535g TL: N47 36 04 W117 17 53 On air date: 2000. 1201 W. Sprague Ave., Spokane, WA, 99201. Phone: (509) 340-3400. Fax: (509) 340-3417. Web Site: www.ionline.tv/stations/list.cfm. Licensee: Paxson Spokane License Inc.
Key Personnel:
Amber Morales. . . . . opns mgr
Mitch Wasson . . . . chief of engrg
Jennifer Perry. . . . . traf mgr

KHQ-TV— Digital Channel: 15. Digital Hrs: 24 1,000 kw vis. ant 2,142t/859g TL: N47 34 52 W117 17 47 On air date: Dec 20, 1952. PO Box 600, Spokane, WA, 99210-0600. 1201 W. Sprague Ave., Spokane, WA 99201-4102. Phone: (509) 448-6000. Fax: (509) 448-4694.E-mail: q6news@khq.com Web Site: www.khq.com. Licensee: KHQ Inc. Group Owner: (group owner) Population Served: 1,500,000 Natl. Network: NBC, . Natl. Rep: Blair Television,. Washington Atty: Skadden, Arps. News staff: 52; News: 26 hrs wkly.
Key Personnel:
Betsy Cowles . . . . chmn
Paula Bauer . . . . pres
Bill Storms . . . . gen sls mgr
Jonathan Mitchell. . . . . prom mgr
Mike Dugger. . . . . progmg mgr
Jonathan Michell . . . . news dir

KLEW-TV— Digital Channel: 32. Digital Hrs: 20 56.2 kw vis, 1.38 kw aur. 1,260t/303 TL: N46 27 25 W117 05 57 On air date: December 1955. PO Box 615, Lewiston, ID, 83501. 2626 17th St., Lewiston, ID 83501. Phone: (208) 746-2636. Fax: (208) 746-4819.E-mail: info@klewtv.com Web Site: www.klewtv.com. Licensee: Fisher Broadcasting - Washington TV L.L.C. Group Owner: Fisher Broadcasting Company (acq 12-4-2001; grpsl). Population Served: 165,000 Natl. Network: CBS, . Natl. Rep: Petry Television Inc.,. Washington Atty: Shaw Pittman. Wire Svc: AP News staff: 4; News: 12 hrs wkly.
Key Personnel:
Fred Fickenwirth. . . . . stn mgr & gen sls mgr
Greg Meyer . . . . news dir
Bill Dunlap. . . . . chief of engrg
Margo Aragon . . . . pub affrs dir & pub svc dir
Ann Fickenwirth . . . . opns
Satellite of KIMA-TV Yakima Wash.

KQUP— Digital Channel: 24. Digital Hrs: 24 1,000 kw vis. ant 1,866t/656g TL: N47 34 44 W117 17 46 On air date: Sept 1, 2003. Stn currently dark 3901 Hwy. 121 S., Bedford, TX, 76021. Phone: (817) 571-1229. Fax: (817) 571-7458. Web Site: www.daystar.com. Licensee: Word of God Fellowship Inc. Group Owner: Equity Broadcasting Corp. (acq 7-31-2009; grpsl). Population Served: 378,500

Key Personnel:
Marcus D. Lamb . . . . pres

KREM— Digital Channel: 20. Digital Hrs: 24 893 kw vis. ant 2,102t/794g TL: N47 35 41 W117 17 53 On air date: Oct 31, 1954. Box 8037, Spokane, WA, 99203. 4103 S. Regal, Spokane, WA 99223. Phone: (509) 448-2000. Fax: (509) 448-6397 (news). Fax: (509) 448-2090 (sales). Web Site: www.krem.com. Licensee: KREM-TV Inc. Group Owner: Belo Corp., Broadcast Division (acq 9-92; grpsl;9-16-91). Population Served: 174,500 Natl. Network: CBS, . Washington Atty: Covington & Burling. News staff: 36; News: 17 hrs wkly.
Key Personnel:
Robert Decherd . . . . CEO
Jim Maroney . . . . exec VP
Jamie Aitken . . . . gen mgr
Amy Warren . . . . gen sls mgr
Bruce Felt . . . . prom dir
Christine Werfelmann . . . . progmg dir
Boyd Lundberg . . . . chief of engrg
Deannie Armstrong . . . . traf mgr

KSKN— Digital Channel: 36.1,860 kw vis. ant 1,958t TL: N47 35 42 W117 17 53 On air date: Oct 1, 1983. 4103 S. Regal, Spokane, WA, 99223-7377. Phone: (509) 448-2000. Fax: (509) 448-2090. Web Site: www.krem.com. Licensee: KSKN Television Inc. Group Owner: Belo Corp., Broadcast Division (acq 8-24-01; $5 million). Natl. Network: CW, . News staff: 5; News: 6 hrs wkly.
Key Personnel:
D.J. Wilson . . . . pres & sr VP
Jamie Aitken . . . . gen mgr
Dan Lamphere . . . . opns dir & opns mgr
Susan Miller . . . . gen sls mgr
Ron Keller . . . . prom dir & prom mgr
Terry Cocker . . . . progmg dir
Noah Cooper . . . . news dir
John Souza . . . . engrg dir
Boyd Lundberg . . . . chief of engrg
Tom Hudson . . . . sports cmtr
Tom Sherry . . . . weather dir

***KSPS-TV—** Digital Channel: 7. Digital Hrs: 24 45.1 kw vis. ant 1,830t/530g TL: N47 34 34 W117 17 58 On air date: Apr 24, 1967. S. 3911 Regal St., Spokane, WA, 99223. Phone: (509) 354-7800. Fax: (509) 354-7757. Web Site: www.ksps.org. Licensee: Spokane School District No. 81. Population Served: 1,200,000 Natl. Network: PBS, . Washington Atty: Garvey, Schubert & Barer.
Key Personnel:
Claude Kistler . . . . gen mgr
Patty Starkey . . . . dev dir
Kerry Faggiano . . . . prom mgr
Cary Balzer . . . . progmg mgr

***KUID-TV—** Digital Channel: 12. Digital Hrs: 24 44 kw vis. ant 971t/148g TL: N46 40 54 W116 58 13 On air date: July 1, 1965. c/o KAID, 1455 N. Orchard St., Boise, ID, 83706. PO Box 443101, University of Idaho, Moscow, ID 83844-3101. Phone: (208) 885-1226. Fax: (208) 885-5711.E-mail: idptv@idahoptv.org Web Site: www.idahoptv.org. Licensee: State Board of Education, State of Idaho. Population Served: 151,000 Natl. Network: PBS, . Washington Atty: Fletcher, Heald & Hildreth.
Key Personnel:
Peter Morrill . . . . gen mgr
Kris Freeland . . . . stn mgr
Kim Philipps . . . . dev dir

***KWSU-TV—** Digital Channel: 10. Digital Hrs: 24 117 kw vis, 11.7 kw aur. 1,350t/300g TL: N46 51 43 W117 10 26 On air date: Sept 24, 1962. Box 642530, Pullman, WA, 99164-2530. Phone: (509) 335-6511. Fax: (509) 335-3772.E-mail: kwsu@wsu.edu Web Site: www.kwsu.org. Licensee: Washington State University. Population Served: 170,000 Natl. Network: PBS, . Washington Atty: Dow, Lohnes & Albertson.
Key Personnel:
Sarah McDaniel . . . . dev dir
Kari Watkins . . . . progmg dir

KXLY-TV— Digital Channel: 13. Digital Hrs: 24 48 kw vis, 4.8 kw aur. ant 3,060t/153g TL: N47 55 18 W117 06 48 On air date: Feb 22, 1953. 500 W. Boone Ave., Spokane, WA, 99201. Phone: (509) 324-4000. Fax: (509) 328-5274. Web Site: www.kxly.com. Licensee: Spokane TV Inc. Group Owner: Evening Telegram Company—Morgan Murphy Stns (acq 1-17-63; grpsl; 1-63). Population Served: 555,400 Natl. Network: ABC, MyNetworkTV, . Natl. Rep: Continental Television Sales,. Washington Atty: Rini, Coran, PC. Wire Svc: AP News: 19 hrs wkly.

Key Personnel:
Elizabeth M. Burns . . . . pres
Steve Herling . . . . gen mgr

Tacoma

see Seattle-Tacoma, WA market

Vancouver

see Portland, OR market

Yakima-Pasco-Richland-Kennewick, WA (DMA 126)

KAPP— Digital Channel: 14. Digital Hrs: 21 646 kw vis, 64.6 kw aur. ant 961t TL: N46 31 57 W120 30 33 On air date: Sept 21, 1970. Box 10208, Yakima, WA, 98909-1208. 1610 S. 24th Ave., Yakima, WA 98902. Phone: (509) 453-0351. Fax: (509) 453-3623.E-mail: comments@kapptv.com Web Site: www.kapptv.com. Licensee: Apple Valley Broadcasting Inc. Group Owner: Morgan Murphy Stations Population Served: 421,000 Natl. Network: ABC, MyNetworkTV, . Washington Atty: Manatt, Phelps & Phillips.
Key Personnel:
Elizabeth Burns . . . . pres
Brian Paul . . . . gen mgr & stn mgr
Shane Pierone . . . . rgnl sls mgr
Mike Balmelli . . . . news dir
Neil Bennett . . . . chief of engrg
Amy Vetsch . . . . traf mgr
Sharon Crawford . . . . financial ed

KEPR-TV— Digital Channel: 18. Digital Hrs: 24 490 kw vis, 88.3 kw aur. 1,203t/354g TL: N46 05 51 W119 11 30 On air date: Dec 28, 1954. Box 2648, Pasco, WA, 99302. 2807 W. Lewis, Pasco, WA 99301. Phone: (509) 547-0547. Fax: (509) 547-2845. Web Site: www.keprtv.com. Licensee: Fisher Broadcasting - Washington TV L.L.C. Group Owner: Fisher Broadcasting Company (acq 12-4-2001; grpsl). Population Served: 260,000 Natl. Network: CBS, . Washington Atty: Winthrope, Shaw, Pittman, LLP. Wire Svc: CBS Wire Svc: Pacifica Network News News staff: 12; News: 17 hrs wkly.
Key Personnel:
Ben Tucker . . . . pres
Ken Messer . . . . gen mgr
David Praga . . . . stn mgr
Brad Gayken . . . . opns mgr
Steve Crow . . . . gen sls mgr & natl sls mgr
Randy Irwin . . . . prom mgr
Cris Headley . . . . pub affrs dir & traf mgr
John Housholder . . . . chief of engrg
Stu Seibel . . . . progmg dir & rsch dir
Scott Shogars . . . . film dir
Ed Dawson . . . . sports cmtr
Fred Rixe . . . . weather dir

KFFX-TV— Digital Channel: 11. Digital Hrs: 6 AM- 12:35 AM 3.16 kw vis. ant 1,043t TL: N45 40 58 W118 46 17 On air date: 1999. 2509 W. Falls Ave., Kennewick, WA, 99336. 4600 S. Regal St., Spokane, WA 99223. Phone: (509) 735-1700. Fax: (509) 735-1004. Web Site: www.fox11tricities.com. Licensee: Mountain Licenses L.P. Group Owner: Northwest Broadcasting Inc. (acq 1-14-2003; $239,659 for CP). Population Served: 211,610 Natl. Network: Fox, . Natl. Rep: Millennium Sales & Marketing,. Washington Atty: Leventhal, Senter & Lerman.
Key Personnel:
Brian Brady . . . . CEO
Bill Quarles . . . . CFO
Jon Rand . . . . gen mgr
Glenn Rousch . . . . stn mgr
Rick Andrycha . . . . opns mgr
Lynn Creager . . . . natl sls mgr
Lonnie Eaton . . . . rgnl sls mgr
Ron Sweatte . . . . chief of engrg
Robin Lennell . . . . traf mgr
Jennifer Ranney . . . . prom

KIMA-TV— Digital Channel: 33. Digital Hrs: 24 490 kw vis, 87.3 kw aur. ant 971t/67g TL: N46 31 58 W120 30 26 On air date: July 19, 1953. Box 702, Yakima, WA, 98907. 2801 Terrace Heights Dr., Yakima, WA 98901. Phone: (509) 575-0029. Fax: (509) 248-1218.E-mail: information@kimatv.com Web Site: www.kimatv.com. Licensee: Fisher Broadcasting - Washington TV L.L.C. Group Owner: Fisher Broadcasting Company (acq 12-4-2001; grpsl). Population Served: 443,000 Natl. Network: CBS, . Natl. Rep: Petry Television Inc.,. Washington Atty: Shaw Pittman. Wire Svc: CBS Wire Svc: CNN Wire Svc: AP News staff: 24; News: 15 hrs wkly.

Key Personnel:
Colleen Brown . . . . CEO & pres
Mr. Phelps Fisher . . . . chmn
Ken Messer . . . . VP & gen mgr
Karla Griffin . . . . opns mgr
Steve Crow . . . . gen sls mgr & natl sls mgr
Cheryl Menke . . . . rgnl sls mgr
Stu Siebel . . . . progmg dir
Robin Wojtanik . . . . news dir
Cliff Grady . . . . chief of engrg

KNDO— Digital Channel: 16. Digital Hrs: 24 501 kw vis, 61 kw aur. 961t/161g TL: N46 31 59 W130 20 36 On air date: Oct 15, 1959. 1608 S. 24th Ave., Yakima, WA, 98902. Phone: (509) 225-2323. Fax: (509) 225-2330.E-mail: news@kndo.com Web Site: www.kndo.com. Licensee: KHQ Inc. Group Owner: (group owner; (acq 6-17-99; $22.25 million with KNDU(TV) Richland). Population Served: 203,195 Natl. Network: NBC, . News staff: 9; News: 27 hrs wkly.
Key Personnel:
Lon Lee . . . . pres
Paul Dughi . . . . gen mgr & stn mgr
Larry Forsgren . . . . gen sls mgr
Scott Morgan . . . . mktg dir
Christine Brown . . . . news dir
Mark Kennedy . . . . engrg dir & chief of engrg
Susan Martinez . . . . progmg dir & traf mgr

KNDU— Digital Channel: 26. Digital Hrs: 24 150 kw vis. ant 1,319t/190g TL: N46 06 12 W119 07 49 On air date: July 1, 1961. 3312 W. Kennewick Ave., Kennewick, WA, 99336. Phone: (509) 737-6700. Phone: (509)737-6725. Fax: (509) 737-6749.E-mail: news@kndu.com Web Site: www.kndu.com. Licensee: KHQ Inc. Group Owner: (group owner; (acq 6-17-99; $22.25 million with KNDO(TV) Yakima). Population Served: 265,600 Natl. Network: NBC, . Washington Atty: Hogan & Hartson. News staff: 22; News: 22.5 hrs wkly.
Key Personnel:
Larry Sorsgren . . . . gen mgr & stn mgr gen sls mgr
Sheri Bissell . . . . natl sls mgr
Randy Brown . . . . rgnl sls mgr
Susan Martinez . . . . progmg dir
Christine Brown . . . . news dir
Satellite of KNDO(TV) Yakima 94%.

***KTNW—** Digital Channel: 38. Digital Hrs: 24 53.5 kw vis, 5.35 kw aur. 1,198t/36g TL: N46 06 23 W119 07 50 On air date: Oct 18, 1987. Box 642530, Pullman, WA, 99164-2530. Phone: (509) 335-6588. Fax: (509) 335-3772.E-mail: nwptv@wsu.edu Web Site: www.kwsu.org. Licensee: Washington State University. Natl. Network: PBS, . Washington Atty: Dow, Lohnes & Albertson.
Key Personnel:
Kari Watkins . . . . stn mgr
Sarah McDaniel . . . . dev dir

KVEW— Digital Channel: 44. Digital Hrs: 24 501 kw vis, 39.8 kw aur. ant 1,280t/205g TL: N46 06 11 W119 07 54 On air date: Oct 30, 1970. 601 N. Edison, Kennewick, WA, 99336. Phone: (509) 735-8369. Fax: (509) 735-1836 (news). Fax: (509) 735-7889. Web Site: www.kvewtv.com. Licensee: Apple Valley Broadcasting Inc. Group Owner: Morgan Murphy Stations Population Served: 163,300 Natl. Network: ABC, MyNetworkTV, .
Key Personnel:
Brian Paul . . . . gen mgr & stn mgr
Mike Balmelli . . . . news dir
Satellite of KAPP Yakima.

***KYVE—** Digital Channel: 21. Digital Hrs: 24 640 kw vis, 64 kw aur. ant 918t/135g TL: N46 31 58 W120 30 33 On air date: Nov 1, 1962. 12 S. 2nd St., Yakima, WA, 98901. Phone: (509) 452-4700. Fax: (509) 452-4704. Web Site: www.kyve.org. Licensee: KCTS Television. Ownership: KCTS Television board of directors (acq 8-1-94;8-22-94). Population Served: 192,000 Natl. Network: PBS, . Washington Atty: Schwartz, Woods & Miller.
Key Personnel:
Bill Mohler . . . . CEO
Mark Leonard . . . . gen mgr
Ken Messer . . . . stn mgr
Brenda Setterlund . . dev mgr & mktg mgr mktg mgr & prom mgr
Chris Splawn . . . . progmg mgr
Rod Venable . . . . stn mgr & chief of engrg

West Virginia

Beckley

see Bluefield-Beckley-Oak Hill, WV market

Bluefield-Beckley-Oak Hill, WV (DMA 155)

WLFB— Digital Channel: 40.2,880 kw vis. ant 1,282t/177g TL: N37 13 08 W81 15 39 On air date: 2001. Box 1867, Abingdon, VA, 24212. 8594 Hidden Valley Rd., Abingdon, VA 24210. Phone: (276) 676-3806. Fax: (276) 676-3572. Licensee: Living Faith Ministries Inc.

Key Personnel:
Micheal D. Smith . . . . CEO
Michael D. Smith . . . . pres & gen mgr
Fredia Keene . . . . CFO
Satellite of WLFG(TV) Grundy, VA.

WOAY-TV— Digital Channel: 50. Digital Hrs: 24 100 kw vis, 20 kw aur. ant 740t/688g TL: N37 57 30 W81 09 03 On air date: Dec 14, 1954. Box 3001, Oak Hill, WV, 25901. Phone: (304) 469-3361. Fax: (304) 465-1420.E-mail: amarra@woay.com Web Site: www.woay.com. Licensee: Thomas Broadcasting Co. Population Served: 332,000 Natl. Network: ABC, . Natl. Rep: Continental Television Sales,. Washington Atty: Fletcher, Heald & Hildreth.
Key Personnel:
Robert R. Thomas III . . . . pres
Al Marra . . . . gen mgr & progmg dir
Joetta Kelly-Oliver . . . . gen sls mgr
Robert Brunner . . . . news dir
TBA . . . . chief of engrg
Joe Wynne . . . . traf mgr

***WSWP-TV—** Digital Channel: 10. Digital Hrs: 24 316 kw vis, 63.2 kw aur. ant 1,000t/488g TL: N37 53 46 W80 59 21 On air date: Nov 1, 1970. PO Box 9004, Beckley, WV, 25802. 124 Industrial Dr., Beaver, WV 25813. Phone: (304) 254-7840. Fax: (304) 254-7879. Web Site: www.wvpubcast.org. Licensee: West Virginia Educational Broadcasting Authority. Population Served: 970,000 Natl. Network: PBS, . News: 5 hrs wkly.
Key Personnel:
Rita Ray . . . . CEO
Dennis Atkins . . . . gen mgr & stn mgr
Marilyn DeVita . . . . dev dir

WVNS-TV— Digital Channel: 8. Digital Hrs: 24 1,923 kw vis. ant 1,863t TL: N37 46 22 W80 42 25 On air date: Jan 1, 1997. Box 509, Ghent, WV, 25843. 141 Old Cline Rd., Ghent, WV 25843. Phone: (304) 787-5959. Fax: (304) 787-2440.E-mail: fbarnes@wvnstv.com Web Site: www.cbs59.com. Licensee: West Virginia Media Holdings LLC. Group Owner: (group owner; (acq 1-9-2003). Population Served: 270,000 Natl. Network: CBS, . Natl. Rep: Petry Television Inc.,. Washington Atty: Borsari & Paxson.
Key Personnel:
Bray Cary. . . . . CEO & pres
Marstow W. Becker. . . . . chmn
Charlie Dusic . . . . CFO
Chris Leister . . . . sr VP
Frank Barnes . . . . gen mgr
Sue Bosio. . . . . opns mgr
Gary Bowden . . . . sls VP
Jack Scott. . . . . gen sls mgr
Robert McCallister . . . . rgnl sls mgr
John Fawcett . . . . prom dir
M.J. Coss . . . . progmg dir
Gary Kirk . . . . chief of engrg

WVVA— Digital Channel: 46. Digital Hrs: 24 50.1 kw vis, 6.03 kw aur. ant 1,220t/185g TL: N37 15 21 W81 10 55 On air date: July 31, 1955. Box 1930, Bluefield, WV, 24701. Phone: (304) 325-5487. Fax: (304) 327-5586. Web Site: www.wvva.com. Licensee: WVVA TV Inc. Group Owner: Quincy Newspapers Inc., see Cross-Ownership (acq 5-1-79; $8 million;4-23-79). Population Served: 325,000 Natl. Network: NBC, CW, . Natl. Rep: Blair Television,. Washington Atty: Wilkinson, Barker, Knauer & Quinn. News staff: 20; News: 27 hrs wkly.
Key Personnel:
Thomas A. Oakley . . . . CEO
Ralph M. Oakley. . . . . COO
Frank Brady. . . . . VP & gen mgr
Jim Briggs . . . . stn mgr & sls dir mktg dir
Danny Via . . . . engrg dir

Charleston-Huntington, WV (DMA 65)

WCHS-TV— Digital Channel: 41. Digital Hrs: 24 49.6 kw vis. ant 1,746t/1,477g TL: N38 24 28 W81 54 13 On air date: Aug 15, 1954. 1301 Piedmont Rd., Charleston, WV, 25301. Phone: (304) 346-5358. Fax: (304) 346-4765.E-mail: info@wchstv.com Web Site: www.wchstv.com. Licensee: WCHS Licensee L.L.C. Group Owner: Sinclair Broadcast Group Inc. (acq 10-8-97). Population Served: 510,000 Natl. Network: ABC, . Washington Atty: Fisher, Wayland, Cooper, Leader & Zaragoza. News staff: 37; News: 19.5 hrs wkly.
Key Personnel:
Harold Cooper . . . . gen mgr
Paul Fox. . . . . prom dir
Lori Marquette . . . . progmg dir
Terry Cole . . . . news dir
Raymon Beckner . . . . chief of engrg
Sherry Allen . . . . traf mgr

***WKAS—** Digital Channel: 26.61.3 kw vis. ant 449t/16g TL: N38 27 44 W82 37 12 On air date: Sept 23, 1968. 600 Cooper Dr., Lexington, KY, 40502. Phone: (859) 258-7000. Fax: (859) 258-7390.E-mail: drbitton@ket.org Web Site: www.ket.org. Licensee: Kentucky Authority for Educational TV. Natl. Network: PBS, . Kentucky Educational Television
Key Personnel:
Craig Cornwell . . . . opns mgr & progmg dir
Tim Bischoff . . . . mktg dir
Robert Ball . . . . engrg dir

***WKPI-TV—** Digital Channel: 24.50.4 kw vis. ant 1,387t/85g TL: N37 17 06 W82 31 28 On air date: Apr 8, 1968. 600 Cooper Dr., Lexington, KY, 40502. Phone: (859) 233-3000. Fax: (859) 258-7399. Web Site: www.ket.org. Licensee: Kentucky Authority for Educational TV. Natl. Network: PBS, . Kentucky Educational Television
Key Personnel:
Craig Cornwell. . . . . opns mgr & progmg dir
Tim Bischoff . . . . mktg mgr
Mike Brower . . . . pub affrs dir & progmg
Robert Ball . . . . engrg dir

WLPX-TV— Digital Channel: 39. Digital Hrs: 24 1,000 kw vis. ant 1,148t/23g TL: N38 28 12 W81 46 35 On air date: Aug 28, 1998. 600 C Prestige Dr., Hurricane, WV, 25526. Phone: (304) 760-1029. Fax: (304) 760-1036. Web Site: www.ionline.tv/stations/list.cfm. Licensee: Paxson Charleston License Inc. Group Owner: Paxson Communications Corp. (acq 10-28-98; $8.25 million). Natl. Network: ION Television, . Washington Atty: Dan J. Alpert.
Key Personnel:
Brandon Burgess. . . . . CEO
Carol Holzhauer . . . . VP
Steven Stanley . . . . gen mgr & stn mgr & stn mgr
Joseph Koker. . . . . opns dir
Gene Monday . . . . chief of engrg

WOWK-TV— Digital Channel: 13. Digital Hrs: 24 141 kw vis, 26.3 kw aur. 1,269t/1,108g TL: N38 30 21 W82 12 33 On air date: Oct 2, 1955. 555 Fifth Ave., Huntington, WV, 25701. Phone: (304) 525-1313. Fax: (304) 529-4910. Web Site: wowktv.com. Licensee: West Virginia Media Holdings LLC. Group Owner: (group owner; (acq 4-8-2002; $40.5 million). Population Served: 667,520 Natl. Network: CBS, . Natl. Rep: TeleRep,. Washington Atty: Bryan Cave.
Key Personnel:
Bray Cary. . . . . pres
John Fawcett. . . . . gen mgr & mktg dir prom dir & pub svc dir
Chris Leister. . . . . gen sls mgr
M.J. Coss . . . . progmg dir
Rod Fowler . . . . news dir
Bill Gallaway. . . . . chief of engrg
Elizabeth Melvin . . . . traf mgr & news cmtr
Sandra Cole . . . . news cmtr

***WPBO—** Digital Channel: 43. Digital Hrs: 24 50 kw vis. ant 1,253t/915g TL: N38 45 42 W83 03 41 On air date: October 1973. 2400 Olentangy River Rd., Columbus, OH, 43210. Phone: (614) 292-9678. Fax: (614) 688-3399. Fax: (614) 688-3343.E-mail: wosu@wosu.org Web Site: www.wosu.org. Licensee: The Ohio State University. Natl. Network: PBS, . Rgnl. Network: CEN. Washington Atty: Dow, Lohnes & Albertson.
Key Personnel:
Thomas Rieland. . . . . gen mgr
Edwin Clay . . . . stn mgr
Janice "Sheri" Walker . . . . opns mgr
Doug Partusch . . . . dev dir
Rebroadcasts WOSU-TV Columbus 100%.

***WPBY-TV—** Digital Channel: 34. Digital Hrs: 24 2,371 kw vis, 105 kw aur. ant 1,243t TL: N38 29 41 W82 12 03 On air date: July 14, 1969. 600 Capitol St., Charleston, WV, 25301. Phone: (304) 556-4900 / (304) 556-4905. Fax: (304) 556-4982. Web Site: www.wvpubcast.org. Licensee: West Virginia Educational Broadcasting Authority. Population Served: 300,000 Natl. Network: PBS, . Rgnl. Network: SECA.
Key Personnel:
Bill Acker . . . . gen mgr & stn mgr
Marilyn DiVita. . . . . dev dir & dev mgr
Craig Lanham. . . . . progmg dir
Greg Collard . . . . news dir & pub affrs dir

WQCW— Digital Channel: 17. Digital Hrs: 24 2,040 kw vis, 204 kw aur. ant 1,174t/850g TL: N38 45 42 W83 03 41 On air date: Oct 5, 1998. 800 Gallia, Suite 430, Portsmouth, OH, 45662. 400 Capitol St., Charleston, OH 25301. Phone: (740) 353-3391. Fax: (740) 353-3372. Web Site: www.tristatescw.com. Licensee: Television Properties Inc. Ownership: Commonwealth Broadcasting Group Inc., 88%; Kenneth Russell, 12% (acq 7-11-2002). Population Served: 298,742 Natl. Network: CW, .
Key Personnel:
Dave Hanna . . . . pres
William White. . . . . gen mgr
Vince Wardell . . . . gen sls mgr

WSAZ-TV— Digital Channel: 23.42.7 kw vis, 7 kw aur. ant 1,273t/1,101g TL: N38 30 34 W82 13 09 On air date: Nov 15, 1949. 645 Fifth Ave., Huntington, WV, 25701. Phone: (304) 697-4780. Fax: (304) 690-3065 (news).E-mail: news@wsaz.com Web Site: www.wsaz.com. Licensee: Gray Television Licensee Inc. Group Owner: Emmis Communications Corp. (acq 11-30-2005; $186 million). Population Served: 1,252,100 Natl. Network: NBC, MyNetworkTV, .
Key Personnel:
Don Ray . . . . gen mgr & stn mgr
Aaron Withrow . . . . opns dir

WTSF— Digital Channel: 44. Digital Hrs: 24 50 kw vis. ant 571t/421g TL: N38 25 11 W82 24 06 On air date: Apr 30, 1983. Box 2320, Ashland, KY, 41105-2320. 3100 Bath Ave., Ashland, KY 41101. Phone: (606) 329-2700. Fax: (606) 324-9256. Web Site: www.wtsftv.com. Licensee: Word of God Fellowship Inc. Ownership: Jimmie F. Lamb, 25%; John T. Calender, 25%; Joni T. Lamb, 25%; and Marcus D. Lamb, 25% (acq 4-18-2003).
Key Personnel:
Richard Clifton . . . . gen mgr & stn mgr
Virgil Adkins . . . . chief of engrg

WVAH-TV— Digital Channel: 19. Digital Hrs: 24 51 kw vis, 5.1 kw aur. ant 1,722t/1,552g TL: N38 25 15 W81 55 27 On air date: Sept 19, 1982. 11 Broadcast Plaza, Hurricane, WV, 25526. Phone: (304) 757-0011. Fax: (304) 757-7533.E-mail: info@wvah.com Web Site: www.wvah.com. Licensee: WVAH Licensee LLC. Group Owner: Cunningham Broadcasting Corporation (acq 11-15-2001; grpsl). Natl. Network: Fox, . Washington Atty: Arter & Hadden. News staff: 38; News: 7 hrs wkly.
Key Personnel:
Harold Cooper . . . . pres & gen mgr
Paul Fox. . . . . prom dir
Lori Marquette . . . . progmg dir
Matt Snyder . . . . news dir
Raymond Beckner. . . . . chief of engrg
Sherry Allen . . . . traf mgr

Clarksburg-Weston, WV (DMA 168)

WBOY-TV— Digital Channel: 12. Digital Hrs: 24 12.25 kw vis. ant 859t/571g TL: N39 17 06 W80 19 46 On air date: Nov 17, 1957. 904 W. Pike St., Clarksburg, WV, 26301. 912 W. Pike St., Clarksburg, WV 26301. Phone: (304) 623-3311. Fax: (304) 624-6152. Web Site: www.wboy.com. Licensee: West Virginia Media Holdings LLC. Group Owner: (group owner; (acq 10-25-2001; $20 million). Population Served: 250,000 Natl. Network: NBC, . Natl. Rep: Petry Television Inc.,. Washington Atty: Cohn & Marks LLP. Wire Svc: AP News staff: 24; News: 24 hrs wkly.
Key Personnel:
Bray Cary. . . . . CEO & pres
Marty Becker . . . . chmn
Charlie Dusic . . . . CFO
Larry Cottrill . . . . gen mgr
Kim Morrison . . . . opns mgr
George Boggs . . . . gen sls mgr
Scott Sterling . . . . natl sls mgr
John Fawcett . . . . mktg mgr
Amanda Leasburg . . . . prom mgr
Gary McNair . . . . progmg dir
Jim Platzer. . . . . news dir
Bob Hardman . . . . chief of engrg
Virginia Richison. . . . . traf mgr

WDTV— Digital Channel: 5. Digital Hrs: 24 10 kw vis. ant 787t/613g TL: N39 18 02 W80 20 37 On air date: June 1, 1960. Box 480, Bridgeport, WV, 26330. Phone: (304) 848-5000. Fax: (304) 842-7501.E-mail: wdtv@wdtv.com Web Site: www.wdtv.com. Licensee: W. Russell Withers Jr. Group Owner: Withers Broadcasting Co. (acq 5-8-73; $600,000;4-16-73). Population Served: 116,000 Natl. Network: CBS, . Washington Atty: Gardner, Carton & Douglas. News staff: 21; News: 18.5 hrs wkly.
Key Personnel:
W. Russell Withers Jr. . . . . pres
Tim Defazio . . . . gen mgr & stn mgr dev dir
John Breen. . . . . opns dir

WVFX— Digital Channel: 10. Digital Hrs: 24 155 kw vis, 15.5 kw aur. ant 800t/632g TL: N39 18 02 W80 20 37 On air date: Jan 1999. Box 480, Bridgeport, WV, 26330. Phone: (304) 848-5000. Fax: (304) 842-7501.E-mail: info@wvfx.com Web Site: www.myfox.com. Licensee: Withers Broadcasting Co. of Clarksburg LLC. (acq 5-6-2008; $5 million). Natl. Network: Fox, CW, . Washington Atty: Law Office of Dennis J. Kelly.

Huntington

see Charleston-Huntington, WV market

Martinsburg

see Washington, DC (Hagerstown, MD) market

Morgantown

see Pittsburgh, PA market

Oak Hill

see Bluefield-Beckley-Oak Hill, WV market

Parkersburg, WV
(DMA 193)

WTAP-TV— Digital Channel: 49. Digital Hrs: 5 AM-2:35 AM (M-F); 6 AM-2:05 AM (S); 6 AM-12:35 AM (Su) 220 kw vis, 41.1 kw aur. ant 630t/440g TL: N39 20 59 W81 33 56 On air date: Oct 8, 1953. One Television Plaza, Parkersburg, WV, 26101. Phone: (304) 485-4588. Fax: (304) 422-3920. E-mail: gm@wtap.com Web Site: www.wtap.com. Licensee: Gray Television Group, Inc. Group Owner: Gray Television Inc. (acq 8-29-2002; grpsl). Population Served: 325,000 Natl. Network: NBC, Fox, MyNetworkTV. Natl. Rep: Continental Television Sales,. Washington Atty: Covington & Burling. Wire Svc: AP Wire Svc: CNN News staff: 15; News: 24 hrs wkly.
Key Personnel:
Roger Sheppard . . . . VP
Jeff Nutter . . . . gen mgr
Joyce Ancrile . . . . prom dir
Shane Vass . . . . rgnl sls mgr & progmg mgr
Bruce Layman . . . . news dir
Kevin Buskirk . . . . chief of engrg & engr
Dirk Kreiss . . . . traf mgr

Weston

see Clarksburg-Weston, WV market

Wheeling, WV-Steubenville, OH
(DMA 159)

WTOV-TV— Digital Channel: 9. Digital Hrs: 24 23 kw vis. ant 925t/869g TL: N40 20 33 W80 37 14 On air date: Dec 24, 1953. Box 9999, Steubenville, OH, 43952. 9 Red Donelly Plaza (also shipping), Mingo Junction, OH 43938. Phone: (740) 282-9999. Phone: (304) 232-6933. Fax: (740) 282-0350. Web Site: www.wtov9.com. Licensee: WTOV Inc. Group Owner: Cox Broadcasting (acq 9-22-2000; $58 million). Population Served: 144,000 Natl. Network: NBC, ABC, . Natl. Rep: TeleRep,. Washington Atty: Dow, Lohnes & Albertson. Wire Svc: AP News staff: 32; News: 22 hrs wkly.
Key Personnel:
Andrew Fisher . . . . pres
Bruce Baker . . . . exec VP
Mike Seachman . . . . opns mgr
Tom Pleva . . . . gen sls mgr
Bill Seifert . . . . prom dir
Melissa Knollinger . . . . news dir
Leonard Smith . . . . chief of engrg

WTRF-TV— Digital Channel: 7. Digital Hrs: 24 316 kw vis, 30.9 kw aur. ant 960t/740g TL: N40 03 41 W80 45 08 On air date: Oct 23, 1953. 96 16th St., Wheeling, WV, 26003. Phone: (304) 232-7777. Fax: (304) 232-4975. Web Site: www.wtrf.com. Licensee: West Virginia Media Holdings LLC. Group Owner: (group owner; (acq 3-12-2002; grpsl). Population Served: 255,000 Natl. Network: CBS, . Natl. Rep: Petry Television Inc.,. Washington Atty: Edmundson & Edmundson. Wire Svc: AP News staff: 28; News: 26 hrs wkly.

Key Personnel:
Roger Lyons . . . . gen mgr
Charlotte Cohen . . . . gen sls mgr
Jane DomBroski. . . . . prom dir
M.J. Coss . . . . progmg dir
Brenda Danehart . . . . news dir
Brad Stanford . . . . chief of engrg

Wisconsin

Appleton

see Green Bay-Appleton, WI market

Eau Claire

see La Crosse-Eau Claire, WI market

Green Bay-Appleton, WI
(DMA 70)

WACY-TV— Digital Channel: 27. Digital Hrs: 24 50 kw vis. ant 975t/785g TL: N44 21 30 W87 58 48 On air date: Mar 7, 1984. 1391 North Rd., Green Bay, WI, 54307-2328. Phone: (920) 490-2647. Fax: (920) 494-9550. E-mail: rbell@mynew32.com Web Site: www.mynew32.com. Licensee: Ace TV Inc. Ownership: Shirley A. Martin (acq 5-25-2000). Natl. Network: MyNetworkTV, . Washington Atty: Davis Wright Tremaine LLP.
Key Personnel:
Robb Bell . . . . gen mgr

WBAY-TV— Digital Channel: 23. Digital Hrs: 24 (Su-Th); 19 (F,S) 100 kw vis, 20 kw aur. ant 1,205t/1,149g TL: N44 24 35 W88 00 05 On air date: Mar 17, 1953. 115 S. Jefferson St., Green Bay, WI, 54301. Phone: (920) 432-3331. Phone: (800) 242-8090. Fax: (920) 432-1190 (news). E-mail: wbay@wbay.com Web Site: www.wbay.com. Licensee: Young Broadcasting of Green Bay Inc. Group Owner: Young Broadcasting Inc. (acq 8-24-94; grpsl;9-12-94). Population Served: 973,000 Natl. Network: ABC, . Natl. Rep: Adam Young,. Washington Atty: Brooks, Pierce, McClendon & Humphry. News staff: 100; News: 19 hrs wkly.
Key Personnel:
Don Carmichael. . . . . gen mgr
Steve Lavin . . . . stn mgr
Richard Millhiser . . . . opns dir

WFRV-TV— Digital Channel: 39. Digital Hrs: 24 100 kw vis, 18.6 kw aur. ant 1,119t/998g TL: N44 24 21 W88 00 19 On air date: May 21, 1955. 1181 E. Mason, Green Bay, WI, 54301. Box 19055, Green Bay, WI 54307. Phone: (920) 437-5411. Fax: (920) 437-4576. E-mail: tips@wfrv.com Web Site: www.wfrv.com. Licensee: WFRV and WJMN Television Station Inc. Group Owner: Viacom Television Stations Group (acq 4-16-2007; with WJMN-TV Escanaba, MI). Population Served: 967,000 Natl. Network: CBS, . Natl. Rep: TeleRep,. News: 24.5 hrs wkly.
Key Personnel:
Perry Kidder. . . . . pres & VP & gen mgr
Jackie Stewart . . . . gen sls mgr
Kristen Kent . . . . mktg mgr
Lee Hitter . . . . news dir
Dale Mitchell . . . . chief of engrg

WGBA-TV— Digital Channel: 41. Digital Hrs: 24 1,000 kw vis, 100 kw aur. ant 975t/785g TL: N44 21 30 W87 58 48 On air date: Dec 31, 1980. 1391 North Rd., Green Bay, WI, 54313. Phone: (920) 494-2626. Fax: (920) 494-9550. Web Site: www.nbc26.com. Licensee: Journal Broadcast Corp. (acq 10-7-2004; $43.25 million). Population Served: 1,930,100 Natl. Network: NBC, . Natl. Rep: Petry Television Inc.,. Washington Atty: Shaw Pittman. Wire Svc: AP News staff: 33; News: 16 hrs wkly.

WIWB— Digital Channel: 21. Digital Hrs: 24 1000 kw vis, 100 kw aur. ant 613t/544g TL: N44 59 30 W88 23 55 On air date: Feb 22, 1984. 975 Parkview Rd., Suite 4, Green Bay, WI, 54304. Phone: (920) 983-9014. Fax: (920) 983-9424. E-mail: promotions@wisconsinscw.com Web Site: www.wisconsinscw.com Licensee: Acme Television Licenses of Wisconsin L.L.C. Group Owner: Acme Communications Inc. (acq 6-1-99; grpsl). Population Served: 1,035,000 Natl. Network: CW, . Natl. Rep: MMT,. Washington Atty: Dickstein, Shapiro, Morin & Oshinsky LLP.

Key Personnel:
Stephen M. Shanks . . . . gen mgr
Stephen Shanks . . . . stn mgr
Todd Zielgler. . . . . gen sls mgr
Peter Marquardt . . . . natl sls mgr
Jeff Bartel . . . . prom mgr
Tim Brusky . . . . chief of engrg
Heidi Gillis . . . . traf mgr

WLUK-TV— Digital Channel: 11. Digital Hrs: 24 316 kw vis, 47.4 kw aur. ant 1,260t/1,159g TL: N44 24 31 W87 59 29 On air date: Sept 11, 1954. Box 19011, 787 Lombardi Ave., Green Bay, WI, 54307-9011. Phone: (920) 494-8711. Fax: (920) 494-8782. E-mail: jlynch@wluk.com Web Site: www.wluk.com. Licensee: LIN of Wisconsin LLC. Group Owner: Emmis Communications Corp. (acq 11-30-2005; grpsl). Population Served: 1,049,000 Natl. Network: Fox, . Natl. Rep: Blair Television,. Wire Svc: AP News staff: 55; News: 32.5 hrs wkly.
Key Personnel:
Jay Zollar . . . . gen mgr
Tori Grant-Welhouse. . . . . gen sls mgr
Pat Krohlow . . . . mktg dir
Juli Buehler . . . . news dir
Mike Nipps . . . . chief of engrg

*WPNE-TV— Digital Channel: 42.200 kw vis. ant 1,230t/1,066g TL: N44 24 34 W88 00 06 On air date: Sept 12, 1972. 821 University Ave., Madison, WI, 53706. Phone: (608) 263-2121. Fax: (608) 263-9763. E-mail: comments@wpt.org Web Site: www.wpt.org. Licensee: State of Wisconsin-Educational Communications Board. Population Served: 4,600,000 Natl. Network: PBS, . Washington Atty: Dow, Lohnes & Albertson.
Key Personnel:
Malcolm Brett . . . . gen mgr & progmg mgr
Mike Edgette . . . . opns dir
Jon Miskowski . . . . dev dir

WWAZ-TV— Digital Channel: 44. Digital Hrs: 24 4,986 kw vis. ant 640t/468g TL: N43 26 20 W88 31 29 On air date: Dec 1, 2000. Box 2326, Fond Du Lac, WI, 54936-2326. Phone: (920) 387-9698. Fax: (920) 387-9660. Licensee: WMMF License LLC. Group Owner: Pappas Telecasting Companies (acq 3-10-2001). Population Served: 1, 913,668 Washington Atty: Paul Hastings.
Key Personnel:
Edward Bok . . . . CEO & chief of engrg
Howard Shrier . . . . gen mgr
Debbie Sweeney . . . . progmg VP

La Crosse-Eau Claire, WI
(DMA 127)

WEAU-TV— Digital Channel: 13. Digital Hrs: 24 316 kw vis, 37 kw aur. ant 1,990t/2,000g TL: N44 39 51 W90 57 41 On air date: Dec 17, 1953. Box 47, Eau Claire, WI, 54702. 1907 S. Hastings Way, Eau Claire, WI 54701. Phone: (715) 835-1313. Fax: (715) 832-0246. E-mail: info@weau.com Web Site: www.weau.com. Licensee: WEAU Licensee Corp. Group Owner: Gray Television Inc. (acq 8-1-98; grpsl). Population Served: 224,000 Natl. Network: NBC, . Natl. Rep: Continental Television Sales,. Washington Atty: Pepper & Corazzini. Wire Svc: Medialink News: 34 hrs wkly.
Key Personnel:
Terry McHugh. . . . . gen mgr
Tom Benson . . . . opns dir
Wendy Gustofson. . . . . gen sls mgr
John Hoffland . . . . news dir

WEUX— Digital Channel: 49.60.3 kw vis, 6 kw aur. 321t TL: N44 52 36 W91 18 22 On air date: February 1993. 800 Wisconsin St., Suite 101, #60, Eau Claire, WI, 54703. Phone: (715) 831-2548. Fax: (715) 831-2550. E-mail: info@fox25fox48.com Web Site: www.fox25fox48.com. Licensee: Grant Media LLC. Group Owner: (group owner; (acq 1996; $6.25 million with WLAX(TV) La Crosse). Natl. Network: Fox, . Natl. Rep: TeleRep,.
Key Personnel:
Steve Roth . . . . rgnl sls mgr
Barb Quillin . . . . prom dir
Mark Burg . . . . chief of engrg
Eric Barczak . . . . traf mgr

*WHLA-TV— Digital Channel: 30. Digital Hrs: 24 307.5 kw vis. ant 1,130t/792g TL: N43 48 17 W91 22 06 On air date: Dec 3, 1973. 3319 W. Beltline Hwy., Madison, WI, 53713. Phone: (608) 264-9600 / (507) 895-2026. Fax: (608) 264-9664 / (507) 895-4147. Web Site: www.ecb.org. Licensee: State of Wisconsin-Educational Communications Board. Natl. Network: PBS, . Washington Atty: Dow, Lohnes & Albertson.
Key Personnel:
Byron Knight . . . . gen mgr & stn mgr
Mike Edgette . . . . opns dir
Jon Miskowski . . . . dev dir
Mary Clare Sorenson . . . . adv dir & progmg mgr
Kathy Bissen . . . . news dir
Dick Taugher . . . . chief of engrg
Irene Ekleberry . . . . traf mgr

WKBT— Digital Channel: 8. Digital Hrs: 24 316 kw vis, 57.5 kw aur. ant 1,625t/1,540g TL: N44 05 28 W91 20 15 On air date: Aug 8, 1954.

141 S. 6th St., La Crosse, WI, 54601. Phone: (608) 782-4678. Fax: (608) 782-4674.E-mail: news8@wkbt.com Web Site: www.wkbt.com. Licensee: QueenB Television L.L.C. Group Owner: Morgan Murphy Stations (acq 3-31-2000; $22 million). Natl. Network: CBS, MyNetworkTV, . Natl. Rep: Harrington, Righter & Parsons,.

Key Personnel:
David Sanks . . . exec VP
Scott Chorski . . . gen mgr
Dennis McSorley . . . opns mgr & chief of engrg
Barb Pervisky . . . gen sls mgr & natl sls mgr
Brian Voigt . . . prom mgr
Maria Roswall . . . progmg dir & progmg mgr
Anne Paape . . . news dir
Larry Johnson . . . traf mgr

WLAX— Digital Channel: 17. Digital Hrs: 24 562 kw vis, 56.2 kw aur. 1,004t/674g TL: N43 48 16 W91 22 18 On air date: Sept 28, 1986. Box 2529, La Crosse, WI, 54602. 1305 Interchange Pl., La Crosse, WI 54603. Phone: (608) 781-0025. Fax: (608) 783-2520.E-mail: info@fox25fox48.com Web Site: www.fox25fox48.com. Licensee: Grant Media LLC. Group Owner: (group owner; (acq 5-15-96; $6.25 million with WEUX(TV) Chippewa Falls). Natl. Network: Fox, . Natl. Rep: TeleRep,. News: 3.5 hrs wkly.

Key Personnel:
Bob Weinstein . . . stn mgr

WQOW-TV— Digital Channel: 15. Digital Hrs: 24 407 kw vis, 40.7 kw aur. 741t/507g TL: N44 57 49 W91 40 05 On air date: Sept 22, 1980. 5545 Hwy. 93 S., Eau Claire, WI, 54701. Phone: (715) 835-1881. Fax: (715) 835-8009.E-mail: info@wqow.com Web Site: www.wqow.com. Licensee: WXOW/WQOW Television Inc. Group Owner: Quincy Newspapers Inc., see Cross-Ownership (acq 6-1-2001; grpsl). Population Served: 214,000 Natl. Network: ABC, CW, . Natl. Rep: Blair Television,. Washington Atty: Wilkinson, Barker, Knauer LLP. News staff: 16; News: 18 hrs wkly.

Key Personnel:
Tom Oakley . . . chmn
Ralph Oakley . . . pres
Charles "Chuck" Roth . . . gen mgr
Mark Golden . . . stn mgr

WXOW-TV— Digital Channel: 48. Digital Hrs: 24 631 kw vis, 63 kw aur. ant 1,138t/790g TL: N43 48 23 W91 22 02 On air date: Mar 7, 1970. Box C-4019, La Crosse, WI, 54602-4019. 3705 County Hwy. 25, La Crescent, MN 55947. Phone: (507) 895-9969. Fax: (507) 895-8124. Web Site: www.wxow.com. Licensee: WXOW-WQOW Television Inc. Group Owner: Quincy Newspapers Inc., see Cross-Ownership (acq 6-1-2001). Population Served: 1,542,600 Natl. Network: ABC, CW, . Natl. Rep: Blair Television,. Washington Atty: Wilkinson, Barker & Knauer, L.L.P. Wire Svc: AP News staff: 24; News: 18 hrs wkly.

Key Personnel:
David Booth . . . gen mgr
Sean Dwyer . . . news dir
Dave White . . . chief of engrg

Madison, WI
(DMA 85)

WBUW— Digital Channel: 32. Digital Hrs: 24 5,000 kw vis, 500 kw aur. ant 1,361t/1,273g TL: N43 03 03 W89 29 13 On air date: June 28, 1999. 2814 Syene Rd., Madison, WI, 53713. Phone: (608) 270-5700. Fax: (608) 270-5717. Web Site: www.madisonscw.com. Licensee: Acme Television Licenses of Madison LLC. Group Owner: Acme Communications Inc. (acq 1-1-2003). Population Served: 750,000 Natl. Network: CW, . Natl. Rep: MMT,. Washington Atty: Dickstein, Shapiro, Morin & Oshinsky LLP.

Key Personnel:
Jamie Kellner . . . CEO
Doug Gealy . . . COO
Tom Allen . . . CFO
Eric Krieghoff . . . dev mgr & natl sls mgr
Sharon Weiler . . . sls VP
Tom Keeler . . . gen mgr & gen sls mgr
Dave Shelly . . . natl sls mgr
Matt Creamer . . . prom mgr
Eugene Cooper . . . progmg mgr
Emmy Fink . . . news dir & pub affrs dir min affrs dir
Brent Stephenson . . . engrg VP
Jeff Juniet . . . chief of engrg
Shani Stewart . . . rsch dir
Mark Albright . . . traf mgr

***WHA-TV—** Digital Channel: 20.140 kw vis. ant 1,486t/1,348g TL: N43 03 21 W89 32 06 On air date: May 3, 1954. 821 University Ave., Madison, WI, 53706. Phone: (608) 263-2121. Fax: (608) 263-9763. Web Site: www.wpt.org. Licensee: University of Wisconsin Board of Regents. Population Served: 210,000 Natl. Network: PBS, . Washington Atty: Dow, Lohnes & Albertson.

Key Personnel:
Malcolm Brett . . . gen mgr & stn mgr
Mike Edgette . . . opns mgr
Jon Miskowski . . . dev dir

WISC-TV— Digital Channel: 50. Digital Hrs: 24 56.2 kw vis, 11 kw aur. ant 1,191t/1,108g TL: N43 01 52 W89 30 18 On air date: June 24, 1956. Box 44965, Madison, WI, 53744-4965. Phone: (608) 271-4321. Fax: (608) 271-6111. Web Site: www.channel3000.com. Licensee: TV Wisconsin Inc. Group Owner: Morgan Murphy Stns. Population Served: 280,000 Natl. Network: CBS, MyNetworkTV, . Natl. Rep: Harrington, Righter & Parsons,. Washington Atty: Rini Coran, PC. News staff: 30; News: 30 hrs wkly.

Key Personnel:
Elizabeth Murphy Burns . . . pres
David Sanks . . . exec VP & gen mgr
Jill Sommers . . . opns dir & gen sls mgr & progmg dir

WKOW-TV— Digital Channel: 27. Analog Hrs: 24 1,000 kw vis, 100 kw aur. 1,250t/1,182g TL: N43 03 09 W89 28 42 (CP: Ant 1,492t/1,424g. TL: N43 03 21 W89 32 06) On air date: July 1953. 5727 Tokay Blvd., Madison, WI, 53719. Phone: (608) 274-1234. Fax: (608) 274-9514. Web Site: www.wkowtv.com. Licensee: WKOW Television Inc. Group Owner: Quincy Newspapers Inc., see Cross-Ownership (acq 5-22-2001; grpsl). Population Served: 214,800 Natl. Network: ABC, . Washington Atty: Rosenman & Colin. News staff: 28; News: 22 hrs wkly.

Key Personnel:
Tom Allen . . . gen mgr

WMSN-TV— Digital Channel: 49. Digital Hrs: 6AM-2AM 1,000 kw vis, 100 kw aur. ant 1,466t TL: N43 03 21 W89 32 06 On air date: June 8, 1986. 7847 Big Sky Dr., Madison, WI, 53719. Phone: (608) 833-0047. Fax: (608) 833-5055. Fax: (608) 833-0665 (Natl Sls).E-mail: comments@fox47.com Web Site: www.fox47.com. Licensee: WMSN Licensee LLC. Group Owner: Sinclair Broadcast Group Inc. (acq 12-10-01; grpsl). Natl. Network: Fox, .

Key Personnel:
Kerry Johnson . . . gen mgr
Ed Woloszyn . . . gen sls mgr & natl sls mgr
Audra Johnson . . . prom dir
Collin Campbell . . . progmg dir & progmg mgr
Al Zobel . . . news dir & engrg mgr
Kerry Maki . . . chief of engrg
Carol Poole . . . traf mgr

WMTV— Digital Channel: 19. Digital Hrs: 24 1,050 kw vis, 105 kw aur. ant 1,161t/1,101g TL: N43 03 01 W89 29 15 On air date: July 1953. 615 Forward Dr., Madison, WI, 53711. Phone: (608) 274-1515/(608) 274-1500 (news). Fax: (608) 271-5193/(608) 271-5194 (news).E-mail: feedback@nbc15.com Web Site: www.nbc15.com. Licensee: Gray Television Licensee Inc. Group Owner: Gray Television Inc. (acq 8-29-2002; grpsl). Population Served: 308,310 Natl. Network: NBC, . Washington Atty: Covington & Burling. Wire Svc: AP Wire Svc: CNN News staff: 36; News: 19 hrs wkly.

Key Personnel:
J. Mack Robinson . . . pres
Jim Ryan . . . CFO
Robert Prather Jr. . . . exec VP
Bob Smith . . . gen mgr
Curt Molander . . . gen sls mgr
Ellen Buss . . . progmg mgr
Chris Gegg . . . news dir
Tom Weeden . . . chief of engrg

Menomonie

see Minneapolis-St. Paul, MN market

Milwaukee, WI
(DMA 35)

WBME-TV— Digital Channel: 48. Digital Hrs: 24 2,690 kw vis, 260 kw aur. ant 435t/405g TL: N42 51 18 W87 50 41 (CP: 5,000 kw vis, ant 895t. TL: N43 05 15 W87 54 01) On air date: Jan 27, 1990. 4311 E. Oakwood Rd., Oak Creek, WI, 53154. Phone: (414) 764-4953. Fax: (414) 764-5190. Web Site: www.metvmilwaukee.com. Licensee: TV-49 Inc. (acq 4-21-2008; $6.5 million).

Key Personnel:
Joe Kinlow. pres & gen mgr stn mgr & dev mgr dev mgr & gen sls mgr progmg dir & news dir
Bruce Herzog . . . chief of engrg

WCGV-TV— Digital Channel: 25. Digital Hrs: 25 3,000 kw vis, 300 kw aur. ant 1,030t/1,039g TL: N43 05 15 W87 54 13 On air date: Mar 17, 1980. 4041 N. 35th St., Milwaukee, WI, 53216. Phone: (414) 442-7050. Fax: (414) 874-1899.E-mail: comments@wcgv24.com Web Site: www.My24Milwaukee.com. Licensee: WCGV Licensee L.L.C. Group Owner: Sinclair Broadcast Group Inc. (acq 5-23-94; grpsl;11-19-90). Population Served: 4,189,000 Natl. Network: MyNetworkTV, . Natl. Rep: Millennium Sales & Marketing,.

Key Personnel:
David Ford . . . gen mgr
Milan Macksimovic . . . opns mgr
Paul Rudolph . . . chief of opns
Jason Van Acker . . . prom mgr
Dennis Brechlin . . . chief of engrg
Kay Mazurkiewicz . . . traf mgr

WDJT-TV— Digital Channel: 46. Digital Hrs: 24 2,820 kw vis, 282 kw aur. 535t TL: N43 02 20 W87 55 04 (CP: 5,000 kw vis, ant 1,112t) On air date: November 1988. 809 S. 60th St., Milwaukee, WI, 53214. Phone: (414) 777-5800. Fax: (414) 777-5802. Web Site: www.cbs58.com. Licensee: WDJT-TV L.P. Group Owner: Weigel Broadcasting Co. Population Served: 762,000 Natl. Network: CBS, . Natl. Rep: Harrington, Righter & Parsons,. Washington Atty: Cohn & Marks.

Key Personnel:
Norman Shapiro . . . pres
Jim Hall . . . gen mgr & stn mgr
Marty Schack . . . gen sls mgr
Grant Uitti . . . news dir

WISN-TV— Digital Channel: 34. Digital Hrs: 24 316 kw vis, 31.6 kw aur. ant 1,000t/1,105g TL: N43 06 41 W87 55 38 On air date: Oct 27, 1954. Box 402, MIlwaukee, WI, 53201. Phone: (414) 342-8812. Fax: (414) 342-4486. Web Site: www.themilwaukeechannel.com. Licensee: WISN Hearst-Argyle Television Inc., a California corp. Group Owner: Hearst-Argyle Television Inc. (acq 7-16-97; grpsl). Population Served: 760,000 Natl. Network: ABC, . Natl. Rep: Continental Television Sales,. Washington Atty: Peper, Martin, Jensen, Maichel & Hetlage. Wire Svc: News 1

Key Personnel:
Jan Wade . . . gen mgr
Pete Monfre . . . gen sls mgr
Dean Maytag . . . progmg dir
Lori Waldon . . . news dir
Tony Coleman . . . chief of engrg
Sue Samuelson . . . traf mgr

WITI— Digital Channel: 33. Digital Hrs: 24 100 kw vis, 10 kw aur. ant 1,000t/1,078g TL: N43 05 24 W87 53 47 On air date: May 21, 1956. 9001 N. Green Bay Rd., Milwaukee, WI, 53209. Phone: (414) 355-6666. Fax: (414) 586-2141.E-mail: fox6news@foxtv.com Web Site: www.myfox.com. Licensee: Community Television of Wisconsin License LLC. Group Owner: Fox Television Stations Inc. (acq 7-14-2008; grpsl). Population Served: 780,000 Natl. Network: Fox, . Washington Atty: Dow Lohnes PLLC.

Key Personnel:
Parveen Hughes . . . CFO
Chuck Steinmetz . . . VP & gen mgr
John Workman . . . opns VP
Mike Neale . . . sls VP
Bob O'Neil . . . natl sls mgr
Sue Swaziek . . . rgnl sls mgr
Lori Wucherer . . . prom VP
Jim Lemon . . . news dir
Kelly Skindzelewski . . . pub affrs dir & pub svc dir
Don Hain . . . engrg VP
Hayley Puffer . . . progmg

***WMVS—** Digital Channel: 8. Digital Hrs: 24 309 kw vis, 30.9 kw aur. 1,010t/1,101g TL: N43 05 48 W87 54 19 On air date: Oct 28, 1957. 1036 N. 8th St., Milwaukee, WI, 53233. Phone: (414) 271-1036. Fax: (414) 297-7536.E-mail: info@mptv.org Web Site: www.mptv.org. Licensee: Milwaukee Area District Board of Vocational, Technical & Adult Education. Population Served: 2,100,000 Natl. Network: PBS, . Rgnl. Network: CEN. Washington Atty: Dow, Lohnes & Albertson.

Key Personnel:
Ellis Bromberg . . . gen mgr
Kate Tierney . . . opns mgr & prom dir
Tom Dvorak . . . progmg dir
Dan Jones . . . news dir
David Felland . . . chief of engrg

***WMVT—** Digital Channel: 35. Digital Hrs: 24 4,790 kw vis. ant 1,115t/1,143g TL: N43 05 46 W87 54 15 On air date: Jan 23, 1963. 4th Fl., 1036 N. 8th St., Milwaukee, WI, 53233. Phone: (414) 271-1036. Fax: (414) 297-7536.E-mail: info@mptv.org Web Site: www.mptv.org. Licensee: Milwaukee Area District Board of Vocational, Technical & Adult Education. Population Served: 2,100,000 Natl. Network: PBS, . Washington Atty: Dow, Lohnes & Albertson. Foreign lang progmg: SpanishS 4

Key Personnel:
Ellis Bromberg . . . gen mgr
Kate Tierney . . . opns VP & prom dir
Tom Dvorak . . . progmg dir
Dan Jones . . . news dir
David Felland . . . engrg dir & chief of engrg

WPXE-TV— Digital Channel: 40. Digital Hrs: 24 830 kw vis. ant 1,174t/1,200g TL: N43 05 44 W87 54 17 On air date: June 1, 1988.

6161 N. Flint Rd., Suite F, Glendale, WI, 53209. Phone: (414) 247-0117. Fax: (414) 247-1302. Web Site: www.ionline.tv. Licensee: ION Media Milwaukee License Inc., debtor-in-possession. Group Owner: Paxson Communications Corp. (acq 2-18-2000; grpsl). Natl. Network: ION Television, . Washington Atty: Gardner, Carton & Douglas. Wire Svc: CNN
Key Personnel:
Joanne Levy . . . . natl sls mgr
Laurie Lau . . . . opns

WTMJ-TV— Digital Channel: 28.100 kw vis, 20 kw aur. ant 1,000t/1,096g TL: N43 05 29 W87 54 07 On air date: December 1947. 720 E. Capitol Dr., Milwaukee, WI, 53212. Phone: (414) 332-9611. Fax: (414) 967-5378.E-mail: tmj4feedback@todaystmj4.com Web Site: www.todaystmj4.com. Licensee: Journal Broadcast Corp. Group Owner: Journal Broadcast Group Inc. Population Served: 2,150,000 Natl. Network: NBC, . Washington Atty: Hogan & Hartson.
Key Personnel:
Mark Strachota . . . . gen mgr & gen sls mgr natl sls mgr
Mar LeGrand . . . . rgnl sls mgr
Sean O'Flaherty . . . . mktg mgr & news dir
Brenda Serio . . . . progmg dir
Kent Aschenbrenner . . . . chief of engrg
Tim McCormack . . . . traf mgr

WVCY-TV— Digital Channel: 22. Digital Hrs: 9 AM-midnight (M-F), 8 AM-midnight (S-Su) 196 kw vis, 22.92 kw aur. ant 938t/965g TL: N43 05 46 W87 54 15 On air date: Jan 11, 1983. 3434 W. Kilbourn Ave., Milwaukee, WI, 53208. Phone: (414) 935-3000. Fax: (414) 935-3015.E-mail: tv30@vcyamerica.org Web Site: www.vcyamerica.org. Licensee: VCY America Inc. Group Owner: (group owner) Washington Atty: Wiley Rein LLP.
Key Personnel:
Dr. Randall Melchert. . . . . pres
Vic Eliason . . . . VP & gen mgr
Jim Cronin . . . . opns mgr
Jim Schneider . . . . progmg dir & pub affrs dir
Andy Eliason. . . . . chief of engrg

WVTV— Digital Channel: 18. Digital Hrs: 24 5,000 kw vis, 500 kw aur. ant 1,008t/1,101g TL: N43 05 48 W87 54 19 On air date: July 1, 1959. 4041 N. 35th St., Milwaukee, WI, 53216. Phone: (414) 442-7050. Fax: (414) 874-1898. Fax: (414) 874-1899. Web Site: www.thattvwebsite.com. Licensee: WVTV Licensee Inc. Group Owner: Glencairn Ltd. (acq 2-1-2002). Population Served: 1,826,000 Natl. Network: CW, . Natl. Rep: Millennium Sales & Marketing,.
Key Personnel:
David Smith. . . . . CEO & pres
David Ford . . . . gen mgr
Milan Macksimovic . . . . opns mgr
Paul Rudulph . . . . chief of opns
Rob Krieghoff . . . . rgnl sls mgr
Jason Van Acker. . . . . prom mgr
Jim Feely . . . . progmg dir
Dennis Brechlin. . . . . chief of engrg
Kay Mazurkiewicz . . . . traf mgr

WWRS-TV— Digital Channel: 43. Digital Hrs: 8:30 am - 5:30 pm 1,000 kw vis. ant 656t/466g TL: N43 26 11 W88 31 34 On air date: 1997. Phone: (920) 387-9052. Fax: (920) 387-9053.E-mail: dcalhoun@tbn.org Web Site: www.tbn.org. Licensee: National Minority T.V. Inc. Ownership: not for profit Corp. (acq 2-16-99; $3,300,000). Washington Atty: Shaw Pittman.
Key Personnel:
Dinah Calhoun . . . . gen mgr & stn mgr

Rhinelander

see Wausau-Rhinelander, WI market

Superior

see Duluth, MN-Superior, WI market

Wausau-Rhinelander, WI (DMA 135)

WAOW-TV— Digital Channel: 9. Digital Hrs: 24 316 kw vis, 31.6 kw aur. ant 1,210t/647g TL: N44 55 14 W89 41 31 On air date: May 7, 1965. 1908 Grand Ave., Wausau, WI, 54403. Phone: (715) 842-2251. Fax: (715) 848-0195. Fax: (715) 842-7808.E-mail: info@waow.com Web Site: www.waow.com. Licensee: WAOW-WYOW Television Inc. Group Owner: Quincy Newspapers Inc., see Cross Ownership (acq 5-22-2001; grpsl). Population Served: 533,000 Natl. Network: ABC, CW, . Natl. Rep: Blair Television,. Washington Atty: Wilkinson, Baker & Knauer, LLP. Wire Svc: AP Wire Svc: CNN News staff: 26; News: 15.5 hrs wkly.
Key Personnel:
Thomas A. Oakley . . . . CEO
Ralph M. Oakley . . . . COO
Laurin Jorstad. . . . . VP & gen mgr stn mgr
Randy Winters . . . . opns mgr
Mark Oliver . . . . mktg dir & prom dir
Tara Marshall . . . . progmg dir & traf mgr
Randy Winter . news dir & consumer affrs dir edit dir & feature ed
Russ Crass . . . . chief of engrg
Tricia Schlarer . . . . min affrs dir
Jean Crooks . . . . pub svc dir
Byron Graff . . . . sports cmtr
Brian Niznansky. . . . . weather dir
Melissa Langbehn . . . . women's int ed
Rebroadcasts WYOW-TV Eagle River 100%.

WBIJ— Digital Channel: 12. Digital Hrs: 24 1.7 kw vis. ant 403t/255g TL: N45 34 23 W88 52 57 (CP: 4.3 kw vis, ant 390t/240g) On air date: 2004. 4529 Hickory Heights Ave., Oshkosh, WI, 54904. Phone: (920) 589-2511. Licensee: Selenka Communications LLC.
Key Personnel:
Dennis Selenka . . . . gen mgr

WFXS— Digital Channel: 31. Digital Hrs: 24 685 kw vis. ant 1,066t/994g TL: N45 03 22 W89 27 54 On air date: Dec 1, 1999. 1000 N. 3rd St., Wausau, WI, 54403. Phone: (715) 847-1155. Fax: (715) 847-1156.E-mail: wfxs@wfxs.com Web Site: www.wfxs.com. Licensee: Davis Television Wausau L.L.C. Population Served: 431,000 Natl. Network: Fox, . Natl. Rep: Millennium Sales & Marketing,. Washington Atty: Leventhal, Senter & Lerhman. News: 5 hrs wkly.
Key Personnel:
Robert Raff. gen mgr
Scott Storkel . . . . opns dir
Jan El Daul . . . . gen sls mgr
Deb Steinfest . . . . prom dir
Randy Winter. news dir

***WHRM-TV—** Digital Channel: 24. Digital Hrs: 24 172 kw vis. ant 1,269t/630g TL: N44 55 14 W89 41 28 On air date: 1975. 3319 W. Beltline Hwy., Madison, WI, 53713. Phone: (608) 264-9600. Web Site: www.ecb.org. Licensee: Wisconsin Educational Communications Board. Natl. Network: PBS, . Washington Atty: Dow, Lohnes & Albertson.
Key Personnel:
Bryon Knight . . . . gen mgr
Mike Edgette . . . . opns dir
Jon Miskowski . . . . dev dir
Michael Bridgeman . . . . mktg dir & prom dir
Mary Clare Sorenson . . . . adv dir
Kathy Bissen. . . . . progmg mgr & news dir
Terry Baun. . . . . chief of engrg
Irene Ekleberry . . . . traf mgr

WJFW-TV— Digital Channel: 16. Digital Hrs: 24 269 kw vis. ant 1,187t/1,168g TL: N45 40 03 W89 12 29 On air date: Oct 20, 1966. Box 858, Rhinelander, WI, 54501. Phone: (715) 365-8812. Fax: (715) 365-8810.E-mail: e-mail@wjfw.com Web Site: www.wjfw.com. Licensee: Northland Television LLC. Group Owner: Rockfleet Broadcasting Inc. Population Served: 657,000 Natl. Network: NBC, . Natl. Rep: Blair Television,. Washington Atty: Wiley, Rein & Fielding. News staff: 13; News: 18.5 hrs wkly.
Key Personnel:
Robert Schmidtbauer . . . . CFO & opns mgr
Robert Krieghoff. . . . . gen mgr & prom mgr progmg dir
Charlotte Berens . . . . natl sls mgr
Heather Schellock . . . . news dir
Greg Buzzell . . . . chief of engrg
Susan Sharkey . . . . traf mgr

***WLEF-TV—** Digital Channel: 36. Digital Hrs: 24 741 kw vis, 74.2 kw aur. 1,468t/1,467g TL: N45 56 43 W90 16 28 On air date: December 1977. 821 University Ave., Madison, WI, 53706. Phone: (608) 263-2121. Fax: (608) 263-9363.E-mail: comments@wpt.org Web Site: www.wpt.org. Licensee: State of Wisconsin-Educational Communications Board. Natl. Network: PBS, . Washington Atty: Dow, Lohnes & Albertson.
Key Personnel:
Mike Edgette . . . . opns dir
Jon Miskowski . . . . dev dir
Michael Bridgeman . . . . mktg dir & prom mgr
Mary Clare Sorenson . . . . adv dir & progmg mgr
Kathy Bissen . . . . news dir
Dick Taugher. . . . . chief of engrg

WSAW-TV— Digital Channel: 7. Digital Hrs: 24 316 kw vis, 63.2 kw aur. ant 1,210t/647g TL: N44 55 14 W89 41 31 On air date: Oct 23, 1954. 1114 Grand Ave., Wausau, WI, 54403. Phone: (715) 845-4211. Fax: (715) 845-2649. Web Site: www.wsaw.com. Licensee: WEAU Licensee Corp. Group Owner: Gray Television Inc. (acq 8-29-2002; grpsl). Population Served: 184,600 Natl. Network: CBS, MyNetworkTV, . Natl. Rep: Continental Television Sales,. Wire Svc: AP News staff: 21; News: 15 hrs wkly.
Key Personnel:
Al Lancaster. . . . . VP & gen mgr
Patti Shook . . . . opns mgr & progmg mgr traf mgr
Judy Stark . . . . rgnl sls mgr
Dan Froelich . . . . prom dir & prom mgr
Susan Ramsett . . . . news dir
Chad Myers . . . . chief of engrg

WTPX-TV— Digital Channel: 46.3,090 kw vis. ant 918t TL: N45 03 33 W89 26 10 On air date: 2006. 720 E. Capitol Dr., Milwaukee, WI, 53212-1308. Phone: (414) 967-5592. Fax: (414) 967-5597. Licensee: ION Media Wausau License Inc., debtor-in-possession. Group Owner: Paxson Communications Corp. (acq 4-18-2000; $887,500 for CP). Natl. Network: ION Television, .

WYOW— Digital Channel: 28. Digital Hrs: 24 2,400 kw vis. ant 1,092t TL: N45 46 30 W89 14 55 On air date: 1997. Box 2705, Eagle River, WI, 54521. 528 W. Pine St., Suite B, Eagle River, WI 54521. Phone: (715) 477-2020. Fax: (715) 477-2438.E-mail: wyowtv34@newnorth.net Web Site: www.wyowt34.com. Licensee: WAOW-WYOW Television Inc. Group Owner: Quincy Newspapers Inc., see Cross-Ownership (acq 5-22-2001; grpsl). Natl. Network: ABC, CW, . Natl. Rep: Blair Television,. Washington Atty: Wilkinson, Barker & Knauer, LLP. Wire Svc: AP Wire Svc: CNN
Key Personnel:
Thomas A. Oakley . . . . CEO
Ralph Oakley . . . . COO
Laurin Jorstad . . . . gen mgr
Carol Kellum. . . . . gen sls mgr
Tim Atterberg . . . . rgnl sls mgr
Mark Oliver . . . . mktg dir & prom mgr
Tricia Atterberg . . . . progmg dir
Randy Winter. . . . . news dir
Russ Crass . . . . chief of engrg
Tracy Lake . . . . traf mgr
Mark Baker . . . . financial ed

Wyoming

Casper-Riverton, WY (DMA 197)

***KCWC-TV—** Digital Channel: 8. Digital Hrs: 24 100 kw vis, 10 kw aur. ant 1,519t/199g TL: N42 34 59 W108 42 36 On air date: January 2002. Wyoming Public Television, 2660 Peck Ave., Riverton, WY, 82501. Phone: (307) 856-6944. Fax: (307) 856-3893. Web Site: wyoptv.org. Licensee: Central Wyoming College. Natl. Network: PBS, . Wyoming Public Television Washington Atty: Fletcher, Heald & Hildreth.
Key Personnel:
Ruby Calvert . . . . gen mgr
J. Amend . . . . prom VP
Michael Dietz . . . . progmg dir
Bob Spain . . . . chief of engrg
Suze Kanack . . . . traf mgr

KCWY-DT— Digital Channel: 12. Digital Hrs: 24 3.2 kw vis. ant 1,875t/220g TL: N42 44 37 W106 18 24 On air date: 2002. Box 1540, Mills, WY, 82644. 141 Progress Circle, Mills, WY 82644. Phone: (307) 577-0013. Fax: (307) 577-5251.E-mail: pporter@kcwy13.com Web Site: kcwy13.com. Licensee: Bozeman Trail Communications Co. Group Owner: Sunbelt Communications Co. Natl. Network: NBC, . Natl. Rep: Petry Television Inc.,. Wire Svc: AP Wire Svc: CNN News staff: 13; News: 20 hrs wkly.
Key Personnel:
Peggy L. Porter. . . . . gen mgr & gen sls mgr
John Ehrhart . . . . news dir
Mark Hildebrand . . . . chief of engrg

KFNB-TV— Digital Channel: 20. Digital Hrs: 24 58.9 kw vis. ant 1,909t TL: N42 44 37 W106 18 31 On air date: Oct 31, 1984. 1856 Skyview Dr., Casper, WY, 82601. Phone: (307) 577-5923. Phone: (307) 577-5924. Fax: (307) 234-4005.E-mail: klwy@coffey.com Licensee: WyoMedia Corp. Population Served: 32,000 Natl. Network: Fox, . Washington Atty: Irwin, Campbell & Tannenwald.
Key Personnel:
Mark Nalboe . . . . gen mgr
Terry Lane . . . . opns mgr & progmg dir
Judie Lewis . . . . gen sls mgr
Joe Lownden . . . . prom mgr
Greg Flabager . . . . news dir
Dave Ericson. . . . . chief of engrg
Tony Lattea . . . . traf mgr

KFNE— Digital Channel: 10. Digital Hrs: 24 11.3 kw vis. ant 1,725t/62g TL: N43 27 26 W108 12 02 On air date: Dec 22, 1957.

1856 Skyview Dr., Casper, WY, 82601. Phone: (307) 577-5923. Fax: (307) 234-4005.E-mail: klwy@coffey.com Licensee: Wyomedia Corp. (acq 2-28-2009; with KFNR(TV) Rawlins). Natl. Network: ABC, .

Key Personnel:

Mark Nalbone	gen mgr
Terry Lane	opns mgr & progmg dir
Tina Nalbone	gen sls mgr
Joe Lowndes	prom dir
Dave Ericson	chief of engrg
Tony Lattea	traf mgr

KGWC-TV— Digital Channel: 14. Digital Hrs: 24 53.3 kw vis. ant 1,843t/164g TL: N42 44 26 W106 21 34 On air date: Aug 12, 1981. 1856 Skyview Dr., Casper, WY, 82601. Phone: (307) 577-5923 / 5924. Fax: (307) 634-7511. Licensee: Mark III Media Inc. Group Owner: Chelsey Broadcasting Co. (acq 5-31-2006; grpsl). Population Served: 59,000 Natl. Network: CBS, Fox, . Washington Atty: Dow, Lohnes & Albertson.

Key Personnel:

Mark Nalbone	gen mgr
Terry Lane	opns mgr & progmg dir
Tina Nalbone	gen sls mgr
Joe Lowden	prom dir
Greg Flabager	news dir
Dave Ericson	chief of engrg
Tony Lattea	traf mgr

KGWL-TV— Digital Channel: 7. Digital Hrs: 24 26.8 kw vis. ant 371t/89g TL: N42 53 43 W108 43 34 On air date: Sept 10, 1982. 1856 Skyview Dr., Casper, WY, 82601. Phone: (307) 234-1111. Fax: (307) 234-4005. Licensee: Mark III Media Inc. Group Owner: Chelsey Broadcasting Co. (acq 5-31-2006; grpsl). Natl. Network: CBS, . Washington Atty: Covington & Burling.

Key Personnel:

Mark Nalbone	gen mgr
Terry Lane	opns mgr

Satellite of KGWC-TV Casper.

*KPTW— Digital Channel: 8.2.3 kw vis. ant 1,863t/190g TL: N42 44 26 W106 21 34 On air date: 2007. Wyoming Public Television, 2660 Peck Ave., Riverton, WY, 82501. Phone: (307) 856-6944. Fax: (307) 856-3893. Web Site: wyoptv.org. Licensee: Central Wyoming College. Natl. Network: PBS, . Wyoming Public Television

Key Personnel:

Ruby Calvert	gen mgr
Michael Dietz	progmg mgr
Bob Spain	chief of engrg

Satellite of KCWC-TV Lander.

KTWO-TV— Digital Channel: 17. Digital Hrs: 24 741 kw vis. ant 1,928t/242g TL: N42 44 03 W106 20 00 On air date: Mar 1, 1957. 1896 Skyview Drive, Casper, WY, 82601-9638. Phone: (307) 237-3711. Fax: (307) 237-4458.E-mail: k2@k2tv.com Web Site: www.k2tv.com. Licensee: Silverton Broadcasting Co. LLC. Ownership: Barry Silverton, 100% Group Owner: Equity Broadcasting Corp. (acq 5-31-2006; $1.2 million). Population Served: 500,000 Natl. Network: ABC, . Natl. Rep: Millennium Sales & Marketing,. News staff: 23; News: 19.5 hrs wkly.

Key Personnel:

Kristi Lockard	gen mgr
Mick Birge	stn mgr
Amie Miller	news dir
Tina Nalbone	sls

Cheyenne, WY-Scottsbluff, NE (DMA 198)

KDUH-TV— Digital Channel: 7. Digital Hrs: 24 100 kw vis, 20 kw aur. 2,001t/1,966g TL: N42 10 21 W103 13 57 On air date: Mar 5, 1958. Box 1529, Scottsbluff, NE, 69363-1529. 1523 1st Ave., Scottsbluff, NE 69361. Phone: (308) 632-3071. Fax: (308) 632-3596. Web Site: www.kduhtv.com. Licensee: Duhamel Broadcasting Enterprises. Group Owner: (group owner) Natl. Network:

ABC, . Washington Atty: Fisher, Wayland, Cooper, Leader & Zaragoza. News staff: 6; News: 2 hrs wkly.

Key Personnel:

Patrick Maag	gen mgr
Monte Loos	progmg mgr
Jerry Dishong	news dir
Teddy Johnson	chief of engrg

KGWN-TV— Digital Channel: 30. Digital Hrs: 24 100 kw vis, 10 kw aur. ant 620t/483g TL: N41 06 01 W105 00 23 On air date: Mar 22, 1954. 2923 E. Lincolnway, Cheyenne, WY, 82001. Phone: (307) 634-7755. Fax: (307) 638-0182.E-mail: news@kgwn.tv Web Site: www.kgwn.tv. Licensee: SagamoreHill Broadcasting Co. of Wyoming/Northern Colorado LLC. Group Owner: (group owner; (acq 3-19-2004; $6.5 million with KSTF(TV) Scottsbluff, NE). Population Served: 65,000 Natl. Network: CBS, CW, . Natl. Rep: Continental Television Sales,. Washington Atty: Dow, Lohnes & Albertson. News staff: 16; News: 15 hrs wkly.

Key Personnel:

Louis Wall	pres
Joan Turner	gen mgr & natl sls mgr
Dusty Thein	gen sls mgr
Keith Lindstrom	rgnl sls mgr
Barbara Parenti	progmg dir & traf mgr
Tregg White	news dir
Tony Schaefer	engrg dir
Keith Yosten	chief of engrg

KLWY— Digital Channel: 27. Digital Hrs: 24 169 kw vis. ant 761t/605g TL: N41 02 55 W104 53 28 On air date: 1992. 1856 Skyview Dr., Casper, WY, 82601. Phone: (307) 577-5923. Fax: (307) 234-4005.E-mail: klwy@coffey.com Licensee: Wyomedia Corp. (acq 12-4-91; $100,000; 1-6-92). Natl. Network: Fox, .

Key Personnel:

Mark Nalbone	gen mgr
Terry Lane	opns mgr & progmg dir
Judie Lewis	gen sls mgr & rgnl sls mgr
Joe Lowndes	prom dir
Greg Flabager	news dir
Dave Ericson	chief of engrg
Tony Lattea	traf mgr

KQCK— Digital Channel: 11. Digital Hrs: 24 251 kw vis, 25.1 kw aur. ant 485t TL: N41 08 55 W104 57 22 On air date: Aug 28, 1987. Phone: (501) 219-2400. Web Site: www.katv.com. Licensee: Denver Broadcasting Inc., debtor in possession. Group Owner: Equity Broadcasting Corp. (acq 3-26-2001; $3.5 million with KTWO-TV Casper). Natl. Network: ABC, . Natl. Rep: Millennium Sales & Marketing,. News staff: 17; News: 15 hrs wkly.

KSTF— Digital Channel: 29. Digital Hrs: 24 240 kw vis, 24 kw aur. ant 840t/674g TL: N41 59 58 W103 39 55 On air date: Aug 7, 1955. 2923 E. Lincoln Way, Cheyenne, NE, 82001. Phone: (308) 632-6107. Fax: (308) 632-3470. Web Site: www.kgwn.tv. Licensee: SagamoreHill Broadcasting Co. of Wyoming/Northern Colorado LLC. Group Owner: (group owner; (acq 3-19-2004; $6.5 million with KGWN-TV Cheyenne, WY). Population Served: 57,000 Natl. Network: CBS, Fox, . Washington Atty: Dow, Lohnes & Albertson. News staff: 6; News: 8 hrs wkly.

Key Personnel:

Joan Turner-Doyle	gen mgr
Barbara Parenti	gen sls mgr & progmg dir progmg mgr & traf mgr
Jon Martin	news dir
Tony Schaefer	chief of engrg
Tricia Murphy	prom mgr & mktg

*KTNE-TV— Digital Channel: 13. Digital Hrs: 18 27 kw vis. ant 1,528t/1,435g TL: N41 50 27 W103 03 18 On air date: Sept 7, 1966. 1800 N. 33rd St., Lincoln, NE, 68503. Phone: (402) 472-3611. Fax: (402) 472-1785.E-mail: net1@unl.edu Web Site: www.netnebraska.org. Licensee: Nebraska Educational Telecommunications Commission.

Natl. Network: PBS, . National Educational Telecommunications Association Washington Atty: Dow, Lohnes & Albertson.

Key Personnel:

Rod Bates	gen mgr

Satellite of *KUON-TV Lincoln.

KTUW— Analog Channel: 16. Digital Channel: 17. Analog Hrs: 24 40 kw vis. ant 554t/69g TL: N41 45 05 W103 53 56 On air date: 2006. 1 Shackleford Dr., Suite 400, Little Rock, AR, 72211. Phone: (501) 219-2400. Fax: (501) 221-1101. Licensee: EBC Scottsbluff Inc., debtor in possession. Group Owner: Equity Broadcasting Corp. Washington Atty: Irwin, Campbell & Tannenwald.

Key Personnel:

Greg Fess	CEO

Jackson
see Idaho Falls-Pocatello, ID market

Laramie
see Denver, CO market

Rawlins
see Denver, CO market

Riverton
see Casper-Riverton, WY market

Rock Springs
see Salt Lake City, UT market

Sheridan
see Rapid City, SD market

American Samoa

*KVZK-2— Analog Channel: 2. Analog Hrs: 24 60 kw vis, 6.0 kw aur. 2,000t/400g TL: N14 16 14 W170 41 12 On air date: 1964. Box 2567, Pago Pago, AS, 96799. Phone: (684) 633-4191. Fax: (684) 633-1044.E-mail: siviapaolo@yahoo.cm Web Site: www.asg-gov.com /agencies/opi.asg.htm. Licensee: The Government of American Samoa. Natl. Network: PBS, .

Key Personnel:

Sivia Paolo	gen mgr

*KVZK-4— Analog Channel: 4. Analog Hrs: 24 72 kw vis, 7.2 kw aur. Box 2567, Pago Pago, AS, 96799. Phone: (684) 633-4191. Fax: (684) 633-1044.E-mail: siviapaolo@yahoo.com Web Site: www.asg-gov.com /agencies/opi.asg.htm. Licensee: The Government of American Samoa. Natl. Network: ABC, CBS, .

Key Personnel:

Sivia Paolo	gen mgr

*KVZK-5— Analog Channel: 5. Analog Hrs: 24 72 kw vis, 7.2 kw aur. 2,000t/400g On air date: Oct 5, 1964. Box 2567, Pago Pago, AS, 96799. Phone: (684) 633-4191. Fax: (684) 633-1044.E-mail: siviapaolo@yahoo.com Web Site: www.asg-gov.com/agencies/opi.asg.htm. Licensee: The Government of American Samoa. Natl. Network: ABC, CBS, .

Key Personnel:

Sivia Paolo	gen mgr

Guam

*KGTF-TV— Digital Channel: 12. Digital Hrs: 18 27.5 kw vis, 5.47 kw aur. ant 297t/196g TL: N13 26 13 E144 48 17 On air date: Oct 30, 1970. Box 21449, GMF, GU, 96921. 194 Sesame St., Washington Dr., Mangilao, GU 96921. Phone: (671) 734-2207. Phone: (671) 734-5788.

Fax: (671) 734-3476.E-mail: kgtf12@kgtf.org Web Site: www.kgtf.org. Licensee: Guam Educational Telecommunications Corp. Population Served: 160,000 Natl. Network: PBS, . Washington Atty: Cohn & Marks.
Key Personnel:
Sam Soza . . . . gen mgr
Benny Flores . . . . opns mgr

KUAM-TV— Digital Channel: 8. Digital Hrs: 24 25.1 kw vis, 2.57 kw aur. ant 140t/320g TL: N13 25 53 W144 42 36 On air date: Aug 5, 1956. Calvo Commercial Ctr., 600 Harmon Loop Rd., Suite 102, Dededo, GU, 96929. United States Minor Outlying Islands. Phone: (671) 637-5826. Fax: (671) 637-9865. Web Site: www.kuam.com. Licensee: Pacific Telestations Inc. Ownership: Edward M. Calvo (acq 1988). Population Served: 150,000 Natl. Network: NBC, CBS, . Washington Atty: Haley, Bader & Potts. News staff: 20; News: 14 hrs wkly.
Key Personnel:
Joseph Calvo . . . . exec VP & gen mgr sls VP
Marie Calvo-Monge . . . . gen mgr
Annie SanNicolas . . . . sls VP & gen sls mgr
Christie San Agustin . . . . prom dir
Annie San Nicolas . . . . progmg mgr
Richard Garman . . . . chief of engrg

KTGM— Digital Channel: 14. Digital Hrs: 6:30 am-midnight 12.5 kw vis. ant 551t/118g TL: N13 29 17 E144 49 30 On air date: Oct 19, 1988. 111 W. Chalan Santo Papa St., Suite 800, Hagatna, GU, 96910. Phone: (671) 477-5700. Fax: (671) 477-3982. Licensee: Sorensen Television Systems Inc. (acq 10-26-2005; $500,000). Natl. Network: ABC, . Washington Atty: Kaye, Scholer LLP. News staff: 10; News: 12 hrs wkly.
Key Personnel:
Rex Sorensen . . . . pres

Puerto Rico

WQHA— Digital Channel: 50. Digital Hrs: 24 501 kw vis, 200 kw aur. ant 1,125t TL: N18 19 06 W67 10 49 On air date: 1995. Box 3869, Carolina, PR, 00984-3869. Phone: (787) 750-4090. Fax: (787) 701-4245.E-mail: conciliofav@hotmail.com Web Site: www.ncntelevision.com. Licensee: Concilio Mision Cristiana Fuente de Agua Viva.
Key Personnel:
Otoniel Font . . . . gen mgr
Edwin Rodriguez . . . . gen sls mgr
Josue Salgado . . . . progmg dir & chief of engrg

***WELU—** Digital Channel: 34.250 kw vis. ant 1,984t/134g TL: N18 09 06 W66 59 23 On air date: 1987. Box 1093, Hormigueros, PR, 00660. Phone: (787) 849-4020. Fax: (787) 849-2092. Licensee: Pabellon Educational Broadcasting Inc. (acq 4-28-2000).
Key Personnel:
Hector Perez . . . . pres & gen mgr
Joel Velez . . . . gen sls mgr
Fabian Rivera . . . . progmg dir
Ramon Rivera . . . . chief of engrg

WOLE-DT— Digital Channel: 12. Digital Hrs: 8 AM-5 PM 275 kw vis, 27.5 kw aur. ant 2,181t TL: N18 09 00 W66 59 00 On air date: May 13, 1960. Box 1200, Mayaguez, PR, 00681-1200. Mckinley Edif. Westerbank Piso 7, Mayaguez, PR 00681-1200. Phone: (787) 833-1200. Phone: (787) 891-8100. Fax: (787) 831-6330. Fax: (787) 891-3380. Licensee: Western Broadcasting Corp. of Puerto Rico. Ownership: Du Art Film Labs Inc., 61.2%; Jose Bechara, 30.6%; Alfonso Giminez-Aguayo, 8.2%. Foreign lang progmg: SpanishS 168
Key Personnel:
Wilson Lugo . . . . gen mgr & gen sls mgr
Santiago Hernandez . . . . progmg mgr
Doel Oriol . . . . chief of engrg
Rebroadcasts WKAQ-TV San Juan.

WVEO— Digital Channel: 17. Digital Hrs: 24 42 kw vis. ant 1,220t/184g TL: N18 19 06 W67 10 42 On air date: October 1974. Southwestern B/C Inc., 1554 Bori St., Rio Piedras, PR, 00927-6113. Phone: (787) 882-0422. Fax: (787) 281-9758. Licensee: International Broadcasting Corp. (acq 10-8-2004; $1,382,961 with WXRF(AM) Guayama). Foreign lang progmg: SpanishS 168
Key Personnel:
Pedro Roman Collazo . . . . gen mgr
Margarita Nazario . . . . progmg dir

WCCV-TV— Digital Channel: 46. Digital Hrs: 24 11.7 kw vis, 2.34 kw aur. ant -220t TL: N18 28 28 W66 43 36 On air date: Nov 15, 1981. Box 949, Camuy, PR, 00627-0949. Puerto Rico. Phone: (787) 262-5400. Phone: (787) 898-5120. Fax: (787) 262-0541.E-mail: plaud@cdminternational.com Web Site: www.cdminternational.com. Licensee: Asociacion Evan. Cristo Viene Inc. Ownership: Francisco Valazquez, 88%; Wilfredo Almodovar, 6%; Juana Roman, 5%; Patricio R. Fermaintt, 2%. Washington Atty: Fletcher, Heald & Hildreth, P.L.C.
Key Personnel:
Marcos Plaud . . . . gen mgr

WMEI— Digital Channel: 14. Digital Hrs: 24 1,000 kw vis. ant 2,322t/141g TL: N18 10 09 W66 34 30 Not on air, target date: unknown: CMCG Puerto Rico License LLC, 900 Laskin Rd., Virginia Beach, VA, 23451. Phone: (757) 437-9800. Fax: (757) 437-0034. Web Site: www.maxmediallc.com. Licensee: CMCG Puerto Rico License LLC. (acq 7-17-2006; $4.25 million).
Key Personnel:
A. Eugene Loving Jr. . . . . gen mgr

WDWL— Digital Channel: 30. Digital Hrs: 24 9.33 kw vis, 933 w aur. ant 1,079t/308g TL: N18 16 40 W66 06 38 On air date: 1991. Box 50615, Levittown Stn, PR, 00950. Phone: (787) 795-8113. Fax: (787) 795-8140.E-mail: jbenle@prtc.net Web Site: www.teleadoracion.com. Licensee: Bayamon Christian Network.. Ownership: Felix Berrios, 20%; Simon Castillo, 20%; Wilfredo Diaz, 20%; David Perez, 20%; Luciano Rodriguez, 20%.
Key Personnel:
Jesus Velez . . . . pres
Zoraida Jostinano . . . . gen mgr
David Baez . . . . chief of engrg

WLII-DT— Digital Channel: 11. Digital Hrs: 24 316 kw vis. ant 1,164t/207g TL: N18 16 54 W66 06 46 On air date: May 27, 1960. Box 7888, Guaynabo, PR, 00970. 64 Calle Carazo, Guaynabo, PR 00969. Phone: (787) 300-5000. Fax: (787) 300-5003. Licensee: WLII/WSUR License Partnership G.P. Group Owner: Raycom Media Inc. (acq 6-30-2005; with WSUR-TV Ponce). Population Served: 3,900,000 Washington Atty: Pillsbury. Foreign lang progmg: SpanishS 140 News staff: 31.
Key Personnel:
Larry Sands . . . . gen mgr
Carlos Pagan . . . . gen sls mgr
Jessica Rodriguez . . . . progmg dir & progmg mgr
Susanne Ramirez de Arellano . . . . news dir
Andres Diaz . . . . chief of engrg

***WUJA—** Digital Channel: 48.55 kw vis, 5.5 kw aur. ant 1,078t/110g TL: N18 16 40 W66 06 38 On air date: September 1985. Box 4039, Valle Arryba Heights Stn, Carolina, PR, 00984. Phone: (787) 625-5858. Fax: (787) 701-4245. Licensee: Caguas Educational TV Inc.
Key Personnel:
Otoniel Font . . . . gen mgr

WRFB— Digital Channel: 51. Digital Hrs: 24 275 kw vis. ant 1,919t/252g TL: N18 16 44 W65 51 12 On air date: August 1998. Box 1833, Carolina, PR, 00984-1833. Phone: (787) 762-5500. Fax: (787) 752-1825. Web Site: videomaxpr.tv. Licensee: R &.F Broadcasting Inc. Ownership: Enrique A. (Rickin) Sanchez, 50%; Blanche Vidal de Sanchez, 50%. Washington Atty: Fletcher, Heald & Hildeth, P.L.C.
Key Personnel:
Rickin Sanchez . . . . gen mgr

***WMTJ—** Digital Channel: 16. Digital Hrs: 24 209 kw vis, 20.9 kw aur. ant 2,750t/259g TL: N18 18 36 W65 47 41 On air date: January 1985. Box 21345, San Juan, PR, 00928-1345. Isadoro Color, Rd. 176, San Juan, PR 00928. Phone: (787) 766-2600. Fax: (787) 250-8546. Web Site: www.suagm.edu. Licensee: Ana G. Mendez Educational Foundation. Washington Atty: Dow, Lohnes & Albertson. Foreign lang progmg: SpanishS 64
Key Personnel:
Migdalia Torres . . . . gen mgr

WORO-DT— Digital Channel: 13.141 kw vis, 14.1 kw aur. ant 2,831t/210g TL: N18 18 36 W65 47 41 On air date: 1991. Box 1967, San Juan, PR, 00902-1967. Margary De Castro, Carolina, PR 00902-1967. Phone: (787) 276-1300. Fax: (787) 276-1307. Licensee: Catholic, Apostolic and Roman Church of Puerto Rico. Washington Atty: Mullin, Rhyne, Emmons & Topel.
Key Personnel:
Juan Miguel Muniz . . . . pres & gen mgr

WRUA— Digital Channel: 33.50.1 kw vis, 5 kw aur. ant 2,781t TL: N18 18 36 W65 47 41 On air date: 1997. Box 310, Bayamon, PR, 00960. Phone: (787) 279-3434. Fax: (787) 279-5549. Licensee: Eastern Television Corp. (acq 2-4-00; $335,000).
Key Personnel:
Rafael Padilla . . . . gen mgr

WIDP— Digital Channel: 45. Digital Hrs: 8:30 AM-11 PM 1,480 kw vis, 151 kw aur. ant 2,070t TL: N18 16 44 W65 51 10 On air date: 1999. Box 21065, San Juan, PR, 00928. Phone: (787) 999-0360. Fax: (787) 999-1560.E-mail: info@teletriunfo.com Web Site: www.teletriunso.com. Licensee: Ebenezer Broadcasting Group Inc. Washington Atty: Shaw Pittman LLP.
Key Personnel:
Alcardo Aponte . . . . gen mgr

WVSN— Digital Channel: 49.46 kw vis. ant 2,043t/210g TL: N18 16 44 W65 51 10 On air date: 1989. Box 949, Camuy, PR, 00627. Phone: (787) 262-5400. Web Site: www.cdminternacional.com. Licensee: La Cadena Del Milagro Inc.. Ownership: Jose J. Avila, 33%; Frank R. Martinez, 33%; Marcos A. Plaud, 33% (acq 7-18-2000).
Key Personnel:
Frank Martinez . . . . gen mgr
Sandra Ramos . . . . progmg dir

***WIPM-TV—** Digital Channel: 35. Digital Hrs: 24 81.3 kw vis, 8.1 kw aur. ant 2,273t/382g TL: N18 09 00 W66 59 00 On air date: Apr 28, 1961. Box 190909, San Juan, PR, 00919. Phone: (787) 834-0164. Fax: (787) 832-9139. Licensee: Puerto Rico Public Broadcasting Corp. Natl. Network: PBS, . Washington Atty: Steptoe & Johnson.
Key Personnel:
Eduardo Bado . . . . gen mgr
Reinaldo Perez . . . . opns dir
Diane Ramos . . . . gen sls mgr
Mirta Rodriguez . . . . progmg dir
Jorge Gonzalez . . . . chief of engrg

WNJX-TV— Digital Channel: 23. Digital Hrs: 24 4,201 kw vis. ant 2,158t/272g TL: N18 09 00 W66 59 00 On air date: Apr 27, 1986. c/o WAPA-TV, Apartado 362052, San Juan, PR, 00936. Phone: (787) 792-4444. Fax: (787) 782-4420. Licensee: WNJX-TV Inc. Group Owner: LIN Television Corporation (acq 3-1-2001; up to $1.075 million for stock). Foreign lang progmg: SpanishS 168
Key Personnel:
Joe Ramos . . . . gen mgr
Jonathan Garcia . . . . gen sls mgr
Margarita Millan . . . . progmg VP
Enrique Cruz . . . . news dir
Jose Guerra . . . . chief of engrg
Aurora Tirado . . . . traf mgr
Satellite of WAPA-TV San Juan.

WORA-TV— Digital Channel: 29. Digital Hrs: 24 100 kw vis, 20 kw aur. 2,001t/241g TL: N18 09 02 W66 59 20 On air date: Oct 1, 1955. Box 43, Mayaguez, PR, 00681. Phone: (787) 831-5555/(787) 721-4054. Fax: (787) 833-0075/(787) 724-1554.E-mail: gatoro@woratv.com Web Site: www.woratv.com. Licensee: Telecinco Inc. Ownership: Alfredo R. deArellano Jr. and family, 100%. Washington Atty: Edward O'Niell. Foreign lang progmg: SpanishS 168
Key Personnel:
Jose Toro . . . . gen mgr & gen sls mgr
Ramon Guzman . . . . progmg dir
Carlos Sepulveda . . . . news dir
Fred Toledo . . . . chief of engrg
Aixa Benejan . . . . traf mgr

WOST— Digital Channel: 22.9.55 kw vis. ant 1,107t/115g TL: N18 18 51 W67 11 24 On air date: November 2006. CMCG Puerto Rico License LLC, 900 Laskin Rd., Virginia Beach, VA, 23451. 1095 Avenida Wilson Edificio Puerta, del Condado, Suite 2, San Juan, PR 00907. Phone: (787) 723-6060. Fax: (787) 723-0087.E-mail: noticias@telemarpr.com Web Site: www.telemarpr.com. Licensee: CMCG Puerto Rico License LLC.. Ownership: Power Television International LLC, 51%; and Max Media IV LLC, 49% (acq 2-17-2006; $4.25 million with WMEI(TV) Arecibo). Population Served: 3,800,000 Foreign lang progmg: SpanishS 168
Key Personnel:
A. Eugene Loving Jr. . . . . gen mgr

WECN— Digital Channel: 18.1,000 kw vis, 100 kw aur. ant 466t/107g TL: N18 17 34 W66 16 02 On air date: April 1986. Box 310, Bayamon, PR, 00960. Hwy. 167, Naranjito, PR 00960. Phone: (787) 799-1480.E-mail: evn@centennialpr.net Licensee: Encuentro Christian Network. Ownership: Rafael Torres Ortega, 11.11%; Iris Padilla, 11.11%; Ramon Luis Acevedo, 11.11%; Jofre Ayala, 11.11%; Daramid Ayala, 11.11% (acq 9-87; $175,000;4-13-87). Washington Atty: Irwin, Campbell & Tannenwald.
Key Personnel:
Rafael Torres Padilla . . . . gen mgr

WKPV— Digital Channel: 19.700 kw vis, 70 kw aur. ant 882t/102g TL: N18 04 49 W66 44 53 On air date: Aug 6, 1985. Box 362050, Attn: Edwin Pujols, San Juan, PR, 00936-2050. Phone: (787) 792-4760. Phone: (787) 705-4153. Fax: (787) 782-7825.E-mail: edwn.pujols@wapa-tv.com Web Site: www.caribevision.com. Licensee: S & E Network Inc. Group Owner: LIN Television Corporation (acq 12-3-2007; grpsl).

Key Personnel:
Joe Ramos. . . . . gen mgr
Satellite of WJPX(TV) San Juan.

*WQTO— Digital Channel: 25. Digital Hrs: 24 1,000 kw vis. ant 991t/213g TL: N18 04 50 W66 44 54 On air date: November 1986. Box 21345, San Juan, PR, 00928-1345. Isadoro Color, Rd. 176, San Juan, PR 00928. Phone: (787) 766-2600. Fax: (787) 250-8546. Web Site: www.suagm.edu. Licensee: Systema Universitario Ana G. Mendez Inc. Washington Atty: Dow, Lohnes & Albertson.
Key Personnel:
Migdalia Torres . . . . gen mgr

WSTE-DT— Digital Channel: 7. Digital Hrs: 24 3.2 kw vis. ant 289t/220g TL: N18 02 52 W66 39 16 On air date: Feb 2, 1958. Box 2528, Guaynavo, PR, 00902. Phone: (787) 724-7777. Fax: (787) 300-5225. Licensee: WLII/WSUR License Partnership G.P. (acq 11-30-2007; $15.5 million). Foreign lang progmg: SpanishS 168
Key Personnel:
Maria Negron . . . . gen sls mgr
Wanda Costanzo . . . . . gen mgr & gen sls mgr & progmg dir
Gilberto Vera . . . . chief of engrg

WSUR-DT— Digital Channel: 9.178 kw vis. ant 2,811t/266g TL: N18 10 09 W66 34 36 On air date: February 1958. Box 7888, Guaynabo, PR, 00970-7888. One 3rd St., San Juan, PR 00908. Phone: (787) 724-1111. Fax: (787) 722-3505. Fax: (787) 723-0094. Licensee: WLII/WSUR License Partnership G.P. Group Owner: Raycom Media Inc. (acq 6-30-2005; with WLII(TV) Caguas). Natl. Network: Univision (Spanish), . Washington Atty: Hamel & Park. Foreign lang progmg: SpanishS 140
Key Personnel:
Larry Sands. . . . . sr VP & sr VP VP & gen mgr
Carlos Pagan . . . . gen sls mgr & mktg dir
Manuel Santiago . . . . prom dir
Jessica Rodriguez . . . . progmg dir
Jose Morales . . . . news dir
Andres Diaz . . . . chief of engrg

WTIN-TV— Analog Channel: 14. Analog Hrs: 24 1070 kw vis, 10 kw aur. ant 2,824t/53g TL: N18 10 11 W66 34 38 On air date: 1998. Box 362050, San Juan, PR, 00936-2050. Phone: (787) 792-4444. Fax: (787) 782-4420. Licensee: Televicentro of Puerto Rico LLC. Group Owner: LIN Television Corporation (acq 5-6-2004; $5 million). Washington Atty: Baraff, Koerner, Olender & Hochberg.
Key Personnel:
Margarita Millan . . . . progmg VP
Jose Guerra . . . . engrg VP

WVOZ-TV— Digital Channel: 47.50.1 kw vis. ant 810t/98g TL: N18 04 50 W66 44 50 On air date: 1994. Bori 1554 St. Urb Point, San Juan, PR, 00927. Phone: (787) 274-1800. Fax: (787) 281-9758. Licensee: International Broadcasting Corp. Group Owner: (group owner; (acq 10-9-2001; grpsl).
Key Personnel:
Margarita Nazario . . . . gen mgr & gen sls mgr
Roman Callazo . . . . progmg dir
Rudi Rivas. . . . . chief of engrg

WAPA-TV— Digital Channel: 27. Digital Hrs: 24 53.7 kw vis, 8.13 kw aur. ant 2,865t/1,094g TL: N18 06 42 W66 03 05 On air date: April 1954. Apartado 362050, San Juan, PR, 00936-2050. Phone: (787) 792-4444. Fax: (787) 782-4420. Web Site: www.televicentropr.com. Licensee: Televicentro of Puerto Rico L.L.C. Group Owner: LIN Television Corporation (acq 7-12-2000; grpsl). Washington Atty: Fletcher, Heald & Hildreth. Foreign lang progmg: SpanishS 133 News staff: 29; News: 20 hrs wkly.
Key Personnel:
Joe Ramos. . . . . gen mgr
Jonathan Garcia . . . . gen sls mgr
Margarita Millan . . . . progmg dir
Enrique Cruz . . . . news dir
Jose Guerra . . . . chief of engrg
Aurora Tirado . . . . traf mgr

*WIPR-TV— Digital Channel: 43. Digital Hrs: 24 53.7 kw vis, 5.4 kw aur. ant 2,860t/1,094g TL: N18 06 42 W66 03 05 On air date: Jan 6, 1958. Box 190909, San Juan, PR, 00919. Phone: (787) 766-0505.

Fax: (787) 753-9846. Licensee: Puerto Rico Public Broadcasting Corp. Natl. Network: PBS, . Washington Atty: Steven Huffines. Foreign lang progmg: SpanishS 40
Key Personnel:
Susanne Marte . . . . VP
Victor Montilla . . . . gen mgr
Rebecca Torres . . . . opns VP
Ebelmiro Torres . . . . progmg dir
Jorge Gonzalez . . . . chief of engrg

WJPX— Digital Channel: 21.676 kw vis. ant 1,909t/220g TL: N18 16 45 W65 51 14 On air date: Feb 15, 1987. Box 362050, Attn: Edwin Pujols, San Juan, PR, 00936. Phone: (787) 792-4444. Phone: (787) 706-4153. Fax: (787) 782-7825.E-mail: edwin.pujols@wapa-tv.com Web Site: www.caribevision.com. Licensee: S&E Network Inc. Group Owner: LIN Television Corporation (acq 12-3-2007; grpsl). Washington Atty: Dow, Lohnes & Albertson.
Key Personnel:
Joe Ramos. . . . . gen mgr
Edwin Pujols . . . . stn mgr
Jonathan Garcia . . . . gen sls mgr
Margarita Millan . . . . progmg dir
Enrique Cruz . . . . news dir
Jose Guerra . . . . chief of engrg
Aurora Tirado . . . . traf mgr

WKAQ-TV— Digital Channel: 28. Digital Hrs: 24 55 kw vis, 10.5 kw aur. ant 2,824t/1,099g TL: N18 06 54 W66 03 10 On air date: Mar 28, 1954. Box 366222, San Juan, PR, 00936-6222. 383 Roosevelt Ave., Hato Rey, PR 00919. Phone: (787) 758-2222. Phone: (787) 641-2222. Fax: (787) 641-2175. Fax: (787) 641-2184. Web Site: www.telemundo.com. Licensee: NBC Telemundo License Co. Group Owner: Telemundo Group Inc. (acq 4-10-2002; grpsl). Population Served: 3,900,000 Natl. Network: Telemundo (Spanish), . Washington Atty: Hogan & Hartson. Foreign lang progmg: SpanishS 130 News staff: 40; News: 10 hrs wkly.
Key Personnel:
Hilary Hattler . . . . gen mgr
Jose Medina. . . . . opns mgr
Raymond Totti . . . . sls dir
Ileana Santiago . . . . progmg dir
Juan Miguel Muniz . . . . news dir

WSJU-TV— Digital Channel: 31. Digital Hrs: 24 2,630 kw vis, 263 kw aur. ant 941t/196g TL: N18 16 30 W66 05 36 On air date: 1985. 1508 Calle Bori, Urb. Antonsanti, San Juan, PR, 00927. Phone: (787) 756-8700. Fax: (787) 765-2965. Web Site: www.canal30pr.com. Licensee: Aerco Broadcasting Corp. Ownership: Angel O. Roman Lopez, 50%; Ruth E. Roman Lopez, 50% (acq 1-11-2005). Washington Atty: Borsari & Assoc.
Key Personnel:
Angel O. Roman Lopez . . . . pres & gen mgr
Sergio Ballesteros . . . . gen sls mgr
Rudi Rivas. . . . . chief of engrg

WTCV— Digital Channel: 32. Digital Hrs: 14 759 kw vis, 75.9 kw aur. ant 2,778t/174g TL: N18 18 36 W65 47 41 On air date: Aug 19, 1984. Bori 1554, San Juan, PR, 00927-6113. Phone: (787) 274-1800. Phone: (787) 203-9178. Fax: (787) 281-9758. Licensee: International Broadcasting Corp. Group Owner: (group owner; (acq 10-9-2001; grpsl). Population Served: 1,500,000 Washington Atty: Marmet & McCombs.
Key Personnel:
Pedro Roman. . . . . pres & pres & gen mgr
Margarita Nazario . . . . gen sls mgr & prom dir

WJWN-TV— Digital Channel: 39. Digital Hrs: 24 700 kw vis. ant 2,057t/171g TL: N18 09 00 W66 59 00 Box 362050, Attn: Edwin Pujols, San Juan, PR, 00936. Phone: (787) 792-4444. Fax: (787) 782-7825.E-mail: edwin.pujols@wapa-tv.com Web Site: www.caribevision.com. Licensee: S&E Network Inc. Group Owner: LIN Television Corporation (acq 12-3-2007; grpsl).
Key Personnel:
Joe Ramos. . . . . gen mgr
Satellite of WJPX(TV) San Juan.

WIRS— Digital Channel: 41.185 kw vis. ant 2,729t/126g TL: N18 10 10 W66 34 36 On air date: Dec 1, 1991. Box 310, Bayamon, PR, 00960-0310. Phone: (787) 799-1480. Licensee: CaribeVision Station Group LLC. Group Owner: LIN Television Corporation (acq 12-3-2007; grpsl).

Key Personnel:
Myriam Guzman Rodriguez . . . . gen mgr
Satellite of WJPX(TV) San Juan.

Virgin Islands

*WTJX-TV— Digital Channel: 44. Digital Hrs: 24 28.8 kw vis, 2.9 kw aur. ant 1,479t TL: N18 21 26 W64 56 50 On air date: 1972. Box 7879, St. Thomas, VI, 00801. Phone: (340) 774-6255. Fax: (340) 774-7092.E-mail: optter@wtixtv.org Web Site: wtjxtv.org. Licensee: Virgin Islands Public Television System Board of Directors. Natl. Network: PBS, . Washington Atty: Schwartz, Woods & Miller.
Key Personnel:
Osbert Potter . . . . stn mgr

WVXF— Digital Channel: 17. Digital Hrs: 24 75.9 kw vis. ant 1,506t/59g TL: N18 21 26 W64 56 50 On air date: 1999. 8000 Nisky Center, Ste. 714, St. Thomas, VI, 00802. Phone: (340) 774-2012 / (800) 511-5899. Fax: (340) 776-5362.E-mail: info@wvxftv.com Web Site: www.wvxftv.com. Licensee: Storefront Television. Ownership: LKK Group Corp., 50%; Bluewater LLC, 50% (acq 9-30-2004; $600,000). Washington Atty: Dow, Lohnes & Albertson.
Key Personnel:
Keith Bass . . . . gen mgr & stn mgr

WZVI— Digital Channel: 43.1.4 kw vis. ant 92t/24g TL: N18 20 43 W64 55 45 On air date: 2006. c/o Thomas J. Dougherty Jr., Kilpatrick, Stockton LLP, 607 14th St. N.W., Washington, DC, 20005. Phone: (202) 508-5836. Fax: (202) 508-5858. Web Site: www.wsvitv.com. Licensee: Marri Broadcasting LP.
Key Personnel:
David P. Lampel. . . . . exec VP

WCVI-TV— Digital Channel: 23. Digital Hrs: 24 26.67 kw vis. ant 440t/59g TL: N17 44 53 W64 43 40 On air date: Mar 1, 2000. Box 24027, Christiansted, VI, 00824. Phone: (340) 713-9927. Fax: (340) 773-0712.E-mail: mbox@wcvi.tv Web Site: www.wcvi.tv. Licensee: Virgin Blue Inc. Natl. Network: CW, .
Key Personnel:
Marty Adamshick . . . . progmg dir
Victor Gold . . . . gen mgr & gen sls mgr & chief of engrg

WSVI— Digital Channel: 20. Digital Hrs: 24 200 kw vis, 20 kw aur. ant 1,144t/265g TL: N17 45 20 W64 47 55 On air date: January 1966. Box 6000, Christiansted, St. Croix, VI, 00823. Sunny Isle Shopping Ctr., Christiansted, St. Croix, VI 00823. Phone: (340) 778-5008; (803) 732-1757. Fax: (340) 778-5011.E-mail: channel&@wsvitv.com Web Site: www.wsvi.tv. Licensee: Alpha Broadcasting Corp. Natl. Network: ABC, . Natl. Rep: Roslin, . Washington Atty: Marmet & McCombs. Foreign lang progmg: SpanishS 5
Key Personnel:
David Lampel. . . . . gen mgr
Glen Dratte . . . . stn mgr
Jackie Schrock . . . . sls dir
Denisha Brown . . . . news dir
Chester Benjamin . . . . chief of engrg

WVIF— Digital Channel: 15. Digital Hrs: 24 16.2 kw vis. ant 971t/51g TL: N17 45 21 W64 47 56 On air date: 2001. 5660 Southwyck Blvd., Toledo, OH, 43614. Phone: (419) 861-3815. Fax: (419) 861-3818. Web Site: www.telostv.com. Licensee: CMCG St. Croix License LLC. Group Owner: MAX Media L.L.C. (acq 2-7-2003; $10 million with WPFO(TV) Waterville, ME).
Key Personnel:
Charles Glover . . . . CEO & gen mgr
Mitch Lambert . . . . gen mgr

Mexico

Ciudad Juarez
see El Paso (Las Cruces, NM), TX market

Tijuana
see San Diego, CA market

Directory of TV Stations in the Canada

Alberta

CFRN-TV-4— Analog Channel: 12.14.6 kw vis, 1.46 kw aur. ant 635t/590g TL: N54 08 07 W111 36 16 On air date: 1966. c/o CTV Edmonton, 18520 Stony Plain Rd., Edmonton, AB, T5S 1A8. Phone: (780) 483-3311. Fax: (780) 484-4426.E-mail: cfrn@ctv.ca Web Site: www.ctvedmonton.ca. Licensee: CFRN-TV, a div. of CTV Television Inc. Natl. Network: CTV, .
Key Personnel:
Lloyd Lewis . . . . VP & gen mgr

CBXFT-1— Analog Channel: 6.67 kw vis, 13.4 kw aur. Box 555, c/o CBXFT, Edmonton, AB, T5J 2P4. c/o CBXFT, Edmonton City Centre, 10062-102 Ave., Suite 123, Edmonton, AB T5J 2Y8. Phone: (780) 468-7500. Fax: (780) 468-7792. Web Site: www.cbc.ca. Licensee: Canadian Broadcasting Corp. Natl. Network: Radio Canada, .
Key Personnel:
Don Orchard . . . . CFO
Lionel Bonneville . . . . gen mgr

CBRT— Analog Channel: 9.178 kw vis, 35.6 kw aur. 1,135t/845g On air date: Sept 1, 1975. 1724 Westmount Blvd. N.W., Calgary, AB, T2P 2M7. Phone: (403) 521-6000. Fax: (403) 521-6007.E-mail: del_simon@cbc.ca Web Site: cbc.ca. Licensee: CBC. Natl. Network: CBC, .
Key Personnel:
Carole Taylor . . . . chmn
Robert Rabinovich . . . . pres
Harold Redekopp . . . . exec VP
Don Orchard . . . . gen mgr & opns dir opns mgr
Wendy Ell . . . . sls dir
Pat Paproski . . . . rgnl sls mgr
Irene Karras . . . . mktg mgr
Del Simon . . . . prom dir
Fred Youngs . . . . progmg dir
Nancy Rose . . . . progmg mgr
Laurie Long . . . . news dir
Lindsay Rutschke . . . . chief of engrg

CFCN-TV— Analog Channel: 4. Digital Channel: 36.100 kw vis, 27.5 kw aur. ant 623t/380g TL: N52 03 37 W114 10 13 On air date: September 1960. Broadcast House, 80 Patina Rise S.W., Calgary, AB, T3H 2W4. Phone: (403) 240-5711.E-mail: cfcnnews@ctv.ca Web Site: www.cfcnplus.ca. Licensee: CTV Television Inc. **Group Owner:** (group owner) Natl. Network: CTV, .
Key Personnel:
Len Perry . . . . gen mgr & stn mgr

CIAN-TV— Analog Channel: 13. Analog Hrs: 24 9.9 kw vis. ant 807t TL: N51 03 54 W114 12 47 On air date: 1989. 3720 76 Ave., Edmonton, AB, T6B 2N9. Phone: (780) 440-7777. Fax: (780) 440-8899. Web Site: www.accesslearning.com/accesstv. Licensee: Learning and Skills Television of Alberta Ltd. Ownership: CHUM Ltd., 60%; Olympus Management, 20%; 1006228 Ontario Inc., 15.5%; and Jay Switzer, 4.5%. (acq 1995).
Key Personnel:
Ron Keast . . . . CEO
Moses Znaimer . . . . chmn
Dr. Ronald Keast . . . . pres
Peter Palframan . . . . CFO & VP
Richard Hiron . . . . adv dir

CICT-TV— Analog Channel: 2. Digital Channel: 41. Analog Hrs: 24 100 kw vis, 20 kw aur. ant 989t/633g On air date: October 1954. 222 23rd St. N.E., Calgary, AB, T2E 7N2. Phone: (403) 235-7777. Fax: (403) 248-0252. Web Site: www.canada.com. Licensee: Canwest Television GP Inc. (the general partner) and Canwest Media Inc. (the limited partner), carrying on business as Canwest Television L.P. News staff: 50; News: 13 hrs wkly.
Key Personnel:
C. McGinley . . . . VP & gen mgr
Norm Michaelis . . . . opns dir
Greg Campbell . . . . gen sls mgr
J. Eisler . . . . mktg dir
Lynda Ritz . . . . prom mgr
Dawna Docherty . . . . progmg dir
Dave Budge . . . . news dir
Jeff Eisler . . . . pub affrs dir
Dan Gold . . . . engrg VP
Rebroadcast CISA-TV Lethbridge 90%.

CJCO-TV— Analog Channel: 38.310 kw vis. ant 1,065t/774g TL: N51 03 54 W114 12 51 On air date: Sept 15, 2008. 10212 Jasper Ave.,

---

Edmonton, AB, T5J 5A3. Phone: (780) 424-2222. Fax: (780) 440-7793.E-mail: info@omniab.ca Web Site: www.omniab.ca. Licensee: Rogers Broadcasting Ltd.

CKAL-TV— Analog Channel: 5.33.6 kw vis. On air date: Sept 20, 1997. 535 7th Ave. S.W., Calgary, AB, T2P 0Y4. Phone: (403) 508-2222. Fax: (403) 508-2224. Web Site: www.a-channel.com. Licensee: Rogers Broadcasting Ltd. Group Owner: (group owner). (acq 10-31-2007; grpsl).
Key Personnel:
Andy Pernal . . . . CFO
Al Thorgeikson . . . . gen mgr
Mike Pietrus . . . . news dir

CKCS-TV— Analog Channel: 32.75 kw vis. TL: N51 03 00 W114 05 00 On air date: Oct 8, 2007. 839 5 Ave. S.W., Suite 100B, Calgary, AB, T2P 3C8. Phone: (403) 263-3191. Fax: (403) 263-3705. Web Site: www.ctstv.com. Licensee: Crossroads Television System. Natl. Rep: Airtime TV,.
Key Personnel:
Glenn Stewart . . . . sls dir & mktg dir
Chris Somerville . . . . prom mgr
Rob Sheppard . . . . progmg mgr
David Storey . . . . engrg dir

CFSO-TV— Analog Channel: 32.20 w. TL: N49 10 40 W113 19 36 On air date: 1996. Box 1238, Cardston, AB, T0K 0K0. Phone: (403) 653-3792. Fax: (403) 653-3792.E-mail: channel32@mac.com Web Site: www.channel32.ca. Licensee: Logan McCarthy.
Key Personnel:
Logan McCarthy . . . . stn mgr

CHCA-TV-1— Analog Channel: 10. Analog Hrs: 6 AM-2 AM 190 kw vis, 19 kw aur. ant 697t/240g TL: N50 09 15 W111 09 30 On air date: 1960. 2840 Bremner Ave., 2nd Fl., Red Deer, AB, T4R 1M9. Phone: (403) 346-2573. Fax: (403) 346-9980.E-mail: chcanews@chcanews.ca Web Site: www.canada.com. Licensee: Canwest Television L.P. Group Owner: CanWest Global Communications Corp. News staff: 12; News: 5 hrs wkly.
Key Personnel:
Stan Schmidt . . . . gen mgr
Rebroadcasts CHCA-TV Red Deer.

CFCN-TV-1— Analog Channel: 12.14.1 kw vis, 7 kw aur. 1,073t TL: N51 33 46 W112 19 44 c/o CFCN-TV, 80 Patina Rise S.W., Calgary, AB, T3H 2W4. Phone: (403) 240-5600. Fax: (403) 240-5773.E-mail: cfcnnews@ctv.ca Web Site: www.cfcn.ca. Licensee: CTV Television Inc. Natl. Network: CTV, .
Key Personnel:
Len Perry . . . . gen mgr

CBXFT— Analog Channel: 11.90 kw vis, 18 kw aur. On air date: 1970. Box 555, Edmonton, AB, T5J 2P4. Edmonton City Centre, 10062-102 Ave., Suite 123, Edmonton, AB T5J 2Y8. Phone: (780) 468-7500. Fax: (780) 468-7868. Web Site: www.cbc.ca. Licensee: CBC. Natl. Network: CBC, . News staff: 15; News: 2 hrs wkly.
Key Personnel:
Don Orchard . . . . CFO & opns dir
Carol Nielsen. . . . . chief of engrg

CBXT— Analog Channel: 5.318 kw vis, 34.3 kw aur. On air date: 1961. Box 555, Edmonton, AB, T5J 2P4. Edmonton City Centre, 10062-102 Ave., Suite 123, Edmonton, AB T5J 2Y8. Phone: (780) 468-7500. Fax: (780) 468-7893. Web Site: www.cbc.ca. Licensee: CBC. Natl. Network: CBC, .
Key Personnel:
Don Orchard . . . . gen mgr & opns dir

CFRN-TV— Analog Channel: 3. Analog Hrs: 5:30 AM-1:30 AM 250 kw vis, 25 kw aur. ant 1,101t/260g TL: N53 23 06 W113 12 48 On air date: Oct 17, 1954. 18520 Stony Plain Rd., Edmonton, AB, T5S 1A8. Phone: (780) 483-3311. Fax: (780) 484-4426. Web Site: www.ctvedmonton.ca. Licensee: CFRN TV, a div. of CTV Television Inc. Group Owner: CTV Inc. (acq 1998). Population Served: 1,200,000 Natl. Network: CTV, . News: 12 hrs wkly.
Key Personnel:
Lloyd Lewis . . . . VP & gen mgr
David Fisher . . . . prom dir

CITV-TV— Analog Channel: 13. Digital Channel: 47.325 kw vis, 32.5 kw aur. ant 900t TL: N53 23 06 W113 12 48 On air date: 1974. 5325 Allard Way, Edmonton, AB, T6H 5B8. Phone: (780) 436-1250. Fax:

---

(780) 989-4613.E-mail: edmonton@globaltv.ca Web Site: www.canada.com. Licensee: Canwest Television GP Inc. (the general partner) and Canwest Media Inc. (the limited partner), carrying on business as Canwest Television L.P. Group Owner: Canwest Global (acq 2-6-91). News staff: 33; News: 11 hrs wkly.
Key Personnel:
Tim Spelliscy . . . . gen mgr
Neill Fitzpatrick . . . . news dir

***CJAL-TV—** Analog Channel: 9. Analog Hrs: 24 8.2 kw vis. TL: N53 24 19 W113 20 38 On air date: Apr 1, 1991. 3720 76th Ave., Edmonton, AB, T6B 2N9. Phone: (780) 440-7777. Fax: (780) 440-8899.E-mail: access@incentre.net Web Site: www.accesslearning.com. Licensee: Learning and Skills Television of Alberta Ltd.. Ownership: CHUM Ltd., 60%; Olympus Management Ltd., 20%; 1006228 Ontario Ltd., 15.5%; Jay Switzer, 5.5%. Group Owner: CHUM Ltd. (acq 9-1-95). Population Served: 2,500,000
Key Personnel:
Moses Znaimer . . . . chmn
Peter Palframan. . . . . exec VP
Richard Hiron . . . . sls dir
Jill Bonenfant . . . . progmg dir
John Wood . . . . engrg dir

CJEO-TV— Analog Channel: 56.340 kw vis. ant 705g TL: N53 27 49 W113 20 11 On air date: Sept 15, 2008. 10212 Jasper Ave., Edmonton, AB, T5J 5A3. Phone: (780) 424-2222. Fax: (780) 440-7793.E-mail: info@omniab.ca Web Site: www.omniab.ca. Licensee: Rogers Broadcasting Ltd.

CKEM-TV— Analog Channel: 51.704 kw vis. On air date: Sept 18, 1997. 10212 Jasper Ave., Edmonton, AB, T5J 5A3. Phone: (780) 424-2222. Fax: (780) 424-0357.E-mail: webmaster@appliedthemalsciences.com Web Site: www.a-channel.com. Licensee: 4384903 Canada Inc. Group Owner: (group owner). (acq 10-31-2007; grpsl).
Key Personnel:
Jim Haskins . . . . gen mgr
John Cuccaro . . . . opns mgr
Art Eden . . . . rgnl sls mgr
Barry Close . . . . prom mgr
Chris Duncan . . . . news dir
Peter Nobel. . . . . engrg mgr
Tania Nease . . . . traf mgr

CKES-TV— Analog Channel: 45.34 kw vis. On air date: Oct 8, 2007. 5330 Calgary Tr., Edmonton, AB, T6H 4J8. Phone: (780) 433-3118. Fax: (780) 433-3248.E-mail: sfraser@ctstv.com Web Site: www.ctstv.com. Licensee: Crossroads Television System. Natl. Rep: Airtime TV,.
Key Personnel:
Glenn Stewart . . . . sls dir & mktg dir
Chris Somerville . . . . prom mgr
Rob Sheppard . . . . progmg mgr
David Storey . . . . engrg dir

CBXFT-6— Analog Channel: 12.5.8 kw vis, 500 w aur. 200t/300g On air date: Mar 1, 1970. Box 555, Edmonton, AB, T5J 2P4. c/o CBC, Edmonton City Centre, 10062-102 Ave., Suite 123, Edmonton, AB T5J 2Y8. Phone: (780) 468-7500. Fax: (780) 468-7792. Web Site: www.cbc.ca. Licensee: Canadian Broadcasting Corp. Natl. Network: Radio Canada, .
Key Personnel:
Don Orchard . . . . opns dir

CBXAT— Analog Channel: 10.36 kw vis, 18 kw aur. Box 555, c/o CBXT, Edmonton, AB, T5J 2P4. 123 Edmonton City Centre, 10062-102 Ave., Suite 123, Edmonton, AB T5J 2Y8. Phone: (780) 468-7500. Fax: (780) 468-7893. Web Site: www.cbc.ca/edmonton. Licensee: CBC. Natl. Network: CBC, .
Key Personnel:
Don Orchard . . . . CFO & opns dir
Carol Nielsen. . . . . chief of engrg

CBXFT-8— Analog Channel: 19.3.3 kw vis, 330 w aur. Box 555, Edmonton, AB, T5J 2P4. Edmonton City Centre, 10062-102 Ave., Suite 123, Edmonton, AB T5J 2Y8. Phone: (780) 468-7500. Fax: (780) 468-7792. Web Site: www.cbc.ca. Licensee: CBC. Natl. Network: Radio Canada, .
Key Personnel:
Don Orchard . . . . opns dir
Carol Nielsen. . . . . chief of engrg

CFRN-TV-1— Analog Channel: 13.32 kw vis, 6.4 kw aur. ant 1,014t/641g TL: N55 27 57 W118 45 32 c/o CTV Edmonton, 18520

Stony Plain Rd., Edmonton, AB, T5S 1A8. Phone: (780) 483-3311. Fax: (780) 484-4426. Web Site: www.ctvedmonton.ca. Licensee: CFRN-TV, a div. of CTV Television Inc. Natl. Network: CTV, .
Key Personnel:
Lloyd Lewis . . . . VP & gen mgr

CFRN-TV-8— Analog Channel: 18.6 kw vis, 600 w aur. ant 549t/369g TL: N55 32 26 W116 07 26 On air date: November 1981. c/o CTV Edmonton, 18520 Stony Plain Rd., Edmonton, AB, T5S 1A8. Phone: (780) 483-3311. Fax: (780) 484-4426.E-mail: cfrn@ctv.ca Web Site: www.ctvedmonton.ca. Licensee: CFRN TV, a div. of CTV Television Inc. Natl. Network: CTV, .
Key Personnel:
Lloyd Lewis . . . . VP & gen mgr
Rebroadcasts CFRN-TV-1 Grande Prairie.

CBXAT-2— Analog Channel: 2.6.2 kw vis, 620 w aur. c/o CBXT, Box 555, Edmonton, AB, T5J 2P4. 123 Edmonton City Centre, 10062-102 Ave., Edmonton, AB T5J 2Y8. Phone: (780) 468-7500. Fax: (780) 468-7893. Web Site: www.cbc.ca/edmonton. Licensee: CBC. Natl. Network: CBC, .
Key Personnel:
Don Orchard . . . . exec VP & opns dir
Carol Nielsen. . . . . chief of engrg

CFRN-TV-5— Analog Channel: 2.2.13 kw vis, 213 w aur. ant 126t/157g TL: N54 45 13 W111 56 26 c/o CTV Edmonton, 18520 Stony Plain Rd., Edmonton, AB, T5S 1A8. Phone: (780) 483-3311. Fax: (780) 484-4426.E-mail: cfrn@ctv.ca Web Site: www.ctvedmonton.ca. Licensee: CFRN-TV, a div. of CTV Television Inc. Natl. Network: CTV, .

Key Personnel:
Lloyd Lewis . . . . VP & gen mgr

CFCN-TV-5— Analog Channel: 13.47 kw vis, 7.34 kw aur. ant 564t TL: N49 43 59 W112 57 36 c/o CFCN-TV, 80 Patina Rise S.W., Calgary, AB, T3H 2W4. Phone: (403) 240-5600. Fax: (403) 240-5773.E-mail: cfcnnews@ctv.ca Web Site: www.cfcnplus.ca. Licensee: CTV Television Inc. Group Owner: (group owner) Natl. Network: CTV, .
Key Personnel:
Len Perry . . . . gen mgr

CISA-TV— Analog Channel: 7.167 kw vis, 33.4 kw aur. 662t/600g TL: N49 47 01 W112 52 01 On air date: 1955. 1401-28 Street N., Lethbridge, AB, T1H 6H9. Phone: (403) 327-1521. Fax: (403) 320-2620.E-mail: cisa@globaltv.ca Web Site: www.canada.com/lethbridge. Licensee: Canwest Television L.P. Group Owner: CanWest Global Communications Corp. (acq 9-1-2000; grpsl). News staff: 19; News: 12 hrs wkly.
Key Personnel:
Peter Deys . . . . gen mgr

CJIL-TV— Analog Channel: 17.31.6 kw vis. On air date: 1995. Box 1566, 450 31st St. N., Lethbridge, AB, T1H 3Z3. Phone: (403) 380-3399. Fax: (403) 380-3322. Licensee: Miracle Channel.
Key Personnel:
Gord Klussen . . . . gen mgr
Len Whyte. . . . . chief of engrg

CITL-TV— Analog Channel: 4.130 kw vis, 13 kw aur. 724t/708g On air date: July 28, 1976. 5026 50th St., Lloydminster, AB, T9V 1P3. Phone: (780) 875-3321. Fax: (780) 875-4704. Web Site: www.ctv.ca. Licensee: NewCap Inc. Group Owner: Midwest Broadcasting. (acq 12-22-2004; C$6,304,000 with CKSA-TV Lloydminster). Natl. Network: CTV, .
Key Personnel:
R.G. Steele . . . . pres
Ken Ruptash . . . . gen mgr

CKSA-TV— Analog Channel: 2.116 kw vis, 23.2 kw aur. On air date: Sept 23, 1960. 5026 50th St., Lloydminster, AB, T9V 1P3. Phone: (780) 875-3321. Fax: (780) 875-4704. Licensee: NewCap Inc. Group Owner: Midwest Broadcasting. (acq 12-22-2004; C$6,304,000 with CITL-TV Lloydminster). Natl. Network: CBC, .
Key Personnel:
R.G. Steele . . . . pres
Ken Ruptash . . . . gen mgr

CFRN-TV-7— Analog Channel: 7.5 kw vis, 500 w aur. ant 723t/517g TL: N52 32 15 W111 31 06 On air date: Sept 7, 1979. c/o CTV Edmonton, 18520 Stony Plain Rd., Edmonton, AB, T5S 1A8. Phone: (780) 483-3311. Fax: (780) 484-4426.E-mail: cfrn@ctv.ca Web Site: www.ctvedmonton.ca. Licensee: CFRN-TV, a div. of CTV Television Inc. Natl. Network: CTV, .

Key Personnel:
Lloyd Lewis . . . . VP & gen mgr
Rebroadcasts CFRN-TV Edmonton.

CBXAT-3— Analog Channel: 12. Analog Hrs: 7 AM-3 AM 1.77 kw vis, 177 w aur. TL: N56 42 20 W117 39 17 On air date: Oct 7, 1968. Box 555, Edmonton, AB, T5J 2P4. c/o CBC, Edmonton City Centre, 10062-102 Ave., Suite 123, Edmonton, AB T5J 2Y8. Phone: (780) 468-7500. Fax: (780) 468-7779. Web Site: www.radio-canada.ca. Licensee: CBC. Population Served: 3,300 Natl. Network: CBC, .
Key Personnel:
Don Orchard . . . . exec VP & opns dir & engrg mgr
Carol Nielsen . . . . chief of engrg

CJTG-TV— Analog Channel: 13.10 w vis. On air date: 1994. Box 1377, High Level, AB, T0H 1Z0. Web Site: www.tachegondihesociety.com. Licensee: Tache Gondihe Society.
Key Personnel:
Camille Piche . . . . gen mgr

CFCN-TV-8— Analog Channel: 8.5.8 kw vis, 600 w aur. ant 315t TL: N50 04 36 W110 47 40 c/o CFCN-TV, 60 Patina Rise S.W., Calgary, AB, T3H 2W4. Phone: (403) 240-5600. Fax: (403) 240-5711.E-mail: cfcnnews@ctv.ca Web Site: www.calgary.ctv.ca. Licensee: CTV Television Inc. Natl. Network: CTV, .
Key Personnel:
Len Perry . . . . gen mgr

CHAT-TV— Analog Channel: 6.58 kw vis, 5.8 kw aur. 700t/559g On air date: 1957. Box 1270, Medicine Hat, AB, T1A 7H5. 10 Boundary Rd. S.E., Red Cliff, AB T0J 2P0. Phone: (403) 529-1270. Fax: (403) 529-1292.E-mail: info@chattv6-3.com Web Site: www.chattv6-3.com. Licensee: Jim Pattison Broadcast Group Ltd. (the general partner) and Jim Pattison Industries Ltd. (the limited partner) carrying on business as Jim Pattison Broadcast Group L.P. Group Owner: The Jim Pattison Broadcast Group (acq 12-21-2000; grpsl). Natl. Rep: Airtime TV,.
Key Personnel:
Dwaine Dietrich . . . . gen mgr
Joel Simmons . . . . chief of engrg

CFRN-TV-2— Analog Channel: 3.2.4 kw vis, 240 w aur. ant 559t/351g TL: N56 08 47 W117 20 15 On air date: 1970. c/o CTV Edmonton, 18520 Stony Plain Rd., Edmonton, AB, T5S 1A8. Phone: (780) 483-3311. Fax: (780) 484-4426.E-mail: cfrn@ctv.ca Web Site: www.ctvedmonton.ca. Licensee: CFRN-TV, a div. of CTV Television Inc. Natl. Network: CTV, .
Key Personnel:
Lloyd Lewis . . . . VP & gen mgr

CHAT-TV-1— Analog Channel: 3.2.75 kw vis, 1.37 kw aur. Box 1270, Medicine Hat, AB, T1A 7H5. 10 Boundary Rd., Red Cliff, AB T0J 2P0.Canada Phone: (403) 529-1270. Fax: (403) 529-1292.E-mail: www.1270chat@monach.net Licensee: Jim Pattison Broadcast Group Ltd. (the general partner) and Jim Pattison Industries Ltd. (the limited partner) carrying on business as Jim Pattison Broadcast Group L.P. Group Owner: The Jim Pattison Broadcast Group (acq 12-21-2000; grpsl).
Key Personnel:
Dwaine Dietrich . . . . gen mgr
Joel Simmons . . . . chief of engrg
Rebroadcasts CHAT-TV Medicine Hat.

CFRN-TV-6— Analog Channel: 8.22 kw vis, 2.2 kw aur. ant 882t/588g TL: N52 19 10 W113 40 37 c/o CTV Edmonton, 18520 Stony Plain Rd., Edmonton, AB, T5S 1A8. Phone: (780) 483-3311. Fax: (780) 484-4426.E-mail: cfrn@ctv.ca Web Site: www.ctvedmonton.ca. Licensee: CFRN-TV, a div. of CTV Television Inc. Natl. Network: CTV, .
Key Personnel:
Lloyd Lewis . . . . VP & gen mgr

CHCA-TV— Analog Channel: 6.100 kw vis, 10 kw aur. 817t/570g On air date: 1956. 2840 Bremner Ave. 2nd Fl., Red Deer, AB, T4R 1M9. Phone: (403) 346-2573. Fax: (403) 346-9980.E-mail: rdtv@globaltv.ca Web Site: www.rdtv.com. Licensee: Canwest Television L.P. Group Owner: CanWest Global Communications Corp. (acq 2000; grpsl). Natl. Network: CBC, .
Key Personnel:
Stan Schmidt . . . . gen mgr

CFRN-TV-9— Analog Channel: 4.320 w vis, 32 w aur. ant 1,101t/260g TL: N55 28 18 W114 47 05 On air date: November 1981. c/o CTV Edmonton, 18520 Stony Plain Rd., Edmonton, AB, T5S 1A8. Phone: (780) 483-3311. Fax: (780) 484-4426.E-mail: cfrn@ctv.ca Web Site: www.ctvedmonton.ca. Licensee: CFRN TV, a div. of CTV Television Inc.

Key Personnel:
Lloyd Lewis . . . . VP & gen mgr
Rebroadcasts CFRN-TV-1 Grande Prairie.

CFRN-TV-3— Analog Channel: 12.9.8 kw vis, 980 w aur. ant 1,308t/160g TL: N54 01 58 W115 43 03 c/o CTV Edmonton, 18520 Stony Plain Rd., Edmonton, AB, T5S 1A8. Phone: (780) 483-3311. Fax: (780) 484-4426.E-mail: cfrn@ctv,ca Web Site: www.ctvedmonton.ca. Licensee: CFRN-TV, a div. of CTV Television Inc. Natl. Network: CTV,

Key Personnel:
Lloyd Lewis . . . . VP & gen mgr

British Columbia

CFEG-TV— Analog Channel: 19.50 w vis. TL: N49 03 07 W122 20 29 On air date: 2000. 2719 Clearbrook Rd., Abbotsford, BC, V2T 2Y9. Phone: (604) 850-6607. Fax: (604) 850-5717.E-mail: clearbrookmbchurch@telus.net Licensee: Clearbrook Mennonite Brethren Church.

CHAN-TV-2— Analog Channel: 3.5 w vis. Global BC, 7850 Enterprise St., Burnaby, BC, V5A 1V7. Phone: (604) 420-2288. Fax: (604) 422-6651. Licensee: Canwest Television L.P. Group Owner: Global BC. Natl. Network: Global, .
Key Personnel:
Roy Gardner . . . . gen mgr
Bob Urban . . . . opns mgr
Brett Monlove . . . . gen sls mgr
Ruth Powell . . . . rgnl sls mgr
John Ridley . . . . prom dir
Ian Mayson . . . . news dir
John O'Connor. . . . . engrg VP

CHAN-TV-5— Analog Channel: 9.21 w vis. Global BC, 7850 Enterprise St., Burnaby, BC, V5A 1V7. Phone: (604) 420-2288. Fax: (604) 421-9427. Licensee: Canwest Television L.P. Group Owner: Global BC. Natl. Network: Global, .
Key Personnel:
Roy Gardner . . . . gen mgr

CHEK-TV-5— Analog Channel: 13.3 kw vis, 300 w aur. 1493t/240g c/o CHEK-TV, 780 King's Rd., Victoria, BC, V8T 5A2. Phone: (250) 383-2435. Fax: (250) 384-7766. Web Site: www.canada.com/victoria/chtv. Licensee: Canwest Television L.P. Group Owner: CanWest Global Communications Corp. Natl. Network: Global, .
Key Personnel:
Ron Eberle. . . . . gen mgr

CBUBT-1— Analog Channel: 12.510 w vis, 51 w aur. Box 4600, c/o CBUT, Vancouver, BC, V6B 4A2. Phone: (604) 662-6000. Fax: (604) 662-6335. Web Site: www.cbc.ca/bc. Licensee: CBC. Natl. Network: CBC, .
CBUT.

CHAN-TV-1— Analog Channel: 11.71 w vis. 7850 Enterprise St., Burnaby, BC, V5A 1V7. Canada. Phone: (604) 420-2288. Fax: (604) 421-9427. Licensee: Canwest Television L.P. Group Owner: Global BC. Natl. Network: Global, .
Key Personnel:
Roy Gardner . . . . gen mgr

CBUBT-7— Analog Channel: 10.900 w vis, 90 w aur. On air date: 1962. Box 4600, c/o CBUT-TV, Vancouver, BC, V6B 4A2. Phone: (604) 662-6000. Fax: (604) 662-6335. Web Site: www.cbc.ca. Licensee: CBC. Natl. Network: CBC, .
CBUT.

CJDC-TV— Analog Channel: 5.10 kw vis, 5 kw aur. ant 1,500t/500g On air date: 1958. CJDC-TV Astral Media GP, 901 102nd Ave., Dawson Creek, BC, V1G 2B6. Phone: (250) 782-3341. Fax: (250) 782-3154. Licensee: Astral Media Radio G.P. Group Owner: Standard Broadcasting Corp. (acq 10-29-2007; grpsl). Natl. Network: CBC, . News staff: 4; News: 10 hrs wkly.
Key Personnel:
Terry Shepherd . . . . gen mgr

CHNU-TV— Analog Channel: 66. Analog Hrs: 6 AM-2 AM 17 kw vis. On air date: Sept 15, 2001. 5668 192 St., Suite 201, Surrey, BC, V3S 2V7. Phone: (604) 575-4112. Fax: (604) 576-6895. Web Site: www.joytv10.ca. Licensee: Christian Channel Inc. (acq 5-26-2008) C$6,247,908 with CIIT-TV Winnipeg, MB). Population Served: 2,200,000

Key Personnel:
Terry Mahoney . . . . gen mgr
Gary Milne . . . . gen sls mgr
Karen Corbeil . . . . prom dir

CBUFT-2— Analog Channel: 50.200 w vis, 20 w aur. On air date: February 1979. 700 Hamilton St., Vancouver, BC, V6B 4A2. Phone: (604) 662-6000. Fax: (604) 662-6161. Web Site: www.radio-canada.ca/c-b. Licensee: Societe Radio Canada. Natl. Network: Radio Canada, .
Key Personnel:
Lionel Bonneville . . . . gen mgr
Rebroadcasts CBUFT Vancouver.

CFJC-TV— Analog Channel: 4. Digital Channel: 7.4.4 kw vis, 2.4 kw aur. 501t/114g On air date: 1957. 460 Pemberton Terr., Kamloops, BC, V2C 1T5. Phone: (250) 372-3322. Fax: (250) 374-0445.E-mail: info@cfjctv.com Web Site: www.cfjctv.com. Licensee: Jim Pattison Broadcast Group Ltd. (the general partner) and Jim Pattison Industries Ltd. (the limited partner) carrying on business as Jim Pattison Broadcast Group L.P. Group Owner: Group owner:The Jim Pattison Broadcast Group (acq 1987). Population Served: 200,000 News staff: 8; News: 14 hrs wkly.
Key Personnel:
Richard W. Arnish . . . . pres & gen mgr
Dave Somerton . . . . opns mgr

CHKM-TV— Analog Channel: 6.4 kw vis. ant 502t TL: N50 40 15 W120 23 50 Global BC, 7850 Enterprise St., Burnaby, BC, V5A 1V7. Phone: (604) 420-2288. Fax: (604) 422-6698. Web Site: www.canada.com /vancouver/globaltv. Licensee: Canwest Television L.P. Group Owner: Global BC. Natl. Network: Global, .
Key Personnel:
Roy Gardner . . . . gen mgr

CHBC-TV— Analog Channel: 2. Analog Hrs: 5 AM-4:37 AM 3.7 kw vis, 460 w aur. 2,704t/77g TL: N49 58 00 W119 31 40 On air date: September 1957. 342 Leon Ave., Kelowna, BC, V1Y 6J2. Phone: (250) 762-4535. Fax: (250) 860-2422. Fax: (250) 868-0662.E-mail: comments@chbc.com Web Site: www.chbc.com. Licensee: Canwest Television L.P. Group Owner: CanWest Global Communications Corp. Population Served: 360,000 News staff: 31; News: 20 hrs wkly.
Key Personnel:
Keith Williams. . . . . gen mgr
Rob Weller . . . . opns mgr

CKPG-TV— Analog Channel: 2.778 w vis, 389 w aur. On air date: 1961. 1810 Third Ave., 2nd Fl, Prince George, BC, V2M 164. Canada. Phone: (250) 564-8861. Web Site: www.ckpgtv.com. Fax: (250) 562-8768.E-mail: ckpgmail@ckpg.bc.ca Licensee: Jim Pattison Broadcast Group LP. (the general partner) and Jim Pattison Industries Ltd. (the limited partner) carrying on business as Jim Pattison Broadcast Group L.P. Group Owner: The Jim Pattison Broadcast Group (acq 12-21-2000; grpsl). Natl. Rep: Airtime TV,.
Key Personnel:
Ken Kilcullen . . . . gen mgr & gen sls mgr

CHAN-TV-3— Analog Channel: 7.62 w vis. Global BC, 7850 Enterprise St., Burnaby, BC, V5A 1V7. Phone: (604) 420-2288. Fax: (604) 422-6651. Licensee: Canwest Television L.P. Group Owner: Global BC. Natl. Network: Global, .
Key Personnel:
Roy Gardner . . . . gen mgr
Bob Urban . . . . opns mgr
Brett Monlove . . . . gen sls mgr
Ruth Powell . . . . rgnl sls mgr
John Ridley . . . . prom dir
Ian Mayson . . . . news dir
John O'Connor . . . . engrg dir

CBUFT-3— Analog Channel: 11.500 w vis, 50 w aur. On air date: Aug 27, 1979. 700 Hamilton St., Vancouver, BC, V6B 4A2. Phone: (604) 662-6000. Fax: (604) 662-6161. Web Site: www.radio-canada.ca/c-b. Licensee: Societe Radio Canada. Natl. Network: Radio Canada, .
Key Personnel:
Lionel Bonneville . . . . gen mgr

CFTK-TV— Analog Channel: 3.13.8 kw vis, 1.38 kw aur. 1,488t/140g On air date: 1962. 4625 Lazelle Ave., Terrace, BC, V8G 1S4. Phone: (250) 635-6316. Fax: (250) 638-6320. Web Site: www.cftk.com. Licensee: Astral Media Radio G.P. Group Owner: Standard Broadcasting Corp. (acq 10-29-2007; grpsl). Natl. Network: CBC, .
Key Personnel:
Brian Langston . . . . gen mgr

CHVC-TV— Analog Channel: 7.10 kw vis. On air date: 1994. Box 922, Valemount, BC, V0E 2Z0. Phone: (250) 566-8288. Fax: (250) 566-4645. Web Site: www.tv@ve. Licensee: The Valemount Entertainment Society.

Key Personnel:
Penni Osadchuk. . . . . gen mgr

CBUFT— Analog Channel: 26.256 kw vis. ant 2,011t TL: N49 21 12 W122 57 18 On air date: Sept 27, 1976. Box 4600, Vancouver, BC, V6B 4A2. Canada. Phone: (604) 662-6000. Fax: (604) 662-6161. Web Site: www.radio-canada.ca/c-b. Licensee: Societe Radio-Canada. Natl. Network: Radio Canada, .
Key Personnel:
Lionel Bonneville . . . . gen mgr
Brigitte Tesniere . . . . prom dir
Michele Smolkin . . . . stn mgr & progmg dir

CBUT— Analog Channel: 2. Digital Channel: 58.47.6 kw vis, 7.6 kw aur. ant 2,400t/190g On air date: Dec 16, 1953. Box 4600, 700 Hamilton St., Vancouver, BC, V6B 4A2. Phone: (604) 662-6000. Fax: (604) 662-6414. Web Site: www.cbc.ca. Licensee: CBC. Natl. Network: CBC, .

CHAN-TV— Analog Channel: 8. Digital Channel: 22. Analog Hrs: 24 193.6 kw vis, 19.4 kw aur. ant 2,315t/250g TL: N49 21 29 W122 57 09 On air date: Oct 31, 1960. 7850 Enterprise St., Burnaby, BC, V5A 1V7. Phone: (604) 420-2288. Fax: (604) 421-9427. Fax: (604) 444-9561. Licensee: Canwest Television L.P. Group Owner: CanWest Global Communications Corp. Natl. Network: Global, .
Key Personnel:
Roy Gardner . . . . gen mgr

CHNM-TV— Analog Channel: 42. Digital Channel: 20.76 kw vis. On air date: June 27, 2003. channel m, 88 E. Pender St., Vancouver, BC, V6A 3X3. Phone: (604) 678-3800. Fax: (604) 678-3810. Web Site: www.channelm.ca. Licensee: Rogers Broadcasting Ltd. (acq 4-30-2008; C$61,291,913). Population Served: 3,000,000
Key Personnel:
Rael Merson. . . . . pres
Bruce Hamlin. . . . . sls dir
Mike Maslenki . . . . prom mgr
Dianne Collins . . . . news dir

CIVT-TV— Analog Channel: 32. Digital Channel: 33.710 kw vis. TL: N49 21 29 W122 57 09 On air date: Sept 22, 1997. 750 Burrard St., Suite 300, Vancouver, BC, V6Z 1X5. Phone: (604) 608-2868. Fax: (604) 608-2698.E-mail: bccomments@ctv.ca Web Site: www.ctv.ca. Licensee: CTV Television Inc. Group Owner: CTV Inc. Population Served: 2,500,000 Natl. Network: CTV, .
Key Personnel:
Ivan Fecan . . . . CEO
Rick Brace . . . . pres
Robin Fillingham . . . . CFO
Jim Rusnak . . . . sr VP & VP gen mgr
Jim Olsen . . . . opns mgr & prom mgr
Louise Clark. . . . . dev dir
Lynne Forbes . . . . gen sls mgr & rgnl sls mgr
Doug Elphick . . . . natl sls mgr
Brenda Vasas . . . . progmg dir & progmg mgr traf mgr
Tom Walters . . . . news dir
Vladimir Rybarczyk. . . . . engrg mgr
M. Jung Lee . . . . news cmtr
Jason Lee . . . . sports cmtr
David Jones . . . . weather dir

CKVU-TV— Analog Channel: 10.325 kw vis, 65 kw aur. 1,959t/159g TL: N48 45 13 W123 29 25 On air date: Sept 1, 1976. 180 W. Second Ave., Vancouver, BC, V5Y 3T9. Phone: (604) 876-1344. Fax: (604) 876-3100. Web Site: www.citytv.com. Licensee: Rogers Broadcasting Ltd. Group Owner: CHUM Ltd. (acq 10-31-2007; grpsl).
Key Personnel:
Geoff Poulton . . . . VP & gen mgr
John Voiles . . . . rgnl sls mgr
Steve Scarrow. . . . . mktg VP & mktg dir
Debbie Millette. . . . . progmg mgr
Manuel Ponseca . . . . news dir

CHEK-TV— Analog Channel: 6. Analog Hrs: 24 100 kw vis, 10 kw aur. 1,628t/380g On air date: 1956. 780 Kings Rd., Victoria, BC, V8T 5A2. Phone: (250) 383-2435. Fax: (250) 384-7766. Licensee: Canwest Television L.P. Group Owner: CanWest Global Communications Corp. Natl. Network: Global, .
Key Personnel:
Ron Eberle. . . . . gen mgr

CIVI-TV— Analog Channel: 53. Analog Hrs: 24 12 kw vis. On air date: Oct 4, 2001. 1420 Broad St., Victoria, BC, V8W 2B1. Phone: (250) 381-2484. Fax: (250) 381-2485.E-mail: islandcontactus@achannel.ca Web Site: www.achannel.ca/victoria. Licensee: CTV Ltd. Group Owner: (group owner).

Key Personnel:
Jen Wong . . . . prom
Brian Gatensby. . . . . engr

CHAN-TV-7— Analog Channel: 9.31 w vis. Global BC, 7850 Enterprise St., Burnaby, BC, V5A 1V7. Phone: (604) 420-2288. Fax: (604) 421-9427. Licensee: Canwest Television L.P. Group Owner: Global BC. Natl. Network: Global, .
Key Personnel:
Roy Gardner . . . . gen mgr

Manitoba

CBWST— Analog Channel: 8. Analog Hrs: 17 120 kw vis, 12 kw aur. c/o CBWT, Box 160, Winnipeg, MB, R3C 2H1. 541 Portage Ave., Winnipeg, MB R3B 2G1. Phone: (204) 788-3222. Phone: (204) 788-3141. Fax: (204) 788-3639.E-mail: info@winnipeg.cbc.ca Web Site: www.winnipeg.cbc.ca. Licensee: CBC. Natl. Network: CBC, .
Key Personnel:
John Bertrand . . . . gen mgr
John Mang . . . . opns mgr

CBWFT-10— Analog Channel: 21.9.4 kw vis, 940 w aur. 340g On air date: Feb 11, 1978. Box 160, Winnipeg, MB, R3C 2H1. c/o CBC, 541 Portage Ave., Winnipeg, MB R3C 2H1. Phone: (204) 788-3222. Phone: (204) 788-3141. Fax: (204) 788-3639. Licensee: CBC. Natl. Network: CBC, .
Key Personnel:
Lionel Bonneville . . . . gen mgr
Richard Augert . . . . stn mgr
Philippe Vrignon . . . . progmg mgr

CKX-TV— Analog Channel: 5. Analog Hrs: 6 AM-2 AM 44 kw vis, 27 kw aur. ant 511t/525g On air date: 1955. 2940 Victoria Ave., Brandon, MB, R7B 3Y3. Phone: (204) 728-1150. Fax: (204) 727-2505.E-mail: feedbackbrandon@chumtv.com Web Site: www.cktv.com. Licensee: CTV Ltd. Group Owner: (group owner). (acq 11-19-2004; grpsl). Natl. Network: CBC, . News staff: 20; News: 15 hrs wkly.
Key Personnel:
Alan Cruise . . . . gen mgr
Brian Atkinson . . . . stn mgr & news dir

CKYB-TV— Analog Channel: 4.55 kw vis. c/o CKY-TV, Polo Park, Winnipeg, MB, R3G 0L7. Phone: (204) 788-3300. Fax: (204) 788-3399. Licensee: CTV Television Inc. Group Owner: CTV Inc. (acq 8-2-01; grpsl). Natl. Network: CTV, .
Key Personnel:
Bill Hanson. . . . . gen mgr

CBWGT— Analog Channel: 10. Analog Hrs: 17 27.4 kw vis, 5.48 kw aur. 559t/548g Box 160, Winnipeg, MB, R3C 2H1. c/o CBWT, 541 Portage Ave., Winnipeg, MB R3B 2G1. Phone: (204) 788-3222. Phone: (204) 788-3141. Fax: (204) 788-3639. Licensee: CBC. Natl. Network: CBC, .
Key Personnel:
John Bertrand . . . . gen mgr
John Mang . . . . opns mgr

CBWBT— Analog Channel: 10. Analog Hrs: 17 7.8 kw vis, 1.6 kw aur. Box 160, c/o CBWT, Winnipeg, MB, R3C 2H1. c/o CBWT, 541 Portage Ave., Winnipeg, MB R3B 2G1. Phone: (204) 788-3222. Phone: (204) 788-3141. Fax: (204) 788-3639.E-mail: info@winnipeg.cbc.ca Web Site: www.winnipeg.cbc.ca. Licensee: CBC. Natl. Network: CBC, .
Key Personnel:
John Bertrand. . . . . opns dir
John Mang . . . . opns mgr

CKX-TV-1— Analog Channel: 11.46.8 kw vis, 3.48 kw aur. (CP: 56.8 kw vis) c/o CKX-TV, 2940 Victoria Ave., Brandon, MB, R7B 3Y3. Phone: (204) 728-1150. Fax: (204) 727-2505.E-mail: feedbackbrandon@chumtv.com Web Site: www.ckxtv.com. Licensee: CTV Ltd. Group Owner: (group owner). (acq 11-19-2004; grpsl). Natl. Network: CBC, .
Key Personnel:
Alan Cruise . . . . gen mgr
Glenn Edmonson . . . . gen sls mgr & consumer affrs ed
Rich Chudley. . . . . progmg dir
Paul Weger . . . . chief of engrg

CBWT-2— Analog Channel: 4.8.4 kw vis, 1.7 kw aur. Box 160, c/o CBWT, Winnipeg, MB, R3C 2H1. c/o CBWT, 541 Portage Ave., Winnipeg, MB R3B 2G1. Phone: (204) 788-3222. Phone: (204) 788-3141. Fax: (204) 788-3639. Licensee: CBC. Natl. Network: CBC, .

Key Personnel:
John Bertrand . . . . . gen mgr
John Mang . . . . . opns mgr

CBWYT— Analog Channel: 2.4 kw vis. 370g On air date: July 14, 1978. Box 160, c/o CBWT, Winnipeg, MB, R3C 2H1. c/o CBC, 541 Portage Ave., Winnipeg, MB R3C 2H1. Phone: (204) 788-3222. Phone: (204) 788-3141. Fax: (204) 788-3639.E-mail: info@winnipeg.cbc.ca Web Site: www.winnipeg.cbc.ca. Licensee: CBC. Natl. Network: CBC, .
Key Personnel:
John Bertrand. . . . . opns dir

CBWFT-4— Analog Channel: 3.1.2 kw. 120g On air date: May 15, 1976. Box 160, Winnipeg, MB, R3C 2H1. c/o CBWFT, 541 Portage Ave., Winnipeg, MB R3C 2H1. Phone: (204) 788-3222. Phone: (204) 788-3141. Fax: (204) 788-3639.E-mail: info@winnipeg.cbc.ca Web Site: www.winnipeg.cbc.ca. Licensee: CBC. Natl. Network: CBC, .
Key Personnel:
Lionel Bonneville . . . . . gen mgr
Richard Augert . . . . . stn mgr
Wayne Yonka. . . . . engrg dir & chief of engrg

CBWFT— Analog Channel: 3.59 kw vis, 7.3 kw aur. 1,027t/1,020g On air date: 1960. Box 160, Winnipeg, MB, R3C 2H1. 541 Portage Ave., Winnipeg, MB R3C 2H1. Phone: (204) 788-3222. Fax: (204) 788-3639. Web Site: www.radio-canada.ca. Licensee: Societe Radio-Canada. Natl. Network: Radio Canada, .
Key Personnel:
Lionel Bonneville . . . . . gen mgr
Richard Augert . . . . . stn mgr
Philippe Vrignon. . . . . progmg dir

CBWT— Analog Channel: 6.100 kw vis, 12 kw aur. 1,027t/1,020g TL: N49 46 15 W97 30 35 On air date: 1954. Box 160, Winnipeg, MB, R3C 2H1. 541 Portage Ave., Winnipeg, MB R3B 2G1. Phone: (204) 788-3222. Fax: (204) 788-3167.E-mail: communications@winnipeg.cbc.ca Web Site: www.winnipeg.cbc.ca. Licensee: CBC. Natl. Network: CBC, .
Key Personnel:
John Bertrand . . . . . gen mgr & opns mgr
John Mang . . . . . opns mgr

CHMI-TV—(Portage la Prarie, Analog Channel: 13. Analog Hrs: 24 325 kw vis, 32.5 kw aur. 1,029t/1,100g On air date: Oct 17, 1986. #8 Forks Market Rd., Winnipeg, MB, R3C 4Y3. Phone: (204) 947-9613. Fax: (204) 956-0811.E-mail: winnipeginteractive@chumtv.com Web Site: www.citytv.com. Licensee: Rogers Broadcasting Ltd. Group Owner: (group owner). (acq 10-31-2007; grpsl). Population Served: 813,000 News staff: 35; News: 34 hrs wkly.
Key Personnel:
Cam Cowie . . . . . VP & gen mgr
Christine Ljungberg . . . . . opns mgr
Glen Cassie . . . . . news dir

CIIT-TV— Analog Channel: 35. On air date: Feb 6, 2006. 171 E. Liberty St., Suite 230, Toronto, ON, M6K 3P6. Canada. Phone: (416) 368-3194. Fax: (416) 368-9774. Web Site: www.joytv11.ca. Licensee: Christian Channel Inc. (acq 6-30-2008; C$6,247,908 with CHNU-TV Fraser Valley, BC).
Key Personnel:
Jennifer Craig. . . . . progmg dir

CKND-TV— Analog Channel: 9. Analog Hrs: 24 325 kw vis, 25 kw aur. ant 500t/600g On air date: Sept 1, 1975. 603 St. Mary's Rd., Winnipeg, MB, R2M 3L8. Phone: (204) 233-3304. Fax: (204) 233-5615. Web Site: www.globaltv.com. Licensee: Canwest Television L.P. Group Owner: CanWest Global Communications Corp. News staff: 19; News: 12 hrs wkly.
Key Personnel:
Tim Schellenberg . . . . . gen mgr
Heather McIntyre. . . . . prom mgr
Jon Lovlin . . . . . news dir
Len Virog . . . . . engrg dir

CKY-TV— Analog Channel: 7.325 kw vis, 65 kw aur. ant 1,000g On air date: 1960. Polo Park, 400-345 Grahm Ave, Winnipeg, MB, R3C 5S6. Phone: (204) 788-3300. Fax: (204) 788-3399. Web Site: www.cky.com. Licensee: CTV Television Inc. Group Owner: CTV Inc. Natl. Network: CTV, .
Key Personnel:
Diane Kashton . . . . . pres & prom dir
Bill Hansen. . . . . VP
Bill Hanson. . . . . gen mgr
Kenneth Peron. . . . . opns mgr
Wally Comrie . . . . . gen sls mgr
Jeff Bollenbach . . . . . news dir
Winnie Navarro . . . . . progmg dir & traf mgr

New Brunswick

CKCD-TV— Analog Channel: 7.920 w vis, 180 w aur. 75t 191 Halifax St., Moncton, NB, E1C 9R7. Phone: (506) 857-2600. Fax: (506) 857-2617.E-mail: ckcw@ctv.ca Web Site: www.ctv.ca. Licensee: CTV Television Inc. Group Owner: CTV Inc. (acq 11-1-97). Natl. Network: CTV, .
Key Personnel:
Ivan Fecan . . . . . CEO
Rick Brace . . . . . pres
Robin Fillingham . . . . . CFO
Elaine Ali . . . . . exec VP
Mike Elgie . . . . . VP & gen mgr
Brian Lewis . . . . . stn mgr & gen sls mgr adv mgr
John Silver . . . . . opns mgr
Jane Hefler . . . . . progmg mgr
Jay Witherbee . . . . . news dir & pub affrs dir
Carson McDavid . . . . . engrg dir & chief of engrg
Rebroadcasts CKCW-TV Moncton 100%.

CBAT— Analog Channel: 4.54.2 kw vis, 7.8 kw aur. 1,268t/1,631g TL: N45 28 39 W66 14 03 On air date: 1954. Box 2200, Fredericton, NB, E3B 5G4. Phone: (506) 451-4000. Fax: (506) 451-4003. Web Site: www.cbc.ca/nb. Licensee: CBC. (acq 4-29-94). Natl. Network: CBC, .
Key Personnel:
Gary Arsenault . . . . . gen mgr

CBAFT— Analog Channel: 11.137.7 kw vis. ant 781t/394g TL: N46 08 41 W64 54 14 On air date: 1959. Box 950, Moncton, NB, E1C 8N8. 250 University Ave., Moncton, NB E1C 5K3. Phone: (506) 853-6666. Phone: (506) 853-6740 (Stn Dir). Fax: (506) 867-8031. Fax: (506) 853-6601 (news). Web Site: www.radio-canada.ca/regions /atlantique/index.shtml. Licensee: Societe Radio-Canada. Natl. Network: Radio Canada, .
Key Personnel:
Louise Imbeault . . . . . gen mgr
Jonna Brewen. . . . . stn mgr

CKCW-TV— Analog Channel: 2.56 kw vis, 9.2 kw aur. On air date: 1954. 191 Halifax St., Moncton, NB, E1C 9R7. Phone: (506) 857-2600. Fax: (506) 857-2617.E-mail: ckcw@ctv.ca Web Site: www.ctv.ca. Licensee: CTV Television Inc. Group Owner: CTV Inc. (acq 11-1-97). Natl. Network: CTV, .
Key Personnel:
Ivan Fecan . . . . . CEO
Rick Brace . . . . . pres
Robin Fillingham . . . . . CFO
Elaine Ali . . . . . exec VP
Mike Elgie . . . . . VP & gen mgr
Brian Lewis . . . . . stn mgr & gen sls mgr adv mgr
John Silver . . . . . opns mgr
Jane Hefler . . . . . progmg mgr
Jay Witherbee . . . . . news dir & pub affrs dir
Carson McDavid . . . . . chief of engrg
Paul Street . . . . . rsch dir
Sharron White. . . . . traf mgr
Steve Murphy . . . . . news cmtr
Paul Hollingsworth. . . . . sports cmtr
Peter Coade . . . . . weather dir

CHCT-TV— Analog Channel: 26.100 w vis. TL: N45 04 54 W67 03 34 On air date: Nov 1, 2006. 24 Reed Ave., Unit 2, St. Andrews, NB, E5B 1A1. Phone: (506) 529-8826. Fax: (506) 529-2601.E-mail: general.mail@chct.ca Web Site: www.chct.ca. Licensee: St. Andrews Community Television.

CKLT-TV— Analog Channel: 9.162 kw vis, 32 kw aur. 1,361t/241g 12 Smythe St., Suite 126, Saint John, NB, E2L 5G5. Canada. Phone: (506) 658-1010. Fax: (506) 658-1208.E-mail: cklt@ctv.ca Web Site: www.ctv.ca. Licensee: CTV Television Inc. Group Owner: CTV Inc. (acq 11-1-97). Natl. Network: CTV, .
Key Personnel:
Mike Elgie . . . . . gen mgr

CKAM-TV— Analog Channel: 12.280 kw vis, 141 kw aur. On air date: unknown. c/o CKCW-TV, 191 Halifax St., Moncton, NB, E1C 9R7. Phone: (506) 857-2600. Fax: (506) 857-2617.E-mail: ckcw@ctv.ca Web Site: www.ctv.ca. Licensee: CTV Television Inc. Group Owner: CTV Inc. (acq 11-1-97). Natl. Network: CTV, . Ottawa Atty: . Ottawa atty: Alexander, Pearson & Dawson
Key Personnel:
Ivan Fecan . . . . . CEO
Rick Brace . . . . . pres
Robin Fillingham . . . . . CFO
Elaine Ali . . . . . exec VP
Mike Elgie . . . . . VP & gen mgr
Brian Lewis . . . . . stn mgr & gen sls mgr adv mgr
John Silver . . . . . opns mgr
Renee Fournier . . . . . progmg mgr
Jay Witherbee . . . . . news dir & pub affrs dir
Carson McDavid . . . . . engrg dir & chief of engrg
Rebroadcasts CKCW-TV Moncton 100%.

Newfoundland

CJOM-TV— Analog Channel: 3. Analog Hrs: 24 6.7 kw vis, 3.4 kw aur. 275g On air date: September 1957. Box 2020, c/o CJON-TV, 446 Logy Bay Rd., St. John's, NF, A1C 5S2. 446 Logy Bay Rd., St. John's , NF A1C 5S2.Canada Phone: (709) 722-5015. Fax: (709) 726-5107.E-mail: ntv@ntv.ca Web Site: www.ntv.ca. Licensee: Newfoundland Broadcasting Co. Ltd. Group Owner: (group owner); (acq 9-1-77). Population Served: 575,000 Natl. Network: CTV, . News staff: 12; News: 11 hrs wkly.
Key Personnel:
Scott Stirling . . . . . pres

CBNAT-1— Analog Channel: 3. Analog Hrs: 24 5 kw vis, 500 w aur. TL: N49 57 34 W56 18 42 On air date: Sept 15, 1968. 95 University Ave., St. John's, NF, A1B 1Z4. Phone: (709) 576-5000. Fax: (709) 576-5011. Web Site: www.cbc.ca/nl. Licensee: CBC. Natl. Network: CBC, .
Key Personnel:
Diane Humber . . . . . gen mgr

CJWB-TV— Analog Channel: 10. Analog Hrs: 24 9.9 kw vis, 990 w aur. 539 TL: N48 37 30 W53 03 45 On air date: 1972. Box 2020, 446 Logy Bay Rd., 446 Logy Bay Rd., St. John's, NF, A1C 5S2. Phone: (709) 722-5015. Fax: (709) 726-5107.E-mail: ntv@ntv.ca Web Site: www.ntv.ca. Licensee: Newfoundland Broadcasting Co. Ltd. Group Owner: (group owner) Population Served: 575,000 Natl. Network: CTV, . News staff: 12; News: 11 hrs wkly.
Key Personnel:
Scott Stirling . . . . . pres

CBYT-3— Analog Channel: 2. Analog Hrs: 24 1 kw vis, 100 w aur. 300t/300g TL: N49 33 12 W57 53 24 On air date: Mar 12, 1971. 95 University Ave., St. John's, NF, A1B 1Z4. Phone: (709) 576-5000. Fax: (709) 576-5011. Licensee: CBC. Natl. Network: CBC, CBC Radio One, . Rgnl. Network: CBC Northern Television Services.
Key Personnel:
Diane Humber . . . . . gen mgr
Satellite of CBNT(TV) Saint John's.

CBNAT— Analog Channel: 11. Analog Hrs: 24 30 kw vis, 3 kw aur. TL: N49 11 51 W55 22 05 On air date: Dec 21, 1967. 95 University Ave., St. John's, NF, A1B 1Z4. Phone: (709) 576-5000. Fax: (709) 576-5011. Web Site: www.cbc.ca/nl. Licensee: CBC. Natl. Network: CBC, . News staff: one.
Key Personnel:
Diane Humber. . . . . engrg mgr

CJWN-TV— Analog Channel: 10. Analog Hrs: 24 6.07 kw vis, 1 kw aur. 364t/300g TL: N48 56 55 W57 58 23 On air date: December 1974. Box 2020, 446 Logy Bay Rd., 446 Logy Bay Rd., St. John's, NF, A1C 5S2. Phone: (709) 722-5015. Fax: (709) 726-5107.E-mail: ntv@ntv.ca Web Site: www.ntv.ca. Licensee: Newfoundland Broadcasting Co. Ltd. Group Owner: (group owner) Natl. Network: CTV, .
Key Personnel:
Jim Furlong . . . . . news dir

CJOX-TV-1— Analog Channel: 2. Analog Hrs: 24 4.67 kw vis, 470 w aur. 387t/287g TL: N47 05 17 W55 46 23 On air date: 1972. Box 2020, 446 Logy Bay Rd., 446 Logy Bay Rd., St. John's, NF, A1C 5S2. Phone: (709) 722-5015. Fax: (709) 726-5107.E-mail: ntv@ntv.ca Web Site: www.ntv.ca. Licensee: Newfoundland Broadcasting Co. Ltd. Group Owner: (group owner) Population Served: 575,000 Natl. Network: CTV, . News staff: 12; News: 11 hrs wkly.
Key Personnel:
Scott Stirling . . . . . pres

CJCN-TV— Analog Channel: 4. Analog Hrs: 24 100 kw vis, 10 kw aur. 602 TL: N49 04 12 W55 16 54 On air date: 1963. Box 2020, 446 Logy Bay Rd., 446 Logy Bay Rd., St. John's, NF, A1C 5S2. Phone: (709) 722-5015. Fax: (709) 726-5107.E-mail: ntv@ntv.ca Web Site: www.nvt.ca. Licensee: Newfoundland Broadcasting Co. Ltd. Group Owner: (group owner) Population Served: 575,000 Natl. Network: CTV, . News staff: 12; News: 11 hrs wkly.
Key Personnel:
Scott Stirling. . . . . pres
Jim Furlong . . . . . news dir

***CBNLT—** Analog Channel: 13. Analog Hrs: 24 250 kw vis, 25 w aur. TL: N52 56 41 W66 54 11 On air date: Nov 7, 1973. 95 University Ave., St. John's, NF, A1B 1Z4. Phone: (709) 576-5000. Fax: (709) 576-5011. Web Site: www.cbc.ca/nl. Licensee: CBC. Natl. Network: CBC, . News staff: one.
Key Personnel:
Diane Humber . . . . . gen mgr

CBNT-3— Analog Channel: 5. Analog Hrs: 24 5 kw vis, 500 w aur. TL: N47 08 39 W55 08 52 On air date: Nov 30, 1965. Box 12010, c/o CBNT, 95 University Ave., St. John's, NF, A1B 3T8. Phone: (709) 576-5000. Fax: (709) 576-5099. Web Site: www.cbc.ca/nl. Licensee: Canadian Broadcasting Corp. Natl. Network: CBC, .

Key Personnel:
Diane Humber . . . . gen mgr
Keith Durnford . . . . engrg mgr & chief of engrg

CBNAT-9— Analog Channel: 9. Analog Hrs: 24 3 kw vis, 300 w aur. TL: N51 01 05 W56 48 47 On air date: Nov 30, 1973. 95 University Ave., St. John's, NF, A1B 1Z4. Phone: (709) 576-5000. Fax: (709) 576-5011. Web Site: www.cbc.ca/nl. Licensee: CBC. Natl. Network: CBC, .
Key Personnel:
Diane Humber . . . . gen mgr

CBNT-2— Analog Channel: 12. Analog Hrs: 24 10.6 kw vis, 100 w aur. TL: N47 13 52 W53 58 56 On air date: Nov 27, 1965. Box 12010, c/o CBNT, 95 University Ave., St. John's, NF, A1B 3T8. Phone: (709) 576-5000. Fax: (709) 576-5099. Web Site: www.cbc.ca/nl. Licensee: Canadian Broadcasting Corp. Natl. Network: CBC, .
Key Personnel:
Diane Humber . . . . gen mgr
Keith Durnford . . . . engrg mgr & chief of engrg

CBNT-1— Analog Channel: 13. Analog Hrs: 24 3 kw vis, 300 w aur. TL: N48 26 27 W53 21 25 On air date: October 1964. Box 12010, c/o CBNT, 95 University Ave., St. John's, NF, A1B 3T8. Phone: (709) 576-5000. Fax: (709) 576-5099. Fax: (709) 576-5144. Web Site: www.cbc.ca/nl. Licensee: Canadian Broadcasting Corp. Natl. Network: CBC, .
Key Personnel:
Keith Durnford . . . . chief of engrg

CBNAT-4— Analog Channel: 6. Analog Hrs: 24 3 kw vis, 300 w aur. TL: N51 21 14 W55 34 00 On air date: Oct 21, 1968. 95 University Ave., St. John's, NF, A1B 1Z4. Phone: (709) 576-5000. Fax: (709) 576-5011. Web Site: www.cbc.ca/nl. Licensee: CBC. Natl. Network: CBC, .
Key Personnel:
Diane Humber . . . . gen mgr

CBNT— Analog Channel: 8. Analog Hrs: 24 3 kw vis, 300 w aur. TL: N48 26 27 W53 21 25 On air date: 1964. Box 12010, Stn A, Saint John's, NF, A1B 3T8. 95 University Ave., Saint John's, NF A1B 1Z4. Phone: (709) 576-5000. Fax: (709) 576-5011. Web Site: www.cbc.ca/nl. Licensee: CBC. Natl. Network: CBC, .
Key Personnel:
Diane Humber . . . . gen mgr

CJON-TV— Analog Channel: 6. Analog Hrs: 24 212 kw vis, 21 kw aur. 825t/301 TL: N47 31 36 W52 42 50 On air date: September 1955. Box 2020, 446 Logy Bay Rd., St John's, NF, A1C 5S2. Phone: (709) 722-5015. Fax: (709) 726-5107. E-mail: ntv@ntv.ca Web Site: www.ntv.ca. Licensee: Newfoundland Broadcasting Co. Ltd. Group Owner: (group owner) Population Served: 575,000 Natl. Network: CTV, . Ottawa Atty: . Ottawa atty: Johnston & Buchan Wire Svc: BN Wire News staff: 12; News: 11 hrs wkly.
Key Personnel:
Scott Stirling . . . . pres & gen mgr
Jim Furlong . . . . news dir

CJSV-TV— Analog Channel: 4. Analog Hrs: 24 5.56 kw vis, 560 w aur. 439 TL: N48 31 09 W58 31 00 On air date: 1973. Box 2020, 446 Logy Bay Rd., 446 Logy Bay Rd., St. John's, NF, A1C 5S2. Phone: (709) 722-5015. Fax: (709) 726-5107. E-mail: ntv@ntv.ca Web Site: www.nvt.ca. Licensee: Newfoundland Broadcasting Co. Ltd. Group Owner: (group owner) Population Served: 575,000 Natl. Network: CTV, . News staff: 12; News: 11 hrs wkly.
Key Personnel:
Scott Stirling . . . . pres
Jim Furlong . . . . news dir

Northwest Territories

*CHAK-TV— Analog Channel: 8. Analog Hrs: 20 3 kw vis, 300 w aur. 443t/360g Bag Service No. 8, 155 Mackenzie Rd., Inuvik, NT, X0E 0T0. Phone: (867) 920-5400. Fax: (867) 920-5489. E-mail: cbcnorth@cbc.ca Web Site: www.cbc.ca/north. Licensee: CBC. Natl. Network: CBC, . News staff: 2.
Key Personnel:
John Agnew . . . . gen mgr
Rebroadcast of CFYK-TV Yellow Knife.

*CFYK-TV— Analog Channel: 6. Analog Hrs: 20 1 kw vis, 100 w aur. On air date: 1968. Box 160, Yellowknife, NT, X1A2N2. Canada. 5002

Forest Dr., Yellowknife, NT X1A2N2.Canada Phone: (867) 920-5400. Fax: (867) 920-5489.E-mail: cbcnorth@cbc.ca Web Site: www.cbc.ca/north. Licensee: CBC. Natl. Network: CBC, .
Key Personnel:
John Agnew . . . . gen mgr

Nova Scotia

CJCB-TV-2— Analog Channel: 9. Analog Hrs: 24 140 kw vis. 500t TL: N45 32 45 W62 15 39 c/o CJCB-TV, 1283 George St., Sydney, NS, B1P 1N7. Phone: (902) 562-5511. Fax: (902) 562-9714.E-mail: cjcb@ctv.ca Web Site: www.ctv.ca. Licensee: ATV Cape Breton. Natl. Network: CTV, .
Key Personnel:
Glenn McLanders . . . . stn mgr
Edgar Bennett . . . . engrg dir

CJCH-TV-6— Analog Channel: 6. Analog Hrs: 24 100 kw vis, 20 kw aur. 630t/400g TL: N44 20 26 W65 06 34 Box 1653, Halifax, NS, B3J 2Z4. 2885 Robie St., Halifax, NS B3J 2Z4. Phone: (902) 453-4000. Fax: (902) 454-3302.E-mail: cjch@ctv.ca Web Site: www.ctv.ca. Licensee: CTV Television Inc. Group Owner: Baton Broadcasting Inc. Natl. Network: CTV, .
Key Personnel:
Michael Elgie . . . . gen mgr
Renee Fournier . . . . mktg mgr

CJCH-TV-1— Analog Channel: 10. Analog Hrs: 24 18.1 kw vis, 3.62 kw aur. ant 886t/300g TL: N45 12 12 W64 24 06 Box 1653, Halifax, NS, B3J 2Z4. Phone: (902) 453-4000. Fax: (902) 454-3302.E-mail: cjch@ctv.ca Web Site: www.ctv.ca. Licensee: Atlantic Television System. Group Owner: CTV Television Inc. Natl. Network: CTV, .
Key Personnel:
Michael Elgie . . . . gen mgr
Ian MacArthur . . . . gen sls mgr
Renee Fournier . . . . mktg mgr
Jane Hefler . . . . progmg mgr
Jay Witherbee . . . . news dir
Gary Robertson . . . . chief of engrg

CBIT-2— Analog Channel: 2. Analog Hrs: 24 2.5 kw vis, 250 w aur. 150g c/o CBIT, 285 Alexandra St., Sydney, NS, B1S 2E8. Phone: (902) 539-5050. Fax: (902) 539-1562.E-mail: cbns@cbc.ca Web Site: www.cbc.ca/ns. Licensee: CBC. Natl. Network: CBC, .
Key Personnel:
Mike Gillis . . . . chief of engrg
CBHT in Halifax.

CBHT— Analog Channel: 3. Analog Hrs: 24 56 kw vis, 11.2 kw aur. 866t/1,620g On air date: 1954. Box 3000, Halifax, NS, B3J 3E9. Phone: (902) 420-8311. Fax: (902) 420-4010.E-mail: cbcns@cbc.ca Web Site: www.cbc.ca/ns. Licensee: CBC. Natl. Network: CBC, .
Key Personnel:
Andrew Cochran . . . . gen mgr
Lenny Jackson . . . . opns mgr
Mary Elizabeth Luka . . . . dev mgr
John Channing . . . . rgnl sls mgr

CIHF-TV— Analog Channel: 8. Analog Hrs: 24 8.2 kw vis, 1.6 aur. 691t/645g TL: N44 39 03 W63 39 28 On air date: Sept 5, 1988. Box 1643 C.R.O., Halifax, NS, B3J 2Z1. Phone: (902) 481-7400. Phone: (506) 632-3400. Fax: (902) 468-2154.E-mail: news@globaltv.com Web Site: www.globalmaritimes.com. Licensee: Canwest Television L.P. Group Owner: CanWest Global System (acq 8-29-94; $11 million). Population Served: 1,500,000 News staff: 40; News: 17 hrs wkly.
Key Personnel:
Leonard Asper . . . . chmn
John Burgis . . . . CFO
Barry Saunders . . . . gen mgr

CJCH-TV— Analog Channel: 9. Analog Hrs: 24 100 kw vis, 10 kw aur. ant 821t/575g TL: N44 39 03 W63 39 28 On air date: Jan 1, 1961. Box 1653, Halifax, NS, B3J 2Z4. 2885 Robie St., Halifax, NS B3K 5Z4. Phone: (902) 453-4000. Fax: (902) 454-3302.E-mail: cjch@ctv.ca Web Site: www.ctv.ca. Licensee: CTV Television Inc. Group Owner: CTV Inc. Natl. Network: CTV, .
Key Personnel:
Michael Elgie . . . . VP & gen mgr
Ian MacArthur . . . . gen sls mgr
Renee Fournier . . . . mktg mgr
Jane Hefler . . . . progmg mgr
Jay Witherbee . . . . news dir
Gary Robertson . . . . chief of engrg

CJCB-TV-1— Analog Channel: 6. Analog Hrs: 24 9.4 kw vis, 4.7 kw aur. c/o CJCB-TV, 1283 George St., Sydney, NS, B1P 1N7. Phone:

(902) 562-5511. Fax: (902) 562-9714.E-mail: cjcb@ctv.ca Web Site: www.ctv.ca. Licensee: ATV Cape Breton. Natl. Network: CTV, .
Key Personnel:
Glenn McLanders . . . . gen mgr & stn mgr

CIMC-TV— Analog Channel: 10. Analog Hrs: 24 450 w vis. On air date: June 2003. Box 87, Arichat, NS, B0E 1A0. 705 Lower Rd., Arichat, NS B0E 1A0. Phone: (902) 226-1928. Fax: (902) 226-1331.E-mail: telile@telile.tv Web Site: www.telile.tv. Licensee: Telile:Isle Madame Community Television Association/Association Television Communautaire de l'Ile Madame.
Key Personnel:
Gloria Hill . . . . gen mgr

CBHT-11— Analog Channel: 12.129 kw vis, 12.9 kw aur. Box 3000, c/o CBHT, 5600 Sackville St., Halifax, NS, B3J 3E9. 1840 Bell Rd., Halifax, NS B3H 2Z5. Phone: (902) 420-8311. Fax: (902) 420-4010.E-mail: cbcns@cbc.ca Web Site: www.cbc.ca/ns/. Licensee: CBC. Natl. Network: CBC, .
Key Personnel:
Andrew Cochran . . . . gen mgr & engrg mgr
Penny Longley . . . . dev mgr
John Channing . . . . rgnl sls mgr

CBHT-4— Analog Channel: 11. Analog Hrs: 24 9.07 kw vis, 1.814 kw aur. Box 3000, c/o CBHT, 5600 Sackville St., Halifax, NS, B3J 3E9. 1840 Bell Rd., Halifax, NS B3H 2Z5.Canada Phone: (902) 420-8311. Fax: (902) 420-4010.E-mail: cbcns@cbc.ca Web Site: www.cbc.ca/ns. Licensee: CBC. Natl. Network: CBC, .
Key Personnel:
Andrew Cochran . . . . gen mgr
Mary Elizabeth Luka . . . . dev mgr

CBIT— Analog Channel: 5. Analog Hrs: 24 54 kw vis, 5.4 kw aur. On air date: 1972. 285 Alexandra St., Sydney, NS, B1S 2E8. Phone: (902) 539-5050; (902) 563-4100. Fax: (902) 539-1562.E-mail: cbns@cbc.ca Web Site: www.cbc.ca/ns. Licensee: CBC. Natl. Network: CBC, .
Key Personnel:
Mike Gillis . . . . chief of engrg
CBHT in Halifax.

CJCB-TV— Analog Channel: 4. Analog Hrs: 24 100 kw vis, 60 kw aur. On air date: 1954. 1283 George St., Sydney, NS, B1P 1N7. Phone: (902) 562-5511. Fax: (902) 562-9714.E-mail: cjcb@ctv.ca Web Site: www.ctv.ca. Licensee: ATV Cape Breton. Group Owner: CTV Inc. Natl. Network: CTV, .
Key Personnel:
Glenn McLanders . . . . stn mgr & gen sls mgr
Gary Robertson . . . . opns dir & chief of engrg
Renee Fournier . . . . mktg mgr & prom mgr
Jane Hefler . . . . progmg mgr
Jay Witherbee . . . . news dir
Edgar Bennett . . . . engrg dir & chief of engrg

CBHT-3— Analog Channel: 11. Analog Hrs: 24 15.7 kw vis, 3.3 kw aur. Box 3000, c/o CBHT, Halifax, NS, B3J 3E9. Phone: (902) 420-8311. Fax: (902) 420-4010.E-mail: cbcns@cbc.ca Web Site: www.cbc.ca/ns. Licensee: CBC. Natl. Network: CBC, .
Key Personnel:
Andrew Cochran . . . . gen mgr
Lenny Jackson . . . . chief of opns
Mary Elizabeth Luka . . . . dev mgr
John Channing . . . . rgnl sls mgr

Ontario

CIII-TV-2— Analog Channel: 2.100 kw vis, 15 kw aur. ant 1,279 On air date: January 1974. 81 Barber Greene Rd., Toronto, ON, M3C 2A2. Phone: (416) 446-5311. Fax: (416) 446-5447.E-mail: newstips@canada.com Web Site: www.canada.com. Licensee: Canwest Television L.P. Group Owner: Global Television Network Natl. Network: Global, .
Key Personnel:
Leonard Asper . . . . chmn
Bill Hunt . . . . gen mgr

CKVR-TV— Analog Channel: 3. Analog Hrs: 24 100 kw vis, 10 kw aur. ant 820t/651g TL: N44 21 05 W79 41 55 On air date: Sept 28, 1955. Box 519, Barrie, ON, L4M 4T9. 33 Beacon Rd., Barrie, ON L4M 4S7. Phone: (705) 734-3300. Fax: (705) 733-0302. Fax: (705) 734-2061.E-mail: achannel@achannel.ca Web Site: www.achannel.ca. Licensee: CTV Ltd. Group Owner: CHUM Ltd. Population Served: 6,000,000 News staff: 30; News: 14 hrs wkly.

Key Personnel:
Jay Switzer . . . . pres
Bob McLaughlin. . . . . opns mgr & news dir
Paul Woodhouse . . . . sls dir
Dan Hamilton . . . . gen sls mgr
Peggy Hebden. . . . . stn mgr & progmg dir & film buyer
Brian Cathline . . . . chief of engrg

***CICO-TV-59—** Analog Channel: 59. Analog Hrs: 24 34.3 kw vis, 3.4 kw aur. 717t/718g On air date: June 1976. Box 200 Stn Q, c/o TV Ontario, Toronto, ON, M4T 2T1. 2180 Yonge St., Toronto, ON M4S 2B9. Phone: (416) 484-2600. Fax: (416) 484-6285.E-mail: asktvo@tvo.org Web Site: www.tvo.org. Licensee: Ontario Educational Communications Authority.
Key Personnel:
Lee Robock . . . . COO & gen mgr
Lisa DeWilde . . . . pres
Ray Newell. . . . . opns dir
Meg Pinto . . . . mktg dir

CJOH-TV-8— Analog Channel: 8. Analog Hrs: 24 260 kw vis. ant 615t TL: N45 10 35 W74 31 38 On air date: 1958. CTV Ottawa, Box 5813, Ottawa, ON, K2C 3G6. Phone: (613) 224-1313. Fax: (613) 274-4215.E-mail: ctvottawa@ctv.ca Web Site: www.ottawa.ctv.ca. Licensee: CTV Television Inc. Group Owner: (group owner) Natl. Network: CTV, .
Key Personnel:
Louis Douville . . . . VP & gen mgr
Rebroadcasts CJOH-TV Ottawa 100%.

CJOH-TV-6— Analog Channel: 6. Analog Hrs: 24 100 kw vis. ant 671t/573g TL: N44 08 30 W77 04 34 On air date: September 1972. CTV Ottawa, Box 5813, Merivale Depot, Ottawa, ON, K2C 3G6. Phone: (613) 224-1313. Fax: (613) 274-4215.E-mail: ctvottawa@ctv.ca Web Site: www.ottawa.ctv.ca. Licensee: CTV Television Inc. Group Owner: CTV Inc. Natl. Network: CTV, .
Key Personnel:
Louis Douville . . . . VP & gen mgr
Rebroadcasts CJOH-TV Ottawa 100%.

CICI-TV-1— Analog Channel: 5.19 kw vis, 1.9 kw aur. 576t/216g On air date: 1958. c/o MC-TV, 699 Frood Rd., Sudbury, ON, P3C 5A3. Phone: (705) 674-8301. Fax: (705) 674-2706.E-mail: newsforthenorth@ctv.ca Web Site: www.ctv.ca. Licensee: CTV Television Inc. Group Owner: Baton Broadcasting Inc. Natl. Network: CTV, . News staff: 15; News: 10 hrs wkly.
Key Personnel:
Scott Lund . . . . VP & gen mgr
John Eddy . . . . opns mgr & engrg mgr
Rick MacKenzie . . . . gen sls mgr
Don Chapman . . . . news dir

CBLAT— Analog Channel: 13.22 kw vis, 4.4 kw aur. 598t/540g Box 500, Stn A, c/o CBLT, Toronto, ON, M5W 1E6. Phone: (416) 205-3311. Web Site: www.cbc.ca. Licensee: CBC. Natl. Network: CBC, .

CHCH-TV— Analog Channel: 11. Digital Channel: 18. Analog Hrs: 24 Digital Hrs: 24 230 kw vis, 23 kw aur. ant 1,173t/1,054g On air date: June 4, 1954. Box 2230, Stn. A, 163 Jackson St. W., Hamilton, ON, L8N 3A6. Phone: (905) 522-1101. Fax: (905) 523-8778.E-mail: newstips@chtv.ca Web Site: www.chtv.ca. Licensee: Canwest Television L.P. Group Owner: CanWest Global Communications Corp. (acq 7-6-2000). Natl. Network: Global, .
Key Personnel:
Patrick O'Hara . . . . gen mgr

CITS-TV— Analog Channel: 36. Digital Channel: 35. Analog Hrs: 24 514 kw vis. On air date: Sept 30, 1998. 1295 N. Service Rd., Burlington, ON, L7R 4X5. Phone: (905) 331-7333. Fax: (905) 332-6005.E-mail: cts@ctstv.com Web Site: www.ctstv.com. Licensee: Crossroads Television System.
Key Personnel:
Fred Vanstone . . . . pres
Terry Maskel. opns mgr
Glenn Stewart . . . . gen sls mgr
Rob Sheppard . . . . progmg mgr
David Storey. . . . . engrg dir

CITO-TV-2— Analog Channel: 11. Analog Hrs: 6am - 2am 325 kw vis, 32.5 kw aur. 734t/396g Box 620, c/o MCTV-CTV, 681 Pine St. N., Timmins, ON, P4N 7G3. Phone: (705) 264-4211. Fax: (705) 264-3266.E-mail: newsforthenorth@ctv.ca Web Site: www.ctv.ca. Licensee: CTV Television Inc. Group Owner: CTV Inc. Natl. Network: CTV, .
Key Personnel:
Scott Lund . . . . gen mgr & stn mgr
Jason Laneville . . . . sls dir

CBWAT— Analog Channel: 8.2 kw vis, 200 w aur. 433t/371g c/o CBC, Box 160, Winnipeg, MB, R3C 2H1. Canada. Phone: (204) 788-3222. Fax: (204) 788-3643. Web Site: www.winnipeg.cbc.ca. Licensee: CBC. Natl. Network: CBC, .

CJBN-TV— Analog Channel: 13.177 kw vis, 35 kw aur. 200g On air date: April 1983. 102 Tenth St., Keewatin, ON, P0X 1C0. 104 Tenth St., Keewatin, ON P9N 3X8. Phone: (807) 547-2852. Fax: (807) 547-2348.E-mail: darrylm@norcomcable.ca Web Site: www.norcomcable.ca. Licensee: Shaw Cablesystems G.P. Natl. Network: CTV, . News staff: 2; News: one hr wkly.
Key Personnel:
Darryl Michaluk. . . . . stn mgr & prom dir

CKWS-TV— Analog Channel: 11. Analog Hrs: 24 325 kw vis, 32.5 kw aur. ant 830t/785g TL: N44 10 02 W76 25 40 On air date: 1954. 170 Queen St., Kingston, ON, K7K 1B2. Phone: (613) 544-2340. Fax: (613) 544-5508.E-mail: newswatch@corusent.com Web Site: www.ckwstv.com. Licensee: 591987 B.C. Ltd. Group Owner: Corus Entertainment Inc. (acq 3-24-2000; grpsl). Natl. Network: CBC, . News: 12 hrs wkly.
Key Personnel:
Mike Ferguson . . . . gen mgr & stn mgr
Tim Wieczorek . . . . gen sls mgr
Alison MacLean . . . . prom dir
Jay Westman. . . . . news dir
Roger Cole . . . . engrg VP & chief of engrg

***CICO-TV-28—** Analog Channel: 28. Analog Hrs: 24 200 kw vis, 20 kw aur. 972t/904g On air date: January 1976. Box 200, sta Q, c/o TV Ontario, Toronto, ON, M4T 2T1. 2180 Yonge St., Toronto, ON M4S 2P9. Phone: (416) 484-2600. Fax: (416) 484-6285.E-mail: asktvo@tvo.org Web Site: www.tvo.org. Licensee: Ontario Educational Communications Authority.
Key Personnel:
Lisa DeWilde . . . . CEO

CKCO-TV— Analog Channel: 13. Analog Hrs: 24 325 kw vis, 32.5 kw aur. 954t/653g TL: N43 24 15 W80 38 05 On air date: Mar 1, 1954. CTV Southwestern Ontario, Box 91026, Kitchener, ON, N2G 4E9. Canada. Phone: (519) 578-1313. Fax: (519) 743-0730 (news).E-mail: viewermail@southwesternontario.ctv.ca Web Site: www.southwesternontario.ctv.ca. Licensee: CKCO-TV Division of CTV Inc. Group Owner: CTV Inc. (acq 8-31-97). Population Served: 2,000,000 Natl. Network: CTV, .
Key Personnel:
Ivan Fecan . . . . CEO
Robin Fillingham . . . . CFO
Dennis Watson. . . . . VP & gen mgr
Dave MacNeill . . . . opns dir
Cameron Crassweller . . . . rgnl sls mgr
Janet Taylor. . . prom mgr & adv mgr progmg mgr & pub affrs dir
Andy LaBlanc. news dir
Dave Melse . . . . chief of engrg

CFTV-TV— Analog Channel: 34.400 w vis. On air date: 2006. 223 Talbot St. W., Leamington, ON, N8H 1N8. Phone: (519) 326-4000.E-mail: info@cftv.ca Web Site: www.cftv.ca. Licensee: Southshore Broadcasting Inc.
Key Personnel:
Tony Vidal. . . . . pres
Ted Mastronardi . . . . VP

CFPL-TV— Analog Channel: 10. Analog Hrs: 24 325 kw vis, 43.2 kw aur. 1,000t/975g On air date: Nov 28, 1953. 1 Communications Road, London, ON, N6J 4Z1. Canada. Phone: (519) 686-8810. Fax: (519) 668-3288. Web Site: www.atv.ca/london. Licensee: CTV Ltd. Group Owner: CHUM Ltd. (acq 1997). Population Served: 500,000
Key Personnel:
Don Mumford . . . . gen mgr & stn mgr

***CICO-TV-18—** Analog Channel: 18. Analog Hrs: 24 34.9 kw vis, 3.5 kw aur. 1,029t/956 On air date: April 1976. Box 200 Stn Q, c/o TV Ontario, Toronto, ON, M4T 2T1. 2180 Yonge St., Toronto, ON M4S 2B9. Phone: (416) 484-2600. Fax: (416) 484-6285.E-mail: asktvo@tvo.org Web Site: www.tvo.org. Licensee: Ontario Educational Communications Authority.
Key Personnel:
Lisa DeWilde . . . . CEO
Lee Robock . . . . gen mgr
Ray Newell. . . . . opns dir
Meg Pinto . . . . mktg dir

CBLAT-4— Analog Channel: 11. Analog Hrs: 17 7.5 kw vis, 1.532 kw aur. 599t TL: N48 44 50 W86 34 00 On air date: May 16, 1968. Box 500, Stn A, c/o CBLT, Toronto, ON, M5W 1E6. Phone: (416) 205-3311. Fax: (416) 205-2552. Web Site: www.cbc.ca. Licensee: Canadian Broadcasting Corp. Natl. Network: CBC, .
Rebroadcast of CBLT Toronto 100%.

CIII-TV-7— Analog Channel: 7.325 kw vis, 48.8 kw aur. 1,132t/1,174g On air date: Nov 24, 1987. 81 Barber Greene Rd., Toronto, ON, M3C 2A2. Phone: (416) 446-5311. Fax: (416) 446-5447.E-mail: newstips@globaltv.com Web Site: www.canada.com. Licensee: Canwest Television L.P. Group Owner: Global Television Network
Key Personnel:
Bill Hunt. . . . . gen mgr

CKNY-TV— Analog Channel: 10. Analog Hrs: 20 70.5 kw vis, 7.1 kw aur. 607t/1,165g On air date: October 1981. 245 Oak St. E., North Bay, ON, P1B 8P8. Phone: (705) 476-3111. Fax: (705) 495-4474. Fax: (705) 495-0922 (news).E-mail: northbaynews@ctv.ca Web Site: www.ctv.ca. Licensee: CTV Television Inc. Group Owner: CTV Inc. (acq 1991). Population Served: 156,000 Natl. Network: CTV, . News: 10 hrs wkly.
Key Personnel:
Scott Lund . . . . pres & gen mgr
Ron Driscoll . . . . gen sls mgr

CIII-TV-29— Analog Channel: 29. Analog Hrs: 5 AM-2 AM 370 kw vis, 55.5 kw aur. 685t/701g On air date: Jan 6, 1974. 81 Barber Greene Rd., Toronto, ON, M3C 2A2. Phone: (416) 446-5311. Fax: (416) 446-5447.E-mail: newstips@globaltv.com Web Site: www.canada.com. Licensee: Canwest Television L.P. Group Owner: Global Television Network
Key Personnel:
Bill Hunt. . . . . gen mgr

CHEX-TV-2— Analog Channel: 22. Analog Hrs: 20 550 kw vis. ant 440t TL: N43 57 15 W78 48 24 On air date: 1993. 500 Wentworth St. E., Unit 7, Oshawa, ON, L1H 3V9. Canada. Phone: (905) 434-2421. Fax: (905) 432-2315. Web Site: www.channel12.ca. Licensee: 591987 B.C. Ltd. Group Owner: Corus Entertainment Inc. (acq 3-24-2000; grpsl). Natl. Network: CBC, .
Key Personnel:
Kathleen McNair. . . . . VP & gen mgr & stn mgr

CBOFT— Analog Channel: 9. Digital Channel: 22. Analog Hrs: 17 128 kw vis, 12.8 kw aur. ant 1,394t/702g Box 3220, Stn C, Ottawa, ON, K1Y 1E4. Ottawa Broadcast Centre, 181 Queen St., Ottawa, ON K1P 1K9. Phone: (613) 288-6000. Phone: (613) 288-6750 (news). Fax: (613) 288-6770.E-mail: tjottawa-gatincau@radio-canada.ca Web Site: www.radio-canada.ca. Licensee: CBC. Natl. Network: Radio Canada, .
Key Personnel:
Richard Simoens . . . . gen mgr

CBOT— Analog Channel: 4. Digital Channel: 25. Analog Hrs: 17 100 kw vis, 10 kw aur. ant 1,310t/618g On air date: 1953. Box 3220, Stn C, Ottawa, ON, K1Y 1E4. Ottawa Broadcast Centre, 181 Queen St., Ottawa, ON K1P 1K9. Phone: (613) 288-6000. Fax: (613) 288-6423.E-mail: newsatsixottawa@cbc.ca Web Site: www.cbc.ca. Licensee: CBC. Natl. Network: CBC, .

CHRO-TV-43— Analog Channel: 43.282 kw vis. TL: N45 13 01 W75 33 51 On air date: 2002. A-Channel Ottawa, 87 George St., Ottawa, ON, K1N 9H7. Phone: (613) 789-0606. Fax: (613) 789-6590.E-mail: ottawa.promotions@Achannel.ca Web Site: www.achannel.ca/ottawa/. Licensee: CTV Ltd.
Key Personnel:
Peter Angione . . . . news dir

***CICO-TV-24—** Analog Channel: 24.427.6 kw vis. ant 1,092t/400g On air date: Oct 17, 1975. Box 200, sta Q, c/o TV Ontario, Toronto, ON, M4T 2T1. 2180 Yonge St., Toronto, ON M4S 2B9. Phone: (416) 484-2600. Fax: (416) 484-6285.E-mail: asktvo@tvo.org Web Site: www.tvo.org. Licensee: Ontario Educational Communications Authority.
Key Personnel:
Lisa DeWilde . . . . CEO

CIII-TV-6— Analog Channel: 6. Analog Hrs: 5 AM-2 AM 50 kw vis, 7.5 kw aur. 843t/750g On air date: Jan 6, 1974. 81 Barber Greene Rd., Toronto, ON, M3C 2A2. Phone: (416) 446-5311. Fax: (416) 446-5447.E-mail: newstips@globaltv.con Web Site: www.canada.com. Licensee: Canwest Television L.P. Group Owner: Global Television Network (acq 3-22-77).
Key Personnel:
Bill Hunt. . . . . gen mgr

CJOH-TV— Analog Channel: 13. Analog Hrs: 24 325 kw vis, 65 kw aur. ant 1,225t/533g TL: N45 30 11 W75 51 02 On air date: March 1961. CTV Ottawa, Box 5813, Merivale Depot, Ottawa, ON, K2C 3G6. 1500 Merivale Rd., Nepean, ON K2E 6Z5. Phone: (613) 224-1313. Fax: (613) 274-4215.E-mail: ctvottawa@ctv.ca Web Site: www.ottawa.ctv.ca. Licensee: CTV Television Inc. Group Owner: (group owner) Population Served: 2,000,000 Natl. Network: CTV, . Natl. Rep: Canadian Broadcast Sales,.
Key Personnel:
Louis Douville . . . . VP & gen mgr
Art Clarke. . . . . opns mgr
Dan Champagne . . . . sls VP & gen sls mgr
Brent Corbeil . . . . prom mgr
Scott Hannant . . . . news dir
Kim Closs . . . . traf mgr

CIII-TV-4— Analog Channel: 4.37 kw vis, 5.5 kw aur. 429t/477g On air date: June 27, 1988. 81 Barber Greene Rd., Toronto, ON, M3C 2A2.

Phone: (416) 446-5311. Fax: (416) 446-5447.E-mail: newstips@globaltv.com Web Site: www.canada.com. Licensee: Canwest Television L.P. Group Owner: Global Television Network
Key Personnel:
Bill Hunt . . . . gen mgr

CHRO-TV— Analog Channel: 5. Analog Hrs: 24 100 kw vis, 10 kw aur. 496t/520g TL: N45 50 02 W77 09 50 On air date: 1961. Box 1010, Pembroke, ON, K8A 6Y6. 87 George St., Ottawa, ON K1N 9H7. Phone: (613) 789-0606. Phone: (613) 735-1036. Fax: (613) 789-6590.E-mail: ottawa@Achannel.ca Web Site: www.Achannel.ca. Licensee: CTV Ltd. Group Owner: (group owner; acq 1997). Population Served: 1,000,000 News: 30 hrs wkly.
Key Personnel:
Greg Orr . . . . gen sls mgr
Peter Angione . . . . news dir
Robert Edgley . . . . chief of engrg

CHEX-TV— Analog Channel: 12. Analog Hrs: 20 185 kw vis, 18.5 kw aur. ant 772t/753g TL: N44 19 45 W78 18 03 On air date: 1955. 743 Monaghan Rd., Peterborough, ON, K9J 5K2. Phone: (705) 742-0451. Fax: (705) 742-7274.E-mail: newswatch@chextv.com Web Site: www.chextv.com. Licensee: 5191987 B.C. Ltd. Group Owner: Corus Entertainment Inc. (acq 3-24-2000; grpsl). Natl. Network: CBC, . Natl. Rep: TeleRep,.
Key Personnel:
John Cassaday . . . . CEO
Ron Johnston . . . . gen mgr & stn mgr
Paul Burke . . . . opns mgr

CIII-TV-27— Analog Channel: 27.2,535 kw vis, 380 aur. 913t/499g On air date: Oct 5, 1988. 81 Barber Greene Rd., Toronto, ON, M3C 2A2. Phone: (416) 446-5311. Fax: (416) 446-5447.E-mail: newstips@globaltv.com Web Site: www.canada.com. Licensee: Canwest Television L.P. Group Owner: Global Television Network.
Key Personnel:
Bill Hunt . . . . gen mgr

CKCO-TV-3— Analog Channel: 42. Analog Hrs: 24 846 kw vis, 84.6 kw aur. 994t/985g TL: N42 42 53 W82 08 12 On air date: November 1975. CTV Southwestern Ontario, Box 91026, c/o CKCO-TV, Kitchener, ON, N2G 4E9. Canada. Phone: (519) 578-1313. Fax: (519) 743-0730.E-mail: viewermail@southwesternontario.ctv.ca   Web   Site: www.southwesternontario.ctv.ca. Licensee: CKCO-TV Division of CTV Inc. Group Owner: CTV Inc. (acq 8-31-97). Population Served: 2,000,000 Natl. Network: CTV, .
Key Personnel:
Ivan Fecan . . . . CEO
Dennis A. Watson . . . . VP
Dennis Watson . . . . gen mgr
Dave MacNeill . . . . opns dir
Cameron Crassweller . . . . rgnl sls mgr
Andy LaBlanc . . . . news dir
Janet Taylor. . . prom mgr & adv mgr progmg mgr & pub affrs dir
Dave Melse . . . . chief of engrg
Rebroadcasts CKCO-TV Kitchener, on 100%.

CHBX-TV— Analog Channel: 2. Analog Hrs: 6 AM-2 AM 100 kw vis, 10 kw aur. 600t/500g On air date: September 1978. 119 East St., Sault Ste. Marie, ON, P6A 3C7. Phone: (705) 759-8232. Fax: (705) 759-7783.E-mail: saultnews@ctv.ca Web Site: www.ctv.ca. Licensee: CTV Television Inc. Group Owner: (group owner) Population Served: 104,000 Natl. Network: CTV, . Natl. Rep: Canadian Broadcast Sales,.
Key Personnel:
Scott Lund . . . . gen mgr

*CICO-TV-20— Analog Channel: 20. Analog Hrs: 24 5.9 kw vis, 590 w aur. 650t/515g On air date: October 1978. Box 200, stn Q, c/o TV Ontario, Toronto, ON, M4T 2T1. 2180 Yonge St., Toronto, ON M4S 2B9. Phone: (416) 484-2600. Fax: (416) 484-6285.E-mail: asktvo@tvo.org Web Site: www.tvo.org. Licensee: Ontario Educational Communications Authority. Group Owner: Baton Broadcasting Inc.
Key Personnel:
Lisa DeWilde . . . . CEO

CIII-TV-22— Analog Channel: 22. On air date: 1974. 81 Barber Greene Rd., Toronto, ON, M3C 2A2. Phone: (416) 446-5311. Fax: (416) 446-5447.E-mail: newstips@globaltv.com Web Site: www.canada.com /toronto/globaltv. Licensee: Canwest Television L.P. Group Owner: Global Television Network. Natl. Network: Global, . Natl. Rep: CanWest Media Sales,.
Key Personnel:
Bill Hunt . . . . gen mgr

CICI-TV— Analog Channel: 5.100 kw vis, 10 kw aur. 1,057t/975g On air date: Oct 25, 1953. 699 Frood Rd., Sudbury, ON, P3C 5A3. Phone: (705) 674-8301. Fax: (705) 674-2706.E-mail: newsforthenorth@ctv.ca

Web Site: www.ctv.ca. Licensee: CTV Television Inc. Group Owner: (group owner; acq 4-1-80). Natl. Network: CTV, . News staff: 15; News: 10 hrs wkly.
Key Personnel:
Scott Lund . . . . VP & gen mgr
John Eddy . . . . opns mgr

*CICO-TV-19— Analog Channel: 19. Analog Hrs: 24 186.5 kw vis, 18.7 kw aur. 564t/497g On air date: June 30, 1978. Box 200 Stn Q, c/o TV Ontario, Toronto, ON, M4T 2T1. 2180 Yonge St., Toronto, ON M4S 2B9. Phone: (416) 484-2600. Fax: (416) 484-6285.E-mail: asktvo@tvo.org Web Site: www.tvo.org. Licensee: Ontario Educational Communications Authority.
Key Personnel:
Lisa DeWilde . . . . CEO
Lee Robock . . . . gen mgr
Ray Newell . . . . opns dir

CHFD-TV— Analog Channel: 4. Analog Hrs: 18 56 kw vis, 10 kw aur. 1,202t/634g TL: N48 31 30 W89 06 50 On air date: 1972. 87 Hill St. N., Thunder Bay, ON, P7A 5V6. Phone: (807) 346-2600. Fax: (807) 345-9923.E-mail: tbtv@tbtv.com Web Site: tbtv.com. Licensee: Thunder Bay Electronics Ltd. Ownership: H.F. Dougall, Esq., 100%. Population Served: 160,000 Natl. Network: CTV, . Natl. Rep: CanWest Media Sales,. Wire Svc: CNW Broadcast
Key Personnel:
H.F. Dougall . . . . pres
D. Caron . . . . CFO
A. Snell . . . . opns dir
P. Bentz . . . . progmg dir

*CICO-TV-9— Analog Channel: 9. Analog Hrs: 24 32 kw vis, 3.2 kw aur. 780t/522g On air date: June 1978. Box 200 Stn Q, c/o TV Ontario, Toronto, ON, M4TT 2T1. 2180 Yonge St., Toronto, ON M4S 2B9. Phone: (416) 484-2600. Fax: (416) 484-6285.E-mail: asktvo@tvo.org Web Site: www.tvo.org. Licensee: Ontario Educational Communications Authority.
Key Personnel:
Lisa DeWilde . . . . CEO
Lee Robock . . . . COO & gen mgr
Ray Newell . . . . opns dir
Meg Pinto . . . . mktg dir

CKPR-TV— Analog Channel: 2. Analog Hrs: 18 56 kw vis, 10 kw aur. ant 1,202t/643g TL: N48 31 30 W89 06 50 On air date: 1954. 87 N. Hill St., Thunder Bay, ON, P7A 5V6. Phone: (807) 346-2600. Fax: (807) 345-9923.E-mail: tbt@tbtv.com Web Site: www.TbTv.com. Licensee: Thunder Bay Electronics Ltd. Ownership: H.F. Dougall, Esq., 100%. Population Served: 160,000 Natl. Network: CBC, . Natl. Rep: CanWest Media Sales,. News: 11 hrs wkly.
Key Personnel:
H.F. Dougall . . . . pres
D. Caron . . . . VP & gen mgr
A. Snell . . . . opns dir & news dir
P. Bentz . . . . progmg dir

CITO-TV— Analog Channel: 3. Analog Hrs: 6am - 2am 100 kw vis, 10 kw aur. 544t/499g Box 620, Timmins, ON, P4N 7G3. Canada. Phone: (705) 264-4211. Fax: (705) 264-3266.E-mail: newsforthenorth@ctv.ca Web Site: www.ctv.ca. Licensee: CTV Television Inc. Group Owner: CTV Inc. Population Served: 132,900 Natl. Network: CTV, .
Key Personnel:
Jason Laneville . . . . VP & sls dir

CBLT— Analog Channel: 5. Digital Channel: 20.77 kw vis, 7 kw aur. ant 444t/541g On air date: Sept 8, 1952. Box 500, Stn A, Toronto, ON, M5W 1E6. 205 Wellington St. W., Toronto, ON M5V 3G7. Phone: (416) 205-3311. Fax: (416) 205-7166. Web Site: www.cbc.ca. Licensee: CBC. Natl. Network: CBC, . News staff: 45; News: 10 hrs wkly.
Key Personnel:
Richard Stursberg . . . . exec VP

CFMT-TV— Analog Channel: 47. Analog Hrs: 24 807 kw vis, 80.7 kw aur. ant 1,600t/1,427g (Digital TV: ch 64; 15,000 w vis) On air date: Sept 3, 1979. Omni Television, 545 Lake Shore Blvd. W., Toronto, ON, M5V 1A3. Canada. Phone: (416) 260-0047. Fax: (416) 260-3621.E-mail: info@omnitv.ca Web Site: www.omnitv.ca. Licensee: Rogers Broadcasting Ltd.
Key Personnel:
Madeline Ziniak . . . . VP & stn mgr
Bill Hope . . . . chief of engrg

CFTO-TV— Analog Channel: 9. Digital Channel: 40. Analog Hrs: 24 325 kw vis, 162 kw aur. ant 1815t/1614g TL: N43 38 33 W79 23 15 On air date: Jan 1, 1961. 9 Channel 9 Ct., Scarborough, ON, M1S 4B5. Phone: (416) 332-5000. Fax: (416) 332-5022.E-mail: cftonews@ctv.ca Web Site: www.ctv.ca. Licensee: CTV Television Inc. Group Owner: (group owner) Natl. Network: CTV, .

Key Personnel:
Paul Rogers . . . . pres & sr VP

*CICA-TV— Analog Channel: 19. Analog Hrs: 24 1080 kw vis, 108 kw aur. 1,605t/1,686g (CP: 1288.2 kw vis) On air date: Sept 27, 1970. Box 200, Stn Q, c/o TV Ontario, Toronto, ON, M4T 2T1. 2180 Yonge St., Toronto, ON M4S 2B9. Phone: (416) 484-2600. Fax: (416) 484-6285.E-mail: asktvo@tvo.org Web Site: www.tvo.org. Licensee: Ontario Educational Communications Authority.
Key Personnel:
Lisa DeWilde . . . . CEO
Lee Robock . . . . COO & gen mgr
Ray Newell . . . . opns dir
Meg Pinto . . . . mktg dir

CIII-TV—(Paris, Analog Channel: 6. Analog Hrs: 5 AM-2 AM 100 kw vis, 15 kw aur. 1,037t/999g On air date: Jan 6, 1974. 81 Barber Greene Rd., Toronto, ON, M3C 2A2. Phone: (416) 446-5311. Fax: (416) 446-5447.E-mail: newstips@globaltv.com Web Site: www.globaltv.com. Licensee: Canwest Television L.P. Group Owner: Global Television Network (acq 3-22-77). Natl. Network: Global, .

CIII-TV-41— Analog Channel: 41. Digital Channel: 65.732 kw vis, 221 kw aur. ant 1,644t/1,779g TL: N43 38 33 W79 23 15 On air date: Oct 22, 1987. 81 Barber Greene Rd., Toronto, ON, M3C 2A2. Phone: (416) 446-5311. Fax: (416) 446-5447.E-mail: newstips@globaltv.com Web Site: www.canada.com. Licensee: Canwest Television L.P. Group Owner: Global Television Network

CITY-TV— Analog Channel: 57. Digital Channel: 53. Analog Hrs: 24 280 kw vis, 28 kw aur. 1,690t/1,780g On air date: Sept 28, 1972. 299 Queen St. W., Toronto, ON, M5V 2Z5. Phone: (416) 591-5757. Fax: (416) 340-7005. Web Site: www.citytv.com. Licensee: Rogers Broadcasting Ltd. Group Owner: CHUM Ltd. (acq 10-31-2007; grpsl). Population Served: 4,000,000 News: 25 hrs wkly.
Key Personnel:
Maria Hale . . . . pres & VP
John Morrison . . . . opns mgr & gen sls mgr
Dan Hamilton . . . . sls VP & prom dir
Susan Arthur . . . . mktg dir
Bev Nenson . . . . prom dir & prom mgr
Jenny Norush . . . . adv dir
Ellen Baine . . . . . . progmg VP & progmg dir film buyer
Stephen Hurlbut . . . . news dir
Sarah Crawford . . . . pub affrs dir
Bruce Cowan . . . . engrg dir

CJMT-TV— Analog Channel: 69. Digital Channel: 66. Analog Hrs: 24 500 kw vis. On air date: Sept 16, 2002. 545 Lake Shore Blvd. W., Toronto, ON, M5V 1A3. Phone: (416) 260-0060. Fax: (416) 260-3621.E-mail: info@omnitv.ca Web Site: www.omnitv.ca. Licensee: Rogers Broadcasting Ltd. Group Owner: (group owner).
Key Personnel:
Leslie Sole . . . . CEO
Madeline Ziniak . . . . gen mgr
Malcolm Dunlop . . . . mktg VP & progmg VP
Kelly Colasanti . . . . engrg VP

CKXT-TV— Analog Channel: 52. Digital Channel: 66. Analog Hrs: 24 Digital Hrs: 24 30 kw vis. ant 1,502t TL: N43 38 33 W79 23 15 On air date: Sept 19, 2003. SUN TV, 25 Ontario St., Toronto, ON, M5A 4L6. Phone: (416) 601-0010. Fax: (416) 601-0004. Web Site: suntv.canoe.ca. Licensee: Sun TV Co. Group Owner: (group owner). (acq 11-19-2004; C$46 million). News staff: 9.
Key Personnel:
Duane Parks . . . . gen sls mgr
Christina Fagan . . . . mktg mgr
Don Gaudet . . . . progmg dir
London, Ottawa.

CKCO-TV-2— Analog Channel: 2. Analog Hrs: 24 100 kw vis, 10 kw aur. 939t/789g TL: N44 56 41 W81 07 55 On air date: June 1, 1971. CTV Southwestern Ontario, Box 91026, c/o CKCO-TV, Kitchener, ON, N2G 4E9. Canada. Phone: (519) 578-1313. Fax: (519) 743-0730.E-mail: viewermail@southwesternontario.ctv.ca   Web   Site: www.southwesternontario.ctv.ca. Licensee: CKCO-TV Div. of CTV. Group Owner: CTV Inc. (acq 8-31-97). Population Served: 2,000,000 Natl. Network: CTV, .
Key Personnel:
Ivan Fecan . . . . CEO
Dennis Watson. . . . . VP & gen mgr
Dave MacNeill . . . . opns dir
Cameron Crassweller . . . . rgnl sls mgr
Andy LaBlanc. . . . . news dir
Janet Taylor. . . prom mgr & adv mgr progmg mgr & pub affrs dir
Dave Melse . . . . chief of engrg
Rebroadcasts CKCO-TV Kitchener, ON 100%..

*CBEFT— Analog Channel: 54. Analog Hrs: 24 62.7 kw vis, 6.3 kw aur. 683g On air date: July 16, 1976. 825 Riverside W., Windsor, ON,

N9A 5K9. Canada. Box 1609, Windsor, ON N9A 1K7.Canada Phone: (519) 255-3411. Fax: (519) 255-3412. Licensee: Societe Radio Canada. Natl. Network: Radio Canada, . News staff: one.
Key Personnel:
Benoit Quenneville . . . . stn mgr

CBET— Analog Channel: 9. Analog Hrs: 24 325 kw vis, 32.5 kw aur. ant 575t/650g TL: N42 18 59 W83 02 58 On air date: Sept 16, 1954. 825 Riverside Dr. W., Windsor, ON, N9A 5K9. Phone: (519) 255-3411. Fax: (519) 255-3412. Web Site: cbc.ca/windsor. Licensee: Canadian Broadcasting Corp. (acq 7-23-75). Natl. Network: CBC, . Natl. Rep: Canadian Broadcast Sales,. News staff: 18; News: 5 hrs wkly.
Key Personnel:
Gary Cunliffe . . . . opns mgr

CHWI-TV— Analog Channel: 16.183 kw vis. On air date: Oct 18, 1993. 300 Ouellette Ave., Suite 200, Windsor, ON, N9A 7B4. Phone: (519) 977-7432. Fax: (519) 977-0564. Web Site: www.atv.ca/windsor. Licensee: CTV Ltd. Group Owner: CHUM Ltd. (acq 1997). Natl. Network: CTV, .
Key Personnel:
Don Mumford . . . . gen mgr
Tom Fitz-Gerald . . . . gen sls mgr
Cal Johnstone . . . . news dir

*CICO-TV-32— Analog Channel: 32. Analog Hrs: 24 180 kw vis, 18 kw aur. 703t/703g On air date: July 1976. Box 200, Stn Q, c/o TV Ontario, Toronto, ON, M4T 2T1. 2180 Yonge St., Toronto, ON M4S 2B9. Phone: (416) 484-2600. Fax: (416) 484-6285.E-mail: asktvo@tvo.org Web Site: www.tvo.org. Licensee: Ontario Educational Communication Authority.
Key Personnel:
Lisa DeWilde . . . . CEO
Lee Robock . . . . gen mgr
Ray Newell . . . . opns dir
Meg Pinto . . . . mktg dir

CKNX-TV— Analog Channel: 8.260 kw vis, 26 kw aur. ant 793t/623g On air date: 1955. 215 Carling Terr., Wingham, ON, N0G 2W0. Phone: (519) 357-4438. Fax: (519) 357-4398. Web Site: www.atv.ca/wingham. Licensee: CTV Ltd. Group Owner: CHUM Ltd. (acq 1997). Population Served: 300,000
Key Personnel:
Don Mumford . . . . gen mgr & progmg mgr
Tom Fitz-Gerald . . . . gen sls mgr
Cal Johnstone . . . . news dir

Prince Edward Island

CBCT— Analog Channel: 13.320 kw vis, 30 kw aur. 918t/720g On air date: 1968. Box 2230, Charlottetown, PE, C1A 8B9. 430 University Ave., Charlottetown, PE C1A 4N6.Canada Phone: (902) 629-6400. Fax: (902) 629-6518. Web Site: www.cbct.ca/pei. Licensee: CBC. Ownership: CBC (Crown Corp). Natl. Network: CBC, .
Key Personnel:
Craig Mackie . . . . gen mgr & stn mgr

CKCW-TV-1— Analog Channel: 8.29 kw vis, 2.9 aur. ant 489t/250g 191 Halifax St., Moncton, NB, E1C 9R7. Canada. Phone: (506) 857-2600. Fax:(506) 857-2617.E-mail: ckcw@ctv.ca Web Site: www.ctv.ca. Licensee: CTV Television Inc. Group Owner: CTV Inc. (acq 11-1-97). Natl. Network: CTV, .
Key Personnel:
Ivan Fecan . . . . CEO
Rick Brace . . . . pres
Robin Fillingham . . . . CFO
Elaine Ali . . . . exec VP
Mike Elgie . . . . VP & gen mgr
Brian Lewis . . . . stn mgr & gen sls mgr adv mgr
John Silver . . . . opns mgr
Renee Fournier . . . . prom dir & progmg mgr
Jane Hefler. . . . . progmg dir
Jay Witherbee . . . . news dir & pub affrs dir
Carson McDavid . . . . chief of engrg
Paul Street . . . . rsch dir
Sharron White. . . . . traf mgr
Steve Murphy . . . . news cmtr
Paul Hollingsworth. . . . . sports cmtr
Peter Coade . . . . weather dir
Rebroadcasts CKCW-TV Moncton, NB 100%.

CKCW-TV-2— Analog Channel: 5.2.5 kw vis, 1.3 kw aur. ant 341t/356g On air date: November 1982. 191 Halifax St., Moncton, NB,

E1C 9R7. Canada. Phone: (506) 857-2600. Fax: (506) 857-2617.E-mail: ckcw@ctv.ca Web Site: www.ctv.ca. Licensee: CTV Television Inc. Group Owner: CTV Inc. (acq 11-1-97). Population Served: 100,000 Natl. Network: CTV, .
Key Personnel:
Ivan Fecan . . . . CEO
Rick Brace . . . . pres
Robin Fillingham . . . . CFO
Elaine Ali . . . . exec VP
Mike Elgie . . . . VP & gen mgr
Brian Lewis . . . . stn mgr & gen sls mgr adv mgr
John Silver . . . . opns dir & opns mgr
Renee Fournier . . . . prom dir & progmg mgr
Jay Witherbee . . . . news dir & pub affrs dir
Carson McDavid . . . . chief of engrg
Paul Street . . . . rsch dir
Sharron White . . . . traf mgr
Steve Murphy . . . . news cmtr
Paul Hollingsworth . . . . sports cmtr
Peter Coade . . . . weather dir
Rebroadcasts CKCW-TV Moncton, NB 100%.

Quebec

*CIVP-TV— Analog Channel: 12. Analog Hrs: 24 62 kw vis. 2,001t TL: N49 23 28 W67 28 18 On air date: Nov 15, 1982. 1000 Fullum, Montreal, PQ, H2K 3L7. Phone: (514) 521-2424. Fax: (514) 873-2601. Fax: (514) 873-4413.E-mail: info@telequebec.qc.ca Web Site: www.telequebec.tv. Licensee: Societe de telediffusion du Quebec. Group Owner: Tele-Quebec.
Key Personnel:
Michele Fortim . . . . pres
Luc Chartier . . . . gen mgr

CKRN-TV-3— Analog Channel: 3.35 kw vis, 3.5 kw aur. 171 A Jean-Proulx St., Gatineau, PQ, J8Z 1W5. Canada. Phone: (819) 770-1040. Fax: (819) 770-0272. Web Site: www.rncmedia.ca. Licensee: RNC MEDIA Inc. Group Owner: (group owner). Natl. Network: Radio Canada, .
Key Personnel:
Pierre R. Brosseau . . . . pres
Michael Noiseux. . . . . gen mgr
Rebroadcasts CKRN-TV Rouyn-Noranda.

*CIVP-TV— Analog Channel: 23. Analog Hrs: 24 8.65 kw vis. TL: N45 55 29 W77 04 23 1000, rue Fullum, Montreal, PQ, H2K 3L7. Phone: (514) 521-2424. Fax: (514) 873-2601. Fax: (514) 864-4222.E-mail: info@telequebec.tv Web Site: www.telequebec.tv. Licensee: Societe de telediffusion du Quebec. Group Owner: Tele-Quebec.
Key Personnel:
Michele Fortim . . . . pres
Luc Chartier . . . . gen mgr

CBJET— Analog Channel: 58.10 kw vis. PO Box 6000, Montreal, PQ, H3C 3A8. Phone: (514) 597-6000. Fax: (514) 597-4537. Web Site: www.cbc.ca/montreal. Licensee: CBC. Natl. Network: CBC, .

*CIVV-TV— Analog Channel: 8. Analog Hrs: 24 278.1 kw vis, 27.8 kw aur. 1,948t/570g TL: N48 36 04 W70 49 46 On air date: November 1982. 1000 Fullum, Montreal, PQ, H2K 3L7. Phone: (514) 521-2424. Fax: (514) 873-2601. Fax: (514) 864-4222.E-mail: info@telequebec.qc.ca Web Site: www.telequebec.tv. Licensee: Societe de telediffusion du Quebec. Group Owner: Tele-Quebec. Natl. Network: TeleFutura (Spanish), .
Key Personnel:
Michele Fortim . . . . pres
Luc Chartier . . . . gen mgr

CJPM-TV— Analog Channel: 6.61 kw vis, 6.7 kw aur. ant 440t/190g On air date: Apr 14, 1963. One Mont Ste-Claire St, Saguenay, PQ, G7H 5G3. Phone: (418) 549-2576. Fax: (418) 549-1130.E-mail: cjpm@saglac.qc.ca Web Site: www.reseau.tva.ca. Licensee: Groupe TVA Inc. Group Owner: (group owner). Natl. Network: TVA, . News: 6 hrs wkly.

Key Personnel:
Pierre Dion . . . . pres
Michel Roberge . . . . prom dir
Roger Jobin . . . . gen mgr & sls dir & progmg dir
Myriam Donaldson. . . . . news dir

CFGS-TV— Analog Channel: 34.117 kw vis. On air date: Sept 7, 1986. 171 A Jean-Proulx St., Gatineau, PQ, J8Z 1W5. Phone: (819) 770-1040. Fax: (819) 770-0272.E-mail: tqs@rncmedia.ca Web Site: www.rncmedia.ca. Licensee: RNC MEDIA Inc. Group Owner: (group owner). Natl. Network: Quatre Saisons, . Natl. Rep: Canadian Broadcast Sales,.
Key Personnel:
Pierre R. Brosseau . . . . CEO & pres
Robert H. Parent . . . . gen mgr
Michel Noiseux . . . . opns dir

CHOT-TV— Analog Channel: 40.498 kw vis. 1,184t On air date: Oct 30, 1978. 171 A Jean-Proulx St., Gatineau, PQ, J8Z 1W5. Phone: (819) 770-1040. Fax: (819) 770-1490 (news).E-mail: chot@radionord.com Web Site: www.radionord.com. Licensee: RNC MEDIA Inc. Group Owner: (group owner). Natl. Network: TVA, .
Key Personnel:
Pierre R. Brosseau . . . . CEO & pres
Robert H. Parent . . . . gen mgr
Michel Noiseux . . . . opns dir
Benoit Pilote . . . . sls dir
Eric Brousseau. . . . . prom dir
Daniele Young . . . . news dir

*CIVO-TV— Analog Channel: 30.1327.4 kw vis, 265.5 kw aur. 1,184t/465g On air date: Aug 14, 1977. 1000 Fullum, Montreal, PQ, H2K 3L7. Phone: (514) 521-2424. Fax: (514) 873-2601. Fax: (514) 873-4413.E-mail: info@telequebec.qc.ca Web Site: www.telequebec.tv. Licensee: Societe de telediffusion du Quebec. Group Owner: Tele-Quebec.
Key Personnel:
Luc Chartier . . . . gen mgr

CBIMT— Analog Channel: 12.3.9 kw vis. 750t/235g On air date: Nov 9, 1964. PO Box 6000, Montreal, PQ, H3C 3A8. Phone: (514) 597-6000. Fax: (514) 597-4537. Web Site: www.cbc.ca. Licensee: CBC. Natl. Network: Radio Canada, .

CFRS-TV— Analog Channel: 4. Analog Hrs: 18 100 kw vis, 10 kw aur. 1,941t/460g On air date: Sept 1, 1986. 2303 rue Sir Wilfred Laurier, Jonquiere, PQ, G7X 5Z2. Phone: (418) 542-4551. Fax: (418) 542-7217. Fax: (418) 542-8319. Web Site: www.cgotv.ca. Licensee: TQS Inc. (acq 6-26-2008; grpsl). Population Served: 300,000 Natl. Network: Quatre Saisons, .
Key Personnel:
Martin Gagnon . . . . gen mgr
Michel Goulet . . . . opns dir
Ammie Tremblay . . . . sls dir
Annie Tremblay . . . . mktg dir

CBVT-2— Analog Channel: 3.15.4 kw vis, 1.54 kw aur. PO Box 6000, 1400 boul. Rene Levesque E., Montreal, PQ, H3C 3A8. Phone: (514) 597-6000. Fax: (514) 597-6510. Web Site: www.cbc.ca. Licensee: CBC. Natl. Network: Radio Canada, .

CBVD-TV— Analog Channel: 5.9.35 kw vis, 4.675 kw aur. CBC Television, 1400 Rene Levesque E., Montreal, PQ, H2L 2M2. Phone: (514) 597-6000. Phone: (514) 597-4537. Web Site: montreal.cbc.ca. Licensee: CBC. Natl. Network: CBC, .
Rebroadcasts CBMT(TV) Montreal 100%.

CBFT-2— Analog Channel: 3.28.2 kw vis, 2.8 kw aur. 509t/400g On air date: Dec 3, 1962. Box 6000, Montreal, PQ, H3C 3A8. Phone: (514) 597-6000. Fax: (514) 597-6354. Web Site: www.cbc.ca. Licensee: Societe Radio Canada. Natl. Network: Radio Canada, .

CBFT— Analog Channel: 2. Digital Channel: 19.100 kw vis, 10 kw aur. ant 905t/252g On air date: 1952. PO Box 6000, 1400 boul. Rene Levesque E., Montreal, PQ, H3C 3A8. Phone: (514) 597-6000. Phone: (514) 597-4282. Fax: (514) 597-4316.E-mail: auditoire@radio-canada.ca Web Site: radio-canada.ca. Licensee: CBC. Ownership: CBC. Natl. Network: Radio Canada, .
Key Personnel:
Daniel Gourd . . . . VP
Richard Portelance . . . . sls dir & gen sls mgr
Loren Thibeault . . . . natl sls mgr
Alain Messier . . . . mktg dir
Danielle Rivard . . . . mktg mgr
Andre Beau det . . . . adv dir
Mario Clement . . . . progmg dir

CBMT— Analog Channel: 6. Digital Channel: 20.100 kw vis, 15 kw aur. ant 820t/167g On air date: 1954. Box 6000, Montreal, ON, H3C

3A8. Canada. Phone: (514) 597-6000. Fax: (514) 597-6354. Web Site: www.cbc.ca/montreal. Licensee: CBC. Natl. Network: CBC, .

CFCF-TV— Analog Channel: 12. Digital Channel: 7.325 kw vis, 33 kw aur. 1,032t/294g On air date: Jan 20, 1961. CTV Television Inc., 1205 Papineau Ave., Montreal, PQ, H2K 4R2. Phone: (514) 273-6311. Fax: (514) 276-9399.E-mail: cfcfpromo@ctv.ca Web Site: www.cfcf.ca. Licensee: CTV Television Inc. Group Owner: (group owner; (acq 9-21-01; C$141.5 million). Natl. Network: CTV, .
Key Personnel:
Mike Piperni . . . . news dir

CFJP-TV— Analog Channel: 35. Digital Channel: 42.697 kw vis, 70 kw aur. ant 900t/335g TL: N45 35 20 W73 35 32 On air date: Sept 7, 1986. 612 Rue St-Jacques Bur 100, Montreal, PQ, H3C 5R1. Phone: (514) 390-6035. Fax: (514) 390-0773.E-mail: tvpublic@tqs.ca Web Site: www.tqs.ca. Licensee: TQS Inc. (acq 6-26-2008; grpsl). News staff: 51; News: 12 hrs wkly.
Key Personnel:
Francois Birtz . . . . opns dir
Annie Villeneuve . . . . dev dir
Louis Trepanier . . . . progmg VP

CFTM-TV— Analog Channel: 10. Digital Channel: 59.365 kw vis, 65 kw aur. ant 325t/1,068g Box 170, Stn C, Montreal, PQ, H2L 4P6. Phone: (514) 790-0461. Phone: (514) 526-9251. Fax: (514) 598-6082. Web Site: www.tva.canoe.com. Licensee: Groupe TVA Inc. Natl. Network: TVA, .
Key Personnel:
Pierre Viem . . . . gen mgr

***CFTU-TV—** Analog Channel: 29. Analog Hrs: 24 10 kw vis, 1 kw aur. 604t/305g On air date: Aug 20, 1985. 4750 Ave. Henri-Julien, Bureau 100, local 0058, Montreal, PQ, H2T 3E4. Phone: (514) 841-2626. Fax: (514) 284-9363.E-mail: info@canal.qc.ca Web Site: www.canal.qc.ca. Licensee: Corp. pour l'Avancement de Nouvelles Applications des Langages. (acq 5-86).
Key Personnel:
Michel Umbriaco . . . . pres
Guy Massicotte . . . . VP
Sylvie Godbout. . . . . chmn & gen mgr

***CIVM-TV—** Analog Channel: 17. Digital Channel: 27. Analog Hrs: 7:00am - 1:30am 889.5 kw vis. On air date: Jan 19, 1975. 1000, rue Fullum, Fort Myers, PQ, H2K 3L7. Phone: (514) 521-2424. Fax: (514) 873-2601. Fax: (514) 873-4413.E-mail: info@telequebec.tv Web Site: www.telequebec.tv. Licensee: Societe de telediffusion du Quebec. Population Served: 7,000,000 News staff: 25; News: 5 hrs wkly.

CJNT-TV— Analog Channel: 62.11 kw vis. On air date: 1997. 1600 Blvd., De Maisonneuve E., 9th Fl., Montreal, PQ, H2L 4P2. Phone: (514) 522-4150. Fax: (514) 522-9579. Web Site: www.cahmontreal.com. Licensee: Canwest Television L.P. Group Owner: CanWest Global Communications Corp. (acq 11-29-2000).
Key Personnel:
Isabella Federigi. . . . . gen mgr

CBVT— Analog Channel: 11. Digital Channel: 12.128.8 kw vis, 12.8 kw aur. ant 657t/541g On air date: 1964. 888 Saint-Jean St., Quebec, PQ, G1R 5H6. Phone: (418) 656-8500. Fax: (418) 656-8505. Web Site: www.cbc.ca. Licensee: CBC. Natl. Network: Radio Canada, .
Key Personnel:
Louise Cordeau . . . . gen mgr

CFAP-TV— Analog Channel: 2. Analog Hrs: 6:00 AM-2:30 AM 70 kw vis, 7 kw aur. 551t/501g TL: N46 48 27 W71 13 02 On air date: Sept 4, 1989. 330 St.-Vallier St. East, Quebec City, PQ, G1K 9C5. Phone: (418) 624-2222. Fax: (418) 624-3099. Fax: (418) 624-0162.E-mail: www@tqs.ca Web Site: www.tqs.ca. Licensee: TQS Inc. Group Owner: Cogeco Radio-Television Inc. (acq 6-26-2008; grpsl). Natl. Network: Quatre Saisons, . News staff: 29; News: 10 hrs wkly.
Key Personnel:
Jean Simard. . . . . opns dir & chief of opns engrg dir
Joel Godin . . . . sls dir & mktg dir
Renaud Francoeur . . . . . . gen mgr & progmg dir & news dir
Pierre Martineau . . . . pub affrs dir
Denise Delisle. engrg mgr
Rebroadcasts CFJP-TV Montreal.

CFCM-TV— Analog Channel: 4. Digital Channel: 7. Analog Hrs: 5:00am - 2:00am 100 kw vis, 15 kw aur. 460t/407g On air date: July 17, 1954. 1000 Ave. Myrand, Quebec City, PQ, G1V 2W3. Canada. Phone: (418) 688-9330. Fax: (418) 681-4239. Web Site: www.tva.ca. Licensee: Tele-Metropole Inc. Group Owner: Groupe TVA Inc.

***CIVQ-TV—** Analog Channel: 15.1,298 kw vis, 259 kw aur. 628t/576g TL: N46 48 27 W71 13 02 On air date: Jan 19, 1975. 1000 Fullum, Montreal, PQ, H2K 3L7. Phone: (514) 521-2424. Fax: (514) 873-2601. Fax: (514) 873-4413.E-mail: info@telequebec.qc.ca Web Site: www.telequebec.tv. Licensee: Societe de telediffusion du Quebec Group Owner: Tele-Quebec.
Key Personnel:
Michele Fortim . . . . pres
Luc Chartier . . . . gen mgr

CKMI-TV— Analog Channel: 20.20.2 kw vis, 3.77 kw aur. ant 460t/407g On air date: 1957. 1000 Myrand Ave., Ste.-Foy, PQ, G1V 2W3. 1600 Boul.de Maisonneuve East, Montreal, PQ H2L 4P2.Canada Phone: (418) 682-2020. Phone: (514) 521-4323. Fax: (418) 682-2620. Fax: (514) 521-2829.E-mail: globalnews.que@globaltv.ca Web Site: www.globaltv.ca. Licensee: Canwest Television GP Inc. (the general partner) and Canwest Media Inc. (the limited partner), carrying on business as Canwest Television L.P. (acq 1997).
Key Personnel:
Marven Rogers . . . . gen mgr
Michel Yeos . . . . opns dir & opns mgr
Suzanne Lapalme . . . . sls dir
Masikc Vergcilles . . . . prom mgr
Karen Macdonald . . . . news dir
Michel Paquet. . . . . engrg mgr

CFER-TV— Analog Channel: 11.325 kw vis, 32.5 kw aur. 1,420t/289g On air date: June 4, 1978. 465 Boul. Ste.-Anne, Rimouski, PQ, G5M 1G1. Canada. Phone: (418) 722-6011. Fax: (418) 724-7810. Fax: (418) 723-0857. Web Site: www.tva.canoe.com. Licensee: Tele-Metropole Inc. Group Owner: Groupe TVA Inc. Natl. Network: TVA, .

***CIVB-TV—** Analog Channel: 22. Analog Hrs: 24 55 kw vis. 300t TL: N48 28 02 W68 12 53 On air date: Oct 15, 1981. 1000 Fullum, Montreal, PQ, H2K 3L7. Phone: (514) 521-2424. Fax: (514) 873-2601. Fax: (514) 873-4413.E-mail: info@telequebec.qc.ca Web Site: www.telequebec.tv. Licensee: Societe de telediffusion du Quebec. Group Owner: Tele-Quebec.
Key Personnel:
Michele Fortim . . . . pres
Luc Chartier . . . . gen mgr

CJBR-TV— Analog Channel: 2.100 kw vis, 10 kw aur. 1,341t/204g On air date: November 1954. 273 St. Jeans Baptiste W., Rimouski, PQ, G5L 4J8. Phone: (418) 723-2217. Phone: (418) 723-4730. Fax: (418) 743-6126. Licensee: CBC. Natl. Network: CBC, .
Key Personnel:
Bernard Lepage. . . . . gen mgr

CFTF-TV— Analog Channel: 29.50 kw vis. ant 1,086t TL: N47 35 03 W69 22 10 On air date: 1988. 103 des Equipements Parc Industriel, Rivieres-du-Loup, PQ, G5R 5W7. 298 Boulevard Armand-Theriault, Bureau 100, Riviere-du-Loup, PQ G5R 4C2. Phone: (418) 862-2909. Fax: (418) 862-8147.E-mail: cftf@qc.aira.com Licensee: Television MBS Inc. Group Owner: Tele Inter-Rives Ltee. Population Served: 600,000
Key Personnel:
Marc Simard. . . . . pres
Catherine Simard . . . . gen mgr & dev VP mktg VP
Michel Belanger . . . . opns VP & progmg VP
Ginette Dumant . . . . sls VP & rgnl sls mgr
Yves Belanger . . . . sls dir
Nancy Fortin . . . . prom VP
Germain Gelinas . . . . engrg VP

CIMT-TV— Analog Channel: 9. Analog Hrs: 24 275.6 kw vis, 2.7 kw aur. ant 1,178t/200g TL: N47 35 03 W69 22 10 On air date: Sept 18, 1978. 15 Rue de la Chute, Riviere-du-Loup, PQ, G5R 5B7. Phone: (418) 867-1341. Fax: (418) 867-4710. Web Site: www.cimt.ca. Licensee: Tele Inter-Rives Ltee. Group Owner: (group owner). Natl. Network: TVA, .

CKRT-TV— Analog Channel: 7. Analog Hrs: 24 49 kw vis, 4.9 kw aur. ant 1,156t/200g TL: N47 35 03 W69 22 10 On air date: 1961. 15 Rue de la Chute, Riviere-du-Loup, PQ, G5R 5B7. Phone: (418) 867-1341. Fax: (418) 867-4710. Licensee: CKRT-TV Ltee. Group Owner: Tele Inter-Rives Ltee. Natl. Network: CBC, .
Key Personnel:
Germain Gelinas . . . . pres

***CIVA-TV—** Analog Channel: 8. Analog Hrs: 24 299.2 kw vis, 28.6 kw aur. On air date: Jan 18, 1980. 1000 Fullum, Montreal, PQ, H2K 3L7. Phone: (514) 521-2424. Fax: (514) 873-2601. Fax: (514) 864-4222.E-mail: info@telequebec.qc.ca Web Site: www.telequebec.tv. Licensee: Societe de telediffusion du Quebec. Group Owner: Tele-Quebec.
Key Personnel:
Michele Fortim . . . . pres
Luc Chartier . . . . gen mgr

CKRN-TV— Analog Channel: 4. Analog Hrs: 24 115 kw vis, 11.5 kw aur. 670g On air date: 1957. 380 Murdoch, Rouyn-Noranda, PQ, J9X 1G5. Phone: (819) 762-0741. Fax: (819) 762-2466. Web Site: www.radionord.com. Licensee: RNC MEDIA Inc. Group Owner: (group owner). Natl. Network: Radio Canada, .
Key Personnel:
Pierre R. Brosseau . . . . pres
Andre Houle . . . . gen mgr
Denis Chenier. opns dir
Nancy Desches . . . . sls dir
Robert Ashby. . . . . news dir
Gerald Landry . . . . chief of engrg

CFER-TV-2— Analog Channel: 5.100 kw vis, 10 kw aur. 706t/495g On air date: Nov 13, 1981. c/o CFER-TV, 465 Boul. Ste. Anne, Rimouski, PQ, G5M 1G1. Canada. Phone: (418) 722-6011. Fax: (418) 724-7810. Fax: (418) 723-0854 (news). Web Site: www.tva.canoe.com. Licensee: Groupe TVA Inc. Group Owner: (group owner). Natl. Network: TVA, .

***CIVG-TV—** Analog Channel: 9. Analog Hrs: 16 246 kw vis, 49.2 kw aur. 943t/500g On air date: Nov 5, 1982. c/o Tele-Quebec, 1000 Fullum, Montreal, PQ, H2K 3L7. Phone: (514) 521-2424. Fax: (514) 873-2601. Fax: (514) 873-7464. Web Site: www.telequebec.tv. Licensee: Societe de telediffusion du Quebec. Group Owner: Tele-Quebec.
Key Personnel:
Michele Fortim . . . . pres
Luc Chartier . . . . gen mgr

CFKS-TV— Analog Channel: 30.92.3 kw vis. 2,011t TL: N45 18 43 W72 14 32 On air date: September 1986. 3720 Boul. Industrial, Sherbrooke, PQ, J1L 1Z9. Canada. Phone: (819) 565-9999. Fax: (819) 822-4205. Web Site: www.cogeco.com. Licensee: TQS Inc. Group Owner: Cogeco Inc. (acq 6-26-2008; grpsl). Natl. Network: Quatre Saisons, .
Key Personnel:
Sophie Ferron . . . . gen mgr
Robert PeRusse . . . . dev dir

CHLT-TV— Analog Channel: 7. Analog Hrs: 5:30am - 2:00am 325 kw vis, 32.5 kw aur. ant 1,920t/106g On air date: Aug 12, 1956. 3330 Ouest Rue King, Sherbrooke, PQ, J1L 1C9. Phone: (819) 565-7777. Fax: (819) 565-4650. Fax: (819) 563-0141. Licensee: Tele-Metropole Inc. Group Owner: Groupe TVA Inc. (acq 7-9-90). Natl. Network: TVA, .
Key Personnel:
Serge Matte . . . . gen mgr

***CIVS-TV—** Analog Channel: 24. Analog Hrs: 24 475 kw vis, 47.5 kw aur. 2,000t/90g On air date: Feb 26, 1982. 1000 Fullum, Montreal, PQ, H2K 3L7. Phone: (514) 521-2424. Fax: (514) 873-2601. Fax: (514) 864-4222.E-mail: info@telequebec.qc.ca Web Site: www.telequebec.tv. Licensee: Societe de telediffusion du Quebec. Group Owner: Tele-Quebec.
Key Personnel:
Michele Fortim . . . . pres
Luc Chartier . . . . gen mgr

CKSH-TV— Analog Channel: 9.325 kw vis, 56 kw aur. On air date: Sept 1, 1974. 3720 Boul. Industrial, Suite 200, Sherbrooke, PQ, J1L 1Z9. Canada. Phone: (819) 565-9999. Fax: (819) 822-4205. Web Site: www.radio-canada.ca. Licensee: Canadian Broadcasting Corp. Group Owner: Cogeco Inc. (acq 6-26-2008; grpsl). Natl. Network: CBC, .

CBFST-2— Analog Channel: 12.6.9 kw vis, 1.416 kw aur. PO Box 6000, Montreal, PQ, H3C 3A8. Phone: (514) 597-6000. Fax: (514) 597-4537. Web Site: www.cbc.ca. Licensee: CBC. Natl. Network: Radio Canada, .

CFKM-TV— Analog Channel: 16.169.5 kw vis,. ant 1,073t/1,071g TL: N46 29 27 W72 39 00 On air date: Sept 7, 1986. Box 277, Trois-Rivieres, PQ, G9A 5G3. Canada. Phone: (819) 377-6053. Fax: (819) 377-5442. Licensee: TQS Inc. Group Owner: Cogeco Inc. (acq 6-26-2008; grpsl). Natl. Network: Quatre Saisons, .
Key Personnel:
Michel Cloutier . . . . dev dir

CHEM-TV— Analog Channel: 8.325 kw vis, 32.5 kw aur. 946t/698g On air date: Aug 29, 1976. 3625 boul. Chanoine-Moreau, Trois-Rivieres, PQ, G8Y 5N6. Phone: (819) 376-8880. Fax: (819) 376-2906. Licensee: Tele-Metropole Inc. Group Owner: Groupe TVA Inc. (acq 7-9-90). Natl. Network: TVA, .
Key Personnel:
Richard Renault . . . . gen mgr & stn mgr
Gerald Trives. . . . . chief of engrg

***CIVC-TV—** Analog Channel: 45. Analog Hrs: 16 651.8 kw vis. ant 1,575t/1,000g TL: N46 29 27 W72 39 00 On air date: Oct 7, 1981. c/o Tele-Quebec, 1000 Fullum, Montreal, PQ, H2K 3L7. Phone: (514) 521-2424. Fax: (514) 873-2601. Fax: (514) 864-4222.E-mail:

info@telequebec.ca Web Site: www.telequebec.tv. Licensee: Societe de telediffusion du Quebec. Group Owner: Tele-Quebec.
Key Personnel:
Luc Chartier . . . pres & gen mgr

CKTM-TV— Analog Channel: 13. Analog Hrs: 6:00am - 2:00am 164.4 kw vis, 65 kw aur. ant 1,660t/1,085g TL: N46 29 27 W72 39 00 On air date: Apr 15, 1958. 4141 boul.St-Jean, Trois-Rivieres, PQ, G9B 2M8. Canada. Phone: (819) 377-4413. Fax: (819) 377-5239.E-mail: paul_rousseau@radiocanada.ca Licensee: Canadian Broadcasting Corp. Group Owner: Cogeco Inc. (acq 6-26-2008; grpsl). Natl. Network: CBC, .
Key Personnel:
Hubert T. Lacroix . . . pres

CFVS-TV— Analog Channel: 25. Digital Channel: 5. Analog Hrs: 24 On air date: Jan 19, 19P7. 1729 3ieme Ave., Val d'Or, PQ, J9P 1W3. Phone: (819) 825-0010. Fax: (819) 825-7313. Web Site: www.radionord.com. Licensee: RNC MEDIA Inc. Group Owner: (group owner)
Key Personnel:
Pierre R. Brosseau . . . pres
Andre Houle . . . gen mgr & gen sls mgr
Nancy Deschenes . . . stn mgr & sls dir
Dennis Chenier . . . opns mgr & prom dir progmg dir
Robert H. Ashey . . . news dir
Gerald Landry . . . chief of engrg

Saskatchewan

CBKFT-9— Analog Channel: 26.11.4 kw vis, 1.1 kw aur. ant 413t/416g On air date: Mar 15, 1980. Box 540, Regina, SK, S4P 4A1. Phone: (306) 347-9540. Fax: (306) 347-9493. Licensee: Societe Radio Canada. Natl. Network: Radio Canada, .
Key Personnel:
David Kyle . . . gen mgr & opns dir
Steve Tomchuck . . . chief of engrg

CKCK-TV-1— Analog Channel: 12. Analog Hrs: 24 84.8 kw vis, 8.5 kw aur. 532t/581g TL: N49 26 16 W103 47 53 On air date: Dec 15, 1962. c/o CKCK-TV, Box 2000, One Hwy. 1 East, Regina, SK, S4P 3E5. Phone: (306) 569-2000. Fax: (306) 522-0090.E-mail: ckck@ctv.ca Web Site: www.ctv.ca. Licensee: CTV Television Inc. Group Owner: (group owner) Natl. Network: CTV, .
Key Personnel:
Dennis Dunlop . . . gen mgr

CBCP-TV-2— Analog Channel: 2.2.45 kw vis, 240 w aur. ant 395g On air date: Oct 1, 1979. c/o CBKT, 2440 Broad St., Regina, SK, S4P 4A1. Phone: (306) 347-9540. Fax: (306) 347-9748. Web Site: www.cbc.ca/sask. Licensee: CBC. Natl. Network: CBC, .
Key Personnel:
Derek Dalton . . . VP
David Kyle . . . opns mgr
Rebroadcasts CBKT(TV) Regina 100%.

CBKFT-3— Analog Channel: 22.2.9 kw vis. ant 306t/310g On air date: Dec 2, 1979. Box 540, 2440 Broad St., Regina, SK, S4P 4A1. Phone: (306) 347-9540. Fax: (306) 347-9635.E-mail: info@radio-canada.ca Web Site: radio-canada.ca. Licensee: Societe Radio Canada. Natl. Network: Radio Canada, .
Key Personnel:
Lionel Bonneville . . . gen mgr
David Kyle . . . opns dir
Steve Tomchuck . . . chief of engrg
Rebroadcasts CBKFT-1 Saskatoon.

CKMC-TV-1— Analog Channel: 10. Analog Hrs: 24 229 kw vis, 22.9 kw aur. 554t/600g TL: N50 12 20 W109 35 43 On air date: Dec 15, 1988. c/o CKCK-TV, Box 2000, One Hwy. 1 East, Regina, SK, S4P 3E5. Phone: (306) 569-2000. Fax: (306) 522-0090. Web Site: www.ctv.ca. Licensee: CTV Television Inc. Group Owner: (group owner) Natl. Network: CTV, .
Key Personnel:
Dennis Dunlop . . . gen mgr
Les Sampson . . . chief of engrg

CBKFT-6— Analog Channel: 39.19 kw vis, 1.9 kw aur. ant 638t/615g On air date: Mar 13, 1980. Box 540, 2440 Broad St., Regina, SK, S4P 4A1. Phone: (306) 347-9540. Fax: (306) 347-9493. Licensee: Societe Radio Canada. Natl. Network: Radio Canada, .
Key Personnel:
Lionel Bonneville . . . gen mgr
David Kyle . . . opns dir
Steve Tomchuck . . . chief of engrg

CKBQ-TV— Analog Channel: 2.15.5 kw vis, 1.55 kw aur. ant 492t/490g On air date: 1973. Box 540, Reginia, SK, S4P 4A1. Phone: (306) 347-9540. Phone: (306) 956-7400. Fax: (306) 347-9635.E-mail: info@saskcbc.ca Web Site: www.saskcbc.ca. Licensee: CTV Television Inc. Group Owner: CTV Inc. Natl. Network: CBC, .
Key Personnel:
Lionel Bonneville . . . gen mgr
David Kyle . . . opns dir

CFQC-TV-2— Analog Channel: 6. Analog Hrs: 24 16.8 kw vis, 1.9 kw aur. 584t/350g On air date: 1972. c/o CFQC-TV, 216 First Ave. N., Saskatoon, SK, S7K 3W3. Phone: (306) 665-8600. Fax: (306) 665-0450. Web Site: www.ctv.ca. Licensee: TV West Inc. Natl. Network: CTV, .
Key Personnel:
Dennis Dunlop . . . gen mgr
Denis Gilbertson . . . opns mgr
Barry Berglund . . . gen sls mgr
Chris Ransom. . . . mktg dir
Geoff Bradley . . . prom mgr
Bonnie MacKenzie . . . progmg mgr
Dale Liebrecht. . . . engrg mgr

CBCP-TV-3— Analog Channel: 3.10.5 kw vis. ant 650t/717g On air date: November 1979. Box 540, c/o CBKT, 2440 Broad St., Regina, SK, S4P 4A1. Phone: (306) 347-9540. Fax: (306) 347-9758. Web Site: http://cbc.ca. Licensee: CBC. Natl. Network: CBC, .
Key Personnel:
Lionel Bonneville . . . gen mgr
David Kyle . . . opns dir
Steve Tomchuck . . . chief of engrg
Rebroadcasts CBKT(TV) Regina 100%.

CIPA-TV— Analog Channel: 9. Analog Hrs: 24 325 kw vis, 32.5 kw aur. 711t/460g On air date: Jan 12, 1987. 22 10th St. W., Prince Albert, SK, S6V 3A5. Phone: (306) 922-6066. Fax: (306) 763-3041.E-mail: cipa@ctv.ca Web Site: www.ctv.ca. Licensee: CTV Television Inc. Group Owner: CTV Inc. (acq 8-1-86). Natl. Network: CTV, . News staff: 5.
Key Personnel:
Dennis Dunlop . . . gen mgr

CBKFT— Analog Channel: 13. Analog Hrs: 18 103 kw vis, 31.3 kw aur. On air date: Sept 27, 1976. Box 540, 2440 Broad St., Regina, SK, S4P 4A1. Phone: (306) 347-9540. Fax: (306) 347-9635.E-mail: info@radio-canada.ca/regions/saskatchewan/index.shtm Web Site: www.radio-canada.ca/regions/saskatchewan/index.shtml. Licensee: Societe Radio Canada. Natl. Network: Radio Canada, .
Key Personnel:
Lionel Bonneville . . . gen mgr

CBKT— Analog Channel: 9.140 kw vis, 20 kw aur. ant 680t/698g On air date: 1969. Box 540, Regina, SK, S4P 4A1. Phone: (306) 347-9540. Fax: (306) 347-9616. Web Site: www.sask.cbc.ca. Licensee: CBC. Natl. Network: CBC, .
Key Personnel:
David Kyle . . . opns mgr
Carley Caverly . . . gen sls mgr
Bob Rankin . . . news dir
Jon Simons . . . mktg

CFRE-TV— Analog Channel: 11. Analog Hrs: 24 146 kw vis. 984t On air date: Sept 6, 1987. 370 Hoffer Dr., Regina, SK, S4N 7A4. Phone: (306) 775-4000. Fax: (306) 721-4817. Web Site: www.canada.com. Licensee: Canwest Television L.P. Group Owner: CanWest Global Communications Corp. Population Served: 320,000
Key Personnel:
Mitch Bozak. . . . gen mgr & stn mgr gen sls mgr
Lyndon Gray . . . prom mgr
Doug Hoover . . . film buyer
Brent Williamson . . . news dir
Paul Godfrey . . . opns mgr & engrg mgr
Len Virog . . . chief of engrg

CKCK-TV— Analog Channel: 2. Analog Hrs: 24 100 kw vis, 10 kw aur. 588t/670g TL: N50 26 52 W104 30 00 On air date: July 28, 1954. Box 2000, Regina, SK, S4P 3E5. One Hwy. 1 East, Regina, SK S4P 3E5. Phone: (306) 569-2000. Fax: (306) 522-0991.E-mail: ckcknews@ctv.ca Web Site: www.ctv.ca. Licensee: CTV Television Inc. Group Owner: (group owner) Natl. Network: CTV, . News: 15.5 hrs local news wkly.
Key Personnel:
Dennis Dunlop . . . gen mgr

CBKFT-4— Analog Channel: 7. Analog Hrs: 18 140 w vis, 14 w aur. ant 200t/185g On air date: Dec 17, 1979. Box 540, 2440 Broad St., Regina, SK, S4P 4A1. Phone: (306) 347-9540. Fax: (306) 347-9635.E-mail: info@radio-canada.regions/saskatchewan/index.shtml Web Site: radio-canada.ca/regions/saskatchewan/index.shtml. Licensee: Societe Radio Canada. Natl. Network: Radio Canada, .
Key Personnel:
Lionel Bonneville . . . gen mgr

CBKST— Analog Channel: 11. Analog Hrs: 20 325 kw vis, 32 kw aur. ant 559t/595g On air date: Oct 17, 1971. 144 Second Ave. South, Saskatoon, SK, S7K 1K5. Phone: (306) 956-7400. Fax: (306) 347-9650 (admin). Web Site: www.cbc.ca/sask. Licensee: CBC. Natl. Network: CBC, .
Key Personnel:
David Kyle . . . gen mgr

CFQC-TV— Analog Channel: 8.325 kw vis, 180 kw aur. 891t/650g TL: N52 07 51 W106 39 49 On air date: 1954. 216 First Ave. N., Saskatoon, SK, S7K 3W3. Phone: (306) 665-8600. Fax: (306) 665-0450.E-mail: cfqcnews@ctv.ca Web Site: www.ctv.ca. Licensee: CFQC Broadcasting Ltd. Group Owner: CTV Inc. (acq 1972). Population Served: 333,400 Natl. Network: CTV, .
Key Personnel:
Dennis Dunlop . . . gen mgr
Denis Gibertson . . . opns VP & opns mgr
Barry Berglund . . . gen sls mgr
Chris Ransom. . . . mktg dir & mktg mgr pub svc dir
Geoff Bradley . . . prom mgr
Bonnie Mackenzie . . . progmg mgr & traf mgr
Dale Neufeld . . . news dir
Les Sampson . . . chief of engrg
Denis Gilbertson . . . film dir
Kevin Waugh . . . sports cmtr
Jeff Rogstad . . . weather dir

CFSK-TV— Analog Channel: 4. Analog Hrs: 24 54 kw vis, 5.4 kw aur. 455t/219g On air date: Sept 6, 1987. 218 Robin Crescent, Saskatoon, SK, S7L 7C3. Phone: (306) 665-6969. Fax: (306) 665-6069. Licensee: Canwest Television L.P. Population Served: 290,000 Natl. Network: Global, . News staff: 17; News: 10 hrs wkly.

CBCP-TV-1— Analog Channel: 7. Analog Hrs: 24 4.5 kw vis. c/o CBKT, Box 540, Regina, SK, S4P 4A1. Phone: (306) 347-9540. Fax: (306) 347-9616. Web Site: www.sask.cbc.ca. Licensee: CBC. Natl. Network: CBC, .
Key Personnel:
David Kyle . . . opns mgr
Rebroadcasts CBKT(TV) Regina 100%.

CBKST-1— Analog Channel: 9. Analog Hrs: 20 323 kw vis, 32.3 kw aur. 2400 Broad St., Regina, SK, S4P 4A1. Phone: (306) 347-9540. Fax: (306) 347-9616 (admin). Fax: (306) 956-9417 (news). Web Site: www.cbc.ca. Licensee: CBC. Natl. Network: CBC, .
Rebroadcasts CBKST Saskatoon 100%.

CKMC-TV— Analog Channel: 12. Analog Hrs: 24 100 kw vis, 10 kw aur. ant 549t/399g TL: N50 18 31 W107 52 35 On air date: Oct 20, 1976. c/o CKCK-TV, Box 2000, Regina, SK, S4P 3E5. c/o CKCK-TV, One Hwy. 1 East, Regina, SK S4P 3E5. Phone: (306) 569-2000. Fax: (306) 522-0090.E-mail: ckck@ctv.ca Web Site: www.ctv.ca. Licensee: CTV Television Inc. Group Owner: (group owner) Natl. Network: CTV, .
Key Personnel:
Dennis Dunlop . . . gen mgr
Rebroadcasts CKCK-TV Regina 100%.

CIEW-TV— Analog Channel: 7.100 kw vis, 10 kw aur. c/o CICC-TV, 95 E. Broadway St., Yorkton, SK, S3N 0L1. Phone: (306) 783-3685. Fax: (306) 782-7212. Web Site: www.ctv.ca. Licensee: CTV Television Inc. Group Owner: Baton Broadcasting Inc. Natl. Network: CTV, .
Key Personnel:
Dennis Dunlop . . . gen mgr
Rebroadcasts CICC-TV Yorkton 100%.

CBKT-2— Analog Channel: 10. Analog Hrs: 24 22.1 kw vis, 2.2 kw aur. CBC TV, Box 540, 2440 Broad St., Regina, SK, S4P 4A1. Phone: (306) 347-9666. Fax: (306) 347-9635.E-mail: info@cbc.ca/sask/ Web Site: www.cbc.ca/sask/. Licensee: CBC. Natl. Network: CBC, .
Key Personnel:
David Kyle . . . gen mgr
Nigel Sims . . . progmg dir
Bob Rankin . . . news dir
Jon Anderson . . . chief of engrg

CKCK-TV-2— Analog Channel: 6.17.5 kw vis, 8.75 kw aur. 864t/677g (CP: 27.1 kw vis) On air date: May 29, 1963. c/o CKCK-TV, Box 2000,

One Hwy. 1 East, Regina, SK, S4P 3E5. Phone: (306) 569-2000. Fax: (306) 522-0090.E-mail: ckck@ctv.ca Web Site: www.ctv.ca. Licensee: CTV Television Inc. Group Owner: (group owner) Natl. Network: CTV, .

Key Personnel:
Dennis Dunlop . . . . gen mgr

CBKFT-5— Analog Channel: 21.3 kw vis, 300 w aur. ant 456t/310g On air date: Feb 19, 1979. 2440 Broad St., c/o CBKFT, 2440 Broad St., Regina, SK, S4P 4A1. Phone: (306) 347-9540. Fax: (306) 347-9493. Fax: (306) 347-9635. Web Site: www.cbc.ca/sask/. Licensee: CBC. Natl. Network: CBC, .
Key Personnel:
David Kyle . . . . gen mgr & progmg dir
Debbie Carpentier . . . . opns mgr

Carly Caverly . . . . gen sls mgr
Jonathan Shanks . . . . progmg dir
Steve Tomchuk . . . . chief of engrg
CBKFT.

CICC-TV— Analog Channel: 10.56 kw vis, 18 kw aur. On air date: 1974. 95 E. Broadway, Yorkton, SK, S3N 0L1. Phone: (306) 786-8400. Fax: (306) 782-7212.E-mail: ctvyorktonnews@ctv.ca Web Site: www.ctv.ca. Licensee: CTV Television Inc. Group Owner: (group owner) Natl. Network: CTV, .
Key Personnel:
Dennis Dunlop . . . . gen mgr
Wade Moffatt . . . . gen sls mgr
Bob Maloney . . . . progmg dir & news dir news dir

Peter Whitehead . . . . chief of engrg

Yukon Territory

CFWH-TV— Analog Channel: 6. Analog Hrs: 24 441 w. vis, 30 w aur. 1,248t/100g 3103 3rd Ave., White Horse, YT, Y1A 1E5. Phone: (867) 668-8400. Fax: (867) 668-8408. Web Site: www.cbc.ca/north. Licensee: CBC. Natl. Network: CBC, .
Key Personnel:
Frank Fry . . . . opns mgr & progmg dir
James Miller . . . . news dir

U.S. Television Stations by Call Letters

*KAAH-TV Honolulu, HI
KAAL Rochester, MN-Mason City, IA-Austin, MN
KAAS-TV Wichita-Hutchinson Plus, KS
KABB San Antonio, TX
KABC-TV Los Angeles
KABY-TV Sioux Falls (Mitchell), SD
*KACV-TV Amarillo, TX
KADN-TV Lafayette, LA
KAEF-TV Eureka, CA
*KAET Phoenix (Prescott), AZ
*KAFT Ft. Smith-Fayetteville -Springdale-Rogers, AR
*KAID Boise, ID
KAII-TV Wailuku HI
KAIL Fresno-Visalia, CA
KAIT Jonesboro, AR
KAJB Yuma, AZ-El Centro, CA
KAKE-TV Wichita-Hutchinson Plus, KS
*KAKM Anchorage, AK
KAKW-DT Waco-Temple-Bryan, TX
KALB-TV Alexandria, LA
*KALO Honolulu, HI
KAMC Lubbock, TX
KAME-TV Reno, NV
KAMR-TV Amarillo, TX
*KAMU-TV Waco-Temple-Bryan, TX
KAPP Yakima-Pasco -Richland-Kennewick, WA
KAQY Monroe, LA-El Dorado, AR
KARD Monroe, LA-El Dorado, AR
KARE Minneapolis-St. Paul, MN
KARK-TV Little Rock-Pine Bluff, AR
KARZ-TV Little Rock-Pine Bluff, AR
KASA-TV Albuquerque-Santa Fe, NM
KASN Little Rock-Pine Bluff, AR
KASW Phoenix (Prescott), AZ
KASY-TV Albuquerque-Santa Fe, NM
KATC Lafayette, LA
KATN Fairbanks, AK
KATU Portland, OR
KATV Little Rock-Pine Bluff, AR
KAUT-TV Oklahoma City, OK
KAUZ-TV Wichita Falls, TX & Lawton, OK
KAVU-TV Victoria, TX
*KAWB Minneapolis-St. Paul, MN
*KAWE Minneapolis-St. Paul, MN
KAYU-TV Spokane, WA
KAZA-TV Los Angeles
KAZH Houston
*KAZQ Albuquerque-Santa Fe, NM
KAZT-TV Phoenix (Prescott), AZ
KBAK-TV Bakersfield, CA
KBAO Great Falls, MT
KBBC-TV Los Angeles
KBBJ Great Falls, MT
KBCA Alexandria, LA
KBCB Seattle-Tacoma, WA
KBCI-TV Boise, ID
KBCJ Salt Lake City, UT
KBCW San Francisco-Oakland-San Jose
*KBDI-TV Denver, CO
*KBDM Medford-Klamath Falls, OR
KBEH Los Angeles
KBEO Idaho Falls-Pocatello, ID
KBFD-DT Honolulu, HI
*KBHE-TV Rapid City, SD
KBIM-TV Albuquerque-Santa Fe, NM
*KBIN-TV Omaha, NE
KBJR-TV Duluth, MN-Superior, WI
KBLN Medford-Klamath Falls, OR
KBLR Las Vegas, NV
*KBME-TV Minot-Bismarck-Dickinson, ND
KBMT Beaumont-Port Arthur, TX
KBMY Minot-Bismarck-Dickinson, ND
KBNY Salt Lake City, UT
KBRR Fargo-Valley City, ND
KBSD-DT Wichita-Hutchinson Plus, KS

KBSH-DT Wichita-Hutchinson Plus, KS
KBSI Paducah, KY-Cape Girardeau, MO-Harrisburg-Mount Vernon, IL
KBSL-DT Wichita-Hutchinson Plus, KS
*KBSV Sacramento-Stockton-Modesto, CA
*KBTC-TV Seattle-Tacoma, WA
KBTV-TV Beaumont-Port Arthur, TX
KBTX-TV Waco-Temple-Bryan, TX
KBTZ Butte-Bozeman, MT
KBVU Eureka, CA
*KBYU-TV Salt Lake City, UT
KBZK Butte-Bozeman, MT
KCAL-TV Los Angeles
KCAU-TV Sioux City, IA
KCBA Monterey-Salinas, CA
KCBD Lubbock, TX
KCBS-TV Los Angeles
KCBU Salt Lake City, UT
KCBY-TV Eugene, OR
KCCI Des Moines-Ames, IA
KCCO-TV Minneapolis-St. Paul, MN
KCCW-TV Minneapolis-St. Paul, MN
KCDO-TV Denver, CO
*KCDT-TV Spokane, WA
KCEB Tyler-Longview (Lufkin & Nacogdoches), TX
KCEC Denver, CO
KCEN-TV Waco-Temple-Bryan, TX
*KCET Los Angeles
KCFG Phoenix (Prescott), AZ
KCFW-TV Missoula, MT
*KCGE-DT Fargo-Valley City, ND
KCHF Albuquerque-Santa Fe, NM
KCIT Amarillo, TX
*KCKA Seattle-Tacoma, WA
KCLO-TV Rapid City, SD
KCNC-TV Denver, CO
KCNS San Francisco-Oakland-San Jose
KCOP Los Angeles
*KCOS El Paso (Las Cruces, NM), TX
KCOY-TV Santa Barbara-Santa Maria-San Luis Obispo, CA
KCPM Fargo-Valley City, ND
KCPQ Seattle-Tacoma, WA
*KCPT Kansas City, MO
KCRA-TV Sacramento -Stockton-Modesto, CA
KCRG-TV Cedar Rapids-Waterloo-Iowa City & Dubuque, IA
*KCSD-TV Sioux Falls (Mitchell), SD
KCSG Salt Lake City, UT
*KCSM-TV San Francisco-Oakland-San Jose
*KCTS-TV Seattle-Tacoma, WA
KCTV Kansas City, MO
KCVU Chico-Redding, CA
*KCWC-TV Casper-Riverton, WY
KCWE Kansas City, MO
KCWI-TV Des Moines-Ames, IA
KCWV Duluth, MN-Superior, WI
KCWX San Antonio, TX
KCWY-DT Casper-Riverton, WY
KDAF Dallas-Ft. Worth
KDBC-TV El Paso (Las Cruces, NM), TX
*KDCK Wichita-Hutchinson Plus, KS
KDCU-DT Wichita-Hutchinson Plus, KS
KDEN Denver, CO
KDFI Dallas-Ft. Worth
KDFW Dallas-Ft. Worth
*KDIN-TV Des Moines-Ames, IA
KDKA-TV Pittsburgh, PA
KDKF Medford-Klamath Falls, OR
KDLH Duluth, MN-Superior, WI
KDLO-TV Sioux Falls (Mitchell), SD
KDLT-TV Sioux Falls (Mitchell), SD
KDLV-TV Sioux Falls (Mitchell), SD
KDMD Anchorage, AK
KDMI Des Moines-Ames, IA

KDNL-TV St. Louis, MO
KDOC-TV Los Angeles
KDOR-TV Tulsa, OK
KDRV Medford-Klamath Falls, OR
*KDSD-TV Sioux Falls (Mitchell), SD
*KDSE Minot-Bismarck-Dickinson, ND
KDSM-TV Des Moines-Ames, IA
*KDTN Dallas-Ft. Worth
*KDTP Phoenix (Prescott), AZ
*KDTV-DT San Francisco-Oakland-San Jose
*KDTX-TV Dallas-Ft. Worth
KDUH-TV Cheyenne, WY-Scottsbluff, NE
KDVR Denver, CO
KECI-TV Missoula, MT
KECY-TV Yuma, AZ-El Centro, CA
*KEDT Corpus Christi, TX
*KEET Eureka, CA
*KEFB Des Moines-Ames, IA
KEGS Reno, NV
KEJB Monroe, LA-El Dorado, AR
KELO-TV Sioux Falls (Mitchell), SD
*KEMV Little Rock-Pine Bluff, AR
KENS San Antonio, TX
KENV-DT Salt Lake City, UT
*KENW Amarillo, TX
*KEPB-TV Eugene, OR
KEPR-TV Yakima-Pasco -Richland-Kennewick, WA
*KERA-TV Dallas-Ft. Worth
KERO-TV Bakersfield, CA
*KESD-TV Sioux Falls (Mitchell), SD
KESQ-TV Palm Springs, CA
*KETA-TV Oklahoma City, OK
*KETC St. Louis, MO
*KETG Little Rock-Pine Bluff, AR
*KETH-TV Houston
KETK-TV Tyler-Longview (Lufkin & Nacogdoches), TX
*KETS Little Rock-Pine Bluff, AR
KETV Omaha, NE
*KETZ Monroe, LA-El Dorado, AR
KEVN-TV Rapid City, SD
KEYC-TV Mankato, MN
KEYE-TV Austin, TX
KEYT-TV Santa Barbara-Santa Maria-San Luis Obispo, CA
KEYU Amarillo, TX
KEZI Eugene, OR
KFBB-TV Great Falls, MT
KFCT Denver, CO
KFDA-TV Amarillo, TX
KFDM-TV Beaumont-Port Arthur, TX
KFDX-TV Wichita Falls, TX & Lawton, OK
KFFX-TV Yakima-Pasco -Richland-Kennewick, WA
KFJX-TV Joplin, MO-Pittsburg, KS
KFMB-TV San Diego, CA
*KFME Fargo-Valley City, ND
KFNB-TV Casper-Riverton, WY
KFNE Casper-Riverton, WY
KFNR Denver, CO
KFOR-TV Oklahoma City, OK
KFOX-TV El Paso (Las Cruces, NM), TX
KFPH-DT Phoenix (Prescott), AZ
KFPX-TV Des Moines-Ames, IA
KFQX Grand Junction-Montrose, CO
KFRE-TV Fresno-Visalia, CA
KFSF-DT San Francisco-Oakland-San Jose
KFSM-TV Ft. Smith-Fayetteville -Springdale-Rogers, AR
KFSN-TV Fresno-Visalia, CA
KFTA-TV Ft. Smith-Fayetteville -Springdale-Rogers, AR
KFTC Minneapolis-St. Paul, MN
KFTH-DT Houston
KFTR-DT Los Angeles
*KFTS Medford-Klamath Falls, OR

KFTU-DT Tucson (Sierra Vista), AZ
KFTV-DT Fresno-Visalia, CA
KFTY San Francisco-Oakland-San Jose
KFVE Honolulu, HI
KFVS-TV Paducah, KY-Cape Girardeau, MO-Harrisburg-Mount Vernon, IL
KFWD Dallas-Ft. Worth
KFXA Cedar Rapids-Waterloo-Iowa City & Dubuque, IA
KFXB-TV Cedar Rapids-Waterloo-Iowa City & Dubuque, IA
KFXF Fairbanks, AK
KFXK-TV Tyler-Longview (Lufkin & Nacogdoches), TX
KFXL-TV Lincoln & Hastings-Kearney, NE
KFXP Idaho Falls-Pocatello, ID
KFYR-TV Minot-Bismarck-Dickinson, ND
KGAN Cedar Rapids-Waterloo-Iowa City & Dubuque, IA
KGBT-TV Harlingen-Weslaco -Brownsville-McAllen, TX
KGCW Davenport, IA-Rock Island-Moline, IL
KGEB Tulsa, OK
KGET-TV Bakersfield, CA
*KGFE Fargo-Valley City, ND
KGIN Lincoln & Hastings-Kearney, NE
KGLA-DT New Orleans, LA
KGMB Honolulu, HI
KGMC Fresno-Visalia, CA
KGMD-TV Hilo HI
KGMV Wailuku HI
KGNS-TV Laredo, TX
KGO-TV San Francisco-Oakland-San Jose
KGPE Fresno-Visalia, CA
KGPX-TV Spokane, WA
*KGTF-TV Hagatna GU
KGTV San Diego, CA
KGUN-TV Tucson (Sierra Vista), AZ
KGW Portland, OR
KGWC-TV Casper-Riverton, WY
KGWL-TV Casper-Riverton, WY
KGWN-TV Cheyenne, WY-Scottsbluff, NE
KGWR-TV Salt Lake City, UT
KHAS-TV Lincoln & Hastings-Kearney, NE
KHAW-TV Hilo HI
KHBC-TV Hilo HI
KHBS Ft. Smith-Fayetteville -Springdale-Rogers, AR
*KHCE-TV San Antonio, TX
KHCV Seattle-Tacoma, WA
*KHET Honolulu, HI
KHGI-TV Lincoln & Hastings-Kearney, NE
*KHIN Omaha, NE
KHIZ Los Angeles
KHMT Billings, MT
*KHNE-TV Lincoln & Hastings-Kearney, NE
KHNL Honolulu, HI
KHOG-TV Ft. Smith-Fayetteville -Springdale-Rogers, AR
KHON-TV Honolulu, HI
KHOU Houston
KHQA-TV Quincy, IL-Hannibal, MO-Keokuk, IA
KHQ-TV Spokane, WA
KHRR Tucson (Sierra Vista), AZ
KHSD-TV Rapid City, SD
KHSL-TV Chico-Redding, CA
KHVO Hilo HI
KIAH Houston
KICU-TV San Francisco-Oakland-San Jose
KIDA Twin Falls, ID

KIDK-TV Idaho Falls-Pocatello, ID
KIDY San Angelo, TX
KIEM-TV Eureka, CA
KIFI-TV Idaho Falls-Pocatello, ID
KIII Corpus Christi, TX
*KIIN Cedar Rapids-Waterloo-Iowa City & Dubuque, IA
KIKU Honolulu, HI
KIMA-TV Yakima-Pasco -Richland-Kennewick, WA
KIMO Anchorage, AK
KIMT Rochester, MN-Mason City, IA-Austin, MN
KINC Las Vegas, NV
KING-TV Seattle-Tacoma, WA
KINT-TV El Paso (Las Cruces, NM), TX
KION-TV Monterey-Salinas, CA
*KIPT-TV Twin Falls, ID
KIRO-TV Seattle-Tacoma, WA
*KISU-TV Idaho Falls-Pocatello, ID
*KITU-TV Beaumont-Port Arthur, TX
KITV Honolulu, HI
KIVI-TV Boise, ID
KIVV-TV Rapid City, SD
*KIXE-TV Chico-Redding, CA
KJCT Grand Junction-Montrose, CO
KJLA Los Angeles
KJNP-TV Fairbanks, AK
*KJRE Fargo-Valley City, ND
KJRH Tulsa, OK
KJRR Fargo-Valley City, ND
KJTL Wichita Falls, TX & Lawton, OK
KJTV-TV Lubbock, TX
KJUD Juneau, AK
KJWY Idaho Falls-Pocatello, ID
KJZZ-TV Salt Lake City, UT
KKAI Honolulu, HI
*KKAP Little Rock-Pine Bluff, AR
KKCO Grand Junction-Montrose, CO
KKJB Boise, ID
KKPX-TV San Francisco-Oakland-San Jose
KKTV Colorado Springs-Pueblo, CO
KKYK-DT Little Rock-Pine Bluff, AR
KLAS-TV Las Vegas, NV
KLAX-TV Alexandria, LA
KLBK-TV Lubbock, TX
KLBY Wichita-Hutchinson Plus, KS
*KLCS Los Angeles
KLCW-TV Lubbock, TX
KLDO-TV Laredo, TX
KLDT Dallas-Ft. Worth
KLEI

KLEW-TV Spokane, WA
KLFY-TV Lafayette, LA
KLJB Davenport, IA-Rock Island-Moline, IL
KLKN Lincoln & Hastings-Kearney, NE
KLMN Great Falls, MT
*KLNE-TV Lincoln & Hastings-Kearney, NE
*KLPA-TV Alexandria, LA
*KLPB-TV Lafayette, LA
*KLRN San Antonio, TX
KLRT-TV Little Rock-Pine Bluff, AR
*KLRU Austin, TX
KLSR-TV Eugene, OR
KLST San Angelo, TX
*KLTJ Houston
*KLTL-TV Lake Charles, LA
*KLTM-TV Monroe, LA-El Dorado, AR
*KLTS-TV Shreveport, LA
KLTV Tyler-Longview (Lufkin & Nacogdoches), LA
*KLUJ-TV Harlingen-Weslaco -Brownsville-McAllen, TX
KLUZ-TV Albuquerque-Santa Fe, NM
*KLVX Las Vegas, NV
KLWB Lafayette, LA

KLWY Cheyenne, WY-Scottsbluff, NE
KMAU Wailuku HI
KMAX-TV Sacramento -Stockton-Modesto, CA
KMBC-TV Kansas City, MO
*KMBH Harlingen-Weslaco -Brownsville-McAllen, TX
KMCB Eugene, OR
KMCC Las Vegas, NV
KMCI Kansas City, MO
KMCT-TV Monroe, LA-El Dorado, AR
KMCY Minot-Bismarck-Dickinson, ND
*KMDE Fargo-Valley City, ND
*KMEB Wailuku HI
KMEG Sioux City, IA
KMEX-DT Los Angeles
KMGH-TV Denver, CO
KMID Odessa-Midland, TX
KMIR-TV Palm Springs, CA
KMIZ Columbia-Jefferson City, MO
KMLM Odessa-Midland, TX
KMMF Missoula, MT
*KMNE-TV Lincoln & Hastings-Kearney, NE
KMOH-TV Phoenix (Prescott), AZ
*KMOS-TV Columbia-Jefferson City, MO
KMOT Minot-Bismarck-Dickinson, ND
KMOV St. Louis, MO
KMPH-TV Fresno-Visalia, CA
KMPX Dallas-Ft. Worth
KMSB Tucson (Sierra Vista), AZ
KMSP-TV Minneapolis-St. Paul, MN
KMSS-TV Shreveport, LA
KMTF Helena, MT
*KMTP-TV San Francisco-Oakland-San Jose
KMTR Eugene, OR
KMTV-TV Omaha, NE
KMTW Wichita-Hutchinson Plus, KS
KMVT Twin Falls, ID
KMVU-DT Medford-Klamath Falls, OR
KMYQ Seattle-Tacoma, WA
KMYS San Antonio, TX
KMYT-TV Tulsa, OK
KNAT-TV Albuquerque-Santa Fe, NM
KNAZ-TV Phoenix (Prescott), AZ
KNBC Los Angeles
KNBN Rapid City, SD
*KNCT Waco-Temple-Bryan, TX
KNDO Yakima-Pasco -Richland-Kennewick, WA
KNDU Yakima-Pasco -Richland-Kennewick, WA
KNDX Minot-Bismarck-Dickinson, ND
KNIC-DT San Antonio, TX
KNIN-TV Boise, ID
KNLC St. Louis, MO
KNLJ Columbia-Jefferson City, MO
*KNMD-TV Albuquerque-Santa Fe, NM
*KNME-TV Albuquerque-Santa Fe, NM
*KNMT Portland, OR
KNOE-TV Monroe, LA-El Dorado, AR
KNOP-TV North Platte, NE
*KNPB Reno, NV
KNRR Fargo-Valley City, ND
KNSD San Diego, CA
KNSO Fresno-Visalia, CA
KNTV San Francisco-Oakland-San Jose
KNVA Austin, TX
KNVN Chico-Redding, CA
KNVO Harlingen-Weslaco -Brownsville-McAllen, TX
KNWA-TV Ft. Smith-Fayetteville -Springdale-Rogers, AR
KNWS-TV Houston
*KNXT Fresno-Visalia, CA
KNXV-TV Phoenix (Prescott), AZ
KOAA-TV Colorado Springs-Pueblo, CO
*KOAB-TV Bend, OR
*KOAC-TV Eugene, OR
KOAM-TV Joplin, MO-Pittsburg, KS
KOAT-TV Albuquerque-Santa Fe, NM
KOB Albuquerque-Santa Fe, NM
KOBF Albuquerque-Santa Fe, NM

KOBG-TV Albuquerque-Santa Fe, NM
KOBI Medford-Klamath Falls, OR
KOBR Albuquerque-Santa Fe, NM
KOCB Oklahoma City, OK
*KOCE-TV Los Angeles
KOCM Oklahoma City, OK
KOCO-TV Oklahoma City, OK
KOCT Albuquerque-Santa Fe, NM
KOCW Wichita-Hutchinson Plus, KS
KODE-TV Joplin, MO-Pittsburg, KS
*KOED-TV Tulsa, OK
*KOET Tulsa, OK
KOFT Albuquerque-Santa Fe, NM
KOFY-TV San Francisco-Oakland-San Jose
KOGG Wailuku HI
KOHD Bend, OR
KOIN Portland, OR
KOKH-TV Oklahoma City, OK
KOKI-TV Tulsa, OK
KOLD-TV Tucson (Sierra Vista), AZ
KOLN Lincoln & Hastings-Kearney, NE
KOLO-TV Reno, NV
KOLR Springfield, MO
KOMO-TV Seattle-Tacoma, WA
KOMU-TV Columbia-Jefferson City, MO
KONG Seattle-Tacoma, WA
*KOOD Wichita-Hutchinson Plus, KS
*KOPB-TV Portland, OR
KOPX-TV Oklahoma City, OK
KORO Corpus Christi, TX
KOSA-TV Odessa-Midland, TX
KOTA-TV Rapid City, SD
KOTI Medford-Klamath Falls, OR
KOTV Tulsa, OK
KOVR Sacramento-Stockton-Modesto, CA
KOVT Albuquerque-Santa Fe, NM
*KOZJ Joplin, MO-Pittsburg, KS
*KOZK Springfield, MO
KPAX-TV Missoula, MT
*KPAZ-TV Phoenix (Prescott), AZ
KPBI Ft. Smith-Fayetteville -Springdale-Rogers, AR
*KPBS San Diego, CA
*KPBT-TV Odessa-Midland, TX
KPCB Abilene-Sweetwater, TX
KPDX Portland, OR
KPEJ-TV Odessa-Midland, TX
KPHO-TV Phoenix (Prescott), AZ
KPIC Eugene, OR
KPIF Idaho Falls-Pocatello, ID
KPIX-TV San Francisco-Oakland-San Jose
KPJR-DT Denver, CO
KPLC Lake Charles, LA
KPLO-TV Sioux Falls (Mitchell), SD
KPLR-TV St. Louis, MO
KPMR Santa Barbara-Santa Maria-San Luis Obispo, CA
*KPNE-TV North Platte, NE
KPNX Phoenix (Prescott), AZ
KPNZ Salt Lake City, UT
KPOB Paducah, KY-Cape Girardeau, MO-Harrisburg-Mount Vernon, IL
KPPX-TV Phoenix (Prescott), AZ
KPRC-TV Houston
KPRY-TV Sioux Falls (Mitchell), SD
*KPSD-TV Minot-Bismarck-Dickinson, ND
KPTB Lubbock, TX
KPTF Amarillo, TX
KPTH Sioux City, IA
KPTM Omaha, NE
*KPTS Wichita-Hutchinson Plus, KS
KPTV Portland, OR
*KPTW Casper-Riverton, WY
KPVI-DT Idaho Falls-Pocatello, ID
KPXB-TV Houston
KPXC-TV Denver, CO
KPXD-TV Dallas-Ft. Worth
KPXE-TV Kansas City, MO
KPXG-TV Portland, OR
KPXJ Shreveport, LA
KPXL-TV San Antonio, TX

KPXM-TV Minneapolis-St. Paul, MN
KPXN-TV Los Angeles
KPXO-TV Honolulu, HI
KPXR-TV Cedar Rapids-Waterloo-Iowa City & Dubuque, IA
KQCA Sacramento-Stockton-Modesto, CA
KQCD-TV Minot-Bismarck-Dickinson, ND
KQCK Cheyenne, WY-Scottsbluff, NE
KQCW Tulsa, OK
KQDS-TV Duluth, MN-Superior, WI
*KQED San Francisco-Oakland-San Jose
*KQET Monterey-Salinas, CA
*KQIN Davenport, IA-Rock Island-Moline, IL
*KQSD-TV Sioux Falls (Mitchell), SD
KQTV St. Joseph, MO
KQUP Spokane, WA
KRBC-TV Abilene-Sweetwater, TX
KRBK Springfield, MO
KRCA Los Angeles
*KRCB San Francisco-Oakland-San Jose
KRCG Columbia-Jefferson City, MO
KRCR-TV Chico-Redding, CA
KRCW-TV Portland, OR
KRDO-TV Colorado Springs-Pueblo, CO
KREG-TV Denver, CO
KREM Spokane, WA
KREN-TV Reno, NV
KREX-TV Grand Junction-Montrose, CO
KREY-TV Grand Junction-Montrose, CO
KREZ-TV Albuquerque-Santa Fe, NM
KRGV-TV Harlingen-Weslaco -Brownsville-McAllen, TX
KRII Duluth, MN-Superior, WI
*KRIN Cedar Rapids-Waterloo-Iowa City & Dubuque, IA
KRIS-TV Corpus Christi, TX
KRIV Houston
KRON-TV San Francisco-Oakland-San Jose
KRPV Albuquerque-Santa Fe, NM
KRQE Albuquerque-Santa Fe, NM
*KRSC-TV Tulsa, OK
KRTV Great Falls, MT
*KRWB-TV Albuquerque-Santa Fe, NM
KRWF Minneapolis-St. Paul, MN
*KRWG-TV El Paso (Las Cruces, NM), TX
KRXI-TV Reno, NV
KSAN-TV San Angelo, TX
KSAS-TV Wichita-Hutchinson Plus, KS
KSAT-TV San Antonio, TX
KSAX Minneapolis-St. Paul, MN
KSAZ-TV Phoenix (Prescott), AZ
KSBI Oklahoma City, OK
KSBW Monterey-Salinas, CA
KSBY Santa Barbara-Santa Maria-San Luis Obispo, CA
*KSCE El Paso (Las Cruces, NM), TX
KSCI Los Angeles
KSCW-DT Wichita-Hutchinson Plus, KS
KSDK St. Louis, MO
KSEE Fresno-Visalia, CA
KSFX-TV Springfield, MO
KSFY-TV Sioux Falls (Mitchell), SD
KSGW-TV Rapid City, SD
KSHB-TV Kansas City, MO
KSHV-TV Shreveport, LA
*KSIN-TV Sioux City, IA
KSKN Spokane, WA
KSLA Shreveport, LA
KSL-TV Salt Lake City, UT

*KSMN Sioux Falls (Mitchell), SD
KSMO-TV Kansas City, MO
*KSMQ-TV Rochester, MN-Mason City, IA-Austin, MN
KSMS-TV Monterey-Salinas, CA
KSNB-TV Lincoln & Hastings-Kearney, NE
KSNC Wichita-Hutchinson Plus, KS
KSNF Joplin, MO-Pittsburg, KS
KSNG Wichita-Hutchinson Plus, KS
KSNK Wichita-Hutchinson Plus, KS
KSNT Topeka, KS
KSNW Wichita-Hutchinson Plus, KS
KSPR Springfield, MO
*KSPS-TV Spokane, WA
KSPX-TV Sacramento -Stockton-Modesto, CA
KSQA Topeka, KS
*KSRE Minot-Bismarck-Dickinson, ND
KSTC-TV Minneapolis-St. Paul, MN
KSTF Cheyenne, WY-Scottsbluff, NE
KSTP-TV Minneapolis-St. Paul, MN
KSTR-DT Dallas-Ft. Worth
KSTS San Francisco-Oakland-San Jose
KSTU Salt Lake City, UT
KSTW Seattle-Tacoma, WA
KSVI Billings, MT
KSWB-TV San Diego, CA
*KSWK Wichita-Hutchinson Plus, KS
KSWO-TV Wichita Falls, TX & Lawton, OK
KSWT Yuma, AZ-El Centro, CA
KSWY Rapid City, SD
*KSYS Medford-Klamath Falls, OR
KTAB-TV Abilene-Sweetwater, TX
KTAJ-TV St. Joseph, MO
KTAL-TV Shreveport, LA
KTAQ Dallas-Ft. Worth
KTAS Santa Barbara-Santa Maria-San Luis Obispo, CA
KTAZ Phoenix (Prescott), AZ
KTBC Austin, TX
KTBN-TV Los Angeles
KTBO-TV Oklahoma City, OK
KTBS-TV Shreveport, LA
KTBU Houston
KTBW-TV Seattle-Tacoma, WA
KTBY Anchorage, AK
*KTCA-TV Minneapolis-St. Paul, MN
*KTCI-TV Minneapolis-St. Paul, MN
KTCW Eugene, OR
KTDO El Paso (Las Cruces, NM), TX
*KTEH San Francisco-Oakland-San Jose
*KTEJ Jonesboro, AR
KTEL-TV Albuquerque-Santa Fe, NM
KTEN Sherman, TX-Ada, OK
KTFD-DT Denver, CO
KTFF-DT Fresno-Visalia, CA
KTFK-DT Sacramento -Stockton-Modesto, CA
KTFN El Paso (Las Cruces, NM), TX
KTFQ-DT Albuquerque-Santa Fe, NM
KTGF Great Falls, MT
KTGM Tamuning GU
KTHV Little Rock-Pine Bluff, AR
*KTIN Des Moines-Ames, IA
KTIV Sioux City, IA
KTKA-TV Topeka, KS
KTLA Los Angeles
KTLL-TV Albuquerque-Santa Fe, NM
*KTLM Harlingen-Weslaco -Brownsville-McAllen, TX
KTLN-TV San Francisco-Oakland-San Jose
KTMD Houston
KTMF Missoula, MT
KTMW Salt Lake City, UT
KTNC-TV San Francisco-Oakland-San Jose
*KTNE-TV Cheyenne, WY-Scottsbluff, NE
KTNL-TV Juneau, AK
KTNV-TV Las Vegas, NV
*KTNW Yakima-Pasco -Richland-Kennewick, WA

*KTOO-TV Juneau, AK
KTPX-TV Tulsa, OK
KTRE Tyler-Longview (Lufkin & Nacogdoches), TX
KTRG San Antonio, TX
KTRK-TV Houston
KTRV-TV Boise, ID
*KTSC Colorado Springs-Pueblo, CO
*KTSD-TV Sioux Falls (Mitchell), SD
KTSF San Francisco-Oakland-San Jose
KTSM-TV El Paso (Las Cruces, NM), TX
KTTC Rochester, MN-Mason City, IA-Austin, MN
KTTM Sioux Falls (Mitchell), SD
KTTU Tucson (Sierra Vista), AZ
KTTV Los Angeles
KTTW Sioux Falls (Mitchell), SD
KTUL Tulsa, OK
KTUU-TV Anchorage, AK
KTUW Cheyenne, WY-Scottsbluff, NE
KTUZ-TV Oklahoma City, OK
KTVA Anchorage, AK
KTVB Boise, ID
KTVC Eugene, OR
KTVD Denver, CO
KTVE Monroe, LA-El Dorado, AR
KTVF Fairbanks, AK
KTVG-TV Lincoln & Hastings-Kearney, NE
KTVH-DT Helena, MT
KTVI St. Louis, MO
KTVK Phoenix (Prescott), AZ
KTVL Medford-Klamath Falls, OR
KTVM Butte-Bozeman, MT
KTVN Reno, NV
KTVO Ottumwa, IA-Kirksville, MO
KTVQ Billings, MT
*KTVR Portland, OR
KTVT Dallas-Ft. Worth
KTVU San Francisco-Oakland-San Jose
KTVW-DT Phoenix (Prescott), AZ
KTVX Salt Lake City, UT
KTVZ Bend, OR
KTWO-TV Casper-Riverton, WY
*KTWU Topeka, KS
KTXA Dallas-Ft. Worth
KTXH Houston
KTXL Sacramento-Stockton-Modesto, CA
KTXS-TV Abilene-Sweetwater, TX
*KTXT-TV Lubbock, TX
*KUAC-TV Fairbanks, AK
KUAM-TV Hagatna GU
*KUAS-TV Tucson (Sierra Vista), AZ
*KUAT-TV Tucson (Sierra Vista), AZ
KUBD Ketchikan AK
KUCW Salt Lake City, UT
*KUED Salt Lake City, UT
*KUEN Salt Lake City, UT
*KUES Salt Lake City, UT
*KUEW Salt Lake City, UT
*KUFM-TV Missoula, MT
*KUHT Houston
*KUID-TV Spokane, WA
KULR-TV Billings, MT
KUMV-TV Minot-Bismarck-Dickinson, ND
KUNO-TV San Francisco-Oakland-San Jose
KUNP Portland, OR
KUNS-TV Seattle-Tacoma, WA
KUOK Oklahoma City, OK
*KUON-TV Lincoln & Hastings-Kearney, NE
KUPB Odessa-Midland, TX
KUPK-TV Wichita-Hutchinson Plus, KS
KUPT Albuquerque-Santa Fe, NM
KUPU Honolulu, HI
KUPX-TV Salt Lake City, UT
KUQI Corpus Christi, TX
KUSA Denver, CO
*KUSD-TV Sioux Falls (Mitchell), SD
KUSG Salt Lake City, UT
KUSI-TV San Diego, CA

*KUSM Butte-Bozeman, MT
KUTF Salt Lake City, UT
KUTH-DT Salt Lake City, UT
KUTP Phoenix (Prescott), AZ
KUTV Salt Lake City, UT
KUVE-DT Tucson (Sierra Vista), AZ
KUVI-DT Bakersfield, CA
KUVN-DT Dallas-Ft. Worth
KUVS-DT Sacramento-Stockton-Modesto, CA
KVAL-TV Eugene, OR
KVAW San Antonio, TX
KVBC-DT Las Vegas, NV
*KVCR-DT Los Angeles
KVCT Victoria, TX
KVCW Las Vegas, NV
KVDA San Antonio, TX
KVEA Los Angeles
KVEO-TV Harlingen-Weslaco-Brownsville-McAllen, TX
KVEW Yakima-Pasco-Richland-Kennewick, WA
KVHP Lake Charles, LA
KVIA-TV El Paso (Las Cruces, NM), TX
*KVIE Sacramento-Stockton-Modesto, CA
KVIH-TV Amarillo, TX
KVII-TV Amarillo, TX
KVIQ Eureka, CA
KVLY-TV Fargo-Valley City, ND
KVMD Los Angeles
KVMY Las Vegas, NV
KVNV Salt Lake City, UT
KVOA Tucson (Sierra Vista), AZ
KVOS-TV Seattle-Tacoma, WA
*KVPT Fresno-Visalia, CA
KVRR Fargo-Valley City, ND
KVSN-DT Colorado Springs-Pueblo, CO
KVTH-DT Little Rock-Pine Bluff, AR
KVTJ-DT Jonesboro, AR
KVTN-DT Little Rock-Pine Bluff, AR
KVTV Laredo, TX
KVUE Austin, TX
KVVU-TV Las Vegas, NV
KVYE Yuma, AZ-El Centro, CA
*KVZK-2 Pago Pago AS
*KVZK-4 Pago Pago AS
*KVZK-5 Pago Pago AS
KWAB-TV Odessa-Midland, TX
KWBA-TV Tucson (Sierra Vista), AZ
KWBM Springfield, MO
*KWBN Honolulu, HI
KWBQ Albuquerque-Santa Fe, NM
*KWBU-TV Waco-Temple-Bryan, TX
KWCH-DT Wichita-Hutchinson Plus, KS
*KWCM-TV Minneapolis-St. Paul, MN
*KWDK Seattle-Tacoma, WA
KWES-TV Odessa-Midland, TX
*KWET Oklahoma City, OK
KWEX-DT San Antonio, TX
KWGN-TV Denver, CO
KWHB Tulsa, OK
KWHD Denver, CO
KWHE Honolulu, HI
KWHH Hilo HI
KWHM Wailuku HI
KWHY-TV Los Angeles
KWKB Cedar Rapids-Waterloo-Iowa City & Dubuque, IA
*KWKS Wichita-Hutchinson Plus, KS
KWKT-TV Waco-Temple-Bryan, TX
KWNB-TV Lincoln & Hastings-Kearney, NE
KWNV Reno, NV
KWOG Ft. Smith-Fayetteville-Springdale-Rogers, AR
KWPX-TV Seattle-Tacoma, WA
KWQC-TV Davenport, IA-Rock Island-Moline, IL
KWSD Sioux Falls (Mitchell), SD
*KWSE Minot-Bismarck-Dickinson, ND
*KWSU-TV Spokane, WA
KWTV Oklahoma City, OK
KWTX-TV Waco-Temple-Bryan, TX

KWWF Cedar Rapids-Waterloo-Iowa City & Dubuque, IA
KWWL Cedar Rapids-Waterloo-Iowa City & Dubuque, IA
KWWT Odessa-Midland, TX
KWYB Butte-Bozeman, MT
*KWYP-TV Denver, CO
KXAM-TV Austin, TX
KXAN-TV Austin, TX
KXAS-TV Dallas-Ft. Worth
KXGN-TV Glendive, MT
KXII Sherman, TX-Ada, OK
KXJB-TV Fargo-Valley City, ND
KXLA Los Angeles
KXLF-TV Butte-Bozeman, MT
KXLN-DT Houston
KXLT-TV Rochester, MN-Mason City, IA-Austin, MN
KXLY-TV Spokane, WA
KXMA-TV Minot-Bismarck-Dickinson, ND
KXMB-TV Minot-Bismarck-Dickinson, ND
KXMC-TV Minot-Bismarck-Dickinson, ND
KXMD-TV Minot-Bismarck-Dickinson, ND
KXND Minot-Bismarck-Dickinson, ND
*KXNE-TV Sioux City, IA
KXRM-TV Colorado Springs-Pueblo, CO
KXTF Twin Falls, ID
KXTV Sacramento-Stockton-Modesto, CA
KXTX-TV Dallas-Ft. Worth
KXVA Abilene-Sweetwater, TX
KXVO Omaha, NE
KXXV Waco-Temple-Bryan, TX
KYES-TV Anchorage, AK
*KYIN Rochester, MN-Mason City, IA-Austin, MN
KYLE-TV Waco-Temple-Bryan, TX
KYMA-DT Yuma, AZ-El Centro, CA
*KYNE-TV Omaha, NE
KYOU-TV Ottumwa, IA-Kirksville, MO
KYTV Springfield, MO
KYTX Tyler-Longview (Lufkin & Nacogdoches), TX
*KYUK-TV Bethel AK
KYUS-TV Billings, MT
*KYVE Yakima-Pasco-Richland-Kennewick, WA
KYW-TV Philadelphia
KZJL Houston
*KZSD-TV Rapid City, SD
KZTV Corpus Christi, TX
WAAY-TV Huntsville-Decatur (Florence), AL
WABC-TV New York
WABG-TV Greenwood-Greenville, MS
WABI-TV Bangor, ME
WABM Birmingham (Anniston, Tuscaloosa), AL
*WABW-TV Albany, GA
WACH Columbia, SC
*WACS-TV Albany, GA
WACX Orlando-Daytona Beach-Melbourne, FL
WACY-TV Green Bay-Appleton, WI
WADL Detroit
WAFB Baton Rouge, LA
WAFF Huntsville-Decatur (Florence), AL
WAGA-TV Atlanta
WAGM-TV Presque Isle, ME
WAGT Augusta, GA
WAGV Knoxville, TN
*WAIQ Montgomery-Selma, AL
WAKA Montgomery-Selma, AL
WALA-TV Mobile, AL-Pensacola (Ft. Walton Beach), FL
WALB Albany, GA
WAMI-DT Miami-Ft. Lauderdale, FL
WAND Champaign & Springfield-Decatur, IL
WANE-TV Ft. Wayne, IN
WAOE Peoria-Bloomington, IL
WAOW-TV Wausau-Rhinelander, WI

WAPA-TV San Juan PR
WAPT Jackson, MS
WAQP Flint-Saginaw-Bay City, MI
*WATC-DT Atlanta
WATE-TV Knoxville, TN
WATL Atlanta
WATM-TV Johnstown-Altoona, PA
WAVE Louisville, KY
WAVY-TV Norfolk-Portsmouth-Newport News, VA
WAWD Mobile, AL-Pensacola (Ft. Walton Beach), FL
WAWS Jacksonville, FL
WAXN-TV Charlotte, NC
WAZE-TV Evansville, IN
WBAL-TV Baltimore, MD
WBAY-TV Green Bay-Appleton, WI
WBBH-TV Ft. Myers-Naples, FL
WBBJ-TV Jackson, TN
WBBM-TV Chicago
*WBCC Orlando-Daytona Beach-Melbourne, FL
WBDT Dayton, OH
*WBEC-TV Miami-Ft. Lauderdale, FL
WBFF Baltimore, MD
WBFS-TV Miami-Ft. Lauderdale, FL
*WBGU-TV Toledo, OH
WBIF Panama City, FL
WBIH Montgomery-Selma, AL
WBIJ Wausau-Rhinelander, WI
*WBIQ Birmingham (Anniston, Tuscaloosa), AL
WBIR-TV Knoxville, TN
WBKB-TV Alpena, MI
WBKI-TV Louisville, KY
WBKO Bowling Green, KY
WBKP Marquette, MI
WBME-TV Milwaukee, WI
WBMM Montgomery-Selma, AL
WBNA Louisville, KY
WBNG-TV Binghamton, NY
WBNS-TV Columbus, OH
WBNX-TV Cleveland-Akron (Canton), OH
WBOC-TV Salisbury, MD
WBOY-TV Clarksburg-Weston, WV
WBPG Mobile, AL-Pensacola (Ft. Walton Beach), FL
WBPH-TV Philadelphia
WBPX-TV Boston (Manchester, NH)
*WBRA-TV Roanoke-Lynchburg, VA
WBRC Birmingham (Anniston, Tuscaloosa), AL
WBRE-TV Wilkes Barre-Scranton, PA
WBRZ-TV Baton Rouge, LA
WBSF Flint-Saginaw-Bay City, MI
WBTV Charlotte, NC
WBTW Myrtle Beach-Florence, SC
WBUI Champaign & Springfield-Decatur, IL
WBUP Marquette, MI
WBUW Madison, WI
WBUY-TV Memphis, TN
WBXX-TV Knoxville, TN
WBZ-TV Boston (Manchester, NH)
WCAU Philadelphia
WCAV Charlottesville, VA
WCAX-TV Burlington, VT-Plattsburgh, NY
*WCBB Portland-Auburn, ME
WCBD-TV Charleston, SC
WCBI-TV Columbus-Tupelo-West Point, MS
WCBS-TV New York
WCCB Charlotte, NC
WCCO-TV Minneapolis-St. Paul, MN
WCCU Champaign & Springfield-Decatur, IL
WCCV-TV Arecibo PR
WCDC Albany-Schenectady-Troy, NY
*WCES-TV Augusta, GA
*WCET Cincinnati, OH
*WCFE-TV Burlington, VT-Plattsburgh, NY
WCFN Champaign & Springfield-Decatur, IL

WCFT-TV Birmingham (Anniston, Tuscaloosa), AL
WCGV-TV Milwaukee, WI
WCHS-TV Charleston-Huntington, WV
WCIA Champaign & Springfield-Decatur, IL
*WCIQ Birmingham (Anniston, Tuscaloosa), AL
WCIU-TV Chicago
WCIV Charleston, SC
WCJB-TV Gainesville, FL
WCLF Tampa-St. Petersburg (Sarasota), FL
WCLJ-TV Indianapolis, IN
WCMH-TV Columbus, OH
*WCML Alpena, MI
*WCMU-TV Flint-Saginaw-Bay City, MI
*WCMV Traverse City-Cadillac, MI
*WCMW Traverse City-Cadillac, MI
WCNC-TV Charlotte, NC
*WCNY-TV Syracuse, NY
WCOV-TV Montgomery-Selma, AL
*WCPB Salisbury, MD
WCPO-TV Cincinnati, OH
WCPX-TV Chicago
WCSC-TV Charleston, SC
WCSH Portland-Auburn, ME
*WCTE Nashville, TN
WCTI-TV Greenville-New Bern-Washington, NC
WCTV Tallahassee, FL-Thomasville, GA
WCTX Hartford & New Haven, CT
WCVB-TV Boston (Manchester, NH)
*WCVE-TV Richmond-Petersburg, VA
WCVI-TV Christiansted VI
*WCVN-TV Cincinnati, OH
*WCVW Richmond-Petersburg, VA
WCWG Greensboro-High Point-Winston Salem, NC
WCWJ Jacksonville, FL
WCWN Albany-Schenectady-Troy, NY
WCYB-TV Tri-Cities, TN-VA
WDAF-TV Kansas City, MO
WDAM-TV Hattiesburg-Laurel, MS
WDAY-TV Fargo-Valley City, ND
WDAZ-TV Fargo-Valley City, ND
WDBB Birmingham (Anniston, Tuscaloosa), AL
WDBD Jackson, MS
WDBJ Roanoke-Lynchburg, VA
WDCA Washington, DC (Hagerstown, MD)
*WDCP-TV Flint-Saginaw-Bay City, MI
*WDCQ-TV Flint-Saginaw-Bay City, MI
WDCW Washington, DC (Hagerstown, MD)
WDEF-TV Chattanooga, TN
WDFX-TV Dothan, AL
WDHN Dothan, AL
WDHS Marquette, MI
WDIO-DT Duluth, MN-Superior, WI
*WDIQ Montgomery-Selma, AL
WDIV-TV Detroit
WDJT-TV Milwaukee, WI
WDKA Paducah, KY-Cape Girardeau, MO-Harrisburg-Mount Vernon, IL
WDKY-TV Lexington, KY
WDLI-TV Cleveland-Akron (Canton), OH
*WDPB Salisbury, MD
WDPM-DT Mobile, AL-Pensacola (Ft. Walton Beach), FL
WDPX-TV Boston (Manchester, NH)
WDRB Louisville, KY
WDRL-TV Roanoke-Lynchburg, VA
*WDSC-TV Orlando-Daytona Beach-Melbourne, FL
*WDSE Duluth, MN-Superior, WI
WDSI-TV Chattanooga, TN
WDSU New Orleans, LA
*WDTI Indianapolis, IN
WDTN Dayton, OH
WDTV Clarksburg-Weston, WV
WDWL Bayamon PR
*WEAO Cleveland-Akron (Canton), OH

WEAR-TV Mobile, AL-Pensacola (Ft. Walton Beach), FL
WEAU-TV La Crosse-Eau Claire, WI
*WEBA-TV Augusta, GA
WECN Naranjito PR
WECT Wilmington, NC
*WEDH Hartford & New Haven, CT
*WEDN Hartford & New Haven, CT
*WEDU Tampa-St. Petersburg (Sarasota), FL
WEDW New York
*WEDY Hartford & New Haven, CT
WEEK-TV Peoria-Bloomington, IL
WEHT Evansville, IN
*WEIQ Mobile, AL-Pensacola (Ft. Walton Beach), FL
*WEIU-TV Champaign & Springfield-Decatur, IL
*WEKW-TV Boston (Manchester, NH)
WELF-TV Chattanooga, TN
*WELU Aguadilla PR
WEMT Tri-Cities, TN-VA
*WENH-TV Boston (Manchester, NH)
WENY-TV Elmira (Corning), NY
WEPX-TV Greenville-New Bern-Washington, NC
WESH Orlando-Daytona Beach-Melbourne, FL
*WETA-TV Washington, DC (Hagerstown, MD)
*WETK Burlington, VT-Plattsburgh, NY
WETM-TV Elmira (Corning), NY
*WETP-TV Knoxville, TN
WEUX La Crosse-Eau Claire, WI
WEVV-TV Evansville, IN
WEWS-TV Cleveland-Akron (Canton), OH
WEYI-TV Flint-Saginaw-Bay City, MI
WFAA Dallas-Ft. Worth
WFBD Mobile, AL-Pensacola (Ft. Walton Beach), FL
WFBT Elmira (Corning), NY
WFDC-DT Washington, DC (Hagerstown, MD)
WFFF-TV Burlington, VT-Plattsburgh, NY
WFFT-TV Ft. Wayne, IN
WFGC West Palm Beach-Ft. Pierce, FL
WFGX Mobile, AL-Pensacola (Ft. Walton Beach), FL
WFIE Evansville, IN
*WFIQ Huntsville-Decatur (Florence), AL
WFLA-TV Tampa-St. Petersburg (Sarasota), FL
WFLD Chicago
WFLI-TV Chattanooga, TN
WFLX West Palm Beach-Ft. Pierce, FL
WFME-TV New York
WFMJ-TV Youngstown, OH
WFMY-TV Greensboro-High Point-Winston Salem, NC
WFMZ-TV Philadelphia
WFOR-TV Miami-Ft. Lauderdale, FL
*WFPT Washington, DC (Hagerstown, MD)
WFPX-TV Raleigh-Durham (Fayetteville), NC
WFQX-TV Traverse City-Cadillac, MI
WFRV-TV Green Bay-Appleton, WI
WFSB Hartford & New Haven, CT
*WFSG Panama City, FL
*WFSU-TV Tallahassee, FL-Thomasville, GA
WFTC Minneapolis-St. Paul, MN
WFTS-TV Tampa-St. Petersburg (Sarasota), FL
WFTT-DT Tampa-St. Petersburg (Sarasota), FL
WFTV Orlando-Daytona Beach-Melbourne, FL
WFTX-TV Ft. Myers-Naples, FL
WFTY-DT New York
*WFUM Flint-Saginaw-Bay City, MI
WFUP Traverse City-Cadillac, MI
WFUT-DT New York
*WFWA Ft. Wayne, IN

WFXB Myrtle Beach-Florence, SC
WFXG Augusta, GA
WFXI Greenville-New Bern-Washington, NC
WFXL Albany, GA
WFXP Erie, PA
WFXR Roanoke-Lynchburg, VA
WFXS Wausau-Rhinelander, WI
WFXT Boston (Manchester, NH)
WFXU Tallahassee, FL-Thomasville, GA
WFXV Utica, NY
WFXW-TV Terre Haute, IN
*WFYI Indianapolis, IN
WGAL Harrisburg -Lancaster-Lebanon-York, PA
WGBA-TV Green Bay-Appleton, WI
*WGBC Meridian, MS
*WGBH-TV Boston (Manchester, NH)
WGBO-DT Chicago
*WGBX-TV Boston (Manchester, NH)
*WGBY-TV Springfield-Holyoke, MA
WGCB-TV Harrisburg -Lancaster-Lebanon-York, PA
WGCL-TV Atlanta
*WGCU Ft. Myers-Naples, FL
WGEM-TV Quincy, IL-Hannibal, MO-Keokuk, IA
WGEN-TV Miami-Ft. Lauderdale, FL
WGFL Gainesville, FL
WGGB-TV Springfield-Holyoke, MA
WGGN-TV Cleveland-Akron (Canton), OH
WGGS-TV Greenville-Spartanburg, SC-Asheville, NC-Anderson, SC
WGHP Greensboro-High Point-Winston Salem, NC
*WGIQ Dothan, AL
WGMB-TV Baton Rouge, LA
WGME-TV Portland-Auburn, ME
WGNM Macon, GA
WGNO New Orleans, LA
WGNT Norfolk-Portsmouth-Newport News, VA
WGN-TV Chicago
*WGPT Pittsburgh, PA
WGPX-TV Greensboro-High Point-Winston Salem, NC
WGRZ Buffalo, NY
WGSA Savannah, GA
*WGTE-TV Toledo, OH
WGTQ Traverse City-Cadillac, MI
WGTU Traverse City-Cadillac, MI
*WGTV Atlanta
WGTW-TV Philadelphia
*WGVK Grand Rapids-Kalamazoo-Battle Creek, MI
*WGVU-TV Grand Rapids-Kalamazoo-Battle Creek, MI
WGXA Macon, GA
WHAG-TV Washington, DC (Hagerstown, MD)
WHAM-TV Rochester, NY
WHAS-TV Louisville, KY
*WHA-TV Madison, WI
WHBF-TV Davenport, IA-Rock Island-Moline, IL
WHBQ-TV Memphis, TN
WHBR Mobile, AL-Pensacola (Ft. Walton Beach), FL
WHDF Huntsville-Decatur (Florence), AL
WHDH-TV Boston (Manchester, NH)
WHEC-TV Rochester, NY
*WHFT-TV Miami-Ft. Lauderdale, FL
WHIO-TV Dayton, OH
*WHIQ Huntsville-Decatur (Florence), AL
WHIZ-TV Zanesville, OH
WHKY-TV Charlotte, NC
*WHLA-TV La Crosse-Eau Claire, WI
WHLT Hattiesburg-Laurel, MS
WHLV-TV Orlando-Daytona Beach-Melbourne, FL
WHMB-TV Indianapolis, IN
*WHMC Myrtle Beach-Florence, SC

WHME-TV South Bend-Elkhart, IN
WHNO New Orleans, LA
WHNS Greenville-Spartanburg, SC-Asheville, NC-Anderson, SC
WHNT-TV Huntsville-Decatur (Florence), AL
WHO-DT Des Moines-Ames, IA
WHOI Peoria-Bloomington, IL
WHP-TV Harrisburg -Lancaster-Lebanon-York, PA
WHPX-TV Hartford & New Haven, CT
WHRE Norfolk-Portsmouth-Newport News, VA
*WHRM-TV Wausau-Rhinelander, WI
*WHRO-TV Norfolk-Portsmouth-Newport News, VA
*WHSG-TV Atlanta
WHSV-TV Harrisonburg, VA
*WHTJ Charlottesville, VA
WHTM-TV Harrisburg -Lancaster-Lebanon-York, PA
WHTN Nashville, TN
WHTV Lansing, MI
*WHUT-TV Washington, DC (Hagerstown, MD)
*WHWC-TV Minneapolis-St. Paul, MN
*WHYY-TV Philadelphia
WIAT Birmingham (Anniston, Tuscaloosa), AL
WIBW-TV Topeka, KS
WICD Champaign & Springfield -Decatur, IL
WICS Champaign & Springfield -Decatur, IL
WICU-TV Erie, PA
WICZ-TV Binghamton, NY
WIDP Guayama PR
WIFR Rockford, IL
*WIIQ Montgomery-Selma, AL
*WILL-TV Champaign & Springfield -Decatur, IL
WILX-TV Lansing, MI
WINK-TV Ft. Myers-Naples, FL
WINM Ft. Wayne, IN
*WIPB Indianapolis, IN
*WIPM-TV Mayaguez PR
*WIPR-TV San Juan PR
WIPX-TV Indianapolis, IN
WIRS Yauco PR
WIRT-DT Duluth, MN-Superior, WI
WIS Columbia, SC
WISC-TV Madison, WI
WISE-TV Ft. Wayne, IN
WISH-TV Indianapolis, IN
WISN-TV Milwaukee, WI
*WITF-TV Harrisburg -Lancaster-Lebanon-York, PA
WITI Milwaukee, WI
WITN-TV Greenville-New Bern-Washington, NC
*WITV Charleston, SC
WIVB-TV Buffalo, NY
WIVT Binghamton, NY
WIWB Green Bay-Appleton, WI
WJAC-TV Johnstown-Altoona, PA
WJAL Washington, DC (Hagerstown, MD)
WJAR Providence, RI-New Bedford, MA
WJBF Augusta, GA
WJBK Detroit
WJCL Savannah, GA
*WJCT Jacksonville, FL
*WJEB-TV Jacksonville, FL
WJET-TV Erie, PA
WJFB Nashville, TN
WJFW-TV Wausau-Rhinelander, WI
WJHG-TV Panama City, FL
WJHL-TV Tri-Cities, TN-VA
WJKT Jackson, TN
WJLA-TV Washington, DC (Hagerstown, MD)
WJMN-TV Marquette, MI
*WJPM-TV Myrtle Beach-Florence, SC
WJPX San Juan PR
WJRT-TV Flint-Saginaw-Bay City, MI
*WJSP-TV Columbus, GA

WJSU-TV Birmingham (Anniston, Tuscaloosa), AL
WJTC Mobile, AL-Pensacola (Ft. Walton Beach), FL
WJTV Jackson, MS
WJW Cleveland-Akron (Canton), OH
*WJWJ-TV Savannah, GA
WJWN-TV San Sebastian PR
WJXT Jacksonville, FL
WJXX Jacksonville, FL
WJYS Chicago
WJZ-TV Baltimore, MD
WJZY Charlotte, NC
WKAQ-TV San Juan PR
*WKAR-TV Lansing, MI
*WKAS Charleston-Huntington, WV
*WKBD-TV Detroit
WKBN-TV Youngstown, OH
WKBS-TV Johnstown-Altoona, PA
WKBT La Crosse-Eau Claire, WI
WKBW-TV Buffalo, NY
WKCF Orlando-Daytona Beach-Melbourne, FL
WKDH Columbus-Tupelo-West Point, MS
WKEF Dayton, OH
*WKGB-TV Bowling Green, KY
*WKHA Lexington, KY
*WKLE Lexington, KY
*WKMA-TV Evansville, IN
WKMG-TV Orlando-Daytona Beach-Melbourne, FL
*WKMJ-TV Louisville, KY
*WKMR Lexington, KY
*WKMU Paducah, KY-Cape Girardeau, MO-Harrisburg-Mount Vernon, IL
*WKNO Memphis, TN
*WKOH Evansville, IN
WKOI-TV Dayton, OH
*WKON Cincinnati, OH
*WKOP-TV Knoxville, TN
WKOW-TV Madison, WI
*WKPC-TV Louisville, KY
*WKPD Paducah, KY-Cape Girardeau, MO-Harrisburg-Mount Vernon, IL
*WKPI-TV Charleston-Huntington, WV
WKPT-TV Tri-Cities, TN-VA
WKPV Ponce PR
WKRC-TV Cincinnati, OH
WKRG-TV Mobile, AL-Pensacola (Ft. Walton Beach), FL
WKRN-TV Nashville, TN
*WKSO-TV Lexington, KY
WKTC Columbia, SC
WKTV Utica, NY
WKYC Cleveland-Akron (Canton), OH
WKYT-TV Lexington, KY
*WKYU-TV Bowling Green, KY
*WKZT-TV Louisville, KY
*WLAE-TV New Orleans, LA
WLAJ Lansing, MI
WLAX La Crosse-Eau Claire, WI
WLBT Jackson, MS
WLBZ Bangor, ME
*WLED-TV Portland-Auburn, ME
*WLEF-TV Wausau-Rhinelander, WI
WLEX-TV Lexington, KY
WLFB Bluefield-Beckley-Oak Hill, WV
WLFG Tri-Cities, TN-VA
WLFI-TV Lafayette, IN
WLFL Raleigh-Durham (Fayetteville), NC
WLGA Columbus, GA
WLII-DT Caguas PR
WLIO Lima, OH
*WLIW New York
WLJC-TV Lexington, KY
*WLJT Jackson, TN
WLKY-TV Louisville, KY
WLLA Grand Rapids-Kalamazoo-Battle Creek, MI
WLMB Toledo, OH
WLMT Memphis, TN
WLNE-TV Providence, RI-New Bedford, MA
WLNS-TV Lansing, MI
*WLNY-TV New York

WLOS Greenville-Spartanburg, SC-Asheville, NC-Anderson, SC
WLOV-TV Columbus-Tupelo-West Point, MS
WLOX Biloxi-Gulfport, MS
*WLPB-TV Baton Rouge, LA
WLPX-TV Charleston-Huntington, WV
*WLRN-TV Miami-Ft. Lauderdale, FL
WLS-TV Chicago
WLTV-DT Miami-Ft. Lauderdale, FL
WLTX Columbia, SC
WLTZ Columbus, GA
WLUC-TV Marquette, MI
WLUK-TV Green Bay-Appleton, WI
*WLVI-TV Boston (Manchester, NH)
*WLVT-TV Philadelphia
WLWC Providence, RI-New Bedford, MA
WLWT Cincinnati, OH
*WLXI Greensboro-High Point-Winston Salem, NC
WLYH-TV Harrisburg -Lancaster-Lebanon-York, PA
*WMAA Columbus-Tupelo-West Point, MS
*WMAB-TV Columbus-Tupelo-West Point, MS
*WMAE-TV Columbus-Tupelo-West Point, MS
*WMAH-TV Biloxi-Gulfport, MS
WMAK Knoxville, TN
*WMAO-TV Greenwood-Greenville, MS
WMAQ-TV Chicago
WMAR-TV Baltimore, MD
*WMAU-TV Jackson, MS
*WMAV-TV Memphis, TN
*WMAW-TV Meridian, MS
WMAZ-TV Macon, GA
WMBB Panama City, FL
WMBC-TV New York
WMBD-TV Peoria-Bloomington, IL
WMBF-TV Myrtle Beach-Florence, SC
WMCF-TV Montgomery-Selma, AL
WMCN-TV Philadelphia
WMC-TV Memphis, TN
WMDN Meridian, MS
WMDT Salisbury, MD
*WMEA-TV Portland-Auburn, ME
*WMEB-TV Bangor, ME
*WMEC Quincy, IL-Hannibal, MO-Keokuk, IA
*WMED-TV Bangor, ME
WMEI Arecibo PR
*WMEM-TV Presque Isle, ME
*WMFD-TV Cleveland-Akron (Canton), OH
*WMFE-TV Orlando-Daytona Beach-Melbourne, FL
WMFP Boston (Manchester, NH)
WMGM-TV Philadelphia
WMGT-TV Macon, GA
*WMHT Albany-Schenectady-Troy, NY
WMMP Charleston, SC
WMOR-TV Tampa-St. Petersburg (Sarasota), FL
*WMPB Baltimore, MD
*WMPN-TV Jackson, MS
*WMPT Baltimore, MD
WMPV-TV Mobile, AL-Pensacola (Ft. Walton Beach), FL
WMSN-TV Madison, WI
*WMSY-TV Tri-Cities, TN-VA
*WMTJ Fajardo PR
WMTV Madison, WI
WMTW Portland-Auburn, ME
*WMUM-TV Macon, GA
*WMUR-TV Boston (Manchester, NH)
*WMVS Milwaukee, WI
*WMVT Milwaukee, WI
WMYA-TV Greenville-Spartanburg, SC-Asheville, NC-Anderson, SC
WMYD Detroit
WMYO Louisville, MY
WMYT-TV Charlotte, NC
WMYV Greensboro-High Point-Winston Salem, NC

WNAC-TV Providence, RI-New Bedford, MA
WNBC New York
WNBW-DT Gainesville, FL
WNCF Montgomery-Selma, AL
WNCN Raleigh-Durham (Fayetteville), NC
WNCT-TV Greenville-New Bern-Washington, NC
WNDU-TV South Bend-Elkhart, IN
WNDY-TV Indianapolis, IN
*WNED-TV Buffalo, NY
WNEG-TV Greenville-Spartanburg, SC-Asheville, NC-Anderson, SC
*WNEH Greenville-Spartanburg, SC-Asheville, NC-Anderson, SC
WNEM-TV Flint-Saginaw-Bay City, MI
*WNEO Youngstown, OH
WNEP-TV Wilkes Barre-Scranton, PA
*WNET New York
WNEU Boston (Manchester, NH)
*WNGH-TV Chattanooga, TN
WNGS Buffalo, NY
*WNIN Evansville, IN
*WNIT South Bend-Elkhart, IN
*WNJB New York
*WNJN New York
*WNJS Philadelphia
*WNJT Philadelphia
WNJU New York
WNJX-TV Mayaguez PR
WNKY Bowling Green, KY
WNLO Buffalo, NY
WNMN Burlington, VT-Plattsburgh, NY
*WNMU Marquette, MI
WNNE Burlington, VT-Plattsburgh, NY
WNOL-TV New Orleans, LA
*WNPB-TV Pittsburgh, PA
*WNPI-DT Watertown, NY
*WNPT Nashville, TN
WNPX-TV Nashville, TN
*WNSC-TV Charlotte, NC
*WNTV Greenville-Spartanburg, SC-Asheville, NC-Anderson, SC
WNTZ-TV Jackson, MS
WNUV Baltimore, MD
*WNVC Washington, DC (Hagerstown, MD)
*WNVT Washington, DC (Hagerstown, MD)
WNWO-TV Toledo, OH
WNYA Albany-Schenectady-Troy, NY
WNYB Buffalo, NY
*WNYE-TV New York
WNYO-TV Buffalo, NY
WNYS-TV Syracuse, NY
WNYT Albany-Schenectady-Troy, NY
WNYW New York
WOAI-TV San Antonio, TX
WOAY-TV Bluefield-Beckley-Oak Hill, WV
WOFL Orlando-Daytona Beach-Melbourne, FL
WOGX Gainesville, FL
WOI-DT Des Moines-Ames, IA
WOIO Cleveland-Akron (Canton), OH
WOLE-DT Aguadilla PR
WOLF-TV Wilkes Barre-Scranton, PA
WOLO-TV Columbia, SC
WOOD-TV Grand Rapids-Kalamazoo-Battle Creek, MI
WOPX-TV Orlando-Daytona Beach-Melbourne, FL
WORA-TV Mayaguez PR
WORO-DT Fajardo PR
WOST Mayaguez PR
*WOSU-TV Columbus, OH
WOTF-DT Orlando-Daytona Beach-Melbourne, FL
WOTV Grand Rapids-Kalamazoo-Battle Creek, MI
*WOUB-TV Columbus, OH
*WOUC-TV Columbus, OH
WOWK-TV Charleston-Huntington, WV
WOWT-TV Omaha, NE

WPAN Mobile, AL-Pensacola (Ft. Walton Beach), FL
*WPBA Atlanta
WPBF West Palm Beach-Ft. Pierce, FL
WPBN-TV Traverse City-Cadillac, MI
*WPBO Charleston-Huntington, WV
*WPBS-DT Watertown, NY
*WPBT Miami-Ft. Lauderdale, FL
*WPBY-TV Charleston-Huntington, WV
WPCB-TV Pittsburgh, PA
WPCH-TV Atlanta
WPCT Panama City, FL
WPCW Pittsburgh, PA
WPDE-TV Myrtle Beach-Florence, SC
WPEC West Palm Beach-Ft. Pierce, FL
WPFO Portland-Auburn, ME
WPGA-TV Macon, GA
WPGD-TV Nashville, TN
WPGH-TV Pittsburgh, PA
WPGX Panama City, FL
WPHL-TV Philadelphia
WPIX New York
WPLG Miami-Ft. Lauderdale, FL
WPME Portland-Auburn, ME
WPMI-TV Mobile, AL-Pensacola (Ft. Walton Beach), FL
WPMT Harrisburg-Lancaster-Lebanon-York, PA
WPMY Pittsburgh, PA
*WPNE-TV Green Bay-Appleton, WI
WPPX-TV Philadelphia
WPRI-TV Providence, RI-New Bedford, MA
WPSD-TV Paducah, KY-Cape Girardeau, MO-Harrisburg-Mount Vernon, IL
WPSG Philadelphia
*WPSU-TV Johnstown-Altoona, PA
WPTA Ft. Wayne, IN
*WPTD Dayton, OH
*WPTO Cincinnati, OH
WPTV West Palm Beach-Ft. Pierce, FL
WPTY-TV Memphis, TN
WPTZ Burlington, VT-Plattsburgh, NY
WPVI-TV Philadelphia
WPWR-TV Chicago
WPXA-TV Atlanta
WPXC-TV Jacksonville, FL
WPXD-TV Detroit
WPXE-TV Milwaukee, WI
WPXG-TV Boston (Manchester, NH)
WPXH-TV Birmingham (Anniston, Tuscaloosa), AL
WPXI Pittsburgh, PA
WPXJ-TV Buffalo, NY
WPXK-TV Knoxville, TN
WPXL-TV New Orleans, LA
WPXM-TV Miami-Ft. Lauderdale, FL
WPXN-TV New York
WPXP-TV West Palm Beach-Ft. Pierce, FL
WPXQ-TV Providence, RI-New Bedford, MA
WPXR-TV Roanoke-Lynchburg, VA
WPXS St. Louis, MO
WPXT Portland-Auburn, ME
WPXU-TV Greenville-New Bern-Washington, NC
WPXV-TV Norfolk-Portsmouth-Newport News, VA
WPXW-TV Washington, DC (Hagerstown, MD)
WPXX-TV Memphis, TN
WQAD-TV Davenport, IA-Rock Island-Moline, IL
WQCW Charleston-Huntington, WV
*WQEC Quincy, IL-Hannibal, MO-Keokuk, IA
*WQED Pittsburgh, PA
WQEX Pittsburgh, PA
WQHA Aguada PR
WQHS-DT Cleveland-Akron (Canton), OH
*WQLN Erie, PA
WQMY Wilkes Barre-Scranton, PA

WQOW-TV La Crosse-Eau Claire, WI
*WQPT-TV Davenport, IA-Rock Island-Moline, IL
WQPX-TV Wilkes Barre-Scranton, PA
WQRF-TV Rockford, IL
*WQTO Ponce PR
WRAL-TV Raleigh-Durham (Fayetteville), NC
WRAY-TV Raleigh-Durham (Fayetteville), NC
WRAZ Raleigh-Durham (Fayetteville), NC
WRBJ Jackson, MS
WRBL Columbus, GA
WRBU St. Louis, MO
WRBW Orlando-Daytona Beach-Melbourne, FL
WRCB Chattanooga, TN
WRC-TV Washington, DC (Hagerstown, MD)
WRDC Raleigh-Durham (Fayetteville), NC
WRDQ Orlando-Daytona Beach-Melbourne, FL
WRDW-TV Augusta, GA
WREG-TV Memphis, TN
*WRET-TV Greenville-Spartanburg, SC-Asheville, NC-Anderson, SC
WREX-TV Rockford, IL
WRFB Carolina PR
WRGB Albany-Schenectady-Troy, NY
WRGT-TV Dayton, OH
WRIC-TV Richmond-Petersburg, VA
*WRJA-TV Columbia, SC
WRJM-TV Montgomery-Selma, AL
WRLH-TV Richmond-Petersburg, VA
*WRLK-TV Columbia, SC
WRLM Cleveland-Akron (Canton), OH
WRNN-TV New York
WROC-TV Rochester, NY
WRPX-TV Raleigh-Durham (Fayetteville), NC
WRSP-TV Champaign & Springfield-Decatur, IL
WRTV Indianapolis, IN
WRUA Fajardo PR
WRXY-TV Ft. Myers-Naples, FL
WSAH New York
WSAV-TV Savannah, GA
WSAW-TV Wausau-Rhinelander, WI
WSAZ-TV Charleston-Huntington, WV
*WSBE-TV Providence, RI-New Bedford, MA
WSBK-TV Boston (Manchester, NH)
*WSBN-TV Tri-Cities, TN-VA
WSBS-TV Miami-Ft. Lauderdale, FL
WSBT-TV South Bend-Elkhart, IN
WSB-TV Atlanta
WSCV Miami-Ft. Lauderdale, FL
*WSEC Champaign & Springfield-Decatur, IL
WSEE-TV Erie, PA
WSET-TV Roanoke-Lynchburg, VA
WSFA Montgomery-Selma, AL
WSFJ-TV Columbus, OH
WSFL-TV Miami-Ft. Lauderdale, FL
WSFX-TV Wilmington, NC
WSIL-TV Paducah, KY-Cape Girardeau, MO-Harrisburg-Mount Vernon, IL
*WSIU-TV Paducah, KY-Cape Girardeau, MO-Harrisburg-Mount Vernon, IL
WSJU-TV San Juan PR
WSJV South Bend-Elkhart, IN
*WSKA Elmira (Corning), NY
*WSKG-TV Binghamton, NY
WSKY-TV Norfolk-Portsmouth-Newport News, VA
WSLS-TV Roanoke-Lynchburg, VA
WSMH Flint-Saginaw-Bay City, MI
WSMV-TV Nashville, TN
WSNS Chicago
WSOC-TV Charlotte, NC
WSPA-TV Greenville-Spartanburg, SC-Asheville, NC-Anderson, SC
WSPX-TV Syracuse, NY

*WSRE Mobile, AL-Pensacola (Ft. Walton Beach), FL
WSST-TV Albany, GA
WSTE-DT Ponce PR
WSTM-TV Syracuse, NY
WSTR-TV Cincinnati, OH
WSUR-DT Ponce PR
WSVI Christiansted VI
WSVN Miami-Ft. Lauderdale, FL
WSWB Wilkes Barre-Scranton, PA
WSWG Tallahassee, FL-Thomasville, GA
*WSWP-TV Bluefield-Beckley-Oak Hill, WV
WSYM-TV Lansing, MI
WSYR-TV Syracuse, NY
WSYT Syracuse, NY
WSYX Columbus, OH
WTAE-TV Pittsburgh, PA
WTAJ-TV Johnstown-Altoona, PA
WTAP-TV Parkersburg, WV
WTAT-TV Charleston, SC
WTBY-TV New York
*WTCE-TV West Palm Beach-Ft. Pierce, FL
*WTCI Chattanooga, TN
WTCT Paducah, KY-Cape Girardeau, MO-Harrisburg-Mount Vernon, IL
WTCV San Juan PR
WTEN Albany-Schenectady-Troy, NY
WTEV-TV Jacksonville, FL
WTGL Orlando-Daytona Beach-Melbourne, FL
WTGS Savannah, GA
WTHI-TV Terre Haute, IN
WTHR Indianapolis, IN
WTIC-TV Hartford & New Haven, CT
WTIN-TV Ponce PR
*WTIU Indianapolis, IN
WTJP-TV Birmingham (Anniston, Tuscaloosa), AL
WTJR Quincy, IL-Hannibal, MO-Keokuk, IA
*WTJX-TV Charlotte Amalie VI
WTKR Norfolk-Portsmouth-Newport News, VA
WTLF Tallahassee, FL-Thomasville, GA
WTLH Tallahassee, FL-Thomasville, GA
WTLJ Grand Rapids-Kalamazoo-Battle Creek, MI
WTLV Jacksonville, FL
WTLW Lima, OH
WTMJ-TV Milwaukee, WI
WTNH Hartford & New Haven, CT
WTNZ Knoxville, TN
WTOC-TV Savannah, GA
WTOG Tampa-St. Petersburg (Sarasota), FL
WTOK-TV Meridian, MS
WTOL Toledo, OH
WTOM-TV Traverse City-Cadillac, MI
WTOV-TV Wheeling, WV-Steubenville, OH
WTPX-TV Wausau-Rhinelander, WI
WTRF-TV Wheeling, WV-Steubenville, OH
WTSF Charleston-Huntington, WV
WTSP Tampa-St. Petersburg (Sarasota), FL
WTTA Tampa-St. Petersburg (Sarasota), FL
WTTE Columbus, OH
WTTG Washington, DC (Hagerstown, MD)
WTTK Indianapolis, IN
WTTO Birmingham (Anniston, Tuscaloosa), AL
WTTV Indianapolis, IN
*WTTW Chicago
WTVA Columbus-Tupelo-West Point, MS
WTVC Chattanooga, TN
WTVD Raleigh-Durham (Fayetteville), NC
WTVE Philadelphia
WTVF Nashville, TN

WTVG Toledo, OH
WTVH Syracuse, NY
*WTVI Charlotte, NC
WTVJ Miami-Ft. Lauderdale, FL
WTVM Columbus, GA
WTVO Rockford, IL
*WTVP Peoria-Bloomington, IL
WTVQ-DT Lexington, KY
WTVR-TV Richmond-Petersburg, VA
*WTVS Detroit
WTVT Tampa-St. Petersburg (Sarasota), FL
WTVW Evansville, IN
WTVX West Palm Beach-Ft. Pierce, FL
WTVY Dothan, AL
WTVZ-TV Norfolk-Portsmouth-Newport News, VA
WTWC-TV Tallahassee, FL-Thomasville, GA
WTWO-TV Terre Haute, IN
*WTWV Memphis, TN
WTXF-TV Philadelphia
WTXL-TV Tallahassee, FL-Thomasville, GA
WTXX Hartford & New Haven, CT
WUAB Cleveland-Akron (Canton), OH
WUCW Minneapolis-St. Paul, MN
*WUFT Gainesville, FL
WUFX Jackson, MS
WUHF Rochester, NY
*WUJA Caguas PR
*WUNC-TV Raleigh-Durham (Fayetteville), NC
*WUND-TV Norfolk-Portsmouth-Newport News, VA
*WUNE-TV Charlotte, NC
*WUNF-TV Greenville-Spartanburg, SC-Asheville, NC-Anderson, SC
*WUNG-TV Charlotte, NC
WUNI Boston (Manchester, NH)
*WUNJ-TV Wilmington, NC
*WUNK-TV Greenville-New Bern-Washington, NC
*WUNL-TV Greensboro-High Point-Winston Salem, NC
*WUNM-TV Greenville-New Bern-Washington, NC
*WUNP-TV Raleigh-Durham (Fayetteville), NC
*WUNU Myrtle Beach-Florence, SC
*WUNW Greenville-Spartanburg, SC-Asheville, NC-Anderson, SC
WUOA Birmingham (Anniston, Tuscaloosa), AL
WUPA Atlanta
WUPL New Orleans, LA
WUPV Richmond-Petersburg, VA
WUPW Toledo, OH
WUPX-TV Lexington, KY
WUSA Washington, DC (Hagerstown, MD)
*WUSF-TV Tampa-St. Petersburg (Sarasota), FL
*WUSI-TV Terre Haute, IN
WUTB Baltimore, MD
WUTF-DT Boston (Manchester, NH)
WUTR Utica, NY
WUTV Buffalo, NY
WUVC-DT Raleigh-Durham (Fayetteville), NC
WUVG-DT Atlanta
WUVN Hartford & New Haven, CT
WUVP-DT Philadelphia
WUXP-TV Nashville, TN
WVAH-TV Charleston-Huntington, WV
*WVAN-TV Savannah, GA
WVBT Norfolk-Portsmouth-Newport News, VA
WVCY-TV Milwaukee, WI
WVEA-TV Tampa-St. Petersburg (Sarasota), FL
WVEC Norfolk-Portsmouth-Newport News, VA
WVEN-TV Orlando-Daytona Beach-Melbourne, FL
WVEO Aguadilla PR

*WVER Burlington, VT-Plattsburgh, NY
WVFX Clarksburg-Weston, WV
*WVIA-TV Wilkes Barre-Scranton, PA
WVIF Christiansted VI
WVII-TV Bangor, ME
WVIR-TV Charlottesville, VA
WVIT Hartford & New Haven, CT
*WVIZ Cleveland-Akron (Canton), OH
WVLA-TV Baton Rouge, LA
WVLR Knoxville, TN
WVLT-TV Knoxville, TN
WVNS-TV Bluefield-Beckley-Oak Hill, WV
WVNY Burlington, VT-Plattsburgh, NY
WVOZ-TV Ponce PR
*WVPT Harrisonburg, VA
WVPX-TV Cleveland-Akron (Canton), OH
*WVPY Washington, DC (Hagerstown, MD)
WVSN Humacao PR
WVTA Burlington, VT-Plattsburgh, NY
*WVTB Burlington, VT-Plattsburgh, NY
WVTM-TV Birmingham (Anniston, Tuscaloosa), AL
WVTV Milwaukee, WI
WVUE-DT New Orleans, LA
*WVUT Terre Haute, IN
WVVA Bluefield-Beckley-Oak Hill, WV
WVXF Charlotte Amalie VI
WWAY Wilmington, NC
WWAZ-TV Green Bay-Appleton, WI
WWBT Richmond-Petersburg, VA
WWCP-TV Johnstown-Altoona, PA
WWCW Roanoke-Lynchburg, VA
WWDP Boston (Manchester, NH)
WWHO Columbus, OH
WWJ-TV Detroit
WWJX Jackson, MS
WWLP Springfield-Holyoke, MA
WWL-TV New Orleans, LA
WWMB Myrtle Beach-Florence, SC
WWMT Grand Rapids-Kalamazoo-Battle Creek, MI
WWNY-TV Watertown, NY
WWOR-TV New York
*WWPB Washington, DC (Hagerstown, MD)
WWPX-TV Washington, DC (Hagerstown, MD)
WWRS-TV Milwaukee, WI
WWSB Tampa-St. Petersburg (Sarasota), FL
WWSI Philadelphia
WWTI Watertown, NY
WWTO-TV Chicago
WWTV Traverse City-Cadillac, MI
WWUP-TV Traverse City-Cadillac, MI
WXCW Ft. Myers-Naples, FL
*WXEL-TV West Palm Beach-Ft. Pierce, FL
WXFT-DT Chicago
*WXGA-TV Jacksonville, FL
WXIA-TV Atlanta
WXII-TV Greensboro-High Point-Winston Salem, NC
WXIN Indianapolis, IN
WXIX-TV Cincinnati, OH
WXLV-TV Greensboro-High Point-Winston Salem, NC
WXMI Grand Rapids-Kalamazoo-Battle Creek, MI
WXOW-TV La Crosse-Eau Claire, WI
WXPX-TV Tampa-St. Petersburg (Sarasota), FL
WXTV-DT New York
WXTX Columbus, GA
WXVT Greenwood-Greenville, MS
WXXA-TV Albany-Schenectady-Troy, NY
*WXXI-TV Rochester, NY
WXXV-TV Biloxi-Gulfport, MS
WXYZ-TV Detroit
*WYBE Philadelphia
*WYCC Chicago

WYCW Greenville-Spartanburg, SC-Asheville, NC-Anderson, SC
WYDC Elmira (Corning), NY
*WYDN Boston (Manchester, NH)
WYDO Greenville-New Bern-Washington, NC
*WYES-TV New Orleans, LA

WYFF Greenville-Spartanburg, SC-Asheville, NC-Anderson, SC
*WYIN Chicago
WYMT-TV Lexington, KY
WYOU Wilkes Barre-Scranton, PA
WYOW Wausau-Rhinelander, WI

WYPX Albany-Schenectady-Troy, NY
WYTV Youngstown, OH
WYZZ-TV Peoria-Bloomington, IL
WZDX Huntsville-Decatur (Florence), AL
WZMQ Marquette, MI

WZMY-TV Boston (Manchester, NH)
WZPX-TV Grand Rapids-Kalamazoo-Battle Creek, MI
WZRB Columbia, SC
WZTV Nashville, TN
WZVI Charlotte Amalie VI

WZVN-TV Ft. Myers-Naples, FL
WZZM Grand Rapids-Kalamazoo-Battle Creek, MI
XETV San Diego, CA
XEWT-TV San Diego, CA
XHIJ El Paso (Las Cruces, NM), TX

Canadian Television Stations by Call Letters

CBAFT Moncton, NB
CBAT Fredericton-Saint John, NB
CBCP-TV-1 Shaunavon, SK
CBCP-TV-2 Cypress Hills, SK
CBCP-TV-3 Ponteix, SK
CBCT Charlottetown, PE
*CBEFT Windsor, ON
CBET Windsor, ON
CBFST-2 Temiscaning, PQ
CBFT Montreal, PQ
CBFT-2 Mont-Laurier, PQ
CBHT Halifax, NS
CBHT-11 Mulgrave, NS
CBHT-3 Yarmouth, NS
CBHT-4 Sheet Harbour, NS
CBIMT Iles-de-la-Madeleine, PQ
CBIT Sydney, NS
CBIT-2 Cheticamp, NS
CBJET Chicoutimi, PQ
CBKFT Regina, SK
CBKFT-3 Debden, SK
CBKFT-4 Saint Brieux, SK
CBKFT-5 Xenon Park, SK
CBKFT-6 Gravelbourg, SK
CBKFT-9 Bellegarde, SK
CBKST Saskatoon, SK
CBKST-1 Stranraer, SK
CBKT Regina, SK
CBKT-2 Willow Bunch, SK
CBLAT Geraldton, ON
CBLAT-4 Marathon, ON
CBLT Toronto, ON
CBMT Montreal, PQ
CBNAT Botwood, NF
CBNAT-1 Baie Verte, NF
CBNAT-4 Saint Anthony, NF
CBNAT-9 Mount St. Margaret, NF
*CBNLT Labrador City, NF
CBNT Saint John's, NF
CBNT-1 Port Rexton, NF
CBNT-2 Placentia, NF
CBNT-3 Marystown, NF
CBOFT Ottawa, ON
CBOT Ottawa, ON
CBRT Calgary, AB
CBUBT-1 Canal Flats, BC
CBUBT-7 Cranbrook, BC
CBUFT Vancouver, BC
CBUFT-2 Kamloops, BC
CBUFT-3 Terrace, BC
CBUT Vancouver, BC
CBVD-TV Malartic, PQ
CBVT Quebec City, PQ

CBVT-2 La Tuque, PQ
CBWAT Kenora, ON
CBWBT Flin Flon, MB
CBWFT Winnipeg, MB
CBWFT-10 Brandon, MB
CBWFT-4 Ste-Rose-du-Lac, MB
CBWGT Fisher Branch, MB
CBWST Baldy Mountain, MB
CBWT Winnipeg, MB
CBWT-2 Lac du Bonnet, MB
CBWYT Mafeking, MB
CBXAT Grande Prairie, AB
CBXAT-2 High Prairie, AB
CBXAT-3 Manning, AB
CBXFT Edmonton, AB
CBXFT-1 Bonnyville, AB
CBXFT-6 Fort McMurray, AB
CBXFT-8 Grande Prairie, AB
CBXT Edmonton, AB
CBYT-3 Bonne Bay, NF
CFAP-TV Quebec City, PQ
CFCF-TV Montreal, PQ
CFCM-TV Quebec City, PQ
CFCN-TV Calgary, AB
CFCN-TV-1 Drumheller, AB
CFCN-TV-5 Lethbridge, AB
CFCN-TV-8 Medicine Hat, AB
CFEG-TV Abbotsford, BC
CFER-TV Rimouski, PQ
CFER-TV-2 Sept-Iles, PQ
CFGS-TV Gatineau, PQ
CFJC-TV Kamloops, BC
CFJP-TV Montreal, PQ
CFKM-TV Trois-Rivieres, PQ
CFKS-TV Sherbrooke, PQ
CFMT-TV Toronto, ON
CFPL-TV London, ON
CFQC-TV Saskatoon, SK
CFQC-TV-2 North Battleford, SK
CFRE-TV Regina, SK
CFRN-TV Edmonton, AB
CFRN-TV-1 Grande Prairie, AB
CFRN-TV-2 Peace River, AB
CFRN-TV-3 Ashmont, AB
CFRN-TV-4 Ashmont, AB
CFRN-TV-5 Lac La Biche, AB
CFRN-TV-6 Red Deer, AB
CFRN-TV-7 Lougheed, AB
CFRN-TV-8 Grouard Mission-High Prairie, AB
CFRN-TV-9 Slave Lake, AB
CFRS-TV Jonquiere, PQ
CFSK-TV Saskatoon, SK

CFSO-TV Cardston, AB
CFTF-TV Riviere-du-Loup, PQ
CFTK-TV Terrace, BC
CFTM-TV Montreal, PQ
CFTO-TV Toronto, ON
*CFTU-TV Montreal, PQ
CFTV-TV Leamington, ON
CFVS-TV Val d'Or, PQ
CFWH-TV White Horse, YT
*CFYK-TV Yellowknife, NT
*CHAK-TV Inuvik, NT
CHAN-TV Vancouver, BC
CHAN-TV-1 Chilliwack, BC
CHAN-TV-2 Bowen Island, BC
CHAN-TV-3 Squamish, BC
CHAN-TV-5 Brackendale, BC
CHAN-TV-7 Whistler, BC
CHAT-TV Medicine Hat, AB
CHAT-TV-1 Pivot, AB
CHAU-TV Carleton, PQ
CHBC-TV Kelowna, BC
CHBX-TV Sault Ste. Marie, ON
CHCA-TV Red Deer, AB
CHCA-TV-1 Coronation, AB
CHCH-TV Hamilton, ON
CHCT-TV Saint Andrews, NB
CHEK-TV Victoria, BC
CHEK-TV-5 Campbell River, BC
CHEM-TV Trois-Rivieres, PQ
CHEX-TV Peterborough, ON
CHEX-TV-2 Oshawa, ON
CHFD-TV Thunder Bay, ON
CHKM-TV Kamloops, BC
CHLT-TV Sherbrooke, PQ
CHMI-TV Portage la Prairie, MB
CHNM-TV Vancouver, BC
CHNU-TV Fraser Valley, BC
CHOT-TV Gatineau, PQ
CHRO-TV Pembroke, ON
CHRO-TV-43 Ottawa, ON
CHVC-TV Valemount, BC
CHWI-TV Windsor, ON
CIAN-TV Calgary, AB
*CICA-TV Toronto, ON
CICC-TV Yorkton, SK
CICI-TV Sudbury, ON
CICI-TV-1 Elliot Lake, ON
*CICO-TV-18 London, ON
*CICO-TV-19 Sudbury, ON
*CICO-TV-20 Sault Ste. Marie, ON
*CICO-TV-24 Ottawa, ON
*CICO-TV-28 Kitchener, ON
*CICO-TV-32 Windsor, ON

*CICO-TV-59 Chatham, ON
*CICO-TV-9 Thunder Bay, ON
CICT-TV Calgary, AB
CIEW-TV Warmley, SK
CIHF-TV Halifax, NS
CIII-TV Paris, ON
CIII-TV-2 Bancroft, ON
CIII-TV-22 Stevenson, ON
CIII-TV-27 Peterborough, ON
CIII-TV-29 Oil Springs, ON
CIII-TV-4 Owen Sound, ON
CIII-TV-41 Toronto, ON
CIII-TV-6 Ottawa, ON
CIII-TV-7 Midland, ON
CIIT-TV Winnipeg, MB
CIMC-TV Isle Madame, NS
CIMT-TV Riviere-du-Loup, PQ
CIPA-TV Prince Albert, SK
CISA-TV Lethbridge, AB
CITL-TV Lloydminster, AB
CITO-TV Timmins, ON
CITO-TV-2 Kearns, ON
CITS-TV Hamilton, ON
CITV-TV Edmonton, AB
CITY-DT Toronto, ON
CITY-TV Toronto, ON
*CIVA-TV Rouyn, PQ
*CIVB-TV Rimouski, PQ
*CIVC-TV Trois-Rivieres, PQ
*CIVF-TV Baie-Trinite, PQ
*CIVG-TV Sept-Iles, PQ
CIVI-TV Victoria, BC
*CIVM-TV Montreal, PQ
*CIVO-TV Gatineau, PQ
*CIVP-TV Chapeau, PQ
*CIVQ-TV Quebec City, PQ
*CIVS-TV Sherbrooke, PQ
CIVT-TV Vancouver, BC
*CIVV-TV Chicoutimi, PQ
*CJAL-TV Rouyn-Noranda, PQ
CJBN-TV Kenora, ON
CJBR-TV Rimouski, PQ
CJCB-TV Sydney, NS
CJCB-TV-1 Inverness, NS
CJCB-TV-2 Antigonish, NS
CJCH-TV Halifax, NS
CJCH-TV-1 Canning, NS
CJCH-TV-6 Caledonia, NS
CJCN-TV Grand Falls, NF
CJCO-TV Calgary, AB
CJDC-TV Dawson Creek, BC
CJEO-TV Edmonton, AB
CJIL-TV Lethbridge, AB

CJMT-TV Toronto, ON
CJNT-TV Montreal, PQ
CJOH-TV Ottawa, ON
CJOH-TV-6 Deseronto, ON
CJOH-TV-8 Cornwall, ON
CJOM-TV Argentia, NF
CJON-TV St John's, NF
CJOX-TV-1 Grand Bank, NF
CJPM-TV Chicoutimi, PQ
CJSV-TV Stephenville, NF
CJTG-TV Meander River, AB
CJWB-TV Bonavista, NF
CJWN-TV Corner Brook, NF
CKAL-TV Calgary, AB
CKAM-TV Upsalquitch Lake, NB
CKBQ-TV Melfort, SK
CKCD-TV Campbellton, NB
CKCK-TV Regina, SK
CKCK-TV-1 Colgate, SK
CKCK-TV-2 Willow Bunch, SK
CKCO-TV Kitchener, ON
CKCO-TV-2 Wiarton, ON
CKCO-TV-3 Sarnia, ON
CKCS-TV Calgary, AB
CKCW-TV Moncton, NB
CKCW-TV-1 Charlottetown, PE
CKCW-TV-2 Saint Edward, PE
CKEM-TV Edmonton, AB
CKES-TV Edmonton, AB
CKLT-TV Saint John, NB
CKMC-TV Swift Current, SK
CKMC-TV-1 Golden Prairie, SK
CKMI-TV Quebec City, PQ
CKND-TV Winnipeg, MB
CKNX-TV Wingham, ON
CKNY-TV North Bay, ON
CKPG-TV Prince George, BC
CKPR-TV Thunder Bay, ON
CKRN-TV Rouyn-Noranda, PQ
CKRN-TV-3 Beam-Fabre, PQ
CKRT-TV Riviere-du-Loup, PQ
CKSA-TV Lloydminster, AB
CKSH-TV Sherbrooke, PQ
CKTM-TV Trois-Rivieres, PQ
CKVR-TV Barrie, ON
CKVU-TV Vancouver, BC
CKWS-TV Kingston, ON
CKXT-TV Toronto, ON
CKX-TV Brandon, MB
CKX-TV-1 Foxwarren, MB
CKYB-TV Brandon, MB
CKY-TV Winnipeg, MB

U.S. Television Stations by Analog Channel

Channel 2

*KVZK-2 Pago Pago, AS

Channel 3

KOFT Farmington, NM

Channel 4

*KYUK-TV Bethel, AK
*KVZK-4 Pago Pago, AS
KHMT Hardin, MT

Channel 5

*KVZK-5 Pago Pago, AS

Channel 6

XETV Tijuana, MEX
KBNY Ely, NV
KBCJ Vernal, UT

Channel 12

XEWT-TV Tijuana, MEX

Channel 22

KSQA Topeka, KS

Channel 44

XHIJ Ciudad Juarez, MEX

Canadian Television Stations by Analog Channel

Channel 2

CICT-TV Calgary AB
CBXAT-2 High Prairie AB
CFRN-TV-5 Lac La Biche AB
CKSA-TV Lloydminster AB
CHBC-TV Kelowna BC
CKPG-TV Prince George BC
CBUT Vancouver BC
CBWYT Mafeking MB
CKCW-TV Moncton NB
CBYT-3 Bonne Bay NF
CJOX-TV-1 Grand Bank NF
CBIT-2 Cheticamp NS
CIII-TV-2 Bancroft ON
CHBX-TV Sault Ste. Marie ON
CKPR-TV Thunder Bay ON
CKCO-TV-2 Wiarton ON
CBFT Montreal PQ
CFAP-TV Quebec City PQ
CJBR-TV Rimouski PQ
CBCP-TV-2 Cypress Hills SK
CKBQ-TV Melfort SK
CKCK-TV Regina SK

Channel 3

CFRN-TV Edmonton AB
CFRN-TV-2 Peace River AB
CHAT-TV-1 Pivot AB
CHAN-TV-2 Bowen Island BC
CFTK-TV Terrace BC
CBWFT-4 Ste-Rose-du-Lac MB
CBWFT Winnipeg MB
CJOM-TV Argentia NF
CBNAT-1 Baie Verte NF
CBHT Halifax NS
CKVR-TV Barrie ON
CITO-TV Timmins ON
CKRN-TV-3 Beam-Fabre PQ
CBVT-2 La Tuque PQ
CBFT-2 Mont-Laurier PQ
CBCP-TV-3 Ponteix SK

Channel 4

CFCN-TV Calgary AB
CITL-TV Lloydminster AB
CFRN-TV-9 Slave Lake AB
CFJC-TV Kamloops BC
CKYB-TV Brandon MB
CBWT-2 Lac du Bonnet MB
CBAT Fredericton-Saint John NB
CJCN-TV Grand Falls NF
CJSV-TV Stephenville NF
CJCB-TV Sydney NS
CBOT Ottawa ON
CIII-TV-4 Owen Sound ON
CHFD-TV Thunder Bay ON
CFRS-TV Jonquiere PQ
CFCM-TV Quebec City PQ
CKRN-TV Rouyn-Noranda PQ
CFSK-TV Saskatoon SK

Channel 5

CKAL-TV Calgary AB
CBXT Edmonton AB
CJDC-TV Dawson Creek BC
CKX-TV Brandon MB
CBNT-3 Marystown NF
CBIT Sydney NS
CICI-TV-1 Elliot Lake ON
CHRO-TV Pembroke ON
CICI-TV Sudbury ON
CBLT Toronto ON

Channel 6

CKCW-TV-2 Saint Edward PE
CHAU-TV Carleton PQ
CBVD-TV Malartic PQ
CFER-TV-2 Sept-Iles PQ

CBXFT-1 Bonnyville AB
CHAT-TV Medicine Hat AB
CHCA-TV Red Deer AB
CHKM-TV Kamloops BC
CHEK-TV Victoria BC
CBWT Winnipeg MB
CBNAT-4 Saint Anthony NF
CJON-TV St John's NF
CJCH-TV-6 Caledonia NS
CJCB-TV-1 Inverness NS
*CFYK-TV Yellowknife NT
CJOH-TV-6 Deseronto ON
CIII-TV-6 Ottawa ON
CIII-TV Paris ON
CJPM-TV Chicoutimi PQ
CBMT Montreal PQ
CFQC-TV-2 North Battleford SK
CKCK-TV-2 Willow Bunch SK
CFWH-TV White Horse YT

Channel 7

CISA-TV Lethbridge AB
CFRN-TV-7 Lougheed AB
CHAN-TV-3 Squamish BC
CHVC-TV Valemount BC
CKY-TV Winnipeg MB
CKCD-TV Campbellton NB
CIII-TV-7 Midland ON
CKRT-TV Riviere-du-Loup PQ
CHLT-TV Sherbrooke PQ
CBKFT-4 Saint Brieux SK
CBCP-TV-1 Shaunavon SK
CIEW-TV Warmley SK

Channel 8

CFCN-TV-8 Medicine Hat AB
CFRN-TV-6 Red Deer AB
CHAN-TV Vancouver BC
CBWST Baldy Mountain MB
CBNT Saint John's NF
CIHF-TV Halifax NS
*CHAK-TV Inuvik NT
CJOH-TV-8 Cornwall ON
CBWAT Kenora ON
CKNX-TV Wingham ON
CKCW-TV-1 Charlottetown PE
*CIVV-TV Chicoutimi PQ
*CIVA-TV Rouyn PQ
CHEM-TV Trois-Rivieres PQ
CFQC-TV Saskatoon SK

Channel 9

CBRT Calgary AB
*CJAL-TV Edmonton AB
CHAN-TV-5 Brackendale BC
CHAN-TV-7 Whistler BC
CKND-TV Winnipeg MB
CKLT-TV Saint John NB
CBNAT-9 Mount St. Margaret NF
CJCB-TV-2 Antigonish NS
CJCH-TV Halifax NS
CBOFT Ottawa ON
*CICO-TV-9 Thunder Bay ON
CFTO-TV Toronto ON
CBET Windsor ON
CIMT-TV Riviere-du-Loup PQ
*CIVG-TV Sept-Iles PQ

CKSH-TV Sherbrooke PQ
CIPA-TV Prince Albert SK
CBKT Regina SK
CBKST-1 Stranraer SK

Channel 10

CHCA-TV-1 Coronation AB
CBXAT Grande Prairie AB
CBUBT-7 Cranbrook BC
CKVU-TV Vancouver BC
CBWGT Fisher Branch MB
CBWBT Flin Flon MB
CJWB-TV Bonavista NF
CJWN-TV Corner Brook NF
CJCH-TV-1 Canning NS
CIMC-TV Isle Madame NS
CFPL-TV London ON
CKNY-TV North Bay ON
CFTM-TV Montreal PQ
CKMC-TV-1 Golden Prairie SK
CBKT-2 Willow Bunch SK
CICC-TV Yorkton SK

Channel 11

CBXFT Edmonton AB
CHAN-TV-1 Chilliwack BC
CBUFT-3 Terrace BC
CKX-TV-1 Foxwarren MB
CBAFT Moncton NB
CBNAT Botwood NF
CBHT-4 Sheet Harbour NS
CBHT-3 Yarmouth NS
CHCH-TV Hamilton ON
CITO-TV-2 Kearns ON
CKWS-TV Kingston ON
CBLAT-4 Marathon ON
CBVT Quebec City PQ
CFER-TV Rimouski PQ
CFRE-TV Regina SK
CBKST Saskatoon SK

Channel 12

CFRN-TV-4 Ashmont AB
CFCN-TV-1 Drumheller AB
CBXFT-6 Fort McMurray AB
CBXAT-3 Manning AB
CFRN-TV-3 Whitecourt AB
CBUBT-1 Canal Flats BC
CKAM-TV Upsalquitch Lake NB
CBNT-2 Placentia NF
CBHT-11 Mulgrave NS
CHEX-TV Peterborough ON
*CIVF-TV Baie-Trinite PQ
CBIMT Iles-de-la-Madeleine PQ
CFCF-TV Montreal PQ
CBFST-2 Temiscaning PQ
CKCK-TV-1 Colgate SK
CKMC-TV Swift Current SK

Channel 13

CIAN-TV Calgary AB
CITV-TV Edmonton AB
CFRN-TV-1 Grande Prairie AB
CFCN-TV-5 Lethbridge AB
CJTG-TV Meander River AB
CHEK-TV-5 Campbell River BC
CHMI-TV Portage la Prarie MB
*CBNLT Labrador City NF
CBNT-1 Port Rexton NF
CBLAT Geraldton ON
CJBN-TV Kenora ON
CKCO-TV Kitchener ON
CJOH-TV Ottawa ON

CBCT Charlottetown PE
CKTM-TV Trois-Rivieres PQ
CBKFT Regina SK

Channel 15

*CIVQ-TV Quebec City PQ

Channel 16

CHWI-TV Windsor ON
CFKM-TV Trois-Rivieres PQ

Channel 17

CJIL-TV Lethbridge AB
*CIVM-TV Montreal PQ

Channel 18

CFRN-TV-8 Grouard Mission-High Prairie AB
*CICO-TV-18 London ON

Channel 19

CBXFT-8 Grande Prairie AB
CFEG-TV Abbotsford BC
*CICO-TV-19 Sudbury ON
*CICA-TV Toronto ON

Channel 20

*CICO-TV-20 Sault Ste. Marie ON
CKMI-TV Quebec City PQ

Channel 21

CBWFT-10 Brandon MB
CBKFT-5 Xenon Park SK

Channel 22

CHEX-TV-2 Oshawa ON
CIII-TV-22 Stevenson ON
*CIVB-TV Rimouski PQ
CBKFT-3 Debden SK

Channel 23

*CIVP-TV Chapeau PQ

Channel 24

*CICO-TV-24 Ottawa ON
*CIVS-TV Sherbrooke PQ

Channel 25

CFVS-TV Val d'Or PQ

Channel 26

CBUFT Vancouver BC
CHCT-TV Saint Andrews NB
CBKFT-9 Bellegarde SK

Channel 27

CIII-TV-27 Peterborough ON

Channel 28

*CICO-TV-28 Kitchener ON

Channel 29

CIII-TV-29 Oil Springs ON
*CFTU-TV Montreal PQ
CFTF-TV Riviere-du-Loup PQ

Channel 30

*CIVO-TV Gatineau PQ
CFKS-TV Sherbrooke PQ

Channel 32

CKCS-TV Calgary AB
CFSO-TV Cardston AB
CIVT-TV Vancouver BC
*CICO-TV-32 Windsor ON

Channel 34

CFTV-TV Leamington ON
CFGS-TV Gatineau PQ

Channel 35

CIIT-TV Winnipeg MB
CFJP-TV Montreal PQ

Channel 36

CITS-TV Hamilton ON

Channel 38

CJCO-TV Calgary AB

Channel 39

CBKFT-6 Gravelbourg SK

Channel 40

CHOT-TV Gatineau PQ

Channel 41

CIII-TV-41 Toronto ON

Channel 42

CHNM-TV Vancouver BC
CKCO-TV-3 Sarnia ON

Channel 43

CHRO-TV-43 Ottawa ON

Channel 45

CKES-TV Edmonton AB
*CIVC-TV Trois-Rivieres PQ

Channel 47

CFMT-TV Toronto ON

Channel 50

CBUFT-2 Kamloops BC

Channel 51

CKEM-TV Edmonton AB

Channel 52

CKXT-TV Toronto ON

Channel 53

CIVI-TV Victoria BC

Channel 54

*CBEFT Windsor ON

Channel 56

CJEO-TV Edmonton AB

Channel 57

CITY-TV Toronto ON

Channel 58

CBJET Chicoutimi PQ

Channel 59

*CICO-TV-59 Chatham ON

Channel 62

CJNT-TV Montreal PQ

Channel 66

CHNU-TV Fraser Valley BC

Channel 69

CJMT-TV Toronto ON

U.S. Television Stations by Digital Channel

Channel 2

KNAZ-TV Flagstaff, AZ
KREX-TV Grand Junction, CO
WLBZ Bangor, ME
KNOP-TV North Platte, NE
KVBC-DT Las Vegas, NV
KOTA-TV Rapid City, SD
KJWY Jackson, WY

Channel 3

KIEM-TV Eureka, CA
WSBS-TV Key West, FL
KYUS-TV Miles City, MT
KVNV Ely, NV
KDLO-TV Florence, SD
*WBRA-TV Roanoke, VA

Channel 4

WHBF-TV Rock Island, IL
KSNB-TV Superior, NE

Channel 5

KYES-TV Anchorage, AK
WOI-DT Ames, IA
KIDA Sun Valley, ID
WBKP Calumet, MI
*WGVK Kalamazoo, MI
KXLF-TV Butte, MT
KXGN-TV Glendive, MT
KHAS-TV Hastings, NE
WLMB Toledo, OH
KOBI Medford, OR
KIVV-TV Lead, SD
WMC-TV Memphis, TN
WTVF Nashville, TN
KCWX Fredericksburg, TX
WCYB-TV Bristol, VA
WDTV Weston, WV

Channel 6

WUOA Tuscaloosa, AL
*WEDY New Haven, CT
*WABW-TV Pelham, GA
*WCES-TV Wrens, GA
KBSD-DT Ensign, KS
KTVM Butte, MT
KWNB-TV Hayes Center, NE
WRGB Schenectady, NY
WPVI-TV Philadelphia, PA

Channel 7

KFXF Fairbanks, AK
KTNL-TV Sitka, AK
*WCIQ Mount Cheaha, AL
*KETS Little Rock, AR
KAZT-TV Prescott, AZ
KAIL Fresno, CA
KABC-TV Los Angeles, CA
KRCR-TV Redding, CA
KGO-TV San Francisco, CA
KMGH-TV Denver, CO
KJCT Grand Junction, CO
WJLA-TV Washington, DC
*WJCT Jacksonville, FL
WSVN Miami, FL
WJHG-TV Panama City, FL
WFLA-TV Tampa, FL
*WMUM-TV Cochran, GA
KAII-TV Wailuku, HI
KWWL Waterloo, IA
KTVB Boise, ID
WLS-TV Chicago, IL
WEHT Evansville, IN
KBSH-DT Hays, KS
KOAM-TV Pittsburg, KS
WLJC-TV Beattyville, KY
KPLC Lake Charles, LA
WHDH-TV Boston, MA
WVII-TV Bangor, ME
WJBK Detroit, MI
WOOD-TV Grand Rapids, MI
WPBN-TV Traverse City, MI

KCCO-TV Alexandria, MN
KHQA-TV Hannibal, MO
KQTV Saint Joseph, MO
WLBT Jackson, MS
KRTV Great Falls, MT
KPAX-TV Missoula, MT
KQCD-TV Dickinson, ND
KJRR Jamestown, ND
*KMNE-TV Bassett, NE
KDUH-TV Scottsbluff, NE
KOAT-TV Albuquerque, NM
KLAS-TV Las Vegas, NV
KRNV-DT Reno, NV
KWNV Winnemucca, NV
WXXA-TV Albany, NY
WBNG-TV Binghamton, NY
WWNY-TV Carthage, NY
WABC-TV New York, NY
WNGS Springville, NY
KOCO-TV Oklahoma City, OK
*KOAC-TV Corvallis, OR
WSTE-DT Ponce, PR
*WITV Charleston, SC
WSPA-TV Spartanburg, SC
KEVN-TV Rapid City, SD
KTTW Sioux Falls, SD
WMAK Knoxville, TN
KVII-TV Amarillo, TX
KTBC Austin, TX
KOSA-TV Odessa, TX
KLTV Tyler, TX
WHRE Virginia Beach, VA
*KSPS-TV Spokane, WA
WSAW-TV Wausau, WI
WTRF-TV Wheeling, WV
KGWL-TV Lander, WY
KSWY Sheridan, WY

Channel 8

*KAKM Anchorage, AK
KAIT Jonesboro, AR
*KAET Phoenix, AZ
KUNO-TV Fort Bragg, CA
KSBW Salinas, CA
*KTSC Pueblo, CO
WGEN-TV Key West, FL
*WGTV Athens, GA
*WACS-TV Dawson, GA
*WXGA-TV Waycross, GA
KUAM-TV Hagatna, GU
KHON-TV Honolulu, HI
KCCI Des Moines, IA
KIFI-TV Idaho Falls, ID
*WSIU-TV Carbondale, IL
*KPTS Hutchinson, KS
*KSWK Lakin, KS
WBNA Louisville, KY
KNOE-TV Monroe, LA
WVUE-DT New Orleans, LA
WMTW Poland Spring, ME
WAGM-TV Presque Isle, ME
WDHS Iron Mountain, MI
WWMT Kalamazoo, MI
WGTQ Sault Ste. Marie, MI
*WDSE Duluth, MN
KOMU-TV Columbia, MO
WTVA Tupelo, MS
*KUSM Bozeman, MT
KFBB-TV Great Falls, MT
WGHP High Point, NC
WFXI Morehead City, NC
WDAZ-TV Devils Lake, ND
KUMV-TV Williston, ND
KLKN Lincoln, NE
*WNJB New Brunswick, NJ
KOFT Farmington, NM
KOBR Roswell, NM
KOLO-TV Reno, NV
WICZ-TV Binghamton, NY
WJW Cleveland, OH
WLIO Lima, OH

*KWET Cheyenne, OK
KJRH Tulsa, OK
*KSYS Medford, OR
KGW Portland, OR
WWCP-TV Johnstown, PA
WGAL Lancaster, PA
WOLO-TV Columbia, SC
*KESD-TV Brookings, SD
*KZSD-TV Martin, SD
*WNPT Nashville, TN
*KACV-TV Amarillo, TX
KIII Corpus Christi, TX
WFAA Dallas, TX
*KUHT Houston, TX
KGNS-TV Laredo, TX
WKBT La Crosse, WI
*WMVS Milwaukee, WI
WVNS-TV Lewisburg, WV
*KPTW Casper, WY
*KCWC-TV Lander, WY
*KWYP-TV Laramie, WY

Channel 9

*KUAC-TV Fairbanks, AK
WJSU-TV Anniston, AL
WALA-TV Mobile, AL
*KAFT Fayetteville, AR
KGUN-TV Tucson, AZ
KECY-TV El Centro, CA
KCAL-TV Los Angeles, CA
*KIXE-TV Redding, CA
*KVIE Sacramento, CA
KUSA Denver, CO
*WEDN Norwich, CT
WUSA Washington, DC
WINK-TV Fort Myers, FL
WNBW-DT Gainesville, FL
WPGX Panama City, FL
*WVAN-TV Savannah, GA
KGMD-TV Hilo, HI
KCRG-TV Cedar Rapids, IA
KCAU-TV Sioux City, IA
*WILL-TV Urbana, IL
*WNIN Evansville, IN
WISH-TV Indianapolis, IN
WAFB Baton Rouge, LA
*WMEB-TV Orono, ME
WWTV Cadillac, MI
*KAWE Bemidji, MN
KMSP-TV Minneapolis, MN
KBBJ Havre, MT
KCFW-TV Kalispell, MT
WSKY-TV Manteo, NC
*KDSE Dickinson, ND
*KPNE-TV North Platte, NE
WMUR-TV Manchester, NH
*KNMD-TV Santa Fe, NM
KVVU-TV Henderson, NV
WTOV-TV Steubenville, OH
KWTV Oklahoma City, OK
KEZI Eugene, OR
WBPH-TV Bethlehem, PA
WSUR-DT Ponce, PR
*WHMC Conway, SC
*WNTV Greenville, SC
KABY-TV Aberdeen, SD
WTVC Chattanooga, TN
KFWD Fort Worth, TX
KTRE Lufkin, TX
KWES-TV Odessa, TX
*KLRN San Antonio, TX
KCEN-TV Temple, TX
KUSG Saint George, UT
*WVER Rutland, VT
*KCTS Seattle, WA
WAOW-TV Wausau, WI
KFNR Rawlins, WY

Channel 10

KTUU-TV Anchorage, AK
*KTOO-TV Juneau, AK
*WBIQ Birmingham, AL
*WDIQ Dozier, AL
KSAZ-TV Phoenix, AZ
KERO-TV Bakersfield, CA
KXTV Sacramento, CA
KGTV San Diego, CA
KKTV Colorado Springs, CO
*KRMZ Steamboat Springs, CO
WTNH New Haven, CT
WPLG Miami, FL
WJXX Orange Park, FL
WTSP Saint Petersburg, FL
WALB Albany, GA
WXIA-TV Atlanta, GA
*KMEB Wailuku, HI
KNIN-TV Caldwell, ID
WWTO-TV LaSalle, IL
WGEM-TV Quincy, IL
WTHI-TV Terre Haute, IN
KBSL-DT Goodland, KS
KAKE-TV Wichita, KS
KLFY-TV Lafayette, LA
WWDP Norwell, MA
*WCBB Augusta, ME
*WMED-TV Calais, ME
*WMEM-TV Presque Isle, ME
WBUP Ishpeming, MI
WILX-TV Onondaga, MI
WWUP-TV Sault Ste. Marie, MI
*KWCM-TV Appleton, MN
WDIO-DT Duluth, MN
KTTC Rochester, MN
KBRR Thief River Falls, MN
KOLR Springfield, MO
*WMAB-TV Mississippi State, MS
KTVQ Billings, MT
WNCT-TV Greenville, NC
KMOT Minot, ND
KOLN Lincoln, NE
KBIM-TV Roswell, NM
KCHF Santa Fe, NM
KOVT Silver City, NM
KENV-DT Elko, NV
WHEC-TV Rochester, NY
WCPO-TV Cincinnati, OH
WOIO Shaker Heights, OH
KTEN Ada, OK
KTUL Tulsa, OK
KTVL Medford, OR
*KOPB-TV Portland, OR
WHTM-TV Harrisburg, PA
WIS Columbia, SC
KHSD-TV Lead, SD
*KTSD-TV Pierre, SD
WBIR-TV Knoxville, TN
WSMV-TV Nashville, TN
KFDA-TV Amarillo, TX
KZTV Corpus Christi, TX
KWTX-TV Waco, TX
*KWSU-TV Pullman, WA
WVFX Clarksburg, WV
*WSWP-TV Grandview, WV
KFNE Riverton, WY

Channel 11

KJUD Juneau, AK
*KDTP Holbrook, AZ
KYMA-DT Yuma, AZ
*KEET Eureka, CA
KTTV Los Angeles, CA
KNSO Merced, CA
WESH Daytona Beach, FL
WTVM Columbus, GA
WTOC-TV Savannah, GA
KHAW-TV Hilo, HI
*KHET Honolulu, HI
*KDIN-TV Des Moines, IA
KMVT Twin Falls, ID

WLFI-TV Lafayette, IN
KSNG Garden City, KS
*KTWU Topeka, KS
WHAS-TV Louisville, KY
KAQY Columbia, LA
*WYES-TV New Orleans, LA
WWLP Springfield, MA
WBAL-TV Baltimore, MD
WBKB-TV Alpena, MI
*WGVU-TV Grand Rapids, MI
KRII Chisholm, MN
KARE Minneapolis, MN
WTOK-TV Meridian, MS
KULR-TV Billings, MT
*KUFM-TV Missoula, MT
*WTVI Charlotte, NC
WTVD Durham, NC
*KWSE Williston, ND
KGIN Grand Island, NE
*WENH-TV Durham, NH
*KLVX Las Vegas, NV
WPIX New York, NY
WTOL Toledo, OH
KSWO-TV Lawton, OK
*KOED-TV Tulsa, OK
*KOAB-TV Bend, OR
KCBY-TV Coos Bay, OR
KFFX-TV Pendleton, OR
WPCW Jeannette, PA
WBRE-TV Wilkes-Barre, PA
WLII-DT Caguas, PR
*KQSD-TV Lowry, SD
KELO-TV Sioux Falls, SD
WJHL-TV Johnson City, TN
KTVT Fort Worth, TX
KHOU Houston, TX
KCBD Lubbock, TX
KVCT Victoria, TX
KCBU Price, UT
*WVPT Staunton, VA
KSTW Tacoma, WA
WLUK-TV Green Bay, WI
KQCK Cheyenne, WY
KBEO Jackson, WY

Channel 12

KIMO Anchorage, AK
WSFA Montgomery, AL
*KETZ El Dorado, AR
KTHV Little Rock, AR
KPNX Mesa, AZ
KNTV San Jose, CA
KKCO Grand Junction, CO
*WHYY-TV Wilmington, DE
WTVT Tampa, FL
WPTV West Palm Beach, FL
WFXL Albany, GA
WRDW-TV Augusta, GA
*KGTF-TV Hagatna, GU
KMAU Wailuku, HI
*KIIN Iowa City, IA
*KUID-TV Moscow, ID
WBBM-TV Chicago, IL
WINM Angola, IN
KWCH-DT Hutchinson, KS
WYMT-TV Hazard, KY
WJRT-TV Flint, MI
KEYC-TV Mankato, MN
KCCW-TV Walker, MN
KFVS-TV Cape Girardeau, MO
KRCG Jefferson City, MO
*WMAE-TV Booneville, MS
WJTV Jackson, MS
KTVH-DT Helena, MT
WCTI-TV New Bern, NC
KXMB-TV Bismarck, ND
*KUON-TV Lincoln, NE
KSNK McCook, NE
*KRNE-TV Merriman, NE
KOBF Farmington, NM
KOBG-TV Silver City, NM

WNYT Albany, NY
WKRC-TV Cincinnati, OH
WMFD-TV Mansfield, OH
KDRV Medford, OR
KPTV Portland, OR
WICU-TV Erie, PA
WOLE-DT Aguadilla, PR
WNAC-TV Providence, RI
KTTM Huron, SD
WDEF-TV Chattanooga, TN
KBMT Beaumont, TX
*KAMU-TV College Station, TX
KSAT-TV San Antonio, TX
KXII Sherman, TX
KUTF Logan, UT
WWBT Richmond, VA
WBIJ Crandon, WI
WBOY-TV Clarksburg, WV
WWPX-TV Martinsburg, WV
KCWY-DT Casper, WY

Channel 13

KUBD Ketchikan, AK
WVTM-TV Birmingham, AL
*KETG Arkadelphia, AR
*KEMV Mountain View, AR
KFPH-DT Flagstaff, AZ
KSWT Yuma, AZ
KCOP Los Angeles, CA
KCBA Salinas, CA
*KBDI-TV Broomfield, CO
KREY-TV Montrose, CO
WTLV Jacksonville, FL
WMBB Panama City, FL
*WEDU Tampa, FL
WPEC West Palm Beach, FL
WMAZ-TV Macon, GA
KHVO Hilo, HI
WHO-DT Des Moines, IA
KTRV-TV Nampa, ID
WREX-TV Rockford, IL
WCFN Springfield, IL
WTHR Indianapolis, IN
KUPK-TV Garden City, KS
KFJX-TV Pittsburg, KS
WIBW-TV Topeka, KS
WBKO Bowling Green, KY
WKYT-TV Lexington, KY
WBRZ-TV Baton Rouge, LA
*KLTM-TV Monroe, LA
WNYA Pittsfield, MA
WJZ-TV Baltimore, MD
WZZM Grand Rapids, MI
*WNMU Marquette, MI
WIRT-DT Hibbing, MN
WLOX Biloxi, MS
KBZK Bozeman, MT
KBAO Lewistown, MT
KECI-TV Missoula, MT
WLOS Asheville, NC
*KFME Fargo, ND
KXMC-TV Minot, ND
*KTNE-TV Alliance, NE
KHGI-TV Kearney, NE
*WNET Newark, NJ
KRQE Albuquerque, NM
KTNV-TV Las Vegas, NV
KTVN Reno, NV
WHAM-TV Rochester, NY
WSYX Columbus, OH
WTVG Toledo, OH
*KETA-TV Oklahoma City, OK
KVAL-TV Eugene, OR
KOTI Klamath Falls, OR
*KTVR La Grande, OR
*WQED Pittsburgh, PA
WYOU Scranton, PA
WORO-DT Fajardo, PR
WPRI-TV Providence, RI
WBTW Florence, SC
*KPSD-TV Eagle Butte, SD
KPLO-TV Reliance, SD
KSFY-TV Sioux Falls, SD
WRCB Chattanooga, TN
WHBQ-TV Memphis, TN
KRIS-TV Corpus Christi, TX

*KCOS El Paso, TX
KTRK-TV Houston, TX
KAKW-DT Killeen, TX
KVTV Laredo, TX
KRGV-TV Weslaco, TX
WVEC Hampton, VA
WSET-TV Lynchburg, VA
WVNY Burlington, VT
KXLY-TV Spokane, WA
KCPQ Tacoma, WA
WEAU-TV Eau Claire, WI
WOWK-TV Huntington, WV
KGWR-TV Rock Springs, WY
KSGW-TV Sheridan, WY

Channel 14

WHDF Florence, AL
KTNC-TV Concord, CA
KTGM Tamuning, GU
*WTIU Bloomington, IN
KOCW Hoisington, KS
*WKSO-TV Somerset, KY
WKBD-TV Detroit, MI
KNLC Saint Louis, MO
WGPX-TV Burlington, NC
KMCY Minot, ND
KXMD-TV Williston, ND
WFBT Bath, NY
WUTV Buffalo, NY
WPTZ North Pole, NY
WCMH-TV Columbus, OH
WMEI Arecibo, PR
WMYA-TV Anderson, SC
*KERA-TV Dallas, TX
KCSG Cedar City, UT
KTBW-TV Tacoma, WA
KAPP Yakima, WA
KGWC-TV Casper, WY

Channel15

WPMI-TV Mobile, AL
KHOG-TV Fayetteville, AR
KNXV-TV Phoenix, AZ
*KBSV Ceres, CA
KSBY San Luis Obispo, CA
KTFD-DT Boulder, CO
KREZ-TV Durango, CO
KFQX Grand Junction, CO
WBBH-TV Fort Myers, FL
WRBL Columbus, GA
KUPU Waimanalo, HI
KYOU-TV Ottumwa, IA
KPIF Pocatello, ID
*WSEC Jacksonville, IL
*WKMR Morehead, KY
WNOL-TV New Orleans, LA
*WDCQ-TV Bad Axe, MI
*KSMN Worthington, MN
KPOB-TV Poplar Bluff, MO
*KMOS-TV Sedalia, MO
WXVT Greenville, MS
WRPX-TV Rocky Mount, NC
*KGFE Grand Forks, ND
KNRR Pembina, ND
*KNPB Reno, NV
WSPX-TV Syracuse, NY
WEWS-TV Cleveland, OH
KTBO-TV Oklahoma City, OK
*WPSU-TV Clearfield, PA
*WNSC-TV Rock Hill, SC
WZTV Nashville, TN
KXVA Abilene, TX
KCIT Amarillo, TX
KFOX-TV El Paso, TX
KTAL-TV Texarkana, TX
KAVU-TV Victoria, TX
KJTL Wichita Falls, TX
WFDC-DT Arlington, VA
WVIF Christiansted, VI
KHQ-TV Spokane, WA
WQOW-TV Eau Claire, WI

Channel 16

WCJB-TV Gainesville, FL
WPBF Tequesta, FL
WELF-TV Dalton, GA
WGXA Macon, GA

KOGG Wailuku, HI
KDSM-TV Des Moines, IA
WTVO Rockford, IL
*KOOD Hays, KS
WNKY Bowling Green, KY
*WKHA Hazard, KY
KADN-TV Lafayette, LA
WSMH Flint, MI
*KCGE-DT Crookston, MN
*WMAH-TV Biloxi, MS
WLOV-TV West Point, MS
KBMY Bismarck, ND
KTVG-TV Grand Island, NE
KINC Las Vegas, NV
*WXXI-TV Rochester, NY
*WPTD Dayton, OH
KUNP La Grande, OR
WSEE-TV Erie, PA
*WMTJ Fajardo, PR
WPDE-TV Florence, SC
WGGS-TV Greenville, SC
KCLO-TV Rapid City, SD
KTSM-TV El Paso, TX
KPTB Lubbock, TX
*KHCE-TV San Antonio, TX
KBCJ Vernal, UT
*WHRO-TV Hampton-Norfolk, VA
KNDO Yakima, WA
WJFW-TV Rhinelander, WI

Channel 17

KPHO-TV Phoenix, AZ
KVIQ Eureka, CA
WKCF Clermont, FL
WEAR-TV Pensacola, FL
*KISU-TV Pocatello, ID
WTCT Marion, IL
*WYIN Gary, IN
KLBY Colby, KS
KAAS-TV Salina, KS
*WKPC-TV Louisville, KY
KSLA Shreveport, LA
*WCMV Cadillac, MI
KQDS-TV Duluth, MN
KMIZ Columbia, MO
KMMF Missoula, MT
WNCN Goldsboro, NC
*WUNE-TV Linville, NC
*KYNE-TV Omaha, NE
KTUW Scottsbluff, NE
*KAZQ Albuquerque, NM
WSYR-TV Syracuse, NY
WKYC Cleveland, OH
WQCW Portsmouth, OH
KDOR-TV Bartlesville, OK
KMTR Eugene, OR
WPHL-TV Philadelphia, PA
WVEO Aguadilla, PR
WPXQ-TV Block Island, RI
WLTX Columbia, SC
*KDSD-TV Aberdeen, SD
*WKOP-TV Knoxville, TN
KVIA-TV El Paso, TX
KPCB Snyder, TX
WFXR Roanoke, VA
WVXF Charlotte Amalie, VI
WLAX La Crosse, WI
KTWO-TV Casper, WY

Channel 18

KATN Fairbanks, AK
WDBB Bessemer, AL
KFSM-TV Fort Smith, AR
KSCI Long Beach, CA
KUVS-DT Modesto, CA
KUSI-TV San Diego, CA
*KRMA-TV Denver, CO
*KRMJ Grand Junction, CO
*WPBT Miami, FL
*KYIN Mason City, IA
WAND Decatur, IL
WISE-TV Fort Wayne, IN
*WKYU-TV Bowling Green, KY
WMFP Lawrence, MA
*WDCP-TV University Center, MI
*KCPT Kansas City, MO
*WMAU-TV Bude, MS

KSVI Billings, MT
WMBC-TV Newton, NJ
WETM-TV Elmira, NY
KTVC Roseburg, OR
WECN Naranjito, PR
*WNEH Greenwood, SC
WFXB Myrtle Beach, SC
KNIC-DT Blanco, TX
KDBC-TV El Paso, TX
KPTF Farwell, TX
KUPB Midland, TX
KYTX Nacogdoches, TX
*KUEW Saint George, UT
WDBJ Roanoke, VA
*WVTB Saint Johnsbury, VT
KEPR-TV Pasco, WA
WVTV Milwaukee, WI

Channel 19

*WIIQ Demopolis, AL
KMOH-TV Kingman, AZ
KTTU Tucson, AZ
KSWB-TV San Diego, CA
KOFY-TV San Francisco, CA
KCOY-TV Santa Maria, CA
KTVD Denver, CO
WTEV-TV Jacksonville, FL
WMOR-TV Lakeland, FL
WSFL-TV Miami, FL
WGCL-TV Atlanta, GA
KIKU Honolulu, HI
KDMI Des Moines, IA
WGN-TV Chicago, IL
*WUSI-TV Olney, IL
WHOI Peoria, IL
*KWKS Colby, KS
KSCW-DT Wichita, KS
WBKI-TV Campbellsville, KY
*WGBH-TV Boston, MA
WABI-TV Bangor, ME
WXMI Grand Rapids, MI
WZMQ Marquette, MI
KSPR Springfield, MO
KWYB Butte, MT
*WUNM-TV Jacksonville, NC
WCWG Lexington, NC
KXMA-TV Dickinson, ND
KVRR Fargo, ND
*KXNE-TV Norfolk, NE
KOCT Carlsbad, NM
WSYT Syracuse, NY
KPIC Roseburg, OR
WKPV Ponce, PR
KPRY-TV Pierre, SD
KAMR-TV Amarillo, TX
KTXA Fort Worth, TX
KTXH Houston, TX
KLDO-TV Laredo, TX
KIDY San Angelo, TX
*KUES Richfield, UT
WCAV Charlottesville, VA
KBCB Bellingham, WA
*KCKA Centralia, WA
WMTV Madison, WI
KBJR-TV Superior, WI
WVAH-TV Charleston, WV

Channel 20

KTBY Anchorage, AK
KJNP-TV North Pole, AK
WMPV-TV Mobile, AL
WCOV-TV Montgomery, AL
*KTEJ Jonesboro, AR
*KPAZ-TV Phoenix, AZ
KBBC-TV Bishop, CA
KFTV-DT Hanford, CA
KCVU Paradise, CA
*KRMU Durango, CO
WTXX Waterbury, CT
*WLRN-TV Miami, FL
WPCH-TV Atlanta, GA
WHMB-TV Indianapolis, IN
WAZE-TV Madisonville, KY
*KLTL-TV Lake Charles, LA
WCVB-TV Boston, MA
WOTV Battle Creek, MI
*KSMQ-TV Austin, MN

KNLJ Jefferson City, MO
*WMPN-TV Jackson, MS
*WUND-TV Edenton, NC
*KJRE Ellendale, ND
KETV Omaha, NE
KVIH-TV Clovis, NM
KAME-TV Reno, NV
WNYI Ithaca, NY
WFMJ-TV Youngstown, OH
KQCW Muskogee, OK
WBXX-TV Crossville, TN
KTXS-TV Sweetwater, TX
*KWBU-TV Waco, TX
KTMW Salt Lake City, UT
WWCW Lynchburg, VA
WSVI Christiansted, VI
KREM Spokane, WA
*WHA-TV Madison, WI
KFNB-TV Casper, WY

Channel 21

WDHN Dothan, AL
KHBS Fort Smith, AR
KMAX-TV Sacramento, CA
KPMR Santa Barbara, CA
KFCT Fort Collins, CO
WCLF Clearwater, FL
*WPBA Atlanta, GA
KWHM Wailuku, HI
*KAID Boise, ID
*WYCC Chicago, IL
*WMEC Macomb, IL
WPXS Mount Vernon, IL
*WFYI Indianapolis, IN
*KDCK Dodge City, KS
WUPX-TV Morehead, KY
KPXJ Minden, LA
WHNO New Orleans, LA
WBOC-TV Salisbury, MD
WMYD Detroit, MI
*WCMW Manistee, MI
KTAJ-TV Saint Joseph, MO
WAPT Jackson, MS
WDAY-TV Fargo, ND
KRWB-TV Roswell, NM
*WLIW Garden City, NY
WWTI Watertown, NY
WBNS-TV Columbus, OH
KTVZ Bend, OR
WHP-TV Harrisburg, PA
WJPX San Juan, PR
*WSBE-TV Providence, RI
WWMB Florence, SC
WHNS Greenville, SC
KNBN Rapid City, SD
WUXP-TV Nashville, TN
KXAN-TV Austin, TX
KFDM-TV Beaumont, TX
*WVPY Front Royal, VA
*KYVE Yakima, WA
WIWB Suring, WI

Channel 22

*WFIQ Florence, AL
WBMM Tuskegee, AL
KATV Little Rock, AR
KAEF-TV Arcata, CA
KVYE El Centro, CA
KXRM-TV Colorado Springs, CO
WFOR-TV Miami, FL
WOFL Orlando, FL
WJCL Savannah, GA
KHBC-TV Hilo, HI
KGMB Honolulu, HI
KWWF Waterloo, IA
*KIPT-TV Twin Falls, ID
WBUI Decatur, IL
WSBT-TV South Bend, IN
*WVUT Vincennes, IN
KSNC Great Bend, KS
WLWC New Bedford, MA
*WGBY-TV Springfield, MA
WNEM-TV Bay City, MI
WUCW Minneapolis, MN
KBSI Cape Girardeau, MO
WHLT Hattiesburg, MS
KHMT Hardin, MT

WCNC-TV Charlotte, NC
*KBME-TV Bismarck, ND
WOWT-TV Omaha, NE
*WNJS Camden, NJ
KTFQ-DT Albuquerque, NM
KVMY Las Vegas, NV
KOKI-TV Tulsa, OK
KMCB Coos Bay, OR
KPXG-TV Salem, OR
WFXP Erie, PA
WOST Mayaguez, PR
*WCTE Cookeville, TN
*KLRU Austin, TX
KETK-TV Jacksonville, TX
KAUZ-TV Wichita Falls, TX
WRIC-TV Petersburg, VA
WCAX-TV Burlington, VT
WVCY-TV Milwaukee, WI

Channel 23

WDPM-DT Mobile, AL
KVOA Tucson, AZ
*KRCB Cotati, CA
KVMD Twentynine Palms, CA
KREG-TV Glenwood Springs, CO
KCDO-TV Sterling, CO
WLTV-DT Miami, FL
*WMFE Orlando, FL
*WJSP-TV Columbus, GA
KWHH Hilo, HI
KFVE Honolulu, HI
KCWI-TV Ames, IA
KPVI-DT Pocatello, ID
*WQPT-TV Moline, IL
*WIPB Muncie, IN
*KLPB-TV Lafayette, LA
WPFO Waterville, ME
*KOZK Springfield, MO
KTMF Missoula, MT
WBTV Charlotte, NC
*WUNK-TV Greenville, NC
*KRWG-TV Las Cruces, NM
WPXJ-TV Batavia, NY
*WNPI-DT Norwood, NY
WFTY-DT Smithtown, NY
WVPX-TV Akron, OH
WLYH-TV Lancaster, PA
WNJX-TV Mayaguez, PR
WPXK-TV Jellico, TN
*WTWV Memphis, TN
WNAB Nashville, TN
*KEDT Corpus Christi, TX
*KLTJ Galveston, TX
KUVN-DT Garland, TX
KPEJ-TV Odessa, TX
WCVI-TV Christiansted, VI
WBAY-TV Green Bay, WI
WSAZ-TV Huntington, WV

Channel 24

*WHIQ Huntsville, AL
KVTN-DT Pine Bluff, AR
KTVK Phoenix, AZ
KNVN Chico, CA
KBEH Oxnard, CA
KRDO-TV Colorado Springs, CO
WWSB Sarasota, FL
WTLF Tallahassee, FL
WPXC-TV Brunswick, GA
WNEG-TV Toccoa, GA
KGMV Wailuku, HI
KIVI-TV Nampa, ID
WPTA Fort Wayne, IN
*WCVN-TV Covington, KY
*WKPI-TV Pikeville, KY
*KLTS-TV Shreveport, LA
WUPL Slidell, LA
*WCML Alpena, MI
WTLJ Muskegon, MI
KCTV Kansas City, MO
KMOV Saint Louis, MO
WMDN Meridian, MS
KBTZ Butte, MT
KXND Minot, ND
KNAT-TV Albuquerque, NM
*WNYE-TV New York, NY
WSTM-TV Syracuse, NY

WSFJ-TV Newark, OH
KOKH-TV Oklahoma City, OK
WATM-TV Altoona, PA
WJET-TV Erie, PA
WTAT-TV Charleston, SC
*KCSD-TV Sioux Falls, SD
KTAB-TV Abilene, TX
KVEO-TV Brownsville, TX
KVAW Eagle Pass, TX
*KETH-TV Houston, TX
KPNZ Ogden, UT
WDRL-TV Danville, VA
*WNVC Fairfax, VA
*WVTA Windsor, VT
KQUP Pullman, WA
*WHRM-TV Wausau, WI

Channel 25

WBPG Gulf Shores, AL
KMSB Tucson, AZ
KGET-TV Bakersfield, CA
KOVR Stockton, CA
*KQET Watsonville, CA
WVEA-TV Venice, FL
WATL Atlanta, GA
KLEI Kailua-Kona, HI
*KTIN Fort Dodge, IA
KWKB Iowa City, IA
WEEK-TV Peoria, IL
WRTV Indianapolis, IN
*WLPB-TV Baton Rouge, LA
*KOZJ Joplin, MO
*WMAO-TV Greenwood, MS
*WUNF-TV Asheville, NC
*WUNC-TV Chapel Hill, NC
*KMDE Devils Lake, ND
KTEL-TV Carlsbad, NM
*WCNY-TV Syracuse, NY
KDKA-TV Pittsburgh, PA
WTVE Reading, PA
*WQTO Ponce, PR
WPTY-TV Memphis, TN
KINT-TV El Paso, TX
WTVR-TV Richmond, VA
WNNE Hartford, VT
KMYQ Seattle, WA
WCGV-TV Milwaukee, WI

Channel 26

KTVF Fairbanks, AK
WTJP-TV Gadsden, AL
KVTH-DT Hot Springs, AR
KUTP Phoenix, AZ
*KVCR-DT San Bernardino, CA
KTFK-DT Stockton, CA
WHPX-TV New London, CT
WKMG-TV Orlando, FL
WCCU Urbana, IL
KSAS-TV Wichita, KS
*WKAS Ashland, KY
WLKY-TV Louisville, KY
*KLPA-TV Alexandria, LA
WGNO New Orleans, LA
WHAG-TV Hagerstown, MD
*WCMU-TV Mount Pleasant, MI
KFTC Bemidji, MN
*KTCI-TV Saint Paul, MN
KPLR-TV Saint Louis, MO
KLMN Great Falls, MT
KNDX Bismarck, ND
*KLNE-TV Lexington, NE
KOB Albuquerque, NM
KREN-TV Reno, NV
WTEN Albany, NY
WNYB Jamestown, NY
*WVIZ Cleveland, OH
WBDT Springfield, OH
KMVU-DT Medford, OR
KYW-TV Philadelphia, PA
KDLV-TV Mitchell, SD
*KBHE-TV Rapid City, SD
WATE-TV Knoxville, TN
KRIV Houston, TX
KMID Midland, TX
KPXL-TV Uvalde, TX
KXXV Waco, TX
WRLH-TV Richmond, VA

KNDU Richland, WA

Channel 27

WKRG-TV Mobile, AL
*WAIQ Montgomery, AL
KTVE El Dorado, AR
KFTA-TV Fort Smith, AR
KTSF San Francisco, CA
KEYT-TV Santa Barbara, CA
*WETA-TV Washington, DC
WRDQ Orlando, FL
WTXL-TV Tallahassee, FL
*WXEL-TV West Palm Beach, FL
WAGA-TV Atlanta, GA
*KAAH-TV Honolulu, HI
KFXA Cedar Rapids, IA
WCIU-TV Chicago, IL
WIPX-TV Bloomington, IN
KSNT Topeka, KS
WUTF-DT Marlborough, MA
KCWV Duluth, MN
KRWF Redwood Falls, MN
WCCB Charlotte, NC
WLFL Raleigh, NC
KCPM Grand Forks, ND
WGTW-TV Burlington, NJ
KRPV Roswell, NM
KASA-TV Santa Fe, NM
KBNY Ely, NV
WTBY-TV Poughkeepsie, NY
WFXV Utica, NY
*WOUB-TV Athens, OH
*WBGU-TV Bowling Green, OH
KFOR-TV Oklahoma City, OK
WAPA-TV San Juan, PR
WKPT-TV Kingsport, TN
WKRN-TV Nashville, TN
KORO Corpus Christi, TX
KXAM-TV Llano, TX
KAMC Lubbock, TX
*KBTC-TV Tacoma, WA
WACY-TV Appleton, WI
WKOW-TV Madison, WI
*WHWC-TV Menomonie, WI
KLWY Cheyenne, WY

Channel 28

KTVA Anchorage, AK
WTTO Homewood, AL
*KUAS-TV Tucson, AZ
KBVU Eureka, CA
*KCET Los Angeles, CA
KMPH-TV Visalia, CA
WGFL High Springs, FL
WFLX West Palm Beach, FL
*KSIN-TV Sioux City, IA
KBCI-TV Boise, ID
WYZZ-TV Bloomington, IL
WSJV Elkhart, IN
WTVW Evansville, IN
KATC Lafayette, LA
KTBS-TV Shreveport, LA
*WFPT Frederick, MD
*WCPB Salisbury, MD
*WFUM Flint, MI
*KAWB Brainerd, MN
KSFX-TV Springfield, MO
WDAM-TV Laurel, MS
WRDC Durham, NC
*KHNE-TV Hastings, NE
WNBC New York, NY
WUHF Rochester, NY
WUAB Lorain, OH
*WPTO Oxford, OH
KTPX-TV Okmulgee, OK
WKAQ-TV San Juan, PR
WTGS Hardeeville, SC
*WRJA-TV Sumter, SC
WREG-TV Memphis, TN
KYLE-TV Bryan, TX
KTRG Del Rio, TX
KFDX-TV Wichita Falls, TX
KSTU Salt Lake City, UT
KAYU-TV Spokane, WA
WYOW Eagle River, WI
WTMJ-TV Milwaukee, WI

Channel 29

WBIH Selma, AL
KFTR-DT Ontario, CA
KPIX-TV San Francisco, CA
KDEN Longmont, CO
WFTS-TV Tampa, FL
WMAQ-TV Chicago, IL
WTTK Kokomo, IN
WXIX-TV Newport, KY
WUNI Worcester, MA
*WMPB Baltimore, MD
WGTU Traverse City, MI
WFTC Minneapolis, MN
KMBC-TV Kansas City, MO
KMTF Helena, MT
*WUNJ-TV Wilmington, NC
WXLV-TV Winston-Salem, NC
KSTF Scottsbluff, NE
WUVP-DT Vineland, NJ
*WFME-TV West Milford, NJ
KUPT Hobbs, NM
KWBQ Santa Fe, NM
KVCW Las Vegas, NV
WKTV Utica, NY
*WGTE-TV Toledo, OH
KTUZ-TV Shawnee, OK
*KEPB-TV Eugene, OR
KDKF Klamath Falls, OR
WQMY Williamsport, PA
WORA-TV Mayaguez, PR
*WTCI Chattanooga, TN
*WKNO Memphis, TN
KRBC-TV Abilene, TX
KUPX-TV Provo, UT
WVBT Virginia Beach, VA

Channel 30

WIAT Birmingham, AL
KLRT-TV Little Rock, AR
*KUAT-TV Tucson, AZ
KFSN-TV Fresno, CA
*KPBS San Diego, CA
*KQED San Francisco, CA
*WBCC Cocoa, FL
WSCV Fort Lauderdale, FL
WAGT Augusta, GA
WMBD-TV Peoria, IL
*WKOH Owensboro, KY
KVHP Lake Charles, LA
WBZ-TV Boston, MA
WEYI-TV Saginaw, MI
WSFX-TV Wilmington, NC
WFUT-DT Newark, NJ
*WSKA Corning, NY
WUTR Utica, NY
WBNX-TV Akron, OH
WRGT-TV Dayton, OH
KBLN Grants Pass, OR
WGCB-TV Red Lion, PA
WDWL Bayamon, PR
WVLT-TV Knoxville, TN
KMPX Decatur, TX
KWWT Odessa, TX
KABB San Antonio, TX
*WNVT Goldvein, VA
WSLS-TV Roanoke, VA
KPDX Vancouver, WA
*WHLA-TV La Crosse, WI
KGWN-TV Cheyenne, WY

Channel 31

KWBM Harrison, AR
KTLA Los Angeles, CA
KSMS-TV Monterey, CA
WTIC-TV Hartford, CT
WPPX-TV Wilmington, DE
*WGCU Fort Myers, FL
WTVJ Miami, FL
WOGX Ocala, FL
*WSRE Pensacola, FL
WFXG Augusta, GA
KWHE Honolulu, HI
KFXP Pocatello, ID
WFLD Chicago, IL
WANE-TV Fort Wayne, IN
KDCU-DT Derby, KS

WDKY-TV Danville, KY
KLAX-TV Alexandria, LA
*WLAE-TV New Orleans, LA
WFXT Boston, MA
WPXD-TV Ann Arbor, MI
KCWE Kansas City, MO
KDNL-TV Saint Louis, MO
*WGBC Meridian, MS
*WUNU Lumberton, NC
WXII-TV Winston-Salem, NC
KFYR-TV Bismarck, ND
WPXN-TV New York, NY
*KOET Eufaula, OK
KLSR-TV Eugene, OR
WSWB Scranton, PA
WSJU-TV San Juan, PR
WLMT Memphis, TN
KEYU Borger, TX
KGBT-TV Harlingen, TX
KFXK-TV Longview, TX
WAVY-TV Portsmouth, VA
KONG Everett, WA
WFXS Wittenberg, WI

Channel 32

KDMD Anchorage, AK
WAAY-TV Huntsville, AL
WNCF Montgomery, AL
KARK-TV Little Rock, AR
KCFG Flagstaff, AZ
KOLD-TV Tucson, AZ
KDOC-TV Anaheim, CA
KION-TV Monterey, CA
KFTY Santa Rosa, CA
KDVR Denver, CO
WAWS Jacksonville, FL
WBFS-TV Miami, FL
*WFSU-TV Tallahassee, FL
WPGA-TV Perry, GA
KLEW-TV Lewiston, ID
WTJR Quincy, IL
WNDY-TV Marion, IN
WPSD-TV Paducah, KY
WBPX-TV Boston, MA
WFQX-TV Cadillac, MI
WCCO-TV Minneapolis, MN
WABG-TV Greenwood, MS
WITN-TV Washington, NC
*WUNL-TV Winston-Salem, NC
*KENW Portales, NM
KMCC Laughlin, NV
WNLO Buffalo, NY
WTAJ-TV Altoona, PA
WPSG Philadelphia, PA
WQPX-TV Scranton, PA
WTCV San Juan, PR
*WRLK-TV Columbia, SC
WMBF-TV Myrtle Beach, SC
KPXB-TV Conroe, TX
KDAF Dallas, TX
KMYS Kerrville, TX
KUTH-DT Provo, UT
WVIR-TV Charlottesville, VA
*WSBN-TV Norton, VA
*WETK Burlington, VT
WBUW Janesville, WI

Channel 33

WDFX-TV Ozark, AL
WCFT-TV Tuscaloosa, AL
KTVW-DT Phoenix, AZ
KBAK-TV Bakersfield, CA
*KMTP-TV San Francisco, CA
KTBN-TV Santa Ana, CA
KTLL-TV Durango, CO
WFSB Hartford, CT
*WHUT-TV Washington, DC
*WDSC-TV New Smyrna Beach, FL
WRXY-TV Tice, FL
*WNGH-TV Chatsworth, GA
KBFD-DT Honolulu, HI
*KBIN-TV Council Bluffs, IA
KDLH Duluth, MN
KTVO Kirksville, MO
WMYV Greensboro, NC
WPXG-TV Concord, NH
WGRZ Buffalo, NY

WCBS-TV New York, NY
WSTR-TV Cincinnati, OH
KOCB Oklahoma City, OK
*KFTS Klamath Falls, OR
KRCW-TV Salem, OR
WRUA Fajardo, PR
*WEBA-TV Allendale, SC
WPGD-TV Hendersonville, TN
KVUE Austin, TX
*KITU-TV Beaumont, TX
KWAB-TV Big Spring, TX
WTVZ-TV Norfolk, VA
KWPX-TV Bellevue, WA
KIMA-TV Yakima, WA
WITI Milwaukee, WI
*WNPB-TV Morgantown, WV

Channel 34

KPBI Eureka Springs, AR
KGPE Fresno, CA
KMEX-DT Los Angeles, CA
KTAS San Luis Obispo, CA
KFSF-DT Vallejo, CA
KWGN-TV Denver, CO
WTVX Fort Pierce, FL
WCWJ Jacksonville, FL
WHBR Pensacola, FL
*WUSF-TV Tampa, FL
*KEFB Ames, IA
*KQIN Davenport, IA
KXTF Twin Falls, ID
WSIL-TV Harrisburg, IL
*WQEC Quincy, IL
WVLA-TV Baton Rouge, LA
KMSS-TV Shreveport, LA
WHTV Jackson, MI
*KTCA-TV Saint Paul, MN
WDAF-TV Kansas City, MO
WRBJ Magee, MS
WSOC-TV Charlotte, NC
WPXU-TV Jacksonville, NC
WNEU Merrimack, NH
WIVT Binghamton, NY
*WMHT Schenectady, NY
*WCET Cincinnati, OH
WQHS-DT Cleveland, OH
WJAC-TV Johnstown, PA
WCAU Philadelphia, PA
*WELU Aguadilla, PR
WCIV Charleston, SC
*KUSD-TV Vermillion, SD
WTNZ Knoxville, TN
*KLUJ-TV Harlingen, TX
KUTV Salt Lake City, UT
WPXW-TV Manassas, VA
KGPX-TV Spokane, WA
WISN-TV Milwaukee, WI
*WPBY-TV Huntington, WV

Channel 35

KCRA-TV Sacramento, CA
KCNC-TV Denver, CO
WVIT New Britain, CT
WDCA Washington, DC
WFTX-TV Cape Coral, FL
WPXM-TV Miami, FL
WGSA Baxley, GA
WLTZ Columbus, GA
KHNL Honolulu, HI
*KHIN Red Oak, IA
*KRIN Waterloo, IA
*WNIT South Bend, IN
KMTW Hutchinson, KS
KALB-TV Alexandria, LA
WPME Lewiston, ME
WTOM-TV Cheboygan, MI
WLUC-TV Marquette, MI
KSTP-TV Saint Paul, MN
KSDK Saint Louis, MO
WCBI-TV Columbus, MS
WZMY-TV Derry, NH
*KNME-TV Albuquerque, NM
*WOUC-TV Cambridge, OH
WLWT Cincinnati, OH
*WYBE Philadelphia, PA
*WIPM-TV Mayaguez, PR
KDFW Dallas, TX

KPRC-TV Houston, TX
KJTV-TV Lubbock, TX
KVOS-TV Bellingham, WA
*WMVT Milwaukee, WI

Channel 36

WABM Birmingham, AL
WTVY Dothan, AL
*KKAP Little Rock, AR
KFTU-DT Douglas, AZ
KAJB Calipatria, CA
KNBC Los Angeles, CA
KICU-TV San Jose, CA
KFRE-TV Sanger, CA
WTTG Washington, DC
*WUFT Gainesville, FL
WPXP-TV Lake Worth, FL
KWQC-TV Davenport, IA
KIDK-TV Idaho Falls, ID
WFFT-TV Fort Wayne, IN
WJYS Hammond, IN
WTWO-TV Terre Haute, IN
*WKMU Murray, KY
WWL-TV New Orleans, LA
KARD West Monroe, LA
WCDC Adams, MA
*WGPT Oakland, MD
WLNS-TV Lansing, MI
KAAL Austin, MN
*WMAV-TV Oxford, MS
WFPX-TV Fayetteville, NC
*WUNP-TV Roanoke Rapids, NC
WNJU Linden, NJ
WMGM-TV Wildwood, NJ
WENY-TV Elmira, NY
WTTE Columbus, OH
WYTV Youngstown, OH
*KRSC-TV Claremore, OK
*WITF-TV Harrisburg, PA
WMMP Charleston, SC
WYFF Greenville, SC
KWSD Sioux Falls, SD
WNPX-TV Cookeville, TN
KFTH-DT Alvin, TX
KDFI Dallas, TX
*KUEN Ogden, UT
WPXR-TV Roanoke, VA
KSKN Spokane, WA
*WLEF-TV Park Falls, WI

Channel 38

KSEE Fresno, CA
KPXN-TV San Bernardino, CA
KRON-TV San Francisco, CA
KPJR-DT Greeley, CO
*WTCE-TV Fort Pierce, FL
*WFSG Panama City, FL
WTTA Saint Petersburg, FL
*KALO Honolulu, HI
WGBO-DT Joliet, IL
WQAD-TV Moline, IL
WKMJ-TV Louisville, KY
KMCT-TV West Monroe, LA
WMAR-TV Baltimore, MD
WGME-TV Portland, ME
WSYM-TV Lansing, MI
WUVC-DT Fayetteville, NC
KXJB-TV Valley City, ND
KXVO Omaha, NE
WWOR-TV Secaucus, NJ
WKBW-TV Buffalo, NY
*WCFE-TV Plattsburgh, NY
*WOSU-TV Columbus, OH
WQEX Pittsburgh, PA
WEMT Greeneville, TN
WHTN Murfreesboro, TN
KUQI Corpus Christi, TX
*KMBH Harlingen, TX
KIAH Houston, TX
*KPBT-TV Odessa, TX
KVDA San Antonio, TX
KSL-TV Salt Lake City, UT
*KTNW Richland, WA
KOMO-TV Seattle, WA

Channel 39

KASN Pine Bluff, AR
KWOG Springdale, AR
KTAZ Phoenix, AZ
KVEA Corona, CA
KCNS San Francisco, CA
WCTX New Haven, CT
WFTV Orlando, FL
WSB-TV Atlanta, GA
WSAV-TV Savannah, GA
KFPX-TV Newton, IA
KMEG Sioux City, IA
KKJB Boise, ID
WAOE Peoria, IL
WKOI-TV Richmond, IN
WFXW-TV Terre Haute, IN
WLEX-TV Lexington, KY
WSBK-TV Boston, MA
WJAL Hagerstown, MD
WADL Mount Clemens, MI
*KETC Saint Louis, MO
WIVB-TV Buffalo, NY
WDLI-TV Canton, OH
*WLVT-TV Allentown, PA
WJWN-TV San Sebastian, PR
WMYT-TV Rock Hill, SC
WKTC Sumter, SC
WJKT Jackson, TN
*KSCE El Paso, TX
KLDT Lake Dallas, TX
*KTXT-TV Lubbock, TX
KENS San Antonio, TX
KIRO-TV Seattle, WA
WFRV-TV Green Bay, WI
WLPX-TV Charleston, WV

Channel 40

KHRR Tucson, AZ
*KVPT Fresno, CA
KTXL Sacramento, CA
KNSD San Diego, CA
*KRMT Denver, CO
*WBEC-TV Boca Raton, FL
WPAN Fort Walton Beach, FL
WACX Leesburg, FL
WTWC-TV Tallahassee, FL
WMGT-TV Macon, GA
KITV Honolulu, HI
*WFWA Fort Wayne, IN
WTVQ-DT Lexington, KY
WGGB-TV Springfield, MA
WDPX-TV Vineyard Haven, MA
WNUV Baltimore, MD
KPXM-TV Saint Cloud, MN
WDBD Jackson, MS
WHKY-TV Hickory, NC
*KSRE Minot, ND
WXTV-DT Paterson, NJ
KBLR Paradise, NV
WNMN Saranac Lake, NY
WHIZ-TV Zanesville, OH
KAUT-TV Oklahoma City, OK
KOIN Portland, OR
WDSI-TV Chattanooga, TN
KXTX-TV Dallas, TX
KLBK-TV Lubbock, TX
KBTV-TV Port Arthur, TX
*KTLM Rio Grande City, TX
KTVX Salt Lake City, UT
WTKR Norfolk, VA
WPXE-TV Kenosha, WI
WLFB Bluefield, WV

Channel 41

WZDX Huntsville, AL
*WEIQ Mobile, AL
KKPX-TV San Jose, CA
WZVN-TV Naples, FL
WRBW Orlando, FL
*WATC-DT Atlanta, GA
KPXO-TV Kaneohe, HI
KGCW Burlington, IA
KTIV Sioux City, IA
WICD Champaign, IL
WIFR Freeport, IL
KMCI Lawrence, KS

*WKPD Paducah, KY
KBCA Alexandria, LA
WLVI-TV Cambridge, MA
WUTB Baltimore, MD
WXYZ-TV Detroit, MI
WBUY-TV Holly Springs, MS
WUFX Vicksburg, MS
*WPBS-DT Watertown, NY
WHIO-TV Dayton, OH
WKBN-TV Youngstown, OH
*WVIA-TV Scranton, PA
WIRS Yauco, PR
*WETP-TV Sneedville, TN
KAZH Baytown, TX
KXAS-TV Fort Worth, TX
KWEX-DT San Antonio, TX
WGBA-TV Green Bay, WI
WCHS-TV Charleston, WV

Channel 42

WAKA Selma, AL
KWHY-TV Los Angeles, CA
KESQ-TV Palm Springs, CA
KOAA-TV Pueblo, CO
WSAH Bridgeport, CT
WXPX-TV Bradenton, FL
WJXT Jacksonville, FL
WJBF Augusta, GA
KIMT Mason City, IA
WQRF-TV Rockford, IL
WICS Springfield, IL
WCLJ-TV Bloomington, IN
WNDU-TV South Bend, IN
*WKLE Lexington, KY
*WKMA-TV Madisonville, KY
KGLA-DT Hammond, LA
*WMPT Annapolis, MD
KSAX Alexandria, MN
KSHB-TV Kansas City, MO
WRAY-TV Wilson, NC
KLUZ-TV Albuquerque, NM
*WSKG-TV Binghamton, NY
WGGN-TV Sandusky, OH
KMYT Tulsa, OK
WTXF-TV Philadelphia, PA
WPMY Pittsburgh, PA
WFLI-TV Cleveland, TN
KPXD-TV Arlington, TX
KTBU Conroe, TX
KMLM Odessa, TX
*KUED Salt Lake City, UT
*WMSY-TV Marion, VA
*WCVE-TV Richmond, VA
*KWDK Tacoma, WA
*WPNE-TV Green Bay, WI

Channel 43

KEJB El Dorado, AR
KHSL-TV Chico, CA
KGMC Clovis, CA
KCBS-TV Los Angeles, CA
*KCSM-TV San Mateo, CA
KPXC-TV Denver, CO
WOTF-DT Melbourne, FL
WUPA Atlanta, GA
WSWG Valdosta, GA
*KWBN Honolulu, HI
KFXB-TV Dubuque, IA
WCPX-TV Chicago, IL
*WKZT-TV Elizabethtown, KY
WDSU New Orleans, LA
*WGBX-TV Boston, MA
WPXT Portland, ME
*WTVS Detroit, MI
KODE-TV Joplin, MO
KTVI Saint Louis, MO
*WMAA Columbus, MS
WLXI Greensboro, NC
KPTM Omaha, NE
*WNJT Trenton, NJ
*WNED-TV Buffalo, NY
WCWN Schenectady, NY
*WPBO Portsmouth, OH
KATU Portland, OR
WPGH-TV Pittsburgh, PA
*WIPR-TV San Juan, PR
*WRET-TV Spartanburg, SC

WBBJ-TV Jackson, TN
KEYE-TV Austin, TX
*KDTN Denton, TX
KLCW-TV Wolfforth, TX
WZVI Charlotte Amalie, VI
WFFF-TV Burlington, VT
WWRS-TV Mayville, WI

Channel 44

*WGIQ Louisville, AL
KARZ-TV Little Rock, AR
KWBA-TV Sierra Vista, AZ
KHIZ Barstow, CA
KTVU Oakland, CA
*WDPB Seaford, DE
*WJEB-TV Jacksonville, FL
WTOG Saint Petersburg, FL
*WHSG-TV Monroe, GA
WRSP-TV Springfield, IL
*WDTI Indianapolis, IN
WTSF Ashland, KY
*WKON Owenton, KY
KSHV-TV Shreveport, LA
*WWPB Hagerstown, MD
WCSH Portland, ME
WZPX-TV Battle Creek, MI
WWJ-TV Detroit, MI
KYTV Springfield, MO
*WMAW-TV Meridian, MS
*WUNG-TV Concord, NC
WECT Wilmington, NC
KVLY-TV Fargo, ND
WMCN-TV Atlantic City, NJ
KRXI-TV Reno, NV
WNYW New York, NY
WNYS-TV Syracuse, NY
WTLW Lima, OH
*WJWJ-TV Beaufort, SC
WJFB Lebanon, TN
KZJL Houston, TX
KWKT-TV Waco, TX
*KBYU-TV Provo, UT
*WCVW Richmond, VA
*WTJX-TV Charlotte Amalie, VI
KVEW Kennewick, WA
KHCV Seattle, WA
WWAZ-TV Fond du Lac, WI

Channel 45

WPXH-TV Gadsden, AL
KUVI-DT Bakersfield, CA
KRCA Riverside, CA
KBCW San Francisco, CA
KWHD Castle Rock, CO
*WEDH Hartford, CT
WXCW Naples, FL
WJTC Pensacola, FL
WGNM Macon, GA
*KCDT Coeur d'Alene, ID
WSNS Chicago, IL
WEVV-TV Evansville, IN
WXIN Indianapolis, IN
KSNW Wichita, KS
WGMB-TV Baton Rouge, LA
*WMEA-TV Biddeford, ME
WDIV-TV Detroit, MI
WLLA Kalamazoo, MI
WFUP Vanderbilt, MI
KSTC-TV Minneapolis, MN
WKDH Houston, MS
KTGF Great Falls, MT
WYCW Asheville, NC
KMTV-TV Omaha, NE
KASY-TV Albuquerque, NM
WROC-TV Rochester, NY
*WNEO Alliance, OH
KOTV Tulsa, OK
*KNMT Portland, OR
KTCW Roseburg, OR
WOLF-TV Hazleton, PA
WIDP Guayama, PR
*WJPM-TV Florence, SC
*KDTX-TV Dallas, TX
KXLN-DT Rosenberg, TX

Channel 46

WHNT-TV Huntsville, AL
WMCF-TV Montgomery, AL
KUVE-DT Green Valley, AZ
KMIR-TV Palm Springs, CA
KQCA Stockton, CA
WUVN Hartford, CT
WTGL Leesburg, FL
*WHFT-TV Miami, FL
WCTV Thomasville, GA
*WTVP Peoria, IL
WFIE Evansville, IN
WHME-TV South Bend, IN
WBFF Baltimore, MD
WBSF Bay City, MI
KXLT-TV Rochester, MN
KSNF Joplin, MO
WWAY Wilmington, NC
WWHO Chillicothe, OH
WUPW Toledo, OH
KOCM Norman, OK
WFMZ-TV Allentown, PA
WKBS-TV Altoona, PA
WCCV-TV Arecibo, PR
*KNCT Belton, TX
KTAQ Greenville, TX
KJZZ-TV Salt Lake City, UT
*WHTJ Charlottesville, VA
WPXV-TV Norfolk, VA
WTPX-TV Antigo, WI
WDJT-TV Milwaukee, WI
WVVA Bluefield, WV

Channel 47

WLGA Opelika, AL
KAZA-TV Avalon, CA
KTLN-TV Novato, CA
WAMI-DT Hollywood, FL
WPCT Panama City Beach, FL

WFTT-DT Tampa, FL
KPXR-TV Cedar Rapids, IA
*WTTW Chicago, IL
WRBU East St. Louis, IL
WAVE Louisville, KY
*WYDN Worcester, MA
WMDT Salisbury, MD
KSMO-TV Kansas City, MO
WJZY Belmont, NC
WYDO Greenville, NC
KTDO Las Cruces, NM
WLNY-TV Riverhead, NY
WTVH Syracuse, NY
WRLM Canton, OH
KWHB Tulsa, OK
WPMT York, PA
WVOZ-TV Ponce, PR
WCSC-TV Charleston, SC
WZRB Columbia, SC
KDLT-TV Sioux Falls, SD
*WLJT Lexington, TN
KNWS-TV Katy, TX
WUPV Ashland, VA

Channel 48

WAFF Huntsville, AL
WRJM-TV Troy, AL
KVTJ-DT Jonesboro, AR
*KOCE-TV Huntington Beach, CA
KTFF-DT Porterville, CA
KSPX-TV Sacramento, CA
KVSN-DT Pueblo, CO
WRC-TV Washington, DC
WFBD Destin, FL
WFXU Live Oak, FL
WOPX-TV Melbourne, FL
WUVG-DT Athens, GA
WCIA Champaign, IL
WTTV Bloomington, IN

*WKGB-TV Bowling Green, KY
WJMN-TV Escanaba, MI
WAQP Saginaw, MI
WXXV-TV Gulfport, MS
WRAL-TV Raleigh, NC
*WLED-TV Littleton, NH
WYDC Corning, NY
WRNN-TV Kingston, NY
WPXI Pittsburgh, PA
*WUJA Caguas, PR
WACH Columbia, SC
WVLR Tazewell, TN
KTMD Galveston, TX
KSTR-DT Irving, TX
WOAI-TV San Antonio, TX
KUCW Ogden, UT
KING-TV Seattle, WA
WXOW-TV La Crosse, WI
WBME-TV Racine, WI

Channel 49

KKYK-DT Camden, AR
KASW Phoenix, AZ
KSTS San Jose, CA
KJLA Ventura, CA
*WEDW Bridgeport, CT
WVEN-TV Daytona Beach, FL
WAWD Fort Walton Beach, FL
WFGC Palm Beach, FL
WXTX Columbus, GA
KLJB Davenport, IA
KPTH Sioux City, IA
KTKA-TV Topeka, KS
WDRB Louisville, KY
WDKA Paducah, KY
WLNE-TV New Bedford, MA
KRBK Osage Beach, MO
WNTZ-TV Natchez, MS
WRAZ Raleigh, NC

*WEKW-TV Keene, NH
WWSI Atlantic City, NJ
WNYO-TV Buffalo, NY
WNWO-TV Toledo, OH
KGEB Tulsa, OK
WVSN Humacao, PR
KNVA Austin, TX
KNVO McAllen, TX
WLFG Grundy, VA
WHSV-TV Harrisonburg, VA
WEUX Chippewa Falls, WI
WMSN-TV Madison, WI
WTAP-TV Parkersburg, WV

Channel 50

WBRC Birmingham, AL
KNWA-TV Rogers, AR
*KTEH San Jose, CA
*KNXT Visalia, CA
WDCW Washington, DC
WFGX Fort Walton Beach, FL
WTLH Bainbridge, GA
KKAI Kailua, HI
WXFT-DT Aurora, IL
*WEIU-TV Charleston, IL
KLWB New Iberia, LA
WPXL-TV New Orleans, LA
WAXN-TV Kannapolis, NC
KEGS Goldfield, NV
WYPX Amsterdam, NY
*WEAO Akron, OH
WDTN Dayton, OH
KOPX-TV Oklahoma City, OK
*WQLN Erie, PA
WPCB-TV Greensburg, PA
WNEP-TV Scranton, PA
WQHA Aguada, PR
WCBD-TV Charleston, SC
KBTX-TV Bryan, TX

WGNT Portsmouth, VA
KUNS-TV Bellevue, WA
WISC-TV Madison, WI
WOAY-TV Oak Hill, WV

Channel 51

KPPX-TV Tolleson, AZ
KXLA Rancho Palos Verdes, CA
KDTV-DT San Francisco, CA
KCEC Denver, CO
WHLV-TV Cocoa, FL
WBIF Marianna, FL
WSST-TV Cordele, GA
WPXA-TV Rome, GA
KGAN Cedar Rapids, IA
WPWR-TV Gary, IN
WMYO Salem, IN
WAGV Harlan, KY
WLAJ Lansing, MI
KPXE-TV Kansas City, MO
WWJX Jackson, MS
WFMY-TV Greensboro, NC
WEPX-TV Greenville, NC
KFXL-TV Lincoln, NE
*WNJN Montclair, NJ
WKEF Dayton, OH
KSBI Oklahoma City, OK
KOHD Bend, OR
WTAE-TV Pittsburgh, PA
WRFB Carolina, PR
WJAR Providence, RI
WPXX-TV Memphis, TN
KTFN El Paso, TX
KCEB Longview, TX

Channel 55

KFMB-TV San Diego, CA
*WKAR-TV East Lansing, MI

Spanish-Language Television Stations

The following Spanish-language television stations operate within the United States or near the U.S. border. Stations are listed by Designated Market Area (DMA), city of license, call letters and channel. Stations in U.S. territories do not fall within any Designated Market Areas. For further information on individual stations, see Directory of Television Stations in the U.S. beginning on page B-13.

Arizona

Phoenix (Prescott), AZ
 KFPH-DT Flagstaff (ch 13)
Phoenix (Prescott), AZ
 KTAZ Phoenix (ch 39)
Phoenix (Prescott), AZ
 KTVW-DT Phoenix (ch 33)
Tucson (Sierra Vista), AZ
 KFTU-DT Douglas (ch 36)
Tucson (Sierra Vista), AZ
 KHRR Tucson (ch 40)

California

Fresno-Visalia, CA
 KFTV-DT Hanford (ch 20)
Fresno-Visalia, CA
 KNSO Merced (ch 11)
Los Angeles
 KAZA-TV Avalon (ch 47)
Los Angeles
 KVEA Corona (ch 39)
Los Angeles
 KMEX-DT Los Angeles (ch 34)
Los Angeles
 KTLA Los Angeles (ch 31)
Los Angeles
 KWHY-TV Los Angeles (ch 42)
Los Angeles
 KFTR-DT Ontario (ch 29)
Los Angeles
 KRCA Riverside (ch 45)
Monterey-Salinas, CA
 KSMS-TV Monterey (ch 31)
Sacramento-Stockton-Modesto, CA
 KUVS-DT Modesto (ch 18)
Sacramento-Stockton-Modesto, CA
 KMAX-TV Sacramento (ch 21)
Sacramento-Stockton-Modesto, CA
 KTFK-DT Stockton (ch 26)
San Francisco-Oakland-San Jose
 KTNC-TV Concord (ch 14)
San Francisco-Oakland-San Jose
 KDTV-DT San Francisco (ch 51)
San Francisco-Oakland-San Jose
 KSTS San Jose (ch 49)
San Francisco-Oakland-San Jose
 KFSF-DT Vallejo (ch 34)
Santa Barbara-Santa Maria-San Luis Obispo, CA
 KTAS San Luis Obispo (ch 34)
Santa Barbara-Santa Maria-San Luis Obispo, CA
 KPMR Santa Barbara (ch 21)
Yuma, AZ-El Centro, CA
 KAJB Calipatria (ch 36)
Yuma, AZ-El Centro, CA
 KVYE El Centro (ch 22)

Colorado

Albuquerque-Santa Fe, NM
 KTLL-TV Durango (ch 33)
Denver, CO
 KTFD-DT Boulder (ch 15)
Denver, CO
 KCEC Denver (ch 51)
Denver, CO
 KDEN Longmont (ch 29)

Florida

Miami-Ft. Lauderdale, FL
 WSCV Fort Lauderdale (ch 30)
Miami-Ft. Lauderdale, FL
 WSBS-TV Key West (ch 3)
Miami-Ft. Lauderdale, FL
 WLTV-DT Miami (ch 23)
Orlando-Daytona Beach-Melbourne, FL
 WVEN-TV Daytona Beach (ch 49)
Orlando-Daytona Beach-Melbourne, FL
 WOTF-DT Melbourne (ch 43)
Tampa-St. Petersburg (Sarasota), FL
 WFTT-DT Tampa {ch 47}
Tampa-St. Petersburg (Sarasota), FL
 WVEA-TV Venice (ch 25)

Georgia

Atlanta
 WUVG-DT Athens (ch 48)

Illinois

Chicago
 WSNS Chicago (ch 45)
Chicago
 WGBO-DT Joliet (ch 38)

Louisiana

New Orleans, LA
 KGLA-DT Hammond Massachusetts (ch 42)

Massachusetts

Boston (Manchester, NH)
 WUTF-DT Marlborough (ch 27)
Boston (Manchester, NH)
 WUNI Worcester (ch 29)

Nevada

Las Vegas, NV
 KINC Las Vegas (ch 16)
Las Vegas, NV
 KBLR Paradise (ch 40)

New Hampshire

Boston (Manchester, NH)
 WNEU Merrimack (ch 34)

New Jersey

New York
 WNJU Linden (ch 36)
New York
 WFUT-DT Newark (ch 30)
New York
 WXTV-DT Paterson (ch 40)
Philadelphia
 WWSI Atlantic City (ch 49)
Philadelphia
 WUVP-DT Vineland (ch 29)

New Mexico

Albuquerque-Santa Fe, NM
 KLUZ-TV Albuquerque (ch 42)
Albuquerque-Santa Fe, NM
 KTFQ-DT Albuquerque (ch 22)
Albuquerque-Santa Fe, NM
 KTEL-TV Carlsbad (ch 25)
El Paso (Las Cruces, NM), TX
 KTDO Las Cruces (ch 47)

North Carolina

Raleigh-Durham (Fayetteville), NC
 WUVC-DT Fayetteville (ch 38)

Ohio

Cleveland-Akron (Canton), OH
 WQHS-DT Cleveland (ch 34)

Oklahoma

Oklahoma City, OK
 KTUZ-TV Shawnee (ch 29)
Oklahoma City, OK
 KUOK Woodward (ch 35)

Oregon

Portland, OR
 KUNP La Grande (ch 16)

Texas

Amarillo, TX
 KEYU Borger (ch 31)
Corpus Christi, TX
 KORO Corpus Christi (ch 27)
Dallas-Ft. Worth
 KXTX-TV Dallas (ch 40)
Dallas-Ft. Worth
 KUVN-DT Garland (ch 23)
El Paso (Las Cruces, NM), TX
 KINT-TV El Paso (ch 25)
El Paso (Las Cruces, NM), TX
 KSCE El Paso (ch 39)
El Paso (Las Cruces, NM), TX
 KTFN El Paso (ch 51)
Harlingen-Weslaco-Brownsville-McAllen, TX
 KNVO McAllen (ch 49)
Harlingen-Weslaco-Brownsville-McAllen, TX
 KTLM Rio Grande City (ch 40)
Houston
 KFTH-DT Alvin (ch 36)
Houston
 KAZH Baytown (ch 41)
Houston
 KTMD Galveston (ch 48)
Houston
 KXLN-DT Rosenberg (ch 45)
Laredo, TX
 KLDO-TV Laredo (ch 19)
Odessa-Midland, TX
 KUPB Midland (ch 18)
San Antonio, TX
 KNIC-DT Blanco (ch 18)
San Antonio, TX
 KTRG Del Rio (ch 28)
San Antonio, TX
 KVDA San Antonio (ch 38)
San Antonio, TX
 KWEX-DT San Antonio (ch 41)
Waco-Temple-Bryan, TX
 KAKW-DT Killeen Utah (ch 13)

Utah

Salt Lake City, UT
 KUTH-DT Provo Virginia (ch 32)

Washington

Washington, DC (Hagerstown, MD)
 WFDC-DT Arlington Washington (ch 15)
Seattle-Tacoma, WA
 KUNS-TV Bellevue (ch 50)
Seattle-Tacoma, WA
 KHCV Seattle (ch 44)

Mexico

El Paso (Las Cruces, NM), TX
 XHIJ Ciudad Juarez (ch 44)
San Diego, CA
 XEWT-TV Tijuana (ch 12)

U.S. TV Stations Providing News Programming

Abilene-Sweetwater, TX
KTAB-TV, 8 hrs weekly

Albany, GA
WALB, 15 hrs weekly
WFXL, 4 hrs weekly

Albany-Schenectady-Troy, NY
WCDC, 15 hrs weekly
WNYT, 27 hrs weekly
WRGB, 26.5 hrs weekly
WTEN, 22 hrs weekly
WXXA-TV, 23.5 hrs weekly
WYPX, 5 hrs weekly

Albuquerque-Santa Fe, NM
KASA-TV, 7 hrs weekly
KBIM-TV, 6 hrs weekly
KLUZ-TV, .5 hr weekly
KOB, 12 hrs weekly
KOBF, 4 hrs weekly
KRQE, 24 hrs weekly

Alexandria, LA
KLAX-TV, 5.5 hrs weekly

Alpena, MI
WBKB-TV, 5.5 hrs weekly

Amarillo, TX
KCIT, 3 hrs weekly
KENW, 3 hrs weekly
KFDA-DT, 2.5 hrs weekly
KFDA-TV, 19.5 hrs weekly
KVII-TV, 36 hrs weekly

Anchorage, AK
KTUU-TV, 12 hrs weekly
KTVA, 7 hrs weekly
KYES-TV, 1 hr weekly

Atlanta
WAGA-TV, 38 hrs weekly
WGCL-DT, 29 hrs weekly
WGCL-TV, 14.5 hrs weekly
WPBA, 1.5 hrs weekly

Augusta, GA
WAGT, 8 hrs weekly
WJBF, 22hrswky hrs weekly
WRDW-TV, 20 hrs weekly

Austin, TX
KEYE-TV, 20 hrs weekly
KTBC, 24 hrs weekly
KVUE, 29.5 hrs weekly
KXAN, 22 hrs weekly

Bakersfield, CA
KBAK-TV, 30.5 hrs weekly
KGET-TV, 27 hrs weekly

Baltimore, MD
WBAL-TV, 24 hrs weekly

Bangor, ME
WABI-TV, 25 hrs weekly
WLBZ, 33 hrs weekly
WVII-TV, 6 hrs weekly

Baton Rouge, LA
WBRZ-TV, 22 hrs weekly
WLPB-TV, 1 hr weekly
WVLA-TV, 6 hrs weekly

Beaumont-Port Arthur, TX
KBMT, 13 hrs weekly

Bend, OR
KTVZ, 20 hrs weekly

Billings, MT
KTVQ, 17 hrs weekly
KULR-TV, 20 hrs weekly

Biloxi-Gulfport, MS
WLOX, 18 hrs weekly

Binghamton, NY
WBNG-TV, 24.5 hrs weekly
WICZ-TV, 2 hrs weekly

Birmingham (Anniston, Tuscaloosa), AL
WBRC, 21 hrs weekly
WDBB, 15 hrs weekly
WIAT, 6 hrs weekly
WJSU-TV, 9 hrs weekly
WPXH-TV, 8 hrs weekly
WVTM-TV, 24 hrs weekly

Bluefield-Beckley-Oak Hill, WV
WSWP-TV, 5 hrs weekly
WVVA, 27 hrs weekly

Boise, ID
KAID, 3 hrs weekly
KBCI-TV, 19 hrs weekly
KIVI-TV, 19.5 hrs weekly
KTRV-TV, 7 hrs weekly
KTVB, 27 hrs weekly

Boston (Manchester, NH)
WBPX-TV, 20 hrs weekly
WBZ-TV, 20 hrs weekly
WCVB-DT, 25 hrs weekly
WCVB-TV, 30 hrs weekly
WENH-TV, 2 hrs weekly
WFXT, 7 hrs weekly
WLVI-TV, 7 hrs weekly
WMUR-TV, 29 hrs weekly
WSBK-TV, 4 hrs weekly
WUNI, 3 hrs weekly
WZMY-TV, 5 hrs weekly

Bowling Green, KY
WBKO, 17 hrs weekly
WKYU-TV, 1 hr weekly

Burlington, VT-Plattsburgh, NY
WCAX-TV, 15 hrs weekly
WFFF-TV, 24.5hrs/week hrs weekly
WPTZ, 23 hrs weekly

Butte-Bozeman, MT
KXLF-TV, 16 hrs weekly

Casper-Riverton, WY
KCWY-DT, 20 hrs weekly
KTWO-TV, 19.5 hrs weekly

Cedar Rapids-Waterloo-Iowa City & Dubuque, IA
KFXA, 13.5 hrs weekly
KGAN, 12 hrs weekly
KWWL, 22 hrs weekly

Champaign & Springfield -Decatur, IL
WEIU-TV, 3 hrs weekly
WICD, 17 hrs weekly
WICS, 22 hrs weekly

Charleston, SC
WCBD-TV, 17 hrs weekly
WCIV, 12 hrs weekly
WCSC-TV, 21 hrs weekly
WTAT-TV, 3.5 hrs weekly

Charleston-Huntington, WV
WCHS-TV, 19.5 hrs weekly
WVAH-TV, 7 hrs weekly

Charlotte, NC
WHKY-TV, 5 hrs weekly

Charlottesville, VA
WVIR-TV, 32 hrs weekly

Chattanooga, TN
WDEF-TV, 19.5 hrs weekly
WDSI-TV, 3.5hrs/week hrs weekly
WRCB, 22 hrs weekly
WTVC, 32 hrs weekly

Cheyenne, WY-Scottsbluff, NE
KDUH-TV, 2 hrs weekly
KGWN-TV, 15 hrs weekly
KQCK, 15 hrs weekly
KSTF, 8 hrs weekly

Chicago
WFLD, 35.5 hrs weekly
WGN-TV, 32 hrs weekly
WLS-TV, 8 hrs weekly
WSNS, 5 hrs weekly
WTTW, 5 hrs weekly

Chico-Redding, CA
KCVU, 0 hrs weekly
KHSL-TV, 20 hrs weekly
KIXE-TV, 1 hr weekly
KRCR-TV, 16 hrs weekly

Cincinnati, OH
WCPO-TV, 24 hrs weekly
WPTO, 1 hr weekly
WXIX-TV, 23 hrs weekly

Clarksburg-Weston, WV
WBOY-TV, 24 hrs weekly
WDTV, 18.5 hrs weekly

Cleveland-Akron (Canton), OH
WEAO, 1 hr weekly
WEWS-TV, 22 hrs weekly
WMFD-TV, 36 hrs weekly

Colorado Springs-Pueblo, CO
KKTV, 27 hrs weekly
KOAA-TV, 7 hrs weekly
KXRM-TV, 3.5 hrs weekly

Columbia, SC
WIS, 26.5 hrs weekly
WLTX, 27 hrs weekly

Columbia-Jefferson City, MO
KMIZ, 19 hrs weekly
KOMU-TV, 20 hrs weekly
KRCG, 14 hrs weekly

Columbus, OH
WBNS-TV, 31 hrs weekly
WCMH-TV, 31.5 hrs weekly
WOUB-TV, 3 hrs weekly

Columbus-Tupelo-West Point, MS
WLOV-TV, 5 hrs weekly
WTVA, 17 hrs weekly

Corpus Christi, TX
KIII, 17.5 hrs weekly
KORO, 5 hrs weekly
KRIS-TV, 14 hrs weekly

Dallas-Ft. Worth
KDAF, 6 hrs weekly
KDFW, 50 hrs weekly
KTVT, 27 hrs weekly
KUVN-DT, 10 hrs weekly
KXAS-TV, 37 hrs weekly
WFAA, 28 hrs weekly

Davenport, IA-Rock Island-Moline, IL
KLJB, 3 hrs weekly
WHBF-TV, 7 hrs weekly
WQAD-TV, 22.5 hrs weekly

Dayton, OH
WKEF, 17 hrs weekly
WPTD, 1 hr weekly
WRGT-TV, 16 hrs weekly

Denver, CO
KCDO-TV, 17 hrs weekly
KCNC-TV, 28.5 hrs weekly
KDEN, 1 hr weekly
KPXC-TV, 24 hrs weekly
KRMA-TV, 1 hr weekly
KWGN-TV, 29.5 hrs weekly

Des Moines-Ames, IA
KCCI, 30 hrs weekly
KDSM-TV, 4 hrs weekly
WHO-DT, 30 hrs weekly
WOI-DT, 15 hrs weekly

Detroit
WJBK, 36 hrs weekly

Dothan, AL
WDHN, 7 hrs weekly
WTVY, 16 hrs weekly

Duluth, MN-Superior, WI
KBJR-TV, 10 hrs weekly
KDLH, 12 hrs weekly
KQDS-TV, 2.5 hrs weekly
WDIO-DT, 9 hrs weekly

El Paso (Las Cruces, NM), TX
KDBC-TV, 15 hrs weekly
KFOX-TV, 6 hrs weekly
KINT-TV, 10 hrs weekly
KRWG-TV, 3 hrs weekly
KTSM-TV, 19.5 hrs weekly
KVIA-TV, 31.5 hrs weekly
XHIJ, 15 hrs weekly

Elmira (Corning), NY
WENY-TV, 10 hrs weekly
WETM-TV, 14 hrs weekly

Erie, PA
WFXP, 3.5 hrs weekly
WICU-TV, 22 hrs weekly
WJET-TV, 3.5 hrs weekly
WSEE-TV, 14 hrs weekly

Eugene, OR
KEZI, newsprogram22 hrs weekly
KMCB, 22 hrs weekly
KMTR, 15 hrs weekly

KPIC, 14 hrs weekly
KTCW, 22 hrs weekly
KVAL-TV, 17 hrs weekly

Eureka, CA
KAEF-TV, 2 hrs weekly

Evansville, IN
WEVV-TV, 9 hrs weekly
WTVW, 22.5 hrs weekly

Fairbanks, AK
KATN, 6p-11pwkly hrs weekly
KFXF, 10 hrs weekly
KTVF, 9 hrs weekly

Fargo-Valley City, ND
KVLY-TV, 16 hrs weekly
KXJB-TV, 10 hrs weekly

Flint-Saginaw-Bay City, MI
WEYI-TV, 19.5 hrs weekly
WJRT-TV, 34 hrs weekly
WSMH, 7 hrs weekly

Fresno-Visalia, CA
KAIL, 5 hrs weekly
KFRE-TV, 2 hrs weekly
KFSN-TV, 30 hrs weekly
KFTV-DT, 8 hrs weekly
KGPE, 28 hrs weekly
KMPH-TV, 7 hrs weekly

Ft. Myers-Naples, FL
WBBH-TV, 32 hrs weekly
WINK-TV, 32 hrs weekly
WXCW, 13.5 hrs weekly
WZVN-TV, 19.5 hrs weekly

Ft. Smith-Fayetteville -Springdale-Rogers, AR
KFSM-TV, 28 hrs weekly
KFTA-TV, 20.5 hrs weekly
KHBS, 15 hrs weekly
KNWA-TV, 17 hrs weekly

Ft. Wayne, IN
WANE-TV, 22 hrs weekly
WISE-TV, 14 hrs weekly
WPTA, 31 hrs weekly

Gainesville, FL
WCJB-TV, 17 hrs weekly
WOGX, 7 hrs weekly
WUFT, 3 hrs weekly

Grand Junction-Montrose, CO
KJCT, 19.5wkly hrs weekly
KKCO, 28 hrs weekly
KREX-TV, 30 hrs weekly

Grand Rapids-Kalamazoo-Battle Creek, MI
WGVK, 1 hr weekly
WOTV, 13 hrs weekly
WWMT, 25 hrs weekly
WXMI, 4 hrs weekly
WZZM, 26 hrs weekly

Great Falls, MT
KFBB-TV, 6 hrs weekly
KRTV, 15 hrs weekly

Green Bay-Appleton, WI
WBAY-TV, 19 hrs weekly
WFRV-TV, 24.5 hrs weekly
WGBA-TV, 16 hrs weekly
WLUK-TV, 32.5 hrs weekly

U.S. TV Stations Providing News Programming

Greensboro-High Point-Winston Salem, NC
WFMY-TV, 32 hrs weekly
WGHP, 39 hrs weekly
WMYV, 7 hrs weekly
WXLV-TV, 2.5 hrs weekly

Greenville-New Bern-Washington, NC
WFXI, 4 hrs weekly
WITN-TV, 27.5 hrs weekly
WUNK-TV, 3 hrs weekly

Greenville-Spartanburg, SC-Asheville, NC-Anderson, SC
WHNS, 27 hrs weekly
WLOS, 24 hrs weekly
WNEG-TV, 13 hrs weekly
WSPA-TV, 26.5 hrs weekly
WYFF, 28 hrs weekly

Greenwood-Greenville, MS
WABG-TV, 13 hrs weekly

Harlingen-Weslaco-Brownsville-McAllen, TX
KGBT-TV, 22 hrs weekly
KRGV-TV, 12 hrs weekly
KTLM, 8 hrs weekly

Harrisburg-Lancaster-Lebanon-York, PA
WGAL, 29 hrs weekly
WHP-TV, 24 hrs weekly
WHTM-TV, 27 hrs weekly
WPMT, 17 hrs weekly

Harrisonburg, VA
WHSV-TV, 16 hrs weekly

Hartford & New Haven, CT
WCTX, 8.5 hrs weekly
WFSB, 36 hrs weekly
WTIC-TV, 6 hrs weekly
WTNH, 32 hrs weekly
WUVN, 5 hrs weekly

Hattiesburg-Laurel, MS
WDAM-TV, 20 hrs weekly

Helena, MT
KTVH-DT, 7 hrs weekly

Honolulu, HI
KBFD-DT, 6 hrs weekly
KFVE, 7 hrs weekly
KHNL, 23 hrs weekly
KHON-TV, 25 hrs weekly
KITV, 20 hrs weekly
KUPU, 14 hrs weekly

Houston
KETH-TV, 3 hrs weekly
KHWB-DT, 4 hrs weekly
KIAH, 4 hrs weekly
KPRC-TV, 34 hrs weekly
KTMD, 7 hrs weekly
KXLN-DT, 7 hrs weekly

Huntsville-Decatur (Florence), AL
WAFF, 26 hrs weekly

Idaho Falls-Pocatello, ID
KIDK-TV, 15 hrs weekly
KIFI-TV, 30 hrs weekly
KJWY, 5 hrs weekly
KPVI-DT, 17 hrs weekly

Indianapolis, IN
WHMB-TV, 1 hr weekly
WTIU, 3 hrs weekly
WXIN, 19 hrs weekly

Jackson, MS
WAPT, 14 hrs weekly
WJTV, 21 hrs weekly

Jacksonville, FL
WJXT, 51 hrs weekly
WTEV-TV, 22 hrs weekly
WTLV, 17 hrs weekly

Johnstown-Altoona, PA
WJAC-TV, 25hrsnewswkly hrs weekly
WTAJ-TV, 29 hrs weekly

Jonesboro, AR
KAIT, 17 hrs weekly

Joplin, MO-Pittsburg, KS
KFJX-TV, 3 hrs weekly
KOAM-TV, 19 hrs weekly
KODE-TV, 16 hrs weekly

Juneau, AK
KJUD, 5 hrs weekly
KTOO-TV, 1 hr weekly

Kansas City, MO
KMBC-TV, 28 hrs weekly
KSHB-TV, 32 hrs weekly
WDAF-TV, 49 hrs weekly

Knoxville, TN
WATE-TV, 24 hrs weekly
WBIR-TV, 24 hrs weekly
WTNZ, 7 hrs weekly
WVLT-TV, 24.5 hrs weekly

La Crosse-Eau Claire, WI
WEAU-TV, 34 hrs weekly
WLAX, 3.5 hrs weekly
WQOW-TV, 18 hrs weekly
WXOW-TV, 18 hrs weekly

Lafayette, IN
WLFI-TV, 22 hrs weekly

Lafayette, LA
KATC, 19.5 hrs weekly
KLFY-TV, 14 hrs weekly

Lake Charles, LA
KVHP, 9 hrs weekly

Lansing, MI
WLAJ, 5 hrs weekly
WSYM-TV, 10 hrs weekly

Laredo, TX
KGNS-TV, 17 hrs weekly

Las Vegas, NV
KBLR, 2 hrs weekly
KBLR-DT, 2 hrs weekly
KINC, 5 hrs weekly
KTNV-TV, 22 hrs weekly
KVBC-DT, 29 hrs weekly

Lexington, KY
WDKY-TV, 7 hrs weekly
WKYT-TV, 43 hrs weekly
WTVQ-DT, 27 hrs weekly

Lima, OH
WLIO, 24 hrs weekly

Lincoln & Hastings-Kearney, NE
KHGI-TV, 17.5 hrs weekly
KHNE-TV, 30min.wkly hrs weekly
KLKN, 22 hrs weekly
KSNB-TV, 13 hrs weekly
KUON-TV, 30min.wkly hrs weekly
KWNB-TV, 17.5 hrs weekly

Little Rock-Pine Bluff, AR
KARK-TV, 22 hrs weekly
KTHV, 20 hrs weekly

Los Angeles
KCBS-TV, 26 hrs weekly
KHIZ, 5 hrs weekly
KLCS, 5 hrs weekly
KMEX-DT, 17 hrs weekly
KOCE-TV, 12.5 hrs weekly
KSCI, 12 hrs weekly
KTLA, 22 hrs weekly
KTTV, 25 hrs weekly
KWHY-TV, 12 hrs weekly

Louisville, KY
WDRB, 35 hrs weekly
WLKY-TV, 37.5 hrs weekly

Lubbock, TX
KAMC, 39 hrs weekly
KJTV-TV, 7 hrs weekly
KLBK-TV, 27 hrs weekly

Macon, GA
WGNM, 1 hr weekly
WMAZ-TV, 27 hrs weekly
WPGA-TV, 3 hrs weekly

Madison, WI
WISC-TV, 30 hrs weekly
WKOW-TV, 22 hrs weekly
WMTV, 19 hrs weekly

Mankato, MN
KEYC-TV, 13 hrs weekly

Marquette, MI
WBKP, 10 hrs weekly
WLUC-TV, 16 hrs weekly
WNMU, 1 hr weekly

Medford-Klamath Falls, OR
KDKF, 12 hrs weekly
KDRV, 20 hrs weekly
KTVL, 16 hrs weekly

Memphis, TN
WHBQ-TV, 27 hrs weekly
WPTY-TV, 7 hrs weekly

Meridian, MS
WTOK-TV, 15 hrs weekly

Miami-Ft. Lauderdale, FL
WAMI-DT, 3 hrs weekly
WBZL-DT, 3.5 hrs weekly
WFOR-TV, 30 hrs weekly
WLTV-DT, 24hrs/week hrs weekly
WSCV, 16 hrs weekly
WSFL-TV, 3.5 hrs weekly

Minneapolis-St. Paul, MN
KAWB, 2.5 hrs weekly
KAWE, 2.5 hrs weekly
KMSP-TV, 19.5 hrs weekly
KSTP-TV, 27.5 hrs weekly
WCCO-TV, 23 hrs weekly
WFTC, 3.5 hrs weekly

Minot-Bismarck-Dickinson, ND
KFYR-TV, 24 hrs weekly
KUMV-TV, 6 hrs weekly
KXMB-TV, 9 hrs weekly
KXMC-TV, 9 hrs weekly

Missoula, MT
KCFW-TV, 6 hrs weekly
KECI-TV, 14 hrs weekly
KPAX-TV, 15 hrs weekly

Mobile, AL-Pensacola (Ft. Walton Beach), FL
WALA-TV, 23hrs weekly
WEAR-TV, 14 hrs weekly
WPMI-TV, 5 hrs weekly

Monroe, LA-El Dorado, AR
KMCT-TV, 6 hrs weekly
KNOE-TV, 22 hrs weekly
KTVE, 13 hrs weekly

Monterey-Salinas, CA
KCBA, 10 hrs weekly
KION-TV, 8 hrs weekly
KSBW, 31 hrs weekly

Montgomery-Selma, AL
WAKA, 9 hrs weekly
WNCF, 1 hr weekly

Myrtle Beach-Florence, SC
WBTW, 78 hrs weekly
WFXB, 2.5 hrs weekly
WMBF-TV, 27 hrs weekly

Nashville, TN
WHTN, 2 hrs weekly
WJFB, 4 hrs weekly
WKRN-TV, 25 hrs weekly
WTVF, 24 hrs weekly
WZTV, 7 hrs weekly

New Orleans, LA
WDSU, 32hrs.wkly hrs weekly
WHNO, 10 hrs weekly
WVUE-DT, 21 hrs weekly

New York
WFTY-DT, 4 hrs weekly
WLNY-TV, 2 hrs weekly
WMBC-TV, 5 hrs weekly
WNET, 5 hrs weekly
WNJB, 2 hrs weekly
WNJN, 3 hrs weekly
WNJN-DT, 3 hrs weekly
WPIX, 19.5 hrs weekly
WRNN-TV, 82 hrs weekly
WWOR-TV, 7 hrs weekly
WXTV-DT, 17 hrs weekly

Norfolk-Portsmouth-Newport News, VA
WAVY-TV, 31 hrs weekly
WHRO-TV, 1 hr weekly
WVEC, 24 hrs weekly

North Platte, NE
KNOP-TV, 15 hrs weekly

Odessa-Midland, TX
KMID, 17 hrs weekly
KOSA-TV, 16 hrs weekly

Oklahoma City, OK
KETA-TV, 3 hrs weekly
KFOR-TV, 29 hrs weekly
KOCO-TV, 30hrsnewsprogrgwkly hrs weekly
KWET, 4 hrs weekly
KWTV, 36 hrs weekly

Omaha, NE
KETV, 28 hrs weekly
KMTV-TV, 23 hrs weekly
KPTM, 7 hrs weekly
KYNE-TV, 30min.wkly hrs weekly
WOWT-TV, 37 hrs weekly

Orlando-Daytona Beach-Melbourne, FL
WFTV, 25 hrs weekly
WKMG-TV, 24 hrs weekly

Ottumwa, IA-Kirksville, MO
KTVO, 14 hrs weekly

Paducah, KY-Cape Girardeau, MO-Harrisburg-Mount Vernon, IL
KFVS-TV, 28 hrs weekly
WPSD-DT, 23 hrs weekly
WPSD-TV, 23 hrs weekly
WSIU-TV, 2 hrs weekly

Palm Springs, CA
KESQ-TV, 17 hrs weekly
KMIR-TV, 27 hrs weekly

Panama City, FL
WMBB, 143 hrs weekly

Parkersburg, WV
WTAP-TV, 24 hrs weekly

Peoria-Bloomington, IL
WEEK-TV, 16 hrs weekly
WHOI, 7 hrs weekly

Philadelphia
WCAU, 21 hrs weekly
WCAU-DT, 21 hrs weekly
WFMZ-DT, 37 hrs weekly
WFMZ-TV, 32 hrs weekly
WHYY-TV, 5 hrs weekly
WMGM-TV, 8 hrs weekly
WNJS, 2 hrs weekly
WNJS-DT, 2 hrs weekly
WNJT, 10 hrs weekly
WTXF-TV, 36.5 hrs weekly
WWSI, 3 hrs weekly

Phoenix (Prescott), AZ
KAET, 3 hrs weekly
KAZT-TV, 11hrs/week hrs weekly
KPHO-DT, 22 hrs weekly
KPHO-TV, 30.5 hrs weekly
KSAZ-TV, 38 hrs weekly
KTVK, 48 hrs weekly

Pittsburgh, PA
WNPB-TV, 1 hr weekly
WPGH-DT, 6 hrs weekly
WTAE-TV, 32 hrs weekly

Portland, OR
KATU, varies hrs weekly
KGW, 35 hrs weekly
KGW-DT, 35 hrs weekly
KOIN, 27 hrs weekly
KPTV, 42.5 hrs weekly
KRCW-TV, 3.5 hrs weekly

Portland-Auburn, ME
WGME-TV, 25 hrs weekly
WMTW, 13.5 hrs weekly
WPFO, 18.5 hrs weekly
WPME, 3.5 hrs weekly
WPXT, 3.5 hrs weekly

Presque Isle, ME
WAGM-TV, 14 hrs weekly

Providence, RI-New Bedford, MA
WPXQ-TV, 5 hrs weekly

Quincy, IL-Hannibal, MO-Keokuk, IA
KHQA-TV, 13 hrs weekly
WGEM-TV, 20 hrs weekly

Raleigh-Durham (Fayetteville), NC
WLFL, 7 hrs weekly
WNCN, 30 hrs weekly
WNCN-DT, 30 hrs weekly
WRAL-TV, 30 hrs weekly

Rapid City, SD
KEVN-TV, 9 hrs weekly
KIVV-TV, 9 hrs weekly
KNBN, 11 hrs weekly
KOTA-TV, 9 hrs weekly
KSGW-TV, 8 hrs weekly

Reno, NV
KOLO-TV, 22 hrs weekly
KRNV-DT, 14 hrs weekly
KTVN, 22.5 hrs weekly

Richmond-Petersburg, VA
WRLH-TV, 3 hrs weekly

Roanoke-Lynchburg, VA
WDBJ, 18 hrs weekly
WFXR, 2 hrs weekly
WSET-TV, 12 hrs weekly
WSLS-TV, 15 hrs weekly
WWCW, 1 hr weekly

Rochester, MN-Mason City, IA-Austin, MN
KAAL, 11 hrs weekly
KIMT, 19 hrs weekly
KTTC, 11 hrs weekly
KXLT-TV, 7 hrs weekly

Rochester, NY
WHAM-TV, 24 hrs weekly
WHEC-TV, 22 hrs weekly
WROC-TV, 14 hrs weekly
WUHF, 3.5 hrs weekly
WXXI-DT, 1 hr weekly
WXXI-TV, 2 hrs weekly

Rockford, IL
WIFR, 19 hrs weekly
WTVO, 7 hrs weekly

Sacramento -Stockton-Modesto, CA
KCRA-TV, 55 hrs weekly
KOVR, 21 hrs weekly
KSPX-TV, 7 hrs weekly
KTXL, 17 hrs weekly
KUVS-DT, 12 hrs weekly

Salisbury, MD
WBOC-TV, 31 hrs weekly
WDPB, 3 hrs weekly
WMDT, 12 hrs weekly

Salt Lake City, UT
KBYU-TV, 3 hrs weekly
KSL-TV, 21 hrs weekly
KSTU, 34 hrs weekly
KTVX, 14 hrs weekly

KUTH-DT, 5 hrs weekly
KUTV, 34.5 hrs weekly

San Angelo, TX
KLST, 17 hrs weekly

San Antonio, TX
KABB, 7 hrs weekly
KENS, 24 hrs weekly
KSAT-TV, 21 hrs weekly
KVDA, 10 hrs weekly
KWEX-DT, 5 hrs weekly
WOAI-TV, 19.5 hrs weekly

San Diego, CA
KGTV, 35 hrs weekly
KSWB-TV, 14 hrs weekly
KUSI-TV, 51 hrs weekly
XETV, 20 hrs weekly
XEWT-TV, 11 hrs weekly

San Francisco-Oakland-San Jose
KDTV-DT, 5 hrs weekly
KFTY, 7 hrs weekly
KICU-TV, .5 hr weekly
KNTV, 20 hrs weekly
KPIX-TV, 20 hrs weekly
KQED, .5 hr weekly
KRON-TV, 42 hrs weekly
KSTS, 3 hrs weekly
KTSF, 24 hrs weekly

Santa Barbara-Santa Maria-San Luis Obispo, CA
KCOY-TV, 28 hrs weekly
KEYT-TV, 21 hrs weekly
KTAS, 3 hrs weekly

Savannah, GA
WJCL, 5 hrs weekly
WTGS, 5 hrs weekly

Seattle-Tacoma, WA
KBCB, 4 hrs weekly
KCPQ, 21 hrs weekly
KIRO-TV, 46 hrs weekly
KVOS-TV, 1 hr weekly

Sherman, TX-Ada, OK
KTEN, 36 hrs weekly
KXII, 30 hrs weekly

Sioux City, IA
KTIV, 19.5 hrs weekly
KXNE-TV, 30min.wkly hrs weekly

Sioux Falls (Mitchell), SD
KDLT-TV, 19 hrs weekly
KDLV-TV, 20 hrs weekly
KPRY-TV, 15 hrs weekly
KSFY-TV, 15 hrs weekly

South Bend-Elkhart, IN
WSBT-TV, 22 hrs weekly
WSJV, 16 hrs weekly

Spokane, WA
KAYU-TV, 8 hrs weekly
KHQ-TV, 26 hrs weekly
KLEW-TV, 12 hrs weekly
KREM, 17 hrs weekly
KSKN, 6 hrs weekly
KXLY-TV, 19 hrs weekly

Springfield, MO
KOLR, 22 hrs weekly
KSFX-TV, 12 hrs weekly
KSPR, 9 hrs weekly
KYTV, 24 hrs weekly

St. Joseph, MO
KQTV, 16 hrs weekly

St. Louis, MO
KMOV, 29 hrs weekly
KPLR-TV, 4 hrs weekly
KTVI, 37.5 hrs weekly
KTVI-DT, 7 hrs weekly

Syracuse, NY
WSTM-TV, 27.5 hrs weekly
WSYR-TV, 22.5 hrs weekly
WSYT, 3.5 hrs weekly
WTVH, 24 hrs weekly

Tallahassee, FL-Thomasville, GA
WTWC-TV, 14 hrs weekly
WTXL-TV, 24 hrs weekly

Tampa-St. Petersburg (Sarasota), FL
WTVT, 46 hrs weekly
WVEA-TV, 3.5 hrs weekly
WWSB, 21 hrs weekly

Terre Haute, IN
WFXW-TV, 2 hrs weekly
WTWO-TV, 20 hrs weekly
WVUT, 5 hrs weekly

Toledo, OH
WNWO-TV, 22 hrs weekly
WTOL, 25 hrs weekly
WTVG, 10 hrs weekly

WUPW, 5 hrs weekly

Topeka, KS
KSNT, 25 hrs weekly
KTKA-TV, 15 hrs weekly
WIBW-TV, 30.5 hrs weekly

Traverse City-Cadillac, MI
WFQX-TV, 3 hrs weekly
WFUP, 3 hrs weekly

Tucson (Sierra Vista), AZ
KGUN-TV, 22 hrs weekly
KHRR, 5 hrs weekly
KOLD-TV, 27 hrs weekly
KVOA, 27 hrs weekly

Tulsa, OK
KJRH, 26.5 hrs weekly
KOKI-TV, 7 hrs weekly
KTPX-DT, 2.5 hrs weekly
KTUL, 17 hrs weekly

Twin Falls, ID
KMVT, 10 hrs weekly
KXTF, 2 hrs weekly

Tyler-Longview (Lufkin & Nacogdoches), TX
KETK-TV, 27 hrs weekly
KTRE, 20 hrs weekly
KYTX, 19.5 hrs weekly

Utica, NY
WKTV, 31.5 hrs weekly

Victoria, TX
KAVU-TV, 29 hrs weekly
KVCT, 2.5 hrs weekly

Waco-Temple-Bryan, TX
KBTX-TV, 19hrs.wkly hrs weekly
KCEN-TV, 17 hrs weekly
KNCT, 1 hr weekly
KWTX-TV, 20 hrs weekly
KXXV, 14.5 hrs weekly

Washington, DC (Hagerstown, MD)
WHAG-TV, 20 hrs weekly
WJAL, 5hrslocalnewswkly hrs weekly
WJLA-TV, 24 hrs weekly
WTTG-DT, 30 hrs weekly
WUSA, 39 hrs weekly

Watertown, NY
WWNY-TV, 19 hrs weekly
WWTI, 5 hrs weekly

Wausau-Rhinelander, WI
WAOW-TV, 15.5 hrs weekly
WFXS, 5 hrs weekly
WJFW-TV, 18.5 hrs weekly
WSAW-TV, 15 hrs weekly

West Palm Beach-Ft. Pierce, FL
WPBF, 25 hrs weekly
WPEC, 24 hrs weekly
WPTV, 27 hrs weekly

Wheeling, WV-Steubenville, OH
WTOV-TV, 22 hrs weekly
WTRF-TV, 26 hrs weekly

Wichita Falls, TX & Lawton, OK
KAUZ-TV, 15 hrs weekly
KFDX-TV, 19.5 hrs weekly

Wichita-Hutchinson Plus, KS
KAKE-TV, 16 hrs weekly
KBSH-DT, 24 hrs weekly
KUPK-DT, 7 hrs weekly
KUPK-TV, 7 hrs weekly
KWCH-DT, 24 hrs weekly

Wilkes Barre-Scranton, PA
WBRE-TV, 24 hrs weekly
WNEP-TV, 36 hrs weekly
WOLF-DT, 3.5 hrs weekly
WOLF-TV, 6.5 hrs weekly
WYOU, 19.5 hrs weekly

Wilmington, NC
WSFX-TV, 3 hrs weekly

Yakima-Pasco -Richland-Kennewick, WA
KEPR-TV, 17 hrs weekly
KIMA-TV, 15 hrs weekly
KNDO, 27 hrs weekly
KNDU, 22.5 hrs weekly

Youngstown, OH
WFMJ-TV, 10 hrs weekly
WKBN-TV, 25 hrs weekly
WNEO, 1 hr weekly
WYTV, 20 hrs weekly

Yuma, AZ-El Centro, CA
KSWT, 5 hrs weekly
KVYE, 5 hrs weekly
KYMA-DT, 12 hrs weekly

Zanesville, OH
WHIZ-TV, 10 hrs weekly

Nielsen DMA Market Atlas

The Designated Market Area (DMA) is a geographic market design that defines each television market exclusive of others, based on measured viewing patterns. Each market's DMA consists of all the counties in which the home market stations receive a preponderance of viewing, and every county is allocated exclusively to one DMA—there is no overlap. The total of all DMAs represents the total television households in the United States.

The DMA is a standard market definition. As a television buying tool, it is a geographical and demographic means for maximum efficiency. As a station tool, it has applications for sales, programming, and promotion planning.

Following, in alphabetical order, are Nielsen's 210 markets for 2009 with coverage maps for each, with county by county breakouts of TV households. Other data include the markets' stations, their cities of license, channel numbers, and network affiliations. An asterisk preceding call letters indicates that it is a noncommercial (ETV) station.

Coverage maps show total survey areas in light shading, the DMAs themselves in dark shading and white, with Nielsen Metro ratings in white. The survey areas consist of all counties in which the home market stations are viewed to a significant extent including via cable. The Metro Areas usually conform to U.S. Census Standard Metropolitan statistical areas.

Non-DMA markets do not meet Nielsen's criteria for having a DMA of their own. They are listed with the DMA of which they are a part.

A cross-reference list of cities in multi-city DMAs appears on page B-228

All maps © 2009 Nielsen Media Research.

Abilene-Sweetwater, TX (165)

DMA TV Households: 115,310
% of U.S. TV Households: .101

KXVA Abilene, TX, ch. 15, Fox
KPCB Snyder, TX, ch. 17, IND
KTXS-TV Sweetwater, TX, ch. 20, ABC, CW
KTAB-TV Abilene, TX, ch. 24, CBS
KRBC-TV Abilene, TX, ch. 29, NBC

DMA Counties	State	TV Households
Brown	TX	14,680
Callahan	TX	5,350
Coleman	TX	3,560
Eastland	TX	7,180
Fisher	TX	1,690
Haskell	TX	2,280
Jones	TX	5,460
Knox	TX	1,480
Mitchell	TX	2,670
Nolan	TX	5,860
Runnels	TX	3,990
Scurry	TX	5,760
Shackelford	TX	1,190
Stephens	TX	3,570
Stonewall	TX	590
Taylor	TX	49,310
Throckmorton	TX	690

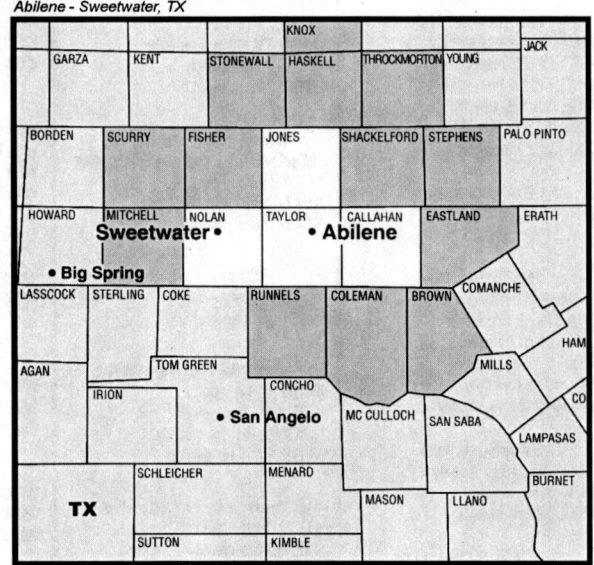

Abilene - Sweetwater, TX

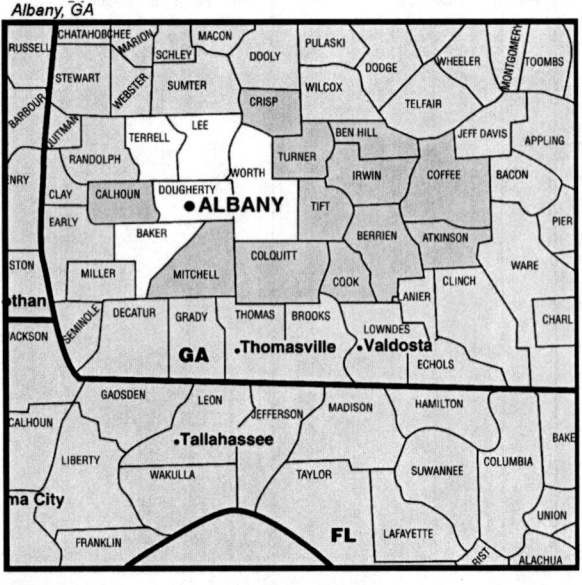

Albany, GA

Albany, GA (147)

DMA TV Households: 156,800
% of U.S. TV Households: .137

*WABW-TV Pelham, GA, ch. 6, ETV
*WACS-TV Dawson, GA, ch. 8, ETV
WALB Albany, GA, ch. 10, NBC
WFXL Albany, GA, ch. 12, Fox
WSST-TV Cordele, GA, ch. 51, IND

DMA Counties	State	TV Households	DMA Counties	State	TV Households
Atkinson	GA	2,950	Dougherty	GA	37,010
Baker	GA	1,380	Irwin	GA	3,570
Ben Hill	GA	6,840	Lee	GA	11,690
Berrien	GA	6,610	Mitchell	GA	8,420
Calhoun	GA	1,870	Terrell	GA	3,660
Coffee	GA	14,170	Tift	GA	15,580
Colquitt	GA	16,860	Turner	GA	3,380
Cook	GA	6,260	Worth	GA	8,020
Crisp	GA	8,530			

Maps courtesy of Nielsen Media Research

Albany - Schenectady - Troy

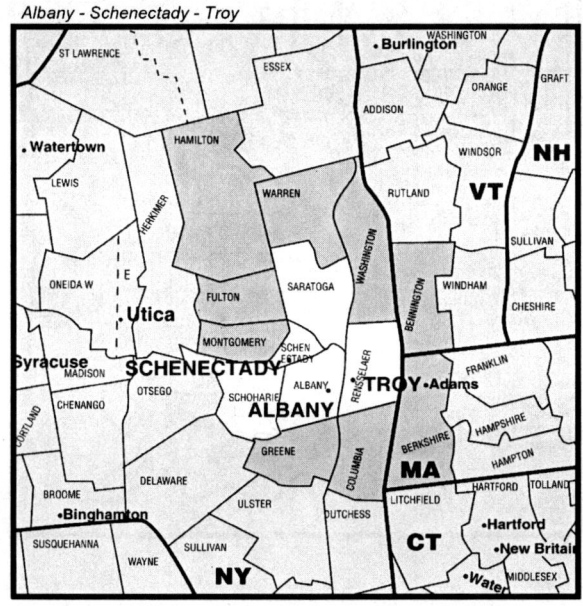

Albany-Schenectady-Troy, NY (57)

DMA TV Households: 556,750
% of U.S. TV Households: .486

WRGB Schenectady, NY, ch. 6, CBS
WXXA-TV Albany, NY, ch. 7, Fox
WNYT Albany, NY, ch. 12, NBC
WNYA Pittsfield, MA, ch. 13, MyNetworkTV
WTEN Albany, NY, ch. 26, ABC
***WMHT** Schenectady, NY, ch. 34, ETV
WCDC Adams, MA, ch. 36, satellite to WTEN
WCWN Schenectady, NY, ch. 43, CW
WYPX Amsterdam, NY, ch. 50, ION Television

DMA Counties	State	TV Households	DMA Counties	State	TV Households
Berkshire	MA	54,410	Rensselaer	NY	62,020
Albany	NY	124,180	Saratoga	NY	85,980
Columbia	NY	25,040	Schenectady	NY	61,450
Fulton	NY	22,440	Schoharie	NY	12,540
Greene	NY	19,060	Warren	NY	28,400
Hamilton	NY	2,290	Washington	NY	24,210
Montgomery	NY	19,950	Bennington	VT	14,780

Albuquerque-Santa Fe (44)

DMA TV Households: 689,120
% of U.S. TV Households: .602

Albuquerque - Santa Fe, NM

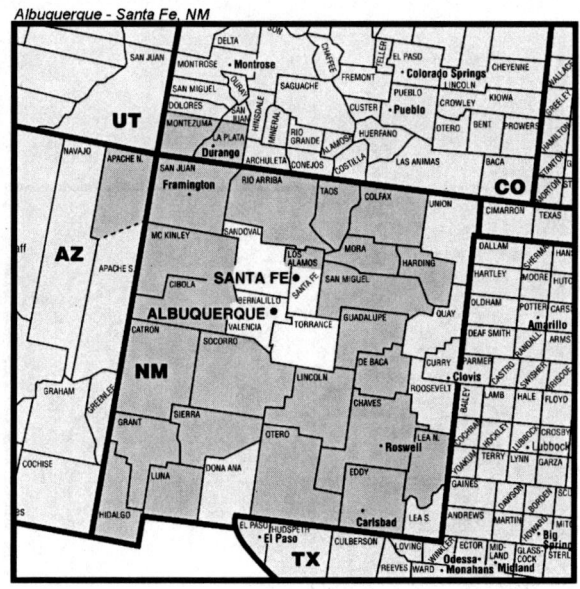

KOFT Farmington, NM, ch. 3, ABC
KOAT-TV Albuquerque, NM, ch. 7, ABC
KOBR Roswell, NM, ch. 8, NBC
KNMD-TV Santa Fe, NM, ch. 9, ETV
KBIM-TV Roswell, NM, ch. 10, CBS
KCHF Santa Fe, NM, ch. 10, IND
KOVT Silver City, NM, ch. 10, ABC
KOBF Farmington, NM, ch. 12, NBC
KOBG-TV Silver City, NM, ch. 12, satellite to KOB
KRQE Albuquerque, NM, ch. 13, CBS
KREZ-TV Durango, CO, ch. 15, satellite to KRQE
***KAZQ** Albuquerque, NM, ch. 17, ETV
KOCT Carlsbad, NM, ch. 19, satellite to KOAT-TV
***KRMU** Durango, CO, ch. 20, ETV

KRWB-TV Roswell, NM, ch. 21, IND
KTFQ-DT Albuquerque, NM, ch. 22, TeleFutura
KNAT-TV Albuquerque, NM, ch. 24, IND
KTEL-TV Carlsbad, NM, ch. 25, Telemundo
KOB Albuquerque, NM, ch. 26, NBC
KRPV Roswell, NM, ch. 27, IND
KASA-TV Santa Fe, NM, ch. 27, Fox
KUPT Hobbs, NM, ch. 29, MyNetworkTV
KWBQ Santa Fe, NM, ch. 29, CW
KTLL-TV Durango, CO, ch. 33, Telemundo
***KNME-TV** Albuquerque, NM, ch. 35, ETV
KLUZ-TV Albuquerque, NM, ch. 42, Univision
KASY-TV Albuquerque, NM, ch. 45, MyNetworkTV

DMA Counties	State	TV Households	DMA Counties	State	TV Households
Apache North	AZ	14,350	Los Almos	NM	7,610
La Plata	CO	19,750	Luna	NM	10,240
Montezuma	CO	10,190	McKinley	NM	19,390
Bernalillo	NM	258,290	Mora	NM	1,980
Catron	NM	1,430	Otero	NM	23,270
Chaves	NM	23,130	Rio Arriba	NM	15,260
Cibola	NM	8,650	Sandoval	NM	43,610
Colfax	NM	5,420	San Juan	NM	40,350
De Baca	NM	750	San Miguel	NM	10,400
Eddy	NM	19,530	Santa Fe	NM	56,220
Grant	NM	12,010	Sierra	NM	5,370
Guadalupe	NM	1,560	Socorro	NM	6,620
Harding	NM	270	Taos	NM	12,990
Hidalgo	NM	1,750	Torrance	NM	5,780
Lea North	NM	19,410	Valencia	NM	24,650
Lincoln	NM	8,890			

Maps courtesy of Nielsen Media Research

Alexandria, LA (179)

DMA TV Households: 89,630
% of U.S. TV Households: .078

KALB-TV Alexandria, LA, ch. 35, NBC, CBS
*KLPA-TV Alexandria, LA, ch. 26, ETV
KLAX-TV Alexandria, LA, ch. 31, ABC
KBCA Alexandria, LA, ch. 41, CW

DMA Counties	State	TV Households
Avoyelles	LA	15,560
Grant	LA	7,810
Rapides	LA	50,030
Vernon	LA	16,230

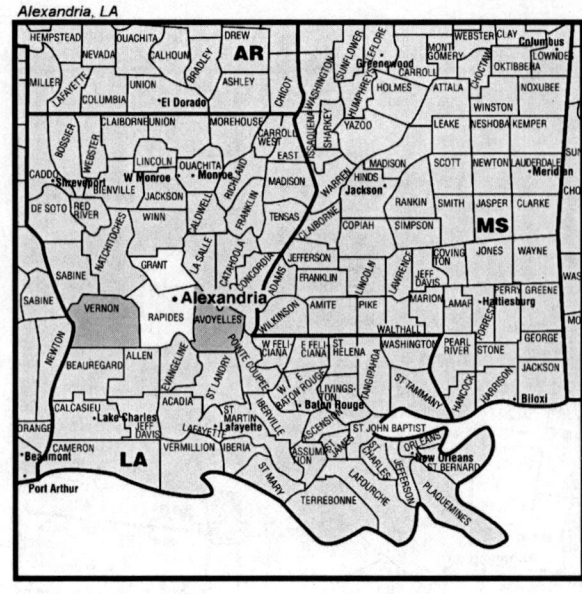

Alexandria, LA

Alpena, MI (208)

DMA TV Households: 17,520
% of U.S. TV Households: .015

WBKB-TV Alpena, MI, ch. 11, CBS
*WCML Alpena, MI, ch. 24, ETV

DMA Counties	State	TV Households
Alcona	MI	5,140
Alpena	MI	12,380

Alpena, MI

Maps courtesy of Nielsen Media Research

Amarillo, TX

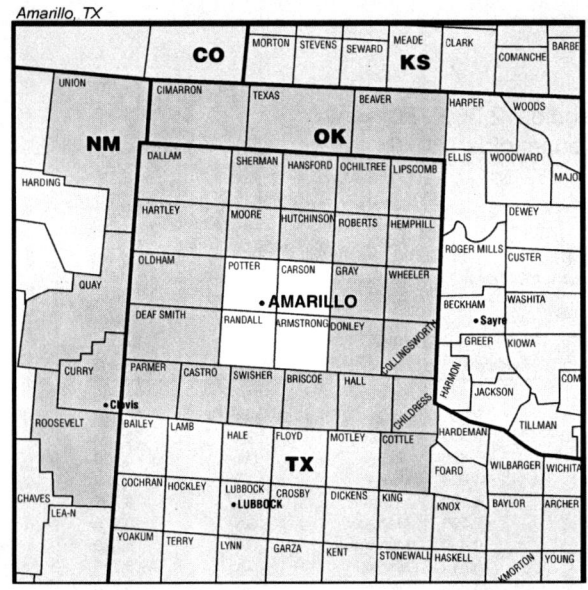

Amarillo, TX (131)

DMA TV Households: 192,090
% of U.S. TV Households: .168

KVII-TV Amarillo, TX, ch. 7, ABC, CW
*KACV-TV Amarillo, TX, ch. 8, ETV
KFDA-TV Amarillo, TX, ch. 10, CBS
KVIH-TV Clovis, NM, ch. 12, satellite to KVII-TV
KCIT Amarillo, TX, ch. 15, Fox
KPTF Farwell, TX, ch. 18, IND
KAMR-TV Amarillo, TX, ch. 19, NBC
KEYU Borger, TX, ch. 31, Univision
*KENW Portales, NM, ch. 32, ETV

DMA Counties	State	TV Households	DMA Counties	State	TV Households
Curry	NM	17,170	Gray	TX	8,750
Quay	NM	3,750	Hall	TX	1,390
Roosevelt	NM	6,780	Hansford	TX	1,980
Union	NM	1,550	Hartley	TX	1,490
Beaver	OK	1,970	Hemphill	TX	1,380
Cimarron	OK	970	Hutchinson	TX	8,660
Texas	OK	6,820	Lipscomb	TX	1,180
Armstrong	TX	790	Moore	TX	6,680
Briscoe	TX	590	Ochiltree	TX	3,460
Carson	TX	2,490	Oldham	TX	690
Castro	TX	2,390	Parmer	TX	3,180
Childress	TX	2,360	Potter	TX	42,420
Collingsworth	TX	1,180	Randall	TX	45,290
Cottle	TX	690	Roberts	TX	400
Dallam	TX	2,210	Sherman	TX	980
Deaf Smith	TX	6,210	Swisher	TX	2,680
Donley	TX	1,580	Wheeler	TX	1,980

Anchorage, AK (150)

DMA TV Households: 150,620
% of U.S. TV Households: .132

KYES-TV Anchorage, ch. 5, MyNetworkTV
*KAKM Anchorage, ch. 8, ETV
KTUU-TV Anchorage, ch. 10, NBC
KIMO Anchorage, ch. 12, ABC, CW
KTBY Anchorage, ch. 20, Fox
KTVA Anchorage, ch. 28, CBS
KDMD Anchorage, ch. 32, IND

DMA Counties	State	TV Households
Anchorage	AK	102,210
Kenai-Pensla	AK	19,560
Matanka-Sustn	AK	28,850

Anchorage, AK

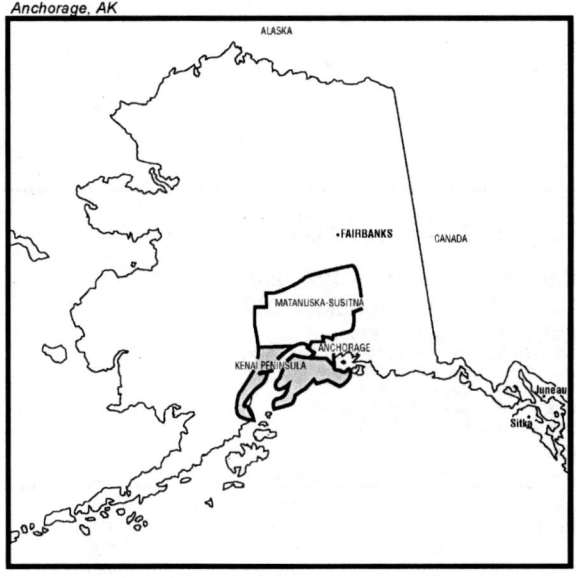

Maps courtesy of Nielsen Media Research

Atlanta, GA

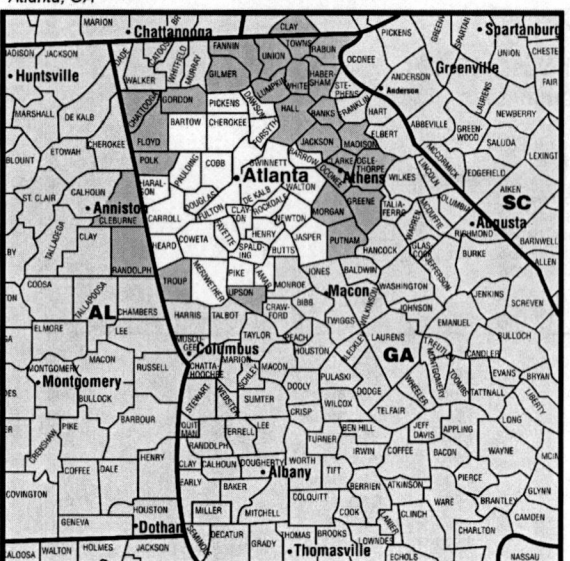

Atlanta (8)

DMA TV Households: 2,369,780
% of U.S. TV Households: 2.070

WSB-TV Atlanta, ch. 39, ABC
WAGA-TV Atlanta, ch. 27, Fox
***WGTV** Athens, GA, ch. 8, ETV
WXIA-TV Atlanta, ch. 10, NBC
WPXA-TV Rome, GA, ch. 51, ION Television
WPCH-TV Atlanta, ch. 20, IND
***WPBA** Atlanta, ch. 21, ETV

WUVG-DT Athens, GA, ch. 48, Univision
WATL Atlanta, ch. 25, MyNetworkTV
WGCL-TV Atlanta, ch. 19, CBS
***WATC-DT** Atlanta, ch. 41, ETV
WHSG-TV Monroe, GA, ch. 63, IND
WUPA Atlanta, ch. 43, CW

DMA Counties	State	TV Households	DMA Counties	State	TV Households
Cleburne	AL	6,040	Heard	GA	4,200
Randolph	AL	8,750	Henry	GA	68,190
Banks	GA	6,330	Jackson	GA	22,890
Barrow	GA	25,420	Jasper	GA	5,150
Bartow	GA	34,020	Lamar	GA	6,230
Butts	GA	8,180	Lumpkin	GA	9,790
Carroll	GA	42,590	Madison	GA	10,970
Chattooga	GA	10,420	Meriwether	GA	8,630
Cherokee	GA	76,810	Morgan	GA	6,750
Clarke	GA	44,850	Newton	GA	36,310
Clayton	GA	93,960	Oconee	GA	11,090
Cobb	GA	259,370	Oglethorpe	GA	5,500
Coweta	GA	44,140	Paulding	GA	47,680
Dawson	GA	8,840	Pickens	GA	12,560
De Kalb	GA	276,460	Pike	GA	6,310
Douglas	GA	47,680	Polk	GA	15,550
Fannin	GA	9,900	Putnam	GA	8,380
Fayette	GA	37,770	Rabun	GA	6,850
Floyd	GA	35,660	Rockdale	GA	28,790
Forsyth	GA	58,530	Spalding	GA	23,780
Fulton	GA	395,850	Towns	GA	4,880
Gilmer	GA	11,180	Troup	GA	23,830
Gordon	GA	19,640	Union	GA	9,200
Greene	GA	6,350	Upson	GA	10,800
Gwinnett	GA	272,980	Walton	GA	30,610
Habersham	GA	16,100	White	GA	10,000
Hall	GA	61,040	Clay	NC	4,800
Haralson	GA	11,200			

Augusta, GA (115)

DMA TV Households: 253,950
% of U.S. TV Households: .222

***WCES-TV** Wrens, GA, ch. 6, ETV
WRDW-TV Augusta, GA, ch. 12, CBS, MyNetworkTV
WAGT Augusta, GA, ch. 30, NBC, CW
WFXG Augusta, GA, ch. 31, Fox
***WEBA-TV** Allendale, SC, ch. 33, ETV
WJBF Augusta, GA, ch 42, ABC

DMA Counties	State	TV Households	DMA Counties	State	TV Households
Burke	GA	8,180	Taliaferro	GA	790
Columbia	GA	40,590	Warren	GA	2,370
Emanuel	GA	8,500	Wilkes	GA	4,230
Glascock	GA	1,190	Aiken	SC	59,940
Jefferson	GA	5,920	Allendale	SC	3,660
Jenkins	GA	3,250	Bamberg	SC	5,900
Lincoln	GA	3,250	Barnwell	SC	9,180
McDuffie	GA	8,220	Edgefield	SC	8,660
Richmond	GA	75,240	McCormick	SC	3,880

Augusta, GA

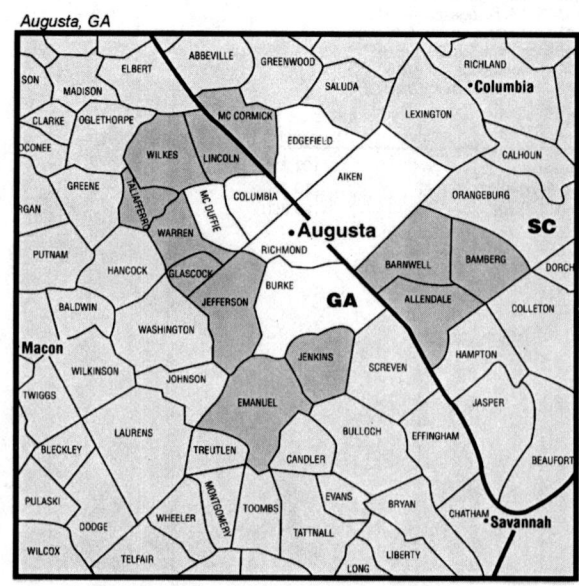

Austin, TX

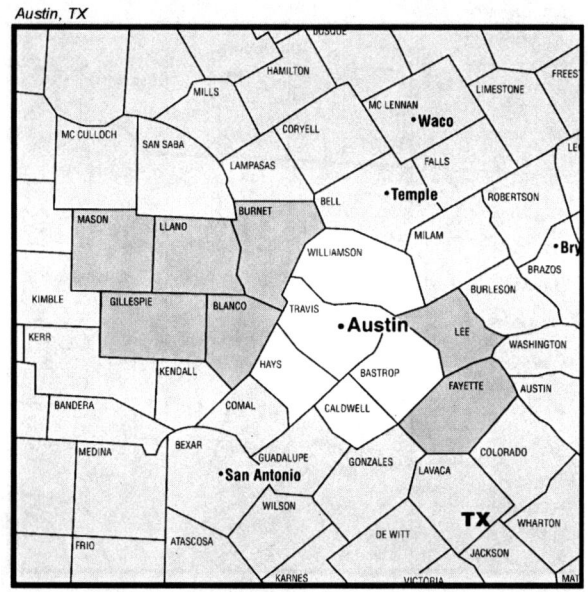

Austin, TX (49)

DMA TV Households: 667,670
% of U.S. TV Households: .583

KTBC Austin, TX, ch. 7, Fox
 KNIC-TV Blanco, TX, ch. 17, TeleFutura
KXAN-TV Austin, TX, ch. 21, NBC
***KLRU** Austin, TX, ch. 22, ETV
KXAM-TV Llano, TX, ch. 27, satellite to KXAN-TV
KVUE Austin, TX, ch. 33, ABC
KEYE-TV Austin, TX, ch. 43, CBS
KNVA Austin, TX, ch. 49, CW

DMA Counties	State	TV Households
Bastrop	TX	25,820
Blanco	TX	3,550
Burnet	TX	16,870
Caldwell	TX	12,470
Fayette	TX	9,240
Gillespie	TX	10,100
Hays	TX	50,350
Lee	TX	5,930
Llano	TX	8,810
Mason	TX	1,640
Travis	TX	388,780
Williamson	TX	134,110

Bakersfield, CA (125)

DMA TV Households: 220,730
% of U.S. TV Households: .193

KERO-TV Bakersfield, CA, ch. 10, ABC
KGET-TV Bakersfield, CA, ch. 25, NBC
KBAK-TV Bakersfield, CA, ch. 33, CBS
KUVI-DT Bakersfield, CA, ch. 45, MyNetworkTV

DMA Counties	State	TV Households
Kern West	CA	220,730

Bakersfield, CA

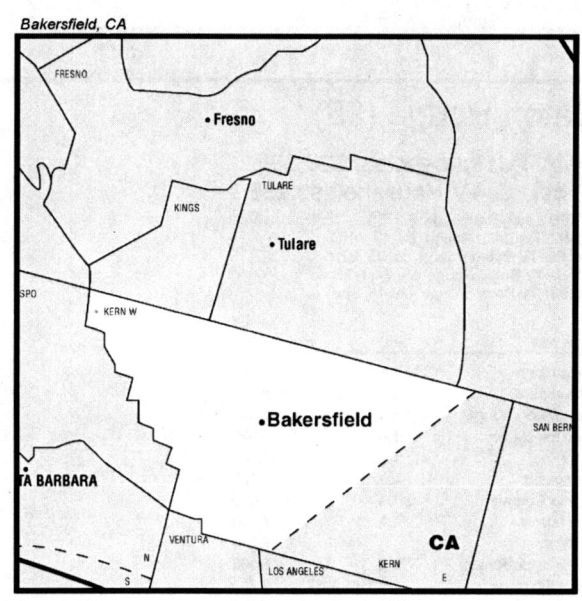

Maps courtesy of Nielsen Media Research

Baltimore (26)

DMA TV Households: 1,102,080
% of U.S. TV Households: .963

WBAL-TV Baltimore, ch. 11, NBC
WJZ-TV Baltimore, ch. 13, CBS
*****WMPB** Baltimore, ch. 29, ETV
WMAR-TV Baltimore, ch. 38, ABC
WNUV Baltimore, ch. 40, CW
WUTB Baltimore, ch. 41, MyNetworkTV
*****WMPT** Annapolis, MD, ch. 42, ETV
WBFF Baltimore, ch. 46, Fox

DMA Counties	State	TV Households	DMA Counties	State	TV Households
Anne Arundel	MD	192,600	Harford	MD	90,900
Baltimore	MD	317,120	Howard	MD	100,980
Baltimore City	MD	249,520	Kent	MD	8,170
Caroline	MD	12,600	Queen Annes	MD	18,120
Carroll	MD	59,400	Talbot	MD	15,530
Cecil	MD	37,140			

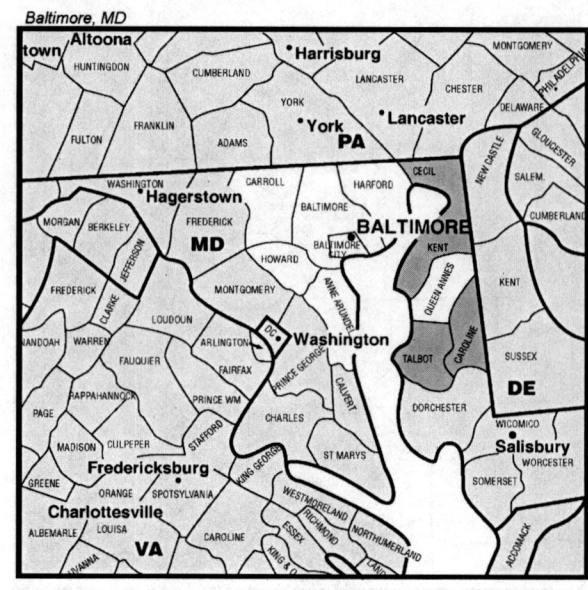

Baltimore, MD

Bangor, ME

Bangor, ME (153)

DMA TV Households: 145,100
% of U.S. TV Households: .127

WLBZ Bangor, ME, ch. 2, NBC
WVII-TV Bangor, ME, ch. 7, ABC
*****WMEB-TV** Orono, ME, ch. 9, ETV
*****WMED-TV** Calais, ME, ch. 10, ETV
WABI-TV Bangor, ME, ch. 19, CBS, CW

DMA Counties	State	TV Households
Hancock	ME	23,270
Penobscot	ME	62,260
Piscataquis	ME	7,510
Somerset	ME	21,740
Waldo	ME	16,200
Washington	ME	14,120

Baton Rouge (95)

DMA TV Households: 326,390
% of U.S. TV Households: .285

WAFB Baton Rouge, ch. 9, CBS
WBRZ-TV Baton Rouge, ch. 13, ABC
*****WLPB-TV** Baton Rouge, ch. 25, ETV
WVLA-TV Baton Rouge, ch. 34, NBC
WGMB-TV Baton Rouge, ch. 45, Fox

DMA Counties	State	TV Households
Ascension	LA	36,690
Assumption	LA	8,460
East Baton Rouge	LA	167,560
East Feliciana	LA	6,820
Iberville	LA	10,630
Livingston	LA	43,130
Pointe Coupee	LA	8,600
St. Helena	LA	4,160
St. Mary	LA	19,270
West Baton Rouge	LA	8,460
West Feliciana	LA	3,750
Amite	MS	5,230
Wilkinson	MS	3,630

Baton Rouge, LA

Maps courtesy of Nielsen Media Research

Beaumont - Port Arthur, TX

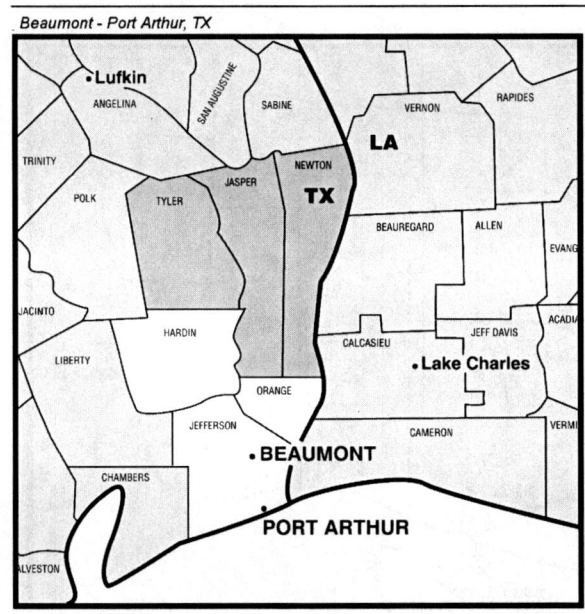

Beaumont-Port Arthur, TX (141)

DMA TV Households: 165,440
% of U.S. TV Households: .145

KBTV-TV Port Arthur, TX, ch. 40, Fox
KFDM-TV Beaumont, TX, ch. 21, CBS, CW
KBMT Beaumont, TX, ch. 12, ABC, NBC
***KITU-TV** Beaumont, TX, ch. 33, ETV

DMA Counties	State	TV Households
Hardin	TX	19,480
Jasper	TX	13,060
Jefferson	TX	88,310
Newton	TX	5,220
Orange	TX	31,700
Tyler	TX	7,670

Bend, OR (192)

DMA TV Households: 64,830
% of U.S. TV Households: .057

***KOAB-TV** Bend, OR, ch. 11, ETV
KTVZ Bend, OR, ch. 21, NBC, CW
KOHD Bend, OR, ch. 51, ABC

DMA Counties	State	TV Households
Deschutes	OR	64,830

Bend, OR

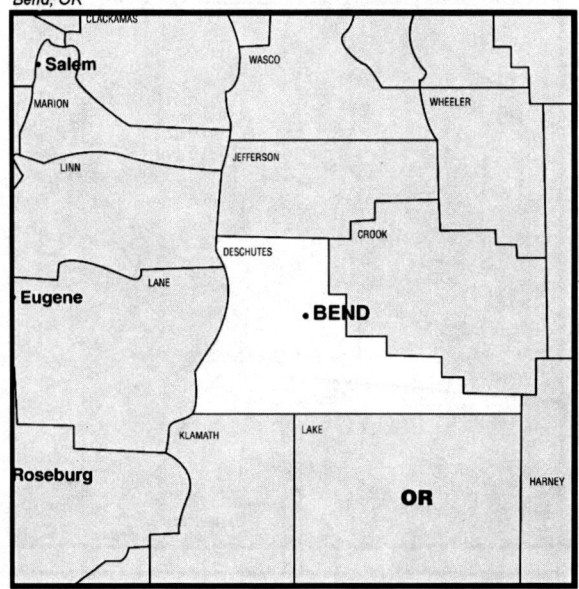

Billings, MT

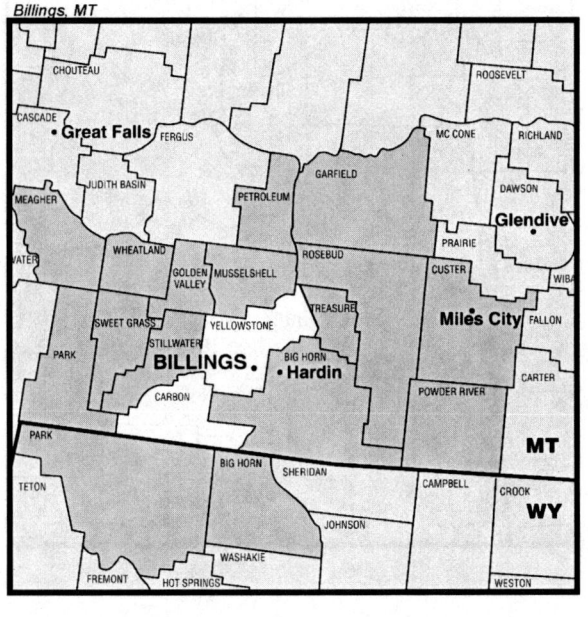

Billings, MT (170)

DMA TV Households: 106,030
% of U.S. TV Households: .093

KTVQ Billings, MT, ch. 10, CBS, CW
KYUS-TV Miles City, MT, ch. 3, satellite to KULR-TV
KULR-TV Billings, MT, ch. 11, NBC
KSVI Billings, MT, ch. 18, ABC
KHMT Hardin, MT, ch. 22, Fox

DMA Counties	State	TV Households	DMA Counties	State	TV Households
Big Horn	MT	3,910	Powder River	MT	690
Carbon	MT	4,210	Rosebud	MT	3,330
Custer	MT	4,530	Stillwater	MT	3,450
Garfield	MT	490	Sweet Grass	MT	1,500
Golden Valley	MT	390	Treasure	MT	290
Meagher	MT	780	Wheatland	MT	690
Musselshell	MT	1,840	Yellowstone	MT	57,250
Park	MT	7,070	Big Horn	WY	4,190
Petroleum	MT	190	Park	WY	11,230

Maps courtesy of Nielsen Media Research

Biloxi-Gulfport, MS (163)

DMA TV Households: 121,750
% of U.S. TV Households: .106

WLOX Biloxi, MS, ch. 13, ABC
*WMAH-TV Biloxi, MS, ch. 16, ETV
WXXV-TV Gulfport, MS, ch. 48, IND

DMA Counties	State	TV Households
Harrison	MS	67,850
Jackson	MS	48,390
Stone	MS	5,510

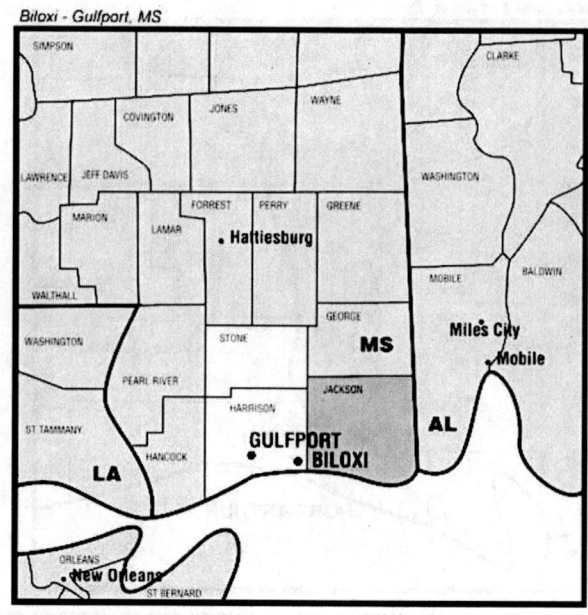

Biloxi - Gulfport, MS

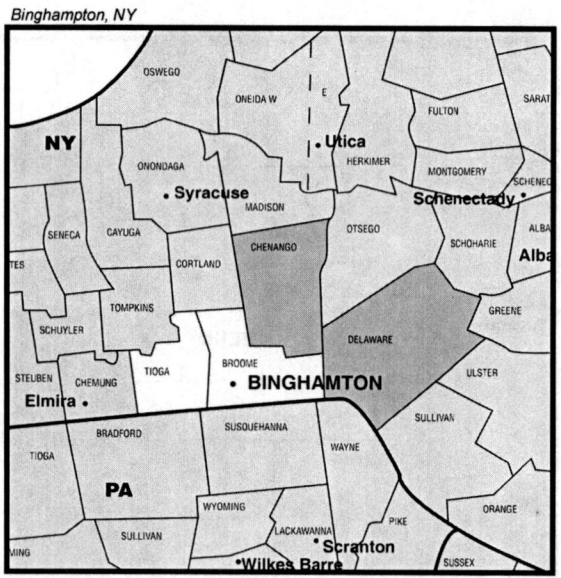

Binghampton, NY

Binghamton, NY (157)

DMA TV Households: 138,930
% of U.S. TV Households: .121

WBNG-TV Binghamton, NY, ch. 7, CBS, CW
WICZ-TV Binghamton, NY, ch. 8, Fox
WIVT Binghamton, NY, ch. 34, ABC
*WSKG-TV Binghamton, NY, ch. 42, ETV

DMA Counties	State	TV Households
Broome	NY	80,250
Chenango	NY	20,310
Delaware	NY	18,730
Tioga	NY	19,640

Birmingham (Anniston and Tuscaloosa), AL (40)

DMA TV Households: 739,750
% of U.S. TV Households: .646

WBRC Birmingham, AL, ch. 50, Fox
*WCIQ Mt. Cheaha, AL, ch. 7, ETV
*WBIQ Birmingham, AL, ch. 10, ETV
WVTM-TV Birmingham, AL, ch. 13, NBC
WDBB Bessemer, AL, ch. 18, Fox
WTTO Homewood, AL, ch. 28, CW
WUOA Tuscaloosa, AL, ch. 6, IND

WTJP-TV Gadsden, AL, ch. 26, IND
WCFT-TV Tuscaloosa, AL, ch. 33, ABC
WJSU-TV Anniston, AL, ch. 9, ABC
WIAT Birmingham, AL, ch. 30, CBS
WPXH-TV Gadsden, AL, ch. 45, ION Television
WABM Birmingham, AL, ch. 36, MyNetworkTV

DMA Counties	State	TV Households	DMA Counties	State	TV Households
Bibb	AL	7,980	Hale	AL	6,530
Blount	AL	21,910	Jefferson	AL	264,960
Calhoun	AL	47,320	Marion	AL	12,310
Cherokee	AL	10,330	Pickens	AL	7,620
Chilton	AL	16,740	St. Clair	AL	29,900
Clay	AL	5,720	Shelby	AL	71,700
Coosa	AL	4,350	Talladega	AL	31,010
Cullman	AL	32,740	Tuscaloosa	AL	72,860
Etowah	AL	42,920	Walker	AL	28,120
Fayette	AL	7,340	Winston	AL	10,030
Greene	AL	3,670			

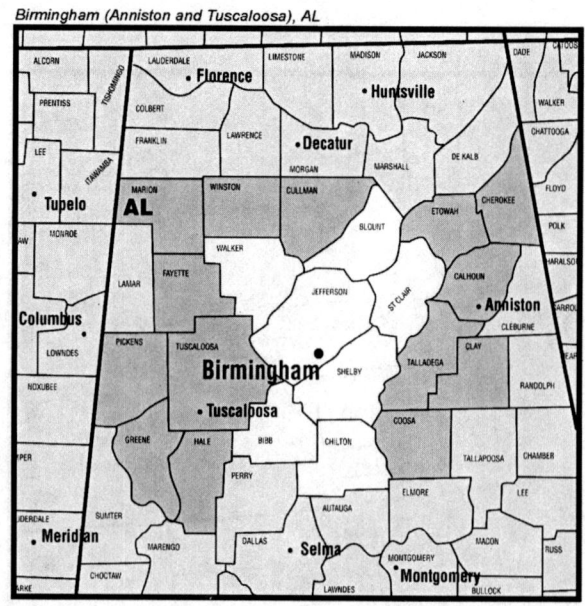

Birmingham (Anniston and Tuscaloosa), AL

Bluefield - Beckley - Oak Hill, WV

Bluefield-Beckley-Oak Hill, WV (155)

DMA TV Households: 142,570
% of U.S. TV Households: .125

WVNS-TV Lewisburg, WV, ch. 8, CBS
*WSWP-TV Grandview, WV, ch. 10, ETV
WLFB Bluefield, WV, ch. 40, IND
WVVA Bluefield, WV, ch. 46, NBC, CW
WOAY-TV Oak Hill, WV, ch. 50, ABC

DMA Counties	State	TV Households
Tazewell	VA	18,570
Fayette	WV	18,740
Greenbrier	WV	15,020
McDowell	WV	9,690
Mercer	WV	26,890
Monroe	WV	5,710
Pocahontas	WV	3,580
Raleigh	WV	32,850
Summers	WV	4,990
Wyoming	WV	10,110

Boise, ID (112)

DMA TV Households: 262,290
% of U.S. TV Households: .229

KTVB Boise, ID, ch. 7, NBC
KNIN-TV Caldwell, ID, ch. 10, CW
KTRV-TV Nampa, ID, ch. 13, Fox
*KAID Boise, ID, ch. 21, ETV
KIVI-TV Nampa, ID, ch. 24, ABC
KBCI-TV Boise, ID, ch. 28, CBS
KKJB Boise, ID, ch. 39, IND

DMA Counties	State	TV Households
Ada	ID	148,490
Adams	ID	1,430
Boise	ID	2,940
Camas	ID	490
Canyon	ID	64,490
Elmore	ID	9,100
Gem	ID	6,020
Owyhee	ID	3,710
Payette	ID	8,120
Valley	ID	3,950
Washington	ID	3,710
Malheur	OR	9,840

Boise, ID

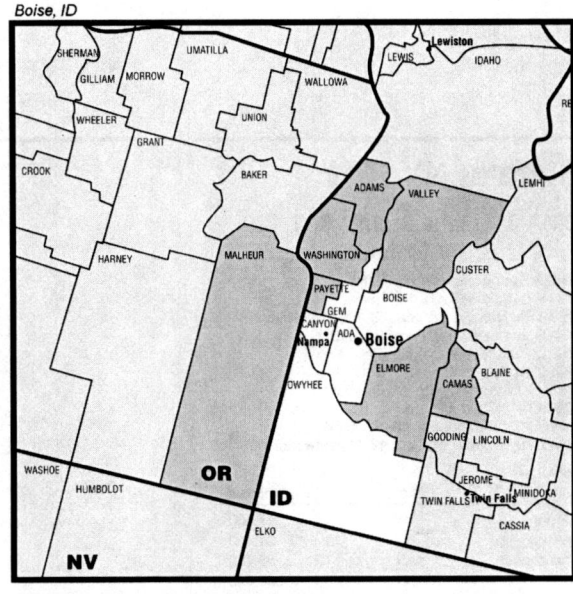

Boston, MA

Boston (Manchester, NH) (7)

DMA TV Households: 2,409,080
% of U.S. TV Households: 2.105

*WGBH-TV Boston, ch. 19, ETV
WBZ-TV Boston, ch. 30, CBS
WCVB-TV Boston, ch. 20, ABC
WHDH-TV Boston, ch. 7, NBC
WMUR-TV Manchester, NH, ch. 9, ABC
WWDP Norwell, MA, ch. 10, IND
*WENH-TV Durham, NH, ch. 11, ETV
WPXG-TV Concord, NH, ch. 33, satellite to WBPX
WFXT Boston, ch. 31, Fox
WUNI Worcester, MA, ch. 29, Univision
WBPX-TV Boston, ch. 32, ION Television

WSBK-TV Boston, ch. 39, IND
WDPX-TV Vineyard Haven, MA, ch. 40,
  satellite to WBPX-TV
*WGBX-TV Boston, ch. 43, ETV
*WYDN Worcester, MA, ch. 47, ETV
WZMY-TV Derry, NH, ch. 35, MyNetworkTV
*WEKW-TV Keene, NH, ch. 49, ETV
WLVI-TV Cambridge, MA, ch. 41, CW
WNEU Merrimack, NH, ch. 34, Telemundo
WMFP Lawrence, MA, ch. 18, IND
WUTF-DT Marlborough, MA, ch. 27, TeleFutura

DMA Counties	State	TV Households	DMA Counties	State	TV Households
Barnstable	MA	95,360	Worcester	MA	297,250
Dukes	MA	6,630	Belknap	NH	25,000
Essex	MA	276,990	Cheshire	NH	29,950
Middlesex	MA	564,860	Hillsborough	NH	153,330
Nantucket	MA	4,060	Merrimack	NH	57,430
Norfolk	MA	254,480	Rockingham	NH	114,740
Plymouth	MA	178,460	Strafford	NH	47,090
Suffolk	MA	285,520	Windham	VT	17,930

Maps courtesy of Nielsen Media Research

Bowling Green, KY

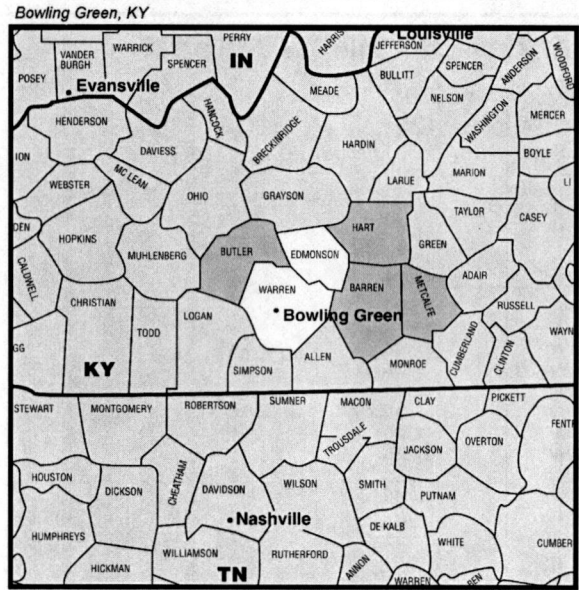

Bowling Green, KY (182)

DMA TV Households: 80,260
% of U.S. TV Households: .070

WBKO Bowling Green, KY, ch. 13, ABC, CW, Fox
WNKY Bowling Green, KY, ch. 16, NBC
***WKYU-TV** Bowling Green, KY, ch. 18, ETV
***WKGB-TV** Bowling Green, KY, ch. 48, ETV

DMA Counties	State	TV Households
Barren	KY	17,250
Butler	KY	5,260
Edmonson	KY	4,910
Hart	KY	7,140
Metcalfe	KY	4,260
Warren	KY	41,440

Buffalo, NY (51)

DMA TV Households: 631,120
% of U.S. TV Households: .551

WNGS Springville, NY, ch. 7, IND
WUTV Buffalo, NY, ch. 14, Fox
WPXJ-TV Batavia, NY, ch. 23, ION Television
WNYB Jamestown, NY, ch. 26, IND
WNLO Buffalo, NY, ch. 32, CW
WGRZ Buffalo, NY, ch. 33, NBC
WKBW-TV Buffalo, NY, ch. 38, ABC
WIVB-TV Buffalo, NY, ch. 39, CBS
***WNED-TV** Buffalo, NY, ch. 43, ETV
WNYO-TV Buffalo, NY, ch. 49, MyNetworkTV

DMA Counties	State	TV Households
Allegany	NY	17,900
Cattaraugus	NY	31,410
Chautauqua	NY	52,150
Erie	NY	368,020
Genesee	NY	22,290
Niagara	NY	86,310
Orleans	NY	14,970
Wyoming	NY	14,730
McKean	PA	16,990
Potter	PA	6,350

Buffalo, NY

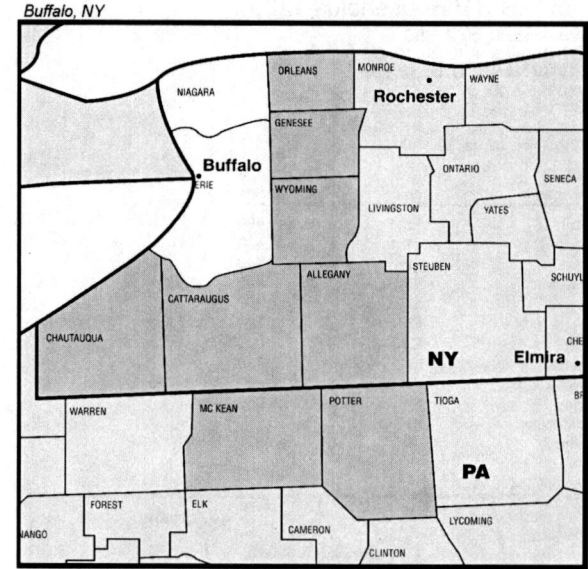

Burlington, VT - Plattsburgh, NY

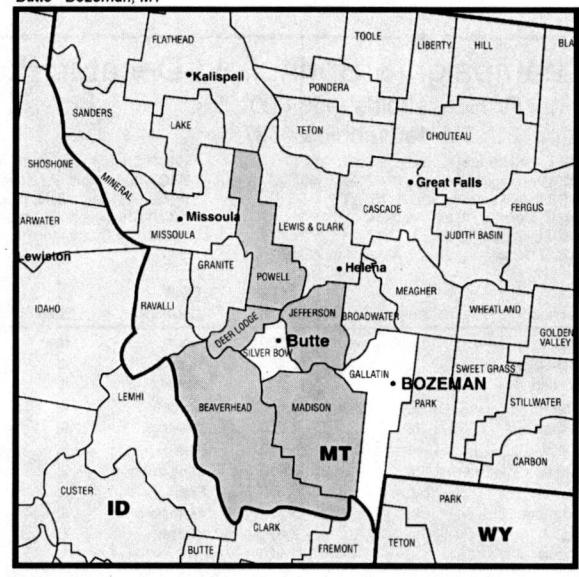

Burlington, VT-Plattsburgh, NY (93)

DMA TV Households: 331,320
% of U.S. TV Households: .289

WCAX-TV Burlington, VT, ch. 3, CBS
***WVER** Rutland, VT, ch. 9, satellite to WETK
WVNY Burlington, VT, ch. 13, ABC
WPTZ North Pole (Plattsburgh), NY, ch. 14, NBC
***WVTB** St. Johnsbury, VT, ch. 18, satellite to WETK
***WVTA** Windsor, VT, ch. 24, satellite to WETK
WNNE Hartford, VT, ch. 25, NBC
***WETK** Burlington, VT, ch. 32, ETV
***WCFE-TV** Plattsburgh, NY, ch. 38, ETV
***WNMN** Saranac Lake, NY, ch. 40, IND
WFFF-TV Burlington, VT, ch 43, Fox, CW
***WLED-TV** Littleton, NH, ch. 48, ETV

DMA Counties	State	TV Households	DMA Counties	State	TV Households
Grafton	NH	32,590	Franklin	VT	18,060
Sullivan	NH	17,870	Grand Isle	VT	3,180
Clinton	NY	31,080	Lamoille	VT	10,020
Essex	NY	15,030	Orange	VT	11,490
Franklin	NY	18,050	Orleans	VT	11,380
Addison	VT	13,560	Rutland	VT	25,970
Caledonia	VT	12,240	Washington	VT	24,380
Chittenden	VT	59,850	Windsor	VT	23,920
Essex	VT	2,650			

Butte-Bozeman, MT (190)

DMA TV Households: 65,480
% of U.S. TV Households: .057

KXLF-TV Butte, MT, ch. 5, CBS, CW
KTVM Butte, MT, ch. 6, satellite to KECI-TV
***KUSM** Bozeman, MT, ch. 8, ETV
KBZK Bozeman, MT, ch. 13, CBS, CW
KWYB Butte, MT, ch. 19, ABC, Fox
KBTZ Butte, MT, ch. 24, IND

DMA Counties	State	TV Households
Beaverhead	MT	3,340
Deer Lodge	MT	3,650
Gallatin	MT	35,050
Jefferson	MT	4,210
Madison	MT	3,320
Powell	MT	2,240
Silver Bow	MT	13,670

Butte - Bozeman, MT

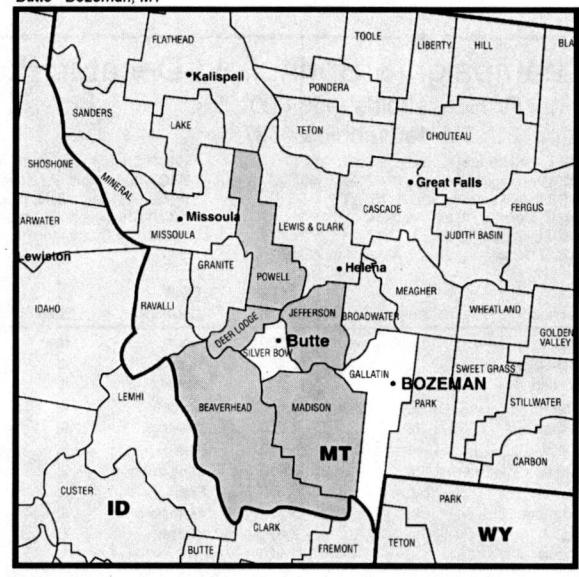

Casper - Riverton, WY

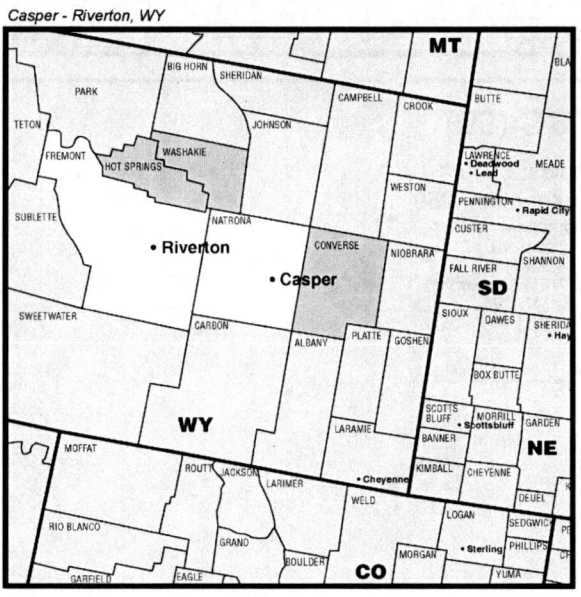

Casper-Riverton, WY (197)

DMA TV Households: 54,340
% of U.S. TV Households: .047

KGWL-TV Lander, WY, ch. 7, CBS
***KPTW** Casper, WY, ch. 8, satellite to KCWC-TV
***KCWC-TV** Lander, WY, ch. 8, ETV
KFNE Riverton, WY, ch. 10, satellite to KFNB
KCWY-DT Casper, WY, ch. 12, NBC
KGWC-TV Casper, WY, ch. 14, CBS
KTWO-TV Casper, WY, ch. 17, ABC
KFNB Casper, WY, ch. 20, Fox

DMA Counties	State	TV Households
Converse	WY	5,190
Fremont	WY	14,550
Hot Springs	WY	1,930
Natrona	WY	29,540
Washakie	WY	3,130

Maps courtesy of Nielsen Media Research

Cedar Rapids - Waterloo - Iowa City & Dubuque

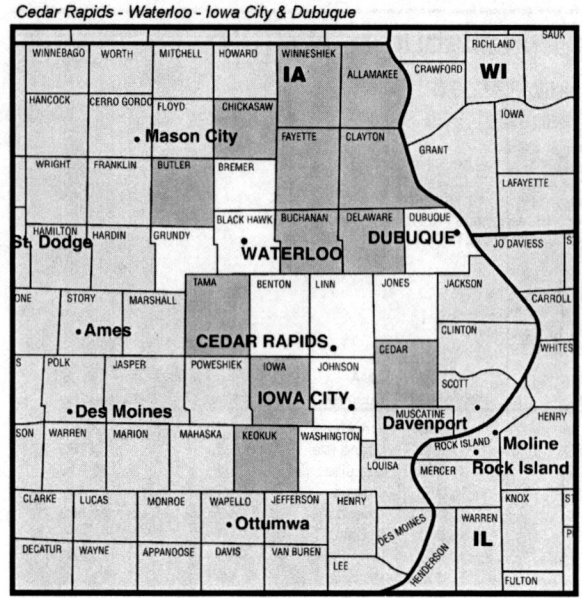

Cedar Rapids-Waterloo-Iowa City & Dubuque, IA (88)

DMA TV Households: 346,330
% of U.S. TV Households: .303

KWWL Waterloo, IA, ch. 7, NBC
KCRG-TV Cedar Rapids, IA, ch. 9, ABC
*****KIIN-TV** Iowa City, IA, ch. 12, ETV
KWWF Waterloo, IA, ch. 22, IND
KWKB Iowa City, IA, ch. 25, CW, MyNetworkTV
KFXA Cedar Rapids, IA, ch. 27, IND
*****KRIN** Waterloo, IA, ch. 35, ETV
KFXB-TV Dubuque, IA, ch. 43, ABC
KPXR-TV Cedar Rapids, IA, ch. 47, ION Television
KGAN Cedar Rapids, IA, ch. 51, CBS

DMA Counties	State	TV Households	DMA Counties	State	TV Households
Allamakee	IA	5,720	Fayette	IA	8,170
Benton	IA	10,260	Grundy	IA	4,880
Black Hawk	IA	50,920	Iowa	IA	6,270
Bremer	IA	9,170	Johnson	IA	53,040
Buchanan	IA	8,060	Jones	IA	7,740
Butler	IA	6,070	Keokuk	IA	4,360
Cedar	IA	7,180	Linn	IA	86,430
Chickasaw	IA	4,860	Tama	IA	6,870
Clayton	IA	7,030	Washington	IA	8,350
Delaware	IA	6,580	Winneshiek	IA	7,750
Dubuque	IA	36,620			

Champaign & Springfield-Decatur, IL (83)

DMA TV Households: 386,000
% of U.S. TV Households: .337

*****WILL-TV** Urbana, IL, ch. 9, ETV
WCFN Springfield, IL, ch. 13, MyNetworkTV
*****WSEC** Jacksonville, IL, ch. 15, ETV
WAND Decatur, IL, ch. 18, NBC
WBUI Decatur, IL, ch. 22, CW
WCCU Urbana, IL, ch. 26, satellite to WRSP-TV

WICD Champaign, IL, ch. 41, satellite to WICS
WICS Springfield, IL, ch. 42, ABC
WRSP-TV Springfield, IL, ch. 44, Fox
WCIA Champaign, IL, ch. 48, CBS
*****WEIU-TV** Charleston, IL, ch. 50, ETV

DMA Counties	State	TV Households	DMA Counties	State	TV Households
Cass	IL	5,360	Logan	IL	10,560
Champaign	IL	76,480	Macon	IL	45,390
Christian	IL	13,730	Menard	IL	4,980
Coles	IL	20,800	Morgan	IL	13,520
Cumberland	IL	4,260	Moultrie	IL	5,470
De Witt	IL	6,670	Piatt	IL	6,680
Douglas	IL	7,410	Sangamon	IL	82,390
Edgar	IL	7,550	Shelby	IL	8,660
Effingham	IL	13,230	Vermilion	IL	32,130
Ford	IL	5,670	Warren	IN	3,260
Iroquois	IL	11,800			

Champaign & Springfield - Decatur - IL

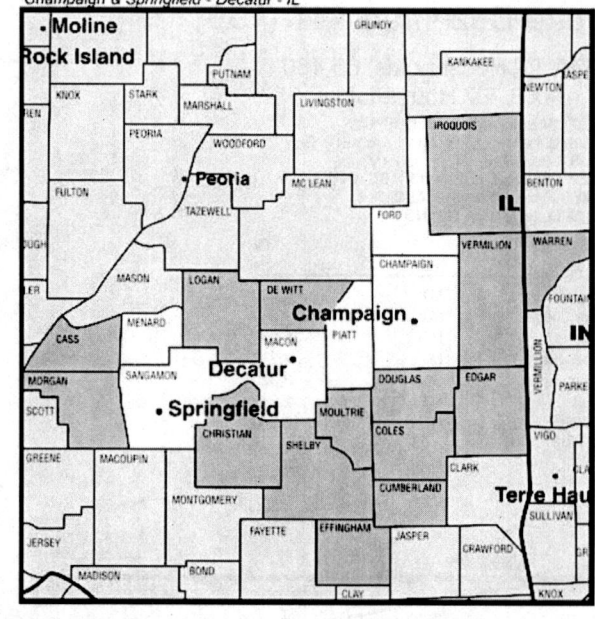

Charleston, SC

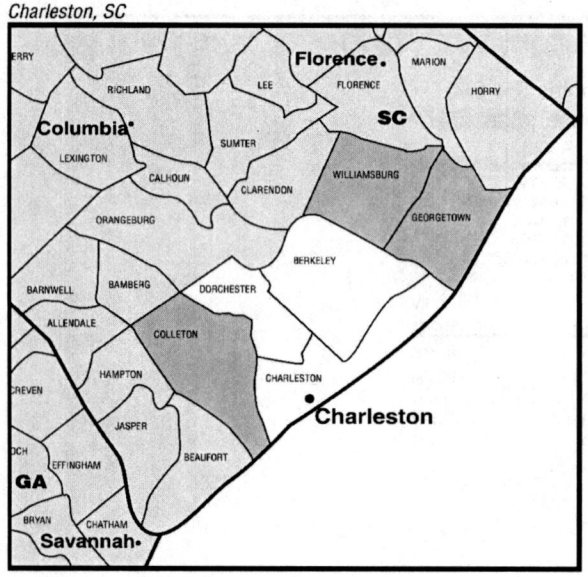

Charleston, SC (99)

DMA TV Households: 307,610
% of U.S. TV Households: .269

*****WITV** Charleston, SC, ch. 7, ETV
WTAT-TV Charleston, SC, ch. 24, Fox
WCIV Charleston, SC, ch. 34, ABC
WMMP Charleston, SC, ch. 36, MyNetworkTV
WCSC-TV Charleston, SC, ch. 47, CBS
WCBD-TV Charleston, SC, ch. 50, NBC, CW

DMA Counties	State	TV Households
Berkeley	SC	62,020
Charleston	SC	144,280
Colleton	SC	15,310
Dorchester	SC	47,700
Georgetown	SC	25,180
Williamsburg	SC	13,120

Maps courtesy of Nielsen Media Research

Charleston - Huntington, WV

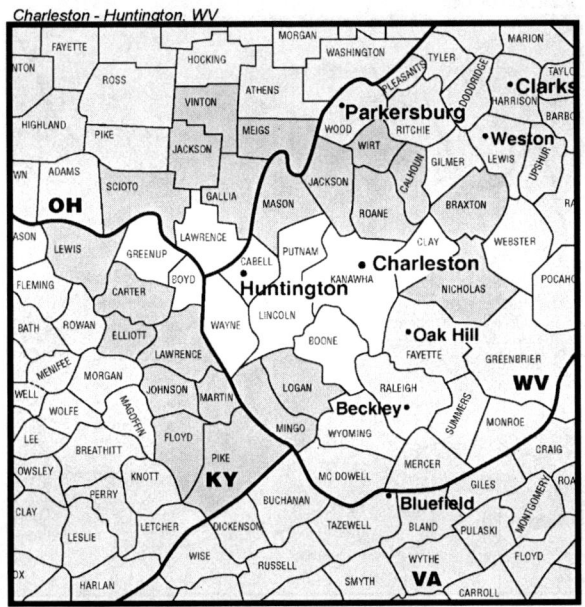

Charleston-Huntington, WV (65)

DMA TV Households: 479,750
% of U.S. TV Households: .419

WOWK-TV Huntington, WV, ch. 13, CBS
WQCW Portsmouth, OH, ch. 17, CW
WVAH-TV Charleston, WV, ch. 19, Fox
WSAZ-TV Huntington, WV, ch. 23, NBC, MyNetworkTV
***WKPI-TV** Pikeville, KY, ch. 24, ETV
***WKAS** Ashland, KY, ch. 26, ETV
***WPBY-TV** Huntington, WV, ch. 34, ETV
WLPX-TV Charleston, WV, ch. 39, ION Television
WCHS-TV Charleston, WV, ch. 41, ABC
***WPBO** Portsmouth, OH, ch. 43, ETV
WTSF Ashland, KY, ch. 44, IND

DMA Counties	State	TV Households	DMA Counties	State	TV Households
Boyd	KY	19,830	Boone	WV	10,490
Carter	KY	11,010	Braxton	WV	5,730
Elliott	KY	2,930	Cabell	WV	40,680
Floyd	KY	17,690	Calhoun	WV	2,890
Greenup	KY	15,410	Clay	WV	4,030
Johnson	KY	9,730	Jackson	WV	11,540
Lawrence	KY	6,510	Kanawha	WV	83,320
Lewis	KY	5,530	Lincoln	WV	9,140
Martin	KY	4,550	Logan	WV	14,780
Pike	KY	27,500	Mason	WV	10,720
Gallia	OH	12,320	Mingo	WV	11,200
Jackson	OH	13,070	Nicholas	WV	10,900
Lawrence	OH	25,800	Putnam	WV	22,210
Meigs	OH	9,390	Roane	WV	6,200
Scioto	OH	30,210	Wayne	WV	16,950
Vinton	OH	5,220	Wirt	WV	2,270

Charlotte, NC (24)

DMA TV Households: 1,122,860
% of U.S. TV Households: .981

***WTVI** Charlotte, NC, ch. 11, ETV
***WNSC-TV** Rock Hill, SC, ch. 15, ETV
***WUNE-TV** Linville, NC, ch. 17, ETV
WCNC-TV Charlotte, NC, ch. 22, NBC
WBTV Charlotte, NC, ch. 23, CBS
WCCB Charlotte, NC, ch. 27, Fox
WSOC-TV Charlotte, NC, ch. 34, ABC
WMYT-TV Rock Hill, SC, ch. 39, MyNetworkTV
WHKY-TV Hickory, NC, ch. 40, IND
***WUNG-TV** Concord, NC, ch. 44, ETV
WJZY Belmont, NC, ch. 47, CW
WAXN-TV Kannapolis, NC, ch. 50, IND

DMA Counties	State	TV Households	DMA Counties	State	TV Households
Alexander	NC	14,170	Lincoln	NC	28,050
Anson	NC	9,020	Mecklenburg	NC	341,690
Ashe	NC	10,960	Richmond	NC	17,820
Avery	NC	6,350	Rowan	NC	52,820
Burke	NC	34,720	Stanly	NC	22,730
Cabarrus	NC	61,740	Union	NC	65,770
Caldwell	NC	32,080	Watauga	NC	16,240
Catawba	NC	61,240	Chester	SC	12,530
Cleveland	NC	38,220	Chesterfield	SC	17,080
Gaston	NC	79,570	Lancaster	SC	24,810
Iredell	NC	58,470	York	SC	79,560

Charlotte, NC

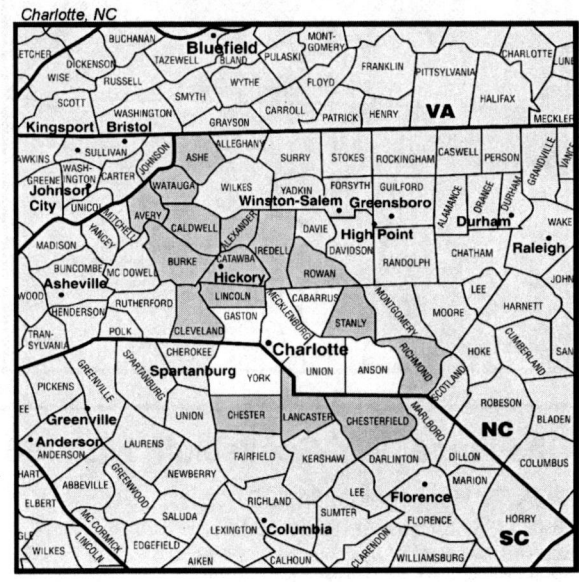

Charlottesville, VA (183)

DMA TV Households: 76,600
% of U.S. TV Households: .067

WCAV Charlottesville, VA, ch. 19, CBS
WVIR-TV Charlottesville, VA, ch. 32, NBC
***WHTJ** Charlottesville, VA, ch. 46, ETV

DMA Counties	State	TV Households
Albemarle	VA	54,720
Fluvanna	VA	9,990
Greene	VA	6,560
Madison	VA	5,330

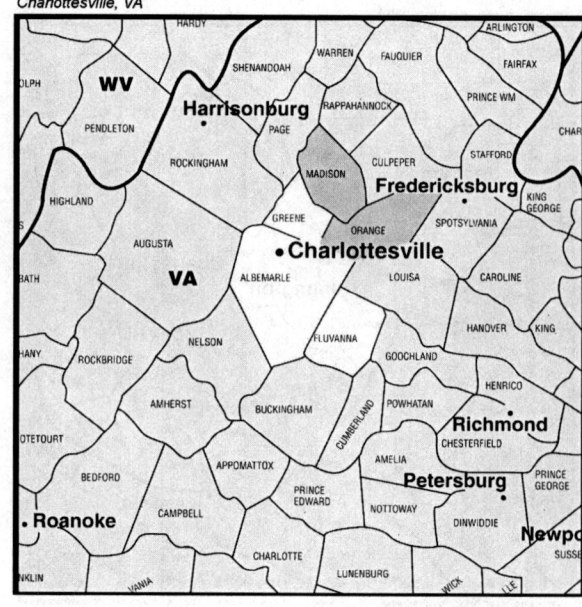
Charlottesville, VA

Chattanooga, TN (86)

DMA TV Households: 366,780
% of U.S. TV Households: .320

WTVC Chattanooga, ch. 9, ABC
WDEF-TV Chattanooga, ch. 12, CBS
WRCB Chattanooga, ch. 13, NBC
WELF-TV Dalton, GA, ch. 16, IND
***WTCI** Chattanooga, ch. 29, ETV
***WNGH-TV** Chatsworth, GA, ch. 33, ETV
WDSI-TV Chattanooga, ch. 40, Fox, MyNetworkTV
WFLI-TV Cleveland, TN, ch. 42, CW

DMA Counties	State	TV Households	DMA Counties	State	TV Households
Catoosa	GA	24,840	Grundy	TN	5,680
Dade	GA	6,100	Hamilton	TN	139,130
Murray	GA	15,010	Marion	TN	11,540
Walker	GA	25,590	McMinn	TN	21,700
Whitfield	GA	32,190	Meigs	TN	4,660
Cherokee	NC	11,920	Polk	TN	6,530
Bledsoe	TN	4,800	Rhea	TN	12,270
Bradley	TN	39,280	Sequatchie	TN	5,540

Chattanooga, TN

Cheyenne, WY-Scottsbluff, NE (198)

DMA TV Households: 54,120
% of U.S. TV Households: .047

KDUH-TV Scottsbluff, NE, ch. 4, satellite to KOTA-TV
KQCK Cheyenne, WY, ch. 11, satellite to KTWO-TV
***KTNE-TV** Alliance, NE, ch. 13, ETV
KTUW Scottsbluff, NE, ch. 17, IND
KLWY Cheyenne, WY, ch. 27, Fox
KSTF Scottsbluff, NE, ch. 29, satellite to KGWN-TV
KGWN-TV Cheyenne, WY, ch. 30, CBS, CW

DMA Counties	State	TV Households
Scotts Bluff	NE	14,770
Goshen	WY	4,950
Laramie	WY	34,400

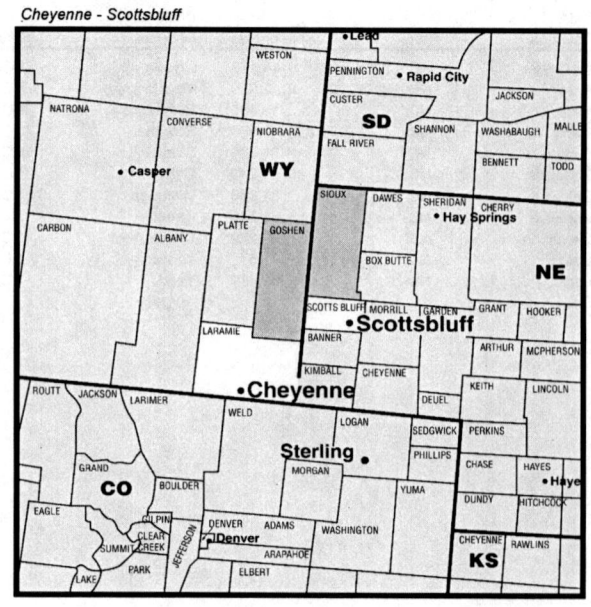
Cheyenne - Scottsbluff

Chicago, IL

Chicago (3)

DMA TV Households: 3,492,850
% of U.S. TV Households: 3.052

WBBM-TV Chicago, ch. 12, CBS
WMAQ-TV Chicago, ch. 29, NBC
WLS-TV Chicago, ch. 7, ABC
WGN-TV Chicago, ch. 19, CW
WWTO-TV La Salle, IL, ch. 10, IND
*****WTTW** Chicago, ch. 47, ETV
*****WYCC** Chicago, ch. 21, ETV
WCIU-TV Chicago, ch. 27, IND

WFLD Chicago, ch. 31, Fox
WCPX-TV Chicago, ch. 43, ION Television
WSNS Chicago, ch. 45, Telemundo
WPWR-TV Gary, IN, ch. 51, MyNetworkTV
*****WYIN** Gary, IN, ch. 56, ETV
WXFT-DT Aurora, IL, ch. 50, TeleFutura
WJYS Hammond, IN, ch. 36, IND
WGBO-DT Joliet, IL, ch. 38, Univision

DMA Counties	State	TV Households	DMA Counties	State	TV Households
Cook	IL	1,914,710	Lake	IL	239,410
De Kalb	IL	37,950	McHenry	IL	111,400
Du Page	IL	336,840	Will	IL	231,280
Grundy	IL	19,000	Jasper	IN	11,820
Kane	IL	169,270	La Porte	IN	42,100
Kankakee	IL	41,820	Lake	IN	186,930
Kendall	IL	37,260	Newton	IN	5,150
La Salle	IL	44,920	Porter	IN	62,990

Chico-Redding, CA (130)

DMA TV Households: 197,280
% of U.S. TV Households: .172

KRCR-TV Redding, CA, ch. 7, ABC
*****KIXE-TV** Redding, CA, ch. 9, ETV
KCVU Paradise, CA, ch. 20, Fox
KNVN Chico, CA, ch. 24, NBC
KHSL-TV Chico, CA, ch. 43, CBS, CW

DMA Counties	State	TV Households
Butte	CA	84,690
Glenn	CA	9,710
Modoc	CA	3,680
Shasta	CA	70,200
Tehama	CA	23,000
Trinity	CA	6,000

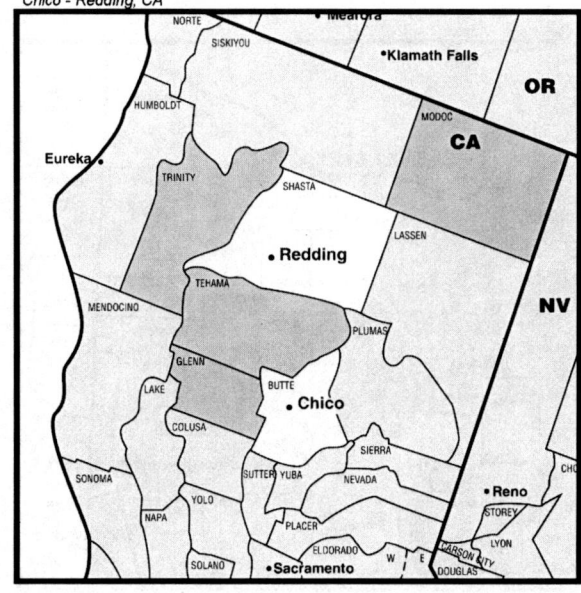

Chico - Redding, CA

Cincinnati, OH

Cincinnati (34)

DMA TV Households: 915,570
% of U.S. TV Households: .800

WLWT Cincinnati, ch. 35, NBC
WCPO-TV Cincinnati, ch. 10, ABC
WKRC-TV Cincinnati, ch. 12, CBS, CW
WXIX-TV Newport, KY, ch. 29, Fox
*****WPTO** Oxford, OH, ch. 28, ETV

*****WCVN-TV** Covington, KY, ch. 24, ETV
*****WCET** Cincinnati, ch. 34, ETV
*****WKON** Owenton, KY, ch. 44, ETV
WSTR-TV Cincinnati, ch. 33, MyNetworkTV

DMA Counties	State	TV Households	DMA Counties	State	TV Households
Dearborn	IN	18,770	Mason	KY	7,240
Franklin	IN	8,470	Owen	KY	4,430
Ohio	IN	2,290	Pendleton	KY	5,480
Ripley	IN	10,320	Robertson	KY	790
Switzerland	IN	3,790	Adams	OH	10,970
Union	IN	2,770	Brown	OH	16,450
Boone	KY	43,370	Butler	OH	135,250
Bracken	KY	3,490	Clermont	OH	73,960
Campbell	KY	35,050	Clinton	OH	16,920
Gallatin	KY	2,970	Hamilton	OH	347,320
Grant	KY	9,430	Highland	OH	16,510
Kenton	KY	63,860	Warren	OH	75,670

Maps courtesy of Nielsen Media Research

Clarksburg-Weston, WV (168)

DMA TV Households: 109,150
% of U.S. TV Households: .095

WDTV Weston, WV, ch. 5, CBS (ABC)
WVFX Clarksburg, WV, ch. 10, Fox, CW
WBOY-TV Clarksburg, WV, ch. 12, NBC (ABC)

DMA Counties	State	TV Households
Barbour	WV	6,230
Doddridge	WV	2,730
Gilmer	WV	2,730
Harrison	WV	27,940
Lewis	WV	7,230
Marion	WV	24,290
Randolph	WV	11,190
Ritchie	WV	4,210
Taylor	WV	6,450
Tucker	WV	2,860
Upshur	WV	9,270
Webster	WV	4,020

Clarksburg - Weston, WV

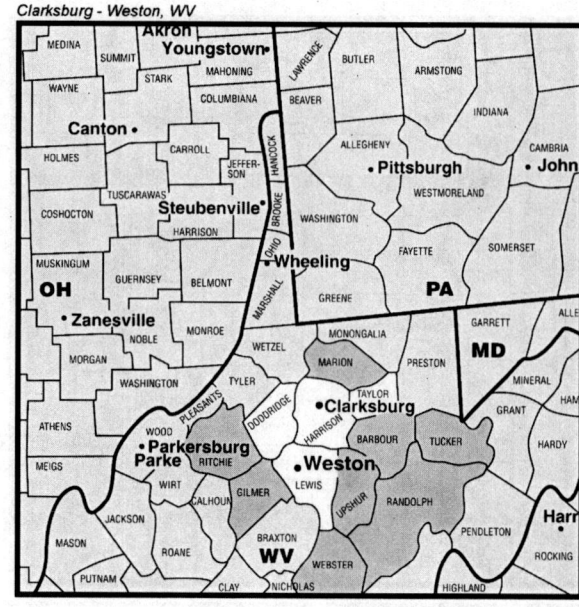

Cleveland - Akron (Canton), OH

Cleveland-Akron (Canton), OH (17)

DMA TV Households: 1,524,930
% of U.S. TV Households: 1.332

WJW Cleveland, ch. 8, Fox
WOIO Shaker Heights, OH, ch. 10, CBS
WMFD-TV Mansfield, OH, ch. 12, IND
WEWS-TV Cleveland, ch. 15, ABC
WKYC Cleveland, ch. 17, NBC
WVPX-TV Akron, OH, ch. 23, ION Television
WVIZ Cleveland, ch. 26, ETV

WUAB Lorain, OH, ch. 28, MyNetworkTV
WBNX-TV Akron, OH, ch. 30, CW
WQHS-DT Cleveland, ch. 34, Univision
WGGN-TV Sandusky, OH, ch. 42, IND
WOAC Canton, OH, ch. 47, IND
***WDLI-TV** Canton, OH, ch. 49, IND
***WEAO** Akron, OH, ch. 50, ETV

DMA Counties	State	TV Households	DMA Counties	State	TV Households
Ashland	OH	20,820	Lorain	OH	115,220
Ashtabula	OH	39,350	Medina	OH	63,960
Carroll	OH	11,220	Portage	OH	59,870
Cuyahoga	OH	525,930	Richland	OH	48,370
Erie	OH	31,480	Stark	OH	150,680
Geauga	OH	33,580	Summit	OH	220,600
Holmes	OH	9,920	Tuscarawas	OH	35,430
Huron	OH	22,910	Wayne	OH	41,290
Lake	OH	94,300			

Colorado Springs-Pueblo, CO (91)

DMA TV Households: 334,390
% of U.S. TV Households: .292

***KTSC** Pueblo, CO, ch. 8, ETV
KKTV Colorado Springs, ch. 10, CBS, MyNetworkTV
KXRM-TV Colorado Springs, ch. 22, Fox
KRDO-TV Colorado Springs, ch. 24, ABC
KOAA-TV Pueblo, CO, ch. 42, NBC
KVSN-DT Pueblo, CO, ch. 48, Univision

DMA Counties	State	TV Households
Baca	CO	1,640
Bent	CO	1,770
Crowley	CO	1,090
Custer	CO	1,730
El Paso	CO	224,470
Fremont	CO	15,810
Huerfano	CO	3,060
Kiowa	CO	590
Las Animas	CO	6,510
Otero	CO	7,540
Pueblo	CO	61,280
Teller	CO	8,900

Colorado Springs - Pueblo, CO

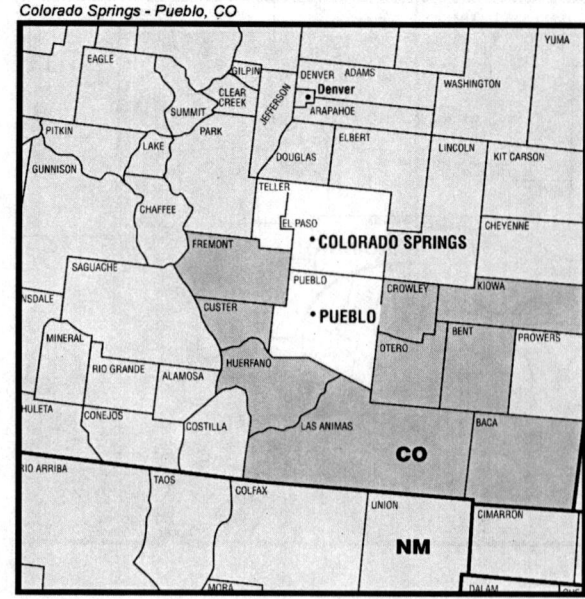

Maps courtesy of Nielsen Media Research

Columbia-Jefferson City, MO (137)

DMA TV Households: 179,010
% of U.S. TV Households: .156

KOMU-TV Columbia, MO, ch. 8, NBC, CW
KRCG Jefferson City, MO, ch. 12, CBS
*KMOS-TV Sedalia, MO, ch. 15, ETV
KMIZ Columbia, MO, ch. 17, ABC, MyNetworkTV
KNLJ Jefferson City, MO, ch. 20, IND

DMA Counties	State	TV Households
Audrain	MO	9,620
Boone	MO	64,140
Callaway	MO	15,870
Chariton	MO	3,160
Cole	MO	29,060
Cooper	MO	6,320
Howard	MO	3,680
Maries	MO	3,660
Miller	MO	10,030
Moniteau	MO	5,330
Montgomery	MO	4,760
Morgan	MO	8,280
Osage	MO	5,290
Randolph	MO	9,830

Columbia - Jefferson City, MO

Columbia, SC (79)

DMA TV Households: 393,170
% of U.S. TV Households: .344

WOLO-TV Columbia, SC, ch. 8, ABC
WIS Columbia, SC, ch. 10, NBC
WLTX Columbia, SC, ch. 17, CBS
*WRJA-TV Sumter, SC, ch. 28, ETV
*WRLK-TV Columbia, SC, ch. 32, ETV
WZRB Columbia, SC, ch. 47, CW
WACH Columbia, SC, ch. 48, IND
WKTC Sumter, SC, ch. 39, MyNetworkTV

DMA Counties	State	TV Households
Calhoun	SC	6,060
Clarendon	SC	12,530
Fairfield	SC	9,210
Kershaw	SC	23,510
Lee	SC	7,090
Lexington	SC	98,750
Newberry	SC	15,080
Orangeburg	SC	34,220
Richland	SC	140,810
Saluda	SC	7,050
Sumter	SC	38,860

Columbia, SC

Columbus, GA (128)

DMA TV Households: 213,980
% of U.S. TV Households: .187

WTVM Columbus, GA, ch. 11, ABC
WRBL Columbus, GA, ch. 15, CBS
*WJSP-TV Columbus, GA, ch. 23, ETV
WLTZ Columbus, GA, ch. 35, NBC
WLGA Opelika, AL, ch. 47, CW
WXTX Columbus, GA, ch. 49, Fox

DMA Counties	State	TV Households	DMA Counties	State	TV Households
Barbour	AL	9,910	Muscogee	GA	73,360
Chambers	AL	14,120	Quitman	GA	1,090
Lee	AL	54,960	Randolph	GA	2,770
Russell	AL	20,700	Schley	GA	1,680
Chattahoochee	GA	2,890	Stewart	GA	1,870
Clay	GA	1,380	Sumter	GA	11,790
Harris	GA	11,240	Talbot	GA	2,670
Marion	GA	2,660	Webster	GA	890

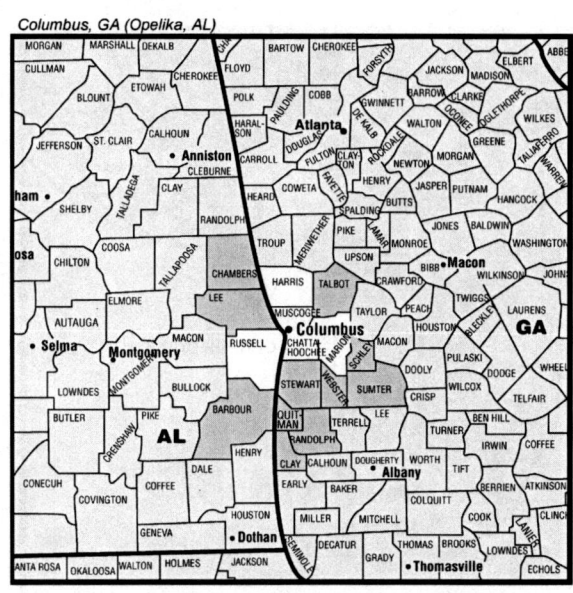

Columbus, GA (Opelika, AL)

Maps courtesy of Nielsen Media Research

Columbus, OH

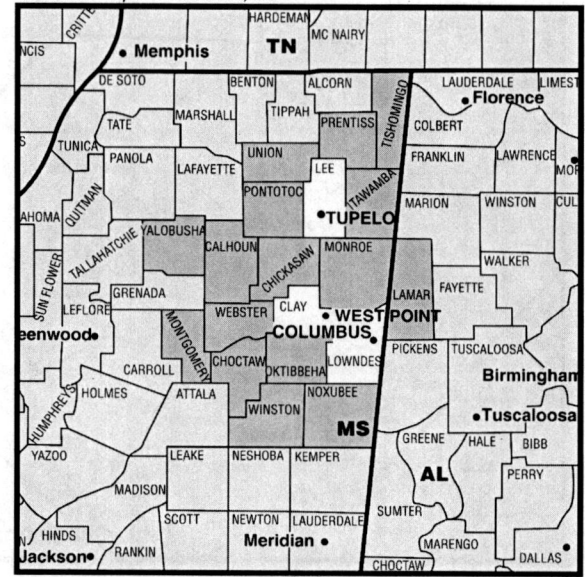

Columbus - Tupelo - West Point, MS

Columbus, OH (32)

DMA TV Households: 925,840
% of U.S. TV Households: .809

WSYX Columbus, OH, ch. 13, ABC, MyNetworkTV
WCMH-TV Columbus, OH, ch. 14, NBC
WBNS-TV Columbus, OH, ch. 21, CBS
WSFJ-TV Newark, OH, ch. 24, IND
***WOUB-TV** Athens, OH, ch. 27, ETV
***WOUC-TV** Cambridge, OH, ch. 35, ETV
WTTE Columbus, OH, ch. 36, Fox
***WOSU-TV** Columbus, OH, ch. 38, ETV
WWHO Chillicothe, OH, ch. 46, CW

DMA Counties	State	TV Households	DMA Counties	State	TV Households
Athens	OH	23,040	Licking	OH	61,600
Coshocton	OH	14,150	Madison	OH	14,550
Crawford	OH	18,080	Marion	OH	24,550
Delaware	OH	62,630	Morgan	OH	5,960
Fairfield	OH	53,460	Morrow	OH	12,990
Fayette	OH	11,230	Noble	OH	4,550
Franklin	OH	470,410	Perry	OH	12,890
Guernsey	OH	15,890	Pickaway	OH	19,300
Hardin	OH	11,920	Pike	OH	10,670
Hocking	OH	11,340	Ross	OH	27,680
Knox	OH	21,890	Union	OH	17,060

Columbus-Tupelo-West Point, MS (133)

DMA TV Households: 188,740
% of U.S. TV Households: .165

WTVA Tupelo, MS, ch. 8, NBC
***WMAB-TV** Mississippi State, MS, ch. 10, ETV
***WMAE-TV** Boonevile, MS, ch. 12, ETV
WLOV-TV West Point, MS, ch. 16, Fox
WCBI-TV Columbus, MS, ch. 35, CBS, CW, MyNetworkTV
***WMAA** Columbus, MS, ch. 43, ETV
WKDH Houston, MS, ch. 45, ABC

DMA Counties	State	TV Households	DMA Counties	State	TV Households
Lamar	AL	5,930	Noxubee	MS	4,000
Calhoun	MS	5,930	Oktibbeha	MS	17,250
Chickasaw	MS	7,100	Pontotoc	MS	10,950
Choctaw	MS	3,430	Prentiss	MS	9,920
Clay	MS	7,920	Tishomingo	MS	7,870
Itawamba	MS	8,920	Union	MS	10,500
Lee	MS	31,240	Webster	MS	3,660
Lowndes	MS	22,180	Winston	MS	7,550
Monroe	MS	14,440	Yalobusha	MS	5,590
Montgomery	MS	4,360			

Corpus Christi, TX

Corpus Christi, TX (129)

DMA TV Households: 197,290
% of U.S. TV Households: .172

KIII Corpus Christi, TX, ch. 8, ABC
KZTV Corpus Christi, TX, ch. 10, CBS
KRIS-TV Corpus Christi, TX, ch. 13, NBC, CW
***KEDT** Corpus Christi, TX, ch. 23, ETV
KORO Corpus Christi, TX, ch. 27, Univision
KUQI Corpus Christi, TX, ch. 38, Fox

DMA Counties	State	TV Households
Aransas	TX	10,350
Bee	TX	9,010
Brooks	TX	2,650
Duval	TX	4,010
Jim Hogg	TX	1,760
Jim Wells	TX	13,790
Kenedy	TX	100
Kleberg	TX	10,490
Live Oak	TX	3,950
Nueces	TX	115,050
Refugio	TX	2,780
San Patricio	TX	23,350

Maps courtesy of Nielsen Media Research

Dallas - Ft. Worth, TX

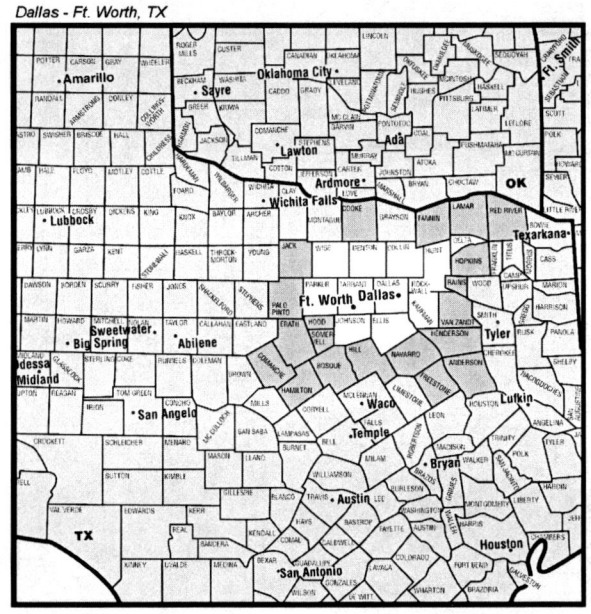

Dallas-Fort Worth, TX (5)

DMA TV Households: 2,489,970
% of U.S. TV Households: 2.175

WFAA Dallas, ch. 8, ABC
KFWD Fort Worth, ch. 9, IND
KTVT Fort Worth, ch. 11, CBS
*KERA-TV Dallas, ch. 14, ETV
KTXA Fort Worth, ch. 19, IND
KUVN-DT Garland, TX, ch. 23, Univision
KMPX Decatur, TX, ch. 30, IND
KDAF Dallas, ch. 32, CW
KDFW Dallas, ch. 35, Fox
KDFI Dallas, ch. 36, MyNetworkTV
KLDT Lake Dallas, TX, ch. 39, IND
KXTX-TV Dallas, ch. 40, Telemundo
KXAS-TV Fort Worth, ch. 41, NBC
KPXD-TV Arlington, TX, ch. 42, ION Television
*KDTN Denton, TX, ch. 43, ETV
KDTX-TV Dallas, ch. 45, IND
KTAQ Greenville, TX, ch. 46, IND
KSTR-DT Irving, TX, ch. 48, TeleFutura

DMA Counties	State	TV Households	DMA Counties	State	TV Households
Anderson	TX	16,190	Hopkins	TX	13,070
Bosque	TX	7,050	Hunt	TX	30,540
Collin	TX	283,580	Jack	TX	3,060
Comanche	TX	5,270	Johnson	TX	52,160
Cooke	TX	14,770	Kaufman	TX	34,780
Dallas	TX	844,220	Lamar	TX	19,300
Delta	TX	2,070	Navarro	TX	17,850
Denton	TX	228,870	Palo Pinto	TX	10,900
Ellis	TX	49,450	Parker	TX	38,500
Erath	TX	13,150	Rains	TX	4,440
Fannin	TX	11,910	Red River	TX	5,340
Freestone	TX	7,110	Rockwall	TX	27,090
Hamilton	TX	3,360	Somervell	TX	2,860
Henderson	TX	30,310	Tarrant	TX	638,460
Hill	TX	13,360	Van Zandt	TX	19,770
Hood	TX	20,390	Wise	TX	20,790

Davenport, IA-Rock Island-Moline, IL (97)

DMA TV Households: 309,600
% of U.S. TV Households: .270

WHBF-TV Rock Island, IL, ch. 4, CBS
*WQPT-TV Moline, IL, ch. 23, ETV
*KQIN Davenport, IA, ch. 34, satellite to *WQPT-TV
KWQC-TV Davenport, IA, ch. 36, NBC
WQAD-TV Moline, IL, ch. 38, ABC
KGCW Burlington, IA, ch. 41, CW
KLJB Davenport, IA, ch. 49, Fox

DMA Counties	State	TV Households	DMA Counties	State	TV Households
Bureau	IL	14,220	Whiteside	IL	23,440
Carroll	IL	6,550	Clinton	IA	19,940
Henderson	IL	3,100	Des Moines	IA	16,660
Henry	IL	19,750	Henry	IA	7,530
Jo Daviess	IL	9,610	Jackson	IA	8,160
Knox	IL	20,350	Louisa	IA	4,270
Mercer	IL	6,480	Muscatine	IA	16,430
Rock Island	IL	60,920	Scott	IA	65,620
Warren	IL	6,580			

Davenport - Rock Island - Moline, IL

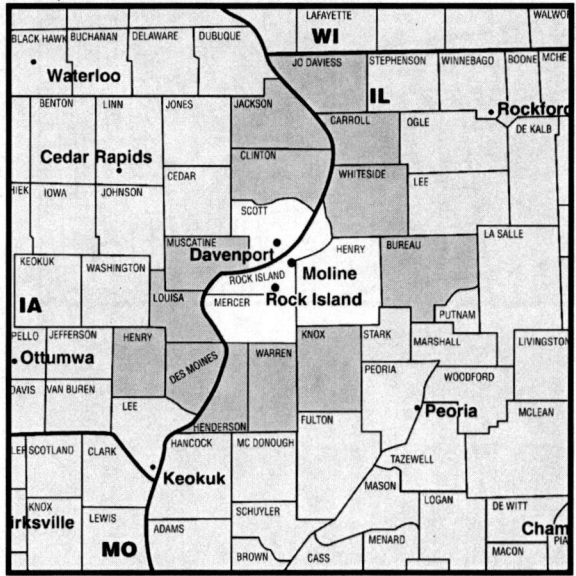

Maps courtesy of Nielsen Media Research

Dayton, OH (64)

DMA TV Households: 483,790
% of U.S. TV Households: .423

*WPTD Dayton, OH, ch. 16, ETV
WBDT Springfield, OH, ch. 26, CW
WRGT-TV Dayton, OH, ch. 30, Fox, MyNetworkTV
WKOI-TV Richmond, IN, ch. 39, IND
WHIO-TV Dayton, OH, ch. 41, CBS
WDTN Dayton, OH, ch. 50, NBC
WKEF Dayton, OH, ch. 51, ABC

DMA Counties	State	TV Households
Champaign	OH	15,480
Clark	OH	56,060
Darke	OH	20,350
Greene	OH	60,530
Logan	OH	18,370
Mercer	OH	15,240
Miami	OH	39,940
Montgomery	OH	223,050
Preble	OH	16,140
Shelby	OH	18,630

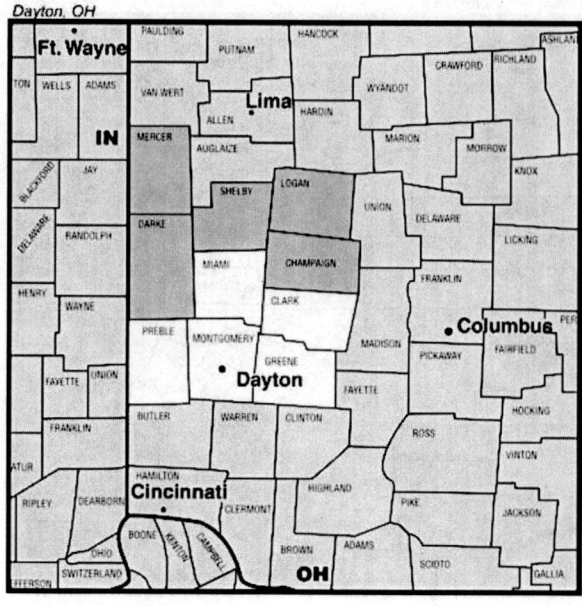

Dayton, OH

Denver, CO

Denver (18)

DMA TV Households: 1,524,210
% of U.S. TV Households: 1.332

KWGN-TV Denver, ch. 34, CW
KREG-TV Glenwood Springs, CO, ch. 23, CBS
KCDO-TV Sterling, CO, ch. 23, satellite to KTVD
KCNC-TV Denver, ch. 35, CBS
*KRMA-TV Denver, ch. 18, ETV
KMGH-TV Denver, ch. 7, ABC
*KWYP-TV Laramie, WY, ch. 8, ETV
KUSA Denver, ch. 9, NBC
KFNR Rawlins, WY, ch. 9, Fox
*KBDI-TV Broomfield, CO, ch. 13, ETV
*KRNE-TV Merriman, NE, ch. 12, ETV
KTFD-DT Boulder, CO, ch. 15,TeleFutura

KTVD Denver, ch. 19, MyNetworkTV
KFCT Fort Collins, CO, ch. 21, satellite to KDVR
*KRMZ Steamboat Springs, CO, ch. 10, satellite to KRMA-TV
KDEN Longmont, CO, ch. 29, Telemundo
KDVR Denver, ch. 32, Fox
KPJR-DT Greeley, CO, ch. 38, IND
*KRMT Denver, ch. 40, ETV
KWHD Castle Rock, CO, ch. 45, IND
KCEC Denver, ch. 51, Univision
KPXC-TV Denver, ch. 43, ION Television

DMA Counties	State	TV Households	DMA Counties	State	TV Households
Adams	CO	148,110	Phillips	CO	1,790
Alamosa	CO	5,700	Pitkin	CO	6,550
Arapahoe	CO	219,540	Prowers	CO	4,750
Archuleta	CO	5,080	Rio Blanco	CO	2,550
Boulder	CO	108,270	Rio Grande	CO	4,640
Broomfield	CO	20,550	Routt	CO	9,250
Chaffee	CO	7,050	Saguache	CO	2,620
Cheyenne	CO	670	San Juan	CO	290
Clear Creek	CO	4,050	San Miguel	CO	3,450
Conejos	CO	2,960	Sedgwick	CO	990
Costilla	CO	1,450	Summit	CO	10,490
Delta	CO	12,330	Washington	CO	1,870
Denver	CO	250,080	Weld	CO	87,980
Dolores	CO	820	Yuma	CO	3,750
Douglas	CO	101,790	Arthur	NE	100
Eagle	CO	18,340	Banner	NE	300
Elbert	CO	7,880	Box Butte	NE	4,390
Garfield	CO	20,410	Cheyenne	NE	4,180
Gilpin	CO	2,220	Dawes	NE	3,440
Grand	CO	5,860	Deuel	NE	800
Gunnison	CO	5,950	Garden	NE	790
Hinsdale	CO	400	Grant	NE	190
Jackson	CO	580	Hooker	NE	290
Jefferson	CO	213,440	Keith	NE	3,380
Kit Carson	CO	2,650	Kimball	NE	1,490
Lake	CO	2,810	Sheridan	NE	2,270
Larimer	CO	114,650	Sioux	NE	590
Lincoln	CO	1,780	Albany	WY	13,260
Logan	CO	7,680	Campbell	WY	15,930
Mineral	CO	490	Carbon	WY	6,420
Moffat	CO	5,220	Johnson	WY	3,600
Morgan	CO	9,650	Niobrara	WY	980
Ouray	CO	1,830	Platte	WY	3,480
Park	CO	7,070			

Maps courtesy of Nielsen Media Research

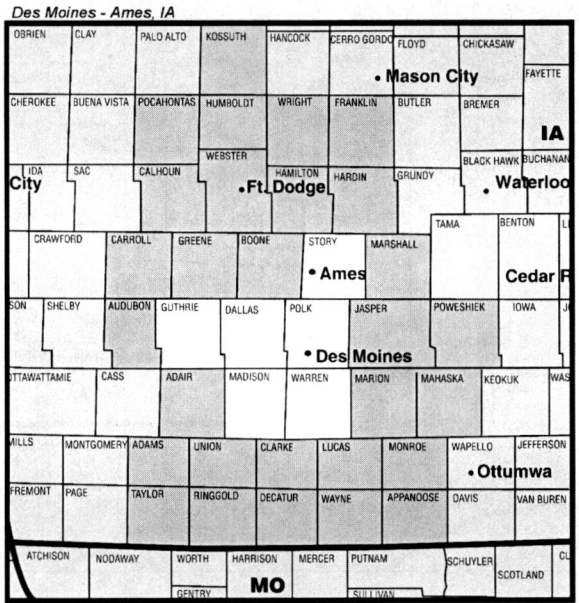

Des Moines - Ames, IA

Des Moines-Ames, IA (71)

DMA TV Households: 432,410
% of U.S. TV Households: .378

WOI-DT Ames, IA, ch. 5, ABC
KCCI Des Moines, IA, ch. 8, CBS
***KDIN-TV** Des Moines, IA, ch. 11, ETV
WHO-DT Des Moines, IA, ch. 13, NBC
KDSM-TV Des Moines, IA, ch. 16, Fox
KDMI Des Moines, IA, ch. 19, CW, MyNetworkTV
KCWI-TV Ames, IA, ch. 23, CW
***KTIN** Fort Dodge, IA, ch. 25, ETV
***KEFB** Ames, IA, ch. 34, ETV
KFPX-TV Newton, IA, ch. 39, ION Television

DMA Counties	State	TV Households	DMA Counties	State	TV Households
Adair	IA	3,090	Lucas	IA	3,780
Adams	IA	1,690	Madison	IA	6,060
Appanoose	IA	5,430	Mahaska	IA	8,910
Audubon	IA	2,380	Marion	IA	12,330
Boone	IA	10,580	Marshall	IA	15,330
Calhoun	IA	3,900	Monroe	IA	3,060
Carroll	IA	8,560	Pocahontas	IA	3,190
Clarke	IA	3,470	Polk	IA	173,600
Dallas	IA	23,340	Poweshiek	IA	7,430
Decatur	IA	3,160	Ringgold	IA	2,080
Franklin	IA	4,290	Story	IA	32,650
Greene	IA	3,690	Taylor	IA	2,570
Guthrie	IA	4,480	Union	IA	5,260
Hamilton	IA	6,380	Warren	IA	16,770
Hardin	IA	7,060	Wayne	IA	2,550
Humboldt	IA	3,960	Webster	IA	15,130
Jasper	IA	14,650	Wright	IA	5,250
Kossuth	IA	6,350			

Detroit (11)

DMA TV Households: 1,926,970
% of U.S. TV Households: 1.684

WJBK Detroit, ch. 7, Fox
CBET Windsor, Ont., ch. 9, CBC
WKBD-TV Detroit, ch. 14, CW
WMYD Detroit, ch. 21, MyNetworkTV
WPXD-TV Ann Arbor, MI, ch. 31, ION Television
WADL Mount Clemens, MI, ch. 39, IND
WXYZ-TV Detroit, ch. 41, ABC
***WTVS** Detroit, ch. 43, ETV
WWJ-TV Detroit, ch. 44, CBS
WDIV-TV Detroit, ch. 45, NBC

DMA Counties	State	TV Households
Lapeer	MI	33,050
Livingston	MI	67,790
Macomb	MI	337,490
Monroe	MI	58,630
Oakland	MI	482,790
Sanilac	MI	16,590
St. Clair	MI	66,330
Washtenaw	MI	139,160
Wayne	MI	725,140

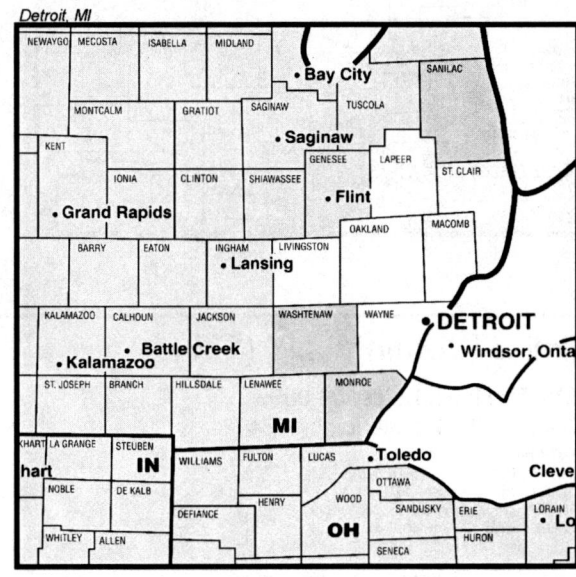

Detroit, MI

Maps courtesy of Nielsen Media Research

Dothan, AL (172)

DMA TV Households: 100,950
% of U.S. TV Households: .088

WDHN Dothan, AL, ch. 21, ABC
WDFX-TV Ozark, AL, ch. 33, Fox
WTVY Dothan, AL, ch. 36, CBS, CW, MyNetworkTV
*WGIQ Louisville, AL, ch. 44, ETV

DMA Counties	State	TV Households
Coffee	AL	19,640
Dale	AL	19,040
Geneva	AL	10,700
Henry	AL	6,950
Houston	AL	40,060
Early	GA	4,560

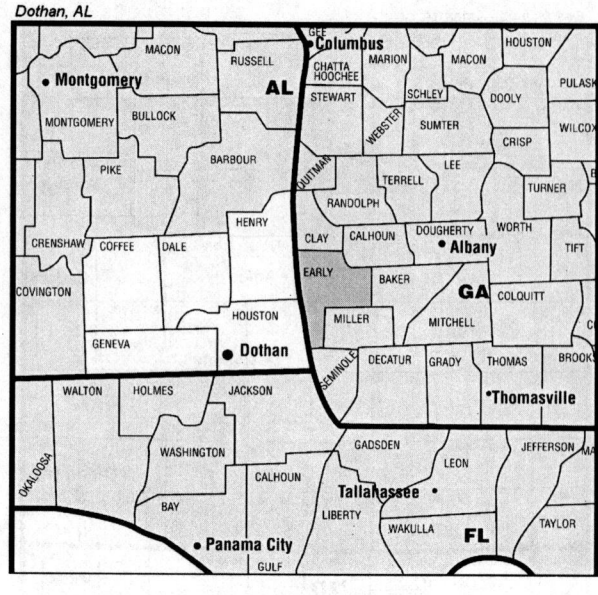

Dothan, AL

Duluth, MN-Superior, WI (139)

DMA TV Households: 173,180
% of U.S. TV Households: .151

*WDSE Duluth, MN, ch. 8, ETV
WDIO-DT Duluth, MN, ch. 10, ABC
KRII Chisholm, MN, ch. 11, satellite to KBJR-TV
WIRT-DT Hibbing, MN, ch. 13, satellite to WDIO-TV
KQDS-TV Duluth, MN, ch. 17, Fox
KBJR-TV Superior, WI, ch. 19, NBC, MyNetworkTV
KCWV Duluth, MN, ch. 27, IND
KDLH Duluth, MN, ch. 33, CBS, CW

DMA Counties	State	TV Households
Gogebic	MI	6,560
Carlton	MN	13,330
Cook	MN	2,490
Itasca	MN	18,500
Koochiching	MN	5,810
Lake	MN	4,570
St. Louis	MN	80,290
Ashland	WI	6,570
Bayfield	WI	6,450
Douglas	WI	18,410
Iron	WI	3,090
Sawyer	WI	7,110

Duluth, MN - Superior, WI

Elmira (Corning), NY (175)

DMA TV Households: 96,090
% of U.S. TV Households: .084

WFBT Bath, NY, ch. 14, IND
WETM-TV Elmira, NY, ch. 18, NBC
*WSKA Corning, NY, ch. 30, ETV
WENY-TV Elmira, NY, ch. 36, ABC, CW
WYDC Corning, NY, ch. 48, Fox

DMA Counties	State	TV Households
Chemung	NY	34,520
Schuyler	NY	7,400
Steuben	NY	38,440
Tioga	PA	15,730

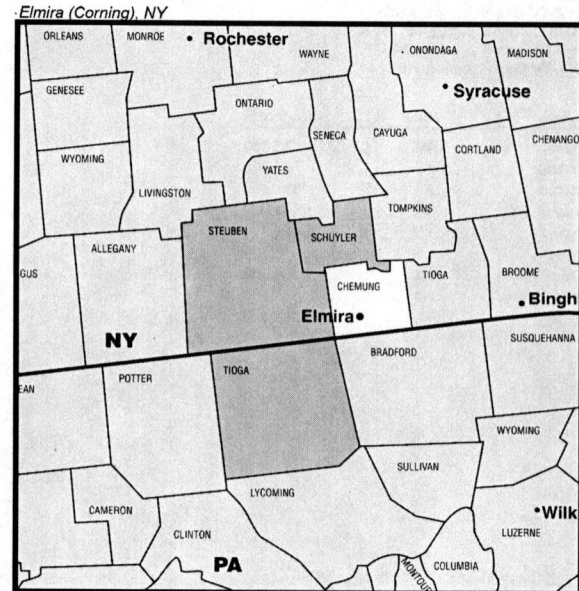

Elmira (Corning), NY

Maps courtesy of Nielsen Media Research

El Paso, TX (Las Cruces, NM)

El Paso, TX (Las Cruces, NM) (98)

DMA TV Households: 308,080
% of U.S. TV Households: .269

KVIA-TV El Paso, ch. 7, ABC, CW
KTSM-TV El Paso, ch. 9, NBC
*****KCOS** El Paso, ch. 13, ETV
KFOX-TV El Paso, ch. 15, Fox
KDBC-TV El Paso, ch. 18, CBS, MyNetworkTV
*****KRWG-TV** Las Cruces, NM, ch. 23, ETV
KINT-TV El Paso, ch. 25, Univision
*****KSCE** El Paso, ch. 39, ETV
KTDO Las Cruces, NM, ch. 47, Telemundo
KTFN El Paso, ch. 51, IND

DMA Counties	State	TV Households
Dona Ana	NM	69,660
Culberson	TX	890
El Paso	TX	236,470
Hudspeth	TX	1,060

Erie, PA (146)

DMA TV Households: 157,610
% of U.S. TV Households: .138

WICU-TV Erie, PA, ch. 12, NBC
WSEE-TV Erie, PA, ch. 16, CBS, CW
WFXP Erie, PA, ch. 22, Fox
WJET-TV Erie, PA, ch. 24, ABC
*****WQLN** Erie, PA, ch. 50, ETV

DMA Counties	State	TV Households
Crawford	PA	33,690
Erie	PA	107,320
Warren	PA	16,600

Erie, PA

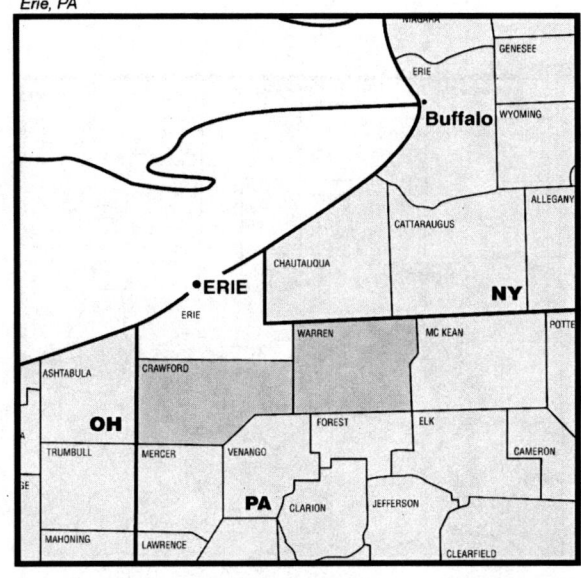

Eugene, OR

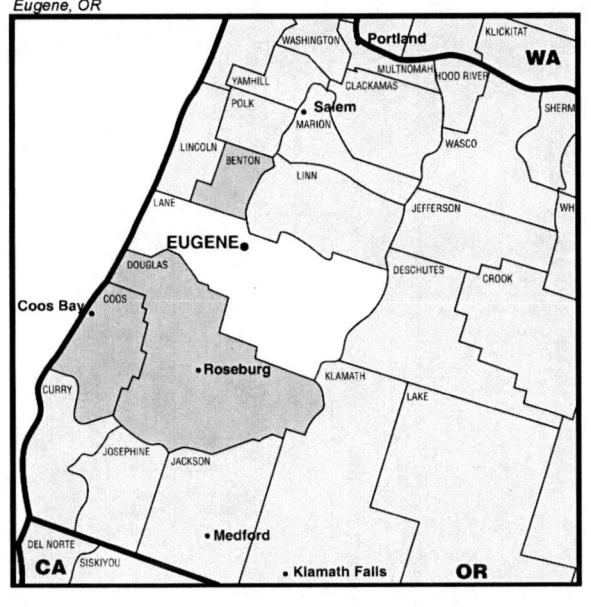

Eugene, OR (119)

DMA TV Households: 242,790
% of U.S. TV Households: .212

*****KOAC-TV** Corvallis, OR, ch. 7, ETV
KEZI Eugene, OR, ch. 9, ABC
KCBY-TV Coos Bay, OR, ch. 11, satellite to KVAL-TV
KVAL-TV Eugene, OR, ch. 13, CBS
KMTR Eugene, OR, ch. 17, NBC, CW
KTVC Roseburg, OR, ch. 18, IND
KPIC Roseburg, OR, ch. 19, satellite to KVAL-TV
KMCB Coos Bay, OR, ch. 22, satellite to KMTR
*****KEPB-TV** Eugene, OR, ch. 29, ETV
KLSR-TV Eugene, OR, ch. 31, Fox
KTCW Roseburg, OR, ch. 45, satellite to KMTR

DMA Counties	State	TV Households
Benton	OR	33,350
Coos	OR	26,610
Douglas	OR	42,180
Lane	OR	140,650

Maps courtesy of Nielsen Media Research

Eureka, CA (195)

DMA TV Households: 60,900
% of U.S. TV Households: .053

KIEM-TV Eureka, CA, ch. 3, NBC
*KEET Eureka, CA, ch. 11, ETV
KVIQ Eureka, CA, ch. 17, CBS
 KAEF-TV Arcata, CA, ch. 22, Fox
KBVU Eureka, CA, ch. 28, Fox

DMA Counties	State	TV Households
Del Norte	CA	9,500
Humboldt	CA	51,400

Eureka, CA

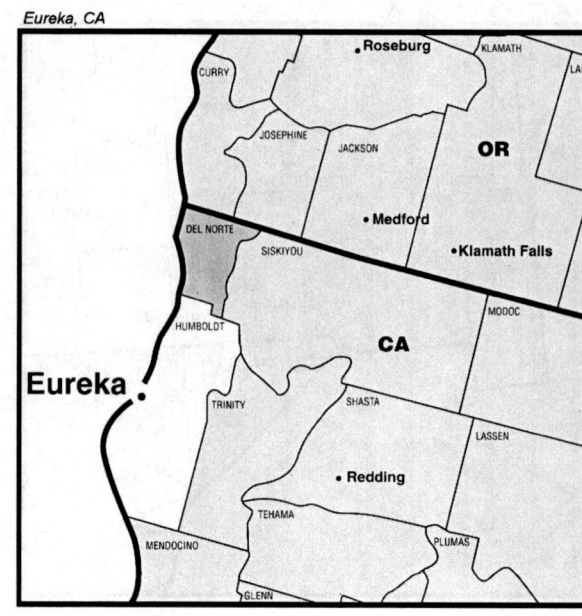

Evansville, IN

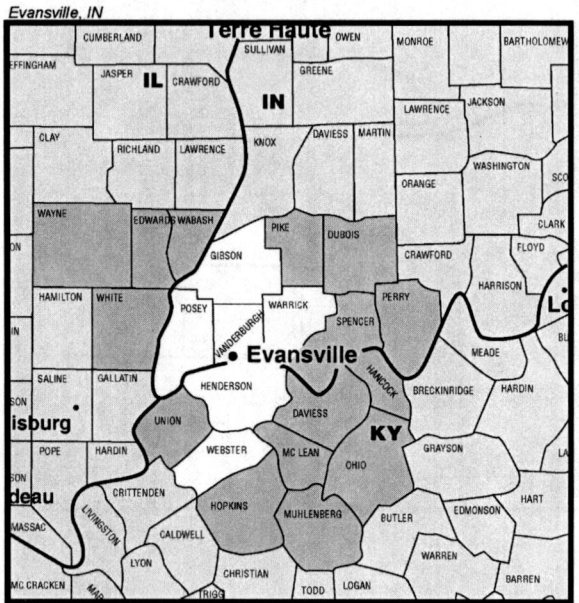

Evansville, IN (102)

DMA TV Households: 292,220
% of U.S. TV Households: .255

WEHT Evansville, IN, ch. 7, ABC
*WNIN Evansville, IN, ch. 9, ETV
WAZE-TV Madisonville, KY, ch. 20, CW
WTVW Evansville, IN, ch. 28, Fox
*WKOH Owensboro, KY, ch. 30, ETV
*WKMA-TV Madisonville, KY, ch. 42, ETV
WEVV-TV Evansville, IN, ch. 45, CBS, MyNetworkTV
WFIE Evansville, IN, ch. 46, NBC

DMA Counties	State	TV Households	DMA Counties	State	TV Households
Edwards	IL	2,790	Warrick	IN	22,190
Wabash	IL	4,870	Daviess	KY	38,250
Wayne	IL	6,900	Hancock	KY	3,460
White	IL	6,260	Henderson	KY	18,820
Dubois	IN	15,930	Hopkins	KY	19,140
Gibson	IN	13,130	McLean	KY	3,960
Perry	IN	7,470	Muhlenberg	KY	12,370
Pike	IN	5,050	Ohio	KY	9,420
Posey	IN	9,950	Union	KY	5,580
Spencer	IN	7,640	Webster	KY	5,420
Vanderburgh	IN	73,620			

Fairbanks, AK

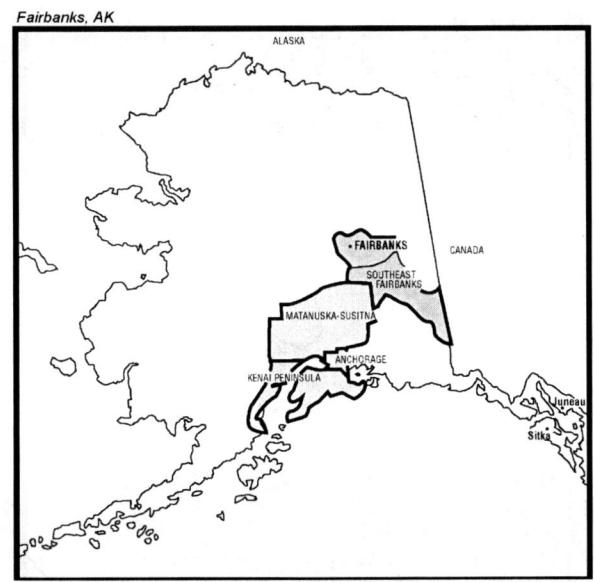

Fairbanks, AK (202)

DMA TV Households: 37,110
% of U.S. TV Households: .032

KFXF Fairbanks, AK, ch. 7, Fox
*KUAC-TV Fairbanks, AK, ch. 9, ETV
KATN Fairbanks, AK, ch. 18, ABC
KJNP-TV North Pole, AK, ch. 20, IND
KTVF Fairbanks, AK, ch. 26, NBC

DMA Counties	State	TV Households
Fairbanks-Plus	AK	37,110

Fargo-Valley City, ND (120)

DMA TV Households: 241,120
% of U.S. TV Households: .211

KJRR Jamestown, ND, ch. 7, satellite to KVRR
WDAZ-TV Devils Lake, ND, ch. 8, satellite to WDAY-TV
KBRR Thief River Falls, MN, ch. 10, satellite to KVRR
KNRR Pembina, ND, ch. 12, IND
*KFME Fargo, ND, ch. 13, ETV
*KGFE Grand Forks, ND, ch. 15, ETV
*KCGE-DT Crookston, MN, ch. 16, ETV
KVRR Fargo, ND, ch. 19, Fox
*KJRE Ellendale, ND, ch. 20, satellite to KFME
WDAY-TV Fargo, ND, ch. 21, ABC, CW
*KMDE Devils Lake, ND, ch. 25, satellite to KFME
KCPM Grand Forks, ND, ch. 27, MyNetworkTV
KXJB-TV Valley City, ND, ch. 38, CBS
KVLY-TV Fargo, ND, ch. 44, NBC

DMA Counties	State	TV Households	DMA Counties	State	TV Households
Becker	MN	13,020	Dickey	ND	2,090
Clay	MN	20,940	Eddy	ND	990
Clearwater	MN	3,300	Foster	ND	1,490
Kittson	MN	1,790	Grand Forks	ND	25,850
Lake of the Woods	MN	1,760	Griggs	ND	1,090
Mahnomen	MN	1,990	La Moure	ND	1,690
Marshall	MN	3,980	Nelson	ND	1,390
Norman	MN	2,680	Pembina	ND	3,030
Otter Tail	MN	22,980	Ramsey	ND	4,680
Pennington	MN	5,660	Ransom	ND	2,280
Polk	MN	12,120	Richland	ND	6,360
Red Lake	MN	1,680	Sargent	ND	1,680
Roseau	MN	6,120	Steele	ND	690
Wilkin	MN	2,490	Stutsman	ND	8,440
Barnes	ND	4,480	Towner	ND	990
Benson	ND	2,280	Traill	ND	3,180
Cass	ND	61,860	Walsh	ND	4,480
Cavalier	ND	1,590			

Fargo - Valley City, ND

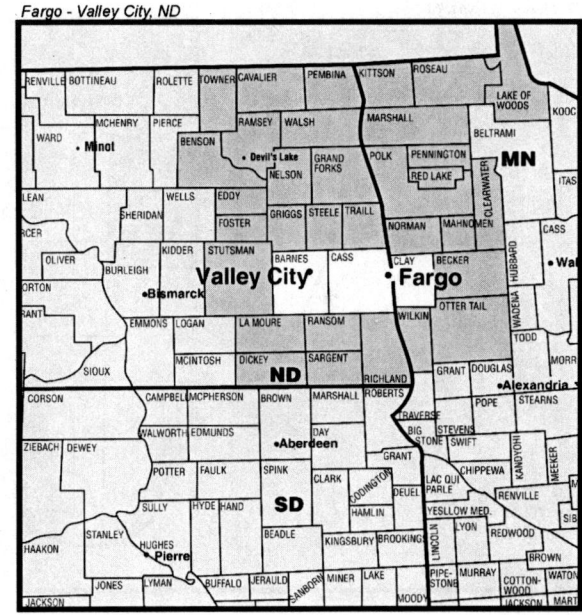

Maps courtesy of Nielsen Media Research

Flint-Saginaw-Bay City, MI (66)

DMA TV Households: 465,790
% of U.S. TV Households: .407

WJRT-TV Flint, MI, ch. 12, ABC
*WDCQ-TV Bad Axe, MI, ch. 15, ETV
WSMH Flint, MI, ch. 16, Fox
*WDCP-TV University Center, MI, ch. 19, ETV
WNEM-TV Bay City, MI, ch. 22, CBS,
   MyNetworkTV
*WCMU-TV Mt. Pleasant, MI, ch. 26, ETV
*WFUM Flint, MI, ch. 28, ETV
WEYI-TV Saginaw, MI, ch. 30, NBC, CW
WBSF Bay City, MI, ch. 46, CW
WAQP Saginaw, MI, ch. 48, IND

DMA Counties	State	TV Households
Arenac	MI	6,550
Bay	MI	44,040
Genesee	MI	172,670
Gladwin	MI	10,910
Gratiot	MI	14,350
Huron	MI	13,680
Iosco	MI	11,720
Isabella	MI	24,350
Midland	MI	32,480
Ogemaw	MI	8,970
Saginaw	MI	77,260
Shiawassee	MI	27,420
Tuscola	MI	21,390

Flint - Saginaw - Bay City, MI

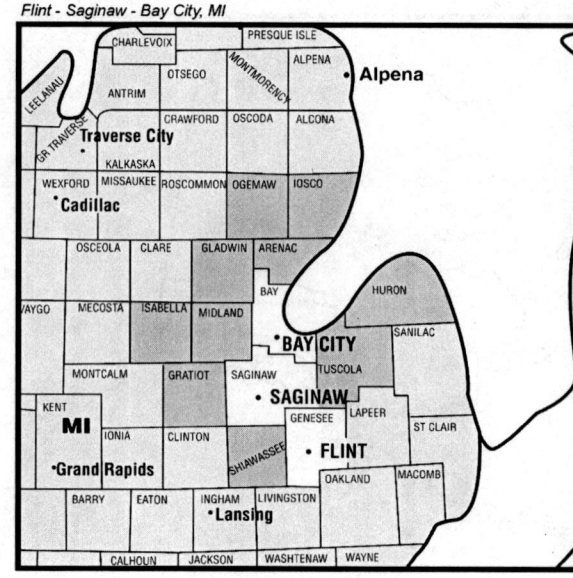

Ft. Myers - Naples, FL

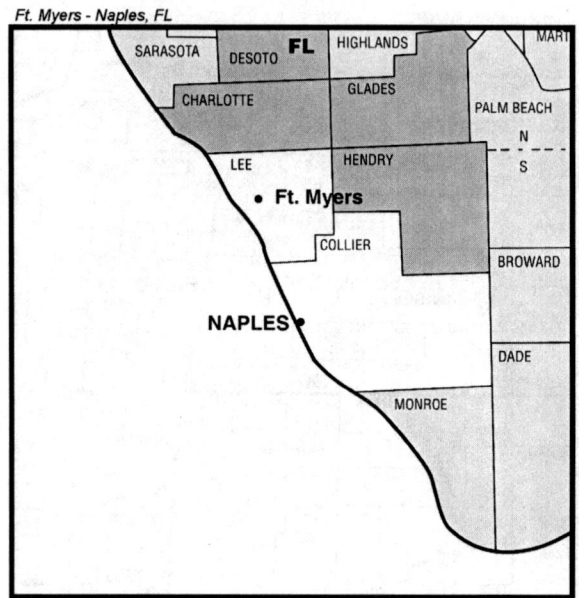

Ft. Myers-Naples, FL (62)

DMA TV Households: 509,530
% of U.S. TV Households: .445

WINK-TV Fort Myers, FL, ch. 9, CBS
WBBH-TV Fort Myers, FL, ch.15, NBC
*WGCU Fort Myers, FL, ch. 31, ETV
WRXY-TV Tice, FL, ch. 33, IND
WFTX-TV Cape Coral, FL, ch. 35, Fox
WZVN-TV Naples, FL, ch. 41, ABC
WXCW Naples, FL, ch. 45, CW

DMA Counties	State	TV Households
Charlotte	FL	73,580
Collier	FL	133,830
De Soto	FL	11,200
Glades	FL	4,010
Hendry	FL	11,900
Lee	FL	275,010

Maps courtesy of Nielsen Media Research

Ft. Smith - Fayetteville - Springdale - Rogers, AR

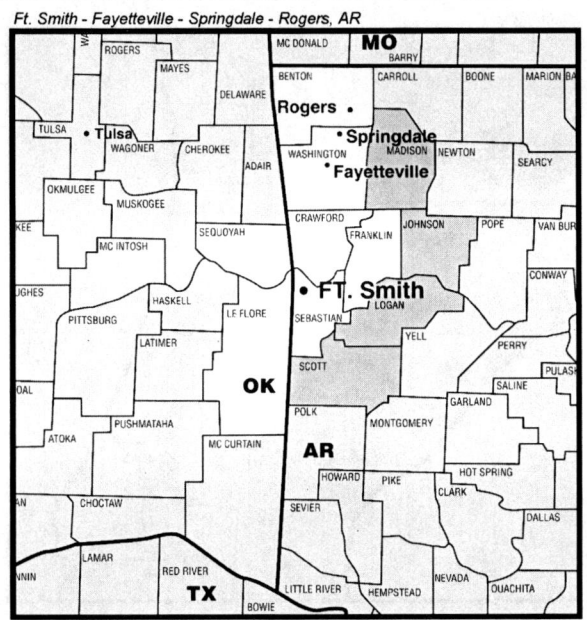

Ft. Smith-Fayetteville-Springdale-Rogers, AR (100)

DMA TV Households: 297,920
% of U.S. TV Households: .260

*KAFT Fayetteville, AR, ch. 9, ETV
KHOG-TV Fayetteville, AR, ch. 15, satellite to KHBS
KFSM-TV Fort Smith, AR, ch. 18, CBS
KHBS Fort Smith, AR, ch. 21, ABC, CW
KFTA-TV Fort Smith, AR, ch. 27, Fox
KWOG Springdale, AR, ch. 39, IND
KNWA-TV Rogers, AR, ch. 50, NBC

DMA Counties	State	TV Households
Benton	AR	80,070
Crawford	AR	22,440
Franklin	AR	7,120
Johnson	AR	9,490
Logan	AR	8,830
Madison	AR	5,950
Scott	AR	4,450
Sebastian	AR	47,970
Washington	AR	77,370
LeFlore	OK	18,530
Sequoyah	OK	15,700

Ft. Wayne, IN

Ft. Wayne, IN (107)

DMA TV Households: 275,350
% of U.S. TV Households: .241

WINM Angola, IN, ch. 12, IND
WISE-TV Fort Wayne, IN, ch. 18, NBC, MyNetworkTV
WPTA Fort Wayne, IN, ch. 24, ABC, CW
WANE-TV Fort Wayne, IN, ch. 31, CBS
WFFT-TV Fort Wayne, IN, ch. 36, Fox
*WFWA Fort Wayne, IN, ch. 40, ETV

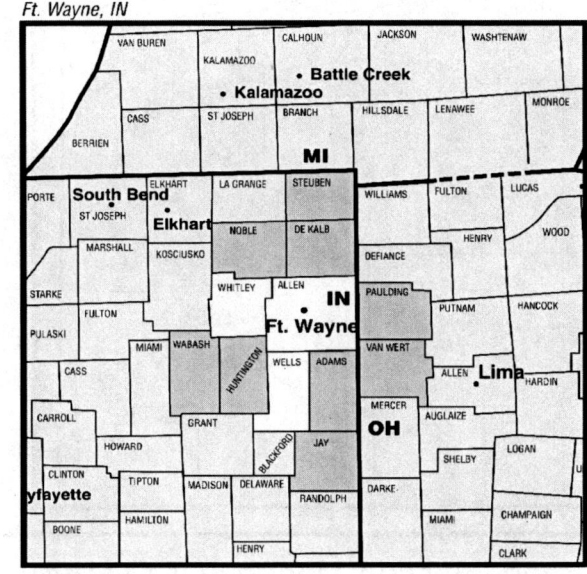

DMA Counties	State	TV Households
Adams	IN	11,970
Allen	IN	139,230
De Kalb	IN	16,100
Huntington	IN	14,250
Jay	IN	8,330
Noble	IN	17,310
Steuben	IN	12,970
Wabash	IN	12,500
Wells	IN	10,650
Whitley	IN	12,960
Paulding	OH	7,510
Van Wert	OH	11,570

Fresno - Visalia, CA

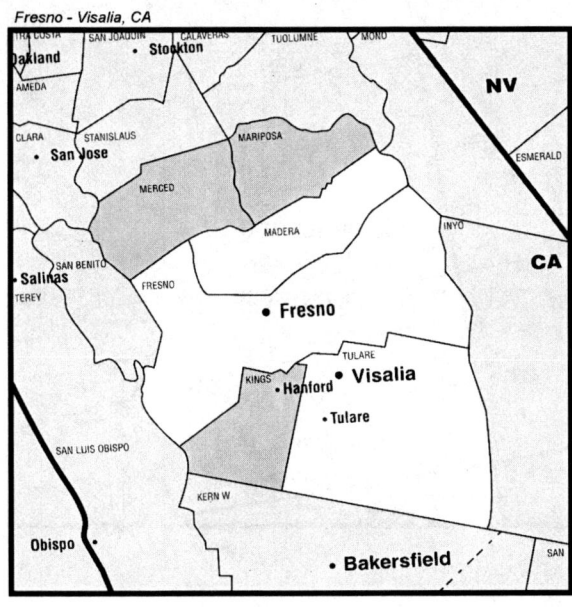

Fresno-Visalia, CA (55)

DMA TV Households: 574,900
% of U.S. TV Households: .502

KAIL Fresno, CA, ch. 7, MyNetworkTV
KNSO Merced, CA, ch. 11, Telemundo
*KVPT Fresno, CA, ch. 18, ETV
KFTV-DT Hanford, CA, ch. 20, Univision
KMPH-TV Visalia, CA, ch. 28, Fox
KFSN-TV Fresno, CA, ch. 30, ABC
KGPE Fresno, CA, ch. 34, CBS
KFRE-TV Sanger, CA, ch. 36, CW
KSEE Fresno, CA, ch. 38, NBC
KGMC Clovis, CA, ch. 43, IND
KTFF-DT Porterville, CA, ch. 48, TeleFutura
*KNXT Visalia, CA, ch. 50, ETV

DMA Counties	State	TV Households
Fresno	CA	284,620
Kings	CA	39,580
Madera	CA	43,260
Mariposa	CA	6,790
Merced	CA	74,330
Tulare	CA	126,320

Maps courtesy of Nielsen Media Research

Gainesville, FL (160)

DMA TV Households: 129,960
% of U.S. TV Households: .114

WNBW-DT Gainesville, FL, ch. 9, NBC
WCJB-TV Gainesville, FL, ch. 16, ABC, CW
WGFL High Springs, FL, ch. 28, CBS, MyNetworkTV
WOGX Ocala, FL, ch. 31, IND
*****WUFT** Gainesville, FL, ch. 36, ETV

DMA Counties	State	TV Households
Alachua	FL	101,470
Dixie	FL	5,900
Gilchrist	FL	6,200
Levy	FL	16,390

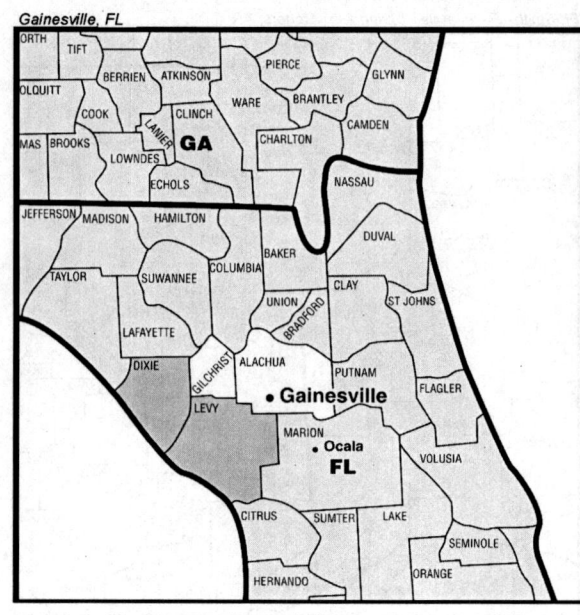

Gainesville, FL

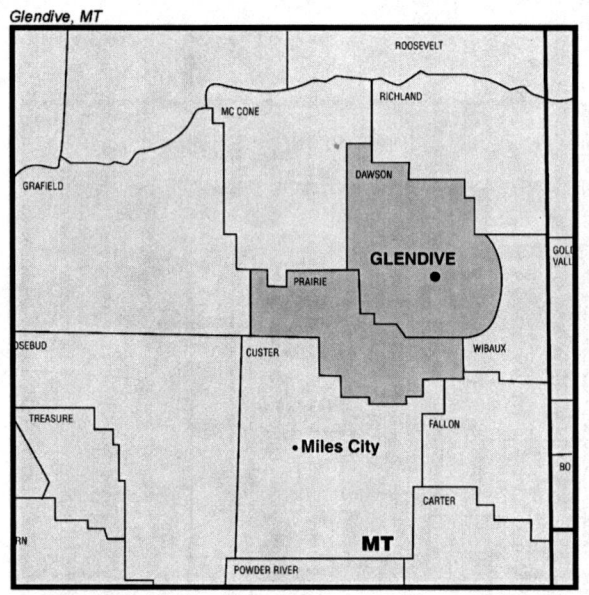

Glendive, MT

Glendive, MT (210)

DMA TV Households: 3,940
% of U.S. TV Households: .003

KXGN-TV Glendive, MT, ch. 5, CBS (NBC)

DMA Counties	State	TV Households
Dawson	MT	3,450
Prairie	MT	490

Grand Junction-Montrose, CO (184)

DMA TV Households: 73,360
% of U.S. TV Households: .064

KREX-TV Grand Junction, CO, ch. 2, CBS
KJCT Grand Junction, CO, ch. 7, ABC
KKCO Grand Junction, CO, ch. 12, NBC, CW
KREY-TV Montrose, CO, ch. 13, satellite to KREX-TV
KFQX Grand Junction, CO, ch. 15, Fox
*****KRMJ** Grand Junction, CO, ch. 18, ETV

DMA Counties	State	TV Households
Mesa	CO	57,410
Montrose	CO	15,950

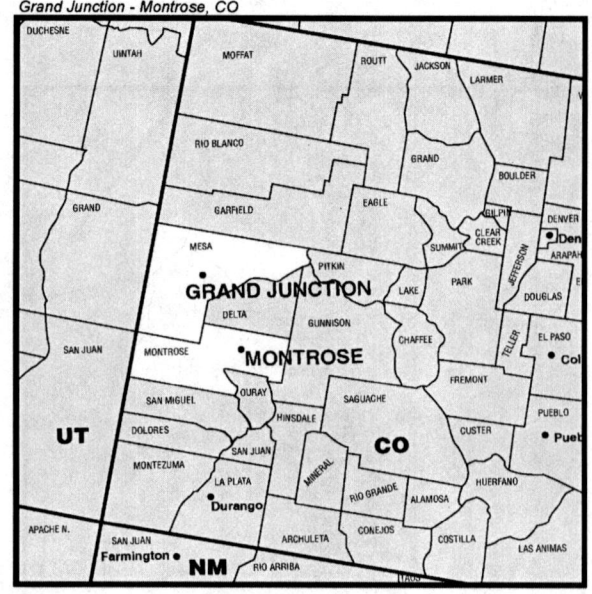

Grand Junction - Montrose, CO

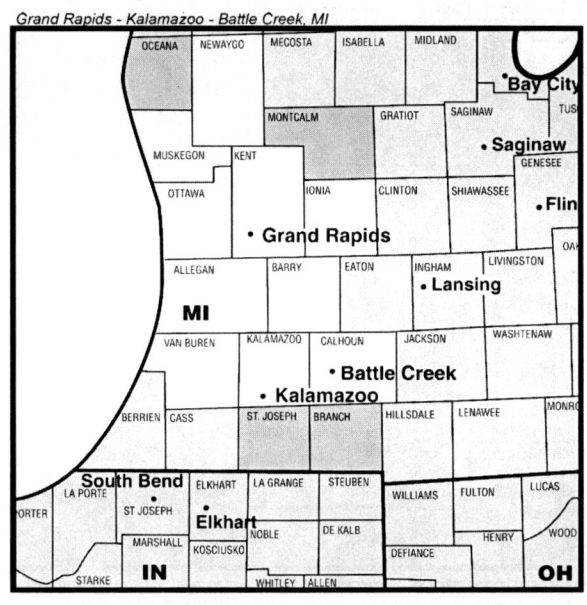

Grand Rapids - Kalamazoo - Battle Creek, MI

Grand Rapids-Kalamazoo-Battle Creek, MI (39)

DMA TV Households: 741,420
% of U.S. TV Households: .648

*WGVK Kalamazoo, MI, ch. 5, ETV
WOOD-TV Grand Rapids, MI, ch. 7, NBC
WWMT Kalamazoo, MI, ch. 8, CBS, CW
*WGVU-TV Grand Rapids, MI, ch. 11, ETV
WZZM Grand Rapids, MI, ch. 13, ABC
WXMI Grand Rapids, MI, ch. 19, Fox
WOTV Battle Creek, MI, ch. 20, ABC
WTLJ Muskegon, MI, ch. 24, IND
WZPX-TV Battle Creek, MI, ch. 44, ION Television
WLLA Kalamazoo, MI, ch. 45, IND

DMA Counties	State	TV Households	DMA Counties	State	TV Households
Allegan	MI	41,550	Montcalm	MI	22,870
Barry	MI	22,460	Muskegon	MI	65,910
Branch	MI	16,150	Newaygo	MI	18,110
Calhoun	MI	53,380	Oceana	MI	10,170
Ionia	MI	21,690	Ottawa	MI	90,110
Kalamazoo	MI	99,400	St. Joseph	MI	23,450
Kent	MI	227,580	Van Buren	MI	28,590

Great Falls, MT (191)

DMA TV Households: 64,910
% of U.S. TV Households: .057

KRTV Great Falls, MT, ch. 7, CBS, CW
KFBB-TV Great Falls, MT, ch. 8, ABC
KBBJ Havre, MT, ch. 9, IND
KBAO Lewistown, MT, ch. 13, NBC
KLMN Great Falls, MT, ch. 26, IND
KTGF Great Falls, MT, ch. 45, Fox

DMA Counties	State	TV Households
Blaine	MT	2,230
Cascade	MT	33,390
Chouteau	MT	1,880
Fergus	MT	4,540
Glacier	MT	4,330
Hill	MT	6,410
Judith Basin	MT	780
Liberty	MT	690
Phillips	MT	1,570
Pondera	MT	2,170
Teton	MT	2,220
Toole	MT	1,750
Valley	MT	2,850

Great Falls, MT

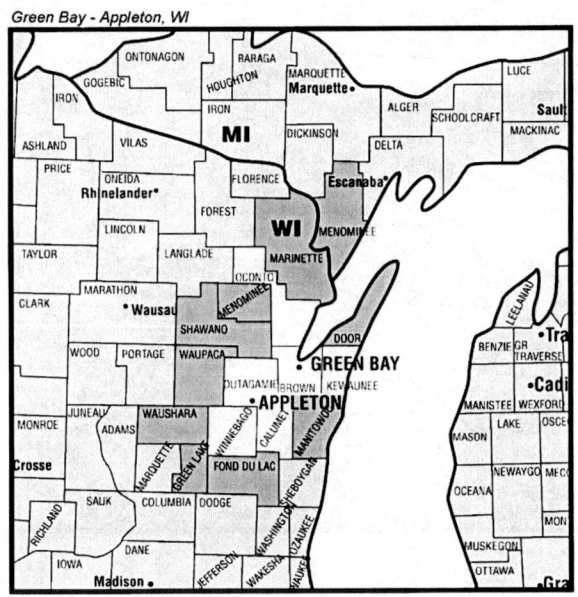

Green Bay - Appleton, WI

Green Bay-Appleton, WI (70)

DMA TV Households: 444,210
% of U.S. TV Households: .388

WLUK-TV Green Bay, WI, ch. 11, Fox
WIWB Suring, WI, ch. 21, CW
WBAY-TV Green Bay, WI, ch. 23, ABC
WACY-TV Appleton, WI, ch. 27, MyNetworkTV
WFRV-TV Green Bay, WI, ch. 39, CBS
WGBA-TV Green Bay, WI, ch. 41, NBC
*WPNE-TV Green Bay, WI, ch. 42, ETV
WWAZ-TV Fond du Lac, WI, ch. 44, IND

DMA Counties	State	TV Households	DMA Counties	State	TV Households
Menominee	MI	10,350	Marinette	WI	18,240
Brown	WI	97,550	Menominee	WI	1,400
Calumet	WI	17,450	Oconto	WI	15,510
Door	WI	12,740	Outagamie	WI	68,470
Fond du Lac	WI	39,180	Shawano	WI	16,700
Green Lake	WI	7,850	Waupaca	WI	20,700
Kewaunee	WI	8,180	Waushara	WI	9,780
Manitowoc	WI	33,590	Winnebago	WI	66,520

Maps courtesy of Nielsen Media Research

Greensboro-High Point-Winston Salem, NC (46)

DMA TV Households: 685,110
% of U.S. TV Households: .599

WGHP High Point, NC, ch. 8, Fox
WGPX-TV Burlington, NC, ch. 14, ION Television
WCWG Lexington, NC, ch. 19, CW
WXLV-TV Winston-Salem, NC, ch. 29, ABC
WXII-TV Winston-Salem, NC, ch. 31, NBC
*WUNL-TV Winston-Salem, NC, ch. 32, ETV
WMYV Greensboro, NC, ch. 33, MyNetworkTV
WLXI Greensboro, NC, ch. 43, IND
WFMY-TV Greensboro, NC, ch. 51, CBS

DMA Counties	State	TV Households	DMA Counties	State	TV Households
Alamance	NC	58,670	Randolph	NC	55,010
Alleghany	NC	4,880	Rockingham	NC	37,860
Caswell	NC	8,840	Stokes	NC	18,800
Davidson	NC	63,080	Surry	NC	28,740
Davie	NC	16,620	Wilkes	NC	27,140
Forsyth	NC	139,600	Yadkin	NC	15,290
Guilford	NC	191,970	Patrick	VA	8,190
Montgomery	NC	10,420			

Greensboro - High Point - Winston Salem, NC

Greenville-New Bern-Washington, NC (103)

DMA TV Households: 289,050
% of U.S. TV Households: .253

*WUND-TV Columbia, NC, ch. 2, ETV
WFXI Morehead City, NC, ch. 8, Fox
WNCT-TV Greenville, NC, ch. 10, CBS, CW
WCTI-TV New Bern, NC, ch. 12, ABC
*WUNM-TV Jacksonville, NC, ch. 19, ETV
*WUNK-TV Greenville, NC, ch. 23, ETV
WITN-TV Washington, NC, ch. 32, NBC
WPXU-TV Jacksonville, NC, ch. 34, MyNetworkTV
WYDO Greenville, NC, ch. 47, Fox
WEPX-TV Greenville, NC, ch. 51, MyNetworkTV

Greenville - New Bern - Washington, NC

DMA Counties	State	TV Households	DMA Counties	State	TV Households
Beaufort	NC	19,540	Lenoir	NC	23,340
Bertie	NC	7,560	Martin	NC	9,430
Carteret	NC	27,920	Onslow	NC	51,970
Craven	NC	39,430	Pamlico	NC	5,160
Duplin	NC	20,030	Pitt	NC	64,600
Greene	NC	7,250	Tyrrell	NC	1,480
Hyde	NC	1,940	Washington	NC	5,250
Jones	NC	4,150			

Greenville-Spartanburg, SC-Asheville, NC-Anderson, SC (36)

DMA TV Households: 858,050
% of U.S. TV Households: .750

WYFF Greenville, SC, ch. 36, NBC
WSPA-TV Spartanburg, SC, ch. 7, CBS
WLOS Asheville, NC, ch. 13, ABC
WGGS-TV Greenville, SC, ch. 16, IND
WHNS Greenville, SC, ch. 21, Fox
*WUNW Canton, NC, ch. 27, satellite to WUNC-TV

*WNTV Greenville, SC, ch. 9, ETV
WNEG-TV Toccoa, GA, ch. 24, CBS
*WUNF-TV Asheville, NC, ch. 25, ETV
*WNEH Greenwood, SC, ch. 18, ETV
WMYA-TV Anderson, SC, ch. 14, MyNetworkTV
*WRET-TV Spartanburg, SC, ch. 43, ETV
WYCW Asheville, NC, ch. 45, CW

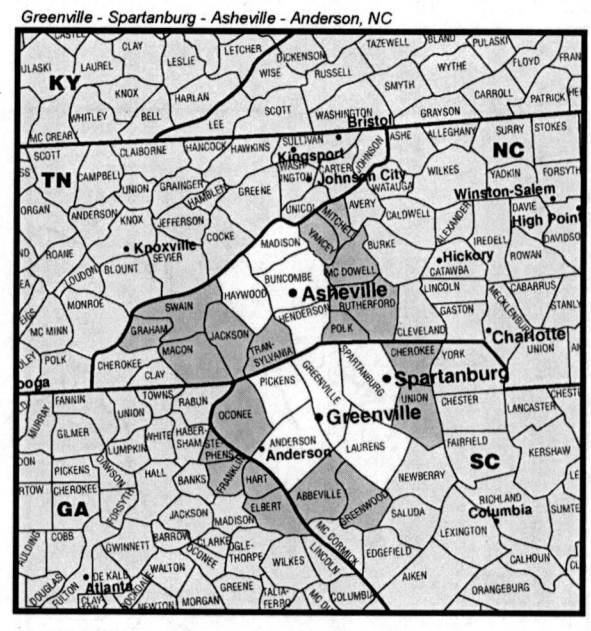

Greenville - Spartanburg - Asheville - Anderson, NC

DMA Counties	State	TV Households	DMA Counties	State	TV Households
Elbert	GA	8,160	Rutherford	NC	25,810
Franklin	GA	8,590	Swain	NC	5,620
Hart	GA	9,960	Transylvania	NC	13,320
Stephens	GA	10,050	Yancey	NC	7,830
Buncombe	NC	95,860	Abbeville	SC	9,900
Graham	NC	3,380	Anderson	SC	73,150
Haywood	NC	24,920	Cherokee	SC	21,770
Henderson	NC	44,190	Greenville	SC	175,220
Jackson	NC	15,080	Greenwood	SC	26,080
Macon	NC	14,410	Laurens	SC	26,780
Madison	NC	8,370	Oconee	SC	29,630
McDowell	NC	17,660	Pickens	SC	45,080
Mitchell	NC	6,740	Spartanburg	SC	110,650
Polk	NC	8,310	Union	SC	11,530

Maps courtesy of Nielsen Media Research

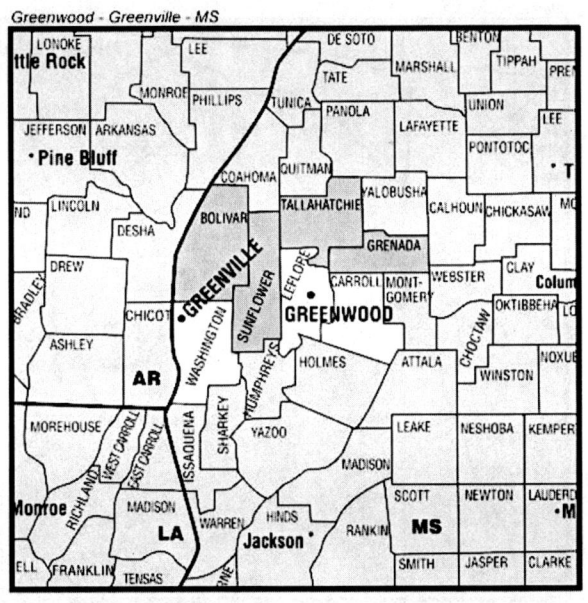

Greenwood - Greenville - MS

Greenwood-Greenville, MS (187)

DMA TV Households: 70,050
% of U.S. TV Households: .061

WXVT Greenville, MS, ch. 15, CBS
***WMAO-TV** Greenwood, MS, ch. 25, ETV
 WABG-TV Greenwood, MS, ch. 32, ABC, Fox

DMA Counties	State	TV Households
Bolivar	MS	12,860
Carroll	MS	3,950
Grenada	MS	8,990
Leflore	MS	11,840
Sunflower	MS	8,400
Tallahatchie	MS	4,600
Washington	MS	19,410

Harlingen-Weslaco-Brownsville-McAllen, TX (87)

DMA TV Households: 349,910
% of U.S. TV Households: .306

KRGV-TV Weslaco, TX, ch. 13, ABC
KVEO-TV Brownsville, TX, ch. 24, NBC
KGBT-TV Harlingen, TX, ch. 31, CBS
***KLUJ-TV** Harlingen, TX, ch. 34, ETV
***KMBH** Harlingen, TX, ch. 38, ETV
KTLM Rio Grande City, TX, ch. 40, Telemundo
KNVO McAllen, TX, ch. 49, Univision

DMA Counties	State	TV Households
Cameron	TX	117,460
Hidalgo	TX	209,330
Starr	TX	17,310
Willacy	TX	5,810

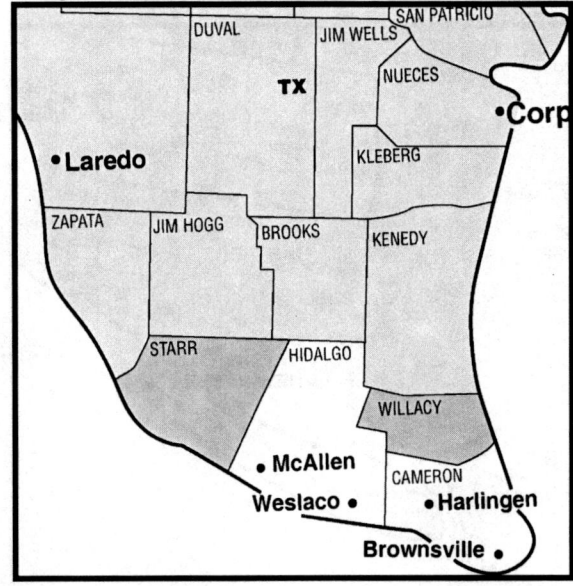

Harlingen - Weslaco - Brownsville - McAllen, TX

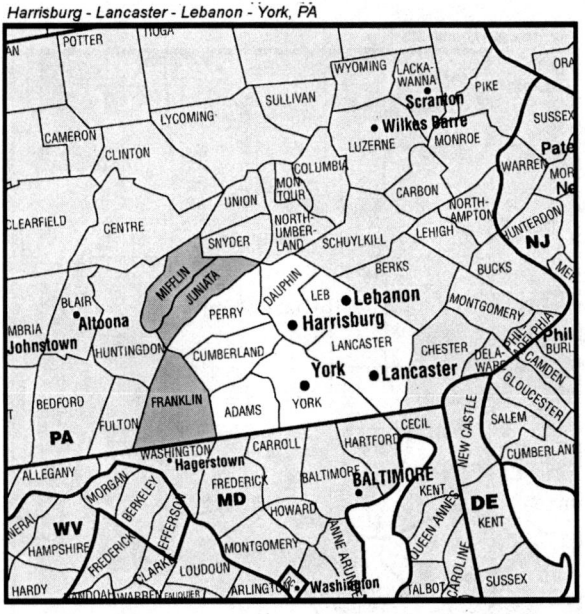

Harrisburg - Lancaster - Lebanon - York, PA

Harrisburg-Lancaster-Lebanon-York, PA (41)

DMA TV Households: 738,880
% of U.S. TV Households: .646

WGAL Lancaster, PA, ch. 8, NBC
WHTM-TV Harrisburg, PA, ch. 10, ABC
WHP-TV Harrisburg, PA, ch. 21, CBS, MyNetworkTV
WLYH-TV Lancaster, PA, ch. 23, CW
WGCB-TV Red Lion, PA, ch. 30, IND
***WITF-TV** Harrisburg, PA, ch. 36, ETV
WPMT York, PA, ch. 47, Fox

DMA Counties	State	TV Households
Adams	PA	37,940
Cumberland	PA	91,460
Dauphin	PA	105,540
Franklin	PA	57,200
Juniata	PA	8,780
Lancaster	PA	183,580
Lebanon	PA	50,070
Mifflin	PA	18,220
Perry	PA	17,690
York	PA	168,400

Maps courtesy of Nielsen Media Research

Harrisonburg, VA (178)

DMA TV Households: 92,900
% of U.S. TV Households: .081

WHSV-TV Harrisonburg, VA, ch. 3, ABC, Fox, MyNetworkTV
*WVPT Staunton, VA, ch. 51, ETV

DMA Counties	State	TV Households
Augusta	VA	47,570
Rockingham	VA	42,290
Pendleton	WV	3,040

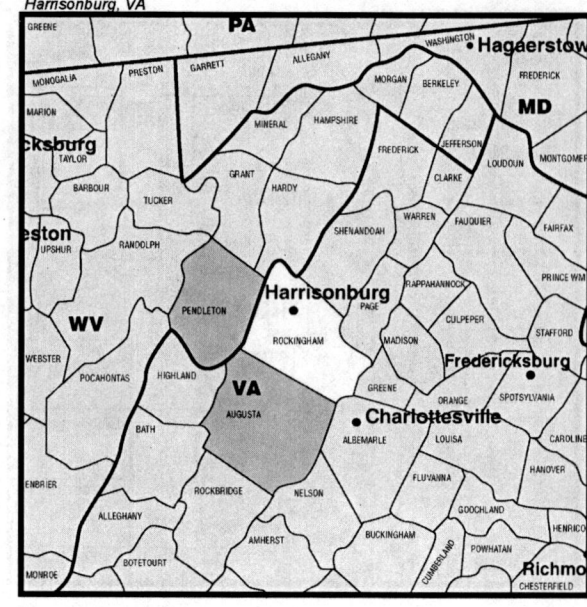

Harrisonburg, VA

Hartford & New Haven, CT (30)

DMA TV Households: 1,014,990
% of U.S. TV Households: .887

WFSB Hartford, CT, ch. 3, CBS
WTNH-TV New Haven, CT, ch. 8, ABC
WUVN Hartford, CT, ch. 18, Univision
WTXX Waterbury, CT, ch. 20, CW
*WEDH Hartford, CT, ch. 24, ETV
WHPX New London, CT, ch. 26, ION Television
WVIT New Britain, CT, ch. 30, NBC
*WEDN Norwich, CT, ch. 53, ETV
WCTX New Haven, CT, ch. 59, MyNetworkTV
WTIC-TV Hartford, CT, ch. 61, Fox
*WEDY New Haven, CT, ch. 65, ETV

DMA Counties	State	TV Households
Hartford	CT	344,280
Litchfield	CT	74,590
Middlesex	CT	66,800
New Haven	CT	326,420
New London	CT	104,040
Tolland	CT	53,960
Windham	CT	44,900

Hartford & New Haven

Hattiesburg-Laurel, MS (167)

DMA TV Households: 110,330
% of U.S. TV Households: .096

WHLT Hattiesburg, MS, ch. 22, CBS
WDAM-TV Laurel, MS, ch. 28, NBC

DMA Counties	State	TV Households
Covington	MS	7,640
Forrest	MS	29,960
Jasper	MS	6,840
Jones	MS	25,510
Lamar	MS	18,430
Marion	MS	9,390
Perry	MS	4,550
Wayne	MS	8,010

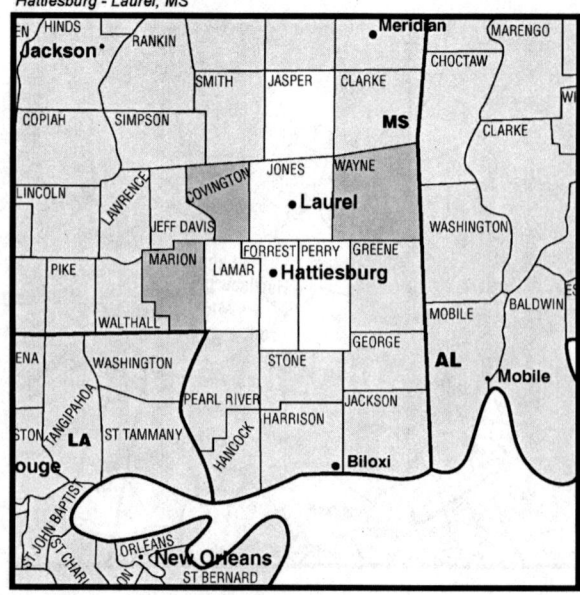

Hattiesburg - Laurel, MS

Maps courtesy of Nielsen Media Research

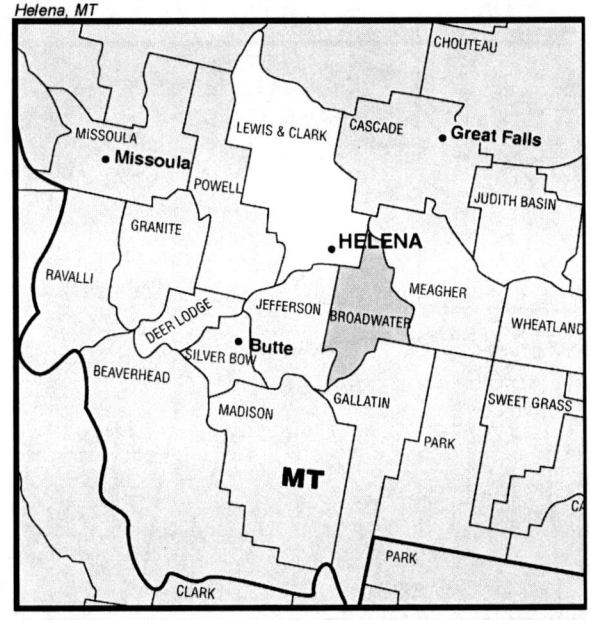

Helena, MT

Helena (206)

DMA TV Households: 27,040
% of U.S. TV Households: .024

KTVH-DT Helena, MT, ch. 12, NBC
KMTF Helena, MT, ch. 29, CW

DMA Counties	State	TV Households
Broadwater	MT	1,840
Lewis and Clark	MT	25,200

Honolulu, HI (72)

DMA TV Households: 429,940
% of U.S. TV Households: .376

KHON-TV Honolulu, ch. 8, Fox, CW
***KHET** Honolulu, ch. 11, ETV
KUPU Waimanalo, HI, ch. 15, IND
KIKU Honolulu, ch. 19, IND
KGMB Honolulu, ch. 22, CBS
KFVE Honolulu, ch. 23, MyNetworkTV
KAAH-TV Honolulu, ch. 27, IND
KWHE Honolulu, ch. 31, IND
KBFD-DT Honolulu, ch. 33, IND
KHNL Honolulu, ch. 35, NBC
***KALO** Honolulu, ch. 38, ETV
KITV Honolulu, ch. 40, ABC
KPXO-TV Kaneohe, HI, ch. 41, ION Television
***KWBN** Honolulu, ch. 43, ETV
KKAI Kailua, HI, ch. 50, IND

DMA Counties	State	TV Households
Hawaii	HI	62,740
Honolulu	HI	297,710
Kauai	HI	22,010
Maui	HI	47,480

Honolulu, HI

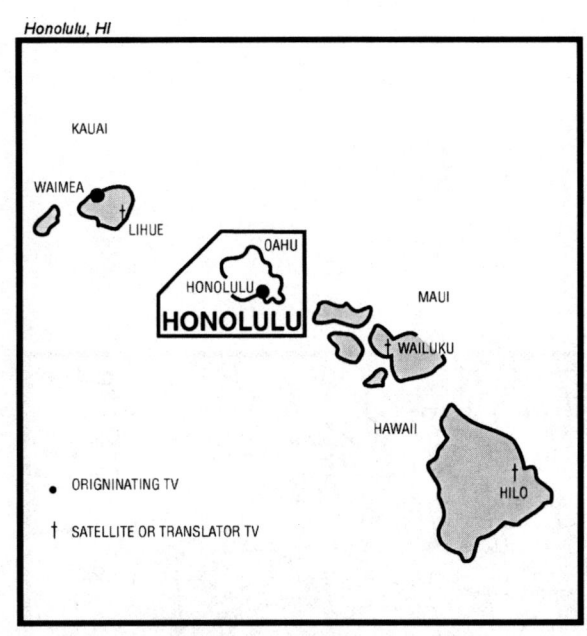

- ● ORGINATING TV
- † SATELLITE OR TRANSLATOR TV

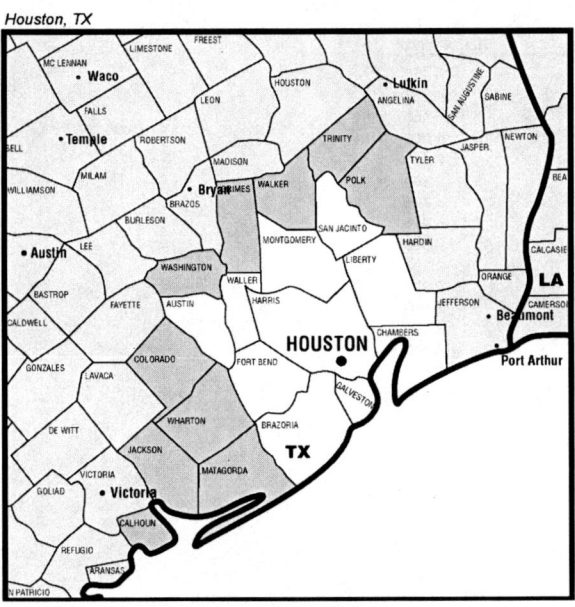

Houston, TX

Houston (10)

DMA TV Households: 2,106,210
% of U.S. TV Households: 1.840

KPRC-TV Houston, ch. 35, NBC
***KUHT** Houston, ch. 8, ETV
KHOU Houston, ch. 11, CBS
KTRK-TV Houston, ch. 13, ABC
***KETH-TV** Houston, ch. 24, ETV
KTXH Houston, ch. 19, MyNetworkTV
***KLTJ** Galveston, TX, ch. 23, ETV
KRIV Houston, ch. 26, Fox
KIAH Houston, ch. 38, CW

KXLN-DT Rosenberg, TX, ch. 45, Univision
KTMD Galveston, TX, ch. 48, Telemundo
KPXB-TV Conroe, TX, ch. 32, ION Television
KNWS-TV Katy, TX, ch. 47, IND
KTBU Conroe, TX, ch. 42, IND
KAZH Baytown, TX, ch. 41, IND
KZJL Houston, ch. 44, IND
KFTH-DT Alvin, TX, ch. 36, TeleFutura

DMA Counties	State	TV Households	DMA Counties	State	TV Households
Austin	TX	9,960	Liberty	TX	24,980
Brazoria	TX	104,460	Matagorda	TX	13,550
Calhoun	TX	7,330	Montgomery	TX	151,480
Chambers	TX	10,900	Polk	TX	17,420
Colorado	TX	7,870	San Jacinto	TX	9,590
Fort Bend	TX	169,140	Trinity	TX	5,880
Galveston	TX	110,130	Walker	TX	18,610
Grimes	TX	8,490	Waller	TX	12,320
Harris	TX	1,392,090	Washington	TX	12,070
Jackson	TX	5,110	Wharton	TX	14,840

Maps courtesy of Nielsen Media Research

Huntsville-Decatur (Florence), AL (82)

DMA TV Households: 386,520
% of U.S. TV Households: .338

WHDF Florence, AL, ch. 15, CW
WHNT-TV Huntsville, AL, ch. 19, CBS
*****WHIQ** Huntsville, AL, ch. 25, ETV
WAAY-TV Huntsville, AL, ch. 31, ABC
*****WFIQ** Florence, AL, ch. 36, ETV
WAFF Huntsville, AL, ch. 48, NBC
WZDX Huntsville, AL, ch. 54, Fox, MyNetworkTV

DMA Counties	State	TV Households
Colbert	AL	22,900
De Kalb	AL	25,960
Franklin	AL	11,900
Jackson	AL	21,900
Lauderdale	AL	37,020
Lawrence	AL	13,770
Limestone	AL	28,850
Madison	AL	129,970
Marshall	AL	34,480
Morgan	AL	46,390
Lincoln	TN	13,380

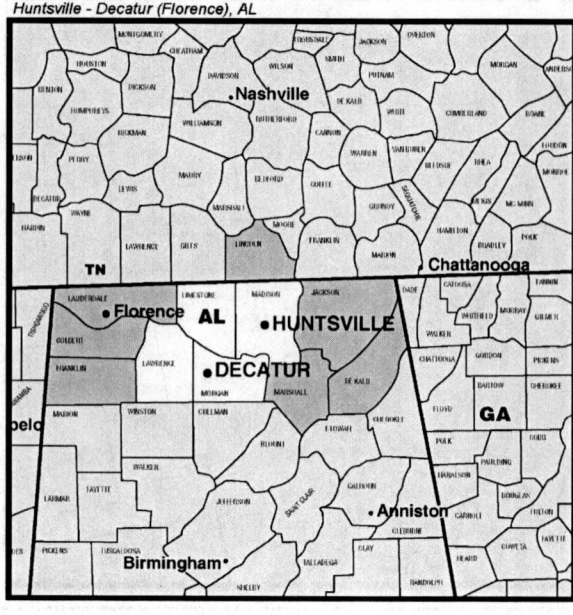

Huntsville - Decatur (Florence), AL

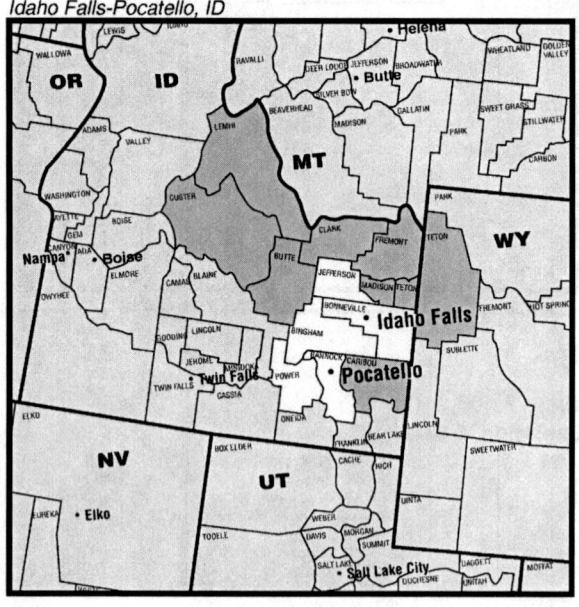

Idaho Falls-Pocatello, ID

Idaho Falls-Pocatello, ID (162)

DMA TV Households: 124,220
% of U.S. TV Households: .109

KJWY Jackson, WY, ch. 2, NBC
KIFI-TV Idaho Falls, ID, ch. 8, ABC, CW, Telemundo
KBEO Jackson, WY, ch. 11, IND
KPIF Pocatello, ID, ch. 15, IND
*****KISU-TV** Pocatello, ID, ch. 17, ETV
KPVI-DT Pocatello, ID, ch. 23, NBC
KFXP Pocatello, ID, ch. 31, Fox
KIDK Idaho Falls, ID, ch. 36, CBS

DMA Counties	State	TV Households
Bannock	ID	29,450
Bingham	ID	14,270
Bonneville	ID	35,450
Butte	ID	1,080
Caribou	ID	2,460
Clark	ID	290
Custer	ID	1,720
Fremont	ID	4,210
Jefferson	ID	7,500
Lemhi	ID	3,190
Madison	ID	10,310
Power	ID	2,660
Teton	ID	3,150
Teton	WY	8,480

Indianapolis, IN

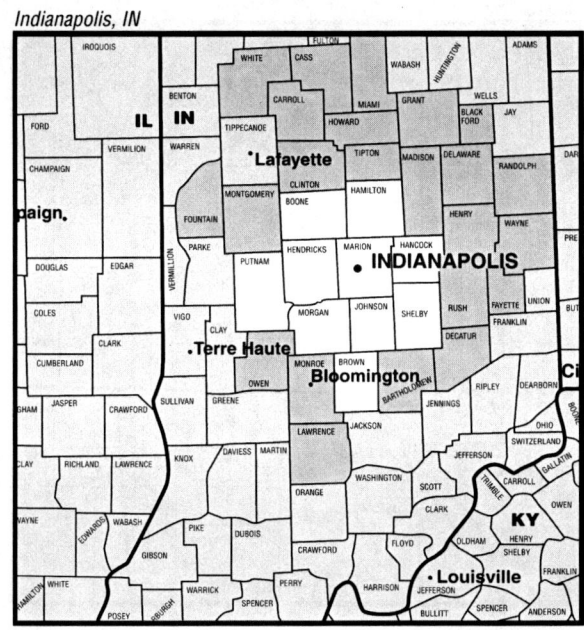

Indianapolis (25)

DMA TV Households: 1,114,970
% of U.S. TV Households: .974

WTTV Bloomington, IN, ch. 48, CW
WRTV Indianapolis, ch. 25, ABC
WISH-TV Indianapolis, ch. 9, CBS
WTHR Indianapolis, ch. 13, NBC
*WFYI Indianapolis, ch. 21, ETV
WNDY-TV Marion, IN, ch. 32, MyNetworkTV
WTTK Kokomo, IN, ch. 29, satellite to WTTV

*WTIU Bloomington, IN, ch. 14, ETV
WHMB-TV Indianapolis, ch. 20, IND
WCLJ-TV Bloomington, IN, ch. 42, IND
*WIPB Muncie, IN, ch. 23, ETV
WXIN Indianapolis, ch. 45, Fox
WIPX-TV Bloomington, IN, ch. 27, ION Television
*WDTI Indianapolis, ch. 44, ETV

DMA Counties	State	TV Households	DMA Counties	State	TV Households
Bartholomew	IN	29,080	Johnson	IN	52,870
Blackford	IN	5,360	Lawrence	IN	19,040
Boone	IN	20,790	Madison	IN	52,800
Brown	IN	5,810	Marion	IN	362,150
Carroll	IN	7,530	Miami	IN	13,480
Cass	IN	14,900	Monroe	IN	50,200
Clinton	IN	12,510	Montgomery	IN	14,730
Decatur	IN	9,850	Morgan	IN	25,640
Delaware	IN	45,880	Owen	IN	8,590
Fayette	IN	9,800	Putnam	IN	12,830
Fountain	IN	6,650	Randolph	IN	10,330
Grant	IN	25,970	Rush	IN	6,620
Hamilton	IN	98,830	Shelby	IN	17,200
Hancock	IN	26,690	Tipton	IN	6,380
Hendricks	IN	52,250	Wayne	IN	27,210
Henry	IN	18,680	White	IN	9,030
Howard	IN	35,290			

Jackson, MS (90)

DMA TV Households: 334,650
% of U.S. TV Households: .292

WLBT Jackson, MS, ch. 7, NBC
WJTV Jackson, MS, ch. 12, CBS
*WMAU-TV Bude, MS, ch. 18, ETV
*WMPN-TV Jackson, MS, ch. 20, ETV
WAPT Jackson, MS, ch. 21, ABC
WRBJ Magee, MS, ch. 34, CW
WDBD Jackson, MS, ch. 40, Fox
WUFX Vicksburg, MS, ch. 41, MyNetworkTV
WNTZ-TV Natchez, MS, ch. 49, Fox, MyNetworkTV
WWJX Jackson, MS, ch. 51, IND

DMA Counties	State	TV Households	DMA Counties	State	TV Households
Adams	MS	12,720	Leake	MS	7,950
Attala	MS	7,610	Lincoln	MS	13,190
Claiborne	MS	3,420	Madison	MS	34,120
Copiah	MS	10,440	Pike	MS	15,380
Franklin	MS	3,140	Rankin	MS	52,600
Hinds	MS	89,070	Scott	MS	10,320
Holmes	MS	6,660	Sharkey	MS	1,780
Humphreys	MS	3,360	Simpson	MS	10,250
Issaquena	MS	490	Smith	MS	6,060
Jeff Davis	MS	4,860	Walthall	MS	5,780
Jefferson	MS	3,060	Warren	MS	18,600
Lawrence	MS	5,130	Yazoo	MS	8,660

Jackson, MS

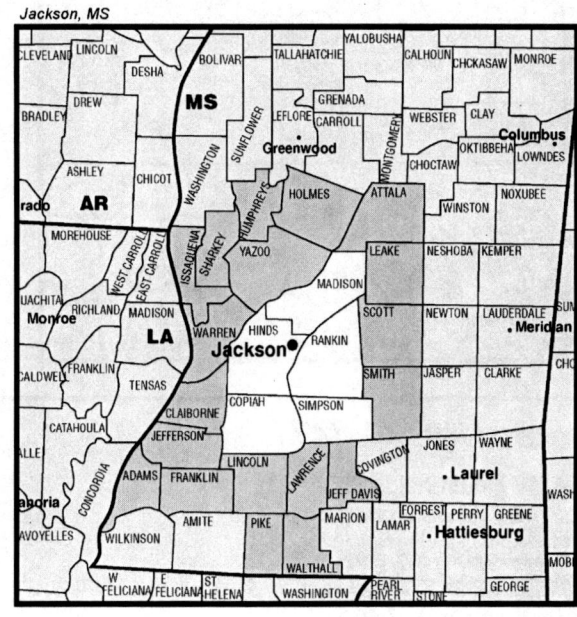

Maps courtesy of Nielsen Media Research

Jackson, TN (173)

DMA TV Households: 98,050
% of U.S. TV Households: .086

WBBJ-TV Jackson, TN, ch. 7, ABC
*WLJT-TV Lexington, TN, ch. 11, ETV
WJKT Jackson, TN, ch. 16, Fox

DMA Counties	State	TV Households
Carroll	TN	11,570
Chester	TN	6,030
Gibson	TN	20,050
Hardin	TN	10,950
Henderson	TN	11,050
Madison	TN	38,400

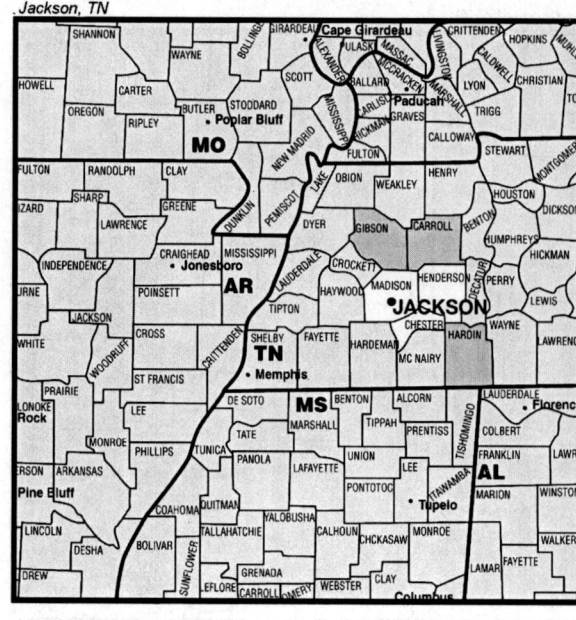

Jackson, TN

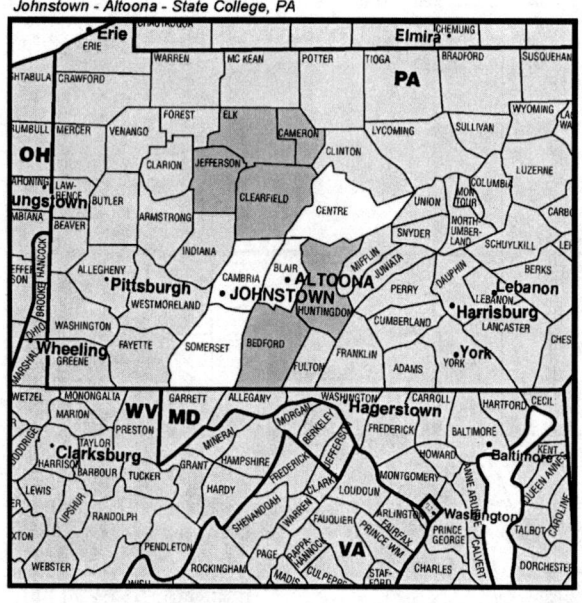

Johnstown - Altoona - State College, PA

Johnstown-Altoona, PA (101)

DMA TV Households: 293,860
% of U.S. TV Households: .257

WJAC-TV Johnstown, PA, ch. 6, NBC
WWCP-TV Johnstown, PA, ch. 8, Fox
WTAJ-TV Altoona, PA, ch. 10, CBS
*WPSU-TV Clearfield, PA, ch. 15, ETV
WATM-TV Altoona, PA, ch. 23, ABC
WKBS-TV Altoona, PA, ch. 46, IND

DMA Counties	State	TV Households
Bedford	PA	19,860
Blair	PA	50,580
Cambria	PA	57,580
Cameron	PA	2,190
Centre	PA	52,240
Clearfield	PA	32,530
Elk	PA	13,430
Huntingdon	PA	16,850
Jefferson	PA	18,370
Somerset	PA	30,230

Jacksonville, FL (47)

DMA TV Households: 674,860
% of U.S. TV Households: .590

WJXT Jacksonville, FL, ch. 4, IND
*WJCT Jacksonville, FL, ch. 7, ETV
*WXGA-TV Waycross, GA, ch. 8, ETV
WTLV Jacksonville, FL, ch. 12, NBC
WCWJ Jacksonville, FL, ch. 17, CW
WPXC-TV Brunswick, GA, ch. 21, ION Television
WJXX Orange Park, FL, ch. 25, ABC
WAWS Jacksonville, FL, ch. 30, Fox, MyNetworkTV
*WJEB-TV Jacksonville, FL, ch. 44, ETV
WTEV-TV Jacksonville, FL, ch. 47, CBS

DMA Counties	State	TV Households	DMA Counties	State	TV Households
Baker	FL	8,550	Union	FL	3,750
Bradford	FL	9,610	Brantley	GA	6,050
Clay	FL	69,490	Camden	GA	16,940
Columbia	FL	25,410	Charlton	GA	3,470
Duval	FL	350,580	Glynn	GA	30,640
Nassau	FL	26,430	Pierce	GA	7,180
Putnam	FL	28,870	Ware	GA	13,930
St. Johns	FL	73,960			

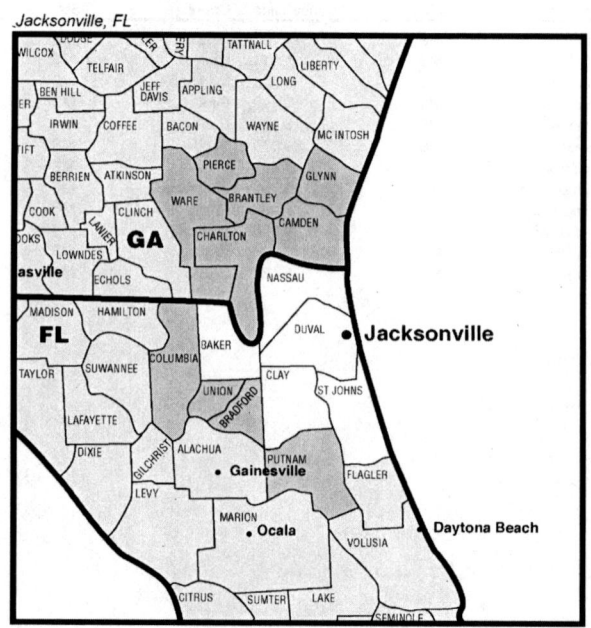

Jacksonville, FL

Maps courtesy of Nielsen Media Research

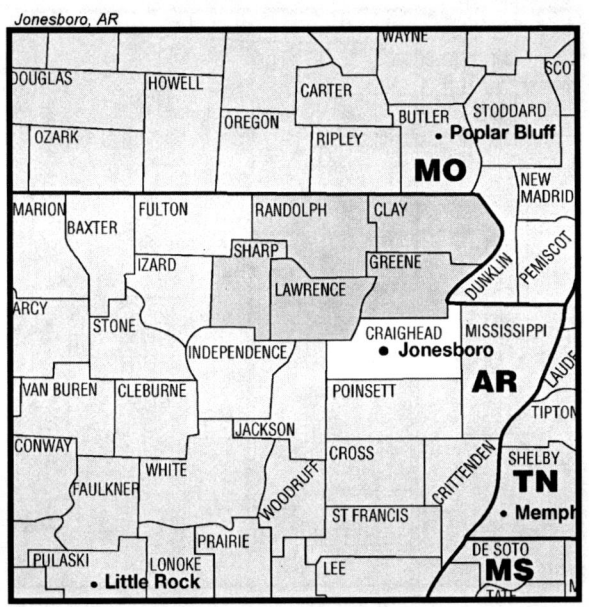

Jonesboro, AR

Jonesboro, AR (181)

DMA TV Households: 80,900
% of U.S. TV Households: .071

KAIT Jonesboro, AR, ch. 8, ABC
*KTEJ Jonesboro, AR, ch. 19, ETV
KVTJ Jonesboro, AR, ch. 48, IND

DMA Counties	State	TV Households
Clay	AR	6,650
Craighead	AR	36,410
Greene	AR	16,400
Lawrence	AR	6,680
Randolph	AR	7,210
Sharp	AR	7,550

Joplin, MO-Pittsburg, KS (148)

DMA TV Households: 156,560
% of U.S. TV Households: .137

KOAM-TV Pittsburg, KS, ch. 7, CBS
KODE-TV Joplin, MO, ch. 12, ABC
KFJX Pittsburg, KS, ch. 14, Fox
*KOZJ Joplin, MO, ch. 25, ETV
KSNF Joplin, MO, ch. 46, NBC

DMA Counties	State	TV Households
Allen	KS	5,350
Bourbon	KS	5,830
Cherokee	KS	8,250
Crawford	KS	15,700
Labette	KS	8,800
Neosho	KS	6,370
Wilson	KS	3,880
Woodson	KS	1,360
Barton	MO	4,830
Jasper	MO	45,990
McDonald	MO	8,480
Newton	MO	21,740
Vernon	MO	7,700
Ottawa	OK	12,280

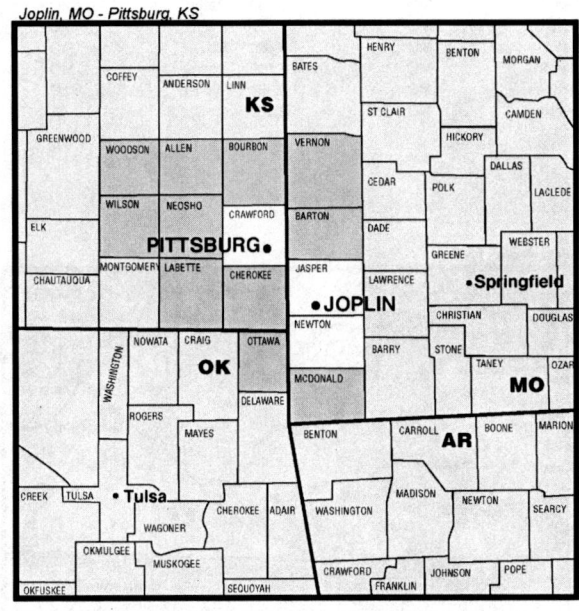

Joplin, MO - Pittsburg, KS

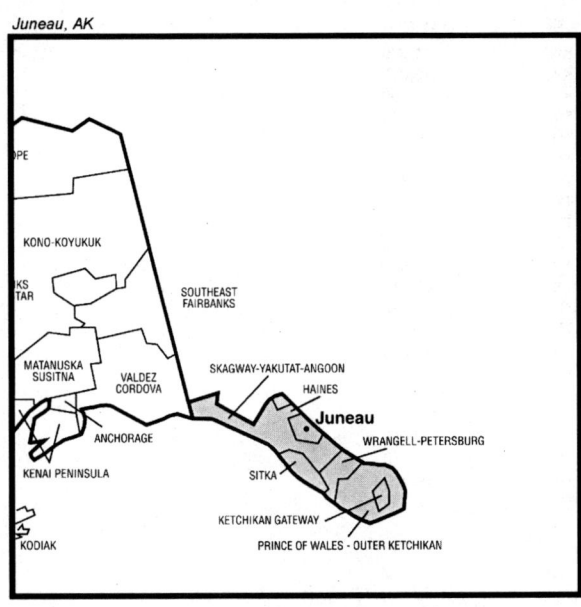

Juneau, AK

Juneau, AK (207)

DMA TV Households: 25,250
% of U.S. TV Households: .022

KTNL-TV Sitka, AK, ch. 7, CBS
*KTOO-TV Juneau, AK, ch. 10, ETV
KJUD Juneau, AK, ch. 11, ABC, CW
KUBD Ketchikan, AK, ch. 13, IND

DMA Counties	State	TV Households
Juneau	AK	25,250

Maps courtesy of Nielsen Media Research

Kansas City, MO (31)

DMA TV Households: 937,970
% of U.S. TV Households: .819

*KCPT Kansas City, MO, ch. 18, ETV
KCTV Kansas City, MO, ch. 24, CBS
KMBC-TV Kansas City, MO, ch. 29, ABC
KCWE Kansas City, MO, ch. 31, CW
WDAF-TV Kansas City, MO, ch. 34, Fox
KMCI Lawrence, KS, ch. 41, IND
KSHB-TV Kansas City, MO, ch. 42, NBC
KSMO-TV Kansas City, MO, ch. 47, MyNetworkTV
KPXE-TV Kansas City, MO, ch. 51, ION Television

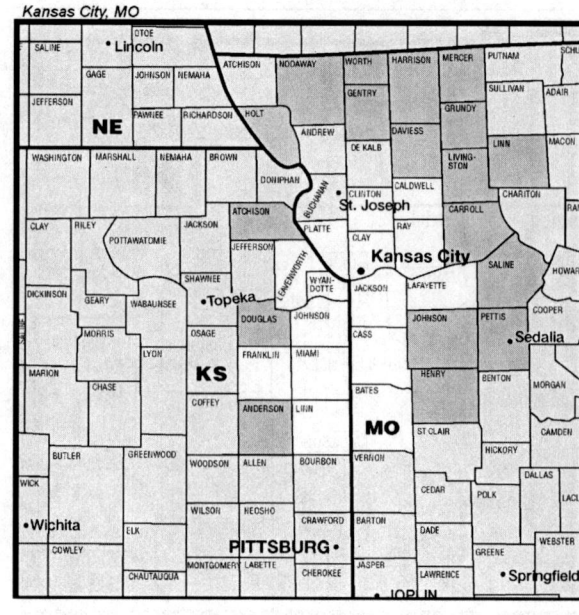

Kansas City, MO

DMA Counties	State	TV Households	DMA Counties	State	TV Households
Anderson	KS	3,030	Grundy	MO	4,260
Atchison	KS	6,270	Harrison	MO	3,660
Douglas	KS	44,330	Henry	MO	9,280
Franklin	KS	10,180	Holt	MO	2,080
Johnson	KS	210,650	Jackson	MO	273,560
Leavenworth	KS	25,240	Johnson	MO	18,880
Linn	KS	3,870	Lafayette	MO	12,430
Miami	KS	11,620	Linn	MO	5,130
Wyandotte	KS	57,580	Livingston	MO	5,640
Bates	MO	6,610	Mercer	MO	1,480
Caldwell	MO	3,660	Nodaway	MO	8,510
Carroll	MO	3,950	Pettis	MO	16,140
Cass	MO	37,310	Platte	MO	34,880
Clay	MO	85,760	Ray	MO	8,850
Clinton	MO	8,160	Saline	MO	8,550
Daviess	MO	3,150	Worth	MO	890
Gentry	MO	2,380			

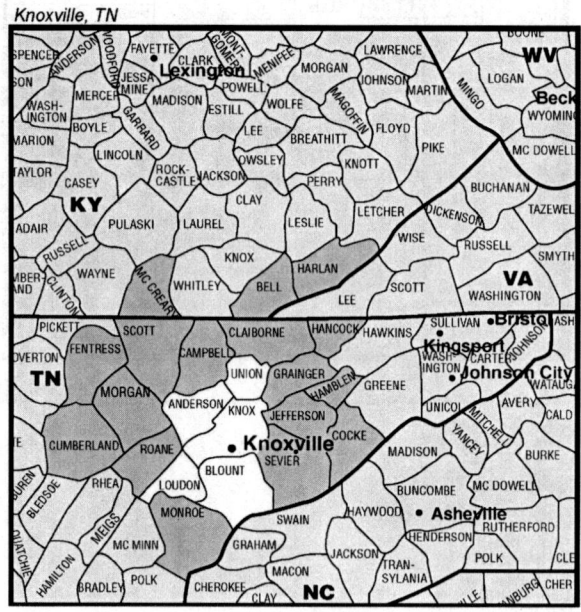

Knoxville, TN

Knoxville, TN (59)

DMA TV Households: 547,930
% of U.S. TV Households: .479

WMAK Knoxville, TN, ch. 7, IND
WBIR-TV Knoxville, TN, ch. 10, NBC
*WKOP-TV Knoxville, TN, ch. 17, ETV
WBXX-TV Crossville, TN, ch. 20, CW
WPXK-TV Jellico, TN, ch. 23, ION
WATE-TV Knoxville, TN, ch. 26, ABC
WVLT-TV Knoxville, TN, ch. 30, CBS, MyNetworkTV
WTNZ Knoxville, TN, ch. 34, Fox
*WETP-TV Sneedville, TN, ch. 41, ETV
WVLR Tazewell, TN, ch. 48, IND
WAGV Harlan, KY, ch. 51, IND

DMA Counties	State	TV Households
Bell	KY	11,970
Harlan	KY	13,010
McCreary	KY	6,800
Anderson	TN	31,300
Blount	TN	49,420
Campbell	TN	17,170
Claiborne	TN	12,850
Cocke	TN	15,090
Cumberland	TN	23,360
Fentress	TN	7,120
Grainger	TN	9,480
Hamblen	TN	25,510
Hancock	TN	2,860
Jefferson	TN	20,220
Knox	TN	183,070
Loudon	TN	19,590
Monroe	TN	18,630
Morgan	TN	7,400
Roane	TN	22,450
Scott	TN	8,970
Sevier	TN	34,310
Union	TN	7,350

Maps courtesy of Nielsen Media Research

La Crosse-Eau Claire, WI (127)

DMA TV Households: 215,610
% of U.S. TV Households: .188

WKBT La Crosse, WI, ch. 8, CBS, MyNetworkTV
WEAU-TV Eau Claire, WI, ch. 13, NBC
WQOW-TV Eau Claire, WI, ch. 18, ABC, CW
WXOW-TV La Crosse, WI, ch. 19, ABC, CW
WLAX La Crosse, WI, ch. 25, Fox
***WHLA-TV** La Crosse, WI, ch. 30, ETV
WEUX Chippewa Falls, WI, ch. 48, Fox

DMA Counties	State	TV Households
Houston	MN	7,750
Winona	MN	18,870
Buffalo	WI	5,750
Chippewa	WI	23,920
Clark	WI	12,110
Crawford	WI	6,720
EauClaire	WI	39,450
Jackson	WI	7,530
La Crosse	WI	44,990
Monroe	WI	16,760
Pepin	WI	2,880
Rusk	WI	6,130
Trempealeau	WI	11,430
Vernon	WI	11,320

La Crosse - Eau Claire, WI

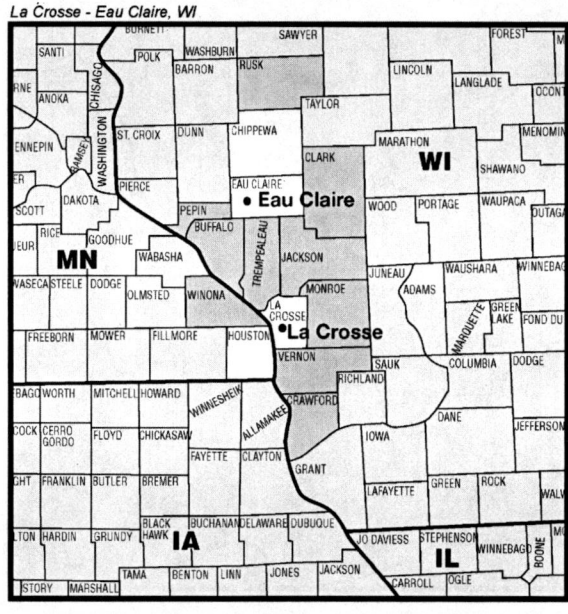

Lafayette, IN

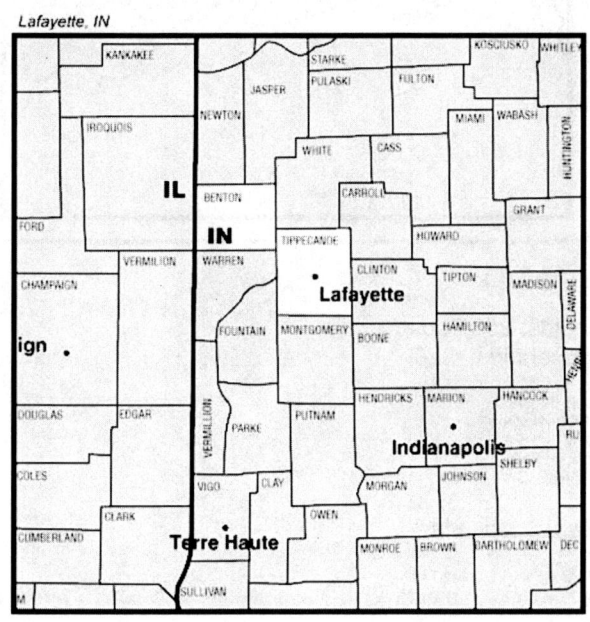

Lafayette, IN (189)

DMA TV Households: 67,070
% of U.S. TV Households: .059

WLFI-TV Lafayette, IN, ch. 18, CBS

DMA Counties	State	TV Households
Benton	IN	3,280
Tippecanoe	IN	63,790

Maps courtesy of Nielsen Media Research

Lafayette, LA

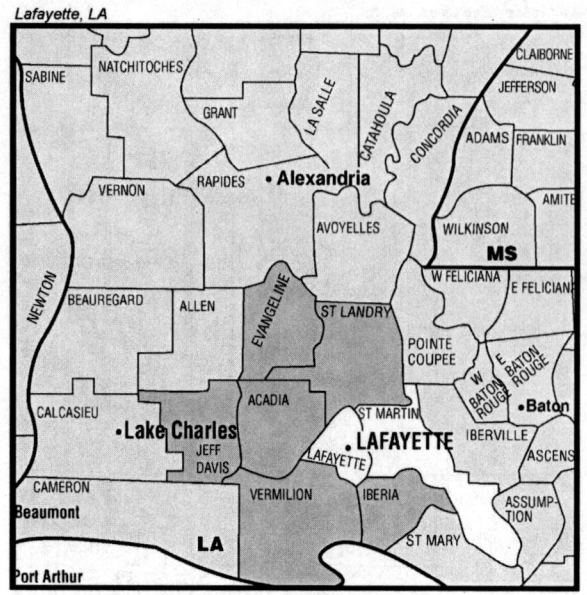

Lafayette, LA (123)

DMA TV Households: 230,670
% of U.S. TV Households: .202

KATC Lafayette, LA, ch. 3, ABC
KLFY-TV Lafayette, LA, ch. 10, CBS
KADN Lafayette, LA, ch. 15, Fox
*KLPB-TV Lafayette, LA, ch. 24, ETV
KLWB New Iberia, LA, ch. 50, CW

DMA Counties	State	TV Households
Acadia	LA	22,230
Evangeline	LA	13,400
Iberia	LA	26,570
Jefferson Davis	LA	11,730
Lafayette	LA	82,200
St. Landry	LA	34,150
St. Martin	LA	19,220
Vermilion	LA	21,170

Lake Charles, LA (176)

DMA TV Households: 95,410
% of U.S. TV Households: .083

KPLC Lake Charles, LA, ch. 7, NBC
*KLTL-TV Lake Charles, LA, ch. 18, ETV
KVHP Lake Charles, LA, ch. 29, Fox

DMA Counties	State	TV Households
Allen	LA	8,370
Beauregard	LA	13,180
Calcasieu	LA	71,090
Cameron	LA	2,770

Lake Charles, LA

Lansing, MI

Lansing, MI (114)

DMA TV Households: 258,650
% of U.S. TV Households: .226

WLNS-TV Lansing, MI, ch. 6, CBS
WILX-TV Onondaga, MI, ch. 10, NBC
WHTV Jackson, MI, ch. 18, MyNetworkTV
*WKAR-TV East Lansing, MI, ch. 23, ETV
WSYM-TV Lansing, MI, ch. 47, Fox
WLAJ Lansing, MI, ch. 53, ABC, CW

DMA Counties	State	TV Households
Clinton	MI	26,710
Eaton	MI	42,740
Hillsdale	MI	17,610
Ingham	MI	110,950
Jackson	MI	60,640

Maps courtesy of Nielsen Media Research

Laredo, TX (188)

DMA TV Households: 68,110
% of U.S. TV Households: .060

KGNS-TV Laredo, TX, ch. 8, NBC
KVTV Laredo, TX, ch. 13, CBS
KLDO-TV Laredo, TX, ch. 27, Univision

DMA Counties	State	TV Households
Webb	TX	63,540
Zapata	TX	4,570

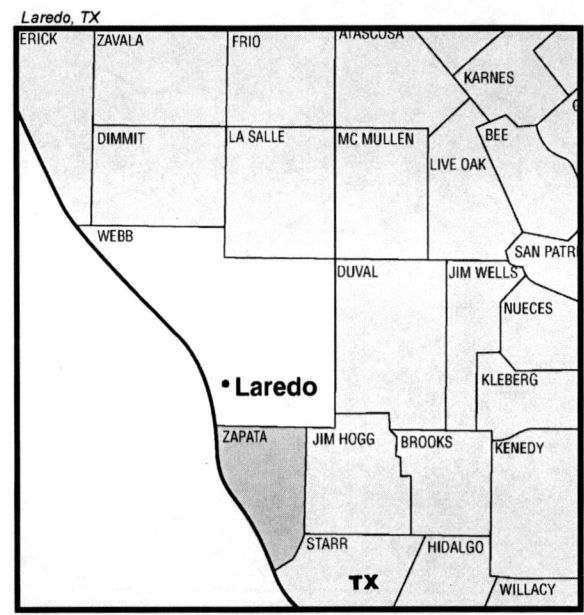

Laredo, TX

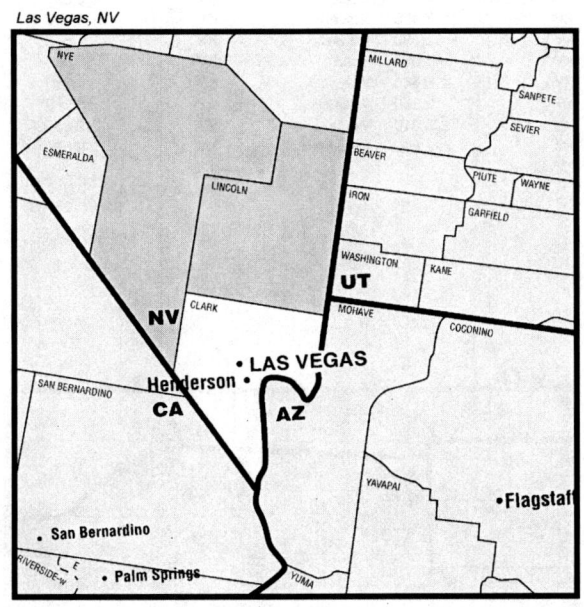

Las Vegas, NV

Las Vegas (42)

DMA TV Households: 728,410
% of U.S. TV Households: .636

KVBC-DT Las Vegas, ch. 2, NBC
KLAS-TV Las Vegas, ch. 7, CBS
KVVU-TV Henderson, NV, ch. 9, Fox
***KLVX** Las Vegas, ch. 11, ETV
KTNV-TV Las Vegas, ch. 13, ABC
KINC Las Vegas, ch. 16, Univision
KVMY Las Vegas, ch. 22, MyNetworkTV
KVCW Las Vegas, ch. 29, CW
KMCC Laughlin, NV, ch. 32, IND
KBLR Paradise, NV, ch. 40, Telemundo

DMA Counties	State	TV Households
Clark	NV	707,520
Lincoln	NV	1,760
Nye	NV	19,130

Maps courtesy of Nielsen Media Research

Lexington, KY

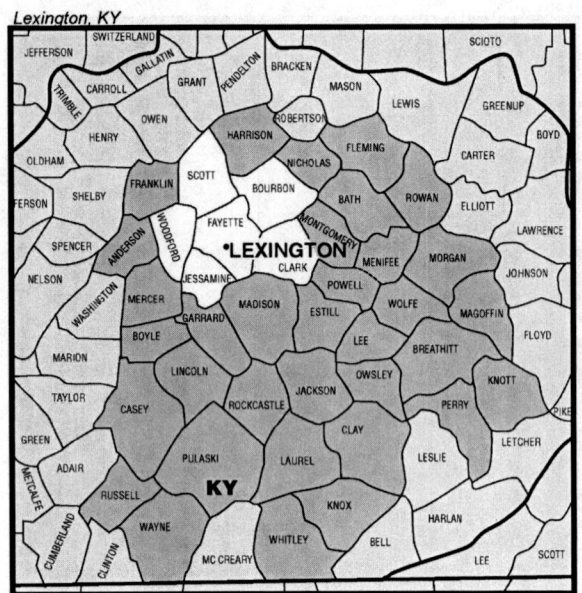

Lexington, KY (63)

DMA TV Households: 503,260
% of U.S. TV Households: .440

WKYT-TV Lexington, KY, ch. 13, CBS, CW
*WKSO-TV Somerset, KY, ch. 14, ETV
*WKMR Morehead, KY, ch. 15, ETV
*WKHA Hazard, KY, ch. 16, ETV
WLEX-TV Lexington, KY, ch. 18, NBC
WTVQ-TV Lexington, KY, ch. 36, ABC
*WKLE Lexington, KY, ch. 42, ETV
WDKY-TV Danville, KY, ch. 56, Fox
WYMT-TV Hazard, KY, ch. 57, CBS
WLJC-TV Beattyville, Ky, ch. 65, IND
WUPX-TV Morehead, KY, ch. 67, ION Television

DMA Counties	State	TV Households	DMA Counties	State	TV Households
Anderson	KY	8,470	Lincoln	KY	10,330
Bath	KY	4,760	Madison	KY	32,050
Bourbon	KY	8,050	Magoffin	KY	5,200
Boyle	KY	11,310	Menifee	KY	2,660
Breathitt	KY	5,960	Mercer	KY	9,120
Casey	KY	6,720	Montgomery	KY	10,510
Clark	KY	14,630	Morgan	KY	4,970
Clay	KY	8,430	Nicholas	KY	2,770
Estill	KY	6,150	Owsley	KY	1,740
Fayette	KY	121,630	Perry	KY	11,960
Fleming	KY	5,780	Powell	KY	5,450
Franklin	KY	20,870	Pulaski	KY	25,230
Garrard	KY	6,760	Rockcastle	KY	6,690
Harrison	KY	7,450	Rowan	KY	8,300
Jackson	KY	5,430	Russell	KY	7,570
Jessamine	KY	16,980	Scott	KY	16,990
Knott	KY	6,840	Wayne	KY	8,380
Knox	KY	13,350	Whitley	KY	15,160
Laurel	KY	23,310	Wolfe	KY	2,850
Lee	KY	2,800	Woodford	KY	9,650

Lima, OH (186)

DMA TV Households: 70,690
% of U.S. TV Households: .062

WLIO Lima, OH, ch. 35, NBC, CW
WTLW Lima, OH, ch. 44, IND

DMA Counties	State	TV Households
Allen	OH	40,320
Auglaize	OH	17,730
Putnam	OH	12,640

Lima, OH

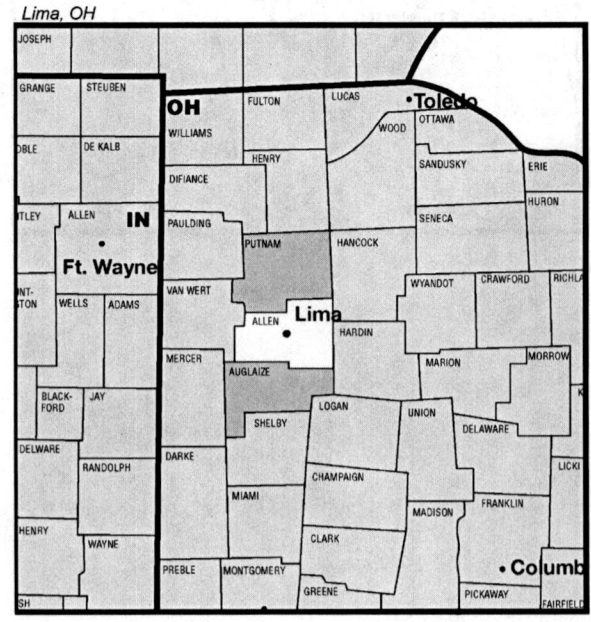

Lincoln & Hastings-Kearney, NE (106)

DMA TV Households: 281,290
% of U.S. TV Households: .246

*KLNE-TV Lexington, NE, ch. 26, ETV
KHAS-TV Hastings, NE, ch. 5, NBC
KSNB-TV Superior, NE, ch. 4, satellite to KTVG
KWNB-TV Hayes Center, NE, ch. 6
*KMNE-TV Bassett, NE, ch. 7, ETV
KLKN Lincoln, NE, ch. 8, ABC
KOLN Lincoln, NE, ch. 10, CBS, MyNetworkTV

KGIN Grand Island, NE, ch. 11, satellite to KOLN
*KUON-TV Lincoln, NE, ch. 12, ETV
KHGI-TV Kearney, NE, ch. 13, ABC
KTVG-TV Grand Island, NE, ch. 16, Fox
*KHNE-TV Hastings, NE, ch. 28, ETV
KFXL-TV Lincoln, NE, ch. 51, Fox

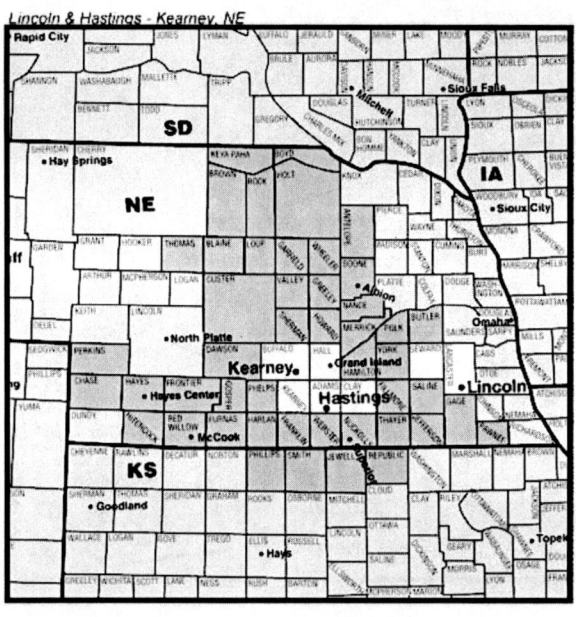

Lincoln & Hastings - Kearney, NE

DMA Counties	State	TV Households	DMA Counties	State	TV Households
Jewell	KS	1,390	Hayes	NE	400
Phillips	KS	2,180	Hitchcock	NE	1,190
Republic	KS	2,080	Holt	NE	4,160
Smith	KS	1,690	Howard	NE	2,580
Adams	NE	12,970	Jefferson	NE	3,080
Antelope	NE	2,680	Kearney	NE	2,490
Blaine	NE	190	Keya Paha	NE	290
Boone	NE	2,090	Lancaster	NE	113,420
Boyd	NE	880	Loup	NE	300
Brown	NE	1,380	Merrick	NE	2,990
Buffalo	NE	17,550	Nance	NE	1,390
Butler	NE	3,280	Nuckolls	NE	1,980
Chase	NE	1,490	Pawnee	NE	1,090
Clay	NE	2,390	Perkins	NE	1,190
Custer	NE	4,370	Phelps	NE	3,580
Dawson	NE	8,630	Polk	NE	2,090
Fillmore	NE	2,380	Red Willow	NE	4,360
Franklin	NE	1,290	Rock	NE	700
Frontier	NE	990	Saline	NE	5,080
Furnas	NE	1,990	Seward	NE	6,050
Gage	NE	9,560	Sherman	NE	1,290
Garfield	NE	700	Thayer	NE	2,090
Gosper	NE	790	Thomas	NE	290
Greeley	NE	890	Valley	NE	1,780
Hall	NE	21,260	Webster	NE	1,490
Hamilton	NE	3,480	Wheeler	NE	300
Harlan	NE	1,390	York	NE	5,680

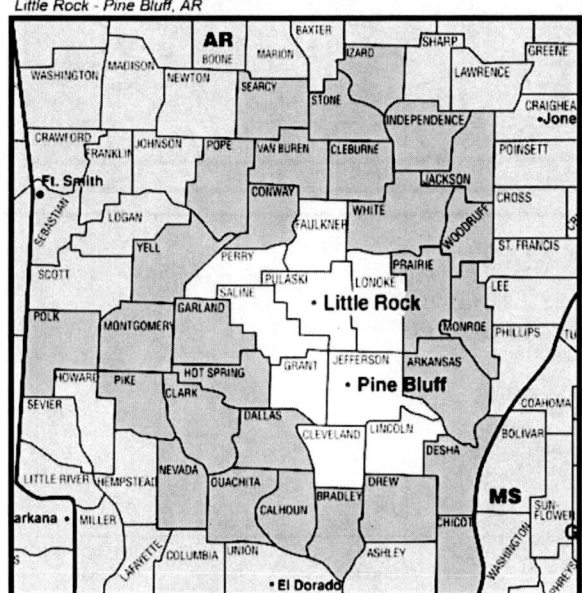

Little Rock - Pine Bluff, AR

Little Rock-Pine Bluff, AR (56)

DMA TV Households: 567,060
% of U.S. TV Households: .495

*KETS Little Rock, AR, ch. 2, ETV
KARK-TV Little Rock, AR, ch. 4, NBC
*KEMV Mountain View, AR, ch. 6, ETV
KATV Little Rock, AR, ch. 7, ABC
*KETG Arkadelphia, AR, ch. 9, ETV
KTHV Little Rock, AR, ch. 11, CBS
KLRT-TV Little Rock, AR, ch. 16, Fox

KVTN Pine Bluff, AR, ch. 25, IND
KVTH Hot Springs, AR, ch. 26, IND
*KKAP Little Rock, AR, ch. 36, ETV
KASN Pine Bluff, AR, ch. 38, CW
KARZ-TV Little Rock, AR, ch. 44, MyNetworkTV
KKYK-DT Camden, AR, ch. 49, IND

DMA Counties	State	TV Households	DMA Counties	State	TV Households
Arkansas	AR	7,820	Lincoln	AR	3,840
Bradley	AR	4,550	Lonoke	AR	24,370
Calhoun	AR	2,260	Monroe	AR	3,420
Chicot	AR	4,510	Montgomery	AR	3,600
Clark	AR	9,020	Nevada	AR	3,650
Cleburne	AR	10,910	Ouachita	AR	10,600
Cleveland	AR	3,340	Perry	AR	4,070
Conway	AR	8,330	Pike	AR	4,360
Dallas	AR	3,180	Polk	AR	7,900
Desha	AR	5,410	Pope	AR	22,540
Drew	AR	7,500	Prairie	AR	3,570
Faulkner	AR	41,150	Pulaski	AR	158,510
Garland	AR	40,980	Saline	AR	39,440
Grant	AR	6,710	Searcy	AR	3,480
Hot Spring	AR	12,370	Stone	AR	5,010
Independence	AR	13,850	Van Buren	AR	7,120
Izard	AR	5,330	White	AR	28,390
Jackson	AR	6,320	Woodruff	AR	3,050
Jefferson	AR	28,570	Yell	AR	8,030

Maps courtesy of Nielsen Media Research

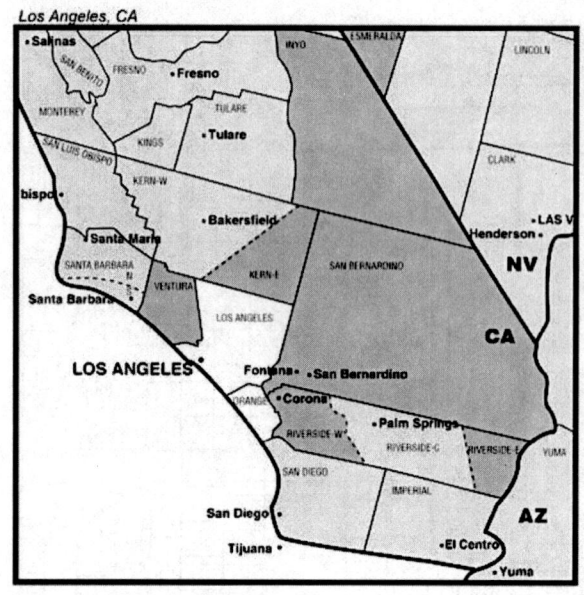

Los Angeles, CA

Los Angeles, CA (2)

DMA TV Households: 5,654,260
% of U.S. TV Households: 4.940

KCBS-TV Los Angeles, ch. 43, CBS
KNBC Los Angeles, ch. 36, NBC
KTLA Los Angeles, ch. 31, CW
KABC-TV Los Angeles, ch. 7, ABC
KCAL-TV Los Angeles, ch. 9, IND
KTTV Los Angeles, ch. 11, Fox
KCOP Los Angeles, ch. 13, MyNetworkTV
KSCI Long Beach, CA, ch. 18, IND
KBBC-TV Bishop, CA, ch. 20, IND
KWHY-TV Los Angeles, ch. 42, IND
***KVCR-DT** San Bernardino, CA, ch. 26, ETV
***KCET** Los Angeles, ch. 28, ETV
KPXN-TV San Bernardino, CA, ch. 38, ION
  Television

KVMD Twentynine Palms, CA, ch. 23, IND
KMEX-DT Los Angeles, ch. 34, Univision
KTBN-TV Santa Ana, CA, ch. 33, IND
KXLA Rancho Palos Verdes, CA, ch. 51, IND
KFTR-DT Ontario, CA, ch. 29, TeleFutura
***KOCE-TV** Huntington Beach, CA, ch. 48, ETV
KVEA Corona, CA, ch. 39, Telemundo
KAZA-TV Avalon, CA, ch. 47, Azteca America
KDOC-TV Anaheim, CA, ch. 32, IND
KJLA Ventura, CA, ch. 49, IND
***KLCS** Los Angeles, ch. 41, ETV
KRCA Riverside, CA, ch. 45, IND
KHIZ Barstow, CA, ch. 44, IND
KBEH Oxnard, CA, ch. 24, IND

DMA Counties	State	TV Households	DMA Counties	State	TV Households
Inyo	CA	7,310	Riverside West	CA	513,540
Kern East	CA	28,260	San Bernardino	CA	613,020
Los Angeles	CA	3,243,060	Ventura	CA	261,430
Orange	CA	981,190	Esmeralda	NV	390
Riverside East	CA	6,060			

Louisville, KY (50)

DMA TV Households: 667,230
% of U.S. TV Households: .583

WAVE Louisville, KY, ch. 3, NBC
WHAS-TV Louisville, KY, ch. 11, ABC
***WKPC-TV** Louisville, KY, ch. 17, ETV
WBNA Louisville, KY, ch. 21, ION Television
***WKZT-TV** Elizabethtown, KY, ch. 43, ETV

WLKY-TV Louisville, KY, ch. 32, CBS
WBKI-TV Campbellsville, KY, ch. 34, CW
WDRB Louisville, KY, ch. 41, Fox
WMYO Salem, IN, ch. 58, MyNetworkTV
***WKMJ** Louisville, KY, ch. 38, ETV

DMA Counties	State	TV Households	DMA Counties	State	TV Households
Clark	IN	45,080	Green	KY	4,750
Crawford	IN	4,230	Hardin	KY	38,270
Floyd	IN	29,110	Henry	KY	6,140
Harrison	IN	14,430	Jefferson	KY	300,940
Jackson	IN	16,720	Larue	KY	5,440
Jefferson	IN	12,800	Marion	KY	7,140
Jennings	IN	10,560	Meade	KY	10,160
Orange	IN	7,910	Nelson	KY	16,740
Scott	IN	9,420	Oldham	KY	19,220
Washington	IN	10730	Shelby	KY	15,410
Adair	KY	7,150	Spencer	KY	6,460
Breckinridge	KY	7,600	Taylor	KY	9,860
Bullitt	KY	28,190	Trimble	KY	3,580
Carroll	KY	4,170	Washington	KY	4,560
Grayson	KY	10,460			

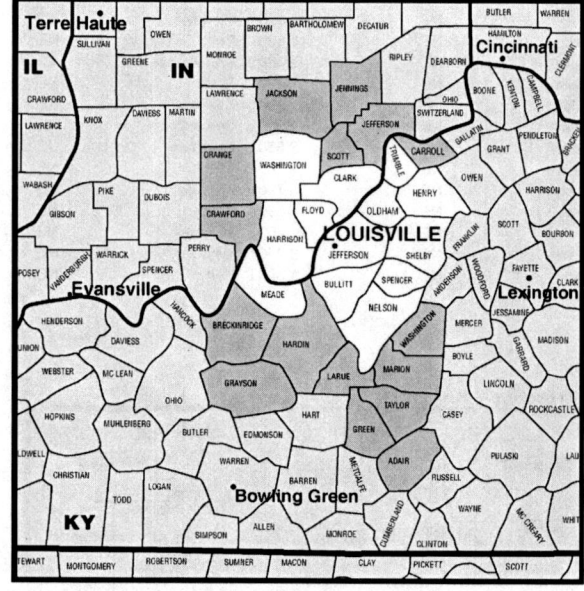

Louisville, KY

Lubbock, TX

Lubbock, TX (143)

DMA TV Households: 158,070
% of U.S. TV Households: .138

***KTXT-TV** Lubbock, TX, ch. 5, ETV
KCBD Lubbock, TX, ch. 11, NBC
KLBK-TV Lubbock, TX, ch. 13, CBS
KPTB Lubbock, TX, ch. 16, IND
KLCW-TV Wolfforth, TX, ch. 22, CW
KAMC Lubbock, TX, ch. 28, ABC
KJTV-TV Lubbock, TX, ch. 34, Fox

DMA Counties	State	TV Households	DMA Counties	State	TV Households
Bailey	TX	2,250	Hale	TX	11,730
Borden	TX	290	Hockley	TX	8,050
Cochran	TX	1,180	Kent	TX	290
Crosby	TX	2,290	Lamb	TX	5,060
Dawson	TX	4,330	Lubbock	TX	103,450
Dickens	TX	870	Lynn	TX	2,090
Floyd	TX	2,360	Motley	TX	590
Gaines	TX	4,800	Terry	TX	4,180
Garza	TX	1,690	Yoakum	TX	2,570

Maps courtesy of Nielsen Media Research

Macon, GA (122)

DMA TV Households: 239,820
% of U.S. TV Households: .210

WMAZ-TV Macon, GA, ch. 13, CBS
WGXA Macon, GA, ch. 24, Fox, MyNetworkTV
***WMUM-TV** Cochran, GA, ch. 29, ETV
WMGT-TV Macon, GA, ch. 41, NBC
WPGA-TV Perry, GA, ch. 58, IND
WGNM Macon, GA, ch. 64, IND

DMA Counties	State	TV Households	DMA Counties	State	TV Households
Baldwin	GA	15,670	Monroe	GA	9,120
Bibb	GA	60,330	Peach	GA	9,530
Bleckley	GA	4,580	Pulaski	GA	3,480
Crawford	GA	4,440	Taylor	GA	3,350
Dodge	GA	7,510	Telfair	GA	4,130
Dooly	GA	3,850	Treutlen	GA	2,660
Hancock	GA	3,150	Twiggs	GA	3,760
Houston	GA	51,450	Washington	GA	7,440
Johnson	GA	3,250	Wheeler	GA	2,080
Jones	GA	10,420	Wilcox	GA	2,690
Laurens	GA	18,440	Wilkinson	GA	3,850
Macon	GA	4,640			

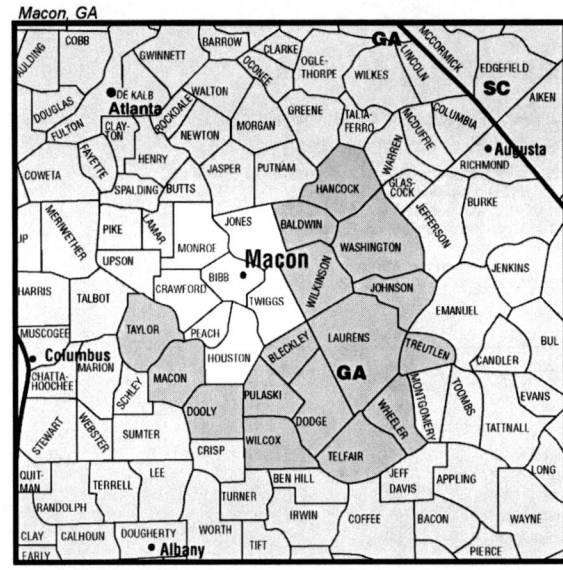

Macon, GA

Madison, WI (85)

DMA TV Households: 378,740
% of U.S. TV Households: .331

WISC-TV Madison, WI, ch. 3, CBS, MyNetworkTV
WMTV Madison, WI, ch. 15, NBC
***WHA-TV** Madison, WI, ch. 20, ETV
WKOW-TV Madison, WI, ch. 27, ABC
WMSN-TV Madison, WI, ch. 47, Fox
WBUW Janesville, WI, ch. 57, CW

DMA Counties	State	TV Households
Columbia	WI	22,090
Dane	WI	196,490
Grant	WI	19,030
Green	WI	14,520
Iowa	WI	9,430
Juneau	WI	10,480
Lafayette	WI	6,270
Marquette	WI	6,340
Richland	WI	7,350
Rock	WI	62,790
Sauk	WI	23,950

Madison, WI

Mankato, MN (199)

DMA TV Households: 52,230
% of U.S. TV Households: .046

KEYC-TV Mankato, MN, ch. 12, CBS, Fox

DMA Counties	State	TV Households
Blue Earth-Nicollet South	MN	28,950
Brown	MN	10,440
Martin	MN	8,560
Watonwan	MN	4,280

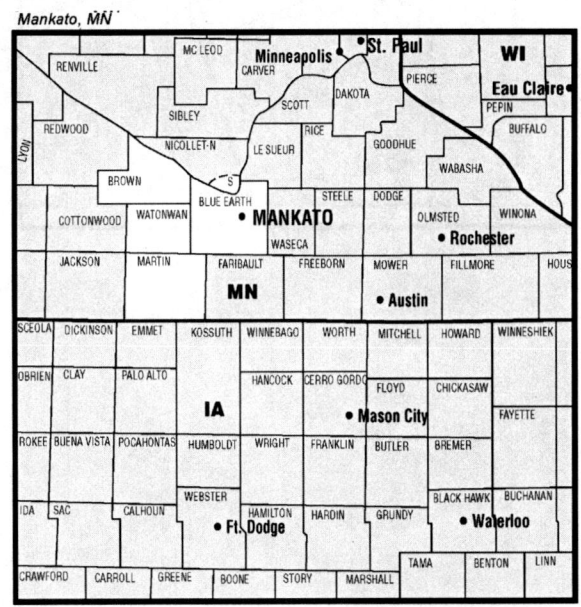

Mankato, MN

Maps courtesy of Nielsen Media Research

Marquette, MI (180)

DMA TV Households: 89,290
% of U.S. TV Households: .078

WJMN-TV Escanaba, MI, ch. 3, satellite to WFRV-TV
WBKP Calumet, MI, ch. 5, CW
WLUC-TV Marquette, MI, ch. 6, NBC
WDHS Iron Mountain, MI, ch. 8, IND
WBUP Ishpeming, MI, ch. 10, ABC
***WNMU-TV** Marquette, MI, ch. 13, ETV
WZMQ Marquette, MI, ch. 19, MyNetworkTV

DMA Counties	State	TV Households
Alger	MI	3,770
Baraga	MI	3,160
Delta	MI	15,810
Dickinson	MI	11,350
Houghton	MI	12,940
Iron	MI	5,230
Keweenaw	MI	990
Marquette	MI	27,330
Ontonagon	MI	3,060
Schoolcraft	MI	3,460
Florence	WI	2,190

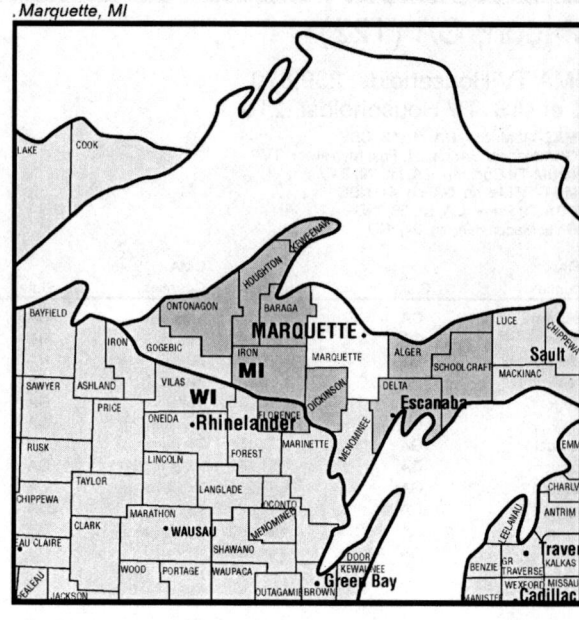

Marquette, MI

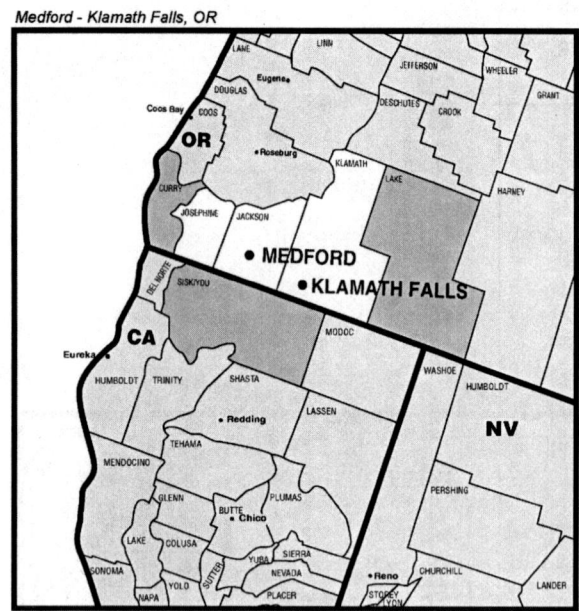

Medford - Klamath Falls, OR

Medford-Klamath Falls, OR (140)

DMA TV Households: 171,830
% of U.S. TV Households: .150

KOTI Klamath Falls, OR, ch. 2, satellite to KOBI
KOBI Medford, OR, ch. 5, NBC
***KSYS** Medford, OR, ch. 8, ETV
KTVL Medford, OR, ch. 10, CBS
KDRV Medford, OR, ch. 12, ABC
***KBDM** Yreka City, CA, ch. 20, ETV
***KFTS** Klamath Falls, OR, ch. 22, satellite to *KSYS
KMVU Medford, OR, ch. 26, IND
KBLN Grants Pass, OR, ch. 30, IND
KDKF Klamath Falls, OR, ch. 31, ABC

DMA Counties	State	TV Households
Siskiyou	CA	18,620
Curry	OR	9,710
Jackson	OR	80,820
Josephine	OR	33,380
Klamath	OR	26,240
Lake	OR	3,060

Maps courtesy of Nielsen Media Research

Memphis, TN

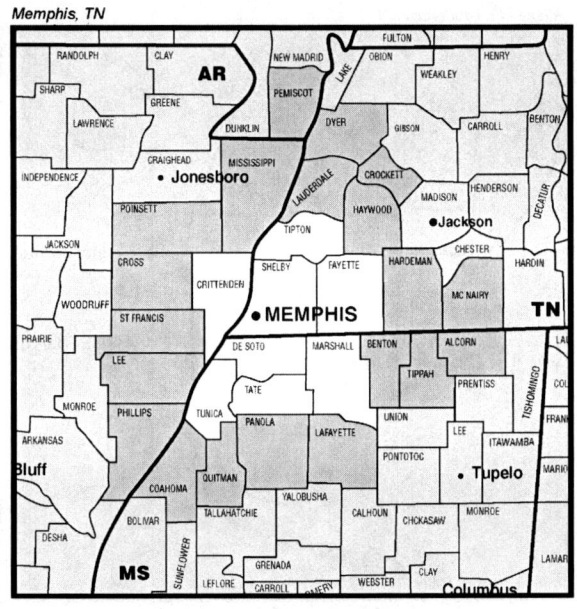

Memphis (48)

DMA TV Households: 673,770
% of U.S. TV Households: .589

WREG-TV Memphis, ch. 3, CBS
WMC-TV Memphis, ch. 5, NBC
WHBQ-TV Memphis, ch. 13, Fox
*****WMAV-TV** Oxford, MS, ch. 18, ETV
*****WTWV** Memphis, ch. 23, ETV
WPTY-TV Memphis, ch. 24, ABC
*****WKNO** Memphis, ch. 29, ETV
WLMT Memphis, ch. 30, CW
WBUY-TV Holly Springs, MS, ch. 41, IND
WPXX-TV Memphis, ch. 50, MyNetworkTV

DMA Counties	State	TV Households	DMA Counties	State	TV Households
Crittenden	AR	19,590	Quitman	MS	3,050
Cross	AR	7,150	Tate	MS	9,710
Lee	AR	3,430	Tippah	MS	8,380
Mississippi	AR	17,430	Tunica	MS	3,890
Phillips	AR	7,870	Pemiscot	MO	7,410
Poinsett	AR	9,800	Crockett	TN	5,470
St. Francis	AR	9,180	Dyer	TN	14,950
Alcorn	MS	15,010	Fayette	TN	14,860
Benton	MS	3,080	Hardeman	TN	9,520
Coahoma	MS	9,220	Haywood	TN	7,410
De Soto	MS	58,400	Lauderdale	TN	9,510
Lafayette	MS	16,790	McNairy	TN	10,560
Marshall	MS	13,170	Shelby	TN	344,860
Panola	MS	12,940	Tipton	TN	21,1300

Meridian, MS (185)

DMA TV Households: 72,280
% of U.S. TV Households: .063

WTOK-TV Meridian, MS, ch. 11, ABC, CW, Fox
*****WMAW-TV** Meridian, MS, ch. 14, ETV
WMDN Meridian, MS, ch. 24, CBS
WGBC Meridian, MS, ch. 30, NBC

DMA Counties	State	TV Households
Choctaw	AL	5,790
Sumter	AL	5,230
Clarke	MS	6,940
Kemper	MS	3,710
Lauderdale	MS	30,440
Neshoba	MS	11,550
Newton	MS	8,620

Meridian, MS

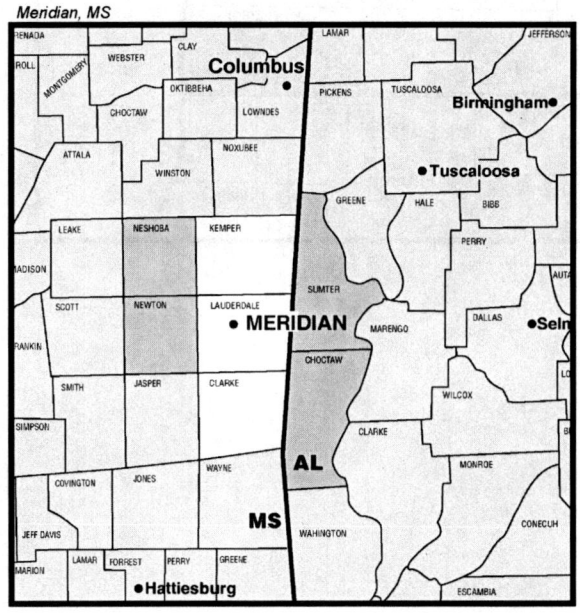

Maps courtesy of Nielsen Media Research

Miami-Ft. Lauderdale, FL (16)

DMA TV Households: 1,546,920
% of U.S. TV Households: 1.352

*WPBT Miami, ch. 2, ETV
WFOR-TV Miami, ch. 4, CBS
WTVJ Miami, ch. 6, NBC
WSVN Miami, ch. 7, Fox
WGEN-TV Key West, FL, ch. 8, IND
WPLG Miami, ch. 10, ABC
*WLRN-TV Miami, ch. 17, ETV
WSBS-TV Key West, FL, ch. 22, IND

WLTV Miami, ch. 23, Univision
WBFS-TV Miami, ch. 33, MyNetworkTV
WPXM Miami, ch. 35, ION Television
WSFL-TV Miami, ch. 39, CW
WHFT-TV Miami, ch. 46, IND
WSCV Fort Lauderdale, FL, ch. 51, Telemundo
WAMI-TV Hollywood, FL, ch. 69, TeleFutura

DMA Counties	State	TV Households
Broward	FL	688,120
Miami-Dade	FL	826,800
Monroe	FL	32,000

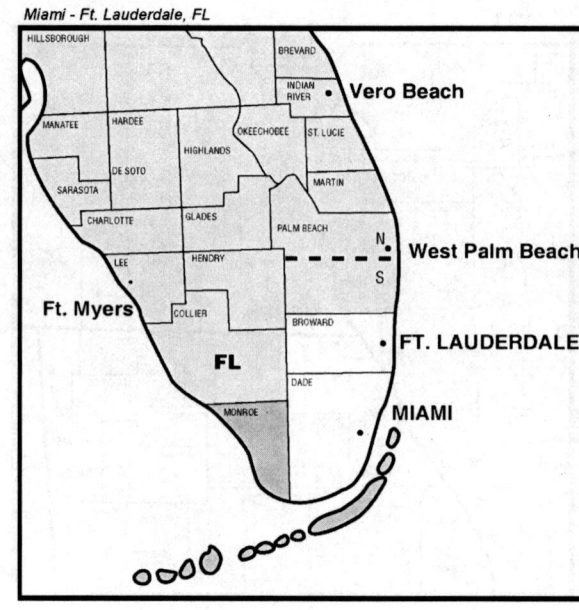

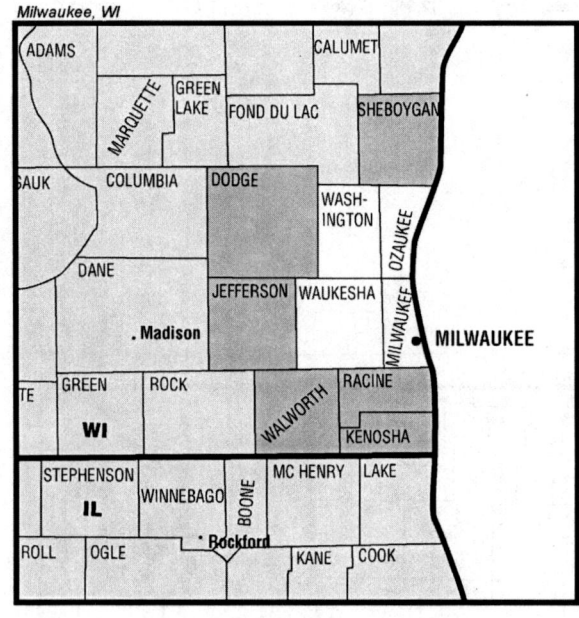

Milwaukee, WI

Milwaukee, WI (35)

DMA TV Households: 905,350
% of U.S. TV Households: .791

WTMJ-TV Milwaukee, ch. 4, NBC
WITI Milwaukee, ch. 6, Fox
*WMVS Milwaukee, ch. 10, ETV
WISN-TV Milwaukee, ch. 12, ABC
WVTV Milwaukee, ch. 18, CW
WVCY-TV Milwaukee, ch. 22, IND
WCGV-TV Milwaukee, ch. 24, MyNetworkTV
*WMVT Milwaukee, ch. 36, ETV
WPXE-TV Kenosha, WI, ch. 40, ION Television
WWRS-TV Mayville, WI, ch. 43, IND
WBME-TV Racine, WI, ch. 49, IND
WDJT-TV Milwaukee, ch. 58, CBS

DMA Counties	State	TV Households
Dodge	WI	33,390
Jefferson	WI	30,620
Kenosha	WI	61,560
Milwaukee	WI	385,750
Ozaukee	WI	33,290
Racine	WI	75,580
Sheboygan	WI	46,510
Walworth	WI	38,300
Washington	WI	51,100
Waukesha	WI	149,250

Maps courtesy of Nielsen Media Research

Minneapolis - St. Paul, MN

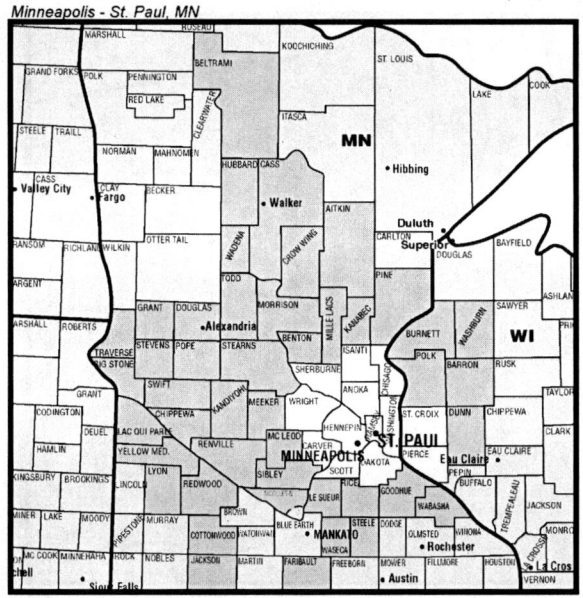

Minneapolis-St. Paul, MN (15)

DMA TV Households: 1,730,530
% of U.S. TV Households: 1.512

*KTCA-TV St. Paul, ch. 2, ETV
WCCO-TV Minneapolis, ch. 4, CBS
KSTP-TV St. Paul, ch. 5, ABC
KCCO-TV Alexandria, MN, ch. 7, CBS
*KAWE Bemidji, MN, ch. 9, ETV
KMSP-TV Minneapolis, ch. 9, Fox
*KWCM-TV Appleton, MN, ch. 10, ETV
KARE Minneapolis, ch. 11, NBC
KCCW-TV Walker, MN, ch. 12, satellite to
   KCCO-TV

*KTCI-TV St. Paul, ch. 17, ETV
*KAWB Brainerd, MN, ch. 22, ETV
WUCW Minneapolis, ch. 23, CW
KFTC Bemidji, MN, ch. 26, IND
*WHWC-TV Menomonie, WI, ch. 28, ETV
WFTC Minneapolis, ch. 29, MyNetworkTV
KPXM-TV St. Cloud, MN, ch. 40, ION Television
KSAX Alexandria, MN, ch. 42, ABC
KRWF Redwood Falls, MN, ch. 43, ABC
KSTC-TV Minneapolis, ch. 45, IND

DMA Counties	State	TV Households	DMA Counties	State	TV Households
Aitkin	MN	7,090	Nicollet-North	MN	6,050
Anoka	MN	121,590	Pine	MN	10,770
Beltrami	MN	16,220	Pope	MN	4,580
Benton	MN	15,830	Ramsey	MN	198,530
Big Stone	MN	2,190	Redwood	MN	6,150
Carver	MN	32,120	Renville	MN	6,360
Cass	MN	11,750	Rice	MN	21,170
Chippewa	MN	5,180	Scott	MN	45,260
Chisago	MN	18,130	Sherburne	MN	30,830
Cottonwood	MN	4,560	Sibley	MN	5,670
Crow Wing	MN	25,520	Stearns	MN	55,970
Dakota	MN	150,670	Steele	MN	14,220
Douglas	MN	15,140	Stevens	MN	3,660
Faribault	MN	6,080	Swift	MN	3,840
Goodhue	MN	17,950	Todd	MN	9,270
Grant	MN	2,390	Traverse	MN	1,490
Hennepin	MN	465,790	Wabasha	MN	8,530
Hubbard	MN	7,650	Wadena	MN	5,280
Isanti	MN	14,700	Waseca	MN	7,050
Jackson	MN	4,480	Washington	MN	85,950
Kanabec	MN	6,330	Wright	MN	44,620
Kandiyohi	MN	16,080	Yellow Medicine	MN	4,060
Lac qui Parle	MN	2,990	Barron	WI	18,740
Le Sueur	MN	10,990	Burnett	WI	7,090
Lyon	MN	9,550	Dunn	WI	15,830
McLeod	MN	14,780	Pierce	WI	14,640
Meeker	MN	8,860	Polk	WI	18,140
Mille Lacs	MN	10,680	St. Croix	WI	31,950
Morrison	MN	12,540	Washburn	WI	7,000

Minot-Bismarck-Dickinson, ND (158)

DMA TV Households: 136,730
% of U.S. TV Households: .119

KXMA-TV Dickinson, ND, ch. 2, satellite to
   KXMC-TV
*KBME-TV Bismarck, ND, ch. 22, ETV
*KWSE Williston, ND, ch.11, ETV
KFYR-TV Bismarck, ND, ch. 5, NBC
*KSRE Minot, ND, ch. 40, ETV
KQCD-TV Dickinson, ND, ch. 7, NBC
KUMV-TV Williston, ND, ch. 8, satellite to
   KFYR-TV
*KDSE Dickinson, ND, ch. 9, ETV
KMOT Minot, ND, ch. 10, satellite to
   KFYR-TV

KXMD-TV Williston, ND, ch. 11, satellite to
   KXMC-TV
*KQSD-TV Lowry, SD, ch. 11, ETV
KXMB-TV Bismarck, ND, ch. 12, satellite to
   KXMC-TV
KXMC-TV Minot, ND, ch. 13, CBS
*KPSD-TV Eagle Butte, SD, ch. 13, ETV
KMCY Minot, ND, ch. 14, ABC
KBMY Bismarck, ND, ch. 17, ABC
KXND Minot, ND, ch. 24, Fox
KNDX Bismarck, ND, ch. 26, Fox

DMA Counties	State	TV Households	DMA Counties	State	TV Households
Daniels	MT	690	Logan	ND	790
Fallon	MT	1,060	McHenry	ND	2,190
McCone	MT	690	McIntosh	ND	1,090
Richland	MT	3,870	McKenzie	ND	2,180
Roosevelt	MT	3,350	McLean	ND	3,480
Sheridan	MT	1,380	Mercer	ND	3,160
Wibaux	MT	390	Morton	ND	10,630
Adams	ND	990	Mountrail	ND	2,580
Billings	ND	400	Oliver	ND	690
Bottineau	ND	2,690	Pierce	ND	1,690
Bowman	ND	1,290	Renville	ND	1,000
Burke	ND	790	Rolette	ND	4,550
Burleigh	ND	32,840	Sheridan	ND	590
Divide	ND	890	Sioux	ND	1,180
Dunn	ND	1,280	Slope	ND	290
Emmons	ND	1,390	Stark	ND	9,260
Golden Valley	ND	700	Ward	ND	22,290
Grant	ND	990	Wells	ND	1,780
Hettinger	ND	990	Williams	ND	8,360
Kidder	ND	1,000	Corson	SD	1,280

Minot - Bismarck - Dickinson (Williston), ND

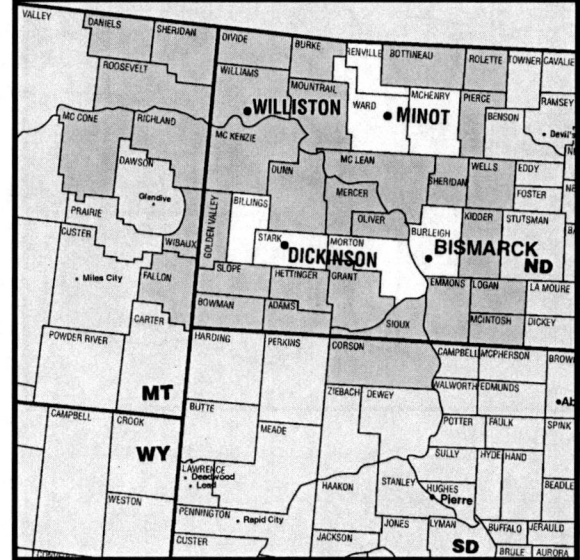

Maps courtesy of Nielsen Media Research

Missoula, MT (166)

DMA TV Households: 111,340
% of U.S. TV Households: .097

KPAX-TV Missoula, MT, ch. 8, satellite to KXLF-TV
KCFW-TV Kalispell, MT, ch. 9, NBC
*****KUFM-TV** Missoula, MT, ch. 11, ETV
KECI-TV Missoula, MT, ch. 13, NBC
KMMF Missoula, MT, ch. 17, IND
KTMF Missoula, MT, ch. 23, ABC, Fox

DMA Counties	State	TV Households
Flathead	MT	33,980
Granite	MT	1,180
Lake	MT	11,100
Mineral	MT	1,560
Missoula	MT	42,500
Ravalli	MT	16,210
Sanders	MT	4,810

Missoula, MT

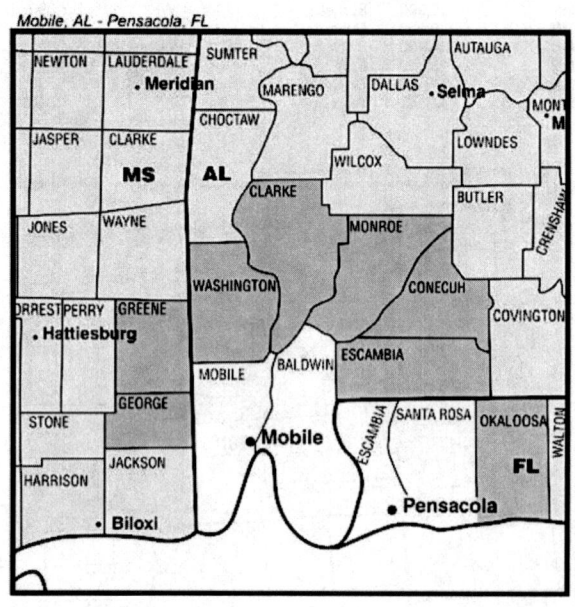

Mobile, AL - Pensacola, FL

Mobile, AL-Pensacola (Ft. Walton Beach), FL (60)

DMA TV Households: 537,810
% of U.S. TV Households: .470

WKRG-TV Mobile, AL, ch. 5, CBS
WALA-TV Mobile, AL, ch. 10, Fox
WPMI-TV Mobile, AL, ch. 15, NBC
WEAR-TV Pensacola, FL, ch. 17, ABC
WMPV-TV Mobile, AL, ch. 20, IND
WDPM-DT Mobile, AL, ch. 23, IND
*****WSRE** Pensacola, FL, ch. 31, ETV
WHBR Pensacola, FL, ch. 33, IND
WFGX Fort Walton Beach, FL, ch. 35, MyNetworkTV
*****WEIQ** Mobile, AL, ch. 42, ETV
WJTC Pensacola, FL, ch. 44, IND
WFBD Destin, FL, ch. 48, IND
WPAN Fort Walton Beach, FL, ch. 53, IND
WBPG Gulf Shores, AL, ch. 55, CW
WAWD Fort Walton Beach, FL, ch. 58, IND

DMA Counties	State	TV Households
Baldwin	AL	72,880
Clarke	AL	10,400
Conecuh	AL	5,610
Escambia	AL	14,140
Mobile	AL	153,590
Monroe	AL	9,070
Washington	AL	6,500
Escambia	FL	120,340
Okaloosa	FL	78,970
Santa Rosa	FL	54,430
George	MS	7,720
Greene	MS	4,160

Maps courtesy of Nielsen Media Research

Monroe, LA-El Dorado, AR (136)

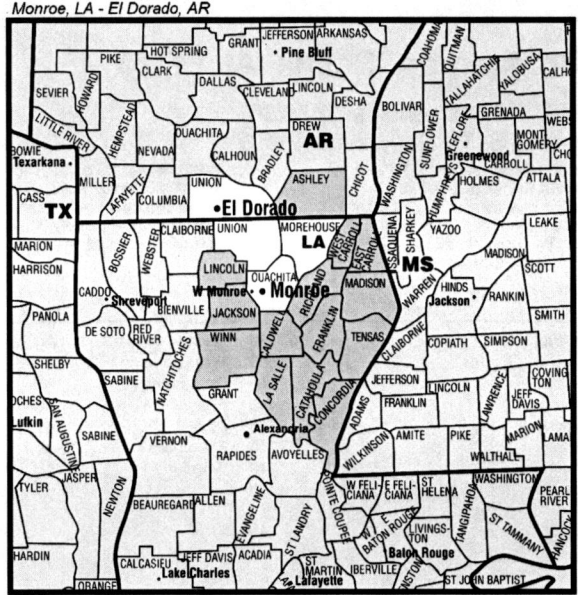

DMA TV Households: 179,190
% of U.S. TV Households: .157

KNOE-TV Monroe, LA, ch. 8, CBS, CW
KAQY Columbia, LA, ch. 11, ABC
***KETZ** El Dorado, AR, ch. 12, ETV
***KLTM-TV** Monroe, LA, ch. 13, ETV
KTVE El Dorado, AR, ch. 27, NBC
KARD West Monroe, LA, ch. 36, Fox
KMCT-TV West Monroe, LA, ch. 39, IND
KEJB El Dorado, AR, ch. 43, MyNetworkTV

DMA Counties	State	TV Households	DMA Counties	State	TV Households
Ashley	AR	8,750	Lincoln	LA	15,910
Union	AR	17,080	Madison	LA	3,960
Caldwell	LA	3,930	Morehouse	LA	10,800
Catahoula	LA	4,040	Ouachita	LA	57,670
Concordia	LA	7,310	Richland	LA	7,520
East Carroll	LA	2,500	Tensas	LA	2,170
Franklin	LA	7,350	Union	LA	9,260
Jackson	LA	6,130	West Carroll	LA	4,160
La Salle	LA	5,220	Winn	LA	5,430

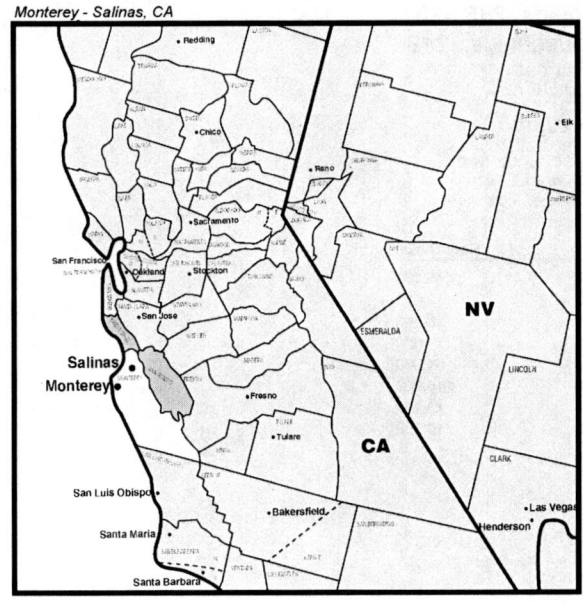

Monterey-Salinas, CA (124)

DMA TV Households: 225,350
% of U.S. TV Households: .197

KSBW Salinas, CA, ch. 8, NBC
***KQET** Watsonville, CA, ch. 25, ETV
KCBA Salinas, CA, ch. 35, Fox
KION-TV Monterey, CA, ch. 46, CBS
KSMS-TV Monterey, CA, ch. 67, Univision

DMA Counties	State	TV Households
Monterey	CA	120,530
San Benito	CA	16,160
Santa Cruz	CA	88,660

Maps courtesy of Nielsen Media Research

Montgomery-Selma, AL (118)

DMA TV Households: 247,230
% of U.S. TV Households: .216

*WDIQ Dozier, AL, ch. 2, ETV
WAKA Selma, AL, ch. 8, CBS
WSFA Montgomery, AL, ch. 12, NBC
WCOV-TV Montgomery, AL, ch. 20, Fox
WBMM Tuskegee, AL, ch. 22, CW
*WAIQ Montgomery, AL, ch. 26, ETV
WBIH Selma, AL, ch. 29, IND
WNCF Montgomery, AL, ch. 32, ABC
*WIIQ Demopolis, AL, ch. 41, ETV
WMCF-TV Montgomery, AL, ch. 46, IND
WRJM-TV Troy, AL, ch. 67, MyNetworkTV

DMA Counties	State	TV Households	DMA Counties	State	TV Households
Autauga	AL	19,390	Macon	AL	8,400
Bullock	AL	3,610	Marengo	AL	8,560
Butler	AL	8,200	Montgomery	AL	89,950
Covington	AL	15,740	Perry	AL	3,900
Crenshaw	AL	5,850	Pike	AL	12,360
Dallas	AL	17,010	Tallapoosa	AL	16,670
Elmore	AL	27,910	Wilcox	AL	4,880
Lowndes	AL	4,800			

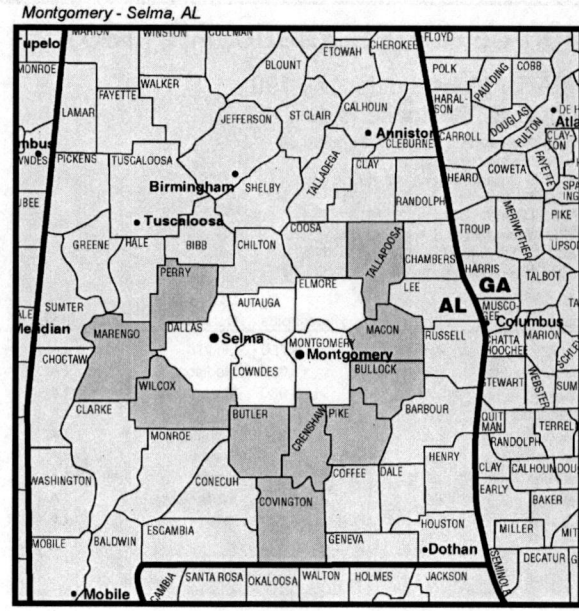

Montgomery - Selma, AL

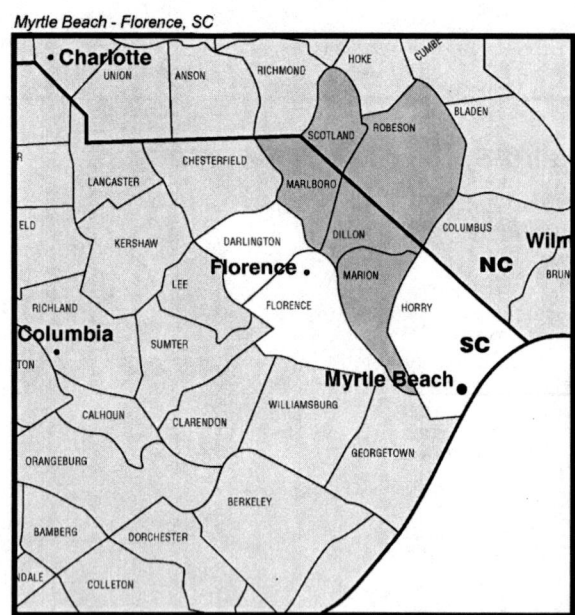

Myrtle Beach - Florence, SC

Myrtle Beach-Florence, SC (104)

DMA TV Households: 285,010
% of U.S. TV Households: .249

WBTW Florence, SC, ch. 13, CBS
WPDE-TV Florence, SC, ch. 15, ABC
WWMB Florence, SC, ch. 21, CW
*WHMC Conway, SC, ch. 23, ETV
*WUNU Lumberton, NC, ch. 31, ETV
WMBF-TV Myrtle Beach, SC, ch. 32, NBC
*WJMP-TV Florence, SC, ch. 33, ETV
WFXB Myrtle Beach, SC, ch. 43, Fox

DMA Counties	State	TV Households
Robeson	NC	45,180
Scotland	NC	13,690
Darlington	SC	25,190
Dillon	SC	11,600
Florence	SC	51,030
Horry	SC	115,000
Marion	SC	13,100
Marlboro	SC	10,220

Maps courtesy of Nielsen Media Research

Nashville (29)

DMA TV Households: 1,016,290
% of U.S. TV Households: .888

WKRN-TV Nashville, ch. 2, ABC
WSMV Nashville, ch. 4, NBC
WTVF Nashville, ch. 5, CBS
*WNPT Nashville, ch. 8, ETV
WZTV Nashville, ch. 17, Fox
*WCTE Cookeville, TN, ch. 22, ETV
WUXP-TV Nashville, ch. 30, MyNetworkTV
WPGD-TV Hendersonville, TN, ch. 33, IND
WNPX-TV Cookeville, TN, ch. 36, ION Television
WHTN Murfreesboro, TN, ch. 39, IND
WNAB Nashville, ch. 58, CW
WJFB Lebanon, TN, ch. 66, IND

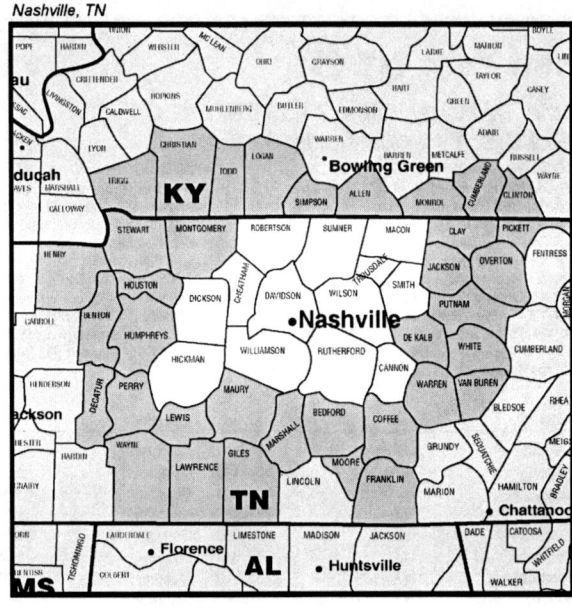

Nashville, TN

DMA Counties	State	TV Households	DMA Counties	State	TV Households
Allen	KY	7,450	Jackson	TN	4,430
Christian	KY	29,170	Lawrence	TN	16,020
Clinton	KY	4,100	Lewis	TN	4,460
Cumberland	KY	2,700	Macon	TN	8,430
Logan	KY	10,960	Marshall	TN	11,390
Monroe	KY	4,760	Maury	TN	32,060
Simpson	KY	6,860	Montgomery	TN	59,100
Todd	KY	4,610	Moore	TN	2,470
Trigg	KY	5,750	Overton	TN	8,680
Bedford	TN	16,540	Perry	TN	3,080
Benton	TN	6,790	Pickett	TN	2,070
Cannon	TN	5,330	Putnam	TN	28,370
Cheatham	TN	14,400	Robertson	TN	24,150
Clay	TN	3,430	Rutherford	TN	95,490
Coffee	TN	20,840	Smith	TN	7,440
Davidson	TN	266,620	Stewart	TN	5,250
Decatur	TN	4,630	Sumner	TN	60,860
De Kalb	TN	7,550	Trousdale	TN	2,980
Dickson	TN	18,580	Van Buren	TN	2,280
Franklin	TN	16,250	Warren	TN	15,940
Giles	TN	11,620	Wayne	TN	5,880
Henry	TN	13,320	White	TN	10,230
Hickman	TN	8,730	Williamson	TN	62,250
Houston	TN	3,260	Wilson	TN	41,180
Humphreys	TN	7,550			

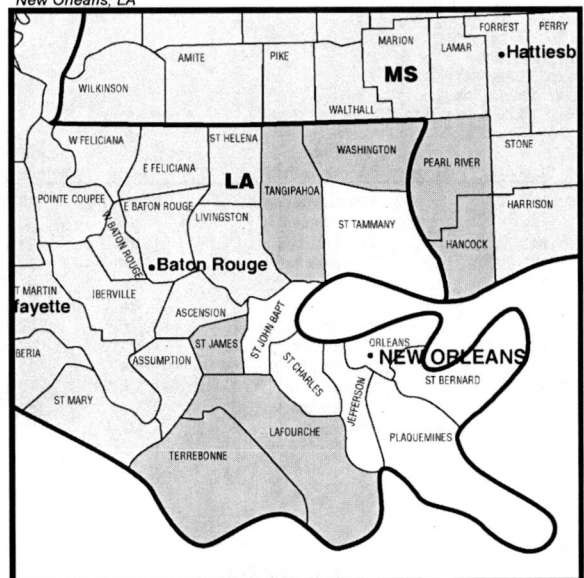

New Orleans, LA

New Orleans (53)

DMA TV Households: 602,740
% of U.S. TV Households: .527

WWL-TV New Orleans, ch. 4, CBS
WDSU-TV New Orleans, ch. 6, NBC
WVUE New Orleans, ch. 8, Fox
*WYES-TV New Orleans, ch. 12, ETV
WHNO New Orleans, ch. 20, IND
WGNO New Orleans, ch. 26, ABC
*WLAE-TV New Orleans, ch. 32, ETV
WNOL-TV New Orleans, ch. 38, CW
KGLA-TV Hammond, LA, ch. 42, Telemundo
WPXL-TV New Orleans, ch. 50, ION Television
WUPL Slidell, LA, ch. 54, MyNetworkTV

DMA Counties	State	TV Households	DMA Counties	State	TV Households
Jefferson	LA	166,330	St. John the Baptist	LA	16,630
Lafourche	LA	34,240	St. Tammany	LA	84,860
Orleans	LA	117,760	Tangipahoa	LA	43,690
Plaquemines	LA	8,230	Terrebonne	LA	38,370
St. Bernard	LA	11,260	Washington	LA	17,250
St. Charles	LA	18,210	Hancock	MS	16,130
St. James	LA	7,450	Pearl River	MS	22,330

Maps courtesy of Nielsen Media Research

New York, NY (1)

DMA TV Households: 7,433,820
% of U.S. TV Households: 6.495

WCBS-TV New York, ch. 2, CBS
WNBC New York, ch. 4, NBC
WNYW New York, ch. 5, Fox
WABC-TV New York, ch. 7, ABC
WWOR-TV Secaucus, NJ, ch. 9, MyNetworkTV
WPIX New York, ch. 11, CW
*****WNET** Newark, NJ, ch. 13, ETV
*****WLIW** Garden City, NY, ch. 21, ETV
*****WNYE-TV** New York, ch. 25, ETV
WPXN-TV New York, ch. 31, ION Television
WXTV Paterson, NJ, ch. 41, Univision
WSAH Bridgeport, CT, ch. 43, Azteca America

WNJU Linden, NJ, ch. 47, Telemundo
*****WEDW** Bridgeport, CT, ch. 49, ETV
*****WNJN** Montclair, NJ, ch. 50, ETV
WTBY-TV Poughkeepsie, NY, ch. 54, IND
WLNY Riverhead, NY, ch. 57, IND
*****WNJB** New Brunswick, NJ, ch. 58, ETV
WMBC-TV Newton, NJ, ch. 63, IND
WRNN-TV Kingston, NY, ch. 63, IND
*****WFME-TV** West Milford, NJ, ch. 66, ETV
WFTY-TV Smithtown, NY, ch. 67, IND
WFUT-TV Newark, NJ, ch. 68, TeleFutura

New York, NY

DMA Counties	State	TV Households	DMA Counties	State	TV Households
Fairfield	CT	325,740	Dutchess	NY	104,230
Bergen	NJ	333,540	Kings	NY	865,890
Essex	NJ	273,970	Nassau	NY	431,640
Hudson	NJ	221,690	New York	NY	744,560
Hunterdon	NJ	46,520	Orange	NY	127,120
Middlesex	NJ	278,160	Putnam	NY	34,240
Monmouth	NJ	235,940	Queens	NY	771,390
Morris	NJ	177,440	Richmond	NY	172,550
5505550cean	NJ	224,690	Rockland	NY	93,860
Passaic	NJ	159,650	Suffolk	NY	481,260
Somerset	NJ	117,740	Sullivan	NY	28,590
Sussex	NJ	54,700	Ulster	NY	69,150
Union	NJ	183,420	Westchester	NY	342,160
Warren	NJ	41,750	Pike	PA	22,870
Bronx	NY	469,360			

Norfolk - Portsmouth - Newport News, VA

Norfolk-Portsmouth-Newport News, VA (43)

DMA TV Households: 718,020
% of U.S. TV Households: .627

WTKR Norfolk, VA, ch. 3, CBS
WSKY-TV Manteo, NC, ch. 4, IND
WAVY-TV Portsmouth, VA, ch. 10, NBC
WVEC Hampton, VA, ch. 13, ABC
*****WHRO-TV** Hampton-Norfolk, VA, ch. 15, ETV
WHRE Virginia Beach, VA, ch. 21, IND
WGNT Portsmouth, VA, ch. 27, CW
WTVZ-TV Norfolk, VA, ch. 33, MyNetworkTV
WVBT Virginia Beach, VA, ch. 43, Fox
WPXV-TV Norfolk, VA, ch. 46, ION Television

DMA Counties	State	TV Households	DMA Counties	State	TV Households
Camden	NC	3,980	Isle of Wight	VA	13,750
Chowan	NC	5,900	James City	VA	30,160
Currituck	NC	9,630	Mathews	VA	3,940
Dare	NC	14,790	Newport News City	VA	73,490
Gates	NC	4,560	Norfolk City	VA	87,790
Hertford	NC	8,870	Northampton	VA	5,550
Pasquotank	NC	15,800	Portsmouth City	VA	38,530
Perquimans	NC	5,430	Southampton	VA	10,560
Accomack	VA	15,270	Suffolk City	VA	31,230
Chesapeake City	VA	78,290	Surry	VA	2,780
Gloucester	VA	14,560	Virginia Beach	VA	162,150
Hampton City	VA	53,700	York	VA	27,310

Maps courtesy of Nielsen Media Research

North Platte, NE (209)

DMA TV Households: 15,250
% of U.S. TV Households: .013

KNOP-TV North Platte, NE, ch. 2, NBC
*KPNE-TV North Platte, NE, ch. 9, ETV

DMA Counties	State	TV Households
Lincoln	NE	14,750
Logan	NE	300
McPherson	NE	200

North Platte, NE

Odessa - Midland, TX

Odessa-Midland, TX (156)

DMA TV Households: 141,560
% of U.S. TV Households: .124

KMID Midland, TX, ch. 2, ABC
KWAB-TV Big Spring, TX, ch. 4, satellite to KWES-TV
KOSA-TV Odessa, TX, ch. 7, CBS, MyNetworkTV
KWES-TV Odessa, TX, ch. 9, NBC
KUPB Midland, TX, ch. 18, Univision
KPEJ Odessa, TX, ch. 24, IND
KWWT Odessa, TX, ch. 30, CW
*KPBT-TV Odessa, TX, ch. 36, ETV
KMLM Odessa, TX, ch. 42, IND

DMA Counties	State	TV Households	DMA Counties	State	TV Households
Lea South	NM	1,990	Midland	TX	48,170
Andrews	TX	4,890	Pecos	TX	5,000
Brewster	TX	3,420	Presidio	TX	2,720
Crane	TX	1,290	Reagan	TX	1,090
Ector	TX	47,600	Reeves	TX	3,460
Glasscock	TX	400	Terrell	TX	380
Howard	TX	11,030	Upton	TX	1,180
Jeff Davis	TX	910	Ward	TX	3,860
Loving	TX	100	Winkler	TX	2,480
Martin	TX	1,590			

Maps courtesy of Nielsen Media Research

Oklahoma City, OK

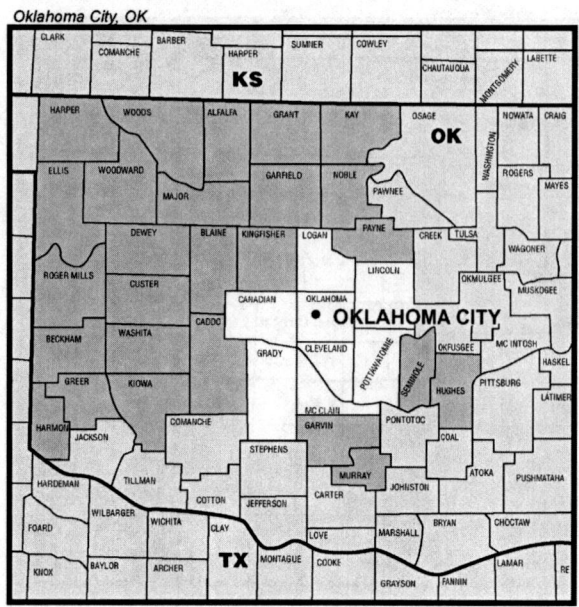

Oklahoma City (45)

DMA TV Households: 687,300
% of U.S. TV Households: .600

KFOR-TV Oklahoma City, ch. 4, NBC
KOCO-TV Oklahoma City, ch. 5, ABC
*****KWET** Cheyenne, OK, ch. 8, ETV
KWTV Oklahoma City, ch. 9, CBS
*****KETA** Oklahoma City, ch. 13, ETV
KTBO-TV Oklahoma City, ch. 15, IND
KOKH-TV Oklahoma City, ch. 25, Fox
KTUZ-TV Shawnee, OK, ch. 30, Telemundo
KOCB Oklahoma City, ch. 34, CW
KUOK Woodward, OK, ch. 35, Univision
KAUT-TV Oklahoma City, ch. 43, MyNetworkTV
KOCM Norman, OK, ch. 46, IND
KOPX-TV Oklahoma City, ch. 50, ION Television
KSBI Oklahoma City, ch. 51, IND

DMA Counties	State	TV Households	DMA Counties	State	TV Households
Alfalfa	OK	1,960	Kay	OK	17,920
Beckham	OK	8,020	Kingfisher	OK	5,450
Blaine	OK	3,960	Kiowa	OK	3,870
Caddo	OK	10,520	Lincoln	OK	12,360
Canadian	OK	39,340	Logan	OK	13,950
Cleveland	OK	94,300	Major	OK	2,950
Custer	OK	10,410	McClain	OK	12,320
Dewey	OK	1,780	Murray	OK	5,070
Ellis	OK	1,760	Noble	OK	4,450
Garfield	OK	23,240	Oklahoma	OK	287,990
Garvin	OK	10,780	Payne	OK	31,610
Grady	OK	19,840	Pottawatomie	OK	25,620
Grant	OK	1,780	Roger Mills	OK	1,470
Greer	OK	2,090	Seminole	OK	9,330
Harmon	OK	1,080	Washita	OK	4,620
Harper	OK	1,370	Woods	OK	3,370
Hughes	OK	5,090	Woodward	OK	7,630

Omaha (76)

DMA TV Households: 411,520
% of U.S. TV Households: .360

WOWT Omaha, ch. 6, NBC
KETV Omaha, ch. 7, ABC
KXVO Omaha, ch. 15, CW
*****KYNE-TV** Omaha, ch. 26, ETV
*****KBIN** Council Bluffs, IA, ch. 32, ETV
*****KHIN** Red Oak, IA, ch. 36, ETV
KPTM Omaha, ch. 42, Fox, MyNetworkTV
KMTV-TV Omaha, ch. 45, CBS

DMA Counties	State	TV Households	DMA Counties	State	TV Households
Cass	IA	5,780	Colfax	NE	3,270
Crawford	IA	6,280	Cuming	NE	3,590
Fremont	IA	3,080	Dodge	NE	14,540
Harrison	IA	6,070	Douglas	NE	198,880
Mills	IA	5,680	Johnson	NE	1,690
Montgomery	IA	4,480	Nemaha	NE	2,880
Page	IA	6,130	Otoe	NE	6,180
Pottawattamie	IA	35,390	Platte	NE	12,540
Shelby	IA	4,880	Richardson	NE	3,360
Atchison	MO	2,570	Sarpy	NE	56,320
Burt	NE	2,790	Saunders	NE	7,680
Cass	NE	9,880	Washington	NE	7,580

Omaha, NE

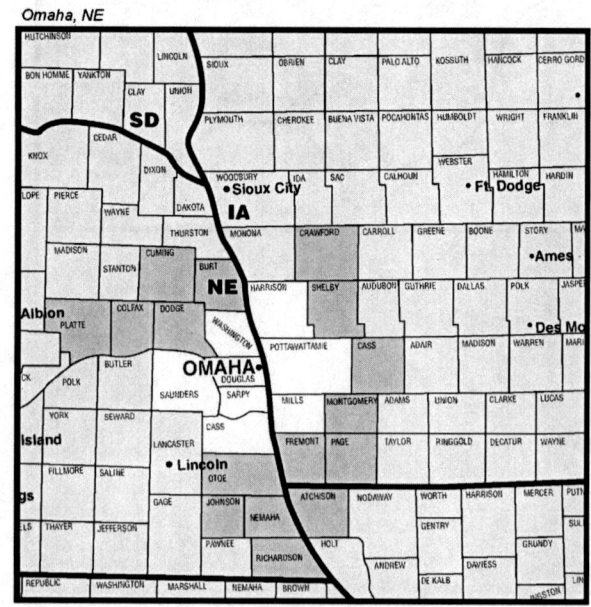

Orlando-Daytona Beach-Melbourne, FL (19)

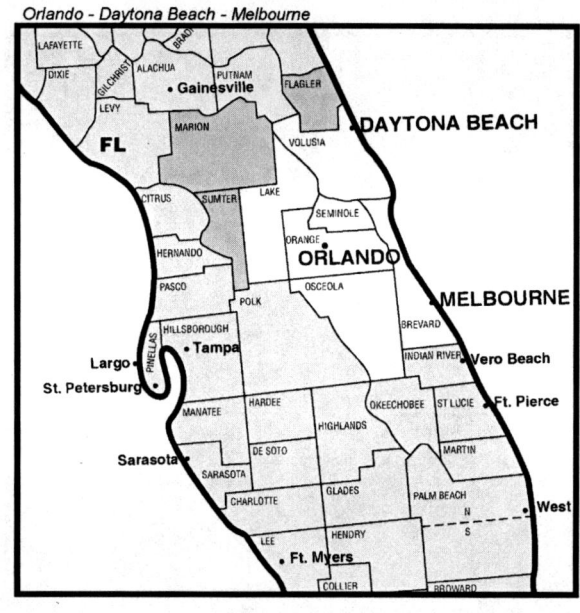

Orlando - Daytona Beach - Melbourne

DMA TV Households: 1,466,420
% of U.S. TV Households: 1.281

WESH Daytona Beach, FL, ch. 2, NBC
WKMG-TV Orlando, FL, ch. 6, CBS
WFTV Orlando, FL, ch. 9, ABC
***WDSC-TV** New Smyrna Beach, FL, ch. 15, ETV
WKCF Clermont, FL, ch. 18, CW
***WMFE-TV** Orlando, FL, ch. 24, ETV
WVEN-TV Daytona Beach, FL, ch. 26, Univision
WRDQ Orlando, FL, ch. 27, IND

WOFL Orlando, FL, ch. 35, Fox
WACX-DT Leesburg, FL, ch. 40, IND
WOTF-TV Melbourne, FL, ch. 43, TeleFutura
WTGL Leesburg, FL, ch. 45, IND
WHLV-TV Cocoa, FL, ch. 52, IND
WOPX-TV Melbourne, FL, ch. 48, ION
WRBW Orlando, FL, ch. 65, MyNetworkTV
***WBCC** Cocoa, FL, ch. 30, ETV

DMA Counties	State	TV Households	DMA Counties	State	TV Households
Brevard	FL	231,480	Osceola	FL	98,440
Flagler	FL	44,100	Seminole	FL	163,810
Lake	FL	126,220	Sumter	FL	34,690
Marion	FL	140,280	Volusia	FL	212,840
Orange	FL	414,560			

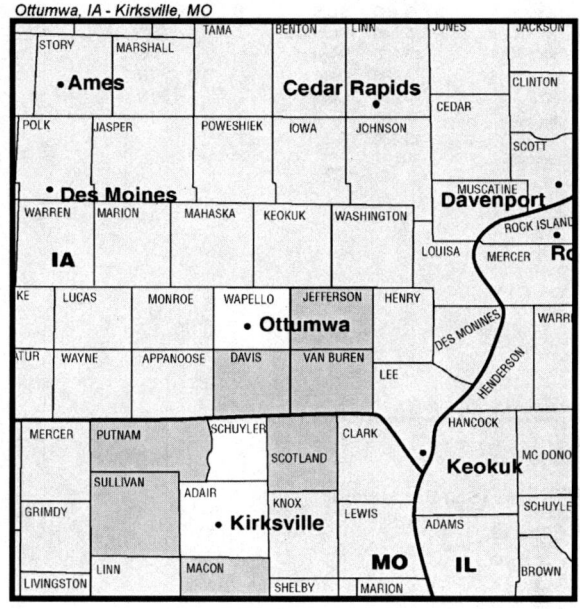

Ottumwa, IA - Kirksville, MO

Ottumwa, Iowa-Kirksville, MO (200)

DMA TV Households: 51,270
% of U.S. TV Households: .045

KTVO Kirksville, MO, ch. 3, ABC
KYOU-TV Ottumwa, IA, ch. 15, IND

DMA Counties	State	TV Households
Davis	IA	3,130
Jefferson	IA	6,350
Van Buren	IA	3,180
Wapello	IA	14,600
Adair	MO	9,520
Macon	MO	6,400
Putnam	MO	2,080
Schuyler	MO	1,690
Scotland	MO	1,760
Sullivan	MO	2,630

Maps courtesy of Nielsen Media Research

Paducah, KY - Cape Girardeau, MO - Harrisburg, IL

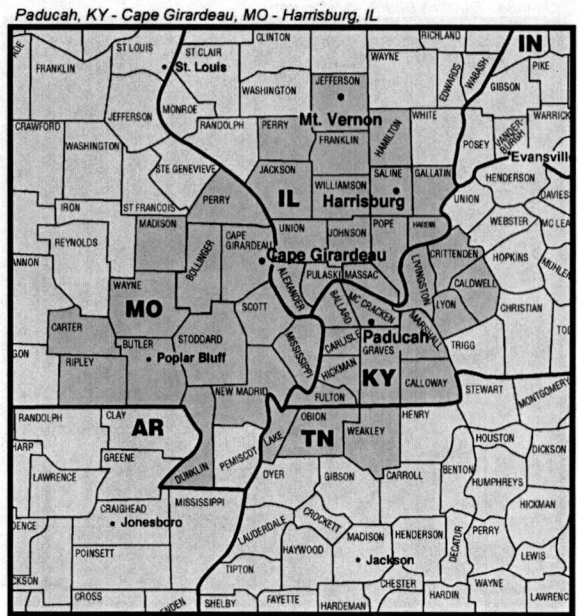

Paducah, KY-Cape Girardeau, MO-Harrisburg, IL (78)

DMA TV Households: 393,260
% of U.S. TV Households: .344

WSIL-TV Harrisburg, IL, ch. 3, ABC
WPSD-TV Paducah, KY, ch. 6, NBC
***WSIU-TV** Carbondale, IL, ch. 8, ETV
KFVS-TV Cape Girardeau, MO, ch. 12, CBS
KPOB-TV Poplar Bluff, MO, ch. 15, satellite to WSIL-TV
KBSI Cape Girardeau, MO, ch. 23, Fox
WTCT Marion, IL, ch. 27, IND
***WKMU** Murray, KY, ch. 36, ETV
***WKPD** Paducah, KY, ch. 41, ETV
WDKA Paducah, KY, ch. 49, MyNetworkTV

DMA Counties	State	TV Households	DMA Counties	State	TV Households
Alexander	IL	3,280	Hickman	KY	2,090
Franklin	IL	16,750	Livingston	KY	3,960
Gallatin	IL	2,580	Lyon	KY	2,980
Hamilton	IL	3,270	Marshall	KY	13,250
Hardin	IL	1,880	McCracken	KY	28,040
Jackson	IL	24,550	Bollinger	MO	4,660
Jefferson	IL	15,600	Butler	MO	17,140
Johnson	IL	4,450	Cape Girardeau	MO	29,720
Massac	IL	6,260	Carter	MO	2,300
Perry	IL	8,440	Dunklin	MO	12,640
Pope	IL	1,690	Madison	MO	4,950
Pulaski	IL	2,470	Mississippi	MO	5,380
Saline	IL	10,720	New Madrid	MO	7,080
Union	IL	7,360	Perry	MO	7,360
Williamson	IL	27,310	Ripley	MO	5,350
Ballard	KY	3,480	Scott	MO	16,000
Caldwell	KY	5,340	Stoddard	MO	12,220
Calloway	KY	15,270	Wayne	MO	5,330
Carlisle	KY	2,190	Lake	TN	2,080
Crittenden	KY	3,780	Obion	TN	13,020
Fulton	KY	2,780	Weakley	TN	13,210
Graves	KY	15,050			

Palm Springs, CA (142)

DMA TV Households: 159,240
% of U.S. TV Households: .139

KMIR-TV Palm Springs, CA, ch. 36, NBC
KESQ-TV Palm Springs, CA, ch. 42, ABC, CW

DMA Counties	State	TV Households
Riverside Central	CA	159,240

Palm Springs, CA

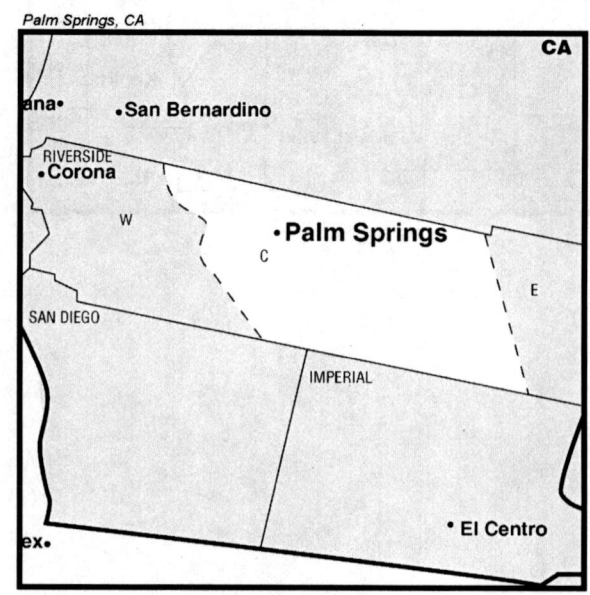

Maps courtesy of Nielsen Media Research

Panama City, FL (151)

DMA TV Households: 147,520
% of U.S. TV Households: .129

WJHG-TV Panama City, FL, ch. 7, NBC, CW, MyNetworkTV
WMBB Panama City, FL, ch. 13, ABC
WPGX Panama City, FL, ch. 28, IND
WPCT Panama City Beach, FL, ch. 46, IND
WBIF Marianna, FL, ch. 51, IND
***WFSG** Panama City, FL, ch. 56, ETV

DMA Counties	State	TV Households
Bay	FL	71,150
Calhoun	FL	4,910
Franklin	FL	4,790
Gulf	FL	5,810
Holmes	FL	7,450
Jackson	FL	17,980
Liberty	FL	2,540
Walton	FL	23,870
Washington	FL	9,020

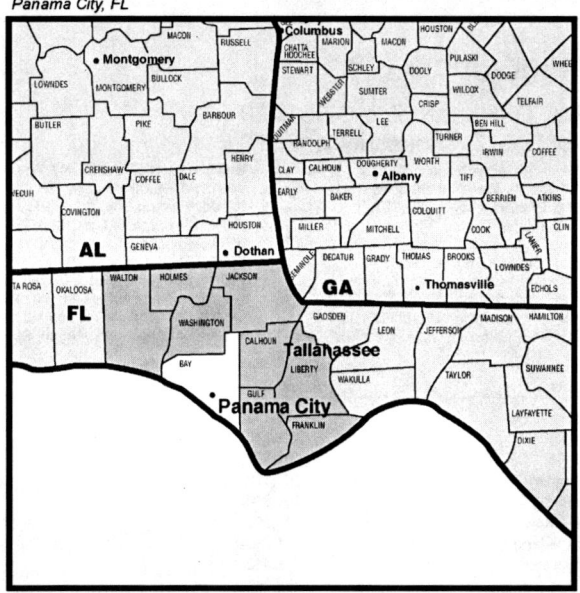

Panama City, FL

Parkersburg, WV (193)

DMA TV Households: 63,760
% of U.S. TV Households: .056

WTAP-TV Parkersburg, WV, ch. 15, NBC, Fox, MyNetworkTV

DMA Counties	State	TV Households
Washington	OH	24,810
Pleasants	WV	2,790
Wood	WV	36,160

Parkersburg, WV

Peoria-Bloomington, IL (116)

DMA TV Households: 248,510
% of U.S. TV Households: .217

WHOI Peoria, IL, ch. 19, ABC, CW
WEEK-TV Peoria, IL, ch. 25, NBC
WMBD-TV Peoria, IL, ch. 31, CBS
WYZZ-TV Bloomington, IL, ch. 43, Fox
***WTVP** Peoria, IL, ch. 47, ETV
WAOE Peoria, IL, ch. 59, MyNetworkTV

DMA Counties	State	TV Households
Fulton	IL	14,340
Livingston	IL	13,690
Marshall	IL	5,150
Mason	IL	5,970
McLean	IL	64,010
Peoria	IL	73,670
Putnam	IL	2,390
Stark	IL	2,480
Tazewell	IL	52,840
Woodford	IL	13,970

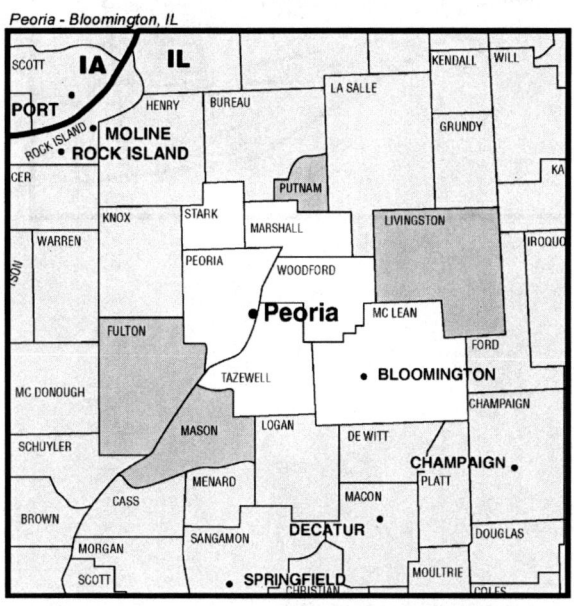

Peoria - Bloomington, IL

Maps courtesy of Nielsen Media Research

Philadelphia (4)

DMA TV Households: 2,950,220
% of U.S. TV Households: 2.578

KYW-TV Philadelphia, ch. 3, CBS
WPVI-TV Philadelphia, ch. 6, ABC
WCAU Philadelphia, ch. 10, NBC
WHYY-TV Wilmington, DE, ch. 12, ETV
WPHL-TV Philadelphia, ch. 17, MyNetworkTV
*****WNJS** Camden, NJ, ch. 23, ETV
WTXF-TV Philadelphia, ch. 42, Fox
*****WYBE** Philadelphia, ch. 35, ETV
*****WLVT-TV** Allentown, PA, ch. 39, ETV
WMGM-TV Wildwood, NJ, ch. 40, NBC

WMCN-TV Atlantic City, NJ, ch. 44, IND
WGTW-TV Burlington, NJ, ch. 27, IND
WTVE Reading, PA, ch. 51, IND
*****WNJT** Trenton, NJ, ch. 52, ETV
WPSG Philadelphia, ch. 57, CW
WBPH-TV Bethlehem, PA, ch. 60, IND
WPPX-TV Wilmington, DE, ch. 31, ION Television
WWSI Atlantic City, NJ, ch. 49, Telemundo
WUVP-TV Vineland, NJ, ch. 65, Univision
WFMZ-TV Allentown, PA, ch. 69, IND

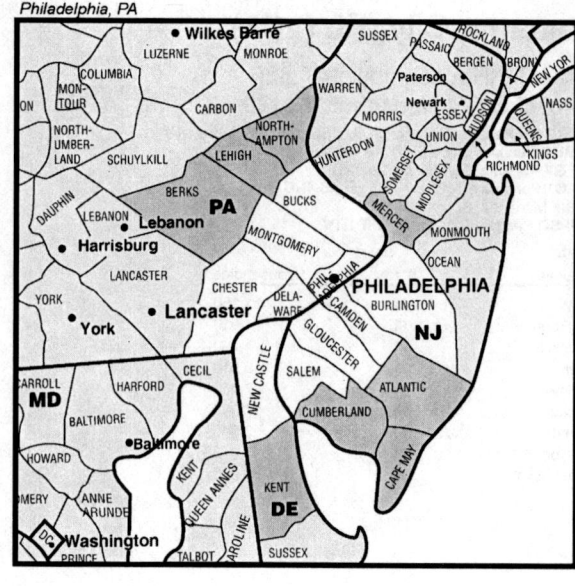

Philadelphia, PA

DMA Counties	State	TV Households
Kent	DE	59,980
New Castle	DE	200,070
Atlantic	NJ	102,780
Burlington	NJ	166,510
Camden	NJ	189,960
Cape May	NJ	40,210
Cumberland	NJ	51,790
Gloucester	NJ	105,440
Mercer	NJ	128,740
Salem	NJ	25,190
Berks	PA	152,880
Bucks	PA	232,190
Chester	PA	182,090
Delaware	PA	207,240
Lehigh	PA	134,210
Montgomery	PA	300,630
Northampton	PA	114,420
Philadelphia	PA	555,890

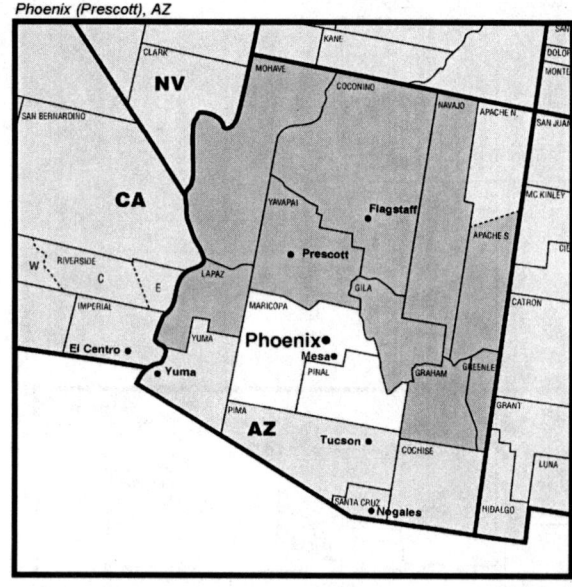

Phoenix (Prescott), AZ

Phoenix (Prescott), AZ (12)

DMA TV Households: 1,855,930
% of U.S. TV Households: 1.622

KNAZ-TV Flagstaff, AZ, ch. 2, NBC
KTVK Phoenix, ch. 3, IND
KPHO-TV Phoenix, ch. 5, CBS
KMOH-TV Kingman, AZ, ch. 6,
  satellite to KBEH
KAZT-TV Prescott, AZ, ch. 7, IND
*****KAET** Phoenix, ch. 8, ETV
KCFG Flagstaff, AZ, ch. 9, IND
KSAZ-TV Phoenix, ch. 10, Fox
*****KDTP** Holbrook, AZ, ch. 11, IND

KPNX Mesa, AZ, ch. 12, NBC
KFPH-TV Flagstaff, AZ, ch. 13, TeleFutura
KNXV-TV Phoenix, ch. 15, ABC
KPAZ-TV Phoenix, ch. 20, IND
KTVW-TV Phoenix, ch. 33, Univision
KTAZ Phoenix, ch. 39, Telemundo
KUTP Phoenix, ch. 45, MyNetworkTV
KPPX Tolleson, AZ, ch. 51, ION Television
KASW Phoenix, ch. 61, CW

DMA Counties	State	TV Households
Apache S.	AZ	4,950
Coconino	AZ	45,880
Gila	AZ	21,140
Graham	AZ	10,800
Greenlee	AZ	3,050
La Paz	AZ	9,010
Maricopa	AZ	1,428,130
Mohave	AZ	82,130
Navajo	AZ	34,330
Pinal	AZ	124,700
Yavapai	AZ	91,810

Pittsburgh, PA

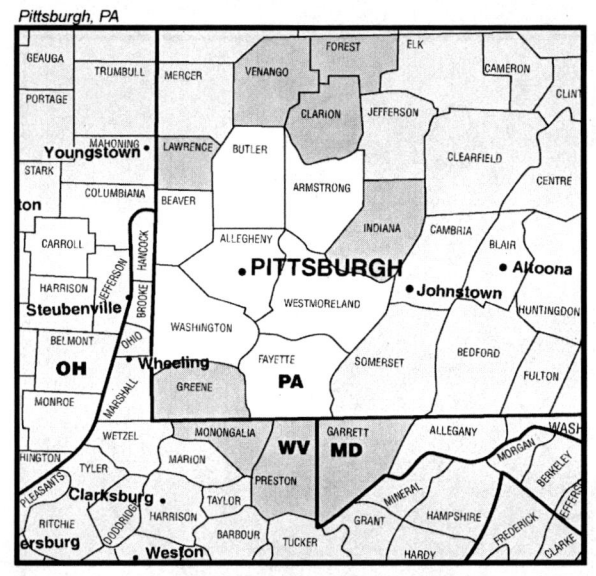

Pittsburgh (23)

DMA TV Households: 1,156,460
% of U.S. TV Households: 1.010

KDKA-TV Pittsburgh, ch. 2, CBS
WTAE-TV Pittsburgh, ch. 4, ABC
WPXI Pittsburgh, ch. 11, NBC
*****WQED** Pittsburgh, ch. 13, ETV
WQEX Pittsburgh, ch. 16, IND
WPCW Jeannette, PA, ch. 19, CW

WPMY Pittsburgh, ch. 22, MyNetworkTV
*****WNPB-TV** Morgantown, WV, ch. 33, ETV
*****WGPT** Oakland, MD, ch. 36, ETV
WPCB-TV Greensburg, PA, ch. 50, IND
WPGH-TV Pittsburgh, ch. 53, Fox

DMA Counties	State	TV Households	DMA Counties	State	TV Households
Garrett	MD	11,400	Greene	PA	14,820
Allegheny	PA	513,180	Indiana	PA	34,500
Armstrong	PA	28,090	Lawrence	PA	35,590
Beaver	PA	69,980	Venango	PA	21,730
Butler	PA	71,060	Washington	PA	83,080
Clarion	PA	15,9190	Westmoreland	PA	148,890
Fayette	PA	58,810	Monongalia	WV	35,040
Forest	PA	2,060	Preston	WV	12,420

Portland-Auburn, ME (77)

DMA TV Households: 410,890
% of U.S. TV Households: .359

WCSH Portland, ME, ch. 6, NBC
WMTW Poland Spring, ME, ch. 8, ABC
*****WCBB** Augusta, ME, ch. 10, ETV
WGME-TV Portland, ME, ch. 13, CBS
WPFO Waterville, ME, ch. 23, Fox
*****WMEA-TV** Biddeford, ME, ch. 26, ETV
WPME Lewiston, ME, ch. 35, MyNetworkTV
WPXT Portland, ME, ch. 51, CW

DMA Counties	State	TV Households
Androscoggin	ME	44,950
Cumberland	ME	113,720
Franklin	ME	12,300
Kennebec	ME	51,280
Knox	ME	17,300
Lincoln	ME	15,170
Oxford	ME	23,850
Sagadahoc	ME	14,970
York	ME	83,310
Carroll	NH	20,100
Coos	NH	13,940

Portland - Auburn, ME

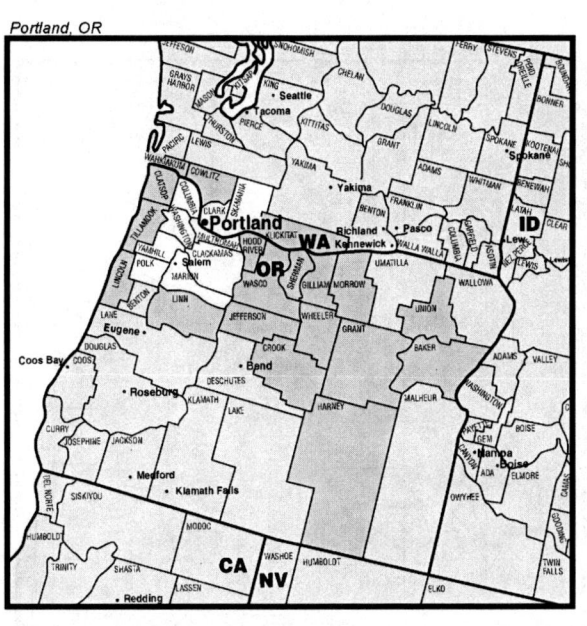

Portland, OR

Portland, OR (22)

DMA TV Households: 1,175,100
% of U.S. TV Households: 1.027

KATU Portland, OR, ch. 2, ABC
KOIN Portland, OR, ch. 6, CBS
KGW-TV Portland, OR, ch. 8, NBC
*****KOPB-TV** Portland, OR, ch. 10, ETV
KPTV Portland, OR, ch. 12, Fox
*****KTVR** La Grande, OR, ch. 13, ETV

KUNP La Grande, OR, ch. 16, Univision
KPXG Salem, OR, ch. 22, ION Television
KNMT Portland, OR, ch. 45, IND
KRCW-TV Salem, OR, ch. 32, CW
KPDX Vancouver, WA, ch. 49, MyNetworkTV

DMA Counties	State	TV Households	DMA Counties	State	TV Households
Baker	OR	6,580	Multnomah	OR	291,700
Clackamas	OR	142,670	Polk	OR	26,300
Clatsop	OR	15,230	Sherman	OR	670
Columbia	OR	18,460	Tillamook	OR	10,610
Crook	OR	9,510	Union	OR	9,890
Gilliam	OR	770	Wasco	OR	9,340
Grant	OR	2,810	Washington	OR	198,580
Harney	OR	2,670	Wheeler	OR	580
Hood River	OR	7,180	Yamhill	OR	32,910
Jefferson	OR	7,630	Clark	WA	153,210
Lincoln	OR	19,550	Cowlitz	WA	38,290
Linn	OR	42,740	Klickitat	WA	7,570
Marion	OR	110,190	Skamania	WA	4,060
Morrow	OR	3,800	Wahkiakum	WA	1,600

Maps courtesy of Nielsen Media Research

Presque Isle, ME (204)

DMA TV Households: 31,270
% of U.S. TV Households: .027

WAGM-TV Presque Isle, ME, ch. 8, CBS, Fox
***WMEM-TV** Presque Isle, ME, ch. 10, ETV

DMA Counties	State	TV Households
Aroostook	ME	31,270

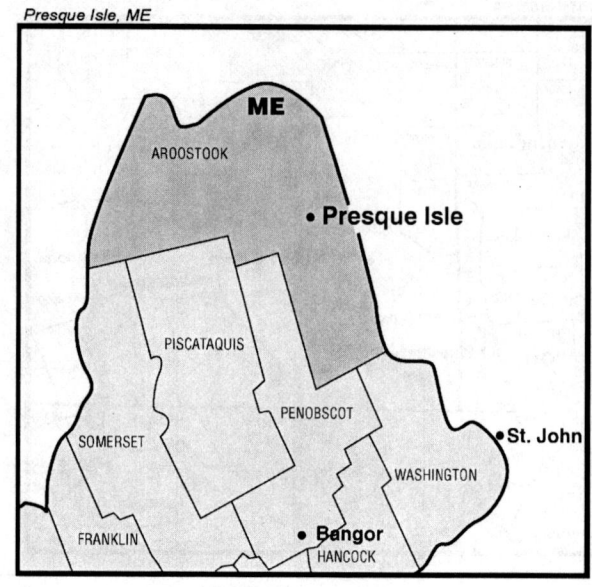

Presque Isle, ME

Providence, RI - New Bedford, MA

Providence, RI-New Bedford, MA (52)

DMA TV Households: 622,580
% of U.S. TV Households: .544

WLNE New Bedford, MA, ch. 6, ABC
WJAR Providence, RI, ch. 10, NBC
WPRI-TV Providence, RI, ch. 12, CBS
WPXQ-TV Block Island, RI, ch. 17, ION Television
WLWC New Bedford, MA, ch. 28, CW
***WSBE-TV** Providence, RI, ch. 36, ETV
WNAC-TV Providence, RI, ch. 64, Fox, MyNetworkTV

DMA Counties	State	TV Households
Bristol	MA	211,320
Bristol	RI	19,220
Kent	RI	68,890
Newport	RI	34,410
Providence	RI	239,000
Washington	RI	49,740

Quincy, IL-Hannibal, MO-Keokuk, IA (171)

DMA TV Households: 103,910
% of U.S. TV Households: .091

KHQA-TV Hannibal, MO, ch. 7, CBS, ABC
WGEM-TV Quincy, IL, ch. 10, NBC, CW, Fox
WTJR Quincy, IL, ch. 16, IND
***WMEC** Macomb, IL, ch. 22, ETV
***WQEC** Quincy, IL, ch. 27, ETV

DMA Counties	State	TV Households	DMA Counties	State	TV Households
Adams	IL	27,190	Clark	MO	2,980
Brown	IL	1,880	Knox	MO	1,650
Hancock	IL	7,550	Lewis	MO	3,770
McDonough	IL	11,930	Marion	MO	11,140
Pike	IL	6,570	Monroe	MO	3,680
Schuyler	IL	2,880	Ralls	MO	3,890
Scott	IL	2,090	Shelby	MO	2,580
Lee	IA	14,130			

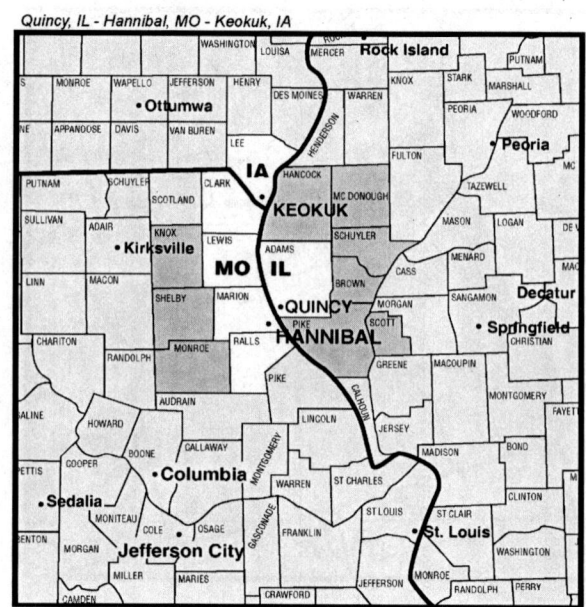

Quincy, IL - Hannibal, MO - Keokuk, IA

Maps courtesy of Nielsen Media Research

Raleigh-Durham (Fayetteville), NC (27)

DMA TV Households: 1,080,680
% of U.S. TV Households: .944

*WUNC-TV Chapel Hill, NC, ch. 4, ETV	WRAY-TV Wilson, NC, ch. 30, IND
WRAL-TV Raleigh, NC, ch. 5, CBS	*WUNP-TV Roanoke Rapids, NC, ch. 36, ETV
WTVD Durham, NC, ch. 11, ABC	WUVC-TV Fayetteville, NC, ch. 40, Univision
WNCN Goldsboro, NC, ch. 17, NBC	WRPX-TV Rocky Mount, NC, ch. 15, ION Television
WLFL Raleigh, NC, ch. 22, CW	WRAZ Raleigh, NC, ch. 50, Fox
WRDC Durham, NC, ch. 28, MyNetworkTV	WFPX-TV Fayetteville, NC, ch. 36, ION Television

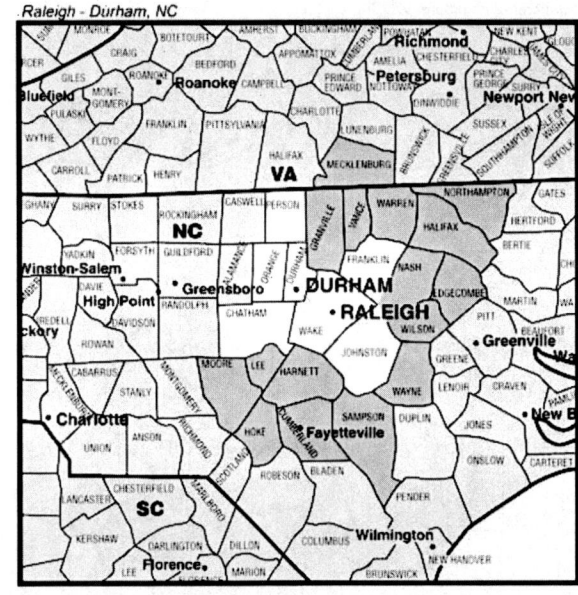

Raleigh - Durham, NC

DMA Counties	State	TV Households	DMA Counties	State	TV Households
Chatham	NC	25,420	Nash	NC	36,600
Cumberland	NC	114,860	Northampton	NC	8,580
Durham	NC	104,910	Orange	NC	49,000
Edgecombe	NC	19,230	Person	NC	15,240
Franklin	NC	22,420	Sampson	NC	24,170
Granville	NC	19,670	Vance	NC	16,700
Halifax	NC	21,790	Wake	NC	332,960
Harnett	NC	40,060	Warren	NC	7,730
Hoke	NC	15,240	Wayne	NC	44,550
Johnston	NC	60,970	Wilson	NC	30,530
Lee	NC	22,180	Mecklenburg	VA	13,370
Moore	NC	34,500			

Rapid City, SD (174)

DMA TV Households: 96,450
% of U.S. TV Households: .084

KOTA-TV Rapid City, SD, ch. 3, ABC	KHSD-TV Lead, SD, ch. 10, satellite to KOTA-TV
KIVV-TV Lead, SD, ch. 5, satellite to KEVN-TV	KSGW-TV Sheridan, WY, ch. 12, satellite to KOTA-TV
KEVN-TV Rapid City, SD, ch. 7, Fox	KCLO-TV Rapid City, SD, ch. 15, IND
KSWY Sheridan, WY, ch. 7, NBC	KNBN Rapid City, SD, ch. 21, NBC
*KZSD-TV Martin, SD, ch. 8, ETV	
*KBHE-TV Rapid City, SD, ch. 9, ETV	

Rapid City, SD

DMA Counties	State	TV Households	DMA Counties	State	TV Households
Carter	MT	490	Lawrence	SD	9,960
Morrill	NE	1,980	Meade	SD	9,130
Bennett	SD	1,080	Pennington	SD	39,120
Butte	SD	3,730	Perkins	SD	1,190
Custer	SD	3,330	Shannon	SD	3,010
Fall River	SD	3,020	Ziebach	SD	780
Haakon	SD	790	Crook	WY	2,650
Harding	SD	480	Sheridan	WY	12,010
Jackson	SD	890	Weston	WY	2,810

Reno, NV (108)

DMA TV Households: 271,080
% of U.S. TV Households: .237

KTVN Reno, ch. 2, CBS
KRNV Reno, ch. 4, NBC
*KNPB Reno, ch. 5, ETV
KWNV Winnemucca, NV, ch. 7, satellite to KRNV
KOLO-TV Reno, ch. 8, ABC
KRXI-TV Reno, ch. 11, Fox
KAME-TV Reno, ch. 21, MyNetworkTV
KREN-TV Reno, ch. 27, CW
KEGS Goldfield, NV, ch. 50, IND

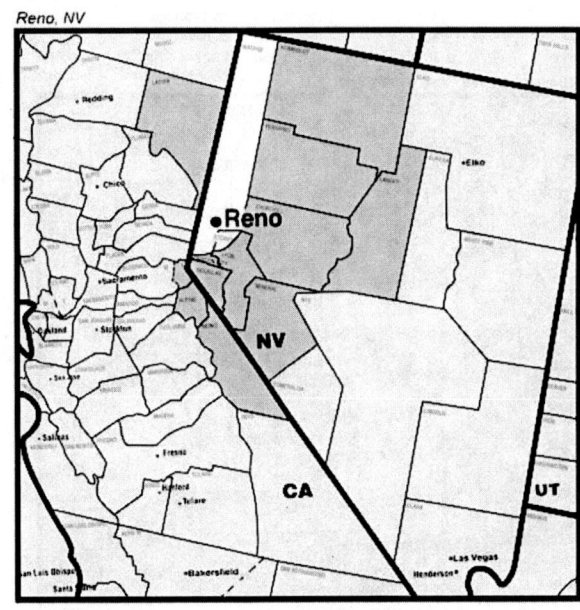

Reno, NV

DMA Counties	State	TV Households	DMA Counties	State	TV Households
Alpine	CA	460	Humboldt	NV	6,160
El Dorado East	CA	13,590	Lander	NV	1,800
Lassen	CA	9,570	Lyon	NV	20,940
Mono	CA	5,040	Mineral	NV	2,040
Carson City	NV	20,660	Pershing	NV	1,780
Churchill	NV	9,360	Storey	NV	1,830
Douglas	NV	18,920	Washoe	NV	158,930

Maps courtesy of Nielsen Media Research

Richmond - Petersburg, VA

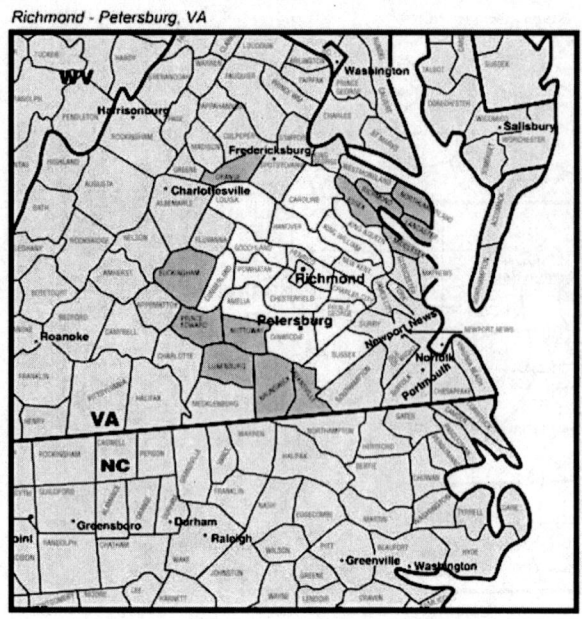

Richmond-Petersburg, VA (58)

DMA TV Households: 550,240
% of U.S. TV Households: .481

WTVR-TV Richmond, VA, ch. 6, CBS
WRIC-TV Petersburg, VA, ch. 8, ABC
WWBT Richmond, VA, ch. 12, NBC
WRLH-TV Richmond, VA, ch. 35, Fox, MyNetworkTV
***WCVE-TV** Richmond, VA, ch. 42, ETV
***WCVW** Richmond, VA, ch. 44, ETV
WUPV Ashland, VA, ch. 65, CW

DMA Counties	State	TV Households	DMA Counties	State	TV Households
Amelia	VA	4,960	Lancaster	VA	5,140
Brunswick	VA	6,250	Louisa	VA	13,020
Buckingham	VA	5,730	Lunenburg	VA	5,150
Caroline	VA	10,490	Middlesex	VA	4,560
Charles City	VA	2,960	New Kent	VA	6,640
Chesterfield	VA	120,120	Northumberland	VA	5,860
Cumberland	VA	3,990	Nottoway	VA	5,650
Dinwiddie	VA	23,450	Orange	VA	13,570
Essex	VA	4,550	Powhatan	VA	9,620
Goochland	VA	8,080	Prince Edward	VA	7,340
Greensville	VA	5,830	Prince George	VA	20,520
Hanover	VA	36,020	Richmond	VA	3,060
Henrico	VA	121,050	Richmond City	VA	83,470
King and Queen	VA	2,960	Sussex	VA	4,170
King William	VA	6,030			

Roanoke-Lynchburg, VA (67)

DMA TV Households: 461,420
% of U.S. TV Households: .403

WDBJ Roanoke, VA, ch. 7, CBS, MyNetworkTV
WSLS-TV Roanoke, VA, ch. 10, NBC
WSET-TV Lynchburg, VA, ch. 13, ABC
***WBRA-TV** Roanoke, VA, ch. 15, ETV
WWCW Lynchburg, VA, ch. 21, Fox, CW
WDRL-TV Danville, VA ch. 24, IND
WFXR-TV Roanoke, VA, ch. 27, satellite to WWCW
WPXR-TV Roanoke, VA, ch. 36, ION Television

DMA Counties	State	TV Households	DMA Counties	State	TV Households
Alleghany	VA	9,530	Giles	VA	7,270
Amherst	VA	12,710	Grayson	VA	7,040
Appomattox	VA	5,770	Halifax	VA	15,010
Bath	VA	1,980	Henry	VA	29,850
Bedford	VA	30,110	Highland	VA	1,080
Bland	VA	2,770	Montgomery	VA	39,990
Botetourt	VA	12,820	Nelson	VA	6,340
Campbell	VA	48,660	Pittsylvania	VA	44,750
Carroll	VA	15,720	Pulaski	VA	15,180
Charlotte	VA	5,150	Roanoke	VA	89,980
Craig	VA	2,140	Rockbridge	VA	14,040
Floyd	VA	6,400	Wythe	VA	12,320
Franklin	VA	21,380	Pocahontas	WV	3,430

Roanoke - Lynchburg, VA

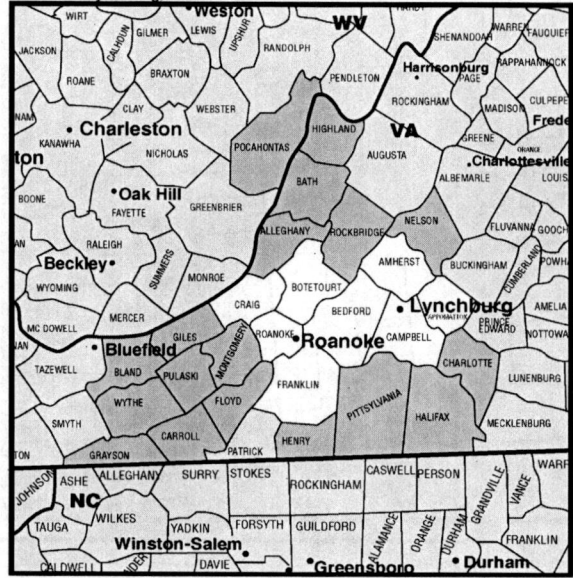

Rochester - Mason City - Austin, MN

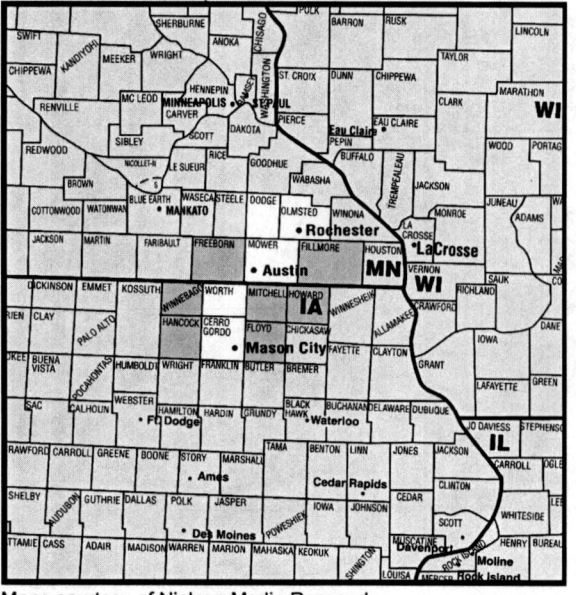

Rochester, MN-Mason City, IA-Austin, MN (154)

DMA TV Households: 144,700
% of U.S. TV Households: .126

KIMT Mason City, IA, ch. 3, CBS
KAAL Austin, MN, ch. 6, ABC
KTTC Rochester, MN, ch. 10, NBC
***KSMQ-TV** Austin, MN, ch. 20, ETV
***KYIN** Mason City, IA, ch. 24, ETV
KXLT-TV Rochester, MN, ch. 47, Fox

DMA Counties	State	TV Households
Cerro Gordo	IA	18,430
Floyd	IA	6,680
Hancock	IA	4,460
Howard	IA	3,770
Mitchell	IA	4,270
Winnebago	IA	4,490
Worth	IA	3,180
Dodge	MN	7,360
Fillmore	MN	8,260
Freeborn	MN	12,960
Mower	MN	15,360
Olmsted	MN	55,480

Maps courtesy of Nielsen Media Research

Rochester, NY (80)

DMA TV Households: 390,590
% of U.S. TV Households: .341

WROC-TV Rochester, NY, ch. 8, CBS
WHEC-TV Rochester, NY, ch. 10, NBC
WHAM-TV Rochester, NY, ch. 13, ABC, CW
*WXXI-TV Rochester, NY, ch. 21, ETV
WUHF Rochester, NY, ch. 31, Fox

DMA Counties	State	TV Households
Livingston	NY	21,860
Monroe	NY	194,490
Ontario	NY	41,030
Rochester City	NY	89,410
Wayne	NY	34,890
Yates	NY	8,910

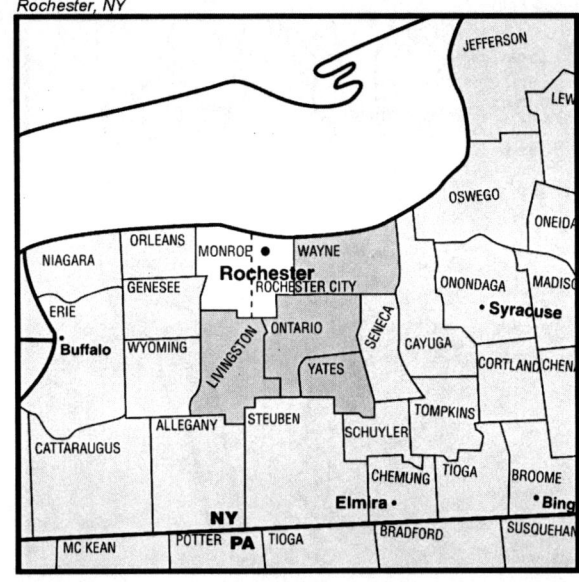

Rochester, NY

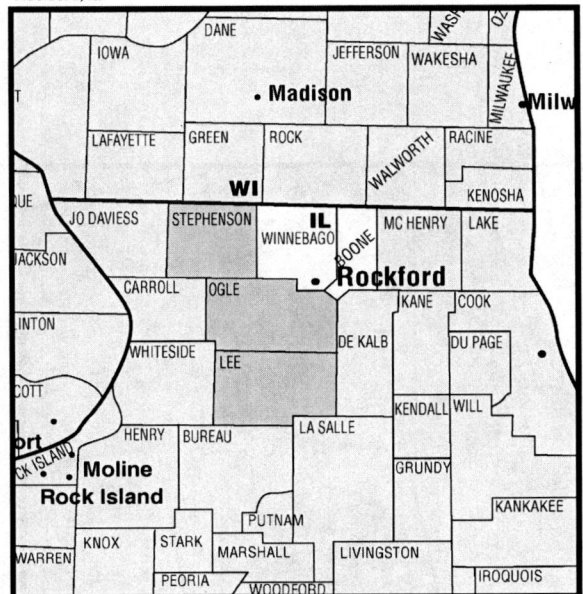

Rockford, IL

Rockford, IL (132)

DMA TV Households: 188,860
% of U.S. TV Households: .165

WREX-TV Rockford, IL, ch. 13, NBC, CW
WTVO Rockford, IL, ch. 17, ABC, MyNetworkTV
WIFR Rockford, IL, ch 23, CBS
WQRF-TV Rockford, IL, ch. 39, Fox

DMA Counties	State	TV Households
Boone	IL	19,270
Lee	IL	13,290
Ogle	IL	21,220
Stephenson	IL	18,850
Winnebago	IL	116,230

Sacramento-Stockton-Modesto, CA (20)

DMA TV Households: 1,399,520
% of U.S. TV Households: 1.223

KCRA-TV Sacramento, CA, ch. 3, NBC
*KVIE Sacramento, CA, ch. 6, ETV
KXTV Sacramento, CA, ch. 10, ABC
KOVR Stockton, CA, ch. 13, CBS
KUVS-TV Modesto, CA, ch. 19, Univision
*KBSV Ceres, CA, ch. 23, ETV

KSPX-TV Sacramento, CA, ch. 48, ION Television
KMAX-TV Sacramento, CA, ch. 31, CW
KTXL Sacramento, CA, ch. 40, Fox
KQCA Stockton, CA, ch. 58, MyNetworkTV
KTFK-TV Stockton, CA, ch. 64, TeleFutura

DMA Counties	State	TV Households	DMA Counties	State	TV Households
Amador	CA	14,030	San Joaquin	CA	218,210
Calaveras	CA	19,080	Sierra	CA	1,480
Colusa	CA	6,910	Solano East	CA	86,320
El Dorado West	CA	51,560	Stanislaus	CA	164,500
Nevada	CA	38,890	Sutter	CA	31,330
Placer	CA	128,430	Tuolumne	CA	22,140
Plumas	CA	8,670	Yolo	CA	68,120
Sacramento	CA	515,010	Yuba	CA	24,840

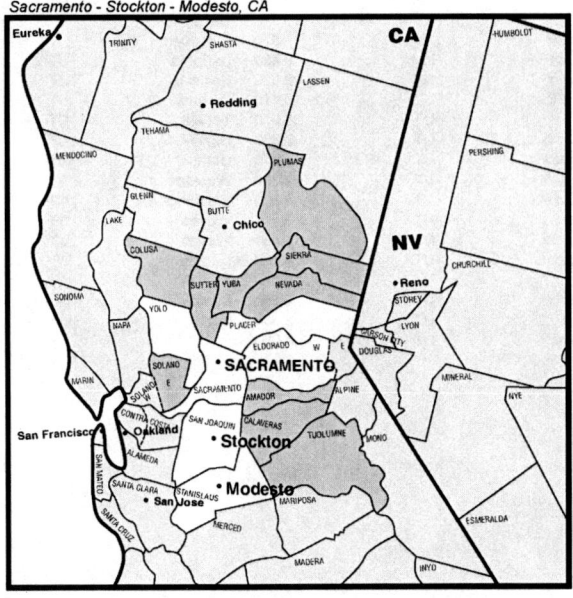

Sacramento - Stockton - Modesto, CA

Maps courtesy of Nielsen Media Research

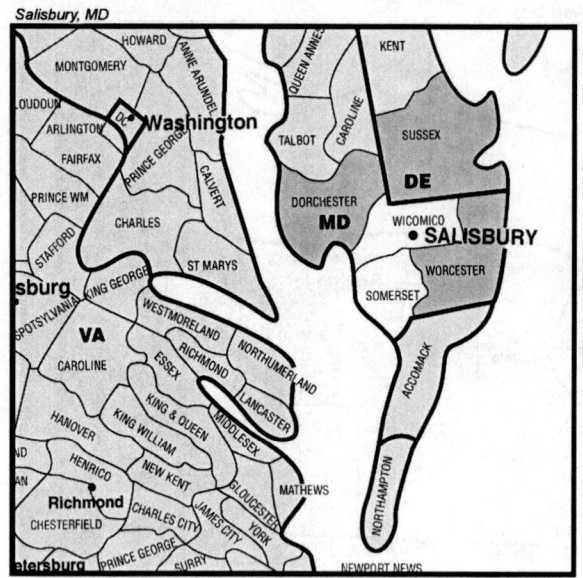

Salisbury, MD

Salisbury, MD (144)

DMA TV Households: 157,940
% of U.S. TV Households: .138

WBOC-TV Salisbury, MD, ch. 16, CBS, Fox
***WCPB** Salisbury, MD, ch. 28, ETV
WMDT Salisbury, MD, ch. 47, ABC, CW
***WDPB** Seaford, DE, ch. 64, ETV

DMA Counties	State	TV Households
Sussex	DE	77,240
Dorchester	MD	13,570
Somerset	MD	8,910
Wicomico	MD	36,820
Worcester	MD	21,400

Salt Lake City, UT (33)

DMA TV Households: 919,390
% of U.S. TV Households: .803

KUTV Salt Lake City, ch. 2, CBS
KVNV Ely, NV, ch. 3, NBC
KCBU Price, UT, ch. 3, TeleFutura
KTVX Salt Lake City, ch. 4, ABC
KSL-TV Salt Lake City, ch. 5, NBC
***KUED** Salt Lake City, ch. 7, ET
***KUEN** Ogden, UT, ch. 9, ETV
KENV Elko, NV, ch. 10, NBC
***KBYU-TV** Provo, UT, ch. 11, ETV
KUTF Logan, UT, ch. 12, IND
KUSG St. George, UT, ch. 12, satellite to KUTV
KSTU Salt Lake City, ch. 13, Fox

KGWR-TV Rock Springs, WY, ch. 13, CBS
KJZZ-TV Salt Lake City, ch. 14, IND
KCSG Cedar City, UT, ch. 14, MyNetworkTV
KBCJ Vernal, UT, ch. 16, IND
KUPX-TV Provo, UT, ch. 29, ION Television
***KUEW** St. George, UT, ch. 18, ETV
***KUES** Richfield, UT, ch. 19, ETV
KTMW Salt Lake City, ch. 20, IND
KPNZ Ogden, UT, ch. 24, IND
KBNY Ely, NV, ch. 27, IND
KUCW Ogden, UT, ch. 30, CW
KUTH Provo, UT, ch. 32, Univision

DMA Counties	State	TV Households	DMA Counties	State	TV Households
Bear Lake	ID	1,990	Morgan	UT	2,550
Franklin	ID	3,780	Piute	UT	490
Oneida	ID	1,470	Rich	UT	780
Elko	NV	15,990	Salt Lake	UT	337,700
Eureka	NV	570	San Juan	UT	4,040
White Pine	NV	3,450	Sanpete	UT	7,270
Beaver	UT	2,030	Sevier	UT	6,640
Box Elder	UT	15,110	Summit	UT	13,130
Cache	UT	33,570	Tooele	UT	17,890
Carbon	UT	7,330	Uintah	UT	10,060
Daggett	UT	370	Utah	UT	138,310
Davis	UT	92,250	Wasatch	UT	6,880
Duchesne	UT	5,530	Washington	UT	49,160
Emery	UT	3,470	Wayne	UT	990
Garfield	UT	1,530	Weber	UT	75,280
Grand	UT	3,430	Lincoln	WY	6,230
Iron	UT	14,520	Sublette	WY	3,380
Juab	UT	2,880	Sweetwater	WY	15,530
Kane	UT	2,380	Uinta	WY	7,350
Millard	UT	4,080			

Salt Lake City, UT

Maps courtesy of Nielsen Media Research

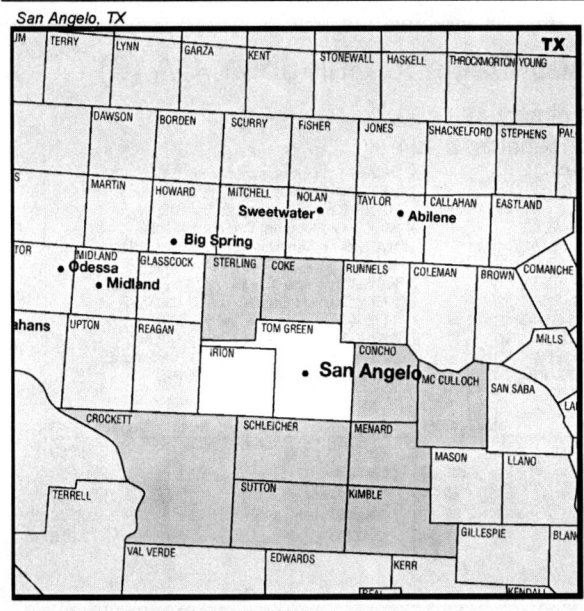

San Angelo, TX

San Angelo, TX (196)

DMA TV Households: 54,980
% of U.S. TV Households: .048

KSAN-TV San Angelo, TX, ch. 3, satellite to KRBC-TV
KIDY San Angelo, TX, ch. 6, Fox
KLST San Angelo, TX, ch. 8, CBS

DMA Counties	State	TV Households
Coke	TX	1,480
Concho	TX	890
Crockett	TX	1,480
Irion	TX	680
Kimble	TX	1,950
McCulloch	TX	3,130
Menard	TX	880
Schleicher	TX	1,090
Sterling	TX	490
Sutton	TX	1,660
Tom Green	TX	41,250

San Antonio, TX (37)

DMA TV Households: 818,560
% of U.S. TV Households: .715

KCWX Fredericksburg, TX, ch. 5, CW
WOAI-TV San Antonio, TX, ch. 4, NBC
KENS San Antonio, TX, ch. 39, CBS
*KLRN San Antonio, TX, ch. 9, ETV
KTRG Del Rio, TX, ch. 10, IND
KSAT-TV San Antonio, TX, ch. 12, ABC
KVAW Eagle Pass, TX, ch. 16, IND

*KHCE-TV San Antonio, TX, ch. 16, ETV
KPXL-TV Uvalde, TX, ch. 26, ION Television
KABB San Antonio, TX, ch. 29, Fox
KMYS Kerrville, TX, ch. 35, MyNetworkTV
KWEX-TV San Antonio, TX, ch. 41, Univision
KVDA San Antonio, TX, ch. 60, Telemundo

DMA Counties	State	TV Households	DMA Counties	State	TV Households
Atascosa	TX	14,640	Kerr	TX	19,650
Bandera	TX	8,020	Kinney	TX	1,260
Bexar	TX	570,620	LaSalle	TX	1,790
Comal	TX	41,170	Lavaca	TX	7,490
DeWitt	TX	7,070	Maverick	TX	14,390
Dimmit	TX	3,260	McMullen	TX	390
Edwards	TX	680	Medina	TX	14,660
Frio	TX	4,790	Real	TX	1,280
Goliad	TX	2,750	Uvalde	TX	8,580
Gonzales	TX	7,040	Val Verde	TX	15,230
Guadalupe	TX	40,060	Wilson	TX	14,150
Karnes	TX	4,450	Zavala	TX	3,400
Kendall	TX	11,740			

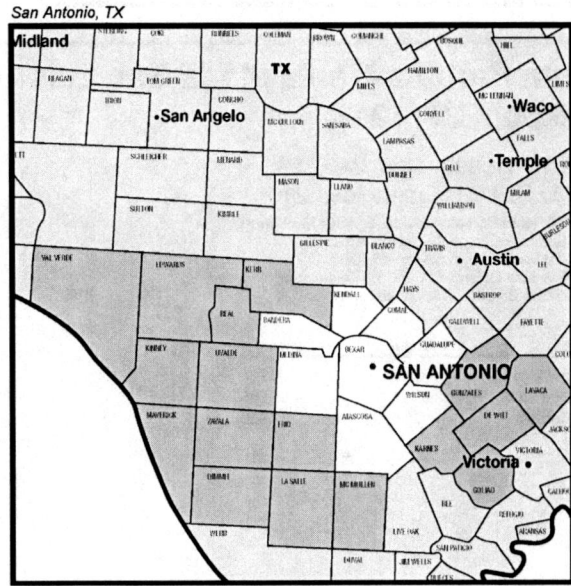

San Antonio, TX

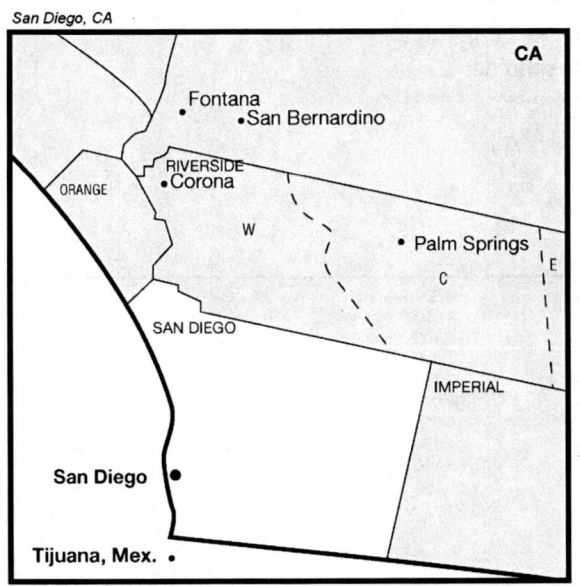

San Diego, CA

San Diego (28)

DMA TV Households: 1,066,680
% of U.S. TV Households: .932

XETV Tijuana, Mexico, ch. 6, CW
KFMB-TV San Diego, ch. 8, CBS
KGTV San Diego, ch. 10, ABC
*KPBS San Diego, ch. 15, ETV
KNSD San Diego, ch. 39, NBC
KUSI-TV San Diego, ch. 51, IND
KSWB-TV San Diego, ch. 69, Fox

DMA Counties	State	TV Households
San Diego	CA	1,066,680

Maps courtesy of Nielsen Media Research

San Francisco - Oakland - San Jose, CA

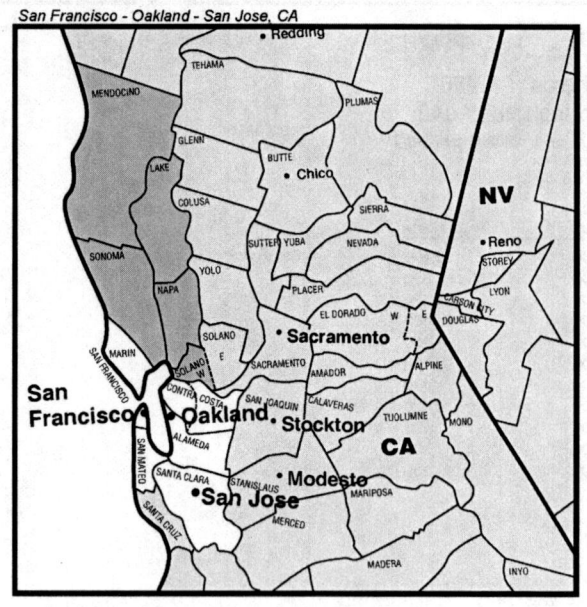

San Francisco-Oakland-San Jose, CA (6)

DMA TV Households: 2,476,450
% of U.S. TV Households: 2.164

KTVU Oakland, CA, ch. 2, Fox
KRON-TV San Francisco, ch. 4, MyNetworkTV
KPIX-TV San Francisco, ch. 5, CBS
KGO-TV San Francisco, ch. 7, ABC
KUNO-TV Fort Bragg, CA, ch. 8, IND
*****KQED** San Francisco, ch. 9, ETV
KNTV San Jose, CA, ch. 11, NBC
KDTV San Francisco, ch. 14, Univision
KOFY-TV San Francisco, ch. 20, IND
*****KRCB** Cotati, CA, ch. 22, ETV
KTSF San Francisco, ch. 26, IND

*****KQEC** San Francisco, ch. 32, ETV
KICU-TV San Jose, CA, ch. 36, IND
KCNS San Francisco, ch. 38, IND
KTNC-TV Concord, CA, ch. 14, IND
*****KCSM-TV** San Mateo, CA, ch. 43, ETV
KBCW San Francisco, ch. 44, CW
KSTS San Jose, CA, ch. 48, Telemundo
KFTY Santa Rosa, CA, ch. 50, IND
*****KTEH** San Jose, CA, ch. 54, ETV
KKPX-TV San Jose, CA, ch. 41, ION
KFSF-TV Vallejo, CA, ch. 66, TeleFutura
KTLN-TV Novato, CA, ch. 68, IND

DMA Counties	State	TV Households	DMA Counties	State	TV Households
Alameda	CA	520,000	San Francisco	CA	322,060
Contra Costa	CA	366,620	San Mateo	CA	250,320
Lake	CA	25,240	Santa Clara	CA	590,100
Marin	CA	99,120	Solano West	CA	50,520
Mendocino	CA	31,340	Sonoma	CA	172,910
Napa	CA	48,220			

Santa Barbara-Santa Maria-San Luis Obispo, CA (121)

DMA TV Households: 240,190
% of U.S. TV Households: .210

KEYT-TV Santa Barbara, CA, ch. 3, ABC, MyNetworkTV
KSBY San Luis Obispo, CA, ch. 6, NBC, CW
KCOY-TV Santa Maria, CA, ch. 12, CBS
KTAS San Luis Obispo, CA, ch. 33, Telemundo
KPMR Santa Barbara, CA, ch. 38, Univision

DMA Counties	State	TV Households
San Luis Obispo	CA	100,760
Santa Barbara N.	CA	67,000
Santa Barbara S.	CA	72,430

Santa Barbara - Santa Maria - San Luis Obispo, CA

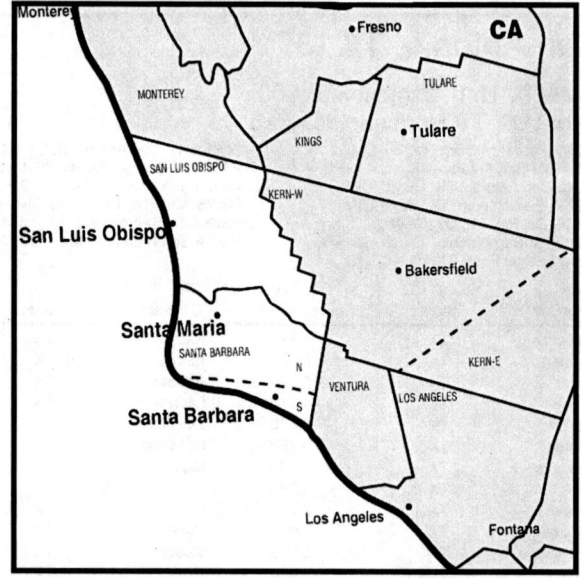

Savannah, GA

Savannah, GA (96)

DMA TV Households: 319,160
% of U.S. TV Households: .279

WSAV-TV Savannah, GA, ch. 3, NBC, MyNetworkTV
*****WVAN-TV** Savannah, GA, ch. 9, ETV
WTOC-TV Savannah, GA, ch. 11, CBS
*****WJWJ-TV** Beaufort, SC, ch. 16, ETV
WJCL Savannah, GA, ch. 22, ABC
WTGS Hardeeville, SC, ch. 28, Fox
WGSA Baxley, GA, ch. 34, CW

DMA Counties	State	TV Households	DMA Counties	State	TV Households
Appling	GA	6,880	Long	GA	3,840
Bacon	GA	4,050	McIntosh	GA	4,610
Bryan	GA	11,190	Montgomery	GA	3,210
Bulloch	GA	25,510	Screven	GA	60
Candler	GA	3,750	Tattnall	GA	7,500
Chatham	GA	98,990	Toombs	GA	10,840
Effingham	GA	19,010	Wayne	GA	10,570
Evans	GA	4,170	Beaufort	SC	59,580
Jeff Davis	GA	5,190	Hampton	SC	7,700
Liberty	GA	19,290	Jasper	SC	7,680

Maps courtesy of Nielsen Media Research

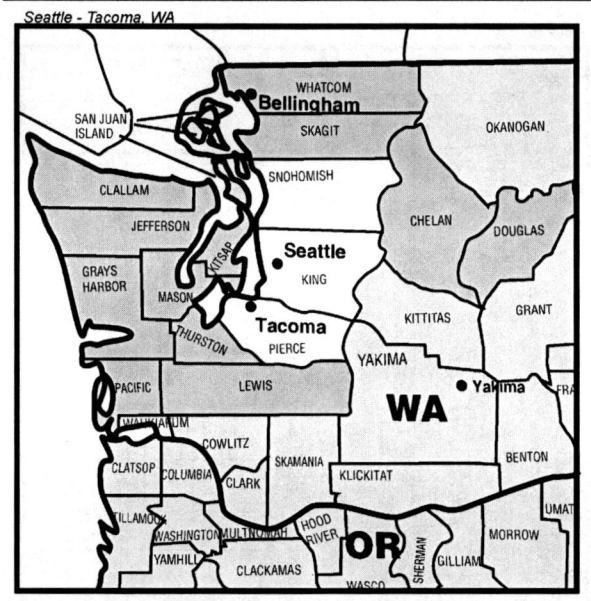

Seattle - Tacoma, WA

Seattle-Tacoma, WA (14)

DMA TV Households: 1,819,970
% of U.S. TV Households: 1.590

KOMO-TV Seattle, ch. 4, ABC
KING-TV Seattle, ch. 5, NBC
KIRO-TV Seattle, ch. 7, CBS
*KCTS-TV Seattle, ch. 9, ETV
KSTW Tacoma, WA, ch. 11, CW
KVOS-TV Bellingham, WA, ch. 12, IND
KCPQ Tacoma, WA, ch. 13, Fox
*KCKA Centralia, WA, ch. 15,
KONG Everett, WA, ch. 31, IND

KTBW-TV Tacoma, WA, ch. 14, IND
KMYQ Seattle, ch. 22, MyNetworkTV
KBCB Bellingham, WA, ch. 24, IND
*KBTC-TV Tacoma, WA, ch. 28, ETV
KWPX Bellevue, WA, ch. 33, ION Television
KHCV Seattle, ch. 45, Azteca America
KUNS-TV Bellevue, WA, ch. 51, Univision
*KWDK Tacoma, WA, ch. 56, ETV

DMA Counties	State	TV Households	DMA Counties	State	TV Households
Chelan	WA	25,430	Mason	WA	21,780
Clallam	WA	29,600	Pacific	WA	9,370
Douglas	WA	12,980	Pierce	WA	294,810
Grays Harbor	WA	27,260	San Juan	WA	7,170
Island	WA	31,250	Skagit	WA	43,020
Jefferson	WA	12,820	Snohomish	WA	257,940
King	WA	759,090	Thurston	WA	95,370
Kitsap	WA	89,900	Whatcom	WA	74,650
Lewis	WA	27,530			

Sherman, TX-Ada, OK (161)

DMA TV Households: 128,100
% of U.S. TV Households: .112

KTEN Ada, OK, ch. 10, NBC, CW
KXII Sherman, TX, ch. 12, CBS, Fox, MyNetworkTV

DMA Counties	State	TV Households
Atoka	OK	5,350
Bryan	OK	15,910
Carter	OK	19,040
Choctaw	OK	6,050
Coal	OK	2,170
Johnston	OK	4,070
Love	OK	3,560
Marshall	OK	6,140
Pontotoc	OK	14,750
Pushmataha	OK	4,630
Grayson	TX	46,430

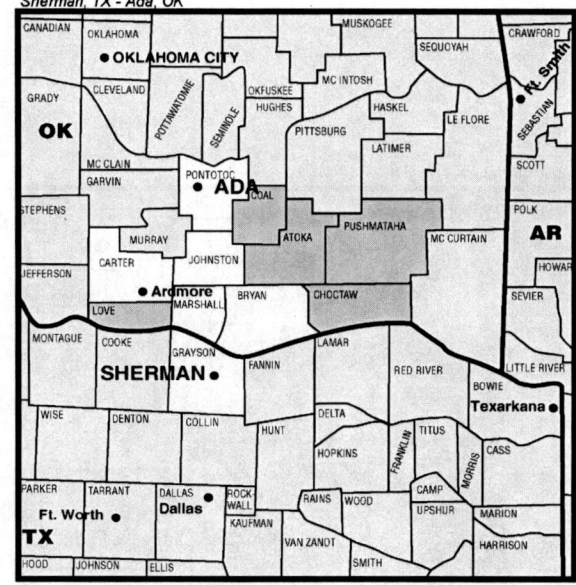

Sherman, TX - Ada, OK

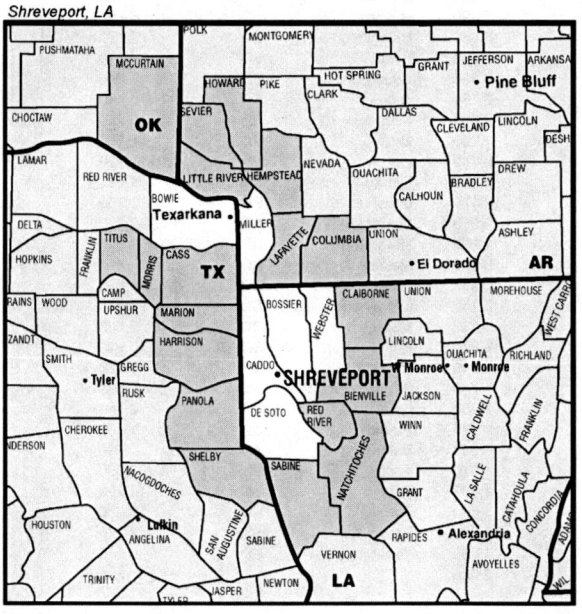

Shreveport, LA

Shreveport, LA (84)

DMA TV Households: 385,770
% of U.S. TV Households: .337

KTBS-TV Shreveport, LA, ch. 3, ABC
KSLA-TV Shreveport, LA, ch. 12, CBS
KTAL-TV Texarkana, TX, ch. 15, NBC
KPXJ Minden, LA, ch. 21, CW
*KLTS-TV Shreveport, LA, ch. 24, ETV
KMSS-TV Shreveport, LA, ch. 33, Fox
KSHV Shreveport, LA, ch. 45, MyNetworkTV

DMA Counties	State	TV Households	DMA Counties	State	TV Households
Columbia	AR	9,480	Red River	LA	3,260
Hempstead	AR	8,700	Sabine	LA	9,560
Howard	AR	5,270	Webster	LA	16,580
Lafayette	AR	3,160	McCurtain	OK	12,850
Little River	AR	5,290	Bowie	TX	34,670
Miller	AR	16,780	Cass	TX	12,280
Sevier	AR	5,730	Harrison	TX	24,090
Bienville	LA	5,850	Marion	TX	4,570
Bossier	LA	42,760	Morris	TX	5,300
Caddo	LA	99,080	Panola	TX	9,090
Claiborne	LA	6,040	Shelby	TX	9,97
DeSoto	LA	10,350	Titus	TX	10,010
Natchitoches	LA	15,050			

Maps courtesy of Nielsen Media Research

Sioux City, IA (149)

DMA TV Households: 154,900
% of U.S. TV Households: .135

*KUSD-TV Vermillion, SD, ch. 2, ETV
KTIV Sioux City, IA, ch. 4, NBC, CW
KCAU-TV Sioux City, IA, ch. 9, ABC
KMEG Sioux City, IA, ch. 14, CBS
*KXNE-TV Norfolk, NE, ch. 19, ETV
*KSIN Sioux City, IA, ch. 27, ETV
KPTH Sioux City, IA, ch. 44, Fox, MyNetworkTV

DMA Counties	State	TV Households	DMA Counties	State	TV Households
Buena Vista	IA	7,170	Woodbury	IA	38,670
Cherokee	IA	4,890	Cedar	NE	3,180
Clay	IA	7,080	Dakota	NE	6,9900
Dickinson	IA	7,380	Dixon	NE	2,390
Emmet	IA	4,280	Knox	NE	3,450
Ida	IA	2,890	Madison	NE	12,820
Monona	IA	3,790	Pierce	NE	2,680
O'Brien	IA	5,580	Stanton	NE	2,280
Palo Alto	IA	3,8750	Thurston	NE	2,190
Plymouth	IA	9,2860	Wayne	NE	3,190
Sac	IA	4,290	Union	SD	5,660
Sioux	IA	10,900			

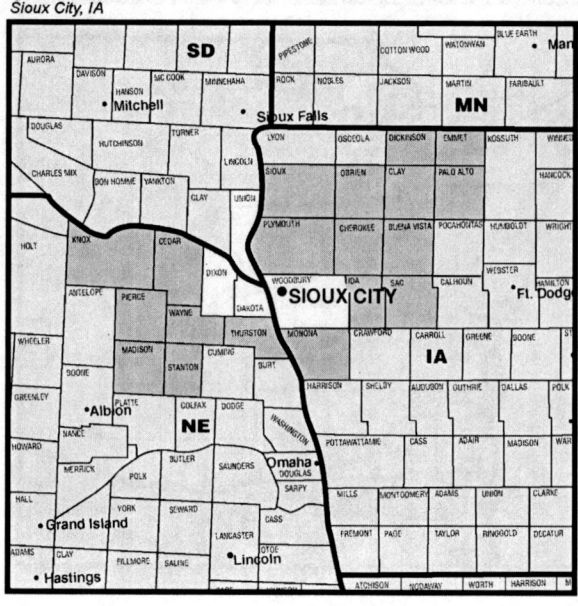

Sioux City, IA

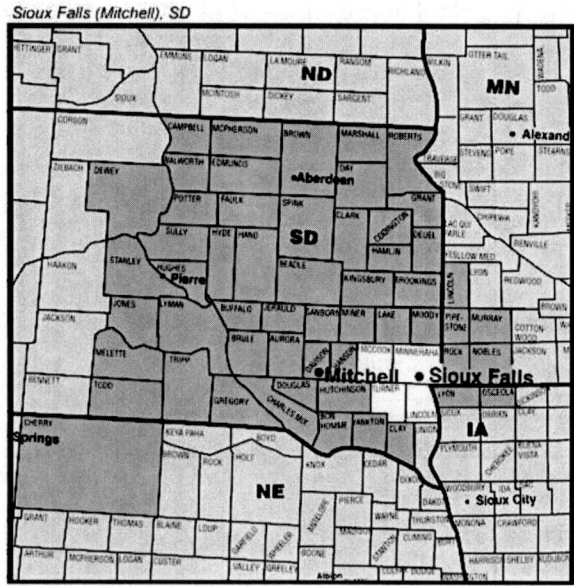

Sioux Falls (Mitchell), SD

Sioux Falls (Mitchell), SD (113)

DMA TV Households: 260,190
% of U.S. TV Households: .227

KDLO-TV Florence, SD, ch. 3, satellite to KELO-TV
KPRY-TV Pierre, SD, ch. 4, satellite to KSFY-TV
KDLV-TV Mitchell, SD, ch. 5, NBC
KPLO-TV Reliance, SD, ch. 6, satellite to KELO-TV
*KESD-TV Brookings, SD, ch. 8, ETV
KABY-TV Aberdeen, SD, ch. 9, satellite to KSFY-TV
*KTSD-TV Pierre, SD, ch. 10, ETV

KELO-TV Sioux Falls, SD, ch. 11, CBS, MyNetworkTV
KTTM Huron, SD, ch. 12, satellite to KTTW
KSFY-TV Sioux Falls, SD, ch. 13, ABC
*KDSD-TV Aberdeen, SD, ch. 16, ETV
KTTW Sioux Falls, SD, ch. 17, Fox
*KSMN Worthington, MN, ch. 20, ETV
*KCSD-TV Sioux Falls, SD, ch. 23, ETV
KWSD Sioux Falls, SD, ch. 36, CW
KDLT-TV Sioux Falls, SD, ch. 46, IND

DMA Counties	State	TV Households	DMA Counties	State	TV Households
Lyon	IA	4,080	Hand	SD	1,390
Osceola	IA	2,480	Hanson	SD	1,290
Lincoln	MN	2,490	Hughes	SD	6,760
Murray	MN	3,480	Hutchinson	SD	2,870
Nobles	MN	7,550	Hyde	SD	590
Pipestone	MN	3,860	Jerauld	SD	890
Rock	MN	3,760	Jones	SD	480
Cherry	NE	2,380	Kingsbury	SD	2,280
Aurora	SD	1,080	Lake	SD	4,580
Beadle	SD	6,740	Lincoln	SD	14,920
Bon Homme	SD	2,390	Lyman	SD	1,390
Brookings	SD	11,170	Marshall	SD	1,780
Brown	SD	15,050	McCook	SD	2,190
Brule	SD	1,990	McPherson	SD	990
Buffalo	SD	580	Mellette	SD	690
Campbell	SD	490	Miner	SD	1,090
Charles Mix	SD	3,180	Minnehaha	SD	71,420
Clark	SD	1,280	Moody	SD	2,600
Clay	SD	4,870	Potter	SD	890
Codington	SD	10,840	Roberts	SD	3,560
Davison	SD	7,740	Sanborn	SD	980
Day	SD	2,380	Spink	SD	2,480
Deuel	SD	1,780	Stanley	SD	1,180
Dewey	SD	1,840	Sully	SD	590
Douglas	SD	1,070	Todd	SD	2,800
Edmunds	SD	1,490	Tripp	SD	2,290
Faulk	SD	890	Turner	SD	3,280
Grant	SD	2,860	Walworth	SD	2,170
Gregory	SD	1,790	Yankton	SD	8,140
Hamlin	SD	2,050			

Maps courtesy of Nielsen Media Research

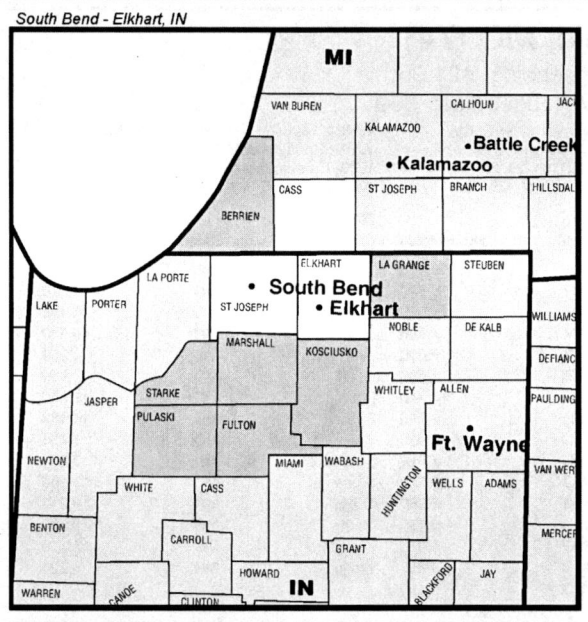

South Bend - Elkhart, IN

South Bend-Elkhart, IN (89)

DMA TV Households: 334,720
% of U.S. TV Households: .292

WNDU-TV South Bend, IN, ch. 16, NBC
WSBT-TV South Bend, IN, ch. 22, CBS
WSJV Elkhart, IN, ch. 28, Fox
*WNIT-TV South Bend, IN, ch. 34, ETV
WHME-TV South Bend, IN, ch. 46, IND

DMA Counties	State	TV Households
Elkhart	IN	71,600
Fulton	IN	8,080
Kosciusko	IN	28,460
Lagrange	IN	11,740
Marshall	IN	17,270
Pulaski	IN	5,260
St. Joseph	IN	101,070
Starke	IN	8,840
Berrien	MI	62,520
Cass	MI	19,880

Spokane, WA (75)

DMA TV Households: 416,630
% of U.S. TV Households: .364

KREM Spokane, WA, ch. 20, CBS
KLEW-TV Lewiston, ID, ch. 3, satellite to KIMA-TV
KXLY-TV Spokane, WA, ch. 4, ABC, MyNetworkTV
*KSPS-TV Spokane, WA, ch. 7, ETV
*KWSU-TV Pullman, WA, ch. 10, ETV

KHQ-TV Spokane, WA, ch. 15, NBC
KSKN Spokane, WA, ch. 22, CW
KQUP Pullman, WA, ch. 24, IND
*KCDT Coeur d'Alene, ID, ch. 26, ETV
KAYU-TV Spokane, WA, ch. 28, Fox
KGPX-TV Spokane, WA, ch. 34, ION
*KUID-TV Moscow, ID, ch. 35, ETV

DMA Counties	State	TV Households	DMA Counties	State	TV Households
Benewah	ID	3,580	Adams	WA	5,270
Bonner	ID	16,370	Asotin	WA	8,680
Boundary	ID	4,030	Columbia	WA	1,630
Clearwater	ID	3,080	Ferry	WA	2,950
Idaho	ID	5,850	Garfield	WA	880
Kootenai	ID	53,100	Grant	WA	27,370
Latah	ID	13,000	Lincoln	WA	4,150
Lewis	ID	1,460	Okanogan	WA	14,620
Nez Perce	ID	16,010	Pend Oreille	WA	5,080
Shoshone	ID	5,570	Spokane	WA	181,740
Lincoln	MT	7,850	Stevens	WA	15,770
Wallowa	OR	2,910	Whitman	WA	15,680

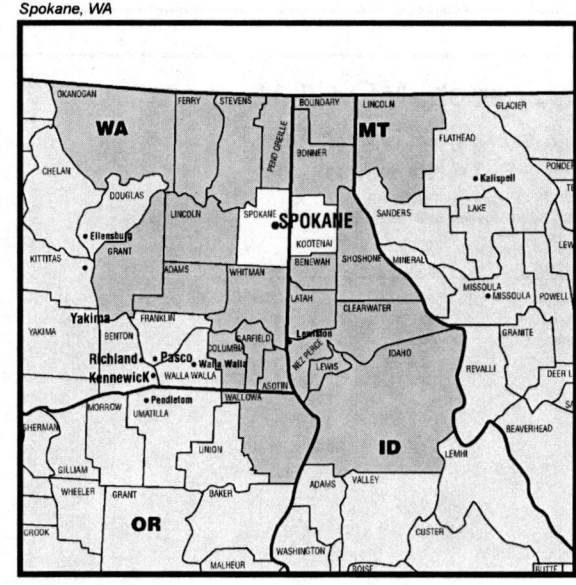

Spokane, WA

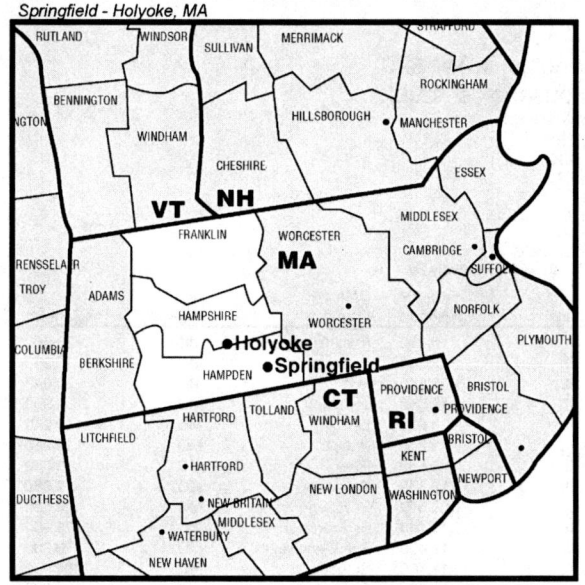

Springfield - Holyoke, MA

Springfield-Holyoke, MA (111)

DMA TV Households: 262,850
% of U.S. TV Households: .230

WWLP Springfield, MA, ch. 22, NBC
WGGB-TV Springfield, MA, ch. 40, ABC, Fox
*WGBY-TV Springfield, MA, ch. 22, ETV

DMA Counties	State	TV Households
Franklin	MA	29,490
Hampden	MA	176,340
Hampshire	MA	57,020

Maps courtesy of Nielsen Media Research

Springfield, MO

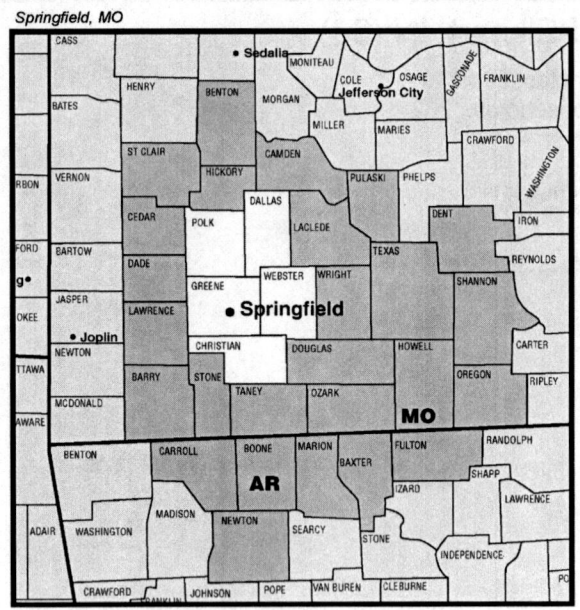

Springfield, MO (74)

DMA TV Households: 421,960
% of U.S. TV Households: .369

KYTV Springfield, MO, ch. 3, NBC, CW
KOLR Springfield, MO, ch. 10, CBS
*KOZK Springfield, MO, ch. 23, ETV
KSFX-TV Springfield, MO, ch. 28, Fox
KWBM Harrison, AR, ch. 31, MyNetworkTV
KSPR Springfield, MO, ch. 33, ABC
KPBI Eureka Springs, AR, ch. 34, IND
KRBK Osage Beach, MO, ch. 49, IND

DMA Counties	State	TV Households	DMA Counties	State	TV Households
Baxter	AR	19,150	Hickory	MO	3,940
Boone	AR	15,440	Howell	MO	15,270
Carroll	AR	11,010	Laclede	MO	14,160
Fulton	AR	4,880	Lawrence	MO	14,540
Marion	AR	7,000	Oregon	MO	4,200
Newton	AR	3,500	Ozark	MO	3,750
Barry	MO	14,340	Polk	MO	11,240
Benton	MO	8,220	Pulaski	MO	14,150
Camden	MO	17,880	Shannon	MO	3,430
Cedar	MO	5,610	St. Clair	MO	3,960
Christian	MO	28,980	Stone	MO	13,180
Dade	MO	2,980	Taney	MO	19,210
Dallas	MO	6,480	Texas	MO	9,580
Dent	MO	6,070	Webster	MO	13,110
Douglas	MO	5,330	Wright	MO	7,220
Greene	MO	114,150			

St. Joseph, MO

St. Joseph, MO (201)

DMA TV Households: 46,840
% of U.S. TV Households: .041

KQTV St. Joseph, MO, ch. 2, ABC
KTAJ-TV St. Joseph, MO, ch. 21, IND

DMA Counties	State	TV Households
Doniphan	KS	2,990
Andrew	MO	6,480
Buchanan	MO	33,890
De Kalb	MO	3,480

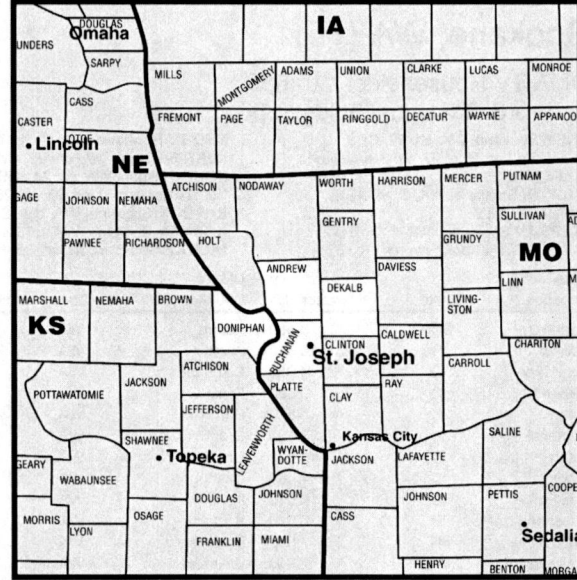

St. Louis (21)

DMA TV Households: 1,249,820
% of U.S. TV Households: 1.092

KTVI St. Louis, ch. 2, Fox
KMOV St. Louis, ch. 4, CBS
KSDK St. Louis, ch. 5, NBC
*KETC St. Louis, ch. 9, ETV
KPLR-TV St. Louis, ch. 11, CW
WPXS Mount Vernon, IL, ch. 21, IND
KNLC St. Louis, ch. 24, IND
KDNL-TV St. Louis, ch. 30, ABC
WRBU East St. Louis, IL, ch. 46, MyNetworkTV

DMA Counties	State	TV Households	DMA Counties	State	TV Households
Bond	IL	6,450	Franklin	MO	38,660
Calhoun	IL	2,090	Gasconade	MO	6,260
Clay	IL	5,540	Iron	MO	3,940
Clinton	IL	13,550	Jefferson	MO	80,900
Fayette	IL	8,020	Lincoln	MO	19,240
Greene	IL	5,350	Phelps	MO	16,910
Jersey	IL	8,660	Pike	MO	6,550
Macoupin	IL	19,150	Reynolds	MO	2,650
Madison	IL	108,570	St. Charles	MO	130,680
Marion	IL	15,780	St. Francois	MO	23,400
Monroe	IL	12,430	Ste. Genevieve	MO	6,660
Montgomery	IL	11,160	St. Louis	MO	401,900
Randolph	IL	11,960	St. Louis-Ind	MO	145,230
St. Clair	IL	101,790	Warren	MO	12,130
Washington	IL	5,600	Washington	MO	9,130
Crawford	MO	9,480			

St. Louis, MO

Maps courtesy of Nielsen Media Research

Syracuse, NY

Syracuse, NY (81)

DMA TV Households: 388,000
% of U.S. TV Households: .339

WSTM-TV Syracuse, NY, ch. 3, NBC
WTVH Syracuse, NY, ch. 5, CBS
WSYR-TV Syracuse, NY, ch. 9, ABC
WNYI Ithaca, NY, ch. 20, IND
*WCNY-TV Syracuse, NY, ch. 24, ETV
WNYS-TV Syracuse, NY, ch. 43, MyNetworkTV
WSPX-TV Syracuse, NY, ch. 56, IND
WSYT Syracuse, NY, ch. 68, Fox

DMA Counties	State	TV Households
Cayuga	NY	30,880
Cortland	NY	18,440
Madison	NY	25,890
Oneida West	NY	34,930
Onondaga	NY	181,940
Oswego	NY	46,170
Seneca	NY	12,610
Tompkins	NY	37,140

Tallahassee, FL-Thomasville, GA (105)

DMA TV Households: 282,390
% of U.S. TV Households: .247

WCTV Thomasville, GA, ch. 6, CBS, MyNetworkTV
*WFSU-TV Tallahassee, FL, ch. 11, ETV
WTLF Tallahassee, FL, ch. 24, CW
WTXL-TV Tallahassee, FL, ch. 27, ABC
WTWC-TV Tallahassee, FL, ch. 40, NBC
WSWG Valdosta, GA, ch. 43, CBS, MyNetworkTV
WTLH Bainbridge, GA, ch. 49, Fox, CW
WFXU Live Oak, FL, ch. 57, IND

DMA Counties	State	TV Households	DMA Counties	State	TV Households
Gadsden	FL	17,430	Clinch	GA	2,680
Hamilton	FL	4,490	Decatur	GA	10,600
Jefferson	FL	5,240	Echols	GA	1,380
Lafayette	FL	2,340	Grady	GA	9,530
Leon	FL	115,380	Lanier	GA	2,970
Madison	FL	7,100	Lowndes	GA	38,260
Suwannee	FL	16,340	Miller	GA	2,470
Taylor	FL	8,140	Seminole	GA	3,470
Wakulla	FL	11,460	Thomas	GA	17,750
Brooks	GA	6,360			

Tallahassee, FL - Thomasville, GA

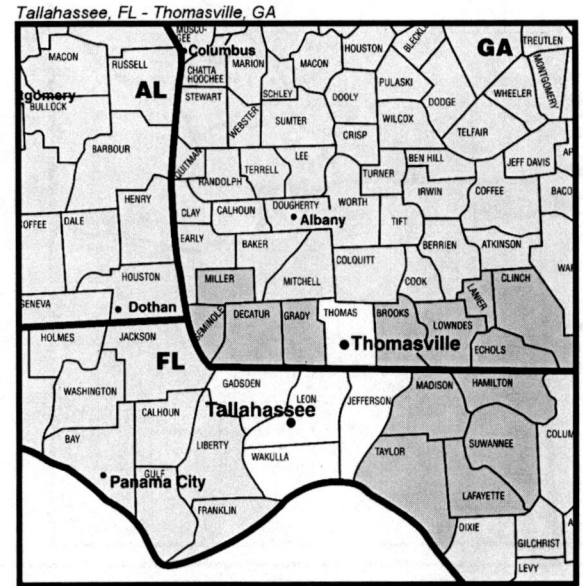

Tampa - St. Petersburg (Sarasota), FL

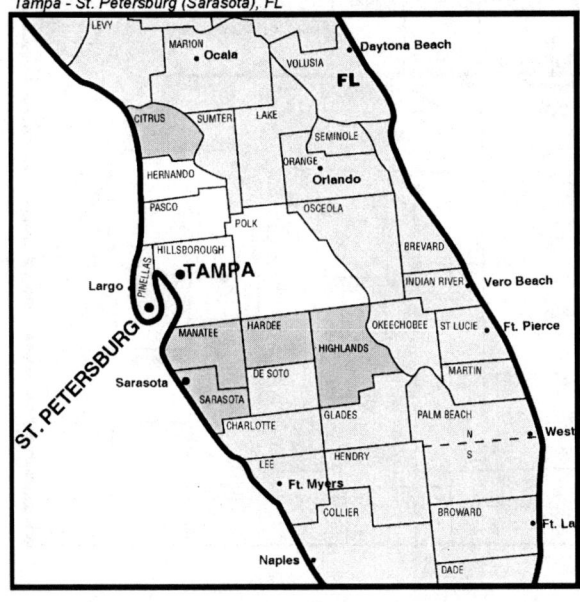

Tampa-St. Petersburg (Sarasota), FL (13)

DMA TV Households: 1,822,160
% of U.S. TV Households: 1.592

*WEDU Tampa, FL, ch. 3,ETV
WFLA-TV Tampa, FL, ch. 8, NBC
WTSP St. Petersburg, FL, ch. 10, CBS
WTVT Tampa, FL, ch. 13, Fox
WCLF Clearwater, FL, ch. 22, IND
WFTS Tampa, FL, ch. 28, ABC
WMOR-TV Lakeland, FL, ch. 32, IND
*WUSF-TV Tampa, FL, ch. 34, ETV

WTTA St. Petersburg, FL, ch. 38, MyNetworkTV
WWSB Sarasota, FL, ch. 40, ABC
WXPX-TV Bradenton, FL, ch. 42, ION Television
WTOG St. Petersburg, FL, ch. 44, CW
WFTT-TV Tampa, FL, ch. 50, TeleFutura
WVEA-TV Venice, FL, ch. 62, Univision

DMA Counties	State	TV Households
Citrus	FL	64,540
Hardee	FL	8,230
Hernando	FL	71,900
Highlands	FL	42,690
Hillsborough	FL	473,520
Manatee	FL	138,420
Pasco	FL	195,460
Pinellas	FL	413,720
Polk	FL	233,710
Sarasota	FL	179,970

Maps courtesy of Nielsen Media Research

Terre Haute, IN (152)

DMA TV Households: 145,450
% of U.S. TV Households: .127

WTWO Terre Haute, IN, ch. 2, NBC
WTHI-TV Terre Haute, IN, ch. 10, CBS
***WUSI-TV** Olney, IL, ch. 16, ETV
***WVUT** Vincennes, IN, ch. 22, ETV
WFXW Terre Haute, IN, ch. 38, Fox

DMA Counties	State	TV Households	DMA Counties	State	TV Households
Clark	IL	6,970	Greene	IN	13,270
Crawford	IL	7,470	Knox	IN	15,280
Jasper	IL	3,770	Martin	IN	4,040
Lawrence	IL	5,930	Parke	IN	6,220
Richland	IL	6,420	Sullivan	IN	7,670
Clay	IN	10,230	Vermillion	IN	6,660
Daviess	IN	10,500	Vigo	IN	41,020

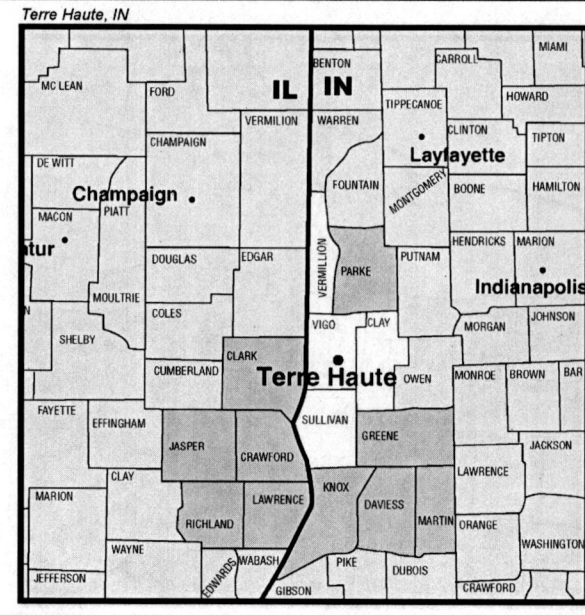
Terre Haute, IN

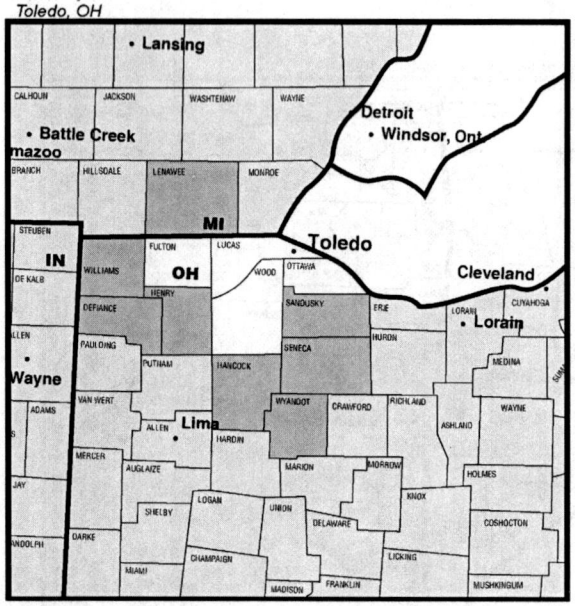
Toledo, OH

Toledo, OH (73)

DMA TV Households: 425,890
% of U.S. TV Households: .372

WTOL Toledo, OH, ch. 11, CBS
WTVG Toledo, OH, ch. 13, ABC
WNWO-TV Toledo, OH, ch. 24, NBC
***WBGU-TV** Bowling Green, OH, ch. 27, ETV
***WGTE-TV** Toledo, OH, ch. 30, ETV
WUPW Toledo, OH, ch. 36, Fox
WLMB Toledo, OH, ch. 40, IND

DMA Counties	State	TV Households
Lenawee	MI	37,510
Defiance	OH	15,220
Fulton	OH	16,010
Hancock	OH	30,490
Henry	OH	11,060
Lucas	OH	179,220
Ottawa	OH	17,030
Sandusky	OH	24,130
Seneca	OH	21,990
Williams	OH	15,080
Wood	OH	49,190
Wyandot	OH	8,960

Topeka, KS (138)

DMA TV Households: 175,940
% of U.S. TV Households: .154

***KTWU** Topeka, KS, ch. 11, ETV
WIBW-TV Topeka, KS, ch. 13, CBS, MyNetworkTV
KSQA Topeka, KS, ch. 22, IND
KSNT Topeka, KS, ch. 27, NBC, CW
KTKA-TV Topeka, KS, ch. 49, ABC

DMA Counties	State	TV Households
Brown	KS	4,040
Clay	KS	3,580
Cloud	KS	3,710
Coffey	KS	3,250
Geary	KS	9,240
Jackson	KS	5,060
Jefferson	KS	6,850
Lyon	KS	13,640
Marshall	KS	4,070
Morris	KS	2,460
Nemaha	KS	3,620
Osage	KS	6,360
Pottawatomie	KS	7,320
Riley	KS	25,830
Shawnee	KS	71,860
Wabaunsee	KS	2,680
Washington	KS	2,370

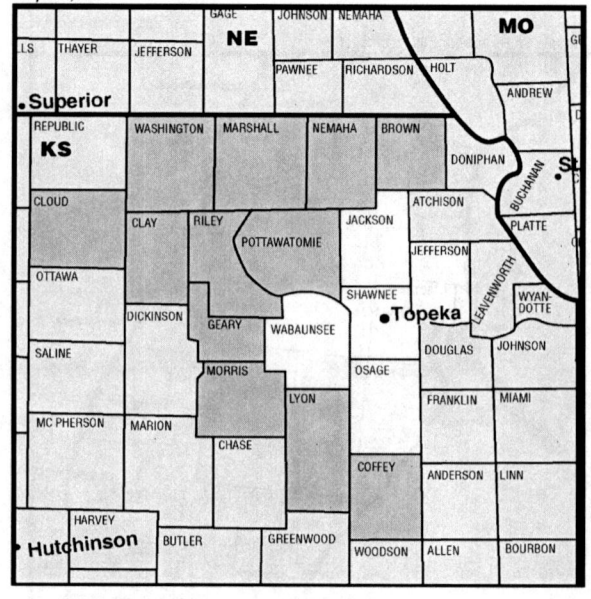
Topeka, KS

Maps courtesy of Nielsen Media Research

Traverse City-Cadillac, MI (117)

DMA TV Households: 247,650
% of U.S. TV Households: .216

WTOM-TV Cheboygan, MI, ch. 4, satellite to WPBN-TV
WPBN-TV Traverse City, MI, ch. 7, NBC
WGTQ Sault Ste. Marie, MI, ch. 8, satellite to WGTU
WWTV Cadillac, MI, ch. 9, CBS
WWUP-TV Sault Ste. Marie, MI, ch. 10, satellite to WWTV
*WCMW Manistee, MI, ch. 21, ETV
*WCMV Cadillac, MI, ch. 27, ETV
WGTU Traverse City, MI, ch. 29, ABC
WFQX-TV Cadillac, MI, ch. 32, Fox
WFUP Vanderbilt, MI, ch. 45, satellite to WFQX-TV

DMA Counties	State	TV Households	DMA Counties	State	TV Households
Antrim	MI	9,840	Mackinac	MI	4,630
Benzie	MI	7,220	Manistee	MI	9,920
Charlevoix	MI	10,620	Mason	MI	11,750
Cheboygan	MI	11,300	Mecosta	MI	16,070
Chippewa	MI	13,750	Missaukee	MI	5,780
Clare	MI	12,620	Montmorency	MI	4,530
Crawford	MI	5,760	Osceola	MI	9,000
Emmet	MI	13,770	Oscoda	MI	3,570
Grand Traverse	MI	34,880	Otsego	MI	9,620
Kalkaska	MI	6,810	Presque Isle	MI	6,080
Lake	MI	4,760	Roscommon	MI	11,330
Leelanau	MI	9,030	Wexford	MI	12,650
Luce	MI	2,360			

Traverse City - Cadillac, MI

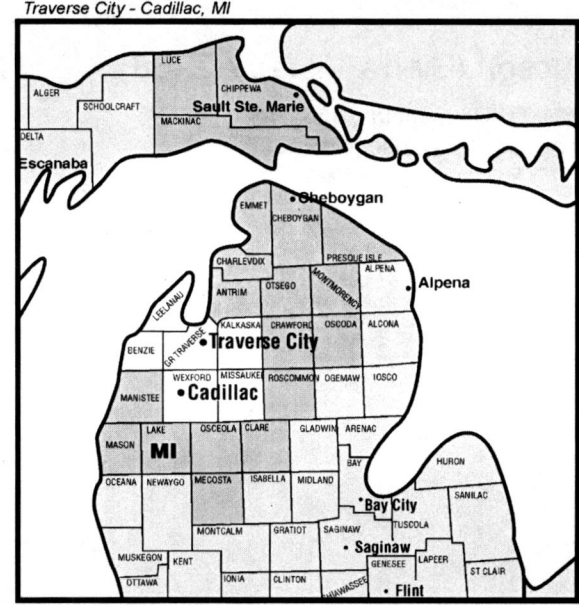

Tri Cities, TN-VA

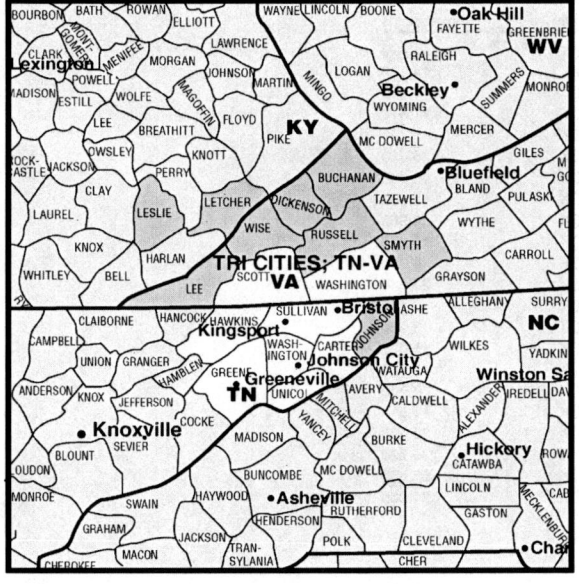

Tri-Cities, TN-VA (92)

DMA TV Households: 332,840
% of U.S. TV Households: .291

WCYB-TV Bristol, VA, ch. 5, NBC, CW, Fox
WJHL-TV Johnson City, TN, ch. 11, CBS
WKPT-TV Kingsport, TN, ch. 19, ABC, MyNetworkTV
WEMT Greeneville, TN, ch. 39, Fox
*WSBN-TV Norton, VA, ch. 47, ETV
*WMSY-TV Marion, VA, ch. 52, ETV
WLFG Grundy, VA, ch. 68, IND

DMA Counties	State	TV Households	DMA Counties	State	TV Households
Leslie	KY	4,780	Buchanan	VA	9,460
Letcher	KY	9,960	Dickenson	VA	6,930
Carter	TN	24,650	Lee	VA	10,120
Greene	TN	27,910	Russell	VA	12,070
Hawkins	TN	24,330	Scott	VA	10,070
Johnson	TN	7,190	Smyth	VA	13,600
Sullivan	TN	66,500	Washington	VA	30,420
Unicoi	TN	7,730	Wise	VA	17,990
Washington	TN	49,130			

Maps courtesy of Nielsen Media Research

Tucson (Sierra Vista), AZ (68)

DMA TV Households: 456,030
% of U.S. TV Households: .398

KFTU-TV Douglas, AZ, ch. 3, TeleFutura
KVOA Tucson, AZ, ch. 4, NBC
KGUN Tucson, AZ, ch. 9, ABC
KOLD-TV Tucson, AZ, ch. 13, CBS
KTTU-TV Tucson, AZ, ch. 18, MyNetworkTV
KMSB Tucson, AZ, ch. 25, Fox
*****KUAS-TV** Tucson, AZ, ch. 27, ETV
*****KUAT-TV** Tucson, AZ, ch. 30, ETV
KHRR Tucson, AZ, ch. 40, Telemundo
KUVE-TV Green Valley, AZ, ch. 46, Univision
KWBA-TV Sierra Vista, AZ, ch. 44, CW

DMA Counties	State	TV Households
Cochise	AZ	50,980
Pima	AZ	390,960
Santa Cruz	AZ	14,090

Tucson (Sierra Vista), AZ

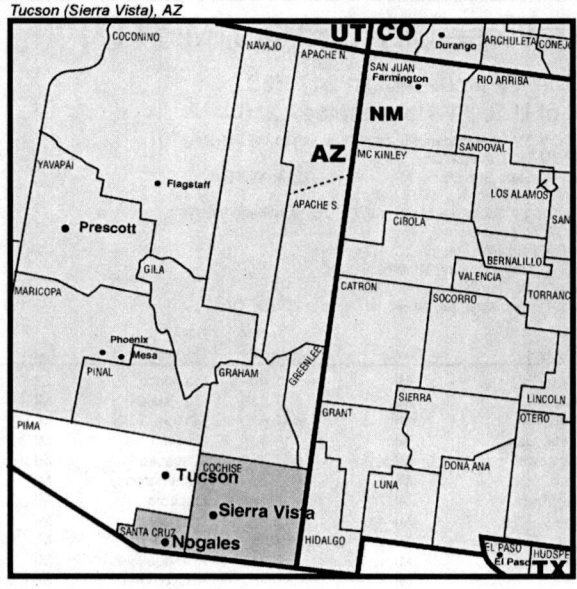

Tulsa, OK (61)

DMA TV Households: 529,540
% of U.S. TV Households: .463

KJRH Tulsa, OK, ch. 2, NBC
KOTV Tulsa, OK, ch. 6, CBS
KTUL Tulsa, OK, ch. 8, ABC
*****KOED-TV** Tulsa, OK, ch. 11, ETV
KDOR-TV Bartlesville, OK, ch. 17, IND
KQCW Muskogee, OK, ch. 19, CW
KOKI-TV Tulsa, OK, ch. 23, Fox
KTPX-TV Okmulgee, OK, ch. 28, ION
   Television
*****KOET** Eufaula, OK, ch. 31, ETV
*****KRSC-TV** Claremore, OK, ch. 35, ETV
KMYT-TV Tulsa, OK, ch. 41, MyNetworkTV
KWHB Tulsa, OK, ch. 47, IND
KGEB Tulsa, OK, ch. 53, IND

Tulsa, OK

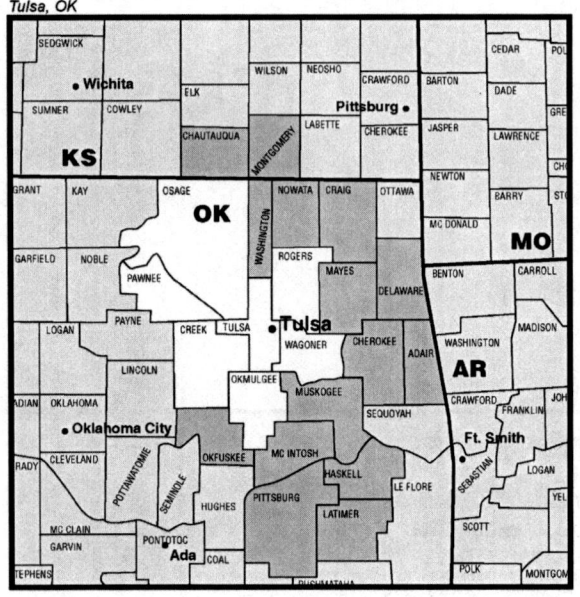

DMA Counties	State	TV Households
Chautauqua	KS	1,470
Montgomery	KS	14,130
Adair	OK	7,850
Cherokee	OK	17,510
Craig	OK	5,740
Creek	OK	26,410
Delaware	OK	16,480
Haskell	OK	4,630
Latimer	OK	3,950
Mayes	OK	15,470
McIntosh	OK	8,300
Muskogee	OK	26,840
Nowata	OK	4,160
Okfuskee	OK	3,950
Okmulgee	OK	15,070
Osage	OK	17,180
Pawnee	OK	6,260
Pittsburg	OK	17,510
Rogers	OK	30,430
Tulsa	OK	239,720
Wagoner	OK	25,480
Washington	OK	21,000

Maps courtesy of Nielsen Media Research

Twin Falls, ID (194)

DMA TV Households: 63,540
% of U.S. TV Households: .056

KIDA Sun Valley, ID, ch. 5, IND
KMVT Twin Falls, ID, ch. 11, CBS
*KIPT Twin Falls, ID, ch. 13, satellite to *KAID
*KBGH Filer, ID, ch. 19, ETV
KXTF Twin Falls, ID, ch. 35, IND

DMA Counties	State	TV Households
Blaine	ID	8,840
Cassia	ID	6,900
Gooding	ID	4,950
Jerome	ID	6,810
Lincoln	ID	1,580
Minidoka	ID	6,410
Twin Falls	ID	28,050

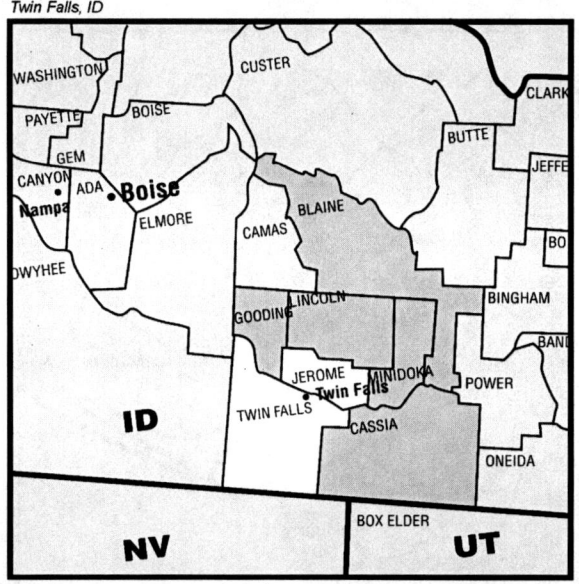

Tyler - Longview (Lufkin & Nacogdoches), TX

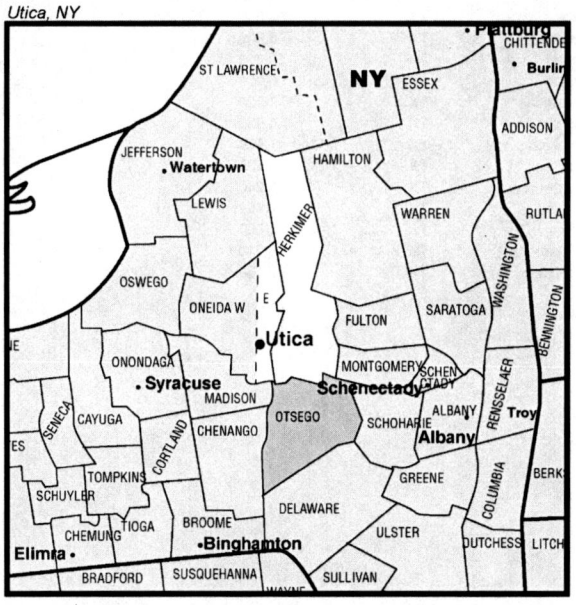

Tyler-Longview (Lufkin & Nacogdoches), TX (110)

DMA TV Households: 265,200
% of U.S. TV Households: .232

KLTV Tyler, TX, ch. 7, ABC
KTRE Lufkin, TX, ch. 9, satellite to KLTV
KYTX Nacogdoches, TX, ch. 19, CBS, MyNetworkTV
KFXK Longview, TX, ch. 51, Fox
KCEB Longview, TX, ch. 54, CW
KETK-TV Jacksonville, TX, ch. 56, NBC

DMA Counties	State	TV Households
Angelina	TX	30,110
Camp	TX	4,750
Cherokee	TX	17,1180
Franklin	TX	4,430
Gregg	TX	45,210
Houston	TX	8,120
Nacogdoches	TX	23,610
Rusk	TX	17,970
Sabine	TX	4,400
San Augustine	TX	3,560
Smith	TX	74,040
Upshur	TX	14,540
Wood	TX	17,350

Utica, NY (169)

DMA TV Households: 106,280
% of U.S. TV Households: .093

WKTV Utica, NY, ch. 2, NBC, CW
WUTR Utica, NY, ch. 20, ABC
WFXV Utica, NY, ch. 33, Fox

DMA Counties	State	TV Households
Herkimer	NY	25,540
Oneida East	NY	57,130
Otsego	NY	23,610

Maps courtesy of Nielsen Media Research

Victoria, TX

Victoria, TX (205)

DMA TV Households: 31,260
% of U.S. TV Households: .027

KVCT Victoria, TX, ch. 19, Fox
KAVU-TV Victoria, TX, ch. 25, ABC

DMA Counties	State	TV Households
Victoria	TX	31,260

Waco-Temple-Bryan, TX (94)

DMA TV Households: 329,690
% of U.S. TV Households: .288

KBTX-TV Bryan, TX, ch. 3, satellite to KWTX-TV
KCEN-TV Temple, TX, ch. 6, ABC
KWTX-TV Waco, TX, ch. 10, CBS, CW
KAKW-DT Killeen, TX, ch. 13, Univision
*__KAMU-TV__ College Station, TX, ch. 15, ETV
KXXV Waco, TX, ch. 25, NBC
KYLE Bryan, TX, ch. 28, satellite to KWKT
*__KWBU-TV__ Waco, TX, ch. 34, ETV
KWKT Waco, TX, ch. 44, Fox, MyNetworkTV
*__KNCT__ Belton, TX, ch. 46, ETV

DMA Counties	State	TV Households
Bell	TX	103,290
Brazos	TX	64,880
Burleson	TX	6,600
Coryell	TX	19,360
Falls	TX	5,900
Lampasas	TX	7,900
Leon	TX	6,650
Limestone	TX	7,950
Madison	TX	4,130
McLennan	TX	83,280
Milam	TX	9,450
Mills	TX	1,960
Robertson	TX	6,210
San Saba	TX	2,130

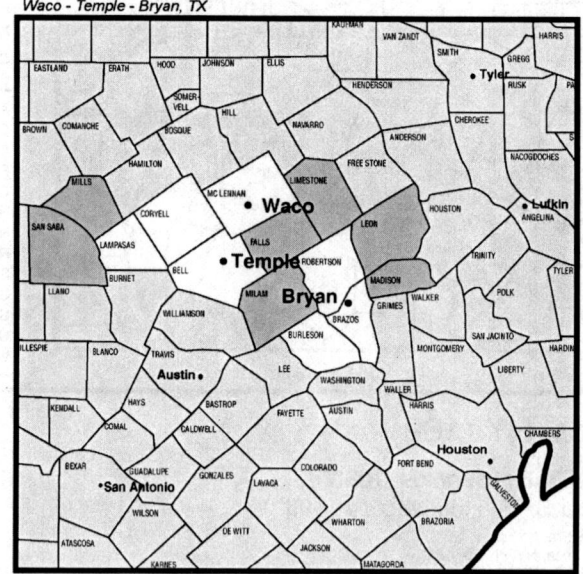

Waco - Temple - Bryan, TX

Washington, DC (Hagerstown, MD) (9)

DMA TV Households: 2,321,610
% of U.S. TV Households: 2.028

WRC-TV Washington, ch. 4, NBC
WTTG Washington, ch. 5, Fox
WJLA-TV Washington, ch. 7, ABC
WUSA Washington, ch. 9, CBS
WFDC-TV Arlington, VA, ch. 14, Univision
WDCA Washington, ch. 20, MyNetworkTV
WHAG-TV Hagerstown, MD, ch. 25, NBC
*WETA-TV Washington, ch. 26, ETV
*WWPB Hagerstown, MD, ch. 31, ETV
*WHUT-TV Washington, ch. 32, ETV

*WVPY Front Royal, VA, ch. 42, ETV
WDCW Washington, ch. 50, CW
*WNVT Goldvein, VA, ch. 53, ETV
*WNVC Fairfax, VA, ch. 56, ETV
WWPX-TV Martinsburg, WV, ch. 12, ION Television
*WFPT Frederick, MD, ch. 28, ETV
WPXW-TV Manassas, VA, ch. 34, ION
WJAL Hagerstown, MD, ch. 68, IND

DMA Counties	State	TV Households	DMA Counties	State	TV Households
Dist of Columbia	DC	257,650	Loudoun	VA	103,700
Allegany	MD	28,630	Page	VA	10,140
Calvert	MD	30,940	Prince William	VA	146,460
Charles	MD	50,670	Rappahannock	VA	2,860
Frederick	MD	82,740	Shenandoah	VA	17,120
Montgomery	MD	345,720	Spotsylvania	VA	53,570
Prince George	MD	295,210	Stafford	VA	41,010
St. Marys	MD	37,400	Warren	VA	13,950
Washington	MD	56,950	Westmoreland	VA	7,120
Fulton	PA	6,220	Berkeley	WV	40,920
Arlington	VA	155,200	Grant	WV	5,030
Clarke	VA	6,010	Hampshire	WV	9,090
Culpeper	VA	17,410	Hardy	WV	5,780
Fairfax	VA	382,320	Jefferson	WV	20,580
Fauquier	VA	24,630	Mineral	WV	10,770
Frederick	VA	40,160	Morgan	WV	6,880
King George	VA	8,770			

Washington, DC (Hagerstown, MD)

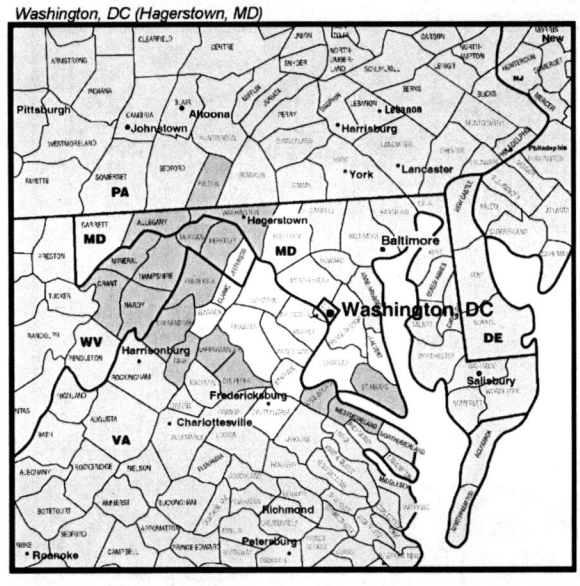

Watertown, NY (177)

DMA TV Households: 94,960
% of U.S. TV Households: .083

WWNY-TV Carthage, NY, ch. 7, CBS
*WNPI-TV Norwood, NY, ch. 23, ETV
*WPBS-TV Watertown, NY, ch. 41, ETV
WWTI Watertown, NY, ch. 50, ABC, CW

DMA Counties	State	TV Households
Jefferson	NY	43,810
Lewis	NY	10,210
St. Lawrence	NY	40,940

Watertown, NY

Maps courtesy of Nielsen Media Research

Wausau - Rhinelander, WI

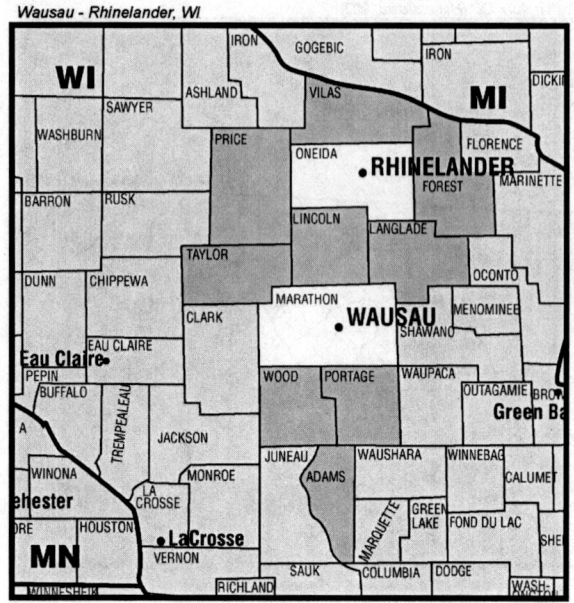

Wausau-Rhinelander, WI (135)

DMA TV Households: 184,220
% of U.S. TV Households: .161

WBIJ Crandon, WI, ch. 4, IND
WSAW-TV Wausau, WI, ch. 7, CBS, MyNetworkTV
WAOW-TV Wausau, WI, ch. 9, ABC, CW
WJFW-TV Rhinelander, WI, ch. 16, NBC
***WHRM-TV** Wausau, WI, ch. 24, ETV
WYOW Eagle River, WI, ch. 28, ABC, CW
WFXS Wittenberg, WI, ch. 31, Fox
***WLEF-TV** Park Falls, WI, ch. 36, ETV
WTPX Antigo, WI, ch. 46, ION Television

DMA Counties	State	TV Households
Adams	WI	8,630
Forest	WI	4,190
Langlade	WI	8,620
Lincoln	WI	12,240
Marathon	WI	52,420
Oneida	WI	15,830
Portage	WI	26,940
Price	WI	6,430
Taylor	WI	7,840
Vilas	WI	9,790
Wood	WI	31,290

West Palm Beach-Ft. Pierce, FL (38)

DMA TV Households: 779,430
% of U.S. TV Households: .681

WPTV West Palm Beach, FL, ch. 5, NBC
WPEC West Palm Beach, FL, ch. 13, CBS
WPBF Tequesta, FL, ch. 25, ABC
WFLX West Palm Beach, FL, ch. 29, Fox
***WXEL-TV** West Palm Beach, FL, ch. 27, ETV
WTVX Ft. Pierce, FL, ch. 34, CW
WPXP-TV Lake Worth, FL, ch. 36, ION Television
***WTCE-TV** Fort Pierce, FL, ch. 38, ETV
WFGC Palm Beach, FL, ch. 61, IND
***WBEC-TV** Boca Raton, FL, ch. 63, ETV

DMA Counties	State	TV Households
Indian River	FL	62,570
Martin	FL	61,450
Okeechobee	FL	14,120
Palm Beach North	FL	321,920
Palm Beach South	FL	206,470
St. Lucie	FL	112,900

West Palm Beach - Ft. Pierce, FL

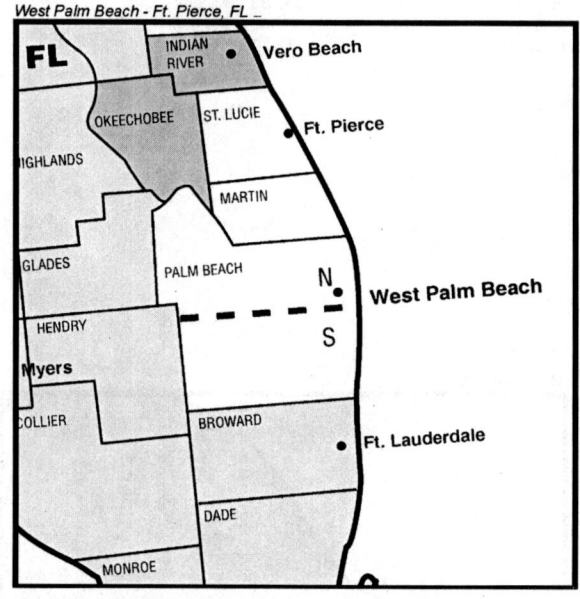

Wheeling, WV - Steubenville, OH

Wheeling, WV-Steubenville, OH (159)

DMA TV Households: 133,700
% of U.S. TV Households: .117

WTRF-TV Wheeling, WV, ch. 7, CBS (ABC)
WTOV-TV Steubenville, OH, ch. 9, NBC

DMA Counties	State	TV Households
Belmont	OH	27,800
Harrison	OH	6,460
Jefferson	OH	28,490
Monroe	OH	5,690
Brooke	WV	9,950
Hancock	WV	12,940
Marshall	WV	13,440
Ohio	WV	18,620
Tyler	WV	3,580
Wetzel	WV	6,730

Maps courtesy of Nielsen Media Research

Wichita Falls, TX & Lawton, OK

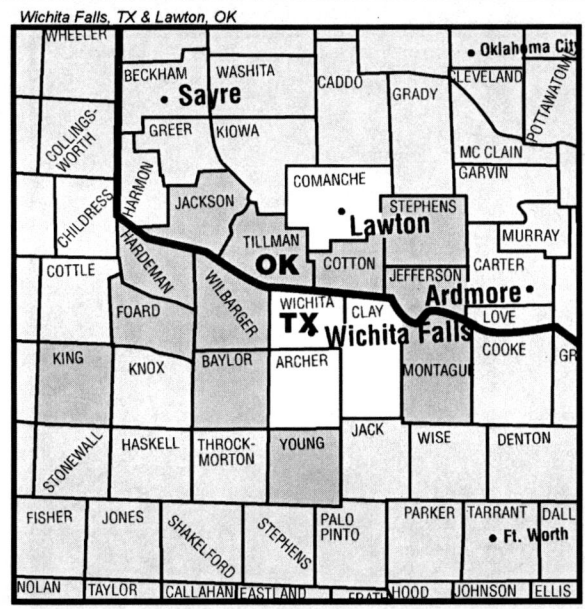

Wichita Falls, TX & Lawton, OK (145)

DMA TV Households: 157,820
% of U.S. TV Households: .138

KFDX-TV Wichita Falls, TX, ch. 3, NBC
KSWO-TV Lawton, OK, ch. 7, ABC
KJTL Wichita Falls, TX, ch. 18, Fox
KAUZ-TV Wichita Falls, TX, ch. 22, CBS, CW

DMA Counties	State	TV Households	DMA Counties	State	TV Households
Comanche	OK	41,370	Clay	TX	4,380
Cotton	OK	2,490	Foard	TX	600
Jackson	OK	9,420	Hardeman	TX	1,690
Jefferson	OK	2,480	King	TX	90
Stephens	OK	17,760	Montague	TX	8,110
Tillman	OK	3,080	Wichita	TX	48,620
Archer	TX	3,480	Wilbarger	TX	5,360
Baylor	TX	1,680	Young	TX	7,210

Wichita - Hutchinson, KS Plus

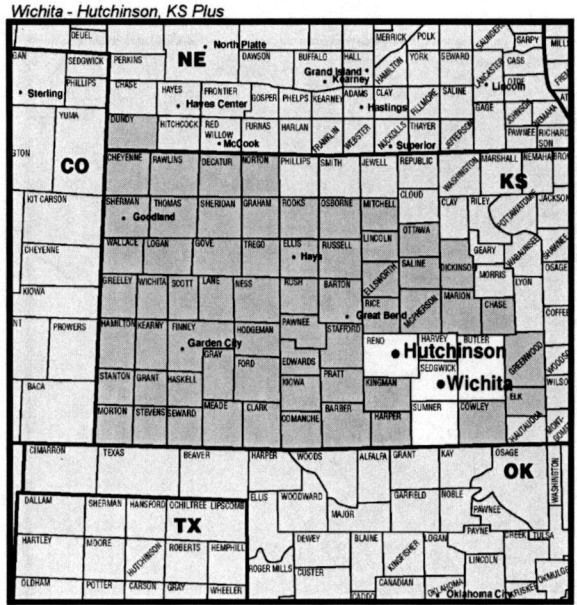

Wichita-Hutchinson Plus, KS (69)

DMA TV Households: 450,930
% of U.S. TV Households: .394

KSNC Great Bend, KS, ch. 2, satellite to KSNW
KSNW Wichita, KS, ch. 3, NBC
*KSWK Lakin, KS, ch. 3, ETV
KLBY Colby, KS, ch. 4, ABC
KSWT Liberal, KS, ch. 5, IND
KBSD-TV Ensign, KS, ch. 6, satellite to KWCH-TV
KBSH-TV Hays, KS, ch. 7, satellite to KWCH-TV
KSNK McCook, NE, ch. 8, satellite to KSNW
*KOOD Hays, KS, ch. 9, ETV
KAKE-TV Wichita, KS, ch. 10, ABC
KBSL-TV Goodland, KS, ch. 10, satellite to KBSH-TV
KSNG Garden City, KS, ch. 11, satellite to KSNW
KWCH-TV Hutchinson, KS, ch. 12, CBS
KUPK-TV Garden City, KS, ch. 13, ABC
KOCW Hoisington, KS, ch. 14, satellite to KSAS-TV
KAAS-TV Salina, KS, ch. 18, satellite to KSAS-TV
KSCW Wichita, KS, ch. 19, CW
*KWKS Colby, KS, ch. 19, ETV
*KDCK Dodge City, KS, ch. 21, ETV
KSAS-TV Wichita, KS, ch. 24, Fox
KDCU-DT Derby, KS, ch. 31, IND
KMTW Hutchinson , KS, ch. 36, MyNetworkTV

DMA Counties	State	TV Households	DMA Counties	State	TV Households
Barber	KS	1,980	McPherson	KS	10,740
Barton	KS	11,360	Marion	KS	4,410
Butler	KS	23,110	Meade	KS	1,590
Chase	KS	1,160	Mitchell	KS	2,560
Cheyenne	KS	1,190	Morton	KS	1,080
Clark	KS	790	Ness	KS	1,290
Comanche	KS	890	Norton	KS	2,000
Cowley	KS	13,060	Osborne	KS	1,680
Decatur	KS	1,290	Ottawa	KS	2,280
Dickinson	KS	7,750	Pawnee	KS	2,290
Edwards	KS	1,290	Pratt	KS	3,860
Elk	KS	1,240	Rawlins	KS	1,090
Ellis	KS	11,440	Reno	KS	24,740
Ellsworth	KS	2,390	Rice	KS	3,690
Finney	KS	11,830	Rooks	KS	2,090
Ford	KS	10,790	Rush	KS	1,390
Gove	KS	960	Russell	KS	2,890
Graham	KS	1,090	Saline	KS	21,810
Grant	KS	2,550	Scott	KS	1,770
Gray	KS	1,840	Sedgwick	KS	189,220
Greeley	KS	490	Seward	KS	7,340
Greenwood	KS	2,860	Sheridan	KS	990
Hamilton	KS	990	Sherman	KS	2,390
Harper	KS	2,360	Stafford	KS	1,790
Harvey	KS	12,780	Stanton	KS	790
Haskell	KS	1,280	Stevens	KS	1,780
Hodgeman	KS	690	Sumner	KS	8,920
Kearny	KS	1,390	Thomas	KS	2,890
Kingman	KS	2,980	Trego	KS	1,280
Kiowa	KS	1,140	Wallace	KS	590
Lane	KS	690	Wichita	KS	790
Lincoln	KS	1,390	Dundy	NE	790
Logan	KS	1,080			

Maps courtesy of Nielsen Media Research

Wilkes Barre-Scranton, PA (54)

DMA TV Households: 594,570
% of U.S. TV Households: .519

WNEP-TV Scranton, PA, ch. 16, ABC
WYOU Scranton, PA, ch. 22, CBS
WBRE-TV Wilkes-Barre, PA, ch. 28, NBC
WSWB Scranton, PA, ch. 31, CW
WQPX-TV Scranton, PA, ch. 32, ION Television
***WVIA-TV** Scranton, PA, ch. 44, ETV
WQMY Williamsport, PA, ch. 53, MyNetworkTV
WOLF-TV Hazleton, PA, ch. 56, Fox

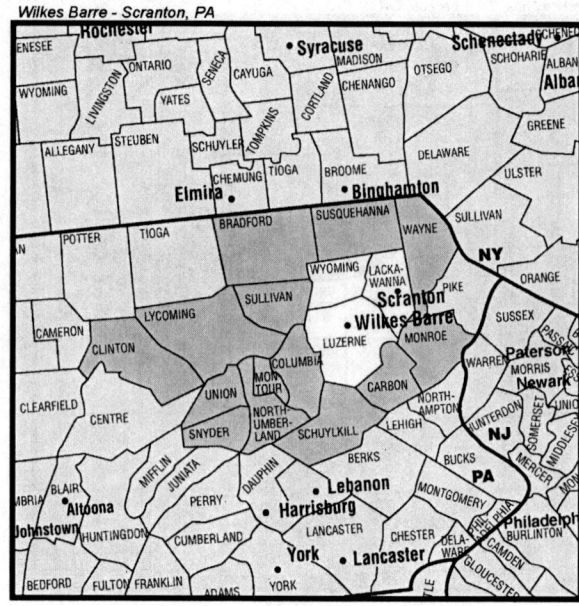

Wilkes Barre - Scranton, PA

DMA Counties	State	TV Households	DMA Counties	State	TV Households
Bradford	PA	24,460	Northumberland	PA	37,360
Carbon	PA	26,550	Schuylkill	PA	59,980
Clinton	PA	14,660	Snyder	PA	13,960
Columbia	PA	25,520	Sullivan	PA	2,520
Lackawanna	PA	86,370	Susquehanna	PA	16,320
Luzerne	PA	130,180	Union	PA	13,630
Lycoming	PA	46,230	Wayne	PA	19,900
Monroe	PA	59,000	Wyoming	PA	10,960
Montour	PA	6,970			

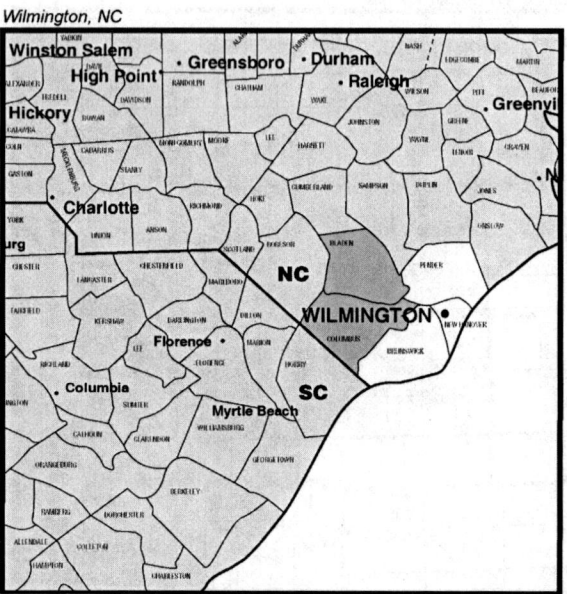

Wilmington, NC

Wilmington, NC (134)

DMA TV Households: 187,480
% of U.S. TV Households: .164

WSFX-TV Wilmington, NC, ch. 30, Fox
***WUNJ-TV** Wilmington, NC, ch. 39, ETV
WECT Wilmington, NC, ch. 44, NBC
WWAY Wilmington, NC, ch. 46, ABC

DMA Counties	State	TV Households
Bladen	NC	13,440
Brunswick	NC	44,530
Columbus	NC	21,790
New Hanover	NC	87,080
Pender	NC	20,640

Yakima-Pasco-Richland-Kennewick, WA (126)

DMA TV Households: 216,780
% of U.S. TV Households: .189

KFFX-TV Pendleton, OR, ch. 11, Fox
KEPR-TV Pasco, WA, ch. 19, satellite to KIMA-TV
KNDO Yakima, WA, ch. 23, NBC
KNDU Richland, WA, ch. 25, satellite to KNDO
KIMA-TV Yakima, WA, ch. 29, CBS
***KTNW** Richland, WA, ch. 31, ETV
KAPP Yakima, WA, ch. 35, ABC, MyNetworkTV
KVEW Kennewick, WA, ch. 42, satellite to KAPP
***KYVE** Yakima, WA, ch. 47, ETV

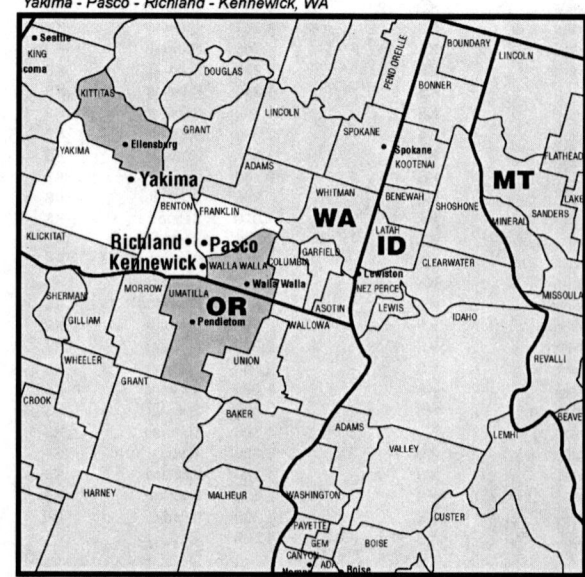

Yakima - Pasco - Richland - Kennewick, WA

DMA Counties	State	TV Households
Umatilla	OR	25,270
Benton	WA	59,430
Franklin	WA	21,100
Kittitas	WA	14,420
Walla Walla	WA	20,210
Yakima	WA	76,350

Youngstown, OH

Youngstown, OH (109)

DMA TV Households: 268,930
% of U.S. TV Households: .235

WFMJ-TV Youngstown, OH, ch. 21, NBC, CW
WKBN-TV Youngstown, OH, ch. 27, CBS
WYTV Youngstown, OH, ch. 33, ABC, MyNetworkTV
***WNEO** Alliance, OH, ch. 45, ETV

DMA Counties	State	TV Households
Columbiana	OH	41,940
Mahoning	OH	95,860
Trumbull	OH	85,290
Mercer	PA	45,840

Yuma, AZ-El Centro, CA (164)

DMA TV Households: 115,650
% of U.S. TV Households: .101

KVYE El Centro, CA, ch. 7, Univision
KECY-TV El Centro, CA, ch. 9, Fox, ABC
KYMA Yuma, AZ, ch. 11, NBC
KSWT Yuma, AZ, ch. 13, CBS, CW
KAJB Calipatria, CA, ch. 54, TeleFutura

DMA Counties	State	TV Households
Yuma	AZ	68,670
Imperial	CA	46,980

Yuma, AZ - El Centro, CA

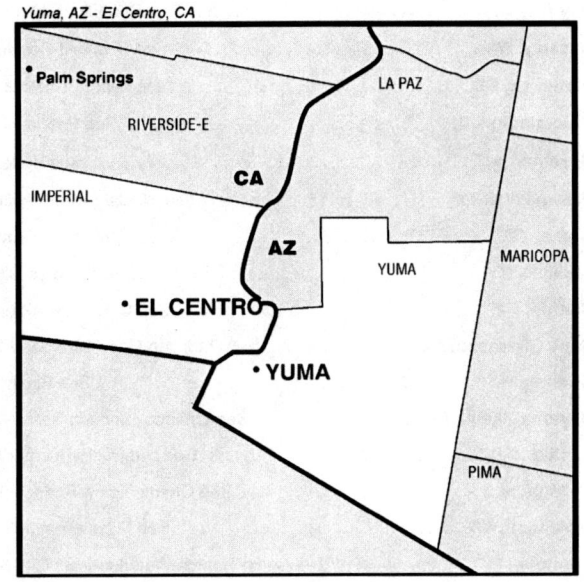

Zanesville, OH

Zanesville, OH (203)

DMA TV Households: 32,550
% of U.S. TV Households: .028

WHIZ-TV Zanesville, OH, ch. 18, NBC

DMA County	State	TV Households
Muskingum	OH	32,550

Maps courtesy of Nielsen Media Research

Multi-City DMA Cross-Reference

The following cities are in hyphenated markets, but are not the first city given in such a market; e.g., Troy in Albany-Schenectady-Troy, NY. They are listed alphabetically.

Ada, OK	See Sherman-Ada
Akron, OH	See Cleveland-Akron (Canton)
Altoona, PA	See Johnstown-Altoona
Ames, IA	See Des Moines-Ames
Anderson, SC	See Greenville-Spartanburg-Asheville-Anderson
Anniston, AL	See Birmingham (Anniston and Tuscaloosa)
Appleton, WI	See Green Bay-Appleton
Asheville, NC	See Greenville-Spartanburg-Asheville-Anderson
Auburn, ME	See Portland-Auburn
Austin, MN	See Rochester-Mason City-Austin
Battle Creek, MI	See Grand Rapids-Kalamazoo-Battle Creek
Bay City, MI	See Flint-Saginaw-Bay City
Beckley, WV	See Bluefield-Beckley-Oak Hill
Bismarck, ND	See Minot-Bismarck-Dickinson
Bloomington, IL	See Peoria-Bloomington
Bozeman, MT	See Butte-Bozeman
Brownsville, TX	See Harlingen-Weslaco-Brownsville-McAllen
Bryan, TX	See Waco-Temple-Bryan
Cadillac, MI	See Traverse City-Cadillac
Canton, OH	See Cleveland-Akron (Canton)
Cape Girardeau, MO	See Paducah-Cape Girardeau-Harrisburg
Corning, NY	See Elmira (Corning)
Daytona Beach, FL	See Orlando-Daytona Beach-Melbourne
Decatur, AL	See Huntsville-Decatur (Florence)
Decatur, IL	See Champaign & Springfield-Decatur
Dickinson, ND	See Minot-Bismarck-Dickinson
Dubuque, IA	See Cedar Rapids-Waterloo-Iowa City & Dubuque
Durham, NC	See Raleigh-Durham (Fayetteville)
Eau Claire, WI	See La Crosse-Eau Claire
El Centro, CA	See Yuma-El Centro
El Dorado, AR	See Monroe-El Dorado
Elkhart, IN	See South Bend-Elkhart
Fayetteville, AR	See Ft. Smith-Fayetteville-Springdale-Rogers
Fayetteville, NC	See Raleigh-Durham (Fayetteville)
Florence, AL	See Huntsville-Decatur (Florence)
Florence, SC	See Myrtle Beach-Florence
Ft. Lauderdale, FL	See Miami-Ft. Lauderdale
Ft. Pierce, FL	See West Palm Beach-Ft. Pierce
Ft. Walton Beach, FL	See Mobile-Pensacola (Ft. Walton Beach)
Ft. Worth, TX	See Dallas-Ft. Worth
Greenville, MS	See Greenwood-Greenville
Gulfport, MS	See Biloxi-Gulfport
Hagerstown, MD	See Washington, DC (Hagerstown)
Hannibal, MO	See Quincy-Hannibal-Keokuk
Harrisburg, IL	See Paducah-Cape Girardeau-Harrisburg
Hastings, NE	See Lincoln & Hastings-Kearney
High Point, NC	See Greensboro-High Point-Winston Salem
Holyoke, MA	See Springfield-Holyoke
Huntington, WV	See Charleston-Huntington
Hutchinson, KS	See Wichita-Hutchinson Plus
Iowa City, IA	See Cedar Rapids-Waterloo-Iowa City & Dubuque
Jefferson City, MO	See Columbia-Jefferson City
Kalamazoo, MI	See Grand Rapids-Kalamazoo-Battle Creek
Kearney, NE	See Lincoln & Hastings-Kearney
Kennewick, WA	See Yakima-Pasco-Richland-Kennewick
Keokuk, IA	See Quincy-Hannibal-Keokuk
Kirksville, MO	See Ottumwa-Kirksville
Klamath Falls, OR	See Medford-Klamath Falls
Lancaster, PA	See Harrisburg-Lancaster-Lebanon-York
Las Cruces, NM	See El Paso (Las Cruces)
Laurel, MS	See Hattiesburg-Laurel
Lawton, OK	See Wichita Falls & Lawton
Lebanon, PA	See Harrisburg-Lancaster-Lebanon-York
Longview, TX	See Tyler-Longview (Lufkin & Nacogdoches)
Lufkin, TX	See Tyler-Longview (Lufkin & Nacogdoches)
Lynchburg, VA	See Roanoke-Lynchburg
Manchester, NH	See Boston (Manchester)
Mason City, IA	See Rochester-Mason City-Austin
McAllen, TX	See Harlingen-Weslaco-Brownsville-McAllen
Melbourne, FL	See Orlando-Daytona Beach-Melbourne
Midland, TX	See Odessa-Midland
Mitchell, SD	See Sioux Falls (Mitchell)
Modesto, CA	See Sacramento-Stockton-Modesto
Moline, IL	See Davenport-Rock Island-Moline
Montrose, CO	See Grand Junction-Montrose
Nacogdoches, TX	See Tyler-Longview (Lufkin & Nacogdoches)
Naples, FL	See Ft. Myers-Naples
New Bedford, MA	See Providence-New Bedford
New Bern, NC	See Greenville-New Bern-Washington
New Haven, CT	See Hartford & New Haven
Newport News, VA	See Norfolk-Portsmouth-Newport News
Oak Hill, WV	See Bluefield-Beckley-Oak Hill
Oakland, CA	See San Francisco-Oakland-San Jose
Pasco, WA	See Yakima-Pasco-Richland-Kennewick
Pensacola, FL	See Mobile-Pensacola
Petersburg, VA	See Richmond-Petersburg
Pine Bluff, AR	See Little Rock-Pine Bluff
Pittsburg, KS	See Joplin-Pittsburg
Plattsburgh, NY	See Burlington-Plattsburgh
Pocatello, ID	See Idaho Falls-Pocatello

Port Arthur, TX . . . . .See Beaumont-Port Arthur

Portsmouth, VA . . . . .See Norfolk-Portsmouth-Newport News

Prescott, AZ . . . . .See Phoenix (Prescott)

Pueblo, CO . . . . .See Colorado Springs-Pueblo

Redding, CA . . . . .See Chico-Redding

Rhinelander, WI . . . . .See Wausau-Rhinelander

Richland, WA . . . . .See Yakima-Pasco-Richland-Kennewick

Riverton, WY . . . . .See Casper-Riverton

Rock Island, IL . . . . .See Davenport-Rock Island-Moline

Rogers, AR .See Ft. Smith-Fayetteville-Springdale-Rogers

Saginaw, MI . . . . .See Flint-Saginaw-Bay City

St. Paul, MN . . . . .See Minneapolis-St. Paul

St. Petersburg, FL . . . . .See Tampa-St. Petersburg (Sarasota)

Salinas, CA . . . . .See Monterey-Salinas

San Jose, CA . . . . .See San Francisco-Oakland-San Jose

San Luis Obispo, CA . . . . .See Santa Barbara-Santa Maria-San Luis Obispo

Santa Fe, NM . . . . .See Albuquerque-Santa Fe

Santa Maria, CA . . . . .See Santa Barbara-Santa Maria-San Luis Obispo

Sarasota, FL . . . . .See Tampa-St. Petersburg (Sarasota)

Schenectady, NY . . . . .See Albany-Schenectady-Troy

Scottsbluff, NE . . . . .See Cheyenne-Scottsbluff

Scranton, PA . . . . .See Wilkes Barre-Scranton

Selma, AL . . . . .See Montgomery-Selma

Sierra Vista, AZ . . . . .See Tucson (Sierra Vista)

Spartanburg, SC . . . . .See Greenville-Spartanburg-Asheville-Anderson

Springdale, AR . . . . .See Ft. Smith-Fayetteville-Springdale-Rogers

Springfield, IL . . . . .See Champaign & Springfield-Decatur

Steubenville, OH . . . . .See Wheeling-Steubenville

Stockton, CA . . . . .See Sacramento-Stockton-Modesto

Superior, WI . . . . .See Duluth-Superior

Sweetwater, TX . . . . .See Abilene-Sweetwater

Tacoma, WA . . . . .See Seattle-Tacoma

Temple, TX . . . . .See Waco-Temple-Bryan

Thomasville, GA . . . . .See Tallahassee-Thomasville

Troy, NY . . . . .See Albany-Schenectady-Troy

Tupelo, MS . . . . .See Columbus-Tupelo-West Point

Tuscaloosa, AL . . . . .See Birmingham (Anniston and Tuscaloosa)

Valley City, ND . . . . .See Fargo-Valley City

Visalia, CA . . . . .See Fresno-Visalia

Washington, NC . . . . .See Greenville-New Bern-Washington

Waterloo, IA . . . . .See Cedar Rapids-Waterloo-Iowa City & Dubuque

Weslaco, TX . . . . .See See Harlingen-Weslaco-Brownsville-McAllen

Weston, WV . . . . .See Clarksburg-Weston

West Point, MS . . . . .See Columbus-Tupelo-West Point

Winston Salem, NC . . . . .See Greensboro-High Point-Winston Salem

York, PA . . . . .See Harrisburg-Lancaster-Lebanon-York

Section C
Cable

Top 25 Cable System Operators

Ranked by Basic Subscribers*

Rank	Company	Subscribers
1	Comcast	24,182.0
2	Time Warner	13,069.0
3	Cox	5,328.3
4	Charter	5,045.7
5	Cablevision Systems	3,108.0
6	Bright House (e)	2,307.8
7	Mediacom	1,318.0
8	Suddenlink Communications	1,268.7
9	Insight Communications	707.6
10	Cable One	669.5
11	RCN	366.0
12	WideOpenWest (e)	363.8
13	Bresnan	309.4
14	Service Electric (e)	290.7
15	Atlantic Broadband	285.5
16	Armstrong	247.3
17	Knology	232.8
18	Midcontinent Communications (&)	206.2
19	MetroCast Cablevision **	188.9
20	Blue Ridge (e)	177.4
21	Broadstripe (e)	158.4
22	Buckeye CableSystem (e)	147.8
23	General Communication	147.7
24	Wave (e)	141.2
25	MidOcean Partners (e)	139.8

* As of December 2008.
** Includes Vista III Media.
(e) Estimate.
(&) Counts include recent sale or acquisition.
Subs in mil. Data actual.
Note: Unless otherwise noted, counts include owned and managed subscribers.

Cable Penetration by DMA

Listed below are the Neilsen Media Research Designated Market Areas (DMAs) with the number of cable homes and the percentage of penetration.

Designated Market Area	Cable Households	Cable Penetration (%)
Abilene-Sweetwater	48,500	42
Albany, GA	93,100	59
Albany-Schenectady-Troy	425,440	76
Albuquerque-Santa Fe	282,200	41
Alexandria, LA	58,190	65
Alpena	10,680	61
Amarillo	89,390	47
Anchorage	101,860	68
Atlanta	1,374,120	58
Augusta	159,290	63
Austin	438,110	66
Bakersfield	119,010	54
Baltimore	772,940	70
Bangor	63,500	44
Baton Rouge	245,730	75
Beaumont-Port Arthur	100,600	61
Bend, OR	42,800	66
Billings	57,230	54
Biloxi-Gulfport	86,400	71
Binghamton	105,640	76
Birmingham (Anniston, Tuscaloosa)	370,910	50
Bluefield-Beckley-Oak Hill	98,350	69
Boise	83,620	32
Boston (Manchester)	2,009,300	83
Bowling Green	54,440	68
Buffalo	390,010	62
Burlington-Plattsburgh	166,340	50
Butte-Bozeman	29,360	45
Casper-Riverton	34,220	63
Cedar Rapids-Waterloo & Dubuque	206,960	60
Champaign & Springfield-Decatur	230,100	60
Charleston, SC	199,390	65
Charleston-Huntington	282,530	59
Charlotte	674,860	60
Charlottesville	42,370	55
Chattanooga	225,510	61
Cheyenne-Scottsbluff	34,810	64
Chicago	2,132,960	61
Chico-Redding	69,830	35
Cincinnati	540,910	59
Clarksburg-Weston	59,890	55
Cleveland	1,066,060	70
Colorado Springs-Pueblo	151,200	45
Columbia, SC	230,720	52
Columbia-Jefferson City	66,200	37
Columbus, GA	154,206	72
Columbus, OH	626,170	68
Columbus-Tupelo-West Point	70,460	37
Corpus Christi	134,850	68
Dallas-Fort Worth	1,043,110	42
Davenport-Rock Island-Moline	176,690	57
Dayton	302,580	63
Denver	831,880	55
Des Moines-Ames	194,410	45
Detroit	1,274,510	66

Designated Market Area	Cable Households	Cable Penetration (%)
Dothan	67,810	67
Duluth-Superior	72,000	42
El Paso	139,620	45
Elmira	69,150	72
Erie	92,330	59
Eugene	118,970	49
Eureka	38,530	63
Evansville	157,300	54
Fairbanks	15,850	43
Fargo-Valley City	135,550	56
Flint-Saginaw-Bay City	281,050	60
Fort Myers-Naples	355,000	70
Fort Smith-Fayetteville-Springdale-Rogers	155,730	52
Fort Wayne	124,130	45
Fresno-Visalia	224,500	39
Gainesville	79,170	61
Glendive	2,910	74
Grand Junction-Montrose	39,840	54
Grand Rapids-Kalamazoo-Battle Creek	399,530	54
Great Falls	30,440	47
Green Bay-Appleton	219,860	49
Greensboro-High Point-Winston Salem	428,550	63
Greenville-New Bern-Washington	164,130	57
Greenville-Spartanburg-Asheville-Anderson	407,080	47
Greenwood-Greenville	44,530	64
Harlingen-Weslaco-Brownsville-McAllen	142,790	41
Harrisburg-Lancaster-Lebanon-York	520,750	70
Harrisonburg	56,980	61
Hartford & New Haven	817,380	81
Hattiesburg-Laurel	52,730	48
Helena	15,140	56
Honolulu	384,720	89
Houston	1,090,680	52
Huntsville-Decatur, Florence	221,930	57
Idaho Falls-Pocatello	45,340	36
Indianapolis	620,830	56
Jackson, MS	150,990	45
Jackson, TN	60,720	62
Jacksonville, Brunswick	413,710	61
Johnstown-Altoona	195,090	66
Jonesboro	49,450	61
Joplin-Pittsburg	59,390	38
Juneau	17,530	69
Kansas City	576,100	61
Knoxville	326,530	60
La Crosse-Eau Claire	116,490	54
Lafayette, IN	48,200	72
Lafayette, LA	142,760	62
Lake Charles	64,020	67
Lansing	138,620	54
Laredo	41,580	61
Las Vegas	494,100	68
Lexington	274,070	54
Lima	50,710	72
Lincoln & Hastings-Kearney	159,500	57
Little Rock-Pine Bluff	245,590	43
Los Angeles	2,853,210	50
Louisville	415,700	62
Lubbock	67,880	43

Designated Market Area	Cable Households	Cable Penetration (%)
Macon	134,020	56
Madison	193,660	51
Mankato	34,220	66
Marquette	62,620	70
Medford-Klamath Falls	76,150	44
Memphis	346,460	51
Meridian	28,580	40
Miami-Fort Lauderdale	990,450	64
Milwaukee	568,860	63
Minneapolis-St. Paul	994,480	57
Minot-Bismarck-Dickinson	87,360	64
Missoula	40,960	37
Mobile-Pensacola (Fort Walton Beach)	324,440	60
Monroe-El Dorado	88,080	49
Monterey-Salinas	128,880	57
Montgomery (Selma)	165,830	67
Myrtle Beach-Florence	185,740	65
Nashville	545,870	54
New Orleans	385,270	64
New York	6,140,730	83
Norfolk-Portsmouth-Newport News	508,080	71
North Platte	10,190	67
Odessa-Midland	95,010	67
Oklahoma City	385,920	56
Omaha	300,530	73
Orlando-Daytona Beach-Melbourne	1,028,710	70
Ottumwa-Kirksville	23,450	46
Paducah-Cape Girardeau-Harrisburg-Mt. Vernon	160,310	41
Palm Springs	129,290	81
Panama City	93,900	64
Parkersburg	45,190	71
Peoria-Bloomington	154,700	62
Philadelphia	2,266,810	77
Phoenix	1,020,380	55
Pittsburgh	837,960	72
Portland, OR	633,090	54
Portland-Auburn	275,600	67
Presque Isle	18,530	59
Providence-New Bedford	519,890	84
Quincy-Hannibal-Keokuk	45,530	44
Raleigh-Durham (Fayetteville)	628,210	58
Rapid City	63,100	65
Reno	140,610	52
Richmond-Petersburg	311,830	57
Roanoke-Lynchburg	218,340	47
Rochester, NY	269,070	69
Rochester-Mason City-Austin	92,990	64
Rockford	110,630	59
Sacramento-Stockton-Modesto	655,360	47
Salisbury	117,190	74
Salt Lake City	360,280	39
San Angelo	32,450	59
San Antonio	498,380	61
San Diego	847,190	79
San Francisco-Oakland-San Jose	1,665,620	67
Santa Barbara-Santa Maria-San Luis Obispo	153,480	64
Savannah	193,440	61
Seattle-Tacoma	1,258,010	69
Sherman, TX-Ada, OK	55,490	43

Designated Market Area	Cable Households	Cable Penetration (%)
Shreveport	151,550	39
Sioux City	88,470	58
Sioux Falls (Mitchell)	165,630	64
South Bend-Elkhart	147,890	44
Spokane	176,510	42
Springfield, MO	122,900	29
Springfield-Holyoke	220,040	84
St. Joseph	29,260	62
St. Louis	600,780	48
Syracuse	286,650	74
Tallahassee-Thomasville	166,120	59
Tampa-St. Petersburg, Sarasota	1,361,340	75
Terre Haute	64,360	44
Toledo	259,930	61
Topeka	105,950	60
Traverse City-Cadillac	118,860	48
Tri-Cities, TN-VA	205,490	62
Tucson (Sierra Vista)	253,250	56
Tulsa	274,740	52
Twin Falls	26,700	42
Tyler-Longview (Lufkin & Nacogdoches)	110,340	42
Utica	79,640	75
Victoria	20,300	65
Waco-Temple-Bryan	180,720	55
Washington, DC (Hagerstown)	1,497,900	65
Watertown	62,620	66
Wausau-Rhinelander	83,300	45
West Palm Beach-Fort Pierce	538,600	69
Wheeling-Steubenville	99,520	74
Wichita Falls & Lawton	75,390	48
Wichita-Hutchinson Plus	280,220	62
Wilkes Barre-Scranton	395,230	66
Wilmington	129,370	69
Yakima-Pasco-Richland-Kennewick	90,510	42
Youngstown	184,990	69
Yuma-El Centro	46,870	41
Zanesville	23,540	72

Top 50 DMA by Cable Penetration

Listed below are the Nielsen Media Research Designated Market Areas (DMAs) ranked by percentage of cable penetration.

Rank	Designated Market Area	Cable Penetration (%)
1	Honolulu	89
2	Providence-New Bedford	84
2	Springfield-Holyoke	84
4	Boston (Manchester)	83
4	New York	83
6	Hartford & New Haven	81
6	Palm Springs	81
8	San Diego	79
9	Philadelphia	77
10	Albany-Schenectady-Troy	76
10	Binghamton	76
12	Baton Rouge	75
12	Tampa-St. Petersburg, Sarasota	75
12	Utica	75
15	Glendive	74
15	Salisbury	74
15	Syracuse	74
15	Wheeling-Steubenville	74
19	Omaha	73
20	Columbus, GA	72
20	Elmira	72
20	Lafayette, IN	72
20	Lima	72
20	Pittsburgh	72
20	Zanesville	72
26	Biloxi-Gulfport	71
26	Norfolk-Portsmouth-Newport News	71
26	Parkersburg	71
29	Baltimore	70
29	Cleveland	70
29	Fort Myers-Naples	70
29	Harrisburg-Lancaster-Lebanon-York	70
29	Marquette	70
29	Orlando-Daytona Beach-Melbourne	70
35	Bluefield-Beckley-Oak Hill	69
35	Juneau	69
35	Rochester, NY	69
35	Seattle-Tacoma	69
35	West Palm Beach-Fort Pierce	69
35	Wilmington	69
35	Youngstown	69
42	Anchorage	68
42	Bowling Green	68
42	Columbus, OH	68
42	Corpus Christi	68
42	Las Vegas	68
47	Dothan	67
47	Lake Charles	67
47	Montgomery (Selma)	67
47	North Platte	67
47	Odessa-Midland	67
47	Portland-Auburn	67
47	San Francisco-Oakland-San Jose	67

Bottom 50 DMA by Cable Penetration

Listed below are the Nielsen Media Research Designated Market Areas (DMAs) ranked by percentage of cable penetration. Boise and Fairbanks have the lowest percentage.

Rank	Designated Market Area	Cable Penetration (%)
210	Springfield, MO	29
209	Boise	32
208	Chico-Redding	35
207	Idaho Falls-Pocatello	36
204	Columbia-Jefferson City	37
204	Columbus-Tupelo-West Point	37
204	Missoula	37
203	Joplin-Pittsburg	38
200	Fresno-Visalia	39
200	Salt Lake City	39
200	Shreveport	39
199	Meridian	40
195	Albuquerque-Santa Fe	41
195	Harlingen-Weslaco-Brownsville-McAllen	41
195	Paducah-Cape Girardeau-Harrisburg-Mt. Vernon	41
195	Yuma-El Centro	41
188	Abilene-Sweetwater	42
188	Dallas-Fort Worth	42
188	Duluth-Superior	42
188	Spokane	42
188	Twin Falls	42
188	Tyler-Longview (Lufkin & Nacogdoches)	42
188	Yakima-Pasco-Richland-Kennewick	42
184	Fairbanks	43
184	Little Rock-Pine Bluff	43
184	Lubbock	43
184	Sherman, TX-Ada, OK	43
179	Bangor	44
179	Medford-Klamath Falls	44
179	Quincy-Hannibal-Keokuk	44
179	South Bend-Elkhart	44
179	Terre Haute	44
172	Butte-Bozeman	45
172	Colorado Springs-Pueblo	45
172	Des Moines-Ames	45
172	El Paso	45
172	Fort Wayne	45
172	Jackson, MS	45
172	Wausau-Rhinelander	45
171	Ottumwa-Kirksville	46
166	Amarillo	47
166	Great Falls	47
166	Greenville-Spartanburg-Asheville-Anderson	47
166	Roanoke-Lynchburg	47
166	Sacramento-Stockton-Modesto	47

Rank	Designated Market Area	Cable Penetration (%)
162	Hattiesburg-Laurel	48
162	St. Louis	48
162	Traverse City-Cadillac	48
162	Wichita Falls & Lawton	48
159	Eugene	49
159	Green Bay-Appleton	49
159	Monroe-El Dorado	49

Top 50 DMA by Cable Households

Listed below are the Nielsen Media Research Designated Market Areas (DMAs) ranked by cable television households.

Rank	Designated Market Area	Cable Penetration (%)	Cable Households
1	New York	83	6,140,730
2	Los Angeles	50	2,853,210
3	Philadelphia	77	2,266,810
4	Chicago	61	2,132,960
5	Boston (Manchester)	83	2,009,300
6	San Francisco-Oakland-San Jose	67	1,665,620
7	Washington, DC (Hagerstown)	65	1,497,900
8	Atlanta	58	1,374,120
9	Tampa-St. Petersburg, Sarasota	75	1,361,340
10	Detroit	66	1,274,510
11	Seattle-Tacoma	69	1,258,010
12	Houston	52	1,090,680
13	Cleveland	70	1,066,060
14	Dallas-Fort Worth	42	1,043,110
15	Orlando-Daytona Beach-Melbourne	70	1,028,710
16	Phoenix	55	1,020,380
17	Minneapolis-St. Paul	57	994,480
18	Miami-Fort Lauderdale	64	990,450
19	San Diego	79	847,190
20	Pittsburgh	72	837,960
21	Denver	55	831,880
22	Hartford & New Haven	81	817,380
23	Baltimore	70	772,940
24	Charlotte	60	674,860
25	Sacramento-Stockton-Modesto	47	655,360
26	Portland, OR	54	633,090
27	Raleigh-Durham (Fayetteville)	58	628,210
28	Columbus, OH	68	626,170
29	Indianapolis	56	620,830
30	St. Louis	48	600,780
31	Kansas City	61	576,100
32	Milwaukee	63	568,860
33	Nashville	54	545,870
34	Cincinnati	59	540,910
35	West Palm Beach-Fort Pierce	69	538,600
36	Harrisburg-Lancaster-Lebanon-York	70	520,750
37	Providence-New Bedford	84	519,890
38	Norfolk-Portsmouth-Newport News	71	508,080
39	San Antonio	61	498,380
40	Las Vegas	68	494,100
41	Austin	66	438,110
42	Greensboro-High Point-Winston Salem	63	428,550
43	Albany-Schenectady-Troy	76	425,440
44	Louisville	62	415,700
45	Jacksonville, Brunswick	61	413,710
46	Greenville-Spartanburg-Asheville-Anderson	47	407,080
47	Grand Rapids-Kalamazoo-Battle Creek	54	399,530
48	Wilkes Barre-Scranton	66	395,230
49	Buffalo	62	390,010
50	Oklahoma City	56	385,920

Section D

Radio

Section D

Radio

Radio Group Ownership

A

ABC Inc., 2300 Riverside Dr., Burbank, CA 91521. Phone: (818) 249-9999. Web Site:www.abc.go.com Ownership ABC Enterprises Inc., 100%. Note: ABC Enterprises Inc. is 100% owned by Disney Enterprises Inc. Disney Enterprises Inc. is 100% owned by The Walt Disney Co.

Stns: 43 AM. 3 FM. KDIS-FM Little Rock, AR; KMIK Tempe, AZ; KSPN(AM) Los Angeles, CA; KMKY Oakland, CA; KDIS(AM) Pasadena, CA; KIID(AM) Sacramento, CA; KDDZ Arvada, CO; WDZK Bloomfield, CT; WBWL Jacksonville, FL; WMYM(AM) Miami, FL; WDYZ(AM) Orlando, FL; WMNE(AM) Riviera Beach, FL; WWMI Saint Petersburg, FL; WDWD Atlanta, GA; WSDZ Belleville, IL; WMVP Chicago, IL; WRDZ La Grange, IL; WRDZ-FM Plainfield, IN; KQAM Wichita, KS; WDRD(AM) Newburg, KY; WBYU New Orleans, LA; WMKI(AM) Boston, MA; WFDF(AM) Farmington Hills, MI; KDIZ Golden Valley, MN; KPHN Kansas City, MO; WGFY Charlotte, NC; WCOG Greensboro, NC; WWJZ Mount Holly, NJ; KALY Los Ranchos de Albuquerque, NM; WDDY(AM) Albany, NY; WEPN(AM) New York, NY; WQEW New York, NY; WWMK Cleveland, OH; KDZR(AM) Lake Oswego, OR; WEAE Pittsburgh, PA; WDDZ(AM) Pawtucket, RI; KESN(FM) Allen, TX; KMIC(AM) Houston, TX; KMKI Plano, TX; KRDY(AM) San Antonio, TX; KWDZ(AM) Salt Lake City, UT; WDZY Colonial Heights, VA; WRJR(AM) Portsmouth, VA; WHKT Portsmouth, VA; KKDZ Seattle, WA; WKSH(AM) Sussex, WI.

Stns: 10 TV. WLS, Chicago; WJRT-TV, Flint-Saginaw-Bay City, MI; KFSN-TV, Fresno-Visalia, CA; KTRK, Houston; KABC, Los Angeles; WABC-TV, New York; WPVI, Philadelphia; WTVD, Raleigh-Durham (Fayetteville), NC; KGO, San Francisco-Oakland-San Jose; WTVG, Toledo, OH.

Robert A. Iger, pres; Phillip J. Meek, pres; Lawrence J. Pollock, chmn owned TV stns.

ARKLATEX Radio Inc., 111 Westwood Dr., De Queen, AR 71832. Phone: (870) 642-2446. Fax: (870) 642-2442. Ownership Jay Wallace Bunyard and Teresa Sharon Bunyard Living Revocable Trust, Jay and Teresa Bunyard sole voting trustees, 100%.

Stns: 1 AM. 2 FM. KMTB-FM Murfreesboro, AR; KNAS-FM Nashville, AR; KBHC Nashville, AR.

Jay Bunyard, pres; Bonita Smith, CFO.

AVC Communications Inc., Box 338, Cambridge, OH 43725. Phone: (740) 432-5605. Fax: (740) 432-1991. Web Site:www.yourradioplace.com Ownership W. Grant Hafley, 100%.

Stns: 1 AM. 2 FM. KMTB-FM Murfreesboro, AR; KNAS-FM Nashville, AR; KBHC Nashville, AR2 FM. WILE-FM Byesville, OH; WCMJ-FM Cambridge, OH.

Grant Hafley, pres; Joel Losego, gen mgr; David Wilson, opns mgr.

Aboriginal Voices Radio Inc., Box 87, Station E, Toronto, ON M6H 4E1. Canada. Phone: (416) 703-1287. Fax: (416) 703-4328.E-mail: info@boriginalvoices.com Web Site:www.aboriginalradio.com

Stns: 1 AM. 2 FM. KMTB-FM Murfreesboro, AR; KNAS-FM Nashville, AR; KBHC Nashville, AR; WILE-FM Byesville, OH; WCMJ-FM Cambridge, OH5 FM. CKAV-FM-3 Calgary, AB; CKAV-FM-4 Edmonton, AB; CKAV-FM-2 Vancouver, BC; CKAV-FM-9 Ottawa, ON; CKAV-FM Toronto, ON.

Absolute Broadcasting LLC, 30 Temple Dr., Litchfield, NH 03052. Phone: (603) 883-9900. Ownership Monahan Family LLC, 98%; and Thomas F. Monahan, 2%.

Stns: 3 AM. WGAM(AM) Manchester, NH; WGHM(AM) Nashua, NH; WSMN Nashua, NH.

Acadia Broadcasting Ltd., Box 2000, Saint John, NB E2L 3T4. Canada. Phone: (506) 648-2100. Fax: (506) 632-3407.E-mail: info@radioabl.ca Web Site:www.acadiabroadcastinglimited.ca Ownership Ocean Capital Investments NB Ltd., 100%.

Stns: 3 AM. WGAM(AM) Manchester, NH; WGHM(AM) Nashua, NH; WSMN Nashua, NH11 FM. CHWV-FM Saint John, NB; CHSJ-FM Saint John, NB; CHTD-FM Saint Stephen, NB; CKBW-FM Bridgewater, NS; CKBW-FM-1 Liverpool, NS; CKBW-FM-2 Shelburne, NS; CKDR-FM Dryden, ON; CFOB-FM Fort Frances, ON; CJRL-FM Kenora, ON; CKDR-FM-5 Red Lake, ON; CKDR-FM-2 Sioux Lookout, ON.

Access.1 Communications Corp., 11 Penn Plaza, 16th Fl., New York, NY 10001. Phone: (212) 714-1000. Fax: (212) 714-1563. Ownership Sydney L. Small, 54.12%;

Black Enterprise/Greenwich Street Capital Partners, 19.47%; MESBIC Ventures Inc., 5.54%; Chesley Maddox-Dorsey, 2.84%; and Adriane Gaines, 1.85%.

Stns: 5 AM. 10 FM. KSYR(FM) Benton, LA; KDKS-FM Blanchard, LA; KBTT(FM) Haughton, LA; KLKL(FM) Minden, LA; KOKA Shreveport, LA; WGYM(AM) Hammonton, NJ; WWRL(AM) New York, NY; KOYE(FM) Frankston, TX; KOOI-FM Jacksonville, TX; KFRO Longview, TX; KYKX-FM Longview, TX; KCUL Marshall, TX; KCUL-FM Marshall, TX; KTAL-FM Texarkana, TX; KKUS(FM) Tyler, TX.

Stns: 1 TV. WMGM-TV, Philadelphia.

Sydney L. Small, chmn/CEO.

Ace Radio Corp., 2801 Via Fortuna Dr., Suite 675, Austin, TX 78746. Ownership Stephen M. Hackerman, 51%; and Spectrum Radio Co., 49%.

Stns: 5 AM. 10 FM. KSYR(FM) Benton, LA; KDKS-FM Blanchard, LA; KBTT(FM) Haughton, LA; KLKL(FM) Minden, LA; KOKA Shreveport, LA; WGYM(AM) Hammonton, NJ; WWRL(AM) New York, NY; KOYE(FM) Frankston, TX; KOOI-FM Jacksonville, TX; KFRO Longview, TX; KYKX-FM Longview, TX; KCUL Marshall, TX; KCUL-FM Marshall, TX; KTAL-FM Texarkana, TX; KKUS(FM) Tyler, TX8 FM. KRPH(FM) Yarnell, AZ; KQNO(FM) Coalinga, CA; KQMX(FM) Lost Hills, CA; KCOO(FM) Dunkerton, IA; WTPO(FM) New Albany, MS; WZHL(FM) New Augusta, MS; KQLP(FM) Gallup, NM; KBWT(FM) Santa Anna, TX.

Gordon Ackley Stns, Box 302179, St. Thomas, VI 00803-2179. Phone: (340) 776-3291. Fax: (340) 776-7060. Ownership Gordon P. Ackley, 100%.

Stns: 1 AM. 2 FM. WVWI Charlotte Amalie, VI; WVJZ-FM Charlotte Amalie, VI; WWKS-FM Cruz Bay, VI.

Ad Astra Per Aspera Broadcasting Inc., 106 N. Main St., Hutchinson, KS 67501-5219. Phone: (620) 665-5758. Fax: (620) 665-6655.E-mail: cliffcshank@yahoo.com Ownership Cliff C. Shank, 71%; Michael G. Hill, 14%.

Stns: 1 AM. 2 FM. WVWI Charlotte Amalie, VI; WVJZ-FM Charlotte Amalie, VI; WWKS-FM Cruz Bay, VI4 FM. KNZS(FM) Arlington, KS; KWHK(FM) Hutchinson, KS; KXKU(FM) Lyons, KS; KSKU(FM) Sterling, KS.

Cliff C. Shank, pres & gen mgr; Michael G. Hill, VP & sls mgr.

Adelman Broadcasting Inc., 731 N. Balsam, Ridgecrest, CA 93555. Phone: (760) 371-1700. Fax: (760) 371-1824. Web Site:adelmanbroadcasting.com Ownership Robert Adelman, 100%.

Stns: 1 AM. 3 FM. KGBB(FM) Edwards, CA; KRAJ(FM) Johannesburg, CA; KLOA Ridgecrest, CA; KEPD(FM) Ridgecrest, CA.

Robert Adelman, owner.

Adonai Radio Group, 2448 E. 81st St., Suite 5500, Tulsa, OK 74137. Phone: (918) 492-2660. Fax: (918) 492-8840.E-mail: mail@kxoj.com Web Site:www.kxoj.com

Stns: 2 AM. 6 FM. KEOJ-FM Caney, KS; KTFR-FM Chelsea, OK; KEMX-FM Locust Grove, OK; KBIX Muskogee, OK; KYAL-FM Muskogee, OK; KYAL(AM) Sapulpa, OK; KXOJ-FM Sapulpa, OK; KCXR(FM) Taft, OK.

Michael P. Stephens, pres.

Air South Radio Inc., Box 2116, Tupelo, MS 38803. Phone: (662) 842-9595. Fax: (662) 842-9568. Ownership Olvie E. Sisk; Kathern Sisk.

Stns: 2 AM. 6 FM. KEOJ-FM Caney, KS; KTFR-FM Chelsea, OK; KEMX-FM Locust Grove, OK; KBIX Muskogee, OK; KYAL-FM Muskogee, OK; KYAL(AM) Sapulpa, OK; KXOJ-FM Sapulpa, OK; KCXR(FM) Taft, OK3 FM. WLZA(FM) Eupora, MS; WFTA-FM Fulton, MS; WCNA-FM Potts Camp, MS.

Olvie E. Sisk, pres; Kathern Sisk, sec/treas.

Alaska Broadcast Communications Inc., 3161 Channel Dr., Suite 2, Juneau, AK 99801. Phone: (907) 586-3630. Fax: (907) 463-3685. Web Site:www.kjno.com

Stns: 3 AM. 3 FM. KJNO(AM) Juneau, AK; KTKU-FM Juneau, AK; KTKN Ketchikan, AK; KGTW-FM Ketchikan, AK; KIFW Sitka, AK; KSBZ-FM Sitka, AK.

Richard Burns, group CEO.

Aleluya Christian Broadcasting Inc., 912 Curtis Ave., Pasadena, TX 77502-2402. Phone: (713) 589-1336. Fax: (713) 589-1335. Ownership Roberto R. Villarreal, 25% votes; Rosalinda A. Villarreal, 25% votes; Ruben Villarreal, 25% votes; Roberta Rose Villarreal, 25% votes.

Stns: 2 AM. 2 FM. KUZN(FM) Centerville, TX; KBRZ(AM)

Missouri City, TX; KFTG-FM Pasadena, TX; KRTX Rosenberg-Richmond, TX.

Alexandra Communications Inc., 1600 Gray Lynn Dr., Walla Walla, WA 99362. Phone: (509) 527-1000. Fax: (509) 529-5534. Ownership Thomas D. Hodgins, 50%; and Cheryl Hodgins, 50%.

Stns: 1 AM. 4 FM. KIXT(FM) Bay City, OR; KDEP(FM) Garibaldi, OR; KLKY(FM) Stanfield, OR; KUJJ(FM) Weston, OR; KUJ Walla Walla, WA.

Allegheny Mountain Network Stations, Box 247, Tyrone, PA 16686. Phone: (814) 684-3200. Fax: (814) 684-1220.E-mail: amnet@aol.com Ownership Cary H. Simpson.

Stns: 4 AM. 4 FM. WFRM Coudersport, PA; WNBQ-FM Mansfield, PA; WEEO-FM McConnellsburg, PA; WKBI Saint Marys, PA; WKBI-FM Saint Marys, PA; WTRN Tyrone, PA; WNBT Wellsboro, PA; WNBT-FM Wellsboro, PA.

Cary Simpson, pres; John F. Simpson, VP.

Alma Corp., 630 W. 8th Ave., Anchorage, AK 99501. Phone: (907) 274-6213. Fax: (907) 272-6308. Ownership Dennis Wallace, 100%.

Stns: 4 AM. 4 FM. WFRM Coudersport, PA; WNBQ-FM Mansfield, PA; WEEO-FM McConnellsburg, PA; WKBI Saint Marys, PA; WKBI-FM Saint Marys, PA; WTRN Tyrone, PA; WNBT Wellsboro, PA; WNBT-FM Wellsboro, PA4 FM. KUMR(FM) Doolittle, MO; KNDH(FM) Hettinger, ND; KQWY(FM) Lusk, WY; KOUZ(FM) Manville, WY.

Amaturo Groups, 3101 N. Federal Hwy., 6th Fl., Fort Lauderdale, FL 33306-1018. Phone: (954) 565-1411. Fax: (954) 565-1311.E-mail: jca@amaturogroups.com Ownership Amaturo Group of L.A. Inc. (Joseph C. Amaturo, gen ptnr): KAJL(FM), KJLL-FM and KHJL(FM).

Stns: 4 AM. 4 FM. WFRM Coudersport, PA; WNBQ-FM Mansfield, PA; WEEO-FM McConnellsburg, PA; WKBI Saint Marys, PA; WKBI-FM Saint Marys, PA; WTRN Tyrone, PA; WNBT Wellsboro, PA; WNBT-FM Wellsboro, PA4 FM. KUMR(FM) Doolittle, MO; KNDH(FM) Hettinger, ND; KQWY(FM) Lusk, WY; KOUZ(FM) Manville, WY3 FM. KAJL(FM) Adelanto, CA; KJLL-FM Fountain Valley, CA; KHJL(FM) Thousand Oaks, CA.

Joseph Amaturo, gen ptnr.

American Family Radio, Box 3206, Tupelo, MS 38803. Phone: (662) 844-8888. Fax: (662) 842-6791.E-mail: comments@afr.net Web Site:www.afr.net Ownership American Family Association, a nonprofit organization.

Stns: 4 AM. 4 FM. WFRM Coudersport, PA; WNBQ-FM Mansfield, PA; WEEO-FM McConnellsburg, PA; WKBI Saint Marys, PA; WKBI-FM Saint Marys, PA; WTRN Tyrone, PA; WNBT Wellsboro, PA; WNBT-FM Wellsboro, PA4 FM. KUMR(FM) Doolittle, MO; KNDH(FM) Hettinger, ND; KQWY(FM) Lusk, WY; KOUZ(FM) Manville, WY3 FM. KAJL(FM) Adelanto, CA; KJLL-FM Fountain Valley, CA; KHJL(FM) Thousand Oaks, CA165 FM. WALN-FM Carrollton, AL; WAQG-FM Ozark, AL; WAQU-FM Selma, AL; WAKD-FM Sheffield, AL; WAXU-FM Troy, AL; KAPG(FM) Bentonville, AR; KBCM(FM) Blytheville, AR; KBDO(FM) Des Arc, AR; KBNV(FM) Fayetteville, AR; KARH(FM) Forrest City, AR; KAOW(FM) Fort Smith, AR; KBPW(FM) Hampton, AR; KBMJ(FM) Heber Springs, AR; KAOG(FM) Jonesboro, AR; KJSB(FM) Jonesboro, AR; KNLL(FM) Nashville, AR; KANX(FM) Sheridan, AR; KBMH(FM) Holbrook, AZ; KCAI(FM) Kingman, AZ; KAWN(FM) Winslow, AZ; WTLG-FM Starke, FL; WBJY-FM Americus, GA; WAEF-FM Cordele, GA; WEBH(FM) Cuthbert, GA; WAWH-FM Dublin, GA; WBKG-FM Macon, GA; WASW-FM Waycross, GA; KAYP(FM) Burlington, IA; KIAD(FM) Dubuque, IA; KBDC(FM) Mason City, IA; KWVI(FM) Waverly, IA; WBEL-FM Cairo, IL; WBMF-FM Crete, IL; WEFI(FM) Effingham, IL; WAXR-FM Geneseo, IL; WAWF-FM Kankakee, IL; WAWJ(FM) Marion, IL; WAPO-FM Mount Vernon, IL; WWGN-FM Ottawa, IL; WZRS(FM) Pana, IL; WSLE-FM Salem, IL; WQSG(FM) Lafayette, IN; KXJH(FM) Linton, IN; WATI-FM Vincennes, IN; KAXR(FM) Arkansas City, KS; KBJQ(FM) Bronson, KS; KBDA(FM) Great Bend, KS; KHYS(FM) Hays, KS; KBQC(FM) Independence, KS; KMLL(FM) Marysville, KS; KSNB(FM) Norton, KS; KRBW-FM Ottawa, KS; KAKA(FM) Salina, KS; KBUZ(FM) Topeka, KS; KCFN(FM) Wichita, KS; WAPD-FM Campbellsville, KY; WBMK-FM Morehead, KY; WAXG-FM Mt. Sterling, KY; WGCF(FM) Paducah, KY; KAPM(FM) Alexandria, LA; KAXV(FM) Bastrop, LA; KBAN(FM) De Ridder, LA; KYLC(FM) Lake Charles, LA;

KAVK(FM) Many, LA; KPAQ(FM) Plaquemine, LA; KSUL(FM) Port Sulphur, LA; KAPI(FM) Ruston, LA; KSJY(FM) Saint Martinville, LA; WMCQ(FM) Muskegon, MI; KBPG(FM) Montevideo, MN; KQRB(FM) Windom, MN; KBOJ(FM) Worthington, MN; KAUF(FM) Kennett, MO; KBGM(FM) Park Hills, MO; WPRG(FM) Columbia, MS; WCSO(FM) Columbus, MS; WAUM-FM Duck Hill, MS; WQVI(FM) Forest, MS; WQST-FM Forest, MS; WAOY-FM Gulfport, MS; WAII-FM Hattiesburg, MS; WYTF(FM) Indianola, MS; WATP-FM Laurel, MS; WAQL-FM McComb, MS; WASM-FM Natchez, MS; WAVI-FM Oxford, MS; WPAS(FM) Pascagoula, MS; WATU-FM Port Gibson, MS; WMSB(FM) Senatobia, MS; WJZB(FM) Starkville, MS; WAQB-FM Tupelo, MS; WAJS-FM Tupelo, MS; WAFR-FM Tupelo, MS; WZKM(FM) Waynesboro, MS; WYAZ(FM) Yazoo City, MS; KAFH(FM) Great Falls, MT; WBKU-FM Ahoskie, NC; WXBE(FM) Beaufort, NC; WRYN(FM) Hickory, NC; WJKA(FM) Jacksonville, NC; WAAE-FM New Bern, NC; WBFY-FM Pinehurst, NC; WRAE(FM) Raeford, NC; KDVI(FM) Devils Lake, ND; KJTW(FM) Jamestown, ND; KNHS(FM) Hastings, NE; KAYA(FM) Hubbard, NE; KKNL(FM) Valentine, NE; KAQF(FM) Clovis, NM; KOBH(FM) Hobbs, NM; WJJE(FM) Delaware, OH; WBIE-FM Delphos, OH; WWGV(FM) Grove City, OH; WAUI-FM Shelby, OH; WBJV-FM Steubenville, OH; WWVY(FM) Waverly, OH; KAKO(FM) Ada, OK; KQPD(FM) Ardmore, OK; KAYC(FM) Durant, OK; KXRT(FM) Idabel, OK; KVRS-FM Lawton, OK; KARG(FM) Poteau, OK; KAYM(FM) Weatherford, OK; KANL(FM) Baker City, OR; KAPK(FM) Grants Pass, OR; WAWN-FM Franklin, PA; WDLL(FM) Dillon, SC; KEEA(FM) Aberdeen, SD; KASD(FM) Rapid City, SD; WAUO-FM Hohenwald, TN; WAMP-FM Jackson, TN; WAWI-FM Lawrenceburg, TN; WIGH-FM Lexington, TN; WPRH(FM) Paris, TN; WAUV-FM Ripley, TN; WAZD-FM Savannah, TN; WBIA-FM Shelbyville, TN; WAUT-FM Tullahoma, TN; KAQD(FM) Abilene, TX; KAVW(FM) Amarillo, TX; KATG(FM) Athens, TX; KBCX(FM) Big Spring, TX; KLGS(FM) College Station, TX; KAFR(FM) Conroe, TX; KCKT(FM) Crockett, TX; KTDA(FM) Dalhart, TX; KDLI(FM) Del Rio, TX; KZFT(FM) Fannett, TX; KTXG(FM) Greenville, TX; KSUR(FM) Mart, TX; KMEO(FM) Mertzon, TX; KBMM(FM) Odessa, TX; KAVO(FM) Pampa, TX; KPKO(FM) Pecos, TX; KBAH(FM) Plainview, TX; KBDE(FM) Temple, TX; KVHR(FM) Van Horn, TX; KAYK(FM) Victoria, TX; WAUQ-FM Charles City, VA; WARN-FM Culpeper, VA; WRIH(FM) Richmond, VA; KAYB(FM) Sunnyside, WA; WWEN(FM) Wentworth, WI; WBHZ-FM Elkins, WV; WPWV(FM) Princeton, WV

Tim Wildmon, pres/CEO.

American General Media, Box 2700, Bakersfield, CA 93303. Phone: (661) 328-0118. Fax: (661) 328-1648. Ownership Anthony S. Brandon, Lawrence Brandon, L. Rogers Brandon.
 Stns: 6 AM. 17 FM. KIQO-FM Atascadero, CA; KISV(FM) Bakersfield, CA; KERI(AM) Bakersfield, CA; KGEO Bakersfield, CA; KGFM-FM Bakersfield, CA; KBOX(FM) Lompoc, CA; KRQK-FM Lompoc, CA; KEBT(FM) Lost Hills, CA; KPAT-FM Orcutt, CA; KKAL(FM) Paso Robles, CA; KKJG-FM San Luis Obispo, CA; KZOZ-FM San Luis Obispo, CA; KKXX-FM Shafter, CA; KERN(AM) Wasco-Greenacres, CA; KKIM Albuquerque, NM; KDLW(FM) Belen, NM; KARS Belen, NM; KLVO(FM) Los Alamos, NM; KABG(FM) Los Alamos, NM; KAGM(FM) Los Lunas, NM; KKIM-FM Santa Fe, NM; KTRC(AM) Santa Fe, NM; KHFM(FM) Santa Fe, NM.

L. Rogers Brandon, VP.

American Media Investments Inc., 1162 E. Hwy. 126, Pittsburg, KS 66762. Phone: (620) 231-7200. Ownership O. Gene Bicknell, 100%.
 Stns: 4 AM. 7 FM. KPGG(FM) Ashdown, AR; KCAR-FM Baxter Springs, KS; KMOQ(FM) Columbus, KS; KBZI(FM) Columbus, KS; KQYX(AM) Galena, KS; KBTN(AM) Neosho, MO; KBTN-FM Neosho, MO; KCAR Clarksville, TX; KGAP-FM Clarksville, TX; KEWL-FM New Boston, TX; KKTK(AM) Texarkana, TX.

O. Gene Bicknell, pres/CEO.

Americom, 11400 W. Olympic Blvd, Suite 780, Los Angeles, CA 90064. Phone: (310) 481-0440. Fax: (310) 481-0445.
 Stns: 2 AM. 3 FM. KLCA-FM Tahoe City, CA; KZTQ(FM) Carson City, NV; KRNO(FM) Incline Village, NV; KJFK(AM) Reno, NV; KBZZ(AM) Sparks, NV.

Tom Quinn, pres/CEO.

Amistad Communications Inc., 7480 Greenwood Rd., Shreveport, LA 71119. Phone: (318) 938-1885. Fax: (318) 425-7507.
 Stns: 2 AM. 1 FM. KBEF(FM) Gibsland, LA; KASO Minden, LA; KSYB(AM) Shreveport, LA.

Anaheim Broadcasting Corp., Box 2668, Del Mar, CA 92014-5668. Phone: (858) 794-1626. Fax: (858) 794-4068. Ownership Tim Sullivan.

 Stns: 2 AM. 1 FM. KBEF(FM) Gibsland, LA; KASO Minden, LA; KSYB(AM) Shreveport, LA2 FM. KCAL-FM Redlands, CA; KOLA(FM) San Bernardino, CA.

Tim Sullivan, pres; Doug Lida, CFO.

Anastos Media Group Inc., 21 Malta Commons, 100 Saratoga Village Blvd, Malta, NY 12020. Phone: (518) 899-3000. Fax: (518) 899-3057.E-mail: star1013fm@aol.com Web Site:www.star1013.com
 Stns: 3 AM. 1 FM. WABY(AM) Mechanicville, NY; WVKZ Schenectady, NY; WQAR-FM Stillwater, NY; WUAM(AM) Watervliet, NY.

Scott Collins, pres.

Anderson Radio Broadcasting Inc., 581 N. Reservoir Rd., Polson, MT 59860. Phone: (406) 883-5255. Fax: (406) 883-4441. Ownership Dennis L. Anderson, 50%; and Nila Y. Anderson, 50%.
 Stns: 2 AM. 5 FM. KIBG(FM) Bigfork, MT; KZXT(FM) Eureka, MT; KQJZ(AM) Evergreen, MT; KKMT(FM) Pablo, MT; KERR Polson, MT; KQRK-FM Ronan, MT; KZJZ(FM) Saint Regis, MT.

Apex Broadcasting Inc., Box 61091, N Charleston, SC 29419-1091. Phone: (843) 852-9003. Fax: (843) 852-9041. Web Site:www.apexbroadcasting.com
 Stns: 1 AM. 4 FM. WSPO(AM) Charleston, SC; WAVF(FM) Hanahan, SC; WXST(FM) Hollywood, SC; WIOP(FM) Isle of Palms, SC; WIHB(FM) Moncks Corner, SC.

Houston L. Pearce, chmn; G. Dean Pearce, pres.

Arkansas County Broadcasters Inc., Box 789, Wynne, AR 72396-0789. Phone: (870) 238-8141. Fax: (870) 238-5997. Ownership Bobby Caldwell, 50%; C.B. Moery Jr., 50%. Note: Bobby Caldwell owns 100% of East Arkansas Broadcasters Inc. (see listing) and 50% of Combined Media Group Inc. (see listing).
 Stns: 1 AM. 3 FM. KDEW-FM De Witt, AR; KAFN(FM) Gould, AR; KWAK Stuttgart, AR; KWAK-FM Stuttgart, AR.

Arklatex LLC, 615 W. Olive, Texarkana, TX 75501. Phone: (903) 793-4671. Fax: (903) 792-4261.E-mail: alex@101jams.com Ownership Sudbury Affiliates LLC, 50%; Malvern Entertainment Corp., 25%; and DTJ Inc., 25%.
 Stns: 2 AM. 3 FM. KBYB(FM) Hope, AR; KTOY(FM) Texarkana, AR; KFYX(FM) Texarkana, AR; KCMC Texarkana, TX; KTFS(AM) Texarkana, TX.

Mike Simpson, gen mgr; Alex Rain, opns mgr.

Armada Media Corp., 1 W. Second St., 2nd Fl., Fond du Lac, WI 54935-4908. Phone: (920) 906-9900. Fax: (920) 906-9800. Web Site:www.armadamedia.com Ownership AMC Partners LLC, Lake Lida LLC, et al.
 Stns: 9 AM. 18 FM. KSTH(FM) Holyoke, CO; KJBL(FM) Julesburg, CO; KFNF-FM Oberlin, KS; WAGN Menominee, MI; WHYB-FM Menominee, MI; KDIO Ortonville, MN; KPHR-FM Ortonville, MN; KUVR Holdrege, NE; KMTY-FM Holdrege, NE; KADL(FM) Imperial, NE; KHAQ(FM) Maxwell, NE; KQHK(FM) McCook, NE; KICX-FM McCook, NE; KBRL McCook, NE; KXNP-FM North Platte, NE; KODY North Platte, NE; KSDN Aberdeen, SD; KSDN-FM Aberdeen, SD; KBFO(FM) Aberdeen, SD; KGIM Aberdeen, SD; KMSD Milbank, SD; KNBZ-FM Redfield, SD; KGIM-FM Redfield, SD; KBWS-FM Sisseton, SD; WLST-FM Marinette, WI; WMAM Marinette, WI; WSFQ-FM Peshtigo, WI.

Chris Bernier, CEO; John R. Larson, sr VP; Terry K. Shockley, chmn/pres.

Arnold Broadcasting Inc., Box 753, Lamar, CO 81052. Phone: (719) 336-4227. Ownership William Arnold, 100%.
 Stns: 1 AM. 3 FM. KECK(FM) Eckley, CO; KNNG(FM) Sterling, CO; KSTC Sterling, CO; KNEC-FM Yuma, CO.

Bill Arnold, pres.

Artistic Media Partners Inc., 5520 E. 75th St., Indianapolis, IN 46250. Phone: (317) 594-0600. Fax: (317) 594-9567.E-mail: artradio@aol.com Web Site:www.artisticradio.com Ownership Arthur A. Angotti.
 Stns: 3 AM. 8 FM. WSHP(FM) Attica, IN; WBWB-FM Bloomington, IN; WBPE(FM) Brookston, IN; WHCC(FM) Ellettsville, IN; WZOW(FM) Goshen, IN; WSHY(AM) Lafayette, IN; WAZY-FM Lafayette, IN; WSMM(FM) New Carlisle, IN; WDND(AM) South Bend, IN; WPNT(AM) South Bend, IN; WNDV-FM South Bend, IN.

Arthur A. Angotti, pres/CEO; Arthur A. Angotti III, sr VP.

Asterisk Inc., 2848 E. Oakland Park Blvd., Fort Lauderdale, FL 33306. Phone: (954) 566-7559. Fax: (954) 564-6753. Ownership Richard S. Ingham, 100%.
 Stns: 3 AM. 8 FM. WSHP(FM) Attica, IN; WBWB-FM Bloomington, IN; WBPE(FM) Brookston, IN; WHCC(FM) Ellettsville, IN; WZOW(FM) Goshen, IN; WSHY(AM) Lafayette, IN; WAZY-FM Lafayette, IN; WSMM(FM) New Carlisle, IN;

WDND(AM) South Bend, IN; WPNT(AM) South Bend, IN; WNDV-FM South Bend, IN3 FM. WXJZ(FM) Gainesville, FL; WYGC(FM) High Springs, FL; WMFQ-FM Ocala, FL.

Frederick H. Ingham, pres.

Astor Broadcast Group, 1835 Aston Ave., Carlsbad, CA 92008. Phone: (760) 729-1000. Fax: (760) 476-9604.
 Stns: 3 AM. KFSD(AM) Escondido, CA; KSPA(AM) Ontario, CA; KCEO Vista, CA.

Peri Corso, gen mgr .

Astral Media Inc., 2100 rue Sainte-Catherine Ouest, Bureau 1000, Montreal, PQ H3H 2T3. Canada. Phone: (514) 939-5000. Fax: (514) 939-1515. Web Site:www.astralmedia.com Ownership Abgreen Holdings Ltd., 55.71% vote; 654625 Ontario Inc., 13.63% vote.
 Stns: 24 AM. 62 FM. CJAY-FM Calgary, AB; CKMX Calgary, AB; CIBK-FM Calgary, AB; CFBR-FM Edmonton, AB; CFRN Edmonton, AB; CFMG-FM Saint Albert, AB; CFKC Creston, BC; CJDC Dawson Creek, BC; CKRX-FM Fort Nelson, BC; CHRX-FM Fort St. John, BC; CKNL-FM Fort St. John, BC; CKGR Golden, BC; CKIR Invermere, BC; CKFR(AM) Kelowna, BC; CHSU-FM Kelowna, BC; CILK-FM Kelowna, BC; CKTK-FM Kitimat, BC; CKKC-FM Nelson, BC; CKZX-FM New Denver, BC; CJOR Osoyoos, BC; CJMG-FM Penticton, BC; CKOR Penticton, BC; CHTK Prince Rupert, BC; CIOR Princeton, BC; CKCR Revelstoke, BC; CISL Richmond, BC; CKXR-FM Salmon Arm, BC; CHOR Summerland, BC; CFTK Terrace, BC; CJFW-FM Terrace, BC; CJAT-FM Trail, BC; CKZZ-FM Vancouver, BC; CICF-FM Vernon, BC; CKX-FM Brandon, MB; CKXA-FM Brandon, MB; CFQX-FM Selkirk, MB; CKMM-FM Winnipeg, MB; CKBC-FM Bathurst, NB; CIBX-FM Fredericton, NB; CKHJ(AM) Fredericton, NB; CFXY-FM Fredericton, NB; CIKX-FM Grand Falls, NB; CJCJ-FM Woodstock, NB; CKTO-FM Truro, NS; CKTY-FM Truro, NS; CHAM Hamilton, ON; CKOC Hamilton, ON; CKLH-FM Hamilton, ON; CKSL London, ON; CJBK(AM) London, ON; CJBX-FM London, ON; CIQM-FM London, ON; CKQB-FM Ottawa, ON; CHVR-FM Pembroke, ON; CHRE-FM Saint Catharines, ON; CHTZ-FM Saint Catharines, ON; CKTB Saint Catharines, ON; CJEZ-FM Toronto, ON; CKFM-FM Toronto, ON; CFRB Toronto, ON; CFVM-FM Amqui, PQ; CFIX-FM Chicoutimi, PQ; CHRD-FM Drummondville, PQ; CJDM-FM Drummondville, PQ; CKTF-FM Gatineau, PQ; CIMF-FM Gatineau, PQ; CIMO-FM Magog, PQ; CITE-FM Montreal, PQ; CHOM-FM Montreal, PQ; CKMF-FM Montreal, PQ; CJFM-FM Montreal, PQ; CJAD Montreal, PQ; CHIK-FM Quebec, PQ; CITF-FM Quebec, PQ; CIKI-FM Rimouski, PQ; CJOI-FM Rimouski, PQ; CJMM-FM Rouyn-Noranda, PQ; CJAB-FM Saguenay, PQ; CFEI-FM Saint Hyacinthe, PQ; CFZZ-FM Saint Jean-Iberville, PQ; CKSM Shawinigan, PQ; CITE-FM-1 Sherbrooke, PQ; CIGB-FM Trois Rivieres, PQ; CHEY-FM Trois Rivieres, PQ; CJMV-FM Val d'Or, PQ; CHBD-FM Regina, SK.
 Stns: 2 TV. CJDC, Dawson Creek, BC; CFTK, Terrace, BC.

Ian Greenberg, pres/CEO.

Astro Tele-Communications Corp. Rhode Island, Box 920365, Needham, MA 02492. Phone: (781) 444-4754. Fax: (781) 444-8630.E-mail: addelco@gis.net Web Site:www.wadk.com Ownership Maurice B. Polayes, 100%.
 Stns: 2 AM. 1 FM. WJZS(FM) Block Island, RI; WKFD(AM) Charlestown, RI; WADK Newport, RI.

Maurice B. Polayes, pres.

Atlantic Broadcasting, 1601 New Rd., Linwood, NJ 08221-1116. Phone: (609) 653-1400. Fax: (609) 601-0450. Ownership Northwood Ventures LLC, 63.29%; Northwood Capital Partners LLC, 11.17%; Brett DeNafo, 6.96%; W. Stewart Cahn, 6.52%; Michael Ferriola, 3.50%; Joseph Borsello Jr., 3.26%; Joseph E. Kane & Anna Marie Kane, jointly, 2.17%; Henry T. Wilson, 1.63%; and Paul Theophall, 1.50%.
 Stns: 2 AM. 3 FM. WMGM(FM) Atlantic City, NJ; WTKU-FM Ocean City, NJ; WJSE-FM Petersburg, NJ; WOND(AM) Pleasantville, NJ; WTAA(AM) Pleasantville, NJ.

Brett DeNafo, CEO.

Atlantic Coast Radio L.L.C., 779 Warren Avenue, Portland, ME 04103. Phone: (207) 773-9695. Fax: (207) 761-4406. Web Site:www.redhot95.com
 Stns: 2 AM. 3 FM. WJJB-FM Gary, ME; WLOB Portland, ME; WPEI(FM) Saco, ME; WLOB-FM Topsham, ME; WRED(AM) Westbrook, ME.

J.J. Jeffrey, pres.

Azteca Broadcasting Corp., 323 E. San Joaquin St., Tulare, CA 93274. Phone: (559) 686-1370. Fax: (559) 685-1394.E-mail: wwwkgen@sbcglobal.net
 Stns: 3 AM. 1 FM. KGEN-FM Hanford, CA; KGEN

Tulare, CA; KXEQ Reno, NV; KSVN Ogden, UT.

Margarita Hernandez, gen mgr .

B

BAS Broadcasting Inc., 1281 N. River Rd., Fremont, OH 43420. Phone: (419) 332-8218. Fax: (419) 333-8226. Ownership James A. Lorenzen, 42.5%; Thomas W. Klein, 23.5%; James A. Lorenzen, trustee Bas Broadcasting Inc. Retirement Plan, 19%; Jeffrey Neidert, 5.3%; Michael Herbert, 3.5%; Anthony Paradiso, 3.5%; and Joseph L. Minnick, 2.7%.

Stns: 3 AM. 6 FM. WOHF(FM) Bellevue, OH; WMJK(FM) Clyde, OH; WFRO-FM Fremont, OH; WMVO(AM) Mount Vernon, OH; WQIO-FM Mount Vernon, OH; WPFX-FM North Baltimore, OH; WLEC Sandusky, OH; WCPZ(FM) Sandusky, OH; WTTF Tiffin, OH.

James A. Lorenzen, pres.

Back Bay Broadcasters LLC, 1110 Central Ave., Pawtucket, RI 02861-2262. Phone: (401) 724-7600. Fax: (401) 728-1865. Ownership Peter H. Ottmar, 40.1%; David J. Ottmar, 26.1%; John Maguire, 19.0%; and Barbara Ottmar, 7.2%.

Stns: 3 AM. 6 FM. WOHF(FM) Bellevue, OH; WMJK(FM) Clyde, OH; WFRO-FM Fremont, OH; WMVO(AM) Mount Vernon, OH; WQIO-FM Mount Vernon, OH; WPFX-FM North Baltimore, OH; WLEC Sandusky, OH; WTTF Tiffin, OH4 FM. WBAZ(FM) Bridgehampton, NY; WEHN(FM) East Hampton, NY; WEHM(FM) Southampton, NY; WBEA(FM) Southold, NY.

Peter H. Ottmar, chmn; John Maguire, CEO.

Backyard Broadcasting LLC, 4237 Salisbury Rd., Suite 225, Jacksonville, FL 32216. Phone: (904) 674-0260. Fax: (904) 854-4596. Web Site:www.bybradio.com Ownership Boston Ventures Limited Partnership VI; PCG Media Investment Partners LLC; Barry Drake.

Stns: 9 AM. 21 FM. WMQX(FM) Alexandria, IN; WHBU Anderson, IN; WURK-FM Elwood, IN; WMXQ(FM) Hartford City, IN; WERK-FM Muncie, IN; WLBC-FM Muncie, IN; WXFN Muncie, IN; WWJK(FM) Jackson, MS; WRXW(FM) Pearl, MS; WNKI-FM Corning, NY; WWLZ Horseheads, NY; WPGI-FM Horseheads, NY; WNGZ-FM Montour Falls, NY; WHDL Olean, NY; WPIG-FM Olean, NY; WRCE(AM) Watkins Glen, NY; WCXR(FM) Lewisburg, PA; WBZD-FM Muncy, PA; WZXR-FM South Williamsport, PA; WWPA Williamsport, PA; WLMY(FM) Williamsport, PA; WILQ-FM Williamsport, PA; KSQB-FM Dell Rapids, SD; KXQL(FM) Flandreau, SD; KTWB(FM) Sioux Falls, SD; KWSN-FM Sioux Falls, SD; KELO(AM) Sioux Falls, SD; KELO-FM Sioux Falls, SD; KRRO(FM) Sioux Falls, SD; KSQB(AM) Sioux Falls, SD.

Barry Drake, pres/CEO; Robin A. Smith, VP/CFO; Tom Atkins, VP & dir engrg.

Bahakel Communications, Box 32488, Charlotte, NC 28232. Phone: (704) 372-4434. Fax: (704) 335-9904. Ownership 2000 Bahakel Descendents Trust, 100%.

Stns: 4 AM. 5 FM. KILO-FM Colorado Springs, CO; KRXP(FM) Pueblo West, CO; KOKZ-FM Waterloo, IA; KWLO(AM) Waterloo, IA; KXEL Waterloo, IA; KFMW-FM Waterloo, IA; WDEF Chattanooga, TN; WDEF-FM Chattanooga, TN; WDOD Chattanooga, TN.

Stns: 8 TV. WCCU, Champaign & Springfield-Decatur, IL; WRSP-TV, Champaign & Springfield-Decatur, IL; WCCB, Charlotte, NC; WOLO, Columbia, SC; WABG-TV, Greenwood-Greenville, MS; WBBJ, Jackson, TN; WAKA, Montgomery-Selma, AL; WFXB, Myrtle Beach-Florence, SC.

Beverly B. Poston, pres; Stephen Bahakel, Sr VP radio div; Russell Schwartz, Sr VP business affrs/gen counsel; Bill Napier, VP eng/tech; Anna Rufty, VP Hum Res.

Baker Family Stations, Box 889, Blacksburg, VA 24063. Phone: (540) 552-4252. Fax: (540) 951-5282. Ownership Principal owners: Vernon H. Baker, Edward A. Baker, Virginia L. Baker.

Stns: 12 AM. 5 FM. WYHY(AM) Cannonsburg, KY; WLGN Logan, OH; WKNA(FM) Logan, OH; WMPO Middleport-Pomeroy, OH; WTGR-FM Union City, OH; WKEX Blacksburg, VA; WFIC(AM) Collinsville, VA; WBNN-FM Dillwyn, VA; WKTR Earlysville, VA; WKNV Fairlawn, VA; WODY Fieldale, VA; WZFM(FM) Narrows, VA; WKGM Smithfield, VA; WAMN Green Valley, WV; WIHY(AM) Hurricane, WV; WBGS Point Pleasant, WV; WCEF-FM Ripley, WV.

Vernon H. Baker, CEO; Edward A. Baker, pres; Virginia L. Baker, treas.

Baldridge-Dumas Communications Inc., 605 San Antonio Ave., Many, LA 71449. Phone: (318) 256-5924. Fax: (318) 256-0950. Web Site:www.bdcradio.com Ownership Tedd

W. Dumas, 50%; Patricia M. Baldridge Declaration of Trust, 50%.

Stns: 2 AM. 6 FM. KBDV(FM) Leesville, LA; KWLA Many, LA; KZBL-FM Natchitoches, LA; KDBH(FM) Natchitoches, LA; KVCL Winnfield, LA; KVCL-FM Winnfield, LA; KTEZ(FM) Zwolle, LA; KTHP(FM) Hemphill, TX.

Tedd Dumas, pres; Rhonda Benson, gen mgr .

Vernon R Baldwin Inc., 8686 Michael Ln., Fairfield, OH 45014. Phone: (513) 829-7700. Ownership Vernon R. Baldwin, 100%.

Stns: 2 AM. 4 FM. WWLT-FM Manchester, KY; WVRB-FM Wilmore, KY; WCNW Fairfield, OH; WMOH Hamilton, OH; WNLT-FM Harrison, OH; WKLN(FM) Wilmington, OH.

Vernon R. Baldwin, pres.

Barnstable Corporation, 2 Newton Executive Park, Suite 302, Newton, MA 02462-1434. Phone: (617) 527-0062. Fax: (617) 630-0960. Ownership Albert J. Kaneb; Michael A. Kaneb.

Stns: 1 AM. 5 FM. WBZO-FM Bay Shore, NY; WLVG-FM Center Moriches, NY; WHLI Hempstead, NY; WKJY-FM Hempstead, NY; WRCN-FM Riverhead, NY; WMJC(FM) Smithtown, NY.

Albert J. Kaneb, chmn/CEO; Michael A. Kaneb, pres/COO; James L. Paglia, VP/CFO.

Bayshore Broadcasting Corp., Box 280, Owen Sound, ON N4K 5P5. Canada. Phone: (519) 376-2030. Fax: (519) 371-4242.E-mail: bayshore@radioowensound.com Web Site:www.radioowensound.com Ownership Controlled by Douglas C. Caldwell.

Stns: 1 AM. 5 FM. CHWC-FM Goderich, ON; CFOS(AM) Owen Sound, ON; CIXK-FM Owen Sound, ON; CKYC-FM Owen Sound, ON; CFPS-FM Port Elgin, ON; CHGB-FM Wasaga Beach, ON.

Ross Kentner, gen mgr .

Beacon Broadcasting Inc., Box 1789, Warren, OH 44482-1790. Phone: (330) 394-7700. Fax: (330) 394-7701. Ownership Harold F. Glunt, 100%.

Stns: 4 AM. 1 FM. WRTK(AM) Niles, OH; WANR Warren, OH; WLOA(AM) Farrell, PA; WEXC-FM Greenville, PA; WGRP Greenville, PA.

Beasley Broadcast Group Inc., 3033 Riviera Dr., Suite 200, Naples, FL 34103. Phone: (239) 263-5000. Fax: (239) 263-8191.E-mail: email@bbgi.com Web Site:www.bbgi.com Ownership George G. Beasley.

Stns: 18 AM. 26 FM. WSBR Boca Raton, FL; WKIS-FM Boca Raton, FL; WRXK-FM Bonita Springs, FL; WXKB-FM Cape Coral, FL; WJBX-FM Fort Myers Beach, FL; WJPT(FM) Fort Myers Villas, FL; WQAM Miami, FL; WPOW-FM Miami, FL; WWCN North Fort Myers, FL; WWNN Pompano Beach, FL; WHSR Pompano Beach, FL; WAEC Atlanta, GA; WGAC Augusta, GA; WRDW(AM) Augusta, GA; WGUS(AM) Augusta, GA; WWWE(AM) Hapeville, GA; WCHZ-FM Harlem, GA; WDRR(FM) Martinez, GA; WGAC-FM Warrenton, GA; WRCA Waltham, MA; WAZZ(AM) Fayetteville, NC; WNCT Greenville, NC; WNCT-FM Greenville, NC; WXNR-FM Grifton, NC; WFLB-FM Laurinburg, NC; WKML-FM Lumberton, NC; WIKS New Bern, NC; WSFL-FM New Bern, NC; WMGV-FM Newport, NC; WTEL(AM) Red Springs, NC; WUKS(FM) Saint Pauls, NC; WZFX-FM Whiteville, NC; WTMR Camden, NJ; KCYE(FM) Boulder City, NV; KKLZ-FM Las Vegas, NV; KDWN Las Vegas, NV; KFRH(FM) North Las Vegas, NV; KBET(AM) Winchester, NV; WXTU-FM Philadelphia, PA; WWDB(AM) Philadelphia, PA; WRDW-FM Philadelphia, PA; WKXC-FM Aiken, SC; WHHD(FM) Clearwater, SC; WGUS-FM New Ellenton, SC.

George G. Beasley, chmn/CEO; Bruce G. Beasley, pres/COO; Caroline Beasley, exec VP/CFO; Brian Beasley, VP opns.

Bee Broadcasting Inc., Box 5409, Kalispell, MT 59903. Phone: (406) 755-8700. Fax: (406) 755-8770. Web Site:www.kbbz.com

Stns: 2 AM. 3 FM. KHNK(FM) Columbia Falls, MT; KBBZ(FM) Kalispell, MT; KDBR(FM) Kalispell, MT; KJJR Whitefish, MT; KSAM(AM) Whitefish, MT.

Benny Bee, pres.

Benton-Weatherford Broadcasting Inc. of Tennessee, 110 India Rd., Paris, TN 38242. Phone: (731) 644-9455. Fax: (731) 644-9421.E-mail: wmuf@bellsouth.net Ownership Gary Benton, Len Watson.

Stns: 2 AM. 2 FM. WMUF-FM Henry, TN; WHDM McKenzie, TN; WLZK-FM Paris, TN; WMUF Paris, TN.

Gary Benton, pres.

Berkshire Broadcasting Corp., WLAD(AM)/WDAQ(FM)/WREF(AM), 198 Main St., Danbury, CT 06810. Phone: (203) 744-4800. Fax: (203) 778-4655.

Web Site:www.98q.com, www.850wref.com

Stns: 2 AM. 1 FM. WDAQ(FM) Danbury, CT; WLAD Danbury, CT; WREF(AM) Ridgefield, CT.

Irv Goldstein, exec VP & gen mgr.

Bernard Radio LLC, 745 Fifth Ave., 18th Fl., New York, NY 10151. Phone: (646) 720-9100. Ownership D.B. Zwirn & Co. L.P., mgng member, 100% of votes; D.B. Zwirn Special Opportunities Fund L.P., 100% of total assets.

Stns: 5 AM. 2 FM. WGFT(AM) Campbell, OH; WVKO Columbus, OH; WRBP(FM) Hubbard, OH; WVKO-FM Johnstown, OH; WASN(AM) Youngstown, OH; KFCD(AM) Farmersville, TX; KHSE(AM) Wylie, TX.

Best Broadcast Group, 107 S. Main St., Brookfield, MO 64628. Phone: (660) 258-3383. Fax: (660) 258-7307.E-mail: corporate@bestbroadcastgroup.com Web Site:www.bestbroadcastgroup.com Ownership Phil Chirillo; Dale Palmer

Stns: 2 AM. 3 FM. KFMZ(AM) Brookfield, MO; KZBK(FM) Brookfield, MO; KLTI Macon, MO; KZZT-FM Moberly, MO; KMCR-FM Montgomery City, MO.

Dale Palmer, VP/gen mgr; Phil Chirillo, pres.

Bethesda Christian Broadcasting, Box 168, Rapid City, SD 57709. Phone: (719) 481-0100. Fax: (719) 481-4649.E-mail: bcbpres@aol.com Web Site:www.klmp.com Ownership Nonprofit bd of directors.

Stns: 2 AM. 3 FM. KFMZ(AM) Brookfield, MO; KZBK(FM) Brookfield, MO; KLTI Macon, MO; KZZT-FM Moberly, MO; KMCR-FM Montgomery City, MO5 FM. KTPT(FM) Rapid City, SD; KLMP(FM) Rapid City, SD; KSLT-FM Spearfish, SD; WNLI(FM) Sturgeon Bay, WI; WPFF(FM) Sturgeon Bay, WI.

Mark Pluimer, pres.

Better Life Ministries, 8320 W. 66th Ave., Arvada, CO 80004. Phone: (303) 431-0103. Ownership Ruth J. Bartel, 16.7% votes; James Gordon, 16.7% votes; Ruth E. Maenpaa, 16.7% votes; Claud M. Pettit, 16.7% votes; Margaret E. Pettit, 16.7% votes; and Clyde O. Speas, 16.7% votes.

Stns: 8 AM. KYNN(AM) Cameron, AZ; KHRJ(AM) Del Norte, CO; KEHT(AM) Eads, CO; KOAH(AM) Comstock, TX; KHTW(AM) Langtry, TX; KHRX(AM) Marathon, TX; KHUA(AM) Presidio, TX; KYHR(AM) Richfield, UT.

Claud Pettit, pres.

Bible Broadcasting Network, 11530 Carmel Commons Blvd., Charlotte, NC 28226. Phone: (704) 523-5555. Fax: (704) 522-1967. Web Site:www.bbnradio.org Ownership Nonprofit, non-stock corporation.

Stns: 4 AM. 29 FM. WYFD-FM Decatur, AL; WYFZ(FM) Belleview, FL; WYFB-FM Gainesville, FL; WYFO-FM Lakeland, FL; WYFE-FM Tarpon Springs, FL; WYFK-FM Columbus, GA; WYFS-FM Savannah, GA; WYFA-FM Waynesboro, GA; WYFW-FM Winder, GA; WYBV(FM) Wakarusa, IN; WYFW-FM Wichita, KS; KYFL-FM Monroe, LA; WYFP-FM Harpswell, ME; WYFQ(AM) Charlotte, NC; WYBH(FM) Fayetteville, NC; WYFL-FM Henderson, NC; WYFQ-FM Wadesboro, NC; KYFG(FM) Omaha, NE; WYBY(AM) Cortland, NY; WYFY Rome, NY; WYFU-FM Masontown, PA; WYFV-FM Cayce, SC; WYFG-FM Gaffney, SC; WYFH-FM North Charleston, SC; WYFC-FM Clinton, TN; WYFN Nashville, TN; KYFB(FM) Denison, TX; KYFP(FM) Palestine, TX; KYFS-FM San Antonio, TX; KYFO-FM Ogden, UT; WYFJ-FM Ashland, VA; WYFT-FM Luray, VA; WYFI-FM Norfolk, VA.

Lowell Davey, pres; Leo Galletta, opns mgr.

Bick Broadcasting Co., Box 711, 119 N. Third St., Hannibal, MO 63401. Phone: (573) 221-3450. Fax: (573) 221-5331.E-mail: kickfm@bickbroadcasting.com Web Site:www.979kickfm.com Ownership Frank C. Bick, 46%; James P. Bick, 46%; James E. Janes, 8%.

Stns: 3 AM. 3 FM. WLIQ(AM) Quincy, IL; KHMO Hannibal, MO; KXKX-FM Knob Noster, MO; KICK-FM Palmyra, MO; KSDL-FM Sedalia, MO; KSIS(AM) Sedalia, MO.

James E. Janes, pres.

Bicoastal Media L.L.C., 140 N. Main St., Lake Port, CA 94953. Phone: (707) 263-6113. Fax: (707) 263-0939. Web Site:www.bicoastalmedia.com

Stns: 18 AM. 28 FM. KATA Arcata, CA; KPOD Crescent City, CA; KPOD-FM Crescent City, CA; KRED-FM Eureka, CA; KFMI-FM Eureka, CA; KGOE Eureka, CA; KKHB-FM Eureka, CA; KNTI-FM Lakeport, CA; KXBX Lakeport, CA; KUKI Ukiah, CA; KUKI-FM Ukiah, CA; KQPM-FM Ukiah, CA; KLLK Willits, CA; KTHH(AM) Albany, OR; KRKT-FM Albany, OR; KIFS(FM) Ashland, OR; KBDN(FM) Bandon, OR; KSHR-FM Coquille, OR; KWRO Coquille, OR; KEJO Corvallis, OR; KLOO Corvallis, OR; KLOO-FM Corvallis, OR; KFLY-FM Corvallis, OR; KZZE-FM Eagle Point, OR;

KPNW Eugene, OR; KODZ-FM Eugene, OR; KDUK-FM Florence, OR; KRWQ-FM Gold Hill, OR; KIHR Hood River, OR; KCGB-FM Hood River, OR; KLDZ(FM) Medford, OR; KMED Medford, OR; KTEE(FM) North Bend, OR; KOOS(FM) North Bend, OR; KBBR(AM) North Bend, OR; KPPK(FM) Rainier, OR; KJMX(FM) Reedsport, OR; KACI-FM The Dalles, OR; KACI The Dalles, OR; KMSW(FM) The Dalles, OR; KRQT-FM Castle Rock, WA; KELA Centralia-Chehalis, WA; KMNT(FM) Chehalis, WA; KLYK(FM) Kelso, WA; KEDO Longview, WA; KBAM Longview, WA.

Ken Dennis, CEO; Mike Wilson, pres.

Big League Broadcasting LLC, 3350 Peachtree Rd., Suite 1610, Atlanta, GA 30326-1040. Phone: (404) 467-1877. Fax: (404) 231-5923. Ownership Andrew Philip Saltzman, 20.435% of votes, 24.375% of equity; Stephen Shapiro, 20.435% of votes, 24.375% of equity; Jeffrey Bloomberg, 16.61% of votes, 16.75% of equity; and others.

Stns: 2 AM. 1 FM. KFNS(AM) Wood River, IL; KRFT(AM) De Soto, MO; KFNS-FM Troy, MO.

Big River Broadcasting Corp., 624 Sam Phillips St., Florence, AL 35630. Phone: (256) 764-8121. Fax: (256) 764-8169.E-mail: nmartin@bigriverbroadcasting.com Web Site:www.wqlt.com

Stns: 1 AM. 2 FM. WXFL(FM) Florence, AL; WSBM(AM) Florence, AL; WQLT-FM Florence, AL.

Knox Phillips, VP; Jerry Phillips, pres.

Birach Broadcasting Corp., 21700 Northwestern Hwy., Suite 1190, Southfield, MI 48075. Phone: (248) 557-3500. Fax: (248) 557-3241.E-mail: sima@birach.com Web Site:www.birach.com Ownership Sima Birach, 100%.

Stns: 19 AM. KTUV(AM) Little Rock, AR; WIJR(AM) Highland, IL; WNWI Oak Lawn, IL; WCND Shelbyville, KY; WNZK Dearborn Heights, MI; WCXI(AM) Fenton, MI; WMJH Rockford, MI; WSDS(AM) Salem Township, MI; WPON Walled Lake, MI; WMFN Zeeland, MI; WEW Saint Louis, MO; WCXN Claremont, NC; WTOR Youngstown, NY; KJMU(AM) Sand Springs, OK; WWCS Canonsburg, PA; WKGE(AM) Johnstown, PA; KOLE Port Arthur, TX; WGOP(AM) Pocomoke City, MD; WDMV(AM) Walkersville, MD.

Sima Birach, pres.

Birch Broadcasting Corp., 11971 Glenmore Dr., Coral Springs, FL 33071-7806. Phone: (954) 323-8531. Ownership Thomas C. Birch, 51%; and Aurora D.P. Birch, 49%.

Stns: 2 AM. 2 FM. KXLQ Indianola, IA; WLUS-FM Clarksville, VA; WSHV(AM) South Hill, VA; WKSK-FM South Hill, VA.

Black Crow Media Group LLC, 126 W. International Speedway Blvd., Daytona Beach, FL 32114. Phone: (386) 255-9300. Ownership J. Michael Linn, 100%.

Stns: 5 AM. 17 FM. WAHR-FM Huntsville, AL; WLOR Huntsville, AL; WRTT-FM Huntsville, AL; WNDB Daytona Beach, FL; WKRO-FM Edgewater, FL; WCJX-FM Five Points, FL; WVYB-FM Holly Hill, FL; WQHL(AM) Live Oak, FL; WQHL-FM Live Oak, FL; WXHT(FM) Madison, FL; WHOG-FM Ormond-by-the-Sea, FL; WVGA(FM) Lakeland, GA; WSTI-FM Quitman, GA; WQPW(FM) Valdosta, GA; WVLD(AM) Valdosta, GA; WWRQ-FM Valdosta, GA; WKAA(FM) Willacoochee, GA; WFKX(FM) Henderson, TN; WHHM-FM Henderson, TN; WZDQ(FM) Humboldt, TN; WJAK Jackson, TN; WWYN(FM) McKenzie, TN.

Mike Linn, pres/CEO.

Black Media Works Inc., 1150 W. King St., Cocoa, FL 32922. Phone: (321) 632-1000. Fax: (321) 636-0000.

Stns: 5 AM. 17 FM. WAHR-FM Huntsville, AL; WLOR Huntsville, AL; WRTT-FM Huntsville, AL; WNDB Daytona Beach, FL; WKRO-FM Edgewater, FL; WCJX-FM Five Points, FL; WVYB-FM Holly Hill, FL; WQHL(AM) Live Oak, FL; WQHL-FM Live Oak, FL; WXHT(FM) Madison, FL; WHOG-FM Ormond-by-the-Sea, FL; WVGA(FM) Lakeland, GA; WSTI-FM Quitman, GA; WQPW(FM) Valdosta, GA; WVLD(AM) Valdosta, GA; WWRQ-FM Valdosta, GA; WKAA(FM) Willacoochee, GA; WFKX(FM) Henderson, TN; WHHM-FM Henderson, TN; WZDQ(FM) Humboldt, TN; WJAK Jackson, TN; WWYN(FM) McKenzie, TN3 FM. WJCB(FM) Clewiston, FL; WJFP-FM Fort Pierce, FL; KAYT(FM) Jena, LA.

Kimberly Holman Kassis, pres.

Blackburn Group Inc., 140 Fullerton, Suite 1905, London, ON N6A 5P2. Canada. Phone: (519) 679-8680. Fax: (519) 679-5321. Web Site:www.blackburnradio.com Ownership Kilbyrne Investments Corp., 100%.

Stns: 3 AM. 8 FM. CFCO Chatham, ON; CKUE-FM Chatham, ON; CKSY-FM Chatham, ON; CHYR-FM Leamington, ON; CJSP-FM Leamington, ON; CFGX-FM Sarnia, ON; CHOK Sarnia, ON; CHKS-FM Sarnia, ON; CIBU-FM Wingham, ON; CKNX Wingham, ON; CKNX-FM Wingham, ON.

Sandy Green, pres.

Blakeney Communications Inc., Box 6408, Laurel, MS 39441. Phone: (601) 649-0095. Fax: (601) 649-8199.E-mail: b95@b95country.com Web Site:www.b95country.com

Stns: 3 AM. 8 FM. CFCO Chatham, ON; CKUE-FM Chatham, ON; CKSY-FM Chatham, ON; CHYR-FM Leamington, ON; CJSP-FM Leamington, ON; CFGX-FM Sarnia, ON; CHOK Sarnia, ON; CHKS-FM Sarnia, ON; CIBU-FM Wingham, ON; CKNX Wingham, ON; CKNX-FM Wingham, ON4 FM. WKZW-FM Bay Springs, MS; WXRR-FM Hattiesburg, MS; WXHB(FM) Richton, MS; WBBN(FM) Taylorsville, MS.

Larry Blakeney, pres/CEO.

Bliss Communications Inc., Box 5001, One S. Parker Dr., Janesville, WI 53547-5001. Phone: (608) 754-3311. Fax: (608) 754-8038.E-mail: sbliss@gazetteextra.com

Stns: 3 AM. 1 FM. WCLO Janesville, WI; WRJN Racine, WI; WBKV(AM) West Bend, WI; WBWI-FM West Bend, WI.

Bliss Communications Inc. publishes *Ironwood* (MI) *Daily Globe, The Delavan* (WI) *Enterprise, The Week* (Delavan, Il), *MidWeek* (Delavan, WI), *The Jotter* (Janesville, WI), the *Janesville* (WI) *Gazette*, the *Eagle Herald* (Marinette, WI), & the *Monroe* (WI) *Times.*

Sidney H. Bliss, pres/CEO.

Blount Communications Group, 8 Lawrence Rd., Derry, NH 03038. Phone: (603) 437-9337. Fax: (603) 434-1035.E-mail: warv@aol.com Web Site:www.lifechangingradio.com Ownership William A. Blount, Deborah C. Blount.

Stns: 5 AM. 1 FM. WFIF Milford, CT; WVNE(AM) Leicester, MA; WNEB Worcester, MA; WBCI-FM Bath, ME; WDER(AM) Derry, NH; WARV Warwick, RI.

William A. Blount, pres; Deborah C. Blount, exec VP; David O. Young, VP.

Blue Ridge Radio Inc., 312 Robin Rd., Mount Airy, NC 27030. Phone: (336) 786-4498. Fax: (336) 789-7792.

Stns: 3 AM. 1 FM. WSYD Mount Airy, NC; WPAQ Mount Airy, NC; WBRF(FM) Galax, VA; WWWJ Galax, VA.

Earlene Epperson, pres; Ralph Epperson, VP; John Mullins, chief engr.

Blueberry Broadcasting LLC, Box 2600, Kennebunkport, ME 04046. Phone: (207) 967-8094. Ownership Louis Vitali, 60% control; Bruce Biette, 40% control; Blueberry Radio LLC, 28% equity.

Stns: 3 AM. 12 FM. WVQM(FM) Augusta, ME; WAEI(AM) Bangor, ME; WAEI-FM Bangor, ME; WLKE-FM Bar Harbor, ME; WBFB-FM Belfast, ME; WTQX(FM) Boothbay Harbor, ME; WQSS-FM Camden, ME; WKSQ-FM Ellsworth, ME; WABK-FM Gardiner, ME; WFAU Gardiner, ME; WLEK(FM) Gouldsboro, ME; WVOM-FM Howland, ME; WIGY-FM Madison, ME; WRKD Rockland, ME; WTOS-FM Skowhegan, ME.

Louis Vitali, pres/CEO.

Bold Gold Media Group LP, 575 Grove St., Honesdale, PA 18431. Phone: (570) 253-1616. Fax: (570) 253-6297.E-mail: vbenedetto@boldgoldmedia.com Web Site:www.boldgoldmedia.com

Stns: 4 AM. 4 FM. WDNB(FM) Jeffersonville, NY; WFBS(AM) Berwick, PA; WYCY-FM Hawley, PA; WPSN(AM) Honesdale, PA; WDNH-FM Honesdale, PA; WYCK Plains, PA; WWRR(FM) Scranton, PA; WICK Scranton, PA.

Vince Benedetto, pres; Robert VanDerneyden, COO.

Bolland Enterprises LLC, 403 Capital St., Lewiston, ID 83501. Phone: (208) 743-6564. Fax: (208) 798-0110.

Stns: 1 AM. 3 FM. KATW(FM) Lewiston, ID; KCLK Asotin, WA; KCLK-FM Clarkston, WA; KVAB-FM Clarkston, WA.

Bonneville International Corporation, Broadcast House, Box 1160, Salt Lake City, UT 84110-1160. Phone: (801) 575-7500. Fax: (801) 575-7521. Web Site:www.bonnint.com Ownership Deseret Management Corp. Deseret Management Corp. owns *The Deseret Morning News,* a Salt Lake City, UT, daily.

Stns: 8 AM. 21 FM. KTAR-FM Glendale, AZ; KPKX(FM) Phoenix, AZ; KMVP Phoenix, AZ; KTAR(AM) Phoenix, AZ; KSWD(FM) Los Angeles, CA; WTOP-FM Washington, DC; WFED(AM) Washington, DC; WDRV(FM) Chicago, IL; WILV(FM) Chicago, IL; WXOS(FM) East St. Louis, IL; WARH(FM) Granite City, IL; WTMX-FM Skokie, IL; WWDV(FM) Zion, IL; WYGY(FM) Fort Thomas, KY; WIL-FM Saint Louis, MO; WKRQ-FM Cincinnati, OH; WUBE-FM Cincinnati, OH; WREW(FM) Fairfield, OH; KSL-FM Midvale, UT; KRSP-FM Salt Lake City, UT; KSFI-FM Salt Lake City, UT; KSL Salt Lake City, UT; WWWT-FM Manassas, VA; KTTH(AM) Seattle, WA; KIRO Seattle, WA; KIRO-FM Tacoma, WA; WTLP(FM) Braddock Heights, MD; WWFD(AM) Frederick, MD; WZAA(AM) Silver Spring, MD.

Stns: 1 TV. KSL, Salt Lake City, UT.

Bruce T. Reese, pres/CEO; Robert A. Johnson, exec VP & COO.

Border Media Partners LLC, 201 Main St., Suite 2001, Fort Worth, TX 76102. Phone: (817) 335-5999. Fax: (817) 335-1197. Web Site:www.bmpradio.com Ownership The Goldman Sachs Group Inc., 48.85%; RGG Radio LLC, 16.29%; DBVA BMP Holdings LLC, 9.32%.

Stns: 8 AM. 14 FM. KJAV-FM Alamo, TX; KFON Austin, TX; KWOW-FM Clifton, TX; KXBT(FM) Dripping Springs, TX; KURV Edinburg, TX; KXXS(FM) Elgin, TX; KTFM(FM) Floresville, TX; KLEY-FM Jourdanton, TX; KLNT Laredo, TX; KNEX-FM Laredo, TX; KHHL(FM) Leander, TX; KBDR(FM) Mirando City, TX; KRIO-FM Pearsall, TX; KVJY Pharr, TX; KSOX Raymondville, TX; KBUC(FM) Raymondville, TX; KJXK(FM) San Antonio, TX; KTSA San Antonio, TX; KZDC San Antonio, TX; KZSP-FM South Padre Island, TX; KESO-FM South Padre Island, TX; KSAH(AM) Universal City, TX.

Bott Radio Network, 10550 Barkley St., Suite 100, Overland Park, KS 66212. Phone: (913) 642-7770. Fax: (913) 642-1319.E-mail: comments@bottradionetwork.com Web Site:www.bottradionetwork.com Ownership Richard P. Bott Sr.

Stns: 12 AM. 22 FM. KAYH(FM) Fayetteville, AR; KOFC Fayetteville, AR; KCIV(FM) Mount Bullion, CA; KTFC-FM Sioux City, IA; KTFG-FM Sioux Rapids, IA; WFCV Fort Wayne, IN; KBMP(FM) Enterprise, KS; KARF(FM) Independence, KS; KCVW(FM) Kingman, KS; KJRG Newton, KS; KCCV-FM Olathe, KS; KCCV Overland Park, KS; KKCV(FM) Rozel, KS; KCVT(FM) Silver Lake, KS; KSIV(AM) Clayton, MO; KJCV(FM) Country Club, MO; KMCV(FM) High Point, MO; KBCV(AM) Hollister, MO; KLTE-FM Kirksville, MO; KLEX Lexington, MO; KCGR(FM) Oran, MO; KAYX(FM) Richmond, MO; KMOZ Rolla, MO; KSIV-FM Saint Louis, MO; KSCV(FM) Springfield, MO; KCRL(FM) Sunrise Beach, MO; KAMI(AM) Cozad, NE; KCVN(FM) Cozad, NE; KLCV-FM Lincoln, NE; KQCV Oklahoma City, OK; KQCV-FM Shawnee, OK; WCRV Collierville, TN; WCRT(AM) Donelson, TN; KTAA(FM) Big Sandy, TX.

Richard P. Bott II, exec VP; Richard P. Bott Sr., pres; Trace Thurlby, COO; Tom Holdeman, CFO.

Bravo Mic Communications LLC, 101 Perkins Dr., Las Cruces, NM 88005. Phone: (505) 527-1111. Fax: (505) 527-1100. Ownership Ned W. Bennett, 50%; and Sandra G. Zane, 50%.

Stns: 1 AM. 3 FM. KVLC(FM) Hatch, NM; KOBE Las Cruces, NM; KXPZ(FM) Las Cruces, NM; KMVR(FM) Mesilla Park, NM.

Brazos Valley Communications Ltd., 1240 E. Villa Maria, Bryan, TX 77802. Phone: (979) 776-1240. Fax: (979) 776-4700. Ownership Brazos Valley Communications GP LLC, 100% votes, 10% equity; Tommy R. Vascocu, 21% equity.

Stns: 1 AM. 4 FM. KORA-FM Bryan, TX; KTAM(AM) Bryan, TX; KAPN(FM) Caldwell, TX; KJXJ(FM) Cameron, TX; KBXT(FM) Franklin, TX.

Tommy R. Vascocu, gen ptnr; Chris Kiske, VP/gen mgr.

Brewer Broadcasting Corp., 1305 Carter St., Chattanooga, TN 37402. Phone: (423) 265-9494. Fax: (423) 266-2335.E-mail: jlb@brewerradio.com Web Site:www.brewerradio.com Ownership Estate of James R. Brewer, James L. Brewer, Maytha N. Brewer.

Stns: 1 AM. 5 FM. WMPZ-FM Ringgold, GA; WHON Centerville, IN; WQLK-FM Richmond, IN; WALV-FM Lakesite, TN; WPLZ(FM) Ooltewah, TN; WJTT-FM Red Bank, TN.

James L. Brewer Sr., pres.

Bristol Broadcasting Co. Inc., Box 1389, Bristol, VA 24203. Phone: (276) 669-8112. Fax: (276) 669-0541. Ownership Lisa Nininger Hale, 100%.

Stns: 8 AM. 11 FM. WKYX-FM Golconda, IL; WLLE(FM) Clinton, KY; WNGO(AM) Mayfield, KY; WQQR(FM) Mayfield, KY; WKYQ-FM Paducah, KY; WKYX(AM) Paducah, KY; WDDJ(FM) Paducah, KY; WDXR Paducah, KY; WPAD Paducah, KY; WXBQ-FM Bristol, TN; WTZR(FM) Elizabethton, TN; WAEZ(FM) Greeneville, TN; WGGQ(AM) Newport, TN; WNPC-FM Newport, TN; WFHG-FM Abingdon, VA; WFHG(AM) Bristol, VA; WVTS(AM) Charleston, WV; WBES(AM) Dunbar, WV; WZJO(FM) Dunbar, WV.

W.L. Nininger, pres & gen mgr .

Broadcast Communications Inc., Box 990, Greensburg, PA 15601. Phone: (724) 853-7000.

Stns: 4 AM. 2 FM. WKHB(AM) Irwin, PA; WKFB(AM)

Jeannette, PA; WKVE(FM) Mount Pleasant, PA; WANB(AM) Waynesburg, PA; WROG-FM Cumberland, MD; WCMD(AM) Cumberland, MD.

Robert M. Stevens, pres; Ashley R. Stevens, VP.

Broadcast South LLC, 1931 Ga. Hwy. 32 East, Douglas, GA 31533. Phone: (912) 389-0995. Fax: (912) 383-8552. Ownership John O. Higgs, 25%; Kerry Van Moore, 25%; B. Gene Waldron, 25%; and Nearly Famous Properties LLC, 25%.

Stns: 2 AM. 3 FM. WDMG-FM Ambrose, GA; WDMG Douglas, GA; WRDO-FM Fitzgerald, GA; WBHB Fitzgerald, GA; WKZZ-FM Tifton, GA.

John Higgs, pres.

Brooke Communications Inc., 1445 W. Harvard Ave., Roseburg, OR 97470. Phone: (541) 672-6641. Fax: (541) 673-7598. Ownership William E. Markham Trust, Patrick A. Markham.

Stns: 2 AM. 3 FM. KQEN(AM) Roseburg, OR; KSKR(AM) Roseburg, OR; KRSB-FM Roseburg, OR; KSKR-FM Sutherlin, OR; KKMX(FM) Tri City, OR.

David Hansen, gen sls mgr; Mike Carter, opns mgr; Patrick A. Markham, pres & gen mgr .

Brothers Broadcasting Corp., Box D, Rensselaer, IN 47978. Phone: (219) 866-4104. Fax: (219) 866-5106.E-mail: wirn@ffni.com Ownership John Balvich, 100%.

Stns: 2 AM. 3 FM. KQEN(AM) Roseburg, OR; KSKR(AM) Roseburg, OR; KRSB-FM Roseburg, OR; KSKR-FM Sutherlin, OR; KKMX(FM) Tri City, OR1 FM. WIBN-FM Earl Park, IN.

John Balvich, pres & gen mgr .

Bryan Broadcasting Corp., Box 3248, Bryan, TX 77805-3248. Phone: (979) 846-1150. Fax: (979) 846-1933. Ownership William R. Hicks, 89%; and Ben D. Downs, 11%.

Stns: 3 AM. 1 FM. KZNE(AM) College Station, TX; WTAW(AM) College Station, TX; KNDE(FM) College Station, TX; KWBC Navasota, TX.

Buckley Broadcasting Corp., 166 West Putnam Ave., Greenwich, CT 06830. Phone: (203) 661-4307. Fax: (203) 622-7341.E-mail: rbuckley@buckleyradio.com Web Site:www.buckleyradio.com Ownership Steven Buckley; Dana Buckley; Richard Buckley; Martha Fahnoe

Stns: 9 AM. 10 FM. KKBB-FM Bakersfield, CA; KNZR Bakersfield, CA; KUBB-FM Mariposa, CA; KWAV-FM Monterey, CA; KIDD Monterey, CA; KLLY-FM Oildale, CA; KHTN(FM) Planada, CA; KIOO-FM Porterville, CA; KYZZ(FM) Salinas, CA; KSMJ(FM) Shafter, CA; KSEQ-FM Visalia, CA; WDRC(AM) Hartford, CT; WDRC-FM Hartford, CT; WMMW Meriden, CT; WSNG Torrington, CT; WWCO(AM) Waterbury, CT; WSEN(AM) Baldwinsville, NY; WOR New York, NY; WFBL(AM) Syracuse, NY.

Richard Buckley, pres; Joseph Bilotta, COO.

Burbach Broadcasting Group, 100 Ryan Ct., Suite 98, Pittsburgh, PA 15205. Phone: (412) 489-1001. Fax: (412) 278-1002. Ownership Estate of John L. Laubach Jr., Nicholas A. Galli, chmn/pres.

Stns: 4 AM. 7 FM. WGIE(FM) Clarksburg, WV; WOBG Clarksburg, WV; WXKX(AM) Clarksburg, WV; WRZZ-FM Elizabeth, WV; WGYE(FM) Mannington, WV; WXIL-FM Parkersburg, WV; WGGE(FM) Parkersburg, WV; WADC Parkersburg, WV; WHBR-FM Parkersburg, WV; WVNT(AM) Parkersburg, WV; WOBG-FM Salem, WV.

Nicholas A. Galli, pres, gen mgr; Thomas Bayer, VP finance.

Burt Broadcasting Inc., Box 1848, Alamogordo, NM 88311. Phone: (505) 434-1414. Fax: (505) 434-2213.E-mail: burtbroadcasting@charter.net Ownership William F. Burt, 50%; Donnie L. Burt, 50%.

Stns: 1 AM. 3 FM. KINN Alamogordo, NM; KYEE-FM Alamogordo, NM; KZZX(FM) Alamogordo, NM; KQEL(FM) Alamogordo, NM.

Bill Burt, gen mgr .

BusinessTalkRadio.Net Inc., Box 4826, Greenwich, CT 06831-9998. Phone: (203) 323-7300. Fax: (203) 323-7302. Web Site:businesstalkradio.net Ownership B. Michael Pisani, 42.1% voiting rights; Michael Metter, 10.1% voting rights; FJL Enterprises Inc., 6.12% voting rights; all 82 other stockholders hold less than 5% of the stock.

Stns: 4 AM. WGCH(AM) Greenwich, CT; WXBR(AM) Brockton, MA; KNUU(AM) Paradise, NV; WLFP(AM) Braddock, PA.

Michael L. Metter, pres/CEO.

Bustos Media LLC, 500 Media Pl., Sacramento, CA 95815. Phone: (916) 368-6300. Fax: (916) 473-0146.E-mail: abustos@bustosmedia.com Web Site:www.bustosmedia.com

Stns: 12 AM. 15 FM. KLMG(FM) Esparto, CA; KBAA(FM) Grass Valley, CA; KTTA(FM) Jackson, CA; KBBU(FM) Modesto, CA; KZSJ(AM) San Martin, CA; KKHI(FM) Centennial, CO; KQTA(FM) Homedale, ID; KSZN(AM) Gresham, OR; KZTB(FM) Milton-Freewater, OR; KOOR(AM) Milwaukie, OR; KGDD(AM) Oregon City, OR; KLPM(AM) Portland, OR; KTXV(AM) Mabank, TX; KREH Pecan Grove, TX; KTUB(AM) Centerville, UT; KDUT(FM) Randolph, UT; KTBK(AM) Auburn-Federal Way, WA; KMMG(FM) Benton City, WA; KDDS-FM Elma, WA; KULE Ephrata, WA; KULE-FM Ephrata, WA; KZTA-FM Naches, WA; KZML(FM) Quincy, WA; KDYM(AM) Sunnyside, WA; KDYK(AM) Union Gap, WA; WDDW(FM) Sturtevant, WI; KBMG(FM) Evanston, WY.

Amador S. Bustos, pres.

Butler County Radio Network Inc., 112 Hollywood Dr., Suite 203, Butler, PA 16001. Phone: (724) 287-5778. Fax: (724) 282-9188. Web Site:www.insidebutlercountry.com Ownership Daniel R. Vernon, 25%; Linda D. Harvey, 25%; Scott W. Briggs, 25%; and Victoria A. Hinterberger, 25%.

Stns: 2 AM. 1 FM. WBUT Butler, PA; WISR Butler, PA; WLER-FM Butler, PA.

Vicki Hinterberger, gen mgr; Scott Briggs, opns mgr; Bill Davis, news dir; Ron Willison, sports dir.

C

CBS Radio, 1515 Broadway, 46th Fl., New York, NY 10036. Phone: (212) 846-3939. Web Site:www.cbsradio.com Ownership Viacom Inc., 100%. Note: Viacom Inc. also owns the CBS Television Stations Group (see listing under TV Group Ownership, Section B).

Stns: 34 AM. 96 FM. KMLE-FM Chandler, AZ; KOOL-FM Phoenix, AZ; KZON(FM) Phoenix, AZ; KRAK(AM) Hesperia, CA; KTWV-FM Los Angeles, CA; KRTH-FM Los Angeles, CA; KNX Los Angeles, CA; KAMP-FM Los Angeles, CA; KFWB Los Angeles, CA; KEZN-FM Palm Desert, CA; KROQ-FM Pasadena, CA; KYMX-FM Sacramento, CA; KZZO-FM Sacramento, CA; KHTK Sacramento, CA; KNCI-FM Sacramento, CA; KFRG-FM San Bernardino, CA; KSCF(FM) San Diego, CA; KYXY-FM San Diego, CA; KFRC(AM) San Francisco, CA; KMVQ-FM San Francisco, CA; KCBS San Francisco, CA; KFRC-FM San Francisco, CA; KITS-FM San Francisco, CA; KLLC-FM San Francisco, CA; KXFG-FM Sun City, CA; KVFG(FM) Victorville, CA; KSFM-FM Woodland, CA; WZMX-FM Hartford, CT; WTIC Hartford, CT; WRCH-FM New Britain, CT; WJHM-FM Daytona Beach, FL; WOCL-FM De Land, FL; WSJT(FM) Holmes Beach, FL; WPBZ-FM Indiantown, FL; WMBX-FM Jensen Beach, FL; WNEW(FM) Jupiter, FL; WLLD(FM) Lakeland, FL; WOMX-FM Orlando, FL; WYUU(FM) Safety Harbor, FL; WQYK-FM Saint Petersburg, FL; WQYK(AM) Seffner, FL; WRBQ-FM Tampa, FL; WIRK-FM West Palm Beach, FL; WEAT-FM West Palm Beach, FL; WAOK Atlanta, GA; WZGC(FM) Atlanta, GA; WXRT-FM Chicago, IL; WUSN-FM Chicago, IL; WBBM(AM) Chicago, IL; WBBM-FM Chicago, IL; WJMK-FM Chicago, IL; WSCR(AM) Chicago, IL; WCFS-FM Elmwood Park, IL; WBMX(FM) Boston, MA; WBZ-FM Boston, MA; WBZ Boston, MA; WZLX-FM Boston, MA; WODS-FM Boston, MA; WOMC-FM Detroit, MI; WWJ Detroit, MI; WVMV-FM Detroit, MI; WYCD-FM Detroit, MI; WXYT Detroit, MI; WXYT-FM Detroit, MI; WCCO Minneapolis, MN; KZJK(FM) Saint Louis Park, MN; KEZK-FM Saint Louis, MO; KMOX Saint Louis, MO; KYKY-FM Saint Louis, MO; WBCN(AM) Charlotte, NC; WFNZ Charlotte, NC; WNKS-FM Charlotte, NC; WKQC(FM) Charlotte, NC; WSOC-FM Charlotte, NC; WPEG-FM Concord, NC; WBAV-FM Gastonia, NC; KMXB(FM) Henderson, NV; KKJJ(FM) Henderson, NV; KLUC-FM Las Vegas, NV; KYDZ(AM) North Las Vegas, NV; KXNT North Las Vegas, NV; KXTE-FM Pahrump, NV; WCBS New York, NY; WCBS-FM New York, NY; WWFS(FM) New York, NY; WINS New York, NY; WFAN New York, NY; WXRK(FM) New York, NY; WQAL-FM Cleveland, OH; WDOK-FM Cleveland, OH; WNCX(FM) Cleveland, OH; WKRK-FM Cleveland Heights, OH; KINK(FM) Portland, OR; KUFO-FM Portland, OR; KCMD(AM) Portland, OR; KUPL-FM Portland, OR; WZPT-FM New Kensington, PA; WYSP-FM Philadelphia, PA; WPHT Philadelphia, PA; WOGL(FM) Philadelphia, PA; KYW Philadelphia, PA; WIP Philadelphia, PA; WDSY-FM Pittsburgh, PA; WBZW-FM Pittsburgh, PA; KDKA Pittsburgh, PA; KJKK(FM) Dallas, TX; KRLD Dallas, TX; KLUV(FM) Dallas, TX; KRLD-FM Dallas, TX; KMVK(FM) Fort Worth, TX; KVIL(FM) Highland Park-Dallas, TX; KHMX-FM Houston, TX; KLOL-FM Houston, TX; KKHH(FM) Houston, TX; KILT Houston, TX; KILT-FM Houston, TX; KIKK Pasadena, TX; WJFK-FM Manassas, VA; KJAQ(FM) Seattle, WA; KZOK-FM Seattle, WA; KPTK(AM) Seattle, WA; KMPS-FM Seattle, WA; WLZL(FM) Annapolis, MD; WJZ(AM) Baltimore, MD; WLIF-FM Baltimore, MD; WWMX-FM Baltimore, MD; WTGB-FM Bethesda, MD; WJZ-FM Catonsville, MD; WHFS(AM) Morningside, MD; WPGC-FM Morningside, MD

Ken O'Keefe, exec VP; Brian Ongaro, sr VP; Clancy Woods, sr VP; Dan Mason, pres/CEO.

CRISTA Broadcasting, 19303 Fremont Ave. N., Seattle, WA 98133. Phone: (206) 546-7350. Fax: (206) 289-7792.E-mail: comments@spirit1053.com Web Site:www.spirit1053.com Ownership CRISTA Ministries.

Stns: 1 AM. 2 FM. KCIS(AM) Edmonds, WA; KCMS(FM) Edmonds, WA; KWPZ(FM) Lynden, WA.

Bob Lonal, pres/CEO; Rick Carter, sr VP.

CSN International, 3232 W. MacArthur Blvd., Santa Ana, CA 92704. Phone: (714) 825-9663. Fax: (714) 825-9660. Web Site:www.csnradio.com

Stns: 1 AM. 70 FM. WJIK(FM) Monroeville, AL; KGSF(FM) Green Forest, AR; KVIR(FM) Bullhead City, AZ; KVJC(FM) Globe, AZ; KJCU(FM) Fort Bragg, CA; KOGR(FM) Rosedale, CA; KJCQ(FM) Westwood, CA; WIGW(FM) Eustis, FL; WYJC(FM) Greenville, FL; WUJC(FM) Saint Marks, FL; KHJC(FM) Lihue, HI; KIHS(FM) Adel, IA; KZJB(FM) Pocatello, ID; KYMS(FM) Rathdrum, ID; KEFX-FM Twin Falls, ID; KTWD(FM) Wallace, ID; WJCZ(FM) Milford, IL; WPJC(FM) Pontiac, IL; WJCY(FM) Cicero, IN; WOJC(FM) Crothersville, IN; WHLP(FM) Hanna, IN; WQKO-FM Howe, IN; WJCJ(FM) Ladoga, IN; WWTS(FM) Logansport, IN; WTMK(FM) Lowell, IN; WJCO(FM) Montpelier, IN; WCJL(FM) Morgantown, IN; WFGL Fitchburg, MA; WJWT(FM) Gardner, MA; WSMA(FM) Scituate, MA; WJCX-FM Pittsfield, ME; WCVM-FM Bronson, MI; WJCE(FM) Elkton, MI; KTBJ(FM) Festus, MO; KRSS(FM) Tarkio, MO; WWUN-FM Friar's Point, MS; KJFT(FM) Arlee, MT; KGFJ(FM) Belt, MT; KYWH(FM) Lockwood, MT; WGPS(FM) Elizabeth City, NC; WJIJ(FM) Norlina, NC; WPGT(FM) Roanoke Rapids, NC; WAJC(FM) Zebulon, NC; WWFP(FM) Brigantine, NJ; KKCJ(FM) Cannon AFB, NM; KPKJ(FM) Mentmore, NM; KNMA(FM) Tularosa, NM; WIFF(FM) Binghamton, NY; WKJA(FM) Brunswick, OH; WTPG(FM) Weston, OH; KJCC(FM) Carnegie, OK; KDJC(FM) Baker City, OR; KJCH(FM) Coos Bay, OR; KPIJ(FM) Junction City, OR; KEFS(FM) North Powder, OR; KKJA(FM) Redmond, OR; KAJC(FM) Salem, OR; WREQ-FM Ridgebury, PA; KWRC(FM) Hermosa, SD; KYJC(FM) Commerce, TX; KDKR(FM) Decatur, TX; KSGR(FM) Portland, TX; KJCF(FM) Asotin, WA; KKRS(FM) Davenport, WA; KTJC(FM) Kelso, WA; KBLD(FM) Kennewick, WA; WJWD(FM) Marshall, WI; KLWD(FM) Gillette, WY; KWYC(FM) Orchard Valley, WY; KWCF(FM) Sheridan, WY; KRWT(FM) West Laramie, WY.

Charles W. Smith, pres; Mike Stocklin, dir opns.

CTC Media Group Inc., Box 353, Royal Oak, MD 21662. Phone: (410) 745-5958.E-mail: mail@ctc-media.com Web Site:www.ctc-media.com Ownership Lee Afflerbach; Mike Afflerbach

Stns: 4 AM. WSME(AM) Camp Lejeune, NC; WNOS New Bern, NC; WWNB New Bern, NC; WECU(AM) Winterville, NC.

Lee Afflerbach, pres/CEO; Mike Afflerbach, VP opns.

CTVglobemedia, 9 Channel Nine Ct., Scarborough, ON M1S 4B5. Canada. Phone: (416) 332-5000. Fax: (416) 332-5283.E-mail: ctvglobemediacommunications @ctvglobemedia.com Web Site:www.ctvglobemedia.com Ownership Ontario Teachers' Plan Board, 25%; The Woodbridge Co. Ltd., 23.59%; Torstar Corp., 20%; 1565117 Ontario Ltd., 16.41%; and BCE Inc., 15%.

Stns: 10 AM. 23 FM. CKCE-FM Calgary, AB; CHBN-FM Edmonton, AB; CFBT-FM Vancouver, BC; CKST Vancouver, BC; CFUN Vancouver, BC; CHQM-FM Vancouver, BC; CFAX Victoria, BC; CHBE-FM Victoria, BC; CFWM-FM Winnipeg, MB; CHIQ-FM Winnipeg, MB; CFRW(AM) Winnipeg, MB; CIOO-FM Halifax, NS; CJCH-FM Halifax, NS; CJPT-FM Brockville, ON; CFLY-FM Kingston, ON; CKLC-FM Kingston, ON; CKKW-FM Kitchener, ON; CFCA-FM Kitchener, ON; CKLY-FM Lindsay (city of Kawartha Lakes), ON; CHST-FM London, ON; CFGO Ottawa, ON; CFRA Ottawa, ON; CJMJ-FM Ottawa, ON; CKKL-FM Ottawa, ON; CKQM-FM Peterborough, ON; CKPT-FM Peterborough, ON; CHUM Toronto, ON; CHUM-FM Toronto, ON; CKLW Windsor, ON; CIDR-FM Windsor, ON; CIMX-FM Windsor, ON; CKWW Windsor, ON; CKGM Montreal, PQ.

Stns: 10 TV. CKVR, Barrie, ON; CKX, Brandon, MB; CJAL, Edmonton, AB; CKX-1, Foxwarren, MB; CFPL-TV, London, ON; CHRO-TV-43, Ottawa, ON; CHRO, Pembroke, ON; CIVI-TV, Victoria, BC; CHWI-TV, Windsor, ON; CKNX, Wingham, ON.

John R. Gossling, CFO; Ivan Fecan, pres/CEO; Paul Sparkes, sr VP; Bonnie Brownlee, sr VP; Chris Gordon, pres, radio division.

CTV Inc., Box 9, Station O, Scarborough, ON M4A 2M9. Canada. Phone: (416) 332-5000. Fax: (416) 332-5283. Web Site:www.ctv.ca Ownership CTVglobemedia Inc., 100% (see listing).

Stns: 10 AM. 23 FM. CKCE-FM Calgary, AB; CHBN-FM Edmonton, AB; CFBT-FM Vancouver, BC; CKST Vancouver, BC; CFUN Vancouver, BC; CHQM-FM Vancouver, BC; CFAX Victoria, BC; CHBE-FM Victoria, BC; CFWM-FM Winnipeg, MB; CHIQ-FM Winnipeg, MB; CFRW(AM) Winnipeg, MB; CIOO-FM Halifax, NS; CJCH-FM Halifax, NS; CJPT-FM Brockville, ON; CFLY-FM Kingston, ON; CKLC-FM Kingston, ON; CKKW-FM Kitchener, ON; CFCA-FM Kitchener, ON; CKLY-FM Lindsay (city of Kawartha Lakes), ON; CHST-FM London, ON; CFGO Ottawa, ON; CFRA Ottawa, ON; CJMJ-FM Ottawa, ON; CKKL-FM Ottawa, ON; CKQM-FM Peterborough, ON; CKPT-FM Peterborough, ON; CHUM Toronto, ON; CHUM-FM Toronto, ON; CKLW Windsor, ON; CIDR-FM Windsor, ON; CIMX-FM Windsor, ON; CKWW Windsor, ON; CKGM Montreal, PQ1 FM. CFJR-FM Brockville, ON.

Stns: 40 TV. CKYB, Brandon, MB; CJCH-6, Caledonia, NS; CFCN, Calgary, AB; CKCD, Campbellton, NB; CJCH-1, Canning, NS; CKCW-1, Charlottetown, PE; CKCK-1, Colgate, SK; CJOH-8, Cornwall, ON; CJOH-6, Deseronto, ON; CFRN, Edmonton, AB; CICI-1, Elliot Lake, ON; CKMC-1, Golden Prairie, SK; CJCH, Halifax, NS; CITO-2, Kearns, ON; CKCO, Kitchener, ON; CFCN-5, Lethbridge, AB; CKBQ, Melfort, SK; CKCW, Moncton, NB; CFCF, Montreal, PQ; CKNY-TV, North Bay, ON; CJOH-TV, Ottawa, ON; CIPA, Prince Albert, SK; CKCK, Regina, SK; CKCW-TV-2, Saint Edward, PE; CKLT, Saint John, NB; CKCO-3, Sarnia, ON; CFQC, Saskatoon, SK; CHBX, Sault Ste. Marie, ON; CICI, Sudbury, ON; CKMC, Swift Current, SK; CJCB, Sydney, NS; CITO, Timmins, ON; CFTO, Toronto, ON; CKAM, Upsalquitch Lake, NB; CIVT, Vancouver, BC; CIEW, Warmley, SK; CKCO-2, Wiarton, ON; CKCK-2, Willow Bunch, SK; CKY, Winnipeg, MB; CICC, Yorkton, SK.

Ivan Fecan, CEO; Rick Brace, pres, revenue, business planning & sports; Susanne Boyce, pres, creative & content & channels.

Sheila Callahan and Friends Inc., Box 309, Missoula, MT 59806-0309. Phone: (406) 542-1025. Fax: (406) 721-1036. Ownership SC&F Inc.

Stns: 10 AM. 23 FM. CKCE-FM Calgary, AB; CHBN-FM Edmonton, AB; CFBT-FM Vancouver, BC; CKST Vancouver, BC; CFUN Vancouver, BC; CHQM-FM Vancouver, BC; CFAX Victoria, BC; CHBE-FM Victoria, BC; CFWM-FM Winnipeg, MB; CHIQ-FM Winnipeg, MB; CFRW(AM) Winnipeg, MB; CIOO-FM Halifax, NS; CJCH-FM Halifax, NS; CJPT-FM Brockville, ON; CFLY-FM Kingston, ON; CKLC-FM Kingston, ON; CKKW-FM Kitchener, ON; CFCA-FM Kitchener, ON; CKLY-FM Lindsay (city of Kawartha Lakes), ON; CHST-FM London, ON; CFGO Ottawa, ON; CFRA Ottawa, ON; CJMJ-FM Ottawa, ON; CKKL-FM Ottawa, ON; CKQM-FM Peterborough, ON; CKPT-FM Peterborough, ON; CHUM Toronto, ON; CHUM-FM Toronto, ON; CKLW Windsor, ON; CIDR-FM Windsor, ON; CIMX-FM Windsor, ON; CKWW Windsor, ON; CKGM Montreal, PQ1 FM. CFJR-FM Brockville, ON4 FM. KHDV(FM) Darby, MT; KDXT(FM) Lolo, MT; KMSO-FM Missoula, MT; KMTZ(FM) Three Forks, MT.

Sheila Callahan, pres; Max Murphy, CFO.

Calvary Evangelistic Mission Inc., Box 367000, San Juan, PR 00936-7000. Phone: (787) 724-1190. Fax: (787) 722-5395.E-mail: radio@therockradio.org Web Site:www.therockradio.org Ownership Dr. James Christensen, 11.1% of votes; Clair D. Miller, 11.1% of votes; James A. Looman, 11.1% of votes; Pablo E. Fernandez, 11.1% of votes; Raul Zevallos, 11.1% of votes; Vernon Green, 11.1% of votes; Wallace B. Bishop Jr., 11.1% of votes; Gwendolyn Santiago, 11.1% of votes; and Ruth Luttrell, 11.1% of votes.

Stns: 3 AM. WCGB Juana Diaz, PR; WBMJ San Juan, PR; WIVV Vieques, PR.

Ruth Lutterall, pres; Janet Luttrell, gen mgr; Nila Luttrell, CFO.

Cameron Broadcasting Inc., 1615 Orange Tree Ln., Suite 102, Redlands, CA 92374. Phone: (909) 793-2233. Fax: (909) 798-6984. Web Site:kflg947.com; lucky98fm.com; theknack107.com Ownership William Jaeger, Don Jaeger.

Stns: 3 AM. 3 FM. KZZZ(AM) Bullhead City, AZ; KFLG(AM) Bullhead City, AZ; KAAA Kingman, AZ; KFLG-FM Big River, CA; KNKK(FM) Needles, CA; KLUK(FM) Needles, CA.

William Jaeger, pres/CEO; Don Jaeger, VP/gen mgr.

Canfin Enterprises Inc., Box 3498, Abilene, TX 79604. Phone: (325) 672-5442. Fax: (325) 672-6128.E-mail: info@radioabilene.com Web Site:radioabilene.com Ownership Parker S. Cannan, 100%.

Stns: 2 AM. 1 FM. KKHR-FM Abilene, TX; KZQQ(AM) Abilene, TX; KWKC(AM) Abilene, TX.

Canxus Broadcasting Corp., 152 E. Green Ridge Rd., Caribou, ME 04736-3737. Phone: (207) 473-7513. Fax: (207) 472-3221. Web Site:www.channelxradio.com Ownership

Dennis Curley, 92%; Richard Chandler, 4%; and Pamela Curley, 4%.

Stns: 2 AM. 1 FM. KKHR-FM Abilene, TX; KZQQ(AM) Abilene, TX; KWKC(AM) Abilene, TX3 FM. WCXU-FM Caribou, ME; WCXX-FM Madawaska, ME; WCXV(FM) Van Buren, ME.

Capital Community Broadcasting Inc., 360 Egan Dr., Juneau, AK 99801-1748. Phone: (907) 586-1670. Fax: (907) 586-3612.

Stns: 2 AM. 1 FM. KKHR-FM Abilene, TX; KZQQ(AM) Abilene, TX; KWKC(AM) Abilene, TX3 FM. WCXU-FM Caribou, ME; WCXX-FM Madawaska, ME; WCXV(FM) Van Buren, ME; KRNN(FM) Juneau, AK; KXLL(FM) Juneau, AK; KTOO-FM Juneau, AK.

Stns: 1 TV. KTOO-TV, Juneau, AK.

Capital Media Corp., 30 Park Ave., Cohoes, NY 12047-3330. Phone: (518) 237-1330. Fax: (518) 235-4468.E-mail: info@whaz.com Web Site:www.whaz.com

Stns: 1 AM. 4 FM. WHAZ-FM Hoosick Falls, NY; WBAR-FM Lake Luzerne, NY; WMYY-FM Schoharie, NY; WHAZ Troy, NY; WMNV-FM Rupert, VT.

Paul F. Lotters, pres, gen mgr; Steve Klob, opns dir.

Capitol Broadcasting Co. Inc., Box 12000, Raleigh, NC 27605. Phone: (919) 821-8555. Fax: (919) 821-8733. Web Site:www.cbc-raleigh.com Ownership Capitol Holding Co. Inc.

Stns: 1 AM. 8 FM. WKXB-FM Burgaw, NC; WCMC-FM Creedmoor, NC; WLGD(FM) Jacksonville, NC; WSFM(FM) Oak Island, NC; WRAL(FM) Raleigh, NC; WNCM(FM) Sharpsburg, NC; WAZO(FM) Southport, NC; WILT(FM) Wilmington, NC; WMFD Wilmington, NC.

Stns: 4 TV. WMYT-TV, Charlotte, NC; WJZY, Charlotte, NC; WRAL-TV, Raleigh-Durham (Fayetteville), NC; WRAZ, Raleigh-Durham (Fayetteville), NC.

James F. Goodmon, pres/CEO; Vicke S. Murray, sec; Daniel P. McGrath, VO/CFO; Michael D. Hill, VP/gen counsel; James R. Hefner, III, VP, tv.

Capps Broadcast Group, 2003 N.W. 56th Dr., Pendleton, OR 97801. Phone: (541) 276-1511. Fax: (541) 276-1480.

Stns: 3 AM. 4 FM. KCMB(FM) Baker City, OR; KWRL-FM La Grande, OR; KTIX Pendleton, OR; KUMA Pendleton, OR; KUMA-FM Pendleton, OR; KWHT-FM Pendleton, OR; KTEL Walla Walla, WA.

Randy McKone, pres & gen mgr .

CapSan Media LLC, 277 Bendix Rd., Suite 411, Virginia Beach, VA 23452. Phone: (757) 497-1415. Fax: (757) 497-2560. Web Site:www.capsanmedia.com Ownership Jason Baker, 42.3%; William Whitlow, 42.3%.

Stns: 3 AM. 4 FM. KCMB(FM) Baker City, OR; KWRL-FM La Grande, OR; KTIX Pendleton, OR; KUMA Pendleton, OR; KUMA-FM Pendleton, OR; KWHT-FM Pendleton, OR; KTEL Walla Walla, WA4 FM. WYND-FM Hatteras, NC; WFMZ(FM) Hertford, NC; WVOD(FM) Manteo, NC; WZPR(FM) Nags Head, NC.

Carlson Communications International, 3606 S. 500 W., Salt Lake City, UT 84115. Phone: (801) 262-5624. Fax: (801) 266-1510. Ownership Ralph J. Carlson, any stockholder with 10% or more.

Stns: 3 AM. 2 FM. KRJC-FM Elko, NV; KTSN Elko, NV; KCYN(FM) Moab, UT; KDYL(AM) South Salt Lake, UT; KCPX(AM) Spanish Valley, UT.

Ralph J. Carlson, pres.

Carolina Christian Radio, Box 957, Wilmington, NC 28402. Phone: (910) 763-2452. Fax: (910) 763-6578.E-mail: life@life905.com Web Site:www.life905.com

Stns: 3 AM. 3 FM. WMYT Carolina Beach, NC; WZDG(FM) Scotts Hill, NC; WWIL Wilmington, NC; WWIL-FM Wilmington, NC; WLSG(AM) Wilmington, NC; WDVV-FM Wilmington, NC.

Jim Stephens, pres/gen mgr.

Carroll Broadcasting Co., 1119 E. Plaza Dr., Carroll, IA 51401. Phone: (712) 792-4321. Fax: (712) 792-6667. Web Site:www.carrollbroadcasting.com

Stns: 1 AM. 2 FM. KCIM Carroll, IA; KKRL-FM Carroll, IA; KIKD-FM Lake City, IA.

Mary Collison, pres.

Carroll Enterprises Inc., Box 549, Tawas City, MI 48764. Phone: (989) 362-3417. Fax: (989) 362-4544.E-mail: wkjc@wkjc.com Web Site:www.wkjc.com

Stns: 1 AM. 2 FM. WKJZ-FM Hillman, MI; WIOS Tawas City, MI; WKJC-FM Tawas City, MI.

John Carroll Jr., pres & gen mgr .

Jimmy Ray Carroll Stns, Box 271, Kemmerer, WY 83101. Phone: (307) 877-0000. Fax: (307) 877-5524.

Stns: 3 AM. 3 FM. KWUD(AM) Woodville, TX; KEVA

Evanston, WY; KWYW(FM) Lost Cabin, WY; KTRZ-FM Riverton, WY; KDNO(FM) Thermopolis, WY; KTHE Thermopolis, WY.

Jimmy Ray Carroll, owner.

Carter Broadcast Group Inc., 11131 Colorado Ave., Kansas City, MO 64137. Phone: (816) 763-2040. Fax: (816) 966-1055. Ownership Michael Carter

Stns: 1 AM. 1 FM. KPRS-FM Kansas City, MO; KPRT Kansas City, MO.

Michael Carter, pres.

Catholic Radio Network Inc., 201 N. Industrial Park Rd., Excelsior Springs, MO 64024-1736. Phone: (816) 630-1090. Ownership Carolyn O'Laughlin, 33.3% votes; James E. O'Laughlin, 33.3% votes; and Jim Kafka, 33.3% votes.

Stns: 4 AM. 1 FM. KPIO(AM) Loveland, CO; KFEL Pueblo, CO; KAHS(AM) El Dorado, KS; KEXS(AM) Excelsior Springs, MO; KEXS-FM Ravenwood, MO.

James E. O'Laughlin, pres.

Cedar Cove Broadcasting Inc., 87 Jasper Lake Rd., Loveland, CO 80537. Phone: (970) 669-9200.

Stns: 4 AM. 1 FM. KPIO(AM) Loveland, CO; KFEL Pueblo, CO; KAHS(AM) El Dorado, KS; KEXS(AM) Excelsior Springs, MO; KEXS-FM Ravenwood, MO8 FM. KDAB(FM) Central City, CO; KEZD(FM) Estes Park, CO; KGQD(FM) Fraser, CO; KMPB(FM) Frisco, CO; KADE(FM) Salida, CO; KEZF(FM) Burns, WY; KGCY(FM) Esterbrook, WY; KDNR(FM) South Greeley, WY.

Victor A. Michael, pres.

Cenla Broadcasting Co. Inc., 1115 Texas Ave., Alexandria, LA 71301. Phone: (318) 445-1234. Fax: (318) 473-1960. Web Site:www.cenlabroadcasting.com Ownership Taylor C. Thompson, 50% votes; and Charles J. Soprano, 50% votes.

Stns: 2 AM. 4 FM. KQID-FM Alexandria, LA; KRRV-FM Alexandria, LA; KSYL Alexandria, LA; KZMZ-FM Alexandria, LA; KDBS Alexandria, LA; KKST-FM Oakdale, LA.

Taylor C. Thompson, pres.

Centennial Broadcasting LLC, 3443 Robinhood Rd., Suite H, Winston-Salem, NC 27106. Phone: (336) 794-7971. Ownership G Force LLC, 73.75%; Centennial Management Inc., 25%; Allen B. Shaw, 0.71%; Steven H. Watts, 0.36%; and Christopher Jarrell, 0.18%.

Stns: 2 AM. 4 FM. KQID-FM Alexandria, LA; KRRV-FM Alexandria, LA; KSYL Alexandria, LA; KZMZ-FM Alexandria, LA; KDBS Alexandria, LA; KKST-FM Oakdale, LA4 FM. WLEQ(FM) Bedford, VA; WZZU(FM) Lynchburg, VA; WLNI-FM Lynchburg, VA; WZZI-FM Vinton, VA.

Center Broadcasting Co. Inc., 307 San Augustine St., Center, TX 75935. Phone: (936) 598-3304. Fax: (936) 598-9537.

Stns: 1 AM. 2 FM. KDET Center, TX; KQBB(FM) Center, TX; KQSI(FM) San Augustine, TX.

Lori Alvis, gen mgr .

Central Wisconsin Broadcasting Inc., Box 387, 1201 E. Division St., Neillsville, WI 54456. Phone: (715) 743-3333. Fax: (715) 743-2288.E-mail: 1075therock@tds.net Web Site:1075therock.com Ownership J. Kevin and Margaret L. Grap, 100%.

Stns: 1 AM. 2 FM. WCCN Neillsville, WI; WCCN-FM Neillsville, WI; WPKG(FM) Neillsville, WI.

J. Kevin Grap, gen mgr .

Cessna Communications Inc., Box 1, Bedford, PA 15522. Phone: (814) 623-1000. Fax: (814) 623-9692.E-mail: cesscomm@earthlink.net Ownership Jay B. Cessna; John H. Cessna.

Stns: 2 AM. 2 FM. WBVE(FM) Bedford, PA; WBFD(AM) Bedford, PA; WAYC-FM Bedford, PA; WHJB(AM) Bedford, PA.

Jay Cessna, pres; John H. Cessna, VP/gen mgr.

Chaparral Communications, Box 100, Jackson, WY 83001. Phone: (307) 733-2120. Fax: (307) 733-4760.E-mail: jacksonholeradio@onewest.net Web Site:www.jacksonholeradio.com Ownership Jerrold Lundquist.

Stns: 3 AM. 8 FM. KLZY(FM) Honokaa, HI; KYZK(FM) Sun Valley, ID; KECH-FM Sun Valley, ID; KSKI-FM Sun Valley, ID; KWMY(FM) Park City, MT; KWYS West Yellowstone, MT; KZJH-FM Jackson, WY; KJAX(FM) Jackson, WY; KSGT Jackson, WY; KMTN-FM Jackson, WY; KPOW Powell, WY.

Scott Anderson, gen mgr .

Cherry Creek Radio LLC, 501 S. Cherry St., Suite 480, Denver, CO 80246. Phone: (303) 468-6500. Fax: (303) 468-6555.E-mail: jschwartz@cherrycreekradio.com Web Site:www.cherrycreekradio.com Ownership Arlington Capital

Partners L.P., 97.716% of votes, 80.131% of total assets; ACP/CCR Holdings LLC, 17.585% of total assets.

Stns: 21 AM. 41 FM. KWCD-FM Bisbee, AZ; KXFF(FM) Colorado City, AZ; KTAN(AM) Sierra Vista, AZ; KZMK(FM) Sierra Vista, AZ; KROP(AM) Brawley, CA; KSIQ-FM Brawley, CA; KRLT-FM South Lake Tahoe, CA; KOWL(AM) South Lake Tahoe, CA; KTHN(FM) La Junta, CO; KBLJ(AM) La Junta, CO; KLMR-FM Lamar, CO; KLMR Lamar, CO; KKXK-FM Montrose, CO; KUBC(AM) Montrose, CO; KBNG(FM) Ridgway, CO; KERT(FM) Alberton, MT; KYYA-FM Billings, MT; KRZN(FM) Billings, MT; KBLG Billings, MT; KRKX(FM) Billings, MT; KMBR-FM Butte, MT; KAAR(FM) Butte, MT; KXTL Butte, MT; KVVR(FM) Dutton, MT; KHKR-FM East Helena, MT; KLFM-FM Great Falls, MT; KMON Great Falls, MT; KMON-FM Great Falls, MT; KAAK(FM) Great Falls, MT; KXDR-FM Hamilton, MT; KZMT-FM Helena, MT; KBLL Helena, MT; KBLL-FM Helena, MT; KCAP Helena, MT; KGGL-FM Missoula, MT; KGRZ Missoula, MT; KZOQ-FM Missoula, MT; KYLT Missoula, MT; KHLN(FM) Montana City, MT; KBQQ(FM) Pinesdale, MT; KTHC-FM Sidney, MT; KYYZ-FM Williston, ND; KEYZ Williston, ND; KCOM Comanche, TX; KYOX(FM) Comanche, TX; KSTV-FM Dublin, TX; KSTV Stephenville, TX; KREC(FM) Brian Head, UT; KXBN(FM) Cedar City, UT; KCIN(FM) Cedar City, UT; KSUB Cedar City, UT; KDXU Saint George, UT; KSNN-FM Saint George, UT; KUNF(AM) Washington, UT; KWWX(FM) Cashmere, WA; KZHR(FM) Dayton, WA; KYSN-FM East Wenatchee, WA; KONA Kennewick, WA; KONA-FM Kennewick, WA; KWWW-FM Quincy, WA; KAAP(FM) Rock Island, WA; KZNW(AM) Wenatchee, WA.

Joe Schwartz, pres/CEO; Dan Gittings, exec VP/dir sls; Dennis Goodman, exec VP/dir opns.

Chesapeake-Portsmouth Broadcasting Corp., 2202 Jolliff Rd., Chesapeake, VA 23321. Phone: (757) 488-1010. Ownership Nancy A. Epperson, 100%. Note: Group also owns 50% of New AM Nassau Village-Ratliff, FL. Group is broker of airtime on WRJR(AM) Portsmouth, VA.

Stns: 5 AM. WBOB(AM) Jacksonville, FL; WLES(AM) Bon Air, VA; WPMH(AM) Claremont, VA; WLVA Lynchburg, VA; WTJZ Newport News, VA.

Henry W. Hoot, .

The Chickasaw Nation, Box 609, Ada, OK 74821-0609. Phone: (580) 332-1212. Fax: (580) 332-0128. Web Site:www.chickasaw.net Ownership The Chickasaw Nation, an Indian tribal government, is governed by a legislature.

Stns: 1 AM. 5 FM. KADA Ada, OK; KADA-FM Ada, OK; KCNP(FM) Ada, OK; KYKC-FM Byng, OK; KXFC(FM) Coalgate, OK; KTLS-FM Holdenville, OK.

Choice Broadcasting Co. LLC, 125 Tun Jesus Cristostomo St., Suite 308, Tamuning, GU 96931. Phone: (671) 648-4262. Ownership Richard C. Yu, 35%; Jeselyn T. Yu, 35%; and Robert F. Kelley Jr., 30%.

Stns: 1 AM. 2 FM. KCNM-FM Garapan-Saipan, NP; KCNM(AM) Garapan-Saipan, NP; KZMI(FM) Garapan-Saipan, NP.

Christian Broadcasting System Ltd., 29200 Vassar Dr. Ste.150, Livonia, MI 48152. Phone: (248) 477-4600. Fax: (248) 477-6911.

Stns: 6 AM. 2 FM. WQRT(AM) Florence, KY; WJMM-FM Keene, KY; WCGW Nicholasville, KY; WLRT(AM) Nicholasville, KY; WSNL(AM) Flint, MI; WLCM(AM) Holt, MI; WJIV-FM Cherry Valley, NY; WCVX(AM) Cincinnati, OH.

Jon R. Yinger, pres/CEO; Ralph Van Luven, VP; Sally Van Luven, sec; Vicky Yinger, treas.

Christian Faith Broadcasting Inc., 3809 Maple Ave., Castalia, OH 44824. Phone: (419) 684-5311. Fax: (419) 684-5378.E-mail: wggn@lrbcg.com

Stns: 6 AM. 2 FM. WQRT(AM) Florence, KY; WJMM-FM Keene, KY; WCGW Nicholasville, KY; WLRT(AM) Nicholasville, KY; WSNL(AM) Flint, MI; WLCM(AM) Holt, MI; WJIV-FM Cherry Valley, NY; WCVX(AM) Cincinnati, OH3 FM. WJKW-FM Athens, OH; WGGN-FM Castalia, OH; WLRD(FM) Willard, OH.

Stns: 2 TV. WGGN, Cleveland-Akron (Canton), OH; WLLA, Grand Rapids-Kalamazoo-Battle Creek, MI.

Shelby Gillam, pres; Rusty Yost, VP.

Christian Listening Network Inc., 996 Helen St., Fayetteville, NC 28303. Phone: (910) 864-5028. Fax: (910) 864-6270. Ownership George E. Wilson, 52%; Michele W. Lhotellier, 12%; Regina W. Parker, 12%; Sharlene W. Tew, 12%; and Jeffrey S. Wilson, 12%.

Stns: 1 AM. 2 FM. WCLN(AM) Clinton, NC; WCLN-FM Clinton, NC; WZKB-FM Wallace, NC.

Christian Voice of Central Ohio Inc., Box 793, New Albany, OH 43054. Phone: (614) 855-9171. Fax: (614) 855-9280. Ownership David R. Kolbe, 9.09% votes; Joe Panzica, 9.09% votes; Cheryl Burket, 9.09% votes; George Cunningham, 9.09% votes; Gary Hosfelt, 9.09% votes; David Humphrey, 9.09% votes; Andrew Lang, 9.09% votes; Matt Levin 9.09% votes; Doug Martin, 9.09% votes; Mark Nicholas, 9.09% votes; and Donald Stillion, 9.09% votes.

Stns: 3 AM. 4 FM. WDPT(AM) Decatur, AL; WTKI(AM) Huntsville, AL; WZRP(FM) Richmond, IN; WZCP(FM) Chillicothe, OH; WRFD(AM) Columbus-Worthington, OH; WCVO-FM Gahanna, OH; WZWP(FM) West Union, OH.

Drenda Keesee, chmn; Dan Baughman, pres.

Churchill Communications LLC, 871 Country Club Rd., Eugene, OR 97401. Phone: (541) 344-5500. Fax: (541) 485-2550. Ownership Suzanne Arlie, 100%.

Stns: 3 AM. KLZS(AM) Eugene, OR; KXOR(AM) Junction City, OR; KXPD(AM) Tigard, OR.

Citadel Broadcasting Corp., 7201 W. Lake Mead Blvd., Suite 400, Las Vegas, NV 89128. Phone: (702) 804-5200. Fax: (702) 804-5936. Web Site:www.citadelbroadcasting.com Ownership Forstmann Little Funds, 58%; and public shareholders, 42%.

Stns: 62 AM. 157 FM. WJOX(FM) Birmingham, AL; WZRR-FM Birmingham, AL; WUHT(FM) Birmingham, AL; WAPI Birmingham, AL; WSPZ(AM) Birmingham, AL; WFFN-FM Cordova, AL; WDGM(FM) Greensboro, AL; WWMM(FM) Northport, AL; WTUG-FM Northport, AL; WBEI(FM) Reform, AL; WTSK(AM) Tuscaloosa, AL; KAAY Little Rock, AR; KARN Little Rock, AR; KURB-FM Little Rock, AR; KPZK(AM) Little Rock, AR; KIPR-FM Pine Bluff, AR; KOKY-FM Sherwood, AR; KLAL-FM Wrightsville, AR; KSZR(FM) Oro Valley, AZ; KHYT-FM Tucson, AZ; KIIM-FM Tucson, AZ; KTUC Tucson, AZ; KCUB Tucson, AZ; KWIN-FM Lodi, CA; KLOS-FM Los Angeles, CA; KABC Los Angeles, CA; KDJK(FM) Mariposa, CA; KHKK-FM Modesto, CA; KATM(FM) Modesto, CA; KESP(AM) Modesto, CA; KHOP-FM Oakdale, CA; KGO San Francisco, CA; KSFO San Francisco, CA; KWYL(FM) South Lake Tahoe, CA; KJOY-FM Stockton, CA; KWNN-FM Turlock, CA; KCSF(AM) Colorado Springs, CO; KVOR Colorado Springs, CO; KKPK(FM) Colorado Springs, CO; KKFM-FM Colorado Springs, CO; KATC-FM Colorado Springs, CO; KKMG-FM Pueblo, CO; WSUB Groton, CT; WMOS(FM) Stonington, CT; WRQX-FM Washington, DC; WMAL Washington, DC; WYAY-FM Gainesville, GA; WKHX-FM Marietta, GA; KWQW(FM) Boone, IA; KGGO-FM Des Moines, IA; KHKI-FM Des Moines, IA; KBGG(AM) Des Moines, IA; KJJY(FM) West Des Moines, IA; KIZN-FM Boise, ID; KQFC-FM Boise, ID; KBOI Boise, ID; KKGL-FM Nampa, ID; KTIK Nampa, ID; KZMG(FM) New Plymouth, ID; WLS-FM Chicago, IL; WLS Chicago, IL; WWKI-FM Kokomo, IN; WMDH New Castle, IN; WMDH-FM New Castle, IN; WIBR Baton Rouge, LA; WXOK Baton Rouge, LA; KKND(FM) Belle Chasse, LA; WCDV(FM) Hammond, LA; WEMX-FM Kentwood, LA; WDVW(FM) La Place, LA; KRRQ-FM Lafayette, LA; KSMB-FM Lafayette, LA; KRDJ(FM) New Iberia, LA; KXKC(FM) New Iberia, LA; KQXL-FM New Roads, LA; KMEZ(FM) Port Sulphur, LA; KNEK Washington, LA; WFHN-FM Fairhaven, MA; WXLO-FM Fitchburg, MA; WBSM New Bedford, MA; WWFX(FM) Southbridge, MA; WHLL(AM) Springfield, MA; WMAS-FM Springfield, MA; WORC-FM Webster, MA; WMME-FM Augusta, ME; WJZN(AM) Augusta, ME; WCYY-FM Biddeford, ME; WSHK(FM) Kittery, ME; WBLM-FM Portland, ME; WJBQ-FM Portland, ME; WBPW(FM) Presque Isle, ME; WQHR-FM Presque Isle, ME; WOZI(FM) Presque Isle, ME; WTVL(AM) Waterville, ME; WEBB-FM Waterville, ME; WIOG(FM) Bay City, MI; WHNN-FM Bay City, MI; WHTS(FM) Coopersville, MI; WDRQ(FM) Detroit, MI; WJR Detroit, MI; WDVD(FM) Detroit, MI; WVFN(AM) East Lansing, MI; WFMK(FM) East Lansing, MI; WFBE-FM Flint, MI; WTRX Flint, MI; WJRW(AM) Grand Rapids, MI; WLAV-FM Grand Rapids, MI; WBBL-FM Greenville, MI; WTNR(FM) Holland, MI; WVIB(FM) Holton, MI; WJIM(AM) Lansing, MI; WJIM-FM Lansing, MI; WITL-FM Lansing, MI; WKQZ-FM Midland, MI; WLAW(FM) Newaygo, MI; WLCS-FM North Muskegon, MI; WILZ-FM Saginaw, MI; WKLQ(AM) Whitehall, MI; WGVY(FM) Cambridge, MN; WGVZ(FM) Eden Prairie, MN; KQRS-FM Golden Valley, MN; WGVX(FM) Lakeville, MN; KXXR(FM) Minneapolis, MN; WRBO(FM) Como, MS; WMTI(FM) Picayune, MS; WOKQ-FM Dover, NH; WSAK(FM) Hampton, NH; WHOM-FM Mt. Washington, NH; WPKQ(FM) North Conway, NH; KNML(AM) Albuquerque, NM; KDRF(FM) Albuquerque, NM; KRST-FM Albuquerque, NM; KKOB(AM) Albuquerque, NM; KKOB-FM Albuquerque, NM; KTBL(AM) Los Ranchos de Albuquerque, NM; KBUL-FM Carson City, NV; KNEV-FM Reno, NV; KKOH Reno, NV; WHWK-FM Binghamton, NY; WYOS(AM) Binghamton, NY; WNBF Binghamton, NY; WBBF(AM) Buffalo, NY; WHTT-FM Buffalo, NY; WGRF-FM Buffalo, NY; WEDG-FM Buffalo, NY; WWYL(FM) Chenango Bridge, NY; WAQX-FM Manlius, NY; WXLM(FM) Montauk, NY; WABC(AM) New York, NY; WPLJ(FM) New York, NY; WHLD Niagara Falls, NY; WNSS(AM) Syracuse, NY; WNTQ(FM) Syracuse, NY; WLTI(FM) Syracuse, NY; WWLS-FM Edmond, OK; WWLS(AM) Moore, OK; KATT-FM Oklahoma City, OK; KYIS(FM) Oklahoma City, OK; WKY Oklahoma City, OK; WLEV-FM Allentown, PA; WCAT-FM Carlisle, PA; WSJR(FM) Dallas, PA; WCTO-FM Easton, PA; WXTA-FM Edinboro, PA; WIOV-FM Ephrata, PA; WQHZ(FM) Erie, PA; WRIE Erie, PA; WBSX(FM) Hazleton, PA; WMHX(FM) Hershey, PA; WBHT-FM Mountain Top, PA; WBHD(FM) Olyphant, PA; WIOV Reading, PA; WARM Scranton, PA; WMGS-FM Wilkes-Barre, PA; WQXA-FM York, PA; WPRO Providence, RI; WWLI-FM Providence, RI; WPRV(AM) Providence, RI; WEAN-FM Wakefield-Peacedale, RI; WWKX-FM Woonsocket, RI; WIWF(FM) Charleston, SC; WSSX-FM Charleston, SC; WTMA Charleston, SC; WLXC(FM) Columbia, SC; WISW Columbia, SC; WNKT(FM) Eastover, SC; WOMG(FM) Lexington, SC; WTCB-FM Orangeburg, SC; WWWZ-FM Summerville, SC; WXSM(AM) Blountville, TN; WGOW Chattanooga, TN; WOGT-FM East Ridge, TN; WGFX-FM Gallatin, TN; WNRX(FM) Jefferson City, TN; WJCW Johnson City, TN; WQUT-FM Johnson City, TN; WKOS-FM Kingsport, TN; WGOC(AM) Kingsport, TN; WNML(AM) Knoxville, TN; WIVK-FM Knoxville, TN; WNML-FM Loudon, TN; WGKX-FM Memphis, TN; WXMX(FM) Millington, TN; WKIM(FM) Munford, TN; WKDF-FM Nashville, TN; WOKI(FM) Oliver Springs, TN; WGOW-FM Soddy-Daisy, TN; KPMZ(FM) Flower Mound, TX; KSCS-FM Fort Worth, TX; WBAP Fort Worth, TX; KJQS(AM) Murray, UT; KENZ(FM) Ogden, UT; KBER(FM) Ogden, UT; KKAT-FM Orem, UT; KHTB(FM) Provo, UT; KFNZ Salt Lake City, UT; KKAT(AM) Salt Lake City, UT; KBEE(FM) Salt Lake City, UT; WJZW-FM Woodbridge, VA

Farid Suleman, chmn/CEO; Judy Ellis, COO.

Clancy-Mance Communications, 199 Wealtha Ave., Watertown, NY 13601. Phone: (315) 782-1240. Fax: (315) 782-0312. Ownership Jack Clancy, David Mance.

Stns: 1 AM. 2 FM. WLYK(FM) Cape Vincent, NY; WCDO Sidney, NY; WCDO-FM Sidney, NY.

David Mance, pres/gen mgr; John Clancy, sec/treas.

Clarion County Broadcasting Corp., 1168 Greenville Pike, Clarion, PA 16214-0688. Phone: (814) 226-4500. Fax: (814) 226-5898.E-mail: clarionradio@comcast.net Web Site:www.clarioncountydailynews.com Ownership William S. Hearst, 100%.

Stns: 2 AM. 2 FM. WWCH Clarion, PA; WCCR-FM Clarion, PA; WKQW Oil City, PA; WKQW-FM Oil City, PA.

William S. Hearst, pres.

Clarke Broadcasting Corp., 1175 Fairview Dr., Suite N, Carson City, NV 89701. Phone: (775) 887-0588. Fax: (775) 887-1752.

Stns: 1 AM. 2 FM. KVML(AM) Sonora, CA; KZSQ-FM Sonora, CA; KKBN(FM) Twain Harte, CA.

H. Randolph Holder, pres; Larry England, gen mgr .

Claro Communications Ltd., 11737 Nelon Dr., Corpus Christi, TX 78410. Phone: (361) 774-4354. Fax: (361) 241-7945. Ownership Gerald Benavides, 100%. Note: Gerald Benavides is a 50% joint venturer in B Communications Joint Venture, licensee of KROB(AM) Robstown, TX.

Stns: 3 AM. 4 FM. KOPY Alice, TX; KOPY-FM Alice, TX; KMZZ(FM) Bishop, TX; KBRN Boerne, TX; KROB(AM) Robstown, TX; KUKA-FM San Diego, TX; KGGB(FM) Yorktown, TX.

Classic Communications Inc., Box 1600, Woodward, OK 73802-1600. Phone: (580) 256-1450. Fax: (580) 254-9102. Ownership Sherre D. House, 50%; Blake Brewer, 25%; and Bret Brewer, 25%.

Stns: 1 AM. 2 FM. KSIW Woodward, OK; KWDQ-FM Woodward, OK; KWFX-FM Woodward, OK.

Sherre House, pres; Bret Brewer, dir opns.

Clear Channel Communications Inc., 200 E. Basse Rd., San Antonio, TX 78209. Phone: (210) 822-2828. Fax: (210) 822-2299.E-mail: markpmays@clearchannel.com Web Site:www.clearchannel.com Ownership Thomas O. Hicks, 6.5%; L. Lowry Mays, 5.2%. Publicly traded company with the majority of its shares owned by the investing public.

Stns: 258 AM. 589 FM. KASH-FM Anchorage, AK; KBFX(FM) Anchorage, AK; KENI Anchorage, AK; KGOT-FM Anchorage, AK; KTZN Anchorage, AK; KYMG-FM Anchorage, AK; KFBX(AM) Fairbanks, AK; KIAK-FM Fairbanks, AK; KKED-FM Fairbanks, AK; KAKQ-FM Fairbanks, AK; WSTH-FM Alexander City, AL; WERC Birmingham, AL; WMJJ-FM Birmingham, AL; WRTR(FM) Brookwood, AL; WZBQ-FM Carrollton, AL; WDRM-FM Decatur, AL; WHOS Decatur, AL; WTXT-FM Fayette, AL; WBFA(FM) Fort Mitchell, AL; WAAX Gadsden, AL; WGMZ-FM Glencoe, AL; WTAK-FM Hartselle, AL; WERC-FM Hoover, AL; WBHP Huntsville, AL; WDXB(FM) Jasper, AL; WHLW(FM) Luverne, AL; WWMG(FM) Millbrook, AL; WKSJ-FM Mobile, AL; WMXC-FM

Mobile, AL; WNTM(AM) Mobile, AL; WRKH-FM Mobile, AL; WHAL(AM) Phenix City, AL; WGSY-FM Phenix City, AL; WAGH(FM) Smiths, AL; WZHT-FM Troy, AL; WQEN(FM) Trussville, AL; WACT(AM) Tuscaloosa, AL; WQRV(FM) Tuscumbia, AL; KHKN(FM) Benton, AR; KMJX-FM Conway, AR; KKIX-FM Fayetteville, AR; KEZA-FM Fayetteville, AR; KYHN(AM) Fort Smith, AR; KMAG-FM Fort Smith, AR; KWHN(AM) Fort Smith, AR; KWHF(FM) Harrisburg, AR; KDJE(FM) Jacksonville, AR; KNEA(AM) Jonesboro, AR; KIYS(FM) Jonesboro, AR; KFIN(FM) Jonesboro, AR; KBTM(AM) Jonesboro, AR; KSSN-FM Little Rock, AR; KMXF(FM) Lowell, AR; KHLR(FM) Maumelle, AR; KFXR-FM Chinle, AZ; KTZR-FM Green Valley, AZ; KOHT-FM Marana, AZ; KZZP-FM Mesa, AZ; KYOT-FM Phoenix, AZ; KOY Phoenix, AZ; KMXP-FM Phoenix, AZ; KNIX-FM Phoenix, AZ; KFYI(AM) Phoenix, AZ; KGME(AM) Phoenix, AZ; KESZ-FM Phoenix, AZ; KXEW South Tucson, AZ; KWFM(AM) Tucson, AZ; KRQQ-FM Tucson, AZ; KWMT-FM Tucson, AZ; KNST Tucson, AZ; KHYL-FM Auburn, CA; KBFP(AM) Bakersfield, CA; KHTY(AM) Bakersfield, CA; KUSS(FM) Carlsbad, CA; KBFP-FM Delano, CA; KDFO(FM) Delano, CA; KRDU Dinuba, CA; KHTS-FM El Cajon, CA; KALZ(FM) Fowler, CA; KHGE(FM) Fresno, CA; KCBL Fresno, CA; KRAB-FM Green Acres, CA; KRZR-FM Hanford, CA; KTLK(AM) Los Angeles, CA; KYSR-FM Los Angeles, CA; KIIS-FM Los Angeles, CA; KHHT(FM) Los Angeles, CA; KLAC Los Angeles, CA; KOST-FM Los Angeles, CA; KBIG-FM Los Angeles, CA; KFI Los Angeles, CA; KMRQ(FM) Manteca, CA; KTOM-FM Marina, CA; KJSN-FM Modesto, CA; KFIV Modesto, CA; KTPI(AM) Mojave, CA; KKGN(AM) Oakland, CA; KNEW Oakland, CA; KOCN-FM Pacific Grove, CA; KOSO-FM Patterson, CA; KHLX(FM) Pollock Pines, CA; KSTE Rancho Cordova, CA; KGGI-FM Riverside, CA; KDIF Riverside, CA; KVVS(FM) Rosamond, CA; KQJK(FM) Roseville, CA; KGBY-FM Sacramento, CA; KFBK Sacramento, CA; KDON-FM Salinas, CA; KION(AM) Salinas, CA; KPRC-FM Salinas, CA; KKDD San Bernardino, CA; KTDD(AM) San Bernardino, CA; KMYI(FM) San Diego, CA; KIOZ-FM San Diego, CA; KGB-FM San Diego, CA; KOGO(AM) San Diego, CA; KLSD(AM) San Diego, CA; KMEL-FM San Francisco, CA; KIOI-FM San Francisco, CA; KISQ-FM San Francisco, CA; KKSF-FM San Francisco, CA; KYLD-FM San Francisco, CA; KWSX(AM) Stockton, CA; KQOD-FM Stockton, CA; KCNL(FM) Sunnyvale, CA; KSRY(FM) Tehachapi, CA; KMYT(FM) Temecula, CA; KTMQ(FM) Temecula, CA; KBOS-FM Tulare, CA; KFSO-FM Visalia, CA; KEZL(AM) Visalia, CA; KBCO(FM) Boulder, CO; KBPI(FM) Denver, CO; KRFX-FM Denver, CO; KOA Denver, CO; KPTT(FM) Denver, CO; KHOW Denver, CO; KPAW-FM Fort Collins, CO; KIIX(AM) Fort Collins, CO; KIBT(FM) Fountain, CO; KSME(FM) Greeley, CO; KDZA(AM) Pueblo, CO; KVUU-FM Pueblo, CO; KCSJ Pueblo, CO; KCCY(FM) Pueblo, CO; KDZA-FM Pueblo, CO; KPHT(FM) Rocky Ford, CO; KKZN(AM) Thornton, CO; KCOL(AM) Wellington, CO; KTCL(FM) Wheat Ridge, CO; KKLI-FM Widefield, CO; WPKX-FM Enfield, CT; WKCI-FM Hamden, CT; WHCN-FM Hartford, CT; WKSS-FM Hartford, CT; WPOP Hartford, CT; WAVZ New Haven, CT; WELI New Haven, CT; WWYZ-FM Waterbury, CT; WWDC-FM Washington, DC; WASH-FM Washington, DC; WBIG-FM Washington, DC; WIHT(FM) Washington, DC; WMZQ-FM Washington, DC; WJBT(FM) Callahan, FL; WXTB-FM Clearwater, FL; WBTP(FM) Clearwater, FL; WMMV Cocoa, FL; WJRR-FM Cocoa Beach, FL; WTKS-FM Cocoa Beach, FL; WSRZ-FM Coral Cove, FL; WTZB(FM) Englewood, FL; WMIB(FM) Fort Lauderdale, FL; WBGG-FM Fort Lauderdale, FL; WHYI-FM Fort Lauderdale, FL; WOLZ-FM Fort Myers, FL; WLDI-FM Fort Pierce, FL; WKGR-FM Fort Pierce, FL; WFUS(FM) Gulfport, FL; WQIK-FM Jacksonville, FL; WPLA(FM) Jacksonville, FL; WFXJ(AM) Jacksonville, FL; WAIL(FM) Key West, FL; WEOW(FM) Key West, FL; WCKT(FM) Lehigh Acres, FL; WMMB Melbourne, FL; WBVD-FM Melbourne, FL; WEBZ(FM) Mexico Beach, FL; WINZ(AM) Miami, FL; WIOD Miami, FL; WMIA-FM Miami Beach, FL; WMGE(FM) Miami Beach, FL; WFLA-FM Midway, FL; WMGF(FM) Mount Dora, FL; WBTT(FM) Naples Park, FL; WFKS(FM) Neptune Beach, FL; WYGM(AM) Orlando, FL; WRUM(FM) Orlando, FL; WPAP-FM Panama City, FL; WFSY-FM Panama City, FL; WDIZ Panama City, FL; WFLF-FM Parker, FL; WTKX-FM Pensacola, FL; WYCL-FM Pensacola, FL; WFLF(AM) Pine Hills, FL; WCTH(FM) Plantation Key, FL; WFKZ(FM) Plantation Key, FL; WZJZ(FM) Port Charlotte, FL; WPBH(FM) Port St. Joe, FL; WCCF(AM) Punta Gorda, FL; WXSR-FM Quincy, FL; WZZR(FM) Riviera Beach, FL; WSDV(AM) Sarasota, FL; WCTQ(FM) Sarasota, FL; WCVU(FM) Solana, FL; WKII(AM) Solana, FL; WAVW(FM) Stuart, FL; WTNT-FM Tallahassee, FL; WNLS Tallahassee, FL; WHNZ(AM) Tampa, FL; WFLA(AM) Tampa, FL; WMTX(FM) Tampa, FL; WXXL-FM Tavares, FL; WDDV(AM) Venice, FL; WLTQ-FM Venice, FL; WZTA(AM) Vero Beach, FL; WQOL-FM Vero Beach, FL; WRLX-FM West Palm Beach, FL; WJNO(AM) West Palm Beach, FL; WBZT(AM) West Palm Beach, FL; WJIZ-FM Albany, GA; WJYZ Albany, GA; WGST Atlanta, GA; WKLS(FM) Atlanta, GA; WUBL(FM) Atlanta, GA; WEKL(FM) Augusta, GA; WSGF(AM) Augusta, GA; WBBQ-FM Augusta, GA; WRAK-FM Bainbridge, GA; WBZY(FM) Bowdon, GA; WSOL-FM Brunswick, GA; WWVA-FM Canton, GA; WDAK Columbus, GA; WSHE(AM) Columbus, GA; WVRK-FM Columbus, GA; WMRZ(FM) Dawson, GA; WFSM(AM) Dry Branch, GA; WQBZ-FM Fort Valley, GA; WIBB-FM Fort Valley, GA; WPCH(FM) Gray, GA; WMGP(FM) Hogansville, GA; WVCC(AM) Hogansville, GA; WIBB(AM) Macon, GA; WPRW-FM Martinez, GA; WCOH Newnan, GA; WWLG(FM) Peachtree City, GA; WRXR-FM Rossville, GA; WTKS(AM) Savannah, GA; WSOK Savannah, GA; WAEV-FM Savannah, GA; WTLY(FM) Thomasville, GA; WOBB-FM Tifton, GA; WRBV-FM Warner Robins, GA; KSSK(AM) Honolulu, HI; KDNN(FM) Honolulu, HI; KHBZ(AM) Honolulu, HI; KIKI-FM Honolulu, HI; KHVH Honolulu, HI; KUCD(FM) Pearl City, HI; KSSK-FM Waipahu, HI; KASI Ames, IA; KCCQ(FM) Ames, IA; KKSY(FM) Anamosa, IA; KPTL(FM) Ankeny, IA; KMJM(AM) Cedar Rapids, IA; WMT Cedar Rapids, IA; WMT-FM Cedar Rapids, IA; KMXG(FM) Clinton, IA; WOC Davenport, IA; KCQQ(FM) Davenport, IA; WLLR-FM Davenport, IA; WHO(AM) Des Moines, IA; KXNO(AM) Des Moines, IA; KDRB(FM) Des Moines, IA; KKDM-FM Des Moines, IA; KXKT(FM) Glenwood, IA; KXIC Iowa City, IA; KKRQ-FM Iowa City, IA; KMNS Sioux City, IA; KGLI-FM Sioux City, IA; KWSL Sioux City, IA; KSEZ-FM Sioux City, IA; KCDA(FM) Post Falls, ID; KATZ-FM Alton, IL; WVON(AM) Berwyn, IL; WGRB(AM) Chicago, IL; WGCI-FM Chicago, IL; WLIT-FM Chicago, IL; WNUA-FM Chicago, IL; WKSC-FM Chicago, IL; KMJM-FM Columbia, IL; KUUL(FM) East Moline, IL; WDDD Johnston City, IL; WFXN(AM) Moline, IL; WVAZ-FM Oak Park, IL; WTFX-FM Clarksville, IN; WRZX-FM Indianapolis, IN; WNDE Indianapolis, IN; WFBQ-FM Indianapolis, IN; WQMF-FM Jeffersonville, IN; WZKF(FM) Salem, IN; KZCH(FM) Derby, KS; KZSN(FM) Hutchinson, KS; KRBB-FM Wichita, KS; KTHR(FM) Wichita, KS; WSEK(FM) Burnside, KY; WSFE(AM) Burnside, KY; WGVN(AM) Georgetown, KY; WBUL-FM Lexington, KY; WLAP Lexington, KY; WMXL-FM Lexington, KY; WLKT-FM Lexington-Fayette, KY; WKJK(AM) Louisville, KY; WHAS Louisville, KY; WAMZ(FM) Louisville, KY; WLUE(FM) Louisville, KY; WKRD(AM) Louisville, KY; WUBT(FM) Russellville, KY; WKRD-FM Shelbyville, KY; WKEQ(FM) Somerset, KY; WSFC Somerset, KY; WLLK-FM Somerset, KY; WKQQ-FM Winchester, KY; WFMF(FM) Baton Rouge, LA; WJBO Baton Rouge, LA; WYNK-FM Baton Rouge, LA; KRVE-FM Brusly, LA; WSKR Denham Springs, LA; KYRK(FM) Houma, LA; WYLD New Orleans, LA; WYLD-FM New Orleans, LA; WQUE-FM New Orleans, LA; WRNO-FM New Orleans, LA; WODT New Orleans, LA; WNOE-FM New Orleans, LA; WRNX-FM Amherst, MA; WJMN-FM Boston, MA; WXKS Everett, MA; WKOX Framingham, MA; WXKS-FM Medford, MA; WHYN Springfield, MA; WHYN-FM Springfield, MA; WSNE-FM Taunton, MA; WNNZ Westfield, MA; WSRS-FM Worcester, MA; WTAG Worcester, MA; WSKX(FM) York Center, ME; WTKA Ann Arbor, MI; WWWW-FM Ann Arbor, MI; WBCK-FM Battle Creek, MI; WNIC-FM Dearborn, MI; WDTW(AM) Dearborn, MI; WMXD-FM Detroit, MI; WDTW-FM Detroit, MI; WKQI-FM Detroit, MI; WDFN Detroit, MI; WJLB-FM Detroit, MI; WBFX(FM) Grand Rapids, MI; WTKG Grand Rapids, MI; WOOD Grand Rapids, MI; WOOD-FM Grand Rapids, MI; WBCT-FM Grand Rapids, MI; WMAX-FM Holland, MI; WBXX(FM) Marshall, MI; WSNX-FM Muskegon, MI; WSHZ(FM) Muskegon, MI; WKBZ(AM) Muskegon, MI; WMUS(FM) Muskegon, MI; WMRR-FM Muskegon Heights, MI; WLBY(AM) Saline, MI; KQQL-FM Anoka, MN; KQHT-FM Crookston, MN; KMFX-FM Lake City, MN; KTCZ-FM Minneapolis, MN; KTLK-FM Minneapolis, MN; KFAN Minneapolis, MN; KFXN Minneapolis, MN; KDWB-FM Richfield, MN; KRCH(FM) Rochester, MN; KWEB(AM) Rochester, MN; KEEY-FM Saint Paul, MN; KSNR-FM Thief River Falls, MN; KMFX Wabasha, MN; KSWF(FM) Aurora, MO; KGBX-FM Nixa, MO; KTOZ-FM Pleasant Hope, MO; KSD(FM) Saint Louis, MO; KSLZ(FM) Saint Louis, MO; KLOU(FM) Saint Louis, MO; KATZ(AM) Saint Louis, MO; KIGL(FM) Seligman, MO; KGMY Springfield, MO; KXUS-FM Springfield, MO; WESE-FM Baldwyn, MS; WMJY-FM Biloxi, MS; WWKZ(FM) Columbus, MS; WJKX-FM Ellisville, MS; WBVV(FM) Guntown, MS; WUSW-FM Hattiesburg, MS; WFOR Hattiesburg, MS; WHER-FM Heidelberg, MS; WHAL-FM Horn Lake, MS; WZRX Jackson, MS; WJDX Jackson, MS; WHLH(FM) Jackson, MS; WMSI-FM Jackson, MS; WQJQ-FM Kosciusko, MS; WNSL-FM Laurel, MS; WHJA(AM) Laurel, MS; WJDQ(FM) Marion, MS; WYHL(AM) Meridian, MS; WMSO(FM) Meridian, MS; WBUV(FM) Moss Point, MS; WWZD-FM New Albany, MS; WHTU(FM) Newton, MS; WQYZ-FM Ocean Springs, MS; KJMS(FM) Olive Branch, MS; WKNN-FM Pascagoula, MS; WZLD(FM) Petal, MS; WKMQ(AM) Tupelo, MS; WTUP Tupelo, MS; WZKS-FM Union, MS; WSTZ-FM Vicksburg, MS; KZIN-FM Shelby, MT; KSEN Shelby, MT; WWNC Asheville, NC; WKSL(FM) Cary, NC; WMKS(FM) Clemmons, NC; WDCG-FM Durham, NC; WGBT(FM) Eden, NC; WPEK(AM) Fairview, NC; WQNQ(FM) Fletcher, NC; WMYI(FM) Hendersonville, NC; WLYT-FM Hickory, NC; WMAG(FM) High Point, NC; WVBZ(FM) High Point, NC; WRFX(FM) Kannapolis, NC; WCDG(FM) Moyock, NC; WRVA-FM Rocky Mount, NC; WEND-FM Salisbury, NC; WIBT(FM) Shelby, NC; WKKT-FM Statesville, NC; WMXF(AM) Waynesville, NC; WQNS-FM Waynesville, NC; WRDU-FM Wilson, NC; WTQR-FM Winston-Salem, NC; KBMR Bismarck, ND; KSSS-FM Bismarck, ND; KXMR Bismarck, ND; KYYY-FM Bismarck, ND; KFYR Bismarck, ND; KQDY(FM) Bismarck, ND; KLTC Dickinson, ND; KZRX-FM Dickinson, ND; KCAD(FM) Dickinson, ND; KJKJ-FM Grand Forks, ND; KKXL Grand Forks, ND; KIZZ-FM Minot, ND; KMXA-FM Minot, ND; KZPR-FM Minot, ND; KYYX-FM Minot, ND; KRRZ Minot, ND; KCJB Minot, ND; KTWI(FM) Bennington, NE; KMCX-FM Ogallala, NE; KOGA Ogallala, NE; KOGA-FM Ogallala, NE; KGOR-FM Omaha, NE; KQBW(FM) Omaha, NE; KFAB Omaha, NE; KSFT-FM South Sioux City, NE; WERZ-FM Exeter, NH; WGIR Manchester, NH; WGIR-FM Manchester, NH; WHEB-FM Portsmouth, NH; WMYF Portsmouth, NH; WGIN Rochester, NH; WQSO-FM Rochester, NH; WHCY-FM Blairstown, NJ; WSUS-FM Franklin, NJ; WHTZ-FM Newark, NJ; WTOC(AM) Newton, NJ; WNNJ(FM) Newton, NJ; KABQ Albuquerque, NM; KBQI(FM) Albuquerque, NM; KZRR-FM Albuquerque, NM; KPEK-FM Albuquerque, NM; KCQL Aztec, NM; KKFG-FM Bloomfield, NM; KSYU-FM Corrales, NM; KTRA-FM Farmington, NM; KDAG(FM) Farmington, NM; KFMQ-FM Gallup, NM; KGLX(FM) Gallup, NM; KAZX(FM) Kirtland, NM; KTEG(FM) Santa Fe, NM; KXTC-FM Thoreau, NM; KWNR-FM Henderson, NV; KSNE-FM Las Vegas, NV; KPLV(FM) Las Vegas, NV; WPYX-FM Albany, NY; WHRL-FM Albany, NY; WPHR-FM Auburn, NY; WKKF(FM) Ballston Spa, NY; WINR Binghamton, NY; WVOR(FM) Canandaigua, NY; WCTW-FM Catskill, NY; WKGB-FM Conklin, NY; WALK(AM) East Patchogue, NY; WRWC(FM) Ellenville, NY; WELG(AM) Ellenville, NY; WENE(AM) Endicott, NY; WMRV-FM Endicott, NY; WBBI(FM) Endwell, NY; WBBS-FM Fulton, NY; WRWD-FM Highland, NY; WFXF(FM) Honeoye Falls, NY; WHUC Hudson, NY; WZCR(FM) Hudson, NY; WKGS-FM Irondequoit, NY; WKTU(FM) Lake Success, NY; WBWZ-FM New Paltz, NY; WAXQ-FM New York, NY; WWPR-FM New York, NY; WLTW-FM New York, NY; WKIP Poughkeepsie, NY; WPKF(FM) Poughkeepsie, NY; WRNQ-FM Poughkeepsie, NY; WDVI(FM) Rochester, NY; WHTK Rochester, NY; WHAM Rochester, NY; WUMX(FM) Rome, NY; WTRY-FM Rotterdam, NY; WRVE-FM Schenectady, NY; WGY Schenectady, NY; WROO(FM) South Bristol Township, NY; WHEN Syracuse, NY; WSYR Syracuse, NY; WWHT-FM Syracuse, NY; WYYY-FM Syracuse, NY; WOFX(AM) Troy, NY; WMXW-FM Vestal, NY; WHLO Akron, OH; WARF(AM) Akron, OH; WNCO Ashland, OH; WNCO-FM Ashland, OH; WXEG-FM Beavercreek, OH; WNUS-FM Belpre, OH; WYNT(FM) Caledonia, OH; WRQK-FM Canton, OH; WKDD(FM) Canton, OH; WKKJ(FM) Chillicothe, OH; WLZT(FM) Chillicothe, OH; WBEX Chillicothe, OH; WCHI Chillicothe, OH; WCKY(AM) Cincinnati, OH; WKRC Cincinnati, OH; WLW Cincinnati, OH; WSAI(AM) Cincinnati, OH; WEBN(FM) Cincinnati, OH; WGAR-FM Cleveland, OH; WMJI-FM Cleveland, OH; WMMS-FM Cleveland, OH; WMVX-FM Cleveland, OH; WTAM Cleveland, OH; WBVB-FM Coal Grove, OH; WTVN(AM) Columbus, OH; WNCI-FM Columbus, OH; WYTS(AM) Columbus, OH; WCOL-FM Columbus, OH; WLWD(FM) Columbus Grove, OH; WMMX-FM Dayton, OH; WTUE-FM Dayton, OH; WONE Dayton, OH; WONW Defiance, OH; WZOM-FM Defiance, OH; WDFM-FM Defiance, OH; WRXS(FM) Dublin, OH; WZRX-FM Fort Shawnee, OH; WXXR(FM) Fredericktown, OH; WFXN-FM Galion, OH; WBWR(FM) Hilliard, OH; WSRW Hillsboro, OH; WSRW-FM Hillsboro, OH; WLQT-FM Kettering, OH; WIMA Lima, OH; WIMT(FM) Lima, OH; WXXF(FM) Loudonville, OH; WMAN Mansfield, OH; WLTP(AM) Marietta, OH; WRVB-FM Marietta, OH; WMRN Marion, OH; WMRN-FM Marion, OH; WKFS-FM Milford, OH; WNDH-FM Napoleon, OH; WBBG(FM) Niles, OH; WHOF(FM) North Canton, OH; WMLX-FM Saint Mary's, OH; WVKF(FM) Shadyside, OH; WSWR-FM Shelby, OH; WIZE Springfield, OH; WCKY-FM Tiffin, OH; WCWA Toledo, OH; WIOT(FM) Toledo, OH; WSPD Toledo, OH; WVKS-FM Toledo, OH; WRVF(FM) Toledo, OH; WCHO(AM) Washington Court House, OH; WNCD(FM) Youngstown, OH; WNIO(AM) Youngstown, OH; WKBN Youngstown, OH; WMXY(FM) Youngstown, OH; KTBT(FM) Broken Arrow, OK; KIZS(FM) Collinsville, OK; KHBZ-FM Oklahoma City, OK; KXXY-FM Oklahoma City, OK; KTOK(AM) Oklahoma City, OK; KTST-FM Oklahoma City, OK; KQLL-FM Owasso, OK; KZBB-FM Poteau, OK; KKBD(FM) Sallisaw, OK; KMOD-FM Tulsa,

OK; KTBZ(AM) Tulsa, OK; KAKC(AM) Tulsa, OK; KXJM(FM) Banks, OR; KKCW-FM Beaverton, OR; KLTH(FM) Lake Oswego, OR; KKRZ-FM Portland, OR; KPOJ(AM) Portland, OR; KEX Portland, OR; WAEB Allentown, PA; WSAN(AM) Allentown, PA; WZZO-FM Bethlehem, PA; WTKT(AM) Harrisburg, PA; WRVV-FM Harrisburg, PA; WRBT-FM Harrisburg, PA; WHP Harrisburg, PA; WKBO Harrisburg, PA; WRKK Hughesville, PA; WLAN Lancaster, PA; WLAN-FM Lancaster, PA; WVRT(FM) Mill Hall, PA; WVRZ(FM) Mount Carmel, PA; WUSL-FM Philadelphia, PA; WRFF(FM) Philadelphia, PA; WISX(FM) Philadelphia, PA; WIOQ-FM Philadelphia, PA; WUBA(AM) Philadelphia, PA; WDAS-FM Philadelphia, PA; WDVE-FM Pittsburgh, PA; WPGB(FM) Pittsburgh, PA; WXDX-FM Pittsburgh, PA; WBGG(AM) Pittsburgh, PA; WWSW-FM Pittsburgh, PA; WKST-FM Pittsburgh, PA; WRFY-FM Reading, PA; WRAW(AM) Reading, PA; WBYL(FM) Salladasburg, PA; WBLJ-FM Shamokin, PA; WAKZ(FM) Sharpsville, PA; WRAK Williamsport, PA; WWBB-FM Providence, RI; WHJJ Providence, RI; WHJY-FM Providence, RI; WKSP(FM) Aiken, SC; WYKZ(FM) Beaufort, SC; WLTY-FM Cayce, SC; WEZL-FM Charleston, SC; WCOS Columbia, SC; WNOK(FM) Columbia, SC; WVOC Columbia, SC; WSCC-FM Goose Creek, SC; WSSL-FM Gray Court, SC; WLFJ(AM) Greenville, SC; WESC-FM Greenville, SC; WGVL Greenville, SC; WLVH-FM Hardeeville, SC; WBZT-FM Mauldin, SC; WRFQ-FM Mt. Pleasant, SC; WYNF(AM) North Augusta, SC; WXLY-FM North Charleston, SC; WXBT(FM) West Columbia, SC; WUSY-FM Cleveland, TN; WRVW-FM Lebanon, TN; WREC(AM) Memphis, TN; WHRK-FM Memphis, TN; WDIA Memphis, TN; WEGR(FM) Memphis, TN; WLAC Nashville, TN; WSIX-FM Nashville, TN; WLND(FM) Signal Mountain, TN; WURV(FM) Walden, TN; KASE-FM Austin, TX; KVET Austin, TX; KVET-FM Austin, TX; KPEZ-FM Austin, TX; KLVI Beaumont, TX; KYKR-FM Beaumont, TX; KVNS(AM) Brownsville, TX; KKYS-FM Bryan, TX; KNFX-FM Bryan, TX; KMXR-FM Corpus Christi, TX; KUNO Corpus Christi, TX; KKTX(AM) Corpus Christi, TX; KRYS-FM Corpus Christi, TX; KZPS-FM Dallas, TX; KFXR(AM) Dallas, TX; KDMX(FM) Dallas, TX; KHKS-FM Denton, TX; KRPT(FM) Devine, TX; KBFM(FM) Edinburg, TX; KHEY(AM) El Paso, TX; KTSM-FM El Paso, TX; KTSM(AM) El Paso, TX; KPRR-FM El Paso, TX; KEGL-FM Fort Worth, TX; KDGE(FM) Fort Worth-Dallas, TX; KHFI-FM Georgetown, TX; KCOL-FM Groves, TX; KTRH Houston, TX; KPRC Houston, TX; KODA-FM Houston, TX; KKRW-FM Houston, TX; KTBZ-FM Houston, TX; KBME Houston, TX; KIIZ-FM Killeen, TX; KAGG(FM) Madisonville, TX; KHKZ(FM) Mercedes, TX; KTEX(FM) Mercedes, TX; KQXX-FM Mission, TX; KLFX-FM Nolanville, TX; KIOC-FM Orange, TX; KKMY-FM Orange, TX; KSAB-FM Robstown, TX; KTKR San Antonio, TX; KZEP-FM San Antonio, TX; KXXM-FM San Antonio, TX; KQXT-FM San Antonio, TX; KAJA(FM) San Antonio, TX; WOAI San Antonio, TX; KNCN-FM Sinton, TX; WACO-FM Waco, TX; KWTX Waco, TX; KWTX-FM Waco, TX; KBGO(FM) Waco, TX; KJMY(FM) Bountiful, UT; KNRS-FM Centerville, UT; KNRS Salt Lake City, UT; KODJ-FM Salt Lake City, UT; KZHT(FM) Salt Lake City, UT; KOSY-FM Spanish Fork, UT; WYYD-FM Amherst, VA; WJJX(FM) Appomattox, VA; WACL-FM Elkton, VA; WFQX-FM Front Royal, VA; WKCY Harrisonburg, VA; WKCY-FM Harrisonburg, VA; WROV-FM Martinsville, VA; WOWI-FM Norfolk, VA; WKUS(FM) Norfolk, VA; WRNL Richmond, VA; WRVQ-FM Richmond, VA; WBTJ(FM) Richmond, VA; WTVR-FM Richmond, VA; WRXL-FM Richmond, VA; WRVA Richmond, VA; WJJS(FM) Roanoke, VA; WSVO-FM Staunton, VA; WKDW Staunton, VA; WKSI-FM Stephens City, VA; WKCI(AM) Waynesboro, VA; WLVE(AM) Winchester, VA; WJCD(FM) Windsor, VA; WAZR-FM Woodstock, VA; KNBQ(FM) Centralia, WA; KFNK(FM) Eatonville, WA; KIXZ-FM Opportunity, WA; KJR Seattle, WA; KJR-FM Seattle, WA; KUBE-FM Seattle, WA; KPTQ(AM) Spokane, WA; KKZX-FM Spokane, WA; KQNT(AM) Spokane, WA; KBKS-FM Tacoma, WA; KHHO Tacoma, WA; KFBW(FM) Vancouver, WA; WQRB(FM) Bloomer, WI; WDUZ-FM Brillion, WI; WATQ(FM) Chetek, WI; WPCK(FM) Denmark, WI; WBIZ Eau Claire, WI; WBIZ-FM Eau Claire, WI; WQLH-FM Green Bay, WI; WDUZ(AM) Green Bay, WI; WOGB-FM Kaukauna, WI; WTSO Madison, WI; WIBA Madison, WI; WIBA-FM Madison, WI; WMEQ(AM) Menomonie, WI; WMEQ-FM Menomonie, WI; WQBW(FM) Milwaukee, WI; WISN Milwaukee, WI; WRIT-FM Milwaukee, WI; WOKY Milwaukee, WI; WKKV-FM Racine, WI; WMAD(FM) Sauk City, WI; WXXM(FM) Sun Prairie, WI; WMIL-FM Waukesha, WI; WMRE Charles Town, WV; WVHU(AM) Huntington, WV; WKEE-FM Huntington, WV; WTCR-FM Huntington, WV; WTCR Kenova, WV; WAMX-FM Milton, WV; WHNK(AM) Parkersburg, WV; WDMX-FM Vienna, WV; WEGW-FM Wheeling, WV; WKWK-FM Wheeling, WV; WBBD Wheeling, WV; WWVA(AM) Wheeling, WV; KXBG(FM) Cheyenne, WY; KOLZ-FM Cheyenne, WY; WCAO Baltimore, MD; WQSR(FM) Baltimore, MD; WCHH(FM) Baltimore, MD; WPOC-FM Baltimore, MD; WWFG-FM Ocean City, MD; WTGM Salisbury, MD; WSBY-FM Salisbury, MD; WJDY(AM) Salisbury, MD; WOSC-FM Bethany Beach, DE; WDSD(FM) Dover, DE; WDOV Dover, DE; WRDX(FM) Smyrna, DE; WWTX(AM) Wilmington, DE; WILM Wilmington, DE

L. Lowry Mays Sr., chmn; Mark P. Mays Sr., CEO; Randall T. Mays Sr., pres; Kenneth E. Wyker Sr., sr VP; Herbert W. Hill Sr., sr VP; Craig Millar, sr VP.

Coast Radio Company Inc., 600 E. Main St., Vacaville, CA 95688. Phone: (707) 446-0200. Fax: (707) 446-0122. Ownership James E. Levitt, 35.3% voting interest; John F. Levitt, 35.3% voting interest; Lauren Leigh Levitt 1996 Trust, James E. Levitt, trustee, 7.35% voting interest; Joseph Curtis Levitt 1996 Trust, James E. Levitt, trustee, 7.35% voting interest; Jessica Nicole Sanders 1996 Trust, John F. Levitt, trustee, 7.35% voting interest; and John Patrick Levitt 1996 Trust, John F. Levitt, trustee, 7.35% voting interest. FM. KKIQ-FM Livermore, CA; KUIC-FM Vacaville, CA; KKDV(FM) Walnut Creek, CA

Cochise Broadcasting LLC, Box 11060, Jackson, WY 83002. Phone: (703) 812-0482. Ownership Jana Tucker, 50%; and Ted Tucker, 50%.

Stns: 2 AM. 12 FM. KCUZ Clifton, AZ; KZXK(FM) Doney Park, AZ; KCDQ(FM) Douglas, AZ; KKYZ-FM Sierra Vista, AZ; KFMM-FM Thatcher, AZ; KTBX(FM) Tubac, AZ; KXZK(FM) Vail, AZ; KOMJ(AM) Omaha, NE; KCDC(FM) Milford, UT; KWYX(FM) Casper, WY; KWXR(FM) Reliance, WY; KTWY(FM) Shoshoni, WY; KWWY(FM) Shoshoni, WY; KXJW(FM) Sinclair, WY.

Cogeco Radio-Television Inc., 612 St. Jacques, Suite 100, Montreal, PQ H3C 5R1. Canada. Phone: (514) 390-6035. Fax: (514) 390-6070. Ownership Cogeco Inc., 100%.

Stns: 2 AM. 12 FM. KCUZ Clifton, AZ; KZXK(FM) Doney Park, AZ; KCDQ(FM) Douglas, AZ; KKYZ-FM Sierra Vista, AZ; KFMM-FM Thatcher, AZ; KTBX(FM) Tubac, AZ; KXZK(FM) Vail, AZ; KOMJ(AM) Omaha, NE; KCDC(FM) Milford, UT; KWYX(FM) Casper, WY; KWXR(FM) Reliance, WY; KTWY(FM) Shoshoni, WY; KWWY(FM) Shoshoni, WY; KXJW(FM) Sinclair, WY5 FM. CFGL-FM Laval, PQ; CJMF-FM Quebec, PQ; CJEC-FM Quebec, PQ; CFGE-FM Sherbrooke, PQ; CJEB-FM Trois Rivieres, PQ.

Rene Guimond, pres/CEO; Luc Doyon, VP; Therese David, VP; Guy Meunier, sls VP; Jacques Boiteau, gen mgr; Geoffrey O. Brow, gen mgr .

Cohan Radio Group Inc., 3750 US 27N, Suite 1, Sebring, FL 33870. Phone: (863) 382-9999. Fax: (863) 382-1982.E-mail: cohanradiogroup@htn.net Web Site:www.cohanradiogroup.com

Stns: 3 AM. 2 FM. WWOJ(FM) Avon Park, FL; WWTK(AM) Lake Placid, FL; WWLL(FM) Sebring, FL; WITS(AM) Sebring, FL; WJCM(AM) Sebring, FL.

Peter L. Coughlin, pres.

College Creek Media LLC, 980 N. Michigan Ave., Suite 1875, Chicago, IL 60611. Phone: (312) 204-9900. Ownership Media Focus LLC, 100% votes, 62.5% total assets; Simmons Media Group LLC (see listing), 37.5% total assets.

Stns: 3 AM. 2 FM. WWOJ(FM) Avon Park, FL; WWTK(AM) Lake Placid, FL; WWLL(FM) Sebring, FL; WITS(AM) Sebring, FL; WJCM(AM) Sebring, FL23 FM. KEEC(FM) Teec Nos Pos, AZ; KCGC(FM) Coarsegold, CA; KAYF(FM) Bayfield, CO; KPAU(FM) Center, CO; KDVC(FM) Dove Creek, CO; KYEN(FM) Severance, CO; KQPI(FM) Aberdeen, ID; KRID(FM) Ashton, ID; KXJO(FM) Saint Maries, ID; KKDT(FM) Burdett, KS; KXNC(FM) Ness City, KS; KEAU(FM) Fairfield, MT; KZUS(FM) Highwood, MT; KUUS(FM) Vaughn, MT; KHSK(FM) Allen, NE; KPHD(FM) Elko, NV; KCLS(FM) Ely, NV; KHIJ(FM) Mesquite, NV; KEMR(FM) Castle Dale, UT; KHUN(FM) Huntington, UT; KRPX(FM) Wellington, UT; KABW(FM) Westport, WA; KADQ-FM Evanston, WY.

Coloff Media LLC, 620 Juanita Ave., Cedar Falls, IA 50613. Phone: (319) 277-1918. Fax: (319) 277-5202. Ownership James A. Coloff, 50%; Anthony G. Coloff, 25%; Susan I. Coloff, 25%.

Stns: 1 AM. 5 FM. KHAM(FM) Britt, IA; KCHA Charles City, IA; KCHA-FM Charles City, IA; KLKK(FM) Clear Lake, IA; KMCH-FM Manchester, IA; KCZE(FM) New Hampton, IA.

Colonial Radio Group Inc., 2086 Old State Rd., Mainesburg, PA 16932-9449. Phone: (814) 837-9564. Fax: (814) 975-1098. Web Site:www.colonial.cc Ownership Jeffrey M. Andrulonis, 100%.

Stns: 1 AM. 5 FM. KHAM(FM) Britt, IA; KCHA Charles City, IA; KCHA-FM Charles City, IA; KLKK(FM) Clear Lake, IA; KMCH-FM Manchester, IA; KCZE(FM) New Hampton, IA3 FM. WBYB(FM) Portville, NY; WLMI-FM Kane, PA; WXMT(FM) Smethport, PA.

Jeffrey M. Andrulonis, pres.

Combined Communications, Box 5037, Bend, OR 97708. Phone: (541) 382-5263. Fax: (541) 388-0456.E-mail: mcheney@bendradio.com Web Site:www.klrr.com

Stns: 1 AM. 3 FM. KBND Bend, OR; KTWS(FM) Bend, OR; KMTK(FM) Bend, OR; KLRR-FM Redmond, OR.

Chuck Chackel, pres.

Combined Media Group Inc., Box 789, Wynne, AR 72396. Phone: (870) 238-8141. Fax: (870) 238-5997. Ownership Bobby Caldwell, 45%; Timothy B. Scott, 45%; and Scott Siler, 10%. Note: Bobby Caldwell owns 50% of Arkansas County Broadcasters Inc. (see listing) and 100% of East Arkansas Broadcasters Inc. (see listing).

Stns: 2 AM. KPOC(AM) Pocahontas, AR; KRLW Walnut Ridge, AR.

Tim Scott, gen mgr .

Commonwealth Broadcasting Corp., 113 W. Public Sq., Suite 400, Glasgow, KY 42141. Phone: (270) 659-2002. Fax: (270) 651-1771. Ownership Steven W. Newberry, Vickie V. Newberry.

Stns: 8 AM. 13 FM. WTCO Campbellsville, KY; WCKQ-FM Campbellsville, KY; WPTQ(FM) Cave City, KY; WIEL Elizabethtown, KY; WTSZ(AM) Eminence, KY; WOVO(FM) Glasgow, KY; WWKU(AM) Glasgow, KY; WGRK(AM) Greensburg, KY; WGRK-FM Greensburg, KY; WTHX(FM) Hodgenville, KY; WHHT(FM) Horse Cave, KY; WLBN Lebanon, KY; WLSK-FM Lebanon, KY; WKMO(FM) Lebanon Junction, KY; WYMV(FM) Madisonville, KY; WTTL Madisonville, KY; WPKY Princeton, KY; WAVJ-FM Princeton, KY; WWKY(FM) Providence, KY; WYSB(FM) Springfield, KY; WRZI-FM Vine Grove, KY.

Steven W. Newberry, pres/CEO; W. Dale Thornhill, exec VP.

Communications Capital Managers LLC, 1111 Michigan Ave., Suite 301, East Lansing, MI 48823-1096. Phone: (517) 351-3333. Fax: (517) 351-4481.

Stns: 2 AM. 3 FM. WUBR(AM) Baton Rouge, LA; KNBB(FM) Dubach, LA; KRUS Ruston, LA; KXKZ-FM Ruston, LA; KPCH(FM) Ruston, LA.

Michael Oesterle, CEO; Deb Grugen, CFO.

Communications Corp. of the Americas Inc., Box 2128, Rock Springs, WY 82902. Phone: (307) 362-3793. Fax: (307) 362-8727. Web Site:www.wyoradio.com Ownership William J. Luzmoor III, 100%.

Stns: 1 AM. 3 FM. KSIT(FM) Rock Springs, WY; KQSW-FM Rock Springs, WY; KRKK Rock Springs, WY; KMRZ-FM Superior, WY.

Communicom Broadcasting LLC, 220 Josephine St., Suite 200, Denver, CO 80206. Phone: (303) 759-8481. Ownership CCA Inc., 100%. Note: CCA Inc. controls 100% of the votes and owns 5% of the total assets of WLNO(AM) New Orleans, LA.

Stns: 3 AM. KXEG(AM) Phoenix, AZ; KXXT(AM) Tolleson, AZ; WLVJ(AM) Boynton Beach, FL.

Community Broadcasters LLC, 199 Wealtha Ave., Watertown, NY 13601. Phone: (315) 782-1240. Ownership James L. Leven, 20% votes; Bruce J. Mittman, 20% votes; Peter G. Schiff, 20% votes; Paul Homer, 20% votes; and Henry T. Wilson, 20% votes.

Stns: 2 AM. 6 FM. WOTT(FM) Calcium, NY; WTOJ(FM) Carthage, NY; WBDR(FM) Copenhagen, NY; WGIX-FM Gouverneur, NY; WEFX(FM) Henderson, NY; WQTK(FM) Ogdensburg, NY; WSLB Ogdensburg, NY; WATN Watertown, NY.

Conner Media Corp., 702 Hartness Rd., Statesville, NC 28677. Phone: (704) 878-9004. Ownership Ronald Benfield, 100%.

Stns: 3 AM. 2 FM. WSTK(FM) Aurora, NC; WJNC Jacksonville, NC; WAVQ(AM) Jacksonville, NC; WZUP(FM) La Grange, NC; WEGG Rose Hill, NC.

Ronald W. Benfield, pres.

Connoisseur Media LLC, 136 Main St., Suite 202, Westport, CT 06880-3304. Phone: (203) 227-1978. Fax: (203) 227-2373. Web Site:www.connoisseurmedia.com Ownership CM Broadcast Management LLC, mgng member, 100% votes.

Stns: 2 AM. 19 FM. KGGG(FM) Pacific Junction, IA; KZWF(FM) Patterson, IA; KZWU(FM) Pleasantville, IA; WBBE(FM) Heyworth, IL; WIHN-FM Normal, IL; WVMG(FM) Normal, IL; KVWF(FM) Augusta, KS; KIBB(FM) Haven, KS; KPBR(FM) Joliet, MT; KPLN(FM) Lockwood, MT; KKBO(FM) Flasher, ND; KBBX-FM Nebraska City, NE; WXBW(FM) Gallipolis, OH; WRTS-FM Erie, PA; WXBB(FM) Erie, PA; WFNN(AM) Erie, PA; WJET(AM) Erie, PA; WTWF(FM) Fairview, PA; WRKT-FM North East, PA;

KXMZ(FM) Box Elder, SD; WMGA(FM) Kenova, WV.

Jeffrey D. Warshaw, CEO; Michael O. Driscoll, exec VP/CFO.

Contemporary Communications, 9408 Grand Gate St., Las Vegas, NV 89143. Phone: (702) 898-4669. Fax: (208) 567-6865.E-mail: contemporary@cox.net Ownership Larry G. Fuss, 100%.

Stns: 3 AM. 2 FM. WVUV(AM) Leone, AS; KKHJ(AM) Leone, AS; KKHJ-FM Pago Pago, AS; WROX Clarksdale, MS; WKXY(FM) Merigold, MS.

Larry Fuss, pres.

Convergent Broadcasting LLC, 1766 Washington Ave., Portland, ME 04103. Phone: (207) 878-0095. Fax: (361) 855-3770. Ownership Housatonic Micro Fund SBIC LP, 58.27%; Housatonic Equity Investors SBIC LP, 36.79%; Daniel Duman, 1.975%; George Silverman, 1.975%; and Bruce A. Biette, .99%.

Stns: 3 AM. 2 FM. WVUV(AM) Leone, AS; KKHJ(AM) Leone, AS; KKHJ-FM Pago Pago, AS; WROX Clarksdale, MS; WKXY(FM) Merigold, MS3 FM. KPUS(FM) Gregory, TX; KRSR(FM) Ingleside, TX; KKPN(FM) Rockport, TX.

Coon Valley Communications Inc., 2260 141st Dr., Perry, IA 50220. Phone: (507) 643-0065. Ownership Patrick Delaney, 100%.

Stns: 1 AM. 2 FM. KGRA-FM Jefferson, IA; KDLS Perry, IA; KKRF-FM Stuart, IA.

Corus Entertainment Inc., 630 3rd Ave. S.W., Suite 105, Calgary, AB T2P 4L4. Canada. Phone: (403) 444-4244. Fax: (403) 444-4242. Web Site:www.corusent.com Ownership J.R. Shaw controls an aggregate of 80% of the voting rights.

Stns: 15 AM. 37 FM. CHQR Calgary, AB; CFGQ-FM Calgary, AB; CKRY-FM Calgary, AB; CKNG-FM Edmonton, AB; CISN-FM Edmonton, AB; CHQT Edmonton, AB; CHED Edmonton, AB; CFMI-FM New Westminster, BC; CKNW New Westminster, BC; CFOX-FM Vancouver, BC; CHMJ(AM) Vancouver, BC; CJKR-FM Winnipeg, MB; CJOB Winnipeg, MB; CJGV-FM Winnipeg, MB; CIQB-FM Barrie, ON; CHAY-FM Barrie, ON; CJXY-FM Burlington, ON; CJDV-FM Cambridge, ON; CKCB-FM Collingwood, ON; CJSS-FM Cornwall, ON; CFLG-FM Cornwall, ON; CJUL(AM) Cornwall, ON; CJOY Guelph, ON; CIMJ-FM Guelph, ON; CING-FM Hamilton, ON; CHML Hamilton, ON; CFMK-FM Kingston, ON; CFFX-FM Kingston, ON; CKBT-FM Kitchener-Waterloo, ON; CFPL London, ON; CFPL-FM London, ON; CILQ-FM North York, ON; CKRU Peterborough, ON; CKWF-FM Peterborough, ON; CFHK-FM St. Thomas, ON; CFMJ(AM) Toronto, ON; CFNY-FM Toronto, ON; CKDK-FM Woodstock, ON; CJRC-FM Gatineau, PQ; CFOM-FM Levis, PQ; CHMP-FM Longueuil, PQ; CFEL-FM Montmagny, PQ; CFQR-FM Montreal, PQ; CKAC Montreal, PQ; CINW(AM) Montreal, PQ; CKRS-FM Saguenay, PQ; CIME-FM Saint Jerome, PQ; CHLT-FM Sherbrooke, PQ; CKOY-FM Sherbrooke, PQ; CHLN-FM Trois Rivieres, PQ; CKOI-FM Verdun, PQ; CINF(AM) Verdun, PQ.

Stns: 3 TV. CKWS, Kingston, ON; CHEX-TV-2, Oshawa, ON; CHEX, Peterborough, ON.

John M. Cassaday, pres.

Coshocton Broadcasting Co., 114 N. Sixth St., Coshocton, OH 43812. Phone: (740) 622-1560. Fax: (740) 622-7940. Ownership Bruce Wallace, 100%.

Stns: 1 AM. 1 FM. WTNS Coshocton, OH; WKLM-FM Millersburg, OH.

Bruce Wallace, pres & gen mgr .

Costa-Eagle Radio Ventures L.P., 462 Merrimack St., Methuen, MA 01844. Phone: (978) 686-9966. Fax: (978) 687-1180.E-mail: pcosta@ceradio.com Ownership Costa Communications, 51%; and Cambridge Acquisitions, 49%.

Stns: 3 AM. WCEC(AM) Haverhill, MA; WNNW(AM) Lawrence, MA; WCCM(AM) Salem, NH.

Country Mountain Airwaves LLC, 1491 W. Thatcher Blvd., Safford, AZ 85546-3306. Phone: (928) 428-2217. Ownership William Konopnicki, 100% votes.

Stns: 1 AM. 3 FM. KJIK(FM) Duncan, AZ; KTHQ-FM Eagar, AZ; KQAZ(FM) Springerville, AZ; KRVZ(AM) Springerville, AZ.

Covenant Network, 4424 Hampton Ave., St. Louis, MO 63109. Phone: (314) 752-7000. Fax: (314) 752-7702. Web Site:www.covenantnet.net

Stns: 5 AM. 3 FM. WRMS Beardstown, IL; WOLG-FM Carlinville, IL; WRYT(AM) Edwardsville, IL; WIHM Taylorville, IL; WHOJ(FM) Terre Haute, IN; WCKW(AM) Garyville, LA; KBKC(FM) Moberly, MO; KHOJ(AM) Saint Charles, MO.

John Anthony Holman, pres.

Cox Radio Inc., 6205 Peachtree Dunwoody Rd., Atlanta, GA 30328. Phone: (678) 645-0000.E-mail: cxr.info@cox.com Web Site:coxradio.com Ownership Cox Enterprises Inc., 100%. Note: Cox Enterprises Inc. also owns 100% of Cox Television (see listing in section B under TV Group Ownership).

Stns: 16 AM. 69 FM. WZZK-FM Birmingham, AL; WAGG(AM) Birmingham, AL; WENN(AM) Birmingham, AL; WNCB(FM) Gardendale, AL; WBPT(FM) Homewood, AL; WBHJ(FM) Midfield, AL; WBHK-FM Warrior, AL; WEZN-FM Bridgeport, CT; WPLR-FM New Haven, CT; WFOX(FM) Norwalk, CT; WNLK(AM) Norwalk, CT; WCTZ(FM) Stamford, CT; WSTC(AM) Stamford, CT; WFYV-FM Atlantic Beach, FL; WHQT-FM Coral Gables, FL; WCFB-FM Daytona Beach, FL; WSUN-FM Holiday, FL; WOKV Jacksonville, FL; WAPE-FM Jacksonville, FL; WJGL(FM) Jacksonville, FL; WXXJ(FM) Jacksonville, FL; WPYO(FM) Maitland, FL; WHDR(FM) Miami, FL; WEDR-FM Miami, FL; WFLC-FM Miami, FL; WDUV-FM New Port Richey, FL; WDBO Orlando, FL; WHTQ-FM Orlando, FL; WMMO-FM Orlando, FL; WOKV-FM Ponte Vedra Beach, FL; WXGL(FM) Saint Petersburg, FL; WPOI(FM) Saint Petersburg, FL; WHPT(FM) Sarasota, FL; WWRM(FM) Tampa, FL; WRFC Athens, GA; WGAU(AM) Athens, GA; WSB Atlanta, GA; WSB-FM Atlanta, GA; WGMG-FM Crawford, GA; WBTS(FM) Doraville, GA; WSRV(FM) Gainesville, GA; WALR-FM La Grange, GA; WXKT(FM) Royston, GA; WNGC(FM) Toccoa, GA; WPUP(FM) Watkinsville, GA; KCCN-FM Honolulu, HI; KRTR(AM) Honolulu, HI; KINE-FM Honolulu, HI; KRTR-FM Kailua, HI; KPHW(FM) Kaneohe, HI; KKNE(AM) Waipahu, HI; WSFR(FM) Corydon, IN; WVEZ(FM) Louisville, KY; WRKA(FM) Louisville, KY; WQNU(FM) Lyndon, KY; WBAB(FM) Babylon, NY; WGBB Freeport, NY; WBLI-FM Patchogue, NY; WHFM-FM Southampton, NY; WHIO Dayton, OH; WHKO-FM Dayton, OH; WHIO-FM Piqua, OH; WZLR(FM) Xenia, OH; KRMG-FM Sand Springs, OK; KWEN-FM Tulsa, OK; KJSR-FM Tulsa, OK; KRAV-FM Tulsa, OK; KRMG Tulsa, OK; WJMZ-FM Anderson, SC; WHZT(FM) Seneca, SC; KTHT(FM) Cleveland, TX; KHPT(FM) Conroe, TX; KONO-FM Helotes, TX; KGLK(FM) Lake Jackson, TX; KKBQ-FM Pasadena, TX; KISS-FM San Antonio, TX; KCYY(FM) San Antonio, TX; KKYX San Antonio, TX; KONO San Antonio, TX; KSMG(FM) Seguin, TX; KPWT(FM) Terrell Hills, TX; WDYL-FM Chester, VA; WKHK-FM Colonial Heights, VA; WKLR-FM Fort Lee, VA; WMXB-FM Richmond, VA.

Cox Enterprises Inc. owns the following daily newspapers: The (Grand Junction, CO) *Daily Sentinel; Palm Beach* (FL) *Daily News* and *The Palm Beach* (FL) *Post; The Atlanta* (GA) *Journal & Constitution; The Daily Advance* (Elizabeth City), *The* (Greenville) *Daily Reflector* and the *Rocky Mount Telegram*, all NC; *Dayton Daily News* and the *Springfield News-Sun*, both OH; *Austin American-Statesman, Longview News-Journal, The Lufkin Daily News, News Messenger* (Marshall), *The* (Nacogdoches) *Daily Sentinel* and the *Waco Tribune-Herald*, all TX. Cox also owns weekly newspapers and shoppers in CO, FL, NC, OH, and TX.

Robert F. Neil, pres/CEO; Marc. W. Morgan, COO; Neil O. Johnston, CFO; Richard A. Reis, group VP.

Crain Media Group LLC, 200 S. Commerce, Suite 702, Little Rock, AR 72201. Phone: (501) 537-0720. Fax: (501) 537-0722. Ownership Crain Investments, 100%.

Stns: 3 AM. 7 FM. KAPZ Bald Knob, AR; KCNY(FM) Bald Knob, AR; KKSP(FM) Bryant, AR; KHTE-FM England, AR; KAWW(AM) Heber Springs, AR; KEAZ(FM) Heber Springs, AR; KOLL(FM) Lonoke, AR; KSMD(FM) Pangburn, AR; KWCK Searcy, AR; KWCK-FM Searcy, AR.

Crain publishes 22 trade magazines including *Advertising Age*.

Paul Coates, gen mgr; Phil Weaver, gen mgr .

Cram Communications LLC, 401 W. Kirkpatrick St., Syracuse, NY 13204. Phone: (315) 468-0908. Ownership Craig L. Fox, 80%; and Samuel J. Furco Jr., 20%.

Stns: 3 AM. WVOA(AM) Dewitt, NY; WSIV East Syracuse, NY; WAMF(AM) Fulton, NY.

Craig L. Fox, pres.

Crawford Broadcasting Co., Box 3003, Blue Bell, PA 19422. Phone: (215) 628-3500. Fax: (215) 628-0818. Web Site:www.crawfordbroadcasting.com Ownership Donald B. Crawford is sole owner of all the stns except WMUZ(FM), WRDT(AM), WEXL(AM), KJSL(AM) and KSTL(AM). WMUZ(FM), WRDT(AM), WEXL(AM), KJSL(AM) and KSTL(AM) are owned by Donald B. Crawford and Dean A. Crawford.

Stns: 17 AM. 11 FM. WYDE(AM) Birmingham, AL; WDJC-FM Birmingham, AL; WXJC(AM) Birmingham, AL; WXJC-FM Cordova, AL; WYDE-FM Cullman, AL; KBRT Avalon, CA; KLVZ(AM) Brighton, CO; KCMN Colorado Springs, CO; KLTT Commerce City, CO; KLZ Denver, CO; KLDC(AM) Denver, CO; KCBR Monument, CO; WYCA(FM) Crete, IL; WYRB(FM) Genoa, IL; WSRB(FM) Lansing, IL; WPWX(FM) Hammond, IN; WMUZ-FM Detroit, MI; WRDT(AM) Monroe, MI; WEXL Royal Oak, MI; KJSL Saint Louis, MO; KSTL Saint Louis, MO; WDCD(AM) Albany, NY; WDCX-FM Buffalo, NY; WPTR(FM) Clifton Park, NY; WDCX(AM) Rochester, NY; WLGZ-FM Webster, NY; KKPZ(AM) Portland, OR; KAAM(AM) Garland, TX.

Donald B. Crawford, pres/CEO.

Criswell Communications, Box 619000, Dallas, TX 75261-9000. Phone: (817) 792-3800. Fax: (817) 277-9929.E-mail: kcbi@kcbi.org Web Site:www.kcbi.org

Stns: 1 AM. 3 FM. KSYE(FM) Frederick, OK; KCBI(FM) Dallas, TX; KCRN San Angelo, TX; KCRN-FM San Angelo, TX.

Ronald L. Harris, exec VP; Dr. Jerry Johnson, pres.

The Cromwell Group Inc., Cromwell Radio Group and Affiliates. Box 150846, Nashville, TN 37215. Phone: (615) 361-7560. Fax: (615) 366-4313.E-mail: bwalters@comwellradio.com Web Site:www.cromwellradio.com Ownership Bayard H. Walters, 100%.

Stns: 6 AM. 15 FM. WCBH-FM Casey, IL; WWGO-FM Charleston, IL; WCRA Effingham, IL; WCRC-FM Effingham, IL; WZUS(FM) Macon, IL; WMCI-FM Mattoon, IL; WHQQ(FM) Neoga, IL; WEJT-FM Shelbyville, IL; WZNX(FM) Sullivan, IL; WPMB Vandalia, IL; WKRV-FM Vandalia, IL; WLME(FM) Lewisport, IN; WTCJ-FM Tell City, IN; WTCJ Tell City, IN; WKCM Hawesville, KY; WVJS(AM) Owensboro, KY; WBIO(FM) Philpot, KY; WXCM(FM) Whitesville, KY; WQZQ(AM) Clarksville, TN; WBUZ(FM) La Vergne, TN; WPRT-FM Pegram, TN.

Bayard H. Walters, pres; Thomas Crocker, CFO.

Crossroads Communications Inc., 1301 Ohio St., Terre Haute, IN 47807. Phone: (812) 234-9770. Fax: (812) 238-1576.E-mail: mike@radioworksforme.com Web Site:www.radioworksforme.com Ownership Michael A. Petersen, 53%; Dan T. Lacy, 47%.

Stns: 2 AM. 3 FM. WSDX(AM) Brazil, IN; WSDM-FM Brazil, IN; WAXI-FM Rockville, IN; WBOW(AM) Terre Haute, IN; WBOW-FM Terre Haute, IN.

Michael A. Petersen, pres/gen mgr; Dan Lacy, CFO.

Cumulus Media Inc., 3535 Piedmont Rd., Atlanta, GA 30305. Phone: (404) 949-0700. Fax: (404) 949-0740.E-mail: bill@cumulusb.com Web Site:www.cumulus.com

ChicagoIL. Cumulus Broadcasting Inc., 875 N. Michigan Ave, Suite 3650. Phone:

Stns: 81 AM. 195 FM. WZYP-FM Athens, AL; WVNN Athens, AL; WYOK-FM Atmore, AL; WDLT-FM Chickasaw, AL; WXQW(AM) Fairhope, AL; WHRP(FM) Gurley, AL; WUMP Madison, AL; WBLX-FM Mobile, AL; WGOK Mobile, AL; WLWI(AM) Montgomery, AL; WHHY-FM Montgomery, AL; WLWI-FM Montgomery, AL; WMSP Montgomery, AL; WNZZ Montgomery, AL; WXFX(FM) Montgomery, AL; WWFF-FM New Market, AL; WVNN-FM Trinity, AL; KKEG(FM) Bentonville, AR; KFAY Farmington, AR; KQSM-FM Fayetteville, AR; KLSZ-FM Fort Smith, AR; KYNF(FM) Prairie Grove, AR; KAMO-FM Rogers, AR; KMCK-FM Siloam Springs, AR; KYNG(AM) Springdale, AR; KBBQ-FM Van Buren, AR; KOAI(AM) Van Buren, AR; KMGQ(FM) Goleta, CA; KRUZ(FM) Santa Barbara, CA; KVYB(FM) Santa Barbara, CA; KVEN Ventura, CA; KHAY-FM Ventura, CA; KBBY-FM Ventura, CA; KKNN-FM Delta, CO; KEKB-FM Fruita, CO; KEXO Grand Junction, CO; KBKL(FM) Grand Junction, CO; KMXY-FM Grand Junction, CO; KENG(FM) Parachute, CO; WICC Bridgeport, CT; WINE Brookfield, CT; WRKI-FM Brookfield, CT; WEBE-FM Westport, CT; WFTW Fort Walton Beach, FL; WZNS-FM Fort Walton Beach, FL; WYZB-FM Mary Esther, FL; WINT(AM) Melbourne, FL; WAOA-FM Melbourne, FL; WCOA Pensacola, FL; WHKR-FM Rockledge, FL; WSJZ-FM Sebastian, FL; WNCV(FM) Shalimar, FL; WBZE(FM) Tallahassee, FL; WGLF(FM) Tallahassee, FL; WHBT(AM) Tallahassee, FL; WHBX(FM) Tallahassee, FL; WGPC Albany, GA; WQVE(FM) Albany, GA; WALG Albany, GA; WWLD(FM) Cairo, GA; WPEZ(FM) Jeffersonville, GA; WJAD-FM Leesburg, GA; WMAC Macon, GA; WDEN-FM Macon, GA; WDDO Macon, GA; WAYS(AM) Macon, GA; WIFN(FM) Macon, GA; WLZN(FM) Macon, GA; WMGB(FM) Montezuma, GA; WEGC-FM Sasser, GA; WJCL-FM Savannah, GA; WJLG Savannah, GA; WIXV-FM Savannah, GA; WBMQ Savannah, GA; WZAT-FM Savannah, GA; WEAS-FM Springfield, GA; WNUQ(FM) Sylvester, GA; WTYB(FM) Tybee Island, GA; WJOD-FM Asbury, IA; KQCS(FM) Bettendorf, IA; KOEL-FM Cedar Falls, IA; KDAT(FM) Cedar Rapids, IA; KHAK(FM) Cedar Rapids, IA; KJOC Davenport, IA; KBOB-FM De Witt, IA; KXGE-FM Dubuque, IA; WDBQ Dubuque, IA; KLYV-FM Dubuque, IA; KCRR(FM) Grundy Center, IA; KRNA(FM) Iowa City, IA; KBEA-FM Muscatine, IA; KOEL(AM) Oelwein, IA; KKHQ-FM Oelwein, IA; WXXQ-FM Freeport, IL; WDBQ-FM Galena, IL; WKGL-FM Loves Park, IL; WXLP-FM Moline, IL;

WZOK-FM Rockford, IL; WROK Rockford, IL; KDVB(FM) Effingham, KS; KQTP-FM Saint Marys, KS; KTOP Topeka, KS; KWIC-FM Topeka, KS; KMAJ Topeka, KS; KDVV-FM Topeka, KS; WCYN-FM Cynthiana, KY; WXZZ-FM Georgetown, KY; WVLK Lexington, KY; WLTO-FM Nicholasville, KY; WVLK-FM Richmond, KY; KQLK(FM) De Ridder, LA; KBIU(FM) Lake Charles, LA; KAOK Lake Charles, LA; KXZZ Lake Charles, LA; KYKZ-FM Lake Charles, LA; KRMD Shreveport, LA; KRMD-FM Shreveport, LA; KVMA-FM Shreveport, LA; KMJJ-FM Shreveport, LA; KKGB-FM Sulphur, LA; WEZQ-FM Bangor, ME; WQCB-FM Brewer, ME; WDEA Ellsworth, ME; WBZN-FM Old Town, ME; WKFR-FM Battle Creek, MI; WDZZ-FM Flint, MI; WWCK Flint, MI; WKMI Kalamazoo, MI; WTWR-FM Luna Pier, MI; WRSR-FM Owosso, MI; WRKR-FM Portage, MI; KLCX(FM) Eyota, MN; KDHL Faribault, MN; KQCL-FM Faribault, MN; KRFO Owatonna, MN; KFIL Preston, MN; KFIL-FM Preston, MN; KOLM(AM) Rochester, MN; KROC(AM) Rochester, MN; KROC-FM Rochester, MN; KWWK(FM) Rochester, MN; KDZZ(FM) Saint Charles, MN; KVGO-FM Spring Valley, MN; KYBA-FM Stewartville, MN; KOQL-FM Ashland, MO; KPLA(FM) Columbia, MO; KBXR(FM) Columbia, MO; KFRU Columbia, MO; KBBM(FM) Jefferson City, MO; KLIK(AM) Jefferson City, MO; KZJF(FM) Jefferson City, MO; KJMO(FM) Linn, MO; KRWP(FM) Stockton, MO; WSMS(FM) Artesia, MS; WNMQ(FM) Columbus, MS; WKOR-FM Columbus, MS; WJWF(AM) Columbus, MS; WKOR(AM) Starkville, MS; WMXU-FM Starkville, MS; WSSO(AM) Starkville, MS; WRCQ-FM Dunn, NC; WFNC Fayetteville, NC; WAAV Leland, NC; WFVL(FM) Lumberton, NC; WMGU(FM) Southern Pines, NC; WGNI-FM Wilmington, NC; WMNX-FM Wilmington, NC; WWQQ-FM Wilmington, NC; KACL(FM) Bismarck, ND; KKCT-FM Bismarck, ND; KBYZ(FM) Bismarck, ND; KLXX Bismarck-Mandan, ND; KUSB(FM) Hazelton, ND; WRRB(FM) Arlington, NY; WPUT(AM) Brewster, NY; WFAS-FM Bronxville, NY; WCZX-FM Hyde Park, NY; WPDA-FM Jeffersonville, NY; WKXP(FM) Kingston, NY; WKNY Kingston, NY; WALL Middletown, NY; WFAF(FM) Mount Kisco, NY; WDBY(FM) Patterson, NY; WEOK Poughkeepsie, NY; WFAS(AM) White Plains, NY; WZAD-FM Wurtsboro, NY; WRQN-FM Bowling Green, OH; WOFX-FM Cincinnati, OH; WNNF(FM) Cincinnati, OH; WLQR-FM Delta, OH; WXKR-FM Port Clinton, OH; WSOM Salem, OH; WWWM-FM Sylvania, OH; WTOD Toledo, OH; WLQR Toledo, OH; WBBW Youngstown, OH; KOMS-FM Poteau, OK; KEHK-FM Brownsville, OR; KUJZ(FM) Creswell, OR; KSCR(AM) Eugene, OR; KUGN Eugene, OR; KZEL-FM Eugene, OR; WHGB(AM) Harrisburg, PA; WTPA-FM Mechanicsburg, PA; WWIZ-FM Mercer, PA; WLLF-FM Mercer, PA; WWKL(FM) Palmyra, PA; WPIC Sharon, PA; WSEA(FM) Atlantic Beach, SC; WIQB(AM) Conway, SC; WJXY-FM Conway, SC; WYNN Florence, SC; WXJY-FM Georgetown, SC; WLFF(FM) Georgetown, SC; WHSC Hartsville, SC; WBZF-FM Hartsville, SC; WWFN-FM Lake City, SC; WCMG-FM Latta, SC; WYMB Manning, SC; WHLZ(FM) Marion, SC; WMXT-FM Pamplico, SC; WDAI-FM Pawley's Island, SC; WSYN(FM) Surfside Beach, SC; KDEZ(FM) Brandon, SD; KYBB(FM) Canton, SD; KSOO-FM Lennox, SD; KIKN-FM Salem, SD; KKLS-FM Sioux Falls, SD; KMXC(FM) Sioux Falls, SD; KXRB(AM) Sioux Falls, SD; KSOO(AM) Sioux Falls, SD; WRQQ(FM) Goodlettsville, TN; WQQK-FM Hendersonville, TN; WWTN-FM Manchester, TN; WNFN(FM) Millersville, TN; WSM-FM Nashville, TN; KPUR Amarillo, TX; KQIZ-FM Amarillo, TX; KTLT(FM) Anson, TX; KIKR Beaumont, TX; KTCX-FM Beaumont, TX; KQXY-FM Beaumont, TX; KOOC(FM) Belton, TX; KYYI-FM Burkburnett, TX; KZRK(AM) Canyon, TX; KZRK-FM Canyon, TX; KPUR-FM Canyon, TX; KARX(FM) Claude, TX; KSSM(FM) Copperas Cove, TX; KSTB-FM Crystal Beach, TX; KOLI-FM Electra, TX; KCDD(FM) Hamlin, TX; KUSJ(FM) Harker Heights, TX; KHXS-FM Merkel, TX; KMND Midland, TX; KZBT(FM) Midland, TX; KBAT(FM) Monahans, TX; KBED(AM) Nederland, TX; KODM-FM Odessa, TX; KRIL Odessa, TX; KGEE(FM) Pecos, TX; KAYD-FM Silsbee, TX; KTEM Temple, TX; KLTD-FM Temple, TX; KBCY(FM) Tye, TX; KQHN(FM) Waskom, TX; KQXC-FM Wichita Falls, TX; KLUR-FM Wichita Falls, TX; WBRW-FM Blacksburg, VA; WFNR Blacksburg, VA; WFNR-FM Christiansburg, VA; WPSK-FM Pulaski, VA; WRAD Radford, VA; WNAM Neenah-Menasha, WI; WPKR-FM Omro, WI; WOSH Oshkosh, WI

Richard W. Denning Jr., chmn; Lewis W. Dickey Jr., VP.

Cumulus Media Partners LLC, 14 Piedmont, 3535 Piedmont Rd., Suite 1400, Atlanta, GA 30305-4601. Phone: (404) 949-0700. Fax: (404) 949-0740. Ownership Cumulus Media Inc., 25% (see listing); Bain Funds, 25%; Blackstone Funds, 25%; and THLee Funds, 25%.

Stns: 9 AM. 26 FM. WMXS-FM Montgomery, AL; KFFG-FM Los Altos, CA; KFOG-FM San Francisco, CA; KNBR San Francisco, CA; KSAN-FM San Mateo, CA; KTCT San Mateo, CA; WWWQ(FM) Atlanta, GA; WNNX(FM) College Park, GA; WFMS-FM Indianapolis, IN; WQKC(AM) Jeffersonville, IN; WRWM(FM) Lawrence, IN; WJJK(FM) Noblesville, IN; WLCL(FM) Sellersville, IN; KCHZ(FM) Ottawa, KS; KCJK(FM) Garden City, MO; KCFX(FM) Harrisonville, MO; KCMO Kansas City, MO; KCMO-FM Kansas City, MO; KMJK(FM) Lexington, MO; WRRM-FM Cincinnati, OH; WGRR-FM Hamilton, OH; WFTK(FM) Lebanon, OH; WGLD(AM) Red Lion, PA; WSOX-FM Red Lion, PA; WSBA York, PA; WARM-FM York, PA; KFNC(FM) Beaumont, TX; KLIF(AM) Dallas, TX; KTCK Dallas, TX; KPLX(FM) Fort Worth, TX; KDBN(FM) Haltom City, TX; KRBE(FM) Houston, TX; KHJK(FM) La Porte, TX; KKLF(AM) Richardson, TX; KTDK(FM) Sanger, TX.

Lew Dickey, chmn/CEO.

The Curators of the University of Missouri, (Business Services Division). University of Missouri, 316 University Hall, Columbia, MO 65211. Phone: (573) 882-2388. Fax: (573) 882-0010. Web Site:www.umsystem.edu Ownership (Business Services Division).

Stns: 9 AM. 26 FM. WMXS-FM Montgomery, AL; KFFG-FM Los Altos, CA; KFOG-FM San Francisco, CA; KNBR San Francisco, CA; KSAN-FM San Mateo, CA; KTCT San Mateo, CA; WWWQ(FM) Atlanta, GA; WNNX(FM) College Park, GA; WFMS-FM Indianapolis, IN; WQKC(AM) Jeffersonville, IN; WRWM(FM) Lawrence, IN; WJJK(FM) Noblesville, IN; WLCL(FM) Sellersville, IN; KCHZ(FM) Ottawa, KS; KCJK(FM) Garden City, MO; KCFX(FM) Harrisonville, MO; KCMO Kansas City, MO; KCMO-FM Kansas City, MO; KMJK(FM) Lexington, MO; WRRM-FM Cincinnati, OH; WGRR-FM Hamilton, OH; WFTK(FM) Lebanon, OH; WGLD(AM) Red Lion, PA; WSOX-FM Red Lion, PA; WSBA York, PA; WARM-FM York, PA; KFNC(FM) Beaumont, TX; KLIF(AM) Dallas, TX; KTCK Dallas, TX; KPLX(FM) Fort Worth, TX; KDBN(FM) Haltom City, TX; KRBE(FM) Houston, TX; KHJK(FM) La Porte, TX; KKLF(AM) Richardson, TX; KTDK(FM) Sanger, TX6 FM. KBIA(FM) Columbia, MO; KCUR-FM Kansas City, MO; KAUD(FM) Mexico, MO; KMNR-FM Rolla, MO; KMST(FM) Rolla, MO; KWMU-FM Saint Louis, MO.

Stns: 1 TV. KOMU, Columbia-Jefferson City, MO.

Michael Dunn, gen mgr; Martin Siddall, gen mgr .

Curtis Media Group, 3012 Highwoods Blvd., Raleigh, NC 27604. Phone: (919) 876-0674. Fax: (919) 790-8369. Web Site:www.curtismedia.com Ownership Donald W. Curtis.

Stns: 14 AM. 11 FM. WZJS-FM Banner Elk, NC; WECR-FM Beech Mountain, NC; WXIT Blowing Rock, NC; WATA Boone, NC; WPCM Burlington, NC; WZTK(FM) Burlington, NC; WDNC(AM) Durham, NC; WYMY(FM) Goldsboro, NC; WKIX(FM) Goldsboro, NC; WFMC(AM) Goldsboro, NC; WGBR Goldsboro, NC; WSML Graham, NC; WMFR High Point, NC; WMMY(FM) Jefferson, NC; WKXU(FM) Louisburg, NC; WYRN(AM) Louisburg, NC; WECR Newland, NC; WWMY(FM) Raleigh, NC; WDOX(AM) Raleigh, NC; WQDR-FM Raleigh, NC; WPTF Raleigh, NC; WBBB-FM Raleigh, NC; WCLY Raleigh, NC; WEQR(FM) Walnut Creek, NC; WSJS Winston-Salem, NC.

Donald Curtis, chmn/CEO; Philip Zachary, pres/COO; Adam Maisano, VP, dir of sls; Allen Sherrill, engrg dir.

D

DCBroadcasting Inc., Box 1009, Jasper, IN 47547-1009. Phone: (812) 634-9232. Fax: (812) 482-3696.E-mail: pknies@psci.net Web Site:www.dcbroadcasting.com Ownership Loc mktg agreement: WRZR(FM) Loogootee, IN. LPTV (class A): WJTS-LP Jasper, IN.

Stns: 1 AM. 3 FM. WBDC(FM) Huntingburg, IN; WXGO Madison, IN; WORX-FM Madison, IN; WAXL-FM Santa Claus, IN.

Paul Knies, pres; Caroline Knies, VP/treas; Giesla Knies Schepers, sec.

DMC Broadcasting Inc., 5542 NDCBU, Taos, NM 87571-6122. Phone: (505) 758-4491. Fax: (505) 758-4452. Ownership Darren Cordova, 100%.

Stns: 1 AM. 3 FM. KKTC(FM) Angel Fire, NM; KKIT(FM) Taos, NM; KVOT(AM) Taos, NM; KXMT(FM) Taos, NM.

Dailey Corp., Box 10, New Martinsviille, WV 26155. Phone: (304) 455-1111. Fax: (304) 455-1170. Web Site:www.powercountry104.com Ownership Calvin E. Dailey Jr., 100%.

Stns: 1 AM. 1 FM. WETZ New Martinsville, WV; WYMJ(FM) New Martinsville, WV.

Calvin Dailey Jr., pres.

Dakota Communications Ltd., Box 364, Pierre, SD 57501. Phone: (605) 224-5434. Fax: (605) 224-5444.E-mail: ddb@eaglecarver.com Web Site:performanceradio.com Ownership Duane D. Butt, 50%; and Barbara G. Butt, 50%.

Stns: 2 AM. 3 FM. KIJV Huron, SD; KOKK Huron, SD; KZKK-FM Huron, SD; KXLG(FM) Milbank, SD; KJRV(FM) Wessington Springs, SD.

Linda Marcus, gen mgr .

Darby Advertising Inc., Box 1766, Gaylord, MI 49734. Phone: (989) 732-2341. Fax: (989) 732-6202. Ownership Kent D. Smith, 100%.

Stns: 2 AM. 3 FM. KIJV Huron, SD; KOKK Huron, SD; KZKK-FM Huron, SD; KXLG(FM) Milbank, SD; KJRV(FM) Wessington Springs, SD3 FM. WGRL(FM) Frederic, MI; WMJZ-FM Gaylord, MI; WUPN(FM) Paradise, MI.

Kent D. Smith, pres.

Davidson Media Group LLC, 709 Peninsula Dr., Davidson, NC 28036-7200. Phone: (704) 987-3585. Fax: (704) 987-3586. Web Site:www.davidsonmediagroup.com Ownership CapStreet II L.P., 38.51% of votes, 38.6% of total assets; Citicorp North America Inc., 32.74% of votes, 32.81% of total assets; Black Enterprise/Greenwich Street Corporate Growth Partners L.P., 10.91% of votes, 10.94% of total assets.

Stns: 32 AM. 7 FM. WAYE Birmingham, AL; KAKS(FM) Huntsville, AR; WXCT(AM) Southington, CT; WNTS Beech Grove, IN; KDTD(AM) Kansas City, KS; KCZZ(AM) Mission, KS; WCVG Covington, KY; WTUV-FM Eminence, KY; WTUV(AM) Louisville, KY; WLLV Louisville, KY; WLOU Louisville, KY; WPYR(AM) Baton Rouge, LA; WFNO Norco, LA; WSPR Springfield, MA; WACM West Springfield, MA; WDRJ(AM) Inkster, MI; KMNQ(AM) Brooklyn Park, MN; KMNV(AM) Saint Paul, MN; WTIK Durham, NC; WRJD(AM) Durham, NC; WSTS-FM Fairmont, NC; WWBG Greensboro, NC; WSGH Lewisville, NC; WNOW Mint Hill, NC; WTOB Winston-Salem, NC; WEMG(AM) Camden, NJ; WKKB(FM) Middletown, RI; WOLI-FM Easley, SC; WNOW-FM Gaffney, SC; WZZQ(AM) Gaffney, SC; WOLT-FM Greer, SC; WOLI(AM) Spartanburg, SC; WNVL(AM) Nashville, TN; WMDB(AM) Nashville, TN; WTOX(AM) Glen Allen, VA; WVXX(AM) Norfolk, VA; WVNZ(AM) Richmond, VA; WREJ(AM) Richmond, VA; WLEE(AM) Richmond, VA.

Russ Jones, opns VP.

Davis Broadcasting Inc., 2203 Wynnton Rd., Columbus, GA 31906. Phone: (706) 576-3565. Fax: (706) 576-3683. Web Site:www.foxie105.com Ownership Gregory A. Davis, 76%.

Stns: 3 AM. 5 FM. WKZJ(FM) Eufaula, AL; WEAM-FM Buena Vista, GA; WLKQ-FM Buford, GA; WCHK Canton, GA; WEAM Columbus, GA; WOKS Columbus, GA; WIOL(FM) Greenville, GA; WNSY-FM Talking Rock, GA.

Gregory A. Davis, pres/CEO.

Debut Broadcasting Corp. Inc., 1209 16th Ave. S., Suite 200, Nashville, TN 37212. Phone: (615) 301-0001. Fax: (615) 301-0002. Ownership Robert Marquitz, 49%; Steven Ludwig, 33.5%; Stephen Rush, 11%; and Garrett L. Cecchini, 6.5%.

Stns: 2 AM. 4 FM. WBAQ-FM Greenville, MS; WNIX(AM) Greenville, MS; WNLA Indianola, MS; WNLA-FM Indianola, MS; WIQQ-FM Leland, MS; WBBV-FM Vicksburg, MS.

Dee Rivers Radio Group, GRAM Corp., 43 Sherman Hill Rd. #204, Woodbury, CT 06798. Phone: (203) 263-1900. Fax: (203) 263-1969. Ownership Georgia R. Salva, trustee, E.D. Rivers Jr. Trust, 50.98%; Robert Salva, 39.22%; and Georgia R. Salva, 9.8%.

Stns: 1 AM. 2 FM. WLYX(FM) Valdosta, GA; WAAC(FM) Valdosta, GA; WGOV(AM) Valdosta, GA.

Georgia Salva, CEO.

Deer Creek Broadcasting LLC, 2225 First Ave., Napa, CA 94558. Phone: (707) 226-2309. Ownership Elliot B. Evers, 43.75% of votes, 12.08% of total assets; Duff Ackerman & Goodrich QP Fund II L.P., 26.89% of votes, 7.43% of total assets; John McSorley, 12.49% of votes, 3.45% of total assets; Greg D. Widroe, 12.49% of votes, 3.45% of total assets; Duff Ackerman & Goodrich II L.P., 2.55% of votes, 0.70% of total assets; DAG GP Fund II LLC, 1.53% of votes, 0.42% of total assets; and DAG II Partners Fund LLC, 0.30% of votes, 0.08% of total assets.

Stns: 2 AM. 3 FM. KMXI-FM Chico, CA; KPAY Chico, CA; KHHZ(FM) Gridley, CA; KEWE(AM) Oroville, CA; KHSL-FM Paradise, CA.

Delmarva Broadcasting Co., Box 7492, 2727 Shipley Rd., Wilmington, DE 19803. Phone: (302) 478-2700. Fax: (302) 478-0100. Web Site:www.delmarvabroadcasting.com Ownership Steinman

Stns: 3 AM. 8 FM. WXCY(FM) Havre de Grace, MD; WQJZ-FM Ocean Pines, MD; WICO-FM Pocomoke City, MD; WICO(AM) Salisbury, MD; WKTT(FM) Salisbury, MD;

WZKT(FM) Lewes, DE; WAFL-FM Milford, DE; WYUS Milford, DE; WNCL(FM) Milford, DE; WSTW-FM Wilmington, DE; WDEL Wilmington, DE.

Lancaster Inteligencer-Journal & *New Era*, Lancaster, PA, have the same ownership (Steinman) as Delmarva Broadcasting Co.

Stations (operated independently).

Julian H. Booker, pres/CEO.

Dickey Broadcasting Co., 3535 Piedmont Rd., Bldg. 14, Suite 1200, Atlanta, GA 30305. Phone: (404) 688-0068. Fax: (404) 995-4045. Web Site:www.680thefan.com

Stns: 3 AM. WALR Atlanta, GA; WFOM Marietta, GA; WCNN North Atlanta, GA.

David W. Dickey, pres/CEO.

Dierking Communications Inc., 937 Jayhawk Rd., Marysville, KS 66508. Phone: (785) 562-2361. Fax: (785) 562-2188.E-mail: kndy@bluevalley.net

Stns: 2 AM. 4 FM. KZDY-FM Cawker City, KS; KDNS(FM) Downs, KS; KNDY Marysville, KS; KNDY-FM Marysville, KS; KQNK Norton, KS; KQNK-FM Norton, KS.

Bruce Dierking, gen mgr & pres.

Digital Radio Broadcasting Inc., 135 White Bridge Rd., Middletown, NY 10940. Phone: (845) 355-4001. Fax: (845) 355-4002. Ownership Charles Williamson, 100%.

Stns: 3 AM. WYNY(AM) Middletown, NY; WMJQ(AM) Ontario, NY; WQCD(AM) Milford, PA.

Charles Williamson, pres.

Dispatch Broadcast Group, 770 Twin Rivers Dr., Columbus, OH 43215. Phone: (614) 460-3700. Fax: (614) 460-2809. Web Site:www.10tv.com Ownership Dispatch Printing Company

Stns: 1 AM. 1 FM. WBNS Columbus, OH; WBNS-FM Columbus, OH.

Stns: 2 TV. WBNS, Columbus, OH; WTHR, Indianapolis, IN.

Owns *The Columbus* (OH) *Dispatch, This Week* & *Ohio Magazine.*

Tamara J. Clapsaddle, controller; Michael J. Fiorile, pres.

Dos Costas Communications Corp., 1818 S. Australian Ave., Suite 102, West Palm Beach, FL 33409. Phone: (561) 655-6615. Ownership Roland A. Ulloa, 100%.

Stns: 1 AM. 1 FM. WBNS Columbus, OH; WBNS-FM Columbus, OH3 FM. KDUC-FM Barstow, CA; KXXZ-FM Barstow, CA; KDUQ-FM Ludlow, CA.

Roland A. Ulloa, pres; Jime Garza, VP/gen mgr.

Double O Radio L.L.C., 1156 Bowman Rd., Suite 200, Mount Pleasant, SC 29464. Phone: (843) 416-1107. Fax: (843) 416-1199.E-mail: info@doubleoradio.com Web Site:doubleoradio.com Ownership Pilot Group LP, 100%.

Stns: 4 AM. 22 FM. WAKT-FM Callaway, FL; WPFM-FM Panama City, FL; WASJ(FM) Panama City Beach, FL; WRBA(FM) Springfield, FL; KRRY(FM) Canton, MO; WDHI-FM Delhi, NY; WTBD-FM Delhi, NY; WIYN-FM Deposit, NY; WBKT-FM Norwich, NY; WCHN Norwich, NY; WKXZ-FM Norwich, NY; WDOS Oneonta, NY; WZOZ-FM Oneonta, NY; WSRK-FM Oneonta, NY; WDLA Walton, NY; WDLA-FM Walton, NY; WWNQ(FM) Forest Acres, SC; WWNU(FM) Irmo, SC; KKCN(FM) Ballinger, TX; KQRX-FM Midland, TX; KHKX(FM) Odessa, TX; KMCM-FM Odessa, TX; KELI-FM San Angelo, TX; KGKL San Angelo, TX; KGKL-FM San Angelo, TX; KNRX(FM) Sterling City, TX.

Terry Bond, CEO.

Dr. Pepper Pepsi-Cola Bottling Co. of Dyersburg, 35 Radio Rd., Dyersburg, TN 38025-0100. Phone: (731) 285-1339. Fax: (731) 287-0100.E-mail: sl100@wasl.net Ownership W.E. Burks, 53.41%; Richard Rodgers, 16.18%; J.L. Jones, 3.15%; and Guy McClain, 1.5%.

Stns: 1 AM. 2 FM. WTRO Dyersburg, TN; WASL-FM Dyersburg, TN; WTNV(FM) Tiptonville, TN.

DreamCatcher Communications Inc., 114 S. Manchester Ave., West Union, OH 45693. Phone: (937) 544-9722. Fax: (937) 544-5523.E-mail: c103@lycos.com Ownership Donald Bowles, 50%; Venita Bowles, 50%.

Stns: 1 AM. 1 FM. WFLE Flemingsburg, KY; WRAC-FM West Union, OH.

Don Bowles, pres/CEO; Ted Foster, stn mgr.

Duhamel Broadcasting Enterprises, Box 1760, Rapid City, SD 57709. Phone: (605) 342-2000. Fax: (605) 342-7305. Web Site:www.kotatv.com Ownership William F. Duhamel, 63%; Peter A. and Lois G. Duhamel, 37%.

Stns: 1 AM. 1 FM. KOTA Rapid City, SD; KDDX(FM) Spearfish, SD.

Stns: 4 TV. KDUH, Cheyenne, WY-Scottsbluff, NE; KHSD-TV, Rapid City, SD; KOTA-TV, Rapid City, SD; KSGW-TV, Rapid City, SD.

William F. Duhamel, pres.

Durham Radio Inc., 1200 Airport Blvd., Suite 207, Oshawa, ON L1J 8P5. Canada. Phone: (905) 428-9600. Fax: (905) 571-1150. Ownership Douglas E. Kirk; 80%, Mary Kirk 15%.

Stns: 1 AM. 3 FM. CJKX-FM Ajax, ON; CIWV-FM Hamilton, ON; CKDO Oshawa, ON; CKGE-FM Oshawa, ON.

Douglas E. Kirk, chmn/pres; Steve Kassay, VP opns; Steve Macaulay, VP sls; Lill Bolton, admin dir.

E

EMF Broadcasting, 2351 Sunset Blvd., Suite 170-218, Rocklin, CA 95765. Phone: (916) 251-1600. Fax: (916) 251-1650. Web Site:www.emfbroadcasting.com Ownership Educational Media Foundation, 100%. Educational Media Foundation is a nonprofit, nonstock corporation, governed by a seven-member board of directors.

Stns: 2 AM. 262 FM. KAKL(FM) Anchorage, AK; KGCF(FM) Juneau, AK; KLSF(FM) Juneau, AK; KOAR(FM) Beebe, AR; KAIA(FM) Blytheville, AR; KAKV(FM) El Dorado, AR; KPOS(FM) Fouke, AR; KALR(FM) Hot Springs, AR; KLRO(FM) Hot Springs, AR; KJLV(FM) Hoxie, AR; KJBR-FM Marked Tree, AR; KLMK(FM) Marvell, AR; KLRM(FM) Melbourne, AR; KKLT(FM) Texarkana, AR; WPLX(AM) Turrell, AR; KKLV(FM) Turrell, AR; KLFS(FM) Van Buren, AR; KLVA(FM) Casa Grande, AZ; KZAI(FM) Coolidge, AZ; KLVK(FM) Fountain Hills, AZ; KAIH(FM) Lake Havasu City, AZ; KAIC(FM) Tucson, AZ; KWLU(FM) Chester, CA; KLVS(FM) Citrus Heights, CA; KARQ(FM) East Sonora, CA; KLVY-FM Fairmead, CA; KLVG(FM) Garberville, CA; KHRI(FM) Hollister, CA; KZLU(FM) Inyokern, CA; KLVJ-FM Julian, CA; KDRH(FM) King City, CA; KHKL(FM) Laytonville, CA; KLVN(FM) Livingston, CA; KLRS(FM) Lodi, CA; KLVC-FM Magalia, CA; KLVR(FM) Middletown, CA; KKLC(FM) Mount Shasta, CA; KGBM(FM) Randsburg, CA; KLVB(FM) Red Bluff, CA; KKRO(FM) Redding, CA; KLVH(FM) San Luis Obispo, CA; KSRI(FM) Santa Cruz, CA; KQKL(FM) Selma, CA; KAIB(FM) Shafter, CA; KJAR(FM) Susanville, CA; KBLV(FM) Tehachapi, CA; KYKL(FM) Tracy, CA; KULV(FM) Ukiah, CA; KXRD(FM) Victorville, CA; KARA(FM) Williams, CA; KLRD(FM) Yucaipa, CA; KGCO(FM) Fort Collins, CO; KLXV(FM) Glenwood Springs, CO; KLFV(FM) Grand Junction, CO; KLRY(FM) Gypsum, CO; KHCO(FM) Hayden, CO; KLDV(FM) Morrison, CO; KLBV(FM) Steamboat Springs, CO; KLZV(FM) Sterling, CO; KDRE(FM) Sterling, CO; WKVH(FM) Monticello, FL; WVKV(FM) Nashville, GA; WGCN(FM) Nashville, GA; WHKV(FM) Sylvester, GA; WQAI(FM) Thomson, GA; WVDA(FM) Valdosta, GA; KHAI(FM) Wahiawa, HI; KILV(FM) Castana, IA; KKLG(FM) Newton, IA; KAIP(FM) Wapello, IA; KAIO(FM) Idaho Falls, ID; KARJ(FM) Kuna, ID; KLRI(FM) Rigby, ID; WCLR(FM) Arlington Heights, IL; WARW(FM) Dorsey, IL; WJKL(FM) Glendale Heights, IL; WGSL-FM Loves Park, IL; WLKU(FM) Rock Island, IL; WQFL-FM Rockford, IL; WSRI(FM) Sugar Grove, IL; WZKL(FM) Woodstock, IL; WIKL(FM) Greencastle, IN; WKMV(FM) Muncie, IN; WARA(FM) New Washington, IN; WIKV(FM) Plymouth, IN; WQKV(FM) Rochester, IN; WJLR-FM Seymour, IN; WKHL(FM) West Lafayette, IN; KAIG(FM) Dodge City, KS; KTLI(FM) El Dorado, KS; KWBI(FM) Great Bend, KS; KGLV(FM) Manhattan, KS; KRLE(FM) Oberlin, KS; WKYB(FM) Burgin, KY; WLAI(FM) Danville, KY; WPRZ-FM Fredonia, KY; WRVG(FM) Georgetown, KY; WKVN(FM) Morganfield, KY; WKVY(FM) Somerset, KY; WXKY-FM Stanford, KY; KLXA-FM Alexandria, LA; WBKL(FM) Clinton, LA; KYLA-FM Homer, LA; KITA(FM) Iota, LA; KIKL(FM) Lafayette, LA; WNKV(FM) Norco, LA; KRLR(FM) Sulphur, LA; WTKL(FM) North Dartmouth, MA; WKMY(FM) Winchendon, MA; WKVZ(FM) Dexter, ME; WARX(FM) Lewiston, ME; WKVV(FM) Searsport, ME; WLKB(FM) Bay City, MI; WAKL(FM) Flint, MI; WTRK(FM) Freeland, MI; WLVM(FM) Ironwood, MI; KMKL(FM) North Branch, MN; KKLW(FM) Willmar, MN; KRLP(FM) Windom, MN; KLRQ(FM) Clinton, MO; WGCQ(FM) Hayti, MO; KOBC-FM Joplin, MO; WKVF(FM) Byhalia, MS; WLVZ(FM) Collins, MS; WLRK(FM) Greenville, MS; WLKO(FM) Quitman, MS; KGCM(FM) Belgrade, MT; KLRV(FM) Billings, MT; KLBZ(FM) Bozeman, MT; KGFA(FM) Great Falls, MT; KHLV(FM) Helena, MT; KLKM(FM) Kalispell, MT; KBIL(FM) Park City, MT; KQLR(FM) Whitehall, MT; WKVK(FM) Semora, NC; WZRI(FM) Spring Lake, NC; WKGV(FM) Swansboro, NC; KNRI(FM) Bismarck, ND; KKLQ(FM) Harwood, ND; KLUU(FM) Jamestown, ND; KGCD(FM) Lincoln, ND; KLNB(FM) Grand Island, NE; KMLV(FM) Ralston, NE; KLJV(FM) Scottsbluff, NE; KDAI(FM) Scottsbluff, NE; KFLV(FM) Wilber, NE; WNHI(FM) Farmington, NH; WKVP(FM) Cherry Hill, NJ; KQGC(FM) Belen, NM; KQRI(FM) Bosque Farms, NM; KELU(FM) Clovis, NM; KGGA(FM) Gallup, NM; KLLU(FM) Gallup, NM; KLGQ(FM) Grants, NM; KLHK(FM) Hobbs, NM; KGCN(FM) Roswell, NM; KQAI(FM) Roswell, NM; KRLU(FM) Roswell, NM; KQLV(FM) Santa Fe, NM; KVLK(FM) Socorro, NM; KVLP(FM) Tucumcari, NM; KAIZ(FM) Mesquite, NV; KLRH(FM) Sparks, NV; WKDL-FM Brockport, NY; WGKV(FM) Pulaski, NY; WYKV(FM) Ravena, NY; WOKR(FM) Remsen, NY; WYAI(FM) Scotia, NY; WKVU(FM) Utica, NY; WRCK-FM Utica, NY; WKWV(FM) Watertown, NY; WLKP(FM) Belpre, OH; WYKL(FM) Crestline, OH; WQRP-FM Dayton, OH; WORI(FM) Delhi Hills, OH; WCVJ-FM Jefferson, OH; WHKU(FM) Proctorville, OH; WNWT(AM) Rossford, OH; WOAR(FM) South Vienna, OH; WEKV(FM) South Webster, OH; WOKL(FM) Troy, OH; WNKL(FM) Wauseon, OH; KKVO-FM Altus, OK; KWRI(FM) Bartlesville, OK; KARU(FM) Cache, OK; KOKF-FM Edmond, OK; KKRD(FM) Enid, OK; KWKL(FM) Grandfield, OK; KYLV-FM Oklahoma City, OK; KKRI(FM) Pocola, OK; KTKL(FM) Stigler, OK; KLOY(FM) Astoria, OR; KVLB(FM) Bend, OR; KGCL(FM) Jordan Valley, OR; KKLJ(FM) Klamath Falls, OR; KKLP(FM) La Pine, OR; KGRI(FM) Lebanon, OR; KLON(FM) Rockaway Beach, OR; KLVP(FM) Sandy, OR; KJKL(FM) Selma, OR; KVRA(FM) Sisters, OR; KLVU-FM Sweet Home, OR; KAIK(FM) Tillamook, OR; KZRI(FM) Welches, OR; KLOV(FM) Winchester, OR; WKEL(FM) Confluence, PA; WLVU(FM) Halifax, PA; WPKV(FM) Nanty Glo, PA; WLKA(FM) Tafton, PA; WKIV(FM) Westerly, RI; WKVC(FM) North Myrtle Beach, SC; KLRJ(FM) Aberdeen, SD; KSFS(FM) Sioux Falls, SD; KJKT(FM) Spearfish, SD; WRRI(FM) Brownsville, TN; WZKV(FM) Dyersburg, TN; WMXK-FM Morristown, TN; WXKV(FM) Selmer, TN; WTAI(FM) Union City, TN; KAGT(FM) Abilene, TX; KXRI(FM) Amarillo, TX; KXLV(FM) Amarillo, TX; KKWV(FM) Aransas Pass, TX; KMLU(FM) Brownfield, TX; KLRW(FM) Byrne, TX; KKLM(FM) Corpus Christi, TX; KLLR(FM) Dripping Springs, TX; KKLY(FM) El Paso, TX; KYAR(FM) Gatesville, TX; KMLR(FM) Gonzales, TX; KZAR(FM) Gonzales, TX; KRLH(FM) Hereford, TX; KYLR(FM) Hutto, TX; KZLO(FM) Kilgore, TX; KKLU(FM) Lubbock, TX; KZLV(FM) Lytle, TX; KPGA(FM) Morton, TX; KLVW(FM) Odessa, TX; KGCE(FM) Post, TX; KNAR(FM) San Angelo, TX; KFRI(FM) West Odessa, TX; KZKL(FM) Wichita Falls, TX; KNKL(FM) North Ogden, UT; KAER(FM) Saint George, UT; KLUW(FM) East Wenatchee, WA; KYKV(FM) Ellensburg, WA; KTSL-FM Medical Lake, WA; KSBC(FM) Nile, WA; KLOP(FM) Ocean Park, WA; KRKL(FM) Walla Walla, WA; WDKV(FM) Fond du Lac, WI; WKMZ(FM) Mukwonago, WI; WCKU(FM) Clarksburg, WV; WDKL(FM) Grafton, WV; WKVW(FM) Marmet, WV; WLVW(FM) Moundsville, WV; WLKV(FM) Ripley, WV; KLWC(FM) Casper, WY; KAIX(FM) Cheyenne, WY; KLWV(FM) Chugwater, WY; KLOF(FM) Gillette, WY; KMLT(FM) Jackson, WY; KAIW(FM) Laramie, WY; KVLZ(FM) Sheridan, WY

Richard Jenkins, pres; Keith Whipple, dev VP; Mike Novak, opns VP; Devona R. Porter, opns VP; David Pierce, progmg dir.

Eagle Bluff Enterprises, 932 County Rd. 448, Poplar Bluff, MO 63901. Phone: (573) 686-3700.

Stns: 1 AM. 2 FM. KFEB(FM) Campbell, MO; KOEA-FM Doniphan, MO; KDFN Doniphan, MO.

Steven C. Fuch, pres.

Eagle Communications Group, 2703 Hall St., Suite 15, Hays, KS 67601. Phone: (785) 625-4000. Fax: (785) 625-8030. Web Site:www.eaglecom.net Ownership Eagle Communications Inc. Employee Stock Ownership Trust. Cable TV.

Stns: 7 AM. 14 FM. KVGB Great Bend, KS; KVGB-FM Great Bend, KS; KJLS-FM Hays, KS; KAYS Hays, KS; KHAZ-FM Hays, KS; KKQY-FM Hill City, KS; KHOK-FM Hoisington, KS; KHUT-FM Hutchinson, KS; KWBW Hutchinson, KS; KHMY(FM) Pratt, KS; KINA Salina, KS; KSKG-FM Salina, KS; KFEQ(AM) Saint Joseph, MO; KESJ(AM) Saint Joseph, MO; KSJQ(FM) Savannah, MO; KAAQ(FM) Alliance, NE; KQSK(FM) Chadron, NE; KCNB(FM) Chadron, NE; KNPQ(FM) Hershey, NE; KOOQ(AM) North Platte, NE; KELN-FM North Platte, NE.

Eagle's Nest Inc., Box 710, Roanoke, AL 36274. Phone: (334) 863-4139. Fax: (334) 863-2540. Web Site:www.eagle1023.com Ownership Jim Vice, 51%; Kay Vice, 49%.

Stns: 2 AM. 1 FM. WELR Roanoke, AL; WELR-FM Roanoke, AL; WLAG La Grange, GA.

Jim Vice, pres.

Earls Broadcasting Co., 202 Courtney St., Branson, MO 65616. Phone: (417) 334-6003. Fax: (417) 334-7141. Web Site:www.komc.com Ownership Charles Earls, Scottie Earls, Scott Earls.

Stns: 3 AM. 7 FM. KHOZ Harrison, AR; KHOZ-FM Harrison, AR; KTLO Mountain Home, AR; KTLO-FM Mountain Home, AR; KHOM(FM) Salem, AR; KCTT-FM Yellville, AR;

KBMV-FM Birch Tree, MO; KRZK-FM Branson, MO; KOMC Branson, MO; KOMC-FM Kimberling City, MO.

Charles C. Earls, CEO; Scottie Earls, gen mgr; Scott Earls, pres.

East Arkansas Broadcasters Inc., Box 789, Wynne, AR 72396. Phone: (870) 238-8141. Fax: (870) 238-5997. Ownership Bobby Caldwell, 100%. Note: Bobby Caldwell owns 50% of Arkansas County Broadcasters Inc. (see listing) and 45% of Combined Media Group Inc. (see listing).

Stns: 2 AM. 2 FM. KBRI Brinkley, AR; KTRQ(FM) Colt, AR; KWYN Wynne, AR; KWYN-FM Wynne, AR.

East Carolina Radio Group, 2422 S. Wrightsville Ave., Nags Head, NC 27959. Phone: (252) 449-8331. Fax: (252) 449-8354. Web Site:www.ecri.net

Stns: 3 AM. 4 FM. WRSF(FM) Columbia, NC; WERX-FM Columbia, NC; WZBO(AM) Edenton, NC; WCNC(AM) Elizabeth City, NC; WKJX(FM) Elizabeth City, NC; WOBX(AM) Wanchese, NC; WOBR-FM Wanchese, NC.

Rick Loesch, pres.

East Kentucky Broadcasting Corp., Box 2200, Pikeville, KY 41502. Phone: (606) 437-4051. Fax: (606) 432-2809.E-mail: wpke@wpke.com Web Site:www.ekbradio.com Ownership Walter E. May; Pamela May; Keith Casebolt

Stns: 3 AM. 3 FM. WPKE-FM Coal Run, KY; WEKB(AM) Elkhorn City, KY; WDHR-FM Pikeville, KY; WLSI Pikeville, KY; WPKE Pikeville, KY; WZLK-FM Virgie, KY.

Walter E. May, pres; Keith Casebolt, gen mgr .

East Kentucky Radio Network Inc., Box 2200, Pikeville, KY 41502. Phone: (606) 437-4051. Fax: (606) 432-2809. Web Site:www.ekbradio.com Ownership Walter E. May; Pamela May; Keith Casebolt.

Stns: 2 AM. WPRT Prestonsburg, KY; WBTH Williamson, WV.

Walter E. May, pres; Keith Casebolt, VP; Pamela May, sec/treas.

East Tennessee Radio Group III L.P., 112 Jordan Dr., Chattanooga, TN 47421. Phone: (423) 485-8987. Ownership Whitfield Communications Inc., 100% of votes.

Stns: 3 AM. 1 FM. WBAC(AM) Cleveland, TN; WDNT(AM) Dayton, TN; WAYA(FM) Decatur, TN; WXQK(AM) Spring City, TN.

East Tennessee Radio Group L.P., 112 Jordan Dr., Chattanooga, TN 37421. Phone: (423) 485-8987. Ownership Whitfield Communications Inc., 100% of votes. Note: Whitfield Communications Inc. also is the gen ptnr and owns 1% of WNOO(AM) Chattanooga, TN.

Stns: 3 AM. 1 FM. WBAC(AM) Cleveland, TN; WDNT(AM) Dayton, TN; WAYA(FM) Decatur, TN; WXQK(AM) Spring City, TN2 FM. WSEV-FM Gatlinburg, TN; WPFT(FM) Pigeon Forge, TN.

East Texas Broadcasting Inc., Box 990, Mount Pleasant, TX 75456. Phone: (903) 572-8726. Fax: (903) 572-7232. Web Site:www.eastexasradio.com Ownership John Mitchell; Bud Kitchens.

Stns: 2 AM. 5 FM. KIMP(AM) Mount Pleasant, TX; KOYN-FM Paris, TX; KPLT Paris, TX; KBUS(FM) Paris, TX; KSCN(FM) Pittsburg, TX; KSCH-FM Sulphur Springs, TX; KALK(FM) Winfield, TX.

John Mitchell, chmn; Bud Kitchens, pres; Bob Gibson, VP.

Edwards Communications L.C., 125 Eagles Nest Dr., Seneca, SC 29678. Phone: (864) 882-3272. Fax: (864) 882-3718. Web Site:www.edwgroupinc.com Ownership Steve Edwards, 50%; Jerry Edwards, 50%

Stns: 3 AM. 5 FM. WHSB-FM Alpena, MI; WIDL-FM Caro, MI; WKYO Caro, MI; WWTH(FM) Oscoda, MI; WHAK Rogers City, MI; WHAK-FM Rogers City, MI; KTAK-FM Riverton, WY; KVOW Riverton, WY.

Jerry Edwards, pres; Steve Edwards Jr., VP.

Electronic Applications Radio Service Inc., 15 Wood St., Greenfield, IN 46140. Phone: (317) 467-1062 .

Stns: 1 AM. 3 FM. WVXI(FM) Cole, IN; WRFM(AM) Muncie, IN; WYJZ(FM) Fearsville, KY; WBOO(FM) Morganfield, KY.

Patrick Diemer, pres.

Ely Radio LLC, 5010 Spencer, Las Vegas, NV 89119. Phone: (702) 740-5588. Ownership Fred Weinberg, 100%.

Stns: 2 AM. 1 FM. KELY Ely, NV; KWNA(AM) Winnemucca, NV; KWNA-FM Winnemucca, NV.

Fred Weinberg, .

Elyria-Lorain Broadcasting Co., Box 4006, Elyria, OH 44036. Phone: (440) 322-3761. Fax: (440) 284-3189. Ownership Lorain County Printing & Publishing Co., 100%.

Stns: 2 AM. 3 FM. WEOL Elyria, OH; WNWV-FM Elyria, OH; WKFM-FM Huron, OH; WLKR-FM Norwalk, OH; WLKR(AM) Norwalk, OH.

Lorain County Printing & Publishing Co. publishes *Chronicle-Telegram* (Elyria) and *Medina Gazette* (Medina), both OH.

Lonnie Gronek, VP/gen mgr.

Emerald Wave Media, 718 E. Chapel St., Santa Maria, CA 93454. Phone: (805) 928-4334. Fax: (805) 349-2765. Ownership August Ruiz, 100%.

Stns: 1 AM. 2 FM. KRTO(FM) Guadalupe, CA; KIDI-FM Lompoc, CA; KTAP Santa Maria, CA.

Emmis Communications Corp., 40 Monument Cir., Suite 700, Indoamopolis, IN 46204-3011. Phone: (317) 266-0100. Fax: (317) 631-3750. Web Site:www.emmis.com Ownership Jeffrey H. Smulyan, approximately 61% votes.

Stns: 2 AM. 21 FM. KPWR-FM Los Angeles, CA; KXOS(FM) Los Angeles, CA; WKQX-FM Chicago, IL; WLUP-FM Chicago, IL; WIBC(FM) Indianapolis, IN; WFNI(AM) Indianapolis, IN; WYXB(FM) Indianapolis, IN; WLHK(FM) Shelbyville, IN; WTHI-FM Terre Haute, IN; WWVR-FM West Terre Haute, IN; KSHE(FM) Crestwood, MO; KFTK(FM) Florissant, MO; KIHT-FM Saint Louis, MO; KPNT-FM Sainte Genevieve, MO; WRKS(FM) New York, NY; WQHT-FM New York, NY; WRXP(FM) New York, NY; KLBJ Austin, TX; KLBJ-FM Austin, TX; KGSR-FM Bastrop, TX; KROX-FM Buda, TX; KDHT(FM) Cedar Park, TX; KBPA(FM) San Marcos, TX.

The publishing unit of Emmis Communications publishes seven magazines: *Allanta Magazine, Cincinnati Magazine, Los Angeles Magazine, Wildlife Journal, Indianapolis Monthly* and *Texas Monthly.*

Jeffrey Smulyan, chmn/CEO; Rick Cummings, pres & progmg; Patrick Walsh, COO/CFO.

Empire Broadcasting Corp., 750 Story Rd., San Jose, CA 95122. Phone: (408) 293-8030. Fax: (408) 293-6124. Web Site:www.kliv.com Ownership Robert Kieve.

Stns: 1 AM. 1 FM. KRTY-FM Los Gatos, CA; KLIV San Jose, CA.

Robert Kieve, pres; John McLeod, progmg VP.

Emporia's Radio Stations Inc., Box 968, Emporia, KS 66801. Phone: (620) 342-1400. Fax: (620) 342-0804. Ownership Steve Sauder, 100%.

Stns: 1 AM. 2 FM. KFFX-FM Emporia, KS; KVOE(AM) Emporia, KS; KVOE-FM Emporia, KS.

Lee Schroeder, gen mgr; Susan Grother, business mgr.

Encino Broadcasting LLC, 9434 Parkfield Dr., Austin, TX 78758. Phone: (512) 453-1491. Fax: (512) 834-1491.E-mail: spots@austintejas.com

Stns: 3 AM. KELG(AM) Manor, TX; KOKE Pflugerville, TX; KTXZ West Lake Hills, TX.

Jose Garcia, gen mgr; Alma Kyle, office mgr.

Entercom Communications Corp., 401 City Ave., Suite 809, Bala-Cynwyd, PA 19004. Phone: (610) 660-5610. Fax: (610) 660-5620. Web Site:www.entercom.com Ownership Joseph M. Field.

Stns: 33 AM. 78 FM. KSSJ-FM Fair Oaks, CA; KRXQ-FM Sacramento, CA; KSEG-FM Sacramento, CA; KBZC(FM) Sacramento, CA; KDND(FM) Sacramento, CA; KDFC-FM San Francisco, CA; KOIT-FM San Francisco, CA; KBWF(FM) San Francisco, CA; KCTC(AM) West Sacramento, CA; KEZW Aurora, CO; KQMT(FM) Denver, CO; KOSI-FM Denver, CO; KALC(FM) Denver, CO; WKTK-FM Crystal River, FL; WSKY-FM Micanopy, FL; WZPL-FM Greenfield, IN; WNTR(FM) Indianapolis, IN; WXNT(AM) Indianapolis, IN; KDGS(FM) Andover, KS; KFH-FM Clearwater, KS; KFBZ(FM) Haysville, KS; KUDL-FM Kansas City, KS; KXTR(AM) Kansas City, KS; KYYS(AM) Kansas City, KS; KQRC-FM Leavenworth, KS; KFH(AM) Wichita, KS; KEYN-FM Wichita, KS; KNSS(AM) Wichita, KS; WWL-FM Kenner, LA; WLMG(FM) New Orleans, LA; WEZB-FM New Orleans, LA; WKBU(FM) New Orleans, LA; WWWL(AM) New Orleans, LA; WWL(AM) New Orleans, LA; WRKO Boston, MA; WEEI Boston, MA; WKAF(FM) Brockton, MA; WVEI-FM Easthampton, MA; WMKK(FM) Lawrence, MA; WAAF(FM) Westborough, MA; WVEI(AM) Worcester, MA; KMBZ Kansas City, MO; KRBZ(FM) Kansas City, MO; KKSN(FM) Kansas City, MO; KCSP(AM) Kansas City, MO; WDAF-FM Liberty, MO; WTPT-FM Forest City, NC; WPET Greensboro, NC; WQMG-FM Greensboro, NC; WEAL Greensboro, NC; WSMW(FM) Greensboro, NC; WJMH-FM Reidsville, NC; WPAW(FM) Winston-Salem, NC; WGR Buffalo, NY; WBEN Buffalo, NY; WWKB Buffalo, NY; WWWS Buffalo, NY; WKSE-FM Niagara Falls, NY; WROC(AM) Rochester, NY; WCMF-FM Rochester, NY; WBZA(FM) Rochester, NY; WBEE-FM Rochester, NY; WPXY-FM Rochester, NY; WLKK(FM) Wethersfield Township, NY; KRSK(FM) Molalla, OR; KFXX(AM) Portland, OR; KWJJ-FM Portland, OR; KYCH-FM Portland, OR; KGON-FM Portland, OR; KWOD(AM) Salem, OR; WILK-FM Avoca, PA; WGGI-FM Benton, PA; WDMT(FM) Pittston, PA; WGGY-FM Scranton, PA; WBZU(AM) Scranton, PA; WKRF(FM) Tobyhanna, PA; WKZN(AM) West Hazleton, PA; WILK Wilkes-Barre, PA; WKRZ-FM Wilkes-Barre, PA; WEEI-FM Westerly, RI; WROQ-FM Anderson, SC; WYRD Greenville, SC; WYRD-FM Simpsonville, SC; WORD(AM) Spartanburg, SC; WSPA-FM Spartanburg, SC; WMFS-FM Bartlett, TN; WKQK(FM) Germantown, TN; WRVR(FM) Memphis, TN; WMC(AM) Memphis, TN; WMC-FM Memphis, TN; WMFS(AM) Memphis, TN; KKMJ-FM Austin, TX; KAMX(FM) Luling, TX; KJCE Rollingwood, TX; KLQB(FM) Taylor, TX; WWDE-FM Hampton, VA; WVKL-FM Norfolk, VA; WNVZ-FM Norfolk, VA; WPTE-FM Virginia Beach, VA; KNRK-FM Camas, WA; KKWF(FM) Seattle, WA; KNDD-FM Seattle, WA; KISW-FM Seattle, WA; KMTT-FM Tacoma, WA; KTRO(AM) Vancouver, WA; WOLX-FM Baraboo, WI; WMYX-FM Milwaukee, WI; WSSP(AM) Milwaukee, WI; WMMM-FM Verona, WI; WCHY(FM) Waunakee, WI; WXSS-FM Wauwatosa, WI

Joseph M. Field, chmn/CEO; David J. Field, pres/COO; John C. Donlevle, exec VP; Steve Fisher, sr VP; Eugene D. Levin, treas; Martin Hadfield, VP engrg; Deborah Kane, VP sls.

Entravision Communications Corp., 2425 Olympic Blvd., Suite 6000W, Santa Monica, CA 90404. Phone: (310) 447-3872. Fax: (310) 447-3899.E-mail: kthompson@entravision.com Web Site:www.entravision.com Ownership Walter F. Ulloa, Philip W. Wilkinson, Paul Zevnik.

Stns: 12 AM. 37 FM. KVVA-FM Apache Junction, AZ; KMIA(AM) Black Canyon City, AZ; KDVA(FM) Buckeye, AZ; KLNZ-FM Glendale, AZ; KRRN(FM) Kingman, AZ; KSSE(FM) Arcadia, CA; KSEH(FM) Brawley, CA; KCVR-FM Columbia, CA; KXSE(FM) Davis, CA; KWST(AM) El Centro, CA; KSSD(FM) Fallbrook, CA; KLOK-FM Greenfield, CA; KMXX-FM Imperial, CA; KCVR Lodi, CA; KRCX-FM Marysville, CA; KDLE(FM) Newport Beach, CA; KTSE-FM Patterson, CA; KLYY(FM) Riverside, CA; KBMB(FM) Sacramento, CA; KDLD(FM) Santa Monica, CA; KSES-FM Seaside, CA; KNTY(FM) Shingle Springs, CA; KMBX(AM) Soledad, CA; KLOB-FM Thousand Palms, CA; KMIX-FM Tracy, CA; KSSC(FM) Ventura, CA; KPVW(FM) Aspen, CO; KMXA Aurora, CO; KJMN-FM Castle Rock, CO; KXPK-FM Evergreen, CO; WLQY Hollywood, FL; WNUE-FM Titusville, FL; KRZY Albuquerque, NM; KRZY-FM Santa Fe, NM; KQRT(FM) Las Vegas, NV; KRNV-FM Reno, NV; KKPS-FM Brownsville, TX; KVLY-FM Edinburg, TX; KHRO(AM) El Paso, TX; KOFX-FM El Paso, TX; KINT-FM El Paso, TX; KSVE(AM) El Paso, TX; KYSE(FM) El Paso, TX; KFRQ-FM Harlingen, TX; KGOL Humble, TX; KBZO Lubbock, TX; KNVO-FM Port Isabel, TX; KAIQ(FM) Wolfforth, TX; WACA Wheaton, MD.

Stns: 20 TV. KLUZ, Albuquerque-Santa Fe, NM; WUNI, Boston (Manchester, NH); KVSN-DT, Colorado Springs-Pueblo, CO; KORO, Corpus Christi, TX; KCEC, Denver, CO; KINT, El Paso (Las Cruces, NM), TX; KTFN, El Paso (Las Cruces, NM), TX; KNVO, Harlingen-Weslaco -Brownsville-McAllen, TX; WUVN, Hartford & New Haven, CT; KLDO, Laredo, TX; KINC, Las Vegas, NV; KSMS, Monterey-Salinas, CA; KUPB, Odessa-Midland, TX; WVEN-TV, Orlando-Daytona Beach-Melbourne, FL; KREN, Reno, NV; KPMR, Santa Barbara-Santa Maria-San Luis Obispo, CA; WVEA-TV, Tampa-St. Petersburg (Sarasota), FL; WJAL, Washington, DC (Hagerstown, MD); KDCU-DT, Wichita-Hutchinson Plus, KS; KVYE, Yuma, AZ-El Centro, CA.

Walter F. Ulloa, chmn/CEO; Philip Wilkinson, pres/COO; Larry Safir, exec VP.

Equity Communications LP, 8025 Black Horse Pike, Bayport One, Suite 100-102, West Atlantic City, NJ 08232. Phone: (609) 484-8444. Fax: (609) 646-6331.E-mail: gfequity@aol.com Web Site:951wayv.com

Stns: 2 AM. 7 FM. WAYV(FM) Atlantic City, NJ; WMID(AM) Atlantic City, NJ; WAIV(FM) Cape May, NJ; WSNQ(FM) Cape May Court House, NJ; WTTH(FM) Margate City, NJ; WZBZ(FM) Pleasantville, NJ; WZXL(FM) Wildwood, NJ; WCMC(AM) Wildwood, NJ; WEZW(FM) Wildwood Crest, NJ.

Gary S. Fisher, pres.

Eureka Broadcasting Co., 1101 Marsh Rd., Eureka, CA 95501. Phone: (707) 442-5744. Ownership Barbara Papstein, 50%; Hugo Papstein, 28%; and Brian Papstein, 22%.

Stns: 3 AM. 3 FM. KEJY(FM) Blue Lake, CA; KWSW Eureka, CA; KEKA-FM Eureka, CA; KINS Eureka, CA; KURY Brookings, OR; KURY-FM Brookings, OR.

Hugo Papstein, gen mgr .

Evangel Ministries Inc., 1909 W. 2nd, Appleton, WI 54914. Phone: (920) 749-9456. Fax: (920) 749-0474. Web Site:www.christianfamilyradio.net

Stns: 3 AM. 3 FM. KEJY(FM) Blue Lake, CA; KWSW Eureka, CA; KEKA-FM Eureka, CA; KINS Eureka, CA; KURY Brookings, OR; KURY-FM Brookings, OR3 FM. WEMI(FM) Appleton, WI; WEMY-FM Green Bay, WI; WGNV(FM) Milladore, WI.

Paul Comeron, exec dir.

Evanov Communications Inc., 5302 Dundas St. W., Toronto, ON M9B 1B2. Canada. Phone: (416) 213-1035. Fax: (416) 233-8617. Web Site:evanovradiogroup.com Ownership William Evanov, 74.26%; Paul Evanov, 25%; and The Bill Evanov Family Trust, 0.74%. Note: Group also owns 50% of CIRR-FM Toronto, ON.

Stns: 1 AM. 6 FM. CKHZ-FM Halifax, NS; CIAO Brampton, ON; CKHK-FM Hawkesbury, ON; CKDX-FM Newmarket, ON; CIDC-FM Orangeville, ON; CJWL-FM Ottawa, ON; CIRR-FM Toronto, ON.

Bill Evanov, pres.

F

FM Idaho Co. LLC, 21361 Hwy. 30, Twin Falls, ID 83301. Phone: (208) 735-8300.

Stns: 2 AM. 4 FM. KPDA(FM) Gooding, ID; KMHI Mountain Home, ID; KQLZ(FM) Mountain Home, ID; KWYD(FM) Parma, ID; KSRV Ontario, OR; KSRV-FM Ontario, OR.

Faith Communications Corp., 2201 S. 6th St., Las Vegas, NV 89104. Phone: (702) 731-5452. Fax: (702) 731-1992. Web Site:www.sosradio.net

Stns: 1 AM. 6 FM. KHMS-FM Victorville, CA; KSQS(FM) Ririe, ID; KCIR(FM) Twin Falls, ID; KMZO(FM) Hamilton, MT; KMZL-FM Missoula, MT; KSOS(FM) Las Vegas, NV; KANN Roy, UT.

Brad Staley, pres.

Family Life Communications Inc., Box 35300, Tucson, AZ 85740. Phone: (520) 742-6976. Fax: (520) 742-6979. Web Site:www.flc.org Ownership All stns are owned by Family Life Communications Inc. A nonprofit, noncommercial Christian organization. No individual stockholders.

Stns: 4 AM. 15 FM. KJTA-FM Flagstaff, AZ; KFLR-FM Phoenix, AZ; KFLT Tucson, AZ; KFLT-FM Tucson, AZ; WJTF-FM Panama City, FL; WJTG(FM) Fort Valley, GA; KJTY-FM Topeka, KS; WUFN(FM) Albion, MI; WUNN(AM) Mason, MI; WUGN-FM Midland, MI; WUFL Sterling Heights, MI; KFLQ(FM) Albuquerque, NM; KWFL-FM Roswell, NM; WJBP(FM) Red Bank, TN; KRGN-FM Amarillo, TX; KAMY(FM) Lubbock, TX; KFLB(AM) Odessa, TX; KFLB-FM Stanton, TX; WJTY-FM Lancaster, WI.

Randy L. Carlson, pres.

Family Life Network, Box 506, Bath, NY 14810. Phone: (607) 776-4151. Fax: (607) 776-6929.E-mail: mail@fln.org Web Site:www.fln.org Ownership Not-for-profit corporation.

Stns: 4 AM. 15 FM. KJTA-FM Flagstaff, AZ; KFLR-FM Phoenix, AZ; KFLT Tucson, AZ; KFLT-FM Tucson, AZ; WJTF-FM Panama City, FL; WJTG(FM) Fort Valley, GA; KJTY-FM Topeka, KS; WUFN(FM) Albion, MI; WUNN(AM) Mason, MI; WUGN-FM Midland, MI; WUFL Sterling Heights, MI; KFLQ(FM) Albuquerque, NM; KWFL-FM Roswell, NM; WJBP(FM) Red Bank, TN; KRGN-FM Amarillo, TX; KAMY(FM) Lubbock, TX; KFLB(AM) Odessa, TX; KFLB-FM Stanton, TX; WJTY-FM Lancaster, WI17 FM. WCOF(FM) Arcade, NY; WCIK-FM Bath, NY; WCOM-FM Belfast, NY; WCIY-FM Canandaigua, NY; WCOV-FM Clyde, NY; WCIH-FM Elmira, NY; WCID-FM Friendship, NY; WCOT-FM Jamestown, NY; WCII-FM Spencer, NY; WCOU-FM Warsaw, NY; WFUZ(FM) Carbondale, PA; WCIG(FM) Dallas, PA; WCOH-FM DuBois, PA; WCOG-FM Galeton, PA; WCIJ(FM) Laporte, PA; WCIM(FM) Shenandoah, PA; WCIT-FM Trout Run, PA.

Rick Snavely, pres/CEO; Dick Snavely, CFO; Cecil VanHouten, progmg dir; Jim Travis, chief engr.

Family Stations Inc., 290 Hegenberger Rd., Oakland, CA 94621. Phone: (510) 568-6200. Fax: (510) 568-6190. Ownership Nonprofit corporation.

Stns: 12 AM. 55 FM. WBFR-FM Birmingham, AL; KEAF(FM) Fort Smith, AR; KPHF-FM Phoenix, AZ; KFRB-FM Bakersfield, CA; KHAP(FM) Chico, CA; KFRJ(FM) China Lake, CA; KFRP(FM) Coalinga, CA; KECR El Cajon, CA; KFNO-FM Fresno, CA; KXBC(FM) Garberville, CA; KEFR-FM Le Grand, CA; KFRN Long Beach, CA; KEBR Rocklin, CA; KEAR-FM Sacramento, CA; KEAR(AM) San Francisco, CA; KHFR(FM) Santa Maria, CA; KFRS-FM Soledad, CA; KPRA-FM Ukiah, CA; KFRY(FM) Pueblo, CO; WCTF Vernon, CT; WMFL-FM Florida City, FL; WFTI-FM Saint Petersburg, FL; WWFR(FM) Stuart, FL; WFRP(FM) Americus, GA; WFRC-FM Columbus, GA; KDFR(FM) Des Moines, IA; KEGR(FM) Fort Dodge, IA; KYFR Shenandoah, IA; WJCH-FM Joliet, IL; KPOR-FM Emporia, KS; WOFR(FM) Schoolcraft, MI; KFRD(FM) Butte, MT; KFRT(FM) Butte, MT; KFRW(FM) Great Falls, MT; KBFR(FM) Bismarck, ND; WKDN-FM Camden, NJ; WFME-FM Newark, NJ; KXFR(FM) Socorro, NM; WFBF-FM Buffalo, NY; WFRH-FM Kingston, NY; WFRS-FM Smithtown, NY; WFRW-FM Webster, NY; WCUE Cuyahoga Falls, OH; WOTL-FM Toledo, OH; WYTN-FM Youngstown, OH; KYOR(FM) Newport, OR; KPFR(FM) Pine Grove, OR; KQFE-FM Springfield, OR; WUFR(FM) Bedford, PA; WEFR-FM Erie, PA; WFRJ-FM Johnstown, PA; WXFR(FM) State College, PA; WFCH-FM Charleston, SC; KKAA(AM) Aberdeen, SD; KQFR(FM) Rapid City, SD; KQKD(AM) Redfield, SD; KIFR(FM) Alice, TX; KEDR(FM) Bay City, TX; KTXB-FM Beaumont, TX; KUFR-FM Salt Lake City, UT; KARR Kirkland, WA; KJVH-FM Longview, WA; WWJA(FM) Janesville, WI; WMWK-FM Milwaukee, WI; WFSI-FM Annapolis, MD; WBGR Baltimore, MD; WBMD Baltimore, MD.

Stns: 1 TV. WFME, New York.

Harold Camping, pres.

Family Worship Center Church Inc., Box 262550, Baton Rouge, LA 70826. Phone: (225) 768-3224. Web Site:www.jsm.org Ownership Jimmy Swaggart, 8.33% vote; Frances Swaggart, 8.33% vote; Donnie Swaggart, 8.33% vote; Harold Lee, 8.33% vote; Peggy Lee, 8.33% vote; Clyde Fuller, 8.33% vote; Elizabeth Fuller, 8.33% vote; Roy Chacon, 8.33% vote; Beulah Chacon, 8.33% vote; Jack Daugherty, 8.33% vote; Barbara Studley, 8.33% vote; and Debbie Swaggart, 8.33% vote.

Stns: 4 AM. 20 FM. WQUA-FM Citronelle, AL; KJSM-FM Augusta, AR; KNHD Camden, AR; KUUZ-FM Lake Village, AR; KSSW(FM) Nashville, AR; KPSH(FM) Coachella, CA; WFFL(FM) Panama City, FL; KBDD(FM) Winfield, KS; WJFM-FM Baton Rouge, LA; KCKR(FM) Church Point, LA; KTOC-FM Jonesboro, LA; KDJR(FM) De Soto, MO; WTGY-FM Charleston, MS; WJNS-FM Yazoo City, MS; KNBE(FM) Beatrice, NE; KNFA(FM) Grand Island, NE; WJCA(FM) Albion, NY; WJYM Bowling Green, OH; KAJT(FM) Ada, OK; KMFS(AM) Guthrie, OK; KSSO(FM) Norman, OK; WAYB-FM Graysville, TN; WSTN Somerville, TN; KNRB(FM) Atlanta, TX.

Jimmy Swaggart, pres; David Whitelaw, opns dir.

Fantasia Broadcasting Inc., 450 Leonard Ave., Fairmont, WV 26554. Phone: (304) 366-3700. Fax: (304) 366-3706. Ownership Nick Fantasia, 100%.

Stns: 2 AM. 2 FM. WTCS Fairmont, WV; WRLF-FM Fairmont, WV; WMMN Fairmont, WV; WZST-FM Westover, WV.

Nick Fantasia, pres.

Federated Media, Box 2500, Elkhart, IN 46515. Phone: (574) 295-2500. Fax: (574) 294-4014.

Stns: 4 AM. 7 FM. WQHK-FM Decatur, IN; WBYT-FM Elkhart, IN; WTRC Elkhart, IN; WMEE-FM Fort Wayne, IN; WFWI-FM Fort Wayne, IN; WKJG(AM) Fort Wayne, IN; WOWO Fort Wayne, IN; WLEG(FM) Ligonier, IN; WAOR-FM Niles, MI; WNIL Niles, MI; WBYR-FM Van Wert, OH.

Federated Media publishes *The* (Elkhart, IN) *Truth.*

John F. Dille III, pres; Robert A. Watson III, treas; Robert A. Watson III, sec.

The Findlay Publishing Co., 701 W. Sandusky St., Findlay, OH 45840. Phone: (419) 422-5151. Fax: (419) 422-2937.E-mail: daveglass@findlayoh.com

Stns: 2 AM. 6 FM. WRBI-FM Batesville, IN; WCSI(AM) Columbus, IN; WINN(FM) Columbus, IN; WKKG-FM Columbus, IN; WWWY(FM) North Vernon, IN; WKXA-FM Findlay, OH; WFIN Findlay, OH; WBUK(FM) Ottawa, OH.

The Findlay Publishing Co. publishes the *Findlay* (OH) *Courier*.

Karl Heminger, pres.

Finger Lakes Radio Group, 3568 Lenox Rd., Geneva, NY 14456. Phone: (315) 781-7000. Fax: (315) 781-7700. Web Site:www.fingerlakes1.com

Stns: 4 AM. 1 FM. WAUB Auburn, NY; WCGR Canandaigua, NY; WFLR Dundee, NY; WFIZ(FM) Odessa, NY; WSFW Seneca Falls, NY.

George Kimble, pres; Alan Bishop, VP/gen mgr.

First Broadcasting Operating Inc., 8300 Douglas Ave., Suite 730, Dallas, TX 75225. Phone: (214) 855-0002. Fax: (214) 855-5145.E-mail: info@firstbroadcasting.com Web Site:www.firstbroadcasting.com Ownership Gary Lawrence, Alta Communications.

Stns: 1 AM. 4 FM. WOXY-FM Oxford, OH; WAOL-FM Ripley, OH; KMCQ-FM The Dalles, OR; KBIS(AM) Forks, WA; KBDB-FM Forks, WA.

Gary Lawrence, pres/CEO; Hal Rose, COO; Neil Read, CFO; Bob Denny, exec VP technology & software dev.

First Media Radio LLC, 306 Port St., Easton, MD 21601. Phone: (410) 822-3301. Fax: (410) 822-0576. Ownership LPTV: WNVN-LP Roanoke Rapids, NC.

Stns: 9 AM. 17 FM. WTRG(FM) Gaston, NC; WWDR(AM) Murfreesboro, NC; WDLZ-FM Murfreesboro, NC; WZAX(FM) Nashville, NC; WPWZ(FM) Pinetops, NC; WPTM-FM Roanoke Rapids, NC; WCBT Roanoke Rapids, NC; WDWG(FM) Rocky Mount, NC; WRMT(AM) Rocky Mount, NC; WSMY Weldon, NC; WZWW-FM Bellefonte, PA; WQYX-FM Clearfield, PA; WCPA Clearfield, PA; WOWQ(FM) DuBois, PA; WLAK-FM Huntingdon, PA; WMRF-FM Lewistown, PA; WIEZ Lewistown, PA; WZDB(FM) Sykesville, PA; WWDW(FM) Alberta, VA; WWZW(FM) Buena Vista, VA; WYTT(FM) Emporia, VA; WREL Lexington, VA; WJLS Beckley, WV; WJLS-FM Beckley, WV; WEMD(AM) Easton, MD; WCEI-FM Easton, MD.

Alex Kolobielski, pres/CEO.

First Natchez Radio Group, Box 768, Natchez, MS 39121. Phone: (601) 442-4895. Fax: (601) 446-8260.

Stns: 1 AM. 3 FM. KTGV(FM) Jonesville, LA; WNAT Natchez, MS; WKSO(FM) Natchez, MS; WQNZ-FM Natchez, MS.

Marie Perkins, pres; Stephen Perkins, VP; Margaret Perkins, gen mgr .

Fisher Communications Inc., 100 4th Ave. N., Suite 440, Suite 1525, Seattle, WA 98109. Phone: (206) 404-7000. Fax: (206) 404-7050. Web Site:www.fsci.com

Stns: 4 AM. 4 FM. KIKF(FM) Cascade, MT; KXGF Great Falls, MT; KINX(FM) Great Falls, MT; KQDI Great Falls, MT; KQDI-FM Great Falls, MT; KVI(AM) Seattle, WA; KOMO(AM) Seattle, WA; KPLZ(FM) Seattle, WA.

Stns: 13 TV. KBAK-TV, Bakersfield, CA; KBCI-TV, Boise, ID; KCBY, Eugene, OR; KPIC, Eugene, OR; KVAL, Eugene, OR; KIDK-TV, Idaho Falls-Pocatello, ID; KATU, Portland, OR; KUNP, Portland, OR; KUNS-TV, Seattle-Tacoma, WA; KOMO, Seattle-Tacoma, WA; KLEW-TV, Spokane, WA; KIMA-TV, Yakima-Pasco-Richland-Kennewick, WA; KEPR, Yakima-Pasco-Richland-Kennewick, WA.

Collen Brown, pres/CEO; Sheri Leonard, asst.

Flint Media Inc., Box 7425, Bainbridge, GA 39818-7425. Phone: (229) 416-6021. Fax: (229) 246-9995. Ownership Kevin Dowdy, 100%.

Stns: 2 AM. 2 FM. WBGE(FM) Bainbridge, GA; WBBK Blakely, GA; WGMK-FM Donalsonville, GA; WSEM Donalsonville, GA.

Foothills Radio Group LLC, Box 1678, Lenoir, NC 28645. Phone: (828) 758-1033. Fax: (828) 757-3300.E-mail: abunch@kicksradio.com Web Site:foothillsradio.com Ownership Donald W. Curtis, 45%; William M. McClatchey Jr., 10%; George A. Bunch Jr. 45%.

Stns: 2 AM. 1 FM. WJRI Lenoir, NC; WKGX Lenoir, NC; WKVS-FM Lenoir, NC.

Al Bunch, pres.

Forever Broadcasting, One Forever Dr., Hollidaysburg, PA 16648. Phone: (814) 941-9800. Fax: (814) 943-2754. Web Site:www.foreverradio.com Ownership Kerby Confer, Donald Alt, Carol Logan, Lynn Deppen.

Stns: 12 AM. 18 FM. WVAM Altoona, PA; WWOT(FM) Altoona, PA; WFBG Altoona, PA; WALY-FM Bellwood, PA; WBUS(FM) Boalsburg, PA; WXMJ(FM) Cambridge Springs, PA; WMAJ-FM Centre Hall, PA; WUUZ(FM) Cooperstown, PA; WRKW(FM) Ebensburg, PA; WFRA Franklin, PA; WHMJ(FM) Franklin, PA; WWGY(FM) Grove City, PA; WRKY-FM Hollidaysburg, PA; WHUN Huntingdon, PA; WFGI-FM Johnstown, PA; WKYE(FM) Johnstown, PA; WJHT(FM) Johnstown, PA; WGYY(FM) Meadville, PA; WMGW Meadville, PA; WBSS(FM) Mount Union, PA; WJST(AM) New Castle, PA; WKST(AM) New Castle, PA; WOYL Oil City, PA; WUZZ(FM) Saegertown, PA; WNTW(AM) Somerset, PA; WRSC State College, PA; WRSC-FM State College, PA; WQWK(AM) State College, PA; WTIV Titusville, PA; WFGE(FM) Tyrone, PA.

Carol Logan, pres.

Forever Communications Inc., 1919 Scottsville Rd., Bowling Green, KY 42104-3303. Phone: (270) 843-3333. Fax: (270) 843-0454.E-mail: chris@forevercomm.com Ownership Kerby E. Confer Grantor Retained Annuity Trust, Kerby E. Confer, trustee; Donald J. Alt Grantor Retained Annuity Trust, Donald J. Alt, trustee; Christine E. Hillard.

Stns: 6 AM. 10 FM. WBVR-FM Auburn, KY; WBGN(AM) Bowling Green, KY; WSTV-FM Frankfort, KY; WFKY(FM) Frankfort, KY; WKYW(AM) Frankfort, KY; WLYE-FM Glasgow, KY; WNBS Murray, KY; WFGS(FM) Murray, KY; WOFC(AM) Murray, KY; WUHU(FM) Smiths Grove, KY; WTJJ(FM)

Dyer, TN; WTJW(FM) Humboldt, TN; WLLI(AM) Humboldt, TN; WOGY(FM) Jackson, TN; WTJS Jackson, TN; WYNU-FM Milan, TN.

Christine Hillard, pres/COO.

Fort Bend Broadcasting Co., 1610 Woodstead Ct., Suite 350, Spring, TX 77380-3414. Phone: (281) 298-6797. Fax: (281) 298-8707. Ownership Roy E. Henderson, owner. Note: Roy E. Henderson also owns WTCU(FM) Fife Lake, MI; and KNUZ(AM) Bellville, TX.

Stns: 1 AM. 8 FM. WCUZ(FM) Bear Lake, MI; WBNZ(FM) Beulah, MI; WARD(AM) Petoskey, MI; WLDR-FM Traverse City, MI; KLTR(FM) Brenham, TX; KULM-FM Columbus, TX; KHTZ(FM) Ganado, TX; KROY(FM) Palacios, TX; KJAZ(FM) Point Comfort, TX.

Roy E. Henderson, pres.

Fort Myers Broadcasting Co., 2824 Palm Beach Blvd., Fort Myers, FL 33916. Phone: (239) 334-1111. Fax: (239) 334-0744.E-mail: manaager@winktv.com Web Site:winktv.com Ownership Brian A. McBride.

Stns: 2 AM. 2 FM. WINK-FM Fort Myers, FL; WNPL(AM) Golden Gate, FL; WPTK(AM) Pine Island Center, FL; WTLQ-FM Punta Rassa, FL.

Stns: 1 TV. WINK-TV, Ft. Myers-Naples, FL.

Brian McBride, pres/CEO; Gary Gardner, VP/gen mgr.

Forum Communications Co., Box 2020, Fargo, ND 58107. Phone: (701) 235-7311. Fax: (701) 241-5406. Web Site:www.in-forum.com

Stns: 1 AM. 1 FM. WZUU-FM Allegan, MI; WDAY Fargo, ND.

Stns: 4 TV. WDAY-TV, Fargo-Valley City, ND; WDAZ-TV, Fargo-Valley City, ND; KBMY, Minot-Bismarck-Dickinson, ND; KMCY, Minot-Bismarck-Dickinson, ND.

Forum Communications Co. owns the *Alexandria* (MN) *Echo Press; The Pioneer,* Bemidj, MN; *Detroit Lakes* (MN) *Tribune; The Becker County Record,* Detroit Lakes, MN; *Park Rapids* (MN) *Enterprise; The Wadena* (MN) *Pioneer Journal; West Central Daily Tribune,* Willmar, MN; *The Daily Globe,* Worthington, MN; *The Daily Republic,* Mitchell SD; *The Dickinson Press,* Dickinson, ND & *The* (ND) *Forum.*

William C. Marcil, pres.

Foster Communications Co. Inc., Box 2191, San Angelo, TX 76902-2191. Phone: (325) 949-2112. Fax: (325) 944-0851. Web Site:www.fostercommunications.us Ownership Fred M. Key, 100% of votes, 95% of total assets.

Stns: 1 AM. 3 FM. KIXY-FM San Angelo, TX; KKSA San Angelo, TX; KWFR-FM San Angelo, TX; KCLL(FM) San Angelo, TX.

Fred M. Key, pres/CEO; Doug Smith, gen sls mgr; Jay Michaels, VP/gen mgr.

Four Corners Broadcasting L.L.C., Drawer P, Durango, CO 81302. Phone: (970) 259-4444. Fax: (970) 247-1005.E-mail: fcb@frontier.net Web Site:www.radiodurango.com Ownership Four Corners Communications L.L.C., Fordstone, IN.

Stns: 1 AM. 3 FM. KKDC(FM) Dolores, CO; KIQX(FM) Durango, CO; KIUP Durango, CO; KRSJ-FM Durango, CO.

Allen Brill, CEO; Ward S. Holmes, gen mgr .

4-K Radio Inc., Box 936, Lewiston, ID 83501. Phone: (208) 743-2502. Fax: (208) 743-1995.E-mail: radiorip@aol.com Web Site:www.koze.com Ownership Eugene Hamblin Trust; Michael R. Ripley.

Stns: 2 AM. 2 FM. KORT Grangeville, ID; KORT-FM Grangeville, ID; KOZE Lewiston, ID; KOZE-FM Lewiston, ID.

Michael R. Ripley, pres.

Four Rivers Broadcasting Inc., Box 1729, Yreka, CA 96097. Phone: (530) 842-4158. Fax: (530) 842-7635. Web Site:www.mtshastalive.com Ownership Alta California Broadcasting Inc., 100%.

Stns: 2 AM. 2 FM. KORT Grangeville, ID; KORT-FM Grangeville, ID; KOZE Lewiston, ID; KOZE-FM Lewiston, ID4 FM. KTDE(FM) Gualala, CA; KMFB-FM Mendocino, CA; KNTK(FM) Weed, CA; KSYC-FM Yreka, CA.

John Anthony, gen mgr .

The Free Lance-Star Publishing Co., 616 Amelia St., Fredericksburg, VA 22401. Phone: (540) 373-1500. Fax: (540) 374-5525. Ownership Josiah P. Rowe III; Anne W. Rowe

Stns: 1 AM. 3 FM. WWUZ(FM) Bowling Green, VA; WFLS-FM Fredericksburg, VA; WYSK Fredericksburg, VA; WVBX(FM) Spotsylvania, VA.

The Free Lance-Star Publishing Co., publishes the *Fredericksburg* (VA) *Free Lance-Star.*

Josiah P. Rowe III, pres; Florence C. Barnick, assoc publisher; Nicholas J. Cadwallender, assoc publisher;

John Moen, gen mgr radio stns.

Freedom Communications of Connecticut Inc., 330 Main St., Hartford, CT 06106. Phone: (860) 524-0001. Fax: (860) 548-1922.E-mail: mssm2115@msn.com Ownership Richard Weaver-Bey, 50% of votes; and Stephen Brisker, 50% of votes.

Stns: 3 AM. WNEZ(AM) Manchester, CT; WLAT(AM) New Britain, CT; WKND(AM) Windsor, CT.

Stephen Brisker, pres/CEO & chmn.

Freeland Broadcasting Stations, Box 387, Benton, KY 42025. Phone: (270) 527-3102. Fax: (270) 527-5606. Ownership Jim W. Freeland, 100%.

Stns: 2 AM. 3 FM. WCBL Benton, KY; WCBL-FM Benton, KY; WCCK-FM Calvert City, KY; WWDX(AM) Huntingdon, TN; WVHR-FM Huntingdon, TN.

Friends Communications Inc., 121 W. Maumee St., Adrian, MI 49221-2019. Phone: (517) 265-1500. Fax: (517) 263-4525.E-mail: friends@tc3net.com Ownership Bob Elliot, 100%.

Stns: 1 AM. 2 FM. WQTE-FM Adrian, MI; WABJ Adrian, MI; WBZV(FM) Hudson, MI.

Bob Elliot, pres; Moneca Morton, gen sls mgr.

Fritz Communications Inc., 1355 N. Dutton Ave. #225, Santa Rosa, CA 95401-7107. Phone: (707) 546-9185. Fax: (707) 546-9188. Ownership KEWB(FM), KNCQ(FM), KESR(FM), KKXS(FM) and KHRD(FM) are licensed to Results Radio of Redding Licensee LLC. KBQB(FM), KKCY(FM), KTHU(FM), KMJE(FM), KCEZ(FM) and KRQR(FM) are licensed to Results Radio of Chico Licensee LLC. KCCL(FM) is licensed to Results Radio of Sacramento LLC.

Stns: 1 AM. 2 FM. WQTE-FM Adrian, MI; WABJ Adrian, MI; WBZV(FM) Hudson, MI12 FM. KEWB-FM Anderson, CA; KBQB(FM) Chico, CA; KKCY-FM Colusa, CA; KTHU(FM) Corning, CA; KMJE-FM Gridley, CA; KCEZ(FM) Los Molinos, CA; KRQR-FM Orland, CA; KCCL(FM) Placerville, CA; KNCQ-FM Redding, CA; KESR(FM) Shasta Lake City, CA; KKXS(FM) Shingletown, CA; KHRD(FM) Weaverville, CA.

Jack Fritz, pres/CEO.

J. & J. Fritz Media Ltd., Box 311, Fredericksburg, TX 78624. Phone: (830) 997-2197. Fax: (830) 997-2198.E-mail: txradio@ktc.com Web Site:www.texasrebelradio.com

Stns: 1 AM. 3 FM. KEEP-FM Bandera, TX; KNAF Fredericksburg, TX; KNAF-FM Fredericksburg, TX; KFAN-FM Johnson City, TX.

Jayson Fritz, gen mgr; Jan Fritz, gen sls mgr.

Frontier Radio Management Inc., 4311 Wilshire Blvd., Suite 412, Los Angeles, CA 90010. Phone: (323) 931-1745. Fax: (323) 931-0925. Ownership Jason R. Wolff, 100%.

Stns: 4 AM. 12 FM. KBLU Yuma, AZ; KTTI-FM Yuma, AZ; KQSR(FM) Yuma, AZ; KZXY-FM Apple Valley, CA; KIXW(AM) Apple Valley, CA; KATJ-FM George, CA; KURQ(FM) Grover Beach, CA; KSMY(FM) Lompoc, CA; KSTT-FM Los Osos-Baywood Park, CA; KIXA-FM Lucerne Valley, CA; KSLY-FM San Luis Obispo, CA; KVEC San Luis Obispo, CA; KXFM-FM Santa Maria, CA; KSMX(AM) Santa Maria, CA; KSNI-FM Santa Maria, CA; KRSX-FM Yermo, CA.

Jason R. Wolff, pres.

Fuchs Radio L.L.C., Box 311, Hobart, OK 73651. Phone: (580) 726-5656. Fax: (580) 726-2222. Ownership Chad Fox, 50%; and Shelley Fox, 50%.

Stns: 1 AM. 3 FM. KTIJ-FM Elk City, OK; KTJS Hobart, OK; KHIM-FM Mangum, OK; KJCM-FM Snyder, OK.

G

GAP Broadcasting LLC, 12900 Preston Rd., Suite 525, Dallas, TX 75230. Phone: (214) 295-3530. Fax: (972) 386-4445. Web Site:www.gapbroadcast.com Ownership GAP Broadcasting Holdings LLC, 100%.

Stns: 14 AM. 45 FM. KMJI(FM) Ashdown, AR; KOSY(AM) Texarkana, AR; KYGL-FM Texarkana, AR; KTSR(FM) De Quincy, LA; KJEF(AM) Jennings, LA; KHLA(FM) Jennings, LA; KJMH(FM) Lake Arthur, LA; KLCL Lake Charles, LA; KNGT(FM) Lake Charles, LA; KEEL(AM) Shreveport, LA; KXKS-FM Shreveport, LA; KRUF(FM) Shreveport, LA; KVKI-FM Shreveport, LA; KWKH(AM) Shreveport, LA; KZCD(FM) Lawton, OK; KVRW(AM) Lawton, OK; KLAW(FM) Lawton, OK; KFGL(FM) Abilene, TX; KULL-FM Abilene, TX; KEYJ-FM Abilene, TX; KSLI(AM) Abilene, TX; KYYW(AM) Abilene, TX; KEAN-FM Abilene, TX; KMXJ-FM Amarillo, TX; KATP(FM) Amarillo, TX; KIXZ Amarillo, TX; KXSS-FM Amarillo, TX; KPRF(FM) Amarillo, TX; KLUB-FM Bloomington, TX; KTUX-FM Carthage, TX; KAFX-FM Diboll, TX; KFZX(FM)

Gardendale, TX; KPWW-FM Hooks, TX; KDOK(AM) Kilgore, TX; KKTX-FM Kilgore, TX; KKCL-FM Lorenzo, TX; KKAM Lubbock, TX; KFMX-FM Lubbock, TX; KFYO Lubbock, TX; KQBR(FM) Lubbock, TX; KZII-FM Lubbock, TX; KYKS-FM Lufkin, TX; KCRS-FM Midland, TX; KCRS(AM) Midland, TX; KCHX(FM) Midland, TX; KSFA(AM) Nacogdoches, TX; KTBQ(FM) Nacogdoches, TX; KMRK-FM Odessa, TX; KKYR-FM Texarkana, TX; KNUE(FM) Tyler, TX; KTYL-FM Tyler, TX; KQVT(FM) Victoria, TX; KIXS-FM Victoria, TX; KVLL-FM Wells, TX; KISX-FM Whitehouse, TX; KNIN-FM Wichita Falls, TX; KWFS Wichita Falls, TX; KWFS-FM Wichita Falls, TX; KBZS(FM) Wichita Falls, TX.

George Laughlin, pres; Shawn Nunn, sls VP; Norman Philips, engrg VP.

GAPWEST Broadcasting, 8480 E. Orchard Rd., Suite 1300, Greenwood Village, CO 80111. Phone: (303) 773-9378. Fax: (303) 221-4794. Web Site:www.gapwest.com Ownership GAP Broadcasting Holdings II LLC, 100%.

Stns: 17 AM. 38 FM. KGRS-FM Burlington, IA; KBKB-FM Fort Madison, IA; KLLP-FM Chubbuck, ID; KID Idaho Falls, ID; KID-FM Idaho Falls, ID; KPKY-FM Pocatello, ID; KWIK Pocatello, ID; KEGE(FM) Pocatello, ID; KEZJ-FM Twin Falls, ID; KLIX Twin Falls, ID; KLIX-FM Twin Falls, ID; KLDJ-FM Duluth, MN; KKCB-FM Duluth, MN; WEBC Duluth, MN; KBMX(FM) Proctor, MN; KISN(FM) Belgrade, MT; KKBR-FM Billings, MT; KBBB(FM) Billings, MT; KBUL Billings, MT; KCTR-FM Billings, MT; KMMS(AM) Bozeman, MT; KMMS-FM Bozeman, MT; KZMY(FM) Bozeman, MT; KMPT(AM) East Missoula, MT; KVWE(FM) Frenchtown, MT; KLYQ Hamilton, MT; KBAZ(FM) Hamilton, MT; KMHK-FM Hardin, MT; KXLB(FM) Livingston, MT; KPRK Livingston, MT; KYSS-FM Missoula, MT; KGVO Missoula, MT; KENR(FM) Superior, MT; KOLW(FM) Basin City, WA; KQMY(FM) Naches, WA; KFLD Pasco, WA; KEYW-FM Pasco, WA; KORD-FM Richland, WA; KDBL(FM) Toppenish, WA; KXRX-FM Walla Walla, WA; KUTI(AM) Yakima, WA; KATS(FM) Yakima, WA; KFFM-FM Yakima, WA; KIT Yakima, WA; KIGN(FM) Burns, WY; KMGW(FM) Casper, WY; KKTL Casper, WY; KTRS-FM Casper, WY; KTWO Casper, WY; KLEN-FM Cheyenne, WY; KOWB(AM) Laramie, WY; KCGY(FM) Laramie, WY; KWYY(FM) Midwest, WY; KGAB Orchard Valley, WY; KRVK(FM) Vista West, WY.

Erik Hellum, pres; Daniel Wilson, CFO; Jack Evans, VP progmg; Jeff Schatz, VP sls; Norman Philips, VP engrg.

GCC Bend LLC, 969 S. W. Colorado, Bend, OR 97702. Phone: (541) 388-3300. Fax: (541) 389-7885. Web Site:www.ksjj.com Ownership Gross Holdings L.P., 100%.

Stns: 1 AM. 3 FM. KMGX(FM) Bend, OR; KXIX-FM Bend, OR; KICE(AM) Bend, OR; KSJJ-FM Redmond, OR.

Dana Horner, COO.

GHB Radio Group, 1776 Briarcliff Rd. N.E., Suite A, Atlanta, GA 30306-2106. Phone: (404) 875-1110. Fax: (404) 875-1186. Ownership George H. Buck Jr.

Stns: 12 AM. 2 FM. WMGY Montgomery, AL; WYZE Atlanta, GA; WIST(AM) New Orleans, LA; WCGC Belmont, NC; WHVN Charlotte, NC; WEGO Concord, NC; WAME(AM) Statesville, NC; WIST-FM Thomasville, NC; WBLO(AM) Thomasville, NC; WSVM(AM) Valdese, NC; WOLS(FM) Waxhaw, NC; WTIX(AM) Winston-Salem, NC; WNAP Norristown, PA; WAVO Rock Hill, SC.

Jacob E. Bogan, COO; George H. Buck Jr., pres.

Galaxy Communications L.P., 235 Walton St., Syracuse, NY 13202. Phone: (315) 472-9111. Fax: (315) 472-1888. Web Site:www.galaxycommunications.com

Stns: 6 AM. 7 FM. WTKW-FM Bridgeport, NY; WKLL-FM Frankfort, NY; WIXT(AM) Little Falls, NY; WKRH-FM Minetto, NY; WKRL-FM North Syracuse, NY; WTLA North Syracuse, NY; WSGO Oswego, NY; WTKV-FM Oswego, NY; WZUN(FM) Phoenix, NY; WRNY Rome, NY; WSCP Sandy Creek-Pulaski, NY; WTLB Utica, NY; WOUR-FM Utica, NY.

Ed Levine, pres; Mimi Griswold, VP progmg; Lisa Morrow, VP sls; Michael Lucarelli, CFO.

Galesburg Broadcasting Co., 154 E. Simmons St., Galesburg, IL 61401. Phone: (309) 342-5131. Fax: (309) 342-0840.E-mail: results@galesburgradio.com Web Site:www.galesburgradio.com Ownership John Pritchard, pres, 100%.

Stns: 1 AM. 3 FM. WAAG-FM Galesburg, IL; WGIL Galesburg, IL; WLSR(FM) Galesburg, IL; WKAY(FM) Knoxville, IL.

John T. Pritchard, pres.

Gateway Radio Works Inc., 22 West Main St., Mount Sterling, KY 40353. Phone: (859) 498-1077. Fax: (859) 498-7930. Ownership Hays McMakin, 100%.

Stns: 1 AM. 3 FM. WIVY(FM) Morehead, KY; WMST(AM) Mt. Sterling, KY; WKYN(FM) Owingsville, KY; WKCA(FM) Salt Lick, KY.

Hays McMakin, pres; Jeff Ray, VP/gen mgr.

Genesis Communications Inc., 2110 Powers Ferry Rd., Suite 198, Atlanta, GA 30339. Phone: (678) 324-0170. Fax: (678) 324-0174.E-mail: ceo@radiogenesis.com Web Site:www.radiogenesis.com Ownership Bruce C. Maduri, J. Donald Childress.
    Stns: 6 AM. WMGG(AM) Dunedin, FL; WHOO(AM) Kissimmee, FL; WWBA(AM) Largo, FL; WAMT(AM) Pine Castle-Sky Lake, FL; WHBO(AM) Pinellas Park, FL; WIXC(AM) Titusville, FL.
    J. Donald Childress, VP; Bruce C. Maduri, pres/CEO.

Georgia-Carolina Radiocasting Companies, Drawer E, Toccoa, GA 30577. Phone: (706) 297-7264. Fax: (706) 297-7266.E-mail: sutton@gacaradio.com Web Site:www.gacaradio.com Ownership Douglas M. Sutton Jr., 100% of all stns except WGHC(AM), WNGA(FM), WLHR-FM, WSNW(AM) and WGOG(FM). M. Terry Carter owns 50% and Douglas M. Sutton Jr. owns 50% of WGHC(AM), WNGA(FM), WLHR-FM, WSNW(AM) and WGOG(FM).
    Stns: 6 AM. 6 FM. WRBN(FM) Clayton, GA; WGHC(AM) Clayton, GA; WSGC-FM Elberton, GA; WSGC(AM) Elberton, GA; WNGA(FM) Helen, GA; WLHR-FM Lavonia, GA; WNEG(AM) Toccoa, GA; WNCC-FM Franklin, NC; WFSC Franklin, NC; WRGC(AM) Sylva, NC; WSNW(AM) Seneca, SC; WGOG(FM) Walhalla, SC.
    M. Terry Carter, pres/COO; Douglas M. (Art) Sutton Jr., chmn/CEO; Tonya Burgess, VP/CFO.

Georgia Eagle Broadcasting Inc., 1350 Radio Loop Rd., Warner Robins, GA 31088. Phone: (478) 923-3416. Fax: (478) 923-3236. Web Site:www.georgiaeagleradio.com Ownership Cecil P. Staton, 50%; and Joe Sam Robinson Jr., 50%. Note: Group also has a loc mktg agreement for WQSA(AM) Unadilla, GA.
    Stns: 6 AM. 8 FM. WMCD(FM) Claxton, GA; WDCO(AM) Cochran, GA; WDXQ-FM Cochran, GA; WQXZ(FM) Hawkinsville, GA; WCEH Hawkinsville, GA; WHKN-FM Millen, GA; WSSY(FM) Pinehurst, GA; WPTB(AM) Statesboro, GA; WPMX-FM Statesboro, GA; WWNS Statesboro, GA; WZBX-FM Sylvania, GA; WSYL Sylvania, GA; WNNG-FM Unadilla, GA; WNNG(AM) Warner Robins, GA.

Geos Communications, Box 701, Tunkhannock, PA 18657. Phone: (570) 836-4200. Fax: (570) 928-2100. Ownership Kevin M. Fitzgerald, gen ptnr, 33.3% interest; Benjamin P. Smith, gen ptnr, 33% interest; and Betty S. Curtin, gen ptnr, 33% interest.
    Stns: 1 AM. 1 FM. WNKZ(FM) Laporte, PA; WGMF(AM) Tunkhannock, PA.
    Kevin M. Fitzgerald, gen ptnr.

Gestion Appalaches inc., C.P. 69, Thetford Mines, PQ G6G 5S3. Canada. Phone: (418) 335-7533. Phone: (819) 752-2785. Fax: (418) 335-9009. Fax: (819) 752-3182. Ownership Francois Labbe, 99.9%; Fiducie familiale F. Labbe, .07%; and Annie Labbie, .03%.
    Stns: 1 AM. 1 FM. WNKZ(FM) Laporte, PA; WGMF(AM) Tunkhannock, PA3 FM. CFJO-FM Thetford Mines, PQ; CKLD-FM Thetford Mines, PQ; CFDA-FM Victoriaville, PQ.
    Annie Labbe, gen mgr .

Gleason Radio Group, 555 Center St., Auburn, ME 04210. Phone: (207) 748-5868. Fax: (207) 784-4700.E-mail: dick@gleasonmedia.com Web Site:www.gleasonmedia.com Ownership Richard D. Gleason, 100%.
    Stns: 3 AM. 2 FM. WEZR(AM) Lewiston, ME; WTBM(FM) Mexico, ME; WOXO-FM Norway, ME; WTME(AM) Rumford, ME; WKTQ South Paris, ME.
    Richard Gleason, pres/gen mgr.

Gleiser Communications LLC, 1001 E. Southeast Loop 323, Suite 455, Tyler, TX 75701. Phone: (903) 593-2519. Fax: (903) 597-4141.E-mail: info@ktbb.com Web Site:www.gleisercom.com Ownership Broadcasting partnors holdings, LP, Paul L. Gleiser.
    Stns: 3 AM. 1 FM. KEES Gladewater, TX; KTBB Tyler, TX; KYZS Tyler, TX; KTBB-FM Tyler, TX.
    Paul Gleiser, pres/CEO.

Glenwood Communications Corp., 222 Commerce St., Kingsport, TN 37660. Phone: (423) 246-9578. Fax: (423) 246-6261.E-mail: golz@wkpttv.com Web Site:www.wkpttv.com Ownership William M. Boyd; Hugh N. Boyd Trust.
    Stns: 4 AM. 4 FM. WOPI Bristol, TN; WRZK-FM Colonial Heights, TN; WKTP Jonesborough, TN; WKPT Kingsport, TN; WTFM-FM Kingsport, TN; WMEV Marion, VA; WMEV-FM Marion, VA; WVEK-FM Weber City, VA.
    Stns: 1 TV. WKPT-TV, Tri-Cities, TN-VA.
    George E. DeVault Jr., pres.

Glory Communications Inc., Box 2355, West Columbia, SC 29171. Phone: (803) 939-9530. Fax: (803) 939-9469. Ownership Alex Snipe, 100%.
    Stns: 4 AM. 5 FM. WSPX-FM Bowman, SC; WEAF(AM) Camden, SC; WTQS(AM) Cameron, SC; WGCV(AM) Cayce, SC; WQXL Columbia, SC; WPDT-FM Johnsonville, SC; WTUA-FM Saint Stephen, SC; WFMV(FM) South Congaree, SC; WLJI-FM Summerton, SC.
    Alex Snipe, pres/CEO.

Goforth Media Inc., Box 1328, Mobile, AL 36633. Phone: (251) 473-8488. Fax: (251) 473-8854.E-mail: wgoforth@goforth.org Web Site:www.goforth.org Ownership No stock. Nonprofit.
    Stns: 1 AM. 1 FM. WBHY Mobile, AL; WBHY-FM Mobile, AL.
    Wilbur Goforth, pres; Steve Riggs, VP; Stephen Goforth, VP.

Gold Coast Broadcasting LLC, 2284 S. Victoria, Suite 2M, Ventura, CA 93003. Phone: (805) 289-1400. Phone: (805) 339-0773. Fax: (805) 644-4257. Ownership Point Broadcasting Company 88.51%, Jeri Lynn Broadcasting 6.32%, August G Inc. 5.17%.
    Stns: 3 AM. 3 FM. KOCP-FM Camarillo, CA; KFYV(FM) Ojai, CA; KCAQ(FM) Oxnard, CA; KVTA Port Hueneme, CA; KKZZ(AM) Santa Paula, CA; KUNX(AM) Ventura, CA.
    John Q. Hearne, chmn; Miles Sexton, pres.

Golden West Broadcasting Ltd., Box 950, Altona, MB R0G 0B0. Canada. Phone: (204) 324-6464. Fax: (204) 324-8918.E-mail: info@cfamradio.com Ownership Elmer Hildebrand Ltd., 50%; Elmer Hildebrand, 13.81%; and others, 36.19%.
    Stns: 13 AM. 17 FM. CHOO-FM Drumheller, AB; CHRB High River, AB; CFXO-FM High River-Okotoks, AB; CKUV-FM High River-Okotoks, AB; CKVN-FM Lethbridge, AB; CFAM Altona, MB; CJRB Boissevain, MB; CFRY Portage la Prairie, MB; CFRY-FM Portage la Prairie, MB; CJPG-FM Portage la Prairie, MB; CHSM Steinbach, MB; CILT-FM Steinbach, MB; CJEL-FM Winkler, MB; CKMW Winkler-Morden, MB; CHVN-FM Winnipeg, MB; CFEQ-FM Winnipeg, MB; CHSN-FM Estevan, SK; CJSL Estevan, SK; CFYM Kindersley, SK; CKVX-FM Kindersley, SK; CILG-FM Moose Jaw, SK; CJAW-FM Moose Jaw, SK; CHAB Moose Jaw, SK; CJYM Rosetown, SK; CJSN Shaunavon, SK; CKSW Swift Current, SK; CIMG-FM Swift Current, SK; CKFI-FM Swift Current, SK; CKRC-FM Weybum, SK; CFSL Weyburn, SK.
    Elmer Hildebrand, pres/CEO; Menno Friesen, VP; Lyndon Friesen, VP.

Good Karma Broadcasting L.L.C., Box 902, Beaver Dam, WI 53916. Phone: (920) 885-4442. Fax: (920) 885-2152. Ownership Craig Karmazin, 100%
    Stns: 8 AM. 3 FM. WEFL(AM) Tequesta, FL; WTJK South Beloit, IL; WKNR(AM) Cleveland, OH; WWGK(AM) Cleveland, OH; WBEV Beaver Dam, WI; WXRO-FM Beaver Dam, WI; WTTN(AM) Columbus, WI; WTLX(FM) Columbus, WI; WWHG(FM) Evansville, WI; WAUK(AM) Jackson, WI; WRRD(AM) Waukesha, WI.
    Rick Armon, opns dir; Chris Hartl, business mgr; Craig Karmazin, gen mgr .

Good News Communications Inc., 3222 S. Richey Ave., Tucson, AZ 85713. Phone: (520) 790-2440. Fax: (520) 790-2937.
    Stns: 5 AM. KVOI(AM) Cortaro, AZ; KAPR Douglas, AZ; KNXN Sierra Vista, AZ; KCEE(AM) Tucson, AZ; KGMS(AM) Tucson, AZ.
    Douglas E. Martin, pres; Mary R. Martin, sec.

Good News Media Inc., Box 1400, Traverse City, MI 49685-1400. Phone: (231) 946-1400. Fax: (231) 946-3959. Web Site:www.wljn.com
    Stns: 2 AM. 1 FM. WLJW(AM) Cadillac, MI; WLJN Elmwood Township, MI; WLJN-FM Traverse City, MI.
    Doug Knorr, pres.

Good News Network, 2278 Wortham Lane, Grovetown, GA 30813-5103. Phone: (706) 309-9610. Fax: (706) 309-9669.E-mail: ctbarinowski@comcast.net Web Site:www.gnnradio.org
    Stns: 1 AM. 8 FM. WQRX Valley Head, AL; WPMA(FM) Buckhead, GA; WPWB(FM) Byron, GA; WWGF-FM Donalsonville, GA; WTHP(FM) Gibson, GA; WLPF-FM Ocilla, GA; WZIQ-FM Smithville, GA; WGPH(FM) Vidalia, GA; WLGP-FM Harkers Island, NC.
    Clarence Barinowski, pres/CEO.

GoodRadio.TV, 777 S. Flagler Dr., Suite 800, West Palm Beach, FL 33401. Phone: (561) 515-6142.E-mail: info@goodradio.tv Web Site:goodradio.tv
    Stns: 11 AM. 12 FM. KKFD-FM Fairfield, IA; KMCD

Fairfield, IA; KGRN Grinnell, IA; KRTI(FM) Grinnell, IA; KCOB Newton, IA; KCOB-FM Newton, IA; KAAN Bethany, MO; KAAN-FM Bethany, MO; KMRN Cameron, MO; KKWK(FM) Cameron, MO; KREI Farmington, MO; KTJJ-FM Farmington, MO; KJFF(AM) Festus, MO; KBNN Lebanon, MO; KJEL-FM Lebanon, MO; KIRK-FM Macon, MO; KCDG(FM) Madison, MO; KWIX Moberly, MO; KRES(FM) Moberly, MO; KJPW Waynesville, MO; KIIK-FM Waynesville, MO; KOZQ Waynesville, MO; KFBD-FM Waynesville, MO.
    Dean Goodman, CEO.

Gore-Overgaard Broadcasting Inc., 11310 E. Arabian Park Dr., Scottsdale, AZ 85259. Phone: (480) 314-0144. Fax: (480) 314-4942. Ownership Cordell Overgaard, Harold Gore.
    Stns: 5 AM. KLHC(AM) Bakersfield, CA; KBIF Fresno, CA; KIRV Fresno, CA; WROD Daytona Beach, FL; WSBB New Smyrna Beach, FL.
    Harold W. Gore, chmn/CEO; Cordell J. Overgaard, pres.

Grace Broadcasting Services Inc., 25 Stonebrook Pl., Suite G, #322, Jackson, TN 38305. Phone: (731) 663-3931. Fax: (731) 663-9804. Web Site:www.gracebroadcasting.com Ownership Charles Ennis, 55.8%; Lacy Ennis, 31.1%; Ray Smith, 7.5%; Dr. Buck Morton, 1.9%; and Phillip Chambers, 0.2%. Note: Group also owns 50% of WTRB(AM) Ripley, TN.
    Stns: 3 AM. 5 FM. WWGM(FM) Alamo, TN; WTKB-FM Atwood, TN; WNKX Centerville, TN; WFGZ-FM Lobelville, TN; WSIB-FM Selmer, TN; WDTM Selmer, TN; WTNE Trenton, TN; WTNE-FM Trenton, TN.

Graham Newspapers Inc., 620 Oak St., Graham, TX 76450. Phone: (940) 549-1330. Fax: (940) 549-8628.E-mail: gm@kwkq-kswa.com
    Stns: 2 AM. 2 FM. KLXK(FM) Breckenridge, TX; KROO(AM) Breckenridge, TX; KSWA(AM) Graham, TX; KWKQ(FM) Graham, TX.
    Joe Graham, gen mgr .

Great Eastern Radio LLC, 35 S. Main St., Suite 300, Hanover, NH 03755. Phone: (603) 643-4007. Ownership Jeffrey D. Shapiro, 51%; and Courtney S. Galluzzo, 49%.
    Stns: 1 AM. 6 FM. WTSL(AM) Hanover, NH; WGXL-FM Hanover, NH; WTPL(FM) Hillsboro, NH; WXXK-FM Lebanon, NH; WEEY(FM) Springfield, VT; WKKN(FM) Westminster, VT; WMXR-FM Woodstock, VT.

Great Lakes Radio Inc., 2025 US 41 W., Marquette, MI 49855. Phone: (906) 227-7777. Phone: (906) 228-6800. Fax: (906) 475-8888. Fax: (906) 228-8128.E-mail: todd@greatlakesradio.org Web Site:www.greatlakesradio.org
    Stns: 1 AM. 4 FM. WPIQ(FM) Manistique, MI; WFXD-FM Marquette, MI; WRUP-FM Munising, MI; WQXO Munising, MI; WKQS-FM Negaunee, MI.
    Todd S. Noordyk, pres.

Great Plains Media Inc., Box 1628, Cape Girardeau, MO 63702-1628. Phone: (573) 651-0707. Ownership Jerome R. Zimmer Revocable Trust U/A/D October 14, 1977, sole trustee, Jerome R. Zimmer, 100%.
    Stns: 3 AM. 7 FM. WRPW(FM) Colfax, IL; WYST(FM) Fairbury, IL; WDQZ(FM) Lexington, IL; KLWN(AM) Lawrence, KS; KLZR(FM) Lawrence, KS; KMXN(FM) Osage City, KS; WPTN Cookeville, TN; WGIC-FM Cookeville, TN; WGSQ-FM Cookeville, TN; WHUB Cookeville, TN.
    Jerome R. Zimmer, pres.

Great Scott Broadcasting, 224 Maugers Mill Rd., Pottstown, PA 19464. Phone: (610) 326-4000. Fax: (610) 326-7984.E-mail: jay.warren@1370wpaz.com Web Site:www.1370wpaz.com Ownership Faye Scott, special trustee, Charles Mott & James Worthington, co-trustees, Family Trust U/D/T dated 11/6/81, 86.72% of total assets; Faye Scott Annuity Trust U/D/T dated 3/6/02, Charles Mott & James Worthington, co-trustees, 6.64% of total assets; Faye Scott & James Worthington, co-trustees, Marital Trust U/D/T dated 11/6/81, 100% of votes, 0.98% of total assets.
    Stns: 3 AM. 8 FM. WPAZ Pottstown, PA; WOCQ-FM Berlin, MD; WKHI(FM) Fruitland, MD; WXSH(FM) Pocomoke City, MD; WJKI(FM) Bethany Beach, DE; WJWL Georgetown, DE; WZBH-FM Georgetown, DE; WKDB(FM) Laurel, DE; WZEB(FM) Ocean View, DE; WGBG-FM Seaford, DE; WJWK Seaford, DE.
    Faye Scott, CEO; Jay Warren, gen mgr .

Greater Media Inc., 35 Braintree Hill Office Park, Suite 300, Braintree, MA 02184. Phone: (781) 348-8600. Fax: (781) 348-8680. Web Site:www.greatermedia.com Ownership Bordes family, 100%.
    Stns: 5 AM. 17 FM. WTKK(FM) Boston, MA; WMJX-FM Boston, MA; WBOS-FM Brookline, MA; WROR-FM Framingham, MA; WKLB-FM Waltham, MA; WCSX-FM

Birmingham, MI; WRIF(FM) Detroit, MI; WMGC-FM Detroit, MI; WBT Charlotte, NC; WLNK(FM) Charlotte, NC; WWTR(AM) Bridgewater, NJ; WNUW(FM) Burlington, NJ; WDHA-FM Dover, NJ; WJRZ-FM Manahawkin, NJ; WMTR(AM) Morristown, NJ; WMGQ(FM) New Brunswick, NJ; WCTC(AM) New Brunswick, NJ; WRAT(FM) Point Pleasant, NJ; WPEN Philadelphia, PA; WBEN-FM Philadelphia, PA; WMMR-FM Philadelphia, PA; WBT-FM Chester, SC.

Greater Media, Inc. owns 100% of The Sentinel Publishing Co., publisher of twelve weekly newspapers: the *Sentinel* of East Brunswick, the *Edison/Metuchen Sentinel*, the *Woodbridge Sentinel*, the *North/South Brunswick Sentinel*, the *Atlanticville* of Long Branch, the *Bulletin* of Brick Township, the *Examiner* of Allentown, the *Hub* of Red Bank, the *Independent* of Middletown, the *News Transcript* of Freehold, the *Suburban* of Sayreville, and the *Tri-Town News* of Howell, Lakewood, Jackson and Plumsted, all NJ.

Peter H. Smyth, chmn.

Greeley Broadcasting Corp., 1020 9th St., Suite 201, Greeley, CO 80631. Phone: (970) 356-1452. Fax: (970) 356-8522. Ownership Ricardo Salazar, 100%. Note: Group has a time brokerage agreement for the operation of KRYE(FM) Rye, CO.
Stns: 1 AM. 2 FM. KGRE Greeley, CO; KFVR-FM La Junta, CO; KLMI(FM) Rock River, WY.

Ricardo Salazar, pres.

Green County Broadcasting, W4765 Radio Ln., Monroe, WI 53566. Phone: (608) 325-2161. Fax: (608) 325-2164. Ownership Scott Thompson, 75%; and Ronald Spielman, 25%. Note: Scott Thompson owns 75% and Ronald Spielman owns 25% of WQLF(FM) Lena, IL.
Stns: 2 AM. 2 FM. WFPS-FM Freeport, IL; WFRL Freeport, IL; WEKZ Monroe, WI; WEKZ-FM Monroe, WI.

Grenax Broadcasting LLC, 10337 Carriage Club Dr., Lone Tree, CO 80124. Phone: (303) 790-4015. Ownership Greg Dinetz, 100% of votes.
Stns: 2 AM. 2 FM. WFPS-FM Freeport, IL; WFRL Freeport, IL; WEKZ Monroe, WI; WEKZ-FM Monroe, WI4 FM. KFLX-FM Kachina Village, AZ; KSED-FM Sedona, AZ; KWMX-FM Williams, AZ; WCFX(FM) Clare, MI.

Greg Dinetz, pres.

Guaranty Broadcasting Co. of Baton Rouge, LLC, Box 2231, Baton Rouge, LA 70821. Phone: (225) 388-9898 ext 148. Fax: (225) 344-3077. E-mail: owen.weber@gbcradio.com Ownership Guaranty Broadcasting Company LLC, 100%.
Stns: 2 AM. 2 FM. WFPS-FM Freeport, IL; WFRL Freeport, IL; WEKZ Monroe, WI; WEKZ-FM Monroe, WI4 FM. KFLX-FM Kachina Village, AZ; KSED-FM Sedona, AZ; KWMX-FM Williams, AZ; WCFX(FM) Clare, MI5 FM. WTGE(FM) Baker, LA; WYPY(FM) Baton Rouge, LA; WDGL(FM) Baton Rouge, LA; KNXX(FM) Donaldsonville, LA; WNXX(FM) Jackson, LA.

Owen Weber, VP.

Guyann Corp., Box 1930, Flagstaff, AZ 86002. Phone: (928) 774-5231. Fax: (928) 779-2988. Web Site:www.kaff.com Ownership Richard D. Guest, 50%; Pamela Flaherty, 50%. Note: Richard D. Guest and Pamela Flaherty are co-special administrators.
Stns: 2 AM. 3 FM. KAFF Flagstaff, AZ; KAFF-FM Flagstaff, AZ; KMGN-FM Flagstaff, AZ; KNOT(AM) Prescott, AZ; KTMG(FM) Prescott, AZ.

H

HRN Broadcasting Inc., Box 430, Lincolnton, NC 28093. Phone: (704) 735-8071. Fax: (704) 732-9567. Web Site:www.hrnb.com
Stns: 6 AM. WZGM(AM) Black Mountain, NC; WCSL Cherryville, NC; WGNC Gastonia, NC; WLON Lincolnton, NC; WOHS Shelby, NC; WADA Shelby, NC.

Haliburton Broadcasting Group Inc., 46 Nanton Ave., Toronto, ON M4W 2Y9. Canada. Phone: (416) 925-0488. Fax: (416) 925-6256. Web Site:www.hbgradio.com Ownership Beaumaris Group Inc., 70.1%; and Standard Radio Inc., 29.9%.
Stns: 6 AM. WZGM(AM) Black Mountain, NC; WCSL Cherryville, NC; WGNC Gastonia, NC; WLON Lincolnton, NC; WOHS Shelby, NC; WADA Shelby, NC12 FM. CHMS-FM Bancroft, ON; CFBG-FM Bracebridge, ON; CHPB-FM Cochrane, ON; CKNR-FM Elliot Lake, ON; CKJN-FM Haldimand County, ON; CFZN-FM Haliburton, ON; CFBK-FM Huntsville, ON; CFIF-FM Iroquois Falls, ON; CKAP-FM Kapuskasing, ON; CFXN-FM North Bay, ON; CKLP-FM Parry Sound, ON; CHMT-FM Timmins, ON.

Christopher Grossman, pres; Kim Ward, VP opns mgr.

Hall Communications Inc., Box 2038, 404 W. Lime St., Lakeland, FL 33806. Phone: (863) 682-8184. Fax: (863) 683-2409. Web Site:www.hallradio.com Ownership Bonnie Hall Rowbotham.
Stns: 8 AM. 13 FM. WNLC-FM East Lyme, CT; WKNL(FM) New London, CT; WICH(AM) Norwich, CT; WCTY(FM) Norwich, CT; WILI-FM Willimantic, CT; WILI(AM) Willimantic, CT; WWRZ-FM Fort Meade, FL; WONN(AM) Lakeland, FL; WLKF(AM) Lakeland, FL; WPCV(FM) Winter Haven, FL; WCTK(FM) New Bedford, MA; WNBH New Bedford, MA; WKOL-FM Plattsburgh, NY; WBTZ-FM Plattsburgh, NY; WROZ-FM Lancaster, PA; WLPA Lancaster, PA; WSJW(FM) Starview, PA; WLKW(AM) West Warwick, RI; WJOY(AM) Burlington, VT; WOKO-FM Burlington, VT; WIZN-FM Vergennes, VT.

Arthur J. Rowbotham, pres; Bonnie Hall Rowbotham, chmn; Bill Baldwin, exec VP.

Harvard Broadcasting Inc., Century Plaza, 1900 Rose Dt., Regina, SK S4P 0A9. Canada. Phone: (306) 546-6200. Fax: (306) 781-7338. E-mail: rpettigrew @harvardbroadcasting.com Web Site:www.harvardbroadcasting.com Ownership Harvard Developments Inc., 100%.
Stns: 1 AM. 5 FM. CFEX-FM Calgary, AB; CFVR-FM Fort McMurray, AB; CFWF-FM Regina, SK; CHMX-FM Regina, SK; CKRM(AM) Regina, SK; CFWD-FM Saskatoon, SK.

Bruce Cowie, VP; Michael Olstrom, gen mgr .

Haugo Broadcasting Inc., Box 1680, Rapid City, SD 57709. Phone: (605) 343-0888. Fax: (605) 342-3075.
Stns: 1 AM. 1 FM. KSQY-FM Deadwood, SD; KTOQ Rapid City, SD.

Chris Haugo, pres.

Heartland Christian Broadcasters Inc., Box 433, International Falls, MN 56649. Phone: (218) 285-7398. Fax: (218) 285-7419. Ownership Chuck Scherer, 20%; Dan Griffith, 20%; Jim Hummel, 20%; Mike Worth, 20%; and Tom Wherley, 20%.
Stns: 1 AM. 1 FM. KSQY-FM Deadwood, SD; KTOQ Rapid City, SD3 FM. KADU(FM) Hibbing, MN; KBHW(FM) International Falls, MN; KXBR(FM) International Falls, MN.

Heartland Communications Group LLC, 4650 W. Spencer St., Appleton, WI 54914. Phone: (920) 882-4750. Fax: (920) 882-4751. Web Site:www.heartlandcomm.com Ownership Granite Equity L.P., 44.05% equity; The Thomas L. Bookey Family L.P., 38.57% equity; Granite/Heartland Co-Investment L.P., 10.57% equity; and James L. Gregori, 6.81% equity. Note: Group is managed by a five-member board of governors.
Stns: 5 AM. 8 FM. WOLV-FM Houghton, MI; WCCY Houghton, MI; WHKB(FM) Houghton, MI; WIKB Iron River, MI; WIKB-FM Iron River, MI; WJJH-FM Ashland, WI; WATW Ashland, WI; WBSZ(FM) Ashland, WI; WRJO-FM Eagle River, WI; WERL Eagle River, WI; WNXR(FM) Iron River, WI; WCQM-FM Park Falls, WI; WNBI Park Falls, WI.

Tom Bookey, CEO; James Gregori, pres.

Charles A. Hecht and Alfredo Alonso Stns, 16 Doe Run, Pittstown, NJ 08867. Phone: (908) 730-7959. Fax: (908) 730-7408. E-mail: hechtassoc@sprintmail.com Ownership Alfredo Alonso, 50%; and Charles A. Hecht, 50%.
Stns: 3 AM. WRME(AM) Hampden, ME; WVNC(AM) Masonboro, NC; WVVT(AM) Essex Junction, VT.

He's Alive Inc., Box 540, Grantsville, MD 21536. Phone: (301) 895-3292. Fax: (301) 895-3293. E-mail: hesalive@hesalive.net Web Site:www.hesalive.net Ownership Non-stock, nonprofit organization.
Stns: 3 AM. WRME(AM) Hampden, ME; WVNC(AM) Masonboro, NC; WVVT(AM) Essex Junction, VT4 FM. WRIJ(FM) Masontown, PA; WPCL(FM) Northern Cambria, PA; WLIC-FM Frostburg, MD; WAIJ-FM Grantsville, MD.

Dewayne Johnson, pres.

Bennie E. Hewett Stns, Box 907670, Gainesville, GA 30501-0911. Phone: (770) 519-0082. Fax: (770) 536-4103. Ownership Bennie Hewett.
Stns: 1 AM. 2 FM. WBMH(FM) Grove Hill, AL; WRJX(AM) Jackson, AL; WHOD(FM) Jackson, AL.

Bennie E. Hewett, pres.

Hi-Favor Broadcasting LLC, 136 S. Oak Knoll Ave., Pasadena, CA 91101. Phone: (626) 356-4230. Fax: (626) 795-9185. Ownership Daisy Publishing Co. Inc., Pasadena, CA, 100%.
Stns: 3 AM. KLTX Long Beach, CA; KEZY(AM) San Bernardino, CA; KSDO San Diego, CA.

High Desert Broadcasting LLC, 570 East Ave. Q9, Palmdale, CA 93550. Phone: (661) 947-3107. Fax: (661) 272-5688. Ownership John Hearne.
Stns: 2 AM. 3 FM. KGMX-FM Lancaster, CA; KOSS(AM) Lancaster, CA; KUTY Palmdale, CA; KLKX-FM Rosamond, CA; KKZQ-FM Tehachapi, CA.

Miles Sexton, pres.

Hispanic Target Media Inc., c/o Lerman Senter PLLC, 2000 K St. N.W., Suite 600, Washington, DC 20006-1809. Phone: (202) 429-8970. Fax: (202) 293-7783. Ownership Francisco San Millan, 80.4%.
Stns: 2 AM. 3 FM. KGMX-FM Lancaster, CA; KOSS(AM) Lancaster, CA; KUTY Palmdale, CA; KLKX-FM Rosamond, CA; KKZQ-FM Tehachapi, CA5 FM. KRIK(FM) Perry, FL; KALN(FM) Dexter, NM; KAJP(FM) Carrizo Springs, TX; KGWT(FM) George West, TX; KJJS(FM) Zapata, TX.

Francisco San Millan, pres.

Holladay Broadcasting of Louisiana LLC, Box 4808, Monroe, LA 71211. Phone: (318) 398-1618. Ownership Robert H. Holladay, 100%.
Stns: 2 AM. 5 FM. KJMG-FM Bastrop, LA; KRVV-FM Bastrop, LA; KJLO-FM Monroe, LA; KLIP-FM Monroe, LA; KMLB(AM) Monroe, LA; KRJO(AM) Monroe, LA; KLSM(FM) Tallulah, LA.

Robert Holladay, member.

Holy Family Communications, 6325 Sheridan Dr., Williamsville, NY 14221. Phone: (716) 839-6117. Fax: (716) 839-0400. Web Site:www.wlof.net Ownership James N. Wright, 33.33%; Joanne Wright, 33.33%; and Mary Ellen Capece, 33.33%.
Stns: 2 AM. 1 FM. WLOF(FM) Attica, NY; WHIC(AM) Rochester, NY; WQOR(AM) Olyphant, PA.

James N. Wright, pres.

Hoosier Broadcasting Corp., 3500 DePauw Blvd., Suite 2085, Indianapolis, IN 46268-6103. Phone: (317) 870-8400. Fax: (317) 870-8404.
Stns: 2 AM. 1 FM. WLOF(FM) Attica, NY; WHIC(AM) Rochester, NY; WQOR(AM) Olyphant, PA3 FM. WSPM(FM) Cloverdale, IN; WCNB(FM) Lebanon, IN; WIRE-FM Lebanon, IN.

William S. Poorman, pres.

Horizon Broadcasting Group LLC, 854 N.E. 4th St., Bend, OR 97701. Phone: (541) 383-3825. Fax: (541) 383-3403. Web Site:www.horizonbroadcasting.com
Stns: 1 AM. 4 FM. KQAK(FM) Bend, OR; KRCO(AM) Prineville, OR; KLTW-FM Prineville, OR; KWPK-FM Sisters, OR; KWLZ-FM Warm Springs, OR.

Keith Shipman, pres/CEO.

Horizon Christian Fellowship, 5331 Mt. Alifan Dr., San Diego, CA 92111. Phone: (858) 277-4991. Fax: (858) 277-1365. Web Site:www.horizonsd.org/radio.asp Ownership Rudy Batiz, 9.09% votes; Jeries El Raheb, 9.09% votes; Gayle Gordon, 9.09% votes; Larry Gordon, 9.09% votes; Michael MacIntosh, 9.09% votes; Phillip MacIntosh, 9.09% votes; Victor Najor, 9.09% votes; Tom Phillips, 9.09% votes; Fred Salley, 9.09% votes; Hank Sybrandy, 9.09% votes; and Mike Turk, 9.09% votes.
Stns: 1 AM. 4 FM. KQAK(FM) Bend, OR; KRCO(AM) Prineville, OR; KLTW-FM Prineville, OR; KWPK-FM Sisters, OR; KWLZ-FM Warm Springs, OR25 FM. KHZK(FM) Kotzebue, AK; KHZX(FM) Yakutat, AK; WVUV-FM Fagaitua, AS; KWDS(FM) Kettleman City, CA; KWDI(FM) Idalia, CO; KWDN(FM) Newell, IA; WDVL(FM) Danville, IN; WWDL(FM) Lebanon, IN; WRYP(FM) Wellfleet, MA; WTNP(FM) Richland, MI; KHZA(FM) Bunker, MO; KSRD(FM) Saint Joseph, MO; WCMR-FM Bruce, MS; KWDV(FM) Valier, MT; KHRU(FM) Beulah, ND; KCVG(FM) Medina, ND; KCVD(FM) New England, ND; KCVF(FM) Sarles, ND; KHZY(FM) Overton, NE; KHZZ(FM) Sargent, NE; KWDC(FM) Coahoma, TX; KWDR(FM) Royal City, WA; WDSW(FM) Westby, WI; KWDU(FM) Upton, WY; KHRW(FM) Wright, WY.

Tom Phillips, COO.

Horne Radio Group, 517 Watt Rd., Knoxville, TN 37922. Phone: (865) 675-4105. Fax: (865) 675-4859. E-mail: knoxvilletalk@aol.com Web Site:www.wkvl.com
Stns: 6 AM. 1 FM. WMTY(AM) Farragut, TN; WKVL(AM) Knoxville, TN; WLOD Loudon, TN; WFIV-FM Loudon, TN; WGAP Maryville, TN; WATO Oak Ridge, TN; WDEH Sweetwater, TN.

Douglas A. Horne, pres.

Houston Christian Broadcasters Inc., KHCB Network, 2424 South Blvd., Houston, TX 77098-5110. Phone: (713) 520-5200. Web Site:www.khcb.org E-mail: email@khcb.org
Stns: 2 AM. 19 FM. KHCX(FM) Soda Springs, ID; KHCL(FM) Arcadia, LA; KHMD(FM) Mansfield, LA; KHIB(FM) Bastrop, TX; KHVT(FM) Bloomington, TX; KHBW(FM)

Brownwood, TX; KALD(FM) Caldwell, TX; KHPS(FM) Camp Wood, TX; KBLC(FM) Fredericksburg, TX; KHCB Galveston, TX; KANJ(FM) Giddings, TX; KHCB-FM Houston, TX; KHCH(AM) Huntsville, TX; KHCJ(FM) Jefferson, TX; KHKV(FM) Kerrville, TX; KKER(FM) Kerrville, TX; KHML(FM) Madisonville, TX; KHCP(FM) Paris, TX; KHPO(FM) Port O'Connor, TX; KCPC(FM) Sealy, TX; KHTA(FM) Wake Village, TX.

Bruce E. Munsterman, pres & gen mgr; Bonnie C. BeMent, asst gen mgr.

Hubbard Broadcasting Inc., 3415 University Ave., St. Paul, MN 55114. Phone: (651) 646-5555. Fax: (651) 642-4103. E-mail: jmahoney@hbi.com

Stns: 2 AM. 2 FM. WFMP(FM) Coon Rapids, MN; KSTP(AM) Saint Paul, MN; KSTP-FM Saint Paul, MN; WIXK(AM) New Richmond, WI.

Stns: 13 TV. WNYT, Albany-Schenectady-Troy, NY; KOBG-TV, Albuquerque-Santa Fe, NM; KOB, Albuquerque-Santa Fe, NM; KOBF, Albuquerque-Santa Fe, NM; KOBR, Albuquerque-Santa Fe, NM; WDIO-DT, Duluth, MN-Superior, WI; WIRT-DT, Duluth, MN-Superior, WI; KRWF, Minneapolis-St. Paul, MN; KSAX, Minneapolis-St. Paul, MN; KSTP, Minneapolis-St. Paul, MN; KSTC-TV, Minneapolis-St. Paul, MN; KAAL, Rochester, MN-Mason City, IA-Austin, MN; WHEC, Rochester, NY.

Stanley E. Hubbard, chmn/pres/CEO; Stanley I. Hubbard II, VP; Virginia H. Morris, VP; Robert W. Hubbard, VP; Julia D. Coyte, VP; Gerald D. Deeney, sr VP/treas/CFO; Harold C. Crump, VP; C. Thomas Newberry, VP; Linda S. Tremere, VP; Sue J. Cook, VP; Edward J. Aiken, VP; Kari Rominski, sec; Gary R. Macomber, asst sec.

Huth Broadcasting, Box 669, Marysville, CA 95901. Phone: (530) 742-5555. Fax: (530) 741-3758. Ownership Tom F. Huth, 100%. Note: Tom F. Huth owns 49.9% of the stock of Sierra Radio Inc., licensee of KTOR(AM) Westwood, CA.

Stns: 4 AM. KMYC(AM) Marysville, CA; KPCO Quincy, CA; KBLF Red Bluff, CA; KOBO Yuba City, CA.

Hutton Broadcasting LLC, 915 Orchid Point Way, Vero Beach, FL 32963-9518. Phone: (772) 559-3790. Ownership Edward B. Hutton, 50%; and George S. Hutton, 50%.

Stns: 1 AM. 4 FM. KBAC(FM) Las Vegas, NM; KQBA(FM) Los Alamos, NM; KLBU(FM) Pecos, NM; KVSF-FM Pecos, NM; KVSF(AM) Santa Fe, NM.

Scott Hutton, gen mgr; Jennifer Owens Hutton, owner/mgr.

I

IHR Educational Broadcasting, Box 180, Tahoma, CA 96142. Phone: (530) 584-5700. Fax: (530) 584-5705. E-mail: info@ihradio.org Web Site:www.ihradio.org

Stns: 10 AM. 2 FM. KAHI Auburn, CA; KCIK(AM) Blue Lake, CA; KIHH(AM) Eureka, CA; KJPG(AM) Frazier Park, CA; KPJP(FM) Greenville, CA; KJOP Lemoore, CA; KSFB(AM) San Francisco, CA; KWG(AM) Stockton, CA; KSMH(AM) West Sacramento, CA; KXXQ(FM) Milan, NM; KIHM(AM) Reno, NV; KIHU(AM) Tooele, UT.

Icicle Broadcasting Inc., 7475 KOHO Pl., Leavenworth, WA 98826. Phone: (509) 548-1011. Fax: (509) 548-3222. Web Site:www.kohoradio.com

Stns: 1 AM. 3 FM. KOZI Chelan, WA; KOZI-FM Chelan, WA; KOHO-FM Leavenworth, WA; KZAL(FM) Manson, WA.

Gary Mathews, gen mgr .

Idaho Wireless Corp., Box 97, Pocatello, ID 83204. Phone: (208) 234-1290. Fax: (208) 234-9451.

Stns: 1 AM. 2 FM. KORR-FM American Falls, ID; KOUU(AM) Pocatello, ID; KZBQ(FM) Pocatello, ID.

Paul Anderson, gen mgr .

IdaVend Broadcasting Inc., 805 Stewart Ave., Lewiston, ID 83501. Phone: (208) 743-1551. Fax: (208) 743-4440. E-mail: rprasil@idavend.com Ownership Robert Prasil; Gary Prasil; Dorothy Prasil.

Stns: 1 AM. 2 FM. KMOK(FM) Lewiston, ID; KRLC Lewiston, ID; KVTY-FM Lewiston, ID.

Robert Prasil, gen mgr; Zoanne Davis, traffic dir; Ben Bonfield, gen sls mgr; Darin Siebert, opns dir; Melva Prasil, stn mgr.

Illinois Bible Institute Inc., Box 140, Carlinville, IL 62626. Phone: (217) 854-4600. Fax: (217) 854-4610. E-mail: rwhitworth@idcag.org Web Site:www.wibi.org

Stns: 1 AM. 7 FM. KMOK(FM) Lewiston, ID; KRLC Lewiston, ID; KVTY-FM Lewiston, ID8 FM. WTSG-FM Carlinville, IL; WIBI-FM Carlinville, IL; WBGL-FM Champaign, IL; WZGL(FM) Charleston, IL; WBMV-FM Mount Vernon, IL; WCIC-FM Pekin, IL; WPRC(FM) Princeton, IL; WCRT-FM

Terre Haute, IN.

Richard C. Whitworth, dir.

Impact Radio LLC, 59750 Constantine Rd., Three Rivers, MI 49093-9303. Phone: (269) 278-1815. Fax: (269) 273-7975. E-mail: drumsey@wlkm.com Ownership Dennis W. Rumsey.

Stns: 2 AM. 2 FM. WRCI(AM) Three Rivers, MI; WLKM-FM Three Rivers, MI; WQCT Bryan, OH; WBNO-FM Bryan, OH.

Dennis W. Rumsey, pres.

Independence Media Holdings LLC, 8226 Douglas Ave., Suite 627, Dallas, TX 75225. Phone: (469) 619-1001. Ownership Seaport Capital Partners III AIV L.P., 33.3% votes, 73.32% total assets; Seaport IMH Blocker Corp., 33.3% votes, 24.58% total assets; David F. Jacobs, 33.3% votes, 1.96% total assets.

Stns: 1 AM. 6 FM. WOCN Miami, FL; WWCT(FM) Bartonville, IL; WPIA(FM) Eureka, IL; WZPN(FM) Farmington, IL; WHPI(FM) Glasford, IL; WNUY(FM) Bluffton, IN; WWKN(FM) Morgantown, KY.

Information Communications Corp., Box 2061, Bristol, TN 37621-2061. Phone: (423) 878-6279. Fax: (423) 878-6520. Ownership Kenneth C. Hill, 51%; and Appalachian Educational Communication Corp., 49%.

Stns: 3 AM. WPWT(AM) Colonial Heights, TN; WHGG(AM) Kingsport, TN; WABN Abingdon, VA.

Dr. Kenneth C. Hill, pres/CEO.

Ingstad Brothers Broadcasting LLC, Box 1248, Minnetonka, MN 55345. Phone: (952) 938-0575. Fax: (952) 938-2295. Ownership Thomas E. Ingstad, 49%; Tor Ingstad, 49%; and Randy K. Holland, 2%.

Stns: 3 AM. 2 FM. KCHK New Prague, MN; KRDS-FM New Prague, MN; KNUJ(AM) New Ulm, MN; KYMN Northfield, MN; KNUJ-FM Sleepy Eye, MN.

Robert Ingstad Broadcast Properties, Box 994, Valley City, ND 58072. Phone: (701) 845-1490. Fax: (701) 845-1245. Ownership the estate of Robert E. Ingstad, Janice M. Ingstad, Robert J. Ingstad and Todd M. Ingstad.

Stns: 8 AM. 14 FM. KSKZ(FM) Copeland, KS; KKJQ-FM Garden City, KS; KBUF(AM) Holcomb, KS; KFXX-FM Hugoton, KS; KSSA-FM Ingalls, KS; KWKR(FM) Leoti, KS; KSKL-FM Scott City, KS; KULY Ulysses, KS; KXGT(FM) Carrington, ND; KDAK Carrington, ND; KQZZ-FM Devils Lake, ND; KQDJ Jamestown, ND; KYNU(FM) Jamestown, ND; KDDR Oakes, ND; KOVC Valley City, ND; KRVX(FM) Wimbledon, ND; KJBI(FM) Fort Pierre, SD; KMLO-FM Lowry, SD; KOLY Mobridge, SD; KGFX Pierre, SD; KGFX-FM Pierre, SD; KPLO-FM Reliance, SD.

Tom Ingstad Broadcasting Group, Box 1248, Minnetonka, MN 55345. Phone: (952) 938-0575. Fax: (952) 938-2295.

Stns: 4 AM. 4 FM. KARP-FM Dassel, MN; KKRC-FM Granite Falls, MN; KDUZ Hutchinson, MN; KDMA Montevideo, MN; KMGM-FM Montevideo, MN; KMRS Morris, MN; KRVY-FM Starbuck, MN; KKAQ Thief River Falls, MN.

Tom Ingstad, pres/CEO.

Inland Northwest Broadcasting LLC, 805 Stewart Ave., Lewiston, ID 83501. Phone: (208) 791-2605. Fax: (208) 743-4440. E-mail: rprasil@idavend.com Ownership Robert Prasil, 50%; and Melva Prasil, 50%.

Stns: 2 AM. 2 FM. KCLX Colfax, WA; KMAX Colfax, WA; KRAO-FM Colfax, WA; KZZL-FM Pullman, WA.

Robert Prasil, pres; Gary Cummings, VP/owner; Michelle King, dir opns; Steve Franko, chief engr.

Inner Banks Media LLC, 408 W. Arlington Blvd., Suite 101-B, Greenville, NC 27834. Phone: (252) 355-8822. Ownership Donald W. Curtis, 50%; Henry Williams Hinton Jr., 40%; and Henry Williams Hinton III, 10%.

Stns: 2 AM. 2 FM. KCLX Colfax, WA; KMAX Colfax, WA; KRAO-FM Colfax, WA; KZZL-FM Pullman, WA WA4 FM. WTIB(AM) Farmville, NC; WRHT-FM Morehead City, NC; WNBU(FM) Oriental, NC; WRHD(FM) Williamston, NC.

Inner City Broadcasting, 3 Park Ave., 41st Fl., New York, NY 10016. Phone: (212) 447-1000. Fax: (212) 447-5197. E-mail: info@wbls.com Web Site:www.wbls.com

Stns: 7 AM. 10 FM. KBLX-FM Berkeley, CA; KVTO Berkeley, CA; KVVN Santa Clara, CA; WJMI-FM Jackson, MS; WJQS(AM) Jackson, MS; WOAD Jackson, MS; WKXI-FM Magee, MS; WJNT Pearl, MS; WZNO(FM) Pickens, MS; WBLS-FM New York, NY; WLIB New York, NY; WZMJ-FM Batesburg, SC; WOIC(AM) Columbia, SC; WARQ(FM) Columbia, SC; WHXT-FM Orangeburg, SC; WMFX(FM) Saint Andrews, SC; WWDM(FM) Sumter, SC.

Pierre Sutton, chmn/CEO.

Inter-Island Communications Inc., 1868 Halsey Dr., Piti, GU 96915. Phone: (671) 477-7108. Fax: (671) 477-6411. Ownership Edward H. Poppe Jr., Frances W. Poppe.

Stns: 1 AM. 2 FM. KSTO(FM) Hagatna, GU; KTWG(AM) Hagatna, GU; KISH(AM) Hagatna, GU.

Edward H. Poppe Jr., pres.

International Broadcasting Corp., 1554 Bori St., San Juan, PR 00927-6113. Phone: (787) 274-1800. Fax: (787) 281-9758. Ownership Pedro Roman Collazo, 100%. Note: Pedro Roman Collazo, as an individual, owns WVOZ(AM) San Juan, PR.

Stns: 7 AM. 1 FM. WRSJ(AM) Bayamon, PR; WGIT(AM) Canovanas, PR; WVOZ-FM Carolina, PR; WIBS Guayama, PR; WXRF Guayama, PR; WTIL Mayaguez, PR; WEKO(AM) Morovis, PR; WCHQ(AM) Quebradillas, PR.

Stns: 3 TV. WVEO, Aguadilla, PR; WVOZ, Ponce, PR; WTCV, San Juan, PR.

Pedro Roman Callazo, pres; Margarita Nazario, gen mgr

Iorio Broadcasting Inc., 1316 7th Ave., Beaver Falls, PA 15010. Phone: (724) 846-4100. Fax: (724) 843-7771. Ownership Frank Iorio Jr., 100%.

Stns: 2 AM. 1 FM. WMBA Ambridge, PA; WBVP(AM) Beaver Falls, PA; WNAE-FM Clarendon, PA.

Frank Iorio, pres.

J

J&V Communications Inc., 222 Hazard St., Orlando, FL 32804. Phone: (407) 841-8282. Fax: (407) 841-8250. Ownership Jesus Torrado, Virgen Torrado.

Stns: 4 AM. WTJV(AM) De Land, FL; WOTS Kissimmee, FL; WSDO(AM) Sanford, FL; WPRD Winter Park, FL.

John Torrado, pres; Frank F. Vaught, opns mgr.

JER Licenses LLC, 194 McGee Rd., Versailles, KY 40383. Phone: (859) 879-0818. Ownership Jon E. Robinson, 100% voting interest, 58% ownership interest; and Allison Robinson, 32% non-voting interest.

Stns: 4 AM. WTJV(AM) De Land, FL; WOTS Kissimmee, FL; WSDO(AM) Sanford, FL; WPRD Winter Park, FL4 FM. KXZT(FM) Newell, SD; KXZS(FM) Wall, SD; KRKP(FM) Leakey, TX; WDTX(FM) Rothschild, WI.

JWC Broadcasting, 259 S. Willow Ave., Cookeville, TN 38501. Phone: (931) 528-6064. Fax: (931) 520-1590. Ownership Joe W. Wilmoth, 99%; and Reba Wilmoth, 1%.

Stns: 1 AM. 3 FM. WATX Algood, TN; WBXE-FM Baxter, TN; WLQK(FM) Livingston, TN; WKXD-FM Monterey, TN.

Joel Wilmoth, gen ptnr.

Jabar Communications Inc., 5081 Rivers Ave., North Charleston, SC 29406. Phone: (843) 554-1063. Fax: (843) 554-1088. E-mail: traffic@jabarcommunications.com Web Site:jabarcommunications.com

Stns: 1 AM. 2 FM. WJNI(FM) Ladson, SC; WWIK(FM) McClellanville, SC; WAZS(AM) Summerville, SC.

Thomas Daniel, pres.

Jackson County Broadcasting Inc., Box 667, 295 E. Main St., Jackson, OH 45640. Phone: (740) 286-3023. Fax: (740) 286-6679. E-mail: jmossbarger@jbiradio.com Ownership Alan Stockmeister

Stns: 1 AM. 2 FM. WCJO-FM Jackson, OH; WKOV-FM Wellston, OH; WYPC Wellston, OH.

Jerry Mossbarger, gen mgr .

Jackson Radio Works Inc., 1700 Glenshire Dr., Jackson, MI 49201. Phone: (517) 787-9546. Fax: (517) 787-7517. E-mail: bgoldsen@wkhm.com Web Site:www.wkhm.com Ownership Bruce & Susan Goldsen, 100%

Stns: 2 AM. 1 FM. WKHM-FM Brooklyn, MI; WIBM Jackson, MI; WKHM(AM) Jackson, MI.

Susan Goldsen; Bruce Goldsen, pres & gen mgr.

Jacobs Media Corp., Box 10, Gainesville, GA 30503. Phone: (770) 532-9921. Fax: (770) 532-0506. E-mail: jayjacobs@wdun.com Web Site:www.wdun.com Ownership Elizabeth Jacobs Carswell.

Stns: 2 AM. 1 FM. WMJE-FM Clarkesville, GA; WDUN Gainesville, GA; WGGA(AM) Gainesville, GA.

John W. Jacobs III, pres/CEO; Jay Andrews, VP bcstg.

James Crystal Inc., 6600 N. Andrews Ave., Suite 160, Fort Lauderdale, FL 33309. Phone: (954) 315-1515. Fax: (954) 315-1555. Ownership James W. Hilliard, Crystal H. Armstrong.

Stns: 5 AM. WFLL(AM) Fort Lauderdale, FL; WMEN(AM) Royal Palm Beach, FL; WFTL(AM) West Palm Beach, FL;

KCKN(AM) Roswell, NM; KNIT(AM) Dallas, TX.

James C. Hilliard, pres.

Jodesha Broadcasting Inc., Box 1198, Aberdeen, WA 98520. Phone: (360) 533-3000. Fax: (360) 532-1456. E-mail: bossbill@jodesha.com Web Site:www.jodesha.com Ownership William J and Susan Wolfenbarger.

Stns: 1 AM. 3 FM. KBKW Aberdeen, WA; KSWW(FM) Montesano, WA; KANY(FM) Ocean Shores, WA; KJET(FM) Raymond, WA.

William J. Wolfenbarger, pres; Susan Wolfenbarger, sec/treas.

Johnson Enterprises Inc., 338 S. KLEY Dr., Wellington, KS 67152. Phone: (620) 326-3341. Fax: (620) 326-8512. E-mail: kley@sutv.com Web Site:www.kleyam.com Ownership E. Gordon Johnson, Susan G. Johnson.

Stns: 2 AM. 1 FM. KLEY(AM) Wellington, KS; KWME-FM Wellington, KS; KKLE(AM) Winfield, KS.

E. Gordon Johnson, pres.

Journal Communications Inc., 333 W. State St., Milwaukee, WI 53203. Phone: (414) 224-2616. Fax: (414) 224-2469. Web Site:www.jc.com

Stns: 9 AM. 26 FM. KGMG-FM Oracle, AZ; KFFN Tucson, AZ; KMXZ-FM Tucson, AZ; KQTH(FM) Tucson, AZ; KJOT(FM) Boise, ID; KGEM(AM) Boise, ID; KCID(AM) Caldwell, ID; KTHI(FM) Caldwell, ID; KRVB(FM) Nampa, ID; KQXR-FM Payette, ID; KYQQ(FM) Arkansas City, KS; KFXJ(FM) Augusta, KS; KFTI-FM Newton, KS; KICT-FM Wichita, KS; KFTI(AM) Wichita, KS; KFDI-FM Wichita, KS; KSGF-FM Ash Grove, MO; KZRQ-FM Mount Vernon, MO; KSPW(FM) Sparta, MO; KSGF(AM) Springfield, MO; KTTS-FM Springfield, MO; KKCD-FM Omaha, NE; KSRZ-FM Omaha, NE; KEZO-FM Omaha, NE; KXSP(AM) Omaha, NE; KQCH(FM) Omaha, NE; KXBL(FM) Henryetta, OK; KFAQ(AM) Tulsa, OK; KVOO-FM Tulsa, OK; WCYQ(FM) Karns, TN; WKHT(FM) Knoxville, TN; WKTI(AM) Powell, TN; WWST(FM) Sevierville, TN; WTMJ Milwaukee, WI; WLWK-FM Milwaukee, WI.

Stns: 11 TV. KIVI-TV, Boise, ID; KNIN, Boise, ID; WFTX-TV, Ft. Myers-Naples, FL; WGBA-TV, Green Bay-Appleton, WI; WSYM, Lansing, MI; KTNV-TV, Las Vegas, NV; WTMJ, Milwaukee, WI; KMTV-TV, Omaha, NE; KMIR-TV, Palm Springs, CA; KGUN-TV, Tucson (Sierra Vista), AZ; KWBA-TV, Tucson (Sierra Vista), AZ.

Journal Communications Inc., publisher of the morning *Milwaukee* (WI) *Journal Sentinel,* owns 100% of Journal Broadcast Corp.

Douglas G. Kiel, pres.

J-Systems Franchising Corp., Hotel Traylor, 1444 Hamilton St., Allentown, PA 18102. Phone: (610) 435-5913. Fax: (610) 435-8918. E-mail: wmgh@ptd.net Web Site:www.wmgh.com Ownership Harold G. Fulmer III, 100%.

Stns: 1 AM. 1 FM. WLSH Lansford, PA; WMGH-FM Tamaqua, PA.

Harold G. Fulmer III, pres.

K

KCD Enterprises Inc., Box 1100, Bartlesville, OK 74005. Phone: (918) 336-1001. Fax: (918) 336-3939. E-mail: radio@bartlesvilleradio.com Web Site:www.bartlesvilleradio.com Ownership Kevin Potter, 50%; Dorea Potter, 50%. Note: KPGM(AM) Pawhuska, OK is licensed to Potter Radio LLC. All of the membership units of Potter Radio LLC are held by the Kevin M. and Dorea S. Potter Trust.

Stns: 2 AM. 2 FM. KWON Bartlesville, OK; KYFM-FM Bartlesville, OK; KRIG-FM Nowata, OK; KPGM(AM) Pawhuska, OK.

Kevin Potter, pres & gen mgr.

KEA Radio Inc., Box 966, Scottsboro, AL 35768. Phone: (256) 259-2341. Fax: (256) 574-2156. Web Site:www.wkeafm.com Ownership Ronald H. Livengood; Gene Sisk; Ivous Sisk; Diane Livengood.

Stns: 2 AM. 2 FM. KWON Bartlesville, OK; KYFM-FM Bartlesville, OK; KRIG-FM Nowata, OK; KPGM(AM) Pawhuska, OK2 FM. WKEA-FM Scottsboro, AL; WMXN-FM Stevenson, AL.

Ronald H. Livengood, pres; Gene Sisk, VP; Diane Livengood, sec; Ivous Sisk, treas.

KERM Inc., 201 W. 2nd, Russellville, AR 72801. Phone: (479) 968-1184. Fax: (479) 967-5278. E-mail: karv610@cei.net

Stns: 2 AM. 2 FM. KURM-FM Gravette, AR; KARV-FM Ola, AR; KURM Rogers, OK; KARV Russellville, AR.

Chris Womack, gen mgr; James K. Womack, pres.

KHWY Inc., 12381 Wilshire Blvd. #105, Los Angeles, CA 90025. Phone: (310) 820-4628. Fax: (310) 826-7866. E-mail: khwyha@earthlink.net Web Site:www.thehighwaystations.com Ownership Howard B. Anderson; Kirk M. Anderson.

Stns: 2 AM. 2 FM. KURM-FM Gravette, AR; KARV-FM Ola, AR; KURM Rogers, AR; KARV Russellville, AR8 FM. KIXF-FM Baker, CA; KHRQ(FM) Baker, CA; KHWY-FM Essex, CA; KIXW-FM Lenwood, CA; KHDR(FM) Lenwood, CA; KHWZ-FM Ludlow, CA; KHYZ-FM Mountain Pass, CA; KRXV-FM Yermo, CA.

Howard B. Anderson, pres/CEO; Kirk M. Anderson, exec VP; Jean Sheranian, sec.

KM Communications Inc., 3654 Jarvis Ave., Skokie, IL 60076. Phone: (847) 674-0864. Fax: (847) 674-9188. Web Site:www.kmcommunications.com

Stns: 3 AM. 9 FM. WPNG(FM) Pearson, GA; KTKB-FM Hagatna, GU; KTKB(AM) Tamuning, GU; KEWA(AM) Ewa Beach, HI; KQMG Independence, IA; KQMG-FM Independence, IA; WLCN(FM) Atlanta, IL; WMKB(FM) Earlville, IL; KBWM(FM) Breckenridge, TX; KKEV(FM) Centerville, TX; KBDK(FM) Leakey, TX; KHMR(FM) Lovelady, TX.

Stns: 3 TV. KWKB, Cedar Rapids-Waterloo-Iowa City & Dubuque, IA; KPIF, Idaho Falls-Pocatello, ID; KEJB, Monroe, LA-El Dorado, AR.

Myoung Hwa Bae, pres; Kevin J. Bae, VP/gen mgr.

KNZA Inc., Box 104, Hiawatha, KS 66434-0104. Phone: (785) 547-3461. Fax: (785) 547-9900. E-mail: knza@rainbowtel.net Web Site:www.knzafm.com Ownership Greg Buser, 51%; Robert Hilton, 45%; Doug Weinberg, 4%.

Stns: 2 AM. 4 FM. KAIR Atchison, KS; KNZA-FM Hiawatha, KS; KAIR-FM Horton, KS; KMZA-FM Seneca, KS; KLZA-FM Falls City, NE; KTNC Falls City, NE.

Greg Buser, pres; Robert Hilton, sec/treas.

K95.5 Inc., 24189 E. 865 Rd., Welling, OK 74471-2245. Phone: (918) 230-2165. Fax: (918) 457-3512. E-mail: Paynewh@aol.com Web Site:www.k955.com Ownership William H. Payne 100% stockholder. Note: William H. Payne also is sole owner of Payne 5 Communications LLC, licensee of KTLQ(AM)-KEOK(FM) Tahlequah, OK.

Stns: 2 AM. 4 FM. KAIR Atchison, KS; KNZA-FM Hiawatha, KS; KAIR-FM Horton, KS; KMZA-FM Seneca, KS; KLZA-FM Falls City, NE; KTNC Falls City, NE3 FM. KTNT-FM Eufaula, OK; KITX(FM) Hugo, OK; KTFX-FM Warner, OK.

William H. Payne, pres.

KOOR Communications Inc., Box 2295, New London, NH 03257. Phone: (603) 448-0500. Fax: (603) 448-6601. E-mail: bob@wntk.com Web Site:www.wntk.com

Stns: 3 AM. 1 FM. WUVR(AM) Lebanon, NH; WNTK-FM New London, NH; WCNL(AM) Newport, NH; WCFR(AM) Springfield, VT.

Robert L. Vinikoor, pres; Sheila E. Vinikoor, VP; Robert L. Vinikoor, gen mgr.

KSPD Inc., (Inspired Family Radio). 1440 S. Weideman Ave., Boise, ID 83709. Phone: (208) 377-3790. Fax: (208) 377-3792. E-mail: info@myfamilyradio.com Web Site:www.myfamilyradio.com Ownership Lee Schafer, 50%; Beth A. Schafer, 50%.

Stns: 1 AM. 2 FM. KSPD Boise, ID; KBXL(FM) Caldwell, ID; KDZY-FM McCall, ID.

Lee Schafer, gen mgr; David Schafer, asst mgr.

KSRM Inc., 40960 K. Beach Rd., Kenai, AK 99611. Phone: (907) 283-5811. Fax: (907) 283-9177. E-mail: info@radiokenai.com Web Site:www.radiokenai.com Ownership John C. Davis.

Stns: 2 AM. 3 FM. KFSE(FM) Kasilof, AK; KWHQ-FM Kenai, AK; KKIS-FM Soldotna, AK; KSLD(AM) Soldotna, AK; KSRM Soldotna, AK.

John Davis, pres; Cherie Curry, gen mgr.

KUTE Inc., Box 737, Ignacio, CO 81137-0737. Phone: (970) 563-0255. Fax: (970) 563-0399. Ownership Robert Baker, 14.29%; Bertha Box, 14.29%; Eddie Box Jr., 14.29%; Marvin Cook, 14.29%; Richard Jefferson, 14.29%; Harald Jordan, 14.29%; and Mike Matheson, 14.29%.

Stns: 2 AM. 3 FM. KFSE(FM) Kasilof, AK; KWHQ-FM Kenai, AK; KKIS-FM Soldotna, AK; KSLD(AM) Soldotna, AK; KSRM Soldotna, AK6 FM. KDNG(FM) Durango, CO; KSUT-FM Ignacio, CO; KUTE-FM Ignacio, CO; KPGS(FM) Pagosa Springs, CO; KUUT(FM) Farmington, NM; KUSW(FM) Flora Vista, NM.

KZLZ LLC, 204 E. 4th St., North Little Rock, AR 72114. Phone: (501) 375-9131. Fax: (520) 325-3495.

Stns: 1 AM. 2 FM. KZLZ-FM Kearny, AZ; KHIL Willcox, AZ; KWCX-FM Willcox, AZ.

Kaspar Broadcasting Group, 1401 W. Barner St., Frankfort, IN 46041. Phone: (765) 659-3338. Fax: (765) 659-3338. Web Site:www.kasparradio.com

Stns: 2 AM. 2 FM. WSHW-FM Frankfort, IN; WILO Frankfort, IN; KFAV-FM Warrenton, MO; KWRE(AM) Warrenton, MO.

Vern Kaspar, pres/CEO; Russ Kaspar, VP.

Kemp Communications Inc., 3800 Howard Hughes Pkwy., Wells Fargo Tower, 17th Fl., Las Vegas, NV 89169. Phone: (702) 385-6000. Fax: (702) 385-6001. Ownership Will Kemp, 100%. Note: Group also is a 49.9% stockholder of KNAN(FM) Nanakuli, HI.

Stns: 1 AM. 5 FM. KMZQ-FM Payson, AZ; KVGG(FM) Salome, AZ; KVGQ(FM) Snowflake, AZ; KMZQ(AM) Las Vegas, NV; KVEG(FM) Mesquite, NV; KONV(FM) Overton, NV.

Will Kemp, pres.

Key Broadcasting Inc., Box 1227, Corbin, KY 40702. Phone: (606) 528-8787. Fax: (606) 528-9928. Ownership Terry E. Forcht.

Stns: 8 AM. 11 FM. WIKK-FM Newton, IL; WVLN Olney, IL; WSEI-FM Olney, IL; WIMC(FM) Crawfordsville, IN; WCVL Crawfordsville, IN; WCDQ(FM) Crawfordsville, IN; WANV(FM) Annville, KY; WAIN Columbia, KY; WAIN-FM Columbia, KY; WHOP(AM) Hopkinsville, KY; WHOP-FM Hopkinsville, KY; WFTG London, KY; WWEL-FM London, KY; WSIP Paintsville, KY; WSIP-FM Paintsville, KY; WYKY(FM) Science Hill, KY; WTLO Somerset, KY; WTCW Whitesburg, KY; WXKQ-FM Whitesburg, KY.

Terry E. Forcht, pres/CEO.

Keymarket Communications LLC, 100 Ryan Ct., Suite 98, Pittsburgh, PA 15205. Phone: (412) 489-1001. Fax: (412) 279-5500. Web Site:www.froggyland.com

Stns: 6 AM. 6 FM. WOMP Bellaire, OH; WYJK-FM Bellaire, OH; WOHI East Liverpool, OH; WOGF(FM) East Liverpool, OH; WSTV Steubenville, OH; WASP Brownsville, PA; WFGI(AM) Charleroi, PA; WYJK(AM) Connellsville, PA; WKPL(FM) Ellwood City, PA; WOGG(FM) Oliver, PA; WPKL(FM) Uniontown, PA; WUKL(FM) Bethlehem, WV.

Gerald Getz, pres/CEO.

Kindred Communications Inc., 401 11th St., Suite 200, Huntington, WV 25701. Phone: (304) 523-8401. Fax: (304) 523-4848. Web Site:www.kindredcom.net

Stns: 2 AM. 2 FM. WCMI Ashland, KY; WDGG-FM Ashland, KY; WCMI-FM Catlettsburg, KY; WRVC Huntington, WV.

Mike Kirtner, pres & gen mgr .

Kirkman Broadcasting Inc., Indigo Executive Park, 60 Markfield Dr., Suite 4, Charleston, SC 29407. Phone: (843) 763-6631. Web Site:www.kirkmanbroadcasting.com

Stns: 4 AM. WQNT(AM) Charleston, SC; WQSC Charleston, SC; WTMZ Dorchester Terrace-Brentwood, SC; WJKB(AM) Moncks Corner, SC.

Gil Kirkman, pres/CEO.

Knight Broadcasting Inc., 1693 Mission Dr., Solvang, CA 93463. Phone: (805) 688-8386. Fax: (805) 688-2271. Ownership Sandra C. Knight, 55%; and Shawn T. Knight, 45%.

Stns: 2 AM. 2 FM. KSMA(AM) Lompoc, CA; KUHL(AM) Santa Maria, CA; KRAZ-FM Santa Ynez, CA; KSYV-FM Solvang, CA.

Kona Coast Radio LLC, 87 Jasper Lake Rd., Loveland, CO 80537. Phone: (970) 669-9200. E-mail: vicmichael@aol.com Ownership Victor A. Michael Jr., 100%.

Stns: 2 AM. 2 FM. KSMA(AM) Lompoc, CA; KUHL(AM) Santa Maria, CA; KRAZ-FM Santa Ynez, CA; KSYV-FM Solvang, CA3 FM. KMAP(FM) Arriba, CO; KHIH(FM) Hugo, CO; KGGY(FM) Stratton, CO.

Koser Radio Group, P.O. Box 352, Rice Lake, WI 54868. Phone: (715) 234-2131. Fax: (715) 234-6942.

Stns: 2 AM. 1 FM. WAQE Rice Lake, WI; WJMC Rice Lake, WI; WJMC-FM Rice Lake, WI.

Thomas A. Koser, pres.

Kuiper Stns, Box 1808, Grand Rapids, MI 49501. Phone: (616) 451-9387. Fax: (616) 451-8460. Ownership William E. Kuiper Sr.

Stns: 2 AM. WFUR Grand Rapids, MI; WKPR Kalamazoo, MI.

William E. Kuiper Sr., gen mgr & pres.

L

LKCM Radio Group L.P., 115 W. 3rd St., Fort Worth, TX 76102. Phone: (817) 332-0959. Fax: (817) 332-4630. E-mail: gerry@lkcmradio.com Ownership LKCM Capital Group

Inc., gen ptnr, 100% of votes.

Stns: 1 AM. 10 FM. KFSZ(FM) Munds Park, AZ; KVSO(AM) Ardmore, OK; KKAJ-FM Ardmore, OK; KTRX(FM) Dickson, OK; KYBE-FM Frederick, OK; KYNZ(FM) Lone Grove, OK; KRVA-FM Campbell, TX; KTFW-FM Glen Rose, TX; KRVF(FM) Kerens, TX; KOME-FM Meridian, TX; KFWR(FM) Mineral Wells, TX.

Gerry Schlegel, pres.

L M Communications Inc., 401 W. Main St., Suite 301, Lexington, KY 40507. Phone: (859) 233-1515. Fax: (859) 233-1517. E-mail: jmac@lmcomm.com Web Site:www.lmcomm.com

Stns: 4 AM. 8 FM. WBVX(FM) Carlisle, KY; WLXG Lexington, KY; WBTF-FM Midway, KY; WGKS-FM Paris, KY; WCDA-FM Versailles, KY; WYBB-FM Folly Beach, SC; WCOO(FM) Kiawah Island, SC; WMON Montgomery, WV; WKLC-FM Saint Albans, WV; WJYP(AM) Saint Albans, WV; WMXE(FM) South Charleston, WV; WSCW South Charleston, WV.

Lynn Martin, pres; James E. MacFarlane, gen mgr .

La Crosse Radio Group, Box 2017, La Crosse, WI 54602. Phone: (608) 782-8335. Fax: (608) 782-8340. Web Site:www.lacrosseradiogroup.net Ownership Howard G. Bill, 45%; TCOM Inc., 45%; and Patrick H. Smith, 10%.

Stns: 1 AM. 4 FM. KQEG-FM La Crescent, MN; WLFN La Crosse, WI; WLXR-FM La Crosse, WI; WQCC-FM La Crosse, WI; WKBH-FM West Salem, WI.

Patrick H. Smith, gen mgr .

La Favorita Inc., Box 746, Austell, GA 30106. Phone: (770) 944-0900. Fax: (770) 944-9794. Web Site:www.radiolafavorita.com Ownership Samuel Zamarron, pres; Graciela Zamarron, VP.

Stns: 3 AM. WAOS(AM) Austell, GA; WXEM Buford, GA; WLBA Gainesville, GA.

Samuel Zamarron, pres/CEO; Graciela Zamarron, VP.

La Promesa Foundation, 1406 E. Garden Ln., Midland, TX 79702. Phone: (432) 682-1485. Fax: (432) 682-5230. Web Site:www.grnonline.com Ownership La Promesa Foundation is a non-stock, non-profit corporation.

Stns: 2 AM. 4 FM. KJMA(FM) Floresville, TX; KBKN(FM) Lamesa, TX; KBMD(FM) Marble Falls, TX; KVDG(FM) Midland, TX; KLPF(FM) Midland, TX; KWMF(AM) Pleasanton, TX.

La Salle County Broadcasting Corp., 1 Broadcast Lane, Oglesby, IL 61348. Phone: (815) 223-3100. Fax: (815) 223-3095. E-mail: joyce@wlpo.net Web Site:www.wlpo.net Ownership Peter Miller.

Stns: 1 AM. 2 FM. WAJK-FM La Salle, IL; WLPO La Salle, IL; WKOT-FM Marseilles, IL.

Peter Miller, pres, owns 95% of Daily News-Tribune Inc., which publishes the *News Tribune*.

Peter Miller, pres; Joyce McCullough, VP/gen mgr; John Spencer, progmg dir; Mark Lippert, sls mgr.

Lake Cities Broadcasting Corp., Box 999, Angola, IN 46703. Phone: (260) 665-9554. Fax: (260) 665-9064. E-mail: wlki@wlki.com Web Site:www.wlki.com Ownership Thomas R. Andrews, William Kerner Jr., David Czurak.

Stns: 1 AM. 4 FM. WLKI-FM Angola, IN; WTHD-FM Lagrange, IN; WMSH Sturgis, MI; WMSH-FM Sturgis, MI; WLZZ(FM) Montpelier, OH.

Thomas R. Andrews, pres; William Kerner Jr., VP.

Lake Michigan Broadcasting Inc., 5941 W. U.S. 10, Ludington, MI 49431. Phone: (231) 843-3438. Fax: (231) 843-1886. Web Site:www.wkla.com Ownership Lynn S. Baerwolf, 40.125%; Scott J. Seeburger, 18%; John J. Hausbeck, 15%.

Stns: 2 AM. 3 FM. WKLA Ludington, MI; WKLA-FM Ludington, MI; WMTE-FM Manistee, MI; WMTE Manistee, MI; WKZC-FM Scottville, MI.

Lynn Barewolf, pres.

Lake Region Radio Works, Box 882, Devils Lake, ND 58301. Phone: (701) 662-7563. Fax: (701) 662-2222. E-mail: kzzyfm@gondtc.com Web Site:www.lrradioworks.com

Stns: 1 AM. 2 FM. KDLR Devils Lake, ND; KDVL-FM Devils Lake, ND; KZZY(FM) Devils Lake, ND.

Curtis D. Teigen, opns mgr.

Lakes Radio Inc., 524 Ludington, Suite 300, Escanaba, MI 49829. Phone: (906) 789-9700. Fax: (906) 789-9700. Web Site:www.radioresultsnetwork.com

Stns: 2 AM. 2 FM. WCHT Escanaba, MI; WGKL-FM Gladstone, MI; WCMM-FM Gulliver, MI; WTIQ Manistique, MI.

Rick Duerson, pres.

Langer Broadcasting Group L.L.C., Box 380699, Murdock, FL 33938-0699. Phone: (508) 820-2430. Ownership Alexander G. Langer, 100%.

BostonMA . Langer Broadcasting Corp., 164 Canal St, Suite 450. Phone:

Stns: 4 AM. WSRO(AM) Ashland, MA; WBIX(AM) Natick, MA; WFYL(AM) King of Prussia, PA; WPYT(AM) Wilkinsburg, PA.

Larche Communications Inc., 355 Cranston Crescent, Midland, ON L4R 4L3. Canada. Phone: (705) 720-1991. Fax: (705) 526-3060.

Stns: 4 AM. WSRO(AM) Ashland, MA; WBIX(AM) Natick, MA; WFYL(AM) King of Prussia, PA; WPYT(AM) Wilkinsburg, PA3 FM. CICZ-FM Midland, ON; CICX-FM Orillia, ON; CICS-FM Sudbury, ON.

Paul Larche, pres.

Latino Communications LLC, 600 Grant St., Suite 600, Denver, CO 80203. Phone: (303) 733-5266. Fax: (303) 733-5242. E-mail: kbno@kbno.net Web Site:www.kbno.net Ownership Alex Cranberg, 49%; Zee Ferrufino, 26%; and Frank Ponce, 25%.

Stns: 3 AM. KBNO(AM) Denver, CO; KXRE(AM) Manitou Springs, CO; KAVA Pueblo, CO.

Zee Ferrufino, pres/CEO.

Lew Latto Group of Northland Radio Stations, 5732 Eagle View Dr., Duluth, MN 55803-9498. Phone: (218) 729-9888. Fax: (218) 729-9888. E-mail: LewLatto@aol.com Ownership Lew Latto, 100%.

Stns: 1 AM. 2 FM. KGPZ-FM Coleraine, MN; KRBT Eveleth, MN; WEVE-FM Eveleth, MN.

Lew Latto, pres.

Lazer Broadcasting Corp., 200 S. A St., 4th Fl., Oxnard, CA 93030. Phone: (805) 240-2070. Fax: (805) 240-5960. Web Site:www.radiolazer.com Ownership Alfredo Plascancia, 100%.

Stns: 4 AM. 14 FM. KXSB-FM Big Bear Lake, CA; KSSB-FM Calipatria, CA; KSRT(FM) Cloverdale, CA; KXZM(FM) Felton, CA; KXRS-FM Hemet, CA; KXSM(FM) Hollister, CA; KSRN(FM) Kings Beach, CA; KBTW(FM) Lenwood, CA; KXTT(FM) Maricopa, CA; KLMM(FM) Morro Bay, CA; KOXR Oxnard, CA; KLUN(FM) Paso Robles, CA; KCAL Redlands, CA; KZER(AM) Santa Barbara, CA; KSBQ Santa Maria, CA; KLJR-FM Santa Paula, CA; KEAL(FM) Taft, CA; KJOR(FM) Windsor, CA.

Alfredo Plascencia, CEO; Terry Janisch, gen mgr .

Le Sea Broadcasting, Box 12, South Bend, IN 46624. Phone: (574) 291-8200. Fax: (574) 291-9043. E-mail: leseabroadcasting@lesea.com Web Site:www.lesea.com

Stns: 4 AM. 14 FM. KXSB-FM Big Bear Lake, CA; KSSB-FM Calipatria, CA; KSRT(FM) Cloverdale, CA; KXZM(FM) Felton, CA; KXRS-FM Hemet, CA; KXSM(FM) Hollister, CA; KSRN(FM) Kings Beach, CA; KBTW(FM) Lenwood, CA; KXTT(FM) Maricopa, CA; KLMM(FM) Morro Bay, CA; KOXR Oxnard, CA; KLUN(FM) Paso Robles, CA; KCAL Redlands, CA; KZER(AM) Santa Barbara, CA; KSBQ Santa Maria, CA; KLJR-FM Santa Paula, CA; KEAL(FM) Taft, CA; KJOR(FM) Windsor, CA3 FM. WHPZ-FM Bremen, IN; WHME-FM South Bend, IN; WHPD(FM) Dowagiac, MI.

Stns: 8 TV. KWHD, Denver, CO; KWHH, Hilo, HI; KWHE, Honolulu, HI; WHMB-TV, Indianapolis, IN; WHNO, New Orleans, LA; WHME, South Bend-Elkhart, IN; KWHB, Tulsa, OK; KWHM, Wailuku, HI.

Peter Sumrall, pres/CEO.

Legacy Communications LLC, 3205 W. North Front St., Grand Island, NE 88803-4024. Phone: (308) 381-0206. Ownership Jay Vavricek, mngg member, 100%.

Stns: 3 AM. 11 FM. KRGY(FM) Aurora, NE; KOZY-FM Bridgeport, NE; KMOR(FM) Gering, NE; KRGI Grand Island, NE; KRGI-FM Grand Island, NE; KSWN-FM McCook, NE; KIOD(FM) McCook, NE; KZMC(FM) McCook, NE; KHYY(FM) Minatare, NE; KETT(FM) Mitchell, NE; KZTL(FM) Paxton, NE; KOLT Scottsbluff, NE; KRNP(FM) Sutherland, NE; KOAQ Terrytown, NE.

Legacy Media Corporation, 210 North 1000 E., Box 1450, St. George, UT 84771-1450. Phone: (435) 628-1000. Fax: (435) 628-6636. E-mail: legacy1@infowest.com Web Site:www.legacy.cc Ownership Bear River Trust (E. Morgan Skinner Jr., trustee), 38.52%; Randall Family Trust (Lavon Randall, trustee), 33.07%; all other shareholders (52), less than 5%.

Stns: 8 AM. 1 FM. KACE(AM) Bishop, CA; KPTO(AM) Pocatello, ID; KITT(FM) Soda Springs, ID; KIFO(AM) Hawthorne, NV; KTNP(AM) Tonopah, NV; KOBY(AM) Cedar City, UT; KOGN(AM) Ogden, UT; KENT(AM) Parowan, UT; KNFL(AM) Tremonton, UT.

R. Michael Bull, principal accounting off; Jeffrey B. Bate, dir; E. Morgan Skinner, pres/CEO, dir; Lavon Randall, sec/dir.

Legend Communications L.L.C., 6805 Douglas Legum Dr., Suite 100, Elkridge, MD 21075. Phone: (410) 799-1740. Fax: (410) 799-1705. E-mail: larry@patcomm.com Web Site:www.patcomm.com Ownership Larry Patrick, Susan Patrick.

Stns: 6 AM. 11 FM. KDKD Clinton, MO; KDKD-FM Clinton, MO; KLGT-FM Buffalo, WY; KBBS Buffalo, WY; KODI Cody, WY; KTAG-FM Cody, WY; KGWY-FM Gillette, WY; KIML Gillette, WY; KAML-FM Gillette, WY; KZMQ Greybull, WY; KZMQ-FM Greybull, WY; KCGL(FM) Powell, WY; KZZS(FM) Story, WY; KYTS(FM) Ten Sleep, WY; KKLX-FM Worland, WY; KWOR Worland, WY; KDDV-FM Wright, WY.

Larry Patrick, mngg ptnr; Susan Patrick, mngg ptnr; Greg Guy, mngg ptnr.

Leighton Enterprises Inc., Box 1458, St. Cloud, MN 56302. Phone: (320) 251-1450. Fax: (320) 251-8952. Web Site:www.1047kcld.com Ownership Thomas H. Graham, trustee, Leighton Children's LP Trust, 27.3%; Thomas H. Graham, trustee, Leighton Grandchildren's LP Trust, 25.7%.

Stns: 4 AM. 7 FM. KYCK-FM Crookston, MN; KDLM Detroit Lakes, MN; KZLT-FM East Grand Forks, MN; KCNN East Grand Forks, MN; KZPK-FM Paynesville, MN; KBOQ(FM) Pelican Rapids, MN; KCLD-FM Saint Cloud, MN; KNSI Saint Cloud, MN; KCML(FM) Saint Joseph, MN; KNOX Grand Forks, ND; KNOX-FM Grand Forks, ND.

Al Leighton, chmn/CEO; John Sowada, pres; Dennis Niess, VP.

Liberman Broadcasting Inc., 1845 Empire Ave., Burbank, CA 91504. Phone: (818) 729-5300. Fax: (818) 729-5678. E-mail: LBinfo@lbimedia.com Web Site:www.lbimedia.com Ownership Lenard D. Liberman, 47.5-49% votes, 40-42.5% equity; Jose Liberman 2003 Annuity Trust, 23.75-24.5% votes, 20-21.25% equity; Esther Liberman 2003 Annuity Trust, 23.75-24.5% votes, 20-21.25% equity; public shareholders of Liberman Broadcasting Inc., 2-5% votes, 15-20% equity.

Stns: 7 AM. 15 FM. KEBN(FM) Garden Grove, CA; KBUE(FM) Long Beach, CA; KHJ(AM) Los Angeles, CA; KBUA(FM) San Fernando, CA; KRQB(FM) San Jacinto, CA; KVNR Santa Ana, CA; KWIZ-FM Santa Ana, CA; KTCY(FM) Azle, TX; KXGJ-FM Bay City, TX; KQQK(FM) Beaumont, TX; KBOC(FM) Bridgeport, TX; KJOJ Conroe, TX; KNTE-FM El Campo, TX; KJOJ-FM Freeport, TX; KEYH Houston, TX; KQUE Houston, TX; KNOR(FM) Krum, TX; KZZA(FM) Muenster, TX; KZMP-FM Pilot Point, TX; KTJM-FM Port Arthur, TX; KSEV(AM) Tomball, TX; KZMP(AM) University Park, TX.

Stns: 4 TV. KMPX, Dallas-Ft. Worth; KZJL, Houston; KRCA, Los Angeles; KPNZ, Salt Lake City, UT.

Lenard Liberman, pres; Brett Zane, CEO.

Liggett Communications L.L.C., 808 Huron Ave., Port Huron, MI 48060. Phone: (810) 982-9000. Fax: (810) 987-9380.

Stns: 2 AM. 1 FM. WBTI-FM Lexington, MI; WHLX(AM) Marine City, MI; WPHM Port Huron, MI.

Larry Smith, VP/gen mgr; Robert Liggett, pres.

Lincoln Financial Media, 100 N. Greene St., Greensboro, NC 27420. Phone: (336) 691-3000. Fax: (336) 691-3222. Web Site:www.lincolnfinancialmedia.com Ownership Lincoln National Corp., 100%.

Stns: 5 AM. 10 FM. KSOQ-FM Escondido, CA; KIFM-FM San Diego, CA; KBZT(FM) San Diego, CA; KNSN(AM) San Diego, CA; KSON(FM) San Diego, CA; KYGO-FM Denver, CO; KRWZ(AM) Denver, CO; KQKS-FM Lakewood, CO; KEPN(AM) Lakewood, CO; KKFN(AM) Longmont, CO; WLYF(FM) Miami, FL; WMXJ-FM Pompano Beach, FL; WAXY South Miami, FL; WQXI Atlanta, GA; WSTR-FM Smyrna, GA.

Ed Hull, pres, Lincoln Financial Sports; John Shreves, pres & Lincoln Financial TV; Don Benson, pres, Lincoln Financial Radio.

Linder Broadcasting Group, Box 1420, Mankato, MN 56002. Phone: (507) 345-4537. Fax: (507) 345-5364. Web Site:www.katoinfo.com Ownership Donald Linder, John Linder.

Stns: 4 AM. 9 FM. KOWZ-FM Blooming Prairie, MN; KTOE(AM) Mankato, MN; KYSM(AM) Mankato, MN; KARZ(FM) Marshall, MN; KMHL Marshall, MN; KATO-FM New Ulm, MN; KDOG(FM) North Mankato, MN; KOLV-FM Olivia, MN; KXAC-FM Saint James, MN; KRRW-FM Saint James, MN; KARL(FM) Tracy, MN; KRUE-FM Waseca, MN; KOWZ(AM) Waseca, MN.

John Linder, pres.

Little Falls Radio Corp., 25801 Nacre St. N.W., St. Francis, MN 55070. Phone: (763) 862-9909.E-mail: rod.grams@att.net Web Site:www.fallsradio.com Ownership Rod Grams, 50%; and Chrstina Rae Grams, 50%.
Stns: 1 AM. 2 FM. WYRQ-FM Little Falls, MN; KFML-FM Little Falls, MN; KLTF Little Falls, MN.

J.R. Livesay Group, Box 322, Mattoon, IL 61938-0322. Phone: (217) 234-6464. Fax: (217) 234-6019.E-mail: wlbh@wlbh.com Ownership J.R. Livesay II owns 50% of WLBH-AM-FM. Shirley L. Herrington owns 35% of WLBH-AM-FM.
Stns: 1 AM. 1 FM. WLBH Mattoon, IL; WLBH-FM Mattoon, IL.

J.R. Livesay II, chmn; Shirley L. Herrington II, CFO.

Locally Owned Radio LLC, 21361 Hwy. 30, Twin Falls, ID 83301. Phone: (208) 735-8300. Fax: (208) 733-4196. Web Site:www.locallyownedradio.com Ownership Porter Hogan Charitable Trust, Jennifer Meeks, trustee; Wendell M. Starke, Lawrence C. Johnson, Stephanie S. Johnson.
Stns: 1 AM. 4 FM. KYUN(FM) Hailey, ID; KTPZ(FM) Hazelton, ID; KIKX-FM Ketchum, ID; KTFI Twin Falls, ID; KIRQ(FM) Twin Falls, ID.

Larry Johnson, pres, gen mgr, gen sls mgr; Jerry Fender, opns mgr; Stephanie Johnson, VP.

Lost Coast Communications Inc., Box 25, Ferndale, CA 95536. Phone: (707) 786-5104. Fax: (707) 786-5100. Web Site:www.khum.com www.kslg.com Ownership Martin and Peggy Cleary, 36.6%; Blue Lake Rancheria, 21.7%; Patrick Cleary, 16.8%; William Thorington, 9.4%; Cliff Berkowitz, 4.4%; and Trust for Rockey Poole and Phoebe Smith, Rockey Poole, dir, 3%.
Stns: 1 AM. 4 FM. KYUN(FM) Hailey, ID; KTPZ(FM) Hazelton, ID; KIKX-FM Ketchum, ID; KTFI Twin Falls, ID; KIRQ(FM) Twin Falls, ID3 FM. KWPT(FM) Fortuna, CA; KHUM(FM) Garberville, CA; KSLG-FM Hydesville, CA.

Patrick Cleary, pres.

Lotus Communications Corp., 3301 Barham Blvd., Suite 200, Los Angeles, CA 90068. Phone: (323) 512-2225. Fax: (323) 512-2224.E-mail: hq@lotuscorp.com Web Site:www.lotuscorp.com Ownership LPTV: KPHE-LD Phoenix, AZ; WTAM-LD Tampa, FL; and KHLM-LD Houston, TX.
Stns: 12 AM. 15 FM. KFMA-FM Green Valley, AZ; KCMT(FM) Oro Valley, AZ; KTKT Tucson, AZ; KLPX-FM Tucson, AZ; KKBZ(FM) Auberry, CA; KPSL-FM Bakersfield, CA; KVMX(FM) Bakersfield, CA; KWAC Bakersfield, CA; KCHJ Delano, CA; KGST Fresno, CA; KLBN(FM) Fresno, CA; KWKW Los Angeles, CA; KHIT-FM Madera, CA; KIWI(FM) McFarland, CA; KWKU(AM) Pomona, CA; KIRN(AM) Simi Valley, CA; KWWN(AM) Las Vegas, NV; KXPT-FM Las Vegas, NV; KOMP-FM Las Vegas, NV; KWID(FM) Las Vegas, NV; KBAD Las Vegas, NV; KENO Las Vegas, NV; KDOT-FM Reno, NV; KHIT Reno, NV; KOZZ-FM Reno, NV; KPLY(AM) Reno, NV; KUUB(FM) Sun Valley, NV.

Howard A. Kalmenson, pres; Jerry Roy, sr VP; Bill Shriftman, sr VP.

Lovcom Inc., Box 5086, Sheridan, WY 82801. Phone: (307) 672-7421. Fax: (307) 672-2933.E-mail: info@sheridanmedia.com Web Site:www.sheridanmedia.com Ownership W.K. Love and family.
Stns: 2 AM. 3 FM. KLQQ(FM) Clearmont, WY; KROE(AM) Sheridan, WY; KWYO Sheridan, WY; KYTI-FM Sheridan, WY; KZWY-FM Sheridan, WY.

Bob Grammens, gen mgr; Kim Love, owner.

Barry P. Lunderville Stns, 195 Main St., Lancaster, NH 03584. Phone: (603) 788-3636. Fax: (603) 788-3536. Ownership Barry P. Lunderville, 100%.
Stns: 4 AM. 2 FM. WMOU Berlin, NH; WKDR(AM) Berlin, NH; WKBR(AM) Lancaster, NH; WXXS-FM Lancaster, NH; WLTN-FM Lisbon, NH; WLTN Littleton, NH.

M

MAX Media L.L.C., 900 Laskin Rd., Virginia Beach, VA 23451. Phone: (757) 437-9800. Fax: (757) 437-0034. Web Site:www.maxmediallc.com Ownership MBG-GG LLC, 42.0345%; MBG Quad-C Investors I Inc., 41.4124%; Aardvarks Also LLC, 6.1967%; Colonnade Max Investors Inc., 4.8671%; Quad-C Max Investors Inc., 4.6799%; MBG Quad-C Investors II Inc., 0.6221%; and Quad-C Max Investors II Inc., 0.1872%.
Stns: 12 AM. 24 FM. KVLD(FM) Atkins, AR; KCJC(FM) Dardanelle, AR; KCAB Dardanelle, AR; KVOM Morrilton, AR; KVOM-FM Morrilton, AR; KWKK-FM Russellville, AR; WCIL Carbondale, IL; WUEZ(FM) Carterville, IL; WXLT(FM) Christopher, IL; WOOZ-FM Harrisburg, IL; WJPF Herrin, IL; KZIM Cape Girardeau, MO; KEZS-FM Cape Girardeau,

MO; KGIR Cape Girardeau, MO; KCGQ-FM Gordonville, MO; KMAL(AM) Malden, MO; KLSC(FM) Malden, MO; KWOC Poplar Bluff, MO; KJEZ-FM Poplar Bluff, MO; KKLR-FM Poplar Bluff, MO; KGKS-FM Scott City, MO; KSIM(AM) Sikeston, MO; WQDK-FM Ahoskie, NC; WGAI(AM) Elizabeth City, NC; WCMS-FM Hatteras, NC; WCXL(FM) Kill Devil Hills, NC; WFYY(FM) Bloomsburg, PA; WYGL-FM Elizabethville, PA; WWBE-FM Mifflinburg, PA; WLGL-FM Riverside, PA; WYGL Selinsgrove, PA; WCMS(AM) Newport News, VA; WGH-FM Newport News, VA; WVHT(FM) Norfolk, VA; WVBW(FM) Suffolk, VA; WXEZ-FM Yorktown, VA.
Stns: 7 TV. WMEI, Arecibo, PR; KULR-TV, Billings, MT; WNKY, Bowling Green, KY; KWYB, Butte-Bozeman, MT; WVIF, Christiansted, VI; KTMF, Missoula, MT; WPFO, Portland-Auburn, ME.

John A. Trinder, pres.

MBC Grand Broadcasting Inc., 1360 E. Sherwood Dr., Grand Junction, CO 81501. Phone: (970) 254-2100. Fax: (970) 245-7551. Web Site:www.gjradio.com Ownership Richard C. Dean.
Stns: 4 AM. 4 FM. KGLN Glenwood Springs, CO; KJYE-FM Grand Junction, CO; KNZZ(AM) Grand Junction, CO; KTMM(AM) Grand Junction, CO; KMGJ(FM) Grand Junction, CO; KMOZ-FM Grand Junction, CO; KSTR-FM Montrose, CO; KNAM(AM) Silt, CO.

Richard C. Dean, chmn/CEO.

M.B. Communications, 481 Hamilton St., Geneva, NY 14456. Phone: (315) 781-1101. Phone: (315) 536-0850. Fax: (315) 781-6666. Fax: (315) 536-3299.E-mail: k1017@fltg.net Web Site:www.k1017.com Ownership Russ Kimble, 100%.
Stns: 1 AM. 1 FM. WFLK-FM Geneva, NY; WYLF(AM) Penn Yan, NY.

Russell Kimble, pres; Deborah Kimble, VP.

M.R.S. Ventures Inc., 100 E. Ferguson, Suite 614, Tyler, TX 75702. Phone: (903) 595-4795. Fax: (903) 593-2666.E-mail: jdonrussell@aol.com Ownership Jerry D. Russell, 100%.
Stns: 3 AM. 7 FM. KRKD(FM) Dermott, AR; KZYQ-FM Lake Village, AR; KOTN Pine Bluff, AR; KPBQ-FM Pine Bluff, AR; KZYP-FM Pine Bluff, AR; KCLA Pine Bluff, AR; WDSK Cleveland, MS; WDTL-FM Cleveland, MS; WRKG(FM) Drew, MS; WZYQ-FM Mound Bayou, MS.

MTD Inc., Box 2010, Ruidoso Downs, NM 88346. Phone: (505) 258-9922. Fax: (505) 258-2363.E-mail: kruikwmw@trailnet.com Web Site:www.ruidoso.net/krui Ownership R.D. Hubbard, 75%; Mike Warren, 25%.
Stns: 1 AM. 4 FM. KNMB(FM) Cloudcroft, NM; KWMW-FM Maljamar, NM; KIDX(FM) Ruidoso, NM; KRUI Ruidoso Downs, NM; KTUM(FM) Tatum, NM.

Bruce Rimbo, pres; Timothy Keithley, gen mgr .

MTS Broadcasting, Box 237, Cambridge, MD 21613. Phone: (410) 228-4800. Fax: (410) 228-0130.E-mail: theheat@intercom.net Web Site:www.mtslive.com
Stns: 1 AM. 2 FM. WCEM Cambridge, MD; WTDK-FM Federalsburg, MD; WAAI(FM) Hurlock, MD.

Thomas C. Mulitz, pres/CEO.

MacDonald Broadcasting Co., Box 1776, Saginaw, MI 48605. Phone: (989) 752-8161. Fax (989) 752-8102.E-mail: wkcq@chartermi.net Web Site:www.98fmkcq.com Ownership Ken MacDonald Jr. Note: Group also owns and operates a Muzak franchise in a six-county area in mid-Michigan.
Stns: 3 AM. 5 FM. WQHH-FM Dewitt, MI; WXLA Dimondale, MI; WMJO(FM) Essexville, MI; WHZZ-FM Lansing, MI; WILS Lansing, MI; WSAG(FM) Linwood, MI; WSAM Saginaw, MI; WKCQ-FM Saginaw, MI.

Kenneth MacDonald Jr., CEO; Duane Alverson, pres.

MacDonald Garber Broadcasting Co., Box 286, Petoskey, MI 49770. Phone: (231) 347-8713. Fax: (231) 347-8782. Web Site:www.lite96.com
Stns: 3 AM. 3 FM. WATT Cadillac, MI; WLXV(FM) Cadillac, MI; WKHQ-FM Charlevoix, MI; WMKT(AM) Charlevoix, MI; WLXT(FM) Petoskey, MI; WMBN(AM) Petoskey, MI.

Trish MacDonold Garber, pres.

Magic Broadcasting LLC, 7106 Laird St., Suite 102, Panama City Beach, FL 32408. Phone: (850) 234-8388. Fax: (850) 230-6988. Web Site:magicbroadcasting.net Ownership Magic Management Co. LLC, mgng member; Donald G. McCoy, 29.57%; Stephen A. Bodzin, trustee of Anne S. Reich 1984 Revocable Trust, 21.13%; Kim Styles DiBacco, 7.75%; Thomas A. DiBacco, 7.75%.
Stns: 1 AM. 11 FM. WTVY-FM Dothan, AL; WKMX-FM Enterprise, AL; WJRL-FM Ozark, AL; WLDA(FM) Slocomb, AL; KWIE(AM) Ontario, CA; KDAY(FM) Redondo Beach,

CA; WYYX-FM Bonifay, FL; WILN-FM Panama City, FL; WPCF(AM) Panama City Beach, FL; WVVE(FM) Panama City Beach, FL; WYOO-FM Springfield, FL; WBBK-FM Blakely, GA.

Kim Styles, gen mgr; Thomas DiBacco, ptnr.

Magnum Broadcasting Inc., Box 436, State College, PA 16804. Phone: (814) 272-1320. Fax: (814) 272-3291. Web Site:www.1059joefm.com Ownership Michael M. Stapleford, 100%.
Stns: 2 AM. 2 FM. WBLF Bellefonte, PA; WJOW(FM) Philipsburg, PA; WPHB Philipsburg, PA; WZYY-FM Renovo, PA.

Diana Albright, gen mgr .

Magnum Communications Inc., 1021 N. Superior Ave., Suite 5, Tomah, WI 54660. Phone: (608) 742-2544. Ownership David R. Magnum, 100%.
Stns: 2 AM. 4 FM. WBKY(FM) Portage, WI; WRDB Reedsburg, WI; WBDL-FM Reedsburg, WI; WNFM-FM Reedsburg, WI; WNNO-FM Wisconsin Dells, WI; WDLS(AM) Wisconsin Dells, WI.

David R. Magnum, pres.

Magnum Radio Inc., 1021 N. Superior Ave., Suite 5, Tomah, WI 54660. Phone: (608) 372-9600. Fax: (608) 372-7566.E-mail: magnumradio@charter.net Ownership David R. Magnum, 87.91%. Note: Sister corporation Magnum Broadcasting Inc. owns WAUN-FM Kewaunee and WSRG(FM) Sturgeon Bay, both WI.
Stns: 1 AM. 2 FM. WXYM(FM) Tomah, WI; WBOG(AM) Tomah, WI; WTMB(FM) Tomah, WI.

Dave Magnum, pres.

Mahaffey Enterprises Inc., Box 4584, Springfield, MO 65808. Phone: (417) 883-9180. Fax: (417) 883-9096. Ownership John B. Mahaffey, Fredna B. Mahaffey, Robert B. Mahaffey.
Stns: 3 AM. 9 FM. KGGF Coffeyville, KS; KKRK(FM) Coffeyville, KS; KUSN(FM) Dearing, KS; KGGF-FM Fredonia, KS; KDAA(FM) Rolla, MO; KTTR Rolla, MO; KZNN-FM Rolla, MO; KTTR-FM Saint James, MO; KSPI Stillwater, OK; KSPI-FM Stillwater, OK; KGFY-FM Stillwater, OK; KVRO-FM Stillwater, OK.

John B. Mahaffey, chmn; Robert B. Mahaffey, pres/CEO.

Mahalo Broadcasting L.L.C., 6890 E. Sunrise Dr., Box 120-40, Tucson, AZ 85750. Phone: (407) 488-2098. Ownership George W. Kimble, 100% votes, 67% total assets.
Stns: 1 AM. 2 FM. KHNU(AM) Hilo, HI; KBGX(FM) Keaau, HI; KKOA(FM) Volcano, HI.

Main Line Broadcasting LLC, 300 Conshohocken State Rd., Suite 380, West Conshohocken, PA 19428-3801. Phone: (610) 825-8101. Fax: (610) 825-8106. Ownership Arlington Capital Partners II L.P., 100%.
Stns: 3 AM. 16 FM. WGZB-FM Lanesville, IN; WMJM-FM Jeffersontown, KY; WXMA(FM) Louisville, KY; WDJX-FM Louisville, KY; WLRS(FM) Shepherdsville, KY; WING Dayton, OH; WGTZ-FM Eaton, OH; WDHT(FM) Springfield, OH; WKSW-FM Urbana, OH; WROU-FM West Carrollton, OH; WCHA Chambersburg, PA; WIKZ-FM Chambersburg, PA; WQCM(FM) Greencastle, PA; WLFV(FM) Ettrick, VA; WWLB(FM) Midlothian, VA; WARV-FM Petersburg, VA; WBBT-FM Powhatan, VA; WHAG Halfway, MD; WDLD(FM) Halfway, MD.

Daniel Savadove, CEO; Marc Guralnick, exec VP sls; J. Edwin Conrad, exec VP/CFO.

Malkan Broadcast Associates, 2117 Leopard St., Corpus Christi, TX 78408-3925. Phone: (361) 883-3516. Fax: (361) 882-9767.E-mail: thechief@star94.net Ownership Malkan Broadcasting Management L.L.C., gen ptnr; Matthew Malkan; Hope Malkan; Glen Powers.
Stns: 1 AM. 2 FM. KEYS(AM) Corpus Christi, TX; KZFM(FM) Corpus Christi, TX; KKBA(FM) Kingsville, TX.

Glen Powers, pres.

Mapleton Communications LLC, 10900 Wilshire Blvd., Suite 1500, Los Angeles, CA 90024. Phone: (310) 209-7221. Fax: (310) 209-7239. Web Site:www.mapletoncomm.com Ownership Mapleton Radio LLC, 100%.
Stns: 11 AM. 30 FM. KBRE(FM) Atwater, CA; KRRX-FM Burney, CA; KKHK(FM) Carmel, CA; KCDU(FM) Carmel, CA; KPYG(FM) Cayucos, CA; KFMF-FM Chico, CA; KQPT(FM) Colusa, CA; KBLO(FM) Corcoran, CA; KPIG-FM Freedom, CA; KHIP(FM) Gonzales, CA; KNAH(FM) Merced, CA; KTIQ(AM) Merced, CA; KABX-FM Merced, CA; KYOS Merced, CA; KZAP-FM Paradise, CA; KPIG(AM) Piedmont, CA; KXTZ-FM Pismo Beach, CA; KALF(FM) Red Bluff, CA; KNRO(AM) Redding, CA; KQMS Redding, CA; KSHA-FM Redding, CA; KYNS(AM) San Luis Obispo, CA; KWWV(FM) Santa Margarita, CA; KBOQ(FM) Seaside, CA; KNNN(FM) Shasta Lake City, CA; KRDG-FM Shingletown, CA; KXDZ(FM)

Templeton, CA; KLOQ-FM Winton, CA; KGAY(AM) Ashland, OR; KCMX-FM Ashland, OR; KBOY-FM Medford, OR; KTMT-FM Medford, OR; KAKT(FM) Phoenix, OR; KCMX Phoenix, OR; KEYF-FM Cheney, WA; KEYF(AM) Dishman, WA; KGA Spokane, WA; KDRK-FM Spokane, WA; KZBD(FM) Spokane, WA; KBBD(FM) Spokane, WA; KJRB Spokane, WA.

Adam Nathanson, pres/CEO; Raul Salvador, VP finance; Mike Anthony, progmg VP; Rich Elmendorf, CFO.

Maritime Broadcasting, 226 Union St., Saint John, NB E2L 1B1. Canada. Phone: (506) 658-2330. Fax: (506) 658-5116.E-mail: mailbag@k100.ca Web Site:www.mbsradio.com

Stns: 8 AM. 15 FM. CKNB Campbellton, NB; CFAN-FM Miramichi City, NB; CHOY-FM Moncton, NB; CKCW-FM Moncton, NB; CFQM-FM Moncton, NB; CFBC Saint John, NB; CIOK-FM Saint John, NB; CJYC-FM Saint John, NB; CJCW Sussex, NB; CKDH Amherst, NS; CKDY Digby, NS; CHFX-FM Halifax, NS; CHNS-FM Halifax, NS; CKWM-FM Kentville, NS; CKEN-FM Kentville, NS; CKAD Middleton, NS; CJCB(AM) Sydney, NS; CKPE-FM Sydney, NS; CHER-FM Sydney, NS; CFAB Windsor, NS; CHLQ-FM Charlottetown, PE; CFCY-FM Charlottetown, PE; CJRW-FM Summerside, PE.

Kelly O'Neill, gen sls mgr; Robert Pace, CEO.

Mark Media Group, Box 607, Burnsville, NC 28714. Phone: (828) 682-6221. Fax: (828) 682-0998.E-mail: mmg@wkyk.com Web Site:www.wkyk.com Ownership J. Ardell Sink and Remelle K. Sink, 100%.

Stns: 3 AM. WKYK Burnsville, NC; WTZQ(AM) Hendersonville, NC; WTOE Spruce Pine, NC.

J. Ardell Sink, chmn/CEO; Remelle K. Sink, exec VP & CFO; Michael A. Sink, pres/COO.

MarMac Communications LLC, 7515 Blythe Island Hwy., Brunswick, GA 31523. Phone: (912) 264-6251. Fax: (912) 264-9991. Ownership Gary P. Marmitt, 50%; and Sharon McKeand, 50%.

Stns: 3 AM. WFNS(AM) Blackshear, GA; WSFN Brunswick, GA; WSEG(AM) Savannah, GA.

Mars Hill Network, 4044 Makyes Rd., Syracuse, NY 13215. Phone: (315) 469-5051. Fax: (315) 469-4066.E-mail: mhn@marshillnetwork.org Web Site:www.marshillnetwork.org Ownership Not-for-profit corporation. Note: Group also has a radio net, 14 translators.

Stns: 3 AM. WFNS(AM) Blackshear, GA; WSFN Brunswick, GA; WSEG(AM) Savannah, GA4 FM. WMHI-FM Cape Vincent, NY; WMHQ(FM) Malone, NY; WMHR-FM Syracuse, NY; WMHN-FM Webster, NY.

Clayton Roberts, pres; Michael Gettman, VP; Wayne Taylor, gen mgr; Jim Stewart, sec; John Seeland, treas.

Martin Broadcasting Inc., 4638 Decker Dr., Baytown, TX 77520. Phone: (210) 333-0050. Fax: (210) 333-0081.E-mail: kchl1480@yahoo.com

Stns: 6 AM. WLVV Mobile, AL; KZZB Beaumont, TX; KYOK(AM) Conroe, TX; KRMY Killeen, TX; KCHL San Antonio, TX; KANI Wharton, TX.

Darrell E. Martin, pres.

Martz Communications Group, 955 S. Virginia St., Reno, NV 89502. Phone: (415) 359-1030. Fax: (415) 359-1050. Ownership Timothy D. Martz, 100%.

Stns: 1 AM. 2 FM. WYUL-FM Chateaugay, NY; WVNV-FM Malone, NY; WICY Malone, NY.

Timothy D. Martz, pres/CEO.

Matinee Radio LLC, 2801 Via Fortuna, Suite 675, Austin, TX 78746. Phone: (512) 329-5843. Fax: (512) 329-5847. Ownership Matinee Broadcasting Corp., 51%; Mark Eckenrode, 12.25%; Katy Gaffney, 12.25%; William M. Smith, 12.25%; and Robert Walker, 12.25%.

Stns: 1 AM. 2 FM. WYUL-FM Chateaugay, NY; WVNV-FM Malone, NY; WICY Malone, NY5 FM. KANM(FM) Magdalena, NM; KNOS(FM) Albany, TX; KTXO(FM) Goldsmith, TX; KKUL-FM Groveton, TX; KRTS(FM) Marfa, TX.

Maverick Media LLC, 136 Main St., Suite 202, Westport, CT 06880. Phone: (203) 227-2800. Fax: (203) 227-4819.

Stns: 5 AM. 14 FM. KVRV(FM) Monte Rio, CA; KMHX(FM) Rohnert Park, CA; KSRO Santa Rosa, CA; KXFX-FM Santa Rosa, CA; WXRX-FM Belvidere, IL; WNTA Rockford, IL; WGFB(FM) Rockton, IL; WRTB(FM) Winnebago, IL; WDOH-FM Delphos, OH; WEGE(FM) Lima, OH; WCIT(AM) Lima, OH; WWSR(FM) Lima, OH; WFGF(FM) Wapakoneta, OH; WEAQ Chippewa Falls, WI; WDRK(FM) Cornell, WI; WIAL-FM Eau Claire, WI; WAXX-FM Eau Claire, WI; WAYY(AM) Eau Claire, WI; WECL-FM Elk Mound, WI.

Gary S. Rozynek, pres/CEO.

William W. McCutchen III Stns, 1551 Queens Rd., Los Angeles, CA 90069. Phone: (323) 656-0796. Ownership William W. McCutchen III, 100%.

Stns: 5 AM. 14 FM. KVRV(FM) Monte Rio, CA; KMHX(FM) Rohnert Park, CA; KSRO Santa Rosa, CA; KXFX-FM Santa Rosa, CA; WXRX-FM Belvidere, IL; WNTA Rockford, IL; WGFB(FM) Rockton, IL; WRTB(FM) Winnebago, IL; WDOH-FM Delphos, OH; WEGE(FM) Lima, OH; WCIT(AM) Lima, OH; WWSR(FM) Lima, OH; WFGF(FM) Wapakoneta, OH; WEAQ Chippewa Falls, WI; WDRK(FM) Cornell, WI; WIAL-FM Eau Claire, WI; WAXX-FM Eau Claire, WI; WAYY(AM) Eau Claire, WI; WECL-FM Elk Mound, WI3 FM. KMDR(FM) McKinleyville, CA; KDRW(FM) Hewitt, TX; KQDR(FM) Savoy, TX.

McKenzie River Broadcasting Company, Inc., 925 Country Club Rd., Suite 200, Eugene, OR 97401. Phone: (541) 484-9400. Fax: (541) 344-9424. Ownership Renate R. Tilson, 50.71%; John Q. Tilson III, 49.29%.

Stns: 5 AM. 14 FM. KVRV(FM) Monte Rio, CA; KMHX(FM) Rohnert Park, CA; KSRO Santa Rosa, CA; KXFX-FM Santa Rosa, CA; WXRX-FM Belvidere, IL; WNTA Rockford, IL; WGFB(FM) Rockton, IL; WRTB(FM) Winnebago, IL; WDOH-FM Delphos, OH; WEGE(FM) Lima, OH; WCIT(AM) Lima, OH; WWSR(FM) Lima, OH; WFGF(FM) Wapakoneta, OH; WEAQ Chippewa Falls, WI; WDRK(FM) Cornell, WI; WIAL-FM Eau Claire, WI; WAXX-FM Eau Claire, WI; WAYY(AM) Eau Claire, WI; WECL-FM Elk Mound, WI3 FM. KMDR(FM) McKinleyville, CA; KDRW(FM) Hewitt, TX; KQDR(FM) Savoy, TX3 FM. KMGE-FM Eugene, OR; KKNU(FM) Springfield-Eugene, OR; KEUG(FM) Veneta, OR.

John Q. Tilson III, pres; Renate R. Tilson, VP.

McMurray Communications Inc., 3335 W. 8th St., Safford, AZ 85546. Phone: (928) 428-1230. Fax: (928) 428-1311.E-mail: traffic@eaznet.com Web Site:www.mysouthernaz.com

Stns: 1 AM. 2 FM. KWRQ-FM Clifton, AZ; KXKQ-FM Safford, AZ; KATO Safford, AZ.

Harry S. McMurray, pres/CEO; David Nathan, gen mgr .

McNaughton-Jakle Stations, 14 Douglas Avenue, Elgin, IL 60120. Phone: (847) 741-7700. Fax: (847) 468-0000.E-mail: mail@wrmn.com Web Site:www.wrmn1410.com Ownership Bradley L. Beesley, K. Richard Jakle

Stns: 3 AM. WBIG Aurora, IL; WRMN Elgin, IL; KSHP North Las Vegas, NV.

(Joseph E. McNaughton & family) identified with *The Davis Enterprise, Fairfield Republic* & the *Placerville Mountain Democrat*, all CA.

K. Richard Jakle, chmn/pres.

Media Logic LLC, Box 430, Fort Morgan, CO 80701-0430. Phone: (970) 867-5674. Fax: (970) 542-1023. Ownership Wayne Johnson, 90%; and Richard Lindsey, 10%.

Stns: 2 AM. 2 FM. KFTM Fort Morgan, CO; KATR-FM Otis, CO; KSRX(FM) Sterling, CO; KRDZ Wray, CO.

Wayne Johnson, gen mgr .

Media One Group, 147 Bell St., Suite 200, Chagrin Falls, OH 44022. Phone: (440) 893-8114.

Stns: 2 AM. 3 FM. WWSE-FM Jamestown, NY; WHUG(FM) Jamestown, NY; WJTN Jamestown, NY; WKSN Jamestown, NY; WQFX-FM Russell, PA.

Media Power Group Inc., 100 Gran Bulevar Paseos, Suite 403A, San Juan, PR 00926. Phone: (787) 292-1700. Fax: (787) 292-1717.E-mail: wskn1320@yahoo.com Ownership PR Grupo Radio Nacional Inc., 25%; Jose Enrique Fernandez, 25%; Arturo Diaz Jr., 25%; and Empresas Bechara Inc., 25%.

Stns: 4 AM. WLEY Cayey, PR; WDEP(AM) Ponce, PR; WSKN(AM) San Juan, PR; WKFE Yauco, PR.

Eduardo Albino Rivero, pres; Ismael Nieves, VP.

Melia Communications Inc., Box 569, Goodland, KS 67735. Phone: (785) 899-2309. Fax: (785) 899-3062.E-mail: kloe@eaglecom.net Web Site:www.kloe.com Ownership Martin K. Melia, 50%; Kathleen J. Melia, 50%.

Stns: 1 AM. 1 FM. KWGB-FM Colby, KS; KLOE Goodland, KS.

Kathleen J. Melia, VP; Martin K. Melia, gen mgr & pres.

Mentor Partners Inc., 18720 16 Mile Rd., Big Rapids, MI 49307. Phone: (231) 796-7000. Fax: (231) 796-7951. Ownership Jeffrey Scarpelli, 100%.

Stns: 1 AM. 2 FM. WYBR-FM Big Rapids, MI; WBRN Big Rapids, MI; WWBR(FM) Big Rapids, MI.

Meredith Broadcasting Group, Meredith Corp., 1716 Locust St., Des Moines, IA 50309-3023. Phone: (515) 284-2159. Fax: (515) 284-2514. Web Site:www.meredith.com Ownership Meredith Broadcasting is an operating group of Meredith Corp., Des Moines, IA.

Stns: 1 AM. WNEM(AM) Bridgeport, MI.

Stns: 11 TV. WGCL-TV, Atlanta; WNEM-TV, Flint-Saginaw-Bay City, MI; WHNS, Greenville-Spartanburg, SC-Asheville, NC-Anderson, SC; WFSB, Hartford & New Haven, CT; KSMO-TV, Kansas City, MO; KCTV, Kansas City, MO; KVVU, Las Vegas, NV; WSMV, Nashville, TN; KPHO-TV, Phoenix (Prescott), AZ; KPTV, Portland, OR; KPDX, Portland, OR.

The publishing group includes:

Magazines: *American Baby, American Patchwork & Quilting, Better Homes & Gardens, Country Home, Country Home Country Gardens, Creative Home, Decorating, Do It Yourself, Garden, Deck, and Landscape, Garden Shed, Ladies' Home Journal, Midwest Living, MORE, Renovation Style, Successful Farming, Traditional Home,* and *Wood*, along with more than 170 special interest titles.

Paul Karpowic, pres; Douglas Lowe, exec VP.

Meridian Broadcasting Inc., 2824 Palm Beach Blvd., Fort Myers, FL 33916. Phone: (239) 337-2346. Fax: (239) 332-0767. Ownership Joseph C. Schwartzel.

Stns: 2 AM. 3 FM. WNTY(FM) Estero, FL; WINK(AM) Fort Myers, FL; WNOG Naples, FL; WTLT-FM Naples, FL; WARO-FM Naples, FL.

Joseph C. Schwartzel, pres.

Metro Radio Inc., 2251 Hunter Mill Rd., Vienna, VA 22181. Phone: (703) 938-1016. Fax: (703) 331-4706. Web Site:www.metroradioinc.com Ownership Bruce A. Houston Trust, Bruce A. Houston, trustee, 60%; Joan H. Houston Trust, Joan H. Houston, trustee, 20%; J. David Houston, 10%; and Robert B. Houston, 10%.

Stns: 3 AM. WKDV Manassas, VA; WKDL(AM) Warrenton, VA; WKCW Warrenton, VA.

Bruce A. Houston, pres.

Metropolitan Radio Group Inc., 318 E. Pershing St., Springfield, MO 65806. Phone: (417) 862-0852. Fax: (417) 862-9079. Ownership Gary L. Acker.

Stns: 5 AM. 3 FM. WBRD Palmetto, FL; WRXB Saint Petersburg Beach, FL; WTMY Sarasota, FL; KJVC-FM Mansfield, LA; KTKC-FM Springhill, LA; KUNQ-FM Houston, MO; KBTC Houston, MO; KIJN Farwell, TX.

Mark L. Acker, pres.

Meyer Communications Inc., Box 3676, Springfield, MO 65808. Phone: (417) 862-3990. Fax: (417) 869-7675. Web Site:www.ktxrfm.com E-mail: manager@radiospringfield.com Ownership Kenneth E. Meyer, 100%.

Stns: 2 AM. 3 FM. KBFL-FM Buffalo, MO; KBFL(AM) Springfield, MO; KTXR-FM Springfield, MO; KWTO Springfield, MO; KWTO-FM Springfield, MO.

Kenneth E. Meyer, pres.

Michael Radio Group, 1063 W Hwy. 34, Apt. F, Loveland, CO 80537-9424. Phone: (307) 778-9318.

Stns: 2 AM. 3 FM. KBFL-FM Buffalo, MO; KBFL(AM) Springfield, MO; KTXR-FM Springfield, MO; KWTO Springfield, MO; KWTO-FM Springfield, MO3 FM. KYOY(FM) Kimball, NE; KGRK(FM) Glenrock, WY; KRKI(FM) Newcastle, WY.

Mid Atlantic Network, Box 3300, Winchester, VA 22604. Phone: (540) 667-2224. Fax: (540) 722-3295. Ownership John P. Lewis, David P. Lewis, Howard P. Lewis.

Stns: 2 AM. 4 FM. WWRE(FM) Berryville, VA; WBQB(FM) Fredericksburg, VA; WFVA(AM) Fredericksburg, VA; WWRT(FM) Strasburg, VA; WINC Winchester, VA; WINC-FM Winchester, VA.

John P. Lewis, pres.

Mid-America Radio Group Inc., Box 1970, Martinsville, IN 46151. Phone: (765) 349-1485. Fax: (765) 342-3569.E-mail: mid-americaradio@scican.net Ownership David Keister, principal owner.

Stns: 6 AM. 9 FM. WZWZ-FM Kokomo, IN; WIOU Kokomo, IN; WXXC(FM) Marion, IN; WBAT Marion, IN; WMRI(AM) Marion, IN; WCBK-FM Martinsville, IN; WMYJ(AM) Martinsville, IN; WVNI-FM Nashville, IN; WARU Peru, IN; WARU-FM Roann, IN; WHZR-FM Royal Center, IN; WCLS(FM) Spencer, IN; WCJC-FM Van Buren, IN; WJOT Wabash, IN; WJOT-FM Wabash, IN.

David C. Keister, pres.

Midwest Communications Inc., Box 23333, Green Bay, WI 54305-3333. Phone: (920) 435-3771. Fax: (920) 321-2300. Web Site:www.mci.fm Ownership D.E. Wright, 100%.

Stns: 16 AM. 26 FM. WPRS Paris, IL; WIBQ(FM) Paris, IL; WWSY(FM) Seelyville, IN; WMGI-FM Terre Haute, IN; WTVB(AM) Coldwater, MI; WNWN-FM Coldwater, MI; WHTC(AM) Holland, MI; WKZO(AM) Kalamazoo, MI; WQLR(AM) Kalamazoo, MI; WVFM(FM) Kalamazoo, MI; WYZO(FM) Portage, MI; WNWN Portage, MI; WYVN(FM) Saugatuck, MI; KDAL Duluth, MN; KDAL-FM Duluth, MN; KTCO-FM Duluth, MN; WTBX-FM Hibbing, MN; WMFG

Hibbing, MN; WMFG-FM Hibbing, MN; WNMT Nashwauk, MN; KMFG(FM) Nashwauk, MN; WUSZ-FM Virginia, MN; WTAQ-FM Glenmore, WI; WNFL Green Bay, WI; WTAQ(AM) Green Bay, WI; WIXX-FM Green Bay, WI; WOFM-FM Mosinee, WI; WNCY-FM Neenah-Menasha, WI; WROE-FM Neenah-Menasha, WI; WOZZ-FM New London, WI; WXER(FM) Plymouth, WI; WIZD-FM Rudolph, WI; WRIG Schofield, WI; WHBL(AM) Sheboygan, WI; WBFM(FM) Sheboygan, WI; WHBZ(FM) Sheboygan Falls, WI; WRQE(FM) Sturgeon Bay, WI; WDSM Superior, WI; WGEE(AM) Superior, WI; KHQG(FM) Superior, WI; WSAU Wausau, WI; WDEZ-FM Wausau, WI.

D.E. Wright, pres.

The Mid-West Family Broadcast Group, Box 44408, Madison, WI 53744. Phone: (608) 273-1000. Fax: (608) 273-3588.E-mail: tom.walker@mwfbg.net Web Site:www.midwestfamilybroadcasting.com Ownership Philip Fisher, Richard T. Record, Thomas A. Walker.

Stns: 8 AM. 21 FM. WLCE(FM) Petersburg, IL; WMAY(AM) Springfield, IL; WNNS(FM) Springfield, IL; WQLZ(FM) Taylorville, IL; WSJM-FM Benton Harbor, MI; WYTZ-FM Bridgman, MI; WCXT(FM) Hartford, MI; WSJM Saint Joseph, MI; WIRX-FM Saint Joseph, MI; WCSY(AM) South Haven, MI; WCSY-FM South Haven, MI; KCLH(FM) Caledonia, MN; KQYB-FM Spring Grove, MN; KQRA(FM) Brookline, MO; KKLH(FM) Marshfield, MO; KOMG(FM) Ozark, MO; KOSP(FM) Willard, MO; WJQM(FM) De Forest, WI; WKTY(AM) La Crosse, WI; WIZM La Crosse, WI; WIZM-FM La Crosse, WI; WRQT(FM) La Crosse, WI; WLMV(AM) Madison, WI; WTDY Madison, WI; WHIT(AM) Madison, WI; WMGN-FM Madison, WI; WWQM-FM Middleton, WI; WWQN(FM) Mount Horeb, WI; WJJO-FM Watertown, WI.

Thomas A. Walker, pres; Richard T. Record, dir; Jason McCutchin, CFO.

Midwestern Broadcasting Co., 314 E. Front St., Traverse City, MI 49684. Phone: (231) 947-7675. Fax: (231) 929-3988. Web Site:www.wtcmi.com Ownership Ross Biederman, 52.5%; William Kiker Estate, 16.25%; William McClay, 15%.

Stns: 3 AM. 5 FM. WATZ Alpena, MI; WATZ-FM Alpena, MI; WBCM(FM) Boyne City, MI; WJZQ(FM) Cadillac, MI; WCZW(FM) Charlevoix, MI; WRGZ(FM) Rogers City, MI; WTCM(AM) Traverse City, MI; WCCW(AM) Traverse City, MI.

Ross Biederman, pres.

Millcreek Broadcasting L.L.C., 980 N. Michigan Ave., Suite 1880, Chicago, IL 60611. Phone: (312) 204-9900. Fax: (312) 587-9466. Ownership Alta Communications VII LP, 79% (percentage of total assets).

Stns: 3 AM. 5 FM. WATZ Alpena, MI; WATZ-FM Alpena, MI; WBCM(FM) Boyne City, MI; WJZQ(FM) Cadillac, MI; WCZW(FM) Charlevoix, MI; WRGZ(FM) Rogers City, MI; WTCM(AM) Traverse City, MI; WCCW(AM) Traverse City, MI4 FM. KAUU(FM) Manti, UT; KUDE(FM) Nephi, UT; KUDD(FM) Roy, UT; KUUU(FM) South Jordan, UT.

Christopher Devine, pres; Bruce Buzil, exec VP.

Millennium Radio Group LLC, 220 Northpointe Pkwy., Suite D, Amherst, NY 14228. Phone: (716) 639-9300. Fax: (719) 639-8782. Ownership UBS Capital Americas; Alta Communications; Mercy Capital Partners LP.

Stns: 3 AM. 8 FM. WADB(AM) Asbury Park, NJ; WJLK(FM) Asbury Park, NJ; WPUR-FM Atlantic City, NJ; WENJ(AM) Atlantic City, NJ; WFPG(FM) Atlantic City, NJ; WSJO(FM) Egg Harbor City, NJ; WOBM(AM) Lakewood, NJ; WCHR-FM Manahawkin, NJ; WENJ-FM Millville, NJ; WOBM-FM Toms River, NJ; WKXW(FM) Trenton, NJ.

Charles W. Banta, chmn; James Donahoe, pres/CEO.

Miller Communications Inc., Box 1269, Sumter, SC 29151. Phone: (803) 775-2321. Fax: (803) 773-4856. Web Site:www.miller.fm Ownership Frank H. Avent, 31.33%; William Duncan, 24.37%; Harold T. Miller Jr., 20.89%; Theresa Miller, 20.89%; and David Baker, 2.5%.

Stns: 5 AM. 7 FM. WGFG-FM Branchville, SC; WOLH(AM) Florence, SC; WDKD Kingstree, SC; WWKT-FM Kingstree, SC; WHYM(AM) Lake City, SC; WSIM(FM) Lamar, SC; WQKI-FM Orangeburg, SC; WIGL(FM) Saint Matthews, SC; WWHM(AM) Sumter, SC; WDXY Sumter, SC; WWBD(FM) Sumter, SC; WIBZ-FM Wedgefield, SC.

Harold T. Miller Jr., pres/CEO; Dave Baker, VP; Theresa Miller, VP/gen mgr.

Miller Media Group, Box 169, 918 East Park, Taylorville, IL 62568-0169. Phone: (217) 824-3395. Fax: (217) 824-3301. Web Site:www.randyradio.com Ownership Randal J. Miller owns 100% of WYEC(FM), WHOW(AM), WHOW-FM, WJRE(FM), WKEI(AM) & translator 104.3 FM, and WRAN(FM); 70% of WMKR(FM) & WTIM-FM. Lawrence Travis owns 30% of WMKR(FM) & WTIM-FM. Note: Group also owns the Hometown Illinois Radio Network, an ad-hoc network of 30 radio stns that bcsts reports from the Illinois State Fair, Illinois Farm Bureau annual meeting & Commodity Classic.

Stns: 2 AM. 6 FM. WYEC(FM) Cambridge, IL; WHOW Clinton, IL; WEZC(FM) Clinton, IL; WJRE(FM) Galva, IL; WKEI(AM) Kewanee, IL; WMKR(FM) Pana, IL; WTIM-FM Taylorville, IL; WRAN(FM) Tower Hill, IL.

Randal J. Miller, pres; Cathaleen R. Miller, sec/treas.

Milner Broadcasting, 292 N. Convent, Bourbonnais, IL 60914. Phone: (815) 933-9287. Fax: (815) 933-8696.

Stns: 2 AM. 6 FM. WYEC(FM) Cambridge, IL; WHOW Clinton, IL; WEZC(FM) Clinton, IL; WJRE(FM) Galva, IL; WKEI(AM) Kewanee, IL; WMKR(FM) Pana, IL; WTIM-FM Taylorville, IL; WRAN(FM) Tower Hill, IL3 FM. WFAV(FM) Gilman, IL; WVLI-FM Kankakee, IL; WIVR(FM) Kentland, IN.

Milwaukee Radio Alliance L.L.C., N72 W12922 Good Hope Rd., Menomonee Falls, WI 53051-4441. Phone: (414) 771-1021. Fax: (414) 771-3036.E-mail: bhurwitz@milwaukeeradio.com Web Site:www.milwaukeeradio.com Ownership All Pro Broadcasting, 50%; Shamrock Communications, 50%.

Stns: 1 AM. 2 FM. WMCS Greenfield, WI; WLDB(FM) Milwaukee, WI; WLUM-FM Milwaukee, WI.

Willie Davis, chmn; William Lynette, pres.

Minn-Iowa Christian Broadcasting Inc., Box 72, Blue Earth, MN 56013. Phone: (507) 526-3233. Fax: (507) 526-3235.E-mail: kjly@kjly.com Web Site:www.kjly.com

Stns: 1 AM. 2 FM. WMCS Greenfield, WI; WLDB(FM) Milwaukee, WI; WLUM-FM Milwaukee, WI5 FM. KJYL-FM Eagle Grove, IA; KJCY(FM) Saint Ansgar, IA; KJIA(FM) Spirit Lake, IA; KJLY-FM Blue Earth, MN; KJWR(FM) Windom, MN.

Matt Dorfner, exec dir.

Miriam Media Inc., 6117 Lemon Thyme Dr., Alexandria, VA 22310. Phone: (571) 228-1258. Fax: (703) 299-6626. Ownership Darryl Delawder, 51%; and Evan Carb, 49%.

Stns: 1 AM. 2 FM. WMCS Greenfield, WI; WLDB(FM) Milwaukee, WI; WLUM-FM Milwaukee, WI5 FM. KJYL-FM Eagle Grove, IA; KJCY(FM) Saint Ansgar, IA; KJIA(FM) Spirit Lake, IA; KJLY-FM Blue Earth, MN; KJWR(FM) Windom, MN2 FM. KBTY(FM) Benjamin, TX; KCHT(FM) Childress, TX.

Darryl Delawder, pres.

Mission Nebraska Inc., Box 30345, Lincoln, NE 68503-0345. Phone: (402) 477-1090. Web Site:www.missionnebraska.org Ownership Ron Brown, 16.67%; Stanley A. Parker, 16.67%; David Chally, 16.67%; Mike Hoefler, 16.67%; Patrick McNair, 16.67%; and David O'Doherty, 16.67%.

Stns: 1 AM. 5 FM. KPNY-FM Alliance, NE; KROA(FM) Grand Island, NE; KMMJ Grand Island, NE; KMHB(FM) Seward, NE; KMBT(FM) Tecumseh, NE; KMBV(FM) Valentine, NE.

Mississippi Broadcasters L.L.C., Box 1699, Meridian, MS 39302. Phone: (601) 693-2661. Fax: (601) 483-0826. Ownership Clay Holladay, 100%.

Stns: 1 AM. 5 FM. KPNY-FM Alliance, NE; KROA(FM) Grand Island, NE; KMMJ Grand Island, NE; KMHB(FM) Seward, NE; KMBT(FM) Tecumseh, NE; KMBV(FM) Valentine, NE4 FM. WMLV(FM) Butler, AL; WJXM(FM) De Kalb, MS; WUCL(FM) Meridian, MS; WKZB(FM) Stonewall, MS.

Clay E. Holladay, pres & gen mgr .

Missouri River Christian Broadcasting Inc., (Good News Voice). Box 187, Washington, MO 63090. Phone: (636) 239-0400. Fax: (636) 293-4448. Web Site:www.goodnewsvoice.org Ownership Group also owns K235AO Salem, MO, translator stn on 94.9 mhz.

Stns: 1 AM. 5 FM. KPNY-FM Alliance, NE; KROA(FM) Grand Island, NE; KMMJ Grand Island, NE; KMHB(FM) Seward, NE; KMBT(FM) Tecumseh, NE; KMBV(FM) Valentine, NE4 FM. WMLV(FM) Butler, AL; WJXM(FM) De Kalb, MS; WUCL(FM) Meridian, MS; WKZB(FM) Stonewall, MS4 FM. KGNA-FM Arnold, MO; KGNN-FM Cuba, MO; KGNY(FM) Dixon, MO; KGNV(FM) Washington, MO.

J.C. Goggan, gen mgr .

Monarch Broadcasting Inc., 212 W. Cypress St., Altus, OK 73521. Phone: (580) 482-1450. Fax: (580) 482-3420. Web Site:www.kwhw.com Ownership Matthew L. Ward and Kristin Ward, 51%; and Deborah Ward-Ingstad, 49%. Note: Matthew L. Ward is sole officer, dir and shareholder of KIMM Radio Inc., licensee of KIMM(AM) Rapid City, SD.

Stns: 1 AM. 1 FM. KWHW Altus, OK; KQTZ-FM Hobart, OK.

Matthew L. Ward, pres.

Monticello Media LLC, 3948 S. Third St., Suite 191, Jacksonville Beach, FL 32250. Phone: (904) 285-3239. Ownership George Reed, 100%.

Stns: 2 AM. 4 FM. WWTJ(FM) Charlottesville, VA; WCHV Charlottesville, VA; WKAV Charlottesville, VA; WZGN(FM) Crozet, VA; WHTE-FM Ruckersville, VA; WCYK-FM Staunton, VA.

George R. Reed, pres.

Montrose Broadcasting Corp., Box 248, 9 Locust St., Montrose, PA 18801. Phone: (570) 278-2811. Fax: (570) 278-1442.E-mail: mail@wpel.org Web Site:www.wpel.org Ownership Non Profit Non Stock Corporation.

Stns: 2 AM. 3 FM. WPGM Danville, PA; WPGM-FM Danville, PA; WPEL Montrose, PA; WPEL-FM Montrose, PA; WBGM-FM New Berlin, PA.

Larry Souder, pres; John Hagenboch, VP; Barbara Snyder, sec; Charles W. Scott, Jr., treas.

The Moody Bible Institute of Chicago, 820 N. LaSalle Blvd., Chicago, IL 60610. Phone: (312) 329-4300. Fax: (312) 329-8980. Web Site:www.mbn.org E-mail: mbn@moody.edu

Stns: 5 AM. 26 FM. WMBV-FM Dixons Mills, AL; WMFT(FM) Tuscaloosa, AL; WRMB-FM Boynton Beach, FL; WHGN(FM) Crystal River, FL; WKES-FM Lakeland, FL; WKZM-FM Sarasota, FL; WMBI(AM) Chicago, IL; WMBI-FM Chicago, IL; WDLM East Moline, IL; WGNR Anderson, IN; WGNR-FM Anderson, IN; WIWC-FM Kokomo, IN; WMBL(FM) Mitchell, IN; WHPL-FM West Lafayette, IN; WJSO-FM Pikeville, KY; WGNB(FM) Zeeland, MI; WMBU-FM Forest, MS; KSPL-FM Kalispell, MT; KJCG(FM) Missoula, MT; KMBN(FM) Las Cruces, NM; WCRF-FM Cleveland, OH; WVML(FM) Millersburg, OH; WVMS-FM Sandusky, OH; WVME(FM) Meadville, PA; WVMN-FM New Castle, PA; WMBW-FM Chattanooga, TN; WFCM Smyrna, TN; KMLW-FM Moses Lake, WA; KMBI Spokane, WA; KMBI-FM Spokane, WA; KMWY(FM) Jackson, WY.

Joseph Stowell, pres; Wayne Pederson, VP bcstg.

Moon Broadcasting, 1200 W. Venice Blvd., Los Angeles, CA 90006. Phone: (213) 745-6224. Fax: (213) 745-7577. Ownership Abel DeLuna, 100%.

Stns: 6 AM. 7 FM. KIQQ Barstow, CA; KAEH(FM) Beaumont, CA; KMQA-FM East Porterville, CA; KDAC Fort Bragg, CA; KMEN(FM) Mendota, CA; KIQQ-FM Newberry Springs, CA; KAAT(FM) Oakhurst, CA; KTNS Oakhurst, CA; KTOB(AM) Petaluma, CA; KRRS Santa Rosa, CA; KMNA(FM) Mabton, WA; KZXR Prosser, WA; KLES(FM) Prosser, WA.

Abel DeLuna, pres.

The Morey Organization Inc., 1103 Stewart Ave., Garden City, NY 11530. Phone: (516) 228-6570. Web Site:www.moreyorg.com

Stns: 6 AM. 7 FM. KIQQ Barstow, CA; KAEH(FM) Beaumont, CA; KMQA-FM East Porterville, CA; KDAC Fort Bragg, CA; KMEN(FM) Mendota, CA; KIQQ-FM Newberry Springs, CA; KAAT(FM) Oakhurst, CA; KTNS Oakhurst, CA; KTOB(AM) Petaluma, CA; KRRS Santa Rosa, CA; KMNA(FM) Mabton, WA; KZXR Prosser, WA; KLES(FM) Prosser, WA3 FM. WDRE(FM) Calverton-Roanoke, NY; WLIR-FM Hampton Bays, NY; WBON(FM) Westhampton, NY.

Jed Morey, COO; John Caracciolo, pres.

Morgan County Industries Inc., 129 College St., West Liberty, KY 41472. Phone: (606) 743-3145. Fax: (606) 743-9557.E-mail: radio41472@yahoo.com

Stns: 3 AM. 4 FM. WCBJ-FM Campton, KY; WMOR Morehead, KY; WMOR-FM Morehead, KY; WRLV Salyersville, KY; WRLV-FM Salyersville, KY; WLKS West Liberty, KY; WLKS-FM West Liberty, KY.

Paul Lyons, COO.

Morris Radio LLC, 725 Broad St., Augusta, GA 30903-0936. Phone: (706) 823-3331. Fax: (706) 823-3212. Web Site:www.morris.com Ownership Owned by Morris Communications Company LLC. Group also owns the Kansas Agriculture Network, Topeka, KS; Kansas Information Network, Topeka, KS; and the Wildcat Sports Network, Topeka, KS.

Stns: 15 AM. 16 FM. KBRJ(FM) Anchorage, AK; KEAG-FM Anchorage, AK; KFQD Anchorage, AK; KHAR Anchorage, AK; KMXS-FM Anchorage, AK; KWHL-FM Anchorage, AK; KAYO(FM) Wasilla, AK; KNWZ(AM) Coachella, CA; KKUU(FM) Indio, CA; KNWQ(AM) Palm Springs, CA; KXPS(AM) Thousand Palms, CA; KFUT(AM) Thousand Palms, CA; KNWH(AM) Twentynine Palms, CA; KDGL(FM) Yucca Valley, CA; KSAJ-FM Abilene, KS; KABI Abilene, KS; KBLS(FM) North Fort Riley, KS; KSAL(AM) Salina, KS; KSAL-FM Salina, KS; KYEZ(FM) Salina, KS; WIBW Topeka, KS; WIBW-FM Topeka, KS; KGNC-FM Amarillo,

TX; KGNC Amarillo, TX; KXRO Aberdeen, WA; KWOK(AM) Hoquiam, WA; KXXK(FM) Hoquiam-Aberdeen, WA; KWIQ-FM Moses Lake, WA; KWIQ(AM) Moses Lake North, WA; KKRT Wenatchee, WA; KWLN(FM) Wilson Creek, WA.

Morris Publishing Group owns the following daily newspapers: *Amarillo* (Texas) *Globe-News, Athens* (GA) *Banner-Herald, The Augusta* (GA) *Chronicle, Brainerd* (MN) *Dispatch, The Daily Ardmoreite*, Ardmore, OK, *Dodge City* (Kan.) *Daily Globe, The Examiner*, Independence, MO, *The Florida Times-Union*, Jacksonville, *The Grand Island* (NE) *Independent, Hannibal* (MO) *Courier-Post, Hillsdale* (MI) *Daily News, The Holland* (MI) *Sentinel, Juneau* (AK) *Empire, Log Cabin Democrat*, Conway, AK, *Lubbock* (Texas) *Avalanche-Journal, The Morning Sun*, Pittsburg, KS, *News Chief*, Winter Haven, FL, *The Newton* (KS) *Kansan, The Oak Ridger*, Oak Ridge, TN, *Peninsula Clarion*, Kenai, AK, *The St. Augustine* (FL) *Record, Savannah* (GA) *Morning News, The Shawnee* (OK) *News-Star, The Topeka* (KS) *Capital-Journal, Yankton* (SD) *Daily Press & Dakotan, York* (NE) *News-Times. Magazines include: Athens Magazine, Augusta Magazine, Coastal Antiques and Art, Coastal Senior, Eco Latino* (Athens), *Eco Latino* (St. Augustine), *Gainesville Life, Her Voice, Hers Kansas, LOUNGE, Savannah Coastal Parent, Savannah Magazine, Senior Living, She's OK!, Skirt!, Water's Edge, West Michigan Senior Times. Other publications include 37 non-daily newspapers and shoppers.*

Michael D. Osterhout, COO.

Mortenson Broadcasting Co., 3270 Blazer Pkwy. #101, Lexington, KY 40509-1847. Phone: (859) 245-1000. Fax: (859) 245-1600. Ownership Jack Mortenson, 100%.

Stns: 7 AM. 1 FM. KGGN Gladstone, MO; KRVA Cockrell Hill, TX; KGGR Dallas, TX; KHVN Fort Worth, TX; KKGM(AM) Fort Worth, TX; KTNO(AM) University Park, TX; WEMM-FM Huntington, WV; WRWB(AM) Huntington, WV.

Jack Mortenson, pres.

Mt. Rushmore Broadcasting Inc., 218 N. Wolcott, Casper, WY 82602. Phone: (307) 265-1984. Fax: (307) 266-3295.E-mail: mtrushmore@wyoming.com Web Site:www.wyomingradio.com

Stns: 5 AM. 8 FM. KAWK(FM) Custer, SD; KFCR Custer, SD; KZMX Hot Springs, SD; KZMX-FM Hot Springs, SD; KASS(FM) Casper, WY; KVOC Casper, WY; KHOC-FM Casper, WY; KMLD(FM) Casper, WY; KQLT-FM Casper, WY; KRAL Rawlins, WY; KIQZ(FM) Rawlins, WY; KGOS Torrington, WY; KERM-FM Torrington, WY.

Jan Charles Gray, pres/CEO.

Mountain Broadcasting Corp., 99 Clinton Rd., West Caldwell, NJ 07006. Phone: (973) 852-0300. Fax: (973) 808-5516. Ownership Sun Young Joo, 66% votes, 35.2% total assets; John H. Joo, 14% votes, 6.3% total assets; Victor C. Joo, 14% votes, 5.6% total assets; Sun Hoo Joo, 6% votes, 2.9% total assets; and Hansen Lau, 5.7% total assets.

Stns: 3 AM. WPWA Chester, PA; WBTK(AM) Richmond, VA; WWGB Indian Head, MD.

Stns: 1 TV. WMBC-TV, New York.

Sun Young Joo, pres.

Mountain Communications, Box 211, Saranac Lake, NY 12983-0211. Phone: (518) 891-1544. Fax: (518) 891-1545. Ownership Prescott House LLC owns 100% of WIRD(AM)-WLPW(FM) and WRGR(FM). Edward S. Morgan, the sole member of Prescott House LLC, is also the controlling stockholder of WNBZ(AM)-WYZY(FM).

Stns: 2 AM. 3 FM. WIRD Lake Placid, NY; WLPW-FM Lake Placid, NY; WNBZ Saranac Lake, NY; WYZY(FM) Saranac Lake, NY; WRGR-FM Tupper Lake, NY.

Ted Morgan, owner.

Mountain Dog Media, 254 Winnebago Dr., Fond du Lac, WI 54935. Phone: (920) 921-1071. Fax: (920) 921-0757.

Stns: 2 AM. 1 FM. KFIZ Fond du Lac, WI; WFON(FM) Fond du Lac, WI; WCLB(AM) Sheboygan, WI.

Randy Hopper, pres.

Mountain Wireless Inc., Box 159, Skowhegan, ME 04976. Phone: (207) 474-5171. Fax: (207) 474-3299.

Stns: 1 AM. 2 FM. WCTB-FM Fairfield, ME; WFMX(FM) Skowhegan, ME; WSKW Skowhegan, ME.

Alan W. Anderson, pres.

Mt. Washington Radio & Gramophone L.L.C., Box 2008, Conway, NH 03818. Phone: (603) 356-8870. Fax: (603) 356-8875.E-mail: office@wmwv.com Web Site:www.wmwv.com Ownership Ronald Frizzell, 51%; Greg Frizzell, 25%; Arnold Lerner, 24%.

Stns: 1 AM. 2 FM. WBNC Conway, NH; WVMJ(FM) Conway, NH; WMWV-FM Conway, NH.

Ron Frizzell, pres.

Muirfield Broadcasting Inc., 200 Short Rd., Southern Pines, NC 28387. Phone: (910) 692-2107. Fax: (910) 692-6849. Web Site:www.star1025fm.com Ownership Walker Morris.

Stns: 1 AM. 1 FM. WIOZ Pinehurst, NC; WIOZ-FM Southern Pines, NC.

Walker Morris, pres.

Multicultural Radio Broadcasting Inc., 449 Broadway, New York, NY 10013. Phone: (212) 966-1059. Fax: (212) 966-9580. Web Site:www.mrbi.net Ownership Arthur S. Liu, 51%; and Yvonne S. Liu, 49%.

Stns: 30 AM. KWRU(AM) Fresno, CA; KYPA Los Angeles, CA; KAZN Pasadena, CA; KATD Pittsburg, CA; KAHZ(AM) Pomona, CA; KIQI San Francisco, CA; KEST San Francisco, CA; KSJX(AM) San Jose, CA; KBLA Santa Monica, CA; KALI West Covina, CA; WNMA Miami Springs, FL; WEXY Wilton Manors, FL; WGFS Covington, GA; WLYN Lynn, MA; WAZN(AM) Watertown, MA; WJDM Elizabeth, NJ; WWRU(AM) Jersey City, NJ; WTTM(AM) Lindenwold, NJ; WNSW Newark, NJ; WPAT Paterson, NJ; WHWH Princeton, NJ; WNYG Babylon, NY; WZRC New York, NY; WKDM(AM) New York, NY; KDFT Ferris, TX; KXYZ Houston, TX; KMNY(AM) Hurst, TX; WZHF Arlington, VA; KXPA Bellevue, WA; WLXE(AM) Rockville, MD.

Arthur S. Liu, pres/CEO.

Munbilla Broadcasting Properties Ltd., 5526 Hwy. 281 N., Marble Falls, TX 78654. Phone: (830) 693-5551. Fax: (830) 693-5107. Ownership B. Shane Fox, 100%.

Stns: 1 AM. 5 FM. KBEY(FM) Burnet, TX; KRHC(AM) Burnet, TX; KRZS(FM) Hunt, TX; KHLE(FM) Kempner, TX; KHLB(FM) Mason, TX; KYRT(FM) Mason, TX.

Duane Fox, gen mgr; Sabrina Preiss, traf mgr; Bill Woleben, chief engr, opns mgr.

Morgan Murphy Media, 7025 W. Raymond Rd., Madison, WI 53719. Phone: (608) 271-4321. Fax: (608) 271-0800.E-mail: tbier@wisctv.com Web Site:www.morganmurphymedia.com Ownership Evening Telegram Co. owns 100% of KVEW(TV), KXLY-AM-FM-TV, KXLY-DT and KAPP(TV). Evening Telegram Co. owns 84.4% of Television Wisconsin Inc., with an additional 15.2% of the stn held by Evening Telegram stockholders.

Stns: 4 AM. 4 FM. KXLX(AM) Airway Heights, WA; KXLY Spokane, WA; KZZU-FM Spokane, WA; KEZE-FM Spokane, WA; WGLR Lancaster, WI; WGLR-FM Lancaster, WI; WPVL Platteville, WI; WPVL-FM Platteville, WI.

Stns: 5 TV. WKBT, La Crosse-Eau Claire, WI; WISC-TV, Madison, WI; KXLY-TV, Spokane, WA; KAPP, Yakima-Pasco -Richland-Kennewick, WA; KVEW, Yakima-Pasco -Richland-Kennewick, WA.

The Evening Telegram principals own *Madison Magazine*, Madison, WI.

Elizabeth Murphy Burns, pres; George Nelson, exec VP; David Sanks, exec VP; Steve Herling, exec VP; Brian Lubarski, gen mgr; Scott Chorski, VP/gen mgr.

Muzzy Broadcasting L.L.C., 500 Division St., Stevens Point, WI 54481. Phone: (715) 341-9800. Fax: (715) 341-0000. Web Site:www.979wspt.com Ownership Richard L. Muzzy.

Stns: 1 AM. 2 FM. WKQH(FM) Marathon, WI; WSPT Stevens Point, WI; WSPT-FM Stevens Point, WI.

Richard L. Muzzy, pres.

My Broadcasting Corp., Box 961, Renfrew, ON K7V 4H4. Canada. Phone: (613) 432-6936. Fax: (613) 432-1086. Web Site:www.myfmradio.ca

Stns: 1 AM. 2 FM. WKQH(FM) Marathon, WI; WSPT Stevens Point, WI; WSPT-FM Stevens Point, WI5 FM. CIYN-FM Kincardine, ON; CKYM-FM Napanee, ON; CIMY-FM Pembroke, ON; CHMY-FM Renfrew, ON; CJMI-FM Strathroy, ON.

My Town Media Inc., 250 N. Water, Suite 300, Wichita, KS 67202. Phone: (620) 431-1333. Fax: (620) 431-4643.E-mail: dave@mytown-media.com Web Site:www.kkoyfm.com Ownership Murfin Inc.

Stns: 1 AM. 5 FM. KSNP(FM) Burlington, KS; KKOY Chanute, KS; KKOY-FM Chanute, KS; KINZ-FM Humboldt, KS; KWXD-FM Asbury, MO; KHST(FM) Lamar, MO.

William Wachter, pres & gen mgr.

N

NL Broadcasting Ltd., 611 Lansdowne St., Kamloops, BC V2C 1Y6. Canada. Phone: (250) 372-2292. Fax: (250) 372-2293. Ownership NL Properties Inc., 37.92%; J. Robert Dunn, 38.61%; and others 13.33%. Note: Group also owns 51% of CJNL(AM) Merritt, BC.

Stns: 1 AM. 2 FM. CHNL(AM) Kamloops, BC; CKRV-FM Kamloops, BC; CJKC-FM Kamloops, BC.

NRC Broadcasting Inc., 1201 Eighteenth St., Suite 250, Denver, CO 80202. Phone: (303) 675-4698. Fax: (303) 296-7030. Web Site:www.nrcbroadcasting.com Ownership Anschutz Co., 60.9%; Tim Brown, 33.5%; Ray Skibitsky, 2.8%; and Dave Rogers, 2.8%. Note: Stns licensed to NRC Broadcasting Mountain Group LLC are owned by Timothy Brown and David Rogers, 100%.

Stns: 1 AM. 11 FM. KSPN-FM Aspen, CO; KNFO-FM Basalt, CO; KSMT-FM Breckenridge, CO; KTUN-FM Eagle, CO; KRKY-FM Estes Park, CO; KKCH(FM) Glenwood Springs, CO; KCUV(FM) Greenwood Village, CO; KQZR(FM) Hayden, CO; KIDN-FM Hayden, CO; KCKK(AM) Littleton, CO; KFMU-FM Oak Creek, CO; KJAC(FM) Timnath, CO.

Tim Brown, chmn/CEO; Ray Skibitsky, pres/COO; Dave Rogers, CFO.

NRG Media LLC, 2875 Mount Vernon Rd. S.E., Cedar Rapids, IA 52403. Phone: (319) 862-0300. Fax: (319) 286-9383.E-mail: jlink@nrgmedia.com Web Site:www.nrgmedia.com Ownership Waitt Media Holdings LLC, 55.1%; and NewRadio Group LLC, 44.9%.

Stns: 14 AM. 27 FM. KLGA Algona, IA; KLGA-FM Algona, IA; KWBG Boone, IA; KHBT-FM Humboldt, IA; KKIA-FM Ida Grove, IA; KAYL Storm Lake, IA; KAYL-FM Storm Lake, IA; KQWC Webster City, IA; KQWC-FM Webster City, IA; WIXN Dixon, IL; WRCV(FM) Dixon, IL; WSEY(FM) Oregon, IL; WRKX(FM) Ottawa, IL; WCMY(AM) Ottawa, IL; WJBD Salem, IL; WJBD-FM Salem, IL; KWBE Beatrice, NE; KHUB Fremont, NE; KFMT-FM Fremont, NE; KSYZ-FM Grand Island, NE; KROR(FM) Hastings, NE; KRNY(FM) Kearney, NE; KQKY(FM) Kearney, NE; KGFW(AM) Kearney, NE; KLNC(FM) Lincoln, NE; KBBK(FM) Lincoln, NE; KLIN Lincoln, NE; KFGE-FM Milford, NE; WRLO-FM Antigo, WI; WSJY-FM Fort Atkinson, WI; WFAW Fort Atkinson, WI; WYTE(FM) Marshfield, WI; WLKD Minocqua, WI; WMQA-FM Minocqua, WI; WHDG-FM Rhinelander, WI; WRHN(FM) Rhinelander, WI; WOBT(AM) Rhinelander, WI; WBCV(FM) Wausau, WI; WKCH-FM Whitewater, WI; WLJY(FM) Whiting, WI; WGLX-FM Wisconsin Rapids, WI.

Mary Quass, pres/CEO; Norman W. Waitt Jr., chmn.

Nassau Broadcasting Partners L.P., 619 Alexander Rd., 3rd Fl., Princeton, NJ 08540. Phone: (609) 452-9696. Fax: 609) 419-0143. Web Site:www.nassaubroadcasting.com

Stns: 15 AM. 35 FM. WFQR(FM) Harwich Port, MA; WPXC-FM Hyannis, MA; WCRB(FM) Lowell, MA; WFRQ(FM) Mashpee, MA; WTHT(FM) Auburn, ME; WBQI(FM) Bar Harbor, ME; WLVP(AM) Gorham, ME; WBYA(FM) Islesboro, ME; WBQQ-FM Kennebunk, ME; WBQW(FM) Kennebunkport, ME; WLAM(AM) Lewiston, ME; WFNK(FM) Lewiston, ME; WHXR(FM) North Windham, ME; WHXQ(FM) Scarborough, ME; WBQX-FM Thomaston, ME; WNHW(FM) Belmont, NH; WHDQ-FM Claremont, NH; WTSV Claremont, NH; WJYY-FM Concord, NH; WNNH-FM Henniker, NH; WLNH-FM Laconia, NH; WEMJ Laconia, NH; WWHQ(FM) Meredith, NH; WFNQ(FM) Nashua, NH; WFYX(FM) Walpole, NH; WLKZ-FM Wolfeboro, NH; WWYY-FM Belvidere, NJ; WNJE(AM) Flemington, NJ; WCHR(AM) Trenton, NJ; WPST(FM) Trenton, NJ; WTKZ Allentown, PA; WODE-FM Easton, PA; WEEX Easton, PA; WBYN(AM) Lehighton, PA; WPLY(AM) Mount Pocono, PA; WVPO Stroudsburg, PA; WORK-FM Barre, VT; WSNO Barre, VT; WZLF(FM) Bellows Falls, VT; WWFY(FM) Berlin, VT; WEXP-FM Brandon, VT; WMOO-FM Derby Center, VT; WWOD(FM) Hartford, VT; WIKE Newport, VT; WXLF(FM) White River Junction, VT; WNHV White River Junction, VT; WTHK(FM) Wilmington, VT; WARK Hagerstown, MD; WWEG(FM) Hagerstown, MD; WAFY-FM Middletown, MD.

Louis F. Mercatani, pres.

Nebraska Rural Radio Association, Box 880, Lexington, NE 68850. Phone: (308) 324-2371. Fax: (308) 324-5786.E-mail: krvnam@krvn.com Web Site:www.krvn.com Ownership Nebraska Rural Radio Association, 100%

Stns: 3 AM. 3 FM. KRVN Lexington, NE; KRVN-FM Lexington, NE; KNEB Scottsbluff, NE; KNEB-FM Scottsbluff, NE; KTIC West Point, NE; KTIC-FM West Point, NE.

Eric Brown, sec/treas; Larry Hudkins, pres; Kevin Cooksley, VP.

Neuhoff Family L.P., 1501 N. Washington Ave., Danville, IL 61832. Phone: (217) 442-1700. Phone: (217) 787-9200. Fax: (217) 431-1489.E-mail: mhulvey@cooketech.net Web Site:neuhoffmedia.com Ownership Neuhoff Corp., North Palm Beach, FL, 100% of votes.

Stns: 4 AM. 8 FM. WRHK-FM Danville, IL; WDAN(AM) Danville, IL; WDNL(FM) Danville, IL; WDZ(AM) Decatur, IL; WDZQ(FM) Decatur, IL; WSOY(AM) Decatur, IL; WSOY-FM Decatur, IL; WXAJ(FM) Hillsboro, IL; WCZQ-FM Monticello, IL; WFMB(AM) Springfield, IL; WFMB-FM Springfield, IL; WCVS-FM Virden, IL.

Stns: 1 TV. KMVT, Twin Falls, ID.

Mike Hulvey, gen mgr; Geoff Neuhoff, pres.

Nevada County Broadcasters Inc., 1255 E. Main St., Suite A, Grass Valley, CA 95945. Phone: (530) 272-3424. Fax: (530) 272-2872.E-mail: knco@nccn.com Web Site:www.knco.com
Stns: 2 AM. 1 FM. KNCO(AM) Grass Valley, CA; KNCO-FM Grass Valley, CA; KUBA(AM) Yuba City, CA.

Bob Breck, CEO.

New Media Broadcasters Inc., 2210 31st St. N., Havre, MT 59501-8003. Phone: (406) 265-7841. Fax: (406) 265-8855.E-mail: nmb@nmbi.com Web Site:www.nmbi.com Ownership C. David Leeds, 100%.
Stns: 1 AM. 2 FM. KRYK(FM) Chinook, MT; KOJM Havre, MT; KPQX(FM) Havre, MT.

C. David Leeds, pres; Cynthia H. Leeds, sec/treas.

New Northwest Broadcasters LLC, 1011 Western Ave., Suite 920, Seattle, WA 98104. Phone: (206) 204-0213. Fax: (206) 204-0214. Web Site:www.nnbradio.com Ownership E. Perot Bissell, 50%; and Bradford N. Creswell, 50%.
Stns: 11 AM. 25 FM. KFAT(FM) Anchorage, AK; KDBZ(FM) Anchorage, AK; KTDZ(FM) College, AK; KWLF-FM Fairbanks, AK; KXLR-FM Fairbanks, AK; KFAR Fairbanks, AK; KCBF Fairbanks, AK; KXLW(FM) Houston, AK; KBBO-FM Houston, AK; KGHL-FM Billings, MT; KRPM(FM) Billings, MT; KQBL(FM) Billings, MT; KGHL Billings, MT; KRSQ-FM Laurel, MT; KKEE(AM) Astoria, OR; KAST Astoria, OR; KYSF-FM Bonanza, OR; KAGO Klamath Falls, OR; KAGO-FM Klamath Falls, OR; KLAD(AM) Klamath Falls, OR; KLAD-FM Klamath Falls, OR; KCRX-FM Seaside, OR; KUJ-FM Burbank, WA; KARY-FM Grandview, WA; KVAS-FM Ilwaco, WA; KTCR Kennewick, WA; KJOX-FM Long Beach, WA; KIOK-FM Richland, WA; KEGX(FM) Richland, WA; KALE Richland, WA; KBBO(AM) Selah, WA; KKSR(FM) Walla Walla, WA; KHHK-FM Yakima, WA; KJOX(AM) Yakima, WA; KRSE-FM Yakima, WA; KXDD-FM Yakima, WA.

Pete Benedetti, CEO.

New South Communications Inc., Box 5797, Meridian, MS 39302. Phone: (601) 693-2661. Fax: (601) 483-0826. Ownership F.E. Holladay, 100%.
Stns: 2 AM. 3 FM. WYOY-FM Gluckstadt, MS; WUSJ(FM) Madison, MS; WALT Meridian, MS; WIIN Ridgeland, MS; WJKK-FM Vicksburg, MS.

F.E. Holladay, pres.

New West Broadcasting Corp., 1145 Kilauea Ave., Hilo, HI 96720. Phone: (808) 935-5461. Fax: (808) 935-7761. Ownership NWB Holdings Inc., 80% stockholder; and Christopher S. Leonard, 20% stockholder.
Stns: 1 AM. 2 FM. KNWB-FM Hilo, HI; KPUA Hilo, HI; KAOY(FM) Kealakekua, HI.

NewCap Inc., 745 Windmill Rd., Dartmouth, NS B3B1C2. Canada. Phone: (902) 468-7557. Fax: (902) 468-7558. Web Site:www.ncc.ca Ownership H.R. Steele, Blavin & Company.
Stns: 22 AM. 42 FM. CKBA-FM Athabasca, AB; CJPR-FM Blairmore, AB; CJEG-FM Bonnyville, AB; CIXF-FM Brooks, AB; CIBQ Brooks, AB; CFXL-FM Calgary, AB; CFUL-FM Calgary, AB; CFCW-FM Camrose, AB; CFCW Camrose, AB; CJXK-FM Cold Lake, AB; CKDQ Drumheller, AB; CKRA-FM Edmonton, AB; CIRK-FM Edmonton, AB; CFXE-FM Edson, AB; CHFT-FM Fort McMurray, AB; CKVH High Prairie, AB; CFXH-FM Hinton, AB; CKSA-FM Lloydminster, AB; CKGY-FM Red Deer, AB; CIZZ-FM Red Deer, AB; CHLW(AM) Saint Paul, AB; CHSL-FM Slave Lake, AB; CKSQ(AM) Stettler, AB; CKKY Wainwright, AB; CKWY-FM Wainwright, AB; CFOK(AM) Westlock, AB; CKJR Wetaskiwin, AB; CFXW-FM Whitecourt, AB; CHNK-FM Winnipeg, MB; CKJS Winnipeg, MB; CFRK-FM Fredericton, NB; CJXL-FM Moncton, NB; CJMO-FM Moncton, NB; CKIM Baie Verte, NF; CHVO-FM Carbonear, NF; CFLC-FM Churchill Falls, NF; CKVO Clarenville, NF; CKXX-FM Corner Brook, NF; CFCB Corner Brook, NF; CKGA Gander, NF; CKXD-FM Gander, NF; CFLN Goose Bay, NF; CKCM Grand Falls, NF; CKXG-FM Grand Falls-Windsor, NF; CHCM Marystown, NF; CFNW Port au Choix, NF; CFCV-FM Saint Andrews, NF; VOCM(AM) Saint John's, NF; CJYQ Saint John's, NF; CKIX-FM Saint John's, NF; CFSX Stephenville, NF; CFLW Wabush, NF; CFRQ-FM Dartmouth, NS; CKUL-FM Halifax, NS; CIJK-FM Kentville, NS; CHRK-FM Sydney, NS; CIHT-FM Ottawa, ON; CILV-FM Ottawa, ON; CHNO-FM Sudbury, ON; CIGM-FM Sudbury, ON; CJUK-FM Thunder Bay, ON; CKTG-FM Thunder Bay, ON; CHTN-FM Charlottetown, PE; CKQK-FM Charlottetown, PE.
Stns: 2 TV. CITL, Lloydminster, AB; CKSA, Lloydminster, AB.

H.R. Steele, chmn; Scott Weatherby, CEO; R.G. Steele, pres/CEO.

Newfoundland Broadcasting Co., (NTV & OZ Networks). Box 2020, St. John's, NF A1C 5S2. Canada. Phone: (709) 722-5015. Fax: (709) 726-5107.E-mail: ozfm@ozfm.com Web Site:www.ntv.ca Ownership Geoffrey W. Stirling, 89.95%; G. Scott Stirling, 10%; and others, 0.05%.
Stns: 22 AM. 42 FM. CKBA-FM Athabasca, AB; CJPR-FM Blairmore, AB; CJEG-FM Bonnyville, AB; CIXF-FM Brooks, AB; CIBQ Brooks, AB; CFXL-FM Calgary, AB; CFUL-FM Calgary, AB; CFCW-FM Camrose, AB; CFCW Camrose, AB; CJXK-FM Cold Lake, AB; CKDQ Drumheller, AB; CKRA-FM Edmonton, AB; CIRK-FM Edmonton, AB; CFXE-FM Edson, AB; CHFT-FM Fort McMurray, AB; CKVH High Prairie, AB; CFXH-FM Hinton, AB; CKSA-FM Lloydminster, AB; CKGY-FM Red Deer, AB; CIZZ-FM Red Deer, AB; CHLW(AM) Saint Paul, AB; CHSL-FM Slave Lake, AB; CKSQ(AM) Stettler, AB; CKKY Wainwright, AB; CKWY-FM Wainwright, AB; CFOK(AM) Westlock, AB; CKJR Wetaskiwin, AB; CFXW-FM Whitecourt, AB; CHNK-FM Winnipeg, MB; CKJS Winnipeg, MB; CFRK-FM Fredericton, NB; CJXL-FM Moncton, NB; CJMO-FM Moncton, NB; CKIM Baie Verte, NF; CHVO-FM Carbonear, NF; CFLC-FM Churchill Falls, NF; CKVO Clarenville, NF; CKXX-FM Corner Brook, NF; CFCB Corner Brook, NF; CKGA Gander, NF; CKXD-FM Gander, NF; CFLN Goose Bay, NF; CKCM Grand Falls, NF; CKXG-FM Grand Falls-Windsor, NF; CHCM Marystown, NF; CFNW Port au Choix, NF; CFCV-FM Saint Andrews, NF; VOCM(AM) Saint John's, NF; CJYQ Saint John's, NF; CKIX-FM Saint John's, NF; CFSX Stephenville, NF; CFLW Wabush, NF; CFRQ-FM Dartmouth, NS; CKUL-FM Halifax, NS; CIJK-FM Kentville, NS; CHRK-FM Sydney, NS; CIHT-FM Ottawa, ON; CILV-FM Ottawa, ON; CHNO-FM Sudbury, ON; CIGM-FM Sudbury, ON; CJUK-FM Thunder Bay, ON; CKTG-FM Thunder Bay, ON; CHTN-FM Charlottetown, PE; CKQK-FM Charlottetown, PE8 FM. CJOZ-FM Bonavista Bay, NF; CJKK-FM Clarenville, NF; CKOZ-FM Corner Brook, NF; CIOZ-FM Marystown, NF; CHOS-FM Rattling Brook, NF; CKSS-FM Red Rocks, NF; CHOZ-FM Saint John's, NF; CIOS-FM Stephenville, NF.
Stns: 6 TV. CJOM, Argentia, NF; CJWB, Bonavista, NF; CJWN, Corner Brook, NF; CJOX-1, Grand Bank, NF; CJCN, Grand Falls, NF; CJSV, Stephenville, NF.

Scott G. Stirling, pres/CEO; Doug Neal, engrg dir.

News-Press & Gazette Co., Box 29, St. Joseph, MO 64502. Phone: (816) 271-8500. Fax: (816) 271-8695. Ownership David R. Bradley Jr., Henry H. Bradley, Lyle E. Leimkuhler. Cable TV: NPG Cable of Arizona.
Stns: 2 AM. 1 FM. KESQ Indio, CA; KUNA-FM La Quinta, CA; KRDO(AM) Colorado Springs, CO.
Stns: 7 TV. KTVZ, Bend, OR; KRDO-TV, Colorado Springs-Pueblo, CO; KVIA-TV, El Paso (Las Cruces, NM), TX; KJCT, Grand Junction-Montrose, CO; KIFI, Idaho Falls-Pocatello, ID; KESQ-TV, Palm Springs, CA; KECY-TV, Yuma, AZ-El Centro, CA.

News-Press & Gazette Co. publishes the *St. Joseph News-Press*, St. Joseph, MO.

John Kueneke, pres.

Newsweb Corp., 1645 W. Fullerton Ave., Chicago, IL 60614. Phone: (773) 975-0401. Fax: (773) 975-1301. Ownership Fred Eychaner, 100%.
Stns: 5 AM. 4 FM. WCPT-FM Arlington Heights, IL; WSBC(AM) Chicago, IL; WCFJ Chicago Heights, IL; WAIT(AM) Crystal Lake, IL; WCPY(FM) De Kalb, IL; WKIF-FM Kankakee, IL; WCPQ(FM) Park Forest, IL; WCPT(AM) Willow Springs, IL; WNDZ Portage, IN.
Stns: 1 TV. KCDO-TV, Denver, CO.

Fred Eychaner, CEO; Charley Gross, COO.

NextMedia Group Inc., 6312 S. Fiddler's Green Cir., Suite 360E, Englewood, CO 80111. Phone: (303) 694-9118. Fax: (303) 694-4940. Web Site:www.nextmediagroup.com Ownership NextMedia Investors LLC, 100% of votes.
Stns: 8 AM. 27 FM. KBAY(FM) Gilroy, CA; KEZR(FM) San Jose, CA; WERV-FM Aurora, IL; WRXQ(FM) Coal City, IL; WCCQ-FM Crest Hill, IL; WWYW(FM) Dundee, IL; WJOL Joliet, IL; WSSR(FM) Joliet, IL; WKRS Waukegan, IL; WXLC-FM Waukegan, IL; WZSR-FM Woodstock, IL; WSGW-FM Carrollton, MI; WCEN-FM Hemlock, MI; WSGW Saginaw, MI; WTLZ-FM Saginaw, MI; WQZL(FM) Belhaven, NC; WANG Havelock, NC; WSSM(FM) Havelock, NC; WQSL-FM Jacksonville, NC; WXQR-FM Jacksonville, NC; WRNS Kinston, NC; WRNS-FM Kinston, NC; WERO(FM) Washington, NC; WHBC Canton, OH; WHBC-FM Canton, OH; WKZQ-FM Forestbrook, SC; WRNN(AM) Myrtle Beach, SC; WMYB(FM) Myrtle Beach, SC; WYAV(FM) Myrtle Beach, SC; WRNN-FM Socastee, SC; KMKT-FM Bells, TX; KLAK(FM) Tom Bean, TX; KMAD-FM Whitesboro, TX; WLIP Kenosha, WI; WJBR-FM Wilmington, DE.

Steven Dinetz, CEO; Skip Weller, pres.

Nicolet Broadcasting Inc., 3030 Park Drive, Suite 3, Sturgeon Bay, WI 54235. Phone: (920) 746-9430. Fax: (920) 746-9433.E-mail: wbbk@doorcountydailynews.com Web Site:www.doorcountydailynews.com Ownership Roger Utnehmer.
Stns: 8 AM. 27 FM. KBAY(FM) Gilroy, CA; KEZR(FM) San Jose, CA; WERV-FM Aurora, IL; WRXQ(FM) Coal City, IL; WCCQ-FM Crest Hill, IL; WWYW(FM) Dundee, IL; WJOL Joliet, IL; WSSR(FM) Joliet, IL; WKRS Waukegan, IL; WXLC-FM Waukegan, IL; WZSR-FM Woodstock, IL; WSGW-FM Carrollton, MI; WCEN-FM Hemlock, MI; WSGW Saginaw, MI; WTLZ-FM Saginaw, MI; WQZL(FM) Belhaven, NC; WANG Havelock, NC; WSSM(FM) Havelock, NC; WQSL-FM Jacksonville, NC; WXQR-FM Jacksonville, NC; WRNS Kinston, NC; WRNS-FM Kinston, NC; WERO(FM) Washington, NC; WHBC Canton, OH; WHBC-FM Canton, OH; WKZQ-FM Forestbrook, SC; WRNN(AM) Myrtle Beach, SC; WMYB(FM) Myrtle Beach, SC; WYAV(FM) Myrtle Beach, SC; WRNN-FM Socastee, SC; KMKT-FM Bells, TX; KLAK(FM) Tom Bean, TX; KMAD-FM Whitesboro, TX; WLIP Kenosha, WI; WJBR-FM Wilmington, DE4 FM. WRLU-FM Algoma, WI; WBDK-FM Algoma, WI; WRKU-FM Forestville, WI; WSBW(FM) Sister Bay, WI.

Roger Utnehmer, pres & gen mgr.

Noalmark Broadcasting Corp., 202 W. 19th St., El Dorado, AR 71730. Phone: (870) 862-7777. Fax: (870) 862-0203. Ownership William C. Nolan Jr., 65%; Edwin B. Alderson Jr., 35%.
Stns: 8 AM. 15 FM. KDEL-FM Arkadelphia, AR; KVRC Arkadelphia, AR; KIXC(FM) Bearden, AR; KELD El Dorado, AR; KMLK(FM) El Dorado, AR; KAGL(FM) El Dorado, AR; KMRX(FM) El Dorado, AR; KIXB-FM El Dorado, AR; KYXK(FM) Gurdon, AR; KELD-FM Hampton, AR; KLAZ-FM Hot Springs, AR; KZHS(AM) Hot Springs, AR; KBHS(AM) Hot Springs, AR; KVMA(AM) Magnolia, AR; KLEZ(FM) Malvern, AR; KBOK(AM) Malvern, AR; KVMZ(FM) Waldo, AR; KYKK(AM) Hobbs, NM; KIXN(FM) Hobbs, NM; KPER(FM) Hobbs, NM; KPZA-FM Jal, NM; KBIM Roswell, NM; KBIM-FM Roswell, NM.

William C. Nolan Jr., pres; Edwin B. Alderson Jr., exec VP; Paul Starr Jr., VP; Anna Canterbury, sec/treas.

Norsan Consulting and Management Inc., Box 2148, Tucker, GA 30085. Phone: (770) 414-5026. Ownership Norberto Sanchez, 100%.
Stns: 9 AM. 1 FM. WEWC(AM) Callahan, FL; WVOJ(AM) Fernandina Beach, FL; WNNR(AM) Jacksonville, FL; WSOS(AM) Saint Augustine Beach, FL; WGSP Charlotte, NC; WFAY(AM) Fayetteville, NC; WXNC(AM) Monroe, NC; WCEO(AM) Columbia, SC; WGSP-FM Pageland, SC; WKGN Knoxville, TN.

North American Broadcasting Co. Inc., 1458 Dublin Rd., Columbus, OH 43215. Phone: (614) 481-7800. Fax: (614) 481-8070. Web Site:www.nabco-inc.com Ownership Norma Mnich; Matthew Mnich.
Stns: 1 AM. 2 FM. WRKZ(FM) Columbus, OH; WMNI Columbus, OH; WTDA(FM) Westerville, OH.

Norma Mnich, chmn; Matthew Mnich, pres/CEO; Mark Jividen, VP; Nick Reed, VP/sec/treas.

North Cascades Broadcasting Inc., Box 151, Omak, WA 98841. Phone: (509) 826-0100. Fax: (509) 826-3929. Web Site:www.komw.net
Stns: 1 AM. 1 FM. KOMW Omak, WA; KZBE-FM Omak, WA.

John Andrist, pres.

North Georgia Radio Group L.P., 112 Jordan Dr., Chattanooga, TN 37421. Phone: (423) 425-8987. Ownership Whitfield Communications Inc., gen ptnr, 100% of votes.
Stns: 2 AM. 2 FM. WYYU-FM Dalton, GA; WBLJ(AM) Dalton, GA; WDAL Dalton, GA; WOCE(FM) Ringgold, GA.

Northeast Broadcasting Company Inc., 288 S. River Rd., Bedford, NH 03110. Phone: (603) 668-9999. Fax: (603) 668-6470. Web Site:www.nebcast.com Ownership Steven A. Silberberg, Ed Flanagan.
Stns: 10 AM. 28 FM. KJMP(AM) Pierce, CO; KVRG(FM) Victor, ID; KRVQ(FM) Victor, ID; WXRV(FM) Andover, MA; WXRG(FM) Athol, MA; WGAW Gardner, MA; WJOE(AM) Orange-Athol, MA; WNYN-FM Whitefield, NH; KVUW(FM) Wendover, NV; WTWK(AM) Plattsburgh, NY; KFMH(FM) Belle Fourche, SD; WUSX(FM) Addison, VT; WCAT(AM) Burlington, VT; WDOT(FM) Danville, VT; WFAD Middlebury, VT; WNCS(FM) Montpelier, VT; WSKI Montpelier, VT; WRJT-FM Royalton, VT; WRSA(AM) Saint Albans, VT; WWMP(FM) Waterbury, VT; KBEN-FM Basin, WY; KRAE Cheyenne, WY; KAZY(FM) Cheyenne, WY; KMJY(FM) Chugwater, WY; KWHO(FM) Cody, WY; KDAD(FM) Douglas, WY; KTED(FM) Evansville, WY; KANT(FM) Guernsey, WY; KTUG(FM) Hudson, WY; KRQU(FM) Laramie, WY; KIMX(FM) Laramie, WY; KHAT(AM) Laramie, WY; KROW(FM) Lovell, WY; KZQL(FM) Mills, WY; KHAD(FM) Upton, WY; KHNA(FM) Wamsutter, WY; KRAN(FM) Warren AFB, WY;

KPAD(FM) Wheatland, WY.

Steven Silberberg, CEO; Edward Flanagan, VP.

Northeast Colorado Broadcasting LLC, 220 State St., Suite 106, Fort Morgan, CO 80701. Phone: (970) 867-7271. Fax: (970) 867-2676.

Stns: 1 AM. 3 FM. KPRB-FM Brush, CO; KSIR Brush, CO; KRFD(FM) Merino, CO; KPMX(FM) Sterling, CO.

Alec L. Creighton, gen mgr .

Northeast Communications Corp., 110 Babbit Rd., Franklin, NH 03235. Phone: (603) 934-2500. Fax: (603) 934-2933. E-mail: onair@mix941fm.com Web Site:www.mix941fm.com Ownership Jeff Fisher, 44.5%; Chris Fisher, 17.5%; and Phil Fisher, 16.5%.

Stns: 2 AM. 1 FM. WFTN Franklin, NH; WSCY-FM Moultonborough, NH; WPNH Plymouth, NH.

Jeff Fisher, pres; Fred Caruso, progmg dir; Rick Ganley, progmg dir; Cathy Keyser, opns mgr.

Northeast Oklahoma Broadcast Network Inc., 1 W. 3rd St., Grove, OK 74344. Phone: (918) 786-2211. Fax: (918) 786-2284. Ownership Janell M. Hestand, 50%; and Larry J. Hestand, 50%.

Stns: 1 AM. 2 FM. KESA(FM) Eureka Springs, AR; KVIS Miami, OK; KGLC-FM Miami, OK.

Larry J. Hestand, pres.

Northern Christian Radio Inc., Box 695, Gaylord, MI 49734-0695. Phone: (800) 545-8857. Phone: (989) 732-6274. Fax: (989) 732-8171. E-mail: ncr@ncradio.org Web Site:www.ncradio.org

Stns: 1 AM. 2 FM. KESA(FM) Eureka Springs, AR; KVIS Miami, OK; KGLC-FM Miami, OK5 FM. WOLW-FM Cadillac, MI; WRQC(FM) East Tawas, MI; WPHN-FM Gaylord, MI; WTHN(FM) Sault Ste. Marie, MI; WHST(FM) Tawas City, MI.

Joe Sereno, chmn; George Lake, chief exec admin; Patrick Green, progmg dir.

Northern Star Broadcasting L.L.C., 1356 Mackinaw Ave., Cheboygan, MI 49721. Phone: (231) 627-2341. Fax: (231) 627-7000. E-mail: cmonk@nsbroadcasting.com Web Site:www.nsbroadcasting.com Ownership Wade Fetzer, 91.7%; W. Palmer Pyle, 7% (nterest held as voting trustee); and George Atkinson III, 1.3%.

Stns: 5 AM. 15 FM. WCKC-FM Cadillac, MI; WCBY Cheboygan, MI; WGFM(FM) Cheboygan, MI; WGFN(FM) Glen Arbor, MI; WJZJ(FM) Glen Arbor, MI; WIMK-FM Iron Mountain, MI; WMIQ Iron Mountain, MI; WJPD-FM Ishpeming, MI; WIAN Ishpeming, MI; WLJZ(FM) Mackinaw City, MI; WDMJ Marquette, MI; WUPK-FM Marquette, MI; WAVC-FM Mio, MI; WNGE-FM Negaunee, MI; WIHC-FM Newberry, MI; WZNL-FM Norway, MI; WMKD(FM) Pickford, MI; WMKC(FM) Saint Ignace, MI; WYSS-FM Sault Ste. Marie, MI; WKNW Sault Ste. Marie, MI.

Chris Monk, VP; Palmer Pyle, pres.

Northwest Indy Radio, 2200 Simpson Ave., Hoquiam, WA 98550. Phone: (360) 705-0619. E-mail: stephenp@otakuworld.com Ownership Northwest Indy Radio is an association operating in Washington state for the advancement of the art and science of independent community media.

Stns: 5 AM. 15 FM. WCKC-FM Cadillac, MI; WCBY Cheboygan, MI; WGFM(FM) Cheboygan, MI; WGFN(FM) Glen Arbor, MI; WJZJ(FM) Glen Arbor, MI; WIMK-FM Iron Mountain, MI; WMIQ Iron Mountain, MI; WJPD-FM Ishpeming, MI; WIAN Ishpeming, MI; WLJZ(FM) Mackinaw City, MI; WDMJ Marquette, MI; WUPK-FM Marquette, MI; WAVC-FM Mio, MI; WNGE-FM Negaunee, MI; WIHC-FM Newberry, MI; WZNL-FM Norway, MI; WMKD(FM) Pickford, MI; WMKC(FM) Saint Ignace, MI; WYSS-FM Sault Ste. Marie, MI; WKNW Sault Ste. Marie, MI4 FM. KCFL(FM) Elma, WA; KZFL(FM) Glenoma, WA; KRYA(FM) Glenoma, WA; KEFL(FM) Westport, WA.

Stephen P. Lepisto, pres.

Northwestern College & Radio, 3003 Snelling Ave. N., St. Paul, MN 55113-1598. Phone: (651) 631-5000. Fax: (651) 631-5086. E-mail: phvirts@nwc.edu Web Site:www.nwc.edu Ownership Non-profit organization. Northwestern College, St. Paul, is the owner and operator of the 15 radio licenses.

Stns: 5 AM. 9 FM. WSMR-FM Sarasota, FL; KNWM(FM) Madrid, IA; KNWI-FM Osceola, IA; KNWS Waterloo, IA; KDNI(FM) Duluth, MN; KDNW(FM) Duluth, MN; KTIS Minneapolis, MN; KTIS-FM Minneapolis, MN; KFNW-FM Fargo, ND; KFNL(FM) Kindred, ND; KFNW(AM) West Fargo, ND; KNWC(AM) Sioux Falls, SD; WNWC-FM Madison, WI; WNWC(AM) Sun Prairie, WI.

Dr. Paul Virts, sr VP; Dr. Alan Cureton, pres.

O

Omni Broadcasting Co., 502 Beltrami Ave. N.W., Bemidji, MN 56601-3010. Phone: (218) 444-1500. Fax: (218) 759-0345. Ownership Louis H. Buron Jr., Mary Campbell, G. Michael Boen.

Stns: 5 AM. 11 FM. KULO(FM) Alexandria, MN; KBHP(FM) Bemidji, MN; KBUN Bemidji, MN; KKZY-FM Bemidji, MN; WQXJ(FM) Blackduck, MN; WJJY-FM Brainerd, MN; KVBR Brainerd, MN; KLIZ(AM) Brainerd, MN; KLIZ-FM Brainerd, MN; KUAL-FM Brainerd, MN; KBLB(FM) Nisswa, MN; KIKV-FM Sauk Centre, MN; KNSP(AM) Staples, MN; KWAD Wadena, MN; KKWS(FM) Wadena, MN; KLLZ-FM Walker, MN.

Louis H. Buron Jr., pres/CEO; Mary Campbell, VP/CFO.

One Ten Broadcast Group Inc., 2 E. Main St., Shawnee, OK 74801-6906. Phone: (405) 878-1803. E-mail: kirc1059@aol.com Ownership Linda D. Jones, 100%.

Stns: 1 AM. 2 FM. KIRC-FM Seminole, OK; KWSH Wewoka, OK; KSLE(FM) Wewoka, OK.

Linda Jones, pres.

1TV.Com Inc., Box 1416, Los Altos, CA 94023. Phone: (650) 520-6002. Ownership John Low, 100%.

Stns: 3 AM. 1 FM. KIKO-FM Claypool, AZ; KJAA Globe, AZ; KIKO Miami, AZ; KBSZ Wickenburg, AZ.

John Low, pres.

Opus Broadcasting Systems Inc., 511 Rossanley Dr., Medford, OR 97501. Phone: (541) 772-0322. Fax: (541) 772-4233. Ownership Henry Flock, 70%; Dean Flock, 20%; Alan Benz, 5%; and John Lavoie, 5%.

Stns: 2 AM. 3 FM. KRVC(FM) Hornbrook, CA; KCNA(FM) Cave Junction, OR; KROG-FM Grants Pass, OR; KRTA Medford, OR; KEZX(AM) Medford, OR.

Dean Flock, gen mgr; Brian Fraser, sls dir.

Opus Media Holdings LLC, 950 Third Ave., 19th Fl., New York, NY 10022. Phone: (212) 634-3376. Ownership Opus Capital LLC, 100% of votes.

Stns: 2 AM. 3 FM. KRVC(FM) Hornbrook, CA; KCNA(FM) Cave Junction, OR; KROG-FM Grants Pass, OR; KRTA Medford, OR; KEZX(AM) Medford, OR11 FM. WHTF-FM Havana, FL; WEGT(FM) Lafayette, FL; WQTL(FM) Tallahassee, FL; WAIB-FM Tallahassee, FL; KBKK(FM) Ball, LA; KEZP-FM Bunkie, LA; KQLQ(FM) Columbia, LA; KXRR(FM) Monroe, LA; KMYY(FM) Rayville, LA; KLAA-FM Tioga, LA; KZRZ(FM) West Monroe, LA.

Richard Linhart, chmn; James Shea, pres/CEO.

The Original Company Inc., Box 242, Vincennes, IN 47591. Phone: (812) 882-6060. Fax: (812) 885-2604. E-mail: marklange@originalcompany.com Web Site:www.originalcompany.com Ownership Mark R. Lange, 50%; Saundra K. Lange, 50%.

Stns: 3 AM. 7 FM. WUZR-FM Bicknell, IN; WREB-FM Greencastle, IN; WQTY-FM Linton, IN; WBTO Linton, IN; WRCY(AM) Mount Vernon, IN; WYFX(FM) Mount Vernon, IN; WBTO-FM Petersburg, IN; WZDM-FM Vincennes, IN; WAOV Vincennes, IN; WWBL-FM Washington, IN.

Mark R. Lange, pres.

O-Town Communications Inc., 416 E. Main St., Ottumwa, IA 52501. Phone: (641) 684-5563. Fax: (641) 684-5832. E-mail: mail@ottumwaradio.com Web Site:www.ottumwaradio.com Ownership Bruce Linder, 51%; and Greg List, 49%.

Stns: 1 AM. 3 FM. KKSI-FM Eddyville, IA; KRKN-FM Eldon, IA; KTWA-FM Ottumwa, IA; KBIZ Ottumwa, IA.

Ouachita Broadcasting Inc., Box 1450, Mena, AR 71953. Phone: (479) 394-1450. Ownership Jay Bunyard, 100%.

Stns: 1 AM. 3 FM. KILX(FM) Hatfield, AR; KQOR(FM) Mena, AR; KENA(AM) Mena, AR; KENA-FM Mena, AR.

Jay Bunyard, pres; Teresa Bunyard, VP.

Our Three Sons Broadcasting L.L.P., Box 307, Rock Hill, SC 29731. Phone: (803) 324-1340. Fax: (803) 324-2860. Web Site:www.wrhi.com Ownership Allan M. Miller, mngng ptnr; Manning Kimmel, ptnr.

Stns: 1 AM. 1 FM. WVSZ-FM Chesterfield, SC; WRHI(AM) Rock Hill, SC.

Allan M. Miller, pres.

Buck Owens Productions Inc., 3223 Sillect, Bakersfield, CA 93308. Phone: (661) 326-1011. Fax: (661) 328-7503. Ownership Buck Owens Revocable Trust II (Michael Owens and Melvin L. Owens Jr., co-trustees), 100%.

Stns: 1 AM. 2 FM. KCWR(FM) Bakersfield, CA; KUZZ Bakersfield, CA; KUZZ-FM Bakersfield, CA.

Ozark Media Inc., 555 Marshall Dr., St. Robert, MO 65584. Phone: (573) 336-5535. Fax: (573) 336-7619. Ownership Dalton C. Wright, 100%.

Stns: 1 AM. 2 FM. KCWR(FM) Bakersfield, CA; KUZZ Bakersfield, CA; KUZZ-FM Bakersfield, CA3 FM. KOZX-FM Cabool, MO; KELE-FM Mountain Grove, MO; KFLW-FM Saint Robert, MO.

Dalton Wright, pres.

P

PMB Broadcasting LLC, c/o Bradley & Hatcher, 33 W. 11th St., Suite 100, Columbus, GA 31901. Phone: (706) 660-9988. Ownership H. Lynn Page, 25%; James R. Martin, 12.5%; Debra H. Martin, 12.5%; Creek Stand Partners LP, 10%; Richard Y. Bradley, 6.67%; and others.

Stns: 1 AM. 3 FM. WRLD-FM Valley, AL; WRCG Columbus, GA; WCGQ-FM Columbus, GA; WKCN-FM Lumpkin, GA.

Pacific Cascade Communications Corp., 1139 Hartnell Ave., Redding, CA 96002-2113. Phone: (530) 222-4455. Fax: (530) 222-4484. Ownership Pacific Cascade Communications Corp. is a non-stock, non-profit corporation.

Stns: 2 AM. 3 FM. KNDZ(FM) McKinleyville, CA; KVIP Redding, CA; KVIP-FM Redding, CA; KMWR(FM) Brookings, OR; KGRV Winston, OR.

David L. Morrow, VP.

Pacific Empire Radio Corp., 228 1st St., Idaho Falls, ID 83401. Phone: (208) 528-6813. Fax: (208) 529-6927. E-mail: kclkam@aol.com Web Site:www.hot106.fm.com Ownership Mark L. Bolland and Mary Bolland, JTWROS, 34.3%; John Taylor and Connie Taylor, JTWROS, 30.7%; AIA Services Corp. 401K & Profit Sharing Plan, FBO John Taylor, 13.6%; Hillcrest Aircraft Co., 6.84%; and Randolph Lamberjack, 6%.

Stns: 4 AM. 6 FM. KSEI Pocatello, ID; KRXK(AM) Rexburg, ID; KGTM(FM) Rexburg, ID; KBJX(FM) Shelley, ID; KQZB(FM) Troy, ID; KBKR Baker City, OR; KKBC-FM Baker City, OR; KRJT(FM) Elgin, OR; KUBQ-FM La Grande, OR; KLBM La Grande, OR.

Mark Bolland, pres/CEO.

Pacific Radio Group Inc., 311 Ano St., Kahului, HI 96732. Phone: (808) 877-5566. Fax: (808) 871-0666. E-mail: bergson@pacificradiogroup.com Web Site:www.pacificradiogroup.com Ownership Ed Johnson, Robert Van Dine, Chuck Bergson.

Stns: 4 AM. 10 FM. KHLO Hilo, HI; KAPA(FM) Hilo, HI; KKBG-FM Hilo, HI; KPVS-FM Hilo, HI; KLEO(FM) Kahaluu, HI; KLHI-FM Kahului, HI; KNUI Kahului, HI; KJKS(FM) Kahului, HI; KLUA(FM) Kailua-Kona, HI; KKON(AM) Kealakekua, HI; KPOA-FM Lahaina, HI; KJMD(FM) Pukalani, HI; KMVI(AM) Wailuku, HI; KAGB(FM) Waimea, HI.

Chuck Bergson, CEO; Robert Van Dine, dir; L.E. Johnson, CFO.

Pacific West Broadcasting Inc., Box 1430, Newport, OR 97365. Phone: (541) 265-2266. Fax: (541) 265-6397. E-mail: info@ybcradio.com Web Site:ybcradio.com Ownership David J. & Linda R. Miller, 100%.

Stns: 1 AM. 2 FM. KBCH Lincoln City, OR; KCRF-FM Lincoln City, OR; KNCU(FM) Newport, OR.

David Miller, pres.

Pacifica Foundation Inc., (dba Pacific Radio). 1925 Martin Luther King Jr. Way, Berkeley, CA 94704. Phone: (510) 849-2590. Web Site:www.pacifica.org Ownership (dba Pacific Radio).

Stns: 1 AM. 2 FM. KBCH Lincoln City, OR; KCRF-FM Lincoln City, OR; KNCU(FM) Newport, OR6 FM. KPFA-FM Berkeley, CA; KPFB-FM Berkeley, CA; KPFK-FM Los Angeles, CA; KPFW-FM Washington, DC; WBAI-FM New York, NY; KPFT-FM Houston, TX.

Dan Cougjhlin, exec dir.

Pamal Broadcasting Ltd., 6 Johnson Rd., Latham, NY 12110. Phone: (518) 786-6600. Fax: (518) 786-6610. Web Site:www.pamal.com Ownership James Morrell, owner.

Stns: 12 AM. 22 FM. WKZY(FM) Cross City, FL; WDVH(AM) Gainesville, FL; WTMN(AM) Gainesville, FL; WRZN Hernando, FL; WXBM-FM Milton, FL; WHHZ(FM) Newberry, FL; WMEZ-FM Pensacola, FL; WDVH-FM Trenton, FL; WTMG-FM Williston, FL; WPNI(AM) Amherst, MA; WYJB(FM) Albany, NY; WROW(AM) Albany, NY; WKLI-FM Albany, NY; WZMR-FM Altamont, NY; WBNR Beacon, NY; WXPK(FM) Briarcliff Manor, NY; WFFG-FM Corinth, NY; WMML Glens Falls, NY; WNYQ(FM) Hudson Falls, NY; WIZR Johnstown, NY; WGHQ Kingston, NY; WLNA(AM) Peekskill, NY; WHUD-FM Peekskill, NY; WSPK-FM Poughkeepsie, NY; WBPM(FM) Saugerties, NY; WENU(AM) South Glens Falls, NY; WFLY-FM Troy, NY; WAJZ(FM) Voorheesville, NY; WKBE-FM Warrensburg, NY; WJEN(FM) Killington, VT; WDVT(FM) Rutland, VT; WJJR-FM Rutland,

VT; WZRT-FM Rutland, VT; WSYB Rutland, VT.

Michael Dufort, CFO; Debbie Grembowicz, gen mgr; Dan Austin, market mgr; Jason Finkelberg, market mgr; Clay Ashworth, market mgr; Dave Lobb, rgnl VP.

Pamplin Broadcasting, 888 S.W. Fifth Ave., Suite 790, Portland, OR 97204. Phone: (503) 223-4321. Fax: (503) 222-2850. E-mail: kpam@kpam.com

Stns: 2 AM. KPAM Troutdale, OR; KKAD(AM) Vancouver, WA.

Andrea Marek, pres; Paul Clithero, gen mgr .

Pappas Telecasting Companies, 500 S. Chinowth Rd., Visalia, CA 93277. Phone: (559) 733-7800. Fax: (559) 733-7878. Web Site:www.pappastv.com Ownership Harry J. Pappas.

Stns: 2 AM. KMPH(AM) Modesto, CA; KTRB(AM) San Francisco, CA.

Stns: 17 TV. WLGA, Columbus, GA; KDMI, Des Moines-Ames, IA; KCWI-TV, Des Moines-Ames, IA; KDBC-TV, El Paso (Las Cruces, NM), TX; KMPH-TV, Fresno-Visalia, CA; KFRE-TV, Fresno-Visalia, CA; WWAZ-TV, Green Bay-Appleton, WI; WCWG, Greensboro-High Point-Winston Salem, NC; KAZH, Houston; KWNB, Lincoln & Hastings-Kearney, NE; KHGI, Lincoln & Hastings-Kearney, NE; KAZA-TV, Los Angeles; KPTM, Omaha, NE; KTNC, San Francisco-Oakland-San Jose; KUNO-TV, San Francisco-Oakland-San Jose; KPTH, Sioux City, IA; KSWT, Yuma, AZ-El Centro, CA.

Harry J. Pappas, chmn/CEO; Dennis J. Davis, pres/COO; Bruce M. Yeager, exec VP/CFO.

Paradis Broadcasting of Alexandria Inc., 1312 Broadway, Alexandria, MN 56308. Phone: (320) 763-3131. Fax: (320) 763-5641. E-mail: thefolks@kxra.com Web Site:www.kxra.com Ownership Mel Paradis, 60%; Brett Paradis, 40%.

Stns: 1 AM. 2 FM. KXRZ(FM) Alexandria, MN; KXRA Alexandria, MN; KXRA-FM Alexandria, MN.

Mel Paradis, CEO; Brett Paradis, pres, gen mgr .

Paragon Communications Inc., Box 945, Elk City, OK 73648. Phone: (580) 225-9696. Fax: (580) 225-9699. E-mail: keco@io2online.com Web Site:www.kecofm.com

Stns: 1 AM. 2 FM. KADS Elk City, OK; KECO(FM) Elk City, OK; KXOO(FM) Elk City, OK.

Blake Brewer, pres & gen mgr .

The Jim Pattison Broadcast Group, 460 Pemberton Terrace, Kamloops, BC V2C 1T5. Canada. Phone: (250) 372-3322. Fax: (250) 374-0445. Web Site:www.jpbroadcast.com Ownership Jim Pattison Group.

Stns: 1 AM. 2 FM. KADS Elk City, OK; KECO(FM) Elk City, OK; KXOO(FM) Elk City, OK29 FM. CIBW-FM Drayton Valley, AB; CJXX-FM Grande Prairie, AB; CHLB-FM Lethbridge, AB; CFMY-FM Medicine Hat, AB; CHAT-FM Medicine Hat, AB; CFDV-FM Red Deer, AB; CHUB-FM Red Deer, AB; CHBW-FM Rocky Mountain House, AB; CJBZ-FM Taber, AB; CKLR-FM Courtenay, BC; CHBZ-FM Cranbrook, BC; CHDR-FM Cranbrook, BC; CJDR-FM Fernie, BC; CKBZ-FM Kamloops, BC; CIFM-FM Kamloops, BC; CKLZ-FM Kelowna, BC; CKOV-FM Kelowna, BC; CKWV-FM Nanaimo, BC; CHWF-FM Nanaimo, BC; CIBH-FM Parksville, BC; CHPQ-FM Parksville, BC; CJAV-FM Port Alberni, BC; CKDV-FM Prince George, BC; CKKN-FM Prince George, BC; CJJR-FM Vancouver, BC; CKPK-FM Vancouver, BC; CKIZ-FM Vernon, BC; CJZN-FM Victoria, BC; CKKQ-FM Victoria, BC.

Stns: 4 TV. CFJC-TV, Kamloops, BC; CHAT, Medicine Hat, AB; CHAT-1, Pivot, AB; CKPG, Prince George, BC.

Rick Arnish, pres; Bill Dinicol, VP Finance; Bruce Davis, VP sls; Loretta Lewis, admin asst.

Peak Broadcasting LLC, 1071 W. Shaw Ave., Fresno, CA 93711. Phone: (559) 490-5800. Fax: (559) 490-5843. Ownership Duff Ackerman & Goodrich QP Fund II L.P., 86.0297% membership interest.

Stns: 4 AM. 8 FM. KFPT(AM) Clovis, CA; KMJ-FM Fresno, CA; KSKS-FM Fresno, CA; KWYE(FM) Fresno, CA; KMGV-FM Fresno, CA; KMJ Fresno, CA; KFXD(AM) Boise, ID; KAWO(FM) Boise, ID; KSAS-FM Caldwell, ID; KXLT-FM Eagle, ID; KCIX(FM) Garden City, ID; KIDO(AM) Nampa, ID.

Todd Lawley, CEO; Tim Lyons, CFO.

Pearson Broadcasting, 9530 Miolothian Pike, Richmond, VA 23235. Phone: (804) 521-0603. Fax: (804) 674-8938. Ownership Max H. Pearson, 100%.

Stns: 4 AM. 8 FM. KFPT(AM) Clovis, CA; KMJ-FM Fresno, CA; KSKS-FM Fresno, CA; KWYE(FM) Fresno, CA; KMGV-FM Fresno, CA; KMJ Fresno, CA; KFXD(AM) Boise, ID; KAWO(FM) Boise, ID; KSAS-FM Caldwell, ID; KXLT-FM Eagle, ID; KCIX(FM) Garden City, ID; KIDO(AM) Nampa, ID4 FM. KBCN-FM Marshall, AR; KTTG-FM Mena, AR; KERX(FM) Paris, AR; KMAC-FM Gainesville, MO.

Max H. Pearson, pres; Bruce W. Hale, VP.

Pecos Valley Broadcasting Co., 317 W. Quay Ave., Artesia, NM 88210. Phone: (505) 746-2751. Fax: (505) 748-3748.

Stns: 1 AM. 3 FM. KSVP Artesia, NM; KTZA(FM) Artesia, NM; KPZE-FM Carlsbad, NM; KEND-FM Roswell, NM.

Sam Beard, pres; David Ruckman, VP; Gene Dow, VP/gen mgr.

Peg Broadcasting Crossville LLC, 961 Miller Ave., Crossville, TN 38555. Phone: (931) 707-1102. Fax: (931) 707-1220. Ownership Jeffrey H. Shaw, 50%; and John T. Crunk Jr., 50%.

Stns: 6 AM. 4 FM. WPBX(FM) Crossville, TN; WOWF-FM Crossville, TN; WAEW Crossville, TN; WCSV(AM) Crossville, TN; WAKI McMinnville, TN; WBMC McMinnville, TN; WOWC(FM) Morrison, TN; WTZX Sparta, TN; WSMT Sparta, TN; WTRZ(FM) Spencer, TN.

Pembrook Pines Media Group, 1705 Lake St., Elmira, NY 14901. Phone: (607) 733-5626. Fax: (607) 733-5627. E-mail: ppinesmedia1@stny.rr.com Web Site:www.pembrookpines.com Ownership Robert J. Pfuntner, 100%. Company also owns Pembrook Pines Media agency.

Stns: 6 AM. 5 FM. WZKZ-FM Alfred, NY; WABH Bath, NY; WELM Elmira, NY; WEHH Elmira Heights-Horseheads, NY; WOEN(AM) Olean, NY; WMXO-FM Olean, NY; WGGO Salamanca, NY; WQRS(FM) Salamanca, NY; WOKN-FM Southport, NY; WPIE Trumansburg, NY; WQRW(FM) Wellsville, NY.

Robert J. Pfuntner, pres/CEO.

Peninsula Communications Inc., Box 109, Homer, AK 99603. Phone: (907) 235-6000. Fax: (907) 235-6683. E-mail: kwavefm@xyz.net Ownership David F. Becker, 50%; Eileen L. Becker, 50%.

Stns: 1 AM. 3 FM. KGTL Homer, AK; KWVV-FM Homer, AK; KXBA(FM) Nikiski, AK; KPEN-FM Soldotna, AK.

Tim White, opns mgr; Dave Webb, production mgr; David Becker, gen mgr .

Perry Publishing & Broadcasting Co., 1457 N.E. 23rd St., Oklahoma City, OK 73111. Phone: (405) 425-4100. Fax: (405) 424-8811. Web Site:www.perry-pub -broadcasting.com

Stns: 6 AM. 9 FM. WTHB Augusta, GA; WFXA-FM Augusta, GA; WAEG-FM Evans, GA; WAKB(FM) Waynesboro, GA; WTHB-FM Wrens, GA; KACO(AM) Apache, OK; KJMM-FM Bixby, OK; KJMZ(FM) Cache, OK; KDDQ(FM) Comanche, OK; KPNS(AM) Duncan, OK; KKRX Lawton, OK; KXCA(AM) Lawton, OK; KVSP(FM) Oklahoma City, OK; KRMP(AM) Oklahoma City, OK; KGTO Tulsa, OK.

Russell Perry, pres/CEO.

Pharis Broadcasting Inc., Box 908, Fort Smith, AR 72902. Phone: (479) 288-1047. Fax: (479) 785-2638. E-mail: ssrg@sbcglobal.net Web Site:www.fortsmithradiogroup.com Ownership William L. Pharis, 51%; Karen Ann Pharis, 49%.

Stns: 2 AM. 3 FM. KFPW-FM Barling, AR; KQBK(FM) Booneville, AR; KFPW Fort Smith, AR; KHGG(AM) Van Buren, AR; KHGG-FM Waldron, AR.

William L. Pharis, pres/CEO; Karen A. Pharis, gen mgr , sec.

Phillips Broadcasting Inc., 100 Fisher Dr., Trinidad, CO 81082. Phone: (719) 846-3355. Fax: (719) 846-4711. E-mail: kcrt@adelphia.net

Stns: 1 AM. 2 FM. KCRT Trinidad, CO; KCRT-FM Trinidad, CO; KBKZ(FM) Raton, NM.

David Phillips, pres.

Phoenix Media Communications Group, 126 Brookline Ave., Boston, MA 02215. Phone: (617) 536-5390. Fax: (617) 859-8201. Web Site:www.thephoenix.com

Stns: 1 AM. 3 FM. WFNX(FM) Lynn, MA; WPHX(AM) Sanford, ME; WPHX-FM Sanford, ME; WFEX(FM) Peterborough, NH.

Barry Morris, pres; Stephen Mindich, CEO.

Piedmont Communications Inc., Box 271, Orange, VA 22960. Phone: (540) 672-1000. Fax: (540) 672-0282. Ownership Thomas D. Bond, 22.6%; A. Pierce Stone & Pamela H. Stone, 11%; The Cook Family Trust, Mrs. Toy E. Cook, trustee, Richard S. Cook, atty in fact, 9.8%; Lloyd M. Garnett & Barbara S. Garnett, 8.6%; Robert F. Gillespie Jr., 8.6%; and Harry B. Sedwick Jr., 8.6%.

Stns: 2 AM. 2 FM. WJMA-FM Culpeper, VA; WCVA Culpeper, VA; WOJL(FM) Louisa, VA; WVCV Orange, VA.

Pilgrim Communications Inc., Box 90, New Palestine, IN 46163. Phone: (317) 894-2000. Ownership P. Gene Hood, 100% votes, 51% total assets; and Randall Hood, 49% total assets.

Stns: 4 AM. 2 FM. KSKE(AM) Buena Vista, CO; KKKK(AM) Colorado Springs, CO; KVLE-FM Gunnison, CO; KRCN(AM) Longmont, CO; KVLE(AM) Vail, CO; WFDM(FM) Franklin, IN.

Pillar of Fire Inc., Box 9058, Weston Canal Rd., Zarephath, NJ 08890. Phone: (732) 469-0991. Fax: (732) 469-2115. E-mail: info@star991fm.com Web Site:www.star991fm.com Ownership No stockholders; non-profit corporation.

Stns: 1 AM. 2 FM. KPOF Denver, CO; WAWZ(FM) Zarephath, NJ; WAKW-FM Cincinnati, OH.

Pillar of Fire Inc. publishes one religious periodical, a semi-monthly for the family *Pillar of Fire*.

Robert B. Dallenbach, pres; Scott Taylor, stn mgr.

Pines Broadcasting Inc., 1255 N. Myrtle St., Warren, AR 71671. Phone: (870) 226-2653. Fax: (870) 226-3039. Ownership Jimmy Sledge, 50%; and Gwen Sledge, 50%.

Stns: 1 AM. 3 FM. KXSA-FM Dermott, AR; KGPQ-FM Monticello, AR; KHBM Monticello, AR; KHBM-FM Monticello, AR.

Jimmy Sledge, pres.

Pittman Broadcasting Services LLC, 307 S. Jefferson Ave., Covington, LA 70433. Phone: (985) 892-3661. Web Site:www.pittmanbroadcasting.com Ownership Marcus Pittman, 50%; and Janet Pittman, 50%.

Stns: 3 AM. 3 FM. WOMN(AM) Franklinton, LA; WUUU(FM) Franklinton, LA; KFXZ(AM) Lafayette, LA; KVOL Lafayette, LA; KYMK-FM Maurice, LA; KFXZ-FM Opelousas, LA.

Marcus Pittman, pres.

Platinum Broadcasting Co., Box 789, Junction City, KS 66441. Phone: (785) 762-5525. Fax: (785) 762-5387. E-mail: platinum@kjck.com Web Site:www.kjck.com

Stns: 1 AM. 2 FM. KJCK(AM) Junction City, KS; KJCK-FM Junction City, KS; KQLA-FM Ogden, KS.

Mark Ediger, gen mgr; Ed Klimek, VP sls.

Platte River Radio Inc., Box 130, Kearney, NE 68848. Phone: (308) 236-9900. Fax: (308) 234-6781. Ownership David Oldfather, 31%; Craig J. Eckert, 30%; Jane O. Light, 19.5%; and Diane H. Oldfather, 19.5%.

Stns: 3 AM. 2 FM. KLIQ(FM) Hastings, NE; KHAS Hastings, NE; KICS Hastings, NE; KXPN(AM) Kearney, NE; KKPR-FM Kearney, NE.

Point Broadcasting Company, 715 Broadway, Suite 320, Santa Monica, CA 90401. Phone: (310) 451-4430. Fax: (310) 451-1423. Ownership John Hearne Revocable Trust. Note: Owns stns through subsidiaries: Gold Coast Broadcasting LLC (see listing) and High Desert Broadcasting LLC (see listing). Also owns 50% of KHRN(FM) Huron, CA and 31.8% of KHRQ(FM) Baker and KHDR(FM) Lenwood, both CA.

Stns: 2 AM. 5 FM. KMVE(FM) California City, CA; KSBL-FM Carpinteria, CA; KSPE-FM Ellwood, CA; KTMS Santa Barbara, CA; KTYD-FM Santa Barbara, CA; KIST-FM Santa Barbara, CA; KIST(AM) Santa Barbara, CA.

John Hearne, chmn/pres.

Pollack Broadcasting Co., 5500 Poplar Ave. #1, Memphis, TN 38119. Phone: (901) 685-3993. Fax: (901) 685-3995. E-mail: wpollack@midsouth.rr.com Ownership William H. Pollack, 100%. Note: Group also owns KWCE-LP Alexandria, LA.

Stns: 3 AM. 3 FM. KBOA-FM Piggott, AR; KCRV Caruthersville, MO; KCRV-FM Caruthersville, MO; KBOA Kennett, MO; KTMO(FM) New Madrid, MO; KMIS Portageville, MO.

Stns: 2 TV. KLAX, Alexandria, LA; KIEM, Eureka, CA.

William H. Pollack, pres.

Polnet Communications Ltd., 3656 W. Belmont Ave., Chicago, IL 60618. Phone: (773) 588-6300. Fax: (773) 588-0834. Web Site:www.pclradio.com

Stns: 6 AM. WKTA Evanston, IL; WEEF Highland Park, IL; WNVR Vernon Hills, IL; WPJX(AM) Zion, IL; WRKL New City, NY; WLIM Patchogue, NY.

Walter Kotaby, pres; Kent D. Gustafson, VP & CEO.

Porter County Broadcasting Corp., 2755 Sager Rd., Valparaiso, IN 46383. Phone: (219) 462-8125. Ownership Leonard J. Ellis Trust, 27.10%; Bernice A. Ellis Trust, 27.10%; Leigh Ellis, 15.25%; Neenah Ellis, 15.25%; and Marissa Wilson, 15.25%.

Stns: 1 AM. 3 FM. WXRD-FM Crown Point, IN; WZVN-FM Lowell, IN; WAKE Valparaiso, IN; WLJE Valparaiso, IN.

Positive Alternative Radio Inc., Box 889, Blacksburg, VA 24063. Phone: (540) 552-4282. Fax: (540) 951-5282. Web Site:www.parfm.com Ownership Vernon H. Baker, 33.33%; Virginia L. Baker, 33.33%; and Edward A. Baker, 33.33%.
　Stns: 1 AM. 3 FM. WXRD-FM Crown Point, IN; WZVN-FM Lowell, IN; WAKE Valparaiso, IN; WLJE-FM Valparaiso, IN22 FM. WKAO(FM) Ashland, KY; WTJY-FM Asheboro, NC; WPIR-FM Hickory, NC; WXRI-FM Winston-Salem, NC; WRFE(FM) Chesterfield, SC; WCQR-FM Kingsport, TN; WTTX-FM Appomattox, VA; WPER-FM Culpeper, VA; WOKD-FM Danville, VA; WPIN-FM Dublin, VA; WJYA-FM Emporia, VA; WJYJ-FM Fredericksburg, VA; WOKG(FM) Galax, VA; WPIM-FM Martinsville, VA; WJCN(FM) Nassawadox, VA; WRXT-FM Roanoke, VA; WPAR-FM Salem, VA; WPVA-FM Waynesboro, VA; WPJY(FM) Blennerhassett, WV; WPIB-FM Bluefield, WV; WPJW(FM) Hurricane, WV; WVRR(FM) Point Pleasant, WV.
　Edward A. Baker, pres.

Powell Broadcasting Co. Inc., 8641 United Plaza Blvd., Suite 300, Baton Rouge, LA 70809. Phone: (225) 922-4662. Fax: (225) 922-4544. Ownership The Powell Group L.L.C., 100%.
　Stns: 2 AM. 4 FM. KKMA(FM) Le Mars, IA; KLEM(AM) Le Mars, IA; KZSR(FM) Onawa, IA; KSCJ Sioux City, IA; KKYY(FM) Whiting, IA; KSUX(FM) Winnebago, NE.
　Thomas J. Spies, COO; Nanette Noland, pres.

Prairie Radio Communications, 2410 Sycamore Rd., Suite C, De Kalb, IL 60115. Phone: (815) 758-8686. Fax: (815) 756-9723. Web Site:www.radiomacomb.com
　Stns: 7 AM. 10 FM. KCLN Clinton, IA; KMCN(FM) Clinton, IA; KMCS-FM Muscatine, IA; KWPC Muscatine, IA; WLMD-FM Bushnell, IL; WCDD(FM) Canton, IL; WBYS(AM) Canton, IL; WLBK(AM) De Kalb, IL; WAIK Galesburg, IL; WLRB Macomb, IL; WKAI-FM Macomb, IL; WMOI-FM Monmouth, IL; WRAM Monmouth, IL; WPWQ(FM) Mount Sterling, IL; WKXQ-FM Rushville, IL; KWBZ(FM) Monroe City, MO; WSLD-FM Whitewater, WI.
　Don Davis, pres/CEO.

Premier Broadcasters, 1133 Kresky, Centralia, WA 98531. Phone: (360) 736-1355. Fax: (360) 736-4761.E-mail: live95@live95.com Web Site:www.live95.com Ownership Rod Etherton.
　Stns: 1 AM. 2 FM. KITI Chehalis-Centralia, WA; KRXY-FM Shelton, WA; KITI-FM Winlock, WA.
　Rod Etherton, pres.

Prescott Valley Broadcasting Co. Inc., Box 26523, Prescott Valley, AZ 86312. Phone: (928) 445-8289. Fax: (928) 442-0448. Ownership Sanford Cohen and Terry Cohen, joint tenants with right of survivorship, 100%.
　Stns: 1 AM. 3 FM. KDDL(FM) Chino Valley, AZ; KPKR(FM) Parker, AZ; KPPV(FM) Prescott Valley, AZ; KQNA(AM) Prescott Valley, AZ.

Press Communications L.L.C., 1329 Campus Pkwy., Suite 106, Wall, NJ 07753-6815. Phone: (732) 751-1119. Fax: (732) 751-1726. Ownership Mark D. Lass, 16.5%; Alfred D. Colantoni, 16.5%; Jules L. Plangere III, 16.5%; Jules Plangere Jr., 16.5%; Robert E. McAllan, 16.5%; Richard T. Morena, 10.5%; and E. Donald Lass, 7%.
　Stns: 1 AM. 5 FM. WBBO(FM) Bass River Township, NJ; WHTG Eatontown, NJ; WHTG-FM Eatontown, NJ; WWZY-FM Long Branch, NJ; WKMK(FM) Ocean Acres, NJ; WBHX-FM Tuckerton, NJ.

Prettyman Broadcasting Co., 1606 W. King St., Martinsburg, WV 25401. Phone: (304) 263-8868. Fax: (304) 263-8906. Web Site:www.wepm.com
　Stns: 1 AM. 2 FM. WEPM Martinsburg, WV; WLTF(FM) Martinsburg, WV; WICL(FM) Williamsport, MD.
　William E. Prettyman, pres/CEO; Norm Slemenda, gen mgr .

Prieto Broadcasting Inc., Box 48122, Doraville, GA 30362. Phone: (770) 825-0095. Fax: (770) 246-0054. Web Site:www.prietobroadcasting.com Ownership Filiberto Prieto, 100%.
　Stns: 3 AM. WFTD Marietta, GA; WDUR Durham, NC; WETC Wendell-Zebulon, NC.
　Filiberto Prieto, pres/CEO; Franco Vera, gen sls mgr.

Priority Communications, 12 W. Long Ave., DuBois, PA 15801-2100. Phone: (814) 375-5260. Fax: (814) 375-5263.
　Stns: 2 AM. 2 FM. WCDK-FM Cadiz, OH; WCED DuBois, PA; WDSN-FM Reynoldsville, PA; WEIR Weirton, WV.
　Jay M. Philippone, pres.

Priority Radio Inc., Box 5204, Wilmington, DE 19808-5204. Phone: (302) 731-7270. Fax: (302) 738-3090. Web Site:www.thereachfm.com Ownership Jennifer Hare, 33.3%; Rev. Steve Hare, 33.3%.
　Stns: 1 AM. 5 FM. KXRL(FM) Cherry Valley, AR; WVBH(FM) Beach Haven West, NJ; WXHZ(FM) Bridgeport, OH; WSRY(AM) Elkton, MD; WXHL-FM Christiana, DE; WXHM(FM) Middletown, DE.

Pritchard Broadcasting Corp., 610 N. 4th St., ite 300, Burlington, IA 52601. Phone: (319) 752-5402. Fax: (319) 752-4715.E-mail: johnp@burlingtonradio.com Ownership John T. Pritchard, 100%.
　Stns: 2 AM. 4 FM. KBUR Burlington, IA; KDMG(FM) Burlington, IA; KKMI-FM Burlington, IA; KBKB Fort Madison, IA; KHDK(FM) New London, IA; WQKQ(FM) Carthage, IL.
　John T. Pritchard, pres.

Programmers Broadcasting Inc., Box 28, Bottineau, ND 58318-0028. Phone: (701) 228-5151. Fax: (701) 228-2483. Ownership John Kircher, 50%; and Jean Kircher, 50%.
　Stns: 2 AM. 4 FM. KBUR Burlington, IA; KDMG(FM) Burlington, IA; KKMI-FM Burlington, IA; KBKB Fort Madison, IA; KHDK(FM) New London, IA; WQKQ(FM) Carthage, IL3 FM. KBTO(FM) Bottineau, ND; KWGO(FM) Burlington, ND; KTZU(FM) Velva, ND.

Progressive Broadcasting System Inc., Box 307, Elkhart, IN 46515. Phone: (574) 875-5166. Fax: (574) 875-6662. Web Site:www.wfrn.com
　Stns: 1 AM. 2 FM. WCMR(AM) Elkhart, IN; WFRN-FM Elkhart, IN; WFRI-FM Winamac, IN.
　Edwin Moore, pres.

Q

Qantum Communications Corp., 1266 E. Main St., 6th Fl., Stamford, CT 06902. Phone: (203) 388-0048. Ownership Frank D. Osborn, 61.74% of votes; Frank Washington, 19.03% of votes; Osborn Family Partners L.P., 15.23% of votes; Michael F. Mangan, 3.85% of votes; William Nelson III and Frank D. Osborn, as trustees of the Osborn 2002 Family Trust, a trust in favor of the children of Frank D. Osborn, 0.15% of votes.
　Stns: 8 AM. 24 FM. WKKR-FM Auburn, AL; WMXA(FM) Opelika, AL; WTLM Opelika, AL; WZMG Pepperell, AL; WMXZ(FM) De Funiak Springs, FL; WFFY(FM) Destin, FL; WWAV-FM Santa Rosa Beach, FL; WMOG Brunswick, GA; WGIG(AM) Brunswick, GA; WHFX(FM) Darien, GA; WBGA(FM) Saint Simons Island, GA; WYNR(FM) Waycross, GA; WWSN-FM Waycross, GA; WPLV West Point, GA; WCJM-FM West Point, GA; WEII(FM) Dennis, MA; WCIB-FM Falmouth, MA; WCOD-FM Hyannis, MA; WXTK-FM West Yarmouth, MA; WYNA-FM Calabash, NC; WLQB(FM) Ocean Isle Beach, NC; WRXZ(FM) Briarcliff Acres, SC; WGTR-FM Bucksport, SC; WJMX-FM Cheraw, SC; WDAR-FM Darlington, SC; WWRK(AM) Darlington, SC; WDSC Dillon, SC; WEGX-FM Dillon, SC; WJMX Florence, SC; WWXM(FM) Garden City, SC; WRZE(FM) Kingstree, SC; WZTF(FM) Scranton, SC.
　Frank Osborn, pres/CEO; Michael Mangan, CFO.

Quarnstrom Media Group LLC, 1104 Cloquet Ave., Cloquet, MN 55720. Phone: (218) 879-4534. Fax: (218) 879-1962. Ownership Alan & Linda Quarnstrom, 100%.
　Stns: 2 AM. 3 FM. WKLK Cloquet, MN; WKLK-FM Cloquet, MN; WMOZ(FM) Moose Lake, MN; WCMP Pine City, MN; WCMP-FM Pine City, MN.
　Aian Quarnstrom, pres; Don Welch, VP.

Quincy Newspapers Inc., 130 S. Fifth St., Quincy, IL 62301. Phone: (217) 223-5100. Fax: (217) 223-5019. Web Site:www.qni.biz
　Stns: 1 AM. 1 FM. WGEM Quincy, IL; WGEM-FM Quincy, IL.
　Stns: 12 TV. WVVA, Bluefield-Beckley-Oak Hill, WV; KWWL, Cedar Rapids-Waterloo-Iowa City & Dubuque, IA; WQOW-TV, La Crosse-Eau Claire, WI; WXOW-TV, La Crosse-Eau Claire, WI; WKOW, Madison, WI; WGEM-TV, Quincy, IL-Hannibal, MO-Keokuk, IA; KTTC, Rochester, MN-Mason City, IA-Austin, MN; WREX-TV, Rockford, IL; KTIV, Sioux City, IA; WSJV, South Bend-Elkhart, IN; WAOW-TV, Wausau-Rhinelander, WI; WYOW, Wausau-Rhinelander, WI.
　Quincy Newspapers Inc. owns the *Quincy* (IL) *Herald-Whig*, and the *New Jersey Herald*, Newton, NJ.
　Thomas A. Oakley, pres.

Quinte Broadcasting Ltd., Box 488, Belleville, ON K8N 5B2. Canada. Phone: (613) 969-5555. Fax: (613) 969-8122. Ownership Herbert M. Morton, 66.67%; and Joyce Mulock, 33.33%.
　Stns: 1 AM. 2 FM. CIGL-FM Belleville, ON; CJBQ Belleville, ON; CJTN-FM Quinte West, ON.

Quorum Radio Partners of Virginia Inc., 8512 Beech Ln., McKinney, TX 75070. Phone: (972) 529-1192. Fax: (972) 540-2454. Ownership Todd W. Fowler, 31.25%; Michael A. Stone, 31.25%; Jevin S. Jensen, 20%; Robert Barnett, 10%; and Kevin T. Lilly, 5%.
　Stns: 2 AM. 1 FM. WIQO-FM Covington, VA; WKEY Covington, VA; WSLW White Sulphur Springs, WV.
　Todd W. Fowler, pres/CEO.

R

The RAFTT Corp., 3633 Farm to Market Rd. 437, Rogers, TX 76569. Phone: (281) 564-7064. Ownership Jerome Friemel, 100%.
　Stns: 3 AM. KBSF Springhill, LA; KYRO Potosi, MO; KTON Belton, TX.
　Jerome Friemel, pres.

RNC MEDIA Inc., 380 av Murdoch, Rouyn-Noranda, PQ J9X 1G5. Canada. Phone: (819) 762-0741. Fax: (819) 762-6331.
　Stns: 3 AM. KBSF Springhill, LA; KYRO Potosi, MO; KTON Belton, TX9 FM. CHPR-FM Hawkesbury, ON; CHXX-FM Donnacona, PQ; CHLX-FM Gatineau, PQ; CFTX-FM Gatineau, PQ; CJLA-FM Lachute, PQ; CKLX-FM Montreal, PQ; CHOI-FM Quebec, PQ; CHOA-FM Rouyn-Noranda, PQ; CHGO-FM Val d'Or, PQ.
　Stns: 5 TV. CKRN-3, Bearn-Fabre, PQ; CFGS-TV, Gatineau, PQ; CHOT-TV, Gatineau, PQ; CKRN-TV, Rouyn-Noranda, PQ; CFVS, Val d'Or, PQ.
　Pierre R. Brosseau, pres.

RNC Media Saguenay-Lac-Saint-Jean, 568 boul. St. Joseph, Roberval, PQ G8H 2K6. Canada. Phone: (418) 275-1831. Fax: (418) 275-2475.E-mail: malevesque@rncmedia.ca Web Site:chrlfm.com Ownership RNC MEDIA Inc., 75% (see listing); 9150-2898 Quebec inc., 25%.
　Stns: 1 AM. 4 FM. CFGT Alma, PQ; CKYK-FM Alma, PQ; CKXO-FM Chibougamau, PQ; CHVD-FM Dolbeau-Mistassini, PQ; CHRL-FM Roberval, PQ.
　Marc-Andre Levesque, pres.

RR Broadcasting, 2100 E. Tahquitz Canyon Way, Palm Springs, CA 92262. Phone: (760) 325-2582. Fax: (760) 322-3562. Web Site:www.rrbroadcasting.com Ownership Rozene R. Supple, 100%.
　Stns: 3 AM. 2 FM. KPTR(AM) Cathedral City, CA; KDES-FM Palm Springs, CA; KGAM Palm Springs, CA; KPSI Palm Springs, CA; KPSI-FM Palm Springs, CA.
　Mike Keane, gen mgr .

Radio Cleveland Inc., Drawer 780, Cleveland, MS 38732. Phone: (662) 843-4091. Fax: (662) 843-9805.E-mail: wcld@tecinfo.com Web Site:www.radiomiss.com Ownership Homer Sledge Jr., pres, 37.1/5%; Kevin W. Cox, treas, 37.1/2%; Clint L. Webster, gen mgr, 37.1/2%.
　Stns: 1 AM. 2 FM. WAID-FM Clarksdale, MS; WCLD Cleveland, MS; WMJW-FM Cleveland, MS.
　Clint L. Webster, gen mgr .

Radio Dubuque Inc., Box 659, Dubuque, IA 52004. Phone: (563) 690-0800. Fax: (563) 588-5688. Ownership Donald L. Rabbitt, 70%; Thomas Parsley, 25%; and Paul Hemmer, 5%.
　Stns: 1 AM. 3 FM. KATF(FM) Dubuque, IA; KDTH Dubuque, IA; KGRR-FM Epworth, IA; WVRE(FM) Dickeyville, WI.
　Thomas Parsley, gen mgr .

Radio Fargo-Moorhead Inc., 1020 25th St. S., Fargo, ND 58103. Phone: (701) 277-4200. Ownership James D. Ingstad, 100%.
　Stns: 2 AM. 4 FM. KBVB(FM) Barnesville, MN; WDAY-FM Fargo, ND; KFGO Fargo, ND; KRWK(FM) Fargo, ND; KVOX(AM) Fargo, ND; KMJO(FM) Hope, ND.

Radio Greeneville Inc., Box 278, Greeneville, TN 37744. Phone: (423) 638-4147. Fax: (423) 638-1979.E-mail: wgrv@greeneville.com Web Site:www.greeneville.com/wgrv Ownership Ronald & Nellie R.Metcalfe; Paul O. Metcalfe.
　Stns: 2 AM. 1 FM. WSMG Greeneville, TN; WGRV Greeneville, TN; WIKQ(FM) Tusculum, TN.
　Ronald Metcalfe, pres.

The Radio Group, Box 1319, Columbia, LA 71418. Phone: (318) 649-7959. Fax: (318) 649-5874.E-mail: radiotom1@yahoo.com Ownership Tom G. Gay, 100%.
　Stns: 2 AM. 1 FM. WSMG Greeneville, TN; WGRV Greeneville, TN; WIKQ(FM) Tusculum, TN5 FM. KFNV-FM Ferriday, LA; KJNA-FM Jena, LA; KAPB-FM Marksville,

LA; KWTG(FM) Vidalia, LA; KMAR-FM Winnsboro, LA.

Tom D. Gay, gen mgr .

Radio La Grande, 1010 Vermont Ave. N.W., Suite 100, Washington, DC 20005. Phone: (202) 638-1959. Fax: (202) 393-7464. E-mail: VALTRAVEL@RCN.com Web Site:radiolagrande.net Ownership Estuardo Valdemar Rodriguez, 50%; Leonor Rodriguez, 50%. Note: Estuardo Valdemar Rodriguez also is the licensee of WLLN(AM) Lillington, NC.

Stns: 7 AM. WLLQ(AM) Chapel Hill, NC; WRTG Garner, NC; WSRP(AM) Jacksonville, NC; WLNR Kinston, NC; WGSB Mebane, NC; WREV Reidsville, NC; WLLY Wilson, NC.

Radio Maria Inc., 601 Washington St., Alexandria, LA 71301. Phone: (318) 561-6145. Fax: (318) 449-9954. E-mail: info.usa@radiomaria.org Web Site:www.radiomaria.us Ownership Radio Maria is a not-for-profit corporation run by a board of directors.

Stns: 4 AM. 3 FM. KJMJ(AM) Alexandria, LA; KOJO-FM Lake Charles, LA; KBIO(FM) Natchitoches, LA; KNIR New Iberia, LA; WHJM(FM) Anna, OH; WULM(AM) Springfield, OH; KDEI(AM) Port Arthur, TX.

Radio One Inc., 5900 Princess Garden Pkwy., Lanham, MD 20706. Phone: (301) 306-1111. Fax: (301) 306-9426. Web Site:www.radio-one.com Ownership Alfred C. Liggins, 39.4% of voting shares; Catherine L. Hughes, 16.7% of voting shares.

Stns: 11 AM. 41 FM. WYCB Washington, DC; WOL Washington, DC; WKYS-FM Washington, DC; WUMJ(FM) Fayetteville, GA; WHTA(FM) Hampton, GA; WPZE(FM) Mableton, GA; WAMJ(FM) Roswell, GA; WFUN-FM Bethalto, IL; WHHL(FM) Jerseyville, IL; WMOJ-FM Connersville, IN; WTLC-FM Greenwood, IN; WTLC Indianapolis, IN; WHHH-FM Indianapolis, IN; WNOU(FM) Speedway, IN; WIZF-FM Erlanger, KY; WILD Boston, MA; WDMK(FM) Detroit, MI; WHTD(FM) Mount Clemens, MI; WCHB Taylor, MI; WPZS(FM) Albemarle, NC; WFXC-FM Durham, NC; WNNL-FM Fuquay-Varina, NC; WQNC(FM) Harrisburg, NC; WFXK-FM Tarboro, NC; WRNB(FM) Pennsauken, NJ; WDBZ(AM) Cincinnati, OH; WENZ-FM Cleveland, OH; WJMO(AM) Cleveland, OH; WZAK-FM Cleveland, OH; WERE(AM) Cleveland Heights, OH; WCKX-FM Columbus, OH; WJYD(FM) London, OH; WXMG-FM Upper Arlington, OH; WPPZ-FM Jenkintown, PA; WPHI-FM Media, PA; KBFB(FM) Dallas, TX; KSOC(FM) Gainesville, TX; KMJQ-FM Houston, TX; KBXX(FM) Houston, TX; KROI(FM) Seabrook, TX; WPZZ(FM) Crewe, VA; WCDX-FM Mechanicsville, VA; WKJM(FM) Petersburg, VA; WTPS(AM) Petersburg, VA; WKJS(FM) Richmond, VA; WQOK-FM South Boston, VA; WOLB(AM) Baltimore, MD; WWIN Baltimore, MD; WERQ-FM Baltimore, MD; WWMJ-FM Bethesda, MD; WWIN-FM Glen Burnie, MD; WPRS-FM Waldorf, MD.

Catherine Hughes, chairperson; Alfred Liggins, pres/CEO; Scott Royster, CFO; Darrell Huckaby, VP progmg; Tony Washington, VP sls; Charles Kinney, engrg dir.

Radio Palouse Inc., Box 1, Pullman, WA 99163. Phone: (509) 332-6551. Fax: (509) 332-5151. E-mail: khtr@aol.com Web Site:www.border104.com

Stns: 2 AM. KQQQ Pullman, WA; KUUX(AM) Pullman, WA.

Bill Weed, gen mgr .

Radio Partners LLC, Box 719, Beaver Falls, PA 15010. Phone: (724) 846-4100. Fax: (724) 843-7771. E-mail: iorio@wbvp-wmba.com Web Site:kibcoradio.com Ownership Frank Iorio, 100%.

Stns: 1 AM. 2 FM. WKNB-FM Clarendon, PA; WNAE Warren, PA; WRRN-FM Warren, PA.

Dave Whipple, sls mgr .

Radio Stations WPAY/WPFB Inc., 4505 Central Ave., Middletown, OH 45044. Phone: (513) 422-3625. Fax: (513) 424-9732. Web Site:www.rebel1059.com Ownership Douglas L. Braden, 100%.

Stns: 2 AM. 2 FM. WPFB Middletown, OH; WPFB-FM Middletown, OH; WPAY Portsmouth, OH; WPAY-FM Portsmouth, OH.

Douglas L. Branden, pres.

Radio Vermont Group Inc., Box 550, Waterbury, VT 05676. Phone: (802) 244-7321. Fax: (802) 244-1771.

Stns: 1 AM. 3 FM. WLVB-FM Morrisville, VT; WCVT-FM Stowe, VT; WDEV-FM Warren, VT; WDEV Waterbury, VT.

Ken Squier, pres; Eric Michaels, VP.

Radio Works Inc., 111 Westwood Dr., De Queen, AR 71832. Phone: (870) 642-3637. Ownership Jay Wallace Bunyard and Teresa Sharon Bunyard Living Revocable Trust, Jay and Teresa Bunyard, sole voting trustees, 100%.

Stns: 1 AM. 3 FM. WLVB-FM Morrisville, VT; WCVT-FM Stowe, VT; WDEV-FM Warren, VT; WDEV Waterbury, VT3 FM. KAMD-FM Camden, AR; KMGC-FM Camden, AR; KCXY(FM) East Camden, AR.

Radioactive LLC, 1717 Dixie Hwy., Suite 650, Fort Wright, KY 41011. Phone: (859) 331-9100. Ownership Benjamin L. Homel, 100%.

Stns: 1 AM. 3 FM. WLVB-FM Morrisville, VT; WCVT-FM Stowe, VT; WDEV-FM Warren, VT; WDEV Waterbury, VT3 FM. KAMD-FM Camden, AR; KMGC-FM Camden, AR; KCXY(FM) East Camden, AR20 FM. KYME(FM) Rockford, IA; KJLN(FM) Sac City, IA; WMLF(FM) Watseka, IL; KMML(FM) Cimarron, KS; KRMR(FM) Hays, KS; KDJM(FM) Lindsborg, KS; WPBK(FM) Crab Orchard, KY; WKFC(FM) North Corbin, KY; WUPZ(FM) Crystal Falls, MI; WUPT(FM) Gwinn, MI; WUPF(FM) Powers, MI; WUPG(FM) Republic, MI; WRAX(FM) Walhalla, MI; KXLP(FM) Eagle Lake, MN; WYME(FM) Au Sable, NY; WBLH(FM) Black River, NY; WNMR(FM) Dannemora, NY; WXMR(FM) Minerva, NY; KSYY(FM) Ingram, TX; WDYK(FM) Ridgeley, WV.

RadioJones LLC, Box 5356, Atlanta, GA 31107-5356. Phone: (404) 432-1450. E-mail: dj@radiojones.com Web Site:www.radiojones.com Ownership Dennis Jones, 100%.

Stns: 2 AM. 2 FM. WEDB(FM) East Dublin, GA; WJAT Swainsboro, GA; WXRS(AM) Swainsboro, GA; WXRS-FM Swainsboro, GA.

Dennis Jones, pres.

RadioStar Inc., 781 Bolsana Dr., Laguna Beach, CA 92651-4124. Phone: (915) 715-9770. Ownership James D. Glassman, 100%.

Stns: 2 AM. 2 FM. WEDB(FM) East Dublin, GA; WJAT Swainsboro, GA; WXRS(AM) Swainsboro, GA; WXRS-FM Swainsboro, GA4 FM. WGKC-FM Mahomet, IL; WLFH(FM) Rantoul, IL; WQQB(FM) Rantoul, IL; WEBX-FM Tuscola, IL.

Jim Glassman, pres.

RadioWorks Inc., 2830 Sandy Hollow Rd., Rockford, IL 61109. Phone: (815) 874-7861. Fax: (815) 874-2202.

Stns: 2 AM. 2 FM. WEDB(FM) East Dublin, GA; WJAT Swainsboro, GA; WXRS(AM) Swainsboro, GA; WXRS-FM Swainsboro, GA4 FM. WGKC-FM Mahomet, IL; WLFH(FM) Rantoul, IL; WQQB(FM) Rantoul, IL; WEBX-FM Tuscola, IL1 FM. WKHY(FM) Lafayette, IN.

Robert E. Rhea Jr., pres; David W. McAley, exec VP.

Rama Communications Inc., 3765 N. John Young Pkwy., Orlando, FL 32804. Phone: (407) 523-2770. Fax: (407) 523-2888. Web Site:www.gospelrama.com

Stns: 7 AM. WNTF Bithlo, FL; WMEL(AM) Cocoa Beach, FL; WKIQ Eustis, FL; WQBQ Leesburg, FL; WLAA(AM) Winter Garden, FL; WOKB(AM) Winter Garden, FL; WRFV(AM) Valdosta, GA.

Sabita Persaud, pres.

Ramar Communications II Ltd., Box 3757, Lubbock, TX 79452. Phone: (806) 745-3434. Fax: (806) 748-1949. Web Site:www.ramarcom.com E-mail: bmoran@ramarcom.com Ownership Ray Moran, 51%; Brad Moran, 49%.

Lubbock TX , 9800 University Ave.

Stns: 1 AM. 3 FM. KTTU-FM Brownfield, TX; KJTV(AM) Lubbock, TX; KXTQ-FM Lubbock, TX; KLZK(FM) New Deal, TX.

Stns: 4 TV. KTLL-TV Albuquerque-Santa Fe, NM; KUPT, Albuquerque- Santa Fe, NM; KTEL-TV, Albuquerque-Santa Fe, NM; KJTV-TV, Lubbock, TX.

Ray Moran, chmn; Brad Moran, pres.

Rawlco Radio Ltd., 715 Saskatchewan Crescent West, Saskatoon, SK S7M 5V7. Canada. Phone: (306) 934-2222. Fax: (306) 933-3300. Ownership Rawlco Inc., 90.1%; and others, 9.9%.

Stns: 5 AM. 11 FM. CIGY-FM Calgary, AB; CHMC-FM Edmonton, AB; CJNS-FM Meadow Lake, SK; CJNS Meadow Lake, SK; CJNB North Battleford, SK; CJCQ-FM North Battleford, SK; CJHD-FM North Battleford, SK; CHQX-FM Prince Albert, SK; CKBI Prince Albert, SK; CFMM-FM Prince Albert, SK; CIZL-FM Regina, SK; CJME(AM) Regina, SK; CKCK-FM Regina, SK; CJDJ-FM Saskatoon, SK; CFMC-FM Saskatoon, SK; CKOM(AM) Saskatoon, SK.

Pam Leyland, pres; Gordon Rawlinson, CEO.

Red Rock Radio Corp., 501 Lake Ave. S., Duluth, MN 55802. Phone: (218) 728-9500. Fax: (218) 723-1499. Ownership Curtis Squire Inc., 85%; Ro D. Grignon, 15%.

Stns: 4 AM. 12 FM. KKIN Aitkin, MN; KKIN-FM Aitkin, MN; KAOD(FM) Babbitt, MN; KFGI(FM) Crosby, MN; KBAJ(FM) Deer River, MN; KQDS Duluth, MN; KQDS-FM Duluth, MN; WXXZ-FM Grand Marais, MN; WWAX-FM Hermantown, MN; KGHS International Falls, MN; KSDM-FM International Falls, MN; KZIO-FM Two Harbors, MN;

WLMX-FM Balsam Lake, WI; WHSM Hayward, WI; WHSM-FM Hayward, WI; WXCX(FM) Siren, WI.

Ro Grignon, pres.

Red Zebra Holdings LLC, 21300 Redskin Park Dr., Ashburn, VA 20147. Phone: (703) 726-7015. Web Site:www.espn980.com Ownership Daniel Snyder, 100% of votes, 38.21% of assets; David Donovan, 0.14% of assets.

Stns: 6 AM. 3 FM. WTEM Washington, DC; WWRC(AM) Washington, DC; WXTR(AM) Alexandria, VA; WXTG(AM) Hampton, VA; WXGI Richmond, VA; WXTG-FM Virginia Beach, VA; WWXX(FM) Warrenton, VA; WTNT(AM) Bethesda, MD; WWXT(FM) Prince Frederick, MD.

Redwood Empire Stereocasters, Box 100, Santa Rosa, CA 95402. Phone: (707) 528-4434. Fax: (707) 527-8216. Ownership Gordon D. Zlot, trustee, The Zlot Living Trust, 98%; and Thomas G. Skinner, 2%.

Stns: 6 AM. 3 FM. WTEM Washington, DC; WWRC(AM) Washington, DC; WXTR(AM) Alexandria, VA; WXTG(AM) Hampton, VA; WXGI Richmond, VA; WXTG-FM Virginia Beach, VA; WWXX(FM) Warrenton, VA; WTNT(AM) Bethesda, MD; WWXT(FM) Prince Frederick, MD3 FM. KGRP(FM) Cazadero, CA; KZST-FM Santa Rosa, CA; KJZY-FM Sebastopol, CA.

Gordon D. Zlot, pres.

Regent Communications Inc., 100 E. River Center Blvd., 9th Fl., Covington, KY 41011. Phone: (859) 292-0030. Fax: (859) 814-0136. E-mail: wstakelin@regentcomm.com

Stns: 13 AM. 46 FM. KTRR-FM Loveland, CO; KMAX-FM Wellington, CO; KUAD-FM Windsor, CO; WBNQ-FM Bloomington, IL; WJBC Bloomington, IL; WJEZ(FM) Dwight, IL; WFYR-FM Elmwood, IL; WBWN-FM Le Roy, IL; WVEL Pekin, IL; WGLO-FM Pekin, IL; WZPW(FM) Peoria, IL; WIXO(FM) Peoria, IL; WTRX-FM Pontiac, IL; WGBF Evansville, IN; WJLT(FM) Evansville, IN; WDKS-FM Newburgh, IN; WGBF-FM Henderson, KY; WKDQ-FM Henderson, KY; WBKR(FM) Owensboro, KY; WOMI(AM) Owensboro, KY; KPEL-FM Abbeville, LA; KROF Abbeville, LA; KFTE-FM Breaux Bridge, LA; KRKA(FM) Erath, LA; KMDL-FM Kaplan, LA; KPEL Lafayette, LA; KTDY-FM Lafayette, LA; WFNT Flint, MI; WRCL(FM) Frankenmuth, MI; WNWZ Grand Rapids, MI; WGRD-FM Grand Rapids, MI; WFGR-FM Grand Rapids, MI; WQUS(FM) Lapeer, MI; WLCO(AM) Lapeer, MI; WWBN-FM Tuscola, MI; WTRV-FM Walker, MI; KMXK-FM Cold Spring, MN; WWJO-FM Saint Cloud, MN; WJON Saint Cloud, MN; KZRV(FM) Sartell, MN; KLZZ-FM Waite Park, MN; KXSS(AM) Waite Park, MN; WGNA-FM Albany, NY; WJYE-FM Buffalo, NY; WBUF(FM) Buffalo, NY; WYRK-FM Buffalo, NY; WQBJ-FM Cobleskill, NY; WBLK-FM Depew, NY; WBZZ(FM) Malta, NY; WTMM-FM Mechanicville, NY; WQBK-FM Rensselaer, NY; WODZ-FM Rome, NY; WFRG-FM Utica, NY; WIBX Utica, NY; WLZW-FM Utica, NY; KSII-FM El Paso, TX; KROD El Paso, TX; KKPL(FM) Cheyenne, WY; KARS-FM Laramie, WY.

Terry S. Jacobs, chmn/CEO; William L. Stakelin, pres/COO; Anthony Vasconcellos, sr VP & CFO.

Regional Radio Group LLC, 128 Glen St., Glens Falls, NY 12801. Phone: (518) 761-9890. Fax: (518) 761-9893. Web Site:www.radiowins.com Ownership Northway Broadcasting LLC, 100%.

Stns: 1 AM. 2 FM. WWSC Glens Falls, NY; WCKM-FM Lake George, NY; WCQL(FM) Queensbury, NY.

Clay Ashworth, gen mgr .

Reier Broadcasting Co. Inc., Box 20, Bozeman, MT 59718. Phone: (406) 587-9999. Fax: (406) 587-5855. Ownership William R. Reier Sr., 100%.

Stns: 2 AM. 3 FM. KBOZ Bozeman, MT; KOBB Bozeman, MT; KOBB-FM Bozeman, MT; KBOZ-FM Bozeman, MT; KOZB(FM) Livingston, MT.

Relevant Radio, 3200 Riverside Dr., Green Bay, WI 54307. Phone: (800) 342-0306. Fax: (920) 469-3023. E-mail: info@relevantradio.com Web Site:www.relevantradio.com Ownership Mark C. Follett, 33.33% of votes; John Cavil, 33.3% of votes; and Robert Atwell, 33.33% of votes.

Stns: 9 AM. 5 FM. WNTD Chicago, IL; WAUR Sandwich, IL; WWCA Gary, IN; WMUP(FM) Carney, MI; WLOL(AM) Minneapolis, MN; KIXL(AM) Del Valle, TX; WOVM(FM) Appleton, WI; WYNW(FM) Birnamwood, WI; WDVM(AM) Eau Claire, WI; WKBH Holmen, WI; WJOK Kaukauna, WI; WMMA(FM) Nekoosa, WI; WPJP(FM) Port Washington, WI; WHFA(AM) Poynette, WI.

Mark Follett, chmn/CEO.

Renda Broadcasting Corp., (Renda Radio Inc.). 900 Parish Street, 4th Fl, Pittsburgh, PA 15220. Phone: (412) 875-1800. Fax: (412) 875-1801. Ownership S.F. Renda, 100%.

Stns: 5 AM. 18 FM. WWGR-FM Fort Myers, FL; WEJZ-FM Jacksonville, FL; WGUF-FM Marco, FL; WSGL-FM Naples, FL; WGNE-FM Palatka, FL; WSOS-FM Saint Augustine, FL; WJGO(FM) Tice, FL; WMUV(FM) Brunswick, GA; KHTT-FM Muskogee, OK; KMGL-FM Oklahoma City, OK; KOKC(AM) Oklahoma City, OK; KOMA(FM) Oklahoma City, OK; KRXO-FM Oklahoma City, OK; KBEZ(FM) Tulsa, OK; WLCY-FM Blairsville, PA; WKQL(FM) Brookville, PA; WGSM(FM) Greensburg, PA; WCCS Homer City, PA; WDAD Indiana, PA; WQMU-FM Indiana, PA; WSHH-FM Pittsburgh, PA; WJAS Pittsburgh, PA; WECZ Punxsutawney, PA.

Anthony F. Renda, pres; Maryann Kelly, VP/controller; Alan Serena, VP opns; Judy Reich, VP sls.

The Result Radio Group, Box 767, Winona, MN 55987-0767. Phone: (507) 452-4000. Fax: (507) 452-9494. E-mail: jpapenfuss@winonaradio.com Web Site:winonaradio.com Ownership Jerry Papenfuss.

Stns: 6 AM. 8 FM. KBEW Blue Earth, MN; KBEW-FM Blue Earth, MN; KBRF Fergus Falls, MN; KJJK Fergus Falls, MN; KJJK-FM Fergus Falls, MN; KZCR(FM) Fergus Falls, MN; KPRW(FM) Perham, MN; KWNO-FM Rushford, MN; KDOM Windom, MN; KDOM-FM Windom, MN; KHME(FM) Winona, MN; KWNO Winona, MN; KAGE Winona, MN; KAGE-FM Winona, MN.

Jerry Papenfuss, owner.

Results Broadcasting, 1456 E. Green Bay St., Shawano, WI 54166. Phone: (715) 524-2194. Fax: (715) 524-9980. Ownership Bruce D. Grassman, 100%.

Stns: 3 AM. 7 FM. WOBE-FM Crystal Falls, MI; WJNR-FM Iron Mountain, MI; WHTO(FM) Iron Mountain, MI; WACD-FM Antigo, WI; WATK Antigo, WI; WOTE(AM) Clintonville, WI; WJMQ(FM) Clintonville, WI; WTCH Shawano, WI; WOWN-FM Shawano, WI; WCYE(FM) Three Lakes, WI.

Bruce Grassman, pres.

Revolution Broadcast Company of the West, 2125 Sidney Baker North, Kerrville, TX 78028. Phone: (830) 896-1230. Fax: (830) 792-4142. Ownership All of the stns are licensed to Foster Charitable Foundation Inc. Ownership of Foster Charitable Foundation Inc.: David L. Greenwald, 50%; and Jana Smith, 50%.

Stns: 2 AM. 4 FM. KMBL Junction, TX; KOOK-FM Junction, TX; KRVL(FM) Kerrville, TX; KERV Kerrville, TX; KYXX(FM) Ozona, TX; KHOS-FM Sonora, TX.

David L. Greenwald, pres.

Reynolds Radio Inc., Box 11196, College Station, TX 77842. Phone: (979) 696-1196. E-mail: rusty@reynoldsradio.com Web Site:www.theblaze.cc

Stns: 2 AM. 4 FM. KMBL Junction, TX; KOOK-FM Junction, TX; KRVL(FM) Kerrville, TX; KERV Kerrville, TX; KYXX(FM) Ozona, TX; KHOS-FM Sonora, TX3 FM. KAZE(FM) Ore City, TX; KZTK(FM) White Oak, TX; KBLZ(FM) Winona, TX.

Kenneth R. Reynolds, pres.

Rhattigan Broadcasting (Texas) LP, Box 1420, Plainview, TX 79073. Phone: (806) 853-9147. Fax: (815) 346-2084. Ownership Michael Rhattigan, 40% votes; Jerome Rhattigan, 30% votes; and Guy Gill, 30% votes.

Stns: 5 AM. 7 FM. KBST Big Spring, TX; KBST-FM Big Spring, TX; KBTS(FM) Big Spring, TX; KEPS Eagle Pass, TX; KINL-FM Eagle Pass, TX; KVOP(AM) Plainview, TX; KKYN-FM Plainview, TX; KREW(AM) Plainview, TX; KRIA(FM) Plainview, TX; KVOU Uvalde, TX; KVOU-FM Uvalde, TX; KUVA-FM Uvalde, TX.

Riverbend Communications LLC, 2880 N. 55th W., Idaho Falls, ID 83402. Phone: (208) 528-6635. Ownership Frank L. VanderSloot Trust, Frank L. VanderSloot, trustee, 90%; and Belinda VanderSloot, 10%.

Stns: 2 AM. 4 FM. KCVI(FM) Blackfoot, ID; KBLI(AM) Blackfoot, ID; KLCE-FM Blackfoot, ID; KTHK(FM) Idaho Falls, ID; KFTZ-FM Idaho Falls, ID; KBLY(AM) Idaho Falls, ID.

Riviera Broadcast Group LLC, 3333 Sierra Oaks Dr., Sacramento, CA 95864-5738. Phone: (916) 768-8049. Fax: (480) 247-5123. Web Site:www.rivierabroadcast.com Ownership VSS Communications Partners IV L.P., 82.5%; Chris Maguire, 8.75%; and Tim Pohlman, 8.75%.

Stns: 2 AM. 4 FM. KCVI(FM) Blackfoot, ID; KBLI(AM) Blackfoot, ID; KLCE-FM Blackfoot, ID; KTHK(FM) Idaho Falls, ID; KFTZ-FM Idaho Falls, ID; KBLY(AM) Idaho Falls, ID4 FM. KOAS(FM) Dolan Springs, AZ; KEDJ(FM) Gilbert, AZ; KKFR(FM) Mayer, AZ; KVGS(FM) Laughlin, NV.

Tim Pohlman, mgng ptnr/CEO; Chris Maguire, mgng ptnr/CFO.

F W Robbert Broadcasting Co. Inc., 2730 Loumor Ave., Metairie, LA 70001. Phone: (504) 831-6941. Web Site:www.wwcr.com Ownership Fred P. Westenberger, 51%; Chris P. Westenberger, 9.75%; Fritz N. Westenberger, 9.75%; Lisa M. Westenberger, 9.75%; Eric M. Westenberger, 9.75%; George McClintock, 10%.

Stns: 3 AM. WVOG New Orleans, LA; WMQM(AM) Lakeland, TN; WNQM Nashville, TN.

Fred P. Westenberger, pres; Eric M. Westenberger, gen mgr .

Robinson Corporation, E7601A County Rd. SS, Viroqua, WI 54665. Phone: (608) 637-7200. Fax: (608) 637-7299. E-mail: wvrq@mwt.net Web Site:www.wqpcradio.com Ownership David Robinson, Jane Robinson.

Stns: 2 AM. 3 FM. WQPC(FM) Prairie du Chien, WI; WPRE(AM) Prairie du Chien, WI; WKPO(FM) Soldiers Grove, WI; WVRQ(AM) Viroqua, WI; WVRQ-FM Viroqua, WI.

David Robinson, pres; Jeff Robinson, gen mgr & gen sls mgr.

Rocking M Radio Inc., 4806 Vue du Lac Place, Suite B, Manhattan, KS 66503. Phone: (785) 565-0406. Fax: (785) 565-0437. Web Site:www.rockingmradio.com Ownership Monte M. Miller, 33.33%; Doris Miller, 33.33%; and Christopher D. Miller, 33.33%.

Stns: 5 AM. 9 FM. KRDQ(FM) Colby, KS; KXXX Colby, KS; KAHE(FM) Dodge City, KS; KZRD(FM) Dodge City, KS; KGNO Dodge City, KS; KZRS(FM) Great Bend, KS; KERP(FM) Ingalls, KS; KNNS Larned, KS; KSOB(FM) Larned, KS; KSMM-FM Liberal, KS; KSMM(AM) Liberal, KS; KVOB(FM) Lindsborg, KS; KZUH(FM) Minneapolis, KS; KMMM(AM) Pratt, KS.

Monte M. Miller, pres.

Rodgers Broadcasting Corp., Box 1646, Richmond, IN 47374. Phone: (765) 962-6533. Fax: (765) 966-1499. Ownership David Rodgers, 100%.

Stns: 3 AM. 3 FM. WBML Macon, GA; WIFE(AM) Connersville, IN; WFMG(FM) Richmond, IN; WKBV(AM) Richmond, IN; WIFE-FM Rushville, IN; WZZY-FM Winchester, IN.

David Rodgers, pres.

Rogers Broadcasting Ltd., 777 Jarvis St., Toronto, ON M4Y 3B7. Canada. Phone: (416) 935-8200. Web Site:www.rogers.com Ownership Rogers Media Inc., 100%. Note: Rogers Media Inc. is 100% owned by Rogers Communications Inc.

Stns: 6 AM. 43 FM. CFFR Calgary, AB; CJAQ-FM Calgary, AB; CHMN-FM Canmore, AB; CKER-FM Edmonton, AB; CHDI-FM Edmonton, AB; CKYX-FM Fort McMurray, AB; CJOK-FM Fort McMurray, AB; CFGP-FM Grande Prairie, AB; CFRV-FM Lethbridge, AB; CJRX-FM Lethbridge, AB; CKMH-FM Medicine Hat, AB; CKQC-FM Abbotsford, BC; CKGO-FM-1 Boston Bar, BC; CKCL-FM Chilliwack, BC; CKSR-FM Chilliwack, BC; CFSR-FM Hope, BC; CISP-FM Pemberton, BC; CKKS-FM Sechelt, BC; CKWX Vancouver, BC; CKLG-FM Vancouver, BC; CHTT-FM Victoria, BC; CIOC-FM Victoria, BC; CISW-FM Whistler, BC; CITI-FM Winnipeg, MB; CKY-FM Winnipeg, MB; CKNI-FM Moncton, NB; CHNI-FM Saint John, NB; CFLT-FM Dartmouth, NS; CJNI-FM Halifax, NS; CKXC-FM Kingston, ON; CIKR-FM Kingston, ON; CKGL Kitchener, ON; CHYM-FM Kitchener, ON; CIKZ-FM Kitchener-Waterloo, ON; CHUR-FM North Bay, ON; CKAT(AM) North Bay, ON; CKFX-FM North Bay, ON; CHEZ-FM Ottawa, ON; CHAS-FM Sault Ste. Marie, ON; CJQM-FM Sault Ste. Marie, ON; CKBY-FM Smiths Falls, ON; CJMX-FM Sudbury, ON; CJRQ-FM Sudbury, ON; CJQQ-FM Timmins, ON; CKGB-FM Timmins, ON; CJCL Toronto, ON; CKIS-FM Toronto, ON; CFTR Toronto, ON; CHFI-FM Toronto, ON.

Stns: 10 TV. CKAL, Calgary, AB; CJCO-TV, Calgary, AB; CKEM, Edmonton, AB; CJEO-TV, Edmonton, AB; CHMI-TV, Portage la Prairie, MB; CITY-TV, Toronto, ON; CFMT, Toronto, ON; CJMT-TV, Toronto, ON; CHNM-TV, Vancouver, BC; CKVU, Vancouver, BC.

Rael Merson, pres.

Rooney Moon Broadcasting Inc., 208 E. Grand Ave., Clovis, NM 88101. Phone: (505) 763-4649. Fax: (505) 763-1693. E-mail: info.rmb@yucca.net Web Site:www.bettermix.com

Stns: 1 AM. 3 FM. KSMX-FM Clovis, NM; KRMQ-FM Clovis, NM; KSEL Portales, NM; KSEL-FM Portales, NM.

Steve Rooney, pres.

Rose City Radio Corp., 0234 Southwest Bancroft St., Portland, OR 97239. Phone: (503) 243-7595. Fax: (503) 417-7662. Web Site:www.kxlradio.com

Stns: 3 AM. 1 FM. WWZN(AM) Boston, MA; WSNR(AM) Jersey City, NJ; KXTG(FM) Portland, OR; KXL Portland, OR.

Tim McNamara, VP/gen mgr.

Roser Communications Network Inc., 185 Genesee St., Suite 1600, Utica, NY 13501-2108. Phone: (315) 734-9245. Fax: (315) 624-9245. Ownership Kenneth F. Roser, 100%.

Stns: 3 AM. 4 FM. WVTL(AM) Amsterdam, NY; WBUG-FM Fort Plain, NY; WSKU(FM) Little Falls, NY; WBGK(FM) Newport Village, NY; WADR Remsen, NY; WUTQ Utica, NY; WSKS(FM) Whitesboro, NY.

Kenneth Roser, pres.

Roswell Radio Inc./Quay Broadcasters Inc., Box 670, Roswell, NM 88202. Phone: (505) 622-6450. Fax: (505) 622-9041. Ownership John M. Dunn, 100%.

Stns: 2 AM. 4 FM. KBCQ-FM Roswell, NM; KMOU(FM) Roswell, NM; KBCQ(AM) Roswell, NM; KSFX(FM) Roswell, NM; KTNM Tucumcari, NM; KQAY-FM Tucumcari, NM.

John M. Dunn, pres.

Rubber City Radio Group Inc., 1795 W. Market St., Akron, OH 44313. Phone: (330) 869-9800. Fax: (330) 864-6799. E-mail: mail@wakr.net Web Site:www.wqmx.com Ownership Thomas Mandel.

Stns: 1 AM. 5 FM. WJZL(FM) Charlotte, MI; WVIC(FM) Jackson, MI; WJXQ-FM Jackson, MI; WQTX(FM) Saint Johns, MI; WAKR Akron, OH; WQMX-FM Medina, OH.

Thomas Mandel, pres; Mark Biviano, VP; Nick Anthony, VP.

Ruby Radio Corp., 1750 Manzanita, Suite 1, Elko, NV 89801. Phone: (775) 777-1196. Fax: (775) 777-9587. Ownership Ken Sutherland, 50%; and Mary A. Sutherland, 50%.

Stns: 1 AM. 5 FM. WJZL(FM) Charlotte, MI; WVIC(FM) Jackson, MI; WJXQ-FM Jackson, MI; WQTX(FM) Saint Johns, MI; WAKR Akron, OH; WQMX-FM Medina, OH3 FM. KHIX-FM Carlin, NV; KOYT(FM) Elko, NV; KEBG(FM) Spring Creek, NV.

Ken Sutherland, pres.

S

SIGA Broadcasting Corp., 1302 N. Shepherd Dr., Houston, TX 77008. Phone: (713) 868-5559. Fax: (713) 868-9631. E-mail: sigabroadcasting@gmail.com Web Site:www.sigabroadcasting.com Ownership Gabriel Arango, 50%; and Silvia Arango 50%.

Stns: 6 AM. KHFX(AM) Cleburne, TX; KTMR(AM) Converse, TX; KFJZ Fort Worth, TX; KGBC Galveston, TX; KAML Kenedy-Karnes City, TX; KLVL Pasadena, TX.

STARadio Corp., 329 Maine St., Quincy, IL 62301-3928. Phone: (217) 224-4102. Fax: (217) 224-4133. E-mail: reception@staradio.com Ownership Howard A. Doss, Derek Parrish and Jack Whitley.

Stns: 2 AM. 6 FM. WKAN Kankakee, IL; WQCY(FM) Quincy, IL; WTAD Quincy, IL; WCOY(FM) Quincy, IL; WXNU(FM) Saint Anne, IL; WYKT-FM Wilmington, IL; KGRC-FM Hannibal, MO; KZZK-FM New London, MO.

Mike Moyers, gen mgr .

Saga Communications Inc., 73 Kercheval Ave., Suite 201, Grosse Pointe Farms, MI 48236. Phone: (313) 886-7070. Fax: (313) 886-7150. E-mail: chapsburg@sagacom.com Web Site:www.sagacommunications.com Ownership Edward K. Christian, 56.5% of the voting stock. Other Interests: Illinois Radio Network, Michigan Radio Network, Michigan Farm Radio Network.

Stns: 28 AM. 59 FM. KEGI(FM) Jonesboro, AR; KDXY(FM) Lake City, AR; KJBX(FM) Trumann, AR; KLTI-FM Ames, IA; KRNT Des Moines, IA; KSTZ(FM) Des Moines, IA; KPSZ(AM) Des Moines, IA; KIOA(FM) Des Moines, IA; KAZR(FM) Pella, IA; KICD Spencer, IA; KICD-FM Spencer, IA; KLLT(FM) Spencer, IA; WIXY-FM Champaign, IL; WLRW-FM Champaign, IL; WXTT(FM) Danville, IL; WYMG(FM) Jacksonville, IL; WABZ(FM) Sherman, IL; WTAX(AM) Springfield, IL; WQQL(FM) Springfield, IL; WDBR(FM) Springfield, IL; WCFF(FM) Urbana, IL; WEGI(AM) Fort Campbell, KY; WCVQ-FM Fort Campbell, KY; WVVR(FM) Hopkinsville, KY; WZZP(FM) Hopkinsville, KY; WEGI-FM Oak Grove, KY; WHNP(AM) East Longmeadow, MA; WPVQ(FM) Greenfield, MA; WHMQ(FM) Greenfield, MA; WHAI(FM) Greenfield, MA; WHMP Northampton, MA; WLZX(FM) Northampton, MA; WAQY-FM Springfield, MA; WRSI(FM) Turners Falls, MA; WVAE(AM) Biddeford, ME; WCLZ(FM) Brunswick, ME; WBAE Portland, ME; WGAN(AM) Portland, ME; WPOR Portland, ME; WZAN Portland, ME; WMGX(FM) Portland, ME; WYNZ-FM Westbrook, ME; WOXL-FM Biltmore Forest, NC; WYSE(AM) Canton, NC; WTMT(FM) Weaverville, NC; WMLL(FM) Bedford, NH; WZBK(AM) Keene, NH; WKBK(AM) Keene, NH;

WKNE(FM) Keene, NH; WZID(FM) Manchester, NH; WFEA Manchester, NH; WSNI(FM) Swanzey, NH; WINQ(FM) Winchester, NH; WIII(FM) Cortland, NY; WHCU Ithaca, NY; WYXL-FM Ithaca, NY; WNYY(AM) Ithaca, NY; WQNY-FM Ithaca, NY; WQEL-FM Bucyrus, OH; WBCO(AM) Bucyrus, OH; WSNY(FM) Columbus, OH; WVMX(FM) Delaware, OH; WJZA(FM) Pickerington, OH; WODB(FM) Richwood, OH; KMIT-FM Mitchell, SD; KUQL(FM) Wessington Springs, SD; WKFN(AM) Clarksville, TN; WINA Charlottesville, VA; WWWV-FM Charlottesville, VA; WQMZ(FM) Charlottesville, VA; WVAX(AM) Charlottesville, VA; WCNR(FM) Keswick, VA; WNOR(FM) Norfolk, VA; WJOI Norfolk, VA; WAFX-FM Suffolk, VA; WKVT Brattleboro, VT; WKVT-FM Brattleboro, VT; WRSY(FM) Marlboro, VT; KGMI Bellingham, WA; KISM-FM Bellingham, WA; KBAI(AM) Bellingham, WA; KPUG Bellingham, WA; WJZX(FM) Brookfield, WI; WJMR-FM Menomonee Falls, WI; WJYI Milwaukee, WI; WKLH-FM Milwaukee, WI; WHQG(FM) Milwaukee, WI.

Stns: 3 TV. WXVT, Greenwood-Greenville, MS; KOAM, Joplin, MO-Pittsburg, KS; KAVU-TV, Victoria, TX.

Edward K. Christian, pres/CEO; Marcia Lobaito, VP business affrs; Sam Bush, CFO; Warren Lada Sr., VP opns.

Salem Communications Corp., 4880 Santa Rosa Rd., Suite 100, Camarillo, CA 93012. Phone: (805) 987-0400. Fax: (805) 384-4511. Web Site:www.salem.cc

Stns: 64 AM. 29 FM. KPXQ(AM) Glendale, AZ; KKNT(AM) Phoenix, AZ; KFSH-FM Anaheim, CA; KXMX(AM) Anaheim, CA; KFIA Carmichael, CA; KSAC-FM Dunnigan, CA; KRLA(AM) Glendale, CA; KKFS(FM) Lincoln, CA; KKLA-FM Los Angeles, CA; KDAR(FM) Oxnard, CA; KDOW(AM) Palo Alto, CA; KTKZ Sacramento, CA; KTIE(AM) San Bernardino, CA; KCBQ San Diego, CA; KFAX San Francisco, CA; KPRZ San Marcos-Poway, CA; KRKS-FM Boulder, CO; KZNT(AM) Colorado Springs, CO; KNUS Denver, CO; KRKS(AM) Denver, CO; KBJD Denver, CO; KBIQ(FM) Manitou Springs, CO; KGFT-FM Pueblo, CO; WORL(AM) Altamonte Springs, FL; WHIM Apopka, FL; WMCU(AM) Coral Gables, FL; WGUL(AM) Dunedin, FL; WZAZ Jacksonville, FL; WKAT North Miami, FL; WTLN(AM) Orlando, FL; WTBN(AM) Pinellas Park, FL; WTWD(AM) Plant City, FL; WLSS(AM) Sarasota, FL; WLTA Alpharetta, GA; WFSH-FM Athens, GA; WGKA(AM) Atlanta, GA; WAFS(AM) Atlanta, GA; WNIV Atlanta, GA; KKOL-FM Aiea, HI; KGU Honolulu, HI; KHCM(AM) Honolulu, HI; KAIM-FM Honolulu, HI; KHUI(FM) Honolulu, HI; KHCM-FM Honolulu, HI; WYLL(AM) Chicago, IL; WIND Chicago, IL; WFIA-FM New Albany, IN; WGTK(AM) Louisville, KY; WFIA Louisville, KY; WEZE Boston, MA; WWDJ(AM) Boston, MA; WROL Boston, MA; WDTK(AM) Detroit, MI; WLQV Detroit, MI; KYCR Golden Valley, MN; WWTC Minneapolis, MN; KKMS Richfield, MN; KGBI-FM Omaha, NE; KOTK(AM) Omaha, NE; KCRO Omaha, NE; WNYM(AM) Hackensack, NJ; WMCA New York, NY; WHKW(AM) Cleveland, OH; WFHM-FM Cleveland, OH; WHK(AM) Cleveland, OH; KRYP(FM) Gladstone, OR; KPDQ Portland, OR; KPDQ-FM Portland, OR; KFIS(FM) Scappoose, OR; WNTP(AM) Philadelphia, PA; WFIL(AM) Philadelphia, PA; WPIT Pittsburgh, PA; WORD-FM Pittsburgh, PA; WFFI(FM) Kingston Springs, TN; WFFH(FM) Smyrna, TN; WVRY-FM Waverly, TN; WBOZ(FM) Woodbury, TN; KLTY(FM) Arlington, TX; KSKY(AM) Balch Springs, TX; KWRD-FM Highland Village, TX; KNTH(AM) Houston, TX; KPXI-FM Overton, TX; KSLR San Antonio, TX; KLUP(AM) Terrell Hills, TX; KKHT-FM Winnie, TX; WAVA-FM Arlington, VA; WAVA(AM) Arlington, VA; KGNW Burien-Seattle, WA; KNTS(AM) Seattle, WA; KKOL Seattle, WA; KLFE Seattle, WA; KKMO Tacoma, WA; WAMD Aberdeen, MD

Edward G. Atsinger III, pres/CEO; Stuart W. Epperson III, chmn; Eric H. Halvorson III, VP/COO.

San Luis Valley Broadcasting Inc., Box 631, Monte Vista, CO 81144. Phone: (719) 852-3581. Fax: (719) 852-3583. Ownership Marion L. Goad, 65.01%; and H. Robert Gourley III, 34.99%.

Stns: 1 AM. 2 FM. KSLV-FM Del Norte, CA; KSLV(AM) Monte Vista, CO; KYDN(FM) Monte Vista, CO.

Sand Hill Media Corp., Box 570, Logan, UT 84323. Phone: (435) 752-1390. Ownership Sand Hill Media 2001, 100%.

Stns: 1 AM. 3 FM. KSPZ(AM) Ammon, ID; KUPI-FM Idaho Falls, ID; KQEO(FM) Idaho Falls, ID; KSNA(FM) Rexburg, ID.

Sandab Communications L.P. II, 2201 Old Court Rd., Baltimore, MD 21208. Phone: (508) 771-1224. Web Site:www.capecodbroadcasting.com Ownership Stephen Seymour

Stns: 1 AM. 3 FM. KSPZ(AM) Ammon, ID; KUPI-FM Idaho Falls, ID; KQEO(FM) Idaho Falls, ID; KSNA(FM) Rexburg, ID4 FM. WQRC(FM) Barnstable, MA; WFCC-FM Chatham, MA; WOCN-FM Orleans, MA; WKPE-FM South Yarmouth, MA.

Stephen Seymour, pres; Scott Frothinghan, VP; Gregory Bone, gen mgr .

Sandusky Radio, 515 Park Ave., Apt. 4A, New York, NY 10022. Phone: (212) 355-3074. Fax: (212) 355-3075. Ownership Alice S. White trust. All 100% owned by the White and Rau families

Stns: 4 AM. 6 FM. KDKB(FM) Mesa, AZ; KAZG(AM) Scottsdale, AZ; KSLX-FM Scottsdale, AZ; KUPD-FM Tempe, AZ; KDUS Tempe, AZ; KQMV(FM) Bellevue, WA; KRWM-FM Bremerton, WA; KIXI Mercer Island-Seattle, WA; KWJZ(FM) Seattle, WA; KKNW(AM) Seattle, WA.

Sandusky Newspapers Inc. publishes the *Sandusky Register, Norwalk Reflector* (OH) *Kingsport Times-News*(TN) *Grand Haven Tribune*(MI)*Ogden Standard-Examiner*(UT)*Johnson City Press, Lebanon Democrat* (TN) and five weekly newspapers,*Erwin Record, Jonesborough Herald & Tribune, Mountain City Tomahawk, Hartsville Vidette* and the*Mt. Juliet News.*

David A. Rau, chmn/CEO; Norman Rau, pres; Peter W. Vogt, CFO.

Sanpete County Broadcasting Co., Box 40, Manti, UT 84642. Phone: (435) 835-7301. Fax: (435) 835-2250. Ownership Douglas Barton, 100%.

Stns: 1 AM. 2 FM. KMTI Manti, UT; KMXD(FM) Monroe, UT; KLGL(FM) Richfield, UT.

Saskatoon Media Group, 366 3rd Ave. South, Saskatoon, SK S7K 1M5. Canada. Phone: (306) 244-1975. Fax: (306) 665-8484.

Stns: 1 AM. 2 FM. CKBL-FM Saskatoon, SK; CJWW Saskatoon, SK; CJMK-FM Saskatoon, SK.

Elmer Hildebrand, CEO; Vic Dubois, gen mgr .

Schurz Communications Inc., 225 W. Colfax Ave., South Bend, IN 46626. Phone: (574) 287-1001. Fax: (574) 287-2257.E-mail: mburdick@schurz.com Web Site:www.schurz.com Ownership Franklin D. Schurz Jr., James M. Schurz, Scott C. Schurz and Mary Schurz, trustees.

Stns: 4 AM. 8 FM. WASK-FM Battle Ground, IN; WXXB(FM) Delphi, IN; WASK Lafayette, IN; WKOA-FM Lafayette, IN; WSBT South Bend, IN; WNSN-FM South Bend, IN; KFXS-FM Rapid City, SD; KKLS Rapid City, SD; KKMK-FM Rapid City, SD; KOUT-FM Rapid City, SD; KRCS-FM Sturgis, SD; KBHB Sturgis, SD.

Stns: 9 TV. WAGT, Augusta, GA; WDBJ, Roanoke-Lynchburg, VA; WSBT, South Bend-Elkhart, IN; KYTV, Springfield, MO; KBSD-DT, Wichita-Hutchinson Plus, KS; KBSH-DT, Wichita-Hutchinson Plus, KS; KBSL-DT, Wichita-Hutchinson Plus, KS; KWCH-DT, Wichita-Hutchinson Plus, KS; KSCW-DT, Wichita-Hutchinson Plus, KS.

Schurz Communications publishes the following nwsprs: *Imperial Valley Press, Southside Times-Beech, Times; Bedford Times-Mail, Bloomington Herald-Times* , & *South Bend Tribune, Martinsville Reporter, Danville Advocate-Messenger, The Herald Mail Co.; Daily American, Somerset, PA.*

Marcia K. Burdick, sr VP bcstg; Franklin D. Schurz Jr., chmn; Todd F. Schurz, pres.

Scott Communications Inc., Box 1150, Selma, AL 36702-1150. Phone: (334) 875-9360. Fax: (334) 875-1340. Ownership Paul Scott Alexander, 100%.

Stns: 1 AM. 2 FM. WALX(FM) Orrville, AL; WJAM(AM) Selma, AL; WMRK-FM Shorter, AL.

Sea-Comm Inc., 122 Cinema Dr., Wilmington, NC 28403. Phone: (910) 772-6300. Fax: (910) 772-6310. Web Site:www.sea-comm.com Ownership N. Eric Jorgensen, 100%.

Stns: 1 AM. 2 FM. WALX(FM) Orrville, AL; WJAM(AM) Selma, AL; WMRK-FM Shorter, AL3 FM. WLTT(FM) Shallotte, NC; WBNE(FM) Shallotte, NC; WNTB(FM) Wrightsville Beach, NC.

Paul Knight, gen mgr; Rick Jorgenson, pres/CEO.

Seaton Stations, Manhattan Broadcasting Inc., 2414 Casement Rd., Manhattan, KS 66502. Phone: (785) 776-1350. Fax: (785) 539-1000.

Stns: 1 AM. 2 FM. KMAN Manhattan, KS; KXBZ-FM Manhattan, KS; KACZ(FM) Riley, KS.

Seaton Goup of newspapers includes the *Manhattan Mercury* & *Winfield Courier,* both KS; *Alliance Times-Herald & Hastings Tribune,* both NE; *The Black Hills Pioneer,* Spearfish, SD; *Sheridan* (WY) *Press.*

Richard Wartell, gen mgr .

Seattle Streaming Radio LLC, Box 1471, Evergreen, CO 80437. Phone: (303) 688-5162. Fax: (303) 660-4930. Ownership David M. Drucker, 80%; and Penny Drucker, 20%.

Stns: 5 AM. KXLJ(AM) Juneau, AK; WKIZ Key West, FL; KBRO Bremerton, WA; KLDY Lacey, WA; KNTB Lakewood, WA.

Seehafer Broadcasting Corp., Box 1385, Manitowoc, WI 54221-1385. Phone: (920) 682-0351. Fax: (920) 682-1008. Ownership Donald W. Seehafer, 100%.

Stns: 4 AM. 3 FM. WQTC-FM Manitowoc, WI; WOMT(AM) Manitowoc, WI; WDLB Marshfield, WI; WRCW(FM) Nekoosa, WI; WOSQ-FM Spencer, WI; WXCO Wausau, WI; WFHR Wisconsin Rapids, WI.

Don Seehafer, pres; Mark Seehafer, VP.

Service Broadcasting Group LLC, 621 N.W. 6th St., Grand Prairie, TX 75050-5555. Phone: (972) 263-9911. Fax: (972) 558-0010. Web Site:www.k104fm.com

Stns: 1 AM. 2 FM. KKDA-FM Dallas, TX; KRNB-FM Decatur, TX; KKDA Grand Prairie, TX.

Hymen Childs, pres; Chuck Smith, gen mgr .

Seward County Broadcasting Co., 1410 N. Western, Liberal, KS 67901. Phone: (620) 624-3891. Fax: (620) 624-7885.E-mail: sales@kscb.net Web Site:www.kscb.net Ownership Jack Landon, Robert Larrabee, Stuart Melchert.

Stns: 1 AM. 2 FM. KLDG-FM Liberal, KS; KSCB Liberal, KS; KSCB-FM Liberal, KS.

Stuart Melchert, gen mgr .

Shamrock Communications Inc., 149 Penn Ave., Scranton, PA 18503. Phone: (570) 348-9108. Fax: (570) 348-9109. Web Site:www.nepanews.com Ownership Principal owners: William R. Lynett, James J. Haggerty, Edward J. Lynett, George V. Lynett. Shamrock Communications owns 50% of the Milwaukee Radio Alliance LLC (see listing).

Stns: 2 AM. 11 FM. KZZD(FM) Fallon, NV; KEHD(FM) Fernley, NV; KZHD(FM) Lovelock, NV; WBZX(FM) Hancock, NY; KTSO(FM) Glenpool, OK; KMYZ-FM Pryor, OK; WQFN(FM) Forest City, PA; WQFM-FM Nanticoke, PA; WPZX(FM) Pocono Pines, PA; WEJL Scranton, PA; WEZX-FM Scranton, PA; WBAX Wilkes-Barre, PA; WZBA(FM) Westminster, MD.

Publications include *Orlando Weekly,* Orlando, FL; *City Paper,* Baltimore, MD; *Metro Times* (Detroit), Detroit, MI; *Owego Pennysaver,* Owego, NY; *Pocono Shopper* (Monroe County Edition), East Stroudsburg, *Susquehanna County Independent, Susquehanna County Weekender,* Montrose, *Pottsville Republican and Evening Herald,* Pottsville, *ADI, Electric City, Good Times, Northeast Pennsylvania Business Journal, Scranton Times-Tribune, Suburban Weekly, Tri-Boro Banner, Valley Advantage,* all Scranton, *News Item, Shamokin, Daily Review, The Bradford Sullivan Pennysaver, The Farmer's Friend,* Towanda, *Troy Pennysaver,* Troy, *New Age-Examiner, Wyoming County Advance,* Tunkhannock, *The Citizen Standard, Valley View, Citizens Voice,* Wilkes-Barre, all PA; *San Antonio Current,* San Antonio, TX.

William R. Lynett, pres; Jim Loftus, COO.

Sheridan Broadcasting Corp., 960 Penn Ave., Suite 200, Pittsburgh, PA 15222. Phone: (412) 456-4000. Fax: (412) 456-4022. Web Site:www.wamo.com Ownership Ronald R. Davenport Sr. and Judith M. Davenport, 96.34%; Ronald R. Davenport Jr., 1.22%; Judith Allison, 1.22%; and Susan Davenport Austin, 1.22%. Note: all stns 100% owned except for WIGO(AM) Morrow, GA. Group owns 75% of WIGO(AM) Morrow, GA.

Stns: 5 AM. 1 FM. WATV(AM) Birmingham, AL; WIGO(AM) Morrow, GA; WUFO Amherst, NY; WAMO-FM Beaver Falls, PA; WAMO(AM) Millvale, PA; WPGR(AM) Monroeville, PA.

Ronald R. Davenport Sr., chmn.

Simmons Broadcasting Inc., 1403 Third St., Langdon, ND 58249. Phone: (701) 256-1080. Fax: (701) 256-1081.E-mail: kndkkicksbs@utma.com Ownership Robert N. Simmons, 50%; and Diane R. Simmons, 50%. Note: Pursuant to a loc mktg agreement, group provides substantially all of the progmg for KXPO(AM)-KAUJ(FM) Grafton, ND.

Stns: 1 AM. 3 FM. KAOC(FM) Cavalier, ND; KNDK Langdon, ND; KNDK-FM Langdon, ND; KYTZ(FM) Walhalla, ND.

Simmons Media Group, 515 South 700 East, Salt Lake City, UT 84102. Phone: (801) 524-2600. Fax: (801) 524-6002. Web Site:www.simmonsmedia.com Ownership The David E. Simmons 201 Trust, The Matthew R. Simmons 201 Trust, The Laurence E. Simmons 201 Trust, The Julia S. Watkins 201 Trust, The Elizabeth S. Hoke 201 Trust and The Harris H. Simmons 201 Trust.

Stns: 12 AM. 10 FM. KDXE(AM) North Little Rock, AR; KQPN(AM) West Memphis, AR; WFFX(AM) East St. Louis, IL; KSLG(AM) Saint Louis, MO; KZNX(AM) Creedmoor, TX; KLRK(FM) Marlin, TX; KRQX Mexia, TX; KRQX-FM Mexia, TX; KWNX(AM) Taylor, TX; KRZI(AM) Waco, TX; KEGH(FM) Brigham City, UT; KXOL Brigham City, UT; KJQN(FM) Coalville, UT; KURR(FM) Hurricane, UT;

KEGA(FM) Oakley, UT; KXRK-FM Provo, UT; KOVO Provo, UT; KZNS(AM) Salt Lake City, UT; KYMV(FM) Woodruff, UT; KDWY(FM) Diamondville, WY; KAOX(FM) Kemmerer, WY; KMER Kemmerer, WY.

David Simmons, chmn; Craig Hanson, pres; Bruce W. Thomas, CFO; Bret Leifson, controller; Alan Hague, opns VP.

Sinclair Communications Inc., 999 Waterside Dr., Suite 500, Norfolk, VA 23510. Phone: (757) 640-8500. Fax: (757) 640-8552. Web Site:www.sinclairstations.com Ownership John L. Sinclair, chmn; Robert Sinclair, J. David Sinclair, Ann Adams. Note: Group also manages KNOB(FM) Healdsburg, CA.
   Stns: 2 AM. 6 FM. KSXY(FM) Calistoga, CA; KXTS(FM) Geyserville, CA; KRSH(FM) Healdsburg, CA; WPYA(FM) Chesapeake, VA; WROX-FM Exmore, VA; WTAR(AM) Norfolk, VA; WNIS Norfolk, VA; WUSH(FM) Poquoson, VA.

John L. Sinclair, chmn; J. David Sinclair, pres; Robert L. Sinclair, sec.

SkyWest Media L.L.C., Box 36148, Tucson, AZ 85740. Phone: (520) 797-4434.E-mail: ttucker@skywestmedia.com Ownership Ted Tucker, 100%.
   Stns: 1 AM. 8 FM. KXML(FM) Salmon, ID; KNFT Bayard, NM; KNFT-FM Bayard, NM; KPSA-FM Lordsburg, NM; KSCQ-FM Silver City, NM; KRZX(FM) Monticello, UT; KXWY(FM) Hudson, WY; KCYA(FM) Kaycee, WY; KFMR(FM) Marbleton, WY.

Smoke and Mirrors LLC, Number 10 Media Center Dr., Lake Havasu City, AZ 86403. Phone: (928) 855-1051. Fax: (928) 855-7996. Ownership Rick L. Murphy, 100%.
   Stns: 1 AM. 8 FM. KXML(FM) Salmon, ID; KNFT Bayard, NM; KNFT-FM Bayard, NM; KPSA-FM Lordsburg, NM; KSCQ-FM Silver City, NM; KRZX(FM) Monticello, UT; KXWY(FM) Hudson, WY; KCYA(FM) Kaycee, WY; KFMR(FM) Marbleton, WY4 FM. KFTT(FM) Bagdad, AZ; KRRK-FM Lake Havasu City, AZ; KVYL(FM) Mohave Valley, AZ; KVAL(FM) Cal-Nev-Ari, NV.

Somar Communications Inc., 28095 Three Notch Rd., Suite 2-B, Mechanicsville, MD 20659. Phone: (301) 870-5550. Fax: (301) 884-0280.
   Stns: 2 AM. 3 FM. WKIK-FM California, MD; WKIK La Plata, MD; WPTX(AM) Lexington Park, MD; WMDM(FM) Lexington Park, MD; WSMD-FM Mechanicsville, MD.

Roy Robertson, pres/CEO.

Sorensen Pacific Broadcasting Inc., 111 W. Chanlan Santo Papa, Suite 800, Hagatna, GU 96910. Phone: (671) 477-5700.   Fax: (671)   477-3982.E-mail: comments@radiopacific.com Web Site: www.radiopacific.com Ownership Rex W. Sorensen, 97.6%.
   Stns: 1 AM. 4 FM. KGUM-FM Dededo, GU; KGUM(AM) Hagatna, GU; KZGZ(FM) Hagatna, GU; KPXP(FM) Garapan-Saipan, NP; KRSI-FM Garapan-Saipan, NP.

Rex Sorensen, chmn/CEO; Jon Anderson, pres.

Sorenson Broadcasting Corp., 2804 S. Ridgeview Way, Sioux Falls, SD 57105. Phone: (605) 334-1117. Fax: (605) 338-0326.E-mail: sorenson@sbcradio.com Ownership Dean P. Sorenson, 100%.
   Stns: 5 AM. 8 FM. KUQQ-FM Milford, IA; KIHK-FM Rock Valley, IA; KSOU Sioux Center, IA; KSOU-FM Sioux Center, IA; KUOO-FM Spirit Lake, IA; KCUE Red Wing, MN; KWNG-FM Red Wing, MN; KORN Mitchell, SD; KQRN(FM) Mitchell, SD; KCCR Pierre, SD; KLXS-FM Pierre, SD; KYNT Yankton, SD; KKYA-FM Yankton, SD.

Dean Sorenson, pres.

South Central Communications Corp., Box 3848, Evansville, IN 47736. Phone: (812) 463-7950. Fax: (812) 463-7915. Web Site:www.southcentralcommunications.net Ownership John D. Engelbrecht, 80%, J.P. Engelbrecht, 20%.
   Stns: 1 AM. 11 FM. WEJK(FM) Boonville, IN; WLFW(FM) Chandler, IN; WEOA Evansville, IN; WIKY-FM Evansville, IN; WABX-FM Evansville, IN; WSTO-FM Owensboro, KY; WIMZ-FM Knoxville, TN; WJXB-FM Knoxville, TN; WQJK(FM) Maryville, TN; WCJK(FM) Murfreesboro, TN; WJXA-FM Nashville, TN; WRJK(FM) Norris, TN.

John D. Engelbrecht, pres; J.P. Engelbrecht, VP.

South Texas FM Investments LLC, Box 880, Roma, TX 78584. Phone: (956) 487-8015. Ownership Judge Eloy Vera, 20%; Mario Mascorro, 20%; Juan Diego Posada, 20%; Eugenio Falcon Jr., 20%; and Jose Vasquez, 20%.
   Stns: 1 AM. 11 FM. WEJK(FM) Boonville, IN; WLFW(FM) Chandler, IN; WEOA Evansville, IN; WIKY-FM Evansville, IN; WABX-FM Evansville, IN; WSTO-FM Owensboro, KY; WIMZ-FM Knoxville, TN; WJXB-FM Knoxville, TN; WQJK(FM) Maryville, TN; WCJK(FM) Murfreesboro, TN; WJXA-FM

Nashville, TN; WRJK(FM) Norris, TN6 FM. KXOW(FM) Eldorado, OK; KTSX(FM) Knox City, TX; KAHA(FM) Olney, TX; KZAM(FM) Pleasant Valley, TX; KZNO(FM) Seymour, TX; KXME(FM) Wellington, TX.

Southeast Kansas Independent Living Resource Center Inc., 202 E. Centennial Ave., Suite 2B, Pittsburg, KS 66762. Phone: (620) 232-9912. Fax: (620) 232-9915. Ownership Officers and bd members: Shari Coatney, pres/CEO; Jeanette Pruitt, bd chmn; Ron Garnett, treas; Faron Morales, John Spillman, Carolyn Freeman, Marty Wooten, Darlene Lomax and Edward Reynolds.
   Stns: 2 AM. 1 FM. KSEK-FM Girard, KS; KLKC(AM) Parsons, KS; KSEK Pittsburg, KS.

Shari Coatney, pres.

Southeastern Oklahoma Radio LLC, Box 1011, Hartshorne, OK 74547. Phone: (918) 297-2501. Ownership Bob and Sheila Turnbow (jointly), 33.33%; Lee Anderson, 33.33%; and Richard C. Lerblance, 33.33%. Note: Richard C. Lerblance also owns 33.33% of KESC(FM) Wilburton, OK.
   Stns: 2 AM. 2 FM. KNED McAlester, OK; KTMC McAlester, OK; KTMC-FM McAlester, OK; KMCO(FM) Wilburton, OK.

Southern Broadcasting Companies Inc., 1010 Tower Pl., Bogart, GA 30622. Phone: (706) 369-7301. Fax: (706) 353-1967. Web Site:www.magic1021.com Ownership Paul C. Stone.
   Stns: 2 AM. 3 FM. WSRM(FM) Coosa, GA; WMGZ(FM) Eatonton, GA; WRGA Rome, GA; WQTU-FM Rome, GA; WLOV Washington, GA.

Paul Stone, pres; Traci Long, gen mgr .

Southern Communications Corp., 306 S. Kanawaha St., Beckley, WV 25801. Phone: (304) 253-7000. Fax: (304) 255-1044. Web Site:www.103cir.com Ownership R. Shane Southern, 50.4%; Karen L. Martin, 24.8%; and Kristin E. Wallace, 24.8%.
   Stns: 3 AM. 4 FM. WCIR-FM Beckley, WV; WIWS Beckley, WV; WWNR Beckley, WV; WMTD Hinton, WV; WMTD-FM Hinton, WV; WTNJ-FM Mount Hope, WV; WAXS-FM Oak Hill, WV.

Jay Quesenberry, gen mgr; R. Shane Southern, pres.

Southern Star Broadcasting of Missouri LLC, 270 Walnut Leaf Dr., Memphis, TN 38018. Phone: (901) 692-3116. Ownership Randolph A. Miller, 60%; Paul Pesce, 40%.
   Stns: 2 AM. 3 FM. KTNX(FM) Arcadia, MO; KYLS Fredericktown, MO; KYLS-FM Ironton, MO; KPWB Piedmont, MO; KPWB-FM Piedmont, MO.

Chip Miller, pres.

Southern Wabash Communications Corp., 435 37th Ave. N., Nashville, TN 37209. Phone: (615) 844-1039. Fax: (615) 777-2284. Web Site:www.wnsr.com
   Stns: 2 AM. 2 FM. WSJD-FM Princeton, IN; WNTC-FM Drakesboro, KY; WNSR Brentwood, TN; WMGC Murfreesboro, TN.

Randy Bell, pres; Ted Johnson, gen mgr .

Southwest Broadcasting Inc., 206 N. Front, McComb, MS 39648. Phone: (601) 684-4116. Fax: (601) 684-4654.E-mail: spots@k106.net Ownership C. Wayne Dowdy, 100%.
   Stns: 2 AM. 6 FM. WTGG-FM Amite, LA; WJSH(FM) Folsom, LA; WKJN(FM) Centreville, MS; WAZA-FM Liberty, MS; WAKH-FM McComb, MS; WAPF(AM) McComb, MS; WAKK(AM) McComb, MS; WFCG(FM) Tylertown, MS.

C. Wayne Dowdy, pres.

Spanish Broadcasting System Inc., 2601 South Bayshore Dr., PH 2, Coconut Grove, FL 33133. Phone: (305) 441-6901. Fax: (305) 446-5148. Web Site:www.spanishbroadcasting.com Ownership Raul Alarcon Jr., Jose Grimalt.
   Stns: 2 AM. 6 FM. WTGG-FM Amite, LA; WJSH(FM) Folsom, LA; WKJN(FM) Centreville, MS; WAZA-FM Liberty, MS; WAKH-FM McComb, MS; WAPF(AM) McComb, MS; WAKK(AM) McComb, MS; WFCG(FM) Tylertown, MS20 FM. KLAX-FM East Los Angeles, CA; KXOL-FM Los Angeles, CA; KRZZ(FM) San Francisco, CA; WRMA-FM Fort Lauderdale, FL; WCMQ-FM Hialeah, FL; WXDJ-FM North Miami Beach, FL; WLEY-FM Aurora, IL; WPAT-FM Paterson, NJ; WSKQ-FM New York, NY; WODA(FM) Bayamon, PR; WRXD(FM) Fajardo, PR; WMEG-FM Guayama, PR; WZET(FM) Hormigueros, PR; WNOD(FM) Mayaguez, PR; WIOB-FM Mayaguez, PR; WIOC-FM Ponce, PR; WZMT-FM Ponce, PR; WEGM(FM) San German, PR; WZNT-FM San Juan, PR; WIOA(FM) San Juan, PR.
   Stns: 1 TV. WSBS-TV, Miami-Ft. Lauderdale, FL.

Raul Alarcon Jr., pres/CEO; Jose Grimalt, exec VP.

Spanish Peaks Broadcasting Inc., 3702 Sunridge Dr., Park City, UT 84098-4618. Phone: (801) 560-9595. Ownership Kevin Terry, 100%.
   Stns: 2 AM. 6 FM. WTGG-FM Amite, LA; WJSH(FM) Folsom, LA; WKJN(FM) Centreville, MS; WAZA-FM Liberty, MS; WAKH-FM McComb, MS; WAPF(AM) McComb, MS; WAKK(AM) McComb, MS; WFCG(FM) Tylertown, MS20 FM. KLAX-FM East Los Angeles, CA; KXOL-FM Los Angeles, CA; KRZZ(FM) San Francisco, CA; WRMA-FM Fort Lauderdale, FL; WCMQ-FM Hialeah, FL; WXDJ-FM North Miami Beach, FL; WLEY-FM Aurora, IL; WPAT-FM Paterson, NJ; WSKQ-FM New York, NY; WODA(FM) Bayamon, PR; WRXD(FM) Fajardo, PR; WMEG-FM Guayama, PR; WZET(FM) Hormigueros, PR; WNOD(FM) Mayaguez, PR; WIOB-FM Mayaguez, PR; WIOC-FM Ponce, PR; WZMT-FM Ponce, PR; WEGM(FM) San German, PR; WZNT-FM San Juan, PR; WIOA(FM) San Juan, PR3 FM. KDTR(FM) Florence, MT; KYJK(FM) Missoula, MT; KKVU(FM) Stevensville, MT.

Sparta-Tomah Broadcasting Co. Inc., 113 W. Oak St., Sparta, WI 54656. Phone: (608) 269-3307. Fax: (608) 269-5170. Ownership Rice Family Trust, 35.73%; David Z. Rice, 18.01%; Patricia R. Hoffman, 15.42%; Barbara Rice, 15.42%; Elizabeth Ecker, 12.48%; and Sarah R. Cooper, 2.94%.
   Stns: 1 AM. 2 FM. WCOW-FM Sparta, WI; WKLJ Sparta, WI; WFBZ-FM Trempealeau, WI.

Jose Grimalt, exec VP; Raul Alarcon, chmn & pres/CEO.

Spotlight Broadcasting LLC, Box 8888, Metairie, LA 70011. Phone: (504) 309-7260. Fax: (504) 309-7262.E-mail: kmrc@kmrc1430.com Web Site:www.kmrc1430.com
   Stns: 3 AM. WABL Amite, LA; KMRC Morgan City, LA; KAGY Port Sulphur, LA.

Patrick Andras, pres.

Stanford Communications Inc., Box 458, Amory, MS 38821. Phone: (662) 256-9726. Fax: (662) 256-9725.E-mail: wamywafm@traceroad.net Web Site:www.fm95radio.com
   Stns: 2 AM. 1 FM. WWZQ Aberdeen, MS; WAFM-FM Amory, MS; WAMY Amory, MS.

Ed Stanford, pres; Teresa Stanford, sec/treas.

Star Broadcasting Inc., 21 Miracle Strip Pkwy., Fort Walton Beach, FL 32548. Phone: (850) 244-1400. Fax: (850) 243-1471. Ownership Ronald E. Hale Jr., 40%; James Franklin Hale, 40%; and Jennifer E. Hale, 20%.
   Stns: 2 AM. 2 FM. WPGG(AM) Evergreen, AL; WZFN(AM) Fort Walton Beach, FL; WTKE-FM Holt, FL; WRKN(FM) Niceville, FL.

Starlight Broadcasting Co., Box 106, 314 Main, Hartford, KY 42347. Phone: (270) 298-3268. Fax: (270) 298-9326. Web Site:www.wxmz.com
   Stns: 1 AM. 1 FM. WAIA(AM) Beaver Dam, KY; WKYA-FM Greenville, KY.

Andy Anderson, pres/CEO.

Steckline Communications Inc., 1632 S. Maize Rd., Wichita, KS 67209. Phone: (316) 721-8484. Fax: (316) 721-8276. Web Site:www.maanradio.com Ownership Gregory R. Steckline, 100%.
   Stns: 4 AM. KIUL Garden City, KS; KGGS(AM) Garden City, KS; KYUL(AM) Scott City, KS; KGSO(AM) Wichita, KS.

Greg Steckline, pres.

Stephens Family L.P., Box 1250, Sapulpa, OK 74067. Phone: (918) 492-2660.
   Stns: 3 AM. 10 FM. WZNE-FM Brighton, NY; WNCQ-FM Canton, NY; WRCD-FM Canton, NY; WFKL(FM) Fairport, NY; WMSA Massena, NY; WYSX(FM) Morristown, NY; WVLF(FM) Norwood, NY; WPAC(FM) Ogdensburg, NY; WRMM-FM Rochester, NY; WNER(AM) Watertown, NY; WTNY Watertown, NY; WCIZ-FM Watertown, NY; WFRY-FM Watertown, NY.

Michael P. Stephens, gen ptnr.

Studstill Broadcasting, 3905 Progress Blvd., Peru, IL 61354. Phone: (815) 224-2100. Phone: (815) 224-2100 (Corp). Fax: (815) 224-2066. Ownership Owen L. Studstill; Lamar Studstill; Cole C. Studstill.
   Stns: 1 AM. 6 FM. WGLC-FM Mendota, IL; WALS(FM) Oglesby, IL; WBZG(FM) Peru, IL; WIVQ(FM) Spring Valley, IL; WYYS(FM) Streator, IL; WSTQ(FM) Streator, IL; WSPL(AM) Streator, IL.

Owen L. Studstill, pres; Lamar Studstill, chmn; Cole C. Studstill, opns off.

Sudbury Services Inc., Box 989, Blytheville, AR 72316. Phone: (870) 762-2093. Fax: (870) 763-8459. Web Site:www.thundercountry963.com Ownership Harold L. Sudbury Jr., Lydia Sudbury Langston, LaNeal Sudbury

Salter. Cable TV: Blytheville TV Cable Co., Blytheville, AR.

Stns: 5 AM. 5 FM. KLCN Blytheville, AR; KHLS-FM Blytheville, AR; KAMJ-FM Gosnell, AR; KXAR Hope, AR; KHPA-FM Hope, AR; KNBY Newport, AR; KOKR(FM) Newport, AR; KQMJ(FM) Osceola, AR; KTPA Prescott, AR; KOSE Wilson, AR.

Harold Sudbury Jr., pres.

Summit City Radio Group, 2000 Lower Huntington Rd., Fort Wayne, IN 46819. Phone: (260) 747-1511. Fax: (260) 747-3999.E-mail: lloyd@summitcityradio.com Web Site:www.summitcityradio.com Ownership Bernard Radio LLC, 30%; Northwest Capital Partners II L.P.,70%, 100% total assets.

Stns: 1 AM. 3 FM. WNHT(FM) Churubusco, IN; WXKE(FM) Fort Wayne, IN; WGL Fort Wayne, IN; WGL-FM Huntington, IN.

Lloyd B. Roach, pres.

Summit Media Broadcasting LLC, 180 Main St., Sutton, WV 26601. Phone: (304) 765-7373. Fax: (304) 765-7836.E-mail: info@theboss97fm.com Web Site:www.theboss97fm.com Ownership Nunzio Aldo Sergi, 100%. Note: Mr. Sergi also owns 51% of WVAR(AM) Richwood and WAFD(FM) Webster Springs, both WV.

Stns: 2 AM. 3 FM. WKQV(FM) Cowen, WV; WVAR Richwood, WV; WSGB(AM) Sutton, WV; WDBS(FM) Sutton, WV; WAFD(FM) Webster Springs, WV.

Al Sergi, owner & gen mgr .

Sumter Broadcasting Co. Inc., Box 727, Americus, GA 31709. Phone: (229) 924-1390. Fax: (229) 928-2337. Web Site:www.americusradio.com

Stns: 1 AM. 2 FM. WDEC-FM Americus, GA; WISK Americus, GA; WISK-FM Americus, GA.

Steve Lashley, pres.

Sun Mountain Inc., 9045 Hobble Creek, Billings, MT 59101. Phone: (406) 665-2828. Fax: (406) 665-2131. Web Site:www.bigskyradio.net Ownership Richard Solberg, 100%.

Stns: 3 AM. KHDN(AM) Hardin, MT; KBSR Laurel, MT; KYLW(AM) Lockwood, MT.

Sun Valley Radio Inc., 810 W. 200 North, Logan, UT 84321. Phone: (435) 752-1390. Fax: (435) 752-1392. Ownership M. Kent Frandsen, owner.

Stns: 2 AM. 4 FM. KKEX-FM Preston, ID; KLZX(FM) Weston, ID; KLGN Logan, UT; KVNU Logan, UT; KZHK-FM Saint George, UT; KGNT(FM) Smithfield, UT.

M. Kent Frandsen, pres.

Sunbelt Broadcasting Corp., Box 351, Columbia, MS 39429. Phone: (601) 731-2298.E-mail: wjdr@zzip.cc

Stns: 2 AM. 4 FM. KKEX-FM Preston, ID; KLZX(FM) Weston, ID; KLGN Logan, UT; KVNU Logan, UT; KZHK-FM Saint George, UT; KGNT(FM) Smithfield, UT2 FM. WCJU-FM Prentiss, MS; WJDR-FM Prentiss, MS.

Thomas F. McDaniel, pres.

Sunburst Media-Louisiana LLC, 300 Crescent Ct., Suite 850, Dallas, TX 75201. Phone: (214) 661-3100. Ownership Momentum Plan I Ltd. LLP, 33.33%; Aldus Sunburst Inc., 33.33%; John M. Borders, 29.7%; Don L. Turner, 3.64%. Note: Sunburst Media Inc. (0% equity and voting control) is the sole manager. Officers of Sunburst Media Inc.: John Borders, pres; Don L. Turner, VP.

Stns: 1 AM. 3 FM. KCIL(FM) Houma, LA; KJIN(AM) Houma, LA; KMYO-FM Morgan City, LA; KXOR-FM Thibodaux, LA.

Sunbury Broadcasting Corp., Box 1070, Sunbury, PA 17801. Phone: (570) 286-5838. Fax: (570) 743-7837.E-mail: wqkx@wqkx.com Web Site:www.wqkx.com Ownership Lois W. Haddon, 90.7%' Dr. Harry H. Haddon Jr., 8%; and Roger S. Haddon Jr., 1.3%.

Stns: 2 AM. 3 FM. WVLY-FM Milton, PA; WMLP(AM) Milton, PA; WEGH(FM) Northumberland, PA; WKOK Sunbury, PA; WQKX(FM) Sunbury, PA.

Roger S. Haddon Jr., pres/CEO.

Sunrise Broadcasting Corp., Box 2307, Newburgh, NY 12550. Phone: (845) 561-2131. Fax: (845) 561-2138. Web Site:www.wgnyfm.com Ownership CVC Capital Corp.

Stns: 3 AM. 2 FM. KSNM(AM) Las Cruces, NM; KGRT-FM Las Cruces, NM; WJGK(AM) Highland, NY; WGNY Newburgh, NY; WGNY-FM Newburgh, NY.

J. Klebe, pres.

Superior Communications, 3302 N. Van Dyke, Imlay City, MI 48444. Phone: (810) 724-2638. Fax (877) 850-0881. Web Site:www.positivehits.com

Stns: 3 AM. 2 FM. KSNM(AM) Las Cruces, NM; KGRT-FM Las Cruces, NM; WJGK(AM) Highland, NY; WGNY Newburgh, NY; WGNY-FM Newburgh, NY8 FM.

WTLI-FM Bear Creek Township, MI; WSLI(FM) Belding, MI; WTAC(FM) Burton, MI; WHYT(FM) Goodland Township, MI; WAIR(FM) Lake City, MI; WLGH-FM Leroy Township, MI; WSIS(FM) Riverside, MI; WEJC-FM White Star, MI.

Edward Czelada, pres.

Sweet Home Ashtabula LLC, Second Generation Place, 3209 Prospect, Cleveland, OH 44115. Phone: (216) 426-1500. Fax: (216) 588-1558. Ownership James T. Embrescia, 47.5%; Second Generation Ltd., 47.5%.

Stns: 1 AM. 4 FM. WREO-FM Ashtabula, OH; WFUN Ashtabula, OH; WYBL(FM) Ashtabula, OH; WZOO-FM Edgewood, OH; WFXJ-FM North Kingsville, OH.

James T. Embrescia, pres.

T

Tackett-Boazman Broadcasting LP, 600 Fisk Ave., Brownwood, TX 76801. Phone: (325) 646-3535. Fax: (325) 646-3535.E-mail: rextackett@wendlee.com Web Site:Wendleebroadcasting.com Ownership Ray L. Boazman, 50%; and Donald Rex Tackett, 50%.

Stns: 2 AM. 2 FM. KXYL(AM) Brownwood, TX; KXYL-FM Brownwood, TX; KSTA Coleman, TX; KQBZ(FM) Coleman, TX.

Rex Tackett, ptnr.

Talking Stick Communications LLC, 421 S. Second St., Elkhart, IN 46514. Phone: (574) 258-5483. Ownership Alec C. Dille, 60%; John F. Dille IV, 20%; and Sarah D. Erlacher, 20%.

Stns: 1 AM. 4 FM. WYPW(FM) Nappanee, IN; WRBR-FM South Bend, IN; WAWC-FM Syracuse, IN; WRSW Warsaw, IN; WRSW-FM Warsaw, IN.

Alec C. Dille, pres.

Talley Radio Stations, Box 10, Litchfield, IL 62056. Phone: (217) 324-5921. Fax: (217) 532-2431.E-mail: wsmi@wsmiradio.com Web Site:wsmiradio.com Ownership Hayward L. Talley, Emma C. Talley.

Stns: 1 AM. 2 FM. WSMI Litchfield, IL; WSMI-FM Litchfield, IL; WAOX-FM Staunton, IL.

Hayward L. Talley, pres; Brian Talley, sr VP.

Tallgrass Broadcasting LLC, 1174 Hunters Ridge East, Hoffman Estates, IL 60192-4540. Phone: (847) 289-8018. Fax: (847) 289-1423. Ownership Joseph E. Walker, 50%; and William H. Kurtis, 50%.

Stns: 3 AM. 5 FM. KIND Independence, KS; KIND-FM Independence, KS; KKYC-FM Clovis, NM; KICA Clovis, NM; KOSG(FM) Pawhuska, OK; KICA-FM Farwell, TX; KMUL(AM) Farwell, TX; KMUL-FM Muleshoe, TX.

Tama Broadcasting Inc., 5207 Washington Blvd., Tampa, FL 33619. Phone: (813) 620-1300. Fax: (813) 628-0713. Web Site:www.wtmp.com Ownership Black Enterprise/Greenwich Street Corporate Growth Partners L.P., 73.89% votes, 78.34% assets; Glenn W. Cherry, 20.89% votes, 17.33% assets; and Charles W. Cherry II, 5.22% votes, 4.33% assets.

Stns: 1 AM. 4 FM. WTMP-FM Dade City, FL; WTMP Egypt Lake, FL; WSGA(FM) Hinesville, GA; WTHG(FM) Hinesville, GA; WSSJ(FM) Rincon, GA.

Glenn W. Cherry, CEO.

Sarkes Tarzian, Box 62, Bloomington, IN 47402. Phone: (812) 332-7251. Fax: (812) 331-4575. Ownership Tom Tarzian; Gray Television Inc.

Stns: 1 AM. 3 FM. WTTS-FM Bloomington, IN; WGCL Bloomington, IN; WLDE-FM Fort Wayne, IN; WAJI(FM) Fort Wayne, IN.

Stns: 2 TV. WRCB, Chattanooga, TN; KTVN, Reno, NV.

Tom Tolar, pres, TV; Tom Tarzian, chmn; Geoff Vargo, pres, radio; Bob Davis, CFO; Valerie Carney, gen counsel.

Team Radio LLC, Box 2509, Ponca City, OK 74602. Phone: (580) 765-2485. Fax: (580) 767-1103. Web Site:www.eteamradio.com Ownership William L. Coleman, 100%.

Stns: 2 AM. 3 FM. KOKB Blackwell, OK; KOKP Perry, OK; KOSB-FM Perry, OK; KPNC(FM) Ponca City, OK; KLOR-FM Ponca City, OK.

Bill Coleman, gen mgr .

Tejas Broadcasting Ltd. LLP, 1227 W. Magnolia Ave., Suite 300, Fort Worth, TX 76104-4400. Phone: (817) 920-7599. Ownership Ultimately controlled by James L. Anderson.

Stns: 1 AM. 8 FM. KBZD(FM) Amarillo, TX; KTNZ Amarillo, TX; KQFX-FM Borger, TX; KKNM(FM) Bovina, TX; KLTG-FM Corpus Christi, TX; KGRW-FM Friona, TX; KLHB(FM) Odem, TX; KMJR(FM) Portland, TX; KOUL-FM

Sinton, TX.

Jim Anderson, CEO.

TeleSouth Communications Inc., 6311 Ridgewood Rd., Jackson, MS 39211. Phone: (601) 957-1700. Fax: (601) 957-2389. Web Site:www.supertalkms.com Ownership Steve Davenport

Stns: 4 AM. 10 FM. WXRZ(FM) Corinth, MS; WKCU Corinth, MS; WFMN-FM Flora, MS; WBLZ(FM) Greenwood, MS; WKXG Greenwood, MS; WYMX-FM Greenwood, MS; WOEG Hazlehurst, MS; WDXO-FM Hazlehurst, MS; WTCD(FM) Indianola, MS; WRQO-FM Monticello, MS; WQLJ-FM Oxford, MS; WFMM-FM Sumrall, MS; WTNM(FM) Water Valley, MS; WROB(AM) West Point, MS.

Stephen C. Davenport, pres/CEO.

3 Daughters Media Inc., c/o Brooks, Pierce, et al, Box 1800, Raleigh, NC 27602. Phone: (919) 839-0300. Ownership Gary E. Burns, 100%.

Stns: 5 AM. 2 FM. WUUS(AM) Rossville, GA; WUUQ(FM) South Pittsburg, TN; WBLT(AM) Bedford, VA; WMNA Gretna, VA; WMNA-FM Gretna, VA; WVGM Lynchburg, VA; WGMN Roanoke, VA.

Three Eagles Communications, 3800 Cornhusker Hwy., Lincoln, NE 68504. Phone: (402) 466-1234. Fax: (402) 467-4095.E-mail: gbuchanan@threeeagles.com Web Site:www.threeeagles.com Ownership Rolland C. Johnson.

Stns: 18 AM. 30 FM. KIAQ-FM Clarion, IA; KKEZ-FM Fort Dodge, IA; KUEL(FM) Fort Dodge, IA; KVFD(AM) Fort Dodge, IA; KWMT Fort Dodge, IA; KXFT(FM) Manson, IA; KLSS-FM Mason City, IA; KRIB(AM) Mason City, IA; KGLO(AM) Mason City, IA; KIAI(FM) Mason City, IA; KYTC-FM Northwood, IA; KTLB-FM Twin Lakes, IA; KATE Albert Lea, MN; KCPI(FM) Albert Lea, MN; KAUS Austin, MN; KAUS-FM Austin, MN; KQYK(FM) Lake Crystal, MN; KQAD(AM) Luverne, MN; KEEZ-FM Mankato, MN; KYSM-FM Mankato, MN; KLGR Redwood Falls, MN; KLGR-FM Redwood Falls, MN; KRBI-FM Saint Peter, MN; KITN-FM Worthington, MN; KWOA Worthington, MN; KWOA-FM Worthington, MN; KTGL-FM Beatrice, NE; KZEN-FM Central City, NE; KTTT Columbus, NE; KKOT-FM Columbus, NE; KLIR-FM Columbus, NE; KJSK(AM) Columbus, NE; KIBZ(FM) Crete, NE; KLMS(AM) Lincoln, NE; KFRX(FM) Lincoln, NE; KFOR(AM) Lincoln, NE; KZKX-FM Seward, NE; KBRK Brookings, SD; KDBX(FM) Clear Lake, SD; KJAM(AM) Madison, SD; KJAM-FM Madison, SD; KKSD-FM Milbank, SD; KKQQ-FM Volga, SD; KJJQ Volga, SD; KIXX-FM Watertown, SD; KDLO-FM Watertown, SD; KSDR Watertown, SD; KWAT Watertown, SD.

Gary Buchanan, pres/COO.

3 Point Media, 980 N. Michigan Ave., Suite 1880, Chicago, IL 60611. Phone: (312) 204-9900. Fax: (312) 587-9466.

Stns: 18 AM. 30 FM. KIAQ-FM Clarion, IA; KKEZ-FM Fort Dodge, IA; KUEL(FM) Fort Dodge, IA; KVFD(AM) Fort Dodge, IA; KWMT Fort Dodge, IA; KXFT(FM) Manson, IA; KLSS-FM Mason City, IA; KRIB(AM) Mason City, IA; KGLO(AM) Mason City, IA; KIAI(FM) Mason City, IA; KYTC-FM Northwood, IA; KTLB-FM Twin Lakes, IA; KATE Albert Lea, MN; KCPI(FM) Albert Lea, MN; KAUS Austin, MN; KAUS-FM Austin, MN; KQYK(FM) Lake Crystal, MN; KQAD(AM) Luverne, MN; KEEZ-FM Mankato, MN; KYSM-FM Mankato, MN; KLGR Redwood Falls, MN; KLGR-FM Redwood Falls, MN; KRBI-FM Saint Peter, MN; KITN-FM Worthington, MN; KWOA Worthington, MN; KWOA-FM Worthington, MN; KTGL-FM Beatrice, NE; KZEN-FM Central City, NE; KTTT Columbus, NE; KKOT-FM Columbus, NE; KLIR-FM Columbus, NE; KJSK(AM) Columbus, NE; KIBZ(FM) Crete, NE; KLMS(AM) Lincoln, NE; KFRX(FM) Lincoln, NE; KFOR(AM) Lincoln, NE; KZKX-FM Seward, NE; KBRK Brookings, SD; KDBX(FM) Clear Lake, SD; KJAM(AM) Madison, SD; KJAM-FM Madison, SD; KKSD-FM Milbank, SD; KKQQ-FM Volga, SD; KJJQ Volga, SD; KIXX-FM Watertown, SD; KDLO-FM Watertown, SD; KSDR Watertown, SD; KWAT Watertown, SD4 FM. KZZQ(FM) Coalville, UT; KMGR(FM) Delta, UT; KCUA(FM) Naples, UT; KYLZ(FM) Lyman, WY.

Three Rivers Media Corp., Box 1247, Wytheville, VA 24382. Phone: (276) 228-3185. Fax: (276) 228-9261. Ownership Anthony Accamando Jr., 39%; James Browne, 39%; and Gary W. Hagerich, 22%.

Stns: 2 AM. 1 FM. WXBX(FM) Rural Retreat, VA; WLOY(AM) Rural Retreat, VA; WYVE Wytheville, VA.

Gary W. Hagerich, pres/COO.

Three Trees Communications Inc., 113 E. College Ave., Ashburn, GA 31714. Phone: (229) 567-9038. Ownership James Andrew Howard, 33.33%; James Thomas Overton, 33.33%; and Andrew H. Reeves, 33.33%.

Stns: 1 AM. 2 FM. WFFM(FM) Ashburn, GA; WTIF-FM Omega, GA; WTIF Tifton, GA.

Thunderbolt Broadcasting Co., Box 318, 1410 N. Lindell St., Martin, TN 38237. Phone: (731) 587-9526. Fax: (731) 587-5079. Ownership Paul Freeman Tinkle, trustee of the Paul Freeman Tinkle Revocable Trust, 40.42%; Jimmy C. Smith, 23.75%; Thomas L. Moore Jr., 19.16%; and Fred C. Stoker, 16.67%.

Stns: 1 AM. 4 FM. WCDZ(FM) Dresden, TN; WCMT(AM) Martin, TN; WCMT-FM South Fulton, TN; WYVY(FM) Union City, TN; WQAK(FM) Union City, TN.

Paul Freeman Tinkle, pres.

Tiger Communications Inc., 2514 S. College St., Suite 104, Auburn, AL 36832-6925. Phone: (334) 887-9999. Fax: (334) 826-9599. Ownership Thomas Haley, 96.5%; and Tracey Ivey, 3.5%.

Stns: 4 AM. 3 FM. WAUD Auburn, AL; WQNR(FM) Tallassee, AL; WTGZ(FM) Tuskegee, AL; WBIL Tuskegee, AL; WQSI(FM) Union Springs, AL; WTRP La Grange, GA; WRLA(AM) West Point, GA.

Touch Canada Broadcasting (2006) Inc., 5316 Calgary Tr., Edmonton, AB T6H 4J8. Canada. Phone: (780) 466-4930. Fax: (780) 469-5335.E-mail: info@shinefm.com Web Site:www.shinefm.com

Stns: 1 AM. 3 FM. CJSI-FM Calgary, AB; CJRY-FM Edmonton, AB; CJCA Edmonton, AB; CJGY-FM Grande Prairie, AB.

Charles Allard, owner.

Tower Investment Trust Inc., 819 S. Federal Hwy., Suite 106, Stuart, FL 34994-2952. Phone: (772) 215-1634. Web Site:www.toweritrust.com Ownership William H. Brothers, 50%; and Gary S. Hess, 50%. Note: Group also has an application for a New FM Pine Knoll Shores, NC. William H. Brothers, as an individual, is the permittee of KDRX(FM) Rocksprings, TX. Gary S. Hess, as an individual, is the licensee of WLEL(FM) Ellaville, GA and permittee of KSAQ(FM) Charlotte and KHES(AM) Rocksprings, both TX.

Stns: 1 AM. 3 FM. CJSI-FM Calgary, AB; CJRY-FM Edmonton, AB; CJCA Edmonton, AB; CJGY-FM Grande Prairie, AB4 FM. WBNK(FM) Pine Knoll Shores, NC; KXXN(FM) Iowa Park, TX; KTTY(FM) New Boston, TX; KLOW(FM) Reno, TX.

Bill Brothers, pres; Gary Hess, VP.

Town and Country Broadcasting Inc., 486 W. 2nd St., Xenia, OH 45385-3610. Phone: (937) 372-3531. Fax: (937) 372-3508. Ownership William J. Mullins, 100%.

Stns: 3 AM. WEDI(AM) Eaton, OH; WKFI(AM) Wilmington, OH; WBZI Xenia, OH.

Tri-Market Radio Broadcasters Inc. & Eagle Rock Broadcasting Inc., 120 South 300 W., Rupert, ID 83350. Phone: (208) 436-4757. Fax: (208) 436-3050.

Stns: 2 AM. 2 FM. KBAR Burley, ID; KZDX-FM Burley, ID; KFTA(AM) Rupert, ID; KKMV(FM) Rupert, ID.

Kim Lee, gen mgr .

Triad Broadcasting Co. L.L.C., 2511 Garden Rd., Bldg. A, Suite 104, Monterey, CA 93940. Phone: (831) 655-6350. Fax: (831) 655-6355.E-mail: jpeterson@triadbroadcasting.com Web Site:www.triadbroadcasting.com Ownership Northwest Equity Partners, Shamrock Capital Advisors, Bank of America Capital Investors.

Stns: 11 AM. 18 FM. WGCO(FM) Midway, GA; WDQX(FM) Morton, IL; WXCL(FM) Pekin, IL; WSWT-FM Peoria, IL; WPBG-FM Peoria, IL; WIRL(AM) Peoria, IL; WMBD Peoria, IL; KBMW Breckenridge, MN; KLTA(FM) Breckenridge, MN; KQWB-FM Moorhead, MN; KVOX-FM Moorhead, MN; WXBD Biloxi, MS; WTNI(AM) Biloxi, MS; WCPR-FM D'Iberville, MS; WXYK-FM Gulfport, MS; WUJM(FM) Gulfport, MS; WHGO(FM) Pascagoula, MS; KPFX(FM) Fargo, ND; KQWB(AM) West Fargo, ND; WGZR(FM) Bluffton, SC; WFXH(AM) Hilton Head Island, SC; WLOW(FM) Port Royal, SC; WBDY Bluefield, VA; WHQX-FM Cedar Bluff, VA; WTZE Tazewell, VA; WHAJ-FM Bluefield, WV; WHIS Bluefield, WV; WKEZ Bluefield, WV; WKOY-FM Princeton, WV.

Judy Peterson, VP; Thomas Douglas, CFO.

Tribune Broadcasting Co., 435 N. Michigan Ave., Suite 1800, Chicago, IL 60611. Phone: (312) 222-3333. Fax: (312) 329-0611. Web Site:www.tribune.com Ownership The Tribune Employee Stock Ownership Plan as implemented through the Tribune Employee Stock Ownership Trust, Oak Brook, IL, 100%.

Stns: 1 AM. WGN(AM) Chicago, IL.

Stns: 24 TV. WGN-TV, Chicago; KDAF, Dallas-Ft. Worth; KWGN, Denver, CO; WXMI, Grand Rapids-Kalamazoo-Battle Creek, MI; WPMT, Harrisburg -Lancaster-Lebanon-York, PA; WTIC, Hartford & New Haven, CT; WTXX, Hartford & New Haven, CT; KIAH, Houston; WTTK, Indianapolis, IN; WTTV, Indianapolis, IN; WXIN, Indianapolis, IN; KTLA, Los Angeles; WSFL-TV, Miami-Ft. Lauderdale, FL; WGNO, New Orleans, LA; WNOL, New Orleans, LA; WPIX, New York; WPHL, Philadelphia; KRCW-TV, Portland, OR; KTXL, Sacramento -Stockton-Modesto, CA; KSWB, San Diego, CA; KCPQ, Seattle-Tacoma, WA; KMYQ, Seattle-Tacoma, WA; KPLR, St. Louis, MO; WDCW, Washington, DC (Hagerstown, MD).

John Vitanovec, exec VP; Ed Wilson, pres.

Tri-County Broadcasting Inc., Box 366, Sauk Rapids, MN 56379. Phone: (320) 252-6200. Fax: (320) 252-9367. Ownership Herbert M. Hoppe, 51% of votes; Valeria Hoppe, 49% of votes. Note: Herbert M. Hoppe owns 100% of WPPI(AM) Sauk Rapids, MN.

Stns: 2 AM. 1 FM. WVAL Sauk Rapids, MN; WBHR Sauk Rapids, MN; WHMH-FM Sauk Rapids, MN.

Truth Broadcasting Corp., 4405 Providence Ln., Suite D, Winston-Salem, NC 27106. Phone: (336) 759-0363. Fax: (336) 759-0366.E-mail: tbooth@830wtru.com Web Site:www.wtru.com Ownership Stuart W. Epperson Jr., 100%. Note: Group also manages WLES(AM) Bon Air, VA.

Stns: 5 AM. WCRU(AM) Dallas, NC; WKEW Greensboro, NC; WTRU(AM) Kernersville, NC; WDRU(AM) Wake Forest, NC; WPOL Winston-Salem, NC.

Stuart Epperson, pres.

Buddy Tucker Association Inc., Box 63, Mobile, AL 36601. Phone: (386) 738-1348. Fax: (251) 432-1396. Ownership Theodore D. Tucker, 100%.

Stns: 3 AM. WTOF(AM) Bay Minette, AL; WMOB Mobile, AL; WYND De Land, FL.

2510 Licenses LLC, 100 Ryan Ct., Suite 98, Pittsburgh, PA 15205. Phone: (412) 489-1001. Fax: (412) 489-1002. Ownership Nicholas A. Galli, 100%.

Stns: 2 AM. 7 FM. WCCL(FM) Central City, PA; WNTJ(AM) Johnstown, PA; WWSH(FM) Pleasant Gap, PA; WKVB(FM) Port Matilda, PA; WLKJ(FM) Portage, PA; WBHV(AM) Somerset, PA; WLKH(FM) Somerset, PA; WBHV-FM State College, PA; WOWY(FM) University Park, PA.

Tyler Media Broadcasting Corp., 5101 S. Shields Blvd., Oklahoma City, OK 73129. Phone: (405) 616-5500. Fax: (405) 616-5505. Web Site:www.kkng.com Ownership Ty A. Tyler, Tony J. Tyler and Tony J. Tyler 2000 Irrevocable Trust, Tony J. Tyler, trustee.

Stns: 2 AM. 3 FM. KOJK(FM) Blanchard, OK; KOCY(AM) Del City, OK; KKNG-FM Newcastle, OK; KTUZ-FM Okarche, OK; KTLR(AM) Oklahoma City, OK.

Stns: 1 TV. KTUZ-TV, Oklahoma City, OK.

Skip Stow, market mgr; Robert De Negri, CFO.

U

US Stations LLC, 125 Corporate Terr., Hot Springs, AR 71913. Phone: (501) 525-9700. Fax: (501) 525-9739. Web Site:www.usstations.com Ownership Charles Shinn, 52%; Gary Terrell, 28%; and Craig Dale, 20%.

Stns: 1 AM. 4 FM. KYDL(FM) Hot Springs, AR; KQUS-FM Hot Springs, AR; KZNG Hot Springs, AR; KLXQ(FM) Mountain Pine, AR; KLBL(FM) Pearcy, AR.

United Ministries, 300 E. Rock Rd., Allentown, PA 18103. Phone: (970) 254-5565. Fax: (970) 254-5550. Ownership Non-stock, not-for-profit corporation.

Stns: 2 AM. 1 FM. KDTA Delta, CO; KJOL(AM) Grand Junction, CO; WBMR-FM Telford, PA.

Universal Broadcasting of New York Inc., Corporate Offices, WTHE Radio 260 E. 2nd St., Mineola, NY 11501. Phone: (516) 742-1520. Fax: (516) 742-2878.E-mail: nygospelradio@aol.com Web Site:www.wthe1520am.com Ownership Howard Warshaw and Miriam Warshaw.

Stns: 2 AM. WVNJ(AM) Oakland, NJ; WTHE(AM) Mineola, NY.

Miriam Warshaw, pres; Howard Warshaw, VP.

Univision Radio, 3102 Oak Lawn, Suite 215, Dallas, TX 75219. Phone: (214) 525-7700. Fax: (214) 525-7750. Web Site:www.univision.net/corp/en/urg.jsp Ownership Univision Communications Inc., 100% (see listing under TV Group Ownership, Section B).

Stns: 16 AM. 53 FM. KKMR(FM) Arizona City, AZ; KQMR(FM) Globe, AZ; KHOT-FM Paradise Valley, AZ; KOMR(FM) Sun City, AZ; KHOV-FM Wickenburg, AZ; KOND(FM) Clovis, CA; KSCA-FM Glendale, CA; KRDA(FM) Hanford, CA; KRCD(FM) Inglewood, CA; KLVE-FM Los Angeles, CA; KTNQ Los Angeles, CA; KLLE(FM) North Fork, CA; KLNV-FM San Diego, CA; KLQV-FM San Diego, CA; KSOL(FM) San Francisco, CA; KLOK San Jose, CA; KBRG(FM) San Jose, CA; KVVZ(FM) San Rafael, CA; KVVF(FM) Santa Clara, CA; KSQL(FM) Santa Cruz, CA; KRCV(FM) West Covina, CA; WRTO-FM Goulds, FL; WQBA Miami, FL; WAMR-FM Miami, FL; WAQI Miami, FL; WRTO(AM) Chicago, IL; WPPN(FM) Des Plaines, IL; WOJO-FM Evanston, IL; WVIV-FM Highland Park, IL; WVIX(FM) Joliet, IL; WCAA-FM Newark, NJ; KKRG(FM) Albuquerque, NM; KJFA(FM) Santa Fe, NM; KKSS-FM Santa Fe, NM; KRGT(FM) Indian Springs, NV; KISF-FM Las Vegas, NV; KLSQ(AM) Whitney, NV; WQBU-FM Garden City, NY; WADO New York, NY; WYEL(AM) Mayaguez, PR; WUKQ-FM Mayaguez, PR; WUKQ(AM) Ponce, PR; WKAQ San Juan, PR; KDXX(FM) Benbrook, TX; KGSX(FM) Comfort, TX; KFZO(FM) Denton, TX; KAMA El Paso, TX; KQBU(AM) El Paso, TX; KBNA-FM El Paso, TX; KFLC(AM) Fort Worth, TX; KLNO(FM) Fort Worth, TX; KOVE-FM Galveston, TX; KHZS(FM) Georgetown, TX; KGBT Harlingen, TX; KBTQ(FM) Harlingen, TX; KLTN(FM) Houston, TX; KLAT Houston, TX; KESS-FM Lewisville, TX; KAJZ(FM) Llano, TX; KGBT-FM McAllen, TX; KLTO-FM McQueeney, TX; KAMA-FM Missouri City, TX; KQBU-FM Port Arthur, TX; KHCK-FM Robinson, TX; KCOR(AM) San Antonio, TX; KXTN-FM San Antonio, TX; KROM(FM) San Antonio, TX; KBBT(FM) Schertz, TX; KPTY(FM) Winnie, TX.

McHenry T. Tichenor Jr., pres/CEO.

Uno Radio Group, Box 363222, San Juan, PR 00936-3222. Phone: (787) 758-1300. Fax: (787) 282-6060.E-mail: lsoto@unoradio.com Web Site:www.unoradio.com Ownership Jesus M. Soto.

Stns: 6 AM. 7 FM. WFDT(FM) Aguada, PR; WIVA-FM Aguadilla, PR; WCMN Arecibo, PR; WCMN-FM Arecibo, PR; WMIO(FM) Cabo Rojo, PR; WNEL Caguas, PR; WORA Mayaguez, PR; WPRP Ponce, PR; WLEO(AM) Ponce, PR; WRIO-FM Ponce, PR; WFID-FM Rio Piedras, PR; WPRM-FM San Juan, PR; WUNO(AM) San Juan, PR.

Jesus M. Soto, CEO; Luis A. Soto, pres; Elba Esmurria, sls VP; Luis Gonzalez, VP finance; Ray Cruz, VP progmg; Alberte Pereira, VP engrg.

Urban Radio Licenses LLC, 273 Azalea Rd., Suite 1-308, Mobile, AL 36609. Phone: (251) 343-4900. Fax: (251) 343-4905.E-mail: info@urbanradio.fm Web Site:www.urbanradio.fm Ownership Urban Radio Communications LLC, 100%. Note: Urban Radio Communications LLC also owns KMXH(FM) Alexandria and KBCE(FM) Boyce, both LA.

Stns: 2 AM. 8 FM. WLAY-FM Littleville, AL; WLAY Muscle Shoals, AL; WVNA-FM Muscle Shoals, AL; WVNA Tuscumbia, AL; WAJV-FM Brooksville, MS; WACR-FM Columbus AFB, MS; WMSU(FM) Starkville, MS; WIMX-FM Gibsonburg, OH; WJZE-FM Oak Harbor, OH; WMXV(FM) Saint Joseph, TN.

V

VCY America Inc., 3434 W. Kilbourn Ave., Milwaukee, WI 53208. Phone: (414) 935-3000. Fax: (414) 935-3015.E-mail: vcy@vcyamerica.org Web Site:www.vcyamerica.org

Stns: 1 AM. 19 FM. KVCY-FM Fort Scott, KS; KCVS(FM) Salina, KS; WVCN(FM) Baraga, MI; WVCM(FM) Iron Mountain, MI; WQRN(FM) Cook, MN; KVCS(FM) Spring Valley, MN; WJIC-FM Zanesville, OH; KVCF(FM) Freeman, SD; KVCX-FM Gregory, SD; KVCH(FM) Huron, SD; KVFL(FM) Pierre, SD; KVSD(FM) Wasta, SD; WVCF-FM Eau Claire, WI; WVFL(FM) Fond du Lac, WI; WVCY-FM Milwaukee, WI; WVCY Oshkosh, WI; WVCS(FM) Owen, WI; WVCX(FM) Tomah, WI; WEGZ(FM) Washburn, WI; WVRN(FM) Wittenberg, WI.

Stns: 1 TV. WVCY, Milwaukee, WI.

Vic Eliason, VP/gen mgr; Jim Schneider, progmg dir.

Vermont Broadcast Associates Inc., Box 97, Lyndonville, VT 05851. Phone: (802) 626-9800. Fax: (802) 626-8500. Ownership Bruce A. James, 100%.

Stns: 1 AM. 4 FM. WMTK-FM Littleton, NH; WJPK(FM) Barton, VT; WGMT-FM Lyndon, VT; WKXH-FM Saint Johnsbury, VT; WSTJ Saint Johnsbury, VT.

Vernal Enterprises Inc., Box 1032, Indiana, PA 15701-1032. Phone: (724) 543-1380. Fax: (724) 543-1140. Ownership Larry L. Schrecongost, 51%; Nancy W. Schrecongost, 49%.

Stns: 3 AM. 1 FM. WRDD Ebensburg, PA; WHPA(FM) Gallitzin, PA; WTYM Kittanning, PA; WNCC(AM) Northern Cambria, PA.

Vero Beach Broadcasters LLC, 1235 16th St., Vero Beach, FL 32960. Phone: (772) 567-0937. Fax: (772) 562-4747. Web Site:wosnfm.com Ownership Mitchell Rubenstein, Laurie Silvers and Robert McAllan.

Stns: 1 AM. 3 FM. WOSN-FM Indian River Shores, FL; WGYL-FM Vero Beach, FL; WTTB Vero Beach, FL;

WJKD(FM) Vero Beach, FL.

Jim Davis, gen mgr .

VerStandig Broadcasting, 4850 Connecticut Ave. N.W., Suite 103, Washington, DC 20008. Phone: (202) 244-1422. Fax: (202) 362-4149. Ownership John VerStandig, 1996 VerStandig Children's Trust, M. Belmont VerStandig Trust.

Stns: 3 AM. 6 FM. WPPT(FM) Mercersburg, PA; WBHB-FM Waynesboro, PA; WCBG(AM) Waynesboro, PA; WTGD(FM) Bridgewater, VA; WJDV(FM) Broadway, VA; WHBG Harrisonburg, VA; WQPO-FM Harrisonburg, VA; WSVA Harrisonburg, VA; WAYZ(FM) Hagerstown, MD.

John VerStandig, CEO.

Victoria RadioWorks Ltd., 8023 Vantage Dr., Suite 840, San Antonio, TX 78230. Phone: (210) 340-7080. Fax: (210) 341-1777. Ownership John W. Barger, pres of gen ptnr 89%; Cindy Cox, 10%.

Stns: 2 AM. 3 FM. KITE(FM) Port Lavaca, TX; KVIC(FM) Victoria, TX; KNAL(AM) Victoria, TX; KVNN(AM) Victoria, TX; KBAR-FM Victoria, TX.

John Barger, pres; Cindy Cox, gen mgr .

Vidalia Communications Corp., Box 900, Vidalia, GA 30475. Phone: (912) 537-9202. Fax: (912) 537-4477. E-mail: wtcq@vidaliacommunications.com   Web Site:www.vidaliacommunications.com

Stns: 1 AM. 1 FM. WYUM-FM Mount Vernon, GA; WVOP Vidalia, GA.

Advance-Progress Newspaper Inc., publisher of the weekly *Advance*, is part of the partnership of Vidalia Communications Corp.

John Ladson III, pres; Zack Fowler III, gen mgr .

Viper Communications Broadcast Group, Box 225, Osage Beach, MO 65065. Phone: (573) 348-2772. Fax: (573) 348-2779 . Web Site:www.krmsradio.com

Stns: 2 AM. 1 FM. WENG Englewood, FL; KRMS Osage Beach, MO; KMYK(FM) Osage Beach, MO.

Dennis Klautzer, VP/gen mgr.

Visionary Related Entertainment L.L.C., Box 1437, Wailuku, HI 96793. Phone: (808) 244-9145. Fax: (808) 244-8247.E-mail: kaoi@kaoi.net Web Site:www.kaoi.net Ownership Visionary Related Entertainment Inc., 50.1% of votes, 40.58% of total assets; Frontier Radio Investors L.L.C., 49.9% of votes, 59.42% of total assets.

Stns: 4 AM. 12 FM. KUAI Eleele, HI; KUMU Honolulu, HI; KUMU-FM Honolulu, HI; KPOI-FM Honolulu, HI; KQMQ-FM Honolulu, HI; KMKK-FM Kaunakakai, HI; KSHK-FM Kekaha, HI; KHEI-FM Kihei, HI; KAOI(AM) Kihei, HI; KTBH-FM Kurtistown, HI; KQNG Lihue, HI; KDLX(FM) Makawao, HI; KNUQ-FM Paauilo, HI; KSRF-FM Poipu, HI; KAOI-FM Wailuku, HI; KDDB(FM) Waipahu, HI.

John Detz, pres; James McKeon, VP.

Vista Broadcast Group Inc., 1940 Third Ave., Prince George, BC V2M 1G7. Canada. Phone: (250) 564-2524. Fax: (250) 562-6611. Web Site:www.vistaradio.ca Ownership Jetport Inc., 21.4%; 49 shareholders holding less than 10% each. Note: Group also owns CFFM-FM-2 Quesnel and CIRX-FM-1 Vanderhoof, both BC (both originating stns).

Stns: 6 AM. 14 FM. CFNA-FM Bonnyville, AB; CFRI-FM Grande Prairie, AB; CKLM-FM Lloydminster, AB; CKBX 100 Mile House, BC; CFLD Burns Lake, BC; CIQC-FM Campbell River, BC; CKQR-FM Castlegar, BC; CFCP-FM Courtenay, BC; CJSU-FM Duncan, BC; CJUI-FM Kelowna, BC; CHNV-FM Nelson, BC; CFNI Port Hardy, BC; CFPW-FM Powell River, BC; CJCI-FM Prince George, BC; CIRX-FM Prince George, BC; CKCQ-FM Quesnel, BC; CFBV Smithers, BC; CIVH Vanderhoof, BC; CFFM-FM Williams Lake, BC; CKWL Williams Lake, BC.

Gary Russell, pres.

Vox AM/FM LLC, 70 Walnut St., Suite 411, Wellesley, MA 02481. Phone: (781) 239-8018. Fax: (781) 239-8007.E-mail: voxmedia@aol.com Ownership Vox Holding Co. LLC, 51.1%; and WB AM/FM Inc., 48.9%.

Stns: 2 AM. 5 FM. WCPV-FM Essex, NY; WEAV Plattsburgh, NY; WVTK(FM) Port Henry, NY; WXZO(FM) Willsboro, NY; WEZF-FM Burlington, VT; WTSJ(AM) Randolph, VT; WCVR-FM Randolph, VT.

Vox Communications, 70 Walnut St., Wellesley, MA 02481. Phone: (781) 239-8018. Fax: (781) 239-8007.E-mail: voxmedia@aol.com Web Site:www.voxcommunicationsllc.com

Stns: 4 AM. 8 FM. WWUS(FM) Big Pine Key, FL; WCNK(FM) Key West, FL; WAVK(FM) Marathon, FL; WSBS Great Barrington, MA; WUPE-FM North Adams, MA; WNAW North Adams, MA; WBEC Pittsfield, MA; WBEC-FM Pittsfield, MA; WUPE(AM) Pittsfield, MA; WWHK(FM) Concord, NH; WBOP(FM) Buffalo Gap, VA; WSIG(FM) Mount Jackson, VA.

Bruce G. Danziger, CEO; Ken Barlow, COO.

W

WAMC/Northeast Public Radio, 318 Central Ave., Albany, NY 12206. Phone: (518) 465-5233. Fax: (518) 432-6974.E-mail: mail@wamc.org Web Site:www.wamc.org Ownership Non-stock educ corporation.

Stns: 2 AM. 9 FM. WAMQ-FM Great Barrington, MA; WAMC(AM) Albany, NY; WAMC-FM Albany, NY; WCAN-FM Canajoharie, NY; WAMK-FM Kingston, NY; WOSR-FM Middletown, NY; WWES(FM) Mount Kisco, NY; WCEL-FM Plattsburgh, NY; WRUN-FM Remsen, NY; WANC-FM Ticonderoga, NY; WRUN(AM) Utica, NY.

Alan Chartock, pres/CEO; David Galletly, sr VP/CFO.

WAY-FM Media Group Inc., 1012 McEwen Dr., Franklin, TN 37067. Phone: (615) 261-9293. Fax: (615) 261-3967. Web Site:www.wayfm.com

Stns: 2 AM. 9 FM. WAMQ-FM Great Barrington, MA; WAMC(AM) Albany, NY; WAMC-FM Albany, NY; WCAN-FM Canajoharie, NY; WAMK-FM Kingston, NY; WOSR-FM Middletown, NY; WWES(FM) Mount Kisco, NY; WCEL-FM Plattsburgh, NY; WRUN-FM Remsen, NY; WANC-FM Ticonderoga, NY; WRUN(AM) Utica, NY; WAYH(FM) Harvest, AL; WAYU(FM) Steele, AL; KBWA(FM) Brush, CO; KXWA(FM) Loveland, CO; KJWA(FM) Rye, CO; KRWA(FM) Rye, CO; WAYJ-FM Fort Myers, FL; WAYP(FM) Marianna, FL; WAYF(FM) West Palm Beach, FL; WAYT(FM) Thomasville, GA; WAYI(FM) Charlestown, IN; KYWA(FM) Wichita, KS; WAYD(FM) Auburn, KY; WRVI-FM Valley Station, KY; KWYA(FM) Astoria, OR; WAYQ(FM) Clarksville, TN; WAYM(FM) Columbia, TN; WAYW(FM) New Johnsonville, TN; KWYQ(FM) Longview, WA.

Bob Augsburg, pres/CEO; Dusty Rhodes, sr VP; Lloyd Parker, COO; Dave Ringing, CFO.

WENK of Union City Inc., 1729 Nailling Dr., Union City, TN 38261. Phone: (731) 885-1240. Fax: (731) 885-3405.E-mail: thailey@wenkwtpr.com Ownership Bill Latimer; Robert Kirkland; Robert Terrell Jr.

Stns: 2 AM. 3 FM. WWKF-FM Fulton, KY; WTPR-FM McKinnon, TN; WAKQ-FM Paris, TN; WTPR(AM) Paris, TN; WENK Union City, TN.

Terry Hailey, pres; Bill Latimer, chmn.

WOLF Radio Inc., 401 W. Kirkpatrick St., Syracuse, NY 13204. Phone: (315) 472-0222. Fax: (315) 478-7745. Ownership Craig S. Fox, 51%; George W. Kimble, 49%.

Stns: 2 AM. 2 FM. WWLF(AM) Auburn, NY; WOLF-FM Oswego, NY; WWLF-FM Sylvan Beach, NY; WOLF Syracuse, NY.

Craig Fox, pres.

WRD Entertainment Inc., Box 2077, Batesville, AR 72503. Phone: (870) 793-4196. Fax: (870) 793-5222.E-mail: rob@maxfm.com Web Site:www.maxfm.com

Stns: 2 AM. 4 FM. KAAB Batesville, AR; KBTA Batesville, AR; KBTA-FM Batesville, AR; KZLE-FM Batesville, AR; KKIK(FM) Horseshoe Bend, AR; KWOZ-FM Mountain View, AR.

John R. Grace, pres; Gary Bridgman, gen mgr .

WS2K Radio LLC dba WS Media, 770 E Market St., Suite 110, West Chester, PA 19382. Phone: (610) 696-5472. Fax: (610) 696-5072.E-mail: ken@ws2kmedia.com Web Site:www.ws2kmedia.com Ownership WallerSutton 2000 L.P., 100%.

Stns: 7 AM. 4 FM. WENI-FM Big Flats, NY; WCBA Corning, NY; WGMM(FM) Corning, NY; WENI(AM) Corning, NY; WENY Elmira, NY; WENY-FM Elmira, NY; WLNP(FM) Carbondale, PA; WCDL(AM) Carbondale, PA; WHYL Carlisle, PA; WAZL Hazleton, PA; WNAK Nanticoke, PA.

Ira Rosenblatt, CEO; Ken Karaszkiewicz, CFO.

WZOE Inc., Box 69, Princeton, IL 61356. Phone: (815) 875-8014. Web Site:www.wzoeradio.com Ownership Steve Samet, 100%.

Stns: 1 AM. 2 FM. WRVY-FM Henry, IL; WZOE Princeton, IL; WZOE-FM Princeton, IL.

Steve Samet, pres/gen mgr.

Wagenvoord Advertising Group Inc., 2360 N.E. Coachman Rd., Clearwater, FL 33765. Phone: (727) 726-8247. Fax: (727) 799-8866. Web Site:www.tantalk1340.com Ownership Dave Wagenvoord, 50%; Lola Wagenvoord, 50%.

Stns: 4 AM. KLRG(AM) Sheridan, AR; WTAN(AM) Clearwater, FL; WDCF Dade City, FL; WZHR(AM) Zephyrhills, FL.

Lola Wagenvoord, gen mgr .

Wagon Wheel Broadcasting LLC, 201 N. Union St., Suite 340, Alexandria, VA 22314. Phone: (703) 519-3703. Fax: (703) 519-9756. Ownership NBC LLC, 49%; Brantley Broadcast Associates LLC, 49% (see listing); and Kenneth S. Johnson, 2%.

Stns: 4 AM. KLRG(AM) Sheridan, AR; WTAN(AM) Clearwater, FL; WDCF Dade City, FL; WZHR(AM) Zephyrhills, FL3. FM. WSCH-FM Aurora, IN; WXCH(FM) Hope, IN; WIKI-FM Carrollton, KY.

Kenneth S. Johnson, .

Wagonwheel Communications Corp., 40 Shoshone Ave., Green River, WY 82935. Phone: (307) 875-6666. Fax: (303) 875-5847.E-mail: kugr@sweetwater.net Web Site:www.theradionetwork.net Ownership Alan W. Harris, trustee of the Alan W. Harris Living Trust, 51%; and Faith R. Harris, trustee of the Faith R. Harris Living Trust, 49%.

Stns: 1 AM. 3 FM. KFRZ-FM Green River, WY; KUGR Green River, WY; KZWB(FM) Green River, WY; KYCS(FM) Rock Springs, WY.

Waitt Omaha LLC, 1125 S. 103rd St., Suite 200, Omaha, NE 68124. Phone: (402) 697-8000. Ownership WaittCorp Investments LLC, 100% of total assets.

Stns: 4 AM. 4 FM. KQKQ-FM Council Bluffs, IA; KOZN(AM) Bellevue, NE; KOIL(AM) Bellevue, NE; KBLR-FM Blair, NE; KOOO(FM) Lincoln, NE; KKAR Omaha, NE; KMMQ(AM) Plattsmouth, NE; KOPW(FM) Plattsmouth, NE.

Walking by Faith Ministries Inc., 336 Rodenberg Ave., Biloxi, MS 39531-3444. Phone: (228) 374-9739. Ownership James L. Black, 50% votes; and Bobbie Black, 50% votes.

Stns: 3 AM. WQFX Gulfport, MS; WAML Laurel, MS; WMLC(AM) Monticello, MS.

James L. Black, pres.

Waller Broadcasting, Box 1648, Jacksonville, TX 75766. Phone: (903) 586-2527. Fax: (903) 586-1394.E-mail: jacksonville@wallerbroadcasting.com   Web Site:www.wallerbroadcasting.com Ownership Dudley Waller, owner.

Stns: 1 AM. 4 FM. KFRO-FM Gilmer, TX; KLJT-FM Jacksonville, TX; KEBE Jacksonville, TX; KDVE(FM) Pittsburg, TX; KXAL-FM Tatum, TX.

Dudley Waller, pres/CEO; Dave Moreland, VP progmg.

Wallingford Broadcasting Co., 128 Big Hill Ave., Richmond, KY 40475. Phone: (859) 623-1340. Fax: (859) 623-1341.E-mail: coyote@chpl.net Web Site:www.wcyo.com

Stns: 3 AM. 2 FM. WKXO Berea, KY; WLFX(FM) Berea, KY; WCYO-FM Irvine, KY; WIRV Irvine, KY; WEKY Richmond, KY.

Kelly Wallingford, pres/CEO; Kendra Steele, opns mgr.

Walton Stns, Box 776, Kermit, TX 79745. Phone: (432) 586-3366. Fax: (432) 586-3958. Ownership John B. Walton, 100%.

Stns: 2 AM. 1 FM. KBUY Ruidoso, NM; KWES-FM Ruidoso, NM; KWES(AM) Ruidoso, NM.

John Walton, pres; Harold Oakes, gen mgr .

Woodrow Michael Warren Stns, Box 106, Alturas, CA 96101. Phone: (530) 233-4842. Fax: (530) 233-4173.

Stns: 2 AM. 1 FM. KBUY Ruidoso, NM; KWES-FM Ruidoso, NM; KWES(AM) Ruidoso, NM3 FM. KALT-FM Alturas, CA; KLCR-FM Lakeview, OR; KWTR-FM Big Lake, TX.

Woodrow Michael Warren, pres; Matt Warren, opns mgr.

Wayne County Broadcasting Co., Box 310, Fairfield, IL 62837. Phone: (618) 842-2159. Fax: (618) 847-5907. Ownership Thomas S. Land; David H. Land; Judith L. Moore; Cynthia L. Cummins.

Stns: 1 AM. 2 FM. WOKZ(FM) Fairfield, IL; WFIW(AM) Fairfield, IL; WFIW-FM Fairfield, IL.

Thomas S. Land, chmn.

West Alabama Radio Inc., Box 938, Demopolis, AL 36732. Phone: (334) 289-9850. Fax: (334) 289-9811. Ownership Amy Ross Ward, 50%; Betty R. Ross, 25%; and Joe M. Ross Jr., 25%.

Stns: 1 AM. 2 FM. WZNJ-FM Demopolis, AL; WXAL Demopolis, AL; WINL-FM Linden, AL.

West Virginia Radio Corp., 1251 Earl L. Core Rd., Morgantown, WV 26505. Phone: (304) 296-0029. Fax: (304) 296-3876. Web Site:wvmetronews.com Ownership John R. Raese, David A. Raese, Dale B. Miller.

Stns: 7 AM. 15 FM. WBRB(FM) Buckhannon, WV; WBTQ-FM Buckhannon, WV; WBUC Buckhannon, WV; WKAZ(AM) Charleston, WV; WCHS Charleston, WV; WVAF-FM Charleston, WV; WSWW Charleston, WV; WKWS-FM Charleston, WV; WWLW(FM) Clarksburg, WV;

WSWW-FM Craigsville, WV; WDNE Elkins, WV; WDNE-FM Elkins, WV; WELK-FM Elkins, WV; WQZK-FM Keyser, WV; WKLP Keyser, WV; WKAZ-FM Miami, WV; WAJR Morgantown, WV; WVAQ-FM Morgantown, WV; WRVZ-FM Pocatalico, WV; WAJR-FM Salem, WV; WFBY(FM) Weston, WV; WVMD(FM) Midland, MD.

Morgantown (WV) *Dominion-Post* is affiliated with Metronews Radio Network and West Virginia Radio Corp.

Dale B. Miller, pres/CEO; Harvey Kercheval, opns VP; Joe Parsons, sls VP.

Westburg Media Capital LP, 530 9th Ave., Kirkland, WA 98033. Phone: (425) 893-9230. Ownership Westburg Media Capital Inc., gen ptnr, 100% voting, 1 equity. Note: Westburg Media Capital Inc. is owned 100% by David Westburg.

Stns: 2 AM. 2 FM. KEPL(AM) Estes Park, CO; KNMZ-FM Alamogordo, NM; KRSY(AM) Alamogordo, NM; KRSY-FM La Luz, NM.

Western Slope Communications LLC, 751 Horizon Court, Suite 225, Grand Junction, CO 81506. Phone: (970) 241-6460. Fax: (970) 241-6452. E-mail: kiss@kissradio.com Web Site:www.kissradio.com

Stns: 2 AM. 3 FM. KAVP(AM) Colona, CO; KRVG(FM) Glenwood Springs, CO; KAYW(FM) Meeker, CO; KRGS(AM) Rifle, CO; KZKS(FM) Rifle, CO.

Steve Wennerstrom, pres; John Monroe, gen mgr.

Weston Entertainment L.P., 112 E. Pecan St., Suite 1212, San Antonio, TX 78205. Phone: (386) 423-3289. E-mail: dennis1@ucnsb.net Web Site:www.westonentertainment.net Ownership Second (2nd) Kings LP, 69.5%; J. Elliott Cunningham, 15%; Michael Wakely, 15%; and Weston Entertainment GP LLC, 0.5%. Note: Weston Entertainment GP LLC is solely made up of Second (2nd) Kings LP.

Stns: 1 AM. 2 FM. KBHT(FM) Crockett, TX; KVRP-FM Haskell, TX; KVRP Stamford, TX.

Dennis W. Goodman, radio mgr.

Wheeler Broadcasting Inc., Box K, Grand Coulee, WA 99133-0841. Phone: (509) 633-2020. Fax: (509) 633-1014. E-mail: keygfm@nwi.net Ownership Deanna D. Wheeler, 30%; Verl D. Wheeler, 30%; Mark Wheeler and Nilufer Wheeler, 23%; Tonya D. Baker and Scott B. Baker, 10%.

Stns: 1 AM. 2 FM. KXAA(FM) Cle Elum, WA; KEYG Grand Coulee, WA; KEYG-FM Grand Coulee, WA.

Verl D. Wheeler, pres/CEO; Mark Wheeler, VP/gen mgr.

Mel Wheeler Inc., 5009 S. Hulen, Suite 101, Fort Worth, TX 76132-1989. Phone: (817) 294-7644. Fax: (817) 294-8519. Ownership Leonard E. Wheeler, 34.73%; Stephen J. Wheeler, 33.63% votes, 33.31% assets; and Clark V. Wheeler, 31.64%.

Stns: 2 AM. 4 FM. WVBE-FM Lynchburg, VA; WXLK-FM Roanoke, VA; WVBE(AM) Roanoke, VA; WSLQ-FM Roanoke, VA; WSLC-FM Roanoke, VA; WFIR(AM) Roanoke, VA.

Stns: 2 TV. KPOB, Paducah, KY-Cape Girardeau, MO-Harrisburg-Mount Vernon, IL; WSIL-TV, Paducah, KY-Cape Girardeau, MO-Harrisburg-Mount Vernon, IL.

Leonard Wheeler, pres; Clark Wheeler, VP; Gretchen Cummings, sec/treas.

White Mountain Radio, 1838 W. Commerce Dr., Suite A, Lakeside, AZ 85929. Phone: (928) 368-8100. Fax: (928) 368-8108. Ownership Henry Ash.

Stns: 3 AM. 3 FM. KDJI Holbrook, AZ; KZUA-FM Holbrook, AZ; KRFM-FM Show Low, AZ; KSNX-FM Show Low, AZ; KVSL Show Low, AZ; KVWM(AM) Show Low, AZ.

Henry A. Ash, pres/CEO; Joseph M. Fry, CFO; F. Lewis Robertson, COO.

Wilkins Communications Network Inc., Box 444, Spartanburg, SC 29304. Phone: (864) 585-1885. Fax: (864) 597-0687. E-mail: info@wilkinsradio.com Web Site:www.wilkinsradio.com Ownership Robert Wilkins; LuAnn Wilkins

Stns: 18 AM. WBXR(AM) Hazel Green, AL; WIJD(AM) Prichard, AL; WNVY Cantonment, FL; WVTJ(AM) Pensacola, FL; WFAM(AM) Augusta, GA; KLNG(AM) Council Bluffs, IA; WBRI(AM) Indianapolis, IN; KCNW(AM) Fairway, KS; KWDF Ball, LA; KIOU Shreveport, LA; WCPC Houston, MS; WSKY(AM) Asheville, NC; KXKS(AM) Albuquerque, NM; WWNL(AM) Pittsburgh, PA; WITK(AM) Pittston, PA; WYYC(AM) York, PA; WELP(AM) Easley, SC; WLMR(AM) Chattanooga, TN.

Robert Wilkins, CEO; Mitchell Mathis, pres; LuAnn Wilkins, exec VP.

Wilks Broadcast Group LLC, 100 North Point Center East, Suite 310, Alpharetta, GA 30022. Phone: (770) 754-3211. Fax: (678) 893-0123. E-mail: info@wilksbroadcasting.com Web Site:wilksbroadcasting.com

Stns: 18 AM. WBXR(AM) Hazel Green, AL; WIJD(AM) Prichard, AL; WNVY Cantonment, FL; WVTJ(AM) Pensacola, FL; WFAM(AM) Augusta, GA; KLNG(AM) Council Bluffs, IA; WBRI(AM) Indianapolis, IN; KCNW(AM) Fairway, KS; KWDF Ball, LA; KIOU Shreveport, LA; WCPC Houston, MS; WSKY(AM) Asheville, NC; KXKS(AM) Albuquerque, NM; WWNL(AM) Pittsburgh, PA; WITK(AM) Pittston, PA; WYYC(AM) York, PA; WELP(AM) Easley, SC; WLMR(AM) Chattanooga, TN21 FM. KJFX-FM Fresno, CA; KJZN(FM) San Joaquin, CA; KFRR-FM Woodlake, CA; KWOF(FM) Broomfield, CO; KIMN-FM Denver, CO; KXKL-FM Denver, CO; KFKF-FM Kansas City, KS; KMXV-FM Kansas City, MO; KBEQ-FM Kansas City, MO; KCKC(FM) Kansas City, MO; KTHX-FM Dayton, NV; KURK(FM) Reno, NV; KRZQ-FM Sparks, NV; KJZS(FM) Sparks, NV; WNKK(FM) Circleville, OH; WLVQ(FM) Columbus, OH; WHOK-FM Lancaster, OH; KONE(FM) Lubbock, TX; KLLL-FM Lubbock, TX; KMMX(FM) Tahoka, TX; KBTE(FM) Tulia, TX.

Jeff Wilks, CEO; Jeff Sanders, exec VP; Lee J. Killian, exec VP; Stephen Bradshaw, CFO.

Williams Communications Inc., 801 Noble St, 8th Fl., Suite 30, Anniston, AL 36201. Phone: (256) 236-1880. Fax: (256) 236-4480. E-mail: whmabig95@cableone.net Web Site:whmabig95.com Ownership Walton E. Williams Jr., 51%; and Melinda Williams, 49%.

Stns: 3 AM. 5 FM. WHMA Anniston, AL; WTXO(FM) Ashland, AL; WFXO(FM) Centre, AL; WFMH-FM Hackleburg, AL; WHMA-FM Hobson City, AL; WZZX Lineville, AL; WFCT(FM) Apalachicola, FL; WLTG Panama City, FL.

Walton E. Williams Jr., pres.

Marion R. Williams Stns, 925 N. 5th St., Niles, MI 49120. Phone: (269) 683-4343. Fax: (269) 683-7759. Web Site:www.wsmkradio.com

Stns: 4 AM. 1 FM. WSTT Thomasville, GA; WSMK-FM Buchanan, MI; WONG Canton, MS.

Marion R. Williams, owner.

Willis Broadcasting Corp., 645 Church St., Suite 400, Norfolk, VA 23510. Phone: (757) 622-4600. Fax: (757) 624-6515.

Stns: 8 AM. 3 FM. WTJH East Point, GA; KDLA De Ridder, LA; KLPL Lake Providence, LA; WGRM Greenwood, MS; WGRM-FM Greenwood, MS; WBXB(FM) Edenton, NC; WGTM Wilson, NC; WCPK Chesapeake, VA; WHFD-FM Lawrenceville, VA; WGPL Portsmouth, VA; WPCE Portsmouth, VA.

Levi Willis, pres.

Wilson Broadcasting Inc., 805 N. Lena St., Suite 13, Dothan, AL 36303. Phone: (334) 671-1753. Fax: (334) 677-6923. Web Site:www.wjjn.greatnow.com

Stns: 1 AM. 2 FM. WJJN-FM Columbia, AL; WAGF Dothan, AL; WAGF-FM Dothan, AL.

James R. Wilson III, gen mgr.

Winton Road Broadcasting Co. LLC, Box 2700, Bakersfield, CA 93303. Phone: (661) 328-0118. Fax: (661) 328-1648. Ownership Anthony S. Brandon, 66%; L. Rogers Brandon, 33%.

Stns: 3 AM. 3 FM. KISZ-FM Cortez, CO; KVFC Cortez, CO; KPTE-FM Durango, CO; KDGO Durango, CO; KENN Farmington, NM; KRWN-FM Farmington, NM.

Rogers Brandon, pres.

The Wireless Group Inc., Box 198, Brownsville, TN 38012. Phone: (731) 772-3700. Ownership Carlton Veirs, pres, 50%; Lyle Reid, 50%. (See also Cross-Ownership, Sect. A.)

Stns: 1 AM. 1 FM. WNWS Brownsville, TN; WNWS-FM Jackson, TN.

The Wireless Group Inc., publishes the weekly magazine *Hunting & Fishing News.*

Carlton Veirs, pres.

Wisdom LLC, Box 861, Rock Hill, SC 29731. Phone: (803) 329-2664. Phone: (803) 329-8652. Fax: (803) 329-3317. Fax: (803) 329-8652. Ownership Rodriguez Neely, 60% equity; Emma Neely, 20% equity; Frank Neely, 10% equity; and Emma Neely, Custodian for Precious Neely under SC UGMA, 10% equity.

Stns: 2 AM. 1 FM. WGIV(AM) Pineline, NC; WGCD Chester, SC; WAAW-FM Williston, SC.

Frank Neely, mgr.

Withers Broadcasting Co., Box 1508, Mount Vernon, IL 62864. Phone: (618) 242-3500. Fax: (618) 242-4444. Ownership W. Russell Withers Jr., 100%.

Stns: 11 AM. 20 FM. KOKX Keokuk, IA; KRNQ(FM) Keokuk, IA; WKIB(FM) Anna, IL; WRUL-FM Carmi, IL; WROY Carmi, IL; WCEZ(FM) Carthage, IL; WILY Centralia, IL; WRXX-FM Centralia, IL; WEBQ-FM Eldorado, IL; WISH-FM Galatia, IL; WEBQ Harrisburg, IL; WTAO-FM Herrin, IL; WDDD-FM Johnston City, IL; WMOK Metropolis, IL; WREZ-FM Metropolis, IL; WZZT-FM Morrison, IL; WYNG(FM) Mount Carmel, IL; WMIX Mount Vernon, IL; WMIX-FM Mount Vernon, IL; WVZA(FM) Murphysboro, IL; WSSQ-FM Sterling, IL; WSDR Sterling, IL; WHET(FM) West Frankfort, IL; WFRX West Frankfort, IL; WZZL-FM Reidland, KY; WGKY-FM Wickliffe, KY; KGMO(FM) Cape Girardeau, MO; KAPE Cape Girardeau, MO; KJXX(AM) Jackson, MO; KRHW Sikeston, MO; KBXB(FM) Sikeston, MO.

Stns: 3 TV. WDTV, Clarksburg-Weston, WV; WVFX, Clarksburg-Weston, WV; WDHS, Marquette, MI.

W. Russell Withers Jr., pres.

Wolf Creek Broadcasting Inc., Box 490, Mineral Bluff, GA 30559-0490. Phone: (706) 379-1970. Ownership A.D. Frazier Jr., 63%; and Clair W. Frazier, 37%.

Stns: 3 AM. 1 FM. WALH Mountain City, GA; WYHG(AM) Young Harris, GA; WACF(FM) Young Harris, GA; WLSB Copperhill, TN.

Wolfhouse Radio Group Inc., 548 E. Alisal St., Salinas, CA 93905. Phone: (831) 757-1910. Fax: (831) 757-8015. Ownership Hector Villalobos, 100% of votes.

Stns: 1 AM. 3 FM. KEXA(FM) King City, CA; KRAY-FM Salinas, CA; KTGE Salinas, CA; KMJV(FM) Soledad, CA.

Hector Villalobos, pres.

Woodward Communications Inc., Box 688, Dubuque, IA 52004-0688. Phone: (563) 588-5687. Fax: (563) 588-5739. Web Site:www.wcinet.com Ownership M. Jeanne Woodward, F. Robert Woodward.

Stns: 2 AM. 4 FM. WSCO(AM) Appleton, WI; WAPL(FM) Appleton, WI; WKSZ(FM) De Pere, WI; WHBY(AM) Kimberly, WI; WZOR(FM) Mishicot, WI; WECB(FM) Seymour, WI.

Woodward Communications Inc. publishes the *Telegraph Herald* and weekly newspapers and shoppers in Dyersville and Cascade, Iowa; Oregon, Fitchburg, Platteville, Prairie du Chien, Richland Center, Verona, Stoughton, Wisconsin.

Tom Yunt, pres.

Wooster Republican Printing Co., (dba Dix Communications). 212 E. Liberty St., Wooster, OH 44691. Phone: (330) 264-3511. Fax: (330) 263-5013. Web Site:www.dixcom.com Ownership (dba Dix Communications).

Stns: 3 AM. 6 FM. WNDT(FM) Alachua, FL; WOGK(FM) Ocala, FL; WNDD-FM Silver Springs, FL; WKVX Wooster, OH; WQKT(FM) Wooster, OH; WTBO Cumberland, MD; WKGO-FM Cumberland, MD; WFRB Frostburg, MD; WFRB-FM Frostburg, MD.

Stns: 1 TV. KFBB, Great Falls, MT.

Wooster Republican Printing Co. publishes *The Daily Record*, Wooster, OH.

Robert C. Dix, TV div chmn; G. Charles Dix, VP; Dale E. Gerber, CFO.

Word Broadcasting Network Inc., Box 19229, Louisville, KY 40259. Phone: (502) 964-3304. Fax: (502) 966-9692. Web Site:www.wbna21.com Ownership Robert W. Rodgers, 20%; Gregory A. Holt, 20%; Melissa Fraser, 20%; Cleddie Kieth, 20%; and Margaret A. Rodgers, 20%.

Stns: 3 AM. WYMM(AM) Jacksonville, FL; WVHI Evansville, IN; WYRM(AM) Norfolk, VA.

Stns: 1 TV. WBNA, Louisville, KY.

Bob Rogers, pres; Greg Holt, VP.

World Radio Link Inc., Box 5429, Twin Falls, ID 83303-5429. Phone: (208) 733-3551. Ownership Clark Parrish, 33.3%; Diana Atkin, 33.3%; and Earl Williamson, 33.3%.

Stns: 3 AM. WYMM(AM) Jacksonville, FL; WVHI Evansville, IN; WYRM(AM) Norfolk, VA4 FM. KMVV(FM) Sterling, AK; WSIZ-FM Jacksonville, GA; KXRV(FM) Cannon Ball, ND; WCOP(FM) Farmington Township, PA.

Earl Williamson, pres.

World Radio Network Inc., Box 3765, McAllen, TX 78502-3765. Phone: (956) 787-9788. Fax: (956) 787-9783. E-mail: wrn@hcjb.org Web Site:www.wrn-rcm.org Ownership Non-profit corporation. Note: World Radio Network Inc. is affiliated with World Radio Missionary Fellowship Inc., which operates international sw missionary stn HCJB in Quito, Ecuador.

Stns: 3 AM. WYMM(AM) Jacksonville, FL; WVHI Evansville, IN; WYRM(AM) Norfolk, VA4 FM. KMVV(FM) Sterling, AK; WSIZ-FM Jacksonville, GA; KXRV(FM) Cannon Ball, ND; WCOP(FM) Farmington Township, PA8 FM. KRMB-FM Bisbee, AZ; KYRM(FM) Yuma, AZ; KRUC-FM Las Cruces, NM; KBNR(FM) Brownsville, TX; KBNJ(FM) Corpus Christi, TX; KVER-FM El Paso, TX; KBNL(FM) Laredo, TX; KVMV-FM McAllen, TX.

Dr. Ted Haney, pres; Glenn Lafitte, dir.

Wright Broadcasting Systems, Box 587, Weatherford, OK 73096. Phone: (580) 772-5939. Fax: (580) 772-1590. E-mail: traffic@wrightradio.com Web

Site:www.wrightwradio.com Ownership G. Harold Wright, 100%.

Stns: 2 AM. 2 FM. KCLI Clinton, OK; KWEY-FM Clinton, OK; KCDL(FM) Cordell, OK; KWEY Weatherford, OK.

G. Harold Wright, pres.

Wynne Enterprises LLC, 1338 Oregon Ave., Klamath Falls, OR 97601. Phone: (541) 882-4656. Fax: (541) 884-2845.E-mail: kflskkrb@aol.com Web Site:www.klamathradio.com Ownership Robert Wynne, Floyd Wynne, Barbara Wynne.

Stns: 1 AM. 2 FM. KFLS-FM Tulelake, CA; KKRB-FM Klamath Falls, OR; KFLS Klamath Falls, OR.

Robert Wynne, pres/CEO; Floyd Wynne, VP.

Y

Yavapai Broadcasting Corp., 3405 E. Hwy. 89-A, Suite A, Cottonwood, AZ 86326. Phone: (928) 634-2286. Fax: (928) 634-2295. Web Site:www.myradioplace.com Ownership W. Grant Hafley.

Stns: 2 AM. 4 FM. KVRD-FM Cottonwood, AZ; KYBC(AM) Cottonwood, AZ; KKLD(FM) Cottonwood, AZ; KVNA-FM Flagstaff, AZ; KVNA(AM) Flagstaff, AZ; KQST-FM Sedona, AZ.

Grant Hafley, pres; David J. Kessel, gen mgr .

Z

Zia Broadcasting Co., Box 1907, Clovis, NM 88102-1907. Phone: (505) 763-4401. Fax: (505) 769-2564.E-mail: kclv@allsups.com Ownership Allsup's Convenience Stores Inc., 100%.

Stns: 3 AM. 3 FM. KCLV(AM) Clovis, NM; KCLV-FM Clovis, NM; KACT Andrews, TX; KACT-FM Andrews, TX; KQTY Borger, TX; KQTY-FM Borger, TX.

Rick Keefer, gen mgr; Lonnie Alsup, pres.

Zimmer Radio Inc., 2702 E. 32nd St., Joplin, MO 64804. Phone: (417) 624-1025. Fax: (417) 781-6842. Web Site:www.joplinradio.com Ownership James L. Zimmer Revocable Trust U/A/D May 24, 2005 (James L. Zimmer, sole trustee), 100%.

Stns: 2 AM. 4 FM. KZRG(AM) Joplin, MO; KSYN-FM Joplin, MO; KZYM(AM) Joplin, MO; KIXQ(FM) Joplin, MO; KJMK-FM Webb City, MO; KXDG-FM Webb City, MO.

James Zimmer, pres; Larry Boyd, gen mgr .

Zoe Communications Inc., Box 190, Shell Lake, WI 54871. Phone: (715) 468-9500. Fax: (715) 468-9505. Web Site:www.zoestations.com

Stns: 3 AM. 2 FM. WQOQ(AM) Durand, WI; WDMO(FM) Durand, WI; WPDR Portage, WI; WPLT(FM) Sarona, WI; WCSW Shell Lake, WI.

Wendy Oberg, gen mgr .

The Zone Corp., Box 1929, Bangor, ME 04402. Phone: (207) 990-2800. Fax: (207) 990-2444. Web Site:www.zoneradio.com Ownership Stephen King is the sole stockholder.

Stns: 1 AM. 2 FM. WZON Bangor, ME; WKIT-FM Brewer, ME; WDME-FM Dover Foxcroft, ME.

Stephen King, pres; Tabitha King, VP; Arthur B. Greene, sec/treas; Bobby Russell, gen mgr .

Key to Radio Listings

(1) WOF(AM)—**(2)** Oct 8, 1946: **(3)** 1000 khz. **(3a)** Stereo. **(3b)** Hrs opn: 24. **(4)** Box 1000 99999. Phone: (909) 555-1000. Fax: (909) 999-9999. E-mail: wof@wofam.com. Web Site: www.wofam.com. **(5)** Licensee: General Broadcasting Corp. (group owner; acq 7-20-69; $255,000 with co-located FM; **(5a)** FTR 2-12-83). **(6)** Population served: 250,000 **(7)** Natl. Network: ABC/E, AP, Mountain State Network. Natl. Rep: Jones & Company, Penn State. Format: MOR, C&W. News staff: one; News: 15 hrs wkly. Target aud: 25-54; baby boomers. Spec prog: Sp 3 hrs wkly. **(8)** John Jones, gen mgr; David Smith, chief engr.

(1a) WOF-FM—**(2)** October 1959: **(9)** 101.1 mhz; 3 kw. Ant 300 ft. **(3a)** Stereo. **(10)** Dups AM 50%. Format: C&W. **(11)** WOF-TV affil.

(1) Station call letters as assigned by the Federal Communications Commission (FCC) or Canadian Radio-television and Telecommunications Commission (CRTC).

(1a) Station call letters for co-owned FM station. WOF-FM has the same ownership as WOF(AM), and the FM listing contains only information different from the AM. Co-owned AM and FM stations are often listed together, even when they have dissimilar call letters. In some instances FM may be listed first.

(2) Date station first went on air (regardless of subsequent ownership changes).

(3) Frequency in kilohertz.

(3a) WOF broadcasts in stereo.

(3b) WOF broadcasts 24 hours daily.

(4) Address and zip code, telephone, fax, web site and e-mail address.

(5) Licensee name and date of acquisition (if not original owner). If the licensee is a group owner—a company with several broadcast properties—it is so identified, as a group owner of which the licensee is a subsidiary. Details on group owners are listed in Section A. If the station has been sold and the sale information is available, it is recorded after the acquisition date, ie. acq. date; purchase price; FTR date.

(5a) FTR date. FTR refers to *Broadcasting & Cable* magazine's weekly For the Record column that appeared in the magazine until June 8, 1998, where station sales were recorded as received from the FCC.

(6) Population served refers to the station's potential market.

(7) Network, representative and programming. WOF national affiliates are ABC Entertainment Network and AP Network. The regional affiliate is Mountain State. The WOF national sales representative is Jones & Company and their regional sales representative is Penn State. The WOF program format is part middle-of-the-road, part country and western, with three hours weekly of special programming in Spanish. They have one staff member covering local news, and provide local news 15 hours per week. Their target audience is baby boomers age 25-54.

(8) Key personnel.

(9) Frequency for WOF-FM is 101.1 megahertz, with 3 kilowatts of effective radiated power and an antenna height of 300 feet above average terrain. WOF-FM broadcasts in stereo (see **(3a)**).

(10) Programming. WOF-FM duplicates WOF(AM) programs 50/% of the time and has a country and western format.

(11) Co-owned TV. WOF-TV has the same licensee as WOF-AM-FM.

Note: Listings for independent AM & FM stations follow the sample shown for WOF(AM).

An asterisk (*) preceding station call letters indicates noncommercial stations.

Directory of Radio Stations in the United States

Alabama

Abbeville

WIZB(FM)— Feb 2, 1968: 94.3 mhz; 19.5 kw. Ant 371 ft TL: N31 26 19 W85 17 22. Stereo. Hrs open: 24 Box 8097, Dothan, 36304-8097. Secondary address: 2563 Montgomery Hwy., Dothan 36303. Phone: (334) 699-5672. Fax: (334) 699-5034.E-mail: ekelley@hisradio943.com Web Site:www.hisradio943.com Licensee: Radio Training Network, Inc. (acq 7-98; $550,000). Gammon & Grange, P.C. Format: Contemp Christian. News: 3 hrs wkly. Target aud: 25-49; women. ◆Jim Campbell, CEO; Earl Kelley, gen mgr, gen sls mgr; K.W. Keene, prom dir; Russell Brooks, progmg dir; Neal Riddle, chief of engrg, engr; Melinda McKenna, traf mgr.

Addison

WQAH-FM— 1996: 105.7 mhz; 6 kw. 328 ft TL: N34 18 19 W87 04 24. Hrs open: 24 Box 1048, Hartselle, 35640. Secondary address: 219 Chestnut St, Hartelle 35640. Phone: (256) 773-2563. Fax: (256) 773-6915.E-mail: radio@hiwaay.net Web Site:www.wqah.com Licensee: Abercrombie Broadcasting FM Inc. (acq 2-7-2000). Format: Classic country. ◆Alvin Abercrombie, pres; Carol Lynn, gen mgr, progmg dir, disc jockey, sls, mktg; Keith Abercrombie, engrg dir; Mark Donovan, disc jockey & sls.

Alabaster

WQCR(AM)— Sept 28, 1981: 1500 khz; 2.3 kw-D (1.2 kw-CH). TL: N33 12 27 W86 45 34. Hrs open: Sunrise-sunset 50 Hwy. 26, 35007. Phone: (205) 613-2108.E-mail: JOELRIVERA1500AM@YAHOO.COM Licensee: Rivera Communications LLC (acq 2-10-2006; $5,000 and assumption of debt). Population served: 275,000 Format: Sp. ◆Maria Esparza, VP; Joel Rivera, gen mgr; Israel deJesus, progmg dir.

Albertville

WAVU(AM)— 1947: 630 khz; 1 kw-D, 28 w-N. TL: N34 14 19 W86 09 59. Hrs open: 24 Box 190, 35950. Secondary address: 3770 US Hwy. 431 35951. Phone: (256) 878-8575. Fax: (256) 878-1051.E-mail: tommylee@wqsb.com Licensee: Sand Mountain Broadcasting Service Inc. Population served: 25,000 Natl. Network: AP Radio, . Fletcher, Heald & Hildreth. Wire Svc: AP Format: Southern gospel, Christian. News staff: one. Target aud: 35 plus. ◆Pat M. Courington Jr., pres; Tommy Lee, gen mgr; Ted McCreless, gen sls mgr; Dale Stallings, progmg dir; Al Taylor, news dir.

WQSB(FM)— 1948: 105.1 mhz; 2.7 kw. Ant 1,000 ft TL: N34 09 27 W86 02 44. Stereo. Hrs open: 24 Prog sep from AM Box 190, 35950. Secondary address: 3770 US Hwy. 431 35951. Phone: (256) 878-8575. Fax: (256) 878-1051.E-mail: wqsb@aol.com Web Site:www.wqsb.com Population served: 220,000 Format: Country. News staff: one. Target aud: 25-54. ◆Ted McCreless, sls dir; Barry Galloway, progmg dir, disc jockey; Dale Stallings, mus dir; Al Taylor, news dir, disc jockey.

WWGC(AM)— April 1982: 1090 khz; 500 w-D. TL: N34 18 02 W86 16 01. Hrs open: 6 AM-7:15 PM 454 Alabamah Hwy 75 N., 35950. Phone: (256) 894-6294. Fax: (256) 894-6495.E-mail: wwgc1090@yahoo.com Licensee: Quality Properties LLC (acq 1-16-2007; $355,000). Population served: 500,000 Format: Sp. ◆Jeff Beck, gen mgr; Joel Arriga, progmg dir.

Alexander City

WBNM(AM)— May 31, 1947: 1050 khz; 1 kw-D; 48 w-N. TL: N32 56 51 W85 59 17. Hrs open: 24 1739 Radio Rd., 35010. Phone: (256) 215-7296. Licensee: William and Margaret Neeck, Co-Trustees (group owner); (acq 12-1-2007). Population served: 60,000 Natl. Network: ABC, . Alabama Radio Net. Haley, Bader & Potts. Format: Southern gospel, sports.

*WJHO(FM)— 2008: 89.7 mhz; 6 kw vert. Ant 256 ft TL: N33 01 42 W85 59 23. Hrs open: 908 Opelika Rd., Auburn, 36830. Phone: (334) 821-0744. Fax: (334) 821-4031.E-mail: jimmy@jimmyscarstereo.com Licensee: Jimmy Jarrell Communications Foundation Inc. ◆Jimmy Jarrell, pres & gen mgr.

WSTH-FM— Sept 30, 1949: 106.1 mhz; 100 kw. 981 ft TL: N32 45 33 W85 28 04. (CP: 85.8 kw, ant 1,047 ft.). Stereo. Hrs open: 24 Box 687, Columbus, GA, 31902. Secondary address: 1501 13th Ave., Columbus, GA 31901. Phone: (706) 576-3000. Fax: (706) 576-3010.E-mail: info@rooster106online.com Web Site:www.rooster106online.com Licensee: CC Licenses LLC. Group owner: Clear Channel Communications Inc. (acq 5-9-2003; $2.73 million with WDAK(AM) Columbus, GA). Natl. Network: ABC, . Format: Country. News staff: one. Target aud: General. ◆Jim Martin, gen mgr; Brian Waters, opns mgr.

Aliceville

WZBQ(FM)—See Carrollton

Andalusia

WAAO-FM— Aug 24, 1987: 103.7 mhz; 3 kw. Ant 328 ft TL: N31 20 27 W86 28 02. Stereo. Hrs open: 24 Box 987, MLK Expressway, 36420. Phone: (334) 222-1166. Fax: (334) 222-1167.E-mail: waao@alaweb.com Web Site:www.waao.com Licensee: Companion Broadcasting Service Inc. Population served: 10,092 Format: Country. Target aud: General. ◆Lee Williams, pres & gen mgr.

*WSTF(FM)— March 1996: 91.5 mhz; 5 kw. Ant 361 ft TL: N31 26 20 W86 30 48. Hrs open: Box 210789, Montgomery, 36121-0789. Phone: (334) 271-8900. Fax: (334) 260-8962.E-mail: mail@faithradio.org Web Site:www.faithradio.org Licensee: Faith Broadcasting Inc. Format: Educ, relg, MOR. ◆Russell Dean, gen mgr; Gary Hundley, dev dir.

Anniston

WDNG(AM)— July 1, 1957: 1450 khz; 1 kw-U. TL: N33 40 01 W85 50 56. Hrs open: 24 1115 Leighton Ave., 36207. Phone: (256) 236-8291. Fax: (256) 236-8292.E-mail: jj@wdng.net Web Site:www.wdng.net Licensee: WDNG Inc. (acq 6-30-87; $500,000; 7-6-87). Population served: 125,000 Natl. Network: CBS, . Format: News/talk. Target aud: General. ◆J.J. Dark, pres & gen mgr.

*WGRW(FM)— July 1999: 90.7 mhz; 3 kw vert. 328 ft TL: N33 29 19 W86 47 58. Hrs open: 24 Word Works Inc., Box 2555, 36202. Secondary address: 4265 Hill St. 36206. Phone: (256) 238-9990. Fax: (256) 237-1102.E-mail: jon@graceradio.com Web Site:www.graceradio.com Licensee: Word Works Inc. Population served: 111,000 Natl. Network: Moody, . Format: Christian. ◆Aaron Acker, pres; Jon Holder, gen mgr.

WHMA(AM)— 1938: 1390 khz; 5 kw-D, 1 kw-N, DA-N. TL: N33 42 31 W85 51 14. Hrs open: 24 801 Noble St., Suite 30, 36201. Phone: (256) 237-8741. Fax: (256) 231-9414. Licensee: Williams Communications Inc. (group owner; acq 8-12-2003; $275,000). Population served: 120,000 Format: Gospel. News staff: one; News: 12 hrs wkly. Target aud: 25-54; those with upscale, mobile, discretionary incomes. ◆Walt Williams, gen mgr; John Goodbread, progmg dir.

WSYA(AM)— August 1954: 1490 khz; 1 kw-U. TL: N33 41 15 W85 49 49. Hrs open: 24 Box 7785, 1913 Barry St., Suite B, Oxford, 36203. Phone: (256) 741-6000. Fax: (256) 741-6080.E-mail: jimj@wtdrthunder.com Web Site:www.wtdrthunder.com Licensee: Jacobs Broadcast Group Inc. (acq 5-1-2006; $330,000). Population served: 200,000 Wire Svc: AP Format: Adult contemp. News staff: one. ◆Jim Jacobs, pres; Laura Jacobs, VP & gen mgr.

Arab

WAFN-FM— Nov 5, 1979: 92.7 mhz; 1.15 kw. Ant 663 ft TL: N34 20 40.5 W86 26 23.4. Stereo. Hrs open: 24 981 N. Brindlee Mt. Pkwy, 35016. Phone: (256) 586-9300. Fax: (256) 586-9301.E-mail: funhouse@fun927.com Web Site:www.fun927.com Licensee: Fun Media Group Inc. (acq 7-31-97; $492,500). Population served: 90,000 Natl. Network: CNN Radio, . Format: Oldies. News staff: one; News: 3 hrs wkly. Target aud: 18-54. ◆Susan E. McKenney, pres; Michael St. John, CFO, VP, gen mgr; Suan McKenney, gen sls mgr.

WRAB(AM)— Oct 25, 1961: 1380 khz; 1 kw-D. TL: N34 20 06 W86 28 07. Hrs open: 6am-6pm Box 625, 35016. Secondary address: 619 S. Brindlee Mountain Pkwy. 35016. Phone: (256) 586-4123. Fax: (256) 586-4124.E-mail: wrab@otclco.net Web Site:www.wrab.net Licensee: Reed Broadcasting LLC (acq 6-22-01; $163,000). Population served: 20,000 Wire Svc: AP Format: Country, relg, gospel. News staff: one; News: 12 hrs. wkly. ◆Ed Reed, pres; Archie Anderson, gen mgr.

Argo

*WKRE(FM)—Not on air, target date: unknown: 88.1 mhz; 1 w horiz, 4 kw vert. Ant 253 ft TL: N33 41 53 W86 31 29. Hrs open: 2101 Executive Park Dr., Suite 103, Opelika, 36801. Phone: (706) 965-2355. Licensee: Wilbur Gospel Communications and Foundation. ◆William Casey Jarrell, pres.

Ashland

WCKF(FM)— Dec 1, 2007: 100.7 mhz; 1.9 kw. Ant 590 ft TL: N33 19 14.2 W85 51 39.2. Hrs open: Box 8, Anniston, 36202. Phone: (256) 282-4338. Fax: (256) 782-2489. Licensee: Alabama 810 LLC. Natl. Network: USA, . Alabama Radio Net. Format: Country. News staff: one; News: 5 hrs wkly. ◆Leslie E. Gradick, gen mgr.

WTXO(FM)— Dec 20, 1959: 98.3 mhz; 1.7 kw. Ant 617 ft TL: N33 18 30 W85 50 58. Stereo. Hrs open: 24 801 Noble St. 8th Fl., Suite 30, Anniston, 36201. Phone: (256) 236-1880. Fax: (256) 236-4480. Fax: (256) 231-9414. Web Site:www.rock983.net Licensee: Williams Communications Inc. (group owner; acq 8-16-2001). Natl. Network: ABC, . Format: Rock. News staff: one. Target aud: 25-54. ◆Eva Gibson, gen mgr.

Athens

WKAC(AM)— September 1964: 1080 khz; 5 kw-D. TL: N34 50 13 W86 58 28. Hrs open: Sunrise-sunset Box 1083, 35612. Secondary address: 19245 Hwy. 127 35614. Phone: (256) 232-6827. Fax: (256) 232-6828.E-mail: wkac@companet.net Web Site:www.wkac1080.com Licensee: Limestone Broadcasting Co. Population served: 750,000 Natl. Network: CNN Radio, . Rgnl. Network: Capitol Radio Net. Format: Oldies. News: 6 hrs wkly. Target aud: 25-54; adults mid/upper income, blue/white collar. Spec prog: Farm 5 hrs. ◆Kenneth A. Casey, pres; Keith Casey, gen mgr; Kirk Harvey, progmg dir; Joyce Casey, traf mgr, women's int ed.

WVNN(AM)— Nov 8, 1948: 770 khz; 10 kw-D, 250 w-N, DA-N. TL: N34 50 21 W86 55 44. Hrs open: 24 1717 Hwy. 72 E., 35611. Phone: (256) 830-8300. Fax: (256) 232-6842. Web Site:www.wvnn.com Licensee: Cumulus Licensing LLC. Group owner: Cumulus Media Inc. (acq 7-21-2003; grpsl). Population served: 450,000 Natl. Network: ABC, . Natl. Rep: Katz Radio, . Format: News/talk. News: 60 hrs wkly. Target aud: 25-64. ◆Bill G. West, VP, gen mgr; Dale Jackson, opns mgr, progmg dir; Tracy Flesch, gen sls mgr; Aaron Hurd, prom dir; Chuck Miller, chief of engrg; Audrey Raines, traf mgr.

WZYP(FM)— Oct 1, 1958: 104.3 mhz; 100 kw. 1,115 ft TL: N34 49 05 W86 44 16. Stereo. Hrs open: 24 Prog sep from AM 1717 Hwy. 72 E., 35611. Phone: (256) 830-8300. Fax: (256) 232-6842. Web Site:www.wzyp.com Population served: 900,000 Natl. Rep: Katz Radio, . Format: Top-40. News: 3 hrs wkly. Target aud: 18-49. ◆Bill West, gen mgr; Aaron Hurd, prom dir; Tracy Flesch, gen sls mgr & progmg dir; Audrey Raines, traf mgr; Chuck Miller, engr.

Atmore

WNSI-FM— June 28, 1991: 105.9 mhz; 3.3 kw. Ant 446 ft TL: N31 00 26 W87 32 15. Stereo. Hrs open: 24
Simulcast with WNSI(AM) Robertsdale 100%.
Box 578, Robertsdale, 36567. Phone: (251) 947-2346. Fax: (251) 947-2347.E-mail: wnsiradio@gulftel.com Web Site:www.wnsiradio.com Licensee: Southern Media Communications Inc. (acq 3-4-98). Format: News, sports. News: 18 hrs wkly. Spec prog: American Indian one hr, Black one hr, farm 5 hrs, gospel 12 hrs wkly. ◆Walter Bowen, gen mgr; Randy Burgan, gen sls mgr, progmg dir.

WYOK(FM)— May 19, 1966: 104.1 mhz; 100 kw. Ant 1,555 ft TL: N30 37 35 W87 38 50. Stereo. Hrs open: 24 2800 Dauphin St., #104, Mobile, 36606-2400. Phone: (251) 652-2000. Fax: (251) 652-2001.E-mail: mobile.prog@cumulus.com Web Site:www.jack104online.com Licensee: Cumulus Licensing Corp. Group owner: Cumulus Media Inc. (acq 10-18-99; grpsl). Population served: 954,300 Cohn & Marks. Format: Adult hits. News staff: one; News: 5 hrs wkly. Target aud: 25-40. ◆Gary Pizzati, gen mgr; Steve Crumbely, opns VP, opns mgr & progmg dir.

Attalla

WKXX(FM)—Licensed to Attalla. See Gadsden

Auburn

WANI(AM)—See Opelika

WAUD(AM)— Dec 22, 1947: 1230 khz; 1 kw-U. TL: N32 37 47 W85 28 08. Hrs open: 24 2514 S. College St., Suite 104, 36830. Phone: (334) 887-3401. Fax: (334) 826-9599.E-mail: info@thetiger.fm Licensee: Tiger Communications Inc. (acq 2-26-98). Population served: 90,000 Natl. Network: CBS Radio, . Natl. Rep: Rgnl Reps,. Alabama Radio Net. Format: Sports, big band, jazz. News staff: one; News: 7 hrs wkly. Target aud: 25 plus. ♦Chris Bailey, gen mgr.

***WEGL(FM)**— Apr 25, 1971: 91.1 mhz; 3 kw. 190 ft TL: N32 36 11 W85 29 12. (CP: Ant 214 ft.). Stereo. Hrs open: 24 116 Foy Union Bldg., Auburn Univ., 36849-5231. Phone: (334) 844-4114. Fax: (334) 844-4118.E-mail: wegl@auburn.edu Web Site:wegl.auburn.edu Licensee: Board of Trustees Auburn University. Population served: 50,000 Format: College alternative. News staff: one; News: 6 hrs wkly. Target aud: College students. Spec prog: Various specialty shows. ♦Elizabeth Kent, gen mgr; Drew McCracken, progmg dir; Chandler White, mus dir.

WKKR(FM)— July 8, 1968: 97.7 mhz; 3.1 kw. 453 ft TL: N32 33 54 W85 22 13. Stereo. Hrs open: 24 Box 2329, Opelika, 36803. Secondary address: 915 Veterans Pkwy., Opelika 36801. Phone: (334) 745-4657. Fax: (334) 749-1520.E-mail: genmorj@charter.net Web Site:www.kickerfm.com Licensee: Qantum of Auburn License Co. LLC. Group owner: Qantum Communications Corp. (acq 7-2-2003; grpsl). Population served: 100,000 Gardner, Carton & Douglas. Format: Country. News staff: 2; News: 7 hrs wkly. Target aud: 25-54. ♦Frank Osborn, pres; Sandy Mathews, sls dir & gen sls mgr; Ruth Law, mktg mgr; Bill Morgan, progmg mgr.

WTLM(AM)—See Opelika

Bay Minette

WNSP(FM)— Oct 1, 1964: 105.5 mhz; 5.3 kw. 348 ft TL: N30 49 34 W87 51 52. (CP: 1.9 kw, ant 410 ft.). Stereo. Hrs open: 24 1100-E Dauphin St., # E, Mobile, 36604-2512. Phone: (251) 438-5460. Fax: (251) 438-5462.E-mail: wnsp@wnsp.com Web Site:www.wnsp.com Licensee: Dot Com+ L.L.C. (acq 7-6-98; $1.05 million). Population served: 190,025 Format: Sports. Target aud: 18-49. ♦Ken Johnson, pres & gen mgr; Clint Crouch, opns mgr.

WTOF(AM)— 1958: 1110 khz; 10 kw-D. TL: N30 52 10 W87 46 09. Hrs open: Box 63, Mobile, 36606. Phone: (386) 738-1348. Licensee: Buddy Tucker Association Inc. (acq 1-16-2007; $300,000). Population served: 7,200 ♦Buddy Tucker, gen mgr.

Bessemer

WZGX(AM)— June 1, 1950: 1450 khz; 1 kw-U. TL: N33 25 23 W86 57 17. Hrs open: 3300 Jaybird Rd., 35020. Phone: (205) 428-0146. Fax: (205) 426-3178. Web Site:www.doblex1450.com Licensee: Bessemer Radio Inc. (acq 9-1-88). Population served: 300,910 Format: Rgnl Mexican. ♦Joel Garcia, gen mgr; Jerry Lopez, progmg dir.

Birmingham

WAGG(AM)— 1927: 610 khz; 5 kw-D, 1 kw-N. TL: N33 29 40 W86 52 30. Hrs open: Dups FM 100% 950 22nd St., N., Suite 1000, 35203. Phone: (205) 322-2987. Fax: (205) 322-2390. Web Site:www.wagg610.com Licensee: Cox Radio Inc. Group owner: Cox Broadcasting (acq 9-9-97). Population served: 300910 Natl. Network: ABC, . Natl. Rep: Christal,. Dow, Lohnes & Albertson. Wire Svc: AP Format: Gospel. News staff: 2; News: 5 hrs wkly. Target aud: 45 plus. ♦David DuBose, gen mgr; David Ellis, gen sls mgr; Mary Kay, progmg dir.

WAPI(AM)— 1922: 1070 khz; 50 kw-D, 5 kw-N, DA-N. TL: N33 33 07 W86 54 40. Hrs open: 24 244 Goodwin Crest Dr., Suite 300, 35209. Phone: (205) 942-1004. Fax: (205) 917-1906. Web Site:www.wapi1070.com Licensee: Citadel Broadcasting Co. Group owner: Citadel Broadcasting Corp. (acq 4-26-2001; grpsl). Population served: 300,910 Natl. Rep: Christal,. Format: News/talk. Target aud: 35 plus. ♦Dale Daniels, gen mgr; Steve Harrison, gen sls mgr; Jennifer Dickson, prom dir; Frank Giardina, progmg dir.

WATV(AM)— May 20, 1946: 900 khz; 1 kw-U. TL: N33 32 14 W86 50 16. Stereo. Hrs open: 24 hrs 3025 Ensley Ave, 35208. Phone: (205) 780-2014. Fax: (205) 780-4034.E-mail: rjanuary@watv900.com Web Site:www.9006060watv.com Licensee: McL/McM Alabama LLC. (group owner; (acq 10-12-2004; $1.5 million). Population served: 865,600 Natl. Network: American Urban, . Natl. Rep: Interep,. Fletcher, Heald & Hildreth, P.L.C. Format: Black, oldies, relg. Target aud: 18 plus. ♦Ron Davenport, pres; Ron January, opns mgr.

WAYE(AM)— Aug 1, 1972: 1220 khz; 1 kw-D, 75 w-N. TL: N33 28 39 W86 50 57. Hrs open: 836 Lomb Ave. S.W., 35211. Phone: (205) 786-9293. Fax: (205) 786-9296.E-mail: WAYEGM@BellSouth.Net Licensee: Davidson Media Station WAYE Licensee LLC. Group owner: Willis Broadcasting Corp. (acq 9-8-2006; $950,000). Population served: 759,000 Format: Gospel. Target aud: 19 plus; loyal, mature & financially stable. ♦Mary Agee, gen mgr & gen sls mgr; Demetrius Roscoe, progmg dir.

***WBFR(FM)**— 1988: 89.5 mhz; 100 w. Ant 672 ft TL: N33 29 02 W86 48 35. Hrs open: 290 Hegenberger Rd., Oakland, CA, 94621. Phone: (510) 568-6200. Fax: (510) 568-6190.E-mail: info@familyradio.com Web Site:www.familyradio.com Licensee: Family Stations Inc. (group owner) Format: Relg, evangelical. ♦Stanley Jackson, gen mgr.

WBHJ(FM)—(Midfield, 1952: 95.7 mhz; 12 kw. Ant 1,004 ft TL: N33 27 37 W86 51 07. Stereo. Hrs open: 24 950 22nd St. N., Suite 1000, 35203. Phone: (205) 322-2987. Fax: (205) 322-2390.E-mail: info@987.q.com Web Site:957jamz.com Licensee: Cox Radio Inc. Group owner: Cox Broadcasting (acq 10-6-98; $17 million with WBHK(FM) Warrior). Population served: 642,000 Natl. Network: Westwood One, . Natl. Rep: Christal,. Dow, Lohnes & Albertson. Format: Hip hop, rhythm and blues. News staff: one; News: one hr wkly. Target aud: 18-34; upscale baby boomers. ♦David DuBose, gen mgr; David Ellis, gen sls mgr; Mickey Johnson, progmg dir.

***WBHM(FM)**— December 1976: 90.3 mhz; 32 kw. 1,214 ft TL: N33 29 19 W86 47 58. Stereo. Hrs open: 24
Rebroadcasts WSGN(FM) Gadsden 100%.
650 11th St. S., 35233-1221. Phone: (205) 934-2606. Fax: (205) 934-5075.E-mail: info@wbhm.org Web Site:www.wbhm.org Licensee: Board of Trustees, University of Alabama. Population served: 780,000 Natl. Network: NPR, PRI, . Wire Svc: AP Format: NPR news. News staff: 3; News: 74 hrs wkly. Target aud: General. Spec prog: New age 6 hrs wkly. ♦Mike Morgan, gen mgr; Mary Hendley, dev dir; Michael Krall, progmg dir; Tanya Ott, news dir.

WBPT(FM)—(Homewood, June 1959: 106.9 mhz; 97 kw. Ant 1,325 ft TL: N33 29 04 W86 48 25. Stereo. Hrs open: 24 301 Beacon Pkwy. W., Suite 200, 35209. Phone: (205) 916-1100. Fax: (205) 916-1151. Web Site:www.birminghampointeagle.com Licensee: Cox Radio Inc. Group owner: Cox Broadcasting (acq 3-28-97; grpsl). Natl. Rep: Katz Radio,. Format: Classic hits. News staff: one; News: 15 hrs wkly. Target aud: 25-54; affluent baby boomers. ♦Ray Nelson, gen mgr; David Wells, progmg dir; Don Daley, news dir; Sherri Clark, traf mgr.

WDJC-FM— Apr 22, 1968: 93.7 mhz; 100 kw. 1,007 ft TL: N33 26 36 W86 52 50. Stereo. Hrs open: 120 Summit Pkwy, Suite 200, Homewood, 35209. Phone: (205) 879-3324. Fax: (205) 802-4555.E-mail: thejunction@wdjconline.com Web Site:www.93.7wdjc.com Licensee: Kimtron Inc. Group owner: Crawford Broadcasting Co. Population served: 1,000,000 Format: Contemp Christian music. Target aud: 25-60; conservative middle income. ♦Steve Armstrong, gen mgr; Tom LoPresti, gen sls mgr.

WENN(AM)— 1950: 1320 khz; 5 kw-D, 111 w-N. TL: N33 33 41 W86 51 37. Hrs open: 301 Beacon Pkwy., Suite 200, 35209. Phone: (205) 916-1100. Fax: (205) 916-1151. Web Site:wzzk.com Licensee: Cox Radio Inc. Group owner: Cox Communications Inc. (acq 3-28-97; grpsl). Population served: 300,910 Natl. Rep: Christal,. Dow, Lohnes & Albertson. Format: Sp. ♦Ray Nelson, gen mgr.

WERC(AM)— May 25, 1925: 960 khz; 5 kw-U, DA-N. TL: N33 32 02 W86 51 07. Hrs open: Prog sep from FM 600 Beacon Pkwy. W., Suite 400, 35209. Phone: (205) 439-9600. Fax: (205) 439-8390. Web Site:www.werctalk.com Licensee: Capstar TX L.P. Format: News/talk. Target aud: Adults. ♦Dennis Cruz, gen sls mgr; Jim Faherty, news dir; Shelia Howell, traf mgr.

***WGIB(FM)**— 1983: 91.9 mhz; 600 w. 679 ft TL: N33 29 02 W86 48 35. Hrs open: 24 1137 10th Pl. S., 35205. Phone: (205) 323-1516. Fax: (205) 323-2747.E-mail: nmills@gleniris.net Web Site:www.gleniris.net Licensee: Glen Iris Baptist School (acq 1-31-02). Format: Christian. ♦Chris Lamb, chmn, gen mgr; Dan Ratje, stn mgr, opns mgr & progmg dir.

WJLD(AM)—(Fairfield, 1942: 1400 khz; 1 kw-U. TL: N33 28 36 W86 53 01. Hrs open: 24 Box 19123, 35219-9123. Secondary address: 1449 Spaulding Ishkooda Rd. 35211-5059. Phone: (205) 942-1776. Fax: (205) 942-4814.E-mail: wjld@juno.com Web Site:www.wjldfm.com Licensee: Richardson Broadcasting Corp. (acq 10-87). Population served: 900,000 Natl. Network: American Urban, CNN Radio, . Format: Blues, takl, gospel. Target aud: 35+; majority Black, adult, blue and white collar working class. ♦Gary R. Richardson, pres & gen mgr; Bob Friedman, opns mgr, sls dir; Gary Richardson, progmg dir; Eloise Gaffney, traf mgr.

WJOX(FM)— 1947: 94.5 mhz; 100 kw. Ant 1,214 ft TL: N33 29 26 W86 47 48. Stereo. Hrs open: 244 Goodwin Crest Dr., Suite 300, 35209. Phone: (205) 942-1004. Fax: (205) 917-1906. Web Site:www.wjoxfm.com Licensee: Citadel Broadcasting Co. Natl. Network: ESPN Radio, . Format: Sports talk. Target aud: 25-54; general.

***WJSR(FM)**— Aug 11, 1977: 91.1 mhz; 100 w. 195 ft TL: N33 39 07 W86 42 20. Stereo. Hrs open: 24 2601 Carson Rd., 35215. Phone: (205) 856-6095. Fax: (205) 856-7702. Web Site:wjsrfm.com Licensee: Jefferson State Community College. Population served: 100,000 Format: Classic rock. News: 4 hrs wkly. Target aud: 24-49; college population. ♦Ray Edwards, gen mgr.

***WLJR(FM)**— 1998: 88.5 mhz; 200 w. 623 ft TL: N33 23 35 W86 39 48. Stereo. Hrs open: 24 Briarwood Presbyterian Church, 2200 Briarwood Way, 35243. Phone: (205) 978-2200. Fax: (205) 824-8419.E-mail: info@wljr.org Web Site:www.wljr.org Licensee: Briarwood Presbyterian Church. Natl. Network: Moody, . Southmayd & Miller. Format: Div, educ, relg. News: 10 hrs wkly. Target aud: General; upper middle class. ♦James Hulgan, gen mgr.

WMJJ(FM)— June 1, 1961: 96.5 mhz; 100 kw. 1,027 ft TL: N33 26 38 W86 42 10. Stereo. Hrs open: 600 Beacon Pkwy. W., Suite 400, 35209. Phone: (205) 439-9600. Fax: (205) 439-8390. Fax: (205) 439-8391. Web Site:www.magic96fm.com Licensee: Capstar TX L.P. Group owner: Clear Channel Communications Inc. (acq 8-30-00; grpsl). Population served: 300,910 Reed, Smith, Shaw & McClay. Format: Adult contemp. Target aud: 25-54. ♦L. Lowry Mays, CEO; Jimmy Vineyard, gen mgr; John Friend, opns mgr, sls dir; Bradley Spears, gen sls mgr; Cindee Standridge, mktg dir; Bob Newberry, chief of engrg; Cynthia Childress, traf mgr; Tom Hanrahan, progmg dir & opns.

WQEN(FM)—(Trussville, Oct 7, 1966: 103.7 mhz; 100 kw. Ant 935 ft TL: N33 26 38 W86 52 47. Stereo. Hrs open: 600 Beacon Pkwy. W., Suite 400, 35209. Phone: (205) 439-9600. Fax: (205) 439-8390. Web Site:www.1037theq.com Licensee: Capstar TX L.P. (acq 8-30-2000; grpsl). Population served: 800,000 Format: CHR, Top-40. ♦Jimmy Vineyard, gen mgr; Keith Allen, progmg dir.

WQOH(AM)—See Irondale

WSPZ(AM)— Oct 15, 1947: 690 khz; 50 kw-D, 500 w-N, DA-N. TL: N33 26 56 W86 55 18. Hrs open: 244 Goodwin Crest Dr., Suite 300, 35209-3714. Phone: (205) 945-4646. Fax: (205) 945-3999. Web Site:www.wjox690.com Licensee: Citadel Broadcasting Co. Group owner: Citadel Broadcasting Corp. (acq 4-26-2001; grpsl). Population served: 375,900 Wire Svc: SportsTicker Format: Sports. Target aud: 25-54. Spec prog: Gospel 5 hrs wkly. ♦Dale Daniels, gen mgr; Kerry Lambert, opns VP; Lenny Frisaro, sls dir; Steve Harrison, natl sls mgr; Jennifer Dickson, prom dir; Ryan Haney, progmg dir, chief of engrg; Lisa Holifield, news dir; Will Berry, pub affrs dir.

WUHT(FM)— Sept 15, 1969: 107.7 mhz; 100 kw. Ant 1,237 ft TL: N33 43 52 W86 37 57. Hrs open: 24 244 Goodwin Crest Dr., Suite 300, 35209. Phone: (205) 945-4646. Fax: (205) 942-3175. Web Site:www.hot1077radio.com Licensee: Citadel Broadcasting Co. Group owner: Citadel Broadcasting Corp. (acq 4-26-2001; grpsl). Population served: 300,910 Format: Hot rhythm and blues. Target aud: 18-34. ♦Dale Daniels, gen mgr; Jane Mitchell, gen sls mgr.

***WVSU-FM**— Apr 6, 1967: 91.1 mhz; 500 w vert. Ant 413 ft TL: N33 27 47 W86 46 08. Stereo. Hrs open: 17 Samford Univ., 35229-2301. Phone: (205) 726-2877. Fax: (205) 726-4032.E-mail: wvsu@samford.edu Web Site:www.samford.edu/wvsu Licensee: Samford University. Population served: 800,000 Format: Smooth jazz. News: one hr wkly. Target aud: General. ♦Andy Parrish, gen mgr.

WXJC(AM)— Apr 1, 1953: 850 khz; 50 kw-D, 1 kw-N, DA-2. TL: N33 37 25 W86 44 45. Hrs open: 120 Summit Pkwy., 35209. Phone: (205) 879-3324. Fax: (205) 802-4555.E-mail: thejunction@wdjconline.com Web Site:www.850wxjc.com Licensee: Kimtron Inc. Group owner: Crawford Broadcasting Co. (acq 11-12-99). Population served: 785,000 Natl. Network: USA, . Format: Talk. Target aud: Under 12. ♦Steve Armstrong, gen mgr; Jennifer Poepcke, gen sls mgr; Todd Dixon, chief of engrg; Melodye Grubb, traf mgr.

WYDE(AM)— Mar 25, 1953: 1260 khz; 5 kw-D, 41 w-N. TL: N33 31 29 W86 47 10. Hrs open: 120 Summit Pkwy., 35209. Phone: (205)

879-3324. Fax: (205) 802-4555.E-mail: thejunction@wdjconline.com Licensee: Kimtron Inc. Group owner: Crawford Broadcasting Co. (acq 1994). Population served: 100,000 Natl. Rep: McGavren Guild,. Format: Classic hits. ◆Steve Armstrong, gen mgr; Jennifer Paepcke, gen sls mgr; Todd Dixon, chief of engrg; Melodye Grubb, traf mgr.

WZGX(AM)—See Bessemer

WZRR(FM)— December 1975: 99.5 mhz; 100 kw. 870 ft TL: N33 26 28 W86 53 00. (CP: Ant 1,000 ft.). Hrs open: Prog sep from AM 244 Goodwin Crest Dr., Suite 300, 35209. Phone: (205) 945-4646. Fax: (205) 942-3175. Web Site:www.wzrr.com Natl. Rep: Christal,. Wire Svc: Accu-Weather Format: Classic rock. ◆Allen Dick, pres; Dave Henderlite, CFO; Davis Hawkins, opns VP; Kerry Lambert, opns mgr.

WZZK-FM— 1948: 104.7 mhz; 100 kw. 1,300 ft TL: N33 29 02 W86 48 21. Stereo. Hrs open: 24 301 Beacon Pkwy. W., Suite 200, 35209. Phone: (205) 916-1100. Fax: (205) 916-1151.E-mail: wzzk@cox.com Web Site:www.wzzk.com Licensee: Cox Radio Inc. Group owner: Cox Broadcasting (acq 3-28-97; grpsl). Population served: 407,400 Dow, Lohnes and Albertson. Format: Country. News staff: 2; News: 10 hrs wkly. Target aud: 25-54. ◆Ray Nelson, gen mgr; David Wells, gen sls mgr; Justin Case, progmg dir.

Boaz

WBSA(AM)— Oct 1, 1959: 1300 khz; 1 kw-D. TL: N34 12 50 W86 09 10. Hrs open: 1525 Wills Rd., 35957. Phone: (256) 593-4264. Fax: (256) 593-4265. Web Site:www.wbsaam.com Licensee: Watkins Broadcasting Inc. (acq 10-4-94) $100,000; 10-17-94). Population served: 9,800 Format: Southern gospel. Target aud: General. ◆Roger Watkins, gen mgr; Dale Johnson, progmg dir.

Brantley

WAOQ(FM)— June 3, 1999: 100.3 mhz; 6 kw. 328 ft TL: N31 42 26 W86 13 12. Stereo. Hrs open: 24 P.O. Box 699, Luverne, 36049. Phone: (334) 335-2877. Fax: (205) 755- 3329.E-mail: waoq@waoq.com Web Site:www.waoq.com Licensee: Alatron Corp. Inc. Format: Classic country. News: 14 hrs wkly. Spec prog: Gospel 14 hrs wkly. ◆Robert E. Williams, pres; Christopher W. Johnson, gen mgr, progmg dir; Ken Lyons, stn mgr, gen sls mgr; Robert Williams, chief of engrg.

Brewton

WEBJ(AM)— Aug 1, 1947: 1240 khz; 1 kw-U. TL: N31 06 35 W87 03 36. Hrs open: 6 AM-8 PM 301 Downing St., 36426. Phone: (251) 867-5717. Fax: (251) 867-5718.E-mail: info@webj.com Licensee: Candy Cashman Smith, individual. (acq 10-2-97). Population served: 25,000 Gardner, Carton & Douglas. Format: Oldies. News staff: one; News: 20 hrs wkly. Target aud: 21 plus; 60% female, 40% male. ◆Dennis Dunnaway, gen mgr.

*WELJ(FM)— 1998: 90.9 mhz; 45 kw. Ant 502 ft TL: N31 18 13 W87 02 50. Stereo. Hrs open: Box 347, 36403. Secondary address: 42676 Hwy. 31 36427. Phone: (251) 809-1915. Fax: (251) 809-1916.E-mail: gradio@bellsouth.net Licensee: Gateway Public Radio (acq 10-12-00; $3,500). Format: Southern gospel, Christian. ◆Debra Johnson, gen mgr, stn mgr.

WKNU(FM)— Aug 19, 1974: 106.3 mhz; 3.8 kw. Ant 417 ft TL: N31 06 42 W87 01 17. Stereo. Hrs open: 24 Box 468, 36427. Secondary address: 2832 Ridge Rd. 36426. Phone: (251) 867-4824. Fax: (251) 867-7003.E-mail: wknubroadcasting@bellsouth.net Licensee: Ellington Radio Inc. (acq 12-28-78). Population served: 35,000 Format: C&W. News: 8 hrs wkly. Target aud: General. Spec prog: Gospel 2 hrs, relg 2 hrs wkly. ◆Jack Floyd, pres; Carol Ellington, gen mgr.

Bridgeport

WGNQ(AM)— Sept 19, 1961: 1480 khz; 1 kw-D, 39 w-N. TL: N34 56 34 W85 42 26. Hrs open: 24 1237 County Rd. 295, Higdon, 35979-6349. Phone: (256) 495-2500. Fax: (914) 730-9820.E-mail: manager@wgnq.net Web Site:www.wgnq.net Licensee: MG Media Inc. (acq 9-29-2005). Population served: 128,730 Natl. Network: Salem Radio Network, . Alabama Radio Net. Donald Martin, P.C. Format: Christian talk and ministry. ◆Marvin Glass, pres, gen mgr, progmg dir & sls.

Brookwood

WRTR(FM)—Licensed to Brookwood. See Tuscaloosa

Brundidge

WTBF-FM— Oct 1, 1997: 94.7 mhz; 14.5 kw. 433 ft TL: N31 40 38 W85 56 43. Stereo. Hrs open: 24 67 Court Sq., Troy, 36081. Phone: (334) 566-0300. Fax: (334) 566-5689.E-mail: wtbf@radio.com Web Site:www.wtbf947.com Licensee: Troy Broadcasting Corp. Population served: 200,000 Natl. Network: Moody, . Rgnl. Network: Alabama Net. Alabama Radio Net. Gardner, Carton & Douglas. Wire Svc: National Weather Network Format: Oldies. News: 20 hrs wkly. Target aud: 28-60. ◆Jim Roling, gen mgr; Doc Kirby, opns mgr.

Butler

WMLV(FM)— Nov 20, 1978: 93.5 mhz; 32 kw. Ant 610 ft TL: N32 09 26 W88 29 17. Stereo. Hrs open: 3436 Hwy. 45 N., Meridian, MS, 39301. Phone: (601) 693-2661. Fax: (601) 483-0826. Licensee: Mississippi Broadcasters L.L.C. (group owner; (acq 10-30-2002; $771,500). Population served: 50,000 Format: Hot adult contemp. ◆Clay Holladay, stn mgr; Scott Stevens, opns mgr.

WPRN(AM)— July 11, 1959: Stn currently dark. 1330 khz; 5 kw-D. TL: N32 06 02 W88 14 07. Hrs open: 909 W. Pushmataha St., 36904-2441. Phone: (205) 459-3222. Fax: (205) 459-4140. Licensee: Butler Broadcasting Corp. (acq 1-75). Population served: 25,000 Format: Country. ◆Daryl Jackson, gen mgr.

Calera

WBYE(AM)— Jan 12, 1958: 1370 khz; 1 kw-D. TL: N33 05 26 W86 46 37. Hrs open: 6 AM-6 PM Box 1727, 35040. Secondary address: 9170 Highway 25 36726. Phone: (205) 668-1370. Fax: (205) 668-7562. Licensee: WBYE Broadcasting Co. Inc. (acq 4-14-89; $100,754; 4-24-89). Population served: 130,000 Format: Gospel. News: 15 hrs wkly. Target aud: 25-65. ◆Frank Cummings, pres & gen mgr.

Carrollton

*WALN(FM)— 1997: 89.3 mhz; 9.5 kw vert. 699 ft TL: N33 13 06 W88 05 46. Hrs open: 24 American Family Radio, Box 3206, Tupelo, MS, 38803. Phone: (662) 844-8888. Fax: (662) 842-6791. Web Site:www.afr.net Licensee: American Family Association. Group owner: American Family Radio Format: Inspirational Christian. ◆Tim Waldmon, pres; Marvin Sanders, gen mgr; John Riley, progmg dir; Fred Jackson, news dir; Joey Moody, engrg dir.

WREN(AM)— Aug 15, 1951: Stn currently dark. 590 khz; 1 kw-D, 185 w-N. TL: N33 13 04 W88 05 48. Hrs open: 11563 Argonne Rd, Festus, MO, 63028-2951. Secondary address: P.O. Box 161, Aliceville Phone: (636) 586-8697. Fax: (636) 586-8697.E-mail: svicomm@hughes.net Web Site:www.svicommunications.com Licensee: Serendipity Ventures II LLC Group owner: Willis Broadcasting Corp. (acq 2006). Population served: 25,000 Natl. Network: USA, . Format: Gospel, rhythm and blues. ◆Steve Vogt, gen mgr.

WZBQ(FM)— February 1970: 94.1 mhz; 98 kw. Ant 1,007 ft TL: N33 13 07 W88 05 47. Stereo. Hrs open: 3900 11th Ave. S., Tuscaloosa, 35401-7056. Phone: (205) 344-4589. Fax: (205) 349-3200. Fax: (205) 752-9269.E-mail: info@941zbq.com Web Site:www.941zbq.com Licensee: Capstar TX L.P. Group owner: Clear Channel Communications Inc. (acq 8-30-2000; grpsl). Population served: 750,000 Format: CHR. Target aud: 18-49. ◆Lori Moore, gen mgr, sls dir; Bill Seckbach, opns mgr; Louis Linguini, progmg dir; Laurie Mundy, news dir; Ross Swaner, chief of engrg.

Carrville

WACQ(AM)—Licensed to Carrville. See Tallassee

Centre

WEIS(AM)— Sept 30, 1961: 990 khz; 1 kw-D, 30 w-N. TL: N34 09 10 W85 40 44. Hrs open: 24 Box 297, 35960. Phone: (256) 927-5152. Fax: (256) 927-6503. Web Site:www.weis990am.com Licensee: Baker Enterprises Inc. (acq 9-8-83; $157,675; 9-26-83). Population served: 450,000 Timothy K. Brady. Format: Country, southern gospel. News staff: one; News: 10 hrs wkly. Target aud: General. ◆Jerry Baker, pres & gen mgr.

WFXO(FM)— Oct 10, 1992: 105.9 mhz; 6 kw. 150 ft TL: N34 12 51 W85 46 20. Hrs open: 24 801 Nobel St., Fl. 8, Anniston, 36201. Phone: (256) 236-1880. Fax: (256) 236-4480. Web Site:www.y-106.com Licensee: Williams Communications Inc. (group owner; (acq 6-99; $380,000). Population served: 440,000 Natl. Network: Motor Racing

Net, PRI, . Rgnl. Network: Motor Racing Net, PRI. Format: Hot country. News: one hr wkly. Target aud: 25-54. ◆Walt Williams, gen mgr; Dan Pullman, gen sls mgr; Tex Carter, progmg dir; Mike Mote, news dir.

WLYJ(AM)— Nov 9, 1962: 1560 khz; 1 kw-D. TL: N34 07 41 W85 38 27. Hrs open: 6 AM-sunset Box 2, 35960. Phone: (256) 927-4027. Fax: (205) 295-1238. Web Site:www.joychristian.com Licensee: Joy Christian Communications Inc. (acq 12-1-2003). Population served: 245,000 Rgnl. Network: Tenn. Radio Net., Tobacco. Tenn. Radio Net. Format: Southern gospel. News staff: one; News: 7 hrs wkly. Target aud: 25-55; working middle class, rural. Spec prog: Farm one hr wkly. ◆Ed Smith, pres, gen mgr; Marie Smith, sr VP.

Centreville

WBIB(AM)— Dec 14, 1964: 1110 khz; 1 kw-D. TL: N32 58 01 W87 09 01. Hrs open: Sunrise-sunset Box 216, 35042. Phone: (205) 926-6286.E-mail: wbibradio@bellsouth.net Licensee: James DeLoach (acq 11-21-2005). Population served: 20,000-30,000 Natl. Rep: Keystone (unwired net),. Format: Gospel, country. Target aud: Adults. ◆Horrace Cruchfield, gen mgr.

Chickasaw

WDLT-FM—Licensed to Chickasaw. See Mobile

Citronelle

WQUA(FM)— June 25, 1989: 102.1 mhz; 15 kw. Ant 426 ft TL: N31 05 04 W88 23 51. Stereo. Hrs open: 24 Box 262550, Baton Rouge, LA, 70826. Secondary address: 8919 World Ministry Ave., Baton Rouge, LA 70810. Phone: (225) 768-3688. Phone: (225) 768-8300. Fax: (225) 768-3729.E-mail: kawikfish@yahoo.com Web Site:www.jsm.org Licensee: Family Worship Center Church Inc. Group owner: ABC Inc. (acq 8-25-2005; $1.25 million). Format: Christian. ◆David Whitelaw, COO; Jimmy Swaggart, pres.

WTLM(AM)—See Opelika

Columbia

WJJN(FM)— September 1992: 92.1 mhz; 2.55 kw. 499 ft TL: N31 10 56 W85 10 59. Hrs open: 1406 Ross Clark Circle, Dothan, 36303. Phone: (334) 671-1753. Fax: (334) 677-6923.E-mail: wtraffic@graceba.net Web Site:www.wjjn.com Licensee: Wilson Broadcasting Inc. (group owner) Format: Urban contemp. ◆James R. Wilson III, gen mgr.

Columbiana

WQEM(FM)— 2000: 101.5 mhz; 1.8 kw. Ant 607 ft TL: N33 13 45 W86 42 56. Hrs open: 1137 Tenth Pl. S., Birmingham, 35205. Phone: (205) 323-1516. Fax: (205) 323-2747 (Phone/Fax). Web Site:www.gleniris.net Licensee: Glen Iris Baptist School (acq 12-24-02). Format: Teaching, gospel. ◆Chris Lamb, chmn & gen mgr.

Cordova

WFFN(FM)— June 22, 1987: Stn currently dark. 95.3 mhz; 5 kw. Ant 354 ft TL: N33 46 11 W87 12 06. (CP: COL Coaling. 17.5 kw, ant 840 ft. TL: N33 03 15 W87 32 57). Stereo. Hrs open: 142 Skyland Blvd., Tuscaloosa, 35405. Phone: (205) 750-0929. Fax: (205) 349-1715.E-mail: greg.thomas@citcomm.com Licensee: Citadel Broadcasting Co. (acq 7-12-2005; grpsl). ◆Gigi South, gen mgr; Brandy Jackson, gen sls mgr; Trey Daniels, progmg dir; Val Goodson, news dir; Herb Connellan, chief of engrg.

WXJC-FM— 1997: 92.5 mhz; 2.2 kw. Ant 548 ft TL: N33 38 55 W87 09 19. Hrs open: 24 120 Summit Pkwy., Birmingham, 35209. Phone: (205) 879-3324. Fax: (205) 802-4555.E-mail: thejunction@wdjconline.com Licensee: Kimtron Inc. Group owner: Crawford Broadcasting Co. (acq 7-15-2004; $1.15 million). Format: Southern gospel. ◆Steve Armstrong, gen mgr; Jennifer Paepcke, gen sls mgr; Todd Dixon, chief of engrg; Melodye Grubb, traf mgr.

Cullman

WFMH(AM)— October 1946: 1340 khz; 670 w-U. TL: N34 10 49 W86 51 59. Hrs open: 24 1707 Warnke Rd, N.W., 35055. Phone: (256) 734-3271. Fax: (256) 734-3622.E-mail: wfmh@adelphia.net Licensee: Walton E. Williams III Group owner: Williams Communications Inc.

(acq 7-1-2008; with WMCJ(AM) Cullman). Population served: 75,000 Natl. Rep: Keystone (unwired net),. Format: News/talk, sports. News: 18 hrs wkly. Target aud: 25-54; middle & upper income adults. ♦Walt Williams, gen mgr; Susan Hackney, progmg dir.

WKUL(FM)— September 1967: 92.1 mhz; 6 kw. 328 ft TL: N34 11 41 W86 43 52. Stereo. Hrs open: Box 803, 214 1st Ave. S.E., 35056. Phone: (256) 734-0183. Fax: (256) 739-2999. Web Site:www.wkul.com Licensee: Jonathan Christian Corp. (acq 3-1-77). Population served: 1,200,000 Format: Country, sports, talk. News staff: one; News: 20 hrs wkly. Target aud: 25-54. Spec prog: Farm 15 hrs wkly. ♦Ron Mosley, pres, gen mgr; Rick Nix, opns mgr; Ron Mosley Jr., gen sls mgr.

WMCJ(AM)— Mar 25, 1950: 1460 khz; 5 kw-D, 500 w-N, DA-N. TL: N34 10 44 W86 51 58. Hrs open: 24 1707 Warnke Rd. N.W., 35055. Phone: (256) 734-3271. Fax: (256) 734-3622. Licensee: Walton E. Williams III (acq 7-1-2008; with WFMH(AM) Cullman). Population served: 138,672 Format: Solid gospel. ♦Walt Williams, gen mgr; Susan Hackney, progmg dir.

WYDE-FM— Aug 6, 1949: 101.1 mhz; 100 kw. Ant 1,345 ft TL: N34 04 56 W86 54 15. Hrs open: 24 120 Summit Pkwy., Birmingham, 35209. Phone: (205) 879-3324. Fax: (205) 802-4555.E-mail: thejunction@wdjconline.com Licensee: Kimtron Inc. Group owner: Crawford Broadcasting Co. (acq 6-14-2002; $8.5 million). Population served: 1,274,627 Format: Adult contemp. ♦Steve Armstrong, gen mgr; Jennifer Paepcke, gen sls mgr; Todd Dexon, chief of engrg; Melodye Grubb, traf mgr.

Dadeville

WDLK(AM)— Aug 11, 1980: 1450 khz; 1 kw-U. TL: N32 50 56 W85 46 10. Hrs open: Box 275, 2015 Hwy. 49 S., 36853. Phone: (256) 825-8313. Fax: (256) 825-8314. Licensee: Progressive United Communications Inc. (group owner; (acq 11-6-2000; $45,000). Population served: 60,000 Format: Gospel. ♦Walter Gilmore, gen mgr.

***WELL-FM**— Mar 1, 1990: 88.7 mhz; 100 kw. 328 ft TL: N32 51 20 W85 46 31. (CP: Ant 305 ft.). Stereo. Hrs open: 24 658 Horseshoe Bend Rd., 36853. Phone: (256) 825-6456. Fax: (256) 825-6426.E-mail: cassiekeyes@hotmail.com Licensee: Jimmy Jarrell Communications Foundation Inc. Natl. Network: USA, . Format: Christian. News staff: one. Target aud: 24 plus. ♦Cassie Keyes, gen mgr.

WGZZ(FM)— July 23, 1989: 100.3 mhz; 2.2 kw. Ant 546 ft TL: N32 52 58 W85 49 16. Stereo. Hrs open: 1261 Jacksons Gap Way, Jacksons Gap, 36861-5760. Secondary address: 13263 Hwy. 280, Jacksons Gap 36861. Phone: (256) 825-4221.E-mail: www.wzlm@charter.net Licensee: Auburn Network Inc. (group owner; (acq 6-28-2007; $1.4 million). Format: Country. Target aud: 18-55. Spec prog: Gospel 3 hrs wkly. ♦Cameron Reynolds, gen mgr.

Daleville

WCMA(AM)— Oct 25, 1983: Stn currently dark. 1560 khz; 50 kw-D, 2.5 kw-CH. TL: N31 16 35 W85 45 54. Hrs open: Box 1969, Santa Rosa Beach, FL, 32459. Phone: (866) 748-7610. Licensee: Perihelion Global Inc. (acq 4-21-2004; $135,000). Population served: 350,000 ♦John Beebe, gen mgr.

Daphne

WASG(AM)— Nov 12, 1981: Stn currently dark. 550 khz; 2.5 kw-D, 19 w-N. TL: N30 44 44 W88 05 40. Stereo. Hrs open: 24 2070 N. Palafax, Pensacola, FL, 32501. Phone: (850) 434-1230. Fax: (850) 469-9698. Licensee: 550 AM Inc. ♦Dara Glinter, exec VP; Michael B. Glinter, pres & gen mgr.

WAVH(FM)— May 15, 1993: 106.5 mhz; 50 kw. Ant 449 ft TL: N30 44 44 W88 05 40. Stereo. Hrs open: 24 900 Western America Cir., Suite 506, Mobile, 36609. Phone: (251) 344-1065. Fax: (251) 316-3733. Web Site:fmtalk1065.com Licensee: Bigler Broadcasting LLC (acq 1-31-2008; $3.6 million). Population served: 470,000 Natl. Rep: McGavren Guild,. Lewis, Rice & Fingersh L.C. Format: Talk. Target aud: 25-64; general. ♦Kevin McLaughlin, gen mgr.

Decatur

WDPT(AM)— Oct 3, 1953: Stn currently dark. 1490 khz; 1 kw-U. TL: N34 35 14 W86 59 13. Hrs open: 401 14th St. S.E., Suite 2A, 35601. Phone: (256) 551-9885.E-mail: dbaughman@1049theriver.com Web Site:protalk1490.com Licensee: Christian Voice of Central Ohio Inc. (acq 6-24-2007; $167,500). Population served: 110,000 ♦Dan Baughman, gen mgr.

WDRM(FM)— September 1951: 102.1 mhz; 100 kw. Ant 981 ft TL: N34 49 08 W86 44 19. Stereo. Hrs open: 24 Box 21008, Huntsville, 35824. Secondary address: 26869 Peoples Rd., Madison 35756. Phone: (205) 353-1750. Fax: (256) 350-2653.E-mail: info@wdrm.com Web Site:www.wdrm.com Licensee: Capstar TX L.P. Format: Country.

WHOS(AM)— October 1948: 800 khz; 1 kw-D, 215 w-N. TL: N34 35 55 W87 00 24. Hrs open: 24 Box 21008, Huntsville, 35824. Secondary address: 26869 Peoples Rd., Madison 35756. Phone: (256) 353-1750. Fax: (256) 350-2653. Licensee: Capstar TX L.P. Group owner: Clear Channel Communications Inc. (acq 7-18-2000; grpsl). Population served: 343,500 Format: 24 hr. News staff: 3. Target aud: 25-54. ♦Rick Brown, gen mgr; Carmelita Palmer, sls dir.

WWTM(AM)— May 1935: 1400 khz; 1 kw-U. TL: N34 36 44 W86 59 28. Hrs open: 1209 Danville Rd. S.W., Suite N, 35601-3853. Phone: (256) 353-1400. Fax: (256) 353-0363.E-mail: jburns@espn1400.info Web Site:www.espn1400.info Licensee: R & B Communications Inc. (acq 3-18-97). Natl. Network: ESPN Radio, . Format: Sports. Target aud: 25-54. ♦Joe Burns, gen mgr.

***WYFD(FM)**— May 7, 1975: 91.7 mhz; 3 kw. 787 ft TL: N34 47 53 W86 38 24. Stereo. Hrs open: 24 11530 Carmel Commons Blvd., Charlotte, NC, 28226. Phone: (704) 523-5555.E-mail: bbn@bbnradio.org Web Site:www.bbnradio.org Licensee: Bible Broadcasting Network. (group owner; acq 10-19-90; $75,000; 11-12-90). Population served: 450,000 Format: Relg, educ. ♦Lowell Davey, pres; Hank Crull, gen mgr; Dave Phillips, stn mgr.

Demopolis

***WMWI(FM)**—Not on air, target date: unknown: 88.7 mhz; 25 kw. Ant 321 ft TL: N32 23 00 W87 54 35. Hrs open: Box 3800, Birmingham, 35208. Phone: (205) 929-1609. Licensee: Miles College. ♦Kenneth Jones, gen mgr.

WXAL(AM)— Nov 9, 1947: 1400 khz; 790 w-U. TL: N32 30 08 W87 49 07. Hrs open: Box 938, 1226 Jefferson Rd., 36732. Phone: (334) 289-1400. Fax: (334) 289-9811.E-mail: valerie@mywin98.com Licensee: West Alabama Radio Inc. (acq 8-18-98; $456,300 with co-located FM). Population served: 75,000 Natl. Network: Westwood One, USA, . Format: News/talk, Black gospel. Target aud: 25-54. ♦Amy Ward, CEO; Larry Carr, chmn, progmg dir; Amy Ross, gen mgr; Sean Park, gen sls mgr; Valerie Webb, news dir.

WZNJ(FM)— 1975: 106.5 mhz; 25 kw. 492 ft TL: N32 20 40 W87 37 43. Stereo. Hrs open: Prog sep from AM Box 938, 1226 Jefferson Rd., 36732. Licensee: West Alabama Radio Inc. Natl. Network: Westwood One, USA, . Format: Oldies, sports. Target aud: 18-49.

Dixons Mills

***WMBV(FM)**— Aug 15, 1988: 91.9 mhz; 62 kw. 613 ft TL: N32 07 45 W87 44 16. Stereo. Hrs open: 24 Box 91.9 FM, 36736-0091. Secondary address: 10564 Marengo County Rd. 30 36736. Phone: (334) 992-2425. Phone: (888) 624-7234. Fax: (334) 992-2637.E-mail: wmbv@moody.edu Web Site:www.wmbv.org Licensee: Moody Bible Institute. Group owner: The Moody Bible Institute of Chicago (acq 3-31-88). Population served: 200,000 Natl. Network: Moody, . Southmayd & Miller. Format: Relg. News: 10 hrs wkly. Target aud: 35-55; general. Spec prog: Financial 3 hrs, children 3 hrs, sports one hr wkly. ♦Rob Moore, gen mgr.

Dora

WCOC(AM)— Apr 1, 1982: Stn currently dark. 1010 khz; 5 kw-D. TL: N33 48 04 W87 06 42. Hrs open: 6475 Hwy. 78, Cordova, 35550. Phone: (619) 929-9186. Licensee: Azteca Communications of Alabama Inc. (acq 4-4-2002; $190,000). ♦Patricia Perez, gen mgr.

Dothan

WAGF(AM)— Sept 29, 1932: 1320 khz; 1 kw-U, DA-N. TL: N31 14 56 W85 23 20. Hrs open: 4106 Rose Clark Circle, 36303. Phone: (334) 671-1753. Fax: (334) 677-6923.E-mail: wtraffic@graceba.net Web Site:www.wjjn.com Licensee: Wilson Broadcasting Inc. (group owner; acq 8-13-92; $60,000; 8-31-92). Format: Gospel. ♦James Wilson III, gen mgr.

WAGF-FM— 1991: 101.3 mhz; 3 kw. 328 ft TL: N31 12 02 W85 20 12. (CP: 820 w, ant 640 ft.). Hrs open: 24 4106 Ross Clark Circle, 36303. Phone: (334) 677-7654. Fax: (334) 677-6923.E-mail: wtraffic@graceba.net Web Site:www.wjjn.com Licensee: Wilson Broadcasting Inc. (group owner) Natl. Network: Jones Radio Networks, . Rgnl. Network: Alabama Net. Natl. Rep: Rgnl Reps,. Alabama Radio Net. Arter & Hadden. Format: Soft hits, lite adult contemp. Target aud: 25-54; female. ♦James R. Wilson III, gen mgr; J.R. Wilson, gen sls mgr; James Wilson, progmg dir.

***WDYF(FM)**— 2004: 90.3 mhz; 9.2 kw. Ant 535 ft TL: N31 19 31 W85 36 02. Hrs open: Box 210789, Montgomery, 36121. Secondary address: 381 Mendel Parkway, Montgomery 36117. Phone: (334) 271-8900. Fax: (334) 260-8962.E-mail: mail@faithradio.org Web Site:www.faithradio.org Licensee: Faith Broadcasting Inc. Format: Educ, relg, MOR. ♦Russell Dean, gen mgr; Andrew Leuthold, opns mgr; Gary Hundley, dev dir; Bob Crittenden, progmg dir.

WEEL(AM)— July 3, 1995: 700 khz; 1.6 kw-D. TL: N31 26 19 W85 17 22. Hrs open: Sunrise-sunset 3385 Reeves St., 36303. Phone: (502) 776-1240. Licensee: Jalo Broadcasting Corp. (acq 12-20-2006; $225,000). ♦Argie Dale Sr., gen mgr.

WESP(FM)— Sept 1, 1989: 102.5 mhz; 16.5 kw. Ant 403 ft TL: N31 15 48 W85 18 24. Stereo. Hrs open: 24 3245 Montgomery Hwy., Suite 1, 36303-2150. Phone: (334) 671-1025. Phone: (334) 712-9233. Fax: (334) 712-0374.E-mail: ron@wdjr.com Web Site:www.rock1025.com Licensee: Gulf South Communications Inc. (acq 1999; $1.4 million). Population served: 450,000 Natl. Rep: McGavren Guild,. Format: Rock. Target aud: 25-54; men. ♦Ron Eubanks, gen mgr; Misty Huff, opns mgr, prom mgr; Bill Moody, gen sls mgr; Jess Bailey, progmg dir; April Granger, traf mgr.

***WGTF(FM)**— September 1988: 89.5 mhz; 19 kw. 213 ft TL: N31 14 02 W85 26 02. Hrs open: 24 107 Wanda Ct., 36303. Phone: (334) 794-4770. Fax: (334) 794-4770.E-mail: wgtf@bbnradio.org Licensee: Dothan Community Educational Radio Inc. Natl. Network: Bible Bcstg Net, . Format: Relg. ♦Raymond Brown, gen mgr.

WOOF(AM)— Feb 17, 1947: 560 khz; 5 kw-D, 117 w-N. TL: N31 13 05 W85 21 10. Stereo. Hrs open: Box 1427, 36302. Secondary address: 2518 Columbia Hwy. 36303. Phone: (334) 792-1149. Fax: (334) 677-4612.E-mail: woof@ala.net Licensee: WOOF Inc. Format: Sports, talk. Spec prog: Black gospel 17 hrs wkly. ♦Leigh Simpson, traf mgr.

WOOF-FM— Sept 18, 1964: 99.7 mhz; 100 kw. 1,021 ft TL: N31 15 07 W85 17 12. Stereo. Hrs open: Box 1427, 36302. Secondary address: 2518 Columbia Hwy. 36303. Phone: (334) 792-1149. Fax: (334) 677-4612.E-mail: info@997wooffm.com Web Site:www.997wooffm.com Licensee: WOOF Inc. Population served: 440,000 Natl. Rep: Christal,. Shaw Pittman. Format: Adult contemp. News staff: 2; News: 3 hrs wkly. Target aud: 25-54; women 18-49 dominant. ♦Leigh Simpson, gen mgr, opns mgr, progmg dir, news dir; Hal Edwards, gen sls mgr; John Daniel, news dir; Laura Pate, disc jockey.

***WRWA(FM)**— December 1985: 88.7 mhz; 50 kw. 500 ft TL: N31 12 30 W85 36 51. Stereo. Hrs open: 6 AM-midnight
Rebroadcasts WTSU(FM) Troy 100%.
Wallace Hall, Troy Univ., Troy, 36082. Phone: (334) 670-3268. Fax: (334) 670-3934.E-mail: wtsu@troy.edu Web Site:wtsu.troy.edu Licensee: Troy State University. Natl. Network: NPR, PRI, . Format: Class, news. News: 25 hrs wkly. Target aud: General. Spec prog: Children one hr wkly. ♦James Clower, gen mgr; Judy Davis, opns mgr; Fred Azbell, progmg dir.

WTVY-FM— Sept 20, 1968: 95.5 mhz; 100 kw. Ant 1,078 ft TL: N31 15 16 W85 15 39. Stereo. Hrs open: 24 Box 889, 36302-2088. Secondary address: 285 N. Foster, 8th Fl. 36303. Phone: (334) 792-0047. Fax: (334) 712-9346.E-mail: sue@stylesmedia.com Web Site:www.955wtvy.com Licensee: Magic Broadcasting Alabama Licensing LLC. (group owner; (acq 7-27-2001). Population served: 417,000 Natl. Rep: Christal,. Kenkel & Associates. Format: Country. News: 5 hrs wkly. Target aud: 25-54. Spec prog: Farm 5 hrs, gospel 4 hrs, religion 3 hrs wkly. ♦Jeff Storey, CEO; Greg Kamishlian, gen mgr; Chris Green, gen sls mgr; Amie Pollard, progmg dir, prom; Mike Casey, mus dir.

***WVOB(FM)**— Dec 8, 1988: 91.3 mhz; 2.5 kw. 328 ft TL: N31 10 57 W85 24 21. Hrs open: 24 Box 1944, 36302. Secondary address: 2573 Hodgesville Rd. 36301. Phone: (334) 671-9862. Fax: (334) 793-4344.E-mail: wvob913fm@bethanybc.edu Web Site:www.bethanyradionetwork.com Licensee: Bethany Divinity College & Seminary Inc. Natl. Network: USA, . Format: Southern gospel music & educ. News staff: one; News: 6 hrs wkly. Target aud: General; college students & relg community. ♦Dr. Steve Shuemake, gen mgr.

WWNT(AM)— Apr 30, 1947: 1450 khz; 1 kw-U. TL: N31 13 10 W85 22 14. Hrs open: 1733 Columbia Hwy., 36303. Phone: (334) 671-0075. Fax: (334) 671-0091. Web Site:www.wwnt1450.com Licensee: WWNT LLC (acq 6-10-83; $115,000;7-4-83). Population served: 36,733 Natl. Network: USA, . Format: Talk/news. News staff: 2. Target aud: 25-54 men; 25-54 males. ♦Larry Williams, gen mgr.

Elba

WELB(AM)— Nov 16, 1958: 1350 khz; 1 kw-D. TL: N31 27 10 W86 04 00. Hrs open: 11 20334 Hwy 87, 36323. Phone: (334) 897-2216. Phone: (334) 897-2217. Fax: (334) 897-3694.E-mail: welbam1350@yahoo.com Licensee: Elba Radio Co. (acq 3-4-76). Population served: 4,634 Format: Classic country. News: 6 hrs wkly. Target aud: General. Spec prog: Gospel 12 hrs wkly. ♦Doug Holderfield, gen mgr; Mike Holderfield, progmg dir; Eddie Phillips, news dir.

WVVL(FM)— Oct 1, 1986: 101.1 mhz; 640 w. 682 ft TL: N31 24 41 W85 57 32. Stereo. Hrs open: 19 100 N. Main St., Enterprise, 36330. Phone: (334) 347-5621. Fax: (334) 347-5631. Format: Country. ♦Doug Holderfielf, gen mgr.

Enterprise

WDJR(FM)— July 1, 1968: 96.9 mhz; 100 kw. 1,515 ft TL: N30 55 11 W85 44 30. Stereo. Hrs open: 3245 Montgomery Hwy Suite 1, Dothan, 36303. Phone: (334) 712-9233. Fax: (334) 712-0374.E-mail: ron@wdjr.com Web Site:www.wdjr.com Licensee: Gulf South Communications Inc. (acq 7-9-92; $700,000; 7-27-92). Natl. Rep: McGavren Guild,. Format: Country. ♦Ron Eubanks, gen mgr; Misty Huff, opns mgr, prom dir; Bill Moody, gen sls mgr; Brett Mason, progmg dir; April Granger, traf mgr.

WKMX(FM)— Nov 27, 1974: 106.7 mhz; 100 kw. Ant 1,068 ft TL: N31 24 41 W85 57 32. Stereo. Hrs open: 24 285 N. Foster St., 8th Fl., Dothan, 36303. Phone: (334) 792-0047. Fax: (334) 712-9346.E-mail: info@wkmx.com Web Site:www.wkmx.com Licensee: Magic Broadcasting Alabama Licensing LLC. (group owner; (acq 9-3-2004; $4.5 million). Population served: 281,400 Format: CHR. News: 2 hrs wkly. Target aud: Females; 18-49. ♦Dan Bradley, gen mgr; Doc Thompson, opns dir; Richard Reomjardt, opns mgr; Chris Green, gen sls mgr; Amie Pollard, natl sls mgr; John Houston, prom dir, progmg dir.

Equality

***WBNB(FM)**—Not on air, target date: unknown: 91.3 mhz; 700 w. Ant 210 ft TL: N32 49 06 W86 03 25. Hrs open: 221 Elm Dr., Montgomery, 36117. Phone: (334) 430-4296. Licensee: Equality Broadcasting Network. ♦Benny Newton, pres & gen mgr.

Eufaula

WKZJ(FM)— 1969: 92.7 mhz; 39 kw. Ant 551 ft TL: N32 07 58 W85 04 13. Stereo. Hrs open: 2203 Wynnton Rd., Columbus, GA, 31906. Phone: (706) 576-3565. Fax: (706) 576-3683.E-mail: riversales@kenology.net Web Site:www.theriverrocks.com Licensee: Davis Broadcasting Inc. (group owner; (acq 7-20-2004; $2.7 million). Population served: 11,000 Leventhal, Senter & Lerman. Format: Adult contemp, CHR. News staff: 2; News: 6 hrs wkly. ♦Gregory A. Davis, pres; Janet Armstead, gen mgr; Bernie Corcoran, opns mgr; Angela Verdejo, gen sls mgr; Carl Conner, progmg VP.

WRVX(FM)— Mar 16, 1992: 97.9 mhz; 6 kw. Ant 328 ft TL: N31 56 04 W85 12 27. Stereo. Hrs open: 24 Box 1419, 36072-1419. Secondary address: 1347 S. Eufaula Ave. 36027. Phone: (334) 616-0097. Fax: (334) 687-3600.E-mail: lake98fm@gmail.com Licensee: River Valley Media L.L.C. (acq 2-28-98; $200,000). Format: Var. Target aud: 24 plus. ♦Clyde Earnest, gen mgr; John Crumpton, progmg dir; Pam Sharp, sls; Terry Harper, engr.

WULA(AM)— 1948: 1240 khz; 1 kw-U. TL: N31 54 30 W85 09 51. Hrs open: Box 1419, 36027-0531. Phone: (334) 616-0097. Fax: (334) 687-3600.E-mail: lake98fm@gmail.com Licensee: River Valley Media LLC (acq 5-21-2004; $95,000). Population served: 20,000 Format: Sports, Talk, News. Target aud: 25-54; adults. Spec prog: Farm 2 hrs, Black 3 hrs wkly. ♦John Burns, pres.

Eutaw

WQZZ(FM)— August 1990: 104.3 mhz; 2.3 kw. 370 ft TL: N32 54 16 W87 50 09. Hrs open: 24 Box 70427, Tuscaloosa, 35407. Secondary address: 601 Greensboro Ave., Suite 507, Tuscaloosa 35401. Phone: (205) 345-4787. Fax: (205) 345-4790.E-mail: jwlawson@bellsouth.net Licensee: Jim Lawson Communications Inc. (acq 3-27-93). Format: Rhythm & blues, urban. ♦Jim Lawson, gen mgr.

Eva

WRJL-FM— 1996: 99.9 mhz; 25 kw. Ant 318 ft TL: N34 18 43 W86 43 54. Hrs open: 24 5610 Hwy. 55 E., 35621. Phone: (256) 796-8000. Fax: (256) 796-8515. Licensee: Rojo Inc. Format: Southern gospel. ♦Jo French, gen mgr; Amy Holland, progmg dir.

Evergreen

WPGG(AM)— July 1, 1957: 1470 khz; 1 kw-D. TL: N31 26 29 W86 56 08. Hrs open: 24 Box 705, 36401. Secondary address: Hwy. 31 S 36401. Phone: (251) 578-2780. Fax: (251) 578-5399.E-mail: powerpig@bellsouth.net Licensee: Star Broadcasting Inc. (acq 4-13-2004; $2.75 million with co-located FM). Population served: 20,000 Putbrese, Hunsaker & Trent P. Format: Country. News staff: 3; News: 20 hrs wkly. Target aud: 34-64. ♦Luther Upton, gen mgr.

Fairfield

WJLD(AM)—Licensed to Fairfield. See Birmingham

Fairhope

WABF(AM)— Aug 12, 1961: 1220 khz; 1 kw-D, 64 w-N, DA-D. TL: N30 30 38 W87 54 13. Hrs open: 24 Box 1220, 36533. Secondary address: 460 S. Section St. 36533. Phone: (251) 928-2384. Fax: (251) 928-9229.E-mail: wabf1220@bellsouth.net Web Site:wabf1220.net Licensee: Gulf Coast Broadcasting Co. Inc. (acq 5-24-99). Population served: 15500 Natl. Network: CBS Radio, . Putbrese, Hunsaker & Trent P. Format: Adult Standards. News: 15 hrs wkly. Target aud: 45 plus; upscale. Spec prog: Farm one hr, Swap Shop 6 hrs, relg 6 hrs wkly. ♦R. Hagan, pres; Lori Dubose, gen mgr; Don Brown, gen sls mgr; Randy Frawley, progmg dir.

WXQW(AM)—Licensed to Fairhope. See Mobile

WZEW(FM)— Aug 28, 1966: 92.1 mhz; 20.5 kw. Ant 363 ft TL: N30 31 23 W88 06 32. Stereo. Hrs open: 24 1100 Dauphin St., Suite E, Mobile, 36604. Phone: (251) 433-9236. Phone: (251) 438-5460. Fax: (251) 438-5462.E-mail: wzewfm@wzewfm.com Web Site:www.92zew.net Licensee: Baldwin Broadcasting Co. (acq 10-1-98; $1.425 million). Population served: 954,300 Format: Adult alternative, blues. News staff: one; News: 6 hrs wkly. Target aud: 25-44. Spec prog: Jazz 6 hrs wkly. ♦Ken Johnson, gen mgr; Gene Murrell, progmg dir.

Fayette

WLDX(AM)— Sept 3, 1949: 990 khz; 1 kw-D, 42 w-N. TL: N33 41 06 W87 49 16. Hrs open: Box 189, 733 Columbus St. E., 35555. Phone: (205) 932-3318. Fax: (205) 932-3318.E-mail: wldx@wldx.com Web Site:www.wldx.com Licensee: Dean Broadcasting Inc. (acq 6-1-2005; $450,000). Population served: 30,000 Fletcher, Heald & Hildreth. Format: Country. Target aud: 25-55; middle-income adults. ♦J. Wiley Dean, pres; Jill Dean, VP, gen mgr; Joe Redker, progmg dir.

WTXT(FM)— Jan 29, 1977: 98.1 mhz; 100 kw. 984 ft TL: N33 34 31 W87 59 27. (CP: TL: N33 31 17 W87 51 38). Stereo. Hrs open: 24 3900 11th Ave. S., Tuscalossa, 35401. Phone: (205) 344-4589. Phone: (205) 349-3200. Fax: (205) 366-9774.E-mail: ddhamric@clearchannel.com Web Site:www.98txt.com Licensee: Clear Channel Communications Group owner: Clear Channel Communications Inc. (acq 8-30-00; grpsl). Population served: 350,000 Natl. Network: ABC, . Natl. Rep: Christal,. Wire Svc: Direct Line Weather Wire Format: Contemp country. News staff: one. Target aud: 25-54. ♦Ray Quinn, gen mgr.

Five Points

***WJBE(FM)**—Not on air, target date: unknown: 88.5 mhz; 500 w vert. Ant 200 ft TL: N33 57 51 W87 12 34. Hrs open: Box 1065, Jasper, 35502. Phone: (205) 295-2055. Licensee: Big South Community Broadcasting Inc. ♦Brett Elmore, pres.

Florala

WKWL(AM)— Nov 3, 1979: 1230 khz; 1 kw-U. TL: N31 00 20 W86 19 53. Hrs open: 6 AM-6 PM Box 159, 36442-0159. Secondary address: 427 S Sixth St 36442. Phone: (334) 858-6162. Fax: (334) 858-6162.E-mail: wkwl@alaweb.com Licensee: Florala Broadcasting Co. Inc. Population served: 100,000 Natl. Network: USA, . Format: Southern gospel, Christian country. News staff: one; News: 15 hrs wkly. Target aud: 5 plus; general. Spec prog: Farm one hr, relg 12 hrs wkly. ♦Robert Williamson, pres & gen mgr.

Florence

WBCF(AM)— 1946: 1240 khz; 1 kw-U. TL: N34 47 02 W87 42 16. Stereo. Hrs open: 24 Box 1316, 35631. Secondary address: 525 E. Tennessee St. 35630. Phone: (256) 764-8170.E-mail: sales@wbcf.com Web Site:www.wbcf.com Licensee: BCB Inc. (acq 8-11-77). Population served: 284,000 Natl. Network: Westwood One, Fox News Radio, CBS Radio, ABC, Talk Radio Network, . Format: News/Talk. News staff: 2; News: 165 hrs wkly. Target aud: 25-64; adult, mature, affluent, educated, family, business. Spec prog: 24 hrs, local news 10 times daily. ♦Benji Carle, pres, pres, news dir; Edward Carter, chief of engrg; Pat Costa, CFO & traf mgr. Co-owned TV: WBCF-LP, WXFL-LP

***WFIX(FM)**— Mar 20, 1988: 91.3 mhz; 30 kw. 600 ft TL: N34 40 24 W87 42 56. Stereo. Hrs open: 5 AM-11 PM 113 N. Seminary St., 35630. Phone: (256) 764-9964. Fax: (256) 764-9154.E-mail: wfix@wfix.net Licensee: Tri-State Inspirational Broadcasting Inc. (acq 10-20-98; $100,000 for stock). Natl. Network: USA, . Format: Adult contemp, Christian. News: 2 hrs wkly. Target aud: 25-54; upscale family oriented women & men. Spec prog: Sports, jazz, gospel 6 hrs wkly. ♦Mark Allen, gen mgr & opns mgr.

WQLT-FM— May 29, 1967: 107.3 mhz; 100 kw. 1,000 ft TL: N34 40 24 W87 42 56. Stereo. Hrs open: 24 Box 932, 35631. Secondary address: 624 Sam Phillips Street 35630. Phone: (256) 764-8121. Fax: (256) 764-8169. Web Site:www.wqlt.com Licensee: Big River Broadcasting Corp. (group owner) Population served: 670,000 Format: Adult contemp. Target aud: 25-54. ♦Nick Martin, gen mgr; Jeff Thomas, opns mgr; Rocky Reich, sls dir; Sharon Brook, gen sls mgr; Jimmy Oliver, prom mgr; Greg Pace, chief of engrg; Leisa Johnson, traf mgr.

WSBM(AM)— Mar 29, 1946: 1340 khz; 1 kw-U. TL: N34 47 50 W87 39 54. Stereo. Hrs open: 24 Prog sep from FM P.O. Box 932, 35631. Secondary address: 624 Sam Phillips Street 35630. Phone: (256) 764-8121. Fax: (256) 764-8169. Web Site:www.1340theref.com Licensee: Big River Broadcasting Corp. (Acq 2-21-73). Population served: 140,000 Natl. Network: Fox Sports, . Format: Sports. ♦Nick Martin, gen mgr; Jeff Thomas, opns mgr; Rocky Reich, sls dir; Sharon Brook, gen sls mgr; Greg Pace, engrg dir; Leisa Johnson, chief of engrg, traf mgr.

WXFL(FM)— February 1992: 96.1 mhz; 20.5 kw. Ant 781 ft TL: N34 54 17 W87 24 02. Stereo. Hrs open: 24 P.O. Box 932, 35631. Secondary address: 624 Phillips Street 35630. Phone: (256) 764-8121. Fax: (256) 764-8169. Web Site:www.kix96country.com Licensee: Big River Broadcasting Corp. (group owner) Population served: 670,000 Format: Country. Target aud: 18-49; general. ♦Knox Phillips, pres; Jerry Phillips, VP; Nick Martin, gen mgr; Jeff Thomas, opns mgr; Rocky Reich, sls dir; Sharon Brook, gen sls mgr; Fletch Brown, progmg dir; Greg Pace, engrg dir; Leisa Johnson, traf mgr.

Foley

WHEP(AM)— May 31, 1953: 1310 khz; 2.5 kw-D, 43 w-N. TL: N30 26 38 W87 40 52. Hrs open: 24 Box 1747, 36536. Secondary address: 20109 Hadley Rd. 36535. Phone: (251) 943-7131. Fax: (251) 943-7031.E-mail: whepsports@yahoo.com Web Site:www.whep1310.com Licensee: Stewart Broadcasting Co. Inc. (acq 5-1-61). Population served: 328,622 Natl. Network: CNN Radio, Talk Radio Network, Westwood One, . Alabama Radio Net. Format: MOR, news/talk, sports. News staff: 2. Target aud: 25 plus. Spec prog: Farm 2 hrs wkly. ♦Clark J. Stewart, pres & gen mgr.

Fort Mitchell

WBFA(FM)— 1988: 98.3 mhz; 6 kw. Ant 328 ft TL: N32 21 48 W85 03 06. Hrs open: 1501 13th Ave., Columbus, 31901. Phone: (706) 576-3000. Fax: (706) 576-3010.E-mail: rasheedaali@clearchannel.com Web Site:1013thebeat.com Licensee: CC Licenses LLC. Group owner: Clear Channel Communications Inc. (acq 2-21-2002; grpsl). Population served: 273,000 Format: Urban mainstream. Spec prog: Relg 6 hrs wkly. ♦James R. Martin, gen mgr; Brian Waters, opns mgr.

Fort Payne

WFPA(AM)— December 1949: 1400 khz; 1 kw-U. TL: N34 26 21 W85 42 09. Stereo. Hrs open: 24 1210 Johnson St. E., 35967. Phone: (256) 845-7721. Fax: (256) 845-6828. Web Site:www.1400wfpa.net Licensee: J.A.R. Services LLC (acq 5-10-2006; $95,000). Population served: 50,000 Natl. Network: CBS Radio, Premiere Radio Networks, Westwood One, . Format: Adult contemp. News staff: one; News: 15 hrs wkly. Target aud: 25-49; women. ♦Joseph Allen Rivera, gen mgr.

WZOB(AM)— July 2, 1950: 1250 khz; 5 kw-U. TL: N34 26 23 W85 45 12. Hrs open: 24 hrs Box 680748, 35968. Secondary address: Hwy. 35 W., Radio Dr. 35968. Phone: (256) 845-2810. Fax: (256) 845-7521.E-mail:

wzobam@windjammer.net Licensee: Central Broadcasting Co. Inc. (acq 8-12-03). Population served: 50,000 Rgnl rep: Dora-Clayton. Wire Svc: NOAA Weather Format: C&W. News staff: one. Spec prog: Farm 2 hrs, gospel 5 hrs, relg 5 hrs wkly. ◆Mike Kirby, pres; Doris Hobbs, stn mgr.

Fruithurst

WCKS(FM)— May 9, 1994: 102.7 mhz; 1.6 kw. 630 ft TL: N33 37 24 W85 20 14. Hrs open: 102 Parkwood Cir., Carrollton, GA, 30117. Phone: (770) 834-5477. Fax: (770) 830-1027.E-mail: info@wcks.com Web Site:www.wcks.com Licensee: WCKS LLC. Format: Adult contemp. Target aud: 25-44. ◆Steve L. Gradick, pres & gen mgr.

Gadsden

WAAX(AM)— Oct 18, 1947: 570 khz; 5 kw-D, 500 w-N. DA-N. TL: N33 58 45 W86 05 15. Hrs open:
Rebroadcasts WERC(AM) Birmingham 80%.
304 S. 4th St., 35902. Phone: (256) 543-9229. Fax: (256) 543-8777.E-mail: gadsdenthoduction@clearcasts.com Web Site:www.waax570.com Licensee: Capstar TX L.P. Group owner: Clear Channel Communications Inc. (acq 8-30-2000; grpsl). Population served: 83,000 Format: News/talk. Target aud: 25-54. ◆Kathy Boggs, gen mgr; Pam Denham, stn mgr; Rick Sisk, progmg dir; Carl Samperi, chief of engrg.

WGAD(AM)—(Rainbow City, 1926: 930 khz; 5 kw-D, 500 w-N, DA-2. TL: N33 59 09 W86 02 15. Hrs open: 17 Box 1350, 35902. Secondary address: 750 Walnut St, Gadsen 35901. Phone: (256) 546-1611. Fax: (256) 547-9062.E-mail: dhedrick@wgad.com Web Site:www.wgad.com Licensee: Coosa River Communications Inc. (acq 2-2-2007; $175,000). Population served: 200,000+ Format: Oldies. News: 16 hrs wkly. Target aud: 25 plus; general. ◆Dave Hedrick, gen mgr; Ron Downey, news dir.

WGMZ(FM)—(Glencoe, Oct 11, 1993: 93.1 mhz; 6 kw. 620 ft TL: N33 57 16 W85 51 40. Stereo. Hrs open: 24 Box 517, 35902. Secondary address: 304 S. 4th St. 35901. Phone: (256) 549-0931. Fax: (256) 543-8777.E-mail: gadsdenthoduction@clearchannel.com   Web Site:www.wgmz.com Licensee: Capstar TX L.P. Group owner: Clear Channel Communications Inc. (acq 8-30-00; grpsl). Population served: 350,000 Format: Classic hits of the 60s, 70s & 80s. News staff: one. Target aud: 35 plus. ◆Mark Mayes, pres; Kathy Boggs, gen mgr, gen sls mgr; Rick Sisk, progmg dir.

WJBY(AM)— May 26, 1947: 1350 khz; 5 kw-D, 1 kw-N, DA-N. TL: N34 01 03 W86 05 15. Hrs open: 24 Box 1350, 35902. Secondary address: 750 Walnut St. 35901. Phone: (256) 546-1611. Fax: (256) 547-9062.E-mail: dhedrick@wgad.com Licensee: The DR Group LLC (acq 11-15-2004; $250,000). Population served: 100,000 Natl. Network: Fox Sports, . Format: Sports. ◆Dave Hedrick, gen mgr.

WKXX(FM)—(Attalla, Aug 31, 1991: 102.9 mhz; 1.1 kw. 702 ft TL: N33 58 28 W86 12 24. Stereo. Hrs open: 24 100 Spurlock St., Rainbow City, 35906. Secondary address: Box 8405 35902. Phone: (256) 442-3944. Fax: (256) 442-7287.E-mail: tommylee@wasc.com Web Site:www.wkxx.com Licensee: Broadcast Media L.L.C. (acq 1-16-98; $650,000). Population served: 300,910 Wire Svc: AP Format: Hot adult contemp. News staff: one; News: 2 hrs wkly. Target aud: 18-49. ◆Pat Courington Jr., CEO; Tommy Lee, gen mgr; Ted McReless, gen sls mgr; Brandon Murray, progmg dir; Dave Fitz, news dir.

WMGJ(AM)— Sept 11, 1985: 1240 khz; 1 kw-U. TL: N34 00 04 W86 01 48. Hrs open: 815 Tuscaloosa Ave., 35901. Phone: (256) 546-4434. Fax: (256) 546-9645.E-mail: floydddonald@aol.com Web Site:www.wmgj.com Licensee: Floyd L. Donald Broadcasting Co. Inc. Natl. Rep: Roslin,. Format: Black, urban contemp. ◆Floyd L. Donald, gen mgr.

***WSGN(FM)—** Feb 11, 1975: 91.5 mhz; 6.3 kw. 520 ft TL: N34 04 29 W86 01 11. Stereo. Hrs open: 24
Rebroadcasts WBHM(FM) Birmingham 80%.
Gadsden State Community College, 1001 George Wallace Dr., 35902. Phone: (256) 549-8439.E-mail: nmullin@gadsdenstate.edu Web Site:www.gadsdenstate.edu Licensee: Gadsden State Community College. Population served: 250,000 Gardner, Carton & Douglas. Format: Class, news. News: 34 hrs wkly. Target aud: General. Spec prog: Folk 2 hrs, new age 10 hrs wkly. ◆Dr. Renee Culverhouse, pres; Neil D. Mullin, gen mgr.

***WTBB(FM)—** July 20, 1999: 89.9 mhz; 4.8 kw. Ant 515 ft TL: N34 06 03 W85 59 37. Stereo. Hrs open: 24
Rebroadcasts WTBJ(FM) Oxford 100%.
Trinity Christian Academy, 1500 Airport Rd., Oxford, 36203. Phone: (256) 831-3333. Fax: (256) 831-5895.E-mail: truth@trinityoxford.org Web Site:www.trinityoxford.org Licensee: Trinity Christian Academy.

Population served: 500,000 Fletcher, Heald & Hildreth. Format: Christian, relg. Spec prog: Sp one hr wkly. ◆Dr. C.O. Grinstead, gen mgr.

Gardendale

WNCB(FM)— 1998: 97.3 mhz; 6.2 kw. Ant 1,325 ft TL: N33 29 04 W86 48 25. Hrs open: 24 301 Beacon Pkwy. W., Suite 200, Birmingham, 35209. Phone: (205) 916-1100. Fax: (205) 916-1151. Web Site:www.newcountry973.com Licensee: Cox Radio Inc. Group owner: Cox Broadcasting (acq 6-8-99). Natl. Network: ABC, . Natl. Rep: Katz Radio,. Dow, Lohnes and Albertson. Format: New country. News staff: one; News: at 2 hrs wkly. ◆Ray Nelson, gen mgr; Justin Case, progmg dir.

Geneva

WGEA(AM)— Mar 17, 1953: 1150 khz; 1 kw-D, 35 w-N. TL: N31 01 21 W85 52 16. Hrs open: Box 339, 36340. Secondary address: 420 Riverside Ave., 36340. Phone: (334) 684-7079. Fax: (334) 684-0329. Licensee: Shelley Broadcasting Co. (acq 10-26-87). Population served: 23,647 Format: Country, gospel, news/talk. Target aud: 30 plus. ◆Jack Mizell, pres; Doc Parker, gen mgr.

WUSD(FM)— Sept 12, 1969: 93.7 mhz; 100 kw. Ant 853 ft TL: N31 02 42 W85 57 33. Hrs open: 24 285 E. Broad St., Ozark, 36360. Phone: (334) 774-7673. Fax: (334) 774-6450.E-mail: hjmizell@wrjm.com Web Site:www.wrjm.com Licensee: Stage Door Development, William C. Carn, Trustee (acq 2-6-2008). Population served: 790,000 Natl. Network: ABC, Westwood One, . Natl. Rep: Rgnl Reps,. Latham & Watkins LLP. Format: Country. Target aud: 30 plus. ◆Jack Mizell, pres, gen mgr; Susannah Hodges, stn mgr, opns mgr & gen sls mgr; Boyd Mizell, engrg mgr, engr.

Georgiana

WFXX(FM)— 1999: 107.7 mhz; 42 kw. 535 ft TL: N31 27 08 W86 37 07. Hrs open: 24 1406 River Falls St., Andalusia, 36420. Phone: (334) 222-2222. Fax: (334) 427-8888.E-mail: wfxx@alaweb.com Web Site:fox107.com Licensee: Star Broadcasting Inc. (acq 3-29-2004; $975,000). Population served: 464,000 Format: Adult Contemp. ◆Jeffrey K. Haynes, pres; Kelly Haynes, gen mgr.

Glencoe

WGMZ(FM)—Licensed to Glencoe. See Gadsden

Goodwater

WKGA(FM)— Apr 4, 1990: 97.5 mhz; 5.1 kw. Ant 354 ft TL: N33 01 42 W85 59 23. Stereo. Hrs open: 24 Box 998, Alexander City, 35011. Secondary address: 1051 Tallapoosa St., Alexander City 35011. Phone: (256) 234-6977. Fax: (256) 234-6976. Web Site:info@wkgacountry.com Licensee: Lake Broadcasting Inc. (group owner; (acq 11-21-2007; $385,000). Population served: 250,000 Format: Country. ◆John Kennedy, pres.

***WTXN(FM)—**Not on air, target date: unknown: 91.1 mhz; 700 w. Ant 220 ft TL: N33 07 01 W86 07 01. Hrs open: 908 Opelika Rd., Auburn, 36830. Phone: (334) 821-0744. Fax: (334) 821-4031.E-mail: jimmy@jimmyscarstereo.com Licensee: Jimmy Jarrell Communications Foundation Inc. ◆Jimmy Jarrell, pres & gen mgr.

Greensboro

WDGM(FM)— 03/03/2002: 99.1 mhz; 25 kw. Ant 328 ft TL: N32 49 46 W87 40 19. Hrs open: 24 142 Skyland Blvd., Tuscaloosa, 35405. Phone: (205) 345-7200. Fax: (205) 349-1715. Licensee: Citadel Broadcasting Co. (acq 7-12-2005; grpsl). Natl. Network: ABC, Jones Radio Networks, . Natl. Rep: Roslin,. Gardner, Carton & Douglas. Format: Oldies. Target aud: 25 plus; male & female. ◆Greg Thomas, progmg mgr.

Greenville

WGYV(AM)— Aug 18, 1948: 1380 khz; 1 kw-D. TL: N31 50 01 W85 52 16. Hrs open: Box 585, 1604 E. Commerce St., 36037. Phone: (334) 382-5444. Fax: (334) 382-5444.E-mail: wgyv@alaweb.com Web Site:www.wgyv.com Licensee: Robert John Williamson (acq 11-29-02).

Population served: 8,033 Format: News/talk, oldies. Target aud: 25-54; general. Spec prog: Black 6 hrs wkly. ◆Robert Williamson, gen mgr; Bob Luman, chief of engrg.

WKXN(FM)— July 18, 1977: 95.9 mhz; 4 kw. 225 ft TL: N31 50 43 W86 38 56. (CP: 2.1 kw, ant 564 ft. TL: N31 56 52 W86 42 09). Hrs open: 24
Simulcasts WKXK(FM) Pine Hill 100%.
Box 369, 36037. Secondary address: 563 Manningham Rd. 36037. Phone: (334) 382-6555. Fax: (334) 382-7770.E-mail: wkxn@wkxn.com Web Site:www.wkxn.com Licensee: Autaugaville Radio Inc. (acq 11-22-94; $287,500; 1-2-95). Population served: 10,000 Format: Urban contemp, blues. ◆Roscoe Miller, gen mgr & stn mgr.

WQZX(FM)— Aug 19, 1985: 94.3 mhz; 3.9 kw. 410 ft TL: N31 54 40 W86 36 19. Stereo. Hrs open: 24 205 W. Commerce, 36037. Phone: (334) 382-6633. Fax: (334) 382-6634.E-mail: q94@q94.net Web Site:www.q94.net Licensee: Haynes Broadcasting Inc. Natl. Network: ABC, . Format: Modern country. ◆Kyle Haynes, pres, gen mgr; Mark Ritchie, progmg dir; Chris Johnson, chief of engrg.

Grove Hill

WBMH(FM)— May 1999: 106.1 mhz; 12 kw. 472 ft TL: N31 43 30 W87 54 58. Hrs open: Box 518, c/o The Radio Center, Jackson, 36545. Secondary address: 4428 N College Ave, Jackson 36545. Phone: (251) 246-4431. Fax: (251) 246-1980.E-mail: bama1061@yahoo.com Licensee: Capital Assets Inc. Group owner: Bennie E. Hewett Stns. Format: Classic country. ◆Benney Hewitt, gen mgr; Paul McVay, opns mgr & progmg dir.

Gulf Shores

WCSN-FM—(Orange Beach, July 2, 1996: 105.7 mhz; 5 kw. 246 ft TL: N30 17 45 W87 33 42. Stereo. Hrs open: 24 Box 1919, 36547. Secondary address: 2421 E. Second St. 36542. Phone: (251) 967-1057. Fax: (251) 967-1050.E-mail: sunny105@gulftel.com Web Site:www.sunny105.com Licensee: Gulf Coast Broadcasting Co. Inc. (acq 10-31-97). Population served: 60,000 Putbrese, Hunsaker & Trent. Format: Adult contemp. Target aud: 25-54; upscale. ◆R. Lee Hagan, pres; Bryant Ellis, gen sls mgr, pub affrs dir; Katie Tyler, prom dir; Ron Wainscott, progmg dir.

Guntersville

WGSV(AM)— Apr 16, 1950: 1270 khz; 1 kw-D. TL: N34 18 31 W86 17 44. Hrs open: Box 220, 35976. Secondary address: 2301 Thomas Ave. Phone: (256) 582-8131. Fax: (256) 582-4347.E-mail: am1270@cwgsv.com Web Site:www.wgsv.com Licensee: Guntersville Broadcasting Co. Inc. Population served: 75,000 Natl. Network: ABC, . Format: News/talk. ◆Lavell Jackson, pres; Kerry Jackson, VP, gen mgr, opns mgr.

***WJIA(FM)—** September 1995: 88.5 mhz; 2.2 kw. 426 ft TL: N34 25 33 W86 18 25. Hrs open: 5025 Spring Creek Dr., 35976. Phone: (256) 505-0885. Fax: (256) 505-0886.E-mail: jfm@wjia.org Web Site:www.wjia.org Licensee: Lake City Educational Broadcasting Inc. Format: Christian. ◆Stan Broadus, gen mgr; Kevin Guffey, stn mgr, progmg dir.

WTWX-FM— Aug 1, 1969: 95.9 mhz; 10.7 kw. 596 ft TL: N34 20 14 W86 16 46. Hrs open: 24 Box 220, 35976. Secondary address: 2301 Thomas Ave. Phone: (256) 582-4946. Fax: (256) 582-4347. Web Site:www.wtwx.com Licensee: Guntersville Broadcasting Co., Inc. Population served: 85,000 Natl. Network: ABC, . Format: C&W. ◆Lavell Jackson, pres.

Gurley

WHRP(FM)— June 8, 1995: 94.1 mhz; 710 w. Ant 945 ft TL: N34 40 50 W86 30 55. Stereo. Hrs open: 24 1717 U.S. Hwy. 72 E., Athens, 35611. Phone: (256) 830-8300. Fax: (256) 232-6842. Web Site:www.whrpfm.com Licensee: Cumulus Licensing LLC. Group owner: Clear Channel Communications Inc. (acq 4-4-2006; $3.3 million with WVNN-FM Trinity). Population served: 800,000 Natl. Rep: Katz Radio,. Format: Urban adult. News: 4 hrs per wk. ◆Bill G. West, gen mgr; Tracy Flesch, gen sls mgr; Aaron Hurd, prom dir; Audrey Raines, traf mgr; Chuck Miller, engr.

Hackleburg

WFMH-FM— 1996: 95.5 mhz; 4.1 kw. Ant 400 ft TL: N34 18 38 W87 56 13. Stereo. Hrs open: 24 16800 Hwy. 129, Brilliant, 35548. Phone: (205) 935-3730. Fax: (205) 935-3734. Licensee: Williams Communications.

Group owner: Williams Communications Inc. (acq 8-18-2004; $2.45 million with WFMH(AM) Cullman). Population served: 65,000 Wire Svc: AP Format: Country. News: 15 hrs wkly. Target aud: 35-64. ♦Bryan Walker, gen mgr & progmg dir.

Haleyville

WJBB(AM)— Apr 1, 1949: 1230 khz; 1 kw-U. TL: N34 14 00 W87 37 32. Hrs open: 24 Drawer 370, 807 Hwy. 13 N., 35565. Phone: (205) 486-2277. Phone: (205) 486-2278. Fax: (205) 486-3905.E-mail: advertising@wjbbfm.com Licensee: Haleyville Broadcasting Co. Inc. (acq 1951). Population served: 87,000 Natl. Rep: Rgnl Reps,. Fletcher, Heald & Hildreth, P.L.C. Format: Southern gospel, loc news. News staff: one; News: 36 hrs wkly. Target aud: 25-55; professionals. Spec prog: Farm 3 hrs wkly.John L. Slatton, pres, edit dir; Terry L. Slatton, gen mgr & opns VP; Debby Aderholt, dev dir, prom dir; Aubrey Haynes, sls VP, adv mgr, sports cmtr, disc jockey; Robert Wakefield, progmg dir, disc jockey; Larry Gardner, mus dir, pub affrs dir, disc jockey; Sherron Hayes, news dir, local news ed; Chester Barber, chief of engrg; Calabe Mayhall, disc jockey

WJBB-FM— July 14, 1979: 92.7 mhz; 3.9 kw. Ant 240 ft TL: N34 14 00 W87 37 32. (CP: Ant 328 ft.). Stereo. Hrs open: Drawer 370, 35565. Secondary address: 807 Hwy. 13 N. 35565. Phone: (205) 486-2277. Phone: (205) 486-2278. Fax: (205) 486-3905.E-mail: wjbb@southnet.net Licensee: Haleyville Broadcasting Co. Inc. Population served: 118,000 Format: Country. Target aud: 24-55. ♦John Slatton, CEO, chmn, edit mgr; Terry Slatton, exec VP; Andy Marbutt, opns mgr, farm dir, disc jockey; Aubrey Haynes, sls dir, disc jockey; Sherron Hayes, local news ed; Keith Page, disc jockey.

Hamilton

WERH(AM)— Aug 24, 1950: 970 khz; 5 kw-D. TL: N34 07 01 W87 59 29. Hrs open: Box 1119, 35570. Phone: (205) 921-3195. Fax: (205) 921-7187.E-mail: werh@sonet.net Licensee: Kate F. Fite. (acq 4-1-58). Population served: 100,000 Format: Country, gospel. Target aud: General. Spec prog: Farm. ♦James B. Fowler, gen mgr; Geraldine Miller, adv mgr; Bryan Williams, mus dir; Bill Moates, chief of engrg.

WERH-FM— Apr 1, 1968: 92.1 mhz; 3 kw. 120 ft TL: N34 07 01 W87 59 29. Stereo. Hrs open: 24 Prog sep from AM 1597 Military St. S., 35570. Phone: (205) 921-3481. Fax: (205) 921-7187. Population served: 50,000 Format: Classic Rock. ♦Mark Burleson, news dir; Geraldine Miller, traf mgr.

Hanceville

WQHC(AM)— April 1986: 1170 khz; 460 w-D. TL: N34 04 28 W86 46 44. Hrs open: Sunrise-sunset 513 19th St. W., Jasper, 35501. Phone: (256) 352-1115. Fax: (205) 295-1238. Licensee: Queen of Heaven Catholic Radio Inc. (acq 2-27-2009; $18,000). Format: Southern gospel. ♦Ralph Jolly, gen mgr.

Hartselle

WTAK-FM— August 1992: 106.1 mhz; 5.4 kw. 725 ft TL: N34 27 54 W86 38 36. Hrs open: 24 Box 21008, Huntsville, 25824. Secondary address: 26869 Peoples Rd., Madison 35756. Phone: (256) 353-1750. Fax: (256) 350-2653.E-mail: info@wtak.com Web Site:www.wtak.com Licensee: Clear Channel Communications Group owner: Clear Channel Communications Inc. (acq 8-30-00; grpsl). Population served: 800,000 Format: Classic rock. ♦Rick Brown, gen mgr; Erich West, opns mgr, progmg dir; Carmelilta Palmer, gen sls mgr; Carl Ampieri, chief of engrg; Stephanie McGee, traf mgr.

WYAM(AM)— Oct 1, 1956: 890 khz; 2.5 kw-D. TL: N34 34 00 W86 54 46. Stereo. Hrs open: 12 1301 Central Pkwy. S.W., Decatur, 35601. Phone: (256) 355-4567. Fax: (256) 351-1234.E-mail: wileywg@acninc.net Licensee: Decatur Communications Properties LLC (acq 8-12-2003). Population served: 800,000 Format: Rgnl Mexican. News staff: 2; News: 6 hrs wkly. Target aud: 18-60; General. ♦William Wiley, pres & gen mgr.

Harvest

***WAYH(FM)**— 2003: 88.1 mhz; 3.5 kw. Ant 669 ft TL: N34 49 08 W86 44 19. Hrs open: 24 9582 Madison Blvd., Suite 8, Madison, 35758. Phone: (256) 837-9293. Fax: (256) 772-6731.E-mail: contact@wayfm.com Web Site:www.wayfm.com Licensee: WAY-FM Media Group Inc. (group owner). Population served: 390,800 Format: Contemp Christian. Target aud: 18-34; youth & young adults. ♦Lloyd Parker, COO; Bob Augsburg, pres; Thom Ewing, gen mgr; Jack Davis, opns dir; Tina Dimarco, prom dir.

Hazel Green

WBXR(AM)— Dec 11, 1970: 1140 khz; 15 kw-D, DA. TL: N34 57 18 W86 38 32. Hrs open: Sunrise-sunset 2926-D Huntsville Hwy., Fayetteville, TN, 37334. Phone: (931) 433-7017. Phone: (888) 570-7286. Fax: (931) 433-8282.E-mail: wbxr@wilkinsradio.com Web Site:wilkinsradio.com Licensee: New England Communications Inc. (acq 9-16-97; $150,000). Population served: 1,000,000 Natl. Network: Salem Radio Network, . Womble, Carlyle, Sandridge & Rice. Format: Christian teaching/talk. Target aud: 35 plus. ♦Robert L. Wilkins, pres; Mitchell Mathis, VP; Carla Payne, gen mgr, stn mgr; Greg Garrett, opns mgr; Kevin Kidd, chief of opns, engr; Don Roden, engr.

Headland

WDBT(FM)— September 1992: 105.3 mhz; 11.5 kw. Ant 485 ft TL: N31 15 48 W85 18 24. Stereo. Hrs open: 24 3245 Montgomery Hwy., Suite 1, Dothan, 36303. Phone: (334) 712-9233. Fax: (334) 712-0374.E-mail: ron@wdjr.com Web Site:www.legends1053.com Licensee: Gulf South Communications Inc. (acq 1-27-97; $745,000). Natl. Rep: McGavren Guild,. Format: News/talk. News staff: 7. ♦Ron Eubanks, gen mgr; Misty Huff, opns mgr, prom dir, progmg dir; April Granger, traf mgr; Bill Moody, sls.

Heflin

***WKNG-FM**— May 2005: 89.1 mhz; 250 w. Ant 718 ft TL: N33 33 18 W85 27 25. Hrs open: 102 Parkwood Cir., Carrollton, GA, 30117. Phone: (770) 834-5477. Fax: (770) 830-1027.E-mail: steve1027@aol.com Licensee: Covenant Communications Inc. Format: Southern gospel. ♦Steven Gradick, pres.

***WPIL(FM)**— 2003: 91.7 mhz; 1 kw. Ant 75 ft TL: N33 36 55 W85 32 41. Hrs open: 256 Brockford Rd., 36264. Phone: (256) 463-4226. Fax: (256) 463-4232.E-mail: wpil@wpilfm.com Web Site:www.wpilfm.com Licensee: Jimmy Jarrell Communications Foundation Inc. (acq 12-31-2002). Format: Country/bluegrass/gospel. ♦Jimmy Jarrell, pres & gen mgr.

Hobson City

WHMA-FM— Oct 4, 1984: 95.5 mhz; 530 w. Ant 1,089 ft TL: N33 37 38 W85 53 25. Stereo. Hrs open: 24 801 Noble St., Suite 30, Anniston, 36201. Phone: (256) 236-1880. Fax: (256) 236-4480. Licensee: Williams Communications Inc. (group owner; (acq 8-2-2002; $2.88 million with WZZX(AM) Lineville). Format: Country. Target aud: 18-54. Spec prog: Black 6 hrs wkly. ♦Walt Williams Jr., pres & gen mgr; Tex Carter, progmg dir.

WHOG(AM)— Apr 15, 1991: 1120 khz; 500 w-D. TL: N33 36 50 W85 51 19. Hrs open: Sunrise-sunset 1330 Noble St., Suite 25, Anniston, 36201. Phone: (256) 236-6484. Fax: (256) 236-6484.E-mail: hog1120@aol.com Licensee: Hobson City Broadcasting Co. Population served: 200,000 Natl. Rep: Dora-Clayton,. Format: Urban contemp. Target aud: General.

Holly Pond

WRSA-FM— Nov 23, 1965: 96.9 mhz; 100 kw. Ant 1,010 ft TL: N34 29 23 W86 37 38. Stereo. Hrs open: 24 8402 Memorial Pkwy SW, Huntsville, 35802. Phone: (256) 885-9797. Fax: (256) 885-9796. Web Site:www.lite969.com Licensee: NCA Inc. (acq 3-18-2002). Population served: 500,000 Natl. Rep: Eastman Radio,. Wire Svc: AP Format: Adult contemp. News staff: one; News: one hr wkly. Target aud: 35 plus. ♦Penny Nielson, CEO, pres; Tom Panucci, gen mgr & gen sls mgr; John Malone, progmg dir; Nate Adams, mus dir; Don Rhoden, chief of engrg.

Homewood

WBPT(FM)—Licensed to Homewood. See Birmingham

Hoover

WERC-FM— September 1993: 105.5 mhz; 29.5 kw. Ant 623 ft TL: N33 29 04 W86 48 25. Hrs open: 24 600 Beacon Pkwy. W., Suite 400, Birmingham, 35209. Phone: (205) 439-9600. Fax: (205) 439-8390. Web Site:www.talkradio1055.com Licensee: Capstar TX L.P. Group owner: Clear Channel Communications Inc. (acq 8-30-2000; grpsl). Format: News/talk. News staff: one. ♦Jimmy Vineyard, gen mgr; Jimbo Wood, progmg dir.

Huntsville

WAHR(FM)— July 28, 1959: 99.1 mhz; 100 kw. 984 ft TL: N34 47 53 W86 38 24. Stereo. Hrs open: 1555 The Boardwalk, Suite 1, 35816. Phone: (256) 536-1568. Fax: (256) 536-4416.E-mail: info@star99.fm Web Site:www.star99.fm Licensee: BCA Radio LLC. Group owner: Black Crow Media Group LLC (acq 11-15-2001; grpsl). Population served: 407,200 Format: Hot Adult contemp. Target aud: 25-55. ♦Davis Hawkins, gen mgr; Eric Jewell, gen sls mgr; Don Phelps, news dir; Brianna Bragdon, traf mgr; Chris Calloway, progmg.

WBHP(AM)— May 23, 1937: 1230 khz; 1 kw-U. TL: N34 43 09 W86 35 42. Hrs open: Box 21008, 35824. Secondary address: 266869 Peoples Rd., Madison 35758. Phone: (256) 309-2400. Fax: (256) 350-2653.E-mail: rbrown@wbhp.com Web Site:www.wbhpam.com Licensee: Capstar TX L.P. Group owner: Clear Channel Communications Inc. (acq 8-30-00; grpsl). Population served: 139,282 Format: Talk. Target aud: General. ♦Rick Brown, gen mgr; Stuart Langston, progmg dir.

WDJL(AM)— Oct 1, 1968: 1000 khz; 10 kw-D, DA. TL: N34 46 47 W86 39 16. Hrs open: Sunrise-sunset 2025 Sparkman Dr., Suite 3, 35810. Phone: (256) 852-1223. Fax: (256) 852-1900.E-mail: info@wjdl.com Licensee: James K. Sharp dba 5th Avenue Broadcasting. (acq 8-95; $300,000). Population served: 450,000 Natl. Network: Westwood One, . Jack Pennington & Associates. Format: Gospel. Target aud: 35-65; upscale decision makers that enjoy hits of the 40s, 50s & 60s. Spec prog: Gospel comedy 6 hrs wkly. ♦Walter Peavy, pres & gen mgr; Marvin Pease, progmg dir.

WEUP(AM)— 2001: 1700 khz; 10 kw-D, 1 kw-N. TL: N34 45 32 W86 38 35. Hrs open: 2609 Jordan Ln. N.W., 35816. Phone: (256) 837-9387. Fax: (256) 837-9404.E-mail: hundley@103weup.com Web Site:www.weupam.com Licensee: Hundley Batts Sr. & Virginia Caples. Format: Gospel. ♦Hundley Batts, gen mgr; Steve Murry, progmg dir.

WHIY(AM)— Mar 20, 1958: 1600 khz; 5 kw-D, 500 w-N, DA-D. TL: N34 45 32 W86 38 35. Hrs open: 2609 Jordan Ln. N.W., 35816. Phone: (256) 837-9387. Fax: (256) 837-9404.E-mail: hundley@103weup.com Web Site:www.whiyam.com Licensee: Hundley Batts Sr. & Virginia Caples. Population served: 325,500 Format: Blues. Target aud: 25-65. ♦Hundley Batts Sr., pres; Hundley Batts, gen mgr; Steve Murry, progmg dir.

***WJAB(FM)**— May 9, 1991: 90.9 mhz; 100 kw. 334 ft TL: N34 47 09 W86 34 00. Stereo. Hrs open: 24 Alabama A&M University, Telecommunications Center, Box1687, Normal, 35762. Secondary address: 3409 Meridian St. 35811. Phone: (256) 372-5795. Phone: (256) 372-5861 (request line). Fax: (256) 372-5907. Web Site:www.aamu.edu/wjab Licensee: Board of Trustees Alabama A&M University. Population served: 600,000 Natl. Network: NPR, PRI, . Wire Svc: AP Format: Jazz, blues. News staff: one. Spec prog: Black 3 hrs, oldies 8 hrs, reggae 4 hrs, Latin one hr, gospel 14 hrs wkly, gospel jazz one hr wkly. ♦Elizabeth Sloan-Ragland, gen mgr; Michael Burns, opns mgr; Erica Fox, news dir, pub affrs dir.

***WJOU(FM)**— Dec 1978: 90.1 mhz; 25 kw. 230 ft TL: N34 45 28 W86 39 44. Stereo. Hrs open: 24 Oakwood College, 4920 University, Suite J, 35896. Phone: (256) 722-9990. Fax: (256) 726-7417.E-mail: wocg@wocg.org Web Site:www.wocg.org Licensee: Oakwood College. Population served: 300,000 Natl. Network: USA, . Donald E. Martin. Format: Inspirational, Christian, lite urban gospel. News: 14 hrs wkly. Target aud: 34-55; families with interest in relg & educ progmg. ♦Delbert Baker, pres; Victoria L. Miller, gen mgr & opns mgr; Dameon Malone, progmg dir.

WLOR(AM)— June 1948: 1550 khz; 50 kw-D, 500 w-N, DA-2. TL: N34 44 36 W86 35 39. Hrs open: 24 1555 The Boardwalk, Suite 1, 35816. Phone: (256) 536-1568. Fax: (256) 536-4416.E-mail: ed@star99.fm Licensee: BCA Radio LLC. Group owner: Black Crow Media Group LLC (acq 11-15-2001; grpsl). Natl. Network: ABC, . Format: Oldies. News staff: one; News: one hr wkly. Target aud: General. ♦Davis Hawkins, gen mgr; Ed Gaines, progmg dir.

***WLRH(FM)**— Oct 13, 1976: 89.3 mhz; 100 kw. 810 ft TL: N34 37 41 W86 30 59. Stereo. Hrs open: 24 UAH Campus, John Wright Dr., 35899. Phone: (256) 895-9574. Fax: (256) 830-4577.E-mail: wlrhnews@highway.net Web Site:www.wlrh.org Licensee: Alabama ETV Commission. (acq 12-14-77). Population served: 600,000 Natl. Network: PRI, NPR, . Format: Class, news, variety. News staff: one; News: 40 hrs wkly. Target aud: General. ♦Cheryl Carlson, gen mgr, stn mgr; Jennifer Jaudon-Johnston, dev dir; Oliver Stultner, progmg dir.

WRSA-FM—See Holly Pond

WRTT-FM— Oct 6, 1960: 95.1 mhz; 50 kw. 110 ft TL: N34 42 56 W86 35 55. Stereo. Hrs open: 24 1555 The Boardwalk, Suite 1, 35816. Phone: (256) 536-1568. Fax: (256) 536-4416.E-mail: info@rocket951.fm

Web Site:www.rocket951.fm Licensee: BCA Radio LLC. Group owner: Black Crow Media Group LLC (acq 11-15-2001; grpsl). Population served: 300500 Format: Active Rock. News staff: one. Target aud: 24-54; male. Spec prog: Relg. ◆Davis Hawkins, gen mgr; Clay Sanders, progmg dir.

WTKI(AM)— November 1946: Stn currently dark. 1450 khz; 1 kw-U. TL: N34 43 30 W86 36 15. Hrs open: 24 2305 Holmes Ave., 35805. Phone: (256) 533-1450. Fax: (256) 551-9865.E-mail: dbaughman@1049theriver.com Web Site:www.protalkradio.com Licensee: Christian Voice of Central Ohio Inc. (acq 3-9-2007; $460,000). Population served: 250,000 ◆Dan Baughman, pres & gen mgr.

WUMP(AM)—See Madison

WZYP(FM)—See Athens

Irondale

WQOH(AM)— Dec 5, 1960: 1480 khz; 5 kw-D. TL: N33 32 54 W86 39 56. Hrs open: 24 40 Park Rd., Suite B, Pleasant Grove, 35127. Phone: (205) 744-4456. Web Site:www.queenofheavenradio.com Licensee: Queen of Heaven Catholic Radio Inc. (acq 6-12-2008; $575,000). Population served: 1,200,000 Natl. Network: EWTN Radio, . Format: Catholic. ◆Marc Corsini, pres.

Jackson

WHOD(FM)— Aug 1, 1964: 94.5 mhz; 30 kw. 640 ft TL: N31 28 59 W87 42 27. Hrs open: 5 AM-midnight Dups AM 99% Box 518 Hwy. 43 N., 36545. Secondary address: 4428 College Ave. 36545. Phone: (251) 246-4431. Phone: (251) 246-5581. Fax: (251) 246-1980. Population served: 100,000 Natl. Network: ABC, . Format: Hot adult contemp. News staff: one; News: 2 hrs wkly.

WRJX(AM)— June 1, 1950: 1230 khz; 1 kw-U. TL: N31 32 38 W87 52 30. (CP: 1190 khz, 10 kw-D, 300 w-N). Hrs open: 5 AM-midnight Box 518, Hwy. 43 N., 36545. Secondary address: 4428 College Ave. 36545. Phone: (251) 246-4431. Phone: (251) 246-5581. Fax: (251) 246-1980.E-mail: radiocenter@starband.com Licensee: Capital Assets Inc. Group owner: Bennie E. Hewett Stations Population served: 6,500 Format: Black gospel. News staff: one. Target aud: 25-54; business minded, baby-boomers. ◆Shirley Chandler, sls VP; Paul McVay, progmg dir; Kelly Snell, traf mgr.

Jacksonville

WCKA(AM)— January 1986: 810 khz; 50 kw-D, 500 w-N, DA-2. TL: N33 50 58 W85 45 46. Hrs open: 24 Box 8, Anniston, 36202. Secondary address: 188 Broadcast Blvd. 36265. Phone: (256) 237-0810. Fax: (256) 782-2489.E-mail: alabama810@alabama810.com Web Site:www.alabama810.com Licensee: Alabama 810 LLC (acq 12-22-2005; $207,940). Population served: 3,234,000 Natl. Network: USA, . Alabama Radio Net. Nall, Estill. Format: Classic Country. News staff: 2; News: 15 hrs wkly. Target aud: 25 plus; adults. Spec prog: Gospel 2 hrs wkly. ◆Leslie E. Gradick, exec VP; Mike Mitchell, gen mgr & news dir.

*WLJS-FM— Sept 29, 1975: 91.9 mhz; 3 kw. 246 ft TL: N33 49 29 W85 45 49. Stereo. Hrs open: 700 Pelham Rd N, 36265. Phone: (256) 782-5300. Phone: (256) 782-5572. Fax: (256) 782-5645.E-mail: info@jsu.edu/92j Web Site:www.jsu.edu/92j Licensee: Board of Trustees-Jacksonville State University. Population served: 90,000 Natl. Network: NPR, . Gardner, Carton & Douglas. Format: Var/div, class. Target aud: 18-34; college, young adult. Spec prog: Relg 3 hrs wkly. ◆Mike Stedham, gen mgr; John Nickolson, progmg dir.

Jasper

WDXB(FM)— Mar 28, 1962: 102.5 mhz; 79 kw. 2,096 ft TL: N33 28 51 W87 24 03. Stereo. Hrs open: 600 Beacon Pkwy. W., Suite 400, Birmingham, 35209. Phone: (205) 439-9600. Fax: (205) 439-8390. Web Site:www.1025thebull.com Licensee: Capstar TX L.P. Group owner: Clear Channel Communications Inc. (acq 8-30-00; grpsl). Population served: 400000 Format: Hit country. ◆Jimmy Vineyard, gen mgr; John Friend, sls dir; Todd Berry, progmg dir; Jim Faherty, news dir; Bob Newberry, chief of engrg; Cynthia Childress, traf mgr.

WIXI(AM)— Nov 2, 1946: 1360 khz; 1 kw-D, 42 w-N. TL: N33 49 12 W87 16 26. Stereo. Hrs open: 14 Box 622, 409 9th Ave., 35501. Phone: (205) 384-1461. Fax: (205) 384-3462.E-mail: wixi@1360wixi.com Licensee: James T. Lee (acq 9-1-99). Population served: 16,000 Fletcher, Heald & Hildreth. Format: Christian, Southern gospel. News:

4 hrs wkly. Target aud: General. Spec prog: Gospel 6 hrs wkly. ◆Joe Cook, gen mgr; Joe Cooke, gen mgr & progmg dir.

WJLX(AM)— Mar 1, 1957: 1240 khz; 1 kw-U. TL: N33 48 54 W87 16 19. Hrs open: 24 Box 1065, 35502. Phone: (205) 221-2222. Licensee: Wal Win LLC (acq 4-11-2008; $300,000). Population served: 70,000 Format: Southern gospel. ◆Brett Elmore, gen mgr.

Jemison

WHPH(FM)— May 15, 1953: 97.7 mhz; 3.1 kw. Ant 459 ft TL: N32 58 12 W86 43 04. Hrs open: 24 6930 Cahaba Valley Rd., Suite 202, Birmingham, 35242. Phone: (205) 755-0980.E-mail: wklf@tridigitalbb.com Web Site:www.peach97.com Licensee: Great South Wireless LLC. (group owner; (acq 2-12-2007;. grpsl). Format: Oldies. ◆Steven Salter, gen mgr.

*WZLM(FM)—Not on air, target date: unknown: 89.3 mhz; 500 w. Ant 187 ft TL: N33 00 25 W86 44 03. Hrs open: 908 Opelika Rd., Auburn, 36830. Phone: (334) 821-0744. Fax: (334) 821-4031. Licensee: Jimmy Jarrell Communications Foundation Inc. ◆Jimmy Jarrell, pres & gen mgr.

Level Plains

WIRB(AM)—Not on air, target date: unknown: 1490 khz; 430 w-U. TL: N31 17 51 W85 47 33. Hrs open: 422 County Rd. 551, New Brockton, 36351. Phone: (334) 894-5047. Fax: (334) 894-6684. Licensee: Virgle Leon Strictland, individually. ◆Virgle Leon Strictland, gen mgr.

Lexington

WJHX(AM)— Feb 20, 1981: 620 khz; 5 kw-D, 99 w-N. TL: N34 58 37 W87 22 10. Hrs open: 1426 5th Ave. S.E., Decatur, 35601. Phone: (256) 353-5959. Licensee: BAR Broadcasting Inc. (acq 12-30-2005). Rgnl. Network: Alabama Net. Format: Sp. ◆Pedro Zamora, pres; Moises Gomez, gen mgr.

Lincoln

*WJAU(FM)—Not on air, target date: unknown: 89.5 mhz; 2.2 kw vert. Ant 259 ft TL: N33 34 51 W86 08 37. Hrs open: 2101 Executive Park Dr., Suite 103, Opelika, 36801. Phone: (706) 965-2355. Licensee: Wilbur Gospel Communications and Foundation. ◆Grey Wilson, VP.

Linden

WINL(FM)— April 1991: 98.5 mhz; 100 kw. 817 ft TL: N32 07 34 W87 44 02. Stereo. Hrs open: 24 Box 938, Demopolis, 36732. Phone: (334) 289-9850. Fax: (334) 289-9811.E-mail: valerie@mywin98.com Web Site:www.bestcountryaround.com Licensee: West Alabama Communications Inc. (acq 2-12-2001; $1.28 million). Population served: 225,000 Natl. Network: ABC, . Natl. Rep: Dora-Clayton,. Format: Country. Target aud: 25-54. Spec prog: Gospel 5 hrs, farm 10 hrs wkly. ◆Amy Douglas, gen mgr & opns mgr.

Lineville

WZZX(AM)— 1967: 780 khz; 5 kw-D. TL: N33 17 04 W85 47 24. Hrs open: 801 Noble St., Suite 30, Anniston, 36201. Phone: (256) 236-1880. Fax: (256) 236-4480. Licensee: Williams Communications Inc. (acq 7-25-2002; $2.88 million). Population served: 20,000 Format: Country. ◆Walt Williams Jr., pres; Eva Gibson, gen mgr.

Lisman

WPRN-FM— 1997: 107.7 mhz; 6 kw. Ant 328 ft TL: N32 05 27 W88 13 57. Hrs open: 909 W. Pushmataha St., Butler, 36904. Phone: (205) 459-3222. Fax: (205) 459-4140.E-mail: wprn@tds.net Licensee: Butler Broadcasting Corp. (acq 11-5-99). Format: Country. ◆Daryl Jackson, gen mgr, gen sls mgr, progmg dir; Virginia Hummer, traf mgr.

Littleville

WLAY-FM— Sept 12, 1986: 103.5 mhz; 3.3 kw. Ant 386 ft TL: N34 40 27 W87 42 48. Stereo. Hrs open: 24 273 Azalea Rd., Suite 1-308, Mobile, 36609. Phone: (251) 343-4900. Fax: (251) 343-4905. Web Site:www.mix1035.com Licensee: Urban Radio Licenses LLC. Group owner: Clear Channel Communications Inc. (acq 5-13-2005; grpsl).

Population served: 180,000 Fletcher, Heald & Hildreth. Format: Oldies. News staff: one. Target aud: 18-49. ◆Kevin Wagner, CEO, pres; Todd Mannesses, opns mgr; Laura Crosby, news dir, pub affrs dir; Rob Green, chief of engrg.

Livingston

WSLY(FM)—See York

WYLS(AM)—See York

Luverne

WHLW(FM)— 1997: 104.3 mhz; 13.5 kw. Ant 1,830 ft TL: N31 58 28 W86 09 44. Hrs open: 203 Gunn Rd., Montgomery, 36117. Phone: (334) 274-6464. Fax: (334) 274-6465. Web Site:www1043hallelujahfm.com Licensee: Capstar TX L.P. Group owner: Clear Channel Communications Inc. (acq 8-30-2000; grpsl). Format: Gospel. Target aud: 18-49. ◆James Belton, gen mgr; Michael Long, opns mgr; Nikita Pogue, prom dir; Connye Bryant, progmg dir.

Madison

WUMP(AM)— Mar 29, 1983: 730 khz; 1 kw-D, 123 w-N. TL: N34 41 46 W86 44 19. Hrs open: 24 1717 Hwy. 72 E., Athens, 35611. Phone: (256) 830-8300. Fax: (256) 232-6842. Web Site:www.730ump.com Licensee: Cumulus Licensing LLC. Group owner: Cumulus Media Inc. (acq 7-21-2003; grpsl). Natl. Network: ESPN Radio, . Natl. Rep: Katz Radio,. Format: Sports. Target aud: 18-54; males. Spec prog: Univ. of Alabama Sports. ◆Bill West, gen mgr; Tracy Flesch, gen sls mgr; Aaron Hurd, prom dir; Zack Bennett, gen sls mgr & progmg dir; Audrey Raines, traf mgr.

Marion

WJUS(AM)— Dec 8, 1951: 1310 khz; 5 kw-D. TL: N32 38 04 W87 17 48. Hrs open: WJUS Radio Station, Hwy. 5, 36756. Phone: (334) 683-2043. Phone: (334) 872-8400. Fax: (334) 872-2329. Licensee: Marion Radio Inc. (acq 6-86; $115,000; 6-30-86). Population served: 4,289 Rgnl. Network: Tobacco. Format: Urban contemp. ◆Rev. Glenn King, gen mgr.

WNPT-FM— Dec 19, 1990: 102.9 mhz; 29 kw. Ant 646 ft TL: N32 40 50 W87 24 22. Stereo. Hrs open: 24 Box 2000, Tuscaloosa, 35403. Phone: (205) 758-5523. Fax: (205) 752-9696.E-mail: wtbc@dbtech.net Licensee: John Sisty Enterprises Inc. (acq 11-28-2003; $450,000). Population served: 75,000 Format: Classic country. ◆John Sisty, pres; Ronnie Quarles, gen mgr; Nancy Wilson, gen sls mgr; Jay Bronson, progmg dir.

Midfield

WBHJ(FM)—Licensed to Midfield. See Birmingham

Millbrook

WWMG(FM)— Aug 1, 1993: 97.1 mhz; 3 kw. 328 ft TL: N32 25 58 W86 20 07. Hrs open: 24 203 Gunn Rd., Montgomery, 36117. Phone: (334) 274-6464. Fax: (334) 274-6465. Web Site:www.mymagic97.com Licensee: Capstar TX L.P. Group owner: Clear Channel Communications Inc. (acq 8-30-2000; grpsl). Natl. Network: American Urban, Westwood One, . Format: Adult contemp. Target aud: 25-54. ◆James Belton, gen mgr, stn mgr; Michael Long, opns mgr; Alberta Jackson, rgnl sls mgr; Nikita Pogue, prom dir; Darryl Elliott, progmg dir.

Mobile

WABB(AM)— November 1948: 1480 khz; 5 kw-U, DA-N. TL: N30 43 11 W88 04 16. Hrs open: 24 Prog sep from FM Box 2148, 36652. Secondary address: 1551 Springhill Ave. 36604. Phone: (251) 432-5572. Fax: (251) 438-4044.E-mail: b.dittman@wabb.com Web Site:www.wabb.com Licensee: WABB-FM Inc. Group owner: Dittman Group Inc. Population served: 303,900 Natl. Rep: Christal,. Format: News/talk. Target aud: 18-49.

WABB-FM— Feb 5, 1973: 97.5 mhz; 100 kw. Ant 1,551 ft TL: N30 41 20 W87 49 49. Stereo. Hrs open: 24 Box 2148, 36652-2148. Secondary address: 1551 Springhill Ave. 36604. Phone: (251) 432-5572. Fax: (251) 438-4044.E-mail: b.dittman@wabb.com Web Site:www.wabb.com Licensee: WABB-FM Inc. (acq 8-30-2000; grpsl). Population served:

1,092,100 Natl. Rep: Christal,. Format: Top-40. ♦Bernard Dittman, pres, gen mgr; Laura English, sls dir.

WAVH(FM)—See Daphne

WBHY(AM)— Dec 9, 1943: 840 khz; 10 kw-D. TL: N30 45 50 W88 06 36. Hrs open: Box 1328, 36633-1328. Secondary address: 6530 Spanish Fort Blvd., Suite B, Spanish Fort 36527. Phone: (251) 473-8488. Web Site:www.goforth.org Licensee: Goforth Media Inc. (Acq 4-11-86). Population served: 500,000 Natl. Rep: Salem,. Format: Christian. Target aud: 34-64; Christians. ♦Wilbur Goforth, pres.

***WBHY-FM**— Mar 20, 1992: 88.5 mhz; 33 kw. 624 ft TL: N30 40 55 W87 49 41. Stereo. Hrs open: 24 Box 1328, 36633-1328. Secondary address: 6530 Spanish Fort Blvd., Suite B, Spanish Fort 36527. Phone: (251) 473-8488.E-mail: power88.5@goforth.org Web Site:www.goforth.org Licensee: Goforth Media Inc. (group owner; acq 6-27-90; 7-30-90). Population served: 1,000,000 Fletcher, Heald & Hildreth. Format: Contemp Christian music. News: 7 hrs wkly. Target aud: 18-34. ♦Robert Barber, CEO, opns mgr; Charles Smith, pres, gen sls mgr; Wilbur Goforth, pres & opns mgr; Steve Riggs, chief of engrg; Jean Williams, traf mgr.

WBLX-FM— April 1976: 92.9 mhz; 98 kw. Ant 1,555 ft TL: N30 37 35 W87 38 50. Stereo. Hrs open: Prog sep from AM 2800 Dauphin St., Suite 104, 36606. Web Site:www.thebigstation9361x.com Natl. Network: ABC, . Format: Urban contemp. Target aud: 12 plus; primarily Black women, 18-34.

WDLT-FM—(Chickasaw, 1980: 98.3 mhz; 40 kw. 548 ft TL: N30 35 05 W88 15 57. Stereo. Hrs open: 24 2800 Dauphin St., Suite 104, 36606. Phone: (251) 652-2000. Fax: (251) 652-2007.E-mail: mobile.prog@cumulus.com Web Site:www.smooth98.com Licensee: April Broadcasting Inc. Group owner: Cumulus Media Inc. (acq 10-18-99; grpsl). Format: Adult Contemp. News staff: one; News: 5 hrs wkly. Target aud: 25-54. Spec prog: Jazz 5 hrs, blues 18 hrs, pub affrs 4 hrs wkly. ♦Gary Pizzati, gen mgr; Steve Crumbely, opns mgr & progmg dir.

WGOK(AM)— Nov 21, 1958: 900 khz; 1 kw-D, 381 w-N, DA-2. TL: N30 42 27 W88 03 55. Stereo. Hrs open: 2800 Dauphin St., Suite 104, 36606. Phone: (251) 652-2000. Fax: (251) 652-2001. Web Site:www.cumulus.com Licensee: Cumulus Licensing Corp. Group owner: Cumulus Media Inc. (acq 10-18-99; $6 million with WYOK(FM) Atmore). Population served: 350,000 Natl. Rep: Roslin,. Format: Gospel. Target aud: 18-54; Black adults. ♦Dickie Roberts, pres; Gary Pizzati, gen mgr; Kevin Wagner, stn mgr, gen sls mgr; Danny Wright, prom dir; Steve Crumbely, progmg dir.

***WHIL-FM**— 1979: 91.3 mhz; 100 kw. 1,066 ft TL: N30 41 20 W87 49 49. Stereo. Hrs open: 24 Box 8509, 36689-0509. Secondary address: 4000 Dauphin St. 36608. Phone: (251) 380-4685. Fax: (251) 460-2189.E-mail: whil@whil.org Web Site:www.whil.org Licensee: Spring Hill College. Population served: 782,000 Natl. Network: PRI, NPR, . Dow, Lohnes & Albertson. Format: Classical/npr. News: 40 hrs wkly. Target aud: 35 plus. ♦Mario Mazza, gen mgr; Kurt Garrett, opns dir; Alan Serotta, dev dir; Kris Pierce, progmg dir.

WIJD(AM)—See Prichard

WKSJ-FM— Apr 12, 1971: 94.9 mhz; 100 kw. 410 ft TL: N30 35 36 W87 39 40. (CP: Ant 1,554 ft. TL: N30 37 35 W87 38 50). Stereo. Hrs open: 555 Broadcast Dr., 3rd Fl., 36606. Phone: (251) 450-0100. Fax: (251) 479-3418.E-mail: stevepowers@clearchannel.com Web Site:www.95ksj.com Licensee: CC Licenses LLC. Group owner: Clear Channel Communications Inc. (acq 11-21-97; grpsl). Population served: 313,000 Rgnl rep: David Coppock Format: Contemp country. News staff: 2; News: 25 hrs wkly. Target aud: 25-54; mid level to high class country music listeners. ♦David Coppock, VP, gen mgr; Jeanie Hufford, stn mgr; Bo Clark, gen sls mgr; Bill Black, progmg dir; Mike Sloan, news dir.

WLPR(AM)—(Prichard, Dec 31, 1986: 960 khz; 5 kw-U, DA-N. TL: N30 45 50 W88 06 36. Hrs open: 24 Box 1328, 36633-1328. Phone: (251) 473-8488.E-mail: info@wlpr.com Web Site:www.goforth.org Licensee: Goforth Media Inc. (acq 1994). Natl. Network: Salem Radio Network, . Natl. Rep: Salem,. Fletcher, Heald & Hildreth. Format: Southern gospel. News: 6 hrs wkly. Target aud: 35 plus. ♦Wilbur Goforth, gen mgr; Robert Barber, opns dir, engrg VP; Charlie Smith, gen sls mgr; Kenny Fowler, mus dir; Steve Riggs, chief of engrg; Jean Williams, traf mgr.

WLVV(AM)— Feb 7, 1930: 1410 khz; 5 kw-U, DA-N. TL: N30 40 52 W88 00 02. Hrs open: 24 1263 Battleship Pkwy., Spanish Fort, 36527. Phone: (251) 626-1090. Fax: (251) 626-1099.E-mail: wlvv@bellsouth.net Licensee: WLVV Inc. Group owner: Martin Broadcasting Inc. (acq 4-14-99; $263,750). Natl. Network: American Urban, . Natl. Rep: Katz Radio,. Format: Gospel, MOR. Target aud: 18-44; Black. ♦Tom Alexander, gen mgr, gen sls mgr & progmg dir.

WMOB(AM)— Jan 25, 1961: 1360 khz; 5 kw-D, 212 w-N, DA-2. TL: N30 41 26 W88 01 33. Hrs open: 24 Box 63, 36601. Secondary address: 200 Addsco Rd. Causeway 36601. Phone: (251) 432-1360. Fax: (251) 432-1396. Licensee: Buddy Tucker Association Inc. (acq 4-84; $395,000; 4-9-84). Format: Relg. ♦Theodore Tucker, pres; LeVaughn Tucker, VP; Buddy Tucker, gen mgr; Don Tucker, opns mgr; Art Taylor, news dir; A.J. Crawford, news rptr.

WMXC(FM)— Oct 16, 1947: 99.9 mhz; 100 kw. Ant 1,755 ft TL: N30 41 20 W87 49 49. Stereo. Hrs open: Prog sep from AM Box 161489, 36616. Phone: (251) 450-0100. Fax: (251) 479-3418.E-mail: stevepowers @clearchannel.com Licensee: CC Licenses LLC Population served: 3,180,000 Format: Adult contemp. Target aud: 25-54. ♦Dan Mason, progmg dir.

WNTM(AM)— 1946: 710 khz; 1 kw-D, 500 w-N. TL: N30 43 13 W88 03 34. Hrs open: Box 161489, 36616. Secondary address: 555 Broadcast Dr. 36606. Phone: (251) 450-0100. Fax: (251) 479-3418.E-mail: stevepowers@clearchannel.com Licensee: CC Licenses LLC. Group owner: Clear Channel Communications Inc. (acq 11-21-97; grpsl). Population served: 375,000 Natl. Network: CBS, . Leventhal, Senter & Lerman. Format: News/talk, sports. Target aud: 25 plus. ♦Dave Cappock, pres; Ronnie Bloodworth, gen mgr; Scott O'Brien, progmg dir; Bill King, news dir.

WRKH(FM)— Dec 5, 1964: 96.1 mhz; 100 kw. 1,342 ft TL: N30 41 20 W87 49 49. Stereo. Hrs open: 24 555 Broadcast Dr., 3rd Fl., 36606. Phone: (251) 450-0100. Phone: (251) 770-9600. Fax: (251) 479-3418.E-mail: stevepowers@clearchannel.com Web Site:www.961therocket.com Licensee: CC Licenses LLC. Group owner: Clear Channel Communications Inc. (acq 11-21-97; grpsl). Natl. Rep: D & R Radio,. Format: Classic rock hits. News staff: 2; News: 2 hrs wkly. Target aud: 25-49; front edge baby boomers. ♦David Coppock, VP, gen mgr; Jeanie Hufford, stn mgr; Steve Powers, progmg dir.

WXQW(AM)—(Fairhope, Apr 22, 1965: 660 khz; 10 kw-D, 850 w-N, DA-N. TL: N30 42 27 W88 03 55. Hrs open: 24
Simulcast with WGOK(AM(Mobile 100%.
2800 Dauphin St.,, Suite 104, 36606. Phone: (251) 652-2000. Fax: (251) 652-2007.E-mail: carmen.brown@cumulus.com Web Site:www.gospel900.com Licensee: Cumulus Licensing Corp. Group owner: Cumulus Media Inc. (acq 10-18-99; grpsl). Format: Gospel. Target aud: 18-54; Black adults. ♦Steve Sandman, gen mgr; James Alexander, opns mgr, progmg dir; Vinny Duncan, prom dir.

Monroeville

WEZZ(AM)— Dec 6, 1982: Stn currently dark. 930 khz; 5 kw-D, 48 w-N. TL: N31 29 40 W87 21 29. Hrs open: 415 N. College St., Greenville, 36037. Phone: (205) 618-2020. Licensee: Brantley Broadcast Associates LLC (acq 6-6-2007; $36,500). ♦Wendy Smith, gen mgr.

***WILF(FM)**—Not on air, target date: unknown: 88.9 mhz; 50 kw. Ant 328 ft TL: N31 28 56 W87 15 01. Hrs open: Box 2400, Pace, FL, 32571. Phone: (850) 994-7911. Licensee: WOW Community Broadcasting Inc. ♦Lawrence Steelman, pres.

***WJIK(FM)**—Not on air, target date: unknown: 89.3 mhz; 3 kw. Ant 435 ft TL: N31 53 28 W87 42 45. Hrs open: CSN International, 4002 N. 3300 E., Twin Falls, ID, 83301. Phone: (208) 734-6633. Fax: (208) 736-1958. Web Site:www.csnradio.com Licensee: CSN International. ♦Michael Kestler, pres; Mike Stockland, gen mgr; Don Mills, progmg dir.

WMFC(AM)— April 1952: 1360 khz; 780 w-D. TL: N31 30 51 W87 17 55. Hrs open: Box 645, 36461. Secondary address: 961 Pineville Rd. 36460. Phone: (251) 575-3281. Phone: (251) 575-4061. Fax: (251) 575-3280.E-mail: nmfc@frontiernet.net Licensee: Monroe Broadcasting Co. Inc. Population served: 18,000 Wire Svc: NOAA Weather Format: Black gospel. Target aud: 25-54. ♦Carolyn Stewart, chmn; David Stewart, pres, stn mgr & gen sls mgr; Carol Casey, progmg dir, chief of engrg.

WMFC-FM— December 1965: 99.3 mhz; 30 kw. Ant 308 ft TL: N31 30 51 W87 17 55. Stereo. Hrs open: 5 AM-midnight Prog sep from AM Box 645, 36460. Phone: (251) 575-3281. Fax: (251) 575-3280. Licensee: Monroe Broadcasting Co. Inc. Population served: 38,450 Natl. Network: Jones Radio Networks, . Rgnl. Network: Alabama Net. Alabama Radio Net. Format: Good time oldies. Target aud: General.

Montgomery

WACV(AM)— Jan 16, 1939: 1170 khz; 10 kw-D, 1 kw-N, DA-2. TL: N32 27 16 W86 17 21. Hrs open: 24
Simulcast with WMRK-FM Shorter 100%.
4101 Wall St., 36106. Phone: (334) 244-0961. Fax: (334) 279-9563. Web Site:www.newstalk1079.com Licensee: Bluewater Broadcasting Co. LLC (group owner; (acq 6-21-2004; grpsl). Population served: 250,000 Natl. Network: CBS, . Format: News/talk. Target aud: 25 plus. ♦Terry Barber, gen mgr; Rick Peters, progmg dir.

WBAM-FM— Jan 1, 1961: 98.9 mhz; 100 kw. 1095 ft TL: N32 24 11 W86 11 48. Stereo. Hrs open: 24 4101-A Wall St., 36106. Phone: (334) 244-0961. Fax: (334) 279-9563. Web Site:www.bamacountry989.com Licensee: Bluewater Broadcasting Co. LLC (group owner; acq 4-19-2004). Population served: 133,386 Natl. Rep: Christal,. Format: Country. News staff: one; News: one hr wkly. Target aud: 12-54. ♦Terry Barber, gen mgr; John Norris, progmg dir.

WHHY-FM— Jan 9, 1962: 101.9 mhz; 100 kw. 1,200 ft TL: N32 29 33 W86 08 50. (CP: TL: N32 24 11 W86 11 48). Stereo. Hrs open: One Commerce St., Suite 300, 36104. Phone: (334) 240-9274. Fax: (334) 240-9219. Web Site:www.y102montgomery.com Licensee: Cumulus Licensing Corp. Group owner: Cumulus Media Inc. (acq 3-12-01; grpsl). Population served: 133,386 Natl. Rep: McGavren Guild,. Format: CHR. News: one hr wkly. Target aud: 18-40. ♦Bernie Barker, gen mgr, natl sls mgr; Bill Jones, opns mgr; Bill Hardin, prom dir, prom mgr; Joy Melton, gen sls mgr & news dir; Herb Connellan, chief of engrg; Crystal Palmer Lund, traf mgr.

***WLBF(FM)**— Apr 4, 1984: 89.1 mhz; 100 kw. 537 ft TL: N32 24 13 W86 11 50. Stereo. Hrs open: 24 Box 210789, 36121-0789. Secondary address: 381 Mendel Parkway 36117. Phone: (334) 271-8900. Fax: (334) 260-8962.E-mail: mail@faithradio.org Web Site:www.faithradio.org Licensee: Faith Broadcasting Inc. Population served: 500,000 Natl. Network: Moody, USA, . Southmayd & Miller. Format: Educ, relg, MOR. News: 14 hrs wkly. Target aud: General. ♦Russell Dean, gen mgr; Gary Hundley, dev dir; Donna Spears, traf mgr.

WLWI(AM)— Apr 30, 1930: 1440 khz; 5 kw-D, 1 kw-N, DA-N. TL: N32 18 24 W86 13 40. (CP: TL: N32 24 11 W86 11 48). Hrs open: One Commerce St., Suite 300, 36104. Phone: (334) 240-9274. Fax: (334) 240-9211. Web Site:www.cumulus.com Licensee: Cumulus Licensing Corp. Population served: 133386 Natl. Network: CNN Radio, . Format: News/talk. News staff: one. Target aud: 18 plus. ♦Bernie Barker, mktg mgr; Steve Smith, progmg dir; Gwen Pierce, traf mgr.

WLWI-FM— July 15, 1969: 92.3 mhz; 100 kw. 1,095 ft TL: N32 24 13 W86 11 50. (CP: TL: N32 24 11 W86 11 48). Stereo. Hrs open: Prog sep from AM One Commerce St., Suite 300, 36104. Phone: (334) 240-9274. Fax: (334) 240-9219. Web Site:www.wlwi.com Licensee: Cumulus Licensing Corp. Population served: 225,000 Natl. Network: CNN Radio, . Format: Country. News staff: one. Target aud: 25-54. Spec prog: Gospel 4 hrs wkly. ♦Bernie Barker, gen mgr; Bill Hardin, prom dir; Bill Dollar, progmg dir; Marcus Hyles, news dir; Herb Connellan, chief of engrg; Gwen Pierce, traf mgr; Barry McKnight, sports cmtr; Andi Scott, disc jockey.

WMGY(AM)— June 1, 1946: 800 khz; 1 kw-D, 193 w-N. TL: N32 24 48 W86 17 25. Hrs open: 6 AM-midnight 2305 Upper Wetumpka Rd., 36107-1345. Phone: (334) 834-3710. Fax: (334) 834-3711.E-mail: davewmgy@aol.com Licensee: WMGY Radio Inc. Group owner: GHB Radio Group (acq 7-75). Population served: 200,000 Natl. Network: USA, . Format: Southern gospel. News: 7 hrs wkly. Target aud: 35 plus. Spec prog: Black 15 hrs, sports 6 hrs wkly. ♦Dane Harris, gen mgr.

WMSP(AM)— 1953: 740 khz; 50 kw-D, 73 w-N, DA-2. TL: N32 18 39 W86 17 25. Hrs open: One Commerce St., Suite 300, 36104. Phone: (334) 240-9274. Fax: (334) 240-9219. Web Site:www.sportsradio740.com Licensee: Cumulus Licensing Corp. Group owner: Cumulus Media Inc. (acq 12-12-98; grpsl). Natl. Network: ESPN Radio, . Gardner, Carton & Douglas. Format: Sports. Target aud: Adults 18 plus. ♦Bernie Barker, gen mgr, mktg mgr; Bill Jones, opns mgr; Bill Hardin, prom dir; Bob Wooddy, progmg dir; Herb Connellan, chief of engrg; Barry McKnight, sports cmtr.

WMXS(FM)— July 9, 1961: 103.3 mhz; 100 kw. 1,007 ft TL: N32 24 48 W86 17 25. (CP: TL: N32 24 11 W86 11 48). Stereo. Hrs open: Prog sep from AM One Commerce Street., Suite 300, 36104. Phone: (334) 240-9274. Fax: (334) 240-9219. Web Site:www.mix103.com Licensee: Cumulus Licensing Corp. Natl. Network: CNN Radio, . Format: Adult contemp. Target aud: 25-54. ♦Bernie Barker, gen mgr; Bill Hardin, prom dir; Brian Roberts, progmg dir; Marcus Hyles, news dir; Herb Connellan, chief of engrg; J.T. Thompson, disc jockey.

WNZZ(AM)— May 8, 1953: 950 khz; 1 kw-U, DA-N. TL: N32 26 23 W86 15 49. Hrs open: One Commerce St., Suite 300, 36104. Phone:

(334) 240-9274. Fax: (334) 240-9219. Web Site:www.cumulus.com Licensee: Cumulus Licensing Corp. Group owner: Cumulus Media Inc. (acq 12-12-98; grpsl). Population served: 133,386 Gardner, Carton & Douglas. Format: American standards, news. News staff: one. ◆Bernie Barker, gen mgr, mktg mgr; Bill Jones, opns dir; Bill Hardin, prom dir; Bob Wooddy, progmg dir; Herb Connellan, chief of engrg.

WQKS-FM— Dec 1, 1990: 96.1 mhz; 900 w. Ant 820 ft TL: N32 22 03 W86 15 42. Stereo. Hrs open: 24 4101-A Wall St., 36106. Phone: (334) 244-0961. Fax: (334) 279-9563. Web Site:www.q961fm.com Licensee: Bluewater Broadcasting Co. LLC (group owner; (acq 6-21-2004; grpsl). Natl. Network: ABC, . Format: Oldies. News: one hr wkly. Target aud: 25-54. ◆Terry Barber, gen mgr, gen sls mgr; Rick Peters, progmg dir; Tom Jones, chief of engrg; Mary Brazell, traf mgr.

*WVAS(FM)— June 15, 1984: 90.7 mhz; 80 kw. Ant 347 ft TL: N32 21 58 W86 17 40. Stereo. Hrs open: 24 Alabama State Univ., 915 S. Jackson St., 36101-0271. Phone: (334) 229-4708. Fax: (334) 269-4995. Web Site:www.wvasfm.org Licensee: Alabama State University. (acq 6-83) Natl. Network: NPR, . Wilkes, Artis, Hedrick & Lane. Wire Svc: AP Format: Jazz. News staff: 5; News: 5 hrs wkly. Target aud: General; African-American community. Spec prog: Gospel 5 hrs, blues 9 hrs, news/talk 7 hrs wkly. ◆John S. Knight, gen mgr; Candy Capel, stn mgr.

WXFX(FM)— August 1977: 95.1 mhz; 50 kw. 492 ft TL: N32 28 01 W86 24 15. Stereo. Hrs open: 24 1 Commerce St., Suite 300, 36104. Phone: (334) 240-9274. Fax: (334) 240-9219. Web Site:www.wxfx.com Licensee: Cumulus Licensing Corp. Group owner: Cumulus Media Inc. (acq 3-12-01; grpsl). Population served: 280,000 Natl. Network: CNN Radio, Motor Racing Net, . Natl. Rep: Katz Radio,. Alabama Radio Net. Format: Classic rock. News staff: one. Target aud: 25-54; upscale adults, two paycheck households. ◆Bernie Barker, gen mgr; Bill Jones, opns mgr; Donna Headley, gen sls mgr; Rick Hendricks, progmg dir; Larry Wilkins, chief of engrg.

WXVI(AM)— May 1947: 1600 khz; 5 kw-D, 1 kw-N, DA-2. TL: N32 23 40 W86 17 21. Hrs open: 24 912 South Perry St., 36104. Phone: (334) 263-4141. Fax: (334) 263-9191. Licensee: New Life Ministries Inc. (acq 9-8-2005). Natl. Network: American Urban, . Natl. Rep: Roslin,. Format: Christian. Target aud: 35 plus; urban. ◆Terry Ellison, CEO; Glenda Perkins, progmg dir.

Montgomery-Troy

*WTSU(FM)— Mar 1, 1977: 89.9 mhz; 100 kw. Ant 754 ft TL: N32 03 40 W86 01 19. Stereo. Hrs open: 24
Rebroadcasts WTJB(FM) Columbus 100%.
Wallace Hall, Troy State Univ., Troy, 36082. Phone: (334) 670-3268. Fax: (334) 670-3934.E-mail: wtsu@troyst.edu Web Site:www.troyst.edu Licensee: Troy State University. Population served: 500,000 Natl. Network: NPR, PRI, . Format: News. Classical. News: 25 hrs wkly. Target aud: General. Spec prog: Children one hr wkly. ◆James Clower, gen mgr; Judy Davis, opns mgr; Fred Azbell, progmg dir, progmg mgr.

Moody

WURL(AM)— October 1984: 760 khz; 1 kw-D. TL: N33 35 13 W86 28 18. Hrs open: 2999 Radio Park Dr., 35004. Phone: (205) 699-9875. Fax: (205) 640-4379.E-mail: wurlradio@aol.com Web Site:www.wurlradio.com Licensee: Bill Davison Evangelistic Assn. (acq 9-89; $175,000; 10-2-89). Natl. Network: USA, . Format: Gospel. Target aud: General. ◆William J. Davison Sr., pres, gen mgr & gen sls mgr.

Moulton

WEUP-FM— Sept 1, 1991: 103.1 mhz; 6 kw. 328 ft TL: N34 32 07 W87 13 31. Stereo. Hrs open: 20 2609 Jordon Ln. N.W., Huntsville, 35816. Phone: (256) 837-9387. Fax: (256) 890-1600.E-mail: info@103weup.com Web:103weup.com Licensee: Hundley Batts Sr. and Virginia Caples (acq 6-7-99; $775,000 with co-located AM). Population served: 30000 Natl. Network: USA, . Natl. Rep: Rgnl Reps,. Wire Svc: NOAA Weather Format: Urban, Hip-Hop. News staff: one. Target aud: 21-55. Spec prog: Relg one hr wkly. ◆Huntley Batts Sr., gen mgr; Huntley Batts, gen sls mgr; Big Ant, progmg dir.

WEUV(AM)— Dec 11, 1963: 1190 khz; 2.5 kw-D. TL: N34 28 55 W87 18 04. Hrs open: Dups FM 75% Box 37, 13471 Court St., 35650. Phone: (256) 974-0681. Phone: (256) 897-0682. Licensee: Hundley Batts Sr. and Virginia Caples Format: Soul gospel. Target aud: General. ◆Steve Murry, progmg dir.

Muscle Shoals

WBCF(AM)—See Florence

WLAY(AM)— Jan 15, 1933: 1450 khz; 1 kw-U. TL: N34 45 23 W87 41 08. Stereo. Hrs open: 509 N. Main St., Tuscumbia, 35674. Phone: (256) 383-2525. Fax: (256) 389-1912.E-mail: donnajohnson @clearchannel.com Web Site:www.wlayfm.com Licensee: Urban Radio Licenses LLC. Group owner: Clear Channel Communications Inc. (acq 5-13-2005; grpsl). Population served: 135,000 M. Scott Johnson. Format: Sports. Target aud: 18-54. ◆Brian Rickman, opns mgr; Cheryl Self, gen sls mgr.

*WQPR(FM)— November 1987: 88.7 mhz; 20 kw. Ant 430 ft TL: N34 34 41 W87 47 02. (CP: Ant 429 ft). Stereo. Hrs open: 24
Rebroadcasts WUAL-FM Tuscaloosa 95%.
Phifer Annex, Suite 166, Tuscaloosa, 35487. Phone: (205) 348-6644. Fax: (205) 348-6648.E-mail: apr@apr.org Web Site:www.apr.org Licensee: Board of Trustees University of Alabama. Population served: 80,000 Natl. Network: PRI, NPR, . Arter & Hadden. Format: Class, jazz, news & info. News staff: one; News: 5 hrs wkly. Spec prog: Bluegrass, blues, folk 5 hrs, new age 19 hrs wkly. ◆Elizabeth Brock, stn mgr.

WSBM(AM)—See Florence

WVNA-FM— Oct 28, 1964: 105.5 mhz; 1.05 w. 741 ft TL: N34 40 24 W87 42 56. Stereo. Hrs open: Dups AM 95% 509 N. Main St., Tusumbia, 35674. Phone: (256) 383-2525. Fax: (256) 389- 1912. Format: Classic rock.

WXFL(FM)—See Florence

New Hope

WHWT(FM)— 2007: 103.5 mhz; 290 w. Ant 1,473 ft TL: N34 38 11 W86 30 42. Hrs open: 1359 Carmichael Way, Montgomery, 36106. Phone: (334) 356-9776. Licensee: Stroh Communications Corp. ◆Allan G. Stroh, pres.

New Market

WWFF-FM— July 1, 1962: 93.3 mhz; 14.5 kw. Ant 913 ft TL: N34 47 37 W86 37 51. Stereo. Hrs open: 24 1717 Hwy. 72 E., Athens, 35611. Phone: (256) 830-8300. Fax: (256) 232-6842. Web Site:www.wolf933.com Licensee: Cumulus Licensing LLC. Group owner: Cumulus Media Inc. (acq 7-21-2003; grpsl). Population served: 600,000 Natl. Rep: Katz Radio,. Format: Country. News staff: 3. Target aud: Adult; 25-54. ◆Bill West, gen mgr; Aaron Hurd, gen sls mgr, prom dir; Buzz Stphens, progmg dir; Chuck Miller, chief of engrg; Audrey Raines, traf mgr, women's int ed.

Northport

*WSJL(FM)— 2008: 88.1 mhz; 10 w horiz 15 kw vert. Ant 492 ft TL: N33 28 51 W87 24 03. Hrs open: 1115 Honeysuckle Dr., Keene, TX, 76059. Phone: (817) 641-3495. Licensee: Mary V. Harris Foundation. ◆Linda De Romanett, pres & gen mgr.

WTUG-FM—Licensed to Northport. See Tuscaloosa

WWMM(FM)— July 15, 1991: 100.5 mhz; 85 kw. Ant 912 ft TL: N33 05 42 W87 15 16. (CP: COL Helena. 93 kw, ant 1,014 ft). Hrs open: 24 244 Goodwin Crest Dr., Suite 300, Birmingham, 35209. Phone: (205) 945-4646. Fax: (205) 945-3999. Web Site:www.live1005online.com Licensee: Citadel Broadcasting Co. (group owner; (acq 7-12-2005; grpsl). Format: AAA. ◆Dale Daniels, gen mgr; Lenny Frisaro, gen sls mgr; Jennifer Dickson, prom dir; Ryan Haney, progmg dir.

Oneonta

WCRL(AM)— July 29, 1952: 1570 khz; 2.5 kw-D. TL: N33 57 16 W87 28 20. Hrs open: Box 490, 35121. Secondary address: 908 2nd Ave. E. 35121. Phone: (205) 625-3333. Fax: (205) 625-5433.E-mail: wkld@wkld.com Web Site:www.wkld.com Licensee: Blount County Broadcasting Service Inc. (acq 9-19-02). Population served: 45,000 Natl. Network: Jones Radio Networks, . Format: Hispanic hits of the 60s. ◆Danny Bentley, gen mgr; L.D. Bentley, pres & farm dir.

WKLD(FM)— July 12, 1968: 97.7 mhz; 3.2 kw. Ant 367 ft TL: N33 56 48 W86 29 06. Hrs open: Box 490, 35121. Secondary address: 908 2nd Ave. E. 35121. Web Site:www.wkld.com Population served: 200,000 Format: Country. Spec prog: Atlanta Braves baseball. ◆L.D. Bentley, farm dir; Danny Bentley, disc jockey.

Opelika

WANI(AM)— June 3, 1940: 1400 khz; 1 kw-U. TL: N32 38 13 W85 24 23. Hrs open: 24 Box 950, Auburn, 36831-0950. Secondary address: 197 E. University Dr., Auburn 36830. Phone: (334) 826-2929. Fax: (334) 826-9151.E-mail: aburcham@aunetwork.com Web Site:www.wani1400.com Licensee: Auburn Network Inc. (acq 11-7-97; $135,000). Population served: 120,000 Natl. Network: ABC, Fox News Radio, Premiere Radio Networks, Radio America, Talk Radio Network, . Wire Svc: AP Format: News/talk. News staff: one. ◆Mike Hubbard, pres; Andy Burcham, gen mgr, progmg dir; Tim Chambliss, gen sls mgr; Julie Burns, news dir; Drew McCracken, traf mgr.

WKKR(FM)—See Auburn

WMXA(FM)— July 1, 1991: 96.7 mhz; 3.5 w. 430 ft TL: N32 33 54 W85 22 13. Stereo. Hrs open: 24 Box 2329, 36803. Secondary address: 915 Veterans Pkwy. 36801. Phone: (334) 745-2067. Fax: (334) 749-1520.E-mail: genmorj@charter.net Web Site:oaadvertising.com Population served: 115,000 Format: Adult contemp. News staff: one; News: 2 hrs wkly. Target aud: 18-49.

WTLM(AM)— Aug 12, 1968: 1520 khz; 1 kw-D. TL: N32 39 13 W85 25 25. Hrs open: Sunrise-sunset Box 2329, 36803-2329. Secondary address: 915 Veterans Pkwy. 36801. Phone: (334) 745-4656. Fax: (334) 749-1520.E-mail: genmorj@charter.net Web Site:oaadvertising.com Licensee: Qantum of Auburn License Co. LLC. Group owner: Qantum Communications Corp. (acq 7-2-03; grpsl). Population served: 100,000 Gardner, Carton & Douglas. Format: Adult standards. News staff: one. Target aud: 35 plus. ◆Jim Powell, gen mgr, mktg mgr; Sandy Matthews, sls dir; Woody Russ, progmg dir.

WZMG(AM)—(Pepperell, Oct 1, 1979: 910 khz; 650 w-D, 56 w-N, DA-1. TL: N32 56 30 W85 24 50. Hrs open: 24 915 Veterans Pkwy., 36803. Phone: (334) 745-4656. Fax: (334) 745-2067. Web Site:www.intouch910am.com Licensee: Qantum of Auburn License Co. LLC. Group owner: Qantum Communications Corp. (acq 7-2-03; grpsl). Population served: 100,000 Natl. Network: ABC, . Format: Urban. Target aud: 25-54; African Americans. ◆Richard LeGrand, progmg dir & news dir.

Opp

WAMI(AM)— Dec 12, 1952: 860 khz; 1 kw-D, 47 w-N. TL: N31 18 54 W86 15 45. Stereo. Hrs open: Box 40, 36467. Phone: (334) 493-3588. Fax: (334) 493-4182.E-mail: wami@oppcatv.com Licensee: Opp Broadcasting Co. Inc. Population served: 150,000 Natl. Network: ABC, . Format: Country classic. Target aud: 25-45; agricultural & garment industry workers. Spec prog: Gospel 15 hrs wkly. ◆Harry Phillips, gen mgr.

WAMI-FM— Nov 9, 1973: 102.3 mhz; 3.4 kw. 230 ft TL: N31 18 54 W86 15 45. Stereo. Hrs open: Dups AM 100% Box 40 , 36467. Secondary address: 1807 N. Main 36467. Phone: (334) 493-3588. Fax: (334) 493-4182.E-mail: wami@oppcatv.com Population served: 175,000

*WJIF(FM)— 1986: 91.9 mhz; 380 w. 164 ft TL: N31 15 50 W86 13 26. Hrs open: 700 Hwy. 52, 36467. Phone: (334) 493-4947. Fax: (334) 493-4947. Licensee: Opp Educational Broadcasting Foundation. Format: Southern gospel. ◆Heywood Nyland, gen mgr.

WOPP(AM)— Sept 19, 1980: 1290 khz; 2.5 kw-D, 500 w-N, DA-2. TL: N31 17 27 W86 13 51. Hrs open: 24 1101 Cameron Rd., 36467-2407. Phone: (334) 493-4545. Phone: (334) 493-1035. Fax: (334) 493-4546.E-mail: wopp@wopp.com Web Site:www.wopp.com Licensee: E & R Broadcasting Inc. (acq 8-87). Population served: 67,000 Natl. Network: Salem Radio Network, . Rgnl rep: Rgnl Reps. Roy F. Perkins. Format: Progsv C&W, oldies mix. News staff: one; News: 16 hrs wkly. Target aud: 19-58; progsv & highly loc. Spec prog: Farm 2 hrs, Black 4 hrs, gospel 19 hrs wkly. ◆Robert Boothe, gen mgr; Ronnie Boothe, traf mgr & engr.

Orange Beach

WCSN-FM—Licensed to Orange Beach. See Gulf Shores

Orrville

WALX(FM)— Dec 12, 1973: 100.9 mhz; 50 kw. Ant 492 ft TL: N32 21 40 W86 52 28. Stereo. Hrs open: Box 1150, Selma, 36702. Phone: (334) 875-9360. Fax: (334) 875-1340. Licensee: Scott Communications Inc. Population served: 27,397 Format: Hot adult contemp. Target aud: 18-40.

Oxford

*WTBJ(FM)— May 29, 1994: 91.3 mhz; 170 w. Ant 1,578 ft TL: N33 29 07 W85 48 33. Stereo. Hrs open: 24 c/o Trinity Christian Academy, 1500 Airport Rd., 36203. Phone: (256) 831-3333. Fax: (256) 831-5895. E-mail: truth@trinityoxford.org Web Site:www.trinityoxford.org Licensee: Trinity Christian Academy. Population served: 500,000 Fletcher, Heald & Hildreth. Format: Educ, relg. Target aud: General. Spec prog: Sp one hr wkly. ◆Dr. C.O. Grinstead, gen mgr.

WVOK(AM)— April 1956: 1580 khz; 2.5 kw-D, 22 w-N. TL: N33 26 55 W86 03 54. Hrs open: 24 PO Box 3770, 36203. Secondary address: 1215 Church St. 36203. Phone: (256) 835-1580. Fax: (256) 831-1500. Licensee: Woodard Broadcasting Co. (acq 5-62). Population served: 40,000 Natl. Network: ABC, . Format: Oldies. Target aud: 25-54. ◆Chuck Woodard, gen mgr, progmg dir; Steve Stevens, opns mgr.

WVOK-FM— Feb 19, 1990: 97.9 mhz; 510 w. Ant 1,109 ft TL: N33 37 20 W85 52 19. Stereo. Hrs open: 24 PO Box 3770, 36203. Secondary address: 1215 Church St. 36203. Phone: (256) 835-1580. Fax: (256) 831-1500. E-mail: productions@979wvok.com Web Site:www.979wvok.com Population served: 40,000 Format: Hot adult contemp. ◆Chuck Woodward, gen mgr; Steve Stevens, opns mgr; Whit McGhee, progmg dir.

Ozark

*WAQG(FM)— June 1998: 91.7 mhz; 3 kw. 321 ft TL: N31 26 25 W85 33 49. Hrs open: Box 3206, American Family Radio, Tupelo, MS, 38803. Phone: (601) 844-8888. Fax: (601) 842-6791. Web Site:www.afr.net Licensee: American Family Radio. (group owner) Format: Inspirational Christian. ◆Marvin Sanders, gen mgr; John Riley, progmg dir; Joe Moody, engrg dir.

WJRL-FM— Oct 5, 1968: 103.9 mhz; 25 kw. Ant 292 ft TL: N31 26 25 W85 33 49. Stereo. Hrs open: 24 285 N. Foster St., Dothan, 36302. Phone: (334) 792-0047. Fax: (334) 712-9346. Licensee: Magic Broadcasting Alabama Licensing LLC. (acq 8-1-2002; $750,000 with co-located AM). Natl. Network: Moody, . Format: Classic hits. News staff: one; News: 15 hrs wkly. Spec prog: Gospel 8 hrs, jazz 4 hrs, oldies 6 hrs wkly. ◆Greg Kamishlian, gen mgr; Chris Green, gen sls mgr; John Houston, progmg dir; Steve Youngblood, chief of engrg.

WOAB(FM)— July 9, 1967: 104.9 mhz; 6.0 kw. 275 ft TL: N31 27 19 W85 40 53. Hrs open: Prog sep from AM Box 1109, 36361. Phone: (334) 774-5600. Fax: (334) 774-1148. Licensee: Ozark Broadcasting Corp. Format: Country.

WOZK(AM)— May 3, 1953: 900 khz; 1 kw-D, 78 w-N. TL: N31 27 19 W85 40 58. Hrs open: Box 1109, 36361. Phone: (334) 774-5600. Fax: (334) 774-1148. E-mail: wozk@alaweb.com Licensee: Ozark Broadcasting Corp. Population served: 100,000 Format: Adult standard. ◆John Stein, gen mgr.

WQLS(AM)— April 1968: 1210 khz; 10 kw-D, 3 w-N, 5 kw-CH. TL: N31 28 40 W85 41 07. Hrs open: Box 250, 36360. Phone: (334) 445-1612. Fax: (334) 445-9266. Licensee: Horizon Broadcasting Co. (group owner; (acq 1-16-2007; $125,000). Format: Gospel. Target aud: 25-64. ◆Wayne North, gen mgr.

Pell City

WFHK(AM)— Jan 7, 1956: 1430 khz; 5 kw-D. TL: N33 35 10 W86 19 35. Hrs open: 6 AM-6 PM 22 Cogswell Ave., 35125. Phone: (205) 338-1430. Fax: (205) 814-1430. Licensee: Stocks Broadcasting Inc. (acq 2-27-01; $275,000). Population served: 35,000 Rgnl. Network: Alaska Radio Net. Alaska Pub. Format: Country. ◆John Simpson, gen mgr.

Pepperell

WZMG(AM)—Licensed to Pepperell. See Opelika

Phenix City

WDAK(AM)—See Columbus, GA

WGSY(FM)—Licensed to Phenix City. See Columbus GA

WHAL(AM)—Licensed to Phenix City. See Columbus GA

Piedmont

*WJCK(FM)— April 1994: 88.3 mhz; 6 kw. 328 ft TL: N34 04 11 W85 14 48. Hrs open: 24 9423 Hwy. 21 N., 36272. Phone: (770) 387-0917. Fax: (770) 387-2856. E-mail: jck95@aol.com Web Site:www.ibn.org Licensee: Immanuel Broadcasting Network. Format: Relg. ◆Ed Tuten, pres, gen mgr; Jane Tuten, VP; Neil Hopper, gen mgr; Jackson Kiruke, progmg dir; Jimmy Hardy, mus dir; Phillip Baker, chief of engrg.

WPID(AM)— June 1953: 1280 khz; 1 kw-D, 84 w-N. TL: N33 55 50 W85 35 00. Hrs open: 6 AM-10 PM 412 Cedartown Hwy., 36272. Phone: (256) 447-9096. Fax: (256) 447-6669. Licensee: Piedmont Radio Co. (acq 6-15-84; $125,000). Population served: 90,000 Format: Adult contemp, oldies. News: 2 hrs wkly. Target aud: 25-55. ◆Jimmy Kennedy, gen mgr; Andy Kennedy, opns mgr.

Pine Hill

WKXK(FM)— 2000: 96.7 mhz; 9 kw. 544 ft TL: N32 04 24 W87 35 27. Hrs open:
Simulcast of WKXN(FM) Greenville 100%.
Box 369, Greenville, 36037. Secondary address: 563 Manningham Rd., Greenville 36037. Phone: (334) 382-6555. Fax: (334) 382-7770. E-mail: wkxn@alaweb.com Web Site:www.wkxn.com Licensee: Autaugaville Radio Inc. Format: Urban contemp, blues, gospel. ◆Roscoe Miller, gen mgr, stn mgr, progmg dir; Mike Morris, gen sls mgr; Bob Luman, chief of engrg; Shelley Merritt, traf mgr.

Pine Level

WVRV(FM)— 2008: 97.5 mhz; 6 kw. Ant 328 ft TL: N31 58 32 W85 58 27. Hrs open: 1359 Carmichael Way, Montgomery, 36106. Phone: (334) 239-9750. Fax: (334) 356-9776. Web Site:www.wvrvfmtheriver.com Licensee: Back Door Broadcasting LLC. Format: Contemp Christian. ◆Allan G. Stroh, pres.

Prattville

WIQR(AM)— March 1969: 1410 khz; 5 kw-D, 1 kw-N, DA-2. TL: N32 25 23 W86 26 21. Hrs open: 921 East Main St., Laurel, 36066. Phone: (334) 358-0410. E-mail: wiqr@hotmail.com Web Site:www.wiqr.net Licensee: Star Power Communications Corp. (acq 2-1-2001; $167,000). Rgnl rep: Alabama Net. Format: Local sports. Target aud: General. ◆Greg Meadows, gen mgr.

Priceville

WKZD(AM)— August 1986: 1310 khz; 1 kw-D. TL: N34 32 32 W86 54 14. Hrs open: Sunrise-sunset Box 150, Decatur, 35602. Secondary address: 303 2nd Ave. S.E., Decatur 35601. Phone: (256) 773-4114. Fax: (256) 773-6915. Web Site:www.wkzd1053.com Licensee: Abercrombie Broadcasting AM Inc. (acq 8-86). Population served: 343,500 Format: Oldies. Target aud: 25-65. ◆Percy Yarbrough, gen mgr.

Prichard

WIJD(AM)— June 13, 1966: 1270 khz; 5 kw-D, 103 w-N. TL: N30 44 44 W88 05 40. Hrs open: 24 273 Azalea Road, Two Office Park Suite 403, Mobile, 36609. Phone: (251) 340-0442. E-mail: wijd@wilkinsradio.com Web Site:www.wilkinsradio.com Licensee: Mobile Bay Corp. (acq 7-18-2006; $450,000). Population served: 313,000 Format: Christian Preaching/Talk. Target aud: 35 plus. ◆Bob Wilkins, CEO, gen mgr; Mike Pickett, stn mgr.

WKSJ-FM—See Mobile

WLPR(AM)—Licensed to Prichard. See Mobile

Rainbow City

WGAD(AM)—Licensed to Rainbow City. See Gadsden

Rainsville

WVSM(AM)— May 16, 1967: 1500 khz; 1 kw-D. TL: N34 29 56 W85 50 34. Hrs open: Sunrise-sunset Box 339, 368 McCurdy Ave. N., 35986. Phone: (256) 638-2137. E-mail: wvsm@farmerstel.com Web Site:www.wvsm.net Licensee: Sand Mountain Advertising Co. Inc. Population served: 60,000 Format: Southern gospel. News staff: 3; News: 9 hrs wkly. Target aud: General. ◆Kayron Guffey, VP; Annie Ruth Huber, gen sls mgr; Ann Spears, disc jockey.

Red Bay

WRMG(AM)— June 29, 1968: 1430 khz; 1 kw-D. TL: N34 24 51 W88 08 11. (CP: 3 kw-D). Hrs open: Box 656, 35582. Phone: (256) 356-4458. Licensee: Jack W. Ivy Sr. (acq 1-9-2002; $42,300). Population served: 10,000 Format: Country, Southern gospel, Bluegrass. ◆Jack W. Ivy Sr., pres & progmg dir.

Reform

WBEI(FM)— May 7, 1991: 101.7 mhz; 22.5 kw. Ant 725 ft TL: N33 13 48 W87 50 50. Hrs open: 24 142 Skyland Blvd., Tuscaloosa, 35405. Phone: (205) 345-7200. Fax: (205) 349-1715. Web Site:www.b1017online.com Licensee: Citadel Broadcasting Co. (group owner; (acq 7-12-2005; grpsl). Format: Hot Adult contemp. Target aud: 18-49. ◆Todd Livingston, gen mgr; Tammy Boyd, gen sls mgr; Meg Summers, prom dir; Greg Thomas, progmg dir.

Repton

WPPG(FM)— Oct 1, 2002: 101.1 mhz; 3.1 kw. Ant 459 ft TL: N31 26 45 W87 16 59. Hrs open: 24 415 N. College St., Greenville, 36037-2005. Phone: (251) 575-7601. Fax: (251) 575-7703. E-mail: fun101@frontiernet.net Licensee: Wolff Broadcasting Corp. (group owner; (acq 6-9-2008; $250,000). Format: Lite rock. ◆Wendy Smith, gen mgr, opns mgr & progmg dir; Robert Williams, chief of engrg.

Roanoke

WELR(AM)— April 1954: 1360 khz; 1 kw-D. TL: N33 09 45 W85 22 30. Hrs open: Box 710, 6855 Hwy. 431, 36274. Phone: (334) 863-4139. Fax: (334) 863-2540. E-mail: jim@eagle1023.com Web Site:www.eagle1023.com Licensee: Eagle's Nest Inc. (group owner) acq 10-15-88). Population served: 25,000 Natl. Network: ESPN Radio, . Gardner, Carton & Douglas. Format: Sports. ◆Jim Vice, pres, gen mgr; Kay Vice, opns mgr; Coleman Vice, gen sls mgr; Don Strength, prom mgr; Al Haynes, news dir.

WELR-FM— Feb 14, 1969: 102.3 mhz; 8.9 kw. Ant 544 ft TL: N33 02 39 W85 20 15. Stereo. Hrs open: 24 304 Broome St., La Grange, GA, 30240. Phone: (334) 863-4139. Fax: (334) 863-2540. Web Site:www.eagle1023.com Licensee: Eagle's Nest Inc. (acq 1988). Population served: 1,000,000 Format: Country. News staff: 2. ◆Jim Vice, gen mgr; Kay Vice, opns mgr; Coleman Vice, gen sls mgr; Don Strength, progmg dir; Al Haynes, news dir.

Robertsdale

WNSI(AM)— Mar 1, 1985: 1000 khz; 1 kw-D. TL: N30 32 10 W87 42 55. Hrs open: 6 am-6 pm
Simulcast with WNSI-FM Atmore 100%.
Box 578, 36567. Phone: (251) 947-2346. Fax: (251) 947-2347. E-mail: wnsiradio@gulftel.com Web Site:www.wnsiradio.com Licensee: Great American Radio Network Inc. (acq 3-16-2001; $180,000). Population served: 40,000 Format: Sports, talk. News staff: one; News: 2 hrs wkly. Target aud: 45 plus; upscale. Spec prog: Religion 6 hrs wkly. ◆Walter Bowen, gen mgr.

Rogersville

WYTK(FM)— January 1994: 93.9 mhz; 2.25 kw. 531 ft TL: N34 51 52 W87 23 43. Hrs open: 24 Box 146, Florence, 35631. Phone: (256) 764-9390. Fax: (256) 764-7760. E-mail: the score@bellsouth.net Web Site:www.939thescore.com Licensee: Valley Broadcasting Inc. (acq 9-18-02; $900,000). Population served: 450,000 Format: Sports. Target aud: 25-54; male. ◆Al Mann, opns mgr, progmg dir; Greg Thornton, pres, gen mgr & gen sls mgr.

Russellville

WGOL(AM)— May 29, 1949: 920 khz; 1 kw-D, 43 w-N. TL: N34 30 50 W87 42 55. Hrs open: 16 113 N. Washington Ave., 35653. Phone: (256) 332-0214. Fax: (256) 332-7430. Licensee: Pilati Investments Corp. (acq 8-31-2005; $171,500). Population served: 30,000 Rgnl. Network: Alaska Radio Net. Alaska Pub. Format: Country. News: 9 hrs wkly. Target aud: 25-60. Spec prog: Black gospel 4 hrs, relg 10 hrs wkly. ◆John Pilati, stn mgr.

WKAX(AM)— Apr 3, 1974: 1500 khz; 1 kw-D. TL: N34 31 42 W87 42 41. Hrs open: 113 Washington Ave. N.W., 35653. Phone: (256) 332-6103. Fax: (256) 332-7430. Licensee: Jamar Communications

Inc. (acq 1999; $65,000). Population served: 30,000 Format: Southern gospel, Sp. Target aud: 21-54. Spec prog: Black 4 hrs wkly. ◆Marshall R. Moore, pres & gen mgr.

Saint Florian

WWFA(FM)—Not on air, target date: unknown: 102.7 mhz; 10 kw. Ant 462 ft TL: N34 45 28 W87 30 06. Hrs open: 188 S. Bellevue, Suite 222, Memphis, TN, 38104. Phone: (901) 516-8970. Licensee: George S. Flinn Jr. ◆George S. Flinn Jr., gen mgr.

Saraland

WHOA(AM)—Not on air, target date: unknown: 770 khz; 38 kw-D, 800 w-N. TL: N30 51 39 W88 05 37. Hrs open: 6930 Cahaba Valley Rd., Suite 202, Birmingham, 35242. Phone: (205) 618-2020. Licensee: Brantley Broadcast Associates LLC. (acq 5-8-2007; $100 for CP). ◆Paul Reynolds, gen mgr.

Scottsboro

WKEA-FM— Nov 3, 1965: 98.3 mhz; 6 kw. 531 ft TL: N34 34 50 W85 47 30. Stereo. Hrs open: 24 19784 John T. Reid Pkwy., 35768. Phone: (256) 259-2341. Fax: (256) 574-2156.E-mail: ron@wkeafm.com Web Site:www.wkeafm.com Licensee: KEA Radio Inc. (group owner) Population served: 125,000 Format: Country. News staff: one; News: 2 hrs wkly. Target aud: 25-54. Spec prog: Farm one hr, relg 4 hrs wkly. ◆Gene Sisk, VP; Ronald H. Livengood, CEO, pres & gen mgr; Campbell Smith, opns mgr.

WWIC(AM)— June 13, 1950: 1050 khz; 1 kw-D, 101 w-N. TL: N34 40 23 W86 03 11. Hrs open: 24 Box 759, 35768. Phone: (256) 259-1050. Fax: (256) 575-2411.E-mail: wwic@scottsboro.org Web Site:www.wwicradio.com Licensee: Scottsboro Broadcasting Co. Inc. (acq 1-14-2005; $88,306 for 50%). Population served: 15,000 Natl. Network: ABC, . Alabama Radio Net. Format: Classic country, sports. ◆Greg Bell, pres & gen mgr.

WZCT(AM)— June 11, 1952: 1330 khz; 5 kw-D, 38 w-N. TL: N34 42 07 W86 00 15. Hrs open: 24 1111 E.Willow St., 35768. Phone: (256) 574-1330. Fax: (256) 218-3013. Licensee: Bonner and Carlile Enterprises. (acq 2-28-90). Population served: 175,000 Natl. Network: Reach Satellite, USA, . Format: Southern gospel. News: 14 hrs wkly. Target aud: 25 plus. Spec prog: Sports 19 hrs wkly. ◆Rob Carlile, gen mgr, stn mgr, opns mgr & gen sls mgr.

Selma

*WAPR(FM)— May 5, 1996: 88.3 mhz; 1.85 kw horiz, 53 kw vert. 1,401 ft TL: N32 08 30 W86 44 43. Hrs open:
Rebroadcasts WUAL-FM Tuscaloosa 100%.
Phifer Hall Annex, Suite 166, Tuscaloosa, 35487. Phone: (205) 348-6644. Fax: (205) 348-6648.E-mail: apr@apr.org Web Site:www.apr.org Licensee: Ua-Asu-Tsu Educational Radio Corp. Population served: 30,000 Natl. Network: NPR, PRI, . Format: Class, jazz, news. ◆Elizabeth Brock, stn mgr.

*WAQU(FM)— March 1998: 91.1 mhz; 21.5 kw. Ant 335 ft TL: N32 24 17 W87 25 32. Hrs open: Box 3206, American Family Radio, Tupelo, MS, 38803. Phone: (662) 844-8888. Fax: (662) 842-6791. Web Site:www.afr.net Licensee: American Family Association. Group owner: American Family Radio Format: Inspirational Christian. ◆Don Wildmon, CEO; Tim Wildmon, exec VP; Marvin Sanders, gen mgr; John Riley, progmg dir; Fred Jackson, news dir; Shan Easterling, chief of engrg.

WBFZ(FM)— 2001: 105.3 mhz; 50 kw. Ant 492 ft TL: N32 16 18 W87 15 28. Hrs open: 2 P.O. Box 369, 36702. Phone: (334) 872-2177. Fax: (334) 872-5577. Licensee: Inami Communications Corp. Inc. Format: Urban contemp. ◆Henry Sanders, pres; Charles Jones, gen mgr; Derriet Moore, progmg dir.

WDXX(FM)— September 1965: 100.1 mhz; 50 kw. Ant 288 ft TL: N32 26 02 W87 00 40. Stereo. Hrs open: 24 Box 1055, 36702. Secondary address: 505 Lauderdale St. 36701. Phone: (334) 875-3350. Fax: (334) 874-6959. Licensee: Broadsouth Communications Inc. Format: Country. News staff: 2; News: 5 hrs wkly.

WHBB(AM)— Nov 11, 1935: 1490 khz; 1 kw-U. TL: N32 26 02 W87 00 40. Hrs open: 24 Box 1055, 36702. Secondary address: 505 Lauderdale St. 36701. Phone: (334) 875-3350. Fax: (334) 874-6959.E-mail: info@wdxx.com Web Site:www.wdxx.com Licensee: Broadsouth Communications Inc. (acq 7-24-92; $400,000 with co-located FM; 8-17-92). Population served: 27,379 Natl. Rep: Rgnl Reps,. Format: News/talk. News staff: one; News: 13 hrs wkly. Target aud: 25-54.

Spec prog: Black 18 hrs, farm 10 hrs wkly. ◆Mike Reynolds, gen mgr; Evelyn Ogle, gen sls mgr; George Henry, progmg dir.

WJAM(AM)— Dec 19, 1946: 1340 khz; 1 kw-U. TL: N32 25 31 W86 59 47. Hrs open: Box 1150, 36702. Phone: (334) 875-9360. Fax: (334) 875-1340. Licensee: Scott Communications Inc. (acq 12-30-2005; $29,500 for 47.2% of stock with co-located FM). Format: Oldies. Target aud: 25-49. ◆Betty Alexander, mus dir; Scott Alexander, pres, gen mgr, progmg dir & chief of engrg.

*WRNF(FM)— 2007: 89.5 mhz; 6 kw vert. Ant 328 ft TL: N32 32 50 W86 55 33. Hrs open: Box 10, 36702-0010. E-mail: wrnf@moody.edu Licensee: The Moody Bible Institute of Chicago. Format: Relg. ◆Rob Moore, gen mgr.

Sheffield

*WAKD(FM)— 1996: 89.9 mhz; 1 kw. 125 ft TL: N34 44 25 W87 42 58. Hrs open: Box 3206, Tupelo, MS, 38803. Phone: (662) 844-8888. Fax: (662) 842-6791. Web Site:www.afr.net Licensee: American Family Association. Group owner: American Family Radio Format: Inspirational Christian. ◆Marvin Sanders, gen mgr; John Riley, progmg dir; Joey Moody, chief of engrg.

WBTG(AM)— Nov 6, 1963: 1290 khz; 1 kw-D, 79 w-N. TL: N34 46 27 W87 40 14. Hrs open: 24 P.O. Box 518, 35660. Secondary address: 1605 Gospel Rd. 35660. Phone: (256) 381-6800. Fax: (256) 381-6801.E-mail: announcements@wbtgradio.com Web Site:www.wbtgradio.com Licensee: Slatton & Associates. (acq 12-17-87). Population served: 150,000 Natl. Network: Salem Radio Network, . Ill. Radio Net. Format: Memory music. Target aud: 25 up; conservative, mainstream family audience. ◆Paul Slatton, pres & gen mgr; Dan Michaels, progmg dir, mus dir; Kerri Melton, traf mgr.

WBTG-FM— July 2, 1969: 106.3 mhz; 6 kw. Ant 682 ft TL: N34 41 34 W87 47 49. Stereo. Hrs open: 24 Prog sep from AM Box 518, 35660. Secondary address: 1605 Gospel Rd. 35660. Phone: (205) 381-6800. Fax: (256) 381-6801. Web Site:www.wbtgradio.com (Acq 1-17-78). Format: Southern gospel. News: 12 hrs wkly. ◆Paul Slatton, gen mgr; Dan Michaels, progmg dir, mus dir; Kerri Melton, traf mgr.

Shorter

WMRK-FM— August 1994: 107.9 mhz; 25 kw. Ant 328 ft TL: N32 21 09 W86 03 06. Hrs open: 4101 Wall St., Montgomery, 36106. Phone: (334) 244-0961. Fax: (334) 279-9563. Web Site:www.newstalk1079.com Licensee: Alexander Broadcasting Co. LLC. (acq 10-13-94). Format: Talk. ◆Terry Barber, gen mgr.

Slocomb

WLDA(FM)— 1991: 100.5 mhz; 16.5 kw. Ant 408 ft TL: N31 11 00 W85 24 23. Stereo. Hrs open: 24 285 N. Foster St., Dothan, 36303. Phone: (334) 792-0049. Fax: (334) 712-9346. Licensee: Magic Broadcasting Alabama Licensing LLC. (group owner; (acq 10-1-2003; $750,000). Population served: 150,000 Format: Adult contemp. News staff: one. Target aud: 25-54; upscale baby boomers, acitive duty & retired military. ◆Dan Bradley, gen mgr; Doc Thompson, opns dir & opns mgr; Chris Green, sls dir, gen sls mgr.

Smiths

WAGH(FM)— 1998: 101.3 mhz; 6 kw. Ant 328 ft TL: N32 25 35 W85 08 20. Hrs open: Box 687, Columbus, GA, 31902. Secondary address: 1501 13th Ave., Columbus, GA 31901. Phone: (706) 576-3000. Fax: (706) 576-3005. Web Site:www.magic98online.com Licensee: CC Licenses LLC. Group owner: Clear Channel Communications Inc. (acq 2-21-2002; grpsl). Format: Urban adult contemp. Target aud: 25-54; working Black adults. ◆Jim Martin, gen mgr; Henry Holt, gen sls mgr; Rasheeda Ali, progmg dir; Frank McLemore, chief of engrg.

Steele

*WAYU(FM)—Not on air, target date: unknown: 91.1 mhz; 117 w horiz, 470 w vert. Ant 754 ft TL: N33 57 29.6 W86 13 01. Hrs open: Box 64500, Colorado Springs, CO, 80962. Phone: (719) 533-0300. Fax: (719) 278-4339. Web Site:www.wayfm.com Licensee: WAY-FM Media Group Inc. ◆Robert Augsburg, pres.

Stevenson

WMXN-FM— June 13, 1977: 101.7 mhz; 2.3 kw. Ant 541 ft TL: N34 41 02 W85 48 04. Stereo. Hrs open: Box 966, 19784 John T. Reid Pkwy., Scottsboro, 35768. Phone: (256) 259-2341. Fax: (256) 574-2156.E-mail: ron@wkeafm.com Web Site:www.wwkeafm.com Licensee: KEA Radio Inc. (group owner; (acq 1996). Fletcher, Heald & Hildreth. Wire Svc: AP Format: Classic rock. ◆Gene Sisk, VP; Ron Livengood, pres & gen mgr; Campbell Smith, opns dir.

Sulligent

WVSA(AM)—See Vernon

Sumiton

WRSM(AM)— June 27, 1978: Stn currently dark. 1540 khz; 1 kw-D. TL: N33 45 50 W87 03 47. Hrs open: Country Box 11385, Birmingham, 35202. Phone: (205) 326-8844. Licensee: Sumiton Broadcasting Co. Inc. ◆Earl F. Hilliard, pres & gen mgr.

Sylacauga

WFEB(AM)— March 1945: 1340 khz; 1 kw-U. TL: N33 10 16 W86 13 57. Hrs open: 16 Box 358, 1209 Millerville Hwy., 35150. Phone: (256) 245-3281. Fax: (256) 245-3050. Licensee: Powers Broadcasting Co LLC (acq 3-18-2008; $184,310). Population served: 500,000 Rgnl rep: Keystone (unwired net). Fletcher, Heald & Hildreth. Format: News/talk, sports. News staff: 3; News: 17 hrs wkly. Target aud: 25-54. Spec prog: Gospel 6 hrs wkly. ◆Bruce C. Carr, gen mgr & gen sls mgr.

WYEA(AM)— May 16, 1948: 1290 khz; 1 kw-D, 50 w-N. TL: N33 11 15 W86 14 06. Hrs open: 6 AM-8 PM Box 629, One Motes Rd., 35150. Phone: (256) 249-4263. Fax: (256) 245-4355.E-mail: wyea@rocketmail.com Web Site:www.wyearadio.com Licensee: Spirit Broadcasting Co. Inc. (acq 4-13-2001). Population served: 62,450 Rgnl. Network: Ill Radio Net. Alabama Radio Net. Format: Christian country. News: 7 hrs wkly. Target aud: General. ◆John Vogel, pres & gen mgr.

Talladega

WNUZ(AM)— 1945: 1230 khz; 1 kw-U. TL: N33 25 16 W86 07 13. Hrs open: 5 AM-11 PM 1301 Fort Lashley Ave., 35160. Phone: (256) 480-6040. Fax: (256) 480-6050. Licensee: Birmingham Christian Radio Inc. (acq 5-13-97; $30,000). Population served: 76,000 Format: Full gospel. News staff: one. Target aud: 25-70; middle/upper middle, blue & white collar. Spec prog: Talk 5 hrs, Gospel 7 hrs, bluegrass 6 hrs wkly. ◆L.E. Willis Sr., pres; Jonnie Luster, gen mgr; Louis Amerson, progmg dir.

WTDR(FM)— Nov 10, 1972: 92.7 mhz; 2.6 kw. Ant 505 ft TL: N33 29 12 W85 59 15. (CP: COL Munford. 250 w, ant 1,578 ft. TL: N33 29 06 W85 48 32). Stereo. Hrs open: 24 Box 7785, 1913 Barry St., Suite B, Oxford, 36203. Phone: (256) 741-6000. Fax: (256) 741-6080.E-mail: jimj@wtdrthunder.com Web Site:www.wtdrthunder.com Licensee: Jacobs Broadcast Group Inc. (acq 9-16-92; $570,000; 10-19-92). Population served: 300,000 Natl. Network: AP Radio, . Wire Svc: AP Format: Country. News staff: one. Target aud: 25-54; adults. ◆Jim Jacobs, pres; Laura Jacobs, VP; Grady Sapp, opns mgr; Bill Moats, chief of engrg; Laura Jacobs, traf mgr.

Tallassee

WACQ(AM)—(Carrville, June 30, 1979: 1130 khz; 1 kw-D. TL: N32 33 22 W85 52 17. (CP: 25 kw-D, 1 kw-CH. TL: N32 27 17 W85 55 57). Hrs open: Sunrise-sunset 320 Barnett Blvd., 36078. Phone: (334) 283-6888. Fax: (334) 283-6358.E-mail: WACQradio@elmore.rr.com Web Site:www.wacqradio.com Licensee: Hughey Communications Inc. (group owner; (acq 12-4-2006; $106,000). Population served: 400,000 Natl. Network: ABC, . Rgnl. Network: N.D. News Net. Alabama Radio Net. Fletcher, Heald & Hildreth. Wire Svc: AP Format: Oldies. News staff: one; News: 7 hrs wkly. Target aud: 25-54; baby boomers. Spec prog: Farmer one hr, gospel 5 hrs wkly. ◆Randall Hughey, gen mgr; Debra Hughey, traf mgr.

WQNR(FM)— Oct 29, 1992: 99.9 mhz; 3.1 kw. Ant 452 ft TL: N32 34 37 W85 51 43. Hrs open: 2514 S. College St., Suite 104, Auburn, 36832. Phone: (334) 887-9999. Fax: (334) 826-9599.E-mail: info@thetiger.fm Web Site:www.wqnr.com Licensee: Tiger Communications Inc. (acq 1999). Gardner, Carton & Douglas. Format: AOR. Target aud: 25-54; adults. ◆Chris Bailey, gen mgr.

WTLS(AM)— June 1, 1954: 1300 khz; 1.2 kw-D, 18 w-N. TL: N32 30 39 W85 53 33. Hrs open: Box 780146, 36078. Secondary address: 2045 Hwy 229 36078. Phone: (334) 283-8200. Fax: (334) 283-8622.E-mail: mbutler@1300wtls.com Web Site:www.1300wtls.com Licensee: Michael Butler Broadcasting LLC (acq 8-24-99). Population served: 138,000 Dan Alpert. Format: Full service, sports, talk. Spec prog: Farm 6 hrs wkly. ♦Michael Butler, pres, gen mgr; Leigh Anne Butler, gen sls mgr; Steve Butler, progmg VP; Terry Harper, chief of engrg; Miles Hathcock, prom.

Thomaston

WTID(FM)— 2001: 103.9 mhz; 500 w. Ant 46 ft TL: N32 16 49 W87 38 06. Hrs open: 6930 Cahaba Valley Rd., Suite 202, Birmingham, 35242. Phone: (205) 949-4586. Licensee: Great South Wireless LLC. (group owner; (acq 2-12-2007; grpsl).

Thomasville

***WDLG(FM)**— 2007: Stn currently dark. 90.1 mhz; 500 w. Ant 249 ft TL: N31 44 24 W87 45 43. Stereo. Hrs open: 2070 N. Palafox, Pensacola, FL, 32501. Phone: (850) 434-1230.E-mail: mglin@aol.com Licensee: Nationwide Inspirational Broadcasting. ♦Michael B. Glinter, pres.

WJDB(AM)— July 16, 1956: 630 khz; 1 kw. TL: N31 52 58 W87 44 42. Hrs open: Sunrise-sunset Box 219, 2211 Hwy. 43 S., 36784. Phone: (334) 636-4438. Fax: (334) 636-4439.E-mail: wjdb@dixienet1.com Licensee: Griffin Broadcasting Corp. (acq 1-4-91; $375,000 with co-located FM; 1-28-91). Population served: 20,000 Natl. Network: CBS, . Rgnl. Network: Ark. Radio Net. Ark. Radio Net. Format: Grooving oldies. News staff: one; News: 10 hrs wkly. Target aud: General. ♦Ivy Griffin, gen mgr, gen sls mgr & gen sls mgr.

WJDB-FM— Nov 2, 1972: 95.5 mhz; 9.6 kw. Ant 525 ft TL: N31 52 58 W87 44 42. Stereo. Hrs open: 24 Box 219, 36784. Secondary address: 2211 Hwy. 43 S. 36784. Phone: (334) 636-4438. Fax: (334) 636-4439.E-mail: wjdb@dixienet1.com Licensee: Griffin Broadcasting Corp. Population served: 100,000 Format: Top 40 country. News: 10 hrs wkly. Target aud: General.

Trinity

WVNN-FM— Oct 4, 1992: 92.5 mhz; 3.1 kw. Ant 423 ft TL: N34 42 36 W87 04 54. Stereo. Hrs open: 24
Simulcasts WVNN-AM 100%.
1717 U.S. Hwy. 72 E., Athens, 35611-4413. Phone: (256) 830-8300. Fax: (256) 232-6842. Web Site:www.wvnn.com Licensee: Cumulus Licensing LLC. Group owner: Clear Channel Communications Inc. (acq 4-4-2006; $3.3 million with WXQW(FM) Meridianville). Population served: 802,300 Natl. Network: ABC, . Natl. Rep: Katz Radio,. Format: News/talk. News staff: 3; News: 7 hrs news prgmg wkly. ♦Bill G. West, gen mgr; Tracy Flesch, gen sls mgr.

Troy

***WAXU(FM)**— 2001: 91.1 mhz; 1.089 kw. Ant 246 ft TL: N31 47 22 W85 58 58. Hrs open: 24 Drawer 3206, American Family Radio, Tupelo, MS, 38803. Phone: (662) 844-8888. Fax: (662) 842-6791. Web Site:www.afr.net Licensee: American Family Association. Group owner: American Family Radio Format: Inspirational Christian. ♦Marvin Sanders, gen mgr; John Riley, progmg dir.

WTBF(AM)— Feb 25, 1947: 970 khz; 5 kw-D, 45 w-N. TL: N31 50 07 W85 55 58. Hrs open: 24 67 Court Sq., 36081. Phone: (334) 566-0300. Fax: (334) 566-5689.E-mail: wtbf@radio.com Web Site:www.wtbf.com Licensee: Troy Broadcasting Corp. Population served: 30,000 Format: Talk, community intensive progmg. News: 20 hrs wkly. Target aud: 35 plus; general. Spec prog: Farm 17 hrs wkly. ♦Joe Gilchrist, pres; Jim Roling, VP, gen mgr; Dave Kirby, opns mgr, progmg dir.

WZHT(FM)— Feb 28, 1973: 105.7 mhz; 100 kw. Ant 1,830 ft TL: N31 58 28 W86 09 44. Stereo. Hrs open: 203 Gunn Rd., Montgomery, 36117. Phone: (334) 274-6464. Fax: (334) 274-6465. Web Site:www.myhot105.com Licensee: Capstar TX L.P. Group owner: Clear Channel Communications Inc. (acq 8-30-00; grpsl). Natl. Network: ABC, Westwood One, . Natl. Rep: McGavren Guild,. Latham & Watkins. Format: Urban. Target aud: 18-49. ♦James Belton, gen mgr; Michael Long, opns mgr, progmg dir; Nikita Pogue, prom dir; Connye Bryant, traf mgr.

Trussville

WQEN(FM)—Licensed to Trussville. See Birmingham

Tuscaloosa

WACT(AM)— September 1958: 1420 khz; 5 kw-D, 108 w-N. TL: N33 10 30 W87 33 18. Hrs open: 24 Box 20126, 35402-0126. Secondary address: 2121 9th St., Suite B 35401. Phone: (205) 344-4589. Fax: (205) 366-9774. Web Site:www.news1420.com Licensee: Capstar TX L.P. Group owner: Clear Channel Communications Inc. (acq 8-30-2000; grpsl). Population served: 75,000 Format: News/talk. Target aud: 35 plus. ♦Ray Quinn, gen mgr; Todd Robins, prom dir; Vince Ferrara, progmg dir; Laurie Mundy, news dir, pub affrs dir; Russ Williams, chief of engrg, opns.

WJRD(AM)— Oct 10, 1936: 1150 khz; 20 kw-D, 1 kw-N, DA-N. TL: N33 15 02 W87 36 35. Hrs open: 24 Box 70937, 35407. Phone: (205) 345-9573. Fax: (205) 366-9480. Licensee: JRD Inc. (group owner; (acq 11-19-2007; $200,000). Population served: 100,000 Natl. Network: ABC, . Format: True Oldies Channel. Target aud: Adults 35 plus. ♦Jimmy Shaw, pres.

***WMFT(FM)**— June 6, 2005: 88.9 mhz; 100 kw vert. Ant 522 ft TL: N33 20 19 W87 21 32. Stereo. Hrs open: 24
Rebroadcasts WMBV(FM) Dixon Mills.
5710 Watermelon Rd., Suite 316, Northport, 35473. Phone: (334) 992-2425. Fax: (334) 992-2637.E-mail: wmft@moody.edu Web Site:www.wmft.fm Licensee: The Moody Bible Institute of Chicago (group owner). Population served: 250,000 Natl. Network: Moody, . Souyhmayd & Miller. Wire Svc: AP Format: Christian. News: 6 hrs wkly. Target aud: 35-54. ♦Rob Moore, stn mgr; John Rogers, progmg dir.

WRTR(FM)—(Brookwood, June 1, 1966: 105.9 mhz; 25 kw. Ant 269 ft TL: N33 14 17 W87 29 06. Stereo. Hrs open: 24 Box 20126, 35401. Secondary address: 3900 11th Ave. S. 35401. Phone: (205) 344-4589. Fax: (205) 366-9774. Web Site:www.news1420.com Licensee: Capstar TX L.P. Natl. Network: USA, . Format: Talk. Target aud: 25 plus. ♦Ray Quinn, gen mgr.

WTBC(AM)— Dec 23, 1946: 1230 khz; 1 kw-U. TL: N33 12 05 W87 32 00. Hrs open: 24 Box 2000, 35403. Secondary address: 2110 McFarland Blvd. E., Suite C 35404. Phone: (205) 758-5523. Phone: (205) 732-9822. Fax: (205) 752-9696.E-mail: wtbc@dbtech.net Web Site:www.wtbc1230.com Licensee: John Sisty Enterprises Inc. (acq 2-14-02). Population served: 116,029 Natl. Network: ABC, ESPN Radio, . Rgnl rep: Alabama Net. Tim K. Brady. Format: News/talk, sports. News: 3 hrs wkly. Target aud: 25-54; upscale, affluent. Spec prog: Relg 3 hrs wkly. ♦John Sisty, CEO, pres; Ronnie Quarles, COO, gen mgr; Dave McDaniel, opns mgr, progmg; Nancy Wilson, gen sls mgr; Tesha Price, traf mgr.

WTSK(AM)— February 1958: 790 khz; 5 kw-D, 36 w-N. TL: N33 11 17 W87 35 23. Hrs open: 142 Skyland Blvd., 35405. Phone: (205) 345-7200. Fax: (205) 349-1715. Licensee: Citadel Broadcasting Co. (group owner; (acq 7-12-2005; grpsl). Format: Gospel. Target aud: 35 plus. ♦Todd Livingston, gen mgr; Charles Anthony, opns mgr, progmg dir; Tammy Boyd, gen sls mgr; Jade Nicole, news dir.

WTUG-FM—(Northport, March 1979: 92.9 mhz; 100 kw. Ant 980 ft TL: N33 03 15 W87 32 57. Stereo. Hrs open: 24 Prog sep from AM 142 Skyland Blvd., 35405. Phone: (205) 345-7200. Fax: (205) 349-1715. Web Site:www.wtug.com Format: Urban Adult contemp. Target aud: 25-54. ♦Todd Livingston, gen mgr; Greg Thomas, opns mgr; Tammy Boyd, gen sls mgr; Meg Summers, prom dir; Charles Anthony, progmg dir.

***WUAL-FM**— Jan 4, 1982: 91.5 mhz; 100 kw. 523 ft TL: N33 05 40 W87 24 47. Stereo. Hrs open: 24 Phifer Annex, Suite 166, 35487. Phone: (205) 348-6644. Fax: (205) 348-6648.E-mail: apr@apr.org Licensee: Board of Trustees of the University of Alabama. Natl. Network: PRI, NPR, . Rgnl rep: Alabama Net. Arter & Hadden. Format: Class, jazz, news/talk. News staff: 3; News: 5 hrs wkly. Target aud: 35 plus. Spec prog: Folk 5 hrs, new age 20 hrs wkly. ♦Elizabeth Brock, gen mgr & stn mgr; Brian Pollnitz, opns mgr; David Duff, mus dir; Butler Cain, news dir.

***WVUA-FM**— Sept 7, 1972: 90.7 mhz; 160 w. 142 ft TL: N33 12 33 W87 32 57. Stereo. Hrs open: Box 870152, 35487-0152. Phone: (205) 348-6461. Fax: (205) 348-0375.E-mail: wvua@sa.ua.edu Web Site:www.newrock907.com Licensee: Board of Trustees University of Alabama. Format: Alternative, rock. Target aud: 18-25; high school & college students. Spec prog: Christian 3 hrs, hardcore 3 hrs, blues 3 hrs, heavy metal 4 hrs, reggae 3 hrs wkly. ♦Loy Singleton, gen mgr; Graham Flaugan, stn mgr.

WWPG(AM)— Dec 10, 1951: 1280 khz; 5 kw-D, 500 w-N, DA-N. TL: N33 13 07 W87 34 05. (CP: COL Eutaw. 7 kw-D, 25 w-N. TL: N32 55 19 W87 49 08). Hrs open: 601 Greensboro Ave., Suite 507, 35401. Phone: (205) 345-4787. Fax: (205) 345-4790.E-mail: jwlawson@bellsouth.net Licensee: Lawson of Tuscaloosa Inc. (acq 3-17-93; $160,000; 4-5-93). Population served: 75,000 Natl. Network: Westwood One, . Taylor, Smith & Parker. Format: Gospel. Target aud: 24-54; mature business audience. Spec prog: Jazz 2 hrs wkly. ♦Jim Lawson, pres, gen mgr; Mildred Porter, opns mgr & gen sls mgr.

Tuscumbia

WQRV(FM)— May 2, 1962: 100.3 mhz; 100 kw. Ant 246 ft TL: N34 45 23 W87 41 08. (CP: COL Meridianville. 8.5 kw, ant 981 ft. TL: N34 47 36 W86 37 51). Stereo. Hrs open: 24 26869 Peoples Rd., Madison, 35756. Phone: (256) 309-2400. Fax: (256) 389-1912. Web Site:www.103theriver.com Licensee: CC Licenses LLC. (acq 12-19-2000; grpsl). Format: Country. News staff: 2; News: 60 hrs wkly. Target aud: 18-34. ♦Rick Brown, gen mgr; Carmelita Palmer, sls dir; Bruce Reynolds, progmg dir; Carl Sampieri, chief of engrg.

WVNA(AM)— Apr 5, 1955: 1590 khz; 5 kw-D, 1 kw-N, DA-N. TL: N34 45 24 W87 36 35. Hrs open: 24 273 Azalea Rd., Suite 1-308, Mobile, 36609. Phone: (251) 343-4900. Fax: (251) 343-4905.E-mail: info@urbanradio.com Web Site:www.wvnafm.com Licensee: Urban Radio Licenses LLC. Group owner: Clear Channel Communications Inc. (acq 5-13-2005; grpsl). Population served: 500,000 Natl. Network: CBS, . Format: News/talk, sports. News staff: 3; News: 60 hrs wkly. Target aud: 25-64. ♦Kevin Wagner, gen mgr.

WZZA(AM)— Apr 17, 1960: 1410 khz; 500 w-D, 51 w-N. TL: N34 42 29 W87 41 35. Hrs open: 24 1570 Woodmont Dr., 35674. Phone: (256) 381-1862. Phone: (256) 383-5810. Fax: (256) 381-6006.E-mail: wzzaradio@aol.com Licensee: Muscle Shoals Broadcasting. (acq 12-1-77). Population served: 250,000 Natl. Network: American Urban, . Fletcher, Heald & Hildreth, PLC. Format: Soul & gospel. News staff: one; News: 15 hrs wkly. Target aud: Black. ♦Jurado Bailey, pres, CFO; Tori Bailey, CEO, gen mgr & gen mgr; Dwight Winston, opns dir; Peter Smith, progmg dir; John Reeder, sls.

Tuskegee

WBIL(AM)— July 1, 1952: 580 khz; 500 w-D, 139 w-N. TL: N32 22 36 W85 39 28. Hrs open: 118 S. Main St., 36083. Phone: (334) 727-2100. Fax: (334) 724-9169. Licensee: Tiger Communications Inc. Group owner: Willis Broadcasting Corp. (acq 4-6-2006; $350,000 with WQSI(FM) Union Springs). Population served: 14,793 Format: Gospel. ♦Bernita Luke, gen mgr, gen sls mgr; Sylvester McPherson, progmg dir; Terry Harper, chief of engrg.

WTGZ(FM)— July 12, 1975: 95.9 mhz; 4.3 kw. 377 ft TL: N32 28 17 W85 34 28. Stereo. Hrs open: 2514 S. College St., Suite 104, Auburn, 36830. Phone: (334) 887-9999. Fax: (334) 826-9599.E-mail: info@thetiger.fm Web Site:www.thetiger.fm Licensee: Tiger Communications Inc. (acq 2-26-98; $450,000). Format: Modern rock. Target aud: 18-34. ♦Chris Bailey, gen mgr.

Union Springs

WQSI(FM)— Oct 15, 1975: 93.9 mhz; 12.5 kw. Ant 469 ft TL: N32 19 04 W85 40 16. Stereo. Hrs open: 24 2514 S. College St., Suite 104, Auburn, 36830. Phone: (334) 887-9999.E-mail: wacqradio@elmore.rr.com Licensee: Tiger Communications Inc. (acq 4-6-2006; $350,000 with WBIL(AM) Tuskegee). Population served: 620,000 Alabama Radio Net. John Trent. Format: Classic country. News: 15 wkly. Target aud: 25-54; 40+ boomers, active, affluent southerners.

Valley

***WEBT(FM)**— Jan 17, 1986: 91.5 mhz; 380 w. 85 ft TL: N32 48 15 W85 10 43. Hrs open: 2615 64th Blvd., 36854. Phone: (334) 756-6923. Fax: (334) 756-8430. Licensee: Langdale Educational Broadcasting Foundation. Population served: 20,000 Format: Southern gospel. Target aud: General. Spec prog: Southern gospel. ♦Tim Foster, stn mgr & progmg dir.

WRLD-FM— May 17, 1993: 95.3 mhz; 25 kw. Ant 328 ft TL: N32 44 03 W85 07 53. Hrs open: 24 1353 13th Ave., Columbus, GA, 31901. Phone: (706) 327-1217. Fax: (706) 596-4600. Web Site:www.boomer.fm Licensee: PMB Broadcasting LLC. Group owner: Archway Broadcasting Group (acq 10-1-2008; grpsl). Fletcher, Heald & Hildreth. Format: Oldies. Target aud: 35 plus. ♦Chuck Thompson, gen mgr & sports cmtr.

Valley Head

WQRX(AM)— Feb 10, 1986: 870 khz; 10 kw-D. TL: N34 33 20 W85 37 12. Hrs open: Sunrise-sunset 2278 Wortham Ln., Grovetown, GA, 30813. Phone: (706) 309-9610.E-mail: cbarinowski@comcast.net Web Site:www.gnnradio.org Licensee: Barinowski Investment Company Group owner: Good News Network (acq 10-13-99). Format: Sp. All Sp. ♦Clarence Barinowski, pres, gen mgr & gen mgr.

Vernon

WJEC(FM)— Apr 1, 1991: 106.5 mhz; 6 kw. 328 ft TL: N33 51 15 W88 01 55. Hrs open: 24 Box 630, 35592. Phone: (205) 695-9191. Fax: (205) 695-9131. Format: Southern gospel. ♦R. William Davis, CEO; Curtis Smith, gen mgr, progmg mgr.

WVSA(AM)— July 4, 1966: 1380 khz; 5 kw-D, 39 w-N. TL: N33 47 45 W88 07 03. Hrs open: Box 630, 35592. Phone: (205) 695-9191. Fax: (205) 695-9131.E-mail: wjec1065@yahoo.com Licensee: Lamar County Broadcasting Co. Inc. Population served: 2,190 Format: All sports. ♦Curtis Smith, gen mgr.

Warrior

WBHK(FM)— Apr 22, 1992: 98.7 mhz; 14 kw. 945 ft TL: N33 27 45 W86 50 59. Hrs open: 950 22nd St. N, Suite 1000, Birmingham, 35203. Phone: (205) 322-2987. Fax: (205) 322-2390. Web Site:www.987kiss.com Yes Licensee: Cox Radio Inc. Group owner: Cox Broadcasting (acq 10-6-98; $17 million with WBHJ(FM) Tuscaloosa). Population served: 1,000,000 Natl. Rep: Christal,. Dow, Lohnes & Albertson. Wire Svc: Metro Weather Service Inc. Format: Classic soul & rhythm and blues. News staff: 2; News: 5 hrs wkly. Target aud: 25-54; general. ♦David DuBose, gen mgr; Tony Walker, gen sls mgr; Darryl Johnson, progmg dir; Reginald Green, news dir; Dan Goodman, chief of engrg.

Wetumpka

WAPZ(AM)— Oct 2, 1954: 1250 khz; 5 kw-D, 80 w-N. TL: N32 29 06 W86 12 25. Hrs open: 24
95.7 FM.
2821 U.S. Hwy. 231, 36093. Phone: (334) 512-1250. Fax: (334) 567-7971.E-mail: wapz@wapz1250.com Web Site:www.wapz1250.com Licensee: J&W L.L.C. (acq 9-1-84; $235,000; 7-23-84). Population served: 450,000 Format: Gospel, Relg, Talk. News: 10 hrs/week. Target aud: 12-100. Spec prog: Hispanic. ♦Johnny Roland, pres; Roz Dorsey, gen mgr; Pat Sullivan, opns mgr, gen sls mgr.

WJWZ(FM)— 1998: 97.9 mhz; 3 kw. 328 ft TL: N32 27 08 W86 12 35. Hrs open: 4101-A Wall St., Montgomery, 36106. Phone: (334) 244-0961. Fax: (334) 279-9563. Web Site:www.979-jamz.com Licensee: Bluewater Broadcasting Co. LLC (group owner; (acq 6-21-2004; grpsl). Format: Urban. ♦Terry Barber, gen mgr; Marvin Nugent, progmg dir.

Winfield

WKXM(AM)— Aug 23, 1965: 1300 khz; 5 kw-D, 30 w-N, DA-D. TL: N33 55 52 W87 48 36. Hrs open: Box 608, 35594. Secondary address: 655 Fairview Rd. 35594. Phone: (205) 487-3261. Fax: (205) 487-6991.E-mail: wkxm@dlis.net Licensee: Ad-Media Management Corp. (acq 12-30-91; $365,000 with co-located FM; 1-27-92). Natl. Network: Westwood One, ESPN Radio, NBC Radio, . Alabama Radio Net. Format: Sports talk. Target aud: General. ♦Maxine Harper, pres, gen mgr, gen sls mgr; Doug Threadgill, news dir; Olen Booth, engrg mgr; Teresa Benton, opns mgr, mus dir & traf mgr.

WKXM-FM— 1991: 97.7 mhz; 3.9 kw. Ant 403 ft TL: N34 01 53 W87 48 06. Hrs open: 24 Box 608, 35594. Secondary address: 655 Fairview Rd. 35594. Phone: (205) 487-3261. Fax: (205) 487-6991. Natl. Network: ABC, . Format: Oldies. Target aud: General. ♦Teresa Benton, traf mgr.

York

WSLY(FM)— September 1976: 104.9 mhz; 50 kw. Ant 492 ft TL: N32 16 54 W88 15 28. Stereo. Hrs open: 24 11474 Hwy. 11 N., 36925. Phone: (205) 392-5234. Web Site:foxsports1049.com Licensee: Sarah P. Grant. Population served: 250,000 Natl. Network: Fox Sports, . Format: Sports. Target aud: 18-54; male & female.

WYLS(AM)— November 1970: 670 khz; 4.8 kw-D. TL: N32 31 24 W88 15 28. Hrs open: 7 AM-4:30 PM 11474 U.S. Hwy. 11, 36925. Phone: (205) 392-5234. Fax: (205) 392-5536.E-mail: ken@1049jackfm.com Licensee: Grantell Broadcasting Co. (acq 11-21-2003; with co-located FM). Population served: 300,000 Format: Gospel. Target aud: 25-54+. ♦Ken Michaels, opns mgr.

Alaska

Akiachak

***KHKY(FM)**— 2007: 92.7 mhz; 50 w vert. Ant 92 ft TL: N60 54 35.6 W161 25 56.6. Hrs open: Box 51101, 99551. Phone: (907) 825-3600. Fax: (907) 825-3655. Web Site:www.yupiit.org Licensee: Yupiit School District. ♦Trevor L. Snyder, gen mgr.

Anchorage

KAFC(FM)— Apr 4, 1999: 93.7 mhz; 27 kw. 663 ft TL: N61 04 02 W149 44 36. Hrs open: Box 210389, 99521. Secondary address: 6401 E. Northern Lights Blvd. 99504. Phone: (907) 333-5282. Fax: (907) 333-9851.E-mail: tom@katb.org Web Site:www.kafc.org Licensee: Christian Broadcasting Inc. Format: Christian contemp music. ♦Tom Steigleman, gen mgr.

***KAKL(FM)**— 2004: 88.5 mhz; 11 kw. Ant -82 ft TL: N61 07 14 W149 53 42. Stereo. Hrs open: 24 2351 Sunset Blvd., Suite 170-218, Rocklin, CA, 95765. Phone: (916) 251-1600. Fax: (916) 251-1650.E-mail: klove@klove.com Web Site:www.klove.com Licensee: Educational Media Foundation. Group owner: EMF Broadcasting. Natl. Network: K-Love, . Shaw Pittman. Format: Contemp Christian. News staff: 3. Target aud: 25-44; Judeo Chrisitan, female. ♦Richard Jenkins, pres; Lloyd Paker, gen mgr; Keith Whipple, dev dir; Eric Allen, natl sls mgr; Mike Novak, progmg dir; David Pierce, progmg mgr; Ed Lenane, news dir; Sam Wallington, engrg dir; Arthur Vassar, traf mgr.

KASH-FM— Dec 1, 1985: 107.5 mhz; 100 kw. 1,014 ft TL: N61 09 53 W149 41 05. Stereo. Hrs open: 24 800 E. Dimond Blvd., Suite 3-370, 99515-2043. Phone: (907) 522-1515. Fax: (907) 743-5184.E-mail: anchorage@clearchannel.com Web Site:www.country1075.com Licensee: Clear Channel Radio Licenses Inc. Group owner: Clear Channel Communications Inc. (acq 8-30-00; grpsl). Format: Country. Target aud: 25-54. ♦Gary Donovan, pres; Andy Lohman, gen mgr; Jimmy O'Brien, progmg dir.

***KATB(FM)**— June 1985: 89.3 mhz; 4.9 kw. 572 ft TL: N61 04 02 W149 44 04. (CP: Ant 344 ft. TL: N61 07 32 W149 42 46). Stereo. Hrs open: 24 Box 210389, 99521. Secondary address: 6401 E. Northern Lights Blvd. 99504. Phone: (907) 333-5282. Fax: (907) 333-9851.E-mail: tom@katb.org Web Site:www.katb.org Licensee: Christian Broadcasting Inc. Natl. Network: Moody, . Format: Relg. News: 5 hrs wkly. Target aud: 25-49; women. ♦Tom Steigleman, gen mgr.

***KAUG(FM)**— 2007: 89.9 mhz; 10 w horiz. Ant 98 ft TL: N61 24 33 W149 25 15. Hrs open: Anchorage School District, 5530 E. Northern Lights Blvd., 99504-3135. Phone: (907) 742-4000. Fax: (907) 742-3545. Licensee: Anchorage School District. ♦Carol Comeau, gen mgr.

KBFX(FM)— Oct 1, 1978: 100.5 mhz; 25 kw. 178 ft TL: N61 11 52 W149 52 31. Stereo. Hrs open: 800 E. Dimond Blvd., Suite 3-370, 99515-2043. Phone: (907) 522-1515. Fax: (907) 743-5184.E-mail: anchorage@clearchannel.com Web Site:www.1005thefox.com Licensee: Capstar TX L.P. Group owner: Clear Channel Communications Inc. (acq 8-7-00; grpsl). Format: Classic rock. ♦Gray Donavan, pres; Andy Lohman, gen mgr; Mark Murphy, opns dir; Kim Williams, gen sls mgr; Jeremy Hegna, progmg dir.

KBRJ(FM)— November 1966: 104.1 mhz; 55 kw. Ant 62 ft TL: N61 07 12 W149 53 43. Stereo. Hrs open: 24 301 Artic Slope Ave., Suite 200, 99518. Phone: (907) 344-9622. Fax: (907) 349-7326.E-mail: news@kfqd.com Web Site:kbrj.com Licensee: MCC Radio LLC. Format: Country. Target aud: 18-49. ♦Matt Valley, progmg dir.

KBYR(AM)— 1948: 700 khz; 10 kw-U. TL: N61 12 25 W149 55 20. Hrs open: 24 1399 W. 34th Ave., Suite 202, 99503. Phone: (907) 278-5297. Fax: (907) 272-5297.E-mail: dubs@kbyram.com Web Site:www.kbyr.com Licensee: Cobb Communications Inc. (acq 5-02.). Population served: 258,000 Natl. Network: ABC, . Format: News/talk. News staff: one. Target aud: 25-54. ♦Justin McDonald, gen mgr, opns dir, progmg dir; Debbie Rinckey, gen sls mgr; Kathy Phillips, news dir.

KDBZ(FM)— Feb 1, 1973: 102.1 mhz; 25 kw. 174 ft TL: N61 20 10 W149 30 46. (CP: 23 kw, ant 82 ft.). Stereo. Hrs open: 833 Gamble St, 99501. Phone: (907) 344-4045. Fax: (907) 522-6053.E-mail: info@buzz1021.com Web Site:www.buzz1021.com Licensee: New Northwest Broadcasters LLC (group owner; acq 8-12-99; $1.3 million). Wire Svc: AP Format: Hot adult contemp. Target aud: 18-44; women. ♦Pete Benedetti, CEO; Trila Bumstead, CFO; Tom Oakes, gen mgr; Carla Wyrick, gen sls mgr; Tom Oaks, progmg dir.

KEAG(FM)— 1987: 97.3 mhz; 100 kw. 593 ft TL: N61 25 22 W149 52 20. Hrs open: 24 301 Arctic Slope Ave., 99518. Phone: (907) 344-9622. Fax: (907) 349-7326.E-mail: news@kqfd.com Web Site:www.kool973.com Licensee: Morris Communications Corp. Group owner: Morris Communications Inc. (acq 10-15-98; grpsl). Format: Oldies. News staff: one; News: 3 hrs wkly. Target aud: 35-49. ♦Scott Smith, gen mgr; Dave Stroh, progmg dir.

KENI(AM)— July 15, 1967: 650 khz; 50 kw-U. TL: N61 09 58 W149 49 34. Stereo. Hrs open: 24 800 E. Dimond Blvd., Suite 3-370, 99515. Phone: (907) 522-1515. Fax: (907) 743-5186.E-mail: info@keni.com Web Site:www.keni650.com Licensee: Capstar TX L.P. Group owner: Clear Channel Communications Inc. (acq 8-30-2000; grpsl). Population served: 250,000 Natl. Rep: Christal,. Format: Talk. News staff: one; News: 5 hrs wkly. Target aud: 25-64. ♦Andy Lowman, gen mgr.

KFAT(FM)— Apr 1, 1997: 92.9 mhz; 100 kw. Ant 1,269 ft TL: N61 21 05 W149 29 10. Stereo. Hrs open: 24 833 Gamble St, 99501. Phone: (907) 344-4045.E-mail: info@kfat929.com Web Site:www.kfat929.com Licensee: New Northwest Broadcasters LLC. (group owner; (acq 7-30-99). Population served: 350,000 Natl. Network: ABC, . Format: Rhythmic CHR. Target aud: 18-34; adults. ♦Pete Benedetti, CEO; Trila Bumstead, CFO; Tom Oakes, gen mgr, opns mgr; McConnell Adams, progmg dir. Co-owned TV: KYES(TV) affil.

KFQD(AM)— 1924: 750 khz; 50 kw-U. TL: N61 08 13 W149 50 06. Hrs open: 301 Artic Slope Ave., Suite 200, 99518. Phone: (907) 344-9622. Fax: (907) 349-7326.E-mail: news@kfqd.com Web Site:www.kfqd.com Licensee: Morris Communications Corp. Group owner: Morris Communications Inc. (acq 12-1-98; grpsl). Population served: 270,000 Natl. Rep: Katz Radio,. Format: News/talk. Target aud: 35 plus; higher income, upper demo. ♦Dennis Bookey, gen mgr; Scott Smith, gen sls mgr, prom mgr; Sharon Leighow, news dir; Paul Jewusiak, chief of engrg.

KGOT(FM)— Sept 15, 1975: 101.3 mhz; 26 kw. -66 ft TL: N61 09 58 W149 49 34. Stereo. Hrs open: 24 Prog sep from AM 800 E. Dimond Blvd., Suite 3-370, 99515. Phone: (907) 522-1515. Fax: (907) 522-0672.E-mail: anchorage@clearchannel.com Web Site:www.kgot.com Licensee: Capstar TX L.P. Format: CHR, btfl music. News: 2 hrs wkly. Target aud: 12-44. ♦Mark Murphy, opns mgr.

KHAR(AM)— Jan 7, 1961: 590 khz; 5 kw-U. TL: N61 07 12 W149 53 43. Hrs open: 24 301 Artic Slope Ave., Suite 200, 99518. Phone: (907) 344-9622. Fax: (907) 349-7326.E-mail: news@kfqd.com Web Site:khar590.com Licensee: MCC Radio LLC. Group owner: Morris Communications Inc. (acq 12-1-98; grpsl). Population served: 250,000 Natl. Rep: International Media,. Wiley, Rein & Fielding. Format: Adult standards. News: 3 hrs wkly. Target aud: 35 plus; white collar, professional, upper-income demographics. ♦Dennis Bookey, gen mgr; Ron Clement, gen sls mgr; Paul Jewusiak, chief of engrg.

KLEF(FM)— Sept 16, 1988: 98.1 mhz; 25 kw. Ant -85 ft TL: N61 11 17 W149 52 57. Stereo. Hrs open: 19 4700 Business Park Blvd, Build 44, 99503. Phone: (907) 561-5556. Fax: (907) 562-4219.E-mail: klef@klef.com Web Site:www.klef.com Licensee: Chinook Concert Broadcasters Inc. (acq 6-87;6-8-87). Population served: 230,000 Rgnl rep: Tacher. Format: Classical. Target aud: 25-64; highly educated, affluent adults. Spec prog: Children one hr wkly. ♦Rick Goodfellow, gen mgr & stn mgr.

KMXS(FM)— Sept 1, 1987: 103.1 mhz; 100 kw. Ant 105 ft TL: N61 11 33 W149 54 01. Stereo. Hrs open: 24 301 Artic Slope Ave., 99518. Phone: (907) 344-9622. Fax: (907) 349-7326.E-mail: news@kftq.com Web Site:www.kmxs.com Licensee: Morris Communications Corp. Group owner: Morris Communications Inc. (acq 10-15-98; grpsl). Natl. Rep: McGavren Guild,. Format: Hot adult contemp. News staff: one; News: 5 hrs wkly. Target aud: 25-44; female listeners. ♦Scott Smith, gen mgr; Roxy Lennox, progmg dir.

***KNBA(FM)**— September 1996: 90.3 mhz; 100 kw. 640 ft TL: N61 25 22 W149 52 20. Stereo. Hrs open: 24 3600 San Jeronimo Ct. Ste 480, 99508-2870. Phone: (907) 793-3500. Fax: (907) 793-3536.E-mail: feedback@knba.org Web Site:www.knba.org Licensee: Koahnic Broadcast Corp. Population served: 250,000 Format: var/div. News staff: 3; News: 8 hrs wkly. Target aud: 20-50; well off, public radio listeners. ♦Jaclyn Sallee, CEO, pres, dev mgr; Loren Dixon, progmg dir.

KNIK-FM— Sept 15, 1960: 105.7 mhz; 51 kw. Ant 1,069 ft TL: N61 20 11 W149 30 48. Stereo. Hrs open: 24 4700 Business Park Blvd., Bldg. E 44A, 99513. Phone: (907) 522-1018. Fax: (907) 522-1027. Web Site:www.knik.com Licensee: Ubik Corp. Population served: 360,000

Natl. Rep: Interep,. Format: Smooth jazz. News staff: one; News: 9 hrs wkly. Target aud: 25-54 plus. ◆Mike Robbins, gen mgr & stn mgr; Dan Thomas, progmg dir.

KOAN(AM)—(Eagle River, Dec 25, 1986: Stn currently dark. 1020 khz; 10 kw-U, DA-N. TL: N61 29 03 W149 45 52. Hrs open: 4700 Business Park Blvd., Bldg. E, Suite 44, 99503. Phone: (907) 522-1018. Fax: (907) 522-1027. Licensee: Tati Broadcasting LLC Group owner: American Radio Brokers Inc./SFO (acq 10-1-2007; $1.5 million with KZND-FM Houston). Population served: 350,000 Format: Busines talk. News staff: . ◆Mike Robbins, gen mgr.

*KRUA(FM)— Feb 14, 1992: 88.1 mhz; 155 w. 292 ft TL: N61 07 32 W149 42 46. Hrs open: 24 PSB Rm 254, 3211 Providence Dr., 99508. Phone: (907) 786-6800. Fax: (907) 786-6806.E-mail: aykrua1@uaa.alaska.edu Web Site:www.krua.uaa.alaska.edu Licensee: University of Alaska-Anchorage. Wilkinson Barker Knauer. Format: Progsv, alternative. News staff: 4; News: 10 hrs wkly. Target aud: General; college community/div. Spec prog: Var/div music 20 hrs, sports one hr wkly. Var/div music 20 hrs, American Indian 3 hrs, sports one hr wkly ◆Neil Torquiano, stn mgr.

*KSKA(FM)— Aug 15, 1978: 91.1 mhz; 36 kw. 190 ft TL: N61 11 25 W149 48 16. (CP: 100 kw, ant 617 ft.). Stereo. Hrs open: 24 3877 University Dr., 99508. Phone: (907) 550-8400. Fax: (907) 550-8401. Fax: (907) 550-8403.E-mail: info@ksml.com Web Site:www.kska.org Licensee: Alaska Public Telecommunications Inc. (acq 1994). Population served: 250,000. Natl. Network: NPR, PRI, . Rgnl. Network: Alaska Pub. Alaska Pub. Format: In-depth news. News staff: 2; News: 70 hrs wkly. Target aud: 24 plus; professionals. ◆Paul Stankavich, pres & gen mgr; Bede Trantina, stn mgr; Duncan Moon, news dir.

KTZN(AM)— May 2, 1948: 550 khz; 5 kw-U. TL: N61 12 25 W149 55 20. Hrs open: 800 E. Dimond Blvd., Suite 3-370, 99515. Phone: (907) 522-1515. Fax: (907) 743-5184.E-mail: anchorage@clearchannel.com Web Site:www.550thezone.com Licensee: Capstar TX L.P. Group owner: Clear Channel Communications Inc. (acq 8-30-00; grpsl). Population served: 250,000 Natl. Rep: D & R Radio,. Haley, Bader & Potts. Format: Sports. Target aud: 25-54. ◆Gary Donovan, pres; Andy Lohman, gen mgr; Kim Williams, gen sls mgr; Mark Murphy, progmg dir.

KUDO(AM)— May 10, 1975: 1080 khz; 10 kw-U. TL: N61 07 12 W149 53 43. Hrs open: 4700 Business Park Blvd, Build 44, 99503. Phone: (907) 561-5556. Fax: (907) 562-4219.E-mail: klef@klef.com Web Site:kudo1080.com Licensee: IBEW Local 1547 Investments LLC (acq 9-19-2005; $244,000). Population served: 250,000 Format: Progsv talk. Target aud: 25 plus. ◆Rich McClear, gen mgr.

KWHL(FM)— Sept 18, 1982: 106.5 mhz; 100 kw. Ant -89 ft TL: N61 08 13 W149 50 06. Stereo. Hrs open: 301 Artic Slope Ave., Suite 200, 99518. Phone: (907) 344-9622. Fax: (907) 349-7326. Web Site:www.kwhl.com Licensee: Morris Communications Corp. Format: Rock/AOR. Target aud: 18-44; medium income adults, mostly men. ◆Larry Snider, progmg dir.

KYMG(FM)— Jan 1, 1989: 98.9 mhz; 100 kw. 499 ft TL: N61 25 22 W149 52 20. Stereo. Hrs open: 24 800 E. Dimond Blvd., Suite 3-370, 99515. Phone: (907) 522-1515. Fax: (907) 743-5184.E-mail: anchorage@clearchannel.com Web Site:www.magic989fm.com Licensee: Clear Channel Radio Licenses Inc. Group owner: Clear Channel Communications Inc. (acq 8-30-00; grpsl). Becker & Finerfrock. Format: Adult contemp. News staff: one; News: 4 hrs wkly. Target aud: 25-49; mostly women. Spec prog: Relg one hr wkly. ◆Gary Donovan, pres; Andy Lohman, gen mgr; Mark Murphy, opns dir; Kim Williams, gen sls mgr; Dave Flavin, progmg dir.

KZND-FM—(Houston, Apr 1, 1998: 94.7 mhz; 50 kw. Ant 371 ft TL: N61 29 03 W149 45 52. Stereo. Hrs open: 24 4700 Business Park Blvd., Bldg. E, Suite 44, 99503. Phone: (907) 522-1018. Fax: (907) 522-1027. Web Site:947theend.fm Licensee: Tati Broadcasting LLC Group owner: American Radio Brokers Inc./SFO. (acq 10-1-2007; $1.5 million with KOAN(AM) Eagle River). Format: Rock. Target aud: 25-44; general. ◆Mike Robbins, gen mgr.

Barrow

*KBRW(AM)— Dec 22, 1975: 680 khz; 10 kw-U. TL: N71 15 24 W156 31 32. Hrs open: 24 Box 109, 1695 Okpik St., 99723. Phone: (907) 852-6811. Fax: (907) 852-2274.E-mail: info@kbrw.org Web Site:www.kbrw.org Licensee: Silakkuagvik Communications Inc. Population served: 10,000. Natl. Network: PRI, NPR, . Rgnl. Network: Alaska Pub. Alaska Pub. Schwartz, Woods & Miller. Format: Var/div. News staff: one; News: 24 hrs wkly. Target aud: General. Spec prog: Class 2 hrs, jazz 6 hrs, relg one hr, Filipino 2 hrs, country 7 hrs wkly. ◆Jim Vorderstrasse, pres; Robert C. Sommer, VP, gen mgr & stn mgr; Isaac Tuckfield, opns dir, progmg dir; Kai Saxton, opns mgr; Jason Gilbert,

dev dir; Janelle Everett, prom dir, news dir; Charles M. Laykatis, chief of engrg; Doreen Simmonds, news rptr; Earl Finkler, reporter, sports cmtr; Bob Thomas, sports cmtr.

*KBRW-FM— Sept 1, 1996: 91.9 mhz; 890 w. 72 ft TL: N71 17 20 W156 45 31. Hrs open: 7 AM-midnight Box 109, 99723. Phone: (907) 852-6811. Fax: (907) 852-2274. Licensee: Silakkuagvik Communications Inc. Natl. Network: NPR, PRI, . Rgnl. Network: Alaska Pub. Alaska Pub. Format: Adult contemp, big band, class. News staff: one; News: 80 hrs wkly. Target aud: General. ◆Jason Gilbert, dev dir; Issac Tuckfield, progmg dir; Diana Gish, news dir; Robert Sommer, chief of engrg.

Bethel

KYKD(FM)— November 1994: 100.1 mhz; 12 kw. 72 ft TL: N60 48 20 W161 47 14. Stereo. Hrs open: 24 P.O. Box 2428, 99559. Phone: (907) 543-5953. Fax: (907) 543-5952.E-mail: kykd@vfcm.org Web Site:www.vfcm.org/kykd Licensee: Voice For Christ Ministries Inc. Natl. Network: Moody, Salem Radio Network, . Format: Christian music, Christian Bible teaching, News. Target aud: Native and Rural Alaskans. Spec prog: Christian Native. ◆Kristan Thieme, CEO.

*KYUK(AM)— May 13, 1971: 640 khz; 10 kw-U. TL: N60 46 57 W161 53 00. Hrs open: Box 468, 640 Radio St., 99559. Phone: (907) 543-3131. Fax: (907) 543-3130.E-mail: webmaster@kyuk.org Web Site:www.kyuk.org Licensee: Bethel Broadcasting Inc. Population served: 15,000. Natl. Network: PRI, NPR, . Rgnl. Network: Alaska Pub. Alaska Pub. Format: Bilingual talk & div mus, public info. Target aud: General. Spec prog: Class 4 hrs, country 4 hrs wkly. ◆Joan Hamilton, chmn, pres; Ronald Daugherty, gen mgr; Angela Denning Barnes, news dir; Joseph Siebert, chief of engrg. Co-owned TV: *KYUK-TV affil

Big Lake

KAGV(AM)— Nov. 1, 2005: 1110 khz; 10 kw-U. TL: N61 38 03 W149 47 36. Hrs open: Box 474, Nenana, 99760. Phone: (907) 832-5426. Web Site:www.vfcm.org/kagv.htm Licensee: Voice for Christ Ministries Inc. Format: News/talk, music, Christian. News: 20 hrs wkly. Spec prog: Native Alaskan 3 hrs wkly. ◆Art Thompson, gen mgr; Karl Thieme, stn mgr.

Chevak

*KCUK(FM)— 1990: 88.1 mhz; 150 w. 75 ft TL: N61 31 46 W165 35 20. (CP: 6 kw, ant 78 ft.). Hrs open: 985 KSD Way, 99563. Phone: (907) 858-7015. Fax: (907) 858-7279.E-mail: Nauliaran@yahoo.com Licensee: Kashunamiut School District. Natl. Network: NPR, . Alaska Pub. Format: Variety/diversified. ◆Peter Tuluk, gen mgr.

Chugiak

KHFT(AM)—Not on air, target date: unknown: 1160 khz; 9.5 kw-D, 410 w-N. TL: N61 26 05 W149 46 43. Hrs open: Box 670361, 99567. Phone: (907) 884-3278. Licensee: Steve King. ◆Steve King, gen mgr.

College

KTDZ(FM)— Sept 6, 1984: 103.9 mhz; 2.95 kw. Ant 823 ft TL: N64 55 20 W147 42 55. Stereo. Hrs open: 819 1st Ave, Ste A, Fairbanks, 99709. Phone: (907) 451-5910. Fax: (907) 451-5999.E-mail: 1039koolfm@nnbradio.com Licensee: New Northwest Broadcasters LLC (group owner; (acq 10-26-99; grpsl). Natl. Rep: Tacher,. Format: Adult hits. ◆Perry Walley, gen mgr; Glenn Anderson, opns mgr.

Cordova

KCDV(FM)—Not on air, target date: unknown: 100.9 mhz; 1.2 kw. -423 ft TL: N60 32 20 W145 45 35. Hrs open: Box 60, 112 Forestry Way, 99574. Phone: (907) 424-3796. Fax: (907) 424-3737. Format: Hot adult contemp.

KLAM(AM)— May 1953: 1450 khz; 250 w-U. TL: N60 32 20 W145 45 35. Hrs open: Box 60, 112 Forestry Way, 99574. Phone: (907) 424-3796. Fax: (907) 424-3737.E-mail: bayside@ctc.net Web Site:bayview@ctcak.net Licensee: Bayview Communications Inc. Population served: 6,000. Natl. Network: ABC, . Haley, Bader & Potts. Format: Country, classic rock, news & info. Target aud: General. ◆J.R. Lewis, gen mgr.

Deadhorse

*KCDS(FM)— 2000: 88.1 mhz; 90 w. Ant 105 ft TL: N70 12 00 W148 28 02. Hrs open: Rebroadcasts KBRW(AM) Barrow 100%. Box 109, Barrow, 99723. Phone: (907) 852-6811. Fax: (907) 852-2274. Web Site:www.kbrw.org Licensee: Silakkuagvik Communications Inc. Format: Var news/talk. ◆Robert Sommer, gen mgr; Isaac Tuckfield, progmg dir.

Dillingham

*KDLG(AM)— July 22, 1975: 670 khz; 10 kw-U. TL: N59 02 43 W158 27 07. Hrs open: 18 Box 670, 99576. Phone: (907) 842-5281. Fax: (907) 842-5645.E-mail: kdlgnews@kdlg.org Licensee: Dillingham City School District. Population served: 30,000 Natl. Network: NPR, . Rgnl. Network: Alaska Pub. Alaska Pub. Format: Adult contemp, country, rock. News staff: one; News: 20 hrs wkly. Spec prog: Yupik one hr wkly. ◆Buchi Lind, pres; Rob Carpenter, gen mgr.

*KDLG-FM—Not on air, target date: unknown: 89.9 mhz; 250 w. Ant 82 ft TL: N59 02 37 W158 27 47. Hrs open: Box 670, 99576. Phone: (907) 842-5281. Fax: (907) 842-5645. Licensee: Dillingham City School District. ◆Rob Carpenter, gen mgr.

KRUP(FM)— August 1995: 99.1 mhz; 6 kw. Ant 128 ft TL: N59 02 31 W158 31 19. Hrs open: 24 Box 157, 99576. Secondary address: 301 Airport Rd. 99576. Phone: (907) 842-5364. Licensee: McCormick Broadcasting. Format: Talk. ◆Jackson McCormick, pres & gen mgr.

Eagle River

KOAN(AM)—Licensed to Eagle River. See Anchorage

Ester

KDJF(FM)— July 1, 2007: 93.5 mhz; 20.5 kw. Ant 1,578 ft TL: N64 52 45 W148 03 14. Hrs open: 3650 Braddock St., Fairbanks, 99701. Phone: (907) 452-3697. Fax: (907) 456-3428.E-mail: tw@tvtv.com Licensee: Tanana Valley Television Co. (acq 1-10-2008; $173,000 for CP). Shainis & Peltzman. ◆William St. Pierre, pres; Terry Walley, gen mgr.

Fairbanks

KAKQ-FM— Apr 4, 1981: 101.1 mhz; 25 kw. 131 ft TL: N64 54 53 W147 38 54. Stereo. Hrs open: 24 546 9th Ave., 99701. Phone: (907) 450-1000. Fax: (907) 457-2128.E-mail: info@101magic.com Web Site:www.101magic.com Licensee: Capstar TX L.P. Group owner: Clear Channel Communications Inc. (acq 8-30-00; grpsl). Natl. Network: Westwood One, . Natl. Rep: Christal,. Format: Top 40. News staff: 2; News: one hr wkly. Target aud: 25-44; working families & adults. ◆Gary Donovan, sr VP; Pete Hutton, gen mgr; Missey Kohler, progmg dir.

KCBF(AM)— 1948: 820 khz; 10 kw-U. TL: N64 51 49 W147 45 06. Hrs open: 24 819 1st Ave, Ste A, 99709. Phone: (907) 451-5910. Fax: (907) 451-5999. Licensee: New Northwest Broadcasters LLC (group owner; acq 8-12-99; grpsl). Population served: 85,000 Natl. Network: CBS, Westwood One, . Format: Sports. News staff: one; News: 4 hrs wkly. Target aud: 35-54. ◆Perry Walley, gen mgr & stn mgr; Glenn Anderson, progmg dir; Paige Smith, chief of engrg.

KFAR(AM)— 1939: 660 khz; 10 kw-U. TL: N64 52 09 W147 49 20. Hrs open: 819 1st Ave, Ste A, 99709. Phone: (907) 451-5910. Fax: (907) 451-5999. Web Site:www.akradio.com Licensee: New Northwest Broadcasters LLC. (group owner; (acq 9-8-81; $675,000; 9-28-81). Population served: 30,000 Shaw Pittman. Format: News/talk. Target aud: 25 plus. Spec prog: Gospel 2 hrs wkly. ◆Perry Walley, gen mgr & gen sls mgr.

KFBX(AM)— Sept 18, 1972: 970 khz; 10 kw-U. TL: N64 52 48 W147 40 29. Hrs open: 24 546 9th Ave., 99701. Phone: (907) 450-1000. Fax: (907) 457-2128.E-mail: info@970kfbx.com Web Site:www.970kfbx.com Licensee: Capstar TX L.P. Group owner: Clear Channel Communications Inc. (acq 8-30-2000; grpsl). Population served: 68,578 Natl. Rep: Christal,. Format: News, talk. News staff: one; News: 30 hrs wkly. Target aud: 35 plus; males. ◆Pete Hutton, gen mgr; Cheys Castle, prom dir, prom mgr; Charlie O'Toole, progmg dir; April LaFever, disc jockey.

KIAK-FM— Sept 21, 1983: 102.5 mhz; 55 kw. Ant 1,620 ft TL: N64 52 45 W148 03 14. Stereo. Hrs open: 546 9th Ave., 99701. Phone: (907)

450-1000. Fax: (907) 457-2128.E-mail: info@kiak.com Web Site:www.kiak.com Licensee: Capstar TX L.P. Format: Country. Target aud: 18 plus; general. ♦Pete Van Nort, progmg dir; Doug Burnside, traf mgr; Monte Brown, local news ed; J.B. Carnahan, disc jockey.

KKED(FM)— Sept 20, 1962: 104.7 mhz; 10.5 kw. 440 ft TL: N64 54 42 W147 46 38. Stereo. Hrs open: 24 546 9th Ave., 99701. Phone: (907) 450-1000. Fax: (907) 457-2128. E-mail: info@1047theedge.com Web Site:www.1047theedge.com Licensee: Capstar TX L.P. Group owner: Clear Channel Communications Inc. (acq 8-30-00; grpsl). Population served: 75,000 Format: Active rock. ♦Pete Hutton, gen mgr; Mike Crosby, progmg dir.

*KSUA(FM)— Oct 10, 1985: 91.5 mhz; 3 kw. -16 ft TL: N64 51 32 W147 49 41. Stereo. Hrs open: 24 Box 750113, Univ. of Alaska, 307 Constitution Hall, 99775. Phone: (907) 474-7054. Fax: (907) 474-6314.E-mail: fyksua@uaf.edu Web Site:www.uaf.edu/ksua Licensee: The University of Alaska Board of Regents. Population served: 80,000 Format: Progsv. Target aud: 14-35. Spec prog: Black 8 hrs, Sp 3 hrs, var/div music 19 hrs wkly. ♦Nick Brewer, gen mgr; Sean Bledsoe, progmg dir.

KTDZ(FM)—See College

*KUAC(FM)— 1962: 89.9 mhz; 38 kw. 1,660 ft TL: N64 52 49 W148 03 08. Stereo. Hrs open: 24 Box 755620, Univ. of Alaska-Fairbanks, 99775-5620. Phone: (907) 474-7491. Fax: (907) 474-5064.E-mail: info@kuac.com Web Site:www.kuac.org Licensee: University of Alaska. Population served: 80,000 Natl. Network: NPR, PRI, . Alaska Pub. Wire Svc: AP Format: Div, class, news/talk. News staff: 3; News: 32 hrs wkly. Target aud: General. Spec prog: Jazz 15 hrs, folk 10 hrs, blues 4 hrs, new age 3 hrs wkly. ♦Greg Petrowich, CEO, gen mgr; Scott Diseth, stn mgr; Gretchen Gordon, dev dir. Co-owned TV: *KUAC-TV affil.

KWLF(FM)— Oct 31, 1987: 98.1 mhz; 25 kw. Ant -7 ft TL: N64 52 38 W147 48 46. (CP: 28 kw). Stereo. Hrs open: 819 1st Ave, Ste A, 99709. Phone: (907) 451-5910. Fax: (907) 451-5999.E-mail: info@akradio.com Web Site:www.akradio.com Licensee: New Northwest Broadcasters LLC. Format: CHR. Target aud: 18 plus; general.

*KWMB(FM)—Not on air, target date: unknown: 90.7 mhz; 4 kw horiz. Ant 1,660 ft TL: N64 52 49 W148 03 08. Hrs open: Box 75, Girdwood, 99587-0075. Phone: (907) 783-2256. Web Site:www.oneskyradio.com Licensee: Alaska Educational Radio System Inc. ♦Jeremy Lansman, gen mgr.

KXLR(FM)— July 1989: 95.9 mhz; 25 kw. 7 ft TL: N64 51 49 W147 45 06. Stereo. Hrs open: 24 Prog sep from AM 819 1st St., Ste. A, 99709. Phone: (907) 451-5910. Fax: (907) 451-5999. Licensee: New Northwest Broadcasters LLC Format: Classic rock. Target aud: 25-49. ♦Crys Castle, progmg mgr. Co-owned TV: KTVF(TV) affil

KYSC(FM)— 2001: 96.9 mhz; 920 w. Ant 1,607 ft TL: N64 52 45 W148 03 14. Hrs open: 24 3650 Braddock St., 99701-7617. Phone: (907) 455-9690. Fax: (907) 456-3428.E-mail: ads@kyscfm.com Licensee: Tanana Valley Radio LLC (acq 9-28-2005; $700,000). Population served: 85,000 Natl. Network: ABC, . Format: Adult contemp. ♦Bill St. Pierre, pres; Terry Walley, stn mgr. Co-owned TV: KFXF(TV) affil

Fort Yukon

*KZPA(AM)— Sept 30, 1993: 900 khz; 5 kw-U. TL: N66 33 24 W145 12 04. Hrs open: P.O. Box 50, 1933 E. 3rd Ave., 99740. Phone: (907) 662-8255. Phone: (907) 662-8255. Fax: (907) 662-2915.E-mail: kzparadio@hotmail.com Licensee: Gwandak Public Broadcasting Inc. Format: Var/div. News: 6 hrs wkly. Target aud: All ages. ♦Arlene Joseph, pres; John Alexander, progmg mgr.

Galena

*KIYU(AM)— July 4, 1986: 910 khz; 5 kw-U. TL: N64 41 18 W156 43 29. Hrs open: 24 Box 165, 99741. Phone: (907) 656-1488. Fax: (907) 656-1734.E-mail: raven@kiyu.com Web Site:www.kiyu.com Licensee: Big River Public Broadcasting Corp. Natl. Network: NPR, . Rgnl. Network: Alaska Pub. Alaska Pub. Format: Var/div. News: 35 hrs wkly. Target aud: General. Spec prog: Jazz 4 hrs, Alaska native 2 hrs wkly. ♦Susie Sam, pres; Shadow Steele, gen mgr; Tim Bodony, opns dir & progmg dir.

*KIYU-FM— 2008: 97.1 mhz; 100 w. Ant 49 ft TL: N64 44 34 W156 50 30. Hrs open: Box 165, 99741. Phone: (907) 656-1488. Fax: (907) 656-1734. Web Site:www.kiyu.com Licensee: Big River Public Broadcasting Corp. Format: Var/div. ♦Shadow Steele, gen mgr; Rex Charger, progmg dir.

Girdwood

*KEUL(FM)— September 1998: 88.9 mhz; 1.4 kw horiz. Ant 636 ft TL: N60 57 44 W149 04 38. Stereo. Hrs open: 24 Box 29, Glacier City Radio, 99587. Phone: (907) 754-2489 .E-mail: radio@glaciercity.us Web Site:http://www.glaciercity.us Licensee: Girdwood Community Club Inc. Format: Free form, free speech, electic. Target aud: Sole service provider. ♦Lewis Leonard, VP & gen mgr.

Glennallen

KCAM(AM)— Apr 16, 1964: 790 khz; 5 kw-U. TL: N62 06 52 W145 32 07. Hrs open: 24 Box 249, 99588. Phone: (907) 822-5226. Fax: (907) 822-3761.E-mail: manager@kcam.org Web Site:www.kcam.org Licensee: Northern Light Network (acq 2-25-92). Population served: 10,000 Natl. Network: Moody, USA, . Format: Diversified. News: 28 hrs wkly. Target aud: General. Spec prog: American Indian one hr, class 10 hrs, contemp Christian 8 hrs wkly. ♦Scott Yahr, stn mgr; George Reichman, gen sls mgr; Michael Eastty, progmg dir; Scott Hill, chief of engrg.

*KLOJ(FM)—Not on air, target date: unknown: 91.3 mhz; 1 kw. Ant 56 ft TL: N62 06 31.7 W145 29 13.3. Hrs open: Box 89, Kasilof, 99610. Phone: (907) 262-0920. Licensee: Blessed Hope Baptist Mission. ♦David McElwain, pres.

KVRM(FM)—Not on air, target date: unknown: 88.7 mhz; 2 kw. Ant 797 ft TL: N62 06 15 W146 10 20. Hrs open: Box 249, 99588-0249. Phone: (907) 822-5226. Fax: (907) 822-3761. Licensee: Northern Light Network. ♦Jasper Hall, pres; Scott Yahr, stn mgr.

*KXGA(FM)— October 1994: 90.5 mhz; 3.2 kw. 219 ft TL: N62 06 31 W146 10 25. (CP: Ant 750 ft.). Hrs open: 24 Rebroadcasts KCHU(AM) Valdez 100%. c/o KCHU(AM), Box 467, Valdez, 99686. Secondary address: c/o KCHU(AM), 128 Pioneer Dr., Valdez 99686. Phone: (907) 835-4665. Fax: (907) 835-2847.E-mail: kchu@cvinternet.net Web Site:www.kchu.org Licensee: Terminal Radio Inc. Format: Div, public radio. ♦John Anderson, gen mgr, opns mgr.

Haines

*KHNS(FM)— Oct 4, 1980: 102.3 mhz; 3 kw. -1,220 ft TL: N59 13 06 W135 25 29. Stereo. Hrs open: 24 Box 1109, One Theater Ln., 99827. Phone: (907) 766-2020. Fax: (907) 766-2022.E-mail: khns@khns.org Web Site:www.khns.org Licensee: Lynn Canal Broadcasting. Population served: 3,000 Natl. Network: NPR, . Rgnl. Network: Alaska Pub. Alaska Pub. Arter & Hadden. Format: Var/div. News staff: 2; News: 21 hrs wkly. Target aud: General. ♦Emily Seward, chmn, pres; Judy Erekson, gen mgr; Mary Giovanini, progmg dir; Steven Scarrott, opns mgr & mus dir.

Homer

*KBBI(AM)— Aug 4, 1979: 890 khz; 10 kw-U. TL: N59 40 14 W151 26 38. Hrs open: 24 3913 Kachemak Way, 99603. Phone: (907) 235-7721. Fax: (907) 235-2357.E-mail: dorle@kbbi.org Web Site:www.kbbi.org Licensee: Kachemak Bay Broadcasting Inc. Population served: 10,000 Natl. Network: PRI, NPR, AP Radio, . Rgnl. Network: Alaska Pub. Alaska Pub. Wire Svc: AP Format: Public radio, educational. News staff: 1.5; News: 84 hrs wkly. Target aud: General. Spec prog: APM, AAA, jazz, rock. ♦David S. Anderson, gen mgr; Jonathan Coke, dev dir; Terry Rensel, progmg dir; Paulette Wellington, mus dir; Mike Mason, news dir.

KGTL(AM)— Feb 11, 1981: 620 khz; 5 kw-U. TL: N59 41 03 W151 37 51. Hrs open: 24 Box 109, 99603-0109. Phone: (907) 235-6000. Fax: (907) 235-6683.E-mail: kwavefm@xyz.net Satcom C-5 Tr. 3 Licensee: Peninsula Communications Inc. (group owner) Population served: 25,000 Natl. Network: USA, . Southmayd & Miller. Format: Adult standards. News: 20 hrs wkly. Target aud: 35 plus; professionals. ♦David F. Becker, pres & gen mgr.

*KHGO(FM)—Not on air, target date: unknown: 89.9 mhz; 3 kw vert. Ant -187 ft TL: N59 42 41 W151 19 58. Hrs open: Box 2418, 99603. Phone: (907) 235-7931. Web Site:homernewlife.org Licensee: New Life Tabernacle Homer AK. ♦Jon R. Springer, pres.

*KMJG(FM)— 2000: 88.9 mhz; 250 w. 666 ft TL: N59 40 19 W151 30 30. Hrs open: Box 1121, Kasilof, 99610. Phone: (907) 260-7702. Fax: (907) 262-1069.E-mail: kwjg915@gci.net Web Site:www.kwjg.org Licensee: Kasilof Public Broadcasting Inc. Format: Div, oldies. ♦William Glynn, pres & gen mgr.

Houston

KBBO-FM— 1997: 92.1 mhz; 10 kw. 810 ft TL: N61 20 10 W149 30 47. Hrs open: 24 833 Gamble St, Anchorage, 99501. Phone: (907) 344-4045. Fax: (907) 522-6053.E-mail: www.921bob.fm Web Site:www.921bob.fm Licensee: New Northwest Broadcasters LLC. (group owner; (acq 8-12-99; $1.1 million). Population served: 260,000 Wire Svc: AP Format: 80s, 90s & whatever. ♦Pete Benedetti, CEO; Trila Bumstead, CFO; Tom Oakes, gen mgr.

*KJHA(FM)— July 8, 1998: 88.7 mhz; 285 w. -161 ft TL: N61 37 50 W149 48 49. Hrs open: 24 Rebroadcasts KJNP-FM North Pole midnight-7 AM and rebroadcasts KJNP(AM) North Pole 7 AM-midnight. Box 56359, North Pole, 99705. Phone: (907) 488-2216. Fax: (907) 488-5246.E-mail: kjnp@mosquitonet.com Web Site:www.mosquitonet.com/~kjnp Licensee: Evangelistic Alaska Missionary Fellowship Inc. Format: Country gospel. Spec prog: Athabaskan Indian 2 hrs, Eskimo one hr wkly. ♦Gen Nelson, CEO; Yuonne L. Carriker, pres; Richard T. Olson, VP.

KXLW(FM)— 2000: 96.3 mhz; 6 kw. Ant 262 ft TL: N61 33 58 W149 42 52. Stereo. Hrs open: 833 Gamble St, Anchorage, 99501. Phone: (907) 344-4045. Fax: (907) 522-6053.E-mail: info@xrock963.com Web Site:www.963thewolf.com Licensee: New Northwest Broadcasters LLC. (group owner; (acq 7-30-99). Wire Svc: AP Format: Rock. Target aud: 20-49; men. ♦Pete Benedetti, CEO; Trila Bumstead, CFO; Tom Oakes, gen mgr.

KZND-FM—Licensed to Houston. See Anchorage

Huslia

*KHUS(FM)— 2009: 98.1 mhz; 36 w. Ant 187 ft TL: N65 41 48 W156 21 52. Hrs open: Box 165, Galena, 99741. Phone: (907) 656-1488. Fax: (907) 656-1734. Licensee: Big River Public Broadcasting Corp. ♦Shadow Steele, gen mgr.

Juneau

*KAIS(FM)—Not on air, target date: unknown: 88.1 mhz; 10 kw vert. Ant -1,214 ft TL: N58 18 05 W134 26 26. Hrs open: 1355 Gordon Ln., Santa Rosa, CA, 95404. Phone: (707) 577-2225. Licensee: One Ministries Inc. ♦Keith J. Leitch, pres.

*KGCF(FM)—Not on air, target date: unknown: 89.7 mhz; 10 kw vert. Ant -1,214 ft TL: N58 18 05 W134 26 26. Hrs open: 2351 Sunset Blvd., Suite 170-218, Rocklin, CA, 95765. Phone: (916) 251-1600. Fax: (916) 251-1650. Licensee: Educational Media Foundation. (acq 12-9-2008; grpsl). ♦Mike Novak, pres.

KINY(AM)— May 28, 1935: 800 khz; 10 kw-D, 8 kw-N. TL: N58 18 05 W134 26 26. Stereo. Hrs open: 24 1107 W. 8th St., Suite 2, 99801. Phone: (907) 586-1800. Fax: (907) 586-3266.E-mail: kiny@ptialaska.net Web Site:www.kinyradio.com Licensee: Alaska-Juneau Communications Inc. Population served: 35,000 Format: Adult contemp. News staff: 2; News: 4 hrs wkly. Target aud: General. ♦Dennis W. Egan, pres, gen mgr; Kelly Peres, opns mgr, disc jockey; Tim Armstrong, gen sls mgr; Jim Morgan, prom dir, disc jockey; Charlie Gray, engrg dir; Christine Personnet, women's int ed; Chris Burns, disc jockey.

KJNO(AM)— Oct 19, 1952: 630 khz; 5 kw-D, 1 kw-N. TL: N58 19 47 W134 28 17. Hrs open: 24 3161 Channel Dr., Suite 2, 99801. Phone: (907) 586-3630. Fax: (907) 586-3685. Web Site:www.kjno.com Licensee: Alaska Broadcast Communications Inc. (group owner; (acq 1972; with co-located FM). Population served: 33,000 Natl. Network: CBS Radio, . Natl. Rep: Tacher,. Rgnl rep: Tacher Garvey, Schubert & Barer. Format: Talk. Target aud: 25-54. ♦Roy Paschal, pres; Richard Burns, VP, gen mgr; Jeff McCoy, progmg dir.

*KLSF(FM)—Not on air, target date: unknown: 90.5 mhz; 10 kw vert. Ant -1,214 ft TL: N58 18 05 W134 26 26. Hrs open: 2351 Sunset Blvd., Suite 170-218, Rocklin, CA, 95765. Phone: (916) 251-1600. Fax: (916) 251-1650. Licensee: Educational Media Foundation. (acq 12-9-2008; $7,500 in exchange of KLSF(FM) and KAIS(FM) Juneau for KORB(FM) Hopland, CA) ♦Mike Novak, pres.

*KNGW(FM)—Not on air, target date: unknown: 88.9 mhz; 10 kw vert. Ant -1,214 ft TL: N58 18 05 W134 26 26. Hrs open: 14820 Sherman Way, Van Nuys, CA, 91405-2233. Phone: (818) 779-8444. Fax: (818) 779-8411. Web Site:www.ktlw.net Licensee: Life On The Way Communications Inc. (acq 3-2-2009). ◆Gary Curtis, gen mgr.

*KRNN(FM)— 1999: 102.7 mhz; 6 kw. Ant -417 ft TL: N58 17 09 W134 25 40. Hrs open: 360 Egan Dr., 99801-1748. Phone: (907) 586-1670. Fax: (907) 586-3612. Web Site:www.ktoo.org Licensee: Capital Community Broadcasting Inc. (acq 12-27-2006; $676,400 with KXLL(FM) Juneau). Population served: 40,000 Format: Diverse. ◆Bill Legere, pres; Cheryl Levitt, stn mgr; John Beiler, dev dir; Jeff Brown, progmg dir; Jeff Brown, mus dir; Rosemarie Alexander, news dir.

KSUP(FM)— Dec 1, 1984: 106.3 mhz; 10 kw. Ant -1,007 ft TL: N58 18 05 W134 26 26. Stereo. Hrs open: 24 1107 W. 8th St., Suite 2, 99801. Phone: (907) 586-1063. Fax: (907) 586-3266.E-mail: ksup@ptialaska.net Web Site:www.ksupradio.com Licensee: Alaska-Juneau Communications Inc. Format: Classic, contemp rock. ◆Kelly Peres, progmg dir.

KTKU(FM)— July 9, 1984: 105.1 mhz; 3.84 kw. Ant -1,057 ft TL: N58 19 47 W134 28 17. Stereo. Hrs open: 24 3161 Channel Dr., Suite 2, 99801. Phone: (907) 586-3630. Fax: (907) 463-3685. Web Site:www.kjno.com Licensee: Alaska Broadcast Communications Inc. Format: Hot country.

*KTOO(FM)— Jan 27, 1974: 104.3 mhz; 1.4 kw. Ant -1,016 ft TL: N58 18 04 W134 25 21. Stereo. Hrs open: 24 360 Egan Dr., 99801-1748. Phone: (907) 586-1670. Fax: (907) 586-3612. Fax: (907) 586-2561 (news).E-mail: info@ktoo.org Web Site:www.ktoo.org Licensee: Capital Community Broadcasting Inc. Population served: 30,000 Natl. Network: NPR, PRI, . Rgnl. Network: Alaska Pub. Alaska Pub. Schwartz, Woods & Miller. Format: Diversified, news. News staff: 14; News: 48 hrs wkly. Target aud: General. Spec prog: Children one hrs, folk 8 hrs, Sp 2 hsr, French 3 hrs, jazz 14 hrs, Alaska native one hr wkly. ◆Bill Legere, pres, gen mgr; Cheryl Levitt, stn mgr; Mike Sakarias, opns dir; Rosemarie Alexander, news dir. Co-owned TV: *KTOO-TV affil.

KXLJ(AM)— 2008: 1330 khz; 10 kw-D, 3 kw-N. TL: N58 18 05 W134 26 26. Hrs open: Box 1471, Evergreen, CO, 80437. Phone: (303) 688-5162. Fax: (303) 660-4930. Web Site:www.kxljradio.com Licensee: Seattle Streaming Radio LLC. (acq 6-24-2006; $150,000 for CP). Natl. Network: Air America, . Format: Talk. ◆David M. Drucker, gen mgr.

*KXLL(FM)— October 1999: 100.7 mhz; 6 kw. Ant -417 ft TL: N58 17 09 W134 25 40. Stereo. Hrs open: 360 Egan Dr., 99801. Phone: (907) 586-1670. Fax: (907) 586-3612.E-mail: whiteoakbroadcasting@gci.net Web Site:www.todaysbesthits.com Licensee: Capital Community Broadcasting Inc. (acq 12-27-2006; $676,400 with KRNN(FM) Juneau). Population served: 40,000 Format: AAA, alternative. ◆Bill Legere, pres; Andy Kline, progmg dir.

Kaltag

*KALG(FM)— 2009: 98.1 mhz; 100 w. Ant -253 ft TL: N64 19 40 W158 43 36. Hrs open: Box 165, Galena, 99741. Phone: (907) 656-1488. Fax: (907) 656-1734. Licensee: Big River Public Broadcasting Corp. ◆Shadow Steel, gen mgr.

Kasilof

*KABN-FM— 2003: 89.5 mhz; 500 w horiz. Ant 197 ft TL: N60 22 44 W151 11 30. Hrs open: Box 75, Girdwood, 99587. Phone: (907) 783-2256. Web Site:www.oneskyradio.com Licensee: Alaska Educational Radio System Inc. ◆Jeremy Lansman, gen mgr.

KFSE(FM)— Nov 22, 2007: 106.9 mhz; 8 kw. Ant 203 ft TL: N60 25 55 W151 08 26. Hrs open: 24 40960 K-Beach Rd., Kenai, 99611. Phone: (907) 283-8700. Fax: (907) 283-9177.E-mail: info@radiokenai.com Licensee: KSRM Inc. (acq 3-22-2007; $210,000 for CP). Format: Rock. ◆John C. Davis, pres; Cherie Curry, gen mgr.

*KWJG(FM)— July 29, 1998: 91.5 mhz; 1 kw. 262 ft TL: N60 22 44 W151 11 30. Stereo. Hrs open: 24 Box 1121, AR, 99610. Phone: (907) 260-7702. Fax: (907) 262-1069.E-mail: info@kwjg.com Licensee: Kasilof Public Broadcasting Inc. Population served: 6,700 Bechtel & Cole. Format: Oldies, variety/diverse. ◆William J. Glynn Jr., pres & gen mgr.

*KWMD(FM)— 2003: 90.5 mhz; 500 w horiz. Ant 197 ft TL: N60 22 44 W151 11 30. Hrs open: 3700 Woodland Dr., Suite 800, Anchorage, 99517. Phone: (800) 974-6525.E-mail: aers@oneskyradio.com Licensee: Alaska Educational Radio System Inc.

Kenai

*KDLL(FM)— 1981: 91.9 mhz; 4.9 kw. 72 ft TL: N60 34 03 W151 07 25. Hrs open: 24 Box 2111, 99611. Phone: (907) 283-8433. Fax: (907) 283-6701.E-mail: allen@kdllradio.org Web Site:www.kdllradio.org Licensee: Pickle Hill Public Broadcasting Inc. Population served: 30,000 Natl. Network: NPR, PRI, . Rgnl. Network: Alaska Pub. Alaska Pub. Format: Var/div, news. News staff: one; News: 60 hrs wkly. Target aud: Affluent. Spec prog: American idian 10 hrs wkly. ◆Dave Anderson, gen mgr; Allen Auxier, stn mgr.

KPEN-FM—See Soldotna

KSRM(AM)—See Soldotna

KWHQ-FM— Nov 18, 1976: 100.1 mhz; 3 kw. Ant 260 ft TL: N60 30 49 W151 11 19. Stereo. Hrs open: 24 40960 K-Beach Rd., 99611. Phone: (907) 283-9430. Fax: (907) 283-9177.E-mail: info@radiokenai.com Web Site:www.radiokenai.com Licensee: KSRM Inc. (group owner). Population served: 45,000 Pepper & Corazzini. Wire Svc: AP Format: Modern country. News staff: 2; News: 12 hrs wkly. Target aud: 18-49. ◆John C. Davis, CEO & pres; J.R. Kitchens, opns mgr; James "Red" Goodwin, mktg dir.

Ketchikan

KFMJ(FM)— Sept 23, 1996: 99.9 mhz; 115 w. Ant 2,234 ft TL: N55 21 40 W131 47 43. Stereo. Hrs open: 24 516 Stedman St., 99901. Phone: (907) 247-3699. Fax: (907) 247-5365.E-mail: kfmj@alaska.fm Web Site:www.kfmj.com Licensee: TLP Communications Inc. Population served: 20,000 Natl. Network: ABC, USA, . Wire Svc: AP Format: Oldies. News: 18.5 hrs wkly. Target aud: 30 plus. ◆Robert J. Kern, chmn, pres; Robert Kern, gen mgr; Julie Slanaker, gen sls mgr; Stewart White, progmg dir.

KGTW(FM)— November 1987: 106.7 mhz; 4 kw. -308 ft TL: N55 20 22 W131 38 12. Stereo. Hrs open: 24 Prog sep from AM 526 Stedman St., 99901. Phone: (907) 225-2193. Fax: (907) 225-0444. Web Site:gateway1067.com Format: Country. Target aud: 18 plus. ◆John Hunt, progmg dir.

*KRBD(FM)— May 1976: 105.3 mhz; 3.4 kw. Ant 69 ft TL: N55 20 23 W131 37 29. Stereo. Hrs open: 24 123 Stedman St., 99901. Phone: (907) 225-9655. Fax: (907) 247-0808. Web Site:www.krbd.org Licensee: Rainbird Community Broadcasting Corp. Population served: 18,000 Natl. Network: NPR, PRI, . Rgnl. Network: Alaska Pub. Alaska Pub. Wire Svc: AP Format: Div. News staff: 2; News: 2 hrs wkly. Target aud: General. Spec prog: Class 11 hrs, C&W 14 hrs, folk 10 hrs, jazz 10 hrs, tribal topics 5 hrs wkly. ◆Jeff Seifert, gen mgr; Maria Dudzak, progmg dir; Deanna Garrison, news dir.

KTKN(AM)— 1942: 930 khz; 5 kw-D, 1 kw-N. TL: N55 20 22 W131 38 12. Hrs open: 24 526 Stedman St., 99901. Phone: (907) 225-2193. Fax: (907) 225-0444.E-mail: bmesser@gci.net Web Site:www.ktkn.com Licensee: Alaska Broadcast Communications Inc. (group owner). Population served: 30,000 Rgnl rep: Tacher. Haley, Bader & Potts. Format: Adult contemp, news/talk. News staff: 5; News: 20 hrs wkly. Target aud: 25 plus. ◆Blake Messer, gen mgr; Jamie Beldo, progmg dir.

Kodiak

*KMXT(FM)— June 1, 1976: 100.1 mhz; 3 kw. 3 ft TL: N57 47 41 W152 23 28. Stereo. Hrs open: 24 620 Egan Way, 99615. Phone: (907) 486-3181. Fax: (907) 486-2733.E-mail: kmxt@kmxt.org Web Site:www.kmxt.org Licensee: Kodiak Public Broadcasting Corp. (acq 10-2-75). Population served: 12,000 Natl. Network: NPR, PRI, . Rgnl. Network: Alaska Pub. Alaska Pub. Format: Div, news. News staff: 2; News: 5 hrs wkly. Target aud: General. ◆Mike Wall, gen mgr; Fred Hawley, dev dir.

KRXX(FM)— 1987: 101.1 mhz; 3.1 kw. 46 ft TL: N57 48 36 W152 20 54. Stereo. Hrs open: Prog sep from AM Box 708, 99615. Secondary address: 1315 Mill Bay Rd. 99615. Phone: (907) 486-5159. Fax: (907) 486-3044.E-mail: kvok@ak.net Web Site:www.jackfmkodiak.com Population served: 14,000 Format: Jack FM. Target aud: 18-56. ◆Ellen Simeonoff, gen mgr; JR Kitchens, opns mgr.

KVOK(AM)— Nov 7, 1974: 560 khz; 1 kw-U. TL: N57 48 36 W152 20 54. Hrs open: 24 Box 708, 99615. Secondary address: 1315 Mill Bay Rd. 99615. Phone: (907) 486-5159. Fax: (907) 486-3044.E-mail: kvok@ak.net Web Site:www.kvok.com Licensee: Kodiak Island Broadcasting Co. Inc. (acq 4-3-00; $500,000 with co-located AM). Population served: 25,000 Natl. Network: ABC, . Wire Svc: AP Format: Country, talk. Target aud: 25-56. ◆Ellen Simeonoff, gen mgr; JR Kitchens, opns mgr.

Kotzebue

*KHZK(FM)— 2007: 103.9 mhz; 200 w. Ant 46 ft TL: N66 54 11 W162 34 16. Hrs open: Rebroadcasts KSRD(FM) Saint Joseph, MO 100%. 5331 Mt. Alifan Dr., San Diego, CA, 92111. Phone: (858) 277-4991. Fax: (858) 277-1365. Web Site:www.horizonradio.org Licensee: Horizon Christian Fellowship. (acq 2-9-2006; grpsl). Format: Christian. ◆Mike MacIntosh, pres.

*KINU(FM)—Not on air, target date: unknown: 89.9 mhz; 100 w. Ant 82 ft TL: N66 53 46 W162 35 46. Hrs open: Box 78, 99752-0078. Phone: (907) 442-3434. Fax: (907) 442-2292. Licensee: Kotzebue Broadcasting Inc. ◆Chester Ballot, chmn.

*KOTZ(AM)— March 1973: 720 khz; 10 kw-U. TL: N66 50 22 W162 34 05. Hrs open: 0600-0000 Box 78, 99752. Phone: (907) 442-3434. Fax: (907) 442-2292. Licensee: Kotzebue Broadcasting Inc. Population served: 8,000 Natl. Network: NPR, . Rgnl. Network: Alaska Pub. Alaska Pub. Format: Var. Target aud: General; 90% rural Eskimo, 10% white-collar caucasian. ◆Suzy Erlich, gen mgr; Johnson Greene, progmg dir; Pierre Lonewolf, chief of engrg.

Koyukuk

*KOYU(FM)—Not on air, target date: unknown: 98.1 mhz; 100 w. Ant -23 ft TL: N64 52 58 W157 42 10. Hrs open: Box 165, Galena, 99741. Phone: (907) 656-1488. Fax: (907) 656-1734. Licensee: Big River Public Broadcasting Corp. ◆Shadow Steele, gen mgr.

McCarthy

*KXKM(FM)— October 1994: 89.7 mhz; 102 w. -169 ft TL: N61 24 58 W143 01 19. Hrs open: 24 Rebroadcasts KCHU(AM) Valdez 100%. c/o KCHU(AM), Box 467, Valdez, 99686. Secondary address: c/o KCHU(AM), 128 Pioneer Dr., Valdez 99686. Phone: (907) 835-4665. Fax: (907) 835-2847.E-mail: kchu@cvinternet.net Web Site:www.kchu.org Licensee: Terminal Radio Inc. Natl. Network: NPR, PRI, . Rgnl. Network: Alaska Radio Net. Alaska Pub. Format: Div, educ, news/talk, public radio. News staff: one; News: 10 hrs wkly. Target aud: General. ◆Lisa West, gen mgr; John Anderson, opns mgr.

McGrath

*KMCG(FM)—Not on air, target date: unknown: 90.3 mhz; 250 w vert. Ant -128 ft TL: N62 57 17 W155 35 49. Hrs open: Box 82, 99627. Phone: (907) 524-3182.E-mail: radiomcgrath@yahoo.com Licensee: McGrath Community Radio. ◆Jack Collins, gen mgr.

*KOGB(FM)—Not on air, target date: unknown: 91.3 mhz; 100 w. Ant 6 ft TL: N62 55 57 W155 31 07. Hrs open: Box 89, Kasilof, 99610. Phone: (907) 262-0920. Licensee: Blessed Hope Baptist Mission. ◆David McElwain, pres.

Naknek

KAKN(FM)— May 1987: 100.9 mhz; 3 kw. 338 ft TL: N58 44 33 W156 58 39. Stereo. Hrs open: 24 Box 0214, 99633. Secondary address: Mile 2 AK Peninsula Hwy. 99633. Phone: (907) 246-7492. Fax: (907) 246-7462.E-mail: studio@victoryradionetwork.com Web Site:www.victoryradionetwork.com Licensee: Association of Free Lutheran Congregations Mission Corp. (acq 5-8-2008). Population served: 15,000 Natl. Network: USA, . Format: Light adult contemp Christian, southern gospel, news. News: 15 hrs wkly. Target aud: General; mobile town/village population & coml fishermen. ◆Richard Long, pres; Michael Johnson, VP; Thomas Olsen, gen mgr; Anita Karlsson, stn mgr.

Nenana

KIAM(AM)— June 28, 1985: 630 khz; 10 kw-D, 3.1 kw-N. TL: N64 28 43 W149 05 10. Hrs open: 24 Box 474, 99760. Phone: (907) 832-5426. Fax: (907) 832-5450.E-mail: Alaskaradio@vfcm.org Web Site:www.vfcm.org Licensee: Voice for Christ Ministries. Natl. Network: USA, . Format: News/talk, Christian music. News: News progm 20 hrs wkly. Target aud: General. Spec prog: American Indian 3 hrs, class one hr wkly. ◆Art Thompson, gen mgr; Brian Blair, stn mgr & mus dir.

Nikiski

KXBA(FM)— March 4, 2000: 93.3 mhz; 50 kw. Ant 243 ft TL: N60 30 39 W151 16 12. Stereo. Hrs open: Box 109, Homer, 99603-0109. Phone: (907) 262-6000. Phone: (907) 283-7423. Fax: (907) 283-8461.E-mail: kpenfm@acsalaska.net Licensee: Peninsula Communications Inc. (group owner) Population served: 60,000 Southmayd & Miller. Format: Oldies. News: 8 hrs wkly. Target aud: 25-54. ◆David F. Becker, pres, gen mgr; Tiarnan "Terry" Coval, gen sls mgr; Tim White, opns mgr & news dir.

Nome

KICY(AM)— Apr 17, 1960: 850 khz; 50 kw-U. TL: N64 29 15 W165 18 53. Hrs open: 24 Box 820, 99762. Secondary address: 408 W. D St. 99762. Phone: (907) 443-2213. Fax: (907) 443-2344.E-mail: office@kicy.org Web Site:www.kicy.org Licensee: Arctic Broadcasting Association (group owner). Population served: 15,000 Natl. Network: ABC, Moody, Salem Radio Network, . Rgnl rep: Alaska Broadcast Media Wombel, Carlyle, Sandridge & Rice. Format: Southern gospel, Russian. Target aud: 25-64. ◆Ted Haney, pres; Dennis Weidler, gen mgr, gen sls mgr.

KICY-FM— Sept 11, 1977: 100.3 mhz; 84 w. Ant 40 ft TL: N64 30 04 W165 24 39. Stereo. Hrs open: 24 Box 820, 99762. Secondary address: 408. W. D St. 99762. Phone: (907) 443-2213. Fax: (907) 443-2344. Web Site:www.kicy.org Licensee: Arctic Broadcasting Association. Population served: 4,500 Wire Svc: AP Format: Christian. Target aud: 18-35.

KNOM(AM)— July 14, 1971: 780 khz; 25 kw-D, 14 kw-N. TL: N64 29 16 W165 17 58. Hrs open: 24 107 W. 3rd Ave., 99762. Phone: (907) 443-5221. Fax: (907) 443-5757.E-mail: info@knom.org Web Site:www.knom.org Licensee: Catholic Bishop of Northern Alaska. Population served: 20,000 Wilkinson, Barker & Knauer. Wire Svc: AP Format: Div, relg, news/talk. News staff: 2; News: 30 hrs wkly. Target aud: General. Spec prog: Eskimo 6 hrs, CHR 12 hrs, relg 20 hrs, class 5 hrs, weather 14 hrs wkly. ◆Kelly Brabec, pres, progmg dir; Thomas Busch, CFO, gen mgr; Ric Schmidt, gen mgr, progmg dir; Thomas A. Busch, dev dir; Paul Korchin, news dir, chief of engrg.

KNOM-FM— May 17, 1993: 96.1 mhz; 88 w. -138 ft TL: N64 29 56 W165 23 56. Stereo. Hrs open: 24 Dups AM 98% 107 W. 3rd Ave., 99762. Phone: (907) 443-5221. Fax: (907) 443-5757. Population served: 4,000 Natl. Network: AP Radio, . Wilkinson, Barker & Knauer. Wire Svc: AP News staff: 2; News: 30 hrs wkly.

North Nenana

*KIAM-FM— 2008: 91.9 mhz; 260 w. Ant -10 ft TL: N64 33 50 W149 05 21. Hrs open: Box 474, Nenana, 99760-0474. Phone: (907) 832-5426. Fax: (907) 832-5450. Web Site:www.vfcm.org Licensee: Voice for Christ Ministries Inc. Format: Christian. ◆Brian Blair, stn mgr.

North Pole

*KJNP(AM)— Oct 11, 1967: 1170 khz; 50 kw-D, 21 kw-N. TL: N64 45 34 W147 19 26. Hrs open: 19 hrs Box 56359, 99705. Phone: (907) 488-2216. Fax: (907) 488-5246.E-mail: kjnp@mosquitonet.com Web Site:www.mosquitonet.com Licensee: Evangelistic Alaska Missionary Fellowship. Population served: 8,100 Format: C&W, relg. Spec prog: Russian 11 hrs, Athabaskan Indian 2 hrs, Eskimo one hr wkly. ◆Gen Nelson, CEO; Yuonne Carriker, pres; Richerd Olson, VP.

*KJNP-FM— Oct 11, 1977: 100.3 mhz; 25 kw. Ant 1,570 ft TL: N64 52 44 W148 03 10. Stereo. Hrs open: Box 56359, 99705. Phone: (907) 488-2216. Fax: (907) 488-5246. Licensee: Evangelistic Alaska Missionary Fellowship. Format: Conservative btfl mus, relg. ◆Leland Carriker, disc jockey. Co-owned TV: *KJNP-TV affil.

Nulato

*KNUL(FM)— 2009: 99.1 mhz; 100 w. Ant 16 ft TL: N64 43 59 W158 06 25. Hrs open: Box 165, Galena, 99741. Phone: (907) 656-1488. Fax: (907) 656-1734. Licensee: Big River Public Broadcasting Corp. ◆Shadow Steel, gen mgr.

Palmer

*KJLP(FM)— August 2005: 88.9 mhz; 250 w. Ant -210 ft TL: N61 37 18 W149 01 16. Hrs open: Box 210389, Anchorage, 99521. Secondary address: 6401 E. Northern Lights, Anchorage 99521. Phone: (907) 333-5282. Fax: (907) 333-5282.E-mail: tom@katb.org Licensee: Christian Broadcasting Inc. Format: Christian. ◆Tom Steigleman, gen mgr.

Petersburg

*KFSK(FM)— September 1977: 100.9 mhz; 2 kw. -482 ft TL: N56 48 55 W132 57 12. Stereo. Hrs open: 24 Box 149, 99833. Secondary address: 404 N Second St Phone: (907) 772-3808. Fax: (907) 772-9296.E-mail: tom@kfsk.org Web Site:www.kfsk.org Licensee: Narrows Broadcasting Corp. Population served: 3,800 Natl. Network: PRI, NPR, AP Network News, . Rgnl. Network: Alaska Pub. Alaska Pub. Wire Svc: AP Format: Var. News staff: 2; News: news prgmg 7 hrs wkly. ◆Tom Abbott, gen mgr; Suzanne Fuqua, dev dir; Matt Lichtenstein, news dir; Joe Viechnicki, news rptr.

KRSA(AM)— Sept 24, 1982: 580 khz; 5 kw-U, DA-1. TL: N56 40 23 W132 55 00. Hrs open: 24 Box 650, 99833. Phone: (907) 772-3891. Fax: (907) 772-4538.E-mail: krsa@krsa.net Web Site:www.krsa.net Licensee: Northern Light Network (acq 2-20-92). Population served: 25,000 Format: Relg, country. News: 20 hrs wkly. Target aud: General. Spec prog: Class 5 hrs, children, oldies 5 hrs wkly. ◆Andrew Mazzella, pres, gen mgr, stn mgr; Daryl Carlson, progmg dir; Joe Garness, mus dir; Scott Hill, chief of engrg.

Port Alsworth

*KGCU(FM)—Not on air, target date: unknown: 90.3 mhz; 250 w vert. Ant -128 ft TL: N60 12 09 W154 18 53. Hrs open: 101 Church Dr., 99653. Phone: (907) 781-2243. Licensee: Lake Clark Bible Church. ◆James Walsh, gen mgr.

Ruby

*KRBY(FM)— 2009: 98.1 mhz; 100 w. Ant -69 ft TL: N64 44 20 W155 28 48. Hrs open: Box 165, Galena, 99741. Phone: (907) 656-1488. Fax: (907) 656-1734. Web Site:www.kiyu.com Licensee: Big River Public Broadcasting Corp. ◆Shadow Steele, gen mgr.

Saint Paul

*KUHB-FM— July 4, 1984: 91.9 mhz; 3 kw. Ant 56 ft TL: N57 07 14 W170 16 45. Stereo. Hrs open: Box 905, Pribios School District, 99660. Phone: (907) 546-2254. Fax: (907) 546-2367.E-mail: gm@ kuhb.org Licensee: Pribilof School District. Natl. Network: NPR, . Format: Anything & everything. ◆Walt Gregg, gen mgr; B.J. Kibbe, news dir.

Sand Point

*KSDP(AM)— Mar 2, 1983: 830 khz; 1 kw-U. TL: N55 21 06 W160 28 02. Hrs open: 24
Rebroadcasts KDLG(AM) Dillingham.
Box 328, City Bldg, 328 Main St., 99661. Phone: (907) 383-5737. Fax: (907) 383-5737.E-mail: gm@ksdpradio.com Web Site:www.ksdpradio.org Licensee: Aleutian Peninsula Broadcasting Inc. Population served: 6,000 Natl. Network: NPR, PRI, . Format: Div. Target aud: General. Spec prog: Gospel. ◆Kells Hetherington, gen mgr; Jeremy Krone, progmg dir.

*KSPM(FM)—Not on air, target date: unknown: 90.3 mhz; 250 w vert. Ant -66 ft TL: N55 20 13 W160 30 01. Hrs open: Box 329, 99661-0329. Phone: (907) 383-4551.E-mail: radiosandpoint@yahoo.com Web Site:www.sandpointchurch.com Licensee: Sand Point Baptist Church. ◆Craig D. Furlough, gen mgr.

Seward

KKNI(FM)— 1998: Stn currently dark. 105.9 mhz; 3 kw. Ant -1,312 ft TL: N60 05 27 W149 20 20. Hrs open: Box 2414, 99664. Phone: (907) 224-5793. Fax: (907) 224-4702. Licensee: Seward Media Partners LLC (acq 9-18-2006; $40,000 with KSEW(AM) Seward). ◆Wolfgang Kurtz, gen mgr; James Spanos, stn mgr.

KSEW(AM)— November 1948: 950 khz; 1 kw-U. TL: N60 06 51 W149 26 44. Hrs open: Box 2414, 99664. Phone: (907) 224-5793. Fax: (907) 224-4702. Web Site:www.sewardradio.com Licensee: Seward Media Partners LLC (acq 9-18-2006; $40,000 with KKNI(FM) Seward). Population served: 3,200 Format: Country. ◆Wolfgang Kurtz, gen mgr; James Spanos, stn mgr.

Sitka

*KCAW(FM)— Feb 19, 1982: 104.7 mhz; 5 kw. -612 ft TL: N57 03 13 W135 21 07. Stereo. Hrs open: 24 2 Lincoln St., Suite B, 99835. Phone: (907) 747-5877. Fax: (907) 747-5977. Web Site:www.ravenradio.org Licensee: Raven Radio Foundation. Natl. Network: NPR, PRI, . Rgnl.

Network: Alaska Pub. Alaska Pub. Format: Div, news. Target aud: General. Spec prog: Class 15 hrs, Indian 3 hrs wkly. ◆Ken Fate, CEO, gen mgr; Steve Will, progmg dir; Robert Woolsey, news dir.

KIFW(AM)— September 1949: 1230 khz; 1 kw-U. TL: N57 03 27 W135 20 02. Hrs open: 24 611 Lake St., 99835. Phone: (907) 747-6626. Phone: (907) 747-5439. Fax: (907) 747-8455.E-mail: kifw@ptialaska.net Web Site:www.kifw.com Licensee: Alaska Broadcast Communications Inc. (group owner; (acq 12-21-2000; grpsl). Population served: 8,700 Haley, Bader & Potts. Format: MOR, oldies, news/talk. News: 60 hrs wkly. Target aud: 18-49; all demographics. ◆Steve Rhyner, pres; Blake Messer, stn mgr; Bobbie Rusk, gen sls mgr; Devin Reiter, progmg dir; Clint Daniels, news dir; Chris Kobger, chief of engrg.

KSBZ(FM)— Oct 18, 1990: 103.1 mhz; 3 kw. Ant 144 ft TL: N57 03 27 W135 20 02. Stereo. Hrs open: 24 611 Lake St., 99835. Phone: (907) 747-6627. Fax: (907) 747-8455. Web Site:www.ksbz.com Licensee: Alaska Broadcast Communications Inc. Format: Country. Target aud: 18-34. ◆Amy Denny, pub affrs dir.

Soldotna

KKIS-FM— Mar 2, 1994: 96.5 mhz; 10 kw. 259 ft TL: N60 31 26 W151 03 23. Stereo. Hrs open: 24 40960 K-Beach Rd., Kenai, 99611. Phone: (907) 283-5821. Fax: (907) 283-9177.E-mail: info@radiokenai.com Web Site:www.radiokenai.com Licensee: KSRM Inc. (group owner; (acq 12-7-2001; $350,000 with co-located AM). Population served: 45,000 Natl. Network: ABC, . Pepper & Corazzini LLP. Format: Adult contemp. News staff: one; News: 2 hrs wkly. Target aud: 18-49. ◆John C. Davis, CEO, pres; Steve Holloway, opns mgr; James "Red" Goodwin, mktg dir; Joe Nicks, news dir.

KPEN-FM— Dec 1, 1984: 101.7 mhz; 25 kw. 240 ft TL: N60 30 40 W151 16 12. Stereo. Hrs open: 24 Box 109, Homer, 99603. Phone: (907) 262-6000. Phone: (907) 283-7451. Fax: (907) 235-6683.E-mail: kwavefm@xyz.net Licensee: Peninsula Communications Inc. (group owner) Population served: 50,000 Natl. Network: USA, . Southmayd & Miller. Format: Country. Target aud: 25-54. ◆David F. Becker, pres, gen mgr; Tim White, opns mgr & news dir.

KSLD(AM)— Apr 6, 1985: 1140 khz; 10 kw-U. TL: N60 31 26 W151 03 23. Stereo. Hrs open: 24 40960 K-Beach Rd., Kenai, 99611. Phone: (907) 283-8700.E-mail: info@radiokenai.com Web Site:www.radiokenai.com Licensee: KSRM Inc. Population served: 45,000 Natl. Network: Westwood One, . Pepper and Corazzini. Format: Classic rock, CHR. News: one hr wkly. Target aud: 25-59.

KSRM(AM)— Sept 27, 1967: 920 khz; 5 kw-U. TL: N60 30 49 W151 11 19. Hrs open: 24 40960 K-Beach Rd., Kenai, 99611. Phone: (907) 283-5959. Fax: (907) 283-5811.E-mail: info@radiokenai.com Web Site:www.radiokenai.com Licensee: KSRM Inc. (group owner; (acq 4-72). Population served: 45,000 Pepper & Corazzini. Format: News/talk. News staff: one; News: 105 hrs wkly. Target aud: 25-54. ◆John C. Davis, CEO, chmn, pres, gen mgr; Dayne Clark, exec VP; Steve Holloway, opns mgr; James "Red" Goodwin, dev dir, mktg dir, prom dir, adv dir; J.R. Kitchens, progmg dir; Joe Nicks, news dir; Paul Jewusiak, engrg dir; Dan Gensel, sports cmtr.

Sterling

KMVV(FM)— Mar 13, 2008: 104.9 mhz; 45 kw. Ant 663 ft TL: N61 04 02 W149 44 36. Hrs open: 4700 Business Park Blvd., Bldg. E, Suite 44, Anchorage, 99503. Phone: (907) 522-1018. Fax: (907) 522-1027. Licensee: World Radio Link Inc. Format: Rhythmic adult contemp. ◆Mike Robbins, gen mgr; Cary Carrigan, progmg dir.

*KRAW(FM)— 2006: 90.1 mhz; 1.2 kw horiz. Ant 20 ft TL: N60 29 16 W150 47 38. Hrs open: 3700 Woodland Dr., Anchorage, 99517. Phone: (800) 974-6525. Licensee: Alaska Educational Radio System Inc. ◆Wolfgang Kurtz, pres.

Talkeetna

*KTNA(FM)— February 1993: 88.9 mhz; 7.2 kw. Ant 72 ft TL: N62 19 05 W150 17 52. Stereo. Hrs open: 24 Box 300, 13764 2nd Ave., Talkeetna, 99676. Phone: (907) 733-1700. Fax: (907) 733-1781.E-mail: info@ktna.org Web Site:www.ktna.org Licensee: Talkeetna Community Radio Inc. Population served: 4,500 Natl. Network: NPR, PRI, . Format: Eclectic, news/talk. News staff: one; News: 15 hrs wkly. Target aud: General; rural Alaskans. Spec prog: Blues 5 hrs, light rock 5 hrs wkly. ◆Robert Ambrose, gen mgr & stn mgr; Kirsten Merkley, gen sls mgr; Deborah Brock, progmg dir; Amanda Stossel, news dir.

Tok

*KUDU(FM)— Mar 3, 1998: 91.9 mhz; 200 w. -121 ft TL: N63 19 53 W143 07 02. Hrs open: Box 661, 99780. Phone: (907) 883-4397. Phone: (907) 883-5855. Fax: (907) 883-5245.E-mail: defiee@oddpost.com Web Site:www.lifetalk.net Licensee: Lifetalk Broadcasting Association. Format: Relg, inspirational music, talk. ◆Francine Lee, gen mgr.

Unalakleet

KNSA(AM)— 1998: 930 khz; 2.5 kw-U. TL: N63 53 17 W160 41 29. Hrs open: Box 178, 99684. Phone: (907) 624-3100. Phone: (907) 624-3101. Fax: (907) 624-3130. Licensee: Unalakleet Broadcasting Inc. Format: Var. ◆Henry Ivanoff, stn mgr.

Unalaska

*KUCB(FM)— October 2008: 89.7 mhz; 1 kw. Ant -308 ft TL: N53 52 35 W166 32 24. Hrs open: Box 181, 99685. Phone: (907) 581-1888. Fax: (907) 581-1634. Web Site:www.kucbradio.org Licensee: Unalaska Community Broadcasting Inc. Natl. Network: NPR, . Alaska Pub. Format: Public radio. ◆Lauren Adams, gen mgr.

Valdez

*KCHU(AM)— Aug 3, 1986: 770 khz; 9.7 kw-U. TL: N61 06 40 W146 15 39. Hrs open: 24 PO Box 467, 99686. Secondary address: 128 Poineer Dr. Phone: (907) 835-4665. Fax: (907) 835-2847.E-mail: gm@kchu.org Web Site:www.kchu.org Licensee: Terminal Radio Inc. (acq 10-84; $250,000; 10-8-84). Natl. Network: NPR, PRI, . Rgnl. Network: Alaska Pub. Alaska Pub. Format: Div. News staff: one; News: 40 hrs wkly. Target aud: General. ◆Danny Sparrell, gen mgr; John Anderson, opns dir.

KVAK(AM)— January 1983: 1230 khz; 1 kw-U. TL: N61 07 16 W146 15 25. Hrs open: 24 Box 367, 99686. Secondary address: 501 E. Bremner St. 99686. Phone: (907) 835-5825. Fax: (907) 835-5158.E-mail: kvak@kvak.com Licensee: North Wave Communications Inc. (acq 1996). Format: Country, talk. News: one hr wkly. Target aud: General. ◆Laurie Prax, pres & traf mgr.

KVAK-FM— May 28, 1999: 93.3 mhz; 6 kw. -1,958 ft TL: N61 07 16 W146 15 25. Hrs open: Box 367, 501 E. Bremner St., Suite 2, 99686. Phone: (907) 835-5825. Fax: (907) 835-5158.E-mail: kvak@kvak.com Format: Hot adult contemp.

Wasilla

KAYO(FM)— Jan 23, 2009: 100.9 mhz; 50 kw. Ant -276 ft TL: N61 38 21 W148 59 56. Hrs open: 5431 E. Mayflower Ln., Unit 3, 99654. Phone: (907) 631-0493. Fax: (907) 631-0483. Web Site:www.countrylegends1009.com Licensee: MCC Radio LLC. Format: Country. ◆Eddie Maxwell, progmg dir.

KMBQ(AM)— 2008: 1430 khz; 1 kw-U. TL: N61 37 09 W149 17 17. Hrs open: 2200 E. Parks Hwy., 99654. Phone: (907) 373-0222. Fax: (907) 376-1575. Web Site:www.kmbq.com Licensee: Spirit of Alaska Broadcasting Inc. (acq 1-29-2007; $70,000 for CP). ◆John Klapperich, pres & gen mgr.

KMBQ-FM— Mar 15, 1985: 99.7 mhz; 51 kw. -187 ft TL: N61 38 03 W149 26 25. Stereo. Hrs open: 24 2200 E. Parks Hwy., 99654. Phone: (907) 373-0222. Fax: (907) 376-1575.E-mail: john@kmbq Web Site:www.kmbq.com Licensee: KMBQ Corp. Population served: 91,000 Natl. Network: CNN Radio, . Garvey, Schukert & Barer. Format: Adult contemp. News staff: 2; News: 13 wkly. Target aud: 25-54; mid-upper class suburbanites & farm community. ◆John Klapperich, CEO, gen mgr; Roxi Lennox, progmg dir; Van Craft, chief of engrg.

Wrangell

*KSTK(FM)— July 2, 1977: 101.7 mhz; 3 kw. -294 ft TL: N56 27 14 W132 22 54. Stereo. Hrs open: 24 Box 1141, 99929. Secondary address: 202 St. Michael's 99929. Phone: (907) 874-2345. Fax: (907) 874-3293.E-mail: info@kstk.com Web Site:kstk.org Licensee: Wrangell Radio Group Inc. Population served: 3,200 Natl. Network: NPR, PRI, . Rgnl. Network: Alaska Pub., Alaska Radio Net. Alaska Pub. Format: Div. News staff: 2; News: 20 hrs wkly. Target aud: General. Spec prog: Class 4 hrs, country 16 hrs, jazz 8 hrs wkly. ◆Peter Helgeson, gen mgr; Cindy Sweat, dev dir; Dawn Stevens, progmg dir.

Yakutat

KHZX(FM)—Not on air, target date: unknown: 103.9 mhz; 170 w. Ant 52 ft TL: N59 33 12 W139 44 47. Hrs open: 5331 Mount Alifan Dr., San Diego, CA, 92111-2622. Phone: (858) 277-4991. Fax: (858) 277-1365. Licensee: Horizon Christian Fellowship. ◆Mike MacIntosh, pres.

Arizona

Apache Junction

KVVA-FM— July 1, 1973: 107.1 mhz; 25 kw. Ant 312 ft TL: N33 26 48 W111 37 32. Stereo. Hrs open: 501 N. 44th St., Suite 425, Phoenix, 85008. Phone: (602) 266-2005. Fax: (602) 279-2921. Licensee: Entravision Holdings LLC. Group owner: Entravision Communications Corp. (acq 7-28-00; grpsl). Cohn & Marks. Format: Sp adult hits. Target aud: 18-49; Hispanic. ◆Tom Duran, gen mgr; Edgar Pineda, progmg dir.

Arizona City

KKMR(FM)— Apr 13, 1985: 106.5 mhz; 6 kw. Ant 292 ft TL: N32 50 04 W111 38 15. Hrs open: 24 4745 N. 7th St., Suite 140, Phoenix, 85014. Phone: (602) 308-7900. Fax: (602) 308-7979. Web Site:www.univision.com Licensee: HBC License Corp. Group owner: Univision Radio (acq 9-22-2003; grpsl). Population served: 3,173,200 Format: Sp adult hits. Target aud: 25-54. ◆Mary McEvilly-Hernandez, VP & gen mgr.

Bagdad

KFTT(FM)— 2002: 103.1 mhz; 900 w horiz. Ant 1,250 ft TL: N34 33 25 W113 16 00. Hrs open: 10 Media Center Dr., Lake Havasu City, 86403. Phone: (928) 855-1051. Fax: (928) 855-7996.E-mail: epress@maddog.net Web Site:www.maddog.net Licensee: Smoke and Mirrors LLC. (acq 4-18-2001). Format: Adult standards. ◆Chris Rolando, gen mgr.

Benson

KAVV(FM)— April 1983: 97.7 mhz; 6 kw. 590 ft TL: N31 54 24 W110 27 08. Stereo. Hrs open: 24 Box 18899, Tucson, 85731-8899. Secondary address: 156 W. 5th St. 85602. Phone: (520) 586-9797.E-mail: cave@gainbroadband.com Web Site:www.cavefm.com Licensee: Stereo 97 Inc. Population served: 60,000 Format: C&W. Target aud: 25-49. Spec prog: Relg 3 hrs wkly. ◆Jack Lotsof, pres; Paul Lotsof, gen mgr, stn mgr, progmg dir & chief of engrg.

Bisbee

*KRMB(FM)— 1997: 90.1 mhz; 47 w. 2,247 ft TL: N31 28 52 W109 57 30. Hrs open:
Rebroadcasts KRMC(FM) Douglas 100%.
Box 2520, Douglas, 85603. Phone: (520) 364-5392. Fax: (520) 364-5392. Licensee: World Radio Network Inc. (group owner) Format: Relg, Sp. ◆Glen Lafitte, gen mgr.

KWCD(FM)— Oct 12, 1979: 92.3 mhz; 90 w. Ant 2,129 ft TL: N31 28 52 W109 57 30. Stereo. Hrs open: 24 Box 2770, 2300 Busby Dr., Sierra Vista, 85636-2770. Phone: (520) 458-4313. Fax: (520) 458-4317.E-mail: ktan@wavmax.com Licensee: CCR-Sierra Vista IV LLC. Group owner: Cherry Creek Radio LLC (acq 12-19-2003; grpsl). Population served: 92,000 Natl. Network: Westwood One, . Natl. Rep: Tacher,. Format: Country. News staff: one; News: one hr wkly. Target aud: 25-54; financially secure adults & military personnel. ◆Paul Orlando, gen mgr; Grady Butler, opns mgr.

*KWRB(FM)— December 1996: 90.9 mhz; 99w. 2,093 ft TL: N31 28 58 W109 57 29. Hrs open: 24 96-C S. Carmichael, Sierra Vista, 85635. Phone: (520) 452-8022. Fax: (520) 452-0927.E-mail: kwrb@lwpn.org Web Site:www.kwrb.org Licensee: World Radio Network Inc. Population served: 115,000 Format: Christian, educ, inspirational. Target aud: Women 35+. ◆Dwight Lind, gen mgr.

Black Canyon City

KMIA(AM)— Sept 1, 1981: 710 khz; 22 kw-D, 3.9 kw-N, DA-2. TL: N34 04 48 W112 09 15. Hrs open: 24 501 N. 44th St., Suite 425, Phoenix, 85008. Phone: (602) 776-1400. Fax: (602) 279-2921.E-mail:

info@entravision.com Licensee: Entravision Holdings LLC. Group owner: Entravision Communications Corp. (acq 7-28-00; grpsl). Format: Sports, Sp. Target aud: 18-54. ◆Tom Duran, gen mgr.

Buckeye

KDVA(FM)— 1993: 106.9 mhz; 6 kw. Ant 305 ft TL: N33 27 01 W112 35 58. Hrs open: 501 N. 44th St., Suite 425, Phoenix, 85008. Phone: (602) 776-1400. Fax: (602) 279-2921. Licensee: Entravision Holdings LLC. Group owner: Entravision Communications Corp. (acq 6-14-2001; $10 million). Format: Latin Contempory, "Radio Romantica". Spec prog: Black 6 hrs, gospel 7 hrs wkly. ◆Tom Duran, gen mgr; Edgar Pineda, progmg dir.

Bullhead City

KFLG(AM)— Oct 1, 1978: 1000 khz; 1 kw-D. TL: N35 10 10 W114 38 02. Hrs open: 1531 Jill Way, Suite 7, 86426-9341. Phone: (928) 763-5586. Fax: (928) 763-3775. Licensee: Cameron Broadcasting Inc. (group owner; acq 11-24-99). Population served: 76,000 Format: Legends/Nostalgia. Target aud: 35 plus; upper demographics. ◆Billy Williams, CEO; Craig Powers, opns mgr; Mike Fletcher, gen sls mgr; Dave Cooper, chief of engrg.

*KVIR(FM)—Not on air, target date: unknown: 89.9 mhz; 38 kw vert. Ant 2,995 ft TL: N35 06 28 W113 52 40. Hrs open: 4002 N. 3300 E., Twin Falls, ID, 83301. Phone: (208) 734-6633. Fax: (208) 736-1958. Web Site:www.csnradio.com Licensee: CSN International. ◆Mike Kestler, pres.

KZZZ(AM)— Nov 15, 1981: 1490 khz; 1 kw-U. TL: N35 05 10 W112 07 40. Hrs open: 1531 Jill Way, Suite 7, 86426-9341. Phone: (928) 763-5586. Fax: (928) 763-3775. Web Site:www.talkatoz.com Licensee: Cameron Broadcasting Inc. (group owner; acq 7-91; $1.28 million with KNKK(FM) Needles, CA; 7-29-91). Population served: 37000 Natl. Network: Fox News Radio, . Format: Talk. News staff: one. Target aud: 35 plus. ◆William Jaeger, CEO; Don Jaeger, gen mgr; Craig Powers, opns mgr; Mike Fletcher, gen sls mgr; Dave Cooper, chief of engrg.

Cameron

KYNN(AM)—Not on air, target date: unknown: 1450 khz; 1 kw-U. TL: N35 51 46 W111 25 52. Hrs open: 8320 W. 66th Ave., Arvada, CO, 80004. Phone: (303) 431-0103. Licensee: Better Life Ministries. ◆Claud Pettit, pres.

Camp Verde

KAJM(FM)— July 4, 1984: 104.3 mhz; 40 kw. Ant 2,647 ft TL: N34 13 47 W112 21 03. Stereo. Hrs open: 24 7434 E. Stetson Dr., Suite 255, Scottsdale, 85251. Phone: (480) 994-9100. Phone: (800) 254-7510. Fax: (480) 423-8770.E-mail: info@mega1043.com Web Site:www.mega1043.com Licensee: Sierra H. Broadcasting Inc. Population served: 3,000,000 Natl. Network: Westwood One, CNN Radio, . Natl. Rep: Roslin,. Format: Old school/rhythm & blues. Target aud: 25-54; general. ◆Michael Mallace, gen mgr; Jack Preda, sls dir; Michael Devitt, prom dir; Rod Carrillo, progmg dir; Alex Santa Maria, mus dir; Steven Szalay, opns mgr & pub affrs dir; Michael Day, chief of engrg.

Casa Grande

*KLVA(FM)— Apr 8, 1976: 105.5 mhz; 50 kw. Ant 492 ft TL: N33 00 14 W111 58 53. Stereo. Hrs open: 24 2351 Sunset Blvd., Suite 170-218, Rocklin, CA, 95765. Phone: (916) 251-1600. Fax: (916) 251-1650-.E-mail: klove@klove.com Web Site:www.klove.com Yes Licensee: Educational Media Foundation. Group owner: EMF Broadcasting (acq 7-19-99). Population served: 1,881,000 Natl. Network: K-Love,. Shaw, Pittman. Format: Contemp Christian. Target aud: 25-44; Judeo-Christian, female. Spec prog: Sports 7 hrs wkly. ◆Richard Jenkins, pres; Mike Novak, VP, progmg dir; Lloyd Parker, gen mgr; Ed Lenane, opns dir, news dir; Keith Whipple, dev dir; Eric Allen, natl sls mgr; David Pierce, progmg mgr; Jon Rivers, mus dir; Sam Wallington, engrg dir; Arthur Vassar, traf mgr; Karen Johnson, news rptr.

Cave Creek

KFNX(AM)— June 27, 1997: 1100 khz; 50 kw-D, 1 kw-N, DA-2. TL: N33 47 52 W111 59 30. Stereo. Hrs open: 24 2001 N. 3rd St., Suite 102, Phoenix, 85004. Phone: (602) 277-1100. Fax: (602) 248-1478.E-mail: info@kfnxam.com Web Site:www.1100kfnx.com Licensee: North American Broadcasting Co. Inc., debtor in possession (acq 8-13-02). Population served: 3,000,000 Format: Talk. News staff: 2. Target aud: 35 plus; Upscale. ◆Francis Battaglia, CEO.

Chandler

KMLE(FM)—Licensed to Chandler. See Phoenix

Chinle

KFXR-FM— August 1995: 107.3 mhz; 3.6 kw. 1,630 ft TL: N36 21 07 W109 49 54. Hrs open: 24 Rebroadcasts KGLX(FM) Gallup. 1632 S. Second St., Gallup, NM, 87301. Phone: (505) 863-9391. Fax: (505) 863-9393. Licensee: CC Licenses LLC. Group owner: Clear Channel Communications Inc. (acq 8-18-2000). Format: Country. ◆Mary Ann Armijo, gen mgr.

Chino Valley

KDDL(FM)— 1999: 94.3 mhz; 4.1 kw. Ant 810 ft TL: N34 49 32 W112 34 09. Hrs open: 8581 E. Florentine, Suite C, Prescott Valley, 86314. Phone: (928) 775-2530. Fax: (928) 775-2532. Web Site:www.kfpbradio.com Licensee: Prescott Valley Broadcasting Co. Inc. (acq 10-15-2007) $1.2 million). Format: Country. ◆Patti Esell, gen mgr.

Claypool

KIKO-FM—Licensed to Claypool. See Miami

Clifton

KCUZ(AM)—Licensed to Clifton. See Safford

KWRQ(FM)—Licensed to Clifton. See Safford

Colorado City

KXFF(FM)— 1993: 107.3 mhz; 35 kw. Ant 1,138 ft TL: N37 05 41 W113 11 06. Hrs open: 24 750 W. Ridgeview Dr., Suite 204, Saint George, UT, 84770. Phone: (435) 673-3579. Fax: (435) 673-8900. Licensee: CCR-St. George IV LLC. (group owner; (acq 5-3-2006; grpsl). Population served: 50,000 Format: Hits of the 80s & 90s. ◆Chris McCarthy, sls dir; Rick Parrish, mktg mgr.

Coolidge

KCKY(AM)— Nov 19, 1964: 1150 khz; 5 kw-D, 1 kw-N, DA-2. TL: N33 00 27 W111 32 54. (CP: COL Apache Junction. 5 kw-D, 185 w-N, DA-2. TL: N33 00 27 W111 32 57). Hrs open: 18 1445 W. Baseline Road, Phoenix, 85041. Phone: (602) 426-1150. Phone: (602) 426-9606. Fax: (602) 426-8119. Licensee: Cortaro Broadcasting Corp. (acq 6-13-2003; exchange agreement with KEVT(AM) Cortaro). Population served: 2,045,000 Format: Sp, Christian contemp. News staff: one. Target aud: General. ◆Moses Herrera, pres; Moses Herrera Jr., stn mgr.

*KZAI(FM)— 2004: 89.9 mhz; 10 w horiz, 10 kw vert. Ant 3,025 ft TL: N33 17 55 W110 50 28. Hrs open: 2351 Sunset Blvd., Suite 170-218, Rocklin, CA, 95765. Phone: (916) 251-1600. Fax: (916) 251-1650. Web Site:www.air1.com Licensee: Educational Media Foundation. (acq 2-10-2006; $2.5 million). Natl. Network: Air 1, . Format: Alternative, Christian. ◆Richard Jenkins, pres; Mike Novak, VP; Keith Whipple, dev dir; David Pierce, progmg mgr; Ed Lenane, news dir; Sam Wallington, engrg dir; Karen Johnson, news rptr.

Cortaro

KVOI(AM)— 1994: 1030 khz; 10 kw-D, 1 kw-N, DA-2. TL: N32 20 51 W111 04 19. Hrs open: 24 3222 S. Richey Ave., Tucson, 85713. Phone: (520) 790-2440. Fax: (520) 790-2937.E-mail: info@kvoi.com Web Site:www.kvoi.com Licensee: Good News Communications Inc. (acq 6-8-2009; $1.3 million). Format: Talk. Target aud: 35 plus. ◆Doug Martin, gen mgr; Ed Alexander, opns mgr; Mary Martin, gen sls mgr.

Cottonwood

KKLD(FM)— August 1983: 95.9 mhz; 21 kw. Ant 2,621 ft TL: N34 41 11 W112 07 02. Stereo. Hrs open: 24 Box 187, 86326. Phone: (928) 634-2286. Fax: (928) 634-2295. Web Site:www.kkld.com Licensee: Yavapai Broadcasting Corp. (group owner; (acq 10-1-2000; grpsl). Population served: 200,000 Format: Oldies. News: 7 hrs wkly. Target aud: 18-49. ◆W. Grant Hafley, pres; David J. Kessel, gen mgr; Rich Malone, opns mgr.

KVRD-FM— July 1991: 105.7 mhz; 380 w. 2,555 ft TL: N34 41 15 W112 07 02. (CP: 300 w, ant 2,545 ft.). Stereo. Hrs open: 24 Box 187 , 86326. Secondary address: 3405 E. Hwy. 89 A, Bldg. A 86326. Phone: (928) 634-2286. Fax: (928) 634-2295. Web Site:www.myradioplace.com Population served: 50,000 Format: Country. News: 2 hrs wkly. Target aud: General. ◆Mark Bachman, progmg dir; Paul David, local news ed.

KYBC(AM)— Dec 20, 1964: 1600 khz; 1 kw-D, 46 w-N. TL: N34 43 15 W109 31 45. Hrs open: 24 Box 187, 86326. Secondary address: 3405 E. Hwy. 89 A, Bldg. A 86326. Phone: (928) 634-2286. Fax: (928) 634-2295.E-mail: kybc@myradioplace.com Web Site:www.myradioplace.com Licensee: Yavapai Broadcasting Corp. (group owner; acq 1-96; $750,000 with co-located FM). Population served: 20,000 Natl. Network: Westwood One, . Format: Adult standards, MOR. News staff: 2. Target aud: 18-plus. ◆W. Grant Hafley, pres; David J. Kessel, gen mgr; Mike Puetz, sls dir; Paul Siabe, progmg dir; Paul David, news dir.

Dewey-Humboldt

KMVA(FM)— Jan 15, 1988: 97.5 mhz; 42 kw. Ant 2,785 ft TL: N34 14 05 W112 22 02. Stereo. Hrs open: 24 Phone: (602) 222-9750. Fax: (602) 222-2297. Web Site:www.movin975.com Licensee: Trumper Communications III License LLC (acq 5-27-2005; $22.6 million). Population served: 300,000 Format: Rhythmic hits from the 80s, 90s and today. ◆Jim Ryan, gen sls mgr; Bob Lewis, progmg dir.

Dolan Springs

KOAS(FM)— Jan 7, 1976: 105.7 mhz; 100 kw horiz. Ant 1,761 ft TL: N35 50 11 W114 19 08. Stereo. Hrs open: 24 2725 E. Desert Inn Rd., Suite 180, Las Vegas, NV, 89121. Phone: (702) 784-4000. Fax: (702) 784-4040.E-mail: info@1057theoasis.com Web Site:www.1057theoasis.com Licensee: RBG Las Vegas Licenses LLC. (acq 10-3-2005; $38 million with KVGS(FM) Laughlin, NV). Population served: 150,000 Format: Smooth jazz. ◆Dave Presher, gen mgr; Joshua Mednick, sls dir; Sharon Ranieri, prom dir; Samantha Pasqual, progmg dir; Ray Fodge, chief of engrg; Theresa Dunbar, traf mgr.

Doney Park

KZXK(FM)— 2009: 97.9 mhz; 140 w. Ant 2,001 ft TL: N35 14 26 W111 35 51. Hrs open: Box 11060, Jackson, WY, 83002. Phone: (703) 812-0482. Licensee: Cochise Broadcasting LLC. ◆Ted Tucker, gen mgr.

Douglas

KAPR(AM)— Mar 8, 1958: 930 khz; 2.5 kw-D. TL: N31 22 08 W109 31 45. Hrs open: 24 KVOI. 3222 S. Richey Ave., Tucson, 85713. Phone: (520) 790-2440. Fax: (520) 790-2937.E-mail: info@kvoi.com Web Site:www.kvoi.com Licensee: Good Music Inc. Group owner: Good News Communications Inc. (acq 6-8-2001; $187,500). Population served: 190,000 Natl. Network: Salem Radio Network, . Natl. Rep: Salem;, Wray Fitch. Format: News/talk. News: 2 hrs wkly. Target aud: General. ◆Doug Martin, CEO, gen mgr; Rhonda Curtis, CFO; Mary Martin, gen sls mgr, mktg VP.

KCDQ(FM)— Mar 15, 1979: 95.3 mhz; 3 kw. Ant 210 ft TL: N31 22 08 W109 31 45. Stereo. Hrs open: 24 500 E. Fry Blvd., Ste L-10, Sierra Vista, 85635. Phone: (520) 459-8201. Fax: (520) 458-7104. Web Site:www.kcdq.com Licensee: Cochise Broadcasting LLC (acq 6-8-2001; $137,500). Population served: 120,000 Natl. Network: Westwood One, . Format: Contemp hits. News: 11 hrs wkly. Target aud: 29-49. ◆Ted Tucker, gen mgr; Jeff Davenport, stn mgr.

KDAP(AM)— 1946: 1450 khz; 1 kw-U. TL: N31 21 18 W109 31 45. Hrs open: Box 1179, 85608. Secondary address: 2031 N. Sulphur Springs St. 85607. Phone: (520) 364-3486. Phone: (520) 364-3484. Fax: (520) 364-3483. Licensee: Howard N. Henderson (group owner; (acq 2-3-2005; $165,800 with co-located FM). Population served: 120,000 Format: Sp. Target aud: General; loc Hispanic & Mexican residents. ◆Howard Henderson, gen mgr, gen sls mgr & progmg dir.

KDAP-FM— Nov 15, 1990: 96.5 mhz; 3 kw. Ant 30 ft TL: N31 21 18 W109 33 06. Stereo. Hrs open: 24 Prog sep from AM Box 1179, 85608. Secondary address: 2031 N. Sulphur Springs St. 85607. Phone: (520) 364-3484. Fax: (520) 364-3483. Licensee: Howard N. Henderson. Population served: 120,000 Format: Country. News staff: one. Target aud: General.

*KRMC(FM)— 1996: 91.7 mhz; 3 kw. 236 ft TL: N31 20 52 W109 28 42. Hrs open: Box 2520, 85608. Phone: (520) 364-5392. Fax: (520) 364-5392. Licensee: World Radio Network Inc. Format: Christian, Sp, educ. ◆David Johnson, pres; Glen Lafitte, gen mgr; James V. Heck, engrg dir.

Drake

*KJZA(FM)—Not on air, target date: unknown: 89.5 mhz; 250 w. 1,702 ft Hrs open: 24 923 E. Gurley St., Suite 202, Prescott, 86301. Phone: (928) 541-1008.E-mail: kjzafm@yahoo.com Web Site:www.kjza.org Licensee: St. Paul Bible College. Natl. Network: NPR, PRI, . Format: Jazz. ◆Tom Erickson, gen mgr.

Duncan

KJIK(FM)— 2003: 100.7 mhz; 9.8 kw. Ant 2,348 ft TL: N32 53 21 W109 19 20. Hrs open: 24 1850 W. Thatcher Blvd., Safford, 85546-3306. Phone: (928) 428-4100. Fax: (928) 348-9581.E-mail: production@kjik.fm Licensee: Country Mountain Airwaves LLC. Format: Adult contemp. ◆Dan Curtis, gen mgr & opns mgr.

Eagar

KTHQ(FM)— 1996: 92.5 mhz; 100 kw. 984 ft TL: N34 05 47 W109 27 52. Hrs open: 24 Box 2020, Show Low, 85902. Phone: (928) 532-1010. Fax: (928) 532-0101. Web Site:www.Qcountry92.com Licensee: Country Mountain Airwaves LLC. Format: Country. ◆Camden Smith, gen mgr, gen sls mgr; Laurie Pogson, traf mgr.

Flagstaff

KAFF(AM)— Oct 15, 1963: 930 khz; 5 kw-D, 50 w-N. TL: N35 11 26 W111 40 37. Hrs open: 5 AM-midnight Box 1930, 86002. Secondary address: 1117 W. Hwy. 66 86001. Phone: (928) 774-5231. Phone: (520) 774-5233. Fax: (928) 779-2988. Licensee: Guyann Inc. Group owner: Guyann Corp. (acq 9-7-2005; grpsl). Population served: 492,000 Wire Svc: AP Format: Country. News staff: 2. Target aud: 25-54. ◆Janie Richardson, gen mgr; Val Barret, prom dir & prom mgr; Chris Halstead, progmg dir; Hugh Morris, mus dir; George Davis, news dir; Jon Swett, chief of engrg.

KAFF-FM— October 1968: 92.9 mhz; 100 kw. 1,512 ft TL: N34 58 07 W111 30 24. Stereo. Hrs open: 24 Dups AM 100% Box 1930, 86002. Phone: (928) 774-5231. Fax: (928) 779-2988.E-mail: production@kaff.com Web Site:www.kaff.com Licensee: Guyann Inc. Population served: 250,000 Natl. Network: ABC, . Wire Svc: AP News staff: 2; News: 4 hrs wkly.

KFLX(FM)—(Kachina Village, February 1995: 105.1 mhz; 1 kw. 1,968 ft TL: N35 14 26 W111 35 48. Stereo. Hrs open: 24 112 E. Rt. 66, Suite 105, 86001. Phone: (928) 779-1177. Fax: (928) 774-5179.E-mail: ann@northlandradio.com Web Site:www.1051thecanyon.com Licensee: Grenax Broadcasting II LLC. (acq 1-6-2006; grpsl). Arent, Fox, Kintner, Plotkin & Kahn. Format: Adult contemp. News staff: one; News: 4 hrs wkly. Target aud: 28-54; males. ◆Greg Dinetz, pres; Jim Shipp, gen mgr, prom VP; Bill McAdams, opns dir, traf mgr; Mike Mentor, progmg dir; Samantha Ward, pub affrs dir; Jon Sweat, chief of engrg.

*KJTA(FM)— Dec 19, 2001: 89.9 mhz; 1 kw. Ant 1,988 ft TL: N35 14 25 W111 35 49. Hrs open: 24 1700 N. 2nd St., 86004. Phone: (928) 774-9514. Fax: (928) 774-9515.E-mail: info@kjtafm.com Web Site:www.myfir.org Licensee: Family Life Broadcasting Inc. (acq 5-23-2007; grpsl). Format: Christian contemporary. ◆Dawn Bumstead, progmg dir.

KMGN(FM)— 1975: 93.9 mhz; 100 kw. 1,509 ft TL: N34 58 08 W111 30 28. Stereo. Hrs open: 24 Box 1930, 86002. Secondary address: 1117 W Rt. 66 86001. Phone: (928) 774-5231. Fax: (928) 779-2988.E-mail: info@kmgn.com Web Site:www.kmgn.com Licensee: Guyann Corp. (group owner; .acq 9-7-2005; grpsl). Population served: 250,000 Natl. Network: ABC, . Wire Svc: AP Format: Classic rock. News staff: 2; News: 4 hrs wkly. Target aud: 25-54; upscale, educated, rgnl audience. ◆Janie Richardson, gen mgr; Rob Dowers, progmg dir.

*KNAU(FM)— Nov 24, 1970: 88.7 mhz; 100 kw. 1,549 ft TL: N34 57 40 W111 31 00. Stereo. Hrs open: 24 Box 5764, Northern Arizona Univ., 86011-5764. Phone: (928) 523-5628. Fax: (928) 523-7647.E-mail: knau@nau.edu Web Site:www.knau.org Licensee: Arizona Board of Regents for and on behalf of Northern Arizona University. Population served: 180,000 Natl. Network: NPR, PRI, . Arter & Hadden. Format: News & info, class. News staff: 3; News: 50 hrs wkly. Target aud: 25-54; educated, socially conscious achievers. ◆John Stark, gen mgr;

Dave Riek, opns mgr; Liz Gumerman, dev dir; Jeff Norcross, progmg dir, mus dir; Dan Kraker, progmg mgr, news dir; Jon Swett, chief of engrg; Lisa Skinner, traf mgr.

*KPUB(FM)— October 1995: 91.7 mhz; 500 w. 1,837 ft TL: N35 14 34 W111 36 40. Hrs open: 24 Box 5764, Northern Arizona Univ., 86011-5764. Phone: (928) 523-5628. Fax: (928) 523-7647.E-mail: knau@nau.edu Web Site:www.knau.org Licensee: Northern Arizona University. Natl. Network: NPR, PRI, . Format: News & info. News: 50 hrs wkly. Target aud: 25-54; educated, socially conscious achievers. ♦John Stark, gen mgr; Dave Riek, opns mgr; Liz Gumerman, dev dir; Jeff Norcross, progmg dir; Don Kraker, news dir; Lisa Skinner, traf mgr.

KVNA(AM)— Aug 8, 1950: 600 khz; 5 kw-D, 500 w-N, DA-N. TL: N35 11 47 W111 40 28. Hrs open: 24 Box 187, Cottonwood, 86326. Phone: (928) 526-2700. Fax: (928) 774-5852.E-mail: am600@radioflagstaff.com Web Site:www.radioflagstaff.com Licensee: Yavapai Broadcasting Corp. (acq 9-30-2000; grpsl). Population served: 300,000 Natl. Network: Westwood One, AP Network News, Jones Radio Networks, . Arizona News Radio Format: Sports, news/talk. News staff: one; News: 25 hrs wkly. Target aud: General. Spec prog: Sp 3 hrs wkly, folk music 4hrs wkly. ♦W. Grant Hafley, pres; David J. Kessel, gen mgr; Mike Dougal, opns mgr, progmg dir; Mike Dougall, news dir.

KVNA-FM— 1999: 100.1 mhz; 5.2 kw. Ant 1,433 ft TL: N34 58 05 W111 30 29. Hrs open: 24 Box 187, Cottonwood, 86326. Phone: (928) 526-2700. Fax: (928) 634-2295. Web Site:www.myradioplace.com Licensee: Yavapai Broadcasting Corp. (acq 5-2-2005; $1.5 million). Format: Adult contemp. ♦Dave Kessel, gen mgr.

KZGL(FM)— 2007: 103.7 mhz; 560 w. Ant 1,958 ft TL: N35 14 25 W111 35 53. Hrs open: 510 N. Humphreys St., Suite 501, 86001. Phone: (928) 779-1037.E-mail: studio@eagle1037.fm Web Site:www.eagle1037.fm Licensee: Walker Radio Inc. (acq 8-1-2007; $2.5 million for CP). Format: Triple A. ♦James R. Walker, pres; Paul Lancaster, gen mgr; Rob Dowers, opns mgr.

Florence

KCDX(FM)— 1999: 103.1 mhz; 2.7 kw. Ant 3,057 ft TL: N33 17 55 W110 50 28. Hrs open: Box 36717, Tucson, 85740. Phone: (520) 459-8201. Fax: (520) 458-7104. Web Site:www.kcdx.com Licensee: Desert West Air Ranchers Corp. Format: Classic rock. ♦Ted Tucker, gen mgr.

Fountain Hills

*KLVK(FM)— May 2000: 89.1 mhz; 1.4 kw. Ant 935 ft TL: N33 29 33 W111 38 23. (CP: 2.5 kw vert). Hrs open: 24 2351 Sunset Blvd., Suite 170-218, Rocklin, CA, 95765. Phone: (916) 251-1600. Fax: (916) 251-1650.E-mail: klove@klove.com Web Site:www.klove.com Licensee: Educational Media Foundation. Group owner: EMF Broadcasting (acq 3-11-03; grpsl). Natl. Network: K-Love, . Shaw Pittman. Format: Contemp Christian. News staff: 3. Target aud: 25-33; Judeo Christian, female. ♦Richard Jenkins, pres; Mike Novak, VP; Keith Whipple, dev dir; David Pierce, progmg mgr; Ed Lenane, news dir; Sam Wallington, engrg dir; Karen Johnson, news rptr.

Gilbert

KEDJ(FM)— Feb 25, 1981: 103.9 mhz; 99.59 kw. Ant 620 ft TL: N33 14 50 W111 31 49. Stereo. Hrs open: 24 7434 E. Stetson Dr., Suite 265, Scottsdale, 85251. Phone: (480) 423-9255. Fax: (480) 423-9382.E-mail: nat@theedge1039.com Web Site:www.theedge1039.com Licensee: RBG Phoenix Licenses LLC (acq 11-21-2005; $30 million). Population served: 1,446,948 Natl. Rep: Roslin,. Format: Alternative. News: 2 hrs wkly. Target aud: 18-34. ♦Tim Pohlman, CEO; Nat Galvin, VP, gen mgr, gen sls mgr.

Glendale

KLNZ(FM)—Licensed to Glendale. See Tempe

KPXQ(AM)—Licensed to Glendale. See Phoenix

KTAR-FM—Licensed to Glendale. See Phoenix

Globe

KIKO(AM)—See Miami

KJAA(AM)— 1971: 1240 khz; 1 kw-U. TL: N33 22 51 W110 45 25. Hrs open: 24
KVOI.
3222 S. Richey Ave., Tucson, 85713. Phone: (520) 790-2440. Fax: (520) 790-2937.E-mail: info@kvoi.com Web Site:www.kvoi.com Licensee: 1TV.Com Inc. Group owner: Good News Communications Inc. (acq 11-7-2008; $300,000). Format: News/talk. News staff: 3; News: 3 hrs wkly. Target aud: 35 plus. ♦Doug Martin, gen mgr.

*KLKA(FM)— 2008: 88.5 mhz; 1.5 kw vert. Ant 2,985 ft TL: N33 17 55 W110 50 28. Hrs open:
Rebroadcasts KVLT(FM) Temple, TX 100%.
3411 Market Loop, Suite 108, Temple, TX, 76502. Phone: (254) 791-5251. Fax: (254) 791-0200. Licensee: American Educational Broadcasting Inc. Natl. Network: K-Love, . Format: Contemp Christian music. ♦James E. Auel, gen mgr.

KQMR(FM)— Sept 25, 1980: 100.3 mhz; 90 kw. 2,047 ft TL: N33 17 23 W110 51 53. Stereo. Hrs open: 24 4745 N. Seventh St., Suite 140, Phoenix, 85014. Phone: (602) 308-7900. Fax: (602) 308-7979. Web Site:www.univision.com Licensee: Univision Radio License Corp. Group owner: Univision Radio (acq 9-22-2003; grpsl). Population served: 3,173,200 Format: Sp adult hits. Target aud: 18-49; upscale, well-educated, affluent adults. ♦Dobby White, pres, traf mgr; Mary McEvilly-Hernandez, VP, gen mgr; Chris Morris, sls dir, gen sls mgr; Nelson Oseida, opns dir & progmg dir; Kevin Norgaard, rsch dir.

KRDE(FM)— Oct 13, 1995: 94.1 mhz; 640 w. Ant 3,408 ft TL: N33 17 37 W110 50 09. Stereo. Hrs open: 24 Box 1660, 85502. Secondary address: 800 N. Main St. 85501. Phone: (928) 402-9222. Fax: (928) 425-5063.E-mail: krde@cableone.net Web Site:www.krde.com Licensee: Linda C. Corso. Population served: 1,800,000 Natl. Network: Fox News Radio, Premiere Radio Networks, Westwood One, . Arizona News Radio Rgnl rep: Arizona News Network John McVeigh, P.C. Format: Country. News staff: one; News: 12 hrs wkly. Target aud: 25-54; active, family building, western suburban. ♦Richard Potyka, gen mgr, prom; Mindy Chansley, opns mgr; Sean Cram, news dir; Brad Hartman, sports cmtr.

*KVJC(FM)— 2003: 91.9 mhz; 660 w. Ant 3,395 ft TL: N33 17 37 W110 50 09. Hrs open: 24 800 N. Main St., 85501-9456. Phone: (928) 402-9222. Phone: (208) 734-6633.E-mail: rich.potika@csnradio.com Web Site:www.csnradio.com Licensee: CSN International (group owner). Format: Christian. ♦Jeffrey W. Smith, VP; Mike Stocklin, gen mgr; Don Mills, progmg dir; Kelly Carlson, chief of engrg.

Grand Canyon

*KNAG(FM)—Not on air, target date: unknown: 90.3 mhz; 3 kw. 295 ft TL: N35 56 44 W112 10 16. Hrs open:
KNAU-FM Flagstaff 100%.
Box 5764, Northern Arizona University, Flagstaff, 86011. Phone: (928) 523-5628. Fax: (928) 523-7647.E-mail: knau@nau.edu Web Site:www.knau.org Licensee: Arizona Board of Regents/Northern Arizona University. Format: Class, news. ♦John Stark, gen mgr; Dave Riek, opns mgr; Liz Gumerman, dev dir.

Green Valley

KFMA(FM)— Feb 20, 1983: 92.1 mhz; 50 kw. 492 ft TL: N32 00 11 W110 47 49. Stereo. Hrs open: 24 3871 N. Commerce Dr., Tucson, 85705. Phone: (520) 407-4500. Fax: (520) 407-4600. Web Site:www.kfma.com Licensee: Arizona Lotus Corp. Group owner: Lotus Communications Corp. (acq 5-10-93; $1.26 million; 5-31-93). Natl. Rep: Christal,. Format: Alternative. Target aud: 18-34. ♦Steve Groesbeck, gen mgr; Cindy Craig, prom mgr; Matt Spry, progmg mgr.

KGVY(AM)—Licensed to Green Valley. See Tucson

KTZR-FM—Licensed to Green Valley. See Tucson

Heber

KZOH(FM)—Not on air, target date: unknown: 105.5 mhz; 100 kw. Ant 410 ft TL: N34 27 43 W110 24 10. Hrs open: 27610 N. Desierto Dr., Rio Verde, 85263. Phone: (970) 302-0161. Licensee: New Directions Media Inc. ♦Robert D. Zellmer, pres.

Holbrook

*KBMH(FM)— 2002: 90.3 mhz; 250 w. Ant 141 ft TL: N34 55 05 W110 08 25. Hrs open: Drawer 2440, Tupelo, MS, 38803. Phone: (601) 844-8888. Fax: (662) 842-6791. Licensee: American Family Association.

Group owner: American Family Radio Format: Christian. ♦Marvin Sanders, gen mgr; John Riley, progmg dir; Joey Moody, chief of engrg.

KDJI(AM)— October 1955: 1270 khz; 5 kw-D, 130 w-N. TL: N34 53 55 W110 11 30. Hrs open: 9 AM-4 PM Prog sep from FM 1838 W. Commerce Dr., Suite A, Lakeside, 85929. Phone: (928) 368-8100. Fax: (928) 368-8108.E-mail: production@whitemountainradio.com Licensee: Petracom of Holbrook L.L.C. Population served: 77,000 Natl. Network: ABC, Westwood One, . Format: News/talk. Target aud: 35-65; 46% female, 54% male. Spec prog: Sports 10 hrs, farm 8 hrs wkly.

KZUA(FM)— Dec 6, 1993: 92.1 mhz; 100 kw. Ant 328 ft TL: N34 52 25 W110 09 56. Stereo. Hrs open: 1838 W. Commerce Dr., Suite A, Lakeside, 85929. Phone: (928) 368-8100. Fax: (928) 368-8108.E-mail: production@whitemountainradio.com Licensee: Petracom of Holbrook L.L.C. (acq 2-26-2002; $650,000 with co-located AM). Population served: 95,000 Natl. Network: Westwood One, CNN Radio, . Format: Mainstream country. Target aud: 18-54; 57% female, 43% male. ♦Steve Johnson, gen mgr, progmg dir & chief of engrg; Lisa Ames, traf mgr.

Hotevilla

*KUYI(FM)— Dec 20, 2000: 88.1 mhz; 69 kw. Ant 407 ft TL: N35 48 29 W110 16 23. Hrs open: 24 Box 1500, Keams Canyon, 86034. Phone: (928) 738-5505. Fax: (928) 738-5501.E-mail: kuyihopiradio@yahoo.com Web Site:www.kuyi.net Licensee: Hopi Foundation. Format: Tribal radio, loc news, cultural events. News staff: 2; News: 6 hrs wkly. Target aud: 30 plus. ♦Katherine Sahmie, stn mgr.

Kachina Village

KFLX(FM)—Licensed to Kachina Village. See Flagstaff

Kaibito

*KCHB(FM)—Not on air, target date: unknown: 90.1 mhz; 100 kw. Ant 223 ft TL: N36 34 33 W111 05 50. Hrs open: 5210 S.E. Washington Blvd., Bartlesville, OK, 74006. Phone: (918) 333-8700. Fax: (918) 333-3526. Licensee: Pearl Communications Group. ♦Danny Hester, pres.

*KECU(FM)—Not on air, target date: unknown: 88.5 mhz; 18 kw. Ant 1,010 ft TL: N36 32 39 W110 29 44. Hrs open: Box 94, Stonewall, OK, 74872. Phone: (580) 265-9475. Licensee: Union Valley Baptist Church Inc. ♦Steve Vandegrift, gen mgr.

Kearny

*KKRY(FM)—Not on air, target date: unknown: 90.9 mhz; 45 w. Ant 882 ft TL: N33 04 10 W111 03 13. Hrs open: 4627 N. 23rd St., Arlington, VA, 22207. Phone: (703) 351-1160. Licensee: St. Paul Cultural Broadcasting Inc. ♦Timothy R. Obitts, pres & gen mgr.

KZLZ(FM)—Licensed to Kearny. See Tucson

Kingman

KAAA(AM)— Oct 7, 1949: 1230 khz; 1 kw-U. TL: N35 09 49 W114 04 12. Hrs open: 1880 Lucille Ave., 86401. Phone: (928) 753-2537. Fax: (928) 753-1551.E-mail: office@cameronbroadcasting.com Web Site:www.cameronbroadcasting.com Licensee: Cameron Broadcasting Inc. (group owner; (acq 11-24-99; grpsl). Population served: 65,000 Cohn & Marks. Format: News/talk. Target aud: 25 plus. Spec prog: Sports. ♦Don Jaeger, gen mgr.

*KCAI(FM)—Not on air, target date: unknown: 91.9 mhz; 30 kw Ant 2,893 ft TL: N35 06 35 W113 52 51. Hrs open: Box 2440, Tupelo, MS, 38801-2440. Phone: (662) 844-8888. Fax: (662) 842-6791. Licensee: American Family Association. ♦Donald E. Wildmon, chmn.

KGMN(FM)— Feb 14, 1984: 100.1 mhz; 360 w. 761 ft TL: N35 11 43 W114 06 51. (CP: 930 w, ant 2,896 ft. TL: N35 06 37 W133 52 55). Stereo. Hrs open: 24 812 E. Beale St., 86401. Phone: (928) 753-9100. Fax: (928) 753-1978. Web Site:www.kgmn.net Licensee: New West Broadcasting Systems Inc. Natl. Network: AP Radio, Jones Radio Networks, . Format: Country. ♦Joe Hart, CEO; Rhonda Hart, VP & gen mgr; Deana Campbell, opns mgr; Brian Winters, progmg dir.

*KJZK(FM)—Not on air, target date: unknown: 90.7 mhz; 4.5 kw. Ant 715 ft TL: N35 10 37 W113 39 57. Hrs open: 923 E. Gurley St., Suite

202, Prescott, 86301. Phone: (928) 541-1008.E-mail: kjzafm@yahoo.com Web Site:www.kjza.org Licensee: St. Paul Bible College. ◆Tom Erickson, gen mgr.

KRRN(FM)— November 1990: 92.7 mhz; 17 kw. Ant 1,889 ft TL: N35 01 58 W114 21 57. (CP: COL Dolan Springs. 100 kw, ant 1,774 ft. TL: N35 39 07 W114 18 42). Hrs open: 500 Pilot Rd., Las Vegas, NV, 89119. Phone: (702) 434-0015. Fax: (323) 900-6108. Licensee: Entravision Holdings LLC. Group owner: Entravision Communications Corp. (acq 8-29-02; $12.43 million). Natl. Network: ABC, . Format: Sp contemp. ◆Rick Murphy, VP.

Lake Havasu City

***KAIH(FM)**— 2008: 89.3 mhz; 1.7 kw vert. Ant -219 ft TL: N34 27 52 W114 16 02. Hrs open:
Rebroadcasts KLRD(FM) Yucaipa, CA 100%.
2351 Sunset Blvd., Suite 170-218, Rocklin, CA, 95765. Phone: (916) 251-1600. Fax: (916) 251-1650. Web Site:www.air1.com Licensee: Educational Media Foundation. Group owner: EMF Broadcasting. Natl. Network: Air 1, . Format: Christian. ◆Richard Jenkins, pres; Mike Novak, VP; Keith Whipple, dev dir; David Pierce, progmg mgr; Ed Lenane, news dir; Sam Wallington, engrg dir; Karen Johnson, news rptr.

KJJJ(FM)— May 24, 1994: 102.3 mhz; 1.05 kw. Ant 2,670 ft TL: N34 33 06 W114 11 37. Hrs open: 1845 McCulloch Blvd., Suite A-14, 86403. Phone: (928) 855-9336. Fax: (928) 855-9333.E-mail: steve@kjjjfm.com Web Site:www.kjjjfm.com Licensee: Steven M. Greeley. Population served: 150,000 Koenen & Olendar. Format: Country. ◆Steve Greeley, gen mgr.

***KNLB(FM)**— July 1983: 91.1 mhz; 8 kw. Ant 453 ft TL: N34 29 10 W114 13 06. Stereo. Hrs open: 24 510 N. Acoma Blvd., 86403. Phone: (928) 855-9110. Fax: (928) 453-2588.E-mail: info@knlb.com Web Site:www.knlb.com Licensee: Advance Ministries. Population served: 1,000,000 Natl. Network: USA, . Arent, Fox, Kintner, Plotkin & Kahn. Format: Relg, Christian. News: 8 hrs wkly. Target aud: General. ◆Richard D. Tatham, pres; Faron Eckelbarger, stn mgr, progmg dir, chief of engrg.

KNTR(AM)— Sept 23, 1970: 980 khz; 1 kw-D, 49 w-N. TL: N34 30 12 W114 21 28. Hrs open: 24 1845 McCulloch Blvd., Suite A 14, 86403. Phone: (928) 855-9336. Fax: (928) 855-9333.E-mail: speakout@kntram.com Web Site:www.kntram.com Licensee: Steven M. Greeley. (acq 12-8-99; $608,000). Population served: 60000 Natl. Network: PRI, . Koerner & Olender PC. Format: News/talk. News staff: one; News: 12 hrs wkly. Target aud: 35-64. ◆Steve Greeley, gen mgr.

KRCY-FM— 1999: 96.7 mhz; 1.05 kw. Ant 2,706 ft TL: N34 33 06 W114 11 37. Hrs open: 10 Media Center Dr., Lake Havasu, 86403. Phone: (928) 855-1051. Fax: (928) 855-7996.E-mail: express@maddog.net Web Site:www.maddog.net Licensee: Rick L. Murphy. Format: Oldies. ◆Rick L. Murphy, pres & gen mgr.

KRRK(FM)— Sept 9, 1974: 101.1 mhz; 20 kw. Ant 2,696 ft TL: N34 33 06 W114 11 37. Hrs open: 24 10 Media Center Dr., 86403. Phone: (928) 855-4560. Phone: (928) 855-1051. Fax: (928) 855-7996.E-mail: epress@maddog.net Web Site:www.maddog.net Licensee: Smoke and Mirrors LLC. (acq 11-29-99). Population served: 60,000 Format: Classic rock. News staff: one; News: 5 hrs wkly. Target aud: 18-34. ◆Chris Rolando, gen mgr.

KZUL-FM— 1986: 104.5 mhz; 230 w. Ant 2,670 ft TL: N34 33 06 W114 11 37. Stereo. Hrs open: 24 10 Media Center Dr., 86403. Phone: (928) 855-4560. Fax: (928) 855-7996.E-mail: epress@maddog.net Web Site:www.maddog.net Licensee: Mad Dog Wireless Inc. Natl. Network: ABC, . Format: Adult contemp, classic rock. Target aud: 25-54. ◆Rick Murphy, pres; Chris Rolando, VP, gen mgr; Mike Anthony, gen sls mgr, progmg dir; Faron Eckelbarger, chief of engrg.

Mammoth

***KLTU(FM)**—Not on air, target date: unknown: 88.1 mhz; 160 w. Ant 3,552 ft TL: N32 24 54 W110 42 56. Hrs open: 3222 S. Richey Ave., Tucson, 85713. Phone: (520) 790-2440. Fax: (520) 790-2937.E-mail: doug@kvoi.com Licensee: Good News Radio Broadcasting Inc. (acq 6-8-2005). ◆Doug Martin, gen mgr.

Many Farms

***KRDC(FM)**—Not on air, target date: unknown: 91.9 mhz; 5.5 kw. Ant 1,627 ft TL: N36 21 06 W109 49 51. Hrs open: Box 126, Tsaile, 86556. Phone: (928) 724-6669. Licensee: Dine College. ◆Ferlin Clark, pres.

Marana

KOHT(FM)— Oct 1, 1984: 98.3 mhz; 6 kw. 200 ft TL: N32 27 09 W111 05 09. Stereo. Hrs open: 24 3202 N. Oracle Rd., Tucson, 85705. Phone: (520) 618-2100. Fax: (520) 618-2200.E-mail: hot983comments@yahoo.com Web Site:www.hot983.com Licensee: CC Licenses LLC. Group owner: Clear Channel Communications Inc. (acq 6-22-2001; grpsl). Population served: 262,933 Format: CHR, rhythm & blues, hip hop. News staff: 2; News: 4 hrs wkly. Target aud: 18-49; Sp, contemp, white collar adults. ◆Debbie Wagner, gen mgr; Tim Richards, opns mgr; Steve Clement, gen sls mgr; Fred Rico, progmg dir; Mike Irby, chief of engrg.

KSAZ(AM)—Licensed to Marana. See Tucson

Mayer

KKFR(FM)— May 24, 1996: 98.3 mhz; 41 kw. Ant 2,795 ft TL: N34 14 03 W112 22 01. Stereo. Hrs open: 24 4745 N. 7th St., Suite 410, Phoenix, 85014. Phone: (602) 682-9200. Fax: (602) 283-0923. Web Site:www.power983fm.com Licensee: RBG Phoenix Licenses LLC. (acq 1-1-2007). Population served: 75,000 Format: Hip hop. ◆Nat Galvin, gen mgr; AmyAnn Rosales, gen sls mgr; Charlie Huero, mktg dir; Matt Kirkpatrick, prom dir; Bruce St. James, progmg dir.

Mesa

KDKB(FM)— Apr 20, 1968: 93.3 mhz; 100 kw. 1,538 ft TL: N33 20 04 W112 03 36. Stereo. Hrs open: 24 1167 W. Javelina, 85210. Phone: (480) 897-9300.E-mail: rock@kdkg.com Web Site:www.kdkb.com Licensee: Mesa Radio Inc. Group owner: Sandusky Radio (acq 1977). Natl. Rep: Christal,. Format: AOR. ◆Norman Rau, pres; Chuck Artigue, gen mgr; Bob Weaver, gen sls mgr; Buzz Casey, prom mgr, progmg dir; Clayton Creekmore, chief of engrg; Kathy Perschke, traf mgr.

KFNN(AM)—Licensed to Mesa. See Phoenix

***KJZZ(FM)**—(Phoenix, 1951: 91.5 mhz; 96 kw. 1,607 ft TL: N33 19 58 W112 03 53. Stereo. Hrs open: 24 2323 W. 14th St., Tempe, 85281. Phone: (480) 834-5627. Web Site:www.kjzz.org Licensee: Maricopa County Community College District. Population served: 4,000,000 Natl. Network: NPR, PRI, . Rgnl rep: Public radio partners Wire Svc: NOAA Weather Wire Svc: AP Format: News, acoustic jazz. News staff: 6; News: 50 hrs wkly. Target aud: 25-54. ◆Carl Matthusen, gen mgr; Bill Shedd, opns mgr; Lou Stanley, dev dir; Scott Williams, progmg dir; Mark Moran, news dir.

KXAM(AM)— 1946: Stn currently dark. 1310 khz; 5 kw-D, 500 w-N, DA-N. TL: N33 26 23 W111 50 09. Hrs open: 4725 N. Scottsdale Rd., Suite 234, Scottsdale, 85251. Phone: (480) 423-1310. Fax: (480) 423-3867.E-mail: kxam@aol.com Web Site:www.kxam.com Licensee: Embee Broadcasting Inc. (acq 9-25-90). Population served: 2,500,000 Hogan & Hartson. ◆Byron Gerson, pres; Don Sandler, gen mgr.

KZZP(FM)— 1967: 104.7 mhz; 100 kw. 1,550 ft TL: N33 20 04 W112 03 35. Stereo. Hrs open: 24 4686 E. Van Buren St., Ste. 300, Phoenix, 85008-6967. Phone: (602) 279-5577. Fax: (602) 230-2781. Web Site:www.1047kissfm.com Licensee: Citicasters Licenses L.P. Group owner Clear Channel Communications Inc. (acq 6-99; grpsl). Population served: 1,811,600 Format: CHR. News staff: one; News: 7 hrs wkly. Target aud: 18-34; women. ◆Lowry Mays, CEO; Randy Michaels, chmn; John Hogan, pres; Susan Karis-Madigan, gen mgr; Alan Sledge, opns dir; Cathy Burau, gen sls mgr.

Miami

KIKO(AM)— June 13, 1958: 1340 khz; 1 kw-U. TL: N33 24 41 W110 50 17. Hrs open: 24 4501 Broadway, 85539. Phone: (928) 425-7500 Business. Phone: (928) 425-4471 Contest. Fax: (928) 425-9393.E-mail: radiokiko@cableone.net Web Site:www.kikonews.blogspot.com Westwood One 6 pm-6 am Licensee: 1TV.com Inc. (acq 4-30-2008; $1.025 million with KIKO-FM Claypool). Population served: 35,000 Natl. Network: Westwood One, ABC, . Shaw Pittman. Format: Sports, oldies, contemp hits. News staff: one; News: 8 hrs wkly. Target aud: 21-70; industrial/blue collar workers in loc copper mines, highest hourly wage earners. ◆John Low, pres; Shelly Harrison, gen mgr; Roland Foster, news dir; Randy Escobedo, sports cmtr.

KIKO-FM—(Claypool, Aug 1, 1991: 106.1 mhz; 6 kw. Ant 297 ft TL: N33 24 23 W110 48 18. Stereo. Hrs open: 24 4501 Broadway, 85539. Phone: (928) 425-7500 Business. Fax: (928) 425-9393.E-mail: radiokiko@cableone.net Westwood One 24 hrs Licensee: 1TV.com Inc. (acq 4-30-2008; $1.025 million with KIKO(AM) Miami). Population served: 35,000 Natl. Network: Jones Radio Networks, . Shaw Pittman

Format: Soft adult contemp. News staff: one; News: 6 hrs wkly. Target aud: 21-55; blue collar, housewives, white collar. ◆Shelly Harrison, gen mgr.

KQSS(FM)— Mar 30, 1987: 98.3 mhz; 6 kw. Ant -279 ft TL: N33 24 30 W110 48 14. Stereo. Hrs open: 24 Box 292, 85539. Secondary address: 5734 McKinney, Globe 85501. Phone: (928) 425-7186. Fax: (928) 425-7982.E-mail: bill@gila1019.com Web Site:www.gila1019.com Licensee: William D. Taylor. Format: Country. News staff: one; News: 5 hrs wkly. Target aud: 25-54. ◆Bill Taylor, gen mgr & sls dir.

Mohave Valley

KVYL(FM)—Not on air, target date: unknown: 93.7 mhz; 6 kw. Ant -25 ft TL: N34 58 06 W114 31 58. Hrs open: Number 10 Media Center Dr., Lake Havasu City, 86403. Phone: (928) 855-1051. Licensee: Smoke and Mirrors LLC. ◆Rick L. Murphy, gen mgr.

Morenci

KCUZ(AM)—See Safford

Munds Park

KFSZ(FM)— 2009: 106.1 mhz; 4.3 kw. Ant 1,535 ft TL: N34 58 06 W111 30 29. Hrs open: 115 W. 3rd St., Fort Worth, TX, 76102. Phone: (817) 332-0959. Fax: (817) 348-8373.E-mail: info@lkcm.com Licensee: LKCM Radio Group LP. ◆Gerry Schlegel, pres; Joel Gough, sls dir; Molly Prince, prom dir; Chuck Taylor, mus dir; Michael Margrave, chief of engrg; Jane Wasson, traf mgr.

Nogales

***KNOG(FM)**— Dec 16, 1995: Stn currently dark. 91.1 mhz; 3 kw. 154 ft TL: N31 21 33 W110 53 54. Hrs open: 24 Box 1614, 85628. Secondary address: 150 W. First St. 85628. Phone: (520) 287-5206. Fax: (520) 287-3606.E-mail: knog@hcjb.org Web Site:www.knog.org Licensee: World Radio Network Inc. Population served: 600,000 Natl. Network: Moody, . Format: Sp contemp Christian, educ. News: 5 hrs wkly. Target aud: 18-55; Hispanics. Spec prog: Btfl music 5 hrs wkly. ◆Marcos Romero, stn mgr; Mariana Romero, progmg dir & pub affrs dir; Concepcion Borrayo, traf mgr.

KOFH(FM)— Apr 1, 1999: 99.1 mhz; 6 kw. Ant 328 ft TL: N31 20 46 W110 53 34. Hrs open: 934N Bejarano St., Suite 2, 85621-1385. Phone: (520) 287-6885. Fax: (520) 287-8290.E-mail: noticieroal maximo@hotmail.com Web Site:www.maxima991.fm Licensee: Felix Corp. Format: Top-40, Sp & English. ◆Oscar Felix Sr., gen mgr; Rene Saylor, progmg dir & news dir.

Oracle

KGMG(FM)— December 1984: 106.3 mhz; 430 w vert, 440 w horiz. 4,172 ft TL: N32 26 26 W110 47 12. Stereo. Hrs open: 24 3438 N. Country Club Rd., Tucson, 85716. Phone: (520) 795-1490. Fax: (520) 327-2260. Licensee: Journal Broadcast Corp. Group owner: Journal Broadcast Group Inc. (acq 4-15-98; $5.8 million). Population served: 600,000 Natl. Rep: Christal,. Format: Oldies. News: 2 hrs wkly. Target aud: 25-54; Hispanic and Anglo adults. ◆Julie Brinks, gen mgr; Larkin Gassman, mktg mgr; Bobby Rich, progmg dir.

Oro Valley

KCMT(FM)— 2003: 102.1 mhz; 100 kw. Ant 266 ft TL: N32 17 23 W111 01 06. Hrs open: 3871 N. Commerce Dr., Tucson, 85705. Phone: (520) 407-4500. Fax: (520) 407-4600. Web Site:www.kcmt.com Licensee: Arizona Lotus Corp. Group owner: Lotus Communications Corp. Format: Rgnl Sp. ◆Steve Groesbeck, gen mgr; Tara Hungate, rgnl sls mgr.

KSZR(FM)— Apr 28, 1992: 97.5 mhz; 3 kw. 299 ft TL: N32 23 28 W111 01 48. (CP: 6 kw, ant 328 ft.). Hrs open: 24 575 W. Roger Rd., Tuscon, 85705. Phone: (520) 887-1000. Fax: (520) 887-6397. Web Site:www.bob975.com Licensee: Citadel Broadcasting Co. Group owner: Citadel Broadcasting Corp. (acq 4-26-01; grpsl). Population served: 800,000 Format: Music of the 70's & 80's. News staff: 2; News: 60 hrs wkly. Target aud: 25-54. ◆Farid Suleman, CEO; Ken Kowalcek, gen mgr & stn mgr; Herb Crowe, opns dir; Keith Rosenblatt, sls dir.

Page

***KNAD(FM)**— 1998: 91.7 mhz; 500 w. 1,509 ft TL: N36 41 51 W111 37 57. Hrs open:
Rebroadcasts KNAU(FM) Flagstaff.
Box 5764, Northern Arizona University, Flagstaff, 86011-5764. Phone: (928) 523-5628. Fax: (928) 523-7647.E-mail: knau@nau.edu Web Site:www.knau.org Licensee: Arizona Board of Regents on behalf of Northern Arizona University. Format: News & info. ♦John Stark, gen mgr; Dave Riek, opns mgr; Jeff Norcross, progmg dir; Don Kraker, news dir; Lisa Skinner, traf mgr.

KPGE(AM)— May 15, 1971: 1340 khz; 1 kw-U. TL: N36 45 23 W111 27 32. Hrs open: 24 Box 1030, 91 7th Ave., 86040. Phone: (928) 645-8181. Fax: (928) 645-3347. Web Site:www.lakepowerlife.com Licensee: Lake Powell Communications Inc. (acq 7-1-91; with co-located FM; 6-17-91). Population served: 41,000 Natl. Network: ABC, . Format: Country. News staff: one; News: 15 hrs wkly. Target aud: 25-54. ♦Dan Brown, gen mgr; Janet Brown, gen sls mgr; Elizabeth Joseph, news dir; Dave Weaver, chief of engrg, progmg.

KXAZ(FM)— Sept 22, 1980: 93.3 mhz; 12.5 kw. 921 ft TL: N36 46 42 W111 25 46. Stereo. Hrs open: 24 Prog sep from AM Box 1030, 91 7th Ave., 86040. Phone: (928) 645-8181. Fax: (928) 645-3347. Web Site:kxaz.com Population served: 41,000 Format: Top-40.

Paradise Valley

KHOT-FM— 1996: 105.9 mhz; 36 kw. Ant 577 ft TL: N33 35 16 W111 45 38. Hrs open: 24 4745 N. 7th St., Suite 140-C, Phoenix, 85014. Phone: (602) 308-7900. Fax: (602) 308-7979. Web Site:www.univision.com Licensee: Univision Radio License Corp. Group owner: Univision Radio (acq 9-22-2003; grpsl). Population served: 3,173,200 Format: Rgnl Mexican. Target aud: 18-49. ♦Mary McEvilly-Hernandez, VP, gen mgr; Chris Morris, sls dir, prom mgr; Nelson Oreida, opns dir & progmg dir; Kevin Norgaard, rsch dir; Dobby White, traf mgr.

Parker

KLPZ(AM)— Sept 7, 1974: 1380 khz; 2.5 kw-D, 58 w-N. TL: N34 09 14 W114 17 15. Hrs open: 24 816 6th St., 85344. Phone: (928) 669-9274. Phone: (928) 669-9275. Fax: (928) 669-9300.E-mail: info@klpz1380.com Web Site:www.klpz1380.com Licensee: Keith Douglas Learn (acq 4-1-00). Population served: 20,000 Natl. Network: Jones Radio Networks, . Format: Country, news/talk. News staff: 2; News: 2 hrs wkly. Target aud: 25-55. Spec prog: Farm one hr wkly. ♦Keith Douglas Learn, pres.

KPKR(FM)— Dec 23, 2007: 97.3 mhz; 9.5 kw. Ant 105 ft TL: N34 00 11 W114 13 40. Hrs open: 24 Box 632, 85344. Secondary address: 1713 S. Kofa Ave., Suite E 85344. Phone: (928) 669-9999. Fax: (928) 442-0448. Web Site:www.riverratradio.com Licensee: Prescott Valley Broadcasting Co. Inc. Natl. Network: Jones Radio Networks, . Format: Classic hits. Target aud: 25-54; fun loving recreationists. ♦Sanford Cohen, pres; Terry Cohen, exec VP.

KRIT(FM)— 2003: 93.9 mhz; 7.6 kw. Ant -154 ft TL: N34 08 30 W114 17 50. Stereo. Hrs open: 24 1301 Arizona Ave., Suite 4, 85344. Phone: (661) 823-6201. Phone: (661) 837-0745. Fax: (661) 837-1612.E-mail: achavez@campesina.com Web Site:www.campesina.com Licensee: Farmworker Educational Radio Network Inc. Format: Rgnl, Sp. ♦Anthony Chavez, exec VP; Kevin Lein, stn mgr; Barbara Lein, natl sls mgr; Cesar Chavez, progmg dir; Dave Whitehead, chief of engrg; Maria Vrrutia, traf mgr.

***KWFH(FM)**— November 1984: 90.1 mhz; 460 w. -184 ft TL: N34 08 53 W114 16 44. Stereo. Hrs open: 24 Box 747, 86405. Phone: (928) 669-5683. Phone: (928) 855-9110. Fax: (928) 669-5683. Web Site:www.kwfh.org Licensee: Desert View Baptist Church. Population served: 12,000 Natl. Network: Moody, . Format: Relg. Target aud: General. ♦Gary Covert, stn mgr & opns mgr; Faron Eckelbarger, progmg dir, mus dir.

Payson

KMOG(AM)— Nov 1, 1983: 1420 khz; 2.5 kw-D, 500 w-N, DA-N. TL: N34 16 00 W111 18 54. Hrs open: 24 500 E. Tyler Pkwy., 85541. Phone: (928) 474-5214. Fax: (928) 474-0236.E-mail: kmog@1420kmog.com Web Site:http://and02.info/index.html Licensee: Farrell Enterprises L.L.C. (acq 3-6-97). Format: Country. News staff: one; News: 2 hrs wkly. Target aud: 25-54; working adults. ♦Mike Farrell, pres; Blaine Kimball, gen mgr.

KMZQ-FM— 2007: 99.3 mhz; 17 kw. Ant 403 ft TL: N34 11 04 W111 20 16. Hrs open: 3999 Las Vegas Blvd., S. Suite K, Las Vegas, NV, 89119. Phone: (702) 736-6161. Licensee: Kemp Communications Inc. ♦Will Kemp, pres.

KNRJ(FM)— 2000: 101.1 mhz; 88 kw. Ant 1,033 ft TL: N34 25 51 W111 30 12. Hrs open: 24 7434 E. Stetson Dr., Suite 255, Scottsdale, 85251. Phone: (480) 994-9100. Phone: (800) 254-7510. Fax: (480) 423-8770.E-mail: info@energyarizonafm.com Web Site:www.azthebeat.com Licensee: Sierra H. Broadcasting Inc. Natl. Network: Westwood One, CNN Radio, . Format: Hip hop. ♦Michael Mallace, gen mgr; Rod Carrillo, progmg dir; Steve Szalay, pub affrs dir.

Phoenix

KASA(AM)— Jan 6, 1967: 1540 khz; 10 kw-D, DA. TL: N33 22 36 W112 05 25. Hrs open: 1445 W. Baseline Rd., 85041. Phone: (602) 276-4241. Phone: (602) 276-5272. Fax: (602) 276-8119. Licensee: KASA Radio Hogar Inc. (group owner; (acq 8-26-92; $475,000;9-14-92). Population served: 2,000,000 Cohn & Marks. Format: Relg. Target aud: General. ♦Moses Herrera, pres, gen mgr & opns mgr.

KAZG(AM)—(Scottsdale, 1956: 1440 khz; 5 kw-D, 52 w-N. TL: N33 28 43 W111 56 24. Hrs open: 8:30 AM - 5:30 PM 4343 E. Camelback Rd., Suite 200, 85018. Phone: (480) 941-1007. Fax: (602) 260-5759.E-mail: kslx@kslx.com Licensee: Cactus Radio Inc. Group owner: Sandusky Radio (acq 6-5-98; with co-located FM). Population served: 250,000 Format: Oldies. ♦Chuck Artigue, gen mgr; Dean Mooney, gen sls mgr; Michael Bradford, prom dir & prom mgr; Dave Cooper, progmg dir.

***KBAQ-FM**— Apr 26, 1993: 89.5 mhz; 91 w. 1,463 ft TL: N33 19 58 W112 03 53. (CP: 12.5 kw, ant 2,316 ft. TL: N33 35 33 W112 34 49). Hrs open: 24 2323 W. 14th St., Tempe, 85281. Phone: (480) 834-5627. Fax: (480) 774-8475.E-mail: kbaq.mail@kbaq.org Web Site:www.kbaq.org Licensee: College District. Population served: 4,000,000 Natl. Network: NPR, PRI, . Rgnl rep: Public Radio Partners Wire Svc: AP Format: Class mus, news. ♦Carl Matthusen, gen mgr; Lou Stanley, dev dir, sls dir; Scott Williams, progmg dir; Sterling Beeaff, mus dir; Ralph Hogan, chief of engrg.

KESZ(FM)— July 1982: 99.9 mhz; 100 kw. 1,702 ft TL: N33 20 01 W112 03 44. Stereo. Hrs open: 24 4686 E. Van Buren St., Ste 300, 85008-6967. Phone: (602) 374-6000. Fax: (602) 374-6035. Web Site:www.kez999.com Licensee: CC Licenses LLC. Group owner: Clear Channel Communications Inc. (acq 5-14-99; $58 million). Natl. Network: AP Radio, . Natl. Rep: Katz Radio,. Format: Adult contemp. Target aud: General. ♦Joe Puglise, gen mgr, rgnl sls mgr; Kevin Gossett, prom dir.

***KFLR-FM**— December 1985: 90.3 mhz; 2.2 kw. 354 ft TL: N33 26 09 W112 06 35. (CP: 28.31 kw, ant 1,555 ft. TL: N33 20 02 W112 03 04). Stereo. Hrs open: 24 PMB 549, 428 E. Thunderbird Rd., 85022. Phone: (602) 978-0903. Fax: (602) 548-8089.E-mail: kflr@flc.org Web Site:www.flc.org Licensee: Family Life Broadcasting Inc. Group owner: Family Life Communications Inc. (acq 7-30-78). Population served: 582,000 Natl. Network: Salem Radio Network, . Format: Christian, inspirational. ♦Randy Carlson, pres; Alan Cook, gen mgr, progmg dir; Fred Morse, opns mgr; Bruce Thurman, prom dir; Walter Ellis, engrg mgr & chief of engrg.

KFNN(AM)—(Mesa, November 1962: 1510 khz; 22 kw-D, 100 w-N. TL: N33 23 30 W111 50 16. Hrs open: 24 4800 N. Central Ave., 85012. Phone: (602) 241-1510. Fax: (602) 241-1540.E-mail: info@kfnn.com Web Site:www.kfnn.com Licensee: CRC Broadcasting Co. Inc. (acq 1988). Population served: 135,600 Natl. Network: CNN Radio, . Akin, Gump, Strauss, Houer & Feld. Wire Svc: Metro Weather Service Inc. Format: News/talk, business news, investment advice. News staff: 3; News: 84 hrs wkly. Target aud: 30 plus; upscale, investment-oriented professionals & entrepreneurs; decision makers. ♦Brian DuBose, VP, progmg dir; Ronald E. Cohen, pres & gen mgr; Renee Yorks, opns mgr; Brian Du Bose, progmg dir.

KFYI(AM)— October 1921: 550 khz; 5 kw-D, 1 kw-N. TL: N33 23 17 W112 00 22. Hrs open: 24 Prog sep from FM 4686 Van Buren St., Suite 300, 85008. Phone: (602) 374-6000. Fax: (602) 374-6032.E-mail: info@kfyi.com Web Site:www.kfyi.com Licensee: AMFM Radio Licenses LLC Natl. Network: Westwood One, . Natl. Rep: Christal,. Format: News/talk. Target aud: 50 plus. Spec prog: Relg 2 hrs wkly. ♦Brad Gould, stn mgr, opns mgr; Laurie Canfillo, progmg dir.

KGME(AM)— 1940: 910 khz; 5 kw-U, DA-N. TL: N33 32 00 W112 07 18. Hrs open: 24 4686 E. Van Buren St., Ste 300, 85008-6967. Phone: (602) 374-6000. Fax: (602) 374-6035. Web Site:www.xtra910.com Licensee: AMFM Radio Licenses L.L.C. Group owner: Clear Channel Communications Inc. (acq 8-30-00; grpsl). Natl. Network: CBS, Westwood One, . Format: Sports/talk. News staff: 7. Target aud: General. ♦Brad Gould, stn mgr & sls VP.

KIDR(AM)— Feb 1, 1958: 740 khz; 1 kw-D, 292 w-N, DA-2. TL: N33 21 55 W112 06 30. Stereo. Hrs open: 24 3030 N. Central Ave., Suite 220, 85012-2784. Phone: (602) 234-8998. Fax: (602) 234-8993.E-mail: info@wradiophx.com Web Site:www.wradio.com.mx Licensee: Force Broadcasting LLC Group owner: Multicultural Radio Broadcasting Inc. (acq 2-25-2009; $1.5 million). Population served: 1,900,000 Format: Sp news, talk, sports. News staff: 2; News: 10 hrs wkly. Target aud: 18-64; Hispanic. ♦Arthur Liu, CFO; Arturo Galvez, gen mgr & news dir.

KJZZ(FM)—Licensed to Phoenix. See Mesa

KKNT(AM)— June 1947: 960 khz; 5 kw-U, DA-N. TL: N33 39 12 W111 55 39. (CP: TL: N33 41 34 W112 00 09). Hrs open: 24 2425 E. Camelback Rd., Suite 570, 85016. Phone: (602) 955-9600. Fax: (602) 955-7860.E-mail: jtimm@kknt960.com Web Site:www.kknt960.com Licensee: Common Ground Broadcasting Inc. Group owner: Salem Communications Corp. (acq 1996; $6.5 million). Population served: 1,874,600 Natl. Network: Salem Radio Network, . Format: News/talk. News staff: 2; News: 6 hrs. wkly. Target aud: 25-54; 35-64; upscale adults. Spec prog: Insight bowl. ♦Edward Atsinger III, CEO, news dir; Stuart Epperson, chmn; Joe D. Davis, exec VP, progmg mgr; Jon Horton, VP; John Timm, gen mgr; Laurie Larson, opns dir; Jim Seemiller, gen sls mgr.

KMIK(AM)—(Tempe, June 23, 1960: 1580 khz; 50 kw-U, DA-N. TL: N33 27 22 W111 50 01. Stereo. Hrs open: 24 2231 E. Camelback, Suite 102, 85016. Phone: (602) 381-1580. Fax: (602) 840-1488.E-mail: marni.gerber@abc.com Web Site:www.radiodisney.com Licensee: Radio Disney Group LLC. Group owner: ABC Inc. (acq 9-10-98; $5.85 million). Population served: 2,000,000 Natl. Network: Radio Disney, . Natl. Rep: McGavren Guild,. Format: Family hits. ♦Marni Gerber, stn mgr; Carl Jimenez, mktg dir, prom dir.

KMLE(FM)—(Chandler, Apr 18, 1980: 107.9 mhz; 100 kw. 1,735 ft TL: N33 20 03 W112 03 43. Stereo. Hrs open: 24 840 N. Central Ave., 85014. Phone: (602) 452-1000. Fax: (602) 230-2116. Web Site:www.kmle108.com Licensee: Infinity Radio Inc. Group owner: Infinity Broadcasting Corp. (acq 8-7-00; grpsl). Population served: 350,000 Format: Country. News staff: 2. Target aud: 25-54. Spec prog: Camel Views one hr wkly. ♦Amy Leimbach, gen sls mgr; Mark Waters, gen mgr & mktg mgr; Kris Abrams, progmg dir; Doc Holiday, mus dir.

KMVP(AM)— Nov 23, 1949: 860 khz; 1 kw-U, DA-N. TL: N33 24 16 W112 07 24. Hrs open: 24 5300 N. Central Ave., 85012-1410. Phone: (602) 274-6200. Fax: (602) 266-3858.E-mail: newsradio620@ktar.com Web Site:www.ktar.com Licensee: Bonneville Holding Co. Group owner: Emmis Communications Corp. (acq 1-14-2005; grpsl). Population served: 1,750,000 Natl. Network: ESPN Radio, . Format: Sports talk. Target aud: 25-54; sports enthusiast. ♦Bruce T. Reese, CEO, pres; David Brown, sls dir; Mike Fadelli, gen sls mgr; Dawn Paugh, natl sls mgr; Randy Eccles, prom mgr; Tisa Vrable, progmg dir; Gary Smith, engrg dir.

KMXP(FM)— October 1964: 96.9 mhz; 100 kw. 1,560 ft TL: N33 20 03 W112 03 36. Stereo. Hrs open: 24 4686 E. Van Buren St., Ste 300, 85008-6967. Phone: (602) 279-5577. Fax: (602) 230-2781. Web Site:www.mix969.com Licensee: Citicasters Licenses L.P. Group owner: Clear Channel Communications Inc. (acq 5-4-99; grpsl). Format: Adult contemp. News staff: one. ♦Lowry Mays, CEO; Randy Michaels, chmn; John Hogan, pres; Susan Karis-Madigan, gen mgr; Alan Sledge, opns dir; Shanna McCoy, sls dir.

KNAI(FM)—Licensed to Phoenix. See Keene CA

KNIX-FM— Sept 1, 1969: 102.5 mhz; 98 kw. 1,620 ft TL: N33 19 58 W112 03 53. Stereo. Hrs open: 24 4686 E. Van Buren St., Suite 300, 85008-6967. Phone: (602) 374-6000. Fax: (602) 374-6035. Web Site:www.knixcountry.com Licensee: CC Licenses LLC. Group owner: Clear Channel Communications Inc. (acq 6-1-99; $84 million). Format: Country. News staff: 3; News: one hr wkly. Target aud: 25-54. ♦Joe Puglise, gen mgr.

KNUV(AM)—See Tolleson

KOMR(FM)—See Sun City

KOOL-FM— May 1956: 94.5 mhz; 100 kw. 1,655 ft TL: N33 20 02 W112 03 42. Stereo. Hrs open: 24 4745 N. 7th St., Suite 210, 85014. Phone: (602) 956-9696. Fax: (602) 285-1450. Web Site:www.koolradio.com Licensee: Infinity Radio Inc. Group owner: Infinity Broadcasting Corp. (acq 8-7-00; grpsl). Natl. Rep: Christal,. Format: Oldies. Target aud: 25-54. ♦Charlie Lake, progmg dir.

KOY(AM)— May 1949: 1230 khz; 1 kw-U. TL: N33 26 09 W112 06 35. Hrs open: 24 4686 E. Van Buren St., Suite 300, 85008. Phone: (602)

374-6000. Fax: (602) 374-6035.E-mail: info@am1230koy.com Web Site:www.am1230koy.com Licensee: AMFM Radio Licenses LLC. Group owner: Clear Channel Communications Inc. (acq 8-30-00; grpsl). Format: Oldies. ♦Susan Karis-Madigan, gen mgr.

***KPHF(FM)**— December 1991: 88.3 mhz; 22.5 kw. 997 ft TL: N33 45 37 W112 05 29. Hrs open: 7:30 PM-4:30 AM c/o 290 Hegenberger Rd., Oakland, CA, 94621. Phone: (602) 272-7220. Phone: (800) 543-1465. Licensee: Family Stations Inc. (group owner; acq 12-91). Format: Relg. ♦Harold Camping, pres & gen mgr; David Manzi, opns mgr.

KPHX(AM)— June 10, 1958: 1480 khz; 5 kw-D, 500 w-N, DA-2. TL: N33 24 02 W112 06 28. Hrs open: 824 E. Washington St., 85034. Phone: (602) 257-1351. Fax: (602) 386-4873. Web Site:www.1480kphx.com Licensee: Continental Broadcasting Corp. of Arizona Inc. (acq 2-80; $650,000; 2-18-80). Population served: 581,562 Format: Progressive talk. ♦Kent Ennoms, CEO; Arthur Mobley, gen mgr; Cam Maxwell, stn mgr, opns mgr; Jonathan Molina, opns VP.

KPKX(FM)— July 1, 1960: 98.7 mhz; 100 kw. 1,680 ft TL: N33 20 00 W112 03 48. Stereo. Hrs open: 24 Prog sep from AM 5300 N. Central Ave., 85012. Phone: (602) 274-6200. Fax: (602) 266-3858.E-mail: newsradio620@ktar.com Web Site:www.987thepeak.com Population served: 3,000,000 Format: Adult contemp. News staff: one; News: 2 hrs wkly. Target aud: Adults 25-54; lite rock. ♦Mark Bentz, gen sls mgr; Jodi Hamilton, prom dir; Gary Smith, engrg dir.

KPXQ(AM)—(Glendale, 1946: 1360 khz; 50 kw-D, 1 kw-N, DA-N. TL: N33 30 28 W112 13 01. Hrs open: 24 2425 E. Camelback Rd., Suite 570, 85016. Phone: (602) 955-9600. Fax: (602) 955-7860.E-mail: info@kpxq1360.com Web Site:www.kpxq1360.com Licensee: Common Ground Broadcasting Inc. Group owner: Salem Communications Corp. (acq 6-23-99; $5 million). Population served: 1800000 Natl. Network: Salem Radio Network, . Rgnl. Network: Salem Natl. Rep: Salem,. Dow, Lohnes & Albertson. Format: Relg talk. News staff: one; News: 6 hrs wkly. Target aud: 25-54; adults. ♦Edward Atsinger III, CEO; Stuart Epperson, pres; Joe D. Davis, exec VP; Jon Horton, VP; John Timm, gen mgr; Laurie Larson, opns mgr; Jim Seemiller, gen sls mgr; Rachel Van Hofwegen, prom dir; John Bortowski, chief of engrg; Diane Johnson, traf mgr; John Gibson, local news ed.

KQMR(FM)—See Globe

KSLX-FM—(Scottsdale, Aug 1, 1969: 100.7 mhz; 100 kw. 1,847 ft TL: N33 19 53 W112 03 47. Stereo. Hrs open: 4343 E. Camelback Rd., Suite 200, 85018. Phone: (480) 941-1007. Fax: (602) 260-5759.E-mail: kslx@kslx.com Web Site:www.kslx.com Licensee: Cactus Radio Inc. Population served: 250,000 Format: Classic rock.

KSUN(AM)— Aug 27, 1954: 1400 khz; 1 kw-U. TL: N33 23 23 W111 59 52. Stereo. Hrs open: 714 N. 3rd St., 85004. Phone: (602) 252-0030. Fax: (602) 252-4211.E-mail: info@ksun.com Web Site:www.radiofiesta.com Licensee: Fiesta Radio Inc. (acq 10-86; $600,000; 12-8-86). Population served: 2,500,000 Format: Adult contemp, Sp. Target aud: 19-45. ♦Pedro Marquez, pres.

KTAR(AM)— June 21, 1922: 620 khz; 5 kw-U, DA-N. TL: N33 28 44 W112 00 06. Hrs open: 24 5300 N. Central Ave., 85012-1410. Phone: (602) 274-6200. Fax: (602) 266-3858.E-mail: newsradio620@ktar.com Web Site:www.ktar.com Licensee: Bonneville Holding Co. Group owner: Emmis Communications Corp. (acq 1-14-2005; grpsl). Population served: 3,000,000 Natl. Rep: Interep, D & R Radio,. Wire Svc: UPI Format: Sports. ♦Dave Brown, gen sls mgr; Ryan Hatch, progmg dir.

KTAR-FM—(Glendale, Dec 19, 1979: 92.3 mhz; 98 kw. Ant 1,788 ft TL: N33 19 58 W112 03 48. Stereo. Hrs open: 5300 N. Central Ave., 85012-1410. Phone: (602) 274-6200. Fax: (602) 266-3858.E-mail: newsradio620@ktar.com Web Site:www.ktar.com Licensee: Bonneville Holding Co. Group owner: Emmis Communications Corp. (acq 7-11-2006; $77.5 million). Population served: 2,500,000 Format: News/talk. Target aud: 18-49. ♦Erik Hellum, VP, mktg mgr; Brett Rogers, gen sls mgr; Russ Hill, progmg dir.

KXAM(AM)—See Mesa

KXEG(AM)— 1956: 1280 khz; 2.5 kw-D, 230 w-N. TL: N33 29 32 W112 08 28. Hrs open: 24 2800 N. 44th St., Suite 100, 85012. Phone: (602) 296-3600. Fax: (602) 296-3624.E-mail: jess@kxeg1280.com Web Site:www.kxeg1280.com Licensee: Communicom Co. of Phoenix L.P. Group owner: James Crystal Inc. (acq 12-14-2005; grpsl). Population served: 2,000,000 Natl. Rep: Salem, Commercial Media Sales,. Wilkinson, Barker, Knauer & Quinn. Format: Christian. Target aud: 25 plus; educated adults with disposable income. Spec prog: Sp 5 hrs wkly. ♦Jess Spurgin, gen mgr.

KXXT(AM)—See Tolleson

KYOT-FM— Oct 31, 1963: 95.5 mhz; 96 kw. 1,570 ft TL: N33 20 06 W112 03 39. Stereo. Hrs open: 24 4686 E. Van Buren St., Suite 300, 85008. Phone: (602) 374-6000. Fax: (602) 374-6035.E-mail: info@am1230koy.com Web Site:www.kyot.com Licensee: AMFM Radio Licenses LLC Group owner: Clear Channel Communications Inc. (acq 8-30-00; grpsl). Dow, Lohnes & Albertson. Format: Smoth jazz. News staff: one. Target aud: 25-54. ♦Susan Karis-Madigan, gen mgr; Angie Handa, mus dir; John Baker, chief of engrg.

KZON(FM)— July 5, 1964: 101.5 mhz; 100 kw. Ant 1,740 ft TL: N33 19 52 W112 03 46. Hrs open: 24 840 N. Central Ave., 85004. Phone: (602) 452-1000. Fax: (602) 420-9916. Fax: (602) 440-6530.E-mail: info@kzon.com Web Site:1015jamz.com Licensee: Infinity Radio Inc. Group owner: Infinity Broadcasting Corp. (acq 12-20-99; grpsl). Population served: 2700000 Leventhal, Senter & Lerman. Format: FM Talk. News staff: one. ♦Greg Garber, gen sls mgr, prom mgr; Mark Waters, mktg mgr; Chris Patyk, progmg dir.

KZZP(FM)—See Mesa

Pinetop

KNKI(FM)—Not on air, target date: unknown: 106.7 mhz; 55 kw. Ant 1,240 ft TL: N34 15 06 W109 35 06. Hrs open: 1491 W. Thatcher Blvd., Safford, 85546-3306. Phone: (928) 428-2217. Licensee: William S. Konopnicki. ♦William S. Konopnicki, gen mgr.

Pinetop-Lakeside

***KRCI(FM)**— 2009: 89.5 mhz; 1 kw. Ant 1,125 ft TL: N34 12 22 W109 58 34. Hrs open: 1201 W. Navajo Ln., Lakeside, 85929-9718. Phone: (928) 368-6766. Licensee: Truth and Life Ministries. ♦Kevin Hansen, gen mgr.

Prescott

KAHM(FM)— Sept 9, 1981: 102.1 mhz; 58 kw. 2,526 ft TL: N34 41 14 W112 07 01. Stereo. Hrs open: 24 Box 2529, 86302. Secondary address: 510 Henry St. 86301. Phone: (928) 445-7800. Fax: (928) 445-5365. Web Site:Kahm.info Licensee: Southwest FM Broadcasting Co. Population served: 2,000,000 Cohn & Marks. Format: Easy lstng. News staff: 3; News: 7 hrs wkly. Target aud: 35-64; mature, affluent. ♦Lou Silverstein, gen mgr, opns dir; Nancy Silverstein, progmg dir; Al Hartsell, engrg dir; Sue Mapp, traf mgr.

***KGCB(FM)**— Dec 5, 1994: 90.9 mhz; 58 kw. 2,532 ft TL: N34 41 15 W112 07 02. Stereo. Hrs open: 24 3741 Karicio Ln., 86303. Phone: (928) 776-0909. Fax: (928) 776-1736.E-mail: info@radioshine.org Web Site:www.radioshine.org Licensee: Grand Canyon Broadcasters Inc. Natl. Network: Salem Radio Network, . Wilkinson, Barker, Knauer, LLP. Format: Contemp Christian, adult contemp, relg. Target aud: 25-54; adult, family audience. ♦Stephen R. White, VP, gen mgr, stn mgr; Daniel White, opns dir; Virginia Rayner, dev mgr; Mike Medlin, progmg dir.

***KJZP(FM)**—Not on air, target date: unknown: 90.1 mhz; 3 kw. Ant -367 ft TL: N34 32 37 W112 27 56. Hrs open: 923 E. Gurley St., Suite 202, 86301. Phone: (928) 541-1008.E-mail: kjzafm@yahoo.com Web Site:www.kjza.org Licensee: St. Paul Bible College. Natl. Network: NPR, . ♦Tom Erickson, gen mgr.

***KNAQ(FM)**— September 1997: 89.3 mhz; 100 w. 1,584 ft TL: N34 29 24 W112 31 59. Hrs open:
Rebroadcasts KNAU-FM Flagstaff 100%.
Box 5764, Northern Arizona University, Flagstaff, 86011-5764. Phone: (928) 523-5628. Fax: (928) 523-7647.E-mail: knau@nau.edu Web Site:www.knau.org Licensee: Northern Arizona University. Format: NPR news, classical, info. ♦John Stark, gen mgr; Dave Riek, opns mgr, progmg mgr; Dan Kraker, news dir; Lisa Skinner, traf mgr.

KNOT(AM)— June 22, 1957: 1450 khz; 1 kw-U. TL: N34 32 42 W112 26 46. Hrs open: 24 Box 151, 86302. Secondary address: 2225 E. Hwy. 69 86301. Phone: (928) 445-6880. Fax: (928) 445-6852.E-mail: pamela.flaherty@kaff.com Web Site:www.magic991.com Licensee: Guyann Corp. (acq 9-7-2005; grpsl). Population served: 100,000 Format: Classic country. News staff: one. Target aud: 35 plus. Spec prog: Jazz 2 hrs, sports 8 hrs wkly. ♦Tamie Phillips, gen mgr, stn mgr & opns mgr; C.J. Murri, progmg dir; Leza La Chapelle Dandos, news dir; Mark Hill, chief of engrg; Leza La Chapple Dandos, local news ed.

KPPV(FM)—See Prescott Valley

KTMG(FM)— Nov 11, 1977: 99.1 mhz; 6 kw. 200 ft TL: N34 34 29 W112 28 45. Stereo. Hrs open: 24 Prog sep from AM Box 151, 86301. Secondary address: 2225 E. Hwy. 69 86301. Phone: (928) 445-6880. Fax: (928) 445-6852.E-mail: pamela.flaherty@kaff.com Natl. Network: ABC, . Format: Adult contemp. News staff: one. Target aud: 35 plus.

KYCA(AM)— August 1940: 1490 khz; 1 kw-U. TL: N34 33 03 W112 27 45. Hrs open: 5 AM-1 AM Box 1631, 86302. Secondary address: 500 Henry St. 86301. Phone: (928) 445-1700. Fax: (928) 445-5365. Web Site:www.kyca.info Licensee: Southwest Broadcasting Co. (acq 9-25-70). Population served: 100,000 Natl. Network: CBS, Westwood One, . Cohn & Marks. Format: News/talk. News staff: 4; News: 20 hrs wkly. Target aud: 35-64; mature adults. ♦Willard Hodgkins III, CEO.

Prescott Valley

KPPV(FM)— Sept 1, 1985: 106.7 mhz; 3.7 kw. 1,627 ft TL: N34 29 25 W112 32 00. Stereo. Hrs open: 24 Box 26523, 86312. Phone: (928) 445-8289, (800) 264-5449. Fax: (928) 442-0448. Web Site:www.kppv.com Population served: 250,000 Natl. Network: Jones Radio Networks, . Arizona News Radio Format: Adult contemp. News staff: 2; News: 6 hrs wkly. Target aud: 25-54; middle to upper income professionals with families and disposable income. ♦Sanford Cohen, pres; Terry Cohen, exec VP.

KQNA(AM)— June 28, 1986: 1130 khz; 1 kw-D. TL: N34 37 46 W112 18 56. Hrs open: Box 26523, 86312. Secondary address: 3755 Karicio Ln., Suite 2-C, Prescott 86303. Phone: (928) 445-8289. Phone: (800) 264-5449. Fax: (928) 442-0448.E-mail: info@kppv.com Web Site:www.kqna.com Licensee: Prescott Valley Broadcasting Co. (group owner; (acq 12-27-93; $75,000; 1-10-94). Population served: 200,000 Natl. Network: Fox News Radio, Salem Radio Network, CNN Radio, . Arizona News Radio David Tillotson. Format: News/talk, sports. News staff: 3; News: 84 hrs wkly. Target aud: 35-64; middle - upper income, professionals & new consumers. ♦Sanford B. Cohen, pres, gen mgr; Terry P. Cohen, exec VP; Allison Flannery, natl sls mgr; Ken Byers, pub affrs dir; Mark Hills, engrg mgr; Bill Monroe, news rptr; Mike Austin, sports cmtr.

Quartzsite

KBUX(FM)— November 1988: 94.3 mhz; 205 w. -161 ft TL: N33 40 58 W114 13 59. Stereo. Hrs open: 6 AM-10 PM Box 40, 85346. Phone: (928) 927-5111.E-mail: kugxradio@hotmail.com Licensee: Maude J. Burdette. Format: Btfl music, country, oldies, diversefied. Target aud: General; retired motor home & trailer owners wintering in warmer climate. ♦Maude J. Burdette, gen mgr; Maude Burdette, stn mgr; Marvin Vosper, progmg dir.

***KEQS(FM)**—Not on air, target date: unknown: 91.7 mhz; 100 w. Ant -207 ft TL: N33 40 19 W114 12 24. Hrs open: Box 3475, 85359-3475. Phone: (928) 927-9420. Fax: (928) 927-9425. Licensee: E.Q. Scholars Inc. ♦Steven McClenning, pres.

Red Mesa

***KRMH(FM)**— 1998: 89.7 mhz; 4.5 kw. 134 ft TL: N36 57 48 W109 22 39. Hrs open: HC 6100 Box 40, Teec Nos Pos, 86514. Phone: (928) 656-4100. Fax: (928) 656-4320. Web Site:www.rmusd.net Licensee: Red Mesa Unified School District No. 27. Format: Native American, var.

Safford

KATO(AM)— May 5, 1961: 1230 khz; 1 kw-U. TL: N32 49 30 W109 45 30. Hrs open: 5 AM-midnight Drawer L, 85548. Secondary address: 3335 W. 8th St., Thatcher 85552. Phone: (928) 428-1230. Fax: (928) 428-1311.E-mail: davis@mcmurrayradio.com Web Site:www.mysouthernaz.com Licensee: McMurray Communications Inc. (group owner; acq 12-17-92; $10,000 with co-located FM; 2-1-93). Population served: 36,000 Natl. Network: ABC, . Format: News/talk, sports. News staff: 7; News: 25 hrs wkly. Target aud: 25-54; upscale, intelligent. ♦Bud McMurray, pres; Davis Nathan, gen mgr, sls dir; Reed Richins, opns mgr, progmg dir & chief of engrg.

KCUZ(AM)—(Clifton, July 31, 1969: 1490 khz; 1 kw-U. TL: N33 02 30 W109 17 40. Hrs open: 24
Rebroadcasts KFMM(FM) Thatcher 100%.
Box 35997, Tucson, 85740. Secondary address: 301 B Hwy. 70 E. 85546. Phone: (928) 428-0916. Fax: (928) 428-7797.E-mail: kfmm@eaznet.com Licensee: Cochise Broadcasting LLC. (acq 6-30-2007; $330,000 with KFMM(FM) Thatcher). Population served: 5,087 Format: Classic rock. News staff: one; News: 7 hrs wkly. Target aud: 25-54. Spec prog: Relg 2 hrs, loc talk 8 hrs wkly. ♦Rick Schneider, gen mgr; Darwin Morris, disc jockey.

KFMM(FM)—(Thatcher, Dec 7, 1981: 99.1 mhz; 50 kw. Ant 2,280 ft TL: N32 53 22 W109 19 23. Stereo. Hrs open: 24 Dups AM 50% Rebroadcasts KCUZ (AM) Safford 100%.
Box 35997, Tucson, 85740. Secondary address: 301 B Hwy. 70 E. 85546. Phone: (928) 428-0916. Fax: (928) 428-7797.E-mail: kfmm@eaznet.com Licensee: Cochise Broadcasting LLC. Population served: 100,000 News staff: one; News: 7 hrs wkly. Spec prog: Children 2 hrs wkly. ◆Darwin Morris, chief of engrg.

KWRQ(FM)—(Clifton, Oct 1, 1986: 102.3 mhz; 2.8 kw. 2,211 ft TL: N32 53 23 W109 19 26. Stereo. Hrs open: 24 Drawer L, 85548-0886. Secondary address: 3335 West 8th St., Thatcher 85552. Phone: (928) 428-1020. Fax: (928) 428-6818. Fax: (928) 428-1311.E-mail: davis@mcmarryradio.com Web Site:www.mysouthernaz.com Licensee: McMurray Communications Inc. (group owner; acq 11-97; $350,000). Natl. Network: Jones Radio Networks, . Format: Hot Adult contemp. Target aud: 20-35; working females. ◆Bud McMurray, pres; Davis Nathan, gen mgr; Reed Richins, opns mgr.

KXKQ(FM)— Aug 11, 1979: 94.1 mhz; 1 kw. Ant 4,287 ft TL: N32 39 01 W109 50 53. Stereo. Hrs open: 24 Prog sep from AM 3335 W. 8th St., Thatcher, 85552. Phone: (928) 428-1230. Fax: (928) 428-1311.E-mail: davis@mcmurrayradio.com Licensee: McMurray Communications Inc. Population served: 40,000 Format: Country. News: one hr wkly. Target aud: 25-54. ◆Reed Richins, engrg dir; Lee Patterson, traf mgr.

Sahuarita

KEVT(AM)— Oct 12, 1985: 1210 khz; 10 kw-D, 1 kw-N, DA-N. TL: N32 02 04 W110 56 45. Hrs open: 2955 E. Broadway Blvd., Tucson, 85716. Phone: (520) 628-1200. Fax: (520) 326-4927.E-mail: contact@kevtradio.net Web Site:www.radiounica.com Licensee: One Mart Corp. Group owner: Multicultural Radio Broadcasting Inc. (acq 4-27-2007; $1.5 million). Format: Rgnl Mexican. ◆Francisco Zazueta, gen mgr.

Saint Johns

KWKM(FM)— 2001: 95.7 mhz; 100 kw. Ant 1,197 ft TL: N34 14 59 W109 35 08. Hrs open: 1520 Commerce Dr., Suite B, Show Low, 85901. Phone: (928) 532-2949. Fax: (928) 532-3176.E-mail: program@kwkm.com Web Site:www.kwkm.com Licensee: KM Radio of St. Johns L.L.C. (acq 5-3-99). Natl. Network: ABC, . Format: Hot adult contemp. News: one hr wkly. Target aud: 18-44. Spec prog: News/talk 2 hrs, blues 2 hrs, alternative rock 2 hrs wkly. ◆Jean Barton, gen mgr.

Salome

KVGG(FM)—Not on air, target date: unknown: 101.9 mhz; 6 kw. Ant 328 ft TL: N33 46 54 W113 36 42. Hrs open: 3800 Howard Hughes Pkwy., Wells Fargo Tower, 17th Fl., Las Vegas, NV, 89169. Phone: (702) 385-6000. Fax: (702) 385-6001. Licensee: Kemp Communications Inc. ◆Will Kemp, pres & gen mgr.

Scottsdale

KAZG(AM)—Licensed to Scottsdale. See Phoenix

KSLX-FM—Licensed to Scottsdale. See Phoenix

Sedona

KAZM(AM)— Nov 1, 1974: 780 khz; 5 kw-D, 250 w-N, DA-N. TL: N34 51 38 W111 49 10. Hrs open: 24 Box 1525, 86339. Phone: (928) 282-4154. Fax: (928) 282-2230.E-mail: info@kazmradio.com Web Site:www.kazmradio.com Licensee: Tabback Broadcasting Co. Population served: 280,000 Natl. Network: Westwood One, ESPN Radio, Fox News Radio, . Brooks, Pierce, McLendon, Humphrey & Leonard. Format: New/talk, sports, music. News staff: 2; News: 16 hrs wkly. Target aud: 25 plus; baby boomers, professions, tourists. ◆Tom N. Tabback, gen mgr.

KQST(FM)— May 1, 1984: 102.9 mhz; 90 kw. 1,433 ft TL: N34 58 05 W111 30 29. Stereo. Hrs open: 24 Box 187, Cottonwood, 86326. Phone: (928) 634-2959. Fax: (928) 634-2295. Web Site:www.myradioplace.com Licensee: Yavapai Broadcasting Corp. (acq 12-1-2004; $3 million). John A. Borsari. Format: Adult contemp, top-40. Target aud: 24-59. ◆W. Grant Hafley, pres; Dave Kessel, gen mgr; Mike Puetz, gen sls mgr, prom dir; John Herring, progmg dir.

KSED(FM)— August 1994: 107.5 mhz; 98.4 kw. 1,463 ft TL: N34 58 07 W111 30 22. Stereo. Hrs open: 24 112 E. Rt. 66, Suite 105,

Flagstaff, 86001. Phone: (928) 779-1177. Fax: (928) 774-5179.E-mail: ann@northlandradio.com Web Site:www.koltcountry.com Licensee: Grenax Broadcasting II LLC. (acq 1-6-2006; grpsl). Natl. Network: NBC, . Format: Special blend, country. News staff: one. ◆Greg Dinetz, pres; Jim Shipp, gen mgr, sls dir, prom dir; Bill McAdams, opns dir; Mike Mentor, progmg dir; Jon Sweat, chief of engrg.

Seligman

KZKE(FM)— 1995: 103.3 mhz; 1.75 kw. 423 ft TL: N35 19 26 W112 45 55. Hrs open: 24 812 E. Beale St., Kingman, 86401. Phone: (928) 753-9100. Fax: (928) 753-1978. Licensee: Route 66 Broadcasting L.L.C. (acq 9-1-98). Format: Good time oldies. ◆Rhonda Hart, VP, gen mgr; JoAnn Oxsen, adv dir; Steve Levin, progmg dir.

Sells

*KOHN(FM)— 2004: 91.9 mhz; 10 kw. Ant 1,656 ft TL: N32 07 59 W112 09 31. Hrs open: P.O. Box 183, 85634. Phone: (520) 361-5011. Fax: (520) 361-3931.E-mail: kohn@hotmail.com Licensee: Tohono O'Odham Nation. Format: Eclectic music, Native American. ◆Sial Thonolig, gen mgr; Mary Lopez, cultural affrs dir.

Show Low

*KNAA(FM)— October 1997: 90.7 mhz; 100 w. 850 ft TL: N34 12 17 W109 56 22. Hrs open:
Rebroadcasts KNAU(FM) Flagstaff 100%.
Box 5764, Northern Arizona University, Flagstaff, 86011-5764. Phone: (928) 523-5628. Fax: (928) 523-7647.E-mail: knau@nau.edu Web Site:www.knau.org Licensee: Arizona Board of Regents. Natl. Network: NPR, . Format: Class, news. ◆John Stark, gen mgr; Dave Riek, opns dir.

KRFM(FM)— July 1, 1983: 96.5 mhz; 100 kw. Ant 994 ft TL: N34 12 20 W109 56 26. Stereo. Hrs open: Prog sep from AM 1838 W. Commerce Dr., Suite A, Lakeside, 85929. Phone: (928) 368-8100. Fax: (928) 368-8108.E-mail: info@krfm965.com Web Site:www.krfm965.com Population served: 80,000 Natl. Network: Jones Radio Networks, . Format: Hot adult contemp. Target aud: 18-34; 65% female & 35% male.

KSNX(FM)— Sept 13, 1964: 93.5 mhz; 25 kw. Ant 150 ft TL: N34 13 14 W110 01 49. Hrs open: 1838 W. Commerce Dr., Suite A, Lakeside, 85929. Phone: (928) 368-8100. Fax: (928) 368-8108.E-mail: info@ksnx.com Web Site:www.ksnx.com Format: Good-time oldies. Target aud: 25-54; 50% female & 50% male.

KVSL(AM)— July 6, 1968: 1450 khz; 1 kw-U. TL: N34 16 00 W110 20 10. Hrs open: 1838 W. Commerce Dr., Suite A, Lakeside, 85929. Phone: (928) 368-8100. Fax: (928) 368-8108.E-mail: production @whitemountainradio.com Web Site:www.kvsl1450.com Licensee: Petracom of Holbrook LLC. (acq 11-17-2005; grpsl). Population served: 50,000 Natl. Network: ABC, Fox News Radio, . Format: Nostalgia oldies. Target aud: 45-65; 46% female, 54% male. Spec prog: Farm 2 hrs wkly. ◆Steve Johnson, gen mgr, gen sls mgr & progmg dir.

KVWM(AM)— May 17, 1957: 970 khz; 5 kw-D, 114 w-N. TL: N34 13 14 W110 01 49. Hrs open: 1838 W. Commerce Dr., Suite A, Lakeside, 85929. Phone: (928) 368-8100. Fax: (928) 368-8108.E-mail: production @whitemountainradio.com Licensee: Petracom of Holbrook LLC. (acq 11-17-2005; grpsl). Population served: 60,000 Natl. Network: ABC, Westwood One, . Format: News/talk. Target aud: 35-65; 46% female & 54% male. ◆Steve Johnson, gen mgr, gen sls mgr & progmg dir; Lisa Ames, traf mgr.

Sierra Vista

KKYZ(FM)— Jan 1, 1995: 101.7 mhz; 3 kw. Ant 328 ft TL: N31 33 59 W110 13 57. Stereo. Hrs open: 24 500 E. Fry Blvd., Suite L-10, 85635. Phone: (520) 459-8201. Fax: (520) 458-7104.E-mail: info@kkyz.com Web Site:www.kkyz.com Licensee: Cochise Broadcasting L.L.C. (acq 1-12-2001). Population served: 97,000 Format: Oldies. Target aud: 25-54. ◆Jeff Davenport, stn mgr; Ted Tucker, gen mgr, opns dir & opns mgr.

KNXN(AM)— June 20, 1980: 1470 khz; 2.5 kw-D, 39 w-N. TL: N31 32 53 W110 14 54. Hrs open: 24 680 Avenida del Sol, 85635. Phone: (520) 790-2440. Fax: (520) 790-2937.E-mail: doug@kvoi.com Web Site:www.kgms.com Licensee: Good News Radio. Group owner: Good News Communications Inc. (acq 4-16-01; $300,000). Population served: 92,000 Format: Inspirational talk, Christian. News staff: one; News: 5 hrs wkly. ◆Doug Martin, gen mgr; Jeff Davenport, gen mgr & opns mgr.

KTAN(AM)— March 1957: 1420 khz; 1.5 kw-D, 500 w-N, DA-N. TL: N31 32 47 W110 16 29. Hrs open: 24 Box 2770, 85636. Secondary address: 2300 Busby Dr. 85636. Phone: (520) 458-4313. Fax: (520) 458-4317.E-mail: ktan@wavmax.com Licensee: CCR-Sierra Vista IV LLC. Group owner: Cherry Creek Radio LLC (acq 12-19-2003; grpsl). Population served: 120,000 Natl. Network: CBS, . Natl. Rep: Tacher,. Baraff, Koerner & Olender. Format: News/talk, sports. News staff: one; News: 20 hrs wkly. Target aud: 25-54. ◆Paul Orlando, gen mgr; Rudy Sueskind, gen sls mgr & rgnl sls mgr; Debbie Simmons, mus dir, traf mgr.

KWCD(FM)—See Bisbee

KZMK(FM)— September 1973: 100.9 mhz; 3 kw. -46 ft TL: N31 32 47 W110 16 29. Stereo. Hrs open: 24 Prog sep from AM Box 2770, 85636. Secondary address: 2300 Busby Dr. 85636. Phone: (520) 458-4313. Fax: (520) 458-4317.E-mail: ktan@wavmax.com Population served: 120,000 Format: Adult contemp. News staff: one; News: one hr wkly. Target aud: 18-49.

Snowflake

KVGQ(FM)—Not on air, target date: unknown: 99.7 mhz; 50 kw. Ant 469 ft TL: N34 38 26 W110 19 16. Hrs open: 3800 Howard Hughes Pkwy., Wells Fargo Tower, 17th Fl., Las Vegas, NV, 89169. Phone: (702) 385-6000. Fax: (702) 385-6001. Licensee: Kemp Communications Inc. ◆Will Kemp, pres.

South Tucson

KJLL(AM)—Licensed to South Tucson. See Tucson

KXEW(AM)—Licensed to South Tucson. See Tucson

Springerville

KQAZ(FM)— July 15, 1984: 101.7 mhz; 3 kw. -97 ft TL: N34 08 17 W109 16 10. (CP: 1.1 kw). Stereo. Hrs open: Box 2020, Show Low, 85902. Secondary address: 691 E. Deuce of Clubs, Show Low 85901. Phone: (928) 532-1010. Fax: (928) 532-0101. Web Site:www.majik101.com Licensee: Country Mountain Airwaves LLC. (acq 7-30-99; $175,000 with KRVZ(AM) Springerville). Natl. Network: AP Radio, . Format: Adult Alternative. ◆Camden Smith, gen mgr, progmg dir; Laurie Pogson, traf mgr; Jack Jacobs, disc jockey.

KRVZ(AM)— June 11, 1982: 1400 khz; 1 kw-U. TL: N34 08 17 W109 16 10. Hrs open: 24 Box 2020, Show Low, 85902. Phone: (928) 532-1010. Fax: (928) 532-0101.E-mail: krvz@frontiernet.net Licensee: Country Mountain Airwaves LLC. (acq 7-30-99; $175,000 with KQAZ(FM) Springerville). Natl. Network: Jones Radio Networks, . Format: Talk radio. ◆William Konopnicki, pres; Camden Smith, gen mgr; Dan Curtis, opns dir; Laurie Pogson, traf mgr.

Sun City

KOMR(FM)— Mar 7, 1975: 106.3 mhz; 2.5 kw. 325 ft TL: N33 36 05 W112 17 31. (CP: 23 kw, ant 725 ft.). Stereo. Hrs open: 24 4745 N. 7th St., Suite 140, Phoenix, 85014. Phone: (602) 308-7900. Fax: (602) 308-7979. Web Site:www.univision.com Licensee: HBC License Corp. Group owner: Univision Radio (acq 9-22-2003; grpsl). Population served: 3,173,200 Dow, Lohnes & Albertson. Format: Spanish Adult Hits. Target aud: 25-54. ◆Mary McEvilly-Hernandez, VP, gen mgr; Nelson Oseida, opns dir; Chris Morris, sls dir; Aide Gonzalez, prom dir; Kevin Norgaard, rsch dir; Dobby White, traf mgr.

Sun City West

KVIB(FM)— 2005: 95.1 mhz; 41 kw. Ant 2,785 ft TL: N34 14 05 W112 22 02. Stereo. Hrs open: 24 4343 N. Scottsdale Rd., #200, Scottsdale, 85251. Phone: (480) 222-3300. Fax: (480) 970-1759. Web Site:www.951latinovibefm.com Licensee: Sun City Licenses LLC (acq 3-10-2005; $18.7 million). Natl. Rep: McGavren Guild,. Latham & Watkins. Format: Sp, CHR. Target aud: 18-34; Hispanic 2nd & 3rd generation. ◆Michael Cutchall, pres; Jose Rodilles, gen mgr; Ellen Cavanaugh, sls VP, mktg VP; Jaque Bosque Diaz, natl sls mgr.

Teec Nos Pos

KEEC(FM)—Not on air, target date: unknown: 95.3 mhz; 100 kw. Ant 163 ft TL: N36 57 44 W109 21 24. Hrs open: 980 N. Michigan Ave., Suite 1880, Chicago, IL, 60611. Phone: (312) 204-9900. Licensee: College Creek Media LLC. ◆Neal J. Robinson, pres.

Tempe

KDUS(AM)— Apr 16, 1960: 1060 khz; 5 kw-D, 500 w-N, DA-N. TL: N33 21 43 W111 58 03. Hrs open: 24 1900 W. Carmen, 85283. Phone: (480) 838-0400. Fax: (480) 820-8469.E-mail: info@kdus.com Web Site:www.kdus.com Licensee: Tempe Radio Inc. Group owner: Sandusky Radio (acq 1994; $20 million with co-located FM). Population served: 50,000 Format: Sports. News staff: one. Target aud: 18-34 males. ♦Chuck Artigue, gen mgr.

KLNZ(FM)—(Glendale, Sept 1, 1997: 103.5 mhz; 62 kw. 2,428 ft TL: N33 35 33 W112 34 49. Stereo. Hrs open: 24 501 N. 44th St., Suite 425, Phoenix, 85008. Phone: (602) 266-2005. Fax: (602) 279-2921.E-mail: info@entravision.com Web Site:www.entravision.com Licensee: Entravision Holdings LLC. Group owner: Entravision Communications Corp. (acq 7-28-00; grpsl). Population served: 2,603,200 Bechtel & Cole. Format: Sp, rgnl Mexican. Target aud: General. ♦Tom Duran, gen mgr; Chris Moncayo, gen sls mgr; Carrie Strait, progmg dir; Ryan Oller, chief of engrg.

KMIK(AM)—Licensed to Tempe. See Phoenix

KNIX-FM—See Phoenix

KUPD-FM— April 1960: 97.9 mhz; 100 kw. 1,620 ft TL: N33 19 57 W112 03 53. Stereo. Hrs open: Prog sep from AM 1900 W. Carmen, 85283. Phone: (480) 838-0400. Fax: (480) 820-8469.E-mail: info@98kupd.com Web Site:www.98kupd.com Licensee: Tempe Radio Inc. Population served: 200,000 Wiley, Rein & Fielding. Format: AOR. ♦J.J. Jeffries, progmg dir.

Thatcher

KFMM(FM)—Licensed to Thatcher. See Safford

Tolleson

KNUV(AM)— Jan 23, 1961: 1190 khz; 5 kw-D, 250 w-N, DA-2. TL: N33 26 42 W112 15 54. Hrs open: 24 8547 E. Arapahoe Rd. #J-451, Greenwood Village, CO, 80112. Phone: (303) 680-3281. Licensee: New Radio Venture Inc. Population served: 2,000,000 Cohn & Marks.

KXXT(AM)— Dec 12, 1962: 1010 khz; 15 kw-D, 250 w-N, DA-D. TL: N33 26 43 W112 12 23. Hrs open: 24 2800 N. 44th St., Suite 100, Phoenix, 85008. Phone: (602) 296-3600. Fax: (602) 296-3624.E-mail: jess@kxeg1280.com Web Site:www.newstalk1010.net Licensee: Communicom Co. of Arizona L.P. Group owner: James Crystal Inc. (acq 12-14-2005; grpsl). Population served: 1,270,000 Format: Relg. News staff: one. ♦Bob Christy, gen mgr; Willis Girdner, chief of engrg.

Tuba City

***KGHR(FM)**— Nov 27, 1991: 91.3 mhz; 100 kw horiz. Ant 1,056 ft TL: N36 21 27 W111 12 12. Stereo. Hrs open: 24 Box 160, 86045. Phone: (928) 283-5555. Fax: (928) 283-5557.E-mail: info@kghr.org Web Site:www.kghr.org Licensee: Tuba City High School Board Inc. Natl. Network: NPR, . Format: Native American, AAA. News: 20 hrs wkly. Target aud: General; Native American/Navajo. Spec prog: Pub affrs 5 hrs wkly. ♦John Bittner, stn mgr.

KTBA(AM)— 1980: 1050 khz; 5 kw-D, 5.2 w-N. TL: N36 07 54 W111 14 59. (CP: 760 khz; 250 w-D, 60 w-N). Hrs open: Box 9090, Window Rock, 86515. Phone: (505) 371-5587. Licensee: Western Indian Ministries Inc. (group owner; (acq 1980). Population served: 70,000 Format: Adult contemp. English & Navajo. ♦Larry Harper, gen mgr.

Tubac

KTBX(FM)—Not on air, target date: unknown: 98.1 mhz; 270 w. Ant 1,512 ft TL: N31 42 17 W110 55 25. Hrs open: Box 11060, Jackson, WY, 83002. Phone: (703) 812-0482. Licensee: Cochise Broadcasting LLC. ♦Ted Tucker, gen mgr.

Tucson

***KAIC(FM)**— 2006: 88.9 mhz; 1.8 kw vert. Ant 26 ft TL: N32 36 56 W110 38 38. Hrs open:
Rebroadcasts KLRD(FM) Yucaipa, CA 100%.
2351 Sunset Blvd., Suite 170-218, Rocklin, CA, 95765. Phone: (916) 251-1600. Fax: (916) 251-1650. Web Site:www.air1.com Licensee: Educational Media Foundation. Natl. Network: Air 1, . Format: Alternative rock, div. ♦Richard Jenkins, pres; Mike Novak, VP; Keith Whipple, dev dir; Eric Allen, natl sls mgr; David Pierce, progmg mgr; Ed Lenane, news dir; Sam Wallington, engrg dir; Karen Johnson, news rptr.

KCEE(AM)— Sept 23, 1953: 690 khz; 250 w-D, DA. TL: N32 15 11 W110 57 44. Hrs open: 3222 S. Richey Blvd., 85713-5453. Phone: (520) 790-2440. Fax: (520) 790-2937.E-mail: info@690kcee.com Web Site:www.690kcee.com Licensee: Good News Broadcasting Inc. Group owner: Good News Communications Inc. (acq 9-53). Population served: 700,000 Natl. Rep: Salem,. Wray Fitch. Format: Pop classics. Target aud: 24-54. ♦Doug Martin, pres, gen mgr; Mary Martin, sls dir, gen sls mgr; Matt Manis, opns mgr & progmg dir; Larry Massey, chief of engrg.

KCUB(AM)— August 1929: 1290 khz; 1 kw-U. TL: N32 16 37 W110 58 50. Hrs open: 24 575 W. Roger Rd., 85705. Phone: (520) 887-1000. Fax: (520) 887-6397. Licensee: Citadel Broadcasting Co. Group owner: Citadel Broadcasting Corp. (acq 4-26-2001; grpsl). Population served: 500,000 Format: Sports, news. News staff: one. Target aud: 25-54. ♦Ken Kowalcek, gen mgr; Herb Crowe, opns VP; Keith Rosenblatt, sls VP.

KFFN(AM)— January 1957: 1490 khz; 1 kw-U. TL: N32 14 56 W110 55 29. Stereo. Hrs open: 24 Prog sep from FM 3438 N. COuntry Club, 85716. Phone: (520) 795-1490. Fax: (520) 327-2260. Licensee: Journal Broadcast Corp. Population served: 714,000 Natl. Network: ESPN Radio, . Format: Sports. News: 2 hrs wkly. Target aud: 18-49. ♦Julie Brinks, gen mgr; Rob Cook, progmg dir.

***KFLT(AM)**— October 1977: 830 khz; 50 kw-D, 1 kw-N, DA-N. TL: N32 26 39 W111 05 27. Hrs open: 24 Box 35300, 85740. Secondary address: 7355 N. Oracle Rd., Suite 102 85704. Phone: (520) 797-3700. Fax: (520) 742-6979.E-mail: abiddel@flr.org Web Site:www.myflr.org Licensee: Family Life Broadcasting System Inc. Group owner: Family Life Communications Inc. (acq 10-86; $125,000; 4-14-86). Population served: 3,000,000 Natl. Network: Moody, . Format: Christian, inspirational. News staff: one; News: 15 hrs wkly. Target aud: 25-45; Christian families. ♦Randy Carlson, pres; Adam Biddell, gen mgr; Dawn Bumsted, progmg dir; Bill Ronning, mus dir; Evan Carlson, pub affrs dir; Joe Rother, chief of engrg.

***KFLT-FM**— 2006: 88.5 mhz; 1.5 kw vert. Ant 377 ft TL: N32 00 11 W110 47 49. Hrs open: Box 35300, 85740. Secondary address: 7355 N. Oracle Rd., Suite 102 85704. Phone: (520) 797-3700. Fax: (520) 742-6979.E-mail: abiddel@flr.org Web Site:www.myflr.org Licensee: Family Life Broadcasting Inc. Format: Christian, inspirational. ♦Randy Carlson, pres; Adam Biddell, gen mgr; Dawn Bumstead, progmg dir; Bill Ronning, mus dir; Evan Carlson, pub affrs dir; Joe Rother, chief of engrg.

KGMS(AM)— Aug 10, 1963: 940 khz; 5 kw-D, 1 kw-N, DA-2. TL: N32 12 04 W111 01 02. Hrs open: 24 3222 S. Richey Ave., 85713. Phone: (520) 790-2440. Fax: (520) 790-2937.E-mail: info@kgms.com Web Site:kgms.com Licensee: Good Music Inc. Group owner: Good News Communications Inc. (acq 11-27-00; swap with KCEE(FM) Green Valley). Population served: 700,000 Natl. Rep: Salem,. Wrey Fitch. Format: Christian talk. Target aud: 25-54. ♦Doug Martin, CEO, pres, gen mgr; Matt Manis, opns mgr.

KGVY(AM)—(Green Valley, Sept 23, 1981: 1080 khz; 1 kw-D. TL: N31 55 34 W110 59 45. Hrs open: 6 AM-sunset Box 767, Green Valley, 85622. Secondary address: 1510 W. Camino Antigua, Sahuarita 85629. Phone: (520) 399-1000. Fax: (520) 399-9300.E-mail: kgvyam@quest.net Licensee: KGVY LLC (acq 6-19-2007; $1.1 million). Population served: 1,000,000 Natl. Network: ABC, . Format: Oldies. News staff: 12; News: 13 hrs wkly. Target aud: 50 plus; mature, well educated, higher income, retired. ♦James Walker, gen mgr.

KHYT(FM)— August 1993: 107.5 mhz; 14.5 kw. 3,526 ft TL: N32 24 54 W110 42 56. (CP: 82 kw, ant 2,027 ft.). Hrs open: 575 W. Roger, 85705. Phone: (520) 887-1000. Fax: (520) 887-6397. Web Site:www.rock1075.com Licensee: Citadel Broadcasting Co. Group owner: Citadel Broadcasting Corp. (acq 4-26-01; grpsl). Format: Classic rock. Target aud: 25-54; adults. ♦Farid Suleman, CEO; Ken Kowalcek, gen mgr; Herb Crowe, opns dir; Keith Rosenblatt, sls dir.

KIIM-FM— March 1954: 99.5 mhz; 90 kw. 2,037 ft TL: N32 14 56 W111 06 59. Stereo. Hrs open: 24 Prog sep from AM 575 W. Roger Rd., 85705. Phone: (520) 887-1000. Fax: (520) 887-6397. Web Site:www.kiimfm.com Licensee: Citadel Broadcasting Co. Natl. Network: ABC, Premiere Radio Networks, . Format: Hot country. Target aud: Adult: 25-54.

KJLL(AM)—(South Tucson, 1957: 1330 khz; 2 kw-D, 5 kw-N, DA-N. TL: N32 18 51 W110 50 17. Hrs open: 4433 E. Broadway, Suite 210, 85711. Phone: (520) 529-5865. Fax: (520) 529-9324.E-mail: info@kjllam.com Web Site:www.tucsonsjolt.com Licensee: Hudson Communications Inc. (acq 1996; $36,000). Population served: 600,000 Format: News/talk. ♦Kimberly Lopez, gen mgr.

KLPX(FM)— June 1, 1967: 96.1 mhz; 82 kw. 1,952 ft TL: N32 14 56 W111 06 59. Stereo. Hrs open: Prog sep from AM 3871 N. Commerce, 85705. Phone: (520) 407-4500. Fax: (520) 407-4600. Web Site:www.klpx.com (Acq 6-79). Population served: 1,000,000 Natl. Rep: D & R Radio,. Bryan Cave. Format: Classic rock. Target aud: 25-54.

KMXZ-FM— Apr 11, 1973: 94.9 mhz; 97 kw. 1,952 ft TL: N32 14 56 W111 06 59. Stereo. Hrs open: 24 3438 N. Country Club, 85716. Phone: (520) 795-1490. Fax: (520) 327-2260.E-mail: mixfm@mixfm.com Web Site:www.mixfm.com Licensee: Journal Broadcast Corp. Group owner: Journal Broadcast Group Inc. (acq 1996; grpsl). Natl. Network: AP Radio, . Crowell & Moring. Wire Svc: AP Format: Adult contemp/soft rock. News staff: one; News: 3 hrs wkly. Target aud: 25-54. ♦Julie Brinks, gen mgr; Darla Thomas, opns mgr; Jennifer Nunn, gen sls mgr; Larkin Gassman, mktg dir; Bobby Rich, progmg dir.

KNST(AM)— Oct 1, 1958: 790 khz; 5 kw-D, 500 w-N. TL: N32 14 54 W111 00 30. Hrs open: 24 3202 N. Oracle Rd., 85705. Phone: (520) 618-2100. Fax: (520) 618-2135.E-mail: info@clearchannel.com Web Site:clearchannel.com Licensee: Capstar TX L.P. Group owner: Clear Channel Communications Inc. (acq 8-30-2000; grpsl). Population served: 262,933 Natl. Network: Moody, . Natl. Rep: McGavren Guild,. Format: News/talk. News staff: 3. Target aud: 25-54. ♦Debbie Wagner, gen mgr; Tim Richards, opns mgr; Tom Zlaket, sls dir; Nikki Van Doran, mktg dir; Mike Irby, chief of engrg; Mary Palin, traf mgr.

KOHT(FM)—See Marana

KQTH(FM)— May 4, 1994: 104.1 mhz; 3 kw. Ant 328 ft TL: N32 17 23 W111 01 06. Hrs open: 24 3438 N. Country Club, 85716. Phone: (520) 795-1490. Fax: (520) 327-2260. Web Site:www.1041thetruth.com Licensee: Journal Broadcast Corp. Group owner: Journal Broadcast Group Inc. Format: News. Target aud: 25-54; males, persons. ♦Julie Brinks, gen mgr; Darla Thomas, opns mgr; Jennifer Nunn, gen sls mgr; Andrew Lee, progmg dir.

KRQQ(FM)— Feb 1, 1971: 93.7 mhz; 91 kw. 2,030 ft TL: N32 14 56 W111 06 57. Stereo. Hrs open: Prog sep from AM 3202 N. Oracle Rd., 85705. Phone: (520) 618-2100. Fax: (520) 618-2135.E-mail: info@clearchannel.com Population served: 640,000 Format: CHR, Top-40. News staff: one. Target aud: 18-54.

KSAZ(AM)—(Marana, 1990: 580 khz; 5 kw-D, 390 w-N, DA-N. TL: N32 27 11 W111 17 04. Hrs open: 1011 N. Craycroft, Suite 400, 85711. Phone: (520) 298-6880. Fax: (520) 298-6077.E-mail: amradio1@cox.com Licensee: Owl Broadcasting & Development Inc. (acq 4-89; $1.05 million; 5-1-89). Natl. Network: ABC, . Hogan & Hartson. Format: Classic country. Target aud: 35 plus. Spec prog: International 2 hrs wkly.

KTKT(AM)— December 1949: 990 khz; 10 kw-D, 1 kw-N, DA-2. TL: N32 15 19 W111 00 32. Hrs open: 3871 N. Commerce, 85705. Phone: (520) 407-4500. Fax: (520) 407-4600. Web Site:www.ktktam.com Licensee: Arizona Lotus Corp. Group owner: Lotus Communications Corp. (acq 1973). Population served: 1,000,000 Natl. Network: AP Radio, . Natl. Rep: Lotus Entravision Reps LLC,. Bryan Cave. Format: Sp, sports. Target aud: 25-54. Spec prog: Black one hr, relg 2 hrs wkly. ♦Steve Groesbeck, gen mgr.

KTUC(AM)— July 10, 1926: 1400 khz; 1 kw-U. TL: N32 08 43 W110 53 38. (CP: TL: N32 14 56 W110 55 29). Hrs open: 575 W. Roger., 85705. Phone: (520) 887-1000. Fax: (520) 887-6397. Licensee: Citadel Broadcasting Co. Group owner: Citadel Broadcasting Corp. (acq 4-26-01; grpsl). Natl. Network: CBS, . Natl. Rep: Katz Radio,. Format: Adult standards. Target aud: General; college educated, upper income, politically active adults. ♦Ken Kowalcek, gen mgr.

KTZR-FM—(Green Valley, Oct 21, 1990: 97.1 mhz; 1.75 kw. Ant 613 ft TL: N31 58 37 W111 06 04. Stereo. Hrs open: 24 3202 N. Oracle Rd., 85705. Phone: (520) 618-2100. Fax: (520) 610-2200.E-mail: info@lapribsa.tucson.com Web Site:tucson.lapreciosa.com Licensee: Capstar TX L.P. Group owner: Clear Channel Communications Inc. Format: Spanish var. News staff: 2; News: 2 hrs wkly. Target aud: 18-35. ♦Debbie Wagner, gen mgr; Tim Richards, opns mgr; Tom Zlaket, sls dir; Nikki Van Doran, mktg dir; Ruppert Pacheco, progmg dir; Mike Irby, chief of engrg.

***KUAT-FM**— May 19, 1975: 90.5 mhz; 12.5 kw. 3,580 ft TL: N32 24 55 W110 42 54. Stereo. Hrs open: 24 Prog sep from AM Arizona Public Media, 85721-0067. Secondary address: Box 2100067 85721-0067. Phone: (520) 621-5828. Fax: (520) 621-3360. Web Site:www.kuatfm.org Licensee: Arizona Board of Regents for the Benefit of The University

of Arizona. Population served: 824,400 Natl. Network: PRI, . Rgnl rep: Dana Horner Wire Svc: AP Format: Classical. Target aud: 35 plus. ♦Jack Gibson, gen mgr & disc jockey.

***KUAZ(AM)—** Oct 7, 1968: 1550 khz; 50 kw-D. TL: N32 22 21 W111 05 52. Hrs open: Sunrise-sunset Arizona Public Media, 85721-0067. Secondary address: Box 210067 Phone: (520) 621-5828. Fax: (520) 621-3360. Web Site:www.kuaz.org Licensee: Arizona Board of Regents for the Benefit of The University of Arizona. Population served: 824,400 Natl. Network: NPR, PRI, . Rgnl rep: Dana Horner Dow, Lohnes & Albertson. Wire Svc: AP Format: News, talk/info, jazz. News staff: 5; News: 95+ hours per week. ♦Jack Gibson, gen mgr & stn mgr.

***KUAZ-FM—** Apr 27, 1992: 89.1 mhz; 1.6 kw. Ant 613 ft TL: N32 12 53 W111 00 21. Hrs open: 24 Arizona Public Media, 85721-0067. Secondary address: Box 210067 Phone: (520) 621-5828. Fax: (520) 621-3360.E-mail: kuaz@arizona.edu kuaz@kuat.org Web Site:www.kuaz.org Licensee: Arizona Board of Regents for Benefit of the University of Arizona. (acq 4-92). Population served: 824,400 Natl. Network: NPR, PRI, . Dow, Lohnes & Albertson. Wire Svc: AP Format: News/talk info/jazz. News staff: 5; News: 95+ hrs wkly. Target aud: General. ♦Jack Gibson, gen mgr; John Kelley, stn mgr; Colleen Greer, prom dir, progmg dir; Lyle Kesterson, progmg dir. Co-owned TV: KUAT-TV affil

KWFM(AM)— Feb 27, 1947: 1450 khz; 1 kw-U. TL: N32 12 04 W110 56 48. Stereo. Hrs open: 3202 N. Oracle Rd., 85705. Phone: (520) 618-2100. Fax: (520) 618-2200. Web Site:www.cool1450am.com Licensee: CC Licenses LLC. Group owner: Clear Channel Communications Inc. (acq 6-28-2001; grpsl). Format: Oldies. ♦Debbie Wagner, gen mgr; Tim Richards, opns mgr; Tom Zlaket, sls dir; Deeanne Thomas, gen sls mgr; Nikki Van Doran, mktg dir; Joan Lee, prom dir; Alan Cook, progmg dir; Mike Irby, chief of engrg; Mary Palin, traf mgr.

KWMT-FM— May 18, 1970: 92.9 mhz; 90 kw. 2,037 ft TL: N32 14 56 W111 06 59. Stereo. Hrs open: 24 3202 N. Oracle Rd., 85705. Phone: (520) 618-2100. Fax: (520) 618-2200. Web Site:www.929themountain.com Licensee: Capstar TX L.P. Group owner: Clear Channel Communications Inc. Population served: 452,000 Format: AAA. News staff: 2; News: 21 hrs wkly. ♦Debbie Wagner, gen mgr; Tim Richards, opns mgr; Deanne Thomas, gen sls mgr, local news ed; Blake Rogers, progmg dir.

***KXCI(FM)—** Dec 17, 1983: 91.3 mhz; 340 w. 3,641 ft TL: N32 24 54 W110 42 56. Stereo. Hrs open: 24 220 S. 4th Ave., 85701. Phone: (520) 623-1000, EXT. 11. Phone: (520) 622-5924. Fax: (520) 623-0758.E-mail: onfo@kxci.org Web Site:www.kxci.org Licensee: Foundation for Creative Broadcasting Inc. (acq 2-17-2004). Format: Eclectic, progsv, AAA. News: 4 hrs wkly. Target aud: 18-49. Spec prog: American Indian 2 hrs, Black 4 hrs, folk 2 hrs, gospel 2 hrs, jazz 2 hrs, Sp 4 hrs wkly. ♦Ryan Bruce, gen mgr; Jill Nunes, sls dir; Ginger Doran, progmg dir; Duncan Hudson, mus dir; Amanda Shauger, pub affrs dir; Doug Groenhoff, chief of engrg.

KXEW(AM)—(South Tucson, May 10, 1963: 1600 khz; 1 kw-U, DA-N. TL: N32 11 46 W110 59 02. Hrs open: 24 3202 N. Oracle Rd., 85705. Phone: (520) 618-2100. Fax: (520) 618-2200. Web Site:www.tejano1600.com Licensee: CC Licenses LLC. Group owner: Clear Channel Communications Inc. (acq 9-25-2003). Population served: 262,933 Cohn & Marks. Format: Tejano. Target aud: 25-54; blue collar Hispanics. ♦Debbie Wagner, gen mgr; Tim Richards, opns mgr; Tom Zlaket, sls dir; Patti Ruiz, gen sls mgr; Nikki Van Doran, mktg dir; Melissa Santa Cruz, prom dir; Rupert Pacheco, progmg dir; Mike Irby, chief of engrg; Mary Palin, traf mgr.

KZLZ(FM)—(Kearny, Aug 31, 1991: 105.3 mhz; 50 kw. 492 ft TL: N32 49 38 W110 34 12. Stereo. Hrs open: 24 2959 E. Grant Rd., 85716. Phone: (520) 325-3054. Fax: (520) 325-3495.E-mail: sonia@kzlzradio.com Licensee: KZLZ LLC. Group owner: Entravision Communications Corp. (acq 12-1-2006; $4.75 million). Arent, Fox, Kintner, Plotkin & Kahn. Format: Sp. Target aud: General. ♦Cesar Zalciora, VP, progmg dir; Sonya Tabanico, gen mgr.

Tusayan

KSGC(FM)— July 1, 1991: 92.1 mhz; 4.1 kw. Ant 335 ft TL: N35 58 14 W112 07 53. Stereo. Hrs open: 24 Box 3346, Grand Canyon, 86023-3346. Phone: (928) 638-9552. Fax: (928) 638-9553. Licensee: Tusayan Broadcasting Co. Natl. Network: ABC, . Format: Adult contemp. Target aud: 18-54; Grand Canyon visitors with disposable vacation income. ♦Brian Ciesielski, gen mgr; Wes Yellowstone, progmg dir.

Vail

KRDX(FM)— June 1978: 98.5 mhz; 3.9 kw. Ant 410 ft TL: N31 55 39 W110 37 57. Stereo. Hrs open: 24 Box 36717, Tucson, 85740. Phone: (520) 459-8201. Fax: (520) 458-7104.E-mail: comments@krdx.com Web Site:www.krdx.com Licensee: Desert West Air Ranchers Corp. (acq 6-24-99). Population served: 20,000 Format: Var. ♦Ted Tucker, gen mgr.

KXZK(FM)— 2008: 103.7 mhz; 790 w. Ant 476 ft TL: N31 55 39 W110 37 57. Hrs open: 500 E. Fry Blvd., Suite L-10, Sierra Vista, 85635. Phone: (520) 459-8201. Fax: (520) 458-7104. Licensee: Cochise Broadcasting LLC. ♦Ted Tucker, gen mgr.

Wellton

KCEC-FM— Oct 1, 2000: 104.5 mhz; 6.1 kw. 1,348 ft TL: N32 40 22 W114 20 14. Hrs open: 24 670 East 32 St., Suite 12 A, Yuma, 85365. Phone: (928) 782-5995. Fax: (928) 782-3874.E-mail: info@kcecfm.com Web Site:www.campesina.com Licensee: Farmworker Educational Radio Network Inc. Borsari & Paxson. Format: Mexican rgnl. Target aud: 25-54; Hispanic market. ♦Anthony Chavez, exec VP; Rosella Lopez, gen mgr; Barbara Lane, gen sls mgr; Pepe Escamilla, progmg dir; Isabel Eggert, news dir; Dave Whitehead, chief of engrg.

KUKY(FM)— 2009: 95.9 mhz; 390 w. Ant 1,263 ft TL: N32 40 22 W114 20 11.2. Hrs open: Lerman Senter PLLC, 2000 K St. N.W., Suite 600, Washington, DC, 20006-1809. Phone: (202) 429-8970. Fax: (202) 293-7783. Licensee: Hispanic Target Media Inc. ♦Meredith Senter, gen mgr.

Whiteriver

***KNNB(FM)—** Sept 11, 1982: 88.1 mhz; 630 w. 600 ft TL: N33 45 47 W109 57 39. (CP: 1.25 kw, ant 640 ft.). Stereo. Hrs open: 18 Box 310, 85941. Phone: (928) 338-5229. Phone: (928) 338-5211. Fax: (928) 338-1744. Licensee: Apache Radio Broadcasting Corp. Population served: 30,000 Format: Div, educ. News staff: one; News: 3 hrs wkly. Target aud: 15-60. Spec prog: Apache 8 hrs wkly. ♦Sylvia Browning, progmg dir; Udell Opah, gen mgr, stn mgr & chief of engrg.

Wickenburg

KBSZ(AM)— Jan 27, 1960: 1250 khz; 350 w-D, 202 w-N. TL: N33 55 32 W112 47 38. Hrs open: 24 340 W. Wickenburg Way, Suite. B, 85390. Phone: (928) 668-1250. Fax: (928) 668-1251.E-mail: amradio1tv@yahoo.com Web Site:www.kbsz-am.com Licensee: 1TV.Com Inc. (acq 3-31-2008; $500,000). Population served: 25,000 Format: Musical mix. ♦Pete Peterson, gen mgr & opns mgr.

KHOV-FM— Dec 2, 1983: 105.3 mhz; 6 kw. -1,364 ft TL: N34 11 32 W112 45 13. Stereo. Hrs open: 24 4745 N. 7th St., Suite 140, Phoenix, 85014. Phone: (602) 308-7900. Fax: (602) 308-7979. Web Site:www.univisionradio.com Licensee: HBC License Corp. Group owner: Univision Radio (acq 9-22-2003; grpsl). Population served: 3,173,200 Natl. Network: Jones Radio Networks, . Wiley, Hein & Fielding. Format: Rgnl Mexican. Target aud: 18-49. ♦Mary McEvilly-Hernandez, VP, gen mgr; Nelson Oseida, opns dir; Chris Morris, sls dir; Kevin Norgaard, rsch dir; Dobby White, traf mgr.

KSWG(FM)— January 1993: 96.3 mhz; 6.4 kw. Ant 646 ft TL: N33 55 34 W112 47 40. Hrs open: 24 801 W. Wickenburg Way, 85390. Phone: (928) 684-7804. Fax: (928) 684-7805.E-mail: kswg@directpc.com Web Site:www.kswgradio.com Licensee: Circle S. Broadcasting Co. Inc. (acq 1990). Population served: 1,000,000 Format: Country. ♦Harold Shumway, pres; Mike Shumway, gen mgr & sls dir.

Willcox

KHIL(AM)— Dec 2, 1959: 1250 khz; 5 kw-D, 196 w-N. TL: N32 16 00 W109 49 58. Hrs open: Box 1250, 85644. Secondary address: 900 West Patte Rd. 85643. Phone: (520) 384-4626. Fax: (520) 384-4627. Licensee: KZLZ LLC. (acq 8-8-2007; $900,000 with KWCX-FM Willcox). Population served: 3,243 Natl. Network: USA, . Format: C&W. ♦Dan Curtis, gen mgr.

KWCX-FM— July 8, 1976: 104.9 mhz; 730 w. Ant 3,175 ft TL: N32 13 01 W109 36 26. Stereo. Hrs open: 24 Box 1250, 85644. Phone: (520) 384-4626. Fax: (520) 384-4627. Licensee: KZLZ LLC. Group owner: Clear Channel Communications Inc. (acq 8-8-2007; $900,000 with KHIL(AM) Willcox). Format: Rock. ♦Dan Curtis, gen mgr; Mark Lucke, progmg dir.

Williams

KWMX(FM)— 1998: 96.7 mhz; 10.5 kw. Ant 1,066 ft TL: N35 07 52 W112 08 03. Hrs open: 112 E. Rt. 66, Suite 105, Flagstaff, 86001. Phone: (928) 779-1177. Fax: (928) 774-5179.E-mail: ann@northlandradio.com Web Site:www.thewolf.com Licensee: Grenax Broadcasting II LLC. (acq 4-14-2005; grpsl). Format: Cllasic rock. ♦Greg Dinetz, pres; Jim Shipp, gen mgr, sls dir, prom dir; Bill McAdams, opns dir; Mike Mentor, progmg dir; Jon Sweat, chief of engrg.

KYET(AM)— Aug 17, 1992: Stn currently dark. 1180 khz; 10 kw-U. TL: N35 15 38 W112 10 55. Hrs open: 24 812 E. Beale St., Kingman, 86401. Phone: (928) 753-9100. Fax: (928) 753-1978. Licensee: Grand Canyon Gateway Broadcasting L.L.C. (acq 9-19-97; $290,000). Population served: 55,000 ♦Rhonda Hart, pres, sls VP; Joe Hart, gen mgr; Steve Levin, prom VP & progmg dir; Dave Hawkins, news dir; Matt Krick, engrg VP; Deana Campbell, traf mgr.

Window Rock

KTNN(AM)— Feb 26, 1986: 660 khz; 50 kw-U, DA-N. TL: N35 53 41 W109 08 29. Hrs open: 12A-12A Box 2569, 86515. Phone: (928) 871-3553. Fax: (928) 871-3479.E-mail: webmaster@ktnonline.com Web Site:www.ktnnonline.com Licensee: The Navajo Nation (acq 1-86). Format: Country. News: 1. Navajo Tribe of Native Americans. Spec prog: Native American. ♦Troy Little, gen mgr; Ray Tsosie, asst music dir; Paul Jones, news dir; L.A. Williams, sports cmtr.

KWIM(FM)— Sept 21, 1995: 104.9 mhz; 30 kw. Ant 298 ft TL: N35 39 19 W109 01 59. Stereo. Hrs open: Box 9090, Western Indian Ministries, 86515. Phone: (505) 371-5587. Fax: (505) 371-5588.E-mail: lharpor@westernindian.net Web Site:www.westernindian.org Licensee: Western Indian Ministries Inc. Format: Adult contemp, Christian, relg. ♦Larry Harpor, gen mgr.

KWRK(FM)— October 1996: 96.1 mhz; 94 kw. Ant 328 ft TL: N35 33 36 W109 06 30. Stereo. Hrs open: 24 Box 2569, 86515. Phone: (928) 871-3553. Fax: (928) 871-3479. Licensee: The Navajo Nation. Natl. Network: Jones Radio Networks, . Wire Svc: AP Format: Country. ♦Troy Little, gen mgr.

Winslow

***KAWN(FM)—**Not on air, target date: unknown: 91.3 mhz; 300 w. Ant 118 ft TL: N35 01 36 W110 41 50. Hrs open: Drawer 2440, Tupelo, MS, 38803-2440. Phone: (662) 844-5036. Fax: (662) 842-7798.E-mail: info@afa.net Web Site:www.afr.net Licensee: American Family Association. ♦Donald E. Wildmon, chmn.

KINO(AM)— Dec 18, 1962: 1230 khz; 1 kw-U. TL: N35 02 15 W110 43 00. Hrs open: Drawer K, East End of Easy St., 86047. Phone: (928) 289-3364. Fax: (928) 289-3366.E-mail: kinoradio@cableone.net Licensee: Sunflower Communications. (acq 1-15-77). Population served: 25,000 Natl. Network: CBS, ESPN Radio, . Arizona News Radio Format: Country. Target aud: General. Spec prog: Sp 4 hrs wkly. ♦Loy Engelhardt, gen mgr.

Yarnell

KRPH(FM)—Not on air, target date: unknown: 99.5 mhz; 45 kw. Ant 518 ft TL: N34 07 56 W112 45 00. Hrs open: 2801 Via Fortuna Dr., Suite 675, Austin, TX, 78746. Phone: (713) 528-2517.E-mail: kdao@kdao.com Licensee: Ace Radio Corp. ♦Stephen Hackerman, pres.

Yuma

***KAWC(AM)—** July 11, 1970: 1320 khz; 1 kw-D, 147 w-N. TL: N32 41 10 W114 29 38. Hrs open: 6 AM-6 PM Box 929, 85364. Secondary address: 2020 S. Ave., # 8E 85366. Phone: (928) 317-7690. Phone: (928) 344-4210. Fax: (928) 317-7740. Web Site:kawcradio.org Licensee: Arizona Western College. Population served: 65,000 Natl. Network: NPR, PRI, . Format: News/talk info. News staff: one. Target aud: General. Spec prog: Sp 15 hrs wkly. ♦Dave Riek, gen mgr.

***KAWC-FM—** Mar 27, 1992: 88.9 mhz; 3 kw. 75 ft TL: N32 41 10 W114 29 38. Stereo. Hrs open: 6 AM-9 PM Prog dups AM 25% Box 929, 85364. Phone: (928) 317-7690. Fax: (928) 317-7740. Web Site:kawcradio.org Licensee: Arizona Western College Format: Class, jazz, news. News staff: one.

KBLU(AM)— March 1940: 560 khz; 1 kw-U, DA-N. TL: N32 43 25 W114 38 39. Hrs open: 24 Prog sep from FM 755 W. 28th St., 85364-7136. Phone: (928) 344-4980. Fax: (928) 344-4983. Web Site:560kblu.com Licensee: EDB Yuma License LLC Natl. Network: ABC, Fox News Radio, Fox Sports, Premiere Radio Networks, . Southwest Agri-Radio Format: News/talk. Target aud: Adults 25-54. ◆ Jeff Harris, gen mgr; Russ Egan, progmg dir; Chris Reichman, traf mgr.

*KCFY(FM)— March 1992: 88.1 mhz; 3 kw. 239 ft TL: N32 38 31 W114 33 34. Stereo. Hrs open: 24 Box 1669, 85366. Secondary address: 1921 S. Rail Ave. 85365. Phone: (928) 341-9730. Fax: (928) 341-9099.E-mail: kcfy@kcfyfm.com Web Site:www.kcfyfm.com Licensee: Relevant Media Inc. (acq 3-7-2005; $636,000). Population served: 175,000 Miller & Neely. Format: Christian. News: 4 hrs wkly. Target aud: 25-45; young to middle aged families. ◆ Greg S. Myers, gen mgr; Lynette Toepfer, dev dir; Mike Bondora, prom dir; Brandon Sweet, mus dir; Mikie Francher, traf mgr.

KJOK(AM)— Dec 11, 1950: 1400 khz; 1 kw. TL: N32 39 06 W114 39 00. Hrs open: 24 949 S. Avenue B, 85364. Phone: (928) 782-4321. Fax: (928) 343-1710.E-mail: oldiesradio@kjokyuma.com Web Site:www.kjokyuma.com Licensee: MonsterMedia L.L.C. (acq 1997; with co-located FM). Population served: 160,000 Natl. Network: Jones Radio Networks, . Natl. Rep: McGavren Guild,. Booth, Freret, Imlay & Tepper. Format: News/talk, sports, oldies. News: 6 hrs wkly. Target aud: 35 plus. ◆ Keith Lewis, CEO, gen mgr & gen sls mgr; Jennifer Blackwell, traf mgr.

KLJZ(FM)— Aug 20, 1972: 93.1 mhz; 100 kw. Ant 82 ft TL: N32 39 06 W114 39 00. Stereo. Hrs open: 24 949 S. Avenue B, 85364. Phone: (928) 782-4321. Fax: (928) 343-1710.E-mail: todaysbestmusic@z93yuma.com Web Site:www.z93yuma.com Licensee: MonsterMedia L.L.C. (acq 1-2-97: w/co-owned AM). Population served: 160,000 Natl. Network: Jones Radio Networks, . Natl. Rep: McGavren Guild,. Booth, Freret, Imlay & Tepper P.C. Format: Hot adult contemp. News: 2 hrs wkly. Target aud: 18-49.

KQSR(FM)— Sept 5, 1986: 100.9 mhz; 3 kw. 274 ft TL: N32 38 31 W114 33 34. (CP: Ant 1,075 ft.). Stereo. Hrs open: 24 755 W. 28th St., 85364. Phone: (928) 344-4980. Fax: (928) 344-4983. Web Site:www.kqsrfm.com Licensee: EDB Yuma License LLC. Group owner: Clear Channel Communications Inc. (acq 11-30-2007; grpsl). Population served: 121,418 Format: Adult contemporary. Target aud: 25-54. ◆ Jeff Harris, gen mgr; Jay Wachs, sls dir; Jeff Edwards, progmg dir.

KTTI(FM)— Nov 6, 1970: 95.1 mhz; 50 kw. Ant 246 ft TL: N32 38 31 W114 33 34. Stereo. Hrs open: 24 755 W. 28th St., 85364-7136. Phone: (928) 344-4980. Fax: (928) 344-4983. Web Site:www.kttifm.com Licensee: EDB Yuma License LLC Group owner: Clear Channel Communications Inc. (acq 11-30-2007; grpsl). Population served: 56,000 Natl. Network: Jones Radio Networks, . Southwest Agri-Radio Format: Country. News staff: 3. Target aud: 25-54; Adults. ◆ Jeff Harris, gen mgr; Jeff Edwards, opns dir.

*KYRM(FM)— April 2000: 91.9 mhz; 6.3 kw. 407 ft TL: N33 03 18 W114 49 37. Stereo. Hrs open: 24 Box 5965, 85366-5965. Secondary address: 2690 3rd Ave. 85364. Phone: (928) 314-4141.E-mail: kyrm@lwrn.org Web Site:www.kyrmradio.org Licensee: World Radio Network. Group owner: World Radio Network Inc. Population served: 1,500,000 Format: Sp, Christian, relg. News: 6 hrs wkly. Hispanic population. Spec prog: Children 6 hrs. ◆ Douglas Swanson, stn mgr, engrg mgr; Rachel Swanson, progmg dir.

Arkansas

Arkadelphia

KDEL-FM— June 12, 1977: 100.9 mhz; 3 kw. Ant 95 ft TL: N34 06 39 W93 03 01. Stereo. Hrs open: 24 Box 40, 71923. Secondary address: 601 S. 7th St. 71923. Phone: (870) 246-9272. Fax: (870) 246-5878. Web Site:www.arkadelphiaradio.com Licensee: Noalmark Broadcasting Corp. Format: Classic rock. ◆ Pete Osteen, gen mgr.

*KHED(FM)— Not on air, target date: unknown: 91.9 mhz; 250 w. Ant 98 ft TL: N34 07 44 W93 03 37. Hrs open: Henderson State University , 1100 Henderson St., 71999-0001. Phone: (870) 230-5091.E-mail: khedfm@kswhgmail.com Licensee: Henderson State University. ◆ Charles Dunn, pres.

*KSWH(FM)— Sept 25, 1969: 99.9 mhz; 10 w. 70 ft TL: N34 07 32 W93 03 48. Stereo. Hrs open: 6 AM-midnight HSU Box 7872, Henderson State Univ., 71999-0001. Phone: (870) 230-5185. Fax:

(870) 230-5144.E-mail: kswh@hsu.edu Web Site:www.kswh.org Licensee: Henderson State University. Population served: 18,000 News staff: 2; News: 2 hrs wkly. Target aud: 18-36; activity-orienated youthful females. Spec prog: Alternative 15 hrs, contemp Christian 2 hrs, rap 15 hrs wkly. ◆ Michael Taggart, gen mgr; Jaris Johnson, opns VP, opns dir; Annie Benoit, dev dir; Cody Graves, news dir.

KVRC(AM)— Sept 25, 1947: 1240 khz; 1 kw-U. TL: N34 06 39 W93 03 01. Hrs open: 24 Box 40, 71923. Secondary address: 601 S. 7th St. 71923. Phone: (870) 246-9272. Fax: (870) 246-5878. Web Site:www.arkadelphiaradio.com Licensee: Noalmark Broadcasting Corp. (group owner; (acq 6-29-2007; grpsl). Population served: 24,000 Format: News/talk. ◆ Pete Osteen, gen mgr; Randy Seale, progmg dir; Ronna Pennington, news dir; Annette Jennings, traf mgr.

KYXK(FM)— See Gurdon

Ashdown

KMJI(FM)— May 25, 1985: 93.3 mhz; 7.4 kw. 597 ft TL: N33 30 24 W94 12 25. Stereo. Hrs open: 24 2324 Arkansas Blvd., Texarkana, 71854. Phone: (870) 772-3771. Fax: (870) 772-0364.E-mail: wesspicher@gapbroadcasting.com Web Site:www.magic933.com Licensee: GAP Broadcasting Texarkana License LLC. Group owner: Clear Channel Communications Inc. (acq 8-3-2007; grpsl). Population served: 100000 Format: Adult contemp. News staff: one; News: 7 hrs wkly. Target aud: General. Spec prog: Relg 4 hrs wkly. ◆ Ron Bird, gen mgr; Wes Spicher, gen mgr & progmg dir.

KPGG(FM)— May 19, 1972: 103.9 mhz; 5.1 kw. Ant 354 ft TL: N33 36 06 W94 04 38. Stereo. Hrs open: 24 1323 College Dr., Texarkana, TX, 75501. Phone: (903) 793-1109. Fax: (903) 794-4717. Licensee: American Media Investments Inc. Group owner: Petracom Media LLC (acq 2-17-2009; grpsl). Natl. Rep: Katz Radio,. Format: Country legends/(classic country). News staff: one. ◆ Charlotte Hartwell, gen mgr.

Atkins

KVLD(FM)— October 1999: 99.3 mhz; 4.1 kw. Ant 394 ft TL: N35 14 41 W92 52 51. Hrs open: 24 Box 10310, Russellville, 72812. Phone: (479) 968-6816. Fax: (479) 968-2946.E-mail: rich@rivervalleyradio.com Web Site:www.oldies993.com Licensee: MMA License LLC. Group owner: MAX Media L.L.C. (acq 6-6-2003; grpsl). Format: Oldies. ◆ Rich Moellers, stn mgr.

Augusta

KJSM-FM— Licensed to Augusta. See Mayflower

Bald Knob

KAPZ(AM)— Aug 18, 1980: 710 khz; 250 w-D, DA. TL: N35 16 32 W91 33 39. Hrs open: 111 N. Spring St., Searcy, 72143. Phone: (501) 268-7123. Fax: (501) 279-2900.E-mail: jrrunyon@crainmedia.com Licensee: Crain Media Group LLC (group owner; (acq 8-7-2002; grpsl). Format: News/talk. Spec prog: Farm 3 hrs wkly. ◆ J.R. Runyon, gen mgr.

KCNY(FM)— Oct 15, 1984: 107.1 mhz; 19 kw. Ant 305 ft TL: N35 17 29 W91 40 24. (CP: COL Greenbrier. 12.5 kw, ant 466 ft. TL: N35 17 47 W92 19 11). Hrs open: Dups AM 100% 111 N. Spring St., Searcy, AZ, 72143. Phone: (501) 832-0925. Fax: (501) 279-2900.E-mail: jrrunyon@crainmedia.com Licensee: Crain Media Group LLC Format: Adult contemp.

KJSM-FM— See Mayflower

Barling

KFPW-FM— Sept 1, 1987: 94.5 mhz; 18.5 kw. Ant 269 ft TL: N35 15 54 W94 21 52. Stereo. Hrs open: 24 Box 908, Fort Smith, 72902. Phone: (479) 288-1047. Fax: (479) 785-2638. Web Site:www.fortsmithradiogroup.com/fort_94.htm Licensee: Pharis Broadcasting Inc. (group owner; (acq 3-14-2002;. $350,000 with KFPW(AM) Fort Smith). Natl. Network: ABC, Fox News Radio, . Natl. Rep: Commercial Media Sales,. Ark. Radio Net. Irwin Campbell & Tannenwald. Format: Classic rock. Target aud: 25-54; general. ◆ William Pharis, pres; Karen Pharis, gen mgr, stn mgr; Ernie Witt Jr., opns VP.

Batesville

KAAB(AM)— August 1980: 1130 khz; 1 kw-D, DA. TL: N35 16 32 W91 38 21. (CP: 20 w-N). Hrs open: 920 Harrison St., Suite C, 72501. Secondary address: Box 2077 72503. Phone: (870) 793-4196. Fax: (870) 793-5222.E-mail: arweekly@cei.net Licensee: WRD Entertainment Inc. (group owner). Rgnl. Network: Ark. Radio Net. Ark. Radio Net. Format: Mexicana. Target aud: 18-44. Spec prog: Farm 5 hrs wkly. ◆ John R. Grace, pres; Gary Bridgman, gen mgr.

KBTA(AM)— June 30, 1950: 1340 khz; 1 kw-U. TL: N35 44 39 W91 38 21. Hrs open: 24 Box 2077, 920 Harrison, Suite C, 72503. Phone: (870) 793-4196. Fax: (870) 793-5222.E-mail: info@maxfm.com Web Site:maxfm.com Licensee: W.R.D. Entertainment Inc. (group owner; acq 12-15-95). Population served: 32,000 Wire Svc: AP Format: Sports. News staff: 2; News: 22 hrs wkly. Target aud: 18 plus. ◆ Rob Grace, pres; Gary Bridgman, gen mgr; Ben Johnson, progmg dir; Dale Johnson, chief of engrg.

KBTA-FM— 1999: 99.5 mhz; 3.4 kw. Ant 426 ft TL: N35 52 07 W91 35 14. Hrs open: 920 Harrison St., Suite C, 72503. Phone: (870) 793-4196. Fax: (870) 793-5222.E-mail: garyb@swbell.net Licensee: W.R.D. Entertainment Inc. (group owner). Format: Adult contemp. ◆ Rob Grace, pres; Gary Bridgman, gen mgr; Matt Johnson, gen sls mgr; Rob Stanley, progmg dir; Bill Beck, news dir; Dale Johnson, chief of engrg.

KZLE(FM)— Mar 3, 1982: 93.1 mhz; 100 kw. 984 ft TL: N35 53 27 W91 44 01. Stereo. Hrs open: Prog sep from AM Box 2077, 72503. Phone: (870) 793-4196. Fax: (870) 793-5222.E-mail: rob@maxfm.com Web Site:maxfm.com Licensee: W.R.D. Entertainment Inc. Population served: 33,200 Fletcher, Heald & Hildreth, P.L.C. Wire Svc: AP Format: Rock. Target aud: 24 plus. ◆ Rob Grace, progmg dir & mus dir; Dale Johnson, engrg dir.

Bearden

KIXC(FM)— Not on air, target date: unknown: 92.7 mhz; 5.5 kw. Ant 341 ft TL: N33 41 23 W92 38 52. Hrs open: 202 W. 19th St., El Dorado, 71730. Phone: (870) 862-7777. Fax: (870) 862-0203. Licensee: Noalmark Broadcasting Corp. ◆ William C. Nolan Jr., pres.

Beebe

*KOAR(FM)— June 22, 1991: 101.5 mhz; 6 kw. Ant 328 ft TL: N35 11 26 W91 54 45. Hrs open: 24 2351 Sunset Blvd., Suite 170-218, Rocklin, CA, 95765. Phone: (916) 251-1600. Fax: (916) 251-1650. Web Site:www.air1.com Licensee: Educational Media Foundation. (group owner; (acq 6-9-2005; $525,000). Population served: 50,000 Natl. Network: Air 1, . Format: Christian hit music. ◆ Mike Novak, pres.

Bella Vista

KBVA(FM)— November 1991: 106.5 mhz; 37 kw. 567 ft TL: N36 18 21 W94 27 29. Hrs open: 24 1655 Hwy. 72 S.E., Gravette, 72736. Phone: (479) 787-6411. Fax: (479) 787-6116. Web Site:www.variety1065.com Licensee: Gayla Joy McKenzie. Format: Var. ◆ Gayla Joy McKenzie, pres & gen mgr.

KREB(AM)— See Bentonville-Bella Vista

Bellefonte

KNWA(AM)— 1986: 1600 khz; 5 kw-D, 50 w-N. TL: N36 14 49 W93 05 06. Hrs open: Box 850, Harrison, 72602. Secondary address: 600 S. Pine, Harrison 72601. Phone: (870) 741-1402. Fax: (870) 741-9702.E-mail: kcwd@all.net Licensee: Harrison Radio Stations Inc. Format: Southern Gospel. ◆ Tom Arnold, gen mgr, sls dir & mktg dir; Phillip Cary, progmg dir.

Benton

KEWI(AM)— June 26, 1953: 690 khz; 250 w-D, 73 w-N. TL: N34 31 57 W92 34 16. Hrs open: 5 AM-10 PM 115 S. Main St., 72015. Phone: (501) 778-6677. Fax: (501) 778-7717.E-mail: kewi690@yahoo.com Web Site:www.kewi690.com Licensee: Landers Broadcasting Co. Inc. (acq 5-95). Population served: 500,000 Natl. Network: USA, . Rgnl. Network: Ark. Radio Net. Ark. Radio Net. Format: Loc news, oldies, sports, country, talk. News staff: one; News: 10 hrs wkly. Target aud: 25-65; all income levels. Spec prog: Farm 4 hrs, gospel 10 hrs, relg 5 hrs wkly. ◆ Doris L. Landers, exec VP; Jim Landers, CEO, gen mgr & opns mgr.

KHKN(FM)— Jan 1, 1979: 106.7 mhz; 16 kw. Ant 866 ft TL: N34 47 56 W92 29 53. Stereo. Hrs open: 24 10800 Colonel Glenn Rd., Little Rock, 72204. Phone: (501) 217-5000. Fax: (501) 228-9547. Fax: (501) 227-5776. Web Site:www.1067hallelujah.com Licensee: CC Licenses LLC. Group owner: Clear Channel Communications Inc. (acq 9-12-97; grpsl). Population served: 490,000 Bryan Cave. Format: Black gospel. Target aud: 18-49. ◆Kim Pyle, gen mgr, progmg dir; Kevin Waltman, gen sls mgr; Sonny Victory, progmg dir; Tom Rusk, chief of engrg.

Bentonville

KAMO-FM—See Rogers

*KAPG(FM)— 2006: 88.1 mhz; 1 kw. Ant 233 ft TL: N36 23 37 W94 10 57. Hrs open: Drawer 2440, Tupelo, MS, 38803. Phone: (662) 844-8888. Fax: (662) 842-6791. Web Site:www.afr.net Licensee: American Family Association. Group owner: American Family Radio. Format: Christian classics. ◆Marvin Sanders, gen mgr; John Riley, progmg dir; Fred Jackson, news dir; Joey Moody, chief of engrg.

KFFK(AM)—See Rogers

KIGL(FM)—See Seligman, MO

KKEG(FM)— Nov 7, 1983: 98.3 mhz; 100 kw. Ant 617 ft TL: N36 07 38 W93 59 23. Stereo. Hrs open: 24 4209 N Frontage Road, Fayetteville, 72703. Phone: (479) 521-5566. Fax: (479) 521-0751. Web Site:www.983thekeg.com Licensee: Cumulus Licensing Corp. Group owner: Cumulus Media Inc. (acq 2-1-99; grpsl). Format: AOR, classic rock. Target aud: 25-54. Spec prog: Class 2 hrs wkly. ◆Joe Conway, gen mgr; Jay Phillips, progmg dir.

KSEC(FM)—Not on air, target date: unknown: 95.7 mhz; 6 kw. Ant 328 ft TL: N36 17 13 W94 12 32. Hrs open: 24 Box 335, Springdale, 72765. Phone: (479) 756-8686. Fax: (479) 756-8687.E-mail: info@ezspanishmedia.com Web Site: www.ezspanishmedia.com Licensee: Lazeta 957 Co. (acq 6-1-2005; $1.99 million). Format: Mexician rgnl. ◆Edwards Vega, gen mgr.

Bentonville-Bella Vista

KREB(AM)— Feb 5, 1979: 1190 khz; 2.5 kw-D. TL: N36 23 17 W94 11 42. Hrs open: Sunrise-sunset 1780 Holly St., Fayetteville, 72703. Phone: (479) 582-3776. Fax: (479) 571-0995. Web Site:www.newrock1049x.com Licensee: Butler Broadcasting Co. LLC (acq 10-13-99; $100,000). Population served: 150000 Natl. Network: USA, . Format: ESPN Sports, talk. Target aud: 35 plus. ◆Steve Butler, gen mgr; Dave Jackson, progmg dir.

Berryville

KTHS(AM)— February 1958: 1480 khz; 5 kw-D, 64 w-N. TL: N36 21 42 W93 33 40. Hrs open: 24 Box 191, 72616. Secondary address: One Radio Dr. 72616. Phone: (870) 423-2147. Fax: (870) 423-2146.E-mail: studio@kthsradio.com Licensee: Carroll County Broadcasting Inc. (acq 6-29-2006; $3.5 million with co-located FM). Population served: 25,000 Natl. Network: ABC, Jones Radio Networks, . Format: Modern country. News staff: one; News: 21.5 hrs. Target aud: General. Spec prog: Farm 15 hrs wkly. ◆Jay Bunyard, pres; Tim Poynter, gen mgr; William C. Autry, gen sls mgr; Linda Boyer, mus dir, news dir; Zeb Huffmaster, chief of engrg; Sherri Linz, traf mgr; Travis Doshier, disc jockey.

KTHS-FM— Dec 19, 1974: 107.1 mhz; 3.6 kw. Ant 627 ft TL: N36 20 45 W93 29 17. Stereo. Hrs open: 24 Dups AM 100% Box 191, 72616. Phone: (870) 423-2147. Fax: (870) 423-2146. Population served: 25,000 Natl. Network: ABC, Jones Radio Networks, . News staff: one; News: 21.5 hrs wkly. Target aud: General. ◆Sherri Linz, traf mgr; Travis Dashier, disc jockey.

Blytheville

*KAIA(FM)—Not on air, target date: unknown: 91.5 mhz; 1 kw. Ant 190 ft TL: N35 54 41 W89 53 28. Hrs open: 5700 West Oaks Blvd., Rocklin, CA, 95765. Phone: (916) 251-1600. Fax: (916) 251-1650. Licensee: Educational Media Foundation. Group owner: American Family Radio. (acq 3-23-2007; grpsl). ◆Richard Jenkins, pres.

*KBCM(FM)— 2000: 88.3 mhz; 500 w. Ant 190 ft TL: N35 54 45 W89 53 28. Hrs open: 24 Drawer 2440, Tupelo, MS, 38803. Phone: (662) 844-8888. Fax: (662) 844-9090.E-mail: info@afa.net Licensee: American Family Association. Group owner: American Family Radio Format: Christian. ◆Marvin Sanders, gen mgr; John Riley, progmg dir.

KHLS(FM)— 1948: 96.3 mhz; 100 kw. 450 ft TL: N35 55 27 W89 52 18. (CP: Ant 351 ft. TL: N35 38 27 W89 56 54). Stereo. Hrs open: Prog sep from AM Box 989 , 72316. Secondary address: 125 S. Second St. 72315. Phone: (870) 762-2093. Fax: (870) 763-8459. Population served: 24,752 Format: C&W.

KLCN(AM)— 1922: 910 khz; 5 kw-D, 85 w-N. TL: N35 55 27 W89 52 18. Hrs open: Box 989, 72316. Secondary address: 125 S. Second St. 72315. Phone: (870) 762-2093. Fax: (870) 763-8459. Licensee: Sudbury Services Inc. Group owner: Sudbury Services Inc. & Newport Broadcasting Co. Population served: 24,752 Format: News/talk. ◆Dave Clark, gen mgr; Tom Hill, news dir & chief of engrg.

Booneville

*KBHN(FM)— 2005: 89.7 mhz; 59 kw. Ant 302 ft TL: N35 08 25 W94 03 43. Hrs open: Box 6210, Fort Smith, 72906. Phone: (479) 646-6700. Fax: (479) 646-1373. Web Site:www.kzfm.com Licensee: Vision Ministries Inc. Format: Christian. ◆Marilyn K. Lynch, pres; Jerry Lynch, gen mgr; Jay Lynch, stn mgr; Al Ross, progmg dir.

KQBK(FM)—Licensed to Booneville. See Fort Smith

Brinkley

KBRI(AM)— Oct 25, 1959: 1570 khz; 250 w-D, 44 w-N. TL: N34 52 02 W91 12 04. Hrs open: 6 AM-10 PM Box 111, Hwy. 70 W., 72021. Phone: (870) 734-1570. Fax: (870) 734-1571. Licensee: East Arkansas Broadcasters Inc. Population served: 30,000 Rgnl. Network: Ark. Radio Net. Ark. Radio Net. Format: Gospel. News staff: one. Target aud: General. ◆Bobby Caldwell, stn mgr; David Sills, gen sls mgr, progmg dir; Lane Goodwin, chief of engrg.

KTRQ(FM)—(Colt, October 1969: 102.3 mhz; 40 kw. Ant 548 ft TL: N35 03 16 W90 44 36. Stereo. Hrs open: Box 111, 72021. Secondary address: Hwy. 70 W. 72021. Phone: (870) 734-1570. Fax: (870) 734-1571. Licensee: East Arkansas Broadcasters Inc. Population served: 100,000 Format: Oldies.

Bryant

KKSP(FM)—Licensed to Bryant. See Malvern

Cabot

KPZK-FM— May 1993: 102.5 mhz; 3 kw. Ant 328 ft TL: N34 55 22 W92 00 32. Stereo. Hrs open: 24 700 Wellington Hills Rd., Little Rock, 72211. Phone: (501) 401-0200 . Fax: (501) 401-0366. Licensee: The Last Bastion Station Trust LLC, as Trustee Group owner: Citadel Broadcasting Corp. (acq 6-12-2007; grpsl). Population served: 525,000 Natl. Network: ABC, . Natl. Rep: McGavren Guild,. Eckert, Seamans, Cherin & Mellot. Format: Gospel. News staff: 4. Target aud: 25-49. ◆Jim Beard, mktg mgr.

KZTD(AM)— Nov 16, 1980: 1350 khz; 2.5 kw-D, 73 w-N. TL: N34 59 59 W92 01 41. Hrs open: 121 Radio Heights Dr., Searcy, 72143. Phone: (501) 378-0104. Fax: (501) 305-2977.E-mail: kztd1350@hotmail.com Web Site:www.lamexicana.com Licensee: New World LLC (group owner; (acq 2-2-2007; $190,000). Format: Sp. Target aud: 18-49. ◆Arik Lev, pres; Phil Hall, gen mgr; Robert Tindle, opns dir; Christy Flynn, sls VP.

Cale

*KEJA(FM)—Not on air, target date: unknown: 91.7 mhz; 20 kw. Ant 446 ft TL: N33 28 34 W93 16 23. Hrs open: 102 Red Branch Ln., Simpsonville, SC, 29681. Phone: (864) 297-0216. Fax: (864) 297-0344.E-mail: info@networkofglory.org Web Site:networkofglory.com Licensee: Network of Glory Inc. ◆Lola Richey, pres.

Calico Rock

KJMT(FM)— Mar 1, 2007: 97.1 mhz; 5.2 kw. Ant 715 ft TL: N36 05 31 W92 15 46. Hrs open: 24 223 Russell Street, Mountain Home, 72653. Phone: (870) 425-4971. Fax: (870) 424-9717. Web Site:www.mountaintalk97.com Licensee: Malvern Entertainment Corp. Population served: 210,527 Natl. Network: Fox News Radio, Premiere Radio Networks, Talk Radio Network, Radio America, . Format: News/talk. News staff: one; News: 29 hrs/week. ◆Scott Gray, CEO; Mike Wiseman, COO; Scott A. Gray, pres.

Camden

KAMD-FM— Dec 1, 1968: 97.1 mhz; 50 kw. Ant 456 ft TL: N33 30 14 W92 48 38. Stereo. Hrs open: 24 612 Fairview Rd, AZ, 71701. Phone: (870) 836-9567. Fax: (870) 836-9500.E-mail: radioworks@cablelynx.com Web Site:www.camdenfm.net Licensee: Radio Works Inc. (acq 12-13-2004; grpsl). Population served: 50,000 Format: Adult contemp. ◆Donna Stewart, stn mgr, sls dir, gen sls mgr; Greg Arnold, opns dir, progmg dir; Helen Aregood, news dir; Steve Halatyn, chief of engrg.

*KCAC(FM)— June 11, 1990: 89.5 mhz; 250 w. 161 ft TL: N33 34 31 W92 49 55. Stereo. Hrs open: 8 AM-midnight Box 3499, 71711. Phone: (870) 836-5289. Fax: (870) 574-4538. Licensee: Southern Arkansas University Tech (acq 8-2-2005). Population served: 30,000 Natl. Network: ABC, . Cohn & Marks. Format: Alternative. Target aud: 18-35. ◆Rachelle Moore, gen mgr; Quintin Green, opns mgr, progmg dir.

KMGC(FM)— Nov 18, 1994: 104.5 mhz; 3 kw. 328 ft TL: N33 30 14 W92 48 38. Stereo. Hrs open: 24 133 Washington St., 71701. Phone: (870) 836-0104. Fax: (870) 836-9500.E-mail: radioworks@cablelynx.com Web Site:www.camdenfm.net Licensee: Radio Works Inc. (acq 12-13-2004; grpsl). Format: Urban contemp. ◆Donna Stewart, stn mgr; Greg Arnold, opns dir & mus dir.

KNHD(AM)— Aug 8, 1963: 1450 khz; 1 kw-U. TL: N33 33 49 W92 50 37. Hrs open: 24 Box 262550, Baton Rouge, LA, 70826. Secondary address: 8917 World Ministry Ave., Baton Rouge, LA 70810. Phone: (225) 768-3688/8300. Fax: (225) 768-3729.E-mail: kawikfish@yahoo.com Web Site:www.jsm.org Licensee: Family Worship Center Church Inc. (group owner; (acq 3-7-2002; grpsl). Population served: 85,000 Format: Southern gospel. News staff: one. Target aud: 35 plus. ◆David Whitelaw, COO; Jimmy Swaggart, pres; John Santiago, progmg dir.

Cave City

*KVMN(FM)— Jan 1, 1981: 89.9 mhz; 3.3 kw. Ant 199 ft TL: N35 57 07 W91 32 58. Stereo. Hrs open: Box 190, 711 N. Main St., 72521. Phone: (870) 283-5331. Fax: (870) 283-3255.E-mail: bsisk@cavecity.ncsc.k12.ar.us Licensee: Cave City Schools. Population served: 10,000 Natl. Network: USA, . Format: Relg, educ, div. Target aud: General. ◆Becky Sisk, gen mgr.

Centerton

KLTK(AM)— Mar 2, 1977: 1140 khz; 700 w-D. TL: N36 21 50 W94 20 53. Hrs open: 1504 W. Persimmon St., Rogers, 72756. Phone: (479) 899-6953. Fax: (479) 899-6953. Licensee: La Mas Mexicana LLC (group owner; (acq 3-21-2008; $100,000). Population served: 100,000 Fletcher, Heald & Hildreth. Format: Sp music. ◆Genaro Salas, pres & gen mgr.

Cherokee Village

KFCM(FM)— May 18, 1981: 98.3 mhz; 3 kw. Ant 298 ft TL: N36 16 29 W91 30 18. Stereo. Hrs open: 24 Box 909, 72525. Phone: (870) 856-4408. Fax: (870) 895-4088.E-mail: hometownradio@centurytel.net Licensee: KFCM Inc. (acq 11-29-89; $174,500; 12-18-89). Format: Oldies. News staff: 3; News: 25 hrs wkly. Target aud: 25-54. ◆James Bragg, pres & gen mgr.

Cherry Valley

KXRL(FM)— 2007: 90.1 mhz; 9 kw. Ant 377 ft TL: N35 22 30.6 W90 43 22.1. Hrs open: Rebroadcasts WXHL-FM Christiana, DE 100%. Box 5204, Wilmington, DE, 19808-5204. Phone: (800) 220-8078. Phone: (302) 540-5690. Fax: (302) 738-3090.E-mail: info@thereachfm.com Web Site:www.thereachfm.com Licensee: Priority Radio Inc. (acq 10-14-2005; $200,000 for CP). Format: Adult contemp Christian music. ◆Steve Hare, pres.

Clarksville

KLYR(AM)— Mar 18, 1957: 1360 khz; 500 w-D, 98 w-N. TL: N35 28 21 W93 29 28. Hrs open: 16 Box 188, Hwy. 64 W., 72830. Phone: (479) 754-3092. Web Site:www.klyr.net Licensee: Randall P. Forrester. (acq 11-81; $31,816; 11-9-81). Population served: 75,000 Format: C&W. News: 12 hrs wkly. Target aud: General. Spec prog: Relg 8 hrs wkly. ◆Randy Forrester, gen mgr.

KLYR-FM— 1974: 92.7 mhz; 3 kw. 292 ft TL: N35 29 38 W93 32 21. Hrs open: 16 Box 188, Hwy. 64 W., 72830. Phone: (479) 754-3092. Population served: 180,000 Format: C & W. ◆Randy Forrester, gen mgr.

KXIO(FM)— April 1991: 106.9 mhz; 5.9 kw. Ant 112 ft TL: N35 33 07 W93 24 33. Hrs open: 901 S. Rogers St., 72830. Phone: (479) 705-1069. Fax: (479) 754-5518.E-mail: office@kxioradio.com Web Site:www.kxio-radio.net Licensee: Jody Copeland (acq 4-15-2008; $449,500). Format: Hot country. ◆Gary Barnett, gen mgr; Kelley Ray, progmg dir & news dir.

Clinton

KGFL(AM)— Oct 1, 1977: 1110 khz; 5 kw-D. TL: N35 33 30 W92 27 32. Hrs open: Box 1349, 72031. Secondary address: Corner of Main & Griggs 72031. Phone: (501) 745-4474. Fax: (501) 745-4084.E-mail: sid@khpq.com Licensee: King-Sulivan Radio (acq 4-3-2001; $75,000 for 26% with co-located FM). Population served: 20,000 Format: Oldies. Target aud: 35 plus. ◆Jerri McCrary, gen mgr; Tim Kelly, progmg dir; Dixie Carter, news dir, pub affrs dir.

KHPQ(FM)— Dec 23, 1982: 92.1 mhz; 10 kw. Ant 571 ft TL: N35 40 44 W92 30 30. Stereo. Hrs open: Box 1349, 72031. Secondary address: Corner of Main & Griggs 72031. Phone: (501) 745-4474. Fax: (501) 745-4084.E-mail: sid@khpq.com Licensee: King-Sulivan Radio. Population served: 40,000 Natl. Network: Jones Radio Networks, . Format: Country. Target aud: 25 plus. ◆Dave Britton, chief of engrg.

Colt

KTRQ(FM)—Licensed to Colt. See Brinkley

Conway

KASR(FM)— April 1984: 92.7 mhz; 3 kw. 282 ft TL: N35 06 46 W92 24 42. Hrs open: Dups AM 75% Box 1266, 117 Oak St., Suite 300, 72032. Phone: (501) 327-6611. Fax: (501) 327-7920.

*KHDX(FM)— May 1973: 93.1 mhz; 8 w. 59 ft TL: N35 06 01 W92 26 29. Stereo. Hrs open: Hendrix College, 1600 Washington Ave., 72032. Phone: (501) 450-1339. Fax: (501) 450-1200.E-mail: khdx@hendrix.edu Web Site:www.hendrix.edu Licensee: Hendrix College. Population served: 1,000 Rgnl. Network: Ark. Radio Net. Ark. Radio Net. Format: Full service. ◆Julie Marvin, gen mgr.

KMJX(FM)— June 1, 1967: 105.1 mhz; 79 kw. Ant 1,053 ft TL: N34 47 53 W92 29 33. Stereo. Hrs open: 24 10800 Colonel Glenn Rd., Little Rock, 72204. Phone: (501) 217-5000. Fax: (501) 228-9547. Web Site:www.classiccountry1067.com Licensee: CC Licenses LLC. Group owner: Clear Channel Communications Inc. (acq 5-5-96; grpsl). Population served: 750,000 Natl. Rep: Clear Channel,. Wiley, Rein & Fielding. Format: Classic country. News staff: one; News: 3 hrs wkly. Target aud: 18-34. ◆Llowrey Mays, chmn; Mark Mays, pres; Randall Mays, CFO; Bruce Demps, sr VP; Jeff Peterson, opns mgr, gen sls mgr, progmg dir; Joe Rook, gen sls mgr, mus dir.

*KUCA(FM)— Oct 10, 1966: 91.3 mhz; 5 kw. 154 ft TL: N35 02 55 W92 27 49. Stereo. Hrs open: 24 Box U-5144, Univ of Central Arkansas, 72035. Secondary address: 201 Donaghey Ave. Phone: (501) 450-3326. Fax: (501) 450-5874.E-mail: Montyr@uca.edu Licensee: University of Central Arkansas. Population served: 80,000 Format: News, adult contemp. News: 10 hrs wkly. Target aud: 18-54; educated adults. ◆Monty Rowell, gen mgr.

KXXA(AM)— May 26, 1961: 1330 khz; 500 w-D, 64 w-N. TL: N35 06 00 W92 26 41. Hrs open: Box 1266, 72033-1266. Phone: (501) 327-6611. Fax: (501) 327-7920. Licensee: Creative Media Inc. (acq 10-1-2004; with co-located FM). Population served: 15,510 Format: All sports. Spec prog: Farm 6 hrs wkly. ◆Elaine Harrison, prom mgr; Michael D. Harrison, pres, gen mgr, sls dir & progmg dir.

Corning

KBKG(FM)— Sept 15, 1983: 93.5 mhz; 3 kw. 138 ft TL: N36 24 00 W90 35 05. Stereo. Hrs open: Prog sep from AM Box 398, 72422. Phone: (870) 857-6646. Fax: (870) 857-6795. Licensee: Shields-Adkins Broadcasting Inc. Natl. Network: ABC, . Format: Adult contemp, oldies. ◆Jim Adkins, CEO.

KCCB(AM)— Feb 19, 1959: 1260 khz; 1 kw-D. TL: N36 24 00 W90 35 05. Hrs open: Box 398, 501 Bryan, 72422. Phone: (870) 857-6646. Fax: (870) 857-6795. Licensee: Shields-Adkins Broadcasting Inc.

Population served: 55,000 Natl. Rep: Keystone (unwired net),. Format: Lite. Target aud: General. ◆Jim Adkins, pres, gen mgr; Tina Privett, gen mgr & gen sls mgr; Neil Raines, progmg dir, news dir; Palmer Johnson, chief of engrg.

Cotton Plant

KAPW(FM)— 2008: 99.3 mhz; 6 kw. Ant 328 ft TL: N34 58 07 W90 59 48. Hrs open: Box 711, Wynne, 72396. Phone: (870) 238-8141. Fax: (870) 238-5997. Licensee: Caldwell Media LLC. Format: Urban adult contemp. ◆Bradford Caldwell, gen mgr.

Crossett

KAGH(AM)— January 1951: 800 khz; 240 w-D, 43 w-N. TL: N33 08 05 W91 56 49. Stereo. Hrs open: 24 Box 697, 117 E. Wellfield Rd., 71635. Phone: (870) 364-2181. Phone: (870) 364-2182. Fax: (501) 364-2183.E-mail: kagh@alltell.net Licensee: Ashley County Broadcasters Inc. (acq 8-1-69). Population served: 18,000 Natl. Network: Westwood One, . Rgnl. Network: Ark. Radio Net. Ark. Radio Net. Format: Country. ◆Kevin Medlin, pres, gen mgr; Bryan Bailey, news dir; Russ Miller, progmg dir & chief of engrg.

KAGH-FM— Mar 16, 1967: 104.9 mhz; 6 kw. 300 ft TL: N33 08 05 W91 56 49. Hrs open: Dups AM 80% Phone: (870) 364-2181. Fax: (501) 364-2183.E-mail: kagh@alltell.net Licensee: Ashley County Broadcasters Inc. Format: Country.

Danville

KYEL(FM)—Not on air, target date: unknown: 105.5 mhz; 4.45 kw. Ant 400 ft TL: N35 07 16 W93 19 34. Hrs open: 5am - 11pm 201 W. 2nd St., Russellville, AZ, 72801. Phone: (479) 890-7207. Fax: (479) 967-5278.E-mail: karv-kyel@yahoo Licensee: Danville FM Inc. Format: Country. Spec prog: Cardinal Baseball. ◆Chris Womack, stn mgr; Diane Womack, gen mgr & sls.

Dardanelle

KCAB(AM)— Mar 24, 1964: 980 khz; 5 kw-D. TL: N35 13 02 W93 10 08. Hrs open: Box 10310, Russellville, 72812. Secondary address: 2705 E. Pkwy., Russellville 72802. Phone: (479) 968-6816. Fax: (479) 968-2946. Web Site:www.rivervalleyradio.com Licensee: MMA License LLC. Group owner: MAX Media L.L.C. (acq 6-6-2003; grpsl). Natl. Network: Premiere Radio Networks, . Natl. Rep: Christal,. Ark. Radio Net. Wire Svc: AP Format: News/talk. Target aud: 25-54; adults. ◆Rich Moellers, gen mgr & stn mgr; Aaron Thomas, opns mgr, news dir; Rhonda Dilbeck, gen sls mgr; Johnny Story, news dir; Jim Alexander, chief of engrg.

KCJC(FM)— Jan 26, 1966: 102.3 mhz; 200 w. 1,227 ft TL: N35 13 41 W93 15 20. (CP: 1.43 kw, ant 1,322 ft.). Hrs open: Box 10310, Russellville, 72802. Phone: (479) 968-6816. Fax: (479) 968-2946. Web Site:www.rivervalleyradio.com Licensee: MMA License LLC. Natl. Network: ABC, . Format: Country.

KWXT(AM)— October 1987: 1490 khz; 1 kw-U. TL: N35 13 08 W93 07 38. Hrs open: 701 E. Main St., Suite 4, Russellville, 72801. Phone: (479) 968-1337. Fax: (479) 968-1337.E-mail: kwxt1490am@ahoo.com Web Site:www.kwxt1490am.com Licensee: George V. Domerese/Sherwood Broadcasting Co. (acq 9-2-92; $60,000; 9-21-92). Format: Christian country, gospel. ◆Tim Domerese, gen mgr; Jim Alexander, chief of engrg.

De Queen

*KBPU(FM)— 2002: 88.7 mhz; 250 w. Ant 122 ft TL: N34 02 38 W94 17 41. Hrs open: Box 5725, Twin Falls, ID, 83303. Phone: (208) 733-3551. Fax: (208) 733-3548. Web Site:www.edgewaterbroadcasting.com Licensee: Edgewater Broadcasting Inc. (group owner; (acq 5-3-2006). Format: Christian programming. ◆Clark Parrish, pres.

KDQN(AM)— Aug 1, 1956: 1390 khz; 500 w-D. TL: N34 01 57 W94 19 43. Hrs open: Box 311, 71832. Secondary address: 921 W Collin Raye Dr, 71832. Phone: (870) 642-2446. Fax: (870) 642-2442.E-mail: numberonecountry@yahoo.com Web Site:www.kdqn.net Licensee: Jay W. Bunyard & Anne W. Bunyard. (acq 6-15-83; $475,000 with co-located FM; 7-4-83). Population served: 4,600 Rgnl. Network: Ark. Radio Net. Ark. Radio Net. Format: Sp. ◆Jay Bunyard, pres; Jon Bunyard, gen mgr; Victor Rojas, gen sls mgr.

KDQN-FM— Oct 6, 1978: 92.1 mhz; 50 kw. Ant 492 ft TL: N34 13 35 W94 17 35. Stereo. Hrs open: Box 311, 71832. Secondary address:

921 West Collin Raye Dr, DeQueen 71832. Phone: (870) 642-2446. Fax: (870) 642-2442. Web Site:www.kdqn.net Licensee: Jay W. Bunyard & Anne W. Bunyard. Format: Country. ◆Jon Bunyard, gen mgr, opns mgr & women's int ed.

De Witt

KDEW-FM— Sept 1, 1970: 97.3 mhz; 50 kw. 272 ft TL: N34 16 09 W91 21 02. Hrs open: 24 c/o KWAK-AM-FM, 1818 S. Buerkle, Stuttgart, 72160. Secondary address: P.O. Box 910, Stuttgart, AZ 72160. Phone: (870) 673-1595. Fax: (870)673-8445.E-mail: kdew973@yahoo.com Licensee: Arkansas County Broadcasters Inc. (group owner; acq 3-5-97; $150,000). Format: Country. News staff: one. ◆Keith Hill, progmg dir; Jonathan Reaves, news dir; Jim Alexander, engrg dir; Sandi Levy, traf mgr; Scott Siler, gen mgr, mktg dir & disc jockey.

Dermott

KRKD(FM)— Apr 1, 2000: 105.7 mhz; 3 kw. Ant 328 ft TL: N33 32 25 W91 22 39. Hrs open: Box 1438, Cleveland, MS, 38732. Phone: (662) 378-4103. Licensee: M.R.S. Ventures Inc. (group owner; (acq 11-1-2003; grpsl). Population served: 90,000 Wood, Maines & Brown, Chartered. ◆Jerry Russell, pres.

KXSA-FM— Aug 24, 1924: 103.1 mhz; 5.5 kw. 328 ft TL: N33 31 56 W91 34 28. Hrs open: 24 279 Midway, Monticello, AZ, 71655. Phone: (870) 367-8528. Fax: (870) 367-9564.E-mail: pinesradio@global.net Licensee: Pines Broadcasting Inc. (group owner; (acq 3-14-2007; grpsl). Format: Classic country. ◆Jimmy Sledge, pres & gen mgr.

Des Arc

*KBDO(FM)— 1999: 91.7 mhz; 56 kw vert. Ant 682 ft TL: N35 00 08 W91 44 41. Hrs open: Box 3206, American Family Radio, Tupelo, MS, 38803. Phone: (662) 844-8888, EXT. 204. Fax: (662) 842-6791. Licensee: American Family Association. Group owner: American Family Radio Format: Relg. ◆Marvin Sanders, gen mgr; Gary Vaile, stn mgr; John Riley, progmg dir; Joey Moody, chief of engrg.

KFLI(FM)— 2003: 104.7 mhz; 25 kw. Ant 328 ft TL: N35 00 23 W91 40 20. Hrs open: 121 Radio Heights Dr., Searcy, 72143. Phone: (501) 268-1047. Fax: (501) 305-2977. Web Site:www.oldiesradioonline.com Licensee: George S. Flinn Jr. Format: Oldies. ◆Ken Madden, gen mgr.

Dumas

KXFE(FM)— Sept 1, 1980: Stn currently dark. 106.9 mhz; 25 kw. Ant 269 ft TL: N33 58 11 W91 32 58. Stereo. Hrs open: Box 789, Wynne, 72396. Phone: (870) 238-8141. Fax: (870) 238-5997. Licensee: Arkansas County Broadcasters Inc. (acq 8-31-2004; $130,000). Population served: 12,500 Format: Country. ◆Bobby Caldwell, CEO; Scott Siler, gen mgr.

Earle

KCJF(FM)— 2004: 103.9 mhz; 12.5 kw. Ant 469 ft TL: N35 27 01 W90 42 11. Hrs open: Box 789, Wynne, 72396. Phone: (870) 238-8141. Fax: (870) 238-5997.E-mail: radiokwyn@cablelynx.com Licensee: Catherine Joanna Flinn. Format: Classic rock.

East Camden

KCXY(FM)— Sept 28, 1987: 95.3 mhz; 100 kw. Ant 456 ft TL: N33 30 14 W92 48 38. Stereo. Hrs open: 24 Box 957, Camden, 71701. Secondary address: 133 Washington St. S.W., Camden 71701. Phone: (870) 836-9567. Fax: (870) 836-9500.E-mail: radioworks@cablelynx.com Web Site:www.camdenfm.net Licensee: Radio Works Inc. (acq 12-13-2004; grpsl). Population served: 50,000 Rgnl. Network: Ark. Radio Net. Ark. Radio Net. Format: C&W. News staff: one; News: 15 hrs wkly. Target aud: 25-54. ◆Donna Stewart, gen mgr, gen sls mgr; Greg Arnold, opns mgr & progmg dir.

El Dorado

KAGL(FM)— Sept 29, 1993: 93.3 mhz; 18 kw. Ant 354 ft TL: N33 16 16 W92 39 17. Stereo. Hrs open: 24 2525 Northwest Ave., 71730. Phone: (870) 863-6126. Fax: (870) 863-4555.E-mail: info@totalradio.com Web Site:www.totalradio.com Licensee: Noalmark Broadcasting Corp. (group owner; acq 1-8-93; $10,000; 3-29-93). Population served:

53,375 Natl. Rep: Target Broadcast Sales,. Format: Classic rock. News staff: one; News: 15 hrs wkly. Target aud: 25-54; general. ♦William C. Nolan, pres; Edwin Alderson, exec VP; Sandy Sanford, gen mgr.

***KAKV(FM)**— 2003: 88.9 mhz; 26 kw. Ant 377 ft TL: N33 12 30 W92 42 30. Hrs open: 24 2351 Sunset Blvd., Suite 170-218, Rocklin, CA, 95765. Phone: (501) 223-6051. Fax: (916) 251-1650. Web Site:www.klove.com Licensee: Educational Media Foundation. (acq 1-23-2008; $320,000 with WLRK(FM) Greenville, MS). Natl. Network: K-Love, . Format: Contemp Christian. ♦David Wolf, gen mgr.

***KBSA(FM)**— December 1987: 90.9 mhz; 3 kw. Ant 581 ft TL: N33 16 19 W92 42 12. Stereo. Hrs open: 24
Rebroadcasts KDAQ(FM) Shreveport, LA 100%.
Box 5250, Shreveport, LA, 71135. Phone: (800) 552-8502. Phone: (318) 797-5150. Fax: (318) 797-5265.E-mail: listenermail@redriverradio.org Web Site:www.redriverradio.org Licensee: Board of Supervisors of Louisiana State University & A&M College. Natl. Network: NPR, PRI, . Format: Classical, jazz, news. Target aud: 25+. ♦Kermit Poling, gen mgr; Rick Shelton, opns dir.

KDMS(AM)— May 8, 1950: 1290 khz; 5 kw-D, 106 w-N. TL: N33 12 27 W92 41 10. Hrs open: 1904 W. Hillsboro, 71730. Phone: (870) 863-5121. Fax: (870) 863-6221.E-mail: klbq@suddenlink.com Web Site:www.klbq99.com Licensee: El Dorado Broadcasting Co. (acq 7-8-87; $950,000 with co-located FM; 4-6-87). Population served: 28,463 Format: Adult contemp. ♦Dan Murphy, opns mgr, progmg dir; Don Travis, gen sls mgr, news dir; Norm Mason, chief of engrg.

KELD(AM)— Oct 17, 1935: 1400 khz; 1 kw-U. TL: N33 12 43 W92 39 48. (CP: TL: N33 14 14 W92 39 54). Stereo. Hrs open: 24 2525 Northwest Ave., 71730. Phone: (870) 863-6126. Phone: (870) 862-1400. Fax: (870) 863-4555.E-mail: info@totalradio.com Web Site:www.totalradio.com Licensee: Noalmark Broadcasting Corp. (group owner; (acq 7-73). Population served: 27,000 Natl. Network: Fox Sports, . Rgnl. Network: Ark. Radio Net. Natl. Rep: Target Broadcast Sales,. Format: Sports. Target aud: General. ♦William C. Nolan Jr., pres; Edwin Alderson, exec VP; Sandy Sanford, gen mgr, sls dir; Patrick Thomas, opns dir, opns mgr, progmg dir; Steven Gray, chief of engrg.

KIXB(FM)— Dec 9, 1963: 103.3 mhz; 100 kw. 571 ft TL: N33 13 20 W92 55 28. Stereo. Hrs open: 24 Prog sep from AM 2525 Northwest Ave., 71730. Phone: (870) 864-0103. Fax: (870) 863-4555.E-mail: kix103@noalmark.com Web Site:www.totalradio.com Licensee: Noalmark Broadcasting Corp. Population served: 50,000 Format: Country. News: 15 hrs wkly. Target aud: 18-54.

KLBQ(FM)— Dec 23, 1963: 98.7 mhz; 14 kw. Ant 298 ft TL: N33 12 30 W92 41 16. Stereo. Hrs open: 1904 W. Hillsboro, 71730. Phone: (870) 863-5121. Fax: (870) 863-6221.E-mail: klbq@suddenlink.com Licensee: El Dorado Broadcasting Co. Population served: 50,000 Format: Top-40, adult contemp. ♦Dan Murphy, disc jockey.

KMLK(FM)— 2000: 101.5 mhz; 6 kw. 328 ft TL: N33 09 32 W92 37 47. Hrs open: 2525 N. West Ave., 71730. Phone: (870) 875-1015. Fax: (870) 863-4555. Licensee: Noalmark Broadcasting Corp. (group owner; acq 6-14-01). Format: Urban adult contemp. ♦Sandy Sanford, gen mgr; Patrick Thomas, opns mgr, progmg dir; Harry Dyer, gen sls mgr; Steven Gay, chief of engrg; Cyndal Thompson, traf mgr.

KMRX(FM)— May 12, 1984: 96.1 mhz; 100 kw. 288 ft TL: N33 16 21 W92 39 25. Stereo. Hrs open: 24 2525 Northwest Ave., 71730. Phone: (870) 863-6126. Fax: (870) 863-4555.E-mail: info@totalradio.com Web Site:www.totalradio.com Licensee: Noalmark Broadcasting Corp. (group owner; acq 7-31-97). Population served: 300,000 Format: Adult contemp, contemp hit. News staff: one; News: 2 hrs wkly. Target aud: 18-34. ♦Sandy Sanford, gen mgr; Chase Roberts, opns mgr.

England

KHTE-FM— Sept 26, 1988: 96.5 mhz; 10.5 kw. Ant 495 ft TL: N34 29 10 W92 09 27. Stereo. Hrs open: 24 400 Hardin Rd., Suite 150, Little Rock, 72211. Phone: (501) 219-1919. Fax: (501) 225-4610.E-mail: donburns@crainmedia.com Web Site:www.khte.com Licensee: Crain Media Group LLC. Group owner: Archway Broadcasting Group (acq 2-1-2008; grpsl). Population served: 300,000 Format: Contemporary hit. ♦David Roederer, gen mgr; Vince Fruge, gen sls mgr; Joe Ratliff, progmg dir, news dir; Chris Duncan, chief of engrg.

KVDW(AM)— Aug 31, 1979: 1530 khz; 250 w-D. TL: N34 32 45 W91 59 04. (CP: COL: Scott, 500 w-D). Hrs open: 24 Vern1530AM, 204 Bucky Beaver, Jacksonville, 72056. Phone: (501) 773-1530. Fax: (501) 842-9308.E-mail: victory1530@yahoo.com Web Site:www.victory1530.com Licensee: Wells Broadcasting Inc. (acq 8-13-02; $35,000). Putbrese, Hunsaker & Trent, P. Format: Gospel hits, inspirational talk. Target aud: 18-54; professionals, farmers, college educated. Spec prog: Farm 5 hrs, talk 10 hrs wkly. ♦Vernon Wells, gen mgr.

Eudora

KAVH(FM)— 2001: 101.5 mhz; 6 kw. Ant 328 ft TL: N33 11 58 W91 15 39. Hrs open: 24 c/o WJJA(TV), 4311 E. Oakwood Rd., Oak Creek, WI, 53154. Phone: (414) 764-4953.E-mail: info@kavh.com Licensee: Joel J. Kinlow. Group owner: Joel J. Kinlow Stns. Format: Var. ♦Bruce Herz, opns dir; Joel Kinlow, gen mgr & progmg dir.

Eureka Springs

KESA(FM)— May 13, 1985: 100.9 mhz; 1.1 kw. 531 ft TL: N36 22 49 W93 44 53. Stereo. Hrs open: 6 AM-10 PM Box 451750, Grove, 74345. Phone: (479) 253-9001. Fax: 4(79) 253-9002. Licensee: Northeast Oklahoma Broadcast Network Inc. (acq 5-7-2008; $302,000). Rgnl. Network: Ark. Radio Net. Ark. Radio Net. Format: Adult contemp. News staff: one; News: 20 hrs wkly. Target aud: 35 plus; upper income & retired. Spec prog: Class 10 hrs, hits of the 50s & 60s 2 hrs wkly. ♦Larry J. Hestand, pres.

Fairfield Bay

KFFB(FM)— Dec 31, 1981: 106.1 mhz; 50 kw. Ant 500 ft TL: N35 45 22 W92 14 49. Stereo. Hrs open: 24 Box 1050, 72088. Phone: (501) 884-6812. Fax: (501) 723-4861.E-mail: kffb@kffb.com Web Site:www.kffb.com Licensee: Freedom Broadcasting Inc. Natl. Network: ABC, . Rgnl. Network: Ark Radio Net. Ark. Radio Net. Smithwick & Belendiuk. Format: MOR. News staff: 2; News: 8 hrs wkly. Target aud: 35 plus; middle & upper income. ♦Bob Connell, pres, gen mgr; Chad Whiteaker, opns dir.

Farmington

KFAY(AM)— Dec 15, 1946: 1030 khz; 10 kw-D, 1 kw-N, DA-2. TL: N36 06 34 W94 10 59. Stereo. Hrs open: 24 4209 Frontage Rd., Fayetteville, 72703. Phone: (479) 521-5566. Fax: (479) 521-4968.E-mail: info@kfayam.com Web Site:www.kfayam.com Licensee: Cumulus Licensing Corp. Group owner: Cumulus Media Inc. (acq 2-1-99; grpsl). Population served: 150,000 Format: News/talk. News staff: 6; News: 20 hrs wkly. Target aud: 25-64; general. ♦Joe Conway, gen mgr; Jay Phillips, progmg dir.

Fayetteville

***KAYH(FM)**— June 26, 2000: 89.3 mhz; 6 kw. Ant 380 ft TL: N36 01 48 W94 05 10. Hrs open: 24 Box 1288, Family FM 89.3, 72702. Phone: (479) 750-7893. Fax: (479) 927-1250. Licensee: Community Broadcasting Inc. (acq 1-14-2008; $450,000). Format: Christian talk/teaching. ♦Mike Disney, gen mgr.

***KBNV(FM)**— 2000: 90.1 mhz; 7.1 kw horiz, 16 kw vert. Ant 466 ft TL: N36 07 38 W93 59 23. Hrs open: 24 Drawer 2440, Tupelo, MS, 38803. Phone: (662) 844-8888. Fax: (662) 844-9090.E-mail: info@afa.net Licensee: American Family Association. Group owner: American Family Radio Format: Christian. ♦John Riley, progmg dir.

KEZA(FM)— Sept 6, 1983: 107.9 mhz; 99 kw. 1,259 ft TL: N35 51 12 W94 01 33. Stereo. Hrs open: 2049 E. Joyce Blvd. F, 72703. Phone: (479) 582-1079. Fax: (479) 582-5302. Web Site:www.magic1079.com Licensee: Capstar TX L.P. Group owner: Clear Channel Communications Inc. (acq 8-30-00; grpsl). Format: Adult contemp. Target aud: 25-54. Spec prog: Jazz, oldies. ♦Tony Beringer, gen mgr; Jim Harvill, progmg dir; Jess Smith, news dir; Zeb Huffmaster, chief of engrg.

KKIX(FM)— Oct 1, 1966: 103.9 mhz; 100 kw. 510 ft TL: N36 01 17 W94 13 04. Stereo. Hrs open: 24 Box 8190, 72703. Phone: (479) 521-0104. Fax: (479) 444-8600.E-mail: info@kkixfm.com Web Site:www.kix104.com Licensee: Capstar TX L.P. Group owner: Clear Channel Communications Inc. (acq 8-30-00; grpsl). Population served: 250,000 Wiley, Rein & Fielding. Format: Country. News staff: one; News: 2 hrs wkly. Target aud: 25-54. ♦Tony Beringer, gen mgr; Jay Steele, progmg dir; Zeb Huffmaster, chief of engrg.

KMXF(FM)—See Lowell

KOFC(AM)— June 10, 1957: 1250 khz; 920 w-D, 45 w-N. TL: N36 04 29 W94 11 00. Hrs open: 16 Box 1288, 72702-1288. Phone: (479) 750-7893. Fax: (479) 927-1250. Licensee: Community Broadcasting Inc. (acq 1-15-2008). Format: Christian talk, teaching. Target aud: 35 plus; traditional Christian families. ♦Michael Disney, opns mgr.

KQSM-FM— Oct 16, 1964: 92.1 mhz; 7.6 kw. Ant 531 ft TL: N36 07 38 W93 59 23. Stereo. Hrs open: 24 4209 N Frontage Road, 72703. Phone: (479) 521-5566. Fax: (479) 521-0751. Licensee: Cumulus Licensing Corp. Group owner: Cumulus Media Inc. (acq 2-1-99; grpsl). Population served: 180,000 Natl. Rep: Roslin,. Format: Sports. News staff: one. Target aud: 18-49. ♦Joe Conway, gen mgr; Becky Dole, gen sls mgr; Chris Baker, progmg dir; Jay Phillips, news dir; Gregg Judd, chief of engrg.

***KUAF(FM)**— Jan 15, 1973: 91.3 mhz; 60 kw. 1,105 ft TL: N35 51 12 W94 01 33. Stereo. Hrs open: 24 747 W. Dickson St., Suite 2, 72701-5023. Phone: (479) 575-2556. Fax: (479) 575-8440.E-mail: kuaf.info@uark.edu Web Site:www.kuaf.com Licensee: Board of Trustees University of Arkansas. Population served: 360,000 Natl. Network: NPR, . Format: News, class, jazz. News staff: 3; News: 45 hrs wkly. Target aud: 25-65. Spec prog: Folk 5 hrs, Black 5 hrs wkly. ♦Rick Stockdell, gen mgr; Rhonda Dillard, gen sls mgr; P.J. Robowski, mus dir; Kyle Kellams, news dir.

***KXUA(FM)**— April 4, 2000: 88.3 mhz; 470 w vert. 262 ft TL: N36 03 56 W94 10 30. Stereo. Hrs open: 24 A 665 Arkansas Union, 72701. Phone: (479) 575-4273. Fax: (479) 575-2019.E-mail: info@kxua.com Web Site:www.kxua.com Licensee: Board of Trustees of University of Arkansas. Population served: 100,000 Format: Var. Target aud: 12-24; high school and colege students. ♦Richard Adams, gen mgr.

Fordyce

KBJT(AM)— Aug 1, 1959: 1590 khz; 4.7 kw-D, 35 w-N. TL: N33 48 10 W92 26 10. Hrs open: 24 303 Spring St., 71742. Phone: (870) 352-7137. Fax: (870) 352-7139.E-mail: kbjt@alltel.net Web Site:kbjtkq.com Licensee: KBJT Inc. (acq 9-1-77). Population served: 11,000 Format: News/talk. Target aud: General. Spec prog: Gospel 11 hrs wkly. ♦Gary Coates, pres, gen mgr; Carna Coates, progmg dir, pub affrs dir; Saxon Coates, news dir, news rptr & reporter.

KQEW(FM)— Feb 23, 1982: 102.3 mhz; 25 kw. 328 ft TL: N33 48 10 W92 26 10. Stereo. Hrs open: Prog sep from AM Licensee: Dallas Properties Inc. Format: C&W. Target aud: General.

Forrest City

***KARH(FM)**— 2000: 88.1 mhz; 3.7 kw. Ant 544 ft TL: N35 12 11 W90 33 57. Hrs open: Drawer 3206, American Family Radio, Tupelo, MS, 38803. Phone: (662) 844-8888. Fax: (662) 842-6791. Web Site:www.afr.net Licensee: American Family Association. Group owner: American Family Radio Format: Relg. ♦Marvin Sanders, gen mgr; John Riley, progmg dir; Joey Moody, chief of engrg.

KBFC(FM)—Listing follows KXJK(AM).

KXJK(AM)— Apr 29, 1949: 950 khz; 5 kw-D, 500 w-N. TL: N34 58 53 W90 51 27. Stereo. Hrs open: 24 Box 707, 501 E. Broadway, 72336. Phone: (870) 633-1252. Fax: (870) 633-1259.E-mail: radio@arkansas.net Web Site:www.kxjk.com Licensee: Forrest City Broadcasting Co. Inc. Population served: 30,000 Rgnl. Network: Ark. Radio Net. Ark. Radio Net. Rgnl rep: Midsouth Gene Smith. Format: Classic rock, news/talk. News staff: 2; News: 24 hrs wkly. Target aud: General. Spec prog: Farm 16 hrs wkly. ♦William Fogg, gen mgr, mus dir & chief of engrg.

Fort Smith

***KAOW(FM)**— 1999: 88.9 mhz; 1 kw. 482 ft TL: N35 26 50 W94 21 54. Hrs open: 24 Box 2440, American Family Radio, Tupelo, MS, 38803. Phone: (662) 844-8888. Fax: (662) 842-6791. Web Site:www.afr.net Licensee: American Family Association. Group owner: American Family Radio Format: Relg. ♦Marvin Sanders, gen mgr; John Riley, progmg dir; Joey Moody, chief of engrg.

KBBQ-FM—See Van Buren

***KEAF(FM)**— 2009: 90.7 mhz; 26 kw vert. Ant 2,086 ft TL: N35 09 56 W93 40 36. Hrs open:
Rebroadcasts WBFR(FM) Birmingham, AL 100%.
c/o WBFR(FM), 244 Goodwin Crest Dr., Suite 118, Birmingham, AL, 35209. Phone: (205) 942-3530. Fax: (510) 568-6190. Web Site:www.familyradio.com Licensee: Family Stations Inc. Format: Relg. ♦Stanley Jackson, gen mgr.

KFPW(AM)— July 27, 1930: 1230 khz; 1 kw-U, DA-1. TL: N35 23 11 W94 21 44. Stereo. Hrs open: 24 Box 908, 72902. Secondary address: 323 N. Greenwood 72902. Phone: (479) 783-5379. Phone: (479) 288-1047. Fax: (479) 785-2638. Web Site:www.kfpwam1230.com Licensee: Pharis Broadcasting Inc. (group owner; (acq 3-14-2002;

$850,000 with KFPW-FM Barling). Population served: 143,800 Natl. Network: ABC, . Rgnl. Network: Ark. Radio Net. Natl. Rep: Commercial Media Sales,. Ark. Radio Net. Campbell & Tannenwald. Format: News/talk. News: 13 hrs wkly. Target aud: 35 plus; affluent. Spec prog: Sp 6 hrs wkly. ◆Bill Pharis, pres, gen mgr; Karen Pharis, VP, progmg dir & news dir.

KFSA(AM)— Feb 13, 1947: 950 khz; 1 kw-D, 500 w-N, DA-2. TL: N35 25 58 W94 28 13. Stereo. Hrs open: Box 6210, 72906. Phone: (501) 646-6700. Fax: (501) 646-1373. Licensee: Fred H. Baker Sr. (acq 11-5-81; $297,000; 11-30-81). Population served: 150,000 Format: Relg teaching. Target aud: General. ◆Fred H. Baker Sr., pres; Jerry Lynch, gen mgr & gen sls mgr; David J. Burdue, progmg dir.

KHGG(AM)—See Van Buren

KISR(FM)— Aug 13, 1971: 93.7 mhz; 100 kw. Ant 1,250 ft TL: N35 31 22 W94 23 32. Stereo. Hrs open: 24 Box 488, 72901. Secondary address: 601 N. Greenwood 72901. Phone: (501) 785-2526. Fax: (479) 782-9127.E-mail: info@kisr.net Web Site:www.kisr.net Licensee: Stereo 93 Inc. Population served: 410,000 Format: CHR. News staff: one. Target aud: 18-39. ◆Fred Baker Jr., gen mgr, progmg dir; Gary Keifer, stn mgr; Carol Patterson, gen sls mgr, traf mgr; Rick Hayes, mus dir; Dale L. Davenport, engrg dir.

KLSZ-FM— July 27, 1978: 100.7 mhz; 50 kw. Ant 459 ft TL: N35 13 32 W94 20 29. Stereo. Hrs open: 24 3104 S. 70th St., 72903. Phone: (479) 452-0681. Fax: (479) 452-0873.E-mail: info@rock1007.com Web Site:www.rock1007.com Licensee: Cumulus Licensing Corp. Group owner: Cumulus Media Inc. (acq 5-1-99; $1 million). Population served: 627,600 Format: Golden oldies. News: 7 hrs wkly. Target aud: 25-64. ◆Smitty O'Loughlin, gen mgr; Geri Richards, progmg dir.

KMAG(FM)— Dec 31, 1964: 99.1 mhz; 100 kw. 1,968 ft TL: N35 09 56 W93 40 35. Stereo. Hrs open: 24 311 Lexington Ave., 72901. Phone: (479) 782-8888. Fax: (479) 785-5946.E-mail: info@kmag991.com Web Site:www.kmag991.com Licensee: Capstar TX L.P. Group owner: Clear Channel Communications Inc. (acq 8-30-00; grpsl). Format: Country. News staff: 2. Target aud: 25-54; females. ◆Paul Swint, gen mgr; Ralph Cherry, opns mgr; Phil Robken, sls dir, progmg dir; Gary Elmore, news dir; Allan Riley, chief of engrg.

KOMS(FM)—See Poteau, OK

KQBK(FM)—(Booneville, Nov 1, 1981: 104.7 mhz; 50 kw. 492 ft TL: N35 11 01 W94 07 44. Stereo. Hrs open: 24 Box 908, 72902. Phone: (479) 288-1047. Fax: (479) 785-2638. Web Site:www.fox94.com Licensee: Pharis Broadcasting Inc. (group owner; acq 11-20-97; $800,000). Population served: 500,000 Rgnl. Network: Ark. Radio Net. Natl. Rep: Commercial Media Sales,. Ark. Radio Net. Rgnl rep: BRI Irwin, Campbell & Tannenwald. Format: Oldies. News staff: one; News: 10 hrs wkly. Target aud: 18-54. ◆Bill Pharis, pres; Karen Pharis, gen mgr; Ernie Witt, opns mgr.

KTCS(AM)— March 1956: 1410 khz; 1 kw-D. TL: N35 16 40 W94 22 35. Hrs open: Prog sep from FM Box 180188, 72918-0188. Secondary address: 5304 Hwy. 45 E 72916. Phone: (479) 646-6151. Fax: (479) 646-3509.E-mail: info@ktcs.com Web Site:www.ktcs.com Licensee: Big Chief Broadcasting Co. (Acq 1961). Population served: 211,000 Format: Southern Gospel. ◆Sandy Hunter, traf mgr.

KTCS-FM— Aug 15, 1964: 99.9 mhz; 100 kw. Ant 1,919 ft TL: N35 04 20 W94 40 50. Stereo. Hrs open: Box 180188, 72918-0188. Secondary address: 5304 Hwy. 45 E. 72916. Phone: (479) 646-6151. Fax: (479) 646-3509.E-mail: info@ktcs.com Web Site:www.ktcs.com Licensee: Big Chief Broadcasting Co. Format: Country. ◆Lee Young, gen mgr, stn mgr, gen sls mgr; Melissa Harper, opns mgr; Darren Minor, progmg dir; Mary Livingston, news dir; Scott Reeves, chief of engrg; Sandy Hunter, traf mgr.

KWHN(AM)— Nov 22, 1947: 1320 khz; 5 kw-U, DA-2. TL: N35 24 36 W94 21 30. Hrs open: 24 311 Lexington Ave., 72901. Phone: (479) 782-8888. Fax: (479) 782-0366. Web Site:www.kwhn.com Licensee: Capstar TX L.P. Population served: 71,515 Format: News/talk. News staff: 6; News: 40 hrs wkly. Target aud: 25-54. ◆Paul Swint, gen mgr; Phil Robken, sls dir.

KYHN(AM)— 2001: 1650 khz; 10 kw-D, 1 kw-N. TL: N35 24 36 W94 21 30. Hrs open: 311 Lexington Ave., 72901. Phone: (479) 782-8888. Fax: (479) 782-0366.E-mail: info@kwhn.com Web Site:www.kwhn.com Licensee: Capstar TX L.P. Group owner: Clear Channel Communications Inc. (acq 1-9-2004). Format: News/talk. ◆Paul Swint, gen mgr; Tony Montgomery, sls dir.

KZBB(FM)—See Poteau, OK

Fouke

*KPOS(FM)— 2001: 104.3 mhz; 5 kw. Ant 361 ft TL: N33 21 05 W93 50 41. Hrs open: 24 2351 Sunset Blvd., Suite 170-218, Rocklin, CA, 95765. Phone: (916) 251-1600. Fax: (916) 251-1650. Web Site:www.air1.com Licensee: Educational Media Foundation. Group owner: EMF Broadcasting (acq 1-15-2004; $500,000). Natl. Network: Air 1, . Shaw Pittman. Format: Christian. News staff: 3. Target aud: 25-44; Judeo Christian, female. ◆Richard Jenkins, pres; Mike Novak, VP; Keith Whipple, dev dir; Eric Allen, natl sls mgr; David Pierce, progmg mgr; Ed Lenane, news dir; Sam Wallington, engrg dir; Karen Johnson, news rptr.

Glenwood

KWXI(AM)— May 12, 1980: 670 khz; 5 kw-D. TL: N34 19 32 W93 33 27. Hrs open: 6 AM-midnight Box 740, 71943. Secondary address: 180 Hwy. 70 E., Suite 11 71943. Phone: (870) 356-2151. Phone: (870) 356-2181. Fax: (870) 356-4684.E-mail: kwxi@alltel.net Licensee: MLS Broadcasting Inc. (acq 5-29-2009; $169,500). Rgnl. Network: Ark. Radio Net. Rgnl rep: Rgnl Reps Format: Souther gospel. News: 8 hrs wkly. Target aud: 34-54; affluent professionals. ◆Lenny Brothers, gen mgr & opns mgr; Doug Dumont, progmg dir, news dir; Danie Appleoff, chief of engrg.

Gosnell

KAMJ-FM— February 1999: 93.9 mhz; 2 kw. 328 ft TL: N35 53 56 W89 52 48. Hrs open: 24 Box 989, Blytheville, 72315-0989. Phone: (870) 762-2093. Fax: (870) 763-8459. Licensee: Phoenix Broadcasting Group Inc. Group owner: Sudbury Services Inc. & Newport Broadcasting Co. Format: Urban contemp. ◆Dave Clark, gen mgr & progmg mgr.

Gould

KAFN(FM)— Apr 15, 1999: 102.5 mhz; 6 kw. Ant 177 ft TL: N33 58 11 W91 32 58. Hrs open: 24 Box 910, Stuttgart, 92160. Secondary address: 1818 S. Buerkle, Stuttgart 92160. Phone: (870) 673-1595. Fax: (870) 673-8445.E-mail: kdew973@yahoo.com Licensee: Arkansas County Broadcasters Inc. (group owner; acq 12-30-2003; $90,000). Format: Country. ◆Scott Siler, stn mgr.

Gravette

KURM-FM— October 1989: 100.3 mhz; 1.75 kw. Ant 610 ft TL: N36 25 54 W94 30 46. Hrs open: 113 E. New Hope Rd., Rogers, 72758. Phone: (479) 633-0790. Fax: (479) 631-9711.E-mail: kurm@kurm.net Web Site:www.kurm.net Licensee: KERM Inc. (acq 4-4-2002; $350,000 with KLTK(AM) Centerton). Rgnl. Network: Missourinet. Law Office of Dan J. Alpert. Format: News/talk. ◆Kermit Womack, gen mgr.

Green Forest

*KGSF(FM)— 2008: 88.7 mhz; 3.55 kw vert. Ant 595 ft TL: N36 21 38 W93 44 54. Hrs open:
Rebroadcasts KAWZ(FM) Twin Falls, ID 100%.
4002 N. 3300 E., Twin Falls, ID, 83301. Phone: (208) 734-6633. Fax: (208) 736-1958. Web Site:www.csnradio.com Licensee: Calvary Chapel of Twin Falls Inc. Format: Christian praise & worship, Bible teaching. ◆Mike Kestler, pres.

Greenwood

KZKZ-FM— December 1981: 106.3 mhz; 1.7 kw. 433 ft TL: N35 13 43 W94 15 45. (CP: 15 kw, and 397 ft.). Stereo. Hrs open: 24 6420 S. Zero St., Fort Smith, 72903. Phone: (479) 646-6700. Fax: (479) 646-1373.E-mail: kzkzfm@kzkzfm.com Web Site:www.kzkzfm.com Licensee: Family Communications Inc. (acq 5-11-93; 6-7-93). Format: Contemp Christian. ◆Jerry Lynch, gen mgr; Jay Lynch, stn mgr; Dave Burdul, progmg dir.

Gurdon

KYXK(FM)— December 1984: 106.9 mhz; 17.5 kw. 298 ft TL: N33 54 42 W93 10 43. Stereo. Hrs open: 24 Box 40, Arkadelphia, 71923. Secondary address: 601 S. 7th St., Arkadelphia 71923. Phone: (870) 246-9272. Fax: (870) 246-5878. Web Site:www.clarkcountybroadcasting.com Licensee: Noalmark Broadcasting Corp. (group owner; (acq 6-29-2007; grpsl). Population served: 170,000 Booth, Freret, Imlay & Tepper. Format: Country. Target aud: 25-54; adults. ◆William Nolan Jr., pres; Stephanie Collie, gen sls mgr; Randy Seale, progmg dir; Ronna Pennington, news dir.

Hamburg

KHMB(FM)— 1996: 99.5 mhz; 3.2 kw. Ant 312 ft TL: N33 17 19 W91 52 45. Hrs open: 24 203 Fairview Rd., Crossett, 71635. Phone: (870) 364-4700. Fax: (870) 364-4770.E-mail: info@khmbfm.com Web Site:www.QLiteradio.com Licensee: R&M Broadcasting (acq 12-28-2005; $131,553). Format: Adult contemp. ◆Dennis Maxwell, gen mgr, progmg dir; Jane Jordan, gen sls mgr.

Hampton

*KBPW(FM)— 2001: 88.1 mhz; 250 w. Ant 259 ft TL: N33 32 11 W92 28 07. Hrs open: Box 2440, Tupelo, MS, 38803. Phone: (662) 844-8888. Fax: (662) 842-6791. Licensee: American Family Association Inc. Group owner: American Family Radio (acq 4-19-01). Format: Christian. ◆Marvin Sanders, gen mgr; John Riley, progmg dir; Joey Moody, chief of engrg.

KELD-FM— Nov 26, 1984: 106.5 mhz; 17.5 kw. 302 ft TL: N33 32 23 W92 34 59. Hrs open: 24 2525 N.W. Ave., El Dorado, 71730. Phone: (870) 863-6126. Fax: (870) 863-4555.E-mail: info@totalradio.com Web Site:www.totalradio.com Licensee: Noalmark Broadcasting Corp. (group owner; acq 2-21-03; $250,000). Natl. Network: ABC, Fox News Radio, . Format: News/talk. ◆Sandy Sanford, gen mgr.

Hardy

KOOU(FM)— Oct 4, 1993: 104.7 mhz; 6 kw. Ant 199 ft TL: N36 18 17 W91 24 38. Stereo. Hrs open: 24 11 FM 101 Rd., 72542. Phone: (870) 856-3240. Fax: (870) 856-4408.E-mail: hometownradio@centurytec.net Licensee: KOOU Inc. (acq 12-10-2003). Rgnl. Network: Ark. Radio Net. Ark. Radio Net. Format: MOR. News staff: 2; News: 10 hrs wkly. Target aud: 25-60; female/professional. ◆James Bragg, gen mgr.

Harrisburg

KWHF(FM)— May 15, 1999: 95.9 mhz; 34 kw. Ant 489 ft TL: N35 47 42 W90 47 35. Hrs open: 24 Box 1737, Jonesboro, 72403-1737. Secondary address: 407 W. Parker Rd., Jonesboro 72404. Phone: (870) 932-8400. Fax: (870) 932-3814.E-mail: larryjames@959thebuzz.com Web Site:www.959thebuzz.com Licensee: CC Licenses LLC. Group owner: Clear Channel Communications Inc. (acq 6-13-2002; $2.05 million with KNEA(AM) Jonesboro). Format: Classic country. News staff: 2; News: 3 hrs wkly. Target aud: 28-65; affluent baby boomers who have spendable income. ◆Scott Silar, gen mgr; Dennis Rogers, news dir.

Harrison

*KBPB(FM)— 2001: 91.9 mhz; 5.5 kw. Ant 341 ft TL: N36 22 12 W93 13 23. Hrs open: 24 1400 Locust St., St. Louis, MO, 63103. Phone: (800) 228-5284. Fax: (573) 896-4376. Licensee: New Life Evangelistic Center Inc. Format: Contemp Christian, southern gospel. ◆Larry Rice, gen mgr.

KCWD(FM)— 1982: 96.1 mhz; 3 kw. 295 ft TL: N36 16 36 W93 05 27. (CP: 8 kw, ant 1,191 ft.). Stereo. Hrs open: 24 Box 850, 72601. Secondary address: 600 S. Pine 72601. Phone: (870) 741-1402. Fax: (870) 741-9702.E-mail: kcwd@all.net Web Site:www.kcwd.com Licensee: Harrison Radio Station Inc. Format: Classic rock. ◆Tom Arnold, gen mgr & chief of opns.

KHOZ(AM)— Sept 28, 1946: 900 khz; 1 kw-D. TL: N36 14 35 W93 06 43. Hrs open: 24 1111 Radio Ave., 72601. Phone: (870) 741-2302. Fax: (870) 741-3299.E-mail: khozradio@khoz.com Web Site:www.khoz.com Licensee: KHOZ LLC. (acq 6-16-2005; $3.7 million with co-located FM). Natl. Network: CBS, . Wire Svc: AP Format: Talk, soft adult contemp. News staff: one; News: 15 hrs wkly. Target aud: General. Spec prog: Gospel 10 hrs wkly. ◆Charles Earls, CEO; Scott Earls, pres; Scottie Earls, gen mgr.

KHOZ-FM— Mar 25, 1963: 102.9 mhz; 100 kw. Ant 981 ft TL: N36 26 11 W93 14 43. Stereo. Hrs open: 24 1111 Radio Ave., 72601. Phone: (870) 741-2301. Fax: (870) 741-3299.E-mail: scottieearls@krzk.com Web Site:www.khoz.com Licensee: KHOZ LLC. Natl. Network: CBS Radio, . Wire Svc: AP Format: Country. News staff: 2; News: 15 hrs wkly. Target aud: 25-54. ◆Jamie Cooleg, mus dir, news rptr; Bill Wilcox, pub affrs dir; Patty Eddings, traf mgr; Tom Parker, reporter; Brent Klein, disc jockey.

Hatfield

KILX(FM)— 2001: 104.1 mhz; 28.5 kw. Ant 469 ft TL: N34 32 42 W94 18 21. Hrs open: 24 1600 S. Reine St., Mena, 71953. Phone: (479) 394-1450. Licensee: Ouachita Broadcasting Inc. (acq 3-8-99). Population served: 60,000 Format: Adult contemp. ♦Dwight Douglas, gen mgr & opns mgr.

Heber Springs

KAWW(AM)— July 15, 1967: 1370 khz; 1 kw-D. TL: N35 29 10 W92 02 05. Hrs open: 6 AM-sunset (2 hrs past) 111 North Spring St., Searcy, 72143. Phone: (501) 268-7123. Fax: (501) 279-2900.E-mail: jrrunyon@crainmedia.com Licensee: Crain Media Group LLC (group owner; acq 8-7-02; grpsl). Population served: 30,000 Rgnl. Network: Ark. Radio Net. Ark. Radio Net. Format: News/talk. News staff: one; News: one hr wkly. Target aud: 25-65. ♦Larry Crain, CEO; J.R. Runyon, gen mgr.

***KBMJ(FM)**— 2002: 89.5 mhz; 70 kw vert. Ant 735 ft TL: N35 44 00 W92 15 37. Hrs open: 24 Drawer 3206, Tupelo, MS, 38803. Phone: (662) 844-8888.E-mail: info@kbmjfm.com Licensee: American Family Association. Group owner: American Family Radio Format: Christian. ♦Marvin Sanders, gen mgr.

KEAZ(FM)— Sept 1, 1972: 100.7 mhz; 50 kw. Ant 328 ft TL: N35 27 26 W92 02 11. Stereo. Hrs open: 24 111 N. Spring St., Searcy, 72143. Phone: (501) 268-7123. Fax: (501) 279-2900.E-mail: jrrunyon@crainmedia.com Licensee: Crain Media Group LLC. (group owner; (acq 8-7-2002; grpsl). Population served: 150,000 Format: Main stream adult contemp. Target aud: 25-54. ♦Larry Crain, CEO; J.R. Runyon, gen mgr.

Helena

KFFA(AM)— Nov 19, 1941: 1360 khz; 1 kw-D, 90 w-N. TL: N34 31 39 W90 37 48. Hrs open: 24 Box 430, 1360 Radio Dr., 72342. Phone: (870) 338-8361. Phone: (870) 338-8331. Fax: (870) 338-8332.E-mail: kffa@arkansas.net Web Site:www.kffa.com Licensee: Delta Broadcasting Inc. (acq 3-80; $445,000; 3-10-80). Population served: 65,000 Rgnl. Network: Prog Farm. Donald E. Martin. Format: Country. News: 25 hrs wkly. Target aud: 18-54. Spec prog: Farm 16 hrs, blues 8 hrs, Black 10 hrs, sports 15 hrs, gospel 4 hrs wkly. ♦Jim Howe, pres, gen sls mgr, mktg dir, adv VP, pub affrs dir; Rose Seaton, opns mgr & prom mgr; Louis Smith, mus dir; Jerry Campbell, engrg mgr; Nancy Howie, traf mgr.

KFFA-FM— 1972: 103.1 mhz; 13 kw. Ant 318 ft TL: N34 31 39 W90 37 46. Stereo. Hrs open: 24 Box 430, 72342. Secondary address: 1360 Radio Dr. 72342. Phone: (870) 338-8361. Phone: (870) 338-8331. Fax: (870) 338-8332.E-mail: kffa@arkansas.net Licensee: Delta Broadcasting Inc. (acq 5-84; grpsl; 5-7-84). Population served: 65,000 Format: Adult contemp, sports. News: 4 hrs wkly. ♦Jim Howe, CEO, rsch dir, farm dir; Rose Seaton, progmg dir; Kacye Patton, traf mgr; Louis Smith, mus critic.

KJIW-FM— Jan 5, 1989: 94.5 mhz; 10 kw. 341 ft TL: N34 31 20 W90 35 47. Hrs open: 24 204 Moore St., Helena-West Helena, 72742. Phone: (870) 338-2700.E-mail: kjiwfm@ipa.net Licensee: Elijah Mondy Jr. (acq 1988). Format: gospel. ♦Elijah Mondy Jr., gen mgr; April Mondy, progmg dir, mus dir; Zipporah Mondy, mus dir.

Hope

KBYB(FM)— Dec 31, 1984: 101.7 mhz; 50 kw. Ant 492 ft TL: N33 41 20 W93 35 55. Stereo. Hrs open: 24 615 Olive St., Texarkana, TX, 75501. Phone: (903) 793-4671. Fax: (903) 792-4261. Licensee: Arklatex LLC. (group owner; (acq 1-3-2007; grpsl). Natl. Rep: Interep,. Format: Adult hits. Target aud: 25-54.

KHPA(FM)— Apr 21, 1977: 104.9 mhz; 3 kw. 298 ft TL: N33 43 10 W93 29 07. (CP: 6 kw, ant 328 ft. TL: N33 43 12 W93 29 11). Stereo. Hrs open: Box 424, 71802. Secondary address: 1600 S. Elm 71801. Phone: (870) 777-8868. Phone: (870) 777-8869. Fax: (870) 777-8888.E-mail: khpafm@supercountry105.com Licensee: Newport Broadcasting Co. Group owner: Sudbury Svcs Inc. & Newport Broadcasting Co. Format: Country. ♦Sonya Odom, gen mgr & sls dir; Alex Rain, chief of engrg; Amanda Smith, traf mgr.

KXAR(AM)— Dec 12, 1947: 1490 khz; 690 w-U. TL: N33 41 20 W93 35 55. Hrs open: Box 424, 71802. Secondary address: 1600 S. Elm 71801. Phone: (870) 777-8868. Fax: (870) 777-8888.E-mail: khpafm@supercountry105.com Licensee: Newport Broadcast Co. (Acq 8-26-99; $51,000). Population served: 35,000 Rgnl. Network: Ark. Radio Net. Ark. Radio Net. Format: Talk. Target aud: General; double income, stable, adult households.

Horseshoe Bend

KKIK(FM)— 2004: 106.5 mhz; 12 kw. Ant 476 ft TL: N36 15 22 W91 55 23. Hrs open: 920 Harrison St., Suite C, Batesville, 72503. Phone: (870) 793-4196. Fax: (870) 793-5222. Licensee: WRD Entertainment Inc. (group owner). Format: Oldies. ♦Gary Bridgman, gen mgr.

Hot Springs

***KALR(FM)**— May 1989: 91.5 mhz; 3 kw. Ant 485 ft TL: N34 37 31 W93 00 37. Hrs open: 24 2351 Sunset Blvd., Suite 170-218, Rocklin, CA, 95765. Phone: (916) 251-1600. Fax: (916) 251-1650. Licensee: Educational Media Foundation. (acq 6-28-2007; $275,000). Format: Christian. ♦Mike Novak, sr VP.

KBHS(AM)— Oct 6, 1966: 1420 khz; 5 kw-D, 87 w-N. TL: N34 27 19 W93 03 26. Hrs open: Box 21430, 71903. Secondary address: 208 Buena Vista Rd. 71902. Phone: (501) 525-1301. Fax: (501) 525-4344.E-mail: klaz@klaz.com Web Site:www.klaz.com Licensee: Noalmark Broadcasting Corp. (group owner; Natl. Rep: Target Broadcast Sales,. Format: Adult contemp. Target aud: 35 plus; upscale, high-income residents & business people. ♦Eddie Tarpley, gen mgr.

KLAZ(FM)— October 1971: 105.9 mhz; 95 kw. 994 ft TL: N34 30 19 W93 05 06. Stereo. Hrs open: Prog sep from AM Box 21430, 71902. Phone: (510) 525-1301. Fax: (501) 525-4344. Licensee: Noalmark Broadcasting Corp. Population served: 150,000 Format: Adult contemp. Target aud: 18-49.

***KLRO(FM)**— Mar 20, 1984: 90.1 mhz; 38 kw. Ant 971 ft TL: N34 30 18 W93 04 42. Stereo. Hrs open: 24 2351 Sunset Blvd., Suite 170-218, Rocklin, CA, 95765. Phone: (916) 251-1600. Fax: (916) 251-1650. Web Site:www.klove.com Licensee: Educational Media Foundation. (acq 9-24-2004; $1.2 million). Natl. Network: K-Love, . Format: Christian contemp, relg. ♦Richard Jenkins, pres, gen mgr; Mike Novak, VP; Keith Whipple, dev dir; Eric Allen, natl sls mgr; David Pierce, progmg mgr; Ed Lenane, news dir; Sam Wallington, engrg dir; Karen Johnson, news rptr.

KQUS-FM— Feb 7, 1969: 97.5 mhz; 100 kw. 860 ft TL: N34 24 11 W93 07 13. Stereo. Hrs open: 24 Prog sep from AM 125 Corporate Terr., 71913. Phone: (501) 525-9700. Fax: (501) 525-9739. Web Site:www.us97country.com Population served: 128,000 Wire Svc: AP Format: C&W. News staff: one. Target aud: 18-54. ♦Gary Terrell, gen mgr, progmg dir; Neal Gladner, gen sls mgr; Craig Dale, progmg dir; Tom Duke, mus dir; Melissa Waters, traf mgr.

KYDL(FM)— June 18, 1965: 96.7 mhz; 940 w. Ant 807 ft TL: N34 24 13 W93 07 14. (CP: 6 kw, ant 308 ft. TL: N34 29 43 W93 01 27). Stereo. Hrs open: 24 125 Corporate Terr., 71913-7248. Phone: (501) 525-9700. Fax: (501) 525-9739. Web Site:www.star96fm.com Licensee: US Stations LLC. Group owner: Powell Broadcasting (acq 2-1-2005; grpsl). Population served: 65,631 Format: Adult contemp. Target aud: 18 plus. ♦Gary Terrell, gen mgr, chief of engrg; Craig Dale, opns dir, progmg dir; Neal Gladner, gen sls mgr; Melissa Waters, traf mgr.

KYXK(FM)—See Gurdon

KZHS(AM)— Mar 10, 1953: 590 khz; 5 kw-D, 67 w-N. TL: N34 29 55 W92 58 45. Stereo. Hrs open: Box 21430, 71903. Phone: (501) 525-4600. Fax: (501) 525-4344. Licensee: Noalmark Broadcasting Corp. (acq 12-13-2004; $140,000). Population served: 35,631 Natl. Network: Fox Sports, . Format: News/talk, sports. ♦Eddie Tarpley, gen mgr.

KZNG(AM)— Jan 1, 1953: 1340 khz; 1 kw-U. TL: N34 29 43 W93 01 27. Hrs open: 24 125 Corporate Terr., 71913-7248. Phone: (501) 525-9700. Fax: (501) 525-9739. Web Site:www.newstalk1340.com Licensee: US Stations LLC. Group owner: Powell Broadcasting (acq 2-1-2005; grpsl). Population served: 138,000 Natl. Network: ABC, Premiere Radio Networks, Westwood One, . Ark. Radio Net. Wire Svc: AP Format: News/talk. News staff: one; News: 10 hrs wkly. Target aud: 18 plus. ♦Gary Terrell, gen mgr, chief of engrg; Neal Gladner, opns dir & gen sls mgr; Craig Dale, progmg dir; Melissa Walters, traf mgr.

Hot Springs Village

KVRE(FM)— February 1994: 92.9 mhz; 25 kw. Ant 328 ft TL: N34 38 34 W93 04 08. Hrs open: 24 122 DeSoto Center Dr., 71909. Phone: (501) 922-5678. Phone: (501) 922-5880. Fax: (501) 922-6626.E-mail: kvre@kvre.com Licensee: Caddo Broadcasting Co. Natl. Network: Music of Your Life, . Format: Adult standards. Target aud: 35 plus; general. ♦Polly Nichols, gen mgr; Alice Bates, opns dir; Cyrie Wright, gen sls mgr; Tom Nichols, opns dir & progmg dir; John Chapman, news dir.

Hoxie

KJLV(FM)— Jan 20, 1988: 105.3 mhz; 25 kw. 328 ft TL: N36 02 24 W90 59 11. Hrs open: 24 2351 Sunset Blvd., Suite 170-218, Rocklin, CA, 95765. Phone: (707) 528-9236. Fax: (707) 528-9246. Fax: (916) 251-1650. Web Site:www.klove.com Licensee: Educational Media Foundation. Group owner: EMF Broadcasting (acq 11-1-01; $1.3 million with KJBR(FM) Marked Tree). Population served: 100,000 Format: Contemp Christian. ♦Richard Jenkins, pres, gen mgr; Mike Novak, VP; Keith Whipple, dev dir; David Pierce, progmg mgr; Ed Lenane, news dir; Sam Wallington, engrg dir; Karen Johnson, news rptr.

Humnoke

KVLO(FM)— 1996: 101.7 mhz; 6 kw. 100 ft TL: N34 32 58 W91 45 26. Hrs open: 700 Wellington Hill Rd., Little Rock, 72211. Phone: (501) 401-0200. Fax: (501) 401-0366. Licensee: The Last Bastion Station Trust LLC, as Trustee Group owner: Citadel Broadcasting Corp. (acq 6-12-2007; grpsl). Rgnl. Network: Simulcast of KARN Format: Gospel. ♦Jim Beard, VP, gen mgr & mktg mgr.

Huntsville

KAKS(FM)— 1955: 99.5 mhz; 13.5 kw. Ant 443 ft TL: N36 07 37 W93 51 57. Hrs open: 70 N. East St., Fayetteville, 72701. Phone: (479) 443-9960. Licensee: Davidson Media Station KREB-FM Licensee LLC. (acq 2-10-2005; $3.9 million with KCZZ(AM) Mission, KS). Population served: 315,000 Natl. Network: ABC, . Format: Sp. Target aud: 25-54; general. ♦Steve Butler, gen mgr.

Jacksonville

KDJE(FM)— Sept 29, 1969: 100.3 mhz; 82.9 kw. 1,054 ft TL: N34 47 53 W92 29 33. Stereo. Hrs open: 24 10800 Colonel Glenn Rd., Little Rock, 72204. Phone: (501) 217-5000. Fax: (501) 228-9547.E-mail: q100@q100fm.com Web Site:www.q1003theedge.com Licensee: CC Licenses LLC. Group owner: Clear Channel Communications Inc. (acq 5-15-96; grpsl). Population served: 500,000 Natl. Rep: Clear Channel,. Arent, Fox, Kintner, Plotkin & Kahn. Format: Alternative rock. News staff: one; News: 3 hrs wkly. Target aud: 18-49. ♦Jeff Peterson, opns dir, progmg dir; Joe Rook, gen sls mgr.

Jonesboro

***KAOG(FM)**— 1999: 90.5 mhz; 1 kw. 243 ft TL: N35 53 06 W90 42 38. Hrs open: Box 2440, American Family Radio, Tupelo, MS, 38803. Phone: (662) 844-8888. Fax: (662) 842-6791. Web Site:www.afr.net Licensee: American Family Association. Group owner: American Family Radio Format: Relg. ♦Marvin Sanders, gen mgr; John Riley, progmg dir; Joey Moody, chief of engrg.

***KASU**— May 17, 1957: 91.9 mhz; 100 kw. 689 ft TL: N35 53 27 W90 40 26. Stereo. Hrs open: 24 Box 2160, Arkansas State University, 104 Cooley, State University, 72467. Phone: (870) 972-2200. Phone: (870) 972-3070. Fax: (870) 972-2997.E-mail: kasu@astate.edu Web Site:www.kasu.org Licensee: Arkansas State University. Population served: 200,000 Natl. Network: PRI, NPR, . Wire Svc: AP Format: News, classical, jazz. News staff: one; News: 45 hrs wkly. Target aud: General. Spec prog: New age, blues, folk 4 hrs, big band 2 hrs wkly. ♦Micheal Doyle, stn mgr; June Taylor, opns mgr; Todd Rutledge, dev dir; Marty Scarbrough, progmg dir; Greg Chance, news dir; Eddy Arnold, chief of engrg.

KBTM(AM)— Mar 15, 1930: 1230 khz; 1 kw-U. TL: N35 50 27 W90 39 44. Hrs open: 24 Prog sep from FM Box 1737, 72403-1737. Secondary address: 407 W. Parker Rd. 72404. Phone: (870) 935-5598. Fax: (870) 932-3814. Licensee: Capstar TX L.P. Population served: 500,000 Rgnl. Network: Ark. Radio Net. Ark. Radio Net. Format: News/talk. News staff: 2; News: 14 hrs wkly. Target aud: 45 plus; upscale adults. ♦Kevin Box, stn mgr & prom mgr; Janice Reid, traf mgr; Barbara Nelson, min affrs dir.

KEGI(FM)— Nov 21, 1986: 100.5 mhz; 38 kw. Ant 558 ft TL: N35 56 59 W90 39 58. Stereo. Hrs open: 24 314 Union Ave., 72401. Phone: (870) 933-8800. Fax: (870) 933-0403.E-mail: trey@triplefm.com Web Site:eagle1005.com Licensee: Saga Communications of Arkansas LLC. Group owner: Saga Communications Inc. (acq 11-8-2002; grpsl). Format: Classic hits. News staff: one; News: one hr wkly. Target aud:

18-49. ♦Trey Stafford, CEO, pres, CFO & gen mgr; Kevin Neathery, sls dir; Bill Pressly, progmg VP; Rick Christian, progmg dir; Al Simpson, chief of engrg; James Dean, traf mgr.

KFIN(FM)— Mar 4, 1974: 107.9 mhz; 100 kw. Ant 600 ft TL: N35 47 56 W90 44 31. Stereo. Hrs open: 24 Box 1737, 72403-1737. Secondary address: 407 W. Parker Rd. 72404. Phone: (870) 932-8400. Fax: (870) 932-3814.E-mail: info@kfin.com Web Site:www.kfin.com Licensee: Capstar TX L.P. Group owner: Clear Channel Communications Inc. (acq 1-18-01; grpsl). Population served: 400,000 Wiley, Rein & Fielding. Format: Country. News staff: one; News: 9 hrs wkly. Target aud: 25-54; broad demographics. Spec prog: Farm 13 hrs wkly. ♦Scott Silar, gen mgr; Brandon Baxter, opns mgr; Dennis Rogers, news dir.

KIYS(FM)— 1947: 101.9 mhz; 100 kw. 1,059 ft TL: N35 57 14 W90 41 41. Stereo. Hrs open: 24 Box 1737, 72403-1737. Secondary address: 407 W. Parker Rd 72404. Phone: (870) 935-5598. Fax: (870) 932-3814. Web Site:www.1019kiysfm.com Licensee: Capstar TX L.P. Group owner: Clear Channel Communications Inc. (acq 1-18-01; grpsl). Population served: 400,000 Fisher, Wayland, Cooper, Leader & Zaragoza. Format: CHR. Target aud: 18-49; middle to upper middle income. ♦Larry James, CEO, gen mgr; Katy Wiliamson, VP, sls dir; Duce Foreman, mktg dir, prom dir; Kevin Box, progmg dir; Troy Owens, engrg VP & chief of engrg; Janice Reed, traf mgr, farm dir.

KJBX(FM)—(Trumann, February 1991: 106.7 mhz; 6 kw. 328 ft TL: N35 44 51 W90 37 49. Stereo. Hrs open: 24 314 Union Ave., 72401. Phone: (870) 933-8800. Fax: (870) 933-0403.E-mail: trey@triplefm.com Web Site:www.themix1067.com Licensee: Saga Communications of Arkansas LLC. Group owner: Saga Communications Inc. (acq 11-8-02; grpsl). Population served: 120,000 Format: Adult contemp. News: 2 hrs wkly. Target aud: 25-54; women. ♦Bill Pressly, pres, stn mgr; Trey Stafford, pres, CFO & gen mgr; Kevin Neathery, sls VP, sls dir; Al Simpson, chief of engrg; James Dean, traf mgr.

***KJSB(FM)**— 2009: 88.3 mhz; 1.9 kw vert. Ant 298 ft TL: N35 48 36 W90 48 45. Hrs open:
Rebroadcasts WAFR(FM) Tupelo, MS 100%.
Drawer 2440, Tupelo, MS, 38803. Phone: (662) 844-8888. Fax: (662) 842-6791. Web Site:www.afr.net Licensee: American Family Association. (acq 3-31-2008). Natl. Network: American Family Radio, . Format: Christian. ♦Donald E. Wildmon, chmn.

KNEA(AM)— Sept 20, 1950: 970 khz; 1 kw-D, 41 w-N. TL: N35 51 17 W90 43 40. Hrs open: 24 Box 1737, 72403. Phone: (870) 932-8400. Fax: (870) 932-3814. Web Site:www.knea970.com Licensee: CC Licenses LLC. Group owner: Clear Channel Communications Inc. (acq 6-13-2002; $2.05 million with KWHF(FM) Harrisburg). Population served: 500,000 Rgnl. Network: Ark. Radio Net. Ark. Radio Net. Format: Gospel. News staff: 5. Target aud: General. Spec prog: Farm 6 hrs wkly. ♦Scott Silar, gen mgr; Ray Sharp, gen sls mgr, progmg dir; Dennis Rogers, news dir.

Judsonia

KVHU(FM)— 2006: 95.3 mhz; 14 kw. Ant 440 ft TL: N35 13 41 W91 29 19. Stereo. Hrs open: 24 Box 10765, Searcy, 72149-0765. Phone: (501) 279-4886. Fax: (501) 279-5152.E-mail: kvhu@harding.edu Web Site:www.kvhu.net Licensee: George S. Flinn Jr. Format: Classic hits. Target aud: 35+. ♦Dutch Hoggatt, gen mgr.

Kensett

KFXV(FM)— 2007: 105.7 mhz; 15 kw. Ant 426 ft TL: N35 17 20 W91 46 17. Hrs open: 401 S. Spring St., Searcy, 72143. Phone: (501) 268-9700. Licensee: Malvern Entertainment Corp. Format: Hot adult contemp. ♦Scott A. Gray, pres; Amber Carson, gen mgr.

Lake City

KDXY(FM)—Licensed to Lake City. See Paragould

Lake Village

KUUZ(FM)— July 30, 1977: 95.9 mhz; 20 kw. Ant 302 ft TL: N33 20 07 W91 07 33. Stereo. Hrs open: 24 Box 262550, Baton Rouge, LA, 70826. Secondary address: 8919 World Ministry Ave. , Baton Rouge, LA 70810. Phone: (225) 768-3688. Phone: (225) 768-8300. Fax: (225) 768-3729.E-mail: kawikfish@yahoo.com Web Site:www.jsm.org Licensee: Family Worship Center Church Inc. (group owner; acq 6-12-02; $500,000). Population served: 100,000 Format: Relg. ♦David Whitelaw, COO; Jimmy Swaggart, pres; John Santiago, gen mgr & progmg mgr.

KZYQ(FM)— Dec 24, 1995: 103.5 mhz; 25 kw. Ant 328 ft TL: N33 17 04 W91 13 03. Stereo. Hrs open: 24 Box 1438, Cleveland, MS, 38732. Phone: (662) 378-4103. Fax: (662) 332-3103 . Licensee: M.R.S. Ventures Inc. (group owner; (acq 11-1-2003; grpsl). Population served: 135,000 Natl. Network: Jones Radio Networks, . Wood, Maines & Brown. Format: Urban contemp. Target aud: 25-54; adults.

Lakeview

KKTZ(FM)— May 1, 1999: 93.5 mhz; 25 kw. 328 ft TL: N36 31 22 W92 40 08. Hrs open: 2352 Hwy. 62B, Mountain Home, 72653. Phone: (870) 492-6022. Fax: (870) 492-2137.E-mail: radio@mountainhome.com Web Site:www.twinlakesradio.com Licensee: John M. Dowdy. Format: Hot adult contemp. Target aud: 24-25. ♦Morgan Dowdy, CEO, pres, gen mgr; Stewart Brunner, VP; Roger Lowery, stn mgr.

Little Rock

KAAY(AM)— Dec 20, 1924: 1090 khz; 50 kw-U, DA-N. TL: N34 46 20 W92 13 30. Hrs open: 700 Wellington Hills Rd., 72211. Phone: (501) 401-0200. Fax: (501) 401-0387.E-mail: info@1060kaay.com Web Site:www.1060kaay.com Licensee: Citadel Broadcasting Co. Group owner: Citadel Broadcasting Corp. (acq 9-30-98; $5 million). Population served: 318,800 Natl. Network: USA, . Latham & Watkins. Format: Relg, southern gospel. Spec prog: Sp 2 hrs wkly. ♦Joe Booker, opns mgr; John Scuderi, gen sls mgr; Jim Beard, mktg mgr.

***KABF(FM)**— Sept 31, 1984: 88.3 mhz; 91 kw. 777 ft TL: N34 47 31 W92 28 38. Stereo. Hrs open: 24 2101 S. Main St., 72206. Phone: (501) 372-6119. Fax: (501) 376-3952.E-mail: kabf@acorn.org Licensee: Arkansas Broadcasting Foundation. Population served: 50,000 Format: Black, jazz, gospel, diversified. News staff: one; News: 12 hrs wkly. Target aud: General; low-moderate income & politically disenfranchised. Spec prog: Sp 10 hrs, folk 10 hrs, American Indian 3 hrs, bluegrass 6 hrs, Caribbean 4 hrs, talk 10 hrs wkly. ♦Pat House, gen mgr; John Cain, stn mgr, progmg dir.

KABZ(FM)— 1967: 103.7 mhz; 100 kw. 1,510 ft TL: N34 47 55 W92 29 58. Stereo. Hrs open: 24 2400 Cottondale Ln., 72202. Phone: (501) 661-1037. Fax: (501) 664-5871. Web Site:www.1037thebuzz.com Licensee: Signal Media of Arkansas Inc. (acq 12-20-93; $2 million; 1-10-94). Population served: 993,600 Natl. Network: Westwood One, ESPN Radio, . Duane Morris LLP. Format: Talk. News staff: one; News: 10 hrs wkly. Target aud: 18-49. ♦Philip Jonsson, pres; Steve Jonsson, gen mgr; Lindy Blackstone, prom dir; Justin Acri, progmg dir.

KARN(AM)— 1928: 920 khz; 5 kw-U, DA-N. TL: N34 46 20 W92 09 30. Hrs open: 24 700 Wellington Hills Rd., 72211. Phone: (501) 401-0200. Fax: (501) 401-0387.E-mail: karn@karnnewsradio.com Web Site:www.920karn.com Licensee: Citadel Broadcasting Co. Group owner: Citadel Broadcasting Corp. (acq 8-27-97; grpsl). Population served: 480,000 Natl. Network: Fox Sports, . Rgnl. Network: Ark. Radio Net. Format: Sports. Target aud: 35-64. ♦Jim Beard, gen mgr & mktg mgr.

KDIS-FM— Aug 14, 1992: 99.5 mhz; 3 kw. Ant 312 ft TL: N34 45 58 W92 17 38. (CP: 6 kw). Hrs open: 415 N. McKinley, Suite 610, 72205. Phone: (501) 663-3300. Fax: (501) 663-3723.E-mail: info@kdis.com Web Site:www.radiodisney.com Licensee: Radio Disney Group LLC. Group owner: ABC Inc. (acq 5-30-03; $2.56 million). Format: Children. ♦John Campbell, stn mgr; Lauren Eddins, gen mgr & prom mgr.

KDJE(FM)—See Jacksonville

KIPR(FM)—See Pine Bluff

KJBN(AM)— 1946: 1050 khz; 1 kw-D, 19 w-N. TL: N34 45 57 W92 17 39. Hrs open: 1800 Maple St., Suite 300, North Little Rock, 72114. Phone: (501) 791-1000. Fax: (501) 791-7121. Licensee: Joshua Ministries and Community Development Corp. (acq 8-26-92; $250,000; 9-21-92). Population served: 60,040 Format: Contemp gospel music, teaching. Target aud: Career-oriented people. ♦Veronica Ayers, gen mgr, gen sls mgr & prom mgr.

KKPT(FM)— Oct 26, 1960: 94.1 mhz; 100 kw. 1,601 ft TL: N34 47 56 W92 29 41. Stereo. Hrs open: 24 2400 Cottondale Ln., 72202. Phone: (501) 664-9410. Fax: (501) 664-5871. Web Site:www.kkpt.com Licensee: Signal Media of Arkansas. (acq 4-30-85; $2.75 million; 3-11-85). Population served: 410,000 Natl. Rep: D & R Radio,. Wire Svc: AP Format: Classic hits. News staff: one; News: one hr wkly. Target aud: 25-54; adults. ♦Philip Jonsson, pres; Mike Kennedy, gen mgr, progmg; Chuck Gatlin, prom dir.

***KLRE-FM**— February 1973: 90.5 mhz; 40 kw. 265 ft TL: N34 40 29 W92 19 04. Stereo. Hrs open: 24 2801 S. University Ave., 72204. Phone: (501) 569-8485. Fax: (501) 569-8488. Web Site:www.ualr.edu Licensee: University of Arkansas. (acq 7-95). Population served: 1,000,000 Natl. Network: PRI, NPR, . Cohn & Marks. Format: Class. Target aud: 35-54. ♦Ben Fry, gen mgr, stn mgr; Mary Waldo, dev dir; Ron Dreeding, progmg dir.

KLRG(AM)—(Sheridan, March 1982: 880 khz; 50 kw-D, 220 w-N. TL: N34 41 36 W92 18 21 (D), N34 18 21 W92 23 06 (N). Hrs open: 24 10000 Warden Rd., North Little Rock, 72120. Phone: (501) 985-0880. Fax: (501) 985-0260. Licensee: Wagenvoord Advertising Group Inc. (group owner; (acq 8-5-2009; $225,000). Natl. Network: Salem Radio Network, . Format: Southern gospel. Target aud: WF 35-64. ♦Larry Skinner, gen mgr, chief of opns; Paula Johnson, disc jockey; Ed Roupe, sls.

KMJX(FM)—See Conway

KPZK(AM)— 1929: 1250 khz; 2.5 kw-D, 1.2 kw-N, DA-2. TL: N34 42 05 W92 13 02. Hrs open: 24 700 Wellington Hills Rd., 72211. Phone: (501) 401-0200. Fax: (501) 401-0366. Licensee: Citadel Broadcasting Co. Group owner: Citadel Broadcasting Corp. (acq 9-19-97; grpsl). Population served: 167,000 Natl. Rep: D & R Radio,. Format: Gospel. News staff: one. Target aud: 50 plus. ♦Jim Beard, mktg mgr.

KSSN(FM)— 1966: 95.7 mhz; 92 kw. 1,663 ft TL: N34 47 57 W92 29 29. Stereo. Hrs open: 24 10800 Colonel Glenn Rd., 72204. Phone: (501) 217-5000. Fax: (501) 228-9547.E-mail: kssn@cei.net Web Site:www.kssn.com Licensee: CC Licenses LLC. Clear Channel Communications Inc. (acq 9-12-97; grpsl). Population served: 490,000 Natl. Rep: Clear Channel,. Format: Contemp country. News staff: one; News: 2 hrs wkly. Target aud: 25-54. ♦Chad Heritage, opns dir, progmg dir; Kevin Waltman, gen sls mgr.

KTUV(AM)— October 1956: 1440 khz; 5 kw-D, 240 w-N. TL: N34 42 46 W92 16 48. Hrs open: 24 723 W. Daisy Bates Dr., 72202. Phone: (501) 375-1440. Fax: (877) 426-1447.E-mail: kita1440@earthlink.net Licensee: Birach Broadcasting Corp. (acq 1-31-2008; $1.5 million with KJMU(AM) Sand Springs, OK). Population served: 450,000 Edmundson & Edmundson. Format: Sp.

***KUAR(FM)**— Sept 16, 1986: 89.1 mhz; 100 kw. 882 ft TL: N34 47 50 W92 29 26. Stereo. Hrs open: 24 2801 S. University Ave., 72204. Phone: (501) 569-8485. Fax: (501) 569-8488. Web Site:www.ualr.edu Licensee: Board of Trustees of the University of Arkansas. Natl. Network: NPR, PRI, . Cohn & Marks. Format: News/talk, jazz. News staff: one; News: 86 hrs wkly. Target aud: 35-54. Spec prog: Folk 3 hrs wkly. ♦Ben Fry, gen mgr, stn mgr; Mary Waldo, dev dir.

KURB(FM)— July 7, 1972: 98.5 mhz; 99 kw. 1,286 ft TL: N34 47 56 W92 29 44. Stereo. Hrs open: 24 700 Wellington Hills Rd., 72211. Phone: (501) 401-0200. Fax: (501) 401-0349.E-mail: info@b98.com Web Site:www.b98.com Licensee: Citadel Broadcasting Co. Group owner: Citadel Broadcasting Corp. Format: Hot adult contemp. ♦Jim Beard, gen sls mgr & mktg mgr.

Lonoke

KOLL(FM)— June 1982: 106.3 mhz; 50 kw. Ant 492 ft TL: N34 46 30 W91 53 33. Hrs open: 400 Hardin Rd., Suite 150, Little Rock, 72211. Phone: (501) 219-1919. Fax: (501) 225-4610.E-mail: donburns@crainmedia.com Web Site:www.koll1063.com Licensee: Crain Media Group LLC. Group owner: Archway Broadcasting Group (acq 2-1-2008; grpsl). Population served: 500,000 Format: Oldies. ♦David Roederer, gen mgr; Don Burns, progmg dir.

Lowell

KMXF(FM)— June 30, 1992: 101.9 mhz; 23 kw. Ant 708 ft TL: N36 26 28 W93 58 22. Stereo. Hrs open: 24 Box 8190, Fayetteville, 72703. Phone: (479) 442-0102. Fax: (479) 587-8255. Web Site:www.hotmix1019.com Licensee: Capstar TX L.P. Group owner: Clear Channel Communications Inc. (acq 8-30-00; grpsl). Population served: 331,000 Dow, Lohnes & Albertson. Wire Svc: AP Format: CHR. News staff: one; News: one hr wkly. Target aud: 18-34; women. ♦Tony Beringer, gen mgr; Dave Ashcraft, opns mgr; Jay Steele, progmg dir.

Magnolia

KVMA(AM)— April 1948: 630 khz; 1 kw-D. TL: N33 17 59 W93 13 57. Hrs open: 24 Box 430, 71754. Secondary address: 131 S. Jackson 71753. Phone: (870) 234-5862. Fax: (870) 234-5865.E-mail: kvmakvmz@suddenlinkmail.com Web Site:www.magnoliaradio.com

Licensee: Noalmark Broadcasting Corp. (acq 8-1-2005; $165,000). Population served: 50,000 Natl. Network: ABC, . Rgnl. Network: Ark. Radio Net. Ark. Radio Net. Borsari & Paxson. Format: C&W/Talk. News: 20 hrs wkly. Target aud: General. Spec prog: Farm 2 hrs wkly. ◆William C. Nolan Jr., pres; Ed Alderson, VP; Ken W. Sibley, gen mgr; Dan Gregory, opns dir.

KZHE(FM)—See Stamps

Malvern

KBOK(AM)— August 1951: 1310 khz; 1 kw-D. TL: N34 22 25 W92 49 52. Hrs open: Sunrise-sunset 302 S. Main St., 72104. Phone: (501) 332-6981. Phone: (501) 332-6982. Fax: (501) 332-6984. Licensee: Noalmark Broadcasting Corp. (group owner; acq 4-1-03; $62,500). Population served: 30,000 Rgnl. Network: Ark. Radio Net. Ark. Radio Net. Format: News, traditional country. News: 20 hrs wkly. Target aud: General. Spec prog: Talk 6 hrs, gospel 8 hrs wkly. ◆Malia Brown, gen mgr.

KKSP(FM)—(Bryant, April 1989: 93.3 mhz; 5.6 kw. Ant 699 ft TL: N34 47 31 W92 28 38. Stereo. Hrs open: 24 400 Hardin Rd., Suite 150, Little Rock, 72211. Phone: (501) 219-1919. Fax: (501) 225-4610.E-mail: donburns@crainmedia.com Web Site:www.spirit933.com Licensee: Crain Media Group LLC. (acq 2-1-2008; grpsl). Population served: 250,000 Format: Contemp Christian. ◆Don Burns, progmg dir.

KLEZ(FM)— Apr 1, 1991: 101.5 mhz; 6 kw. Ant 322 ft TL: N34 28 24 W92 55 51. Stereo. Hrs open: 24 208 Buena Vista Rd., Hot Springs, 71913. Phone: (501) 525-4600. Fax: (501) 525-4344.E-mail: pob@klaz.com Web Site:www.klez.com Licensee: Noalmark Broadcasting Corp. (group owner; acq 1-21-2003; $437,500). Population served: 120,000 Miller & Miller, P.C. Format: Easy lstng. News: 3 hrs wkly. Target aud: 35-60. ◆William C. Nolan Jr., pres; Brad Hutcheson, gen mgr, stn mgr; Kevin Krebbs, gen sls mgr; Larry K, progmg dir; Doc Bryce, chief of engrg.

Mammoth Spring

KALM(AM)—See Thayer, MO

KAMS(FM)— Jan 1, 1956: 95.1 mhz; 100 kw. 650 ft TL: N36 32 58 W91 33 05. Stereo. Hrs open: 24 Box 193, 72554. Secondary address: N. Hwy. 63, Thayer, MO 65791. Phone: (417) 264-7211. Fax: (417) 264-7212.E-mail: kkountry@kkountry.com Web Site:www.kkountry.com Licensee: E-Communications LLC (acq 4-24-2008; $830,000 with KALM(AM) Thayer, MO). Population served: 360,000 Greg Skall. Format: Today's country/True Country. News staff: one; News: 11 hrs wkly. Target aud: General. ◆Robert Eckman, pres & gen mgr.

Marianna

KAKJ(FM)— 1994: 105.3 mhz; 6 kw. Ant 328 ft TL: N34 47 14 W90 46 03. Stereo. Hrs open: 24
Rebroadcasts KCLT(FM) West Helena 90%.
Box 2870, West Helena, 72390. Phone: (870) 572-9506. Phone: (870) 633-9000. Fax: (870) 572-1845.E-mail: force2@sbcglobal.net Web Site:www.force2radio.com Licensee: Raymond & L.T. Simes II. Population served: 1,200,000 Natl. Network: ABC, . Rgnl. Network: Ark. Radio Net. Format: Black, urban contemp. News staff: one. Target aud: All ages. ◆L.T. Simes II, VP; Elaine Simes, stn mgr; Larry Evans, opns mgr; Raymond Simes, pres, gen mgr & gen sls mgr; Elaine Sims, mktg dir; Peter Turner, prom dir, progmg dir.

Marion

KXHT(FM)— February 1986: 107.1 mhz; 3 kw. Ant 328 ft TL: N35 09 23 W90 05 46. (CP: 2.75 kw, ant 479 ft.). Hrs open: 6080 Mt. Mariah Rd. Ext., Memphis, TN, 38115. Phone: (901) 375-9324. Fax: (901) 375-9331.E-mail: info@kxht.com Web Site:www.flinn.com Licensee: Flinn Broadcasting Corp. Format: Rap, hip hop. ◆Lloyd Hetzer, gen mgr; Duane Hargrove, stn mgr.

Marked Tree

KJBR(FM)— 1993: 93.7 mhz; 3 kw. Ant 288 ft TL: N35 32 22 W90 26 35. Hrs open: 24 2351 Sunset Blvd., Suite 170-218, Rocklin, CA, 95765. Phone: (916) 251-1600. Fax: (916) 251-1650. Web Site:www.klove.com Licensee: Educational Media Foundation. Group owner: EMF Broadcasting (acq 11-1-01; $1.3 million with KJLV(FM) Hoxie). Population served: 250,000 Natl. Network: Air 1, . Format: Contemp Christian. ◆Richard Jenkins, pres; Mike Novak, VP; Keith

Whipple, dev dir; Eric Allen, natl sls mgr; David Pierce, progmg mgr; Ed Lenane, news dir; Sam Wallington, engrg dir; Karen Johnson, news rptr.

Marshall

KBCN-FM— Apr 25, 1983: 104.3 mhz; 100 kw. 820 ft TL: N35 52 17 W92 39 10. (CP: Ant 1,016 ft.). Stereo. Hrs open: 24 100 Blue Bird St., Harrison, 72601. Phone: (870) 743-1157. Fax: (870) 743-1168. Licensee: Pearson Broadcasting of Marshall Inc. Group owner: Pearson Broadcasting (acq 4-30-93; $450,000; 5-24-93). Format: Country. ◆David Fransen, gen mgr.

***CAV(FM)**— 2009: 90.3 mhz; 57 w. Ant 676 ft TL: N35 52 16 W92 39 10. Hrs open: 126 S. Church St., Mountain Home, 72653. Phone: (870) 425-2525. Fax: (870) 424-2626. Web Site:www.kcmhradio.com Licensee: Christian Broadcasting Group of Mountain Home Inc. ◆Carl Albright, pres; Lorra Shaw, stn mgr.

KCGS(AM)— May 24, 1975: 960 khz; 5 kw-D. TL: N35 54 56 W92 38 20. Hrs open: 24 Box 1044, 72650. Secondary address: 208 Battle St. 72650. Phone: (870) 448-5567. Fax: (870) 448-5384.E-mail: kcgs@alltel.net Web Site:www.kcgs.com Licensee: Southland Broadcasting Corp. (acq 8-20-2003). Population served: 71,550 Natl. Network: USA, . Format: Bluegrass gospel. News staff: 2; News: 10 hrs wkly. Target aud: General. Spec prog: Bible answers live 7 hrs wkly. ◆ Karl Leukert, gen mgr, opns VP; Ronald Woolsey, pres, dev VP & sls VP.

Marvell

***LMK(FM)**— 1999: 90.7 mhz; 50 kw. Ant 495 ft TL: N34 36 29 W90 58 47. Stereo. Hrs open: 24
Rebroadcasts KLVR(FM) Middletown, CA 100%.
2351 Sunset Blvd., Suite 170-218, Rocklin, CA, 95765. Phone: (916) 251-1600. Fax: (916) 251-1650. Web Site:www.klove.com Licensee: Educational Media Foundation. (acq 8-28-2007; $300,000). Natl. Network: K-Love, . Format: Contemp Christian. ◆Mike Novak, sr VP.

Maumelle

KHLR(FM)— 1971: 94.9 mhz; 96 kw. Ant 1,843 ft TL: N34 26 31 W92 13 03. Stereo. Hrs open: 24 10800 Colonel Glenn Rd., Little Rock, 72204. Phone: (501) 217-5000. Fax: (501) 228-9547. Web Site:www.949tomfm.com Licensee: CC Licenses LLC. Group owner: Clear Channel Communications Inc. (acq 9-12-97; grpsl). Natl. Rep: D & R Radio,. Format: Adult hits. News staff: one; News: 5 hrs wkly. Target aud: 25-54; baby boomers. ◆Kim Pyle, gen mgr; Jeff Peterson, opns dir; Keli Williams, gen sls mgr; Torrez Harris, progmg dir.

KWLR(FM)— 1998: 96.9 mhz; 4.6 kw. 377 ft TL: N34 53 33 W92 24 50. Hrs open: 5700 West Oaks Blvd., Rocklin, CA, 95765. Phone: (707) 528-9236. Fax: (707) 528-9246.E-mail: kwlrword97@aol.com Web Site:www.klove.com Licensee: Flinn Broadcasting Corp. Format: Contemp inspirational.

Mayflower

***KJSM-FM**—(Augusta, Aug 27, 1979: 97.7 mhz; 100 kw. Ant 620 ft TL: N35 10 36 W91 23 49. Stereo. Hrs open: Box 262550, Baton Rouge, LA, 70826. Secondary address: 8919 World Ministry Ave., Baton Rouge, LA 70810. Phone: (225) 768-3688. Phone: (225) 768-8300.E-mail: kawikfish@yahoo.com Web Site:www.jsm.org Licensee: Family Worship Center Church Inc. (group owner; acq 3-4-2003; $2.75 million). Population served: 55,000 Format: Christian. ◆David Whitelaw, COO, gen mgr; Jimmy Swaggart, pres; John Santiago, progmg dir.

McGehee

KVSA(AM)— June 29, 1953: 1220 khz; 1 kw-D, 54 w-N. TL: N33 33 39 W91 23 06. Hrs open: 6 AM-6:30 PM Box 110, Hwy. 65, 71654. Phone: (870) 222-4200. Phone: (870) 538-5200. Fax: (870) 538-3389.E-mail: kvsa1220@yahoo.com Licensee: Southeast Arkansas Broadcasters Inc. Population served: 60,000 Natl. Rep: Keystone (unwired net),. Ark. Radio Net. Format: Div. News staff: 2; News: 10 hrs wkly. Spec prog: Farm 5 hrs wkly. ◆Dale Jones, progmg dir, sls, mktg; Joyce Kinney, pres, gen mgr, sls & mktg.

Melbourne

***KLRM(FM)**— 2008: 90.7 mhz; 7 kw vert. Ant 617 ft TL: N36 05 31 W92 15 46. Hrs open:
Rebroadcasts KLVR(FM) Middletown, CA 100%.

5700 West Oaks Blvd., Rocklin, CA, 95765. Phone: (916) 251-1600. Fax: (916) 251-1650. Web Site:www.klove.com Licensee: Educational Media Foundation. (acq 3-23-2007). grpsl). Natl. Network: K-Love, . Format: Contemp Christian. ◆Richard Jenkins, pres.

Mena

KENA(AM)— July 1950: 1450 khz; 1 kw-U. TL: N34 34 23 W94 14 55. Hrs open: 24 Box 1450, 71953. Secondary address: 1600 S. Reine St. 71953. Phone: (479) 394-1450. Licensee: Ouachita Broadcasting Inc. (acq 1-14-99; $750,000 with co-located FM). Population served: 5,000 Format: Gospel. News staff: one; News: 10 hrs wkly. Target aud: 18 plus; industrial & agricultural workers, retirees, tourists & professionals. ◆Dwight Douglas, gen mgr, stn mgr, mktg dir; Sue Canner, prom dir & mus dir; Matt Stone, news dir, local news ed, news rptr.

KENA-FM— 1969: 102.1 mhz; 12.5 kw. Ant 469 ft TL: N34 32 42 W94 18 21. Hrs open: 24 Box 1450, 71953. Secondary address: 1600 S. Reine St. 71953. Phone: (479) 394-1450. Licensee: Ouachita Broadcasting Inc. Population served: 60,000 Natl. Network: ABC, . Format: Country. News staff: one; News: 6 hrs wkly. ◆Dwight Douglas, stn mgr, opns mgr, progmg mgr; Bevona Williams, traf mgr; Matt Stone, local news ed & news rptr; Curt Teasdale, disc jockey.

KQOR(FM)— 2001: 105.3 mhz; 8.1 kw. 564 ft TL: N34 36 31 W94 12 19. Hrs open: Box 1450, 71953. Phone: (479) 394-1450. Licensee: Ouachita Broadcasting Inc. (acq 3-8-99). Format: Oldies. ◆Dwight Douglas, gen mgr & opns mgr.

KTTG(FM)— December 1994: 96.3 mhz; 100 kw. 1,314 ft TL: N34 36 40 W94 16 20. Stereo. Hrs open: 24 2937 Hwy. 71 N., 71953. Phone: (479) 394-6198. Fax: (479) 784-7290.E-mail: info@kttg.com Web Site:www.espnradio.com Licensee: Pearson Broadcasting of Mena Inc. Group owner: Pearson Broadcasting (acq 1995; $175,000). Population served: 150,000 Natl. Network: ESPN Radio, . Natl. Rep: ABC Radio Sales,. Format: Sports, talk. News staff: one. Target aud: 18-49. ◆Max Pearson, CEO, chmn; Bruce Hale, CFO; Tommy Craft, gen mgr; Jason Wade, progmg dir.

Monticello

KGPQ(FM)— May 1, 1997: 99.9 mhz; 25 kw. 328 ft TL: N33 43 25 W91 48 28. Hrs open: 279 Midway Rt., 71655. Phone: (870) 367-8525. Fax: (870) 367-9564.E-mail: pinesradio@sbcglobal.net Licensee: Pines Broadcasting Inc. (acq 3-14-2007; grpsl). Format: Adult contemp. ◆Jimmy Sledge, pres & gen mgr.

KHBM(AM)— April 1955: 1430 khz; 1 kw-D, 30 w-N. TL: N33 36 18 W91 47 14. Hrs open: 24 279 Midway Rte, AZ, 71655-8605. Phone: (870) 367-6854. Fax: (870) 367-9564.E-mail: pinesradio@sbcglobal.net Licensee: Pines Broadcasting Inc. (group owner; acq 3-14-2007; grpsl). Population served: 76,388 Rgnl. Network: Ark. Radio Net. Ark. Radio Net. Format: Music of Your Life. News staff: one; News: 10 hrs wkly. Target aud: General. ◆Jimmy Sledge, pres; Bonnie Ellis, gen mgr.

KHBM-FM— Sept 1, 1967: 93.7 mhz; 6 kw. 341 ft TL: N33 36 18 W91 47 14. (CP: 93.7 mhz, 25 kw). Stereo. Hrs open: 24 279 Midway Rt., 71655. Phone: (870) 367-6854. Fax: (870) 367-9564.E-mail: pinesradio@sbcglobal.net Licensee: Pines Broadcasting Inc. (acq 3-14-2007; grpsl). Rgnl. Network: Ark. Radio Net. Ark. Radio Net. Format: Classic Hits. News staff: one; News: 8 hrs wkly. ◆Jimmy Sledge, pres & gen mgr.

KXSA-FM—See Dermott

Morrilton

KVOM(AM)— Dec 25, 1952: 800 khz; 250 w-D, 42 w-N. TL: N35 09 32 W92 46 13. Hrs open: Box 541, 1835 Hwy. 113 W., 72110. Phone: (501) 354-2484. Fax: (501) 354-5629.E-mail: kvom@kvom.com Web Site:www.kvom.com Licensee: MMA License LLC. Group owner: MAX Media L.L.C. (acq 6-6-2003; grpsl). Population served: 125,000 Natl. Network: ESPN Radio, . Natl. Rep: Christal,. Ark. Radio Net. Wire Svc: AP Format: Sports. News staff: 2; News: 20 hrs wkly. Target aud: General. ◆Rich Moellers, gen mgr.

KVOM-FM— 1981: 101.7 mhz; 6 kw. Ant 226 ft TL: N35 09 32 W92 46 13. Stereo. Hrs open: 24 Prog sep from AM Box 541, 1835 Hwy. 113 W., 72110. Phone: (501) 354-2484. Fax: (501) 354-5629. Web Site:www.kvom.com Natl. Rep: Christal,. Format: Country. News staff: 2; News: 5 hrs wkly. Target aud: General. ◆Rich Moellers, gen mgr; Ken Eubanks, opns mgr.

Mountain Home

*KCMH(FM)— June 28, 1988: 91.5 mhz; 26 kw. Ant 472 ft TL: N36 16 17 W92 25 20. Stereo. Hrs open: 24 126 S. Church St., 72653. Phone: (870) 425-2525. Fax: (870) 424-2626.E-mail: lorra@kcmhradio.com Web Site:www.kcmhradio.com Licensee: Christian Broadcasting Group of Mountain Home Inc. Natl. Network: Moody, USA, . Format: Educ, relg. News: 9 hrs wkly. Target aud: General. ♦Carl Albright, pres; Lorra Shaw, stn mgr, progmg dir; Michael Coolidge, VP & opns VP.

KOMT(FM)— Oct 25, 1985: 107.5 mhz; 100 kw. Ant 1,017 ft TL: N36 29 13 W92 29 39. Hrs open: 24 2352 Hwy. 62 B, 72653. Phone: (870) 492-6022. Fax: (870) 492-2137.E-mail: radio @mountainhome.com Web Site:www.twinlakesradio.com Licensee: MAC Partners. Natl. Network: ABC, . Format: Adult contemp. Target aud: 25-54; females. ♦Morgan Dowdy, CEO; Stewart Brunner, VP & gen mgr; Roger Lowery, stn mgr, news dir.

KPFM(FM)— June 6, 1984: 105.5 mhz; 19 kw. Ant 797 ft TL: N36 29 13 W92 29 39. Stereo. Hrs open: 24 2352 Hwy. 62 B, 72653. Phone: (870) 492-6022. Fax: (870) 492-2137.E-mail: radio@mountainhome.com Web Site:www.twinlakesradio.com Licensee: Mountain Home Radio Station Inc. Natl. Network: ABC, . Format: Country. News staff: one; News: 15 hrs wkly. Target aud: 24-54. ♦Morgan Dowdy, CEO; Stewart Brunner, VP, VP & gen mgr; Roger Lowery, stn mgr.

KTLO(AM)— May 30, 1953: 1240 khz; 1 kw-U. TL: N36 20 43 W92 23 40. Hrs open: 24 Box 2010, 72654. Secondary address: 620 Hwy. 5 N. 72654. Phone: (870) 425-3101. Fax: (870) 424-4314.E-mail: bob@ktlo.com Web Site:www.ktlo.com Licensee: KTLO L.L.C. (group owner; acq 5-1-91). Population served: 45,000 Format: Country. News staff: 3; News: 11 hrs wkly. Target aud: 18-55; general. ♦Bob Knight, gen mgr.

KTLO-FM— Jan 11, 1971: 97.9 mhz; 30 kw. Ant 636 ft TL: N36 20 55 W92 23 59. Stereo. Hrs open: Prog sep from AM Box 2010, 72654. Secondary address: 620 Hwy. 5 N. 72654. Phone: (870) 425-3101. Fax: (870) 424-4314.E-mail: bob@ktlo.com Rgnl. Network: Ark. Radio Net. Ark. Radio Net. Format: Easy lstng, MOR. Target aud: 40 plus.

Mountain Pine

KLXQ(FM)— 1996: 101.9 mhz; 3.1 kw. Ant 407 ft TL: N34 26 56 W93 15 59. Stereo. Hrs open: 125 Corporate Terr., Hot Springs, 71913. Phone: (501) 525-9700. Fax: (501) 525-9739. Web Site:www.1019therocket.com Licensee: US Stations LLC. Group owner: Powell Broadcasting (acq 2-1-2005; grpsl). Format: Classic rock. Target aud: 25-54. ♦Gary Terrell, gen mgr, chief of engrg; Neal Gladner, gen sls mgr; Craig Dale, progmg dir; Melissa Walters, traf mgr.

Mountain View

KWOZ(FM)— Dec 1, 1981: 103.3 mhz; 100 kw. 987 ft TL: N35 47 06 W91 57 44. Stereo. Hrs open: 920 Harrison St., Suite C, Batesville, 72503. Phone: (870) 793-4196. Fax: (870) 793-5222.E-mail: arkansas103@hotmail.com Web Site:www.arkansas103.com Licensee: WRD Entertainment Inc. (group owner). Natl. Network: ABC, . Letcher, Heald, & Hildreth, P.L.C. Wire Svc: AP Format: C&W. News staff: 2; News: 3 hrs wkly. Target aud: 18-54. ♦Matt Johnson, sls dir; Rob Stanley, stn mgr & progmg dir; Bill Beck, news dir.

Murfreesboro

KMTB(FM)— May 18, 1983: 99.5 mhz; 20.5 kw. 358 ft TL: N34 05 44 W93 41 31. Stereo. Hrs open: 24 1513 S. 4th, Nashville, 71852. Phone: (870) 845-3601. Fax: (870) 845-3680.E-mail: operations @southwestarkansasradio.com Licensee: ARKLATEX Radio Inc. (group owner; acq 8-28-2001; grpsl). Format: Country. ♦Brent Pinkerton, gen mgr; Scott Dunson, opns dir.

Nashville

KBHC(AM)— May 1959: 1260 khz; 500 w-D. TL: N33 55 45 W93 51 01. Hrs open: 1513 S. 4th St., 71852. Phone: (870) 845-3601. Fax: (870) 845-3680.E-mail: operations@southwestarkansasradio.com Licensee: ARKLATEX Radio Inc. (group owner; (acq 8-23-2001; grpsl). Population served: 4,016 Rgnl. Network: Ark. Radio Net. Natl. Rep: Keystone (unwired net),. Ark. Radio Net. Format: Mexican rgnl. ♦Brent Pinkerton, gen mgr, news dir; Scott Dunson, opns dir, mus dir & disc jockey.

KNAS(FM)— Feb 14, 1977: 105.5 mhz; 3 kw. 85 ft TL: N33 55 45 W93 51 01. Stereo. Hrs open: Prog sep from AM 1513 S. 4th St.,

71853. Phone: (870) 845-3601. Fax: (870) 845-9012. Licensee: ARKLATEX Radio Inc. Format: Adult contemp.

*KNLL(FM)— 2008: 90.5 mhz; 100 kw vert. Ant 481 ft TL: N33 30 17 W93 34 47. Hrs open:
Rebroadcasts WAFR(FM) Tupelo, MS 100%.
Drawer 2440, Tupelo, MS, 38801-2440. Phone: (662) 844-8888. Fax: (662) 842-6791. Web Site:www.afr.net Licensee: American Family Association. Natl. Network: American Family Radio, . Format: Christian. ♦Marvin Sanders, gen mgr.

KSSW(FM)— 2003: 96.9 mhz; 6 kw. Ant 328 ft TL: N34 00 41 W93 52 03. Hrs open: 8919 World Ministry Ave., Baton Rouge, 70810. Phone: (225) 768-3688. Fax: (870) 845-3680. Fax: (225) 768-3729. Web Site:www.jsm.org Licensee: Family Worship Center Church Inc. Group owner: Sudbury Services Inc. (acq 9-15-2005; $400,000). Format: Relg teaching. ♦John Santiago, gen mgr.

Newark

*KLLN(FM)— Jan 1, 1985: 90.9 mhz; 4 kw. 456 ft TL: N35 43 25 W91 26 40. Hrs open: 1502 N. Hill St., 72562. Phone: (870) 799-8969. Phone: (870) 799-8691. Fax: (870) 799-8647.E-mail: kllnfm@yahoo.com Web Site:www.klln.fm Licensee: Newark Public School. Format: Southern gospel. ♦Fred Ahlborn, gen mgr.

Newport

KNBY(AM)— Oct 12, 1949: 1280 khz; 1 kw-D, 87 w-N. TL: N35 36 38 W91 15 02. Hrs open: 24 Box 768, 72112. Secondary address: 2025 McCarty Dr. 72112. Phone: (870) 523-5891. Fax: (870) 523-2967.E-mail: daleturner@suddenlinkmail.com Licensee: Newport Broadcasting Co. Group owner: Sudbury Svcs. Inc. & Newport Broadcasting Co. Population served: 21,700 Format: News/talk info. ♦Harold Sudbury, pres; Dale Turner, gen mgr, news dir; Doug Holt, progmg dir, progmg mgr.

KOKR(FM)— Sept 1, 1966: 96.7 mhz; 35 kw. 548 ft TL: N35 29 16 W91 26 13. Stereo. Hrs open: Prog sep from AM Box 768 , 72112. Secondary address: 401 S. Spring Street, Searcy 72143. Phone: (870) 523-5891. Fax: (870) 523_2967.E-mail: rhondap@searcyradiogroup.com Population served: 45,000 Format: Country.

North Crossett

KWLT(FM)— May 1, 1995: 102.7 mhz; 25 kw. Ant 328 ft TL: N33 12 58 W91 55 42. Stereo. Hrs open: 24 Box 697, 117 E. Wellfield Rd., Crosset, 71635. Phone: (870) 364-2181. Fax: (870) 364-2183.E-mail: kagh@alltel.net Web Site:www.crossettradio.com Licensee: South Ark Broadcasting Inc. Population served: 85,000 Natl. Network: ABC, . Format: Classic rock. News: 2 hrs wkly. Target aud: General. ♦Kevin Medlin, pres, gen mgr; Barry Medlin, gen sls mgr; Russell Miller, progmg dir; Brian Bailey, news dir.

North Little Rock

KDXE(AM)— May 9, 1957: 1380 khz; 5 kw-D, 2.5 kw-N, DA-2. TL: N34 52 49 W92 14 01. Hrs open: 24 2902 E. Kiehl Ave., Suite 1D, Sherwood, 72120. Phone: (501) 835-4402. Fax: (501) 835-4992.E-mail: kdxe1380@sbcglobal.net Licensee: Simmons Austin, LS LLC. (acq 3-8-2006; $350,000). Natl. Network: ESPN Radio, . Dow, Lohnes & Albertson. Format: Sports. News staff: 1; News: 2 hrs. Target aud: 25-54; men. Spec prog: 3 hrs wkly. ♦Albert Phipps, pres; Arlen Horn, gen mgr; Lee Malcolm, opns VP; Eric Kailin, gen sls mgr; Mark Hill, engrg VP; David Graves, engr.

KWBF-FM— 1995: 101.1 mhz; 6 kw. Ant 328 ft TL: N34 49 52 W92 19 18. Stereo. Hrs open: 24 1 Shackleford Dr., Suite 400, Little Rock, 72211. Phone: (501) 219-2400. Fax: (501) 604-8004. Licensee: Flinn Broadcasting Corp. Population served: 500,000 Format: Adult album alternative. News staff: one; News: 15 hrs wkly. Target aud: 35-54. Spec prog: News 15 hrs wkly.

Ola

KARV-FM— Jan 1, 1998: 101.3 mhz; 850 w. 856 ft TL: N34 59 46 W93 13 22. Hrs open: 201 W. 2nd, Russellville, 72801. Phone: (479) 968-1184. Fax: (479) 967-5278.E-mail: karv-kyel@yahoo.com Licensee: KERM Inc. (group owner) Format: News/talk. News staff: 2; News: 20 hrs wkly. ♦Kermit Womack, pres; Chris Womack, gen mgr.

Osceola

KOSE(AM)— (Wilson, Oct 11, 1949: 860 khz; 1 kw-D, 21 w-N. TL: N35 41 03 W89 58 57. Hrs open: Box 989, Blytheville, 72316. Phone: (870) 762-2093. Fax: (870) 763-8459. Licensee: Newport Broadcasting Co. (acq 1996). Population served: 1,500,000 Rgnl. Network: Ark. Radio Net. Natl. Rep: Roslin,. Ark. Radio Net. Format: Southern gospel. Target aud: 24-55; middle-class, blue/white collar workers. Spec prog: Black 6 hrs, farm 5 hrs wkly. ♦Tom Hill, chief of engrg.

KQMJ(FM)— Sept 1, 1996: 107.3 mhz; 1.6 kw. Ant 335 ft TL: N35 45 59 W89 55 43. Hrs open: Box 989, Blytheville, 72316. Phone: (870) 762-2093. Fax: (870) 763-8459. Licensee: Phoenix Broadcasting Group Inc. Format: Classic hits.

Ozark

KDYN(AM)— Feb 5, 1969: 1540 khz; 500 w-D. TL: N35 29 16 W93 48 43. Hrs open: Sunrise-sunset Box 1086, 9331 Puddin Ridge Rd., 72949. Phone: (479) 667-4567. Fax: (479) 667-5214.E-mail: kdyn@centurytel.net Web Site:www.realcountryonline.com Licensee: Ozark Communications Inc. (acq 9-15-85). Population served: 300,000 Rgnl. Network: Ark. Radio Net. Ark. Radio Net. Format: Country. News staff: one; News: 20 hrs wkly. Target aud: General. ♦Marc Dietz, pres, gen mgr, sls dir, mktg mgr & progmg dir.

KDYN-FM— Oct 2, 1980: 96.7 mhz; 10 kw. Ant 485 ft TL: N35 29 09.11 W93 53 29.49. Stereo. Hrs open: 24 Box 1086, 72949. Secondary address: 9331 Puddin Ridge Rd. 72949. Phone: (479) 667-4567. Fax: (479) 667-5214. Licensee: Ozark Communications Inc.

Pangburn

KSMD(FM)— Nov 2, 2003: 99.1 mhz; 25 kw. Ant 328 ft TL: N35 23 43 W91 44 17. Hrs open: 24 111 N. Spring St., Searcy, 72143. Phone: (501) 268-7123. Fax: (501) 279-2900.E-mail: production@heartarkansas.com Licensee: Crain Media Group LLC (group owner; acq 10-15-02; $180,000 for CP). Format: News/talk. ♦J.R. Runyon, opns dir & progmg dir; Dave Clark, chief of engrg.

Paragould

KDRS(AM)— Jan 1, 1947: 1490 khz; 1 kw-U. TL: N36 02 56 W90 27 44. Hrs open: 24 400 Tower Dr., 72450. Phone: (870) 236-7627. Fax: (870) 239-4583.E-mail: dina@kdrs.com Web Site:www.kdrs.com Licensee: MOR Media Inc. (acq 7-2-2002; $500,000 with co-located FM). Population served: 50,000 Ark. Radio Net. Fletcher, Heald & Hildreth. Format: Sports news radio. News: 7 hrs wkly. ♦Dina Mason, pres & gen mgr; Brian Osborn, opns mgr.

KDRS-FM— Mar 5, 1983: 107.1 mhz; 3 kw. 410 ft TL: N36 01 48 W90 35 49. Stereo. Hrs open: 24 Dups AM 98% 400 Tower Dr., 72450. Phone: (870) 236-7627. Fax: (870) 239-4583. Web Site:www.kdrs.com Licensee: MOR Media Inc. Fletcher, Heald & Hildreth. Format: Adult contemp. Target aud: 18-44.

KDXY(FM)— (Lake City, Oct 4, 1971: 104.9 mhz; 25 kw. 480 ft TL: N35 49 29 W90 33 54. Stereo. Hrs open: 24 314 Union Ave., Jonesboro, 72401. Phone: (870) 933-8800. Fax: (870) 933-0403.E-mail: trey@triplefm.com Web Site:www.thefox1049.com Licensee: Saga Communications of Arkansas LLC. Group owner: Saga Communications Inc. (acq 11-8-02; grpsl). Population served: 120,000 Format: Country. News staff: one; News: 6 hrs wkly. Target aud: 25-49. ♦Christy Matthews, pres, progmg dir; Trey Stafford, CEO, pres, CFO & gen mgr; Kevin Neathery, sls VP, sls dir; Al Simpson, chief of engrg; James Dean, traf mgr.

Paris

KERX(FM)— May 1981: 95.3 mhz; 50 kw. Ant 459 ft TL: N35 17 13 W94 02 51. Hrs open: 1912 Church St., Barling, 72923. Phone: (479) 484-7285. Fax: (479) 784-7390.E-mail: tommy@pearsonbroadcasting.com Licensee: Pearson Broadcasting of Paris Inc. Group owner: Pearson Broadcasting (acq 10-18-93; $42,000; 11-8-93). Population served: 187,000 Wire Svc: AP Format: AOR. Target aud: 18-44; men & women. Spec prog: Blues 3 hrs wkly. ♦Bruce Hale, CFO; Tommy Craft, gen mgr; Ray Miller, opns dir, progmg dir, news dir; Jeff Clunn, gen sls mgr.

Pearcy

KLBL(FM)— Nov 18, 1991: 104.5 mhz; 3 kw. Ant 407 ft TL: N34 26 56 W93 15 59. Stereo. Hrs open: 24 125 Corporate Terr., Hot Springs, 71913. Phone: (501) 525-9700. Fax: (501) 525-9739.E-mail: gterrel@usstations.com Licensee: US Stations LLC. Natl. Network: CBS Radio, . Rgnl rep: Rgnl Reps Format: Country. News: 7 hrs wkly. Target aud: 25-50; general. ♦Gary Terrel, gen mgr.

Piggott

KBOA-FM— Oct 15, 1983: 105.5 mhz; 6 kw. Ant 298 ft TL: N36 19 50 W90 07 24. Stereo. Hrs open: 24 Box 509, 1303 Southwest Dr., Kennett, MO, 63857. Phone: (573) 888-4616. Fax: (573) 888-4890.E-mail: perry@semoradio.com Web Site:www.semoradio.com Licensee: Pollack Broadcasting Co. (group owner; acq 9-25-98; $450,000 with KBOA(AM) Kennett, MO). Population served: 150,000 Format: Adult standards. News staff: one; News: 5 hrs wkly. Target aud: 18-55; young adults, young professionals, farmers. Spec prog: Farm 5 hrs wkly. ♦William H. Pollack, pres; Perry Jones, gen mgr, gen sls mgr; Monte Lyons, progmg dir; Charles Isbell, news dir; Palmer Johnson, chief of engrg.

Pine Bluff

***KCAT(AM)—** April 1963: 1340 khz; 1 kw-U. TL: N34 12 47 W92 01 53. Hrs open: 1207 W. 6th, 71601-3993. Phone: (870) 534-5001. Licensee: Monday Burke Smith Broadcasting Network (acq 7-15-2004; $150,000). Population served: 185,000 Format: Gospel. Target aud: 18-55. ♦Darren Smith, gen sls mgr; Elijah Mondy, gen mgr & progmg dir; Belinda Mondy, chief of engrg, traf mgr.

KCLA(AM)— Jan 16, 1947: 1400 khz; 1 kw-U. TL: N34 11 33 W92 02 42. Hrs open: 920 Commerce Rd., 71601-7605. Phone: (870) 534-8978. Fax: (870) 534-8984. Licensee: M.R.S. Ventures Inc. (group owner; (acq 4-29-2003; grpsl). Population served: 57,389 Format: News/talk. News staff: 2. Target aud: 35 plus; lower to middle income. ♦J. Don Russell, pres; Dawn Deane, gen mgr; Craig Eastham, sls VP, news dir; Floyd Donald, mus dir.

KIPR(FM)— 1963: 92.3 mhz; 100 kw. Ant 938 ft TL: N34 22 12 W92 10 07. Stereo. Hrs open: 700 Wellington Hills Rd., Little Rock, 72211. Phone: (501) 401-0200. Fax: (501) 401-0366. Web Site:www.power923.com Licensee: Citadel Broadcasting Co. Group owner: Citadel Broadcasting Corp. (acq 7-29-97; grpsl). Population served: 200,000 Format: Urban contemp. Target aud: 18-44. ♦Jim Beard, gen mgr & mktg mgr.

KOTN(AM)— Mar 12, 1934: 1490 khz; 1 kw-U. TL: N34 13 15 W91 58 20. Hrs open: 24 920 Commerce Rd., 71601. Phone: (870) 534-8911. Phone: (501) 534-8978. Fax: (870) 534-8984. Licensee: M.R.S. Ventures Inc. (group owner; (acq 4-29-2003; $350,000). Population served: 60,000 Natl. Network: Westwood One, . Format: Adult contemp, news/talk, sports. News staff: one; News: 7 hrs wkly. Target aud: 25-54. ♦Andy Hodges, gen mgr & mktg VP.

KPBQ-FM— Dec 23, 1991: 101.3 mhz; 25 kw. Ant 328 ft TL: N34 15 13 W92 03 58. Stereo. Hrs open: 24 920 Commerce Rd., 71601. Phone: (870) 534-8911. Fax: (870) 534-8984.E-mail: delta4radio@netscape.net Licensee: M.R.S. Ventures Inc. (group owner; (acq 4-29-2003; grpsl). Population served: 150,000 Natl. Network: ABC, . Format: Country. Target aud: 12-60. Spec prog: Farm 2 hrs wkly. ♦Andy Hodges, gen mgr.

***KUAP(FM)—** 1995: 89.7 mhz; 6 kw. 285 ft TL: N34 14 33 W92 01 02. Hrs open: 1200 N. University Dr., Suite 4948, Thoatre Masscom, 71601. Phone: (870) 575-8272. Fax: (870) 575-4666. Web Site:www.uapb.edu Licensee: Board of Trustees of Univ. of Arkansas. Format: Smooth jazz. ♦Finley Hill, stn mgr.

KZYP(FM)— Nov 1, 1984: 99.3 mhz; 3 kw. Ant 200 ft TL: N34 11 33 W92 02 42. Stereo. Hrs open: Prog sep from AM 920 Commerce Rd., 71601. Phone: (870) 534-8978. Fax: (870) 534-8984. Licensee: M.R.S. Ventures Inc. Format: Urban contemp. Target aud: 25-45; middle to upper income.

Pocahontas

KPOC(AM)— Nov 15, 1950: 1420 khz; 1 kw-D, 118 w-N. TL: N36 16 38 W90 57 16. Hrs open: 24 Box 508, 72455. Secondary address: One Radio Dr. 72455. Phone: (870) 892-5234. Fax: (870) 892-5235.E-mail: info@kpoc.com Licensee: Combined Media Group Inc. (group owner; (acq 12-20-2001; $410,000 with co-located FM). Population served: 6,800 Rgnl. Network: Ark. Radio Net. Ark. Radio Net. Format: Light adult contemp. News staff: one. Target aud: 25-54; general. Spec prog: Farm 10 hrs wkly. ♦Jamie Ward, gen sls mgr; Timothy Scott, pres, gen mgr & progmg dir; Larry Caldwell, chief of engrg.

KPOC-FM— Apr 25, 1969: 104.1 mhz; 6 kw. Ant 144 ft TL: N36 16 38 W90 57 16. Hrs open: 24 Dups AM 100% One Radio Dr., 72455. Phone: (870) 892-5234. Fax: (870) 892-5235.E-mail: info@kpoc.com Population served: 17,000

Prairie Grove

KYNF(FM)— November 1999: 94.9 mhz; 21 kw. 761 ft TL: N35 51 00 W94 23 00. Stereo. Hrs open: 24 4209 N Frontage Rosd, Fayetteville, 72703. Phone: (479) 521-5566. Fax: (479) 521-0751. Web Site:www.y949.com Licensee: Cumulus Licensing Corp. Group owner: Cumulus Media Inc. (acq 3-12-01; $2 million). Population served: 1,250,000 Natl. Network: USA, . Format: Adult contemp. News: 2 hrs wkly. Target aud: 30 plus; listeners who like positive, inspirational progmg. ♦Joe Conway, gen mgr; Becky Dole, gen sls mgr; Bryan Matthews, progmg dir; Jay Phillips, news dir; Greg Judd, chief of engrg.

Prescott

KHPA(FM)—See Hope

KTPA(AM)— Dec 1, 1959: 1370 khz; 1 kw-D, 49 w-N. TL: N36 20 04 W94 10 41. Hrs open: Box 424, Hope, 71802. Secondary address: 1600 So. Elm St., Hope, AZ 71802. Phone: (870) 777-8868. Phone: (870) 777-8869. Fax: (870) 777-8888.E-mail: khpafm@supercountry105.com Licensee: Newport Broadcasting Co. Group owner: Sudbury Services Inc. & Newport Broadcasting Co. (acq 5-14-66). Population served: 3,921 Rgnl. Network: Ark. Radio Net. Ark. Radio Net. Format: Gospel. ♦Sonya Odom, gen mgr, stn mgr & sls dir; Alex Rain, chief of engrg; Amanda Smith, traf mgr.

Rogers

KAMO-FM— 1971: 94.3 mhz; 5.2 kw. 709 ft TL: N36 26 30 W93 58 26. Stereo. Hrs open: 24 4209 Frontage Rd., Fayetteville, 72703. Phone: (479) 521-5566. Fax: (479) 521 4968.E-mail: info@us94.com Web Site:www.us94.com Licensee: Cumulus Licensing Corp. Group owner: Cumulus Media Inc. (acq 12-10-98; grpsl). Format: Oldies. ♦Joe Conway, gen mgr; Dan Hinschell, progmg dir.

KFFK(AM)— Sept 16, 1954: 1390 khz; 5 kw-D, 30 w-N. TL: N36 23 18 W94 11 34. Hrs open: 24 Butler Broadcasting LLC, 1780 Holly St., Fayetteville, 72701. Phone: (479) 582-3776. Fax: (479) 571-0995. Licensee: Butler Broadcasting Co. LLC (acq 10-13-99; grpsl). Population served: 315,000 Natl. Network: Fox Sports, . Format: ESPN Deportes/Urban. Target aud: 25-54. ♦Steve Butler, pres; Steve Bulter, gen mgr; Dave Jackson, progmg dir.

KURM(AM)— Nov 9, 1979: 790 khz; 5 kw-D, 500 w-N, DA-N. TL: N36 18 10 W94 06 47. Hrs open: 5 AM-11 PM 113 E. New Hope Rd., 72758. Phone: (479) 633-0790. Fax: (479) 631-9711.E-mail: kurm@kurm.net Web Site:www.kurm.net Licensee: KERM Inc. (group owner) Population served: 250,000 Natl. Network: CBS, . Okla. News Net. Dan Alpert Law Firm. Format: Var/div. News staff: 2; News: 15 hrs wkly. Target aud: +35. Spec prog: Farm 10 hrs wkly. ♦Kermit Womack, pres & gen mgr; Diane Womack, sls VP, chief of engrg.

Russellville

KARV(AM)— Feb 25, 1947: 610 khz; 1 kw-D, 500 w-N, DA-2. TL: N35 17 56 W93 09 09. Hrs open: 24 201 W. 2nd, 72801. Phone: (479) 968-1184. Fax: (479) 967-5278.E-mail: karv-kyet@yahoo.com Licensee: KERM Inc. (group owner; acq 10-22-92; $250,000;11-23-92). Population served: 70,000 Natl. Network: CBS, . Rgnl. Network: Ark. Radio Net. Ark. Radio Net. Format: New/talk, sports. News staff: 4; News: 38 hrs wkly. Target aud: 35 plus; affluent adults. Spec prog: Farm 5 hrs wkly. ♦Chris Womack, gen mgr.

***KMTC(FM)—** June 1987: 91.1 mhz; 360 w. 62 ft TL: N35 18 11 W93 08 42. Hrs open: 24 Box 570, 72811-0570. Secondary address: 305 Lake Front Dr. 72802. Phone: (479) 967-7400. Fax: (479) 967-7894. Licensee: Russellville Educational Broadcasting Foundation. Population served: 30,000 Natl. Network: USA, . Format: Christian contemp. News: one hr wkly. Target aud: 18-55; Christian. ♦Tom Underhill, CEO; Debbie Bewley, gen mgr; Melissa Krueger, stn mgr, progmg dir.

KWKK(FM)— Sept 29, 1985: 100.9 mhz; 6 kw. 295 ft TL: N35 17 37 W93 10 39. Stereo. Hrs open: 24 Box 10310, 72812. Phone: (479) 968-6816. Fax: (479) 968-2946.E-mail: traffic@rivervalleyradio.com Web Site:www.rivervalleyradio.com Licensee: MMA License LLC. Group owner: MAX Media L.L.C. (acq 6-6-2003; grpsl). Natl. Network: ABC, . Natl. Rep: Christal,. Wire Svc: AP Format: Adult contemp. News staff: one; News: 5 hrs wkly. Target aud: 18-49; young adults. Spec prog: Arkansas Tech University Sports. ♦Rich Moellers, gen mgr; Aaron Thomas, opns mgr; Rhonda Dilbeck, gen sls mgr; Johnny Story, news dir; Jim Alexander, chief of engrg.

***KXRJ(FM)—** Apr 3, 1989: 91.9 mhz; 100 w. -92 ft TL: N35 17 47 W93 08 18. Hrs open: 24 Arkansas Tech Univ., Hwy. 7 N., 72801. Phone: (479) 964-0806. Phone: (479) 964-3282. Fax: (479) 498-6024.E-mail: info@kxrj.edu Web Site:www.broadcast.atu.edu Licensee: Arkansas Tech University. Format: Div, Jazz. News: 10 hrs wkly. Target aud: General. Spec prog: Educ, jazz 15 hrs wkly. ♦George Cotton, chief of engrg.

Salem

KCAB(AM)—See Dardanelle

KHOM(FM)— September 1977: 100.9 mhz; 50 kw. Ant 492 ft TL: N36 35 38 W91 40 03. Stereo. Hrs open: Box 107, West Plains, MO, 65775. Phone: (417) 255-0427. Fax: (417) 255-2907.E-mail: khom@khom.net Web Site:www.khom.net Licensee: Mountain Lakes Broadcasting Corp. (acq 12-14-99). Population served: 75000 Natl. Network: ABC, . Rgnl. Network: Ark. Radio Net. Ark. Radio Net. Format: Traditional country. News staff: one. Target aud: 35-54; adults. ♦Bob Knight, gen mgr; John Thomason, gen mgr & stn mgr.

KSAR(FM)—See Thayer, MO

Searcy

KAPZ(AM)—See Bald Knob

KCNY(FM)—See Bald Knob

KWCK(AM)— Aug 25, 1951: 1300 khz; 5 kw-D, 30 w-N. TL: N35 15 27 W91 43 49. Hrs open: 111 N. Spring St., 72143. Phone: (501) 268-7123. Fax: (501) 279-2900.E-mail: jrrunyon@crainmedia.com Licensee: Crain Media Group LLC. (group owner; (acq 10-21-2002; grpsl). Population served: 13,650 Format: Talk. Target aud: 25-64. Spec prog: Farm 10 hrs wkly. ♦J.R. Runyon, gen mgr.

KWCK-FM— October 1973: 99.9 mhz; 50 kw. 492 ft TL: N35 26 50 W91 56 52. Stereo. Hrs open: 24 Dups AM 95% 111 N. Spring St., 72143. Phone: (501) 268-7123. Fax: (501) 279-2900.E-mail: jrrunyon@crainmedia.com Web Site:www.kwck999.com Format: Country. News staff: one; News: 3 hrs wkly. Target aud: 18-49.

Sheridan

***KANX(FM)—** 1999: 91.1 mhz; 16.5 kw. 522 ft TL: N34 17 26 W92 29 36. (CP: 40 kw). Hrs open: Box 2440, American Family Radio, Tupelo, MS, 38803. Phone: (662) 844-8888. Fax: (662) 842-6791. Web Site:www.afr.net Licensee: American Family Association. Group owner: American Family Radio Format: Relg. ♦Marvin Sanders, gen mgr; John Riley, progmg dir.

KARN-FM— Nov 1, 1984: 102.9 mhz; 50 kw. Ant 488 ft TL: N34 25 08 W92 22 17. Stereo. Hrs open: 24 700 Wellington Hills Rd., Little Rock, 72211. Phone: (501) 401-0200. Fax: (501) 401-0387.E-mail: info@920karn.com Web Site:www.920karn.com Licensee: The Last Bastion Station Trust LLC, as Trustee Group owner: Citadel Broadcasting Corp. (acq 6-12-2007; grpsl). Population served: 248,000 Format: News, talk. News staff: one; News: 2 hrs wkly. Target aud: 35-64. ♦Jim Beard, gen mgr, mktg mgr; John Scuderi, gen sls mgr; Dave Elswick, progmg dir.

KLRG(AM)—Licensed to Sheridan. See Little Rock

Sherwood

KMTL(AM)— Oct 31, 1983: 760 khz; 10 kw-D. TL: N34 49 34 W92 12 19. Hrs open: Box 6460, North Little Rock, 72124. Phone: (501) 835-1554.E-mail: kmtl76am@bcglobal Licensee: George V. Domerese. Format: Relg. ♦George Domerese, gen mgr, progmg dir; Tom Rusk, chief of engrg.

KOKY(FM)— 1994: 102.1 mhz; 4.1 kw. 387 ft TL: N34 44 38 W92 16 32. Hrs open: 700 Wellington Hills Rd., Little Rock, 72211. Phone: (501) 401-0200. Fax: (501) 401-0366. Web Site:www.koky.com Licensee: Citadel Broadcasting Co. Group owner: Citadel Broadcasting Corp. (acq 10-23-97; grpsl). Population served: 525,000 Cohn & Marks. Format: Adult contemp, soul. ♦Jim Beard, gen mgr & mktg mgr.

Siloam Springs

*KLRC(FM)— Oct 1, 1981: 101.1 mhz; 3.1 kw. 459 ft TL: N36 11 25 W94 33 55. Stereo. Hrs open: John Brown Univ., 2000 W. University, 72761. Phone: (479) 524-7101. Phone: (877) KLRC-101. Fax: (479) 524-7451.E-mail: klrc@klrc.edu Web Site:www.klrc.com klrc.com Licensee: John Brown University. Population served: 309,000 Natl. Network: USA, . Wire Svc: UPI Format: Christian, relg. News: 2 hrs wkly. Target aud: 25-49. ◆Charles W. Pollard, pres, chief of engrg; Sean Sawatzky, gen mgr; Mark Michaels, progmg dir.

KMCK(FM)— 1947: 105.7 mhz; 100 kw. 476 ft TL: N36 11 07 W94 17 49. Stereo. Hrs open: 4209 N Frontage Road, Fayetteville, 72703. Phone:(479) 521-5566. Fax: (479) 521-0751. Web Site:www.power1057.com Licensee: Cumulus Licensing Corp. Group owner: Cumulus Media Inc. (acq 12-10-98; grpsl). Population served: 300,000 Natl. Rep: Christal,. Richard Hayes. Format: CHR. Target aud: 18-49; contemp adults. ◆Joe Conway, gen mgr; J.J. Ryan, progmg dir, news dir.

KUOA(AM)— Apr 12, 1923: 1290 khz; 5 kw-D. TL: N36 11 25 W94 33 55. Hrs open: 24 Box 191, Berryville, 72616. Phone: (870) 423-2147. Fax: (870) 423-2146. Licensee: Hog Radio Inc. (acq 8-13-2008; $355,000). Population served: 330,000 Format: All sports. ◆Jay Bunyard, pres; Grant Merrill, gen mgr, gen sls mgr.

Springdale

KXNA(FM)— Sept 19, 1968: 104.9 mhz; 1 kw. 479 ft TL: N36 10 48 W94 05 07. (CP: 2.75 kw). Stereo. Hrs open: Bulter Broadcasting LLC, 1780 Holly St., Fayetteville, 72703. Phone: (479) 582-3776. Fax: (479) 571-0995. Licensee: Bulter Broadcasting LLC. (acq 10-13-99; grpsl). Population served: 35,200 Natl. Rep: Christal,. Format: Alternative. ◆Steve Butler, gen mgr & mus dir.

KYNG(AM)— July 15, 1966: 1590 khz; 2.5 kw-D, 58 w-N. TL: N36 12 21 W94 07 11. Hrs open: 4209 N Frontage Road, Fayetteville, 72703. Phone: (479) 521-5566. Fax: (479) 521-0751. Licensee: Cumulus Licensing Corp. Group owner: Cumulus Media Inc. (acq 12-10-98; grpsl). Population served: 16,783 Richard Hayes. Format: Sp. Target aud: 18-54. ◆Joe Conway, gen mgr; Mariposa Salas, progmg dir.

Stamps

KZHE(FM)— October 1980: 100.5 mhz; 50 kw. 500 ft TL: N33 26 01 W93 27 49. Stereo. Hrs open: 24 406 W. Union St., Magnolia, 71753-3708. Phone: (870) 234-7790. Fax: (870) 234-7791.E-mail: kzhe@kzhe.com Web Site:www.kzhe.com Licensee: A-1 Communications Inc. (acq 5-20-92; $85,000; 6-8-92). Format: Classic country. Target aud: 25-54. Spec prog: Gospel 8 hrs wkly. ◆Troy Alphin, pres; Sharon Alphin, VP; Dave Sehon, gen mgr, opns mgr.

Stuttgart

KWAK(AM)— May 15, 1948: 1240 khz; 1 kw-U. TL: N34 29 27 W91 33 45. Hrs open: 24 Box 910, 1818 S. Buerkle, 72160. Phone: (870) 673-1595. Fax: (870) 673-8445.E-mail: kdew973@yahoo.com Licensee: Arkansas County Broadcasters Inc. (group owner) Population served: 25,000 Natl. Network: ESPN Radio, . Rgnl. Network: Prog Farm. Format: Loc news, sports. News staff: one. Target aud: General. Spec prog: Farm 6 hrs wkly. ◆Bobby Caldwell, pres; Scott Siler, stn mgr, gen sls mgr & progmg dir; Sandi Levey, mus dir, women's int ed; Johnathan Reaves, news dir; Sandy Levey, traf mgr.

KWAK-FM— Dec 15, 1987: 105.5 mhz; 3 kw. 325 ft TL: N34 25 52 W91 26 08. Stereo. Hrs open: 24 Dups AM 15% Box 910, 1818 S. Buerkle, 72160. Phone: (870) 673-1595. Fax: (870) 673-8445.E-mail: kdew973@yahoo.com Population served: 25,000 Natl. Network: ABC, . Format: Oldies. News: one. ◆Scott Siler, gen mgr; Johnathan Reaves, news dir.

Texarkana

KCMC(AM)—See Texarkana, TX

KFYX(FM)— June 11, 1968: 107.1 mhz; 2.9 kw. Ant 479 ft TL: N33 25 45 W94 07 11. Hrs open: 24 615 Olive St., TX, 75501. Phone: (903) 793-4671. Fax: (903) 792-4261. Licensee: ArkLaTex LLC. (group owner) (acq 1-3-2007; grpsl). Population served: 150,000 Format: CHR. News staff: 0. Target aud: 18-34. ◆Harold Sudbury, CEO & gen mgr.

KHTA(FM)—See Wake Village TX

---

*KKLT(FM)— 2004: 89.3 mhz; 1 w horiz, 5.7 kw vert. Ant 505 ft TL: N33 23 36 W93 51 34. (CP: 1 w horiz, 23 kw vert). Hrs open: Rebroadcasts KLVR(FM) Santa Rosa, CA 100%. 2351 Sunset Blvd., Suite 170-218, Rocklin, CA, 95765. Phone: (916) 251-1600. Fax: (916) 251-1650. Web Site:www.klove.com Licensee: Educational Media Foundation. (acq 1-11-2005; $125,000 for CP). Natl. Network: K-Love, . Format: Christian. ◆Richard Jenkins, pres; Mike Novak, VP; Keith Whipple, dev dir; Eric Allen, natl sls mgr; David Pierce, progmg mgr; Ed Lenane, news dir; Sam Wallington, engrg dir; Karen Johnson, news rptr.

KKYR-FM—See Texarkana, TX

KOSY(AM)— Nov 15, 1951: 790 khz; 1 kw-D, 500 w-N, DA-N. TL: N33 22 30 W94 01 00. Hrs open: 24 2324 Arkansas Blvd., 71854. Phone: (870) 772-3771. Fax: (870) 772-0364.E-mail: wesspicher @gapbroadcasting.com Web Site:www.kkyr.com Licensee: GAP Broadcasting Texarkana License LLC. Group owner: Clear Channel Communications Inc. (acq 8-3-2007; grpsl). Population served: 150,000 Format: Modern country. News staff: one. Target aud: General. ◆Ron Bird, gen mgr; Wes Spicher, progmg dir.

KTFS(AM)—See Texarkana, TX

KTOY(FM)— 1993: 104.7 mhz; 3.1 kw. Ant 453 ft TL: N33 25 45 W94 07 11. Stereo. Hrs open: 24 615 Olive St., TX, 75501. Phone: (903) 793-4671. Fax: (903) 792-4261. Licensee: Jo-Al Broadcasting Inc. (acq 1-3-2007; grpsl). Natl. Network: ABC, . Natl. Rep: Interep,. Format: Urban adult contemp. Target aud: 25-54; blacks.

KYGL(FM)— 1995: 106.3 mhz; 3 kw. 328 ft TL: N33 22 39 W93 56 38. Hrs open: 2324 Arkansas Blvd., 71854. Phone: (870) 772-3771. Fax: (870) 770-0364. Format: Classic rock. ◆Wes Spicher, chief of engrg.

Trumann

KJBX(FM)—Licensed to Trumann. See Jonesboro

Turrell

KKLV(FM)— Sept 1, 1999: 94.7 mhz; 6 kw. 328 ft TL: N35 18 04 W90 19 34. Hrs open: 2351 Sunset Blvd., Suuite 170-218, Rockin, CA, 95765. Phone: (916) 251-1600. Fax: (916) 251-1650. Web Site:www.klove.com Licensee: Educational Media Foundation. Group owner: EMF Broadcasting (acq 10-20-2000; grpsl). Population served: 1,000,000 Natl. Network: K-Love, . Format: Contemp Christian. ◆Richard Jenkins, pres; Lloyd Parker, gen mgr; Keith Whipple, dev dir; Mike Novak, progmg VP; David Pierce, progmg dir; Ed Lenane, news dir, news dir; Sam Wallington, engrg dir.

WPLX(AM)—Licensed to Turrell. See Memphis TN

Van Buren

KBBQ-FM— May 22, 1983: 102.7 mhz; 17 kw. Ant 574 ft TL: N35 26 51 W94 21 54. Stereo. Hrs open: 3104 S. 70th St., Suite 103, Fort Smith, AZ, 72903. Phone: (479) 452-0681. Fax: (479) 452-0873.E-mail: info@102thevib.com Web Site:www.102thevib.com Licensee: Cumulus Licensing Corp. Group owner: Cumulus Media Inc. (acq 8-99; $1.15 million). Format: Rock. ◆Smitty O'Loughlin, gen mgr; Rahm Cunningham, progmg dir; Don Jones, chief of engrg; Wendy Wiseman, traf mgr.

KHGG(AM)— Nov 24, 1958: 1580 khz; 1 kw-D, 45 w-N. TL: N35 25 58 W94 19 47. Hrs open: 24 Box 908, Fort Smith, 72902. Phone: (479) 288-1047. Fax: (479) 785-2638.E-mail: koolproduction@sbcglobal.net Web Site:www.sportshog1031.com Licensee: Pharis Broadcasting Inc. (group owner) (acq 9-20-93; $110,000; 10-11-93). Population served: 200,000 Natl. Network: Fox Sports, . Rgnl. Network: Ark. Radio Net. Natl. Rep: Commercial Media Sales,. Ark. Radio Net. Irwin, Campbell and Tannenwold. Format: Sports talk. Target aud: General. ◆William Pharis, CEO & pres; Karen Pharis, exec VP, gen mgr; Ernie Witt, progmg dir.

*KLFS(FM)— 2004: 90.3 mhz; 2.4 kw vert. Ant 256 ft TL: N35 23 37 W94 33 07. Stereo. Hrs open: 24 2351 Sunset Blvd., Suite 170-218, Rocklin, CA, 95765. Phone: (916) 251-1600. Fax: (916) 251-1650.E-mail: klove@klove.com Web Site:www.klove.com Licensee: Educational Media Foundation. Group owner: EMF Broadcasting. Population served: 160,000 Natl. Network: K-Love, . Shaw Pittman. Format: Chrisitan. News staff: 3. Target aud: 25-44; Judeo Chrisitan, female. ◆Richard Jenkins, pres; Mike Novak, VP; Keith Whipple, dev dir; David Pierce, progmg dir; Ed Lenane, news dir; Sam Wallington, engrg dir; Karen Johnson, news rptr.

KOAI(AM)— Sept 6, 1979: 1060 khz; 500 w-D, DA. TL: N35 25 36 W94 18 11. Hrs open: 3104 S. 70th St., Fort Smith, 72903. Phone: (479) 452-0681. Fax: (479) 452-0873.E-mail: info@fortsmithradio.com Web Site:www.fortsmithradio.com Licensee: Cumulus Licensing Corp. Format: Sp. ◆Smitty O'Loughlin, gen mgr.

Viola

KSMZ(FM)— May 1, 2007: 94.3 mhz; 8.1 kw. Ant 571 ft TL: N36 19 30 W91 58 41. Stereo. Hrs open: 24 223 Russell St., Mountain Home, 72653. Phone: (870) 425-4971. Fax: (870) 424-9717. Licensee: MJFM LLC. Population served: 219,194 Format: Adult hits. Target aud: 25-54. ◆Mike Wiseman, COO; Scott Gray, gen mgr.

Waldo

KVMZ(FM)— 2002: 99.1 mhz; 6 kw. Ant 410 ft TL: N33 24 17 W93 12 07. Stereo. Hrs open: Box 430, Magnolia, 71754. Phone: (870) 234-9901. Fax: (870) 234-5865.E-mail: kvmakvmz@suddenlinkmail.com Web Site:www.magnoliaradio.com Licensee: Noalmark Broadcasting Corp. (acq 8-1-2005; $430,000). Ark. Radio Net. Format: Today's Country. ◆Ken Sibley, gen mgr.

Waldron

KHGG-FM— May 18, 1982: 103.1 mhz; 6.1 kw. Ant 1,351 ft TL: N34 58 44 W93 56 42. Stereo. Hrs open: Rebroadcasts KHGG(AM) 100%. Box 908, Fort Smith, 72902. Phone: (479) 288-1047. Fax: (479) 288-0942. Web Site:www.sportshog1031.com Licensee: Pharis Broadcasting Inc. (group owner; (acq 6-1-2003; $360,000). Natl. Network: Fox Sports, . Natl. Rep: Commercial Media Sales,. Rgnl rep: BRI Irwin, Campbell & Tannenwald. Format: Sports talk. News staff: one; News: 10 hrs wkly. Target aud: 25-54. ◆William Pharis, pres; Karen Pharis, gen mgr, stn mgr; Ernie Witt Jr., opns dir.

Walnut Ridge

KRLW(AM)— June 29, 1951: 1320 khz; 1 kw-D. TL: N36 03 58 W90 56 24. Hrs open: 12 1 Radio Dr., Pocohantas, 72455. Phone: (870) 886-6666. Fax: (870) 886-5719.E-mail: krlw@nex.net Licensee: Combined Media Group Inc. (group owner; acq 7-25-01; with co-located FM). Population served: 18,000 Natl. Network: CBS, . Rgnl. Network: Ark. Radio Net. Ark. Radio Net. Format: Oldies. ◆Tim Scott, pres & gen mgr.

KRLW-FM— Mar 27, 1977: 106.3 mhz; 3 kw. 328 ft TL: N36 03 58 W90 56 24. Stereo. Hrs open: 24 1 Radio Dr., Pocohantas, 72455. Phone: (870) 886-6666. Fax: (870) 886-5719.E-mail: info@krlw.com Population served: 20,000 Natl. Network: CBS, . Rgnl. Network: Ark. Radio Net. Ark. Radio Net. Format: Country.

Warren

KWRF(AM)— August 1953: 860 khz; 250 w-D, 55 w-N. TL: N33 37 59 W92 03 51. Hrs open: 24 1255 N. Myrtle, 71671. Phone: (870) 226-2653. Fax: (870) 226-3039.E-mail: pines.broadcasting@sbcglobal.net Licensee: Pines Broadcasting Inc. (acq 4-12-91; $125,000 with co-located FM; 5-6-91). Population served: 31,258 Rgnl. Network: Ark. Radio Net. Ark. Radio Net. Format: Timeless classics. News staff: one; News: 10 hrs wkly. Target aud: General. Spec prog: Gospel 8 hrs wkly. ◆Jimmy Sledge, pres, gen mgr, gen sls mgr, mus dir, news dir, chief of engrg; Gwen Sledge, opns VP; Richard Garrison, disc jockey.

KWRF-FM— June 21, 1976: 105.5 mhz; 3 kw. Ant 250 ft TL: N33 37 59 W92 03 51. Stereo. Hrs open: 24 Dups AM 100% 1255 N. Myrtle, 71671. Phone: (870) 226-2653. Fax: (870) 226-3039. Population served: 31,258 ◆Gwen Sledge, exec VP; Judy Moore, women's int ed; Allen Weise, disc jockey.

West Helena

KCLT(FM)— Dec 17, 1984: 104.9 mhz; 3 kw. 328 ft TL: N34 30 56 W90 40 13. Stereo. Hrs open: 24 Box 2870, 72390. Secondary address: 700 Dr. Martin Luther King Dr., Suite 1 72390. Phone: (870) 572-9506. Fax: (870) 572-1845.E-mail: force2@sbcglobal.net Web Site:www.force2radio.com Licensee: West Helena Broadcasters Inc. (acq 8-8-84). Population served: 1,200,000 Format: Adult urban contemp. News staff: one; News: one hr wkly. Target aud: 25-54; general, mainly African-Americans. Spec prog: Gospel 15 hrs wkly. ◆Raymond Simes, pres & gen mgr; Elaine Sims, stn mgr; Larry Evans, opns mgr.

KFFA-FM—See Helena

West Memphis

KQPN(AM)— Dec 1, 1961: 730 khz; 250 w-U, DA-N. TL: N35 08 31 W90 08 05. Hrs open: 24 203 Beale St., Memphis, TN, 38103. Phone: (901) 522-1919. Fax: (901) 522-1920. E-mail: Harry.Long@730espn.com Web Site:www.730espn.com Licensee: Simmons Austin, LS LLC. Group owner: K-Love Radio Network (acq 6-14-2006; $2 million). Population served: 1,000,000 Natl. Network: ESPN Radio, . Format: Sports. Target aud: 25-54; family types.

White Hall

KTRN(FM)— November 1997: 104.5 mhz; 3 kw. 289 ft TL: N34 13 13 W92 04 37. Hrs open: 24 2215 E. Harding, Suite 7, Pine Bluff, 71601. Phone: (870) 536-5876 (on air). Phone: (870) 536 3282 (office). Fax: (870) 536-3475. Licensee: Bayou Broadcasting Inc. Format: Soft rock. Target aud: Women; 20 & up. ◆Vickie Hooker, gen mgr & opns mgr.

Wilson

KOSE(AM)—Licensed to Wilson. See Osceola

Wrightsville

KLAL(FM)— March 1992: 107.7 mhz; 100 kw. Ant 741 ft TL: N34 36 34 W92 14 14. Hrs open: 700 Wellington Hills Rd., Little Rock, 72211. Phone: (501) 401-0200. Fax: (501) 401-0349. E-mail: info@alice1077.com Web Site:www.alice1077.com Licensee: Citadel Broadcasting Co. Group owner: Citadel Broadcasting Corp. (acq 9-4-97). Format: Hot adult contemp. ◆Jim Beard, gen mgr & mktg mgr.

Wynne

KWYN(AM)— Sept 28, 1956: 1400 khz; 1 kw-U. TL: N35 15 21 W90 47 49. Hrs open: 24 Box 789, 2758 Hwy. 64, 72396. Phone: (870) 238-8141. Fax: (870) 238-5997. E-mail: radiokwyn@cablelynx.com Licensee: East Arkansas Broadcasters Inc. Population served: 21,000 Natl. Network: CBS, Westwood One, . Ark. Radio Net. Format: Talk, C&W, info. Target aud: General. Spec prog: Farm 6 hrs wkly. ◆Bobby Caldwell, CEO; David Sills, sls dir; Lindell Staggs, news dir; Jim Alexander, chief of engrg, engr; Jennifer Lynch, traf mgr; Lane Goodwin, engr.

KWYN-FM— May 15, 1969: 92.5 mhz; 35 kw. Ant 328 ft TL: N35 11 59 W90 43 23. Stereo. Hrs open: 24 Box 789, 2758 Hwy. 64, 72396. Phone: (870) 238-8141. Fax: (870) 238-5997. E-mail: radiokwyn@cablelynx.com Licensee: East Arkansas Broadcasters Inc. Ark. Radio Net. Format: Country. ◆Bobby Caldwell, CEO; David Sills, gen sls mgr; Lindell Staggs, news dir; Jennifer Lynch, traf mgr; Jim Alexander, engr.

Yellville

KCTT-FM— 1986: 101.7 mhz; 2.45 kw. 331 ft TL: N36 15 39 W92 41 42. Stereo. Hrs open: Box 2010, Mountain Home, 72654. Phone: (870) 449-4001. Phone: (870) 425-3101. Fax: (870) 424-4314. E-mail: bob@ktlo.com Web Site:www.ktlo.com Licensee: KTLO L.L.C. (group owner; (acq 5-29-98; $215,000). Natl. Network: ABC, . Format: Oldies. Spec prog: Folk 10 hrs wkly. ◆Bob Knight, CEO, gen mgr; Danny Ward, stn mgr; Brad Haworth, opns VP.

California

Adelanto

KAJL(FM)— 1959: 92.7 mhz; 280 w. Ant 1,473 ft TL: N34 36 44 W117 17 27. Stereo. Hrs open: 24
Rebroadcasts KHJL (FM) Thousand Oaks.
99 Long Ct., Suite 200, Thousand Oaks, 91360. Phone: (805) 497-8511. Fax: (805) 497-8514. E-mail: reception@927jillfm.com Web Site:www.927jillfm.com Licensee: Amaturo Group of L.A. Ltd. Group owner: Amaturo Group Ltd. (acq 1-6-93; $3.25 million; 2-1-93). Population served: 2,100,000 Wire Svc: Metro Weather Service Inc. Format: Adult contemp. Target aud: 25-54. ◆Robert J. Christy, gen mgr & sls dir.

Alameda

KNGY(FM)—Licensed to Alameda. See San Francisco

Alisal

KPRC-FM—See Salinas

Alturas

KALT-FM— July 2002: 106.5 mhz; 500 w. Ant 272 ft TL: N41 29 57 W120 37 30. Hrs open: 215 W. 2nd St., 96101. Phone: (530) 233-4842. Fax: (530) 233-4842. E-mail: kalt@hdo.net Licensee: Woodrow Michael Warren. Group owner: Woodrow Michael Warren Stns. Format: Classic rock. ◆Mike Warren, gen mgr.

KCFJ(AM)— June 4, 1951: 570 khz; 5 kw-D, 200 w-N. TL: N41 30 07 W120 30 01. (CP: 5 kw-U, DA-N). Hrs open: 6 AM-10 PM Box 580, 96101. Phone: (530) 233-3570. Fax: (530) 233-5470. Licensee: EDI Media Inc. (acq 6-5-02; with co-located FM). Population served: 100,000 Natl. Network: USA, . Cohn & Marks. Format: Adult contemp. News staff: one; News: 3 hrs wkly. Target aud: General. Spec prog: Farm one hr wkly. ◆Bill Hansen, gen mgr; Dodie McGouegh, traf mgr.

KCNO(FM)— Dec 4, 1990: 94.5 mhz; 100 kw. 106 ft TL: N41 33 50 W120 24 55. (CP: 52 kw., ant -78 ft.). Hrs open: 14 Box 580, 96101. Phone: (530) 233-3570. Fax: (530) 233-5470. Licensee: EDI Media Inc. Format: Country. News: 17 hrs wkly. Target aud: General. ◆Bill Hansen, gen mgr, sls dir; Dodie McGoregh, traf mgr.

Anaheim

KFSH-FM— Apr 16, 1961: 95.9 mhz; 6 kw. 328 ft TL: N33 49 50 W117 48 39. Stereo. Hrs open: Prog sep from AM Box 29023, Glendale, 91209. Phone: (818) 956-5552. Fax: (818) 551-1110. Web Site:www.thefish959.com Population served: 200,000 Wiley, Rein & Fielding. Format: Contemp Christian music. Target aud: 18-49.

KXMX(AM)— May 18, 1959: 1190 khz; 10 kw-D, 1.3 kw-N, DA-2. TL: N33 56 42 W117 51 44. (CP: 20 kw-D). Hrs open: 24 Box 29023, Glendale, 91209. Phone: (818) 956-5552. Fax: (818) 551-1110. E-mail: info@kkla.com Licensee: Chase Radio Properties L.L.C. Group owner: Salem Communications Corp. (acq 8-24-00; grpsl). Population served: 166,408 Format: Talk, Korean, Arabic. Target aud: Specialized ethnic groups. Spec prog: Gospel, relg, Pol, Sp, Vietnamese 2 hrs wkly. ◆Terry Fahy, gen mgr; Dawn McKahan, gen sls mgr; Bob Hastings, prom mgr, progmg dir; Mark Pollock, chief of engrg.

Anderson

KEWB(FM)— Mar 20, 1983: 94.7 mhz; 4.2 kw. 1,565 ft TL: N40 39 06 W122 31 32. Stereo. Hrs open: 1588 Charles Dr., Redding, 96003. Phone: (530) 244-9700. Fax: (530) 244-9707. E-mail: rhealy@resultsradiomail.com Web Site:www.power94booty.com Licensee: Results Radio of Redding Licensee LLC. Group owner: Fritz Communications Inc. (acq 6-28-2000; grpsl). Arent, Fox, Kintner, Plotkin & Kahn. Format: CHR. Target aud: 18-49. ◆Beth Tappan, gen mgr; Laurie Curto, gen sls mgr; Jacob Font, progmg dir; Rico Garcia, news dir.

Angwin

*KNDL(FM)— May 20, 1961: 89.9 mhz; 794 w. Ant 3,010 ft TL: N38 40 09 W122 37 53. Stereo. Hrs open: 24 95 La Jota Dr., 94508. Phone: (707) 965-4155. Fax: (707) 965-4161. E-mail: kndl@thecandle.com Web Site:www.thecandle.com Licensee: Howell Mountain Broadcasting Co. Inc. Format: Relg. Target aud: 35-49; general. ◆David Shantz, gen mgr.

Apple Valley

KIXW(AM)— June 5, 1954: 960 khz; 5 kw-D, 400 w-N, DA-2. TL: N34 31 00 W117 13 35. Hrs open: 8:30 AM-5:30 PM 12370 Hesperia Rd., Suite 16, Victorville, 92395. Phone: (760) 241-1313. Fax: (760) 241-0205. E-mail: kimjennings@edbroadcasters.com Web Site:www.talk960.com Licensee: EDB VV License LLC. Group owner: Clear Channel Communications Inc. (acq 11-30-2007; grpsl). Population served: 300,000 Natl. Rep: Christal,. Format: Talk. Target aud: 35+. ◆Joe Pagano, progmg dir; Tom Hoyt, VP, mktg mgr & news dir.

KWRN(AM)— Jan 26, 1991: 1550 khz; 5 kw-D, 500 w-N, DA-N. TL: N34 32 12 W117 09 22. Hrs open: 24

Rebroadcasts KWRM(AM) Corona 100%.
Box 1283, Victorville, 92393. Secondary address: 15165 7th St., Ste D, Victorville 92392. Phone: (760) 955-8722. Fax: (760) 955-5751. Web Site:www.kwrn1550am.com Licensee: Major Market Stations Inc. (acq 9-24-2007; with KWRM(AM) Corona). Population served: 500,000 Natl. Network: ABC, . Format: Sp Top-40 hits. Target aud: 34-54; adults with a stable job and disposable income. ◆Marilynn Kramar, pres; Dick Vosper, chief of engrg; kathy DeCastro, traf mgr.

KZXY-FM— May 17, 1968: 102.3 mhz; 6 kw. Ant 328 ft TL: N34 24 40 W117 11 09. Stereo. Hrs open: 12370 Hesperia Rd., Suite 16, Victorville, 92395. Phone: (760) 241-1313. Fax: (760) 241-0205. E-mail: kimjennings@edbroadcasters.com Web Site:www.y102fm.com Licensee: EDB VV License LLC. Population served: 300,000 Natl. Rep: Christal,. Format: Adult contemp. Target aud: 25-54; women. ◆Tom Hoyt, VP & mktg mgr; Colleen Quinn, progmg dir.

Arcadia

KSSE(FM)— Dec 3, 1960: 107.1 mhz; 3 kw. 240 ft TL: N34 10 51 W118 01 38. (CP: 6 kw, ant -43 ft.). Hrs open: 24 5700 Wilshire Blvd., Suite 250, Los Angeles, 90036. Phone: (323) 900-6100. Fax: (323) 900-6200. E-mail: info@viva1071.com Web Site:www.viva1071.com Licensee: Entravision Holdings LLC. Group owner: Entravision Communications Corp. (acq 4-1-03; grpsl). Population served: 6,000,000 Latham & Watkins. Wire Svc: SportsTicker Format: Sp. Target aud: 24-39; general. ◆Karl Meyer, gen mgr; Elias Autran, progmg dir; Nestor Rocha, progmg VP & engrg dir.

Arcata

KATA(AM)— Nov 15, 1957: 1340 khz; 1 kw-U. TL: N40 51 12 W124 05 00. Hrs open: 5640 S. Broadway St., Eureka, 95503-6905. Phone: (707) 442-2000. Fax: (707) 443-6848. Web Site:www.kata1340.com Licensee: Bicoastal Media LLC. (group owner; acq 7-28-99; grpsl). Population served: 120,000 Natl. Network: ESPN Radio, Westwood One, . Format: Sports, News, Talk. Target aud: 25-54; upscale adults. ◆Mike Wilson, pres; Laurie Tate, gen mgr, opns dir; Victoria Bennington, gen sls mgr; Tom Sebourn, progmg dir.

*KHSU-FM— October 1960: 90.5 mhz; 8.8 kw. 1,506 ft TL: N40 43 36 W123 58 19. Stereo. Hrs open: 24 Humboldt State Univ., 1 Harpst St., 95521. Phone: (707) 826-4807. Fax: (707) 826-6082. E-mail: khsu@humboldt.edu Web Site:www.khsu.org Licensee: Humboldt State University. Population served: 125,000 Natl. Network: NPR, PRI, . Format: Var, news, NPR. News: 28 hrs wkly. Spec prog: World 14 hrs, jazz 10 hrs wkly. ◆Patrick Cleary, gen mgr; Katie Whiteside, opns mgr, progmg dir; David Reed, dev dir; Kevin Sanders, chief of engrg.

KXGO(FM)—Licensed to Arcata. See Eureka

Arnold

KBYN(FM)— Sept 1, 1995: 95.9 mhz; 860 w. Ant 863 ft TL: N38 22 40 W120 11 33. Stereo. Hrs open: 24 4043 Geer Rd, Hughson, 95326. Phone: (209) 883-8760. Fax: (209) 883-8769. E-mail: ngomez@lafavorita.net Web Site:www.lafavorita.net Licensee: KBYN Inc. (acq 3-28-01). Natl. Network: CBS, . Shaw Pittman. Format: Sp, country. News staff: one; News: 3 hrs wkly. Target aud: 25-54; general. ◆Nelson Gomez, gen mgr.

*KCFA(FM)— Oct 2, 1995: 106.1 mhz; 3.8 kw. 840 ft TL: N38 22 42 W120 11 36. Hrs open: 24 4043 Geer Rd., Hughson, 95326. Phone: (209) 883-8760. Fax: (209) 883-8769. E-mail: ngomez@lafavorita.net Web Site:www.lafavorita.net Licensee: KCFA Inc. (acq 3-21-02). Format: Sp-Ethnic. News staff: one; News: 5 hrs wkly. Target aud: 30-50; Families. ◆Nelson Gomez, gen mgr & gen sls mgr; Freddy Lopez, news dir; Chuck Hughes, chief of engrg; Armida Marquez, traf mgr.

Arroyo Grande

KLFF(AM)— Sept 1, 2002: 890 khz; 5 kw-U, DA-N. TL: N35 08 44 W120 31 15. Hrs open: Box 1561, San Luis Obispo, 93406. Phone: (805) 541-4343. Fax: (805) 541-9101. E-mail: info@klfie.org Web Site:www.890online.com Licensee: Jerry J. Collins. Format: Relg. ◆Jerry J. Collins, pres; Joel Riley, gen mgr; Noonie Fugler, prom dir.

KXTK(AM)—Licensed to Arroyo Grande. See San Luis Obispo

Arvin

KMYX-FM— June 30, 1999: 92.5 mhz; 1.15 kw. 751 ft TL: N35 11 45 W118 42 30. Hrs open: 24 6313 Schirra Ct., Bakersfield, 93313. Phone: (661) 837-0745. Fax: (661) 837-1612.E-mail: achavez@campesina.com Web Site:www.campesina.com Licensee: Farmworker Educ. Radio Network Inc. Population served: 400,000 Borsari & Paxson. Format: Sp, rgnl Mexican. Target aud: 25-54; Hispanic market. ♦Anthony Chavez, pres, gen mgr; Cesar Chavez, progmg dir; Dave Whitehead, chief of engrg; Maria Urrutia, traf mgr.

Atascadero

KIQO(FM)— May 19, 1979: 104.5 mhz; 5.6 kw. 1,410 ft TL: N35 21 38 W120 39 21. Stereo. Hrs open: 24 3620 Sacramento Dr., Suite 204, San Luis Obispo, 93401. Phone: (805) 781-2750. Fax: (805) 781-2758.E-mail: info@kiqo104.5.com Web Site:www.kiqo104.5.com Licensee: AGM California. Group owner: American General Media (acq 2-10-99; $1.5 million). Population served: 400,000 Natl. Network: ABC, . Format: Oldies. Target aud: 25-55. ♦Kathy Signorelli, gen mgr; Mark Tobin, gen sls mgr, chief of engrg; Seth Blackburn, progmg dir; Pat Mallon, news dir; Bill Bordeaux, chief of engrg.

Atherton

***KCEA(FM)—** June 2, 1979: 89.1 mhz; 100 w. -216 ft TL: N37 27 41 W122 10 30. (CP: Ant 5 ft.). Stereo. Hrs open: 24 555 Middle Field Rd., 94027. Phone: (650) 306-8823. Phone: (650) 306-8822. Fax: (650) 328-8706.E-mail: info@kcea.org Web Site:www.kcea.org Licensee: Sequoia Union High School District. Population served: 200,000 Format: Big band, Nostalgia, adult standards. Target aud: General. ♦Michael Isaacs, gen mgr; John Mylod, sports cmtr, disc jockey; Trish Millet, pub affrs dir & disc jockey.

Atwater

KBRE(FM)— Oct 1, 1995: 92.5 mhz; 6 kw. 328 ft TL: N37 16 42 W120 37 33. Stereo. Hrs open: 24 1020 W. Main St., Merced, 95340-4521. Phone: (209) 723-2191. Fax: (209) 383-2950.E-mail: info@925thebear.com Web Site:www.925thebear.com Licensee: Mapleton License of Merced LLC. (group owner; (acq 6-1-2002; grpsl). Population served: 200,000 Leventhal, Senter & Lerman. Format: Active rock. News staff: one; News: 3 hrs wkly. Men 25-49. ♦Andrew Adams, gen mgr, gen sls mgr, pub affrs dir; Jason LaChance, progmg dir.

Auberry

KKBZ(FM)— July 12, 1992: 105.1 mhz; 600 w. Ant 1,870 ft TL: N37 04 25 W119 25 52. Stereo. Hrs open: 24 1110 E. Olive Ave., Fresno, 93728. Phone: (559) 497-1100. Fax: (559) 497-1125.E-mail: mginsburg@lotusfresno.com Licensee: Lotus Communications Corp. (group owner) Population served: 1,500,000 Natl. Rep: Lotus Entravision Reps LLC,. Format: Classic rock. ♦Howard Kalmenson, pres; Mike Ginsburg, gen mgr.

Auburn

KAHI(AM)— Nov 13, 1957: 950 khz; 5 kw-D, 4.2 kw-N, DA-2. TL: N38 51 28 W121 01 39. Hrs open: 24 985 Lincoln Way, Suite 103, 95603. Phone: (530) 885-5636. Fax: (530) 885-0166.E-mail: info@KAHI.com Web Site:www.kahi.com Licensee: IHR Educational Broadcasting. (group owner; (acq 4-28-99; $475,000 with KSMH(AM) West Sacramento). Population served: 65,700 Natl. Network: Radio America, . Fletcher, Heald & Hildreth. Format: Var. News: 6-9am, 12-1pm, 4-7pm. Target aud: 25-54; Community focused. Spec prog: Community. ♦Jerry Henry, gen mgr & opns mgr; Dave Rosenthal, opns.

KHYL(FM)— Dec 21, 1961: 101.1 mhz; 36.3 kw. 577 ft TL: N38 51 28 W121 01 39. Stereo. Hrs open: 24 1440 Ethan Way, Suite 200, Sacramento, 95825. Phone: (916) 929-5325. Fax: (916) 925-0128.E-mail: info@khylfm.com Web Site:www.v101fm.com Licensee: AMFM Broadcasting Licenses LLC. Group owner: Clear Channel Communications Inc. (acq 8-30-2000; grpsl). Population served: 230,400 Format: Oldies, urban adult contemp. News: one hr wkly. Target aud: 25-54. ♦Jeff Holden, gen mgr & sls dir; Amy Bingham, mktg dir; Don Alias, progmg dir.

Avalon

KBRT(AM)— June 1, 1952: 740 khz; 10 kw-D, DA. TL: N33 21 36 W118 22 18. Stereo. Hrs open: 3183 D Airway Ave., Costa Mesa, 92626. Phone: (714) 754-4450. Fax: (714) 754-0735.E-mail: kbrtinfo@crawfordbroadcasting.com Web Site:www.kbrt740.com Licensee: Kierton Inc. Group owner: Crawford Broadcasting Co. (acq 5-21-80). Population served: 15,961,663 Format: Relg, talk. Target aud: Christian adult. ♦Todd Stickler, opns mgr.

***KISL(FM)—** 2000: 88.7 mhz; 200 w. Ant 20 ft TL: N33 20 32 W118 19 11. Hrs open: 707 Crescent Ave., 90704. Phone: (310) 510-7469. Fax: (310) 510-1025.E-mail: arts@cipas.org Web Site:www.kisl.org Licensee: Catalina Island Performing Arts Foundation (acq 3-15-2000). Format: Var. ♦Aaron Pitts, stn mgr.

Avenal

***KAAX(FM)—**Not on air, target date: unknown: Stn currently dark. 95.1 mhz; 920 w. Ant 656 ft TL: N36 00 40 W120 04 26. Hrs open: 12550 Brookhurst St., Suite A, Garden Grove, 92840. Licensee: Avenal Educational Services Inc.

Baker

KHRQ(FM)— 2002: 94.9 mhz; 1.4 kw. Ant 1,288 ft TL: N35 26 09 W115 55 22. Hrs open: 1611 E. Main St., Barstow, 92311. Phone: (760) 256-0326. Fax: (760) 256-9507.E-mail: tim@highwayradio.com Licensee: The Drive LLC. Group owner: KHWY Inc. (acq 5-31-2003). Natl. Network: Jones Radio Networks, . Hogan & Hartson. Format: Classic rock. ♦Howard Anderson, CEO, pres; Kirk Anderson, exec VP; Timothy Anderson, VP & gen mgr; Judy Robinson, sls VP; John Gregg, prom dir; Lance Todd, progmg dir; Thomas J. McNeill, engrg mgr.

KIXF(FM)— Mar 1, 1994: 101.5 mhz; 4.3 kw. Ant 1,322 ft TL: N35 26 00 W115 55 25. Stereo. Hrs open: 24
Rebroadcasts KIXW-FM Lenwood 100%.
1611 E. Main St., Barstow, 92311. Phone: (760) 256-0326. Fax: (760) 256-9507.E-mail: time@highwayradio.com Web Site:www.thehighwaystations.com Licensee: KHWY Inc. (group owner; (acq 2-18-98; $1,741,444 with KIXW-FM Lenwood). Natl. Network: Westwood One, CNN Radio, . Hogan & Hartson. Format: Country. News staff: one. Target aud: 25-54; interstate travelers to Las Vegas & Laughlin, NV. Spec prog: Hourly traf report to service interstate travelers. ♦Howard B. Anderson, CEO, pres; Kirk Anderson, exec VP; Timothy B. Anderson, VP & gen mgr; Judy Robinson, sls VP; John Gregg, prom dir; Lance Todd, progmg dir; Keith Hayes, news dir; Thomas J. McNeill, engrg mgr.

Bakersfield

KAFY(AM)— 2000: 1100 khz; 4.2 kw-D, 800 w-N, DA-N. TL: N35 27 00 W118 56 48. Hrs open: 24 4043 Green Rd., Hughson, 95326. Phone: (209) 883-8760. Fax: (209) 883-8769.E-mail: ngomez@lafavorita.net Web Site:www.lafavorita.net Licensee: KAFY Inc. (acq 3-28-01). Format: Sp talk. ♦Nelson Gomez, gen mgr.

KBFP(AM)— 1959: 800 khz; 1 kw-D, 440 w-N, DA-2. TL: N35 20 44 W118 59 33. Hrs open: 6 AM-12 AM 1100 Mohawk St., Suite 280, 93309. Phone: (661) 322-9929. Fax: (661) 322-9239.E-mail: A jimbell@clearchannel.com Web Site:www.foxsportsradio800.com Licensee: CC Licenses LLC. Group owner: Clear Channel Communications Inc. (acq 10-11-2000; grpsl). Population served: 500,000 Format: Sports. Target aud: 25-54; adults. ♦Jim Bell, VP; Tony Manes, progmg dir; Steve Mull, chief of engrg.

KBFP-FM—See Delano

KCWR(FM)— Mar 21, 1990: 107.1 mhz; 6 kw. 164 ft TL: N35 22 08 W119 00 14. Hrs open: 24 3223 Sillect Ave., 93308. Phone: (661) 326-1011. Fax: (661) 328-7503. Fax: (661) 328-7537(news). Licensee: Owens One Co. Inc. (acq 5-24-2006; grpsl). Format: Country. ♦Mel Owens Jr., CEO, gen mgr, opns mgr & dev mgr; Julie Randolph, gen sls mgr, mktg mgr.

KERI(AM)— Jan 3, 1932: 1410 khz; 1 kw-U. TL: N35 21 07 W118 56 48. Hrs open: 24 Box 2700, 93303-2700. Secondary address: 1400 Easton Dr., Suite 144 93309. Phone: (661) 328-1410. Fax: (661) 328-0873. Web Site:www.keri.com Licensee: AGM California. Group owner: American General Media (acq 5-1-75). Population served: 584,000 Natl. Rep: Christal,. Wire Svc: AP Format: Christian. Target aud: 25-54. ♦Roger Fessler, exec VP, gen mgr; Toni Snyder, gen sls mgr; D.C. Carter, progmg dir.

***KFRB(FM)—** August 1996: 91.3 mhz; 115 w. 1,368 ft TL: N35 26 17 W118 44 22. Hrs open: 24 c/o Family Stations, 290 Hegenberger Rd., Oakland, 94621. Phone: (209) 389-4659. Web Site:www.familyradio.com Licensee: Family Stations Inc. (group owner) Format: Relg. ♦Harold Camping, pres & gen mgr; David Manzi, opns mgr.

KGEO(AM)— Jan 1, 1946: 1230 khz; 1 kw-U. TL: N35 20 53 W119 00 33. Stereo. Hrs open: 1400 Easton Dr., Suite 144, 93309. Phone: (661) 631-1230. Phone: (661) 328-1410. Fax: (661) 328-0873.E-mail: ccostelloe@americangeneralmedia.com Web Site:www.espnbakersfield.com Licensee: AGM California. Group owner: American General Media (acq 12-9-92; $1.75 million with co-located FM; 1-4-93). Population served: 355,000 Natl. Network: Westwood One, ESPN Radio, CBS, . Natl. Rep: McGavren Guild,. Cohn & Marks. Format: Sports. ♦Roger Fessler, gen mgr.

KGFM(FM)— October 1964: 101.5 mhz; 6.7 kw. Ant 1,299 ft TL: N35 26 17 W118 44 22. Stereo. Hrs open: 1400 Easton Dr., Suite 144, 93309. Phone: (661) 631-1230. Phone: (661) 328-1410. Fax: (661) 328-0873. Licensee: AGM California. Population served: 500,000 Format: Adult Contemp. ♦Roger Fessler, gen mgr; Toni Snyder, gen sls mgr; Chris Edwards, progmg dir.

KHTY(AM)— October 1946: 970 khz; 1 kw-D, 5 kw-N, DA-2. TL: N35 27 00 W118 56 48. Hrs open: 24 1100 Mohawk St., Ste 280, 93309. Phone: (661) 322-9929. Fax: (661) 322-7239. Fax: (661) 283-2963.E-mail: A Jimbell@clearchannel.com Web Site:www.foxsports970am.com Licensee: AMFM Radio Licenses LLC. Group owner: Clear Channel Communications Inc. (acq 12-22-2000; $1.4 million). Population served: 160,000 Natl. Network: Fox Sports, . Format: Sports. ♦Jim Bell, VP, gen mgr; Ron Fisher, gen sls mgr; Steve King, progmg dir; Steve Mull, chief of engrg.

KISV(FM)— 1948: 94.1 mhz; 4.5 kw. 1,312 ft TL: N35 26 20 W118 44 23. Stereo. Hrs open: 24 Box 2700, 93303-2700. Secondary address: 1400 Easton Dr., Suite 144 93309. Phone: (661) 328-1410. Phone: (661) 326-1410. Fax: (661) 328-0873. Web Site:hot941.com Licensee: AGM California. Population served: 500,000 Format: CHR rhythmic. Spec prog: Farm one hr, relg one hr wkly.

KIWI(FM)—(McFarland, July 11, 1989: 102.9 mhz; 25 kw. Ant 321 ft TL: N35 19 16 W119 42 26. Stereo. Hrs open: 24 5100 Commerce Dr., 93309. Phone: (661) 327-9711. Fax: (661) 327-0797.E-mail: napo@radiolobo.com Web Site:radiolobo.com (Acq 12-18-00; $2.5 million including a $10,000 three-year noncompete agreement). Population served: 650,000 Natl. Rep: Lotus Entravision Reps LLC,. Format: Mexican regional. Target aud: General.

KKBB(FM)— November 1991: 99.3 mhz; 1.2 kw. 1,345 ft TL: N35 26 17 W118 44 22. Stereo. Hrs open: 24 Box 80658, 93380. Secondary address: 3651 Pegasus Dr., Suite 107 93380. Phone: (661) 393-1900. Fax: (661) 393-1915.E-mail: jlove@kkbb.com Web Site:www.groove993.com Licensee: Buckley Communications Inc. Group owner: Buckley Broadcasting Corp. (acq 10-3-94; $1 million; 10-17-94). Population served: 480,000 Natl. Rep: D & R Radio,. Format: Rhythmic Oldies. Target aud: 25-54; adults. ♦Steve Darnell, gen mgr; Otis Warren, gen sls mgr; Kathy King, news dir; Bob Turner, chief of engrg.

KLHC(AM)— February 1958: 1350 khz; 1 kw-D, 33 w-N. TL: N35 21 00 W119 58 58. Hrs open: 24 3817 Wilson Rd., Suite E, 93309. Phone: (661) 847-1450. Fax: (661) 847-1452.E-mail: klhc@klhcradio.com Web Site:www.klhcradio.com Licensee: Force Broadcasting LLC. Group owner: American General Media (acq 1-6-2006; $925,000). Population served: 300,000 Format: Sp relg. ♦Maria Ochoa, gen mgr.

KNZR(AM)— 1933: 1560 khz; 25 kw-D, 10 kw-N, DA-N. TL: N35 18 30 W119 02 09. Hrs open: 24 Box 80658, 93308. Secondary address: 3651 Pegasus Dr., Suite 107 93380. Phone: (661) 393-1900. Fax: (661) 393-1915.E-mail: info@knzr.com Web Site:www.knzr.com Licensee: Buckley Broadcasting of California LLC. Group owner: Buckley Broadcasting Corp. (acq 1-25-90; $1 million;2-19-90). Population served: 770,000 Natl. Network: CBS, . Natl. Rep: D & R Radio,. Shaw Pittman. Format: News/talk. News staff: 4; News: 40 hrs wkly. Target aud: 25-54. Spec prog: L.A. Dodgers. ♦Steve Darnell, gen mgr.

***KPRX(FM)—** Feb 28, 1987: 89.1 mhz; 12 kw. 500 ft TL: N35 29 10 W118 53 20. Hrs open: 3437 W. Shaw Ave., Suite 101, Fresno, 93711. Phone: (559) 275-0764. Fax: (559) 275-2202.E-mail: kvpr@kvpr.org Web Site:www.kvpr.org Licensee: White Ash Broadcasting Inc. Natl. Network: NPR, . Format: Class, news & info. ♦Mariam Stepanian, pres, gen mgr; Jim Meyers, stn mgr, progmg dir; Steve Mull, chief of engrg.

KPSL-FM— Dec 15, 1985: 92.1 mhz; 2 kw. Ant 567 ft TL: N35 29 11 W118 53 21. Stereo. Hrs open: 24 5100 Commerce Dr., 93309-0684. Phone: (661) 327-9711. Fax: (661) 327-0797.E-mail: info@thespanishradio.com Web Site:www.thespanishradio.com Licensee: Illinois Lotus Corp. Group owner: Lotus Communications Corp. (acq 8-24-99; grpsl). Population served: 650,000 Format: Sp pop. ♦Mike Allen, gen mgr; Isidro Roman, progmg dir.

KRAB(FM)—(Green Acres, Oct 1, 1991: 106.1 mhz; 25 kw. 410 ft TL: N35 28 17 W119 01 38. Hrs open: 24 1100 Mohawk St., Suite 280, 93309. Phone: (661) 322-9929. Fax: (661) 322-9239.E-mail: A

jimbell@clearchannel.com Web Site:www.krab.com Licensee: CC Licenses LLC. Population served: 460,000 Natl. Rep: McGavren Guild,. Arter & Hadden. Format: AOR. Target aud: 18-49; predominantly male. ♦Jim Bell, VP, gen mgr; Ron Fisher, gen sls mgr; Danny Spanks, progmg dir; Steve Mull, chief of engrg.

KSMJ(FM)—(Shafter, Mar 3, 1978: 97.7 mhz; 4.1 kw. Ant 397 ft TL: N35 27 33 W119 01 13. Stereo. Hrs open: 24 Box 80658, 93380. Phone: (661) 393-1900. Fax: (661) 393-1915.E-mail: info@977thebreeze.com Web Site:www.977thebreeze.com Licensee: Buckley Broadcasting of California LLC. Group owner: Buckley Broadcasting Corp. (acq 2-1-2001; $2 million). Population served: 378,000 Format: Lite rock. Target aud: 18-49. ♦Steve Darnell, gen mgr; E.J. Tyler, opns dir, opns mgr.

***KTQX(FM)**— Apr 14, 1989: 90.1 mhz; 590 w. 3,572 ft TL: N35 27 05 W118 35 10. Hrs open: 24 5005 E. Belmont Ave., Fresno, 93727. Phone: (559) 455-5777. Fax: (559) 455-5778.E-mail: mail@radiobilingue.org Web Site:www.radiobilingue.org Licensee: Radio Bilingue Inc. Format: Ethnic, multilingual, Sp. News staff: 5; News: 11 hrs wkly. Target aud: 16-60; Latino. ♦Hugo Morales, CEO; Maria Erana, gen mgr, opns mgr, gen sls mgr, progmg dir; Phil Traynor, dev VP; Samuel Cozco, news dir; Bill Bach, chief of engrg.

KUZZ(AM)— October 1946: 550 khz; 5 kw-U, DA-N. TL: N35 20 25 W118 56 14. Stereo. Hrs open: 3223 Sillect Ave., 93308. Phone: (661) 326-1011. Fax: (661) 328-7503. Web Site:www.kuzz.com Licensee: Owens One Co. (group owner; (acq 5-24-2006; grpsl). Population served: 100,000 Format: Country. Target aud: 25-54. ♦Mel Owens Jr., CEO, gen mgr; Julie Randolph, gen sls mgr; Harvey Campbell, natl sls mgr; Jerry Hufford, prom dir; Evan Bridwell, progmg dir; Donna James, mus dir; Mark Howell, news dir, local news ed; Sylvia Cariker, pub affrs dir; Terry Gaiser, chief of engrg; Casey McBride, women's int ed, disc jockey; Chris Conner, disc jockey.

KUZZ-FM— 1968: 107.9 mhz; 6 kw. 1,364 ft TL: N35 26 20 W118 44 24. Stereo. Hrs open: Dups AM 100% 3223 Sillect Ave., 93308. Phone: (661) 326-1011. Fax: (661)328-7503. Web Site:www.kuzz.com ♦Retta Smith, traf mgr; Peter Samore, news rptr; Casey McBride, disc jockey.

KVMX(FM)— Aug 24, 1963: 96.5 mhz; 50 kw. Ant 550 ft TL: N35 29 08 W118 53 19. Stereo. Hrs open: 1100 Mohawk St., Suite 280, 93309. Phone: (661) 322-9929. Fax: (661) 322-9239. Web Site:www.965maxfm.com Licensee: Texas Lotus Corp. (acq 7-29-2008; with KWID(FM) Las Vegas, NV in exchange for KZEP-FM San Antonio, TX). Population served: 460,000 Natl. Rep: McGavren Guild,. Bryan Cave LLP. Format: Classic rock. ♦Greg Holcomb, gen mgr; Sandy Ozuna, gen sls mgr; Kenn McCloud, progmg dir.

KWAC(AM)— 1954: 1490 khz; 1 kw-U. TL: N35 24 07 W119 02 45. Stereo. Hrs open: 24 5100 Commerce Dr., 93309. Phone: (661) 327-9711. Fax: (661) 327-0797.E-mail: info@thespanishradio.com Web Site:kwac.com Licensee: Illinois Lotus Corp. Group owner: Lotus Communications Corp. (acq 8-24-99; grpsl). Population served: 1,056,270 Natl. Network: ESPN Radio, . Natl. Rep: Lotus Entravision Reps LLC,. Format: Mexican rgnl. News: 5 hrs wkly. Target aud: General. ♦Howard Kalmenson, pres; Mike Allen, gen mgr; Juan M. Martinez, progmg dir, news dir, disc jockey; Anna Gallegos, pub affrs dir; Lloyd Moss, chief of engrg; Jesus Valdez, disc jockey.

Banning

KMET(AM)— 1948: 1490 khz; 1 kw-U. TL: N33 55 49 W116 55 20. Hrs open: 24 700 E. Redlands Blvd., Suite U, PMB 323, Redlands, 92373. Phone: (951) 849-4644. Phone: (909) 319-1177. Fax: (951) 849-3114.E-mail: kmet1490talkradio@yahoo.com Licensee: Sunset Broadcasting Inc. (acq 3-31-2003). Population served: 375,000 Natl. Network: Talk Radio Network, . Format: News/talk, sports. News: 3 hrs wkly. Target aud: General; 25-54, 35-65. ♦Richard Nuthmann, pres; Mitch McClellan, gen mgr, stn mgr, opns dir.

Barstow

KDUC(FM)— June 4, 1986: 94.3 mhz; 4.6 kw. 783 ft TL: N34 58 15 W117 02 22. Stereo. Hrs open: 29000 Radio Road, 92311. Phone: (760) 256-2121. Fax: (760) 256-5090.E-mail: doscostascommunications@yahoo.com Licensee: Dos Costas Communications Corp. (group owner; acq 6-18-03; grpsl). Format: Top 40, CHR Rythmic. Target aud: 12-44. ♦Manny Lopez, gen sls mgr; Mike Garcia, progmg dir; Roland Ulloa, gen mgr & mus dir.

KIQQ(AM)— Sept 29, 1960: 1310 khz; 5 kw-D, 118 w-N, DA-1. TL: N34 54 51 W117 00 59. Hrs open: 24
Simulcast with KAEH(FM) Beaumont 100%.
710 W. Old Hwy. 58, 92311. Phone: (760) 255-2636. Fax: (760) 255-3236.E-mail: jramirez@lamaquinaamusical.net Web Site:moonbroadcasting.com Licensee: MBR Licensee LLC. Group owner: Moon Broadcasting (acq 8-7-2000). Natl. Network: Westwood One, . Arent, Fox, Kintner, Plotkin & Kahn. Format: Sp, regnl Mexican. Target aud: 45 plus. ♦Alicia Avila, gen mgr.

***KODV(FM)**— 2005: 89.1 mhz; 260 w. Ant 725 ft TL: N34 58 17 W117 02 22. Hrs open: Box 94, Hesperia, 92340-1136. Secondary address: 18280 Atlantic St., Hesperia 92345. Phone: (760) 947-4300. Fax: (760) 956-2427.E-mail: comentarios@ondadevida.net Web Site:www.ondasdevida.net Licensee: Ondas de Vida Network Inc. (acq 12-7-2005; $100,000 for CP). Format: Sp. ♦Hector E. Manzo, CEO.

KRXV(FM)—See Yermo

KSZL(AM)— June 25, 1986: 1230 khz; 1 kw-U. TL: N34 54 44 W117 01 39. Stereo. Hrs open: 24 29000 Radio Rd., 92311. Phone: (760) 256-2121. Phone: (760) 256-5382. Fax: (760) 256-5090.E-mail: am1230kszl@yahoo.com ABC/SMN Stardust Licensee: Dos Costas Communications Corp. (group owner; acq 6-18-03; grpsl). Population served: 220,000 Natl. Network: Westwood One, . Natl. Rep: Western Regional Broadcast Sales,. Fleischman & Walsh, L.L.P. Format: News, Talk, Air America. News staff: 2; News: 12 hrs wkly. Target aud: 25 plus; Adults 35 years +. ♦Manny Lopez, gen mgr, gen sls mgr; Michael Garcia, opns mgr, progmg dir; Steve Hastings, traf mgr.

***KWTH(FM)**— 2006: 91.3 mhz; 1.55 kw. Ant 2,296 ft TL: N34 38 39 W116 37 38. Stereo. Hrs open:
Rebroadcasts KWTW(FM) Bishop 100%.
Box 637, Bishop, 93515. Phone: (760) 872-4225. Phone: (866) 466-5989. Fax: (760) 872-4155.E-mail: friar@schat.com Web Site:www.kwtw.org Licensee: Living Proof Inc. Format: Christian, relg. ♦Daniel McClenaghan, pres & gen mgr.

KXXZ(FM)— 1989: 95.9 mhz; 8.9 kw. Ant 485 ft TL: N34 51 22 W117 03 00. Stereo. Hrs open: 24 29000 Radio Rd., 92311. Phone: (760) 256-2121. Fax: (760) 256-5090.E-mail: doscostas@yahoo.com Licensee: Dos Costas Communications Corp. (group owner; acq 6-18-03; grpsl). Format: Mexican/Regional. ♦Roland Ulloa, gen mgr; Manny Lopez, gen sls mgr; Mike Garcia, progmg dir; Steve Hastings, traf mgr.

Bayside

***KNHM(FM)**— Apr 15, 1992: 91.5 mhz; 550 w. Ant 508 ft TL: N40 47 49 W124 02 47. Hrs open: 24 Jefferson Public Radio, 1250 Siskiyou Blvd., Ashland, OR, 97520. Phone: (541) 552-6301. Fax: (541) 552-8565.E-mail: info@ijpr.org Web Site:www.ijpr.org Licensee: JPR Foundation Inc. (acq 3-24-2004; $130,000). ♦Ronald Kramer, gen mgr & stn mgr; Paul Westhelle, dev mgr, mus dir.

Beaumont

KAEH(FM)— 1996: 100.9 mhz; 1.5 kw. Ant 479 ft TL: N33 54 29 W116 59 45. Hrs open: 24 Moon Broadcasting Riverside LLC, 1200 W. Venice Blvd., Los Angeles, 90006. Phone: (909) 381-0969. Fax: (909) 381-0943.E-mail: postmaster@manbroadcasting.com Web Site:www.moonbroadcasting.com/kaeh Licensee: MBR Licensee LLC. Group owner: Moon Broadcasting (acq 2-13-2002; $1.7 million). Format: Rgnl Mexican. ♦Abel A. DeLuna, pres; Alicia Avila, gen mgr; Juan Ramirez, progmg dir; Manuel Garcia, news dir; Rick Hunt, chief of engrg.

Bella Vista

***KKRN(FM)**—Not on air, target date: unknown: 88.5 mhz; 590 w. Ant 2,034 ft TL: N40 54 21 W121 49 38. Hrs open: Box 188, Montgomery Creek, 96065. Phone: (530) 337-6736. Fax: (530) 337-6567. Web Site:www.acorncafe.org Licensee: Acorn Community Enterprises. ♦Staci Wadley, gen mgr.

Berkeley

***KALX(FM)**— October 1967: 90.7 mhz; 500 w. Ant 778 ft TL: N37 52 40 W122 14 44. Stereo. Hrs open: 24 26 Barrows #5650, 94720-5650. Phone: (510) 642-1111.E-mail: mail@kalx.berkeley.edu Web Site:kalx.berkeley.edu Licensee: The Regents of the University of California. Population served: 1,000,000 Format: Educ, div. News: 4 hrs wkly. ♦Sandra Wasson, gen mgr; Mona Dehghan, opns mgr; James Croft, mus dir; Zaheem Cassim, news dir; Bill Jones, engrg mgr, chief of engrg.

KBLX-FM— Apr 29, 1949: 102.9 mhz; 50 kw. 1,290 ft TL: N37 41 20 W122 26 07. Stereo. Hrs open: 24 55 Hawthorne St., Suite 900, San Francisco, 94105. Phone: ((415) 284-1029. Fax: (415) 764-4959.E-mail: info@kblx.com Web Site:www.kblx.com Population served: 400,000 Wire Svc: Bay City News Service Format: Adult Contemporary. News staff: one; News: feature only. Target aud: 25-54; adults. ♦Harvey Stone, opns mgr; Barry Rose, sls VP; Michelle Heller, natl sls mgr, mktg mgr; Kevin Brown, progmg dir; Kimmie Taylor, mus dir; Aaron Jones, pub affrs dir; Paul Marks, chief of engrg; Renee Guillory, traf mgr; Susie Lee, pub svc dir & disc jockey.

***KPFA(FM)**— April 1949: 94.1 mhz; 59 kw. 1,330 ft TL: N37 51 55 W122 13 12. Stereo. Hrs open: 24 1929 Martin Luther King Jr. Way, 94704. Phone: (510) 848-6767. Fax: (510) 848-3812.E-mail: info@kpfa.org Web Site:www.kpfa.org Licensee: Pacifica Foundation. Group owner: Pacifica Foundations Inc. dba Pacifica Radio Population served: 200,000 Haley, Bader & Potts. Wire Svc: Reuters Wire Svc: Pacifica Network News Format: Div mus, pub affrs. News staff: 4; News: 11 hrs wkly. Target aud: 25-50. Spec prog: C&W 18 hrs, Black 18 hrs, jazz 15 hrs, folk 10 hrs, women 10 hrs, world 18 hrs wkly. ♦Lem Lem Rigio, gen mgr; Luis Medina, mus dir; Mark Mericle, news dir; Michael Yoshida, chief of engrg.

***KPFB(FM)**— February 1954: 89.3 mhz; 460 w. Ant -98 ft TL: N37 52 20 W122 16 18. Hrs open:
Simulcasts with *KPFA(FM) Berkeley except for pub affrs & special events progmg.
Licensee: Pacifica Foundation Inc.

KVTO(AM)— May 22, 1922: 1400 khz; 1 kw-U. TL: N37 50 58 W122 17 44. Hrs open: 24 55 Hawthorne St., Suite 900, San Francisco, 94105. Phone: (415) 284-1029. Fax: (415) 764-4959.E-mail: info@kblx.com Licensee: Urban Radio III L.L.C. Group owner: Inner City Broadcasting (acq 1979). Natl. Rep: D & R Radio,. Format: Asian. Target aud: 25-54. ♦Harvey Stone, pres, gen mgr; Barry Rose, gen sls mgr; Rhonda Amiz, natl sls mgr; Jamie Arbona, progmg dir; Paul Marks, chief of engrg.

Beverly Hills

KGIL(AM)— October 1947: 1260 khz; 5 kw-U, DA-2. TL: N34 14 58 W118 27 15. Hrs open: 24 1500 Cotner Ave., Los Angeles, 90025. Phone: (310) 478-5540. Fax: (310) 445-1439.E-mail: info@1260am.com Web Site:www.1260.am Licensee: Mount Wilson FM Broadcasters Inc. (acq 11-20-92; $2.5 million; 12-14-92). Population served: 400,000 Natl. Network: AP Radio, . Natl. Rep: D & R Radio,. Fisher, Wayland, Cooper, Leader & Zaragoza L.L.P. Format: News/talk, standards. ♦Saul Levine, pres & gen mgr; Mike Johnson, opns dir; Kane Biscaya, gen sls mgr.

Big Bear City

KBHR(FM)— Dec 17, 1995: 93.3 mhz; 1.3 kw. Ant 702 ft TL: N34 16 41 W116 47 31. Stereo. Hrs open: 24 Box 2979, ., 92314. Phone: (909) 584-5247. Fax: (909) 584-5347.E-mail: info@kbhr933.com Web Site:www.kbhr933.com Licensee: Parallel Broadcasting Inc. (acq 1-17-95; 3-13-95). Population served: 25,000 Natl. Network: CNN Radio, . Format: Triple A. News staff: one; News: 11 hrs wkly. Target aud: 25-54; upscale second home owners, resort visitors. Spec prog: CNN news 8 hrs, ski report one hr, fish report one hr wkly. ♦Cathy Herrick, VP, opns dir; Jay Tunnell, sls dir; Rick Herrick, pres, gen mgr & progmg dir; Catherine Sandstrom, news dir.

Big Bear Lake

KXSB(FM)— May 1, 1975: 101.7 mhz; 90 w. 1,500 ft TL: N34 12 47 W116 51 59. (CP: 300 w). Stereo. Hrs open: 24
Rebroadcasts KXLM(FM) Oxnard 80%.
1950 S. Sunwest Ln., #302, San Bernarino, 92408. Phone: (909) 825-5020. Fax: (909) 884-5844. Fax: (909) 890-3849.E-mail: edith@radiolazer.com Web Site:www.radiolazer.com Licensee: Lazer Broadcasting Corp. (group owner; acq 1995; $750,000). Population served: 1,500,000 Natl. Rep: Lotus Entravision Reps LLC,. Fletcher, Heald & Hildreth. Format: CHR, Sp. News staff: one; News: 2 hrs wkly. Target aud: 25-54; adults, serious minded. ♦Alfredo Plascencia, CEO, pres; Vicki Bails, VP, VP, gen mgr & gen sls mgr; Gerardo Palafox, prom dir; Salvador Prieto, progmg dir, news dir; Ralph Jones, chief of engrg.

Big Pine

KRHV(FM)— 1999: 93.3 mhz; 890 w. Ant 2,903 ft TL: N37 24 48 W118 11 08. Hrs open: Box 1284, Mammoth Lakes, 93546. Secondary address: 94 Laurel Mountain Rd., Mammoth Lakes 93546. Phone: (760) 934-8888. Fax: (760) 934-2429.E-mail: kmmtradioworks@yahoo.com Web Site:www.kmmtradio.com Licensee: David & Mary Digerness. Format: Classic rock. ♦David A. Digerness, pres, chief of engrg;

Shellie Woods, gen mgr, gen sls mgr, mktg dir, adv dir, traf mgr; Maryanne Digerness, stn mgr, gen sls mgr, mktg dir, adv dir; Spencer Myers, progmg dir.

Big River

KFLG-FM— Dec 6, 1974: 94.7 mhz; 19.5 kw. Ant 2,736 ft TL: N34 33 06 W114 11 37. Stereo. Hrs open: 24 1531 Jill Way, Suite 7, Bullhead City, AZ, 86426-9341. Phone: (928) 763-5586. Fax: (928) 763-3775. Web Site:www.kflg947.com Licensee: Cameron Broadcasting Inc. Population served: 130,000 Format: Country. News staff: one. Target aud: 25-54. ◆William Jaeger, CEO; Craig Powers, opns mgr; Mike Fletcher, gen sls mgr; Dave Cooper, chief of engrg.

Bishop

KACE(AM)—Not on air, target date: unknown: 1340 khz; 1 kw-U. TL: N37 22 42 W118 23 43. Hrs open: Box 1450, St. George, UT, 84771-1450. Secondary address: 210 North 1000 East, St. George, UT 84770-3155. Phone: (435) 628-1000. Fax: (435) 628-6636. Licensee: Radio 1340 LLC. (acq 4-14-2006). Population served: 15,313 Dan J. Alpert. ◆E. Morgan Skinner Jr., pres.

KBOV(AM)— Apr 1, 1953: 1230 khz; 1 kw-U. TL: N37 20 44 W118 23 43. Hrs open: Box 757, S. Hwy.395, 93515. Phone: (760) 873-6324. Phone: (760) 873-5427. Fax: (760) 872-2639.E-mail: kibskbov@qnet.com Web Site:www.kibskbov.com Licensee: Great Country Broadcasting Inc. (acq 7-6-2004; $965,000 with co-located FM). Population served: 13,000 Natl. Rep: Western Regional Broadcast Sales,. Format: Oldies. News staff: one; News: 8 hrs wkly. Target aud: General. ◆Lauren Brandt, gen mgr.

KIBS(FM)— Nov 1, 1974: 100.7 mhz; 1 kw. 2,960 ft TL: N37 25 00 W118 11 00. Stereo. Hrs open: 24 Prog sep from AM Box 757, S. Hwy. 395, 93515. Phone: (760) 873-6324. Fax: (760) 872-2639.E-mail: kibskbov@qnet.com Web Site:www.kibskbov.com Licensee: Great Country Broadcasting Inc. Population served: 50,000 Format: Country. News staff: one; News: 8 hrs wkly. ◆Steve Miller, gen mgr.

***KWTW(FM)—** 2002: 88.5 mhz; 900 w. Ant 2,916 ft TL: N37 24 48 W118 11 08. Stereo. Hrs open: 24 Box 637, 93515. Secondary address: 125 S. Main St. 93514. Phone: (760) 872-4225. Phone: (866) 466-5989. Fax: (760) 872-4155.E-mail: friar@schat.com Web Site:www.kwtw.org Licensee: Living Proof Inc. Population served: 40,000 Format: Christian, relg. Target aud: General; all who want to hear the gospel. ◆Daniel McClenaghan, pres & gen mgr.

Blue Lake

KCIK(AM)—Not on air, target date: unknown: 1450 khz; 250 w-U. TL: N40 52 52 W123 59 58. Hrs open: Box 180, Tahoma, 96142. Phone: (530) 584-5700. Fax: (530) 584-5705 .E-mail: info@ihradio.org Web Site:www.ihradio.org Licensee: IHR Educational Broadcasting. (group owner; acq 3-28-2003). Format: Relg/Catholic. ◆Douglas M. Sherman, pres; Steve Wise, gen mgr.

KEJY(FM)— 2007: 106.3 mhz; 3.3 kw. Ant 1,692 ft TL: N40 43 38.9 W123 58 17. Hrs open: 1101 Marsh Rd., Eureka, 95501. Phone: (707) 442-5744. Licensee: Eureka Broadcasting Co. Inc. ◆Hugo Papstein, pres.

Blythe

KJMB(FM)— April 1975: 100.3 mhz; 36.4 kw. 174 ft TL: N33 37 16 W114 35 28. Stereo. Hrs open: 24 681 N. 4th St., 92225. Phone: (760) 922-7143. Fax: (760) 922-2844.E-mail: info@kjmbfm.com Licensee: Blythe Radio Inc. Population served: 40,000 Natl. Network: USA, . Format: Adult contemp. News staff: one; News: 10 hrs wkly. Target aud: 18-40; adults. Spec prog: Farm 5 hrs wkly. ◆Jim Mayson, pres; James M. Morris, gen mgr.

Brawley

KROP(AM)—Licensed to Brawley. See El Centro

KSEH(FM)— April 4, 1988: 94.5 mhz; 50 kw. Ant 302 ft TL: N32 54 40 W115 31 40. Stereo. Hrs open: 24 Box 2830, El Centro, 92244. Phone: (760) 482-7777. Fax: (760) 482-0099. Licensee: Entravision Holdings LLC. Group owner: Entravision Communications Corp. Population served: 950,000 Natl. Network: ABC, . Format: Latin pop. Target aud: 25-54. ◆Eric Chavez, gen mgr.

KSIQ(FM)—Licensed to Brawley. See El Centro

Buena Park

***KBPK(FM)—** July 6, 1970: 90.1 mhz; 20 w. 130 ft TL: N33 51 35 W118 00 53. Stereo. Hrs open: 321 E. Chapman Ave., Fullerton, 92832. Phone: (714) 732-5459. Web Site:kbpk-fm.com Licensee: Buena Park School District. Population served: 450,000 Booth, Freret, Imlay & Tepper. Wire Svc: AP Format: Adult contemp. Target aud: 25-54. ◆Edward Ford, opns mgr; Peg Stewart Berger, progmg dir, news dir, sports cmtr; Tracy Thackrah, mus dir.

Burney

***KIBC(FM)—** Nov 15, 1985: 90.5 mhz; 3 kw. 1,456 ft TL: N40 52 29 W121 46 13. Hrs open: 24 Box 1717, 20410 Marquette St., 96013. Phone: (530) 335-5422.E-mail: pastorbud@kibcfm.org Web Site:www.kibcfm.org Licensee: Burney Educational Broadcasting Foundation. Format: Educ, relg mus. Target aud: General. ◆Wayne Hennessey, gen mgr; Jack Drake, chief of engrg.

***KNCA(FM)—** July 1992: 89.7 mhz; 2.28 kw. 1,465 ft TL: N40 52 30 W121 46 14. Stereo. Hrs open: 5 AM-2 AM Southern Oregon State University, 1250 Siskiyou Blvd., Ashland, OR, 97520. Phone: (541) 552-6301. Phone: (541) 552-8565.E-mail: info@ijpr.org Web Site:www.ijpr.org Licensee: The State of Oregon, acting by and through the State Board of Higher Education. Natl. Network: NPR, PRI, . Ernest Sanchez. Format: Jazz, AAA, news. News staff: one; News: 45 hrs wkly. Target aud: General. Spec prog: Blues 6 hrs, folk 3 hrs, pub affrs 7 hrs wkly. ◆Mitchell Christian, CFO; Ronald Kramer, CEO & gen mgr; Bryon Lambert, opns dir; Paul Westhelle, dev dir.

KRRX(FM)—Licensed to Burney. See Redding

Butte City

***KRNR(FM)—**Not on air, target date: unknown: 91.3 mhz; 50 kw. Ant 72 ft TL: N39 16 49 W122 10 38. Hrs open: 3723 Ashley Ave., Oroville, 95966. Phone: (530) 872-8629. Fax: (530) 533-2949. Web Site:www.calvarychapel.com/oroville/ Licensee: Calvary Chapel Oroville. ◆Robert Scott, pres.

Calexico

KGBA(AM)— Apr 6, 1946: 1490 khz; 1 kw-U. TL: N32 41 58 W115 30 10. (CP: COL Heber. 500 w-U. TL: N32 44 32 W115 33 11). Hrs open: 24 Box 232, 695 Hwy. 111, 92231. Phone: (760) 357-5055. Fax: (760) 357-4168. Licensee: The Voice of International Christian Evangelism Inc. (acq 1-31-2008; $350,000). Population served: 1,440,000 Format: Sp. Target aud: 18-49; Hispanic. ◆Douglas Hanson, gen mgr; Paul Raine, gen sls mgr; Noe Diaz, progmg mgr.

***KQVO(FM)—** March 1984: 97.7 mhz; 6 kw. Ant 305 ft TL: N32 40 48 W115 25 36. Stereo. Hrs open: 24 Rebroadcasts KPBS-FM San Diego 100%. c/o KPBS-FM, 5200 Campanile Dr., San Diego, 92182-5400. Phone: (619) 594-1515. Fax: (619) 594-3812. Web Site:www.kpbs.org Licensee: State of California, San Diego State University (acq 5-10-2005; $1.1 million). Natl. Network: NPR, . Format: News/talk, classical. ◆Doug Myrland, gen mgr.

***KUBO(FM)—** 1989: 88.7 mhz; 3 kw. 272 ft TL: N32 47 57 W115 30 12. Hrs open: 24 531 Main St., #2, El Centro, 92243. Phone: (760) 337-8053. Fax: (760) 337-8519.E-mail: carlosleon@radiobilingue.org Web Site:www.radiobilingue.org Licensee: Radio Bilingue Inc. Format: Multilingual, Ethnic, Sp. News staff: 5; News: 3 hrs wkly. Target aud: 16-60; Latino. ◆Hugo Morales, CEO; Maria Erana, opns dir; Maria Esana, progmg dir.

California City

KMVE(FM)— May 22, 1999: 106.9 mhz; 2.35 kw. Ant 522 ft TL: N35 12 44 W117 45 11. Hrs open: 24 Aloha Plaza, 8401 Calif. City Blvd., # 9, 93505. Phone: (760) 373-1069. Fax: (760) 373-8808. Licensee: Point Broadcasting Co. Group owner: Point Broadcasting Company (acq 12-29-2003; $500,000). Population served: 750,000 Natl. Network: ABC, . Format: Rgnl Sp. News staff: one. Target aud: General. Spec prog: Gospel 3 hrs wkly.

Calipatria

KSSB(FM)— Feb 8, 1997: 100.9 mhz; 3 kw. Ant 148 ft TL: N33 07 12 W115 30 47. Hrs open: 24 1950 S. Sunwest Ln., Suite 302, San Bernadino, 92408. Phone: (909) 825-5020. Fax: (909) 884-5844. Licensee: Lazer Licenses LLC. (acq 9-22-2006; $925,000). Format: Rgnl Mexican. News staff: one; News: 6 hrs wkly. Target aud: 25 plus; female/male. Spec prog: Religious 6 hrs wkly. ◆Alfredo Plascencia, CEO; Vickie Balesz, gen mgr.

Calistoga

***KBBF(FM)—** May 30, 1973: 89.1 mhz; 420 w. Ant 2,766 ft TL: N38 39 23 W122 36 54. Hrs open: Box 7189, Santa Rosa, 95407. Phone: (707) 545-8833. Fax: (707) 545-6244. Web Site:www.kbbf-radio.com Licensee: Bilingual Broadcasting Foundation Inc. Population served: 50,006 Format: Educ, Sp, bilingual. ◆Joseph Slali, gen mgr; Roy Brown, opns dir; Roy Brown, prom VP.

KSXY(FM)— 1996: 100.9 mhz; 64 w. 2,945 ft TL: N38 40 10 W122 37 52. Hrs open: 3565 Standish Ave., Santa Rosa, 95407. Phone: (707) 588-0707. Fax: (707) 588-0777. Licensee: Sinclair Telecable Inc. Group owner: Sinclair Communications Inc. (acq 8-3-2001; $3.5 million). Format: Hot adult contemp. Target aud: 25-52; upscale - 60% female. ◆Bob Sinclair, pres; Debbie Morton, gen mgr.

Camarillo

***KMRO(FM)—** Jan 19, 1987: 90.3 mhz; 4.43 kw. Ant 1,250 ft TL: N34 24 47 W119 11 10. Stereo. Hrs open: 24 2310 Ponderosa Dr., Suite 28, 93010. Phone: (805) 482-4797. Fax: (805) 388-5202.E-mail: info@nuevavida.com Web Site:www.nuevavida.com Licensee: The Association for Community Education Inc. Population served: 800,000 Miller & Neely. Format: Relg, Sp. Target aud: General; Hispanics. ◆Phil Guthrie, pres; Mary Guthrie, gen mgr.

KOCP(FM)— Aug 15, 1972: 95.9 mhz; 5 kw. 813 ft TL: N34 06 47 W119 03 34. (CP: 1.25 kw, ant 1,440 ft. TL: 34 20 55 W119 20 13). Stereo. Hrs open: 24 2284 S. Victoria, Suite 2-G, Ventura, 93003. Phone: (805) 289-1400. Fax: (805) 644-7906.E-mail: perryinthemorning@yahoo.com Web Site:www.theoctopus959.com Licensee: Gold Coast Broadcasting LLC (group owner; acq 1995; $1.2 million with KMXO(AM) Santa Paula). Population served: 55,000 Natl. Rep: Katz Radio,. Format: Classic rock. Target aud: 25-54. ◆Chip Ehrhardt, gen mgr; Perry Van Houten, progmg dir.

Cambria

KTEA(FM)— Nov 9, 2003: 103.5 mhz; 6 kw. Ant 322 ft TL: N35 31 26.1 W121 03 40.3. Stereo. Hrs open: 7 AM-midnight 2976 Burton Dr., 93428. Phone: (805) 924-0103.E-mail: jim@ktea-fm.com Licensee: KTEA-FM LLC. Format: Big band 30's through 50's broad spectrum. Target aud: 50+. ◆James Robert Kampschroer, pres, gen mgr; Lee Went, progmg dir.

Camino

***KYCJ(FM)—** 2005: 88.3 mhz; 50 w vert. Ant 508 ft TL: N38 44 18 W120 42 10. Hrs open: 24 Rebroadcasts KYCC(FM) Stockton 100%. 9019 N. West Ln., Stockton, 95210-1401. Phone: (209) 477-3690. Fax: (209) 477-2762.E-mail: kycc@kycc.org Web Site:www.kycc.org Licensee: Your Christian Companion Network Inc. Format: Gospel, inspirational, adult contemp. Target aud: 35-55. ◆Shirley Garner, gen mgr.

Canyon Country

KHTS(AM)— June 1989: 1220 khz; 1 kw-D, 500 w-N, DA-2. TL: N34 27 55 W118 24 08. Stereo. Hrs open: 24 27225 Camp Plenty Rd., Suite 8, Santa Clarita, 91351. Phone: (661) 298-1220. Fax: (661) 298-2020. Web Site:www.hometownstation.com Licensee: Jeri Lyn Broadcasting Inc. (acq 10-24-2003; $900,000). Format: Full svc. ◆Carl Goldman, gen mgr; Shaun Valentine, progmg dir; Jon Dell, news dir; Bruce Smith, chief of engrg.

Carlsbad

KUSS(FM)— Aug 22, 1965: 95.7 mhz; 29 kw. 639 ft TL: N32 50 24 W117 14 52. Stereo. Hrs open: 24 9660 Granite Ridge Rd., San Diego, 92123. Phone: (858) 292-2000. Fax: (858) 278-7957.E-mail: info@kussfm.com Web Site:www.us957.com Licensee: Citicasters

Licenses L.P. Group owner: Clear Channel Communications Inc. (acq 5-4-99; grpsl). Population served: 600,000 Natl. Network: ABC, . Hogan and Hartson. Format: Sixties and Seventies. Target aud: 25-54; general. ◆Bob Bolinger, gen mgr; Geoff Alan, prom dir; Mike O'Brian, progmg dir.

Carmel

KCDU(FM)— Apr 29, 1971: 101.7 mhz; 800 w. 590 ft TL: N36 33 12 W121 47 05. Stereo. Hrs open: 24 60 Garden Ct., Suite 300, Monterey, 93940-5341. Phone: (831) 658-5200. Fax: (831) 658-5299.E-mail: info@1017thebeach.com Web Site:www.1017thebeach.com Licensee: Mapleton License of Monterey LLC. (group owner; (acq 1-17-2002; grpsl). Population served: 500,000 Natl. Rep: McGavren Guild,. Leventhal, Senter & Lerman. Format: Adult contemp 80s & 90s. Target aud: Women 25-54; upscale, educated, above average income. ◆Adam Nathanson, pres; Raul Salvador, CFO; Dale Hendry, gen mgr; Mike Anthony, opns VP; Jodi Morgan, sls dir, gen sls mgr; Sybil DeAngelo, prom dir.

KKHK(FM)—Licensed to Carmel. See Monterey

KRML(AM)— Dec 25, 1957: 1410 khz; 500 w-D, 16 w-N, 2.5 kw-U. TL: N36 32 06 W121 53 34. Stereo. Hrs open: 24 live streaming from www.krmlradio.com Box 7300, The Eastwood Bldg., Carmel-By-The-Sea, 93921. Secondary address: San Carlos near 5th 93921. Phone: (831) 624-6431. Phone: (831) 624-6432. Fax: (831) 625-2417.E-mail: info@thejazzandbluescompany.com Web Site:www.krmlradio.com Licensee: Wisdom Broadcasting Co. Inc. (acq 4-23-2004; $725,000). Population served: 700,000 Rgnl rep: McGavern Guild Putbrese, Hunsaker & Trent, P. Format: Blues, jazz. News: 10.5 hrs wkly. Target aud: 35+. Spec prog: Gospel 6 hrs wkly. ◆David Kimball, CFO & gen mgr.

Carmel Valley

KRXA(AM)— July 10, 1989: 540 khz; 10 kw-D, 500 w-N, DA-2. TL: N36 39 38 W121 32 29. Stereo. Hrs open: 18 495 Elder Ave., Suite 7, Sand City, 93955. Phone: (831) 394-5792. Fax: (831) 899-7600.E-mail: info@kexaam.com Web Site:www.krxa540.com Licensee: KRFA-AM LLC (group owner; (acq 7-8-2005; $800,000). Format: Talk. ◆Hal Ginsberg, gen mgr; Matt Renner, opns dir; Peter B. Collins, progmg mgr.

Carmichael

KFIA(AM)— Jan 11, 1979: 710 khz; 25 kw-D, 1 kw-N, DA-2. TL: N38 49 58 W121 19 03. Hrs open: 1425 River Park Dr., Suite 520, Sacramento, 95815. Phone: (916) 924-0710. Fax: (916) 924-1587.E-mail: info@kfia.com Licensee: New Inspiration Broadcasting Co. Inc. Group owner: Salem Communications Corp. (acq 2-15-95; 5-8-95). Population served: 7,000,000 Format: Relg. Target aud: 35 plus; general. ◆Edward Atsinger III, pres; James Rowten, gen mgr; Steve Gasser, opns mgr; Laurie Larson, progmg dir.

Carnelian Bay

KODS(FM)—Licensed to Carnelian Bay. See Reno NV

Carpinteria

KSBL(FM)— June 1, 1981: 101.7 mhz; 310 w. 810 ft TL: N34 27 55 W119 40 37. Stereo. Hrs open: 24 414 E. Cota St., Santa Barbara, 93101. Phone: (805) 879-8300. Fax: (805) 879-8430. Web Site:www.ksbl.com Licensee: Rincon License Subsidiary LLC. Group owner: Clear Channel Communications Inc. (acq 7-11-2007; grpsl). Format: Adult contemp. News staff: news progmg 2 hrs wkly News: one;. Target aud: 25-54; women. ◆Tom Baker, gen mgr; Keith Royer, opns dir; Vince Hollian, rgnl sls mgr; Lin Aubuchon, prom dir; Peter Bie, news dir; Andrea Shaparenko, traf mgr.

Cartago

KWTY(FM)— November 1989: 94.5 mhz; 2 kw horiz. Ant -1,788 ft TL: N36 19 16 W118 01 22. Stereo. Hrs open: 24 Box 91, Olancha, 93549. Phone: (760) 764-1111. Fax: (760) 764-1111.E-mail: gm@kwty.com Licensee: Mark A. Miller (acq 7-25-2005). Population served: 29,000 Wire Svc: UPI Format: Classic rock, rock. News: 7 hrs wkly. Target aud: General; 15-55 years (M-F), recreation/resort commuters. ◆Dan Owen, sls dir; Mark Miller, gen mgr, stn mgr & chief of engrg.

Cathedral City

KPTR(AM)—Licensed to Cathedral City. See Palm Springs

KWXY-FM—Licensed to Cathedral City. See Palm Springs

Cayucos

KPYG(FM)— Oct 1, 1984: 94.9 mhz; 25 kw. Ant 328 ft TL: N35 31 26 W121 03 40. Stereo. Hrs open: 24 396 Buckley Rd., Suite 2, San Luis Obispo, 93401. Phone: (805) 786-2570. Fax: (805) 547-9860. Web Site:www.mapletoncommunications.com Licensee: Mapleton License of San Luis Obispo LLC (group owner; (acq 7-19-2002; grpsl). Population served: 300,000 Haley, Bader & Potts. Format: AAA. Target aud: 25-54. ◆Adam Nathanson, pres; Bill Heirendt, progmg dir; David Atwood, news dir; Tom Hughes, chief of engrg.

Cazadero

KGRP(FM)— 2007: 106.3 mhz; 1.62 kw. Ant 636 ft TL: N38 29 20 W121 01 53. Stereo. Hrs open: Box 100, Santa Rosa, 95402. Phone: (707) 528-4434. Fax: (707) 527-8216. Web Site:www.k1063.fm Licensee: Redwood Empire Stereocasters. (acq 11-15-2007; $2.9 million). Natl. Rep: McGavren Guild,. Format: Country. ◆Gordon D. Zlot, pres.

Cedarville

*KDUP(FM)— 2008: 88.1 mhz; 130 w. Ant -676 ft TL: N41 31 41 W120 10 14. Hrs open: 42528 Rd. 1, Lake City, 96115. Phone: (530) 279-6262.E-mail: info@openskyradio.org Web Site:opensky.radio.org Licensee: OpenSkyRadio Corp. ◆Jeffrey M. Cotton, gen mgr.

Ceres

*KBES(FM)— Sept 1, 1979: 89.5 mhz; 150 w horiz. 131 ft TL: N37 35 21 W120 57 23. Hrs open: Box 4116, Modesto, 95352. Phone: (209) 538-4130. Fax: (209) 538-2795.E-mail: info@kbesfm.com Web Site:www.betnahrain.org Licensee: Bet Nahrain Inc. Format: Syrian. ◆Dr. Sargon Dadisho, gen mgr; Janet Shamon, progmg dir; Seimon Mamio, chief of engrg.

KVIN(AM)— Sept 15, 1963: 920 khz; 2.5 kw-U, DA-2. TL: N37 35 49 W121 04 15. Hrs open: 961 N. Emerald Ave., Ste A, Modesto, 95351. Phone: (209) 544-1055. Fax: (209) 544-1055.E-mail: theriver@krvr.com Web Site:www.krvr.com Licensee: Threshold Communications (acq 9-5-01; $400,000). Population served: 1,000,000 Natl. Rep: Interep,. Donald E. Martin P.C. Format: Adult standards. Target aud: 35-64. ◆Jim Bryan, gen mgr; Doug Wulff, opns mgr; Brian Henry, chief of engrg.

Chester

KWLU(FM)— Apr 6, 1989: 98.9 mhz; 12 kw. Ant 2,427 ft TL: N40 14 00 W121 01 11. Stereo. Hrs open: 24 2351 Sunset Blvd., Suite 170-218, Rocklin, 95765. Phone: (916) 251-1600. Fax: (916) 251-1650. Licensee: Educational Media Foundation. (acq 6-30-2005; $900,000 with KPCO(AM) Quincy). Population served: 55,851 Format: Christian. ◆Richard Jenkins, pres; Mike Novak, VP; Keith Whipple, dev dir; Ed Lenane, news dir; Sam Wallington, engrg dir; Karen Johnson, news rptr.

Chico

KBQB(FM)— June 1993: 92.7 mhz; 1.5 kw. Ant 643 ft TL: N39 48 25 W121 37 35. Hrs open: 856 Manzanita Ct., 95926. Phone: (530) 342-2200. Fax: (530) 342-2260.E-mail: bob@927bobfm.com Web Site:www.927bobfm.com Licensee: Results Radio Licensee L.L.C. Group owner: Fritz Communications (acq 6-11-99; grpsl). Format: Adult hits. ◆John Graham, gen mgr; Dave Pack, gen sls mgr; Chad Perry, progmg dir; J.D. Davis, chief of engrg; Candy Mason, traf mgr.

*KCHO(FM)— Apr 22, 1969: 91.7 mhz; 7.71 kw. Ant 1,219 ft TL: N39 57 30 W121 42 48. Stereo. Hrs open: 24 California State Univ., 95929-0500. Phone: (530) 898-5896. Fax: (530) 898-4348.E-mail: info@kcho.org Web Site:www.kcho.org Licensee: California State University, Chico Research Foundation. Population served: 234,281 Natl. Network: PRI, NPR, . Cohn & Marks. Format: Class, jazz, news & info. News staff: one; News: 37 hrs wkly. Target aud: General. ◆Brian Terhorst, gen mgr; Beth Heberle, mktg dir; Joe Oleksiewicz, progmg dir; Lorraine Dechter, news dir; Mike Birdsill, chief of engrg.

KFMF(FM)— Feb 1, 1974: 93.9 mhz; 2 kw. 1,128 ft TL: N39 56 46 W121 43 17. Stereo. Hrs open: 24 1459 Humboldt Rd., Suite D, 95928. Phone: (530) 899-3600. Fax: (530) 343-0243. Web Site:www.kfm.com Licensee: Mapleton License of Chico LLC. Group owner: Regent Communications Inc. (acq 11-30-2006; grpsl). Population served: 317,000 Natl. Rep: Christal,. Format: Active rock. News staff: one; News: one hr wkly. Target aud: 18-44. ◆Chad Gammage, gen mgr, mktg mgr; Coyote McGee, opns mgr, prom dir; Kenny Allen, progmg dir & disc jockey.

*KHAP(FM)— 1999: 89.1 mhz; 12 kw. 285 ft TL: N39 43 37 W121 40 45. Hrs open: 290 Hergenberger Rd., Oakland, 94621. Phone: (530) 877-5650. Fax: (916) 641-8238.E-mail: kebr@jps.net Web Site:www.familyradio.com yes Licensee: Family Stations Inc. (group owner) Population served: 85,000 Format: Relg, educ. ◆Harold Camping, pres; Thad McKinney, gen mgr.

KHSL-FM—See Paradise

KKXX(AM)—See Paradise

KMXI(FM)— Nov 16, 1972: 95.1 mhz; 8.7 kw. 1,171 ft TL: N39 56 46 W121 43 17. Stereo. Hrs open: 2654 Cramer Ln., 95928. Phone: (530) 893-0021. Fax: (530) 893-2121. Population served: 25,254 Format: Adult contemp.

KPAY(AM)— Apr 17, 1935: 1290 khz; 5 kw-U, DA-N. TL: N39 44 00 W121 44 10. Stereo. Hrs open: 2654 Cramer Ln., 95928. Phone: (530) 345-0021. Fax: (530) 893-2121.E-mail: info@kpay.com Web Site:www.kpay.com Licensee: Deer Creek Broadcasting LLC. (group owner; (acq 9-8-2004; grpsl). Population served: 350,000 Natl. Rep: Katz Radio,. Format: News/talk. Target aud: 25 plus. ◆Dino Corbin, gen mgr, progmg mgr; Lisa Fitzgerald, mktg dir; Larry Scott, progmg dir; Matt Ray, news dir.

KQPT(FM)—(Colusa, September 1986: 107.5 mhz; 28 kw. 600 ft TL: N39 17 17 W122 20 02. Stereo. Hrs open: 1459 Humboldt Rd., Suite D, 95928-9100. Phone: (530) 899-3600. Fax: (530) 343-0243. Web Site:www.107thepoint.com Licensee: Mapleton License of Chico LLC. Group owner: Regent Communications Inc. (acq 11-30-2006; grpsl). Natl. Rep: Christal,. Format: Modern adult contemp. Target aud: 24-48. ◆Chad Gammage, VP, mktg mgr; Coyote McGee, gen mgr, opns mgr; Kenny Allen, progmg dir.

KZAP(FM)—See Paradise

*KZFR(FM)— July 6, 1990: 90.1 mhz; 6.3 kw. 587 ft TL: N39 48 25 W121 37 35. Stereo. Hrs open: 24 Box 3173, 95927. Secondary address: 341 Broadway, Suite 411 95928. Phone: (530) 895-0706/895-0788. Fax: (530) 895-0775. Web Site:www.kzfr.org Licensee: Golden Valley Community Broadcasters. Format: Div, news/talk. News: 8 hrs wkly. Spec prog: American Indian 2 hrs, Sp 6 hrs wkly. ◆Jill L. Paydon, gen mgr.

China Lake

*KFRJ(FM)— June 2005: 91.1 mhz; 3 kw. Ant 1,282 ft TL: N35 28 41 W117 41 58. Hrs open: 24 Family Stations Inc., 4135 Northgate Blvd., Suite 1, Sacramento, 95834. Phone: (916) 641-8191. Fax: (916) 641-8238. Licensee: Family Stations Inc. (group owner). Format: Relg. ◆Harold Camping, pres.

KSSI(FM)— 1995: 102.7 mhz; 3 kw. -22 ft TL: N35 39 06 W117 40 58. Hrs open: 24 701 Inyokern Rd., Suite C, Ridgecrest, 93555. Phone: (760) 446-5774. Fax: (760) 446-5774.E-mail: jon@kssifm.com Web Site:www.kssifm.com Licensee: Sound Enterprises. Population served: 40,000 Format: AOR. Target aud: 25-54; general. ◆John Perrige, gen mgr; Lisa Garcia, traf mgr.

Chowchilla

KNTO(FM)— Aug 1, 1992: 93.3 mhz; 2.95 kw. 335 ft TL: N37 13 01 W120 11 57. Hrs open: 24 4043 Geer Rd., Hughson, 95326. Phone: (209) 883-8760. Fax: (209) 883-8769.E-mail: ngomez@lafavorita.net Web Site:www.lafavorita.net Licensee: KSKD Inc. (acq 4-17-01; $450,000). Population served: 140,000 Format: Sp, Mexican music. Target aud: 18-35; teens, young adults. ◆Nelson Gomez, pres & gen mgr; Freddy Lopez, news dir.

Chualar

KHDC(FM)—Licensed to Chualar. See Salinas

Citrus Heights

*KLVS(FM)— September 1997: 99.5 mhz; 5.1 kw. Ant 358 ft TL: N38 38 32 W121 05 25. Stereo. Hrs open: 24 Rebroadcasts KLVR(FM) Middletown, CA 100%. 2351 Sunset Blvd., Suite 170-218, Rocklin, 95765. Phone: (916) 251-1600. Fax: (916) 251-1650.E-mail: klove@klove.com Web Site:www.klove.com Licensee: Educational Media Foundation. Group owner: EMF Broadcasting (acq 9-12-96; $65,000). Population served: 336,000 Natl. Network: K-Love, . Shaw Pittman. Format: Contemp Christian. News staff: 3. Target aud: 25-44; Judeo-Christian, female. ◆Richard Jenkins, pres; Mike Novak, VP, chief of engrg; Keith Whipple, dev dir; David Pierce, prom mgr, progmg mgr; Ed Lenane, news dir; Sam Wallington, engrg dir; Karen Johnson, news rptr.

Claremont

*KSPC(FM)— February 1956: 88.7 mhz; 3 kw. Ant -282 ft TL: N34 05 51 W117 42 35. Stereo. Hrs open: Pomona College, 340 N. College Ave., 91711-6340. Phone: (909) 621-8157.E-mail: director@kspc.org Web Site:www.kspc.org Licensee: Pomona College. Format: Alternative rock, div, jazz. Target aud: General. Spec prog: Pol 3 hrs, reggae 4 hrs, blues 4 hrs, pub affrs 3 hrs, hip hop/rap 6 hrs wkly. ◆Roxy Cruz, progmg dir; Stacy Wood, mus dir.

KWKU(AM)—See Pomona

Cloverdale

KSRT(FM)— 2002: 107.1 mhz; 3.5 kw. Ant 430 ft TL: N38 48 34 W123 02 56. Hrs open: 24 5510 Skylane Blvd., Suite 102, Santa Rosa, 95403. Phone: (707) 284-3069. Fax: (707) 284-3174. Web Site:www.radiolazer.com Licensee: Lazer Licenses LLC. (acq 6-29-2006; $6.85 million with KJOR(FM) Windsor). Format: Mexican regional. ◆Ken Kuhl, gen mgr, gen sls mgr; Salvador Prieto, progmg dir.

Clovis

KFPT(AM)— May 2, 1977: 790 khz; 5 kw-D, 2.5 kw-N, DA-2. TL: N36 50 39 W119 41 13. Hrs open: 24 351 W. Cromwell Ave., Suite 108, Fresno, 93711. Phone: (559) 447-3570. Fax: (559) 447-3579. Web Site:www.1430espn.com Licensee: Peak Broadcasting of Fresno Licenses LLC. Group owner: Infinity Broadcasting Corp. (acq 3-30-2007; grpsl). Population served: 1,200,000 Natl. Network: ESPN Radio, . Format: Sports. ◆Paul Swearengin, gen mgr.

KOND(FM)—Licensed to Clovis. See Madera

Coachella

KCLB-FM— Sept 1, 1960: 93.7 mhz; 26.5 kw. 640 ft TL: N33 44 07 W116 13 27. Stereo. Hrs open: Prog sep from AM 1321 North Gene Autry Tr., Palm Springs, 92262. Phone: (760) 322-7890. Fax: (760) 322-5493.E-mail: info@desertfun.com Population served: 200,000 Format: Rock (AOR). Target aud: 18-54. ◆Dave Sparks, progmg dir; Angela Terry, traf mgr.

KNWZ(AM)— 1954: 970 khz; 5 kw-D, 1 kw-N, DA-2. TL: N33 41 12 W116 09 34. Hrs open: 1321 North Gene Autry Tr., Palm Springs, 92262. Phone: (760) 322-7890. Fax: (760) 322-5493.E-mail: info@desertfun.com Licensee: Morris Communications Corp. Group owner: Morris Communications Inc. (acq 1998; $7 million with co-located FM). Format: Talk. Target aud: 18-49. ◆Gary Demardney, opns dir; David Nola, sls dir; Virgina Nelson, gen mgr & gen sls mgr; Pete Fox, prom mgr; Brian Long, progmg mgr; Angela Terry, traf mgr.

*KPCV(FM)— February 2005: 90.3 mhz; 340 w. Ant 574 ft TL: N33 48 08 W116 13 30. Stereo. Hrs open: 24 Rebroadcasts KPCC(FM) Pasadena 100%. Southern California Public Radio, 1570 E. Colorado Blvd., Pasadena, 91106-2003. Phone: (626) 585-7000. Fax: (626) 585-7916.E-mail: mail@kpcc.org Web Site:www.scpr.org Licensee: American Public Media Group (acq 8-22-2008; $1 million). Natl. Network: NPR, PRI, . Format: New/talk/information. Target aud: General. ◆Mark Crowley, gen mgr.

*KPSH(FM)—Not on air, target date: January 2005: 90.9 mhz; 230 w. Ant 623 ft TL: N33 52 03 W116 25 58. Hrs open: 24 5119 McKinley, Baton Rouge, LA, 70826. Secondary address: 8919 World Ministry Ave. , Baton Rouge, LA 70826. Phone: (225) 768-3688. Fax: (225) 768-8300. Fax: (225) 768-3729.E-mail: kawikfish@yahoo.com Web Site:www.jsm.org Licensee: Family Worship Center Church Inc. (group

owner; acq 2-18-2004; $750,000 for CP). Format: Relg, christian. ◆David Whitelow, COO; Jimmy Swaggart, pres; John Santiago, progmg dir.

Coalinga

*KDKL(FM)— 1999: 88.3 mhz; 1.45 kw vert. 2,329 ft TL: N36 22 11 W120 38 37. Hrs open: 2351 Sunset Blvd., Suite 170-218, Rocklin, 95765. Phone: (800) 372-0888. Fax: (916) 251-1650. Web Site:www.klove.com Licensee: Educational Media Foundation (acq 10-20-00; $80,000 for CP). Format: Contemp Christian. ◆Richard Jenkins, pres; Mike Novak, VP; Ed Lenane, opns dir, news dir; Keith Whipple, dev dir; David Pierce, progmg mgr; Sam Wallington, engrg dir; Arthur Vassar, traf mgr; Karen Johnson, news rptr.

*KFRP(FM)— November 2005: 90.7 mhz; 2.5 kw vert. Ant 1,253 ft TL: N35 55 39 W120 22 46. Hrs open: Family Stations Inc., 4135 Northgate Blvd., Suite 1, Sacramento, 95834. Phone: (916) 641-8191. Fax: (916) 641-8238. Licensee: Family Stations Inc. (group owner). Format: Relg. ◆Harold Camping, pres.

KNGS(FM)—Not on air, target date: unknown: 100.1 mhz; 19 kw. Ant 794 ft TL: N36 00 40 W120 04 26. Hrs open: c/o William L. Zawilla, 12550 Brookhurst, Garden Grove, 92640. Licensee: William L. Zawila. ◆William Zawila, gen mgr.

KQNO(FM)—Not on air, target date: unknown: Stn currently dark. 97.3 mhz; 6 kw. Ant 328 ft TL: N36 16 32 W120 19 45. Hrs open: 2801 Via Fortuna Dr., Suite 675, Austin, TX, 78746. Phone: (512) 329-5843. Web Site:www.matineemedia.com Licensee: Ace Radio Corp. ◆Stephen Hackerman, pres.

Coarsegold

KCGC(FM)—Not on air, target date: unknown: 94.5 mhz; 6 kw. Ant 103 ft TL: N37 15 56 W119 41 11. Hrs open: 980 N. Michigan Ave., Suite 1880, Chicago, IL, 60611. Phone: (312) 204-9900. Licensee: College Creek Media LLC. ◆Neal J. Robinson, pres.

Columbia

KCVR-FM— August 1995: 98.9 mhz; 6 kw. Ant 328 ft TL: N38 02 15 W120 22 05. Hrs open: 6820 Pacific Ave., Suite 3A, Stockton, 95207. Phone: (209) 474-0154. Fax: (209) 474-0316.E-mail: info@entravision.com Web Site:www.entravision.com Licensee: Entravision Holdings LLC. Group owner: Entravision Communications Corp. (acq 7-28-2000; grpsl). Format: Sp adult hits. ◆Lisa Sunday, gen mgr; Edgar Pineda, progmg dir.

Colusa

KKCY(FM)— May 1990: 103.1 mhz; 135 w. 1,964 ft TL: N39 12 21 W121 49 11. Stereo. Hrs open: 24 861 Gray Ave., Suite K, Yuba City, 95991. Phone: (530) 673-2200. Fax: (530) 673-3010.E-mail: resultsradio@syix.com Web Site:www.kkcy.com Licensee: Results Radio of Chico Licensee LLC. Group owner: Fritz Communications Inc. (acq 6-11-99; grpsl). Natl. Rep: Katz Radio,. Kaye, Scholer, Fierman, Hays & Handler. Format: Country. News staff: one; News: 7 hrs wkly. Target aud: 18-64. Spec prog: Sp one hr wkly. ◆Jack Fritz, pres; Michael Berry, sls dir & gen sls mgr; Dave Logasa, progmg dir.

KQPT(FM)—Licensed to Colusa. See Chico

Compton

KJLH-FM— April 1965: 102.3 mhz; 5.6 kw. Ant 338 ft TL: N33 59 52 W118 21 32. Stereo. Hrs open: 24 161 N. La Brea Ave., Inglewood, 90301. Phone: (310) 330-2200. Fax: (310) 330-5555. Fax: (310) 330-2244.E-mail: sales@kjlhradio.com Web Site:www.kjlhradio.com Licensee: TAXI Productions Inc. (acq 6-79). Population served: 340,000 Natl. Network: American Urban, ABC, . Natl. Rep: McGavren Guild,. Irwin, Campbell & Tannenwald. Format: Urban contemp, rhythm and blues. News staff: 2; News: 8.5 hrs wkly. Target aud: 25-49; African-American audience. Spec prog: Relg 7 hrs, gospel 6 hrs, talk 8.5 hrs, Christian 6 hrs wkly. ◆Stevland Morris, CEO; Karen Slade, gen mgr; Lawrence Williams, opns dir; Aundrae Russell, progmg dir; Jacquie Stephens, news dir; Barry Clark, chief of engrg; Carrie Haynes, traf mgr.

Concord

*KVHS(FM)— May 16, 1969: 90.5 mhz; 410 w. 450 ft TL: N39 01 49 W122 00 04. Stereo. Hrs open: 24/7 1101 Alberta Way, Suite #S-2, 94521. Phone: (925) 609-5847.E-mail: kvhsgm@mail.com Web Site:www.kvhs.com Licensee: Clayton Valley High School. Population served: 1,001,136 Wire Svc: Bay City News Service Format: Active/New rock. Target aud: 18-34.(P-1) 18-49(P-2) 12+. Spec prog: Flashback Show(Classic Rock); Punk & SKA Show; Metal Show(Hard Rock), Klub KVHS (Dance Mix). ◆Melissa McConnell Wilson, gen mgr.

Copperopolis

KRVR(FM)— Jan 1, 1995: 105.5 mhz; 1 kw. 781 ft TL: N37 56 55 W120 42 16. Stereo. Hrs open: 24 961 N. Emerald Ave., Suite A, Modesto, 95351. Phone: (209) 544-1055. Fax: (209) 544-8105.E-mail: TheRiver@krvr.com Web Site:krvr.com Licensee: Threshold Communications. Population served: 750,000 Natl. Rep: Interep,. Donald E. Martin. Format: Smooth Jazz. Target aud: 35-64. ◆Jim Bryan, gen mgr; Doug Wulff, opns mgr, mus dir; Cheryl Miller, rgnl sls mgr; James Arata, progmg dir; Sally Waterman, traf mgr.

Corcoran

KBLO(FM)— 1999: 102.3 mhz; 19.5 kw. Ant 380 ft TL: N36 11 04 W119 24 01. Hrs open: 24 113 N. Church St., Suite 511, Visalia, 93291. Phone: (559) 740-4172. Fax: (559) 740-4177. Web Site:www.radiolobo987.com Licensee: Mapleton License of Visalia LLC (acq 2-27-2009; $8 million). Format: Sp. ◆Andrew Adams, gen mgr; Dora Deltora, gen sls mgr; Jaun Davbla, prom mgr; Rick McMillion, chief of engrg.

Corning

KTHU(FM)— Apr 8, 1988: 100.7 mhz; 50 kw. 272 ft TL: N39 53 17 W122 37 38. (CP: 20.5 kw, ant 1,742 ft.). Stereo. Hrs open: 24 856 Manzanita Ct., Chico, 95926. Phone: (530) 342-2200. Fax: (530) 342-2260.E-mail: kthu1007@sunset.net Web Site:www.chicothunderheads.com Licensee: Results Radio Licensee L.L.C. Group owner: Fritz Communications Inc. (acq 6-11-99; grpsl). Kaye, Scholer, Fierman, Hays & Handler. Format: Classic rock. News staff: one. Target aud: 25-54. Spec prog: Sp one hr wkly. ◆Jack Fritz, pres; John Graham, gen mgr; dave Pack, gen sls mgr; J. D. Davis, engrg VP; Candy Mason, traf mgr.

Corona

KWRM(AM)— 1948: 1370 khz; 5 kw-D, 2.5 kw-N, DA-2. TL: N33 52 52 W117 32 33. Hrs open: 24 Box 100, 92878. Secondary address: 210 Radio Rd. 92879. Phone: (951) 737-1370. Fax: (951) 735-9572.E-mail: lori@major-market.com Web Site:kwrrm1370am.com Licensee: Major Market Stations Inc. (acq 9-24-2007; with KWRN(AM) Apple Valley). Population served: 10,000,000 Hardy & Carey. Format: Multilingual, sports, var/div. News staff: 2; News: 20 hrs wkly. Target aud: 18-49; young Hispanic adults. ◆Marilynn Kramar, pres & gen mgr; Damian Vasquez, opns dir.

Covelo

KQZT(FM)—Not on air, target date: unknown: 96.9 mhz; 1 kw. Ant 795 ft TL: N39 47 08 W123 05 46. Hrs open: 110 S. Franklin St., Fort Bragg, 95437. Phone: (707) 964-7277. Fax: (707) 964-9536. Licensee: California Radio Partners Inc. ◆Tom Yates, pres & gen mgr.

Crescent City

KCRE-FM— Mar 21, 1980: 94.3 mhz; 25 kw. Ant -305 ft TL: N41 45 35 W124 09 49. Stereo. Hrs open: Box 1089, 95531. Secondary address: 1345 Northcrest Dr. 95531. Phone: (707) 464-9561. Fax: (707) 464-4303.E-mail: kcre@charter.net Web Site:www.historicalfavorites.com Licensee: KPOD L.L.C. (acq 7-30-02; $692,000). Population served: 35,000 Format: Adult contemp. ◆Kelly Schellong, gen sls mgr; Renee Shanle-Hutzell, gen mgr & progmg dir; Kevin Sanders, chief of engrg.

KFVR(AM)— July 1950: 1310 khz; 1 kw-D. TL: N41 45 35 W124 09 49. Hrs open: 24 Box 109, Eureka, 95502-0109. Phone: (707) 725-9363. Fax: (707) 726-9446. Web Site:www.lanueva1090.com Licensee: Del Rosario Talpa Inc. (acq 5-29-2003; $54,000). Format: Rgn Mexican. ◆Mario Meza, gen mgr.

*KHEC(FM)—Not on air, target date: unknown: 91.1 mhz; 4 kw vert. Ant 177 ft TL: N41 48 11 W124 04 09. Hrs open: 8823 Frey Rd., Houston, TX, 77034. Phone: (713) 944-8181. Licensee: Centro Cristiano Cosecha Final. ◆Francisco Diaz, pres.

*KHSR(FM)— July 1999: 91.9 mhz; 800 w. 226 ft TL: N41 50 36 W124 07 55. Stereo. Hrs open: 24
Rebroadcasts KHSU-FM Arcata 100%.
Humboldt State University, 1 Harpst St., Arcata, 95521. Phone: (707) 826-4807. Fax: (707) 826-6082.E-mail: khsu@humboldt.edu Web Site:www.khsu.org Licensee: Humboldt State University. Population served: 22,000 Natl. Network: NPR, PRI, . Format: Var, news. Spec prog: World 14 hrs, jazz 10 hrs wkly. ◆Elizabeth Hans-McCrone, gen mgr; Charles Horn, dev dir; Katie Whiteside, progmg dir; Kevin Sanders, chief of engrg.

KPOD(AM)— Dec 5, 1959: 1240 khz; 778 w-U. TL: N41 45 35 W124 11 28. Hrs open: 24 Box 1089, 1345 Northcrest Dr., 95531. Phone: (707) 464-3183. Fax: (707) 464-4303.E-mail: kcre@charter.net Licensee: KPOD LLC. Group owner: Bicoastal Media LLC (acq 3-31-00; $850,000 with co-located FM). Population served: 60,000 Natl. Network: ABC, . Format: Timeless music. ◆Mike Wilson, pres, gen mgr; Kelly Schellong, gen sls mgr, disc jockey; Renee Shanle-Hutzell, gen mgr & progmg dir; Kevin Sanders, chief of engrg, disc jockey.

KPOD-FM— January 1989: 97.9 mhz; 6 kw. Ant -128 ft TL: N41 45 35 W124 11 28. Hrs open: 24 Prog sep from AM Box 1089, 1345 Northcrest Dr., 95531. Phone: (707) 464-1000. Fax: (707) 464-4303.E-mail: kcre@charter.net Web Site:www.kpod.com Natl. Network: ABC, . Cohn & Marks. Format: Hot country. ◆Chuck Blackburn, sports cmtr; Chuck Clifford, opns mgr & disc jockey.

Culver City

KIEV(AM)—Licensed to Culver City. See Los Angeles

Cupertino

*KKUP(FM)— May 15, 1972: 91.5 mhz; 200 w. 2,294 ft TL: N37 06 40 W121 50 36. Stereo. Hrs open: 24 933 Monroe St., P.O. Box 9150, Santa Clara, 95050-4808. Phone: (408) 260-2999. Phone: (408) 260-2997. Web Site:www.kkup.org Licensee: Assurance Sciences Foundation Inc. Population served: 2,000,000 Format: Eclectic, alternative, blues. Target aud: General. Spec prog: Brazilian 2 hrs, African 6 hrs, Indian 3 hrs, Sp 3 hrs, Latin American 8 hrs wkly. ◆Jim Thomas, chmn; Dan Kind, gen mgr; Tim Alderman, progmg dir; Peter Schwartz, mus dir, chief of engrg.

Davis

*KDVS(FM)— Jan 1, 1968: 90.3 mhz; 9.2 kw. 105 ft TL: N38 32 29 W121 45 03. Stereo. Hrs open: 24 c/o KDVS-FM, Univ. of California, 14 Lower Freeborn Hall, 95616. Phone: (530) 752-0728. Fax: (530) 752-8548.E-mail: gm@kdvs.org Web Site:www.kdvs.org Licensee: Regents of the University of California. Population served: 310,000 Format: Eclectic rock, var, free form radio. News: 13 hrs wkly. Target aud: General; loc community. ◆Benjamin Johnson, gen mgr; Bryce Fsch, progmg dir; A.J. Ramirez, mus dir; Lindsay Schrupp, news dir; Rich Lusch, chief of engrg.

KXSE(FM)— February 1979: 104.3 mhz; 3.4 kw. Ant 436 ft TL: N38 39 26 W121 43 12. Hrs open: 24 1436 Auburn Blvd., Sacramento, 95815. Phone: (916) 646-4000. Fax: (916) 646-1958.E-mail: jverdier@entravision.com Web Site:www.entravision.com Licensee: Entravision Holdings LLC. Group owner: Entravision Communications Corp. (acq 7-28-2000; grpsl). Natl. Network: ABC, Westwood One, CBS, . Mullin, Rhyne, Emmons & Topel. Format: Sp adult contemp. Target aud: 25-54. ◆Larry Lamanski, gen mgr; Joni Verdier, gen sls mgr; Salvador Lopez, prom mgr; Edgar Pineda, progmg dir.

Del Norte

KSLV-FM—Not on air, target date: unknown: 96.5 mhz; 930 w. Ant 1,589 ft TL: N37 43 47 W106 35 18. Hrs open: Box 631, Monte Vista, 81144. Phone: (719) 852-3581. Fax: (719) 852-3583. Licensee: San Luis Valley Broadcasting Inc. ◆H. Robert Gourley III, pres.

Delano

KBFP-FM— Oct 2, 1986: 105.3 mhz; 50 kw. 547 ft TL: N35 30 53 W119 03 41. Stereo. Hrs open: 1100 Mohawk St., Suite 280, Bakersfield, 93309. Phone: (661) 322-9929. Fax: (661) 283-2963.E-mail: A jimbell@clearchannel.com Web Site:www.klite1053.com Licensee:

CC Licenses LLC. (acq 4-94). Population served: 460,000 Natl. Rep: McGavren Guild,. Arter & Hadden. Format: Adult contemp. Target aud: 18-44. ◆Jim Bell, VP, gen mgr; Jim Bell, gen mgr; Steve King, stn mgr, progmg dir; Ron Fisher, gen sls mgr; Steve Mull, chief of engrg.

KCHJ(AM)—Dec 1, 1951: 1010 khz; 5 kw-D, 1 kw-N, DA-2. TL: N35 48 40 W119 19 18. Hrs open: 24 5100 Commerce Dr., Bakersfield, 93309-0684. Phone: (661) 327-9711. Fax: (661) 327-0797.E-mail: info@thespanishradio.com Web Site:www.thespanishradio.com Licensee: Illinois Lotus Corp. Group owner: Lotus Communications Corp. (acq 8-24-99; grpsl). Population served: 1,500,000 Borsari & Paxson. Wire Svc: UPI Format: Sp 24 hrs, 7days a wk. News staff: 2. Target aud: 18 plus; Sp speaking adults. ◆Howard Kalmenson, pres; Mike Allen, gen mgr; Bruce Thompson, stn mgr.

KDFO(FM)— November 1968: 98.5 mhz; 50 kw. Ant 499 ft TL: N35 42 46 W118 47 22. Hrs open: 24 1100 Mohawk St., Suite 280, Bakersfield, 93309. Phone: (661) 322-9929. Fax: (661) 283-2963.E-mail: jimbell@clearchannel.com Web Site:www.985thefox.com Licensee: CC Licenses LLC. Group owner: Clear Channel Communications Inc. (acq 10-16-2000; grpsl). Population served: 1,500,000 Format: Classic rock. Target aud: 18-44. ◆Jim Bell, VP, gen mgr, gen mgr; Steve King, stn mgr; Ron Fisher, gen sls mgr; Kenn McCloud, progmg dir; Steve Mull, chief of engrg.

Desert Hot Springs

KJML(AM)—Not on air, target date: unknown: 1220 khz; 1.4 kw-D, 1.2 kw-N, DA-2. TL: N33 55 51 W116 36 12 (day), N33 59 28 W116 29 28 (night). Hrs open: 24 12272 Sarazen Pl., Granada Hills, 91344. Phone: (213) 494-3377. Licensee: Ether Mining Corp. ◆Mark A. Mueller, VP.

Dinuba

KRDU(AM)— Dec 26, 1946: 1130 khz; 5 kw-D, 6.2 kw-N, DA-2. TL: N36 29 03 W119 15 57. Hrs open: 24 597 N. Alta Ave., 93618. Secondary address: 83 East Shaw, Fresno 93727. Phone: (559) 591-1130. Fax: (559) 591-4822. Licensee: Capstar TX L.P. Group owner: Clear Channel Communications Inc. (acq 8-30-00; grpsl). Population served: 1,000,000 Fletcher, Heald & Hildreth. Format: Relg. News staff: one; News: 7 hrs wkly. Target aud: 18-65. ◆Jim Tuck, gen mgr; Doug Diedrich, progmg dir; Mike Hauber, chief of engrg, chief of engrg, local news ed, local news ed; Steve Carloon, local news ed.

KSOF(FM)— June 5, 1975: 98.9 mhz; 19 kw. 820 ft TL: N36 38 15 W118 56 35. Stereo. Hrs open: 24 Prog sep from AM 4991 E. McKinley, Suite 124, Fresno, 93727. Phone: (559) 243-4300. Population served: 1,193,000 Format: Soft rock. News: 2 hrs wkly. Target aud: 25-54; women. ◆Darrel Goodin, gen mgr; May Lou Goodin, opns VP; Dave Butler, gen sls mgr; Scott Keith, progmg dir; Dave Case, chief of engrg.

Dunnigan

KSAC-FM— Sept 1, 1983: 105.5 mhz; 2.55 kw. Ant 1,010 ft TL: N38 47 17 W122 06 52. Stereo. Hrs open: 24 1425 River Park Dr., Suite 520, Sacramento, 95815. Phone: (916) 924-0710. Fax: (916) 924-1587. Web Site:www.radioluz1055.com Licensee: Caron Broadcasting Inc. Group owner: Salem Communications Corp. (acq 1-11-2002; $8 million). Population served: 1,500,000 Format: Sp relg. ◆James Rowten, gen mgr; Laurie Larson, progmg dir; Dave Fortenberry, engrg dir.

Dunsmuir

KZRO(FM)— Dec 8, 1992: 100.1 mhz; 12.5 kw. 213 ft TL: N41 17 20 W122 14 25. Stereo. Hrs open: 24 Box 1234, Mt. Shasta, 96067. Secondary address: 113 E. Alma St., Mt. Shasta 96067. Phone: (530) 926-1332. Fax: (530) 926-0737.E-mail: zmail@zchannelradio.com Web Site:www.zchannelradio.com Licensee: Dennis Michael Crepps dba Big Tree Communications (acq 6-24-97). Population served: 194,000 Natl. Network: Westwood One, . Format: Classic rock, oldies. News staff: one. Target aud: 18-55; general. Spec prog: Children 2 hrs wkly. ◆Dennis Michaels, gen mgr, gen sls mgr, mktg dir, adv dir, progmg dir; Rob Hanson, chief of engrg.

Earlimart

KNAC(FM)—Not on air, target date: unknown: 93.5 mhz; 6 kw. Ant 177 ft TL: N35 57 30 W119 15 00. Hrs open: 12550 Brookhurst St., Garden Grove, 92640. Web Site:www.knac.com Licensee: Earlimart Educational Foundation Inc. ◆William Zawila, gen mgr.

East Los Angeles

KLAX-FM— Apr 22, 1949: 97.9 mhz; 50 kw. 390 ft TL: N34 00 24 W118 21 52. Stereo. Hrs open: 10281 W. Pico Blvd., Los Angeles, 90064. Phone: (310) 203-0900. Fax: (310) 843-4961.E-mail: info@979laraza.com Web Site:www.979laraza.com Licensee: KLAX Licensing Inc. Group owner: Spanish Broadcasting System Inc. (acq 2-87). Format: Sp, Rgnl Mexican. Target aud: 18-34. ◆Raul Alarcon Jr., CEO & pres; Peter Remington, gen mgr; Juan Carlos Hidalog, dev dir, progmg dir; Jason Wilberding, gen sls mgr; Patty Castor, prom dir.

East Porterville

KMQA(FM)— Dec 1, 1989: 100.5 mhz; 1.5 kw. 465 ft TL: N36 02 37 W118 56 08. (CP: 2.1 kw, ant 1,109 ft.). Hrs open: 1450 E. Bardsley Ave., Tulare, 93274. Phone: (559) 687-3170. Fax: (559) 687-3175.E-mail: traffic@lunacommunications.net Web Site:www.lamaquinamusical.net Licensee: MBP Licensee LLC. Group owner: Moon Broadcasting (acq 12-29-98). Natl. Network: CNN Radio, . Format: Mexican rgnl. Target aud: 25-40. ◆George Rayo, opns mgr, gen sls mgr; Rey Ponce, prom dir.

East Sonora

*KARQ(FM)— 2005: 89.5 mhz; 1.3 kw vert. Ant 1,661 ft TL: N38 03 46 W120 14 45. Hrs open: 24
Rebroadcasts KLRD(FM) Yucaipa 100%.
2351 Sunset Blvd., Suite 170-218, Rocklin, 95765. Phone: (916) 251-1600. Fax: (916) 251-1650. Web Site:www.air1.com Licensee: Educational Media Foundation. Group owner: EMF Broadcasting. Natl. Network: Air 1, . Shaw Pittman. Format: Christian. News staff: 3. Target aud: 25-44; Judeo Christian, female. ◆Richard Jenkins, pres; Mike Novak, VP; Keith Whipple, dev dir; David Pierce, progmg dir; Ed Lenane, news dir; Sam Wallington, engrg dir; Arthur Vassar, traf mgr.

Edwards

KGBB(FM)— March 1990: 103.9 mhz; 6 kw. Ant 328 ft TL: N34 58 45 W118 10 02. Hrs open: 24 731 N. Balsam St., Ridgecrest, 93555. Phone: (760) 371-1700. Fax: (760) 371-1824.E-mail: radio@iwvisp.com Web Site:www.bobfm1039.com Licensee: Adelman Broadcasting Inc. (group owner). Population served: 500,000 Format: Rock, adult contemp. Target aud: 18-54. ◆Robert Adelman, pres.

El Cajon

*KECR(AM)— 1955: 910 khz; 5 kw-U, DA-2. TL: N32 53 38 W116 55 35. Hrs open: 24 11865 Moreno Ave., Lakeside, 92040. Phone: (619) 390-3481. Fax: (619) 443-7693.E-mail: kecr@nethere.com Web Site:www.familyradio.com Licensee: Family Stations Inc. (group owner: Family Stations Inc. acq 6-9-63). Population served: 796,769 Format: Relg. Target aud: All ages; families. ◆Bill Babcock, gen mgr, opns mgr; Jeff Zimmer, chief of engrg.

KHTS-FM—Licensed to El Cajon. See San Diego

El Centro

KGBA(AM)—See Calexico

KGBA-FM—See Holtville

KROP(AM)—(Brawley, November 1946: 1300 khz; 1 kw-D, 500 w-N. TL: N33 00 40 W115 31 16. Hrs open: 24 Box 238, 120 S. Plaza, Brawley, 92227. Phone: (760) 344-1300. Fax: (760) 344-1763.E-mail: q96radio@yahoo.com Licensee: CCR-Brawley IV LLC. Group owner: Cherry Creek Radio LLC acq 6-99; $2 million with co-located FM). Population served: 150,000 Miller & Miller. Format: Country. Target aud: 25-54; male. ◆Tony Driskill, gen mgr; Lisa Aguirre, gen sls mgr.

KSIQ(FM)—(Brawley, Sept 10, 1981: 96.1 mhz; 50 kw. 340 ft TL: N32 57 12 W115 30 05. Stereo. Hrs open: 24 Prog sep from AM Box 238, 120 S. Plaza, Brawley, 92227. Phone: (760) 344-1300. Fax: (760) 344-1763. Format: Mainstream top-40. News one hr wkly. Target aud: 25-49; female. ◆Vincent Salgalo, mktg mgr, prom mgr, adv mgr & progmg mgr; Dean Imhof, engrg dir.

KWST(AM)— June 21, 1958: 1430 khz; 1 kw-U. TL: N32 48 27 W115 32 18. Stereo. Hrs open: 24 Box 2830, 92244. Phone: (760) 337-8707. Fax: (760) 337-8012.E-mail: info@univision.com Web Site:www.univision.com Licensee: Entravision Holding L.L.C. Group owner: Entravision Communications Co. L.L.C. (acq 1998; $4.8 million). Population

served: 950,000 Format: Country. Target aud: 25-49. ◆Albert Valdez, pres, opns mgr; Eric Chavez, gen mgr.

KXO(AM)— January 1927: 1230 khz; 1 kw-U. TL: N32 46 34 W115 32 58. Hrs open: 24 Box 140, 92244. Phone: (760) 352-1230.E-mail: kxoamfm@kxoradio.com Web Site:www.kxoradio.com Licensee: KXO Inc. (acq 1961). Population served: 145,000 Natl. Network: CBS, . Rgnl. Network: Calif. Farm. Natl. Rep: McGavren Guild,. Format: Oldies. News staff: one; News: 10 hrs wkly. Target aud: 18-49. Spec prog: Farm 7 hrs wkly. ◆Caroll Buckley, VP, gen sls mgr, prom mgr, progmg dir; Gene Brister, pres & gen mgr; Doug Melanson, chief of engrg.

KXO-FM— Aug 2, 1976: 107.5 mhz; 25.5 kw. 155 ft TL: N32 46 35 W115 32 58. Stereo. Hrs open: 24 Box 140, 91209. Phone: (760) 352-1230. Fax: (760) 352-0858.E-mail: kxoamfm@kxoradio.com Web Site:www.kxoradio.com (Acq 1976.). Population served: 145,000 Format: Adult contemp. News: 3 hrs wkly. Target aud: 25-49. ◆Gene Brister, gen mgr.

El Cerrito

*KECG(FM)— September 1978: 88.1 mhz; 17 w. Ant -66 ft TL: N37 54 30 W122 17 39. Stereo. Hrs open: 24 540 Ashbury Ave., 94530. Phone: (510) 525-4472. Fax: (510) 525-0554.E-mail: kecg88@aol.com Licensee: West Contra Costa Unified School District. Natl. Network: USA, . Format: Div, educ, jazz. News: 5 hrs wkly. Target aud: General. Spec prog: Gospel 5 hrs, Sp 3 hrs, Filipino 2 hrs wkly. ◆Philip H. Morgan Jr., stn mgr.

El Rio

KMLA(FM)— October 1996: 103.7 mhz; 1 kw. Ant 804 ft TL: N34 18 10 W119 13 41. Hrs open: 355 S. A St., Suite 103, Oxnard, 93030. Phone: (805) 385-5656. Fax: (805) 385-5690.E-mail: willy@lam1037.com Web Site:www.lam1037.com Licensee: Gold Coast Radio L.L.C. (acq 12-6-96; $550,000). Format: Rgnl Mexican. ◆Guillermo Gonzalez, gen mgr, gen sls mgr; Sonia Lopez, stn mgr; Rosa Rodriguez, prom dir; Gerardo Ceja, progmg dir, news dir; Charles Hastings, chief of engrg.

Ellwood

KSPE-FM—Licensed to Ellwood. See Santa Barbara

Encinitas

KPRI(FM)— Jan 20, 1962: 102.1 mhz; 14.5 kw. Ant 817 ft TL: N33 06 40 W117 12 05. Stereo. Hrs open: 24 9710 Scranton Rd., Suite 200, San Diego, 92121. Phone: (858) 678-0102. Fax: (858) 320-7024.E-mail: ilisten@kprifm.com Web Site:www.kprifm.com Licensee: Compass Radio of San Diego Inc. (acq 1996). Population served: 700,000 Natl. Rep: Katz Radio,. Shaw Pittman. Format: Triple A. News staff: one; News: 2 hrs wkly. Target aud: 18-34; upscale, well educated, young adult contemp mus fans. ◆Jonathan D. Schwartz, CFO, sr VP; Bob Hughes, gen mgr, opns mgr; Robert Burch, stn mgr; Patrick Osburn, sls dir; Keith Miller, mktg dir, prom dir.

Escondido

KFSD(AM)— June 1958: 1450 khz; 1 kw-U. TL: N33 07 11 W117 07 07. Hrs open: 24 1835 Aston Ave., Carlsbad, 92008. Phone: (760) 729-1000. Fax: (760) 476-9604.E-mail: reception@astorbroadcastgroup.com Web Site:www.am1510kspa.com Licensee: North County Broadcasting Corp. Group owner: Astor Broadcast Group (acq 9-15-87; $3 million with co-located FM; 6-29-87). Population served: 150,000 Format: Adult standards. News: 2 hrs wkly. Target aud: 35-64. ◆Arthur Astor, CEO, pres; Rick Roome, gen mgr.

KSOQ-FM— July 1966: 92.1 mhz; 580 w. Ant 1,024 ft TL: N33 06 39 W117 09 13. Stereo. Hrs open: 24
Rebroadcasts KSON-FM San Diego 100%.
Box 889004, San Diego, 92168-9004. Secondary address: 1615 Murray Canyon Rd., Suite 710, San Diego 92108-4321. Phone: (619) 291-9797. Phone: (619) 297-3698. Fax: (619) 543-1353. Web Site:www.kson.com Licensee: Jefferson-Pilot Communications Co. of California. Group owner: Jefferson-Pilot Communications Co. (acq 4-1-2004; $18 million). Population served: 1,500,000 Format: Country. ◆Darrel Goodin, gen mgr; Dave Saunders, gen sls mgr; John Marks, progmg dir; Eric Schecter, chief of engrg.

Esparto

KLMG(FM)— 1996: 97.9 mhz; 6 kw. Ant 328 ft TL: N38 45 33 W121 52 33. Hrs open:
Simulcast with KBBU(FM) Modesto 100%.
500 Media Pl., Sacramento, 95815. Phone: (916) 368-6300. Fax: (916) 473-0146.E-mail: azteca16@aol.com Web Site:www.lakebuena.com Licensee: Bustos Media of California License LLC. (acq 12-15-2004; $21.7 million with KBBU(FM) Modesto). Format: Rgnl Mexican. ◆Amparo Perez-Cook, gen mgr; Javier Gonzalez, prom dir; Juan Gonzalez, progmg dir; Mark Sedaka, chief of engrg; Cynthia Sanchez, traf mgr.

Essex

KHWY(FM)— May 1, 1991: 98.9 mhz; 10 kw. Ant 1,073 ft TL: N34 52 50 W115 04 05. Hrs open: 24
Rebroadcasts KRXV(FM) Yermo 100%.
Box 1668, 1611 E. Main St., Barstow, 92312. Phone: (760) 256-0326. Fax: (760) 256-9507.E-mail: tim@highwayradio.com Web Site:www.thehighwaystations.com Licensee: KHWY Inc. Natl. Network: AP Radio, . Hogan & Hartson. Format: Adult contemp. News staff: one; News: 28 hrs wkly. Target aud: 35 plus; travelers on I-40 & I-15 & Mojave Desert residents. ◆Howard B. Anderson, CEO, pres; Kirk M. Anderson, exec VP; Timothy B. Anderson, VP & gen mgr; Judy Robinson, sls VP; John Gregg, prom dir, prom mgr; Lance Todd, progmg dir; Keith Hayes, news dir; Thomas J. McNeill, engrg mgr.

Eureka

KATA(AM)—See Arcata

KEKA-FM— Nov 1, 1983: 101.5 mhz; 100 kw. 3,200 ft TL: N40 25 12 W124 05 00. Stereo. Hrs open: 1101 Marsh Rd., 95501. Phone: (707) 442-5744. Licensee: Eureka Broadcasting. (acq 12-13-90; $430,189;1-7-91). Population served: 150,000 Natl. Network: ABC, . Natl. Rep: Katz Radio,. Format: Modern country. Target aud: 25-54. ◆Hugo Papstein, gen mgr.

KFMI(FM)— 1973: 96.3 mhz; 30 kw. 1,580 ft TL: N40 43 36 W123 58 18. (CP: 100 kw). Stereo. Hrs open: 5640 S. Broadway, 95503. Phone: (707) 442-2000. Fax: (707) 443-6848.E-mail: power963@hotmail.com Web Site:www.power963.com Licensee: Bicoastal Media LLC. (group owner; acq 7-28-99; grpsl). Population served: 120,000 Natl. Network: Westwood One, . Format: Hot adult contemp, CHR. Target aud: 18-36; upscale adults. ◆Ken Dennis, CEO; Mike Wilson, pres; Laurie Tate, gen mgr, opns mgr; Victoria Bennington, gen sls mgr; Tom Sebourn, progmg dir.

KGOE(AM)— May 12, 1933: 1480 khz; 5 kw-D, 1 kw-N. TL: N40 44 28 W124 12 05. Hrs open: 24 5640 S. Broadway, 95503. Phone: (707) 442-2000. Fax: (707) 443-6848.E-mail: tsebourn@bicoastalmedia.com Web Site:www.kgoe1480.com Licensee: Bicoastal Media LLC. (group owner; acq 7-28-99; grpsl). Population served: 125,000 Natl. Network: ABC, Premiere Radio Networks, . Format: News/talk. News staff: one; News: one hr wkly. Target aud: 25-54. ◆Laurie Tate, gen mgr; Victoria Bennington, gen sls mgr; Rollin Treehearn, prom dir; Tom Sebourn, progmg dir; Kevin Sanders, chief of engrg.

KIHH(AM)— July 26, 2008: 1400 khz; 790 w-U. TL: N40 48 09 W124 08 20. Hrs open: 7956 California Ave., Fair Oaks, 95628. Phone: (916) 535-0500. Fax: (916) 535-0504. Web Site:www.ihradio.org Licensee: IHR Educational Broadcasting. Natl. Network: EWTN Radio, . Format: Catholic. ◆Douglas M. Sherman, pres.

KINS(AM)— January 1946: 980 khz; 5 kw-D, 500 w-N, DA-N. TL: N40 48 02 W124 07 39. Hrs open: 24 1101 Marsh Rd., 95501. Phone: (707) 442-5744. Licensee: Eureka Broadcasting Co. (acq 3-1-58). Population served: 28,936 Natl. Network: CBS, Wall Street, . Format: News/talk. News staff: 2. Target aud: 35 plus; upscale, educated. ◆Hugo Papstein, pres, gen mgr, gen sls mgr, progmg dir; Mark Householter, chief of engrg.

KKHB(FM)— 1994: 105.5 mhz; 28 kw. 1,588 ft TL: N40 43 52 W123 57 06. Hrs open:
Rebroadcasts KGO(AM) San Francisco.
5640 S. Broadway, 95503. Phone: (707) 442-2000. Fax: (707) 443-6848. Web Site:www.cool1055.com Licensee: Bicoastal Media L.L.C. (group owner; acq 11-9-98; grpsl). Format: Oldies. ◆Laurie Tate, gen mgr, opns dir; Victoria Bennington, gen sls mgr; Tom Sebourn, progmg dir.

*KMUE(FM)— Aug 9, 1996: 88.3 mhz; 1.25 kw. 1,446 ft TL: N40 43 52 W123 57 06. Hrs open: Box 135, Redway, 95560-0135. Secondary address: 1144 Redway Dr., Redway 95560. Phone: (707) 923-2513. Fax: (707) 923-2501.E-mail: kmud@kmud.org Web Site:www.kmud.org

Licensee: Redwood Community Radio Inc. Population served: 50,000 Format: Talk, div, educ. ◆David Lippe, dev dir, adv mgr; Michael Jacinto, progmg dir.

KNCR(AM)—See Fortuna

KRED-FM— Dec 17, 1979: 92.3 mhz; 25 kw. Ant 1,544 ft TL: N40 43 37 W123 58 25. Stereo. Hrs open: 5640 S. Broadway, 95503. Phone: (707) 442-2000. Fax: (707) 443-6848.E-mail: mail@kred923.com Web Site:www.kred923.com Licensee: Bicoastal Media LLC. Population served: 125,000 Format: Hot country. News staff: one; News: 7 hrs wkly. ◆Laurie Tate, gen mgr; Victoria Bennington, gen sls mgr & prom dir; Rollin Treehearn, progmg dir.

KWSW(AM)— Dec 20, 1979: 790 khz; 5 kw-D, 112 w-N. TL: N40 48 09 W124 08 20. Hrs open: 1101 Marsh Rd., 95501. Phone: (707) 442-5744. Licensee: Eureka Broadcasting Co. Inc. (acq 11-30-92; $105,000;12-21-92). Population served: 150,000 Format: Talk. Target aud: 35 plus; baby boomers with discretionary income. ◆Hugo Papstein, pres, gen mgr, progmg dir; Brian Papstein, gen sls mgr; Mark Householter, chief of engrg.

KXGO(FM)—(Arcata, 1970: 93.1 mhz; 50 kw. Ant 1,666 ft TL: N40 43 38 W123 58 22. Stereo. Hrs open: 603 F. St., 95501. Phone: (707) 445-8104. Fax: (707) 445-3906.E-mail: operations@kxgo.com Web Site:theclassicrockexperience.com Licensee: Miller Broadcasting Co. (acq 11-1-97). Population served: 210,000 Natl. Rep: Christal,. Format: Classic rock. Target aud: 25-54; upscale adults. ◆Becky Collins, opns mgr; Pattison Christensen, pres, stn mgr & natl sls mgr; Carole Arrington, rgnl sls mgr, prom dir; Danny King, progmg dir.

Fair Oaks

KSSJ(FM)— Nov 25, 1970: 94.7 mhz; 86.6 kw. 2,072 ft TL: N39 15 30 W119 42 36. Stereo. Hrs open: 5345 Madison Ave., Sacramento, 95841-3141. Phone: (916) 334-7777. Fax: (916) 339-4281.E-mail: info@kssj.com Web Site:www.kssj.com Licensee: Entercom Sacramento License L.L.C. Group owner: Entercom Communications Corp. (acq 11-4-97; $15.9 million). Format: Smooth jazz. ◆David Lichtman, gen mgr; Lee Hansen, stn mgr & progmg dir.

Fairfield

*KASK(FM)—Not on air, target date: unknown: 91.5 mhz; 75 w. 649 ft TL: N38 19 09 W121 59 30. Hrs open: Maranatha Broadcasting, 130 Portsmouth Ave., Vacaville, 95687. Phone: (707) 449-4059. Fax: (707) 447-0680.E-mail: info@kaskfm.com Licensee: Maranatha Broadcasting. Format: Relg. ◆Michel Mace, pres & stn mgr.

KUIC(FM)—See Vacaville

Fairmead

*KLVY(FM)— 1998: 91.1 mhz; 3.4 kw. 256 ft TL: N37 13 01 W120 11 57. Stereo. Hrs open: 24
Rebroadcasts KLVN(FM) Livingston 100%.
2351 Sunset Blvd., Suite 170-218, Rocklin, 95765. Phone: (916) 251-1600. Fax: (916) 251-1650.E-mail: klove@klove.com Web Site:www.klove.com Licensee: Educational Media Foundation Inc. Group owner: EMF Broadcasting. Population served: 770,000 Natl. Network: K-Love, . Shaw Pittman. Format: Contemp Christian music. News staff: 3. Target aud: 25-44; Judeo-Christian, female. ◆Richard Jenkins, pres; Mike Novak, VP; Keith Whipple, dev dir; David Pierce, prom mgr, progmg mgr; Ed Lenane, news dir; Sam Wallington, engrg dir; Karen Johnson, news rptr.

Fallbrook

KSSD(FM)— Nov 22, 1977: 107.1 mhz; 3 kw. 300 ft TL: N33 23 01 W117 11 20. Stereo. Hrs open: 24 5700 Wilshire Blvd., Suite 250, Los Angeles, 90036. Phone: (323) 900-6100. Fax: (323) 900-6127. Web Site:www.superestrella.com Licensee: Entravision Holdings LLC. Group owner: Entravision Communications Corp. (acq 4-1-03; grpsl). Natl. Rep: Lotus Entravision Reps LLC,. Cohn & Marks. Format: Sp, CHR. Target aud: 18-34. ◆Jeff Liberman, VP, gen mgr; Karl Meyer, gen mgr; Elias Autran, progmg dir; Eugene McAffe, chief of engrg, engr; Pam McCaffrey, traf mgr.

Felton

KXZM(FM)— 1999: 93.7 mhz; 28 w. Ant 1,260 ft TL: N37 03 43 W122 07 14. Hrs open: 200 South St., Suite 400, Oxnard, 93030. Phone: (805) 240-2070. Fax: (805) 240-5960. Licensee: Lazer Broadcasting

Corp. (group owner; (acq 7-25-2005; $2.88 million with KXSM(FM) Hollister). Format: Rgnl Mexican. ♦Alfredo Plascencia, pres; Daniel Osuna, gen mgr.

Ferndale

KJNY(FM)— Apr 1, 1993: 99.1 mhz; 6 kw. 1,715 ft TL: N40 30 03 W124 17 08. Stereo. Hrs open: 24 603 F St., Eureka, 95501. Phone: (707) 445-3699. Fax: (707) 445-3906.E-mail: operations@kxgo.com Web Site:www.kjny.net Licensee: Redwood Broadcasting Co. Inc. (acq 1999). Rosenman & Colin. News staff: one; News: 3 hrs wkly. Target aud: 25-54; upscale adults. ♦Pattison Christensen, pres & stn mgr; Danny King, progmg dir.

Firebaugh

***KYAF(FM)**— 2006: 94.7 mhz; 900 w. Ant 66 ft TL: N36 51 37 W120 27 19. Hrs open: 1572 10th St., 93622. Phone: (559) 659-0100.E-mail: info@kayfm.com Web Site:kyafm.com Licensee: Central Valley Educational Services Inc. Format: Oldies. ♦Verne White, pres.

***KYCI(FM)**— 2008: 90.5 mhz; 395 w. Ant 1,089 ft TL: N36 43 32 W120 45 49. Hrs open: 9019 West Ln., Stockton, 95210-1401. Phone: (209) 477-3690. Fax: (209) 477-2762.E-mail: kycc@kycc.org Web Site:www.kycc.org Licensee: Your Christian Companion Network Inc. Format: Christian. ♦Shirley Garner, exec VP & gen mgr.

Ford City

KZPE(FM)—Not on air, target date: unknown: 102.1 mhz; 6 kw. Ant 128 ft TL: N35 00 02 W119 22 29. Hrs open: c/o William Zawila, Esq., 12600 Brookhurst St., Suite 105, Garden Grove, 92840. Phone: (714) 636-5040. Fax: (714) 636-5042. Licensee: Estate of H.L. Charles, Robert Willing, executor (acq 6-4-2004).

Fort Bragg

KDAC(AM)— June 1948: 1230 khz; 1 kw-U. TL: N39 26 35 W123 46 48. Hrs open: 24
Rebroadcasts KUKI(AM)UKiah 100%.
1400 Kuki Ln., Ukiah, 95482. Phone: (707) 263-6113. Fax: (707) 466-5852.E-mail: ykiah@bicoasyals[\] Population served: 8,000 Natl. Network: ABC, CBS, . Format: Mexican/Rgnl. News staff: one; News: 24 hrs wkly. Target aud: 35 plus. ♦George Feola, gen mgr; Tove Sorensen, opns mgr.

***KJCU(FM)**— 2004: 89.9 mhz; 130 w. Ant 348 ft TL: N39 26 35 W123 43 58. Hrs open: 474 S. Franklin St., 95437. Phone: (707) 964-2170. Licensee: Calvary Chapel of Costa Mesa Inc. (group owner). Format: Relg. ♦Dan Gillman, gen mgr & progmg dir.

KOZT(FM)— Dec 5, 1981: 95.3 mhz; 35 kw. Ant 515 ft TL: N39 24 24 W123 44 04. Stereo. Hrs open: 24 110 S. Franklin, 95437. Phone: (707) 964-7277. Fax: (707) 964-9536.E-mail: thecoast@kozt.com Web Site:www.kozt.com Licensee: California Radio Partners Inc. (acq 12-1-90; 12-17-90). Population served: 100,000 Miller & Neely P.C. Format: AAA. News staff: one; News: one hr wkly. Target aud: 25-49; affluent, educated consumers. ♦Tom Yates, CEO, gen mgr, opns dir; Vicky Watts, chmn & CFO.

KPMO(AM)—See Mendocino

KSAY(FM)— November 1988: Stn currently dark. 98.5 mhz; 3500 w. 453 ft TL: N39 26 08 W123 48 15. Stereo. Hrs open: 24 Box 2269, 95437. Phone: (707) 964-5729. Fax: (707) 964-5729.E-mail: ksayfm@yahoo.com Licensee: Axell Broadcasting. Population served: 100,000 Format: Adult contemp. News staff: one; News: 9 hrs wkly. Target aud: 18-49; primarily women. ♦Wade Axell, gen mgr.

Fortuna

KNCR(AM)— Oct 31, 1966: 1090 khz; 10 kw-D. TL: N40 33 30 W124 07 24. Hrs open: Sunrise-sunset Box 109, Eureka, 95502-0109. Phone: (707) 725-9363. Fax: (707) 726-9446.E-mail: mario@lanueva1090.com Web Site:www.lanueva1090.com Licensee: Del Rosario Talpa Inc. (acq 5-17-2004; $37,500). Rosenman & Colin L.L.P. Format: Rgnl Mexican. News: 2 hrs wkly. Target aud: 25-54. ♦Mario Meza, gen mgr; Sylvia Meza, gen sls mgr.

KWPT(FM)— May 15, 1992: 100.3 mhz; 12 kw. Ant 1,807 ft TL: N40 25 23 W124 06 21. Hrs open: 24 Box 25, Ferndale, 95536. Phone: (707) 786-5104. Fax: (707) 786-5100.E-mail: studio@kwpt.com Web Site:www.kwpt.com Licensee: KWPT Inc. (acq 5-12-2005; $650,000). Population served: 126,000 Law Office of Dan J. Alpert. Format: Classic hits. Target aud: 30-54; affluent, college educated. ♦Patrick Cleary, gen mgr; Jennefer White, natl sls mgr; Gregg Foster, mktg dir; Kara Hochner, prom dir; Cliff Berkowitz, progmg dir, mus dir.

Fountain Valley

KJLL-FM— 1993: 92.7 mhz; 690 w. Ant 961 ft TL: N33 36 20 W117 48 35. Stereo. Hrs open: 24
Rebroadcasts KHJL(FM) Thousand Oaks 100%.
99 Long Ct., Suite 200, Thousand Oaks, 91360. Phone: (805) 497-8511. Fax: (805) 497-8514.E-mail: reception@927jillfm.com Web Site:www.927jillfm.com Licensee: Amaturo Group of L.A. Ltd. Group owner: Amaturo Groups (acq 1996; $5.5 million). Population served: 4,000,000 Natl. Network: ABC, . Rgnl. Network: Metronews Radio Net. Format: Adult contemp. Target aud: 25-54. ♦Joseph Amaturo, CEO, VP; Robert J. Christy, gen mgr; Robert Christy, gen sls mgr; Aaron Fonesca, progmg dir.

Fowler

KALZ(FM)— Nov 7, 1980: 96.7 mhz; 22 kw. Ant 348 ft TL: N36 41 39 W119 43 57. Stereo. Hrs open: 24 83 E. Shaw Ave., Suite 150, Fresno, 93710-7616. Phone: (559) 230-4300. Fax: (559) 243-4301.E-mail: info@myalice967.com Web Site:www.myalice967.com Licensee: Clear Channel Radio Licenses Inc. Group owner: Clear Channel Communications Inc. (acq 8-30-2000; grpsl). Population served: 650,000 Format: Adult contemp. Target aud: 25-54; women. ♦Jeff Negrete, gen mgr; Paul Wilson, opns mgr; Tony Rainaldi, gen sls mgr; Chris Miller, prom dir; Paul Wilson, progmg dir; Dave Case, chief of engrg; Michelle Howes-Appleton, traf mgr.

KQEQ(AM)— July 1, 1962: 1210 khz; 370 w-U. TL: N36 39 37 W119 41 01. Hrs open: 139 W. Olive Ave., Fresno, 93728. Phone: (559) 499-1210. Fax: (559) 499-1212.E-mail: rak@computermail.net Web Site:www.thehmongradio.com Licensee: RAK Communications Inc. (acq 9-30-94;7-4-94). Population served: 600,000 Format: Hmong. News staff: 1; News: 10 hrs wkly. Target aud: 13-Senior; Hmong and Lao. ♦Pahoua Moua, gen mgr & mktg mgr.

Frazier Park

KJPG(AM)— 1994: 1050 khz; 10 kw-D, 7 w-N, DA-D. TL: N35 01 28 W118 55 05 (D), N35 24 07 W119 02 47 (N). Hrs open: Box 180, Tahoma, 96142. Phone: (530) 584-5700. Fax: (530) 584-5705.E-mail: info@ihradio.org Web Site:www.ihradio.org Licensee: IHR Educational Broadcasting. (group owner; (acq 11-15-2003; $700,000). Format: Catholic/relg. ♦Douglas M. Sherman, pres & VP.

Freedom

KPIG-FM— Dec 1, 1987: 107.5 mhz; 5.4 kw. Ant 338 ft TL: N36 50 06 W121 42 22. Stereo. Hrs open: 24 60 Garden Ct., Suite 300, Monterey, 93940. Secondary address: 1110 Main St., Suite 16, Watsonville 95076-3700. Phone: (831) 722-9000. Fax: (831) 722-7548.E-mail: frank@kpig.com Web Site:www.kpig.com Licensee: Mapleton License of Monterey LLC. (group owner; (acq 11-16-2001; grpsl). Natl. Rep: McGavren Guild,. Leventhal, Senter & Lerman. Format: AAA "Americana". Target aud: 25-54. ♦Dale Hendry, gen mgr; Frank Caprista, opns mgr, progmg dir; Jodi Morgan, gen sls mgr; Sybil DeAngelo, prom dir; Velden Levirich, chief of engrg.

Fremont

***KOHL(FM)**— Sept 23, 1974: 89.3 mhz; 145 w. 407 ft TL: N37 32 00 W121 54 35. Stereo. Hrs open: 24 43600 Mission Blvd., 94539. Phone: (510) 659-6221. Fax: (510) 659-6001.E-mail: kohl@kohlradio.com Web Site:www.kohlradio.com Licensee: Fremont-Newark Community College Dist. Format: Contemp hit/Top 40. News: one hr wkly. Target aud: 18-34. ♦Robert Dochterman, gen mgr; Tom Gomez, progmg dir; Matthew Karl, news dir, pub affrs dir.

Fresno

KBIF(AM)— Nov 17, 1947: 900 khz; 1000 kw-D, 500 w-N, DA-N. TL: N36 41 30 W119 40 46. Hrs open: 24 3401 W. Holland Ave., 93722. Phone: (559) 222-0900. Fax: (559) 222-1573.E-mail: kbifkirv@aol.com Web Site:www.kbif900am.com Licensee: Gore-Overgaard Broadcasting Inc. (group owner) Population served: 1,000,000 Natl. Network: USA, . Format: Asian. News staff: 4; News: 10 hrs wkly. Target aud: 25 plus; Asian adults. Spec prog: Sp 6 hrs, Punjabi 16 hrs wkly. ♦Dana Kennon, VP, gen mgr; Tony Donato, opns dir & gen sls mgr.

KBOS-FM—(Tulare, 1965: 94.9 mhz; 16.4 kw. 847 ft TL: N36 38 15 W118 56 35. Stereo. Hrs open: 24 83 East Shaw Ave., Ste. 150, 93710. Phone: (559) 230-4300. Fax: (559) 243-4301.E-mail: info@95forlife.com Web Site:www.b95forlife.com Licensee: Capstar TX L.P. Group owner: Clear Channel Communications Inc. (acq 8-30-00; grpsl). Population served: 918,900 Natl. Network: CBS Radio, . Format: Rhythmic CHR. Target aud: 12-34. ♦Jeff Negrete, VP, gen mgr; Paul Wilson, opns dir & opns mgr; Joni Norvell, gen sls mgr, traf mgr; Greg Hoffman, progmg dir; Dave Case, chief of engrg.

KCBL(AM)— June 26, 1953: 1340 khz; 1 kw-U. TL: N36 45 51 W119 47 08. Hrs open: 83 E. Shaw Ave., Suite 150, 93710. Phone: (559) 243-4300. Fax: (559) 243-4301.E-mail: info@foxsportsradio1340.com Web Site:www.foxsportsradio1340.com Licensee: Capstar TX L.P. Group owner: Clear Channel Communications Inc. (acq 8-30-00; grpsl). Population served: 500,000 Natl. Network: CBS, . Natl. Rep: CBS Radio,. Format: All sports. Target aud: 18-49. ♦Jeff Negrete, VP; Paul Wilson, opns mgr; Brian Noe, progmg dir.

KCIV(FM)—See Mount Bullion

***KEYQ(AM)**— Oct 14, 1957: 980 khz; 500 w-D, 48 w-N. TL: N36 44 28 W119 51 12. Hrs open: 24
Rebroadcasts KMRO(FM) Camarillo 100%.
2310 Ponderosa Dr., Suite 28, Camarillo, 93010. Phone: (805) 482-4797. Fax: (805) 388-5202.E-mail: info@nuevavida.com Web Site:www.nuevavida.com Licensee: The Association for Community Education Inc. Population served: 1,000,000 Miller & Neely. Format: Relg, Sp. Target aud: General; Sp-speaking. ♦Phil Guthrie, pres; Mary Guthrie, gen mgr.

***KFCF(FM)**— June 9, 1975: 88.1 mhz; 2.4 kw. Ant 1,899 ft TL: N37 04 23 W119 25 51. Stereo. Hrs open: 24
Rebroadcasts KPFA(FM) Berkeley 85%.
Box 4364, 93744. Secondary address: 1449 N. Wishon Ave. 93728. Phone: (559) 233-2221. Fax: (559) 233-5776.E-mail: kfcf@kfcf.org Web Site:www.kfcf.org Licensee: Fresno Free College Foundation. Population served: 1,200,000 Arent, Fox, Kintner, Plotkin & Kahn. Format: Var. News staff: 2; News: 12 hrs wkly. Target aud: General; intelligent, discerning, questioning. Spec prog: Southeast Asian languages one hr, American Indian 2 hrs, Sp 5 hrs wkly. ♦Rebecca Caraveo, opns VP; Frank Delgado, prom dir; Rick Flores, mus dir; Rychard Withers, gen mgr, progmg dir & chief of engrg.

KFIG(AM)— January 1938: 1430 khz; 5 kw-U, DA-1. TL: N36 50 49 W119 40 46. Hrs open: 351 W. Cromwell, Suite 108, 93711. Phone: (559) 447-3570. Fax: (559) 447-3579.E-mail: postmaster@1430espn.com Web Site:www.1430espn.com Licensee: Fat Dawgs 7 Broadcasting LLC (acq 7-28-2005; $2.5 million). Population served: 500,000 Natl. Network: ESPN Radio, . Format: All sports. Target aud: 25 plus. ♦Joe Pacheco, pres; Paul Swearengin, gen mgr; Nick Washington, progmg dir; Paul Kleinkramer, chief of engrg.

***KFNO(FM)**— Feb 12, 1992: 90.3 mhz; 1.35 kw. 1,971 ft TL: N37 04 26 W119 25 52. Hrs open: 706 W. Herndon Ave., 93650. Phone: (559) 435-4996. Fax: (916) 641-8238. Licensee: Family Stations Inc. (group owner) Format: Relg. ♦Harold Camping, pres; Peggy Renschler, gen mgr.

KFPT(AM)—See Clovis

***KFSR(FM)**— Oct 30, 1982: 90.7 mhz; 2.55 kw. 66 ft TL: N36 48 42 W119 44 43. Stereo. Hrs open: 24 California State Univ. of Fresno, 5201 N. Maple, MS SA#119, 93740-8027. Phone: (559) 278-2598. Phone: (559) 278-4500. Fax: (559) 278-6985.E-mail: kfsrfresno@hotmail.com Web Site:www.csufresno.edu/kfsr/ Licensee: California State University Fresno. Population served: 500,000 Format: Jazz, alternative rock, div. News: 2 hrs wkly. Target aud: General. Spec prog: Blues 6 hrs, reggae 6 hrs, world 9 hrs, folk 3 hrs, western one hr wkly. ♦Don Priest, gen mgr; Joe Moore, stn mgr; Frank Delgado, progmg dir, progmg mgr; Matt Garcia, mus dir; Matthew Boan, pub affrs dir.

KGED(AM)— 2003: 1680 khz; 10 kw-D, 1 kw-N. TL: N36 46 14 W119 55 20. Hrs open: 139 W. Olive Ave., 93728. Phone: (559) 233-8803. Fax: (559) 233-8871.E-mail: rakradio@comcast.net Licensee: RAK Communications Inc. Format: Sp relg. ♦Albert R. Perez, gen mgr; Albert Perez, gen sls mgr; Paul Klein Kramer, chief of engrg.

KGST(AM)— 1949: 1600 khz; 5 kw-U, DA-N. TL: N36 29 20 W119 19 33. Hrs open: 1110 E. Olive Ave., 93728. Phone: (559) 497-1100. Fax: (559) 497-1125.E-mail: mginsburg@lotusfresno.com Licensee: Lotus Communications Inc. (group owner; (acq 8-1-85; $1.76 million; 4-22-85). Population served: 1,500,000 Natl. Rep: Lotus Entravision Reps LLC,. Format: Sp/ESPN sports. News staff: one; News: 2 hrs wkly. Target aud: 18 plus; Hispanic adults. ♦Howard Kalmenson, pres; Daniel Crotty, gen mgr.

KHGE(FM)— Jan 6, 1962: 102.7 mhz; 50 kw. Ant 500 ft TL: N36 49 07 W119 30 33. Stereo. Hrs open: 24 83 E. Shaw Ave., Suite 150, 93710. Phone: (559) 230-4300. Fax: (559) 243-4301.E-mail: info@bigcountry1027.com Web Site:www.bigcountry1027.com Licensee: Capstar TX L.P. Group owner: Clear Channel Communications Inc. (acq 8-30-2000; grpsl). Population served: 500,000 Natl. Rep: Clear Channel,. Format: Adult contemp. News staff: one; News: 20 hrs wkly. Target aud: 25-54; women. ♦Jeff Negrete, VP, gen mgr; Chris Hansen, gen sls mgr; Rita Walls, rgnl sls mgr; Chris Miller, prom dir; Chuck Geiger, progmg dir.

KIRV(AM)— Oct 1, 1962: 1510 khz; 10,000 kw-D. TL: N36 42 36 W119 50 06. Hrs open: 3401 W. Holland Ave., 93722. Phone: (559) 222-0900. Fax: (559) 222-1573. Web Site:www.kirv.com Licensee: Gore-Overgaard Broadcasting Inc. (acq 4-24-99). Population served: 800,000 Format: Christian talk, Sp Christian talk. Target aud: 25-54. ♦Dana Kennon, VP, stn mgr; Tony Donato, opns dir & gen sls mgr.

KJFX(FM)— May 15, 1970: 95.7 mhz; 17.5 kw. 850 ft TL: N36 56 55 W119 29 09. Stereo. Hrs open: 24 1066 E. Shaw Ave., 93710. Phone: (559) 255-1041. Fax: (559) 230-0177. Web Site:www.957thefox.com Licensee: Wilks License Co.-Fresno LLC. (acq 6-1-2005; grpsl). Natl. Rep: McGavren Guild,. Format: Classic rock. ♦Kevin O'Rorke, gen mgr; Rob Hasson, gen sls mgr; Andrea Carter, progmg dir.

KJWL(FM)— Apr 29, 1994: 99.3 mhz; 5.03 kw. 349 ft TL: N36 44 07 W119 47 10. Hrs open: 675 Santa Fe Ave., 93721. Phone: (559) 497-5118. Fax: (559) 497-9760.E-mail: info@kjwl.com Web Site:www.kjwl.com Licensee: John E. Ostlund. Natl. Network: CNN Radio, . Format: Adult standards. Target aud: 35 plus; upscale. ♦John E. Ostlund, pres, gen mgr; Bruce Campbell, opns mgr; Jennifer Books, dev mgr; Eric McCormick, gen sls mgr; Chris Nieto, prom dir; Jim Roberts, progmg dir; Juanita Stevenson, news dir; Joe Garcia, traf mgr, traf mgr.

KLBN(FM)— Mar 15, 1948: 101.9 mhz; 2.25 kw. Ant 1,958 ft TL: N37 04 22 W119 25 53. Hrs open: 24 1110 E. Olive, 93728. Phone: (559) 497-1100. Fax: (559) 497-1125. Licensee: Lotus Fresno Corp. Group owner: Infinity Broadcasting Corp. (acq 11-1-2007; $8.4 million). Population served: 1,200,000 Natl. Rep: Lotus Entravision Reps LLC,. Format: Classic rock. News staff: one; News: one hr wkly. Target aud: 25-54; adults. ♦Howard Kalmenson, pres; Tony Bonnici, VP; Mike Ginsburg, gen mgr; Vince Cantu, traf mgr; Stella Romo, local news ed.

KMGV(FM)— Mar 15, 1948: 97.9 mhz; 2.07 kw. 1,987 ft TL: N36 44 09 W119 47 59. (CP: 10.5 kw, ant 1,076 ft.). Stereo. Hrs open: 1071 W. Shaw Ave., 93711. Phone: (559) 490-9800. Fax: (559) 490-4199. Licensee: Peak Broadcasting of Fresno Licenses LLC. Group owner: Infinity Broadcasting Corp. (acq 3-30-2007; grpsl). Wire Svc: UPI Format: Rhythm oldies. Target aud: 25-54. ♦Patty Hixson, gen mgr.

KMJ(AM)— June 1925: 580 khz; 5 kw-U. TL: N36 41 37 W120 03 16. Hrs open: 24 1071 W. Shaw Ave., 93711. Phone: (559) 490-5800. Fax: (559) 490-5977.E-mail: info@kmjam.com Web Site:www.kmjnow.com Licensee: Peak Broadcasting of Fresno Licenses LLC. Group owner: Infinity Broadcasting Corp. (acq 3-30-2007; grpsl). Population served: 520,000 Natl. Network: ABC, . Format: News/talk. News staff: 13; News: 44 hrs wkly. Target aud: 25-64. ♦Joe Mauk, CEO, chief of engrg; Patty Hixson, gen mgr.

KMJ-FM— Dec 8, 1979: 105.9 mhz; 2.4 kw. Ant 1,960 ft TL: N37 04 23 W119 25 51. Stereo. Hrs open: 24 1071 W. Shaw Ave., 93711. Phone: (559) 490-5800. Fax: (559) 490-5889. Web Site:www.kmjnow.com Licensee: Peak Broadcasting of Fresno Licenses LLC. Group owner: Infinity Broadcasting Corp. (acq 3-30-2007; grpsl). Leventhal, Senter & Lerman. Format: News/talk, classic hits. ♦Patty Hixson, gen mgr.

KRZR(FM)—See Hanford

***KSJV(FM)**— July 4, 1980: 91.5 mhz; 16 kw. Ant 870 ft TL: N35 38 15 W118 56 35. Stereo. Hrs open: 24 5005 E. Belmont Ave., 93727. Phone: (559) 455-5777. Fax: (559) 455-5778.E-mail: mail@radiobilingue.org Web Site:www.radiobilingue.org Licensee: Radio Bilingue Inc. Population served: 350,000 Format: Ethnic, Sp. News staff: 5; News: 11 hrs wkly. Target aud: 16-60; Latino. ♦Hugo Morales, CEO; Maria Erana, gen mgr, opns dir, gen sls mgr, progmg dir; Phil Traynor, dev dir; Samuel Cozco, news dir; Bill Bach, chief of engrg.

KSKS(FM)— 1946: 93.7 mhz; 68 kw. 1,912 ft TL: N37 04 44 W119 25 47. Stereo. Hrs open: Prog sep from AM 1071 W. Shaw Ave., 93711. Phone: (559) 490-5800. Fax: (559) 490-5944. Web Site:www.ksks.com Population served: 160,600 Format: Modern country. ♦Karen Franz, gen sls mgr.

KSOF(FM)—See Dinuba

***KVPR(FM)**— Oct 15, 1978: 89.3 mhz; 2.45 kw. 1,890 ft TL: N37 04 25 W119 25 52. Stereo. Hrs open: 24 3437 W. Shaw Ave., Suite 101, 93711. Phone: (559) 275-0764. Fax: (559) 275-2202.E-mail: kvpr@kvpr.org Web Site:www.kvpr.org Licensee: White Ash Broadcasting Inc. Population served: 979,500 Natl. Network: NPR, . Format: Class, news. News: 52 hrs wkly. ♦Mariam Stepanian, pres & gen mgr; Jim Meyers, stn mgr.

KWRU(AM)— 1937: 940 khz; 50 kw-U, DA-2. TL: N36 50 49 W119 39 46. Hrs open: 4910 E. Clinton Ave., Suite 107, 93727. Phone: (559) 251-6128. Fax: (559) 452-0948.E-mail: info@kwruam.com Web Site:www.radiovidaabundante.com Licensee: Multicultural Radio Broadcasting Licensee LLC. Group owner: Multicultural Radio Broadcasting Inc. (acq 2-4-2004; grpsl). Population served: 180500 Format: Sp, Christian. Target aud: 25-54. ♦Arthur S. Liu, pres; Alberto Felix, gen mgr, progmg dir.

KWYE(FM)— 1963: 101.1 mhz; 50 kw. 310 ft TL: N36 44 10 W119 47 13. (CP: 10 kw, ant 1,076 ft.). Stereo. Hrs open: 24 1071 W. Shaw, 93711. Phone: (559) 490-1011.E-mail: info@kwye.com Web Site:www.y101hits.com Licensee: Peak Broadcasting of Fresno Licenses LLC. Group owner: Infinity Broadcasting Corp. (acq 3-30-2007; grpsl). Population served: 500,000 Natl. Rep: Katz Radio,. Leventhal, Senter & Lerman,p. Format: CHR. Target aud: 18-49; emphasis on women. ♦Todd Lauley, CEO; Tim Lyons, CFO; Patty Hixson, gen mgr.

KXEX(AM)— September 1962: 1550 khz; 5 kw-D, 2.5 kw-N, DA-2. TL: N36 46 14 W119 55 20. Hrs open: 139 W. Olive Ave., 93728. Phone: (559) 233-8803. Fax: (559) 233-8871.E-mail: rakradio@comcast.net Web Site:www.1550snr.com Licensee: RAK Communications Inc. (acq 8-10-94; $212,000; 8-22-94). Population served: 197,840 Format: Sp. ♦Albert R. Perez, VP, gen mgr; Abel Perez, gen sls mgr; Paul Klein Kramer, chief of engrg.

KYNO(AM)— October 1947: 1300 khz; 5 kw-D, 1 kw-N, DA-N. TL: N36 46 14 W119 45 00. Hrs open: 24 2125 N. Barton Ave., 93703. Phone: (559) 454-1300. Fax: (559) 453-2430.E-mail: info@kyno.com Licensee: John Ostlund and Katrina Ostlund (acq 9-23-2008; $1.6 million). Population served: 165,972 Format: News/talk. ♦Ray Carrasco, gen mgr.

Garberville

KHUM(FM)— 1996: 104.7 mhz; 50 kw. 2,650 ft TL: N40 07 15 W123 41 27. Hrs open: 24 Box 25, Ferndale, 95536-0025. Secondary address: 1400 Main St., Suite 104, Ferndale 95536. Phone: (707) 786-5104. Fax: (707) 786-5100.E-mail: studio@khum.com Web Site:www.khum.com Licensee: Lost Coast Communications Inc. (acq 11-5-2001). Population served: 150,000 Natl. Rep: McGavren Guild,. Dan J. Alpert. Format: AAA. Target aud: 25-54; general. ♦Patrick Cleary, gen mgr; Cliff Berkowitz, opns VP; Jennefer White, natl sls mgr; Gregg Foster, mktg dir; Kara Hochner, prom dir; Mike Dronkers, mus dir; Kevin Sanders, chief of engrg.

***KLVG(FM)**— 1999: 103.7 mhz; 11 kw. Ant 2,348 ft TL: N40 20 05 W124 06 32. Stereo. Hrs open: 24 5700 W. Oak Blvd., Rocklin, 95765. Phone: (916) 251-1600. Fax: (916) 251-1650.E-mail: klove@klove.com Web Site:www.klove.com Licensee: Educational Media Foundation. Group owner: EMF Broadcasting. Population served: 120,000 Natl. Network: K-Love, . Shaw Pittman. Format: Contemp Christian music. News staff: 3. Target aud: 25-44; female (Judeo-Christian). ♦Richard Jenkins, pres; Mike Novak, VP, progmg dir; Lloyd Parker, gen mgr; Ed Lenane, opns dir, news dir; Keith Whipple, dev dir; Eric Allen, natl sls mgr; David Pierce, prom mgr, progmg mgr; Jon Rivers, mus dir; Sam Wallington, engrg dir; Arthur Vassar, traf mgr; Karen Johnson, news rptr.

***KMUD(FM)**— May 28, 1987: 91.1 mhz; 180 w. 2,490 ft TL: N40 07 13 W123 41 32. (CP: 5.5 kw, ant 2,601 ft). Hrs open: 24 Box 135, 1144 Redway Dr., Redway, 95560-0135. Phone: (707) 923-2513. Phone: (707) 923-3911 (STUDIO). Fax: (707) 923-2501.E-mail: kmud@kmud.org Web Site:www.kmud.org Licensee: Redwood Community Radio Inc. Population served: 20,000 Michael Couzens. Format: Educ, div, talk. News staff: one; News: 6 hrs wkly. Target aud: General. Spec prog: Black 3 hrs, ethnic one hr, jazz 6 hrs, Sp 2 hrs, American Indian one hr wkly. ♦David Lippe, dev dir; Michael Jacinto, progmg dir, progmg mgr; Estelle Fennell, news dir; Simon Frech, chief of engrg.

***KXBC(FM)**— 2009: 89.1 mhz; 1.3 kw vert. Ant 2,509 ft TL: N40 07 14 W123 41 31. Hrs open:
Rebroadcasts KEAR-FM Sacramento 100%.
4135 Northgate Blvd., Suite 1, Sacramento, 95834-1226. Phone: (916) 641-8191. Web Site:www.familyradio.com Licensee: Family Stations Inc. Natl. Network: Family Radio, . Format: Relg. ♦David Becker, pres.

Garden Grove

KEBN(FM)— June 21, 1961: 94.3 mhz; 3 kw. Ant 246 ft TL: N33 46 51 W117 53 33. Stereo. Hrs open: 24 QueBuena, 1845 Empire Ave., Burbank, 91504. Phone: (818) 729-5300. Fax: (818) 729-5683.E-mail: advertising@aquisuena.com Web Site:www.aquisuena.com Licensee: LBI Radio License Corp. Group owner: Liberman Broadcasting Inc. (acq 5-15-03; $35 million). Format: Sp. ♦Andrew Mars, gen mgr; Daisy Ortiz, gen sls mgr; Edward Leon, progmg dir; Shannon Murdock, chief of engrg; Gustave Aviles, traf mgr.

George

KATJ-FM— June 29, 1989: 100.7 mhz; 260 w. 1,548 ft TL: N34 36 38 W117 17 18. Stereo. Hrs open: 12370 Hesperia Rd., Suite 16, Victorville, 92395. Phone: (760) 241-1313. Fax: (760) 241-0205.E-mail: kimjennings@edbroadcasters.com Web Site:www.katcountry1007.com Licensee: EDB VV License LLC. Group owner: Clear Channel Communications Inc. (acq 11-30-2007; grpsl). Population served: 300,000 Natl. Network: CNN Radio, . Natl. Rep: Christal,. Latham & Watkins. Format: Country. Target aud: 25-54; adults. ♦Kari Lynn, stn mgr, progmg dir; Tom Hoyt, VP, gen mgr & mktg mgr.

Geyserville

KXTS(FM)— December 1993: 98.7 mhz; 2.65 kw. Ant 503 ft TL: N38 44 08 W122 50 55. Hrs open: 3565 Standish Ave., Santa Rosa, 95407. Phone: (707) 588-0707. Fax: (707) 588-0777. Web Site:www.exitos98.7.fm Licensee: Commonwealth Broadcasting LLC. Group owner: Sinclair Communications Inc. (acq 8-3-2001; $5.5 million). Format: Mexican Regional. ♦Debbie Morton, gen mgr; Alex Ballesteros, progmg dir.

Gilroy

KAZA(AM)— September 1957: 1290 khz; 5 kw-D, DA. TL: N37 09 48 W121 38 28. Hrs open: 6 AM-midnight Box 1290, San Jose, 95108. Phone: (408) 776-3090. Fax: (408) 881-1292.E-mail: sakes@kazaradio.com Web Site:www.kazaradio.com Licensee: Radio Fiesta Corp. (acq 5-14-73). Population served: 200,000 Format: Oldies, Sp. ♦Sonia Rodriquez, pres; Juan Sidhu, VP, opns mgr.

KBAY(FM)— Jan 1, 1970: 94.5 mhz; 1.23 kw. 2,535 ft TL: N37 06 39 W121 50 37. Hrs open: 24 190 Park Center Plaza, Suite 200, San Jose, 95113. Phone: (408) 287-5775. Fax: (408) 293-3341.E-mail: jleathers@kbay-kezr.com Web Site:www.kbay.com Licensee: NM Licensing LLC. Group owner: Infinity Broadcasting Corp. (acq 12-6-2005; $80 million with KEZR(FM) San Jose). Population served: 150,000 Natl. Rep: D & R Radio,. Format: Soft Rock. News staff: one; News: 4 hrs wkly. Target aud: 35-54. ♦John Leathers, gen mgr; Judy Dixon, gen sls mgr; Dana Jang, progmg dir; Lissa Kreisler, news dir; Michael Stockwell, chief of engrg.

Glendale

KRLA(AM)— 1928: 870 khz; 20 kw-D, 3 kw-N, DA-2. TL: N34 08 13 W118 13 34. Stereo. Hrs open: 24 701 N. Brand Blvd., Suite 550, 91203. Phone: (818) 956-5552. Fax: (818) 551-1110. Web Site:www.krla870.com Licensee: New Inspiration Broadcasting Co. Inc. Group owner: Salem Communications Corp. (acq 6-23-98; $33.4 million). Population served: 12,000,000 Natl. Network: Salem Radio Network, . Natl. Rep: Christal,. Rgnl rep: SRR Haley, Bader & Potts. Wire Svc: Metro Weather Service Inc. Format: News/talk. News: 35 hrs wkly. Target aud: 35 plus. ♦Jim Tinker, opns VP; Mark Pennington, gen sls mgr & natl sls mgr; Chuck Tyler, progmg dir; Bill Sheets, chief of engrg; Kristi Charley, traf mgr.

KSCA(FM)— March 1951: 101.9 mhz; 2.4 kw. 2,848 ft TL: N34 13 26 W118 03 45. (CP: 4.8 kw). Stereo. Hrs open: 24 655 N. Central Ave., Suite 2500, 91203. Phone: (818) 500-4500. Fax: (818) 500-4580. Web Site:www.univision.com Licensee: HBC License Corp. Group owner: Univision Radio (acq 9-22-2003; grpsl). Population served: 486,000 Irving Gastfreund. Format: Sp, Mexican rgnl. Target aud: 25-54. ♦Michelle Hohman, VP, gen mgr, adv dir; Haz Montana, opns dir; Victor Camino, gen sls mgr; Veronica Nava, progmg dir; Tom Koza, chief of engrg.

Goleta

KMGQ(FM)— Jan 30, 1982: 106.3 mhz; 250 w. 827 ft TL: N34 27 55 W119 40 38. Stereo. Hrs open: 24 403 E. Montecito St., Suite A, Santa Barbara, 93101-1759. Phone: (805) 966-1755.E-mail: pat.cantwell@cumulus.com Web Site:www.kmgq1063.com Licensee: Cumulus Licensing Corp. Group owner: Cumulus Media Inc. (acq

3-12-2001; grpsl). Population served: 350,000 Natl. Rep: McGavren Guild,. Fletcher, Heald & Hildreth. Format: Jazz, adult contemp. Target aud: 35-64; upscale, educated, professional, affluent. ♦Gail Surrillo, gen mgr; Brandon Randazzo, prom dir; John D. Strakler, chief of engrg; Mark Deanba, progmg.

Gonzales

KHIP(FM)— Oct 25, 1990: 104.3 mhz; 2.6 kw. 508 ft TL: N36 40 06 W121 31 09. Stereo. Hrs open: 24 60 Garden Court, Suite 300, Monterey, 93940. Phone: (831) 658-5200. Fax: (831) 658-5299.E-mail: info@thehippo.com Web Site:www.thehippo.com Licensee: Mapleton License of Monterey LLC. (group owner; (acq 11-16-2001; grpsl). Population served: 500,000 Natl. Rep: McGavren Guild,. Leventhal, Senter & Lerman. Format: Classic rock. Target aud: 18-49; upscale, active young professionals. ♦Dale Hendry, gen mgr; Jodi Morgan, gen sls mgr; Sybil DeAngelo, prom dir; Kenny Allen, progmg dir.

KKMC(AM)— Sept 22, 1984: 880 khz; 10 kw-U, DA-2. TL: N36 33 46 W121 26 05. Hrs open: 24 30 E. San Joaquin St., Suite 105, Salinas, 93901. Phone: (831) 424-5562. Fax: (831) 424-6437.E-mail: info@kkmc.com Web Site:www.kkmc.com SatcomIIIr Licensee: Monterey County Broadcasters Inc. Population served: 500,000 Natl. Network: USA, . Natl. Rep: Salem,. Format: Relg, Christian teaching and talk. News: 7 hrs wkly. Target aud: 25 plus; family oriented. Spec prog: Sp 3 hrs wkly. ♦Carl J. Auel, pres; John N. Dick, gen mgr; John Dick, progmg dir; Lorraine Dick, gen sls mgr & sls.

Grass Valley

KBAA(FM)— May 3, 2004: 103.3 mhz; 530 w. Ant 1,102 ft TL: N39 14 45 W120 57 56. Stereo. Hrs open: 24 500 Media Pl., Sacramento, 95815. Phone: (916) 368-6300. Fax: (916) 473-0146. Web Site:www.lakebuena.com Licensee: Bustos Media of California License LLC. Group owner: Salem Communications Corp. (acq 5-12-2006; $500,000). Format: Mexican rgnl. ♦Amparo Perez-Cook, gen mgr.

KNCO(AM)— Oct 1, 1978: 830 khz; 5 kw-U, DA-N. TL: N39 12 52 W121 00 55. Hrs open: 24 1255 E. Main St., Suite A, 95945. Phone: (530) 272-3424. Fax: (530) 272-2872.E-mail: info@knco.com Web Site:www.knco.com Licensee: Nevada County Broadcasters Inc. (group owner). Population served: 75,000 Natl. Network: CNN Radio, ABC, CBS Radio, . Fletcher, Heald & Hildreth. Wire Svc: AP Format: News/talk. News staff: 4; News: 30 hrs wkly. Target aud: 35 plus; adults of western Nevada County. Spec prog: Christian 4 hrs wkly. ♦Bob Breck, CEO, gen mgr; Edward Sylvester, chmn; Scott Robertson, pres; Tom Fitzsimmons, opns mgr & progmg dir; Tim Parish, chief of engrg; Barbara Juneau, traf mgr.

KNCO-FM— Sept 7, 1982: 94.1 mhz; 660 w. Ant 980 ft TL: N39 14 44 W120 57 52. Stereo. Hrs open: 24 Prog sep from AM 1255 E. Main St., 95945. Secondary address: 1479 Sanborn Rd., Yuba City 95993. Phone: (530) 272-3424. Fax: (530) 272-2872.E-mail: info@mystarradio.com Web Site:www.mystarradio.com Population served: 75,000 Natl. Network: Westwood One, . Format: Adult contemp. News staff: one; News: 2 hrs wkly. Target aud: 25-54; residents of western Nevada County. ♦Hollie Grimaldi-Flores, prom dir; Tom Fitzsimmons, progmg dir.

Green Acres

***KAXL(FM)**— May 4, 1994: 88.3 mhz; 21 kw. Ant 328 ft TL: N35 24 55 W119 14 01. Hrs open: 24 110 S. Montclair, Suite 205, Bakersfield, 93309. Phone: (661) 832-2800. Fax: (661) 832-3164.E-mail: kaxl@kaxl.com Web Site:www.kaxl.com Licensee: Skyride Unlimted Inc. (acq 7-8-91; $4,000; 7-29-91). Leventhal, Senter & Lerman. Format: Contemp inspirational. News: 4 hrs wkly. Target aud: 35 plus; women. ♦Terri Blankenship, stn mgr; Dan Schaffer, opns mgr; Sheryl Giesbrecht, prom dir.

KRAB(FM)—Licensed to Green Acres. See Bakersfield

Greenfield

KLOK-FM— Aug 7, 1989: 99.5 mhz; 50 kw. 492 ft TL: N36 27 51 W121 17 52. (CP: 30 kw, ant 640 ft.). Hrs open: 67 Garden Ct., Monterey, 93940-5302. Phone: (831) 771-9950. Fax: (831) 373-6700.E-mail: valenca@intervision.com Web Site:www.entravision.com Licensee: Entravision Holdings LLC. Group owner: Entravision Communications Corp. (acq 3-14-00; grpsl). Format: Rgnl Mexican. ♦Aaron Scoby, gen mgr; Fidel Soto, news dir; Marcello Soto, chief of engrg; Tony Valencia, progmg dir & sls.

KSEA(FM)— 1998: 107.9 mhz; 870 w. 1,637 ft TL: N36 23 00 W121 25 40. Hrs open: 24 229 Pajaro St. 302 D., Salinas, 93901. Phone: (831) 754-1469. Fax: (831) 754-1563.E-mail: kseaproduction@campesina.com Web Site:www.campesina.com Licensee: Farmworker Educational Radio Network Inc. (acq 3-13-97; $600,000). Population served: 540,000 Borsari & Paxson. Format: Sp Mexican rgnl. Target aud: 18-54; Hispanic market. ♦Juan Zamora, gen mgr.

Greenville

***KPJP(FM)**— Sept 15, 2004: 89.3 mhz; 4.5 kw vert. Ant 2,348 ft TL: N40 13 59 W121 01 08. Hrs open: Box 180, Tahoma, 96142. Phone: (530) 584-5700. Fax: (530) 584-5705.E-mail: info@ihradio.org Web Site:www.ihradio.org Licensee: IHR Educational Broadcasting (group owner). Format: Relg, catholic. ♦Douglas M. Sherman, pres; Steve Wise, gen mgr.

Gridley

KHHZ(FM)— July 6, 1979: 97.7 mhz; 1.5 kw. Ant 1,276 ft TL: N39 30 18 W121 18 35. Stereo. Hrs open: 24 2654 Cramer Ln., Chico, 95928. Phone: (530) 345-0021. Fax: (530) 893-2121. Licensee: Deer Creek Broadcasting LLC. (group owner; (acq 9-8-2004; grpsl). Population served: 650,000 Natl. Rep: Katz Radio,. Format: Hispanic. Target aud: 18-49. ♦Dino Corbin, gen mgr; Bill Meyer, sls dir; Juan Villagrana, progmg dir; Matt Ray, news dir; Mark Miller, chief of engrg; Cheryl Grant, traf mgr.

KMJE(FM)— Oct 1, 1996: 101.5 mhz; 140 w. 1,975 ft TL: N39 12 21 W121 49 11. Hrs open: 861 Gray Ave., Suite K, Yuba City, 95991. Phone: (530) 673-2200. Fax: (530) 673-3010.E-mail: info@gosunny.com Web Site:www.gosunny.com Licensee: Results Radio Licensee L.L.C. Group owner: Fritz Communications Inc. (acq 6-11-99; grpsl). Format: Hot adult contemp. News staff: one; News: 7 hrs wkly. ♦Jack Fritz, pres, gen mgr; Michael Berry, gen sls mgr & engrg VP.

Groveland

***KXSR(FM)**— May 8, 1992: 91.7 mhz; 4 kw. Ant 1,591 ft TL: N38 03 46 W120 14 45. Hrs open: 24 7055 Folsom Blvd., Sacramento, 95826. Phone: (916) 480-5900. Fax: (916) 487-3348.E-mail: npr@csus.edu Web Site:www.capradio.org Licensee: California State University Sacramento. Population served: 100,000 Natl. Network: NPR, PRI, . Duane Morris LLP. Format: Class. Target aud: General; NPR listeners, eg. professionals, educators & administrators. ♦Carl Watanabe, stn mgr, progmg dir, progmg mgr; John Brenneise, opns mgr; Joe Barr, news dir, local news ed, political ed, relg ed; Jeff Browne, engrg dir; Michael Frost, prom dir & traf mgr.

Grover Beach

KURQ(FM)— July 4, 1984: 107.3 mhz; 3.5 kw. Ant 1,650 ft TL: N35 21 37 W120 39 18. Stereo. Hrs open: 24 51 Zaca Ln., Suite 110, San Luis Obispo, 93401. Phone: (805) 545-0101. Fax: (805) 541-5303.E-mail: info@107therock.com Web Site:www.107therock.com Licensee: EDB SLO License LLC. (acq 11-30-2007; grpsl). Population served: 250000 Wiley, Rein & Fielding. Format: Active rock. News staff: one; News: 8 hrs wkly. Target aud: 18-44; emphasis on 25-34 year olds. ♦Rich Hawkins, gen mgr; Pattie Wagner, gen sls mgr; Adam Burns, progmg dir.

Guadalupe

KRTO(FM)— 1992: 105.5 mhz; 350 w. Ant 1,342 ft TL: N34 53 54 W120 35 28. Hrs open: 24 718 E. Chapel St., Santa Maria, 93454-4524. Phone: (805) 928-4334. Fax: (805) 349-2765. Licensee: Emerald Wave Media. (acq 5-1-97; $475,000 with KTAP(AM) Santa Maria). Population served: 60,000 Format: Sp. ♦August Ruiz, gen mgr.

Gualala

***KGUA(FM)**—Not on air, target date: unknown: 88.3 mhz; 1.7 kw. Ant 850 ft TL: N38 50 54 W123 34 46. Hrs open: 35501 S. Hwy One, Unit 50, 95445. Phone: (707) 884-9957. Licensee: Native Media Resource Center. ♦Peggy Berryhill, pres.

KTDE(FM)— August 1993: 100.5 mhz; 6 kw. 669 ft TL: N38 49 33 W123 34 12. Hrs open: 24 Box 1557, 95445. Secondary address: 38958 Cypress Way 95445. Phone: (707) 884-1000. Fax: (707) 884-1229.E-mail: thetide@men.org Web Site:www.ktde.com Licensee: Four Rivers Broadcasting Inc. (group owner; (acq 7-21-2005; grpsl). Population served: 50000 Natl. Network: CBS, . Cole, Raywid & Braverman. Format: Hot adult contemp, var/div. Target aud: 30-55. Spec prog: Gospel one hr wkly. ♦John Power, CEO; Amy Heath, gen mgr; Patricia Weber, opns mgr; Pam Knutson, rgnl sls mgr, prom dir.

Hamilton City

KRER(FM)— 2005: 101.7 mhz; 530 w. Ant 1,099 ft TL: N39 56 46 W121 43 17. Hrs open: 2654 Cramer Ln., Chico, 95928-8838. Phone: (530) 345-0021. Fax: (530) 893-2121. Licensee: Coloma Hamilton City LLC. Natl. Network: ESPN Radio, . Format: Sports. ♦Scott Donohue, pres; Dino Corbin, gen mgr; Larry Scott, progmg dir.

Hanford

KGEN-FM— Jan 1, 1997: 94.5 mhz; 3.3 kw. 443 ft TL: N36 12 16 W119 33 52. Hrs open: 24 Box 2040, Tulare, 93275. Phone: (559) 686-1370. Fax: (559) 685-1394.E-mail: kgen@sbcglobal.net Licensee: Azteca Broadcasting Corp. (group owner) Format: Sp, Rgnl Mexician. Target aud: 18 plus. ♦Margreta Hernandez, gen mgr; Isabel Duran, gen sls mgr; Ernesto Gaytan, progmg dir.

KIGS(AM)— Feb 1, 1948: 620 khz; 1 kw-U, DA-N. TL: N36 19 37 W119 33 58. Hrs open: 24 6165 E. Lacey Blvd., 93230. Phone: (559) 582-0361. Fax: (559) 582-3981.E-mail: info@kigs.com Web Site:www.kigs.com Licensee: Perreira Broadcasting (acq 7-15-90). Population served: 657,000 Allan E. Aronowitz. Format: Foreign languages. News: 35 hrs wkly. Target aud: 18-49. ♦Tony Vieira, gen mgr, gen sls mgr & progmg dir.

KRDA(FM)— September 1976: 107.5 mhz; 20.3 kw. Ant 784 ft TL: N36 38 12 W118 56 34. Stereo. Hrs open: 24 1981 No. Gateway Blvd., Suite 101, Fresno, 93727. Phone: (559) 456-4000. Fax: (559) 251-9555. Licensee: Univision Radio License Corp. Group owner: Pappas Telecasting Companies (acq 1-3-2006; $10 million). Natl. Rep: Lotus Entravision Reps LLC,. Fletcher, Heald & Hildreth. Format: Sp Adult Contemp. Target aud: 35-54; high quality FM oriented news/talk listeners. ♦Angela Navarrete, gen mgr.

KRZR(FM)— Dec 24, 1976: 103.7 mhz; 50 kw. 499 ft TL: N36 33 36 W119 45 20. Stereo. Hrs open: 24 83 E. Shaw Ave., Suite 150, Fresno, 93710. Phone: (559) 230-4300. Fax: (559) 243-4301.E-mail: info@krzr.com Web Site:www.krzr.com Licensee: Capstar TX L.P. Group owner: Clear Channel Communications Inc. (acq 8-30-00; grpsl). Population served: 1,000,000 Natl. Network: ABC, AP Radio, . Dow, Lohnes & Albertson. Format: AOR. News: one hr wkly. Target aud: 18-34; male. ♦Jeff Megrete, gen mgr; Joni Norvell, gen sls mgr; Paul Wilson, progmg dir; Dave Case, chief of engrg, disc jockey.

Happy Camp

***KRUK(FM)**—Not on air, target date: unknown: 90.7 mhz; 340 w. Ant 1,922 ft TL: N41 51 29 W123 21 09. Hrs open: 64236 Second Ave., 96039-1016. Phone: (530) 493-1600. Fax: (530) 493-5322. Licensee: Karuk Tribe of California. ♦Leaf Hillman, gen mgr.

Hayward

***KCRH(FM)**— Apr 10, 1981: 89.9 mhz; 18 w. Ant -134 ft TL: N37 38 23 W122 06 16. Hrs open: 25555 Hesperian Blvd., 94545. Phone: (510) 723-6954.E-mail: cglen@clpccd.cc.ca.us Web Site:www.kcrhradio.com Licensee: South County Community College District. Population served: 130,000 Format: Var, urban contemp. News: 5 hrs wkly. Target aud: 17-35; general. Spec prog: Instructional one hr, pub affrs 5 hrs wkly. ♦Chad Mark Glen, gen mgr; Bernard Bautista, progmg dir.

Healdsburg

KFGY(FM)—Licensed to Healdsburg. See Santa Rosa

KNOB(FM)— 2002: 96.7 mhz; 2.4 kw. Ant 525 ft TL: N38 44 08 W122 50 55. Hrs open: 3565 Standish Ave., Santa Rosa, 95407. Phone: (707) 588-0707. Fax: (707) 588-0777. Web Site:www.967bobfm.com Licensee: JYH Broadcasting. Format: Adult hits. ♦Judy Hughes, gen mgr; Nate Campbell, progmg dir; Dan Ethan, chief of engrg.

KRSH(FM)— Feb 1, 1996: 95.9 mhz; 2.65 kw. Ant 502 ft TL: N38 44 08 W122 50 55. Hrs open: 3565 Standish Ave., Santa Rosa, 95407. Phone: (707) 588-0707. Fax: (707) 588-0777.E-mail: studio@krsh.com Web Site:www.krsh.com Licensee: Deas Communications Inc. Group owner: Sinclair Communications Inc. (acq 8-3-2001; $2.1 million). Format: AAA. Target aud: 25-49. ♦Debbie Morton, gen mgr; Dan Ethan, chief of engrg.

Hemet

KSDT(AM)— Apr 10, 1959: 1320 khz; 500 w-D, 300 w-N, DA-2. TL: N33 44 59 W116 59 53. Hrs open: 24 15700 Village Dr., Suite A, Victorville, 92392. Phone: (760) 243-7903. Fax: (706) 243-7183. Licensee: Rudex Broadcasting Ltd. (acq 9-30-2002; $250,000). Population served: 250,000 Format: Christian. ◆ John Cooper, pres & gen mgr.

KXRS(FM)— Nov 9, 1963: 105.7 mhz; 170 w. Ant 1,023 ft TL: N33 44 59 W116 59 53. Stereo. Hrs open: 24 1950 S. Sunwest Ln., Suite 302, San Bernardino, 92408. Phone: (909) 825-5020. Fax: (909) 884-5844.E-mail: vb@radiolazer.com Web Site:www.radiolazer.com Licensee: Lazer Broadcasting Corp. (group owner; acq 2-94). Format: Rgnl Mexician. ◆ Vicki Bails, gen mgr; Armando Gutierrez, prom dir; Salvador Prieto, progmg dir, news dir.

Hesperia

KRAK(AM)— Feb 1, 1990: 910 khz; 700 w-D, 500 w-N, DA-2. TL: N34 23 19 W117 23 29. Stereo. Hrs open: 24 11920 Hesperia Rd., 92345. Phone: (760) 244-2000. Fax: (760) 244-1198. Web Site:www.stardust910.com Licensee: CBS Radio Stations Inc. Group owner: Infinity Broadcasting Corp. (acq 7-19-2000; $3,537,500 with KVFG(FM) Victorville). Population served: 250,000 Natl. Network: ABC, . Fleischman & Walsh L. Format: Nostalgic/adult standards. Target aud: 40 plus. ◆ Tom Hoyt, gen mgr; Bill Pettus, stn mgr.

Hollister

*KHRI(FM)— Dec 17, 2000: 90.7 mhz; 170 w. Ant -364 ft TL: N36 52 02 W121 23 58. Stereo. Hrs open: 24
Rebroadcasts KLRD(FM) Yucaipa 100%.
2351 Sunset Blvd., Suite 170-218, Rocklin, 95765. Phone: (916) 251-1600. Fax: (916) 251-1650.E-mail: info@air1.com Web Site:www.air1.com Licensee: Educational Media Foundation. Group owner: EMF Broadcasting (acq 11-7-00; $30,000 for CP). Population served: 27,000 Natl. Network: Air 1, . Shaw Pittman. Format: Contemp Christian. News staff: 3. Target aud: 18-35; Judeo-Christian, female. ◆ Richard Jenkins, pres; Mike Novak, VP, progmg dir; Lloyd Parker, gen mgr; Ed Lenane, opns dir, news dir; Keith Whipple, dev dir; Eric Allen, natl sls mgr; David Pierce, progmg dir; Jon Rivers, mus dir; Sam Wallington, engrg dir; Arthur Vassar, traf mgr; Karen Johnson, news rptr.

KMPG(AM)— 1966: 1520 khz; 5 kw-D, DA-2. TL: N36 50 16 W121 25 01. Hrs open: 14 Box 369, 910 Monterey St., 95023. Phone: (831) 722-4477. Fax: (831) 637-4031.E-mail: info@kmpgam.com Web Site:www.kmpgradio@netzero.net Licensee: Promo Radio Corp. (acq 12-19-2003). Population served: 217,000 Format: Sp rgnl Mexican. Target aud: 18-49. ◆ Rafael Meza, pres & gen mgr.

KXSM(FM)— 1979: 93.5 mhz; 110 w. Ant 2,296 ft TL: N36 45 22 W121 30 06. Stereo. Hrs open: 200 South A St., Suite 400, Oxnard, 93030. Phone: (805) 240-2070. Fax: (805) 240-5960. Licensee: Lazer Broadcasting Corp. (group owner; (acq 7-25-2005; $2.88 million with KXZM(FM) Felton). Population served: 1,100,000 Format: Rgnl Mexican. ◆ Alfredo Plascencia, pres; Daniel Osuna, gen mgr.

Holtville

KGBA-FM— Aug 8, 1983: 100.1 mhz; 3 kw. 331 ft TL: N32 48 10 W115 29 53. Stereo. Hrs open: 24 Studio, 605 State St., El Centro, 92243. Phone: (760) 352-9860. Fax: (760) 352-1883.E-mail: kgba@kgba.org Web Site:www.kgba.org Licensee: The Voice of International Christian Evangelism Inc. (acq 11-1-86; $350,000; 9-15-86). Population served: 250,000 Miller & Miller. Format: Relg talk. News: 3 hrs wkly. Target aud: 25-55; adult family Christian conservatives. Spec prog: Chinese 14 hrs, children 4 hrs, gospel 7 hrs wkly. ◆ Robert Sager, gen mgr; Mike Leonard, gen sls mgr; Sara Mae, progmg dir; Dean Imhof, chief of engrg.

Hoopa

*KIDE(FM)— December 1980: 91.3 mhz; 195 w. -1,560 ft TL: N41 03 51 W123 41 05. (CP: 305 w). Stereo. Hrs open: 24
Phone: (530) 625-4245. Fax: (530) 625-4046.E-mail: info@kidefm.org Web Site:www.kidefm.org Licensee: Hoopa Valley Tribe. Format: Country. Spec prog: Hoopa Indian language, history & culture 20 hrs wkly. ◆ Joseph Orozco, gen mgr & progmg dir.

Hopland

*KORB(FM)— 2009: 88.7 mhz; 100 w vert. Ant -1,086 ft TL: N38 58 15 W123 06 50. Hrs open: Box 1118, Santa Rosa, 95402. Phone: (707) 526-2765. Web Site:www.broken.fm Licensee: One Ministries Inc. (acq 12-9-2008; $7,500 for CP). Format: Alternative, Christian. ◆ Keith J. Leitch, pres.

Hornbrook

KRVC(FM)— 2007: 98.9 mhz; 1.25 kw. Ant 2,483 ft TL: N42 05 00 W122 42 00. Hrs open: 511 Rossanley Dr., Medford, OR, 97501. Phone: (541) 772-0322. Fax: (541) 772-4233. Licensee: Opus Broadcasting Systems Inc. Natl. Rep: Tacher,. Format: Top-40. ◆ Dean Flock, gen mgr; Brian Fraser, sls dir.

Huron

KZLA(FM)— 2003: Stn currently dark. 98.3 mhz; 100 w. Ant 43 ft TL: N36 12 05 W120 05 53. Hrs open: 152 E. Elm St., Coalinga, 93210. Phone: (559) 935-4191. Fax: (559) 935-4191. Licensee: Huron Broadcasting LLC. ◆ Rebecca Sexton, gen mgr.

Hydesville

KSLG-FM— Apr 13, 2001: 94.1 mhz; 4.5 kw. 1,784 ft TL: N40 30 04 W124 17 05. Hrs open: Box 25, Ferndale, 95536-0025. Secondary address: 1400 Main St., Suite 104, Ferndale 95536. Phone: (707) 786-5104. Fax: (707) 786-5100.E-mail: 941@kslg.com Web Site:www.kslg.com Licensee: Lost Coast Communications Inc. (acq 11-5-2001). Population served: 125,000 Natl. Rep: McGavren Guild,. Dan J. Alpert. Format: Modern rock. Target aud: 18-49. ◆ Patrick Cleary, gen mgr; Cliff Berkowitz, opns VP; Jennefer White, natl sls mgr; Gregg Foster, mktg dir; Kara Hochner, prom dir; Mike Dronkers, progmg dir; Kevin Sanders, chief of engrg.

Idyllwild

KATY-FM— Dec 1, 1989: 101.3 mhz; 1.55 kw. Ant 656 ft TL: N33 43 31 W116 44 58. Stereo. Hrs open: 24 27431 Enterprise Cir. W., Suite 101, Temecula, 92590. Phone: (951) 506-1222. Fax: (951) 506-1213.E-mail: katytraffic@linkline.com Web Site:www.katyfm.com Licensee: All Pro Broadcasting Inc. (acq 3-21-01; $3.5 million plus $100,000 for option to purchase for 51%). Leventhal, Senter & Lerman. Format: Adult contemp. News staff: one; News: 2 hrs wkly. Target aud: 25-49; affluent, upwardly mobile. ◆ Duane Davis, exec VP, gen sls mgr; Bill McNulty, gen mgr; Kevin Watson, stn mgr, gen sls mgr; Willie D. Davis, CEO & opns mgr; Tom Lazar, progmg dir, news dir.

Imperial

KMXX(FM)— Sept 17, 1980: 99.3 mhz; 3 kw. 200 ft TL: N32 51 44 W115 33 41. (CP 6 kw, ant 302 ft. TL: N32 54 W115 31 40). Stereo. Hrs open: 24 Box 2830, El Centro, 92244. Phone: (760) 352-2277. Fax: (760) 482-0099. Web Site:www.entravision.com Licensee: Entravision Holdings LLC. Group owner: Entravision Communications Corp. (acq 7-31-00; grpsl). Population served: 950,000 Format: Rgnl Mexican. Target aud: 18-49. ◆ Eric Chavez, gen mgr.

Independence

KSRW(FM)— Apr 12, 1996: 92.5 mhz; 870 w. 2,949 ft TL: N36 58 38 W118 07 13. Hrs open: 24 1280 N. Main St., Suite J, Bishop, 93514. Phone: (760) 873-5329. Fax: (760) 873-5328.E-mail: kday@schat.com Licensee: Ms. Benett Kessler (acq 3-14-91;4-1-91). Natl. Network: CNN Radio, . Format: Adult contemp. News staff: one; News: 10 hrs wkly. Target aud: 30-65; professionals & retirees with average to above average buying power. ◆ Benett Kessler, CEO & gen mgr.

Indian Wells

KAJR(FM)— Aug 25, 2007: 95.9 mhz; 1.75 kw. Ant 620 ft TL: N33 48 04 W116 13 28. Hrs open: 836 Prospect St., Suite 202, La Jolla, 92037. Secondary address: 441 S. Calle Encilia, Palm Springs 92262. Phone: (858) 459-2631. Phone: (760) 320-4550. Licensee: A & J Media LLC. Format: Adult hits. ◆ Arthur L. Rivkin, gen mgr.

Indio

KCLB-FM— See Coachella

*KCRI(FM)—

*KCRI(FM)— 1995: 89.3 mhz; 3.3 kw. Ant 561 ft TL: N33 48 07 W116 13 28. Hrs open:
Rebroadcasts KCRW(FM) Santa Monica 100%.
1900 Pico Blvd., Santa Monica, 90405. Phone: (310) 450-5183. Phone: (888) 600-kcrw. Fax: (310) 450-7172.E-mail: mail@kcrw.org Web Site:www.kcrw.com Licensee: Santa Monica Community College. Natl. Network: NPR, . Wire Svc: AP Format: Eclectic, news. ◆ Ruth Seymour, gen mgr; Jennifer Ferro, stn mgr; Mike Newport, opns mgr; David Kleinbart, dev dir.

KESQ(AM)— 1946: 1400 khz; 1 kw-U. TL: N33 43 37 W116 15 10. Stereo. Hrs open: 24 42650 Melanie Pl., Palm Desert, 92211-5170. Phone: (760) 568-6830. Fax: (760) 568-3984. Licensee: Gulf-California Broadcast Co. Population served: 80,000 Format: Regl, Sp. News staff: one; News: 7 hrs wkly. Target aud: General. ◆ Martin Serna, gen mgr.

KJJZ(FM)— March 1993: 102.3 mhz; 600 w. 587 ft TL: N33 48 07 W116 13 29. Hrs open: 24 Box 1825, Palm Springs, 92263. Phone: (760) 320-4550. Fax: (760) 320-3037. Web Site:www.102kjjz.com Licensee: R.M. Broadcasting L.L.C. (acq 1-97; $1,231 million). Population served: 250,000 Natl. Network: Westwood One, . Natl. Rep: McGavren Guild,. Fletcher, Heald & Hildreth. Format: Smooth jazz. News staff: one; News: 3 hrs wkly. Target aud: 25-49; Palm Springs baby boomers. ◆ Todd Marker, VP & gen mgr; Hughes Hilles, gen sls mgr; Cary James, prom dir; Jim Fitzgerald, progmg dir; Jeff Michaels, news dir; Ben Manierre, chief of engrg.

KKUU(FM)— Apr 13, 1984: 92.7 mhz; 4.2 kw. Ant 394 ft TL: N33 52 15 W116 13 37. Stereo. Hrs open: 24 1321 N. Gene Autry Tr., Palm Springs, 92262. Phone: (760) 322-7890. Fax: (760) 322-5493.E-mail: keith.martin@morris.com Licensee: MCC Radio LLC. Group owner: Morris Radio LLC (acq 1998; $4.5 million). Population served: 330,000 Natl. Rep: Christal,. Format: Hip hop. News staff: one; News: 2 hrs wkly. Target aud: 25-54. ◆ Michael Ostehaut, VP; Anthony Quiroz, gen mgr, opns dir.

KNWZ(AM)— See Coachella

Inglewood

KRCD(FM)— 1959: 103.9 mhz; 4.1 kw. Ant 387 ft TL: N34 00 26 W118 21 54. Stereo. Hrs open: 24 655 N Central Ave, Suite 2500, Glendale, 91203-1422. Phone: (818) 500-4500. Fax: (818) 500-4560. Web Site:www.univision.com Licensee: Univision Radio License Corp. Group owner: Univision Radio (acq 9-22-2003; grpsl). Population served: 500000 Natl. Network: CBC, . Rgnl. Network: CBS, Unistar. Format: Adult contemp, Sp. Target aud: 25-44; women, 60% African-American, 30% Hispanic. ◆ Michelle Hohman, gen mgr; Haz Montana, opns mgr; Jim Coronado, gen sls mgr; Offad Vallejo, mktg dir; Amalia Gonzalez, progmg dir; Tom Koza, chief of engrg.

KTYM(AM)— Feb 14, 1958: 1460 khz; 5 kw-D, 500 w-N, DA-2. TL: N34 00 24 W118 21 52. Hrs open: 24 6803 West Blvd., 90302. Phone: (310) 672-3700. Fax: (310) 673-2259.E-mail: gray@ktym.com Web Site:www.ktym1460.com Licensee: Trans America Broadcasting Corp. Population served: 89,985 Miller & Miller, P.C. Format: Black, var/div. News staff: 2; News: 2 hrs wkly. Target aud: 18-54. Spec prog: Japanese one hr, Pol 2 hrs, Russian 2 hrs wkly. ◆ Gerardo Borrego, pres, VP, gen mgr; Gary Rehers, gen sls mgr, progmg dir; Paul Wiren, chief of engrg. Co-owned TV: KAIL(TV) affil

Inyokern

*KZLU(FM)— 2008: 88.5 mhz; 1 kw. Ant 1,299 ft TL: N35 28 39 W117 41 58. Hrs open:
Rebroadcasts KLVR(FM) Middletown 100%.
2351 Sunset Blvd., Suite 170-218, Rocklin, 95765. Phone: (916) 251-1600. Fax: (916) 251-1650. Web Site:www.klove.com Licensee: Educational Media Foundation. (acq 9-14-2005). Natl. Network: K-Love, . Format: Contemp Christian. ◆ Richard Jenkins, pres; Mike Novak, VP; Keith Whipple, dev dir; David Pierce, progmg mgr; Ed Lenane, news dir; Sam Wallington, engrg dir; Karen Johnson, news rptr.

Irvine

*KUCI(FM)— Oct 1, 1969: 88.9 mhz; 200 w. -10 ft TL: N33 38 41 W117 50 36. Stereo. Hrs open: 24 Box 4362, 92616-4362. Phone: (949) 824-6868. Fax: (949) 824-3741.E-mail: kuci@kuci.org Web Site:www.kuci.org Licensee: Regents of the University of California. Population served: 1,000,000 Format: Div. ◆ Kevin Stockdale, dev dir; Scarlett Davis, prom dir; Emilio Nunez, mus dir; Mike Casper, pub affrs dir; Mike Boyle, engrg mgr; Elaine Hawkes, chief of engrg.

Jackson

KTTA(FM)— Aug 16, 1973: Stn currently dark. 94.3 mhz; 4.3 kw. Ant 790 ft TL: N38 24 10 W120 39 15. Stereo. Hrs open: 500 Media Place, Sacramento, 95815. Phone: (916) 368-6300. Fax: (916) 441-6480. Licensee: Bustos Media of California License LLC. Group owner: Univision Radio (acq 5-12-2006; swap for KKFS(FM) Lincoln). Population served: 60,000 Format: Sp. ♦Amparo Perez-Cook, gen mgr; Bobby Reynoso, prom dir; Juan Gonzalez, progmg dir; Mark Sedaka, chief of engrg; Cynthia Sanchez, traf mgr.

Johannesburg

KRAJ(FM)— October 1998: 100.9 mhz; 1.5 kw. Ant 1,312 ft TL: N35 28 41 W117 41 58. Hrs open: 24 731 N. Balsam, Ridgecrest, 93555. Phone: (760) 371-1700. Fax: (760) 371-1824.E-mail: radio@iwvisp.com Web Site:www.krajfm.com Licensee: Adelman Broadcasting Inc. (group owner; (acq 12-28-99; $45,000). Population served: 500,000 Natl. Network: Jones Radio Networks, . Format: Urban CHR. Target aud: 18-54. ♦Robert Adelman, pres.

Joshua Tree

KQCM(FM)— Nov 2, 1995: 92.1 mhz; 6 kw. Ant 230 ft TL: N34 09 16 W116 12 04. Stereo. Hrs open: Box 1437, 92252. Phone: (760) 362-4264.E-mail: coppermountainbroadcasting@yahoo.com Web Site:www.kqcmradio.com Licensee: Copper Mountain Broadcasting Co. (acq 7-14-2004; $575,000 with KXCM(FM) Twentynine Palms). Population served: 85,000 Natl. Network: Westwood One, Jones Radio Networks, . Natl. Rep: Interep,. Leventhal, Senter, & Lerman, PLLC. Format: CHR. Target aud: 18-34. ♦Gary DeMaroney, gen mgr; Carol Vaughn, traf mgr.

Julian

***KLVJ(FM)**— Oct 23, 1991: 100.1 mhz; 110 w. Ant 2,286 ft TL: N33 09 33 W116 36 53. Stereo. Hrs open: 24 2351 Sunset Blvd., Suite 170-218, Rocklin, 95765. Phone: (916) 251-1600. Fax: (916) 251-1650.E-mail: klove@klove.com Web Site:www.klove.com Licensee: Educational Media Foundation. Group owner: EMF Broadcasting (acq 1-30-97; $34,168). Population served: 1,088,000 Natl. Network: K-Love, . Shaw Pittman. Format: Contemp Christian. News staff: 3. Target aud: 25-44; Judeo-Christian, female. ♦Richard Jenkins, pres; Mike Novak, VP; Keith Whipple, dev dir; David Pierce, progmg mgr; Ed Lenane, news dir; Sam Wallington, engrg dir; Karen Johnson, news rptr.

June Lake

***KWTM(FM)**— 2002: 90.9 mhz; 910 w. Ant 344 ft TL: N38 05 14 W119 10 31. (CP: 32 kw, ant 3,221 ft. TL: N38 27 28 W118 45 51). Stereo. Hrs open: 24
Rebroadcasts KWTW(FM) Bishop 100%.
Box 637, Living Proof Inc., Bishop, 93515. Secondary address: 125 S. Main St., Bishop 93514. Phone: (760) 872-4225. Phone: (866) 466-5989. Fax: (760) 872-4155.E-mail: friar@schat.com Web Site:www.kwtw.org Licensee: Living Proof Inc. (acq 4-19-00; $250,000). Population served: 10,000 Format: Christian. ♦Daniel McClenaghan, pres, gen mgr; Brian Law, opns mgr, progmg dir; Robert Branch, chief of engrg.

Keene

***KNAI(FM)**—(Phoenix, AZ) Oct 23, 1991: 88.3 mhz; 22.5 kw ST: *WPHF-FM. 997 ft TL: N33 35 47 W112 05 29. Stereo. Hrs open: 4 AM-7:30 PM 3602 W. Thomas Rd., Suite 6, Phoenix, AZ, 85019. Phone: (602) 269-3121. Fax: (602) 269-3020.E-mail: info@campesinainfo.com Web Site:www.campesina.com Licensee: National Farm Workers Service Center Inc. Population served: 825,000 Rgnl rep: Vision Marketing Borsari & Paxson. Format: Sp, community pub affrs, music. Target aud: 24-54; Hispanic market. ♦Paul Chavez, chmn & pres; Anthony Chavez, VP; Michael Nowakowski, gen mgr; Maria Barquin, prom mgr; Cesar Chavez, progmg dir.

Kerman

KBHH(FM)— March 2001: 95.3 mhz; 6 kw. 328 ft TL: N36 39 40 W120 09 59. Hrs open: 24 2502 Merced St., Fresno, 93721. Phone: (661) 837-0745. Fax: (661) 837-1612.E-mail: Achavez@campesina.com Web Site:www.campesina.com Licensee: Farmworker Educational Radio Network Inc. Population served: 600,000 Borsari & Paxson. Format: Sp rgnl Mexican. Target aud: 25-54; Hispanic market. ♦Anthony Chavez, pres, gen mgr; Cesar Chavez, progmg dir; Dave Whitehead, chief of engrg; Maria Vrrutia, traf mgr.

KOKO-FM— Apr 16, 1990: 94.3 mhz; 3 kw. 328 ft TL: N36 44 29 W120 05 08. Stereo. Hrs open: 24 2775 E. Shaw Ave., Fresno, 93710. Phone: (559) 292-9494. Fax: (559) 294-7041.E-mail: info@kokofm.com Web Site:www.kok94.com Licensee: Big Broadcasting Inc. (acq 1999; $1.14 million). Population served: 600,000 Haley, Bader & Potts. Format: CHR, rhythm oldies. News staff: 4; News: 14 hrs wkly. Target aud: 18-54; Hispanic men & women. ♦Art Laboe, pres, gen mgr; Anna Marie Avila, gen sls mgr, disc jockey; Paul Mendoza, progmg dir & news dir.

Kernville

KCNQ(FM)— November 1985: 102.5 mhz; 130 w. 1,230 ft TL: N35 37 21 W118 26 16. Stereo. Hrs open: 24 Box 2008, 93238-2008. Secondary address: 14 Sierra Dr. 93238. Phone: (760) 379-4500. Fax: (760) 376-3119. Web Site:todaysbestcountryonline.com Licensee: Robert J. Bohn & Katherine M. Bohn. (acq 7-28-97). Population served: 25,000 Natl. Network: ABC, . Format: C&W. News staff: one; News: 18 hrs wkly. Target aud: General. Spec prog: Relg one hr wkly. ♦Anthony M. Bohn, CEO; Robert J. Bohn, pres; Gary Huff, sls dir; Bob Jamison, progmg mgr, chief of engrg; Scott Costa, news dir; Jullian King, traf mgr.

Kettleman City

***KWDS(FM)**— 2006: 89.9 mhz; 50 kw vert. Ant 251 ft TL: N35 59 42 W119 58 06. Hrs open: 5331 Mt. Alifan Dr., San Diego, 92111. Phone: (858) 277-4991. Fax: (858) 277-1365.E-mail: kwoods@horizonsd.org Web Site:www.horizonradio.org Licensee: Horizon Christian Fellowship (acq 5-21-2004; $150,000 for CP). Format: Christian. ♦Mike MacIntosh, pres.

King City

***KDRH(FM)**— 2001: 91.3 mhz; 300 w vert. Ant 75 ft TL: N36 16 22 W121 05 02. Hrs open: 2351 Sunset Blvd., Suite 170-218, Rocklin, 95765-3719. Phone: (916) 251-1600. Fax: (916) 251-1650.E-mail: info@air1.com Web Site:www.air1.com Licensee: Educational Media Foundation. Group owner: EMF Broadcasting (acq 11-7-00; $30,000 for CP). Natl. Network: Air 1, . Shaw Pittman. Format: Contemp Christian. News: one hr wkly. Target aud: 18-25; teen, young adult. ♦Richard Jenkins, pres; Mike Novak, VP; Keith Whipple, dev dir; David Pierce, progmg mgr; Ed Lenane, news dir; Sam Wallington, engrg dir; Arthur Vassar, traf mgr; Karen Johnson, news rptr.

KEXA(FM)— 1981: 93.9 mhz; 5.4 kw. Ant 719 ft TL: N36 22 48 W121 12 57. Stereo. Hrs open: 24 Box 1939, Salinas, 93902. Secondary address: 548 Alisal St., Salinas 93905. Phone: (831) 757-1910. Fax: (831) 757-8015.E-mail: wolfhouseradio@yahoo.es Licensee: Wolfhouse Radio Group Inc. (group owner; (acq 8-31-2001; grpsl). Format: Rhythmic adult contemp. Target aud: General. ♦Ramon Castro, gen mgr.

KRKC(AM)— Sept 21, 1958: 1490 khz; 1 kw-U. TL: N36 13 34 W121 07 26. Hrs open: 24 Box 628, 93930. Secondary address: 1134 San Antonio Dr. 93930. Phone: (831) 385-5421. Phone: (831) 674-2278. Fax: (831) 385-0635.E-mail: bill@krkc.com Web Site:www.krkc.com Licensee: Radio Del Rey. (acq 9-2-82; $270,000; 9-13-82). Population served: 50,000 Natl. Network: CBS, . Natl. Rep: Farmakis, Katz Radio,. Pepper & Corazzini. Format: Country. News staff: one. Target aud: 25-54. Spec prog: Farm 10 hrs, sports 9 hrs wkly. ♦Bill Gittler, pres & gen mgr.

KRKC-FM— Jan 30, 1989: 102.1 mhz; 2.6 kw. Ant 1,820 ft TL: N35 57 06 W121 00 03. Stereo. Hrs open: 24 1134 San Antonio Dr., 93930. Phone: (831) 385-5421. Fax: (831) 385-0635.E-mail: bill@krkc.com Web Site:www.krkc.com Licensee: King City Communications Corp. Natl. Network: AP Radio, . Pepper & Corazzini. Format: Adult contemp. News staff: one; News: 1 hr wkly. Target aud: 18-49; men and women. ♦Bill Gittler, pres, gen mgr; Jim Barker, opns mgr, mus dir; David Magnum, news dir; Ron Warren, chief of engrg.

Kings Beach

KSRN(FM)— 1990: 107.7 mhz; 230 w. 2,883 ft TL: N39 18 47 W119 53 00. Stereo. Hrs open: 1465 Terminal Way, Suite 3, Reno, NV, 89502. Phone: (775) 324-4819. Fax: (775) 324-4832.E-mail: vickyo@radiolazer.com Licensee: Lazer Broadcasting Corp. (group owner; (acq 12-12-2003; $2.5 million). Natl. Network: ABC, . Natl. Rep: Katz Radio,. Format: Sp, rgnl Mexican. News: 5 hrs wkly. Target aud: 35-54; affluent, business professionals. Spec prog: Gospel one hr wkly. ♦Eduardo Rios, opns mgr, prom dir; Vicky Orozco, gen mgr & gen sls mgr; Salvador Prieto, progmg dir.

Kingsburg

KVPW(FM)— 1992: 106.3 mhz; 16 kw. Ant 420 ft TL: N36 26 50 W119 37 10. Stereo. Hrs open: 24 2110 Tulare St., Fresno, 93721. Phone: (559) 237-8767. Fax: (559) 237-8788 . Web Site:www.power1063.fm Licensee: Pro-Active Communications-Fresno LLC (group owner; (acq 7-17-2006; $2.75 million). Population served: 666,000 Format: Rymthmic contemporary. ♦Gerald Clifton, CEO; Brenda Brown, gen mgr.

La Jolla

KIFM(FM)—See San Diego

La Quinta

KUNA-FM— Aug 1, 1987: 96.7 mhz; 650 w. 578 ft TL: N33 48 08 W116 13 30. Stereo. Hrs open: 24 42650 Melanie Pl., Palm Desert, 92211-5170. Phone: (760) 568-6830. Fax: (760) 568-3984. Licensee: Gulf California Broadcasting Co. Group owner: News-Press & Gazette Co. Population served: 280,000 Natl. Rep: Univision Radio National Sales,. Format: Rgnl Mexican. News staff: one; News: 25 hrs wkly. Target aud: 25-54. ♦Martin Serna, gen mgr; Adolpho Iniguez, opns mgr.

La Selva Beach

KOMY(AM)— 1937: 1340 khz; 1 kw-D, 850 w-N. TL: N36 57 43 W121 58 51. Hrs open: 5 AM-midnight (M-S) 2300 Portola Dr., Santa Cruz, 95062. Phone: (831) 475-1080. Fax: (831) 475-2967.E-mail: risie@komy.com Web Site:www.1340komy.com Licensee: Zwerling Broadcasting System Ltd. (acq 6-5-97). Population served: 500,000 Format: Oldies. Target aud: 25-64; people with an investment at risk in the community. ♦Michael Zwerling, CEO, pres; Ron Stevens, pres; Michael Olson, gen mgr.

Lake Arrowhead

KCXX(FM)— June 1978: 103.9 mhz; 180 w. Ant 1,797 ft TL: N34 14 03 W117 08 25. Stereo. Hrs open: 24 242 E. Airport Dr., Suite 106, San Bernardino, 92408. Phone: (909) 890-5904. Fax: (909) 890-9035. Web Site:www.x1039.com Licensee: All-Pro Broadcasting Inc. (acq 9-10-92; $5 million with KCKC(AM) San Bernardino;9-28-92). Population served: 1,300,000 Natl. Rep: Christal,. Leventhal, Senter & Lerman. Format: Alternative rock. Target aud: 18-49. ♦Willie Davis, CEO & pres; Bill McNulty, gen mgr, opns mgr; Lee Weiman, gen sls mgr; Jim Daniels, prom mgr; John DeSantis, progmg dir.

Lake Isabella

KQAB(AM)— July 15, 1977: 1140 khz; 1 kw-D. TL: N35 38 20 W118 28 22. Hrs open: Sunrise-sunset Box 2008, 14 Sierra Dr., Kernville, 93238. Phone: (760) 376-4500. Fax: (760) 376-3119. Licensee: Robert J. and Katherine M. Bohn. (acq 7-24-97; $300,000 with co-located FM). Population served: 29,000 Natl. Network: ABC, . Format: News/talk. News staff: one; News: 14 hrs wkly. Target aud: 40 plus; mature. ♦Anthony Bohn, gen mgr; Gary Huff, gen sls mgr; Bob Jamison, progmg dir; Scott Costa, news dir; Jillian King, traf mgr.

KVLI-FM— Oct 29, 1992: 104.5 mhz; 200 w. 1,260 ft TL: N35 37 21 W118 26 16. Stereo. Hrs open: 24 Box 2008, 14 Sierra Dr., Kernville, 93238. Phone: (760) 376-4500. Fax: (760) 376-3119. Web Site:www.oldiesradioonline.com Population served: 29,000 Natl. Network: ABC, . Format: Oldies. News staff: one; News: 12 hrs wkly. Target aud: 25-54. ♦Anthony Bohn, stn mgr; Scott Cosa, news dir; Jillian King, traf mgr; Bob Jamison, engr.

Lakeport

KNTI(FM)— Oct 21, 1984: 99.5 mhz; 2.5 kw. Ant 1,920 ft TL: N39 07 50 W123 04 32. Stereo. Hrs open: 24 140 N. Main St., 95453. Phone: (707) 263-6113. Fax: (707) 263-0939.E-mail: mwilson@9tbicoastalmedia.com Web Site:www.knti.com Licensee: Bicoastal Media L.L.C. (group owner; acq 7-28-99; grpsl). Population served: 160,000 Natl. Network: CNN Radio, . Keck, Mahin & Cate. Format: Classic hits. News staff: one; News: 8 hrs wkly. Target aud: 25-54; family oriented, upscale, professional adults. Spec prog: Sp 3 hrs, new adult contemp 3 hrs wkly. ♦Ken Dennis, CEO; Mike Wilson, pres; Tony Calumet, gen mgr; Eric Patrick, opns dir, progmg dir; Alan Mathews, gen sls mgr; Paul Reading, news dir; Kevin Mostyn, pub affrs dir, chief of engrg.

***KPFZ-FM**— 2008: 88.1 mhz; 100 w vert. Ant 2,184 ft TL: N38 59 23 W122 46 05. Hrs open: Box 446, 95453. Phone: (707) 274-2152.E-mail:

aw@mchsi.com Web Site:www.kpfz.org Licensee: Lake County Community Radio Inc. ♦Andy Weiss, stn mgr.

KXBX(AM)— June 17, 1966: 1270 khz; 500 w-D, 97 w-N. TL: N39 00 50 W122 53 39. Hrs open: 24 Box 759, 140 N. Main St., 95453. Phone: (707) 263-6113. Fax: (707) 263-0939.E-mail: mwilson@ncradio.com Licensee: Bicoastal Media LLC. (group owner; acq 7-28-99; grpsl). Population served: 55,000 Natl. Network: Westwood One, . Format: MOR, nostalgia. News staff: one; News: 4 hrs wkly. Target aud: 40 plus; retirees. Spec prog: Sp 3 hrs, loc talk & info 5 hrs wkly. ♦Mike Wilson, pres & gen mgr; Alan Matthews, gen sls mgr; Kevin Mostyn, engrg VP, chief of engrg; Juan Huerta, min affrs dir, spanish dir; Bill Moen, disc jockey.

KXBX-FM— Aug 31, 1984: 98.3 mhz; 3 kw. 300 ft TL: N39 02 54 W122 45 59. Stereo. Hrs open: Box 759, 140 N. Main St., 95453. Phone: (707) 263-6113. Fax: (707) 263-0939. Format: Hot adult contemp.

Lancaster

KAVL(AM)— Sept 8, 1950: 610 khz; 4.9 kw-D, 4 kw-N, DA-2. TL: N34 42 22 W118 10 36. Stereo. Hrs open: 24 352 East Ave. K-4, 93535. Phone: (661) 942-1121. Fax: (661) 723-5512.E-mail: info@foxsports610.com Web Site:www.foxsports610.com Licensee: Aloha Station Trust LLC, as Trustee Group owner: Clear Channel Communications Inc. (acq 7-30-2008). Population served: 400,000 Natl. Network: USA, . Thompson Hine LLP. Format: Sports. News staff: 2. Target aud: 25-44; predominantly male, commuters, sports fans. ♦Jim Bell, gen mgr; Mark Mitchell, opns mgr, progmg dir; Shaun Palmer, gen sls mgr.

KGMX(FM)— Oct 28, 1970: 106.3 mhz; 3 kw. 210 ft TL: N34 44 41 W118 07 30. (CP: 3.66 kw, ant 256 ft.). Hrs open: 24 Q-9, 570 East Ave., Palmdale, 93550. Phone: (661) 947-3107. Fax: (661) 272-5688. Licensee: High Desert Broadcasting LLC. Population served: 400,000 Format: Hot adult contemp. Target aud: 24-54. ♦Nelson Rasse, gen mgr.

KOSS(AM)— August 1956: 1380 khz; 1 kw-D, DA. TL: N34 42 43 W118 10 34. Hrs open: 24 Q-9, 570 East Ave., Palmdale, 93550. Phone: (661) 947-3107. Fax: (661) 272-5688. Licensee: High Desert Broadcasting LLC. (group owner; (acq 1-21-97; with co-located FM). Population served: 200,000 Format: News/talk. Target aud: 18-49; homeowners, married couples with discretionary income. ♦Nelson Rasse, gen mgr; Gary Wilson, opns mgr; Jeff McElfresh, prom dir; Bob Montague, news dir; Ella Rice, traf mgr.

***KTLW(FM)**— July 3, 1997: 88.9 mhz; 5.8 kw. Ant 272 ft TL: N34 51 03 W118 09 22. Stereo. Hrs open: 24 14820 Sherman Way, Life On The Way Communications, Van Nuys, 91405. Phone: (818) 779-8444.E-mail: ktlwinfo@ktlw.net Web Site:www.ktlw.net Licensee: Life On The Way Communications Inc. (acq 5-23-2003). Population served: 4,500,000 Natl. Network: AP Network News, . Format: Inspirational, Christian music & teaching. News: 6 hrs wkly. Target aud: 25-54; 50% male, 50% female. ♦Gary Curtis, exec VP, VP; Gary C. Curtis, gen mgr; Rita Medall, opns dir & opns mgr.

KUTY(AM)—See Palmdale

Laytonville

***KHKL(FM)**— 2002: 91.9 mhz; 125 w. Ant 2,184 ft TL: N39 41 41 W123 34 36. Stereo. Hrs open: 24 2351 Sunset Blvd., Suite 170-218, Rocklin, 95765. Phone: (916) 251-1600. Fax: (916) 251-1650.E-mail: klove@klove.com Web Site:www.klove.com Licensee: Educational Media Foundation. Group owner: EMF Broadcasting. Natl. Network: K-Love, . Shaw Pittman. Format: Contemp Christian. News staff: 3. Target aud: 25-44; Judeo Christian, female. ♦Richard Jenkins, pres; Mike Novak, VP, progmg dir; Lloyd Parker, gen mgr; Ed Lenane, opns dir, news dir; Keith Whipple, dev dir; Eric Allen, natl sls mgr; David Pierce, progmg mgr; Jon Rivers, mus dir; Sam Wallington, engrg dir; Arthur Vassar, traf mgr; Karen Johnson, news rptr.

***KLAI(FM)**— 2006: 90.3 mhz; 500 w vert. Ant 2,430 ft TL: N39 41 38 W123 34 43. Hrs open: Secondary address: 1144 Redway Drive, Redway 95560. Phone: (707) 923-2513. Fax: (707) 923-2501.E-mail: kmud@kmud.org Web Site:www.kmud.org Licensee: Redwood Community Radio Inc. Format: Div. ♦Brenda Starr, gen mgr; Michael Jacinto, opns mgr; Kate Klein, mus dir; Estelle Fennell, news dir; Simon Frech, chief of engrg.

***KVUH(FM)**— 2005: 88.5 mhz; 1.2 kw vert. Ant 2,335 ft TL: N39 41 38 W123 34 43. Hrs open:
Rebroadcasts KSJV(FM) Fresno 100%.
5005 E. Belmont Ave., Fresno, 93727. Phone: (559) 455-5777. Fax: (559) 455-5778.E-mail: mail@radiobilingue.org Web Site:www.radiobilingue.org Licensee: Radio Bilingue Inc. (group owner). (acq 6-29-2005; $50,000 for CP). Format: Ethnic, multilingual, Sp. ♦Hugo Morales, CEO; Maria Erana, gen mgr, opns dir, gen sls mgr, progmg dir; Phil Traynor, dev dir; Samuel Cozco, news dir; Bill Bach, chief of engrg.

Le Grand

***KEFR(FM)**— Jan 11, 1985: 89.9 mhz; 1.8 kw. 2,142 ft TL: N37 32 01 W120 01 50. Stereo. Hrs open: Box 52, 13306 Jefferson St., 95333. Phone: (209) 389-4659. Fax: (209) 389-0215.E-mail: kefr@k66.com Web Site:www.familyradio.com Licensee: Family Stations Inc. (group owner) Format: Educ, relg. Target aud: General. ♦Harold Camping, pres; Craig Hulsebos, progmg dir; Larry Milliken, stn mgr & chief of engrg.

Lemoore

KJOP(AM)— Dec 23, 1963: 1240 khz; 1 kw-U. TL: N36 18 47 W119 43 51. Hrs open: Box 180, Tahoma, 96142. Phone: (530) 584-5700. Fax: (530) 584-5705.E-mail: info@ihradio.org Web Site:www.ihradio.org Licensee: IHR Educational Broadcasting. (group owner; (acq 12-22-2000; $125,000). Format: Catholic/religious. ♦Doug Sherman, pres.

Lenwood

KBTW(FM)— April 2001: 104.5 mhz; 2.5 kw. 515 ft TL: N34 51 20 W117 02 59. Hrs open: 24
Rebroadcasts KXLM (FM) Oxnard 80%.
1950 S. Sunwest Ln., Suite 300, San Bernardino, 92408. Secondary address: 125 E. Fredericks St., Barstow 92311. Phone: (909) 825-5020. Phone: (760) 255-4246. Fax: (909) 884-5844. Fax: (760) 255-2406.E-mail: info@radiolazer.com Web Site:www.radiolazer.com Licensee: Lazer Broadcasting Corp. (group owner; (acq 10-27-99; 450,000). Natl. Rep: Lotus Entravision Reps LLC,. Fletcher, Heald & Hildreth. Format: Sp, rgnl Mexican. News: 2 hrs wkly. Target aud: 25-54; adult. ♦Armando Gutierrez, gen mgr, prom dir; Vicki Bails, gen sls mgr; Salvador Prieto, progmg dir; Ralph Jones, chief of engrg.

KHDR(FM)— Dec 20, 2002: 96.9 mhz; 1 kw. Ant 797 ft TL: N34 58 15 W117 02 22. Hrs open: 24
Rebroadcasts KHRQ(FM) Baker 100%.
Box 1668, Barstow, 92312. Phone: (760) 256-0326. Fax: (760) 256-9507.E-mail: tim@highwayradio.com Web Site:www.thehighwaystations.com Licensee: The Drive LLC. Group owner: KHWY Inc. (acq 2-25-2003). Natl. Network: AP Radio, . Hogan & Hartson. Format: Classic rock, AOR. News staff: one. Target aud: General; travelers on I-15 and I-40. ♦Howard B. Anderson, CEO, pres; Kirk M. Anderson, exec VP; Judy Robinson, gen sls mgr; Lance Todd, progmg dir.

KIXW-FM— November 1994: 107.3 mhz; 440 w. Ant 771 ft TL: N34 58 13 W117 02 19. Hrs open: 1611 E. Main St., Barstow, 92311. Phone: (760) 256-0326. Fax: (760) 256-9507.E-mail: tim@highwayradio.com Web Site:www.thehighwaystations.com Licensee: KHWY Inc. (group owner; (acq 2-18-98; $1,741,444 with KIXF(FM) Baker). Natl. Network: CNN Radio, Westwood One, . Hogan & Hartson. Format: Country. ♦Howard Anderson, CEO, pres; Kirk Anderson, exec VP; Timothy Anderson, VP & gen mgr; Judy Robinson, sls VP; John Gregg, prom dir; Lance Todd, progmg dir; Keith Hayes, news dir; Thomas J. McNeill, engrg mgr.

Lincoln

KKFS(FM)— Nov 8, 1974: 103.9 mhz; 6 kw. Ant 328 ft TL: N38 52 33 W121 07 30. Stereo. Hrs open: 24 1425 River Park Dr., Suite 520, Sacramento, 95815. Phone: (916) 924-0710. Fax: (916) 924-1587.E-mail: info@1039thefish.com Web Site:www.1039thefish.com Licensee: Golden Gate Broadcasting Co. Inc. Group owner: First Broadcasting Investment Partners LLC (acq 5-12-2006; swap for KTTA(FM) Jackson). Population served: 750,000 Format: Contemp Christian. ♦James Rowten, gen mgr; Laurie Larson, progmg dir; Dave Fortenberry, engrg dir.

Livermore

KKIQ(FM)— May 1969: 101.7 mhz; 4.5 kw. 382 ft TL: N37 35 42 W121 39 42. Stereo. Hrs open: 24 7901 Stoneridge Dr., Suite 525, Pleasanton, 94588. Phone: (925) 455-4500. Fax: (925) 416-1211.E-mail: info@kkiqfm.com Web Site:www.kkiq.com Licensee: KKIQ Inc. (acq 6-19-98; $9 million). Population served: 500,000 Natl. Network: AP Radio, . Haley, Bader & Potts. Format: Adult contemp. News staff: one; News: 28 hrs wkly. Target aud: 25-54; high income & highly educated adults. ♦John Levitt, gen mgr; David Louie, gen mgr; Sylvia Manker, mktg dir; Jim Hampton, progmg dir; John Higden, chief of engrg.

Livingston

***KCJH(FM)**— 1997: 89.1 mhz; 13.5 kw vert. Ant 305 ft TL: N37 18 57 W120 43 20. Hrs open: 24
Rebroadcasts KYCC(FM) Stockton 100%.
9019 N. West Ln., Stockton, 95210. Phone: (209) 477-3690. Fax: (209) 477-2762.E-mail: kycc@kycc.org Web Site:www.kycc.org Licensee: Your Christian Companion Network Inc. (acq 7-20-98). Cohn & Marks. Format: Gospel, inspirational, adult contemp. Target aud: 35-55. ♦Kenneth F. Haney, pres; Shirley Garner, exec VP & gen mgr; Scott Mearns, progmg mgr, chief of engrg; Marina Tahod, mus dir.

***KLVN(FM)**— 1998: 88.3 mhz; 1.8 kw. 148 ft TL: N37 18 57 W120 43 20. Stereo. Hrs open: 24
Rebroadcasts KLVY(FM) Fairmead 100%.
2351 Sunset Blvd., Suite 170-218, Rocklin, 95765. Phone: (916) 251-1600. Fax: (916) 251-1650.E-mail: klove@klove.com Web Site:www.klove.com Licensee: Educational Media Foundation. Group owner: EMF Broadcasting. Population served: 207,000 Natl. Network: K-Love, . Shaw Pittman. Format: Contemp Christian music. News staff: 3. Target aud: 25-44; female (Judeo-Christian). ♦Richard Jenkins, pres; Mike Novak, VP; Keith Whipple, dev dir; David Pierce, progmg dir; Ed Lenane, news dir; Sam Wallington, engrg dir; Karen Johnson, news rptr.

KSKD(FM)— Nov 1, 1984: 95.9 mhz; 3 kw. Ant 305 ft TL: N37 18 57 W120 43 20. (CP: COL Dos Palos. 6 kw, ant 318 ft. TL: N36 55 35 W120 50 42). Stereo. Hrs open: 4043 Geer Rd., Hughson, 95326. Phone: (209) 883-8760. Fax: (209) 883-8769.E-mail: ngomez@lafavorita.net Web Site:www.lafavorita.net Licensee: All American Broadcasting Co. (acq 2-3-93; $198,000; 3-8-93). Natl. Rep: Lotus Entravision Reps LLC,. Format: Sp, adult contemp. ♦Nelson Gomez, pres & gen mgr.

Lodi

KCVR(AM)— 1946: 1570 khz; 5 kw-D, 500 w-N, DA-2. TL: N38 05 10 W121 12 57. Hrs open: 6820 Pacific Ave., Suite 3 A, Stockton, 95207. Phone: (209) 474-0154. Fax: (209) 474-0316.E-mail: info@entravision.com Web Site:www.entravision.com Licensee: Entravision Holdings LLC. Group owner: Entravision Communications Corp. (acq 7-28-2000; grpsl). Format: Sp. ♦Lisa Sunday, gen mgr, stn mgr; Valentina Rupic, traf mgr.

***KLRS(FM)**—Not on air, target date: unknown: 89.7 mhz; 6.8 kw vert. Ant 396 ft TL: N38 23 01 W121 17 15. Hrs open: 2351 Sunset Blvd., Suite 170-218, Rocklin, 95765. Phone: (916) 251-1600. Fax: (916) 251-1650. Licensee: Educational Media Foundation.

KWIN(FM)— Dec 24, 1959: 97.7 mhz; 3 kw. 300 ft TL: N38 03 05 W121 15 05. Stereo. Hrs open: 24 4643 Quail Lakes Dr., Suite 100, Stockton, 95207-1833. Secondary address: 1581 Cummins Dr., Suite 135, Modesto 95358. Phone: (209) 476-1230. Fax: (209) 957-1833.E-mail: info@kwin.com Web Site:www.kwin.com Licensee: Citadel Broadcasting Co. Group owner: Citadel Broadcasting Corp. (acq 5-9-03; grpsl). Population served: 128,400 Format: CHR. ♦Joanne Matteri, CFO; Roy Williams, gen mgr; Jean Western, sls dir; Raymond Baca, chief of engrg.

Loma Linda

KCAA(AM)— Nov 1, 1964: 1050 khz; 1.4 kw-D, 35 w-N, DA-2. TL: N33 59 22 W117 11 10. BP-20070529ACI. Hrs open: 24 254 Carousel Mall, San Bernardino, 92401. Secondary address: 19939 Gatling Ct., Katy, TX 77449. Phone: (281) 599-9800. Fax: (909) 381-8935.E-mail: ceowon@comcast.net Web Site:www.KCAAradio.com Licensee: Broadcast Management Services Inc. (acq 2-97; $30,000). Population served: 3,000,000 Natl. Network: NBC Radio, . Fletcher Heald. Format: talk/news. News staff: 3; News: 15 hrs wkly. Target aud: General. Spec prog: Polka, swing era, sports. ♦Fred Lundgren, CEO; Jim Hill, VP; Dennis Baxter, gen mgr, news dir; Bill Bruns, opns mgr.

KSGN(FM)—See Riverside

Lompoc

KBOX(FM)—Licensed to Lompoc. See Santa Maria

KIDI-FM— 1999: 105.1 mhz; 420 w. Ant 1,217 ft TL: N34 41 28 W120 15 58. Hrs open: 24 718 E. Chapel St., Santa Maria, 93454-4524. Phone: (805) 928-4334. Fax: (805) 349-2765. Licensee: Emerald Wave Media. (group owner; (acq 7-7-2006; $1.5 million). Format: Sp, Mexican rgnl. News staff: one; News: 5 hrs wkly. Target aud: 18-45; second generation bilingual Mexican Americans. ♦August Ruiz, gen mgr, gen sls mgr; Sofia Lariz, rgnl sls mgr.

***KLWG(FM)—** 2006: 88.1 mhz; 20 w vert. Ant 1,128 ft TL: N34 36 13 W120 29 17. Hrs open: 24 Box 1241, 93438. Phone: (805) 736-3741. Web Site:www.calvarychapellompoc.com/radio_ministry.htm Licensee: Calvary Chapel of Lompoc. Format: Relg. ♦Mark Galvan, gen mgr; Landon Galvan, progmg dir.

KRQK(FM)— Dec 18, 1979: 100.3 mhz; 3.65 kw. 863 ft TL: N34 44 24 W120 26 42. Stereo. Hrs open: 24 2325 Skyway Dr., Suite J, Santa Maria, 93455. Phone: (805) 922-1041. Fax: (805) 928-3069. Licensee: AGM-Santa Maria LP. Group owner: American General Media (acq 10-29-99; $1.3 million). Population served: 51,000 Format: Rgnl Mexican. Target aud: 18-49. ♦Rich Watson, gen mgr; Emily Stich, gen sls mgr, rgnl sls mgr, prom mgr; Salvador Ponce, progmg dir.

***KRQZ(FM)—** Sept 3, 2000: 91.5 mhz; 2 kw vert. Ant 1,050 ft TL: N34 36 13 W120 29 17. Stereo. Hrs open: 24
Rebroadcasts WUFM(FM) Columbus, OH 60%.
Trinity Church of the Nazarene, 500 E. North Ave., 93436. Phone: (805) 736-6415. Fax: (805) 736-2642.E-mail: krqz@trinaz.com Web Site:www.radiou.com Sky Angel Licensee: Trinity Church of the Nazarene. Gammon & Grange. Format: Christian rock. Target aud: 12-24 years. ♦Mark Hostand, stn mgr & gen sls mgr; Chris Hill, chief of engrg.

KSMA(AM)— May 25, 1963: 1410 khz; 500 w-D, 77 w-N, DA-2. TL: N34 39 47 W120 22 58. Hrs open: 24
Rebroadcasts KUHL(AM) Santa Maria 100%.
1101 S Broadway Street, Suite C, Santa Maria, 93454. Phone: (805) 922-7727. Fax: (805) 349-0265.E-mail: Shawn@knightbroadcasting.com Web Site:www.am1410.com Licensee: Knight Broadcasting Inc. (group owner; (acq 7-31-2006; $1.2 million with KUHL(AM) Santa Maria). Population served: 90,000 Natl. Network: ABC, . Format: News/talk. Target aud: 25-54. ♦Jeff Williams, gen mgr.

KSMY(FM)— 1997: 106.7 mhz; 3.5 kw. Ant 879 ft TL: N34 44 31 W120 26 46. Hrs open: 2215 Skyway Dr., Santa Maria, 93455-1118. Phone: (805) 925-2582. Fax: (805) 928-1544. Web Site:www.lapreciosa.com Licensee: EDB SLO License LLC. Group owner: Clear Channel Communications Inc. (acq 11-30-2007; grpsl). Format: Sp rgnl Mexican. ♦Rich Hawkins, gen mgr; Pattie Wagner, gen sls mgr; Jennifer Grant, progmg dir; Milos Nemicik, chief of engrg.

Long Beach

KBUE(FM)— August 1961: 105.5 mhz; 3 kw. Ant 466 ft TL: N33 51 29 W118 13 24. Stereo. Hrs open: 24 1845 Empire Ave., Burbank, 91504. Phone: (818) 729-5300. Fax: (818) 729-5678.E-mail: info@lbimedia.com Web Site:www.aquisuena.com Licensee: LBI Radio License Corp. Group owner: Liberman Broadcasting Inc. (acq 1995; $13 million). Population served: 6,500,000 Format: Sp Mexican rgnl. Target aud: 18-49; Spanish speaking adults. ♦Andy Mars, gen mgr; Daisy Ortiz, gen sls mgr, engrg VP; Xavier Ortiz, natl sls mgr; Luis Hernandez, rgnl sls mgr; Pepe Garza, progmg dir; Chris Buchanan, chief of engrg.

***KFRN(AM)—** March 1924: 1280 khz; 1 kw-D, 690 w-N, DA-2. TL: N33 47 54 W118 14 47. Stereo. Hrs open: 24 3550 Longbeach Blvd., Suite D 4, 90807. Phone: (562) 427-7773. Fax: (562) 427-7723.E-mail: kfrn@familyradio.com Web Site:www.familyradio.com Licensee: Family Stations Inc. (group owner; acq 9-19-77). Natl. Network: Family Radio, . Format: Christian, edu, news. News: 70 hrs wkly. Target aud: Family spectrum. ♦Harold Camping, pres, gen mgr; Ward Cayot, opns mgr; Suong Tran, pub affrs dir.

***KKJZ(FM)—** Jan 3, 1950: 88.1 mhz; 30 kw. Ant 449 ft TL: N33 47 58 W118 09 43. Stereo. Hrs open: 24 1288 N. Bellflower Blvd., 90815-4198. Phone: (562) 985-2999. Fax: (562) 985-2982.E-mail: veronicaj@kkjz.org Web Site:www.jazzandblues.org Telstar7, transponder 15, subcarriers 5.58 & 5.76 Licensee: California State University, Long Beach Foundation (acq 6-18-81; $15,000;4-27-81). Population served: 6,000,000 Natl. Network: NPR, . Fletcher, Heald & Hildreth. Format: Jazz, info. News staff: one; News: 5 hrs wkly. Target aud: 25-64; educated, opinion leaders, jazz & mus lovers. Spec prog: Blues 15 hrs wkly. ♦Stephanie Levine-Fried, gen mgr; Mike Johnson, opns mgr; Denise Maynard, sls dir, mktg dir; Michael Levine, news dir.

KLTX(AM)— 1926: 1390 khz; 5 kw-D, 3.6 w-N, DA-2. TL: N33 53 30 W118 11 03. Hrs open: 24 136 S. Oak Knoll Ave. #202, Pasadena, 91101. Phone: (626) 356-4235. Phone: (626) 356-4230. Fax: (626) 817-9851.E-mail: info@kltxam.com Web Site:www.nuevavida.com Licensee: Hi-Favor Broadcasting LLC (group owner; acq 8-4-00; $30 million). Population served: 450,000 Miller & Miller. Format: Relg, Sp. Target aud: 35 plus; mature audience. ♦Sergio Martinez, opns dir & gen sls mgr.

Los Altos

KFFG(FM)— Oct 17, 1960: 97.7 mhz; 3.3 kw. Ant 445 ft TL: N37 18 27 W122 05 41. Stereo. Hrs open:
Rebroadcasts KFOG(FM) San Francisco 100%.
c/o KFOG, 55 Hawthorne St., Suite 1000, San Francisco, 94105. Phone: (415) 817-5364. Fax: (415) 995-7006.E-mail: info@kffgfm.com Web Site:www.kfog.com Licensee: KFFG Lico Inc. Group owner: Susquehanna Radio Corp. (acq 1995; $8.25 million). Format: AOR. Target aud: 18-49. ♦Tony Salvadore, gen mgr & stn mgr; Omari Patterson, sls dir; Sheri Nelson, prom dir; Dave Benson, progmg dir; Kelly Ransford, mus dir.

***KFJC(FM)—** Dec 4, 1959: 89.7 mhz; 250 w. 1,845 ft TL: N37 19 14 W122 08 29. Stereo. Hrs open: 24 12345 El Monte Rd., Los Altos Hills, 94022. Phone: (650) 949-7260. Fax: (650) 948-1085.E-mail: info@kfjc.org Web Site:www.kfjc.org Licensee: Foothill Community College Board of Trustees. Population served: 2,500,000 Format: Free-form, eclectic. News: 9 hrs wkly. Target aud: 8-80; psychedelic speed freaks, radicals & other social outcasts. Spec prog: Country 8 hrs, bluegrass 8 hrs, jazz 7 hrs, progsv 4 hrs wkly. ♦Eric Johnson, gen mgr; John Burns, sls dir, mus dir; Liz Clark, prom dir; Karin Shriver, progmg dir; Mark Laubach, engrg mgr.

Los Angeles

KABC(AM)— Nov 15, 1929: 790 khz; 5 kw-U, DA-N. TL: N34 01 40 W118 22 20. Hrs open: 3321 S. La Cienega Blvd., 90016. Phone: (310) 840-4912. Fax: (310) 558-5635. Web Site:www.kabc.com Licensee: Radio License Holding VI LLC. Group owner: ABC Inc. (acq 6-12-2007; grpsl). Population served: 9,600,000 Natl. Network: ABC, . Format: Talk. Target aud: 35 plus; upscale, affluent, college educated. ♦John H. Davidson, pres, gen mgr; Joe Schwartz, gen sls mgr, prom mgr; Pete Dominguez, natl sls mgr; Shelley Wagner, mktg dir & prom dir; Erik Braverman, progmg dir; Nelkane Benton, pub affrs dir; Norm Avery, chief of engrg.

KAMP-FM— 1954: 97.1 mhz; 29.5 kw. Ant 2,998 ft TL: N34 09 50 W118 11 46. Stereo. Hrs open: 5670 Wilshire Blvd., Suite 200, 90036. Phone: (323) 971-9710. Fax: (323) 954-0971.E-mail: amp@ampradio.com Web Site:www.ampradio.com Licensee: CBS Radio East Inc. Group owner: Infinity Broadcasting Corp. (acq 7-23-97). Population served: 281,606 Natl. Rep: CBS Radio,. Format: Top-40. Target aud: 25-54; adults. ♦Bob Moore, gen mgr; Ron Escarsega, opns mgr; David Severino, gen sls mgr; Michael Olson, prom dir; Jack Silver, progmg dir.

KBIG-FM— Feb 15, 1959: 104.3 mhz; 65 kw. Ant 3,044 ft TL: N34 13 36 W118 03 59. Stereo. Hrs open: 3400 W. Olive Ave., Suite 550, Burbank, 91505. Phone: (818) 559-2252. Fax: (818) 637-2267. Fax: (818) 559-2252. Web Site:www.kbig.com Population served: 1,000,000 Format: Adult contemp. Target aud: 25-54. ♦Bruce Reese, CEO; Tracy Barrios, traf mgr.

KBLA(AM)—See Santa Monica

KBRT(AM)—See Avalon

KCBS-FM— 1948: 93.1 mhz; 54 kw. 5,000 ft TL: N34 13 57 W118 04 18. Stereo. Hrs open: 24 5670 Wilshire Blvd., 90036. Phone: (323) 569-1070. Fax: (323) 463-9270.E-mail: arrow93@arrowfm.com Web Site:www.arrowfm.com Population served: 12,000,000 Natl. Network: Westwood One, . Natl. Rep: Interep,. Format: Rock and roll classics, mus from the 70s. News staff: one; News: 3 hrs wkly. Target aud: 25-49. ♦Mel Karmazin, CEO & chmn; Dan Mason, pres; Fario Suledian, CFO; Brad West, gen sls mgr; Jaime Korzenieski, prom mgr. Co-owned TV: KCBS-TV affil

KDIS(AM)—See Pasadena

KFI(AM)— Apr 16, 1922: 640 khz; 50 kw-U. TL: N33 52 48 W118 00 48. Hrs open: 3400 W. Olive Ave., Suite 550, Burbank, 91505. Phone: (818) 559-2252. Web Site:www.kfi640.com Licensee: Capstar TX L.P. Group owner: Clear Channel Communications Inc. (acq 8-7-2000; grpsl). Population served: 1,058,900 Natl. Rep: Christal,. Format: Talk. Target aud: 25-54. ♦Greg Ashlock, gen mgr.

KFWB(AM)— Mar 25, 1925: 980 khz; 5 kw-U. TL: N34 04 11 W118 11 36. Stereo. Hrs open: 24 5670 Wilshire Blvd., Suite 200, 90036. Phone: (323) 525-0980. Phone: (323) 871-4612. Fax: (323) 930-8729. Fax: (323) 871-4681. Web Site:www.kfwb.com Licensee: Infinity Broadcasting East Inc. Group owner: Infinity Broadcasting Corp. (acq 11-13-98; grpsl). Population served: 9,500,000 Natl. Network: CNN Radio, . Natl. Rep: CBS Radio,. Wire Svc: AP Wire Svc: Bloomberg News Format: News. News staff: 60; News: 168 hrs wkly. Target aud: 25-54. ♦Pat Duffy, VP, gen mgr; Sean O'Neil, gen sls mgr; Andy Ludlum, progmg dir; Paul Gomez, news dir; Paul Sakrison, chief of engrg.

KHHT(FM)— Dec 29, 1948: 92.3 mhz; 43 kw. 2,910 ft TL: N34 13 36 W118 03 57. Stereo. Hrs open: 24 3400 W. Olive Ave., Suite 550, Burbank, 91505. Phone: (818) 559-2252. Fax: (818) 566-4517.E-mail: info@hot92jamz.com Web Site:info@hot92jams.com Licensee: AMFM Broadcasting Licenses LLC. Group owner: Clear Channel Communications Inc. (acq 8-30-2000; grpsl). Population served: 9,741,200 Format: Urban contemp. Target aud: 18-49; females. ♦Val Maki, gen mgr; Mike Marino, progmg dir.

KHJ(AM)— Apr 13, 1922: 930 khz; 5 kw-U, DA-N. TL: N34 02 26 W118 22 14. Stereo. Hrs open: 24 1845 Empire Ave., Burbank, 91504. Phone: (818) 729-5300. Fax: (818) 729-5678.E-mail: info@lbimedia.com Licensee: LBI Radio License Corp. Group owner: Liberman Broadcasting Inc. (acq 3-27-90). Population served: 11901290 Wiley, Rein & Fielding. Format: Sp. News staff: one. Target aud: 18-49. ♦Jose Liberman, pres; Andy Mars, gen mgr; Disy Ortiz, gen sls mgr; Eddie Leon, progmg dir.

KIEV(AM)—(Culver City, January 1986: Stn currently dark. 1500 khz; 50 kw-D, 4.3 kw-N, DA-2. TL: N34 01 47 W118 05 58. Stereo. Hrs open: 73-733 Fred Waring Dr., Royce International Broadcasting Co., Palm Beach, 92260. Phone: (916) 813-1065. Licensee: Royce International Broadcasting Co. (acq 1984). Population served: 12,000,000 Natl. Rep: McGavren Guild,. Verner, Liipfert, Bernhard, McPherson & Hand. ♦Edward R. Stolz II, pres & gen mgr.

KIIS-FM— 1948: 102.7 mhz; 8 kw. Ant 2,960 ft TL: N34 13 36 W118 03 57. Stereo. Hrs open: 3400 W. Olive Ave., 91505. Phone: (818) 559-2252. Fax: (818) 295-6466. Web Site:www.kiisfm.com Format: CHR. Target aud: 18-34. ♦Roy Laughlin, gen mgr.

KKGO(FM)— Feb 18, 1959: 105.1 mhz; 18 kw. Ant 2,900 ft TL: N34 13 45 W118 04 04. Stereo. Hrs open: 24 Box 250028, 90025. Phone: (310) 478-5540. Fax: (310) 445-1439.E-mail: info@gocountry105.com Web Site:gocountry.am Licensee: Mt. Wilson FM Broadcasters Inc. Population served: 600,000 Natl. Network: AP Radio, . Cohn & Marks. Format: Country. ♦Saul Levine, pres, gen mgr; Linda Vali, sls dir; Michael Levine, mktg dir; Susan Foreman, prom dir; Dave Wagner, progmg VP.

KKLA-FM— 1985: 99.5 mhz; 10.5 kw. 2,880 ft TL: N34 13 26 W118 03 44. Stereo. Hrs open: 24 Box 29023, Glendale, 91209. Secondary address: 701 N. Brand Blvd., Suite 550, Glendale 91203. Phone: (818) 956-5552. Fax: (818) 551-1110.E-mail: info@kkla.com Web Site:www.kkla.com Licensee: New Inspiration Broadcasting Inc. Group owner: Salem Communications Corp. Population served: 8,000,000 Natl. Network: Salem Radio Network, . Natl. Rep: Salem,. Wire Svc: Metro Weather Service Inc. Format: Christian. Target aud: 25-55. ♦Terry Fahy, gen mgr; Jim Tinker, opns VP; Larry Marino, opns dir, chief of engrg; Bill Price, gen sls mgr, pub affrs dir; Chuck Tyler, progmg dir.

KLAC(AM)— 1924: 570 khz; 5 kw-U, DA-N. TL: N34 04 11 W118 11 36. Stereo. Hrs open: 24 3400 W. Olive Ave., Suite 550, Burbank, 91505. Phone: (818) 559-2252.E-mail: info@klacam.com Web Site:www.xtrasportsradio.com Licensee: AMFM Broadcasting Licenses LLC. Group owner: Clear Channel Communications Inc. (acq 8-30-2000; grpsl). Population served: 2,966,763 Format: Sports. Target aud: 35-54. ♦Mark Austin Thomas, VP, opns VP; Ed Krampf, gen mgr; Jeff Thomas, gen sls mgr; V. Freeman, mktg VP; Bill Lewis, mktg dir; Andrea Garcia, prom dir; Robin Bertoluci, progmg VP; Chris Little, news dir; John Paoli, engrg dir.

KLOS(FM)— Dec 30, 1947: 95.5 mhz; 68 kw. 2,920 ft TL: N34 13 37 W118 03 58. Stereo. Hrs open: 3321 S. La Cienega Blvd., 90016. Phone: (310) 840-4800. Fax: (310) 558-7685.E-mail: john.h.davison@citcomm.com Web Site:www.955klos.com Licensee: Radio License Holding XII LLC. Population served: 1,200,000 Format: Classic Rock. ♦John Davison, gen mgr, mktg dir; Leonard Madrid, gen sls mgr; C.W. West, adv dir; Rita Wilde, progmg dir; Jim Villanueva, mus dir; Norm Avery, engrg dir.

KLVE(FM)— May 2, 1959: 107.5 mhz; 29.5 kw. 3,100 ft TL: N34 13 44 W118 04 02. Hrs open: 24 Prog sep from AM 655 N. Central Ave., Suite 2500, Glendale, 91203. Phone: (818) 500-4500. Fax: (818) 500-4307. Wire Svc: Reuters Format: Adult contemp. Target aud: 18-49. ♦Bill Shadorf, sls dir; Jose Santos, progmg dir; Georgia Carrera, pub affrs dir.

KMPC(AM)— Sept 22, 1952: 1540 khz; 50 kw-D, 10 kw-N, DA-2. TL: N34 04 43 W118 11 05. Stereo. Hrs open: 2800 28th St., Suite 308, Santa Monica, 90405. Phone: (310) 452-7100. Fax: (310) 452-7880.E-mail: rnadel@sportingnews.com Licensee: P&Y Broadcasting Inc. (group

owner; (acq 5-30-2007; $33 million). Population served: 2900000 Format: Korean. ♦Chris Canning, pres.

KMRB(AM)—See San Gabriel

KNX(AM)— Sept 10, 1920: 1070 khz; 50 kw-U. TL: N33 51 35 W118 20 56. Stereo. Hrs open: 24 5670 Wilshire Blvd., Suite 200, 90036. Phone: (323) 569-1070. Fax: (323) 930-8798. Web Site:www.knx1070.com Licensee: CBS Radio East Inc. Group owner: Infinity Broadcasting Corp. (acq 9-36). Population served: 13,500,000 Natl. Network: CBS, . Natl. Rep: CBS Radio,. Wire Svc: Reuters Format: News. News staff: 40. Target aud: General.Pat Duffy, VP; Rosemary Hernadez, gen sls mgr; Amanda Arrington, natl sls mgr; Howard Freshman, rgnl sls mgr, mktg dir; David G. Hall, progmg VP, progmg dir; Julie Chin, news dir; Vivian Porter, pub affrs dir; Paul Sakrison, engrg mgr, chief of engrg; Terri Boysaw, traf mgr; Randy Kerdoon, edit dir, sports cmtr; Dick Helton, political ed; Steve Grad, sports cmtr

KOST(FM)— Oct 9, 1957: 103.5 mhz; 12.5 kw. Ant 3,100 ft TL: N34 13 34 W118 03 55. Hrs open: 3400 W. Olive Ave., Suite 550, Burbank, 91505. Phone: (818) 559-2252. Fax: (818) 637-2267. Web Site:www.kost1035.com Licensee: AMFM Broadcasting Licenses LLC. Population served: 1,400,000 Format: Adult contemp. ♦Craig Rossi, stn mgr; Stella Schwartz, progmg dir.

***KPFK(FM)**— July 26, 1959: 90.7 mhz; 110 kw. Ant 2,831 ft TL: N34 13 45 W118 04 03. Stereo. Hrs open: 24 3729 Cahuenga Blvd. W., North Hollywood, 91604. Phone: (818) 985-2711. Fax: (818) 763-7526.E-mail: gm@kpfk.org Web Site:www.kpfk.org Licensee: Pacifica Foundation. Group owner: Pacifica Foundation Inc. dba Pacifica Radio Garvey, Schubert, Barer. Wire Svc: AP Wire Svc: Catholic News Service Wire Svc: Reuters Format: Div, news/talk. News staff: 4; News: 11 hrs wkly. Target aud: 25-55. Spec prog: Children one hr, jazz 5 hrs, gospel 2 hrs, Sp 15 hrs wkly. ♦Eva Georgia, stn mgr; Zuberi Fields, opns mgr; Sue A. Welsh, dev dir; Armando Gudino, progmg dir; Fernando Velasquez, news dir.

KPWR(FM)— Dec. 20, 1956: 105.9 mhz; 25 kw. Ant 3,034 ft TL: N34 13 38 W118 04 00. Stereo. Hrs open: 24 2600 W. Olive Ave., Suite 850, Burbank, 91505. Phone: (818) 953-4200. Fax: (818) 848-0961. Web Site:www.power106.fm Licensee: Emmis Radio License LLC. Group owner: Emmis Communications Corp. (acq 1-84; grpsl;1-30-84). Population served: 8,000,000 Natl. Rep: D & R Radio,. Format: Rhythmic CHR. Target aud: 18-34; males. ♦Val Maki, VP; Janet Brainin, sls dir; Dianna Jason, mktg dir, prom dir; Jimmy Steal, progmg VP; Dennis Martin, chief of engrg.

KRCD(FM)—See Inglewood

KRLA(AM)—See Glendale

KRTH(FM)— 1941: 101.1 mhz; 51 kw. 3,130 ft TL: N34 13 38 W118 04 00. (CP: 53.6 kw). Stereo. Hrs open: 5670 Wilshire, Suite 200, 90036. Phone: (323) 936-5784. Fax: (323) 464-6101. Web Site:www.kearth101.com Licensee: Infinity Broadcasting East Inc. Group owner: Infinity Broadcasting Corp. (acq 2-2-94; $116 million;4-18-94). Population served: 9,607,400 Natl. Network: AP Network News, . Natl. Rep: CBS Radio,. Format: Oldies. Target aud: 25-64. ♦Maureen Lesourd, VP, gen mgr; Tracy Gilliam, sls VP & gen sls mgr; Karen Tobin, prom dir, prom mgr; Jahni Kaye, progmg dir; Lynn Duke, chief of engrg. Co-owned TV: KCBS-TV affil

KSCA(FM)—See Glendale

KSPN(AM)— Feb 18, 1927: 710 khz; 50 kw-D, 10 kw-N, DA-N. TL: N34 10 24 W118 24 24. Hrs open: 24 3321 S. La Cienega Blvd., 90016. Phone: (310) 840-2800. Fax: (310) 840-2848.E-mail: info@kspnam.com Web Site:www.espnradio710.com Licensee: KABC-AM Radio Inc. Group owner: ABC Inc. (acq 2-27-95; $17.5 million). Population served: 9,600,000 Natl. Network: ABC, . Format: Sports. News staff: 2. Target aud: General; famlies and moms. ♦John Davison, pres & gen mgr.

KSWD(FM)— June 1, 1957: 100.3 mhz; 5.3 kw. Ant 3,005 ft TL: N34 13 37 W118 03 58. Stereo. Hrs open: 24 Box 1710, Hollywood, 90078. Secondary address: 5900 Wilshire Blvd., 19th Floor 90036. Phone: (323) 634-1800. Fax: (323) 634-1888. Web Site:www.thesoundla.com Licensee: Bonneville Holding Co. Group owner: Radio One Inc. (acq 5-30-2008; $137.5 million). Population served: 13,000,000 Format: Triple A. Target aud: 25-54. ♦Peter Burton, gen mgr; Ron Turner, gen sls mgr; Leonard McGee, prom dir; Dave Beasing, progmg dir.

KTLK(AM)— 1927: 1150 khz; 50 kw-D, 44 kw-N, DA-2. TL: N34 02 00 W117 59 00. Stereo. Hrs open: 3400 W. Olive Ave., Suite 550, Burbank, 91505. Phone: (818) 559-2252. Licensee: Citicasters Licenses L.P. Group owner: Clear Channel Communications Inc. (acq 5-4-99; grpsl). Format: Progressive talk. ♦Greg Ashlock, gen mgr; Don Martin, stn mgr.

KTNQ(AM)— 1925: 1020 khz; 50 kw-U, DA-2. TL: N34 02 00 W117 59 00. Stereo. Hrs open: 24 655 N. Central Ave., Suite 2500, Glendale, 91203. Phone: (818) 500-4500. Fax: (818) 500-4307. Web Site:www.ktnq.com Licensee: KTNQ-AM License Corp. Group owner: Univision Radio (acq 9-22-2003; grpsl). Population served: 11,765,000 Wire Svc: Reuters Format: Sp, news/talk. Target aud: 25-54. ♦Michelle Hohman, gen mgr; Haz Montana, opns mgr; Eric Osuna, natl sls mgr; Offad Vallejo, mktg dir; Santiago Nieto, progmg dir.

KTWV(FM)— Mar 7, 1961: 94.7 mhz; 58 kw. 2,835 ft TL: N34 13 29 W118 03 47. Stereo. Hrs open: 24 5670 Wilshire Blvd., Suite 200, 90036. Phone: (323) 937-9283. Fax: (323) 634-0947.E-mail: wave@ktwv.cbs.com Web Site:www.947wave.com Licensee: Infinity Broadcasting East Inc. Group owner: Infinity Broadcasting Corp. (acq 11-13-98; grpsl). Population served: 9,500,000 Format: Smooth jazz. Target aud: 25-54. ♦Bob Moore, VP; Dan Weiner, gen mgr; Pat Amsbry, gen sls mgr; Jamie Kanai, mktg dir, prom dir; Paul Goldstein, progmg dir; Ricci Filiar, mus dir; Lynn Duke, engrg mgr, chief of engrg.

***KUSC(FM)**— Oct 24, 1946: 91.5 mhz; 39 kw. Ant 2,922 ft TL: N34 12 48 W118 03 41. Stereo. Hrs open: 24 Box 77913, 90007. Secondary address: 515 S. Figueroa St., Suite 2050 90071. Phone: (213) 225-7400. Fax: (213) 225-7410.E-mail: kusc@kusc.org Web Site:www.kusc.org Licensee: University of Southern California. Population served: 650,000 Natl. Network: PRI, NPR, . Lawrence Bernstein. Format: Class. Target aud: 35 plus. ♦Brenda Barnes, pres; Eric DeWeese, gen mgr; Janet McIntyre, dev dir.

KWKW(AM)— Apr 14, 1931: 1330 khz; 5 kw-U, DA-N. TL: N34 01 10 W118 20 42. Hrs open: 24 3301 Barham Blvd., Suite 201, 90068. Phone: (323) 851-5959. Fax: (323) 512-7460.E-mail: kwkw1330@aol.com Web Site:www.kwkw1330.com Licensee: Lotus Communications Corp. (group owner; (acq 1962). Population served: 1,200,000 Natl. Rep: Lotus Entravision Reps LLC,. Format: Sports/ESPN Desportes radio. News staff: 30. Target aud: 18-34 and 25-54; males. ♦Jim Kalmenson, pres, gen mgr; Mike Addison, gen sls mgr; Juan Rodriguez, progmg dir.

***KXLU(FM)**— February 1957: 88.9 mhz; 3 kw. 12 ft TL: N33 58 16 W118 24 56. Stereo. Hrs open: 24 1 LMU Drive, 90045. Phone: (310) 338-2866. Phone: (310) 338-5958. Fax: (310) 338-5959.E-mail: kxlu889fm@hotmail.com Web Site:www.kxlu.com Licensee: Loyola Marymount University Board of Trustees. Population served: 150,000 Format: Rock. News: 2 hrs wkly. Target aud: 16-30. Spec prog: Black 10 hrs, Children one hr, folk one hr wkly. ♦Justin Bates, gen mgr; Daisy Buchanan, prom dir; Michael Schuman, progmg dir; Maki Tamura, chief of engrg.

KXOL-FM— 1949: 96.3 mhz; 6.6 kw. Ant 1,305 ft TL: N34 11 48 W118 15 30. Stereo. Hrs open: 24 10281 W. Pico Blvd., 90064. Phone: (310) 203-0900. Fax: (310) 843-4961.E-mail: info@elsol963.com Web Site:www.elsol963.com Licensee: KXOL Licensing Inc. Group owner: Spanish Broadcasting System Inc. (acq 10-30-2003; $250 million). Population served: 12,000,000 Format: Sp. Target aud: 18-54. ♦Raul Alcarcon Jr., CEO; Raul Alarcon Jr., pres; Peter Remington, gen mgr; Jason Wilberding, gen sls mgr; Patty Castor, prom dir; Juan Carlos Hidalgo, progmg dir.

KXOS(FM)— Aug 7, 1957: 93.9 mhz; 18.5 kw horiz, 16 kw vert. Ant 3,008 ft TL: N34 13 36 W118 03 59. Stereo. Hrs open: 24 2600 W Olive Ave., 8th Fl., Burbank, 91505. Phone: (818) 525-5000. Fax: (818) 525-5002.E-mail: contacto@exitos939.com Web Site:www.exitos939.com Licensee: KMVN License LLC. Group owner: Emmis Communicationsl Corp. (acq 9-26-2000; grpsl). Format: Sp. ♦Janet Brainin, sls dir; Dean Carter, gen sls mgr; Dianna Jason, mktg dir, prom dir; Jimmy Steal, progmg dir.

KYPA(AM)— 1926: 1230 khz; 1 kw-U. TL: N34 02 15 W118 16 35. Hrs open: 24 747 E. Green St., Suite 400, Pasadena, 91101. Phone: (626) 844-8882. Fax: (626) 844-0156.E-mail: info@mrbi.net Licensee: Multicultural Radio Broadcasting Licensee LLC. Group owner: Multicultural Radio Broadcasting Inc. (acq 2-20-98; grpsl). Natl. Network: ABC, . Fleischman & Walsh L. Format: Korean. ♦David Sweeney, gen mgr & opns mgr.

KYSR(FM)— June 30, 1954: 98.7 mhz; 75 kw. Ant 1,180 ft TL: N34 07 08 W118 23 30. Stereo. Hrs open: 24 3400 W. Olive, Suite 550, Burbank, 91505. Phone: (818) 559-2252. Fax: (818) 566-4517.E-mail: starprogramming@clearchannel.com Web Site:www.star987.com Licensee: AMFM Broadcasting Licenses LLC. Group owner: Clear Channel Communications Inc. (acq 8-30-2000; grpsl). Population served: 49,200 Format: Hot adult contemp. Target aud: 25-54. Spec prog: Pub affrs 2 hrs wkly. ♦Greg Ashlock, gen mgr.

Los Banos

KLBS(AM)— May 1961: 1330 khz; 500 w-D, 5 kw-N, DA-N. TL: N37 05 51 W120 49 51. Stereo. Hrs open: 24 hrs. a day 401 Pacheco Blvd., 93635. Phone: (209) 826-0578/826-4996. Fax: (209) 826-1906.E-mail: pr@klbs.com Web Site:www.klbs.com Licensee: Ethnic Radio Los Banos Inc. (acq 5-82). Population served: 250,000 Format: Portuguese. Spec prog: Relg 8 hrs wkly. ♦Jose Encarnacao, gen mgr.

KQLB(FM)— November 1992: 106.9 mhz; 6 kw. 328 ft TL: N36 55 35 W120 50 42. Stereo. Hrs open: 24 401 Pacheco Blvd., 93635. Phone: (209) 827-0101. Fax: (209) 826-1906.E-mail: pr@kqlb.com Web Site:www.kqlb.com Licensee: VLB Broadcasting Inc. (acq 12-26-91). Population served: 250,000 Format: Sp/Mexican rgnl. ♦Batista Vieira, chmn; J.J. Encarnacao, gen mgr; Cidalia Sequeira, opns mgr; Jose Berumen, progmg dir.

Los Gatos

KRTY(FM)— July 9, 1966: 95.3 mhz; 880 w. 860 ft TL: N37 12 17 W121 56 56. Stereo. Hrs open: 24 Box 995, San Jose, 95108. Phone: (408) 293-8030. Fax: (408) 293-6124. Fax: (408) 995-0823.E-mail: dreyna@empirebroadcasting.com Web Site:www.krty.com Licensee: KRTY Ltd. Group owner: Empire Broadcasting Corp. (acq 2-93; $3.31 million; 1-18-93). Population served: 1,800,000 Format: Country. News staff: one. Target aud: 25-54. ♦Bob Kieve, pres; Nate Deaton, gen mgr, mktg dir; Stuart Hinkle, natl sls mgr; Jan Brock, rgnl sls mgr; Jamie Van Der Veen, prom dir; Julie Stevens, progmg dir; George Sampson, news dir; Mike Danberger, chief of engrg.

Los Molinos

KCEZ(FM)— 1999: 102.1 mhz; 25 kw. Ant 220 ft TL: N39 53 17 W122 37 38. Hrs open: 856 Manzanita Ct., Chico, 95926. Phone: (530) 342-2200. Fax: (530) 342-2260. Web Site:www.chicooldies.com Licensee: Results Radio Licensee L.L.C. Group owner: Fritz Communications Inc. (acq 6-11-99; grpsl). Format: Oldies. ♦John Graham, gen mgr; Dave Pack, gen sls mgr; Steve Michaels, progmg dir; J.D. Davis, chief of engrg; Candy Mason, traf mgr.

Los Osos-Baywood Park

KSTT-FM— 1987: 101.3 mhz; 4.86 kw. 1,506 ft TL: N35 21 38 W120 39 21. (CP: 3.4 kw, ant 1,685 ft.). Hrs open: 24 51 Zaca Ln., Suite 100, San Luis Obispo, 93401. Phone: (805) 545-0101. Fax: (805) 541-5303.E-mail: info@kstt.com Web Site:www.kstt.com Licensee: EDB SLO License LLC. Group owner: Clear Channel Communications Inc. (acq 11-30-2007; grpsl). Population served: 200,000 Format: Soft adult contemp. News staff: one; News: 5 hrs wkly. Target aud: 25-54. ♦Rich Hawkins, gen mgr; Andrew Winford, opns mgr, progmg dir; Pattie Wagner, natl sls mgr; Greg Russo, mktg dir, prom dir.

Lost Hills

KEBT(FM)— Dec 10, 1995: 96.9 mhz; 15.5 kw. Ant 413 ft TL: N35 19 40 W119 42 58. Hrs open: 1400 Easton Dr., Suite 144, Bakersfield, 93309. Phone: (661) 328-1410. Fax: (661) 328-0873. Licensee: AGM California. American General Media (acq 6-5-2006; $2.05 million). Format: Rgnl Mexican. Target aud: 25-54. Spec prog: Piolin Por La Manana. ♦Roger Fessler, gen mgr; Toni Snyder, gen sls mgr; Ricky Perez, progmg dir.

KQMX(FM)—Not on air, target date: unknown: 105.7 mhz; 24.46 kw. Ant 331 ft TL: N35 30 54 W119 57 30. Hrs open: 2801 Via Fortuna Dr., Suite 675, Austin, TX, 78746. Phone: (512) 329-5843. Fax: (512) 329-5847. Web Site:www.matineemedia.com Licensee: Ace Radio Corp. ♦Stephen Hackerman, pres.

Lucerne Valley

KIXA(FM)— November 1992: 106.5 mhz; 150 w. 1,066 ft TL: N34 23 08 W117 03 25. Hrs open: 24 12370 Hesperia Rd., Suite 16, Victorville, 92395. Phone: (760) 241-1313. Fax: (760) 241-0205.E-mail: kimjennings@edbroadcasters.com Web Site:www.thefox1065.com Licensee: EDB VV License LLC. Group owner: Clear Channel Communications Inc. (acq 11-30-2007; grpsl). Population served: 300,000 Natl. Rep: Christal,. Format: Classic Rock. News: 18 hrs wkly. Target aud: 16-45. ♦Tom Hoyt, VP, gen sls mgr & mktg mgr; Joe Pagano, progmg dir.

Ludlow

KDUQ(FM)— July 7, 1995: 102.5 mhz; 6 kw. Ant -164 ft TL: N34 43 21 W116 10 04. Stereo. Hrs open: 24
Rebroadcasts KDUC(FM) Barstow 100%.
29000 Radio Rd., Barstow, 92311. Phone: (760) 256-2121. Fax: (760) 256-5090.E-mail: doscostas@yahoo.com ABC/SMN Pine Gold Licensee: Dos Costas Communications Corp. (group owner; acq 6-18-03; grpsl). Population served: 220,000 Natl. Network: ABC, CBS, . Natl. Rep: Western Regional Broadcast Sales,. Fleischmann & Walsh. Format: CHR rhythmic. News staff: one; News: 7 hrs wkly. Target aud: 25-54; adults. Spec prog: Relg one hr wkly. ◆Roland Ulloa, stn mgr; Manny Lopez, opns mgr, gen sls mgr; Mike Garcia, progmg dir; Brad Sobel, news dir, chief of engrg.

KHWZ(FM)— 1992: 100.1 mhz; 25 kw. Ant -216 ft TL: N34 43 29 W116 09 24. Hrs open: 24
Rebroadcasts KHDR 100%.
Box 1668, Barstow, 90025. Phone: (760) 256-0326. Fax: (760) 256-9507.E-mail: tim@highwayradio.com Web Site:www.thehighwaystations.com Licensee: KHWY Inc. (group owner). Natl. Network: Jones Radio Networks, . Format: AOR. Target aud: 35 plus; travelers on I-15 & I-40. ◆Gary Shorman, pres; Kirk M. Anderson, exec VP; Timothy B. Anderson, VP & gen mgr; Judy Robinson, gen sls mgr, rgnl sls mgr.

Madera

KHIT-FM— October 1992: 107.1 mhz; 9.9 kw. Ant 515 ft TL: N37 07 40 W119 40 38. Hrs open: 1110 E. Olive Ave., Fresno, 93728. Phone: (559) 497-1100. Fax: (559) 497-1125.E-mail: mginsburg@lotsusfresno.com Licensee: Lotus Communications Corp. Group owner: Lotus Communications Corp. (acq 3-10-99). Population served: 1,500,000 Natl. Rep: Lotus Entravision Reps LLC,. Leventhal, Senter & Lerman. Format: Sp contemp hits music. Target aud: 18-49. ◆Dan Crotty, gen mgr; Mike Ginsburg, gen sls mgr, prom mgr; Jose Berumen, progmg dir; Paul Klein Kramer, chief of engrg.

KHOT(AM)— Dec 31, 1956: 1250 khz; 1.5 kw-D, 1 kw-N, DA-2. TL: N36 57 58 W120 02 06. Hrs open: 24 Box 180, Tahoma, 96142. Phone: (530) 584-5700. Fax: (530) 584-5705.E-mail: info@ihradio.org Web Site:www.ihradio.org Licensee: Redwood Family Services Inc. Population served: 500,000 Format: Relg-Catholic. News staff: one; News: 30 hrs wkly. Target aud: 25-54. ◆Doug Sherman, pres.

KOND(FM)—(Clovis, Sept 30, 1974): 92.1 mhz; 36.9 kw. Ant 567 ft TL: N37 07 40 W119 40 38. Stereo. Hrs open: 1981 N. Gateway Blvd., Suite 101, Fresno, 93727. Phone: (559) 456-4000. Fax: (559) 251-9555. Web Site:www.univision.com Licensee: Univision Radio License Corp. Group owner: Univision Radio (acq 2-18-2004; $8 million). Format: Rgnl Mexican. ◆Angela Navarrete, gen mgr.

Magalia

***KLVC(FM)**— Jan 1, 1993: 88.3 mhz; 5.7 kw. Ant 1,184 ft TL: N39 57 45 W121 42 52. Stereo. Hrs open: 24
Rebroadcasts KLVB-FM Red Bluff 100%.
2351 Sunset Blvd., Suite 170-218, Rocklin, 95765. Phone: (916) 251-1600. Fax: (916) 251-1650.E-mail: klove@klove.com Web Site:www.klove.com Licensee: Educational Media Foundation Inc. Group owner: EMF Broadcasting. Population served: 357,000 Natl. Network: K-Love, . Shaw Pittman. Format: Contemp music. News staff: 3. Target aud: 33—40; Judeo-Christian, female. ◆Richard Jenkins, pres; Mike Novak, VP; Keith Whipple, dev dir; Sam Wallington, engrg dir; Karen Johson, news rptr.

Mammoth Lakes

KMMT(FM)— Apr 3, 1973: 106.5 mhz; 360 w. Ant 2,371 ft TL: N37 37 42 W119 01 47. Stereo. Hrs open: 24 Box 1284, 94 Laurel Mountain Rd., 93546. Phone: (760) 934-8888. Fax: (760) 934-2429.E-mail: kmmtradioworks@yahoo.com Licensee: Mammoth Mountain F.M. Associates Inc. Population served: 100,000 Format: Modern adult contemp. News staff: one; News: 2 hrs wkly. Target aud: 18-54; active, athletic, affluent adults. Spec prog: Jazz 2 hrs, classic rock 4 hrs wkly. ◆David A. Digerness, pres; Shellie Woods, gen mgr.

Manteca

KMRQ(FM)— Jan 15, 1979: 96.7 mhz; 1.5 kw. Ant 466 ft TL: N37 43 44 W121 07 34. Stereo. Hrs open: 24 2121 Lancey Dr., Modesto, 95355. Phone: (209) 551-1306. Fax: (209) 551-1359. Web Site:www.rock967.com Licensee: Capstar TX L.P. Group owner: Clear Channel Communications Inc. (acq 8-30-2000; grpsl). Mullin, Rhyne,

Emmons & Topel. Format: Active rock. News staff: one. Target aud: 25-54. ◆Bill Mick, progmg VP & progmg dir.

Maricopa

KXTT(FM)— 2009: 94.9 mhz; 6 kw. Ant 312 ft TL: N35 05 39 W119 27 40. Hrs open: 6901 McDivitt Dr., Suite D, Bakersfield, 93313-2047. Phone: (805) 240-2070. Fax: (805) 240-5960. Web Site:www.radiolazer.com Licensee: Lazer Licenses LLC. (acq 6-11-2007; $3.85 million with KEAL(FM) Taft). ◆Neal Robinson, pres.

Marina

KTOM-FM— Apr 6, 1982: 92.7 mhz; 6.9 kw. 567 ft TL: N36 33 12 W121 47 05. Stereo. Hrs open: 24 903 N. Main St., Salinas, 93906. Phone: (831) 755-8181. Fax: (831) 755-8193. Web Site:www.ktom.com Licensee: CC Licenses LLC. Group owner: Clear Channel Communications Inc. (acq 9-22-97; grpsl). Natl. Rep: D & R Radio,. Format: Country. News staff: one; News: 5 hrs wkly. Target aud: 25-54; men. ◆Rhonda McCormack, gen mgr; Jen Taylor, prom dir; Johnny Morgan, progmg dir.

Mariposa

KDJK(FM)— 1994: 103.9 mhz; 71 w. 2,047 ft TL: N37 32 00 W120 01 29. Stereo. Hrs open: 24 1581 Cummins Dr., Suite 135, Modesto, 95358-6402. Phone: (209) 572-0104. Fax: (209) 522-2061.E-mail: info@104thehawk.com Web Site:www.104thehawk.com Licensee: Citadel Broadcasting Co. Group owner: Citadel Broadcasting Corp. (acq 7-30-93; $6 million;8-23-93). Natl. Rep: Christal,. Format: Classic Rock. Target aud: 18-54. ◆Roy Williams, gen mgr; Richard Perry, opns dir, progmg dir; Jean Western, gen sls mgr; Gary Williams, engrg mgr, chief of engrg.

KUBB(FM)— July 4, 1977: 96.3 mhz; 1.9 kw. 2,112 ft TL: N37 32 00 W120 01 29. Stereo. Hrs open: 24 Box 429, 510 W. 19th St., Merced, 95340. Phone: (209) 383-7900. Fax: (209) 723-8461.E-mail: mcadam@kubb.com Web Site:www.kubb.com Licensee: Buckley Broadcasting of Monterey. Group owner: Buckley Broadcasting Corp. (acq 7-1-85; $640,000; 5-20-85). Population served: 1,000,000 Natl. Network: Westwood One, . Natl. Rep: D & R Radio,. Format: Country. News staff: one; News: 2 hrs wkly. Target aud: 25-54. Spec prog: Farm 2 hrs wkly. ◆Mike McAdam, VP, gen mgr; Mike Peters, gen sls mgr, rgnl sls mgr; Rene Roberts, opns dir & progmg dir.

Marysville

KKCY(FM)—See Colusa

KMYC(AM)— 1940: 1410 khz; 5 kw-D, 1 kw-N, DA-2. TL: N39 08 18 W121 33 15. Hrs open: 6 AM-midnight Box 669, 95901. Phone: (530) 742-5555. Fax: (530) 741-3758.E-mail: kmyc@xyix.com Licensee: Thomas Huth. Group owner: Huth Broadcasting. . Population served: 300,000 Format: Talk radio. News staff: one. Target aud: 18 plus; general. Spec prog: Indian/Punjabi 2 hrs wkly. ◆Thomas Huth, CEO, gen mgr & rgnl sls mgr; Jerry Snaper, engrg VP, chief of engrg.

KOBO(AM)—See Yuba City

KRCX-FM— Oct 12, 1994: 99.9 mhz; 1.74 kw. Ant 2,181 ft TL: N39 12 20 W121 49 10. Stereo. Hrs open: 24 1436 Auburn Blvd., Sacramento, 95815. Phone: (916) 646-4000. Fax: (916) 646-1958.E-mail: jverdier@entravision.com Web Site:www.entravision.com Licensee: Entravision Holdings LLC. Group owner: Entravision Communications Corp. (acq 3-14-2000; grpsl). Population served: 1,500,000 Format: Mexican rgnl, Sp. News staff: 2. Target aud: 18-49. ◆Larry Lamanski, gen mgr; Salvador Lopez, prom dir; Juan Carlos Sanchez, progmg dir.

KUBA(AM)—See Yuba City

McCloud

***KLDD(FM)**— 2008: 91.9 mhz; 35 w. Ant 2,374 ft TL: N41 20 43 W122 11 42. Hrs open: Jefferson Public Radio, 1250 Siskiyou Blvd., Ashland, OR, 97520. Phone: (541) 552-6301. Fax: (541) 552-8565. Web Site:www.ijpr.org Licensee: The State of Oregon Acting By and Through the Oregon State Board of Higher Education for Southern Oregon University. Natl. Network: NPR, . Format: Classics and news. ◆Ron Kramer, gen mgr.

McFarland

KBQF(FM)—Not on air, target date: unknown: 104.3 mhz; 6 kw. Ant 327 ft TL: N35 31 35 W119 18 43. Hrs open: 977 W. 7th St., Oxnard, 93030-6757. Phone: (805) 486-4400. Licensee: JAB Broadcasting LLC. ◆Javier Orosco, gen mgr.

KIWI(FM)—Licensed to McFarland. See Bakersfield

McKinleyville

KMDR(FM)—Not on air, target date: unknown: 95.1 mhz; 2.45 kw. Ant 1,040 ft TL: N40 49 32 W124 00 05. Hrs open: 1551 Queens Rd., Los Angeles, 90069. Phone: (323) 656-0796. Licensee: William W. McCutchen III. ◆William W. McCutchen III, gen mgr.

***KNDZ(FM)**— 2009: Stn currently dark. 89.3 mhz; 750 w vert. Ant 1,005 ft TL: N40 49 32 W124 00 05. Hrs open:
Rebroadcasts KVIP-FM Redding 100%.
1139 Hartnell Ave., Redding, 96002-2113. Phone: (530) 222-4455. Fax: (530) 222-4484.E-mail: info@kvip.org Web Site:www.kvip.org Licensee: Pacific Cascade Communications Corp. (acq 2-9-2009; $62,500 for CP). ◆David L. Morrow, VP.

Mecca

KRCK-FM— 2001: 97.7 mhz; 1.25 kw. Ant 718 ft TL: N33 39 18 W115 59 16. Hrs open: 73-733 Fred Waring Dr., Suite 201, Palm Desert, 92260. Phone: (760) 341-0123. Fax: (760) 341-7455.E-mail: sales@krck.com Web Site:www.krck.com Licensee: Playa Del Sol Broadcasters. Format: Rock of the 80s. ◆Edward Stolz, gen mgr; Kevin Childs, stn mgr.

Mendocino

***KAKX(FM)**— Jan 15, 1997: 89.3 mhz; 250 w. 7 ft TL: N39 18 30 W123 48 02. Stereo. Hrs open: 24 Box 1154, 95460. Phone: (707) 937-1200.E-mail: audio@mcn.org Web Site:www.kakx.org Licensee: Mendocino Unified School District. Population served: 10,000 Format: Educ, var, Rock. ◆Peter Davidson, pres; Marshall Brown, gen mgr.

KMFB(FM)— November 1966: 92.7 mhz; 3 kw. 165 ft TL: N39 20 33 W123 46 51. Stereo. Hrs open: 24 101-E Boatyard Dr., Fort Bragg, 95437. Phone: (707) 964-5307. Fax: (707) 964-3299.E-mail: generalmail@kmfb-fm.com Web Site:www.kmfb-fm.com Licensee: Four Rivers Broadcasting Inc. (group owner; (acq 7-21-2005; grpsl). Population served: 75,000 Wire Svc: Agence France-Presse (AFP) Format: Vintage rock, professional sports. News staff: 4. Target aud: 35-54. ◆Bob Woelfel, gen mgr, gen sls mgr, progmg dir, progmg mgr, mus dir; Liz Helenchild, mus dir; Ed Kowas, news dir.

***KPMO(AM)**— Nov 16, 1966: 1300 khz; 5 kw-D, 77 w-N. TL: N39 20 33 W123 46 51. Hrs open: 24 hrs Jefferson Public Radio, 1250 Siskiyou Blvd., Ashland, OR, 97520. Phone: (541) 552-6301. Fax: (541) 552-8565.E-mail: info@ijpr.org Web Site:www.ijpr.org Licensee: JPR Foundation Inc. (acq 8-8-02). Population served: 25,000 Natl. Network: NPR, PRI, . Ernest Sanchez. Wire Svc: AP Format: News/talk. News staff: one. Target aud: General. ◆Ronald Kramer, CEO; Ronald Kramer, gen mgr; Bryon Lambert, opns dir.

Mendota

KMEN(FM)— 2007: 100.5 mhz; 6 kw. Ant 144 ft TL: N36 38 50 W120 21 02. Hrs open: 1450 E. Bardsley Ave., Tulare, 93274. Phone: (213) 745-6224. Fax: (213) 745-7577.E-mail: mmartinez@lunacommunication.net Licensee: MBP Licensee LLC. Group owner: Moon Broadcasting (acq 3-30-2001; $350,000). Format: Rgnl Mexican. ◆Abel de Luna, pres; Angelica Figueroa, gen sls mgr; Yesenia de Luna, progmg dir.

Merced

KABX-FM— Dec 18, 1975: 97.5 mhz; 50 kw. 490 ft TL: N37 22 31 W120 27 37. Stereo. Hrs open: 24 Prog sep from AM 1020 W. Main, 95340. Phone: (209) 723-2191. Fax: (209) 383-2950. Format: Oldies. ◆Dave Luna, progmg dir.

***KAMB(FM)**— Nov 6, 1967: 101.5 mhz; 1.85 kw. 2,093 ft TL: N37 32 01 W120 01 46. Stereo. Hrs open: 24 90 E. 16th St., 95340-5099. Phone: (209) 723-1015. Fax: (209) 723-1945.E-mail: kamb@celebrationradio.com Web Site:www.celebrationradio.com Licensee: Central Valley Broadcasting Co. Inc. Population served: 1,500,000 Natl. Network: AP Radio, Moody, . Fletcher, Heald & Hildreth. Format:

Contemp Christian. News staff: one; News: 5 hrs wkly. Target aud: 29-54; Christian adults in central California. ♦Dan Finn, pres; Tim Land, CEO & gen mgr; Mark Murdock, opns dir; Jinous Vartan, mktg dir, prom mgr; Dave Benton, progmg dir, mus dir.

KBKY(FM)— January 2002: 94.1 mhz; 6 kw. Ant 328 ft TL: N37 27 59 W120 14 09. Hrs open: 450 Grogan Ave., Suite A, 95340. Phone: (209) 385-9994. Fax: (209) 385-9982.E-mail: mmeroney941@mercednet.com Web Site:www.kbky.com Licensee: KM Radio of Merced L.L.C. (acq 9-30-99). Format: Adult contemp. ♦Dave Putonen, gen sls mgr; Mike Meroney, gen mgr & prom mgr; Matthew Stone, progmg dir; Chuck Hughes, chief of engrg; Jim Wells, traf mgr.

KNAH(FM)— May 14, 1992: 106.3 mhz; 4 kw. Ant 403 ft TL: N37 25 35 W120 26 25. Hrs open: 24 1020 W. Main St., 95340-4521. Phone: (209) 723-2191. Fax: (209) 383-2950.E-mail: info@radiomerced.com Web Site:www.radiomerced.com Licensee: Mapleton License of Merced LLC. (group owner; (acq 6-1-2002; grpsl). Format: Classic hits. Target aud: 25-54; upscale professionals. ♦Andrew Adams, gen mgr; Chad Gammage, gen sls mgr; Chris Ashton, progmg dir; Rick McMillion, chief of engrg.

KTIQ(AM)— Nov 1, 1999: 1660 khz; 10 kw-D, 1 kw-N. TL: N37 16 41 W120 37 35. Hrs open: 24 1020 Main St., 95340. Phone: (209) 723-21911. Fax: (209) 383-2950. Licensee: Mapleton License of Merced LLC. (group owner; (acq 6-1-2002; grpsl). Population served: 202,000 Format: News/talk, Sp. Target aud: 25-54. ♦Andrew Adams, gen mgr & opns VP.

KUBB(FM)—See Mariposa

KYOS(AM)— October 1936: 1480 khz; 5 kw-U, DA-N. TL: N37 22 30 W120 27 37. Hrs open: 24 1020 W. Main, 95340. Phone: (209) 723-2191. Fax: (209) 383-2950. Licensee: Mapleton License of Merced LLC. (group owner; acq 6-5-2002; grpsl). Population served: 186,000 Natl. Network: CBS, . Natl. Rep: Christal,. Format: News/talk. News staff: 2; News: 20 hrs wkly. Target aud: 25-54. Spec prog: Farm 5 hrs, gospel one hr wkly. ♦Adam Nathanson, pres; Andrew Adams, gen mgr, progmg mgr; Dennis Daily, progmg dir.

Middletown

***KLVR(FM)**— Oct 15, 1982: 91.9 mhz; 830 w. Ant 2,988 ft TL: N38 40 09 W122 37 53. Stereo. Hrs open: 24 2351 Sunset Blvd., Sute 170-218, Rocklin, 95765. Phone: (916) 251-1600. Fax: (916) 251-1650.E-mail: klove@klove.com Web Site:www.klove.com Licensee: Educational Media Foundation. Group owner: EMF Broadcasting (acq 1986). Population served: 775,000 Natl. Network: K-Love, . Shaw Pittman. Format: Contemp Christian. News staff: 3. Target aud: 25-44; Judeo-Christian females. ♦Richard Jenkins, pres; Mike Novak, VP; Keith Whipple, dev dir; David Pierce, progmg dir; Ed Lenane, news dir; Sam Wallington, engrg dir; Arthur Vassar, traf mgr.

Mission Viejo

***KSBR(FM)**— May 7, 1979: 88.5 mhz; 620 w. 600 ft TL: N33 30 10 W117 36 06. Stereo. Hrs open: 28000 Marguerite Pkwy., 92692. Phone: (949) 582-5727. Fax: (949) 347-9693. Web Site:www.ksbr.net Licensee: South Orange County Community College District. Population served: 500,000 Natl. Network: AP Network News, . Wire Svc: AP Format: Jazz. News staff: one. Target aud: 25-54. Spec prog: Latin 3 hrs, blues 3 hrs, reggae 3 hrs, electronic 4 hrs, ragtime 2 hrs, folk 2 hrs wkly. ♦Terry Wedel, opns dir; Dawn Kamber, news dir; Mark Schiffelbein, engrg dir.

Modesto

***KADV(FM)**— November 1988: 90.5 mhz; 1.5 kw. 200 ft TL: N37 36 26 W120 57 26. Stereo. Hrs open: 24 2031 Academy Pl., Ceres, 95307. Phone: (209) 537-1201. Fax: (209) 537-1945.E-mail: kadv@sbcglobal.net Web Site:www.kadv.org Licensee: Modesto Adventist Academy. Population served: 500,000 Natl. Network: Moody, . Format: Educ, relg, music. News: 14 hrs wkly. Target aud: 30 plus. Spec prog: Sp one hr wkly. ♦Jerry Moore, gen mgr; Steve White, stn mgr & progmg dir.

KATM(FM)— 1948: 103.3 mhz; 50 kw. Ant 500 ft TL: N37 34 30 W121 21 13. Stereo. Hrs open: 1581 Cummins Dr., Suite 135, 95358. Phone: (209) 523-7756. Fax: (209) 522-2061.E-mail: info@katmfm.com Web Site:www.katmfm.com Licensee: Citadel Broadcasting Co. Format: Country. Target aud: 25-64; mass appeal. ♦Bubba Black, progmg dir.

KBBU(FM)— 1999: 93.9 mhz; 4 kw. Ant 403 ft TL: N37 39 00 W121 01 24. Hrs open: 24

Simulcast with KTTA(FM) Esparto 100%.

500 Media Place, Sacramento, 95815. Phone: (916) 368-6300. Fax: (916) 441-6480.E-mail: abalderas@bustosmedia.com Web Site:www.lakebuena.com Licensee: Bustos Media of California License LLC. (acq 12-15-2004; $21.7 million with KLMG(FM) Esparto). Format: Rgnl Mexican. ♦Amparo Perez-Cook, gen mgr, stn mgr; Javier Gonzalez, prom dir; Juan Gonzalez, progmg dir; Adela Garcia, news dir; Mark Sedaka, chief of engrg; Cynthia Sanchez, traf mgr.

KCIV(FM)—See Mount Bullion

KESP(AM)— 1951: 970 khz; 1 kw-U, DA-2. TL: N37 41 28 W120 57 11. Stereo. Hrs open: 24 1581 Cummins Dr., Suite 135, 95358. Phone: (209) 523-7756. Fax: (209) 522-2061.E-mail: info@espnradio970.com Web Site:www.espnradio970.com Licensee: Citadel Broadcasting Co. Group owner: Citadel Broadcasting Corp. (acq 5-18-92; $12.5 million grpsl, including co-located FM;6-8-92) Population served: 274300 Natl. Network: ABC, CBS, . Natl. Rep: McGavren Guild,. Format: MOR, sports. Target aud: 35 plus. ♦Roy Williams, gen mgr; Jean Western, gen sls mgr; Eric Nelson, news dir; Jeff Silvius, progmg.

KFIV(AM)— 1950: 1360 khz; 4 kw-D, 950 w-N, DA-2. TL: N37 39 52 W120 57 00. Hrs open: 2121 Lancey Dr., 95355. Phone: (209) 551-1306. Fax: (209) 551-1359. Web Site:www.kfiv1360.com Licensee: Capstar TX L.P. Group owner: Clear Channel Communiications Inc. (acq 8-30-2000; grpsl). Population served: 375,000 Natl. Network: ABC, . Format: News/talk. Target aud: 25-54. ♦Gary Granger, gen mgr; Rick Myers, gen sls mgr; Leslie Davidson, prom dir; Bill Mick, progmg dir.

KHKK(FM)— 1949: 104.1 mhz; 50 kw. 500 ft TL: N37 39 10 W121 28 38. Stereo. Hrs open: 24 1581 Cummins Dr., Suite 135, 95358-6402. Phone: (209) 572-0104. Fax: (209) 522-2061.E-mail: info@104thehawk.com Web Site:www.104thehawk.com Licensee: Citadel Broadcasting Co. Group owner: Citadel Broadcasting Corp. (acq 10-1-93). Population served: 250,000 Natl. Rep: McGavren Guild,. Format: Rock/AOR, classic rock. News staff: one; News: 5 hrs wkly. Target aud: 25-49; baby boomers who grew up with rock and roll. ♦Roy Williams, VP & gen mgr; Richard Perry, progmg dir; Farid Suleman, engrg mgr, chief of engrg.

KHTN(FM)—See Planada

KJSN(FM)— July 4, 1977: 102.3 mhz; 6 kw. 300 ft TL: N37 40 47 W120 55 28. Stereo. Hrs open: Prog sep from AM Box 3408, 95353. Phone: (209) 551-1306. Fax: (209) 551-1359. Web Site:www.sunny102fm.com Licensee: Capstar TX L.P. Population served: 100,000 Format: Adult contemp. Target aud: 25-49. ♦Gary Michaels, progmg dir; Steve Minshall, engrg mgr.

KMPH(AM)— July 10, 2006: 840 khz; 5 kw-U, DA-2. TL: N37 42 34 W120 43 34. Hrs open: 1192 Norwegian Ave., 95350. Phone: (209) 527-8400. Phone: (415) 362-8686. Fax: (209) 526-0820.E-mail: jpappas@kmph840.com Web Site:www.kmph840.com Licensee: Pappas Radio of Modesto LLC. Group owner: Pappas Telecasting Companies (acq 11-5-2003). Population served: 774,926 Format: Talk/personality. Target aud: 35-64; Adults:. ♦Harry J. Pappas, CEO; Jim Pappas, VP; Jim P. Pappas, gen mgr; Kevin Barrett, progmg dir.

***KMPO(FM)**— January 1984: 88.7 mhz; 2 kw. 1,500 ft TL: N37 32 00 W120 01 29. Stereo. Hrs open: 24 5005 E. Belmont Ave., Fresno, 93727. Phone: (559) 455-5777. Fax: (559) 455-5778.E-mail: mail@radiobilingue.org Web Site:www.radiobilingue.org Licensee: Radio Bilingue Inc. Format: Ethnic. News staff: 5; News: 11 hrs wkly. Target aud: 16 plus; Latinos. Spec prog: Black 3 hrs, folk 4 hrs, Filipino one hr wkly. ♦Hugo Morales, CEO; Maria Erana, gen mgr, opns dir; Phil Traynor, dev dir; Samuel Cozco, news dir; Bill Bach, chief of engrg.

KOSO(FM)—(Patterson, June 6, 1966: 92.9 mhz; 6 kw. Ant 328 ft TL: N37 36 24.2 W121 02 37.2. Stereo. Hrs open: 24 2121 Lancey Dr., 95355. Phone: (209) 551-1306. Fax: (209) 551-1359. Web Site:www.b931.com Licensee: Capstar TX L.P. Group owner: Clear Channel Communications Inc. (acq 8-30-2000; grpsl). Population served: 900,000 Format: Adult contemp. News staff: one; News: 5 hrs wkly. Target aud: 25-54. ♦Gary Granger, gen mgr; Mark Granger, sls dir; Zack Davis, progmg dir.

KVIN(AM)—See Ceres

Mojave

KCEL(FM)— 2009: 96.1 mhz; 5.4 kw. Ant -10 ft TL: N35 07 23 W118 12 06. Hrs open: Coloma Mojave LLC, 601 Belvedere St., San Francisco, 94117. Phone: (415) 391-2234. Fax: (415) 391-4912. Licensee: Coloma Mojave LLC. ♦Scott Donohue, CEO & pres.

***KCRY(FM)**— June 2000: 88.1 mhz; 10.5 kw. Ant -95 ft TL: N35 07 20 W118 12 25. Hrs open:

Rebroadcasts KCRW(FM) Santa Monica 100%.

c/o KCRW(FM), 1900 Pico Blvd., Santa Monica, 90405. Phone: (310) 450-5183. Phone: (888) 600-kcrw. Fax: (310) 450-7172.E-mail: mail@kcrw.org Web Site:www.kcrw.com Licensee: Santa Monica Community College District. Natl. Network: NPR, . Wire Svc: AP Format: Eclectic, news. ♦Ruth Seymour, gen mgr; Mike Newport, opns mgr; David Kleinbart, dev dir; Nic Harcourt, mus dir; Steve Herbert, chief of engrg.

KSRY(FM)—See Tehachapi

KTPI(AM)— May 1, 1958: 1340 khz; 1 kw-U. TL: N35 02 23 W118 08 57. Hrs open: 24 348 East Avenue K-4, Lancaster, 93535. Phone: (661) 942-1121. Fax: (661) 723-5512. Licensee: CC Licenses LLC. Group owner: Clear Channel Communications Inc. (acq 11-21-2003; grpsl). Population served: 400,000 Natl. Rep: Christal,. Latham & Watkins. Target aud: 35 plus; Adult Christian community. ♦Larry Thornhill, gen mgr; Shaun Palmer, gen sls mgr.

KTPI-FM— May 1966: 97.7 mhz; 3 kw. Ant 298 ft TL: N34 58 45 W118 10 02. Stereo. Hrs open: 24 352 East Ave. K4, Lancaster, 93535. Phone: (661) 942-1121. Fax: (661) 723-5512.E-mail: info@ktpi.com Web Site:www.ktpi.com Licensee: Aloha Station Trust LLC, as Trustee Group owner: Clear Channel Communications Inc. (acq 7-30-2008). Population served: 300,000 Thompson Hine LLP. Format: Country. News staff: one. Target aud: 25-54. ♦Jim Bell, gen mgr; Ron Vacchina, gen sls mgr; John Ivey, progmg dir.

Monte Rio

KVRV(FM)—Licensed to Monte Rio. See Santa Rosa

Montecito

KJEE(FM)— March 1994: 92.9 mhz; 820 w. 886 ft TL: N34 27 57 W119 40 37. Hrs open: 302 W. Carrillo St., 2nd Fl., Santa Barbara, 93101. Phone: (805) 963-4676. Fax: (805) 963-8166.E-mail: sales@kjee.com Web Site:www.kjee.com Licensee: Montecito FM Inc. Format: Modern rock. Target aud: 18-34; general. ♦Eddie Gutierrez, gen mgr, progmg dir; Steve Meade, rgnl sls mgr; Ryan Zoldas, prom dir; John Palmmentari, news dir; Dean Burt, chief of engrg.

Monterey

KIDD(AM)— 1955: 630 khz; 1 kw-U, DA-2. TL: N36 41 28 W121 48 00. Hrs open: Box 1391, 93942. Phone: (831) 649-0969. Fax: (831) 649-3335.E-mail: jsouza@oldies630.com Web Site:www.oldies630.com Licensee: Buckley Communications Inc. (acq 1995; $200,000). Format: Oldies. ♦Jim Souza, sls dir; Kevin Kahl, progmg dir.

KKHK(FM)—(Carmel, Dec 4, 1993: 95.5 mhz; 1.7 kw. Ant 630 ft TL: N36 33 09 W121 47 17. Hrs open: 24 60 Garden Ct., Suite 300, 93940-5370. Phone: (831) 658-5200. Fax: (831) 658-5299. Licensee: Mapleton License of Monterey LLC. (acq 6-7-2005; $3.75 million). Population served: 527,900 Natl. Rep: McGavren Guild,. Leventhal, Senter & Lerman. Format: Country. ♦Adam Nathanson, pres; Dale Hendry, gen mgr; Jodi Morgan, gen sls mgr; Sybil DeAngelo, prom dir; Kenny Allen, progmg dir, progmg mgr; Veldon Leverich, chief of engrg.

KNRY(AM)— October 1935: 1240 khz; 1 kw-U. TL: N36 36 56 W121 53 53. Hrs open: 24 651 Cannery Row, Suite 1, 93940. Phone: (831) 372-1074. Fax: (831) 372-3585.E-mail: Natalie@knry.com Web Site:www.knry.com Licensee: People's Radio Inc. (group owner; (acq 8-31-2000; $1.1 million with KRXA(AM) Carmel Valley). Population served: 650,000 Natl. Network: CBS, . Haley, Bader & Potts. Format: News/talk. Target aud: 35 plus. ♦Jim Vossen, chief of opns & progmg dir.

KOCN(FM)—See Pacific Grove

KPRC-FM—See Salinas

KSES-FM—See Seaside

KTOM-FM—See Marina

KWAV(FM)— Oct 14, 1961: 96.9 mhz; 18 kw. 2,450 ft TL: N36 32 05 W121 37 14. Stereo. Hrs open: Box 1391, 5 Harris Court Bldg. C., 93942. Phone: (831) 649-0969. Fax: (831) 649-3335.E-mail: kwav97fm@kwav.com Web Site:www.kwav.com Licensee: Buckley Broadcasting Corp. of Monterey Group owner: Buckley Broadcasting Corp. (acq 5-1-80; $700,000; 3-17-80). Population served: 97,600

Natl. Rep: Eastman Radio,. Wire Svc: AP Format: Adult contemp. Target aud: 18-54; primarily women. ◆ Kathy Baker, gen mgr; Sean Stade, gen sls mgr; Bernie Moody, progmg dir; Karen Hamilton, news dir; Ron Warren, chief of engrg; Melanie Swain, traf mgr.

Moraga

*KSMC(FM)— Sept 22, 1977: 89.5 mhz; 800 w. 95 ft TL: N37 50 25 W122 06 36. Stereo. Hrs open: 24 Box 3223, St. Mary's College, 94575. Phone: (925) 631-4252. Phone: (925) 631-4772. Fax: (925) 376-5766.E-mail: ksmc@stmarys-ca.edu Web Site:www.ksmc895.com Licensee: Associated Students of St. Mary's College of California. Population served: 15,000 Wire Svc: Dow Jones News Service Format: CHR, educ, country. Target aud: 15-30; young, urban & willing to experiment. Spec prog: Relg 2 hrs, class 4 hrs, Sp 3 hrs, jazz 5 hrs wkly. ◆ Noel Cilker, gen mgr; Jessica Fajardo, prom dir, sports cmtr; Will McCoster, progmg dir; Nick McAlpine, mus dir; Ed Tywoniak, chief of engrg.

Moreno Valley

KHPI(AM)— 1991: Stn currently dark. 1530 khz; 10 kw-D, DA-3. TL: N34 00 42 W117 11 03. Hrs open: Box 909, 92556. Secondary address: 24490 Sunnymead Blvd., #215 92553. Phone: (951) 247-5479. Fax: (951) 247-2790.E-mail: info@khpyam.com Licensee: Dr. D.L. Van Voorhis. Population served: 1,900,000 Fletcher, Heald & Hildreth. ◆ Dr. D.L. Van Voorhis, pres; Bill DeGeorge, gen mgr.

KHPY(AM)— Jan 16, 2003: 1670 khz; 10 kw-D, 9 kw-N. TL: N34 00 42 W117 11 03. Hrs open: Box 909, 92556. Phone: (909) 247-5479. Fax: (909) 247-2790. Licensee: Delbert L. Van Voorhis. Format: Sp relg. ◆ Bill DeGeorge, gen mgr.

Morgan Hill

KSQQ(FM)— December 1990: 96.1 mhz; 530 w. 781 ft TL: N37 10 03 W121 34 20. (CP: 1 kw). Hrs open: 1629-C Alum Rock Ave., San Jose, 95116. Phone: (408) 258-9699. Fax: (408) 258-9770.E-mail: pr@ksqq.com Web Site:www.ksqq.com Licensee: Coyote Communications Inc. Population served: 10,000,000 Format: Ethnic. ◆ Batista Vieira, pres, gen mgr; Peter Mieuli, VP; Aida Barbosa, sls dir; Joao Manuel, progmg dir.

Morro Bay

*KESC(FM)— May 1, 1991: 99.7 mhz; 285 w. Ant 1,489 ft TL: N35 21 40 W120 39 21. Hrs open: 24 Box 77913, Los Angeles, 90007-0913. Phone: (213) 225-7400. Fax: (213) 225-7410. Web Site:www.kusc.org Licensee: University of Southern California (acq 5-1-2009; $1.2 million). Population served: 275,000 Format: Classical. ◆ Brenda Barnes, pres; Eric DeWeese, gen mgr.

KLMM(FM)— September 1997: 94.1 mhz; 890 w. Ant 863 ft TL: N35 15 11 W120 45 42. Hrs open: 24 300 E. Mill St., Suite 301, Santa Maria, 93454-4467. Phone: (805) 928-9796. Fax: (805) 928-3367.E-mail: lazer94@acninc.net Web Site:www.radiolazer.com Licensee: Lazer Broadcasting Corp. (group owner; (acq 8-7-2000; $1.115 million with KLUN(FM) Paso Robles). Booth, Freret, Imlay & Tepper. Format: Adult contemp, Sp. News: 6 hrs wkly. Target aud: 25-54; general. ◆ Jose Guzman, gen mgr, gen sls mgr; Salvador Prieto, chief of opns & progmg dir.

Moss Beach

*KLSI(FM)— May 1, 2006: 89.3 mhz; 1 w horiz, 8 w vert. Ant 1,635 ft TL: N37 33 44 W122 28 46. Stereo. Hrs open: 24 Rebroadcasts WAZQ(FM) Layton, FL 100%. Educational Public Radio Inc., 6910 N.W. 2nd Terr., Boca Raton, FL, 33487-2325. Phone: (561) 912-9002.E-mail: bill@qfmmusic.com Web Site:qfmonline.com Licensee: Educational Public Radio Inc. Format: Hot adult contemp. Target aud: 18-54; adults. ◆ Bill Lacy, pres.

Mount Bullion

KCIV(FM)— Apr 24, 1989: 99.9 mhz; 1.9 kw. Ant 2,094 ft TL: N37 32 00 W120 01 29. Hrs open: 24 1031 15th St., Suite One, Modesto, 95354. Phone: (209) 524-8999. Fax: (209) 524-9088.E-mail: kciv@bottradionetwork.com Web Site:bottradionetwork.com Licensee: Bott Communications Inc. Group owner: Bott Radio Network Format: Christian info. Target aud: 25-54; Christian family audience. ◆ Richard P. Bott, pres; Richard Bott II, VP; Kathleen Reynolds, stn mgr.

Mount Shasta

*KKLC(FM)— Nov 26, 1977: 107.9 mhz; 20 kw horiz. Ant 815 ft TL: N41 13 37 W122 14 23. Hrs open: 24 Rebroadcasts KLVR(FM) Santa Rosa 100%. 2351 Sunset Blvd., Suite 170-218, Rocklin, 95765. Phone: (916) 251-1600. Fax: (916) 251-1650.E-mail: klove@klove.com Web Site:www.klove.com Licensee: Educational Media Foundation Group owner: EMF Broadcasting (acq 12-27-2002; $400,000). Natl. Network: K-Love, . Shaw Pittman. Format: Contemp Christian. News staff: 3. Target aud: 25-44; Judeo Christian, female. ◆ Richard Jenkins, pres; Mike Novak, VP; Keith Whipple, dev dir; David Pierce, progmg dir; Ed Lenane, news dir; Sam Wallington, engrg dir; Marya Morgan, news rptr.

KMJC(AM)— June 12, 1947: 620 khz; 1 kw-D, 290 w-N. TL: N41 19 09 W122 18 35. Hrs open: 24 Jefferson Public Radio, 1250 Siskiyou Blvd., Ashland, OR, 97520. Phone: (541) 552-6301. Fax: (541) 552-8565.E-mail: info@ijpr.org Web Site:www.ijpr.org Licensee: JPR Foundation Inc. (acq 8-8-02; $300,000 with KSYC(AM) Yreka). Population served: 56,000 Natl. Network: NPR, PRI, . Sanchez. Wire Svc: AP Format: News/talk. News staff: one. Target aud: General. ◆ Ronald Kramer, gen mgr; Bryon Lambert, opns dir; Paul Westhelle, dev dir.

*KNSQ(FM)— 1994: 88.1 mhz; 2.28 kw. 2,385 ft TL: N41 20 46 W122 11 42. (CP: 5 kw, ant 890 ft.). Stereo. Hrs open: 5 AM-2 AM Jefferson Public Radio, 1250 Siskiyou Blvd., Ashland, OR, 97520. Phone: (541) 552-6301. Fax: (541) 552-8565.E-mail: info@ijpr.org Web Site:www.ijpr.org Licensee: The State of Oregon, acting by and through the State Board of Higher Education, for the benefit of Southern Oregon University. (acq 1991; 4-1-91). Natl. Network: NPR, PRI, . Ernest Sanchez. Format: Jazz, AAA, news. News staff: one; News: 45 hrs wkly. Target aud: General. Spec prog: Blues 6 hrs, folk 3 hrs, pub affrs 7 hrs wkly. ◆ Mitchell Christian, CFO; Ronald Kramer, CEO & gen mgr; Bryon Lambert, opns dir; Paul Westhelle, dev dir.

Mountain Pass

KHYZ(FM)— April 1980: 99.5 mhz; 10 kw. Ant 1,710 ft TL: N35 29 27 W115 33 27. (CP: 8.4 kw, ant 1,807 ft.). Stereo. Hrs open: 24 Box 1668, 1611 E. Main St., Barstow, 92312. Phone: (760) 256-0326. Fax: (760) 256-9507.E-mail: tim@highwayradio.com Web Site:www.thehighwaystations.com Licensee: KHWY Inc. Natl. Network: AP Radio, . Hogan & Hartson. Format: Adult contemp. News staff: one; News: 16 hrs wkly. Target aud: 35 plus; travelers & loc communities. ◆ Howard B. Anderson, CEO, pres; Kirk Anderson, exec VP; Timothy Anderson, VP & gen mgr; Judy Robinson, sls VP; John Gregg, prom dir; Lance Todd, progmg dir; Keith Hayes, news dir; Thomas J. McNeill, engrg mgr.

Mountain View

*KSFH(FM)— 1974: 87.9 mhz; 10 w. 100 ft TL: N37 22 09 W122 05 00. (CP: 100 w, -246 ft.). Hrs open: 1 PM-9 PM (M-F) 1885 Miramonte Ave., 94040. Phone: (650) 210-2435. Fax: (650) 968-1706. Web Site:www.ksfh.com Licensee: St. Francis High School of Mountain View California Inc. Format: Contemp hits, rock/AOR, urban contemp. News: 5 hrs wkly. Target aud: General; young adult, high school, college. ◆ Lizzy Grandsaert, gen mgr.

Napa

KVON(AM)— Dec 17, 1947: 1440 khz; 5 kw-D, 1 kw-N, DA-2. TL: N38 16 47 W122 18 06. Hrs open: 24 1124 Foster Rd., 94558. Phone: (707) 252-1440. Fax: (707) 226-7544. Web Site:www.kvon.com Licensee: Wine Country Broadcasting Co. (acq 8-11-03; $3 million with KVYN(FM) St. Helena). Natl. Rep: Christal,. Format: News/talk. News staff: 3; News: 30 hrs wkly. Target aud: 35 plus. Spec prog: Sp 2 hrs. ◆ Jeff Schechtman, gen mgr, opns dir; Dan Darnelle, sls dir; Erica Pickett, prom dir; Lesley Lotto, news dir; Ben Webster, chief of engrg.

KVYN(FM)—See Saint Helena

Needles

KLUK(FM)— May 1984: 97.9 mhz; 2.8 kw. 1,571 ft TL: N35 02 06 W114 22 09. (CP: 29.5 kw). Stereo. Hrs open: 1531 Jill Way, Suite 7, Bullhead City, AZ, 86426-9341. Phone: (928) 763-5586. Fax: (928) 763-3775. Web Site:www.lucky98fm.com Licensee: Cameron Broadcasting Inc. (group owner; acq 1-18-02; grpsl). Population served: 70000 Format: Classic rock. News staff: one. Target aud: 25-54. ◆ William Jaeger, CEO & gen mgr; Craig Powers, opns mgr; Mike Fletcher, gen sls mgr; Dave Cooper, chief of engrg.

Mount Shasta (column 3)

KNKK(FM)— 107.1 mhz; 17 kw. Ant 1,909 ft TL: N35 01 57 W114 21 57. Hrs open: 24 1531 Jill Way, Suite 7, Bullhead City, AZ, 86426-9341. Phone: (928) 763-5586. Fax: (928) 763-3775. Web Site:www.theknack107.com Licensee: Cameron Broadcasting Inc. (group owner; acq 3-13-01). Format: Top 40 Hits. Target aud: 18-49. ◆ William Jaeger, CEO; Craig Powers, opns mgr; Mike Fletcher, gen sls mgr; Dave Cooper, chief of engrg.

KTOX(AM)— October 1952: 1340 khz; 1 kw-U. TL: N34 51 10 W114 37 19. Hrs open: 24 100 Balboa Pl., 92363. Secondary address: P.O. Box 8766, Ft. Mahaur, AZ 86427. Phone: (760) 326-4500. Fax: (760) 326-6849.E-mail: ktox1340@citlink.net Web Site:www.ktox1340am.com Licensee: Creative Broadcasting Services Inc. (acq 12-7-00; $200,000). Population served: 80,000 Natl. Network: Jones Radio Networks, Premiere Radio Networks, . Womble, Carlyle, Sandridgee & Rice. Format: News/talk. News staff: one; News: 24 hrs wkly. Target aud: 18 plus. Spec prog: Rt 66 program, 22 hrs of personalities and live local programming wkly. ◆ Robert T. Hayes, CEO; David T. Hayes, pres, gen mgr; Paul Fix, opns mgr; Kelly Hayes, gen sls mgr.

Nevada City

*KVMR(FM)— July 17, 1978: 89.5 mhz; 1.96 kw. 3900 ft TL: N39 14 47 W120 57 48. Stereo. Hrs open: 24 401 Spring St., 95959. Phone: (530) 265-9073. Fax: (530) 265-9077. Web Site:www.kvmr.org Licensee: Nevada City Community Broadcast Group. (acq 7-11-89; $32,000; 5-29-89). Population served: 1,100,000 Format: Var. News staff: 2; News: 1 hr daily mon-fri. Full spectrum community radio. Spec prog: Country 7 hrs, Black 4 hrs, folk 13 hrs, blues 7 hrs, foreign/ethnic 20 hrs wkly. ◆ David Levin, gen mgr, stn mgr; Brianna Caldwell, dev dir; Steve Baker, progmg dir; Alice MacAllister, mus dir; Paul Patterson, chief of engrg.

Newberry Springs

KIQQ-FM— January 2001: 103.7 mhz; 6 kw. Ant 246 ft TL: N34 53 19 W116 53 39. Hrs open: 24 Simulcast with KAEH(FM) Beaumont 100%. 710 W. Old Hwy. 58, Barstow, 92311. Phone: (760) 255-2636. Fax: (760) 255-3236.E-mail: jramirez@lamaquinamusical.net Web Site:www.moonbroadcasting.com; www.lamequinamusical.net Licensee: MBR Licensee LLC. Group owner: Moon Broadcasting (acq 11-5-99). Format: Rgnl Mexican. ◆ Alicia Avila, gen mgr.

Newport Beach

KDLE(FM)— Jan 31, 1964: 103.1 mhz; 300 w. Ant 964 ft TL: N33 36 19 W117 48 38. Stereo. Hrs open: 24 Simulcast with KDLD(FM) Santa Monica 100%. 5700 Wilshire Blvd., Suite 250, Los Angeles, 90036. Phone: (323) 900-6100. Fax: (323) 900-6127. Web Site:www.elgato1031.com Licensee: Entravision Holdings LLC. Group owner: Entravision Communications Corp. (acq 2000; grpsl). Population served: 250,000 Latham & Watkins. Format: Rgnl Mexican. ◆ Karl Meyer, gen mgr.

North Fork

KLLE(FM)— 1996: 107.9 mhz; 1.75 kw. Ant 1,227 ft TL: N37 17 42 W119 33 51. Hrs open: 1981 N. Gateway, Suite 101, Fresno, 93727. Phone: (559) 456-4000. Fax: (559) 251-9555. Web Site:www.univision.com Licensee: Univision Radio License Corp. Group owner: Univision Radio (acq 9-22-2003; grpsl). Format: Spanish rock/pop. ◆ Angela Navarrete, gen mgr.

North Highlands

*KQEI-FM— Feb 21, 1992: 89.3 mhz; 3.1 kw vert. Ant 354 ft TL: N38 42 38 W121 28 54. Stereo. Hrs open: 24 2601 Mariposa St., San Francisco, 94110. Phone: (415) 553-2129. Fax: (415) 553-2241.E-mail: fm@kqed.org Web Site:www.kqed.org Licensee: KQED Inc. (acq 5-9-03; $3 million). Format: News/talk. ◆ Jo Anne Wallace, gen mgr; Traci A. Eckels, dev dir; Paul Ramirez, news dir.

Northridge

*KCSN(FM)— November 1963: 88.5 mhz; 320 w. 1,643 ft TL: N34 19 11 W118 33 14. Hrs open: 24 18111 Nordhoff St., 91330-8312. Phone: (818) 677-3090. Fax: (818) 677-3069.E-mail: info@kcsn.org Web Site:www.kcsn.org Licensee: California State University Northridge. Population served: 3,000,000 Natl. Network: PRI, NPR, . Arter & Hadden. Format: Class, var/div. News staff: one; News: 12 hrs wkly. Target aud: 35 plus; middle/upper middle-class, well educated. Spec prog: German 3 hrs, Jewish 3 hrs, bluegrass 5 hrs wkly. ◆ Fred

Johnson, gen mgr; Martin Perlich, opns mgr, progmg dir; Laura Kelly, dev dir; Keith Goldstein, news dir; Michael Worrall, chief of engrg.

Oakdale

KHOP(FM)— Mar 11, 1985: 95.1 mhz; 29.5 kw. 633 ft TL: N37 47 34 W120 31 08. (CP: 16 kw, ant 876 ft. TL: N37 49 39 W120 34 03). Stereo. Hrs open: 24 1581 Cummins Dr., Suite 135, Modesto, 95358. Phone: (209) 766-5000. Fax: (209) 522-2061.E-mail: info@planet95.com Web Site:www.planet95.com Licensee: Citadel Broadcasting Co. Group owner: Citadel Broadcasting Corp. (acq 1996; $5 million). Fletcher, Heald & Hildreth. Format: 80s & beyond. News staff: one; News: 3 hrs wkly. Target aud: 18-49. Spec prog: Jazz 2 hrs, blues 2 hrs wkly. ◆Roy Williams, VP & gen mgr; Richard Perry, progmg dir.

Oakhurst

KAAT(FM)— Nov 1, 1982: 103.1 mhz; 25 kw. Ant 125 ft TL: N37 25 08 W119 44 40. Stereo. Hrs open: 24 40356 Oak Park Way, Suites E & F, 93644. Phone: (559) 683-1031. Fax: (559) 683-5488.E-mail: mtkaat@sierratel.com Web Site:www.kaat.com Licensee: California Sierra Corp. (acq 3-3-2005); $4.75 million with co-located AM). Population served: 48,685 Format: Hispanic. Target aud: 25-54; general. Spec prog: Relg 2 hrs wkly. ◆Abel DeLuna, pres, stn mgr; Denny Jackson, progmg dir.

KTNS(AM)— Nov 20, 1982: 1060 khz; 5 kw-D, 55 w-N. TL: N37 17 46 W119 36 23. Hrs open: 24 40356 Oak Park Way, Suites E & F, 93644. Phone: (559) 683-1060. Fax: (559) 683-5488.E-mail: tammy@kaat.com Web Site:www.ktnsradio.com Licensee: California Sierra Corp. Natl. Network: CNN Radio, Westwood One, . Format: Adult contemp. News staff: 3. Target aud: 25-49. ◆Becky Deaver, gen sls mgr; Jesse Taylor, progmg dir.

Oakland

KISQ(FM)—See San Francisco

KKGN(AM)— 1925: 960 khz; 5 kw-U, DA-1. TL: N37 49 40 W122 18 53. Hrs open: 24 340 Townsend St., Suite 4-960, San Francisco, 94107. Phone: (415) 977-0960. Fax: (415) 972-1107.E-mail: John@Green960.com Web Site:www.green960.com Licensee: AMFM Broadcasting Licenses LLC. Group owner: Clear Channel Communications Inc. (acq 8-30-2000; grpsl). Population served: 715,674 Natl. Rep: Christal,. Format: Talk. ◆Anna Eppinger, gen mgr; Michael Martin, opns mgr; John Scott, progmg dir.

KMKY(AM)— July 1922: 1310 khz; 5 kw-U, DA-1. TL: N37 49 27 W122 19 10. Hrs open: 24 963 Industrial Rd., Suite 1, San Carlos, 94070. Phone: (650) 637-8800. Web Site:www.radiodisney.com Licensee: KGO-AM Radio Inc. Group owner: ABC Inc. (acq 12-18-97; $6.25 million). Population served: 4,889,900 Natl. Network: Radio Disney, . Natl. Rep: Interep,. Format: Children. Target aud: 2-14; kids, tweens & moms 25-54. ◆Martin Spisak, stn mgr; Shalon Rogers, prom dir.

KNEW(AM)— July 2, 1921: 910 khz; 20 kw-D, 5 kw-N, DA-2. TL: N37 53 45 W122 19 25. Hrs open: 24 340 Townsend St., San Francisco, 94107. Phone: (415) 538-1013. Fax: (415) 975-5573.E-mail: kenjones@clearchannel.com Web Site:www.910wnew.com Licensee: AMFM Broadcasting Licenses LLC. Group owner: Clear Channel Communications Inc. (acq 8-30-2000; grpsl). Population served: 200,000 Format: News/talk. News staff: 8; News: 65 hrs wkly. Target aud: 25-54. ◆Anna Eppinger, gen mgr; Lucia Vandenhof, prom dir; Bob Agnew, progmg dir.

Oceanside

*KKSM(AM)— July 4, 1956: 1320 khz; 500 w-U, DA-1. TL: N33 12 08 W117 36 46. Hrs open: 24 c/o Communications Dept. Palmer College, 1140 W. Mission Rd., San Marcos, 92069. Phone: (760) 744-1150, EXT. 5576 and 3149. Web Site:www.kksm.palomar.edu Licensee: Palomar Community College District. (acq 4-1-96). Population served: 468,400 Format: Eclectic, div. News staff: one; News: 10 hrs wkly. Target aud: 18-25; college age, mid-upper income, diverse ethnic. ◆Zeb Navarro, gen mgr; Christa Lynch, prom dir; Matt O'Brien, progmg dir; David Quera, mus dir; Josh Diaz, news dir.

Oildale

KGDP(AM)—Licensed to Oildale. See Santa Maria

KLLY(FM)— January 1985: 95.3 mhz; 12.5 kw. 394 ft TL: N35 27 55 W119 01 04. Stereo. Hrs open: 24 Box 80658, Bakersfield, 93308.

Secondary address: 3651 Pegasus, Suite 107, Bakersfield 93308. Phone: (661) 393-1900. Fax: (661) 393-1915.E-mail: info@klly.com Web Site:www.klly.com Licensee: Buckley Broadcasting of California LLC. Group owner: Buckley Broadcasting Corp. (acq 12-86; $1.3 million;11-10-86). Population served: 420,000 Natl. Rep: D & R Radio,. Format: Adult contemp. Target aud: 25-44; adults. ◆Steve Darnell, gen mgr; Otis Warren, sls dir; E.J. Tyler, progmg dir.

Ojai

KFYV(FM)— Jan 4, 1972: 105.5 mhz; 310 w. 1,437 ft TL: N34 20 57 W119 20 07. Stereo. Hrs open: 24 2284 S. Victoria, Suite 2G, Ventura, 93003. Phone: (805) 289-1400. Fax: (805) 644-7906.E-mail: info@live1055.fm Web Site:www.live1055.fm Licensee: Gold Coast Broadcasting LLC (group owner; (acq 5-15-97; $2 million with KUNX(AM) Ventura). Natl. Network: AP Radio, . Natl. Rep: Katz Radio,. Format: Hot adult contemp. News staff: one; News: 3 hrs wkly. Target aud: 25-49; fun, upscale, classy adults. ◆Chip Ehrhardt, gen mgr; Mark Elliot, progmg dir.

*KLFH(FM)— 2003: 89.5 mhz; 97 w. Ant 1,322 ft TL: N34 24 45 W119 11 16. Hrs open: 560 Higuera St., suite G, San Luis Obispo, 93401. Phone: (805) 541-4343. Fax: (805) 541-9101.E-mail: info@klife.org Web Site:www.klife.org Licensee: Logos Broadcasting Corp. (acq 2-18-2009; $1.35 million). Format: CHR, Christian hits. ◆Jim Fugler, gen mgr; Noonie Fugler, prom dir.

Ontario

KSPA(AM)— Jan 26, 1947: 1510 khz; 10 kw-D, 1 kw-N, DA-2. TL: N34 05 41 W117 36 46. Hrs open: 24 1045 S. East St., Anaheim, 92805. Phone: (909) 483-1500. Fax: (909) 483-1515.E-mail: kspa1510@aol.com Web Site:www.thesparadio.com Licensee: Ontario Broadcasting L.L.C. Group owner: Astor Broadcast Group. (acq 11-4-99). Population served: 731,000 Format: Adult standards. News staff: one. Target aud: 18-49. ◆Art Astor, pres; Peri Corso, gen mgr; Joe Lyons, opns mgr.

KWIE(FM)— Jan 26, 1947: 93.5 mhz; 5 kw. Ant -131 ft TL: N34 10 32 W117 34 26. Stereo. Hrs open: 24 5055 Wilshire Blvd., Suite 720, Los Angeles, 90036. Phone: (323) 337-1600. Fax: (323) 337-1633.E-mail: info@935kwie.com Web Site:www.935kday.com Licensee: KDAI Licensing LLC. Group owner: Spanish Broadcasting System Inc. (acq 1-31-2006; $120 million with KDAY(FM) Redondo Beach). Population served: 2,000,000 Format: Hip-hop. ◆Kimberly Fletcher, gen mgr.

Orange

KLAA(AM)— Jan 13, 1992: 830 khz; 50 kw-D, 20 kw-N, DA-N. TL: N33 55 43 W117 36 57. Hrs open: 24 15301 Ventura Blvd., Bldg. D, Suite 200, Sherman Oaks, 91403. Phone: (818) 528-2050. Fax: (818) 784-8824. Web Site:www.830am.com Licensee: LAA 1 LLC (acq 5-23-2006; $41 million). Natl. Network: NBC Radio, . Format: News, talk, sports. News: 28 hrs wkly. Target aud: 25-54; Male & female, high income, professionals. Spec prog: Sports. ◆Alan L. Fuller, gen mgr.

Orange Cove

KMAK(FM)— Oct 27, 1990: 100.3 mhz; 72 w. 2,073 ft TL: N36 44 45 W119 16 58. Stereo. Hrs open: 24 PO Box 5, Selma, 93662-0005. Secondary address: 640 Park Blvd. 93662. Phone: (559) 626-7922. Fax: (559) 896-1631.E-mail: kmakfm@sbcglobal.net Licensee: Richard B. Smith. Population served: 475,000 Natl. Network: CNN Radio, . Fletcher Heald. Format: Rgnl Mexican. News staff: one. Target aud: 18-54. ◆Nelson Gomez, mktg dir, progmg dir; Sue Jones, gen mgr & progmg dir; Richard Smith, chief of engrg.

Orcutt

KPAT(FM)—Licensed to Orcutt. See Santa Maria

Orland

KRQR(FM)— January 1994: 106.7 mhz; 25 kw. 56 ft TL: N39 53 17 W122 37 38. Hrs open: 24 856 Manzanita Court, Chico, 95926. Phone: (530) 342-2200. Fax: (530) 342-2260.E-mail: info@zrockfm.com Web Site:www.zrockfm.com Licensee: Results Radio Licensee L.L.C. Group owner: Fritz Communications Inc. (acq 6-11-99; grpsl). Brown, Nietert & Kaufman. Format: Active rock/extreme alternative. ◆Jack Fritz, pres; John Graham, gen mgr; Dave Pack, gen sls mgr; Neil Randall, progmg mgr; J.D. Davis, chief of engrg; Candy Mason, traf mgr.

Orleans

*KHAA(FM)—Not on air, target date: unknown: 89.5 mhz; 15 w. Ant 1,850 ft TL: N41 17 06 W123 29 46. Hrs open: 64236 Second Ave., Happy Camp, 96039-1016. Phone: (530) 493-1600. Fax: (530) 493-5322. Licensee: Karuk Tribe of California. ◆Arch Super, gen mgr.

Oroville

KEWE(AM)— Aug 4, 1962: 1340 khz; 1 kw-U. TL: N39 30 34 W121 35 55. Hrs open: 24 Dups 100% FM 2654 Cramer Ln., Chico, 95928. Phone: (530) 345-0021. Fax: (530) 893-2121. Licensee: Deer Creek Broadcasting LLC Population served: 320000 Format: Sp. ◆Rosa Ramos, progmg dir.

Oxnard

KCAQ(FM)— Sept 27, 1958: 104.7 mhz; 5.1 kw. 1,580 ft TL: N34 20 53 W119 20 07. Hrs open: 2284 S. Victoria, Suite 2G, Ventura, 93003. Phone: (805) 289-1400. Fax: (805) 644-7906.E-mail: info@q1047.com Web Site:www.q1047.com Licensee: Gold Coast Broadcasting LLC (group owner; acq 1996; $3.65 million with KVTA(AM) Port Hueneme). Population served: 636,500 Natl. Rep: Katz Radio,. Format: CHR Rhythmic. Target aud: 18-44. ◆Chip Ehrhardt, gen mgr; Brian Davis, progmg dir.

*KCRU(FM)— 1993: 89.1 mhz; 200 w. 853 ft TL: N34 06 47 W119 03 34. Hrs open: Rebroadcasts KCRW(FM) Santa Monica 98%. 1900 Pico Blvd., Santa Monica, 90405. Phone: (310) 450-5183. Phone: (888) 660-kcrw. Fax: (310) 450-7172.E-mail: mail@kcrw.org Web Site:www.kcrw.com Licensee: Santa Monica Community College District. Format: Eclectic, news. ◆Ruth Seymour, gen mgr; Jennifer Ferro, stn mgr; Mike Newport, opns mgr; David Kleinbart, dev dir; Ariana Morgenstern, asst music dir; Steve Herbert, chief of engrg.

KDAR(FM)— Oct 28, 1974: 98.3 mhz; 1.5 kw. Ant 1,289 ft TL: N34 20 55 W119 19 57. Stereo. Hrs open: 24 Box 5626, 93031. Secondary address: 500 Esplanade Dr., Suite 1500 93036. Phone: (805) 485-8881. Fax: (805) 656-5330.E-mail: radiomail@kdar.com Web Site:www.kdar.com Licensee: New Inspiration Broadcasting Co. Inc. Group owner: Salem Communications Corp. Format: Christian talk & mus. News: 2 hrs wkly. Target aud: 25-54; upscale adults with large families. ◆Ed Atsinger, pres; Richard Trejo, gen mgr; Roy Bach, progmg dir.

KKZZ(AM)—See Santa Paula

KLJR-FM—See Santa Paula

KOCP(FM)—See Camarillo

KOXR(AM)— June 11, 1955: 910 khz; 5 kw-D, 1 kw-N, DA-2. TL: N34 16 58 W119 07 36. Hrs open: 24 200 S. A St., Suite 400, 93030. Phone: (805) 240-2070. Fax: (805) 240-5960. Licensee: Lazer Broadcasting Co. (group owner; acq 1-11-99). Population served: 250,000 Natl. Rep: Lotus Entravision Reps LLC,. Fletcher, Heald & Hildredth. Format: Sp. Target aud: 25-54. ◆Alfredo Plascencia, CEO, pres; Salvador Prieto, opns mgr & progmg dir.

KUNX(AM)—See Ventura

KVEN(AM)—See Ventura

KXLM(FM)— 1991: 102.9 mhz; 5.5 kw. Ant 112 ft TL: N34 14 12 W119 12 11. Hrs open: 24 200 S. A St., Suite 400, 93030. Secondary address: Box 6940 93030. Phone: (805) 240-2070. Fax: (805) 240-5960.E-mail: info@radiolazer.com Web Site:radiolazer.com Licensee: Kext Broadcasters Inc. Format: Sp, adult contemp. News staff: one; News: 2 hrs wkly. Target aud: 25-59. ◆Alfredo Plascencia, pres, gen mgr; Terry Janisch, gen sls mgr.

Pacific Grove

*KAZU(FM)— Oct 1, 1977: 90.3 mhz; 3.7 kw. Ant 522 ft TL: N36 33 09 W121 47 17. Stereo. Hrs open: 24 167 Central Ave. #B, 93950-3060. Phone: (831) 582-5298. Fax: (831) 375-0235.E-mail: mail@kazu.org Web Site:www.kazu.org Licensee: Foundation of California State University Monterey Bay (acq 11-30-00; $150,000). Population served: 500,000 Natl. Network: NPR, . Garvey, Schubert & Barer. Format: News, info. News: 8 hrs wkly. Target aud: 25-65; general. Spec prog: Country 6 hrs, women's mus 6 hrs, gospel 4 hrs, folk 6 hrs, class 3 hrs, oldies 5 hrs wkly. ◆Ducan Lively, gen mgr; Douglas McKnight, dev dir; Ben Adler, progmg dir, news dir.

KOCN(FM)— Apr 10, 1977: 105.1 mhz; 1.8 kw. 600 ft TL: N36 33 09 W121 47 17. (CP: 402 kw, ant 790 ft. TL: N36 30 38 W121 43 57). Stereo. Hrs open: 24 903 N. Main St., Salinas, 93906. Phone: (831) 755-8181. Fax: (831) 755-8191. Licensee: CC Licenses LLC. Group owner: Clear Channel Communications Inc. (acq 9-22-97; grpsl). Population served: 600,000 Natl. Network: Westwood One, . Natl. Rep: Clear Channel,. Format: Oldies. News staff: one. Target aud: 25-54; at work, double income households. ♦Rhonda McCormack, gen mgr & sls dir; Joey Martinez, prom dir, progmg dir.

Pala

***KOPA(FM)**—Not on air, target date: unknown: 91.3 mhz; 100 w. Ant -1,066 ft TL: N33 22 00 W117 04 05. Hrs open: 35008 Pala Temecula Rd., 92059. Phone: (760) 891-3500. Web Site:www.palatribe.com Licensee: Pala Band of Mission Indians. ♦Robert H. Smith, chmn.

Palm Desert

KEZN(FM)— Nov 28, 1977: 103.1 mhz; 1.9 kw. 590 ft TL: N33 51 58 W116 25 56. Stereo. Hrs open: 24 72-915 Parkview Dr., 92260. Secondary address: Box 291 92260. Phone: (760) 340-9383. Fax: (760) 340-5756.E-mail: info@ez103.com Web Site:www.ez103.com Licensee: Infinity Radio Holdings Inc. Group owner: Infinity Broadcasting Corp. (acq 11-13-98; grpsl). Population served: 250,000 Natl. Network: Westwood One, . Leventhal, Senter & Lerman. Format: Adult contemp. News staff: one. Target aud: 25-64. ♦Doug Kratky, gen sls mgr; Frank Torok, prom dir; Rick Shaw, progmg dir.

***KHCS(FM)**— January 1993: 91.7 mhz; 960 w. 574 ft TL: N33 41 25 W116 17 14. Stereo. Hrs open: 24 2341 Duane Rd., Palm Springs, 92262. Phone: (760) 864-9620. Fax: (760) 864-9633.E-mail: Khcs@juno.com Web Site:www.joy92.org Licensee: Prairie Avenue Gospel Center. Lauren A. Colby. Format: Inspirational, Christian. Target aud: 20-85. ♦Dan Pike, pres; R.F. Watts, chief of engrg.

Palm Springs

KDES-FM— Feb 10, 1963: 104.7 mhz; 42 kw. 540 ft TL: N33 51 56 W116 26 04. Stereo. Hrs open: 2100 E. Tahquitz Canyon Way, 510308. Phone: (760) 325-2582. Fax: (760) 322-3562.E-mail: kdes@aol.com Web Site:www.kdes.com Cohn & Marks. Format: Oldies. ♦Kacy Consiglio, progmg mgr & traf mgr.

KGAM(AM)— 1969: 1450 khz; 1 kw-U. TL: N33 48 02 W116 30 25. Hrs open: 24 2100 E. Tahquitz Canyon Way, 92262. Phone: (760) 325-2582. Phone: (760) 320-8255. Fax: (760) 322-3562.E-mail: info@kgam.com Web Site:www.kgam.com Licensee: R & R Radio Corp. Group owner: RR Broadcasting (acq 4-8-2002; with co-located FM). Population served: 100,000 Natl. Rep: Christal,. Cohn & Marks. Format: News/talk, talk. News staff: 2; News: 5 hrs wkly. Target aud: 25 plus; upscale, informed, involved adults. ♦Rozene Supple, pres; Gene Nichols, CFO, news dir; Mike Keane, gen mgr; Mel Hill, rgnl sls mgr; Geoff Allan, prom dir; Steve Kelly, progmg dir; Barry O'Connor, chief of engrg.

KNWQ(AM)— Feb 12, 1946: 1140 khz; 10 kw-D, 2.5 kw-N, DA-2. TL: N33 51 39 W116 28 20. Stereo. Hrs open: 1321 N. Gene Autry Trail, 92262. Phone: (760) 322-7890. Fax: (760) 322-5493.E-mail: info@desertfun.com Web Site:www.desertfun.com Licensee: Morris Communications Corp. Group owner: Morris Communications Inc. (acq 12-24-97; $4.5 million). Population served: 300,000 Natl. Network: CBS, . Natl. Rep: McGavren Guild,. Format: News/talk. Target aud: 35-65. ♦William S. Morris IV, chmn; William S. Morris III, pres; Darrel Fry, CFO; Michael Osterhaut, VP; Keith Martin, gen mgr; Gary Demaroney, opns dir.

KPLM(FM)— Jan 24, 1983: 106.1 mhz; 50 kw. 391 ft TL: N33 52 14 W116 13 39. Stereo. Hrs open: 24 Box 1825, 92263. Phone: (760) 320-4550. Fax: (760) 320-3037.E-mail: kplm@dc.rr.com Web Site:thebig106.com Licensee: RM Broadcasting L.L.C. (acq 9-10-98). Population served: 3,700,000 Natl. Rep: Katz Radio,. Koteen & Naftalin. Format: Country. News staff: one; News: 9 hrs wkly. Target aud: 25-54. ♦Todd Marker, gen mgr; Kory James, opns mgr, prom dir; Hughes Hilles, gen sls mgr; Al Gordon, progmg dir.

***KPSC(FM)**— April 1978: 88.5 mhz; 3 kw. 266 ft TL: N33 52 14 W116 13 39. Stereo. Hrs open: 24
Rebroadcasts KUSC 100%.
Box 77913, Los Angeles, 90007. Secondary address: 515 S. Figueroa St., Suite 2050, Los Angeles 90071. Phone: (213) 225-7400. Fax: (213) 225-7410.E-mail: kusc@kusc.org Web Site:www.kusc.org Licensee: University of Southern California. (acq 9-9-86). Natl. Network: PRI, NPR, . Lawrence Bernstein. Format: Class. Target aud: 35 plus; general. ♦Brenda Barnes, pres; Eric DeWeese, gen mgr; Janet McIntyre, dev VP, dev dir; Stephanie Ross, mktg dir.

KPSI(AM)— Oct 29, 1956: 920 khz; 5 kw-D, 1 kw-N, DA-2. TL: N33 51 29 W116 29 39. Stereo. Hrs open: 2100 E. Tahquitz Canyon Way, 92262. Phone: (760) 325-2582. Fax: (760) 322-3562.E-mail: info@newstalk920.com Web Site:www.newstalk920.com Licensee: R & R Radio Corp. Group owner: RR Broadcasting. Population served: 245,000 Natl. Rep: Christal,. Format: News, talk. News staff: 4; News: 16 hrs wkly. Target aud: 25-54. Spec prog: American Indian 2 hrs wkly. ♦Mike Keane, gen mgr; Gregg Aratin, gen sls mgr; Lisa Giles, prom dir; Steve Kelly, progmg dir; Gregg Nichols, news dir.

KPSI-FM— June 1980: 100.5 mhz; 25 kw. Ant 121 ft TL: N33 56 44 W116 24 34. Stereo. Hrs open: 2100 E. Tahquitz Canyon Way, 92262. Phone: (760) 325-2582. Fax: (760) 320-4632. Web Site:www.mix1005.fm Licensee: R & R Radio Corp. Population served: 250,000 Format: CHR, contemp hit. ♦Gregg Aratin, gen sls mgr; Lisa Giles, prom dir; Connie Breeze, progmg dir.

KPTR(AM)—(Cathedral City, Oct 4, 1964: 1340 khz; 1 kw-U. TL: N33 48 07 W116 27 44. Hrs open: 24 2100 Tahquitz Canyon Way, 92262. Phone: (760) 325-2582. Fax: (760) 325-2582.E-mail: mkeane@rrbroadcasting.com Licensee: R & R Radio Corp. (acq 7-27-2006; $2.3 million). Population served: 180,000 Format: Progressive talk. News staff: one. ♦Mike Keane, gen mgr; Lisa Childs, prom dir; Steve Kelly, progmg dir.

KWXY-FM—(Cathedral City, Jan 19, 1969: 98.5 mhz; 50 kw. 499 ft TL: N33 51 55 W116 26 10. Stereo. Hrs open: 24 KWXY Broadcast Centre, Box 5470, 92263. Phone: (760) 328-1104. Fax: (760) 328-7814. Web Site:www.kwxy.com Licensee: Glen Barnett Inc. Population served: 688,000 Garvey, Schubert & Barer. Wire Svc: AP Format: Btfl mus, adult standards. News staff: one; News: 16 hrs wkly. Target aud: 35 plus; affluent adults. Spec prog: Canadian news 2 hrs wkly. ♦Estelle Layton, exec VP; Bob Wetherall, opns mgr; Glen Barnett, pres, gen mgr & chief of engrg.

Palmdale

KUTY(AM)— August 1957: 1470 khz; 5 kw-U, DA-2. TL: N34 39 55 W118 00 40. Hrs open: 24 Q-9, 570 East Ave., 93550. Phone: (661) 947-3107. Fax: (661) 272-5688.E-mail: info@lameramera1470.com Web Site:www.lameramera1470.com Licensee: High Desert Broadcasting LLC. (group owner; (acq 3-5-97). Population served: 300,000 Format: Rgnl Mexican. ♦Nelson Rasse, gen mgr.

Palo Alto

KDFC-FM—See San Francisco

KDOW(AM)— 1947: 1220 khz; 5 kw-D, 147 w-N. TL: N37 29 04 W122 08 04. Hrs open: 24 39138 Fremont Blvd., 3rd Fl., Freemont, 94538. Phone: (510) 713-1100. Fax: (510) 505-1448. Licensee: SCA-Palo Alto LLC. Group owner: Salem Communications Corp. (acq 6-28-2001; $9 million). Population served: 5,500,000 Natl. Network: CBS, . Natl. Rep: Salem,. Format: News, talk, sports. News staff: 5; News: 70 hrs wkly. Target aud: 25-54; general. ♦Ken Miller, gen mgr; Kelly Chrivtian, gen sls mgr; Amy Nyquist, mktg dir, prom dir; Craig Roberts, chief of engrg.

KZSU(FM)—See Stanford

Paradise

KHSL-FM— Oct 15, 1983: 103.5 mhz; 1.6 kw. 1,250 ft TL: N39 57 29 W121 42 50. Stereo. Hrs open: 24 2654 Cramer Ln., Chico, 95928-8838. Phone: (530) 345-0021. Fax: (530) 893-2121.E-mail: info@khsl.com Web Site:www.khsl.com Licensee: Deer Creek Broadcasting LLC. (group owner; (acq 9-8-2004; grpsl). Population served: 310,000 Natl. Rep: Katz Radio,. Haley, Bader & Potts. Format: Country. News staff: one; News: 6 hrs wkly. Target aud: 25-54; active. ♦Dino Corbin, VP, gen mgr, mktg mgr; Bill Meyer, gen sls mgr; Lisa Fitzgerald, prom mgr.

KKXX(AM)— September 1960: 930 khz; 1 kw-D, 37 w-N. TL: N39 43 37 W121 40 45. (CP: 500 w-N). Hrs open: 1363 Longfellow, Chico, 95926-7319. Phone: (530) 894-7325.E-mail: info@kkxx.net Web Site:www.kkxx.net Licensee: Butte Broadcasting Co. (acq 12-21-66). Population served: 300,000 Format: News/talk, relg. ♦Carl J. Auel, pres; Andrew Palmquist, gen mgr.

KZAP(FM)— June 4, 1977: 96.7 mhz; 1.5 kw. Ant 1,289 ft TL: N39 57 45 W121 42 40. Stereo. Hrs open: 24
Simulcast with KPIG-FM Freedom 100%.
1459 Humbolt Rd., Suite D, Chico, 95928. Phone: (530) 899-3600. Fax: (530) 343-0243.E-mail: info@club967.com Web Site:www.club967.com Licensee: Mapleton License of Chico LLC. Group owner: Regent Communications Inc. (acq 11-30-2006; grpsl). Population served: 250,000 Format: AAA :"Americana". Target aud: 25-49. ♦Coyote McGee, opns mgr; Chad Gammage, mktg mgr; Keriann Brennan, prom dir.

Pasadena

KAZN(AM)— Sept 12, 1942: 1300 khz; 5 kw-D, 1 kw-N, DA-2. TL: N34 09 38 W118 04 46. Stereo. Hrs open: 24 747 E. Green, Suite 101, 91101. Phone: (626) 568-1300. Fax: (626) 568-3666. Web Site:www.mrbi.net Licensee: Multicultural Radio Broadcasting Licensee LLC. Group owner: Multicultural Radio Broadcasting Inc. (acq 5-11-98; $12 million). Format: Chinese. News: 90 hrs wkly. Target aud: Chinese. ♦Arthur S. Liu, pres; Hsiang Lee, progmg dir.

KDIS(AM)— Feb 7, 1942: 1110 khz; 50 kw-D, 20 kw-N, DA-2. TL: N34 06 50 W117 59 51. Stereo. Hrs open: 500 S. Buena Vista St., MC 6325, Burbank, 91505. Phone: (818) 569-5035. Web Site:www.radiodisney.com/kdisam1110 Licensee: KABC-AM Radio Inc. Group owner: ABC Inc. (acq 12-19-00; $65 million). Population served: 10,162,200 Natl. Network: Radio Disney, . Format: Children's progmg. ♦John Davison, pres; Natalie Eig, gen mgr.

***KPCC(FM)**— September 1957: 89.3 mhz; 680 w. 2,922 ft TL: N34 13 35 W118 03 58. Stereo. Hrs open: 24 1570 E. Colorado Blvd., 91106. Phone: (626) 585-7000. Fax: (626) 585-7916.E-mail: mail@kpcc.org Web Site:www.kpcc.org Licensee: Pasadena Area Community College District Board of Trustees. Population served: 342,000 Natl. Network: NPR, PRI, CBC Radio One, . Format: New/talk/information. News: 6 hrs wkly. Target aud: 25-55. ♦Bill Davis, CEO, gen mgr; Doug Johnson, opns dir, opns mgr; Julie Allen, gen sls mgr; Craig Curtis, progmg dir; Paul Glickman, news dir.

KROQ-FM— 1974: 106.7 mhz; 5.6 kw. 2,000 ft TL: N34 11 47 W118 15 30. Hrs open: 24 5901 Venice Blvd., Los Angeles, 90034. Phone: (323) 930-1067. Fax: (323) 931-1067. Web Site:www.kroq.com Licensee: Infinity Broadcasting of Los Angeles Inc. Group owner: Infinity Broadcasting Corp. (acq 11-13-98; grpsl). Population served: 13,000,000 Format: Alternative rock. Target aud: 18-34. ♦Jeff Federman, gen mgr; Kevin Weatherly, progmg dir.

KSSE(FM)—See Arcadia

Paso Robles

KKAL(FM)— Nov 20, 1972: 92.5 mhz; 4.8 kw. Ant 1,486 ft TL: N35 21 40 W120 39 21. Stereo. Hrs open: 24 3620 Sacramento Dr., Suite 204, San Luis Obispo, 93401. Phone: (805) 781-2750. Fax: (805) 781-2758. Web Site:www.kkalonline.com Licensee: AGM California. Group owner: American General Media (acq 1997; $675,000). Population served: 285,000 Format: Hot adult contemp. News staff: one; News: 12 hrs wkly. Target aud: 18 plus. ♦Kathy Signorelli, gen mgr; Mark Tobin, gen sls mgr; Pepper Daniels, progmg dir.

KLUN(FM)— August 1995: 103.1 mhz; 1.2 kw. 761 ft TL: N35 38 45 W120 44 16. Stereo. Hrs open: 24 312 E. Mill St., Suite 301, Santa Maria, 93454. Phone: (805) 928-9796. Fax: (805) 928-3367.E-mail: joseg@radiolazer.com Web Site:www.radiolazer.com Licensee: Lazer Broadcasting Corp. (group owner; acq 8-7-00; $1.115 million with KLMM(FM) Morro Bay). Booth, Freret, Imlay & Tepper. Format: Rgnl Mexican music. Target aud: 18-49; general. ♦Alfredo Placencia, pres; Jose Guzman, gen mgr; Salvador Prieto, progmg dir; Bill Bordoux, chief of engrg.

KPRL(AM)— Oct 1, 1946: 1230 khz; 1 kw-U. TL: N35 39 15 W120 40 52. Hrs open: Box 7, 93447. Phone: (805) 238-1230. Fax: (805) 238-5332.E-mail: kprl@tcsn.net Web Site:www.kprl.com Licensee: North County Communications LLC (acq 5-1-2003; $900,000). Population served: 112,000 Natl. Rep: Western Regional Broadcast Sales,. Garvey, Schubert & Barer. Format: News/talk, sports. News staff: one; News: one hr wkly. Target aud: 25 plus. ♦Kevin Will, CEO, pres & opns mgr.

Patterson

KOSO(FM)—Licensed to Patterson. See Modesto

KTSE-FM— 1996: 97.1 mhz; 3 kw. 328 ft TL: N37 29 26 W121 13 16. Stereo. Hrs open: 24 6820 Pacific Ave., Suite 3A, Stockton, 95207. Phone: (209) 474-0154. Fax: (209) 474-0316.E-mail: info@entravision.com Web Site:www.entravision.com Licensee: Entravision Holdings LLC. Group owner: Entravision Communications Corp. (acq 7-28-00; grpsl). Format: Sp. ♦Lisa Sunday, CFO, gen mgr, opns mgr, gen sls mgr; Jorge Moreno, prom dir; Homero Campos, progmg VP; Jeff Paz, news dir; Paul Shin, chief of engrg; Valentina Rupio, mus dir & traf mgr.

Pebble Beach

*KSPB(FM)— Sept 22, 1978: 91.9 mhz; 1 kw. 485 ft TL: N36 35 11 W121 55 21. Hrs open: 3152 Forest Lake Rd., 93953. Phone: (831) 626-5300. Phone: (831) 625-5078. Fax: (831) 625-5208.E-mail: webmaster@kspb.org Web Site:www.kspb.org Licensee: Robert Louis Stevenson School. Format: Progsv. Spec prog: Black 18 hrs, oldies 4 hrs, reggae 2 hrs, hard rock 2 hrs wkly. ◆Matthew Arruda, gen mgr.

Pescadero

*KPDO(FM)— 2006: 89.3 mhz; 100 w. Ant -141 ft TL: N37 15 23 W122 24 33. Hrs open: 20748 Powder Horn Rd., Hidden Valley Lake, 95467. Phone: (707) 987-9761. Licensee: Pescadero Public Radio Service Inc. ◆Celeste Klienfelder, pres.

Petaluma

KTOB(AM)— Jan 10, 1950: 1490 khz; 1 kw-U. TL: N35 39 15 W120 40 52. Hrs open: 24 c/o Radio Station KRRS(AM), Box 2277, Santa Rosa, 95405. Secondary address: c/o Radio Station KRRS(AM), 1410 Neotomas Ave., Suite 104, Santa Rosa 95405. Phone: (707) 545-1460. Fax: (707) 545-0112.E-mail: krrs@sonic.net Web Site:www.moonradios.com Licensee: Moon Broadcasting Licensee LLC. Group owner: Moon Broadcasting (acq 12-13-2001; $1.28 million). Population served: 1,000,000 Natl. Rep: Interep,. Format: Sp rgnl. Target aud: 15-54; contemporary Hispanic families. ◆Abel DeLuna Sr., CEO; Abel DeLuna, pres; Arelia DeLuna, CFO; Maggie LeClerc, gen mgr; Benoit LeClerc, opns mgr.

Philo

*KZYX(FM)— October 1989: 90.7 mhz; 3.41 kw. 1,686 ft TL: N39 01 22 W123 31 17. Hrs open: Box 1, 95466. Phone: (707) 895-2324. Fax: (707) 895-2451. Web Site:www.kzyx.org Licensee: Mendocino County Public Broadcasting. Population served: 80,000 Natl. Network: NPR, . Format: News, talk radio, div music. Target aud: General. Spec prog: Black 8 hrs, class 14 hrs, folk 8 hrs, gospel 2 hrs, jazz 11 hrs, blues 3 hrs. ◆Belinda Rawlins, gen mgr, dev dir; Burton Segall, opns dir; Vance Crowe, prom dir; Mary Aigner, progmg dir; Annie Esposito, news dir.

Piedmont

KPIG(AM)— May 1947: 1510 khz; 8 kw-D, 230 w-N, DA-2. TL: N37 49 02 W122 17 10. Hrs open: 24
Simulcast with KPIG-FM Freedom 100%.
28 Second St., Suite 501, San Francisco, 94105. Secondary address: 1110 Main St., Suite 16, Watsonville 95076. Phone: (415) 744-1510. Fax: (415) 495-1510.E-mail: sty@kpig.com Web Site:www.kpig.com Licensee: Mapleton License of San Francisco LLC. (acq 7-27-2005; $5.1 million). Population served: 245,000 Natl. Rep: McGavren Guild,. Levental, Senter & Lerman. Format: AAA, Americana. ◆Ed Monroe, gen mgr; Frank Caprista, opns mgr; Mike Martindale, chief of engrg.

Pismo Beach

KXTZ(FM)— Dec 7, 1974: 95.3 mhz; 4.2 kw. 390 ft TL: N35 09 24 W120 38 11. Stereo. Hrs open: 24 396 Buckley Rd., Suite 2, San Luis Obispo, 93401. Phone: (805) 786-2570. Fax: (805) 547-9860. Web Site:www.mapletoncommunications.com Licensee: Mapleton License of San Luis Obispo LLC. (group owner; (acq 7-19-2002; grpsl). Population served: 250,000 Haley, Bader & Potts. Format: Classic hits. News staff: one; News: one hr wkly. Target aud: 18-49. Spec prog: Talk one hr wkly. ◆Adam Nathanson, pres; Bill Heirendt, gen mgr; Drew Ross, progmg dir; David Atwood, news dir; Tom Hughes, chief of engrg.

Pittsburg

KATD(AM)— September 1949: 990 khz; 5 kw-U. TL: N38 04 49 W121 50 33. Stereo. Hrs open: 24 145 Natoma St., 4th Fl., San Francisco, 94105. Phone: (415) 978-5378. Fax: (415) 978-5380. Licensee: Way Broadcasting Licensee LLC. Group owner: Multicultural Radio Broadcasting Inc. (acq 2-4-2004; grpsl). Population served: 250,000 Keck, Mahin & Cate. Format: Sp. News: 50 hrs wkly. Target aud: 25-54; middle upper income. ◆Arthur Liu, pres; Judy Re, gen mgr.

Placerville

KCCL(FM)— Dec 9, 1982: 92.1 mhz; 2.95 kw. Ant 331 ft TL: N38 45 31 W120 44 59. Stereo. Hrs open: 24 298 Commerce Cir., Sacramento,

95815. Phone: (916) 576-7333. Fax: (916) 929-5330.E-mail: swright@khits921.com Web Site:www.khits921.com Licensee: Results Radio of Sacramento LLC. Group owner: First Broadcasting Investment Partners LLC (acq 6-18-2008). Natl. Rep: McGavren Guild,. Format: Oldies. ◆Jack Fritz, pres, gen mgr; Rico Garcia, progmg dir.

Planada

KHTN(FM)— 1966: 104.7 mhz; 1.95 kw. Ant 2,080 ft TL: N37 32 01 W120 01 46. Stereo. Hrs open: 24 510 W. 19th St., Merced, 95340. Phone: (209) 383-7900. Fax: (209) 723-8461. Web Site:www.hot1047fm.com Licensee: Buckley Communications Inc. Group owner: Buckley Broadcasting Corp. (acq 9-21-95; $500,000). Natl. Rep: D & R Radio,. Format: Contemp hit. Target aud: 21-34; women. ◆Mike McAdam, VP, gen mgr; Rene Roberts, opns mgr; Mike Peters, gen sls mgr.

Point Arena

KYOE(FM)— 2003: 102.3 mhz; 1.2 kw. Ant 1,417 ft TL: N38 53 44 W123 32 34. Hrs open: Box 366, 95468. Phone: (707) 882-2323. Fax: (707) 882-3258. Licensee: Del Mar Trust. Format: Country. ◆Karen J. Hay, gen mgr.

Point Reyes Station

*KWMR(FM)— May 2, 1999: 90.5 mhz; 235 w. Ant 1,076 ft TL: N38 04 48 W122 51 57. Hrs open: 7 AM-12 AM Box 1262, 94956. Secondary address: 11431 State Rte. One #8 94956. Phone: (415) 663-8068. Fax: (415) 663-0746.E-mail: kay@kwmr.org Web Site:www.kwmr.org Licensee: West Marin Community Radio Inc. Format: Community radio. ◆Kay Clements, gen mgr; Adrienne Pfeiffer, dev dir; Lyons Filmer, progmg dir; Andrew Shaw, news dir.

Pollock Pines

KHLX(FM)— Aug 19, 1976: 93.1 mhz; 20.5 kw. Ant 364 ft TL: N38 38 10.5 W120 38 14. Stereo. Hrs open: 1440 Ethan Way, Suite 200, Sacramento, 95825. Phone: (916) 929-5325. Fax: (916) 646-9409. Web Site:www.classic931.com Licensee: CC Licenses LLC. (acq 3-6-2008; $2.75 million). ◆Jeff Holden, gen mgr.

Pomona

KAHZ(AM)— May 12, 1947: 1600 khz; 5 kw-U, DA-N. TL: N34 01 48 W117 43 35. Hrs open: 24 747 E. Green St., Floor 4, Pasadena, 91101. Phone: (626) 844-8882. Fax: (626) 844-2928.E-mail: infor@kahzam.com Web Site:www.mrbi.net Licensee: Multicultural Radio Broadcasting Licensee LLC. Group owner: Multicultural Radio Broadcasting Inc. (acq 11-17-98; $7.55 million). Population served: 2,000,000 Format: Business news/talk, Chinese. Target aud: 30 plus; money oriented. ◆Arthur Liu, pres.

KWKU(AM)— Dec 23, 1960: 1220 khz; 250 w-U, DA-2. TL: N34 01 11 W117 43 03. (CP: 930 w-D). Hrs open: 20
Rebroadcasts KWKW(AM) Los Angeles 60%.
363 S. Park Ave., Suite 105, 91766. Phone: (909) 865-3323. Fax: (909) 865-0342.E-mail: jrodriguez@kwkuradio.com Web Site:www.kwkuradio.com Licensee: Lotus Communications Corp. (group owner; acq 2-00; $750,000). Population served: 3500000 Gammon & Grange. Format: Sp, news/talk, sports. News staff: one; News: 7 hrs wkly. Target aud: 24-64. Spec prog: Relg 15 hrs wkly. ◆Juan Rodriguez, gen mgr, progmg dir; Maria Diaz, news dir.

Port Hueneme

KCAQ(FM)—See Oxnard

KVTA(AM)— July 1958: 1520 khz; 10 kw-D, 1 kw-N, DA-2. TL: N34 10 02 W119 08 02. Hrs open: 2284 S. Victoria Ave., Suite 2 G, Ventura, 93003. Phone: (805) 289-1400. Fax: (805) 644-7906.E-mail: info@kvtaam1520.com Web Site:www.kvtaam1520.com Licensee: Gold Coast Broadcasting LLC (group owner; (acq 1996; $3.65 million with KCAQ Oxnard). Population served: 150,000 Leibowitz & Spencer. Format: News/talk. Target aud: 25-54. ◆Chip Ehrhardt, gen mgr; Tom Spence, progmg dir.

Porterville

KIOO(FM)— Aug 1, 1972: 99.7 mhz; 24 kw. 690 ft TL: N36 06 26 W119 01 45. Stereo. Hrs open: 24 617 W. Tulare Ave., Visalia, 93277. Phone: (559) 627-9710. Fax: (559) 627-1590.E-mail:

ino@997classicrock.com Web Site:www.997classicrock.com Licensee: Buckley Broadcasting Corp. (group owner; acq 3-1-94; $360,000; 5-2-94). Population served: 24,000 Natl. Rep: D & R Radio,. Format: Adult classic rock. News staff: one. Target aud: 25-44. ◆Rick Buckley, pres; Ray McCarty, VP, gen mgr; Tommy Del Rio, opns mgr.

KTIP(AM)— 1947: 1450 khz; 1 kw-U. TL: N36 05 44 W119 03 10. Hrs open: 24 1660 N. Newcomb, 93257. Phone: (559) 784-1450. Fax: (559) 784-2482.E-mail: live@ktip.com Web Site:www.ktip.com Licensee: Mayberry Broadcasting Co. Inc. (acq 9-14-00; $130,000 for 51%). Population served: 400,000 Natl. Network: ABC, Westwood One, . Rgnl rep: Rgnl Reps. Dow, Lohnes & Albertson. Format: News/talk. News staff: 2; News: 23 hrs wkly. Target aud: 25 plus. Spec prog: Health show one hr, loc travel one hr wkly, national health 3hrs., Trader's Market. ◆Larry Stoneburner, pres; Larry & Mimi Stoneburner, gen mgr; Kent Hopper, chief of opns, progmg dir, news dir; Michael Partipilo, sls dir; Mimi Stoneburner, mktg dir; P.K. Whitmire, news dir; Ron Neil, chief of engrg; Janice Dawson, traf mgr.

Prunedale

*KLVM(FM)— Feb 28, 1986: 89.7 mhz; 210 w. Ant 2,053 ft TL: N36 45 22 W121 30 05. Stereo. Hrs open: 24
Rebroadcasts KLVR(FM) Santa Rosa 100%.
8145 Prunedale N. Rd., Salinas, 93907. Phone: (800) 525-5683. Fax: (831) 663-1663.E-mail: klove@klove.com Web Site:www.klove.com Licensee: Prunedale Educational Foundation. Natl. Network: K-Love, . Format: Adult contemp, Christian. Target aud: 25-35; Judeo-Christian female. ◆Dr. E.L. Moon, pres & gen mgr.

Quincy

KHGQ(FM)— 1997: Stn currently dark. 100.3 mhz; 900 w. Ant -1,125 ft TL: N39 56 14 W120 56 51. Hrs open: 24 250 W. Nopah Vista Ave., Parump, NV, 89060. Phone: (775) 751-9709. Fax: (775) 751-3624.E-mail: info@khgo.com Licensee: Hilltop Church (acq 7-18-2005). Format: News/talk. ◆Keily Miller, gen mgr, opns mgr; Randy Creff, chief of engrg.

KNLF(FM)— June 10, 1996: 95.9 mhz; 500 w. -499 ft TL: N39 58 03 W120 53 34. Hrs open: 24 Box 117, 440 Lawrence St., 95971. Phone: (530) 283-4145. Fax: (530) 283-5135.E-mail: rtrumbo@excite.com Web Site:www.knlfradio.com Licensee: New Life Broadcasting. Population served: 20,000 Natl. Network: American Family Radio, . Format: Sports, talk, Christian, Contemp. News: 10 hrs wkly. Target aud: 18-54. ◆Ron Trumbo, pres.

KPCO(AM)— Aug 16, 1963: 1370 khz; 5 kw-D, 500 w-N, DA-2. TL: N39 56 54 W120 53 54. Stereo. Hrs open: 24 395 Main St., 95971. Phone: (530) 256-2400. Fax: (530) 283-5117. Licensee: Tom F. Huth (acq 2-2-2006; $100,000). Population served: 52,000 Format: News/talk, hits from 40's, 50's, & 60's. ◆Bob Fink, pres; Bob Darling, VP, gen mgr; Will Taylor, news dir.

*KQNC(FM)— 2005: 88.1 mhz; 500 w. Ant 1,135 ft TL: N39 56 14 W120 56 51. Hrs open:
Simulcast with KXJZ(FM) Sacramento 100%.
Capital Public Radio Inc., 7055 Folsom Blvd., Sacramento, 95826. Phone: (916) 278-8900. Fax: (916) 278-8989.E-mail: npr@csus.edu Web Site:www.csus.edu/npr Licensee: California State University, Sacramento. Natl. Network: NPR, . Duane Morris LLP. Format: Jazz, news & info. ◆Carl Watanabe, stn mgr, prom mgr; John Brenneise, opns mgr; Joe Barr, news dir, local news ed, relg ed; Jeff Browne, engrg dir.

*KQNY(FM)—Not on air, target date: unknown; 91.9 mhz; 2.7 kw. Ant -1,122 ft TL: N39 56 15 W120 56 49. Hrs open: Box 350, 95971. Phone: (530) 283-0202. Licensee: Plumas Community Radio. ◆Michael Presnell, pres.

Rancho Cordova

KSTE(AM)— Apr 19, 1990: 650 khz; 21.4 kw-D, 920 w-N, DA-2. TL: N38 28 47 W121 16 38. Hrs open: 24 1440 Ethan Way, # 200, Sacramento, 95825. Phone: (916) 929-5325. Fax: (916) 929-2236.E-mail: info@kste.com Web Site:www.talk650kste.com Licensee: AMFM Broadcasting Licenses LLC. Group owner: Clear Channel Communications Inc. (acq 8-30-2000; grpsl). Natl. Network: ABC, Westwood One, . Format: Talk. News staff: 4; News: 15 hrs wkly. Target aud: 25-54. ◆Jeff Holden, gen mgr; Alan Eisenson, opns dir, progmg dir.

Rancho Mirage

KMRJ(FM)— July 17, 1998: 99.5 mhz; 3 kw. Ant 328 ft TL: N33 52 15 W116 13 37. Stereo. Hrs open: 24 1061 S. Palm Canyon Dr., Palm Springs, 92264. Phone: (760) 778-6995. Fax: (760) 778-1249.E-mail: info@995theheat.com Web Site:www.995theheat.com Licensee: Mitchell Media Inc. Natl. Rep: Katz Radio,. Dickstein Shapiro Morin & Oshinsky. Format: Classic rock. News: 2 hrs wkly. Target aud: 35-64; mid age families, working adults. ♦Veronica Ochoa, dev VP & prom mgr; Carolina O'Connel, traf mgr.

Randsburg

***KGBM(FM)**— December 2001: 89.7 mhz; 2 kw. Ant 1,269 ft TL: N35 28 41 W117 41 58. Hrs open: 24 2351 Sunset Blvd., Suite 170-218, Rocklin, 95765. Phone: (916) 251-1600. Fax: (916) 251-1650.E-mail: info@air1.com Web Site:www.air1.com Licensee: Educational Media Foundation. Group owner: EMF Broadcasting (acq 4-19-02). Natl. Network: Air 1, . Shaw Pittman. Format: Contemp Christian. News staff: 3. Target aud: 18-35; Judeo-Christian female. ♦Richard Jenkins, pres; Mike Novak, VP; Ed Lenane, opns dir, news dir; Keith Whipple, dev dir; David Pierce, progmg mgr; Sam Wallington, engrg dir; Karen Johnson, news rptr.

Red Bluff

KALF(FM)— 1978: 95.7 mhz; 7 kw. 1,265 ft TL: N39 55 03 W122 40 12. Stereo. Hrs open: 24 1459 Humboldt Rd., Suite D, Chico, 95928-9100. Phone: (530) 899-3600. Fax: (530) 343-0243. Web Site:www.kalf.com Licensee: Mapleton License of Chico LLC. Group owner: Regent Communications Inc. (acq 11-30-2006; grpsl). Population served: 325,000 Natl. Rep: Christal,. Smithwick & Belendiuk. Format: Country. News staff: one; News: 10 hrs wkly. Target aud: 25-54. ♦Chad Gammage, gen mgr, mktg mgr; Coyote McGee, opns mgr & progmg dir.

KBLF(AM)— 1946: 1490 khz; 1 kw-U. TL: N40 11 28 W122 12 54. Stereo. Hrs open: 756 Hickory St., 96080. Phone: (530) 527-1490. Fax: (530) 527-3525.E-mail: kblfam@yahoo.com Web Site:www.kblf.com Licensee: Tom Huth. Group owner: Huth Broadcasting (acq 8-11-98; $5,000). Population served: 50,000 Natl. Network: Westwood One, PRI, . Format: Memories. Target aud: 35-64. Spec prog: Farm 5 hrs, Sp 4 hrs wkly. ♦Cal Hunter, gen mgr.

***KLVB(FM)**— November 1985: 102.7 mhz; 5.5 kw. Ant 1,414 ft TL: N40 20 41 W121 56 48. Stereo. Hrs open: 24
Rebroadcasts KLVC(FM) Magalia 100%.
2351 Sunset Blvd., Suite 170-218, Rocklin, 95765. Phone: (916) 251-1600. Fax: (916) 251-1650.E-mail: klove@klove.com Web Site:www.klove.com Licensee: Educational Media Foundation. Group owner: EMF Broadcasting (acq 1-11-2001; $750,000). Population served: 211,000 Natl. Network: K-Love, . Natl. Rep: D & R Radio,. Shaw Pittman. Format: Christian contemp. News staff: 3. Target aud: 25-44; Judeo Christian, female. ♦Richard Jenkins, pres; Mike Novak, VP; Keith Whipple, dev dir; David Pierce, progmg mgr; Ed Lenane, news dir; Sam Wallington, engrg dir; Arthur Vassar, traf mgr; Karen Johnson, news rptr.

***KTHM(FM)**—Not on air, target date: unknown: 90.7 mhz; 2.5 kw. Ant 328 ft TL: N40 12 31 W122 07 27. Hrs open: Box 981, 96080. Phone: (530) 347-0138. Licensee: Tehama County Community Broadcasters. ♦Erik Mathisen, pres.

Redding

KEWB(FM)—See Anderson

***KFPR(FM)**— Nov 17, 1994: 88.9 mhz; 750 w. Ant 3,578 ft TL: N40 36 10 W122 38 58. Stereo. Hrs open:
Rebroadcasts KCHO(FM) Chico 75%.
603 N. Market, 96003. Secondary address: Box 990061 95929. Phone: (530) 241-5246. Fax: (530) 241-5246.E-mail: npr@awwwsome.com Web Site:www.wfpr.org Licensee: California State University, Chico Research Foundation. Population served: 200,000 Natl. Network: NPR, PRI, . Cohn & Marks. Format: Var/div. Target aud: General. Spec prog: Sp 4 hrs wkly. ♦Jack Brown, gen mgr; Mike Birdsill, opns dir.

***KKRO(FM)**— Nov 15, 2002: 91.5 mhz; 370 w. Ant 1,315 ft TL: N40 54 53 W122 26 37. Stereo. Hrs open: 24
Rebroadcasts KLRD(FM) Yucaipa 100%.
2351 Sunset Blvd., Suite 170-218, Rocklin, 95765. Phone: (916) 251-1600. Fax: (916) 251-1650.E-mail: info@air1.com Web Site:www.air1.com Licensee: Educational Media Foundation Inc. Group owner: EMF Broadcasting. Population served: 211,000 Natl. Network: Air 1, . Format: Contemp Christian. News staff: 3. Target aud: 27-33; Judeo-Christian female. ♦Richard Jenkins, pres; Mike Novak, VP; Keith Whipple, dev dir; David Pierce, progmg mgr; Ed Lenane, news dir; Sam Wallington, engrg dir; Karen Johnson, news rptr.

KLXR(AM)— August 1956: 1230 khz; 1 kw-U. TL: N40 33 14 W122 22 53. Hrs open: 24 1326 Market St., 96001. Phone: (530) 244-5082. Fax: (530) 244-5698.E-mail: KLXR1230@yahoo.com Licensee: Michael R. Quinn (acq 12-31-99; $125,000). Population served: 139,000 Natl. Network: Jones Radio Networks, . Wombley, Carlyle, Sandbridge & Rice LLC. Wire Svc: AP Format: Adult Standards. Target aud: 35 plus. ♦Mike Quinn, gen mgr, progmg dir, opns, sls; MIke Quinn, prom; Mike Quinn, adv.

KNCQ(FM)— Oct 29, 1985: 97.3 mhz; 100 kw. 3,569 ft TL: N40 36 10 W122 38 58. Stereo. Hrs open: 1588 Charles Dr., 96003-1459. Phone: (530) 244-9700. Fax: (530) 244-9707.E-mail: rhealy@resultsradiomail.com Web Site:www.q97country.com Licensee: Results Radio of Redding Licensee LLC. Group owner: Fritz Communications Inc. Natl. Rep: D & R Radio,. Format: Country. Target aud: 25-54. ♦Beth Tappan, gen mgr; Laurie Curto, gen sls mgr; Patrick John, progmg dir & news dir.

KNRO(AM)— 2001: 1670 khz; 10 kw-D, 1 kw-N. TL: N40 33 14 W122 22 53. Hrs open: 3360 Alta Mesa Dr., 96002-2831. Phone: (530) 226-9500. Fax: (530) 221-4940.E-mail: info@espn1670.com Web Site:www.kpig.com Licensee: Mapleton License of Redding LLC. Group owner: Regent Communications Inc. (acq 11-30-2006; grpsl). Format: AAA Americana. ♦Ron Hren, gen mgr.

KQMS(AM)— Sept 14, 1954: 1400 khz; 1 kw-U. TL: N40 33 33 W122 19 42. Hrs open: 3360 Alta Mesa Dr., 96002. Phone: (530) 226-9500. Fax: (530) 221-4940.E-mail: lisag@reddingradio.com Web Site:www.kqms.com Licensee: Mapleton License of Redding LLC. Group owner: Regent Communications Inc. (acq 11-30-2006; grpsl). Population served: 150,000 Natl. Rep: McGavren Guild,. Format: News/talk. ♦Adam Nathanson, pres; Lisa Geraci, gen mgr; Don Burton, opns mgr, progmg dir; Rich Kipp, gen sls mgr; Shellie Sutter, prom dir; Erin Myers, news dir.

KRRX(FM)—(Burney, May 1985: 106.1 mhz; 100 kw. 2,000 ft TL: N40 54 21 W121 49 38. Stereo. Hrs open: 24 3360 Alta Mesa Dr., 96002. Phone: (530) 226-9500. Fax: (530) 221-4940.E-mail: krrx@reddingradio.com Web Site:106x.com Licensee: Mapleton License of Redding LLC. Group owner: Regent Communications Inc. (acq 11-30-2006; grpsl). Population served: 486,000 Grif Johnson. Format: Rock/AOR. News staff: 2. Target aud: 25-54; upscale. ♦Lisa Geraci, gen mgr; Clark Schopslin, progmg dir.

KSHA(FM)— Sept 1, 1981: 104.3 mhz; 100 kw. 1,560 ft TL: N40 39 14 W122 31 12. Stereo. Hrs open: Prog sep from AM 3360 Alta Mesa Dr., 96002. Phone: (530) 226-9500. Fax: (530) 221-4940. Format: Adult contemp. ♦Dennis Kennedy, progmg dir.

***KVIP(AM)**— Jan 4, 1970: 540 khz; 2.5 kw-D, 17 w-N. TL: N40 37 25 W122 16 49. Hrs open: 24 1139 Hartnell Ave., 96002. Phone: (530) 222-4455.E-mail: info@kvip.org Web Site:www.kvip.org Licensee: Pacific Cascade Communications Corp. (acq 12-69). Population served: 200,000 Natl. Network: Moody, Salem Radio Network, . Format: Inspirational, traditional Christian, talk. News staff: 2; News: 14 hrs wkly. Target aud: General. ♦David L. Morrow, VP; Steve Hafen, gen mgr, news dir, pub affrs dir; Ted Hering, progmg dir; Larry Cardoza, engrg dir; Paul Brown, chief of engrg.

***KVIP-FM**— Oct 19, 1975: 98.1 mhz; 30 kw. Ant 1,710 ft TL: N40 36 10 W122 38 58. Stereo. Hrs open: 24 1139 Hartnell Ave., 96002. Phone: (530) 222-4455.E-mail: info@kvip.org Web Site:www.kvip.org Licensee: Pacific Cascade Communications Corp. Population served: 250,000 Natl. Network: Moody, Salem Radio Network, . Wire Svc: AP Format: Inspirational, traditional Christian. News staff: 2. ♦David Morrow, VP; Steve Hafen, gen mgr, news dir; Ted Hering, progmg dir; Paul Brown, chief of engrg.

Redlands

KCAL(AM)— April 1959: 1410 khz; 5 kw-D, 4 kw-N, DA-N. TL: N34 04 08 W117 12 06. Hrs open: 24 1950 S. Sunwest, San Bernardino, 92408. Phone: (909) 825-5020. Fax: (909) 884-5844.E-mail: edith@radiolazer.com Web Site:www.radiolazer.com Licensee: Lazer Broadcasting Corp. (group owner; acq 8-7-01; $2.35 million). Population served: 680,000 Format: Sp. News staff: 2. Target aud: 18-49, 25-64; Mexican origin, Latin American. ♦Alfredo Plascencia, CEO, chmn, exec VP; Vicki Bails, VP & gen mgr; Armando Gutierrez, prom dir.

KCAL-FM— 1965: 96.7 mhz; 3 kw. 377 ft TL: N34 11 51 W117 17 10. Stereo. Hrs open: 1940 Orange Tree Ln., Suite 200, 92374. Phone: (909) 793-3554. Fax: (909) 798-6627.E-mail: info@kcalfm.com Web Site:www.kcalfm.com Licensee: Anaheim Broadcasting Corp. (group owner) Population served: 3,000,000 Natl. Rep: D & R Radio,. Format: Adult rock. Target aud: 16-30. ♦Jeff Parke, VP, gen mgr; Steve Hoffman, opns mgr & progmg dir.

***KUOR-FM**— October 1966: 89.1 mhz; 35 w. Ant 2,781 ft TL: N34 11 47 W117 02 56. Hrs open:
Rebroadcasts KPCC(FM) Pasadena 100%.
1200 E. Colton Ave., 92374. Web Site:www.scpr.org Licensee: University of Redlands. Natl. Network: NPR, .

Redondo Beach

KDAY(FM)— Aug 4, 1961: 93.5 mhz; 3.4 kw. Ant 433 ft TL: N33 51 35 W118 20 56. Stereo. Hrs open: 24 5055 Wilshire Blvd., Suite 720, Los Angeles, 90036. Phone: (323) 337-1600. Fax: (323) 337-1633.E-mail: info@kday.com Web Site:www.935kday.com Licensee: KDAY Licensing LLC. Group owner: Spanish Broadcasting System Inc. (acq 1-31-2006; $120 million with KDAI(FM) Ontario). Population served: 500,000 Format: Hip-hop. ♦Kimberly Fletcher, gen mgr; Lisa Alta Moreno, gen sls mgr; Anthony Acampora, progmg dir; Larry Slover, chief of engrg.

Ridgecrest

KEPD(FM)— 1979: 104.9 mhz; 1.5 kw. Ant 1,289 ft TL: N35 28 38 W117 41 59. Stereo. Hrs open: 731 N. Balsam St., 93555. Phone: (760) 375-8888. Fax: (760) 371-1824.E-mail: info@kloafm.com Web Site:www.kloafm.com Licensee: Adelman Broadcasting Inc. Population served: 70,000 Format: Country.

KLOA(AM)— Dec 11, 1956: 1240 khz; 250 w-U. TL: N35 37 24 W117 41 10. Hrs open: 731 N. Balsam St., 93555. Phone: (760) 375-8888. Fax: (760) 371-1824.E-mail: radio@iwvisp.com Web Site:www.kloaam.com Licensee: Adelman Broadcasting Inc. (group owner). Population served: 50,000 Format: Oldies. ♦Robert Adelman, pres; Eric Kauffman, progmg dir; James Rowles, chief of engrg.

***KRSF(FM)**—Not on air, target date: unknown: 89.3 mhz; 5 kw. Ant 1,466 ft TL: N35 53 54 W117 17 14. Hrs open: Box 716, 93556-0716. Secondary address: 1209 W. Robert Ave. 93555-5936. Phone: (760) 375-2355. Web Site:www.radio74.net Licensee: Radio 74 Internationale. ♦Everet Witzel, pres.

KWDJ(AM)— Apr 7, 1974: 1360 khz; 1 kw-D, 38 w-N. TL: N35 36 58 W117 38 35. Hrs open: 24 121 W. Ridgecrest Blvd., 93555-2606. Phone: (760) 384-4937. Fax: (760) 384-4978.E-mail: eric@kziq.com Web Site:foxtalk1360.com Licensee: James & Donna Knudsen. (acq 9-30-91; $250,000 with co-located FM; 10-28-91). Population served: 60,000 Natl. Network: Fox News Radio, Jones Radio Networks, Premiere Radio Networks, . Rgnl rep: Kim Kauffman Pepper & Corazzini. Format: Newstalk, sports. News staff: one; News: 168 hrs wkly. Target aud: 25-54; educated adults with high disposable income. ♦James L. Knudsen, pres; Eric Kauffman, gen mgr, opns VP; Kim Kauffman, gen sls mgr.

***KWTD(FM)**— May 2005: 91.9 mhz; 7 kw. Ant 1,280 ft TL: N35 28 38 W117 41 58. Stereo. Hrs open:
Rebroadcasts KWTW(FM) Bishop 100%.
Box 637, Bishop, 93515. Phone: (760) 872-6215. Phone: (866) 466-5989. Fax: (760) 872-4155. Licensee: Living Proof Inc. Format: Christian. ♦Daniel McClenaghan, pres & gen mgr.

KZIQ-FM— Jan 1, 1978: 92.7 mhz; 3 kw. Ant -131 ft TL: N35 36 58 W117 38 35. Stereo. Hrs open: 24 121 W. Ridgecrest Blvd., 93555-2606. Phone: (760) 384-4937.E-mail: eric@kziq.com Licensee: James & Donna Knudsen. Population served: 300,000 Format: Country. News: 2 hrs wkly. ♦Eric Kauffman, gen mgr & stn mgr.

Rio Dell

***KNHT(FM)**— 1999: 107.3 mhz; 3.3 kw. Ant 1,702 ft TL: N40 30 03 W124 17 10. Hrs open: 5AM-2AM Jefferson Public Radio, 1250 Siskiyou Blvd., Ashland, OR, 97520. Phone: (541) 552-6301. Fax: (541) 552-8565.E-mail: info@ijpr.org Web Site:www.ijpr.org Licensee: The State of Oregon, acting by and through the State Board of Higher Education, for the benefit of Southern Oregon University. (acq 1-6-00). Natl. Network: NPR, PRI, . Ernest Sanchez. Wire Svc: AP Format: Classical music, news. News staff: one; News: 35 hrs wkly. ♦Mitchell Christian, CFO; Ronald Kramer, CEO & gen mgr; Bryon Lambert, opns dir; Paul Westhelle, dev dir.

Rio Vista

***KRVH(FM)**— Nov 7, 1972: 101.5 mhz; 10 w. 60 ft TL: N38 09 17 W121 41 48. Hrs open: 410 S. 4th St., 94571. Phone: (707) 374-6336.

Fax: (707) 374-6810. Licensee: River Delta Unified School District. Population served: 3,200 Format: CHR. Target aud: 13-19; young adult. ♦William Fulk, gen mgr.

Riverbank

KCBC(AM)— Apr 5, 1987: 770 khz; 50 kw-D, 1 kw-N, DA-2. TL: N37 47 51 W120 53 01. Stereo. Hrs open: 24 10948 Cleveland Ave., Oakdale, 95361. Phone: (209) 847-7700. Fax: (209) 847-1769.E-mail: kcbcradio@surfside.net Web Site:www.770kcbc.com Licensee: Kiertron Inc. (acq 12-30-92; $1 million; 1-25-93). Population served: 12,000,000 Format: Relg. News staff: one; News: 25 hrs wkly. Target aud: 25-49. ♦Don Crawford Sr., pres; Don Crawford Jr., gen mgr; Virginia Marsau, opns VP & opns mgr; Steve Minshall, chief of engrg.

Riverside

KDIF(AM)— Nov 15, 1941: 1440 khz; 1 kw-U. TL: N34 01 37 W117 21 27. Stereo. Hrs open: 24 2030 Iowa Ave., Ste A, 92507. Phone: (951) 684-1991. Fax: (951) 274-4949.E-mail: info@kdifam.com Licensee: Citicasters Licenses L.P. Group owner: Clear Channel Communications Inc. (acq 5-4-99; grpsl). Verner, Liipfert, Bernhard, McPherson & Hand. Format: Sp. News staff: 2; News: 7 hrs wkly. Target aud: 25-54; Hispanic. Spec prog: Hablando Claro one hr wkly. ♦Bob Ridzak, pres, gen mgr & opns dir.

KFRG(FM)—See San Bernardino

KGGI(FM)— Jan 23, 1965: 99.1 mhz; 2.55 kw. 1,843 ft TL: N34 14 04 W117 08 24. Stereo. Hrs open: 24 2030 Iowa Ave., Suite A, 92507. Phone: (951) 684-1991. Fax: (951) 274-4911.E-mail: info@991kggifm.com Web Site:www.991kggifm.com Licensee: AMFM Broadcasting Licenses LLC. Group owner: Clear Channel Communications Inc. (acq 8-30-2000; grpsl). Population served: 2,300,000 Natl. Rep: McGavren Guild,. Format: CHR. Target aud: 18-49. ♦Bob Ridzak, gen mgr; Scott Welsh, gen sls mgr; Justin Garcia, mktg dir; Jesse Garcia, prom dir; Jesse Duran, progmg dir; Rich Mena, chief of engrg.

KLYY(FM)— Mar 17, 1959: 97.5 mhz; 72 kw. 1,571 ft TL: N33 57 57 W117 17 21. (CP: Ant 1,827 ft.). Stereo. Hrs open: 24 5700 Wilshire Blvd., Suite 250, Los Angeles, 90036. Phone: (323) 900-6100. Fax: (323) 900-6127. Web Site:www.oye975.com Licensee: Entravision Holdings LLC. Group owner: Entravision Communications Corp. (acq 4-20-00; grpsl). Population served: 6,500,000 Natl. Rep: Lotus Entravision Reps LLC,. Format: Cumbia. Target aud: 18-49. ♦Jeff Liberman, VP; Karl Meyer, gen mgr; Nestor Rocha, progmg VP, progmg dir; Elias Autran, progmg dir; Eugene McAfel, chief of engrg, engr; Pam McCaffrey, traf mgr.

KPRO(AM)— June 22, 1957: 1570 khz; 5 kw-D, 194 w-N, DA-2. TL: N33 55 54 W117 23 47. Hrs open: 24 7351 Lincoln Ave., 92504. Phone: (951) 688-1570. Fax: (951) 688-7009.E-mail: kproval@aol.com Licensee: Impact Radio Inc. 1957 Population served: 2,500,000 Pepper & Corazzini. Format: Relg. Target aud: General. ♦Ronnie Olenick, pres; Valorie Stitely, gen mgr & stn mgr.

***KSGN(FM)**— January 1970: 89.7 mhz; 3 kw. Ant 300 ft TL: N34 11 51 W117 17 10. Stereo. Hrs open: 24 2048 Orange Tree Ln., Suite 200, Redlands, 92374. Phone: (909) 583-2150. Fax: (909) 583-2170.E-mail: info@ksgn.com Web Site:www.ksgn.com Licensee: Good News Radio. Population served: 2,000,000 Format: Christian educ, relg. News: 12 hrs wkly. Target aud: General; Christians & church goers. ♦Charles Keyes, chmn, pres, CFO; Dawn Hibbard, gen mgr; Bryan O'Neal, progmg dir; Brandi Lanai, news dir; Bruce Potterton, chief of engrg; Holly Higens, traf mgr.

***KUCR(FM)**— October 1966: 88.3 mhz; 750 w. 291 ft TL: N33 58 11 W117 17 50. (CP: 150 w, ant 1,620 ft.). Stereo. Hrs open: 691 Linden St., 92521. Phone: (951) 827-3737. Fax: (951) 827-3240.E-mail: kucrinfo@kucr.org Web Site:www.kucr.org Licensee: The Regents of the University of California. Population served: 1,000,000 Format: Div, alternative rock. Spec prog: Black 18 hrs, class 14 hrs, jazz 6 hrs wkly. ♦Louis Vandenberg, gen mgr; Walter Douglas, prom dir, progmg dir & news dir; Jeff Armantrout, pub affrs dir; Bill Elledge, chief of engrg.

Rocklin

***KEBR(AM)**— July 27, 1988: 1210 khz; 5 kw-D, 500 w-N, DA-D. TL: N38 27 46 W121 07 49. Hrs open: 24 Family Stations Inc., 4135 Northgate Blvd., Suite 1, Sacramento, 95834-1226. Phone: (916) 641-8191. Fax: (916) 641-8238. Licensee: Family Stations Inc. (group owner) Population served: 254,413 Format: Relg. Target aud: General. ♦Harold Camping, pres; Peggy Renschler, stn mgr & opns mgr.

Rohnert Park

KMHX(FM)— Mar 4, 1986: 104.9 mhz; 6.6 kw. Ant 548 ft TL: N38 23 31 W122 40 40. Stereo. Hrs open: 24 1410 Neotomas Ave., Suite 200, Santa Rosa, 95405. Phone: (707) 543-0100. Fax: (707) 543-1097.E-mail: dannywright@maverick-media.ws Web Site:www.mix1049fm.com Licensee: Maverick Media of Santa Rosa Licensee LLC. Group owner: Fritz Communications Inc. (acq 6-5-2006; $7.7 million). Population served: 416,600 Covington & Burling. Format: Hot adult contemp. Target aud: 25-54. ♦Jeff Clark, gen mgr; Danny Wright, opns mgr, progmg dir.

Rosamond

KLKX(FM)— Sept 1, 1993: 93.5 mhz; 3 kw. Ant 207 ft TL: N34 51 03 W118 09 22. Hrs open: 24 Q-9, 570 East Ave., Palmdale, 93550. Phone: (661) 947-3107. Fax: (661) 272-5688.E-mail: info@thequake.com Web Site:www.935thequake.com Licensee: High Desert Broadcasting LLC (group owner; acq 3-7-2002; grpsl). Population served: 300,000 Natl. Network: Westwood One, . Arent, Fox, Kintner, Plotkin & Kahn. Format: Classic rock, news, interviews. Target aud: 25-54. ♦Nelson Rosse, gen mgr; Gary Wilson, opns mgr, progmg dir; Jeff McElfresh, mktg dir, prom dir; Amir Raheem, news dir.

KVVS(FM)— Mar 1, 1985: 105.5 mhz; 3 kw. Ant 328 ft TL: N34 51 03 W118 09 22. Stereo. Hrs open: 24
Simulcast with KIIS-FM Los Angeles 100%.
3400 W. Olive Ave., Suite 500, Burbank, 91505. Phone: (818) 559-2252. Fax: (818) 729-2502. Web Site:www.kiisfm.com Licensee: CC Licenses LLC. Group owner: Clear Channel Communications Inc. (acq 11-21-2003; grpsl). Format: CHR. ♦Greg Ashlock, gen mgr.

Rosedale

***KOGR(FM)**—Not on air, target date: unknown: 88.9 mhz; 3.6 kw. Ant 1,653 ft TL: N35 03 00 W120 02 23. Hrs open: CSN International, 3232 W. MacArthur Blvd., Santa Ana, 92704. Licensee: CSN International. (group owner).

Roseville

KFSG(AM)— 2001: 1690 khz; 10 kw-D, 1 kw-N. TL: N38 44 22 W121 12 50. Hrs open: 3463 Ramona Ave., Suite 15, Sacramento, 95826. Phone: (916) 456-3288. Fax: (916) 456-3324.E-mail: delatorre@mrbi.net Licensee: Way Broadcasting Licensee LLC (acq 6-13-00; grpsl). Format: Sp. ♦Rosario Delatorre, gen mgr; Yuri Reyes, progmg dir.

KLIB(AM)— Apr 1, 1968: 1110 khz; 5 kw-D, 500 w-N, DA-2. TL: N38 44 22 W121 12 48. Hrs open: 24 3463 Romona Ave., Suite 15, Sacramento, 95826. Phone: (916) 456-3288. Fax: (916) 456-3324.E-mail: info@klib.com Licensee: Way Broadcasting Licensee LLC (acq 4-20-2000; grpsl). Format: Ethnic. Target aud: 18 plus; Hispanic.

KQJK(FM)—Licensed to Roseville. See Sacramento

Sacramento

KBMB(FM)— October 1996: 103.5 mhz; 6 kw. 312 ft TL: N38 33 59 W121 28 47. (CP: Ant 308 ft). Hrs open: 24 1436 Auburn Blvd., 95815. Phone: (916) 646-4000. Fax: (916) 927-7376.E-mail: info@kbmb.com Web Site:www.1035thebomb.com Licensee: Entravision Holdings LLC. Group owner: Entravision Communications Corp. (acq 9-30-2004; $16.1 million). Format: Urban. Target aud: 18-49. ♦Larry LeManski, gen mgr; Larry Prater, gen sls mgr; Don Langford, prom dir; Patti Moreno, progmg dir; Paul Waegele, chief of engrg.

KBZC(FM)— Apr 1, 1957: 106.5 mhz; 50 kw. Ant 410 ft TL: N38 38 30 W121 05 25. Stereo. Hrs open: 24 5345 Madison Ave., 95841. Phone: (916) 334-7777. Fax: (916) 339-5668.E-mail: info@kwod.com Web Site:90sbuzz.com Licensee: Entercom Sacramento License LLC. Group owner: Entercom Communications Corp. (acq 5-19-2003; $25 million). Population served: 4,500,000 Format: 90s var. Target aud: 18-49. ♦John Geary, VP; David Lichtman, gen mgr; Curtiss Johnson, stn mgr, progmg dir.

KCBC(AM)—See Riverbank

KCCL(FM)—See Placerville

KDND(FM)— Aug 1, 1945: 107.9 mhz; 50 kw. 403 ft TL: N38 42 38 W121 28 54. Stereo. Hrs open: 24 5345 Madison Ave., 95841. Phone: (916) 334-7777. Fax: (916) 334-1092. Web Site:www.endonline.com Licensee: Entercom Sacramento License L.L.C. Group owner: Entercom Communications Corp. (acq 6-3-97; $27.5 million). Natl. Rep: D & R Radio,. Format: CHR. News staff: one. Target aud: 25-44. ♦David Lichtman, VP, gen mgr; John Geary, gen mgr, mktg mgr; Dan Mason, stn mgr, progmg dir; Butch Mitchell, sls dir; Sara McLure, gen sls mgr; Dayne Damme, prom dir; Kat Maudru, news dir; Mick Rush, engrg dir.

***KEAR-FM**— May 1997: 88.1 mhz; 8.4 kw. Ant 994 ft TL: N38 14 50 W121 30 03. Stereo. Hrs open: 24 4135 Northgate Blvd., Suite One, 95834-1226. Phone: (916) 641-8191. Fax: (916) 641-8238. Licensee: Family Stations Inc. (group owner) Population served: 25,000 Format: Relg. ♦Harold Camping, pres; Peggy Renschler, gen mgr & opns mgr.

KFBK(AM)— 1922: 1530 khz; 50 kw-U, DA-2. TL: N38 50 54 W121 28 58. Hrs open: 24 1440 Ethan Way, Suite 200, 95825. Phone: (916) 929-5325. Fax: (916) 925-6326.E-mail: info@kfbk.com Web Site:www.kfbk.com Licensee: AMFM Broadcasting Licenses LLC. Group owner: Clear Channel Communications Inc. (acq 8-30-2000; grpsl). Population served: 2,825,300 Wire Svc: PR Newswire Format: News/talk. News staff: 8; News: 45 hrs wkly. ♦Jeff Holden, pres; Alan Eisenson, opns dir, opns mgr, natl sls mgr, progmg dir; Sarah Simpson, sls dir; Amy Bingham, prom dir, prom mgr; Drew Sandsor, news dir; Zachary Rukstela, chief of engrg.

KFIA(AM)—See Carmichael

KGBY(FM)— 1946: 92.5 mhz; 50 kw. Ant 499 ft TL: N38 42 26 W121 28 33. Stereo. Hrs open: 24 1440 Ethan Way, Suite 200, 95825. Phone: (916) 929-5325. Fax: (916) 925-9292.E-mail: info@kgryfm.com Web Site:www.my925radio.com Licensee: AMFM Broadcasting Licenses LLC. Format: Adult contemp. News: one hr wkly. ♦Amy Bingham, prom dir, prom mgr; Sonia Jimenez, progmg dir; Elizabeth Xiong, traf mgr.

KHTK(AM)— November 1926: 1140 khz; 50 kw-U, DA-2. TL: N38 23 34 W121 11 51. Hrs open: 24 5244 Madison Ave, 95841. Phone: (916) 338-9200. Fax: (916) 338-9208. Web Site:www.khtk.com Licensee: CBS Radio Holdings Inc. Group owner: Infinity Broadcasting Corp. (acq 11-13-98; grpsl). Population served: 286,000 Natl. Network: Fox Sports, Westwood One, . Format: Sports. News: 10 hrs wkly. Target aud: 25-44. ♦Steve Cottingim, gen mgr; Scott Marsh, gen sls mgr, sports cmtr; Jeff McMurray, progmg dir.

KIID(AM)— Aug 1, 1945: 1470 khz; 5 kw-D, 1 kw-N, DA-2. TL: N38 35 30 W121 27 47. Hrs open: 8265 Sierra College Blvd., Suite 312, Roseville, 95661. Phone: (916) 780-1470. Fax: (916) 780-1493. Web Site:www.radiodisney.com Licensee: Radio Disney Group LLC. Group owner: ABC Inc. (acq 12-19-00; $3.31 million). Population served: 1,200,000 Natl. Network: Radio Disney, . Format: Children. ♦Judy Remy, stn mgr.

KJAY(AM)— May 23, 1963: 1430 khz; 500 w-D, DA. TL: N38 29 39 W121 32 47. Hrs open: 6 AM-8 PM 5030 S. River Rd., West Sacramento, 95691. Phone: (916) 371-5101. Phone: (916) 371-5104. Fax: (916) 371-1459.E-mail: info@kjay.com Licensee: KJAY L.L.C. (acq 11-94). Population served: 2,500,000 Natl. Network: USA, . Shaw Pittman. Format: International. Target aud: 25-64. ♦Trudi Powell, pres; Jerry Sieber, gen mgr.

KNCI(FM)— Feb 21, 1960: 105.1 mhz; 50 kw. Ant 500 ft TL: N38 38 31 W121 05 25. Stereo. Hrs open: 5244 Madison Ave., 95841. Phone: (916) 338-9200. Fax: (916) 338-9208.E-mail: info@kncifm.com Web Site:www.kncifm.com Licensee: CBS Radio Holdings Inc. Population served: 254,413 Format: Country. ♦Steve Cottingim, stn mgr; Mark Evans, opns dir, progmg dir; J.C. Swan, gen sls mgr; Walt Shaw, news dir; Bruce Hirsch, chief of engrg.

KQJK(FM)—(Roseville, June 1970: 93.7 mhz; 25 kw. Ant 328 ft TL: N38 44 22 W121 12 50. Stereo. Hrs open: 24 1440 Ethan Way, Suite 200, 95825. Phone: (916) 929-5325. Fax: (916) 925-0118. Web Site:www.jackdotcom.com Licensee: AMFM Texas Licenses L.P. Group owner: Infinity Broadcasting Corp. (acq 4-1-2009; grpsl). Population served: 150,000 Wiley Rein LLP. Format: Adult hits. News staff: one; News: 2 hrs wkly. Target aud: 25-54. ♦Jeff Holden, gen mgr & chief of engrg.

KRJY(AM)— 1938: 1240 khz; 1 kw-U. TL: N38 35 17 W121 28 05. Hrs open: 24 1017 Front St., 2nd Fl., 95814. Secondary address: Box 1228 95812. Phone: (916) 553-3000. Fax: (916) 553-3013. Licensee: Diamond Broadcasting Group owner: Moon Broadcasting (acq 11-19-2004; $3 million). Population served: 1,000,000 Natl. Network: CBS Radio, . Format: Hip hop gospel, contemp inspiritional. Target aud: 18 plus. ♦Paula Nelson, gen mgr; Frank Redfield, chief of opns; Tony Williams, prom dir; Kydd Mossie, progmg dir.

KRXQ(FM)— Nov 1, 1959: 98.5 mhz; 50 kw. 500 ft TL: N38 38 35 W121 05 51. Stereo. Hrs open: 24 5345 Madison Ave., 95841. Phone: (916) 334-7777. Fax: (916) 339-4277. Web Site:www.krxq.net Licensee: Entercom Sacramento License L.L.C. Group owner: Entercom

Communications Corp. (acq 7-28-98; grpsl). Population served: 300,000 Natl. Rep: McGavren Guild,. Fletcher, Heald & Hildreth. Format: Active rock. News staff: one. Target aud: 25-40; males. Spec prog: Blues one hr wkly. ♦John Geary, pres & VP; David Lichtman, gen mgr; Jim Fox, progmg dir.

KSEG(FM)— 1959: 96.9 mhz; 50 kw. 500 ft TL: N38 38 54 W121 28 40. Stereo. Hrs open: 5345 Madison Ave., 95841-3141. Phone: (916) 334-7777. Fax: (916) 339-4280. Web Site:www.eagle969.com Licensee: Entercom Sacramento License L.L.C. Group owner: Entercom Communications Corp. (acq 1-7-97; $45 million with KRAK(FM) Roseville). Population served: 1,500,000 Natl. Rep: D & R Radio,. Format: Classic rock. Target aud: 18-49. ♦John Geary, pres & VP; David Lichtman, gen mgr; Curtis Johnson, progmg dir.

KSFM(FM)—(Woodland, Feb 4, 1961: 102.5 mhz; 50 kw. 500 ft TL: N38 35 20 W121 43 30. Stereo. Hrs open: 1750 Howe Ave., Suite 500, 95825. Phone: (916) 920-1025. Fax: (916) 929-5341.E-mail: info@ksfm.com Web Site:www.ksfm.com Licensee: Infinity Radio of Sacramento Inc. Group owner: Infinity Broadcasting Corp. (acq 11-13-98; grpsl). Population served: 254,413 Natl. Network: Westwood One, . Leventhal, Senter & Lerman. Format: Rhythm and blues. Target aud: 12-44. ♦Steve Cottingin, gen mgr; Dell Goetz, gen sls mgr; Marcos Montes, prom dir; Byron Kennedy, progmg dir; Mike DaSilva, chief of engrg.

KSMH(AM)—See West Sacramento

KTKZ(AM)— 1952: 1380 khz; 5 kw-U, DA-2. TL: N38 33 19 W121 10 51. Hrs open: 1425 River Park Dr., Suite 520, 95815. Phone: (916) 924-0710. Fax: (916) 924-1587.E-mail: info@ktkz.com Web Site:www.ktkz.com Licensee: New Inspiration Broadcasting Co. Inc. Group owner: Salem Communications Corp. (acq 3-11-97; $1.5 million). Population served: 1,110,000 Format: Talk. Target aud: 35 plus; general. ♦James Rowten, gen mgr; Steve Gasser, opns mgr; Laurie Larson, progmg dir.

***KXJZ(FM)**— October 1964: 90.9 mhz; 50 kw. Ant 500 ft TL: N38 42 38 W121 28 54. Stereo. Hrs open: 24 7055 Folsom Blvd., 95826. Phone: (916) 278-8900. Fax: (916) 278-8989.E-mail: npr@csus.edu Web Site:www.capradio.org Licensee: California State University, Sacramento. Population served: 3,000,000 Natl. Network: NPR, PRI, AP Radio, . Duane Morris, LLP. Format: Jazz, news & info. News staff: 5; News: 90 hrs wkly. Target aud: General; NPR listeners,ex. professionals, educators & administrators. Spec prog: World mus 2 hrs, blues 7 hrs wkly. ♦Carl Watanabe, stn mgr, progmg dir, progmg mgr; John Brenneise, opns mgr; Joe Barr, news dir; Jeff Browne, engrg dir.

***KXPR(FM)**— July 1, 1991: 88.9 mhz; 50 kw. Ant 492 ft TL: N38 16 25 W121 30 11. Stereo. Hrs open: 24 7055 Folsom Blvd., 95826. Phone: (916) 278-8900. Fax: (916) 278-8989.E-mail: npr@csus.edu Web Site:www.capradio.org Licensee: California State University, Sacramento. Population served: 3,000,000 Natl. Network: NPR, PRI, . Duane Morris LLP. Format: Classical. Target aud: General; NPR Listeners, eg. professionals, educators, administrators. ♦Carl Watanabe, pres, stn mgr, progmg mgr; Tom Livingston, gen mgr; John Brenneise, opns mgr; Cheryl Dring, mus dir; Joe Barr, news dir; Jeff Brown, engrg dir.

***KYDS(FM)**— Jan 24, 1979: 91.5 mhz; 410 w. 108 ft TL: N38 36 33 W121 21 38. Hrs open: 7 AM-3:30 PM 4300 El Camino Ave., 95821. Phone: (916) 971-7453. Fax: (916) 971-7429.E-mail: ammaaikido@yahoo.com Licensee: San Juan Unified School District. Population served: 20,000 Format: Var. ♦Ed Santillanes, gen mgr.

KYMX(FM)— 1947: 96.1 mhz; 50 kw. 476 ft TL: N38 38 09 W121 33 11. Stereo. Hrs open: 280 Commerce Cir., 95815. Phone: (916) 923-6800. Fax: (916) 922-2830.E-mail: info@kymx.com Web Site:www.kymx.com Licensee: Infinity Radio Inc. Group owner: Infinity Broadcasting Corp. (acq 11-13-98; grpsl). Format: Adult contemp. News staff: one; News: 3 hrs wkly. Target aud: 25-54; Women ages 25-54. ♦Joel Hollander, pres; Jacque Tortorolli, CFO; Lisa Decker, sr VP; Dale Well, gen sls mgr; Rouna Daouk, prom dir; Bryan Jackson, progmg dir; Jacqui Freeman, news dir.

KZZO(FM)— October 1958: 100.5 mhz; 115 kw. 328 ft TL: N38 38 30 W121 05 25. Stereo. Hrs open: 280 Commerce Cir., 95815. Phone: (916) 923-6800. Fax: (916) 922-2830.E-mail: info@kzzo.com Web Site:www.radiozone.com Licensee: Infinity Radio Inc. Group owner: Infinity Broadcasting Corp. (acq 11-13-98; grpsl). Natl. Rep: Christal,. Format: Adult contemp. News staff: one; News: 3 hrs wkly. Target aud: 25-44. ♦Gavin Mahsman, gen sls mgr; Steve Cottingim, gen mgr, gen mgr & mktg mgr; Sam Sacco, prom dir; Byran Kennedy, progmg dir.

Saint Helena

KVYN(FM)— November 1976: 99.3 mhz; 3 kw. 226 ft TL: N38 25 34 W122 19 33. (CP: Ant 259 ft.). Stereo. Hrs open: 1124 Foster Rd., Napa, 94558. Phone: (707) 252-1440. Phone: (707) 258-1111. Fax: (707) 226-7544. Web Site:www.kvyn.com Licensee: Wine Country Broadcasting Co. (acq 8-11-03; $3 million with KVON(AM) Napa). Population served: 110,000 Natl. Network: ABC, . Natl. Rep: Christal,. Robinson Silverman Pearce Aronsohn & Berman. Format: Adult contemp. Target aud: 25-45. Spec prog: Folk 2 hrs wkly. ♦Roger O. Walther, pres; Jeff Schechtman, gen mgr, progmg dir; Dan Darnelle, sls dir; Erica Pickett, prom dir; Rob Douguty, mus dir; Lesley Lotto, news dir; Ben Webster, chief of engrg.

Salinas

KDBV(AM)— July 17, 1963: 980 khz; 10 kw-U, DA-2. TL: N36 43 58 W121 35 32. Hrs open: 24 604 E. Chapel St., Santa Maria, 93454. Phone: (805) 406-9157.E-mail: info@kdbvam.com Licensee: Centro Cristiano Vida Abundante Inc. (acq 5-21-2004; $850,000). Population served: 183,085 Brown, Nietert & Kaufman. Wire Svc: Accu-Weather Format: Sp, Christian. Target aud: 18-49; Hispanics. ♦Ronald Stevens, gen mgr.

KDON-FM— December 1959: 102.5 mhz; 15 kw. Ant 2,371 ft TL: N36 45 23 W121 30 05. Stereo. Hrs open: 903 N. Main St., 93906. Phone: (831) 755-8181. Fax: (831) 755-8193. Web Site:www.kdon.com Licensee: CC Licenses LLC. Group owner: Clear Channel Communications Inc. (acq 9-22-97; grpsl). Natl. Rep: Christal,. Format: Hip hop. News staff: one. Target aud: 18-54. ♦Rhonda McCormack, gen mgr, gen sls mgr; Nancy Nevarez, prom dir; Sam Diggedy, progmg dir; Jim Sohn, chief of engrg; Irma Gonzalez, traf mgr.

***KHDC(FM)**—(Chualar, June 28, 1981: 90.9 mhz; 3 kw. 194 ft TL: N36 32 54 W121 26 34. Stereo. Hrs open: 161 Main St., 93901. Phone: (831) 757-8039. Fax: (831) 757-9854.E-mail: info@khdcfm.com Web Site:www.radiobilingue.org Licensee: Radio Bilingue Inc. (acq 11-86; $70,000; 5-12-86). Format: Multilingual, ethnic, Sp. ♦Delia Saldivar, gen mgr, progmg dir.

KION(AM)— 1947: 1460 khz; 10 kw-U, DA-1. TL: N36 43 59 W121 35 32. Hrs open: 24 903 N. Main St., 93906. Phone: (831) 755-8181. Fax: (831) 755-8193. Licensee: CC Licenses LLC. Group owner: Clear Channel Communications Inc. Population served: 500,400 Format: News/talk. ♦Mark Carbonera, progmg dir.

KKHK(FM)—See Monterey

KNRY(AM)—See Monterey

KPRC-FM— Sept 16, 1964: 100.7 mhz; 1.4 kw. Ant 2,385 ft TL: N36 32 05 W121 37 14. Stereo. Hrs open: 903 N. Main St., 93906. Phone: (831) 755-8181. Fax: (831) 755-8193. Web Site:salinas.lapreciosa.com/main.html Licensee: CC Licenses LLC. (acq 9-22-97; grpsl). Format: Sp. ♦Rhonda mcCormack, gen mgr; Maggie Fernandez, prom dir; Alex Luca, progmg dir.

KRAY-FM— Dec 5, 1977: 103.5 mhz; 6 kw. Ant 512 ft TL: N36 42 32 W121 36 46. Stereo. Hrs open: 24 Box 1939, 93902. Secondary address: 548 Alisal St. 93905. Phone: (831) 757-1910. Fax: (831) 757-8015. Licensee: Wolfhouse Radio Group Inc. (group owner; (acq 7-13-2001; grpsl). Population served: 560,000 Format: LaBuena. ♦Ramon Castro, gen mgr & chief of engrg.

KTGE(AM)— July 4, 1963: 1570 khz; 500 w-D. TL: N36 41 49 W121 37 22. (CP: 5 kw-D, 500 w-N, DA-2. TL: N36 39 38 W121 32 29). Hrs open: 24 Box 1939, 93901. Secondary address: 548 Alisal St. 93905. Phone: (831) 757-5911. Fax: (831) 757-8015.E-mail: wolfhouseradio@yahoo.es Licensee: Wolfhouse Radio Group Inc. (group owner; (acq 7-13-2001; grpsl). Population served: 503,590 Format: Sp, rgnl Mexican. Target aud: Adults 24-54. ♦Ramon Castro, gen mgr, gen sls mgr; Vicente Romero, progmg dir.

KWAV(FM)—See Monterey

KYZZ(FM)— Mar 10, 1997: 97.9 mhz; 2.9 kw. Ant 112 ft TL: N36 36 32 W121 40 59. Hrs open: 24 Box 1391, Monterey, 93942. Phone: (831) 649-0969. Fax: (831) 642-9304.E-mail: info@kyzzfm.com Licensee: Buckley Broadcasting Corp. of Salinas. (group owner; (acq 12-21-2005; $3 million). . Population served: 250,000 Format: CHR, pop. Target aud: 18-34; women. ♦Kathy Baker, gen mgr; Tommy Del Rio, progmg dir; Jeff Mitchell, sls.

San Ardo

***KBDH(FM)**— Jan 21, 2001: 91.7 mhz; 2.7 kw. Ant 1,781 ft TL: N35 57 06 W121 00 03. Stereo. Hrs open:
Rebroadcasts KUSP(FM) Santa Cruz 100%.
203 8th Ave, Santa Cruz, 95062. Phone: (831) 476-2800. Fax: (831) 476-2802.E-mail: kusp@kusp.org Web Site:www.kusp.org Licensee: Pataphysical Broadcasting Foundation. Natl. Network: NPR, . Format: Div. News: 44 hrs wkly. ♦Terry Green, gen mgr & stn mgr; Paula Kenyon, dev dir; Rob Mullen, mus dir.

San Bernardino

KEZY(AM)— August 1947: 1240 khz; 1 kw-U. TL: N34 04 55 W117 18 17. Hrs open: 24 Box 500, Camarillo, 93011. Phone: (626) 356-4230. Fax: (626) 795-9185.E-mail: info@enuevavida.com Licensee: Hi-Favor Broadcasting LLC (group owner; acq 8-27-01; $4 million). Natl. Network: USA, . Miller & Miller. Format: Sp, relg. News: 2 hrs wkly. Target aud: 30 plus. ♦Roland Hinz, pres; Sergio Martinez, stn mgr & gen sls mgr; Mary Guthrie, progmg dir.

KFRG(FM)— August 1974: 95.1 mhz; 50 kw. 489 ft TL: N34 11 51 W117 17 10. Stereo. Hrs open: 24 900 E. Washington St., Suite 315, Colton, 92324. Phone: (909) 825-9525. Fax: (909) 825-0441. Web Site:www.kfrog.com Licensee: Infinity Radio Inc. Group owner: Infinity Broadcasting Corp. (acq 11-13-98; grpsl). Population served: 2,100,000 Natl. Rep: McGavren Guild,. Format: Country. News staff: one; News: 3 hrs wkly. Target aud: 25-54; dual income families. ♦Tom Hoyt, VP & gen mgr; Lee Douglas, opns mgr.

KKDD(AM)— 1947: 1290 khz; 5 kw-U, DA-2. TL: N34 07 27 W117 17 57. Hrs open: 24 2030 Iowa Ave., Suite A, Riverside, 92507. Phone: (951) 684-1991. Fax: (951) 274-4911.E-mail: info@radiodisney.com Web Site:www.radiodisney.com Licensee: AMFM Broadcasting Licenses LLC. Group owner: Clear Channel Communications Inc. (acq 8-30-2000; grpsl). Population served: 106,869 Format: Radio Disney. News staff: one; News: 10 hrs wkly. ♦Bob Ridzak, gen mgr; Scott Welsh, progmg dir.

KLYY(FM)—See Riverside

KOLA(FM)— June 15, 1959: 99.9 mhz; 29.5 kw. 1,663 ft TL: N33 57 55 W117 16 59. Stereo. Hrs open: 24 1940 Orange Tree Ln., Suite 200, Redlands, 92374. Phone: (909) 793-3554. Fax: (909) 798-6627.E-mail: info@imakolanut.com Web Site:www.imakolanut.com Licensee: Anaheim Broadcasting Corp. (group owner; acq 1995; $5 million). Population served: 3,000,000 Format: Oldies. News: one hr wkly. Target aud: 25-54. ♦Jeff Parke, gen mgr & opns mgr; Gary Springfield, progmg dir.

KTDD(AM)— Oct 15, 1947: 1350 khz; 5 kw-D, 500 w-N, DA-2. TL: N34 05 37 W117 17 57. (CP: 600 w-N). Hrs open: 24 2030 Iowa Ave., Suite A, Riverside, 92507. Phone: (951) 684-1991. Fax: (951) 274-4911.E-mail: info@thetoad1350.com Web Site:www.thetoad1350.com Licensee: Citicasters Licenses L.P. Group owner: Clear Channel Communications Inc. (acq 5-4-99; grpsl). Population served: 1,343,000 Natl. Rep: McGavren Guild,. Leventhal, Senter & Lerman. Format: Country. News: 15 hrs wkly. Target aud: 25-64. ♦Bob Ridzak, gen mgr; Bill Georgi, progmg dir.

KTIE(AM)— 1929: 590 khz; 1 kw-U, DA-2. TL: N34 04 18 W117 17 50. Hrs open: 24 992 Inland Ctr. Dr., 92408. Phone: (909) 885-6555 Ext. 101. Fax: (909) 383-8889. Web Site:www.ktie590.com Licensee: Caron Broadcasting Inc. Group owner: Salem Communications Corp. (acq 8-29-2001; $7 million). Population served: 1,500,000 Format: News/talk. Target aud: 35-54; male /female upscale, educated, home owners, business decision makers. ♦Terry Fahy, gen mgr; Jim Tinker, opns VP; Brad Anderson, gen sls mgr; Pamela Tyus, prom dir; Chuck Tyler, progmg dir.

***KVCR(FM)**— December 1953: 91.9 mhz; 3.8 kw. 1,605 ft TL: N33 57 57 W117 17 05. (CP.3.8. kw, ant 1,620 ft.). Stereo. Hrs open: 24 701 S. Mt. Vernon Ave., 92410. Phone: (909) 384-4444. Fax: (909) 885-2116.E-mail: info@kvcr.org Web Site:www.kvcr.org Licensee: San Bernardino Community College Dist. Population served: 820,784 Natl. Network: NPR, . Format: News, talk. News staff: 3; News: 50 hrs wkly. Target aud: General. ♦Larry Ciecalone, gen mgr; Duncan Lively, stn mgr; Lillian Vasquez, mktg dir; Steve Ward, opns mgr, progmg dir & progmg dir. Co-owned TV: *KVCR-DT affil

San Clemente

KWVE(FM)— Nov 16, 1971: 107.9 mhz; 530 w. Ant 3,792 ft TL: N33 42 40 W117 31 55. Stereo. Hrs open: 24 3000 W. MacArthur Blvd., Suite 500, Santa Ana, 92704. Phone: (714) 918-6207. Fax: (714) 918-6256.E-mail: kwve@kwve.com Web Site:www.kwve.com Licensee: Calvary Chapel of Costa Mesa Inc. (acq 4-15-85). Population served: 15,030,000 Latham & Watkins. Format: Relg, Christian talk. News staff: 2; News: 3-5 hrs wkly. Target aud: General. Spec prog: Children 3 hrs wkly. ♦Charles W. Smith, pres; Jeffrey Dorman, gen mgr, opns dir & opns mgr.

San Diego

KBZT(FM)— Mar 6, 1960: 94.9 mhz; 21.8 kw. 710 ft TL: N32 50 21 W117 14 57. Stereo. Hrs open: 1615 Murray Canyon Rd., Suite 710, 92108. Phone: (619) 297-3698. Fax: (619) 543-1353. Web Site:www.fm49sd.com Licensee: Lincoln Financial Media Co. of California. Group owner: Jefferson-Pilot Communications Co. (acq 9-13-96; $25 million for stock). Format: Alt. Target aud: 18-49. ♦Darrel Goodin, gen mgr, stn mgr; Chris Turner, mktg dir; Copeland Isaac, prom mgr; John Marks, progmg dir; Eric Schecter, chief of engrg.

KCBQ(AM)— 1946: 1170 khz; 50 kw-D, 4.5 kw-N, DA-2. TL: N32 54 29 W116 54 34. Hrs open: 24 9255 Towne Centre Dr., Suite 535, 92121. Phone: (858) 535-1210. Fax: (858) 535-1212. E-mail: info@kcbq.com Web Site:www.kcbq.com Licensee: New Inspiration Broadcasting Co. Inc. Group owner: Salem Communications Corp. (acq 8-23-2000; $5 million). Population served: 2,648,600 Natl. Network: AP Radio, ABC, . Format: News/talk. News: 5 hrs wkly. Target aud: 35-64; baby boomers that grew up in the 50s & early 60s. ♦Dave Armstrong, gen mgr; Dawn Hockaday, prom dir; Heather Lloyd, opns mgr & progmg dir; Craig Caston, chief of engrg.

KECR(AM)—See El Cajon

KFMB(AM)— May 19, 1941: 760 khz; 50 kw-U, DA-N. TL: N32 50 32 W117 01 29. (CP: TL: N32 50 36 W117 01 28). Stereo. Hrs open: 24 Box 85888, 92186. Secondary address: 7677 Engineer Rd. 92186. Phone: (858) 292-7600. Fax: (858) 279-7676. E-mail: info@kdmbam.com Web Site:www.760kfmb.com Licensee: Midwest Television Inc. (group owner; (acq 4-17-2007 with co-located FM and KFMB-TV San Diego). Population served: 2,100,000 Natl. Network: CBS, . Natl. Rep: McGavren Guild,. Covington & Burling. Format: News/talk. News staff: 10. Target aud: 25-54. ♦August C. Meyer Jr., CEO; Ed Trimble, pres; Tracy D. Johnson, gen mgr & opns dir; John Marquiss, gen sls mgr; Dave Sniff, progmg dir; Fred D'Ambrosi, news dir; Dayna Monroe, pub affrs dir; Mike Sommerville, chief of engrg; Melanie Kartalija, rsch dir.

KFMB-FM— Sept 21, 1959: 100.7 mhz; 30 kw horiz, 26.5 kw vert. Ant 620 ft TL: N32 50 17 W117 14 56. (CP: 38.4 kw, ant 536 ft.). Stereo. Hrs open: Box 85888, 92186. Secondary address: 7677 Engineer Rd. 92186. Phone: (858) 292-7600. Fax: (858) 279-3380. E-mail: info@kfmbfm.com Licensee: Midwest Television Inc. Format: Hot adult contemp. ♦Gina Landau, gen sls mgr; Kim Leeds, prom mgr; Scott Sands, progmg dir; Jen Sewell, mus dir; Lynn Yuen, rsch dir. Co-owned TV: KFMB-TV affil.

KGB-FM— 1956: 101.5 mhz; 50 kw. 500 ft TL: N32 43 49 W117 05 01. Stereo. Hrs open: 24 Prog sep from AM 9660 Granite Ridge Dr., 92123. Phone: (292-2000. Fax: (858) 715-3372. Web Site:www.101kgb.com Population served: 2,800,000 Hogan & Hartson. Format: Classic rock. Target aud: 25-54. ♦Dave Saunders, gen sls mgr; Jay Isbell, prom dir; Jim Richards, progmg dir.

KHTS-FM—(El Cajon, 1961: 93.3 mhz; 1.8 kw. Ant 1,885 ft TL: N32 41 48 W116 56 10. Stereo. Hrs open: 24 9660 Granite Ridge Dr., 92123. Phone: (858) 292-2000. Fax: (858) 522-5707. E-mail: info@khtsfm.com Web Site:www.channel933.com Licensee: Citicasters Licenses L.P. Group owner: Clear Channel Communications Inc. (acq 5-4-99; grpsl). Population served: 2,800,000 Hogan & Hartson. Format: CHR. Target aud: 18-34. ♦Bob Bolinger, gen mgr, sls dir; Brad SAmuel, gen sls mgr; Jean Arrollado, mktg dir; Geoff Alan, prom dir, prom mgr; Jimmy Steele, progmg dir, progmg mgr; Mary Ayala, news dir; John Rigg, chief of engrg.

KIFM(FM)— Feb 4, 1960: 98.1 mhz; 28 kw. 640 ft TL: N32 50 17 W117 14 56. Stereo. Hrs open: 24 1615 Murray Canyon Rd., Suite 710, 92108-4321. Phone: (619) 297-3698. Fax: (619) 543-1353. Web Site:www.kifm.com Licensee: Lincoln Financial Media Co. of California. Group owner: Jefferson-Pilot Communications Co. (acq 8-1-96; $28.75 million). Population served: 2,500,000 Natl. Rep: CBS Radio,. Format: Smooth Jazz. News: 2 hrs wkly. Target aud: 25-54; upscale adults. ♦Darrel Goodin, gen mgr, gen mgr, stn mgr; Dave Saunders, gen sls mgr; Chris Turner, mktg dir; Copeland Isaac, prom mgr; John Marks, progmg dir; Eric Schecter, chief of engrg.

KIOZ(FM)— 1954: 105.3 mhz; 26 kw. Ant 689 ft TL: N32 50 20 W117 14 56. Stereo. Hrs open: 24 9660 Granite Ridge Dr., 92123. Phone: (858) 292-2000. Fax: (858) 715-3180. E-mail: info@kiozfm.com Web Site:www.rock1053.com Licensee: Citicasters Licenses L.P. Group owner: Clear Channel Communications Inc. (acq 5-4-99; grpsl). Hagan and Hartson. Format: Rock. News staff: one; News: one hr wkly. Target aud: 18-49; upscale, well educated, young adult rock fans. ♦Bob Bolinger, gen mgr; Jay Isbell, prom dir; Shauna Moran, progmg dir.

KLNV(FM)— June 26, 1960: 106.5 mhz; 50 kw. 440 ft TL: N32 43 17 W117 04 11. Stereo. Hrs open: 600 W. Broadway, Suite 2150, 92101. Phone: (619) 235-0600. Fax: (619) 744-4300. Web Site:www.lanueva1065.com Licensee: HBC San Diego License Corp. Group owner: Univision Radio (acq 9-22-2003; grpsl). Wire Svc: UPI Format: Regional Mexican. Target aud: 18-49; young adult, contemp mus fans, upscale, well-educated. ♦Peter Moore, gen mgr; Michael Donavan, gen sls mgr; Nate Mendez, prom dir; Jose Gadea, progmg dir; Angel Ramos, chief of engrg.

KLQV(FM)— May 20, 1963: 102.9 mhz; 32 kw. Ant 617 ft TL: N32 50 24 W117 14 52. Stereo. Hrs open: 24 600 W. Broadway, Suite 2150, 92101. Phone: (619) 235-0600. Fax: (619) 744-4300. Web Site:www.univison.com Licensee: HBC San Diego License Corp. Group owner: Univision Radio (acq 9-22-2003; grpsl). Population served: 2,700,000 Format: Sp. Target aud: 25-44. ♦Peter Moore, gen mgr.

KLSD(AM)— July 14, 1922: 1360 khz; 5 kw-D, 1 kw-N. TL: N32 43 49 W117 05 01. Hrs open: 9660 Granite Ridge Dr., 92123. Phone: (858) 292-2000. Fax: (858) 715-3372. E-mail: cliffalbert@clearchannel.com Web Site:www.am1360klsd.com Licensee: Citicasters Licenses L.P. Group owner: Clear Channel Communications Inc. (acq 1999; grpsl). Population served: 697,027 Natl. Rep: CBS Radio,. Format: Sports. ♦Cliff Albert, stn mgr, progmg dir; Scotty Morache, gen sls mgr; Sherry Toennies, prom dir; Mary Ayala, news dir; Bill Thompson, chief of engrg.

KMYI(FM)— 1949: 94.1 mhz; 77 kw. Ant 689 ft TL: N32 50 20 W117 14 56. Hrs open: 24 9660 Granite Ridge Dr., 92123. Phone: (858) 292-2000. Fax: (858) 715-3336. E-mail: info@kmyifm.com Web Site:www.my941.com Licensee: Citicasters Licenses L.P. Group owner: Clear Channel Communications Inc. (acq 5-4-99; grpsl). Population served: 2,800,000 Hogan and Hartson. Format: Hot adult contemp. Target aud: 35-54; general, women. ♦Bob Bolinger, gen mgr; Jim Richards, opns VP; Kristin Ferguson, prom dir; Jimmy Steele, progmg dir.

KNSN(AM)— 1946: 1240 khz; 1 kw-U. TL: N32 41 40 W117 07 17. Stereo. Hrs open: 1615 Murray Canyon Rd., Ste 710, 92108-4321. Phone: (619) 291-9797. Licensee: Lincoln Financial Media Co. of California. Group owner: Jefferson-Pilot Communications Co. (acq 4-3-2006; grpsl). Population served: 760,000 Format: Chinese. ♦Darrel Goodin, gen mgr; Eric Schecter, chief of engrg.

KOGO(AM)— 1926: 600 khz; 5 kw-U, DA-1. TL: N32 43 17 W117 04 11. Hrs open: 24 9660 Granite Ridge Dr., 92123-2657. Phone: (858) 292-2000. Fax: (858) 715-3379. E-mail: kogo@clearchannel.com Web Site:www.kogo.com Licensee: Citicasters Licenses L.P. Group owner: Clear Channel Communications Inc. (acq 1999; grpsl). Population served: 2,416,100 Natl. Network: ABC, . Kaye, Scholer, Fierman, Hays & Handler. Wire Svc: UPI Format: News/talk. News staff: 10; News: 22 hrs wkly. Target aud: 25-54; issue oriented talk radio listeners. ♦Bob Bolinger, gen mgr; Sherry Toennies, prom dir; Cliff Albert, progmg dir; John Rigg, chief of engrg.

***KPBS-FM**— Sept 12, 1960: 89.5 mhz; 2.7 kw. Ant 1,804 ft TL: N32 41 53 W116 56 03. Stereo. Hrs open: 24 5200 Campanile Dr., 92182-5400. Phone: (619) 594-8100. Phone: (619) 594-2580. Fax: (619) 594-3812. E-mail: letters@kpbs.org Web Site:www.kpbs.org Licensee: San Diego State University. Population served: 2,212,500 Natl. Network: PRI, NPR, . Dow, Lohnes & Albertson. Wire Svc: AP Format: News/talk, class. News staff: 15; News: 11 hrs wkly. Target aud: 35 plus. ♦Tom Karlo, CFO; Doug Myrland, gen mgr; John Decker, opns dir, progmg dir.

KPRI(FM)—See Encinitas

KSCF(FM)— 1965: 103.7 mhz; 26.5 kw. Ant 689 ft TL: N32 50 20 W117 14 56. Stereo. Hrs open: 24 8033 Linda Vista Rd., 92111-5108. Phone: (858) 560-1037. Fax: (858) 571-0326. Web Site:www.radiosophie.com Licensee: CBS Stations Inc. Group owner: Infinity Broadcasting Corp. (acq 8-7-2000; grpsl). Population served: 300,000 Natl. Rep: Christal,. Format: Adult contemp. ♦Peter Schwartz, gen mgr; Charlie Quinn, opns mgr, progmg dir.

KSDO(AM)— October 1947: 1130 khz; 10 kw-U, DA-2. TL: N32 51 04 W117 57 51. Hrs open: 24 136 S. Oak Knoll Ave., Suite 302, Pasadena, 91101. Phone: (626) 356-4230. Fax: (626) 795-9185. E-mail: info@enuevavida.com Web Site:www.ksdo.com Licensee: Hi-Favor Broadcasting LLC (group owner; acq 4-1-03; $10 million). . Population served: 260,000 Natl. Network: ABC, . Format: Sp-relg. News staff: 10. Target aud: 25-54. ♦Mary Guthrie, gen mgr, progmg dir; Carlos Ortega, news dir; Rudy Agus, chief of engrg.

***KSDS(FM)**— December 1951: 88.3 mhz; 22 kw vert. Ant 246 ft TL: N32 48 19 W117 10 09. Stereo. Hrs open: 24 1313 Park Blvd., 92101. Phone: (619) 388-3037. Fax: (619) 388-3928. E-mail: markd@jazz88.org Web Site:www.jazzs88.org Licensee: San Diego Community College District. Population served: 696,679 Natl. Network: NPR, . James S. Bubar. Format: Jazz, blues. News staff: one; News: 7 hrs wkly. Target aud: 25-65 plus; affluent, professional adults. ♦Mark DeBoskey, stn mgr; Jennifer Weddel, dev dir; Ann Bauer, sls dir; Claudia Russell, progmg dir; Bob Broms, mus dir, news dir; Larry Quick, chief of engrg.

KSON(FM)— Jan 15, 1964: 97.3 mhz; 50 kw. Ant 440 ft TL: N32 43 13 W117 04 14. Stereo. Hrs open: 1615 Murray Canyon Rd., Suite 710, 92108. Phone: (619) 291-9797. Fax: (619) 543-1353. Web Site:www.kson.com Licensee: Lincoln Financial Media Co. of California. Group owner: Jefferson-Pilot Communications Co. (acq 2-7-85). Format: Country. ♦Darrel Goodin, gen mgr, opns dir; Chris Turner, mktg dir; Copeland Isaac, prom mgr; John Marks, progmg dir; Eric Schecter, chief of engrg.

KSSD(FM)—See Fallbrook

KURS(AM)— Nov 1, 1992: 1040 khz; 9.5 kw-D, 4.5 kw-N, DA-2. TL: N32 54 21 W116 55 40. Hrs open: 24 296 H St., Suite 300, Chula Vista, 91910. Phone: (619) 426-5645. Fax: (619) 425-1000. E-mail: jc@psnradio.com Web Site:www.espnradio620am.com Licensee: Quetzal Bilingual Communications Inc. Population served: 580,000 Wire Svc: UPI Format: Oldies. ♦Jaime Bonilla, pres; Jose Carbajal, gen mgr.

KYXY(FM)— 1960: 96.5 mhz; 26.5 kw. Ant 689 ft TL: N32 50 20 W117 14 56. Stereo. Hrs open: 24 8033 Linda Vista Rd., 92111-5108. Phone: (858) 571-7600. Fax: (858) 571-0326. Web Site:www.kyxy.com Licensee: CBS Stations Inc. Group owner: Infinity Broadcasting Corp. (acq 8-7-00; grpsl). Population served: 300,000 Natl. Rep: Christal,. Format: Soft rock. Target aud: 25-54; adults, women. ♦Peter Schwartz, gen mgr; Charlie Quinn, opns mgr, progmg dir.

XETRA(AM)—(Tijuana, MEX) 1934: 690 khz; 77 kw-D, 50 kw-N. Hrs open: 24 3400 W. Olive Ave., Suite 550, Burbank, 91505. Phone: (818) 559-2252. Fax: (818) 260-9961. Licensee: Clear Channel Communications Inc. (group owner; (acq 1999; grpsl). Natl. Network: ABC, . Format: Adult standards. Target aud: 25-54; men. ♦Kevin McCarthy, exec VP & gen mgr; Dan Weiner, sls dir.

XETRA-FM—(Tijuana, MEX) 1978: 91.1 mhz; 100 kw. Ant 1,000 ft Stereo. Hrs open: 24 3400 W. Olive Ave., Suite 550, Burbank, MEX, 91505. Phone: (818) 559-2252. Fax: (818) 260-9961. Web Site:www.91x.com Licensee: Clear Channel Communications Inc. Haley, Bader & Potts. Format: Alternative. News staff: one. Target aud: 18-49; very active, college educated, above market average income, single. ♦Mike Glickenhaus, exec VP; Bill Lipis, stn mgr, mktg dir; Tim Dukes, opns VP.

XHRM-FM—(Tijuana, MEX) January 1981: 92.5 mhz; 100 kw. 548 ft Stereo. Hrs open: 24 9660 Granite Ridge Dr., 92123. Phone: (858) 495-9100. Fax: 858) 522-5717. E-mail: info@magic925.com Web Site:www.magic925.com Licensee: The Rivas Kaloyan Family. Format: Adult contemp, rhythmic oldies, today's rhythm and blues. Target aud: 18-49. ♦Mike Glickenhouse, gen mgr & disc jockey.

San Fernando

KBUA(FM)— Nov 14, 1958: 94.3 mhz; 3 kw. 95 ft TL: N34 17 03 W118 28 17. Stereo. Hrs open: 24
Rebroadcasts KBUE(FM) Long Beach 100%.
1845 Empire Ave., Burbank, 91504. Phone: (818) 729-5300. Fax: (818) 729-5678. Web Site:www.aquisuena.com Licensee: LBI Radio License Corp. Group owner: Liberman Broadcasting Inc. (acq 1997; $10.8 million). Population served: 1,500,000 Format: Mexican rgnl. ♦Lenard Liberman, pres, VP; Pepe Garza, stn mgr & progmg dir; Chris Buchanan, chief of engrg.

San Francisco

***KALW(FM)**— Mar 20, 1941: 91.7 mhz; 1.9 kw. 920 ft TL: N37 45 17 W122 26 44. Stereo. Hrs open: 24 500 Mansell, 94134. Phone: (415) 841-4121. Fax: (415) 841-4125. E-mail: kalw@kalw.org Web Site:www.kalw.org Licensee: San Francisco Unified School District. Population served: 2,500,000 Natl. Network: PRI, NPR, . Format: NPR, BBC, Local. News: 68 hrs wkly. Target aud: General; news & info-oriented listeners. Spec prog: Diversified. ♦Matt Martin, gen mgr; William Helgeson, opns mgr; Dianne Keogh, dev dir.

KBWF(FM)— 1959: 95.7 mhz; 6.9 kw. Ant 1,500 ft TL: N37 41 23 W122 26 12. Stereo. Hrs open: 24 201 3rd St., 94103. Phone: (415) 957-0957. Fax: (415) 356-8394. E-mail: kbwf.radiotown@radio.com Web Site:www.957thewolf.com Licensee: Entercom San Francisco License LLC. Group owner: Bonneville International Corp. (acq 3-14-2008; grpsl). Format: Country. Target aud: 25-54. ♦John Parish, gen sls mgr.

KCBC(AM)—See Riverbank

KCBS(AM)— April 1909: 740 khz; 50 kw, DA-2. TL: N38 08 23 W122 31 45. Hrs open: 865 Battery St., 3rd Fl., 94111. Phone: (415) 765-4000. Fax: (415) 765-4080.E-mail: info@kcbs.com Web Site:www.kcbs.com Licensee: CBS Radio East Inc. Group owner: Infinity Broadcasting Corp. (acq 1996). Population served: 1,000,000 Natl. Network: CBS, . Wire Svc: Reuters Wire Svc: Bay City News Service Wire Svc: U.S. Weather Service Format: News. Target aud: 25-54. ♦Doug Harvill, gen mgr.

KCNL(FM)—See Sunnyvale

KDFC-FM— Sept 1, 1947: 102.1 mhz; 33 kw. 1,050 ft TL: N37 50 57 W122 29 56. Hrs open: 24 201 Third St., Suite 1200, 94103. Phone: (415) 764-1021. Fax: (415) 777-2291.E-mail: info@kdfc.com Web Site:www.kdfc.com Licensee: Entercom San Francisco License LLC. Group owner: Bonneville International Corp. (acq 3-14-2008; grpsl). Population served: 5,000,000 Natl. Rep: CBS Radio,. Format: Class. Target aud: 25-54; educated, upscale. ♦Dwight Walker, gen mgr; Bill Lueth, opns mgr, progmg dir; Joe Schembri, gen sls mgr.

KEAR(AM)— Sept 24, 1924: 610 khz; 5 kw-U. TL: N37 50 58 W122 17 44. Stereo. Hrs open: 290 Hegenberger Rd., Oakland, 94621-1436. Phone: (510) 568-6200. Fax: (510) 568-6190. Web Site:www.familyradio.com Licensee: Family Stations Inc. Group owner: CBS Radio (acq 4-28-2005; $35 million). Population served: 5,330,000 Natl. Network: Family Radio, . Format: Relg. Target aud: General. ♦Harold Camping, pres, gen mgr; Thad McKinney, gen mgr.

KEST(AM)— 1926: 1450 khz; 1 kw-U. TL: N37 46 41 W122 23 16. (CP: TL: N37 45 37 W122 22 56). Hrs open: 24 145 Natoma St., Suite 400, 94105. Phone: (415) 978-5378. Fax: (415) 978-5380.E-mail: info@kestradio.com Web Site:www.kestradio.com Licensee: Multicultural Radio Broadcasting Licensee LLC. Group owner: Multicultural Radio Broadcasting Inc. (acq 3-31-98; grpsl). Population served: 7,500,000 Format: Personal growth talk, foreign language. News staff: one; News: 6 hrs wkly. Target aud: 25 plus. Spec prog: Chinese, Japanese, Indian, gospel, new age. ♦Arthur S. Liu, pres; Judy Re, gen mgr & opns mgr.

KFAX(AM)— 1925: 1100 khz; 50 kw-U, DA-1. TL: N37 37 56 W122 07 49. Hrs open: 24 Box 8125, Fremont, 94537. Phone: (510) 713-1100. Fax: (510) 505-1448.E-mail: info@kfax.com Web Site:www.kfax.com Licensee: Golden Gate Broadcasting Co. Inc. Group owner: Salem Communications Corp. (acq 9-1-84). Population served: 9,000,000 Natl. Network: Salem Radio Network, . Natl. Rep: Salem,. Format: Relg, talk. News: 4 hrs wkly. Target aud: 25-54; females, families, college educated. Spec prog: Contemp Christian music 5 hrs weekly, children one hr wkly. ♦Ken Miller, gen mgr; Peter Thiele, opns dir & opns mgr; Kelly Christian, gen sls mgr; Amy Nyquist, mktg dir, prom dir, progmg dir; Craig Roberts, news dir, chief of engrg.

KFOG(FM)— Mar 1, 1963: 104.5 mhz; 7.9 kw. 1,454 ft TL: N37 45 20 W122 27 05. Stereo. Hrs open: 24 Prog sep from AM 55 Hawthorne St., Suite 1000, 94105. Phone: (415) 817-5364. Fax: (415) 995-7029.E-mail: kfog@kfog.com Web Site:www.kfog.com Licensee: KFFG Lico Inc. Format: Rock. News staff: one; News: 4 hrs wkly. ♦Tony Salvadore, gen mgr; Sheri Nelson, prom dir; David Benson, progmg dir.

KFRC(AM)— 1947: 1550 khz; 10 kw-U, DA-2. TL: N37 31 49 W122 16 29. Stereo. Hrs open: 24 865 Battery St., 2nd Fl., 4th floor, 94111. Phone: (415) 391-9970. Fax: (415) 397-7655. Web Site:www.kfrc.com Licensee: CBS Radio East Inc. Group owner: Infinity Broadcasting Corp. (acq 12-14-2000; grpsl). Population served: 715,674 Format: Oldies. Target aud: 12 plus; affluent, home-owning, highly educated, business professionals. Spec prog: Jazz. ♦Greg Nemitz, gen mgr; Steven Page, stn mgr.

KFRC-FM— 1958: 106.9 mhz; 80 kw. Ant 1,120 ft TL: N37 50 58 W122 29 56. Stereo. Hrs open: 24
Simulcast with KCBS(AM) San Francisco 100%.
865 Battery St., 3rd Fl., 94111. Phone: (415) 765-4000. Fax: (415) 765-4080. Web Site:www.kcbs.com Licensee: CBS Radio Stations Inc. (group owner; (acq 12-7-2005; $95 million). Natl. Network: CBS Radio, . Natl. Rep: CBS Radio,. Format: News. News staff: 2. ♦Doug Harvill, gen mgr.

KGO(AM)— Jan 8, 1924: 810 khz; 50 kw-U, DA-1. TL: N37 31 39 W122 06 05. Hrs open: 900 Front St., 94111-1450. Phone: (415) 398-5600. Fax: (415) 391-2795.E-mail: info@kgo.com Web Site:www.kgo.com Licensee: Radio License Holding VIII LLC. Group owner: ABC Inc. (acq 6-12-2007; grpsl). Population served: 1,000,000 Natl. Rep: ABC Radio Sales, Interep,. Wilmer, Cutler & Pickering. Wire Svc: Weather Wire Svc: Bay City News Service Format: News/talk. Target aud: 25-54; general. ♦Michael Luckoff, pres, gen mgr; Jack Swanson, opns dir, progmg dir; Paul Hosley, news dir; Joe Talbot, chief of engrg.

KIOI(FM)— Oct 27, 1957: 101.3 mhz; 125 kw. Ant 1,160 ft TL: N37 41 24 W122 26 13. Stereo. Hrs open: 24 340 Townsend St., Suite 5-101, 94107. Phone: (415) 538-1013. Fax: (415) 975-5573. Licensee: AMFM Broadcasting Licenses LLC. Group owner: Clear Channel Communications Inc. (acq 8-30-2000; grpsl). Population served: 7,000,000 Natl. Rep: Christal,. Latham & Watkins. Format: Adult contemp. News staff: one; News: one hr wkly. Target aud: 25-54. ♦Anna Eppinger, gen sls mgr, rgnl sls mgr; Tony Ng, prom dir; Stacy Cunningham, progmg dir; John Scott, news dir; David Williams, chief of engrg.

KIQI(AM)— 1957: 1010 khz; 10 kw-D, 500 w-N, DA-2. TL: N37 49 33 W122 18 39. (CP: COL: Sunnyvale, 15 kw-D, 1.5 kw-N). Hrs open: 24 145 Natoma St., 4th Fl., 94105. Phone: (415) 978-5378. Fax: (415) 978-5380. Licensee: Multicultural Radio Broadcasting Licensee LLC. Group owner: Multicultural Radio Broadcasting Inc. (acq 2-4-2004; grpsl). Population served: 715,674 Format: Sp, talk/news. News staff: 3. Target aud: 24-54. ♦Arthur Liu, pres, prom mgr; Judy Re, gen mgr & progmg dir.

KISQ(FM)— July 17, 1958: 98.1 mhz; 75 kw. Ant 1,015 ft TL: N37 51 04 W122 29 50. Stereo. Hrs open: 8 AM-5:30 PM 340 Townsend St., 94107. Phone: (415) 975-5555. Fax: (877) 547-7329.E-mail: info@kisqfm.com Web Site:www.981kissfm.com Licensee: AMFM Broadcasting Licenses LLC. Group owner: AMFM Inc. (acq 8-30-2000; grpsl). Population served: 715,674 Natl. Rep: McGavren Guild,. Format: Oldies. Target aud: 25-54; women. Spec prog: Gospel 3 hrs wkly. ♦Anna Eppinger, gen mgr; Michael Erickson, progmg dir; David Williams, chief of engrg.

KITS(FM)— June 1, 1964: 105.3 mhz; 15 kw. 1,200 ft TL: N37 41 20 W122 26 07. Stereo. Hrs open: 865 Battery St., 3rd Fl., 94111-1513. Phone: (415) 512-1053. Phone: (415) 402-6700. Fax: (415) 777-0608.E-mail: info@kitsfm.com Web Site:www.live105.com Licensee: Infinity Broadcasting East Inc. Group owner: Infinity Broadcasting Corp. (acq 5-7-97). Population served: 715,684 Format: New rock alternative. ♦Steve DiNardo, gen mgr; Karl Isotalo, gen sls mgr; Dave Numme, progmg dir.

KKGN(AM)—See Oakland

KKSF(FM)— Nov 3, 1947: 103.7 mhz; 7.2 kw. Ant 1,470 ft TL: N37 45 19 W122 27 05. Stereo. Hrs open: 24 4th Fl., 340 Townsend St., 94107. Phone: (415) 975-5555. Fax: (415) 975-5573. Web Site:www.1037theband.com Licensee: AMFM Broadcasting Licenses LLC. Group owner: Clear Channel Communications Inc. (acq 8-30-2000; grpsl). Population served: 6,000,000 Format: Hits from the 60s, 70s and 80s. News staff: one; News: 5 hrs wkly. Target aud: 25-49. ♦Anna Eppinger, gen mgr; Ken Jones, opns mgr, progmg dir; Ramona Gutierrez, prom dir.

KLLC(FM)— Feb 1, 1948: 97.3 mhz; 82 kw. 1,014 ft TL: N37 50 57 W122 29 56. Stereo. Hrs open: 24 865 Battery St., 3rd Fl., 94111. Phone: (415) 765-4097. Fax: (415) 765-4084.E-mail: studio@radioalice.com Web Site:www.radioalice.com Licensee: Infinity Broadcasting East Inc. Natl. Rep: CBS Radio,. Format: Modern adult contemp. Target aud: 18-54.

KLOK(AM)—See San Jose

KMEL(FM)— Nov 30, 1960: 106.1 mhz; 69 kw. 1,290 ft TL: N37 41 24 W122 26 13. Stereo. Hrs open: 24 340 Townsend St., 94107. Phone: (415) 538-1061. Fax: (415) 975-5573. Licensee: AMFM Broadcasting Licenses LLC. Group owner: Clear Channel Communications Inc. (acq 8-30-2000; grpsl). Natl. Rep: Christal,. Format: CHR. ♦Anna Eppinger, gen mgr, gen sls mgr; Tony Ng, prom dir; Stacy Cunningham, progmg dir.

KMKY(AM)—See Oakland

KMVQ-FM— 1949: 99.7 mhz; 40 kw. Ant 1,299 ft TL: N37 41 15 W122 26 04. Stereo. Hrs open: 865 Battery St., 3rd Fl., 94111. Phone: (415) 391-9970. Fax: (415) 951-2329.E-mail: cat.ong@movin997.com Web Site:www.movin997.com Licensee: CBS Radio KFRC-FM Inc. (acq 1-96; grpsl). Format: Rhythmic adult contemp. ♦Doug Harvill, gen mgr; Larry Blumhagen, gen sls mgr; Cat Ong, mktg dir; Mike Preston, progmg VP; Phil Lerza, chief of engrg.

KNBR(AM)— 1922: 680 khz; 50 kw-U. TL: N37 31 49 W122 16 29. Hrs open: 24 55 Hawthorne St., Suite 1100, 94105. Phone: (415) 995-6800. Fax: (415) 995-6867.E-mail: sports@knbr.com Web Site:www.knbr.com Licensee: KNBR Lico Inc. Group owner: Susquehanna Radio Corp. (acq 5-24-89; $17.5 million; 6-12-89). Population served: 715,674 Natl. Network: ABC, Westwood One, . Format: Sports talk, personality. Target aud: 18 plus; predominently men. ♦Lee Hammer, VP, opns mgr; Lyell Perry, opns mgr, prom dir; Peter Schwartz, sls dir; Daniel Erman, gen sls mgr; Sheri Nelson, gen mgr & mktg dir.

KNEW(AM)—See Oakland

KNGY(FM)—(Alameda, Aug 1, 1959: 92.7 mhz; 3.6 kw. Ant 420 ft TL: N37 47 54 W122 24 59. Stereo. Hrs open: 400 Second St., Suite 300, 94107. Phone: (415) 356-1600.E-mail: admin@energy927fm.com Web Site:www.energy92fm.com Licensee: Flying Bear Licensing LLC (acq 12-23-2004; $33.64 million). Population served: 250,000 Format: Urban contemp. ♦Brad Bludau, gen mgr, gen sls mgr; Julie Johnson, mktg dir, prom dir; John Peake, progmg dir; Michelle Bayliss, pub svc dir.

KOHL(FM)—See Fremont

KOIT-FM— 1959: 96.5 mhz; 33 kw. Ant 1,410 ft TL: N37 45 20 W122 27 05. Hrs open: 201 3rd St., #1200, 94103-3143. Phone: (415) 777-0965. Fax: (415) 896-0965.E-mail: koit@koit.com Licensee: Entercom San Francisco License LLC. (acq 3-14-2008; grpsl). Format: Adult contemp. Target aud: 25-54; upscale adults who earn an average of $30,000. ♦Dwight Walker, gen mgr; Bill Conway, stn mgr, progmg dir; Scotty Bastable, gen sls mgr; Maribeth Doran, natl sls mgr; Jude Heller, mktg dir, prom dir; Julie Deppish, asst music dir; Sherry Brown, news dir; Shingo Kamada, chief of engrg; Debi Mechanic, traf mgr.

***KPOO(FM)**— April 1971: 89.5 mhz; 270 w. 540 ft TL: N37 47 33 W122 24 52. Stereo. Hrs open: Box 423030, 94142. Secondary address: 1329 Divisadero St. 94142. Phone: (415) 346-5373. Fax: (415) 346-5173.E-mail: 895fm@kpoofmsf.com Web Site:www.kpoofmsf.com Licensee: Poor Peoples' Radio Inc. Population served: 715,674 Format: Div. ♦Terry Collins, pres; Jerome Parsons, gen mgr, progmg dir; Harrison Chastang, news dir; Marilyn Fowler, pub affrs dir; Dave Billicci, chief of engrg.

***KQED-FM**— June 1969: 88.5 mhz; 110 w. Ant 1,270 ft TL: N37 41 23 W177 26 12. Stereo. Hrs open: 24
Rebroadcasts KQEI-FM North Highlands 98%.
2601 Mariposa St., 94110. Phone: (415) 553-2316. Fax: (415) 553-2241.E-mail: fm@kqed.org Web Site:www.kqed.org Licensee: KQED Inc. Population served: 455,300 Natl. Network: NPR, PRI, . Wire Svc: Bay City News Service Format: News/talk. News staff: 9; News: 160 hrs wkly. Target aud: General. ♦Jack Clarke, chmn; Jo Anne Wallace, gen mgr; Monty Carlos, opns mgr; Traci A. Eckels, dev dir; Paul Ramirez, news dir. Co-owned TV: KQED(TV) affil.

KRZZ(FM)— February 1959: 93.3 mhz; 50 kw horiz, 47 kw vert. Ant 492 ft TL: N37 43 27 W122 07 07. Stereo. Hrs open: 24 455 Market St., Suite 2300, 94105. Fax: (415) 543-3753. Web Site:www.yosoyraza.com Licensee: KRZZ Licensing LLC. Group owner: Infinity Broadcasting Corp. (acq 12-7-2004). Format: rgnl Mexican. Target aud: 18-49; Hispanics. ♦Joe Cunningham, gen mgr.

KSFB(AM)— 1926: 1260 khz; 5 kw-D, 1 kw-N. TL: N37 42 59 W122 23 38. Hrs open: 7956 California Ave., Fair Oaks, 95628. Phone: (916) 535-0500. Fax: (916) 535-0504.E-mail: info@ihradio.org Web Site:www.ihradio.org Licensee: IHR Educational Broadcasting. Group owner: Bonneville International Corp. (acq 7-16-2007; $14 million). Population served: 5,200,000 Format: Catholic. ♦Douglas M. Sherman, pres.

KSFO(AM)— Aug 1, 1925: 560 khz; 5 kw-U, DA-N. TL: N37 44 44 W122 22 40. Hrs open: 900 Front St., 94111. Phone: (415) 398-5600. Fax: (415) 658-5401.E-mail: info@ksgl.com Web Site:www.ksfo560.com Licensee: Radio License Holding VIII LLC. (acq 6-12-2007; grpsl). Population served: 715,674 Format: Talk/News. Target aud: 25-54. ♦Michael Luckoff, pres, gen mgr; Ken Berry, progmg dir; Paul Hosley, news dir.

KSOL(FM)— Dec 10, 1959: 98.9 mhz; 6 kw. 1,143 ft TL: N37 45 20 W122 27 05. Stereo. Hrs open: 24 750 Battery St. # 200, 94111. Phone: (415) 989-5765. Fax: (415) 733-5766. Web Site:www.univision.com Licensee: TMS License California Inc. Group owner: Univision Radio (acq 9-22-2003; grpsl). Format: Sp, Mexican rgnl. News staff: one. Target aud: 18-54. ♦Tony Perlongo, gen mgr; Luz Maria Rodriguez, mktg dir; Jose Luis Gonzalez, progmg dir.

KTRB(AM)— June 18, 1933: 860 khz; 50 kw-U, DA-2. TL: N37 35 34 W121 46 27. Stereo. Hrs open: 1700 Montgomery St., Suite 490, 94111. Phone: (415) 362-8686. Fax: (415) 391-6860.E-mail: jpappas@ktrb860.com Web Site:www.ktrb860.com Licensee: Pappas Radio of California, a California L.P. Group owner: Pappas Telecasting Companies (acq 3-30-2000). Population served: 6,923,401 Format: Talk/personality. Target aud: Adults: 35-64. ♦Harry J. Pappas, CEO; Jim P. Pappas, VP, gen mgr; Georgette Rodarakis, prom dir; Kevin Barrett, progmg dir; John Burger, chief of engrg.

***KUSF(FM)**— April 1964: 90.3 mhz; 3 kw. 300 ft TL: N37 46 34 W122 26 54. Stereo. Hrs open: 24 2130 Fulton St., University of San Francisco, 94117-1080. Phone: (415) 386-5873. Fax: (415) 386-6469.E-mail:

kusf@usfca.edu Web Site:www.kusf.org Licensee: University of San Francisco. (acq 1973). Population served: 715,674 Format: Alternative mus, div, educ. Target aud: College educated, affluent, multicultural. Spec prog: Chinese 7.5 hrs, Fr 1 hr, Turkish 2 hrs, It one hr, Pol one hr, Armenian one hr, Finnish one hr, Irish one hr wkly, New York Metropolitan Opera Live, Iranian 1 hr, German 1.5 hrs, Brazilian 1 hr. ♦Steve Runyon, gen mgr; Trista Bernasconi, progmg dir; Bill Ruck, chief of engrg.

KYLD(FM)— Mar 12, 1958: 94.9 mhz; 35 kw. 1,290 ft TL: N37 41 22 W122 26 10. Stereo. Hrs open: 340 Townsend St., 94107. Phone: (415) 975-5555. Fax: (415) 975-5573. Web Site:www.wild949.com Licensee: AMFM Broadcasting Licenses LLC. Group owner: Clear Channel Communications Inc. (acq 8-30-2000; grpsl). Population served: 398,000 Format: Urban contemp, CHR. Target aud: 25-54. ♦Anna Eppinger, gen mgr; Jason Chin, prom dir; Jlm Archer, progmg dir.

San Gabriel

KMRB(AM)— 1942: 1430 khz; 5 kw-U, DA-2. TL: N34 07 10 W118 04 57. Hrs open: 24 2nd Fl., 747 E. Green St., Pasadena, 91101. Phone: (626) 844-8882. Fax: (626) 792-8890.E-mail: info@kmrbam.com Licensee: Polyethnic Broadcasting Licensee LLC (acq 1994). Population served: 100,000 Format: Asian. Target aud: General. Spec prog: Thai 2 hrs, Ethiopian 2 hrs wkly. ♦Arthur Liu, pres; David Sweeney, exec VP, gen mgr; Kevin Chu, stn mgr; Katherine Lieu, gen sls mgr; Alan Mok, progmg dir; Hon Vu, chief of engrg.

San Jacinto

KRQB(FM)— Sept 23, 1990: 96.1 mhz; 1.4 kw. Ant 686 ft TL: N34 02 13 W116 58 07. Stereo. Hrs open: 24 1845 Business Ctr. Dr., Suite 106, San Bernardino, 92408. Phone: (909) 663-1961. Fax: (909) 663-1996.E-mail: advertising@quebuena961.com Web Site:qubuna961.com Licensee: LBI Radio License LLC. (acq 9-6-2007; $25 million). Population served: 1,000,000 Format: Rgnl Mexican. ♦Jose Liberman, pres; Winter Horton, gen mgr; Cristian Garcia, opns mgr; Carlos Santos, gen sls mgr, prom mgr; Pepe Garza, progmg dir.

San Joaquin

KJZN(FM)— 1999: 105.5 mhz; 25 kw. Ant 328 ft TL: N36 36 28 W119 59 49. Hrs open: 24 1066 E. Shaw Ave., Fresno, 93710. Phone: (559) 230-0104. Fax: (559) 230-0177. Licensee: Wilks License Co.-Fresno LLC. Group owner: The Mondosphere Broadcasting Group. (acq 6-1-2005; grpsl). Natl. Rep: McGavren Guild,. Format: Talk. Target aud: Adults 25-54. ♦Kevin O'Rorke, gen mgr; Stephen Mikal Brown, progmg dir.

San Jose

KAZA(AM)—See Gilroy

KBRG(FM)— Mar 4, 1963: 100.3 mhz; 14.5 kw. Ant 2,580 ft TL: N37 06 40 W121 50 34. Stereo. Hrs open: 24 750 Battery St., Suite 200, San Francisco, 94111. Phone: (415) 989-5765. Fax: (415) 675-7126. Fax: (415) 733-5766. Web Site:www.univision.com Licensee: Univision Radio License Corp. Group owner: Entravision Communications Corp. (acq 1-1-2006; $90 million with KLOK(AM) San Jose). Population served: 5,000,000 Format: Sp. ♦Tony Perlongo, gen mgr; Luz Maria Rodriguez, mktg dir; Ramon Lopez, progmg dir.

KEZR(FM)— July 3, 1967: 106.5 mhz; 42 kw. Ant 535 ft TL: N37 12 32 W121 46 27. Stereo. Hrs open: 190 Park Ctr. Plaza, Suite 200, 95113-2223. Phone: (408) 287-5775. Fax: (408) 293-3341. Web Site:www.todaysbestmix.com Licensee: NM Licensing LLC. Group owner: Infinity Broadcasting Corp. (acq 12-6-2005; $80 million with KBAY(FM) Gilroy). Population served: 213,000 Natl. Rep: Christal,. Format: Adult contemp. News staff: one; News: 4 hrs wkly. Target aud: 25-44. ♦John Leathers, gen mgr.

KFAX(AM)—See San Francisco

KFFG(FM)—See Los Altos

KKSF(FM)—See San Francisco

KLIV(AM)— 1946: 1590 khz; 5 kw-U, DA-N. TL: N37 19 45 W121 51 23. Hrs open: 24 Box 995, 95108. Secondary address: 750 Story Rd. 95122. Phone: (408) 293-8030. Fax: (408) 293-6124.E-mail: dreyna@empirebroadcasting.com Web Site:www.kliv.com Licensee: Empire Broadcasting Corp. (group owner; acq 7-1-67). Population served: 1,500,000 Natl. Network: CNN Radio, . Natl. Rep: Christal,. Wire Svc: AP Wire Svc: Bay City News Service Format: News. News staff: 8. Target aud: General. Spec prog: San Jose soccer earthquakes. ♦Robert S. Kieve, pres, gen mgr; George Sampson, progmg dir, news dir; Tina Ferguson, gen sls mgr & chief of engrg.

KLOK(AM)— Oct 19, 1946: 1170 khz; 50 kw-D, 5 kw-N, DA-2. TL: N37 18 41 W121 48 58. Hrs open: 24 750 Battery St., Suite 200, San Francisco, 94111. Phone: (415) 362-1170. Fax: (415) 675-7126. Licensee: Univision Radio License Corp. Group owner: Entravision Communications Corp. (acq 1-1-2006; $90 million with KBRG(FM) San Jose). Population served: 5,262,000 Format: Cumbia. Target aud: 18-49. ♦Tony Perlongo, gen mgr.

***KMTG(FM)**— May 17, 1977: 89.3 mhz; 300 w. Ant -312 ft TL: N37 12 06 W121 51 42. Hrs open: 855 Linden Ave., 95126. Phone: (408) 535-6000.E-mail: info@kmtg.com Licensee: San Jose Unified School District. Population served: 5,000 ♦Brent Pinkerton, gen mgr; Scott Dunson, opns dir.

KSJO(FM)— December 1946: 92.3 mhz; 50 kw. 464 ft TL: N37 12 33 W121 46 30. Stereo. Hrs open: 1420 Koll Cir., Suite A, 95112. Phone: (408) 453-5400. Fax: (408) 452-1330. Web Site:www.ksjo.com Licensee: Aloha Station Trust LLC, as Trustee Group owner: Clear Channel Communications Inc. (acq 7-30-2008). Natl. Rep: McGavren Guild,. Format: Sp. Target aud: 18-49; active adults. ♦Kim Bryant, gen mgr; Monica Novoa, progmg dir.

***KSJS(FM)**— Feb 22, 1963: 90.5 mhz; 235 w. 407 ft TL: N37 12 33 W121 46 30. Stereo. Hrs open: 24 San Jose State Univ., Theater Arts Dept., HGH 126, 95192-0094. Phone: (408) 924-4549. Phone: (408) 924-4545. Fax: (408) 924-4558.E-mail: martinez@ksjs.org Web Site:www.ksjs.org Licensee: San Jose State University. Population served: 2,000,000 Format: Diversified. Target aud: 18-34; students & community members. ♦Nick Martinez, gen mgr; Joey De la Plane, prom dir; Rob Soul, progmg dir.

KSJX(AM)— June 24, 1948: 1500 khz; 10 kw-D, 5 kw-N, DA-2. TL: N37 21 28 W121 52 17. Hrs open: 24 501 Wooster Ave., 95116. Phone: (408) 280-1515. Fax: (408) 280-1585.E-mail: ksjx1500@sbcglobal.net Licensee: Multicultural Radio Broadcasting Licensee LLC. Group owner: Multicultural Radio Broadcasting Inc. (acq 2-20-98; grpsl). Population served: 1,162,700 Format: Asian, Vietnamese. News staff: 2. Target aud: 25-54; managerial, professional, homeowners. Spec prog: Mandarin Chinese 10 hrs, Vietnamese. ♦Arthur Liu, pres; Andrea Yamazaki, gen mgr, stn mgr; Victor Nguyen, opns mgr.

KUFX(FM)— July 1, 1959: 98.5 mhz; 12.5 kw. 880 ft TL: N37 12 17 W121 56 56. Stereo. Hrs open: 24 1420 Koll Cir., Suite A, 95112. Phone: (408) 452-5400. Fax: (408) 452-1330. Web Site:www.kfox.com Licensee: Aloha Station Trust LLC, as Trustee Group owner: Clear Channel Communications Inc. (acq 7-30-2008). Population served: 1,177,300 Natl. Rep: CBS Radio,. Thompson Hine LLP. Format: Classic rock. Target aud: 18-49; general. ♦Kim Bryant, gen mgr; Laurie Roberts, progmg dir.

KVVF(FM)—See Santa Clara

KVVN(AM)—(Santa Clara, Dec 18, 1964: 1430 khz; 1 kw-D, 2.5 kw-N, DA-2. TL: N37 19 47 W121 51 58. Hrs open: 24 1125 E. Santa Clara St., Suite 1, 95116. Phone: (415) 648-7980. Fax: (415) 695-9055.E-mail: sales@inlanguageradio.com Licensee: Urban Radio III L.L.C. Group owner: Inner City Broadcasting (acq 3-24-97; $2.2 million). Population served: 800,000 Koteen & Naftalin. Format: Vietnamese. News staff: one; News: 14 hrs wkly. Target aud: 23-34; Hispanic. ♦Harvey Stone, gen mgr; Andrew Luu, stn mgr; Phung Dang, opns dir; Paul Marks, chief of engrg.

KZSF(AM)— June 21, 1947: 1370 khz; 5 kw-U, DA-2. TL: N37 21 28 W121 52 17. Stereo. Hrs open: 24 3031 Tisch Way, Suite 3, Plaza W., 95128. Phone: (408) 247-0100. Fax: (408) 247-4353.E-mail: info@kzsf.com Web Site:www.1370am.com Licensee: Carlos A. Duharte (acq 7-31-01; $5 million). Population served: 4,500,000 Rgnl rep: Interep Format: Sp; regional Mexican. Target aud: 18-49. ♦Carlos A. Duharte, CEO, chmn, pres, sr VP & gen mgr.

San Luis Obispo

***KCBX(FM)**— July 25, 1975: 90.1 mhz; 5.3 kw. 1,420 ft TL: N35 21 38 W120 39 21. Stereo. Hrs open: 24
Rebroadcasts KSBX(FM) Santa Barbara 100%.
4100 Vachell Ln., 93401. Phone: (805) 549-8855. Fax: (805) 781-3025.E-mail: kcbx@kcbx.org Web Site:www.kcbx.org Licensee: KCBX Inc. Population served: 625,000 Natl. Network: NPR, . Cohn & Marks. Format: Class, jazz, news. News: 32 hrs wkly. Target aud: General. Spec prog: Folk 15 hrs wkly. ♦Frank Lanzone, pres, gen mgr; Hank Hadley, opns mgr; Paul Severtson, dev dir; Guy Rathbun, progmg dir.

***KCPR(FM)**— 1968: 91.3 mhz; 2 kw. -350 ft TL: N35 17 58 W120 40 26. Stereo. Hrs open: 24 Graphic Arts Bldg 26, Rm 301, California Polytechnic State Univ., 93407. Phone: (805) 756-5998. Web Site:www.kcpr.org Licensee: California Polytechnic State University. Population served: 40,000 Format: Div. News: 4 hrs wkly. Target aud: General; Cal Poly students, San Luis Obispo community. Spec prog: Sp 3 hrs, metal 3 hrs, blues 3 hrs. ♦Alyssa Duhe, gen mgr.

KIQO(FM)—See Atascadero

KJDJ(AM)— Feb 8, 1988: 1030 khz; 2.5 kw-D, 700 w-N. TL: N35 17 58 W120 40 24. Hrs open: 604 E. Chapel St., Santa Maria, 93454. Phone: (805) 928-1030.E-mail: oracion@radiovidaabundante.com Web Site:www.radiovidaabundante.com Licensee: Padre Serra Communications Inc. (acq 4-94). Population served: 250,000 Format: Religious. ♦Manuel Salvador, gen mgr; Manny Aram, progmg dir.

KKJG(FM)— Jan 1, 1984: 98.1 mhz; 3.6 kw. 1,624 ft TL: N35 21 37 W120 39 18. Stereo. Hrs open: 3620 Sacramento Dr., Suite 204, 93401. Phone: (805) 781-2750. Fax: (805) 781-2758. Web Site:www.jugcountry.com Licensee: AGM San Luis Obispo L.P. Group owner: American General Media (acq 7-1-97; $1.5 million). Format: Country. Target aud: 25-54. ♦Kathy Signorelli, gen mgr; Pepper Daniels, progmg dir.

KKJL(AM)— Feb 6, 1960: 1400 khz; 1 kw-U. TL: N35 15 51 W120 39 56. Hrs open: 24 Box 1400, 93406. Secondary address: 51 Zaca Ln., Suite 90 93401. Phone: (805) 543-9400. Fax: (805) 543-0787.E-mail: info@kkjl1400.com Web Site:www.kkjl1400.com Licensee: San Luis Obispo Broadcasting Inc. (acq 9-9-86). Population served: 38,000 Natl. Network: CNN Radio, . Leventhal, Senter & Lerman. Format: Adult standards, sports. Target aud: 35 plus; adults males & females. Spec prog: SF Giants, SF 49ers, LA Lakers. ♦Guy Hackman, pres, gen mgr; Kyle Ronemus, VP, stn mgr; Mary S. Brown, opns mgr.

***KLFF-FM**— Sept 26, 1995: 89.3 mhz; 4.4 kw. Ant 1,430 ft TL: N35 21 37 W120 39 17. Stereo. Hrs open: 24 560 Higuera St., Suite G, 93401. Phone: (805) 541-4343. Fax: (805) 541-9101.E-mail: info@klife.org Web Site:www.klife.org Licensee: Logos Broadcasting Corp. Population served: 250,000 Natl. Network: Salem Radio Network, . Joseph E. Dunne III. Format: Christian hit music. Target aud: 18-34; Christians. ♦Dan M. Lemburg, pres; Dr. Daniel Woods, CFO; Jon Fugler, gen mgr; Noonie Fugler, prom dir.

***KLVH(FM)**— Mar 25, 1999: 88.5 mhz; 3 kw. Ant 1,401 ft TL: N35 21 38 W120 39 21. Hrs open: 24 2351 Sunset Blvd., Suite 170-218, Rocklin, 95765. Phone: (916) 251-1600. Fax: (916) 251-1650.E-mail: klove@klove.com Web Site:www.klove.com Licensee: Educational Media Foundation. Group owner: EMF Broadcasting (acq 5-12-99). Population served: 315,000 Natl. Network: K-Love, . Shaw Pittman. Format: Contemp Christian music. News staff: 3. Target aud: 25-44; Judeo Christian, female. ♦Richard Jenkins, pres; Mike Novak, VP; Keith Whipple, dev dir; David Pierce, progmg mgr; Ed Lenane, news dir; Sam Wallington, engrg dir; Karen Johnson, news rptr.

KSLY-FM— December 1959: 96.1 mhz; 3.4 kw. Ant 1,686 ft TL: N35 21 37 W120 39 18. Stereo. Hrs open: 51 Zaca Ln., Suite 110, 93401. Phone: (805) 545-0101. Fax: (805) 541-5303.E-mail: info@ksly.com Web Site:www.ksly.com Licensee: EDB SLO License LLC. Group owner: Clear Channel Communications Inc. (acq 11-30-2007; grpsl). Format: Country. ♦Rich Hawkins, gen mgr; Pattie Wagner, sls dir; Teresa Lara, prom dir; Andy Morris, progmg dir; Ben Grenaway, news dir.

KURQ(FM)—See Grover Beach

KVEC(AM)— May 1937: 920 khz; 1 kw-D, 500 w-N. TL: N35 17 58 W120 40 24. Hrs open: 24 51 Zaca Ln., Suite 100, 93401. Phone: (805) 545-0101. Fax: (805) 541-5303.E-mail: info@920kvec.com Web Site:www.920kvec.com Licensee: EDB SLO License LLC. Group owner: Clear Channel Communications Inc. (acq 11-30-2007; grpsl). Population served: 300,000 Natl. Network: ABC, Fox News Radio, . Format: News/talk, info. News staff: 4; News: 45 hrs wkly. Target aud: 35 plus; affluent decision & newsmakers, sports fans, business owners & retirees. Spec prog: Dodgers baseball, NFL/NCAA football, finance, senior focus, health, real estate. ♦Rich Hawkins, gen mgr.

KXTK(AM)—(Arroyo Grande, June 29, 1962: 1280 khz; 10 kw-D, 2.5 kw-N, DA-2. TL: N35 08 44 W120 31 15. Hrs open: 24 Box 14910, 93406. Phone: (805) 547-1280. Fax: (805) 543-1508.E-mail: sports@espnradio1280.com Web Site:espnradio1280.com Licensee: Pacific Coast Media LLC (acq 10-20-2004; $700,000). Population served: 400,000 Natl. Network: ESPN Radio, Westwood One, . Rgnl. Network: Jones Satellite Radio. Format: Sports. Target aud: 25 plus. ♦Mike Chellsen, gen mgr, gen sls mgr & progmg dir; Bill Bordeaux, engr.

KYNS(AM)— Dec 13, 1949: 1340 khz; 790 w-U. TL: N35 14 03 W120 40 33. Hrs open: 24 396 Buckley Rd., Suite 2, 93401. Phone: (805) 786-2570. Fax: (805) 547-9860. Web Site:www.mapletoncommunications.com.com Licensee: Mapleton License of San Luis Obispo LLC. (group owner; (acq 3-19-2003; $370,000). Population served: 37,500 Format: Progressive news/talk. ♦Adam Nathanson, pres; Nancy Leichter, gen mgr.

KZOZ(FM)— 1962: 93.3 mhz; 29.5 kw. 1,470 ft TL: N35 21 38 W120 39 21. Stereo. Hrs open: 3620 Sacramento Dr., Suite 204, 93401. Phone: (805) 781-2750. Fax: (805) 781-2758.E-mail: sales@americangeneralmedia.com Web Site:www.kzoz.com Licensee: AGM California. Group owner: American General Media (acq 6-89; grpsl). Population served: 191,000 Format: Classic rock, AOR. ♦Bill Heirendt, gen mgr, opns dir, gen sls mgr; David Atwood, progmg dir.

San Marcos-Poway

KPRZ(AM)— 1986: 1210 khz; 20 kw-D, 5 kw-N, DA-2. TL: N33 04 12 W117 11 35. Hrs open: 24 9255 Towne Centre Dr., Suite 535, San Diego, 92121. Phone: (858) 535-1210. Fax: (858) 535-1212.E-mail: kprz@kprz.com Web Site:www.kprz.com Licensee: New Inspiration Broadcasting Co. Inc. Group owner: Salem Communications Corp. (acq 1986). Population served: 2,700,000 Natl. Network: Salem Radio Network, . Format: Christian, talk. News: 15 hrs wkly. Target aud: 25-54; conservative, pro-family. Spec prog: Sp 22 hrs wkly. ♦Edward G. Astinger III, CEO, pres; David Evans, CFO; Dave Armstrong, gen mgr; Dawn Hockaday, prom dir; Heather Lloyd, opns mgr & progmg dir; Craig Caston, chief of engrg.

San Martin

KZSJ(AM)— November 1995: 1120 khz; 5 kw-D, 150 w-N. TL: N36 57 49 W121 29 22. Hrs open: 24 2670 S. White Rd., Suite 165, San Jose, 95148. Phone: (408) 223-3130. Fax: (408) 223-3131.E-mail: qhradio@aol.com Web Site:www.quehuongmedia.com Licensee: KZSJ Radio LLC. Group owner: Bustos Media Holdings (acq 2-26-99). Format: Vietnamese. Hispanic. ♦Amador Bustos, chmn; Raul Salvador, CFO; John Bustos, exec VP, opns mgr; Khoi Nguyen, gen mgr.

San Mateo

***KCSM(FM)**— October 1964: 91.1 mhz; 11.5 kw. 371 ft TL: N37 32 12 W122 20 02. Hrs open: 1700 W. Hillsdale Blvd., 94402. Phone: (650) 524-6905. Fax: (650) 524-6975. Web Site:www.kcsm.org Licensee: San Mateo County Community College District. Population served: 161,000 Natl. Network: PRI, . Format: Jazz. Target aud: 40 plus; males. Spec prog: Blues 3 hrs wkly. ♦Marilyn Lawrence, gen mgr; Alisa Clancy, opns dir; Melanie Berson, progmg dir. Co-owned TV: *KCSM-TV affil.

KSAN(FM)— September 1963: 107.7 mhz; 8.9 kw. 1,162 ft TL: N37 41 20 W122 26 07. Stereo. Hrs open: 55 Hawthorne, Suite1000, San Francisco, 94105. Phone: (415) 981-5726. Fax: (415) 995-7061. Web Site:www.1077thebone.com Licensee: Susquehanna Radio Corp. (group owner; acq 5-29-97; $44 million). Population served: 4,625,300 Natl. Rep: McGavren Guild,. Format: Classic rock. Target aud: 25-54. ♦Tony Salvadore, VP & gen mgr; Michael Seghieri, gen sls mgr; Larry Sharpe, progmg dir; Eric Steinberg, engrg dir, chief of engrg; Sara Bronson, traf mgr.

KTCT(AM)— 1948: 1050 khz; 50 kw-D, 10 kw-N, DA-2. TL: N37 39 02 W122 09 08. Stereo. Hrs open: 24 55 Hawthorne, Suite 1000, San Francisco, 94105. Phone: (415) 864-1050. Fax: (415) 995-6867. Web Site:www.theticket1050.com Licensee: Susquehanna Radio Corp. (Acq 7-21-97; $15 million). Population served: 750,000 Natl. Network: Westwood One, . Format: Sports. Target aud: 25-54. ♦Rich Zirkel, gen sls mgr; Lee Hammer, progmg mgr.

San Rafael

***KSRH(FM)**— May 1, 1980: 88.1 mhz; 10 w. 66 ft TL: N37 58 16 W122 30 47. Hrs open: 9 AM-3 PM 185 Mission Ave., AR 101, 94901. Phone: (415) 457-5314.E-mail: info@ksrh.com Licensee: San Rafael High School District. Format: Div, Black. News: 5 hrs wkly. Target aud: 12-29. Spec prog: Fr one hr wkly. ♦Chris Russo, gen mgr.

KVVZ(FM)— June 1, 1961: 100.7 mhz; 910 w. Ant 810 ft TL: N37 59 25 W122 29 58. Stereo. Hrs open: 750 Battery St., Suite 200, San Francisco, 94111. Phone: (415) 733-5765. Fax: (415) 733-5766. Web Site:www.univision.com Licensee: Univision Radio License Corp. Group owner: Salem Communications Corp. (acq 3-1-2005; exchange for KOSL(FM) Jackson). Format: Sp pop. ♦Tony Perlongo, gen mgr.

Santa Ana

KALI-FM— Feb 6, 1980: 106.3 mhz; 3 kw. 130 ft TL: N33 45 21 W117 51 16. (CP: Ant 203 ft. TL: N33 45 21 W117 51 17). Stereo. Hrs open: 747 E. Green St., Suite 400, Pasadena, 91101. Phone: (626) 844-8882. Fax: (626) 844-0156.E-mail: info@mrbi.net Licensee: KALI-FM Licensee LLC. Population served: 155,710 Format: Asian. Target aud: 18-44. ♦Arthur Liu, pres; David Sweeney, gen mgr; Alan Mok, progmg dir.

KVNR(AM)— Nov 26, 1926: 1480 khz; 5 kw-U, DA-2. TL: N33 45 06 W117 54 36. Hrs open: 15781 Brookhurst St., Suite 101, Westminster, 92683. Phone: (714) 918-4444. Fax: (714) 918-4445.E-mail: radio@littlesoigonradio.com Web Site:www.littlesoiganradio.com Licensee: LBI Radio License Corp. (Acq 1-88; $6.25 million with co-located FM; 1-4-88). Population served: 100,000 Format: Vietnamese. Target aud: 18-49. ♦Ninh Vu, pres; Kathleen Bui, gen mgr; Joe Dinh, chief of engrg.

KWIZ(FM)— 1947: 96.7 mhz; 3 kw. 206 ft TL: N33 48 08 W117 47 43. Stereo. Hrs open: 24 3101 W. 5th St., 92703. Phone: (714) 554-5000. Fax: (714) 554-9362. Web Site:www.sonido967.com Licensee: LBI Radio License Corp. Group owner: Liberman Broadcasting Inc. (acq 1997; $11.2 million). Population served: 200,000 Format: Sp, Tropical. Target aud: 18 plus; Asian. ♦Winnie Coombs, stn mgr; Francisco Morales, prom dir; Edwardo Leon, progmg dir; Jesus Mar, mus dir; Shannon Murdock, chief of engrg; Patty Diaz, traf mgr.

Santa Barbara

KCLU(AM)— 1946: 1340 khz; 650 w-U. TL: N34 25 07 W119 41 10. Stereo. Hrs open:
Simulcast with KCLU-FM Thousand Oaks 100%.
60 W. Olsen Rd., Suite 4400, Thousand Oaks, 91360. Phone: (805) 493-3900. Fax: (805) 493-3982. Web Site:www.kclu.org Licensee: California Lutheran University Group owner: Clear Channel Communications Inc. (acq 10-7-2008; $1.44 million). Population served: 140,757 Natl. Network: NPR, . Format: News/talk. ♦Mary Olson, gen mgr.

***KCSB-FM**— November 1964: 91.9 mhz; 620 w. 2,910 ft TL: N34 31 31 W119 57 29. (CP: Ant 1,879 ft.). Stereo. Hrs open: 24 Box 13401, 93107-3401. Phone: (805) 893-3757. Fax: (805) 893-7832.E-mail: info@kcsb.org Web Site:www.kcsb.org Licensee: Regents of the University of California. Population served: 100,000 Format: Var. News staff: 2; News: 9 hrs wkly. Community radio/college radio. Spec prog: Sp 12 hrs, Japanese pop one hr, East Indian 2 hrs, reggae 6 hrs, American Indian 3 hrs wkly. ♦Erin Fleming, gen mgr; Elizabeth Robinson, stn mgr; Rebecca Redman, progmg dir.

KDB(FM)— Feb 14, 1960: 93.7 mhz; 12.5 kw. 870 ft TL: N34 27 58 W119 40 37. Stereo. Hrs open: 24 Box 91660, 93190. Phone: (805) 966-4131. Fax: (805) 966-4788.E-mail: kdb@kdb.com Web Site:www.kdb.com Licensee: Pacific Broadcasting Co. (acq 11-6-2003; transfer of stock). Population served: 600,000 Fletcher, Heald & Hildreth. Format: Classical music. News: one hr wkly. Target aud: Adults; affluent, influential & educated. ♦Roby Scott, gen mgr; Richard Bickle, opns dir, progmg dir; Bob Scott, sls dir, progmg dir.

KIST(AM)—April 1926: 1490 khz; 1 kw-U. TL: N34 24 57 W119 41 10. Stereo. Hrs open: 24 414 East Cota St., 93101. Phone: (805) 879-8300. Fax: (805) 879-8430. Licensee: Rincon License Subsidiary LLC. Group owner: Clear Channel Communications Inc. (acq 7-11-2007; grpsl). Population served: 300,000 Farrand, Cooper & Bruiniers. Format: Mexican. News staff: one; News: 7 hrs wkly. Target aud: 16-65; Hispanic. ♦J.D. Freedman, gen mgr; Marlene Huddy, opns dir; Jose Fierroz, progmg VP, progmg dir; Ransom Bullard, chief of engrg; Alfredo Quezada, disc jockey.

KIST-FM— 1998: 107.7 mhz; 930 w. Ant 1,627 ft TL: N34 30 10 W119 50 56. Hrs open: 24 414 E. Cota St., 93101. Phone: (805) 879-8300. Fax: (805) 879-8430. Licensee: Rincon License Subsidiary LLC. Group owner: Clear Channel Communications Inc. (acq 7-11-2007; grpsl). Natl. Rep: Katz Radio,. Format: Rgnl Mexican. ♦Tom Baker, gen mgr; Keith Royer, opns dir, progmg dir; Vince Holian, gen sls mgr; Peter Bie, news dir; Andrea Shaparenko, traf mgr.

KMGQ(FM)—See Goleta

***KQSC(FM)**— July 1985: 88.7 mhz; 12 kw. 866 ft TL: N34 27 55 W119 40 37. Stereo. Hrs open: 24
Rebroadcasts KUSC 100%.
Box 77913, Los Angeles, 90007. Phone: (213) 225-7400. Fax: (213) 225-7410.E-mail: kusc@kusc.org Web Site:www.kusc.org Licensee: University of Southern California. Natl. Network: PRI, NPR, . Lawrence Bernstein. Format: Class. News: 3 hrs wkly. Target aud: 35 plus. ♦Brenda Barnes, pres; Eric DeWeese, gen mgr.

KRUZ(FM)— Sept 1, 1957: 97.5 mhz; 17.5 kw. 2,920 ft TL: N34 31 31 W119 57 29. Hrs open: 24 403 E. Montecito St., 93101-1759. Phone: (805) 966-1755. Web Site:www.cumulus.com Licensee: Cumulus Licensing Corp. Group owner: Cumulus Media Inc. (acq 3-12-2001; grpsl). Population served: 650,000 Natl. Rep: McGavren Guild,. Wire Svc: AP Format: Smooth Jazz. Target aud: 35-64; young, educated, upscale adults. ♦Gail Surrillo, gen mgr; Brandon Randazzo, prom dir; John D. Straker, chief of engrg; Mark Deanba, progmg.

KSBL(FM)—See Carpinteria

***KSBX(FM)**— Apr 1, 2003: 89.5 mhz; 50 w. Ant 899 ft TL: N34 27 57 W119 40 37. Stereo. Hrs open: 24
Rebroadcassts KCBX(FM) San Luis Obispo 99%.
KCBX Public Radio, 4100 Vachell Ln., San Luis Obispo, 93401. Phone: (805) 549-8855. Phone: (805) 781-3025.E-mail: kcbx@kccbx.org Web Site:www.kcbx.org Licensee: KCBX Inc. Natl. Network: NPR, . Rgnl rep: Margaret Merisante Format: Class, jazz. News: 30 hrs wkly. ♦Frank Lanzone, gen mgr; Hank Hadley, opns mgr; Paul Severtson, dev dir; Guy Rathbun, progmg dir.

KSPE-FM—(Ellwood, Feb 6, 1989: 94.5 mhz; 81 kw. Ant 2,949 ft TL: N34 31 32 W119 57 28. Hrs open: 24 414 E. Cota St., 93101. Phone: (805) 879-8300. Fax: (805) 879-8430. Licensee: Rincon License Subsidiary LLC. (acq 7-11-2007; grpsl). Format: Sp oldies.

KTMS(AM)— Aug 11, 1962: 990 khz; 5 kw-D, 500 w-N, DA-2. TL: N34 28 15 W119 40 33. Hrs open: 24 414 E. Cota St., 93101. Phone: (805) 879-8300.E-mail: info@990am.com Web Site:www.990am.com Licensee: Rincon Broadcasting LS LLC. (acq 7-11-2007; grpsl). Population served: 250,000 Natl. Network: ABC, CNN Radio, . Format: Talk. News staff: 2; News: 4 hrs wkly. Target aud: 25 plus; upscale adults. ♦Tom Baker, gen mgr; Keith Royer, opns mgr; Lin Aubuchon, prom dir.

KTYD(FM)— Aug 11, 1972: 99.9 mhz; 34 kw. 1,278 ft TL: N34 28 15 W119 40 33. Stereo. Hrs open: 24 414 E. Cota St., 93101. Phone: (805) 879-8300. Fax: (805)879-8430.E-mail: info@ktyd.com Web Site:www.ktyd.com Licensee: Rincon License Subsidiary LLC. Group owner: Clear Channel Communications Inc. (acq 7-11-2007; grpsl). Population served: 170,000 Natl. Rep: Katz Radio,. Wiley, Rein & Fielding. Format: AOR. News staff: one; News: 3 hrs wkly. Target aud: 18-49; upscale adults. Spec prog: Pub affrs one hr wkly. ♦Keith Royer, VP, opns mgr, progmg dir; Tom Baker, gen mgr; Vince Hollian, gen sls mgr; Lin Aubuchon, mktg dir, prom dir; Peter Bie, news dir; Ran Bullard, chief of engrg; Andrea Shaparenko, traf mgr.

KVYB(FM)— Aug 8, 1961: 103.3 mhz; 105 kw. 2,980 ft TL: N34 31 30 W119 57 10. Stereo. Hrs open: 24 1376 Walter St., Ventura, 93003. Phone: (805) 642-8595. Fax: (805) 656-5838.E-mail: info@1033thevibe.com Web Site:www.1033thevibe.com Licensee: Cumulus Licensing Corp. Group owner: Cumulus Media inc. (acq 4-2000). Population served: 1,150,000 Natl. Rep: McGavren Guild,. Format: Hip hop and more. Target aud: 18-54; general. ♦Jonathon Pinch, COO; Lewis W. Dickey Jr., pres; Martin Gausvik, CFO; John W. Dickey, exec VP; Gail Furillo, gen sls mgr, prom dir; Daniel Herejon, progmg dir; J.D. Strahler, chief of engrg; Barbara Haser, traf mgr.

KZER(AM)— Oct 31, 1937: 1250 khz; 2.5 kw-D, 1 kw-N, DA-2. TL: N34 25 06 W119 49 05. Hrs open: 24 200 South A St., Suite 400, Oxnard, 93030. Phone: (805) 240-2070. Fax: (805) 240-7658.E-mail: terryj@radiolazer.com Licensee: Lazer Broadcasting Corp. (group owner; acq 12-18-2003; $1.5 million). Population served: 250,000 Hogan & Hartson. Format: Sp. News staff: 5; News: 140 hrs wkly. Target aud: 25 plus; upscale, educated listeners. ♦Terry Janisch, gen mgr & stn mgr; Salvador Prieto, progmg dir.

KZSB(AM)— March 1961: 1290 khz; 500 w-D, 122 w-N. TL: N34 25 07 W119 41 10. Stereo. Hrs open: 24 1317 Santa Barbara St., 93101. Phone: (805) 568-1444. Fax: (805) 966-3530.E-mail: kzsb@mediasb.com Web Site:www.newspress.com Licensee: Santa Barbara Broadcasting Inc. (acq 3-1-2005; $750,000). Population served: 190,900 Natl. Network: Westwood One, . Format: News/talk. Target aud: 35-64. ♦Dennis M. Weibling, pres; Les Carroll, gen mgr, natl sls mgr; Richard Dugan, opns mgr, progmg dir & news dir; Patrice Cardenas, pub affrs dir.

Santa Clara

KLIV(AM)—See San Jose

***KSCU(FM)**— July 1, 1978: 103.3 mhz; 30 w. 179 ft TL: N37 20 53 W121 56 25. Stereo. Hrs open: 24 Santa Clara Univ., 500 El Camino Real 3207, 95053. Phone: (408) 554-4413. Fax: (408) 554-5738.E-mail: music@kscu.org Web Site:www.kscu.org Licensee: President and Board of Trustees of Santa Clara University. Format: Modern alternative rock. News: one hr wkly. Target aud: 14-34; Young adult who like

modern music. Spec prog: Hip-hop 15 hrs, Blues 3 hrs, loud rock 6 hrs, world one hr wkly. ♦Allyson Harrison, gen mgr; Gordon Young, news dir; Bill Orr, engrg dir, chief of engrg.

KVVF(FM)— Sept 25, 1964: 105.7 mhz; 50 kw. Ant 500 ft TL: N37 21 32 W121 45 22. Stereo. Hrs open: 24 750 Battery St., Suite 200, San Francisco, 94111. Phone: (415) 733-5765. Fax: (415) 733-5766. Web Site:www.univision.com Licensee: Univision Radio License Corp. Group owner: Univision Radio (acq 9-22-2003; grpsl). Population served: 1,400,000 Format: Sp pop. ♦Tony Perlongo, gen mgr.

KVVN(AM)—Licensed to Santa Clara. See San Jose

Santa Cruz

***KFER(FM)**— 1992: 89.9 mhz; 200 w. 26 ft TL: N37 00 45 W121 58 25. Hrs open: 24 Box 13, 95063. Phone: (831) 475-6651. Fax: (831) 464-8427.E-mail: info@kferfm.com Licensee: Santa Cruz Educational Broadcasting Foundation. Rgnl rep: Moody. Format: Var. News: 15 hrs wkly. Target aud: General. ♦Mildred Holmes, pres; Dr. Stan Monteith, gen mgr.

KKHK(FM)—See Monterey

KSCO(AM)— Sept 21, 1947: 1080 khz; 10 kw-D, 5 kw-N, DA-2. TL: N36 57 43 W121 58 51. Hrs open: 24 2300 Portola Dr., 95062. Phone: (831) 475-1080. Fax: (831) 475-2967. Web Site:www.ksco.com Licensee: Zwerling Broadcasting System Ltd. (acq 1-31-91; $600,000; 12-31-90). Population served: 500,000 Format: News/talk. News staff: 8; News: 35 hrs wkly. Target aud: 25 plus; well educated professionals, managers. ♦Michael Zwerling, CEO; Michael Olson, gen mgr.

KSQL(FM)— Sept 2, 1961: 99.1 mhz; 1.1 kw. 2,487 ft TL: N37 06 40 W121 50 34. Stereo. Hrs open: 24 750 Battery St., Suite 200, San Francisco, 94111-1412. Phone: (415) 989-5765. Fax: (415) 733-5766.E-mail: estereosole@univision.com Web Site:www.univision.com Licensee: TMS License California Inc. Group owner: Univision Radio (acq 9-22-2003; grpsl). Format: Sp, Mexican rgnl. News staff: one; News: 4 hrs wkly. Target aud: 25-54. ♦Tony Perlongo, gen mgr.

***KSRI(FM)**— Feb 28, 2001: 90.7 mhz; 316 w. Ant 364 ft TL: N37 00 10 W122 03 05. Stereo. Hrs open: 24
Rebroadcasts KHRI(FM) Hollister 100%.
2351 Sunset Blvd., Suite 170-218, Rocklin, 95765. Phone: (916) 251-1600. Fax: (916) 251-1650.E-mail: info@air1.com Web Site:www.air1.com Licensee: Educational Media Foundation. Group owner: EMF Broadcasting (acq 8-17-00; $295,000). Population served: 160,000 Natl. Network: Air 1, . Shaw Pittman. Format: Contemp Christian. News staff: 3. Target aud: 18-35; Judeo-Christian, female. ♦Richard Jenkins, pres; Mike Novak, VP; Keith Whipple, dev dir; David Pierce, progmg dir; Ed Lenane, news dir; Sam Wallington, engrg dir; Arthur Vassar, traf mgr; Karen Johnson, news rptr.

***KUSP(FM)**— Apr 14, 1972: 88.9 mhz; 1.25 kw. 2,496 ft TL: N36 32 05 W121 37 14. Stereo. Hrs open: 203 8th Ave., 95062. Phone: (831) 476-2800. Fax: (831) 476-2802.E-mail: kusp@kusp.org Web Site:www.kusp.org Licensee: Pataphysical Broadcasting Foundation Inc. Population served: 750,000 Natl. Network: NPR, . Format: Div. News: 44 hrs wkly. ♦Terry Green, gen mgr & stn mgr; Paula Kenyon, dev dir, sls dir; Rob Mullen, mus dir.

***KZSC(FM)**— August 1974: 88.1 mhz; 20 kw. Ant 436 ft TL: N37 00 10 W122 03 04. Stereo. Hrs open: 24 1156 High St., 95064. Phone: (831) 459-2811. Fax: (831) 459-4734.E-mail: stationmanager@kzsc.org Web Site:www.kzsc.org Licensee: Regents of University of California. Population served: 1,400,000 Format: Div. News: 40 hrs wkly. Target aud: 18-plus; college students up till late 30's. ♦Michael Bryant, gen mgr; Kristen Sarton, stn mgr.

Santa Margarita

KWWV(FM)— July 21, 1986: 106.1 mhz; 1.1 kw. Ant 1,446 ft TL: N35 21 40 W120 39 21. Stereo. Hrs open: 24 795 Buckley Rd., Suite 2, San Luis Obispo, 93401. Phone: (805) 786-2570. Fax: (805) 547-9860. Web Site:www.wild1061.com Licensee: Mapleton License of San Luis Obispo LLC. (acq 1-1-2007). Population served: 300000 Format: CHR/top40. News staff: 2; News: 6 hrs wkly. Target aud: 18-34; upscale homeowners. ♦Bill Heirendt, gen mgr.

Santa Maria

KBOX(FM)—(Lompoc, Dec 24, 1968: 104.1 mhz; 3.3 kw. Ant 899 ft TL: N34 44 30 W120 26 45. Stereo. Hrs open: 24 2325 Skyway Dr., Suite J, 93455. Phone: (805) 922-1041. Fax: (805) 928-3069. Licensee: AGM-Santa Maria LP. Group owner: American General Media (acq 2-1-2000). Population served: 200,000 Hogan & Hartson. Format: Adult hits. News staff: one. Target aud: 25-54. ♦Rich Watson, pres & gen mgr; luis Diaz, opns mgr, progmg dir; Emily Stich, gen sls mgr, natl sls mgr; John Bartel, chief of engrg.

KGDP(AM)—(Oildale, July 4, 1988: 660 khz; 10 kw-D, 1 kw-N, DA-2. TL: N34 57 04 W120 22 38. (CP: COL Oildale. 5 kw-U, DA-2. TL: N35 27 10 W118 56 40). Hrs open: 24 2225 Skyway Dr., Suite B, 93455. Phone: (805) 928-7707. Fax: (805) 922-8582.E-mail: kgdp660@yahoo.com Web Site:www.kgdp660.com Licensee: Radio Representatives Inc. Group owner: Norwood J. Patterson Population served: 650,000 Natl. Network: USA, . Format: Christian, talk. Target aud: 35-65. ♦Steve Cox, gen mgr; Bill Greenelsh, prom dir; Gretchen England, traf mgr.

***KGDP-FM**— 2003: 90.5 mhz; 17.5 kw. Ant 846 ft TL: N34 44 30 W120 26 45. Hrs open: 1416 Hollister Ln., Los Osos, 93402. Phone: (805) 528-1996. Fax: (805) 922-8582.E-mail: jp805@msn.com Web Site:kgdp660.com Licensee: People of Action. Format: Christian talk radio. ♦Steve Cox, gen mgr.

***KHFR(FM)**— June 21, 2005: 89.7 mhz; 2.45 kw vert. Ant 1,866 ft TL: N34 54 37 W120 11 08. Hrs open: 24 Family Stations Inc., 4135 Northgate Blvd., Suite 1, Sacramento, 95834. Phone: (916) 641-8191. Fax: (916) 641-8238. Licensee: Family Stations Inc. (group owner). Format: Relg. ♦Harol Camping, pres.

KPAT(FM)—(Orcutt, 1993: 95.7 mhz; 3.3 kw. 735 ft TL: N34 44 20 W120 26 41. Hrs open: 2325 Skyway Dr., Suite J, 93455. Phone: (805) 922-1041. Fax: (805) 928-3069.E-mail: info@957thebeatfm.com Web Site:www.957thebeatfm.com Licensee: AGM-Santa Maria LP. Group owner: American General Media (acq 12-1-99; $900,000). Natl. Network: USA, . Format: Rhythm and blues, hip hop, old school. ♦Emily Stich, gen sls mgr; Jeff Lyons, prom dir; Luis Diaz, progmg dir; Rich Watson, gen mgr & pub affrs dir.

KSBQ(AM)— Sept 1, 1961: 1480 khz; 1 kw-D, 61 w-N. TL: N34 57 02 W120 29 22. Hrs open: 24 200 E. Fesler St., Suites 101 & 201, 93454. Phone: (805) 240-2070. Phone: (805) 928-9796. Fax: (805) 240-5960. Fax: (805) 928-3367. Licensee: Lazer Broadcasting Corp. (group owner; acq 12-29-99; $225,000). Population served: 200,000 Natl. Rep: Lotus Entravision Reps LLC,. Fletcher Heald & Hildreth. Format: Christian. Target aud: 18-49; adults. ♦Alfredo Plascencia, CEO, pres, gen mgr; Salvador Prieto, opns mgr & progmg dir.

KSMX(AM)— 1946: 1240 khz; 1 kw-U. TL: N34 57 02 W120 29 27. Hrs open: 2215 Skyway Dr., 93456. Phone: (805) 925-2582. Fax: (805) 928-1544. Web Site:www.1240ksmx.com Licensee: EDB SLO License LLC. (acq 11-30-2007; grpsl). Population served: 400,000 Natl. Network: Premiere Radio Networks, Westwood One, Talk Radio Network, . Format: News/talk. ♦Ron Roy, gen mgr; Kathy Mansell, gen sls mgr; Nickle Duff, progmg dir.

KSNI-FM— 1960: 102.5 mhz; 17.5 kw. Ant 774 ft TL: N34 50 08 W120 24 06. Stereo. Hrs open: 2215 Skyway Dr., 93456. Phone: (805) 925-2582. Fax: (805) 928-1544. Web Site:www.sunnycountry.com Licensee: EDB SLO License LLC. Population served: 400,000 Format: Contemp country.

KTAP(AM)— June 10, 1962: 1600 khz; 470 w-D. TL: N34 58 48 W120 27 12. Hrs open: 6 AM-midnight 718 E. Chapel St., 93454. Phone: (805) 928-4334. Fax: (805) 349-2765. Licensee: Emerald Wave Media. (acq 3-6-97; $475,000 with KRTO(FM) Guadalupe). Population served: 60,000 Mark Van Burgh. Format: Sp, Mexican. News staff: one; News: 4 hrs wkly. Target aud: General; first generation Mexicans. ♦August Ruiz, gen mgr.

KUHL(AM)— April 1946: 1440 khz; 5 kw-D, 1 kw-N, DA-N. TL: N34 59 02 W120 27 10. Hrs open: 1101 S Broadway Street, Suite C, 93454. Phone: (805) 922-7727. Fax: (805) 349-0265.E-mail: Shawn@knightbroadcasting.com Web Site:www.am1440.com Licensee: Knight Broadcasting Inc. (group owner; (acq 7-31-2006; $1.2 million with KSMA(AM) Lompoc). Population served: 285,000 Format: News/talk. Target aud: 35-64; upscale news & sports listeners. ♦Shawn Knight, gen mgr; Jeff Williams, opns dir.

KURQ(FM)—See Grover Beach

KXFM(FM)— 1959: 99.1 mhz; 1.8 kw. 1,905 ft TL: N34 54 37 W120 11 08. Stereo. Hrs open: 2215 Skyway Dr., 93454. Phone: (805) 925-2582. Fax: (805) 928-1544. Web Site:www.991thefox.com Licensee: EDB SLO License LLC. (acq 11-30-2007; grpsl). Population served: 243,000 Format: Classic rock. Target aud: 18-49; contemp, active adults. ♦Rich Hawkins, gen mgr; Jennifer Grant, opns dir; Pattie Wagner, gen sls mgr; Milos Nemicik, chief of engrg.

KXTK(AM)—See San Luis Obispo

KZOZ(FM)—See San Luis Obispo

Santa Monica

KBLA(AM)— 1947: 1580 khz; 50 kw-U, DA-2. TL: N34 05 08 W118 15 24. Stereo. Hrs open: 747 E. Green St., Suite 400, Pasadena, 91101. Phone: (626) 844-8882. Fax: (626) 844-0156.E-mail: info@mrbi.net Web Site:www.mrbi.net Licensee: Multicultural Radio Broadcasting Licensee LLC. Group owner: Multicultural Radio Broadcasting Inc. (acq 2-4-2004; grpsl). Population served: 500,000 Format: Spanish Christian. News staff: one. ♦David Sweeney, gen mgr; Jose Calles, stn mgr.

***KCRW(FM)**— Jan 1, 1946: 89.9 mhz; 6.9 kw. 1,110 ft TL: N34 07 08 W118 23 30. Stereo. Hrs open: 24 1900 Pico Blvd., 90405. Phone: (310) 450-5183. Fax: (310) 450-7172.E-mail: mail@kcrw.org Web Site:www.kcrw.org Licensee: Santa Monica College District. (acq 8-3-76). Population served: 10,000,000 Natl. Network: NPR, PRI, . Dickstein Shapiro LLP. Wire Svc: AP Format: Indie rock, Latino, news. News staff: 3; News: 14 hrs wkly. Target aud: General; 18-55 year old consumers. ♦Ruth Seymour, gen mgr; Mike Newport, opns dir; David Kleinbart, dev dir; Nic Harcourt, mus dir; Steve Herbert, chief of engrg.

KDLD(FM)— 1963: 103.1 mhz; 3.7 kw. Ant 269 ft TL: N34 00 53 W118 22 50. Stereo. Hrs open: 24
Simulcast with KDLE(FM) Newport Beach 100%.
5700 Wilshire Blvd., Suite 250, Los Angeles, 90036. Phone: (323) 900-6100. Fax: (323) 900-6127. Web Site:www.elgato1031.com Licensee: Entravision Holdings LLC. Group owner: Entravision Communications Corp. (acq 2000). Population served: 6,000,000 Format: Rgnl Mexican. Target aud: 25-54; upscale adults in Los Angeles' westside. ♦Karl Meyer, gen mgr.

Santa Paula

KKZZ(AM)— 1948: 1400 khz; 1 kw-U. TL: N34 19 48 W119 05 31. Stereo. Hrs open: 2284 S. Victoria Ave., Suite 2 G, Ventura, 93003. Phone: (805) 289-1400. Fax: (805) 644-7906.E-mail: info@1590kkzz.com Licensee: Gold Coast Broadcasting LLC (group owner; (acq 8-18-99; grpsl). Format: News/talk. Target aud: 25-54. ♦Chip Ehrhardt, gen mgr; Mark Elliott, progmg dir.

KLJR-FM— Oct 4, 1976: 96.7 mhz; 87 w. 1,500 ft TL: N34 19 33 W119 02 18. (CP: 278 w). Stereo. Hrs open: 24 200 S. A St., Suite 400, Oxnard, 93030. Phone: (805) 240-2070. Fax: (805) 240-5960. Licensee: Lazer Broadcasting Corp. (acq 3-31-98; $925,000;11-4-91). Population served: 55,797 Natl. Rep: Lotus Entravision Reps LLC,. Fletcher, Heald & Hildreth. Format: Sp, adult contemp, CHR. Target aud: 25-54; general. ♦Alfredo Plascencia, CEO, pres, gen mgr; Salvador Prieto, progmg dir.

Santa Rosa

KFGY(FM)—(Healdsburg, Dec 21, 1979: 92.9 mhz; 2.3 kw. Ant 1,800 ft TL: N38 45 45 W122 50 24. Stereo. Hrs open: Box 2158, 95405. Phone: (707) 543-0100. Fax: (707) 571-1097. Web Site:froggy929.com Format: Country. Target aud: 18-44. Spec prog: Jazz 5 hrs wkly.

***KRCB-FM**— September 1993: 91.1 mhz; 120 w. 731 ft TL: N38 44 25 W122 50 46. Stereo. Hrs open: 24 5850 Labath Ave., Rohnert Park, 94928. Phone: (707) 584-2000. Fax: (707) 585-1363. Web Site:www.krcb.org Licensee: Rural California Broadcasting Corp. Population served: 70,000 Natl. Network: NPR, PRI, . Wire Svc: DAC Format: Class, progsv, news/talk. News staff: one; News: 15 hrs wkly. Target aud: General. Spec prog: Folk 6 hrs, jazz 6 hrs wkly. ♦Nancy Dobbs, CEO & pres. Co-owned TV: *KRCB-TV affil.

KRRS(AM)— Apr 1, 1962: 1460 khz; 1 kw-D, 33 w-N, DA-2. TL: N38 22 13 W122 43 39. Stereo. Hrs open: 24 Box 2277, 95405. Phone: (707) 545-1460. Fax: (707) 545-0112.E-mail: krrs@sonic.net Web Site:www.moonradios.com Licensee: Moon Broadcasting Licensee LLC. Group owner: Moon Broadcasting (acq 1993; $400,000;9-6-93). Population served: 500,000 Natl. Rep: Interep,. Format: Sp. Target aud: 25-54; contemporary Hispanic families. ♦Abel DeLuna Sr., CEO; Abel A. DeLuna, pres; Arelia DeLuna, CFO; Maggie LeClerc, gen mgr; Benoit LeClerc, opns mgr.

KSRO(AM)— May 1937: 1350 khz; 5 kw-U, DA-N. TL: N38 26 22 W122 44 51. Hrs open: Box 2158, 95405. Secondary address: 1315 Hwy. 93 N., Suite 200 95405. Phone: (707) 543-0100. Fax: (707) 571-1097. Web Site:www.ksro.com Licensee: Maverick Media of Santa Rosa License LLC. Group owner: Maverick Media LLC (acq 12-16-02; grpsl). Population served: 337,000 Format: News/talk.

Target aud: 35-64. ♦Gary Rozynek, pres; Diane Hubel, gen mgr, gen sls mgr; Michelle Marquis, progmg dir; George Bright, news dir; Virgil Scigla, chief of engrg.

KVRV(FM)—(Monte Rio, Nov 20, 1977: 97.7 mhz; 250 w. 1,122 ft TL: N38 29 08 W123 02 05. Stereo. Hrs open: 24 Box 2158, 95405. Secondary address: 1410 Neotomas Ave., Suite 200 95405. Phone: (707) 543-0100. Fax: (707) 571-1097. Web Site:www.977theriver.com Licensee: Maverick Media of Santa Rosa License LLC. Group owner: Maverick Media LLC (acq 12-16-02; grpsl). Population served: 360,000 Format: Classic rock. Target aud: 25-54. ♦Diane Hubel, gen mgr.

KXFX(FM)— Dec 23, 1974: 101.7 mhz; 2.2 kw. 1,056 ft TL: N38 30 31 W122 39 41. Stereo. Hrs open: Box 2158, 95405. Secondary address: 1410 Neotomas Ave., Suite 200 95405. Phone: (707) 543-0100. Fax: (707) 571-1097. Web Site:www.kxfx.com Licensee: Maverick Media of Santa Rosa License LLC. Group owner: Maverick Media LLC (acq 12-16-02; grpsl). Population served: 380,000 Pepper & Corazzini. Format: Hard rock. Target aud: General. ♦Diane Hubel, gen mgr & prom mgr.

KZST(FM)— Apr 18, 1971: 100.1 mhz; 6 kw. 240 ft TL: N38 25 07 W122 40 33. Stereo. Hrs open: 24 Box 100, 95402. Secondary address: 3392 Mendocino Ave. 95403. Phone: (707) 528-4434. Fax: (707) 527-8216. Web Site:www.kzst.com Licensee: Redwood Empire Stereocasters. Population served: 412,000 Natl. Rep: McGavren Guild,. Haley, Bader & Potts. Wire Svc: Reuters Wire Svc: Bay City News Service Format: Adult contemp. News staff: 2. Target aud: 25-54. ♦Tom Skinner, gen mgr.

Santa Ynez

KRAZ(FM)— 2001: 105.9 mhz; 65 w. Ant 2,932 ft TL: N34 31 32 W119 57 00. Hrs open: 24 1101 S Broadway Street, Suite C, Santa Maria, 93454. Phone: (805) 688-8386. Fax: (805) 688-2271.E-mail: kathy@knightbroadcasting.com Web Site:www.krazfm.com Licensee: Knight Broadcasting Inc. (acq 5-21-2001; $325,000 for CP). Natl. Network: ABC, . Format: Country. ♦Shawn Knight, gen mgr.

Seaside

KBOQ(FM)— October 1996: 103.9 mhz; 1.4 kw. Ant 604 ft TL: N36 30 17 W121 54 21. Stereo. Hrs open: 24 60 Garden Court, Suite 300, Monterey, 93940-5341. Phone: (831) 658-5200. Fax: (831) 658-5299.E-mail: kallen@radiocentralcoast.com Web Site:www.kbach.com Licensee: Mapleton License of Monterey LLC. (group owner; (acq 1-24-2002; $1.85 million). Population served: 500,000 Natl. Rep: McGavren Guild,. Leventhal, Senter & Lerman. Format: Classical. ♦Adam Nathanson, pres; Mike Anthony, gen mgr; Kenny Allen, opns mgr, progmg dir; Jodi Morgan, gen sls mgr; Sybil D'Angelo, prom dir.

KSES-FM— Nov 22, 1972: 107.1 mhz; 1.85 kw. 587 ft TL: N36 33 12 W121 47 05. Stereo. Hrs open: 67 Garden Ct., Monterey, 93940. Phone: (831) 333-9735. Fax: (831) 333-9750. Web Site:www.1071se.com Licensee: Entravision Holdings LLC. Group owner: Entravision Communications Corp. (acq 3-14-00; grpsl). Population served: 565000 Format: Contemp Sp hits. Target aud: 18-49. ♦Aaron Scoby, gen mgr; Tony Valencia, progmg dir.

Sebastopol

KJZY(FM)— Nov 5, 1995: 93.7 mhz; 6 kw. 216 ft TL: N38 25 07 W122 40 33. Stereo. Hrs open: 24 Box 100, Santa Rosa, 95402. Phone: (707) 528-4434. Fax: (707) 527-8216.E-mail: gz@kjzy.com Web Site:www.kjzy.com Licensee: Redwood Empire Stereocasters. Natl. Rep: McGavren Guild,. Format: Smooth. ♦Tom Skinner, gen mgr.

Selma

***KQKL(FM)**— Aug 6, 2003: 88.5 mhz; 17 kw. Ant 397 ft TL: N36 26 50 W119 37 10. Stereo. Hrs open: 24 2351 Sunset Blvd., Suite 170-218, Rocklin, 95765. Phone: (916) 251-1600. Fax: (916) 251-1650.E-mail: klove@klove.com Web Site:www.klove.com Licensee: Educational Media Foundation. Group owner: EMF Broadcasting. Natl. Network: K-Love, . Shaw Pittman. Format: Contemp Christian. News staff: 3. Target aud: 25-44; Judeo Christian, female. ♦Richard Jenkins, pres; Mike Novak, VP; Keith Whipple, dev dir; David Pierce, progmg mgr; Ed Lenane, news dir; Sam Wallington, engrg dir; Karen Johnson, news rptr.

Shafter

***KAIB(FM)**— 2006: 89.5 mhz; 50 kw. Ant 358 ft TL: N35 36 53 W119 28 16. Hrs open:
Rebroadcasts KLRD(FM) Yucaipa 100%.
2351 Sunset Blvd., Suite 170-218, Rocklin, 95765. Phone: (916) 251-1600. Fax: (916) 251-1650. Web Site:www.air1.com Licensee: Educational Media Foundation. Group owner: EMF Broadcasting (acq 1-14-2005). Natl. Network: Air 1, . Format: Alternative rock, div. ♦Richard Jenkins, pres; Lloyd Parker, gen mgr; Keith Whipple, dev dir; David Pierce, progmg mgr; Ed Lenane, news dir; Sam Wallington, engrg dir; Arthur Vassar, traf mgr.

***KGZO(FM)**— June 6, 1996: 90.9 mhz; 1.9 kw. 2070 ft TL: N35 16 51 W119 44 52. Stereo. Hrs open: 24
Rebroadcasts KMRO(FM) Camarillo 100%.
2310 Ponderosa Dr., Suite 28, Camarillo, 93010. Phone: (805) 482-4797. Fax: (805) 388-5202.E-mail: info@nuevavida.com Web Site:www.nuevavida.com Licensee: The Association for Community Education Inc. (acq 7-30-97;). Population served: 500,000 Miller & Neely. Format: Relg, Sp. Target aud: General. ♦Phil Guthrie, pres; Mary Guthrie, gen mgr.

KKXX-FM— 1994: 93.1 mhz; 4 kw. Ant 403 ft TL: N35 28 21 W119 01 40. Stereo. Hrs open: 24 1400 Easton Dr., Suite 144, Bakersfield, 93309. Phone: (661) 328-1410. Fax: (661) 328-0873. Web Site:www.bakersfieldpirateradio.com Licensee: AGM California. Group owner: American General Media (acq 7-25-97; $1.5 million with KBID(AM) Bakersfield). Format: Adult hits. News staff: 4; News: 2 hrs wkly. Target aud: 18-49; men. ♦Roger Fessler, gen mgr; Toni Snyder, gen sls mgr; Chris Edwards, progmg dir.

KSMJ(FM)—Licensed to Shafter. See Bakersfield

Shasta

KCNR(AM)— Aug 13, 1967: 1460 khz; 750 w-U. TL: N40 33 14 W122 22 53. Hrs open: 1326 Market St., Redding, 96001. Phone: (530) 244-5082. Fax: (530) 244-5698. Licensee: M C Allen Productions (acq 10-9-96; $35,000). Population served: 20,000 Womble, Carlyle,Sandbridge & Rice, LLC. Format: Talk, Sports. Target aud: 24-55. ♦Mike Quinn, gen mgr, progmg dir & chief of engrg.

Shasta Lake City

KESR(FM)— 1998: 107.1 mhz; 1.4 kw. 1,361 ft TL: N40 39 06 W122 31 32. Hrs open: 24 1588 Charles Dr., Redding, 96003. Phone: (530) 244-9700. Fax: (530) 244-9707.E-mail: rhealy@resultsradiomail.com Licensee: Results Radio of Redding Licensee LLC. Group owner: Fritz Communications Inc. (acq 5-28-2000; grpsl). Format: Adult contemp. ♦Jack Fritz, pres, gen mgr; Beth Tappan, gen mgr; Rick Healy, opns mgr, progmg dir; Laurie Curto, gen sls mgr; Rob Reid, news dir; Bryant Smith, chief of engrg.

KJPR(AM)— 2005: 1330 khz; 1 kw-U, DA-2. TL: N40 40 48 W122 16 01. Hrs open: 24 hrs Jefferson Public Radio, 1250 Siskiyou Blvd., Ashland, OR, 97520. Phone: (541) 552-6301. Fax: (541) 552-8565.E-mail: info@ijpr.org Web Site:www.ijpr.org Licensee: JPR Foundation Inc. (acq 2-9-2004). Format: News, information. ♦Ronald Kramer, gen mgr; Bryon Lambert, opns dir; Paul Westhelle, dev dir.

KNNN(FM)— Oct 26, 1989: 99.3 mhz; 1.6 kw. Ant 1,525 ft TL: N40 39 15 W122 31 12. Hrs open: 3360 Alta Mesa Dr., Redding, 96002. Phone: (530) 226-9500. Fax: (530) 221-4940.E-mail: knnn@reddingradio.com Web Site:www.mix993fm.com Licensee: Mapleton License of Redding LLC. Group owner: Regent Communications Inc. (acq 11-30-2006; grpsl). Format: CHR. Target aud: 25-54. Spec prog: Jazz 3 hrs wkly. ♦Lisa Geraci, gen mgr; Justin Paul, progmg dir.

Shingle Springs

KNTY(FM)— May 1, 1989: 101.9 mhz; 47 kw. Ant 505 ft TL: N38 51 12 W120 56 23. Stereo. Hrs open: 24 1436 Auburn Blvd., Sacramento, 95815. Phone: (916) 646-4000. Phone: (916) 648-6013. Fax: (916) 646-6020. Web Site:www.kcclbossradio.com Licensee: Entravision Holdings LLC. Group owner: Entravision Communications Corp. (acq 3-14-2000; grpsl). Population served: 3,000,000 Thompson, Hine & Flory L.L.P. Format: Country. Target aud: 25-54. ♦Larry Lemanski, gen mgr; Bob McNeill, prom dir.

Shingletown

KKXS(FM)— January 2001: 96.1 mhz; 1.9 kw. Ant 1,174 ft TL: N40 29 18 W121 53 58. Hrs open: Fritz Communications Inc., 1355 N. Dutton Ave. #225, Santa Rosa, 95401-7107. Phone: (530) 244-9700. Fax: (530) 244-9707.E-mail: rhealy@resultsradiomail.com Web Site:www.smoothjazz961.com Licensee: Results Radio of Redding Licensee LLC. Group owner: Fritz Communications Inc. (acq 3-29-99; $125,000 for 50%). Format: Smooth jazz. ♦Beth Tappan, gen mgr; Laurie Curto, gen sls mgr; Rick Healy, opns dir & progmg dir.

KRDG(FM)— Aug 1, 1995: 105.3 mhz; 10 kw. 1,056 ft TL: N40 29 54 W121 53 25. Stereo. Hrs open: 24 3360 Alta Mesa Dr., Reading, 96002. Phone: (530) 226-9500. Fax: (530) 221-4940.E-mail: info@readingradio.cpm Web Site:www.readingradio.com Licensee: Mapleton License of Redding LLC. Group owner: Regent Communications Inc. (acq 11-30-2006; grpsl). Population served: 1,000,000 Bechtel & Cole. Format: Good time oldies. Target aud: 25-54; active adults with families. ♦Lisa Geraci, gen mgr; Jim Albertson, progmg dir.

Simi Valley

KIRN(AM)— Sept 21, 1984: 670 khz; 5 kw-D, 3 kw-N, DA-1. TL: N34 19 10 W118 42 56. Hrs open: 24 3301 Barham Blvd. #300, Los Angeles, 90068. Phone: (323) 851-5476. Fax: (323) 512-7452.E-mail: pomzaffari@670amkirn.com Web Site:www.670amkirn.com Licensee: Lotus Oxnard Corp. Group owner: Lotus Communications Corp. (acq 12-11-96; $4.2 million). Population served: 900,000 Jerome Boros, Bryan Caves, Robinson Silverman. Format: Farsi (Persian) MOR, news/talk, sports. News staff: 3; News: 14 hrs wkly. Persian, Irawian, Farsi Speaking Middle Eastern. ♦Howard Kalmenson, pres; John Paley, VP, progmg VP; Jason Houts, chief of engrg; Poopak Mozaffari, mktg.

Soledad

***KFRS(FM)**— April 4, 2002: 89.9 mhz; 250 w vert. Ant 305 ft TL: N36 16 25 W121 16 12. Hrs open: Family Stations Inc., 4135 Northgate Blvd., Suite 1, Sacramento, 95834. Phone: (916) 641-8191. Fax: (916) 641-8238. Licensee: Family Stations Inc. (group owner) Format: Relg. ♦Thad McKinney, gen mgr.

KMBX(AM)— 1992: 700 khz; 2.5 kw-D, 700 w-N. TL: N36 27 51 W121 17 52. Hrs open: 67 Garden Ct., Monterey, 93940. Phone: (831) 333-9735. Fax: (831) 333-9750. Web Site:www.jose700.com Licensee: Entravision Holdings LLC. Group owner: Entravision Communications Corp. (acq 3-14-2000; grpsl). Format: Contemp Sp mus. Target aud: 18-49. ♦Aaron Scoby, gen mgr; Jeff Liberman, opns VP; Fidel Soto, news dir; Marcello Soto, chief of engrg.

KMJV(FM)— Oct 1, 1991: 106.3 mhz; 6 kw. 1,720 ft TL: N36 22 48 W121 12 57. Stereo. Hrs open: 24 PO Box 1939, Salinas, 93902. Phone: (831) 757-1910. Fax: (831) 771-1685.E-mail: info@kmjvfm.com Licensee: Wolfhouse Radio Group Inc. (group owner); (acq 7-13-2001; grpsl). Format: Mexican rgnl. Target aud: 18-44. ♦Roman Castro, gen mgr.

Solvang

KSYV(FM)— Sept 22, 1982: 96.7 mhz; 420 w. Ant 1,217 ft TL: N34 41 28 W120 15 58. Stereo. Hrs open: 24 1101 S Broadway Street, Suite C, Santa Maria, 93454. Phone: (805) 688-5798. Fax: (805) 688-2271.E-mail: kathy@knightbroadcasting.com Web Site:www.mix96.com Licensee: Knight Broadcasting Inc. (acq 2-8-2002). Population served: 60,000 Natl. Network: AP Network News, . Format: Adult contemp. News: 126 hrs wkly. Target aud: 24-54; female 60%, male 40%. ♦Shawn Knight, gen mgr; Jeff Williams, opns dir.

Sonoma

***KSVY(FM)**— 2005: 91.3 mhz; 2.5 kw vert. Ant -305 ft TL: N38 16 47 W122 26 47. Hrs open: 168 W. Napa St., 95476. Phone: (707) 933-0808. Fax: (707) 933-1573.E-mail: ksvy@ksvy.org Web Site:www.ksvy.org Licensee: Commonbond Foundation. Format: Community radio. ♦Bill Hammett, pres & gen mgr.

Sonora

KVML(AM)— 1949: 1450 khz; 1 kw-U. TL: N38 00 30 W120 21 45. Hrs open: 24 342 S. Washington, 95370. Phone: (209) 533-1450. Fax: (209) 533-9520. Web Site:www.kvml.com Licensee: Clarke Broadcasting Corp. (group owner; acq 12-86; with co-located FM; 10-6-86). Population served: 200,000 Natl. Network: ABC, CNN Radio, Fox News Radio, . Leventhal, Senter & Lerman. Format: News/talk. News staff: 3; News: 25 hrs wkly. Target aud: 25 plus; general. Spec prog: Relg 3 hrs, sports 15 hrs wkly. ♦H. Randolph Holder Jr., pres; Larry England, gen mgr; Mark Truppner, progmg dir; Bill Johnson, news dir; John Petter, chief of engrg; D.J. Riendeau, traf mgr.

KZSQ-FM— Oct 3, 1973: 92.7 mhz; 380 w. Ant 1,289 ft TL: N38 00 30 W120 21 45. Stereo. Hrs open: 24 342 S. Washington, 95370. Phone: (209) 533-1450. Fax: (209) 533-9520. Licensee: Clarke Broadcasting Corp. (acq 1986). Population served: 500,000 Natl. Network: Fox News Radio, . Format: Adult contemp. News staff: 3; News: 4 hrs wkly. Target aud: 25-54. ♦Justin Flores, progmg dir.

Soquel

KYAA(AM)— 2001: 1200 khz; 25 kw-D, 10 kw-N. TL: N36 39 38 W121 32 29. Hrs open:
Simulcast with KEBV(FM) Salinas 100%.
651 Cannery Row, Monterey, 93940. Phone: (831) 372-1074. Fax: (831) 372-3585.E-mail: kyaknry@aol.com Web Site:www.knry.com Licensee: People's Radio Inc. (group owner). Format: East Indian. ♦Jim Vossen, chief of opns & progmg dir.

South Lake Tahoe

KOWL(AM)— November 1956: 1490 khz; 1 kw-U. TL: N38 56 34 W119 57 25. Hrs open: 2435 E. Venice Dr., Suite 120, 96150. Phone: (530) 541-6681. Fax: (530) 541-4822.E-mail: kowl@krltfm.com Web Site:www.krltfm.com Licensee: CCR-Lake Tahoe IV LLC. Group owner: Cherry Creek Radio LLC (acq 12-19-2003; grpsl). Format: News/talk, sports. ♦Betsy Miller, gen mgr.

KRLT(FM)— June 23, 1976: 93.9 mhz; 6 kw. -190 ft TL: N38 57 38 W119 56 26. Stereo. Hrs open: 24 2435 E. Venice Dr., Suite 120, 96150. Phone: (530) 541-6681. Fax: (530) 541-4822.E-mail: krlt@krltfm.com Web Site:www.krltfm.com Licensee: CCR-Lake Tahoe IV LLC. Group owner: Cherry Creek Radio LLC (acq 12-19-2003; grpsl). Format: 80s, 90s & today. News: 10 hrs wkly. Target aud: 25-54. ♦Betsy Miller, gen mgr.

KTHO(AM)— Mar 17, 1963: 590 khz; 2.5 kw-D, 500 w-N, DA-N. TL: N38 55 00 W119 57 46. Hrs open: 24 Box 5686, State Line, NV, 89449. Secondary address: 2520 Lake Tahoe Blvd., Ste 5 96150. Phone: (530) 543-0590. Fax: (530) 543-1101.E-mail: ed@590ktho.com Licensee: International Aerospace Solutions Inc. (acq 5-1-2009; $125,000). Population served: 825,000 Natl. Network: ABC, . Format: Timeless Favorites. News staff: one; News: 40 hrs wkly. Target aud: 35-55; locals & visitors, working population and retired. Spec prog: Jazz Trax Sundays 8pm. ♦Ed Crook, stn mgr.

KWYL(FM)— 1995: 102.9 mhz; 39 kw. Ant 2,926 ft TL: N39 18 38 W119 53 01. Stereo. Hrs open: 24 595 E. Plumb Ln., Reno, NV, 89502. Phone: (775) 789-6700. Fax: (775) 789-6767. Web Site:www.wild1029.com Licensee: Citadel Broadcasting Co. Group owner: Citadel Broadcasting Corp. (acq 5-9-03; grpsl). Population served: 75,000 Format: Urban, rap, hip hop. Target aud: 25-54. ♦Andrew Perini, gen mgr; Kathy Williams, gen sls mgr; Nick Elliott, progmg dir; Martin Stabbert, chief of engrg.

South Oroville

KYIX(FM)— Feb 1, 1994: 104.9 mhz; 260 w. Ant 1,548 ft TL: N39 39 04 W121 27 43. Hrs open: 1363 Longfellow, Chico, 95926-7319. Phone: (530) 894-7325.E-mail: info@kkxx.net Web Site:www.air1.com Licensee: Butte Broadcasting Co. (acq 1994). Format: Christian hit radio. ♦Andrew Palmquist, gen mgr.

Stanford

*__KZSU(FM)__— Oct 10, 1964: 90.1 mhz; 500 w. -10 ft TL: N37 24 42 W122 10 41. Stereo. Hrs open: 24 Box 20190, 94309. Phone: (650) 725-4868. Fax: (650) 725-5865.E-mail: gm@kzsustanford.edu Web Site:www.kzsu.stanford.edu Licensee: Trustees of Leland Stanford Jr. University. Population served: 13,000 Crowell & Moring. Format: Progressive, educ. Target aud: 13-plus; independent-thinking individuals who value unique programming. ♦Kyle Wulff, gen mgr; Ben Levitti, progmg dir; Anthony Sanchez, news dir; Lisa Dornell, pub affrs dir; Mark Lawrence, chief of engrg.

Stockton

KHKK(FM)—See Modesto

KJOY(FM)— June 15, 1968: 99.3 mhz; 2.35 kw. 330 ft TL: N38 01 21 W121 16 03. Stereo. Hrs open: 24 4643 Quail Lakes Dr., Suite 100, 95207-1833. Secondary address: 1581 Cummins Dr. #135, Modesto 95358. Phone: (209) 476-1230. Fax: (209) 957-1833.E-mail: info@993kjoy.com Web Site:www.993kjoy.com Licensee: Citadel

Broadcasting Co. Group owner: Citadel Broadcasting Corp. (acq 5-9-03; grpsl). Format: Adult contemp. Target aud: 25-54. ♦Roy Williams, gen mgr.

KMIX(FM)—See Tracy

KQOD(FM)— Jan 24, 1980: 100.1 mhz; 6 kw. 285 ft TL: N38 01 21 W121 16 03. Stereo. Hrs open: 2121 Lancey Dr., Modesto, 95355. Phone: (209) 551-1306. Fax: (209) 551-1359. Web Site:www.mega100online.com Licensee: Capstar TX L.P. Group owner: Clear Channel Communications Inc. (acq 11-18-99). Population served: 450,000 Format: Oldies. Target aud: 25-54. ♦Greg Granger, gen mgr, mktg mgr; Leslie Davisson, prom dir; D. Ferrevia, progmg dir; Kacie Marshall, traf mgr.

KSTN(AM)— November 1949: 1420 khz; 5 kw-D, 1 kw-N, DA-2. TL: N37 55 32 W121 14 44. Hrs open: 24 2171 Ralph Ave., 95206. Phone: (209) 948-5786. Licensee: San Joaquin Broadcasting Co. Population served: 3,400,000 Format: Oldies. News staff: one; News: 20 hrs wkly. Target aud: 18-40. Spec prog: Farm 3 hrs, relg 5 hrs wkly. ♦Knox LaRue, pres, stn mgr & progmg mgr; John Hampton, mus dir.

KSTN-FM— 1962: 107.3 mhz; 8.1 kw. Ant 1,610 ft TL: N37 49 17 W121 46 49. Hrs open: 2171 Ralph Ave., 95206. Phone: (209) 948-5786. Population served: 7,000,000 Format: Sp. Target aud: General. Spec prog: Sp, Por 4 hrs wkly. ♦Julio Barrios, progmg dir, disc jockey; Lupe Esquer, disc jockey.

*__KUOP(FM)__— Sept 22, 1947: 91.3 mhz; 7 kw. 1,220 ft TL: N37 28 48 W121 21 02. Stereo. Hrs open: 24 7055 Folsom Blvd., Sacramento, 95826. Phone: (916) 278-8900. Fax: (916) 278-8989.E-mail: npr@csus.edu Web Site:www.capradio.org Licensee: University of the Pacific. Population served: 1,100,000 Natl. Network: NPR, PRI, . Dow, Lohnes & Albertson. Format: News info, class. News staff: one; News: 90 hrs wkly. Target aud: General; NPR listeners, eg. professionals, educators, administrators. ♦John Brenneise, opns dir; Cheryl Dring, progmg dir, mus dir; Joe Barr, news dir, local news ed, edit dir, political ed, relg ed; Jeff Browne, chief of engrg.

*__KWG(AM)__— Nov 22, 1921: 1230 khz; 900 w-U. TL: N37 57 34 W121 15 28. Hrs open: 2280 E. Weber Ave., 95205-5051. Phone: (209) 462-8307.E-mail: info@ihradio.org Web Site:www.ihradio.org Licensee: IHR Educational Broadcasting (group owner; acq 10-18-99; $441,227). Population served: 400,000 Wire Svc: Dow Jones News Service Format: Catholic/relg. Target aud: 25-54. ♦Joseph Nesta, gen mgr & stn mgr; Dale Harry, chief of engrg.

KWIN(FM)—See Lodi

KWSX(AM)— 1947: 1280 khz; 1 kw-U, DA-N. TL: N37 58 55 W121 13 44. Stereo. Hrs open: 24 2121 Lancey Dr., Modesto, 95355. Phone: (209) 551-1306. Fax: (209) 551-1359. Web Site:www.rock967.com Licensee: Capstar TX L.P. Group owner: Clear Channel Communications Inc. (acq 8-30-2000; grpsl). Population served: 471,600 Format: Active rock. Target aud: 25-64. ♦Gary Granger, gen mgr; Bill Mick, progmg dir.

*__KYCC(FM)__— Feb 24, 1975: 90.1 mhz; 26 kw. Ant 230 ft TL: N37 57 10 W121 17 11. Stereo. Hrs open: 9019 N. West Ln., 95210. Phone: (209) 477-3690. Fax: (209) 477-2762.E-mail: kycc@kycc.org Web Site:www.kycc.org Licensee: Your Christian Companion Network Inc. (acq 7-20-98). Population served: 20000 Natl. Network: USA, . Cohn & Marks. Format: Gospel, inspirational, adult contemp. Target aud: 35-55. Spec prog: Black 6 hrs, health one hr wkly. ♦Shirley Garner, exec VP & gen mgr; Adam Biddell, opns mgr.

Sun City

KXFG(FM)— March 1997: 92.9 mhz; 6 kw. 328 ft TL: N33 35 36 W117 08 50. Hrs open:
Rebroadcasts KFRG(FM) San Bernardino 100%.
900 E. Washington St., Suite 315, Colton, 92324. Phone: (909) 825-9525. Fax: (909) 825-0441. Web Site:www.kfrog.com Licensee: Infinity Radio Inc. Group owner: Infinity Broadcasting Corp. (acq 11-13-98; grpsl). Format: Country. ♦Tom Hoyt, gen mgr; Lee Douglas, opns mgr.

Sunnyvale

KCNL(FM)— January 1961: 104.9 mhz; 6 kw. Ant -154 ft TL: N37 19 23 W121 45 15. (CP: Ant -79 ft. TL: N37 19 22 W121 45 15). Stereo. Hrs open: 1420 Koll Cir., Suite A, San Jose, 95112. Phone: (408) 453-5400. Fax: (408) 452-1330.E-mail: johnallers@channel1049.com Web Site:www.channel1049.com Licensee: CC Licenses LLC. Group owner: Clear Channel Communications Inc. (acq 2-2-2004; grpsl).

Format: Alternative rock. Target aud: 18-49. ♦Kim Bryant, gen mgr; John Bassanelli, gen sls mgr; Michael Solari, prom dir; Jeanine Calhoun, progmg dir; Fred Reiss, news dir; David Williams, chief of engrg.

Susanville

*__KJAR(FM)__— 2006: 88.1 mhz; 30 w. Ant 1,141 ft TL: N40 27 12 W120 34 13. Hrs open: 2351 Sunset Blvd., Suite 170-218, Rocklin, 95765. Phone: (916) 251-1600. Fax: (916) 251-1650. Licensee: Educational Media Foundation. (acq 11-1-2006; grpsl). ♦Richard Jenkins, pres.

*__KJDX(FM)__— May 25, 1983: 93.3 mhz; 8.7 kw. Ant 1,155 ft TL: N40 27 13 W120 34 14. Stereo. Hrs open: 24 3015 Johnstonville Rd., 96130. Phone: (530) 257-2121. Fax: (530) 257-6955. Web Site:www.theradionetwork.com Licensee: Sierra Broadcasting Corp. (group owner; (acq 1-7-97; $50,000). Format: Country. Spec prog: Class 5 hrs wkly. ♦Rodney Chambers, gen mgr.

*__KJLC(FM)__—Not on air, target date: unknown: 90.9 mhz; 12 kw. Ant 2,266 ft TL: N40 26 48 W120 21 27. Hrs open: 478-200 Hwy. 139, 96130. Phone: (530) 310-3303. Licensee: Lassen Community College. ♦Kam Vento, gen mgr.

KLZN(FM)— 2006: 96.3 mhz; 1.5 kw. Ant -528 ft TL: N40 26 36 W120 38 35. Hrs open: 2100 Main St., Suite A, 96130. Phone: (530) 257-6100. Fax: (530) 257-6107. Licensee: Gary Katz. Format: Adult hits. ♦Gary Katz, pres; Dennis Carlson, gen mgr.

KSUE(AM)— Apr 22, 1948: 1240 khz; 1 kw-U. TL: N40 23 43 W120 37 32. Hrs open: 3015 Johnstonville Rd., 96130. Phone: (530) 257-2121. Fax: (530) 257-6955.E-mail: radiorodll@aol.com Web Site:www.theradionetwork.com Licensee: Sierra Broadcasting Corp. (group owner) Population served: 45,000 Pepper & Corazzini. Format: News/talk. Target aud: 35-54. Spec prog: Relg 3 hrs wkly. ♦Rod Chambers, pres, gen mgr; Scott Blackwood, opns dir & progmg dir; Mike Smith, news dir; Kristin Volberg, pub affrs dir; Mike Martindale, chief of engrg.

Sutter

*__KXJS(FM)__— 2004: 88.7 mhz; 550 w. Ant 1,978 ft TL: N39 12 20 W121 49 10. Hrs open: Capital Public Radio Inc., 7055 Folsom Blvd., Sacramento, 95826. Phone: (916) 278-8900. Fax: (916) 278-8989.E-mail: npr@csus.edu Web Site:www.csus.edu/npr Licensee: California State University, Sacramento. Duane Morris, LLP. Format: Jazz, news & info. ♦Carl Watanabe, stn mgr, progmg mgr; John Brenneise, opns mgr; Joe Barr, news dir, local news ed, edit dir, political ed; Jeff Browne, engrg dir.

Sutter Creek

KTTA(FM)—See Jackson

Taft

KBDS(FM)— June 1986: Stn currently dark. 103.9 mhz; 6 kw. Ant 328 ft TL: N35 07 04 W119 27 33. Stereo. Hrs open: 24 6313 Schirra Ct., Bakersfield, 93313. Phone: (661) 837-0745. Fax: (661) 837-1612.E-mail: achavez@campesina.com Licensee: Radio Campesina Bakersfield Inc. (acq 1994; $135,000 plus assumption of debt valued at $283,000 with co-located AM) Population served: 300,000 Borsari & Paxson. ♦Anthony Chavez, gen mgr.

KEAL(FM)— 2009: 106.5 mhz; 6 kw. Ant 285 ft TL: N35 05 39 W119 27 40. Hrs open: 200 S. A St., Suite 400, Oxnard, 93030. Phone: (805) 240-2070. Fax: (805) 240-5960. Web Site:www.radiolazer.com Licensee: Lazer Licenses LLC. (acq 6-11-2007; $3.85 million with KXTT(FM) Maricopa). ♦Neal Robinson, pres.

Tahoe City

*__KKTO(FM)__— Oct 3, 1997: 90.5 mhz; 38 kw vert. 2,939 ft TL: N39 18 38 W119 53 01. Stereo. Hrs open: 24 7055 Folsom Blvd., Sacramento, 95826. Phone: (916) 278-8900. Fax: (916) 278-8989.E-mail: npr@csus.edu Web Site:www.capradio.org Licensee: California State University, Sacramento. Population served: 500,000 Natl. Network: NPR, PRI, . Duane Morris LLP. Format: Class, info, news. News staff: 4; News: 90 hrs wkly. Target aud: General; NPR listeners, eg. professionals, educators, administrators. ♦Rick Eytcheson, gen mgr; Carl Watanabe, stn mgr, progmg dir, progmg mgr; John Brenneise, opns mgr; Arla Gibson, dev dir, mktg dir; Linda Onstad, adv dir; Cheryl Dring, mus dir; Joe Barr, news dir; Jeff Browne, engrg dir.

KLCA(FM)—Licensed to Tahoe City. See Reno NV

Tehachapi

*KBLV(FM)— 2006: 88.7 mhz; 140 w. Ant 3,693 ft TL: N35 27 10 W118 35 25. Hrs open:
Rebroadcasts KLVR(FM) Middletown 100%.
2351 Sunset Blvd., Suite 170-218, Rocklin, 95765. Phone: (916) 251-1600. Fax: (916) 251-1650. Web Site:www.klove.com Licensee: Educational Media Foundation. Natl. Network: K-Love, . Format: Contemp Christian. ◆Richard Jenkins, pres; Mike Novak, VP; Keith Whipple, dev dir; David Pierce, progmg mgr; Ed Lenane, news dir; Sam Wallington, engrg dir; Karen Johnson, news rptr.

KKZQ(FM)— 2001: 100.1 mhz; 340 w. Ant 620 ft TL: N35 04 30 W118 22 07. Hrs open: 570 East Ave. Q-9, Palmdale, 93550. Phone: (661) 947-3107. Fax: (661) 272-5688.E-mail: info@edge100.com Web Site:www.edge100.com Licensee: High Desert Broadcasting LLC (group owner). Format: Alternative modern rock. Target aud: 18-49. ◆Gary Wilson, opns mgr; Jeff McElfresh, mktg dir, prom dir; Nelson Rasse, gen mgr & progmg dir; Amir Raheem, news dir.

KSRY(FM)— Jan 8, 1982: 103.1 mhz; 1.9 kw. Ant 577 ft TL: N35 04 30 W118 22 08. Stereo. Hrs open: 24 3400 W. Olive Ave., Suite 550, Burbank, 91505. Phone: (818) 559-2252. Fax: (818) 729-2502. Licensee: CC Licenses LLC. Group owner: Clear Channel Communications Inc. (acq 11-21-2003; grpsl). Population served: 400,000 Natl. Rep: Christal,. Latham & Watkins. Format: Alternative. News staff: one; News: 2 hrs wkly. ◆Greg Ashlock, gen mgr & sls dir.

Temecula

KMYT(FM)— 2000: 94.5 mhz; 320 w. 771 ft TL: N33 28 51 W117 10 58. Hrs open: 24
Rebroadcasts KOGO(AM) San Diego.
27349 Jefferson Ave., Suite 116, 92590. Phone: (951) 296-9050. Fax: (951) 296-9077.E-mail: michaeldellinger@clearchannel.com Web Site:www.kmyt945.com Licensee: CC Licenses LLC. Group owner: Clear Channel Communications Inc. (acq 6-11-2001; $4.5 million including five-year noncompete agreement). Format: Smooth jazz. ◆Bob Ridzak, gen mgr; Robyn Bedessem, gen sls mgr; Mike Dellinger, prom dir; Allen Keppler, mus dir; Rich Mena, chief of engrg.

*KRTM(FM)— Jan 1, 1989: 88.9 mhz; 1.15 kw. 453 ft TL: N33 27 59 W117 08 29. Hrs open: 24 27314 Jefferson Ave., Ste. 4, 92590. Phone: (951) 296-9694.E-mail: steve@krtmradio.com Web Site:www.krtmradio.com Licensee: Penfold Communications Inc. (acq 6-11-98; $234,788). Format: Christian. Target aud: 25-54. ◆Chuck Smith, pres; Jeff Smith, VP; Steve Bessette, gen mgr.

KTMQ(FM)— 2001: 103.3 mhz; 1.25 kw. Ant 715 ft TL: N33 28 51 W117 10 58. Hrs open: 27349 Jefferson Ave., Suite 116, 92590. Phone: (951) 296-9050. Fax: (951) 296-9077.E-mail: michaeldellinger @clearchannel.com Web Site:www.q1033.com Licensee: CC Licenses LLC. Group owner: Clear Channel Communications Inc. (acq 7-31-2001; $6.225 million). Hogan and Hartson. Format: Classic rock. ◆Bob Ridzak, gen mgr; Mike Dellinger, prom dir.

Templeton

KXDZ(FM)— 2004: 100.5 mhz; 1.35 kw. Ant 361 ft TL: N35 30 19 W120 37 18. Hrs open: 396 Buckley Rd., Suite 2, San Luis Obispo, 93401. Phone: (805) 786-2570. Fax: (805) 547-9860. Web Site:www.mapletoncommunications.com Licensee: Mapleton License of San Luis Obispo LLC. (group owner; (acq 7-19-2002;. grpsl). Format: Classic Hits. ◆Adam Nathanson, pres; Bill Heirendt, gen mgr; Drew Ross, progmg mgr; David Atwood, news dir; Tom Hughes, chief of engrg.

Thousand Oaks

*KCLU-FM— Oct 20, 1994: 88.3 mhz; 3.2 kw. Ant 518 ft TL: N34 13 05 W118 56 42. Stereo. Hrs open: 24 60 W. Olsen Rd., Suite 4400, 91360. Phone: (805) 493-3900. Fax: (805) 493-3982.E-mail: kclu@clunet.edu Web Site:www.kclu.org Licensee: California Lutheran University. Population served: 800,000 Natl. Network: NPR, PRI, . Leventhal, Senter & Lerman. Wire Svc: AP Format: News. News staff: 2; News: 125 hrs wkly. Target aud: General. Spec prog: Jazz & blues 5 hrs wkly. ◆Mary Olson, gen mgr & stn mgr; Jim Rondeau, opns dir, progmg dir; Lance Orozco, news dir.

*KDSC(FM)— Dec 4, 1979: 91.1 mhz; 4.8 kw. Ant 1,279 ft TL: N34 24 47 W119 11 10. Stereo. Hrs open: 24
Rebroadcasts KUSC(FM) Los Angeles 100%.

Box 77913, Los Angeles, 90007. Secondary address: 515 S. Figueroa St., Suite 2050, Los Angeles 90071. Phone: (213) 225-7400. Fax: (213) 225-7410.E-mail: kusc@kusc.org Web Site:www.kusc.org Licensee: University of Southern California (acq 3-17-82). Natl. Network: PRI, NPR, . Format: Class. Target aud: 35 plus. ◆Brenda Barnes, pres; Eric DeWeese, gen mgr; Janet McIntyre, dev dir.

KHJL(FM)— Apr 1, 1963: 92.7 mhz; 3.1 kw. Ant 462 ft TL: N34 12 21 W118 49 04. Stereo. Hrs open: 24 99 Long Court, Suite 200, 91360. Phone: (805) 497-8511. Fax: (805) 497-8514.E-mail: reception@927jillfm.com Web Site:www.927jillfm.com Licensee: Amaturo Group of L.A. Ltd. Group owner: Amaturo Group Ltd. (acq 1996; $2 million). Population served: 700,000 Rgnl. Network: Metronews Radio Net. Pepper & Corazzini. Format: Adult contemp. News staff: one. Target aud: 25-54; employed professional adults, especially women. ◆Joseph Amaturo, CEO, progmg dir; Robert J. Christy, gen mgr.

Thousand Palms

KFUT(AM)— Dec 7, 1963: 1270 khz; 5 kw-D, 750 w-N, DA-2. TL: N33 51 04 W116 23 36. Hrs open: 24 1321 N. Gene Autry Trail, Palm Springs, 92262. Phone: (760) 322-7890. Fax: (760) 322-5493.E-mail: info@desertfun.com Web Site:www.desertfun.com Licensee: MCC Radio LLC. Group owner: Morris Radio LLC (acq 12-24-97; $2.25 million with KDGL(FM) Yucca Valley). Population served: 1,500,000 Format: Talk. News staff: 3; News: 20 hrs wkly. Target aud: 25 plus. ◆William S. Morris IV, chmn; William S. Morris III, pres; Darrell Fry, CFO; Michael Ostehaut, VP; Keith Martin, gen mgr; Larry Snider, opns dir.

KLOB(FM)— Apr 21, 1994: 94.7 mhz; 1.8 kw. 606 ft TL: N33 52 07 W116 25 58. Hrs open: 41601 Corporate Way, Palm Desert, 92260-1986. Phone: (760) 341-5837. Fax: (760) 341-0951.E-mail: klobtraffic@entravision.com Web Site:www.entravision.com Licensee: Entravision Holdings LLC. Group owner: Entravision Communications Corp. (acq 2-27-97). Format: Adult latin contemporary. ◆Philip Wilkinson, pres; Ray Nieves, gen mgr, gen sls mgr; Grace Escobar, prom dir; Edgar Pineda, progmg dir; Martha Saldana, news dir; Sergio De la Torre, chief of engrg.

KXPS(AM)— Nov 14, 1992: 1010 khz; 3.6 kw-D, 400 w-N, DA-2. TL: N33 50 35 W116 25 39. Stereo. Hrs open: 24 1321 N. Gene Autry Tr., Palm Springs, 92262. Phone: (760) 322-7890. Fax: (760) 322-5493.E-mail: info@desertfun.com Web Site:www.1010kxps.com Licensee: Morris Communications Corp. Group owner: Morris Communications Inc. (acq 12-24-97; $2.25 million with KDGL(FM) Yucca Valley). Haley, Bader & Potts. Format: Talk, sports. Spec prog: Relg 17 hrs wkly. ◆William Morris, CEO; Michael Ostehaut, VP; Keith Martin, gen mgr; Larry Snider, chief of opns, chief of engrg.

Tipton

KCRZ(FM)— 1997: 104.9 mhz; 2.3 kw. 528 ft TL: N36 10 07 W119 15 04. Stereo. Hrs open: 24 1401 W. Caldwell Ave., Visalia, 93277. Phone: (559) 553-1500. Fax: (559) 627-1496. Web Site:www.z1049.com Licensee: Lemoore Wireless Co. Inc. Natl. Network: ABC, . Format: Hot adult contemp. Target aud: 25-54. ◆Wayne B. Foster, gen mgr; Randy Hendrix, progmg dir.

Torrance

KFOX(AM)— January 1998: 1650 khz; 10 kw-D, 490 w-N. TL: N33 53 30 W118 11 03 (D), N33 53 30 W118 11 03 (N). Hrs open: 4525 Wilshire Blvd., 3rd Fl., Los Angeles, 90010. Phone: (323) 935-0606. Fax: (323) 935-8885.E-mail: info@kfoxam.com Web Site:www.koreatimes.com Licensee: Chagal Communications Inc. (acq 5-25-00; $30 million). Format: Adult contemp, Korean. ◆Grant Chang, gen mgr.

Tracy

KMIX(FM)— Dec 14, 1966: 100.9 mhz; 6 kw. 328 ft TL: N37 37 32 W121 23 58. Stereo. Hrs open: 6820 Pacific Ave., Suite 3A, Stockton, 95207. Phone: (209) 474-0154. Fax: (209) 474-0316.E-mail: info@lavuena.com Web Site:www.lavuena.com Licensee: Entravision Holdings LLC. Group owner: Entravision Communications Corp. (acq 7-28-00; grpsl). Format: Sp. ◆Lisa Sunday, gen mgr; Cesar Medina, stn mgr.

*KYKL(FM)— 2004: 90.7 mhz; 210 w. Ant 1,745 ft TL: N37 33 37 W121 36 19. Stereo. Hrs open: 24 2351 Sunset Blvd., Suite 170-218, Rocklin, 95765. Phone: (916) 251-1600. Fax: (916) 251-1650.E-mail: klove@klove.com Web Site:www.klove.com Licensee: Educational Media Foundation. Group owner: EMF Broadcasting. Natl. Network: K-Love, . Shaw Pittman. Format: Contemp Christian. News staff: 3.

Target aud: 25-44; Judeo Christian, female. ◆Richard Jenkins, pres; Mike Novak, VP; Keith Whipple, dev dir; David Pierce, progmg mgr; Ed Lenane, news dir; Sam Wallington, engrg dir; Karen Johnson, news rptr.

Trinidad

KZCC(FM)—Not on air, target date: unknown: 95.5 mhz; 5 kw. Ant 728 ft TL: N40 58 43 W124 00 36. Hrs open: Airen Broadcasting Company, KZCC (FM, 428 C Street, Ste. K, Eureka, 95501. Secondary address: 455 Capitol Mall, , Suite 210 , Sacramento 95814. Phone: (916) 448-8800. Fax: (916) 448-6455. Licensee: Airen Broadcasting Co. ◆Suzanne E. Rogers, pres.

Truckee

KTKE(FM)— 2003: 101.5 mhz; 140 w. Ant 1,988 ft TL: N39 14 29 W120 08 20. Hrs open: 24 12030 Donner Pass Rd., 96161. Phone: (530) 587-9999. Phone: (530) 587-9330. Fax: (530) 587-9119.E-mail: ktkeradio@yahoo.com Web Site:www.ktke1015.com Licensee: Todd Robinson, Inc Format: AAA. ◆Jon Robinson, gen mgr; Lindsay Romack, stn mgr.

Tulare

KBOS-FM—Licensed to Tulare. See Fresno

KGEN(AM)— 1957: 1370 khz; 1 kw-D, 136 w-N. TL: N36 10 51 W119 19 44. Hrs open: 24 Box 2040, 93275. Secondary address: 323 E. San Joaquin Ave. 93274. Phone: (559) 686-1370. Fax: (559) 685-1394. Licensee: Azteca Broadcasting Corp. (group owner) Population served: 276,700 Format: Sp, Mexican. Target aud: General. ◆Margaretia Hernandez, gen mgr.

KJUG(AM)—Licensed to Tulare. See Visalia

KJUG-FM—Licensed to Tulare. See Visalia

Tulelake

KFLS-FM— July 23, 1993: 96.5 mhz; 20 kw. 2,155 ft TL: N42 05 50 W121 37 59. Stereo. Hrs open: 24 Box 1450, Klamath Falls, OR, 97601. Secondary address: 1338 Oregon Ave., Klamath Falls, OR 97601. Phone: (541) 882-4656. Fax: (541) 884-2845.E-mail: traffic@klamathradio.com Web Site:www.klamathradio.com Licensee: Wynne Enterprises LLC (group owner). Population served: 60,000 Rgnl rep: Tacher. Format: Country. Target aud: 18-49. ◆Robert Wynne, CEO, chmn, pres, gen mgr; Leslie Hougan, gen sls mgr; Randy Adams, progmg dir; Lyle Ahrens, news dir; Russ Jump, chief of engrg; Carol Fritch, traf mgr.

Turlock

*KBDG(FM)— January 1977: 90.9 mhz; 150 w. 94 ft TL: N37 29 59 W120 49 41. (CP: 780 w). Hrs open: 24 Box 192, 95381. Secondary address: 1600 E. Canal Dr. 95380. Phone: (209) 668-7176. Fax: (209) 668-2322. Licensee: Assyrian American Civic Club. (acq 1-7-94; $17,000; 1-31-94). Format: Assyrian music, talk. ◆Zaya Sargis, stn mgr.

*KCSS(FM)— Aug 13, 1975: 91.9 mhz; 400 w. 112 ft TL: N37 31 35 W120 51 25. Hrs open: 20 801 W. Monte Vista Ave., 95382. Phone: (209) 667-3378 (office). Phone: (209) 667-3900 (stn). Fax: (209) 667-3901.E-mail: info@kcss.net Web Site:www.kcss.net Licensee: California State University, Stanislaus. Population served: 700,000 Format: Div. Target aud: 18-54. Spec prog: Class 9 hrs, jazz 4 hrs, Americana 10 hrs, wkly. ◆Greg Jacquay, gen mgr.

KLOC(AM)— October 1949: 1390 khz; 5 kw-U, DA-2. TL: N37 31 48 W120 41 37. Hrs open: 4043 Geer Rd., Hughson, 95326. Phone: (209) 883-8760. Fax: (209) 883-8769.E-mail: ngomez@lafavorita.net Web Site:www.lafavorita.net Licensee: La Favorita Broadcasting Inc. (acq 5-16-03; $500,000). Population served: 2,000,000. Format: Sp. ◆Nelson Gomez, gen mgr; Saul Fiallo, progmg dir.

KWNN(FM)— Mar 3, 1978: 98.3 mhz; 1.6 kw. 390 ft TL: N37 34 46 W120 50 48. (CP: 2 kw). Stereo. Hrs open: 24 1581 Cummins Dr., Suite 100, Modesto, 95358. Phone: (209) 476-1230. Fax: (209) 957-1833. Licensee: Citadel Broadcasting Co. Group owner: Citadel Broadcasting Corp. (acq 12-12-03). Population served: 61,712 Natl. Rep: Christal,. Format: CHR. ◆Roy Williams, gen mgr; Jean Western, sls VP, gen sls mgr.

Twain Harte

KKBN(FM)— Oct 19, 1985: 93.5 mhz; 400 w. Ant 1,262 ft TL: N38 00 30 W120 21 44. Stereo. Hrs open: 24 342 S. Washington St., Sonora, 95370. Phone: (209) 533-1450. Fax: (209) 533-9520.E-mail: lenglandcbc@mlode.com Web Site:www.kkbn.com Licensee: Clarke Broadcasting Corp. (group owner; (acq 3-1-2000; $2.2 million). Population served: 500,000 Natl. Network: Fox News Radio, . Leventhal, Senter & Lerman. Wire Svc: AP Format: Country. News staff: 3; News: 4 hrs wkly. Target aud: 25-54; general. ♦H. Randolph Holder Jr., pres; Joe Marshall, progmg dir.

Twentynine Palms

KCDZ(FM)— July 15, 1989: 107.7 mhz; 6.7 kw. Ant 305 ft TL: N34 09 15 W116 11 50. Stereo. Hrs open: 24 6448 Hallee, Suite 5, Joshua Tree, 92252. Phone: (760) 366-8471. Fax: (760) 366-2976.E-mail: z107@cci-29palms.com Web Site:www.kcdzfm.com Licensee: Morongo Basin Broadcasting Corp. Population served: 393,800 Natl. Network: ABC, . Richard S. Becker & Associates. Wire Svc: AP Format: Adult contemp / CHR. News staff: 6; News: 10 hrs wkly. Target aud: 25-54; baby boomers. ♦Cynthia M. Daigneault, pres, gen mgr; Gary Daigneault, exec VP, VP, progmg dir; Ken Brown, chief of engrg.

KNWH(AM)— Apr 3, 1961: 1250 khz; 1 kw-D, 105 w-N. TL: N34 08 11 W116 10 07. (CP: COL Yucca Valley. 800 w-D, 77 w-N. TL: N34 07 51 W116 22 12). Hrs open:
Rebroadcasts KNWQ(AM) Palm Springs 100%.
1321 N. Gene Autry Trail, Palm Springs, 92262. Phone: (760) 322-7890. Fax: (760) 322-5493.E-mail: info@desertfun.com Web Site:www.desertfun.com Licensee: MCC Radio LLC. (acq 1-12-2005; $100,000). Population served: 90,000 Format: News/talk. News staff: 4; News: 4.5 hrs. wkly. Target aud: 25-54. ♦William S. Morris IV, pres.

KXCM(FM)— Apr 1, 1965: 96.3 mhz; 6 kw. Ant 243 ft TL: N34 09 15 W116 11 50. Stereo. Hrs open: 24 Box 1437, Joshua Tree, 92252. Phone: (760) 362-4264.E-mail: coppermountainbroadcasting@yahoo.com Web Site:www.kxcmradio.com Licensee: Copper Mountain Broadcasting Co. (acq 7-14-2004; $575,000 with KQCM(FM) Joshua Tree). Population served: 100,000 Natl. Network: Westwood One, Jones Radio Networks, . Natl. Rep: Interep,. Leventhal, Senter & Lerman. Format: Country. ♦Gary De Maroney, gen mgr.

Ukiah

***KPRA(FM)**— May 1987: 89.5 mhz; 1.6 kw. 1,135 ft TL: N39 07 01 W123 13 54. Hrs open: 24 Family Stations Inc., 4135 Northgate Blvd., Sacramento, 95834. Phone: (916) 641-8191. Fax: (916) 641-8238. Licensee: Family Stations Inc. (group owner; acq 2-3-86). Format: Relg.

KQPM(FM)— February 1989: 105.9 mhz; 2.9 kw. 2,017 ft TL: N39 09 00 W123 12 30. Hrs open: 24 140 N. Main St., Lakeport, 95453. Phone: (707) 263-6113. Phone: (707) 468-5336. Fax: (707) 263-0939. Licensee: Bicoastal Media L.L.C. (group owner; acq 7-28-99; grpsl). Format: Country. ♦Ken Dennis, CEO; Mike Wilson, pres & gen mgr; Eric Patrick, opns mgr, progmg dir; Alan Mathews, gen sls mgr; Kevin Mostyn, chief of engrg.

KUKI(AM)— Oct 1, 1950: 1400 khz; 1 kw-U. TL: N39 10 03 W123 13 02. Hrs open: 24 1400 KUKI Ln., 95482. Phone: (707) 263-6113. Fax: (707) 466-5852.E-mail: ykiah@bicoastalspots.com Licensee: Bicoastal Media LLC. Group owner: Moon Broadcasting (acq 7-28-2006; grpsl). Population served: 70,000 Pepper & Corazzini. Format: Mexican/rgnl. News staff: 2; News: 25 hrs wkly. Target aud: 25 plus; upwardly mobile adults. ♦Tove Sorensen, opns dir, chief of opns, progmg dir & mus dir.

KUKI-FM— Oct 16, 1974: 103.3 mhz; 2.8 kw. Ant 1,791 ft TL: N39 19 36 W123 16 12. Stereo. Hrs open: 1400 KUKI Ln., 95482. Phone: (707) 263-6113. Fax: (707) 466-5852.E-mail: ykiah@bicoastalspots.com Web Site:www.kukifm.com Population served: 180,000 Natl. Network: ABC, . Format: Country. News staff: one; News: 7 hrs wkly. Target aud: 25-54.

***KULV(FM)**— Sept 22, 2003: 97.1 mhz; 130 w. Ant 1,978 ft TL: N39 07 50 W123 04 32. Stereo. Hrs open: 24 2351 Sunset Blvd., Suite 170-218, Rocklin, 95765. Phone: (916) 251-1600. Fax: (916) 251-1650.E-mail: klove@klove.com Web Site:www.klove.com Licensee: Educational Media Foundation. Group owner: EMF Broadcasting. Natl. Network: K-Love, . Shaw Pittman. Format: Contemp Chrisitan. News staff: 3. Target aud: 25-44; Judeo Christian, female. ♦Richard Jenkins, pres; Mike Novak, VP; Keith Whipple, dev dir; Eric Allen, natl sls mgr; David Pierce, progmg mgr; Ed Lenane, news dir; Sam Wallington, engrg dir; Karen Johnson, news rptr.

KWNE(FM)— 1968: 94.5 mhz; 2.2 kw. 1,965 ft TL: N39 07 50 W123 04 32. Stereo. Hrs open: 24 Box 1056, 95482. Secondary address: 1100 Hastings Rd., Suite B 95482. Phone: (707) 462-1451. Phone: (707) 462-0945. Fax: (707) 462-4670.E-mail: kwine@kwine.com Web Site:www.kwine.com Licensee: Broadcasting Corp of Mendocino County. (acq 10-1-78). Population served: 150,000 Borsari & Paxson. Format: Hot adult contemp. News staff: one; News: 12 hrs wkly. Target aud: 18-54; young adult. Spec prog: Sp 4 hrs, farm one hr wkly. ♦Guilford Dye, pres, gen mgr; Gudrun Dye, VP; Mike Spencer, stn mgr.

Vacaville

KUIC(FM)— Nov 1, 1968: 95.3 mhz; 4.3 kw. 280 ft TL: N38 17 56 W121 59 54. (CP: 594 w, ant 1,948 ft. TL: N38 23 48 W122 06 03). Stereo. Hrs open: 24 KUIC Plaza, 600 E. Main St., 95688. Phone: (707) 446-0200. Fax: (707) 446-0122.E-mail: info@kuic.com Web Site:www.kuic.com Licensee: KUIC Inc. (acq 10-6-98). Population served: 200,000 Garvey, Schubert & Barer. Format: Adult contemp. News staff: 3; News: one hr wkly. Target aud: General; middle class, professionals. ♦Jim Levitt, CEO; John Levitt, pres, CFO & gen mgr.

Vallejo

KDIA(AM)— Mar 19, 1996: 1640 khz; 10 kw-U, DA-N. TL: N37 53 44 W122 19 27 (day), N38 08 03 W122 25 32 (night). Stereo. Hrs open: 24 3260 Blume Dr., Richmond, 95806. Phone: (510) 222-4242. Fax: (510) 262-9054.E-mail: andy.santamaria@kdia.com Web Site:www.kdia.com Licensee: Baybridge Communications L.L.C. Population served: 2,500,000 Format: Teaching ministries. News: 5 hrs wkly. Target aud: 25-54. Spec prog: Relg 5 hrs, Black 2 hrs, gospel 7 hrs wkly. ♦Andy Santamaria, gen mgr.

KDYA(AM)— Aug 1, 1947: 1190 khz; 1 kw-D. TL: N38 07 04 W122 15 24. (Also 1640 khz; 10 kw-D, 1 kw-N). Stereo. Hrs open: 24 3260 Blume Dr., Richmond, 95806. Phone: (510) 222-4242. Fax: (510) 262-9054.E-mail: andy.santamaria@gospel1190.net Web Site:www.gospel1190.net Licensee: Baybridge Communications L.L.C. (acq 1-29-99). Population served: 2,500,000 Format: Gospel. News: 5 hrs wkly. Target aud: 25-54. Spec prog: Relg 5 hrs, Black 2 hrs, gospel 7 hrs wkly. ♦Andy Santamaria, pres, gen mgr; Clifford Brown, opns mgr.

Ventura

KBBY-FM— Dec 27, 1962: 95.1 mhz; 10.8 kw. 925 ft TL: N34 14 12 W119 12 11. Hrs open: 1376 Walters St., 93003. Phone: (805) 642-8595. Fax: (805) 656-5838.E-mail: info@cumulus.com Web Site:www.b951.com Licensee: Cumulus Licensing Corp. Group owner: Cumulus Media Inc. (acq 9-22-00; grpsl). Natl. Network: Westwood One, . Format: Hot Adult Contemp. Target aud: 18-54. ♦Gail Furillo, gen mgr; Tom Watson, opns mgr; Todd Violet, progmg dir.

KCAQ(FM)—See Oxnard

KHAY(FM)— Jan 1, 1962: 100.7 mhz; 39 kw. 1,210 ft TL: N34 20 55 W119 19 57. Stereo. Hrs open: Prog sep from AM 1376 Walter St., 93003. Phone: (805) 642-8595. Fax: (805) 656-5838.E-mail: info@cumulus.com Web Site:www.khay.com Population served: 800,000 Format: Country. Target aud: 18-54. ♦Tom Watson, progmg dir.

KKZZ(AM)—See Santa Paula

KLJR-FM—See Santa Paula

KOCP(FM)—See Camarillo

KSSC(FM)— November 1989: 107.1 mhz; 280 w. 872 ft TL: N34 18 10 W119 13 45. (CP: 420 w). Stereo. Hrs open: 24 5700 Wilshire Blvd., Suite 250, Los Angeles, 90036. Phone: (805) 648-2807. Fax: (323) 900-6200.E-mail: info@1071superstriella.com Web Site:www.1071superstriella.com Licensee: Entravision Holdings LLC. Group owner: Entravision Communications Corp. (acq 4-1-03; grpsl). Format: Contemp Sp. ♦Karl Meyer, gen mgr.

KUNX(AM)— Oct 15, 1994: 1590 khz; 5 kw-U, DA-2. TL: N34 14 12 W119 12 11. Hrs open: 2284 S. Victoria, Suite 2G, 93003. Phone: (805) 289-1400. Fax: (805) 644-7906.E-mail: info@kunx.com Licensee: Gold Coast Broadcasting LLC. (group owner; (acq 2-10-97; $2 million with KFYV(FM) Ojai). Population served: 750,000 Format: Sp news/talk. Target aud: 35 plus. ♦Chip Ehrhardt, gen mgr; Mark Elliott, progmg dir.

KVEN(AM)— March 1948: 1450 khz; 1 kw-U. TL: N34 15 39 W119 14 28. Hrs open: 1376 Walter St., 93003. Phone: (805) 642-8595. Fax: (805) 656-5838.E-mail: info@cumulus.com Web Site:www.kven.com Licensee: Cumulus Licensing Corp. Group owner: Cumulus Media Inc. (acq 9-22-00; grpsl). Population served: 67,000 Erwin Krasnow. Format: Hits of the 50s & 60s. Target aud: 25 plus; affluent, educated, professional with above average income. ♦Gail Furillo, gen mgr; Ernie Bingham, gen sls mgr; Tammy Meyers, prom mgr; Lee Marshall, progmg dir; Cyndy Abarre, news dir; J.D. Strahler, chief of engrg.

KVTA(AM)—See Port Hueneme

Victorville

KATJ-FM—See George

***KHMS(FM)**— Jan 3, 1993: 88.5 mhz; 200 w. 1,512 ft TL: N34 36 40 W117 17 20. Stereo. Hrs open: 24
Rebroadcasts KSOS(FM) Las Vegas 100%.
c/o Faith Communications Corp., 2201 S. 6th St., Las Vegas, NV, 89104. Phone: (702) 731-5452. Fax: (702) 731-1992. Web Site:www.sosradio.net Licensee: Faith Communications Corp. (acq 4-5-91; 4-22-91). Cohn & Marks. Format: Adult contemp, Christian. Target aud: 25-44; young families. ♦Jack French, CEO; Brad Staley, gen mgr; Chris Staley, prom dir; Scott Herrold, progmg dir.

KIXW(AM)—See Apple Valley

KRSX(AM)— Sept 1, 1961: 1590 khz; 500 w-D, 135 w-N. TL: N34 32 15 W117 18 42. Hrs open: 24 15700 Village Dr., Suite A, 92394. Phone: (760) 243-7903. Fax: (760) 243-7183. Licensee: Rudex Broadcasting Limited Corp. (acq 3-19-2004; $176,005). Format: Sp Catholic. Target aud: 18-34 & 14-57. ♦John Cooper, pres; Dino Mercado, gen sls mgr.

KVFG(FM)— Aug 18, 1980: 103.1 mhz; 95 w. 1,424 ft TL: N34 36 45 W117 17 31. (CP; 310 w, ant 1,401 ft.). Stereo. Hrs open: 24 11920 Hesperia Rd., Hesperia, 92345. Phone: (760) 244-2000. Fax: (760) 244-1198. Web Site:www.kfrog103.com Licensee: CBS Radio Station Inc. Group owner: Infinity Broadcasting Corp. (acq 7-19-00; $3,537,500 with KRAK(AM) Hesperia). Population served: 200,000 Natl. Network: ABC, . Fleischman & Walsh. Format: Country. Target aud: 25-54. ♦Bill Pettus, stn mgr; Tom Hoyt, gen mgr & opns mgr.

***KXRD(FM)**— Oct 18, 1994: 89.5 mhz; 1.25 kw. Ant 1,410 ft TL: N34 36 44 W117 17 27. Hrs open: 24
Rebroadcasts KLRD(FM) Yucaipa 100%.
2351 Sunset Blvd., Suite 170-218, Rocklin, 95765. Phone: (700) 528-9236. Fax: (700) 528-9246. Web Site:www.air1.com Licensee: Educational Media Foundation. Group owner: EMF Broadcasting (acq 1-22-99). Natl. Network: Air 1, . Format: Contemp Christian. News: 7 hrs wkly. Target aud: 18-34. ♦Richard Jenkins, pres; Mike Novak, VP; Keith Whipple, dev dir; David Pierce, progmg mgr; Ed Lenane, news dir; Sam Wallington, engrg dir; Karen Johnson, news rptr.

KZXY-FM—See Apple Valley

Visalia

***KARM(FM)**— 1990: 89.7 mhz; 1 kw. 810 ft TL: N36 38 10 W118 56 32. Hrs open: 1300 S. Woodland Dr., 93277. Phone: (559) 627-5276. Fax: (559) 627-5288.E-mail: karm@karm.com Web Site:www.karm.com Licensee: Harvest Broadcasting Co. Natl. Network: ABC, . Format: Inspirational, Christian. ♦Dr. Richard Dunn, chmn; Loren Olson, gen mgr.

***KDUV(FM)**— Jan 1, 1992: 88.9 mhz; 1 kw. 2,647 ft TL: N36 17 14 W118 50 17. Hrs open: 130 N. Kelsey, Suite H-1, 93291. Phone: (559) 651-4111. Fax: (559) 651-4115.E-mail: info@kduvfm.com Web Site:www.kduvfm.com Licensee: Community Educational Broadcasting Inc. Format: Christian hit radio. ♦Bob Croft, gen mgr.

KEZL(AM)— January 1948: 1400 khz; 1 kw-U. TL: N36 21 14 W119 17 02. Hrs open: 83 E. Shaw Ave, Suite 150, Fresno, 93710-7616. Phone: (559) 230-4300. Fax: (209) 591-1130. Licensee: Capstar TX L.P. Group owner: Clear Channel Communications Inc. (acq 8-30-2000; grpsl). Natl. Rep: McGavren Guild,. Format: Sports. Target aud: 25-64; general. ♦Tony Rinaldi, gen sls mgr; Brian Noe, progmg dir; Kristine Kelley, news dir; Michelle Howe, traf mgr.

KFSO-FM— Sept 1, 1951: 92.9 mhz; 18.5 kw horiz, 17 kw vert. 820 ft TL: N36 38 10 W118 56 33. (CP: 17.5 kw, ant 853 ft. TL: N36 38 10 W118 56 34). Stereo. Hrs open: Prog sep from AM 83 E. Shaw Ave., Suite 150, Fresno, 93710-7616. Phone: (559) 230-4300. Fax: (209) 591-1130. Web Site:www.kfso.com Licensee: Capstar TX L.P.

(acq 2-4-2009). Population served: 1,300,000 Format: Oldies. ◆Jeff Negrete, gen mgr; Humberto Avila, sls; Paul Wilson, progmg.

KJUG(AM)—(Tulare, Aug 1, 1946: 1270 khz; 5 kw-D, 1 kw-N, DA-N. TL: N36 13 10 W119 18 51. Hrs open: 24 1401 W. Caldwell Ave., 93277. Phone: (559) 553-1500. Fax: (559) 627-1496. Web Site:www.kjugam.com Licensee: Westcoast Broadcasting Inc. (acq 5-1-81). Population served: 351,300 Natl. Network: ABC, . Natl. Rep: Interep,. Format: Classic country. News staff: one; News: 7 hrs wkly. Target aud: 25-64. Spec prog: Farm 5 hrs wkly. ◆Wayne Foster, gen mgr; Dave Daniels, prom dir, progmg dir; Darrin Cantrell, news dir; Jamie Moore, traf mgr; Wayne Foster, sls.

KJUG-FM—(Tulare, May 6, 1965: 106.7 mhz; 1.2 kw. 6,100 ft TL: N36 17 08 W118 50 17. Stereo. Hrs open: 24 Prog dups AM 90% 1401 W. Caldwell Ave., 93277. Phone: (559) 553-1500. Fax: (559) 627-1496.E-mail: studio@kjug.com Web Site:www.kjug.com Licensee: Westcoast Broadcasting Inc. Format: Today's country. Target aud: 18-54.

KSEQ(FM)— October 1984: 97.1 mhz; 17 kw. 777 ft TL: N36 38 08 W118 56 32. Stereo. Hrs open: 617 W. Tulare Ave., 93277. Phone: (559) 627-9710. Fax: (559) 627-1590.E-mail: raym@q97.com Web Site:www.q97.com Licensee: Buckley Broadcasting of Monterey. Group owner: Buckley Broadcasting Corp. (acq 12-87). Natl. Rep: D & R Radio,. Format: CHR. Target aud: 18-49. ◆Rick Buckley, pres; Ray McCarty, VP, gen mgr; Tommy Del Rio, opns mgr.

KSLK(FM)— Nov 22, 1994: 96.1 mhz; 4.8 kw. Ant 360 ft TL: N36 21 59 W119 10 46. Stereo. Hrs open: 24 7179 N. Van Ness Blvd., Fresno, 93711. Phone: (559) 635-0961. Fax: (559) 439-5714.E-mail: bobeurich@aol.com Licensee: New Visalia Broadcasting Inc. Population served: 1,000,000 Natl. Network: Sporting News Radio Network, . Format: All sports. News staff: 2. ◆Robert Eurich, pres.

Vista

KCEO(AM)— Nov 3, 1967: 1000 khz; 2.5 kw-D, 250 w-N, DA-2. TL: N33 13 59 W117 16 09. Hrs open: 24 1835 Aston Ave., Carlsbad, 92008. Phone: (760) 729-1000. Fax: (760) 476-9604.E-mail: reception@astorbroadcastgroup.com Web Site:www.kceoradio.com Licensee: North County Broadcasting Corp. Group owner: Astor Broadcast Group (acq 4-30-97; $2.6 million). Population served: 1,000,000 Natl. Network: Westwood One, . Format: Talk. News: 20 hrs wkly. Target aud: 35 plus. ◆Arthur Astor, pres; Susan E. Burke, exec VP; Rick Roome, opns dir, opns mgr.

Walnut

*KSAK(FM)— Jan 10, 1974: 90.1 mhz; 3.5 w. 460 ft TL: N34 02 53 W117 51 43. (CP: Ant 410 ft.). Hrs open: 24 1100 N. Grand Ave., 91789. Phone: (909) 594-5611, EXT. 4678.E-mail: ksak@mtsac.edu Web Site:www.ksak.com Licensee: Mount San Antonio Community College District. Population served: 10,000 Wire Svc: UPI Format: Urban rhythmic, Christian. Target aud: 18-25; students. ◆Cason Smith, gen mgr & opns mgr.

Walnut Creek

KKDV(FM)— Dec 10, 1959: 92.1 mhz; 3 kw. Ant 89 ft TL: N37 53 59 W122 05 38. Stereo. Hrs open: 1660 Olympic Blvd., Suite 215, 94596. Phone: (925) 944-6300. Fax: (925) 977-9684.E-mail: info@kkdv.com Web Site:www.kkdv.com Licensee: Contra Costa County Radio Inc. (acq 7-29-2005; $7 million). Population served: 200,000 Rgnl rep: Lotus. Format: Adult contemp. Target aud: Adults; 25-54. ◆John Levitt, gen mgr; Phil DeAngelo, gen sls mgr, natl sls mgr; Scott Ingram, rgnl sls mgr; Jim Hampton, progmg dir.

Wasco

*KFHL(FM)— 2005: 91.7 mhz; 6 kw. Ant 289 ft TL: N35 24 55 W119 14 01. Hrs open: Hillcrest Seventh-day Adventist Church, 2801 Bernard St., Bakersfield, 93306. Phone: (661) 872-0030.E-mail: kfhlradio@yahoo.com Licensee: Mary V. Harris Foundation. Format: Christian talk. ◆Robin Wade, progmg mgr.

Wasco-Greenacres

KERN(AM)— May 17, 1950: 1180 khz; 50 kw-D, 10 kw-N, DA-2. TL: N35 34 17 W119 19 26. Hrs open: 24 1100 N. Grand Ave., 93303. Secondary address: 1400 Easton Dr. , Suite 144, Bakersfield 93309. Phone: (661) 328-1410. Fax: (661) 283-7992.E-mail: news@kernradio.com Web Site:www.kernradio.com Licensee: AGM California. Group owner: American General Media (acq 9-27-2004;

$1.83 million). Population served: 5,600,000 Natl. Rep: Salem,. Format: News/talk. ◆Roger Fessler, gen mgr; Toni Snyder, sls dir; Chris Squires, progmg dir.

Weaverville

KHRD(FM)— 2000: 103.1 mhz; 600 w. Ant 3,592 ft TL: N40 36 10 W122 38 58. Hrs open: 24 1588 Charles Dr., Redding, 96003. Phone: (530) 244-9700. Fax: (530) 244-9707.E-mail: rhealy@resultsradiomail.com Web Site:www.red1031.com Licensee: Results Radio of Redding Licensee LLC. Group owner: Fritz Communications Inc. (acq 6-11-99; grpsl). Format: Classic rock. ◆Beth Tappan, gen mgr; Laurie Curto, gen sls mgr; Don Wilson, progmg dir; JD Suino, news dir; Bryant Smith, chief of engrg.

KWCA(FM)—Not on air, target date: unknown: 101.1 mhz; 250 w. Ant 1,555 ft TL: N40 41 05 W122 44 56. Hrs open: 1784 California Street, Redding, 96001. Phone: (530) 243-5111.E-mail: radio@megafornia.com Licensee: George S. Flinn Jr. Format: Spanish. ◆George S. Flinn Jr., gen mgr.

Weed

KNTK(FM)— November 1983: 102.3 mhz; 5.5 kw. 1,437 ft TL: N41 21 12 W122 15 35. Stereo. Hrs open: 24 1934 S. Mt. Shasta Blvd., Mount Shasta, 96094. Phone: (530) 926-5946. Fax: (530) 926-0830.E-mail: kntk@sbcglobal.net Licensee: Four Rivers Broadcasting Inc. (group owner; (acq 7-21-2005; grpsl). Format: News/talk. News staff: one; News: 6 hrs wkly. Target aud: 25-54. Spec prog: Nostalgia 2 hrs wkly. ◆John Anthony, gen mgr, gen sls mgr; Rick Martin, progmg dir.

West Covina

KALI(AM)— Sept 25, 1963: 900 khz; 500 w-D, DA. TL: N34 01 54 W117 56 06. Hrs open: 24 747 E. Green St., Suite 400, Pasadena, 91101. Phone: (626) 844-8882. Fax: (626) 844-0156.E-mail: info@mrbi.net Web Site:www.mrbi.net Licensee: Multicultural Radio Broadcasting Licensee LLC. Group owner: Multicultural Radio Broadcasting Inc. (acq 10-5-98; $9 million). Population served: 688,108 Format: Sp Christian. ◆Arthur S. Liu, pres; David Sweeney, VP, gen mgr, opns VP & opns VP; Alan Mok, progmg dir.

KRCV(FM)— Nov 18, 1957: 98.3 mhz; 2.3 w. 328 ft TL: N34 01 22 W117 56 15. (CP: 650 w, ant 971 ft.). Stereo. Hrs open: 24 655 N Central Ave, Suite 2500, Glendale, 91203-1422. Phone: (818) 500-4500. Fax: (818) 500-4560. Licensee: HBC License Corp. Group owner: Univision Radio (acq 9-22-2003; grpsl). Format: Sp oldies. News: 3 hrs wkly. Target aud: 18-49; Sp speaking Hispanics, primarily of Mexican origin. ◆Jim Coronado, gen sls mgr; Amalia Gonzalez, progmg dir; Tom Koza, chief of engrg.

West Sacramento

KCTC(AM)— April 1945: 1320 khz; 5 kw-D, 500 w-N, DA-2. TL: N38 38 11 W121 33 09. Stereo. Hrs open: 24 5345 Madison Ave., Sacramento, 95841. Phone: (916) 334-7777. Fax: (916) 339-4572. Web Site:www.kctc.com Licensee: Entercom Sacramento License LLC. Group owner: Entercom Communications Corp. (acq 10-17-97). Population served: 1,300,000 Natl. Network: ESPN Radio, . Format: Sports. ◆John Geary, VP; David Lichtman, gen mgr; Brian Lopez, progmg dir.

KSMH(AM)— February 1999: 1620 khz; 10 kw-D, 1 kw-N. TL: N38 35 17 W121 28 05. Hrs open: 24 2280 E. Weber Ave., Stockton, 95205-5051. Phone: (209) 462-8307.E-mail: info@ihradio.org Web Site:www.ihradio.org Licensee: IHR Educational Broadcasting. (group owner; (acq 4-28-99; $475,000 with KAHI(AM) Auburn). Format: Relg/Catholic. ◆Joseph Nesta, stn mgr.

Westwood

*KJCQ(FM)— 2006: 88.5 mhz; 800 w. Ant 2,352 ft TL: N40 14 00 W121 01 11. Hrs open: Rebroadcasts KJCU(FM) Fort Bragg 100%. 3000 W. MacArthur Blvd., Suite 500, Santa Ana, 92704. Phone: (714) 918-6207. Licensee: Calvary Chapel of Costa Mesa Inc. (group owner). ◆Charles W. Smith, pres.

KTOR(FM)— 2003: 99.7 mhz; 90 w. Ant 2,483 ft TL: N40 14 21 W121 01 52. Hrs open: 24 Box 2371, Chico, 95927. Phone: (530) 256-2400. Fax: (530) 256-3780.E-mail: ktor@frontiernet.net Licensee: Sierra

Radio Inc. (acq 9-4-2002; for 51% of CP). Natl. Network: ABC, . Format: Classic rock. ◆Cari Catron, rgnl sls mgr; Greg Heller, gen mgr, opns mgr & traf mgr.

Williams

*KARA(FM)— Oct 28, 2003: 99.1 mhz; 900 w. Ant 108 ft TL: N39 08 07 W122 07 58. Stereo. Hrs open: 24 2351 Sunset Blvd., Suite 170-218, Rocklin, 95765. Phone: (916) 251-1600. Fax: (916) 251-1650.E-mail: klove@klove.com Web Site:www.klove.com Licensee: Educational Media Foundation. Group owner: EMF Broadcasting. Natl. Network: Air 1, . Shaw Pittman. Format: Contemp Christian. News staff: 3. Target aud: 18-35; Judeo-Christian, female. ◆Richard Jenkins, pres; Mike Novak, VP; Keith Whipple, dev dir; David Pierce, progmg mgr; Ed Lenane, news dir; Sam Wallington, engrg dir; Arthur Vassar, traf mgr.

Willits

KLLK(AM)— Aug 5, 1985: 1250 khz; 5.4 kw-D, 2.7 kw-N, DA-2. TL: N39 23 58 W123 19 20. Hrs open: 5 AM-midnight Rebroadcasts KUKI(AM) Ukiah 100%. 1400 Kuki Ln., Ukiah, 95482. Phone: (707) 263-6113. Fax: (707) 466-5852.E-mail: ykiah@bicoastalspots.com Licensee: Bicoastal Media LLC. Group owner: Moon Broadcasting (acq 7-28-2006; grpsl). Population served: 50,000 Haley, Bader & Potts. Format: Regional Mexican. News: 8 hrs wkly. Target aud: 18-49; adults who like a progsv mix of modern rock mus. ◆Tove Sorensen, opns dir.

KMKX(FM)— Feb 19, 2000: 93.5 mhz; 89 kw. 2,873 ft TL: N39 30 59 W123 05 21. Stereo. Hrs open: 24 Box 1056, Ukiah, 95482. Phone: (707) 462-1483. Phone: (707) 459-6629. Fax: (707) 462-4670.E-mail: info@maxrock.com Web Site:www.maxrock.com Licensee: Radio Millennium L L C (acq 2-3-00). Population served: 150,000 Natl. Network: Westwood One, . Borsari & Paxson. Format: Adult rock. News staff: one; News: 1 hr wkly. Target aud: 18-60; adults. ◆Guilford Dye, pres, gen mgr; Gudrun Dye, VP; Mike Spencer, stn mgr.

*KZYZ(FM)— 1995: 91.5 mhz; 600 w. 1,820 ft Stereo. Hrs open: 18 Rebroadcasts KZYX(FM) Philo 100%. Box 1, Philo, 95466. Phone: (707) 895-2324. Fax: (707) 895-2451.E-mail: kzyx@pacific.net Web Site:www.kzyx.org Licensee: Mendocino County Public Broadcasting. Format: News, talk radio, div music. ◆Mitchell Holman, gen mgr; Burton Segall, opns dir; Mary Aigner, dev dir, sls dir.

Willows

KCHC(FM)—Not on air, target date: unknown: 106.3 mhz; 6 kw. Ant 328 ft TL: N39 29 30 W121 56 51. Hrs open: Pacific Spanish Network Inc., 296 H St., 2nd Fl., Chula Vista, 91910. Phone: (858) 279-9844. Licensee: Pacific Spanish Network Inc.

KIQS(AM)— Dec 29, 1961: 1560 khz; 250 w-D. TL: N39 31 44 W122 10 09. Hrs open: 1564 Arlington Ct., Turlock, 95382. Phone: (209) 277-8433. Fax: (209) 430-2733.E-mail: avianhelpprogramcoordinator@yahoo.com Licensee: Radio Pan de Vida LLC Group owner: Huth Broadcasting (acq 1-14-2005; $400,000). Population served: 22,500 Law office of Dennis J. Kelly. Format: Sp Christian. ◆Martin Alberto Godinez, gen mgr.

Windsor

KJOR(FM)— June 20, 1997: 104.1 mhz; 250 w. 1,105 ft TL: N38 32 24 W122 57 39. Stereo. Hrs open: 24 200 South "A" St., Suite 300, Oxnard, 93030. Secondary address: P.O. Box 6940 , Oxnard 93031. Phone: (805) 240-2070. Fax: (805) 240-5960.E-mail: alfredop@radiolazer.com Web Site:www.radiolazer.com Licensee: Lazer Licenses LLC. Group owner: Fritz Communications Inc. (acq 6-29-2006; $6.85 million with KSRT(FM) Cloverdale). Population served: 400,000 Natl. Rep: Christal,. Covington & Burling. Format: Sp oldies. Target aud: 25-54. ◆Alfredo Plascencia, CEO, pres & gen mgr.

Winton

KLOQ-FM— 1994: 98.7 mhz; 6 kw. 246 ft TL: N37 16 42 W120 37 33. (CP: Ant 298 ft.: TL: N37 16 41 W120 37 35). Hrs open: 24 1020 W. Main St., Merced, 95340. Phone: (209) 723-2191. Fax: (209) 383-2950.E-mail: ynavarro@radiomerced.com Licensee: Mapleton License of Merced LLC. (group owner; acq 6-1-2002; grpsl). Population served: 210,000 Leventhal, Senter & Lerman. Format: Mexican rgnl. Target aud: 25-49; Hispanic. ◆Kelly Leonard, gen mgr & opns mgr.

Woodlake

KFRR(FM)— September 1994: 104.1 mhz; 17 kw. 853 ft TL: N36 38 12 W118 56 34. Hrs open: 24 1066 E. Shaw Ave., Fresno, 93710. Phone: (559) 230-0104. Fax: (559) 230-0177. Licensee: Wilks License Co.-Fresno LLC. (acq 6-1-2005; grpsl). Natl. Rep: McGavren Guild,. Arter & Hadden. Format: Alternative. Target aud: 18-34; young affluent adults. ♦Kevin O'Rorke, gen mgr; Jason Squires, progmg dir.

Woodland

KSFM(FM)—Licensed to Woodland. See Sacramento

KTKZ(AM)—See Sacramento

Yermo

KRSX-FM— December 1996: 105.3 mhz; 400 w. Ant 1,037 ft TL: N34 48 30 W116 41 01. Hrs open: 24 12370 Hesperia Rd, Suite 16, Victorville, 92395. Phone: (760) 241-1313. Fax: (760) 241-0205. Web Site:www.cruisinoldies1053.com Licensee: EDB VV License LLC. Group owner: Clear Channel Communications Inc. (acq 11-30-2007; grpsl). Population served: 100,000 Natl. Rep: Christal,. Pepper & Corazzini. Format: Oldies. News staff: one. Target aud: 18-49; young adults, families. ♦Tom Hoyt, VP & mktg mgr; Joe Pagano, progmg dir.

KRXV(FM)— April 1980: 98.1 mhz; 1.1 kw. Ant 2,280 ft TL: N34 59 43 W116 50 15. Stereo. Hrs open: 24 Box 1668, 1611 E. Main St., Barstow, 92312. Phone: (760) 256-0326. Fax: (760) 256-9507.E-mail: tim@highwayradio.com Web Site:www.thehighwaystations.com Licensee: KHWY Inc. Natl. Network: AP Radio, . Hogan & Hartson. Format: Adult contemp. Target aud: 25-54; travelers on I-15 & I-40 & loc communities. ♦Howard B. Anderson, CEO, pres; Kirk M. Anderson, exec VP, VP; Timothy B. Anderson, VP; Timothy B. Anderson, gen mgr; Judy Robinson, sls VP, gen sls mgr; Thomas McNeill, mktg mgr, chief of engrg; Lance Todd, progmg dir.

Yreka

***KNYR(FM)**— 1995: 91.3 mhz; 400 w. Ant 2,365 ft TL: N41 36 36 W122 37 26. Hrs open: 5AM-2am Jefferson Public Radio, 1250 Siskiyou Blvd., Ashland, OR, 97520. Phone: (541) 552-6301. Fax: (541) 552-8565.E-mail: info@ijpr.org Web Site:www.ijpr.org Licensee: The State of Oregon, Acting By and Through the State Board of Higher Education for the Benefit of Southern Oregon University. Natl. Network: NPR, PRI, . Ernest Sanchez. Format: Class, news. News staff: one; News: 35 hrs wkly. ♦Ronald Kramer, CEO, gen mgr; Bryon Lambert, opns dir; Paul Westhelle, dev dir, mktg dir; Eric Teel, progmg dir, disc jockey; Eric Alan, mus dir, disc jockey; Darin Ransom, engrg dir; Kurt Katzmar, disc jockey.

***KSYC(AM)**— July 27, 1947: 1490 khz; 1 kw-U. TL: N41 43 28 W122 39 00. Hrs open: 24 hrs Jefferson Public Radio, 1250 Siskiyou Blvd., Ashland, OR, 97520. Phone: (541) 552-6301. Fax: (541) 552-8565.E-mail: info@ijpr.org Web Site:www.ijpr.org Licensee: JPR Foundation Inc. (acq 8-8-02; $300,000 with KMJC(AM) Mount Shasta). Population served: 47,000 Natl. Network: NPR, PRI, . Ernest Sanchez. News staff: one; News: 35 hrs wkly. ♦Mitchell Christian, CFO; Ronald Kramer, CEO & gen mgr; Bryon Lambert, opns dir; Paul Westhelle, dev dir, mktg dir; Eric Teel, progmg dir; Eric Alan, mus dir; Darin Ransom, engrg dir.

KSYC-FM— June 1, 1983: 103.9 mhz; 10 kw. 2,364 ft TL: N41 43 28 W122 37 46. Stereo. Hrs open: Box 1729, 96097. Secondary address: 316 Lawrence Ln. 96097. Phone: (530) 842-4158. Fax: (530) 842-7635.E-mail: traffic@ksyc.net Licensee: Four Rivers Broadcasting Inc. (group owner; (acq 7-21-2005; grpsl). Baraff, Koerner & Olender. Format: Country. ♦John Anthony, gen mgr; Andy Eagan, progmg dir.

Yuba City

KMYC(AM)—See Marysville

KOBO(AM)— June 1953: 1450 khz; 500 w-D, 1 kw-N. TL: N39 08 07 W121 36 41. Hrs open: Box 669, Marysville, 95901. Phone: (530) 742-5555. Fax: (530) 741-3758. Licensee: Tom F. Huth. Group owner: Huth Broadcasting (acq 12-17-2003; $200,000). Format: Sp, ethnic. Spec prog: East Indian 3 hrs wkly. ♦Thomas Huth, CEO & gen mgr.

KUBA(AM)— January 1948: 1600 khz; 5 kw-D, 2.5 kw-N, DA-N. TL: N39 06 22 W121 39 18. Hrs open: 24 1479 Sanborn Rd., 95993-6042. Phone: (530) 673-1600. Fax: (530) 673-4768.E-mail: info@lbimedia.com Web Site:www.kubaradio.com Licensee: Nevada County Broadcasters Inc. Group owner: Nevada County Broadcasting Inc. (acq 8-9-2004; $500,000). Population served: 180,000 Natl. Network: CBS Radio, . Rgnl. Network: Calif. Agri-Radio, Calif. Farm. Calif. Agri-Radio Wire Svc: AP Format: Classic hits, news/talk. News staff: 2; News: 15 hrs wkly. Target aud: 35-64; community oriented. Spec prog: Farm 4 hrs, gospel 2 hrs, relg 2 hrs wkly. ♦Dave Bear, opns mgr, progmg dir, chief of engrg; John Black, prom dir; Chris Gilbert, news dir; Lucy Spears, pub affrs dir; Robert R. Harlan, gen mgr, sls dir, gen sls mgr, mktg dir & farm dir.

Yucaipa

***KLRD(FM)**— July 15, 1986: 90.1 mhz; 300 w. Ant 1,024 ft TL: N34 02 19 W116 57 09. Hrs open: 24 2351 Sunset Blvd., Suite 170-218, Rocklin, 95765. Phone: (707) 528-9236.E-mail: aramirez@emfbroadcasting.com Licensee: Educational Media Foundation. Group owner: EMF Broadcasting (acq 1-22-99). Population served: 2,500,000 Natl. Network: Air 1, . Shaw Pittman. Format: Alternative rock, Christian music, div. News: 7 hrs wkly. Target aud: 18-34; Christians. ♦Richard Jenkins, pres; Mike Novak, VP; Keith Whipple, dev dir; Tanya Bohannon, natl sls mgr; David Pierce, progmg dir; Eric Allen, mus dir; Ed Lenane, news dir; Sam Wallington, engrg dir.

Yucca Valley

KDGL(FM)— August 1988: 106.9 mhz; 4 kw. 1,371 ft TL: N34 04 55 W116 20 32. Stereo. Hrs open: 24 1321 N. Gene Autry Trail, Palm Springs, 92262. Phone: (760) 322-9890. Fax: (760) 322-5493.E-mail: info@desertfun.com Web Site:www.desertfun.com Licensee: MCC Radio LLC. Group owner: Morris Radio LLC (acq 1998; $2.25 million with KXPS(AM) Thousand Palms). Population served: 250,000 Natl. Network: USA, . Format: Classic Hits. Target aud: 25 plus. ♦William Morris III, chmn & pres; Darrel Fry, CFO; Michael Oslehaut, sr VP, VP; Keith Martin, gen mgr; Larry Snider, opns dir.

Colorado

Alamosa

KALQ-FM— June 26, 1969: 93.5 mhz; 2.8 kw. Ant 130 ft TL: N37 28 20 W105 51 13. Stereo. Hrs open: Box 179, 81101. Secondary address: 292 Santa Fe 81101. Phone: (719) 589-6644. Phone: (719) 589-6645. Fax: (719) 589-0993.E-mail: info@kgiwkalq.com Web Site:kgiwkalq.com Licensee: Community Broadcasting Corp. Population served: 30,000 Natl. Network: ABC, . Format: Country. ♦Dale Burns, pres, opns mgr; Marilyn Burns, VP; Neil Hammer, gen mgr; Mark Beatty, news dir; Helen Lozoya, pub affrs dir; Will Williams, chief of engrg; Evan Slack, farm dir.

***KASF(FM)**— 1967: 90.9 mhz; 17 w. 121 ft TL: N37 28 20 W105 52 39. Stereo. Hrs open: 24 Adams State College, 110 Richardson Ave., 81101. Phone: (719) 587-7871. Phone: (719) 587-7872. Fax: (719) 587-7522. Web Site:www.adams.edu Licensee: Adams State College. Population served: 8,000 Format: Pop contemp hit. News: one hr wkly. Target aud: Community; college and local. Spec prog: Gospel 4 hrs, talk 6 hrs, blues/jazz 6 hrs, reggae 5 hrs wkly. ♦Beth Dussault, gen mgr.

KGIW(AM)— Feb 27, 1929: 1450 khz; 1 kw-U. TL: N37 28 20 W105 51 13. Hrs open: 6 AM-11 PM Box 179, 292 Santa Fe, 81101. Phone: (719) 589-6644. Phone: (719) 589-6645. Fax: (719) 589-0993.E-mail: info@kgiwkalq.com Web Site:www.kgiwkalq.com Licensee: Community Broadcasting Corp. (acq 1964). Population served: 42,000 Natl. Network: ABC, . Format: Adult contemp. News staff: one; News: 25 hrs wkly. Target aud: 18-60. Spec prog: Sp 6 hrs, farm 6 hrs wkly. ♦Dale K. Burns, pres; Marilyn Burns, exec VP; Neil J. Hammer, gen mgr, progmg dir; Helen Lozoya, gen sls mgr, min affrs dir; Mark Beatty, news dir, local news ed; Will Williams, chief of engrg; Evan Slack, farm dir.

***KRZA(FM)**— Oct 26, 1985: 88.7 mhz; 9.8 kw. 2,076 ft TL: N36 51 32 W106 00 28. Stereo. Hrs open: 5 AM-midnight 528 9th St., 81101. Phone: (719) 589-8844. Fax: (719) 587-0032.E-mail: manager@krza.org Web Site:www.krza.org Licensee: Equal Representation of Media Advocacy Corp. Natl. Network: NPR, . Format: News, jazz,various. News staff: one; News: 18 hrs wkly. Target aud: General; adult progsv community oriented rural area. Spec prog: Sp 14 hrs, Latin American 3 hrs, news 4 hrs wkly. ♦Kristine Taylor, gen mgr & stn mgr.

Arriba

KMAP(FM)—Not on air, target date: unknown: 95.9 mhz; 6.5 kw. Ant 207 ft TL: N39 18 52 W103 18 22. Hrs open: 87 Jasper Lake Rd., Loveland, 80537. Phone: (970) 669-9200. Licensee: Kona Coast Radio LLC. ♦Victor A. Michael Jr., gen mgr.

Arvada

KDDZ(AM)— June 1998: 1690 khz; 10 kw-D, 1 kw-N. TL: N39 39 21 W105 04 27. Hrs open: 12136 W. Bayaud Ave., Suite 125, Lakewood, 80228. Phone: (303) 783-0880. Fax: (303) 761-1774.E-mail: info@kddzam.com Web Site:www.radiodisney.com Licensee: Radio Disney Group LLC. Group owner: ABC Inc. (acq 7-16-98; $3.5 million with KADZ Arvada). Natl. Network: Radio Disney, . Format: Children. ♦Tracy Wells, gen mgr.

Aspen

***KAJX(FM)**— July 7, 1987: 91.5 mhz; 380 w horiz, 370 w vert. Ant -987 ft TL: N39 11 48 W106 48 14. Stereo. Hrs open: 24 110 E. Hallam St., Suite 134, 81611. Phone: (970) 920-9000. Fax: (970) 544-8002.E-mail: info@kajx.org Web Site:www.kajx.org Licensee: Roaring Fork Public Radio Inc. (acq 1996). Population served: 65,000 Natl. Network: NPR, PRI, . Wire Svc: AP Format: Class, jazz, news. News staff: 3; News: 50 hrs wkly. Target aud: General; Aspen residents & tourists. Spec prog: Bluegrass 2 hrs wkly. ♦Brent Gardner-Smith, gen mgr; Steve Cole, progmg dir; Kirk Siegler, news dir.

KPVW(FM)— 2000: 107.1 mhz; 20.5 kw. Ant 361 ft TL: N39 18 56 W106 57 32. Stereo. Hrs open: 24 20 Sunset Dr., Suite 6-A, Basalt, 81621. Phone: (970) 927-7600. Fax: (970) 927-8001.E-mail: jeloy@entravision.com Licensee: Entravision Holdings LLC. Group owner: Entravision Communications Corp. (acq 12-13-01; $57,500). Format: Mexican rgnl. Target aud: Latino; 18-34. ♦Philip Wilkinson, COO; Walter Ulloa, CEO & chmn; Jeffery A. Liberman, pres; John DeLorenzo, CFO; Mario Carrera, gen mgr.

KSNO-FM—See Snowmass Village

KSPN-FM— Feb 14, 1970: 103.1 mhz; 3 kw. Ant -85 ft TL: N39 13 33 W106 50 00. Stereo. Hrs open: 24 Bldg 402 D, Aspen Airport Business Center, 81611. Phone: (970) 925-5776. Fax: (970) 925-1142.E-mail: studio@kspnradio.com Web Site:www.kspnradio.com Licensee: NRC Broadcasting Mountain Group LLC. (group owner; (acq 5-1-2007; grpsl). Population served: 50,473 Natl. Rep: Christal,. Rosenman & Colin. Format: AAA. News staff: 2; News: 6 hrs wkly. Target aud: 25-49; affluent, well educated people who live in resort areas. ♦Colleen Barill, gen mgr; David Bach, chief of opns.

Aurora

KEZW(AM)— 1954: 1430 khz; 5 kw-U, DA-N. TL: N39 12 28 W104 55 46. Stereo. Hrs open: 24 4700 S. Syracuse St., Suite 1050, Denver, 80237. Phone: (303) 967-2700. Fax: (303) 967-2747.E-mail: info@kezw.com Web Site:KEZW.com Licensee: Entercom Denver License LLC. Group owner: Entercom Communications Corp. (acq 7-24-02; with KOSI(FM) Denver). Natl. Rep: Katz Radio,. Format: Nostalgia, big band, MOR. News: 4 hrs wkly. Target aud: 35 plus; general. ♦Jeff Brown, gen sls mgr, rgnl sls mgr; Rick Crandall, progmg dir, progmg mgr; Jeff Garrett, chief of engrg; Stephanie Walrath, traf mgr.

KMXA(AM)—Licensed to Aurora. See Denver

KOSI(FM)—See Denver

Avon

KZYR(FM)— Dec 24, 1984: 97.7 mhz; 15 kw. Ant 440 ft TL: N39 38 05 W106 26 47. Stereo. Hrs open: 24 275 Main St., Unit 0-201, Edwards, 81632-7812. Phone: (970) 845-8565. Fax: (970) 926-7635.E-mail: tony@kzyr.com Web Site:www.kzyr.com Licensee: Cool Radio LLC (acq 12-3-2001; $1.5 million with KSNO-FM Snowmass Village). Cole, Raywid & Braverman. Format: AAA. Target aud: 18-54. ♦Thomas Dobrez, CEO, pres; Tony Mauro, gen mgr.

Basalt

KNFO(FM)— July 1995: 106.1 mhz; 2 kw. 364 ft TL: N39 18 55 W106 57 36. Hrs open: 24 402D AABC, Aspen, 81611. Phone: (970) 544-9100. Fax: (970) 544-9101. Licensee: NRC Broadcasting Mountain Group LLC. (group owner; (acq 5-1-2007; grpsl). Population served: 50,473 Natl. Network: CBS, . Rosenman & Colin. Format: News, talk, sports. News staff: 2; News: 13 hrs wkly. Target aud: 35-64. ♦Tim Brown, CEO & pres; Dave Rogers, CFO; Colleen Barill, gen mgr; David Bach, chief of opns.

Bayfield

KAYF(FM)— 2008: Stn currently dark. 92.5 mhz; 100 w horiz. Ant -272 ft TL: N37 13 51 W107 35 11. Hrs open: 980 N. Michigan Ave., Suite 1880, Chicago, IL, 60611. Phone: (312) 204-9900. Licensee: College Creek Media LLC. ◆Neal J. Robinson, pres.

KLJH(FM)— July 2003: 107.1 mhz; 100 kw horiz. Ant 1,870 ft TL: N37 21 49 W107 47 30. (CP: Ant 1,883 ft. TL: N37 21 46 W107 47 40). Hrs open: Voice Ministries of Farmington Inc., 1105 W. Apache, Farmington, NM, 87401. Phone: (505) 327-7202. Fax: (505) 327-2163.E-mail: kljh@kljh.org Web Site:www.kljh.org Licensee: Voice Ministries of Farmington Inc. Natl. Rep: Salem,. Format: Praise & worship-Christian. ◆Fareed W. Ayoub, gen mgr.

Bennett

KONN-FM— 1978: 107.1 mhz; 100 kw. Ant 1,932 ft TL: N39 55 22 W103 58 18. Hrs open: 24 3033 S. Parker Rd., Suite 700, Aurora, 80014. Phone: (303) 872-1500. Fax: (303) 872-1501. Web Site:hot1071denver.com/info.php Licensee: KSIR-FM LLC (acq 10-24-2005; $14 million). Population served: 300,000 Format: Var. ◆Luis G. Nogales, CEO; Steve Keeney, gen mgr; Tim Maranville, opns dir & progmg dir.

*KZWD(FM)—Not on air, target date: unknown: 91.7 mhz; 50 kw. Ant 210 ft TL: N39 37 30 W104 02 04. Hrs open: 18900 E. Hampden Ave., Aurora, 80013. Phone: (303) 628-7200. Fax: (303) 628-7205.E-mail: info@calvaryaurora.org Web Site:www.calvaryaurora.org Licensee: Calvary Chapel Aurora. ◆Ed Taylor, pres.

Boulder

KBCO(FM)— Oct 1, 1955: 97.3 mhz; 100 kw. Ant 1,541 ft TL: N39 54 48 W105 17 32. Stereo. Hrs open: 2500 Pearl St., Suite 315, 80302. Phone: (303) 444-5600. Fax: (303) 449-3057.E-mail: kbco@kbco.com Web Site:www.kbco.com Licensee: Citicasters Licenses L.P. Group owner: Clear Channel Communications Inc. Population served: 200,000 Format: AAA. ◆Mark Remington, gen mgr; Kenny Marks, natl sls mgr.

KCFC(AM)— Feb 15, 1947: 1490 khz; 1 kw-U. TL: N40 01 42 W105 15 06. Hrs open: Colorado Public Radio, 7409 S. Alton Ct., Centennial, 80112. Phone: (303) 871-9191. Fax: (303) 733-3319. Web Site:www.cpr.org Licensee: Public Broadcasting of Colorado Inc. (acq 8-17-01; $1.1 million). Population served: 250,000 Natl. Network: NPR, . Format: News. Target aud: General. ◆Max Wycisk, pres, gen mgr; Sue Coughlin, dev VP & reporter.

*KGNU-FM— May 22, 1978: 88.5 mhz; 1.3 kw. 215 ft TL: N39 59 32 W105 09 10. Stereo. Hrs open: 24 4700 Walnut St., 80301-2548. Phone: (303) 449-4885.E-mail: marty@kgnu.org Web Site:www.kgnu.org Licensee: Boulder Community Broadcast Association Inc. Population served: 2,500,000 Natl. Network: PRI, NPR, . Rgnl. Network: Colo. Pub. Colo. Pub. Garvey, Schubert, Barer. Format: Var/div. News staff: one; News: 30 hrs wkly. Target aud: General. Spec prog: Black 7 hrs, folk 20 hrs, Sp 3 hrs, jazz 15 hrs, class 13 hrs wkly. ◆Marty Durlin, gen mgr, stn mgr; Evan Perkins, opns mgr; Faye Lamb, dev dir; John Schaefer, mus dir; Sam Fugua, news dir.

KRCN(AM)—See Longmont

KRKS-FM— Mar 15, 1971: 94.7 mhz; 100 kw. 984 ft TL: N40 04 19 W105 21 14. (CP: Ant 1,745 ft. TL: N39 40 33 W105 29 07). Stereo. Hrs open: 24 3131 S. Vaughn Way, Suite 601, Aurora, 80014-3510. Phone: (303) 750-5687. Fax: (303) 696-8063. Web Site:www.krks.com Licensee: Salem Media of Colorado Inc. Group owner: Salem Communications Corp. (acq 12-15-93; $5 million; 11-15-93). Population served: 100,000 Format: Relg. ◆Edward Atsinger, pres; Joe Davis, VP; Brian Taylor, gen mgr.

KVCU(AM)— Nov 14, 1973: 1190 khz; 5 kw-D. TL: N39 57 54 W105 14 05. Stereo. Hrs open: 24 Box 207, University of Colorado, 80309. Phone: (303) 492-5031. Fax: (303) 492-1369.E-mail: ej@radio1190.org Web Site:www.radio1190.org Licensee: The University of Colorado Foundation. Population served: 228,000 Haley, Bader & Potts. Format: Eclectic, diverse. News staff: 3; News: 3 hrs wkly. Target aud: 25-44. Spec prog: Jazz 3 hrs wkly. ◆Conor Walker, gen mgr; Mike Flanagan, stn mgr.

Breckenridge

*KRKM(FM)—Not on air, target date: unknown: 88.7 mhz; 250 w. Ant -249 ft TL: N39 29 44 W106 01 44. Hrs open: 5944 Kenosha St.,

Cheyenne, WY, 82001. Phone: (307) 460-4224. Licensee: Wren Communications Inc. ◆Tara D. Parker, pres.

KSMT(FM)— Sept 12, 1975: 102.3 mhz; 6 kw. Ant -210 ft TL: N39 29 44 W106 01 44. Stereo. Hrs open: 24 Box 7069, 80424. Secondary address: 130 Ski Hill Rd., Suite 240 80424. Phone: (970) 453-2234. Fax: (970) 453-5425.E-mail: ksmtstudio@nrcbroadcasting.com Web Site:www.ksmtradio.com Licensee: NRC Broadcasting Mountain Group LLC. Group owner: American General Media (acq 5-1-2007; grpsl). Format: Triple-A. News staff: one; News: 12 hrs wkly. Target aud: 18-44; upscale adults, heavy ski & outdoor industry consumers. Spec prog: Sp 2 hrs, Reggae 2 hrs wkly. ◆Lisa Korry-Cheek, gen mgr & stn mgr.

Breen

KLLV(AM)—Licensed to Breen. See Durango

Brighton

KLVZ(AM)— Apr 26, 1956: 810 khz; 2.2 kw-D, 430 w-N, DA-2. TL: N40 01 41 W104 49 21 (day), N39 50 36 W104 57 14 (night). Hrs open: 2150 W. 29th Ave., Suite 300, Denver, 80211. Phone: (303) 433-5500. Fax: (303) 433-1555.E-mail: klvz@crawfordbroadcasting.com Web Site:www.810klvz.com Licensee: KLZ Radio Inc. Group owner: Crawford Broadcasting Co. (acq 12-10-93; $700,000; 1-10-94). Population served: 1,500,000 Format: Hispanic Christian. Target aud: 18-49. ◆Donald B. Crawford, pres; Mike Triem, gen mgr; Teresa Johnston, stn mgr.

Broomfield

KWOF(FM)— June 1967: 92.5 mhz; 57 kw. Ant 1,237 ft TL: N40 05 47 W104 54 04. Stereo. Hrs open: 24 1560 Broadway, Suite 1100, Denver, 80202. Phone: (303) 832-5665. Fax: (303) 832-7000.E-mail: info@925thewolf.com Web Site:www.925thewolf.com Licensee: Wilks License Co.-Denver LLC. Group owner: Infinity Broadcasting Corp. (acq 3-5-2009; grpsl). Format: New country choice. News staff: one; News: 2 hrs wkly. Target aud: 35-64; educated, upscale, active professionals, ethnic. ◆Don Howe, gen mgr, mus dir; Lisa Petrone, gen sls mgr; Barry Walters, chief of engrg.

Brush

*KBWA(FM)— 2006: 89.1 mhz; 6 kw vert. Ant 145 ft TL: N40 13 02.1 W103 41 46.2. Hrs open:
Rebroadcasts KXWA(FM) Loveland 100%.
Box 64500, Colorado Springs, 80962. Phone: (719) 533-0300. Fax: (719) 278-4339.E-mail: wxwa@wayfm.com Web Site:kxwa.wayfm.com Licensee: WAY-FM Media Group Inc. (acq 2-23-2005; $25,000 for CP). Format: Contemp Christian. ◆Robert D. Augsburg, pres.

KPRB(FM)— Nov 2, 1998: 106.3 mhz; 6 kw. 201 ft TL: N40 18 50 W103 35 30. Stereo. Hrs open: 24 Box 917, Fort Morgan, 80701. Secondary address: 220 State St., Suite 106, Fort Morgan 80701. Phone: (970) 867-7271. Fax (970) 867-2676.E-mail: b106@necolorado.com Web Site:www.b106.com Population served: 50,000 Natl. Network: ABC, . Wire Svc: AP Format: Adult contemp. News staff: one; News: one hr wkly. Target aud: 18-45; females. ◆Alec Creighton, CEO & progmg dir.

KSIR(AM)— Aug 1, 1977: 1010 khz; 25 kw-D, 280 w-N. TL: N40 18 50 W103 35 30. Hrs open: 24 Box 917, Fort Morgan, 80701. Secondary address: 220 State St., Suite 106, Fort Morgan 80701. Phone: (970) 867-7271. Fax: (970) 867-2676.E-mail: ksir@necolorado.com Web Site:www.ksir.com Licensee: Northeast Colorado Broadcasting LLC (group owner; acq 7-1-2003; grpsl). Population served: 2,500,000 Natl. Network: ABC, . Wire Svc: AP Format: Talk, agriculture, sports. News staff: 2; News: 5 hrs wkly. Target aud: 25-65; farmers, ranchers, sports fans. ◆Alec Creighton, gen mgr; Lorrie Boyer, progmg dir.

Buena Vista

KBVC(FM)— Jan 1, 1997: 104.1 mhz; 600 w. Ant 1,187 ft TL: N38 44 45 W106 11 55. Hrs open: 7600 County Rd. 120, Salida, 81201. Phone: (719) 539-2575. Fax: (719) 539-4851.E-mail: kvrh@kvrh.com Web Site:www.kbvcfm.com Licensee: Three Eagles Communications of Colorado LLC (acq 9-1-2006; swap for KVRH(AM) Salida). Format: Country. ◆Cristy Carothers, gen mgr; Doug Vollertsen, opns mgr, progmg dir, mus dir; Norm Veasman, news dir.

KSKE(AM)— Aug 22, 1986: 1450 khz; 250 w-U. TL: N38 49 07 W106 09 34. Hrs open: 24

Simulcasts KVLE(AM) Vail.
614 Kimbark St., Longmont, 80501. Phone: (303) 776-2323. Fax: (303) 776-1377.E-mail: cduncan@bcdworldwide.com Licensee: Pilgrim Communications Inc. (acq 12-11-97). Natl. Network: NBC Radio, . Natl. Rep: Interep,. Format: Business talk. News staff: 3; News: 12 hrs wkly. Target aud: Adults 25-54. ◆Chuck Duncan, CEO, pres; Gene Hood, pres; Roger Cridelbaugh, pub affrs dir.

Burlington

KNAB(AM)— July 11, 1967: 1140 khz; 1 kw-D. TL: N39 17 28 W102 15 45. Hrs open: Box 516, 17534 County Rd., No. 49, 80807. Phone: (719) 346-8600. Fax: (719) 346-8656.E-mail: knab@centurytel.net Web Site:www.knabradio.com Licensee: KNAB Inc. (acq 9-6-91). Population served: 35,100 Fletcher, Heald & Hildreth. Format: Adult standards. Target aud: 18 plus. ◆Bette Bailly, CEO, pres, gen mgr, chief of engrg; Beverly Schott, traf mgr; Bobby Maze, disc jockey.

KNAB-FM— Mar 7, 1980: 104.1 mhz; 50.7 kw. 358 ft TL: N39 17 41 W102 15 37. Stereo. Hrs open: 24 Box 516, 17534 County Rd. No. 49, 80807. Phone: (719) 346-8600. Fax: (719) 346-8656. Web Site:www.knabradio.com Population served: 30,000 Format: Country. ◆Bette Bailly, gen mgr; Bobby Maze, disc jockey.

KPCR(FM)—Not on air, target date: unknown: 99.3 mhz; 55 kw. Ant 315 ft TL: N39 15 34 W102 24 35. Hrs open: 1951 28th Ave., Unit 29, Greeley, 80634-5755. Phone: (970) 302-8444. Licensee: Youngers Colorado Broadcasting LLC. ◆Kevin J. Youngers, gen mgr.

Calhan

KKHN(FM)—Not on air, target date: unknown: 104.7 mhz; 400 w horiz. Ant 476 ft TL: N38 59 57 W104 18 47. Hrs open: 980 N. Michigan Ave., Suite 1880, Chicago, IL, 60611. Phone: (312) 204-9900. Licensee: Superior Broadcasting of Denver LLC. ◆Christopher F. Devine, pres & gen mgr.

Canon City

KRLN(AM)— Aug 15, 1947: 1400 khz; 1 kw-U. TL: N38 27 35 W105 13 26. Hrs open: 24 1615 Central, 81212. Phone: (719) 275-7488. Fax: (719) 275-5132.E-mail: starads@krln.cc Licensee: Royal Gorge Broadcasting LLC. (acq 3-31-2000; $715,000 with co-located FM). Population served: 35,000 Natl. Network: CBS, . Format: News/talk. News staff: one; News: 25 hrs wkly. Target aud: 25-54; two income families & older discretionary income. ◆Joan Wood, gen mgr; Rosemary Lamberson, gen sls mgr; Melissa Nunn, traf mgr.

KSTY(FM)— June 1, 1975: 104.5 mhz; 6 kw. Ant 46 ft TL: N38 18 54 W105 12 40. Stereo. Hrs open: 1615 Central, 81212. Phone: (719) 275-7488. Fax: (719) 275-5132. Licensee: Royal Gorge Broadcasting LLC. Population served: 100,000 Format: Country. Target aud: 25-60. ◆Rosemary Lamberson, gen sls mgr; Tanner Brandt, mus dir; Dennis Bloomquist, news dir; Ed Norden, chief of engrg; Missi Nunn, traf mgr; Harry Russell, engr.

*KTLC(FM)— May 2001: 89.1 mhz; 1.15 kw. Ant 1,476 ft TL: N38 45 21 W105 13 02. Stereo. Hrs open: 24
Rebroadcasts KTLF(FM) Colorado Springs 100%.
1665 Briargate Blvd., Suite 100, Colorado Springs, 80920. Phone: (719) 593-0600. Fax: (719) 593-2399.E-mail: lightpraise@ktlf.org Web Site:www.ktlf.org Licensee: Make a Difference Foundation Inc. (acq 12-27-01). Format: Christian music. Target aud: 45-60; Christian. ◆Lynn Carmichael, progmg dir.

Carbondale

*KCJX(FM)— Sept 6, 2004: 88.9 mhz; 4 kw horiz, 3.5 kw vert. Ant 2,542 ft TL: N39 25 08 W107 22 10. Hrs open: 110 E. Hallam St., Suite 134, Aspen, 81611. Phone: (970) 925-6445. Fax: (970) 544-8002.E-mail: info@kajx.org Web Site:www.kajx.org Licensee: Roaring Fork Public Radio Inc. (acq 4-16-2002). Population served: 67,000 Wire Svc: AP Format: News, class, jazz. News staff: 3. ◆Brent Gardner-Smith, gen mgr; Kirk Siegler, news dir.

KUUR(FM)— 2007: 96.7 mhz; 90 w. Ant 2,507 ft TL: N39 25 08 W107 22 10. Hrs open: Box 11657, Aspen, 81612. Secondary address: 132 W. Main St. , Aspen 81611. Phone: (970) 920-9600. Fax: (970) 544-5239.E-mail: sales@aspenglenwood.com Web Site:www.aspenglenwood.com Licensee: Colorado Radio Marketing LLC. Format: Cool contemp. ◆Marcos Rodriguez, gen mgr.

*KVOV(FM)— Apr 15, 1983: 90.5 mhz; 215 w. Ant 2,798 ft TL: N39 25 35 W107 22 48. Hrs open:

Rebroadcasts KVOD(FM) Denver 100%.
7409 S. Alton Ct., Centennial, 80112. Phone: (303) 871-9191. Fax: (303) 733-3319. Web Site:www.cpr.org Licensee: Public Broadcasting of Colorado Inc. (acq 10-29-2004; exchange for KDNK(FM) Glenwood Springs). Population served: 45,000 Colo. Pub. Format: Classical music. ♦Max Wycisk, pres.

Castle Rock

KJMN(FM)— Feb 26, 1978: 92.1 mhz; 42 kw. Ant 535 ft TL: N39 23 07 W105 02 52. Stereo. Hrs open: 24 777 Grant St., 5th Fl., Denver, 80203. Phone: (303) 721-9210. Fax: (303) 832-3410. Licensee: Entravision Holdings LLC. Group owner: Entravision Communications Corp. (acq 3-14-00; grpsl). Population served: 2,000,000 Wiley, Rein & Fielding. Format: Sp. Target aud: 25-54. ♦Mario Carrera, gen mgr.

Centennial

KKHI(FM)— Jan 28, 1967: 101.9 mhz; 9.5 kw. Ant 535 ft TL: N39 23 07 W105 02 52. Stereo. Hrs open: 8975 E. Kenyon Ave., Denver, 80237. Phone: (303) 889-1019.E-mail: smooth1019@gmail.com Web Site:www.smooth1019.net Licensee: Bustos Media of Colorado License Corp. (group owner; (acq 9-29-2006; $17.5 million). Format: Smooth jazz. ♦Chuck Lontine, VP & gen mgr.

Center

KPAU(FM)—Not on air, target date: unknown: 105.3 mhz; 25 kw. Ant 280 ft TL: N37 37 17 W106 15 20. Hrs open: 980 N. Michigan Ave., Suite 1880, Chicago, IL, 60611. Phone: (312) 204-9900. Licensee: College Creek Media LLC. ♦Neal J. Robinson, pres.

Central City

***KDAB(FM)**—Not on air, target date: unknown: 88.9 mhz; 130 w. Ant 1,302 ft TL: N39 51 58 W105 32 39. Hrs open: 87 Jasper Lake Rd., Loveland, 80537. Phone: (970) 669-9200. Licensee: Cedar Cove Broadcasting Inc. ♦Victor A. Michael Jr., pres.

Colona

KAVP(AM)— Sept 30, 2000: 1450 khz; I kw-U. TL: N38 15 59 W107 51 07. Hrs open: 24
Rebroadcasts KWGL(FM) Ouray 100%.
751 Horizon Ct. , Suite 225, Grand Junction, 81506. Phone: (970) 241-6460. Fax: (970) 241-6452. Licensee: WS Communications LLC. Group owner: Western Slope Communications LLC. Population served: 140,000 Format: Legendary Country. ♦Merle Allen, gen mgr.

***KTMH(FM)**— 2005: 89.9 mhz; 4 kw vert. Ant 1,633 ft TL: N38 23 15 W107 40 31. Stereo. Hrs open:
Rebroadcasts KTLF(FM) Colorado Springs 100%.
1665 Briargate Blvd., Suite 100, Colorado Springs, 80920. Phone: (719) 593-0600. Fax: (719) 593-2399.E-mail: lightpraise@ktlf.org Web Site:www.ktlf.org Licensee: Educational Communications of Colorado Springs Inc. Format: Christian music. Target aud: 45-60; Christian. ♦Lynn Carmichael, progmg dir.

Colorado Springs

KATC-FM— Oct 1, 1969: 95.1 mhz; 58 kw. Ant 2,280 ft TL: N38 44 43 W104 51 39. Stereo. Hrs open: 24 6805 Corporate Dr., Suite 130, 80919. Phone: (719) 593-2700. Fax: (719) 593-2727.E-mail: info@katcountry951.com Web Site:www.katcountry951.com Licensee: Citadel Broadcasting Co. (acq 8-25-2006; $8.5 million). Population served: 82,000 Format: Country. ♦Bobby Irwin, opns mgr; Jim Miller, progmg dir.

KBIQ(FM)—See Manitou Springs

KCCY(FM)—See Pueblo

KCMN(AM)— Feb 9, 1964: 1530 khz; 15 kw-D, 15 w-N, 1 kw-CH. TL: N38 49 08 W104 46 32. Hrs open: 24 5050 Edison Ave., Suite 218, 80915. Phone: (719) 570-1530. Fax: (719) 570-1007. Web Site:www.1530kcmn.com Licensee: KLZ Radio Inc. Group owner: Crawford Broadcasting Co. (acq 1999; $750,000 with KCBR(AM) Monument). Population served: 400,000 Natl. Network: CNN Radio, Westwood One, . Format: Oldies. Target aud: 40 plus. Spec prog: Relg 3 hrs wkly. ♦Don Crawford Jr., CEO, pres, VP, gen mgr; Tron Simpson, opns mgr.

KCSF(AM)— Sept 22, 1922: 1300 khz; 5 kw-D, 1 kw-N. TL: N38 48 46 W104 48 51. Hrs open: 24 6805 Corporate Dr., Suite 130, 80919-1977. Phone: (719) 593-2700. Web Site:www.kcs1300am.com Licensee: Citadel Broadcasting Co. Group owner: Citadel Broadcasting Corp. (acq 1999; grpsl). Population served: 350,000 Natl. Rep: McGavren Guild,. Format: Classic country. ♦Farid Suleman, CEO; Bobby Irwin, opns mgr.

***KEPC(FM)**— Feb 15, 1957: 89.7 mhz; 10 kw. Ant -256 ft TL: N38 45 41 W104 47 04. Stereo. Hrs open: 24 5675 S. Academy Blvd., 80906. Phone: (719) 502-3128.E-mail: kepc@ppcc.edu Licensee: Pikes Peak Community College. Population served: 350,000 Format: Var/div. Target aud: General. ♦Sharon Hogg, gen mgr & pub affrs dir.

KILO(FM)— Jan 21, 1966: 94.3 mhz; 83 kw. 2,110 ft TL: N38 44 44 W104 51 43. (CP: 94.3 mhz). Stereo. Hrs open: Box 2080, 80901. Secondary address: 1805 E. Cheyenne Rd. 80906. Phone: (719) 634-4896. Fax: (719) 634-5837. Web Site:www.kilo943.com Licensee: Bahakel Communications. (group owner; acq 8-14-84). Population served: 334,000 Format: Active Rock. ♦Lou Mellini, gen mgr.

KKFM(FM)— 1958: 98.1 mhz; 72 kw. 2,300 ft TL: N38 44 36 W104 51 44. Stereo. Hrs open: 24 6805 Corporate Dr., Suite 130, 80919-1977. Phone: (719) 593-2700. Fax: (719) 593-2727.E-mail: info@kkfm.com Web Site:www.kkfm.com Licensee: Citadel Broadcasting Co. Group owner: Citadel Broadcasting Corp. (acq 1-86; $2.5 million;8-16-82). Population served: 500,000 Natl. Rep: McGavren Guild,. Format: Classic rock. News: one hr wkly. Target aud: 25-54. ♦Farid Suleman, CEO; Judy Ellis, COO; Bobby Irwin, gen mgr, opns mgr, progmg dir.

KKKK(AM)— June 22, 1957: 1580 khz; 10 kw-D. TL: N38 43 11 W104 43 16. Hrs open: 24 614 Kimbark St., Longmont, 80501. Phone: (303) 776-2323. Fax: (303) 776-1377.E-mail: cduncan@bcdworldwide.com Licensee: Pilgrim Communications Inc. (acq 6-1-98; $450,000). Population served: 597,000 Natl. Network: ABC, . Format: Business talk. News staff: 3; News: 12 hrs wkly. Target aud: 25-65. ♦Lee Thompson, CEO; Chuck Duncan, pres; Chuck Baker, gen mgr; Gene Hood, progmg dir; Roger Cridelbaugh, pub affrs dir.

KKLI(FM)—(Widefield, Mar 23, 1987: 106.3 mhz; 1.6 kw. 2,224 ft TL: N38 44 41 W104 51 46. Stereo. Hrs open: 24 2864 S. Circle Dr., Suite 150, 80906. Phone: (719) 540-9200. Fax: (719) 579-0882.E-mail: info@kkli.com Web Site:www.kkli.com Licensee: Capstar TX L.P. Group owner: Clear Channel Communications Inc. (acq 8-30-00; grpsl). Natl. Rep: Clear Channel,. Format: Soft adult contemp. News staff: one; News: 4 hrs wkly. Target aud: 25-54; family-oriented, educated. ♦Bob Richards, gen mgr; Scott Jones, gen sls mgr; Nancia Warren, prom dir; Paul Richards, news dir.

KKPK(FM)— Feb 1, 1960: 92.9 mhz; 53 kw. Ant 2,130 ft TL: N38 44 44 W104 51 39. Stereo. Hrs open: 6805 Corporate Dr., 80919. Phone: (719) 593-2700. Fax: (719) 593-2727.E-mail: info@929peakfm.com Web Site:www.929peakfm.com Population served: 350,000 Wire Svc: UPI Format: Hot adult contemp. Target aud: 25-54. ♦Jim Berry, progmg dir.

***KRCC(FM)**— Oct 2, 1951: 91.5 mhz; 2.1 kw. 2,103 ft TL: N38 44 43 W104 51 42. Stereo. Hrs open: 24 912 N. Weber St., 80903. Phone: (719) 473-4801. Fax: (719) 473-7863.E-mail: info@krcc.org Web Site:www.krcc.org Licensee: The Colorado College. Population served: 500,000 Natl. Network: NPR, PRI, . Garvey, Schubert & Barer. Format: Div, news. News: 42 hrs wkly. Target aud: 25-54; general. Spec prog: Celtic 5 hrs, reggae 6 hrs, jazz 15 hrs, blues 5 hrs wkly. ♦Delaney Utterback, gen mgr; Mike Procell, opns mgr; Jeff Bieri, prom dir, progmg dir.

KRDO(AM)— March 1947: 1240 khz; 1 kw-U. TL: N38 49 42 W104 50 15. Hrs open: 24 399 S. 8th St., 80905. Phone: (719) 632-1515. Phone: (719) 473-1240.E-mail: m.lewis@krdotv.com Web Site:www.krdo.com Licensee: Pikes Peak Radio LLC. (group owner) (acq 6-26-2006; grpsl). Population served: 500,000 Natl. Rep: D & R Radio,. Fletcher, Heald & Hildreth. Format: News/talk. ♦David Bradley Jr., pres; Neil O. Klockziem, gen mgr; Ron Mitchell, gen sls mgr & natl sls mgr; Mike Lewis, progmg mgr; J.R. Reed, chief of engrg. Co-owned TV: KRDO-TV affil.

KRDO-FM—See Security

***KTLF(FM)**— Feb 27, 1989: 90.5 mhz; 20 kw. Ant 2,178 ft TL: N38 44 43 W104 51 39. Stereo. Hrs open: 24 1665 Briargate Blvd., Suite 100, 80920. Phone: (719) 593-0600. Fax: (719) 593-2399.E-mail: lightpraise@ktlf.org Web Site:www.ktlf.org Licensee: Educational Communications of Colorado Springs Inc. Population served: 1,000,000 Format: Christian music. Target aud: 45-60; Christian. ♦Dr. Ron Johnson, chmn; Sharick Wade, opns mgr; Lynn Carmichael, progmg dir.

KVOR(AM)— Sept 22, 1922: 740 khz; 3.3 kw-D, 1.5 kw-N, DA-2. TL: N39 05 02 W104 42 41. Stereo. Hrs open: 6805 Corporate Dr., Suite 130, 80919-1977. Phone: (719) 593-2700. Fax: (719) 593-2727.E-mail: info@kvor.com Web Site:www.kvor.com Licensee: Citadel Broadcasting Co. Group owner: Citadel Broadcasting Corp. (acq 1999; grpsl). Population served: 250,000 Natl. Network: CBS, Wall Street, . Format: News/talk, sports. Target aud: General. ♦Bobby Irwin, gen mgr, opns mgr; Dan Mandis, progmg dir.

KZNT(AM)— Dec 15, 1956: 1460 khz; 5 kw-D, 500 w-N, DA-N. TL: N38 49 36 W104 44 30. Hrs open: 24 7150 Campus Dr., Suite 150, 80920. Phone: (719) 531-5438. Fax: (719) 531-5588.E-mail: info@kznt.com Web Site:www.newstalk1460.com Licensee: Bison Media Inc. Group owner: Salem Communications Corp. (acq 10-6-03; $1.5 million). Population served: 350,000 Format: News/talk. ♦Henry Tippie, gen mgr.

Commerce City

KLTT(AM)— 1996: 670 khz; 50 kw-D, 1.4 kw-N, DA-2. TL: N39 57 20 W104 43 50. Hrs open: 2150 W. 29th Ave., Suite 300, Denver, 80211. Phone: (303) 433-5500. Fax: (303) 433-1555.E-mail: kltt@crawfordbroadcasting.com Web Site:www.670kltt.com Licensee: KLZ Radio Inc. Group owner: Crawford Broadcasting Co. (acq 1995; $750,000). Format: Relg, Christian/talk & teaching, conservative talk. Target aud: 30 plus; general. ♦Mike Triem, gen mgr.

Cortez

KISZ-FM— Sept 28, 1978: 97.9 mhz; 100 kw. 1,360 ft TL: N37 21 48 W108 09 00. Stereo. Hrs open: 20 212 W. Apache St., Farmington, NM, 87401-6235. Secondary address: 2402 Hawkins 81321. Phone: (505) 325-3541. Fax: (505) 327-5796. Web Site:www.kisscountry979fm.com Licensee: Winton Road Broadcasting Co. LLC (group owner; (acq 5-3-01; grpsl). Population served: 250,000 Fleischman & Walsh. Format: Country. News staff: one; News: 4 hrs wkly. Target aud: 18-49; young sophisticated adults. ♦Dan Buchta, gen mgr; Randy KLock, gen sls mgr.

KRTZ(FM)— December 1981: 98.7 mhz; 27 kw. 2,900 ft TL: N37 13 10 W108 48 26. Stereo. Hrs open: 24 2402 Hawkins, 81321. Phone: (970) 565-6565. Fax: (970) 565-8567.E-mail: radio@krtzradio.com Web Site:krtzradio.com Population served: 20,000 Format: Adult contemp. News staff: one; News: 3 hrs wkly. Target aud: 20-55. Spec prog: Americian Indian one hr, gospel one hr wkly. ♦Desiree Burnham, prom mgr; Kelly Truner, progmg dir; Jim Burt, engrg dir; Kelly Turner, local news ed & sports cmtr.

***KSJD(FM)**— July 1990: 91.5 mhz; 1.2 kw. Ant 312 ft TL: N37 28 57 W108 30 34. Stereo. Hrs open: 24 33057 Hwy. 160, Mancos, 81328. Phone: (970) 564-0808. Fax: (970) 564-0434.E-mail: ifo@ksjd.com Web Site:www.ksjd.org Licensee: San Juan Basin Technical School. Format: Diverse public radio. News staff: one. Target aud: 16-30; college level. Spec prog: Relg one hr wkly. ♦Jeff Pope, gen mgr; John Hall, progmg dir.

KVFC(AM)— Feb 27, 1955: 740 khz; 1 kw-D, 250 w-N, DA-N. TL: N37 20 58 W108 32 29. Hrs open: 24 2402 Hawkins, 81321. Phone: (970) 565-6565. Fax: (970) 565-8567.E-mail: feedback@kvfcradio.com Web Site:www.kvfcradio.com Licensee: Winton Road Broadcasting Co. LLC (group owner; acq 12-18-01; with co-located FM). Population served: 10,000 Natl. Network: ABC, CNN Radio, Westwood One, . Format: News/talk. News staff: 2; News: 15 hrs wkly. Target aud: 18-54; young adults. ♦Anthony Brandon, CEO; L. Rogers Brandon, COO; Dan Buchta, gen mgr; Kelly Turner, opns mgr, news dir, pub affrs dir; Keri-Lyn Riley, gen sls mgr; Jim Burt, chief of engrg.

***KZET(FM)**—Not on air, target date: unknown: 90.3 mhz; 100 w. Ant 328 ft TL: N37 28 57 W108 30 34. Hrs open: Box 116, 81321. Phone: (970) 749-9117. Licensee: Community Radio Project. ♦Jeffery Pope, gen mgr.

Craig

***KPYR(FM)**— 2005: 88.3 mhz; 250 w. Ant 889 ft TL: N40 33 50 W107 36 40. Hrs open:
Rebroadcasts KCFR(AM) Denver 100%.
Colorado Public Radio, 7409 S. Alton Ct., Centennial, 80112. Phone: (303) 871-9191. Fax: (303) 733-3319. Web Site:www.cpr.org Licensee: Public Broadcasting of Colorado Inc. Format: News. ♦Max Wycisk, pres.

KRAI(AM)— 1948: 550 khz; 5 kw-D, 500 w-N, DA-N. TL: N40 32 45 W107 31 52. Hrs open: 19 Box 65, 81626. Secondary address: 1111 W. Victory Way. 81626. Phone: (970) 824-6574. Fax: (970) 826-4581.E-mail:

frank@krai.com Web Site:www.krai.com Licensee: Wild West Radio Inc. (acq 5-89). Population served: 50,000 Natl. Network: Westwood One, CNN Radio, . Wire Svc: AP Format: Country. News staff: 3; News: 12 hrs wkly. Target aud: 25-54. Spec prog: Farm one hr wkly. ♦Tammie Hanel, pres & stn mgr.

KRAI-FM— April 1976: 93.7 mhz; 100 kw. 980 ft TL: N40 34 35 W107 36 29. Stereo. Hrs open: 24 Box 65, 81626. Secondary address: 1111 W. Victory Way. 81626. Phone: (970) 824-6574. Fax: (970) 826-4581. Web Site:www.krai.com Population served: 45,000 Wire Svc: AP Format: Adult contemp. News staff: 3; News: 4 hrs wkly. Target aud: 18-49. ♦Frank Hanel Jr., gen mgr; Tammie Hannel, stn mgr.

Crested Butte

***KBUT(FM)—** Dec 20, 1986: 90.3 mhz; 250 w. -667 ft TL: N38 52 19 W106 58 44. Stereo. Hrs open: 24 Box 308, 81224. Secondary address: 508 Maroon Ave. 81224. Phone: (970) 349-5225. Phone: (970) 349-7444. Fax: (970) 349-6440.E-mail: kbut@kbut.org Web Site:www.kbut.org Licensee: Crested Butte Mountain Educational Radio Inc. Population served: 2,500 Natl. Network: NPR, PRI, . Garvey, Schubert & Barer. Format: Educational, diversified music, news/talk. News staff: one; News: 72 hrs wkly. Target aud: General. ♦Dave Clayton, gen mgr; Kim Carroll-Bosler, stn mgr & dev dir; Erin Roberts, progmg dir; Chad Reich, mus dir.

Crook

***KOOW(FM)—**Not on air, target date: unknown: 88.1 mhz; 50 kw vert. Ant 403 ft TL: N40 45 51 W102 42 42. Hrs open: 282 Country Estate Dr., Springer, OK, 73458. Phone: (580) 653-2777. Licensee: Ron Elmore Ministries Inc. ♦Ron Elmore, pres.

Del Norte

KHRJ(AM)—Not on air, target date: unknown: 1490 khz; 1 kw-U. TL: N37 40 21 W106 21 12. Hrs open: 8320 W. 66th Ave., Arvada, 80004. Phone: (303) 431-0103. Licensee: Better Life Ministries. ♦Claud M. Pettit, pres.

Delta

KDTA(AM)— Jan 14, 1955: 1400 khz; 1 kw-U. TL: N38 45 38 W108 05 28. Hrs open: 24
Simulcast of KJOL(AM) Grand Junction 100%.
1354 E. Sherwood Dr., Grand Junction, 81501. Phone: (970) 254-5565. Fax: (970) 254-5550.E-mail: info@kjol.org Web Site:www.kjol.org Licensee: United Ministries. (group owner; (acq 11-16-2004; $88,000). Population served: 30,000 Format: Christian talk, music. ♦Ken Andrews, gen mgr.

KKNN(FM)— December 1985: 95.1 mhz; 100 kw. 969 ft TL: N38 52 40 W108 13 30. Stereo. Hrs open: 24 315 Kennedy Ave., Grand Junction, 81501. Phone: (970) 242-7788. Fax: (970) 243-0567.E-mail: info@95rock.com Web Site:www.95rock.com Licensee: Cumulus Licensing Corp. Group owner: Cumulus Media Inc. (acq 1-00). Population served: 225,000 Natl. Rep: Katz Radio,. Format: Classic rock. News staff: one; News: 6 hrs wkly. Target aud: 18-49; men. ♦Lewis Dickey Jr., CEO, pres; John Dickey, exec VP; Kevin Wodlinger, gen mgr; Mike Shafer, opns mgr.

***KPRU(FM)—** 2001: 103.3 mhz; 12 kw. Ant 987 ft TL: N38 52 40 W108 13 32. Hrs open: Colorado Public Radio, 7409 S. Alton Ct., Centennial, 80112. Phone: (303) 871-9191. Fax: (303) 733-3319. Web Site:www.cpr.org Licensee: Public Broadcasting of Colorado Inc. Format: Classical. ♦Max Wycisk, pres; Sue Coughlin, dev VP; Sean Nethery, progmg dir; Bob Hensler, chief of engrg; David Gomez, traf mgr.

Denver

KALC(FM)— June 21, 1965: 105.9 mhz; 100 kw. 900 ft TL: N39 43 59 W105 14 12. Stereo. Hrs open: 4700 S. Syracuse St., Suite 1050, 80237. Phone: (303) 967-2700. Fax: (303) 967-2747.E-mail: info@alice106.com Web Site:www.alice106.com Licensee: Entercom Denver License LLC. Group owner: Entercom Communications Corp. (acq 5-1-2002; $88 million). Population served: 1,534,800 Natl. Rep: Christal,. Format: Hot adult contemp. Target aud: 18-34; women. ♦Mikey Goldenberg, progmg dir; Jeff Garrett, chief of engrg; Stephanie Walrath, traf mgr.

KBJD(AM)— 2001: 1650 khz; 10 kw-D, 1 kw-N. TL: N39 47 56 W104 58 12. Hrs open: 24 3131 S. Vaughn Way, Suite 601, Aurora, 80114. Phone: (303) 750-5687. Fax: (303) 696-8063.E-mail: production @salemdenver.com Web Site:www.710knus.com Licensee: Salem Media of Colorado Inc. Group owner: Salem Communications Corp. Format: religious talk in Spanish. News staff: 3; News: 15 hrs wkly. ♦Brian Taylor, gen mgr.

KBNO(AM)— May 15, 1948: 1280 khz; 5 kw-U, DA-2. TL: N39 36 05 W104 58 49. Hrs open: 24 600 Grant St., Suite 600, 80203. Phone: (303) 733-5266. Fax: (303) 733-5242.E-mail: kbno@kbno.net Web Site:www.kbno.net Licensee: Latino Communications LLC (group owner; acq 11-21-00; $3.3 million). Population served: 1,650,000 Format: Sp. News staff: 27; News: 21 hrs wkly. Target aud: 25-54; male. ♦Michael Ferrufino, VP, opns VP; Zee Ferrufino, CEO, CFO & gen mgr.

KBPI(FM)— June 19, 1962: 106.7 mhz; 100 kw. 987 ft TL: N39 43 59 W105 14 12. Stereo. Hrs open: 24 4695 S. Monaco St., 80237. Phone: (303) 713-8000. Fax: (303) 713-8744.E-mail: info@kbpi.com Web Site:www.kbpi.com Licensee: Citicasters Licenses Inc. (NEW). Group owner: Clear Channel Communications Inc. (acq 5-4-99; grpsl). Population served: 514,678 Natl. Network: ABC, . Format: AOR. Target aud: 25-34; men. ♦Lee Larsen, gen mgr, gen sls mgr; Willie Hung, progmg dir; Karl Schipper, chief of engrg.

***KCFR(AM)—** Mar 4, 1956: 1340 khz; 1 kw-U. TL: N39 39 34 W105 00 44. (CP: TL: N39 41 01 W105 00 25). Hrs open: 24 7409 S. Alton Ct., Centennial, 80112. Phone: (303) 871-9191. Fax: (303) 733-3319. Web Site:www.cpr.org Licensee: Public Broadcasting of Colorado Inc. (acq 11-30-2000; $4.2 million). Population served: 1,250,000 Format: NPR news. ♦Max Wycisk, pres, gen mgr; Sue Coughlin, dev VP.

***KCFR-FM—** November 1970: 90.1 mhz; 50 kw. Ant 910 ft TL: N39 43 49 W105 14 59. Stereo. Hrs open: 24 7409 S.Alton Ct., Centennial, 80112. Phone: (303) 871-9191. Fax: (303) 733-3319.E-mail: info@cpr.org Web Site:www.cpr.org Licensee: Public Broadcasting of Colorado Inc. (acq 1991; 10-28-91). Population served: 2,100,000 Natl. Network: NPR, . Arter & Hadden. Format: News/talk. News staff: 8; News: 50 hrs wkly. Target aud: General. ♦Max Wycisk, pres; Jenny Gentry, exec VP; Sue Coughlin, dev VP; Sean Nethery, progmg dir; Robert Hensler, engrg VP.

KEZW(AM)—See Aurora

***KGNU(AM)—** Jan 1, 1954: 1390 khz; 5 kw-D, DA. TL: N39 39 29 W105 00 49. Stereo. Hrs open: 24
Simulcast of KGNU-FM, Boulder 95%.
4700 Walnut St., Boulder, 80301. Phone: (303) 449-4885.E-mail: info@kgnuam.com Web Site:www.kgnu.org Licensee: Boulder Community Broadcast Association Inc. (acq 11-26-2004; $4.2 million). Format: Eclectic. ♦Marty Durlin, gen mgr.

KHOW(AM)— 1925: 630 khz; 5 kw-U, DA-2. TL: N39 54 36 W104 54 50. Stereo. Hrs open: 24 4695 S. Monaco, 80237. Phone: (303) 713-8000. Fax: (303) 713-8738.E-mail: info@khow.com Web Site:www.khow.com Licensee: Citicasters Licenses L.P. Group owner: Clear Channel Communications Inc. (acq 5-4-99; grpsl). Population served: 100,000 Format: Talk. Target aud: 25-54. ♦Lee Larsen, gen mgr; Ron Smith, opns mgr; Jan Whitbeck, prom dir, prom mgr; Kristine Olinger, progmg dir; Jan Chadwell, chief of engrg.

KIMN(FM)— Aug 1, 1959: 100.3 mhz; 100 kw. 331 ft TL: N39 41 06 W105 04 05. (CP: Ant 1,705 ft. TL: N39 54 48 W105 17 32). Stereo. Hrs open: 24 1560 Broadway, Suite 1100, 80202. Phone: (303) 832-5665. Fax: (303) 832-7000.E-mail: info@mix100.com Web Site:www.mix100.com Licensee: Wilks License Co.-Denver LLC. Group owner: Infinity Broadcasting Corp. (acq 3-5-2009; grpsl). Population served: 514,678 Natl. Rep: Christal,. Format: Hot adult contemp. Target aud: 35-44; women. Spec prog: Pub affrs 2 hrs wkly. ♦Don Howe, gen mgr.

KKZN(AM)—See Thornton

KLDC(AM)— June 5, 1954: 1220 khz; 660 w-D, 11 w-N. TL: N39 41 00 W105 00 24. Hrs open: 2150 W. 29th Ave., Suite 300, 80211. Phone: (303) 433-5500. Fax: (303) 433-1555.E-mail: info@crawfordbroadcasting.com Web Site:www.crawfordbroadcasting.com Licensee: KLZ Radio Inc. Group owner: Crawford Broadcasting Co. (acq 8-11-99; $1.5 million). Population served: 280,000 Fisher, Wayland, Cooper, Leader & Zaragoza L.L.P. Format: Gospel. Target aud: 24-55; general. Spec prog: Black 2 hrs wkly. ♦Mike Triem, gen mgr.

KLDV(FM)—See Morrison

KLVZ(AM)—See Brighton

KLZ(AM)— Mar 10, 1922: 560 khz; 5 kw-U, DA-1. TL: N39 50 36 W104 57 14. Hrs open: 24 2150 W. 29th Ave., Suite 300, 80211. Phone: (303) 433-5500. Fax: (303) 433-1555.E-mail: klzinfo@crawfordbroadcasting.com Web Site:www.crawfordbroadcasting.com Licensee: KLZ Radio Inc. Group owner: Crawford Broadcasting Co. (acq 6-30-92; $1.5 million; 7-20-92). Population served: 2,000,000 Format: Christian music. Target aud: 25-54; men. ♦Mike Triem, gen mgr.

KMXA(AM)—(Aurora, Sept 12, 1972: 1090 khz; 50 kw-D, 500 w-N, DA-2. TL: N39 39 53 W104 39 24. Stereo. Hrs open: 777 Grant St., 5th Floor, 80203. Phone: (303) 721-9210. Fax: (303) 832-3410. Licensee: Entravision Holdings LLC. Group owner: Entravision Communications Corp. (acq 3-14-2000; grpsl). Format: Sp adult hits. Target aud: 18-54; Hispanics. ♦Mario Carrera, gen mgr.

KNRV(AM)—See Englewood

KNUS(AM)— 1941: 710 khz; 5 kw-U, DA-1. TL: N39 57 19 W104 51 01. Hrs open: 24 3131 S. Vaughn Way, Suite 601, Aurora, 80014. Phone: (303) 750-5687. Fax: (303) 696-8063.E-mail: production @salemdenver.com Web Site:www.710knus.com Licensee: Salem Media of Colorado Inc. Group owner: Salem Communications Corp. (acq 1996; $1.2 million). Population served: 1,568,200 Format: News/talk. News staff: 3; News: 15 hrs wkly. Target aud: 35-54; Adults. ♦Brian Taylor, gen mgr.

KOA(AM)— Dec 15, 1924: 850 khz; 50 kw-U. TL: N39 30 22 W104 45 57. Hrs open: 24 4695 S. Monaco St., 80237. Phone: (303) 713-8000. Fax: (303) 713-8735.E-mail: info@850koa.com Web Site:www.850koa.com Licensee: Citicasters Licenses Inc. (NEW). Group owner: Clear Channel Communications Inc. (acq 5-4-99; grpsl). Population served: 514,678 Natl. Network: CBS, . Wire Svc: CBS Format: News/talk, sports. Target aud: 25-54. ♦Lee Larsen, gen mgr; Ron Smith, opns mgr; Kristine Olinger, progmg dir; Jan Chadwell, chief of engrg.

KOSI(FM)— Mar 3, 1968: 101.1 mhz; 100 kw. 1,624 ft TL: N39 43 45 W105 14 06. Stereo. Hrs open: 24 4700 S. Syracuse, Suite 1050, 80237. Phone: (303) 967-2700. Fax: (303) 967-2747.E-mail: info@kosi101.com Web Site:www.kosi101.com Licensee: Entercom Denver License LLC. Group owner: Entercom Communications Corp. (acq 7-24-02; with KEZW(AM) Aurora). Population served: 300,000 Format: Adult contemp. News staff: one; News: 5 hrs wkly. Target aud: 25-54; women/families. ♦Glynn Alan, gen sls mgr; Dave Symonds, progmg dir.

***KPOF(AM)—** Mar 9, 1928: 910 khz; 5 kw-D, 1 kw-N. TL: N39 50 47 W105 01 59. Hrs open: 24 3455 W. 83rd Ave., Westminster, 80031. Phone: (303) 428-0910. Fax: (303) 429-0910.E-mail: info@am91.org Web Site:www.am91.org Licensee: Pillar of Fire Corp. (group owner; acq 1928). Population served: 2,000,000 Natl. Network: Moody, . Format: Christian. Target aud: 18-plus; mature adult and families. ♦Robert Dallenbach, pres; Jack H. Pelon, gen mgr; Jerry Bauer, opns mgr.

KPTT(FM)— Mar 31, 1968: 95.7 mhz; 100 kw. Ant 725 ft TL: N39 43 59 W105 14 10. Stereo. Hrs open: 4695 S. Monaco, 80237. Phone: (303) 713-8000. Fax: (303) 713-8738.E-mail: info@kpttfm.theparty.com Web Site:www.theparty.com Licensee: Citicasters Licenses L.P. Population served: 180,000 Format: Adult contemp 70s, 80s & 90s. Target aud: General. ♦Joe Bevilacqua, progmg dir.

KQKS(FM)—See Lakewood

KQMT(FM)— Oct 2, 1959: 99.5 mhz; 100 kw. 279 ft TL: N39 41 01 W105 00 25. (CP: Ant 1,311 ft.). Stereo. Hrs open: 24 4700 S, Syracuse St., Suite 1050, 80237. Phone: (303) 967-2700. Fax: (303) 967-2747.E-mail: info@995themountain.com Web Site:www.995themountain.com Licensee: Entercom Denver License LLC. Group owner: Entercom Communications Corp. (acq 3-21-03). Population served: 150,000 Format: Timeless rock. News: 4 hrs wkly. Target aud: 25-54; upscale, educated. ♦Ray Quinn, gen mgr; Beau Raines, progmg dir.

KRFX(FM)— June 1, 1961: 103.5 mhz; 100 kw. 1,045 ft TL: N39 43 50 W105 14 07. Stereo. Hrs open: Prog sep from AM 4695 S. Monaco St., 80237. Phone: (303) 713-8000. Fax: (303) 713-8744.E-mail: info@krfxfm@thefox.com Web Site:www.thefox.com Format: Classic rock. Target aud: 25-54. ♦Garner Goin, progmg dir; Karl Schipper, chief of engrg.

KRKS(AM)— Aug 1, 1953: 990 khz; 5 kw-D, 390 w-N, DA-N. TL: N39 41 06 W105 04 05. Hrs open: 24 3131 S. Vaughn Way, Suite 601, Aurora, 80114. Phone: (303) 750-5687. Fax: (303) 696-8063. Web Site:www.krks.com Licensee: Salem Media of Colorado Inc. Group owner: Salem Communications Corp. (acq 10-93; $400,000). Format: Relg. Target aud: 25 plus. ♦Brian Taylor, gen mgr & stn mgr.

KRWZ(AM)— July 4, 1922: 950 khz; 5 kw-U, DA-1. TL: N39 52 30 W104 56 00. Stereo. Hrs open: 24 7800 E. Orchard Rd., Suite 400, Greenwood Village, 80111. Phone: (303) 321-0950. Fax: (303) 321-3383. Licensee: Lincoln Financial Media Co. of Colorado. (group owner) (acq 4-3-2006; grpsl). Population served: 1,700,000 Natl. Rep: CBS Radio,. Format: Oldies. ♦Robert Call, sr VP, VP, gen mgr; Steve Price, sls dir, gen sls mgr; Randy Weidner, natl sls mgr, rgnl sls mgr; Dwayne Taylor, mktg dir, prom dir; Tim Spence, progmg dir; Simone Seikaly, news dir, pub affrs dir; Brad Hart, engrg dir.

***KUVO(FM)**— Aug 29, 1985: 89.3 mhz; 22.5 kw. 910 ft TL: N39 43 49 W105 14 59. Stereo. Hrs open: 24 PO Box 2040, 80201-2040. Secondary address: 2900 Welton St., Suite 200 80205. Phone: (303) 480-9272. Fax: (303) 291-0757.E-mail: info@kuvo.org Web Site:www.kuvo.org Licensee: Denver Educational Broadcasting. Natl. Network: NPR, PRI, . Haley, Bader & Potts. Format: Jazz. Target aud: 25-49. Spec prog: Sp 15 hrs wkly. ♦Carlos Lando, COO, gen mgr, progmg dir; Gene Craven, CEO & pres.

KXKL-FM— Dec 1, 1956: 105.1 mhz; 100 kw. 1,200 ft TL: N39 36 00 W105 12 35. (CP: Ant 1,168 ft.). Hrs open: 24 1560 Broadway, Suite 1100, 80202. Phone: (303) 832-5665. Fax: (303) 832-7000.E-mail: info@kool105.com Web Site:www.kool105.com Licensee: Wilks License Co.-Denver LLC. Group owner: Infinity Broadcasting Corp. (acq 3-5-2009; grpsl). Format: Oldies. ♦Don Howe, gen mgr; Brenda Egger, gen sls mgr; Keith Abrams, progmg VP & progmg dir; Barry Walters, chief of engrg.

KYGO-FM— Dec 1, 1953: 98.5 mhz; 100 kw. 1,820 ft TL: N39 40 35 W105 29 09. Stereo. Hrs open: 24 Prog sep from AM 7800 E. Orchard Rd., Suite 400, Greenwood Village, 80111. Phone: (303) 321—0950. Fax: (303) 321-3383.E-mail: info@kygo.com Web Site:www.kygo.com Format: Country. Target aud: 25-54. ♦Joel Burke, progmg dir; Garrott Doll, mus dir.

Dolores

KKDC(FM)— Jan 6, 2004: 93.3 mhz; 50 kw. Ant 338 ft TL: N37 27 59 W108 31 28. Stereo. Hrs open: P.O. Drawer P, Durango, 81302. Secondary address: 310 Railroad Phone: (970) 259-4444. Fax: (970) 247-1005. Web Site:www.radiodolores.com Licensee: Four Corners Broadcasting L.L.C. (group owner). Format: Classic rock. News staff: 1. Target aud: 35-54. ♦Allen Brill, CEO; Ward Holmes, VP; Ray McDonnell, stn mgr.

***KTCF(FM)**— 2004: 89.5 mhz; 500 w. Ant 174 ft TL: N37 28 07 W108 32 48. Stereo. Hrs open:
Rebroadcasts KTLF(FM) Colorado Springs 100%.
1665 Briargate Blvd., Suite 100, Colorado Springs, 80920. Phone: (719) 593-0600. Fax: (719) 593-2399.E-mail: lightpraise@ktlf.org Web Site:www.ktlf.org Licensee: Educational Communications of Colorado Springs Inc. Format: Christian music. Target aud: 45-60; Christian. ♦Lynn Carmichael, progmg dir.

Dove Creek

KDVC(FM)— 2008: Stn currently dark. 102.5 mhz; 3.8 kw horiz. Ant 1,046 ft TL: N37 56 29 W108 54 27. Hrs open: 980 N. Michigan Ave., Suite 1880, Chicago, IL, 60611. Phone: (312) 204-9900. Licensee: College Creek Media LLC. ♦Neal J. Robinson, pres.

Durango

KDGO(AM)— Apr 18, 1958: 1240 khz; 1 kw-U. TL: N37 18 17 W107 51 10. Hrs open: 24 1911 Main Ave., Suite 100, 81301. Phone: (970) 247-1240. Fax: (970) 247-1771.E-mail: dina@997thepoint.com Web Site:www.kdgoam.com Licensee: Winton Road Broadcasting Co. LLC. (group owner; (acq 6-1-2001; grpsl). Population served: 28,000 Natl. Network: ABC, . Format: News/talk. News staff: one. Target aud: 35-55. ♦Dan Buchta, gen mgr, opns mgr; Ryan Nutter, progmg dir.

***KDNG(FM)**—Not on air, target date: unknown: 89.3 mhz; 200 w. Ant 321 ft TL: N37 15 44 W107 53 58. Hrs open: Box 737, Ignacio, 81137-0737. Phone: (970) 563-0255. Fax: (970) 563-0399.E-mail: info@ksut.org Licensee: KUTE Inc. ♦Eddie Box Jr., pres.

***KDUR(FM)**— 1975: 91.9 mhz; 225 w. -447 ft TL: N37 16 31 W107 52 00. Stereo. Hrs open: Fort Lewis College, 1000 Rim Dr., 81301. Phone: (970) 247-7262.E-mail: stoffer_n@fortlewis.edu Web Site:www.kdur.org Licensee: Board of Trustees for Fort Lewis College. Population served: 12,000 Natl. Network: PRI, . Format: Div. Spec prog: Bluegrass 6 hrs, blues 6 hrs, class 6 hrs, jazz 9 hrs, Native American folk 3 hrs wkly. ♦Nancy Stoffer, stn mgr.

KIQX(FM)— Oct 15, 1982: 101.3 mhz; 100 kw. 439 ft TL: N37 15 45 W107 54 07. Stereo. Hrs open: 24 P.O. Drawer P, 81302. Secondary address: 190 Turner Drive, Suite G 81303. Phone: (970) 259-4444. Fax: (970) 247-1005.E-mail: fcb@frontier.net Web Site:www.radiodurango.com Licensee: Four Corners Broadcasting L.L.C. (group owner) Population served: 39,300 Natl. Network: CBS, . Akin, Gump, Strauss, Hauer & Feld. Format: Adult contemp. News staff: 2; News: 5 hrs wkly. Target aud: 25-54; mainstream business professionals & families. Spec prog: Jazz 7 hrs wkly. ♦Allen H. Brill, chmn; Ward Holmes, VP.

KIUP(AM)— Dec 10, 1935: 930 khz; 5 kw-D, 1 kw-N, DA-N. TL: N37 13 45 W107 51 49. Hrs open: 24 Drawer P, 81302. Secondary address: 190 Turner Drive, Suite G 81303. Phone: (970) 259-4444. Fax: (970) 247-1005.E-mail: fcb@frontier.net Web Site:www.radiodurango.com Licensee: Four Corners Broadcasting LLC. (group owner; (acq 4-1-96; with co-located FM). Population served: 150,000 Natl. Network: ESPN Radio, . Akin, Gump, Strauss, Hauer & Feld. Wire Svc: AP Format: Sports. News staff: 2; News: 5 hrs wkly. Target aud: 12 plus. Spec prog: Rockies-AV's-Flc sports. ♦Allen Brill, CEO; Ward S. Holmes, VP.

KLLV(AM)—(Breen, Sept 19, 1984: 550 khz; 1.8 kw-D. TL: N37 11 02 W108 04 54. Hrs open: 24 Box 2220, 81302. Secondary address: 14780 Hwy. 140, Breen 81326. Phone: (970) 247-8955. Licensee: Daystar Radio Ltd. Population served: 2,000,000 Format: Inspirational. News: New progmg 2 hrs wkly. Target aud: General. ♦Sharon Harper, gen mgr; Debbie Baker, progmg dir; Jim Alexander, chief of engrg.

KPTE(FM)— July 1, 1995: 99.7 mhz; 9.2 kw. 1,128 ft TL: N37 19 59 W107 49 13. Hrs open: 1911 Main Ave., Suite 100, 81301. Phone: (970) 247-1240. Fax: (970) 247-1771.E-mail: dina@997thepoint.com Web Site:997thepoint.com Licensee: Winton Road Broadcasting Co. LLC. Population served: 70,000 Format: Hot adult contemp. Target aud: 18-44.

KRSJ(FM)— Dec 4, 1972: 100.5 mhz; 29.7 kw. Ant 1,994 ft TL: N37 21 46 W107 47 37. Stereo. Hrs open: 24 Drawer P, 81302. Secondary address: 190 Turner Drive, Suite G 81303. Phone: (970) 259-4444. Fax: (970) 247-1005. Web Site:www.radiodurango.com Licensee: Four Corners Broadcasting LLC. Population served: 170,000 Natl. Network: Fox News Radio, . Wire Svc: AP Format: C&W. News staff: 2; News: 6 hrs wkly. Target aud: 25 plus. ♦Allen Brill, CEO; Ward Holmes, VP.

***KTDU(FM)**— May 2, 2005: 88.5 mhz; 4 kw vert. Ant 371 ft TL: N37 15 43 W107 54 24. Stereo. Hrs open:
Rebroadcasts KTLF(FM) Colorado Springs 100%.
1665 Briargate Blvd., Suite 100, Colorado Springs, 80920. Phone: (719) 593-0600. Fax: (719) 593-2399.E-mail: lightpraise@ktcf.org Web Site:www.ktlf.org Licensee: Educational Communications of Colorado Springs Inc. Format: Christian music. Target aud: 45-60; Christian. ♦Lynn Carmichael, progmg dir.

Eads

KEHT(AM)—Not on air, target date: unknown: 1450 khz; 250 w-U. TL: N38 29 22 W102 45 17. Hrs open: 8320 W. 66th Ave., Arvada, 80004. Phone: (303) 431-0103. Licensee: Better Life Ministries. ♦Claud M. Pettit, pres.

Eagle

KTUN(FM)— Apr 16, 1984: 101.7 mhz; 12 kw. Ant 2,211 ft TL: N39 44 18 W106 47 58. Stereo. Hrs open: 24 Box 7205, Avon, 81620. Phone: (970) 949-0140. Fax: (970) 949-1464.E-mail: info@kskeradio.com Licensee: NRC Broadcasting Mountain Group LLC. (group owner; (acq 5-1-2007; grpsl). Arter & Hadden. Format: Classic rock. News staff: 2; News: 4 hrs wkly. Target aud: 25-63; affluent locals & tourists. ♦Meredith Fox, opns mgr, progmg dir; Steve Wodlinger, gen mgr & pub affrs dir.

Eckley

KECK(FM)—Not on air, target date: unknown: 95.3 mhz; 100 kw. Ant 339 ft TL: N40 00 33 W102 45 35. Hrs open: Box 753, Lamar, 81052-0753. Phone: (719) 336-4227. Licensee: Arnold Broadcasting Inc. (acq 7-31-2008; grpsl). ♦William Arnold, gen mgr.

El Jebel

KCUF(FM)— 2006: 100.5 mhz; 6 kw. Ant 295 ft TL: N39 18 56 W106 57 32. Hrs open: 5551 Ridgewood Dr., Suite 501, Naples, FL, 34108. Phone: (239) 263-7700. Fax: (239) 263-0998. Licensee: BS&T Wireless Inc. Leventhal, Senter & Lerman. ♦David G. Budd, gen mgr.

Englewood

KNRV(AM)— 1951: 1150 khz; 10 kw-D, 1 kw-N, DA-2. TL: N39 36 18 W104 50 25. Hrs open: 24 2821 So. Parker Rd., Suite 1205, Aurora, 80014. Phone: (303) 696-5970. Fax: (303) 696-5966.E-mail: info@knrvam.com Web Site:www.onda115am.com Licensee: New Radio Venture Inc. (group owner; Population served: 400,000 Format: Sp/news/talk. ♦Annette Lavina, gen sls mgr; Julio Parra, chief of engrg.

Estes Park

KEPL(AM)— Aug 19, 1967: 1470 khz; 1 kw-D, 53 w-N. TL: N40 20 15 W105 31 36. Hrs open: 24 Box 2810, 80517. Secondary address: 184 E. Elkhorn Ave. 80517. Phone: (970) 586-9555. Fax: (970) 586-9561.E-mail: keplradio@yahoo.com Licensee: WP Broadcasting of Colorado LLC. (acq 6-30-2007). Population served: 10,000 Format: Talk. Target aud: General. ♦Vince Lupo, gen mgr.

***KEZD(FM)**—Not on air, target date: unknown: 90.7 mhz; 200 w. Ant 43 ft TL: N40 21 38 W105 31 12. Hrs open: 87 Jasper Lake Rd., Loveland, 80537. Phone: (970) 669-9200. Licensee: Cedar Cove Broadcasting Inc. ♦Victor A. Michael Jr., pres.

KRKY-FM— Apr 6, 1998: 102.1 mhz; 175 w. Ant 1,007 ft TL: N40 04 19 W105 21 11. Hrs open: 24 1130 Ski Hill Rd., Suite 240, Breckenridge, 80424. Phone: (970) 453-2234. Fax: (970) 453-5425. Licensee: NRC Broadcasting Inc. (group owner; (acq 8-31-2006; exchange for KSKE-FM Vail). Natl. Network: ABC, . Format: Triple A. Target aud: Urban adults 19-34; Black, Hispanic, White. ♦Lisa Korry Cheek, gen mgr.

Evergreen

KXPK(FM)— June 8, 1994: 96.5 mhz; 93 kw. 328 ft TL: N39 40 18 W105 13 12. Hrs open: 24 777 Grant St., 5th Fl., Denver, 80203. Phone: (303) 721-9210. Fax: (303) 832-3410. Licensee: Entravision Holdings LLC. Group owner: Entravision Communications Corp. (acq 5-1-02; $47.5 million). Format: Rgnl Mexican. News staff: one. ♦Mario Carrera, gen mgr.

Fort Collins

KCOL(AM)—(Wellington, Jan 12, 1959: 600 khz; 1 kw-D, 100 w-N, DA-2. TL: N40 35 34 W105 06 18. Hrs open: 4270 Bryd Dr., Loveland, 80538. Phone: (970) 482-5991. Fax: (970) 482-5994.E-mail: info@kcol.com Web Site:www.kcol.com Licensee: Jacor Broadcasting of Colorado Inc. Group owner: Clear Channel Communications Inc. (acq 5-8-98; $6.1 million with co-located FM). Population served: 200000 Natl. Rep: McGavren Guild,. Format: News/talk. Target aud: 35 plus. Spec prog: Farm 2 hrs, relg one hr, sports talk 7 hrs wkly. ♦Stu Haskell, stn mgr; Amy White, prom dir; Rich Bircumshaw, news dir; Dave Agnew, chief of engrg.

***KCSU-FM**— Sept 20, 1964: 90.5 mhz; 10 kw. -355 ft TL: N40 36 00 W105 09 21. Stereo. Hrs open: 24 Lory Student Ctr., Box 13, 80523. Phone: (970) 491-7611. Fax: (970) 491-1690.E-mail: program@colostate.edu Web Site:www.kcsufm.com Licensee: Colorado State Board of Agriculture. Population served: 250,000 Arter & Hadden. Format: Progsv. News: 3 hrs wkly. Target aud: 18-34; general. Spec prog: Hip-hop 3 hrs, jazz 3 hrs, Black 3 hrs wkly. ♦Christina Dickinson, gen mgr & stn mgr.

***KGCO(FM)**— 2005: 88.3 mhz; 1 w horiz, 90 w vert. Ant 941 ft TL: N40 29 36 W105 10 52. Hrs open: 24
Rebroadcasts KLVR(FM) Middletown, CA 100%.
2351 Sunset Blvd., Suite 170-218, Rocklin, CA, 95765. Phone: (916) 251-1600. Fax: (916) 251-1650.E-mail: klove@klove.com Web Site:www.klove.com Licensee: Educational Media Foundation. Group owner: EMF Broadcasting (acq 10-2-2003; grpsl). Natl. Network: K-Love, . Shaw Pittman. Format: Contemp Christian. News staff: 3. Target aud: 25-44; Judeo Christian female. ♦Richard Jenkins, pres; Mike Novak, VP, progmg dir; Lloyd Parker, gen mgr; Ed Lenane, opns dir; Keith Whipple, dev dir; Eric Allen, natl sls mgr; David Pierce, progmg mgr; Jon Rivers, mus dir; Ed Lenane, news dir; Sam Wallington, engrg dir; Arthur Vassar, traf mgr; Karen Johnson, news rptr.

KIIX(AM)— Mar 1, 1947: 1410 khz; 1 kw-U, DA-N. TL: N40 35 34 W105 06 18. Hrs open: 24 4270 Byrd Dr., Loveland, 80538. Phone: (970) 482-5991. Fax: (970) 482-5994.E-mail: info@1410kiix.com Web Site:www.1410kiix.com Licensee: Citicasters Licenses Inc. (NEW).

Group owner: Clear Channel Communications Inc. (acq 5-4-99; grpsl). Population served: 150000 Format: Sports. News staff: 2; News: 35 hrs wkly. Target aud: 18-54; educated, affluent, professional. ♦Stu Haskell, VP & gen mgr; Kathy Arias, gen sls mgr, rgnl sls mgr; Amy White, prom VP, prom dir; Randy Barnard, progmg dir; Rich Bircumshaw, news dir; Dave Agnew, chief of engrg.

KPAW(FM)— July 27, 1975: 107.9 mhz; 100 kw. Ant 470 ft TL: N40 40 50 W104 56 32. Stereo. Hrs open: 24 4270 Byrd Dr., Loveland, 80538. Phone: (970) 482-5991. Fax: (970) 482-5994. Web Site:www.1079thebear.com Licensee: Citicasters Licenses Inc. (NEW). Format: Classic rock. Target aud: 25-54; men. ♦Stu Haskell, stn mgr; Jefferson Chase, opns VP, progmg dir; Collen Taylor, prom dir; Rich Bircumshaw, news dir.

***KRFC(FM)**—Not on air, target date: 3/1/03: 88.9 mhz; 10 w horiz, 3 kw vert. Ant 216 ft TL: N40 34 53 W104 54 20. Hrs open: 24 619 S. College Ave., Suite #4, 80524. Phone: (970) 221-5075. Fax: (970) 221-5075.E-mail: pam@krfcfm.org Web Site:www.krfcfm.org Licensee: Public Radio for the Front Range. Format: Var/div. ♦Pam Turner, stn mgr; Carole Lundgren, dev dir; Dennis Bigelow, mus dir.

Fort Morgan

KFTM(AM)— May 22, 1949: 1400 khz; 1 kw-U. TL: N40 15 31 W103 51 07. Hrs open: Box 430, 80701. Secondary address: 16041 Hwy. 34 80701. Phone: (970) 867-5674. Fax: (970) 542-1023.E-mail: kftm@aginformation.com Web Site:www.kftm.net Licensee: Media Logic LLC (group owner; acq 9-29-03; $415,000). Population served: 55,000 Natl. Network: AP Radio, Jones Radio Networks, . Wire Svc: AP Format: Adult contemporary, Sp, news/talk. News staff: one; News: 16 hrs wkly. Target aud: General; the people of (Morgan county) Colorado. Spec prog: Farm news 6 hrs, talk 5 hrs, sports 10 hrs, Christian progmg 6 hrs, Spanish 9 hrs wkly. ♦Wayne Johnson, pres & gen mgr; Dana Marini, gen sls mgr; John Waters, progmg dir; Carol Howard, traf mgr.

KSIR(AM)—See Brush

Fountain

KIBT(FM)— Sept 25, 1992: 96.1 mhz; 460 w. Ant 2,168 ft TL: N38 44 44 W104 51 42. Stereo. Hrs open: 24 2864 So. Circle Dr., Suite 150, Colorado Springs, 80906. Phone: (719) 540-9200. Fax: (719) 579-0882.E-mail: info@beatcolorado.com Web Site:www.beatcolorado.com Licensee: AMFM Radio Licenses LLC. Group owner: Clear Channel Communications Inc. (acq 7-1-2000; grpsl). Population served: 500,000 Natl. Rep: Clear Channel,. Format: Urban. News staff: one; News: 4 hrs wkly. Target aud: 25-44; men. Spec prog: Blues 3 hrs wkly. ♦Bob Richards, gen mgr; Scott Jones, gen sls mgr; Nancia Warren, prom dir; Jared Goldberg, progmg dir.

Fraser

***KGQD(FM)**—Not on air, target date: unknown: 89.1 mhz; 150 w vert. Ant -1,007 ft TL: N39 56 49 W105 48 57. Hrs open: 87 Jasper Lake Rd., Loveland, 80537. Phone: (970) 669-9200. Fax: (970) 669-0800. Licensee: Cedar Cove Broadcasting Inc. ♦Victor A. Michael Jr., pres.

Frisco

***KMPB(FM)**— June 1, 2008: 90.3 mhz; 400 w. Ant -293 ft TL: N39 29 47 W106 01 43. Stereo. Hrs open: 24 Box 2409, Dillon, 80435-2409. Phone: (970) 468-0905. Fax: (970) 468-0286.E-mail: comments@mountainpublicradio.org Web Site:www.mountainpublicradio.org Licensee: Cedar Cove Broadcasting Inc. (acq 8-10-2007; $280,000). Population served: 50,000 Natl. Network: AP Network News, . Wire Svc: AP Format: Loc progmg/music. News staff: 2; News: 3 hrs wkly. Target aud: 29-54. ♦M.R. Murray, pres, gen mgr; Victor A. Michael Jr., VP.

KYSL(FM)— May 27, 1988: 93.9 mhz; 560 w. 1,050 ft TL: N39 33 22 W106 06 53. Stereo. Hrs open: 24 P.O. Box 27, 80443. Phone: (970) 513-9393. Fax: (970) 262-3677.E-mail: feedback@krystal93.com Web Site:www.krystal93.com Licensee: Krystal Broadcasting Inc. Natl. Network: AP Radio, . Natl. Rep: Interep,. Format: AAA. News staff: one; News: 8 hrs wkly. Target aud: 25-49; upscale adults. ♦Ann Penny, pres; Maureen Bennett, gen mgr.

Fruita

KEKB(FM)—Licensed to Fruita. See Grand Junction

Glenwood Springs

***KDNK(FM)**— 2004: 88.1 mhz; 1.2 kw. Ant 2,542 ft TL: N39 25 08 W107 22 10. Hrs open: 6 AM-1 AM (M-F); 7 AM-1 AM (S, Su) Box 1388, Carbondale, 81623. Phone: (970) 963-0139. Fax: (970) 963-0810.E-mail: kdnk@kdnk.org Web Site:www.kdnk.org Licensee: Carbondale Community Access Radio Inc. (acq 10-29-2004; exchange for KVOV(FM) Carbondale). Natl. Network: NPR, . Haley, Bader & Potts. Format: Eclectic, news. News: 21 hrs wkly. ♦Steve Skinner, stn mgr; Amy Kimberly, dev dir; Wick Moses, adv dir; Luke Nestler, mus dir.

KGLN(AM)— May 14, 1950: 980 khz; 1 kw-D, 225 w-N. TL: N39 33 10 W107 19 48. Hrs open: 24 1360 E. Sherwood Dr., Grand Junction, 81501. Phone: (970) 254-2100. Fax: (970) 245-7551. Web Site:www.kgln.com Licensee: MBC Grand Broadcasting Inc. (acq 1-16-2008; $250,000). Population served: 4,106 Natl. Network: Fox News Radio, . Format: New talk. News staff: one. ♦David G. Hinson, pres.

KKCH(FM)— Sept 1, 1997: 92.7 mhz; 58 kw. 2,470 ft TL: N39 25 05 W107 22 01. Hrs open: Box 7205, Avon, 81620. Phone: (970) 949-0140. Fax: (970) 949-1464.E-mail: mfox@rcbroadcasting.com Licensee: NRC Broadcasting Mountain Group LLC. (group owner; (acq 5-1-2007; grpsl). Format: Jack. ♦Steve Wodlinger, gen mgr.

***KLXV(FM)**— August 1995: 91.9 mhz; 1 w horiz, 250 w vert. Ant 2,660 ft TL: N39 25 30 W107 22 46. Hrs open: 24 2351 Sunset Blvd., Suite 170-218, Rocklin, CA, 95765. Phone: (916) 251-1600. Fax: (916) 251-1650.E-mail: klove@klove.com Web Site:www.klove.com Licensee: Educational Media Foundation. Group owner: EMF Broadcasting (acq 12-28-00; grpsl). Natl. Network: K-Love, . Shaw Pittman. Format: Contemp Christian. News staff: 3. Target aud: 25-44; Judeo Christian, female. ♦Richard Jenkins, pres; Mike Novak, VP; Keith Whipple, dev dir; David Pierce, progmg mgr; Ed Lenane, news dir; Sam Wallington, engrg dir; Arthur Vassar, traf mgr; Karen Johnson, news rptr.

KMTS(FM)— June 6, 1977: 99.1 mhz; 10 kw. Ant -226 ft TL: N39 31 57 W107 20 30. Stereo. Hrs open: Prog sep from AM Box 1028, 81602. Phone: (970) 945-9124. Fax: (970) 945-5409.E-mail: kmts@kmts.com Web Site:www.kmts.com Licensee: Colorado West Broadcasting Inc. (acq 6-93). Population served: 30,000 Format: Country. Target aud: 25-50. ♦Gabe Chenoweth, pres, gen mgr, opns dir, progmg dir, chief of engrg; Kimberly Henrie, sls dir, prom dir; Ron Milhorn, news dir.

KRVG(FM)— Oct. 1, 2000: 95.5 mhz; 1 kw. Ant 2,415 ft TL: N39 25 05 W107 22 01. Hrs open: 24 751 Horizon Ct., Suite 225, Grand Junction, 81506. Phone: (970) 241-6460. Fax: (970) 241-6452.E-mail: info@wscradio.net Jones Rock Classics Licensee: Western Slope Communications LLC. (group owner) Population served: 175,000. Format: Classic Rock. News staff: one; News: 20 hrs wkly. ♦Merle Allen, gen mgr.

Granby

KRKY(AM)— July 3, 1986: 930 khz; 4.5 kw-D. TL: N40 02 26 W105 56 11. Hrs open: 24 Box 7069, Breckenridge, 80424. Phone: (970) 887-1100. Fax: (970) 468-2384.E-mail: bspence@nrcbroadcasting.com Web Site:www.highcountryradio.com Licensee: New Field Broadcasting LLC Group owner: Kona Coast Radio LLC (acq 12-14-2005; $750,000 with KZMV(FM) Kremmling). Population served: 25,000 Natl. Network: ABC, . Format: Country. News staff: 2; News: 5 hrs wkly. Target aud: 24-49; adults. Spec prog: Agriculture one hr, Sp one hr wkly. ♦Lisa Korry Cheek, gen mgr; Sam Scholl, progmg dir.

KSPN-FM—See Aspen

Grand Junction

***KAFM(FM)**— 1999: 88.1 mhz; 20 w. 1,240 ft TL: N39 04 00 W108 44 41. Stereo. Hrs open: 24 1310 Ute Ave., 81501. Phone: (970) 241-8801.E-mail: kafm@kafmradio.org Web Site:www.kafmradio.org Licensee: Grand Valley Public Radio Co. Inc. Population served: 100,000 Format: Community radio, educ. News: 20 hrs wkly. Target aud: 25-80. ♦Marc Foster, stn mgr, mus dir; Tracy Baker, opns mgr; Jon Rizzo, dev mgr, progmg dir.

KBKL(FM)— 1993: 107.9 mhz; 100 kw. 1,305 ft TL: N39 04 00 W108 44 41. (CP: Ant 1,460 ft.). Stereo. Hrs open: 24 315 Kennedy Ave., 81501. Phone: (970) 242-7788. Fax: (970) 243-0567.E-mail: info@kool1079.com Web Site:www.kool1079.com Licensee: Cumulus Licensing Corp. Group owner: Cumulus Media LLC (acq 3-10-98; grpsl). Format: Oldies. Target aud: 25-54. ♦Lewis Dickey Jr., CEO; Jonathan Pinch, COO; Marty Gausvik, CFO; John Dickey, exec VP; Kevin Wodlinger, gen mgr; Mike Shafer, opns mgr.

***KCIC(FM)**— Mar 4, 1979: 88.5 mhz; 450 w. -431 ft TL: N39 04 38 W108 30 38. Stereo. Hrs open: 24 3102 E Rd., 81504. Phone: (970) 434-4113. Phone: (970) 434-8391.E-mail: info@kcicfm.com Licensee: Pear Park Baptist Schools. Format: Educ, relg. News: 2 hrs wkly. Spec prog: Class 14 hrs wkly. ♦Randy David, pres; Glenn Gardner, gen mgr.

KEKB(FM)—(Fruita, May 24, 1984: 99.9 mhz; 79 kw. 1,380 ft TL: N39 03 56 W108 44 52. (CP: Ant 1,542 ft.). Stereo. Hrs open: 24 315 Kennedy Ave., 81501. Phone: (970) 242-7788. Fax: (970) 243-0567.E-mail: info@kekbfm.com Web Site:www.kekbfm.com Licensee: Cumulus Licensing Corp. Group owner: Cumulus Media Inc. (acq 7-9-98; grpsl). Population served: 100,000 Format: Country. News staff: 2; News: 6 hrs wkly. Target aud: 25-54. ♦Lewis Dickey Jr., CEO; Marty Gausvik, CFO; John Dickey, exec VP; Dave Noll, VP; Kevin Wodlinger, gen mgr; Mike Shafer, opns mgr.

KEXO(AM)— 1942: 1230 khz; 1 kw-U. TL: N39 05 41 W108 34 41. Hrs open: 24 315 Kennedy Ave., 81501. Phone: (970) 242-7788. Fax: (970) 243-0567. Web Site:www.kexo1230.com La Maguina Musical Licensee: Cumulus Licensing Corp. Group owner: Cumulus Media Inc. (acq 1-2000). Population served: 130,000 Format: Talk. News staff: one. Target aud: General. ♦Lewis Dickey Jr., CEO; Marty Gausvik, CFO; Kevin Wodlinger, exec VP; Pat Cantwell, gen mgr; Mike Shafer, opns mgr.

KJOL(AM)— June 19, 1957: 620 khz; 5 kw-U. TL: N39 07 35 W108 38 13. Hrs open: 24 1354 E. Sherwood Dr., 81501. Phone: (970) 254-5565. Fax: (970) 254-5550.E-mail: info@kjol.org Web Site:www.kjol.org Licensee: United Ministries. (acq 5-1-2003). Population served: 350,000 Format: Christian, talk, music. ♦Ken Andrews, gen mgr.

KJYE(FM)— May 1, 1960: 92.3 mhz; 100 kw. 1,378 ft TL: N39 04 00 W108 44 41. Stereo. Hrs open: 24 1360 E. Sherwood Dr., 81501. Phone: (970) 254-2100. Fax: (970) 245-7551. Web Site:www.gjradio.com Population served: 240,000 Wire Svc: AP Format: Adult contemp. News: 8 hrs wkly. Target aud: Adults; 25-54. ♦David Hinson, pres.

***KLFV(FM)**— Apr 24, 1982: 90.3 mhz; 1.5 kw. 1,296 ft TL: N30 03 57 W108 44 48. Stereo. Hrs open: 24 2351 Sunset Blvd., Suite 170-218, Rocklin, CA, 95765. Phone: (916) 251-1600. Fax: (916) 251-1650.E-mail: klove@klove.com Web Site:www.klove.com Licensee: Educational Media Foundation. Group owner: EMF Broadcasting (acq 12-28-00; grpsl). Population served: 92,000 Natl. Network: K-Love, . Shaw Pittman. Format: Contemp Christian. News staff: 3. Target aud: 25-44; Judeo Christian, female. Spec prog: Sp 2 hrs wkly. ♦Richard Jenkins, pres; Mike Novak, VP; Ed Lenane, opns dir, news dir; Keith Whipple, dev dir; David Pierce, progmg mgr; Sam Wallington, engrg dir; Karen Johnson, news rptr.

KMGJ(FM)— Nov 1, 1973: 93.1 mhz; 100 kw. 1,433 ft TL: N39 03 59 W108 44 41. Stereo. Hrs open: 24 1360 E. Sherwood Dr., 81501. Phone: (970) 254-2100. Fax: (970) 245-7551. Web Site:gjradio.com Licensee: MBC Grand Broadcasting, Inc. (group owner; acq 5-94; with co-located AM). Population served: 230,000 Format: CHR. News staff: one; News: 6 hrs wkly. Target aud: 18-49; women. ♦Jim Terlouw, gen mgr; Robert St. John, opns mgr; Dave Beck, natl sls mgr; Chris Britt, progmg dir.

KMOZ-FM— Mar 27, 1999: 100.7 mhz; 42 kw. 1,302 ft TL: N39 04 00 W108 44 41. Stereo. Hrs open: 24 1360 E. Sherwood Dr., 81501. Phone: (970) 254-2100. Fax: (970) 245-7551. Web Site:www.gjradio.com Licensee: MBC Grand Broadcasting Inc. (group owner) Population served: 150,000 Format: Country. News staff: 2; News: 2 hrs wkly. Target aud: 25-54. ♦Jim Terlouw, gen mgr.

***KMSA(FM)**— Feb 18, 1975: 91.3 mhz; 3 kw. Ant -382 ft TL: N39 04 48 W108 33 09. Stereo. Hrs open: 24 1100 North Ave., 81501. Phone: (970) 248-1442. Fax: (970) 248-1834.E-mail: rtucci@mesastate.edu Web Site:www.mesastate.edu Licensee: Mesa State College. Population served: 100,000 Format: Adult alternative, hip hop, reggae. News staff: 2; News: 10 hrs wkly. Target aud: 18-60; college students and gen pub. Spec prog: Black 6 hrs, folk 2 hrs, jazz 12 hrs wkly. ♦Regis Tucci, pres.

KMXY(FM)— 1996: 104.3 mhz; 100 kw. 1,296 ft (CP: Ant 1,460 ft.). Hrs open: 315 Kennedy Ave., 81501. Phone: (970) 242-7788. Fax: (970) 243-0567.E-mail: info@mix1043.com Web Site:www.mix1043.com Licensee: Cumulus Licensing Corp. Group owner: Cumulus Media Inc. (acq 7-9-98; grpsl). Format: Adult contemp. ♦Lewis Dickey Jr., CEO; Marty Gausvik, CFO; John Dickey, exec VP; Dave Noll, VP; Kevin Wodlinger, gen mgr.

KNZZ(AM)— May 1, 1926: 1100 khz; 50 kw-D, 10 kw-N, DA-N. TL: N38 57 06 W108 25 10. Hrs open: 24 1360 E. Sherwood Dr., 81501. Phone: (970) 254-2100. Fax: (970) 245-7551. Web Site:www.gjradio.com Licensee: MBC Grand Broadcasting Inc. (group owner; (acq 8-30-89). Population served: 230,000 Natl. Network: Fox News Radio, . Wire

Svc: AP Format: News/talk. News staff: 3; News: 44 hrs wkly. Target aud: 25-64. ◆David Hinson, pres; Jim TerLouw, gen mgr, progmg mgr; Dave Beck, gen sls mgr; Libby Jackson, news dir; Robert Bowe, engrg dir & chief of engrg.

*KPRN(FM)— April 1985: 89.5 mhz; 10 kw. 1,191 ft TL: N39 03 57 W108 44 45. (CP: Ant 1,233 ft.). Stereo. Hrs open: 24 7409 S. Alton Ct., Centennial, 80112. Phone: (303) 871-9191. Fax: (303) 733-3319.E-mail: info@cpr.org Web Site:www.cpr.org Licensee: Public Broadcasting of Colorado Inc. Natl. Network: NPR, . Rgnl. Network: Colo. Pub. Colo. Pub. Arter & Hadden. Format: News. News staff: one; News: 28 hrs wkly. Target aud: 25 plus. ◆Max Wycisk, pres; Jenny Gentry, exec VP; Sue Coughlin, dev VP; Sean Nethery, progmg dir; Robert Hensler, engrg VP, chief of engrg.

KTMM(AM)— 1959: 1340 khz; 1 kw-U. TL: N39 05 35 W108 35 51. Hrs open: 24 1360 E. Sherwood Dr., 81501. Phone: (970) 254-2100. Fax: (970) 245-7551 . Web Site:gjradio.com Licensee: MBC Grand Broadcasting Inc. Population served: 130000 Natl. Network: ESPN Radio, . Format: Sports. News staff: one; News: 10 hrs wkly. Target aud: 25-54; men. ◆Jim Davis, progmg dir.

Greeley

KFKA(AM)— May 21, 1921: 1310 khz; 5 kw-D, 1 kw-N, DA-N. TL: N40 21 56 W104 43 56. Hrs open: 24 820 11th Ave, 80631. Phone: (970) 356-1310. Fax: (970) 356-1314.E-mail: info@1310kfka.com Web Site:www.1310kfka.com Licensee: Music Ventures LLC dba Broadcast Media LLC (acq 11-1-2002; $1.6 million). Population served: 347,500 Natl. Network: CBS Radio, . Format: News/talk. News staff: 2; News: 25 hrs wkly. Target aud: 25-54; community-minded, active people. Spec prog: Farm 15 hrs, Ger one hr, relg 4 hrs wkly. ◆Damon Sasso, pres, opns mgr; Justin Sasso, gen mgr.

KGRE(AM)— Aug 24, 1948: 1450 khz; 1 kw-U. TL: N40 26 15 W104 43 25. Hrs open: 24 1020 9th St., Suite 201, 80631. Phone: (970) 356-1452. Fax: (970) 356-8522.E-mail: kgre@msn.com Web Site:www.tigre1450.com Licensee: Greeley Broadcasting Corp. (acq 3-24-98). Population served: 250,000 Format: Sp. Target aud: 25-54; Hispanic. Spec prog: Bienvenidos a America one hr wkly. ◆Ricardo Salazar, pres & gen mgr.

KSME(FM)— Dec 25, 1975: 96.1 mhz; 100 kw. 660 ft TL: N40 40 50 W104 56 32. Stereo. Hrs open: 24 4270 Byrd Dr., Loveland, 80538. Phone: (970) 482-5991. Fax: (970) 482-5994.E-mail: info@kissfmcolorado.com Web Site:www.kissfmcolorado.com Licensee: Citicasters Licenses Inc. (NEW). Group owner: Clear Channel Communications Inc. (acq 5-4-99; grpsl). Natl. Network: ABC, . Format: Top-40. News staff: 2. Target aud: 10-44. ◆Stu Haskell, VP & gen mgr; Kathy Arias, sls dir, gen sls mgr.

*KUNC(FM)— Jan 1, 1967: 91.5 mhz; 81 kw. Ant 692 ft TL: N40 38 31 W104 49 03. Stereo. Hrs open: 24 822 Seventh St., Suite 530, 80631. Phone: (970) 378-2579. Fax: (970) 378-2580.E-mail: mailbag@kunc.org Web Site:www.kunc.org Licensee: Community Radio for Northern Colorado (acq 8-2001; $1.9 million). Population served: 500,000 Natl. Network: NPR, PRI, . Wire Svc: AP Format: Div, news. News staff: 5; News: 65 hrs wkly. Target aud: General. ◆Neil Best, gen mgr & stn mgr; Michelle Korrnich, dev dir; Kirk Mowens, progmg dir; Jim Beers, news dir; Larry Selzle, chief of engrg.

Greenwood Village

KCUV(FM)— July 19, 1995: 102.3 mhz; 6 kw. Ant 210 ft TL: N39 39 55 W104 51 38. Stereo. Hrs open: 24
Simulcast with KJAC(FM) Timnath 100%.
1201 18th St., Suite 250, Denver, 80202. Phone: (303) 296-7025. Fax: (303) 296-7030.E-mail: info@kcuvradio.com Web Site:www.kcuvradio.com Licensee: NRC Broadcasting Inc. (acq 11-9-2005; $16 million). Format: Adult hits. ◆Timothy Brown, CEO & gen mgr.

Gunnison

KEJJ(FM)— 1980: 98.3 mhz; 25 kw. Ant 304 ft TL: N38 31 22 W106 54 28. Stereo. Hrs open: 24/7
at crested butte/lake city.
Box 1288, 219 N. Iowa Street, 81230. Phone: (970) 641-4000. Fax: (970) 641-3300.E-mail: kpkeharv@hotmail.com Licensee: John Harvey Rees (acq 2-6-2001; $275,000). Population served: 20,000 Natl. Network: Fox News Radio, . Format: Oldies. News staff: 2. Target aud: 25-54. ◆John Harvey Rees, CEO, pres; Matt Rees, opns mgr.

KPKE(AM)— Aug 23, 1960: 1490 khz; 1 kw-U. TL: N38 33 57 W106 55 32. Hrs open: 24 Box 1288, 81230. Phone: (970) 641-4000. Fax: (970) 641-3300.E-mail: kpkeharv@hotmail.com Licensee: John Harvey

Rees. Population served: 20,000 Natl. Network: Fox News Radio, . Format: Country. News staff: one; News: 2 hrs wkly. Target aud: 25-54. Spec prog: Den Broncos. ◆John Harvey Rees, CEO, gen mgr; Matt Rees, opns VP.

KVLE-FM— Apr 18, 1980: 102.3 mhz; 3 kw. 200 ft TL: N38 33 53 W106 55 38. Stereo. Hrs open: 24 50; 50; 50; 42 614 Kimbark St., Longmont, 80501. Phone: (303) 776-2323. Fax: (303) 776-1377.E-mail: cduncan@bcdworldwide.com Web Site:www.radiocoloradonetwork.com Licensee: Pilgrim Communications Inc. (acq 4-30-98; $300,000). Population served: 12,000 Natl. Network: ABC, . Wire Svc: CBS Format: Classic rock "The Storm". News: 12 hrs wkly. Target aud: 25-54; males: 35-54. ◆Chuck Duncan, CEO, pres; Gary Montgomery, gen mgr, gen sls mgr; Roger Cridelbaugh, pub affrs dir.

*KWSB-FM— Jan 26, 1968: 91.1 mhz; 135 w. 304 ft TL: N38 31 22 W106 54 28. Stereo. Hrs open: 18 Taylor Hall, 116 Western State College, 81231. Phone: (970) 943-2158. Fax: (970) 943-2117. Fax: (970) 943-7069. Web Site:www.kwsb.org Licensee: Western State College of Colorado. Population served: 6,000 Natl. Network: AP Radio, . Format: Var. News: 2 hrs wkly. Target aud: 18-25. Spec prog: Jazz 3 hrs, reggae 6 hrs, blues 3 hrs, 60s hits 3 hrs, Sp one hr wkly. ◆Frank Venturo, gen mgr.

Gypsum

*KLRY(FM)— 2003: 91.3 mhz; 110 w. Ant 2,818 ft TL: N39 46 30 W106 50 45. Hrs open: 24
Rebroadcasts KLVR(FM) Santa Rosa, CA 100%.
2351 Sunset Blvd., Suite 170-218, Rocklin, CA, 95765. Phone: (916) 251-1600. Fax: (916) 251-1650.E-mail: klove@klove.com Web Site:www.klove.com Licensee: Educational Media Foundation. Group owner: EMF Broadcasting (acq 10-2-2003; grpsl). Natl. Network: K-Love, . Shaw Pittman. Format: Contemp Christian. News staff: 3. Target aud: 25-44; Judeo Christian female. ◆Richard Jenkins, pres; Mike Novak, VP, progmg dir; Lloyd Parker, gen mgr; Ed Lenane, opns dir, news dir; Keith Whipple, dev dir; David Pierce, progmg mgr; Jon Rivers, mus dir; Sam Wallington, engrg dir; Arthur Vassar, traf mgr; Karen Johnson, news rptr.

KQSE(FM)— Mar 1, 2005: 102.5 mhz; 480 w. Ant 2,165 ft TL: N39 44 18 W106 47 58. Hrs open: Box 7205, Avon, 81620. Phone: (970) 949-0140. Fax: (970) 949-1464.E-mail: info@kskeradio.com Licensee: Wildcat Communications L.L.C. (acq 10-28-2005; $160,000). Format: Sp. ◆Holli Snyder, gen sls mgr.

Hayden

*KHCO(FM)— 2005: 90.1 mhz; 1.9 kw vert. Ant 1,699 ft TL: N40 27 04 W106 45 06. Hrs open:
Rebroadcasts KLRD(FM) Yucaipa, CA 100%.
2351 Sunset Blvd., Suite 170-218, Rocklin, CA, 95765. Phone: (916) 251-1600. Fax: (916) 251-1650. Licensee: Educational Media Foundation. (acq 6-8-2005; $25,000 for CP). Natl. Network: Air 1, . ◆Richard Jenkins, pres; Mike Novak, VP; Keith Whipple, dev dir; David Pierce, progmg mgr; Ed Lenane, news dir; Sam Wallington, engrg dir; Karen Johnson, news rptr.

KIDN-FM— Feb 15, 1985: 95.9 mhz; 1.8 kw. Ant 1,181 ft TL: N40 25 46 W107 05 34. Stereo. Hrs open: Box 772850, Steamboat Springs, 80477. Phone: (970) 879-5368. Fax: (970) 879-5843. Web Site:www.jackintheboat.com Licensee: NRC Broadcasting Mountain Group LLC. Group owner: American General Media (acq 5-1-2007; grpsl). Format: Jack. Target aud: 21-54. ◆Steve Wodlinger, gen mgr & stn mgr.

KQZR(FM)— 2000: 107.3 mhz; 29 kw. Ant 649 ft TL: N40 31 16 W107 17 46. Hrs open: Box 772850, Steamboat Springs, 80477. Phone: (970) 879-5368. Fax: (970) 879-5843. Web Site:www.therangefm.com Licensee: NRC Broadcasting Mountain Group LLC. (group owner) (acq 5-1-2007; grpsl). Format: Country. ◆Steve Wodlinger, gen mgr; Julia Arrotti, opns mgr; David Wittlinger, gen sls mgr; Eli Campbell, prom dir; John Johnston, progmg dir.

Holyoke

KSTH(FM)— 2002: 92.3 mhz; 100 kw. Ant 567 ft TL: N40 51 42 W103 23 35. Hrs open: Box 333, McCook, NE, 69001. Phone: (308) 345-5400. Fax: (308) 345-4720. Licensee: Armada Media - McCook Inc. (acq 1-17-2007; grpsl). Format: Adult contemp. ◆Bryan Loker, gen mgr, sls dir; Clint Bradbury, opns mgr.

Hugo

KHIH(FM)—Not on air, target date: unknown: 92.3 mhz; 26 kw horiz. Ant 269 ft TL: N39 06 20 W103 40 30. Hrs open: 87 Jasper Lake Rd., Loveland, 80537. Phone: (970) 669-9200. Licensee: Kona Coast Radio LLC. ◆Victor A. Michael Jr., gen mgr.

Idalia

KWDI(FM)—Not on air, target date: unknown: 94.1 mhz; 50 kw. Ant 298 ft TL: N39 40 22 W102 15 18. Hrs open: 5331 Mt. Alifan Dr., San Diego, CA, 92111. Phone: (858) 277-4991. Fax: (858) 277-1365. Licensee: Horizon Christian Fellowship. (acq 2-9-2006; grpsl). ◆Mike MacIntosh, pres.

Ignacio

*KSUT(FM)— June 9, 1976: 91.3 mhz; 425 w. Ant 18 ft TL: N37 05 51 W107 37 32. Stereo. Hrs open: 24 Box 737, 81137. Secondary address: 123 Capote Dr. 81137. Phone: (970) 563-0255. Fax: (970) 563-0399.E-mail: info@ksut.org Web Site:www.ksut.org Licensee: Kute Inc. Population served: 200,000 Natl. Network: NPR, PRI, . Format: Native American. News: 30 hrs wkly. Target aud: 24 plus; public radio audience. Spec prog: American Indian 7 hrs, class 8 hrs, jazz 15 hrs wkly. ◆Beth Warren, gen mgr.

*KUTE(FM)— June 1998: 90.1 mhz; 3 kw. Ant 1,965 ft TL: N37 21 51 W107 46 56. Hrs open: Box 737, 81137. Phone: (970) 563-0255. Fax: (970) 563-0399.E-mail: info@ksut.org Web Site:www.ksut.org Licensee: KUTE Inc. Natl. Network: NPR, PRI, . Format: Triple A, americana. ◆Beth Warren, gen mgr.

Johnstown

KHNC(AM)— January 1993: 1360 khz; 10 w-D, 450 w-N, DA-N. TL: N40 23 11 W104 54 19. (CP: 10 kw-D, 1 kw-N, DA-N). Hrs open: Box 1750, 80534-1750. Phone: (970) 587-5175. Fax: (970) 587-5450.E-mail: comments@americanewsnet.com Web Site:www.americanewsnet.com Licensee: Donald A. and Sharon A. Wiedeman. Format: Conservative news/talk. ◆Donald Wiedeman, pres, gen mgr; Michael Golden, opns mgr.

Julesburg

KJBL(FM)— 2002: 96.5 mhz; 100 kw. Ant 567 ft TL: N40 51 42 W103 23 35. Hrs open: Box 333, McCook, NE, 69001. Phone: (308) 345-5400. Fax: (308) 345-4720. Licensee: Armada Media - McCook Inc. (acq 1-17-2007; grpsl). Format: Country. ◆Bryan Loker, gen mgr.

Keystone

KWLW(AM)—Not on air, target date: unknown: 1320 khz; 1 kw-D, 500 w-N, DA-2. TL: N39 36 46 W106 00 05. Hrs open: 87 Jasper Lake Rd., Loveland, 80537. Phone: (970) 669-9200. Licensee: Advanced Modulation Broadcasting LLC. ◆Victor A. Michael Jr., gen mgr.

Kremmling

KZMV(FM)— Nov 1, 1987: 106.3 mhz; 2.5 kw. 1,050 ft TL: N40 00 18 W106 26 57. Stereo. Hrs open: 24 Box 7069, Breckenridge, 80424. Phone: (970) 887-1100. Fax: (970) 468-2384.E-mail: bspence@nrcbroadcasting.com Web Site:www.highcountryradio.com Licensee: New Field Broadcasting LLC Group owner: Kona Coast Radio LLC (acq 12-14-2005; $750,000 with KRKY(AM) Granby). Population served: 25,000 Natl. Network: Jones Satellite Audio. Format: Oldies. News staff: 2; News: 5 hrs wkly. Target aud: 24-49. ◆Lisa Cheek, gen mgr; Sam Scholl, progmg dir.

La Jara

KZBR(FM)—Not on air, target date: unknown: 97.1 mhz; 25 kw. Ant 180 ft TL: N37 22 05 W106 06 44. Hrs open: 1102 Newitt Vick Dr., Vicksburg, MS, 39183-8755. Phone: (601) 883-0848.E-mail: info@kzbrfm.com Licensee: Lendsi Radio LLC. ◆Lina H. Jones, gen mgr.

La Junta

KBLJ(AM)— July 23, 1937: 1400 khz; 1 kw-U. TL: N37 59 14 W103 34 01. Hrs open: 116 Dalton, 81050. Phone: (719) 384-5456. Fax:

(719) 384-5450.E-mail: kblj@rural-com.com Licensee: CCR-La Junta IV LLC. Group owner: Cherry Creek Radio LLC (acq 12-19-2003; grpsl). Population served: 7938 Natl. Network: Westwood One, . Format: Oldies. Target aud: 30 plus; general. ◆Pat Gittings, gen mgr; Pat McGee, progmg dir.

*KECC(FM)— August 2002: 89.1 mhz; 740 w. 298 ft TL: N37 58 43 W103 34 48. Hrs open: 24
Rebroadcasts KRCC(FM) Colorado Springs 100%.
c/o KRCC(FM), 912 N. Weber St., Colorado Springs, 80903. Phone: (719) 473-4801. Fax: (719) 473-7863.E-mail: info@krcc.org Web Site:www.krcc.org Licensee: The Colorado College. Format: Diversified, news. ◆Delaney Utterback, gen mgr; Mike Procell, opns mgr; Jeff Bieri, prom dir; Joel Belik, chief of engrg.

KFVR-FM— 2001: 106.5 mhz; 100 kw. Ant 512 ft TL: N37 39 31 W103 27 55. Hrs open: 24 920 Elm Ave., Rocky Ford, 81067-1249. Phone: (970) 356-1452. Fax: (719) 254-6303. Licensee: Greeley Broadcasting Corp. (group owner; (acq 11-30-2006; $125,000). Format: Mexican rgnl. ◆Ricardo Salazar, gen mgr.

*KJLI(FM)— Not on air, target date: unknown: 90.1 mhz; 25 kw. Ant 341 ft TL: N37 58 43 W103 34 48. Hrs open: Box 991, Meade, KS, 67864-0991. Phone: (620) 873-2991. Fax: (620) 873-2755.E-mail: kjil@kjil.com Web Site:www.kjil.com Licensee: Great Plains Christian Radio Inc. ◆Robert D. Hughes, CEO.

KTHN(FM)— Aug 28, 1974: 92.1 mhz; 3 kw. 300 ft TL: N37 59 15 W103 34 02. Stereo. Hrs open: Prog sep from AM 116 Dalton, 81050. Phone: (719) 384-5456. Fax: (719) 384-5450. Licensee: CCR-La Junta IV LLC Format: Country.

La Veta

KJQY(FM)— Not on air, target date: unknown: 103.3 mhz; 100 kw. Ant 380 ft TL: N37 37 39 W104 49 17. Hrs open: 11 Pheasant Hill Rd., Canton, CT, 06019-3042. Phone: (860) 693-3336. Licensee: Steven R. Bartholomew. ◆Steven R. Bartholomew, gen mgr.

Lakewood

KEPN(AM)— Jan 8, 1955: 1600 khz; 5 kw-U, DA-N. TL: N39 39 20 W105 04 28. Stereo. Hrs open: 7800 E. Orchard Rd., Suite 400, Greenwood Village, 80111. Phone: (303) 321-0950. Fax: (303) 321-3383.E-mail: info@espnradio1600.com Web Site:www.espnradio1600.com Licensee: Lincoln Financial Media Co. of Colorado. (group owner; (acq 4-3-2006; grpsl). Population served: 1,700,000 Natl. Network: ESPN Radio,. Natl. Rep: CBS Radio,. Format: Sports. ◆Clarke Brown, pres; Robert Call, sr VP, gen mgr; John St. John, opns dir; Steve Price, sls dir; Randy Weidner, natl sls mgr; Dwayne Taylor, mktg dir; J.J. Pelini, prom dir; Tim Spence, progmg dir; Simone Seiklay, news dir; Simone Seikaly, pub affrs dir; Brad Hart, engrg dir.

KQKS(FM)— July 9, 1966: 107.5 mhz; 100 kw. 670 ft TL: N39 41 45 W105 09 54. Stereo. Hrs open: Dups AM 100% 7800 E. Orchard Rd., Suite 400, Greenwood Village, 80111. Phone: (303) 321-0950. Fax: (303) 321-3383.E-mail: info@ks1075.com Web Site:www.ks1075.com Licensee: Lincoln Financial Media Co. of Colorado. Format: Hip-hop, rhythm and blues. Target aud: 12-34. ◆Cat Collins, progmg dir.

*KVOD(FM)— 2005: 88.1 mhz; 1.2 kw vert. Ant 1,053 ft TL: N39 40 18 W105 13 05. Hrs open: Bridges Broadcast Center, 7409 S. Alton Ct., Centennial, 80112. Phone: (303) 871-9191. Fax: (303) 733-3319.E-mail: info@cpr.org Web Site:www.cpr.org Licensee: PRC Denver-I LLC Group owner: EMF Broadcasting (acq 7-2-2008; $8.2 million). Population served: 2,548,279 Colo. Pub. Garvey Schubert Barer. Format: Classical.

Lamar

KLMR(AM)— December 1948: 920 khz; 5 kw-D, 500 w-N, DA-N. TL: N38 06 53 W102 37 16. Hrs open: 24 Box 890, 81052. Secondary address: 7350 US Hwy. 50 81052. Phone: (719) 336-2206. Fax: (719) 336-7973.E-mail: klmraudio@yahoo.com Licensee: CCR-Lamar IV LLC. Group owner: Cherry Creek Radio LLC (acq 12-19-2003; grpsl). Population served: 50,000 Natl. Network: ABC, . Format: Classic country. News: 12 hrs wkly. Target aud: 25-54. ◆Pat Gittings, gen mgr, stn mgr; Ty Harmon, gen sls mgr & progmg dir; Eric Stone, news dir.

KLMR-FM— November 1978: 93.3 mhz; 100 kw. 498 ft TL: N38 02 10 W102 35 58. Stereo. Hrs open: 24 7350 U.S. Hwy. 50, 81052. Phone: (719) 336-2206. Fax: (719) 336-7973.E-mail: audio@yahoo.com Population served: 50,000 Natl. Network: CBS, . Format: Classic rock. Target aud: 25-54. ◆Pat Gittings, gen mgr.

KVAY(FM)— Aug 5, 1991: 105.7 mhz; 100 kw. 545 ft TL: N38 06 44 W102 57 37. (CP: Ant 479 ft). Stereo. Hrs open: 24 Box 1176, 224 S. Main, 81052. Phone: (719) 336-8734. Fax: (719) 336-5977. Web Site:www.kvay.com Licensee: Beacon Broadcasting LLC (acq 1-3-03; $825,000). Population served: 100,000 Natl. Network: AP Radio, . Leventhal, Senter & Lerman. Format: Country. News staff: one. Target aud: 25-55. Spec prog: Gospel 4 hrs, classic rock 4 hrs wkly. ◆Debbie Ellis, gen mgr.

Las Animas

KRKV(FM)— July 2008: 107.3 mhz; 100 kw. Ant 384 ft TL: N38 06 44 W102 57 39. Stereo. Hrs open: Box 563, Tanner, AL, 35671. Secondary address: 709 Coleman Ave., Athens, AL 35611. Phone: (256) 497-4502. Fax: (443) 342-2478.E-mail: varietyrock@hotmail.com Licensee: Alleycat Communications. Format: Var rock. Target aud: 18-54. ◆Richard W. Dabney, gen mgr.

Leadville

*KTOL(FM)— 2006: 90.9 mhz; 450 w horiz. Ant -630 ft TL: N39 14 05 W106 17 59. Stereo. Hrs open:
Rebroadcasts KTLF(FM) Colorado Springs 100%.
1665 Briargate Blvd., Suite 100, Colorado Springs, 80920-3400. Phone: (719) 593-0600. Fax: (719) 593-2399.E-mail: lightpraise@ktlf.org Web Site:www.ktlf.org Licensee: Educational Communications of Colorado Springs Inc. Format: Christian music. Target aud: 45-60; Christian. ◆Lynn Carmichael, progmg dir.

Limon

KAVD(FM)— 2003: Stn currently dark. 103.1 mhz; 100 kw. Ant 443 ft TL: N39 28 12 W103 38 14. Stereo. Hrs open: 1211 Chuck Dawley Blvd., Suite 202, Mount Pleasant, SC, 29464. Phone: (843) 849-0076. Licensee: Coloradio Inc. Fletcher, Heald & Hildreth. ◆Edward F. Seeger, gen mgr.

KLIM(AM)— May 8, 1984: Stn currently dark. 1120 khz; 250 w-D. TL: N39 16 27 W103 42 49. Hrs open: 6 AM-sunset 165 E Ave., 80828. Phone: (719) 775-8199. Phone: (719) 964-5804. Licensee: Roger L. Hoppe II (acq 3-7-96; $8,000). Miller & Neely. Format: Oldies. ◆Roger Hoppe II, pres; Alan Olson, gen mgr.

*KYCO(FM)— Not on air, target date: unknown: 89.1 mhz; 1.8 kw. Ant 328 ft TL: N39 22 13 W103 42 50. Hrs open: Box 4872, East Lansing, MI, 48826. Phone: (517) 999-3737. Web Site:www.foundationradio.org Licensee: Saidnewsfoundation. ◆David C. Schaberg, gen mgr.

Littleton

KCKK(AM)— Aug 22, 1957: 1510 khz; 10 kw-D, 1.3 kw-N, DA-2. TL: N39 33 08 W105 02 00. Hrs open: 1201 18th St., Suite 250, Denver, 80202. Phone: (303) 650-1795. Fax: (303) 524-3410. Licensee: People's Wireless Inc. Group owner: NRC Broadcasting Inc. (acq 4-26-2002; $2.7 million). Population served: 150,000 Format: Sports. ◆Kevin Medina, gen mgr.

Longmont

*KGUD(FM)— September 1975: 90.7 mhz; 100 w. Ant 270 ft TL: N40 14 24 W105 03 19. Stereo. Hrs open: 24 Box 1534, 80502-1534. Secondary address: Studio: 457 Fourth Ave. 80501. Phone: (303) 485-9811.E-mail: kgud907@gmail.com Licensee: Longmont Community Radio (acq 10-31-2003). Population served: 180,000 Format: Easy Listening. News staff: 2. Target aud: 45 plus; retirees. ◆George N. Baskos, gen mgr; James R. Boynton Sr., stn mgr.

KKFN(FM)— September 1964: 104.3 mhz; 5.8 kw. Ant 1,204 ft TL: N40 05 47 W104 54 04. Stereo. Hrs open: 24 Jefferson-Pilot Communications, 7800 E. Orchard Rd., Suite 400, Greenwood Village, 80111. Phone: (303) 321-0950. Fax: (303) 321-3383. Web Site:fm1043thefan.com Licensee: Lincoln Financial Media Co. of Colorado. (group owner; (acq 4-3-2006; grpsl). Population served: 2,100,000 Natl. Network: Fox Sports, . Wiley, Rein & Fielding. Format: Sports. Target aud: 18-34; hip. ◆Bob Call, sr VP, gen mgr; Jay Kisskalt, gen sls mgr; Dwayne Taylor, mktg dir; Tim Spence, opns mgr & progmg dir; Brad Hart, chief of engrg.

KRCN(AM)— December 1949: 1060 khz; 50 kw-D, 111 w-N. TL: N40 16 51 W104 56 25 (day), N40 11 28 W105 07 35 (night). Hrs open: 15; 18 (summer) 614 Kimbark St., 80501. Phone: (303) 776-2323. Fax: (303) 776-1377. Licensee: Pilgrim Communications Inc. (acq 5-27-98; $575,000). Population served: 3,000,000 Natl. Network: ABC,

. Natl. Rep: McGavren Guild,. Format: Business talk. News staff: 3; News: 12 hrs wkly. Target aud: 25-64; news & sports listeners. ◆Chuck Duncan, CEO, pres, stn mgr; Roger Cridelbaugh, pub affrs dir.

Loveland

KPIO(AM)— Jan 21, 1955: 1570 khz; 7 kw-D, 18 w-N. TL: N40 23 31 W105 05 51. Hrs open: 24 201 N. Industrial Park Rd., Excelsior Springs, MO, 64024. Phone: (816) 630-1090.E-mail: catholicradionetwork@gmail.com Web Site:www.thecatholicradionetwork.com Licensee: Catholic Radio Network Inc. (acq 1-28-2009; $740,000). Population served: 250,000 Natl. Network: EWTN Radio, . Format: Catholic radio. ◆James O'Laughlin, gen mgr.

KTRR(FM)— Feb 5, 1966: 102.5 mhz; 50 kw. 410 ft TL: N40 27 19 W104 55 25. Stereo. Hrs open: 600 Main St., Windsor, 80550. Phone: (970) 674-2700. Fax: (970) 686-7491.E-mail: chall@regentcomm.com Web Site:www.tri1025.com Licensee: Regent Broadcasting of Ft. Collins Inc. Group owner: Regent Communications Inc. (acq 2-25-03). Population served: 173,000 Format: Adult contemp. Target aud: 25-54. ◆Cal Hall, gen mgr; Mark Callaghan, opns mgr; Miles Schallert, sls dir & gen sls mgr.

*KXWA(FM)— Mar 11, 2004: 89.7 mhz; 80 kw. Ant 1,220 ft TL: N40 37 03 W105 19 40. Stereo. Hrs open: 24 1707 N. Main, Suite 302, Longmont, 80501. Phone: (303) 702-9293. Fax: (303) 485-1929.E-mail: info@wayfm.com Web Site:wayfm.com Licensee: WAY-FM Media Group Inc. (group owner; (acq 11-19-2002). Population served: 2,300,000 Format: Contemp Christian. Target aud: 18-34. ◆Lloyd Parker, COO; Robert D. Augsburg, pres; Zach Cochran, gen mgr; Scott Veigel, progmg dir.

Manitou Springs

KBIQ(FM)— May 1952: 102.7 mhz; 57 kw. Ant 2,280 ft TL: N38 44 43 W104 51 39. Stereo. Hrs open: 24 7150 Campus Dr., Suite 150, Colorado Springs, 80920. Phone: (719) 531-5438. Fax: (719) 531-5588.E-mail: henry@kbiqradio.com Web Site:www.kbiqradio.com Licensee: Bison Media Inc. Group owner: Salem Communications Corp. (acq 10-8-96; $2.825 million). Population served: 350,000 Format: Christian, adult contemp. News staff: one. Target aud: 18-54. ◆Henry Tippie, gen mgr.

*KCME(FM)— Sept 1, 1979: 88.7 mhz; 8.9 kw. 9,570 ft TL: N38 44 40 W104 51 41. Stereo. Hrs open: 24 1921 N. Weber St., Colorado Springs, 80907-6903. Phone: (719) 578-5263. Fax: (719) 578-1033.E-mail: kcme@kcme.org Web Site:www.kcme.org Licensee: Cheyenne Mt. Public Broadcast House Inc. Population served: 1,200,000 Scott Cinnamon. Format: Classical. Target aud: 45 plus; upper-middle class, mostly college graduates. ◆Arthur Aikin Jr., pres; Jeanna Wearing, gen mgr, opns dir; Suzanne Zimmerman, dev dir; Tom White, dev VP & sls.

KXRE(AM)— November 1956: 1490 khz; 500 w-D, 250 w-N. TL: N38 51 43 W104 55 32. Hrs open: 24 600 Grant St., Denver, 80203. Phone: (303) 733-5266. Fax: (303) 733-5242.E-mail: kbno@kbno.com Web Site:www.kbno.net Licensee: Latino Communications LLC (group owner; acq 1-23-03; $350,000 with KAVA(AM) Pueblo). Population served: 350,000 Format: Rgnl Mexican. News staff: 5; News: 21 hrs wkly. Target aud: 25-54. ◆Zee Ferrufino, gen mgr.

Meeker

KAYW(FM)— Sept 30, 2000: 98.1 mhz; 100 kw. Ant 1,145 ft TL: N40 11 45 W107 56 00. Hrs open: 24
Rebroadcasts KZKS(FM) Rifle 100%.
751 Horizon Ct., Suite 225, Grand Junction, 81506. Phone: (970) 241-6460. Fax: (970) 241-6452. Licensee: Western Slope Communications LLC. (group owner) Population served: 60,000 Format: Adult favorites. News: 20 hrs wkly. ◆Merle Allen, gen mgr.

Merino

KRFD(FM)— 2008: 94.5 mhz; 15 kw. Ant 407 ft TL: N40 31 57 W103 07 22. Hrs open: Box 917, Fort Morgan, 80701. Phone: (970) 867-7271. Fax: (970) 867-2676. Licensee: Northeast Colorado Broadcasting LLC. (acq 5-14-2009; $175,000 for CP). ◆Alexander L. Creighton, gen mgr.

Monte Vista

KSLV(AM)— February 1954: 1240 khz; 1 kw-U. TL: N37 36 10 W106 08 58. Hrs open: 24 Box 631, 109 Adams St., 81144. Phone: (719) 852-3581. Fax: (719) 852-3583.E-mail: kslv@amigo.net Web Site:www.kslvradio.com Licensee: San Luis Valley Broadcasting Inc. (acq 4-1-79). Population served: 45,000 Natl. Network: Jones Radio Networks, . Cohn & Marks. Wire Svc: AP Format: Classic Country. News staff: one; News: 1 hr wkly. Target aud: 25-54. Spec prog: Sp 10 hrs, farm one hr, gospel 4 hrs wkly. ◆Gerald Vigil, gen mgr; Linda Pacheco, news dir.

KYDN(FM)— 1986: 95.3 mhz; 6 kw. Ant 89 ft TL: N37 36 10 W106 08 58. Stereo. Hrs open: 24 Box 631, 109 Adams St., 81144. Phone: (719) 852-3581. Fax: (719) 852-3583.E-mail: kslv@amigo.net Web Site:www.kslvradio.com Licensee: San Luis Valley Broadcasting Inc. Natl. Network: Jones Radio Networks, . Wire Svc: AP Format: New Country. News: 6 hrs wkly. ◆Gerald Vigil, gen mgr; Michael Clifford, traf mgr.

Montrose

*KJOL-FM—Not on air, target date: unknown: 91.9 mhz; 150 w vert. Ant -213 ft TL: N38 28 29 W107 54 41. Hrs open: 1360 E. Sherwood Dr., Grand Junction, 81501-7575. Phone: (970) 254-5565. Fax: (970) 254-5550.E-mail: info@kjol.org Web Site:www.kjol.org Licensee: United Ministries. ◆Ken Andrews, gen mgr.

KKXK(FM)— December 1976: 94.1 mhz; 90 kw. 1,748 ft TL: N38 20 16 W107 38 23. Stereo. Hrs open: 24 Box 970, 81402. Secondary address: 106 Rose Ln. 81401. Phone: (970) 249-4546. Fax: (970) 249-2229. Web Site:www.coloradoradio.com Natl. Network: ABC, . Format: Contemp country. News staff: one; News: 4 hrs wkly. Target aud: 25-54. ◆Joe Schwartz, pres.

*KPRH(FM)— October 1998: 88.3 mhz; 5 kw. 1,535 ft TL: N38 20 01 W107 39 52. Hrs open:
Rebroadcasts KCFR(FM) Denver 100%.
Colorado Public Radio, 7409 S. Alton Ct., Centennial, 80112. Phone: (303) 871-9191. Phone: (800) 722-4449. Fax: (303) 733-3319. Web Site:www.cpr.org Licensee: Public Broadcasting of Colorado Inc. Natl. Network: NPR, . Arter & Hadden. Format: News. Target aud: General. ◆Max Wycisk, pres; Sue Coughlin, dev VP; Sean Nethery, progmg dir; Robert Hensler, engrg VP; David Gomez, traf mgr.

KSTR-FM— Apr 10, 1980: 96.1 mhz; 91 kw. Ant 1,099 ft TL: N38 52 40 W108 13 33. Stereo. Hrs open: 1360 E. Sherwood Dr., Grand Junction, 81501. Phone: (970) 254-2100. Fax: (970) 245-7551. Web Site:www.gjradio.com Licensee: MBC Grand Broadcasting Inc. (acq 5-25-2005; $600,000). Population served: 350,000 Format: Rock. ◆David G. Hinson, pres; Jim Terlouw, gen mgr; Dave Beck, gen sls mgr.

KUBC(AM)— Sept 25, 1947: 580 khz; 5 kw-D, 1 kw-N, DA-N. TL: N38 25 32 W107 52 57. Hrs open: 24 Box 970, 81402. Secondary address: 106 Rose Ln. 81401. Phone: (970) 249-4546. Fax: (970) 249-2229. Web Site:www.coloradoradio.com Licensee: CCR-Montrose IV LLC. (group owner; (acq 8-19-2004; grpsl). Population served: 150,000 Natl. Network: ABC, . Garvey, Schubert & Barer. Format: News / Talk. News: 4 hrs wkly. Target aud: 35+. Spec prog: Sports 5 hrs, relg 3 hrs wkly. ◆Joseph D. Schwartz, pres; Jay Austin, gen mgr; Scott Staley, progmg mgr; Janine Mayfield, news dir; Heather Glassman, traf mgr.

*KVMT(FM)— 1999: 89.1 mhz; 3 kw. Ant 1,748 ft TL: N38 18 52 W108 12 02. Hrs open: 24
Rebroadcasts KVNF (FM) Paonia 100%.
Box 1350, Paonia, 81428. Phone: (970) 527-4866. Fax: (970) 527-4865.E-mail: sally@kvnf.org Web Site:www.kvnf.org Licensee: North Fork Valley Public Radio Inc. Format: News, music, pub affrs. News: 35 hrs wkly. ◆Sally Kane, gen mgr.

Monument

KCBR(AM)— July 20, 1986: 1040 khz; 15 kw-D. TL: N38 49 08 W104 46 32. Stereo. Hrs open: Sunrise-sunset 5050 Edison Ave., Suite 218, Colorado Springs, 80915. Phone: (719) 570-1530. Fax: (719) 570-1007. Web Site:www.1040kcbr.com Licensee: KLZ Radio Inc. Group owner: Crawford Broadcasting Co. (acq 1999; $750,000 with KCMN(AM) Colorado Springs). Population served: 400,000 Format: Christian talk. Target aud: 25-54; 70% male, upper-middle income or higher. ◆Don Crawford Jr., CEO, VP, gen mgr; Don Crawford, Sr., pres.

Morrison

*KLDV(FM)— Mar 27, 1971: 91.1 mhz; 100 kw. Ant 1,168 ft TL: N39 36 00 W105 12 35. Stereo. Hrs open: 24
Rebroadcasts KLVR(FM) Middletown, CA 100%.
2351 Sunset Blvd., Suite 170-218, Rocklin, CA, 95765. Phone: (916) 251-1600. Fax: (916) 251-1650.E-mail: klove@klove.com Web Site:www.klove.com Licensee: Educational Media Foundation. Group owner: EMF Broadcasting (acq 12-28-2000; grpsl). Population served: 1,500,000 Natl. Network: K-Love, . Shaw Pittman. Format: Contemp Christian. News staff: 3. Target aud: 25-44; Judeo Christian, female. ◆Richard Jenkins, pres; Mike Novak, VP; Keith Whipple, dev dir.

Mountain Village

KRKQ(FM)—Not on air, target date: unknown: 95.5 mhz; 6 kw. Ant -302 ft TL: N37 56 02 W107 50 03. Hrs open: 911 Colonial Dr., Cheyenne, WY, 82001-7415. Licensee: Lorenz E. Proietti. ◆Lorenz E. Proietti, gen mgr.

New Castle

KJEB(FM)— 2005: 94.5 mhz; 25 kw. Ant -397 ft TL: N39 33 56 W107 32 01. Hrs open: 307 14th St., Glenwood Springs, 81601-3949. Phone: (970) 384-2160. Fax: (970) 384-0783. Licensee: Wildcat Communications LLC. Format: Oldies. ◆Colleen Barill, gen mgr.

Norwood

KRYD(FM)— January 1998: 104.9 mhz; 24 kw. Ant 1,672 ft TL: N38 18 57 W108 11 47. Stereo. Hrs open: 24 444 Seasons Dr., Grand Junction, 81503. Secondary address: 475 Water St., Monrose 81401. Phone: (970) 263-4100. Fax: (970) 263-9600.E-mail: billv@taousa.tv Web Site:www.krydfm.com Licensee: Rocky III Investments Inc. Population served: 225,000 Wood, Maine & Brown, Chartered. Format: Country. News staff: 3; News: one hr wkly. Target aud: 18 plus. ◆Bill Varecha, CEO; Debbie Varecha, CFO; Jon Donofrio, opns mgr; Paul Varecha, gen sls mgr.

Oak Creek

KFMU-FM— Sept 22, 1975: 104.1 mhz; 1.4 kw. 1,073 ft TL: N40 14 10 W106 52 30. Stereo. Hrs open: 24 Box 772850, 2955 Village Dr., Steamboat Springs, 80477. Phone: (970) 879-5368. Fax: (970) 879-5843. Web Site:www.kfmu.com Licensee: NRC Broadcasting Mountain Group LLC. (group owner; (acq 5-1-2007; grpsl). Population served: 40,000 Natl. Network: CBS, . Format: Triple A. News staff: 2; News: 10 hrs wkly. Target aud: 21-54. Spec prog: Jazz 4 hrs, modern mus 4 hrs wkly. ◆Steve Wodlinger, gen mgr.

Otis

KATR-FM— Sept 1, 1983: 98.3 mhz; 100 kw. Ant 554 ft TL: N40 25 13 W102 58 10. Stereo. Hrs open: 24 Box 354, Wray, 80758. Phone: (970) 332-4171. Fax: (970) 332-4172.E-mail: krdz@mediamagicradio.net Web Site:www.katcountry983.com Licensee: Media Logic LLC (group owner; acq 10-28-2002; $700,000). Format: Country. News staff: 3; News: 15 hrs wkly. Target aud: 16-70; males & females. ◆Wayne Johnson, gen mgr & opns mgr.

Ouray

KWGL(FM)— June 16, 1986: 105.7 mhz; 60 kw horiz. Ant 1,752 ft TL: N38 23 16 W107 40 28. Stereo. Hrs open: 24 751 Horizon Ct., Suite 225, Grand Junction, 81506. Phone: (970) 241-6460. Fax: (970) 241-6452. Licensee: WS Communications L.L.C. (acq 1-95; 5-22-95). Population served: 200,000 Natl. Network: Jones Radio Networks, . Format: Legendary Country. News staff: one; News: 15 hrs wkly. ◆Merle Allen, gen mgr; Michael Johnson, progmg dir.

Pagosa Springs

*KPGS(FM)— 2008: 88.1 mhz; 1 kw vert. Ant 1,364 ft TL: N37 11 48 W107 07 01. Hrs open:
Rebroadcasts KUTE(FM) Ignacio 100%.
Box 737, Ignacio, 81137-0737. Phone: (970) 563-0255. Fax: (970) 563-0399. E-mail: info@ksut.org Web Site:www.ksut.org Licensee: KUTE Inc. Natl. Network: NPR, . Format: Triple A, Americana. ◆Eddie Box Jr., pres; Beth Warren, gen mgr.

*KTPS(FM)— 2003: 89.7 mhz; 200 w. Ant 1,273 ft TL: N37 11 35 W107 05 58. Stereo. Hrs open:
Rebroadcasts KTLF(FM) Colorado Springs 100%.
1665 Briargate Blvd., Suite 100, Colorado Springs, 80920. Phone: (719) 593-0600. Fax: (719) 593-2399.E-mail: lightpraise@ktlf.org Web Site:www.ktlf.org Licensee: Educational Communications of Colorado Springs Inc. Format: Christian music. Target aud: 45-60; Christian. ◆Lynn Carmichael, progmg dir.

KWUF(AM)— Aug 27, 1975: 1400 khz; 1 kw-U. TL: N37 15 24 W107 01 06. Hrs open: 24 Box 780, 81147. Secondary address: 702 S. 10th St. 81147. Phone: (970) 264-5983. Fax: (970) 264-5129.E-mail: info@kwuf.com Web Site:www.kwuf.com Licensee: Wolf Creek Broadcasting L.L.C. Population served: 10,000 Natl. Network: Westwood One, . Format: Country, news/talk, sports. News: 10 hrs wkly. Target aud: General. ◆Chris Olivarez, sports cmtr & disc jockey.

KWUF-FM— May 1, 1986: 106.3 mhz; 255 w. Ant 1,280 ft TL: N37 11 32 W107 05 55. Stereo. Hrs open: 24 Box 780, 81147. Secondary address: 702 S. 10th St. 81147. Phone: (970) 264-5983. Fax: (970) 264-5129.E-mail: admin@kwuf.com Web Site:www.kwuf.com Licensee: Wolf Creek Broadcasting L.L.C. (acq 1999; with co-located AM). Population served: 10,000 Natl. Network: Westwood One, . Format: Adult contemp. News: 10 hrs wkly. Target aud: 18 plus. Spec prog: Blues 10 hrs, jazz 10 hrs wkly. ◆Christie Spears, VP; Beth Porter, sls dir; Jodie Blankenship, news dir; Will Spears, CEO, pres, gen mgr, progmg mgr & chief of engrg; Chris Olivarez, sports cmtr; Chris Olivarez, disc jockey.

Palisade

*KAAI(FM)— 2007: 98.5 mhz; 215 w. Ant 2,988 ft TL: N39 03 14 W108 15 13. Hrs open: 2351 Sunset Blvd., Suite 170-218, Rocklin, 95765. Phone: (303) 470-5907. Phone: (888) 937-2471. Fax: (916) 251-1650.E-mail: info@air1.com Web Site:www.air1.com Licensee: Covenant Educational Media Inc. (acq 12-18-2007; $800,000 for CP). ◆A. Fletcher Anderson, pres; Doug Price, gen mgr.

Paonia

*KVNF(FM)— Oct 5, 1979: 90.9 mhz; 3 kw. Ant -171 ft TL: N38 52 20 W107 39 45. Stereo. Hrs open: 18 233 Grand Ave., 81428. Phone: (970) 527-4866. Fax: (970) 527-4865.E-mail: sally@kvnf.org Web Site:www.kvnf.org Licensee: North Fork Valley Public Radio Inc. (acq 1-27-78). Population served: 50,000 Natl. Network: NPR, . Format: News, music, pub affrs. Spec prog: Class 15 hrs, jazz 17 hrs, blues 3 hrs, C&W 5 hrs, new age 6 hrs, Sp 2 hrs, gospel 3 hrs wkly. ◆Sally Kane, gen mgr.

Parachute

KENG(FM)— 2008: 101.1 mhz; 200 w. Ant -1,397 ft TL: N39 26 31 W108 01 15. Hrs open: 315 Kennedy Ave., Grand Junction, 81501. Phone: (970) 242-7788. Fax: (970) 243-0567. Licensee: Cumulus Licensing LLC. Format: Rock. ◆Kevin Wodlinger, gen mgr.

Pierce

KJMP(AM)— 2004: 870 khz; 1.2 kw-D, 320 w-N, DA-2. TL: N40 36 25 W104 41 19. Hrs open: 1063 Big Thompson Rd., Apt F, Loveland, 80537-9424. Phone: (307) 638-8921. Licensee: Brahmin Broadcasting Corp. (acq 2-1-2006; $350,000). Format: Sports. ◆Steven Silverburg., gen mgr.

Pitkin

*KPKN(FM)—Not on air, target date: unknown: 90.1 mhz; 1 kw vert. Ant 1,522 ft TL: N38 29 46 W106 19 05. Hrs open: Box 217, Gainesville, TX, 76241. Phone: (940) 668-7971. Licensee: 1 A Chord Inc. ◆Mary Fay Jackson, gen mgr.

Placerville

*KTEI(FM)—Not on air, target date: 2: 90.7 mhz; 250 w. Ant 1,486 ft TL: N37 59 29 W107 58 21. Stereo. Hrs open:
KTLF (FM) Colorado Springs 100%.
1665 Briargate Blvd., Suite 100, Colorado Springs, 80920. Phone: (719) 593-0600. Fax: (719) 593-2399.E-mail: lightpraise@ktlf.org Web Site:www.ktlf.org Licensee: Educational Communications of Colorado Springs Inc. Format: Christian music. Target aud: 45-60; Christian. ◆Lynn Carmichael, progmg dir.

Poncha Springs

KWUZ(FM)— 2008: 97.5 mhz; 29 w. Ant 2,927 ft TL: N38 27 11 W106 01 02. Hrs open: 4687 Triple Eagle Tr., Larkspur, 80118. Secondary address: 7600 Country Rd., 120, Selida 81201. Phone: (719) 539-2575. Licensee: Three Eagles Communications of Colorado LLC (acq 12-28-2007; $300,000 plus assumption of bank debt for CP). ♦Rolland C. Johnson, CEO.

Pueblo

KAVA(AM)— June 1963: 1480 khz; 1 kw-D, DA. TL: N38 18 56 W104 37 03. Hrs open: 600 Grant St., Denver, 80203. Phone: (303) 733-5266. Fax: (303) 733-5242.E-mail: kbno@kbno.net Web Site:www.kbno.net Licensee: Latino Communications LLC (group owner; acq 1-23-03; $350,000 with KXRE(AM) Manitou Springs). Population served: 110,000 Format: Rgnl Mexican. News staff: 6; News: 21 hrs wkly. Target aud: 25-54. ♦Zee Ferrufino, gen mgr & opns dir.

KCCY(FM)— Aug 23, 1975: 96.9 mhz; 100 kw. 320 ft TL: N38 21 32 W104 58 13. Stereo. Hrs open: 2864 S. Circle Dr., Suite 150, 80906. Phone: (719) 540-9200. Fax: (719) 543-9898. Web Site:www.y969.com Licensee: Clear Channel Radio Licenses, Inc. Group owner: Clear Channel Communications Inc. (acq 11-22-00; with KDZA-FM Pueblo). Population served: 100,000 Natl. Rep: Christal,. Format: C&W. Target aud: 25-54; general. ♦Bob Richards, gen mgr, opns mgr; Mark Warren, gen sls mgr; Robert Vargas, prom dir; Paul Richards, news dir.

***KCFP(FM)**— June 1986: 91.9 mhz; 600 w. 633 ft TL: N38 22 23 W104 33 42. Stereo. Hrs open: 24
Rebroadcasts KCFR(FM) Denver 100%.
Colorado Public Radio, 7409 S. Alton Ct., Centennial, 80112. Phone: (303) 871-9191. Fax: (303) 733-3319. Web Site:www.cpr.org Licensee: Public Broadcasting of Colorado Inc. Natl. Network: NPR, . Arter & Hadden. Format: Class, news. News staff: 8; News: 50 hrs wkly. Target aud: General. ♦Max Wycisk, pres; Sue Coughlin, dev VP.

KCSJ(AM)— 1947: 590 khz; 1 kw-U, DA-N. TL: N38 21 30 W104 38 13. Hrs open: 24 106 W. 24th St., 81003. Phone: (719) 545-2080. Fax: (719) 543-9898.E-mail: webmaster@590kcsj.com Web Site:www.590kcsj.com Licensee: CC Licenses LLC. Group owner: Clear Channel Communications Inc. (acq 6-14-2001; with KDZA(AM) Pueblo). Population served: 150,000 Natl. Network: ABC, . Natl. Rep: Christal,. Format: News/talk. News staff: 2; News: 41 hrs wkly. Target aud: 35-64; upscale. ♦Olene Greenwood, gen mgr.

KDZA(AM)— February 1928: 1350 khz; 5 kw-D, 1 kw-N, DA-N. TL: N38 18 29 W104 38 24. Stereo. Hrs open: 24 106 W. 24th St., 81003. Phone: (719) 545-2080. Fax: (719) 543-9898. Licensee: CC Licenses LLC. Group owner: Clear Channel Communications Inc. (acq 6-14-2001; with KCSJ(AM) Pueblo). Population served: 130,000 Natl. Network: Fox Sports, . Haley, Bader & Potts. Format: Sports. Target aud: 35 plus. ♦Olene Greenwood, gen mgr.

KDZA-FM— Mar 3, 1987: 107.9 mhz; 100 kw. Ant 239 ft TL: N37 56 40 W104 59 56. Stereo. Hrs open: 106 W. 24th St., 81003. Phone: (719) 545-2080. Fax: (719) 543-9898.E-mail: webmaster@kdzafm.com Web Site:www.kdzafm.com Licensee: Capstar TX L.P. Group owner: Clear Channel Communications Inc. (acq 11-22-2000; with KCCY(FM) Pueblo). Population served: 532,300 Format: Rock. ♦Olene Greenwood, gen mgr.

KFEL(AM)— August 1956: 970 khz; 3.2 kw-D, 184 w-N. TL: N38 15 57 W104 40 44. Hrs open: Box 8055, 81008. Phone: (719) 543-7506. Fax: (719) 543—0432.E-mail: kfel970am@aol.com Licensee: Catholic Radio Network Inc. (acq 11-3-2006; $475,000). Population served: 509,500 Format: Relg. Target aud: 25 plus. ♦Allen Bickle, gen mgr.

***KFRY(FM)**— 2006: 89.9 mhz; 870 w. Ant 2,122 ft TL: N38 02 29 W105 11 05. Hrs open:
Rebroadcasts KUFR(FM) Salt Lake City, UT 100%.
c/o KUFR(FM), 136 E.S. Temple, Suite 1630, Salt Lake City, UT, 84111. Phone: (801) 359-3147. Fax: (801) 359-8112.E-mail: info@familyradio.com Web Site:www.familyradio.com Licensee: Family Stations Inc. Format: Christian relg. ♦Harold Camping, pres & gen mgr.

KGFT(FM)— Mar 31, 1988: 100.7 mhz; 72.4 kw. Ant 2,217 ft TL: N38 44 44 W104 51 39. Stereo. Hrs open: 24 7150 Campus Drive, Ste 150, Colorado Springs, 80920. Phone: (719) 531-5438. Fax: (719) 531-5588.E-mail: info@kgft.com Web Site:www.kgftradio.com Licensee: Salem Communications Corp. (group owner; (acq 1996; $3 million). Population served: 800,000 Natl. Network: AP Radio, . Format: Christian, news/talk, relg. News staff: one; News: 4 hrs wkly. Target aud: 25 plus; Christian. Spec prog: Gospel 3 hrs, old time radio 11 hrs wkly. ♦Henry Tippie, gen mgr.

KILO(FM)—See Colorado Springs

KIQN(FM)— November 1979: 106.9 mhz; 27.5 kw. Ant 666 ft TL: N38 06 22 W104 29 18. Stereo. Hrs open: 30 N. Electronic Dr., Pueblo West, 81007. Phone: (719) 547-0411. Fax: (719) 547-9301.E-mail: knfoffice@qwestoffice.net Licensee: Exodus Broadcasting LLC (group owner; (acq 8-7-2009; $500,000 with KWRP(AM) Pueblo). Population served: 159,361 Format: Sp Contemp. Target aud: 18-54. ♦Lupe Brown, gen mgr.

KKMG(FM)— Jan 1, 1967: 98.9 mhz; 100 kw. 1,715 ft TL: N38 44 32 W104 51 41. (CP: 56 kw, ant 2,299 ft.). Stereo. Hrs open: 24 6805 Corporate Dr., Suite 130, Colorado Springs, 80919-1977. Phone: (719) 593-2700. Fax: (719) 593-2727.E-mail: info@989magicfm.com Web Site:www.989magicfm.com Licensee: Citadel Broadcasting Co. Group owner: Citadel Broadcasting Corp. (acq 3-21-94; $912,500;4-18-94). Population served: 500,000 Natl. Rep: McGavren Guild,. Reed, Smith, Shaw & McClay. Format: Top-40. Target aud: 18-44. ♦Bobby Irwin, opns mgr; John Fox, gen mgr & progmg dir.

KKPC(AM)— Dec 29, 1947: 1230 khz; 1 kw-U. TL: N38 16 38 W104 39 13. Hrs open: 24 Colorado Public Radio, 7409 S. Alton Ct., Centennial, 80112. Phone: (303) 871-9191. Fax: (303) 733-3319.E-mail: info@cpr.org Web Site:www.cpr.org Licensee: Public Broadcasting of Colorado Inc. (acq 6-21-01; $275,000). Format: News and info. ♦Max Wycisk, pres; Jenny Gentry, exec VP; Sean Nethery, progmg VP.

KRXP(FM)—(Pueblo West, 1993: 103.9 mhz; 1.75 kw. Ant 2,158 ft. TL: N38 44 40 W104 51 41. Stereo. Hrs open: 24 1805 E. Cheyenne Rd., Colorado Springs, 80906. Phone: (719) 634-4896. Fax: (719) 634-5837. Web Site:www.1039rxp.com Licensee: Colorado Springs Radio Broadcasters Inc. Group owner: Bahakel Communications (acq 2-22-99; grpsl). Population served: 300,000 Format: Rock. News staff: one; News: one hr wkly. Target aud: 25-49; general. ♦Lou Mellini, gen mgr; Jason Janc, opns mgr, progmg dir.

***KTPL(FM)**— 2005: 88.3 mhz; 65 kw. Ant 226 ft TL: N37 56 40 W104 59 56. Stereo. Hrs open: 1665 Briargate Blvd., Suite 100, Colorado Springs, 80920. Phone: (719) 593-0600. Fax: (719) 593-2399.E-mail: power88@power88.org Web Site:www.power88.org Licensee: Educational Communications of Colorado Springs Inc. (acq 12-2-02; $6,251 for CP). Format: Inspirational Christian. Target aud: 18-35; Christian. ♦Sharick Wade, progmg dir.

***KTSC-FM**— October 1970: 89.5 mhz; 9.8 kw. 165 ft TL: N38 18 38 W104 34 40. Stereo. Hrs open: Colorado State University-Pueblo, 2200 Bonforte Blvd. Rm #120, 81001. Phone: (719) 549-2822. Fax: (719) 549-2120.E-mail: info@ktsc.com Licensee: University of Southern Colorado. Population served: 123,000 Format: Hip hop, rhythm and blues. ♦Mike Atencio, stn mgr.

KVUU(FM)— 1976: 99.9 mhz; 57. 2,200 ft TL: N33 44 47 W104 51 37. Stereo. Hrs open: 24 2864 S. Circle Dr., Suite 150, Colorado Springs, 80906. Phone: (719) 540-9200. Fax: (719) 579-0882.E-mail: info@my999radio.com Web Site:www.my999radio.com Licensee: Capstar TX L.P. Group owner: Clear Channel Communications Inc. (acq 8-30-00; grpsl). Natl. Rep: Clear Channel,. Format: Hits of the 90s. News staff: one; News: 3 hrs wkly. Target aud: 25-54; upscale young adults. ♦Bob Richards, chmn, gen mgr; Scott Jones, gen sls mgr; Robert Vargas, prom dir; Paul Richards, news dir.

KWRP(AM)— 1958: 690 khz; 250 w-D, 24 w-N. TL: N38 17 48 W104 38 47. Stereo. Hrs open: 24 30 N. Electronic Dr., Pueblo West, 81007. Phone: (719) 545-2883. Fax: (719) 547-9301.E-mail: knfoffice@qwestoffice.net Licensee: Exodus Broadcasting LLC (group owner; (acq 8-7-2009; $500,000 with KIQN(FM) Pueblo). Population served: 159,000 Format: Rgnl Mexican. Target aud: General; Hispanic families. ♦Lupe Brown, gen mgr.

Pueblo West

KRXP(FM)—Licensed to Pueblo West. See Pueblo

Red Feather Lakes

***KEZC(FM)**—Not on air, target date: unknown: 88.7 mhz; 26 w. Ant 853 ft TL: N40 52 04 W105 38 33. Hrs open: 5944 Kenosha St., Cheyenne, WY, 82001. Phone: (307) 460-4224. Licensee: Wren Communications Inc. ♦Tara D. Parker, pres.

Rico

***KICO(FM)**—Not on air, target date: unknown: 89.5 mhz; 250 w. Ant -997 ft TL: N37 41 34.94 W108 01 40.34. Hrs open: Box 116, Cortez, 81321. Phone: (970) 749-9117. Licensee: Community Radio Project. ♦Tom Yoder, pres.

Ridgway

KBNG(FM)— 2002: 103.7 mhz; 4.1 kw. Ant 1,574 ft TL: N38 23 15 W107 40 31. Stereo. Hrs open: 24 Box 970, Montrose, 81402. Secondary address: 106 Rose Lane, Montrose 81401. Phone: (970) 249-4546. Fax: (970) 249-2229. Web Site:www.coloradoradio.com Licensee: CCR-Montrose IV, LLC. (group owner; (acq 8-19-2004; grpsl). Format: Hot adult contemp. News staff: 1.5. Target aud: 18-44; Adults. ♦Joseph D. Schwartz, pres; Jay Austin, gen mgr; Scott Staley, progmg dir.

Rifle

KRGS(AM)— June 9, 1967: 690 khz; 1 kw-D. TL: N39 32 55 W107 46 10. Hrs open: 24 751 Horizon Ct., Suite 225, Grand Junction, 81506. Phone: (970) 241-6460. Fax: (970) 241-6452. Licensee: Western Slope Communications L.L.C. (group owner) Population served: 40,000 Akin, Gump, Strauss, Hauer & Feld. Format: Sports. Target aud: 18-54; males. ♦Merle Allen, gen mgr & gen sls mgr.

KZKS(FM)— 1994: 105.3 mhz; 60 kw. 2,437 ft TL: N39 25 57 W108 07 46. Stereo. Hrs open: 24 751 Horizon Ct., Suite 225, Grand Junction, 81506. Phone: (970) 241-6460. Fax: (970) 241-6452. Population served: 320,000 Format: Adult favorites. News staff: one; News: 20 hrs wkly. ♦Merle Allen, gen mgr.

Rocky Ford

KPHT(FM)— 2002: 95.5 mhz; 100 kw. Ant 735 ft TL: N37 54 08 W104 16 00. Hrs open: 106 W. 24th St., Pueblo, 81003. Phone: (719) 545-2080. Fax: (719) 543-9898.E-mail: webmaster@hot955.com Web Site:www.hot955.com Licensee: Capstar TX L.P. Group owner: Clear Channel Communications Inc. (acq 2-12-2001; $1 million). Format: Adult contemp, 80s, 90s. ♦Olene Greenwood, gen mgr.

Rye

***KJWA(FM)**—Not on air, target date: unknown: 89.7 mhz; 9.8 kw. Ant 679 ft TL: N37 32 34 W104 22 31. Hrs open:
Rebroadcasts KXWA(FM) Loveland 100%.
1707 N. Main, Suite 302, Longmont, 80501. Phone: (303) 702-9293. Fax: (303) 485-1929.E-mail: info@wayfm.com Web Site:kxwa.wayfm.com/contact-us/ Licensee: WAY-FM Media Group Inc. (acq 6-19-2007). Format: Christian rock. ♦Zach Cochran, gen mgr.

***KRWA(FM)**— Aug 24, 2007: 90.9 mhz; 11.5 kw. Ant 113 ft TL: N37 56 40 W104 59 56. Hrs open: Box 64500, Colorado Springs, 80962. Phone: (719) 533-0300. Fax: (719) 278-4339.E-mail: wxwa@wayfm.com Web Site:www.kxwy.net Licensee: WAY-FM Media Group Inc. (acq 6-17-2005; $200,000 for CP). Format: Christian. ♦Robert Augsburg, pres.

KRYE(FM)— 2008: 104.9 mhz; 25 kw. Ant 180 ft TL: N37 56 40 W104 59 56. Hrs open: 2099 U.S. Hwy 50 W., #130A, Pueblo, 81008. Phone: (719) 253-3777. Fax: (719) 562-4947. Licensee: United States CP LLC. Format: Rgnl Mexican. ♦Ricardo Salazar, gen mgr.

Salida

***KADE(FM)**—Not on air, target date: unknown: 89.7 mhz; 33 w. Ant 2,711 ft TL: N38 26 47 W106 00 37. Hrs open: 87 Jasper Lake Rd., Loveland, 80537. Phone: (970) 669-9200. Licensee: Cedar Cove Broadcasting Inc. ♦Victor A. Michael Jr., pres.

***KMPZ(FM)**—Not on air, target date: unknown: 88.1 mhz; 200 w. Ant 2,713 ft TL: N38 26 48 W106 00 36. Hrs open: c/o Ms. Jeanna Wearing, 1921 N. Weber St., Colorado Springs, 80907-6903. Phone: (719) 578-5263. Licensee: Cheyenne Mountain Public Broadcast House Inc. (acq 12-5-2008). ♦John W. Haralson, pres.

KSBV(FM)— 2002: 93.7 mhz; 1 kw. Ant 2,722 ft TL: N38 26 47 W106 00 37. Stereo. Hrs open: 24 228 East St., 81211. Phone: (719) 539-9377. Fax: (719) 539-7904.E-mail: ksbvradio@chaffee.net Web Site:www.ksbv.com Licensee: Arkansas Valley Broadcasting L.L.C.

Gammon & Grange. Format: Classic rock. Target aud: 25-65. ◆Marc Scott, pres, gen mgr; Melissa Scott, traf mgr.

*KTPF(FM)— 2007: 91.3 mhz; 385 w. Ant 2,952 ft TL: N38 26 48 W106 00 36. Stereo. Hrs open:
Rebroadcasts KTLF(FM) Colorado Springs 100%.
1665 Briargate Blvd., Suite 100, Colorado Springs, 80920-3400. Phone: (719) 593-0600. Fax: (719) 593-2399. Web Site:www.ktlf.org Licensee: Educational Communications of Colorado Springs Inc. Format: Christian music. Target aud: 45-60; Christian. ◆Lynn Carmichael, progmg dir.

KVRH(AM)— Dec 10, 1948: 1340 khz; 1 kw-U. TL: N38 31 55 W106 00 54. Hrs open: 24 7600 County Rd. 120, 81201. Phone: (719) 539-2575. Fax: (719) 539-4851.E-mail: kvrh@kvrh.com Web Site:www.kvrham.com Licensee: Headwaters Media L.L.C. (acq 9-1-2006; swap for KBVC(FM) Buena Vista). Population served: 20,000 Format: News/talk. News staff: one; News: 10 hrs wkly. Target aud: 25-54; general. ◆Jim Berry, gen mgr; Tim Ward, gen sls mgr; Kim Kreiss, progmg dir; Joseph Kreiss, news dir.

KVRH-FM— 1971: 92.3 mhz; 13.5 kw. Ant -656 ft TL: N38 30 26 W106 01 22. Stereo. Hrs open: 24 7600 CR 120, 81201. Phone: (719) 539-2575. Fax: (719) 539-4851.E-mail: kvrh@kvrh.com Web Site:www.kvrh.com Licensee: Three Eagles Communications of Colorado LLC (acq 4-12-2000; with co-located AM). Population served: 20,000 Format: Hot adult contemp. News staff: one; News: 10 hrs wkly. ◆Cristy Carothers, gen mgr, gen sls mgr; Jen Jackson, traf mgr.

Security

KRDO-FM— Apr 8, 1973: 105.5 mhz; 1.6 kw horiz, 1.47 kw vert. Ant 2,237 ft TL: N38 44 40 W104 51 41. Stereo. Hrs open: 24 Simulcasts KRDO(AM) Colorado Springs 100%.
399 S. 8th St., Colorado Springs, 80905. Phone: (719) 578-1055. Fax: (719) 475-0815.E-mail: m.lewis@krdotv.com Web Site:www.krdo.com Licensee: Optima Communications Inc. (acq 1989). Population served: 500,000 Mullin, Rhyne, Emmons & Topel. Format: News/talk. ◆J.B. McCoy III, pres; James R. Bond Jr., CFO; Edward L. Klimek, VP; Neil O. Klockziem, gen mgr.

Severance

KYEN(FM)— Mar 13, 2008: Stn currently dark. 103.9 mhz; 16.5 kw. Ant 1,220 ft TL: N40 37 03 W105 19 40. Hrs open: 980 N. Michigan Ave., Suite 1880, Chicago, IL, 60611. Phone: (312) 204-9900. Licensee: College Creek Media LLC. ◆Neal J. Robinson, pres.

Silt

KNAM(AM)—Not on air, target date: unknown: 1490 khz; 1 kw-U. TL: N39 33 37 W107 39 05. Hrs open: 1360 E. Sherwood Dr., Grand Junction, 81501. Phone: (970) 241-9230. Licensee: MBC Grand Broadcasting Inc. ◆David G. Hinson, pres.

Snowmass Village

KSNO-FM— April 1985: 103.9 mhz; 6 kw. Ant 325 ft TL: N39 14 51 W106 55 13. Stereo. Hrs open: 24 225 N. Mill St., Aspen, 81611. Phone: (970) 925-4111. Fax: (970) 925-7190.E-mail: don@thesoundfm.com Web Site:www.ksno.us Licensee: Cool Radio LLC. Population served: 20,000 Natl. Rep: Katz Radio,. Cole, Raywid & Braverman. Wire Svc: AP Format: AAA. News staff: one; News: 2 hrs wkly. Target aud: 25-54. ◆Don Chaney, gen mgr.

South Fork

*KTML(FM)— 2009: 91.5 mhz; 280 w vert. Ant 1,614 ft TL: N37 43 47 W106 35 18. Hrs open:
Rebroadcasts KTLF(FM) Colorado Springs 100%.
1665 Briargate Blvd., Suite 100, Colorado Springs, 80920. Phone: (719) 593-0600. Fax: (719) 593-2399. Web Site:www.ktlf.org Licensee: Educational Communications of Colorado Springs Inc. Format: Christian music. ◆Lynn Carmichael, gen mgr.

Springfield

*KLXD(FM)—Not on air, target date: unknown: 91.7 mhz; 1 kw. Ant 105 ft TL: N37 24 33 W102 37 40. Hrs open: 116 Hillcrest Dr., Seminole, OK, 74868. Phone: (405) 380-3516.E-mail: info@bpba.us Web Site:www.bpba.us Licensee: Better Public Broadcasting Association. ◆Dennis Burton, gen mgr.

Starkville

*KCCS(FM)— 2008: 91.7 mhz; 370 w. Ant 994 ft TL: N36 59 33 W104 28 24. Hrs open: 912 N. Weber St., Colorado Springs, 80903. Phone: (719) 473-4801. Fax: (719) 473-7863.E-mail: info@krcc.org Web Site:www.krcc.org Licensee: The Colorado College. Natl. Network: NPR, . Format: Div, news. ◆Thomas G. Nycum, VP; Delaney Utterback, gen mgr.

Steamboat Springs

KBCR(AM)— Aug 1, 1976: 1230 khz; 1 kw-U. TL: N40 29 19 W106 50 57. Hrs open: 24 Box 774050, 80477. Secondary address: 2110 Mt. Werner Rd. 80487. Phone: (970) 879-2270. Fax: (970) 879-1404.E-mail: kbcr@nctelecom.net Web Site:kbcr.com Licensee: Cool Radio LLC. (acq 1-30-2006; grpsl). Population served: 25,000 Natl. Network: ESPN Radio, . Format: Sports. News staff: one. Target aud: 24-55. ◆Brian Harvey, gen mgr, prom mgr, progmg dir; Dave Lancaster, sports cmtr.

KBCR-FM— July 25, 1974: 96.9 mhz; 10 kw. Ant 666 ft TL: N40 27 43 W106 50 57. Stereo. Hrs open: Prog sep from AM Box 774050, 80477. Phone: (970) 879-2270. Fax: (970) 879-1404.E-mail: kbcr@nctelecom.net Web Site:kbcr.com Licensee: Cool Radio LLC Population served: 25,000 Natl. Network: ABC, . Format: Country. ◆Brian Harvey, gen mgr; Gabriel Hibby, sls dir; Tony Marko, progmg dir; Debbie Duncan, mus dir.

KFMU-FM—See Oak Creek

*KLBV(FM)— 2005: 89.3 mhz; 2.6 kw vert. Ant 1,699 ft TL: N40 27 04 W106 45 06. Hrs open: 24 2351 Sunset Blvd., Suite 170-218, Rocklin, CA, 95765. Phone: (916) 251-1600. Fax: (916) 251-1650.E-mail: klove@klove.com Web Site:www.klove.com Licensee: Educational Media Foundation. Group owner: EMF Broadcasting (acq 10-2-03; grpsl). Natl. Network: K-Love, . Shaw Pittman. Format: Contemp Christian. News staff: 3. Target aud: 25-44; Judeo Christian, female. ◆Richard Jenkins, pres; Mike Novak, VP; Keith Whipple, dev dir; David Pierce, progmg mgr; Ed Lenane, news dir; Sam Wallington, engrg dir; Karen Johnson, news rptr.

*KRNC(FM)— Jan 23, 2006: 88.5 mhz; 240 w. Ant 600 ft TL: N40 27 43 W106 50 57. Hrs open:
Rebroadcasts KUNC(FM) Greeley 100%.
822 Seventh St., Suite 530, Greeley, 80631-3945. Phone: (970) 378-2579. Fax: (970) 378-2580.E-mail: mailbag@kunc.org Web Site:www.kunc.org Licensee: Community Radio of Northern Colorado (acq 1-5-2006; $50,000 for CP). Natl. Network: NPR, PRI, . Wire Svc: AP Format: Div, news. ◆Neil Best, gen mgr; Michelle Komanich, dev dir; Kirk Mowers, progmg dir; Jim Beers, news dir.

*KTSG(FM)— 2006: 91.7 mhz; 2.5 kw horiz. Ant 610 ft TL: N40 27 43 W106 50 58. Stereo. Hrs open:
Rebroadcasts KTLF(FM) Colorado Springs 100%.
1665 Briargate Blvd., Suite 100, Colorado Springs, 80920-3400. Phone: (719) 593-0600. Fax: (719) 593-2399.E-mail: lightpraise@ktlf.org Web Site:www.ktlf.org Licensee: Educational Communications of Colorado Springs Inc. Format: Christian music. Target aud: 45-60; Christian. ◆Lynn Carmichael, progmg dir.

Sterling

*KDRE(FM)— 2005: Stn currently dark. 90.7 mhz; 1.6 kw vert. Ant 506 ft TL: N40 36 56 W103 02 02. Hrs open:
Rebroadcasts KLRD(FM) Yucaipa, CA 100%.
2351 Sunset Blvd., Suite 170-218, Rocklin, CA, 95765. Phone: (916) 251-1600. Fax: (916) 251-1650. Web Site:www.air1.com Licensee: Educational Media Foundation. (acq 9-22-2005; $17,000 for CP). Natl. Network: Air 1, . Format: Christian rock. ◆Richard Jenkins, pres; Mike Novak, VP; Keith Whipple, dev dir; David Pierce, progmg mgr; Ed Lenane, news dir; Sam Wallington, engrg dir; Arthur Vassar, traf mgr; Karen Johnson, news rptr.

*KLZV(FM)—Not on air, target date: unknown: 91.3 mhz; 6 kw. Ant 423 ft TL: N40 08 56 W103 17 04. Hrs open: 2351 Sunset Blvd., Suite 170-218, Rocklin, CA, 95765. Phone: (916) 251-1600. Fax: (916) 251-1650.E-mail: klove@klove.com Web Site:www.klove.com Licensee: Educational Media Foundation. Group owner: EMF Broadcasting (acq 10-2-2003; grpsl). Natl. Network: K-Love, . Shaw Pittman. Format: Contemp Christian. News staff: 3. Target aud: 25-44; Judeo Christian, female. ◆Richard Jenkins, pres; Mike Novak, VP, progmg dir; Lloyd Parker, gen mgr; Ed Lenane, opns dir, news dir; Keith Whipple, dev dir; Eric Allen, natl sls mgr; David Pierce, progmg dir; Jon Rivers, mus dir; Sam Wallington, engrg dir; Arthur Vassar, traf mgr; Karen Johnson, news rptr.

KNNG(FM)— Feb 8, 1974: 104.7 mhz; 100 kw. Ant 500 ft TL: N40 34 57 W103 01 56. (CP: 1.8 kw, ant 424 ft.). Stereo. Hrs open: 24 Box 830, 803 W. Main, 80751. Phone: (970) 522-1607. Fax: (970) 522-1322.E-mail: montica07@hotmail.com Web Site:www.kingfmonline.com Licensee: Arnold Broadcasting Inc. (acq 7-31-2008; grpsl). Population served: 230,000 Natl. Network: Jones Radio Networks, ABC, . Format: Colorado country. News staff: one; News: 10 hrs wkly. Target aud: General; country listeners. ◆Betty Carlson, gen mgr; Mike Walker, progmg dir.

KPMX(FM)— Aug 19, 1983: 105.7 mhz; 12 kw. Ant 479 ft TL: N40 31 57 W103 07 22. Stereo. Hrs open: 24 117 Main St., 80751. Phone: (970) 522-4800. Fax: (970) 522-3994.E-mail: kpmx@necolorado.com Web Site:www.kpmx.com Jones Licensee: Northeast Colorado Broadcasting LLC (group owner; acq 7-1-2003; grpsl). Population served: 18,000 Booth, Freret, Imlay & Tepper. Format: Adult contemp. Target aud: 18-54. ◆Alec Creighton, gen mgr.

KSRX(FM)— 2008: 97.5 mhz; 17 kw. Ant 561 ft TL: N40 27 15.1 W103 09 6.1. Hrs open: P.O. Box 430, Fort Morgan, 80701-0430. Phone: (970) 867-5674. Fax: (970) 542-1023. Licensee: Media Logic LLC. Target aud: 18-45; female, male. ◆Wayne Johnson, pres; Marc Romero, stn mgr.

KSTC(AM)— Jan 3, 1925: 1230 khz; 1 kw-U. TL: N40 37 04 W103 10 31. Hrs open: 24 Box 830, 803 W. Main, 80751. Phone: (970) 522-1607. Fax: (970) 522-1322.E-mail: montica07@hotmail.com Web Site:www.kingfmonline.com Licensee: Arnold Broadcasting Inc. (group owner; (acq 7-31-2008; grpsl). Population served: 95,000 Natl. Network: ABC, Jones Radio Networks, . Format: Classic oldies. News staff: one; News: 12 hrs wkly. Target aud: General. Spec prog: Farm 15 hrs wkly. ◆Betty Carlson, gen mgr; Mike Walker, progmg dir.

*KTAD(FM)— 2005: 89.9 mhz; 5 kw vert. Ant 407 ft TL: N40 28 48 W103 05 47. Hrs open:
Rebroadcasts KTPL(FM) Pueblo 100%.
1665 Briargate Blvd., Suite 100, Colorado Springs, 80920. Phone: (719) 593-0600. Fax: (719) 593-2399.E-mail: power88@power88.org Web Site:www.power88.org Licensee: Educational Communications of Colorado Springs Inc. Format: Christian, inspirational. Target aud: 18-35; Christian. ◆Sharick Wade, progmg dir.

Strasburg

*KSJL(FM)—Not on air, target date: unknown: 97.7 mhz; 25 kw. Ant 328 ft TL: N39 42 50 W104 11 50. Hrs open: 1115 Honeysuckle Dr., Keene, TX, 76059. Phone: (817) 641-3495. Licensee: Mary V. Harris Foundation. ◆Linda De Romanett, pres.

KTNI-FM— May 1, 1968: 101.5 mhz; 97 kw horiz. Ant 2,050 ft TL: N39 55 22 W103 58 18. Stereo. Hrs open: 24 3033 S. Parker Rd., Suite 700, Aurora, 80014. Phone: (303) 872-1500. Fax: (303) 872-1501.E-mail: info@ktnifm.com Web Site:truthdenver.com Licensee: KBRU-FM LLC (group owner; (acq 10-24-2005; $15.5 million). Format: Talk. ◆Luis G. Nogales, CEO; Steve Keeney, gen mgr; Tim Maranville, opns dir & progmg dir.

Stratton

KGGY(FM)—Not on air, target date: unknown: 97.1 mhz; 51 kw horiz. Ant 164 ft TL: N39 11 00 W102 46 00. Hrs open: 87 Jasper Lake Rd., Loveland, 80537. Phone: (970) 669-9200.E-mail: vicmichael@aol.com Licensee: Kona Coast Radio LLC. ◆Victor A. Michael Jr., gen mgr.

Telluride

*KOTO(FM)— October 1975: 91.7 mhz; 2.35 kw. -187 ft TL: N37 55 59 W107 49 59. Stereo. Hrs open: Box 1069, 207 N. Pine St., 81435. Phone: (970) 728-4334. Fax: (970) 728-4326.E-mail: koto@tellurideacolorado.net Web Site:www.koto.com Licensee: San Miguel Educational Fund. (acq 7-22-86). Population served: 2,500 Natl. Network: NPR, PRI, . Format: Free-form. News staff: 2; News: 2 hrs wkly. Target aud: General; community. Spec prog: Class 9 hrs, country 12 hrs, jazz 9 hrs, blues 7 hrs, drama 3 hrs wkly. ◆Bob Biener, chmn, pres; Ben Kerr, gen mgr, stn mgr, progmg dir; Suzanne Cheavens, mus dir; Stephen Barrett, news dir; Janice Zink, spec ev coord.

Thornton

KKZN(AM)— May 30, 1987: 760 khz; 5 kw-D, 1 kw-N, DA-2. TL: N39 36 18 W104 50 25. Hrs open: 4695 S. Monaco St., Denver, 80237. Phone: (303) 713-8000. Fax: (303) 713-8736.E-mail: info@kkzn.com Web Site:www.am760.net Licensee: Citicasters Licenses Inc. (NEW).

Group owner: Clear Channel Communications Inc. (acq 5-4-99; grpsl). Population served: 514,678 Format: Progressive talk. ◆Lee Larsen, gen mgr; Ron Smith, opns mgr; Kristine Olinger, progmg dir; Jan Chadwell, chief of engrg.

Timnath

KJAC(FM)— Apr 10, 1989: 105.5 mhz; 58 kw. Ant 1,217 ft TL: N40 37 03 W105 19 40. Stereo. Hrs open: 24 1201 18th St., Suite 250, Denver, 80202. Phone: (303) 296-7025. Fax: (303) 296-7030.E-mail: info@1055jackfm.com Web Site:www.1055jackfm.com Licensee: NRC Broadcasting Inc. (group owner; (acq 4-13-2004; $15 million). Population served: 50,000 Natl. Network: Westwood One, . Natl. Rep: Target Broadcast Sales,. Eugene T. Smith. Format: Jack. News: 10 hrs wkly. Target aud: 18-54; general. ◆Timothy Brown, gen mgr; Roger Tighe, chief of engrg.

Trinidad

KCRT(AM)— May 21, 1946: 1240 khz; 250 w-U. TL: N37 08 45 W104 30 42. Hrs open: 24 100 Fisher Dr., 81082. Phone: (719) 846-3355. Fax: (719) 846-4711.E-mail: kcrt@comcast.net Licensee: Phillips Broadcasting Inc. (group owner; (acq 3-30-92; $235,000 with co-located FM; 4-20-92). Population served: 12,000 Natl. Network: ABC, Jones Radio Networks, . Format: Country. News staff: one; News: 15 hrs wkly. Target aud: General. Spec prog: Farm one hr, relg 5 hrs wkly. ◆Anita Phillips, pres, opns VP; Lory Phillips, gen mgr, gen sls mgr; David Phillips, stn mgr, mktg dir, progmg VP, news dir, pub affrs dir; Rick Neurauter, adv dir.

KCRT-FM— August 1981: 92.5 mhz; 38.5 kw. Ant 1,020 ft TL: N36 59 33 W104 28 24. Stereo. Hrs open: 24 Prog sep from AM 100 Fisher Dr., 81082. Phone: (719) 846-3355. Fax: (719) 846-4711.E-mail: krct@comcast.net Licensee: Phillips Broadcasting Inc. Population served: 30,000 Format: Classic rock. Target aud: 25-54.

*KTDL(FM)— 2007: 90.7 mhz; 450 w. Ant 971 ft TL: N36 59 33 W104 28 24. Stereo. Hrs open:
Rebroadcasts KTLF(FM) Colorado Springs 100%.
1665 Briargate Blvd., Suite 100, Colorado Springs, 80920-3400. Phone: (719) 593-0600. Fax: (719) 593-2399. Web Site:www.ktlf.org Licensee: Educational Communications of Colorado Springs Inc. Format: Christian music. Target aud: 45-60; Christian. ◆Lynn Carmichael, progmg dir.

Vail

*KPRE(FM)— Sept 1, 1994: 89.9 mhz; 1.5 kw. 295 ft TL: N39 38 05 W106 26 47. Hrs open: 24
Rebroadcasts KCFR(FM) Denver 100%.
7409 S. Alton Ct., Centennial, 80112. Phone: (303) 871-9191. Fax: (303) 733-3319.E-mail: info@cpr.org Web Site:cpr.org Licensee: Public Broadcasting of Colorado Inc. Population served: 25,000 Natl. Network: NPR, . Arter & Hadden. Format: Class, news, info. News staff: 8; News: 50 hrs wkly. Target aud: General. ◆Max Wycisk, pres; Sue Coughlin, dev VP.

KSKE-FM— 1997: 104.7 mhz; 100 kw. 394 ft TL: N39 38 08 W106 26 46. Stereo. Hrs open: 24 Box 7205, Avon, 81620. Secondary address: 182 Avon Rd., Avon 81620. Phone: (970) 949-0140. Fax: (970) 949-1464.E-mail: info@kskeradio.com Web Site:www.kskeradio.com Licensee: Superior Broadcasting of Denver LLC (group owner; acq 8-31-2006; exchange for KRKY-FM Estes Park). Population served: 12,000 Format: Country. ◆Steve Wodlinger, gen mgr; Meredith Fox, opns mgr; Holli Snyder, gen sls mgr; David Bach, news dir; Ken Laughlin, chief of engrg.

*KVJZ(FM)—Not on air, target date: Sep 1, 2009: 88.5 mhz; 1.9 kw. Ant 197 ft TL: N39 38 05 W106 26 47. Hrs open: 2900 Welton St., Suite 200, Denver, 80205. Phone: (303) 480-9272. Fax: (303) 291-0757.E-mail: info@kuvo.org Web Site:www.kuvo.org Licensee: Denver Educational Broadcasting Inc. ◆Carlos Lando, COO; Gene Craven, pres.

KVLE(AM)— July 25, 1983: 610 khz; 5 kw-D, 217 w-N. TL: N39 34 47 W106 24 54. Hrs open:
Simulcasts KSKE(AM) Buena Vista.
614 Kimbark St., Longmont, 80501. Phone: (303) 776-2323. Fax: (303) 776-1377.E-mail: cduncan@bcdworldwide.com Licensee: Pilgrim Communications Inc. (group owner; (acq 3-2-2000; $150,000). Natl. Network: ABC, . Format: Business talk. News staff: 3; News: 12 hrs wkly. Target aud: 25-65. ◆Chuck Duncan, CEO, pres, gen mgr; Gene Hood, pres; Roger Cridelbaugh, pub affrs dir.

Walden

KEZZ(FM)—Not on air, target date: unknown: 94.1 mhz; 44 kw horiz. Ant 492 ft TL: N40 39 51 W106 24 44. Hrs open: 1951 28th Ave., Unit 29, Greeley, 80634-5755. Phone: (970) 302-8444. Licensee: Youngers Colorado Broadcasting LLC. ◆Kevin J. Youngers, gen mgr.

Walsenburg

KOCK(FM)— 2009: 101.3 mhz; 95.5 kw. Ant 1,000 ft TL: N37 47 20 W104 29 12. Hrs open: 516 Main St., 81089. Phone: (773) 592-9800. Licensee: Edward Magnus. ◆Edward Magnus, gen mgr.

KSPK(FM)— March 1985: 102.3 mhz; 100 kw. Ant 430 ft TL: N37 37 39 W104 49 17. Stereo. Hrs open: 24 516 Main, 81089. Phone: (719) 738-3636. Fax: (719) 738-2010.E-mail: info@kspk.com Web Site:www.kspk.com Licensee: Mainstreet Broadcasting Co. Inc. (acq 9-12-90; $275,000; 10-8-90). Population served: 250,000 Natl. Network: ABC, . Denise B. Moline, P.C. Wire Svc: ABC Format: Country, farm, sports. News staff: 2; News: 3 hrs wkly. Target aud: 24-59; upwardly mobile, two-income families. Spec prog: Relg 2 hrs wkly. ◆Paul Richards, gen mgr; Paul Bossert, chief of engrg; Michelle Lessar, traf mgr. Co-owned TV: KSPK-LP affil

*KTAW(FM)— 2008: 89.3 mhz; 500 w vert. Ant 377 ft TL: N37 37 39 W104 49 17. Hrs open:
Rebroadcasts KTLF(FM) Colorado Springs 100%.
1665 Briargate Blvd., Suite 100, Colorado Springs, 80920-3400. Phone: (719) 593-0600. Fax: (719) 593-2399.E-mail: litepraise@ktlf.org Web Site:www.ktlf.org Licensee: Educational Communications of Colorado Springs Inc. Format: Christian music. ◆Karen Veazey, gen mgr.

Wellington

KCOL(AM)—Licensed to Wellington. See Fort Collins

KMAX-FM— 2003: 94.3 mhz; 8.7 kw. Ant 551 ft TL: N40 55 41 W105 08 36. Hrs open: 24 600 Main St., Windsor, 80550. Phone: (970) 674-2700. Fax: (970) 686-7491.E-mail: chall@regentcomm.com Web Site:www.943maxfm.com Licensee: Regent Broadcasting of Ft. Collins Inc. Group owner: Regent Communications Inc. (acq 2-25-2003). Format: Rock of the 80's and more. ◆Cal Hall, gen mgr; Mark Callaghan, opns mgr; Miles Schallert, sls dir; Ted Rose, progmg dir; Susan Moore, news dir; Quin Morrison, chief of engrg.

Westcliffe

KXCL(FM)— 2008: 101.7 mhz; 180 w. Ant -413 ft TL: N38 08 09 W105 27 07. Hrs open: 2099 U.S. Hwy 50 W., Suite 130A, Pueblo, 81008. Phone: (719) 253-3777. Fax: (719) 562-4947. Licensee: United States CP LLC. Format: Rgnl Mexican. ◆Ricardo Salazar, gen mgr.

Wheat Ridge

KTCL(FM)— September 1965: 93.3 mhz; 71 kw. Ant 1,135 ft TL: N39 43 59 W105 14 10. Stereo. Hrs open: 4695 S. Monaco St., Denver, 80237. Phone: (303) 713-8000. Fax: (303) 713-8743.E-mail: info@ktcl.com Web Site:www.area93.com Licensee: Jacor Broadcasting of Colorado Inc. (acq 5-8-98; $6.1 million with co-located AM). Population served: 160,000 Format: Alternative. Target aud: 18 plus. Spec prog: Comedy one hr, loc bands one hr, reggae 2 hrs wkly. ◆Lee Larsen, gen mgr; Ron Smith, opns mgr; Willie Hung, progmg dir; Karl Schipper, chief of engrg.

Widefield

KKLI(FM)—Licensed to Widefield. See Colorado Springs

Wiggins

*KHWD(FM)—Not on air, target date: unknown: 90.7 mhz; 3.8 kw. Ant 902 ft TL: N40 16 29 W104 06 17. Hrs open: 18900 E. Hampden Ave., Aurora, 80013. Phone: (303) 628-7200. Fax: (303) 628-7205.E-mail: info@calvaryaurora.org Web Site:www.calvaryaurora.org Licensee: Calvary Chapel Aurora. ◆Ed Taylor, pres.

Windsor

KJJD(AM)— Apr 12, 1969: 1170 khz; 1 kw-D. TL: N40 27 46 W104 54 47. Hrs open: Sunrise-sunset 624 N. Main St., Longmont, 80501. Phone: (303) 651-1199. Fax: (303) 651-2244. Web Site:www.laley1170.com Licensee: Rodriguez-Gallegos Broadcasting Corporation. (acq 3-19-85). Population served: 500000 Shaw Pittman. Format: Sp, music. News: 5 hrs wkly. Target aud: 18-54; general. Spec prog: Pub affrs. ◆Jesse Rodriguez, gen mgr; Danny Casas, stn mgr.

KUAD-FM— May 31, 1975: 99.1 mhz; 100 kw. Ant 836 ft TL: N40 38 31 W104 49 03. Stereo. Hrs open: 600 Main St., 80550. Phone: (970) 674-2700. Fax: (970) 686-7491.E-mail: chall@regentcomm.com Web Site:www.k99.com Licensee: Regent Broadcasting of Ft. Collins Inc. Group owner: Regent Communications Inc. (acq 2-25-03). Population served: 295,000 Dow, Lohnes & Albertson. Format: Country. Target aud: 25-54; upscale country listeners, 60% women. ◆Cal Hall, gen mgr; Mark Callaghan, opns mgr, progmg dir; Shelley Heier, gen sls mgr, mktg dir & prom dir; Brian Gary, mus dir; Meg Sprague, traf mgr.

Winter Park

KZMV(FM)—See Kremmling

Woodland Park

*KILE-FM—Not on air, target date: unknown: 89.5 mhz; 100 w vert. Ant -407 ft TL: N38 59 37 W105 02 21. Hrs open: 4703 Orkney Dr., Missouri City, TX, 77459. Phone: (281) 923-7100. Fax: (281) 403-6314. Licensee: Grace Public Radio. ◆Fred R. Morton, gen mgr.

Wray

KRDZ(AM)— Jan 11, 1978: 1440 khz; 5 kw-D, 200 w-N. TL: N56 04 00 W102 11 25. Hrs open: 4:50 AM-midnight Box 354, 80758. Phone: (970) 332-4171. Fax: (970) 332-4172.E-mail: krdz@mediamagicradio.com Web Site:www.krdz.com Licensee: Media Logic LLC (group owner; acq 10-31-2002). Natl. Network: Jones Radio Networks, . Rgnl. Network: Brownfield. Brownfield Format: Classic hits. News: 10 hrs wkly. Target aud: Farmers & ranchers. Spec prog: Focus on family 2 hrs, farm 10 hrs wkly. ◆Wayne Johnson, gen mgr & opns mgr.

Yuma

KNEC(FM)— 1999: 100.9 mhz; 23 kw. Ant 348 ft TL: N40 00 33 W102 45 35. Hrs open: 205 S. Main St., 80759. Phone: (970) 848-2302. Fax: (970) 848-2240.E-mail: knec@plains.net Licensee: Arnold Broadcasting Inc. (group owner; (acq 7-31-2008; grpsl). Format: Hot adult contemp. ◆Tammy Sewell, gen mgr.

Connecticut

Ansonia

WADS(AM)— May 8, 1956: 690 khz; 1 kw-D, 33 w-N, DA-2. TL: N41 20 48 W73 06 56. (CP: 3.5 kw-D, 200 w-N). Hrs open: 261 Portsea St., New Haven, 06519. Phone: (203) 777-7690. Phone: (203) 782-3564. Fax: (203) 782-3565.E-mail: radioamorwad@sbcglobal.net Web Site:www.radioamor690.com Licensee: Radio Amor Inc. (acq 12-30-93; $450,000; 1-17-94). Population served: 85,000 Shaw Pittman. Format: Relg, educ, Sp. News: 3.5 hrs wkly. Target aud: General. ◆Rev. Moses Mercedes, pres; Rev. Luis Rivera, VP; Abraham Hernandez, gen mgr.

Berlin

*WERB(FM)— Jan 12, 1979: 94.5 mhz; 27.5 w. 95 ft TL: N41 37 18 W72 45 13. (CP: 94.5 mhz). Stereo. Hrs open: 24 Berlin High School Media Center, 139 Patterson Way, 06037. Phone: (860) 828-0606. Phone: (860) 828-6577. Fax: (860) 829-0526.E-mail: werb@berlinschools.org Web Site:www.berlinwall.org Licensee: Berlin Board of Education. Format: Educ/Rock. Teenage listeners from Berlin High School. ◆Chris Wolfe, gen mgr.

Bloomfield

WDZK(AM)— February 1964: 1550 khz; 5 kw-D, 2 kw-N, DA-2. TL: N41 51 47 W72 44 01. Hrs open: 24 160 Chapel Rd., Manchester,

06040. Phone: (860) 643-3912. Fax: (860) 643-3910.E-mail: paul.o.robertson.@disney.com Web Site:www.radiodisney.com Licensee: Radio Disney Group LLC. Group owner: ABC Inc. (acq 11-21-00; grpsl). Natl. Network: ABC, . Format: Children. News staff: one; News: 11 hrs wkly. Target aud: 18-80; general. ♦Paul Robertson, gen mgr.

Bridgeport

WCUM(AM)— September 1941: 1450 khz; 1 kw-U. TL: N41 12 40 W73 11 28. Hrs open: 24 1862 Commerce Drive, 06605. Phone: (203) 335-1450. Fax: (203) 337-1220.E-mail: oficina@cumbre.com Web Site:www.wcum1450.com Licensee: Radio Cumbre Broadcasting Inc. (acq 4-89; $550,000; 4-24-89). Population served: 156,542 Natl. Network: CNN Radio, . Format: Sp, tropical. News staff: 2; News: 14 hrs wkly. Target aud: 25 plus. ♦Pablo De Jesus Colon Hijo, CEO & pres; Migdalia Ramos Colon, VP; Allison Sheahan, gen mgr.

WDJZ(AM)— Apr 30, 1977: 1530 khz; 5 kw-D, DA. TL: N41 10 09 W73 13 14. Hrs open: 177 State St., 06604. Phone: (203) 368-4392. Fax: (203) 367-4551.E-mail: wdjzradio@sbcglobal.net Web Site:www.wdjzradio.com Licensee: People's Broadcast Network LLC (acq 6-19-2007). Format: Foreign/Ethnic, gospel. Target aud: 35 plus. ♦Milford Edwards Sr., gen mgr.

WEZN-FM— Oct 24, 1960: 99.9 mhz; 27.6 kw. 669 ft TL: N41 16 46 W73 11 09. Stereo. Hrs open: 440 Wheelers Farms Rd., Suite 302, Milford, 06461. Phone: (203) 783-8200. Fax: (203) 783-8373. Web Site:www.star999.com Licensee: Cox Radio Inc. Group owner: Cox Broadcasting (acq 3-28-97; grpsl). Population served: 350,000 Format: Adult contemp. Target aud: 25-54. ♦Kim Guthrie, exec VP, gen mgr; Helaine Greenbaum, natl sls mgr; Stuart Gorlick, gen sls mgr & rgnl sls mgr; Stephen Donnarummo, prom dir; Samantha Stevens, progmg dir; Dom Bordonaro, chief of engrg; Carol Roberts, traf mgr.

WICC(AM)— 1926: 600 khz; 1 kw-D, 500 w-N, DA-2. TL: N41 09 36 W73 09 53. Stereo. Hrs open: 24 2 Lafayette Sq., 06604-6000. Phone: (203) 366-6000. Fax: (203) 384-0600. Fax: (203) 394-6000. Web Site:www.wicc600.com Licensee: Cumulus Licensing Corp. Group owner: Cumulus Media Inc. (acq 3-14-02; grpsl). Population served: 450,000 Natl. Rep: Christal,. Wiley, Rein & Fielding. Format: Talk. News staff: 5; News: 25 hrs wkly. Target aud: 35-64. Spec prog: It 5 hrs wkly. ♦Ann McManus, VP, gen mgr; Curt Hansen, opns VP.

***WPKN(FM)**— Oct 10, 1963: 89.5 mhz; 10 kw. 550 ft TL: N41 16 43 W73 11 08. Stereo. Hrs open: 24 244 University Ave., 06604. Phone: (203) 331-9756.E-mail: wpkn@wpkn.org Web Site:www.wpkn.org Licensee: WPKN Inc. (acq 12-10-97). Population served: 30,000 Format: Div. Spec prog: Class 2 hrs, Sp 4 hrs, Black 4 hrs, Fr 2 hrs, jazz 16 hrs wkly. ♦Henry Minot, gen mgr.

Bristol

WPRX(AM)— 11/22/1993: 1120 khz; 1 kw-D, 500 w-N, DA-N. TL: N41 39 29 W72 56 51. Hrs open: 24 321 Ellis St., New Britian, 06051. Phone: (860) 348-0667. Fax: (860) 348-0711.E-mail: wprx1120@comcast.net Web Site:www.wprx1120.net Licensee: Nievezquez Production Inc. (acq 4-28-99; $925,000). Population served: 300,000 Format: News/talk, Sp tropical. News staff: 2; News: 12 hrs wkly. Target aud: 23-54; Hispanic adults. Spec prog: Pol 2 hrs wkly. ♦Oscar Nieves, gen mgr.

Brookfield

WINE(AM)— May 9, 1966: 940 khz; 1 kw-D, 4 w-N. TL: N41 29 35 W73 25 47. Hrs open: 1004 Federal Rd., 06804. Phone: (203) 775-1212. Fax: (203) 775-6452.E-mail: info@cumulus.com Web Site:www.cumulus.com Licensee: Cumulus Licensing Corp. Group owner: Cumulus Media Inc. (acq 1-23-2002; grpsl). Population served: 165,000 Natl. Network: ESPN Radio, . Haley, Bader & Potts. Format: Sports. Target aud: 25-54. ♦Brett Beshore, gen mgr; Matt Carey, prom dir, progmg dir; Tim Sheehan, opns mgr & progmg dir; Lisa Harris, news dir; Peter Partenio, chief of engrg.

WRKI(FM)— Dec 24, 1976: 95.1 mhz; 50 kw. Ant 500 ft TL: N41 29 35 W73 25 47. Stereo. Hrs open: 1004 Federal Rd., 06804. Phone: (203) 775-1212. Fax: (203) 775-6452.E-mail: info@i95rock.com Web Site:www.i95rock.com Licensee: Cumulus Licensing Corp. Population served: 75,000 Format: Classic rock. ♦Tom Principi, gen sls mgr; Taryn Polites, prom dir.

Danbury

WDAQ(FM)— December 1953: 98.3 mhz; 1.3 kw. 460 ft TL: N41 22 27 W73 26 47. Stereo. Hrs open: 24 Prog sep from AM 198 Main St., 06810. Phone: (203) 744-4800. Fax: (203) 778-4655. Web Site:www.98q.com Licensee: Berkshire Broadcasting Corp. Population served: 250,000 Natl. Rep: D & R Radio,. Format: Hot A/C.

***WFAR(FM)**— July 19, 1981: 93.3 mhz; 18 w. Ant 210 ft TL: N41 23 44 W73 25 24. Stereo. Hrs open: 25 Chestnut St., 06810. Phone: (203) 748-0001. Fax: (203) 746-4262. Web Site:www.radiofamilia.com Licensee: Danbury Community Radio Inc. (acq 7-81). Format: Educ, Portuguese, relg. News staff: one. Portuguese, Sp & It. Spec prog: Sp 2 hrs wkly. ♦David Abrantes, pres, gen mgr; Helena Abrantes, opns mgr; Joe Mingachos, news dir.

WINE(AM)—See Brookfield

WLAD(AM)— October 1947: 800 khz; 1 kw-D, 287 w-N. TL: N41 22 27 W73 26 47. Stereo. Hrs open: 24 198 Main St., 06810. Phone: (203) 744-4800. Fax: (203)778-4655.E-mail: radio80wlad@aol.com Web Site:www.wlad.com Licensee: Berkshire Broadcasting Corp. (group owner) Population served: 250,000 Natl. Network: CNN Radio, . Natl. Rep: D & R Radio,. Cohn & Marks. Format: News/talk. ♦Irv Goldstein, exec VP; Irving J. Goldstein, gen mgr.

WREF(AM)—See Ridgefield

WRKI(FM)—See Brookfield

***WXCI(FM)**— Feb 10, 1973: 91.7 mhz; 1.2 kw. 205 ft TL: N41 23 44 W73 25 24. (CP: 3 kw, ant 201 ft.). Stereo. Hrs open: 6 AM-2 AM Student Ctr., 181 White St., 06810. Phone: (203) 837-9924.E-mail: wxci@yahoo.com Web Site:www.wxci.org Licensee: Western Connecticut State University Board of Trustees. (acq 3-73). Format: Alternative. News: 3 hrs wkly. Target aud: 14-25. Spec prog: Club mus 3 hrs, jazz 3 hrs, reggae 2 hrs, new age 3 hrs, metal 3 hrs, classic rock 3 hrs wkly. ♦Justin Mazzarese, gen mgr; Chris Merkle, prom dir; John Selwyn, progmg dir; Tom Carpenter, mus dir; Travis Cuddy, chief of engrg.

East Lyme

WNLC(FM)— Apr 1, 1994: 98.7 mhz; 5.5 kw. 269 ft TL: N41 20 48 W72 06 50. Stereo. Hrs open: 24 Box 1031, New London, 06320. Secondary address: 89 Broad St., New London 06320. Phone: (860) 442-5328. Fax: (860) 442-6532.E-mail: arussell@hallradio.com Web Site:www.wnlc.com Licensee: Hall Communication Inc. (group owner; acq 6-16-97; $2 million). Population served: 350,000 Rgnl. Network: CRN. Natl. Rep: Eastman Radio,. Fletcher, Heald & Hildreth. Format: Classic Hits. Target aud: Adults 25-49. ♦Bonnie H. Rowbotham, chmn; Arthur J. Rowbotham, pres; Bill Baldwin, sr VP; Andy Russell, stn mgr.

Enfield

WPKX(FM)— July 1990: 97.9 mhz; 2.22 kw. 528 ft TL: N42 05 05 W72 42 14. Hrs open: 1331 Main St., Springfield, MA, 01103. Phone: (413) 781-1011. Fax: (413) 734-4434. Web Site:www.kix979.com Licensee: Capstar TX L.P. Group owner: Clear Channel Communications Inc. (acq 8-30-00; grpsl). Format: Contemp country. Target aud: 25-54. ♦Sean Davey, gen mgr; Pat McKay, opns mgr.

Fairfield

***WSHU(FM)**— February 1964: 91.1 mhz; 20 kw. Ant 624 ft TL: N41 16 45 W73 11 09. Stereo. Hrs open: 24 5151 Park Ave., 06825. Phone: (203) 365-6604. Fax: (203) 371-7991.E-mail: lombardi@wshu.org Web Site:www.wshu.org Licensee: Sacred Heart University Inc. (acq 1-5-90). Population served: 156,542 Natl. Network: NPR, PRI, . Wire Svc: AP Format: Class, news. News staff: 4; News: 43 hrs wkly. Target aud: General; all ages. Spec prog: Folk 5 hrs, new age 6 hrs wkly. ♦George Lombardi, gen mgr; Barbara Bashar, opns mgr; Gillian Anderson, dev dir.

***WVOF(FM)**— Sept 1, 1970: 88.5 mhz; 100 w. 35 ft TL: N41 09 32 W73 15 35. Stereo. Hrs open: 5 AM-2 AM Box R, Campus Ctr., N. Benson Rd., 06824. Phone: (203) 254-4144. Fax: (203) 254-4224.E-mail: centralstaff@wvof.org Web Site:www.wvof.org Licensee: Fairfield University. Population served: 55,000 Format: Var/div, progsv. News staff: 5; News: 4 hrs wkly. Target aud: 18-35. ♦Matt Dinnan, gen mgr; Mark Gajda, stn mgr; Kim Gryzbala, mktg dir, rsch dir; James Maresca, progmg dir.

Greenwich

WGCH(AM)— Sept 14, 1964: 1490 khz; 1 kw-U. TL: N41 01 37 W73 37 59. Hrs open: 24 71 Lewis St., 06830. Phone: (203) 869-1490. Fax: (203) 869-3636. Web Site:www.wgch.com Licensee: BTR Greenwich Inc. (acq 6-18-2003; $1.1 million). Population served: 361,000 Natl. Network: Fox News Radio, . Rgnl. Network: Capitol Radio Net. Format: News, business talk. News staff: 2; News: 35 hrs wkly. Target aud: 35 plus; very upscale, active, athletic, community-minded. Spec prog: High school sports 6 hrs, educ 2 hrs, Pol one hr, relg 3 hrs, It one hr wkly. ♦Michael Metter, CEO, chmn, pres, gen mgr; Jeff Weber, exec VP, progmg dir; Bob Small, opns mgr; Tony Savino, news dir; Rob Adams, sports cmtr.

Groton

WQGN-FM— 1971: 105.5 mhz; 3 kw. 275 ft TL: N41 23 05 W72 04 13. Stereo. Hrs open: 7 Governor Winthrop Blvd., New London, 06320. Phone: (860) 443-1980. Fax: (860) 444-7970.E-mail: info@q105.fm.com Web Site:www.q105.fm Population served: 300,000 Format: CHR. Target aud: 18-49. ♦Shawn Murphy, mus dir.

WSUB(AM)— July 26, 1958: 980 khz; 1 kw-D. TL: N41 23 05 W72 04 13. Hrs open: 7 Governor Winthrop Blvd., New London, 06320-6437. Phone: (860) 443-1980. Fax: (860) 444-7970.E-mail: info@caliente980.com Web Site:www.caliente980am.com Licensee: Citadel Broadcasting Co. Group owner: Citadel Broadcasting Corp. (acq 4-26-2001; grpsl). Population served: 43,000 Natl. Network: ABC, . Format: Sp. Target aud: 25-49; middle income professionals. ♦Wayne Leland, exec VP; Bonnie Gomes, gen mgr, stn mgr; Kevin Palana, progmg VP, progmg dir; Frank Doremus, chief of engrg.

Guilford

***WGRS(FM)**— Dec 27, 1993: 91.5 mhz; 3.1 kw. 82 ft TL: N41 17 19 W72 39 32. (CP: 6 kw). Stereo. Hrs open: 24
Rebroadcasts WMNR(FM) Monroe 100%.
Box 920, Monroe, 06468. Phone: (203) 268-9667.E-mail: info@wmnr.org Web Site:www.wmnr.org Licensee: Monroe Board of Education. Population served: 60,000 Natl. Network: PRI, . Format: Class. Spec prog: Big band 8 hrs, folk 2 hrs, new age one hr, Broadway one hr wkly. ♦Kurt Anderson, gen mgr; Jane Stadler, opns dir; Carol Babina, dev dir.

Hamden

WAVZ(AM)—See New Haven

WKCI-FM—Licensed to Hamden. See New Haven

***WQAQ(FM)**— February 1973: 98.1 mhz; 16 w. -82 ft TL: N41 25 10 W72 53 41. Stereo. Hrs open: Noon-2 AM (S-Su); 8 AM-2 AM (M-F) Box 59, Quinnipiac Univ., 275 Mt. Casnad Ave., 06518. Phone: (203) 582-5278. Fax: (203) 582-8098. Web Site:www.angelfire.com/ct2/wqaqradio/ Format: AOR, news/talk, alternative rock. News: 10 hrs wkly. Target aud: 18-30. ♦Chris Cooper, gen mgr; Carlos Lanesee, prom dir; Sally Densa, adv VP; Glenn Giangrande, progmg dir; Jessie Elgarten, progmg mgr; Alison Keller, news dir; Bill Shoulders, pub affrs dir.

WQUN(AM)— July 17, 1960: 1220 khz; 1 kw-D, 305 w-N, DA-1. TL: N41 22 32 W72 55 54. Stereo. Hrs open: 24 Quinnipiac University, 275 Mt. Carmel Ave., 06518. Phone: (203) 582-8984. Fax: (203) 582-5372.E-mail: ray.andrewsen@quinnipiac.edu Web Site:www.wqun.com Licensee: Quinnipiac University (acq 9-12-96; $500,000). Population served: 400,000 Natl. Network: CBS, Jones Radio Networks, . Garvey, Schubert, Barer. Format: News, loc info, adult standards. News staff: 2. Target aud: General; community, business & cultural leaders. Spec prog: Irish 2 hrs, Broadway 2hrs, big bands 4 hrs wkly. ♦Ray Andrewsen, gen mgr & opns dir; Greg Little, news dir, pub affrs dir; Bob Radil, chief of engrg.

Hartford

WCCC(AM)—(West Hartford, 1947: 1290 khz; 490 w-D, 11 w-N. TL: N41 47 48 W72 47 50. Hrs open: 24 1039 Asylum Ave., 06105. Phone: (860) 525-1069. Fax: (860) 246-9084.E-mail: info@wccc.com Licensee: Marlin Broadcasting of Hartford LLC (acq 5-18-2000; grpsl). Population served: 200,000 Natl. Rep: Eastman Radio,. Akin, Gump, Strauss, Hauer & Feld. Format: Class. Target aud: 18-54. ♦Woody Tanger, CEO; Boyd E. Arnold, VP, gen mgr; Michael Picozzi, opns mgr; Jay Schultz, sls dir, gen sls mgr; Michelle Bassoss, natl sls mgr; Nicole Godburn, prom dir; John Ramsey, chief of engrg.

WCCC-FM— June 7, 1960: 106.9 mhz; 23 kw. 730 ft TL: N41 47 51 W72 47 52. Stereo. Hrs open: 24 1039 Asylum Ave., 06105. Phone: (860) 525-1069. Fax: (860) 246-9084. Web Site:www.wccc.com Population served: 1,000,000 Natl. Rep: Eastman Radio,. Akin, Gump, Strauss, Hauer & Feld. Format: Active rock. Target aud: 18-49; adult men. ♦Jon Skonieczny, prom mgr.

WDRC(AM)— Dec 10, 1922: 1360 khz; 5 kw-U, DA-N. TL: N41 48 45 W72 41 44. Hrs open: 24 869 Blue Hills Ave., Bloomfield, 06002. Phone: (860) 243-1115. Fax: (860) 286-8257.E-mail: wdrc@talkofconnecticut.com Web Site:talkofconnecticut.com Licensee: Buckley Broadcasting of Connecticut LLC. Group owner: Buckley Broadcasting Corp. (acq 8-1-59). Population served: 1,030,500 Natl. Network: Westwood One, AP Radio, . Natl. Rep: McGavren Guild,. CRN Wire Svc: AP Format: News/talk. News staff: one. Target aud: 40+. ♦Richard D. Buckley, pres; Eric D. Fahnoe, VP, gen mgr; Laura Kittell, opns mgr; Byron McClanahan, gen sls mgr; Grahame Winters, prom dir; Dave Nagel, progmg dir.

WDRC-FM— 1939: 102.9 mhz; 19.5 kw. Ant 810 ft TL: N41 33 44 W72 50 40. Stereo. Hrs open: 24 Prog sep from AM 869 Blue Hills Ave., Bloomfield, 06002. Phone: (860) 243-1115. Fax: (860) 286-8257.E-mail: info@drcfm.com Web Site:drcfm.com Population served: 1,030,500 Natl. Network: AP Radio, . Natl. Rep: McGavren Guild,. Wire Svc: AP Wire Svc: Metro Weather Service Inc. Format: Classic hits. News staff: one. Target aud: 25-64. ♦Grahame Winters, prom mgr.

WHCN(FM)— 1939: 105.9 mhz; 16 kw. Ant 867 ft TL: N41 33 47 W72 50 42. Stereo. Hrs open: 24 10 Columbus Blvd., 06106. Phone: (860) 723-6000. Fax: (860) 723-7090. Web Site:www.theriver1059.com Licensee: Capstar TX L.P. Group owner: Clear Channel Communications Inc. (acq 8-30-00; grpsl). Population served: 2,415,700 Natl. Rep: Christal,. Format: Rock/AOR. ♦Tom McConnell, gen mgr; Steve Honeycomb, sls dir; Todd Thomas, prom dir, progmg dir; Rick Walsh, engrg VP, chief of engrg.

***WJMJ(FM)**— Oct 18, 1976: 88.9 mhz; 7.2 kw. 580 ft TL: N41 45 09 W72 59 40. Stereo. Hrs open: 5 am-Midnight St. Thomas Seminary, 467 Bloomfield Ave., Bloomfield, 06002. Phone: (860) 242-8800. Fax: (860) 242-4886.E-mail: info@wjmj.org Web Site:wjmj.org Licensee: St. Thomas Seminary-Archdiocese of Hartford. Population served: 300,000 Natl. Network: ABC, . Garvey, Schubert & Barer. Wire Svc: AP Format: Btfl music, class, relg. News staff: one; News: 10 hrs wkly. Target aud: 40-65; working, middle-class, family group. Spec prog: Educ, foreign one hr wkly. ♦Archbishop Henry Mansell, pres; John L. Ellinger, gen mgr; John P. Masternak, progmg dir; Ivor Hugh, mus dir.

WKND(AM)—See Windsor

WKSS(FM)— June 1947: 95.7 mhz; 16.5 kw. 880 ft TL: N41 33 41 W72 50 39. Stereo. Hrs open: Hartford Sq. N., 10 Columbus Blvd., 06106-1944. Phone: (860) 723-6000. Fax: (860) 493-7090. Web Site:kiss957.com Licensee: Capstar TX L.P. Group owner: Clear Channel Communications Inc. (acq 8-30-00; grpsl). Population served: 350,000 Rgnl. Network: Conn. Radio Net. Natl. Rep: Christal,. Conn. Radio Net. Format: CHR. Target aud: 18-34. ♦Tom McConnell, gen mgr; Stan Priest, progmg dir.

WLAT(AM)—See New Britain

WMRQ-FM—See Waterbury

WNEZ(AM)—See Manchester

WPOP(AM)— July 1935: 1410 khz; 5 kw-U, DA-2. TL: N41 41 35 W72 45 30. Hrs open: 24 10 Columbus Blvd., 06106. Phone: (860) 723-6000. Fax: (860) 723-7090. Web Site:www.espnradio1410.com Licensee: Capstar TX L.P. Population served: 1,135,000 Natl. Network: ESPN Radio, . Format: Sports. News staff: 8; News: 25 hrs wkly. Target aud: 35 plus.

***WQTQ(FM)**— November 1971: 89.9 mhz; 120 w. 86 ft TL: N41 47 47 W72 41 42. Hrs open: 24 Weaver High School, 415 Granby St., 06112. Phone: (860) 722-8661. Phone: (860) 695-1899. Fax: (860) 242-6241.E-mail: wqtqfm@yahoo.com Web Site:www.wqtq.com/wqtq Licensee: Hartford Board of Education. Population served: 158,017 Format: Educ, urban contemp, ballads. Target aud: 15-45; literate, professional, quality mus listeners. Spec prog: Gospel 12 hrs, clean hip hop rap 19 hrs, reggae/calypso 4 hrs, jazz 12 hrs, Rhythm and blues 18 hrs wkly. ♦Thomas G. Smith, CEO; Connie Coles, pres, gen mgr; Shirley Minnifield, CFO; Tom Smith, chief of opns.

WRCH(FM)—See New Britain

***WRTC-FM**— February 1958: 89.3 mhz; 300 w. 95 ft TL: N41 45 06 W72 41 29. Stereo. Hrs open: 24 c/o Trinity College, 300 Summit St., 06106. Phone: (860) 297-2450. Phone: (860) 297-2439. Fax: (860) 987-6214. Web Site:www.wrtcfm.com Licensee: Trustees of Trinity College. Population served: 158,017 Format: Div. Target aud: 15 plus. Spec prog: Class 4 hrs, gospel 6 hrs, West Indian 6 hrs, Pol 3 hrs, Por 8 hrs, Sp 6 hrs wkly. ♦Zee Santiago, stn mgr.

WTIC(AM)— Feb 10, 1925: 1080 khz; 50 kw-U, DA-N. TL: N41 46 39 W72 48 19. Stereo. Hrs open: 24 10 Executive Dr., Farmington, 06032. Phone: (860) 677-6700. Fax: (860) 284-9842.E-mail: info@wtic.com Web Site:www.wtic.com Licensee: Infinity Radio Inc. Group owner: Infinity Broadcasting Corp. (acq 11-13-98; grpsl). Population served: 469,000 Natl. Network: CBS, . Format: Full service, news/talk. News: 30 hrs wkly. Target aud: 35-59; intelligent, mature adults. ♦Suzanne McDonald, VP, gen mgr; Steve Salhany, opns mgr; Stephanie McNamara, gen sls mgr; Geri DeRosa, natl sls mgr; Tristano Korlou, mktg dir & prom dir; Dana Whalen, news dir, chief of engrg; Jeff Hugabone, chief of engrg, sports cmtr.

WTIC-FM— Feb 5, 1940: 96.5 mhz; 20 kw. 810 ft TL: N41 46 27 W72 48 20. Stereo. Hrs open: 24 10 Executive Dr., Farmington, 06032. Phone: (860) 677-6700. Fax: (860) 678-3952. Web Site:www.ticfm.com Population served: 425,500 Format: Hot adult contemp. News: 8 hrs wkly. Target aud: 18-34; intelligent, spirited, youthful adults.

WWUH(FM)—See West Hartford

WWYZ(FM)—See Waterbury

WZMX(FM)— 1939: 93.7 mhz; 17 kw. Ant 850 ft TL: N41 33 42 W72 50 41. Stereo. Hrs open: 24 10 Executive Dr., Farmington, 06032. Phone: (860) 677-6700. Fax: (860) 674-8427.E-mail: info@hot937.com Web Site:www.hot937.com Licensee: Infinity Radio Inc. Group owner: Infinity Broadcasting Corp. (acq 6-8-98; grpsl). Population served: 158,017 Format: Hip-hop. Target aud: 18-34; adults in Hartford & New Haven. ♦Suzanne McDonald, VP & gen mgr; Steve Salhany, opns mgr.

Ledyard

WBMW(FM)— Dec 24, 1992: 106.5 mhz; 3.1 kw. Ant 459 ft TL: N41 27 43 W72 01 27. Stereo. Hrs open: 24 758 Colonel Ledyard Hwy., 06339. Phone: (860) 464-1065. Fax: (860) 464-8143.E-mail: wbmwandwjjf@aol.com Web Site:www.wbmw.com Licensee: Redwolf Broadcasting Corp. (acq 1-25-94). Natl. Network: USA, . Smithwick & Belendiuk. Format: Hot adult contemp. News staff: one. Target aud: 20-49. ♦John J. Fuller, gen mgr; Scott Bradshaw, opns mgr.

Litchfield

WZBG(FM)— July 8, 1992: 97.3 mhz; 3 kw. 328 ft TL: N41 48 08 W73 09 50. Hrs open: 24 Box 1497, Litchfield Commons, 49 Commons Dr., 06759. Phone: (860) 567-3697. Fax: (860) 567-3292.E-mail: info@wzbg.com Web Site:www.wzbg.com Licensee: Local Girls & Boys Broadcasting Corp. Natl. Network: CBS, . Format: News & info, adult contemp. News staff: 3. Target aud: 25-54. Spec prog: Jazz 2 hrs wkly. ♦Jennifer L. Parsons, gen mgr.

Manchester

WNEZ(AM)— May 18, 1958: 1230 khz; 1 kw-U. TL: N41 46 34 W72 33 27. Hrs open: 24 138 Burnside Ave., East Hartford, 06108. Phone: (860) 524-0001. Fax: (860) 548-1922.E-mail: mtanderson2942@sbcglobal.net Licensee: Freedom Communications of Connecticut Inc. (acq 6-1-2004; $3 million with WLAT(AM) New Britain). Format: Sp news/talk.

Meriden

WMMW(AM)— 1946: 1470 khz; 2.5 kw, DA-2. TL: N41 33 14 W72 48 07. Hrs open: 24
Rebroadcast WDRC (AM) Hartford 100%.
869 Blue Hills Ave., Bloomfield, 06002. Phone: (860) 243-1115. Fax: (860) 286-8257. Web Site:www.talkofconnecticut.com Licensee: Buckley Broadcasting of Connecticut LLC. Group owner: Buckley Broadcasting Corp. (acq 10-21-98; $630,000). Population served: 1,182,000 Natl. Network: Westwood One, AP Radio, ABC, . Natl. Rep: McGavren Guild,. CRN Wire Svc: ABC Format: News, talk. Target aud: 40 plus; middle income, grassroots America. ♦Richard D. Buckley, pres; Wayne Mulligan, VP & gen mgr; Laura Kittell, opns mgr; Eric Fahnoe, sls VP; Grahame Winters, prom dir; Dave Nagel, progmg dir; Dan Lovallo, news dir, news rptr, sports cmtr; Scott Baron, chief of engrg; Joe Orlando, traf mgr.

***WPKT(FM)**— June 11, 1978: 90.5 mhz; 18.5 kw horiz, 13.5 kw vert. Ant 1,148 ft TL: N41 33 42 W72 50 41. Stereo. Hrs open: 24 1049 Asylum Ave., Hartford, 06105. Phone: (860) 278-5310. Fax: (860) 275-7403.E-mail: info@wnpr.org Web Site:www.wnpr.org Licensee: Connecticut Public Television & Radio. Population served: 2,000,000 Natl. Network: NPR, PRI, . Schwartz, Woods and Miller. Format: News/talk. News staff: 5; News: 26 hrs wkly. ♦Jerry Franklin, CEO, pres; Kim Grehn, VP, stn mgr, progmg dir; Nancy Bauer, mktg VP; John Dankosky, news dir; Joseph Zareski, chief of engrg.

Middlefield

WPKT(FM)—See Meriden

Middletown

***WESU(FM)**— September 1939: 88.1 mhz; 1.5 kw. 38 ft TL: N41 33 16 W72 39 30. Stereo. Hrs open: 24 45 Broad St., 2nd floor, 06457. Phone: (860) 685-7703/685-7700/685-7707. Fax: (860) 704-0608.E-mail: wesu@wesufm.org Web Site:www.wesufm.org Licensee: Wesleyan University (acq 3-27-2003). Population served: 900,000 Natl. Network: NPR, . Wire Svc: UPI Format: Free-form. News: News prgmg 12 hrs/day. Target aud: Discerning listeners. Spec prog: NPR, Pacifica and Local Public Affairs by day, Free form music at night and weekends, Blues 10 hrs, gospel 6 hrs, reggae 10 hrs, metal 5 hrs wkly. ♦Benjamin Michael, gen mgr.

***WIHS(FM)**— Oct 11, 1969: 104.9 mhz; 3 kw. 300 ft TL: N41 30 18 W72 39 32. Hrs open: 24 1933 S. Main St., 06457. Phone: (860) 346-1049. Fax: (860) 347-1049.E-mail: wihs@snet.net Web Site:www.wihsradio.org Licensee: Connecticut Radio Fellowship Inc. Population served: 2,000,000 Natl. Network: Moody, . Format: Christian. News: 18 hrs wkly. Target aud: General. Spec prog: Children 9 hrs wkly. ♦William Bacon, pres; G.J. Gerard, gen mgr; Paul A. Kretschmer, opns mgr.

WMRD(AM)— Dec 12, 1948: 1150 khz; 2.5 kw-D, 46 w-N. TL: N41 11 33 W72 37 13. Hrs open: 24 P.O. Box 1150, 777 River Road, 06457. Phone: (860) 347-9673. Phone: (860) 347-2565. Fax: (860) 347-7704.E-mail: radio@wliswmrd.net Web Site:www.wliswmrd.net Licensee: Crossroads Communications L.L.C. (acq 1996). Population served: 200,000 Natl. Network: Westwood One, CBS Radio, Jones Radio Networks, . Rgnl. Network: Conn. Radio Net. Conn. Radio Net. Vinson & Elkins. Format: Talk personalities. News staff: one; News: 8 hrs wkly. Target aud: 25-54; adults. Spec prog: Pol 2 hrs, It 2 hrs, Celtic one hr, Caribbean one hr, Jewish one hr wkly. ♦Don DeCesare, pres & gen mgr.

Milford

WADS(AM)—See Ansonia

WFIF(AM)— Sept 4, 1965: 1500 khz; 5 kw-D, DA. TL: N41 11 33 W73 06 05. Hrs open: Sunrise-sunset 90 Kay Ave., 06460. Phone: (203) 878-5915.E-mail: info@wfif.net Web Site:www.wfif.net Licensee: K.W. Dolmar Broadcasting Co. Inc. Group owner: Blount Communications Group (acq 4-82; $425,000; 1-19-81). Population served: 1,500,000 Natl. Network: Salem Radio Network, . Format: Relg. Target aud: General. Spec prog: Black 6 hrs wkly. ♦Dave Young, exec VP, opns VP; William Blount, pres & gen mgr; Jon Vaught, stn mgr; William Barnett, mus dir, chief of engrg.

Monroe

***WMNR(FM)**— Jan 31, 1974: 88.1 mhz; 5 kw. Ant 403 ft TL: N41 19 08 W73 15 13. Stereo. Hrs open: 24 Box 920, 06468. Phone: (203) 268-9667.E-mail: info@wmnr.org Web Site:www.wmnr.org Licensee: Monroe Board of Education. Population served: 510,000 Natl. Network: PRI, . Format: Class. Spec prog: Big band 8 hrs, folk 2 hrs, new age one hr, Broadway one hr wkly. ♦Kurt Anderson, gen mgr; Jane Stadler, opns dir; Carol Babina, dev dir.

Naugatuck

WFNW(AM)— Feb 26, 1961: 1380 khz; 5 kw-D, 500 w-N, DA-2. TL: N41 30 35 W73 03 20. Stereo. Hrs open: 182 Grand St., Suite 215, Waterbury, 06702. Phone: (203) 755-4960. Fax: (203) 755-4957.E-mail: galaxia1380@yahoo.com Web Site:www.galaxia1380.com Licensee: Candido Dias Carrelo. (acq 6-90; $350,000; 6-25-90). Format: Sp, tropical. ♦Placido Acevedo, pres; Candido Carrelo, gen mgr.

New Britain

***WFCS(FM)**— Oct 17, 1972: 107.7 mhz; 50 w. 160 ft TL: N41 41 36 W72 45 49. Stereo. Hrs open: 24 Student Center, 1615 Stanley St., 06050-4010. Phone: (860) 832-1883. Fax: (860) 832-3757. Web Site:www.wfcs.ccsu.edu Licensee: Trustees of Central Connecticut State University. Population served: 600,000 Format: Educational. News staff: 4; News: 10 hrs wkly. Target aud: 14-50. Spec prog: Blues 12 hrs, Sp 2 hrs wkly. ♦Adam Morgan, gen mgr; Mike McDonald, dev dir; Matt Rockwell, progmg dir; John Ramsey, chief of engrg.

WLAT(AM)— May 20, 1949: 910 khz; 5 kw-U, DA-N. TL: N41 42 58 W72 48 38. Stereo. Hrs open: 24 138 Burnside Ave., East Hartford,

06108. Phone: (860) 524-0001. Fax: (860) 548-1922.E-mail: mtanderson2942@sbcglobal.net Licensee: Freedom Communications of Connecticut Inc. (acq 6-1-2004; $3 million with WNEZ(AM) Manchester). Population served: 701,900 Format: Spanish tropical.

WRCH(FM)— July 1, 1968: 100.5 mhz; 7.5 kw. Ant 1,250 ft TL: N41 42 13 W72 49 57. Stereo. Hrs open: 24 10 Executive Dr., Farmington, 06032. Phone: (860) 677-6700. Fax: (860) 677-5483.E-mail: wrch@cbs.com Web Site:www.wrch.com Licensee: Infinity Radio Inc. Group owner: Infinity Broadcasting corp. (acq 6-8-98; grpsl). Format: Soft adult contemp. Target aud: 25-54; women, adults. ◆Suzanne McDonald, VP & gen mgr; Steve Salhany, opns mgr.

WRYM(AM)— August 1946: 840 khz; 1 kw-D, 208 w-N. TL: N41 41 15 W72 43 46. Hrs open: 24 1056 Willard Ave., Newington, 06111. Phone: (860) 666-5646. Fax: (860) 666-5647.E-mail: radio@wyrm840.com Web Site:www.wrymradio.com Licensee: Eight Forty Broadcasting Corp. (acq 4-8-2004; $1.06 million). Population served: 400,000 Natl. Network: CNN Radio, . Natl. Rep: McGavren Guild,. Cohn & Marks, LLP. Format: Sp. News staff: 4; News: 8 hrs wkly. Target aud: General; Hispanic. Spec prog: Pol 5 hrs wkly, Italian 2 hrs wkly. ◆Walter Martinez, gen mgr; Danny Delgado, news dir; Silvina Martinez, traf mgr.

New Canaan

*WSLX(FM)— 1975: 91.9 mhz; 10 w horiz. 518 ft TL: N41 11 32 W73 29 46. (CP: 19 w vert, ant 171 ft.). Stereo. Hrs open: 377 N. Wilton Rd., 06840. Phone: (203) 972-3894. Licensee: St. Luke's Foundation Inc. Format: Class, div. ◆Dan Mecca, gen mgr.

New Fairfield

WDBY(FM)—See Patterson, NY

New Haven

WAVZ(AM)— September 1947: 1300 khz; 1 kw-U, DA-N. TL: N41 17 16 W72 56 48. Hrs open: 24 495 Benham St., Hamden, 06514. Phone: (203) 281-9600. Fax: (203) 407-4652.E-mail: info@espnradio1300.com Web Site:www.espnradio1300.com Licensee: CC Licenses LLC. Group owner: Clear Channel Communications Inc. (acq 12-18-92; $10 with WKCI-FM Hamden; 1-11-93). Population served: 155,000 Natl. Network: ESPN Radio, . Natl. Rep: Clear Channel,. Format: Sports. News staff: one; News: 14 hrs wkly. Target aud: 35 plus. ◆ Tom McConnel, gen mgr; Gloria Shapiro, sls dir; Brian Zullo, gen sls mgr; David McLaine, prom dir; Jerry Kristafer, progmg dir.

WELI(AM)— October 1935: 960 khz; 5 kw-U, DA-N. TL: N41 22 14 W72 56 15. Stereo. Hrs open: 495 Benham St., Hamden, 06514. Phone: (203) 281-9600. Fax: (203) 407-4652.E-mail: comments@weli.com Web Site:www.960weli.com Licensee: CC Licenses LLC. (group owner; acq 8-5-85). Population served: 200,000 Rgnl. Network: Conn. Radio Net. Natl. Rep: Katz Radio,. Conn. Radio Net. Format: News/talk. Target aud: 18 plus. ◆ L. Lowry Mays, pres; Tom McConnel, gen mgr; Jerry Kristafer, progmg dir.

WKCI-FM—(Hamden, Feb 10, 1969: 101.3 mhz; 15 kw. 876 ft TL: N41 25 22 W72 57 06. Stereo. Hrs open: 495 Benham St., Hamden, 06514. Phone: (203) 281-9600. Fax: (203) 407-4652.E-mail: comments@kc101.com Web Site:www.kc101.com (Acq 7-24-92). Population served: 49,357 Format: CHR,top 40. ◆Chaz Kelly, progmg dir.

WPLR(FM)— 1944: 99.1 mhz; 15 kw. 905 ft TL: N41 25 23 W72 57 06. Stereo. Hrs open: 440 Wheelers Farms Rd., Suite 302, Milford, 06461. Phone: (203) 783-8200. Fax: (203) 783-8373. Web Site:www.wplr.com Licensee: CXR Holdings Inc. Group owner: Cox Broadcasting corp. (acq 8-2000; grpsl). Population served: 200,000 Format: Rock/AOR. ◆Stu Gorlick, gen sls mgr; Samuel Tilery, prom mgr; Ed Sabatino, progmg dir.

WQUN(AM)—See Hamden

WYBC(AM)— 1944: 1340 khz; 1 kw-U. TL: N41 17 32 W72 57 12. Hrs open: 142 Temple St., Suite 203, 06510. Phone: (203) 776-4118. Fax: (203) 776-2446.E-mail: info@wybc.com Web Site:www.wybc.com Licensee: Yale Broadcasting Co. Inc. (acq 7-24-98; $775,000). Population served: 50,000 Rgnl. Network: Conn. Radio Net. Conn. Radio Net. Format: Eclectic. Spec prog: Sp one hr wkly. ◆ Alexandria Newman, gen mgr; Wayne Schmidt, opns mgr; Julia Galeota, progmg dir; Clif Mills, chief of engrg.

WYBC-FM— Mar 9, 1959: 94.3 mhz; 1.8 kw. 325 ft TL: N41 20 58 W72 58 27. Stereo. Hrs open: 24 142 Temple St., Suite 203, 06510. Web Site:www.943wybc.com Licensee: Yale Broadcasting Co. Population served: 550,000 Natl. Network: ABC, . Format: Urban contemp. News: 10 hrs wkly. Target aud: Urban & college age listeners. Spec prog: Gospel 8 hrs, jazz 8 hrs, folk 3 hrs wkly. ◆Juan Castillo, progmg dir & pub affrs dir.

New London

*WCNI(FM)— 1974: 90.9 mhz; 2 kw vert. Ant 187 ft TL: N41 22 53 W72 06 28. Stereo. Hrs open: 1 PM-5 PM (M-F) Box 4972, Connecticut College, 270 Mohegan Ave., 06320. Phone: (860) 439-2853 (office). Phone: (860) 439-2850 ext 52 (studio). Fax: (860) 439-2805.E-mail: wnci@conncoll.edu Web Site:www.wcniradio.org Licensee: Connecticut College Broadcasting Association Inc. Format: Var/div. Target aud: General; all musical audiences except pop. Spec prog: Black 3 hrs, class 6 hrs, folk 9 hrs, gospel 3 hrs, jazz 9 hrs, Pol 3 hrs, Sp 3 hrs, women's 3 hrs wkly. ◆Bridgett Ellis, gen mgr; John Tyler, chief of engrg.

WKNL(FM)— Jan 1, 1970: 100.9 mhz; 3 kw. 328 ft TL: N41 26 27 W72 08 29. Stereo. Hrs open: 24 Box 1031, 06320. Secondary address: 89 Broad St. 06320. Phone: (860) 442-5328. Fax: (860) 442-6532.E-mail: arussell@hallradio.com Web Site:www.kool101fm.com Licensee: Hall Communications Inc. (group owner; acq 1-19-95; $3.5 million with co-located AM; 3-20-95). Natl. Rep: Eastman Radio,. Fletcher, Heald & Hildreth. Format: Oldies. News: 2 hrs wkly. Target aud: 25-54. ◆Bonnie Rowbotham, chmn; Arthur J. Rowbotham, pres; Bill Baldwin, sr VP; Andy Russell, stn mgr.

WQGN-FM—See Groton

WSUB(AM)—See Groton

Norfolk

*WSGG(FM)— May 17, 2001: 89.3 mhz; 100 w. Ant 167 ft TL: N41 59 30 W73 12 46. Hrs open: 24 Box 4594, Hartford, 06147. Phone: (860) 243-5630. Web Site:www.revivalfm.com Licensee: Revival Christian Ministries Inc. Format: Christian. ◆Samuel Girona, gen mgr & progmg dir.

Norwalk

WFOX(FM)— 1966: 95.9 mhz; 3 kw. 299 ft TL: N41 06 54 W73 26 06. Stereo. Hrs open: Prog sep from AM 444 Westport Ave., 06851. Phone: (203) 845-3030. Fax: (203) 845-3097.E-mail: info@thefoxonline.com Web Site:thefoxonline.com Licensee: Cox Radio Inc. Population served: 78,000 Format: Classic rock.

WNLK(AM)— 1948: 1350 khz; 1 kw-D, 500 w-N, DA-N. TL: N41 06 54 W73 26 06. Hrs open: 24 Rebroadcasts WSTC(AM) Stamford 100%. 444 Westport Ave., 06851. Phone: (203) 845-3030. Fax: (203) 845-3097.E-mail: info@wstcwnlk.com Web Site:www.wstcwnlk.com Licensee: Cox Radio Inc. Group owner: Clear Channel Communications Inc. (acq 8-25-2000; grpsl). Population served: 78,000 Conn. Radio Net. Format: News/talk. News staff: 4; News: 20 hrs wkly. Target aud: 25-54. ◆ Robin Faller, gen mgr.

Norwich

WCTY(FM)— May 1968: 97.7 mhz; 1.9 kw. Ant 410 ft TL: N41 28 28 W72 06 14. Stereo. Hrs open: 24 Box 551, 06360-0551. Secondary address: 40 Cuprak Rd. 06360. Phone: (860) 887-3511. Fax: (860) 886-7649. Web Site:www.wcty.com Licensee: WICH Inc. Population served: 219,000 Natl. Rep: Eastman Radio,. Wire Svc: AP Format: Country. Target aud: 25-54. ◆Andy Russell, VP, gen mgr, prom dir; Dave Elder, progmg dir.

WICH(AM)— September 1946: 1310 khz; 5 kw-U, DA-2. TL: N41 33 10 W72 04 34. Hrs open: 24 Box 551, 40 Cuprak Rd., 06360. Phone: (860) 887-3511. Fax: (860) 886-7649. Web Site:www.wich.com Licensee: WICH Inc. Group owner: Hall Communications Inc. (acq 7-1-65). Population served: 220,000 Natl. Network: ABC, . Rgnl. Network: Conn. Radio Net. Natl. Rep: Eastman Radio,. Conn. Radio Net. Fletcher, Heald & Hildreth. Wire Svc: AP Format: Full service. News staff: 2; News: 5. Target aud: 35 plus. Spec prog: Pol 2 hrs wkly. ◆Bonnie H. Rowbotham, chmn; Arthur J. Rowbotham, pres; Bill Baldwin, sr VP; Andy Russell, VP; Bob Reed, stn mgr, prom dir; Karen Dole, opns dir, pub affrs dir; Stu Bryer, progmg dir; Roger Arnold, chief of engrg.

*WNPR(FM)— Oct 17, 1981: 89.1 mhz; 5.1 kw. Ant 590 ft TL: N41 31 11 W72 10 04. Stereo. Hrs open: 24 Rebroadcasts WPKT(FM) Meriden 100%. 1049 Asylum Ave., Hartford, 06105. Phone: (860) 278-5310. Fax: (860) 244-9624. Fax: (860) 275-7403.E-mail: info@wnpr.org Web Site:www.wnpr.org Licensee: Connecticut Public Television & Radio. Natl. Network: NPR, PRI, AP Radio, . Schwartz, Woods and Miller. Format: News/talk. News staff: 13; News: 38 hrs wkly. Target aud: General. ◆ Jerry Franklin, CEO, pres; Kim Grehn, VP, stn mgr, progmg dir; Nancy Bauer, mktg VP; John Dankosky, news dir; Joe Zareski, chief of engrg; Gene Amatruda, opns.

Old Saybrook

WLIS(AM)— Sept 27, 1956: 1420 khz; 5 kw-D, 500 w-N, DA-N. TL: N41 19 38 W72 23 21. Hrs open: 24 hrs Rebroadcasts WMRD(AM) Middletown 90%. P.O. Box 1150, 777 River Road, Middletown, 06457. Phone: (860) 347-9673. Fax: (860) 347-7704.E-mail: radio@wliswmrd.net Web Site:www.wliswmrd.net Licensee: Crossroads Communications of Old Saybrook L.L.C. (acq 10-96). Population served: 200,000 Natl. Network: Westwood One, CNN Radio, Talk Radio Network, . Conn. Radio Net. Vinson & Elkins. Format: Talk personalities. News staff: one; News: 8 hrs wkly. Target aud: 25-64; Adults. Spec prog: Jazz 4 hrs wkly. ◆Don DeCesare, pres & gen mgr.

Pawcatuck

WWRX(FM)— Nov 30, 1995: 107.7 mhz; 1.4 kw. Ant 492 ft TL: N41 27 35 W71 55 40. Stereo. Hrs open: 24 758 Colonel Ledyard Hwy., Ledyard, 06339. Phone: (860) 464-1065. Fax: (860) 464-8143. Web Site:www.jammin1077.com Licensee: Fuller Broadcasting International LLC (acq 12-13-2002; $3.75 million). Population served: 300,000 Shaw Pittman. Format: Top 40 hits. News: one hr wkly. Target aud: 25-54; mobile, upscale. ◆John J. Fuller, pres, gen mgr; Scott Bradshaw, opns mgr.

Pomfret

*WBVC(FM)— 2001: 91.1 mhz; 100 w. Ant 289 ft TL: N41 53 27 W71 57 24. Hrs open: 398 Pomfret St., Box 128, 06258. Phone: (860) 963-5919. Fax: (860) 963-2086.E-mail: info@wbvc.com Web Site:www.pomfretschool.org Licensee: Pomfret School. Format: Var. ◆Tim Peck, gen mgr.

Putnam

WINY(AM)— May 3, 1953: 1350 khz; 5 kw-D, 79 w-N. TL: N41 54 10 W71 53 43. Stereo. Hrs open: 24 Box 231, 45 Pomfret St., 06260. Phone: (860) 928-1350. Fax: (860) 928-7878.E-mail: info@winyradio.com Web Site:www.winyradio.com Licensee: Osbrey Broadcasting Co. (acq 5-31-01; $2 million). Population served: 250,000 Natl. Network: AP Radio, Jones Radio Networks, . Miller & Miller. Wire Svc: AP Format: Adult contemp. News staff: 3; News: 18 hrs wkly. Target aud: 25-54 plus; adults. Spec prog: Talk 11 hrs wkly. ◆Gary W. Osbrey, pres, gen mgr; Karen Osbrey, VP; Andrew Morrison, news dir; Kerri LeClerc, traf mgr; John Wilbur, sports cmtr.

Ridgefield

WREF(AM)— Mar 15, 1985: 850 khz; 2.5 kw. TL: N41 17 27 W73 29 16. Stereo. Hrs open: 6 AM-10 PM 198 Main St., Danbury, 06810. Phone: (203) 744-4800. Fax: (203) 778-4655.E-mail: trueoldies850@hotmail.com Licensee: Berkshire Broadcasting Corp. Group owner: Berkshire Broadcasting Corp. (acq 3-31-97; $550,000). Population served: 500,000 Natl. Network: ABC, . Natl. Rep: D & R Radio,. Cohn & Marks. Format: Classic Hits. ◆Irv Goldstein, exec VP & gen mgr.

Salisbury

WKZE-FM— Sept 1, 1992: 98.1 mhz; 1.8 kw. Ant 604 ft TL: N41 58 35 W73 31 27. Stereo. Hrs open: 24 7392 S. Broadway, Red Hook, NY, 12571. Phone: (845) 758-9810. Fax: (845) 758-9819.E-mail: info@wkze.com Web Site:www.wkze.com Licensee: Willpower Radio L.L.C. (acq 4-7-2005; $1.4 million with WHDD(AM) Sharon). Population served: 650,000 Natl. Network: AP Radio, . Rgnl. Network: CRN. Format: AAA. News staff: one; News: 2 hrs wkly. Target aud: 25-54. ◆Dave Doud, gen mgr; Pete Nugent, sls VP & gen sls mgr; Paul Higgins, sls.

Sharon

WHDD(AM)— Dec 23, 1986: 1020 khz; 2.5 kw-D. TL: N41 58 35 W73 31 27. Stereo. Hrs open: 6 AM-6 PM 67 Main St., 06069. Phone: (860) 364-4640. Fax: (860) 364-7035. Web Site:www.am1020whdd.com Licensee: Willpower Radio L.L.C. (acq 4-7-2005; $1.4 million with WKZE-FM Salisbury). Population served: 650,000 Rgnl. Network: Conn. Radio Net. Format: Talk. ◆Marshall Miles, gen mgr.

*WHDD-FM— May 5, 2008: 91.9 mhz; 650 w. Ant -49 TL: N41 53 32 W73 27 16. Hrs open: 24 67 Main St., 06069. Phone: (860) 364-4640. Fax: (860) 364-7035. Web Site:www.robinhoodradio.com Licensee: Tri-State Public Communications Inc. Natl. Network: NPR, PRI, . ◆Marshall Miles, pres & gen mgr.

WQQQ(FM)— Oct 3, 1994: 103.3 mhz; 1.5 kw. 640 ft TL: N41 55 03 W73 33 32. Stereo. Hrs open: 24 Box 446, Lakeville, 06039-0446. Phone: (860) 435-3333. Fax: (860) 435-3334.E-mail: q103fm@yahoo.com Web Site:www.wqqq.com Licensee: The Ridgefield Broadcasting Corp. (acq 7-20-01). Population served: 350,000 Cohn & Marks. Format: Adult contemp, hits of the 70s, 80s & 90s. News staff: one; News: 14 hrs wkly. Target aud: Upscale adults; 25-54. ◆Dennis Jackson, chmn; Joe Loverro, exec VP & gen mgr.

Shelton

*WRXC(FM)— 1977: 90.1 mhz; 45 w. 482 ft TL: N41 21 43 W73 06 48. Stereo. Hrs open: 24
Rebroadcasts WMNR(FM) Monroe 100%.
Box 920, Monroe, 06468. Phone: (203) 268-9667.E-mail: info@wmnr.org Web Site:www.wmnr.org Licensee: Monroe Board of Education. Population served: 132,000 Natl. Network: PRI, . Format: Class. Spec prog: Big band 8 hrs, folk 2 hrs, new age one hr, Broadway one hr wkly. ◆Kurt Anderson, gen mgr; Jane Stadler, opns dir; Carol Babina, dev dir.

Somers

*WDJW(FM)— Oct 6, 1986: 89.7 mhz; 9.2 w. -58 TL: N41 57 43 W72 27 51. Hrs open:
Rebroadcasts WWUH(FM) West Hartford.
Somers High School, 9th District Rd., 06071. Phone: (860) 749-2501. Phone: (860) 749-0719. Fax: (860) 749-9264. Licensee: Somers Board of Education. Population served: 10,000 Format: Jazz, folk, alternative. ◆Peter Stone, pres & gen mgr.

South Kent

*WGSK(FM)— Dec 25, 1987: 90.1 mhz; 77 w. Ant 128 ft TL: N41 40 54 W73 29 13. Stereo. Hrs open: 24
Rebroadcasts WMNR(FM) Monroe 100%.
Box 920, Monroe, 06468. Phone: (203) 268-9667.E-mail: info@wmnr.org Web Site:www.wmnr.org Licensee: Monroe Board of Education. Population served: 8,000 Natl. Network: PRI, . Format: Class. Spec prog: Big band 8 hrs, folk 2 hrs, new age one hr, Broadway one hr wkly. ◆Kurt Anderson, gen mgr; Jane Stadler, opns dir; Carol Babina, dev dir.

Southington

WXCT(AM)— Sept 2, 1969: 990 khz; 2.5 kw-D, 80 w-N, DA-2. TL: N41 34 59 W72 53 01. Hrs open: 24 Box 488, 440 Old Turnpike Rd., Plantsville, 06479. Phone: (860) 621-1754. Fax: (860) 426-1172. Web Site:www.canticonuevoradio.com Licensee: Davidson Media Station WXCT LLC. Group owner: Davidson Media Group LLC (acq 4-30-2004; $1.4 million). Population served: 350,000 Format: Sp Christian. ◆Eric Salgado, pres; Alejandro Torres, stn mgr.

Stamford

WCTZ(FM)— Oct. 18, 1974: 96.7 mhz; 3 kw. Ant 328 ft TL: N41 02 49 W73 31 36. Stereo. Hrs open: 24 444 Westport Ave., Norwalk, 06851. Phone: (203) 845-3030. Fax: (203) 845-3097.E-mail: eric.mcdonald@coxradio.com Web Site:967thecoast.com Licensee: Cox Radio Inc. Group owner: Cox Broadcasting (acq 8-25-2000; grpsl). Population served: 123,000 Natl. Rep: Katz Radio,. Format: Adult contemp, Greatest Hits. Target aud: 25-54; upscale. ◆Robin Faller, gen mgr; Jim Stagnitti, gen sls mgr; Helaine Greenbaum, natl sls mgr; Kelli McLaughlin, rgnl sls mgr; Steve Soyland, prom dir; Eric McDonald, progmg dir; Clark Burgard, chief of engrg; Steve Rugh, traf mgr.

*WEDW-FM— Feb 17, 1992: 88.5 mhz; 2 kw horiz, 1.8 kw vert. Ant 302 ft TL: N41 02 49 W73 31 36. Stereo. Hrs open:
Rebroadcasts WPKT (FM) Meriden100%.
1049 Asylum Ave., Hartford, 06105. Phone: (860) 278-5310. Fax: (860) 244-9624.E-mail: info@wnpr.org Web Site:www.wnpr.org Licensee: Connecticut Public Broadcasting Inc. Format: News/talk. ◆Kim Grehn, gen mgr, stn mgr, progmg dir; Nancy Bauer, mktg VP; John Dankosky, news dir; Joe Zareski, chief of engrg.

WSTC(AM)— Sept 18, 1941: 1400 khz; 1 kw-U. TL: N41 02 49 W73 31 36. Stereo. Hrs open: 24 Prog sep from FM 444 Westport Ave., Norwalk, 06851. Phone: (203) 845-3030. Fax: (203) 229-1765.E-mail: info@wstc.com Web Site:wstcwnlk.com Licensee: Cox Radio Inc. Population served: 123,000 Natl. Network: CNN Radio, Westwood One, . Rgnl. Network: Conn. Radio Net. Natl. Rep: Katz Radio,. Conn. Radio Net. Format: News/talk. News staff: 4; News: 16 hrs wkly. Target aud: 25-54. ◆Robin Faller, VP; Eric McDonald, progmg dir; Dawn Wachner, prom.

Stonington

WMOS(FM)— November 1981: 102.3 mhz; 3 kw. Ant 328 ft TL: N41 24 23 W71 50 15. Stereo. Hrs open: 24 7 Governor Winthrop Blvd., New London, 06320. Phone: (860) 443-1980. Fax: (860) 444-7970.E-mail: info@thewolf.mohegansun.com Web Site:www.1023thewolf.com Licensee: Citadel Broadcasting Co. Group owner: Citadel Broadcasting Corp. (acq 4-26-2001; grpsl). Population served: 300,000 Natl. Rep: D & R Radio,. Bryan Cave. Format: Classic rock. News staff: one. Target aud: 25-45. ◆Fahrid Soleman, pres; Judy Ellis, CFO, VP; Bonnie Gomes, gen mgr; Dave Holmes, sls VP, traf mgr; Matt Chase, sls dir & gen sls mgr; Jackie Steele, prom mgr; Frank Doremus, chief of engrg.

Storrs

*WHUS(FM)— 1956: 91.7 mhz; 3.16 kw. 360 ft TL: N41 48 48 W72 15 33. Stereo. Hrs open: 24 University of Connecticut, 211 Hillside Rd. Suite 412, 06269-3008. Phone: (860) 486-4007. Fax: (860) 486-2955.E-mail: info@whus.org Web Site:www.whus.org Licensee: Board of Trustees University of Connecticut. Population served: 500,000 Natl. Network: AP Radio, NPR, . Wire Svc: AP Format: Free from /Americana. News staff: 2; News: 18 hrs wkly. Spec prog: Sp 3 hrs wkly. ◆John Murphy, gen mgr; Ben Shaiken, opns mgr.

Torrington

*WAPJ(FM)— 1997: 89.9 mhz; 40 w. Ant 276 ft TL: N41 48 08 W73 09 50. Hrs open:
WWUH(FM) West Hartford.
40 Water St., 06790. Phone: (860) 489-9033. Fax: (860) 482-7614.E-mail: wapjfm@sbcglobal.net Licensee: The I.B. and Zena H. Temkin Foundation Inc. (acq 9-30-2004). Format: Variety. News: 10 hrs wkly. Target aud: General; any and all. ◆Dick Williams, gen mgr.

WSNG(AM)— Jan 29, 1948: 610 khz; 1 kw-D, 500 w-N, DA-2. TL: N41 45 28 W73 03 06. Hrs open: 24 869 Blue Hills Ave., Bloomfield, 06002. Phone: (860) 689-8050. Fax: (860) 286-8257.E-mail: wsng@talkofconnecticut.com Web Site:www.talkofconnecticut.com Licensee: Buckley Broadcasting of Connecticut LLC. Group owner: Buckley Broadcasting Corp. (acq 12-18-96; $425,000). Population served: 70,600 Natl. Network: Westwood One, . Natl. Rep: McGavren Guild,. CRN Erwin Krasnow. Format: Talk. News staff: 3; News: 25 hrs wkly. Target aud: 25-54. ◆Eric D. Fahnoe, VP, gen mgr; Laura Kittell, opns mgr; Byron McClanahan, gen sls mgr; Dave Nagel, progmg dir; Scott Baron, chief of engrg.

Vernon

*WCTF(AM)— Nov 21, 1982: 1170 khz; 1 kw-D, DA. TL: N41 52 38 W72 28 43. (CP: 2.5 kw-D). Hrs open: 45 1/2 East St., 06066. Phone: (201) 736-3600. Phone: (800) 878-0787. Fax: (201) 736-4832. Web Site:www.familyradio.com Licensee: Family Stations Inc. (group owner; acq 1-86; $136,000; 9-23-85). Format: Relg. ◆Harold Camping, pres.

Wallingford

*WWEB(FM)— Nov 10, 1976: 89.9 mhz; 10 w. 230 ft TL: N41 27 34 W72 48 48. Hrs open:
Rebroadcasts WWUH (FM) West Hartford 80%.
Choate Rosemary Hall Foundation, 333 Christian St., 06492. Phone: (203) 697-2506. Fax: (203) 697-2186.E-mail: eb@choate.edu Web Site:www.student.choate.edu/wweb Licensee: Choate Rosemary Hall Foundation. Format: Var/div. Target aud: High school students. Spec prog: Class 2 hrs, C&W 2 hrs wkly. ◆Chris Bielizna, gen mgr.

Warren

*WXRN(FM)—Not on air, target date: unknown: 91.5 mhz; 7 w. Ant 528 ft TL: N41 44 11 W73 21 16. Hrs open: 375 Monroe Tpke., Monroe, 06468. Phone: (203) 268-9667.E-mail: info@wmnr.org Web Site:www.wmnr.org Licensee: Monroe Board of Education. ◆Kurt Anderson, gen mgr.

Waterbury

WATR(AM)— June 15, 1934: 1320 khz; 5 kw-D, 1 kw-N, DA-2. TL: N41 32 12 W73 01 52. Hrs open: 24 One Broadcast Ln., 06706. Phone: (203) 755-1121. Fax: (203) 574-3025.E-mail: talkback@watr.com Web Site:www.watr.com Licensee: WATR Inc. Population served: 275,000 Natl. Network: AP Radio, . Format: News/talk, good time oldies. News staff: 2; News: 15 hrs wkly. Target aud: 35-64. Spec prog: Pol 2 hrs, It 3 hrs wkly. ◆Tom Chute, gen mgr, progmg dir; Trish Torello, gen sls mgr.

WMRQ-FM— Dec 25, 1967: 104.1 mhz; 50 kw. Ant 859 ft TL: N41 33 41 W72 50 39. Stereo. Hrs open: 24 10 Columbus Blvd., Hartford, 06106. Phone: (860) 723-6000. Fax: (860) 493-7090. Web Site:www.radio1041.fm Licensee: Red Wolf Broadcasting Corp. Group owner: Clear Channel Communications Inc. (acq 5-13-2009; $7.9 million). Population served: 900,000 Natl. Network: ABC, . Natl. Rep: Christal,. Format: Modern rock. Target aud: 18-49. ◆Tom McConnell, gen mgr; Michael Maguire, progmg dir.

WWCO(AM)— 1946: 1240 khz; 1 kw-U. TL: N41 33 59 W73 03 23. Hrs open: 24
Rebroadcasts WDRC(AM) Bloomfield 90%.
869 Bluehills Ave., Bloomfield, 06002. Phone: (860) 243-1115. Fax: (860) 274-9734.E-mail: wwco@talkofconnecticut.com Web Site:www.talkofconnecticut.com Licensee: Buckley Broadcasting of Connecticut LLC. Group owner: Buckley Broadcasting Corp. (acq 4-97; $500,000). Population served: 500,000 Format: News/talk. News staff: 2. Target aud: 35 plus. ◆Richard Buckley, pres; Wayne Mulligan, gen mgr; Laura Kittell, opns mgr.

WWYZ(FM)— Aug 1, 1961: 92.5 mhz; 17.8 kw. 879 ft TL: N41 33 43 W72 50 41. Stereo. Hrs open: 24 10 Columbus Blvd., Hartford, 06106. Phone: (860) 723-6000. Fax: (860) 493-7090. Web Site:www.country925.com Licensee: Capstar TX L.P. Group owner: Clear Channel Communications Inc. (acq 8-30-00; grpsl). Population served: 300,000 Natl. Network: Westwood One, . Natl. Rep: Christal,. Format: Country. News staff: one; News: 5 hrs wkly. Target aud: 25-54. ◆Tom McConnell, gen mgr; Todd Thomas, opns mgr; Pete Salant, progmg dir.

West Hartford

WCCC(AM)—Licensed to West Hartford. See Hartford

WRYM(AM)—See New Britain

*WWUH(FM)— July 15, 1968: 91.3 mhz; 440 w. 784 ft TL: N41 46 27 W72 48 20. Stereo. Hrs open: 24 Univ. of Hartford, 200 Bloomfield Ave., 06117. Phone: (860) 768-4701. Phone: (860) 768-4703. Fax: (860) 768-5701.E-mail: wwuh@hartford.edu Web Site:www.wwuh.org Licensee: University of Hartford. Population served: 804,380 Format: Var/div. News: 8 hrs wkly. Target aud: General. Spec prog: It 3 hrs, Por 3 hrs, Pol 3 hrs, It 3 hrs, foreign/ethnic 14 hrs wkly. ◆John N. Ramsey, pres, gen mgr; Stephanie Lloukis, opns dir; Susan Mullis, dev dir; Joe Rush, progmg dir; Andy Taylor, mus dir; Mike DeRosa, pub affrs dir; John Ramsey, chief of engrg.

West Haven

*WNHU(FM)— 1973: 88.7 mhz; 1.7 kw. 150 ft TL: N41 17 29 W72 57 40. Stereo. Hrs open: 6 AM-2 AM Maxy Hall, 300 Boston Post Rd., 06516. Phone: (203) 479-8800.E-mail: hyaggi@newhaven.edu Web Site:www.wnhu.net Licensee: University of New Haven Inc. Population served: 1,200,000 Dow, Lohnes & Albertson. Format: Diverse. News: 12 hrs wkly. Target aud: General. Spec prog: Jazz 12 hrs, folk 6 hrs, Irish 5 hrs, metal 9 hrs, class 9 hrs, gospel 4 hrs wkly. ◆Hank Yaggi, gen mgr.

Westport

WEBE(FM)— Sept 1, 1962: 107.9 mhz; 50 kw. 383 ft TL: N41 10 14 W73 11 05. Stereo. Hrs open: 24 2 Lafayette Sq., Bridgeport, 06604-6000. Phone: (203) 333-9108. Fax: (203) 384-0600. Fax: (203) 394-6000. Web Site:www.webe108.com Licensee: Cumulus Licensing Corp. Group owner: Cumulus Media Inc. (acq 3-14-02; grpsl). Population served: 1,100,000 Natl. Rep: Christal,. Format: Adult

contemp. News staff: one; News: 3 hrs wkly. Target aud: 25-54; upscale females. Spec prog: Talk one hr wkly. ◆Ann Surface McManus, gen mgr; Curtis Hansen, opns VP, opns mgr; Valerie Thompson, traf mgr.

*WSHU(AM)— Apr 15, 1959: 1260 khz; 1 kw-D, DA. TL: N41 07 44 W73 23 20. Stereo. Hrs open: 6 AM-7 PM
Rebroadcasts WSHU(FM) Fairfield 30%.
5151 Park Ave., Fairfield, 06825. Phone: (203) 365-6604. Fax: (203) 371-7991.E-mail: lombardi@wshu.org Web Site:www.wshu.org Licensee: Sacred Heart University Inc. (acq 11-28-97; $325,000 as donation). Population served: 600,000 Natl. Network: NPR, PRI, . Wire Svc: AP Format: News/talk. News staff: 2; News: 45 hrs wkly. Target aud: General. ◆George Lombardi, gen mgr; Julie Freddino, opns mgr; Gillian Anderson, dev dir.

*WWPT(FM)— 1975: 90.3 mhz; 330 w. 110 ft TL: N41 10 19 W73 19 43. Stereo. Hrs open: Staples High School, 70 N. Ave., 06880. Secondary address: 110 Myrtle Ave. 06880. Phone: (203) 341-1381. Phone: (203) 341-1380. Fax: (203) 226-6875. Licensee: Board of Education, Town of Westport. Population served: 100,000 Format: Free-form. Target aud: 14-24; youth. Spec prog: Slovak 3 hrs wkly. ◆Jim Honeycutt, gen mgr.

Willimantic

*WECS(FM)— Feb 6, 1982: 90.1 mhz; 421 w. 380 ft TL: N41 41 00 W72 12 59. Hrs open: 83 Windham St., 06226. Phone: (860) 465-5354. Fax: (860) 465-5073.E-mail: wecs@hotmail.com Web Site:www.easternct.edu/depts/wecs Licensee: Eastern Connecticut State University. Population served: 200,000 Format: Urban contemp, Rock/AOR. Spec prog: Jazz 16 hrs, relg 3 hrs, Sp 9 hrs wkly. ◆John L. Zatowski, gen mgr.

WILI(AM)— Oct 5, 1957: 1400 khz; 1 kw-U. TL: N41 42 55 W72 11 23. Hrs open: 24 720 Main St., 06226. Phone: (860) 456-1111. Fax: (860) 456-9501. Web Site:www.wili.com E-mail: donna@wili.com Licensee: Nutmeg Broadcasting Co. (acq 7-11-2005; $1.8 million with co-located AM). Population served: 75,000 Natl. Network: ABC, . Rgnl. Network: Conn. Radio Net. Natl. Rep: Eastman Radio,. Conn. Radio Net. Wire Svc: AP Format: Full service, adult contemp, news/talk. News staff: 3; News: 10 hrs wkly. Target aud: 25 plus; general. Spec prog: Ukrainian one hr, Sp one hr, relg 2 hrs. ◆Colin K. Rice, VP; Donna Evan, gen sls mgr.

WILI-FM— June 16, 1975: 98.3 mhz; 1.05 kw. Ant 525 ft TL: N41 41 00 W72 13 01. Stereo. Hrs open: 24 720 Main St., 06226. Phone: (860) 456-1111. Fax: (860) 456-9501.E-mail: donna@wili.com Web Site:www.wili.com Licensee: Nutmeg Broadcasting Co. Population served: 125,000 Rgnl. Network: Conn. Radio Net. Natl. Rep: Eastman Radio,. Wire Svc: AP Format: CHR. News staff: one; News: 6 hrs wkly. Target aud: 22-44; college students, young married couples, young families. ◆Colin Rice, exec VP; Donna Evan, gen sls mgr.

Windsor

WKND(AM)— May 4, 1961: 1480 khz; 500 w-D, DA. TL: N41 51 10 W72 40 43. Hrs open: 138 Burnside Ave., East Hartford, 06108. Phone: (860) 524-0001. Fax: (860) 524-0336.E-mail: mtanderson2942@sbcglobal.net Licensee: Freedom Communications of Connecticut Inc. (acq 11-29-2004). Population served: 636,000 Natl. Network: ABC, . Format: Talk, rhythm and blues. Spec prog: Gospel 5 hrs, jazz 3 hrs wkly. ◆Richard Weaver-Bey, pres; Marion Anderson, gen mgr.

Delaware

Bethany Beach

WJKI(FM)— 1996: 103.5 mhz; 1.45 kw. Ant 479 ft TL: N38 34 21 W75 06 58. Hrs open:
Simulcast w/ WGBG (FM) Seaford 100%.
20200 DuPont Blvd., Georgetown, 19947. Phone: (302) 856-2567. Fax: (302) 856-7633. Web Site:www.bigclassicrock.com Licensee: Great Scott Broadcasting. (group owner) Format: Classic rock. ◆Sue Timmons, gen mgr; Sean McHugh, progmg dir; Tracy Baker, traf mgr.

WOSC(FM)— 1974: 95.9 mhz; 10.5 kw. Ant 469 ft TL: N38 25 20 W75 08 23. Stereo. Hrs open: Gateway Crossing, 351 Tilghman Rd., Salisbury, MD, 21804. Phone: (410) 742-1923. Fax: (410) 742-2329. Web Site:www.96rocksyou.com Licensee: Capstar TX L.P. Group owner: Clear Channel Communications Inc. (acq 8-7-2000; grpsl). Natl. Rep: Clear Channel,. Format: Active rock. Target aud: 18-34.

◆Frank Hamilton, gen mgr; Brian Cleary, opns mgr, progmg dir; Dixie Penner, prom dir; Marie Merrill, traf mgr.

Christiana

*WXHL-FM— Aug 1, 1994: 89.1 mhz; 1 w horiz, 1.2 kw vert. Ant 67 ft TL: N39 40 38 W75 39 47. Hrs open: 24 179 Stanton-Christiana Rd., Newark, 19702. Phone: (302) 731-0690. Fax: (302) 738-3090. Web Site:www.thereachfm.com Licensee: Priority Radio Inc. (group owner; (acq 12-10-99). Format: Adult contemp Christian mus. ◆Steve Hare, gen mgr; Dan Edwards, opns mgr; Larry Humm, gen sls mgr; Dave Kirby, progmg dir.

Dover

WDOV(AM)— 1948: 1410 khz; 5.4 kw, DA-2. TL: N39 12 03 W75 33 13. Hrs open: 24 1575 McKee Rd., Suite 206, 19904. Phone: (302) 678-5300. Fax: (302) 674-5978.E-mail: wdov@clearchannel.com Web Site:www.wdov.com Licensee: Capstar TX L.P. Group owner: Clear Channel Communications Inc. (acq 8-30-2000; grpsl). Population served: 100,200 Natl. Network: Westwood One, . Natl. Rep: Clear Channel,. Format: News/talk, sports. News: 162 hrs wkly. Target aud: 25-54. ◆Bob Walton, opns dir, opns mgr; Paige Lamers, mktg mgr; Andy Harris, progmg dir; Phil Feliciangeli, news dir & pub affrs dir.

*WDPZ(AM)— Aug 2, 1957: 1600 khz; 5 kw-D, 1 kw-N, DA-2. TL: N39 10 11 W75 33 13. Hrs open: 24 300 Philadelphia Ave., 2nd Fl., Egg Harbor City, NJ, 08215-1444. Phone: (609) 420-5410. Licensee: WXXY Broadcasting Inc. (acq 10-11-2005). Population served: 125,000 Format: Black gospel. ◆George Krementz, gen mgr.

WDSD(FM)— 1956: 94.7 mhz; 50 kw. Ant 377 ft TL: N39 12 03 W75 33 55. Stereo. Hrs open: 920 W. Basin Rd., Suite 400, New Castle, 19720. Phone: (302) 395-9800. Fax: (302) 395-9808.E-mail: wdsd@clearchannel.com Web Site:www.wdsd.com Licensee: Capstar TX L.P. Natl. Network: Jones Radio Networks, . Latham & Watkins. Format: Country. News staff: one; News: 2 hrs wkly. Target aud: 18-49. ◆Joe Puglise, gen sls mgr; Rob Reb, chief of engrg & disc jockey.

*WRTX(FM)— Apr 5, 1995: 91.7 mhz; 580 w. Ant 315 ft TL: N39 12 03 W75 33 55. Stereo. Hrs open: 24
Rebroadcasts WRTI(FM) Philadelphia, PA 100%.
1509 Cecil B. Moore Ave., Philadelphia, PA, 19121. Phone: (215) 204-8405. Fax: (215) 204-7027.E-mail: comments@wrti.org Web Site:www.wrti.org Licensee: Temple University of the Commonwealth System of Higher Education. Population served: 150,000 Natl. Network: NPR, AP Radio, . Rgnl. Network: Radio Pa. Radio Pa. Format: Jazz, class. News staff: one. Target aud: 30-65. ◆Tobias Poole, opns dir; Brick Torpey, gen sls mgr.

Fenwick Island

WLBW(FM)— Apr 1, 1994: 92.1 mhz; 3 kw. Ant 469 ft TL: N38 25 20 W75 08 23. Stereo. Hrs open: 351 Tilghman Rd., Salisbury, MD, 21804. Phone: (410) 742-1923. Fax: (410) 742-2329.E-mail: wave@intercom.net Web Site:www.isurfthewave.com Licensee: Aloha Station Trust LLC Group owner: Clear Channel Communications Inc. (acq 7-30-2008; grpsl). Format: Oldies. Target aud: 25-54. ◆Frank Hamilton, gen mgr; Marie Merrill, traf mgr.

Georgetown

WJWL(AM)— June 23, 1951: 900 khz; 10 kw-D, 1 w-N, DA-1. TL: N38 42 31 W75 24 25. Hrs open: 24 233 N.E. Front St., Milford, 19963. Phone: (302) 422-2600. Fax: (302) 424-1630.E-mail: digital900@aol.com Web Site:www.digital900.com Licensee: Great Scott Broadcasting Ltd. Group owner: Great Scott Broadcasting Population served: 38,000 Natl. Network: CNN Radio, . Natl. Rep: ABC Radio Sales,. Cohn & Marks. Format: Sp var. News staff: 11; News: 10 hrs wkly. Target aud: 25-54; mature adults. Spec prog: Relg 6 hrs wkly. ◆Faye Scott, pres; Danny Perez, gen mgr; Lisette Perez, progmg dir & farm dir.

WZBH(FM)— July 4, 1969: 93.5 mhz; 11 kw. Ant 485 ft TL: N38 31 24 W75 17 55. (CP: COL Millsboro. 50 kw, ant 492 ft.). Hrs open: 24 20200 DuPont Blvd., 19947. Phone: (302) 856-2567. Fax: (302) 856-7633. Population served: 100,000 Format: Contemp rock. Target aud: Adults; baby boomers. ◆Shawn Murphy, progmg dir; Terry Dalton, chief of engrg; C. Marcus, farm dir; Donna Cavender, women's int ed, disc jockey; B. Graxston, disc jockey.

Harrington

*WKNZ(FM)—Not on air, target date: unknown: 88.7 mhz; 25 kw vert. Ant 322 ft TL: N38 53 30 W75 34 48. Hrs open: Box 129, Milton, 19968. Phone: (302) 684-3149. Fax: (302) 684-2905. Licensee: Eagle's Nest Fellowship Church. ◆William T. Sammons Sr., pres.

Laurel

WKDB(FM)— Nov 19, 1991: 95.3 mhz; 6 kw. Ant 328 ft TL: N38 30 12 W75 39 39. Stereo. Hrs open: 24 20200 DuPont Blvd., Georgetown, 19947. Phone: (302) 856-2567. Fax: (302) 856-7633. Web Site:www.musicontheb.com Licensee: Great Scott Broadcasting. (group owner; (acq 2-13-98; $1.5 million). Population served: 200,000 Format: Adult contemp. News: 6 hrs wkly. Target aud: 25-49. ◆Sue Timmons, gen mgr, stn mgr; Tracy Baker, traf mgr.

Lewes

WZKT(FM)— June 1, 1991: 105.9 mhz; 6 kw. Ant 341 ft TL: N38 38 36 W75 13 00. Stereo. Hrs open: 24
Rebroadcasts WKTT(FM) Salisbury, MD 100%.
Box 909, Salisbury, MD, 21803. Phone: (410) 219-3500. Phone: (410) 548-1543. Fax: (410) 548-1543.E-mail: catcountry@radiocenter.com Web Site:www.catcountryradio.com Licensee: Delmarva Broadcasting Co. (group owner; (acq 6-26-97; grpsl). Population served: 225,000 Natl. Rep: Katz Radio,. Hogan & Hartson. Wire Svc: AP Format: Country. News staff: one; News: 3 hrs wkly. Target aud: 25-54. Spec prog: NASCAR. ◆Joe Beail, gen mgr, gen sls mgr; Joe Edwards, opns mgr; Jeff Twilley, engrg dir, chief of engrg.

Middletown

*WXHM(FM)—Not on air, target date: unknown: 91.9 mhz; 280 w vert. Ant 319 ft TL: N39 26 37 W75 43 24. Hrs open: 179 Stanton-Christiana Rd., Newark, 19702. Phone: (302) 731-0690. Fax: (302) 738-3090. Web Site:www.thereachfm.com Licensee: Priority Radio Inc. ◆Steve Hare, gen mgr.

Milford

WAFL(FM)— May 19, 1973: 97.7 mhz; 6 kw. 328 ft TL: N38 55 39 W75 29 20. Stereo. Hrs open: Box 808, 19963. Secondary address: 1666 Blairs Pond Rd. 19963. Phone: (302) 422-7575. Fax: (302) 422-3069.E-mail: staff@eagle977.com Web Site:www.eagle977.com Licensee: Delmarva Broadcasting Co. (group owner; (acq 6-26-97; grpsl). Population served: 210,000 Natl. Network: Westwood One, . Hogan & Hartson. Format: Adult contemp. Target aud: 18-49; active, affluent adults in central & southern Delaware. Spec prog: Southern gospel 2 hrs wkly. ◆Melody Booker, gen mgr; Steve Monz, opns mgr; Jody Trinsey, gen sls mgr; Gary John, progmg dir; Jeff Twilly, chief of engrg.

WNCL(FM)— Nov 5, 1990: 101.3 mhz; 3 kw. Ant 328 ft TL: N38 51 21 W75 32 09. Stereo. Hrs open: 24 Box 808, 19963-0808. Secondary address: 1666 Blairs Pond Rd. 19963-5263. Phone: (302) 422-7575. Fax: (302) 422-3069.E-mail: cool@cool1013.com Web Site:www.cool1013.com Licensee: Delmarva Broadcasting Co. (group owner; acq 1-17-2003; $1.6 million). Population served: 300,000 Gammon & Grange. Format: Greatest hits of the 60s & 70s. News: 7 hrs wkly. Target aud: 35-54; adults. ◆Melody Booker, gen mgr; Jody Trinsey, gen sls mgr; Steve Monz, progmg dir; Jeff Twilly, chief of engrg.

WYUS(AM)— 1953: 930 khz; 500 w-D, 100 w-N, DA-1. TL: N38 55 39 W75 29 20. Hrs open: 6 AM-midnight Prog sep from FM Box 808, 19963. Secondary address: 1666 Blairs Pond Rd. 19963. Phone: (302) 422-2428.E-mail: rafael@wyusam.com Web Site:www.laexitosa.com Licensee: Delmarva Broadcasting Co. Format: Sp. Target aud: 18 plus; Hispanic. Spec prog: Relg 10 hrs, Haitian 3 hrs wkly. ◆Rafael Dosman, progmg dir.

Newark

WNWK(AM)— Aug 17, 1964: 1260 khz; 1 kw-D, 42 w-N, DA-2. TL: N39 38 39 W75 41 33. Hrs open: 1076 S. Chaple St., 19702. Phone: (240) 481-8242.E-mail: info@sadrosaradio.com Licensee: Jose Roberto Ekonomo and Aida Esperanza Ekonomo (acq 5-4-2007). Format: Sp. ◆Jose Roberto Ekonomo, pres & gen mgr.

*WVUD(FM)— Oct 4, 1976: 91.3 mhz; 1 kw. 135 ft TL: N39 41 26 W75 45 23. Stereo. Hrs open: Univ. of Delaware, Perkins Student Ctr., 19716. Phone: (302) 831-2701. Fax: (302) 831-1399. Web

Site:www.wvud.org Licensee: University of Delaware. Population served: 243,601 Natl. Network: AP Radio, . Format: Progsv, div, educ. Target aud: General. Spec prog: Class 10 hrs, black 10 hrs, jazz 15 hrs, folk 15 hrs, Sp 2 hrs wkly. ♦Chuck Tarver, gen mgr, stn mgr; David Mackenzie, chief of engrg.

Ocean View

WZEB(FM)— Jan 12, 1986: 101.7 mhz; 3 kw. 328 ft TL: N38 29 20 W75 12 01. Stereo. Hrs open:
Simulcast of WKDB (FM) Laurel 100%.
20200 DuPont Blvd., Georgetown, 19947. Phone: (302) 856-2567. Fax: (302) 856-7633. Web Site:www.musicontheb.com Licensee: Great Scott Broadcasting. (group owner; acq 5-29-98; $1.5 million). Format: Adult contemp. ♦Sue Timmons, gen mgr; Tracy Baker, traf mgr.

Pike Creek

***WMHS(FM)—** April 2000: 88.1 mhz; 90 w vert. 121 ft TL: N39 45 27 W75 40 02. Hrs open: 24 4550 New Linden Hill Rd., Suite 117, Wilmington, 19808. Secondary address: 301 McKennans Church Rd., Wilmington 19808. Phone: (302) 992-5520. Fax: (302) 992-5525.E-mail: eric.stancell@redclay.k12.de.us Web Site:www.mckeanradio.com Licensee: Red Clay Consolidated School District. Wire Svc: AP Format: Oldies. News staff: 11; News: 20 hrs wkly. Target aud: 25-54; adults-baby boomers.

Rehoboth Beach

WGMD(FM)— Sept 21, 1975: 92.7 mhz; 2.6 kw. Ant 433 ft TL: N38 42 14.4 W75 12 00.6. Stereo. Hrs open: 24 Box 530, 19971. Phone: (302) 945-2050. Fax: (302) 945-3781.E-mail: wgmd@wgmd.com Web Site:www.wgmd.com Licensee: Resort Broadcasting Co. L.L.C. (acq 7-25-80). Population served: 500,000 Natl. Rep: ABC Radio Sales,. Format: News/talk. News staff: 3; News: 16 hrs wkly. Target aud: 35 plus. Spec prog: Farm 2 hrs, jazz 2 hrs, relg 2 hrs wkly. ♦Dan Gaffney, gen mgr; Jared Morris, opns mgr; Marie Moulinier, gen sls mgr.

Seaford

WGBG(FM)— February 1972: 98.5 mhz; 6 kw. Ant 321 ft TL: N38 36 47 W75 35 12. Stereo. Hrs open: 24 20200 DuPont Blvd., Georgetown, 19947. Phone: (302) 856-2567. Fax: (302) 856-7633. Web Site:www.bigclassicrock.com Licensee: Great Scott Broadcasting (group owner; (acq 4-27-98; $1.2 million with co-located AM). Natl. Network: CBS, . Mullin, Rhyne, Emmons & Topel. Format: Classic rock. News: 4 hrs wkly. Target aud: 18-49; secondary 25-54, tertiary 35 plus. Spec prog: Farm one hr wkly. ♦Sue Timmons, gen mgr, gen sls mgr; Sean McHugh, progmg dir; Terry Dalton, chief of engrg; Tracy Baker, traf mgr.

WJWK(AM)— 1955: 1280 khz; 840 w-D, 250 w-N. TL: N38 37 03 W75 35 09. Hrs open: 6 AM-midnight
Simulcast with WKHI(FM) Fruitland 100%.
20200 DuPont Blvd., Georgetown, 19947. Phone: (302) 856-2567. Fax: (302) 856-7633. Licensee: Great Scott Broadcasting Population served: 10,000 Format: Joe. News: 4 hrs wkly. Target aud: Black adults. ♦Adam Davis, progmg dir; Tracy Baker, traf mgr.

Selbyville

WOCM(FM)— March 1993: 98.1 mhz; 3 kw. Ant 469 ft TL: N38 25 20 W75 08 23. Hrs open: 24 117th W. 49th St., Ocean City, MD, 21842. Phone: (410) 723-3683. Fax: (410) 723-4347. Web Site:www.irieradio.com Licensee: Irie Radio Inc. (acq 9-27-02; $1.08 million). Population served: 50,000 Leventhal, Senter & Lerman. Format: AAA. Target aud: 25-54; seasonal, beach residents & loc urban/farm. ♦Leighton Moore, pres; David Rothner, stn mgr, chief of engrg; Leslie Bunting, prom dir.

Smyrna

WRDX(FM)— Nov 10, 1993: 92.9 mhz; 1.7 kw. Ant 377 ft TL: N39 16 08 W75 31 28. Stereo. Hrs open: 24 920 W. Basin Rd., Suite 400, New Castle, 19720. Phone: (302) 395-9800. Fax: (302) 395-9808.E-mail: wrdx@clearchannel.com Web Site:929tomfm.com Licensee: Capstar TX L.P. Group owner: Clear Channel Communications Inc. (acq 8-30-2000; grpsl). Natl. Network: Westwood One, . Natl. Rep: Clear Channel,. Latham & Watkins. Format: Classic hits. Target aud: 25-54. ♦Bob Walton, opns mgr; Paige Lamers, mktg mgr.

Wilmington

WDEL(AM)— 1922: 1150 khz; 5 kw-U, DA-2. TL: N39 48 54 W75 31 47. Hrs open: 24 Box 7492, 2727 Shipley Rd., 19803. Phone: (302) 478-2700. Fax: (302) 478-0100.E-mail: wdel@wdel.com Licensee: Delmarva Broadcasting Co. Inc. (group owner) Population served: 595,000 Natl. Network: Westwood One, . Natl. Rep: Katz Radio,. Hogan & Hartson. Format: Full service, news/talk. News staff: 10; News: 70 hrs wkly. Target aud: 35-64. Spec prog: Sp 2 hrs wkly. ♦Julian H. Booker, CEO, pres; Michael G. Reath, gen mgr.

WFAI(AM)—(Salem, NJ) Sept 1, 1966: 1510 khz; 2.5 kw-D, DA. TL: N39 34 58 W75 27 39. Hrs open: 6 AM-6 PM First Federal Plaza Bldg., 704 King St., Suite 604, 19801. Phone: (302) 622-8895. Fax: (302) 622-8678.E-mail: tonya@faith1510.com Web Site:www.faith1510.com Licensee: QC Communication Inc. (acq 3-17-97; $1.8 million with WJKS(FM) Canton). Population served: 150,000 Format: Gospel. News staff: 2; News: 3 hrs wkly. Target aud: 18 plus. Spec prog: Farm 8 hrs wkly. ♦Tony Quartarone, gen mgr; Manuel Mena, progmg dir.

WILM(AM)— Oct 1, 1923: 1450 khz; 1 kw-U. TL: N39 43 46 W75 33 07. Hrs open: 24 920 W. Basin Rd., Suite 400, New Castle, 19720. Phone: (302) 395-9800. Fax: (302) 395-9808.E-mail: mail@wilm.com Web Site:www.wilm.com Licensee: Citicasters Licenses L.P. (acq 10-29-2004; $3,986,000). Population served: 426,000 Natl. Network: Wall Street, Fox News Radio, . Natl. Rep: Clear Channel,. Wire Svc: AP Format: All news/talk. News staff: 6; News: 168 hrs wkly. Target aud: Adults 25-54. Spec prog: Community Spotlight, Delaware Radio Magazine. ♦Paige Lamers, gen mgr; Martha Burns, sls dir; Eric Fendt, prom dir; Mark Fowser, progmg dir.

WJBR-FM— January 1957: 99.5 mhz; 50 kw. Ant 499 ft TL: N39 50 03 W75 31 25. Stereo. Hrs open: 24 812 Philadelphia Pike, 19809. Phone: (302) 765-1160. Fax: (302) 765-1192.E-mail: info@wjbr.com Web Site:www.wjbr.com Licensee: NM Licensing LLC. Group owner: NextMedia Group L.L.C. (acq 3-7-00; $32.4 million). Population served: 500,000 Natl. Rep: Christal,. Liebowitz & Associates. Format: Adult contemp. News staff: one. Target aud: 25-54. ♦Bruce Beasley, pres; Jane E. Bartsch, VP; Jane Bartsch, gen mgr; Michael Waite, opns VP.

***WMPH(FM)—** October 1969: 91.7 mhz; 100 w. 143 ft TL: N39 46 23 W75 30 25. Stereo. Hrs open: 24 5201 Washington St. Ext., 19809. Phone: (302) 762-7199.E-mail: radio@wmph.org Web Site:www.wmph.org Licensee: Brandywine School District, Brd of Educ Population served: 500,000 Format: Dance CHR. News staff: one; News: 2 hrs wkly. Target aud: 13-27; high school & college students. ♦Clint Dantinne, gen mgr.

WSTW(FM)— 1950: 93.7 mhz; 50 kw. 490 ft TL: N39 48 57 W75 31 31. Stereo. Hrs open: 24 Prog sep from AM Box 7492, 2727 Shipley Rd., 19803. Phone: (302) 478-2700. Fax: (302) 478-0100.E-mail: info@wstwfm.com Format: Hot adult contemp. News: 10 hrs wkly. Target aud: 25-54. Spec prog: Relg one hr, pub affrs one hr wkly.

WTMC(AM)— 1947: 1380 khz; 5 kw-D, 1 kw-N. TL: N39 48 12 W75 37 42. (CP: 520 w-D, 4.2 kw-N. TL: N39 43 46 W75 33 07 day, N39 48 41 W75 46 20 night). Hrs open: Box 778, Dover, 19901. Phone: (302) 659-2400. Fax: (302) 659-6128.E-mail: info@wtmc.net Web Site:www.deldot.net Licensee: State of Delaware Department of Transportation. (acq 11-4-99). Format: Talk. ♦Jonathan Weishaupt, pres; William Brooks, gen mgr.

WWTX(AM)— Apr 21, 1947: 1290 khz; 2.5 kw-U. TL: N39 44 03 W75 31 44. Hrs open: 24 920 W. Basin Rd., Suite 400, New Castle, 19720. Phone: (302) 395-9800. Fax: (302) 395-9808.E-mail: wwtx@clearchannel.com Web Site:www.1290theticket.com Licensee: Capstar TX L.P. Group owner: Clear Channel Communications Inc. Population served: 70,000 Natl. Rep: Clear Channel,. Format: Sports/sports talk. Target aud: Males: 18-45. ♦Paige Lamers, gen mgr; Martha Burns, gen sls mgr.

District of Columbia

Washington

WACA(AM)—See Wheaton, MD

***WAMU(FM)—** Oct 23, 1961: 88.5 mhz; 50 kw. 500 ft TL: N38 56 09 W77 05 33. Stereo. Hrs open: 24 The American Univ., Brandywine Bldg., 4000 Brandyine St., N.W., 20016. Phone: (202) 885-1200. Fax: (202) 885-1269.E-mail: feedback@wamu.org Web Site:www.wamu.org Licensee: American University. Population served: 3,434,300 Natl. Network: NPR, PRI, . Format: News/talk, bluegrass, culture. News staff: 6; News: 120 hrs wkly. Target aud: 25-54. Spec prog: Vintage radio 4 hrs, country 4 hrs, jazz 3 hrs wkly. ♦Caryn Mathes, gen mgr; Mark McDonald, progmg dir; Jim Asendio, news dir.

WASH(FM)— 1948: 97.1 mhz; 26 kw. 690 ft TL: N38 57 21 W77 04 57. Stereo. Hrs open: 1801 Rockville Pike, 6th Floor, Rockville, MD, 20852. Phone: (301) 984-9710. Fax: (301) 255-4314.E-mail: info@wash.com Web Site:www.washfm.com Licensee: AMFM Radio Licenses LLC. Group owner: Clear Channel Communications Inc. (acq 8-30-00; grpsl). Format: Adult Contemp. ♦Dave Pugh, pres, gen mgr; Bill Hess, opns mgr, progmg dir; Loretta Lage, gen sls mgr.

WAVA(AM)—See Arlington, VA

WAVA-FM—(Arlington, VA) Aug 1, 1948: 105.1 mhz; 41 kw. 541 ft TL: N38 53 44 W77 08 04. Stereo. Hrs open: 1901 N. Moore St., Suite 200, Arlington, VA, 22209. Phone: (703) 807-2266. Fax: (703) 807-2248.E-mail: comment@wava.com Web Site:www.wava.com Licensee: Salem Media of Virginia Inc. Group owner: Salem Communications Corp. (acq 2-13-92; $20 million; 11-18-91). Population served: 8,000,000 Natl. Network: Salem Radio Network, . Natl. Rep: Salem,. Fletcher, Heald & Hildreth. Format: Adult contemp, Christian, talk. News: 4 hrs wkly. Target aud: 25-54. ♦Edward Atsinger, CEO, chief of engrg; Stu Epperson, chmn, disc jockey; David Ruleman, VP, gen mgr; Tom Moyer, stn mgr; Joe Davis, disc jockey.

WBIG-FM— June 3, 1994: 100.3 mhz; 50 kw. Ant 489 ft TL: N38 53 13 W77 12 03. Stereo. Hrs open: 24 6th Fl., 1801 Rockville Pike, Rockville, MD, 20852. Phone: (301) 468-1800. Fax: (301) 770-0236. Web Site:www.idigbig.com Licensee: AMFM Radio Licenses LLC. Group owner: Clear Channel Communications Inc. (acq 8-30-2000; grpsl). Population served: 3,184,600 Format: Oldies. News staff: 2; News: one hr wkly. Target aud: 35-54; professional, college, upscale. ♦Dave Pugh, gen mgr.

***WCSP-FM—** May 8, 1982: 90.1 mhz; 50 kw. 450 ft TL: N38 57 44 W77 01 36. Hrs open: 24 400 N. Capitol St. N.W., Suite 650, 20001. Phone: (202) 737-3220. Fax: (202) 737-5554.E-mail: radio@c-span.org Web Site:www.c-span.org Licensee: National Cable Satellite Corp. (acq 1997). Population served: 3,500,000 Format: Pub affrs. Target aud: General. ♦Brian P. Lamb, CEO; Kate Mills, gen mgr.

WCTN(AM)—See Potomac-Cabin John, MD

WDCT(AM)—See Fairfax, VA

***WETA(FM)—** Apr 19, 1970: 90.9 mhz; 75 kw. Ant 610 ft TL: N38 53 30 W77 07 55. Stereo. Hrs open: 24 2775 S. Quincy St., Arlington, VA, 22206-2269. Phone: (703) 998-2600.E-mail: radio@weta.com Web Site:www.weta.org/fm Licensee: Greater Washington Educational Telecommunications Association Inc. Population served: 4,500,000 Natl. Network: NPR, PRI, . Dow, Lohnes & Albertson. Format: Class. Target aud: General; educated adults. ♦Dan Devany, gen mgr. Co-owned TV: *WETA-TV affil

WFAX(AM)—(Falls Church, VA) Sept. 15, 1948: 1220 khz; 5 kw-D, 100 w-N. TL: N38 52 47 W77 10 18. Hrs open: 6 am-midnight 161 Hillwood Ave., Suite B, Falls Church, VA, 22046-2983. Phone: (703) 532-1220. Fax: (703) 533-7572.E-mail: wfax@wfaxam.com Web Site:www.wfax.com Licensee: Newcomb Broadcasting Corp. Population served: 3,000,000 Arent, Fox, Kintner, Plotkin & Kahn. Format: Relg. News: one hr wkly. Target aud: 34-54. Spec prog: Black 15 hrs, It one hr wkly. ♦Doris N. Newcomb, pres, gen mgr; R. C. Woolfenden, opns dir.

WFED(AM)— Sept 25, 1926: 1500 khz; 50 kw-U, DA-2. TL: N39 02 30 W77 02 45. Hrs open: 24 3400 Idaho Ave. N.W., 20016. Phone: (202) 895-5000. Fax: (202) 895-5144.E-mail: info@federalnewsradio.com Web Site:www.federalnewsradio.com Licensee: Bonneville Holding Co. Group owner: Bonneville International Corp. (acq 4-27-98; grpsl). Population served: 3,451,000 Wilkinson, Barker, Knauer & Quinn. Format: Federal news. Target aud: General. ♦Bruce Reese, pres, VP; Joel Oxley, gen mgr; Lisa Wolfe, progmg dir.

WGTS(FM)—See Takoma Park, MD

WHFS(AM)—See Morningside, MD

WHUR-FM— Dec 10, 1971: 96.3 mhz; 16.5 kw. Ant 800 ft TL: N38 57 01 W77 04 47. Stereo. Hrs open: 24 529 Bryant St. N.W., 20059. Phone: (202) 806-3500. Fax: (202) 806-3522.E-mail: dickinson@whur.com Web Site:www.whur.com Licensee: Howard University Board of Trustees. Population served: 2,275,248 Natl. Network: CNN Radio, ABC, . Natl. Rep: D & R Radio,. Wire Svc: UPI Format: Urban adult contemp. News staff: 3; News: 7 hrs wkly. Target aud: 25-54. Spec

prog: Gospel 14 hrs, Caribbean 6 hrs wkly. ♦Dr. H. Patrick Swygert, pres; Millard J. Watkins III, gen mgr; Jeanette Tyce, gen sls mgr; David Dickinson, progmg dir.

WIHT(FM)— 1960: 99.5 mhz; 22 kw. Ant 751 ft TL: N38 57 49 W77 06 18. Hrs open: 24 1801 Rockville Pike, 6th Fl., Rockville, MD, 20852. Phone: (301) 255-4300. Fax: (301) 770-3541.E-mail: info@hot995.com Web Site:www.hot995.com Licensee: AMFM Radio Licenses L.L.C. Group owner: Clear Channel Communications Inc. (acq 9-00). Population served: 81,000 Format: CHR. ♦Dave Pugh, gen mgr; Bill Hess, opns mgr; Melissa Kelly, gen sls mgr; Jessica Ritch, prom dir; Sarah Fraser, progmg dir.

WILC(AM)—See Laurel, MD

WJFK-FM—(Manassas, VA) Apr 8, 1968: 106.7 mhz; 22.5 kw. Ant 731 ft TL: N38 52 28 W77 13 24. Stereo. Hrs open: 24 10800 Main St., Fairfax, VA, 22030. Phone: (703) 691-1900. Fax: (703) 934-9896. Web Site:www.cbssports.com/local/dc Licensee: CBS Radio Inc. of Washington, DC. Group owner: Infinity Broadcasting Corp. (acq 10-86; $13 million; 9-22-86). Population served: 3,400,000 Format: Sports. Target aud: 25-54. ♦Michael Hughs, gen mgr; Lisa Broyhill, opns mgr; Ernie Fears, gen sls mgr; Leo Donohoe, natl sls mgr; Megan McCluskie, prom dir; Tony Diggs, chief of engrg.

WJZW(FM)—(Woodbridge, VA) Dec 25, 1958: 105.9 mhz; 28 kw. Ant 648 ft TL: N38 52 28 W77 13 24. Stereo. Hrs open: 4400 Jenifer St. NW, Suite 400, 20015. Phone: (202) 686-3100. Fax: (202) 686-3064.E-mail: info@trueoldies1059.com Web Site:www.trueoldies1059.com Licensee: Radio License Holding VII LLC. Group owner: ABC Inc. (acq 6-12-2007; grpsl). Population served: 426,800 Format: Oldies. ♦Jeff Boden, gen mgr; Kenny King, opns dir; Cathy Whissel, gen sls mgr; Steve Allan, progmg dir.

WKIK(AM)—See La Plata, MD

WKYS(FM)— Aug 1, 1947: 93.9 mhz; 24 kw. 707 ft TL: N38 56 24 W77 04 54. Stereo. Hrs open: 24 5900 Princess Garden Pkwy., 8th Fl., Lanham, MD, 20706. Phone: (301) 306-1111. Fax: (301) 306-9510.E-mail: info@939wkys.com Web Site:www.939wkys.com Licensee: Radio One Licenses LLC Group owner: Radio One Inc. (acq 6-95; $34 million;2-27-95). Population served: 4,920,600 Natl. Rep: McGavren Guild,. Format: Hip-hop, rhythm and blues. News staff: 3; News: 4 hrs wkly. Target aud: 25-54; upscale Black adults. ♦Michele Williams, gen mgr; Jack Murray, sls dir; Ezio Torres, natl sls mgr; Steve Hegwood, progmg dir; Paul Stewart, mus dir; Sheila Stewart, news dir, pub svc dir; Scott Tanner, chief of engrg; Cynthia Bullock, traf mgr; Russ Parr, disc jockey.

WLXE(AM)—See Rockville, MD

WMAL(AM)— Oct 12, 1925: 630 khz; 5 kw-U, DA-2. TL: N39 00 55 W77 08 30. Stereo. Hrs open: 24 4400 Jenifer St. N.W., Suite 400, 20015. Phone: (202) 686-3100. Fax: (202) 686-3061.E-mail: info@wmal.com Web Site:www.wmal.com Licensee: Radio License Holding VII LLC. Group owner: ABC Inc. (acq 6-12-2007; grpsl). Population served: 696,800 Natl. Rep: ABC Radio Sales,. Format: News/talk. ♦Chris Berry, pres, gen mgr; Paul Duckworth, opns dir; Ernie Fears Jr., sls dir; John Matthews, news dir; David Sproul, engrg dir; Chuck Eisenhauer, traf mgr; Bryan Nehman, news rptr.

WMMJ(FM)—See Bethesda, MD

WMZQ-FM— September 1968: 98.7 mhz; 50 kw. 490 ft TL: N38 53 12 W77 12 05. Stereo. Hrs open: 24 1801 Rockville Pike, 6th Fl., Rockville, MD, 20852. Phone: (240) 747-2700. Fax: (301) 984-4895. Web Site:www.wmzq.com Licensee: Clear Channel Radio Licenses, Inc. Group owner: Clear Channel Communications Inc. (acq 8-30-00; grpsl). Population served: 4,000,000 Natl. Rep: Christal,. Latham & Watkins. Format: Country. News staff: one. Target aud: 25-54. ♦Dave Pugh, gen mgr; Bill Hess, opns mgr; Meg Stevens, rgnl sls mgr, progmg dir, mus dir; Kim Saver, prom dir; Oswald Pinott, engrg mgr & chief of engrg.

WOL(AM)— 1924: 1450 khz; 1 kw-U. TL: N38 54 16 W77 00 25. Hrs open: 5900 Princess Garden Pkwy., 8th Fl., Lanham, 20706. Web Site:www.1450wolam.com Licensee: Radio One Licenses LLC (Acq 6-95). Population served: 3,500,000 Format: News/talk. ♦Karen Jackson, gen sls mgr; Tobi Davis, mktg dir; Ron Thompson, progmg dir.

***WPFW(FM)**— Feb 28, 1977: 89.3 mhz; 50 kw. 410 ft TL: N38 56 09 W77 05 33. Stereo. Hrs open: 24 2390 Champlain St. N.W., 20009. Phone: (202) 588-0999. Fax: (202) 588-0561.E-mail: bmwpfw@aol.com Web Site:www.wpfw.org Licensee: Pacifica Foundation Inc. Group owner: Pacifica Radio Population served: 3,800,000 Haley, Bader & Potts. Format: Jazz, news/talk, world music. News: 9 hrs wkly. Target aud: 25-55. Spec prog: Oldies 3 hrs, women 3 hrs, health one hr wkly. ♦Ron Pinchback, gen mgr; Tiffany Jordan, dev dir.

WPGC-FM—See Morningside, MD

WPRS-FM—See Waldorf, MD

WRQX(FM)— May 15, 1948: 107.3 mhz; 19.5 kw. Ant 807 ft TL: N38 57 01 W77 04 47. Stereo. Hrs open: Prog sep from AM 4400 Jenifer St. N.W., Suite 400, 20015. Phone: (202) 686-3100. Fax: (202) 686-3091. Web Site:www.mix1073fm.com Licensee: Radio License Holding VII LLC Population served: 676,000 Natl. Network: ABC, . Natl. Rep: Christal,. Format: Hot adult contemp. Target aud: 25-54. ♦Jeff Boden, pres, gen mgr; Carol Parker, mus dir; Tom Grooms, pub affrs dir; David Sproul, engrg mgr; Stella Pressley, traf mgr, disc jockey.

WTEM(AM)— Aug 1, 1923: 980 khz; 50 kw-D, 5 kw-N, DA-2. TL: N38 57 43 W76 58 24. Hrs open: 24 1801 Rockville Pike, 4th Fl., Rockville, MD, 20852. Phone: (301) 255-4300. Fax: (301) 255-4314. Web Site:www.espn980.com Licensee: Red Zebra Broadcasting Licensee LLC. Group owner: Clear Channel Communications Inc. (acq 7-29-2008; grpsl). Natl. Network: ESPN Radio, . Wire Svc: The Sports Network Format: Sports/talk. Target aud: 25-54; men. ♦Bruce Gilbert, pres, VP; Hartley Adkins, gen mgr.

WTGB-FM—See Bethesda, MD

WTNT(AM)—See Bethesda, MD

WTOP-FM— September 1948: 103.5 mhz; 44 kw. Ant 518 ft TL: N38 56 09 W77 05 33. Stereo. Hrs open: 24 3400 Idaho Ave. N.W., 20016. Phone: (202) 895-5000. Fax: (202) 895-5016.E-mail: info@wtop.com Web Site:www.wtop.com Licensee: Bonneville Holding Co. Group owner: Bonneville International Corp. (acq 1-30-98; grpsl). Population served: 3,184,600 Natl. Network: CBS Radio, . Natl. Rep: Katz Radio,. Wire Svc: Reuters Format: News. Target aud: General. ♦Bruce Reese, pres; Joel Oxley, gen mgr; Matt Mills, sls dir & gen sls mgr; Jeff Sisk, progmg dir.

WUST(AM)— 1949: 1120 khz; 20 kw-D, 3 kw-CH. TL: N38 54 15 W77 09 54. Hrs open: 2131 Crimmins Ln., Falls Church, VA, 22043. Phone: (703) 532-0400.E-mail: contactwithwust@wust1120.com Web Site:www.wust1120.com Licensee: New World Radio Inc. (acq 10-26-92; $1.15 million; 8-24-92). Population served: 1,400,000 Format: Multicultural, ethnic. Spec prog: Fr 15 hrs, Sp 15 hrs, Ger 7 hrs, Ethiopian 6 hrs, Farsi 5 hrs, Russian 5 hrs wkly. ♦Alan Pendleton, gen mgr; Brian Edwards, opns mgr.

WWDC-FM— 1947: 101.1 mhz; 22.5 kw. 760 ft TL: N38 59 59 W77 03 27. Stereo. Hrs open: 24 1801 Rockville Pike, Suite 405, Rockville, MD, 20852. Phone: (301) 587-7100. Fax: (301) 587-0225. Web Site:www.dc101.com Licensee: AMFM Radio Licenses L.L.C. Group owner: Clear Channel Communications Inc. (acq 8-30-00; grpsl). Format: Rock. ♦Dave Pugh, gen mgr; Chris Cruze, progmg dir; Oswald Pinott, chief of engrg.

WWGB(AM)—See Indian Head, MD

WWRC(AM)— 1941: 1260 khz; 5 kw-U, DA-2. TL: N38 59 59 W77 03 27. Stereo. Hrs open: 24 1801 Rockville Pike, Rockville, MD, 20852. Phone: (301)231-7798. Fax: (301)881-8030.E-mail: redzebea@broadcasting.com Web Site:www.money1260.com Licensee: Red Zebra Broadcasting Licensee LLC. Group owner: Clear Channel Communications Inc. (acq 7-29-2008; grpsl). Population served: 3,535,000 Natl. Network: Westwood One, . Natl. Rep: Clear Channel,. Format: Business talk. Target aud: 25-54; adults. ♦Dave Pugh, gen mgr, mktg mgr; Bill Hess, opns mgr; Heather Steffan, gen sls mgr; Kathy Lennhoff, prom dir; Jerry Phillips, mus dir, news dir, pub affrs dir; Shaun Sandoval, chief of engrg.

WXTR(AM)—(Alexandria, VA) Dec 10, 1945: 730 khz; 8 kw-D, 25 w-N. TL: N38 44 43 W77 05 58. Stereo. Hrs open: 24 8121 Georgia Ave., Suite 1050, Silver Spring, MD, 20910. Phone: (301) 562-5800. Fax: (301) 562-5850. Web Site:espndeportes.espn.go.com Licensee: Red Zebra Broadcasting Licensee LLC. Group owner: Mega Communications Inc. (acq 5-9-2006; grpsl). Population served: 55,500 Natl. Network: ESPN Deportes, . Format: Sp sports. ♦Bruce Gilbert, CEO.

WYCB(AM)— 1978: 1340 khz; 1 kw-U. TL: N38 55 04 W77 01 27. (CP: TL: N38 51 50 W76 54 38). Hrs open: 5900 Princess Garden Pkwy., 8th Floor, Lanham, MD, 20706. Phone: (301) 306-1111. Fax: (301) 306-9510.E-mail: info@1340wycb.com Web Site:www.1340wycb.com Licensee: Radio One Licenses LLC. Group owner: Radio One Inc. (acq 11-8-01; grpsl). Population served: 15,000 Natl. Network: American Urban, . Format: Gospel. ♦Alfred Liggins, CEO; Cathy Hughes, chmn; Alfred Liggins, pres; Scott Royster, CFO; Michele Williams, gen mgr; Karen Jackson, gen sls mgr; Scott Tanner, chief of engrg.

WZAA(AM)—(Silver Spring, MD) Dec 7, 1946: 1050 khz; 1 kw-D, 44 w-N. TL: N39 00 50 W77 01 46. Hrs open: 24 3400 Idaho Ave. N.W., 20016. Phone: (202) 895-5000. Fax: (202) 895-5016. Web Site:airamerica.com/washington/ Licensee: Bonneville Holding Co. (group owner; (acq 12-13-2004; $4 million). Population served: 3,500,000 Natl. Network: Air America, . Wire Svc: AP Format: Talk. ♦Bruce Reese, pres; Joel Oxley, gen mgr; Jim Farley, progmg VP.

WZHF(AM)—See Arlington, VA

Florida

Alachua

WNDT(FM)— 1996: 92.5 mhz; 3.2 kw. Ant 443 ft TL: N29 44 22 W82 23 09. Hrs open: 24
Rebroadcasts WNDD(FM) Silver Springs 100%.
4020 Newberry Rd., Suite 100, Gainesville, 32607. Phone: (352) 373-6644. Fax: (352) 375-1700.E-mail: windfm.@aol.com Web Site:www.windfm.com Licensee: Ocala Broadcasting Corp. L.L.C. Group owner: Wooster Republican Printing Co. (acq 10-22-97; $675,000 for stock). Population served: 700,000 Natl. Rep: Katz Radio,. Baker & Hostetler. Format: Classic Rock. Target aud: Adults; 25-54. ♦Jim Robertson, VP, gen mgr; Robert Kassi, gen sls mgr; Kevin Davis, progmg dir; Cheree Carr, traf mgr.

Altamonte Springs

WORL(AM)— 1986: 660 khz; 1 kw-U, DA-1. TL: N28 41 35 W81 20 57. Hrs open: 24 1188 Lake View Dr., 32714-2713. Phone: (407) 682-9494. Fax: (407) 682-7005. Web Site:www.worl660.com Licensee: Salem Media of Illinois LLC. Group owner: James Crystal Inc. (acq 2-3-2006; swap in exchange for KNIT(AM) Dallas, TX). Population served: 1,400,000 Natl. Rep: Salem,. Fletcher, Heald & Hildreth. Format: News/talk. Target aud: 35-64; adult, male. ♦Edward Atsinger III, CEO; David Koon, gen mgr; Dale Forbis, opns mgr.

Apalachicola

WFCT(FM)— November 1997: 105.5 mhz; 50 kw. 315 ft TL: N29 45 02 W84 52 18. Stereo. Hrs open: 24 2911 Long Ave., Port St. Joe, 32456. Phone: (850) 227-9048. Fax: (850) 227-1101.E-mail: wfct@gtcom.net Licensee: Williams Communications Inc. (group owner; acq 3-27-02; $650,000). Format: Adult standards, contemp. ♦John Nichols, gen mgr; Ken Carey, news dir.

WOYS(FM)— July 1988: 100.5 mhz; 12 kw. Ant 476 ft TL: N29 43 57 W84 53 24. Stereo. Hrs open: 24 Point Mall 35 Island Dr. #16, Eastpoint, 32328-3264. Phone: (850) 670-8450. Fax: (850) 670-8492.E-mail: manager@oysterradio.com Web Site:www.oysterradio.com Licensee: Oyster Radio Inc. Group owner: Plessinger Radio Group (R.L. Plessinger Holding Co.). (acq 8-30-2007; with WOCY(FM) Carrabelle). Format: Adult contemp/beach music. News staff: one. Target aud: General. ♦Clair D. Plessinger, pres; Rick Plessinger, gen mgr; Michael Allen, stn mgr, prom mgr, news dir; William Denton, gen sls mgr.

Apopka

WHIM(AM)— May 4, 1964: 1520 khz; 5 kw-D, 350 w-N, DA. TL: N28 39 08 W81 29 40. Hrs open: 24 1188 Lake View Dr., Altamonte Springs, 32714. Phone: (407) 682-9494. Phone: (407) 682-9595. Fax: (407) 682-7005.E-mail: whim@salemorlando.com Web Site:www.1520whim.com Licensee: Pennsylvania Media Associates Inc. (acq 1-23-2006; $600,000). Population served: 1,000,000 Natl. Rep: Salem,. Holland & Knight. Format: Christian/family talk. Target aud: 35-64. ♦Edward G. Atsinger III, pres; David Koon, gen mgr; Dale Forbis, opns dir, opns mgr.

Arcadia

WFLN(AM)— Sept 3, 1955: 1480 khz; 1 kw-D. TL: N27 13 43 W81 51 28. Hrs open: 24 201 Asbury St., 34266-8830. Phone: (863) 993-1480. Fax: (863) 499-1489.E-mail: wflnradio@aol.com Licensee: Integrity Radio of Florida LLC. Population served: 100,000 Natl. Network: CBS Radio, CNN Radio, . Florida's Radio Networks Format: News/talk. Target aud: 25-65; upscale adults. ♦George Kalman, pres, gen mgr; Jack Welch, progmg dir; Phill Scott, engr.

Atlantic Beach

WFYV-FM— Mar 10, 1980: 104.5 mhz; 100 kw. 984 ft TL: N30 16 34 W81 33 53. Stereo. Hrs open: 24 8000 Belfort Pkwy., Jacksonville, 32256. Phone: (904) 245-8500. Fax: (904) 245-8501. Web Site:www.rock105i.com Licensee: Cox Radio Inc. Group owner: Cox Broadcasting (acq 2000; grpsl). Population served: 1,200,00 Natl. Network: AP Radio, . Natl. Rep: Christal, Katz Radio,. Format: Classic Rock. News staff: one; News: 20 hrs wkly. Target aud: 18-49; male oriented. ◆David Israel, gen mgr.

WQOP(AM)— Jan 30, 1958: 1600 khz; 5 kw-D, 90 w-N. TL: N30 19 30 W81 25 42. Hrs open: Box 51585, Jacksonville Beach, 32240. Secondary address: 391 S. 14th Ave., Jacksonville Beach 32250. Phone: (904) 241-3311. Fax: (904) 241-1402.E-mail: radioqop@aol.com Web Site:www.qopradio.com Licensee: Queen of Peace Radio, Inc. (acq 6-5-97; $350,000). Natl. Network: USA, . Format: Talk, relg. ◆C. Williams, pres; Tom Moran, gen mgr.

Auburndale

WTWB(AM)— Oct 10, 1956: 1570 khz; 5 kw-D, 13 w-N. TL: N28 04 32 W81 49 19. Hrs open: 24 127 Glenn Road, 33823. Phone: (863) 967-1570. Fax: (206) 350-6874.E-mail: wtwb@talks1570.com Licensee: La Raza Media Group LLC LMA - Breidenbach Media Group (acq 6-16-2008; $385,000). Population served: 300,000 Format: Christian news/talk , politics. News staff: one; News: 13 hrs wkly. Target aud: 30 plus; middle income, 2-income family. ◆Lynne Breidenbach, pres & gen mgr; Justin Sargent, progmg dir.

Avon Park

WFHT(AM)— Oct 1, 1970: 1390 khz; 1 kw-D, 770 w-N. TL: N27 37 08 W81 29 27. Hrs open: 6 AM-10 PM Stn currently dark 801 Hwy. 27 S., Suite 5, 33825. Phone: (863) 453-3423. Fax: (863) 453-3423.E-mail: WSHT1390@USA.COM Licensee: Odyssey Broadcasting Co. Inc. (acq 9-15-2006; $225,000). Population served: 52,000 Natl. Network: Jones Radio Networks, . Format: Oldies/Gospel. News staff: one; News: 12 hrs wkly. Target aud: 18-54; Sp audience. ◆Michael Cardillo, pres; T.J. Reno, gen mgr & chief of engrg.

WWOJ(FM)— August 1982: 99.1 mhz; 10 kw. Ant 515 ft TL: N27 30 39 W81 31 54. Stereo. Hrs open: 24 3750 U.S. 27 N., Suite One, Sebring, 33870. Phone: (863) 382-9999. Fax: (863) 382-1982.E-mail: cohanradiogroup@htn.net Web Site:www.cohanradiogroup.com Licensee: Cohan Radio Group Inc. (group owner; acq 11-1-98; $910,000 with WWTK(AM) Lake Placid). Population served: 80,000 Natl. Network: ABC, . Rgnl. Network: Florida Radio Network. Natl. Rep: Interep,. Florida's Radio Networks Latham & Watkins. Wire Svc: AP Four Country. News staff: one; News: 7 hrs wkly. Target aud: 18 plus. Spec prog: Bluegrass 2 hrs wkly. ◆Peter L. Coughlin, pres; Rob Ellis, opns dir & progmg dir.

Baker

*WTJT(FM)— May 1987: 90.1 mhz; 50 kw. Ant 417 ft TL: N30 49 19 W86 42 37. Hrs open: 24 957 Hwy. C-4A, 32531. Phone: (850) 537-2009. Fax: (850) 537-4663.E-mail: wtjtradio@yahoo.com Licensee: Okaloosa Public Radio Inc. Natl. Network: USA, . Format: Educ. Target aud: 35 plus. ◆ Earl Thompson, pres, gen mgr; Jessica Walker, stn mgr; Ruth Thompson, mus dir; Randy Henry, chief of engrg.

Baldwin

WHJX(FM)— July 30, 1992: 105.7 mhz; 25 kw. Ant 328 ft TL: N30 22 28 W82 01 42. Stereo. Hrs open: 9090 Hogan Rd., Suite B, Jacksonville, 32216. Phone: (904) 425-3482. Web Site:www.radiofreejax.com Licensee: Scott Savage, receiver Group owner: Tama Broadcasting Inc. (acq 2-26-2009). Format: Talk. ◆Andy Johnson, gen mgr.

Bartow

WQXM(AM)— Sept 28, 1953: 1460 khz; 1 kw-D, 155 w-N. TL: N27 54 34 W81 51 29. Hrs open: 6 AM-6 PM Box 452905, Miami, 33245. Phone: (305) 270-1244. Fax: (305) 270-1255. Licensee: Florida Broadcasting Media LLC (acq 5-17-2004; $325,000). Population served: 350,000 Natl. Network: CBS, . Format: Traditional country. Target aud: General. ◆Armando Gutierrez, gen mgr.

WWBF(AM)— Sept 16, 1969: 1130 khz; 2.5 kw-D, 500 w-N. DA-N. TL: N27 54 34 W81 49 35. Stereo. Hrs open: 24 1130 Radio Rd., 33830. Phone: (863) 533-0744. Fax: (863) 533-8546.E-mail: tom@wwbf.com Web Site:www.wwbf.com Licensee: Thornburg Communications Inc. (acq 1-27-84; $220,000; 2-6-84). Population served: 414,700 Natl. Network: CNN Radio, . Rgnl. Network: Florida Radio Net. Florida's Radio Networks Format: Oldies. News staff: one; News: 10 hrs wkly. Target aud: 35-54; affluent adults. Spec prog: Sports. ◆Jeffrey A. Thornburg, VP; Thomas N. Thornburg, pres & gen mgr; Susan E. Thornburg, stn mgr.

Belle Glade

WBGF(FM)— May 31, 1965: 93.5 mhz; 5 kw. 269 ft TL: N26 42 43 W80 40 59. Stereo. Hrs open: Box 1505, 33430. Secondary address: 2001 State Rd. 715 33430. Phone: (561) 996-2063. Fax: (561) 996-1852.E-mail: wswnwbgf@bellsouth.net Web Site:bigdawg935.com Licensee: BGI Broadcasting LP. Population served: 25,000 Natl. Network: ABC, . Florida's Radio Networks Rgnl rep: Interep Format: Sports. Target aud: 25-54. Spec prog: Farm 5 hrs wkly. ◆Mike Diagostine, progmg dir.

WSWN(AM)— Oct 7, 1947: 900 khz; 1 kw-D, 26 w-N. TL: N26 42 54 W80 40 58. (CP: TL: N26 42 56 W80 40 58). Hrs open: Box 1505, 33430. Secondary address: 2001 State Rd. 715 33430. Phone: (561) 996-2063. Fax: (561) 996-1852.E-mail: wswnwbgfa@bellsouth.net Licensee: BGI Inc. (acq 1996). Population served: 806,000 Natl. Network: ABC, Jones Radio Networks, . Rgnl. Network: S.E.Agri., Florida Radio Net. Natl. Rep: Interep,. Southeast AgNet Format: Relg, Gospel. Target aud: 25-54. Spec prog: Sports. ◆David Lampel, gen mgr; Harvey J. Poole Jr., progmg dir; Rick Rieke, chief of engrg.

Belleview

*WYFZ(FM)— Apr 2001: 91.3 mhz; 200 w horiz, 1.1 kw vert. Ant 328 ft TL: N29 10 31 W82 09 09. Hrs open: 24 Box 7300, Charlotte, NC, 28241. Fax: (704) 522-1967. Web Site:bbnradio.org Licensee: Bible Broadcasting Network Inc. (acq 12-1-2005; $250,000). Population served: 350,000 Format: Relg. ◆Lowell L. Davey, pres.

Beverly Beach

WBHQ(FM)— 1978: 92.7 mhz; 5.5 kw. Ant 341 ft TL: N29 32 07 W81 15 50. Stereo. Hrs open: 24 2405 E. Moody Blvd., Suite 402, Bunnell, 32110. Phone: (386) 437-1992. Web Site:www.beach927.com Licensee: Flagler County Broadcasting LLC Group owner: Clear Channel Communications Inc. (acq 2-20-2009; $350,000). Format: Variety hits.

Beverly Hills

WINV(AM)— Sept 1, 1965: Stn currently dark. 1560 khz; 5 kw-D, 4.1 kw-CH. TL: N28 50 30 W82 22 16. Stereo. Hrs open: 4554 S. Suncoast Blvd., Homosassa, 34446. Phone: (352) 628-4444.E-mail: staff@citrus953.com Licensee: WGUL-FM Inc. (acq 11-26-97; $5,000). Michael Wilhelm. ◆Richard Spires, gen mgr.

Big Pine Key

WWUS(FM)— Sept 22, 1980: 104.1 mhz; 100 kw. 433 ft TL: N24 39 38 W81 25 10. Stereo. Hrs open: 24 30336 Overseas Hwy., 33043. Phone: (305) 872-9100. Fax: (305) 872-8930.E-mail: us1radio@aol.com Web Site:www.us1radio.com Licensee: Vox Communications Group LLC. (acq 8-31-2005; grpsl). Natl. Network: AP Radio, . Katten Muchin Rosenman LLP. Format: Classic hits. News staff: one; News: 2 hrs wkly. Target aud: 30-50. Spec prog: Island mus 4 hrs wkly. ◆Kevin LeRoux, gen mgr, gen sls mgr; Race Ashlyn, stn mgr, progmg dir; Bill Becker, news dir; Randy Perry, chief of engrg; Kim Casey, traf mgr.

Bithlo

WNTF(AM)— July 31, 1974: 1580 khz; 2.1 kw-D. TL: N28 32 11 W81 05 06. Hrs open: 3765 N. John Young Pkwy., Orlando, 23804. Phone: (407) 291-1395. Fax: (407) 293-2870. Licensee: Rama Communications Inc. (group owner; acq 10-29-2002; $600,000 with WGAF(AM) Alachua). Population served: 2,000,000 Format: Sp. ◆Sabita Persaud, pres; Steve January, gen mgr; Steve De Lay, chief of engrg.

Blountstown

WPHK(FM)— Dec 18, 1968: 102.7 mhz; 13 kw. Ant 318 ft TL: N30 27 15 W85 02 32. Hrs open: 20872 N.E. Kelley Ave., 32424. Licensee: Blountstown Communications Format: Modern country. Spec prog: Black 12 hrs wkly. ◆Harry S. Hagen, gen mgr.

WYBT(AM)— Sept 8, 1962: 1000 khz; 5 kw-D. TL: N30 27 15 W85 02 32. Hrs open: 20872 N.E. Kelley Ave., 32424. Phone: (850) 674-5101. Fax: (850) 674-2965. Licensee: Blountstown Communications (acq 6-26-86; $103,000;4-14-86). Format: Golden oldies. Spec prog: Gospel & relg 15 hrs wkly. ◆Harry S. Hagen, pres; Cathy Hagen, progmg dir.

Boca Raton

WKIS(FM)—Licensed to Boca Raton. See Miami

WSBR(AM)— April 1965: 740 khz; 2.5 kw-D, 940 w-N, DA-2. TL: N26 20 06 W80 15 55. Hrs open: 6699 N. Federal Hwy., Suite 200, 33487. Phone: (561) 997-0074. Fax: (561) 997-0476.E-mail: info@wsbr.com Web Site:www.wsbradio.com Licensee: WWNN License LLC. Group owner: Beasley Broadcast Group (acq 3-14-2000; grpsl). Population served: 999,700 Format: Financial talk. ◆Bob Morency, VP, gen mgr; Greg Cooper, opns mgr.

Bonifay

WYYX(FM)— Apr 23, 1983: 97.7 mhz; 100 kw. 830 ft TL: N30 30 41 W85 29 24. Stereo. Hrs open: 24 7106 Laird St., Suite 200, Panama City Beach, 32408. Phone: (850) 233-6606. Fax: (850) 233-1541.E-mail: info@wyyx.com Web Site:www.wyyx.com Licensee: Magic Broadcasting Florida Licensing LLC. (group owner; (acq 9-30-2002; grpsl). Format: Active rock, AOR. News staff: one. Target aud: 18-49. ◆ Jim Storey, COO, exec VP, gen mgr, engrg mgr; J.P. Ferrell, gen sls mgr; Karla Melvin, traf mgr.

Bonita Springs

WRXK-FM— Sept 1, 1974: 96.1 mhz; 100 kw. 1,122 ft TL: N26 26 53 W81 48 54. Stereo. Hrs open: 20125 S. Tamiami Tr., Estero, 33928. Phone: (239) 495-2100. Fax: (239) 992-8165.E-mail: info@96krock.com Web Site:www.96krock.com Licensee: Beasley Broadcasting of Western Florida Inc. Group owner: Beasley Broadcast Group (acq 8-12-86). Population served: 800,000 Natl. Network: ABC, . Natl. Rep: Katz Radio,. Format: Classic rock. Target aud: 18-49. ◆ George G. Beasley, pres; Brad Beasley, gen mgr; Shane Reilly, opns mgr; Robert Hallman, gen sls mgr.

Boynton Beach

WLVJ(AM)— Jan 23, 1973: 1040 khz; 25 kw-D, 1.2 kw-N, DA-2. TL: N26 28 26 W80 12 11. Stereo. Hrs open: 24 6600 N. Andrews Ave., Suite 160, Fort Lauderdale, 33309. Phone: (954) 315-1515 / 1539. Fax: (954) 315-1555.E-mail: info@wlvj.com Web Site:www.wlvj.com Licensee: Communicom Co. of Florida L.P. Group owner: James Crystal Inc. (acq 12-14-2005; grpsl). Population served: 950,000 Format: Relg. ◆Rick Hindes, CFO; Steve Lapa, gen mgr.

*WRMB(FM)— Apr 15, 1979: 89.3 mhz; 100 kw. 500 ft TL: N26 31 07 W80 10 17. Stereo. Hrs open: 24 1511 W. Boynton Beach Blvd., 33436. Phone: (561) 737-9762. Fax: (561) 737-9899.E-mail: wrmb@moody.edu Web Site:www.wrmb.org Licensee: Moody Bible Institute of Chicago. (group owner) Natl. Network: Moody, . Wire Svc: AP Format: Relg. News staff: one. Target aud: General. ◆Dr. Paul Nyquist, pres; Jennifer Epperson, stn mgr, mus dir.

WXEL(FM)—See West Palm Beach

Bradenton

*WJIS(FM)— 1989: 88.1 mhz; 100 kw. 397 ft TL: N27 07 54 W82 23 29. Hrs open: 6469 Parkland Dr., Sarasota, 34243. Phone: (941) 753-0401. Fax: (941) 753-2963.E-mail: thejoyfm@thejoyfm.com Web Site:www.thejoyfm.com Licensee: WJIS FM Radio. (acq 8-17-89; grpsl; 9-11-89). Format: Adult Contemp Christian music. ◆Jeff McFarlane, gen mgr, stn mgr; Carmen Brown, prom dir; Steve Swanson, progmg dir; Steve Rieker, chief of engrg.

WSJT(FM)—See Holmes Beach

WWPR(AM)— 1946: 1490 khz; 1 kw-U. TL: N27 30 00 W82 34 25. Hrs open: 24 5910 Cortez Rd. W., Suite 130, 34210. Phone: (941) 761-8843. Fax: (941) 761-8683.E-mail: manager@1490wwpr.com Web Site:www.1490wwpr.com Licensee: Greenrose Broadcasting Services Inc. (acq 9-19-97; $265,000). Natl. Network: Talk Radio Network. . Pepper & Corazzini. Format: Talk. News staff: one; News: 15 hrs wkly. Target aud: 35-64; general. Spec prog: Community talk15 hrs, relg 6 hrs, gospel 6 hrs, sports 5 hrs, Hispanic progmg 40 hrs wkly. ◆Valerie Silver, gen mgr.

Brandon

WLCC(AM)— February 1988: 760 khz; 10 kw-D, 1 kw-N, DA-2. TL: N28 01 29 W82 17 02. Hrs open: 1915 N. Dale Mabry Hwy., Suite 200, Tampa, 33607. Phone: (813) 871-1819. Fax: (813) 871-1155. Web Site:www.laleytampa.com Licensee: Minority Media and Telecommunications Council Inc. Group owner: Mega Communications Inc. (acq 1-22-2009; donation). Format: Rgnl Mexican. Target aud: 25-54. ◆Rafael Grullon, pres & gen mgr.

Brooksville

WWJB(AM)— Oct 11, 1958: 1450 khz; 1 kw-U. TL: N28 33 02 W82 25 02. Hrs open: 24 Box 1507, 34605. Secondary address: 55 W. Fort Dade Ave. 34605-1507. Phone: (352) 796-7469. Fax: (352) 796-5074.E-mail: info@wwjb.com Web Site:www.wwjb.com Licensee: Hernando Broadcasting Co. (acq 3-1-82; 4-5-82). Population served: 150,000 Natl. Network: Westwood One, ABC, . Natl. Rep: Dora-Clayton,. Florida's Radio Networks Format: News/talk, sports. News staff: one. Target aud: 25 plus. ◆Bill Willamson, gen sls mgr; Peggy Hope, prom dir, prom mgr, traf mgr; Bob Haa, news dir; Steve Manuel, pres, gen mgr & political ed.

Bunnell

WNZF(AM)— 2008: 1550 khz; 8.7 kw-D, 250 w-N, DA-N. TL: N29 28 09 W81 16 00. Hrs open: 24 2405 E. Moody Blvd., Suite 402, 32110. Phone: (386) 437-1992.E-mail: newsradio@wnzf.com Web Site:wnzf.com Licensee: Flagler County Broadcasting LLC (acq 8-7-2007; $150,000 for CP). Natl. Network: Fox Sports, . Format: News/talk. ◆David Ayers, gen mgr; Ron Charles, news dir.

Bushnell

WKFL(AM)— Jan 1, 1987: 1170 khz; 1 kw-D. TL: N28 42 31 W82 07 36. Hrs open: 6 AM-9 PM varies by season 5224 State Rt. 46, Ste. 354, Sanford, 32771. Phone: (352) 568-3204. Fax: (407) 322-0431. Web Site:www.talknsports.net Licensee: TalknSports Inc. (acq 6-22-2004). Population served: 375,000 Natl. Network: Salem Radio Network, . Format: Sports, news/talk. News staff: one; News: 8 hrs wkly. Target aud: 18-54; those who enjoy family progmg. ◆Bruce Cox, pres; Jan Hall, gen mgr.

Callahan

WEWC(AM)— 1999: 1160 khz; 5 kw-D, 250 w-N, DA-D. TL: N30 34 47 W87 17 18. Hrs open: 8384 Baymeadows Rd., Suite 1, Jacksonville, 32256. Phone: (904) 549-2218. Fax: (904) 359-0070. Web Site:www.1160latinohits.com Licensee: Norsan Consulting and Management Inc. (acq 9-25-2007; $650,000). Format: Sp. ◆George Lopez, gen mgr.

WJBT(FM)—Licensed to Callahan. See Jacksonville

Callaway

WAKT-FM— February 1990: 103.5 mhz; 100 kw. 475 ft TL: N30 03 18 W85 18 09. (CP: Ant 748 ft. TL: N30 13 45 W85 23 20). Stereo. Hrs open: 24 118 Gwyn Dr., Panama City Beach, 32408. Phone: (850) 234-8858. Fax: (850) 234-1181. Web Site:www.maxcountry1035.com Licensee: Double O Radio Corp. (group owner; acq 3-10-2004; grpsl). Population served: 135,000 Natl. Rep: Christal,. Format: Country. ◆Harry Finch, gen mgr.

Cantonment

WNVY(AM)—Licensed to Cantonment. See Pensacola

Cape Coral

WXKB(FM)— 1975: 103.9 mhz; 100 kw. 981 ft TL: N26 47 43 W81 48 04. Stereo. Hrs open: 20125 S. Tamiami Tr., Estero, 33928. Phone: (239) 495-2100. Fax: (239) 948-0785.E-mail: info@bbgi.com Web Site:www.b103.com Licensee: Beasley Broadcasting. Group owner: Beasley Broadcast Group (acq 11-18-94; $3.7 million;1-2-95). Population served: 31,000 Format: CHR. Target aud: General. ◆George G. Beasley, pres; Brad Beasley, gen mgr; Shane Reilly, opns mgr; Matt Johnson, progmg dir.

Carrabelle

WOCY(FM)— 1999: 106.5 mhz; 100 kw. Ant 361 ft TL: N29 43 57 W84 53 24. Stereo. Hrs open: Point Mall 35 Island Dr. #16, Eastpoint, 32328-3264. Phone: (850) 670-8450. Fax: (850) 670-8492.E-mail: manager@oysterradio.com Web Site:www.woyswocy.homestead.com Licensee: Oyster Radio Inc. Group owner: Plessinger Radio Group (acq 8-30-2007; with WOYS(FM) Apalachicola). Rgnl. Network: Florida Radio Net. Florida's Radio Networks Format: Country. ◆Clair D. Plessinger, pres; Michael Allen, stn mgr, news dir; William Denton, gen sls mgr & mus dir.

Cedar Creek

*****WKSG(FM)—** 1999: 89.5 mhz; 2 kw. Ant 308 ft TL: N29 11 20 W81 52 52. (CP: 30 kw vert, ant 341 ft). Hrs open: 7 E. Silver Springs Blvd., Suite 102, Ocala, 34471. Phone: (352) 369-8950. Fax: (352) 369-1109.E-mail: daystar@ocalapro.com Web Site:www.daystarradio.com Licensee: Daystar Public Radio Inc. (acq 1-5-98). Format: Adult Contemp Christian. ◆Gary Linkus, gen mgr.

Cedar Key

WRGO(FM)— Sept 1996: 102.7 mhz; 12.5 kw. Ant 459 ft TL: N29 11 45 W82 59 46. Hrs open: 24 1929 N.W. Hwy. 19, Crystal River, 34428. Phone: (352) 795-1027. Fax: (352) 795-0002. Licensee: WRGO Radio LLC. (group owner; (acq 9-12-2007; $900,000 with WZCC(AM) Cross City). Population served: 200,000 Natl. Network: Jones Radio Networks, . Booth, Freret, Imlay & Tepper. Format: Oldies. Target aud: 25-64. ◆Lou Cerra, gen mgr.

Century

WPFL(FM)— July 1989: 105.1 mhz; 25 kw. 328 ft TL: N30 52 12 W87 20 05. Hrs open: Box 967, Flomaton, AL, 36441. Secondary address: 2059 Old Fannie Rd., Flomaton, AL 36441. Phone: (251) 296-1051. Fax: (251) 296-1055.E-mail: wpflradio@bellsouth.net Web Site:www.oldiesradioonline.com Licensee: Tri-County Broadcasting Inc. (acq 4-10-01; $575,000 including $50,000 ad credit). Format: Oldies. ◆Ronnie Hammond, gen mgr & progmg; Howard Macht, chief of engrg.

Charlotte Harbor

WIKX(FM)—Licensed to Charlotte Harbor. See Punta Gorda

Chattahoochee

WTCL(AM)— Nov 1, 1963: 1580 khz; 5 kw-D. TL: N30 40 14 W84 50 08. (CP: 10 kw-D, 500 w-N, DA-N). Hrs open: 7175 Bonnie Hill Rd., 32324. Phone: (850) 663-3857. Phone: (850) 663-3857. Fax: (850) 663-8543.E-mail: info@wtcl.com Licensee: Metz Inc. (acq 1-9-97; $55,000). Natl. Network: USA, . Rgnl. Network: Florida Radio Net. Florida's Radio Networks Format: Gospel, ministries. Target aud: General. ◆Don Metz, pres; David Garcia, gen mgr.

Chiefland

WLQH(AM)— June 6, 1968: 940 khz; 1 kw-D. TL: N29 31 00 W82 53 11. Stereo. Hrs open: Sunrise-sunset 12750 Old Fanning Springs Rd., 32626. Phone: (352) 493-4940. Fax: (352) 493-9909. Licensee: Ocala Broadcasting Corp. (acq 11-2-99; with co-located FM). Population served: 35,000 Format: Music of your life. Spec prog: Relg 9 hrs wkly. ◆Bob Moody, stn mgr.

WNDN(FM)— 1991: 107.9 mhz; 6 kw. Ant 328 ft TL: N29 31 00 W82 53 11. Hrs open: 6 AM-midnight Dups AM 100% 12750 Old Fanning Springs Rd., 32626. Phone: (352) 493-4940. Fax: (352) 493-9909. Licensee: Ocala Broadcasting Corp. Natl. Network: Jones Radio Networks, . Format: Plastic Rock.

Chipley

WBGC(AM)— Apr 10, 1956: 1240 khz; 1 kw-U. TL: N30 46 19 W85 33 31. Hrs open: 1513 S. Blvd., 32428. Phone: (850) 638-0234. Fax: (850) 638-4333. Licensee: Jacquelyn Collier Pembroke (acq 5-28-02; with WALD(AM) Walterboro). Population served: 5,441 Rgnl. Network: Florida Radio Net. Natl. Rep: Keystone (unwired net),. Florida's Radio Networks Format: Var. ◆Todd Burnett, gen mgr.

Clearwater

WBTP(FM)— Aug 19, 1963: 95.7 mhz; 100 kw. Ant 607 ft TL: N27 52 00 W82 37 27. Stereo. Hrs open: 24 4002 Gandy Blvd., Tampa, 33611. Phone: (813) 832-1000. Fax: (813) 832-1090. Web Site:www.957thebeat.com Licensee: Clear Channel Broadcasting Licenses Inc. Group owner: Clear Channel Communications Inc. (acq 10-94). Natl. Rep: Katz Radio,. Wire Svc: AP Format: Hot adult contemp/urban. Target aud: 18-49; upwardly mobile adults. ◆Dan DiLoreto, VP, gen mgr; Doug Hammond, opns mgr; Ron Shepard, progmg dir; John McMartin, engrg dir; Misty Pittman, traf mgr.

WMGG(AM)—See Dunedin

WTAN(AM)— June 1948: 1340 khz; 1 kw-U. TL: N27 57 49 W82 24 14. Hrs open: 24 706 N. Myrtle Ave., 33755. Phone: (727) 441-3311. Fax (727) 441-1300.E-mail: lola@tantalk.net Web Site:www.tantalk1340.com Licensee: Wagenvoord Advertising Group Inc. (group owner; acq 12-29-99; $100,000). Population served: 2,500,000 Format: Talk/news, Music of Your Life. News staff: 2; News: 12 hrs wkly. Target aud: 35-64. Spec prog: Big band 40 hrs wkly. ◆Dave Wagenvoord, CEO, pres; Lola Wagenvoord, gen mgr.

WXTB(FM)— Dec 1, 1967: 97.9 mhz; 100 kw. 1,345 ft TL: N28 10 56 W82 46 06. Stereo. Hrs open: 24 4002 Gandy Blvd., Tampa, 33611. Phone: (813) 832-1000. Fax: (813) 831-9898.E-mail: doubledon @clearchannel.com Web Site:www.98rock.com Licensee: Citicasters Licenses L.P. Group owner: Clear Channel Communications Inc. (acq 5-6-99; grpsl). Natl. Network: Premiere Radio Networks, . Natl. Rep: Katz Radio,. Wire Svc: AP Format: Rock. News staff: one; News: 2 hrs wkly. Target aud: 18-49; men. Spec prog: Pub affrs 4 hrs wkly. ◆Daniel DiLoreto, pres, VP, gen mgr; James Howard, opns dir, progmg dir; Doug Hamand, opns mgr; Chris Soechtig, sls dir; John McMartin, engrg dir; Anqunette Wilson, traf mgr.

WYUU(FM)—See Tampa

Clermont

*****WMYZ(FM)—** July 18, 1997: 88.7 mhz; 5.5 kw vert. Ant 384 ft TL: N28 38 56 W81 43 56. Stereo. Hrs open: 24 Rebroadcasts WPOZ(FM) Union Park 100%. 1065 Rainer Dr., Altamonte Springs, 32714-3847. Phone: (407) 869-8000. Fax: (407) 869-0380.E-mail: zcrew@zradio.org Web Site:www.zradio.org Licensee: Central Florida Educational Foundation Inc. (acq 9-20-2005; $1.77 million). Fletcher, Heald & Hildreth. Format: Contemp Christian. ◆James S. Hoge, pres & gen mgr.

WWFL(AM)— 1962: 1340 khz; 1 kw-U. TL: N28 33 06 W81 46 45. Hrs open: 24 Central Florida Investments Inc., 5601 Windover Dr., Suite 102, Orlando, 32819. Phone: (407) 351-3350. Fax: (407) 370-3524. Web Site:www.cflradio.net Licensee: Central Florida Investments Inc. Format: MOR. ◆David Siegal, pres.

Clewiston

WAFC(AM)— Feb 16, 1988: 590 khz; 930 w-D, 470 w-N. TL: N26 43 47 W80 54 45. Hrs open: 24 530 E. Alverdez Ave., 33440-3901. Phone: (863) 983-5900. Fax: (863) 983-6109. Web Site:www.radiofiesta.com Licensee: Glades Media Company LLP Population served: 165,000 Natl. Rep: Interep,. Leibowitz & Associates. Format: Rgnl Mexican. News: 10 hrs wkly. Target aud: General. ◆Jim Johnson, CFO; Robert Castellanos, CEO & gen mgr; Larry Parrish, sls dir; Francisco Sangabriel, progmg dir; Debbie Pattison, traf mgr.

WAFC-FM— July 2, 1979: 99.5 mhz; 12 kw. Ant 472 ft TL: N26 41 27 W80 47 18. Stereo. Hrs open: 24 530 E. Alverdez Ave., 33440. Phone: (863) 902-0995. Fax: (863) 983-6109. Web Site:www.radiofiesta.com Licensee: Glades Media Co. LLP. Population served: 77,000 Rgnl. Network: Florida Radio Net. Leibowitz & Associates. Format: Rgnl Mexican. Target aud: 18-49. ◆Robbie Castellanos, gen mgr; Francisco Sangabriel, progmg dir.

*****WJCB(FM)—**Not on air, target date: unknown: 88.5 mhz; 3 kw. Ant 292 ft TL: N26 43 46 W80 54 49. Hrs open: 1150 W. King St., Cocoa, 32922. Phone: (321) 632-1000. Fax: (321) 636-0000.E-mail: paul@wmiefm.com Licensee: Black Media Works Inc. (group owner). Format: Urban Contemp, Gospel. ◆Ray Kassis, gen mgr.

*****WPSF(FM)—** 2008: 91.5 mhz; 700 w vert. Ant 387 ft TL: N26 41 27 W80 47 18. Hrs open: 3185 S. Highland Dr., Suite 13, Las Vegas, NV, 89109-1029. Phone: (702) 731-5588. Fax: (305) 251-2293. Web Site:www.callfm.com Licensee: American Educational Broadcasting Inc. Format: Christian. ◆Carl J. Auel, pres; Rob Robbins, gen mgr.

Cocoa

WLRQ-FM—Listing follows WMMV(AM).

***WMIE(FM)**— December 1984: 91.5 mhz; 20 kw horiz, 19 kw vert. 98 ft TL: N28 21 21 W80 44 47. Stereo. Hrs open: 24 1150 W. King St., 32922. Phone: (321) 632-1000. Fax: (321) 636-0000. Web Site:www.wjfp.com Licensee: National Christian Network. Population served: 450,000 Format: Modern worship. Target aud: 18-49. ♦Raymond A. Kassis, pres; Paul Esposito, gen mgr; Jim Conn, progmg dir; Jan Ferguson, chief of engrg.

WMMV(AM)— Oct 4, 1957: 1350 khz; 1 kw-U, DA-N. TL: N28 21 58 W80 45 08. Stereo. Hrs open: 1388 S. Babcock St., Melbourne, 32901. Phone: (321) 733-1000. Fax: (321) 733-0904. Web Site:www.wmmvdm.com Licensee: Capstar TX L.P. Group owner: Clear Channel Communications Inc. (acq 8-30-00; grpsl). Population served: 312,000 Natl. Network: ABC, Westwood One, . Rgnl. Network: Florida Radio Net. Florida's Radio Networks Format: Adult standards, news/talk radio. ♦Barbara Latham, gen mgr.

WWBC(AM)— July 1965: 1510 khz; 1 kw-D. TL: N28 21 30 W80 42 38. (CP: COL: Rockledge, 770 khz, 1 kw-D, 480 w-N, DA-2, TL: N28 20 05 W80 46 56). Hrs open: Sunrise-sunset 1150 W. King St., 32922. Phone: (321) 632-1000. Fax: (321) 636-0000.E-mail: paul@wmiefm.com Web Site:www.wmiefm.com Licensee: Astro Enterprises. (acq 3-1-76). Population served: 350,000 Format: Relg/Talk. Target aud: 25 plus. ♦Ray Kassis, pres; Paul Esposito, gen mgr.

Cocoa Beach

WJRR(FM)— July 19, 1962: 101.1 mhz; 100 kw. 1,598 ft TL: N28 34 51 W81 04 32. Stereo. Hrs open: 2500 Maitland Ctr. Pkwy., Suite 401, Maitland, 32751. Phone: (407) 916-7800. Phone: (407) 916-1011. Fax: (407) 916-7407.E-mail: info@realrock1011.com Web Site:www.realrock1011.com Licensee: Clear Channel Broadcasting Licenses Inc. Group owner: Clear Channel Communications Inc. (acq 1-27-2009; with KYRK(FM) Houma, LA). Thompson Hine LLP. Format: Modern Rock. Target aud: 18-34; men. ♦Linda Byrd, pres, gen mgr; Chris Kampmeier, opns VP, progmg dir; Aaron Miller, gen sls mgr; Pat Lynch, natl sls mgr, progmg dir; Rick Everett, mktg dir; Josh Egolf, prom mgr.

WMEL(AM)— June 22, 1959: 1300 khz; 5 kw-D, 1 kw-N, DA-2. TL: N28 20 38 W80 46 06. Hrs open: 24 2355 Pluckebaum Rd., Cocoa, 32936. Phone: (321) 631-9755. Fax: (321) 631-9113.E-mail: Paul@920wmel.com Web Site:www.1300wmel.com Licensee: Rama Communications Inc. (group owner; (acq 10-13-93; $950,000 with WLAA(AM) Winter Garden;11-8-93) Natl. Network: ABC, Talk Radio Network, . Putbrese, Hunsaker & Trent. Format: News/talk, sports. News staff: 2; News: 144 hrs wky. Target aud: 35-64; decision making men & women. ♦John Harper, pres.

WTKS-FM—Licensed to Cocoa Beach. See Orlando

Columbia City

WJTK(FM)— 2006: 96.5 mhz; 5 kw. Ant 359 ft TL: N30 09 20 W82 38 14. Hrs open: 229 S.W. Main Blvd., Lake City, 32025. Phone: (386) 758-9696. Fax: (386) 269-4361.E-mail: cest@965wjtkfm.com Licensee: ABC Media Inc. Format: News/talk. ♦Cesta Newman, pres & gen mgr.

Coral Cove

WSRZ-FM— Mar 25, 1995: 107.9 mhz; 47 kw. Ant 508 ft TL: N27 09 03 W82 27 51. Stereo. Hrs open: 24 1779 Independence Blvd., Sarasota, 34234. Phone: (941) 552-4800. Fax: (941) 552-4900.E-mail: info@oldies108.com Web Site:www.oldies108.com Licensee: Citicasters Licenses L.P. Group owner: Clear Channel Communications Inc. (acq 5-4-99; grpsl). Population served: 902,200 Format: Oldies. Target aud: 25-54. ♦Buddy Lee, gen mgr.

Coral Gables

WHQT(FM)— Nov 15, 1958: 105.1 mhz; 100 kw. 1,049 ft TL: N25 57 59 W80 12 33. (CP: Ant 1,007 ft.). Stereo. Hrs open: 2741 N. 29th Ave., Hollywood, 33020. Phone: (305) 444-4404. Fax: (954) 847-3240 /(954) 584-7117. Web Site:www.hot105fm.com Licensee: Cox Radio Inc. Group owner: Cox Broadcasting (acq 12-28-92; 1-11-93). Population served: 42,494 Natl. Rep: Christal,. Dow, Lohnes & Albertson. Format: Urban adult contemp. Target aud: 18-49. ♦Jerry Rushin, gen mgr; Janine DuPont, prom mgr; Derrick Brown, progmg dir.

WMCU(AM)— Feb 18, 1949: 1080 khz; 50 kw-D, 20 kw-N, DA-2. TL: N25 44 53 W80 32 47. Hrs open: 24 2828 W. Flagler St., Miami, 33135. Phone: (305) 503-1340. Fax: (305) 677-7585.E-mail: info@wkat.com Web Site:1360wkat.com Licensee: Caron Broadcasting Inc. Group owner: Radio One Inc. (acq 4-11-2008; $12.25 million). Format: Christian. ♦Tony Calatayud, gen mgr.

WRHC(AM)— 1963: 1550 khz; 10 kw-D, 500 k-N, DA-2. TL: N25 51 27 W80 28 52. Hrs open: 24 330 S.W. 27th Ave., Suite 207, Miami, 33135. Phone: (305) 541-3300. Fax: (305) 541-7470.E-mail: anavidal@lapoderosa.com Web Site:www.wrhc.com Licensee: WRHC Broadcasting Corp. (acq 3-23-93; 4-5-93). Population served: 1,800,000 Natl. Rep: Lotus Entravision Reps LLC,. Leventhal, Senter & Lerman, P.L.L.C. Format: Sp, news/talk, entertainment, sports. News staff: 4; News: 4 hrs wkly. Central & South Americans. ♦Ana M. Vidal Rodriguez, VP, gen mgr; Jorge Rodriguez, pres & gen sls mgr.

***WVUM(FM)**— May 1968: 90.5 mhz; 100 w horiz, 1.3 kw vert. 175 ft TL: N25 43 02 W80 16 48. Stereo. Hrs open: 24 Box 248191, 33124. Phone: (305) 284-3131. Fax: (305) 284-3132.E-mail: info@wvum.org Web Site:www.wvum.org Licensee: WVUM Inc. Format: Diversified, alternative. News staff: one; News: 3 hrs wkly. Target aud: 13-plus. Spec prog: Sports 5 hrs, Black 7 hrs, relg 6 hrs, Sp 2 hrs, oldies 5 hrs wkly. ♦Benton Galgay, gen mgr; Jay Drybourgh, progmg dir.

Crawfordville

WAKU(FM)— January 1996: 94.1 mhz; 3 kw. 459 ft TL: N30 04 34 W84 18 05. Stereo. Hrs open: 24 Box 4105, Tallahassee, 32315. Secondary address: 3225 Harstfield Rd., Tallahassee 32303. Phone: (850) 926-8000. Fax: (850) 926-2000.E-mail: dougapple@wave94.com Web Site:www.wave94.com Licensee: Altrua Investments International Corp. (acq 7-14-98; $550,000). Population served: 200,000 Natl. Network: Salem Radio Network, . Koteen & Naftalin. Format: Contemp christian. News: 10 hrs wkly. Target aud: 35-54; Adults. ♦Mike Floyd, CEO; Doug Apple, gen mgr.

Crestview

WAAZ-FM— July 15, 1965: 104.7 mhz; 100 kw. Ant 485 ft TL: N30 46 01 W86 35 07. Hrs open: 5 AM - MIDNIGHT
Simulcast with WJSB(AM) Crestview 100%.
P.O. Box 267, 506 W. FIRST AVE., 32536. Secondary address: 506 W. First Ave. 32536. Phone: (850) 682-3040. Phone: (850) 682-4623. Fax: (850) 682-5232.E-mail: waazwjsb@embarqmail.com Licensee: Crestview Broadcasting Co. Natl. Network: CBS Radio, . Format: Country. News staff: one. Spec prog: ATLANTA BRAVES BASEBALL. ♦CAL ZETHMAYER, gen sls mgr; CLAUDE T. STRICKLAND, news dir.

WJSB(AM)— Sept 15, 1954: 1050 khz; 3.1 kw D 500w night. TL: N30 45 56 W86 35 06. (CP: 3.1 kw-D, 500 w-N, DA-N, TL: N30 46 00 W86 35 08). Hrs open: Daytime only Box 267, 32536. Secondary address: 506 W. First Ave. 32536. Phone: (850) 682-3040. Phone: (850) 682-4623. Fax: (850) 682-5232.E-mail: waazwjsb@embarqmail.com Licensee: Crestview Broadcasting Co. (acq 8-11-98). Population served: 16,000 Natl. Network: CBS, . Format: Country. News staff: 3. ♦Claude T. Strickland, news dir, women's int ed; James T. Whitaker, pres & chief of engrg.

Cross City

WKZY(FM)— Nov 16, 1987: 106.9 mhz; 100 kw. Ant 469 ft TL: N29 36 29 W82 51 01. Stereo. Hrs open: 100 N.W. 76th Dr., Suite 2, Gainesville, 32607. Phone: (352) 313-3150. Fax: (352) 313-3166. Web Site:www.1069kzy.com Licensee: 6 Johnson Road Licenses Inc. (acq 1-5-2007; grpsl). Format: Adult contemp 80s based. ♦Jeanie Edwards, gen sls mgr; Alan Ritchie, natl sls mgr.

***WWLC(FM)**— 2006: 88.5 mhz; 425 w. Ant 193 ft TL: N29 39 09 W83 10 08. (CP: 100 kw, ant 338 ft. TL: N29 31 35 W83 14 17). Hrs open: 24 Spirit Radio of North Florida Inc., 412 N.E. 16th Ave., Gainesville, 32601. Phone: (352) 372-4641. Fax: (352) 376-0575. Web Site:www.sprintradio.org Licensee: Spirit Radio of North Florida Inc. Format: Christian. ♦Fr. Roland M. Julien, gen mgr.

WZCC(AM)— November 1985: 1240 khz; 1 kw-U. TL: N29 36 35 W83 08 03. Hrs open: 24 1929 N.W. Hwy. 19, Crystal River, 34428. Phone: (352) 795-1027. Fax: (352) 795-0002. Licensee: WRGO Radio LLC (group owner; (acq 9-12-2007; $900,000 with WRGO(FM) Cedar Key). Format: Country. ♦Lou Cerra, gen mgr.

Crystal River

***WAQV(FM)**— 1999: 90.9 mhz; 3 kw. 331 ft TL: N29 01 52 W82 27 05. Hrs open: 24
Rebroadcasts WHIJ(FM) Ocala 100%.
408 W. University, Suite 206, Gainsville, 32601. Phone: (352) 351-8810. Fax: (352) 351-8917.E-mail: thejoyfm@thejoy.com Web Site:www.thejoyfm.com Licensee: Radio Training Network Inc. (acq 10-5-2001; $80,000 with WHIJ(FM) Ocala). Format: Adult contemp, christian. ♦Jeff MacFarlane, gen mgr & progmg mgr.

***WHGN(FM)**— November 1992: 91.9 mhz; 41 kw horiz, 39.3 kw vert. Ant 541 ft TL: N28 50 29 W82 30 21. (CP: 41 kw). Hrs open: 24 5800 100th Way North, St. Petersburg, 33708. Secondary address: P.O. Box 8889, St. Petersburg 33738. Phone: (727) 391-9994. Fax: (727) 397-6425.E-mail: wkes@moody.com Licensee: The Moody Bible Institute of Chicago (group owner; acq 4-11-03; $500,000). Format: Christian. ♦David Boyer, gen mgr; Mike Gleichman, opns mgr; Pierre Chestang, stn mgr & progmg dir; John Stortz, chief of engrg.

WKTK(FM)— Feb 13, 1976: 98.5 mhz; 100 kw. 1,332 ft TL: N29 15 32 W82 34 03. (CP: 44 kw). Stereo. Hrs open: 24 3600 N.W. 43rd St., Suite B, Gainesville, 32606-8127. Phone: (352) 377-0985. Fax: (352) 377-1884.E-mail: dickoneil@entercom.com Web Site:www.ktk985.com Licensee: Entercom Gainesville License LLC. Group owner: Entercom Communications Corp. (acq 11-13-86; $3.6 million; 7-21-86). Population served: 748,000 Leventhal, Senter & Lerman. Format: Adult contemp. News staff: one; News: 6 hrs wkly. Target aud: 25-54. ♦David Field, CEO, pres; Joseph Field, chmn; Dick O'Neil, VP, gen mgr; Chris Malone, progmg dir.

WXCV(FM)—See Homosassa Springs

Cypress Gardens

WHNR(AM)—Licensed to Cypress Gardens. See Winter Haven

Cypress Quarters

***WREH(FM)**— 2004: 90.5 mhz; 100 kw horiz, 91.7 kw vert. Ant 249 ft TL: N27 20 51 W80 57 04. Hrs open: Reach Communications Inc., 2701 W. Cypress Creek Rd., Fort Lauderdale, 33309. Phone: (954) 315-4315. Fax: (954) 315-4231. Web Site:www.reachfm.org Licensee: Reach Communications Inc. (acq 4-2-2003; $1 million for CP). Format: Christian. ♦Carl Mims, gen mgr; John Boone, progmg dir & mus dir.

Dade City

WDCF(AM)— December 1954: 1350 khz; 1 kw-D, 500 w-N, DA-N. TL: N28 20 04 W82 11 23. Hrs open: 2360 N.E. Coachman Rd., Clearwater, 33765. Phone: (727) 441-3311. Fax: (727) 441-1300.E-mail: lola@tantalk1340.com Web Site:www.tantalk1340.com Licensee: Wagenvoord Advertising Group Inc. (group owner; acq 2-13-02). Population served: 35,000 Natl. Network: ABC, . Rgnl. Network: Florida Radio Net. Florida's Radio Networks Format: Sp relg. Target aud: 25 plus; basic country demographics. ♦Dave Wagenvoord, pres; Lola Wagenvoord, sr VP & gen mgr.

WTMP-FM— Sept 3, 1993: 96.1 mhz; 2.8 kw. 413 ft TL: N28 28 22 W82 17 45. (CP: 2.75 kw, ant 485 ft.). Hrs open: 24 407 N. Howard Ave.,, Suite 200, Tampa, 33606. Phone: (813) 259-9867. Fax: (813) 254-9867.E-mail: info@tamabroadcasting.com Web Site:www.wtmp.com Licensee: Tama Radio Licenses of Tampa, FL, Inc. Group owner: Tama Broadcasting Inc. (acq 12-21-2001; $4.1 million). Format: Urban adult contemp. Target aud: 35 plus; general. ♦Dr. Glenn W. Cherry, CEO; Chris McMurray, gen mgr; Lynn Tolliver, progmg dir.

Davie

WAVS(AM)— Aug 21, 1970: 1170 khz; 5 kw-D, 250 w-N, DA-N. TL: N26 04 39 W80 13 03. Hrs open: 24 6360 S.W. 41st Pl., 33314. Phone: (954) 584-1170. Fax: (954) 581-6441.E-mail: info@wavs1170.com Web Site:www.wavs1170.com Licensee: Alliance Broadcasting Inc. (acq 7-28-2004; $2 million). Population served: 4,500,000 Koerner & Olender PC. Format: Caribbean. News staff: one; News: 5 hrs wkly. Target aud: General; West Indians/Dade, Broward, Palm Beach Counties, Bahamas. Spec prog: Black. ♦Emmanuel Cherubin, pres; Jean Cherubin, gen mgr; Dean Hooper, stn mgr.

Daytona Beach

WCFB(FM)— March 1947: 94.5 mhz; 97.5 kw horiz, 100 kw vert. Ant 1,479 ft TL: N28 58 47 W81 27 20. Stereo. Hrs open: 24 4192 John

Young Pkwy., Orlando, 32804. Phone: (407) 422-9696. Fax: (407) 422-5883. Fax: (407) 422-6538.E-mail: info@star94fm.com Web Site:www.star94fm.com Licensee: Cox Radio Inc. Group owner: Cox Broadcasting (acq 3-28-97; grpsl). Population served: 2,200,000 Format: Adult contemp, urban contemp. ◆Brian Elam, gen mgr; Steve Holbrook, opns dir.

WELE(AM)—See Ormond Beach

WJHM(FM)— Nov 1, 1967: 101.9 mhz; 28 kw. 1,584 ft TL: N28 55 16 W81 19 09. (CP: 61 kw). Stereo. Hrs open: 1800 Pembrook Dr., Suite 400, Orlando, 32810. Phone: (407) 919-1000. Fax: (407) 919-1190. Web Site:www.102jamzorlando.com Licensee: Infinity Radio Inc. Group owner: Infinity Broadcasting Corp. (acq 8-7-00; grpsl). Natl. Network: AP Radio, . Format: Rhythmic CHR. Target aud: 18-34. ◆Earnest James, sr VP, gen mgr, mktg mgr; James Black, gen sls mgr; Dawn Campbell, prom dir; Stevie DeMann, progmg dir.

WMFJ(AM)— Apr 16, 1935: 1450 khz; 1 kw-U. TL: N29 13 30 W81 01 30. Hrs open: 24 4295 Ridgewood Ave., Port Orange, 32127. Phone: (386) 756-9000. Fax: (386) 760-7107.E-mail: thecornerstone @cornerstoneministry.org Web Site:www.cornerstoneministry.org Licensee: Cornerstone Broadcasting Corp. (acq 1996; $225,000). Population served: 400,000 Natl. Network: Moody, USA, . Format: Relg. Target aud: General. ◆William Powell, gen mgr.

WNDB(AM)— April 1948: 1150 khz; 1 kw-U, DA-N. TL: N29 14 06 W81 04 19. Hrs open: 24 126 W. International Speedway Blvd., 32174. Phone: (386) 255-9300 / (386) 257-1150. Fax: (386) 238-6071. Web Site:www.wndb.am Licensee: Black Crow LLC. Group owner: Black Crow Media Group LLC (acq 9-21-2001; grpsl). Population served: 325,000 Natl. Network: CBS, Motor Racing Net, . Dow, Lohnes & Albertson. Wire Svc: UPI Format: News/talk, sports. News staff: 2. Target aud: 25-64; general. Spec prog: Relg 5 hrs, NASCAR auto racing wkly. ◆J. Michael Linn, pres; Stacey Knerler, gen mgr; Frank Scott, opns mgr.

WNUE-FM—(Titusville, September 1968: 98.1 mhz; 100 kw. 462 ft TL: N28 50 54 W80 51 44. Stereo. Hrs open: 24 337 S North Lake Blvd., Ste. 1024, Altamonte Springs, 32701. Phone: (407) 331-1777. Fax: (407) 830-6223.E-mail: jstein@megastations.net Web Site:www.mega981.com Licensee: Entravision Holdings LLC. Group owner: Mega Communications Inc. (acq 3-24-2008; $24 million). Population served: 402800 Natl. Rep: SBS/Interep,. Format: Sp contemp. News staff: one; News: 2 hrs wkly. Target aud: 25-54; Hispanic adults 25-54. ◆Walter F. Ulloa, CEO; Rafael Grullon, exec VP, gen mgr; Jeff Stein, gen mgr, sls VP.

WPUL(AM)—See South Daytona

WROD(AM)— 1947: 1340 khz; 1 kw-U. TL: N29 11 19 W81 00 28. Hrs open: 24 Box 211340, South Daytona, 32121-1340. Secondary address: 2400 S. Ridgewood Ave., Suite 51, South Daytona 32119. Phone: (386) 253-0000. Fax: (386) 255-3178.E-mail: production@wrodam.com Web Site:www.wrod.net Licensee: Gore-Overgaard Broadcasting (group owner; acq 1-8-99; $1.01 million). Population served: 450,000 Natl. Network: ABC, . Haley, Bader & Potts. Format: America's Best Music, adult standards. News staff: one; News: 15 hrs wkly. Target aud: 50 plus; senior community. ◆Hal Gore, CEO & chmn; Cordell Overgaard, pres; George Winslow, gen mgr.

De Funiak Springs

*WAKJ(FM)— January 1996: 91.3 mhz; 1.2 kw. Ant 226 ft TL: N30 41 05 W86 08 28. Stereo. Hrs open: 24 216 East Live Oak Ave., 32435. Secondary address: 295 Hwy. 90 W. 32435. Phone: (850) 892-2107. Fax: (850) 892-2507.E-mail: wakj913@embarqmail.com Web Site:www.wakj.org Licensee: First Baptist Church Inc. Population served: 25,000 Format: Christian. ◆Zane Welch, gen mgr; John Gradick, prom mgr.

WDSP(AM)— Mar 1, 1956: 1280 khz; 5 kw-D, 46 w-N. TL: N30 42 41 W86 06 25. (CP: 9 kw-D, 46 w-N, DA-D). Hrs open: 24 Box 459, 32435. Phone: (850) 951-1280. Fax: (850) 951-1282.E-mail: info@wdsp1280.com Licensee: The Sportzmax Inc. (acq 1-30-2006; $325,000). Population served: 152,200 Natl. Network: ABC, . Format: Classic hit country. Target aud: 25-54. Spec prog: High School Sports. ◆Max Howell, VP; Arty Goodman, gen mgr; Stephen C. Riggs III, pres & progmg dir; Carolyn Mora, sls.

WMXZ(FM)— November 1974: 103.1 mhz; 50 kw. 482 ft TL: N30 30 53 W86 13 12. Stereo. Hrs open: 24 743 Harbor Blvd., Suite 6, Destin, 32541. Phone: (850) 654-1031. Fax: (850) 654-6510. Web Site:mix1031online.com Licensee: Qantum of Fort Walton Beach License Co. LLC. Group owner: Qantum Communications Corp. (acq 7-2-2003; grpsl). Natl. Rep: Katz Radio,. Gravey, Schubert & Barer.

Format: Hot adult contemp. News staff: one; News: 20 hrs wkly. Target aud: 25-54; general. ◆Frank Osborne, pres, gen mgr; Georgia Edmiston, gen mgr; Allyson Buckner, sls dir, natl sls mgr.

WZEP(AM)— October 1955: 1460 khz; 10 kw-D, 186 w-N. TL: N30 43 45 W86 07 04. Hrs open: 24 449 N. 12th St., 32433. Secondary address: Box 627 32435-0627. Phone: (850) 892-3158. Phone: (800) 881-1460. Fax: (850) 892-9675.E-mail: wzep@wzep1460.com Web Site:www.wzep1460.com Licensee: Walton County Broadcasting Inc. (acq 6-1-93; $60,000; 6-21-93). Population served: 58,000 Natl. Network: CBS, . Rgnl. Network: Florida Radio Net. Florida's Radio Networks Timothy K. Brady. Format: Full service, news/talk, country, oldies. News staff: one; News: 47 hrs wkly. Target aud: General; residents & visitors to Walton & Holmes counties. Spec prog: Gospel 13 hrs wkly. ◆Arthur F. Dees, pres, gen mgr; Martha K. Dees, VP; Marty Dees, stn mgr; Kevin Chilcutt, news dir; Tina Martin, traf mgr.

De Land

WOCL(FM)— July 10, 1967: 105.9 mhz; 96 kw. Ant 1,581 ft TL: N28 55 16 W81 19 09. Stereo. Hrs open: 24 1800 Pembrook Dr., Suite 400, Orlando, 32810. Phone: (407) 919-1000. Fax: (407) 919-1190. Web Site:www.sunny1059.com Licensee: CBS Radio Stations Inc. Group owner: Infinity Broadcasting Corp. (acq 8-7-2000; grpsl). Population served: 300,000 Natl. Rep: Christal,. Leibowitz & Associates. Format: Classic hits. News staff: one; News: 20 hrs wkly. Target aud: 25-54. ◆Earnest James, sr VP; Evelyn Pacheo, gen mgr & gen sls mgr; April Reynolds, prom dir, disc jockey; Bobby Smith, progmg dir, disc jockey.

WTJV(AM)— Sept 10, 1948: 1490 khz; 1 kw-U. TL: N29 00 58 W81 17 10. Hrs open: 126 W. International Speedway Blvd., Daytona Beach, 32114. Phone: (386) 255-9300. Fax: (386) 239-0966. Licensee: J&V Communications Inc. Group owner: Black Crow Media Group LLC (acq 12-7-2005; $370,000). Population served: 80,000 Rgnl. Network: Florida Radio Net. Florida's Radio Networks Format: News/talk, community affrs, sports. Target aud: 35 plus. ◆Stacey Knerler, gen mgr; Frank Scott, stn mgr, opns mgr.

WYND(AM)— Dec 7, 1956: 1310 khz; 5 kw-D, 95 w-N. TL: N28 59 57 W81 17 55. Hrs open: 24 316 E. Taylor Rd., 32724. Phone: (386) 734-1310. Fax: (386) 734-8885. Licensee: Buddy Tucker Association Inc. (acq 12-30-86; $255,000; 12-1-86). Population served: 760,000 Natl. Network: USA, . Format: Christian, news/talk. News staff: one; News: 45 hrs wkly. Target aud: 25-55. ◆Buddy Tucker, gen mgr; Art Taylor, chief of engrg.

Delray Beach

WDJA(AM)— February 1952: 1420 khz; 5 kw-D, 500 w-N, DA-2. TL: N26 27 22 W80 05 58. Hrs open: 24 2710 W. Atlantic Ave., 33445. Phone: (561) 278-1420. Fax: (561) 278-7815.E-mail: wjda1420am@yahoo.com Web Site:www.jammin1420.com Licensee: Professional Broadcasting LLC Group owner: James Crystal Inc. (acq 5-18-2007; $2.1 million). Population served: 19,366 Format: Reggae. ◆Roy Bresky, gen mgr; Stan Rain, opns mgr.

Destin

WFFY(FM)— Sept 24, 1981: 92.1 mhz; 25 kw. 279 ft TL: N30 31 06 W86 28 01. Stereo. Hrs open: 743 Harbor Blvd., Suite 6, 32541. Phone: (850) 654-1031. Fax: (850) 654-6510. Web Site:www.fly921online.com Licensee: Qantum of Ft. Walton Beach License Company LLC. Natl. Rep: Katz Radio,. Format: Rhythmic CHR. Target aud: 18-49; general. ◆Frank Osborne, pres; Georgia Edmiston, gen mgr; Allyson Buckner, sls dir.

WNWF(AM)— 2000: 1120 khz; 1 kw-D. TL: N30 30 34 W86 28 34. Hrs open: 6 AM-6 PM Box 1120, 32540. Secondary address: 415 Mountain Dr., Suite 7 32541. Phone: (850) 654-4040. Fax: (850) 650-9440.E-mail: dale@fox1120.com Web Site:www.fox1120.com Licensee: Flagship Communications Inc. (acq 8-24-03; $400,000). Population served: 153,000 Format: News/talk. News staff: one. Target aud: 35-64. ◆Dale Riddick, gen mgr & progmg dir.

Dogwood Lakes Estate

*WJED(FM)— Jan 15, 1992: 91.1 mhz; 700 w. 180 ft TL: N30 51 34 W85 47 45. Hrs open: Box 1944, Dothan, AL, 36302. Secondary address: 2573 Hodgesville Rd, Dothan, AL 36302. Phone: (334) 793-3189. Fax: (334) 793-4344.E-mail: wjed911fm@bethanybc.edu Licensee: Bethany Bible College & Bethany Theological Seminary Inc. Natl. Network: USA, . Format: Educ, relg, gospel. Target aud: General; college students & relg community. ◆Dr. H.D. Shuemake, CEO; Dr. Steve Shuemake, stn mgr; Sylvia Green, opns mgr & progmg dir.

Dunedin

WGUL(AM)—Licensed to Dunedin. See Tampa

WMGG(AM)— 1955: 1470 khz; 5 kw-D, 500 w-N. TL: N28 03 24 W82 44 16. Hrs open: 4300 W. Cypress St., # 1040, Tampa, 33607. Phone: (813) 281-1040. Fax: (813) 281-1948.E-mail: contactus@baybiz1470.com Web Site:www.bayblz1470.com Licensee: Genesis Communications of Tampa Bay Inc. Group owner: Genesis Communications Inc. (acq 3-5-2001; $2 million). Population served: 200,000 Natl. Rep: Interep, McGavren Guild,. Florida's Radio Networks Wire Svc: AP Format: Business talk/news. Spec prog: Relg 2 hrs wkly. ◆Bruce Maduri, CEO; Paul DeFazio, gen mgr; Allan Davis, progmg dir; Wilson Welch, chief of engrg; Cindy Scheffer, traf mgr.

Dunnellon

WTRS(FM)— Mar 11, 1969: 102.3 mhz; 3 kw. 300 ft TL: N29 11 16 W82 23 39. (CP: 50 kw, ant 489 ft.). Stereo. Hrs open: 24 3357 S.W. 7th St., Ocala, 34474. Phone: (352) 732-9877. Fax: (352) 622-6675. Web Site:www.wtrs.fm Licensee: Asterisk Communications Inc. Format: Country. ◆Dean Johnson, gen mgr & pub affrs dir.

Eatonville

WRLZ(AM)—Licensed to Eatonville. See Orlando

Eau Gallie

WBVD(FM)—See Melbourne

WDMC(AM)—See Melbourne

WINT(AM)—See Melbourne

WMMB(AM)—See Melbourne

Ebro

WBPC(FM)— July 15, 2005: 95.1 mhz; 25 kw. Ant 285 ft TL: N30 34 06 W85 48 28. Stereo. Hrs open: 24 Box 27272, Panama City Beach, 32411. Phone: (850) 235-2195. Fax: (850) 235-2795. Web Site:www.beach951.com Licensee: Bay Broadcasting LLC. Natl. Network: Fox News Radio, . Format: Oldies. Target aud: 35-64; adults. ◆Charles Shapiro, gen mgr.

Edgewater

WKRO-FM— 1993: 93.1 mhz; 14.9 kw. 427 ft TL: N28 54 52 W80 53 48. Hrs open: 24 126 W. International Speedway Blvd., Daytona Beach, 32114. Phone: (386) 255-9300. Fax: (386) 238-6071. Web Site:www.wkro.fm Licensee: Black Crow LLC. Group owner: Black Crow Media Group LLC (acq 9-21-2001; grpsl). Population served: 750,000 Format: Country. ◆Stacey Knerler, gen mgr.

*WKTO(FM)— November 1997: 88.7 mhz; 5 kw vert. Ant 298 ft TL: N29 02 29 W81 03 23. (CP: 88.9 mhz; 25 kw, ant 354 ft TL: N29 01 37 W81 07 18). Hrs open: 24 900 Old Mission Rd., New Smyrna Beach, 32168. Phone: (386) 427-1095. Fax: (386) 427-8970.E-mail: wkto@bellsouth.net Web Site:www.wkto.net Licensee: Mims Community Radio Inc. Format: Relg. Target aud: 18-50. Spec prog: Jazz 4 hrs, Pol 1.5 hrs, Ger 1.5 hrs, Sp 2 hr wkly. ◆Carol Henry, CEO, chmn, pres, CFO & gen mgr.

Egypt Lake

WTMP(AM)—Licensed to Egypt Lake. See Tampa

Emeralda

*WGTT(FM)—Not on air, target date: unknown: 91.5 mhz; 700 w. Ant 180 ft TL: N28 56 52 W81 47 45. Hrs open: 1441 Lavender St., Deltona, 32725. Licensee: Sunbelt Educational Broadcasting Inc. ◆Raul Ortiz, pres.

Englewood

WENG(AM)— Nov 15, 1964: 1530 khz; 1 kw-D. TL: N26 58 15 W82 19 24. Hrs open: 24 Box 2908, 34295-2908. Secondary address: 1355 S. River Rd. 34223. Phone: (941) 474-3231. Fax: (941) 475-2205.E-mail: kenb@1530weng.com Web Site:www.1530weng.com Licensee: Viper Communications Inc. Group owner: Viper Communications Broadcast Group (acq 10-21-02). Population served: 217,300 Natl. Network: ABC, . Rgnl. Network: Florida Radio Net. Florida's Radio Networks Pepper & Corazzini. Format: News/talk, listener participation. News staff: one; News: 50 hrs wkly. Target aud: 18 plus; securely established, financially independent. Spec prog: Religious 2 hrs wkly. ♦Kenneth W. Kuenzie, pres; Dennis Klautzer, exec VP; Kenneth A. Birdsong, gen mgr; Scott Holcomb, opns dir & opns mgr.

***WSEB(FM)**— May 1989: 91.3 mhz; 62 kw horiz, 60 kw vert. 282 ft TL: N26 51 48 W87 17 54. Stereo. Hrs open: 24 135 W. Dearborne St., 34223. Phone: (941) 475-9732. Fax: (941) 473-7308.E-mail: comments@wsebfm.com Web Site:www.wsebfm.net Licensee: Suncoast Educational Broadcasting Corp. Format: Christian. Target aud: 35 plus; Christian families. ♦Dr. Kenneth Lindow, pres; Joy Clark, gen mgr; Roger Johnson, progmg dir & mus dir.

WTZB(FM)— Apr 5, 1999: 105.9 mhz; 4.3 kw. 394 ft TL: N27 06 01 W82 22 18. Hrs open: 1779 Independence Blvd., Sarasota, 34236. Phone: (941) 552-4800. Fax: (941) 552-4900.E-mail: info@1059thebuzz.com Web Site:www.1059thebuzz.com Licensee: Citicasters Licenses L.P. Group owner: Clear Channel Communications Inc. (acq 5-4-99; grpsl). Format: Alternative rock. ♦Buddy Lee, gen mgr; Ron White, opns mgr.

Estero

WNTY(FM)— Dec 16, 1978: 92.5 mhz; 25 kw. Ant 620 ft TL: N26 19 00 W81 47 13. Stereo. Hrs open: 24 2824 Palm Beach Blvd., Ft. Myers, 33916. Phone: (239) 337-2346. Fax: (239) 332-0767 / (239) 479-5553.E-mail: randy.marsh@us985.com Web Site:us985.com Licensee: Meridian Broadcasting Inc. (group owner; (acq 9-14-2000; $7 million). Natl. Rep: McGavren Guild,. Leibowitz & Associates. Wire Svc: AP Format: Oldies. Target aud: 25-44. ♦Joseph C. Schwartzel, chmn, pres, gen mgr; Jim Schwartzel, exec VP, sls dir; Lance Hale, progmg dir; Keith Stuhlman, engrg dir; Randy Marsh, progmg.

Eustis

***WIGW(FM)**—Not on air, target date: unknown: 90.3 mhz; 10 w horiz, 8.25 kw vert. Ant 240 ft TL: N28 58 18 W81 45 15. Hrs open: 2521 W. Sunflower N3, Santa Ana, CA, 92704. Phone: (714) 545-7868. Fax: (208) 736-1958. Web Site:www.csnradio.com Licensee: CSN International. ♦Jeffrey W. Smith, pres.

WKIQ(AM)— June 1955: 1240 khz; 790 w-U. TL: N28 50 19 W81 41 46. Hrs open: Rama Communications Inc., 3765 N. John Young Pkwy., Orlando, 32804. Phone: (407) 291-1395. Fax: (407) 293-2870. Licensee: Rama Communications Inc. (group owner; (acq 10-15-2004; $180,000 with WQBQ(AM) Leesburg). Rgnl. Network: Florida Radio Net. Format: Urban contemp. ♦Sabeta Persaud, pres; Steve January, gen mgr.

WLBE(AM)—See Leesburg

Fernandina Beach

***WJBC-FM**— Oct 6, 1985: 91.7 mhz; 32 kw. Ant 223 ft TL: N30 37 23 W81 31 49. Stereo. Hrs open: 5634 Normandy Blvd., Jacksonville, 32205-6249. Phone: (904) 781-4321.E-mail: info@wjbcfm.com Web Site:www.wjbcfm.com Licensee: West Jacksonville Baptist Church Inc. (acq 8-31-2006; $1 million). Population served: 500,000 Format: Southern gospel. Target aud: General. ♦Rodney Kelley, pres.

WJSJ(FM)— 2000: 105.3 mhz; 3.9 kw. Ant 410 ft TL: N30 30 04 W81 35 14. Hrs open:
Simulcast with WJXL(AM) Jacksonville Beach 100%.
9090 Hogan Rd., Jacksonville, 32216. Phone: (904) 641-1011. Fax: (904) 641-1022.E-mail: info@smoothjazz.com Web Site:www.1010xl.com Licensee: Scott Savage, receiver Group owner: Tama Broadcasting Inc. (acq 2-26-2009). Natl. Network: ESPN Radio, . Format: Sports. ♦Steve Griffin, gen mgr; Jack O'Brien, gen sls mgr; Jason Dixon, progmg dir.

WVOJ(AM)— 1955: 1570 khz; 10 kw-D, 30 w-N. TL: N30 40 33 W81 27 35. Hrs open: 24 8384 Baymeadows Rd., Suite 1, Jacksonville, 32256. Phone: (904) 739-3660. Phone: (904) 743-1234. Fax: (904) 739-9409. Licensee: Norsan Consulting and Management Inc. (acq 9-14-2005; $2.1 million with WNNR(AM) Jacksonville). Rgnl. Network: Florida Radio Net. Format: Sp CHR. ♦Norberto Sanchez, pres; Bernie Daigle, gen mgr.

Five Points

WCJX(FM)— 1996: 106.5 mhz; 4.2 kw. 328 ft TL: N30 14 40 W82 40 11. Stereo. Hrs open: 24 1305 Helvenston St., Live Oak, 32064. Secondary address: 5348 NW US Highway 41, Lake City 32055. Phone: (386) 755-9259. Fax: (386) 755-1557.E-mail: audio@wcjx106.5.com Web Site:www.wcjx.com Licensee: RTG Radio LLC. Group owner: Black Crow Media Group LLC (acq 11-9-2001; grpsl). Population served: 55,000 Natl. Network: ABC, Premiere Radio Networks, . Format: Classic rock. ♦Dean Blackwell, gen mgr; Steve Johnson, stn mgr.

Flagler Beach

***WJLH(FM)**— Aug 23, 1996: 90.3 mhz; 2 kw vert. 184 ft TL: N29 22 18 W81 10 45. Hrs open:
Rebroadcasts WJLU(FM) New Smyrna Beach 100%.
4295 Ridgewood Ave., Port Orange, 32127. Phone: (386) 756-9094. Fax: (386) 760-7107.E-mail: thecornerstone@cornerstoneministry.org Web Site:www.cornerstoneministry.org Licensee: Cornerstone Broadcasting Corp. (acq 3-20-97; $27,044). Format: Christian. ♦William Powell, gen mgr & progmg dir; Sandra Leisner, pub affrs dir.

Florida City

***WMFL(FM)**— Oct 1, 1998: 88.5 mhz; 8 kw vert. Ant 134 ft TL: N25 05 50 W80 26 12. Hrs open: 24 Family Stations Inc., 290 Hegenberger Rd., Oakland, CA, 94621. Phone: (510) 568-6200. Fax: (510) 568-6190. Web Site:www.familyradio.com Licensee: Family Stations Inc. (group owner; acq 11-15-00; $75,000). Natl. Network: Family Radio, . Format: Christian, relg. ♦Harold Camping, pres; Stanley Jackson, gen mgr; Rob Robbins, opns mgr.

Fort Lauderdale

***WAFG(FM)**— 1974: 90.3 mhz; 3 kw. 280 ft TL: N26 11 48 W80 06 45. Stereo. Hrs open: 24 5555 N. Federal Hwy., 33308. Phone: (954) 776-7705. Fax: (954) 771-2633.E-mail: wafg@wafg.org Web Site:www.wafg.org Licensee: Westminster Academy. Population served: 1,700,000 Natl. Network: USA, Salem Radio Network, . Gammon & Grange. Format: Christian, news/talk, relg. News: 10 hrs wkly. Target aud: 30 plus; general. ♦Dolores King-St.George, gen mgr, dev dir; Kyle Kirkman, opns mgr; Lesley Hurst, progmg dir; Ken Vaughn, mus dir.

WBGG-FM— July 1960: 105.9 mhz; 100 kw. Ant 1,030 ft TL: N25 59 34 W80 10 27. Stereo. Hrs open: 7601 Riviera Blvd., Miramar, 33023. Phone: (954) 862-2000. Fax: (954) 862-4012.E-mail: info@ccmiami.com Web Site:www.big1059.com Licensee: Clear Channel Radio Licenses Inc. Group owner: Clear Channel Communications Inc. (acq 2-24-94; $14 million; 3-14-94). Format: Classic rock. ♦Todd Winick, gen mgr & gen sls mgr.

WEXY(AM)—See Wilton Manors

WFLL(AM)— Sept 16, 1946: 1400 khz; 1 kw-U. TL: N26 09 13 W80 10 11. Hrs open: 24 6600 N. Andrews Ave., Suite 160, 33309. Phone: (954) 315-1515. Fax: (954) 315-1555.E-mail: info@1400espn.com Web Site:www.1400espn.com Licensee: James Crystal Licenses L.L.C. Group owner: James Crystal Inc. (acq 6-17-98; grpsl). Population served: 1,336,632 Natl. Network: ESPN Radio, . Format: Sports. Target aud: 25 plus. ♦Steve Lapa, gen mgr.

WHSR(AM)—See Pompano Beach

WHYI-FM— July 31, 1960: 100.7 mhz; 100 kw. 928 ft TL: N25 59 34 W80 10 27. (CP: Ant 1,007 ft. TL: N25 57 59 W80 12 33). Hrs open: 7601 Riviera Blvd., Miramar, 33023. Phone: (954) 862-2000. Fax: (954) 862-4012.E-mail: info@y100.7miami.com Web Site:www.y100.7miami.com Licensee: Clear Channel Radio Licenses Inc. Group owner: Clear Channel Communications Inc. (acq 11-94; grpsl). Population served: 500,000 Natl. Rep: McGavren Guild,. Format: Top-40. ♦David D'Dugenio, gen mgr & gen sls mgr.

WMIB(FM)— Oct 17, 1959: 103.5 mhz; 100 kw. 1,007 ft TL: N25 57 59 W80 12 33. Stereo. Hrs open: 7601 Riviera Blvd., Miramar, 33023. Phone: (954) 862-2000. Fax: (954) 862-4012.E-mail: info@thebeatmiami.com Web Site:www.thebeatmiami.com Licensee: Clear Channel Broadcasting Licenses Inc. Group owner: Clear Channel Communications Inc. (acq 11-21-97; grpsl). Population served: 3,000,000 Format: Hip hop, rhythm and blues. ♦Kevin Hemmings, gen mgr & gen sls mgr.

WMXJ(FM)—See Pompano Beach

WRMA(FM)— Aug 15, 1962: 106.7 mhz; 100 kw. 984 ft TL: N25 59 34 W80 10 27. Stereo. Hrs open: 24 1001 Ponce DeLeon Blvd., Coral Gables, 33134. Phone: (305) 444-9292. Fax: (305) 461-4466. Web Site:www.romance106fm.com Licensee: WRMA Licensing Inc. Group owner: Spanish Broadcasting System Inc. (acq 7-11-97; $110 million with WXDJ(FM) North Miami Beach). Population served: 345,730 Natl. Rep: D & R Radio,. Format: Pop latin ballads. News staff: one. Target aud: 18-54; Hispanic adults. ♦Raoul Alarcon, pres; Albert Rodriguez, gen mgr, gen sls mgr; John Caride, prom dir; Tony Campos, progmg dir; Tomas Regalado, news dir; Ralph Chambers, chief of engrg; Yoli Machado, pub affrs dir & traf mgr.

WSRF(AM)— 1955: 1580 khz; 10 kw-D, 5 kw-N, DA-2. TL: N26 04 54 W80 13 34. Hrs open: 24 1510 N.E. 162 St., Miami, 33162-4716. Phone: (305) 944-8383.E-mail: info@wsrf.com Licensee: Niche Radio Inc. Group owner: Inner City Broadcasting (acq 10-14-2005; $1.75 million). Population served: 2,000,000 Format: Ethnic. News staff: 2. ♦Emmanuel Cherubin, pres & gen mgr.

WWNN(AM)—See Pompano Beach

Fort Meade

WWRZ(FM)— Mar 7, 1977: 98.3 mhz; 26 kw. 686 ft TL: N27 38 38 W81 48 00. Stereo. Hrs open: 24 P.O. Box 2038, Lakeland, 33806. Secondary address: 404 West Lime Street, Lakeland 33815-4651. Phone: (863) 682-8184. Fax: (863) 683-2409.E-mail: mjames@halllakeland.com Web Site:www.max983fm.com Licensee: Hall Communications Inc. (group owner; acq 10-1-96; $1,750,000). Population served: 500,000 Natl. Rep: D & R Radio,. Fletcher, Heald & Hildreth. Wire Svc: AP Format: Adult hits. News staff: 2; News: 2 hrs wkly. Target aud: 25-54; women. ♦Bonnie Rowbotham, chmn, pres; Art Rowbotham, sr VP; Nancy Cattarius, stn mgr; Tunie Moss, prom dir; Mike James, progmg dir.

Fort Myers

WARO(FM)—See Naples

***WAYJ(FM)**— October 1987: 88.7 mhz; 75 kw. Ant 1,007 ft TL: N26 25 22 W81 37 49. Stereo. Hrs open: 24 Box 61275, 33906. Secondary address: 1860 Boy Scout Dr., Suite 202 33906. Phone: (239) 936-1929. Fax: (239) 936-5433. Web Site:www.wayfm.com Licensee: WAY-FM Media Group Inc. (group owner). Natl. Network: USA, . Gammon & Grange. Format: Contemp Christian. News staff: one; News: one hr wkly. Target aud: 18-34. ♦Bob Augsburg, pres; Jeff Taylor, gen mgr.

WCKT(FM)—See Lehigh Acres

WCRM(AM)— Aug 22, 1964: 1350 khz; 1 kw-D, 150 w-N. TL: N26 37 31 W81 50 29. (CP: 5 kw-D). Hrs open: 19 3448 Canal St., 33916. Phone: (239) 334-1350 / (941) 332-1350. Fax: (239) 332-8890.E-mail: radio1350office@aol.com Web Site:www.aleluya.com/1350_am.htm Licensee: Manna Christian Missions Inc. (acq 6-89). Population served: 400,000 Natl. Network: USA, . Schwartz, Woods & Miller. Format: Sp, Christian. News staff: one; News: 5 hrs wkly. Target aud: General. ♦Salvador Santana, gen mgr.

***WGCU-FM**— Sept 12, 1983: 90.1 mhz; 100 kw. 813 ft TL: N26 48 54 W81 45 44. Stereo. Hrs open: 24 10501 FGCU Blvd., 33965-6565. Phone: (239) 590-2500. Phone: (239) 590-2300. Fax: (239) 590-2520. Web Site:www.wgcu.org Licensee: Board of Trustees, Florida Gulf Coast University (acq 11-16-2001). Population served: 830,000 Natl. Network: NPR, PRI, . Rgnl. Network: Fla. Pub. Fla. Pub. Cohn & Marks. Format: News, class, jazz. News staff: 4. Target aud: 24 plus. ♦Amy Tardif, stn mgr, progmg dir, news dir, news dir.

WINK(AM)— Mar 1, 1940: 1240 khz; 1 kw-U. TL: N26 37 28 W81 49 52. Hrs open:
Rebroadcasts WNOG(AM) Naples 100%.
2824 Palm Beach Blvd., 33916. Phone: (239) 337-2346. Fax: (239) 334-0744. Web Site:www.winkwnog.com Licensee: Meridian Broadcasting Inc. (group owner) Population served: 516,200 Natl. Network: Jones Radio Networks, . Natl. Rep: McGavren Guild,. Leibowitz & Spencer. Format: News/talk. Target aud: 35 plus. ♦Joe Schwartzel, pres; Randy Marsh, gen mgr & progmg dir.

WINK-FM— Oct 10, 1964: 96.9 mhz; 100 kw. 1,322 ft TL: N26 38 40 W081 52 10. Stereo. Hrs open: 24 Prog sep from AM 2824 Palm

Beach Blvd., 33916. Phone: (239) 334-1111. Fax: (239) 334-0744. Web Site:www.winkfm.com Licensee: Fort Myers Broadcasting Co. Population served: 634,800 Natl. Rep: McGavren Guild,. Leibowitz & Associates. Format: Hot adult contemp. Target aud: 25-54; females. ♦Chad Rufer, prom mgr. Co-owned TV: WINK-TV affil.

***WJYO(FM)**— 1988: 91.5 mhz; 3 kw. 285 ft TL: N26 30 18 W81 51 14. Stereo. Hrs open: 24
Rebroadcasts WBIY(FM) LaBelle 100%.
Box 61721, 33906. Phone: (239) 274-9150. Fax: (239) 274-0191.E-mail: wjyo@aol.com Web Site:airwavesforJesus.com Licensee: Airwaves for Jesus Inc. (acq 3-8-2004; $500,000 with WBIY(FM) La Belle). Format: Bible teaching, light Christian Praise/worship music. News: 10 hrs wkly. Target aud: 44 plus; traditional minded persons. Spec prog: Children 5 hrs wkly. ♦Art Ramos, CEO, pres, gen mgr; Jasmin Ramos, VP.

***WMYE(FM)**— 2008: 91.9 mhz; 1.2 kw. Ant 328 ft TL: N26 47 07.5 W81 47 46.6. Hrs open: Box 507, 8900 South West 168 Street, Florida, 33157. Phone: (239) 652-0567. Fax: (305) 251-2293.E-mail: callfm@callfm.com Web Site:www.callfm.com Licensee: Call Communications Group Inc. Format: Christian. Target aud: 13-25. ♦Rob Robbins, gen mgr.

WMYR(AM)— Nov 11, 1952: 1410 khz; 5 kw-U, DA-N. TL: N26 37 24.9 W81 51 16.7. Hrs open: 24 5043 Tamiami Tr. E., Naples, 34113. Phone: (239) 732-9369. Fax: (239) 732-7267.E-mail: wmyr@relevantradio.com Web Site:www.relevantradio.com Licensee: Sovereign City Radio Services LLC Group owner: Relevant Radio (acq 2-6-2009; grpsl). Population served: 27,351 Format: Catholic talk. ♦Bob Ladd, gen mgr & opns mgr.

WOLZ(FM)— January 1970: 95.3 mhz; 79 kw. 453 ft TL: N26 37 25 W82 06 56. Stereo. Hrs open: 24 13320 Metro Pkwy., 33912. Phone: (239) 225-4300. Phone: (800) 226-3695. Fax: (239) 225-4329.E-mail: info@wolz.com Web Site:www.wolz.com Licensee: Clear Channel Radio Licenses Inc. Group owner: Clear Channel Communications Inc. (acq 2-18-97; grpsl). Population served: 700,000 Natl. Rep: Clear Channel,. Format: Oldies. News staff: one; News: 2 hrs wkly. Target aud: 35-54; upbeat, fun oldies, strong at work and in-car listening. ♦Jim Keating, gen mgr.

WPTK(AM)—(Pine Island Center, Feb 20, 1986: 1200 khz; 10 kw-D, 2.5 kw-N. TL: N26 42 52 W82 02 46. Hrs open: 24 2824 Palm Beach Blvd., 33916. Phone: (239) 337-2346. Phone: (239) 338-4325. Fax: (239) 332-0767. Web Site:www.foxsportsradio1200.com Licensee: Fort Myers Broadcasting Co. (group owner) Population served: 516,200 Natl. Network: Fox Sports, . Rgnl. Network: Florida Radio Net. Natl. Rep: McGavren Guild,. Leibowitz & Associates. Format: Sports. ♦Wayne Simons, VP & gen mgr; Brad Foster, sls dir, gen sls mgr, prom mgr; Chad Rufer, progmg dir; Keith Stuhlmann, engrg dir.

WRXK-FM—See Bonita Springs

WWGR(FM)— Dec 2, 1969: 101.9 mhz; 100 kw. Ant 1,118 ft TL: N26 25 22 W81 37 49. Stereo. Hrs open: 24 10915 K-Nine Dr., 2nd Fl., Bonita Springs, 34135. Phone: (239) 495-8383. Fax: (239) 495-0883.E-mail: wwgr@rendabroadcasting.com Web Site:www.gatorcountry1019.com Licensee: Renda Broadcast Corp. Group owner: Renda Broadcasting Corp.-Renda Radio Inc. (acq 7-13-94; $4 million; 8-1-94). Population served: 549,000 Format: Country. ♦Tony Renda Jr., gen mgr.

Fort Myers Beach

WJBX(FM)— 1983: 99.3 mhz; 50 kw. 476 ft TL: N26 30 18 W81 51 14. Stereo. Hrs open: 20125 S. Tamiami Tr., Estero, 33928. Phone: (239) 495-2100. Fax: (239) 992-8165.E-mail: info@99xwjbx.com Web Site:www.99xwjbx.com Licensee: Dillon License L.P. Group owner: Beasley Broadcast Group (acq 10-16-97; $6 million). Leventhal, Senter & Lerman. Format: Alternative/new rock. Target aud: 18-49; adults. ♦Brad Beasley, gen mgr.

Fort Myers Villas

WJPT(FM)— July 31, 1991: 106.3 mhz; 50 kw. Ant 472 ft TL: N26 29 16 W81 55 49. Hrs open: 20125 S. Tamiami Tr., Estero, 33928. Phone: (239) 495-2100. Fax: (239) 992-8165.E-mail: randy@morningshow.net Web Site:www.sunny1063.com Licensee: WJST License L.P. Group owner: Beasley Broadcast Group (acq 12-11-97; $5 million). Format: Soft adult contemp. Target aud: 45 plus. ♦Brad Beasley, gen mgr; Shane Reilly, opns mgr.

Fort Pierce

WIRA(AM)— May 18, 1946: 1400 khz; 1 kw-U. TL: N27 26 07 W80 21 41. Hrs open: 24 6803 So. Federal Hwy., Port St. Lucie, 34952. Phone: (772) 460-9356. Fax: (772) 460-2700. Web Site:www.1400wira.com Licensee: Team One Media LLC (acq 2-11-2004; $375,000). Population served: 330,400 Natl. Network: ABC, . Rgnl. Network: Westwood One. Format: Urban gospel. Target aud: 45 plus; male & female. Spec prog: Relg one hr, pub affrs one hr wkly. ♦Al Richards, gen mgr.

***WJFP(FM)**— Jan 15, 1995: 91.1 mhz; 6 kw. 157 ft Hrs open: 6 AM-midnight 2284 North U.S. Hwy #1., Ft. Pierce, 34946. Phone: (772) 467-2400. Fax: (772) 467-9400. Web Site:www.wjfp.com Licensee: Black Media Works Inc. (group owner; acq 1-21-98). Population served: 175,000 Format: Urban contemp, relg, educ. Target aud: 12-49. Spec prog: Sp 2 hrs, Haitian 8 hrs wkly. ♦Kimberly Kassis, pres.

WJNX(AM)— Dec 24, 1952: 1330 khz; 5 kw-D, 1 kw-N, DA-2. TL: N27 27 20 W80 22 02. Stereo. Hrs open: 24 4100 Metzger Rd., 34947. Phone: (772) 340-1590. Fax: (772) 340-3245.E-mail: wpsl@wpsl.com Web Site:www.lagigante1330.com Licensee: Port St. Lucie Broadcasters Inc. (acq 3-31-2004; $400,000). Population served: 1,000,000 Natl. Network: ESPN Deportes, . Leventhal, Senter & Lerman. Format: Sp news/talk. News staff: one. Target aud: 25-54. ♦Carol Wyatt, CEO, pres; Greg Wyatt, gen mgr.

WKGR(FM)— May 1, 1961: 98.7 mhz; 100 kw. 1,381 ft TL: N27 07 20 W80 23 21. Stereo. Hrs open: 3071 Continental Dr., West Palm Beach, 33407. Phone: (561) 616-6600. Fax: (561) 616-6677.E-mail: info@gator.com Web Site:www.gater.com Licensee: Clear Channel Radio Licenses Inc. Group owner: Clear Channel Communications Inc. (acq 9-16-97; grpsl). Format: Classic rock. Target aud: 25-54. ♦John Hunt, gen mgr; Dave Denver, opns dir, opns mgr; Roger Koch, sls dir.

WLDI(FM)— Oct 30, 1969: 95.5 mhz; 100 kw. 981 ft TL: N27 07 20 W80 23 21. Stereo. Hrs open: 3071 Continental Dr., West Palm Beach, 33407. Phone: (561) 616-6600. Fax: (561) 616-6677.E-mail: info@wild955.com Web Site:www.wild955.com Licensee: Clear Channel Radio Licenses Inc. Group owner: Clear Channel Communications Inc. (acq 6-17-98; grpsl). Population served: 271,000 Format: CHR. Target aud: 18-49; active, contemp. ♦John Hunt, gen mgr; Dave Denver, opns dir.

***WQCS(FM)**— April 1982: 88.9 mhz; 100 kw. 436 ft TL: N27 25 17 W80 21 23. Stereo. Hrs open: 3209 Virginia Ave., 34981. Phone: (772) 465-8989. Fax: (772) 462-4743.E-mail: info@wqcs.org Web Site:www.wqcs.org Licensee: Indian River State College. Natl. Network: NPR, PRI, . Format: Class, news. ♦Madison Hodges, gen mgr, stn mgr; Michelle Rhinesmith, opns mgr.

Fort Walton Beach

WFSH(AM)—See Valparaiso-Niceville

WFTW(AM)— Nov 20, 1953: 1260 khz; 2.5 kw-D, 131 w-N. TL: N30 24 49 W86 37 40. Hrs open: 24 Box 2347, 225 N.W. Hollywood Blvd., 32548. Phone: (850) 243-7676. Fax: (850) 243-6806. Fax: (850) 664-0202.E-mail: wftw@radiopeople.net Web Site:www.wftw.com Licensee: Cumulus Licensing Corp. Group owner: Cumulus Media Inc. (acq 1-10-03; grpsl). Population served: 27,000 Rgnl. Network: Florida Radio Net. Florida's Radio Networks Format: News/talk. ♦Lou Dickey, pres; Ron Raybourne, gen mgr; Georgia Edmiston, gen sls mgr; Lisa Captain, prom dir, prom mgr; Bruce Campbell, chief of engrg; Gerald Lee, traf mgr; Steve Williams, progmg dir & spec ev coord.

WKSM(FM)— May 28, 1965: 99.5 mhz; 50 kw. Ant 440 ft TL: N30 24 50 W86 37 40. (CP: ant 438 ft). Stereo. Hrs open: Prog sep from AM Box 2347, 225 N.W. Hollywood Blvd., 32548. Phone: (850) 243-7676. Fax: (850) 243-6806. Fax: (850) 664-0202.E-mail: info@wksm.com Web Site:www.wksm.com Population served: 130,000 Format: Rock. ♦Lee Leonard, rgnl sls mgr; Steve O'Day, prom mgr; Nicci Garmon, progmg dir; Anthony Proffitt, mus dir; Aimee Shaffer, news dir, pub affrs dir; Gerald Lee, traf mgr; Steve Williams, spec ev coord.

***WPSM(FM)**— July 1, 1985: 91.1 mhz; 383 w. 120 ft TL: N30 25 14 W86 36 43. Stereo. Hrs open: 24 Box 10, 32549. Secondary address: 233 N. Hill Ave. 32548. Phone: (850) 244-7667. Fax: (850) 244-3254.E-mail: contact@wpsm.com Web Site:www.wpsm.com Licensee: Fort Walton Beach Educ. Broadcasting Corp. Natl. Network: USA, . Format: Christian. News staff: one; News: 14 hrs wkly. Target aud: 25-55; young to middle-age adult Christians. ♦Terry Thorne, gen mgr.

WTKE-FM—(Holt, July 1950: 98.1 mhz; 100 kw. Ant 482 ft TL: N30 24 38 W86 37 22. Stereo. Hrs open: 21 Miracle Strip Pkwy. S.E., 32548. Phone: (850) 244-1400. Fax: (850) 243-1471.E-mail: info@sportstalktheticket.com Web Site:www.sportstalktheticket.com Licensee: Star Broadcasting Inc. Group owner: Qantum Communications Corp. (acq 2-14-2003). Natl. Rep: Roslin,. Wiley, Rein & Fielding. Format: Sports, talk. Target aud: 25-54. ♦Ron Hale, Sr., gen mgr; David Kuntz, gen sls mgr; Frank Hale, prom dir, progmg dir, chief of engrg.

WZFN(AM)— 1956: 1400 khz; 1 kw-U. TL: N30 24 38 W86 37 23. Hrs open: 21 Miracle Strip Pkwy. S.E., 32548. Phone: (850) 244-1400. Fax: (850) 243-1471. Licensee: Star Broadcasting Inc. (acq 7-11-2005). Population served: 37,750 Format: Memories. Target aud: 50 plus. Spec prog: Church program one hr wkly. ♦Ron Hale Sr., gen mgr; David Kuntz, gen sls mgr; Frank Hale, progmg dir, chief of engrg.

WZNS(FM)— 1997: 96.5 mhz; 100 kw. 440 ft TL: N30 24 50 W86 37 40. Hrs open: 24 225 N.W. Hollywood Blvd., 32548. Phone: (850) 664-0665 / 0965. Fax: (850) 243-6806.E-mail: sales@z96.com Web Site:www.z96.com Licensee: Cumulus Licensing Corp. Group owner: Cumulus Media Inc. (acq 1-10-03; grpsl). Format: CHR. ♦Hayden Green, progmg mgr.

Frostproof

***WFLJ(FM)**—Not on air, target date: unknown: 89.3 mhz; 10 kw vert. Ant 371 ft TL: N27 33 37 W81 29 36. Hrs open: Box 7217, Lakeland, 33807-7217. Phone: (863) 644-3464. Licensee: Radio Training Network Inc. ♦James L. Campbell, pres.

Gainesville

WAJD(AM)— May 31, 1961: 1390 khz; 5 kw-D, 51 w-N. TL: N29 39 56 W82 17 26. Hrs open: 7120 S.W. 24th Ave., 32607. Phone: (352) 331-2200. Fax: (352) 331-0401.E-mail: info@kiss1053.com Web Site:www.kiss1053.com Licensee: Gillen Broadcasting Corp. (acq 9-22-87; $1.9 million with co-located FM; 8-17-87). Population served: 90,000 Format: Radio Disney. Target aud: 12-49. ♦Douglas Gillen, pres, gen mgr & gen sls mgr.

WDVH(AM)— October 1954: 980 khz; 5 kw-D, 166 w-N. TL: N29 37 26 W82 17 19. Hrs open: 6 AM-10 PM 100 N.W. 76th Dr., Suite 2, 32607. Phone: (352) 313-3150. Fax: (352) 313-3166.E-mail: jbrand@sunshinebroadcasting.com Web Site:wdvh.net Licensee: 6 Johnson Road Licenses Inc. (group owner; (acq 1-5-2007; grpsl). Natl. Rep: Roslin,. Format: Country legends. News: 2 hrs wkly. Target aud: 35 plus. ♦Richard Hinshaw, gen mgr.

WGGG(AM)— February 1948: 1230 khz; 1 kw-U. TL: N29 40 56 W82 24 48. Hrs open: Box 2930, Ocala, 34478. Secondary address: 101 S.E. 2nd Pl., Grainesville 32601. Phone: (352) 378-7378. Fax: (352) 629-1614.E-mail: sales@floridasportstalk.com Web Site:www.floridasportstalk.com Licensee: Florida Sportstalk Inc. (acq 2-5-97; $300,000). Population served: 175,000 Format: All sports. ♦Doug Gillen, gen mgr.

***WJLF(FM)**— Aug 26, 1990: 91.7 mhz; 2 kw. 400 ft TL: N29 38 34 W82 25 13. Stereo. Hrs open: 24
Rebroadcasts WJIS(FM) Brandenton.
408 West Univ. Ave., Suite 206, 32601. Phone: (352) 373-9553. Fax: (352) 373-9888 / (352) 375-1700.E-mail: thejoyfm@thejoyfm.com Web Site:thejoyfm.com Licensee: Radio Training Network Inc. (acq 10-1-2004; $1 million). Population served: 250,000 Gammon & Grange. Format: Christian. News staff: one; News: 2 hrs wkly. Target aud: 18-49; young adults & young families. Spec prog: Youth 5 hrs, jazz 2 hrs, children 1 hr wkly. ♦James L. Campbell, pres; Andy Haynes, gen mgr, stn mgr.

WKTK(FM)—See Crystal River

WNDD(FM)—(Silver Springs, Feb 1, 1991: 95.5 mhz; 6 kw. 340 ft TL: N29 16 55 W82 02 50. Stereo. Hrs open: 24 3602 N.E. 20th Pl., Ocala, 34470. Phone: (352) 622-9500. Fax: (352) 622-1900. Web Site:www.windfm.com Licensee: Ocala Broadcasting Corp. L.L.C. Group owner: Wooster Republican Printing Co. (acq 9-1-97). Population served: 701,258 Natl. Rep: Katz Radio,. Baker & Hostetler. Format: Classic rock. Target aud: 25-54; adults. ♦Jim Robertson, gen mgr; Bob Kassi, gen sls mgr; Kevin Davis, progmg dir.

WRUF(AM)— 1928: 850 khz; 5 kw-U, DA-N. TL: N29 38 34 W82 25 13. Hrs open: 24 Prog sep from FM Box 14444, 32604. Secondary address: Univ. Of Florida, 3200 Wiemer Hall 32611. Phone: (352) 392-0771. Fax: (352) 392-0519.E-mail: info@am850.com Web Site:www.am850.com Licensee: University of Florida, Board of Trustees Natl. Network: CBS, Westwood One, . Rgnl. Network: Florida Radio Net. Florida's Radio Networks Wire Svc: CBS Format: News/talk, sports. News staff: 3; News: 54 hrs wkly. Target aud: 35-54; middle-to-upper income, decision makers. Spec prog: Black 4 hrs wkly. ♦Robert Lawrence, opns mgr; Larry Dankner, dev dir, mktg dir,

progmg mgr; Tom Ksynski, news dir & pub affrs dir; Don Rice, chief of engrg; Steve Russell, sports cmtr. Co-owned TV: WUFT-TV, WLUF-TV affils.

WRUF-FM— 1948: 103.7 mhz; 100 kw. 768 ft TL: N29 42 34 W82 23 40. Stereo. Hrs open: 24 Box 14444, 32604. Secondary address: Univ. of Florida, 3200 Wiemer Hall 32611. Phone: (352) 392-0771. Fax: (352) 392-0519.E-mail: info@rock104.com Web Site:www.rock104.com Licensee: University of Florida, Board of Trustees Population served: 645,100 Format: Contemp rock. News staff: 3; News: 5 hrs wkly. Target aud: 25-34; urban rockers. Spec prog: Alternative 6 hrs wkly. ◆Larry Dankner, gen mgr, gen sls mgr; Harry Guscott, opns mgr, progmg dir; Cathy Ferguson, news dir, traf mgr; Don Rice, chief of engrg; Matt Lehtola, disc jockey.

WTMG(FM)—See Williston

WTMN(AM)— January 1990: 1430 khz; 10 kw-D, 45 w-N. TL: N29 37 26 W82 17 19. Hrs open: 100 NW 76th Dr., Ste 2, 32607-6659. Phone: (352) 313-3150. Fax: (352) 338-0566.E-mail: rejoice@musicalsoulfood.com Licensee: 6 Johnson Road Licenses Inc. (group owner; (acq 1-5-2007; grpsl). Irwin, Campbell, Crowe & Tannenwald. Format: Gospel. ◆Benjamin Hill, gen mgr.

*WUFT-FM— Sept 27, 1981: 89.1 mhz; 100 kw. 771 ft TL: N29 42 34 W82 23 40. Stereo. Hrs open: 24 Box 118405, 32611. Phone: (352) 392-5200. Fax: (352) 392-5741.E-mail: radio@wuft.org Web Site:www.wuft.org Licensee: Board of Trustees, University of Florida. Population served: 500,000 Natl. Network: NPR, PRI, . Rgnl. Network: Fla. Pub. Fla. Pub. Schwartz, Woods & Miller. Format: Class, jazz, pub affrs. News staff: 3; News: 15 hrs wkly. Target aud: 35-65; general, educated (some college or degree). Spec prog: Black 4 hrs, folk one hr, wkly. ◆Larry Dankner, gen mgr; Henri Pensis, stn mgr; Steve Seipp, opns mgr; Bill Beckett, progmg dir; Richard Drake, mus dir; Kevin Allen, news dir; Manis Samons, chief of engrg. Co-owned TV: *WUFT-TV affil.

WXJZ(FM)— May 1, 1982: 100.9 mhz; 6 kw. Ant 298 ft TL: N29 38 03 W82 18 50. Stereo. Hrs open: 24 4424 N.W. 13th St., Suite C-5, 32609. Phone: (352) 375-1317. Fax: (352) 375-6961.E-mail: feedback@wxjz.fm Web Site:www.wxjz.fm Licensee: Asterisk Communications Inc. Group owner: Asterisk Inc. (acq 10-4-93; $1.4 million;10-25-93). Natl. Network: Jones Radio Networks, . Natl. Rep: McGavren Guild,. Format: Smooth jazz. Target aud: 25-54; upscale, affluent, sophisticated. ◆John Starr, gen mgr & adv mgr; Bill Elliott, progmg dir.

*WYFB(FM)— Aug 4, 1985: 90.5 mhz; 100 kw. 679 ft TL: N29 52 08 W82 12 04. (CP: 96.81 kw). Stereo. Hrs open: 24 11530 Carmel Commons Blvd., Charlotte, NC, 28226. Phone: (704) 523-5555. Fax: (704) 522-1967.E-mail: bbn@bbnradio.org Web Site:www.bbnradio.org Licensee: Bible Broadcasting Network Inc. (group owner) Population served: 1,400,000 Natl. Network: Bible Bcstg Net, USA, . Format: Relg. News: 12 hrs wkly. Target aud: General. ◆Lowell Davey, pres; David Nichols, gen mgr, chief of opns.

WYGC(FM)—(High Springs, Jan 31, 1984: 104.9 mhz; 3.2 kw. Ant 450 ft TL: N29 49 16 W82 34 28. Stereo. Hrs open: 24 4424 N.W. 13th St., Suite C-5, 32609. Phone: (352) 375-1317. Fax: (352) 375-6961. Web Site:www.105thegame.com Licensee: Asterisk Communications Inc. Group owner: Asterisk Inc. (acq 2-99; $825,000). Natl. Network: Fox Sports, . Larry Perry. Format: Sports. Target aud: 25-54. ◆John Starr, gen mgr & gen sls mgr.

WYKS(FM)— May 4, 1970: 105.3 mhz; 3 kw. 466 ft TL: N29 37 52 W82 25 18. (CP: 105.3 mhz, 6 kw). Hrs open: Dups AM 100% 7120 S.W. 24th Ave., 32607. Phone: (352)331-2200. Fax: (352) 331-0401.E-mail: info@kiss1053.com Web Site:www.kiss1053.com Population served: 180,000 Format: Top 40.

Gibsonia

WJWB(AM)—Not on air, target date: unknown: 700 khz; 2.5 kw-D, 250 w-N, DA-2. TL: N28 08 33 W81 52 41. Hrs open: 571 N.W. McClurg Ct., White Springs, 32096-7308. Phone: (386) 397-4489. Licensee: People's Network. ◆Chuck Harder, gen mgr.

Gifford

WSYR-FM— June 1994: 94.7 mhz; 25 kw. 295 ft TL: N27 33 21 W80 22 08. Hrs open: Box 0093, Port St. Lucie, 34985. Phone: (561) 616-6600. Fax: (772) 335-3291.E-mail: star947@clearchannel.com Web Site:www.star947.com Licensee: Aloha Station Trust LLC Group owner: Clear Channel Communications Inc. (acq 7-30-2008; grpsl). Format: Adult contemp. Target aud: 25-54. ◆John Hunt, gen mgr; Andrew Bednar, prom dir; Mike Michaels, opns mgr & progmg dir.

Golden Gate

WNPL(AM)— September 2008: 1460 khz; 7 kw-D, 2 kw-N, DA-2. TL: N26 15 26 W81 40 33. Hrs open: 2824 Palm Beach Blvd., Fort Myers, 33916. Phone: (239) 334-1111. Fax: (239) 332-0767. Web Site:www.foxsportsradio1200.com Licensee: Fort Myers Broadcasting Co. (acq 6-18-2007; $975,000 for CP). Natl. Network: Fox Sports, . Natl. Rep: McGavren Guild,. Format: Sports. ◆Wayne Simons, VP & gen mgr; Brad Foster, sls dir.

Goulds

WRTO-FM—Licensed to Goulds. See Miami

Graceville

WTOT-FM— 1996: 101.7 mhz; 6 kw. 328 ft TL: N30 57 21 W85 29 53. Hrs open: 24 Box 569, Marianna, 32447. Phone: (850) 482-3046. Fax: (850) 482-3049. Licensee: GFR Inc. Population served: 250,000 Natl. Network: ABC, . Format: Adult standards. Target aud: 25+; female. ◆Ed Cearley, gen mgr.

Greenville

*WYJC(FM)— 2005: 90.3 mhz; 325 w. Ant 184 ft TL: N30 23 56 W83 39 24. Hrs open:
Rebroadcasts WUJC(FM) Saint Marks 100%.
8747 Miles Johnson Rd., Tallahassee, 32309. Phone: (850) 514-1929. Fax: (850) 514-1927. Web Site:www.csnradio.com Licensee: CSN International (group owner). Format: Christian. ◆Michael Kestler, pres.

Gretna

WGWD(FM)— Oct 2, 1989: 93.3 mhz; 3 kw. 328 ft TL: N30 33 24 W84 36 05. (CP: 6 kw). Stereo. Hrs open: 24 Box 919, Quincy, 32353. Secondary address: 8 W. Washington, Quincy 32351. Phone: (850) 627-7086. Fax: (850) 627-3422. Licensee: De Col Inc. (acq 9-18-91; $75,000; 10-7-91). Natl. Network: USA, . Format: Classic country. News: 21 hrs wkly. Target aud: 25-54. Spec prog: Black 20 hrs wkly. ◆Monte Bitner, gen mgr, gen sls mgr, progmg dir; Jan Rogers, news dir; Jeff Fallaway, chief of engrg; Pat Bitner, opns mgr & traf mgr.

Gulf Breeze

WNRP(AM)— Feb 1, 1998: 1620 khz; 10 kw-D, 1 kw-N. TL: N30 26 12 W87 13 13. Hrs open: 7251 Plantation Rd., Pensacola, 32504. Phone: (850) 494-2800. Fax: (850) 494-0778. Web Site:www.newsradio1620.com Licensee: ADX Communications of Escambia (acq 11-16-2000). Format: News/talk. Target aud: 35-64; 60% male, 40% female. ◆Mary Hoxeng, gen mgr; Bob Nieman, stn mgr; Jeff Wayne, gen sls mgr; Tracey Castillo, prom dir; Tim McEvoy, engrg dir.

WRNE(AM)— November 1957: 980 khz; 4 kw-D, 1 kw-N, DA-N. TL: N30 29 08 W87 05 01. Stereo. Hrs open: 24 312 E. Nine Mile Rd., Suite 27-D, Pensacola, 32514. Phone: (850) 478-6000. Fax: (850) 484-8080.E-mail: hill@wrne980.com Web Site:www.wrne980.com Licensee: Media One Communications Inc. (acq 11-15-90;11-19-90). Population served: 59,507 Natl. Rep: Dora-Clayton,. Dennis J. Kelly. Format: Urban contemp, gospel, Hispanic. News staff: one; News: 5 hrs wkly. Target aud: 25-54; minorities. Spec prog: Gospel, talk. ◆Robert Hill, pres & gen mgr.

WRRX(FM)—Not on air, target date: unknown: 106.1 mhz; Hrs open: 6565 N. W St., Pensacola, PA, 32505. Phone: (850) 478-6011. Fax: (850) 478-3971.E-mail: info@cumulus.com Web Site:www.cumulus.com Licensee: Cumulus Licensing Corp. Format: Urban contemp. ◆Liz Hanlon, gen mgr; Debbie Dingwall, opns mgr.

Gulfport

WFUS(FM)— October 1963: 103.5 mhz; 98 kw. Ant 1,358 ft TL: N27 50 32 W82 15 45. Stereo. Hrs open: 4002 W. Gandy Blvd., Tampa, 33611. Phone: (813) 832-1000. Fax: (813) 832-1943. Licensee: Citicasters Licenses L.P. Group owner: Clear Channel Communications Inc. (acq 6-99; grpsl). Population served: 1,500,000 Wire Svc: AP Format: Country. Target aud: 25-54; men. ◆Dan DiLoreto, VP, gen mgr; Chris Soechtig, sls dir; John McMartin, chief of engrg; Sandra Ambrosino, traf mgr.

Haines City

WLVF(AM)— Sept 9, 1960: 930 khz; 500 w-D, DA. TL: N28 04 52 W81 38 23. Hrs open: 7 AM-sunset 810 E. Hinson Ave., 33844. Phone: (863) 422-5175. Fax: (863) 422-0110.E-mail: infor@gospel1903.com Licensee: Landmark Baptist Church Population served: 60,000 Format: Southern gospel. Target aud: General. ◆Jonathan Marshall, disc jockey.

*WLVF-FM— Apr 11, 1986: 90.3 mhz; 800 w. 265 ft TL: N28 09 28 W81 37 34. (CP: 1.2 kw, ant 308 ft). Stereo. Hrs open: 24 810 E. Hinson Ave, 33844. Phone: (863) 422-9583. Fax: (863) 422-0110.E-mail: wlvf@gate.net Web Site:www.gospel903.com Licensee: Landmark Baptist Church Population served: 80,000 Natl. Network: USA, . Format: Southern gospel. ◆Steven Carter, gen mgr; Lewis Cruz, opns mgr, progmg dir; Bobby Ogden, gen sls mgr; Jeff Crews, chief of engrg.

Havana

WHTF(FM)— 1986: 104.9 mhz; 47 kw. 494 ft TL: N30 35 11 W84 14 11. Stereo. Hrs open: 24 3000 Olson Rd., Tallahassee, 32308. Phone: (850) 386-8004. Fax: (850) 442-1897. Web Site:www.hot1049.com Licensee: Opus Broadcasting Tallahassee LLC. Group owner: Triad Broadcasting Co. LLC (acq 9-2-2005; grpsl). Population served: 485,000 Natl. Rep: McGavren Guild,. Format: CHR. Target aud: 18-49. ◆Hank Kestenbaum, gen mgr; Doug Purtee, opns mgr.

Hernando

WRZN(AM)— June 1989: 720 khz; 10 kw-D, 250 w-N, DA-N. TL: N28 55 21 W82 22 21. Hrs open: 100 N.W. 76th Dr., Suite 2, Suite B, Gainsville, 32607. Secondary address: 3938 N. Roscoe Rd. 34442. Phone: (352) 726-7221. Fax: (352) 313-3150. Fax: (352) 726-3172. Licensee: 6 Johnson Road Licenses Inc. (group owner; (acq 1-5-2007; grpsl). Format: Adult standards. Target aud: 45 plus. Spec prog: Loc news 4 hrs wkly. ◆Ben Hill, gen mgr; Reggie Thomas, gen sls mgr; Jim Brand, progmg dir.

Hialeah

WACC(AM)—Licensed to Hialeah. See Miami

WCMQ-FM— Dec 22, 1969: 92.3 mhz; 31 kw. 617 ft TL: N25 46 29 W80 11 19. Stereo. Hrs open: 1001 Ponce De Leon Blvd., Coral Gables, 33134. Phone: (305) 444-9292. Fax: (305) 461-4466. Web Site:www.lamusica.com Licensee: WCMQ Licensing Inc. Group owner: Spanish Broadcasting System Inc. (acq 12-22-86; grpsl; 9-29-86). Format: Adult contemp, Sp. ◆Jackie Nosti-Combo, gen mgr; Tony Campos, opns mgr; Albert Rodriguez, gen sls mgr; John Caride, prom dir.

High Springs

WYGC(FM)—Licensed to High Springs. See Gainesville

Hilliard

WJFA(AM)—Not on air, target date: unknown: 830 khz; 50 kw-D, 4 kw-N, DA-2. TL: N30 43 41 W81 59 37. Hrs open: 571 N.W. McClurg Ct., White Springs, 32096. Phone: (386) 397-4489. Licensee: The Dianne A. Mayfield-Harder Trust. ◆Charles Harder, gen mgr.

Hobe Sound

WOLL(FM)— 2002: 105.5 mhz; 50 kw. Ant 456 ft TL: N26 45 42 W80 04 42. Hrs open: 3071 Continental Dr., West Palm Beach, 33407. Phone: (561) 616-6600. Fax: (561) 616-6677.E-mail: info@1055online.com Web Site:www.1055online.com Licensee: Aloha Station Trust LLC, as Trustee Group owner: Clear Channel Communications Inc. (acq 7-30-2008). Format: Oldies. Target aud: 25-54. ◆John Hunt, gen mgr; Dave Denver, opns dir.

Holiday

WSUN-FM— 1979: 97.1 mhz; 3.3 kw. 300 ft TL: N28 16 51 W82 42 52. Stereo. Hrs open: 24 11300 4th St. N., Suite 300, St. Petersburg, 33716. Phone: (727) 579-2000. Fax: (727) 579-2662. Fax: (727) 579-2271.E-mail: 97xcomments@97xonline.com Web Site:www.97xonline.com Licensee: Cox Radio Inc. Group owner: Cox Broadcasting (acq 11-20-98). Reddy, Begley & McCormick. Format:

Alternative/new rock. Target aud: 35 plus. ◆Bob Neil, CEO, pres; Keith Lawless, VP, gen mgr; Tom Paleveda, opns mgr; Dan Connelly, prom mgr.

Holly Hill

*WAPN(FM)— October 1985: 91.5 mhz; 1.8 kw. 285 ft TL: N29 15 06 W81 02 53. Stereo. Hrs open: 24 Box 250, Daytona Beach, 32125. Secondary address: 1508 State Ave., Daytona Beach 32125. Phone: (386) 677-4272. Phone: (386) 672-3333. Fax: (386) 673-3715.E-mail: wapn@wapn.net Web Site:www.wapn.net Licensee: Public Radio Capital Florida (acq 5-16-03; $1.5 million). Format: Word & praise. Target aud: General. Spec prog: Sp 4 hrs wkly. ◆Shellye Lund-Vallance, gen mgr.

*WEAZ(FM)— Aug 20, 1999: 88.1 mhz; 4.2 kw vert. Ant 148 ft TL: N29 22 26 W81 10 49. Hrs open:
Rebroadcasts WPOZ(FM) Union Park 100%.
1065 Rainer Dr., Altamonte Springs, 32714-3847. Phone: (407) 869-8000. Fax: (407) 869-0380.E-mail: zcrew@zradio.org Web Site:www.zradio.org Licensee: Central Florida Educational Foundation Inc. (acq 6-8-99; $75,000). Population served: 250,000 Format: Contemp Christian. ◆James Hoge, gen mgr; Dean O'Neal, opns mgr.

WVYB(FM)— 1997: 103.3 mhz; 3 kw. 328 ft TL: N29 15 05 W81 07 23. (CP: Ant 315 ft.). Hrs open: 24 126 W. International Speedway Blvd., Daytona Beach, 32114. Phone: (386) 255-9300. Fax: (386) 238-6071. Web Site:www.wvyb.fm Licensee: Black Crow LLC. Group owner: Black Crow Media Group LLC (acq 9-21-2001; grpsl). Format: Hot adult contemp, CHR. News: 2 hrs wkly. Target aud: 18-49. ◆Stacey Knerler, gen mgr.

Hollywood

WLQY(AM)— April 1953: 1320 khz; 5 kw-U, DA-2. TL: N26 01 53 W80 16 42. Hrs open: 10800 Biscayne Blvd., Suite 810, Miami, 33161. Phone: (305) 891-1729. Fax: (305) 891-1583.E-mail: wlqy@bellsouth.net Web Site:www.entravision.com Licensee: Entravision Holdings LLC. Group owner: Entravision Communications Corp. (acq 7-28-00; grpsl). Format: Ethnic. Target aud: 35 plus; female. ◆Jeff Liberman, pres; Rick Santos, gen mgr.

Holmes Beach

WSJT(FM)— Jan 27, 1992: 98.7 mhz; 3 kw. Ant 328 ft TL: N27 27 49 W82 35 32. Stereo. Hrs open: 24 9721 Executive Center Dr. N., Suite 200, St. Petersburg, 33702-2439. Phone: (727) 579-1925. Fax: (727) 568-9758.E-mail: smoothjazz@wsjt.com Web Site:www.wsjt.com Licensee: CBS Radio Stations Inc. Group owner: Infinity Broadcasting Corp. (acq 11-13-98; grpsl). Population served: 456,000 Leventhal, Senter & Lerman. Format: Smooth jazz. Target aud: 25-54; middle to upper income adults, skews towards females. ◆Don Howe, gen mgr; Marvin Kopman, gen sls mgr; Heidi Heinz, prom dir; Kathy Curtis, mus dir.

Holt

WTKE-FM—Licensed to Holt. See Fort Walton Beach

Homestead

WOIR(AM)— Nov 4, 1957: 1430 khz; 5 kw-D, 500 w-N, DA-N. TL: N25 27 09 W80 30 57. Hrs open: 10661 N Kendall Dr, Suite 112, Miami, 33176. Phone: (305) 270-1430.E-mail: lenriquez@vida1430am.com Web Site:www.vida1430am.com Licensee: Amanecer Christian Network Inc. (acq 5-17-2001; $2.58 million). Format: Sp, news/talk. ◆Laura Enriquez, gen mgr.

*WRGP(FM)— 1999: 88.1 mhz; 165 w. Ant 423 ft TL: N25 32 24 W80 28 07. Hrs open: 24 Florida International Univ., 11200 S.W. Univ. Park - GC 210, Miami, 33199. Phone: (305) 348-3071. Fax: (305) 348-6665.E-mail: wrgp@fiu.edu Web Site:wrgp.org Licensee: Florida International University. Population served: 1,300,000 Format: Var. News: 4 hrs wkly. Target aud: General; young adults, mainly university students. Spec prog: Hip hop 12 hrs, news 3 hrs, raggae 3 hrs wkly. ◆Brennan Forsyth, gen mgr; Jennifer Mojena, progmg dir.

Homosassa Springs

WXCV(FM)— March 1983: 95.3 mhz; 6 kw. 328 ft TL: N28 53 14 W82 31 39. Stereo. Hrs open: 24 4554 S. Suncoast Blvd., 34446. Phone: (352) 628-4444.E-mail: staff@citrus.com Web Site:www.citrus953.com Licensee: Westwind Broadcasting Inc. Gardner, Carton & Douglas.

Format: Classic rock. News staff: one; News: 7 hrs wkly. Target aud: 25-54. Spec prog: Jazz 7 hrs, oldies 6 hrs wkly. ◆Richard Spires, gen mgr.

Immokalee

WAFZ(AM)— Oct 14, 1964: 1490 khz; 1 kw-U. TL: N26 25 27 W81 26 32. Hrs open: 24 2105 Immokalee Dr., 34142. Phone: (239) 657-9210. Fax: (239) 658-6109.E-mail: robbie@gladesmedia.com Web Site:www.radiofiesta.com Licensee: Glades Media Company LLP. Natl. Network: CNN Radio, . Natl. Rep: Univision Radio National Sales,. Format: Rgnl Mexican. Sp. ◆Robbie Castellanos, pres; Alredo Hernandez, gen mgr; Ricardo Chairez, opns mgr, engrg dir.

WAFZ-FM— 1995: 92.1 mhz; 5.6 kw. Ant 328 ft TL: N26 26 54 W81 16 17. Stereo. Hrs open: 24 2105 Immokalee Dr., 34142. Phone: (239) 657-9210. Fax: (239) 658-6109.E-mail: robbie@gladesmedia.com Web Site:www.radiofiesta.com Licensee: Glades Media Co. LLC (acq 7-14-2004). Natl. Network: CNN Radio, . Natl. Rep: Univision Radio National Sales,. Format: Regional Mex. Target aud: 18 plus; general. ◆Alfredo Hernandez, gen mgr; Ricardlo Chairez, opns mgr; Robbie Castellanos, pres & sls dir.

Indian River Shores

WOSN(FM)— 1996: 97.1 mhz; 6 kw. 328 ft TL: N27 44 06 W80 27 27. Hrs open: 1235 16th Street, Vero Beach, 32960. Phone: (772) 567-0937. Fax: (772) 562-4747. Web Site:www.wosnfm.com Licensee: Vero Beach Broadcasters LLC (group owner; acq 2-15-01; $4.1 million). Format: Adult standards. ◆Jim Davis, gen mgr; Hamp Elliott, progmg dir; John Rotolante, opns mgr & prom.

Indian Rocks Beach

WPOI(FM)—See Saint Petersburg

WXYB(AM)— May 11, 1963: 1520 khz; 1 kw-D, DA. TL: N27 50 26 W82 46 10. (CP: 600 w. TL: N27 50 45 W82 46 21). Hrs open: Sunrise-sunset 109 Bayview Blvd., Suite A, Oldsmar, 34677. Phone: (727) 725-5555. Phone: (813) 814-7575. Fax: (813) 814-7500.E-mail: wpso@wpso.com Web Site:www.wpso.com Licensee: ASA Broadcasting Inc. (acq 5-24-93; $31,000; 6-14-93). Population served: 100,000 Format: Ethnic, Greek, news/talk, educ. News: 7 hrs wkly. Target aud: General; international, ethnic. Spec prog: Indian 3 hrs, It 2 hrs, Pol 2 hrs, East Indian one hr, relg 8 hrs wkly. ◆Sam Agelatos, pres; Angelo Agelatos, gen mgr, stn mgr, opns dir.

Indiantown

WPBZ(FM)— July 4, 1965: 103.1 mhz; 90 kw. 974 ft TL: N27 01 32 W80 10 43. Stereo. Hrs open: 24 701 Northpoint Pkwy., Suite 400, West Palm Beach, 33407. Phone: (561) 616-4600. Fax: (561) 684-6311.E-mail: mcmeatal169@buzz103.com Web Site:www.buzz103.com Licensee: Infinity Radio Inc. Group owner: Infinity Broadcasting Corp. (acq 12-14-00; grpsl). Rosenman & Colin. Format: Alternative. News staff: one; News: 12 hrs wkly. Target aud: 18-34; men. ◆Lee K. Strasser, gen mgr; John O'Connell, opns dir, progmg dir; Fran Marcone, gen sls mgr; Susan Oland, natl sls mgr; Lynette Shady, prom dir; Nik Rivers, mus dir; Chuck Herlihey, engrg dir, chief of engrg; Lane Racette, traf mgr; Jason Davis, disc jockey.

Inglis

WIFL(FM)— Oct 1, 1994: 104.3 mhz; 4.4 kw. Ant 380 ft TL: N29 01 18 W82 41 20. Stereo. Hrs open: 24 11928 N. William St., Dunnellon, 34432. Phone: (352) 522-0172. Fax: (352) 564-8750.E-mail: wifl@xtalwind.net Web Site:www.wow104.com Licensee: Nature Coast Broadcasting Inc. (acq 2-9-2004; $525,000). Population served: 350,000 Florida's Radio Networks Gammon & Grange. Format: Mix adult contemp, CHR. News: one hr wkly. Target aud: 25-54. ◆Lisa Cuppelli, CEO, gen mgr, stn mgr; Sab Cupelli, pres; Marc Tyll, VP, gen mgr; Jon Kay, opns mgr; Jeremy Howard, gen sls mgr.

WXRA(FM)— 2008: 99.3 mhz; 3.7 kw. Ant 420 ft TL: N29 09 19 W82 27 01. Hrs open: 188 S. Bellevue, Suite 222, Memphis, TN, 38104. Phone: (901) 375-9324. Fax: (901) 375-5889. Web Site:www.flinn.com Licensee: George S. Flinn Jr. ◆George S. Flinn Jr., gen mgr.

Inverness

*WJUF(FM)— Oct 1, 1995: 90.1 mhz; 21 kw. Ant 397 ft TL: N28 46 39 W82 28 05. Hrs open: 24

Rebroadcasts WUFT-FM Gainesville 100%.
Weimer Hall Univ. of Florida, Gainesville, 32611. Phone: (352) 392-5200. Fax: (352) 392-5741.E-mail: info@wuft.org Web Site:www.wuft.org Licensee: Board of Trustees, University of Florida. (acq 10-14-94; 12-5-94). Population served: 200,000 Natl. Network: NPR, PRI, . Rgnl. Network: Fla Pub. Fla. Pub. Schwartz, Woods & Miller. Format: Classical, jazz, news and pub affrs. News staff: 3; News: 15 hrs wkly. Target aud: General. ◆Larry Dankner, gen mgr; Henri Pensis, stn mgr. Co-owned TV: *WUFT-TV affil.

Islamorada

*WAZQ(FM)—Not on air, target date: unknown: 89.3 mhz; 3.2 kw vert. Ant 115 ft TL: N24 52 34 W80 42 05. Stereo. Hrs open: 6910 N.W. 2nd Terr., Boca Raton, 33487. Phone: (561) 912-9002. Licensee: Educational Public Radio Inc. Format: Hot adult contemp. News staff: 12. Target aud: 18-54; adults. ◆Bill Lacy, pres.

WWWK(FM)— Oct 15, 1984: 105.5 mhz; 50 kw. Ant 430 ft TL: N25 05 29 W80 26 37. Stereo. Hrs open: 27501 S. Dixie Hwy., Suite 208, Homestead, 33032-8219. Phone: (305) 398-3362.E-mail: LISERRA@MYRADIOEXITO.COM Web Site:www.myradioexito.com Licensee: LSM Radio Partners LLC (acq 6-24-2004; with WAVK(FM) Marathon). Format: Bilingual, Sp. ◆Lilliam M. Sierra, gen mgr.

Jacksonville

WAPE-FM— April 1949: 95.1 mhz; 100 kw. 460 ft TL: N30 17 09 W81 44 52. Stereo. Hrs open: 8000 Belfort Pkwy, 32256. Phone: (904) 245-8500. Fax: (904) 245-8501.E-mail: contest@wape951.com Web Site:www.wape951.com Licensee: Cox Radio Inc. Group owner: Cox Broadcasting (acq 8-00; grpsl). Population served: 528,865 Natl. Rep: Christal,. Format: CHR. ◆Bill Hendrichs, gen mgr.

WAYR(AM)—See Orange Park

WBOB(AM)— 1945: 1320 khz; 50 kw-D, 5 kw-N, DA-N. TL: N30 17 42 W81 44 33. Stereo. Hrs open: 4190 Belfort Rd., Suite 450, 32216. Phone: (904) 470-4615. Fax: (904) 296-1683.E-mail: robin719@comes.net Web Site:www.1320thepatriotr.com Licensee: Chesapeake-Portsmouth Broadcasting Corp. Group owner: Salem Communications Corp. (acq 12-5-2006; $1.8 million with WZNZ(AM) Jacksonville). Population served: 686,000 Fletcher, Heald & Hildreth. Format: News/talk. Target aud: 25-54. ◆Henry Hoot, gen mgr; Calvin Grabau, opns mgr.

WBWL(AM)— Dec 9, 1933: 600 khz; 5 kw-D, 5.4 kw-N, DA-N. TL: N30 18 00 W81 45 34. Hrs open: 24 10245 Centurion Pkwy., Suite 109, 32256. Phone: (904) 646-1100. Phone: (904) 783-3711. Fax: (904) 646-1117. Web Site:www.radiodisney.com Licensee: Radio Disney Group LLC. Group owner: ABC Inc. (acq 8-1-02; $2.5 million). Population served: 751,000 Natl. Network: Radio Disney, . Rgnl. Network: Florida Radio Net. Format: Children. ◆Jay Schneider, stn mgr.

WCGL(AM)— 1948: 1360 khz; 5 kw-D, 89 w-N. TL: N30 16 33 W81 38 12. Hrs open: 24 3890 Dunn Ave., Suite 804, 32218. Phone: (904) 766-9955. Fax: (904) 765-9214.E-mail: wcgl@aol.com Web Site:www.wcgl1360.com Licensee: JBD Communications Inc. (acq 12-27-89; $510,000; 1-15-90). Population served: 528,865 Pepper & Corazzini. Format: Relg. Target aud: 25 plus. ◆Deborah Maiden, pres, gen mgr; Kelvin Postell, opns mgr.

*WCRJ(FM)— Mar 16, 1984: 88.1 mhz; 8 kw. Ant 495 ft TL: N30 16 34 W81 33 53. Stereo. Hrs open: 24 Box 551379, 32255. Phone: (904) 641-9626. Fax: (904) 645-9626.E-mail: calvin@fm88.org Web Site:www.ILoveThePromise.org Licensee: The River Educational Media Inc. Format: Christian contemp. Target aud: 25-55; women. ◆Calvin Grabau, gen mgr; Roger Henderson, opns mgr.

WEJZ(FM)— 1949: 96.1 mhz; 100 kw. 984 ft TL: N30 19 22 W81 38 34. Stereo. Hrs open: 6440 Atlantic Blvd., 32211. Phone: (904) 727-9696. Fax: (904) 721-9322. Web Site:www.wejz.com Licensee: Renda Broadcasting Corp. (group owner; acq 6-90; grpsl; 6-25-90). Population served: 1,000,000 Natl. Rep: McGavren Guild,. Wire Svc: Metro Weather Service Inc. Format: Lite adult contemp. Target aud: 25-54; office, home & in-the-car audience. ◆Tony Renda Sr., CEO, pres; Bill Scull, gen mgr; Bill Reese, gen sls mgr; Woody Carlson, prom dir; Ed Fairbanks, progmg dir; Bob Dillehay, chief of engrg; Brenda McArthur, traf mgr; Jim Byard, pub svc dir.

WFXJ(AM)— November 1925: 930 khz; 5 kw-U, DA-N. TL: N30 17 09 W81 44 52. Hrs open: 24 11700 Central Pkwy, 32224-2600. Phone: (904) 636-0507. Phone: (904) 642-3030. Fax: (904) 997-7713.E-mail: victoriagowan@clearchannel.com Web Site:www.930thefox.com Licensee: Clear Channel Radio Licenses Inc. Group owner: Clear Channel

Communications Inc. Format: Sports. Target aud: 25-49; men. ♦Norm Feuer, gen mgr; Gail Austin, opns mgr; Victoria Gowan, gen sls mgr.

WJAX(AM)— 1958: 1220 khz; 1 kw-D, 37 w-N. TL: N30 19 30 W81 34 15. Hrs open: 24 Prog sep from FM 5353 Arlington Expwy., 32211. Phone: (904) 680-1220.E-mail: kjones@jones.edu Web Site:www.wktz.jones.edu Licensee: Jones College Natl. Network: CNN Radio, . Format: Swing mus. Target aud: 40 plus.

WJBT(FM)—(Callahan, June 1, 1983: 93.3 mhz; 50 kw. Ant 462 ft TL: N30 33 22 W81 33 13. Stereo. Hrs open: 24 11700 Central Pkwy., 32224. Phone: (904) 636-0507. Fax: (904) 997-7713.E-mail: rhondagroff @clearchannel.com Web Site:www.wjbt.com Licensee: Clear Channel Radio Licenses Inc. Group owner: Clear Channel Communications Inc. (acq 11-21-97; grpsl). Format: Urban contemp. Target aud: 12-54; the young & young-at-heart. ♦Norm Feuer, gen mgr; Gail Austin, opns dir; Chad Chumley, progmg dir.

***WJCT-FM**— Apr 17, 1972: 89.9 mhz; 100 kw. 835 ft TL: N30 16 53 W81 34 15. Stereo. Hrs open: 100 Festival Park Ave., 32202. Phone: (904) 353-7770. Fax: (904) 358-6352.E-mail: wjct@wjct.org Web Site:www.wjct.org Licensee: WJCT Inc. Population served: 528,865 Natl. Network: NPR, PRI, . Rgnl. Network: Fla. Pub. Fla. Pub. Schwartz, Woods & Miller. Format: News/talk, class. ♦Michael Boylan, CEO, pres; Tom Patton, stn mgr & news dir. Co-owned TV: *WJCT-TV affil.

***WJFR(FM)**— Sept 15, 1987: 88.7 mhz; 8 kw. 380 ft TL: N30 16 53 W81 34 15. Stereo. Hrs open: 2771-29 Monument Rd. , #318, 32225. Phone: (904) 389-9088. Web Site:www.familyradio.com Licensee: Family Stations Inc. Format: Relg. Target aud: Conservative Christians. ♦Harold Camping, pres; Harold Camping, gen mgr; Marcy Morrison-Pearce, progmg dir, news dir; Phyllis Johnston, mus dir.

WJGL(FM)— July 1, 1969: 96.9 mhz; 98 kw. Ant 1,014 ft TL: N30 16 34 W81 33 53. Stereo. Hrs open: 24 Prog sep from AM 8000 Belfort Pkwy., 32206. Phone: (904) 245-8500. Fax: (904) 245-8501.E-mail: contest@wape951.com Web Site:www.cool969.com Licensee: Cox Radio Inc. Population served: 751,000 Format: Oldies. News staff: one. Target aud: 25-54. ♦Scott Walker, progmg dir.

WJXL(AM)—See Jacksonville Beach

WJXR(FM)—(Macclenny, September 1978: 92.1 mhz; 25 kw. 328 ft TL: N30 17 54 W82 00 55. Stereo. Hrs open: 24 Box One, 32234. Phone: (904) 259-2292. Phone: (904) 358-2265. Fax: (904) 259-4488. Web Site:www.wjxr.com Licensee: WJXR Inc. (acq 1-8-85; $335,000; 2-4-85). Natl. Network: ABC, . Rgnl. Network: Florida Radio Net. Florida's Radio Networks Polner Law Firm. Format: Talk. News staff: one; News: 7 hrs wkly. Target aud: 25-54; middle class & upscale families. ♦Gregory G. Perich, CEO, pres, gen mgr; Doug Rudowich, stn mgr, sls VP; Sarah Perich, opns mgr; Jerry Smith, chief of engrg.

***WKTZ-FM**— Feb 8, 1973: 90.9 mhz; 50 kw. Ant 500 ft TL: N30 16 36 W81 33 47. Stereo. Hrs open: 24 5353 Arlington Expwy., 32211. Phone: (904) 731-1184. Web Site:wktz.jones.edu Licensee: Jones College (acq 2-7-86). Natl. Network: AP Network News, . Format: Beautiful music. Target aud: 40+. ♦Kenneth Jones, gen mgr, gen sls mgr, progmg dir; Tom Buetow, mus dir; Dick Jones, chief of engrg.

WNNR(AM)— Jan 1, 1969: 970 khz; 1 kw-U, DA-1. TL: N30 23 08 W81 40 04. Hrs open: 8384 Baymeadow Rd., Suite 1, 32256. Phone: (904) 739-3660. Fax: (904) 739-9409. Web Site:www.970thewinner.com Licensee: Norsan Consulting and Management Inc. (acq 9-15-2005; $2.1 million with WVOJ(AM) Fernandina Beach). Population served: 1,058,500 Format: Sports. Target aud: General. ♦Norberto Sanchez, pres; Bernie Daigle, gen mgr, stn mgr; Marci Koziolek, news dir, pub affrs dir.

WOKV(AM)— November 1925: 690 khz; 50 kw-D, 10 w-N, DA-N. TL: N30 18 27 W81 56 28. Hrs open: 24 8000 Belfort Pkwy., 32206. Phone: (904) 245-8500. Fax: (904) 245-8501.E-mail: wokv.news@cox.com Web Site:www.wokv.com Licensee: Cox Radio Inc. Group owner: Cox Broadcasting (acq 2-28-2000; grpsl). Population served: 500,000 Natl. Network: CBS, . Cohn & Marks. Format: News/talk. ♦Dick Williams, gen mgr; Cat Thomas, opns mgr; Lindley Tolbert, sls dir; Allison Misora, prom dir; Mike Dorwart, progmg dir; Roxy Tyler, pub affrs dir; Dick Jones, engrg dir; Betty Glover, traf mgr.

WPLA(FM)— May 9, 1977: 107.3 mhz; 100 kw. Ant 705 ft TL: N30 21 48 W81 45 09. Stereo. Hrs open: 24 11700 Central Pkwy, 32224-2600. Phone: (904) 636-0507. Fax: (904) 997-7713. Licensee: Clear Channel Radio Licenses Inc. Group owner: Clear Channel Communications Inc. (acq 11-21-97; grpsl). Population served: 1,000,000 Rgnl. Network: Florida Radio Net. Natl. Rep: Clear Channel,. Florida's Radio Networks Format: Country. News staff: one. Target aud: 25-49. Spec prog: Relg 2 hrs wkly. ♦Norm Feuer, gen mgr; Gail Austin, opns mgr. Co-owned TV: WAWS(TV) affil

WQIK-FM— September 1964: 99.1 mhz; 100 kw. 1,050 ft TL: N30 16 34 W81 33 53. Stereo. Hrs open: 24 Norm Feuer, 11700 Central Pkwy., 32224. Phone: (904) 642-3030. Fax: (904) 997-7707.E-mail: tanderson@ccjax.com Web Site:www.wqik.com Licensee: Citicasters Licenses L.P. Group owner: Clear Channel Communications Inc. (acq 5-4-99; grpsl). Population served: 770,000 Natl. Network: ABC, . Format: Country. News staff: one; News: 4 hrs wkly. Target aud: 18-54. ♦John Hogan, sr VP; Norm Feuer, gen mgr; Gail Austin, opns dir, progmg dir; Tony Anderson, prom dir.

WROS(AM)— July 1955: 1050 khz; 5 kw-D, DA. TL: N30 21 14 W81 44 21. Hrs open: 6 AM-sunset 5590 Rio Grande Ave., 32254. Phone: (904) 353-1050. Fax: (904) 353-7076.E-mail: wros@wros.net Web Site:www.wros.net Licensee: The Rose of Jacksonville (acq 6-1-85;4-1-85). Population served: 1,000,000 Natl. Network: USA, . Rgnl rep: NRB Format: Family oriented, Christian. News staff: one; News: 7 hrs wkly. Target aud: 25-65; Christians & secular. ♦Elwyn V. Hall, CEO, pres; Robyne Hall, gen mgr; Yisrael Freedman, progmg dir; Jerry Smith, chief of engrg.

WSOL-FM—(Brunswick, GA) Sept 1, 1966: 101.5 mhz; 100 kw. 239 ft TL: N31 08 40 W81 34 56. (CP: Ant 1,463 ft.). Stereo. Hrs open: 24 11700 Central Pkwy., 32224. Phone: (904) 996-0400 / (904) 642-3030. Fax: (904) 997-7713.E-mail: karmenbrooks@clearchannel.com Web Site:www.v1015.com Licensee: Citicasters Licenses L.P. Group owner: Clear Channel Communications Inc. (acq 5-4-99; grpsl). Format: Adult urban contemp. ♦Norm Fever, gen mgr.

WXXJ(FM)— November 1965: 102.9 mhz; 100 kw. Ant 984 ft TL: N30 16 34 W81 33 53. Stereo. Hrs open: 24 8000 Belfort Pky., 32256. Phone: (904) 245-8500. Fax: (904) 245-8501. Web Site:x1029.com Licensee: Cox Radio Inc. Group owner: Cox Communications Inc. (acq 2-23-2000; grpsl). Natl. Rep: Christal,. Format: Modern rock. News staff: one; News: 7 hrs wkly. Target aud: 25-49. ♦David Israel, gen mgr.

WYMM(AM)— Nov 18, 1976: 1530 khz; 50 kw-D, DA. TL: N30 21 50 W81 44 54. Hrs open: 6 AM-6 PM 5900 Pickettville Rd., 32254. Phone: (904) 786-2820. Fax: (904) 786-2661. Web Site:www.wymm1530.com Licensee: Word Broadcasting Network Inc. (group owner; (acq 7-29-2003; $1.25 million with WYRM(AM) Norfolk, VA). Format: Talk. ♦Patrick Archuleta, gen mgr.

WZAZ(AM)— July 4, 1950: 1400 khz; 1 kw-U. TL: N30 19 43 W81 41 42. Stereo. Hrs open: 24 4190 Belfort Rd., Suite 450, 32216. Phone: (904) 470-4615. Fax: (904) 296-1683.E-mail: ronin719@comes.net Web Site:www.1400wzaz.com Licensee: Caron Broadcasting Inc. Group owner: Salem Communications Corp. (acq 5-30-03; grpsl). Population served: 6,000,000 Natl. Rep: Roslin,. Format: Gospel. News staff: 2; News: 5 hrs wkly. Target aud: 25-54; adult Black listeners. ♦Henry Hoot, gen mgr; Calvin Grabau, progmg dir.

WZNZ(AM)— August 1942: 1460 khz; 15 kw-D, 5 kw-N, DA-N. TL: N30 19 40 W81 44 49. Stereo. Hrs open: Box 51585, Jacksonville Beach, 32240-1585. Phone: (904) 241-3311. Fax: (904) 241-1402. Web Site:www.qopradio.com Licensee: Queen of Peace Radio Inc. Group owner: Salem Communications Corp. (acq 7-29-2008; $1.6 million). Population served: 40,000 Natl. Network: EWTN Radio, . Law office of Dennis J. Kelly. Format: Catholic. Target aud: 25-54. ♦Tom Moran, gen mgr.

Jacksonville Beach

WJXL(AM)— 1946: 1010 khz; 50 kw-D, 30 kw-N, DA-2. TL: N30 17 57 W82 00 26. Hrs open: 24 9090 Hogan Rd., Jacksonville, 32216. Phone: (904) 641-1011. Fax: (904) 641-1022.E-mail: JasonD@1010XL.com Web Site:www.1010xl.com Licensee: Seven Bridges Radio LLC (acq 2-9-2007; $3,825,000). Population served: 1,000,000 Natl. Network: ESPN Radio, Motor Racing Net, . Garvey, Schubert & Barer. Wire Svc: AP Format: Sports. Target aud: M 25-54. Spec prog: NASCAR (MRN, PRN) Jacksonville University. ♦Steven L. Griffin, pres; Steven Griffin, gen mgr; Jack O'Brien, gen sls mgr; Jason Dixon, progmg dir.

Jensen Beach

WMBX(FM)— Dec 10, 1980: 102.3 mhz; 100 kw. 974 ft TL: N27 01 32 W80 10 43. (CP: 100 kw). Stereo. Hrs open: 24 701 Northpoint Pkwy., Suite 400, West Palm Beach, 33407. Phone: (561) 616-4600. Fax: (561) 684-6311.E-mail: mcmeatal69@buzz103.com Web Site:www.mix1023.com Licensee: Infinity Radio Operations Inc. Group owner: Infinity Broadcasting Corp. (acq 12-14-00; grpsl). Rosenman & Colin. Format: Modern adult contemp. News staff: one; News: 17 hrs wkly. Target aud: 25-54; women. ♦Patricia A. Larschan, VP, gen mgr; John O'Connell, opns mgr, progmg dir; Mark Krieger, gen sls mgr, natl sls mgr; Danelle Sarvas, prom mgr; Jeff Clarke, mus dir; Pam Crosby, news dir, pub affrs dir; Scott Paxson, chief of engrg.

Jupiter

WJBW(AM)— 1997: 1000 khz; 650 w-D, DA. TL: N26 56 40 W80 05 30. Hrs open: 24 1235 16th St., Vero Beach, 32960. Phone: (772) 567-0937. Fax: (772) 562-4747. Licensee: AM of Palm Beach Inc. Group owner: James Crystal Inc. (acq 4-13-2006). Format: News/talk. ♦Laurie S. Silvers, pres; Jim Davis, gen mgr.

WNEW(FM)— Oct 15, 1971: 106.3 mhz; 19 kw. Ant 374 ft TL: N26 47 59 W80 04 33. Hrs open: 701 Northpoint Pkwy., Suite 500, West Palm Beach, 33407. Phone: (561) 684-7400. Fax: (561) 686-9505. Web Site:www.b1063fm.com Licensee: CBS Radio Stations Inc. Group owner: Infinity Broadcasting Corp. (acq 8-30-2001; $20 million). Format: Urban adult contemp. ♦Lee Strasser, sr VP, gen mgr; Mark McCray, opns mgr.

Kendall

WURN(AM)— August 1999: 1020 khz; 8.9 kw-D, 980 w-N, DA-2. TL: N25 37 09 W80 31 00. Hrs open: 75 NW 167th St., N. Miami Beach, 33169. Phone: (305) 446-5444 / (305) 493-1020. Fax: (305) 446-1009 / (305) 493-1111. Web Site:www.radiomega.net Licensee: New World Broadcasting Inc. (acq 12-20-2001; $260,000 for stock for 52%). Format: Ethnic. Target aud: 25-55; adult. ♦Alex Saintsuin, gen mgr.

Key Colony Beach

WKYZ(FM)— April 15, 1999: 101.7 mhz; 100 kw horiz, 90.25 kw vert. Ant 453 ft TL: N24 39 39.8 W81 25 10.4. Hrs open: 24 Box 500940, Marathon, 33050. Phone: (305) 289-1013. Fax: (305) 743-9441.E-mail: keysradiogroup@aol.com Licensee: Keys Media Co. Inc. Format: Classic rock. Target aud: 25-54. ♦Joe Nascone, gen mgr.

Key Largo

***WGES-FM**— 2004: 90.9 mhz; 33 kw. Ant 308 ft TL: N25 14 07 W80 19 35. Hrs open: 11890 S. W. 8th St., Suite 504, South Florida, 33082. Phone: (305) 551-6590. Fax: (305) 551-2737.E-mail: info@wges.com Licensee: Genesis License Subsidiary LLC. Format: Christian, Sp. ♦Edwin Lemuel Ortiz, pres; Kenny Reyes, gen mgr.

***WMKL(FM)**— Oct 1, 1998: 91.9 mhz; 50 kw vert. Ant 308 ft TL: N25 14 07 W80 19 35. Stereo. Hrs open: 24 Box 561832, 8900 South West 168 Street, Florida, 33157. Phone: (305) 662-7736. Fax: (305) 251-2293.E-mail: callfm@callfm.com Web Site:www.callfm.com Licensee: Call Communications Group Inc. (acq 11-4-99; $295,000). Population served: 220,000 Gammon & Grange. Format: Christian. Target aud: 13-25. ♦Robert Robbins, pres & gen mgr; Kelly Downing, mus dir; Jim Sorensen, chief of engrg.

Key West

WAIL(FM)— December 1978: 99.5 mhz; 100 kw. 991 ft TL: N24 39 25 W81 32 18. (CP: Ant 239 ft.). Stereo. Hrs open: 24 5450 McDonald Ave, Suite 10, 33040. Phone: (305) 296-7511. Fax: (305) 296-0358.E-mail: kenmackenzie@clearchannel.com Web Site:www.wail995.com Licensee: Clear Channel Radio Licenses Inc. Group owner: Clear Channel Communications Inc. (acq 6-5-98; $2.6 million with WEOW(FM) Key West). Rgnl. Network: Florida Radio Net. Florida's Radio Networks Format: Classic rock. Target aud: 25-54; men. ♦Greg Capogna, VP, gen mgr, gen mgr; Sherry Russo, stn mgr; Ken MacKenzie, opns dir.

WCNK(FM)— January 1986: 98.7 mhz; 100 kw. Ant 300 ft TL: N24 34 42 W81 44 49. Stereo. Hrs open: 24 30336 Overseas Hwy., Big Pine Key, 33043. Phone: (305) 872-9100. Fax: (305) 872-8930.E-mail: info@conchcountry.com Web Site:www.conchcountry.com Licensee: Vox Communications Group LLC. (acq 8-31-2005; grpsl). Format: Country. News: one hr wkly. Target aud: 24-55; military, baby boomers & largest income holders. Spec prog: Armed Forces news one hr wkly. ♦Kevin LeRoux, gen mgr & stn mgr.

WEOW(FM)— February 1967: 92.7 mhz; 100 kw. Ant 551 ft TL: N24 40 35 W81 30 41. Stereo. Hrs open: 24 5450 MacDonald Ave., Suite 10, 33040. Phone: (305) 296-7511. Fax: (305) 296-0358.E-mail: kenmackenzie@clearchannel.com Web Site:www.weow927.com Licensee: Clear Channel Radio Licenses Inc. Group owner: Clear Channel Communications Inc. (acq 6-5-98; $2.6 million with WAIL(FM) Key

West). Population served: 76,000 Rgnl. Network: Florida Radio Net. Florida's Radio Networks Format: CHR, Top-40. ♦Mark Mays, pres; Sherry Russo, gen mgr.

WIIS(FM)— June 1978: 107.1 mhz; 3 kw. 200 ft TL: N24 33 18 W81 48 07. Stereo. Hrs open: 24 1075 Duval St., Suite 17, 33040. Phone: (305) 292-1133. Phone: (305) 292-1071. Fax: (305) 292-6936.E-mail: johnrussin@hotmail.com Web Site:www.radiokeywest.com Licensee: The Keyed Up Communications Co. (acq 1995; $275,000). Population served: 35,000 Fletcher, Heald & Hildreth. Format: Alternative. News staff: one; News: 5 hrs wkly. Target aud: 18-44; young, educated, active spenders for goods & svcs. Spec prog: Reggae 4 hrs, Metropolitan opera 4 hrs wkly. ♦John Russin, CEO, sls dir, traf mgr; Linda Russin, COO.

***WJIR(FM)**— December 1986: 90.9 mhz; 390 w. Ant 121 ft TL: N24 33 07 W81 47 53. Stereo. Hrs open: 24 1209 United St., 33040. Phone: (305) 296-4306. Fax: (305) 294-9547.E-mail: pastorernie@bellsouth Licensee: Key West Educational Broadcasting. (acq 12-15-85). Format: Relg, educ, Christian. News: 12 hrs wkly. Target aud: General. ♦Ernie DeLoach, stn mgr & opns mgr.

WKEY-FM— Nov 17, 1985: 93.5 mhz; 32 kw. Ant 138 ft TL: N24 34 17 W81 44 25. Stereo. Hrs open: 24 5450 MacDonald Ave., 33040. Phone: (305) 296-7511. Fax: (305) 296-0358.E-mail: kenmackenzie @clearchannel.com Web Site:www.key93.com Licensee: Aloha Station Trust LLC, as Trustee Group owner: Clear Channel Communications Inc. (acq 7-30-2008). Population served: 33,000 Rgnl. Network: Florida Radio Net. Natl. Rep: Clear Channel,. Florida's Radio Networks Format: Adult contemp. News staff: one; News: 8 hrs wkly. Target aud: 25-54; affluent, upscale, culturally supportive. Spec prog: Classical 4 hrs, Sp 3 hrs wkly. ♦Greg Capogna, gen mgr; John Stuempfig, prom dir; Sherry Russo, stn mgr, gen sls mgr & adv mgr.

WKIZ(AM)— Feb 2, 1959: 1500 khz; 250 w-U, DA-1. TL: N24 34 01 W81 44 54. Stereo. Hrs open: 24 5016 5th Ave., 33040. Phone: (305) 293-9536. Fax: (305) 293-1793.E-mail: wkizradio@aol.com Web Site:www.wkizradio.com Licensee: Seattle Streaming Radio L.L.C. Population served: 30,803 Natl. Network: CBS, . Format: Spanish, religious. ♦Jim Spreitzer, gen sls mgr.

WKWF(AM)— October 1945: 1600 khz; 500 w-U. TL: N24 34 30 W81 44 01. Hrs open: 24 5450 MacDonald Ave., Ste. 10, 33040. Phone: (305) 296-7511. Fax: (305) 296-0358.E-mail: Toddswofford @clearchannel.com Web Site:www.keysradio.com Licensee: Spottswood Partners II Ltd. (acq 10-27-97; with co-located FM). Population served: 35,000 Format: Prime sports. ♦Greg Capogna, VP, gen mgr; Sherry Russo, stn mgr, sls dir; Todd Swofford, progmg dir.

***WKWR(FM)**— 2005: 90.1 mhz; 250 w. Ant 69 ft TL: N24 34 05 W81 44 53. Hrs open: Broadcasting for the Challenged Inc., 6080 Mount Moriah Ext., Memphis, TN, 38115. Phone: (901) 375-9324. Fax: (901) 375-0041.E-mail: mail@flinn.com Licensee: Broadcasting for the Challenged Inc. Natl. Network: K-Love, . Format: Contemp Christian. ♦George Flinn Jr., gen mgr.

***WKZG(FM)**— June 1, 2005: 88.3 mhz; 740 w. Ant 112 ft TL: N24 33 07 W81 47 53. Stereo. Hrs open:
Rebroadcasts WAFG(FM) Fort Lauderdale 100%.
5555 N. Federal Hwy., Fort Lauderdale, 33308. Phone: (954) 776-7705. Fax: (954) 771-2633.E-mail: wafg@wafg.org Web Site:www.wafg.org Licensee: Westminster Academy (acq 3-19-2009; $135,233). Format: Contemp Christian. ♦Dolores King-St. George, gen mgr.

***WLSZ(FM)**—Not on air, target date: unknown: 89.1 mhz; 50 kw vert. Ant 495 ft TL: N24 40 35 W81 30 41. Hrs open: 6910 N.W. 2nd Terr., Boca Raton, 33487. Phone: (561) 912-9002. Licensee: Educational Public Radio Inc. ♦Bill Lacy, pres.

WMFM(FM)— 1995: 107.9 mhz; 100 kw. 548 ft TL: N24 39 08 W81 32 04. Hrs open:
Rebroadcasts WXDJ (FM) North Miami Beach 100%.
1001 Ponce de Leon Blvd., Coral Gables, 33134. Phone: (305) 447-9292. Fax: (305) 461-4466. Web Site:www.lamusica.com Licensee: South Broadcasting System Inc. (acq 1-27-2000; $1million with WRAZ-FM Key Largo). Format: Salsa. ♦Jackie Nosti-Combo, gen mgr; Albert Rodriguez, gen sls mgr.

Kissimmee

WHOO(AM)— April 1965: 1080 khz; 19 kw-D, 190 w-N, 10 kw-CH, DA-3. TL: N28 20 30 W81 20 26. Hrs open: 18 1160 S Semoran Blvd., Suite A, Orlando, 32807. Phone: (407) 380-9255. Fax: (407) 382-7565.E-mail: mytake@espnflorida.com Web Site:espn1080.com Licensee: Genesis Communications I Inc. Group owner: Genesis Communications Inc. (acq 10-19-99). Population served: 1,500,000 Natl. Network: ESPN Radio, . Natl. Rep: Interep,. Florida's Radio Networks Booth, Freret, Imlay & Tepper. Format: Sports talk. Target aud: 25-54; men. ♦Bruce Maduri, pres; Colin Cantwell, VP, gen mgr; Simon Luke, opns mgr; Sabrina Lavender, gen sls mgr; Jerry O'Neill, progmg dir.

***WLAZ(FM)**— 2000: 89.1 mhz; 1.1 kw vert. Ant 535 ft TL: N28 10 27 W81 17 01. Hrs open: 24 415 W. Vine St., 34741. Phone: (407) 518-7150. Phone: (407) 208-0333. Fax: (407) 518-0062.E-mail: contacto@gensis89.com Web Site:www.genesis89.net Licensee: Caguas Educational TV Inc. (acq 5-3-02; $1.5 million). James L. Oyster. Format: Christian, Sp. News staff: 2; News: 10 hrs wkly. ♦William Gutierrez, pres & gen mgr.

WOTS(AM)— Oct 23, 1978: 1220 khz; 1 kw-D. TL: N28 19 27 W81 23 44. Hrs open: 24 222 Hazard St., Orlando, 32804-3030. Phone: (407) 841-8282. Fax: (407) 841-8250. Licensee: J&V Communications Inc. (group owner; acq 1-12-99). Leibowitz & Associates. Format: Sp, relg. News staff: one. Tourists. Spec prog: Imus in the Morning. ♦John Torrado, CEO; Jocelyn Torrado, VP; Hector Reyes, gen mgr.

La Belle

***WBIY(FM)**— 1999: 88.3 mhz; 3 kw. Ant 161 ft TL: N26 44 26 W81 27 46. Hrs open: 24 500 W. Hickpochee Ave., 33935. Phone: (863) 674-0033. Fax: (863) 675-7584. Licensee: Oscar Aguero Ministry Inc. (acq 6-13-2006; $900,000). Format: Sp contemp Christian. ♦Oscar Aguero, pres; Roger Martinez, stn mgr.

La Crosse

WBXY(FM)— October 1993: 99.5 mhz; 2.2 kw. 472 ft TL: N29 44 22 W82 23 09. Stereo. Hrs open: 24 4424 N.W.13th St., Suite C-5, Gainesville, 32609. Phone: (352) 375-1317. Fax: (352) 375-6961.E-mail: feedback@thestar.com Web Site:www.thestar.fm Licensee: Asterisk Communications Inc. (acq 7-23-98; $1.15 million). Natl. Network: Westwood One, Talk Radio Network, ABC, Fox Sports, . Natl. Rep: McGavren Guild,. Format: Talk, news, sports. Target aud: 25-54; primarily baby boomers-upscale. ♦John Starr, gen mgr, adv mgr; Steve Cox, progmg dir.

Lafayette

WEGT(FM)—Licensed to Lafayette. See Tallahassee

Lake City

WDSR(AM)— May 6, 1946: 1340 khz; 1 kw-U. TL: N30 09 20 W82 38 14. Hrs open: 24 2485 S. Marion St., 32025. Phone: (386) 752-1340. Fax: (386) 755-9369.E-mail: wnfb@mix943.com Web Site:www.mix943.com Licensee: Newman Media Inc. (acq 9-3-98; $750,000 with co-located FM). Population served: 34,950 Natl. Network: CBS, . Florida's Radio Networks Rgnl rep: Florida's Radio Net. Format: Oldies. Target aud: 40-65. Spec prog: Black 1 hr wkly. ♦John Newman, pres, gen mgr & gen sls mgr; Barry Cole, progmg dir.

WNFB(FM)— May 28, 1969: 94.3 mhz; May 28, 1969. May 28, 1969 TL: May 28, 1969. May 28, 1969. Stereo. 24 2485 S. Marion St., 32025. Phone: (386) 961-9494. Fax: (386)755-9369. Web Site:www.mix943.com Licensee: Newman Media Inc. (acq 11-30-98). Population served: 50,000 Format: Adult contemp. Target aud: 25-54. ♦John Newman, pres; Barry Cole, progmg dir; Jack Wiley, mus dir.

WGRO(AM)— Nov 14, 1958: 960 khz; 500 w-D, 1 kw-N, DA-N. TL: N30 11 47 W82 40 48. (CP: 1 kw-U, DA-N). Hrs open: 6 AM-midnight (M-S); 7 AM-11 PM (Su) 9206 US Hwy. 90 W., 32055. Phone: (386) 755-4102. Fax: (386) 752-9861.E-mail: bandk@ISgroup.net Licensee: Power Country Inc. (acq 9-20-95). Population served: 10,575 Rgnl. Network: Florida Radio Net. Florida's Radio Networks Format: Country gospel. ♦Louis Bolton II, pres; Bob Hendrickson, gen mgr.

WNFB(FM)— May 28, 1969: 94.3 mhz; 50 kw. Ant 492 ft TL: N30 07 44 W82 52 49. Stereo. Hrs open: 24 2485 S. Marion St., 32025. Phone: (386) 961-9494. Fax: (386)755-9369. Web Site:www.mix943.com Licensee: Newman Media Inc. (acq 11-30-98). Population served: 50,000 Format: Adult contemp. Target aud: 25-54. ♦John Newman, pres; Barry Cole, progmg dir; Jack Wiley, mus dir.

***WOLR(FM)**— Sept 11, 1986: 91.3 mhz; 18 kw vert. 285 ft TL: N30 02 56 W82 48 44. Hrs open: 3332 220th Pl., 32024. Phone: (386) 935-3300. Fax: (386) 935-2684. Web Site:www.christianhitradio.net Licensee: WOLR 91.3 FM Inc. (acq 6-25-93; $75,000; 7-19-93). Format: Christian. ♦Rita Loos, gen mgr; Chris Hall, chief of engrg.

Lake Placid

WWTK(AM)— 1989: 730 khz; 500 w-D, 340 w-N, DA-1. TL: N27 24 25 W81 25 56. Hrs open: 24 3750 U.S. 27 N., Suite One, Sebring, 33870. Phone: (863) 382-9999. Fax: (863) 382-1982.E-mail: cohanradiogroup@htn.net Web Site:www.cohanradiogroup.com Licensee: Cohan Radio Group Inc. (group owner; (acq 11-1-98; $910,000 with WWOJ(FM) Avon Park). Population served: 80,000 Natl. Network: USA, CBS Radio, ABC, Premiere Radio Networks, Talk Radio Network, Westwood One, . Rgnl. Network: Florida Radio Net. Natl. Rep: Interep,. Florida's Radio Networks Latham & Watkins. Wire Svc: AP Format: Talk. News staff: one; News: 120 hrs wkly. Target aud: 35 plus. ♦Peter L. Coughlin, pres, gen sls mgr; Libby Coughlin, rgnl sls mgr; Barry Foster, news dir; Phil Scott, chief of engrg; Kim McPherson, traf mgr.

Lake Wales

WIPC(AM)— July 1951: 1280 khz; 1 kw-D, 500 w-N, DA-N. TL: N27 55 34 W81 36 04 (D), N27 55 30 W81 36 16 (N). Hrs open: 24 630 Mountain Lake Cut/Off Rd., Suite A, 33859. Phone: (863) 679-7178. Fax: (863) 679-9395.E-mail: wipc1280@yahoo.com Licensee: Super W Media Group Inc. (acq 9-19-2005). Population served: 485,000 Donald E. Martin. Format: Sp. News staff: one; News: 10 hrs wkly. Target aud: 18+ Hispanics. ♦Carl Czuchaj, VP; Guadalupe Gonzalez, opns mgr; Robert Cubero, pres, gen mgr & gen sls mgr; Raul Centeno, progmg dir; Linda Perez, mus dir; Guadalupe Gonzales, traf mgr.

Lake Worth

WWRF(AM)— May 1, 1959: 1380 khz; 1 kw-D, 500 w-N. TL: N26 37 23 W80 04 20. Hrs open: 24 2326 S. Congress Ave., Suite 2A, W. Palm Beach, 33406-7614. Phone: (561) 585-1380. Phone: (561) 721-9950. Fax: (561) 721-9973.E-mail: info@gladesmedia.com Web Site:www.gladesmedia.com Licensee: Radio Fiesta Inc. (acq 2-24-00; $400,000). Population served: 1225000 Format: Regional Mexican. News staff: one. Target aud: 25-54; Hispanic. Spec prog: Sp relg 4 hrs wkly. ♦Liza Flores, pres, gen mgr; Robbie Castellanos, pres & stn mgr.

Lakeland

***WKES(FM)**— May 20, 1975: 91.1 mhz; 100 kw. 500 ft TL: N28 04 46 W82 02 27. (CP: 420 ft.). Stereo. Hrs open: 24 5800 100th Way N., St. Petersburg, 33708. Phone: (727) 391-9994. Fax: (727) 397-6425.E-mail: wkes@moody.edu Web Site:www.wkes.fm Licensee: The Moody Bible Institute of Chicago. (group owner; acq 10-10-96; $5 million). Population served: 3,600,000 Southmayd & Miller. Format: Relg, educ. ♦Michael Easley, pres; Michael Gleichman, opns mgr, pub affrs dir; Pierre Chestang, stn mgr & progmg dir; John Stortz, chief of engrg.

WLKF(AM)— 1936: 1430 khz; 5 kw-D, 1 kw-N. TL: N28 02 27 W81 56 08. Hrs open: 24 Box 2038, 33806. Secondary address: 404 W. Lime St. 33815-4651. Phone: (863) 682-8184. Fax: (863) 683-2409.E-mail: talk1430@wlkf.com Web Site:www.wlkf.com Licensee: Hall Communications Ltd. Group owner: Hall Communications Inc. (acq 10-1-96; $550,000). Population served: 580,000 Natl. Network: ABC, . Rgnl. Network: Florida Radio Net. Natl. Rep: Eastman Radio,. Florida's Radio Networks Fletcher, Heald & Hildreth. Wire Svc: AP Format: News/talk. News staff: 3; News: 15 hrs wkly. Target aud: 35 plus; middle to upper income adults. ♦Bonnie H. Rowbotham, chmn; Arthur J. Rowbotham, pres; Bill Baldwin, exec VP, sr VP; Nancy Cattarius, stn mgr.

WLLD(FM)— Sept 11, 1967: 94.1 mhz; 100 kw. Ant 1,492 ft TL: N27 40 23 W82 06 35. Stereo. Hrs open: 24 9721 Executive Center Dr. N., Suite 200, St. Petersburg, 33702-2439. Phone: (727) 579-1925. Fax: (727) 568-9758. Web Site:www.wild941.com Licensee: CBS Radio Stations Inc. Group owner: Infinity Broadcasting Corp. (acq 1999; grpsl). Population served: 4,000,000 Natl. Rep: CBS Radio,. Format: Rhythmic CHR. News staff: one. Target aud: 25 plus; professional, educated, upscale audience. ♦Don Howe, gen mgr, sls dir; Marvin Kopman, gen sls mgr; Orlando Davis, progmg dir.

WONN(AM)— Sept 15, 1949: 1230 khz; 1 kw-U. TL: N28 02 23 W81 57 39. Stereo. Hrs open: 24 Box 2038, 33806. Secondary address: 404 W. Lime St. 33815-4651. Phone: (863) 682-8184. Phone: (407) 297-1201. Fax: (863) 683-2409.E-mail: wonn@wonn.com Web Site:www.wonn.com Licensee: Hall Communications Inc. (group owner; acq 10-1-81; $2 million with co-located FM; 8-10-81). Population served: 580,000 Natl. Network: CNN Radio, . Natl. Rep: Eastman Radio,. Fletcher, Heald & Hildreth. Format: MOR. News staff: 3; News: 20 hrs wkly. Target aud: 35 plus. Spec prog: Relg 2 hrs wkly. ♦Bonnie H. Rowbotham, chmn; Arthur J. Rowbotham, pres; Bill Baldwin, sr VP; Nancy Cattarius, gen mgr & stn mgr.

WPCV(FM)—(Winter Haven, 1962: 97.5 mhz; 100 kw. 1,017 ft TL: N28 07 35 W81 33 03. Stereo. Hrs open: 24 Prog sep from AM Box 2038, 33806. Secondary address: 404 W. Lime St. 33815-4651. Phone: (863) 682-8184. Fax: (863) 683-2409.E-mail: wpcv@wpcv.com Web Site:www.wpcv.com Licensee: Hall Communications Inc. Population served: 580,000 Natl. Rep: Eastman Radio,. Wire Svc: AP Format: Country. News staff: 3; News: 4 hrs wkly. Target aud: 25-54. ♦Bonnie Rowbotham, chmn; Art Rowbotham, pres; Nancy Cattarius, stn mgr; Jeff Crews, chief of engrg.

WWAB(AM)— September 1957: 1330 khz; 1 kw-D. TL: N28 02 40 W81 58 28. Hrs open: Box 65, 33802. Secondary address: 1203 Chase St. 33802. Phone: (863) 682-2998. Fax: (863) 683-9922.E-mail: wwab@verizon.net Web Site:www.wwab1330.com Licensee: WWAB Inc. (acq 1-16-73). Population served: 60,000 Format: Rhythm and blues, talk. Target aud: 18-49. Spec prog: Gospel 12 hrs wkly. ♦Jerry Hughes, gen mgr; Hugh Hughes, stn mgr, gen sls mgr; Frank Clark, opns mgr.

***WYFO(FM)**— March 1988: 91.9 mhz; 25 kw horiz, 23 kw vert. 328 ft TL: N27 56 35 W81 54 45. Hrs open: Box 7300, Charlotte, NC, 28241. Phone: (704) 523-5555. Fax: (704) 522-1967.E-mail: wyfo@bbnradio.org Web Site:www.bbnradio.org Licensee: Bible Broadcasting Network Inc. (group owner; acq 9-21-89; $200,000; 10-16-89). Format: Christian, educ. ♦Doug Roby, stn mgr.

Lantana

WPBR(AM)— 1941: 1340 khz; 1 kw-U. TL: N26 36 41 W80 02 17. (CP: TL: N26 33 26 W80 04 20). Hrs open: 24-7 1217 S. Military Trail, Suite E, West Palm Beach, 33415-4600. Phone: (561) 641-8882. Fax: (561) 641-8629.E-mail: adminandsales@1340wpbr.com Web Site:www.talk1340wpbram.com Licensee: Omni-Lingual Broadcasting Corp. (acq 3-4-94; $700,000;5-9-94). Population served: 740,000 Natl. Network: USA, . Format: News/talk, community progmg. Target aud: 35-64. Spec prog: Financial 9 hrs, medical 8 hrs, Jewish 3 hrs, Creole 30 hrs wkly. ♦Emil Antonoff, pres; Markes Pierre Louis, gen mgr.

Largo

WWBA(AM)— May 29, 1972: 820 khz; 50 kw-D, 1 kw-N, DA-2. TL: N27 54 30 W82 46 51. Hrs open: 24 4300 W. Cypress St., Suite 1040, Tampa, 33607. Phone: (813) 281-1040. Fax: (813) 281-1948. Web Site:www.newstalk820.com Licensee: Genesis Communications of Tampa Bay Inc. Group owner: Mega Communications Inc. (acq 1-13-2009; $3 million). Population served: 2,800,000 Natl. Network: ABC, . Format: News/talk. News staff: 3. Target aud: 25-54. ♦Luis Diaz-Albertini, gen mgr; Roger P. Schulman, news dir.

Layton

***WRTH(FM)**—Not on air, target date: unknown: 88.7 nhz; 1.9 kw vert. Ant 117 ft TL: N24 48 20.3 W80 50 38.1. Hrs open: 6910 N.W. 2nd Terr., Boca Raton, 33487. Phone: (561) 912-9002. Licensee: Educational Public Radio Inc. ♦Bill Lacy, pres.

Lecanto

***WLMS(FM)**— September 1992: 88.3 mhz; 3.8 kw. Ant 259 ft TL: N28 52 55 W82 31 30. Hrs open:
Rebroadcasts WBVM(FM) Tampa 100% (simulcast).
Box 18081, Tampa, 33629. Secondary address: 3816 Morrison Ave., Tampa 33629. Phone: (813) 289-8040. Fax: (813) 282-3580. Web Site:zradio.org Licensee: Central Florida Educational Foundation Inc. (acq 10-10-2008; $2 million). Format: Contemp Christian Music. ♦John Morris, gen mgr; Chris Sampson, opns mgr.

Leesburg

WLBE(AM)— August 1949: 790 khz; 5 kw-D, 1 kw-N, DA-N. TL: N28 49 00 W81 46 45. Hrs open: 24 32900 Radio Rd., 34788. Phone: (352) 787-7900. Fax: (352) 787-1402.E-mail: info@am790wlbe.com Licensee: WLBE 790 Inc. Population served: 140,000 Natl. Network: CBS, . Rgnl. Network: Florida Radio Net. Natl. Rep: Dora-Clayton,. Florida's Radio Networks Format: Talk & music. News: 25 hrs wkly. Target aud: 45 plus. Spec prog: Black 3 hrs, farm 3 hrs, gospel 4 hrs, Pol 2 hrs wkly. ♦MJ McNair, gen mgr.

WQBQ(AM)— Sept 12, 1962: 1410 khz; 5 kw-D, 90 w-N. TL: N28 47 13 W81 53 26. Stereo. Hrs open: Box 723, Ocoee, 34761. Phone: (407) 222-6628. Fax: (407) 656-3487. Licensee: Rama Communications Inc. (group owner; (acq 10-15-2004; $180,000 with WKIQ(AM) Eustis). Population served: 200,000 Format: Spanish. ♦Sabeta Persaud, pres; Jose Lopez, gen mgr.

WVLG(AM)—(Wildwood, September 1987: 640 khz; 930 w-D, 860 w-N. TL: N28 54 16 W81 57 36. Hrs open: 6 AM-midnight 1161 Main St., The Villages, 32159. Phone: (352) 753-1119. Fax: (352) 259-4819. Web Site:thevillagesdailysun.com/wvlg/WVLG.html Licensee: Senior Broadcasting Corp. (acq 9-12-00; $1.05 million). Rgnl. Network: S.E. Agri. Southeast AgNet Format: Var/div. Target aud: 18 plus; general. ♦Skip Diegel, gen mgr.

WXXL(FM)—(Tavares, Feb 12, 1969: 106.7 mhz; 100 kw. 823 ft TL: N28 33 31 W81 35 38. Stereo. Hrs open: 24 2500 Maitland Center Pkwy., Suite 401, Maitland, 32751-7407. Phone: (407) 916-7800. Fax: (407) 916-7510.E-mail: info@wxxl.com Web Site:www.wxxl.com Licensee: AMFM Radio Licenses L.L.C. Group owner: Clear Channel Communications Inc. (acq 8-30-00; grpsl). Population served: 1,000,000 Wiley, Rein and Fielding. Format: CHR. News staff: one. Target aud: 18-49; general. Spec prog: Alternative 6 hrs wkly. ♦Linda Byrd, VP, gen mgr; Sam Nein, sls dir; Shannon Fraser, gen sls mgr; Frank Celebre, natl sls mgr; Rick Everett, mktg dir; Glory Adona, prom mgr; Chris Kampmeier, progmg dir; Donna Carmichael, traf mgr.

Lehigh Acres

WCKT(FM)— Jan 1, 1976: 107.1 mhz; 23.5 kw. Ant 722 ft TL: N26 19 00 W81 47 13. Stereo. Hrs open: 24 13320 Metro Pkwy., Fort Myers, 33912. Phone: (239) 225-4300. Phone: (800) 827-1071. Fax: (239) 275-4669. Web Site:www.wckt.com Licensee: Clear Channel Broadcasting Licenses Inc. Group owner: Clear Channel Communications Inc. (acq 1996; grpsl). Population served: 750,000 Natl. Rep: Clear Channel,. Format: Country. News staff: one; News: 20 hrs wkly. Target aud: 25-54. ♦Lowry Mays, chmn; Mark Mays, pres; Randall Mays, CFO; Jay Meyers, sr VP; Jim Keating, gen mgr; Steve Amari, opns dir; Robin Craig, sls dir; Dave Logan, mus dir; Church Morgan, news dir; Dick Parrish, chief of engrg; Debie Lummus, traf mgr.

WWCL(AM)— Apr 29, 1970: Stn currently dark. 1440 khz; 5 kw-D, 1 kw-N, DA-2. TL: N26 36 05 W81 33 30. Hrs open: 7573 N.W. First St., 33972. Phone: (239) 337-1440. Fax: (239) 369-3386.E-mail: energi1440@aol.com Licensee: Latino Media Corp. (acq 10-12-2006; $1.4 million). Population served: 16,000 ♦Angel Ramos, gen mgr.

Leisure City

WRAZ-FM— Jan 20, 1990: 106.3 mhz; 50 kw. Ant 308 ft TL: N25 14 07 W80 19 35. Stereo. Hrs open: 1001 Ponce De Leon Blvd., Coral Gables, 33134. Phone: (305) 444-9292. Fax: (305) 461-4466. Licensee: South Broadcasting System Inc. (acq 1-27-2000; $1 million with WMFM(FM) Key West). Format: Rgnl Mexican. ♦Raoul Alarcon, pres; Jackie Nosti-Cambo, gen mgr; John Caride, prom dir; Ralph Chambers, chief of engrg.

Live Oak

WQHL(AM)— June 16, 1949: 1250 khz; 1 kw-D, 83 w-N. TL: N30 17 14 W82 57 56. Hrs open: 24 1305 Helvenston St. SE, 32064. Phone: (386) 362-1250. Phone: (386) 364-3502. Fax: (386) 364-3504.E-mail: audio@wqhl981.com Web Site:www.wqhl981.com Licensee: RTG Radio LLC. Group owner: Black Crow Media Group LLC (acq 11-9-2001; grpsl). Population served: 46,000 Natl. Network: ABC, . Rgnl. Network: Florida Radio Net. Florida's Radio Networks Format: Classic Hits. News: 12 hrs wkly. Target aud: General. Spec prog: Gospel 7 hrs, relg 6 hrs wkly. ♦Dean Blackwell, gen mgr.

WQHL-FM— October 1973: 98.1 mhz; 50 kw. 420 ft TL: N30 17 14 W82 57 56. Stereo. Hrs open: 24 Prog sep from AM 1305 Helvenston St. SE, 32064. Phone: (386) 362-1250. Phone: (386) 364-3502. Fax: (386) 364-3504.E-mail: audio@wqhl981.com Web Site:wqhl981.com Population served: 250,000 Natl. Network: ABC, . Southeast AgNet Format: Country. Target aud: General. Spec prog: Nascar Racing, High School Football. ♦Dean Blackwell, gen mgr; Rob Harder, progmg dir; Jim Smith, chief of engrg.

Lynn Haven

WWHV(FM)—Not on air, target date: unknown: 104.3 mhz; 6 kw. Ant 249 ft TL: N30 10 47 W85 38 11. Hrs open: 1670 N.W. Federal Hwy., Stuart, 34994. Phone: (772) 692-9454. Fax: (772) 692-0258. Licensee: Hroton Broadcasting Co. Inc. ♦George Metcalf, pres.

Macclenny

WJXR(FM)—Licensed to Macclenny. See Jacksonville

Madison

***WAPB(FM)**— 2005: 91.7 mhz; 200 w. Ant 224 ft TL: N30 27 13 W83 24 17. Hrs open: Box 250, Dayton Beach, 32125. Secondary address: 1508 State Ave., Dayton Beach 32125. Phone: (386) 677-4272. Fax: (386) 673-3715.E-mail: wapn@wapn.net Web Site:www.wapb.net Licensee: Public Radio Inc. Format: Word & praise. ♦Shellye Lund-Vallance, pres.

WMAF(AM)— Dec 6, 1956: 1230 khz; 1 kw-U. TL: N30 28 23 W83 26 09. Hrs open: Box 621, 32341. Secondary address: 2 Captain Brown Rd. 32341. Phone: (850) 973-3233. Fax: (850) 973-3097.E-mail: countrywmaf@embarkmail.com Web Site:www.wmafcountry.com Licensee: Geneva Walker. (acq 1996). Population served: 75,000 Rgnl. Network: Florida Radio Net. Florida's Radio Networks Format: Classic country. Spec prog: Oldies, gospel. ♦Betty Evertt, gen mgr.

WXHT(FM)— November 2000: 102.7 mhz; 19 kw. Ant 377 ft TL: N30 38 23 W83 26 52. Stereo. Hrs open: 1711 Ellis Dr., Valdosta, GA, 31602. Phone: (229) 244-8642. Fax: (229) 242-7620.E-mail: info@hot10227wxnt.com Web Site:www.hot10227wxnt.com Licensee: RTG Radio L.L.C. Group owner: Black Crow Media Group LLC (acq 6-4-2004; $3.4 million with WSTI-FM Quitman, GA). Rini Coran PC. Format: Contemp hits. Target aud: Adults 18-49. ♦Robert Ganzak, pres & gen mgr.

Maitland

WPYO(FM)— Sept 1, 1968: 95.3 mhz; 12 kw. Ant 472 ft TL: N28 34 27 W81 27 46. Hrs open: 24 4192 N. John Young Pkwy., Orlando, 32804. Phone: (407) 422-9696. Fax: (407) 422-5883.E-mail: info@power953.com Web Site:www.power953.com Licensee: Cox Radio Inc. Group owner: Cox Broadcasting (acq 1999; $14.5 million). Population served: 1,500,000 Format: Hip hop. Target aud: General. ♦Brian Elam, gen mgr.

Marathon

WAVK(FM)— 2002: 97.7 mhz; 50 kw horiz, 49 kw vert. Ant 213 ft TL: N24 46 02 W80 56 42. Stereo. Hrs open: 24 30336 Overseas Hwy., Big Pine Key, 33043. Phone: (305) 872-9100. Fax: (305) 872-1603.E-mail: mail@wave-fm.com Licensee: Vox Communications Group LLC. (acq 8-31-2005; grpsl). Format: Hot adult contemp. ♦Kevin LeRoux, gen mgr.

WFFG(AM)— Apr 7, 1962: 1300 khz; 2.5 kw-U, DA-1. TL: N24 41 28 W81 06 30. Hrs open: 24 Box 500940, One Boot Key, 33050. Phone: (305) 743-5563. Phone: (305) 743-5564. Fax: (305) 743-9441.E-mail: keysradiogroup@aol.com Licensee: The Great Marathon Radio Co. (acq 11-5-90; grpsl; 11-26-90). Population served: 82,000 Natl. Network: Westwood One, . Format: News/talk, sports. News: 10 hrs wkly. Target aud: 25-54; general. ♦Joe Mascone, pres, gen mgr; Vince Cacone, engrg dir & chief of engrg; Jane Martin, traf mgr.

WGMX(FM)— December 1976: 94.3 mhz; 50 kw. 276 ft TL: N24 41 28 W81 06 30. (CP: 3.1 kw). Stereo. Hrs open: 24 Box 500940, One Boot Key, 33050. Phone: (305) 743-5563. Phone: (305) 743-5564. Fax: (305) 743-9441.E-mail: keysradiogroup@aol.com (Acq 11-5-90; grpsl; 11-26-90). Natl. Network: Westwood One, . Format: Adult contemp. ♦John Bartus, spec ev coord; John Perry, local news ed & sports cmtr; Dannielle Alderman, women's int ed, women's cmtr.

***WKWM(FM)**— 2008: 91.5 mhz; 12 kw. Ant 462 ft TL: N24 39 38 W81 25 10. Stereo. Hrs open: 24
Rebroadcasts WLRN-FM Miami 100%.
172 N.E. 15th St., Miami, 33132-1348. Phone: (305) 995-1717. Fax: (305) 995-2221.E-mail: radio@wlrn.org Web Site:www.wlrn.org Licensee: The School Board of Miami-Dade County, FL. Population served: 85,000 Natl. Network: NPR, PRI, AP Network News, Premiere Radio Networks, . Fla. Pub. Leibowitz & Associates, P.A. Wire Svc: AP Format: News/talk-info. News staff: 7; News: 111 hrs wkly. Target aud: General; well educated, moderate to high income bracket. Spec prog: Haitian 3 hrs wkly. ♦John LaBonia, gen mgr; Ted Eldredge, stn mgr; Peter J. Moerz, progmg mgr.

Marco

WGUF(FM)— 1990: 98.9 mhz; 6 kw. Ant 328 ft TL: N26 01 50 W81 38 33. Stereo. Hrs open: 24 10915 K-Nine Dr., 2nd Fl., Bonita Springs, 34135. Phone: (239) 495-8383. Fax: (239) 495-0883.E-mail: wguf@rendabroadcasting.com Web Site:www.thegulf989.com Licensee: Renda Broadcasting Corp. of Nevada. Group owner: Renda Broadcasting Corp. (acq 4-17-97; $2 million). Population served: 300,000 Format: News/talk. News: 7 hrs wkly. Target aud: 35 plus; affluent southwest FL residents. ♦Tony Renda Jr., gen mgr; Randy Savage, progmg dir.

***WMKO(FM)—** Feb 8, 1999: 91.7 mhz; 6.9 kw. Ant 369 ft TL: N26 03 10 W81 42 11. Hrs open: 24
Rebroadcasts WGCU-FM Fort Myers100%.
Florida Gulf Coast University, 10501 FGCU Blvd., Fort Myers, 33965. Phone: (239) 590-2500. Fax: (239) 590-2511.E-mail: wgcufm@fgcu.edu Web Site:wgcu.org Licensee: Board of Trustees, Florida Gulf Coast University (acq 11-16-01). Natl. Network: NPR, . Format: Great music, class, jazz & news. ♦Kathleen Davey, gen mgr & stn mgr.

Marco Island

***WCNZ(AM)—** May 1999: 1660 khz; 10 kw-D, 1 kw-N. TL: N25 59 30 W81 37 30. Stereo. Hrs open: 24 5043 E. Tamiami Tr., Naples, 34113. Phone: (239) 732-9369. Fax: (239) 732-7267.E-mail: bladd@mail.com Web Site:www.relevantradio.com Licensee: Sovereign City Radio Services LLC (acq 2-6-2009; grpsl). Population served: 250,000 Rgnl. Network: Florida Radio Network Arter & Hadden. Format: Catholic talk. News staff: 2; News: 10 hrs wkly. Spec prog: Vintage Radio. ♦Robert Ladd, stn mgr.

WTLT(FM)—See Naples

WVOI(AM)— Jan 1, 1975: 1480 khz; 1 kw-U, DA-2. TL: N25 59 30 W81 37 30. Hrs open: 24 5043 E. Tamiami Tr., Naples, 34113. Phone: (239) 732-9369. Fax: (239) 732-7267.E-mail: bladd@relevantradio.com Licensee: Sovereign City Radio Services LLC (acq 2-6-2009; grpsl). Population served: 250,000 Natl. Network: Jones Radio Networks, USA, . Rgnl. Network: Florida Radio Net. Arter & Hadden. Format: Btfl music. News staff: 2; News: 5.5 hrs wkly. Target aud: 45 plus; upscale & professional adults. ♦Robert Ladd, opns VP.

Marianna

***WAYP(FM)—** May 1985: 88.3 mhz; 750 w horiz, 70 kw vert. Ant 344 ft TL: N30 26 18.1 W85 25 27. Stereo. Hrs open: 24 Box 4188, Tallahassee, 32315. Phone: (850) 422-1929. Fax: (850) 297-1888. Web Site:wayp.wayfm.com Licensee: WAY-FM Media Group Inc. (acq 11-13-2007; $210,000). Population served: 823,000 Format: Christian. ♦Steve Young, gen mgr.

***WHMF(FM)**—Not on air, target date: unknown: 91.1 mhz; 1.5 kw vert. Ant 89 ft TL: N30 45 23 W85 11 42. Hrs open: 2327 W. Orlando Rd., Panama City, 32405. Phone: (850) 763-6489. Licensee: Health and Happiness Radio Inc. ♦Leonard Moore, pres.

WJAQ(FM)— Sept 1, 1964: 100.9 mhz; 5.9 kw horiz. 331 ft TL: N30 47 01 W85 15 18. Stereo. Hrs open: 24 Prog sep from AM 4376 Lafayette St., Suite A, 32446. Phone: (850) 482-3046. Fax: (850) 482-3049.E-mail: wjaq@phon1.com Population served: 100,000 Natl. Network: ABC, . Wire Svc: UPI Format: Country. News staff: one; News: 3 hrs wkly. Target aud: General.

WTOT(AM)— Sept 24, 1958: 980 khz; 1 kw-D, 500 w-N. TL: N30 47 01 W85 15 18. Hrs open: 24 Box 569, 32447-0569. Secondary address: 4376 Lafayette St., Suite A 32446-3300. Phone: (850) 482-3046. Fax: (850) 482-3049.E-mail: wjaq@phon1.com Licensee: MFR Inc. (acq 10-8-96; with co-located FM). Population served: 75,000 Natl. Network: ABC, . Format: Adult standards. Target aud: 25 plus. ♦John Biddinger, CEO; Ed Cearley, pres, gen mgr, gen mgr; Don Moore, sls dir, news dir, pub affrs dir; Curtis Blount, chief of engrg.

WTYS(AM)— Apr 3, 1947: 1340 khz; 1 kw-U. TL: N30 45 49 W85 13 52. Hrs open: 24 Box 777, 32447. Secondary address: 2725 Jefferson St. 32448. Phone: (850) 482-2131. Fax: (850) 526-3687.E-mail: wtysradio@embarqmail.com Web Site:www.wtys.cc Licensee: James L. Adams Jr. (acq 12-1-98; $250,000 with WTYS-FM Marianna). Population served: 42,000 Rgnl. Network: Florida Radio Net. Florida's Radio Networks Format: Classic country. News staff: one; News: 7 hrs wkly. Target aud: 25-64; adults in Jackson County & the surrounding area. Spec prog: Farm one hr, gospel 11 hrs wkly. ♦James Adams, gen mgr; Jerry Jackson, opns dir.

WTYS-FM— Aug 4, 1995: 94.1 mhz; 4.4 kw. Ant 384 ft TL: N30 45 47 W85 13 52. Stereo. Hrs open: 24 Box 777, 32447. Secondary address: 2725 Jefferson St. 32448. Phone: (850) 482-2131. Fax: (850) 526-3687.E-mail: wtysradio@embarqmail.com Web Site:www.wtys.cc Licensee: James L. Adams Jr. (acq 12-1-98; with WTYS(AM) Marianna). Population served: 350000 Natl. Network: CBS, . Rgnl. Network: Florida Radio Net. Florida's Radio Networks Format: Southern gospel. News staff: one; News: 5 hrs wkly. Target aud: 25-64; adults in Jackson county, FL & surrounding area. ♦James Adams, gen mgr; Jerry Jackson, opns mgr; Tom O'Brien, news dir.

Mary Esther

WYZB(FM)— May 1986: 105.5 mhz; 25 kw. Ant 305 ft TL: N30 24 42 W86 37 14. Stereo. Hrs open: 225 N.W. Hollywood Blvd., Fort Walton Beach, 32548. Phone: (850) 244-1055 (studio).E-mail: sales@wyzb.com Web Site:www.wyzb.com Licensee: Cumulus Licensing Corp. Group owner: Cumulus Media Inc. (acq 1-10-2003; grpsl). Format: Country. Target aud: 25-54. ♦Georgia Edmiston, gen mgr.

Mayo

***WGSG(FM)—** 1991: 89.5 mhz; 2.5 kw horiz, 20 kw vert. 249 ft TL: N30 02 30 W83 07 45. Hrs open: Box 644, Whispering Oaks, 32066. Phone: (386) 294-2525. Fax: (386) 294-2525. Licensee: True Concepts of Levy County Inc. Format: Relg. ♦Terri Simmons, gen mgr.

Melbourne

WAOA-FM— Nov 9, 1972: 107.1 mhz; 100 kw. Ant 500 ft TL: N28 08 14 W80 42 11. Stereo. Hrs open: 1775 W. Hibiscus Blvd., Suite 301, 32901. Phone: (321) 984-1000. Fax: (321) 724-1565. Web Site:www.wa1a.com Licensee: Cumulus Licensing Corp. Population served: 750000 Format: CHR. Target aud: 25-54.

WBVD(FM)— Dec 25, 1965: 95.1 mhz; 1.2 kw. Ant 210 ft TL: N28 04 41 W80 35 57. Stereo. Hrs open: 24 Prog sep from AM 1388 S. Babcock St., 32901. Phone: (321) 733-1000. Fax: (321) 725-6821.E-mail: info@951thebeat.com Web Site:www.951thebeat.com Licensee: Capstar TX LP Format: Top-40. News: one hr wkly. ♦Jeff McKeel, sls dir; Doug Remington, engrg dir.

WCIF(FM)— Jan 1, 1980: 106.3 mhz; 3 kw. 230 ft TL: N28 04 40 W80 39 26. Stereo. Hrs open: Box 366, 32902. Secondary address: 3301 Dairy Rd. 32904. Phone: (321) 725-9243.E-mail: info@wcif.com Web Site:www.wcif.com Licensee: First Baptist Church Inc. Format: Relg. ♦Lee J. Martinez, gen mgr; Martha Root, opns mgr.

WDMC(AM)— Jan 4, 1956: 920 khz; 5 kw-D, 1 kw-N, DA-3. TL: N28 08 11 W80 41 20. Stereo. Hrs open: 24 1800 Turtle Mound Rd., 32934-8105. Phone: (321) 757-7717. Fax: (321) 757-7705.E-mail: info@divinemercyradio.com Licensee: Divine Mercy Communications Inc. (acq 3-25-2008; $650,000). Population served: 500,000 Rgnl. Network: S.E. Agri. Format: Catholic. ♦Robert G. Groppe, pres.

***WFIT(FM)—** April 1975: 89.5 mhz; 900 w horiz, 4.6 kw vert. 112 ft TL: N28 03 51 W80 37 25. (CP: 700 w, ant 151 ft.). Stereo. Hrs open: 24 150 W. University Blvd., 32901. Phone: (321) 674-8140. Fax: (321) 674-8139.E-mail: wfit@fit.edu Web Site:www.wfit.org Licensee: Florida Institute of Technology. Population served: 400,000 Format: News, AAA. News: 40 hrs wkly. Target aud: 25-54; pub radio listeners. ♦Terri Wright, gen mgr.

WINT(AM)— Mar 8, 1968: 1560 khz; 5 kw-D. TL: N28 07 40 W80 42 29. Hrs open: 6 AM-7 PM 1775 W. Hibiscus Blvd., Suite 301, 32901. Phone: (321) 984-1000. Fax: (321) 724-1565. Licensee: Cumulus Licensing Corp. Group owner:Cumulus Media Inc. (acq 5-23-2001; with co-located FM). Population served: 40,236 Natl. Network: ESPN Radio, . Erwin Krasnow. Format: Sports. Target aud: 35-64. ♦Sue Garrett, gen mgr.

WMMB(AM)— 1947: 1240 khz; 1 kw-U. TL: N28 04 40 W80 35 55. (CP: 940 w-U. TL: N28 04 42 W80 35 56). Hrs open: 24 1388 S. Babcock St., 32901. Phone: (321) 733-1000. Fax: (321) 725-6821.E-mail: wmmb1240@aol.com Web Site:www.wmmbam.com Licensee: Capstar TX L.P. Group owner: Clear Channel Communications Inc. (acq 8-30-00; grpsl). Population served: 200,000 Natl. Network: Westwood One, . Rgnl. Network: Florida Radio Net. Florida's Radio Networks Robert A. DePont. Format: Adult standards, swing. News staff: 3; News: 4 hrs wkly. Target aud: 35 plus. ♦Barbara Latham, gen mgr; Larry Brewer, progmg dir.

Merritt Island

WWBC(AM)—See Cocoa

Mexico Beach

WEBZ(FM)— Nov 28, 1990: 99.3 mhz; 50 kw. Ant 519 ft TL: N30 00 21 W85 20 36. Stereo. Hrs open: 24 1834 Lisenby Ave., Panama City, 32405. Phone: (850) 769-1408. Fax: (850) 769-0659.E-mail: info@panamacity@clearchannel.com Licensee: Clear Channel Broadcasting Licenses Inc. Group owner: Clear Channel Communications Inc. (acq 11-21-97; grpsl). Lukas, McGowan, Nace & Gutierrez. Format: Oldies. Target aud: 30 plus; professional adults. ♦Pete Norden, gen mgr.

Miami

WACC(AM)—(Hialeah, Dec 1, 1987: 830 khz; 1 kw-U, DA-2. TL: N25 46 22 W80 25 16. Stereo. Hrs open: 24 1779 N.W. 28th St., 33142. Phone: (305) 638-9729. Fax: (305) 638-0571.E-mail: isaul@paxcc.org Web Site:www.paxcc.org Licensee: Radio Peace Catholic Broadcasting Inc. (acq 11-27-96; $2.55 million). Thiemain & Evenas. Format: Relg, talk, Sp. News staff: one; News: 18 hrs wkly. Target aud: 25-54; adults. ♦Reverend Jose L. Hernando, pres.

WAMR-FM— June 7, 1974: 107.5 mhz; 95 kw horiz, 80 kw vert. 1,007 ft TL: N25 57 59 W80 12 33. Stereo. Hrs open: 800 Douglas Rd., Suite 111, Coral Gables, 33134. Phone: (305) 447-1140. Fax: (305) 643-1075.E-mail: info@wamr.com Web Site:www.univision.com Licensee: WQBA-FM License Corp. Group owner: Univision Radio (acq 9-22-2003; grpsl). Format: Sp, adult contemp. ♦Claudia Puig, gen mgr.

WAQI(AM)— 1939: 710 khz; 50 kw-U, DA-2. TL: N25 58 07 W80 22 44. Hrs open: 800 Douglas Rd., Suite 111, Coral Gables, 33134. Phone: (305) 447-1140. Fax: (305) 442-7676.E-mail: gfernandez@univisionradio.com Web Site:www.univisionradio.com Licensee: Licensee Corporation #1. Group owner: Univision Radio (acq 9-22-2003; grpsl). Population served: 334,859 Format: Sp, news/talk, entertainment. ♦Claudia Puig, sr VP, gen mgr; Yvette Sanguilty, sls dir; Monica Rabassa, mktg dir, prom dir; Armando Perez-Roura, progmg dir; Max Fitero, chief of engrg.

WAXY(AM)—See South Miami

WBGG-FM—See Fort Lauderdale

WCMQ-FM—See Hialeah

***WDNA(FM)—** June 10, 1980: 88.9 mhz; 7.4 kw. 1,145 ft TL: N25 32 24 W80 28 07. Stereo. Hrs open: 24 2921 Coral Way, 33145. Phone: (305) 662-8889. Fax: (305) 662-1975.E-mail: feedback@wdna.org Web Site:www.wdna.org Licensee: Bascomb Memorial Broadcasting Foundation Inc. (acq 1971). Population served: 1,500,000 Haley, Bader & Potts. Format: Jazz, Sp. News: 10 hrs wkly. Target aud: General; minorities. Spec prog: World music 10 hrs wkly. ♦Maggie Pelleya, gen mgr & stn mgr.

WEDR(FM)— May 18, 1963: 99.1 mhz; 100 kw. 926 ft TL: N25 57 30 W80 12 44. (CP: TL: N25 57 59 W80 12 33). Stereo. Hrs open: 2741 N. 29th Ave., Hollywood, 33020. Phone: (305) 623-7711 / (305) 444-4404. Fax: (305) 624-2736.E-mail: info@wedr.com Web Site:www.wedr.com Licensee: Cox Radio Inc. Group owner: Cox Broadcasting (acq 8-00; grpsl). Population served: 700,000 Smithwick & Belendiuk. Format: Hip-hop. ♦Jerry Rushin, gen mgr; Maestro Powell, prom dir; Tony Field, progmg dir.

WFLC(FM)— July 20, 1951: 97.3 mhz; 100 kw. 800 ft TL: N25 57 30 W80 12 44. Stereo. Hrs open: 2741 N. 29th Ave., Hollywood, 33020. Phone: (305) 444-4404. Fax: (954) 847-3223.E-mail: mike.disney@cox.com Web Site:www.coastfm.com Licensee: Cox Radio Inc. Group owner: Cox Communications Inc. Natl. Rep: Christal,. Format: Old school, rhythm & blues. Target aud: 25-54. ♦Mike G. Disney, gen mgr.

WHDR(FM)— Nov 1, 1960: 93.1 mhz; 100 kw. Ant 1,007 ft TL: N25 58 03 W80 12 34. Stereo. Hrs open: 24 2741 N. 29th Ave., Hollywood, 33020. Phone: (305) 444-4404. Fax: (954) 847-3223. Web Site:93rock.com Licensee: Cox Radio Inc. Group owner: Cox Communications Inc. (acq 5-18-2000; grpsl). Population served: 397,900 Natl. Rep: Christal,. Format: Active rock. Target aud: 18-49; upscale, educ adults with hip active lifestyles. ♦Michael Disney, gen mgr.

WHYI-FM—See Fort Lauderdale

WINZ(AM)— 1946: 940 khz; 50 kw-D, 10 kw-N. TL: N25 57 36 W80 16 13. Hrs open: 24 7601 Riviera Blvd., Miramar, 33023. Phone: (954) 862-2000. Fax: (954) 862-4012.E-mail: info@am940southflorida.com Web Site:www.am940southflorida.com Licensee: Clear Channel Broadcasting Licenses Inc. Group owner: Clear Channel Communications Inc. (acq 11-21-97; grpsl). Population served: 3,000,000 Natl. Network: Fox Sports, . Rgnl. Network: Florida Radio Net. Natl. Rep: Clear Channel,. Format: Sports. News staff: 20. Target aud: 35-64; upscale, professional, managerial adults. ♦Ken Brady, gen mgr & gen sls mgr.

WIOD(AM)— Jan 19, 1926: 610 khz; 10 kw-U, DA-N. TL: N25 50 58 W80 09 18. Stereo. Hrs open: 7601 Riviera Blvd, Miramar, 33023. Phone: (954) 862-2000. Fax: (954) 862-4012. Fax: (954) 862-4015.E-mail: newsradio610@ccmiami.com Web Site:www.newsradio610.com Licensee: Clear Channel Radio Licenses Inc. Group owner: Clear Channel

Communications Inc. (acq 11-21-97; grpsl). Population served: 334,859 Wire Svc: UPI Format: News/talk. Target aud: 25-64. ♦Michael Crusham, opns VP; Ken Brady, gen sls mgr; Peter Bolger, progmg dir.

WKAT(AM)—See North Miami

***WKCP(FM)**— Aug 24, 1970: 89.7 mhz; 100 kw. Ant 1,014 ft TL: N25 32 24 W80 28 07. Stereo. Hrs open: 24 330 S.W. Second St., Suite 207, Fort Lauderdale, 33312. Phone: (866) 592-4160. Web Site:classicalsouthflorida.publicradio.org Licensee: American Public Media Group (acq 3-14-2008; $20 million). Population served: 3,500,000 Wiley Rein LLP. Format: Classical. ♦Douglas C. Evans, gen mgr.

WKIS(FM)—(Boca Raton, October 1965: 99.9 mhz; 100 kw. 986 ft TL: N25 59 34 W80 10 27. Stereo. Hrs open: 24 Prog sep from AM 194 N.W.187th St., 33169. Phone: (305) 654-1700. Fax: (305) 654-1715.E-mail: info@wkis.com Web Site:www.wkis.com Natl. Network: Westwood One, . Format: Country. News staff: one; News: 2 hrs wkly. Target aud: 25-54. ♦George Corso, CEO; Joe Bell, VP; Carole Bowen, gen sls mgr; Bob Barnett, progmg dir.

***WLRN-FM**— February 1948: 91.3 mhz; 47 kw. Ant 935 ft TL: N25 58 46 W80 11 46. Stereo. Hrs open: 24 172 N.E. 15th St., 33132. Phone: (305) 995-1717. Fax: (305) 995-2221.E-mail: radio@wlrn.org Web Site:www.wlrn.org Licensee: School Board of Miami Dade County Florida. Population served: 2,600,000 Natl. Network: NPR, PRI, AP Network News, Premiere Radio Networks, . Fla. Pub. Leibowitz & Associates, P.A. Wire Svc: AP Format: News/talk info. News staff: 7; News: 111 hrs wkly. Target aud: General; well educated, moderate to high income bracket. Spec prog: Haitian 3 hrs wkly. ♦Karen Echols, CFO; John Labonia, gen mgr; Ted Eldredge, stn mgr; Peter J. Maerz, progmg mgr; Mario Burrios, chief of engrg. Co-owned TV: *WLRN-TV affil.

WLYF(FM)— 1948: 101.5 mhz; 100 kw. 810 ft TL: N25 57 59 W80 12 44. Stereo. Hrs open: 24 20450 N.W. 2nd Ave., 33169-2505. Phone: (305) 521-5100. Fax: (305) 652-0098.E-mail: litefm@litemiami.com Web Site:www.litemiami.com Licensee: Lincoln Financial Media Co. of Florida. Group owner: Jefferson-Pilot Communications Co. (acq 4-3-2006; grpsl). Population served: 3,111,400 Natl. Rep: Interep,. Wire Svc: AP Format: Adult contemp. News: 2 hrs wkly. Target aud: 25-54; women. ♦Jon Boscia, CEO; Don Benson, pres; Dennis P. Collins, sr VP, gen mgr; Rob Sidney, opns dir, sls dir, progmg dir; Rosemary Zimmerman, natl sls mgr; Danielle Webb, rgnl sls mgr; Nicole Gates, mktg dir, prom dir; Gary Blau, engrg dir; Tina Marcos, traf mgr.

WMBM(AM)—See Miami Beach

WMGE(FM)—See Miami Beach

WMIB(FM)—See Fort Lauderdale

WMYM(AM)— Aug 15, 1997: 990 khz; 5 kw-U. TL: N25 50 34 W80 25 12. Hrs open: 24 2150 W. 68th St., Suite 202, Hialeah, 33016. Phone: (305) 823-0990. Fax: (305) 823-9322. Licensee: Radio Disney Group LLC. Group owner: ABC Inc. (acq 7-30-99; $7.4 million). Format: Radio Disney, top 40. Kids and families. ♦Gilbert Salguero, gen mgr; Jeff Schwartz, opns dir; John Craveno, sls dir; John Hurni, chief of engrg.

WNMA(AM)—(Miami Springs, May 18, 1958: 1210 khz; 25 kw-D, 2.5 kw-N, DA-2. TL: N25 54 00 W80 21 49. Hrs open: 24 7250 N.W. 58th St., 33166. Phone: (786) 497-3414. Fax: (786) 497-3412.E-mail: eduardor@mrbi.net Web Site:www.mrbi.net Licensee: Multicultural Radio Broadcasting Licensee LLC. Group owner: Multicultural Radio Broadcasting Inc. (acq 2-4-2004; grpsl). Format: Sp, talk, sports. ♦Eduardo Rueda, gen mgr.

WOCN(AM)— Dec 22, 1956: 1450 khz; 1 kw-U. TL: N25 50 24 W80 11 20. Hrs open: 24 350 N.E. 71 St., 33138. Phone: (305) 759-7280. Fax: (305) 759-2276.E-mail: Daniel@1450espndeportes.com Web Site:www.wocn.net Licensee: IM FL Licenses LLC. (acq 7-12-2006; $6 million). Population served: 334,859 Natl. Network: ESPN Deportes, . Gunsten, Yonkley. Wire Svc: AP Format: Sp sports. Target aud: General. ♦David Jacobs, pres, VP; Richard Vega, gen mgr.

WPOW(FM)— June 15, 1985: 96.5 mhz; 100 kw. 1,007 ft TL: N25 57 59 W80 12 33. Stereo. Hrs open: 20295 N.W. 2nd Ave., Suite 300, 33169. Phone: (305) 653-6796. Fax: (305) 770-1456. Web Site:www.power96.com Licensee: Beasley FM Acquisition Corp. Group owner: Beasley Broadcast Group (acq 8-94). Population served: 3,000,000 Format: CHR. ♦George Beasley, pres; Matthew Bell, gen mgr; John Jaras, gen sls mgr; Ira Wolf, natl sls mgr, opns.

WQAM(AM)— May 1921: 560 khz; 5 kw-D, 1 kw-N. TL: N25 44 36 W80 09 14. Stereo. Hrs open: 24 194 NW 187th Street, 33169. Phone: (305) 654-1700. Fax: (305) 654-1717.E-mail: info@wqam.com Web Site:www.wqam.com Licensee: Beasley-Reed Broadcasting. Group owner: Beasley Broadcast Group Population served: 1,100,000 Natl. Network: Sporting News Radio Network, . Natl. Rep: Eastman Radio,. Winston & Strawn. Format: Sports. Target aud: 25-54; males. ♦Joe Bell, gen mgr; Chris Jones, gen sls mgr; Lisa Blum, natl sls mgr; Josh Darrow, progmg dir; George Corso, chief of engrg.

WQBA(AM)— 1947: 1140 khz; 50 kw-D, 10 kw-N, DA-2. TL: N25 45 46 W80 29 03. Hrs open: 800 Douglas Rd., Annex 1, Suite 111, Coral Gables, 33134. Phone: (305) 447-1140. Fax: (305) 441-2454. Web Site:www.wqba.com Licensee: WQBA-AM License Corp. Group owner: Univision Radio (acq 9-22-2003; grpsl). Population served: 1,000,000 Format: News/talk, Sp. ♦Claudia Puig, sr VP, VP & gen mgr.

WRHC(AM)—See Coral Gables

WRMA(FM)—See Fort Lauderdale

WRTO-FM—(Goulds, February 1976: 98.3 mhz; 1.1 kw. 462 ft TL: N25 32 24 W80 28 07. (CP: 100 kw, ant 1,627 ft.). Stereo. Hrs open: 24 800 Douglas Rd., Suite 111, Coral Gables, 33134. Phone: (305) 447-1140. Fax: (305) 529-6631. Web Site:www.univision.com Licensee: License Corp. #2. Group owner: Univision Radio (acq 9-22-2003; grpsl). Population served: 365,000 Format: Latin/tropical, Sp. ♦Claudia Puig, gen mgr; Monica Rabassa, mktg dir.

WSUA(AM)— June 20, 1969: 1260 khz; 5 kw-U, DA-2. TL: N25 46 23 W80 25 17. Hrs open: 24 2100 Coral Way, Suite 201, 33145. Phone: (305) 285-1260. Fax: (305) 858-5907.E-mail: info@wsua.com Web Site:www.caracolusa.com Licensee: WSUA Broadcasting Corp. (acq 7-28-2005; $72,000 for 24% of stock). Population served: 106,873 Format: Sp, News/talk. News staff: 7; News: 31 hrs wkly. Target aud: 18-54; Latin American audience. ♦Tomas Martinez, gen mgr.

WVUM(FM)—See Coral Gables

WWFE(AM)— July 1989: 670 khz; 50 kw-D, 2.5 kw-N, DA-2. TL: N25 51 27 W80 28 52. Stereo. Hrs open: 24 330 S.W. 27th Ave., Suite 207, 33135. Phone: (305) 541-3300. Fax: (305) 541-7470.E-mail: anavidal@lapoderosa.com Web Site:www.lapoderosa.com Licensee: Fenix Broadcasting Corp. (acq 6-22-93; $2.7 million; 7-12-93). Population served: 1,800,000 Natl. Rep: Lotus Entravision Reps LLC,. Leventhal, Senter & Lerman, P.L.L.C. Format: Sp, var/div, news/talk. News staff: 4; News: 27 hrs wkly. Target aud: 25-54. ♦Ana M. Vidal Rodriguez, VP; Ana Vidal Rodriguez, gen mgr; Jorge A. Rodriguez, pres & gen sls mgr.

Miami Beach

WMBM(AM)— 1949: 1490 khz; 1 kw-U. TL: N25 46 10 W80 08 11. Hrs open: 24 13242 NW 7 Ave., North Miami, 33168. Phone: (305) 769-1100. Fax: (305) 769-9975.E-mail: wmbm@wmbm.com Web Site:www.wmbm.com Licensee: New Birth Broadcasting Corp. (acq 3-8-95; 5-8-95). Population served: 50,000 Natl. Network: American Urban, Westwood One, . Pepper & Corazzini. Format: Gospel, community talk. News staff: one; News: 3 hrs wkly. Target aud: 25 plus; mature Black, self-motivated, Christian, professionals. ♦Caroline Kelly, sr VP; Victor T. Curry, pres & gen mgr; Greyory Cooper, progmg mgr.

WMGE(FM)— 1961: 94.9 mhz; 100 kw. 1,007 ft TL: N25 46 29 W80 11 19. Stereo. Hrs open: 7601 Riviera Blvd., Miramar, 33023. Phone: (954) 862-2000. Fax: (305) 862-4012.E-mail: info@mega949.com Web Site:www.mega949.com Licensee: Clear Channel Broadcasting Licenses Inc. Group owner: Clear Channel Communications Inc. (acq 11-21-97; grpsl). Population served: 3,000,000 Natl. Network: Westwood One, . Format: Latino. Target aud: 18-34. ♦Desi Hernandez, gen sls mgr.

WMIA-FM— July 1, 1968: 93.9 mhz; 98 kw. Ant 1,007 ft TL: N25 58 02 W80 12 34. Stereo. Hrs open: 7601 Riviera Blvd, Miramar, 33023. Phone: (954) 862-2000. Fax: (954) 862-4012. Web Site:www.939mia.com Licensee: Clear Channel Radio Licenses Inc. Group owner: Clear Channel Communications Inc. (acq 11-21-97; grpsl). Population served: 3,000,000 Wiley, Rein & Fielding. Format: Rhythmic adult contemp. Target aud: 25-54. ♦Jamie Kaufman, gen mgr.

Miami Springs

WNMA(AM)—Licensed to Miami Springs. See Miami

Micanopy

WSKY-FM— Sept 7, 1985: 97.3 mhz; 50 kw. Ant 492 ft TL: N29 32 09 W82 19 18. Stereo. Hrs open: 24 3600 N.W. 43rd St., Suite B, Gainesville, 32606-8127. Phone: (352) 377-0985. Fax: (352) 337-2968. Web Site:www.thesky973.com Licensee: Entercom Gainesville License L.L.C. Group owner: Entercom Communications Corp. (acq 3-18-98; $2.8 million). Natl. Rep: Christal,. Fisher, Wayland, Cooper, Leader & Zaragoza. Format: News/talk. Target aud: 18-54. ♦David Field, CEO, pres, progmg dir; Mark Leopold, VP, gen mgr & gen sls mgr.

Midway

WFLA-FM— 1996: 100.7 mhz; 11.5 kw. Ant 489 ft TL: N30 29 32 W84 17 13. Hrs open: Bldg. G, 325 John Knox Rd., Tallahassee, 32303. Phone: (850) 422-3107. Fax: (850) 383-0747.E-mail: mattmillar@clearchannel.com Web Site:www.1270wfla.com Licensee: Clear Channel Broadcasting Licenses Inc. Group owner: Clear Channel Communications Inc. (acq 11-21-97; grpsl). Format: Talk radio. ♦Lisa Rice, gen mgr; Jeff Horn, opns mgr; Jason Sauer, prom dir.

Milton

WEBY(AM)— 1978: 1330 khz; 25 kw-D, 79 w-N, DA-D. TL: N30 31 05 W87 04 56. Hrs open: 24 7179 Printers Alley, 32583. Phone: (850) 983-2242. Fax: (850) 983-3231.E-mail: weby@1330weby.com Web Site:www.1330weby.com Licensee: Spinnaker License Corp. (acq 5-28-2002). Population served: 500,000 Natl. Network: Jones Radio Networks, . Format: Talk, news. News staff: one; News: 15 hrs wkly. Target aud: 35 plus; affuent, educated adults. Spec prog: Christian 7 hrs wkly / Florida State football. ♦Mike Bates, pres & gen mgr; Anthony Daughtery, opns mgr; Dave Daughtry, news dir.

WECM(AM)— Dec 18, 1957: 1490 khz; 1 kw-U. TL: N30 37 30 W87 02 54. Hrs open: 24 6583 Berryhill Rd., 32570. Phone: (850) 623-1490. Fax: (850) 623-6818.E-mail: station@memories1490.com Licensee: Camax Communications Group Inc. (acq 9-29-2003). Population served: 50,000 Format: Sp. ♦The Baron of Fulwood, COO, VP & gen mgr; Steve Walker, progmg dir.

***WEGS(FM)**— Oct 15, 1985: 91.7 mhz; 20 kw. Ant 367 ft TL: N30 37 20 W87 05 12. Stereo. Hrs open: 1836 Olive Rd., Pensacola, 32514. Secondary address: 505 Josephine St., Titusville 32796. Phone: (850) 476-1932. Fax: (850) 447-9650.E-mail: wegs917@aol.com Web Site:www.olivebaptist.org Licensee: Florida Public Radio Inc. Format: Talk, adult Christian contemp. ♦Dave Talley, gen mgr & chief of engrg.

WXBM-FM— Apr 28, 1964: 102.7 mhz; 100 kw. 1,328 ft TL: N30 35 18 W87 33 16. Stereo. Hrs open: 6085 Quintet Rd., Pace, 32571. Phone: (850) 994-5357. Fax: (850) 994-7191.E-mail: feedback@wxbm.com Web Site:www.wxbm.com Licensee: 6 Johnson Road Licenses Inc. Group owner: Pamal Broadcasting Ltd. (acq 10-19-2001; grpsl). Population served: 850,000 Format: Country. ♦Dave Cobb, gen mgr.

Mims

WPGS(AM)— May 5, 1986: 840 khz; 1 kw-D. TL: N28 44 20 W80 53 02. Stereo. Hrs open: Sunrise-sunset 805 N. Dixie Ave., Titusville, 32796. Phone: (321) 383-1000.E-mail: wpgs840@aol.com Web Site:www.talkstar840.com Licensee: WPGS Inc. (acq 3-93; $65,000; 3-29-93). Population served: 75,000 Natl. Network: USA, . Format: Talk. ♦Ed Shiflett, pres, gen mgr; Jay Rowan, chief of engrg.

Miramar Beach

WSBZ(FM)— Oct 18, 1994: 106.3 mhz; 3 kw. 328 ft TL: N30 23 07 W86 18 03. Hrs open: 10859 Emerald Coast Pkwy. W., Destin, 32541. Phone: (850) 267-3279. Fax: (850) 231-1775.E-mail: office@wsbz.com Web Site:www.wsbz.com Licensee: Carter Broadcasting Inc. (acq 9-10-99). Format: Smooth jazz (new adult contemp). ♦Renee Carter, CFO; Mark Carter, gen mgr.

Monticello

***WFRF-FM**— December 1996: 105.7 mhz; 16 kw. Ant 410 ft TL: N30 23 08 W83 50 05. Hrs open: 24 Box 181000, Tallahassee, 32318-0009. Phone: (850) 201-1070. Fax: (850) 201-1071.E-mail: mailbox@faithradio.us Web Site:www.faithradio.us Licensee: Faith Radio Network Inc. (acq 1-26-2004; $800,000). Population served: 200,000 Natl. Network: CBS, . Format: Relg. Target aud: 12+. ♦Scott Beigle, gen mgr.

***WKVH(FM)**— March 2003: 91.9 mhz; 1.5 kw. Ant 1,322 ft TL: N30 40 13 W83 56 26. Stereo. Hrs open: 24 2351 Sunset Blvd., Suite

170-218, Rocklin, CA, 95765. Phone: (916) 251-1600. Fax: (916) 251-1650.E-mail: klove@klove.com Web Site:www.klove.com Licensee: Educational Media Foundation. Group owner: EMF Broadcasting. Natl. Network: K-Love, . Shaw Pittman. Format: Contemp Christian. News staff: 3. Target aud: 25-44; Judeo Christian, female. ♦Richard Jenkins, pres; Keith Whipple, dev dir; Eric Allen, natl sls mgr; David Pierce, progmg mgr; Ed Lenane, news dir; Sam Wallington, engrg dir; Karen Johnson, news rptr.

Mount Dora

WMGF(FM)— 1966: 107.7 mhz; 100 kw. 1,584 ft TL: N28 55 16 W81 19 09. Stereo. Hrs open: 24 2500 Maitland Ctr. Pkwy., Suite 401, Maitland, 32751. Phone: (407) 916-7800. Fax: (407) 916-0329.E-mail: info@magic107.com Web Site:www.magic107.com Licensee: Clear Channel Radio Licenses Inc. Group owner: Clear Channel Communications Inc. (acq 11-21-97; grpsl). Population served: 3,442,300 Rgnl rep: Paul Rogers Wiley, Rein and Fielding. Format: Soft adult contemp. News staff: one; News: 2 hrs wkly. Target aud: 25-54; working women. Spec prog: Contemp Christian mus 20 hrs wkly. ♦Linda Byrd, gen mgr; Rochelle Rich, gen sls mgr; Chris Kampmeier, progmg dir; Shawn Williams, traf mgr; Rick Everett, mktg.

Murdock

WBCG(FM)— Oct 22, 2001: 98.9 mhz; 5.5 kw. Ant 341 ft TL: N27 00 09 W82 10 54. Hrs open: 24 24100 Tiseo Blvd., Unit 10, Port Charlotte, 33980. Phone: (941) 639-1112. Fax: (941) 206-9296.E-mail: wbcgbeachradio@cs.com Licensee: Concord Media Group Inc. (acq 8-28-2001). Population served: 65,000 Rgnl. Network: Florida Radio Net. Florida's Radio Networks Rosenman & Colin, L.L.P. Format: Adult contemp. News: 2 hrs wkly. Target aud: Adults 25+; core 35-54 female. ♦Mark Jorgenson, gen mgr; Michael G. Keating, progmg dir.

Naples

WARO(FM)— May 8, 1962: 94.5 mhz; 100 kw. 1,049 ft TL: N26 20 26 W81 42 48. Stereo. Hrs open: 24 Prog sep from AM 2824 Palm Beach Blvd., Fort Myers, 33916. Phone: (239) 337-2346. Fax: (239) 479-5581. Web Site:www.classicrock945.com Licensee: Meridian Broadcasting Inc. Format: Classic rock. Target aud: 25-54; men. Spec prog: Relg 2 hrs wkly. ♦Mike Allen, progmg dir.

***WBGY(FM)**— August 2004: 88.1 mhz; 110 w vert. Ant 59 ft TL: N25 51 56 W81 23 09. Hrs open: 297 Fillmore St., 34104. Phone: (239) 404-9849.E-mail: wbby@earthlink.net Licensee: Everglades City Broadcasting Co. Inc. (acq 3-30-2004; $25,000). Format: Country. ♦Robert Ladd, pres.

WNOG(AM)— Oct 14, 1954: 1270 khz; 5 kw-D, 1.9 kw-N, DA-2. TL: N26 15 26 W81 40 33. Hrs open: 24
Rebroadcasts WINK(AM) Fort Myers 100%.
2824 Palm Beach Blvd., Fort Myers, 33916. Phone: (239) 337-2346. Fax: (239) 337-2346. Web Site:www.winkwnog.com Licensee: Meridian Broadcasting Inc. (group owner; (acq 12-1-96; grpsl). Population served: 516,200 Natl. Network: CBS, . Natl. Rep: McGavren Guild,. Leibowitz & Associates. Format: News/talk. Target aud: 35 plus. ♦Joseph C. Schwantzel, pres; Paul Thomas, gen mgr; Wayne Simons, sls dir; Jim Watkins, progmg dir; Keith Stulhmann, engrg dir.

WSGL(FM)— May 10, 1980: 104.7 mhz; 14 kw. 450 ft TL: N26 07 34 W81 43 18. Stereo. Hrs open: 24 10915 K-Nine Dr., 2nd Fl., Bonita Springs, 34135. Phone: (239) 495-8383. Fax: (239) 495-0883.E-mail: wsgl@rendabroadcasting.com Web Site:www.wsgl1047.com Licensee: Renda Broadcasting Corp. of Nevada. Group owner: Renda Broadcasting Corp. (acq 11-10-98; $3.65 million). Population served: 300,000 Format: Hot adult contemp. News: one hr wkly. Target aud: 25-54; women. Spec prog: Classic rock 70s & 80s music 5 hrs wkly. ♦Tony Renda Jr., gen mgr; Randy Savage, progmg dir.

***WSOR(FM)**— 1989: 90.9 mhz; 36 kw. Ant 902 ft TL: N26 20 29 W81 42 38. Stereo. Hrs open: 24 5800 100th Way N. St, Saint Peterburgs, 33708. Phone: (727) 391-9994. Fax: (727) 397-6425.E-mail: wkes@moody.edu Web Site:www.wkes.fm Licensee: Moody Bible Institute. (acq 1996). Population served: 650,000 Natl. Network: Salem Radio Network, . Wire Svc: AP Format: Christian teaching, talk, music. News staff: one. Target aud: 40 plus. ♦Mike Gleichman, opns mgr, mus dir; Pierre Chestang, gen mgr & progmg dir; John Stortz, chief of engrg.

***WSRX(FM)**— August 1988: 89.5 mhz; 100 kw. Ant 309 ft TL: N26 07 12 W81 40 58. Hrs open: 24 3805 The Lords Way, 34114. Phone: (239) 775-8950. Fax: (239) 774-5889.E-mail: praisefm895@msn.com Web Site:www.praisefm.com Licensee: Shadowlawn Association Inc. (acq 1-95; $236,000; 2-27-95). Format: Christian. Target aud: 18-40. ♦Arnie Coones, gen mgr.

WTLT(FM)— Dec 1, 1971: 93.7 mhz; 21 kw. 328 ft TL: N26 19 00 W81 47 13. Stereo. Hrs open: 24 2824 Palm Beach Blvd., Fort Myers, 33916. Phone: (239) 337-2346. Fax: (239) 332-0767. Web Site:www.lite973.com Licensee: Meridian Broadcasting Inc. (group owner; acq 12-1-96; grpsl). Population served: 532,600 Natl. Rep: McGavren Guild,. Leibowitz & Associates. Wire Svc: AP Format: Adult contemp. News staff: 3; News: 2 hrs wkly. Target aud: 25-54; women. ♦Joseph C. Schwartzel, CEO, gen mgr; Jim Schwartzel, sls dir; Keith Stuhlmann, engrg dir; Randy Marsh, progmg.

Naples Park

WAVV(FM)— May 30, 1987: 101.1 mhz; 100 kw. Ant 980 ft TL: N26 10 58 W81 34 30. Stereo. Hrs open: 24 11800 Tamiami Tr. E., Naples, 34113. Phone: (239) 793-1011. Fax: (239) 793-7000.E-mail: w.tiburski@wavv101.com Web Site:wavv101.com Licensee: Alpine Broadcasting Corp. (group owner; (acq 4-84; $95,000;4-23-84). Natl. Network: AP Radio, . Natl. Rep: Christal,. Format: Modern, easy lstng. News: 8 hrs wkly. Target aud: 35 plus; an economically qualified audience that is somewhat more affluent. Spec prog: Jazz 3 hrs wkly. ♦Norman Alpert, pres; Donna Alpert, CFO; Jeff Alpert, VP, gen mgr; Walt Tiburski, gen mgr & opns mgr.

WBTT(FM)— Oct 22, 1987: 105.5 mhz; 950 w. 584 ft TL: N26 19 00 W81 47 13. (CP: 6.3 kw, ant 649 ft.). Stereo. Hrs open: 13320 Metro Pkwy., Suite 1, Fort Myers, 33912. Phone: (914) 225-4300. Phone: (866) 843-2328. Fax: (239) 225-4329. Web Site:www.1055thebeat.com Licensee: Clear Channel Radio Licenses Inc. Group owner: Clear Channel Communications Inc. (acq 1996; grpsl). Format: Rhythmic CHR. Target aud: 18-34. ♦Jim Keating, gen mgr.

Navarre

WKFP(FM)— 1999: 95.7 mhz; 25 kw. Ant 282 ft TL: N30 27 02 W86 51 59. Hrs open: 2070 N. Palafox St., Pensacola, 32501-2145. Phone: (850) 434-1230. Fax: (850) 469-9698.E-mail: praise957@hotmail.com Web Site:www.praise95.net Licensee: 550 AM Inc. Format: Christian. ♦Dara Glinter, exec VP, opns VP; Michael Glinter, pres, gen mgr & progmg VP.

Neptune Beach

WFKS(FM)— August 1965: 97.9 mhz; 12.5 kw. Ant 991 ft TL: N30 16 51 W81 34 12. Stereo. Hrs open: 24 11700 Central Parkway, Jacksonville, 32224. Phone: (904) 636-0507. Fax: (904) 997-7713.E-mail: info@979kissfm.com Web Site:www.979kissfm.com Licensee: Clear Channel Broadcasting Licenses Inc. Group owner: Clear Channel Communications Inc. (acq 11-21-97; grpsl). Population served: 1,064,400 Format: Top 40. News staff: one; News: one hr wkly. Target aud: 35-54; general. ♦Norm Feuer, stn mgr; Gail Austin, opns mgr.

New Port Richey

***WCIE(FM)**— Apr 10, 1985: 91.5 mhz; 22 kw. Ant 230 ft TL: N28 16 41 W82 43 06. Stereo. Hrs open: 24 6214 Springer Dr., 34668. Phone: (727) 848-9150. Fax: (727) 848-1233.E-mail: jeff@thejoyfm.com Web Site:www.thejoyfm.com Licensee: Radio Training Network Inc. (acq 1995; $100,000). Gammond & Grange. Format: Adult contemp, Christian. ♦James L. Campbell, pres; Jeff MacFarlane, gen mgr; Carmen Brown, prom dir; Steve Rieker, chief of engrg.

WDUV(FM)—Licensed to New Port Richey. See Tampa

WPSO(AM)— Oct 31, 1963: 1500 khz; 250 w-D. TL: N28 15 32 W82 43 54. Hrs open: Sunrise-sunset 109 Bayview Blvd., #A, Oldsmar, 34677. Phone: (727) 725-3500. Phone: (727) 725-5555. Fax: (813) 814-7500.E-mail: wzra48@yahoo.com Web Site:www.wpso.com Licensee: AKMA Broadcast Network Inc. (acq 1993; $250,000; 9-13-93). Population served: 500,000 Format: News/talk, Greek. News staff: one; News: 35 hrs wkly. Target aud: General; international, ethnic. Spec prog: Pol two hrs, quiz/trivia program, relg 8 hrs, East Indian one hr, It 3 hrs wkly, Ethnic. ♦Sam Agelatos, pres & gen mgr; Angelo Agelatos, chief of opns.

New Smyrna Beach

***WJLU(FM)**— Sept 7, 1989: 89.7 mhz; 5 kw. 328 ft TL: N29 00 32 W80 58 27. (CP: 10 kw). Stereo. Hrs open: 24 4295 Ridgewood Ave., Port Orange, 32127. Phone: (386) 756-9094. Fax: (386) 760-7107.E-mail: thecornerstone@cornerstoneministry.org Web Site:www.cornerstoneministry.org Licensee: Cornerstone Broadcasting Corp. Population served: 350,000 Natl. Network: USA, Moody, . Format: Relg. News: 18 hrs wkly. Target aud: General; families. ♦William Powell, gen mgr & progmg dir; Sandra Leisner, pub affrs dir.

WSBB(AM)— 1950: 1230 khz; 1 kw-U. TL: N29 01 57 W80 55 03. Hrs open: 24 229 Canal St., 32168. Phone: (386) 428-9091. Fax: (386) 428-1924. Licensee: Gore-Overgaard Broadcasting Inc. (acq 3-21-2006; $450,000). Population served: 240,000 Format: Adult standards. News: 120 hrs wkly. Target aud: 45 plus. ♦Cordell J. Overgaard, pres; Skip Diegel, gen mgr.

Newberry

WHHZ(FM)— February 1999: 100.5 mhz; 44 kw. Ant 469 ft TL: N29 36 29 W82 51 01. Hrs open: 100 N.W. 76th Dr., Suite 2, Gainesville, 32607. Phone: (352) 313-3130 / 3135. Fax: (352) 313-3166.E-mail: themorningbuzz2004@yahoo.com Web Site:www.1005thebuzz.com Licensee: 6 Johnson Road Licenses Inc. (group owner; (acq 1-5-2007; grpsl). Format: Modern rock. ♦Benjamin Hill, gen mgr.

Niceville

WRKN(FM)— May 1, 1993: 100.3 mhz; 3.5 kw. Ant 440 ft TL: N30 29 20 W86 25 16. Hrs open: 24 21 Miracle Strip Pkwy., Fort Walton Beach, 32548. Phone: (850) 244-1400. Fax: (850) 243-1471.E-mail: info@krocksu.com Web Site:www.krocksu.com Licensee: Star Broadcasting Inc. Group owner: Cumulus Media Inc. (acq 8-2-2006; swap for WNCV(FM) Evergreen, AL). Population served: 150,000 Natl. Network: Jones Radio Networks, . Format: Classic rock. ♦Ron Hale Sr., gen mgr & stn mgr.

Nocatee

WZSP(FM)— Aug 27, 1998: 105.3 mhz; 6 kw. 400 ft TL: N27 11 01 W81 56 57. Stereo. Hrs open: 24 Heartland Broadcasting Corp., 7891 U.S. Highway 17 S., Zolfo Springs, 33890. Phone: (863) 494-4111. Fax: (863) 494-4443.E-mail: wzsp@desoto.net Web Site:www.lazeta.fm Licensee: Heartland Broadcasting Corp. Population served: 200,000 Natl. Network: CNN Radio, . Florida's Radio Networks Rgnl rep: Lotus-Entravision Kaye, Scholer, Fierman, Hays & Handler. Format: Rgnl Mexican. Target aud: General; Sp speaking audience, Charlotte, Desto, Hardee, Sarasota, Polk & Highlands counties. ♦Harold (Hal) Kneller Jr., pres.

North Fort Myers

WWCN(AM)— Dec 17, 1983: 770 khz; 10 kw-D, 1 kw-N, DA-2. TL: N26 46 30 W81 50 51. Stereo. Hrs open: 20125 S. Tamiami Tr., Estero, 33928. Phone: (239) 495-2100. Fax: (239) 992-8165.E-mail: info@am770.com Web Site:www.am770.com Licensee: Beasley Radio Co. Group owner: Beasley Broadcast Group (acq 12-16-87). Format: Talk, sports. ♦George Beasley, pres; Bradley C. Beasley, gen mgr; John Rozz, opns mgr.

North Miami

WKAT(AM)— November 1937: 1360 khz; 5 kw-D, 1 kw-N. TL: N25 44 36 W80 09 14. Hrs open: 2828 W. Flagler St., Miami, 33135. Phone: (305) 503-1340. Fax: (305) 677-7585.E-mail: info@qwkat.com Web Site:1360wkat.com Licensee: Caron Broadcasting Inc. (acq 1-31-2005; $10 million). Population served: 334,859 Fletcher, Heald & Hildreth. Format: News/talk, classical. ♦Tony Calatayud, gen mgr; Stephen James, opns mgr.

North Miami Beach

WXDJ(FM)— 1986: 95.7 mhz; 40 kw. 531 ft TL: N25 46 29 W80 11 19. Stereo. Hrs open: 24 1001 Ponce deLeon Blvd., Coral Gables, 33134. Phone: (305) 444-9292. Fax: (305) 447-4466. Web Site:www.lamusica.com Licensee: WXDJ Licensing Inc. Group owner: Spanish Broadcasting System Inc. (acq 7-11-97; $110 million with WRMA(FM) Fort Lauderdale). Wiley, Rein & Fielding. Format: Salsa. News: 4 hrs wkly. Target aud: 18-54; Hispanic Adults. ♦Jackie Nosti-Combo, gen mgr; John Caride, prom dir.

North Palm Beach

WSVU(AM)— 2006: 960 khz; 1.2 kw-D, 1.4 kw-N, DA-2. TL: N26 49 01 W80 15 07. Hrs open: Phone: (561) 627-9966. Web Site:www.seaviewam960.com Licensee: North Palm Beach Broadcasting Inc. Natl. Network: CBS Radio, . Format: Gold standards. ♦Chet Tart, gen mgr.

Ocala

***WHIJ(FM)**— Mar 30, 1990: 88.1 mhz; 1.25 kw. 394 ft TL: N29 14 17 W82 07 17. Stereo. Hrs open: 24 408 University, Suite 206, Gainsville, 32601. Phone: (352) 351-8810. Fax: (352) 351-8917.E-mail: thejoyfm@thejoyfm.com Web Site:www.thejoyfm.com Licensee: Radio Training Network Inc. (acq 10-5-01; $80,000 with WAQV(FM) Crystal River). Population served: 300,000 Gammon & Grange. Format: Adult contemp, educ, Christian. Target aud: 20-50. ♦Jeff MacFarlane, gen mgr.

WMFQ(FM)— July 11, 1977: 92.9 mhz; 50 kw. 476 ft TL: N29 04 45 W82 05 35. Stereo. Hrs open: 24 3357 S.W. 7th St., 34474. Phone: (352) 732-9877. Fax: (352) 622-6675. Web Site:www.wmfq.fm Licensee: Asterisk Communications Inc. Group owner: Asterisk Inc. (acq 1995; $2.1 million). Population served: 300,000 Natl. Rep: McGavren Guild,. Reddy, Begley & McCormick. Format: Oldies. News staff: one; News: 5 hrs wkly. Target aud: 35 plus; upscale. ♦Dean Johnson, gen mgr.

WMOP(AM)— Dec 18, 1953: 900 khz; 5 kw-D, 23 w-N. TL: N29 14 17 W82 07 17. Stereo. Hrs open: 24 101 S.E. 2nd Pl., Gainesville, 32601. Phone: (352) 378-7378. Fax: (352) 629-1614.E-mail: sales@floridasportstalk.com Web Site:www.floridasportstalk.com Licensee: Florida Sportstalk Inc. (acq 11-14-96; $350,000). Population served: 213,300 Natl. Network: ABC, . Natl. Rep: Dora-Clayton,. Pepper & Corazzini. Format: Sports, talk. News staff: one; News: 3 hrs wkly. Target aud: 35 plus. ♦Tom Catalano, gen mgr.

WOCA(AM)— May 1957: 1370 khz; 5 kw-D. TL: N29 12 04 W82 09 07. Hrs open: 6 AM-8 PM Box 1056, 34478. Secondary address: 1515 E. Silver Springs Blvd., Suite 134 34470. Phone: (352) 732-8000. Phone: (352) 622-9622. Fax: (352) 732-0174.E-mail: woca@woca.com Web Site:www.woca.com Licensee: Westshore Broadcasting Inc. Population served: 300,000 Natl. Network: ABC, . Florida's Radio Networks Format: News/talk. News staff: two; News: 16 hrs wkly. Target aud: 35 plus. Spec prog: Black 2 hrs wkly. ♦Tishia A. Moeller, gen mgr & stn mgr.

WOGK(FM)— Nov 7, 1960: 93.7 mhz; 100 kw. 1,348 ft TL: N29 16 06 W82 04 51. Stereo. Hrs open: 3602 N.E. 20th Pl., 34470. Phone: (352) 622-5600. Fax: (352) 622-3998.E-mail: ncfmrbob@earthlink.net Web Site:www.93kcountry.com Licensee: Ocala Broadcasting L.L.C. Group owner: Wooster Republican Printing Co. (acq 9-27-86). Population served: 700,000 Natl. Rep: Katz Radio,. Baker & Hostetler. Format: Country. News staff: one; News: 3 hrs wkly. Target aud: 25-54; general. ♦Bob Kassi, pres, gen sls mgr; Jim Robertson, VP, gen mgr & gen mgr; Bob Forster, progmg dir.

Ocoee

WUNA(AM)— Oct 25, 1962: 1480 khz; 1 kw-D, 71 w-N. TL: N28 33 27 W81 32 29. Stereo. Hrs open: 749 S. Bluford Ave., 34761. Phone: (407) 656-9823. Fax: (407) 656-2092. Licensee: Way Broadcasting Licensee LLC (acq 4-20-2000; grpsl). Rgnl. Network: Florida Radio Net. Florida's Radio Networks Format: Sp contemp. ♦Juan Nieves, gen mgr; Lou Muller, chief of engrg; Sheila Rodriguez, sls dir & traf mgr.

Okeechobee

WOKC(AM)— Feb 6, 1962: 1570 khz; 1 kw-D, 14 w-N. TL: N27 12 59 W80 49 53. Stereo. Hrs open: 6 AM-11 PM 210 W. North Park St., Suite 102, 34974. Phone: (863) 467-1570. Fax: (863) 763-3171.E-mail: wokc@gladesmedia.com Web Site:www.gladesmedia.com Licensee: Glades Media Co. LLC (acq 7-31-01; $200,000). Population served: 50,000 Rgnl. Network: Florida Radio Net., S.E. Agri. Southeast AgNet Format: Classic country. News staff: one; News: 10 hrs wkly. Target aud: General. ♦Will Skinner, gen mgr.

Orange Park

***WAYR(AM)**— May 28, 1960: 550 khz; 5 kw-D, 500 w-N, DA-1. TL: N30 04 21 W81 47 24. Hrs open: 24 2500 Russell Rd., Green Cove Springs, 32043-9492. Phone: (904) 284-1111. Phone: (904) 284-2500. Fax: (904) 284-2501.E-mail: lstephens@wayradio.org Web Site:www.wayradio.org Licensee: Good Tidings Trust Inc. Population served: 1,100,000 Wiley, Rein & Fielding. Format: Christian. Target aud: 45 plus; mature Christian. ♦Bill Tidwell, pres, chief of engrg; Luke Stephens, gen mgr.

Orlando

WAMT(AM)—See Pine Castle-Sky Lake

WDBO(AM)— May 24, 1924: 580 khz; 5 kw-U, DA-N. TL: N28 37 12 W81 24 34. Hrs open: 4192 John Young Pkwy., 32804. Phone: (407) 295-5858. Phone: (321) 281-2000. Fax: (407) 291-4879.E-mail: info@wdbo.com Web Site:www.wdbo.com Licensee: Cox Radio Inc. Group owner: Cox Broadcasting (acq 3-28-97; grpsl). Population served: 1,104,600 Format: News/talk. ♦Bill Hendrich, gen mgr; Steve Holbrook, opns mgr; Tom Interrante, gen sls mgr; Steve Avellone, natl sls mgr; Rich Mastroberte, prom dir; Kipper McGee, progmg dir; Marsha Taylor, news dir; Steve Fluker, chief of engrg.

WDYZ(AM)— Dec 5, 1947: 990 khz; 50 kw-D, 5 kw-N, DA-2. TL: N28 34 28 W81 27 48. Stereo. Hrs open: 610 Sycamore St., Suite 220, Celebration, 34747. Phone: (407) 566-2033. Fax: (407) 566-2034.E-mail: MICHELE.BASTONE@DISNEY.COM Web Site:www.radiodisney.com Licensee: Radio Disney Group LLC. Group owner: ABC Inc. (acq 1-23-01; $5 million cash). Population served: 3,000,000 Natl. Network: Radio Disney, . Natl. Rep: Interep,. Format: Children/families. Target aud: 4-16;25-49; children; mothers. ♦Paul T. Proly, stn mgr; Pren Rashbury, mktg VP; Robin Jones, progmg VP.

WFLF(AM)—See Pine Hills

WHTQ(FM)— 1952: 96.5 mhz; 100 kw. 1,600 ft TL: N28 34 51 W81 04 32. Stereo. Hrs open: 24 4192 John Young Pkwy, 32804. Phone: (407) 422-9696. Fax: (407) 422-5883. Fax: (407) 422-0917.E-mail: info@whtq.com Web Site:www.whtq.com Licensee: Cox Radio Inc. Group owner: Cox Broadcasting (acq 1997). Population served: 99,006 Natl. Rep: Christal,. Format: Classic rock. News staff: one; News: 2 hrs wkly. Target aud: 25-54; adult male. ♦Debbie Morel, VP & gen mgr.

WLAA(AM)—See Winter Garden

***WMFE-FM**— July 14, 1980: 90.7 mhz; 100 kw. 731 ft TL: N28 36 08 W81 05 37. Stereo. Hrs open: 24 11510 E. Colonial Dr., 32817-4699. Phone: (407) 273-2300. Fax: (407) 273-8462. Fax: (407) 273-3613.E-mail: info@wmfe.org Web Site:www.wmfe.org Licensee: Community Communications Inc. Natl. Network: PRI, NPR, . Format: Class, news & info. News staff: 4; News: 48 hrs wkly. Target aud: 35 plus; well-educated, executive, professional, upper-income. Spec prog: New instrumental 4 hrs wkly. ♦Jose Fajardo, pres.

WMGF(FM)—See Mount Dora

WMMO(FM)— Aug 19, 1990: 98.9 mhz; 44 kw. 522 ft TL: N28 34 27 W81 27 46. Stereo. Hrs open: 24 4192 John Young Pkwy., 32804. Phone: (407) 422-9696. Fax: (407) 422-5883.E-mail: info@wmmo.com Web Site:www.wmmo.com Licensee: Cox Radio Inc. Group owner: Cox Broadcasting Population served: 150,000 Natl. Rep: Christal,. Format: Adult contemp, soft rock. News: one hr wkly. Target aud: 25-49. ♦Debbie Morel, VP & gen mgr.

WOMX-FM— Aug 15, 1967: 105.1 mhz; 95 kw. 1,309 ft TL: N28 36 17 W81 05 13. (CP: Ant 1,597 ft.). Stereo. Hrs open: 24 1800 Pembrook Dr., Suite 400, 32810. Phone: (407) 919-1000. Fax: (407) 919-1190. Web Site:www.mix1051.com Licensee: Infinity Radio Inc. Group owner: Infinity Broadcasting Corp. (acq 12-14-00; grpsl). Population served: 1,235,340 Leibowitz & Associates. Format: Hot adult contemp. News staff: one. ♦Earnest James, sr VP; Michele Holland, CEO & gen sls mgr; Angela Schlesman, prom dir; Jeff Cushman, progmg dir.

WPCV(FM)—See Lakeland

WPRD(AM)—See Winter Park

WRLZ(AM)—(Eatonville, 1957: 1270 khz; 5 kw-U, DA-N. TL: N28 34 03 W81 25 38. Hrs open: 24 Box 593642, 32859-3642. Secondary address: 6106 B Hoffner Ave. 32822. Phone: (407) 345-0700. Fax: (407) 345-1492.E-mail: info@radioluz1270.com Web Site:www.radioluz1270.com Licensee: Radio Luz Inc. (acq 1996; $378,500). Population served: 99,006 Format: Sp, contemp. Target aud: General; Family. ♦Saturnino Gonzalez, pres; John Maldonado, gen mgr.

WRMQ(AM)— Oct 21, 1985: 1140 khz; 4.1 kw-D. TL: N28 30 42 W81 14 09. Hrs open: 1033 Semoran Blvd., Suite 253, Casselberry, 32707. Phone: (407) 830-0800. Fax: (407) 260-6100.E-mail: mannyarroyo@qbcflorida.com Licensee: Florida Broadcasters. Population served: 1,200,000 Roy F. Perkins. Format: Gospel. Target aud: 25-54. ♦George M. Arroyo, pres & gen mgr.

WRUM(FM)— July 1, 1971: 100.3 mhz; 100 kw. Ant 1,597 ft TL: N28 36 08 W81 05 37. Stereo. Hrs open: 24 2500 Maitland Ctr. Pkwy., Suite 401, Maitland, 32751. Phone: (407) 916-7800 / (407) 916-1003. Fax: (407) 916-7400. Web Site:www.rumba1003.com Licensee: Clear Channel Broadcasting Licenses Inc. Group owner: Clear Channel Communications Inc. (acq 1997; grpsl). Population served: 99,006 Wiley, Rein & Fielding. Format: Sp/tropical. Target aud: 18-49. ♦Linda Byrd, pres, gen mgr; Fernando Bauermeister, gen sls mgr; Rick Everett, mktg dir; Suheily Gonzales, prom mgr; Chris Kampmeier, progmg dir; Donna Carmichael, traf mgr.

WSDO(AM)—See Sanford

WTKS-FM—(Cocoa Beach, May 8, 1962: 104.1 mhz; 100 kw. 1,609 ft TL: N28 34 51 W81 04 32. Stereo. Hrs open: 24 2500 Maitland Ctr. Pkwy., Suite 401, Maitland, 32751. Phone: (407) 916-7800. Fax: (407) 916-7511.E-mail: info@wtks.com Web Site:www.wtks.com Licensee: Clear Channel Broadcasting Licenses Inc. Group owner: Clear Channel Communications Inc. (acq 11-21-97; grpsl). Population served: 1,402,300 Natl. Network: Premiere Radio Networks, . Natl. Rep: Clear Channel,. Wiley, Rein & Fielding. Format: Entertainment talk. Target aud: Adults; 25-54. ♦Linda Byrd, gen mgr, chief of engrg; Sam Nein, sls dir; Ed Kennedy, gen sls mgr; Frank Celebre, natl sls mgr; Erika Plak, prom mgr; Chris Kampmeier, progmg dir; Rick Everett, mktg.

WTLN(AM)— April 1, 1940: 950 khz; 12 kw-U, DA-N. TL: N28 32 08 W81 26 55. Hrs open: 24 1188 Lake View Dr., Altamonte Springs, 32714. Phone: (407) 682-9494. Fax: (407) 682-7005.E-mail: wtln@salemorlando.com Web Site:www.wtln.com Licensee: Pennsylvania Media Associates Inc. (acq 12-7-2005; $9.4 million). Population served: 140,000 Natl. Rep: Salem,. Holland & Knight. Format: Christian, talk. Target aud: 35-64. ♦Edward Atsinger III, pres; David Koon, gen mgr; Dale Forbis, stn mgr, opns mgr; Allan Dempsey, progmg dir.

***WUCF-FM**— Jan 30, 1978: 89.9 mhz; 40 kw. 194 ft TL: N28 36 00 W81 12 05. Stereo. Hrs open: 24 P.O. Box 162199, 32816-2199. Secondary address: 4000 Central Florida Blvd., Bldg. 75, Rm. 130 32816. Phone: (407) 823-0899. Fax: (407) 823-6364.E-mail: wucfhost@mail.ucf.edu Web Site:wucf.org Licensee: University of Central Florida. Natl. Network: NPR, PRI, . Cohn & Marks. Format: Jazz. News staff: 10; News: 16 hrs wkly. Spec prog: blues 4 hrs; seasonal opera. ♦John Hitt, pres; Kayonne Riley, gen mgr; Bruce Doerle, engrg dir, chief of engrg.

WWKA(FM)— Apr 24, 1952: 92.3 mhz; 98 kw. 1,380 ft TL: N28 36 08 W81 05 37. Stereo. Hrs open: 24 Prog sep from AM 4192 John Young Pkwy., 32804. Phone: (407) 298-9292. Fax: (407) 291-4879.E-mail: info@wwka.com Web Site:www.wwka.com Format: Country. ♦Kimberly Hellstrom, prom dir; Len Shackelford, progmg mgr; Shadow Stevens, mus dir; Steve Fluker, engrg dir.

WXXL(FM)—See Leesburg

WYGM(AM)— 1947: 740 khz; 50 kw-U, DA-2. TL: N28 28 53 W81 39 43. Hrs open: 24/7 2500 Maitland Center Pkwy., Suite 401, Maitland, 32751. Phone: (407) 916-7800. Fax: (407) 916-0329. Web Site:www.740thegame.com Licensee: Clear Channel Radio Licenses Inc. Group owner: Clear Channel Communications Inc. (acq 11-21-97; grpsl). Population served: 1,000,000 Wiley, Rein and Fielding. Wire Svc: AP Format: Sports. ♦Linda Byrd, VP, gen mgr; Pam Volkman, gen sls mgr; Jimmy D., prom mgr; Rick Everett, mktg dir & progmg dir.

Orlovista

WEUS(AM)— 2006: 810 khz; 10 kw-D, 400 w-N, DA-2. TL: N28 34 18 W81 26 02. Hrs open: 24 hrs 999 Douglas Ave., Attamonte, 32714. Phone: (407) 774-8810. Fax: (407) 774-8895. Licensee: Star Over Orlando Inc. Format: Relg. ♦Carl Como Tutera, pres.

Ormond Beach

WELE(AM)— Aug 1, 1957: 1380 khz; 5 kw-D, 2.5 kw-N, DA-2. TL: N29 16 09 W81 04 54. Hrs open: 432 S. Nova Rd., 32174. Phone: (386) 677-4122. Fax: (386) 677-4123.E-mail: doug@wele1380.com Web Site:www.wele1380.com wele1380.com Licensee: Wings Communications Inc. (acq 9-90; $175,000; 9-24-90). Population served: 90,000 Natl. Network: CNN Radio, Westwood One, . Format: News/talk. Target aud: General; mature, adults interested in sports & local current events. ♦F. Douglas Wilhite, pres, gen mgr; Kristin Cobb, opns mgr; Mike Johnson, progmg dir; Doug Wilhite, engr.

Ormond-by-the-Sea

WHOG-FM— 1995: 95.7 mhz; 25 kw. 328 ft TL: N29 14 10 W81 04 23. Hrs open: 126 W. International Speedway Blvd., Daytona Beach, 32114. Phone: (386) 255-9300. Fax: (386) 238-6071. Web Site:www.whog.fm Licensee: Black Crow LLC. Group owner: Black Crow Media Group LLC (acq 9-21-2001; grpsl). Format: Classic rock, AOR. ♦Stacey Knerler, gen mgr; Donna Fillion, sls dir, progmg dir.

Oviedo

WONQ(AM)— Nov 21, 1992: 1030 khz; 10 kw-D, 1.7 kw-N, DA-2. TL: N28 40 31 W81 10 01. Hrs open: 24 1033 Semoran Blvd., Suite 253, Casselberry, 32707. Phone: (407) 830-0800. Fax: (407) 260-6100.E-mail: mannyarroyo@qbcflorida.com Licensee: Florida Broadcasters. Population served: 1,200,000 Roy F. Perkins. Format: Sp music, news, contemp Latin hits. Target aud: 25-54. ♦George M. Arroyo, pres & gen mgr; George Mier, opns VP.

Palatka

WGNE-FM— Dec 13, 1973: 99.9 mhz; 100 kw. Ant 1,201 ft TL: N29 31 08 W81 19 02. Stereo. Hrs open: 6444 Atlantic Blvd., Jacksonville, 32211. Phone: (904) 727-9696. Fax: (904) 721-9322.E-mail: info@gatercountry.com Web Site:www.gatercountry.com Licensee: Renda Broadcasting Corp. Group owner: Renda Broadcasting Corp.-Renda Radio Inc. (acq 1996; $6.5 million with WMUV(FM) Brunswick, GA). Population served: 2000000 Haley, Bader & Potts. Format: Country. Target aud: 18-49. ♦Toney Renda, pres; Gary Spurgeon, gen mgr; Randy Hill, progmg dir.

***WHIF(FM)**— Mar 29, 1996: 91.3 mhz; 1.7 kw. 318 ft TL: N29 38 54 W81 39 42. Hrs open: 201 S. Palm Ave., 32177. Phone: (386) 325-3334. Fax: (386) 325-0934.E-mail: whif@gbso.net Web Site:www.whif.org Licensee: Putnam Radio Ministries Inc. Population served: 75,000 Format: Adult contemp, Christian. Target aud: 25-54; family-oriented, middle-class. Spec prog: Relg educ 10 hrs wkly. ♦Robin Toole, gen mgr & progmg dir.

WIYD(AM)— Feb 14, 1947: 1260 khz; 400 w-D, 135 w-N. TL: N29 39 07 W81 35 32. Hrs open: 24 Box 918, 32178-0918. Phone: (386) 325-4556. Fax: (386) 328-5161.E-mail: wiyd@atlantic.net Licensee: Hall Broadcasting Co. (acq 2-14-57; $100,000). Population served: 25,000 Natl. Network: ABC, . Rgnl. Network: Florida Radio Net. Florida's Radio Networks Format: C&W. News staff: one; News: 6 hrs wkly. Target aud: 18-49; rich & powerful. Spec prog: Relg 5 hrs wkly. ♦Wayne Bullock, pres & gen mgr; Mary Makie Connor, stn mgr.

WPLK(AM)— 1957: 800 khz; 1 kw-D, 334 w-N. TL: N29 37 40 W81 34 35. (CP: TL: N29 39 07 W81 35 32). Hrs open: 24 Box 335, 32178. Secondary address: 1428 St. John's Ave. 32177. Phone: (386) 325-5800. Fax: (386) 328-8725.E-mail: wplk@wplk.com Web Site:wplk.com Licensee: Radio Palatka Inc. (acq 4-28-98; $250,000 for stock). Natl. Network: ABC, . Format: Oldies, Greatest Music ever Made. News staff: one; News: 2 hrs wkly. Target aud: General. ♦Wayne Bullock, pres & gen mgr.

Palm Bay

***WEJF(FM)**— 1993: 90.3 mhz; 2 kw. 295 ft TL: N28 02 54 W80 40 34. Hrs open: 2824B Palm Bay Rd., 32905. Phone: (321) 722-9998. Fax: (321) 724-0845.E-mail: wejf@bellsouth.net Web Site:www.wejf.com Licensee: Florida Public Radio Inc. (acq 7-95; $40,000). Format: Adult contemp, Christian, var. ♦Eric Sabo, gen mgr & opns mgr.

***WRYZ(FM)**— July 1997: 88.5 mhz; 600 w vert. Ant 108 ft TL: N28 02 54 W80 40 34. Stereo. Hrs open: 24 1065 Rainer Dr., Altamonte Springs, 32714-3847. Phone: (407) 869-8000. Fax: (407) 869-0380. Web Site:www.zradio.org Licensee: Central Florida Educational Foundation Inc. (acq 1-31-2007; $400,000). Format: Contemp Christian. Target aud: Christian. ♦James S. Hoge, pres.

Palm Beach

WBZT(AM)—See West Palm Beach

WRMF(FM)—Licensed to Palm Beach. See West Palm Beach

Palm City

***WCNO(FM)**— Apr 1, 1990: 89.9 mhz; 100 kw. 613 ft TL: N27 07 20 W80 23 21. Hrs open: 2960 S.W. Mapp Rd., 34990-2737. Phone: (772) 221-1100. Fax: (772) 221-8716.E-mail: wcno@wcno.com Web Site:www.wcno.com Licensee: National Christian Network Inc. Format: Christian, adult contemp. ♦Ray Kassis, pres; Tom Craton, gen mgr.

Palm Coast

***WHYZ(FM)**—Not on air, target date: unknown: 91.1 mhz; 2.1 kw vert. Ant 174 ft TL: N29 29 44 W81 08 08. Hrs open: Box 607883, Orlando, 32860-7883. Phone: (407) 869-8000. Fax: (407) 869-0380. Web Site:www.zradio.org Licensee: Central Florida Educational Foundation Inc. ♦James S. Hoge, pres.

Palm Springs

WVAA(AM)—Not on air, target date: unknown: 1500 khz; 5 kw-D, 250 w-N, DA-2. TL: N26 45 18 W80 22 00 (day), N26 37 22 W80 04 20 (night). Hrs open: 3790 Dogwood Ave., Palm Beach Gardens, 33410. Phone: (561) 776-0515. Licensee: Brian M. Johnson. ♦Brian Johnson, gen mgr.

Palmetto

WBRD(AM)— October 1957: 1420 khz; 2.5 kw-D, 1 kw-N, DA-2. TL: N27 32 42 W82 34 28. Stereo. Hrs open: Box 826, Ellenton, 34222. Phone: (941) 955-1420. Fax: (941) 723-9831.E-mail: wbrdradio@aol.com Web Site:www.wbrd.com Licensee: Metropolitan Radio Group Inc. (group owner; acq 6-96). Population served: 2,500,000 Format: Southern Gospel. Target aud: 35 plus. ♦Bill Bailey, gen mgr & opns dir.

Panama City

WDIZ(AM)— April 1940: 590 khz; 1.7 kw-D, 2.5 kw-N, DA-N. TL: N30 10 20 W85 36 49. Stereo. Hrs open: 1834 Lisenby Ave., 32412. Secondary address: 1834 Lisenby Ave. 32405. Phone: (850) 769-1408. Fax: (850) 769-0659.E-mail: info@panamacity@clearchannel.com Licensee: Clear Channel Broadcasting Licenses Inc. Group owner: Clear Channel Communications Inc. (acq 11-21-97; grpsl). Population served: 40,000 Format: Nostalgia. ♦Peter Norden, gen mgr.

WEBZ(FM)—See Mexico Beach

***WFFL(FM)**— 2007: 91.7 mhz; 310 w. Ant 207 ft TL: N30 10 48 W85 38 10. Hrs open:
Rebroadcasts WJFM(FM) Baton Rouge, LA 100%.
Box 262550, Baton Rouge, LA, 70826. Secondary address: 8919 World Ministry Ave., Baton Rouge 70810. Phone: (225) 768-3224. Web Site:www.jsm.org Licensee: Family Worship Center Church Inc. (acq 10-12-2006; grpsl). Format: Christian. ♦David Whitelaw, COO.

***WFSW(FM)**— 1995: 89.1 mhz; 100 kw. 403 ft TL: N30 22 02 W85 55 29. Hrs open: 1600 Red Barber Plaza, Tallahassee, 32310. Phone: (850) 487-3086. Fax: (850) 487-3293. Web Site:www.wfsu.org Licensee: Florida State University. Natl. Network: NPR, . Format: News, talk. ♦Pat Keating, gen mgr; Caroline Austin, stn mgr; Aron Myers, prom dir; Tom Flanigan, news dir; Andy Hanus, engrg dir.

WFSY(FM)— October 1971: 98.5 mhz; 100 kw. Ant 1,090 ft TL: N30 30 41 W85 29 24. Stereo. Hrs open: 1834 Lisenby Ave., 32405. Secondary address: 1834 Lisenby Ave. 32405. Phone: (850) 769-1408. Fax: (850) 769-0659.E-mail: info@panamacity@clearchannel.com Web Site:www.beachfm.com Licensee: Clear Channel Broadcasting Licenses Inc. Population served: 40,000 Format: Adult contemp. Target aud: 25-54.

WILN(FM)— Apr 11, 1985: 105.9 mhz; 50 kw. Ant 406 ft TL: N30 10 44 W85 46 55. Stereo. Hrs open: 24 7106 Laird St., Suite 102, Panama City Beach, 32408. Phone: (850) 230-5855. Fax: (850) 230-6988. Web Site:www.island106.com Licensee: Magic Broadcasting Florida Licensing LLC. (group owner; (acq 1-31-2003; grpsl). Format: CHR. News staff: one; News: 2 hrs wkly. Target aud: 18-49. ♦Jeff Storey, COO, exec VP, gen mgr; Mike Preble, opns VP.

***WJTF(FM)**— Oct 15, 1998: 89.9 mhz; 100 kw. 213 ft TL: N30 10 20 W85 40 20. Hrs open: 835A S. Berthe, 32404. Phone: (850) 874-9900. Fax: (850) 874-9930.E-mail: wjtf@bellsouth.net Web Site:www.myfln.org Licensee: Family Life Broadcasting Inc (acq 5-23-2007; grpsl). Natl. Network: Moody, . Hill & Welch. Format: Relg, educ. Target aud: 35-90; general. ♦Tom Bush, gen mgr; Kelly Dickson, opns mgr; Mickey Jacobs, dev dir, progmg dir.

***WKGC-FM**— October 1982: 90.7 mhz; 100 kw. 336 ft TL: N30 13 05 W85 51 16. Stereo. Hrs open: 5230 W. Hwy. 98, 32401. Phone: (850) 873-3500. Fax: (850) 913-3299.E-mail: fsundram@gulfcoast.edu Web Site:www.wkgc.org Licensee: Gulf Coast Community College. Population served: 150,000 Natl. Network: NPR, PRI, . Rgnl. Network: Fla. Pub. Fla. Pub. Dow, Lohnes & Albertson. Format: News. Target aud: General. Spec prog: Black 6 hrs wkly. ♦Robert Spadden, pres; Frank Sundram, gen mgr; Reed Kinney, opns mgr.

WLTG(AM)— Dec 11, 1949: 1430 khz; 5 kw-U, DA-2. TL: N30 09 55 W85 35 19. Hrs open: Box 15635, 32406. Secondary address: 3100 E. 15th St., Springfield 32405. Phone: (850) 784-9873. Fax: (850) 784-6908.E-mail: wltg@bellsouth.net Licensee: Williams Communications Inc. (group owner; acq 8-12-03; $500,000). Population served: 120,000 Natl. Network: Premiere Radio Networks, Salem Radio Network, . Natl. Rep: Commercial Media Sales,. Format: News/talk, sports, info. Target aud: General. Spec prog: Black gospel 7 hrs wkly. ♦John Gay, gen mgr, sls dir & progmg dir.

WPAP-FM— Mar 30, 1967: 92.5 mhz; 100 kw. 930 ft TL: N30 22 05 W85 12 24. Stereo. Hrs open: 24 1834 Lisenby Ave., 32405. Phone: (850) 769-1408. Fax: (850) 769-0659.E-mail: info@panamacity @clearchannel.com Web Site:www.wpapfm.com Licensee: Clear Channel Radio Licenses Inc. Group owner: Clear Channel Communications Inc. (acq 11-21-97; grpsl). Population served: 250,000 Natl. Rep: McGavren Guild,. Format: Country. Target aud: 25-54. ♦Pete Norton, gen mgr.

WPFM-FM— September 1963: 107.9 mhz; 100 kw. 781 ft TL: N30 26 00 W85 24 51. (CP: 98.4 kw, ant 954 ft. TL: N30 13 45 W85 23 20). Stereo. Hrs open: 24 118 Gwyn Dr., Panama City Beach, 32407. Phone: (850) 234-8858. Fax: (850) 234-6592. Licensee: Double O Radio Corp. (group owner; acq 3-10-2004; grpsl). Population served: 120,000 Natl. Rep: Christal,. Format: Contemp hit/Top-40. Target aud: 18-49; active lifestyle, young adult audience. ♦Harry Finch, gen mgr.

WYOO(FM)—(Springfield, Mar 2, 1993: 101.1 mhz; 5.2 kw. 236 ft TL: N30 12 12 W85 36 57. (CP: 25 kw). Stereo. Hrs open: 24 7106 Laird St., Suite 102, Panama City Beach, 32408. Phone: (850) 230-5855. Fax: (850) 230-6988. Web Site:www.talkradio101.com Licensee: Magic Broadcasting Florida Licensing LLC. (group owner; (acq 9-30-2002; grpsl). Population served: 165,000 Rgnl. Network: Florida Radio Net. Natl. Rep: Christal,. Florida's Radio Networks Richard Hayes. Format: Talk. News staff: one; News: 28 hrs wkly. Target aud: 25-54; educated, upscale. ♦Jeff Storey, COO, pres, exec VP; Mike Preble, opns dir & adv mgr.

Panama City Beach

WASJ(FM)— January 1993: 105.1 mhz; 50 kw. Ant 335 ft TL: N30 10 44 W85 46 55. Stereo. Hrs open: 24 118 Gwyn Dr., Panama City, 32408. Phone: (850) 234-8858. Fax: (850) 234-6592.E-mail: stevegreen @panamacityradio.com Licensee: Double O Radio Corp. (group owner; acq 3-10-2004; grpsl). Population served: 135,000 Natl. Network: ESPN Radio, . Natl. Rep: Christal,. Format: Sports. ♦Harry Finch, gen mgr.

WFSY(FM)—See Panama City

***WKGC(AM)**— June 25, 1965: 1480 khz; 500 w-D, 87 w-N. TL: N30 10 33 W85 48 03. Hrs open: 6 AM-9 PM 5230 W. Hwy. 98, Panama City, 32401. Phone: (850) 873-3500. Fax: (850) 913-3299.E-mail: fsundram@gnfcoast.edu Web Site:www.wkgc.org Licensee: Gulf Coast Community College. (acq 12-1-72). Population served: 150,000 Natl. Network: NPR, . Format: Easy listening. News: 25 hrs wkly. Target aud: General; college students & older high school students. Spec prog: Folk 2 hrs, educ 8 hrs wkly. ♦Robert McSpadden, pres; Frank Sundram, gen mgr, stn mgr; Reed Kinney, opns mgr.

WPCF(AM)— Sept 23, 1958: 1290 khz; 270 w-D, 1 kw-N. TL: N30 10 44 W85 46 55. Hrs open: 7106 Laird St., Ste. 102, 32408. Phone: (850) 230-5855. Fax: (850) 230-6988.E-mail: jeffstorey@stylesmedia.com Licensee: Magic Broadcasting Florida Licensing LLC. (group owner; (acq 9-30-2002; grpsl). Population served: 150000 Format: Country. ♦Jeff Storey, CEO, gen mgr; Kim Styles, gen mgr; Joe Valentine, stn mgr; Mike Preble, opns mgr.

WVVE(FM)— June 1988: 100.1 mhz; 12 kw. Ant 403 ft TL: N30 10 44 W85 46 55. Stereo. Hrs open: 24 7106 Laird St., Suite 102, 32408. Phone: (850) 230-5855. Fax: (850) 230-6988. Licensee: Magic Broadcasting Florida Licensing LLC. (group owner; (acq 9-30-2002; grpsl). Format: Adult contemp. ♦Jeff Storey, CEO, CEO, exec VP; Mike Prebke, opns mgr.

Parker

WFLF-FM— August 1977: 94.5 mhz; 100 kw. Ant 994 ft TL: N29 49 09 W85 15 34. Stereo. Hrs open: 24 1834 Lisenby Ave., Panama City, 32405. Phone: (850) 769-1408. Fax: (850) 769-0659.E-mail: info@panamacity@clearchannel.com Web Site:www.945thefox.com Licensee: Clear Channel Broadcasting Licenses Inc. Group owner: Clear Channel Communications Inc. (acq 11-21-97; grpsl). Population served: 200,000 Natl. Network: Fox News Radio, . Format: News/talk. Spec prog: Relg 5 hrs wkly. ♦Pete Norden, gen mgr.

Pennsuco

***WGNK(FM)**— 1999: 88.3 mhz; 2.25 kw. Ant 282 ft TL: N25 52 24 W80 28 59. (CP: 6 kw). Stereo. Hrs open: 24 19626 Pines Blvd., Ste. 114, Pembroke Pines, 33029. Phone: (305) 406-2883. Fax: (305) 406-3030.E-mail: LANUEVA@FM.COM Web Site:www.lanueva883fm.com Licensee: Genesis License Subsidiary LLC (acq 5-5-2005; $1.69 million). Format: Christian, Sp. News staff: one; News: 3 hrs wkly. Target aud: 18-35; Hispanic Christians. Spec prog: Children 6 hrs. ♦Edwin L. Ortiz, pres; Mauricio Quintana, gen mgr.

Pensacola

WBSR(AM)— Sept 1, 1946: 1450 khz; 1 kw-U. TL: N30 25 44 W87 14 27. Hrs open: 24 Box 19047, 32523. Secondary address: 1601 N. Pace Blvd. 32505. Phone: (850) 438-4982. Fax: (850) 433-7932.E-mail: wbsr@wbsr.com Web Site:www.wbsr.com Licensee: Easy Media Inc. (acq 3-22-85; $330,000; 2-25-85). Population served: 280,000 Format: Soft adult contemp. Target aud: 35-54. ♦Frederic T.C. Brewer, pres; Gene Pfalzer, stn mgr.

WCOA(AM)— Feb 3, 1926: 1370 khz; 5 kw-U, DA-N. TL: N30 26 57 W87 15 46. Hrs open: 24 6565 N. W St., 32505. Phone: (850) 478-6011. Fax: (850) 478-3971. Licensee: Cumulus Licensing Corp. Group owner: Cumulus Media Inc. (acq 10-25-99; with co-located FM). Population served: 160,000 Natl. Network: ABC, . Natl. Rep: Katz Radio,. Format: News/talk. Target aud: 25-54. Spec prog: Relg 3 hrs wkly. ♦Brian Weil, gen mgr; Luke McCoy, progmg dir; Jim Roberts, news dir; Yancy McNair, chief of engrg.

WDWR(AM)— 1947: 1230 khz; 1 kw-U. TL: N30 25 57 W87 13 07. Hrs open: 24 Box 866, 32591. Phone: (850) 777-1568. Fax: (850) 437-3733.E-mail: info@divinewordradio.com Web Site:www.divinewordradio.com Licensee: Divine Word Communications (acq 2-22-2007; $375,000). Natl. Network: EWTN Radio, . Rgnl. Network: Florida Radio Net. Format: Catholic radio. ♦Gene Church, pres & gen mgr.

WJLQ(FM)— Sept 1, 1965: 100.7 mhz; 100 kw. 1,555 ft TL: N30 37 35 W87 38 50. Stereo. Hrs open: Prog sep from AM 6565 N. W St., 32505. Phone: (850) 478-6011. Fax: (850) 478-3971. Population served: 60,000 Format: Music, hot adult comtemp. Target aud: 25-44. ♦John Stuart, progmg dir.

WMEZ(FM)— Nov 11, 1960: 94.1 mhz; 77 kw. Ant 1,601 ft TL: N30 36 40 W87 36 26. Stereo. Hrs open: 6085 Quintette Rd., Pace, 32571. Phone: (850) 916-9222. Phone: (850) 994-5357. Fax: (850) 916-9266.E-mail: info@softrock941.com Web Site:www.softrock941.com Licensee: 6 Johnson Road Licenses Inc. Group owner: Pamal Broadcasting Ltd. (acq 10-19-2001; grpsl). Population served: 250,000 Natl. Network: Westwood One, . Format: Soft rock, adult contemp. Target aud: 25-54. ♦Dave Cobb, gen mgr; Kevin Peterson, progmg mgr; Gerald Wilson, chief of engrg.

WNVY(AM)—(Cantonment, December 1955: 1090 khz; 10 kw-D (2.3 kw-CH). TL: N30 34 47 W87 17 18. Hrs open: 2070 N. Palafox St., 32501. Phone: (850) 435-1115. Licensee: Pensacola Radio Corp. (acq 11-30-2006; $430,000). Format: Relg teaching. ♦Robert Wilkins, gen mgr.

***WPCS(FM)**— June 22, 1971: 89.5 mhz; 95 kw. Ant 1,358 ft TL: N30 35 16 W87 33 13. Stereo. Hrs open: 24 Box 18000, 32523. Phone: (850) 479-6570. Fax: (850) 969-1638.E-mail: rbn@rejoice.org Web Site:www.rejoice.org Licensee: Pensacola Christian College Inc. Population served: 1,025,018 Format: Relg, educ. ♦Arlin Horton, pres, gen mgr; Caleb Keener, stn mgr & chief of engrg.

WPNN(AM)— October 1956: 790 khz; 1 kw-D. TL: N30 27 18 W87 14 22. Hrs open: 3801 N. Pace Blvd., 32505. Phone: (850) 433-1141. Fax: (850) 433-1142. Web Site:www.cnnpensacola.com Licensee: Miracle Radio Inc. (acq 4-1-81). Population served: 62,507 Smithwick & Belendiuk. Format: Local news, CNN Headline News. ♦Gerald Schroeder, pres; Don Schroeder, gen mgr; Michael Schroeder, stn mgr.

WTKX-FM— 1971: 101.5 mhz; 100 kw. Ant 1,328 ft TL: N30 35 18 W87 33 16. Stereo. Hrs open: 24 6485 Pensacola Blvd., 32505. Phone: (850) 473-0400. Fax: (850) 473-0907.E-mail: radio@tk101.com Web Site:www.tk101.com Licensee: Clear Channel Broadcasting Licenses Inc. Group owner: Clear Channel Communications Inc. (acq 11-21-97; grpsl). Population served: 350,000 Wiley, Rein & Fielding. Format: Active rock. Target aud: 18-49; general. ♦Lowry Mays, CEO, chmn; Mark Mays, pres; Randall Mays, CFO.

***WUWF(FM)**— January 1981: 88.1 mhz; 100 kw. 617 ft TL: N30 24 09 W86 59 35. Stereo. Hrs open: 24 11000 University Pkwy., GA, 32514. Phone: (850) 474-2787.E-mail: wuwf@wuwf.org Web Site:www.wuwf.org Licensee: Board of Trustees, University of West Florida (acq 12-4-01). Population served: 400,000 Natl. Network: PRI, NPR, . Rgnl. Network: Fla. Pub. Fla. Pub. Format: Class, news, adult alternative. News staff: one; News: 34 hrs wkly. Target aud: General. ♦Joe Vincenza, gen mgr; Sandra Averhart, news dir.

WVTJ(AM)— Nov 1, 1959: 610 khz; 500 w-D, 157 w-N. TL: N30 27 18 W87 14 22. Hrs open: 24 2070 N. Palafox St., 32501. Phone: (850) 432-3658. Fax: (850) 432-3659.E-mail: wvtj@wilkinsradio.com Web Site:www.wilkinsradio.com Licensee: Pensacola Radio Corp. (acq 4-23-2007; $545,000). Population served: 480,000 Format: Black gospel, Christian. Target aud: 18-64. ♦Robert L. Wilkins, pres; Jessica Jordan, gen mgr.

WXBM-FM—See Milton

WYCL(FM)— Nov 10, 1976: 107.3 mhz; 100 kw. Ant 1,407 ft TL: N30 42 20 W87 19 00. Stereo. Hrs open: 24 6485 Pensacola Blvd., 32505. Phone: (850) 473-0400. Fax: (850) 473-0907. Web Site:www.my107.com Licensee: Clear Channel Broadcasting Licenses Inc. Group owner: Clear Channel Communications Inc. (acq 9-30-2003; $2.2 million). Population served: 350,000 Natl. Rep: McGavren Guild,. Format: 70's & 80's. News staff: 2; News: 15 hrs wkly. Target aud: 25-54. ♦Jeanie Hufford, gen mgr; Eddie Hill, stn mgr, gen sls mgr; Steve Powers, opns dir.

WYCT(FM)— Nov 28, 2003: 98.7 mhz; 100 kw. Ant 981 ft TL: N30 37 30 W87 26 39. Stereo. Hrs open: 7251 Plantation Rd., 32504. Phone: (850) 494-2800. Fax: (850) 494-0778.E-mail: hr@catcountry987.com Web Site:www.catcountry987.com Licensee: ADX Communications of Pensacola. Population served: 450,000 Dan Alpert. Format: Country. ♦David E. Hoxeng, CEO; Mary Hoxeng, gen mgr; Susan Nieman, sls dir; Kevin King, opns.

Perry

KRIK(FM)—Not on air, target date: unknown: 107.7 mhz; 21 kw. Ant 328 ft TL: N30 02 58 W83 41 01. Hrs open: Lerman Senter PLLC, 2000 K St. N.W., Suite 600, Washington, DC, 20006-1809. Phone: (202) 429-8970. Fax: (202) 293-7783. Licensee: Hispanic Target Media Inc. ♦Francisco San Millan, pres; Meredith S. Senter Jr., gen mgr.

WFDZ(FM)—Not on air, target date: unknown: 93.5 mhz; 6 kw. Ant 252 ft TL: N30 08 00 W83 35 45. Hrs open: 2001 S. Jefferson St., 32348. Phone: (573) 701-4708. Licensee: Dockins Telecommunications Inc. ♦Fred Dockins, gen mgr.

WNFK(FM)— December 1989: 92.1 mhz; 2.45 kw. 345 ft TL: N30 07 36 W83 36 28. Stereo. Hrs open: Stn currently dark 5450 Hwy. 27 E., 32347. Phone: (850) 584-9210. Fax: (850) 223-3492.E-mail: powercountry921@wildblue.net Licensee: Taylor County Broadcasting Inc. (acq 4-19-00). Format: Country. ♦Bob Hendrickson, gen mgr; Keith Conway, progmg dir.

WPRY(AM)— 1953: 1400 khz; 1 kw-U. TL: N30 06 27 W83 34 00. Hrs open: 24 2001 S. Jefferson St, 32348. Phone: (850) 223-1400. Fax: (850) 223-3501. Web Site:www.wpry.com Licensee: HF Broadcasting Perry LC (acq 4-1-2004; $150,000). Format: Classic hits. News: 15 hrs wkly. Target aud: 18 plus. Spec prog: Black 2 hrs wkly. ♦Gary Williams, gen mgr.

Pine Castle-Sky Lake

WAMT(AM)— Jan 28, 1977: 1190 khz; 5 kw-D. TL: N28 27 58 W81 22 30. Hrs open: 24 1160 S. Semoran Blvd., Suite A, Orlando, 32807. Phone: (407) 380-9255. Fax: (407) 382-7565.E-mail: studio@wamt1190.com Web Site:www.wamt1190.com Licensee: Genesis Communications I Inc. Group owner: Genesis Communications Inc. (acq 3-20-2000; $2.1 million). Population served: 1,500,000 Natl. Network: ABC, Westwood One, . Natl. Rep: Interep,. Florida's Radio Networks Booth, Freret, Imlay, & Tepper. Wire Svc: AP Wire Svc: Metro Weather Service Inc. Format: News/talk. Target aud: 25-65; general. ♦Bruce Maduri, pres; Colin Cantwell, VP, gen mgr; Sabrina Lavender, gen sls mgr.

Pine Hills

WFLF(AM)— Sept 9, 1955: 540 khz; 50 kw-U, DA-2. TL: N28 07 57 W81 43 16. Hrs open: 24 2500 Maitland Center Pkwy., Suite 407, Maitland, 32751. Phone: (407) 916-7800. Fax: (407) 661-1940.E-mail: kaystelling@clearchannel.com Web Site:www.540wfla.com Licensee: Clear Channel Radio Licenses Inc. Group owner: Clear Channel Communications Inc. (acq 11-21-97; grpsl). Population served: 100,000 Natl. Network: Fox News Radio, . Rgnl. Network: Florida Radio Net. Florida's Radio Networks Wiley, Rein & Fielding. Wire Svc: AP Format: News/talk. News staff: 5; News: 168 hrs wkly. Target aud: 35-64. Spec prog: Florida Gaton football & basketball, Florida Marlins, Miami Dolphins. ♦Linda Byrd, gen mgr; Kay Stelling, sls VP, gen sls mgr; Rick Everett, mktg dir; Chris Kampmeier, progmg dir.

Pine Island Center

WPTK(AM)—Licensed to Pine Island Center. See Fort Myers

Pinellas Park

WHBO(AM)—Licensed to Pinellas Park. See Tampa

WTBN(AM)— Nov 12, 1966: 570 khz; 5 kw-U, DA-2. TL: N28 12 40 W82 31 46. Hrs open: 24 5211 W. Laurel St., # 101, Tampa, 33607. Phone: (813) 639-1903. Fax: (813) 639-1272.E-mail: info@bayword.com Web Site:www.bayword.com Licensee: Common Ground Broadcasting Inc. Group owner: Salem Communications Corp. (acq 8-7-2001; $6.75 million). Population served: 1500000 Natl. Network: Salem Radio Network, . Rgnl. Network: Florida Radio Net. Natl. Rep: Salem,. Format: Christian Talk Radio. News staff: 2; News: 30 hrs wkly. Target aud: 25-64. Spec prog: College (USF) sports football & basketball. ♦Chris Gould, gen mgr; Mike Serio, opns mgr; Rey Noriega, traf mgr.

Plant City

WTWD(AM)— July 1949: 910 khz; 5 kw-U, DA-1. TL: N27 59 26 W82 12 31. Hrs open: 24
Rebroadcasts WTBN Pinnellas Park 100%.
5211 Laurel St., # 101, Tampa, 33607. Phone: (813) 639-1903. Fax: (813) 639-1272.E-mail: info@bayword.com Web Site:www.bayword.com Licensee: South Texas Broadcasting Inc. Group owner: Salem Communications Corp. (acq 7-27-00; grpsl). Population served: 2,100,000 Natl. Network: Salem Radio Network, . Natl. Rep: Salem,. Format: Christian talk. Target aud: 25-54. ♦Christopher Gould, Sr., gen mgr; Mike Serio, opns mgr.

Plantation Key

WCTH(FM)— July 1969: 100.3 mhz; 100 kw. Ant 462 ft TL: N24 57 34 W80 34 30. Stereo. Hrs open: 24 93351 Overseas Hwy., Tavernier, 33070. Phone: (305) 852-9085. Fax: (305) 852-5586. Web Site:www.thundercountry.com Licensee: Clear Channel Radio Licenses Inc. Group owner: Clear Channel Communications Inc. (acq 2-99; $1.8 million). Population served: 150,000 Natl. Network: Westwood One, Motor Racing Net, . Rgnl. Network: Florida Radio Net. Natl. Rep: Clear Channel,. Florida's Radio Networks Format: Country. News staff: one; News: 4 hrs wkly. Target aud: 25-54; residents & tourists. Spec prog: NASCAR 3 hrs wkly. ♦John Hogan, CEO; Greg Capgna, VP; Mark Mills, gen mgr; Scott Hamilton, progmg dir & progmg mgr.

WFKZ(FM)— Jan 2, 1984: 103.1 mhz; 50 kw. 449 ft TL: N25 01 35 W80 30 30. Hrs open: 24 93351 Overseas Hwy., Tavernier, 33070. Phone: (305) 852-9085. Fax: (305) 852-5586. Web Site:www.sun103.com Licensee: Clear Channel Radio Licenses Inc. Group owner: Clear Channel Communications Inc. (acq 11-21-97; grpsl). Population served: 150,000 Format: Adult rock. News staff: 2; News: 8 hrs wkly. Target aud: 25-54; adults. ♦Greg Capgna, VP; Mark Mills, gen mgr & stn mgr.

Pompano Beach

WHSR(AM)— 1959: 980 khz; 5 kw-D, 1 kw-N, DA-D. TL: N26 14 26 W80 10 07. Hrs open: 6699 N. Federal Hwy., Ste 200, Boca Raton, 33487. Phone: (561) 997-0074. Fax: (561) 997-0476.E-mail: info@wshr.com Web Site:www.whsrentertainmentradio.com Licensee: WWNN License L.L.C. Group owner: Beasley Broadcast Group (acq 3-17-2000; grpsl). Population served: 2,500,000 Jason Shrinsky. Format: Foreign, ethnic, talk. Target aud: 25-54; baby boomers weaned on electronic media as an info source. ♦Bob Morency, VP, gen mgr; Greg Cooper, opns mgr.

WMXJ(FM)— 1960: 102.7 mhz; 100 kw. 1,007 ft TL: N25 57 59 W80 12 33. Stereo. Hrs open: 20450 N.W. 2nd Ave., Miami, 33169-2505. Phone: (305) 521-5100. Fax: (305) 652-1888. Web Site:www.majic1027.com Licensee: Lincoln Financial Media Co. of Florida. (acq 4-3-2006; grpsl). Population served: 3,111,400 Natl. Rep: CBS Radio,. Wire Svc: AP Format: Classic hits. Target aud: 35-64. ♦Dennis Collins, sr VP, gen mgr; Daryl Leoce, sls dir, gen sls mgr; Connie Estopinan, prom dir; Robert Hamilton, progmg dir; Gary Blau, engrg dir.

WWNN(AM)— 1959: 1470 khz; 5 kw-D, 2.5 kw-N, DA-1. TL: N26 10 46 W80 13 15. (CP: 50 kw-D). Hrs open: 24 6699 N. Federal Hwy., Suite 200, Boca Raton, 33487. Phone: (561) 997-0074. Fax: (561)

997-0476.E-mail: info@wwnn.com Web Site:www.wwnnradio.com Licensee: WWNN License LLC. Group owner: Beasley Broadcast Group (acq 3-14-2000; grpsl). Population served: 139,590 Format: Health & wealth. ♦Bob Morency, VP, gen mgr; Greg Cooper, opns mgr.

Ponte Vedra Beach

WOKV-FM— 1996: 106.5 mhz; 6 kw. Ant 328 ft TL: N30 16 34 W81 33 58. Stereo. Hrs open: 24 4190 Belfort Rd., Suite 450, Jacksonville, 32216. Phone: (904) 470-4615. Fax: (904) 296-1683. Licensee: Cox Radio Inc. Group owner: Salem Communications Corp. (acq 9-18-2006; $7.65 million). Format: Christian. Target aud: 25-44. ♦Calvin Grabau, gen mgr.

Port Charlotte

WKII(AM)—(Solana, Nov 19, 1986: 1070 khz; 1.8 kw-D, 233 w-N. TL: N26 53 37 W82 03 03. Stereo. Hrs open: 24 24100 Tiseo Blvd., Suite 10, 33980. Phone: (941) 206-1188. Fax: (941) 206-9296. Web Site:www.wkii.com Licensee: Clear Channel Broadcasting Licenses Inc. Rgnl. Network: Florida Radio Net. Florida's Radio Networks Format: Adult standards. News staff: one; News: 2 hrs wkly. Target aud: 35 plus. ♦Mike Moody, stn mgr, progmg dir, news dir; David Ayres, sls dir; Paul Wolf, chief of engrg; Ron Bigley, traf mgr.

***WVIJ(FM)**— July 26, 1987: 91.7 mhz; 1.9 kw. Ant 207 ft TL: N26 58 49 W82 04 03. Stereo. Hrs open: 3279 Sherwood Rd., 33980. Phone: (941) 624-5000. Fax: (775) 243-0586.E-mail: wvij@wvij.com Web Site:www.wvij.com Licensee: Port Charlotte Educational Broadcasting Foundation Inc. Format: Educ, relg. Target aud: 35 plus. ♦Daniel P. Kolenda Jr., gen mgr.

WZJZ(FM)— Oct 1, 1976: 100.1 mhz; 100 kw. Ant 476 ft TL: N26 37 25 W82 06 58. Stereo. Hrs open: 24 13320 Metro Pkwy., Suite 1, Fort Myers, 33966-4804. Phone: (239) 225-4300. Fax: (293) 225-4329. Web Site:www.movetoz100.com Licensee: Clear Channel Broadcasting Licenses Inc. Group owner: Clear Channel Communications Inc. (acq 2-18-97; grpsl). Population served: 450,000 Kaye, Scholer, Fierman, Hays & Handler L.L.P. Format: Hot adult contemp. Target aud: 25-54. ♦Jim Keating, gen mgr.

Port Richey

WSUN-FM—See Holiday

Port St. Joe

WPBH(FM)— Mar 12, 1990: 93.5 mhz; 14.5 kw. 659 ft TL: N29 49 09 W85 15 34. Hrs open: 24 1834 Lisenby Ave., Panama City, 32405. Phone: (850) 769-1408. Fax: (850) 769-0659.E-mail: info@panamacity@clearchannel.com Web Site:www.935thebeat.com Licensee: Citicasters Licenses L.P. Group owner: Clear Channel Communications Inc. (acq 8-26-99; $1 million). Format: Urban. Target aud: 35 plus; upscale, white collar professionals. ♦Pete Norton, stn mgr; Eddie Rupp, opns mgr.

Port St. Lucie

WHLG(FM)— Nov 16, 1998: 101.3 mhz; 6 kw. 328 ft TL: N27 16 04 W80 16 49. Stereo. Hrs open: 24 Horton Broadcasting Co. Inc., 1670 N.W. Federal Hwy., Stuart, 34994. Phone: (772) 692-9454. Fax: (772) 692-0258.E-mail: info@coast1013.com Web Site:www.coast1013.com Licensee: Horton Broadcasting Co. Inc. Population served: 205,900 Natl. Network: Jones Radio Networks, . Natl. Rep: Interep,. Format: Adult contemp. News staff: 10. Target aud: 25-54; female/male 60/40%, 35 years old. ♦George Metcalf, CEO; Lorna Potter, gen mgr.

WPSL(AM)— Oct 26, 1985: 1590 khz; 5 kw-D, 64 w-N. TL: N27 18 28 W80 18 26. Stereo. Hrs open: 24 4100 Metzger Rd., Fort Pierce, 34947. Phone: (772) 340-1590. Fax: (772) 340-3245.E-mail: wpsl@wpsl.com Web Site:www.wpsl.com Licensee: Port St. Lucie Broadcasters Inc. (acq 4-12-93; $200,000;4-26-93). Population served: 1,000,000 Natl. Network: CBS, ESPN Radio, . Rgnl. Network: Florida Radio Net. Florida's Radio Networks Leventhal, Senter & Lerman. Format: News/talk, sports. News staff: one; News: 4 hrs wkly. Target aud: 45 plus; established families. Spec prog: Relg 6 hrs wkly. ♦Carol Wyatt, CEO, pres; Greg Wyatt, VP & gen mgr.

Punta Gorda

WCCF(AM)— Sept 15, 1961: 1580 khz; 1.25 kw-D, 122 w-N. TL: N26 53 37 W82 03 01. Hrs open: 24100 Tiseo Blvd. #10, Port Charlotte, 33980. Phone: (941) 206-1188. Fax: (941) 206-9296.E-mail: info@wccfam.com Web Site:www.wccfam.com Licensee: Citicasters Licenses L.P. Group owner: Clear Channel Communications Inc. (acq 2-1-99; grpsl). Population served: 106,000 Format: News/talk. Target aud: 45 plus. ♦Chris Monk, VP; Mike Moody, gen mgr.

WIKX(FM)—(Charlotte Harbor, Sept 1, 1970: 92.9 mhz; 100 kw. 807 ft TL: N26 53 47 W82 14 27. Stereo. Hrs open: 24 Program sep from AM 24100 Tiseo Blvd. #10, Port Charlotte, 33980. Phone: (941) 206-1188. Fax: (941) 206-9296.E-mail: kixcountry@hotmail.com Web Site:www.wikx.com Population served: 250,000 Format: Country. News: 10 hrs wkly. Target aud: 25-54.

Punta Rassa

WTLQ-FM— May 3, 1999: 97.7 mhz; 14.5 kw. 430 ft TL: N26 29 16 W81 55 46. Stereo. Hrs open: 24 2824 Palm Beach Blvd., Ft. Myers, 33916. Phone: (239) 334-1111 / (239) 338-4325. Fax: (239) 334-0744. Web Site:www.latino977.com Licensee: Fort Myers Broadcasting Co. (group owner; acq 9-13-00; $7 million). Population served: 600,000 Natl. Rep: McGavren Guild,. Liebowitz & Associates. Format: Sp. Target aud: 18-49; adults. ♦Wayne Simons, gen mgr; Brad Foster, sls dir, rgnl sls mgr; Hector Velazquez, progmg dir; Keith Stuhlmann, engrg dir.

Quincy

***WFRU(FM)**— June 25, 2008: 90.1 mhz; 32 kw vert. Ant 328 ft TL: N30 42 22 W84 37 39. Hrs open: Box 181000, Tallahassee, 32318-0009. Phone: (850) 201-1070. Fax: (850) 201-1071. Web Site:www.faithradio.us Licensee: Okaloosa Public Radio Inc. Format: Relg. ♦Scott Beigle, gen mgr.

WWSD(AM)— Mar 15, 1948: 1230 khz; 1 kw-U. TL: N30 34 55 W84 35 59. Hrs open: 1732 W. Elm St., 32351. Phone: (850) 627-4390. Licensee: Tuff-Starr Jam Commuication Inc. ♦Reverend Milton Donato, pres.

WXSR(FM)— December 1966: 101.5 mhz; 50 kw. 476 ft TL: N30 31 08 W84 27 04. Hrs open: 325 John Knox Rd., Bldg. G, Tallahassee, 32303. Phone: (850) 422-3107. Fax: (850) 383-0747. Web Site:www.x1015.com Licensee: Clear Channel Radio Licenses Inc. Group owner: Clear Channel Communications Inc. (acq 11-21-97; grpsl). Format: Alternative, new rock. Target aud: 18-34. ♦Lisa Rice, VP & gen mgr; Jeff Horn, opns mgr, gen sls mgr.

Riviera Beach

WMNE(AM)— Aug 17, 1959: 1600 khz; 5 kw-D, 4.7 kw-N, DA-2. TL: N26 44 55 W80 08 02. Stereo. Hrs open: 24 824 US Hwy. 1, North Palm Beach, 33408. Phone: (561) 694-7636. Fax: (561) 694-7574. Web Site:www.radiodisney.com Licensee: Radio Disney Group LLC. Group owner: ABC Inc. (acq 8-22-00; grpsl). Natl. Rep: Roslin,. Format: Family. News staff: 2; News: 30 hrs wkly. Local Blacks & Hispanics. Spec prog: Sp. ♦Neil Orlikoff, gen mgr.

WZZR(FM)—Licensed to Riviera Beach. See West Palm Beach

Rock Harbor

WKLG(FM)— Nov 1, 1984: 102.1 mhz; 100 kw. Ant 430 ft TL: N25 05 29 W80 26 37. Stereo. Hrs open: 24 Box 0457, Key Largo, 33037. Secondary address: 1452 N. Krome Ave. , Suite 103 E., Florida City 33034. Phone: (305) 451-2202. Fax: (305) 453-2265.E-mail: wklg@bellcell.net Licensee: WKLG Inc. Leibowitz & Associates. Format: Adult contemp. Target aud: 25-54; majority are female 18 plus. ♦Douglas D. LaRue, pres & gen mgr.

Rockledge

WHKR(FM)— Nov 25, 1989: 102.7 mhz; 50 kw. 492 ft TL: N28 35 03 W80 50 56. Stereo. Hrs open: 24 1775 W. Hibiscus Blvd., Suite 101, Melbourne, 32901. Phone: (321) 984-1000. Fax: (321) 724-1565. Web Site:www.thehitkicker.com Licensee: Cumulus Licensing Corp. Group owner: Cumulus Media Inc. (acq 8-7-2000; grpsl). Format: Modern country. News staff: 2; News: 6 hrs wkly. Target aud: 25-54. Spec prog: Pub service one hr wkly. ♦Dan Carelli, gen mgr.

Royal Palm Beach

WMEN(AM)— April 1987: 640 khz; 7.5 kw-D, 460 w-N, DA-2. TL: N26 45 18 W80 22 00. (CP: COL Boca Raton. 50 kw-D, 25 kw-N, DA-2. TL: N26 32 30 W80 44 30). Hrs open: 24 6600 N. Andrews Ave., Suite 160, Fort Lauderdale, 33309. Phone: (954) 315-1515 / 1539. Fax: (954) 315-1555.E-mail: info@wlvj.com Licensee: JCE Licenses L.L.C. Group owner: James Crystal Inc. (acq 11-18-99; $3,945,500 for stock). Population served: 6,000,000 Natl. Network: Fox Sports, . Format: Sports. ♦Steve Lapa, gen mgr.

WPSP(AM)— February 1991: 1190 khz; 1 kw-U, DA-N. TL: N26 44 14 W80 16 23. Hrs open: 18 5730 Corporate Way, Suite 210, West Palm Beach, 33407. Phone: (561) 681-9777. Fax: (561) 687-3398.E-mail: diaz1190am@aol.com Licensee: George M. Arroyo. (acq 5-87; $75,000; 5-11-87). Roy F. Perkins. Format: Sp hits. News staff: 2; News: 20 hrs wkly. Target aud: 25-54. ♦George M. Arroyo, pres; Lissette M. Diaz, gen mgr & opns dir.

Safety Harbor

WYUU(FM)—Licensed to Safety Harbor. See Tampa

Saint Augustine

WAOC(AM)— December 1953: 1420 khz; 2.18 kw-D, 250 w-N. TL: N29 51 00 W81 19 50. Hrs open: 24 Box 3847, 32085. Secondary address: 567 Lewis Point Rd. Ext. 32086. Phone: (904) 797-4444. Fax: (904) 797-3446.E-mail: kris@1420sports.com Web Site:www.1420sports.com Licensee: Phillips Broadcasting LLC (acq 7-1-2006; $1 million with WFOY(AM) Saint Augustine). Population served: 150,000 Natl. Network: ESPN Radio, . Natl. Rep: Rgnl Reps,. Rgnl rep: Rgnl Reps Alan Campbell. Format: Sports. News staff: 1; News: 8 hrs wkly. Target aud: 26 plus; affluent adults. Spec prog: University of Florida sports, NFL Jaguar affiliate, NASCAR. ♦Kristine Phillips, pres; Jenny Hayes, gen mgr.

***WAYL(FM)**— May 22, 1994: 91.9 mhz; 5 kw. 200 ft TL: N29 54 26 W81 18 51. Hrs open: 24 Box 127, 32085. Secondary address: 1485 US Rt. 1 S. 32086. Phone: (904) 829-9200. Fax: (904) 829-9202.E-mail: david@fm88.org Web Site:www.riverradio.org Licensee: New Covenant Educational Ministries Inc. (acq 6-14-02). Population served: 250,000 Natl. Network: Salem Radio Network, . Fletcher, Heald & Hildreth. Format: Contemp Christian. News staff: 2; News: 10 hrs wkly. Target aud: 25-45. ♦David Oglesby, stn mgr; Jerry Smith, engrg mgr.

***WFCF(FM)**— Nov 1, 1993: 88.5 mhz; 6 kw. 141 ft TL: N29 54 27 W81 18 49. Hrs open: 7 AM-midnight Box 1027, Flagler College, St. Augustine, 32085-1027. Phone: (904) 819-6449. Phone: (904) 819-6313. Fax: (904) 826-3471.E-mail: wfcf@flagler.edu Web Site:www.flagler.edu Licensee: Flagler College. Population served: 88,000 Caressa D. Bennet. Format: Div. News: one hr wkly. Target aud: General. Spec prog: Sp 4 hrs, new age 4 hrs, folk 3 hrs, reggae 4 hrs, world 4 hrs, blues 4 hrs wkly. ♦Donna DeLorenzo Webb, gen mgr; Daniel McCook, stn mgr.

WFOY(AM)— July 7, 1936: 1240 khz; 1 kw-U. TL: N29 54 26 W81 18 51. Hrs open: 24 Box 3847, 32085. Secondary address: 567 Lewis Point Rd. Ext. 32086. Phone: (904) 797-1955. Phone: (904) 797-4444. Fax: (904) 797-3446.E-mail: kris@1240news.com Web Site:www.1420sports.com Licensee: Phillips Broadcasting LLC (acq 7-1-2006; $1 million with WAOC(AM) Saint Augustine). Population served: 150,000 Natl. Network: Fox News Radio, Westwood One, Talk Radio Network, . Rgnl. Network: Florida Radio Net. Natl. Rep: Rgnl Reps,. Florida's Radio Networks Rgnl rep: Rgnl Reps Alan Campbell. Format: News/talk, sports. News staff: one; News: 8 hrs wkly. Target aud: 26 plus; affluent adults. Spec prog: Rush Limbaugh affiliate. ♦Kristine Phillips, pres; Jenny Hayes, gen mgr.

WSOS-FM— July 17, 1982: 94.1 mhz; 25 kw. Ant 302 ft TL: N29 57 57 W81 28 36. (CP: COL Fruit Cove). Stereo. Hrs open: 24 2715 Stratton Blvd., 32084. Phone: (904) 824-0833. Phone: (904) 722-9606. Fax: (904) 721-9322.E-mail: tbryan@rendabroadcasting.com Web Site:www.wsosfm.com Licensee: Renda Broadcasting Corp. of Nevada. (acq 4-27-2005; $7.75 million). Population served: 500,000 Natl. Rep: McGavren Guild,. Format: Soft adult contemp. Target aud: 25-54; upscale audience. ♦Tony Renda, CEO; Tim Bryan, gen mgr; Don Runk, gen sls mgr; Stacey Steiner, prom dir; Briggs Bickley, progmg dir; Bob Dillehay, chief of engrg; Brenda McArthur, traf mgr; Jim Byard, pub svc dir.

Saint Augustine Beach

WSJF(FM)— Sept 1, 1995: 105.5 mhz; 16 kw. Ant 410 ft TL: N29 51 00 W81 19 50. Stereo. Hrs open: 24 9550 Regency Sq. Blvd., Suite 200, Jacksonville, 32225. Phone: (904) 680-1050. Fax: (904) 680-1051.E-mail: jaxproduction@tamabroadcasting.com Licensee: Scott Savage, receiver Group owner: Tama Broadcasting Inc. (acq 2-26-2009).

Population served: 175,000 Format: Oldies. Target aud: 20-45; general. ♦Linda Fructuoso, gen mgr; Joel Widdows, opns mgr, prom dir; Gerry Smith, chief of engrg.

WSOS(AM)— Oct 15, 1986: 1170 khz; 710 w-D. TL: N29 55 05 W81 23 26. Hrs open: 6 AM-9 PM 8384 Baymeadows Rd., Suite 1, Jacksonville, 32256-7486. Phone: (904) 739-3660. Fax: (904) 739-9409. Licensee: Norsan Consulting and Management Inc. (acq 1-13-2006; $300,000). Format: Tropical. ♦Jorge Lopez, gen mgr.

Saint Catherine

***WKFA(FM)**— 2005: 89.3 mhz; 100 w. Ant 295 ft TL: N28 32 22 W82 04 48. Hrs open: 505 Josephine St., Titusville, 32796. Phone: (321) 267-3000. Fax: (321) 264-9370.E-mail: wpio@gate.net Web Site:www.noncomradio.com Licensee: Florida Public Radio Inc. (acq 4-12-2003). Format: Inspirational music, Public affairs. ♦Randy Henry, pres & gen mgr.

Saint Cloud

WIWA(AM)— 2005: 1160 khz; 2.5 kw-D, 500 w-N, DA-2. TL: N28 16 15 W81 20 00. Hrs open: 4540 Curry Ford Rd., Orlando, 32812. Phone: (407) 770-2500. Fax: (407) 770-2503.E-mail: info@viva1160.com Web Site:www.viva1160.com Licensee: Centro de la Familia Cristiana Inc. (acq 3-20-2006; $562,800). Format: Spanish news/talk. ♦Roberto Candelario, pres.

Saint Marks

***WUJC(FM)**— 2005: 91.1 mhz; 7 kw vert. Ant 312 ft TL: N30 08 32 W83 54 58. Hrs open: 8747 Miles Johnson Rd., Tallahassee, 32309. Phone: (850) 514-1929. Fax: (850) 514-1927. Web Site:www.csnradio.com Licensee: CSN International (group owner). Format: Relg. ♦Michael Kestler, pres; Don Mills, progmg dir, mus dir.

Saint Petersburg

WDAE(AM)— Nov 1, 1927: 620 khz; 5.6 kw-D, 5.5 kw-N, DA-N. TL: N27 52 37 W82 35 26 (day), N27 52 37 W82 35 25 (night). Stereo. Hrs open: 24 4002 Gandy Blvd., Tampa, 33611. Phone: (813) 832-1000. Fax: (813) 831-3299. Web Site:www.620wdae.com Licensee: Clear Channel Broadcasting Licenses Inc. (acq 11-20-98; $9.75 million). Population served: 2300000 Natl. Network: Fox Sports, . Natl. Rep: Katz Radio,. Wire Svc: AP Format: Sports. ♦Dan Diloreto, VP, gen mgr; Chris Soechtig, sls dir; Mike Killabrew, progmg dir; John McMartin, chief of engrg; Gwen Shuler, traf mgr.

WFLA(AM)—See Tampa

WFLZ-FM—See Tampa

***WFTI-FM**— June 1988: 91.7 mhz; 3 kw. 282 ft TL: N27 46 15 W82 38 19. Stereo. Hrs open: 24 360 Central Ave., Suite 1240, 33701. Phone: (727) 823-1140. Fax: (727) 823-5753.E-mail: WFTIFM@hotmail.com Web Site:www.familyradio.com Licensee: Family Stations Inc. (group owner; acq 11-19-88). Natl. Network: Family Radio, . Format: Relg. News: 9 hrs wkly. Target aud: General. ♦Bob Barnes, stn mgr.

WGES(AM)— May 5, 1950: 680 khz; 690 w-D, 125 w-N. TL: N27 51 24 W82 37 26. Hrs open: 402 N. Reo Street, Suite 218, Tampa, 33609. Phone: (813) 319-5757. Phone: (813) 637-8000. Fax: (813) 319-0029. Fax: (813) 637-8001.E-mail: info@genesis680.com Web Site:www.genesis680.com Licensee: ZGS Broadcasting of Tampa Inc. (acq 1-18-91; $200,000; 2-4-91). Population served: 300,000 Rgnl rep: Katz Hispanic Media Format: Tropical/Spanish. Target aud: General; adults 18-49. ♦Patricia Omana, gen mgr.

WHPT(FM)—See Sarasota

WMTX(FM)—See Tampa

WPOI(FM)— July 1, 1961: 101.5 mhz; 100 kw. 1,358 ft TL: N27 50 32 W82 15 46. Stereo. Hrs open: 24 Cox Radio Inc., 11300 4th St. N., Suite 300, 33716-2941. Phone: (727) 579-2000. Fax: (727) 579-2662. Fax: (727) 579-2271.E-mail: info@doxradio.com Web Site:www.1015thepoint.com Licensee: Cox Radio Inc. Group owner: Cox Communications Inc. (acq 1999; grpsl). Population served: 4,000,000 Natl. Rep: Clear Channel,. Format: Hits of the 80s. Target aud: 25-54. ♦Howard Tuuri, VP, gen mgr, stn mgr; Tom Paleveda, opns mgr; Bernadette Van Osdal, gen sls mgr; Gerry Brauer, prom mgr.

WQYK-FM— May 1958: 99.5 mhz; 100 kw. Ant 590 ft TL: N27 56 50 W82 27 35. Stereo. Hrs open: 24 9721 Executive Center Dr. N., Suite 200, 33702. Phone: (727) 579-1925. Web Site:www.wqyk.com Licensee: CBS Radio Inc. of Florida. Group owner: Infinity Broadcasting Corp. (acq 12-1-86; 10-6-86). Natl. Network: CBS, . Natl. Rep: Interep,. Leventhal, Senter & Lerman. Format: Contemp country. News staff: one; News: 6 hrs wkly. Target aud: 25-54. ♦Charlie Ochs, sr VP; Luis Albertini, VP, gen mgr, progmg dir; Mike Culotta, gen mgr & opns mgr. Co-owned TV: WTOG(TV) affil

WRBQ-FM—See Tampa

WWMI(AM)— 1939: 1380 khz; 5 kw-U, DA-N. TL: N27 52 15 W82 37 03. Hrs open: 24 11300 4th St. N., Suite 143, St. Petersburg, 33716. Phone: (727) 577-4500. Fax: (727) 579-1340. Web Site:www.radiodisney.com Licensee: Radio Disney Group LLC. Group owner: ABC Inc. (acq 1999; grpsl). Population served: 3,102,000 Natl. Rep: Clear Channel,. Wire Svc: NOAA Weather Format: Top- 40. News staff: 2. Target aud: 25-54. ♦Drew Rashbaum, gen mgr; Ted Wolfe, stn mgr.

WWRM(FM)—(Tampa, 1958: 94.9 mhz; 100 kw. 1,289 ft TL: N27 49 09 W82 14 26. Stereo. Hrs open: 24 11300 4th St. N., Suite 300, St. Petersburg, 33716-2941. Phone: (727) 579-2000. Fax: (727) 579-2662.E-mail: info@coxradio.com Web Site:www.949online.com Licensee: Cox Radio Inc. Group owner: Cox Communications Inc. (acq 7-1-88). Natl. Rep: Christal,. Format: Adult contemp. Target aud: 25-54. ♦Howard Tuuri, gen mgr; Tom Paleveda, opns mgr; Mark Kanak, gen sls mgr, natl sls mgr; Julia Freeman, prom mgr.

WXGL(FM)— 1958: 107.3 mhz; 100 kw. 649 ft TL: N27 51 24 W82 37 26. Stereo. Hrs open: 24 11300 4th St. N., Suite 300, 33716. Phone: (727) 579-2000. Fax: (727) 579-2662. Fax: (727) 579-2662.E-mail: info@coxradio.com Web Site:www.1073theeagle.com Licensee: Cox Radio Inc. Group owner: Cox Communications Inc. (acq 7-1-88). Population served: 2,300,000 Natl. Rep: Commercial Media Sales,. Format: Classic Hits. ♦Keith Lawless, VP, gen mgr; Shane Reeve, gen sls mgr; Tom Paleveda, opns mgr & natl sls mgr.

Saint Petersburg Beach

WRXB(AM)— 1957: 1590 khz; 5 kw-D, 1 kw-N, DA-2. TL: N27 44 03 W82 41 08. Hrs open: 2060 First Ave. N., St. Petersburg, 33713. Phone: (727) 821-9967. Fax: (727) 321-3025.E-mail: wrxb@juno.com Web Site:www.wrxb.com Licensee: Metropolitan Radio Group of Florida Inc. Group owner: Metropolitan Radio Group Inc. Population served: 160,000 Format: Adult contemp, urban contemp. Target aud: 23-54; urban contemp. Spec prog: Jazz 15 hrs wkly. ♦Juanita Dials, gen mgr.

San Carlos Park

WDEO-FM— 1995: 98.5 mhz; 18.5 kw. Ant 371 ft TL: N26 30 18 W81 51 14. Stereo. Hrs open: 24 Box 504, Ann Arbor, MI, 48106. Phone: (734) 930-5200. Fax: (734) 930-3179. Web Site:www.avemariaradio.net Licensee: Ave Maria University Inc. (acq 2-9-2004; $4.9 million). Population served: 516,200 Format: Catholic news/talk. Target aud: 21 plus; adult Christian. ♦Michael Jones, gen mgr.

Sanford

WSDO(AM)— May 20, 1947: 1400 khz; 1 kw-U. TL: N28 48 04 W81 15 06. Hrs open: 24 222 Hazard St., Orlando, 32804-3030. Phone: (407) 841-8282. Fax: (407) 841-8250. Licensee: J & V Communications Co. (acq 6-5-92; $300,000; 6-22-92). Natl. Network: Westwood One, . Rgnl. Network: Florida Radio Net. Florida's Radio Networks Format: Sp news/talk. Target aud: 21 plus. Spec prog: Relg 3 hrs wkly. ♦John Torrado, CEO; Jocelyn Torrado, VP, gen mgr; Hector Reyes, gen mgr.

Santa Rosa Beach

WWAV-FM— Apr 3, 1985: 102.1 mhz; 18 kw. TL: N30 23 17 W86 17 55. Hrs open: 24 743 Harbor Blvd., Suite 6, Destin, 32541-2574. Phone: (850) 654-1031. Fax: (850) 654-6510. Web Site:www.wave1021.com Licensee: Qantum of Fort Walton Beach License Co. LLC. Group owner: Root Communications (acq 7-2-2003; grpsl). Population served: 185,000 Natl. Rep: Katz Radio,. Garvey, Schubert & Barer. Format: Adult hits. News: one hr wkly. Target aud: 25-54; general. ♦Frank Osborne, pres; Allyson Buckner, sls dir; Georgia Edmiston, gen mgr & disc jockey.

Sarasota

WBRD(AM)—See Palmetto

WCTQ(FM)— June 30, 1965: 106.5 mhz; 25 kw. 280 ft TL: N27 20 12 W82 34 25. Stereo. Hrs open: 24 1779 Independence Blvd., 34234. Phone: (941) 388-3936. Fax: (941) 55-4900. Web Site:www.1065ctq.com Population served: 600,000 Format: Country. News: one hr wkly. Target aud: 25-54. ♦Mark Wilson, opns mgr, progmg dir; Tracy Black, pub affrs dir; Matt Howell, engrg dir; Maverick Johnson, chief of engrg, disc jockey; Heidi Decker, disc jockey.

WHPT(FM)— 1973: 102.5 mhz; 100 kw. 1,776 ft TL: N27 29 08 W82 32 00. Stereo. Hrs open: 24 11300 4th St. N., Suite 300, St. Petersburg, 33716. Phone: (727) 579-2000. Fax: (727) 579-2662. Fax: (727) 579-2271.E-mail: info@coxradio.com Web Site:theboneonline.com Licensee: Cox Radio Inc. Group owner: Cox Broadcasting (acq 5-99; grpsl). Population served: 200,000 Natl. Rep: Clear Channel,. Format: Class rock. Target aud: 25-54. ♦Keith Lawless, VP & gen mgr.

***WKZM(FM)**— Oct 21, 1974: 104.3 mhz; 6 kw. Ant 266 ft TL: N27 16 30 W82 28 54. Hrs open: 24
Rebroadcasts WKES(FM) Lakeland 100%.
Box 8889, St. Petersburg, 33738. Phone: (727) 391-9994. Fax: (727) 397-6425.E-mail: wkes@moody.edu Web Site:www.wkes.org Licensee: The Moody Bible Institute of Chicago. (group owner; acq 10-15-99). Population served: 500,000 Southmayd & Miller. Format: Inspirational, educ. News: 14 hrs wkly. Target aud: General. ♦Pierre Chestang, gen mgr.

WLSS(AM)— May 23, 1949: 930 khz; 5 kw-D, 3 kw-N, DA-2. TL: N27 21 17 W82 23 06. Hrs open: 24 5211 W. Laurel St., # 101, Tampa, 33607. Phone: (813) 639-1903. Fax: (813) 639-1272.E-mail: wlss@wlssradio.com Web Site:www.wlssradio.com Licensee: Caron Broadcasting Inc. Group owner: WGUL-FM, Inc. (acq 8-12-2005; $9.5 million with WGUL(AM) Dunedin). Population served: 357,700 Natl. Network: Salem Radio Network, . Natl. Rep: Salem,. Format: News/talk. ♦Chris Gould, gen mgr; Mike Serio, opns mgr; Casey Bell, prom.

WSDV(AM)— Dec 7, 1939: 1450 khz; 1 kw-ND. TL: N27 20 12 W82 34 25. Hrs open: 24 1779 Independence Blvd., 34234. Phone: (941) 552-4800. Fax: (941) 552-4900.E-mail: nancylee@doveradio.com Web Site:www.doveradio.com Licensee: Citicasters Licenses L.P. Group owner: Clear Channel Communications Inc. (acq 5-4-99; grpsl). Population served: 700,000 Format: Adult standards. News staff: 3; News: 40 hrs wkly. Target aud: 25-54; general. ♦Sherri Carlson, VP & gen mgr.

WSJT(FM)—See Holmes Beach

***WSMR(FM)**— 1993: 89.1 mhz; 50 kw. 462 ft TL: N27 06 00 W82 22 19. Hrs open: 24 240 N. Washington Blvd., Suite 490, 34236. Phone: (941) 906-9767. Fax: (941) 362-0377. Web Site:www.wsmr.org Licensee: Northwestern College. Group owner: Northwestern College & Radio (acq 10-4-96; $400,000). Format: Christian lite contemp. News: 6 hrs wkly. Target aud: 30-55; with kids still at home. ♦Dr. Alan Cureton, CEO, pres; Harv Hendrickson, gen mgr; Douglas Poll, stn mgr.

WSRQ(AM)— Jan 1, 1961: 1220 khz; 1 kw-D, 600 w-N, DA. TL: N27 19 27 W82 29 47. Hrs open: 8201 S. Tamiami Tr. #54, 34238. Phone: (941) 952-1220. Fax: (941) 365-2900.E-mail: 1220@newstalk1220.com Web Site:www.newstalk1220.com Licensee: SRQ Radio LLC (acq 8-21-2006; $450,000). Population served: 350,000 Rgnl. Network: Florida Radio Net. Florida's Radio Networks Format: News/talk, sports. Target aud: 25-64; men. ♦James Grady, gen mgr.

WTMY(AM)— Dec 2, 1961: 1280 khz; 500 w-D, 340 w-N, DA-2. TL: N27 21 21 W82 29 13. Hrs open: 24 2101 Hammock Pl., 34235. Phone: (941) 954-1280. Fax: (941) 955-9062.E-mail: wtmy@juno.com Web Site:www.wtmy.com Licensee: Metropolitan Radio Group Inc. (group owner; acq 8-96). Population served: 300,000 Format: Money talk, health talk, talk. Target aud: 40 plus; wealth & health oriented. Spec prog: Pol one hr, gospel 6 hrs, full service 2 hrs wkly. ♦Mark Acker, pres; Greg Durkin, gen mgr.

Satellite Beach

WSBH(FM)—Not on air, target date: unknown: 98.5 mhz; 6 kw. Ant 328 ft TL: N28 08 11 W80 42 12. Hrs open: 1670 N.W. Federal Hwy., Stuart, 34994-1006. Phone: (321) 752-9850. Fax: (772) 692-0258. Licensee: Horton Broadcasting Co. Inc. ♦George Metcalf, pres.

Sebastian

WSJZ-FM— 2001: 95.9 mhz; 25 kw. Ant 289 ft TL: N27 49 05 W80 37 18. Hrs open: 24 1775 W. Hibiscus Blvd., Suite 101, Melbourne, 32901. Phone: (321) 984-1000. Fax: (321) 724-1565. Web Site:www.pirate959.com Licensee: Cumulus Licensing LLC. (acq 11-8-2004; $5 million). Format: Rock. ♦Dan Carelli, gen mgr.

Sebring

WFHT(AM)—See Avon Park

WITS(AM)—Nov 24, 1959: 1340 khz; 1 kw-U. TL: N27 30 30 W81 25 20. Hrs open: 24 3750 U.S. 27 N., Suite 1, 33870. Phone: (863) 382-9999. Fax: (863) 382-1982.E-mail: cohanradiogroup@htn.net Web Site:www.cohanradiogroup.com Licensee: Cohan Radio Group Inc. (group owner; (acq 11-1-98; $735,000 with co-located FM plus WJCM(AM) Sebring). Population served: 56,000 Natl. Network: ABC, . Natl. Rep: Interep,. Latham & Watkins. Wire Svc: AP Format: MOR. News staff: one; News: 5 hrs wkly. Target aud: 40 plus; mature adults. ♦ Peter Coughlin, pres & gen mgr; Libby Coughlin, gen sls mgr; Kim McPherson, traf mgr.

WJCM(AM)— May 22, 1950: 1050 khz; 1 kw-D, 11 w-N. TL: N27 30 30 W81 25 20. Hrs open: 24 3750 U.S. 27 N., 33870. Phone: (863) 382-9999. Fax: (863) 382-1982.E-mail: cohanradiogroup@htn.net Web Site:www.cohanradiogroup.com Licensee: Cohan Radio Group Inc. (group owner; (acq 11-1-98; $150,000). Population served: 70,000 Rgnl. Network: Florida Radio Net. Natl. Rep: Interep,. Florida's Radio Networks Rgnl rep: Interep Latham & Watkins. Wire Svc: AP Format: Oldies. News staff: one; News: 8 hrs wkly. Target aud: 45+. ♦ Peter Coughlin, gen mgr, gen sls mgr; Libby Coughlin, rgnl sls mgr; Alan Gray, progmg mgr; Barry Foster, news dir; Stacy Clark, pub affrs dir; Phil Scott, chief of engrg.

*WJFH(FM)— 2007: 91.5 mhz; 16 kw. Ant 454 ft TL: N27 22 52 W81 29 28. Hrs open: Box 7217, Lakeland, 33807-7217. Phone: (863) 644-3464. Fax: (863) 646-5326. Licensee: Radio Training Network Inc. ♦ James L. Campbell, pres.

WWLL(FM)— July 1967: 105.7 mhz; 19 kw. Ant 351 ft TL: N27 21 29 W81 28 22. Stereo. Hrs open: 24 3750 U.S. 27 N., Suite 1, 33870. Phone: (863) 382-9999. Fax: (863) 382-1982. Web Site:www.cohanradiogroup.com Licensee: Cohan Radio Group Inc. (acq 11-1-98). Population served: 90,000+ Natl. Network: NBC Radio, . Rgnl. Network: Florida Radio Net. Natl. Rep: Interep,. Wire Svc: AP Format: Adult contemp. News staff: one; News: 2 hrs wkly. Target aud: 25-54; adults. ♦ Peter Coughlin, pres; Les Howard Jacoby, progmg dir.

WWOJ(FM)—See Avon Park

WWTK(AM)—See Lake Placid

Seffner

WQYK(AM)—Licensed to Seffner. See Tampa

Shalimar

WNCV(FM)— Oct 25, 1982: 93.3 mhz; 50 kw. Ant 469 ft TL: N30 24 38 W86 37 22. Hrs open: 24 225 N.W. Hollywood Blvd., Fort Walton Beach, 32548-4725. Phone: (850) 243-7676. Fax: (850) 243-6806.E-mail: coastoffice@wncv.com Web Site:www.wncv.com Licensee: Cumulus Licensing LLC. (acq 8-2-2006; swap for WRKN(FM) Niceville). Population served: 65,000 Putbrese, Hunsaker & Trent. Format: Adult contemp, soft hits. ♦ Mike DeMarco, gen mgr; Skip Davis, progmg dir.

Silver Springs

WNDD(FM)—Licensed to Silver Springs. See Gainesville

Solana

WCVU(FM)— 1994: 104.9 mhz; 6 kw. Ant 318 ft TL: N26 53 37 W82 03 03. Hrs open: 24100 Tiseo Blvd., Unit 10, Port Charlotte, 33980. Phone: (941) 206-1188. Fax: (941) 206-9296.E-mail: info@clearchannel.com Web Site:www.clearchannel.com Licensee: Citicasters Licenses L.P. Group owner: Clear Channel Communications Inc. (acq 2-1-99; grpsl). Population served: 106,000 Natl. Network: CNN Radio, . Format: Soft adult contemp. ♦ Michael Moody, gen mgr; David Ayres, sls dir; Todd Matthews, progmg mgr.

WKII(AM)—Licensed to Solana. See Port Charlotte

South Daytona

WPUL(AM)— June 13, 1957: 1590 khz; 1 kw-D. TL: N29 09 16 W81 01 20. Hrs open: 6 am-12 pm 427 S. Martin L. King Blvd., Daytona Beach, 32114. Phone: (386) 239-7080 (Studio). Phone: (386) 226-2398. Fax: (386) 254-7510.E-mail: ccherry2@aol.com Licensee: PSI

Communications Inc. (acq 2-1-89; $250,000; 1-23-89). Natl. Network: American Urban, . Format: Gospel, talk. Target aud: General. ♦ Charles W. Cherry II, CEO, gen mgr; Phinesse Demps, progmg mgr.

South Miami

WAXY(AM)— Sept 15, 1947: 790 khz; 25 kw-U, DA-2. TL: N25 46 25 W80 38 13. Stereo. Hrs open: 24 20450 N.W. 2nd Ave., Miami, 33169. Phone: (305) 521-5100 / (887) 790-1015. Fax: (305) 521-1416. Web Site:www.waxy.com Licensee: Lincoln Financial Media Co. of Florida. (group owner; (acq 4-3-2006; grpsl). Population served: 2,800,000 Natl. Rep: CBS Radio,. Format: Sports talk. Target aud: 35 plus. ♦ Dennis P. Collins, gen mgr; Gary Aybar, opns mgr.

Sparr

*WTYG(FM)—Not on air, target date: unknown: 91.5 mhz; 100 w. Ant 95 ft TL: N29 20 21 W82 06 10. Hrs open: 401 Groveland Rd., Mount Dora, 32757. Phone: (913) 669-8101. Licensee: Arts for the Community Inc. ♦ De Miller, pres.

Spring Hill

WJQB(FM)— October 1992: 106.3 mhz; 25 kw. Ant 315 ft TL: N28 31 41 W82 32 45. Hrs open: 35048 US Hwy. 19 N., Palm Harbor, 34684. Phone: (727) 442-4027. Fax: (727) 781-4375.E-mail: staff@wjqb.com Web Site:www.wjqb.com Licensee: WGUL-FM Inc. Format: Oldies. ♦ Steve Schurdell, VP & gen mgr.

Springfield

WRBA(FM)— June 1986: 95.9 mhz; 50 kw. Ant 300 ft TL: N30 12 12 W85 36 57. Hrs open: 24 118 Gwyn Dr., Panama City Beach, 32408. Phone: (850) 234-8858. Fax: (850) 234-6592.E-mail: billyoung@panamacityradio.com Web Site:www.arrow959.com Licensee: Double O Radio Corp. (group owner; acq 3-10-2004; grpsl). Population served: 135,000 Format: Classic rock. Target aud: 30-54; general. ♦ Harry Finch, gen mgr.

WYOO(FM)—Licensed to Springfield. See Panama City

Starke

*WTLG(FM)— 1982: 88.3 mhz; 7 kw. Ant 285 ft TL: N29 54 34 W82 06 02. Stereo. Hrs open: 24 Drawer 2440, Tupelo, MS, 38803. Phone: (662) 844-5036. Fax: (662) 842-6791. Web Site:www.afr.net Licensee: American Family Association. (acq 3-31-2008; $225,000). Natl. Network: American Family Radio, . Format: Christian. ♦ Donald E. Wildmon, chmn.

Stuart

WAVW(FM)— Dec 24, 1964: 92.7 mhz; 50 kw. Ant 482 ft TL: N27 16 30 W80 17 12. Stereo. Hrs open: Box 0093, Port St. Lucie, 34985. Phone: (772) 335-9300. Fax: (772) 335-3291.E-mail: info@wavw.com Web Site:www.wavw.com Licensee: Capstar TX L.P. Group owner: Clear Channel Communications Inc. (acq 8-30-00; grpsl). Population served: 50,000 Format: Country. ♦ John Hunt, gen mgr; Heath West, progmg dir; Mike Kerley, chief of engrg.

WSTU(AM)— Dec 9, 1954: 1450 khz; 1 kw-U. TL: N27 12 53 W80 15 24. Hrs open: 24 4100 Metzger Rd., Fort Pierce, 34947. Phone: (772) 220-9788. Fax: (772) 340-3245.E-mail: wpsl@wpsl.com Web Site:www.wstu1450.com Licensee: Treasure Coast Broadcasters Inc. (acq 2-13-02; $500,000). Population served: 600,000 Natl. Network: ESPN Radio, ABC, . Florida's Radio Networks Leventhal, Senter & Lerman. Format: News/talk, sports. News staff: 2. Target aud: 35 plus. ♦ Carol Wyatt, pres.

*WWFR(FM)— 1988: 91.7 mhz; 2.65 kw. Ant 499 ft TL: N27 07 14 W80 23 59. Stereo. Hrs open: 24 Box 277, Okeechobee, 34973. Secondary address: 10400 NW 240th St., Okeechobee 34973. Phone: (863) 763-5454. Fax: (863) 763-7729.E-mail: wwfrfm@earthlink.net Web Site:www.familyradio.com Licensee: Family Stations Inc. (group owner) Population served: 70,000 Natl. Network: Family Radio, . Format: Relg. News: 11 hrs wkly. Target aud: General. Spec prog: Pub affrs 2 hrs wkly. ♦ Ed Dearborn, chief of opns.

Summerland Key

WPIK(FM)— December 1991: 102.5 mhz; 50 kw. Ant 413 ft TL: N24 40 35 W81 30 41. Stereo. Hrs open: 24 Box 420249, 33042. Secondary address: 22500 Pieces of Eight Rd., Cudjoe Key 33042. Phone: (305) 745-9988. Fax: (305) 745-4165.E-mail: info@myradioritmo.com Web Site:www.myradioritmo.com Licensee: Summerland Media LLC (acq 10-7-2005; $1.85 million). Population served: 75,000 Format: Bilingual music. ♦ Lilliam M. Sierra, gen mgr; Pepin Navarro, progmg dir.

Sunrise

*WKPX(FM)— Feb 14, 1983: 88.5 mhz; 3 kw. 100 ft TL: N26 10 38 W80 15 23. Stereo. Hrs open: 12 8000 N.W. 44th St., 33351. Phone: (754) 321-1000. Fax: (754) 321-1180.E-mail: info@becon.tv Web Site:www.becon.tv Licensee: School Board of Broward County. Format: Modern rock, alternative. Target aud: 15-35; people interested in alternative progmg. Spec prog: Black 3 hrs, blues 3 hrs wkly. ♦ Pat Swank, stn mgr; Jim Sorensen, chief of engrg.

Sweetwater

WZAB(AM)— 2008: 880 khz; 4 kw-D, 5 kw-N, DA-2. TL: N25 44 56 W80 32 50. Hrs open: 2828 W. Flagler St., Miami, 33135. Phone: (305) 503-1340. Fax: (305) 677-7585. Licensee: Florida City Radio. Format: All business. ♦ Tony Calatayud, gen mgr.

Tallahassee

WAIB(FM)— June 17, 1976: 103.1 mhz; 50 kw. 295 ft TL: N30 29 43 W84 13 51. (CP: 42 kw, ant 541 ft. TL: N30 29 39 W84 14 00). Stereo. Hrs open: 24 Opus Broadcasting, 3000 Olson Rd., 32308. Phone: (850) 386-8004. Fax: (850) 422-1897.E-mail: hkestenbaum @opusbroadcasting.com Web Site:www.newcountryb103.com Licensee: Opus Broadcasting Tallahassee LLC. Group owner: Triad Broadcasting Co. LLC (acq 9-2-2005; grpsl). Population served: 350,000 Natl. Rep: McGavren Guild,. Format: Country. Target aud: 25-54. ♦ Hank Kestenbaum, gen mgr; Doug Purtee, opns dir.

*WANM(FM)— November 1976: 90.5 mhz; 1.6 w. 167 ft TL: N30 25 49 W84 17 27. Stereo. Hrs open: 24 Florida A&M Univ., 510 Orr Dr., Ste 3056, 32307. Phone: (850) 599-3083. Fax: (850) 561-2829.E-mail: info@wanm.com Web Site:www.famu.edu/famcast Licensee: The Board of Trustees of Florida A&M University. Population served: 195,000 Natl. Network: AP Radio, . Wire Svc: AP Format: News, sports. News: 5 hrs wkly. Target aud: General; urban African-American in area. Spec prog: Reggae 3 hrs wkly, Gospel 18 hrs wkly, Jazz 15 hrs wkly. ♦ Keith Miles, gen mgr; Greg Bishop, opns mgr.

WBZE(FM)— July 15, 1962: 98.9 mhz; 100 kw. Ant 390 ft TL: N30 29 35 W84 16 55. Stereo. Hrs open: 24 3411 W. Tharpe St., 32303. Phone: (850) 201-3000. Fax (850) 561-8903. Web Site:www.mystar98.com Licensee: Cumulus Licensing Corp. Population served: 320,304 Natl. Rep: Katz Radio,. Wiley & Rein. Format: Adult contemp. Target aud: 25-54. ♦ John Dawson, progmg dir.

WCVC(AM)— Nov 5, 1953: 1330 khz; 5 kw-D. TL: N30 29 03 W84 17 13. Hrs open: 6:30 AM-7 PM 117 1/2 Henderson Rd., 32312. Phone: (850) 386-1330.E-mail: wcvc65@hotmail.com Web Site:www.lordoflorida.com Licensee: WCVC Inc. (acq 10-4-85; $500,000; 8-12-85). Population served: 190,000 ♦ Wendell H. Borrink, pres; Erwin O'Conner, gen mgr, opns mgr, progmg dir.

WEGT(FM)—(Lafayette, Dec 17, 1989): 99.9 mhz; 50 kw. 492 ft TL: N30 20 59 W83 59 53. Stereo. Hrs open: 24 Opus Broadcasting, 3000 Olson Rd., 32308. Phone: (850) 386-8004. Fax: (850) 422-1897. Licensee: Opus Broadcasting Tallahassee LLC. Group owner: Triad Broadcasting Co. LLC (acq 9-2-2005; grpsl). Population served: 350,000 Natl. Rep: McGavren Guild,. Format: Classic hits of the 60s, 70s, etc. News: 2 hrs wkly. Target aud: 25-54. ♦ Hank Kestenbaum, gen mgr; Dooug Purtee, opns dir.

*WFRF(AM)— August 1974: 1070 khz; 10 kw-D. TL: N30 30 34 W84 20 07. Hrs open: Sunrise-sunset Box 181000, 32318. Secondary address: 4015 N. Monroe St. 32303. Phone: (850) 201-7000. Fax: (850) 201-1071.E-mail: mailbox@faithradio.us Web Site:www.faithradio.us Licensee: Faith Radio Network Inc. (acq 9-30-97; $150,000). Population served: 120,200 Format: Christian. Target aud: 12 plus. ♦ Scott Beigle, gen mgr & progmg dir.

*WFSQ(FM)— May 1954: 91.5 mhz; 100 kw. 663 ft TL: N30 21 29 W84 36 39. Stereo. Hrs open: 24 Public Broadcast Ctr., 1600 Red Barber Plaza, 32310. Phone: (850) 487-3086. Fax: (850) 487-2611. Web Site:www.wfsu.org Licensee: The Board of Regents of Florida

acting for and on behalf of Florida State University. Population served: 305,517 Natl. Network: NPR, PRI, . Format: Class. News: one hr wkly. Target aud: 35 plus; highly educated. ♦Patrick Keating, gen mgr; Caroline Austin, stn mgr, prom dir; Cary Martin, engrg dir.

***WFSU-FM—** Oct 14, 1990: 88.9 mhz; 95 kw. 1,243 ft TL: N30 40 13 W83 56 26. Stereo. Hrs open: 24 Public Broadcast Ctr., 1600 Red Barber Plaza, 32310. Phone: (850) 487-3086. Fax: (850) 487-2611. Web Site:www.wfsu.org Licensee: The Board of Regents of Florida acting for and on behalf of Florida State University. Population served: 161,500 Natl. Network: NPR, PRI, . Rgnl. Network: Fla. Pub. Fla. Pub. Cohn & Marks. Format: News/talk. News staff: 9. Target aud: 35-54; highly educated. Spec prog: Jazz 8 hrs wkly. ♦Pat Keating, gen mgr; Caroline Austin, stn mgr; Ann Meyers, prom dir; Cary Martin, chief of engrg.

WGLF(FM)— December 1967: 104.1 mhz; 100 kw. 1,359 ft TL: N30 27 09 W84 00 50. Stereo. Hrs open: 24 3411 W. Tharpe St., Tallahasse, 32303. Phone: (850) 201-3000. Fax: (850) 561-8903. Web Site:www.gulf104.com Licensee: Cumulus Licensing Corp. Group owner: Cumulus Media Inc. (acq 6-22-99; $4 million). Population served: 320,304 Natl. Rep: Katz Radio,. Wiley Rein. Format: Classic rock, AOR. Target aud: 25-54. ♦Barry Kaye, gen mgr; Mark Thompson, progmg dir.

WHBT(AM)— Aug 6, 1959: 1410 khz; 5 kw-D, 18 w-N. TL: N30 29 03 W84 17 13. Hrs open: 24 3411 W. Tharpe St., 32303. Phone: (850) 201-3000. Fax: (850) 561-8903. Web Site:www.1410thefan.com Licensee: Cumulus Licensing Corp. Group owner: Cumulus Media Inc. (acq 10-28-97; grpsl). Population served: 239,452 Natl. Rep: Katz Radio,. Wiley & Rein. Format: Gospel. Target aud: 18-54. ♦Barry Kaye, gen mgr; Peter Walkowiak, chief of engrg.

WHBX(FM)— June 28, 1982: 96.1 mhz; 37 kw. 479 ft TL: N30 16 08 W84 16 32. Stereo. Hrs open: 24 3411 West Tharpe St., 32303. Phone: (850) 201-3000. Fax: (850) 561-8903. Web Site:961jamz.com Licensee: Cumulus Licensing Corp. Group owner: Cumulus Media Inc. (acq 10-28-97; grpsl). Population served: 320,304 Natl. Rep: Katz Radio,. Wiley Rein. Format: Urban contemp. Target aud: 25-54. ♦Barry Kaye, gen mgr; Joe Bullard, opns mgr & progmg dir.

WHTF(FM)—See Havana

WNLS(AM)— Oct 15, 1946: 1270 khz; 5 kw-U, DA-N. TL: N30 25 38 W84 19 46. Hrs open: 24 Prog sep from FM 325 John Knox Rd., Bldg. G, 32303. Phone: (850) 422-3107. Fax: (850) 383-0747.E-mail: mattmillar@clearchannel.com Web Site:www.wnls.com Licensee: Clear Channel Radio Licenses Inc. Population served: 148,000 Format: Sports. News staff: one; News: 25 hrs wkly. ♦Matt Millar, progmg dir; Sandra Lee, traf mgr.

WQTL(FM)— May 1992: 106.1 mhz; 3 kw. Ant 328 ft TL: N30 28 37 W84 20 07. Hrs open: 24 Opus Broadcasting, 3000 Olson Rd., 32308. Phone: (850) 386-8004. Fax: (850) 422-1897.E-mail: hkestenbaum @opusbroadcasting.com Licensee: Opus Broadcasting Tallahassee LLC. Group owner: Triad Broadcasting Co. LLC (acq 9-2-2005;. grpsl). Format: News/talk. Target aud: 18-49. ♦Hank Kestenbaum, VP & gen mgr; Doug Purtee, opns mgr.

WTAL(AM)— 1935: 1450 khz; 1 kw-U. TL: N30 26 20 W84 15 30. Hrs open: 24 1363 E. Tennesse Street, 32308. Phone: (850) 671-1450. Phone: (850) 877-0105. Fax: (850) 877-5110.E-mail: wtaal@nettally.com Web Site:www.wtal1450.com Licensee: Live Communications Inc. (acq 9-14-01; $400,000). Population served: 210,000 Natl. Network: CBS, . Natl. Rep: Roslin,. Reddy, Begley & McCormick. Format: News/talk, Christian, relig. News staff: 4; News: 21 hrs wkly. Target aud: 25-54; educated, intelligent, affluent, involved, conservative. ♦Dr. R.B. Holmes Jr., CEO, pres; Richard Henderson, gen mgr.

WTLY(FM)—(Thomasville, GA) 1971: 107.1 mhz; 100 kw. 981 ft TL: N30 43 55 W84 08 45. Stereo. Hrs open: 24 Bldg. G, 325 John Knox Rd., 32303. Phone: (850) 422-3107. Fax: (850) 383-0747. Fax: (850) 514-4443.E-mail: jeffhorn@clearchannel.com Web Site:www.magic1071.com Licensee: CC Licenses LLC. Group owner: Clear Channel Communications Inc. (acq 11-21-97; grpsl). Population served: 400000 Format: Adult Contempory. News staff: one; News: 5 hrs wkly. Target aud: 25-54. ♦Lisa Rice, gen mgr; Jeff Horn, opns mgr; Randall Moore, chief of engrg.

WTNT-FM— July 24, 1967: 94.9 mhz; 100 kw. 840 ft TL: N30 34 43 W84 15 49. Stereo. Hrs open: 325 John Knox Rd., Bldg. G, 32303. Phone: (850) 422-3107. Fax: (850) 383-0747. Web Site:www.wtntfm.com Licensee: Clear Channel Radio Licenses Inc. Group owner: Clear Channel Communications Inc. (acq 11-21-97; grpsl). Population served: 330,000 Natl. Rep: Christal,. Format: Country. News: one hr wkly. Target aud: 25-54. ♦Lisa Rice, gen mgr; Jeff Horn, opns mgr; Woody Hayes, progmg dir & mus dir; Randy Moore, engrg dir; Sandra Lee, traf mgr.

***WVFS(FM)—** September 1987: 89.7 mhz; 2.7 kw. 174 ft TL: N30 26 22 W84 17 29. Hrs open: 24 420 Diffenbaugh Bldg., Florida State University, 32306. Phone: (850) 644-9692. Fax: (850) 644-8753.E-mail: wvfs@wvfs.fsu.edu Web Site:www.wvfs.fsu.edu Licensee: Florida State University. Population served: 200,000 Format: Alternative. News: 2 hrs wkly. Target aud: General. Spec prog: Black 8 hrs, folk 3 hrs, Sp 2 hrs wkly. ♦Misha Laurents, Ph.D., gen mgr.

Tampa

WAMA(AM)— 1961: 1550 khz; 10 kw-D, 125 w-N. TL: N27 55 16 W82 23 41. Hrs open: 24 4107 W. Spruce St., Suite 26, 33607. Phone: (813) 289-1552. Fax: (813) 289-1554.E-mail: trafficlainvasora@gmail.com Web Site:www.lainvasora1550.com Licensee: WAMA Inc. (acq 10-15-97; $2 million). Natl. Rep: Univision Radio National Sales,. Drinker, Biddle & Reath. Wire Svc: UPI Format: Mexican. News staff: one. Target aud: 25-54; Hispanic Adults. ♦Ron Gordon, chmn; Norberto Vallejo, pres.

WBTP(FM)—See Clearwater

***WBVM(FM)—** May 27, 1986: 90.5 mhz; 75.5 kw vert. Ant 964 ft TL: N27 50 53 W82 15 48. Stereo. Hrs open: 24 Box 18081, 33679. Secondary address: 3816 Morrison Ave. 33629. Phone: (813) 289-8040. Fax: (813) 282-3580.E-mail: contact@spiritfm905.com Web Site:www.spiritfm905.com Licensee: The Bishop of the Diocese of St. Petersburg. Format: Contemp Christian. Target aud: 35 plus; families. Spec prog: Black 4 hrs, children 4 hrs, Sp 4 hrs wkly. ♦John Morris, VP & gen mgr; Chris Sampson, opns mgr.

WDAE(AM)—See Saint Petersburg

WDUV(FM)—(New Port Richey, Sept 19, 1969: 105.5 mhz; 46 kw. Ant 1,345 ft TL: N28 10 56 W82 46 06. (CP: 6.7 kw, ant 1,050 ft.). Stereo. Hrs open: 24 11300 4th St. N., Suite 300, St. Petersburg, 33716-2941. Phone: (727) 579-2000. Fax: (727) 579-2662. Fax: (727) 579-2271.E-mail: info@coxradio.com Web Site:www.wduv.com Licensee: Cox Radio Inc. Group owner: Cox Communications Inc. (acq 5-99). Format: Soft adult contemp. Target aud: 25-54. Spec prog: It one hr wkly. ♦Howard Tuuri, VP, gen mgr; Tom Paleveda, opns mgr & gen sls mgr.

WFLA(AM)— 1924: 970 khz; 25 kw-D, 1 kw-N, DA-2. TL: N28 01 14 W82 36 34. Hrs open: 4002A Gandy Blvd., 33611. Phone: (813) 839-9393. Fax: (813) 831-4475. Fax: (813) 837-0300. Web Site:www.970wfla.com Licensee: Citicasters Licenses L.P. Group owner: Clear Channel Communications Inc. (acq 5-4-99; grpsl). Population served: 1,865,800 Natl. Network: Fox News Radio, . Natl. Rep: Katz Radio,. Hogan & Hartson. Wire Svc: AP Format: News/talk. News staff: 5. Target aud: 25-54. ♦Dan Diloreto, VP; Dan Deloreto, gen mgr; R.C. Bauer, opns mgr; Chris Soechtig, sls dir; John McMartin, chief of engrg; Gwen Shuller, traf mgr.

WFLZ-FM— 1948: 93.3 mhz; 99 kw. Ant 1,358 ft TL: N27 50 32 W82 15 45. Stereo. Hrs open: 4002A Gandy Blvd., 33611. Phone: (813) 839-9393. Fax: (813) 831-4475. Web Site:www.933flz.com Natl. Rep: Katz Radio,. Wire Svc: AP Format: CHR. Target aud: 18-34. ♦Dan Diloreto, gen mgr; Doug Hamand, opns mgr; Chris Soechtig, sls dir; John McMartin, chief of engrg; Misty Pittman, traf mgr.

WGUL(AM)—(Dunedin, Nov 21, 1959: 860 khz; 5 kw-D, 1.5 kw-N, DA-2. TL: N27 59 55 W82 42 01. Hrs open: 24 5211 W. Laurel St., # 101, 33607. Phone: (813) 639-1903. Fax: (813) 639-1272.E-mail: cgould@salemtampa.com Web Site:www.860wgul.com Licensee: Caron Broadcasting Inc. WGUL FM Inc. (acq 8-12-2005; $9.5 million with WLSS(AM) Sarasota). Population served: 4,000,000 Natl. Network: Salem Radio Network, . Natl. Rep: Salem,. Format: News/talk. ♦Chris Gould, gen mgr; Mike Serio, opns mgr.

WHBO(AM)—(Pinellas Park, November 1948: 1040 khz; 5 kw-D, 500 w-N, DA-N. TL: N27 50 50 W82 46 21. Hrs open: 4300 W. Cypress St., Suite 1040, 33607. Phone: (813) 281-1040. Fax: (813) 281-1948.E-mail: contactus@espn1040.com Web Site:www.espn1040.com Licensee: Genesis Communications of Tampa Bay Inc. Group owner: Genesis Communications Inc. (acq 12-17-97; $1.5 million). Population served: 300,000 Natl. Network: ESPN Radio, . Natl. Rep: Interep, McGavren Guild,. Florida's Radio Networks Wire Svc: AP Format: All sports. Target aud: 25-54. ♦Bruce Maduri, CEO; Paul DeFazio, gen mgr; Allan Davis, progmg mgr.

WHNZ(AM)— May 15, 1922: 1250 khz; 25 kw-D, 5.9 kw-N, DA-2. TL: N28 01 14 W82 36 34. Hrs open: 4002 Gandy Blvd., 33611. Phone: (813) 839-9393. Fax: (813) 831-3299. Web Site:www.whnz.com Licensee: Citicasters Licenses L.P. Group owner: Clear Channel Communications Inc. (acq 5-4-99; grpsl). Population served: 277767 Natl. Rep: Katz Radio,. Format: News/talk. Target aud: 25-54. ♦Dan DiLorette, pres, VP, gen mgr; Chris Soechtig, sls dir; Mike Killabrew, progmg dir; John McMartin, chief of engrg; Misty Pittman, traf mgr.

WHPT(FM)—See Sarasota

***WMNF(FM)—** Sept 14, 1979: 88.5 mhz; 70 kw. 520 ft TL: N27 49 04 W82 14 31. Hrs open: 24 1210 E. Martin Luther King Jr. Blvd., 33603. Phone: (813) 238-8001.E-mail: wmnf@wmnf.org Web Site:www.wmnf.org Licensee: The Nathan B. Stubblefield Foundation. Population served: 2,800,000 Natl. Network: NPR, . Haley, Bader & Potts. Format: Div. News staff: 2; News: 15 hrs wkly. Target aud: General. ♦Sheila Cowley, opns mgr; Vicki Santa, stn mgr & dev dir; Randy Wynne, progmg dir; Bill Brown, chief of engrg.

WMTX(FM)— November 1947: 100.7 mhz; 98 kw. Ant 1,358 ft TL: N27 50 32 W82 15 45. Stereo. Hrs open: 24 4002 Gandy Blvd., 33611. Phone: (813) 839-9393. Fax: (813) 831-3299. Web Site:www.wmtx.com Licensee: Citicasters Licenses L.P. Natl. Network: Premiere Radio Networks, . Natl. Rep: Katz Radio,. Wire Svc: AP Format: Adult contemp. ♦Dan DiLoreto, VP, gen mgr; Doug Hamand, opns mgr; Chris Soechtig, sls dir; John McMartin, chief of engrg; Sandra Ambrosino, traf mgr.

WQBN(AM)—(Temple Terrace, 1956: 1300 khz; 5 kw-D, 1 kw-N, DA-2. TL: N28 03 44 W82 19 44. Hrs open: 6 AM-midnight Box 151300, 33684. Secondary address: 5203 N. Armenia Ave. 33603. Phone: (813) 871-1333. Fax: (813) 876-1333.E-mail: superq1300@hotmail.com Web Site:www.superq1300am.com Licensee: Radio Tropical Inc. Population served: 453,000 Format: Sp, variety. News staff: 3; News: 20 hrs wkly. Target aud: 25 plus; Hispanics. ♦Efrain Archilla, pres; Marc L. Vila, VP & gen mgr.

WQYK(AM)—(Seffner, Nov 7, 1960: 1010 khz; 50 kw-D, 5 kw-N, DA-2. TL: N27 59 25 W82 15 06. Stereo. Hrs open: 24 9721 Executive Center Dr. N., Suite 200, Saint Petersburg, 33702. Phone: (727) 579-1925. Fax: (727) 563-8204. Web Site:www.1010sportsonline.com Licensee: CBS Radio Inc. of Tampa. Group owner: Infinity Broadcasting Corp. (acq 11-21-87). Natl. Network: Sporting News Radio Network, Westwood One, . Natl. Rep: CBS Radio,. Leventhal, Senter & Lerman. Format: All sports. News staff: . ♦Don Howe, sr VP; Mike Culotta, gen mgr & opns mgr.

WRBQ-FM— 1954: 104.7 mhz; 100 kw. Ant 561 ft TL: N27 56 50 W82 27 35. Stereo. Hrs open: 9721 Executive Center Dr. N., Suite 200, Saint Petersburg, 33702. Phone: (727) 579-1925. Fax: (727) 579-8888. Web Site:www.tampabaysq105.com Licensee: Infinity Radio Inc. Group owner: Infinity Broadcasting Corp. (acq 5-99). Format: Oldies. Target aud: 18-49. ♦Charlie Ochs, gen mgr; Mason Dixon, progmg dir.

WTIS(AM)— 1946: 1110 khz; 10 kw-D, DA. TL: N27 52 26 W82 37 53. Hrs open: 311 112th Ave. N.E., St. Petersburg, 33716. Phone: (727) 576-2234. Fax: (727) 577-3814. Licensee: WTIS-AM Inc. (acq 12-13-89; $1.7 million;1-1-90). Population served: 1,904,100 Format: Relg, ethnic. Target aud: 25-54. Spec prog: Sp one hr wkly. ♦Ron Roseman, pres; Ed Roseman, exec VP; Mike Smith, gen mgr, opns mgr; Robert Kansnicki, progmg dir.

WTMP(AM)—(Egypt Lake, 1954: 1150 khz; 10 kw-D, 500 w-N. TL: N28 00 42 W82 29 53. Hrs open: 24 407 N. Howard Ave., Suite 200, 33619. Phone: (813) 259-9867. Fax: (813) 254-9867.E-mail: info@tamabroadcasting.com Web Site:www.wtmp.com Licensee: Tama Radio Licenses of Tampa, FL, Inc. Group owner: Tama Broadcasting Inc. (acq 12-18-2001). Population served: 1,800,000 Natl. Network: American Urban, . Format: Urban adult contemp. Target aud: 18-49; urban contemporary music listeners & adults. ♦Dr. Glenn W. Cherry, CEO, pres, CFO, gen mgr; Louis Muhammad, opns mgr; Lynn Tolliver, progmg dir.

***WUSF(FM)—** September 1963: 89.7 mhz; 71 kw. Ant 941 ft TL: N27 50 53 W82 15 48. Stereo. Hrs open: 24 4202 E. Fowler Ave., TVB100, 33620-6870. Phone: (813) 974-8700. Fax: (813) 974-5016.E-mail: jurofsky@wusf.org Web Site:www.wusf.org Licensee: Board of Trustees, University of South Florida. Population served: 3,500,000 Natl. Network: NPR, PRI, . Rgnl. Network: Fla. Pub. Fla. Pub. Cohn & Marks. Wire Svc: AP Format: Class, news, jazz. News staff: 6; News: 38 hrs wkly. Target aud: General. ♦Jo Ann Urofsky, gen mgr; Tom Dollenmayer, stn mgr; Cathy Coccia, dev mgr. Co-owned TV: *WUSF-TV affil

WWRM(FM)—Licensed to Tampa. See Saint Petersburg

WXGL(FM)—See Saint Petersburg

WXTB(FM)—See Clearwater

WYUU(FM)—(Safety Harbor, October 1983: 92.5 mhz; 50 kw. Ant 489 ft TL: N27 50 32 W82 48 52. Stereo. Hrs open: 9721 Executive Center Dr., Suite 200, Saint Petersburg, 33702. Phone: (727) 579-1925. Fax: (813) 287-1833.E-mail: info@lanueva925.com Web Site:lanueva925.com

Licensee: CBS Radio Stations Inc. (acq 10-15-98; $75 million with WLLD(FM) Holmes Beach). Population served: 2,800,000 Leventhal, Senter & Lerman. Format: Sp tropical. Target aud: 18-49. ◆John Fennessy, gen sls mgr.

Tarpon Springs

*WYFE(FM)— June 14, 1988: 88.9 mhz; 50 kw. 500 ft TL: N28 24 07 W82 36 30. (CP: 60 kw, ant 449 ft.). Stereo. Hrs open: 11530 Carmel Commons Blvd., Charlotte, NC, 28226. Phone: (704) 523-5555. Fax: (704) 522-1967.E-mail: bbn@bbnradio.org Web Site:www.bbnradio.org Licensee: Bible Broadcasting Network Inc. (group owner; acq 8-11-89). Format: Relg. Target aud: General; Christians. ◆Lowell Davey, pres; Jack Long, gen mgr.

Tavares

WXXL(FM)—Licensed to Tavares. See Leesburg

Tavenier

WKEZ-FM— 1999: 96.9 mhz; 6 kw. 220 ft TL: N25 01 35 W80 30 30. Hrs open: 93351 Overseas Hwy., 33070. Phone: (305) 852-9085. Fax: (305) 852-5586. Fax: (305) 852-2304. Web Site:www.easy969.com Licensee: Aloha Station Trust LLC, as Trustee Group owner: Clear Channel Communications Inc. (acq 7-30-2008). Format: Easy lstng. ◆Mark Mills, stn mgr; Scott Hamilton, opns mgr; Greg Capgna, mktg mgr.

Temple Terrace

WQBN(AM)—Licensed to Temple Terrace. See Tampa

Tequesta

WEFL(AM)— Aug 1, 2002: 760 khz; 3 kw-D, 1.5 kw-N, DA-2. TL: N26 59 43 W80 11 34. Hrs open: 24 2090 Palm Beach Lakes Blvd., Ste 701, West Palm Beach, 33409. Phone: (561) 697-8353. Fax: (561) 697-8525.E-mail: sports@espn760.com Web Site: www.@espn760.com Licensee: Good Karma Broadcasting L.L.C. (acq 1-3-2006; $2.8 million). Natl. Network: ESPN Radio, Westwood One, . Format: Sports. ◆Craig Karmazin, CEO; Steve Politziner, gen mgr; Lance Davis, opns dir.

Tice

WJGO(FM)— March 2000: 102.9 mhz; 50 kw horiz, 48 kw vert. Ant 466 ft TL: N26 29 16 W81 55 46. Hrs open: 10915 K-Nine Dr., 2nd Fl., Bonita Springs, 34135. Phone: (239) 495-8383. Fax: (239) 495-0883.E-mail: wjgo@rendabroadcasting.com Web Site:www.1029bobfm.com Licensee: Renda Broadcasting Corp. of Nevada. Group owner: Renda Broadcasting Corp. (acq 10-5-2000; $7 million). Format: Adult hits. ◆Tony Renda Jr., gen mgr; Randy Savage, progmg dir.

Titusville

WIXC(AM)— Nov 20, 1957: 1060 khz; 50 kw-D, 5 kw-N, 17 kw-CH, DA-3. TL: N28 39 47 W80 55 17. Hrs open: 24 6305 Hwy. 46, Mims, 32754. Phone: (321) 264-1060. Phone: (321) 264-9700. Fax: (321) 264-4246.E-mail: gregsherlock@espn1060.com Web Site:www.wixc1060.com Licensee: Genesis Communications I Inc. Group owner: Genesis Communications Inc. (acq 4-19-2000; $650,000). Format: News/talk. Target aud: 35 plus. ◆Bruce C. Maouri, CEO; Kevin Fennessy, gen mgr; Steve Potter, gen sls mgr; Greg Sherlock, news dir; Jerry Smith, chief of engrg.

WNUE-FM—Licensed to Titusville. See Daytona Beach

WORL(AM)—See Altamonte Springs

*WPIO(FM)— Oct 19, 1975: 89.3 mhz; 5.8 kw horiz, 7.1 kw vert. Ant 335 ft TL: N28 34 49 W80 51 00. Stereo. Hrs open: 505 Josephine St., 32796. Phone: (321) 267-3000. Fax: (321) 269-9370. Web Site:www.noncomradio.net Licensee: Florida Public Radio Inc. Population served: 200,000 Format: Inspirational mus, pub affrs. ◆Randy Henry, pres & gen mgr.

Trailtown

*WPDJ(FM)—Not on air, target date: unknown: 91.5 mhz; 7 kw. Ant 207 ft TL: N25 51 59 W81 06 46. Hrs open: 860 S.E. 12th St., Miami, 33010. Phone: (305) 558-7003. Licensee: Iglesia Misionera Pregoneros de Justicia de Florida Inc. ◆Reinaldo Medina, pres & gen mgr.

Trenton

WDVH-FM— February 1988: 101.7 mhz; 3 kw. 328 ft TL: N29 36 40 W82 51 14. Stereo. Hrs open: 24 100 N.W. 76th Dr., Suite 2, Gainesville, 32607. Phone: (352) 313-3150. Fax: (352) 313-3166. Licensee: 6 Johnson Road Licenses Inc. (group owner; acq 1-5-2007; grpsl). Format: Country. News: 7 hrs wkly. Target aud: 25 plus; working class & professionals. Spec prog: Farm 2 hrs wkly. ◆Richard Hinshaw, gen mgr & mus dir.

Union Park

*WPOZ(FM)— Aug 9, 1995: 88.3 mhz; 2.5 kw. Ant 1,469 ft TL: N28 36 08 W81 05 37. (CP: 14.5 kw, ant 1,273 ft.). Hrs open: 24 1065 Rainer Dr., Altamonte Springs, 32714. Phone: (407) 869-8000. Fax: (407) 869-0380.E-mail: zcrew@zradio.org Web Site:www.zradio.org Licensee: Central Florida Educational Foundation Inc. Population served: 1,137,888 Joseph E. Dunne III. Format: Contemp Christian. Target aud: 25-44. ◆James S. Hoge, chmn, pres & gen mgr.

Valparaiso-Niceville

WFSH(AM)— November 1958: Stn currently dark. 1340 khz; 1 kw-U. TL: N30 30 34 W86 28 34. Hrs open: 6 AM-6 PM Box 1120, Destin, 32540. Secondary address: 415 Mountain Dr., Suite 7, Destin 32541. Phone: (850) 654-4040. Fax: (850) 650-9440.E-mail: dale@fox1120.com Licensee: Flagship Communications Inc. (acq 8-28-2003; $225,000). Population served: 153,000 ◆Dale Riddick, gen mgr; Max Howell, gen sls mgr; Steve Williams, news dir.

Venice

WDDV(AM)— Feb 1, 1960: 1320 khz; 5 kw-D, 1 kw-N, DA-4. TL: N27 06 20 W82 24 01. Hrs open: 1779 Independence Blvd., Sarasota, 34234. Phone: (941) 552-4800. Fax: (941) 552-4900.E-mail: info@doveradio.com Web Site:www.doveradio.com Licensee: Citicasters Licenses L.P. Group owner: Clear Channel Communications Inc. (acq 5-4-99; grpsl). Population served: 700,000 Rgnl. Network: Florida Radio Net. Format: Adult standards. Target aud: 25-54; active, upscale, affluent. ◆Sherri Carlson, gen mgr & mktg mgr.

WLTQ-FM— Mar 1, 1974: 92.1 mhz; 11.5 kw. Ant 476 ft TL: N27 09 03 W82 27 51. Stereo. Hrs open: 24 Prog sep from AM 1779 Independence Blvd., 34234. Phone: (941)552-4800. Fax: (941) 552-4900.E-mail: info@921online.com Web Site:www.921online.com Population served: 135,000 Format: Rock of 80's. Target aud: 25-54; female. ◆Randy Wanek, sls dir; Jeff Lynn, progmg dir; Joanne Jelinek, traf mgr.

Vero Beach

WCZR(FM)— May 29, 1986: 101.7 mhz; 1.48 kw. 471 ft TL: N27 32 46 W80 22 08. Hrs open: Box 0093, Port St. Lucie, 34985. Phone: (772) 335-9300. Fax: (772) 335-3291. Web Site:www.wzzr.com Licensee: Aloha Station Trust LLC Group owner: Clear Channel Communications Inc. (acq 7-30-2008; grpsl). Population served: 250,000 Format: Talk. ◆John Hunt, gen mgr.

WGYL(FM)— November 1970: 93.7 mhz; 50 kw. 475 ft TL: N27 36 04 W80 23 33. Stereo. Hrs open: Dups AM 10% 1235 16th St., 32960. Phone: (772) 567-0937. Fax: (772) 562-4747. Web Site:www.wgylfm.com Population served: 350,000 Format: Soft adult contemp, smooth jazz. Target aud: 35-64; upscale adult. ◆Jim Davis, opns mgr.

WJKD(FM)— 1995: 99.7 mhz; 50 kw. Ant 321 ft TL: N27 46 38 W80 27 17. Hrs open: 1235 16th St., 32960. Phone: (772) 567-0937. Fax: (772) 562-4747.E-mail: jake@997jackfm.com Web Site:www.997jackfm.com Licensee: Vero Beach FM Radio Partnership. (acq 2-11-2002). Format: 80s, 90s & now. ◆Jim Davis, gen mgr.

WQOL(FM)— Sept 1, 1979: 103.7 mhz; 50 kw. 476 ft TL: N27 33 21 W80 22 08. Stereo. Hrs open: Box 0093, Port St. Lucie, 34985. Phone: (772) 335-9300. Fax: (772) 335-3291. Web Site:www.wqolfm.com Licensee: Capstar TX L.P. Group owner: Clear Channel Communications Inc. (acq 8-30-00; grpsl). Natl. Network: Westwood One, . Format:

Oldies. Target aud: 35-64; baby boomers. ◆Mike Michaels, opns mgr & chief of opns; Heath West, progmg dir; Mike Kerley, engrg mgr.

*WSCF-FM— Feb 1, 1990: 91.9 mhz; 15.5 kw. 305 ft TL: N27 38 10 W80 27 59. Hrs open: 24 6767 20th St., 32966. Phone: (772) 569-0919. Phone: (800) 780-0919. Fax: (772) 562-4892. Web Site:www.wscf.com Licensee: Central Educational Broadcasting Inc. (acq 2-15-89). Natl. Network: USA, . Format: Christian, hit radio. ◆Jon Hamilton, gen mgr; Brad Bacon, dev VP; Paul Tipton, progmg dir; Bruce Douglas, news dir.

WTTB(AM)— June 7, 1954: 1490 khz; 1 kw-U. TL: N27 37 12 W80 25 01. Hrs open: 1235 16th St., 32960. Phone: (772) 569-1490. Fax: (772) 562-4747. Web Site:www.wttbam.com Licensee: Vero Beach Broadcasters LLC (group owner; acq 6-19-00; $5.15 million with co-located FM). Population served: 120,000 Natl. Network: ABC, . Rgnl. Network: Florida Radio Net. Florida's Radio Networks Format: Music of Your Life, talk. Target aud: General. ◆Jim Davis, gen mgr.

WZTA(AM)— May 1954: 1370 khz; 1 kw-D. TL: N27 36 01 W80 23 33. Hrs open: Box 0093, Port St. Lucie, 34985. Phone: (772) 335-9300. Fax: (772) 335-3291. Licensee: Capstar TX L.P. Group owner: Clear Channel Communications Inc. (acq 8-30-2000; grpsl). Population served: 11,908 Format: Talk. ◆John Hunt, gen mgr; Mike Michaels, opns mgr.

Watertown

WQLC(FM)— Oct 6, 1990: 102.1 mhz; 9-kw. 531 ft TL: N30 13 58 W82 48 18. Hrs open: 9206 US Hwy. 90 W., Lake City, 32055. Phone: (386) 755-4102. Fax: (386) 752-9861.E-mail: bandk@ISgroup.net Web Site:www.powercountry102.com Licensee: Power Country Inc. Population served: 512,000 Format: Hot country. Target aud: 18-54. Spec prog: Gospel 4 hrs wkly. ◆Louis Bolton II, CEO & pres; Bob Hendrickson, gen mgr.

Wauchula

WAUC(AM)— Jan 7, 1958: 1310 khz; 5 kw-D, 500 w-N, DA-2. TL: N27 31 48 W81 49 08. Hrs open: 6 AM-midnight Box 471, 33873. Secondary address: 1310 S. Florida Ave. 33873. Phone: (863) 773-5008. Phone: (863) 773-9282. Fax: (863) 773-2032.E-mail: wauc.radiostation@earthlink.net Licensee: Dora A. Cruz. (acq 12-1-97; $25,000). Population served: 200,000 Rgnl. Network: Florida Radio Net. Florida's Radio Networks Format: Mexican. Target aud: 35-54. ◆Robert Ayala, gen mgr.

West Palm Beach

*WAYF(FM)— Nov 11, 1993: 88.1 mhz; 50 w horiz, 50 kw vert. Ant 1,053 ft TL: N26 35 20 W80 12 44. Hrs open: 24 800 Northpoint Pkwy., 33407. Phone: (561) 881-1929. Fax: (561) 840-1929.E-mail: jim@wayfm.com Web Site:www.wayfm.com Licensee: WAY-FM Media Group Inc. (group owner). Population served: 3,700,000. Format: Contemp Christian. Target aud: 18-34; teens, young adults & young families. ◆Bob Augsburg, pres; Jim Marshall, stn mgr.

WBZT(AM)— July 31, 1936: 1230 khz; 1 kw-U. TL: N26 43 36 W80 03 03. (CP: 800 w-N). Hrs open: 24 3071 Continental Dr., 33407. Phone: (561) 616-6600. Fax: (561) 616-6677.E-mail: info@wbzt.com Web Site:www.wbzt.com Licensee: Capstar TX L.P. Group owner Clear Channel Communications Inc. (acq 9-27-00; grpsl). Population served: 350,000 Format: Talk. ◆John Hunt, gen mgr.

WEAT-FM— Aug 30, 1969: 104.3 mhz; 100 kw. 1,273 ft TL: N26 34 37 W80 14 32. Stereo. Hrs open: 701 Northpoint Pkwy., Suite 500, Phone: (561) 686-9505. Fax: (561) 686-0157. Fax: (561) 686-4043.E-mail: info@sunny1043.com Web Site:www.sunny1043.com Licensee: CBS Radio Inc. Group owner: Infinity Broadcasting Corp. (acq 11-13-98; grpsl). Population served: 800,000 Natl. Rep: Katz Radio,. Format: Adult contemp. Target aud: 25-54. ◆Lee K. Strasser, sr VP & gen mgr.

WFTL(AM)— 1948: 850 khz; 50 kw-D, 24 kw-N, DA-2. TL: N26 32 30 W80 44 30. Hrs open: 24 6600 N. Andrews Ave., Fort Lauderdale, 33309. Phone: (954) 315-1515. Fax: (954) 315-1555.E-mail: info@850wftl.com Web Site:www.850wftl.com Licensee: JCE Licenses L.L.C. Group owner: James Crystal Inc. (acq 5-15-98; $1.5 million). Format: News/talk. Target aud: 35 plus. ◆James C. Hilliard, pres; Rick Hindes, CFO; Steve Lapa, gen mgr; Ken Pauli, gen mgr; Tim Reever, gen sls mgr.

WIRK-FM— Aug 1, 1965: 107.9 mhz; 100 kw. Ant 426 ft TL: N26 45 47 W80 12 19. Stereo. Hrs open: 701 Northpoint Pkwy., Suite 500,

33407. Phone: (561) 686-9505. Fax: (561) 686-0157.E-mail: info@wirk.com Web Site:www.wirk.com Licensee: CBS Radio Inc. Group owner: Infinity Broadcasting Corp. (acq 11-13-98; grpsl). Format: Hot new country. ◆Lee Strasser, sr VP; Tony Bonvini, gen sls mgr.

WJNO(AM)— July 15, 1947: 1290 khz; 5 kw-U, DA-N. TL:N26 37 55 W80 07 07. (CP: 10 kw-D, 4.9 kw-N. TL: N26 45 50 W80 12 17). Hrs open: 3071 Continental Drive, 33407. Phone: (561) 616-6600. Fax: (561) 616-6677.E-mail: info@wjno.com Web Site:www.wjno.com Licensee: Clear Channel Radio Licenses Inc. Group owner: Clear Channel Communications Inc. (acq 9-16-97; grpsl). Population served: 800,000 Natl. Rep: Clear Channel,. Format: News/talk, sports. Target aud: Adults; 25-64. ◆John Hunt, gen mgr; Dave Denver, opns dir; Bill Brady, gen sls mgr; Brian Mudd, progmg dir, progmg mgr; Jim Leifer, chief of engrg.

WKGR(FM)—See Fort Pierce

WLVJ(AM)—See Boynton Beach

WRLX(FM)— Dec 13, 1975: 92.1 mhz; 7.2 kw. Ant 498 ft TL: N26 47 58 W80 04 33. Stereo. Hrs open: 3071 Continental Dr., 33407. Phone: (561) 616-6600. Fax: (561) 616-6677.E-mail: info@mia921.com Web Site:www.mia921.com Licensee: Clear Channel Broadcasting Licenses Group owner: Clear Channel Communications Inc. (acq 9-27-2000; grpsl). Population served: 800,000 Natl. Rep: Clear Channel,. Format: Sp. ◆John Hunt, pres & gen mgr; Dave Denver, opns dir, opns mgr.

WRMF(FM)—(Palm Beach, 1957): 97.9 mhz; 100 kw. 1,350 ft TL: N26 34 37 W80 14 32. (CP: Ant 417 ft.). Hrs open: 24 477 S. Rosemary Ave., Suite 302, 33401-5758. Phone: (561) 868-1100. Fax: (561) 868-1111. Web Site:www.wrmf.com Licensee: Cobalt Broadcasting LLC. Natl. Rep: McGavren Guild,. Latham & Watkins. Format: Hot adult contemp. Target aud: 25-54; general. ◆Mike Catchall, CEO; Elizabeth Hamma, pres, gen mgr; Doris Dupee, CFO; Mark Krieger, sls VP; Bob Neumann, progmg dir.

***WXEL(FM)**— Nov 24, 1969: 90.7 mhz; 38 kw. Ant 1,115 ft TL: N26 35 20 W80 12 44. Stereo. Hrs open: 24 Box 6607, 33405. Secondary address: 3401 S. Congress Ave., Boynton Beach 33426. Phone: (561) 737-8000. Fax: (561) 369-3067.E-mail: jcarr@wxel.org Web Site:www.wxel.org Licensee: Barry Telecommunications Inc. (acq 4-16-97). Population served: 684,000 Natl. Network: NPR, . Rgnl. Network: Fla. Pub. Fla. Pub. Schwartz, Woods & Miller. Wire Svc: AP Format: Class, news info. News staff: 7. Target aud: 35 plus; career oriented (news & info). ◆Jerry Carr, CEO, pres; Bernard Henneberg, CFO, exec VP; Joanna Marie, opns mgr.

WZZR(FM)—(Riviera Beach, 1971): 94.3 mhz; 50 kw. Ant 456 ft TL: N26 45 42 W80 04 42. Hrs open: Box 0093, Port St. Lucie, 34985. Phone: (561) 616-6600. Fax: (772) 335-3291. Web Site:www.wzzr.com Licensee: Clear Channel Broadcasting Licenses Inc. Group owner: Clear Channel Communications Inc. (acq 11-21-97; grpsl). Population served: 83,700 Format: Talk. Target aud: 25-54. ◆Mark Bass, gen mgr; Mike Michaels, opns mgr.

White City

WFLM(FM)— Dec 1, 1993: 104.7 mhz; 25 kw. 328 ft TL: N27 26 05 W80 21 42. Hrs open: 24 6803 S. Federal Hwy., Port St. Lucie, 34952. Phone: (772) 460-9356. Fax: (772) 460-2700. Licensee: Midway Broadcasting Co. Population served: 500,000 Format: Rhythm and blues. Target aud: 18-54. Spec prog: Gospel 20 hrs, jazz 4 hrs, reggae 4 hrs wkly. ◆Alice Lee, pres.

White Springs

WNFS(AM)—Not on air, target date: unknown: Stn currently dark. 660 khz; 50 kw-D, 250 w-N, DA-2. TL: N30 19 43 W82 49 35. Hrs open: 605 N.W. McClurg Ct., 32096. Phone: (386) 397-4489. Licensee: The Dianne A. Mayfield-Harder Trust. ◆Charles Harder, gen mgr.

Wildwood

WVLG(AM)—Licensed to Wildwood. See Leesburg

Williston

WTMG(FM)— July 1, 1983: 101.3 mhz; 3.5 kw. 433 ft TL: N29 25 04 W82 32 58. Stereo. Hrs open: 24 100 N.W. 76th Dr., Suite 2, Gainesville, 32607. Phone: (352) 313-3110. Fax: (352) 313-3166 / 3199.E-mail: info@magic1013.com Web Site:www.magic1013.com

Licensee: 6 Johnson Road Licenses Inc. (group owner; (acq 1-5-2007; grpsl). Format: Urban adult contemp. News staff: one; News: 2 hrs wkly. ◆Benjamin Hill, gen mgr.

Wilton Manors

WEXY(AM)— June 1963: 1520 khz; 3.5 kw-D, 250 w-N, DA-N. TL: N26 10 26 W80 09 27. Hrs open: 412 W. Oakland Park Blvd., Fort Lauderdale, 33311. Phone: (954) 561-1520. Fax: (954) 561-9830. Licensee: Multicultural Radio Broadcasting Licensee LLC. Group owner: Multicultural Radio Broadcasting Inc. (acq 4-4-03; $2.75 million). Population served: 3,000,000 Natl. Network: American Urban, . Format: Gospel. ◆Arthur Liu, CEO, pres; Jim Glogowski, VP; Doug DeVos, gen mgr, opns mgr.

Windermere

WUNA(AM)—See Ocoee

Winter Garden

WLAA(AM)— Jan 1, 1958: 1600 khz; 2.2 kw-D, 35 w-N. TL: N28 34 05 W81 31 08. Hrs open: 24 1801 Clark Rd., Ocoee, 34761. Phone: (407) 296-4747. Fax: (407) 293-2870. Licensee: Rama Communications Inc. (group owner; (acq 10-13-93; $950,000 with WMEL(AM) Cocoa Beach; 11-8-93). Population served: 99,006 Cohn & Marks. Format: Rgnl Mexican. ◆Shanti Persaud, gen mgr.

WOKB(AM)— Feb 22, 2000: 1680 khz; 10 kw-D, 1 kw-N. TL: N28 34 08 W81 31 08. Hrs open: 1801 Clark Rd., Ocoee, 34761. Phone: (407) 291-1395. Fax: (407) 293-2870.E-mail: info@wokbradio.com Web Site:www.wokbradio.com Licensee: Rama Communications Inc. (group owner). Format: Gospel. Target aud: 25-54; adults. ◆Joel Marquez, pres; Shanti Persaud, gen mgr.

Winter Haven

WHNR(AM)—(Cypress Gardens, Nov 29, 1958: 1360 khz; 5 kw-D, 2.5 kw-N, DA-2. TL: N28 01 16 W81 42 02. Hrs open: 6 AM-midnight Box 7742, 1505 Dundee Rd., 33883. Phone: (863) 299-1141. Fax: (863) 293-6397.E-mail: info@whnr1360.com Web Site:www.whnr1360.com Licensee: GB Enterprises Communication Corp. (acq 1-9-2007; $665,000). Population served: 350,000 Rgnl. Network: Florida Radio Net. Florida's Radio Networks Format: Urban AC. News staff: one; News: 20 hrs wkly. Target aud: 55 plus. Spec prog: Relg 10 hrs wkly. ◆P.J. Allen, stn mgr & gen sls mgr.

WLKF(AM)—See Lakeland

WPCV(FM)—Licensed to Winter Haven. See Lakeland

WSIR(AM)— Feb 14, 1947: 1490 khz; 1 kw-U. TL: N28 00 50 W81 45 02. Hrs open: 24 665 Southwest Lake Howard Dr., 33880. Phone: (863) 295-9411. Fax: (863) 401-9365. Web Site:www.rejoice1490.com Licensee: Anscombe Broadcasting Group Ltd. (acq 9-5-01). Population served: 250,000 Rgnl. Network: Florida Radio Net. Florida's Radio Networks Format: Gospel / Urban. News: 5 hrs wkly. Target aud: 25 plus. Spec prog: Relg 14 hrs. ◆Steve Reszka, CEO, pres; Joe Fisher, VP, gen mgr, gen mgr; Tony Charles, mus dir.

Winter Park

WLOQ(FM)— 1966: 103.1 mhz; 2.65 kw. 351 ft TL: N28 32 22 W81 26 46. Stereo. Hrs open: 24 2301 Lucien Way, Suite 180, Maitland, 32751. Phone: (407) 647-5557. Fax: (407) 647-4495.E-mail: frontdesk@wloq.com Web Site:www.wloq.com Licensee: Gross Communications Corp. (group owner; (acq 1977). Natl. Rep: Interep,. Pepper & Corazzini. Format: Jazz. Target aud: 25-54; white collar/professionals. ◆Herbert Paul Gross, pres; John Gross, CFO; Rick Weinkauf, VP & gen mgr; Ken Marks, sls dir, gen sls mgr.

WPRD(AM)— September 1954: 1440 khz; 5 kw-D, 1 kw-N, DA-N. TL: N28 35 18 W81 22 53. Stereo. Hrs open: 24 222 Hazard St., Orlando, 32804-3030. Phone: (407) 841-8282. Fax: (407) 841-8250.E-mail: wprd1440@hotmail.com Licensee: J & V Communications Inc. (group owner; acq 11-94; $300,000). Larry Perry. Format: Sp, news/talk. Target aud: 25-64; upscale. ◆John Torrado, CEO; Virgen Torrado, CEO & pres; Jocelyn Torrado, VP, gen mgr; Hector Reyes, gen mgr, opns mgr.

***WPRK(FM)**— Dec 10, 1952: 91.5 mhz; 1.32 kw. 89 ft TL: N28 35 40 W81 20 07. Stereo. Hrs open: 24 Box 2745, Rollins College, 1000 Holt

Ave., 32789-4499. Phone: (407) 646-2915. Phone: (407) 646-2241. Web Site:www.rollins.edu/wprk Licensee: Rollins College. Population served: 300,000 Format: Class, progsv, urban contemp. News: 2 hrs wkly. Target aud: General; non-traditional class and/or rock listeners. Spec prog: Jazz 3 hrs wkly. ◆Dan Seeger, gen mgr; Whitney Coulter, pub affrs dir.

Woodville

WJZT(FM)— September 2003: 97.9 mhz; 6 kw. Ant 328 ft TL: N30 16 30 W84 07 39. Stereo. Hrs open: 8:30 AM-5:30 PM 435 St. Francis St., Tallahassee, 32301. Phone: (850) 561-8400 (studio). Phone: (407) 227-3642. Fax: (850) 224-1553.E-mail: epetrone@wjztfm.com Web Site:www.wjztfm.com Licensee: 97.9 WJZTFM Inc. Population served: 124,000 Format: Smooth jazz. Target aud: 25-55. ◆Ernest Petrone, gen mgr; Chris Cooper, stn mgr.

Yankeetown

WXOF(FM)— 1998: 96.3 mhz; 6 kw. 285 ft TL: N29 01 18 W82 41 20. Hrs open: 4554 S. Suncoast Blvd., Homosassa Springs, 34446. Phone: (352) 628-4444.E-mail: staff@citrus95radio.com Web Site:www.citrus953.com Licensee: WGUL-FM Inc. (acq 1-22-99). Format: Classic rock. ◆Richard Spires, gen mgr.

Zephyrhills

WZHR(AM)— May 9, 1962: 1400 khz; 1 kw-U. TL: N28 16 54 W82 12 30. Hrs open: 24 2360 N.E. Coachman Rd., Clearwater, 33765. Phone: (727) 441-3311. Fax: (727) 441-1300.E-mail: lola@tantalk1340.com Web Site:www.tantalk1340.com Licensee: Wagenvoord Advertising Group Inc. (group owner; acq 2-13-02). Population served: 2,000,000+ Natl. Network: CNN Radio, CBS Radio, . Format: Talk/Gospel. Target aud: 35-64; men & women. Spec prog: CHR 10 hrs wkly. ◆Dave Wagenvoord, CEO, pres; Lola Wagenvoord, VP & gen mgr.

Zolfo Springs

WZZS(FM)— November 1992: 106.9 mhz; 6 kw. 328 ft TL: N27 21 59 W81 47 52. Stereo. Hrs open: 24 7891 U.S. Hwy. 17 S., 33890. Phone: (863) 494-4111. Fax: (863) 494-4443.E-mail: wzzs@desoto.net Web Site:www.bull.fm Licensee: Heartland Broadcasting Corp. Population served: 150,000 Rgnl. Network: Florida Radio Net. Florida's Radio Networks Format: Country. News staff: one; News: one hr wkly. Target aud: General; DeSoto, Hardee and Highlands counties. Spec prog: Gospel 2 hrs, farm one hr wkly. ◆Harold Hal Kneller Jr. Jr., pres.

Georgia

Adel

WDDQ(FM)— October 1979: 92.1 mhz; 6 kw. Ant 298 ft TL: N31 08 15 W83 23 41. Stereo. Hrs open: 24 3766 Old Clyattvile Rd., Valdosta, 31601. Phone: (229) 896-4572. Fax: (229) 559-1332. Licensee: Adventure Radio Group LLC (acq 12-30-2002; $435,000). Format: Talk. Target aud: 18-50. ◆Ron Hester, gen mgr & progmg mgr.

Albany

WALG(AM)— 1940: 1590 khz; 5 kw-D, 1 kw-N, DA-2. TL: N31 37 19 W84 09 09. Hrs open: 24 1104 W. Broad Ave., 31707. Phone: (229) 888-5000. Fax: (912) 888-5960.E-mail: matt.patrick@cumulus.com Web Site:www.1590walg.com Licensee: Cumulus Licensing Corp. Group owner: Cumulus Media Inc. (acq 11-3-98; grpsl). Population served: 150,000 Natl. Network: ABC, . Rgnl. Network: Southern Farm. Natl. Rep: Katz Radio,. Southern Farm Format: News/talk. Target aud: General. ◆George Francis, pres, VP; Bill Jones, progmg dir; Jenna McKay, pub affrs dir; Joey Falgout, chief of engrg.

WEGC(FM)—(Sasser, 1995): 107.7 mhz; 11.5 kw. 312 ft TL: N31 38 42 W84 21 15. Hrs open: 1104 W. Broad Ave., 31707. Phone: (229) 888-5000. Fax: (229) 878-1077. Fax: (229) 888-5960. Web Site:www.mix107albany.com Licensee: Cumulus Licensing Corp. Group owner: Cumulus Media Inc. (acq 7-7-98). Natl. Rep: Katz Radio,. Format: Adult contemp, lite rock favorites. ◆Gregory Kamishlian, gen mgr.

WGPC(AM)— 1933: 1450 khz; 1 kw-U. TL: N31 34 55 W84 11 58. Stereo. Hrs open: 24 1104 W. Broad Ave., 31707. Phone: (229) 888-5000. Fax: (229) 888-5960. Web Site:www.thefanalbany.com

Licensee: Cumulus Licensing Corp. Group owner: Cumulus Media Inc. (acq 11-3-98; $2.25 million with co-locatd FM). Population served: 150,000 Natl. Network: CBS, Fox Sports, . Rgnl. Network: Ga. Net. Ga. News Net. Holland & Knight. Format: Easy lstng, all sports. News: 20 hrs wkly. Target aud: 25 plus; middle to upper income. ♦George Francis, pres, gen mgr; Bill Jones, progmg dir; Joey Falgout, chief of engrg.

WJIZ-FM— January 1965: 96.3 mhz; 100 kw. Ant 466 ft TL: N31 39 16 W84 10 36. Stereo. Hrs open: Prog sep from AM 809 S. Westover Blvd., 31707. Fax: (912) 439-1509. Web Site:www.wjiz.com Population served: 100,000 Natl. Network: American Urban, . Format: Urban contemp. Target aud: 18-54. ♦John Richards, gen mgr; Adrian Guyton, progmg dir.

WJYZ(AM)— November 1952: 960 khz; 5 kw-D, DA. TL: N31 37 06 W84 10 33. Stereo. Hrs open: 24 809 S. Westover Blvd., 31707. Phone: (229) 439-9704. Fax: (229) 439-1509.E-mail: frankc@wjyz.com Web Site:www.wjyz.com Licensee: CC Licenses LLC. Group owner: Clear Channel Communications Inc. (acq 7-12-2000; grpsl). Population served: 115,000 Natl. Network: American Urban, . Natl. Rep: D & R Radio,. Format: Gospel. News: 3.5 hrs wkly. Target aud: 25-54. ♦John Richards, gen mgr; Frank Crapp, progmg dir.

WKAK(FM)— Feb 22, 1963: 104.5 mhz; 100 kw. Ant 981 ft TL: N31 32 57 W84 00 19. Stereo. Hrs open: 24 Dups AM 100% 1104 W. Broad Ave., 31707. Phone: (229) 888-5000. Fax: (229) 888-5960. Web Site:www.cumulus.com Population served: 340,590 Format: Country. News: 25 hrs wkly. ♦Claire Peeples, gen sls mgr; Candy O'Reilley, disc jockey.

WOBB(FM)—(Tifton, 1975: 100.3 mhz; 100 kw. 1,100 ft TL: N31 25 49 W83 45 22. Stereo. Hrs open: 24 809 S. Westover Blvd., 31707. Phone: (229) 439-9704. Fax: (229) 439-1509.E-mail: kurtbaker@clearchannel.com Web Site:www.b100wobb.com Licensee: CC Licenses LLC. Group owner: Clear Channel Communications Inc. (acq 7-12-2000; grpsl). Population served: 600,000 Natl. Rep: Christal,. Bechtel & Cole. Format: Country. News: 2 hrs wkly. Target aud: 25-49. ♦John Richards, gen mgr; Kurt Baker, progmg dir.

WQVE(FM)— Dec 17, 1972: 101.7 mhz; 3 kw. Ant 300 ft TL: N31 37 15 W84 09 11. Stereo. Hrs open: Prog sep from AM 1104 W. Broad Ave., 31707. Phone: (229) 888-5000. Fax: (912) 888-5960.E-mail: matt.patrick@cumulus.com Web Site:www.wqvealbany.com Population served: 250,000 Format: CHR. ♦Ken O'Brien, opns mgr; Mark McGee, progmg dir; Jenna McKay, news dir; Al Crumpton, disc jockey.

WSRA(AM)— July 10, 1962: 1250 khz; 1 kw-D, 53 w-N. TL: N31 37 00 W84 09 32. Hrs open: 2804 N. Jefferson St., 31701. Phone: (229) 432-1250. Fax: (229) 432-1927.E-mail: info@wsra.com Licensee: Livingston Fulton (acq 8-11-2004; $150,000). Population served: 88,000 Format: Sports radio. Target aud: 25-54. ♦Livingston W. Fulton, pres.

***WUNV(FM)—** 1990: 91.7 mhz; 3 kw. Ant 328 ft TL: N31 40 20 W84 03 27. Stereo. Hrs open: 24
Rebroadcasts WJSP-FM Warm Springs 100%.
260 14th St. N.W., Atlanta, 30318-5360. Phone: (404) 685-2690. Fax: (404) 685-2684.E-mail: ask@gpb.org Web Site:www.gpb.org Licensee: Georgia Public Telecommunications Commission. Natl. Network: PRI, NPR, . Wire Svc: AP Format: Class, news. News staff: 10; News: 40 hrs wkly. Target aud: Adults: 35 plus. ♦Nancy Hall, CEO; Bonnie Bean, CFO; Bob Houghton, gen mgr; Tom Barclay, opns mgr; Rob Maynard, progmg dir; Susanna Capelouto, news dir.

***WWVO(FM)—** July 12, 1990: 90.7 mhz; 5.5 kw. Ant 305 ft TL: N31 38 42 W84 21 15. Hrs open: 16 Box 9, Sasser, 39885. Phone: (229) 698-3473. Fax: (229) 874-5015. Licensee: Lamad Ministries Inc. (acq 7-89). Format: Relg. News: 4 hrs wkly. Target aud: 35 plus. ♦C. William Eidenire, pres; Eric Eidenire, gen mgr.

Alma

WAJQ(AM)— October 1957: 1400 khz; 1 kw-U. TL: N31 31 50 W82 27 45. Hrs open: 24 Drawer F, 208 Douglas St., 31510. Phone: (912) 632-1000. Fax: (912) 632-9696. Licensee: Blueberry Broadcasting Co. Inc. (acq 10-5-94; $12,000 with co-located FM; 10-31-94). Population served: 35,000 Natl. Network: CNN Radio, . Rgnl. Network: Ga. Net. Ga. News Net. Format: Southern gospel. News staff: one; News: 6 hrs wkly. Target aud: General. Spec prog: Farm 2 hrs wkly. ♦Debra Deen, gen mgr.

WAJQ-FM— May 14, 1987: 104.3 mhz; 4.5 kw. 371 ft TL: N31 36 26 W82 32 46. Stereo. Hrs open: Drawer F, 208 Douglas St., 31510. Phone: (912) 632-1000. Fax: (912) 632-9696. Format: Country. Target aud: General. ♦Bob Sass, prom dir.

Alpharetta

WLTA(AM)— Aug 25, 1986: 1400 khz; 1 kw-U. TL: N34 03 49 W84 16 34. Hrs open:
Rebroadcasts WNIV(AM) Atlanta 80%.
2970 Peachtree Rd. N.W., Suite 700, Atlanta, 30305. Phone: (404) 995-7300. Fax: (404) 816-0748.E-mail: wniv@wniv.com Web Site:www.wniv.com Licensee: South Texas Broadcasting Inc. Group owner: Salem Communications Corp. (acq 11-17-99; $8 million with WNIV(AM) Atlanta). Population served: 300,000 Booth, Freret, Imlay & Tepper. Format: Relg, talk/news. Target aud: 25-49; upper middle to upper income. ♦Mike Moran, gen mgr; Jeff Carter, opns dir.

Ambrose

WDMG-FM— December 1983: 97.9 mhz; 3.5 kw. Ant 316 ft TL: N31 31 51 W82 54 34. Stereo. Hrs open: 24 1931 GA Hwy. 32 E., Douglas, 31533. Phone: (912) 389-0995. Fax: (912) 383-8552.E-mail: traffic@charter.net Licensee: Broadcast South LLC. Group owner: Black Crow Media Group LLC (acq 11-15-2006; grpsl). Rgnl. Network: Jones Satellite Audio, ABC. Format: Classic rock. ♦John Higgs, gen mgr.

Americus

***WBJY(FM)—** 2002: 89.3 mhz; 65 kw vert. Ant 613 ft TL: N31 38 22 W83 44 58. Hrs open: P O Drawer 2440, Tupelo, MS, 38803. Phone: (662) 844-8888. Fax: (229) 567-9045. Web Site:www.afr.net Licensee: American Family Association. Group owner: American Family Radio Format: Christian. ♦Marvin Sanders, gen mgr.

WDEC-FM— Sept 12, 1964: 94.7 mhz; 25 kw. 328 ft TL: N31 53 52 W84 18 53. Stereo. Hrs open: Box 727, 31709. Secondary address: 1028 Adderton St. 31719. Phone: (229) 924-1390. Fax: (229) 928-2337.E-mail: wisk.wdec@mehsi.com Web Site:www.americusradio.com Licensee: Sumter Broadcasting Co. Group owner: Sumter Broadcasting Co. Inc. (acq 1994; with co-located AM). Population served: 70,000 Natl. Rep: Rgnl Reps,. Format: Hot adult contemp. News staff: 2; News: 2 hrs wkly. Spec prog: Black 5 hrs, farm one hr wkly. ♦Steve Lashley, pres, gen mgr; Thurston Clary, progmg dir.

***WFRP(FM)—** 2005: 88.7 mhz; 4.2 kw. Ant 230 ft TL: N32 05 34 W84 16 56. Hrs open:
Rebroadcasts WBFR(FM) Birmingham, AL 100%.
290 Hegenberger Rd., Oakland, CA, 94621. Phone: (510) 568-6200. Fax: (510) 633-7983. Web Site:www.familyradio.com Licensee: Family Stations Inc. Format: Relg. ♦Stanley Jackson, gen mgr.

WISK(AM)— Aug 28, 1962: 1390 khz; 5 kw-D. TL: N32 04 51 W84 15 20. Hrs open: Sunrise-sunset Box 727, 1028 Adderton St., 31709. Phone: (229) 924-1390. Phone: (229) 924-6500. Fax: (229) 928-2337. Web Site:www.americusradio.com Licensee: Sumter Broadcasting Co. Inc. (group owner) Population served: 28,000 Rgnl. Network: Ga. Net. Ga. News Net. Format: Oldies. News staff: one. Target aud: 19-65. ♦Steve Lashley, gen mgr; Donnie McCreary, news dir.

WISK-FM— September 1973: 98.7 mhz; 25 kw. Ant 302 ft TL: N32 04 51 W84 15 20. Stereo. Hrs open: 24 Box 727, 31709. Secondary address: 1028 Adderton St. 31709. Phone: (229) 924-1390. Phone: (229) 924-6500. Fax: (229) 928-2337.E-mail: wisk.wdec@mehsi.com Licensee: Sumter Broadcasting Co. Inc. Population served: 60,000 Natl. Rep: Rgnl Reps,. Format: Country.

Ashburn

***WFFM(FM)—** December 1989: 105.7 mhz; 6 kw. Ant 328 ft TL: N31 41 17 W83 38 38. Hrs open: 458 Virginia Ave., Suite 26, Tifton, 31794. Phone: (229) 382-1340. Fax: (229) 386-8658. Web Site:www.hookfmoline.com Licensee: Three Trees Communications Inc. (group owner; (acq 10-31-2007; $150,000). Format: Christian. ♦James Andrew Howard, pres.

Athens

WFSH-FM—Licensed to Athens. See Atlanta

WGAU(AM)— May 1, 1938: 1340 khz; 1 kw-U. TL: N33 56 28 W83 24 13. Hrs open: 24 850 Bobbin Mill Rd., 30606. Phone: (706) 549-1340. Fax: (706) 353-1220.E-mail: matt.cesar@coxradio.com Web Site:www.1340wgau.com Licensee: Cox Radio Inc. Group owner: Southern Broadcasting Companies Inc. (acq 8-1-2008; grpsl). Population served: 175,000 Natl. Network: ABC, CNN Radio, . Ga. News Net. Dow Lohnes PLLC. Format: News/talk. News staff: 3. Target aud: 25 plus; educated, middle to upper-income, news & info oriented. ♦Robert F. Neil, pres, VP; Scott Smith, gen mgr, opns mgr; Matt Caesar, progmg dir; Tim Bryant, news dir.

***WMSL(FM)—** October 1987: 88.9 mhz; 20 kw. 315 ft TL: N33 54 25 W83 29 35. Stereo. Hrs open: 24 2121 Ruth Jackson Rd., Bogart, 30622. Phone: (770) 725-8890. Fax: (770) 725-0889.E-mail: gm@wmsl.fm Web Site:www.wmsl.fm Licensee: Prince Avenue Baptist Christian School. Population served: 144,000 Natl. Network: USA, . Garvey, Schubert & Barer. Format: Contemp Christian. News staff: one; News: 11 hrs wkly. Target aud: 25-54; women. ♦Jim Hutto, gen mgr; George McKay, opns dir; Dianne Hutto, mktg dir; Nathan Collins, progmg dir; James Hutto, mus dir; Mitch Kimbrell, news dir.

WRFC(AM)— May 1, 1948: 960 khz; 5 kw-D, 2.5 kw-N, DA-N. TL: N33 59 58 W83 26 00. Stereo. Hrs open: 24 1010 Tower Pl., Bogart, 30622. Phone: (706) 549-6222. Fax: (706) 353-1967. Web Site:www.960theref.com Licensee: Cox Radio Inc. Group owner: Southern Broadcasting Companies Inc. (acq 8-1-2008; grpsl). Population served: 250,000 Natl. Network: ESPN Radio, . Format: Sports, Talk. News staff: 3; News: 10 hrs wkly. Target aud: 25-54; community-minded adults. Spec prog: Black 15 hrs wkly. ♦Robert F. Neil, pres, gen mgr; David Johnston, progmg dir; Scott Smith, opns mgr & chief of engrg.

***WUGA(FM)—** Aug 28, 1987: 91.7 mhz; 6 kw. 328 ft TL: N33 55 13 W83 14 46. Stereo. Hrs open: 24 1197 S. Lumpkin St., Ste. 138, 30602. Secondary address: Georgia Public Radio (HQ), 260 14th St. N.W., Atlanta 30318. Phone: (706) 542-9842. Fax: (706) 542-6718.E-mail: wuga@uga.edu Web Site:www.wuga.org Licensee: Georgia Public Telecommunications Commission. Natl. Network: PRI, NPR, . Rgnl. Network: Peach State Public Radio. Georgia Public Radio Wire Svc: AP Format: Class, news. News staff: 3; News: 5 hrs wkly. Target aud: Adults: 35 plus. Spec prog: Folk 4 hrs, jazz 4 hrs wkly. ♦Nancy Hall, CEO; Bonnie Bean, CFO; Bob Houghton, gen mgr; Steve Bell, stn mgr; Michael Cardin, opns mgr; Rob Maynard, progmg dir; Robb Holmes, progmg mgr; Mary K. Mitchell, news dir.

***WUOG(FM)—** Oct 16, 1972: 90.5 mhz; 9.5 kw. 180 ft TL: N33 57 00 W83 22 02. (CP: 26 kw, ant 179 ft. TL: N33 56 59 W83 22 58). Stereo. Hrs open: 24 Box 2065, Tate Student Ctr., University of Georgia, 30602. Phone: (706) 542-7100. Fax: (706) 542-0070. Web Site:www.wuog.org Licensee: University of Georgia. Population served: 49,457 Rgnl. Network: Ga. Net. Ga. News Net. Format: Alternative. News staff: 3; News: 4 hrs wkly. Target aud: 18-25; students & faculty of Univ. ♦Erin White, gen mgr; Carrie Mumah, prom dir; Mary Beth Ross, news dir; Steven Swigart, pub affrs dir; Wilbur Harrington, chief of engrg.

WXAG(AM)— June 10, 1957: 1470 khz; 1 kw-D, 176 w-N. TL: N33 59 14 W83 20 17 (D), N33 55 03 W83 22 39 (N). Hrs open: 855 Sunset Dr., Suite 16, 30606. Phone: (706) 552-1470. Fax: (706) 425-0847. Licensee: Mecca Communications Inc. (acq 9-8-94; 9-26-94). Format: Gospel. ♦Michael Thurmond, gen mgr.

WXKT(FM)—(Royston, Dec 1, 1988: 103.7 mhz; 25 kw. Ant 328 ft TL: N34 14 13 W83 16 03. (CP: COL Arcade. TL: N34 14 13 W83 31 48). Stereo. Hrs open: 24 1010 Tower Pl., Bogart, 30622. Phone: (706) 549-6222. Fax: (706) 353-1967. Web Site:www.bulldog1037.com Licensee: Cox Radio Inc. Group owner: Southern Broadcasting Companies Inc. (acq 8-1-2008; grpsl). Population served: 190,000 Format: Classic rock. ♦Robert F. Neil, pres; Scott Smith, opns mgr; Kevin Steele, progmg dir.

Atlanta

***WABE(FM)—** Sept 13, 1948: 90.1 mhz; 96 kw. Ant 821 ft TL: N33 45 32 W84 20 07. Stereo. Hrs open: 24 740 Bismark Rd. N.E., 30324. Phone: (678) 686-0321. Fax: (678) 686-0356.E-mail: info@wabe.org Web Site:www.wabe.org Licensee: Board of Education of the City of Atlanta. Population served: 2,950,000 Natl. Network: NPR, PRI, . Schwartz, Woods & Miller. Wire Svc: AP Format: News/talk, class. News staff: 3; News: 9 hrs wkly. Target aud: 35-54; news advocates, class music enthusiasts. Spec prog: Jazz 5 hrs wkly. ♦Milton Clipper, CEO & pres; Irene Wreen, CFO; Earl Johnson, VP, gen mgr, stn mgr; Lisa Williams, dev dir, traf mgr. Co-owned TV: *WPBA-TV affil

WAEC(AM)— 1947: 860 khz; 5 kw-D, 500 w-N. TL: N33 43 45 W84 19 19. Hrs open: 1465 Northside Dr., Suite 218, 30318. Phone: (404) 355-8600. Fax: (404) 355-4156.E-mail: info@waec.com Web Site:www.love860.com Licensee: WAEC License L.P. (acq 10-29-99). Population served: 3,000,000 Format: Contemp Christian, Relg. Total Christian community. ♦George Beasley, chmn; Brian Beasley, pres, exec VP; Caroline Beasley, CFO; Chris Edmonds, gen mgr.

WAFS(AM)— Sept 1, 1955: 1190 khz; 10 kw-D. TL: N33 48 35 W84 21 14. Hrs open: Sunrise-sunset 2970 Peachtree Rd. N.W., Suite 700, 30305. Phone: (404) 995-7300. Fax: (404) 816-0748.E-mail: wniv@wniv.com Licensee: South Texas Broadcasting Inc. Group owner: Salem Communications Corp. (acq 4-4-2000; $8 million).

Population served: 1,495,039 Format: Southern gospel. Target aud: 35-64. ♦Mike Marmon, gen mgr; Jeff Carter, opns mgr.

WALR(AM)— Nov 20, 1965: 1340 khz; 1 kw-U. TL: N33 44 56 W84 24 26. Hrs open: 24 3535 Piedmont Rd., Bldg. 14, Suite 1200, 30305. Phone: (404) 688-0068. Fax: (404) 995-4045.E-mail: scottmcfarlane@680thefan.com Web Site:www.talkradio1340.com Licensee: Dickey Broadcasting Co. (group owner; (acq 8-31-2000; grpsl). Population served: 496,973 Natl. Network: Fox Sports, . Natl. Rep: McGavren Guild,. Holland & Knight. Wire Svc: AP Format: Sports. ♦David Dickey, gen mgr; Scott McFarlane, opns dir; Rob Hasson, sls dir.

WALR-FM—See La Grange

WAOK(AM)— Mar 15, 1954: 1380 khz; 5 kw-U, DA-N. TL: N33 45 36 W84 28 45. (CP: 4.2 kw-N). Hrs open: 1201 Peachtree St., Suite 800, 30361. Phone: (404) 898-8900. Fax: (404) 898-8915.E-mail: slgosnell@cbs.com Web Site:www.waok.com Licensee: Infinity Broadcasting East Inc. Group owner: Infinity Broadcasting Corp. (acq 1996; grpsl). Population served: 444,700 Natl. Network: CBS, . Format: News/talk. News staff: 5; News: 50 hrs wkly. Target aud: 25-54. ♦Mel Karmazin, CEO, pres; Monique McCoy, VP, prom mgr; Val Carolin, gen mgr & sls dir; Rick Caffey, mktg mgr; Tasha Brown, prom dir, pub affrs dir; Tasha Love, progmg dir; Sid Daniel, chief of engrg; Brenda Yelling, rsch dir; Manny Danaie, traf mgr; Katrina Noles, spec ev coord; Jean Ross, news rptr; Linda Looney, reporter.

WATB(AM)—See Cumming

***WCLK(FM)**— Apr 10, 1974: 91.9 mhz; 6 kw. Ant 308 ft TL: N33 44 56 W84 24 26. Stereo. Hrs open: 111 James P. Brawley Dr. S.W., 30314. Phone: (404) 880-8284. Phone: (404) 880-8278. Fax: (404) 880-8869.E-mail: wclkfm@cau.edu Web Site:www.wclk.com Licensee: Clark Atlanta University. Population served: 180,000 Natl. Network: NPR, PRI, . Format: Jazz. News staff: 16. Target aud: 25-49; upscale, college educated, primarily African American. Spec prog: Gospel 17 hrs, reggae 3 hrs, blues 3 hrs, info/talk 12 hrs wkly. ♦Wendy Williams, gen mgr; Tammy Nobles, stn mgr; Glen Simmonds, opns mgr; Shelley Trotter, prom mgr, pub affrs dir; John Armwood, progmg dir; Renee Williams, mus dir; Gary Owens, chief of engrg; Traci Ross, traf mgr; Rose Holmes, edit mgr.

WCNN(AM)—(North Atlanta, Dec 4, 1967: 680 khz; 50 kw-D, 10 kw-N, DA-2. TL: N33 57 42 W84 15 48. Hrs open: 24 3535 Piedmont Rd., Bldg. 14, Suite 1200, 30305. Phone: (404) 688-0068. Fax: (404) 995-4045.E-mail: scottmcfarlane@680t.com Web Site:www.680thefan.com Licensee: Dickey Broadcasting Co. (group owner; acq 8-31-00; grpsl). Population served: 496,973 Rgnl. Network: New Nebraska Public Radio Format: News, sports. ♦David Dickey, pres, gen mgr; Robert Hasson, gen sls mgr; Scott McFarlane, progmg dir.

WDWD(AM)— July 1, 1938: 590 khz; 5 kw-U, DA-N. TL: N33 49 34 W84 18 56. (CP: 4.5 kw-N, DA-2). Hrs open: 6th Fl., 210 Interstate Pkwy. N., 30339. Phone: (770) 541-0590. Fax: (770) 952-7461. Web Site:www.radiodisney.com/atlanta Licensee: Radio Disney Atlanta LLC. Group owner: ABC Inc. (acq 5-17-85; $6.85 million; 6-3-85). Population served: 496,973 Natl. Network: ABC, . Natl. Rep: Interep,. Format: Radio Disney. Target aud: Children 6-14 Adults 25-54. ♦Shawn Serra, stn mgr; Melissa Munro, opns mgr.

WFOM(AM)—See Marietta

WFSH-FM—(Athens, January 1964: 104.7 mhz; 24 kw. Ant 1,656 ft TL: N33 52 02 W83 49 44. Stereo. Hrs open: 24 2970 Peachtree Rd. N.W., Suite 700, 30305. Phone: (404) 995-7300. Fax: (404) 816-0748. Web Site:www.thefishatlanta.com Licensee: South Texas Broadcasting Inc. Group owner: Salem Communications Corp. (acq 7-27-2000; grpsl). Population served: 300,000 Holland & Knight. Format: Contemp. Christian Music. Spec prog: Gospel 2 hrs wkly. ♦David Koon, gen sls mgr; Mike Stoudt, natl sls mgr, mus dir; Taylor Scott, prom dir & prom mgr; Kevin Avery, progmg dir; C. J. Jackson, chief of engrg.

WFTD(AM)—See Marietta

WGKA(AM)— Mar 17, 1922: 920 khz; 5 kw-D, 488 w-N. TL: N33 48 35 W84 21 23. Hrs open: 2970 Peachtree Rd. N.W., Suite 700, 30305. Phone: (404) 995-7300. Fax: (404) 816-0748. Web Site:www.themighty1190.com Licensee: Pennsylvania Media Associates Inc. Group owner: Salem Communications Corp. (acq 6-28-2004; $16.4 million). Format: News/talk. Target aud: General. ♦Mike Moran, gen mgr; Jeff Carter, opns mgr; David Koon, gen sls mgr.

WGST(AM)— Apr 7, 1988: 640 khz; 50 kw-D, 1 kw-N, DA-2. TL: N33 45 43 W84 27 29. Hrs open: 24
Rebroadcasts WHEL(FM) Helen 100%.
1819 Peachtree Rd., Suite 700, 30309. Phone: (404) 367-0640. Fax: (404) 367-1100. Web Site:www.wgst.com Licensee: Citicasters Licenses L.P. Group owner: Clear Channel Communications Inc. Rgnl. Network: Ga. Net. Wire Svc: AP Format: News/talk. Target aud: 25-54. ♦Pat McDonnell, VP, gen mgr; Tim Dukes, opns mgr; Jared Blass, gen sls mgr; Jim Oktavec, mktg dir; Pam Rahal, prom dir, prom mgr; Tom Parker, progmg dir; Paul Mann, news dir; Mike Lawing, chief of engrg.

WGUN(AM)—Licensed to Atlanta. See Tucker

***WJSP-FM**—(Warm Springs, Feb 3, 1985: 88.1 mhz; 100 kw. 975 ft TL: N32 51 08 W84 42 04. Stereo. Hrs open: 24 260 14th St. N.W., 30318-5360. Phone: (404) 685-2690. Fax: (404) 685-2684.E-mail: ask@gpb.org Web Site:www.gpb.org Licensee: Georgia Public Telecommunications Commission. Natl. Network: NPR, PRI, . Wire Svc: AP Format: News, class, talk. News staff: 10; News: 40 hrs wkly. Target aud: 35-54; NPR-demo. Spec prog: Jazz 18 hrs wkly. ♦Nancy Hall, CEO; Bonnie Bean, CFO; Bob Houghton, gen mgr, progmg dir; Tom Barclay, opns mgr; Rob Maynard, progmg dir; Susanna Capelouto, news dir, chief of engrg.

WKHX-FM—(Marietta, November 1960: 101.5 mhz; 100 kw. Ant 1,079 ft TL: N33 48 26 W84 20 22. Stereo. Hrs open: 24 210 Interstate North, Suite 100, 30339. Phone: (404) 521-1015. Fax: (404) 499-1015 (news/on-air).E-mail: info@kicks1015.com Web Site:www.kicks1015.com Licensee: Radio License Holding II LLC. (acq 6-12-2007; grpsl). Population served: 413,800 Natl. Rep: ABC Radio Sales,. Format: Country. News staff: one. Target aud: 25-54. ♦Victor Sansone, pres & gen mgr; Mark Richards, opns mgr; Rick Mack, sls dir; Matt Scarano, gen sls mgr; Nancy Barre, natl sls mgr; Mary Gordon, rgnl sls mgr; Christy Ullman, prom mgr; Mike Macho, mus dir; Glenda Sanders, traf mgr.

WKLS(FM)— Dec 2, 1960: 96.1 mhz; 99 kw. Ant 984 ft TL: N33 48 27 W84 20 26. Stereo. Hrs open: 24 1819 Peachtree St., Suite 700, 30309. Phone: (404) 325-0960. Fax: (404) 367-1155.E-mail: info@project961.com Web Site:www.project961.com Licensee: Citicasters Licenses L.P. Group owner: Clear Channel Communications Inc. (acq 5-4-99; grpsl). Population served: 3,500,000 Format: AOR. News: 7 hrs wkly. Target aud: 25-49; primarily male. ♦Jerry Del Core, gen mgr, gen sls mgr; Mike Wheeler, opns mgr, prom dir; Jeff McMurray, progmg dir; Susan De Bonis, mktg dir & pub affrs dir.

WNIV(AM)— 1948: 970 khz; 5 kw-D, 39 w-N. TL: N33 48 35 W84 21 14. Hrs open: 24 2970 Peachtree Rd. N.W., Suite 700, 30305. Phone: (404) 995-7300. Fax: (404) 816-0748.E-mail: wniv@wniv.com Web Site:www.wniv.com Licensee: South Texas Broadcasting Inc. Group owner: Salem Communications Corp. (acq 11-17-99; $8 million with WLTA(AM) Alpharetta). Population served: 3,500,000 Cohn & Marks. Format: Christian, talk. News staff: one; News: 7 hrs wkly. Target aud: 25-49; educated adults, upper middle to upper income. ♦Stuart W. Epperson, chmn; Edward G. Atsinger III, pres; Mike Moran, gen mgr; Jeff Carter, opns VP, opns mgr, progmg dir, progmg mgr; David Koon, sls VP, gen sls mgr; Joel Foster, prom dir; C. J. Jackson, chief of engrg; Cynthia Weaver, traf mgr.

WQXI(AM)— October 1947: 790 khz; 28 kw-D, 1 kw-N, DA-N. TL: N33 48 42 W84 21 13. Stereo. Hrs open: 3350 Peachtree Rd. N.E., Suite 1610, 30326. Phone: (404) 237-0079. Fax: (404) 231-5923.E-mail: feedback@790thezone.com Web Site:www.790thezone.com Licensee: Jefferson Pilot Communications Co. (group owner: Big League Broadcasting (acq 3-1-74). Population served: 500,000 Format: Talk, sports. Target aud: 18-54; men. ♦Andrew Saltzman, pres, gen mgr; Neal Maziar, VP; Neal Maziiar, gen mgr; Eric Tepe, opns mgr; Chris Young, gen sls mgr; Jim Heilman, natl sls mgr; Leslie Rosetta Smith, mktg dir; Leslie Hoar, prom mgr; Matt Edgar, progmg dir; Tracie Hardy, traf mgr.

***WRAS(FM)**— Jan 18, 1971: 88.5 mhz; 100 kw. 436 ft TL: N33 41 04 W84 17 23. Stereo. Hrs open: 24 Box 4048, 30302-4048. Phone: (404) 413-1630. Fax: (404) 463-9535. Web Site:www.wras.org Licensee: Georgia State University. Population served: 3,500,000 Format: College rock. News: 6 hrs wkly. Target aud: 18-34; college students. Spec prog: Classical 3 hrs, world 3 hrs, reggae 4 hrs, new age 3 hrs, rap/hip-hop 6 hrs wkly. ♦Dr. Kurt Keppler, CEO; Brady Rainey, gen mgr; Michael Valania, prom dir; Andy Hawley, progmg dir; Todd Wiese, mus dir; Tom Taylor, chief of engrg.

***WREK(FM)**— Apr 1, 1968: 91.1 mhz; 40 kw. 340 ft TL: N33 46 41 W84 24 22. Stereo. Hrs open: 24 Georgia Tech., 350 Ferst Dr., Suite 2224, 30332. Phone: (404) 894-2468. Fax: (404) 894-6872.E-mail: wrek@gatech.edu Web Site:www.wrek.org Licensee: Radio Communications Board, Georgia Institute of Technology. Population served: 3,500,000 Rgnl. Network: Ga. Net. Ga. News Net. Format: Progsv, div, Ethnic music. Target aud: General. Spec prog: Experimental 18 hrs, jazz 15 hrs, class 15 hrs wkly. ♦Aakash Jariwala, gen mgr; Jeremy Varner, opns mgr; Steve Fenton, progmg dir.

***WRFG(FM)**— July 15, 1973: 89.3 mhz; 65 kw. Ant 485 ft TL: N33 48 26 W84 20 22. Stereo. Hrs open: 24 1083 Austin Ave. N.E., 30307. Phone: (404) 523-3471. Fax: (404) 523-8990.E-mail: info@wrfg.org Web Site:www.wrfg.org Licensee: Radio Free Georgia Broadcasting Foundation Inc. Population served: 496,973 Haley, Bader & Potts. Format: Eclectic. News: 3 hrs wkly. Target aud: 18-45; socially conscious African-Americans. Spec prog: , Indian 3 hrs, Sp 5 hrs wkly. ♦Joan Baptist, stn mgr; Wanique Shabazz, opns dir.

WSB(AM)— Mar 15, 1922: 750 khz; 50 kw-U. TL: N33 50 43 W84 15 12. Hrs open: 24 1601 W. Peachtree St. N.E., 30309. Phone: (404) 897-7500. Fax: (404) 897-7363. Licensee: Cox Radio Inc. Group owner: Cox Broadcasting Population served: 3,500,000 Natl. Rep: Christal,. Dow, Lohnes & Albertson. Format: News/talk. News staff: 9; News: 168 hrs wkly. Target aud: 25-54. ♦Dan Kearney, VP, gen mgr, mktg mgr; Tony Kidd, VP & mktg mgr; Charles Kinney, chief of engrg.

WSB-FM— Nov 10, 1944: 98.5 mhz; 100 kw. 1,027 ft TL: N33 45 33 W84 20 05. Stereo. Hrs open: 1601 W. Peachtree St. N.E., 30309. Phone: (404) 897-7500. Fax: (404) 897-6211. Web Site:www.b985.com Format: Adult contemp. News staff: one; News: 3.5 hrs wkly. Target aud: 25-54. ♦Dan Kearney, VP, mktg mgr; Tony Kidd, VP, mktg mgr & progmg dir. Co-owned TV: WSB-TV affil

WSTR(FM)—See Smyrna

WTJH(AM)—See East Point

WUBL(FM)— Feb 18, 1962: 94.9 mhz; 100 kw. Ant 984 ft TL: N33 48 27 W84 20 26. Stereo. Hrs open: 24 Prog sep from AM 1819 Peachtree Rd., Suite 700, 30309. Phone: (404) 367-0949. Fax: (404) 367-9490.E-mail: info@bullatlanta.com Web Site:www.bullatlanta.com Population served: 2,000,000 Natl. Network: ABC, . Format: Country. ♦Cheryl Ervin, gen sls mgr; Scott Baker, mktg mgr; Louis Kaplan, progmg dir; Steve Goss, mus dir.

WVEE(FM)— July 1, 1948: 103.3 mhz; 100 kw. 1,022 ft TL: N33 45 35 W84 20 07. Stereo. Hrs open: 1201 Peachtree St., Suite 800, 30361. Phone: (404) 898-8900. Fax: (404) 898-8915. Web Site:www.v-103.com Population served: 496,973 Natl. Network: Westwood One, . Format: Urban contemp. News staff: 2. Target aud: 18-49. ♦Monique McCoy, prom mgr; Denise Dunbar, progmg dir, reporter; Linda Looney, mus dir, news rptr; Jean Ross, news dir; Manny Danaie, traf mgr; Katrina Noles, spec ev coord.

WWWQ(FM)— November 1963: 99.7 mhz; 100 kw. 1,032 ft TL: N33 46 57 W84 23 20. Stereo. Hrs open: 780 Johnson Ferry Rd., Suite 500, 30342. Phone: (404) 497-4700. Fax: (404) 497-4735. Web Site:www.99x.com Licensee: WNNX Lico Inc. Group owner: Susquehanna Radio Corp. (acq 2-28-74). Natl. Rep: McGavren Guild,. Format: Top-40. ♦Mark Fowler, gen mgr; Lisa Kelly, opns dir, natl sls mgr; Leslie Fram, gen sls mgr, progmg dir.

WYZE(AM)— June 1957: 1480 khz; 5 kw-D, 44 w-N. TL: N33 43 25 W84 22 08. Hrs open: 1111 Boulevard S.E., 30312. Phone: (404) 622-7802. Fax: (404) 622-6767.E-mail: am1480wyze@aol.com Web Site:www.wyze1480.com Licensee: GHB Broadcasting Inc. Group owner: GHB Radio Group Population served: 350,000 Rgnl. Network: Ga. Net. Ga. News Net. Format: Black gospel. ♦George H. Buck Jr., pres; Jacob E. Bogan, stn mgr.

WZGC(FM)— Sept 1, 1965: 92.9 mhz; 100 kw. 910 ft TL: N33 45 34 W84 23 19. Stereo. Hrs open: 24 1201 Peachtree St., Suite 800, 30361. Phone: (404) 898-8900. Fax: (404) 843-3541.E-mail: info@929dave.fm Web Site:www.929dave.fm Licensee: CBS Radio Inc. of Atlanta. Group owner: CBS Radio (acq 11-13-98; grpsl). Population served: 750,000 Natl. Network: Westwood One, . Natl. Rep: Katz Radio,. Format: AAA. News staff: one; News: 2 hrs wkly. Target aud: 25-54; upscale baby boomers. ♦Rick Caffey, sr VP, gen mgr; John Riemenschneider, gen sls mgr; Scott Jameson, natl sls mgr, progmg dir; Robert Lafore, chief of engrg; Sully, disc jockey.

Augusta

***WACG-FM**— June 2, 1970: 90.7 mhz; 25 kw. Ant 400 ft TL: N33 24 15 W81 50 19. Stereo. Hrs open: 24
Rebroadcasts WJSP-FM Warm Springs 75%.
260 14th St. N.W., Atlanta, 30318-5360. Secondary address: 2500 Walton Way 30904. Phone: (404) 685-2690. Fax: (404) 685-2684.E-mail: ask@gpb.org Web Site:www.gpb.org Licensee: Georgia Public Telecommunications Commission. (acq 4-87). Population served: 615,000 Natl. Network: PRI, NPR, . Wire Svc: AP Format: Classical, news. News staff: 6; News: 40 hrs wkly. Target aud: 35 plus; upscale, professional, educated, affluent. Spec prog: Jazz 18 hrs wkly. ♦Nancy G. Hall, CEO; Bonnie Bean, CFO; Bob Houghton, gen mgr; Tom Barclay, opns mgr; Rob Maynard, progmg dir; Susanna Capelouto, news dir.

WBBQ-FM— March 1955: 104.3 mhz; 100 kw. 1,003 ft TL: N33 36 41 W81 56 30. Stereo. Hrs open: 24 2743 Perimeter Pkwy., Bldg. 100, Suite 200, 30909. Phone: (706) 396-6000. Fax: (706) 396-6010. Web Site:www.wbbq.com Licensee: Clear Channel Broadcasting Licenses Inc. Group owner: Clear Channel Communications Inc. (acq 12-19-2000; grpsl). Population served: 700,000 Format: Adult contemp, loc news. News staff: 8; News: 7 hrs wkly. Target aud: General. ♦Mark Bass, gen mgr; Mike Kramer, opns mgr; Bobby Boggs, gen sls mgr; Steve Cherry, progmg dir; Earl Welch, chief of engrg; Rob Collins, traf mgr.

WDRR(FM)—See Martinez

WEKL(FM)— Mar 10, 1952: 105.7 mhz; 100 kw. Ant 1,168 ft TL: N33 25 15 W81 50 19. Stereo. Hrs open: 24 2743 Perimeter Pkwy., Suite 300, 30909. Phone: (706) 396-6000. Fax: (706) 396-6010. Web Site:eagle102.com Licensee: Clear Channel Broadcasting Licenses Inc. Group owner: Clear Channel Communications Inc. (acq 12-19-2000; grpsl). Population served: 700,000 Holland & Knight. Format: Classic rock. Target aud: 18-44. ♦Mark Bass, gen mgr; Tim Lawandus, gen sls mgr; Amanda Washington, prom dir; Steve Burke, progmg dir.

WFAM(AM)— Mar 10, 1952: 1050 khz; 5 kw. TL: N33 27 21 W81 56 20. Hrs open: 24 552 Laney-Walker Blvd. Ext., 30901. Phone: (706) 722-6077. Fax: (706) 722-7066.E-mail: wfam@wilkinsradio.com Web Site:www.wilkinsradio.com Licensee: J.J. & B. Broadcasting Inc. Group owner: Wilkins Communications Network Inc. (acq 11-22-96; $330,000). Population served: 1,300,000 Natl. Network: Salem Radio Network, . Natl. Rep: Salem,. Womble, Carlyle, Sandridge & Rice. Format: Relg. News: 2 hrs wkly. Target aud: 35 plus. ♦Robert L. Wilkins, pres; LuAnn Wilkins, exec VP; Mitchell Mathis, VP; Paul Lindsey, stn mgr; Greg Garrett, opns mgr.

WFXA-FM— July 11, 1968: 103.1 mhz; 3 kw. 299 ft TL: N33 30 00 W81 56 03. Stereo. Hrs open: 24 Box 1584, 411 Radio Station Road, 30903. Secondary address: 104 Bennett Ln., North Augusta, SC 29841. Phone: (803) 279-2330. Fax: (803) 279-8149.E-mail: info@perrybroadcasting.net Licensee: Perry Broadcasting of Augusta Inc. Group owner: Radio One Inc. (acq 12-12-2007; grpsl). Population served: 350,000 Format: Black, urban contemp. Target aud: 25-34; females. ♦Dennis Jackson, gen mgr; Ron Thomas, opns mgr, progmg dir; Dianne Mutimer, gen sls mgr; Lakeshia Collins, news dir; Walter Brumbeloe, chief of engrg; Jamie Langley, traf mgr.

WGAC(AM)— 1940: 580 khz; 5 kw-D, 840 w-N, DA-N. TL: N33 30 44 W82 04 48. Hrs open:
Simulcast with WGAC-FM Warrenton.
4051 Jimmie Dyess Pkwy., Agusta, 30909. Phone: (706) 396-7000. Fax: (706) 396-7092.E-mail: wgac@wgac.com Web Site:www.wgac.com Licensee: WGAC License LLC. Group owner: Beasley Broadcast Group (acq 5-19-92; assumption of debt; 6-8-92). Population served: 480,000 Natl. Network: CBS, . Rgnl. Network: Ga. Net. Natl. Rep: D & R Radio,. Format: News/talk, sports. News staff: 5. Target aud: 35-65. Spec prog: Farm 4 hrs, military 3 hrs wkly. ♦George Beasley, chmn; Kent Dunn, VP, gen mgr; Harley Drew, opns dir, progmg dir; Terry Kellems, gen sls mgr; Mary Liz Nolan, news dir; Charlie McCoy, chief of engrg; Diane Underwood, traf mgr; Keith Beckum, farm dir.

***WGPH(FM)**—(Vidalia, 1988: 91.5 mhz; 40 kw. 508 ft TL: N32 14 02 W82 28 52. Stereo. Hrs open: 24 2278 Wortham Ln, Grovetown, 30813. Phone: (706) 309-9610.E-mail: ctbarinowski@comcast.net Web Site:www.gnnradio.org Licensee: Augusta Radio Fellowship Institute Inc. Population served: 210,000 Format: Christian. News: 12 hrs wkly. Target aud: General. ♦Clarence Barinowski, pres & gen mgr.

WGUS(AM)— July 1930: 1480 khz; 5 kw-U, DA-N. TL: N33 31 00 W82 00 36. Stereo. Hrs open:
Simulcast WGUS-FM.
4051 Jimmie Dyess Pkwy., 30909. Phone: (706) 396-7000. Fax: (706) 396-7100.E-mail: info@wgus.com Licensee: WCHZ License LLC. Group owner: Beasley Broadcast Group Inc. (acq 5-3-2000; $800,000 with WGAC-FM Warrenton). Population served: 66,800 Format: Southern Gospel. Target aud: 18-49; well educated. ♦Kent Dunn, gen mgr, chief of opns; Chris O'Kelley, progmg dir.

WIBL(FM)— Nov 11, 1967: 102.3 mhz; 1.5 kw. Ant 666 ft TL: N33 26 15 W82 05 27. Stereo. Hrs open: 24 2743 Perimeter Pkwy., Bldg. 100, Suite 200, 30909. Web Site:www.bullcountry.com Licensee: Aloha Station Trust LLC (acq 7-30-2008; grpsl). Format: Country. News staff: one; News: 3 hrs wkly. Target aud: 18-34. ♦Tim Lawandus, gen sls mgr; Robb Tomas, prom dir; Bill West, progmg dir.

WKSP(FM)—See Aiken, SC

WKXC-FM—See Aiken, SC

WKZK(AM)—See North Augusta, SC

***WLPE(FM)**— Nov 17, 1984: 91.7 mhz; 1.15 kw. Ant 589 ft TL: N33 34 21 W81 55 23. Stereo. Hrs open: 24 2278 Wortham Ln., Grovetown, 30813. Phone: (706) 309-9610.E-mail: ctbarinowski@comcast.net Web Site:www.gnnradio.org Licensee: Augusta Radio Fellowship Institute Inc. Population served: 400,000 Format: Christian. News: 12 hrs wkly. Target aud: General. ♦Clarence Barinowski, pres & gen mgr.

WNRR(AM)— November 1993: 1230 khz; 1 kw-U. TL: N33 27 14 W82 01 47. Hrs open: 24 1286 Broad St., 30901. Phone: (706) 922-3834. Fax: (706) 922-3831.E-mail: will@newsradio1230.com Web Site:www.newsradio1230.com Licensee: Will Nunley Broadcasting LLC (group owner; (acq 11-24-2007; $650,000). Population served: 350,000 Natl. Network: CNN Radio, Premiere Radio Networks, Westwood One, . Ga. News Net. Format: Talk, sports, news. News staff: 3; News: 24 hrs wkly. Target aud: 25- women; 25+ men. ♦Will Nunley, gen mgr; Teri Exrleben, gen sls mgr.

WRDW(AM)— 2001: 1630 khz; 10 kw-D, 1 kw-N. TL: N33 31 00 W82 00 36. Hrs open: 4051 Jimmie Dyess Parkway, 30909. Phone: (706) 396-7000. Fax: (706) 396-7092. Web Site:wrdw.com Licensee: WCHZ License LLC. Group owner: Beasley Broadcast Group Inc. (acq 2-23-2000). Format: Sports, news/talk. ♦Kent Dunn, gen mgr; Harley Drew, opns mgr.

WSGF(AM)— Jan 12, 1947: 1340 khz; 1 kw-U. TL: N33 27 46 W82 00 29. Hrs open: 24 2743 Perimeter Pkwy., Bldg. 100, 30909. Phone: (706) 396-6000. Fax: (706) 396-6010. Licensee: Clear Channel Broadcasting Licenses Inc. Population served: 425,000 Holland & Knight. Format: All sports. Target aud: Children.

WTHB(AM)— May 1960: 1550 khz; 5 kw-D. TL: N33 30 00 W81 56 03. Hrs open: Prog sep from FM Box 1584, 411 Radio Station Road, 30903. Secondary address: 104 Bennett Ln., North Augusta 29841. Phone: (803) 279-2330. Fax: (803) 279-8149.E-mail: info@perrybroadcasting.net Licensee: Perry Broadcasting of Augusta Inc. Population served: 21,200 Natl. Network: American Urban, . Format: Gospel. ♦Mary Kingcannon, progmg dir.

WYFA(FM)—(Waynesboro, Aug 1, 1991: 107.1 mhz; 6 kw. 328 ft TL: N33 10 42 W81 59 24. Stereo. Hrs open: 24 Box 7300, Charlotte, 28241. Secondary address: Bible Broadcasting Network, 11530 Carmel Commons Blvd., Charlotte 28226. Phone: (704) 523-5555. Fax: (704) 522-1967. Web Site:www.bbnradio.org Licensee: Bible Broadcasting Network Inc. (group owner; acq 8-26-92; $225,000; 9-21-92). Format: Relg. ♦Scott Curtis, gen mgr & opns mgr.

WYNF(AM)—(North Augusta, SC) July 30, 1958: 1380 khz; 4 kw-D, 70 w-N. TL: N33 29 17 W81 56 46. Hrs open: 24 2743 Perimeter Pkwy., Bldg. 100, Suite 200, 30909. Phone: (706) 396-6000. Fax: (706) 396-6010. Licensee: Capstar TX L.P. Group owner: Clear Channel Communications Inc. (acq 12-19-2000; grpsl). Population served: 72,000 Wiley, Rein & Fielding. Format: Classic country. News staff: one; News: 7 hrs wkly. ♦Mark Bass, gen mgr.

Austell

WAOS(AM)— Apr 16, 1968: 1600 khz; 20 kw-D, 67 w-N. TL: N33 48 34 W84 39 25. Hrs open: 24 hrs 5815 Westside Rd., 30106. Phone: (770) 944-0900. Fax: (770) 944-9794.E-mail: gracie@radiolafavorita.com Web Site:www.radiolafavorita.com Licensee: La Favorita Inc. (group owner; acq 1-24-90). Population served: 600,000 Format: Sp. Target aud: 18 plus; Hispanics in metro Atlanta & northeast GA. ♦Samuel Zamarron, pres & gen mgr; Gracie Zamarron, stn mgr.

WXEM(AM)—(Buford, Dec 12, 1957: 1460 khz; 5 kw-D. TL: N34 07 15 W83 58 35. Hrs open: 5815 Westside Rd., 30106. Phone: (770) 944-0900. Fax: (770) 944-9794.E-mail: sammy@radiolafavoita.com Web Site:www.radiolafavorita.com Licensee: La Favorita Inc. (group owner; acq 6-12-91; 7-1-91). Population served: 200,000 Format: Sp. Target aud: Hispanic. ♦Samuel Zamarron, CEO, pres & gen mgr; Gracie Zamarron, stn mgr.

Avondale Estates

WMLB(AM)— November 2003: 1690 khz; 10 kw-D, 1 kw-N. TL: N33 48 42 W84 21 37. Stereo. Hrs open: 24 1100 Spring St., Suite 610, Atlanta, 30309. Phone: (404) 681-9307. Fax: (404) 870-8859.E-mail: listeners@jwbroadcasting.com Web Site:www.1690wmlb.com Licensee: JW Broadcasting Inc. (acq 5-18-2006; $12 million). Format: Var. ♦Jeff Davis, gen mgr & chief of opns.

Bainbridge

WBGE(FM)— May 2001: 101.9 mhz; 5.3 kw. Ant 351 ft TL: N30 54 36 W84 33 45. Hrs open: 521 S. Scott St., 39819. Phone: (229) 246-7776. Fax: (229) 246-9995.E-mail: kevin @live1019.com Web Site:www.live1019.com Licensee: Flint Media Inc. (acq 7-15-2005; $485,000). Format: Hot adult contemp. ♦Kevin Dowdy, gen mgr.

WMGR(AM)— Aug 17, 1947: 930 khz; 5 kw-D, 500 w-N. TL: N30 54 25 W84 33 02. Hrs open: 18 203 W. Shotwell St., 39819. Phone: (229) 246-1650. Fax: (229) 246-1403.E-mail: wmgr@wmgr.net Web Site:www.wmgr.net Licensee: Decatur Broadcasting Inc. (acq 6-10-2005; for 50% of stock). Population served: 100,000 Rgnl. Network: Ga. Net. Ga. News Net. Format: Memories from the 60s, 70s, & 80s. News: 10 hrs wkly. Target aud: 30 plus. ♦Coley Voyles, pres & gen mgr.

WRAK-FM— Dec 20, 1967: 97.3 mhz; 100 kw. 1,200 ft TL: N31 09 12 W84 32 42. Hrs open: 24 809 S. Westover Blvd., Albany, 31707. Phone: (229) 439-9704. Fax: (229) 439-1509. Web Site:www.magic973radio.com Licensee: CC Licenses LLC. Group owner: Clear Channel Communications Inc. (acq 7-11-2000; grpsl). Population served: 900,000 Natl. Rep: Christal,. Format: Adult contemp. News: 2 hrs wkly. Target aud: 18-49. ♦John Richards, gen mgr; Jasmine Phoenix, progmg dir.

Barnesville

WBAF(AM)— July 23, 1966: 1090 khz; 1 kw-D. TL: N33 03 13 W84 08 07. Hrs open: 645 Forsyth St., 30204. Phone: (770) 358-1090. Fax: (770) 358-1090. Licensee: Barnesville Broadcasting Inc. Population served: 56,000 Rgnl. Network: Ga. Net. Ga. News Net. Reddy, Begley & McCormick. Format: C&W, relg. Spec prog: Loc 5 hrs wkly. ♦Charles Waters, pres & gen mgr.

Baxley

WBYZ(FM)— July 1983: 94.5 mhz; 100 kw. Ant 1,014 ft TL: N31 47 10 W82 27 03. Stereo. Hrs open: 24 Box 390, 31515. Secondary address: 4005 Golden Isles W. 31515. Phone: (912) 367-3000. Fax: (912) 367-9779.E-mail: peggy@wbyz94.com Web Site:www.wbyz.com Natl. Network: ABC, . Ga. News Net. Format: Modern country. Target aud: 20-55; those with buying power. ♦Peggy C. Miles, mktg mgr; Al Graham, progmg mgr; Cody West, mus dir; Cole Younger, news dir, traf mgr.

WUFE(AM)— December 1954: 1260 khz; 5 kw-D. TL: N31 48 00 W82 24 40. Hrs open: 6 AM-sunset Box 390, 31515. Secondary address: Hwy. 341 W. 31515. Phone: (912) 367-3000. Fax: (912) 367-9779. Licensee: South Georgia Broadcasters Inc. (acq 1-19-82; $240,000;2-8-82). Population served: 75,000 Ga. News Net. Fletcher, Heald & Hildreth. Format: Relg. News: 6 hrs wkly. Target aud: General. ♦Al Graham, pres, pub affrs dir; Peggy C. Miles, gen mgr, gen sls mgr, prom mgr & adv mgr; Larry Ring, chief of engrg.

Blackshear

WFNS(AM)— Mar 10, 1961: 1350 khz; 2.5 kw-D, 125-N. TL: N31 18 44 W82 14 00. Hrs open: 1766 Memorial Dr. Suite 1, Waycross, 31501. Phone: (912) 285-5002. Fax: (912) 285-3877.E-mail: wgaradio@yahoo.com Web Site:www.fandog.net Licensee: MarMac Communications LLC. (acq 7-19-2001; $60,000). Natl. Network: CNN Radio, . Ga. News Net. Format: All sports. Target aud: General; families. Spec prog: Atlanta Braves, Hawks, Falcons, Ga Tech. ♦Gary Moss Marmitt, pres & gen mgr.

Blackshear/Waycross

WKUB(FM)— Dec 1, 1979: 105.1 mhz; 50 kw. Ant 308 ft TL: N31 15 49 W82 17 30. Stereo. Hrs open: 24 Box 112, 2132 Hwy. 84, 31516. Secondary address: Box 1472, Waycross 31502. Phone: (912) 449-3391. Fax: (912) 449-6284.E-mail: wkub@almatel.net Licensee: Mattox Broadcasting Inc. Population served: 140,000 Natl. Network: ABC, . Rgnl. Network: Ga. Net. Natl. Rep: Dora-Clayton,. Ga. News Net. Fletcher, Heald & Hildreth. Format: Country. News: 4 hrs wkly. Target aud: 25 plus. ♦G. Troy Mattox, pres, gen mgr; Jim MIller, gen sls mgr.

Blakely

WBBK(AM)— Oct 22, 1959: 1260 khz; 1 kw-D. TL: N31 21 11 W84 56 50. Hrs open: Box 87, Donalsonville, 31745. Secondary address: Hwy. 62 W. 31745. Phone: (229) 723-2677. Phone: (229) 524-5123. Fax: (229) 723-2678. Fax: (229) 524-2265.E-mail: wbbk@alltel.net

Licensee: Styles Media Group LLC. (group owner; acq 5-13-2004; grpsl). Population served: 50,000 Format: Talk. Target aud: 25-49. ◆Gil Kelley, gen mgr.

WBBK-FM— November 1984: 93.1 mhz; 45 kw. Ant 328 ft TL: N31 17 55 W85 03 18. Stereo. Hrs open: Box 889, Dothan, 36302. Phone: (334) 792-0047. Fax: (334) 712-9346. Licensee: Magic Broadcasting Alabama Licensing LLC. (acq 5-13-2004; grpsl). Population served: 50,000 Format: Urban contemp. ◆Dan Bradley, gen mgr; J.J. Davis, progmg dir.

Blue Ridge

WPPL(FM)— 1971: 103.9 mhz; 6 kw. 400 ft TL: N34 52 03 W84 20 02. (CP: 6 kw, ant 400 ft.). Stereo. Hrs open: 24 Box 938, 30513. Secondary address: 333 W. Highland St. 35013. Phone: (706) 632-9775. Fax: (706) 632-5922.E-mail: mcwolf@etcmail.com Web Site:www.mountaincountryradio.com Licensee: Fannin County Broadcasting Co. Inc. (acq 12-12-97; $200,000 for stock). Population served: 50,000 Natl. Network: AP Radio, . Rgnl. Network: Ga. Net. Ga. News Net. Format: Country. News staff: 9. Target aud: 25-54; adults. ◆Tim White, pres; Vicky Pulliam, gen mgr; Jim Quinton, opns dir.

Bolingbroke

WWWD(FM)— 2005: 102.1 mhz; 4.5 kw. Ant 377 ft TL: N32 54 30 W83 46 37. Hrs open: 6080 Mount Moriah Ext., Memphis, TN, 38115. Phone: (901) 375-9324. Fax: (901) 375-0041.E-mail: info@flinn.com Web Site:www.flinn.com Licensee: George S. Flinn Jr. ◆George S. Flinn Jr., gen mgr.

Boston

WTUF(FM)— July 18, 1988: 106.3 mhz; 6 kw. 328 ft TL: N30 47 40 W83 46 54. Stereo. Hrs open: 24 Box 129, Thomasville, 31799. Secondary address: 117 Remington Ave., Thomasville 31792. Phone: (229) 225-1063. Fax: (229) 226-1361.E-mail: lenrob@rose.net Web Site:www.wtufradio.com Licensee: Boston Radio Co. Population served: 72,000 Natl. Network: AP Network News, . Rgnl. Network: Ga. Net. Agri-Net. Natl. Rep: Rgnl Reps,. Ga. News Net. Format: Classic country. Target aud: 18-65; adults. Spec prog: Bluegrass 5 hrs, gospel 7 hrs wkly. ◆Len Robinson, pres, gen mgr & opns mgr.

Bostwick

WKUN(AM)— Feb 4, 1971: 1490 khz; 1 kw-U. TL: N33 48 37 W83 42 01. Hrs open: 6 AM-6 PM Box 649, Monroe, 30655. Secondary address: 1610 Launius Rd., Good Hope 30641. Phone: (770) 267-0923. Fax: (706) 342-8135.E-mail: wmoq@wmoqfm.com Licensee: B.R. Anderson Sr. dba Radio Station WKUN (acq 6-96). Population served: 10,300 Rgnl. Network: Ga. Net. Ga. News Net. Format: Southern gospel. News: 3 hrs wkly. Target aud: 25-65. ◆B. R. Anderson Sr., pres; David Malcom, opns mgr.

WMOQ(FM)— 1994: 92.3 mhz; 3 kw. 328 ft TL: N33 44 58 W83 33 30. Hrs open: Box 649, Monroe, 30655. Secondary address: 1610 Launius Rd., Good Hope Phone: (770) 267-0923. Fax: (770) 342-8135. Web Site:www.wmoqfm.com Licensee: Bostwick Broadcasting Group Inc. Format: Classic country. ◆B.R. Anderson, Sr., pres, gen mgr; David Malcolm, gen mgr & opns mgr.

Bowdon

WBZY(FM)— Dec 9, 1996: 105.3 mhz; 61 kw. Ant 1,204 ft TL: N33 24 41 W84 49 48. Hrs open: 1819 Peachtree Rd., N.E., Ste 700, Atlanta, 30309. Phone: (404)741-1053. Fax: (404) 367-1111. Web Site:1053elpatron.com Licensee: CC Licenses LLC. Group owner: Clear Channel Communications Inc. (acq 11-24-2000; at least $7 million). Format: Rgnl Mexican. ◆Jerry DelCore, gen mgr.

Bremen

WGMI(AM)— October 1957: 1440 khz; 2.5 kw-D. TL: N33 42 56 W85 09 34. Hrs open: 24 613 Tallapoosa St., 30110. Phone: (770) 537-0840. Phone: (770) 537-9464. Fax: (770) 406-2324.E-mail: wgmi1440@yahoo.com Web Site:www.wgmiradio.com Licensee: Garner Ministries Inc. (acq 11-10-93; $150,000; 11-29-93). Population served: 116,492 Reddy, Begley & McCormick. Format: Relg, southern gospel, Christian country. News staff: one; News: 3 hrs wkly. Target aud: 25-54; majority married women with children. Spec prog: High School Sports. ◆Horace Garner, CEO, stn mgr; Peggy Garner, opns mgr.

Brooklet

WQQT(AM)—Not on air, target date: unknown: 1450 khz; 1 kw-U. TL: N32 24 19 W81 42 26. Hrs open: Drawer 90, Hawkinsville, 31036. Phone: (478) 893-6614. Licensee: Great Southern Radiocasting. ◆Jerry D. Braswell, gen mgr.

Broxton

WULS(FM)— Nov 1, 1993: 103.7 mhz; 6 kw. 328 ft TL: N31 33 26 W82 52 10. Hrs open: 702 N. Madison Ave., Douglas, 31533. Phone: (912) 384-9857. Fax: (912) 384-0016.E-mail: info@wuls.com Licensee: WULS Inc. Format: Southern gospel. ◆Wyndel Bunnsed, gen mgr.

Brunswick

*WAYR-FM— 1996: 90.7 mhz; 2.3 kw. 312 ft TL: N31 11 39 W81 29 30. Stereo. Hrs open: 1426 New Castle St. #200, 31520. Phone: (904) 272-1111. Fax: (904) 284-2501.E-mail: lstephens@wayradio.org Web Site:www.wayradio.org Licensee: Good Tidings Trust Inc. (acq 3-13-98; $100,000). Format: Christian. Target aud: 45-70. ◆Bill Tidwell, pres, gen mgr; Luke Stephens, gen mgr.

WBGA(FM)—(Saint Simons Island, Jan 1, 1990: 92.7 mhz; 6 kw. 340 ft TL: N31 09 55 W81 28 28. Stereo. Hrs open: 24 Prog sep from AM 3833 Hwy. 82, 31523. Phone: (912) 265-9300. Fax: (912) 264-5462.E-mail: scottrysun@gmail.com Licensee: Quantum of Brunswick License Co. LLC Natl. Network: ABC, . Format: Urban. Target aud: 24-45. ◆Jonthan Havens, gen mgr.

WGIG(AM)— Mar 5, 1949: 1440 khz; 5 kw-D, 1 kw-N, DA-N. TL: N31 10 07 W81 32 14. Hrs open: 3833 U.S. Hwy. 82, 31523. Phone: (912) 267-1025. Fax: (912) 264-5462.E-mail: ryfun@adelphia.net Web Site:www.1440wgig.net Licensee: Qantum of Brunswick License Co. LLC. Group owner: Qantum Communications Corp. (acq 7-2-03; grpsl). Population served: 75,000 Natl. Network: CBS, . Rgnl. Network: Ga. Net. Ga. News Net. Format: News/talk. ◆Jonathan Havens, gen mgr; Scott Rygun, opns dir & opns mgr.

WHFX(FM)—See Darien

WMOG(AM)— June 1940: 1490 khz; 1 kw-U. TL: N31 09 55 W81 28 28. (CP: 600 w-U, TL: N31 09 42 W81 28 28). Hrs open: 24 3833 Hwy. 82, 31523. Phone: (912) 267-1025. Fax: (912) 264-5462.E-mail: scottrysun@gmail.com Licensee: Qantum of Brunswick License Co. LLC. Group owner: Qantum Communications Corp. (acq 7-2-2003; grpsl). Population served: 94,000 Natl. Rep: McGavren Guild,. Format: Nostalgia, news/talk, sports. News staff: one; News: 20 hrs wkly. Target aud: 35 plus. Spec prog: Black 8 hrs, class one hr wkly. ◆Larry Landrum, gen mgr; Scott Ryfun, progmg dir.

WMUV(FM)— Nov 8, 1965: 100.7 mhz; 62 kw. Ant 1,473 ft TL: N30 49 16 W81 44 14. Stereo. Hrs open: 24 6440 Atlantic Blvd., Jacksonville, FL, 32216. Phone: (904) 727-9696. Fax: (904) 721-9322.E-mail: info@kool1007.com Web Site:www.countrylegends1007.com Licensee: Renda Broadcasting Corp. Group owner: Renda Broadcasting Corp.-Renda Radio Inc. (acq 1996; $6.5 million with WGNE-FM Palatka, FL). Population served: 1,200,000 Natl. Rep: McGavren Guild,. Format: Classic country. ◆Tony Renda Sr., CEO; Bill Scull, gen mgr; George Sample, gen sls mgr; Stacey Steiner, prom dir; Briggs Bickley, progmg dir; Bob Dillehay, chief of engrg; Judy Riley, traf mgr; Jim Byard, pub svc dir.

WRJY(FM)— June 30, 1994: 104.1 mhz; 4.2 kw. 390 ft TL: N31 11 39 W81 29 30. Hrs open: 24 185 Benedict Rd., 31520. Phone: (912) 261-1000. Fax: (912) 265-8391. Web Site:www.coastalcountry1041.com Licensee: Golden Isles Broadcasting LLC (acq 3-23-2001; $2.8 million with WXMK(FM) Dock Junction). Natl. Rep: Rgnl Reps,. Format: Country. News: 168 hrs wkly. Target aud: 25-54; urban female. ◆Traci Long, gen mgr.

WSFN(AM)— Sept 1, 1966: 790 khz; 500 w-D, 115 w-N, DA-2. TL: N31 08 40 W81 34 56. Hrs open: 7515 Blythe Island Hwy., 31523. Phone: (912) 264-6251. Fax: (912) 264-9991.E-mail: thefanradio@aol.com Web Site:www.fandog.net Licensee: MarMac Communications L.L.C. (acq 4-98; $350,000). Natl. Network: ABC, . Rgnl. Network: Ga. Net. Ga. News Net. Format: Sports. ◆Gary Moss Marmitt, pres & gen mgr.

WSOL-FM—Licensed to Brunswick. See Jacksonville FL

*WWIO-FM— Feb 28, 1993: 88.9 mhz; 11.5 kw. Ant 151 ft TL: N31 11 20 W81 29 05. Stereo. Hrs open: 24 Rebroadcasts WSVH(FM) Savannah 100%. 260 14th St. N.W., Atlanta, 30318-5360. Phone: (404) 685-2690. Fax: (404) 685-2684.E-mail: ask@gpb.org Web Site:www.gpb.org Licensee: Georgia Public Telecommunications Commission. Natl. Network: NPR, PRI, . Wire Svc: AP Format: Classical, news. News staff: 10; News: 51 hrs wkly. Target aud: Adults: 35 plus. ◆Nancy G. Hall, CEO; Bonnie Bean, CFO; Bob Houghton, gen mgr; Eric Nauert, stn mgr; Russell Wells, opns mgr; Rob Maynard, progmg dir; Susanna Capelouto, news dir.

WWSN(FM)—(Waycross, June 3, 1972: 103.3 mhz; 100 kw. 1,100 ft TL: N31 15 42 W82 19 26. (CP: TL: N31 09 22 W81 58 19). Stereo. Hrs open: 3833 US Hwy. 82, 31525. Phone: (912) 267-1025. Fax: (912) 264-5462.E-mail: ryfun@adelphia.net Web Site:www.sunny103.net Licensee: Qantum of Brunswick License Co. LLC. Group owner: Qantum Communications Corp. (acq 7-2-03; grpsl). Population served: 250,000 Natl. Rep: McGavren Guild,. Format: Adult contemp. Target aud: 25-54. Spec prog: Jazz 5 hrs wkly. ◆Jonathan Havens, gen mgr; Scott Ryfun, opns mgr.

WYNR(FM)—(Waycross, Oct 10, 1971: 102.5 mhz; 100 kw. 980 ft TL: N31 09 13 W81 58 00. Stereo. Hrs open: 24 3833 Hwy. 82, 31525. Phone: (912) 267-1025. Fax: (912) 264-5462.E-mail: joepportagee@hotmail.com Web Site:www.1025wynr.net Licensee: Qantum of Brunswick License Co. LLC. Group owner: Qantum Communications Corp. (acq 7-2-03; grpsl). Population served: 250,000 Natl. Rep: McGavren Guild,. Smithwick & Belendiuk. Format: Country. News staff: one; News: one hr wkly. Target aud: 25-54. ◆Frank Osborne, pres, exec VP; Mike Mangen, CFO; Jonathan Brewster, exec VP; Jonathan Havens, gen mgr; Joe Sousa, stn mgr, opns mgr.

Buckhead

WPMA(FM)— December 2002: 102.7 mhz; 7.5 kw. Ant 594 ft TL: N33 30 10 W83 15 37. Stereo. Hrs open: 24 2278 Wortham Ln, Grovetown, 30813. Phone: (706) 309-9610.E-mail: ctbarinowski@comcast.net Web Site:www.gnnradio.org Licensee: Barinowski Investment Co. L.P. Group owner: Good News Network. Population served: 100,000 Format: Christian. ◆Clarence Barinowski, gen mgr.

Buena Vista

WEAM-FM— June 21, 2001: 100.7 mhz; 2.6 kw. Ant 502 ft TL: N32 20 33 W84 39 18. Hrs open: 24 Box 1998, Columbus, 31902-1998. Phone: (706) 576-3565. Fax: (706) 576-3683.E-mail: info@dbicolumbus.com Licensee: Davis Broadcasting Inc. of Columbus. Group owner: Davis Broadcasting Inc. (acq 7-30-2003). Format: Gospel. ◆Gregory Davis, CEO, CFO & gen mgr.

Buford

WLKQ-FM— Jan 1, 1970: 102.3 mhz; 4.2 kw. Ant 390 ft TL: N34 07 16 W83 58 35. Stereo. Hrs open: 24 3235 Satellite Blvd., Suite 230, Duluth, 30096. Phone: (770) 623-8772. Fax: (770) 623-4722.E-mail: info@laraza1023.com Web Site:www.laraza1023.com Licensee: Davis Broadcasting of Atlanta L.L.C. Group owner: Davis Broadcasting Inc. (acq 9-30-2003; $5.25 million). Population served: 2,000,000 Rgnl. Network: Ga. Net. Ga. News Net. Kenkel & Associates. Format: Sp. News staff: 2; News: 6 hrs wkly. Target aud: 35-54; upper-middle class professionals. ◆Gregory A. Davis, pres; Brian Barber, gen mgr.

WXEM(AM)—Licensed to Buford. See Austell

Byron

*WPWB(FM)— 1988: 90.5 mhz; 16.5 kw. 453 ft TL: N32 40 56 W83 22 11. Stereo. Hrs open: 24 2278 Wortham Ln., Grovetown, 30813-5103. Phone: (706) 309-9610. Fax: (706) 309-9669.E-mail: ctbarinowski@comcast.net Web Site:www.gnnradio.org Licensee: Augusta Radio Fellowship Institute Inc. Population served: 325,000 Format: Christian. News: 12 hrs wkly. Target aud: General. ◆Clarence Barinowski, pres & gen mgr.

Cairo

WGRA(AM)— October 1949: 790 khz; 1 kw-D. TL: N30 54 08 W84 14 03. Hrs open: Box 120, 39828. Secondary address: 1809 U.S. 84 W 39828. Phone: (229) 377-4392. Fax: (229) 377-4564.E-mail: jeff@wgra.net Web Site:www.wgra.net Licensee: Lovett Broadcasting Enterprises Inc. (acq 1-84; $450,000;4-23-84). Population served: 35,000 Rgnl. Network: Ga. Net. Ga. News Net. Natl. Rep: Rgnl Reps,. Ga. News Net. Format: News/talk. Target aud: 30 plus; mainly women. Spec prog: Black 6 hrs wkly. ◆Jeffrey Lovett, pres & gen mgr.

WWLD(FM)— June 1983: 102.3 mhz; 27 kw. Ant 604 ft TL: N30 29 32 W84 17 02. Stereo. Hrs open: 3411 W. Tharpe St., Tallahassee, FL,

32303-1139. Phone: (850) 201-3000. Fax: (850) 561-8903. Web Site:blazin1023.com Licensee: Cumulus Licensing LLC. Group owner: Cumulus Media Inc. (acq 10-10-01; $1.5 million including noncompete agreement). Population served: 320,304 Natl. Rep: Katz Radio,. Wiley Rein. Format: Black, hip hop/rhythm and blues. Target aud: 18-34. ♦Barry Kaye, gen mgr; Jay Blaze, progmg dir.

Calhoun

***WCGN(FM)**—Not on air, target date: unknown: 91.3 mhz; 3 kw. Ant 98 ft TL: N34 32 54 W84 51 56. Hrs open: Box 3006, Collegedale, TN, 37315. Phone: (423) 238-4240. Fax: (423) 238-6642. Web Site:www.lifetalk.net Licensee: Lifetalk Radio Inc. ♦Steven Gallimore, pres.

WEBS(AM)— Nov 1, 1966: 1030 khz; 5 kw-D, 3 w-N. TL: N34 29 25 W84 55 04. Hrs open: Box 1299, 30703. Secondary address: 427 S. Wall St. 30703. Phone: (706) 629-2238. Fax: (706) 629-7092. Licensee: Radio WEBS Inc. (acq 7-1-80). Population served: 50,000 Natl. Network: Jones Radio Networks, . Format: Oldies. Target aud: 18-52. Spec prog: Black 2 hrs wkly. ♦Ken D. Payne, pres & gen mgr.

WJTH(AM)— June 16, 1977: 900 khz; 1 kw-D, 266 w-N. TL: N34 27 40 W84 53 44. Hrs open: 24 Box 1119, 30703. Secondary address: 329 Richardson Rd. S.E. 30701. Phone: (706) 629-6397. Fax: (706) 629-8463.E-mail: am900@wjth.com Web Site:www.wjth.com Licensee: Cherokee Broadcasting Co. Population served: 38,000 Natl. Network: ABC, . Rgnl. Network: Ga. Net. Natl. Rep: Rgnl Reps,. Ga. News Net. Format: C&W, loc news & info. News staff: one; News: 20 hrs wkly. Target aud: 18-64; general. Spec prog: Farm one hr, gospel 2 hrs, relg 16 hrs wkly. ♦Sam Thomas, gen mgr; Keith Thomas, stn mgr; Gloria Cooley, gen sls mgr.

Camilla

WZBN(FM)— April 1977: 105.5 mhz; 6 kw. Ant 300 ft TL: N31 18 51 W84 12 18. Stereo. Hrs open: 24 1104 W. Broad Ave., Albany, 31707. Phone: (229) 888-5000. Fax: (912) 888-5960.E-mail: matt.patrick@cumulus.com Licensee: Extreme Media Group LLC Group owner: Cumulus Media Inc. (acq 3-31-2009; exchange for FM translator W250BC Riverdale). Population served: 200,000 Rgnl. Network: Ga. Net. Natl. Rep: Katz Radio,. Ga. News Net. Format: Urban contemp. News staff: one; News: 3 hrs wkly. Target aud: 25-54; female. Spec prog: Blues 5 hrs, gospel 16 hrs wkly. ♦Paul Bucurel, gen mgr.

Canton

WCHK(AM)— Apr 11, 1957: Stn currently dark. 1290 khz; 5 kw-D, 500 w-N, DA-N. TL: N34 15 08 W84 27 49. Hrs open: 3235 Satellite Blvd., Suite 230, Duluth, 30096. Phone: (770) 623-8772. Fax: (770) 623-4722. Licensee: Davis Broadcasting of Atlanta L.L.C. (acq 1-17-2007; $3.8 million with WNSY(FM) Talking Rock). Rgnl. Network: Ga. Net. ♦Brian Barber, gen mgr.

WWVA-FM— Aug 1, 1964: 105.7 mhz; 20 kw. Ant 781 ft TL: N34 03 58 W84 27 15. Stereo. Hrs open: 24 1819 Peachtree Rd., N.E., Suite 700, Atlanta, 30309. Phone: (404) 607-1336. Fax: (404) 367-1105. Web Site:www.vivaatlanta.com Licensee: CC Licenses LLC. Group owner: Clear Channel Communications Inc. (acq 3-29-2004; $31 million). Format: Sp contemp. ♦Ricardo Villalona, gen mgr.

Carrollton

WBTR-FM— 1964: 92.1 mhz; 580 w. 636 ft TL: N33 33 54 W85 01 02. Stereo. Hrs open: 24 102 Parkwood Cir., 30117-8353. Phone: (770) 832-9685. Fax: (770) 830-1027. Web Site:www.b92country.com Licensee: WYAI Inc. (acq 6-7-01). Population served: 150,000 Rgnl. Network: Ga. Net. Ga. News Net. Format: Country. News staff: one; News: 3 hrs wkly. Target aud: 25-49. Spec prog: Black 5 hrs wkly. ♦Steven L. Gradick, pres & gen mgr.

WLBB(AM)— Nov 19, 1975: 1330 khz; 500 w-D. TL: N33 34 17 W85 03 02. Hrs open: 24 808 Newnan Rd., 30117. Phone: (678) 601-1330. Fax: (678) 601-8256.E-mail: info@wlbb.com Web Site:www.newstalk1330.com Licensee: WYAI Inc. (acq 6-7-01; Population served: 16,500 Natl. Network: CBS, . Format: News/talk. News staff: 2. ♦Steve Gradick, pres & gen mgr.

***WUWG(FM)**— Feb 19, 1973: 90.7 mhz; 500 w. 494 ft TL: N33 33 50 W85 01 04. Stereo. Hrs open: 24
WJSP, Warm Springs/Columbus, GA, 75%.
260 14th St. N.W., Atlanta, 30318-5360. Phone: (404) 685-2690. Fax: (404) 685-2684.E-mail: ask@gpb.org Web Site:www.gpb.org Licensee: Georgia Public Telecommunications Commission (acq 8-9-2004). Population served: 35,000 Natl. Network: NPR, PRI, . Rgnl. Network: Peach State Public Radio. Wire Svc: AP Format: Classical, News. News staff: 10; News: 25-30 hrs wkly. Target aud: General; students & area residents. Spec prog: Folk 2 hrs, bluegrass 2 hrs, new age 3 hrs. ♦Nancy G. Hall, CEO; Bonnie Bean, CFO; Bob Houghton, gen mgr; Tom Barclay, opns mgr; Rob Maynard, progmg dir; Nancy Zintak, progmg mgr; Susanna Capelouto, news dir.

Cartersville

WBHF(AM)— July 17, 1946: 1450 khz; 1 kw-U. TL: N34 11 09 W84 48 13. Hrs open: 24 7 N. Wall St., 30120. Phone: (770) 386-1450. Fax: (770) 382-5390.E-mail: news@wbhfradio.org Licensee: Anverse Inc. (acq 7-5-00). Population served: 15600 Natl. Network: ABC, AP Radio, . Wire Svc: AP Format: Oldies, loc news/sports. News staff: 3; News: 10 hrs wkly. ♦Matt Santini, gen mgr; Ernestine Young Jones, opns mgr.

***WCCV(FM)**— Jan 24, 1983: 91.7 mhz; 910 w. 537 ft TL: N34 11 35 W84 45 31. Stereo. Hrs open: Box 1000, 30120-1000. Phone: (770) 387-0917. Fax: (770) 387-2856. Web Site:www.ibn.org Licensee: Immanuel Broadcasting. Format: Relg. ♦Ed Tuten, pres; Howard Tuten, gen mgr & progmg dir.

WYXC(AM)— Sept 21, 1961: 1270 khz; 2 kw-D, 187 w-N. TL: N34 12 34 W84 47 49. Hrs open: 24 Box 200399, 30121. Phone: (770) 382-1306.E-mail: info@newstalk1270.com Web Site:www.newstalk1270.com Licensee: Clarion Communications Inc. (acq 6-14-2005; $500,000). Population served: 15600 Format: News, talk, sports. News staff: one; News: 15 hrs. wkly. Target aud: 25-55. ♦Charles Shiflett, pres; Jim Adams, gen mgr, stn mgr; Connie Dixon, gen sls mgr, prom dir; Charles Brachel, progmg dir, news dir, traf mgr, sports cmtr; Allen Schmelz, chief of engrg.

Chatsworth

***WNGH-FM**— Nov 13, 1976: 98.9 mhz; 6 kw. Ant 312 ft TL: N34 49 42 W84 53 41. Hrs open: 24 Georgia Public Broadcasting, 260 14th St. N.W., Atlanta, 30318. Phone: (404) 685-2415. Web Site:www.gpb.org Licensee: The Foundation for Public Broadcasting in Georgia Inc. Group owner: Clear Channel Communications Inc. (acq 4-18-2008; $3.2 million). Population served: 350,000 Natl. Network: NPR, PRI, . Arnold & Porter LLP. Wire Svc: AP Format: News, classical. News staff: 10; News: 41 hrs wkly. Target aud: 35 plus; adults. Spec prog: Jazz 16 hrs wkly. ♦Nancy G. Hall, CEO; Bonnie Bean, CFO; Bob Houghton, gen mgr, gen mgr; Tom Barclay, opns mgr; Rob Maynard, progmg mgr; Susanna Capelouto, news dir. Co-owned TV: WNGH-TV affil

Chauncey

WQIL(FM)— Oct 20, 1995: 101.3 mhz; 50 kw. 492 ft TL: N32 21 37 W83 08 28. (CP: 33 kw, ant 413 ft.). Stereo. Hrs open: 24 Box 130, Dublin, 31040-0130. Phone: (478) 272-4422. Fax: (478) 275-4657.E-mail: webmaster@1013wqil.com Licensee: GSW Inc. (acq 1994; $95,000). Rgnl rep: Regional Reps Format: Southern Gospel. News: one hr wkly. Target aud: 30 plus; Christians. ♦Rick Humphrey, gen mgr.

Clarkesville

WCHM(AM)— December 1989: 1490 khz; 1 kw-U. TL: N34 36 27 W83 32 15. Hrs open: 24 Box 368, 30523. Secondary address: 1331 Washington St. 30523. Phone: (706) 754-6272. Fax: (706) 754-8621.E-mail: northgeorgiaradio@hemc.net Licensee: Brian Rothell. (acq 11-21-95; $70,000). Population served: 57,000 Natl. Network: USA, . Reynolds & Manning. Format: Contemp Christian. News staff: one; News: 5 hrs wkly. Target aud: 25-62. ♦Brian Rothell, gen mgr.

WMJE(FM)— 1990: 102.9 mhz; 16 kw. 413 ft TL: N34 29 05 W83 38 24. Stereo. Hrs open: 24 PO Box 10, Gainesville, 30503. Secondary address: 1102 Thompson Bridge Rd. N.E., Gainesville 30501. Phone: (770) 532-9921. Fax: (770) 532-0459.E-mail: jay.jacobs@jacobsmedia.net Web Site:MAJIC1029.com Licensee: JWJ Properties Inc. Group owner: Jacobs Media Corp. (acq 3-19-92). Population served: 500,000 Natl. Network: Westwood One, . Wire Svc: AP Format: Var. Target aud: 25-54; females with a median age of 41. ♦John W. Jacobs III, CEO, pres; John W. Jacobs Jr., chmn; Joel Williams, gen mgr, gen sls mgr; Bill Maine, progmg mgr.

Claxton

WCLA(AM)— July 20, 1958: 1470 khz; 1 kw-D, 260 w-N. TL: N32 10 01 W81 54 07. Hrs open: 24 316 N. River St., P.O. Box 637, 30417-5920. Phone: (912) 739-9252. Fax: (912) 739-0050.E-mail: radioevans@bellsouth.net Web Site:wclaradio.net Licensee: W. Danny Swain (group owner; (acq 2-2-2007; $230,000). Population served: 14,000 Natl. Network: ABC, . Ga. News Net. Format: Classic hits/oldies. News staff: one. Target aud: 35-64; adults. Spec prog: Farm 1.5 hrs, Hispanic 6 hrs, relg 4 hrs wkly. ♦W. Danny Smith, gen mgr, traf mgr; Herman Moody, opns mgr; W. Danny Swain, pres & gen sls mgr; Martin Foglia, chief of engrg.

WMCD(FM)— Sept 15, 1972: 107.3 mhz; 25 kw. Ant 328 ft TL: N32 10 01 W81 54 07. Stereo. Hrs open: 24 Box 958, Statesboro, 30459. Secondary address: 561 E. Olliff St., Statesboro 30458. Phone: (912) 764-5446. Fax: (912) 764-8827.E-mail: spots@georgiaeagleradio.com Licensee: Georgia Eagle Broadcasting Inc. Group owner: Communications Capital Managers LLC (acq 5-21-2007; grpsl). Population served: 25,000 Natl. Network: Westwood One, . Rgnl. Network: Ga. Net. Rgnl rep: Rgnl Reps Richard Helmick. Format: Adult contemp. News staff: one; News: 7 hrs wkly. Target aud: 25-50; general. ♦Buddy Horne, gen mgr, progmg dir; Cornell Burgess, traf mgr.

Clayton

WGHC(AM)— 2009: 1400 khz; 1 kw-U. TL: M34 51 41 W83 24 25. Hrs open: 6 AM-sunset Box 1149, 30525. Secondary address: 18 Radio Ln. 30525. Phone: (706) 782-4251. Phone: (706) 782-1041. Fax: (706) 782-4252.E-mail: rabunradio@alltel.net Web Site:www.rabunradio.com Licensee: Tugart Properties LLC. Natl. Network: CBS Radio, . Ga. News Net. Wire Svc: AP Format: Talk, MOR. News staff: one; News: 5 hrs wkly. Target aud: 35 plus. ♦Douglas M. Sutton Jr., pres; Vicki Childs, VP & gen mgr; John Durham, opns mgr; Scott Kimbler, news dir.

WRBN(FM)— June 11, 1990: 104.1 mhz; 370 w. Ant 1,296 ft TL: N34 54 24 W83 24 56. 96.3 mHz; 370 w DA. Hrs open: 24 P O Box 1149, 30525. Secondary address: 18 Radio Lane 30525. Phone: (706) 782-4251. Phone: (706) 782-1041. Fax: (706) 782-4252.E-mail: sky104@rabun.net Licensee: Sutton Radiocasting Corp. Population served: 37,158 Natl. Network: ABC, . Format: Adult contemp/Local News/Community Involvement. News staff: one; News: 2 hrs wkly. Target aud: 25 plus. Spec prog: NASCAR/Local Sports. ♦Douglas M. Sutton Jr., pres; M. Terry Carter, VP; John Durham, opns mgr; Robin Dake, news dir; Marty Lee, chief of engrg.

Cleveland

WAZX-FM— 1989: Stn currently dark. 101.9 mhz; 3.2 kw. Ant 453 ft TL: N34 33 49 W83 38 26. Stereo. Hrs open: 1800 Lake Park Dr., Smyrna, 30080. Phone: (770) 436-6171. Fax: (770) 436-0100. Licensee: WAZX-FM Inc. (acq 4-20-2001; $60,000 for 80%). ♦Javier Macias, pres.

WRWH(AM)— Sept 27, 1958: 1350 khz; 1 kw-D. TL: N34 35 11 W83 46 01. Hrs open: 6 AM-sunset Box 181, 30528. Secondary address: 681 Hood St. 30528. Phone: (706) 865-3181. Fax: (706) 865-0421.E-mail: wrwh@alltel.net Web Site:wrwh.com Licensee: White County Media LLC (acq 5-17-89). Population served: 13,500 Rgnl. Network: Ga. Net. Ga. News Net. Reddy, Begley & McCormick. Format: Country, gospel. Target aud: 35 plus. ♦Dean Dyer, pres, gen mgr & gen sls mgr.

Cochran

WDCO(AM)— July 4, 1965: 1440 khz; 1 kw-D. TL: N32 24 43 W83 21 42. Hrs open: 24 157 Jac Arts Rd., 31014. Phone: (478) 934-6337. Fax: (478) 934-0929.E-mail: taylor@ham.net Licensee: Georgia Eagle Broadcasting Co. Group owner: Communications Capital Managers LLC (acq 5-21-2007; grpsl). Population served: 30,000 Format: Country. Target aud: 18-54; adults. Spec prog: Black 6 hrs, farm 3 hrs, gospel 6 hrs wkly. ♦Tommy Palmer, gen mgr; James Gay, chief of engrg.

WDXQ-FM— July 4, 1968: 96.7 mhz; 3 kw. 319 ft TL: N32 24 43 W83 21 42. Stereo. Hrs open: Box 766, 157 Jac Arts Rd., 31014. Phone: (478) 934-6337. Fax: (478) 934-0929. Population served: 10,291 Natl. Network: ABC, . Natl. Rep: Clear Channel,. Wire Svc: UPI Target aud: Adults 18-54. ♦Carl Strandell, sls VP.

***WMUM-FM**— Feb 4, 1985: 89.7 mhz; 100 kw. Ant 1,010 ft TL: N32 28 11 W83 15 17. Stereo. Hrs open: 24
Rebroadcasts WJSP-FM Warm Springs 80%.
260 14th St. N.W., Atlanta, 30318-5360. Phone: (404) 685-2690. Fax: (404) 685-2684.E-mail: ask@gpb.org Web Site:www.gpb.org Licensee: Georgia Public Telecommunications Commission. Natl. Network: NPR, PRI, . Wire Svc: AP Format: Classical, news. News staff: 10; News: 40 hrs wkly. Adults 35+. Spec prog: Jazz 18 hrs wkly. ♦Nancy G. Hall,

CEO; Bonnie Bean, CFO; Bob Houghton, gen mgr; Tom Barclay, opns mgr; Rob Maynard, progmg dir; Susanna Capelonto, news dir. Co-owned TV: WMUM-TV affil

College Park

WNNX(FM)— April 1947: 100.5 mhz; 12.5 kw. Ant 977 ft TL: N33 45 34 W84 23 19. Stereo. Hrs open: 24 780 Johnson Ferry Rd., Suite 500, Atlanta, 30342. Phone: (404) 497-4700. Fax: (404) 497-4735. Web Site:www.allthehitsq100.com Licensee: WNNX Lico Inc. Group owner: Susquehanna Radio Corp. (acq 1-27-97; with co-located AM). Format: Top-40. ◆Mike Fowler, gen mgr; Lisa Kelly, opns mgr; Rob Roberts, progmg dir.

Colquitt

*WCOQ(FM)— 2008: 90.5 mhz; 4.5 kw vert. Ant 171 ft TL: N31 09 58 W84 43 15. Hrs open: Box 504, Columbia, AL, 36319-0504. Phone: (334) 798-6664.E-mail: wcoqfm@yahoo.com Licensee: D & K Communications Inc. ◆Robert Rogers, pres.

Columbus

WCGQ(FM)— July 15, 1966: 107.3 mhz; 100 kw. 1,011 ft TL: N32 27 59 W85 03 23. Stereo. Hrs open: 24 1353 13th Ave., 31901. Phone: (706) 327-1217. Fax: (706) 596-4600.E-mail: info@q1073.com Web Site:www.q1073.com Licensee: PMB Broadcasting LLC. (acq 10-1-2008; grpsl). Population served: 471,800 Format: Top 40. Target aud: 18-49. ◆Chuck Thompson, mktg dir; Al Haynes, progmg dir.

WDAK(AM)— August 1940: 540 khz; 4 kw-D, 38 w-N. TL: N32 25 58 W84 57 02. Stereo. Hrs open: Box 687, 31902. Secondary address: 1501 13th Ave. 31901. Phone: (706) 576-3000. Fax: (706) 576-3010.E-mail: scottmiller@clearchannel.com Web Site:wdakonline.com Licensee: CC Licenses LLC. Group owner: Clear Channel Communications Inc. (acq 5-9-2003; $2.73 million with WSTH-FM Alexander City, AL). Natl. Network: USA, Westwood One, . Format: News. Target aud: 18-49; men. ◆Jim Martin, gen mgr; Brian Waters, opns mgr.

WEAM(AM)— December 1954: 1580 khz; 2.3 kw-D, 1 kw-N, DA-N. TL: N32 27 55 W85 01 22. Hrs open: 20 Box 1998, 31902-1998. Phone: (706) 576-3565. Fax: (706) 576-3683.E-mail: INFO@DBICOLUMBUS.COM Licensee: Davis Broadcasting Inc. of Columbus. Group owner: Davis Broadcasting Inc. (acq 4-20-01; $400,000). Population served: 250,000 Natl. Network: USA, . Reddy, Begley & McCormick. Format: Sports. News: 15 hrs wkly. Target aud: General. ◆Gregory Davis, CFO & gen mgr.

*WFRC(FM)— June 14, 1985: 90.5 mhz; 8.5 kw. 248 ft TL: N32 27 37 W85 00 30. Stereo. Hrs open: 1010 7th Pl., Phenix City, AL, 36867. Phone: (334) 291-0399. Fax: (510) 633-7983. Web Site:www.familyradio.com Licensee: Family Stations Inc. (group owner) Format: Relg. Spec prog: Call-in 8 hrs wkly. ◆Harold Camping, pres; Sandra Salewski, opns mgr.

WFXE(FM)— Sept 22, 1969: 104.9 mhz; 6 kw. 289 ft TL: N32 27 37 W85 00 30. Stereo. Hrs open: Prog sep from AM Box 1998, 2203 Wynnton Rd., 31906. Phone: (706) 576-3565. Fax: (706) 576-3683.E-mail: info@dbicolumbus.com Licensee: Davis Broadcasting Inc. Population served: 166,565 Format: Urban contemp. ◆Gregory A. Davis, CEO; Bernie Corcoran, CFO.

WGSY(FM)—(Phenix City, AL) Mar 4, 1971: 100.1 mhz; 6 kw. 328 ft TL: N32 30 42 W85 00 41. Stereo. Hrs open: 24 Box 687, 39102. Secondary address: 1501 13th Ave. 31901. Phone: (706) 576-3000. Fax: (706) 576-3010.E-mail: info@sunny100columbus.com Web Site:www.sunny100columbus.com Licensee: CC Licenses LLC. Group owner: Clear Channel Communications Inc. (acq 2-21-2002; grpsl). Population served: 250,000 Natl. Rep: McGavren Guild,. Reddy, Begley & McCormick. Format: Adult contemp. Target aud: 25-54; women. ◆Jim Martin, gen mgr; Brian Waters, opns mgr.

WHAL(AM)—(Phenix City, AL) 1951: 1460 khz; 4 kw-D, 140 w-N. TL: N32 25 58 W84 57 02. Hrs open: 1501 13th Ave., 31901. Secondary address: Box 687 31902. Phone: (706) 576-3000. Fax: (706) 576-3010.E-mail: marshawhitney@clearchannel.com Web Site:www.foxsports1460.com Licensee: CC Licenses LLC. Group owner: Clear Channel Communications Inc. (acq 2-21-2002; grpsl). Population served: 220,000 Natl. Network: Fox Sports, . Natl. Rep: McGavren Guild,. Format: Sports. Target aud: 25 plus. ◆Jim Martin, gen mgr.

WJSP-FM—See Atlanta

WOKS(AM)— Mar 2, 1959: 1340 khz; 1 kw-U. TL: N32 27 07 W84 58 25. Hrs open: Box 1998, 31902-1998. Secondary address: 2203 Wynnton Rd. 31906. Phone: (706) 576-3565. Fax: (706) 576-3683.E-mail: info@dbicolumbus.com Licensee: Davis Broadcasting Inc. (group owner; acq 7-24-92). Natl. Network: American Urban, . Natl. Rep: Katz Radio,. Format: Black gold & gospel. Target aud: 35-64. ◆Gregory Davis, pres, gen mgr; Bernie Corcoran, stn mgr; Cheryl Davis, opns VP; Angela Verdejo, gen sls mgr; Michael Soul, progmg dir; Nicole Gates, prom VP & news dir.

WRCG(AM)— May 10, 1928: 1420 khz; 5 kw-U, DA-N. TL: N32 29 52 W85 02 48. Hrs open: 24 1353 13th Ave., 31901. Phone: (706) 327-1217. Fax: (706) 596-4600.E-mail: info@wrcg.com Web Site:www.wrcg.com Licensee: PMB Broadcasting LLC. Group owner: Archway Broadcasting Group (acq 10-1-2008; grpsl). Population served: 206,000 Natl. Network: CBS, . Natl. Rep: Christal,. Ga. News Net. Format: Sports, news/talk. News staff: one; News: 24 hrs wkly. Target aud: 35 plus; adults with discretionary income. Spec prog: Farm 3 hrs wkly. ◆Chuck Thompson, gen mgr; Bob Quick, opns dir.

WSHE(AM)— 1947: 1270 khz; 5 kw. TL: N32 26 16 W85 01 10. Hrs open: 19 Box 687, 31902. Secondary address: 1501 13th Ave. 31901. Phone: (706) 576-3000. Fax: (706) 576-3010.E-mail: scottmiller @clearchannel.com Web Site:www.wmlfonline.com Licensee: CC Licenses LLC. Group owner: Clear Channel Communications Inc. (acq 2-21-2002; grpsl). Population served: 300,000 Natl. Rep: McGavren Guild,. Reddy, Begley & McCormick. Format: Gospel, sports, Latino. News: 20 hrs wkly. Target aud: 35-60. ◆Jim Martin, gen mgr; Brian Waters, opns mgr.

WSTH-FM—See Alexander City, AL

*WTJB(FM)— Dec 15, 1984: 91.7 mhz; 5 kw. 298 ft TL: N32 25 20 W85 01 50. Hrs open: 6 AM-midnight
Rebroadcasts WTSU(FM) Troy 100%.
Wallace Hall, Troy State Univ., Troy, AL, 36082. Phone: (334) 670-3268. Fax: (334) 670-3934.E-mail: wtsu@troy.edu Web Site:www.troy.edu Licensee: Troy State University. Natl. Network: NPR, PRI, . Format: Class, news. News: 25 hrs wkly. Target aud: General. Spec prog: Children one hr wkly. ◆James Clower, gen mgr; Judy Davis, opns mgr; Fred Azbell, progmg dir.

WVRK(FM)— Nov 16, 1946: 102.9 mhz; 100 kw. Ant 1,521 ft TL: N32 19 25 W84 46 46. Stereo. Hrs open: Prog sep from AM 1501 13th Ave., 31901. Secondary address: Box 687 31902. Phone: (706) 576-3000. Fax: (706) 576-3010.E-mail: brianwaters@clearchannel.com Web Site:www.rock103online.com Format: AOR, classic rock. ◆Jerri Northington, gen sls mgr; Brian Waters, progmg dir.

*WYFK(FM)— July 1987: 89.5 mhz; 50 kw. 439 ft TL: N32 40 03 W84 57 19. Stereo. Hrs open: 11530 Carmel Commons Blvd., Charlotte, NC, 28226. Phone: (800) 888-7077. Phone: (704) 523-5555. Fax: (704) 522-1967.E-mail: bbn@bnnradio.org Web Site:www.bbnradio.org Licensee: Bible Broadcasting Network Inc. (group owner) Format: Relg. Target aud: General. ◆Lowell Davey, pres.

Commerce

WJJC(AM)— June 27, 1957: 1270 khz; 5 kw-D. TL: N34 12 57 W83 26 09. Hrs open: 24 Box 379, 30529. Secondary address: 1801 N. Elm St. 30529. Phone: (706) 335-1270. Fax: (706) 335-1905.E-mail: wjjc@windstream.net Web Site:www.wjjc.net Licensee: Side Communications Inc. (acq 7-31-2007; $240,000). Population served: 100,000 Rgnl. Network: Ga. Net. Natl. Rep: Rgnl Reps,. Ga. News Net. Format: Talk. Target aud: 25-55. Spec prog: Glenn Beck, Jim Rome, Dr. Laura. ◆Rob Jordan, gen mgr.

Conyers

WPBS(AM)— November 1979: 1040 khz; 12 kw-D, 5 kw-CH. TL: N33 40 48 W84 01 44. Hrs open: 12 6171 Neely Farm Dr., Norcross, 30092. Phone: (404) 932-5006. Licensee: PacificStar Media Corp. (acq 5-11-2005; $5.25 million). Population served: 4,000,000 Format: Spanish, Christian. ◆Charles Kim, gen mgr.

Coosa

WSRM(FM)— 2005: 93.5 mhz; 1.2 kw. Ant 741 ft TL: N34 14 02 W85 13 50. Hrs open: 20 John Davenport Dr., Rome, 30165. Phone: (706) 291-9496. Fax: (706) 235-7107.E-mail: info@wrgarome.com Licensee: Coosa Broadcasting Corp. (acq 7-21-2005; $1.1 million). Format: Contemp Christian. ◆Paul Stone, pres; Randy Quick, gen mgr.

Cordele

*WAEF(FM)— 2001: 90.3 mhz; 11 kw vert. Ant 505 ft TL: N31 38 22 W83 44 58. Hrs open: Box 3206, American Family Radio, Tupelo, MS, 38803. Phone: (662) 844-8888. Fax: (662) 842-6791. Web Site:www.afr.net Licensee: American Family Association. Group owner: American Family Radio Format: Inspirational Christian. ◆Marvin Sanders, gen mgr.

Cornelia

WCON(AM)— Mar 28, 1953: 1450 khz; 1 kw-U. TL: N34 30 57 W83 32 20. Hrs open: 24 Box 100, 30531. Secondary address: 540 N. Main St. 30531. Phone: (706) 778-2241. Fax: (706) 778-0576.E-mail: wcon@alltel.net Web Site:www.wconfm.com Licensee: Habersham Broadcasting Co. (acq 2-1-61). Population served: 50,000 Natl. Network: ABC, . Rgnl. Network: Ga. Net. Ga. News Net. Format: Gospel, country. News staff: one. Target aud: Adults. ◆Bobbie C. Foster, pres, gen mgr; John C. Foster, VP; Michael Harvey, news dir; Jimmy Dillard, chief of engrg.

WCON-FM— Mar 27, 1965: 99.3 mhz; 50 kw. Ant 808 ft TL: N34 31 24 W83 40 46. Stereo. Hrs open: 24 Box 100, 30531. Secondary address: 540 N. Main St. 30531. Phone: (706) 778-2241. Fax: (706) 778-0576.E-mail: bobbiefoster @alltel.net Web Site:www.wconfm.com Licensee: Habersham Broadcasting Co. Population served: 1,500,000 Format: Country. News staff: one. Target aud: 18 plus.

Covington

WGFS(AM)— Oct 9, 1946: 1430 khz; 3.9 kw-D, 212 w-N. TL: N33 37 14 W83 53 04. Stereo. Hrs open: 6 AM-7 PM Box 2419, 30015. Secondary address: 1151 Hendricks St. 30014. Phone: (770) 786-1430. Fax: (770) 784-9892. Licensee: Multicultural Radio Broadcasting Licensee LLC. Group owner: Multicultural Radio Broadcasting Inc. (acq 11-21-03; $700,000). Population served: 16,000 Natl. Network: CBS, . Rgnl. Network: Ga. Net. Ga. News Net. Mullin, Rhyne, Emmons & Topel. Wire Svc: CBS Format: Oldies of 50s & 60s. News staff: one; News: 20 hrs wkly. Target aud: General. ◆Arthur Liu, pres; Mike Shumate, stn mgr.

Crawford

WGMG(FM)— April 1990: 102.1 mhz; 10 kw. 328 ft TL: N33 55 18 W83 14 14. Hrs open: 10 Tower Pl., Bogart, 30622. Phone: (706) 369-7223. Fax: (706) 353-1967. Web Site:www.magic1021fm.com Licensee: Cox Radio Inc. Group owner: Southern Broadcasting Companies Inc. (acq 8-1-2008; grpsl). Format: Adult contemp. Target aud: 18-49; general. ◆Robert F. Neil, pres; Scott Smith, opns mgr; Kevin Steele, progmg dir.

Cumming

WATB(AM)—(Decatur, July 19, 1958: 1420 khz; 1 kw-D, 51 w-N, DA-D. TL: N33 47 13 W84 14 53. (CP: 1430 khz; 50 kw-D, 160 w-N, DA-D. Hrs open: 3589 N. Decatur Rd., Scottdale, 30079. Phone: (404) 508-1420. Fax: (404) 508-8930.E-mail: watb1420@yahoo.com Licensee: Way Broadcasting Licensee LLC (acq 6-13-00; grpsl). Format: Multi-cultural. Target aud: General; ethnic groups from around the world. ◆Benjamin F. Vannoy Jr., gen mgr.

*WWEV-FM— Dec 4, 1981: 91.5 mhz; 8.9 kw. Ant 960 ft TL: N34 14 13 W84 09 36. Stereo. Hrs open: 24 Box 248, 30028. Secondary address: 1705 Sawnee Dr. 30040. Phone: (770) 781-9150. Fax: (770) 781-5003.E-mail: wwev@wwev.org Web Site:www.wwev.org Licensee: Curriculum Development Foundation Inc. Format: Relg. Target aud: 18-49; the family unit. ◆N. Barry Holt, gen mgr, progmg dir; Ray Haynes, prom dir.

Cusseta

WBOJ(FM)—Not on air, target date: unknown: 103.7 mhz; 6 kw. Ant 328 ft TL: N32 18 39 W84 45 45. Hrs open: 1820 Wynnton Rd Suite B, Columbus, 31906. Phone: (706) 324-5850. Fax: (706) 256-2984. Web Site:1037thetruth.com Licensee: Signature Broadcasting Ltd. ◆Shirley H. Thrasher, gen mgr.

*WJEP(FM)—Not on air, target date: unknown: 91.1 mhz; 2 kw. Ant 420 ft TL: N32 08 05 W84 40 59. Hrs open: Box 5725, Twin Falls, ID, 83303-5725. Phone: (208) 733-3551. Fax: (208) 733-3548. Web Site:www.edgewaterbroadcasting.com Licensee: Edgewater Broadcasting Inc. (acq 10-15-2008; $21,000 for CP). ◆Clark Parrish, pres; Jim Long, gen mgr.

Cuthbert

WCUG(AM)— Dec 1, 1971: 850 khz; 500 w-D. TL: N31 46 26 W84 50 16. Hrs open: Box 348, 39840. Phone: (229) 732-3725. Licensee: Mullis Communications Inc. Population served: 3,972 Rgnl. Network: Ga. Net. Ga. News Net. Format: Country, Gospel, Oldies. Spec prog: Black 4 hrs, farm 8 hrs wkly. ◆N. Scott Mullis, gen mgr.

*WEBH(FM)—Not on air, target date: unknown: 91.9 mhz; 6 kw. Ant 203 ft TL: N31 45 18 W84 47 26. Hrs open: Box 2440, Tupelo, MS, 38803-2440. Phone: (662) 844-5036. Fax: (662) 842-7798.E-mail: info@afa.net Licensee: American Family Association.

Dahlonega

WDGR(AM)— Mar 1, 1982: Stn currently dark. 1210 khz; 10 kw-D. TL: N34 31 45 W84 00 23. Hrs open: USK Broadcasting, 4325 Steve Reynolds Blvd., Norcross, 30093. Phone: (770) 300-0999. Fax: (770) 300-3082. Licensee: USK Broadcasting Inc. (acq 11-25-2003; $500,000). Population served: 400,000 ◆Hye Kim, gen mgr.

*WNGU(FM)— 1998: 89.5 mhz; 750 w. 459 ft TL: N34 31 29 W83 59 50. Stereo. Hrs open: 24
Rebroadcast WJSP, Warm Springs, Colombus, 100%.
260 14th St. N.W., Atlanta, 30318-5360. Phone: (404) 685-2690. Fax: (404) 685-2684.E-mail ask@gpb.org Web Site:www.gpb.org Licensee: Georgia Public Telecommunications Commission. Natl. Network: NPR, PRI, . Wire Svc: AP Format: Classical, News. News staff: 10; News: 40 hrs wkly. Spec prog: Jazz. ◆Nancy Hall, CEO; Bonnie Bean, CFO; Bob Houghton, gen mgr; Tom Barclay, opns mgr; Rob Maynard, progmg dir; Susanna Capelonto, news dir.

WZTR(FM)— Dec 16, 1996: 104.3 mhz; 3.7 kw. Ant 417 ft TL: N34 29 56 W84 08 32. Stereo. Hrs open: 24 1376 Ben Higgins Rd., 30533. Phone: (706) 867-9542. Fax: (706) 864-4364. Web Site:www.thunder1043fm.com Licensee: Grady W. Turner (group owner; acq 2-9-2006; $1.3 million). Population served: 250,000 Natl. Network: ABC, . Ga. News Net. Format: Country, classic rock. News staff: one; News: 4 hrs wkly. Target aud: 25-54; general. ◆Bo Wilson, stn mgr.

Dallas

WDPC(AM)— Sept 21, 1979: 1500 khz; 1 kw-D, DA. TL: N33 56 40 W84 49 28. Hrs open: 8451 S. Cherokee Blvd., Suite B, Douglasville, 30134. Phone: (770) 920-1520. Fax: (770) 920-4600. Web Site:www.wordchristianbroadcasting.com Licensee: Word Christian Broadcasting Inc. (acq 7-96; $25,000). Population served: 600,000 Format: Old time relg, Southern gospel. Target aud: General. ◆Ken Johns, pres, gen mgr, opns dir & progmg dir.

Dalton

WBLJ(AM)— Apr 8, 1940: 1230 khz; 1 kw-U. TL: N34 45 23 W84 57 02. Hrs open: 24 613 Silver Cir., 30721. Phone: (706) 278-5511. Fax: (706) 226-8766.E-mail: inform@wblj.com Web Site:wblj1230.com Licensee: North Georgia Radio Group L.P. Group owner: Clear Channel Communications Inc. (acq 3-20-2006; grpsl). Population served: 84,000 Natl. Network: CBS Radio, . Rgnl. Network: Ga. Net. Ga. News Net. Format: News/talk. News staff: 28 hrs wkly. Target aud: 18-54. Spec prog: Relg mus. ◆Mark Cooper, gen mgr; Larry Gibson, progmg mgr.

WDAL(AM)— Oct 1, 1954: 1430 khz; 2.5 kw-D, 72 w-N. TL: N34 47 23 W84 57 12. Stereo. Hrs open: 24 Box 1284, 30722. Secondary address: 613 Silver Cir. 30721. Phone: (706) 278-5511. Phone: (706) 278-3300. Fax: (706) 278-7966. Licensee: North Georgia Radio Group L.P. Group owner: Clear Channel Communications Inc. (acq 3-20-2006; grpsl). Population served: 100,000 Natl. Network: CBS, . Natl. Rep: Rgnl Reps,. Leventhal, Senter & Lerman. Format: Mexican. News staff: 3; News: 30 hrs wkly. Target aud: 25-45. ◆Rich Phillips, gen mgr.

WTTI(AM)— June 17, 1965: 1530 khz; 10 kw-D, 10 kw-CH, DA-D. TL: N34 47 09 W85 02 40. Hrs open: Box 216, 30722. Secondary address: 111 W. Crawford St. 30720. Phone: (706) 277-7117. Fax: (706) 277-7180. Licensee: Troy L. Hall. Format: Southern gospel. Target aud: 25-54; family, relg. ◆Troy Hall, CEO & gen mgr; C.W. Queen, stn mgr.

WYYU(FM)— August 1995: 104.5 mhz; 3 kw. Ant 328 ft TL: N34 49 42 W84 53 41. Hrs open: 24 Box 1284, 30722. Secondary address: 613 Silver Cir 30721. Phone: (706) 278-5511. Phone: (706) 278-3300. Fax: (706) 278-7966. Population served: 200,000 Format: Adult contemp. News staff: 3.

Damascus

*WGIA(FM)—Not on air, target date: unknown: 89.7 mhz; 1.5 kw. Ant 207 ft TL: N31 21 25 W84 48 31. Hrs open: 102 Red Branch Ln., Simpsonville, SC, 29681. Phone: (864) 297-0216. Fax: (864) 297-0344.E-mail: info@networkofglory.org Web Site:networkofglory.org Licensee: Network of Glory Inc. (acq 5-27-2008); $7,000 for CP). ◆Lola Richey, pres.

Darien

WHFX(FM)— May 13, 1993: 107.7 mhz; 50 kw. 403 ft TL: N31 10 09 W81 32 14. Stereo. Hrs open: 24 3833 Hwy. 82, Brunswick, 31523. Phone: (912) 267-1025. Fax: (912) 264-5462.E-mail: scottrysun@gmail.com Web Site:1077thefox.net Licensee: Qantum of Brunswick License Co. LLC. Group owner: Qantum Communications Corp. (acq 7-2-2003; grpsl). Population served: 150,000 Natl. Rep: McGavren Guild,. Format: Rock. News staff: one; News: 4 hrs wkly. Target aud: 25 plus; general. ◆Jonathan Havens, gen mgr, min affrs dir; Joe Sousa, opns mgr, mus critic; Jim Hendrick, sls dir; Mike Hamens, news dir; Dick Boekeloo, chief of engrg; Robin Rowe, spec ev coord; Kat Blackstone, disc jockey.

Dawson

WMRZ(FM)— June 2005: 98.1 mhz; 25 kw. Ant 262 ft TL: N31 37 29 W84 19 20. Hrs open: 809 S. Westover Blvd., Albany, 31707. Phone: (229) 439-9704. Fax: (229) 439-1509.E-mail: pauledwards @clearchannel.com Web Site:www.kissalbany.com Licensee: CC Licenses LLC. (group owner; (acq 11-16-2005; $875,000). Format: Rhythm and blues, oldies. ◆John Richards, gen mgr; Paul Edwards, progmg dir.

Decatur

WATB(AM)—Licensed to Decatur. See Cumming

WPBC(AM)— Aug 11, 1964: 1310 khz; 2.5 kw-D, 31 w-N. TL: N33 46 22 W84 16 55. Hrs open: 24 3684 Stewart Rd., Suite A-3, Doraville, 30340. Phone: (678) 200-8540. Licensee: Hanmi Broadcasting Inc. (acq 2-28-2005; $3.3 million). Population served: 80,000 ◆Chang Soo Kim, gen mgr.

WUBL(FM)—See Atlanta

Demorest

*WPPR(FM)— 1997: 88.3 mhz; 6 kw. 640 ft TL: N34 31 24 W83 40 46. Stereo. Hrs open: 24
Rebroadcasts WJSP-FM Warm Springs 85%.
260 14th St. N.W., Atlanta, 30318-5360. Phone: (404) 685-2690. Fax: (404) 685-2684.E-mail: ask@spb.org Web Site:www.gpb.org Licensee: Georgia Public Telecommunications Commission. Natl. Network: NPR, PRI, . Wire Svc: AP Format: News, class. News staff: 10; News: 40 hrs wkly. Adults 35+. Spec prog: Jazz. ◆Nancy G. Hall, CEO; Bonnie Bean, CFO; Bob Houghton, gen mgr; Tom Barclay, opns mgr; Rob Maynard, progmg dir; Susanna Capelouto, news dir.

Dock Junction

WXMK(FM)— May 1, 1991: 105.9 mhz; 15 kw. 489 ft TL: N31 10 09 W81 32 14. Stereo. Hrs open: 24 185 Benedict Rd., Brunswick, 31520. Phone: (912) 261-1000. Fax: (912) 265-8391.E-mail: info@magic1059.com Web Site:www.magic1059.com Licensee: Golden Isles Broadcasting L.L.C. (acq 3-23-2001; $2.8 million with WRJY(FM) Brunswick). Population served: 100,000 Pepper & Corazzini. Format: CHR, adult contemp. Target aud: 25-54; women. ◆Traci Long, gen mgr.

Donalsonville

WGMK(FM)— Sept 1, 1980: 106.3 mhz; 5.9 kw. Ant 331 ft TL: N31 04 26 W84 52 47. Hrs open: Box 87, 31743. Secondary address: 91 North Way 31743. Phone: (229) 524-5123. Fax: (229) 524-2265. Format: Hot adult contemp.

WSEM(AM)— Feb 12, 1963: 1500 khz; 1 kw-D. TL: N31 04 26 W84 52 47. Hrs open: Box 87, 31745. Secondary address: 91 North Way 31743. Phone: (229) 524-5123. Fax: (229) 524-2265.E-mail: wgmk@alltel.net Licensee: Flint Media Inc. (group owner; (acq 6-22-2006; grpsl). Population served: 43,500 Rgnl. Network: Ga. Net. Ga. News Net.

Doraville

Format: Country, talk, Black gospel. Target aud: 25-49. ◆Kevin Dowdy, pres; Gilbert M. Kelley Jr., gen mgr, progmg dir, news dir; Grace Kelley, gen sls mgr.

WWGF(FM)— Aug 1, 1998: 107.5 mhz; 6 kw. 315 ft TL: N30 58 36 W84 55 51. Stereo. Hrs open: 24 2278 Wortham Lane, Grovetown, 30813-5103. Phone: (706) 309-9610.E-mail: ctbarinowski@comcast.net Web Site:www.gnnradio.org Licensee: Barinowski Investment Co. Group owner: Good News Network (acq 1-21-99). Population served: 80,000 Format: Christian. Target aud: All. ◆Clarence Barinowski, gen mgr.

Doraville

WBTS(FM)— May 1948: 95.5 mhz; 40 kw. Ant 1,417 ft TL: N34 07 32 W83 51 32. Stereo. Hrs open: 24 1601 W. Peachtree St. N.E., Atlanta, 30309. Phone: (404) 897-7500. Fax: (404) 897-6211. Web Site:www.955thebeat.com Licensee: Cox Radio Inc. Group owner: Cox Broadcasting (acq 7-19-99; $78 million). Population served: 2,500,000 Format: Rhythmic CHR. Target aud: 25-54; blue collar to executive, modern country mus lovers. ◆Dan Kearney, VP, gen mgr, mktg mgr; Tony Kidd, mktg mgr.

Douglas

WDMG(AM)— March 1947: 860 khz; 5 kw-U, DA-N. TL: N31 30 23 W82 49 10. Hrs open: 1931 GA Hwy. 32 E., 31533. Phone: (912) 389-0995. Fax: (912) 383-8552.E-mail: traffic@charter.net Licensee: Broadcast South LLC. Group owner: Black Crow Media Group LLC (acq 11-15-2006; grpsl). Population served: 100,137 Natl. Network: USA, . Rgnl. Network: GNN Format: Sports. News staff: one; News: 20 hrs wkly. Target aud: 25-54. Spec prog: Farm 4 hrs, relg 6 hrs wkly. ◆John Higgs, stn mgr.

WOKA(AM)— Dec 10, 1962: 1310 khz; 3.9 kw-D, 39 w-N. TL: N31 31 24 W82 52 22. Hrs open: 6 AM-midnight 1310 W. Walker St., 31533. Phone: (912) 384-1310. Phone: (912) 384-8153. Fax: (912) 383-6328. Licensee: Coffee County Broadcasters Inc. (acq 2-13-98; with co-located FM). Population served: 42,000 Format: Solid gold oldies. Target aud: General. ◆Jim Squires, CEO, gen mgr, gen sls mgr; Dwayne Gillis, pres; Paul Sullivan, opns mgr; Michael Van Cleave, news dir; Jim Edwards, relg ed.

WOKA-FM— July 1971: 106.7 mhz; 100 kw. 1,000 ft TL: N31 31 24 W82 52 22. Hrs open: 1310 W. Walker St., 31533. Phone: (912) 384-8153. Phone: (912) 389-1067. Fax: (912) 383-6328.E-mail: production@accessatc.net Web Site:www.dixiecountry.com Licensee: Coffee County Broadcasters Inc. Population served: 120,000 Format: Country. Target aud: Adults 25-54. Spec prog: Gospel 4 hrs wkly. ◆Jim Edwards, relg ed; Paul Sullivan, disc jockey.

Douglasville

WDCY(AM)— May 5, 1993: 1520 khz; 2.5 kw-D, 800 w-N. TL: N33 45 48 W84 44 28. Hrs open: Sunrise-sunset 8451 S. Cherokee Blvd., Suite B, 30134. Phone: (770) 920-1520. Fax: (770) 920-4600.E-mail: info@wordchristianbroadcasting.com Web Site:www.wordchristianbroadcasting.com Licensee: Word Christian Broadcasting Inc. (acq 5-7-93; $95,000; 4-12-93). Population served: 1,400,000 Format: Old time relg. News: 10 hrs wkly. Target aud: General. ◆Ken Johns, pres, gen mgr, opns mgr & progmg dir.

WXJO(AM)— Sept 1, 1969: Stn currently dark. 1120 khz; 1 kw-D. TL: N33 45 48 W84 44 28. Hrs open: 134 S. Main St., Jasper, 30143. Phone: (706) 276-2016. Fax: (706) 635-1018. Licensee: Exponent Broadcasting Inc. (group owner; (acq 5-16-2007; $80,000). Rgnl. Network: Ga. Net. Format: Oldies. ◆Randy Gravley, pres & gen mgr.

Dry Branch

WFSM(AM)— Apr 15, 1998: 1670 khz; 10 kw-D, 1 kw-N. TL: N32 48 16 W83 36 16. Hrs open: 24 7080 Industrial Hwy., Macon, 31216. Phone: (478) 781-1063. Fax: (478) 781-6711.E-mail: huston@965thebuzz.net Licensee: AMFM Radio Licenses LLC. Group owner: Clear Channel Communications Inc. (acq. 2-15-2001; grpsl). Population served: 250,000 Natl. Rep: Clear Channel,. Format: Latino. Target aud: General; adults. ◆Bill Clark, gen mgr.

Dublin

*WAWH(FM)— 2000: 88.3 mhz; 400 w. Ant 82 ft TL: N32 32 27 W82 57 27. Hrs open: Box 3206, American Family Radio, Tupelo, MS,

38803. Phone: (662) 844-8888. Fax: (662) 842-6791. Web Site:www.afr.net Licensee: American Family Association. Group owner: American Family Radio Format: Inspirational Christian. ◆Marvin Sanders, gen mgr.

WKKZ(FM)— Apr 4, 1967: 92.7 mhz; 50 kw. 417 ft TL: N32 31 21 W82 54 00. Stereo. Hrs open: 24 Box 967, 31040. Secondary address: 1006 Martin Luther King Blvd. 31021. Phone: (478) 272-9270. Fax: (478) 275-3592. Licensee: Kirby Broadcasting Co. (acq 9-18-2003). Population served: 750,000 Natl. Network: ABC, . Natl. Rep: Dora-Clayton,. Format: CHR. ◆Ray Beck, gen mgr.

WMLT(AM)— Jan 12, 1945: 1330 khz; 5 kw-D, 500 w-N, DA-N. TL: N32 33 50 W82 52 00. Hrs open: 24 Box 130, 31040. Secondary address: 807 Bellevue Ave. 31021. Phone: (478) 272-4422. Fax: (478) 275-4657.E-mail: richhumphrey@wqzy.com Web Site:www.1330wmlt.com Licensee: State Broadcasting Corporation. Population served: 75,151 Rgnl. Network: Ga. Net. Natl. Rep: Rgnl Reps,. Ga. News Net. Rgnl rep: Regional Reps Format: Urban gospel. News staff: 2. Target aud: 25-54. ◆J. Morgan Dowdy, pres; Rick Humphrey, gen mgr.

WQZY(FM)— 1978: 95.9 mhz; 88 kw. 1,023 ft TL: N32 33 51 W82 52 18. Stereo. Hrs open: 24 Box 130, 31040. Phone: (478) 272-4422. Fax: (478) 275-4657.E-mail: webmaster@wqzy.com Web Site:www.wqzy.com Licensee: State Broadcasting Corporation Population served: 600,000 Rgnl. Network: Ga. Net. Ga. News Net. Rgnl rep: Regional Reps Format: Hit country. Target aud: 18-54. ◆J. Morgan Dowdy, pres; Rick Humphrey, gen mgr; Robert Whitt, progmg dir.

WXLI(AM)— Mar 16, 1958: 1230 khz; 1 kw-U. TL: N32 31 21 W82 54 00. Hrs open: Box 967, 31040. Secondary address: 1006 Martin Luther King Blvd. 31021. Phone: (478) 272-4282. Fax: (478) 275-3592. Licensee: Laurens County Broadcasting Co. (acq 8-10-03). Population served: 250,000 Natl. Network: CBS, . Natl. Rep: Dora-Clayton,. Format: Country. ◆Ray Beck, gen mgr.

East Dublin

WEDB(FM)—Licensed to East Dublin. See Swainsboro

East Point

WCFO(AM)— Oct 9, 1994: 1160 khz; 50 kw-D, 160 w-N, DA-2. TL: N33 49 34 W84 36 20. Hrs open: 24 1100 Spring St., Suite 610, Atlanta, 30309. Phone: (404) 681-9307. Fax: (404) 870-8859.E-mail: listeners@jwbroadcasting.com Web Site:www.newstalk1160.com Licensee: JW Broadcasting. (acq 8-11-2004; $10.4 million). Format: News/talk. ◆Jeff Davis, VP & gen mgr.

WTJH(AM)— December 1949: 1260 khz; 5 kw-D. TL: N33 41 47 W84 28 29. Hrs open: 3079 Campbellton Rd. S.W., Suite 104, Atlanta, 30311. Phone: (404) 344-2233. Fax: (404) 346-0647. Licensee: Christian Broadcasting of East Point Inc. Group owner: Willis Broadcasting Corp. Population served: 45,000 Format: Inspirational, gospel. ◆Christine Willis-Wiggs, gen mgr.

Eastman

WUFF(AM)— Sept 1, 1961: 710 khz; 2.5 kw-D. TL: N32 13 18 W83 13 04. Hrs open: Box 4097, 31023. Secondary address: 855 College St. Phone: (478) 374-3437. Fax: (478) 374-3585.E-mail: wuff radio@nlamerica.com Licensee: Dodge Broadcasting Inc. Population served: 5,416 Format: Country. Spec prog: Black 5 hrs wkly. ◆Gene Rogers, gen mgr; Dale Jones, gen sls mgr, progmg dir, sls; Don Jones, chief of engrg, farm dir.

WUFF-FM— 1976: 97.5 mhz; 2 kw. 371 ft TL: N32 13 35 W83 13 10. (CP: 4.6 kw, ant 364 ft.). Stereo. Hrs open: Box 4097, 31023. Secondary address: 855 College St. 31023. Phone: (478) 374-3437. Fax: (478) 374-3585. Format: Southern gospel, news. ◆Gene Rogers, news dir.

Eatonton

WKVQ(AM)— Dec 15, 1966: 1520 khz; 1 kw-D. TL: N33 19 19 W83 25 03. Hrs open:
Simulcast with WKRR(FM) Milledgeville.
Box 3965, 31024. Phone: (706) 485-8792. Fax: (706) 485-3555.E-mail: starstation@bellsouth.net Licensee: Craig Baker. Population served: 4,125 Format: Adult standards. Target aud: General. ◆Craig Baker, pres & gen mgr.

WMGZ(FM)— Feb 8, 1988: 97.7 mhz; 8.5 kw. 554 ft TL: N33 20 41 W83 13 41. Stereo. Hrs open: 24 Box 832, Milledgeville, 31061. Secondary address: 156 Lake Laurel Rd., Milledgeville 31061. Phone: (478) 453-9406. Fax: (478) 453-3298.E-mail: z97mail@yahoo.com Web Site:todaysbesthits.com Licensee: Southern Stone Broadcasting Inc. (acq 7-6-2005; $1.1 million with WKGQ(AM) Milledgeville). Population served: 125,000 Natl. Network: ABC, . Format: Hot adult contemp. News staff: one; News: 4 hrs wkly. Target aud: 18-49. ◆Tom Ptak, gen mgr.

Elberton

WSGC(AM)— Jan 1, 1947: 1400 khz; 1 kw-U. TL: N34 06 45 W82 52 52. Hrs open: 24 Box 340, 562 Jones St., 30635. Phone: (706) 283-1400. Fax: (706) 283-8710.E-mail: pundt@gacaradio.com Web Site:www.elbertonradio.com Licensee: Georgia-Carolina Radiocasting Co. LLC. Group owner: Georgia-Carolina Radiocasting Companies (acq 7-25-2002; grpsl). Population served: 22,560 Natl. Network: CBS Radio, . Ga. News Net. Dan J. Alpert. Format: MOR, talk. News staff: 2; News: 12 hrs wkly. Target aud: 35+. ◆Art Sutton, pres; Carl Pundt, VP, gen mgr; Ron Shuller, opns mgr; Marty Lee, chief of engrg.

WSGC-FM— 9/1/1973: 105.1 mhz; 6 kw. Ant 328 ft TL: N33 59 22 W82 46 23. Stereo. Hrs open: 24 Box 340, 30635. Secondary address: 562 Jones St. 30635. Phone: (706) 213-1051. Fax: (706) 283-8710.E-mail: pundt@gacaradio.com Web Site:www.elbertonradio.com Licensee: Georgia-Carolina Radiocasting Co. LLC. Group owner: Georgia-Carolina Radiocasting Companies (acq 7-25-2002; grpsl). Population served: 164,296 Natl. Network: ABC, . Dan J. Alpert. Format: Country. News staff: one; News: 5 hrs wkly. Target aud: 25-54; general. ◆Art Sutton, pres; Carl Pundt, VP, gen mgr; Ron Shuller, opns mgr; Marty Lee, chief of engrg.

Ellaville

WLEL(FM)— 2009: 94.3 mhz; 4.8 kw. Ant 328 ft TL: N32 15 10 W84 13 50. Hrs open: 11700 S.W. Tangerine Ct., Palm City, FL, 34990-5801. Phone: (772) 215-1634. Licensee: Gary S. Hess (acq 11-7-2008; grpsl). ◆Gary S. Hess, gen mgr.

Ellijay

WLJA-FM— Nov 1, 1985: 93.5 mhz; 19 kw. Ant 276 ft TL: N34 42 59 W84 30 50. Hrs open: 6 AM-10 PM 134 S. Main St., Jasper, 30143. Phone: (706) 276-2016. Fax: (706) 635-1018. Licensee: Tri-State Communications Inc. (acq 10-21-98; $500,000 with co-located AM). Format: Country & gospel. Target aud: 18-75.

WPGY(AM)— May 10, 1978: 1560 khz; 1 kw-D. TL: N34 42 14 W84 28 35. Hrs open: 134 S. Main St., Jasper, 30143. Phone: (706) 276-2016. Fax: (706) 635-1018.E-mail: wlja@ellijay.com Licensee: Exponent Broadcasting Inc. (acq 9-10-2007; $50,000). Format: Classic country. Target aud: 18-75. ◆Byron Dobbs, gen mgr, news dir; Randy D. Gravley, VP, gen mgr & stn mgr.

Evans

WAEG(FM)— November 1991: 92.3 mhz; 3 kw. Ant 328 ft TL: N33 35 25 W82 13 52. Hrs open: Box 1584, 411 Radio Station Road, Augusta, 30903-2429. Secondary address: 104 Bennett Ln., North Augusta, SC 29841. Phone: (803) 279-2330. Fax: (803) 279-8149.E-mail: info@perrybroadcasting.net Web Site:www.waeg923.com Licensee: Perry Broadcasting of Augusta Inc. Group owner: Radio One Inc. (acq 12-12-2007; grpsl). Population served: 450,000 Natl. Rep: Christal,. Shaw Pittman. Format: Smooth jazz. ◆Ron Tomel, opns mgr & prom dir.

Fargo

*WREE(FM)—Not on air, target date: unknown: 91.1 mhz; 5 kw. Ant 156 ft TL: N30 40 31 W82 40 40. Hrs open: 2701 W. Cypress Creek Rd., Fort Lauderdale, FL, 33309. Phone: (954) 556-4635.E-mail: info@reachfm.org Web Site:www.reachfm.org Licensee: Reach Communications Inc. ◆Robert J. Coy, pres.

Fayetteville

WUMJ(FM)—Licensed to Fayetteville. See Griffin

Fitzgerald

WBHB(AM)— Oct 8, 1946: 1240 khz; 1 kw-U. TL: N31 42 23 W83 15 40. Hrs open: 601 W. Roanoke Dr., 31750. Phone: (229) 423-2077. Fax: (229) 423-8313.E-mail: jank@rtgmedia.net Licensee: Broadcast South LLC. Group owner: Black Crow Media Group LLC (acq 11-15-2006; grpsl). Population served: 50,000 Natl. Network: Westwood One, . Format: Black gospel. Target aud: General. ◆John Higgs, gen mgr & stn mgr.

WRDO(FM)— 1991: 96.9 mhz; 6 kw. Ant 328 ft TL: N31 44 33 W83 14 41. Hrs open: 24 1931 GA Hwy. 32 E., Douglas, 31533. Phone: (912) 389-0995. Fax: (912) 383-8552.E-mail: traffic@charter.net Licensee: Broadcast South LLC. Group owner: Black Crow Media Group LLC (acq 11-15-2006; grpsl). Population served: 30,000 Natl. Network: USA, . Roy F. Perkins. Format: Adult contemp-soft hits. News staff: one. Target aud: 25-55; baby boomers. Spec prog: Gospel 6 hrs wkly. ◆John Higgs, gen mgr.

Folkston

*WATY(FM)— 2000: 91.3 mhz; 600 w. Ant 321 ft TL: N30 52 29 W82 01 10. Stereo. Hrs open: 24 Georgia Public Broadcasting, 260 14th St. N.W., Atlanta, 30318. Phone: (404) 685-2415. Fax: (404) 685-2684. Web Site:www.gpb.org Licensee: The Foundation for Public Broadcasting in Georgia Inc. (acq 6-17-2008; $350,000). ◆Nancy Hall, pres; Bob Houghton, gen mgr.

*WECC-FM— Mar 17, 2002: 89.3 mhz; 30 kw. Ant 489 ft TL: N30 55 54 W81 42 30. Hrs open: 5465 Hwy. 40 E., St. Marys, 31558. Phone: (912) 882-8930. Fax: (912) 882-9322.E-mail: mail@thelighthousefm.org Web Site:www.thelighthousefm.org Licensee: Lighthouse Christian Broadcasting Corp. Natl. Network: Salem Radio Network, . Format: Christian. ◆Paul Hafer, gen mgr.

WFJO(FM)— November 1989: 92.5 mhz; 3.2 kw. Ant 459 ft TL: N30 43 38 W81 56 14. Stereo. Hrs open: 24 9090 Hogan Rd., Suite 14, Jacksonville, FL, 32216. Phone: (904) 425-3482. Web Site:www.radiofreejax.com Licensee: Scott Savage, receiver Group owner: Tama Broadcasting Inc. (acq 2-26-2009). Rgnl. Network: Ga. Net. Format: Talk. Target aud: General. ◆Andy Johnson, gen mgr.

Forsyth

*WBIB-FM—Not on air, target date: unknown: 89.1 mhz; 60 w. Ant 249 ft TL: N33 03 01 W83 57 10. Hrs open: 1100 Fortville Milledgeville Rd., Haddock, 31033-2305. Phone: (478) 932-0036. Licensee: Believers in Broadcasting Inc. ◆Travis M. Nunn, pres.

WQMJ(FM)— Nov 22, 1973: 100.1 mhz; 3 kw. 209 ft TL: N32 58 31 W83 52 11. (CP: 2 kw, ant 574 ft. TL: N32 55 41 W83 52 37). Stereo. Hrs open: 6174 Hwy. 57, Macon, 31217. Phone: (478) 745-3301. Fax: (478) 742-2293.E-mail: productionrci@aol.com Licensee: Roberts Communications Inc. (group owner; acq 5-23-97; $550,000 with WXKO(AM) Fort Valley). Population served: 250000 Format: Mainstream urban. ◆Mike Roberts, gen mgr & stn mgr.

Fort Gaines

*WJWV(FM)— Feb 28, 1993: 90.9 mhz; 85 kw. 267 ft TL: N31 36 16 W85 02 02. Hrs open: 24
Rebroadcasts WJSP-FM Warm Springs 100%.
260 14th St. N.W., Atlanta, 30318-5360. Phone: (404) 685-2690. Fax: (404) 685-2684.E-mail: ask@gpb.org Web Site:www.gpb.org Licensee: Georgia Public Telecommunications Commission. (group owner) Format: Class, news. News staff: 10. Spec prog: Jazz 16 hrs wkly. ◆Nancy Hall, CEO; Bonnie Bean, CFO; Bob Houghton, gen mgr; Tom Barclay, opns mgr; Rob Maynard, progmg dir; Susanna Capelouto, news dir.

Fort Valley

WIBB-FM—Licensed to Fort Valley. See Macon

*WJTG(FM)— Mar 1, 1989: 91.3 mhz; 100 kw. 459 ft TL: N32 41 27 W83 51 45. Stereo. Hrs open: 24 101 Graylane Dr., Byron, 31008. Phone: (478) 956-0085. Fax: (478) 956-0913.E-mail: wjtg913@aol.com Web Site:www.wjtg.org Licensee: Family Life Broadcasting Inc. (acq 5-23-2007; grpsl). Population served: 250,000 Natl. Network: USA, . Format: Southern gospel. Target aud: General. ◆Tracy O. Wells, gen mgr & opns mgr.

WQBZ(FM)—Licensed to Fort Valley. See Macon

WXKO(AM)— June 1951: 1150 khz; 1 kw-D, 60 w-N. TL: N32 34 34 W83 54 17. Hrs open: 24 6070 Rock Springs Rd., Lithonia, 30038. Phone: (912) 825-5547. Fax: (912) 827-1273.E-mail: clmurray11@aol.com Licensee: WVKX-FM Radio LLC (group owner; (acq 7-15-2008; $11,600). Population served: 30,000 Rgnl. Network: Ga. Net. Ga. News Net. Format: Gospel. News staff: one; News: 10 hrs wkly. Target aud: 25 plus; Black. ◆Christopher Murray, pres.

Gainesville

*WBCX(FM)— 1977: 89.1 mhz; 875 w. 544 ft TL: N34 19 01 W83 49 45. Stereo. Hrs open: 24 Brenau Univ., 500 Washington St. S.E., 30501. Phone: (770) 538-4708. Fax: (770) 538-4558.E-mail: sfugate@lib.brenau.edu Web Site:www.brenau.edu Licensee: Brenau University. Population served: 1,000,000 Natl. Network: PRI, Jones Radio Networks, . Format: Eclectic. Target aud: 14-85. Spec prog: Black 12 hrs, class 20 hrs, world 6 hrs, American Indian 4 hrs, Gospel 6 hrs wkly. ◆J. Scott Fugate, gen mgr, opns dir & dev dir.

WDUN(AM)— Apr 2, 1949: 550 khz; 5 kw-D, 2.5 kw-N, DA-N. TL: N34 20 11 W83 47 41. Stereo. Hrs open: Box 10, 30503. Secondary address: 1102 Thompson Bridge Rd. N.E. 30501. Phone: (770) 532-9921. Fax: (770) 532-0506.E-mail: news@wdun.com Web Site:www.wdun.com Licensee: JWJ Properties Inc. Group owner: Jacobs Media Corp. (acq 9-83;9-5-83). Population served: 2,000,000 Natl. Network: CBS, . Rgnl. Network: Ga. Net. Ga. News Net. Format: News/talk. Target aud: 25-65. ◆John W. Jacobs III, CEO, pres; John W. Jacobs Jr., chmn; Jones P. Andrews, gen mgr.

WGGA(AM)— Oct 10, 1941: 1240 khz; 1 kw-U. TL: N34 19 01 W83 49 45. Stereo. Hrs open: 24 PO Box 10, 30503. Secondary address: 1102 Thompson Bridge Rd. N.E. 30501. Phone: (770) 532-9921. Fax: (770) 532-0459.E-mail: jay.jacobs@jacobsmedia.net Web Site:1240Theticket.com Licensee: JWJ Properties Inc. Group owner: Jacobs Media Corp. (acq 4-20-93; $360,000;5-10-93). Population served: 180,000 Natl. Network: NBC Radio, . Ga. News Net. Format: Sports Talk / ESPN. News staff: one; News: hourly. Target aud: 18-49; men. ◆John W. Jacobs III, CEO, pres; John W. Jacobs Jr., chmn; Joel Williams, gen mgr.

WGTJ(AM)—(Murrayville, Nov 1, 1986: 1330 khz; 1 kw-D. TL: N34 22 16 W83 56 47. Hrs open: 6 AM-sunset Box 907038, 30501. Secondary address: 1716 Cleveland Hwy. 30501. Phone: (770) 297-7485. Fax: (770) 297-8030.E-mail: mail@glory1330.com Web Site:www.glory1330.com Licensee: Vision Communications Inc. (acq 1999; $120,000). Format: Christian music. News staff: one. Target aud: General. ◆Mike Wofford, pres & gen mgr.

WLBA(AM)— Jan 26, 1957: 1130 khz; 10 kw-D. TL: N34 16 45 W83 46 33. Hrs open: Sunrise-sunset 5815 Westside Rd., Austell, 30106. Phone: (770) 944-0900. Fax: (770) 944-9794.E-mail: ariel@radiolafavorita.com Web Site:www.radiolafavorita.com Licensee: La Favorita Inc. (group owner; acq 2-18-97; $275,000). Population served: 200,000 Format: Sp. ◆Samuel Zamarron, pres & gen mgr; Ariel Zamarron, stn mgr.

WMJE(FM)—See Clarkesville

WSRV(FM)— Nov 1, 1965: 97.1 mhz; 97 kw. Ant 1,571 ft TL: N34 07 32 W83 51 31. Stereo. Hrs open: 1601 W. Peachtree St. N.E., Atlanta, 30309. Phone: (404) 897-7500. Fax: (404) 876-5126. Web Site:971theriver.com Licensee: Cox Radio Inc. Group owner: Cox Broadcasting (acq 8-16-2000; grpsl). Population served: 3,750,700 Format: Classic hits. News: 3 hrs wkly. Target aud: 35-54; baby boomers. ◆Dan Kearney, VP; Tony Kidd, VP & gen mgr.

WYAY(FM)— Apr 3, 1949: 106.7 mhz; 77 kw. Ant 1,656 ft TL: N33 52 02 W83 49 44. Stereo. Hrs open: 6th Fl., 210 Interstate N., Atlanta, 30339. Phone: (404) 521-1007. Fax: (404) 499-1067 (NEWS FAX). Licensee: Radio License Holding II LLC. Group owner: ABC Inc. (acq 6-12-2007; grpsl). Population served: 500,000 Natl. Network: ABC, . Natl. Rep: ABC Radio Sales,. Format: Country. Target aud: 25-54. ◆Mark Richards, opns mgr; Rick Mack, sls dir; Matt Scarano, gen sls mgr; Nancy Barre, natl sls mgr; Mary Gordon, rgnl sls mgr; Christy Ullman, prom dir; Victor Sansone, pres, gen mgr & progmg dir; Sandy Weaver, mus dir; Glenda Dodd, traf mgr.

Gibson

WTHP(FM)— 2006: 94.3 mhz; 2.05 kw. Ant 571 ft TL: N33 17 05 W82 35 45. Hrs open: 2278 Wortham Ln., Grovetown, 30813-5103. Phone: (706) 309-9610.E-mail: ctbarinowski@comcast.net Web Site:www.gnnradio.org Licensee: Barinowski Investment Co. L.P. (acq 2-15-2006). Format: Christian. ◆Clarence Barinowski, gen mgr.

Glennville

WOAH(FM)— Nov 18, 1977: 106.3 mhz; 6 kw. Ant 394 ft TL: N32 00 27 W81 54 51. Stereo. Hrs open: 24 25 Bristlecone Dr., Savannah, 31419-9506. Phone: (912) 408-1063. Fax: (912) 876-6920.E-mail: jimlewis@coastalnow.net Web Site:www.hotkiss1063.com Licensee: Broadcast Executives Corp. (acq 3-29-2002; $250,000). Format: Contemp hits. ◆James Lewis, gen mgr.

Gordon

WFXM(FM)— Mar 30, 1976: 107.1 mhz; 3 kw. Ant 466 ft TL: N32 50 55 W83 28 29. Stereo. Hrs open: 24 6174 Georgia Hwy. 57, Macon, 31217. Phone: (478) 745-3301. Fax: (478) 745-1077. Fax: (478) 742-2293.E-mail: productionrci@aol.com Licensee: WFXM-FM Radio LLC (acq 7-31-2006; $808,500). Population served: 150000 Format: Mainstream urban contemp. Middle & upper class Georgians. Spec prog: Jazz 3 hrs wkly. ◆Mike Roberts, gen mgr.

Gray

WPCH(FM)— January 1994: 96.5 mhz; 7.6 kw. Ant 414 ft TL: N32 59 03 W83 33 16. Stereo. Hrs open: 24 7080 Industrial Hwy., Macon, 31216. Phone: (478) 781-1063. Fax: (478) 781-6711. Web Site:www.peach965.com Licensee: AMFM Radio Licenses LLC. Group owner: Clear Channel Communications Inc. (acq 2-1-2001; grpsl). Population served: 251,300 Format: Classic hits. Target aud: 18-54; adults. ◆Bill Clark, gen mgr; John Lund, opns mgr.

Grayson

WPLO(AM)—Licensed to Grayson. See Lawrenceville

Greensboro

WDDK(FM)— July 12, 1980: 103.9 mhz; 5.3 kw. 328 ft TL: N33 28 29 W83 14 46. Hrs open: 24 1271-B E. Broad St., 30642. Phone: (706) 453-4140. Fax: (706) 453-7179. Licensee: Wyche Services Corp. (acq 2-28-2005). Population served: 70,000 Natl. Network: ABC, . Rgnl. Network: Ga. Net. Ga. News Net. Format: Talk, oldies. News staff: one; News: 4 hrs wkly. Target aud: 24-60. ◆Chip Lyness, VP, gen mgr; K.B. Travis, opns dir.

Greenville

WIOL(FM)— July 4, 1994: 95.7 mhz; 3.4 kw. Ant 876 ft TL: N32 50 48 W84 41 27. Hrs open: 24 Box 1998, Columbus, 31902. Phone: (706) 576-3565. Fax: (706) 576-3683.E-mail: info@dbicolumbus.com Licensee: Davis Broadcasting of Columbus Inc. Group owner: Davis Broadcasting Inc. (acq 11-4-97; $450,000). Population served: 250,000 Natl. Network: CBS, . McCampbell & Young, P. Format: Classic rock. News staff: 2; News: 6 hrs wkly. Target aud: 18-49; females 18-35 specifically. ◆Gregory A. Davis, CEO, CFO & gen mgr.

Griffin

WEKS(FM)—See Zebulon

WHIE(AM)— Dec 15, 1952: 1320 khz; 5 kw-D, 83 w-N. TL: N33 14 30 W84 18 17. Hrs open: 1000 Memorial Dr., 30223. Phone: (770) 227-9451. Fax: (770) 229-2291. Licensee: Chappell Communications L.L.C. (acq 6-30-98; $240,000). Population served: 30,000 Format: Country, news/talk, sports. ◆Robert E. Chappell Jr., pres & gen mgr.

WKEU(AM)— 1933: 1450 khz; 1 kw-U. TL: N33 14 25 W84 14 54. Hrs open: Box 997, 30224. Secondary address: 1000 Memorial Dr. 30224. Phone: (770) 227-5507. Fax: (770) 229-2291.E-mail: wkeu@aol.com Web Site:www.wkeuradio.com Licensee: WLT & Associates L.P. Population served: 25,000 Rgnl. Network: Ga. Net. Natl. Rep: Rgnl Reps,. Ga. News Net. Format: Oldies, news. Target aud: 25 plus. ◆William Taylor, pres & gen mgr.

*WMVV(FM)— Apr 16, 1995: 90.7 mhz; 18 kw. Ant 472 ft TL: N33 22 12 W84 08 00. Stereo. Hrs open: 24 Box 2020, 30224. Secondary address: 100 S. Hill St., Suite 100 30223. Phone: (770) 229-2020. Licensee: Life Radio Ministries Inc. (acq 1996; $75,000). Population served: 1,200,000 Natl. Network: American Family Radio, . Wire Svc: AP Format: Relg, Christian. ◆Joseph C. Emert, pres; James Stewart, opns mgr.

WUMJ(FM)—(Fayetteville, Mar 8, 1966: 97.5 mhz; 7.9 kw. Ant 574 ft TL: N33 29 29 W84 35 00. Stereo. Hrs open: 101 Marietta St. 12th Floor, Atlanta, 30303. Phone: (404) 765-9750. Fax: (404) 688-7686. Web Site:www.majicatl.com Licensee: Radio One Inc. Group owner: Radio One Inc. (acq 11-8-2001; grpsl). Population served: 50,000 Format: Adult rhythm and blues. ◆Corey Punzi, prom dir; Derek Harper, progmg dir.

Hahira

WTHV(AM)— 1990: 810 khz; 2.5 kw-D. TL: N30 52 25 W83 15 07. Stereo. Hrs open: 15 4198 Rebecca Circle, Valdosta, 31606. Phone: (229) 245-9848. Fax: (229) 242-0809.E-mail: wthv810am@yahoo.com Licensee: Eternal Life Ministries Inc. (acq 8-13-2003; $180,000). Population served: 90,000 Natl. Network: Salem Radio Network, . Format: Southern gospel. Target aud: 24-55. Spec prog: Spanish 5 hrs wkly. ◆Cody Fender, pres, gen mgr, stn mgr; Phyllis Fender, VP.

Hampton

WHTA(FM)— Oct 19, 1973: 107.9 mhz; 27 kw. Ant 577 ft TL: N33 29 24 W84 34 07. Stereo. Hrs open: 101 Marietta St. 12th Floor, Atlanta, 30303. Phone: (404) 765-9750. Fax: (404) 688-7686. Web Site:www.hot1079atl.com Licensee: Radio One Licenses LLC. Group owner: Radio One Inc. (acq 8-20-01; $60 million). Population served: 400,000 Format: Hip hop. ◆Wayne Brown, gen mgr.

Hapeville

WWWE(AM)— Jan 7, 1947: 1100 khz; 1 kw-D. TL: N33 36 34 W85 05 13. (CP: COL: Hapeville. 5 kw-D, 3.8 kw-CH. TL: N33 43 43 W84 19 20). Hrs open: Sunrise-sunset 1465 North Side Dr., Suite 218, Atlanta, 30318. Phone: (404) 352-9993. Fax: (404) 355-0291. Web Site:www.radiovidaatlanta.org Licensee: WAEC License L.P. Group owner: Beasley Broadcast Group (acq 10-29-99; $10 million with WAEC(AM) Atlanta). Population served: 100,000 Format: Sp, relg. News staff: one; News: 8 hrs wkly. Target aud: 35 plus; mature audience. Spec prog: Relg 12 hrs, news/talk 14 hrs, Ethiopian 2 hrs wkly. ◆George Beasley, chmn; Bruce Beasley, pres; Caroline Beasley, CFO; Brian Beasley, exec VP; Chris Edmonds, gen mgr.

Harlem

WCHZ(FM)— Nov 23, 1992: 95.1 mhz; 5.7 kw. 440 ft TL: N33 31 34 W82 15 55. Hrs open: 4051 Jimmie Dyess Pkwy., Augusta, 30909-9469. Phone: (706) 396-7000. Fax: (706) 396-7100.E-mail: info@wchz.com Web Site:www.95rock.com Licensee: WCHZ License LLC Group owner: Beasley Broadcast Group Inc. (acq 1-13-97; $1.2 million). Format: Rock. Target aud: 18-34; well-educated adults, upper demographics. ◆Kent Dunn, gen mgr; Greg Mclaughlin, gen sls mgr.

Hartwell

WKLY(AM)— Sept 5, 1947: 980 khz; 1 kw-D, 140 w-N. TL: N34 21 28 W82 58 35. (CP: 149 w-N). Hrs open: 18 P.O. Box 636, 30643. Secondary address: 2235 Bowersville Hwy. 30643. Phone: (706) 376-2233. Fax: (706) 376-3100.E-mail: wklyradio@hartcom.net Web Site:www.wklyradio.com Licensee: WKLY Broadcasting Co. (acq 11-18-88;12-19-88). Population served: 86,000 Natl. Network: ABC, . Rgnl. Network: Ga. Net. Ga. News Net. Format: Mainstream country, southern gospel, talk. News staff: 2; News: 18 hrs wkly. Target aud: 30 plus; middle class, working adults. ◆Bruce Hicks, CFO; Bryan Hicks, gen mgr & opns mgr.

Hawkinsville

WCEH(AM)— Dec 11, 1952: 610 khz; 500 w-D. TL: N32 16 50 W83 26 37. Hrs open: 24 218 Eastman Hwy, 31036. Phone: (478) 892-9061. Fax: (478) 892-9063. Licensee: Georgia Eagle Broadcasting Inc. (acq 1-12-2007; grpsl). Population served: 143,000 Rgnl. Network: Ga. Net. Dan Alpert. Format: News/Sports. News: News prgmg 7 hrs/week. Target aud: Men 24-65. ◆Jay Braswell, gen mgr; Cecil Staton, progmg dir.

WQXZ(FM)— Sept 26, 1968: 103.9 mhz; 10.5 kw. Ant 495 ft TL: N32 10 03 W83 37 51. Stereo. Hrs open: Box 1398, 31036. Phone: (478) 892-9061. Fax: (478) 892-8663.E-mail: qwixie983@yahoo.com Licensee: Georgia Eagle Broadcasting Inc. Population served: 143,000 Format: News/talk. ◆Hank Brigmond, gen mgr.

Hazlehurst

WVOH(AM)— Sept 6, 1962: 920 khz; 500 w-D, 39 w-N. TL: N31 51 02 W82 33 19. Hrs open: 24 Box 645, 546 Baxley Hwy., 31539. Phone: (912) 375-4511. Fax: (912) 375-4512.E-mail: wvoh@wvohradio.com Web Site:www.wvohradio.com Licensee: Jeff Davis Broadcasters Inc. Population served: 10,000 Natl. Network: Salem Radio Network, . Ga. News Net. Format: Gospel. News staff: 1. Spec prog: Farm 2 hrs wkly. Co-owned TV: WVOH-LP affil

WVOH-FM— Dec 9, 1975: 93.5 mhz; 50 kw. 315 ft TL: N31 51 15 W82 34 00. Hrs open: Dups AM 50% Box 645, 546 Baxley Hwy., 31539. Phone: (912) 835-1580. Fax: (912) 375-4512. Format: Classic country. ◆Tony DeLoach, gen mgr & traf mgr.

Helen

WNGA(FM)— Dec 6, 1993: 105.1 mhz; 1.7 kw. Ant 613 ft TL: N34 44 55 W83 43 43. Stereo. Hrs open: 24 Box 256, 30545. Phone: (706) 878-1051. Fax: (706) 878-1433.E-mail: kjallen@oconeecomm.com Web Site:www.georgia105.com Licensee: Tugart Properties LLC. Group owner: Clear Channel Communications Inc. (acq 6-1-2009; $705,000). Population served: 345,000 Natl. Network: Fox News Radio, . Format: Country. Target aud: 25-54. ◆K.J. Allen, gen mgr.

*WTFH(FM)— February 2001: 89.9 mhz; 10 w. Ant 561 ft TL: N34 44 55 W83 43 43. Stereo. Hrs open: 24 Box 780, TFC Radio Network, Toccoa Falls, 30598. Secondary address: 292 Old Clarksville Hwy., Toccoa Falls 30577. Phone: (706) 282-6030. Phone: (800) 251-8326. Fax: (706) 282-6090.E-mail: radio@tfc.edu Licensee: Toccoa Falls College. Population served: 10,000 Format: Christian. ◆David Cornelius, gen mgr.

Hiawassee

WNGM(AM)—Not on air, target date: unknown: 1230 khz; 1 kw-U. TL: N34 56 34 W83 46 27. Hrs open: 101 S. Main St., Ste 6, 30546. Secondary address: 38 Kenmare Hall, N.E., Atlanta 30324. Phone: (706 896-1230. Phone: (404) 266-2257.E-mail: info@wngm1230.com Licensee: BMG Broadcasting Inc. (acq 7-28-2006). Format: Classic Oldies. ◆Rick Morris, gen mgr; John Allen, mus dir; Jackie Grizzle, chief of engrg.

Hinesville

WGML(AM)— Dec 9, 1958: 990 khz; 250 w-D, 76 w-N. TL: N31 51 01 W81 36 04. Hrs open: Sunrise-sunset Box 615, 31310. Secondary address: 308 Rolland St. 31313. Phone: (912) 368-3399. Fax: (912) 368-4191.E-mail: wgml@coastalnow.net Licensee: Powerhouse of Deliverance Church Inc. (acq 10-12-94; 10-31-94). Population served: 32,000 Borsari & Paxson. Format: Gospel, relg. News: 10 hrs wkly. Target aud: General. Spec prog: Sp one hr wkly. ◆Bishop Raymond Napper, CEO, pres; Elder Mary Napper, exec VP; Emanuel White, gen mgr.

WSGA(FM)— Aug 2, 1982: 92.3 mhz; 50 kw. Ant 482 ft TL: N31 41 37 W81 23 27. Stereo. Hrs open: 24 Box 29, 31310. Secondary address: 120 D Liberty St. 31313. Phone: (912) 368-9258. Fax: (912) 368-5526.E-mail: rjp106@aol.com Web Site:www.freedom923.com Licensee: Tama Radio Licenses of Savannah, GA, Inc. Group owner: Tama Broadcasting Inc. (acq 4-8-2004; $2.79 million). Population served: 250,000 Natl. Rep: Rgnl Reps,. Miller & Miller. Format: Adult hits. News: 2 hrs wkly. Target aud: 25-54; Savannah, Hinesville, Brunswick, 15 county area. ◆Yvonne Clark, gen mgr.

WTHG(FM)— 1994: 104.7 mhz; 12 kw. Ant 469 ft TL: N31 51 18 W81 44 28. Stereo. Hrs open: 24 Box 29, 31310. Secondary address: 120 D Liberty St. 31313. Phone: (912) 368-9258. Fax: (912) 368-5526.E-mail: rjp106@aol.com Web Site:thehawk1047.com Licensee: Tama Radio Licenses of Savannah, GA Inc. (group owner; acq 4-8-2004). Population served: 300,000 Format: Classic rock. ◆Yvonne Clark, gen mgr.

Hogansville

WMGP(FM)— Sept 3, 1992: 98.1 mhz; 25 kw. 328 ft TL: N33 03 54 W84 57 23. (CP: 25 kw). Hrs open: 24 154 Boone Dr., Newnan, 30263. Phone: (770) 683-7234. Fax: (770) 683-9846. Licensee: Citicasters Licenses L.P. Group owner: Clear Channel Communications Inc. (acq 1999; grpsl). Format: Classic hits. Target aud: 17-64; non-country listeners. ◆Bill Clark, gen mgr & mktg mgr.

WVCC(AM)— Aug 12, 1985: 720 khz; 7.97 kw-D. TL: N33 03 54 W84 57 23. Hrs open: Sunrise-sunset 154 Boone Dr., Newnan, 30263.

Phone: (770) 683-7234. Fax: (770) 683-9846. Web Site:www.720thevoice.com Licensee: Citicasters Licenses L.P. Natl. Network: Premiere Radio Networks, Salem Radio Network, Fox News Radio, . Ga. News Net. Format: News/talk info. ◆Bill Clark, pres & mktg mgr.

Homerville

WBTY(FM)— December 1980: 98.7 mhz; 6 kw. Ant 298 ft TL: N31 02 04 W82 51 50. Stereo. Hrs open: Box 9, Dupont, 31630-0009. Secondary address: Intersection of Hwy's 168 & 37 31634. Phone: (912) 487-3412. Fax: (912) 487-3414. Licensee: Southern Broadcasting & Investments. (acq 3-9-90; $100,000; 4-30-90). Population served: 70,000 Format: Classic Hits. Target aud: General. ◆Jim Strickland, opns mgr, chief of engrg; Nancy K. Strickland, pres, gen mgr & gen sls mgr.

Irwinton

WVKX(FM)— September 1995: 103.7 mhz; 3 kw. 328 ft TL: N32 52 48 W83 11 07. Hrs open: Box 569, 31042. Phone: (478) 946-3445. Fax: (478) 946-2406.E-mail: love1037@alltel.net Licensee: Wilkinson Broadcasting Inc. (acq 8-10-92; $60,000; 8-31-92). Format: Rhythm and blues, gospel, urban contemp. ◆Stan Carter, gen mgr.

Jackson

WJGA-FM— Apr 24, 1967: 92.1 mhz; 2.15 kw. Ant 374 ft TL: N33 16 37 W83 57 59. Stereo. Hrs open: 24 Box 878, 940 Brownlee Rd., 30233. Phone: (770) 775-3151. Fax: (770) 775-3153. Licensee: Earnhart Broadcasting Co. Inc. (acq 8-90; $800,000; 8-27-90). Population served: 40,000 Natl. Rep: Keystone (unwired net),. Rgnl rep: Rgnl Reps. Wire Svc: AP Format: Adult contemp, Black. News staff: one; News: 20 hrs wkly. Target aud: General. Spec prog: Gospel 15 hrs wkly. ◆Don Earnhart, pres & gen mgr.

Jacksonville

WSIZ-FM—Not on air, target date: unknown: 102.3 mhz; 5.5 kw. Ant 335 ft TL: N31 46 42 W83 05 07. Hrs open: Box 5429, Twin Falls, ID, 83303-5429. Phone: (208) 733-3551. Licensee: World Radio Link Inc. ◆Earl Williamson, pres.

Jasper

*WIVL(FM)— 1999: 88.3 mhz; 200 w. Ant 3 ft TL: N34 28 01 W84 25 49. Stereo. Hrs open: 24 Box 6767, Athens, 30604. Phone: (706) 425-1830. Fax: (706) 425-1868.E-mail: communitypublicradio@prodigy.net Licensee: Community Public Radio Inc. Format: Btfl music, Christian. Target aud: 35-55; upper middle class, educated, Christian. ◆Penny Jackson, pres.

WYYZ(AM)— May 25, 1973: 1490 khz; 1 kw-U. TL: N34 28 32 W84 26 13. Hrs open: 268 Hood Road, 30143. Phone: (706) 692-4100. Fax: (706) 692-4012. Licensee: Enlightment LLC (acq 5-23-2007; $600,000). Natl. Network: CBS, . Format: Classic rock. ◆Mark Hellinger, gen mgr.

Jeffersonville

WPEZ(FM)— Sept 27, 1993: 93.7 mhz; 50 kw. 490 ft TL: N32 54 49 W83 29 47. Stereo. Hrs open: 24 544 Mulberry St., Macon, 31202. Phone: (478) 746-6286. Fax: (478) 745-4383.E-mail: info@z937.com Web Site:www.z937.com Licensee: Cumulus Licensing Corp. Group owner: Cumulus Media Inc. (acq 12-20-02; grpsl). Population served: 300,000 Format: Lite Rock. News: one hr wkly. Target aud: 25-54. ◆John Sheftic, gen mgr.

Jesup

WIFO-FM— July 1, 1968: 105.5 mhz; 25 kw. Ant 308 ft TL: N31 36 06 W81 56 00. Stereo. Hrs open: 24 Dups AM 20% P.O. Box 647, 31598. Phone: (912) 427-3711. Fax: (912) 530-7717.E-mail: bigdogstaff @bellsouth.net Web Site:www.bigdogcountry.com Licensee: Jesup Broadcasting Corp. Natl. Network: ABC, . Natl. Rep: Rgnl Reps,. Ga. News Net. Format: Country. News staff: one. Target aud: General. ◆Matt Hubbard, gen mgr.

WLOP(AM)— July 12, 1949: 1370 khz; 5 kw-D, 36 w-N. TL: N31 36 06 W81 56 00. Hrs open: Box 647, 31598. Secondary address: 2420 Waycross Hwy 31545. Phone: (912) 427-3711. Fax: (912) 530-7717.E-mail:

bigdogstaff@bellsouth.net Licensee: Jesup Broadcasting Corp. (group owner; (acq 3-31-92). Population served: 24,000 Natl. Network: Fox Sports, . Rgnl. Network: Ga. Net., Tobacco. Natl. Rep: Rgnl Reps,. Ga. News Net. Format: Sports. Target aud: General. ◆Charles Hubbard Jr., pres; Matt Hubbard, gen mgr.

*WLPT(FM)— 1988: 88.3 mhz; 20 kw. Ant 800 ft TL: N31 40 27 W81 53 12. Stereo. Hrs open: 24 2278 Wortham Ln, Grovetown, 30813. Phone: (706) 309-9610.E-mail: ctbarinowski@comcast.net Web Site:www.gnnradio.org Licensee: Augusta Radio Fellowship Institute Inc. Population served: 175,000 Format: Christian. News: 12 hrs wkly. Target aud: General. ◆Clarence Barinowski, gen mgr.

*WTLD(FM)— January 2004: 90.5 mhz; 6 kw. Ant 171 ft TL: N31 35 49 W81 56 14. Stereo. Hrs open: 24 Box 515, Jessup, 31598. Phone: (912) 695-7169. Phone: (912) 588-1821. Fax: (912) 588-1822.E-mail: lsmall7629@aol.com Licensee: Resurrection House Ministries Inc. Format: Gospel. News: 12 hrs wkly. Target aud: 18 plus. ◆Dr. Leonard Small, CEO; Marie Butler, gen mgr.

Kings Bay

*WREI(FM)—Not on air, target date: unknown: 88.5 mhz; 100 w horiz, 1 kw vert. Ant 377 ft TL: N30 50 02 W81 33 57. Hrs open: 2401 W. Cypress Creek Rd., Fort Lauderdale, FL, 33309. Phone: (954) 315-4315. Fax: (954) 315-4231.E-mail: info@reachfm.org Web Site:www.reachfm.org Licensee: Reach Communications Inc. ◆Robert J. Coy, pres.

Kingsland

WKBX(FM)— Feb 23, 1987: 106.3 mhz; 6 kw. 330 ft TL: N30 48 04 W81 40 43. Stereo. Hrs open: 24 Box 2525, 111 N. Grove Blvd., 31548. Phone: (912) 729-6106. Phone: (912) 729-5229. Fax: (912) 729-4106.E-mail: wkbx@k-bay106.com Web Site:www.k-bay106.com Licensee: Radio Kings Bay Inc. (acq 7-1-89; $1 million; 5-29-89). Population served: 49,000 Natl. Network: ABC, . Wolf, Block, Schorr, & Solis-Cohen. Format: Country. News staff: one; News: one hr wkly. Target aud: 18-54; contemp country audience. ◆James Steele, pres, gen mgr; Wendy Steele, exec VP; John Fluery, progmg dir, progmg mgr; Jason Bishop, news dir; Susan Pope, traf mgr.

La Fayette

WQCH(AM)— November 1954: 1590 khz; 5 kw-D. TL: N34 42 57 W83 16 06. Hrs open: 12 Box 746, 30728. Phone: (706) 638-3276. Fax: (706) 638-3896.E-mail: WQCHRadio@aol.com Web Site:www.wqch.net Licensee: Radix Broadcasting Inc. (acq 6-1-88). Natl. Network: AP Network News, . Rgnl. Network: Ga. Net. Natl. Rep: Rgnl Reps,. Ga. News Net. Format: Country, news. News staff: one; News: 10 hrs wkly. Target aud: 25 plus. Spec prog: Farm 2 hrs wkly. ◆Rich Gwyn, pres & gen mgr.

La Grange

WALR-FM— Sept 1, 1947: 104.1 mhz; 60 kw. Ant 1,217 ft TL: N33 24 43 W84 50 03. Stereo. Hrs open: 1601 W. Peachtree St., Atlanta, 30309. Phone: (404) 897-7500. Fax: (404) 897-6495. Web Site:www.kiss1041fm.com Licensee: Cox Radio Inc. Group owner: Cox Broadcasting (acq 8-2000; $280 million). Natl. Rep: McGavren Guild,. Format: Urban & adult contemp. Target aud: 25-54. ◆Tony Kidd, gen mgr.

*WBRQ(FM)—Not on air, target date: unknown: 91.9 mhz; 3 kw. Ant 328 ft TL: N32 52 33 W84 57 20. Hrs open: Box 371177, Cayey, PR, 00737. Phone: (787) 529-8917. Licensee: Family Educational Association Inc. (acq 8-8-2008; swap of CP for CP of KYRQ(FM) Natalia, TX). ◆Juan Carlos Matos, pres.

WELR-FM—See Roanoke, AL

WLAG(AM)— May 1, 1941: 1240 khz; 1 kw-U. TL: N33 02 24 W85 01 27. Hrs open: 24 Box 1429, 30241. Secondary address: 304 Broome St. 30240. Phone: (706) 845-1023. Fax: (706) 845-8642.E-mail: wlag@eagle1023.com Web Site:www.eagle1023.com Licensee: Eagle's Nest Inc. (group owner; acq 4-3-92; $10; 4-27-92). Population served: 100,000 Format: Sports. News staff: one; News: 4 hrs wkly. Target aud: 25-54; general. ◆Jim Vice, gen mgr & stn mgr.

*WOAK(FM)— June 11, 1984: 90.9 mhz; 3.4 kw. Ant 299 ft TL: N32 57 57 W84 59 08. Hrs open: 1921 Hamilton Rd., 30241. Phone: (706) 884-2950. Fax: (706) 884-2930.E-mail: woak@woak.org Web Site:woak.org Licensee: Oakside Christian School. Natl. Network: USA, . Format: Educ, relg. ◆Rick Varnum, gen mgr.

WTRP(AM)— Jan 9, 1953: Stn currently dark. 620 khz; 1 kw-D, 127 w-N. TL: N33 03 33 W85 01 40. Hrs open: 806 New Franklin Rd., Lagrange, 30240. Phone: (706) 884-7022. Fax: (706) 884-7806. Licensee: Tiger Communications Inc. (group owner; (acq 10-19-2006; $279,000 with WRLA(AM) West Point). Population served: 35,000 Format: Timeless classics. ♦Larry Fairall, gen mgr.

Lakeland

WVGA(FM)— 1994: 105.9 mhz; 6 kw. 328 ft TL: N31 04 55 W83 10 47. Stereo. Hrs open: 1711 Ellis Dr., Valdosta, 31601. Phone: (229) 244-8642. Phone: (229) 241-1059. Fax: (229) 242-7620.E-mail: info@newstalk1059wvga.com Web Site:www.newstalk1059wvga.com Licensee: RTG Radio LLC. Group owner: Black Crow Media Group LLC (acq 11-9-2001; grpsl). Population served: 150,000 Format: News/talk. ♦Robert Ganzak, pres; Robert T. Ganzak, gen mgr.

Lavonia

WLHR-FM— 1973: 92.1 mhz; 5.6 kw. Ant 338 ft TL: N34 22 51 W83 07 28. Stereo. Hrs open: P.O. Box 340, 30553. Secondary address: 12715 Augusta Road 30553. Phone: (706) 356-5921. Fax: (706) 356-5921.E-mail: dbrown@gacaradio.com Web Site:www.921wlhr.com Licensee: Lake Hartwell Radio Inc. Group owner: Georgia-Carolina Radiocasting Companies (acq 12-31-2008; $158,185 assumption of debt). Population served: 329,553 Natl. Network: AP Network News, . Dan J. Alpert. Format: Country/community involvement. News staff: 2; News: local 11 hrs wkly. Target aud: 25 plus. ♦Art Sutton, pres; Daniel Brown, VP, gen mgr; Randall Albertson, opns mgr; MJ Kneiser, news dir; Marty Lee, chief of engrg.

Lawrenceville

WPLO(AM)—(Grayson, Jan 7, 1959: 610 khz; 1.5 kw-D, 225 w-N. TL: N33 57 11 W83 58 15. Stereo. Hrs open: 24 2865 Amwiler Rd., Suite 650, Doraville, 30360. Phone: (770) 237-9897. Fax: (770) 246-0054.E-mail: laleysales@covat.net Web Site:www.radiomex610atlanta.com Licensee: Teresa Prieto (acq 6-1-96). Population served: 250,000 Rgnl. Network: Ga. Net. Format: Sp, Mexican rgnl music. ♦Franca Vera, gen mgr.

Leesburg

WJAD(FM)— October 1989: 103.5 mhz; 12.5 kw. 460 ft TL: N31 39 09 W84 05 20. Hrs open: 1104 W. Broad Ave., Albany, 31707. Phone: (229) 888-5000. Fax: (229) 888-5960. Web Site:www.wjad.com Licensee: Cumulus Licensing Corp. Group owner: Cumulus Media Inc. (acq 7-7-98). Population served: 160,000 Natl. Rep: Katz Radio,. Format: Rock. Target aud: 25-40; Generation X, tail end of baby boomers. ♦Bill Jones, opns mgr; Gregory Kamishlian, mktg mgr.

Louisville

WPEH(AM)— Sept 10, 1960: 1420 khz; 1 kw-D, 159 w-N. TL: N33 00 48 W82 23 33. Hrs open: 6 AM-midnight Box 425, 30434. Phone: (912) 625-7248. Fax: (912) 625-7249. Web Site:www.wpeh.com Licensee: Peach Broadcasting Co. Inc. Rgnl. Network: Ga. Net. Ga. News Net. Holland & Knight. Format: Country, oldies. News: 11 hrs wkly. Target aud: General. ♦Ottis G. Stephens, pres; Ottis Stephens, gen mgr, gen sls mgr; Wendell F. Stephens, progmg dir.

WPEH-FM— May 6, 1971: 92.1 mhz; 3 kw. 296 ft TL: N33 00 48 W82 23 33. Hrs open: Dups AM 100% Box 425, 30434. Phone: (912) 625-7248. Fax: (912) 625-7249.E-mail: wpeh@classicsouth.net Licensee: Peach Broadcasting Co. Inc. Target aud: 25 plus. ♦Otis Stephens, gen mgr.

Lumber City

***WMOC(FM)**— April 1997: 88.7 mhz; 50 kw. Ant 210 ft TL: N31 55 48 W82 41 06. Hrs open: Box 520, 31549-0520. Secondary address: 412 Renwick St. 31549. Phone: (912) 363-2203. Fax: (912) 363-2106.E-mail: wmoc887@yahoo.com Web Site:www.wmoc887fm.com Licensee: Full Gospel Church of God Written in Heaven. Format: Gospel. ♦Eddie Conaway, gen mgr & progmg dir.

Lumpkin

WKCN(FM)— Nov 6, 1992: 99.3 mhz; 50 kw. 492 ft TL: N32 09 25 W85 05 51. Stereo. Hrs open: 24 1353 13th Ave., Columbus, 31901. Phone: (706) 596-9000. Fax: (706) 596-4600.E-mail: info@kissin993.com Web Site:www.kissin993.com Licensee: PMB Broadcasting LLC. Group owner: Archway Broadcasting Group (acq 10-1-2008; grpsl). Natl. Rep: Christal,. Fletcher, Heald & Hildreth. Format: New hot country. Target aud: 25-54; general. ♦Chuck Thompson, gen mgr.

***WTMQ(FM)**— 2008: 88.5 mhz; 23 kw. Ant 538 ft TL: N31 59 19 W84 55 59. Hrs open: Box 9382, Columbus, 31908-9382. Phone: (706) 413-0342. Web Site:www.wtmq.com Licensee: Spanish Cultural Education Inc. Format: Sp. ♦Victor Molina, pres.

***WXIV(FM)**—Not on air, target date: unknown: 90.1 mhz; 8 kw. Ant 236 ft TL: N32 00 43 W84 39 42. Hrs open: 5704 Pineglen Ln., Irondale, AL, 35210. Phone: (205) 951-3700. Licensee: TBTA Ministries. ♦Kenneth M. Layton, pres.

Lyons

WBBT(AM)— Mar 12, 1959: 1340 khz; 1 kw-U. TL: N32 12 50 W82 19 51. Stereo. Hrs open: 24 P.O. Box 629, 473 N. Victory Dr., 30436. Phone: (912) 526-8122. Phone: (912) 526-6333. Fax: (912) 526-9155.E-mail: rday@tcbbroadcasting.com Web Site:www.tcbbroadcasting.com ABC Classic R&B Licensee: T.C.B. Broadcasting Inc. (acq 6-16-97; $400,000 with co-located FM). Population served: 85,000 Natl. Network: ABC, . Format: Classic rhythm and blues, Black. News staff: 2; News: 20 hrs wkly. Target aud: General. ♦Ray Bilbrey, CEO, pres, gen mgr, stn mgr, gen sls mgr; Robin Watson, progmg dir.

WLYU(FM)— Jan 1, 1989: 100.9 mhz; 6 kw. Ant 328 ft TL: N32 06 48 W82 23 52. Stereo. Hrs open: 24 Prog sep from AM Box 629, 473 N. Victory Dr., 30436. Phone: (912) 526-8122. Phone: (912) 526-6333. Fax: (912) 526-9155. Web Site:www.tcbbroadcasting.com Population served: 185,000 Format: Modern country. News staff: 3; News: 8 hrs wkly. Target aud: General. ♦Ralph Trapnell, exec VP; Debra Burke, opns mgr, sls VP; Ray Bilbrey, chief of engrg; Robin Watson, traf mgr.

Mableton

WPZE(FM)— 2001: 102.5 mhz; 3 kw. Ant 469 ft TL: N33 41 20 W84 30 38. Hrs open: 101 Marietta St. 12th Floor, Atlanta, 30303. Phone: (404) 765-9750. Fax: (404) 688-7686. Web Site:www.praise1025.com Licensee: ROA Licenses LLC. Group owner: Radio One Inc. (acq 7-8-2004; $31.5 million). Format: Gospel. ♦Tim Davies, gen mgr; Cie Cie Wilson-McGhee, prom dir; Derek Harper, progmg dir, mus dir.

Macon

WAYS(AM)— August 1967: 1500 khz; 1 kw-D. TL: N32 48 47 W83 37 36. Hrs open: 544 Mulberry St., Suite 500, 31201. Phone: (478) 746-6286. Fax: (478) 742-8061.E-mail: info@ways.com Licensee: Cumulus Licensing Corp. Group owner: Cumulus Media Inc. (acq 12-20-2002; grpsl). Population served: 148,000 Natl. Network: Westwood One, . Natl. Rep: Christal,. Format: Oldies. Target aud: 25-54. ♦Steve Hazen, exec VP; John Sheftic, gen mgr.

***WBKG(FM)**— 2002: 88.9 mhz; 5.5 kw. Ant 502 ft TL: N32 45 51 W83 33 32. Hrs open: Box Drawer 2440, Tupelo, MS, 38803-2440. Phone: (662) 844-8888. Fax: (662) 842-6791. Web Site:www.afr.net Licensee: American Family Association. Group owner: American Family Radio Format: Adult contemp. ♦Marvin Sanders, gen mgr; John Riley, progmg dir.

WBML(AM)— Oct 15, 1940: 900 khz; 2 kw-D, 145 w-N. TL: N32 50 58 W83 36 06. Hrs open: Box 6298, 31208. Secondary address: 735 Reese St. 31217. Phone: (478) 743-5453. Fax: (478) 743-9265.E-mail: info@wbml.com Licensee: WBML Inc. Group owner: Rodgers Broadcasting Corp. Population served: 435,000 Format: Relg. Target aud: 35 plus. ♦David A. Rogers, pres.

WDDO(AM)— Nov 25, 1957: 1240 khz; 1 kw-U. TL: N32 50 18 W83 39 02. Hrs open: 24 544 Mulberry St., Suite 500, 31201. Phone: (478) 746-6286. Fax: (478) 745-4383.E-mail: willie.collins@cumulus.com Licensee: Cumulus Licensing Corp. Group owner: Cumulus Media Inc. (acq 12-20-02; grpsl). Population served: 122,423 Natl. Network: American Urban, . Natl. Rep: Christal,. Format: Black gospel. ♦John Sheftic, gen mgr.

WDEN-FM— Feb 17, 1947: 99.1 mhz; 100 kw. Ant 581 ft TL: N32 45 51 W83 33 32. Stereo. Hrs open: 24 Dups AM 90% 544 Mulberry St., Suite 500, 31201. Phone: (478) 746-6286. Fax: (478) 742-8061.E-mail: info@middlegeorgia.com Web Site:Middlegeorgia.com Licensee: Cumulus Licensing Corp. Population served: 300,000 Natl. Rep: Christal,. Format: Country. News staff: one; News: 4 hrs wkly. Target aud: 25-54; female/male split.

WFSM(AM)—See Dry Branch

WIBB(AM)— November 1948: 1280 khz; 5 kw-D, 99 w-N. TL: N32 48 16 W83 36 16. Hrs open: 24 7080 Industrial Hwy., 31216-7538. Phone: (478) 781-1063. Fax: (478) 781-6711.E-mail: ccw@clearchannel.com Licensee: AMFM Radio Licenses LLC. Group owner: Clear Channel Communications Inc. (acq 2-15-2001; grpsl). Population served: 508,300 Natl. Rep: Clear Channel,. Format: Black talk. Target aud: General. ♦Bill Clark, gen mgr.

WIBB-FM—(Fort Valley, Mar 3, 1993: 97.9 mhz; 10.5 kw. 499 ft TL: N32 34 12 W83 45 26. Stereo. Hrs open: 24 7080 Industrial Hwy., 31216. Phone: (478) 781-1063. Fax: (478) 781-6711.E-mail: info@wibb.com Web Site:www.wibb.com Licensee: AMFM Radio Licenses LLC. Group owner: Clear Channel Communications Inc. (acq 2-15-2001; grpsl). Population served: 508,300 Format: Hip hop & rhythm and blues. News staff: one; News: 14 hrs wkly. Target aud: 18-44. ♦Bill Clark, gen mgr.

WIFN(FM)— June 10, 1968: 105.5 mhz; 6.1 kw. Ant 659 ft TL: N32 53 48 W83 32 05. Stereo. Hrs open: 24 Prog sep from AM 544 Mulberry St., Suite 500, 31201. Phone: (478) 746-6286.E-mail: info@wifn.com Population served: 300,000 Natl. Network: ESPN Radio, . Format: Sports. ♦David Nolin, mus dir, disc jockey; Jim Jones, rgnl sls mgr & disc jockey.

WLZN(FM)— August 1992: 92.3 mhz; 3 kw. 328 ft TL: N32 46 26 W83 38 15. Hrs open: 24 544 Mulberry St., 5th Fl., 31021. Phone: (478) 746-6286. Fax: (478) 742-8061.E-mail: info@middlegeorgia.com Licensee: Cumulus Licensing Corp. Group owner: Cumulus Media Inc. (acq 12-20-2002; grpsl). Population served: 300,000 Format: Urban contemp. News: one hr wkly. ♦Bill Hazen, gen mgr; Doug Rice, gen sls mgr; Brian Rayes, progmg dir; Joe Meredith, engrg VP & chief of engrg.

WMAC(AM)— Oct 30, 1922: 940 khz; 50 kw-D, 10 kw-N, DA-N. TL: N32 53 06 W83 43 50. Stereo. Hrs open: 24 544 Mulberry St., Suite 500, 31201. Phone: (478) 746-6286. Fax: (478) 742-8061.E-mail: info@middlegeorgia.com Web Site:www.wmac-am.com Licensee: Cumulus Licensing Corp. Group owner: Cumulus Media Inc. (acq 12-20-02; grpsl). Population served: 300,000 Natl. Network: ABC, Westwood One, . Natl. Rep: McGavren Guild,. Format: News/talk. News staff: 2; News: 40 hrs wkly. Target aud: 40 plus; upscale, college educated, household income $50K plus. Spec prog: Relg 4 hrs wkly. ♦Bill Hazen, gen mgr.

WNEX(AM)— April 1945: 1400 khz; 1 kw-U. TL: N32 51 07 W83 39 12. Hrs open: 1691 Forsyth St., 31201. Phone: (478) 745-5858. Fax: (478) 745-0500.E-mail: phil@upga.tv Web Site:www.radiodisney.com Licensee: Radio Peach Inc. (acq 1-31-00). Population served: 122,423 Natl. Network: Radio Disney, . Format: Children. ♦Lowell Register, CEO & pres; Debbie Hart, gen mgr.

WNNG(AM)—See Warner Robins

WQBZ(FM)—(Fort Valley, Apr 6, 1981: 106.3 mhz; 50 kw. 426 ft TL: N32 45 31 W83 44 49. Stereo. Hrs open: 24 7080 Industrial Hwy., 31216. Phone: (478) 781-1063. Fax: (478) 781-6711.E-mail: info@q106.fm Web Site:www.q106.fm Licensee: AMFM Radio Licenses LLC. Group owner: Clear Channel Communications Inc. (acq 2-15-2001; grpsl). Population served: 508,300 Format: Classic rock. Target aud: 18-49. ♦Bill Clark, gen mgr.

WRBV(FM)—See Warner Robins

Madison

WYTH(AM)— June 1955: 1250 khz; 1 kw-D. TL: N33 34 45 W83 28 40. Hrs open: 6 AM-sunset Box 3965, Eatonton, 31024. Secondary address: 869 Church St., Eaton 31024. Phone: (706) 485-8792. Fax: (706) 485-3555.E-mail: starstation@bellsouth.net Licensee: Craig Baker and Debra Baker (acq 5-15-2005; $63,000). Population served: 272,440 Rgnl. Network: Ga. Net. Ga. News Net. Format: Adult standards. News staff: one; News: 15 hrs wkly. Target aud: General. ♦Craig Baker, pres & gen mgr.

Manchester

WFDR(AM)— June 1957: 1370 khz; 1 kw-D. TL: N32 53 14 W84 35 54. Hrs open: 6 AM-6 PM 129 W. Main St., 31816. Phone: (706) 846-3016. Fax: (706) 866-3494. Licensee: Ploener Radio Group LLC (acq 10-11-2007). Population served: 4,779 Rgnl. Network: Ga. Net. Format: Gospel. ♦Paul Ploener, pres.

WVFJ-FM— 1967: 93.3 mhz; 27 kw. Ant 1,610 ft TL: N33 05 10 W84 46 10. Stereo. Hrs open: 24 120 Peachtree E. Shopping Ctr., Peachtree City, 30269. Phone: (770) 487-4500. Fax: (770) 486-6400. Web Site:www.j933.com Licensee: Provident Broadcasting Co. (acq

8-81; $790,000 with co-located AM; 9-7-81). Population served: 3,185,000 Natl. Rep: Rgnl Reps,. Brown, Nietert & Kaufman. Format: Contemporary, Christian. News staff: one. Target aud: 25-45; women. ◆Rick Davison, gen mgr, opns mgr; John Zeiler, rgnl sls mgr; Steve Williams, mktg dir; Don Schaeffer, progmg mgr; Susan Ricards, news dir; Brian Chin, chief of engrg, traf mgr; Dian Pena, traf mgr.

Marietta

WFOM(AM)— Oct 13, 1946: 1230 khz; 1 kw-U. TL: N33 55 38 W84 30 08. Hrs open: 24 3535 Piedmont Rd., Bldg. 14, Suite 1200, Atlanta, 30305. Phone: (404) 688-0068. Fax: (404) 995-4045. Licensee: Dickey Broadcasting Co. (group owner; (acq 8-31-2000; grpsl). Population served: 18,000 Natl. Network: . Natl. Rep: McGavren Guild,. Holland & Knight. Wire Svc: AP Format: Sports. Target aud: 25-64. Spec prog: Notre Dame football (fall). ◆David Dickey, gen mgr; Jim Mahanay, opns mgr; Tim McCarthy, sls dir.

WFTD(AM)— Nov 14, 1955: 1080 khz; 50 kw-D, 30 kw-CH, DA-2. TL: N34 01 24 W84 40 05. Hrs open: Sunrise-sunset 2865 Amwiler Rd., Suite 650, Doraville, 30360. Phone: (770) 825-0095. Fax: (770) 246-0054. Web Site:www.radiolaley.com Licensee: Prieto Enterprises Inc. (acq 12-20-2001). David Tillotson. Format: Sp. Target aud: 21-45. ◆Filiberto Prieto, pres & gen mgr.

WKHX-FM—Licensed to Marietta. See Atlanta

Martinez

WDRR(FM)— May 31, 1984: 93.9 mhz; 25 kw. Ant 328 ft TL: N33 26 17 W82 05 19. Stereo. Hrs open: 24 4051 Jimmie Dyess Pkwy., Augusta, 30909. Phone: (706) 396-7000 . Fax: (706) 396-7092. Web Site:www.939thedrive.com Licensee: WGOR License LLC. (acq 11-10-92; $810,000; 11-30-92). Population served: 400,000 Format: Classic hits. Target aud: 25 plus. ◆Kent Dunn, VP, gen mgr; Kent Murphy, gen sls mgr; Chris O'Kelley, progmg dir.

WPRW-FM— 1994: 107.7 mhz; 50 kw. Ant 492 ft TL: N33 38 35 W82 19 50. Hrs open: 2743 Perimeter Pky. Bldg. 100, Suite 300, Augusta, 30909. Phone: (706) 396-6000. Fax: (706) 396-6010. Web Site:www.power107.net Licensee: Capstar TX L.P. Group owner: Cumulus Media Inc. (acq 6-30-97; grpsl). Format: Urban contemp. ◆Mark Bass, gen mgr.

McDonough

WKKP(AM)— Apr 2, 1979: 1410 khz; 2.5 kw-D. TL: N33 25 47 W84 07 52. Hrs open: 24
Solid Gospel Network.
Box 878, Jackson, 30233. Secondary address: 940 Brownlee Rd., Jackson 30233. Phone: (770) 504-8410. Fax: (770) 775-3153.E-mail: donaldwearnhart@bellsouth.net Licensee: Henry County Radio Co. Inc. (acq 3-30-92; $65,000;4-20-92). Population served: 65,000 Natl. Network: Jones Radio Networks, . Rgnl. Network: Ga. Net. Natl. Rep: Rgnl Reps,. Format: Classic Country. News: 20 hrs wkly. Target aud: General. ◆Susanne Earnhart, pres; Don Earnhardt, gen mgr; Tom Lynde, opns dir.

McRae

WYIS(AM)— July 27, 1957: 1410 khz; 1 kw-D. TL: N32 03 25 W82 51 56. Hrs open: Box 247, Hwy. 341 S., 31055. Phone: (229) 868-5611. Fax: (229) 868-7552. Licensee: Cinecom Broadcasting Systems Inc. (acq 8-31-99; $220,000 with co-located FM). Natl. Rep: Rgnl Reps,. Format: Oldies. Target aud: 25-50; mature, wage earners. Spec prog: Black 4 hrs wkly. ◆Jimmy Hussey, gen mgr.

WYSC(FM)—Listing follows WYIS(AM).

Meigs

WQLI(FM)— Sept 8, 2000: 92.3 mhz; 6 kw. Ant 328 ft TL: N31 05 12 W84 12 10. Hrs open: 2586 Old Pelham Rd., Pelham, 31779. Phone: (229) 294-1909. Licensee: Mitchell County Television. Format: Adult contemp.

Metter

WBMZ(FM)— Aug 1, 1971: 103.7 mhz; 3 kw. Ant 299 ft TL: N32 23 56 W82 02 36. Stereo. Hrs open: 24 Box 238, 30439. Secondary address: 1075 E. Lillian St. 30439. Phone: (912) 685-2136. Fax: (912)

685-2137. Licensee: Radio Metter Inc. Rgnl. Network: Ga. Net. Ga. News Net. Format: Classic hits. Target aud: General. ◆Jimmy Page, CEO.

WHCG(AM)— Dec 22, 1961: 1360 khz; 1 kw-D. TL: N32 23 56 W82 02 36. Hrs open: Box 238, 30439. Secondary address: 1075 E. Lillian St. 30439. Phone: (912) 685-2136. Fax: (912) 685-2137. Web Site:www.wbmzfm.com Licensee: Radio Metter Inc. Population served: 75,000 Reddy, Begley & McCormick. Format: Southern gospel. Target aud: General. ◆Jimmy Page, pres, gen mgr & gen sls mgr.

Midway

WGCO(FM)—Licensed to Midway. See Savannah

Milan

WMCG(FM)— 1982: 104.9 mhz; 36 kw. Ant 564 ft TL: N32 07 16 W83 16 05. Stereo. Hrs open: 24 Box 130, Dublin, 31040-0130. Phone: (478) 272-4422. Fax: (478) 275-4657.E-mail: webmaster@1049wmcg.com Web Site:www.1049wmcg.com Licensee: Tel-Dodge Broadcasting Inc. Rgnl rep: Dora-Clayton Format: Classic country. News: 1 hr wkly. Target aud: 35+. Spec prog: Farm one hr wkly. ◆J. Morgan Dowdy, gen mgr.

Milledgeville

*WGUR(FM)— August 1975: 88.9 mhz; 37 w horiz. Ant 3 ft TL: N33 04 44 W83 13 55. Hrs open: Box 3124, Georgia College & State University, 31061. Phone: (478) 445-8256. Licensee: Georgia College & State University (acq 8-75). Population served: 4,500 Format: Alternative. Target aud: 18-24; college students. ◆Sonya Barnes, gen mgr.

WKZR(FM)— June 30, 1966: 102.3 mhz; 3.3 kw. 300 ft TL: N33 04 58 W83 15 01. Stereo. Hrs open: Prog sep from AM Box 519, 1250 W. charlton St., 31061. Phone: (478) 452-0586. Fax: (478) 452-5886. Licensee: WMVG Inc. Population served: 80,000 Format: Country.

WLRR(FM)— July 24, 1990: 100.7 mhz; 3 kw. Ant 328 ft TL: N33 06 50 W83 13 08. Hrs open:
Rebroadcasts WKVQ(AM) Eatonton 100%.
Box 3965, Eatonton, 31024. Phone: (706) 485-8792. Fax: (706) 485-3555. Licensee: Preston W. Small. Format: Adult standards. Target aud: 18-35. ◆Craig Baker, pres, gen mgr & opns VP.

WMVG(AM)— Mar 29, 1946: 1450 khz; 1 kw-U. TL: N33 04 58 W83 15 01. Hrs open: 24 Box 519, 1250 W. Charlton St., 31061. Phone: (478) 452-0586. Fax: (478) 452-5886. Licensee: WMVG Inc. (acq 7-8-99; $258,230 for 80% with co-located FM). Population served: 40,000 Natl. Rep: Rgnl Reps,. Format: Sports, news. News staff: one; News: 25 hrs wkly. Target aud: 18-49. Spec prog: Black 4 hrs wkly. ◆Randy Beasley, pres, gen mgr & edit dir.

*WRGC-FM—Not on air, target date: unknown: 88.3 mhz; 4.8 kw. Ant 384 ft TL: N33 04 05 W83 16 30. Hrs open: Campus Box 97, 31061-3375. Phone: (478) 445-6804. Fax: (478) 445-2364. Licensee: Georgia College & State University. ◆Dorothy J. Leland, pres; Angela Criscoe, gen mgr.

Millen

WHKN(FM)— Dec 4, 1989: 94.9 mhz; 14.5 kw. Ant 400 ft TL: N32 43 57 W81 51 43. Stereo. Hrs open: 24 Box 958, Statesboro, 30459. Phone: (912) 764-5496. Fax: (912) 764-8827.E-mail: radiocenter @frontiernet.net Licensee: Georgia Eagle Broadcasting Inc. (group owner; acq 1-12-2007; grpsl). Natl. Network: ABC, . Dan Alpert. Format: Country. News staff: one; News: 8 hrs wkly. Target aud: 25-54; adults. Spec prog: Farm 10 hrs, relg 2 hrs wkly. ◆Buddy Horne, pres, progmg mgr; Jeff Anderson, gen mgr.

Montezuma

WMGB(FM)— Aug 10, 2001: 95.1 mhz; 46 kw. 390 ft TL: N32 33 20 W83 44 14. Stereo. Hrs open: 24 544 Mulberry St., Suite 500, Macon, 31201. Phone: (478) 746-6286. Fax: (478) 745-4383.E-mail: info@allthehitsB951.com Web Site:www. all the hitsB951.com Licensee: Cumulus Licensing Corp. Group owner: Cumulus Media Inc. (acq 12-20-02; grpsl). Population served: 300,000 Natl. Network: Westwood One, . Format: CHR. ◆John Sheftic, gen mgr.

WMNZ(AM)— Nov 29, 1961: 1050 khz; 250 w-D, 42 w-N. TL: N32 17 58 W84 01 34. (CP: TL: N32 17 53 W84 02 02). Hrs open: Box 610, 31063. Secondary address: 115 1/2 Cherry St. 31063. Phone: (478) 472-8286. Fax: (478) 472-8296. Licensee: Macon County Broadcasting Co. Population served: 4,125 Format: Country, oldies, gospel. ◆Danny Blizzard, pres & gen mgr.

Morrow

WIGO(AM)— November 1956: 1570 khz; 5 kw-D, 50 w-N. TL: N33 36 05 W84 18 40. Hrs open: 2424 Old Rex Morrow Rd., Ellenwood, 30296. Phone: (404) 361-1570. Fax: (404) 366-9772.E-mail: info@wigo.com Web Site:www.wssathelight1570am.com Licensee: MCL/MCM Georgia LLC. (acq 12-29-2006; $1.75 million). Population served: 100,000 Format: Gospel, Christian. Target aud: 24-55. ◆Paul Ploener, gen mgr; Leah St. Cyr, stn mgr.

Moultrie

WHBS(AM)— 2002: 1400 khz; 1 kw-U. TL: N31 09 56 W83 46 01. Hrs open: 24 1643 South Blvd., 31768. Phone: (229) 890-2900. Fax: (229) 890-1497. Web Site:whbsam1400.com Licensee: Sailor Broadcasting of Georgia Inc. (acq 3-3-2005; $195,000). Format: Urban contemp, Black gospel. ◆Ronnie Barnes, gen mgr.

WMTM(AM)— Nov 10, 1953: 1300 khz; 5 kw-D. TL: N31 12 54 W83 47 13. Stereo. Hrs open: 6 AM-sunset Box 788, 31776. Secondary address: 100 WMTM Rd. 31768. Phone: (229) 985-1300. Fax: (229) 890-0905.E-mail: jay@cruisin9.4.com Licensee: Colquitt Broadcasting Co. L.L.C. Population served: 14,302 Natl. Rep: Rgnl Reps,. Smithwick & Belendiuk. Format: Southern gospel. News staff: one. Target aud: General. Spec prog: Farm 16 hrs wkly. ◆Jim Turner, pres & gen mgr.

WMTM-FM— Nov 17, 1964: 93.9 mhz; 100 kw. 555 ft TL: N31 12 54 W83 47 13. Stereo. Hrs open: 6 AM-midnight Prog sep from AM Box 788, 31768. Phone: (229) 985-1300. Fax: (229) 890-0905. Licensee: Colquitt Broadcasting Co. LLC Format: Oldies. ◆Jim Turner, opns mgr, mktg mgr & traf mgr.

Mount Vernon

WYUM(FM)— Aug 3, 1998: 101.7 mhz; 6 kw. 325 ft TL: N32 12 44 W82 27 48. Hrs open: Box 900, Vidalia, 30475. Phone: (912) 537-9202. Fax: (912) 537-4477.E-mail: zfowler@vidaliacommunications.com Web Site:www.vidaliacommunications.com Licensee: Vidalia Communications Corp. (group owner) Population served: 30,000 Rgnl. Network: Ga. Net. Ga. News Net. Rgnl rep: Rgnl Reps. Format: Country. Target aud: 25-49. ◆John Ladson III, pres; Zack Fowler, gen mgr; Collins Knightor, opns dir.

Mountain City

WALH(AM)— May 1, 1986: 1340 khz; 1 kw-U. TL: N34 56 16 W83 23 27. Hrs open: Box F, 30562. Phone: (706) 746-2256. Fax: (706) 746-2259.E-mail: walh@alltel.net Web Site:www.wolfcreekbroadcasting.com Licensee: Mountain City Broadcasting Inc. (acq 1-19-2005; $275,000). Format: Country, bluegrass, gospel. Target aud: 30-50; blue collar. Spec prog: Farm 2 hrs wkly. ◆Rebecca St. John, gen mgr.

Murrayville

WGTJ(AM)—Licensed to Murrayville. See Gainesville

Nashville

*WGCN(FM)— 2005: 90.5 mhz; 1 w horiz, 50 kw vert. Ant 292 ft vert TL: N31 09 26 W83 22 28. Hrs open:
Rebroadcasts KLRD(FM) Yucaipa, CA 100%.
2351 Sunset Blvd., Suite 170-218, Rocklin, CA, 95765. Phone: (916) 251-1600. Fax: (916) 251-1650.E-mail: info@air1.com Web Site:www.air1.com Licensee: Educational Media Foundation. Group owner: EMF Broadcasting. (acq 1-7-2004). Natl. Network: Air 1, . Format: Christian. ◆Mike Novak, pres.

WVKV(FM)—Licensed to Nashville. See Tifton

Newnan

WCOH(AM)— December 1947: 1400 khz; 1 kw-U. TL: N33 21 53 W84 48 42. Hrs open: 154 Boone Dr., 30263. Phone: (770) 683-7234. Fax: (770) 683-9846. Web Site:www.foxsports1400.com Licensee: Citicasters

Licenses L.P. Group owner: Clear Channel Communications Inc. (acq 5-4-99; grpsl). Population served: 57,000 Natl. Network: Fox Sports, . Rgnl. Network: Ga. Net. Ga. News Net. Miller & Miller, P.C. Format: Sports. Target aud: 25-54. ◆Bill Clark, gen mgr & mktg mgr.

WNEA(AM)— Apr 18, 1962: 1300 khz; 1 kw-D. TL: N33 22 31 W84 47 08. Hrs open: 8451 South Cherokee Blvd., Suite B, Douglasville, 30134. Phone: (770) 920-1520. Fax: (770) 920-4600. Web Site:www.wordchristianbroadcasting.com Licensee: Word Christian Broadcasting Inc. (acq 2-28-96; 3-11-96). Population served: 40,000 Rgnl. Network: Ga. Net. Ga. News Net. Format: Old time relg. Target aud: 18-64. Spec prog: Black, relg, gospel 15 hrs wkly. ◆Ken Johns, CEO, gen mgr, opns dir & progmg dir.

North Atlanta

WCNN(AM)—Licensed to North Atlanta. See Atlanta

Ochlocknee

WSBX(AM)— June 4, 1984: 1020 khz; 10 kw-D. TL: N30 54 00 W83 59 55. Hrs open: Sunrise-sunset Box 90, Thomasville, 31799. Secondary address: 540 Daisy Ln., Thomasville 31792. Phone: (912) 228-5683. Fax: (912) 436-0544.E-mail: radioelchongo@aol.com Web Site:www.radioelchongo.com Licensee: Doreen A. Blood (acq 10-28-2008; $280,000). Format: Sp music. ◆ Jimmy Bennett, pres & gen mgr.

Ocilla

WLPF(FM)— December 1993: 98.5 mhz; 2.3 kw. 521 ft TL: N31 28 11 W83 14 11. Stereo. Hrs open: 24 2278 Wortham Ln., Grovetown, 30813. Phone: (706) 309-9610. Fax: (706) 309-9669.E-mail: ctbarinowski@comcast.net Web Site:www.gnnradio.org Licensee: Barinowski Investment Co. Group owner: Good News Network (acq 11-17-92; for CP; 12-7-92). Population served: 65,000 Format: Christian. News: 12 hrs wkly. Target aud: General. ◆Clarence Barinowski, gen mgr.

Omega

WTIF-FM— April 1993: 107.5 mhz; 4 kw. Ant 400 ft TL: N31 27 17 W83 33 37. Hrs open: 24 Box 968, Tifton, 31793. Phone: (229) 382-1340. Fax: (229) 386-8658. Licensee: Three Trees Communications Inc. (group owner; (acq 6-28-2004; grpsl). Population served: 100,000 Rgnl. Network: Ga. Net. Ga. News Net. Format: Christian music. News staff: 6; News: 5 hrs wkly. Target aud: 18 plus. ◆ Matt Baldrich, pres & gen mgr.

Patterson

***WNEE(FM)—**Not on air, target date: unknown: 88.1 mhz; 600 w. Ant 174 ft TL: N34 01 15 W83 16 33. Hrs open: Box 6767, Athens, 30604. Phone: (770) 596-0739. Licensee: Community Public Radio Inc. ◆Penny Jackson, pres.

Peachtree City

***WMVW(FM)—**Not on air, target date: unknown: 91.7 mhz; 10 kw. Ant 328 ft TL: N33 16 03 W84 33 20. Hrs open: 100 S. Hill St., Suite 100, Griffin, 30223. Phone: (770) 229-2020. Fax: (770) 229-4820. Licensee: Life Radio Ministries Inc. ◆Joseph Emert, pres.

WWLG(FM)— 1948: 96.7 mhz; 1 kw. Ant 545 ft TL: N33 26 22 W84 42 42. Stereo. Hrs open: 1819 Peachtree Rd. N.E., Suite 700, Atlanta, 30309. Phone: (404) 367-0949. Fax: (404) 367-9490.E-mail: info@976thelegend.com Web Site:967thelegend.com Licensee: Citicasters Licenses L.P. Group owner: Clear Channel Communications Inc. (acq 5-4-99; grpsl). Population served: 200,000 Miller & Miller. Format: Country. ◆Chuck Deskins, gen mgr; Mike Lawing, chief of engrg.

Pearson

WPNG(FM)— August 1999: 101.9 mhz; 12.9 kw. Ant 459 ft TL: N31 19 36 W82 51 54. Stereo. Hrs open: 24 Box 823, 31642. Secondary address: 2232 Old Douglas Hwy. 31642. Phone: (912) 422-6122. Fax: (912) 422-7840.E-mail: freedom1019@planttel.net Web Site:www.hitsandfavorites.com Licensee: KM Radio of Pearson L.L.C. Group owner: KM Communications Inc. (acq 5-3-99). Population served: 532,000 Cohen, Dipple & Everist. Format: Adult contemp. Target aud: 25-49; women ages 25-49. ◆Myoung Hwa Bae, pres; Kevin Bae, gen mgr.

Pelham

WZBN(FM)—See Camilla

Pembroke

WBAW-FM— Aug 31, 1966: Stn currently dark. 99.3 mhz; 100 kw. Ant 869 ft TL: N32 07 15 W81 47 56. Stereo. Hrs open: 321 Fraser Dr., Hinesville, 31313. Licensee: Bullie Broadcasting Corp. (acq 2-5-99; $475,000). Population served: 62,000 Target aud: General.

Perry

WPGA(AM)— 1955: 980 khz; 5 kw-D, 270 w-N. TL: N32 26 40 W83 45 00. Stereo. Hrs open: 24 1691 Forsyth St., Macon, 31201. Phone: (478) 745-5858. Fax: (478) 745-5800.E-mail: info@58abc.com Web Site:www.58abc.com Licensee: Register Communications Inc. (acq 1996). Population served: 80,000 Format: Children. News staff: one. Target aud: Children up to 12. ◆Debbie Hart, gen mgr; Loel Register, pres & gen sls mgr; Janice J. Register, women's int ed.

WPGA-FM— May 3, 1966: 100.9 mhz; 3 kw. 345 ft TL: N32 33 20 W83 44 14. (CP: 2.15 kw, ant 551 ft.). Stereo. Hrs open: Prog sep from AM 1691 Forsyth St., Macon, 31201. Phone: (478) 745-5500. Fax: (478) 745-5800.E-mail: info@58abc.com Web Site:www.58abc.com Licensee: Register Communications Inc. Population served: 250,000 Format: Adult contemp. News staff: one. ◆Kristy Turner, gen sls mgr; Janice J. Register, women's int ed. Co-owned TV: WPGA-TV affil

Pinehurst

WSSY(FM)— Feb 22, 1969: 98.3 mhz; 3.1 kw. Ant 459 ft TL: N32 10 03 W83 37 51. Stereo. Hrs open: 24 Box 667, Cordele, 31010. Phone: (229) 271-3500. Fax: (229) 273-4900.E-mail: qwixie983@yahoo.com Licensee: Georgia Eagle Broadcasting Inc. (group owner; (acq 1-12-2007; grpsl). Population served: 40,000 Natl. Network: Jones Radio Networks, . Dan Alpert. Format: Oldies. News staff: one; News: 15 hrs wkly. Target aud: 35-64. ◆Cecil Staton, pres.

Plainville

WRBF(FM)—Not on air, target date: unknown: 104.9 mhz; 1.8 kw. Ant 606 ft TL: N34 20 35 W85 02 20. Hrs open: 150 Westpark Dr. #320, Athens, 30606. Phone: (817) 846-9535. Licensee: Howard C. Toole. ◆Howard C. Toole, gen mgr.

Port Wentworth

***WLFS(FM)—** 2001: 91.9 mhz; 6 kw. Ant 180 ft TL: N32 09 17 W81 09 55. Hrs open: 5859 Abeerorn St., Suite 3, Savannah, 31405. Phone: (912) 353-9226. Fax: (912) 353-9325.E-mail: Jody @HisRadio.Net Web Site:www.hisradio.com Licensee: Radio Training Network Inc. Format: Christian contemp. ◆Allen Henderson, gen mgr.

Quitman

WSFB(AM)— Nov 19, 1955: 1490 khz; 1 kw-U. TL: N30 46 51 W83 34 30. Hrs open: Box 632, 31643. Phone: (229) 263-4373. Fax: (229) 263-7693. Licensee: Scott Matheson (acq 11-1-2005; $10,000). Population served: 63,462 Format: Adult standards. Target aud: 30+. ◆Scott Matheson, gen mgr.

WSTI-FM— Sept 12, 1986: 105.3 mhz; 3 kw. 300 ft TL: N30 48 45 W83 31 18. Stereo. Hrs open: 1711 Ellis Dr., Valdosta, 31601. Phone: (229) 244-8642. Fax: (229) 242-7620. Licensee: RTG Radio L.L.C. Group owner: Black Crow Media Group LLC (acq 6-4-2004; $3.4 million with WXHT(FM) Madison, FL). Format: Urban contemp. Target aud: 25-54; white collar. Spec prog: Farm 5 hrs wkly. ◆Scott James, gen mgr.

Reidsville

WRBX(FM)— July 1993: 104.1 mhz; 3 kw. 187 ft TL: N32 05 14 W82 07 47. Hrs open: 24 Box 69, 30453. Phone: (912) 557-4140. Population served: 160,000 Natl. Network: USA, . Format: Southern gospel. Target aud: 8 plus; religious. ◆William Keith Register, gen mgr.

WTNL(AM)— June 25, 1976: 1390 khz; 500 w-D. TL: N32 05 14 W82 07 47. Hrs open: 6 AM-sunset Box 69, 30453. Phone: (912) 557-3777.

Fax: (912) 557-6956. Licensee: WRBX/WTNL L.L.C. (acq 3-93; $35,000 with co-located FM; 2-15-93). Population served: 18,000 Natl. Network: USA, . Format: Southern gospel. Target aud: General.

Richmond Hill

WRHQ(FM)— May 13, 1991: 105.3 mhz; 11 kw. 485 ft TL: N32 02 52 W81 07 26. Stereo. Hrs open: 24 1102 E. 52nd St., Savannah, 31404. Phone: (912) 234-1053. Fax: (912) 354-6600.E-mail: qualityrock@wrhq.com Web Site:www.wrhq.com Licensee: Thoroughbred Communications Inc. Group owner: Thoroughbred Communications Natl. Network: AP Radio, . Natl. Rep: Christal,. Shook, Hardy & Bacon. Format: Rock, adult contemp. News: 2 hrs wkly. Target aud: 25-54; 35-64; affluent. ◆Jerry Rogers, pres, gen mgr, gen sls mgr, adv mgr, edit dir; Ray Williams, rgnl sls mgr, prom mgr; Mike Roberts, progmg dir, mus critic, disc jockey; Lyndy Brannan, pub affrs dir; Marty Foglia, chief of engrg; Phyllis Bright, traf mgr; Rusty Fredrich, sports cmtr; Brady McGraw, disc jockey.

Rincon

WSSJ(FM)— May 1, 1967: 100.1 mhz; 50 kw. Ant 492 ft TL: N32 16 49 W81 11 40. Stereo. Hrs open: 24 Box 79, Hinesville, 31313. Secondary address: 120 D. Liberty, Hinesville 31313. Phone: (912) 368-9258. Fax: (912) 368-5526.E-mail: rjp106@aol.com Licensee: Tama Radio Licenses of Savannah, GA Inc. Group owner: Tama Broadcasting Inc. (acq 4-28-2004). Population served: 108,000 Format: Gospel. News staff: one. Target aud: 18-45. ◆ Yvonne Clark, gen mgr.

Ringgold

WMPZ(FM)—Licensed to Ringgold. See Chattanooga TN

WOCE(FM)— March 1989: 101.9 mhz; 1.32 kw. Ant 702 ft TL: N34 58 11 W85 05 10. Hrs open: 613 Silver Cir., Dalton, 30721. Phone: (706) 278-5511. Fax: (423) 553-9490. Licensee: North Georgia Radio Group L.P. Group owner: Clear Channel Communications Inc. (acq 7-28-2006; $2.15 milion). Format: Rgnl Mexican. ◆Paul Fink, gen mgr.

Rockmart

WTSH-FM— August 1989: 107.1 mhz; 45 kw. Ant 518 ft TL: N34 15 03 W84 59 05. Hrs open: 20 John Davenport Dr., Rome, 3016s. Phone: (706) 291-9496. Fax: (706) 235-7107. Web Site:www.south107.com Licensee: Woman's World Broadcasting Inc. (acq 11-14-2003; $5.4 million). Population served: 496,000 Format: Country. Target aud: 25-54. ◆ Randy Quick, gen mgr.

WZOT(AM)— Aug 28, 1959: 1220 khz; 500 w-D, 150 w-N. TL: N34 00 14 W85 03 22. Hrs open: 602 W. Elm St., 30153. Phone: (770) 684-7848. Fax: (770) 684-7848.E-mail: am1220wzot@peoplepc.com Licensee: Triple J's Broadcasting LLC (acq 9-1-2004; $346,804 with WGJK(AM) Rome). Rgnl. Network: Ga. Net. Ga. News Net. Format: Southern gospel. Target aud: 18-45. ◆Paul Stone, pres; Randy Quick, gen mgr.

Rome

WGJK(AM)— Aug 1, 1962: 1360 khz; 500 w-D, 150 w-N. TL: N34 16 15 W85 11 00. Hrs open: 6 AM-12 PM 1010 Tower Pl., Bogart, 30622. Phone: (706) 549-6222. Fax: (706) 353-1967. Licensee: Woman's World Broadcasting Inc. (acq 11-17-2006). Population served: 96,000 ◆Suzanne Stone, pres.

***WGPB(FM)—** May 22, 1965: 97.7 mhz; 25 kw. Ant 790 ft TL: N34 14 00 W85 14 02. Stereo. Hrs open: 24 260 14th St. NW, Atlanta, 30318. Secondary address: Heritage Hall, 415 E. Third Ave. 30162. Phone: (706) 204-2276.E-mail: ask@gpb.org Web Site:www.gpb.org /public/radio/wgpb/ Licensee: Georgia Public Telecommunications Commission (acq 9-24-2007). Population served: 265,000 Natl. Network: NPR, PRI, . Arnold & Porter. Wire Svc: AP Format: News, classical music. News staff: 10; News: 40 hrs wkly. Target aud: Adults: 35 plus. Spec prog: Jazz 16 hrs wkly. ◆Nancy Hall, CEO; Bonnie Bean, CFO; Bob Houghton, gen mgr; Tom Barclay, opns mgr; Rob Maynard, progmg dir; Susanna Capelouto, news dir.

WLAQ(AM)— 1947: 1410 khz; 1 kw-U, DA-N. TL: N34 15 43 W85 12 22. Hrs open: 2 Mount Alto Rd., 30165. Phone: (706) 232-7767. Fax: (706) 295-9225.E-mail: wlaq1410am@hotmail.com Web Site:www.wlaq.com Licensee: Cripple Creek Broadcasting Co. (acq 4-1-87). Population served: 80,000 Natl. Network: CBS, . Format: News/talk, sports. ◆Randy Davis, pres & gen mgr.

WQTU(FM)— May 2, 1966: 102.3 mhz; 6 kw. Ant 804 ft TL: N34 14 02 W85 13 50. Stereo. Hrs open: 24 20 John Davenport Dr., 301645. Phone: (706) 295-1023. Fax: (706) 235-7107.E-mail: q102rome@q102rome.com Web Site:q102rome.com Licensee: McDougald Broadcasting Corp. Population served: 98,000 Wire Svc: National Weather Network Format: Hot adult contemp. News staff: one; News: 6 hrs wkly. Target aud: 25-54; upscale. ♦Randy Quick, gen mgr.

WRGA(AM)— November 1929: 1470 khz; 5 kw-U, DA-N. TL: N34 18 05 W85 09 19. Hrs open: 24 20 John Davenport Dr., 30165. Phone: (706) 291-9496. Fax: (706) 235-7107.E-mail: south107@aol.com Web Site:www.wrgarome.com Licensee: McDougald Broadcasting Corp. Group owner: Southern Broadcasting Companies Inc. (acq 1-28-2002; $1.6 million with co-located FM). Population served: 98,000 Natl. Network: ABC, CNN Radio, . Rgnl. Network: Ga. Net. Ga. News Net. Fletcher, Heald & Hildreth. Wire Svc: National Weather Network Format: News/talk. News staff: 2; News: 168 hrs wkly. Target aud: General; upscale, involved, upwardly mobile. ♦Paul Stone, pres; Gregory Kamishlian, gen mgr.

WROM(AM)— Dec 26, 1946: 710 khz; 1 kw-D. TL: N34 15 30 W85 09 15. Hrs open: Sunrise-sunset 1105 Calhoun Ave., 30162. Phone: (706) 234-7171. Fax: (706) 234-8043.E-mail: wromradio@comcast.net Web Site:www.wromradio.com Licensee: LGV Broadcasting Inc. (acq 1999; $150,000). Population served: 149,000 Natl. Network: USA, . Maupin, Taylor, Ellis & Adams. Format: Southern gospel. News staff: one; News: 14 hrs wkly. Target aud: 35 plus; middle class families, women, homeowners. Spec prog: Christian teaching, contemp Christian mus. ♦Mark Lumpkin, gen mgr.

Rossville

WRXR-FM— June 8, 1966: 105.5 mhz; 1.8 kw. Ant 604 ft TL: N34 57 23 W85 17 32. Stereo. Hrs open: 24 Prog sep from AM 7413 Old Lee Hwy., Chattanooga, TN, 37421. Phone: (423) 892-3333. Fax: (423) 899-7224.E-mail: jcruze@clearchannel.com Licensee: Capstar TX L.P. (acq 8-7-2000; grpsl). Population served: 366000 Natl. Rep: Clear Channel,. Format: Active rock. News: one hr wkly. ♦Sammy George, gen mgr.

WUUS(AM)— Nov 11, 1958: 980 khz; 500 w-D. TL: N34 58 03 W85 18 00. Hrs open: Sunrise-sunset 7413 Old Lee Hwy., Chattanooga, TN, 37421. Phone: (423) 892-3333. Fax: (423) 899-7224. Licensee: 3 Daughters Media Inc. Group owner: Clear Channel Communications Inc. (acq 6-22-2007; grpsl). Natl. Rep: Clear Channel,. Format: Oldies. News staff: one; News: 4 hrs wkly. Target aud: 35-64; adults. ♦Sammy George, gen mgr.

Roswell

WAMJ(FM)— 1997: 107.5 mhz; 21.5 kw. Ant 361 ft TL: N33 55 54 W84 20 43. (CP: 50 kw, ant 351 ft. TL: N33 55 52 W84 14 40). Hrs open: 101 Marietta St. 12th Floor, Atlanta, 30303. Phone: (404) 765-9750. Fax: (404) 688-7686. Web Site:www.majicatl.com Licensee: ROA Licenses LLC. Group owner: Radio One Inc. (acq 11-8-2001; grpsl). Format: Adult rhythm and blues. ♦Tim Davies, gen mgr; Corey Punzi, prom dir; Derek Harper, progmg dir.

Royston

WXFO(AM)— January 1971: 810 khz; 250 w-D. TL: N34 16 50 W83 07 09. Hrs open: Sunrise-sunset 259 Turner St., 30662. Phone: (706) 246-0059. Fax: (706) 245-0890.E-mail: studio@familycountry.com Web Site:www.foxnewsradio810.com Licensee: Oconee River Broadcasting LLC (acq 3-17-2008). . Population served: 99,300 Natl. Network: Fox News Radio, . Rgnl. Network: Ga. Net. Ga. News Net. Format: Talk. News staff: 3; News: 7 hrs wkly. Target aud: General. ♦KJ Allen, gen mgr.

WXKT(FM)—Licensed to Royston. See Athens

Saint Mary's

WWIO(AM)— Oct 15, 1985: 1190 khz; 2.5 kw-D. TL: N30 45 48 W81 36 40. Hrs open: Daytime 2101 Hwy 40E, St. Mary's, 31558. Phone: (404) 685-2527. Web Site:www.gpb.org Licensee: Lighthouse Christian Broadcasting Corp. (acq 12-21-99). Natl. Network: USA, NPR, . Natl. Rep: Rgnl Reps,. Georgia Public Radio Wire Svc: AP Format: News/Classical. News staff: 6; News: 40 hrs wkly. Target aud: General; 35 yrs +. ♦Taylor Lewis, opns mgr; St. John Flynn, progmg dir; Mark Sehlig, chief of engrg.

Saint Simons Island

WBGA(FM)—Licensed to Saint Simons Island. See Brunswick

WGIG(AM)—See Brunswick

WMUV(FM)—See Brunswick

WSOL-FM—See Jacksonville, FL

Sandersville

WSNT(AM)— May 11, 1956: 1490 khz; 1 kw-U. TL: N32 58 23 W82 48 34. Hrs open: Box 150, 31082. Secondary address: 312 Morningside Dr. 31082. Phone: (478) 552-5182. Fax: (478) 553-0800.E-mail: sales@waco100fm.com Licensee: Radio Station WSNT Inc. Natl. Network: ESPN Radio, . Natl. Rep: Rgnl Reps,. Ga. News Net. Rgnl rep: Rgnl Reps Format: Sports. ♦Capers Brazzell, gen mgr.

WSNT-FM— 1975: 99.9 mhz; 3 kw. Ant 184 ft TL: N32 58 23 W82 48 34. Hrs open: Box 150, 31082. Secondary address: 312 Morningside Dr. 31082. Phone: (478) 552-5182. Fax: (478) 553-0800.E-mail: sales@waco100fm.com Web Site:www.realcountryonline.com /home.asp?callsign=WSNT-FM Format: Country.

Sandy Springs

WFGM(AM)—Not on air, target date: unknown: 830 khz; 50 kw-D, 2.4 kw-N, DA-2. TL: N34 02 00 W84 19 09. Hrs open: 1311 Chuck Dawley Blvd., Mount Pleasant, SC, 29464. Phone: (843) 972-2200.E-mail: wfgm@ams.fm Licensee: Frank McCoy. ♦Frank McCoy, gen mgr.

Sasser

WEGC(FM)—Licensed to Sasser. See Albany

Savannah

WAEV(FM)— Feb 4, 1969: 97.3 mhz; 100 kw. 1,000 ft TL: N32 03 30 W81 20 20. Stereo. Hrs open: Prog sep from AM 245 Alfred St., 31408. Phone: (912) 964-7794. Fax: (912) 964-9414. Population served: 118,349 Natl. Network: Westwood One, . Format: CHR. Target aud: 25-54; affluent. ♦Steve Richards, opns mgr; Sheryl Collison, sls dir, rgnl sls mgr; Craig Scott, progmg mgr; Marty Foglia, disc jockey.

WBMQ(AM)— Dec 29, 1939: 630 khz; 5 kw-U, DA-N. TL: N32 03 51 W81 00 52. Hrs open: 214 Television Cir., 31406. Phone: (912) 961-9000. Fax: (912) 961-7070.E-mail: info@diane.hubelcumulus.com Web Site:www.wbmq.com Licensee: Cumulus Licensing Corp. Group owner: Cumulus Media Inc. (acq 3-26-98; grpsl). Population served: 47,000 Natl. Network: CBS, . Format: News/talk. Target aud: 35 plus. ♦Dale Powers, gen mgr.

WEAS-FM—(Springfield, August 1967: 93.1 mhz; 96.64 kw. Ant 981 ft TL: N32 02 45 W81 20 27. Stereo. Hrs open: 214 Television Cir., 31406. Phone: (912) 961-9000. Fax: (912) 961-7070.E-mail: info@diane.hubelcumulus.com Web Site:www.e93jamz.com Licensee: Cumulus Licensing Corp. Population served: 118,349 Format: Urban contemp.

WGCO(FM)—(Midway, 1974: 98.3 mhz; 100 kw. Ant 1,047 ft TL: N31 36 45 W81 21 37. Stereo. Hrs open: 24 401 Mall Blvd., Suite 101 D, 31406. Phone: (912) 351-9830. Fax: (912) 352-4821.E-mail: info@oldies983fm.com Web Site:www.oldies983fm.com Licensee: Monterey Licenses LLC. Group owner: Triad Broadcasting Co. LLC (acq 9-1-2000; grpsl). Population served: 500,000 Natl. Rep: Christal,. Format: Oldies. News staff: 3; News: 2 hrs wkly. Target aud: 25-54; yuppies. ♦Robert Leonard, gen mgr & rgnl sls mgr.

***WHCJ(FM)**— Aug 18, 1975: 90.3 mhz; 6 kw. Ant 223 ft TL: N32 01 28 W81 03 23. Hrs open: 16 Savannah State Univ., 3219 College St., 31404. Phone: (912) 356-2399/356-2381. Fax: (912) 356-2041.E-mail: WHCJ@savstate.edu Web Site:www.savstate.edu/whcj Licensee: Savannah State University. Population served: 150,000 Format: Var/div. Target aud: 17-65; interested in jazz, reggae, blues & gospel. ♦Theron Ike Carter, gen mgr.

WIXV(FM)— Apr 24, 1972: 95.5 mhz; 100 kw. 900 ft TL: N32 03 30 W81 20 20. Stereo. Hrs open: Prog sep from AM 214 Television Cir., 31406. Phone: (912) 961-9000. Fax: (912) 961-7070.E-mail: info@diane.hubelcumulus.com Web Site:www.rockofsavannah.com Population served: 86,200 Format: Classic rock. Target aud: 18-49.

WJCL-FM— June 18, 1972: 96.5 mhz; 100 kw. 1,232 ft TL: N32 03 30 W81 20 20. Stereo. Hrs open: 24 214 Television Cir., 31406. Phone: (912) 961-9000. Fax: (912) 961-7070.E-mail: boomer.lee@cumulus.com Web Site:www.kix96.com Licensee: Cumulus Licensing Corp. Group owner: Cumulus Media LLC (acq 3-12-98; $7.25 million). Population served: 118,349 Format: Country. News staff: one. Target aud: 25-54. ♦Lewis W. Dickey Jr., CEO, pres; Martin R. Gausvik, CFO; Dale Powers, gen mgr; Sam Nelson, opns dir; Tom Hennessey, sls dir.

WJLG(AM)— Oct 6, 1950: 900 khz; 4.35 kw-D, 152 w-N. TL: N32 04 29 W81 04 17. Hrs open: 214 Television Cir., 31406. Phone: (912) 961-9000. Fax: (912) 961-7070.E-mail: info@diane.hubelcumulus.com Web Site:www.cumulus.com Licensee: Cumulus Licensing Corp. Group owner: Cumulus Media Inc. (acq 7-29-98; $5.25 million with co-located FM). Natl. Network: Fox Sports, . Format: Sports. ♦Dale Power, gen mgr.

***WLXP(FM)**— Jan 1, 2002: 88.1 mhz; 1.5 kw. Ant 361 ft TL: N32 02 49 W81 04 42. Stereo. Hrs open: 24 2351 Sunset Blvd., Suite 170-218, Air 1 Radio Network, Rocklin, CA, 95765. Phone: (916) 251-1600. Fax: (916) 251-1650.E-mail: info@air1.com Web Site:www.air1.com Licensee: Christian Multimedia Network Inc. Population served: 237,000 Natl. Network: Air 1, . Shaw Pittman. Format: Contemp Christian. News staff: 3. Target aud: 18-35; Judeo-Christian, female. ♦Joe Miller, CFO; Keith Whipple, gen mgr.

WQBT(FM)— Nov 29, 1946: 94.1 mhz; 100 kw. 1,320 ft TL: N32 03 14 W81 21 01. Stereo. Hrs open: 245 Alfred St., 31408. Phone: (912) 964-7794. Fax: (912) 964-9414. Population served: 566,300 Format: Urban contemp. ♦Steve Richards, opns mgr; Sheryl Collison, sls dir; Chase, progmg dir; Marty Foglia, chief of engrg.

WSEG(AM)— May 1956: 1400 khz; 650 w-U. TL: N32 04 29 W81 04 17. Hrs open: 24 7515 Blythe Island Hwy., Brunswick, 31523. Phone: (912) 264-6251. Licensee: MarMac Communications LLC. (acq 6-26-2007; $300,000). Population served: 277,000 ♦Gary P. Marmitt, gen mgr.

WSOK(AM)— October 1946: 1230 khz; 1 kw-U. TL: N32 04 20 W81 04 35. Hrs open: 245 Alfred St., 31408. Phone: (912) 964-7794. Fax: (912) 964-9414. Licensee: Capstar TX L.P. Group owner: Clear Channel Communications Inc. (acq 8-30-00; grpsl). Population served: 142,400 Natl. Network: American Urban, . Format: Gospel. ♦Craig Scott, CEO; Steve Richards, opns mgr; Sheryl Collison, sls dir; Gary Young, progmg dir; Marty Foglia, chief of engrg; E. Larry McDuffie, disc jockey.

***WSVH(FM)**— Apr 20, 1981: 91.1 mhz; 100 kw. 1,068 ft TL: N32 03 32 W81 17 57. Stereo. Hrs open: 24
WJSP, Warm Springs, GA, 50-60%.
260 14th St. N.W., Atlanta, 30318-5360. Secondary address: 12 Ocean Science Cir. 30602. Phone: (404) 685-2690 HQ. Fax: (404) 685-2684 HQ.E-mail: ask@gpb.org Web Site:www.gpb.org Licensee: Georgia Public Telecommunications Commission. Population served: 231,000 Natl. Network: PRI, NPR, . Wire Svc: AP Format: Class, news, jazz. News staff: 10; News: 51 hrs wkly. Target aud: Adults: 35 plus. ♦Nancy G. Hall, CEO; Bonnie Bean, CFO; Bob Houghton, gen mgr; Eric Nauert, stn mgr; Tom Barclay, opns mgr; Rob Maynard, progmg dir; Susanna Capelouto, news dir; Orlando Montoya, news rptr.

WTKS(AM)— Oct 15, 1929: 1290 khz; 5 kw-U, DA-N. TL: N32 05 26 W81 08 55. Stereo. Hrs open: 245 Alfred St., 31408-3205. Phone: (912) 964-7794. Fax: (912) 964-9414. Licensee: Capstar TX L.P. Group owner: Clear Channel Communications Inc. (acq 8-30-00; grpsl). Population served: 550,000 Wiley, Rein & Fielding. Format: Talk. Target aud: 25-64. ♦Craig Scott, gen mgr; Steve Richards, opns mgr; Sheryl Collison, sls dir; Bill Edwards, news dir; Marty Foglia, chief of engrg.

***WYFS(FM)**— Nov 1, 1986: 89.5 mhz; 100 kw. 630 ft TL: N32 04 04 W81 21 17. Stereo. Hrs open: 24 1388 Old Waynesboro Rd., Waynesboro, 30830. Secondary address: Bible Broadcasting Network, Charlotte 28241-7300. Phone: (877) 554-8226. Phone: (704) 523-5555. Web Site:www.bbnradio.org Licensee: Bible Broadcasting Network Inc. (group owner) Format: Educ, relg, Christian. Target aud: General; christian progmg for the entire family. ♦Lowell Davey, pres; Rob Ferguson, gen mgr & stn mgr.

WZAT(FM)— Oct 19, 1971: 102.1 mhz; 98 kw. Ant 1,328 ft TL: N32 03 29 W81 20 19. Stereo. Hrs open: 24 214 Television Cir., 31406. Phone: (912) 961-9000. Fax: (912) 961-7070.E-mail: brian.rickman@z102.net Web Site:www.z102.net Licensee: Cumulus Licensing Corp. Group owner: Cumulus Media Inc. (acq 7-29-98; $3.5 million). Population served: 560,000 Format: CHR, var. ♦Lewis W. Dickey Jr., CEO, pres; Martin R. Gausvik, CFO; Dale Powers, gen mgr; Sam Nelson, opns dir; Robert Combs, sls dir, engr.

Smithboro

*WAKP(FM)—Not on air, target date: unknown: 89.1 mhz; 3 kw. Ant 79 ft TL: N33 16 55 W83 32 48. Hrs open: 102 Red Branch Ln., Simpsonville, SC, 29681. Phone: (864) 297-0216.E-mail: info@networkofglory.org Licensee: Network of Glory Inc. (acq 8-5-2008; $25,000 for CP). ◆Lola Richey, gen mgr.

Smithville

WUCN(AM)—Not on air, target date: unknown: 1230 khz; 1 kw-U. TL: N31 56 10 W84 15 15. Hrs open: Box 11024, Fort Lauderdale, FL, 33339. Phone: (954) 630-9037. Licensee: Dan Bohanan. ◆Dan Bohanan, gen mgr.

WZIQ(FM)— 1996: 106.5 mhz; 2.45 kw. 515 ft TL: N31 47 59 W84 14 54. Stereo. Hrs open: 24 2278 Wortham Ln., Grovetown, 30813. Phone: (706) 309-9610.E-mail: ctbarinowski@comcast.net Web Site:www.gnnradio.org Group owner: Good News Network (acq 1-21-98). Population served: 110,000 Format: Christian. ◆Clarence Barinowski, gen mgr.

Smyrna

WAZX(AM)— March 1962: 1550 khz; 50 kw-D, 500 w-N, DA-2. TL: N33 53 29 W84 31 19. Stereo. Hrs open: 24 1800 Lake Park Dr., 30080. Phone: (770) 436-6171. Fax: (770) 436-0100.E-mail: pattycool100@hotmail.com Web Site:www.radiolaquebuena.com Licensee: GA-MEX Broadcasting Inc. (acq 7-29-93; $1.1 million; 8-23-93). Population served: 250,000 Format: Rgnl Mexican. Target aud: 12 plus; Sp. ◆Javier Macias, CEO, pres; Patty Perez, gen mgr.

WSTR(FM)— May 1966: 94.1 mhz; 100 kw. Ant 1,018 ft TL: N33 45 33 W84 20 05. Hrs open: Penthouse, 3350 Peachtree Rd., Suite 1800, Atlanta, 30326. Phone: (404) 261-2970. Fax: (404) 365-9026.E-mail: star94frontdesk@star94.com Web Site:www.star94.com Licensee: Jefferson Pilot Communications Co. (group owner; acq 3-1-74). Population served: 750,000 Format: CHR. Target aud: 18-49; general. ◆Don Benson, pres; Mark Kanov, gen mgr; Dan Bowen, progmg dir.

Soperton

WKTM(FM)— Nov 23, 1982: 106.1 mhz; 6 kw. 298 ft TL: N32 25 31 W82 33 26. Stereo. Hrs open: 24 2278 Wortham Ln., Grovetown, 30813. Phone: (706) 309-9610.E-mail: ctbarinowski@comcast.net Web Site:www.gnnradio.org Licensee: Barinowski Investment Co. Group owner: Good News Network (acq 1-21-99). Population served: 150,000 Format: Sp. ◆Clarence Barinowski, gen mgr.

Sparta

*WJDS(FM)—Not on air, target date: unknown: 88.7 mhz; 2 kw vert. 134 ft TL: N33 18 48 W83 00 05. Hrs open: 2278 Wortham Ln, Grovetown, 30813. Phone: (706) 309-9610.E-mail: ctbarinowski@comcast.net Web Site:www.gnnradio.org Licensee: Augusta Radio Fellowship Institute Inc. Population served: 20,000 Format: Sp. ◆Clarence Barinowski, gen mgr.

Springfield

WEAS-FM—Licensed to Springfield. See Savannah

Statenville

WHLJ(FM)— 1999: 97.5 mhz; 6 kw. Ant 328 ft TL: N30 46 47 W82 52 43. Hrs open: LaTaurus Productions Inc., Box 1305, Valdosta, 31605. Phone: (229) 242-9997. Fax: (229) 249-9765.E-mail: WHLJ@BELLSOUTH.NET Licensee: LaTaurus Productions Inc. Format: Rhythm and blues, hip-hop, urban contemp. ◆Warren Lee, gen mgr.

Statesboro

WPMX(FM)— 1995: 102.9 mhz; 25 kw. Ant 328 ft TL: N32 26 43 W81 58 07. Hrs open: 24 Box 958, 30459. Phone: (912) 764-6000. Fax: (912) 764-8827.E-mail: radiocenter@frontiernet.net Licensee: Georgia Eagle Broadcasting Inc. (group owner; acq 1-12-2007; grpsl). Natl. Network: ABC, . Rgnl. Network: Ga. News Net. Ga. News Net. Format: Adult contemp. Target aud: General. ◆Buddy Horne, gen mgr, progmg mgr.

WPTB(AM)— Apr 4, 1976: 850 khz; 1 kw-U, DA-N. TL: N32 28 02 W81 50 07. Hrs open: 24 Box 958, 30458. Phone: (912) 764-6621. Fax: (912) 764-6622.E-mail: espn850@frontiernet.net Web Site:www.radiostatesboro.com Licensee: Georgia Eagle Broadcasting Inc. Group owner: Communications Capital Managers LLC (acq 5-21-2007; grpsl). Population served: 17,000 Natl. Network: ESPN Radio, . Natl. Rep: Dora-Clayton,. Rgnl rep: Regional Reps Richard Helmick. Format: Sports. News staff: one; News: 7 hrs wkly. Target aud: General. Spec prog: Gospel 6 hrs wkly. ◆Nate Hirsch, gen mgr; Bill Kent, stn mgr, progmg dir.

*WSLT(FM)—Not on air, target date: unknown: 88.5 mhz; 4.8 kw. Ant 249 ft TL: N32 37 10 W81 40 25. Hrs open: 265 Cantebury St., Rincon, 31326. Phone: (912) 826-3833. Licensee: Salt and Light Communications Inc. ◆Linda Hand, CEO & pres.

*WVGS(FM)— 1975: 91.9 mhz; 1 kw. 161 ft TL: N32 25 32 W81 46 58. Stereo. Hrs open: 24 Georgia Southern University, Box 8016, 30460. Phone: (912) 681-0877. Fax: (912) 486-7113. Fax: (912) 681-0822.E-mail: wvgs@georgiasouthern.edu Web Site:www.919thebuzz.com Licensee: Georgia Southern University Population served: 27,000 Format: Alternative. Target aud: 18-25; college kids. ◆Melonie Stone, gen mgr & opns mgr.

WWNS(AM)— Dec 1, 1946: 1240 khz; 1 kw-U. TL: N32 27 21 W81 46 27. Hrs open: 24 Box 958, 30459. Secondary address: 561 E. Olliff St. 30458. Phone: (912) 764-5446. Fax: (912) 764-8827.E-mail: spots@georgiaeagleradio.com Licensee: Georgia Eagle Broadcasting Inc. Group owner: Communications Capital Managers LLC (acq 5-21-2007; grpsl). Population served: 50,000 Natl. Network: USA, . Rgnl rep: Rgnl Reps Richard Helnick. Format: News/talk, sports. News staff: one; News: 20 hrs wkly. Target aud: 25-death. ◆Jeff Anderson, gen mgr; Buddy Horne, opns dir, progmg dir.

Summerville

WGTA(AM)— Aug 27, 1950: Stn currently dark. 950 khz; 5 kw-D, 140 w-N. TL: N34 27 53 W85 21 12. Hrs open: 6 AM-7 PM 339 Hwy. 100, 30747. Phone: (770) 436-6171. Fax: (770) 436-0100. Licensee: Azteca Communications Inc. (acq 1-24-2001). Population served: 25,043 Rgnl. Network: Ga. Net. Law Office of Dan J. Alpert. ◆Javier Macias, pres; Patty Perez, gen mgr.

WZQZ(AM)—(Trion, Apr 1, 1985: 1180 khz; 5 kw-D. TL: N34 28 22 W85 19 31. Hrs open: 6am-10pm Box 735, 30747. Secondary address: 4689 US Hwy. 27 30747. Phone: (706) 857-5555. Fax: (706) 857-2006.E-mail: wzqz@alltel.net Licensee: HS Productions Inc. Group owner: Good News Network. (acq 5-12-2008; $65,000). Natl. Network: USA, CNN Radio, . Ga. News Net. Format: Talk shows. Target aud: All ages; Northwest Georgia. ◆Lebron Jimmy Charles Holbrook Jr., pres; Terry Adams, gen mgr & opns dir.

Swainsboro

WEDB(FM)—(East Dublin, Dec 18, 1966: 98.1 mhz; 9.6 kw. Ant 525 ft TL: N32 32 55 W82 38 49. Stereo. Hrs open: 2 Radio Loop, 30401. Phone: (478) 237-1590. Fax: (478) 237-3559. Licensee: RadioJones LLC. Population served: 110,000 Format: Contemp hit. News staff: one; News: 10 hrs wkly. Target aud: 18-50. ◆John Wagner, opns mgr; Jolly Martin, gen sls mgr; Bobby Duncan, progmg dir.

WJAT(AM)— Jan 1, 1950: 800 khz; 1 kw-D, 500 w-N. TL: N32 35 08 W82 21 42. Hrs open: 24 2 Radio Loop, 30401. Phone: (478) 237-1590. Fax: (478) 237-3559. Licensee: RadioJones LLC. (group owner; (acq 4-2-2004; grpsl). Population served: 75,000 Format: News, talk, sports. News staff: one; News: 10 hrs wkly. Target aud: 25-64. Spec prog: Farm 5 hrs wkly; high school sports. ◆Dennis Jones, gen mgr; Jolly Martin, sls dir, gen sls mgr; John Wagner, progmg dir, news dir; Marty Foglia, engrg dir.

WXRS(AM)— Mar 10, 1978: 1590 khz; 2.5 kw-D, 25 w-N. TL: N32 33 25 W82 20 29. Hrs open: 24 2 Radio Loop, 30401. Phone: (478) 237-1590. Fax: (478) 237-3559. Web Site:www.radiojones.com Licensee: RadioJones LLC. (group owner; (acq 4-2-2004; grpsl). Population served: 40,000 Format: Black gospel. News staff: one; News: 56 hrs wkly. Target aud: 25-64. ◆Earl Welch, progmg dir, engr; John Wagner, opns mgr & news dir.

WXRS-FM—Aug 2, 1982: 100.5 mhz; 3 kw. 300 ft TL: N32 34 52 W82 23 14. Stereo. Hrs open: 24 Prog sep from AM 2 Radio Loop, 30401. Phone: (478) 237-1590. Fax: (478) 237-3559. Population served: 75,000 Format: Contemp country. News staff: one; News: 10 hrs wkly. Target aud: 25 plus. ◆John Wagner, opns mgr, progmg dir; Jolly Martin, gen sls mgr; Marty Foglia, chief of engrg.

Sylvania

WSYL(AM)— Dec 1, 1955: 1490 khz; 1 kw-U. TL: N32 43 51 W81 37 04. Hrs open: 24 Box 519, 1526 Savannah Hwy., 30467. Phone: (912) 564-7461. Fax: (912) 564-7462.E-mail: info@wsyl.com Licensee: Georgia Eagle Broadcasting Inc. Group owner: Communications Capital Managers LLC (acq 5-21-2007; grpsl). Rgnl. Network: Ga. Net., Tobocco. Natl. Rep: Rgnl Reps,. Ga. News Net. Spec prog: Farm 5 hrs wkly. ◆Nathan Hirsch, gen mgr; David Hartley, traf mgr, edit mgr; Mary Lou Clontz, relg ed.

WZBX(FM)— Sept 6, 1991: 106.5 mhz; 6 kw. Ant 328 ft TL: N32 43 53 W81 37 03. Hrs open: Box 519, 1526 Savannah Hwy.30467 Phone: (912) 564-7461. Fax: (912) 564-7462.E-mail: info@wzbx.com Population served: 57,000 Format: Rock classics. ◆Nate Hirsch, stn mgr; Scott Kidd, farm dir.

Sylvester

*WHKV(FM)— Jan 27, 1993: 106.1 mhz; 6 kw. Ant 328 ft TL: N31 30 15 W83 55 46. Hrs open: 5700 West Oaks Blvd., Rocklin, CA, 95765. Phone: (916) 251-1600. Fax: (916) 251-1650. Web Site:www.klove.com Licensee: Educational Media Foundation. (group owner; (acq 4-30-2007; $615,000 with WFFM(FM) Ashburn). Natl. Network: K-Love, . Format: Contemp Christian. ◆Mike Novak, sr VP.

WNUQ(FM)— Aug 1, 1999: 102.1 mhz; 6 kw. Ant 276 ft TL: N31 31 42 W83 50 29. Hrs open: 1104 W. Broad Ave., Albany, 31707. Phone: (229) 888-5000. Fax: (229) 888-5960.E-mail: info18@cumulus.com Web Site:www.v102albany.com Licensee: Cumulus Licensing Corp. Group owner: Cumulus Media Inc. (acq 3-12-2001; $550,000). Natl. Rep: Katz Radio,. Format: Blues, urban ceontemp. ◆Gregory Kamishlian, gen mgr, mktg mgr; Roshon Vance, progmg dir.

Talking Rock

WNSY(FM)— 1999: 100.1 mhz; 7 kw. Ant 617 ft TL: N34 37 50 W84 29 29. Hrs open: Rebroadcasts WLKQ-FM Buford 100%. 3235 Satellite Blvd., Suite 230, Duluth, 30096. Phone: (770) 623-8772. Fax: (770) 623-4722. Web Site:www.laraza1023.com Licensee: Davis Broadcasting of Atlanta L.L.C. (acq 1-17-2007; $3.8 million with WCHK(AM) Canton). Format: Rgnl Mexican. ◆Brian Barber, gen mgr.

Tallapoosa

*WEYY(FM)—Not on air, target date: unknown: 88.7 mhz; 125 w. Ant 200 ft TL: N33 44 33 W85 17 11. Hrs open: 150 Ross Rd., Heflin, AL, 36264. Phone: (706) 965-2355. Licensee: Old Time Gospel Ministries. ◆Robert Jarrell, pres.

WKNG(AM)— Sept 1, 1977: 1060 khz; 11 kw-D, 5 kw-CH. TL: N33 44 06 W85 15 08. Hrs open: Box 626, 30176. Secondary address: Hwy. 78, Golf Course Rd. 30176. Phone: (770) 574-1060. Fax: (770) 574-1062.E-mail: info@wkng.com Web Site:www.wkng.com Licensee: WKNG LLC. Population served: 250,000 Natl. Network: ABC, . Rgnl. Network: Ga. Net. Ga. News Net. Format: Classic country. Target aud: 25-54. ◆Steven L. Gradick, pres & gen mgr.

Tallulah Falls

*WVNG(FM)—Not on air, target date: unknown: 91.7 mhz; 65 w. Ant 1,246 ft TL: N34 50 52 W83 30 01. Hrs open: 179 Cross Creek Dr., Toccoa, 30577. Phone: (706) 491-4457. Licensee: Toccoa Foundation Inc. ◆Douglas M. Sutton, pres.

Tennille

WJFL(FM)— Oct 14, 1993: 101.9 mhz; 6 kw. 328 ft TL: N32 54 49 W82 53 06. Hrs open: Box 36, 31089. Phone: (478) 553-1019. Fax: (478) 553-1123.E-mail: wjfl@wjfl.com Web Site:www.wjfl.com Licensee: Fall Line Media Inc. (group owner; (acq 1996; $225,000). Format: Today's hits & yesterdays favorites. ◆Michael Cowan, gen mgr.

The Rock

*WKEU-FM— 2000: 88.9 mhz; 5 kw. Ant 764 ft TL: N32 59 11 W84 21 56. Hrs open: Box 997, Griffin, 30224. Secondary address: 1000 Memorial Dr., Griffin 30224. Phone: (770) 227-5507. Fax: (770) 229-2291.E-mail: wkeu@aol.com Web Site:www.wkeuradio.com Licensee: Georgia Public Radio Inc. Format: Classic rock. ◆William Taylor, Jr., pres; William Taylor Jr., gen mgr.

Thomaston

WTGA(AM)— Nov 1, 1962: 1590 khz; 500 w-D, 25 w-N. TL: N32 53 45 W84 18 10. Hrs open: 208 S. Center St., 30286. Secondary address: Box 550 Phone: (706) 647-7121. Fax: (706) 647-7122. Web Site:www.wtga.com Licensee: Radio Georgia Inc. (acq 1972). Population served: 10,024 Format: Soft hits. Spec prog: Black 4 hrs wkly. ◆David L. Piper, pres, gen mgr, progmg dir; Bill Bailey, gen sls mgr; Robert Lyons, chief of engrg.

WTGA-FM— Nov 15, 1982: 101.1 mhz; 6 kw. 308 ft TL: N32 51 49 W84 25 10. Hrs open: Prog sep from AM 208 S. Center St., 30286. Secondary address: Box 550 30286. Phone: (706) 647-7121. Fax: (706) 647-7122. Web Site:www.wtga.com Population served: 15,000 Format: Soft hits.

Thomasville

*WAYT(FM)— 2003: 88.1 mhz; 35 kw. Ant 1,332 ft TL: N30 40 06 W83 58 10. Hrs open: Box 4188, Tallahassee, FL, 32315. Phone: (850) 422-1929. Fax: (850) 297-1888.E-mail: wayt@wayfm.com Web Site:wayt.wayfm.com Licensee: WAY-FM Media Group Inc. (group owner; acq 10-24-02). Format: Christian. ◆Steve Young, stn mgr.

*WFSL(FM)— Mar 1, 2005: 90.7 mhz; 250 w. Ant 154 ft TL: N30 50 12 W83 58 57. Hrs open: Florida State University, FSU Broadcasting Ctr., 1600 Red Barber Plaza, Tallahassee, FL, 32310-6068. Phone: (850) 487-3086. Fax: (850) 487-3293.E-mail: wfsufm@wfsu.org Web Site:www.wfsu.org Licensee: Florida State University Board of Trustees. Format: Class. ◆Patrick Keating, gen mgr; Caroline Austin, stn mgr.

WHGH(AM)— Dec 15, 1987: 840 khz; 10 kw-D. TL: N30 47 54 W83 56 22. Hrs open: Box 2218, 31799. Secondary address: 221 Pallbearer Rd.31792. Phone: (229) 228-4124. Fax: (229) 225-9508.E-mail: WHGH@ROSE.NET Licensee: H.G.H. Investment Corp. Format: Hip hop, gospel. Target aud: 12 plus; Blacks. ◆Moses Gross, pres, gen mgr & stn mgr.

WPAX(AM)— Dec 27, 1922: 1240 khz; 1 kw-U. TL: N30 50 10 W83 59 19. Stereo. Hrs open: 24 Box 129, 31799. Secondary address: 117 Remington Ave. 31799. Phone: (229) 226-1240. Fax: (229) 226-1361.E-mail: lenrob@rose.net Web Site:www.wpaxradio.com Licensee: LenRob Inc. (acq 10-85). Population served: 41,500 Natl. Network: CBS, . Rgnl. Network: Ga. Net., Tobacco. Natl. Rep: Rgnl Reps,. Ga. News Net. Miller & Fields, P.C. Format: Music of your Life. News staff: one; News: 20 hrs wkly. Target aud: 25 plus; mature with disposable income. ◆Len Robinson, pres & gen mgr.

WSTT(AM)— 1947: 730 khz; 5 kw-D, 27 w-N. TL: N30 48 50 W84 00 48. Hrs open: 5:30 AM-9 PM 2194 Hwy. 319 S., 31792. Phone: (229) 377-2337. Fax: (229) 377-0023.E-mail: sgulfbroadcasting@att.net Licensee: Marion R. Williams. (acq 7-26-99; $300,000). Population served: 500,000 Natl. Network: CBS, . Matthew McCormick. Format: Gospel. Target aud: 25-54; general. ◆Marion Williams, VP & gen mgr.

WTLY(FM)—Licensed to Thomasville. See Tallahassee FL

Thomson

*WQAI(FM)—Not on air, target date: unknown: 89.5 mhz; 1 w horiz, 34 kw vert. Ant 590 ft TL: N33 44 32 W82 31 17. Hrs open: Rebroadcasts KLRD(FM) Yucaipa, CA 100%. 5700 West Oaks Blvd., Rocklin, CA, 95765. Phone: (916) 251-1600. Fax: (916) 251-1650. Web Site:www.air1.com Licensee: Educational Media Foundation. (acq 3-23-2007; grpsl). Natl. Network: Air 1, . Format: Alternative rock, Christian music, div. ◆Mike Novak, pres.

WTHO-FM— Feb 22, 1971: 101.7 mhz; 3 kw. 300 ft TL: N33 28 21 W82 30 00. Stereo. Hrs open: Box 900, 788 Cedar Rock Rd. N.W., 30824. Phone: (706) 595-5122. Fax: (706) 595-3021.E-mail: wtho@classicsouth.net Licensee: Camellia City Communications Inc. (acq 2-5-93; $110,000 with co-located AM; 3-1-93). Population served: 30,000 Rgnl. Network: Ga. Net. Natl. Rep: Rgnl Reps,. Ga. News Net. Covington & Burling. Format: C&W. Target aud: 25-54. Spec prog: Farm 3 hrs, gospel one hr, relg 6 hrs wkly. ◆Lisa Kitchens, news dir; Mike Wall, gen mgr, opns dir, gen sls mgr, adv mgr, progmg dir, mus dir, news dir & chief of engrg; Mary Thomaston, traf mgr.

WTWA(AM)— Jan 10, 1948: 1240 khz; 1 kw-U. TL: N33 28 20 W82 31 02. Hrs open: 19 Prog sep from FM Box 900, 788 Cedar Rock Rd., 30824. Phone: (706) 595-1561. Fax: (706) 595-3021.E-mail: wtwa@classicsouth.net Licensee: Camellia City Communications Inc. Population served: 7,500 Format: Adult Contemporary. Target aud: 35 plus.

Tifton

*WABR(FM)— December 1973: 91.1 mhz; 30 kw. Ant 249 ft TL: N31 29 30 W83 31 49. Stereo. Hrs open: Rebroadcasts WJSP-FM Warm Springs 100%. 260 14th St. N.W., Atlanta, 30318-5360. Phone: (404) 685-4788. Fax: (404) 685-2684.E-mail: ask@gpb.org Web Site:www.gpb.org Licensee: Georgia Public Telecommunications Commission. Population served: 10,000 Natl. Network: NPR, . Georgia Public Radio Wire Svc: AP Format: News, class. News staff: 6; News: 40 hrs wkly. ◆Nancy Hall, CEO; Bonnie Bean, CFO; Bob Houghton, gen mgr; Tom Barclay, opns mgr; Rob Maynard, progmg dir; Susanna Capelouto, news dir.

WKZZ(FM)— 2000: 92.5 mhz; 20.5 kw. Ant 361 ft TL: N31 31 40 W83 20 01. Hrs open: 1931 GA Hwy. 32 E., Douglas, 31533. Phone: (912) 389-0995. Fax: (912) 383-8552.E-mail: traffic@charter.net Licensee: Broadcast South LLC. Group owner: Black Crow Media Group LLC (acq 11-15-2006; grpsl). Population served: 50,000 McCampbell & Young. Format: Adult contemp. ◆John Higgs, CEO & gen mgr.

WOBB(FM)—Licensed to Tifton. See Albany

*WPLH(FM)— January 1988: 103.1 mhz; 29 w. 177 ft TL: N31 28 51 W83 31 38. Stereo. Hrs open: Box 36, Abraham Baldwin Agricultural College, 31793. Secondary address: 2802 Moore Hwy 31793. Phone: (229) 391-4977. Phone: (229) 391-4957. Fax: (229) 386-7158.E-mail: wplh@abac.edu Licensee: Abraham Baldwin Agriculture College. (acq 4-1-88). Rgnl. Network: Peach State Public Radio. Georgia Public Radio Format: Alternative. ◆Eric Cash, gen mgr.

WTIF(AM)— 1957: 1340 khz; 1 kw-U. TL: N31 28 16 W83 29 12. Hrs open: 24 Box 968, 31793. Secondary address: 104 E. 7th St. 31794. Phone: (229) 382-1340. Fax: (229) 386-8658. Licensee: Three Trees Communications Inc. (group owner; (acq 6-28-2004); grpsl). Population served: 12,179 Natl. Network: CBS, . Rgnl. Network: Ga. Net. Ga. News Net. Format: Country. News staff: one; News: 15 hrs wkly. Target aud: 18 plus. Spec prog: Farm 5 hrs wkly. ◆James Andrew Howard, pres; Ron Yontz, gen mgr; Andy Reeves, stn mgr.

WVKV(FM)—(Nashville, Nov 26, 1986: 95.3 mhz; 29 kw. Ant 522 ft TL: N31 10 18 W83 21 57. Stereo. Hrs open: 24 2351 Sunset Blvd., Suite 170-218, Rocklin, CA, 95765. Phone: (916) 251-1600. Fax: (916) 251-1650. Web Site:www.klove.com Licensee: Educational Media Foundation. (acq 5-10-2007; $1.3 million). Natl. Network: K-Love, . Format: Contemp Christian.

Tignall

*WEZG(FM)—Not on air, target date: unknown: 90.3 mhz; 5 kw vert. Ant 269 ft TL: N33 40 33 W82 37 15.3. Hrs open: 179 Cross Creek Dr., Toccoa, 30577. Phone: (706) 491-4457. Licensee: Toccoa Foundation Inc. ◆Douglas M. Sutton Jr., VP.

Toccoa

WLET(AM)— May 1, 1941: 1420 khz; 5 kw-D. TL: N34 35 23 W85 19 11. Hrs open: 24 Box 780, TFC Radio Network, Toccoa Falls, 30598. Secondary address: 292 Old Clarkesville Hwy. 30577. Phone: (706) 282-6030. Phone: (800) 251-8326. Fax: (706) 282-6090.E-mail: radio@tfc.edu Licensee: Toccoa Falls College. (acq 11-3-99). Population served: 150,000 Format: Gospel. News staff: one; News: 10 hrs wkly. Target aud: 35 plus; Stephens county residents seeking news & community info. Spec prog: Black, gospel, relg. ◆David Cornelius, gen mgr.

WNEG(AM)— Apr 21, 1956: 630 khz; 500 w-D, 44 w-N. TL: N34 34 15 W83 19 35. Hrs open: 24 Box 1159, 30577-0907. Phone: (706) 886-2191. Fax: (706) 282-0189.E-mail: hobbs@gacaradio.com Web Site:www.wnegradio.com Licensee: Georgia-Carolina Radiocasting Co. LLC. Group owner: Georgia-Carolina Radiocasting Companies (acq 7-25-2002; grpsl). Population served: 297,285. Natl. Network: CBS Radio, . Rgnl. Network: Ga. Net. Ga. News Net. Dan J. Alpert. Format: MOR, local news. News staff: one; News: 18 hrs wkly. Target aud: General; adult working class. ◆Douglas M. Sutton Jr., pres; Phil Hobbs, VP, gen mgr; Connie Gaines, opns mgr; M.J. Kneiser, news dir; Tim Stephens, chief of engrg.

WNGC(FM)— November 1947: 106.1 mhz; 100 kw. 1,132 ft TL: N34 43 46 W83 29 29. Stereo. Hrs open: 24 850 Bobbin Mill Rd., Athens, 30606. Phone: (706) 549-1340. Phone: (706) 549-6222. Fax: (706) 546-0441.E-mail: wngc@negia.net Web Site:www.1061wngc.com Licensee: Cox Radio Inc. Group owner: Southern Broadcasting Companies Inc. (acq 8-1-2008; grpsl). Population served: 850000 Format: Country. News staff: one; News: 10 hrs wkly. Target aud: 25-54; adults with disposable income. ◆Robert F. Neil, pres; Scott Smith, opns mgr; Kevin Steele, progmg dir.

Toccoa Falls

*WRAF-FM— Sept 4, 1980: 90.9 mhz; 100 kw. 564 ft TL: N34 35 57 W83 21 55. Stereo. Hrs open: 24 Box 780, TFC Radio Network, 30598. Secondary address: 292 Old Clarksville Hwy., Toccoa 30577. Phone: (800) 251-8326. Phone: (706) 282-6030. Fax: (706) 282-6090.E-mail: radio@tfc.edu Web Site:www.myfavoritestation.net Licensee: Toccoa Falls College. Population served: 500,000 Natl. Network: USA, . Wiley, Rein & Fielding. Format: Relg, MOR. Target aud: General; families. ◆David Cornelius, gen mgr & stn mgr.

*WTXR(FM)— September 1996: 89.7 mhz; 100 w. -190 ft Stereo. Hrs open: 24 Box 780, TFC Radio Network, 30598. Secondary address: 292 Old Clarkesville Hwy., Toccoa 30577. Phone: (706) 282-6030. Phone: (800) 251-8326. Fax: (706) 282-6090.E-mail: radio@tfc.edu Web Site:www.wtxr.com Licensee: Toccoa Falls College. Population served: 25,000 Format: Christian. Target aud: 18-35; college students, young adults. ◆David Cornelius, gen mgr.

Toomsboro

*WZZG(FM)— 2009: 91.9 mhz; 2.3 kw. Ant 479 ft TL: N33 04 37.78 W83 08 48.25. Hrs open: 2278 Wortham Ln., Grovetown, 30813-5103. Phone: (706) 309-9610. Fax: (706) 309-9669. Web Site:www.gnnradio.org Licensee: Augusta Radio Fellowship Institute Inc. ◆C.T. Barinowski, pres.

Trenton

WBDX(FM)— 1989: 102.7 mhz; 320 w. 1,374 ft TL: N34 51 48 W85 23 35. Stereo. Hrs open: 24 Box 9396, Chattanooga, TN, 37412. Phone: (423) 892-1200. Fax: (423) 892-1633.E-mail: mailbag@j103.com Web Site:www.j103.com Licensee: Partners for Christian Media Inc. (acq 5-7-98; $1,189,395). Format: Adult contemp, Christian. Target aud: 18-54. ◆Bob Lubell, CEO, pres, gen mgr; David Skinner, CFO; Debbie Lubell, natl sls mgr; Richard Carlisle, rgnl sls mgr.

WKWN(AM)— Apr 4, 1982: 1420 khz; 2.5 w-D, 112 w-N. TL: N34 51 43 W85 29 59. Hrs open: 24 Box 829, 30752. Secondary address: 12544 N. Main St. 30752. Phone: (706) 657-7594. Fax: (706) 657-6767. Licensee: Dade County Broadcasting Inc. (acq 11-20-97; $63,000). Rgnl. Network: Ga. Net. Ga. News Net. Format: News/talk radio. Target aud: 25-54; locals. ◆Evan Stone, CEO, chmn, pres, gen mgr & stn mgr.

Trion

WATG(FM)— January 1997: 95.7 mhz; 6 kw. Ant 699 ft TL: N34 28 10 W85 17 48. Hrs open: 24 Box 200, Summerville, 30747. Secondary address: 10143 Commerce St., Summerville 30747. Phone: (706) 857-2000. Fax: (706) 857-3652.E-mail: oldies957@aol.com Licensee: TTA Broadcasting Inc. (acq 10-19-99; up to $296,530). Natl. Network: ABC, . Natl. Rep: Rgnl Reps,. Cordon & Kelly. Format: Oldies. News: one hr wkly. Target aud: 25-54; general. ◆Randy Davis, pres; Jim Bojo, CFO, gen mgr.

WZQZ(AM)—Licensed to Trion. See Summerville

Tucker

WGUN(AM)—(Atlanta, July 1947: 1010 khz; 50 kw-D, 300 w-N. TL: N33 41 55 W84 17 23. Hrs open: 24 2901 Mountain Industrial Blvd., 30084. Phone: (770) 491-1010. Fax: (770) 491-3019.E-mail: WGUNSTUDIO@BELLSOUTH.NET Licensee: Dee Rivers Group. Population served: 3,095,278 Format: relg talk, info & inspiration. News: one hr wkly. Target aud: 25-54; working class. ◆Georgia Salva, CEO; Darrell Vick, gen mgr; Erwin Hill, opns mgr.

Tybee Island

WTYB(FM)— Oct 1, 1977: 103.9 mhz; 50 kw. Ant 344 ft TL: N32 03 33 W81 00 57. Hrs open: 214 Television Cir., Savannah, 31406. Phone: (912) 961-9000. Fax: (912) 961-7070.E-mail: info@diane.hubelcumulus.com Web Site:www.cumulus.com Licensee: Cumulus Licensing Corp. Group owner: Cumulus Media Inc. (acq 3-26-98; grpsl). Format: Classic soul & today's rhythm and blues. ◆Diane Hubel, gen mgr.

Unadilla

WNNG-FM— June 1995: 99.9 mhz; 6 kw. Ant 328 ft TL: N32 18 29 W83 46 30. Stereo. Hrs open: 24 1350 Radio Loop Rd., Warner

Robins, 31088. Phone: (478) 923-3416.E-mail: information @houstoncountyradio.com Web Site:www.houstoncountyradio.com Licensee: Georgia Eagle Broadcasting Inc (acq 10-8-2007; $350,000). Format: Adult contemp.

Valdosta

WAAC(FM)— 1968: 92.9 mhz; 100 kw. Ant 502 ft TL: N30 48 13 W83 21 20. Stereo. Hrs open: Prog sep from AM Box 1207, 31603. Secondary address: 2973 Hwy. 84 W. 31601. Phone: (229) 242-4513. Fax: (229) 247-7676.E-mail: mail@waacradio.com Web Site:www.waacradio.com Population served: 200,000 Natl. Network: ABC, . Anthony Lepore. Format: Country. Target aud: 25-54. ♦Robert Whitt, opns mgr & progmg dir.

WAFT(FM)— Nov 25, 1971: 101.1 mhz; 100 kw. 558 ft TL: N30 51 50 W83 23 39. Stereo. Hrs open: 24 215 Waft Hill Ln., 31602. Phone: (229) 244-5180. Fax: (229) 242-8808.E-mail: mail@waft.org Web Site:www.waft.org Licensee: Christian Radio Fellowship Inc. Population served: 700,000 Format: Relg. News: 3 hrs wkly. Target aud: General. ♦Bill Tidwell, pres & gen mgr.

WGOV(AM)— 1939: 950 khz; 3.5 kw-D, 63 w-N. TL: N30 48 13 W83 21 20. Hrs open: 24 Box 1207, 31603. Secondary address: 2973 Hwy. 84 W. 31601. Phone: (229) 244-9590. Fax: (229) 247-7676.E-mail: wgovradio@bellsouth.net Web Site:www.wgovradio.com Licensee: WGOV Inc. Group owner: Dee Rivers Group Population served: 104,500 Natl. Rep: Rgnl Reps,. Format: Rhythm and blues, relg. News staff: one; News: 3 hrs wkly. Target aud: 18-45; Black. Spec prog: Gospel 14 hrs, oldies 10 hrs wkly. ♦Lamar Freeman, opns mgr, progmg dir; Loretta Grecco, gen sls mgr; Jammie Brooks, mus dir.

WJEM(AM)— August 1955: 1150 khz; 5 kw-D, 101 w-N, DA-2. TL: N30 50 49 W83 14 14. Hrs open: Box 961808, Riverdale, 30296. Phone: (229) 241-9797. Licensee: WJEM Inc. (acq 2-18-94; $230,000; 3-21-94). Format: Gospel.

WLYX(FM)— June 1985: 96.7 mhz; 50 kw. Ant 328 ft TL: N30 48 13 W83 21 20. Stereo. Hrs open: 24 Box 1207, 31603. Secondary address: 2973 Hwy. 84 W. 31601. Phone: (229) 242-4513. Fax: (229) 247-7676.E-mail: info@govradio.com Web Site:www.wgovradio.com Licensee: W.G.O.V. Inc. (acq 4-19-2006; $2 million). Format: Urban. Target aud: 18-49. ♦Lamar Freeman, gen mgr; Joseph Jones, opns mgr, progmg dir; Loretta Grecco, gen sls mgr.

WQPW(FM)— September 1977: 95.7 mhz; 35.9 kw. 606 ft TL: N30 50 11 W83 17 56. Stereo. Hrs open: 24 1711 Ellis Dr., 31601. Phone: (229) 244-8642. Fax: (229) 242-7620.E-mail: info@957themix.com Web Site:www.957themix.com Licensee: RTG Radio LLC. Group owner: Black Crow Media Group LLC (acq 11-9-2001; grpsl). Population served: 75,000 Borsari & Paxson. Format: Adult contemp. News staff: 14. Target aud: 18-44. ♦Scott James, gen mgr.

WRFV(AM)— Nov 3, 1951: Stn currently dark. 910 khz; 5 kw-U, DA-N. TL: N30 52 21 W83 20 36. (CP: COL Wellborn, FL. 35 kw-D, 5 kw-N, DA-2. TL: N30 12 59 W82 51 39). Hrs open: 3765 N. John Young Pkwy., Orlando, 32804. Phone: (407) 291-1395. Licensee: Rama Communications Inc. (group owner; (acq 2-28-2002; $255,000). Population served: 32,303 ♦Sabeta Persaud, pres.

***WVDA(FM)**— 2006: 88.5 mhz; 18.5 kw vert. Ant 216 ft TL: N30 47 50 W83 01 01. Hrs open:
Rebroadcasts KLRD(FM) Yucaipa, CA 100%.
5700 West Oaks Blvd., Rocklin, CA, 95765. Phone: (916) 251-1600. Fax: (916) 251-1650. Web Site:www.air1.com Licensee: Educational Media Foundation. (acq 5-10-2007; $350,000). Natl. Network: Air 1, . Format: Alternative rock, div. ♦Mike Novak, sr VP.

WVLD(AM)— Sept 3, 1959: 1450 khz; 1 kw-U. TL: N30 50 11 W83 17 56. Hrs open: 24 1711 Ellis Dr., 31601. Phone: (229) 244-8642. Fax: (229) 242-7620. Licensee: RTG Media. Group owner: Black Crow Media Group LLC (acq 11-9-2001; grpsl). Population served: 42,500 Natl. Network: CBS, . Borsari & Paxson. Format: Sports. News: 10 hrs wkly. Target aud: 35 plus. Spec prog: Gospel 2 hrs wkly. ♦Robert Ganzack, pres & gen mgr.

***WVVS(FM)**— July 26, 1971: 90.9 mhz; 5.3 kw. 68 ft TL: N30 50 50 W83 17 26. Stereo. Hrs open: Valdosta State Univ., 1500 N. Patterson, 31698. Phone: (229) 259-2015. Web Site:www.valdosta.edu/wvvs/ Licensee: Valdosta State University. Population served: 100,000 Format: Alternative & urban. Target aud: 18-25; students of VSU, population at large. ♦Michael Taylor, gen mgr.

***WWET(FM)**— December 1989: 91.7 mhz; 430 w vert. Ant 85 ft TL: N30 49 35 W83 16 40. Stereo. Hrs open: 24
Rebroadcasts WJSP-FM Warm Springs 100%.
260 14th St. N.W., Atlanta, 30318-5360. Phone: (404) 685-2690. Fax: (404) 685-2684.E-mail: ask@gpb.org Web Site:www.gpb.org Licensee: Georgia Public Telecommunications Commission. Natl. Network: NPR, PRI, . Wire Svc: AP Format: Class, news. News staff: 10; News: 40 hrs wkly. Target aud: Adults: 35 plus. Spec prog: Jazz 16 hrs. ♦Nancy G. Hall, CEO; Bonnie Bean, CFO; Bob Houghton, gen mgr; Tom Barclay, opns mgr; Rob Maynard, progmg dir; Susanna Capelouto, news dir.

WWRQ-FM— Feb 1, 1992: 107.9 mhz; 14 kw. Ant 315 ft TL: N30 50 11 W83 17 56. (CP: 50 kw, ant 449 ft. TL: N31 03 46 W83 04 21). Hrs open: 1711 Ellis Dr., 31601. Phone: (229) 244-8642. Fax: (229) 247-7620.E-mail: cjohnson@blackcrowfm.com Licensee: RTG Radio LLC. Group owner: Black Crow Media Group LLC (acq 11-9-2001; grpsl). Miller & Miller. Format: Classic rock, AOR. Target aud: 25-49; upscale suburban couples. ♦Scott James, gen mgr & progmg dir.

Vidalia

WBBT(AM)—See Lyons

WGPH(FM)—Licensed to Vidalia. See Augusta

WLYU(FM)—See Lyons

WTCQ(FM)— Mar 5, 1969: 97.7 mhz; 6 kw. 300 ft TL: N32 13 12 W82 26 13. Stereo. Hrs open: Prog sep from AM Box 900, 30475. Secondary address: 1501 Mt. Vernon Rd. 30474. Phone: (912) 537-9202. Fax: (912) 537-4477. Natl. Rep: Rgnl Reps,. Format: Adult contemp. Target aud: 18-34. ♦Zack Fowler, gen mgr; Marvin McIntyre, rgnl sls mgr; Joyce Foskey, traf mgr.

WVOP(AM)— Dec 2, 1946: 970 khz; 5 kw-U. TL: N32 13 12 W82 26 13. Stereo. Hrs open: 24 Box 900, 30475. Secondary address: 1501 Mt. Vernon Rd. 30474. Phone: (912) 537-9202. Fax: (912) 537-4477.E-mail: zfowler@vidaliacommunications.com Licensee: Vidalia Communications Corp. (group owner) Population served: 25,000 Rgnl. Network: Ga. Net. Natl. Rep: Rgnl Reps,. Ga. News Net. Fletcher, Heald & Hildreth. Format: Oldies, news, sports. News staff: one; News: 18 hrs wkly. Target aud: 25-54. Spec prog: Pub affrs 2 hrs, relg 8 hrs wkly. ♦John Ladson, pres; Zack Fowler, stn mgr; Jim Perry, opns mgr; Marvin McIntyre, gen sls mgr; Dick Boekeloo, chief of engrg; Joyce Foskey, traf mgr.

Vienna

WHHR(FM)—Not on air, target date: 12/4/2007: 92.1 mhz; 5.1 kw. Ant 348 ft TL: N32 09 16 W83 47 55. Hrs open: Box 5459, Twin Falls, ID, 83303. Phone: (208) 733-3551. Fax: (208) 734-0674. Web Site:www.edgewaterbroadcasting.com Licensee: Radio Assist Ministry Inc. (acq 8-22-2006; $150,000 for CP). ♦Clark Parrish, pres.

WKTF(AM)— Nov 17, 1979: 1550 khz; 1 kw-D, 23 w-N. TL: N32 07 44 W83 47 46. Hrs open: 24 12165 Ocean Dr., Sparks, NV, 89441. Phone: (229) 268-1550. Licensee: LEN Radio Broadcasting of Vienna, Georgia LLC. (acq 5-17-2005; $230,000). Population served: 30000 Rgnl. Network: Ga. Net. Format: Contemp Christian. ♦Thomas McCoy, gen mgr.

Wadley

***WZAE(FM)**—Not on air, target date: unknown: 93.3 mhz; 6 kw. Ant 298 ft TL: N32 50 55 W82 24 10. Hrs open: Box 7217, Lakeland, FL, 33080-7217. Phone: (863) 644-3464. Fax: (863) 646-5326. Licensee: Radio Training Network Inc. ♦James L. Campbell, pres.

Warm Springs

WJSP-FM—Licensed to Warm Springs. See Atlanta

Warner Robins

WNNG(AM)— Oct 13, 1954: 1350 khz; 15 kw-D, 500 w-N, DA-N. TL: N32 37 00 W83 39 00. Hrs open: 24 1350 Radio Loop, 31088. Phone: (478) 923-3416. Fax: (478) 923-3236. Web Site:www.wnngthepatriot.com Licensee: Georgia Eagle Broadcasting Inc. (acq 1-3-2007; $650,000). Population served: 200,000 Natl. Network: Talk Radio Network, Salem Radio Network, Fox News Radio, . Rgnl. Network: Ga. Net. Ga. News Net. Format: News/talk, sports. News staff: 2; News: news prgmg 12 hr/week. Target aud: 35-74; middle to upper class, working class, miltary, retired, business owners. ♦Cecil P. Staton, pres; Jeff Scott, progmg dir.

WRBV(FM)— August 1969: 101.7 mhz; 4.9 kw. 350 ft TL: N32 38 19 W83 38 33. Stereo. Hrs open: 24 7080 Industrial Hwy., Macon, 31216. Phone: (478) 781-1063. Fax: (478) 781-6711.E-mail: info@1017.com Web Site:www.1017.com Licensee: AMFM Radio Licenses LLC. Group owner: Clear Channel Communications Inc. (acq 2-1-2001; grpsl). Population served: 250,000 Natl. Network: ABC, . Format: Today's rhythm and blues & favorite old school. News: one hr wkly. Target aud: 21-54. ♦Bill Clark, gen mgr.

WZCH(FM)— September 1994: 102.5 mhz; 4 kw. Ant 328 ft TL: N32 34 20 W83 40 13. Stereo. Hrs open: 24 7080 Industrial Hwy., Macon, 31216. Phone: (478) 781-1063. Fax: (478) 781-6711. Web Site:www.peach965.com Licensee: Aloha Station Trust LLC, as Trustee Group owner: Clear Channel Communications Inc. (acq 7-30-2008). Format: Classic hits. Target aud: 25-64. ♦Bill Clark, gen mgr; John Lund, opns mgr.

Warrenton

WGAC-FM— 1998: 93.1 mhz; 4.1 kw. Ant 400 ft TL: N33 29 59 W82 37 09. Hrs open:
Simulcast with WGAC(AM) Augusta.
4051 Jimmie Dyess Pkwy., Augusta, 30909. Phone: (706) 396-7000. Fax: (706) 396-7092.E-mail: wgac@wgac.com Web Site:www.wgac.com Licensee: WCHZ License LLC. Group owner: Beasley Broadcast Group Inc. (acq 5-3-2000; $800,000 with WGUS(AM) Augusta). Format: News/talk. News staff: 5. ♦Kent Dunn, gen mgr; Kent Murphy, gen sls mgr; Harley Drew, progmg dir.

Washington

WLOV(AM)— Sept 1, 1955: 1370 khz; 1 kw-D. TL: N33 43 50 W82 43 10. Hrs open: 823 Berkshire Dr., 30673. Secondary address: 312 Old First National Bank Bldg., Elberton 30635. Phone: (706) 678-0100. Fax: (706) 678-3394. Licensee: Southern Stone Broadcasting Inc. Population served: 4,094 Rgnl. Network: Ga. Net. Ga. News Net. Format: Timeless classics. ♦Leisa McCurley, traf mgr.

Watkinsville

WPUP(FM)— June 1, 1970: 100.1 mhz; 4.3 kw. Ant 289 ft TL: N33 56 28 W83 23 55. Stereo. Hrs open: 24 850 Bobbin Mill Rd., Athens, 30606. Phone: (706) 549-6222. Fax: (706) 353-1967. Web Site:www.bulldog1037.com Licensee: Cox Radio Inc. (group owner; (acq 8-1-2008; grpsl). Population served: 4,094 Format: Classic rock. ♦Scott Smith, opns mgr; Kevin Steele, progmg dir.

Waycross

***WASW(FM)**— June 1998: 91.9 mhz; 1 kw. 148 ft TL: N31 13 07 W82 21 34. Hrs open: Box 3206, American Family Radio, Tupelo, MS, 38803. Phone: (662) 844-8888. Fax: (662) 842-6791. Web Site:www.afr.net Licensee: American Family Radio. (group owner) Format: Inspirational Christian. ♦Marvin Sanders, gen mgr; Rick Robertson, progmg dir.

WAYX(AM)— 2004: 1230 khz; 1 kw-U. TL: N31 12 45 W82 22 20. Hrs open: 24 1766 Memorial Dr., Suite 1, 31501. Phone: (912) 285-5002. Fax: (912) 264-1991.E-mail: wgaradio@yahoo.com Web Site:www.wgaradio.com Licensee: Satilla Broadcast Properties LLC (acq 5-21-2009; $125,000). Format: News/talk. ♦Gary Marmitt, gen mgr, gen sls mgr & progmg dir; Dick Eoekeloo, chief of engrg.

WKUB(FM)—See Blackshear/Waycross

WWSN(FM)—Licensed to Waycross. See Brunswick

WWUF(FM)— Jan 25, 1986: 97.7 mhz; 6 kw. Ant 325 ft TL: N31 11 05 W82 15 24. Stereo. Hrs open: 24 Box 1472, 31501. Secondary address: 2132 Hwy. 84, Blackshear 31516. Phone: (912) 449-3391. Fax: (912) 449-6284.E-mail: wkub@almatel.net Licensee: Mattox Broadcasting Inc. (acq 5-16-2000). Natl. Network: ABC, . Natl. Rep: Dora-Clayton,. Ga. News Net. Fletcher, Heald & Hildreth. Format: classic hits. Target aud: 25-54; general. ♦Troy Mattox, pres & gen mgr; Ray Williamson, opns dir; Jim Miller, gen sls mgr.

***WXVS(FM)**— December 1985: 90.1 mhz; 79 kw horiz, 71 kw vert. 918 ft TL: N31 13 17 W82 34 24. Stereo. Hrs open: 24
WJSP, Warm Springs/Columbus, GA, 100%.
260 14th St. N.W., Atlanta, 30318-5360. Phone: (404) 685-2690. Fax: (404) 685-2684.E-mail: ask@gpb.org Web Site:www.gpb.org Licensee: Georgia Public Telecommunications Commission. Natl. Network: NPR, PRI, . Wire Svc: AP Format: Classical, News. News staff: 10; News: 40 hrs wkly. Spec prog: Jazz 16 hrs. ♦Nancy G. Hall, CEO; Bonnie

Bean, CFO; Bob Houghton, gen mgr; Tom Barclay, opns mgr; Rob Maynard, progmg dir; Susanna Capelouto, news dir.

WYNR(FM)—Licensed to Waycross. See Brunswick

Waynesboro

WAKB(FM)— 1975: 100.9 mhz; 6 kw. Ant 279 ft TL: N33 05 15 W82 02 17. Stereo. Hrs open: 24 Box 1584, 411 Radio Station Road, Augusta, 30903. Secondary address: 104 Bennett Ln., North Augusta, SC 29841. Phone: (803) 279-2330. Fax: (803) 279-8149.E-mail: info@perrybroadcasting.net Licensee: Perry Broadcasting of Augusta Inc. Group owner: Radio One Inc. (acq 12-12-2007; grpsl). Population served: 450,000 Fisher, Wayland, Cooper, Leader & Zaragoza. Format: Urban contemp. News staff: 2; News: 5 hrs wkly. ◆Ron Tomel, opns mgr.

WYFA(FM)—Licensed to Waynesboro. See Augusta

West Point

WCJM-FM— July 18, 1966: 100.9 mhz; 1.85 kw. 235 ft TL: N32 53 42 W85 09 32. (CP: 6 kw, ant 177 ft., TL: N32 53 48 W85 09 24). Hrs open: 705 W. 4th Ave., 31833. Phone: (706) 645-2991. Fax: (706) 645-3364.E-mail: wjcm@qantumofauburn.com Licensee: Qantum of Auburn License Co. LLC. Group owner: Qantum Communications Corp. (acq 7-2-03; grpsl). Population served: 45,000 Rgnl. Network: Ga. Net. Ga. News Net. Format: Country. ◆Steve Wheeler, gen mgr; Anthony Lovelady, progmg dir.

WPLV(AM)— August 1958: 1310 khz; 1 kw-D. TL: N32 53 42 W85 09 32. (CP: TL: N32 53 48 W85 09 24). Hrs open: 24 705 W. Fourth Ave., Westpoint, 31833. Phone: (706) 645-1310. Fax: (706) 645-3364.E-mail: wcjm@quantumofauburn.com Licensee: Qantum of Auburn License Co. LLC. Group owner: Qantum Communications Corp. (acq 7-2-03; grpsl). Population served: 21,000 Rgnl. Network: Keystone (unwired net.). Format: Talk radio. ◆Steve Wheeler, gen mgr; Terry Harper, chief of engrg.

WRLA(AM)— May 1944: 1490 khz; 1 kw-U. TL: N32 52 26 W85 11 32. Hrs open: 24 503 W. 8th St., Suite 102, 31833. Phone: (706) 645-1490. Fax: (706) 645-1497.E-mail: wrla@wrla1490.com Licensee: Tiger Communications Inc. (group owner; acq 10-19-2006; $279,000 with WTRP(AM) La Grange). Population served: 35,000 Rgnl. Network: Ga. Net. Ga. News Net. Gardner, Carton & Douglas. Format: Oldies. News staff: one; News: 9 hrs wkly. Target aud: 18-55. ◆Vince Smith, gen mgr.

Willacoochee

WKAA(FM)— Apr 7, 1978: 99.5 mhz; 43 kw. Ant 755 ft TL: N31 10 18 W83 21 57. Hrs open: 24 1711 Ellis Dr., Valdosta, 31601. Phone: (229) 244-8642. Fax: (229) 242-7620.E-mail: info@995kixcountry.com Web Site:www.995kixcountry.com Licensee: RTG Radio LLC. (acq 11-9-2001; grpsl). Population served: 100,000 Format: Country. News staff: one; News: 10 hrs wkly. Target aud: 25-54. ◆Robert Ganzak, pres & gen mgr.

Winder

WIMO(AM)— Nov 4, 1952: 1300 khz; 1 kw-D, 59 w-N. TL: N33 58 22 W83 42 40. Hrs open: 850 Arch Tanner Rd., Bethlehem, 30620. Phone: (770) 867-1300. Fax: (770) 868-1962.E-mail: quincos@aol.com Web Site:www.wimo1300am.com Licensee: Mark Myers (acq 4-21-2004; $75,000). Population served: 60,000 Natl. Network: Salem Radio Network, Radio America, Fox News Radio, . Rgnl. Network: Ga. Net. Ga. News Net. Format: Talk, gospel. Target aud: General. ◆John Boyd, gen mgr; Jon Graham, opns dir, progmg dir; Kurt Andrews, progmg dir.

*WYFW(FM)— December 1987: 89.5 mhz; 530 w. 130 ft TL: N33 59 32 W83 45 15. (CP: 6 kw). Stereo. Hrs open: 24 11530 Carmel Commons Blvd., Charlotte, NC, 28226. Phone: (800) 888-7077.E-mail: wyfw@bbnradio.org Web Site:www.bbnradio.org Licensee: Bible Broadcasting Network Inc. (group owner; acq 6-24-93; $104,000; 6-28-93). Format: Relg, MOR. News: 7 hrs wkly. Target aud: 35-44. ◆Lowell Davey, pres; Paul D. Montgomery, gen mgr.

Woodbine

WCGA(AM)— June 15, 1987: 1100 khz; 10 kw-D. TL: N30 55 54 W81 42 31. Hrs open: 714 Narrow Way, St. Simons Island, 31522. Phone: (912) 634-1100.E-mail: wescox@adelphia.net Licensee: Cox Broadcast

Group Inc. Format: News/talk. News staff: 2; News: 2 hrs wkly. Target aud: Adults; 35-64. ◆Wesley Cox, gen mgr.

Woodbury

WFDR-FM— 2007: 94.5 mhz; 2.75 kw. Ant 492 ft TL: N32 50 40 W84 37 25. Hrs open: 185 Melody Ln., Fayetteville, 30215. Phone: (706) 846-3016. Fax: (706) 846-3494. Web Site:www.mountain945.com Licensee: Ploener Radio Group LLC. Format: Country. ◆Paul W. Ploener, gen mgr.

Wrens

WTHB-FM— June 10, 1979: 96.9 mhz; 6.2 kw. Ant 397 ft TL: N33 15 32.2 W82 19 10.1. Stereo. Hrs open: 411 Radiostation Rd, North Augusta, SC, 29841. Secondary address: Box 1584, Augusta 30903. Phone: (803) 279-2330. Fax: (803) 819-3781.E-mail: info@wthb.com Licensee: Perry Broadcasting of Augusta Inc. Group owner: Radio One Inc. (acq 12-12-2007; grpsl). Format: Gospel. Target aud: Teen-49. ◆Dennis Jackson, gen mgr.

Wrightsville

WDBN(FM)— May 27, 1986: 107.5 mhz; 3 kw. 295 ft TL: N32 42 24 W82 43 08. 25,000 watts. Stereo. Hrs open: 24 Box 130, Dublin, 31040. Phone: (478) 272-4422. Fax: (478) 275-4657.E-mail: webmaster@wqzy.com Licensee: State Broadcasting Corp. (acq 5-29-89; $160,000; 5-29-89). Population served: 250,000 Rgnl rep: Regional Reps Format: Classic rock. Target aud: 12 plus. ◆J. Morgan Dowdy, pres, gen mgr; Rick Humphrey, gen mgr.

Yates

*WWBM(FM)— 2004: 89.7 mhz; 1 kw. Ant 321 ft TL: N33 27 47 W84 53 35. Hrs open: Best Media Inc., 3601 36th Ave., Long Island City, NY, 11106. Phone: (718) 784-8555, ext 112. Fax: (718) 784-8901. Licensee: Best Media Inc. Scott Cinnamon Law Office. Format: South Asian music news, educational, cultural programs. News staff: one; News: 5 hrs wkly. Asian, Indian, Pakistani, Bengladeshi, and other audience. This rebroadcasts in our translator FM stations in Chicago, Houston, Detroit, & Long Island New York. ◆Banad Visuianatu, pres; Karamjit Nandha, gen mgr.

Young Harris

WACF(FM)— 2007: 95.1 mhz; 200 w. Ant 1,584 ft TL: N34 56 26 W83 55 08. Hrs open: Box 410, 30582. Phone: (706) 379-9770. Fax: (706) 379-4104. Licensee: Wolf Creek Broadcasting Inc. Format: Rock. ◆A.D. Frazier, pres; Rebecca St. John, gen mgr.

*WBTB(FM)—Not on air, target date: unknown: 90.3 mhz; 97 w. Ant 2,318 ft TL: N34 52 27 W83 48 38. Hrs open: Georgia Public Broadcasting, 260 14th St. N.W., Atlanta, 30318. Phone: (404) 685-2690. Fax: (404) 685-2684. Web Site:www.gpb.org Licensee: Georgia Public Telecommunications Commission. ◆Bob Houghton, gen mgr.

WYHG(AM)— May 1984: 770 khz; 750 w-D. TL: N34 56 26 W83 51 13. Hrs open: 12
Simulcast with WLSB(AM) Copperhill, TN.
1352 Main St., Suite 6, 30582. Phone: (706) 379-3169. Fax: (706) 379-4104.E-mail: wyhg@brmemc.net Web Site:www.wolkcreekbroadcasting.com Solid Gospel Network Licensee: Young Harris Broadcasting Corp. (acq 4-30-2003; $120,000). Format: Country, bluegrass, gospel. News staff: 2. Target aud: 30-60; mature adults. ◆Ad Frazier, pres; Rebecca St. John, gen mgr.

Zebulon

WEKS(FM)— February 1994: 92.5 mhz; 12 kw. Ant 476 ft TL: N33 08 20 W84 31 31. Stereo. Hrs open: 24 c/o Stephen D. Tarkenton, 1523 Kell Ln., Suite 1, Griffin, 30224. Phone: (770) 412-8080.E-mail: bear925@bellsouth.net Web Site:www.bear92.com Licensee: Spalding Broadcasting Inc. Population served: 1,000,000. Miller & Miller. Format: C&W. News staff: one. Target aud: 25-54. ◆Stephen D. Tarkenton, CEO; Les Reed, gen mgr, opns VP.

Hawaii

Aiea

KKOL-FM— September 1992: 107.9 mhz; 100 kw-horiz, 79 kw-vert. 1,965 ft TL: N21 23 51 W158 06 01. Stereo. Hrs open: 24 1160 N. King St., 2nd Fl., Honolulu, 96817. Phone: (808) 275-1079. Fax: (808) 536-2528.E-mail: onair@oldiesradio.net Web Site:www.oldiesradio.net Licensee: Salem Media of Hawaii Inc. (acq 1-3-2005 in exchange for KRTR(AM) Honolulu and KKNE(AM) Waipahu). Format: Oldies. News staff: one. Target aud: 35-54; adults. ◆Steve Miller, gen mgr; Bill Davis, gen sls mgr, chief of engrg; Jenny Clipse, progmg dir, traf mgr.

Captain Cook

KMWB(FM)— 2007: 93.1 mhz; 10 kw. Ant 3,234 ft TL: N19 43 14.9 W155 55 16. Hrs open: 8215 Birch St., New Orleans, LA, 70118. Phone: (504) 866-3017. Fax: (504) 865-1714. Licensee: Captain Cook Broadcasting Inc. ◆Joel Sellers, pres & gen mgr.

Eleele

KUAI(AM)— June 30, 1965: 720 khz; 5 kw-U. TL: N21 53 37 W159 33 27. Hrs open: 5 AM-midnight Box 1748, Lihue, 96766. Phone: (808) 245-9527. Fax: (808) 245-3563.E-mail: kuai@hawaiian.net Licensee: Visionary Related Entertainment L.L.C. (group owner; acq 2-10-2004; grpsl). Population served: 56,000 Format: Adult contemp, country, Hawaiian. News: 21 hrs wkly. Target aud: 25-65; loc long-time residents, blue & white collar. Spec prog: Hawaiian 5 hrs, jazz 4 hrs wkly. ◆John Detz, pres & gen mgr.

Ewa Beach

KEWA(AM)—Not on air, target date: unknown: 1320 khz; 5 kw-U, DA-2. TL: N21 19 16 W158 00 40. Hrs open: KM Communications Inc., 3654 W. Jarvis Ave., Skokie, IL, 60076. Phone: (847) 674-0864. Fax: (847) 674-9188. Licensee: KM Communications Inc. ◆Kevin Joel Bae, gen mgr.

Haiku

KUAU(AM)— 1995: Stn currently dark. 1570 khz; 1 kw-D, 500 w-N. TL: N20 54 37 W156 17 15. Hrs open: 24 777 Mokulele Hwy., Kahului, 96732. Phone: (808) 871-7311. Fax: (808) 871-9708. Web Site:www.kingscathedral.com Licensee: First Assembly of God-Kahului, Maui Inc. (acq 6-30-99). Baraff, Koerner & Olender. ◆Ron Moody, gen mgr & stn mgr.

KUHI(FM)—Not on air, target date: unknown: 106.5 mhz; 72 kw. Ant 2,283 ft TL: N20 39 36 W156 21 50. Hrs open: Big Island Broadcasting Inc., 8215 Birch St., New Orleans, LA, 70118. Phone: (504) 458-5976. Licensee: Big Island Broadcasting Inc. ◆Joel Sellers, pres & gen mgr.

Haliimaile

KPMW(FM)— 1994: 105.5 mhz; 9 kw. Ant 541 ft TL: N20 44 40 W156 18 39. Hrs open: 230 Hana Hwy. #2, Kahului, 96732. Phone: (808) 871-6251. Fax: (808) 871-5670.E-mail: wild105@maui.net Web Site:www.wild105.net Licensee: Rey-Cel Broadcasting Inc. Format: CHR/rhythmic top 40. ◆Cecille Piros, gen mgr; Cecile Pirose, gen sls mgr; Bryan Pirose, progmg dir; Ray Piros, news dir.

Hanalei

*KKCR(FM)— Aug 2, 1997: 90.9 mhz; 950 w. Ant -308 ft TL: N22 13 02 W159 28 53. Stereo. Hrs open: 24 Box 825, 96714. Phone: (808) 826-7774. Fax: (808) 826-7977.E-mail: kkcr@kkcr.org Web Site:www.kkcr.org Licensee: Kekahu Foundation Inc. Population served: 53,000 Format: Hawaiian Pacifica, eclectic, educ. News: 5 hrs wkly. Target aud: General; Kauai County residents. ◆Harvey Cohen, pres, CFO; Gwen Squyres, gen mgr; Jessica Dofflemyer, dev dir; Donna Lewis Giarman, engrg VP.

Hilo

*KANO(FM)— 2001: 91.1 mhz; 100 kw. 592 ft TL: N19 47 02 W155 05 23. Hrs open: 24 738 Kaheka St., Honolulu, 96814. Phone: (808) 955-8821. Fax: (808) 942-5477. Web Site:www.hawaiipublicradio.org Licensee: Hawaii Public Radio. Natl. Network: NPR, PRI, . Paul,

Hastings, Janofsky & Walker, L.L.P. Format: Class. News staff: 3; News: 35 hrs wkly. ♦Valerie Yee, VP; Michael Titterton, gen mgr, progmg dir; Charles Husson, opns dir, chief of engrg; Gene Schiller, mus dir; Kayla Rosenfeld, news dir.

KAPA(FM)— December 1988: 100.3 mhz; 74 kw. Ant -515 ft TL: N19 50 19 W155 06 43. Stereo. Hrs open: 24 913 Kanoelehua St., 96720. Phone: (808) 961-0651. Fax: (808) 934-8088.E-mail: jatebara@pacificradiogroup.com Licensee: Pacific Radio Group Inc. (group owner; (acq 8-11-2005; grpsl). Population served: 75000 Format: Hawaiian. Target aud: 18-49. ♦Jeanine Atebara, gen mgr; Jason Iglesias, progmg dir; Russ Roberts, news dir; Aaron Savage, chief of engrg; Cobey Patolo, traf mgr.

***KCIF(FM)**— July 1, 1998: 90.3 mhz; 14 kw. 164 ft TL: N19 30 17 W155 10 40. Hrs open: 180 Kinoole St., Suite 310, 96720. Phone: (808) 935-7434. Fax: (808) 961-6022.E-mail: kcifradio@turquoise.net Licensee: Hilo Christian Broadcasting. Format: Christian, relg, educ. ♦Pastor David Shotwell, chmn & pres.

KHBC(FM)— Sept 20, 1992: Stn currently dark. 92.7 mhz; 7.5 kw. Ant -256 ft TL: N19 50 19 W155 06 43. Hrs open: 24 Box 2936, Sun Valley, ID, 83353. Phone: (808) 443-0292. Fax: (808) 934-9448. Licensee: Parrott Broadcasting L.P. (acq 7-2-2007; $375,000). Population served: 75,000 ♦Scott D. Parker, pres & gen mgr.

KHLO(AM)— Apr 1, 1950: 850 khz; 5 kw-U. TL: N19 44 11 W155 02 07. Hrs open: 24 913 Kanoelehua Ave., 96720. Phone: (808) 961-0651. Fax: (808) 934-8088.E-mail: jatebare@pacificradiogroup.com Licensee: Pacific Radio Group Inc. (group owner; acq 9-17-03; grpsl). Population served: 75,000 Format: Sports. News staff: 2; News: 7 hrs wkly. Target aud: 25-54. ♦Jeanine Atebare, gen mgr.

KHNU(AM)— Sept 10, 1947: 620 khz; 5 kw-U. TL: N19 51 03 W155 05 09. Hrs open: 24 74-5605 Luhia St., B-7, Kailua-Kona, 96740. Phone: (808) 329-8090. Fax: (808) 443-0888.E-mail: info@lava105.com Web Site:www.lava105.com Licensee: Mahalo Broadcasting L.L.C. (acq 8-31-2007; grpsl). Population served: 135,000 Natl. Network: ABC, . Format: News-talk. News staff: 9. Target aud: 35 plus. ♦Chip Begay, opns mgr.

KILE(AM)—Not on air, target date: unknown: 1590 khz; 10 kw-U, DA-2. TL: N19 47 02 W155 05 25. Hrs open: 4703 Orkney Dr., Missouri City, TX, 77459. Phone: (281) 923-7100.E-mail: radioguy@neosoft.com Licensee: Fred R. and Evelyn Morton. ♦Fred R. Morton, gen mgr.

KIPA(AM)— October 1986: Stn currently dark. 1060 khz; 5 kw-U. TL: N19 41 48 W155 03 05. Hrs open: Box 515, 96721. Phone: (808) 959-5700. Fax: (808) 959-5800.E-mail: happenings@khbcradio.com Web Site:www.khbcradio.com Licensee: Parrott Broadcasting L.P. (acq 11-30-2007; $450,000). ♦Buddy Gordon, gen mgr, stn mgr; Robert Turner, chief of engrg.

KKBG(FM)— Aug 5, 1980: 97.9 mhz; 51 kw. Ant -65 ft TL: N19 50 19 W155 06 43. Hrs open: 913 Kanoelehua, 96720. Phone: (808) 961-0651. Fax: (808) 934-8088.E-mail: jatebara@pacificradiogroup.com Licensee: Pacific Radio Group Inc. (group owner; (acq 9-17-2003; grpsl). Population served: 90,000 Format: Adult contemp. News staff: one; News: 10 hrs wkly. ♦Jeanine Atebara, gen mgr.

KNWB(FM)— Aug 3, 1985: 97.1 mhz; 38 kw. Ant -823 ft TL: N19 47 02 W155 05 25. Stereo. Hrs open: 5 AM-10:30 PM 1145 Kilauea Ave., 96720. Phone: (808) 935-5461. Fax: (808) 935-7761.E-mail: sales@kwxx.com Web Site:www.B97Hawaii.com Licensee: New West Broadcasting Corp. (group owner; acq 1995; $270,000). Format: Classic hits. News staff: one; News: 8 hrs wkly. Target aud: 25-45. ♦Chris Leonard, pres, gen mgr; Gavin Tanouye, stn mgr.

KPUA(AM)— 1936: 670 khz; 10 kw-U. TL: N19 47 02 W155 05 25. (CP: 50 kw-U, DA-N). Stereo. Hrs open: 24 1145 Kilauea Ave., 96720. Phone: (808) 935-5461. Fax: (808) 935-7761.E-mail: info@kpua.net Web Site:www.kpua.net Licensee: New West Broadcasting Corp. (group owner; acq 5-18-92; $370,000 with co-located FM;6-8-92). Population served: 64,000 Natl. Network: CBS, Westwood One, . Dan Alpert. Format: News/talk, sports. News staff: 3; News: 22 hrs wkly. Target aud: 25 plus; upscale adults with interest in news. Spec prog: Japanese 6 hrs wkly. ♦Christopher Leonard, gen mgr, sls dir, mktg mgr, prom dir; John Orozco, rgnl sls mgr; Ken Hupp, progmg dir, news dir.

KPVS(FM)— 1995: 95.9 mhz; 50 kw. 230 ft TL: N19 41 12 W155 09 04. (CP: 27 kw, ant -361 ft.). Hrs open: 24
Rebroadcasts KLUA(FM) Kailua-Kona 100%.
913 Kanoelehua Ave., 96720. Phone: (808) 961-0651. Fax: (808) 934-8088.E-mail: jatebare@pacificradiogroup.com Licensee: Pacific Radio Group Inc. (group owner; (acq 8-11-2005; grpsl). Population served: 75,000 Cohen & Berfield. Format: Rhythmic adult contemp. Target aud: 25-54; women. ♦Jeanine Atebara, gen mgr; Darin Gumbs, progmg dir; Russ Roberts, news dir; Aaron Savage, chief of engrg; Cobey Patolo, traf mgr.

KWXX-FM— Dec 16, 1984: 94.7 mhz; 100 kw. -330 ft TL: N19 43 02 W155 08 13. Stereo. Hrs open: 24 Prog sep from AM 1145 Kilauea Ave., 96720. Phone: (808) 935-5461. Fax: (808) 935-7761.E-mail: info@kwxx.com Web Site:www.kwxx.com Natl. Network: Westwood One, . Format: Hot adult contemp, Hawaiian. News staff: one; News: 3 hrs wkly. Target aud: 25 plus; upscale adults. Spec prog: Contemp Hawaiian 20 hrs, reggae 20 hrs wkly. ♦Gavin Tawouye, progmg dir; G. Kruz, disc jockey.

Holualoa

KHWI(FM)— 2008: 92.1 mhz; 4.5 kw. Ant 3,113 ft TL: N19 43 15 W155 55 16. Hrs open: Box 515, Hilo, 96721. Phone: (808) 959-5700. Fax: (808) 959-5800.E-mail: scott@kona.sm Licensee: Parrott Broadcasting L.P. (acq 6-11-2007; $356,250 for CP). Format: Classic rock. ♦Buddy Gordon, gen mgr.

Honokaa

KLZY(FM)—Not on air, target date: 3/08: 102.9 mhz; 100 kw. Ant 1,535 ft TL: N19 53 08 W155 22 05. Hrs open: 14 Cockenoe Dr., Westport, CT, 06880-6908. Licensee: Chaparral Broadcasting Inc. ♦Jerrold T. Lundquist, pres & gen mgr.

Honolulu

KAIM-FM— Nov 1, 1953: 95.5 mhz; 100 kw. Ant 1,853 ft TL: N21 23 45 W158 05 58. Stereo. Hrs open: 24 1160 N. King St., 2nd Fl., 96817. Phone: (808) 533-0065. Fax: (808) 524-2104. Web Site:www.thefishhawaii.com Licensee: Salem Media of Hawaii Inc. (acq 11-10-99; with co-located AM). Population served: 324,871 Natl. Network: Salem Radio Network, . Format: Contemp Christian music. Target aud: 25-49; female. ♦Steve Miller, gen mgr; Corry Reynolds, progmg dir.

KCCN-FM— May 21, 1990: 100.3 mhz; 100 kw horiz, 81 kw vert. 1,965 ft TL: N21 23 51 W158 06 01. Hrs open: 900 Fort St., Suite 700, 96813. Phone: (808) 536-2728. Fax: (808) 536-2528.E-mail: info@kccnfm100.com Web Site:kccnfm100.com Licensee: Cox Radio Inc. Group owner: Cox Broadcasting (acq 3-15-2000; grpsl). Format: Contemp Hawaiian mus. ♦Mike Kelly, gen mgr; David Daniels, opns mgr, progmg dir, progmg dir; Stuart Chang, gen sls mgr; Scott MacKenzie, mktg dir.

KDNN(FM)— July 4, 1988: 98.5 mhz; 51 kw. Ant 59 ft TL: N21 18 49 W157 51 43. Stereo. Hrs open: 24 650 Iwilei Rd., Suite 400, 96817. Phone: (808) 550-9200. Fax: (808) 550-9510.E-mail: info@island985.com Web Site:www.island985.com Licensee: Capstar TX L.P. Group owner: Clear Channel Communications Inc. (acq 8-30-00; grpsl). Population served: 900,000 Natl. Rep: Clear Channel,. Ginsburg, Feldman & Bress. Format: Island Rhythm. Target aud: 25-54; upscale, white collar, college educated. ♦John Hogan, CEO & pres; Charlie Rahilly, sr VP; Chuck Cotton, gen mgr.

KGU(AM)— May 11, 1922: 760 khz; 10 kw-U. TL: N21 17 41 W157 51 49. Hrs open: 24 560 N. Nimitz Hwy., Suite 109, 96817. Phone: (808) 533-0065. Fax: (808) 524-2104.E-mail: info@kguradio.com Web Site:www.kguradio.com Licensee: Salem Media of Hawaii Inc. Group owner: Salem Communications Corp. (acq 2-16-00). Population served: 800,000 Natl. Network: Salem Radio Network, . Natl. Rep: Salem,. Fletcher, Heald & Hildreth. Format: Christian talk & teaching. News: 5 hrs wkly. Target aud: 35-54; general. ♦T.J. Malievsky, gen mgr; Jack Waters, opns mgr.

KHBZ(AM)— Mar 18, 1957: 990 khz; 5 kw-U. TL: N21 17 59 W157 51 33. Hrs open: 24 650 Iwilei Rd., Suite 400, 96817. Phone: (808) 550-9200. Fax: (808) 550-9510.E-mail: info@khbz.com Web Site:khbz.com Licensee: Capstar TX L.P. Population served: 900,000 Natl. Network: ABC, . Natl. Rep: Clear Channel,. Ginsburg, Feldman & Bress. Format: News/talk. News: 20 hrs wkly. Target aud: 25-54.

KHCM(AM)— Aug 31, 1956: 880 khz; 2 kw-U. TL: N21 17 41 W157 51 49. Hrs open: 24 1160 N. King St., 2nd Fl., 96817. Phone: (808) 533-0065. Fax: (808) 524-2104.E-mail: radio88@am880.net Web Site:am880.net Licensee: Salem Media of Hawaii Inc. Group owner: Salem Communications Corp. (acq 11-10-99; with co-located FM). Population served: 324,871 Format: Chinese.

KHCM-FM— Mar 6, 1962: 97.5 mhz; 80 kw. Ant 46 ft TL: N21 17 37 W157 50 32. Stereo. Hrs open: 24 1160 N. King St., 2nd Fl., 96817. Phone: (808) 533-0065. Fax: (808) 524-2104.E-mail: mtshawaii@yahoo.com Web Site:www.hawaiiscountrymusic.com Licensee: Salem Media of Hawaii Inc. Group owner: Salem Communications Corp. (acq 8-13-2004; $3.7 million with KHUI(FM) Honolulu). Population served: 622,900 Shaw Pittman. Format: Country. ♦Steve Miller, gen mgr; Corry Reynolds, progmg dir.

KHNR(AM)— May 14, 1947: 690 khz; 10 kw-U. TL: N21 17 41 W157 51 49. Stereo. Hrs open: 24 1160 N. King St., 2nd Fl., 96817. Phone: (808) 533-0065. Fax: (808) 524-2104.E-mail: info@khnr.com Web Site:www.khnr.com Licensee: Salem Media of Hawaii Inc. (acq 10-1-2006; exchange for KORL(AM) Honolulu). Population served: 1,000,000 Natl. Network: CNN Radio, Fox News Radio, Salem Radio Network, . Fletcher, Heald & Hildreth. Format: Conservative news/talk. ♦Steve Miller, gen mgr; Jack Waters, progmg dir.

***KHPR(FM)**— Nov 13, 1981: 88.1 mhz; 44 kw. 2,000 ft TL: N21 24 03 W158 06 10. Stereo. Hrs open: 24 738 Kaheka St., 96814. Phone: (808) 955-8821. Fax: (808) 946-3863. Web Site:www.hawaiipublicradio.org Licensee: Hawaii Public Radio. Population served: 800,000 Natl. Network: NPR, PRI, . Paul, Hastings, Janofsky & Walker. Format: Class, news, info. News staff: 3; News: 35 hrs wkly. Target aud: General. ♦Valerie Yee, VP; Michael Titterton, gen mgr, progmg dir; Charles Husson, opns mgr, chief of engrg; Gene schiller, mus dir; Kayla Rosenfeld, news dir.

KHRA(AM)— March 1992: Stn currently dark. 1460 khz; 5 kw-U. TL: N21 19 26 W157 52 47. Stereo. Hrs open: 320 Ward Ave., Suite 207, 96814. Phone: (808) 593-1460. Fax: (808) 591-1986. Fax: (808) 591-1120. Licensee: KMC Broadcasting L.L.C. (acq 9-23-2003; $680,000). Population served: 1,000,000 Format: Korean. ♦Tony Young Ho Kim, pres; Chung Sangkit, gen mgr.

KHUI(FM)— Mar 1, 1993: 99.5 mhz; 100 kw. Ant -386 ft TL: N21 18 02 W157 51 53. Stereo. Hrs open: 24 1160 N. King St., 2nd Fl., 96817. Phone: (808) 533-0065. Fax: (808) 524-2104. Web Site:www.khuiradio.com Licensee: Salem Media of Hawaii Inc. Group owner: Salem Communications Corp. (acq 8-13-2004; $3.7 million with KHNR-FM Honolulu). Natl. Rep: McGavren Guild,. Format: Music of Hawaii. ♦Steve Miller, gen mgr; Rudi Camello, gen sls mgr.

KHVH(AM)— April 1951: 830 khz; 10 kw-U. TL: N21 19 26 W157 52 32. Stereo. Hrs open: 24 650 Iwilei Rd., Suite 400, 96817. Phone: (808) 550-9200. Fax: (808) 550-9510.E-mail: info@khvh830am.com Web Site:www.khvh830am.com Licensee: Capstar TX L.P. Group owner: Clear Channel Communications Inc. (acq 8-30-2000; grpsl). Population served: 900,000 Natl. Rep: Clear Channel,. Ginsburg, Feldman & Bress. Wire Svc: AP Format: News/talk, weather, traffic. News staff: 5; News: 21 hrs wkly. Target aud: 25-54. ♦John Hogan, CEO; Charlie Ramilly, sr VP; Chuck Cotton, gen mgr; Patti Milburn, gen sls mgr; Jamie Hartnett, prom dir; Paul Wilson, progmg dir; Dave Curtis, news dir, reporter; Jerry Varoujean, chief of engrg.

KIKI-FM— Feb 14, 1979: 93.9 mhz; 100 kw. Ant -44 ft TL: N21 19 26 W157 52 32. Stereo. Hrs open: 24 650 Iwilei Rd., Suite 400, 96817. Phone: (808) 550-9200. Fax: (808) 550-9510.E-mail: info@hot939.com Web Site:www.hot939.com Licensee: Capstar TX L.P. Wire Svc: AP Format: Rhythmic CHR. News staff: one; News: hrs wkly. Target aud: 18-34. ♦Paul Wilson, opns dir; Laurie Mizuno, gen sls mgr; Kamu Kanekoa, prom dir; Fred Rico, progmg dir; Dave Curtis, pub affrs dir, reporter; Dale Machado, chief of engrg, traf mgr.

KINE-FM— November 1988: 105.1 mhz; 100 kw. 1,948 ft TL: N21 23 51 W158 06 01. Stereo. Hrs open: 900 Fort St. Mall, Suite 700, 96813-3797. Phone: (808) 275-1000. Fax: (808) 536-2528.E-mail: info@hawaiian105.com Web Site:www.hawaiian105.com Licensee: Cox Radio Inc. Group owner: Cox Broadcasting (acq 3-15-2000; grpsl). Format: Contemp & traditional Hawaiian. Target aud: 25-44. ♦Michael Kelly, VP, gen mgr; John Aeto, sls dir; Ann Boots, rgnl sls mgr; Scott MacKenzie, mktg dir; Wade Faildo, prom mgr; David Daniels, progmg dir; Jane Pascual, news dir.

***KIPO(FM)**— 1989: 89.3 mhz; 3.3 kw. 1,968 ft TL: N21 24 03 W158 06 10. Stereo. Hrs open: 24 738 Kaheka St., 96814. Phone: (808) 955-8821. Fax: (808) 946-3863. Web Site:www.hawaiipublicradio.org Licensee: Hawaii Public Radio. Natl. Network: PRI, NPR, . Paul, Hastings, Janofsky & Walker. Format: News & info, jazz, international mus. News staff: 3; News: 50 hrs wkly. Target aud: General. ♦Valerie Yee, VP; Michael Titterton, gen mgr, progmg dir; Charles Husson, opns dir, chief of engrg; Gene Schiller, mus dir; Kayla Rosenfeld, news dir.

KKEA(AM)— Nov 1, 1966: 1420 khz; 5 kw-U. TL: N21 19 26 W157 52 47. Hrs open: 900 Fort St., Suite 700, 96813. Phone: (808) 275-1047. Phone: (808) 296-1420. Fax: (808) 275-1197. Fax: (808) 548-0608.E-mail: info@kkea1420am.com Web Site:www.kkea1420am.com Licensee: Blow Up LLC (acq 5-31-02; $750,000). Population served:

800,000 Natl. Network: CNN Radio, ESPN Radio, . Natl. Rep: Katz Radio,. Format: Talk, sports. Target aud: 25-54; Male. ♦Randall Ikeda, gen mgr; Chris Hart, progmg dir.

***KKUA(FM)**—(Wailuku, Apr 15, 1988: 90.7 mhz; 7 kw. 5,533 ft TL: N20 42 41 W156 15 26. Hrs open: 24
Rebroadcasts KHPR(FM) Honolulu 100%.
738 Kaheka St., 96814. Phone: (808) 955-8821. Fax: (808) 942-5477. Web Site:www.hawaiipublicradio.org Licensee: Hawaii Public Radio Inc. Natl. Network: PRI, NPR, . Format: Class, news, info. News staff: 3; News: 35 hrs wkly. Target aud: General. Spec prog: Hawaiian one hr, Pacific Island 2 hrs wkly. ♦Valerie Yee, VP; Michael Titterton, gen mgr, progmg dir; Charles Husson, opns dir; Gene Schiller, mus dir; Kayla Rosenfeld, news dir.

KLHT(AM)— 1946: 1040 khz; 10 kw-U. TL: N21 20 10 W157 53 33. Hrs open: 24 98-1016 Komo Mai Dr., Aiea, 96701. Phone: (808) 524-1040. Fax: (808) 487-1040.E-mail: klht@hawaii.rr.com Web Site:www.klight.org Licensee: Calvary Chapel of Honolulu Inc. (acq 5-85). Format: Bible teaching. Target aud: General. ♦Jake O'Neil, gen mgr; Peter Scott, progmg dir.

KNDI(AM)— July 11, 1960: 1270 khz; 5 kw-U. TL: N21 19 26 W157 52 47. Hrs open: 24 1734 S. King St., 96826. Phone: (808) 946-2844. Fax: (808) 947-3531.E-mail: kndiradio@hawaii.rr.com Web Site:www.kndi.com Licensee: Leona Jona dba KNDI Radio. Population served: 350,000 Format: Ethnic, Filipino & 10 other ethnic groups. Target aud: Limited english proficiency. ♦Harvey Weinstein, VP, opns mgr, mus dir; Leona Jona, pres & gen mgr.

KORL(AM)— December 1959: 1180 khz; 1 kw-U. TL: N21 26 18 W157 59 29. Hrs open: 24 900 Fort St. Mall, Suite 450, 96813. Phone: (808) 875-8868. Fax: (808) 875-8870. Web Site:www.korlam.com Licensee: Hochman-McCann Hawaii Inc. Group owner: Salem Communications Corp. (acq 10-1-2006; exchange for KHCM(AM) Honolulu). Population served: 95,000 Format: World Ethnic. Target aud: 25 plus. ♦George Hochman, CEO & gen mgr.

KPHI(AM)—2008: 1130 khz; 1 kw-U. TL: N21 26 18 W157 59 29. Hrs open: 900 Fort Street Mall, Suite 450, 96813. Phone: (808) 538-1180. Fax: (808) 538-9548. Web Site:www.hhawaiimedia.com Licensee: Hochman-McCann Hawaii Inc. (acq 12-2-2005; $60,000 for CP). Format: Ethnic. Target aud: 25 plus. ♦George Hochman, pres & gen mgr.

KPOI-FM— Aug 3, 2000: 105.9 mhz; 97 kw. 1,968 ft TL: N21 23 50 W158 06 06. Stereo. Hrs open: 24 765 Amana, 96814. Phone: (808) 947-1500. Fax: (808) 947-1506.E-mail: kumu@kumu.com Web Site:www.lavarock1059.com Licensee: Visionary Related Entertainment LLC. (group owner; (acq 3-17-2004; grpsl). Thompson, Hine & Flory. Format: Classic rock. News staff: one; News: 23 hrs wkly. Target aud: 24-54; families, including single-parent families. ♦John Detz, gen mgr; Greg Everett, gen sls mgr; Dale Parsons, progmg dir; Gary Forsberg, traf mgr.

KQMQ-FM— Oct 1, 1967: 93.1 mhz; 100 kw. Ant 1,853 ft TL: N21 23 45 W158 05 58. Stereo. Hrs open: 765 Amana St., 96814. Phone: (808) 947-1500. Fax: (808) 947-1506. Web Site:www.kqmq.net Licensee: Visionary Related Entertainment L.L.C. (group owner; acq 7-1-2004; grpsl). Population served: 1,000,000 Format: Hits of the 80s. ♦John Detz, gen mgr; Joshua Flemming, gen sls mgr; Sean Lynch, progmg dir; Ryan Sean, mus dir.

KREA(AM)— Apr 24, 1973: 1540 khz; 5 kw-D. TL: N21 19 27 W157 52 47. Hrs open: 24 1839 S. King St., 96826. Phone: (808) 955-1234. Fax: (808) 946-9637. Licensee: JMK Communications Inc. (acq 3-10-00; $575,000). Population served: 90000 Format: Korean language stn. ♦Young Ho Lee, gen mgr.

KRTR(AM)— 1946: 650 khz; 10 kw-U. TL: N21 26 43 W158 03 49. Hrs open: 24 560 N. Nimitz Hwy., Suite109, 96817. Phone: (808) 533-0065. Fax: (808) 524-2104. Web Site:www.khnr.com Licensee: Cox Radio Inc. Group owner: Salem Communications Corp. (acq 1-3-2005 with KKNE(AM) Waipahu in exchange for KKOL-FM Aiea). Natl. Network: CNN Radio, CBS Radio, . Natl. Rep: Salem,. Fletcher, Heald & Hildreth. Wire Svc: AP Format: News, talk. News: 55 hrs wkly. Target aud: 25-54. ♦T.J. Malievsky, gen mgr; Jack Walters, chief of opns; Wayne Marla, progmg dir.

KRTR-FM—See Kailua

KSHK(FM)—(Kekaha, Aug 10, 1999: 103.3 mhz; 100 kw. 918 ft TL: N21 56 11 W159 26 43. Hrs open: Box 1748, Lihue, 96766. Phone: (808) 245-9527.E-mail: knog@hawaiian.net Web Site:www.kongradio.com Licensee: Visionary Related Entertainment L.L.C. (group owner; acq 2-10-2004; grpsl). Format: Top-40. ♦John Detz, pres; Jim McKeon, opns dir, progmg dir; Denise Roberts, prom dir, traf mgr; Ron Middag, chief of engrg.

KSSK(AM)— 1929: 590 khz; 7.5 kw-U. TL: N21 19 26 W157 52 32. Hrs open: 24 650 Iwilei Rd., Suite 400, 96817. Phone: (808) 550-9200. Fax: (808) 550-9507.E-mail: info@ksskradio.com Web Site:www.ksskradio.com Licensee: Capstar TX L.P. Group owner: Clear Channel (acq 3-12-99; grpsl). Population served: 900,000 Natl. Rep: Clear Channel,. Ginsburg, Feldman & Bress. Wire Svc: AP Format: Adult contemp, personalities. News staff: 5; News: 15 hrs wkly. Target aud: 25-54. ♦Chuck Cotton, gen mgr.

KSSK-FM—See Waipahu

***KTUH(FM)**— Jan 1, 1969: 90.3 mhz; 3kw. -82 ft TL: N21 18 14 W157 49 22. Stereo. Hrs open: 24 2445 Campus Rd., Suite 203, 96822. Phone: (808) 956-7431. Phone: (808) 956-5288. Fax: (808) 956-5271.E-mail: gm@ktuh.org Web Site:www.ktuh.org Licensee: University of Hawaii. Population served: 324,871 Target aud: 18-59; no target, all kinds of people listen. ♦Monty Anderson, gen mgr; Loriel Macalma, prom dir, prom mgr; Travis Tokuyama, mus dir; Dale Machado, chief of engrg; Katie McClellen, traf mgr.

KUMU(AM)— Mar 1, 1963: 1500 khz; 10 kw-U. TL: N21 17 08 W157 48 08. Hrs open: 24 765 Amana St., Suite 206, 96814. Phone: (808) 947-1500. Fax: (808) 947-1506. Licensee: Visionary Related Entertainment LLC Natl. Network: Westwood One, . Format: Talk. Target aud: 35-64.

KUMU-FM— Sept 1, 1967: 94.7 mhz; 100 kw. 78 ft TL: N21 17 09 W157 50 19. Stereo. Hrs open: 765 Amana St., Suite 206, 96814. Phone: (808) 947-1500. Fax: (808) 947-1506.E-mail: kumu@kumu.com Licensee: Visionary Related Entertainment LLC (group owner; (acq 3-17-2004; grpsl). Population served: 705,900 Format: Lite rock, adult contemporary. Target aud: 25-54. ♦Bonnie Craig, pres, gen sls mgr; Jeff Coelho, gen mgr; Sumee Mikkelson, prom dir; Ed Kanoi, progmg dir; Ernie Nearman, chief of engrg; Lilly Yamachika, traf mgr.

KUPA(AM)—(Pearl City, May 2, 1990: 1370 khz; 6.2 kw-U. TL: N21 26 18 W157 59 29. Hrs open: 24 Broadcasting Corp. of America, 4766 Holladay Blvd., Holladay, UT, 84117. Phone: (801) 273-9200. Licensee: Broadcasting Corp. of America. Group owner: Diamond Broadcasting Corp. (acq 4-12-2006; $650,000). Natl. Network: Fox Sports, . Format: Sports. ♦Nathan W. Drage, pres.

KWAI(AM)— Jan 21, 1972: 1080 khz; 5 kw-U. TL: N21 17 41 W157 51 49. Hrs open: 24 100 N. Beretania St., Suite 401, 96817. Phone: (808) 523-3868. Fax: (808) 531-6532.E-mail: radio@hawaii.com Licensee: Radio Hawaii Inc. (acq 2-85). Population served: 800,000 Natl. Network: USA, . Format: News/talk. News: 72 hrs wkly. Target aud: 25-64; general. Spec prog: Fillpino 7 hrs, Hawaiian 3hrs wkly, Samoan 14 hrs wkly. ♦Barry Wagenvoord, pres, gen mgr; Sam Wagenvoord, VP; Renee Rosehill, opns VP, opns dir.

KZOO(AM)— Oct 18, 1963: 1210 khz; 1 kw-U. TL: N21 17 59 W157 51 33. (CP: TL: N21 17 41 W157 51 49). Hrs open: 2752 Woodlawn Dr. 5-204, 96822. Phone: (808) 988-8828. Fax: (808) 988-5882.E-mail: radio@am1210kzoo.com Web Site:www.kzoohawaii.com Licensee: Polynesian Broadcasting Inc. (acq 8-4-2005). Population served: 700,000 Format: Japanese, English. ♦David Furuya, pres & gen mgr.

Kahaluu

KLEO(FM)— 1992: 106.1 mhz; 7.3 kw. Ant 2,995 ft TL: N19 43 16 W155 55 15. Hrs open: 913 Kanaoelehua Ave., Hilo, 96720. Phone: (808) 961-0651. Fax: (808) 934-8088.E-mail: jatebare@pacificradiogroup.com Licensee: Pacific Radio Group Inc. (group owner; acq 9-17-03; grpsl). Format: Adult contemp. ♦Jeanine Atebara, gen mgr; J.E. Orozco, gen sls mgr, progmg dir; Russ Roberts, news dir; Aaron Savage, chief of engrg; Cobey Patolo, traf mgr.

Kahului

KAOI(AM)—(Kihei, Oct 11, 1979: 1110 khz; 5 kw-U. TL: N20 47 30 W156 28 21. Stereo. Hrs open: Prog sep from FM 1900 Main St., Wailuku, 96793. Secondary address: Box 1437, Wailuku 96793. Phone: (808) 244-9145. Licensee: Visionary Related Entertainment L.L.C. Natl. Network: CBS, Westwood One, . Format: Talk/news, sports. Target aud: 25-54. ♦J. Detz, news dir; Alex Kowalski, chief of engrg.

KAOI-FM—(Wailuku, June 1974: 95.1 mhz; 100 kw. 1,227 ft TL: N20 38 12 W156 23 24. Stereo. Hrs open: 24 Box 1437, Wailuku, 96793. Phone: (808) 244-9145. Licensee: Visionary Related Entertainment L.L.C. (group owner; (acq 2-10-2004; grpsl). Format: Adult contemp. News staff: one; News: 5 hrs wkly. Target aud: General. ♦Jim McKeon, opns mgr; Dale Parsons, progmg dir; Gary Forsberg, news dir; Alex Kowalski, chief of engrg.

KJKS(FM)— June 22, 1984: 99.9 mhz; 100 kw. -540 ft TL: N20 47 30 W156 28 21. Hrs open: Prog sep from AM 311 Ano St., 96732. Phone: (808) 877-5566. Fax: (808) 877-288. Population served: 100,000 Natl. Network: Westwood One, . Format: Adult contemp. News staff: one. Target aud: 25-49. ♦Sherri Grimes, prom dir; Jeff Hunter, progmg dir; Dorene Moniz, traf mgr; Kopaa Tita, disc jockey.

KLHI-FM— 2007: 92.5 mhz; 1.7 kw. Ant 2,211 ft TL: N20 39 36 W156 21 50. Hrs open: 311 Ano St., 96732. Phone: (808) 877-5566. Fax: (808) 871-0666. Licensee: Pacific Radio Group Inc. (acq 6-29-2007; swap for KORL-FM Waianae). Format: CHR. ♦Pamela Tsutsui, gen mgr; Kawika Duey, progmg dir, mus dir.

KNUI(AM)— Sept 14, 1962: 900 khz; 5 kw-U. TL: N20 47 30 W156 28 21. Hrs open: 24 311 Ano St., 96732. Phone: (808) 877-5566. Fax: (808) 877-2888. Fax: (808) 871-0666.E-mail: onair@knuiam900.com Web Site:www.foxnews900.com Licensee: Pacific Radio Group Inc. (group owner; (acq 12-10-99; grpsl). Population served: 100,000 Natl. Network: Fox News Radio, . Format: News/talk. ♦Eddie Johnson, CEO, CFO; Chuck Bergson, pres, CFO; Pamela Tsutsui, gen mgr; Jeff Hunter, opns mgr; Debbie Probst, gen sls mgr, rgnl sls mgr; Sherri Grimes, prom mgr; Fred Guzman, progmg dir; Earl Tolley, chief of engrg; Dorene Moniz, traf mgr.

Kailua

KRTR-FM— Oct 9, 1978: 96.3 mhz; 75 kw. 2,120 ft TL: N21 19 49 W157 45 24. Stereo. Hrs open: 24 900 Fort St., 7th Fl., Honolulu, 96813. Phone: (808) 275-1000. Fax: (808) 536-2528. Web Site:www.krater96.com Licensee: Cox Radio Inc. Group owner: Cox Broadcasting (acq 11-10-99; grpsl). Format: Adult contemp. Target aud: 25-54.Bob Neil, CEO, pres; Marc Morgan, COO; Neil Johnston, CFO; Richard Ferguson, exec VP; Mike Kelly, gen mgr; John Aeto, sls dir; Mimi Beams, gen sls mgr; Corinne Webb, natl sls mgr, mus dir; Scott McKenzie, mktg dir; Aron Dotes, prom mgr; Wayne Maria, opns mgr & progmg dir; Jane Pascual, news dir; Chris Caughill, chief of engrg; Alexa Dahlquist, traf mgr

Kailua-Kona

KLUA(FM)— 1991: 93.9 mhz; 5.3 kw. 2,831 ft TL: N19 43 15 W155 55 16. Stereo. Hrs open: 24
Rebroadcasts KPVS(FM) Hilo 100%.
913 Kanoelehua Ave., Hilo, 96720. Phone: (808) 961-0651. Fax: (808) 934-8088.E-mail: jatebara@pacificradiogroup.com Licensee: Pacific Radio Group Inc. (group owner; (acq 8-11-2005; grpsl). Population served: 60,000 Format: Rhythmic adult contemp. Target aud: 25-54; women. ♦Jeanine Atebara, gen mgr, gen sls mgr; Darin Gumbs, progmg dir; Russ Roberts, news dir; Aaron Savage, chief of engrg; Cobey Patolo, traf mgr.

Kalaheo

KTOH(FM)— June 1, 2002: 99.9 mhz; 51 kw. Ant 892 ft TL: N21 56 11 W159 26 43. Hrs open: Box 929, 96741. Phone: (808) 332-7976. Fax: (808) 332-7830. Web Site:www.hhawaiimedia.com Licensee: Hochman Hawaii-One Inc. group owner: Hochman Hawaii-One Inc. (acq 6-23-2000; $125,000 for CP). Population served: 60,000 Wire Svc: AP Format: Classic hits. Target aud: 25-54; adults. ♦Dianna Hochman, gen mgr, sls dir; George Hochman, mktg mgr; Mark James, progmg dir.

Kaneohe

KPHW(FM)— Oct 17, 1997: 104.3 mhz; 73.5 kw. 2,116 ft TL: N21 19 49 W157 45 24. Hrs open: 24 900 Fort St., 7th Fl., Honolulu, 96813. Phone: (808) 275-1000. Fax: (808) 536-2528.E-mail: info@1043xme.com Web Site:www.1043xme.com Licensee: Cox Radio Inc. Group owner: Cox Broadcasting (acq 11-10-99; grpsl). Format: CHR. Target aud: 18-34. ♦Bob Neil, CEO, pres, pres; Marc Morgan, COO, VP; Neil Johnston, CFO; Mike Kelly, gen mgr; Wayne Maria, opns mgr; Mark Haworth, gen sls mgr; Corinne Webb, natl sls mgr; Scott McKenzie, mktg dir, prom dir; Aron Dote, prom mgr; K.C. Bejerana, progmg dir; Jane Pascual, news dir; Chris Caughill, engrg mgr.

Kapaa

KITH(FM)— 1999: 98.9 mhz; 51 kw. Ant 918 ft TL: N21 56 10 W159 26 43. Stereo. Hrs open: 4334 Rice St., Suite 204-B, Lihue, 96766.

Phone: (808) 246-4444. Fax: (808) 246-4405. Web Site:www.hhawaiimedia.com Licensee: Hochman Hawaii-Two Inc. (acq 7-14-2000; $110,000 for CP). Wire Svc: AP Format: Hawaiian hit music. News: 10 hrs wkly. Target aud: 18-44; adults. ◆Dianna Hochman, gen mgr.

Kaunakakai

KMKK-FM— Mar 19, 2007: 102.3 mhz; 1.9 kw. Ant 1,181 ft TL: N21 07 55 W157 11 31. Hrs open: Box 1437, Wailuku, 96793. Phone: (808) 553-8300. Fax: (808) 244-8247. Licensee: Visionary Related Entertainment LLC. Format: Hawaiian. ◆John Detz, gen mgr; Jim McKeon, opns mgr.

Kawaihae

KWYI(FM)— November 1993: 106.9 mhz; 5.5 kw. 341 ft TL: N19 53 09 W155 39 28. Hrs open: 6 AM-10 PM Box 6540, 64-1040 Mamalahoa Hwy., Suite 4, Kamuela, 96743. Phone: (808) 885-9866. Fax: (808) 885-6480.E-mail: info@kwyi.com Web Site:www.kwyi.com Licensee: Colin H. Naito. Format: Adult contemp. Target aud: 25-54. ◆Colin H. Naito, gen mgr.

Keaau

KBGX(FM)— Apr 16, 2004: 105.3 mhz; 25.26 kw. Ant 92 ft TL: N19 43 18 W155 27 23. Hrs open: 24 74-5605 Luhia St. B-7, Kailua-Kona, 96740. Phone: (808) 329-8090. Fax: (808) 443-0888.E-mail: info@lava105.com Web Site:www.lava105.com Licensee: Mahalo Broadcasting L.L.C. (acq 8-31-2007; grpsl). Population served: 160,000 Natl. Network: ABC, . Shook, Hardy & Bacon- Erwin Krasnow. Format: Oldies. Target aud: Adults; 25-54. ◆Chip Begay, opns mgr.

Kealakekua

KAOY(FM)— Nov 11, 1982: 101.5 mhz; 6 kw. Ant 2,052 ft TL: N19 31 10 W155 55 08. Stereo. Hrs open: c/o KWXX-FM, 1145 Kilauea Ave., Hilo, 96720. Phone: (808) 935-5461. Fax: (808) 935-7761.E-mail: studio@kwxx.com Web Site:www.kwxx.com Licensee: New West Broadcasting Corp. (group owner; acq 4-16-2004; $500,000). Format: Adult contemp. Target aud: 18-49. ◆Christopher Leonard, gen mgr; Trisha LaRochelle, gen sls mgr; Gavin Panouye, progmg mgr; Ken Hupp, news dir; Yisa Var, traf mgr.

KKON(AM)— October 1963: 790 khz; 5 kw-U. TL: N19 31 10 W155 55 08. Hrs open: 24
Rebroadcasts Khlo(AM) Hilo 100%.
913 Kanoelehua Ave., Hilo, 96720. Phone: (808) 961-0651. Fax: (808) 935-0396.E-mail: info@kkonam.com Web Site:www.pacificradiogroup.com Licensee: Pacific Radio Group Inc. (group owner; (acq 8-11-2005; grpsl). Population served: 60,000 Format: Sports. Target aud: 35 plus; general. Spec prog: Hawaiian mus. ◆Jeanine Atebara, gen mgr.

Kekaha

KSHK(FM)—Licensed to Kekaha. See Honolulu

Kihei

KAOI(AM)—Licensed to Kihei. See Kahului

KHEI-FM— 2009: 107.5 mhz; 750 w horiz. Ant 3,132 ft TL: N20 46 31 W156 14 49. Hrs open: 24 Box 1437, Wailuku, 96793. Secondary address: 1900 Main St., Suite 6, Wailuku 96793. Phone: (808) 244-9145. Fax: (808) 244-8247.E-mail: kaoi@kaoi.net Web Site:www.vremaui.com Licensee: Visionary Related Entertainment LLC. ◆John Detz, gen mgr; Jim McKeon, stn mgr.

Kilauea

*KAQA(FM)— July 3, 1997: 91.9 mhz; 950 w. Ant 1,607 ft TL: N21 58 41 W159 29 55. Stereo. Hrs open: Box 825, Hanalei, 96714. Phone: (808) 826-7774. Fax: (808) 826-7977.E-mail: kkcr@kkcr.org Web Site:www.kkcr.org Licensee: Kekahu Foundation Inc. Population served: 6,000 Format: Hawaiian Pacifica, eclectic, educ. Target aud: General; Kauai County residents. ◆ Harvey Cohen, pres; Larry Lasota, gen mgr & stn mgr; Douvn Jewell, dev VP, engrg VP; Ken Jannelli, progmg dir; Donna Lewis, news dir; Dean Rogers, chief of engrg.

Kurtistown

KTBH-FM— 2008: 102.1 mhz; 50 kw horiz. Ant -207 ft TL: N19 41 48 W155 03 05. Hrs open: Box 1437, Wailuku, 96793. Phone: (808) 935-2924. Fax: (808) 244-8247. Licensee: Visionary Related Entertainment LLC. Format: Adult contemp. ◆John Detz, pres & gen mgr.

Lahaina

KPOA(FM)— October 1984: 93.5 mhz; 1.4 kw. 1,305 ft TL: N20 50 43 W156 54 04. (CP: 346 w, ant 2,421 ft.). Stereo. Hrs open: 24 311 Ano St., Kahului, 96732. Phone: (808) 877-5566. Fax: (808) 871-0666. Web Site:www.kpoa.com Licensee: Pacific Radio Group Inc. (group owner; acq 12-10-99; grpsl). Population served: 100,000 Kenkel & Associates. Format: Contemp Hawaiian Island sounds. News staff: one; News: one hr wkly. Target aud: Adults; 25-54. ◆Eddie Johnson, CFO; Pamela Tsutsui, gen mgr.

Lanai City

KONI(FM)— Nov 1, 1993: 104.7 mhz; 69 kw. Ant 2,283 ft TL: N20 39 36 W156 21 50. Hrs open: 24 300 Ohukai Rd., Suite C-318, Kihei, 96753. Phone: (808) 875-8866. Fax: (808) 875-8870.E-mail: koni@hawaii.rr.com Web Site:www.hhawaiimedia.net Licensee: Hochman Hawaii Publishing Inc. (acq 6-17-2002; $1.15 million). Wire Svc: AP Format: Oldies. News: one hr wkly. Target aud: 25-54; Maui county residents. ◆George Hochman, COO, chmn, pres, CFO, VP; Jim Carroll, gen mgr; Adrienne Owens, gen sls mgr; Joe Hawkins, progmg dir & news dir; Byron McCann, chief of engrg.

Lihue

KFMN(FM)— Mar 7, 1988: 96.9 mhz; 100 kw. 400 ft TL: N21 59 54 W159 25 35. Stereo. Hrs open: 24 Box 1566, 1860 Leleiona St., 96766-5566. Phone: (808) 246-1197. Fax: (808) 246-9697.E-mail: john.wada@fm97radio.com Licensee: FM 97 Associates. (acq 6-7-88; $600,000). Population served: 75,000 Mullin, Rhyne, Emmons & Topel. Format: Adult contemp. News staff: one; News: 4 hrs wkly. Target aud: 25-54; island residents & visitors. ◆John Wada, gen mgr & progmg dir; Jason Fujinaka, news dir.

*KHJC(FM)—Not on air, target date: unknown: 88.9 mhz; 100 kw. 892 ft TL: N21 56 11 W159 26 43. Stereo. Hrs open: 2970 Kele St., Suite 117, 96766. Secondary address: CSN International, 3000 W. MacArthur Blvd., 3rd Fl, Santa Ana, CA 92704. Phone: (808) 245-9696. Fax: (808) 245-9898.E-mail: pastorsteve@khjcradio.com Web Site:www.khjcradio.com Licensee: CSN International (group owner) Format: Teaching/music.

KJMQ(FM)— 2001: 98.1 mhz; 51 kw. Ant 13 ft TL: N21 59 41 W159 24 36. Hrs open: Box 929, Kalaheo, 96741. Phone: (808) 332-7976. Fax: (808) 246-4405. Licensee: Hochman Hawaii Four Inc. (acq 9-25-2007; $400,000). Format: Rhythmic contemp hit radio. ◆George Hochman, pres; Dianna Hochman, gen mgr.

KQNG(AM)— 1939: 570 khz; 1 kw-U. TL: N21 59 33 W159 24 24. Hrs open: Box 1748, KQNG Radio Bldg., 4271 Halenani St., 96766. Phone: (808) 245-9527. Fax: (808) 245-3563.E-mail: kong@hawaiian.net Web Site:www.kongradio.com Licensee: Visionary Related Entertainment L.L.C. (group owner; (acq 2-10-2004; grpsl). Population served: 60,000 Format: News/talk, sports. Target aud: 25-54. ◆John Detz, CEO, gen mgr; Ron Middac, progmg dir & chief of engrg.

KQNG-FM— Oct 17, 1983: 93.5 mhz; 100 kw. 226 ft TL: N21 59 33 W159 24 24. Stereo. Hrs open: Box 1748, KQNG Radio Bldg., 96766. Phone: (808) 245-9527. Fax: (808) 245-3563.E-mail: kong@hawaiian.net Web Site:www.kongradio.com Format: Hot adult Comtemp. Target aud: 18-49. ◆John Detz, pres; Ron Wiley, opns mgr.

Makawao

KDLX(FM)— Dec 31, 1980: 94.3 mhz; 3 kw. -22 ft TL: N20 50 48 W156 19 35. Stereo. Hrs open: 24 Box 1437, Wailuku, 96793. Phone: (808) 244-9145. Fax: (808) 244-8247. Licensee: Visionary Related Entertainment L.L.C. (group owner; acq 2-10-2004; grpsl). Format: Country. ◆John Detz, pres & gen mgr; Jack Gist, progmg dir; Alex Kowalski, chief of engrg; Gary Forsberg, traf mgr.

Nanakuli

KNAN(FM)— 2009: Stn currently dark. 106.7 mhz; 25 kw. Ant -23 ft TL: N21 18 46 W158 05 51. Hrs open: 2550 5th Ave., Suite 600, San Diego, CA, 92103-6624. Phone: (702) 385-6000. Fax: (619) 232-7317. Licensee: Big D Consulting Inc. ◆Donald F. Hildre, pres.

Paauilo

KNUQ(FM)— 1995: 103.7 mhz; 100 kw. 1,209 ft TL: N20 38 18 W156 23 01. Hrs open: 24 Box 1437, Wailuku, 96793. Phone: (808) 244-9145. Fax: (808) 244-8247. Web Site:www.q103maui.com Licensee: Visionary Related Entertainment LLC (group owner; acq 2-10-2004; grpsl). Population served: 90,000 Format: Contemp island music. News staff: one. Target aud: 18-49; young active adults. ◆John Detz, CEO, gen mgr; Alex Kowalski, opns mgr, chief of engrg; Jim McKeon, prom mgr, opns; Shaggy Jenkins, progmg dir; Gary Forsberg, traf mgr.

Pahala

*KAHU(FM)—Not on air, target date: unknown: 91.7 mhz; 1 kw. Ant -1,122 ft TL: N19 11 55 W155 28 55. Hrs open: Box 5054, Hilo, 96720-1054. Phone: (808) 959-2726. Licensee: Haola Inc. ◆Wendell J. Kaehuaea, VP.

*KPHL(FM)— 2006: 90.5 mhz; 250 w. Ant -39 ft TL: N19 06 02 W155 34 09. Hrs open: 935 Dillingham Blvd., Suite One, Honolulu, 96817. Phone: (808) 294-4575. Fax: (808) 923-7723. Licensee: Vineyard Christian Fellowship of Honolulu Inc. (acq 1-26-2007; $1,500). ◆Timothy J. Malievsky, gen mgr.

Pearl City

KUCD(FM)— Feb 14, 1995: 101.9 mhz; 100 kw. 1,948 ft TL: N21 23 51 W158 06 01. Stereo. Hrs open: 24 650 Iwilei Rd, Suite 400, Honolulu, 96817. Phone: (808) 550-9200. Fax: (808) 550-9510.E-mail: info@star1019fm.com Web Site:www.star1019fm.com Licensee: Capstar TX L.P. Group owner: Clear Channel Communications Inc. (acq 8-30-00; grpsl). Population served: 900,000 Natl. Rep: Clear Channel,. Ginsburg, Feldman & Bress. Format: Alternative. Target aud: 25-54; boomers & yuppies. ◆Chuck Cotton, VP, gen mgr; Laurie Mizuno, gen sls mgr; Damian Balinowski, news dir; Dale Costales, chief of engrg; Iwalani Costales, traf mgr; Jamie Hyatt, progmg.

KUPA(AM)—Licensed to Pearl City. See Honolulu

Poipu

KSRF(FM)— Aug 14, 1999: 95.9 mhz; 100 kw. 918 ft TL: N21 56 11 W159 26 43. Hrs open: Box 1748, Lihue, 96766. Phone: (808) 245-9527.E-mail: kong@hawaiian.net Web Site:www.kongradio.com Licensee: Visionary Related Entertainment L.L.C. (group owner; acq 2-10-2004; grpsl). Format: Contemp Hawaiian. ◆John Detz, pres, gen mgr; Shelly Cobb, progmg dir & engrg dir; Ron Middag, chief of engrg; Denise Roberts, traf mgr.

Pukalani

KJMD(FM)— June 15, 1984: 98.3 mhz; 50 kw. 102 ft TL: N20 42 19 W156 21 54. Stereo. Hrs open: 24 311 Ano St., Kahului, 96732. Phone: (808) 877-5566. Fax: (808) 871-0666. Web Site:www.dajam983.com Licensee: Pacific Radio Group Inc. (group owner; acq 12-10-99; grpsl). Population served: 120,000 Format: CHR. News staff: one. Target aud: 18-34; young active adults. ◆Chuck Bergson, CEO; Pamela Tsutsui, gen mgr; Trance, progmg dir.

Volcano

KKOA(FM)— 1996: 107.7 mhz; 25.5 kw. Ant 92 ft TL: N19 43 18 W155 27 23. Hrs open: 24 74-5605 Luhia St., B-7, Kailua-Kona, 96740. Phone: (808) 329-8090. Fax: (808) 443-0888.E-mail: info@KOACountry.com Web Site:www.KOACountry.com Licensee: Mahalo Broadcasting L.L.C. (acq 9-1-2007; grpsl). Population served: 160,000 Natl. Network: ABC, . Erwin Krabnox. Format: Country. Target aud: Adults 18-64. ◆Chip Begay, opns mgr.

Wahiawa

*KHAI(FM)— 2007: 103.5 mhz; 2.2 kw horiz, 1.9 kw vert. Ant 1,958 ft TL: N21 23 51 W158 06 01. Hrs open:
Rebroadcasts KLRD(FM) Yucaipa, CA 100%.
5700 West Oaks Blvd., Rocklin, CA, 95765. Phone: (916) 251-1600. Fax: (916) 251-1650. Web Site:www.air1.com Licensee: Educational Media Foundation. (acq 12-19-2005; $2 million for CP). Natl. Network: Air 1, . Format: Alternative rock, div. ◆Richard Jenkins, pres.

Waianae

KORL-FM— May 1984: 101.1 mhz; 100 kw horiz, 81 kw vert. Ant 1,942 ft TL: N21 23 45 W158 05 58. Stereo. Hrs open: 900 Fort Street Mall, Suite 450, Honolulu, 96813. Phone: (808) 538-1180. Fax: (808) 538-9548. Web Site:www.hhawaiimedia.com Licensee: Hochman Hawaii-Three Inc. (group owner; (acq 6-29-2007; $520,000 plus swap for CP for KLHI-FM Kahului). Dan Alpert. Format: Smooth jazz. News staff: one; News: one hr wkly. Target aud: 18-49; general. ◆Pamela Tsutsui, gen mgr & stn mgr; Jeff Hunter, opns mgr.

Wailea-Makena

KRKH(FM)— June 4, 2008: 97.3 mhz; 1.5 kw. Ant 2,283 ft TL: N20 39 36 W156 21 50. Hrs open: 300 Ohukai Rd., Suite C-318, Kihei, 96753. Phone: (808) 875-8866. Fax: (808) 875-8870. Web Site:www.hhawaiimedia.com Licensee: Hochman Hawaii Publishing Inc. (acq 4-4-2008; $600,000 for CP). Format: Classic rock. ◆George Hochman, pres; Jim Carroll, gen mgr.

Wailuku

KAOI-FM—Licensed to Wailuku. See Kahului

KJMD(FM)—See Pukalani

KKUA(FM)—Licensed to Wailuku. See Honolulu

KMVI(AM)— Mar 17, 1947: 550 khz; 5 kw-U. TL: N20 53 29 W156 29 23. Hrs open: 24 311 Ano St., Kahului, 96732. Phone: (808) 877-5566. Fax: (808) 871-0666. Web Site:www.espn550.com Licensee: Pacific Radio Group Inc. (group owner; acq 12-10-99; grpsl). Population served: 120,000 Natl. Network: ESPN Radio, ABC, . Format: Sports radio. News staff: one. Target aud: 18 plus; men, residents/tourists, educated professionals. ◆Chuck Bergson, pres; Pamela Tsutsui, gen mgr.

Waimea

KAGB(FM)— 2000: 99.1 mhz; 7.3 kw. Ant 2,990 ft TL: N19 43 16 W155 55 15. Hrs open: 913 Kanoelehua Ave., Hilo, 96720. Phone: (808) 961-0651. Fax: (808) 934-8088.E-mail: jatebara@pacificradiogroup.com Licensee: Pacific Radio Group Inc. (group owner; (acq 8-11-2005; grpsl). Format: Hawaiian. ◆Jeanina Atebara, gen mgr; J.E. Orozco, stn mgr, gen sls mgr, progmg dir; Russ Roberts, news dir; Aaron Savage, chief of engrg; Cobey Patolo, traf mgr.

Waipahu

KDDB(FM)— Nov 23, 1988: 102.7 mhz; 61 kw. 1,893 ft TL: N21 23 49 W158 05 58. Stereo. Hrs open: 765 Amana St., Suite 200, Honolulu, 96814. Phone: (808) 947-1500. Fax: (808) 947-1506. Licensee: Visionary Related Entertainment L.L.C. (group owner; acq 7-1-2004; grpsl). Natl. Rep: McGavren Guild,. Format: Top 40 hits. Target aud: 18-34; young adults who enjoy many different types of music. ◆John Detz, gen mgr & stn mgr.

KKNE(AM)— Sept 20, 1950: 940 khz; 10 kw-U. TL: N21 26 43 W158 03 49. Hrs open: 24 900 Fort St., Suite 700, Honolulu, 96813. Phone: (808) 533-0065 Ext. 731. Phone: (808) 257-1000. Fax: (808) 275-1195.E-mail: info@kkneam.com Licensee: Cox Radio Inc. Group owner: Salem Communications Corp. (acq 1-3-2005 with KRTR(AM) Honolulu in exchange for KKOL-FM Aiea). Population served: 1,000,000 Waitt Farm Net. Format: Country. Target aud: 25-44. ◆John Aeto, sls dir; David Daniels, progmg dir.

KSSK-FM— Dec 30, 1976: 92.3 mhz; 100 kw. Ant 1,948 ft TL: N21 23 49 W158 05 58. Stereo. Hrs open: 24 650 Iwilei Rd., Suite 400, Honolulu, 96817-5319. Phone: (808) 550-9200. Fax:(808) 550-9510.E-mail: info@ksskradio.com Web Site:ksskradio.com Licensee: Clear Channel Broadcasting Licenses Inc. Clear Channel Communications Inc. (acq 9-1-00; grpsl). Population served: 900,000 Natl. Rep: Clear Channel,. Ginsburg, Feldman & Bress. Wire Svc: AP Wire Svc: Metro Weather Service Inc. Format: Adult contemp. News staff: 3; News: 6 hrs wkly. Target aud: 25-54. ◆Chuck Cotton, gen mgr; Scott Hogle, opns dir & sls dir; Patti Milburn, gen sls dir; Christine Yasuma, prom dir, prom mgr; Jamie Hyatt, progmg dir; Damian Balinowski, news dir; Dale Machado, chief of engrg; Larry Price, traf mgr, disc jockey.

Idaho

Aberdeen

KQPI(FM)— 2008: 99.5 mhz; 2.2 kw. Ant 1,958 ft TL: N42 48 31 W112 29 10. Hrs open: 980 N. Michigan Ave., Suite 1880, Chicago, IL, 60611. Phone: (312) 204-9900. Licensee: College Creek Media LLC. ◆Neal J. Robinson, pres.

American Falls

KORR(FM)— 1995: 104.1 mhz; 3 kw. 328 ft TL: N42 45 24 W112 48 38. Hrs open: 24 Box 97, Pocatello, 83204-0097. Secondary address: 436 N. Main St., Pocatello 83204. Phone: (208) 234-1290. Fax: (208) 234-9451.E-mail: spots@kzbq.com Licensee: Idaho Wireless Corp. (group owner; acq 1996). Format: Adult contemp. ◆Paul E. Anderson, gen mgr; Harry Neuhardt, gen sls mgr; Paul Anderson, progmg dir.

Ammon

KSPZ(AM)—Licensed to Ammon. See Idaho Falls

Ashton

KRID(FM)—Not on air, target date: unknown: 96.5 mhz; 28 kw. Ant 656 ft TL: N44 10 35 W111 25 51. Hrs open: 980 N. Michigan Ave., Suite 1880, Chicago, IL, 60611. Phone: (312) 204-9900. Licensee: College Creek Media LLC. ◆Bruce Buzil, gen mgr.

Blackfoot

KBLI(AM)— November 1951: 690 khz; 1 kw-D, 43 w-N. TL: N43 10 70 W112 22 10. Hrs open: Box 699, 83221. Phone: (208) 785-1400. Fax: (208) 785-0184. Licensee: Riverbend Communications LLC. Group owner: Bonneville International Corp. (acq 4-17-2006; grpsl). Population served: 9,556 Format: Talk. ◆Delyn Hendricks, gen mgr.

KCVI(FM)— Sept 22, 1994: 101.5 mhz; 100 kw. 1,512 ft TL: N43 30 03 W112 39 43. Stereo. Hrs open: 24 Box 699, 83221. Phone: (208) 785-1400. Fax: (208) 785-0184.E-mail: scott@kbear.fm Web Site:www.kbear.fm Licensee: Riverbend Communications LLC. Group owner: Bonneville International Corp. (acq 4-17-2006; grpsl). Natl. Rep: McGavren Guild,. Format: Active rock. News staff: one; News: 3 hrs wkly. Target aud: 25-44; male. ◆Jim Burgoyne, pres; Delyn Hendricks, gen mgr; Matt Burgoyne, sls dir; Scott Taylor, progmg dir; Tisa Cudmore, traf mgr.

KLCE(FM)— Oct 15, 1975: 97.3 mhz; 100 kw. 1,512 ft TL: N43 30 03 W112 39 43. Stereo. Hrs open: Prog sep from AM Box 699, 83221. Phone: (208) 785-1400. Fax: (208) 785-0184.E-mail: info@klce.com Web Site:www.klce.com Licensee: Riverbend Communications LLC Population served: 9,556 Natl. Rep: McGavren Guild,. Format: Adult contemp. Target aud: 18-49.

Boise

KAWO(FM)— Nov 2, 1979: 104.3 mhz; 52 kw. Ant 2,574 ft TL: N43 45 18 W116 05 52. Stereo. Hrs open: 827 E. Park Blvd., 83712-7782. Phone: (208) 344-6363. Fax: (208) 385-9064. Web Site:www.koololdies1043.com Licensee: Peak Broadcasting of Boise Licenses LLC. Format: Classic oldies. Target aud: 25-54; affluent, managerial, professional. ◆Jack Armstrong, progmg dir.

KBOI(AM)— May 1, 1947: 670 khz; 50 kw-U, DA-N. TL: N43 25 44 W116 19 43. Stereo. Hrs open: 24 Box 1280, 83701. Secondary address: 1419 W. Bannock 83702. Phone: (208) 336-3670. Fax: (208) 336-3734 (Main). Fax: (208) 336-3735 (News).E-mail: andrew.paul@citcomm.com Web Site:www.670kboi.com Licensee: Citadel Broadcasting Co. Group owner: Citadel Broadcasting Corp. (acq 12-10-97; grpsl). Population served: 250,000 Natl. Rep: Katz Radio,. Rgnl rep: Allied Radio Partners Format: News/talk. News staff: 3. Target aud: 25-54; white collar, upper income. ◆Kevin Godwin, gen mgr; Ken Weaver, sls dir, news dir; Linda Rupe, prom dir; Andrew Paul, progmg dir; Mike Owens, gen sls mgr & chief of engrg.

*KBSU(AM)— Dec 4, 1955: 730 khz; 15 kw-D, 500 w-N, DA-2. TL: N43 34 13 W116 20 45. Stereo. Hrs open: 213 SMITC, 1910 University Dr., 83725. Phone: (208) 426-3663. Fax: (208) 344-6631. Web Site:radio.boisestate.edu/AM730.html Licensee: Idaho State Board of Education (Boise State University) (acq 12-30-91; donation;

1-20-92). Population served: 250,000 Dow, Lohnes & Albertson. Format: News/talk, jazz. Spec prog: Folk. ◆John Hess, gen mgr; Brad Campbell, opns mgr; Hy Kloc, dev dir; Ele Ellis, progmg dir; Sadie Babits, news dir; Tom Taylor, chief of engrg.

*KBSU-FM— Jan 16, 1977: 90.3 mhz; 19 kw. Ant 2,637 ft TL: N43 35 41 W116 08 39. Stereo. Hrs open: 24 Boise State Radio, 1910 University Dr., 83725. Phone: (208) 426-3663. Fax: (208) 344-6631. Web Site:radio.boisestate.edu Licensee: Boise State Board of Education. (acq 12-30-91). Population served: 600,000 Natl. Network: PRI, NPR, . Format: Class. News: 15 hrs wkly. Target aud: General. ◆John Hess, gen mgr, chief of engrg; Erik Jones, opns mgr; Ele Ellis, progmg dir; Sadie Babits, news dir.

*KBSX(FM)— 1994: 91.5 mhz; 4 kw. 2,581 ft TL: N43 45 18 W116 05 52. Hrs open: Boise State Radio, 1910 University Dr., 83725. Phone: (208) 426-3663. Fax: (208) 344-6631. Web Site:www.radio.boisestate.edu Licensee: Idaho State Board of Education. Population served: 650,000 Natl. Network: NPR, . Wire Svc: AP Format: News. News staff: 4. ◆John Hess, gen mgr; Erik Jones, opns mgr; Tom Taylor, chief of engrg.

KBXL(FM)—See Caldwell

KCIX(FM)—(Garden City, Jan 1, 1985: 105.9 mhz; 50 kw. 2,700 ft TL: N43 45 18 W116 05 52. Stereo. Hrs open: 827 Park Blvd., Suite 201, 83712. Phone: (208) 344-6363. Fax: (208) 385-9064. Web Site:www.mix106radio.com Licensee: Peak Broadcasting of Boise Licenses LLC. Group owner: Clear Channel Communications Inc. (acq 6-28-2007; grpsl). Natl. Rep: McGavren Guild,. Format: Adult contemp. Target aud: 25-54. ◆Terry Tario, gen mgr; Susan Green, opns mgr, traf mgr; Brent Carey, progmg dir; Dave Burnett, news dir.

KCMW(AM)—Not on air, target date: unknown: 1430 khz; 50 kw-D, 1 kw-N, DA-2. TL: N43 32 44 W116 20 41. Hrs open: 12272 Sarazen Pl., Granada Hills, CA, 91344. Phone: (213) 494-3377. Licensee: Ether Mining Corp. ◆John Cooper, pres; Mark A. Mueller, VP.

KFXD(AM)— Nov 9, 1928: 630 khz; 5 kw-U, DA-2. TL: N43 30 56 W116 19 43. Hrs open: 827 E. Park Blvd., Suite 201, 83712. Phone: (208) 344-6363. Fax: (208) 344-1134. Web Site:www.kidoam.com Licensee: Peak Broadcasting of Boise Licenses LLC. Group owner: Clear Channel Communications Inc. (acq 6-28-2007; grpsl). Population served: 225,000 Format: Talk. ◆Kevin Godwin, gen mgr; Dave Burnett, progmg dir.

KGEM(AM)— 1945: 1140 khz; 10 kw-U, DA-N. TL: N43 35 54 W116 15 14. Stereo. Hrs open: 24 5257 Fairview Ave., Suite 260, 83706. Phone: (208) 344-3511. Fax: (208) 947-6765. Licensee: Journal Broadcast Corp. Group owner: Journal Broadcast Group Inc. (acq 5-13-98; grpsl). Population served: 600,000 Natl. Rep: Katz Radio. Format: Oldies. Target aud: 25-54. ◆Bob Rosenthal, VP, gen mgr, opns mgr; Dan McColly, opns mgr; Kristine Simoni, prom mgr; Rick Kemp, engrg dir; Paula Jensen, traf mgr.

KIDO(AM)—See Nampa

KIZN(FM)— Aug 1, 1968: 92.3 mhz; 44 kw. 2,500 ft TL: N43 45 19 W116 05 52. Stereo. Hrs open: 24 1419 W. Bannock St., 83701. Phone: (208) 336-3670. Fax: (208) 336-3736.E-mail: rich.summers@citicomm.com Web Site:www.kizn.com Licensee: Citadel Broadcasting Co. Group owner: Citadel Broadcasting Corp. (acq 12-24-97; grpsl). Population served: 150,000 Format: Country. News staff: one. Target aud: 25-54. ◆Adella Stauffer, gen sls mgr; Don Morin, mktg mgr; Rich Summers, opns VP & progmg dir; Brenda Mee, news dir; Bill Frahm, chief of engrg; Patti Hull, traf mgr.

KJOT(FM)— 1979: 105.1 mhz; 53 kw. Ant 2,588 ft TL: N43 45 18 W116 05 52. Stereo. Hrs open: 24 5257 Fairview Ave., Suite 260, 83706. Phone: (208) 344-3511. Fax: (208) 947-6765. Licensee: Journal Broadcast Corp. Population served: 600,000 Natl. Rep: Katz Radio,. Format: Classic rock. Target aud: 25-49. ◆Bob Rosenthal, VP, gen mgr; Dan McColly, opns mgr, progmg mgr; Kristine Simoni, prom mgr; Rick Kemp, engrg dir; Paula Jensen, traf mgr.

KNJY(AM)— Apr 8, 1961: 950 khz; 5 kw-D, 35 w-N. TL: N43 37 14 W116 17 57. Hrs open: Box 1600, Nampa, 83653. Phone: (208) 463-1900.E-mail: info@knjyam.com Licensee: First Western Inc. (acq 8-4-03; $150,000). Format: Relg. Spec prog: Farm 5 hrs wkly. ◆Steve Sumner, gen mgr.

KQFC(FM)— Nov 1, 1960: 97.9 mhz; 47 kw. 2,499 ft TL: N43 45 12 W116 06 08. (CP: 58 kw). Stereo. Hrs open: 24 Prog sep from AM Box 1280, 83701. Phone: (208) 336-3670. Fax: (208) 336-3734.E-mail: andrew.paul@citcomm.com Licensee: Citadel Broadcasting Co. Format: Country. Target aud: 25-54; country lifestyle.

KSAS-FM—See Nampa

KSPD(AM)— Apr 29, 1959: 790 khz; 1 kw-D, 61 w-N. TL: N43 33 57 W116 20 13. Hrs open: 24 1440 S. Weideman Ave., 83709. Phone: (208) 377-3790. Fax: (208) 377-3792.E-mail: info@myfamilyradio.com Web Site:www.myfamilyradio.com Licensee: KSPD Inc. (group owner; acq 3-24-83;4-18-83). Population served: 450,000 Natl. Network: Salem Radio Network, . Wiley, Rein & Fielding. Format: Christian, talk. Target aud: 18-54. ◆Beth Schafer, exec VP; Lee Schafer, pres & gen mgr; David Schafer, stn mgr.

KZMG(FM)—(New Plymouth, Mar 17, 1982: 93.1 mhz; 50 kw. 2,630 ft TL: N43 45 19 W116 05 52. Stereo. Hrs open: 24 Box 1280, 83701-1280. Secondary address: 1419 W. Bannock 83701. Phone: (208) 336-3670. Fax: (208) 336-3734.E-mail: andrew.paul@citcomm.com Web Site:www.magic93.com Licensee: Citadel Broadcasting Co. Group owner: Citadel Broadcasting Corp. (acq 12-24-97; grpsl). Population served: 560,000 Natl. Rep: D & R Radio,. Wiley, Rein, Fielding. Format: Contemporary hit/Top-40. News: 6 hrs wkly. Target aud: 18-34; women. ◆Kevin Godwin, gen mgr, stn mgr; Mike Owens, gen sls mgr; Brad Collins, progmg dir; Bill Frahm, chief of engrg.

Bonners Ferry

KBFI(AM)— Sept 1, 1977: 1450 khz; 1 kw-U. TL: N48 41 20 W116 20 04. Hrs open: 327 S. Marion Ave., Sandpoint, 83864. Phone: (208) 263-2179. Fax: (208) 265-5440.E-mail: prod@953kpnd.com Licensee: Blue Sky Broadcasting. (acq 1996). Population served: 12,000 Format: News/talk, sports. News staff: one. Target aud: General. ◆Dylan Benefield, gen mgr, opns mgr; Jim Tomchek, progmg dir.

*KIBX(FM)— 2000: 92.1 mhz; 74 w. Ant 2,749 ft TL: N48 36 37 W116 15 24. Hrs open: Spokane Public Radio Inc., 2319 N. Monroe St., Spokane, WA, 99205-4586. Phone: (509) 328-5729. Fax: (509) 328-5764.E-mail: rkunkel@kpbx.org Web Site:kpbx.org Licensee: Spokane Public Radio Inc. Format: Classical, news, jazz. ◆Richard Kunkel, gen mgr; Brian Flick, progmg dir; Verne Windham, mus dir; Doug Nadvornick, news dir.

Buhl

*KTFY(FM)— Aug 2005: 88.1 mhz; 60 kw vert. Ant 653 ft TL: N42 43 48 W114 25 06. Stereo. Hrs open: 24 16115 S. Montana Ave., Caldwell, 83605. Phone: (208) 459-5879. Fax: (208) 459-3144.E-mail: fun@ktfy.org Web Site:www.881ktfy.org Licensee: Southern Idaho Corp. of Seventh-Day Adventists dba Gem State Academy. Population served: 200,000 Donald Martin. Format: Christian. Target aud: 25-54; women. ◆Donald Klinger, chmn; Stephen L. McPherson, pres; Michael Agee, gen mgr; Jerry Woods, progmg dir.

Burley

KBAR(AM)— Aug 31, 1946: 1230 khz; 1 kw-U. TL: N42 32 05 W113 48 54. Stereo. Hrs open: 120 S. 300 W., Rupert, 83350. Phone: (208) 678-2244. Fax: (208) 678-2246.E-mail: kimlee@cableone.net Licensee: KART Broadcasting Co. Inc. and Eagle Rock Broadcasting Inc. as tenants-in-common. Group owner: Tri-Market Radio Broadcasters Inc. & Eagle Rock Broadcasting Inc. (acq 1-30-98; with co-located FM). Population served: 42,000 Format: Oldies, talk. ◆Kim Lee, gen mgr; Chris Kinzel, gen sls mgr; Ben Reed, progmg dir, news dir.

*KBSY(FM)— October 1998: 88.5 mhz; 440 w vert. 2,083 ft TL: N42 21 42 W113 27 17. Hrs open: Rebroadcasts KBSX(FM) Boise 100%. Boise State Radio, 1910 University Dr., Boise, 83725. Phone: (208) 426-3663. Fax: (208) 344-6631. Web Site:radio.boisestate.edu Licensee: Idaho State Board of Education. Natl. Network: NPR, . Format: News/talk. ◆John Hess, gen mgr; Erik Jones, opns mgr; Ele Ellis, progmg dir; Tom Taylor, engrg dir.

KZDX(FM)— Feb 15, 1975: 99.9 mhz; 27 kw. Ant 2,450 ft TL: N42 20 06 W113 36 15. Stereo. Hrs open: Prog sep from AM 120 S. 300 W., Rupert, 83350. Phone: (208) 678-2244. Fax: (208) 678-2246. Licensee: KART Broadcasting Co. Inc. Population served: 90,050 Format: AOR.

Caldwell

KBGN(AM)— Oct 5, 1960: 1060 khz; 10 kw-D. TL: N43 43 13 W116 31 58. Hrs open: 3303 E. Chicago, 83605. Phone: (208) 459-3635.E-mail: kbgn@kbgnradio.com Web Site:www.kbgnradio.com Licensee: Nelson M. Wilson & Karen E. Wilson. (acq 8-25-89; $188,000; 9-11-89). Natl. Network: USA, . Format: Inspirational, Christian, talk. Target aud: General. Spec prog: Sp 5 hrs wkly. ◆Nelson Wilson, gen mgr; Marnie Fillmore, opns dir.

KBXL(FM)— Feb 22, 1961: 94.1 mhz; 40 kw. Ant 2,634 ft TL: N43 45 18 W116 05 52. Stereo. Hrs open: 24 1440 S. Weideman Ave., Boise, 83709. Phone: (208) 377-3790. Fax: (208) 377-3792.E-mail: info@myfamilyradio.com Web Site:www.myfamilyradio.com Licensee: KSPD Inc. (group owner; acq 4-26-89;7-10-89). Population served: 600,000 Natl. Network: AP Network News, . Natl. Rep: Salem,. Rgnl rep: Tacher Wiley, Rein & Fielding. Format: Relg, Christian talk. Target aud: 25-54. ◆Lee Schafer, pres & gen mgr.

KCID(AM)— 1947: 1490 khz; 1 kw-U. TL: N43 39 51 W116 38 10. Hrs open: 24 5257 Fairview Ave., Suite 260, Boise, 83706. Phone: (208) 344-3511. Fax: (208) 947-6765. Licensee: Journal Broadcast Corp. Group owner: Journal Broadcast Group Inc. (acq 5-13-98; grpsl). Population served: 600,000 Natl. Rep: Katz Radio,. Format: Oldies. Target aud: 35 plus. ◆Bob Rosenthal, VP, gen mgr, chief of engrg; Dan McColly, opns mgr; Kristine Simoni, prom mgr; Rick Kemp, engrg dir; Paula Jensen, traf mgr.

KSAS-FM—Licensed to Caldwell. See Nampa

KTHI(FM)— Dec 1, 1983: 107.1 mhz; 52 kw. Ant 2,578 ft TL: N43 45 18 W116 05 52. Stereo. Hrs open: 24 5257 Fairview Ave., Suite 260, Boise, 83706. Phone: (208) 344-3511. Fax: (208) 947-6765. Licensee: Journal Broadcast Corp. Population served: 600,000 Natl. Rep: Katz Radio,. Format: Super hits of 60's & 70's. Target aud: General. ◆Bob Rosenthal, VP, gen mgr; Dan McColly, opns mgr; Kristine Simoni, prom mgr; KJ Mac, progmg dir; Rick Kemp, engrg dir; Paula Jensen, traf mgr.

*KTSY(FM)— Oct 14, 1990: 89.5 mhz; 8.3 kw. 2,601 ft TL: N43 45 18 W116 05 52. (CP: Ant 2,594 ft.). Stereo. Hrs open: 24 16115 S. Montana Ave., 83607. Phone: (208) 459-5879. Fax: (208) 459-3144.E-mail: fun@ktfy.org Web Site:www.ktsy.org Licensee: Gem State Adventist Academy. Population served: 400,000 Donald E. Martin. Format: Contemp Christian mus. News: 4 hrs wkly. Target aud: 25-45. ◆Donald Klinger, chmn; Stephen McPherson, pres; Michael Agee, gen mgr; Jerry Woods, progmg dir.

Chubbuck

KLLP(FM)— Nov 10, 1984: 98.5 mhz; 7 kw. Ant 987 ft TL: N42 52 26 W112 30 47. Hrs open: 24 Rebroadcasts KAWZ(FM) Twin Falls 65%. 259 E. Center St., Pocatello, 83204. Phone: (208) 233-1133. Fax: (208) 232-1240.E-mail: kellymartinez@gapbroadcasting.com Web Site:www.985klite.com Licensee: GAP Broadcasting Pocatello License LLC. Group owner: Clear Channel Communications Inc. (acq 2-13-2008; grpsl). Population served: 400,000 Format: Adult contemp. Target aud: General. Spec prog: Sp 4 hrs wkly. ◆Neica Kinney, gen mgr; Jeff Evans, opns mgr; Kelly Martinez, progmg dir; Rhett Downing, chief of engrg; Cami Chopski, traf mgr.

KRTK(AM)— 1981: 1490 khz; 1 kw-U. TL: N42 55 38 W112 30 03. Stereo. Hrs open: 24 1633 Olympus Dr., Pocatello, 83201. Phone: (208) 237-9500. Fax: (208) 237-4600.E-mail: krtk@ltlink.com Licensee: Broken Chains Inc. (acq 8-25-00). Population served: 110,000 Natl. Network: ABC, . Format: Christian. Target aud: 35-55. ◆Stacy Dare, stn mgr & chief of opns.

Coeur d'Alene

KHTQ(FM)—(Hayden, Nov 1, 1991: 94.5 mhz; 100 kw. 1,883 ft TL: N47 39 34 W116 57 48. Stereo. Hrs open: 24 Prog sep from AM 504 E. Sherman, 83814. Secondary address: 500 W. Boone Ave., Spokane, WA 99201. Phone: (208) 664-9271. Fax: (208) 667-0945. Web Site:rock945.com Population served: 464,000 Format: Active rock. Target aud: 24-54. ◆Roger Nelson, gen mgr; Barry Hawbaker, progmg dir; Kris Siebers, mus dir, disc jockey; Jolene Longwill, traf mgr; Barry Bennet, disc jockey.

KICR(FM)— Oct 12, 2001: 102.3 mhz; 6 kw. 1,843 ft TL: N47 39 35 W116 57 12. Stereo. Hrs open: 24 Rebroadcasts KIBR-FM Sandpoint 100%. 327 S. Marion Ave., Sandpoint, 83864. Phone: (208) 663-2179. Fax: (208) 265-5440.E-mail: dylanb@a53kpwd.com Web Site:www.k102radio.com Licensee: Great Northern Broadcasting Inc. (acq 8-17-2001; $550,000). Population served: 500,000 Smithwick & Belendiuk, PC. Format: Country. ◆Dylan Benefield, gen mgr, opns dir, gen sls mgr; Jimmy Silver, progmg dir; Mike Brown, news dir.

KVNI(AM)— Nov 1, 1946: 1080 khz; 10 kw-D, 1 kw-N, DA-N. TL: N47 36 57 W116 43 07. Hrs open: 24 504 E. Sherman, 83814. Secondary address: 500 W. Boone Ave., Spokane, WA 99201. Phone: (208) 664-9271. Fax: (208) 667-0945. Licensee: QueenB Radio Inc. Population served: 65,000 Natl. Rep: Katz Radio,. Format: Doo Whoppin' Oldies,

news. News staff: 2. Target aud: 25 plus. Spec prog: Relg 3 hrs wkly. ◆Roger Nelson, gen mgr; Kris Siebers, progmg dir, news dir, pub affrs dir; Tim Anderson, chief of engrg.

Cottonwood

*KNWO(FM)— January 1994: 90.1 mhz; 250 w. 612 ft TL: N46 04 09 W116 27 54. Hrs open: 24 Rebroadcasts KRFA-FM Moscow, ID. c/o Radio Stn KRFA-FM, Box 642530, 382 Murrow Communications Ctr., Pullman, WA, 99164. Phone: (509) 335-6500. Fax: (509) 335-3772.E-mail: nwpr@wsu.edu Web Site:www.nwpr.org Licensee: Washington State University. Dow, Lohnes & Albertson. Format: Class, news. News staff: one; News: 37 hrs wkly. Target aud: 25 plus. ◆Karen Olstad, COO, gen mgr; Dennis Haarsager, gen mgr; Roger Johnson, stn mgr, sls dir; Scott Weatherly, opns mgr; Sarah McDaniel, dev dir; Mary Hawkins, progmg dir; Robin Rilette, mus dir; Ralph Hogan, engrg dir; Rachael McDonald, news rptr.

Donnelly

KMCL(AM)—Licensed to Donnelly. See McCall

Driggs

KCHQ(FM)— Feb 12, 2004: 102.1 mhz; 4 kw. Ant 1899 ft TL: N43 42 42 W111 20 56. Stereo. Hrs open: 24 Box 548, 1152 Bond Avenue, Rexburg, 83440. Secondary address: P.O. Box 54 83422. Phone: (208) 354-4102. Fax: (208) 356-6111.E-mail: ted@q102fm.net Web Site:www.q102country.com Licensee: Ted W. Austin Jr. Population served: 95,000 Natl. Rep: Interep,. Wood, Maines & Nolan. Format: Country. News: 8 hrs wkly. Target aud: 25-54; adults. ◆Ted W. Austin Jr., pres & gen mgr; Connie Austin, gen sls mgr; Dennis Miller, progmg dir; Dave Plourde, news dir.

Eagle

KXLT-FM— September 1994: 107.9 mhz; 45 kw. 2,683 ft TL: N43 45 18 W116 05 52. Hrs open: 827 E. Park Blvd., Suite 201, Boise, 83712. Phone: (208) 344-6363. Fax: (208) 327-8800.E-mail: brent.carey @peakbroadcasting.com Web Site:www.lite108.com Licensee: Peak Broadcasting of Boise Licenses LLC. Group owner: Clear Channel Communications Inc. (acq 6-28-2007; grpsl). Natl. Rep: McGavren Guild,. Format: Soft adult contemp, lite music. Target aud: 25-54. ◆Kevin Godwin, gen mgr, stn mgr; Dave Burnett, gen sls mgr, news dir; Susan Green, prom dir, traf mgr; Tobin Jeffries, progmg dir.

Emmett

KDBI(FM)— Mar 12, 1973: 101.9 mhz; 57 kw. Ant 2,532 ft TL: N43 45 18 W116 05 52. Stereo. Hrs open: 2722 S. Redwood Rd., Salt Lake City, UT, 84119. Phone: (208) 463-2900.E-mail: jtovar@bustomedia.com Web Site:www.bustosmedia.com Licensee: First Western Inc. (acq 11-1-2003; $1.05 million). Population served: 3,945 Format: Rgnl Mexican. ◆Ed Distel, gen mgr.

Fruitland

KWEI-FM—Licensed to Fruitland. See Weiser

Garden City

KCIX(FM)—Licensed to Garden City. See Boise

Gooding

KPDA(FM)— Dec 2, 1996: 100.7 mhz; 73 kw. Ant 2,191 ft TL: N43 14 43 W115 26 12. Hrs open: 24 5660 E. Franklin Rd., Suite 200, Nampa, 83687. Phone: (208) 465-9966. Fax: (208) 465-2922. Licensee: FM Idaho Co. LLC. (group owner; acq 12-31-2006; grpsl). Format: Rgnl Mexican. ◆Larry Johnson, pres; Elliott Klein, gen mgr.

KRXR(AM)— 1992: 1480 khz; 1 kw-D. TL: N42 54 54 W114 42 41. Hrs open: 501 S. Lincoln Ave., Jerome, 83338. Fax: (208) 934-8630.E-mail: krxr@cableone.net Licensee: Maria Elena Juarez. (acq 1999; $200,000). Format: Sp. ◆Efrain Ortega, gen mgr.

Grangeville

*KKAG(FM)—Not on air, target date: unknown: 90.9 mhz; 1.9 kw. Ant 2,324 ft TL: N45 51 42 W116 07 25. Hrs open: 519 Dawn Dr., 83530. Phone: (208) 983-5433.E-mail: calvarychapel@mtida.net Web Site:www.calvarychapelgrangeville.com Licensee: Calvary Chapel of Grangeville Inc. ◆Dean Huibregtse, pres.

*KKRH(FM)—Not on air, target date: unknown: 88.3 mhz; 485 w. Ant 2,353 ft TL: N45 51 42 W116 07 25. Hrs open: 519 Dawn Dr., 83530. Phone: (208) 983-5433. Web Site:www.calvarychapelgrangeville.com Licensee: Calvary Chapel of Grangeville Inc. ◆Dean Huibregtse, pres.

KORT(AM)— Oct 8, 1954: 1230 khz; 1 kw-U. TL: N45 55 52 W116 07 50. Hrs open: Box 510, 83530. Phone: (208) 983-1230. Fax: (208) 983-2744. Licensee: 4-K Radio Inc. (group owner; acq 6-1-71). Population served: 12,500 Format: Today's C&W. News staff: one; News: 8 hrs wkly. Target aud: General. Spec prog: Farm 2 hrs wkly. ◆Mike Ripley, pres; Melinda Hall, gen mgr, opns mgr, gen sls mgr, progmg dir, traf mgr; David Forsman, chief of engrg; Josh Campbell, disc jockey.

KORT-FM— Dec 1, 1979: 92.7 mhz; 360 w. 2,352 ft TL: N45 51 48 W116 07 24. Stereo. Hrs open: Prog sep from AM Box 510, 83530. Phone: (208) 983-1230. Fax: (208) 983-2744. Population served: 8,500 Natl. Network: ABC, . Format: Country.

Hailey

KSKI-FM—See Sun Valley

KYUN(FM)— 2006: 106.7 mhz; 97 kw. Ant 1,578 ft TL: N43 16 45 W114 09 14. Hrs open: 21361 Hwy. 30, Twin Falls, 83301-0197. Phone: (208) 735-8300. Fax: (208) 733-4196.E-mail: lorproduction@gmail.com Web Site:www.canyoncountryonline.com Licensee: Locally Owned Radio LLC. Format: Country. ◆Larry Johnson, pres & gen mgr; Jerre Fender, opns dir, progmg dir; Deb Uvieu, gen sls mgr; Denis Jeffs, traf mgr.

Hayden

KHTQ(FM)—Licensed to Hayden. See Coeur d'Alene

Hazelton

KTPZ(FM)— 2007: 94.3 mhz; 4.9 kw. Ant 741 ft TL: N42 43 54 W114 25 04. Hrs open: 21361 Hwy. 30, Twin Falls, 83301-0197. Phone: (208) 735-8300. Fax: (208) 733-4196.E-mail: lorproduction@gmail.com Licensee: Locally Owned Radio LLC. (acq 9-8-2006; $2,911,000 with KIRQ(FM) Twin Falls). Format: Hot CHR. ◆Larry Johnson, pres & gen mgr; Jerre Fender, opns dir, progmg dir; Deb Uvieu, gen sls mgr; Denis Jeffs, traf mgr.

Homedale

KQTA(FM)— December 2004: 106.3 mhz; 100 kw. Ant 1,028 ft TL: N43 37 15 W117 12 35. Hrs open: 500 Media Place, Sacramento, CA, 95815. Phone: (916) 368-6300. Fax: (916) 283-9614.E-mail: info@bustosmedia.com Web Site:www.bustomedia.com Licensee: Bustos Media of Idaho License LLC. (acq 10-28-2005; $2.25 million). Format: Sp.

Hope

*KZRP(FM)—Not on air, target date: unknown: 90.7 mhz; 160 w horiz. Ant -226 ft TL: N48 13 56.9 W116 15 06.2. Hrs open: Box 1, 83836-0001. Phone: (208) 264-5611. Licensee: Community Development Initiative of North Idaho Inc. ◆Bruce K. Bishop, VP.

Idaho Falls

*KAIO(FM)— 2006: 90.5 mhz; 500 w vert. Ant 528 ft TL: N43 32 37 W111 53 07. Hrs open: Rebroadcasts KLRD(FM) Yucaipa, CA 100%. 2351 Sunset Blvd., Suite 170-218, Rocklin, CA, 95765. Phone: (916) 251-1600. Fax: (916) 251-1650. Web Site:www.air1.com Licensee: Educational Media Foundation. Natl. Network: Air 1, . Format: Christian. ◆Richard Jenkins, pres; Mike Novak, VP; Keith Whipple, dev dir; David Pierce, progmg mgr; Ed Lenane, news dir; Sam Wallington, engrg dir; Karen Johnson, news rptr.

KBLY(AM)— Sept 10, 1960: 1260 khz; 5 kw-D, 64 w-N. TL: N43 31 15 W111 59 33. Hrs open: Box 699, Blackfoot, 83221. Phone: (208) 785-1400. Fax: (208) 785-0184. Licensee: Riverbend Communications LLC. Group owner: Bonneville International Corp. (acq 4-17-2006; grpsl). Population served: 38,987 Format: Talk. Target aud: 35 plus; upscale, mature adults. ◆Jim Burgoyne, pres, chief of engrg; Delyn Hendricks, gen mgr; Matt Burgoyne, sls dir, women's int ed; Neal Larson, progmg dir.

KFTZ(FM)— May 24, 1986: 103.3 mhz; 100 kw. 659 ft TL: N43 32 34 W111 53 07. Stereo. Hrs open: 24 Box 699, Blackfoot, 83221. Secondary address: 1190 Lincoln Rd. 83401. Phone: (208) 785-1400. Fax: (208) 785-0184.E-mail: info@z103.fm Web Site:www.z103.fm Licensee: Riverbend Communications LLC. Group owner: Bonneville International Corp. (acq 4-17-2006; grpsl). Rgnl rep: Christal Radio Format: CHR top-40. Target aud: 18-34. ◆Jim Burgoyne, pres; Delyn Hendricks, gen mgr; Matt Burgoyne, sls dir; Jeremy Dresen, progmg dir; Tisa Cudmore, traf mgr.

KID(AM)— 1928: 590 khz; 5 kw-D, 1 kw-N, DA-N. TL: N43 33 35 W111 55 15. Hrs open: 1406 Commerce Way, 83404. Phone: (208) 524-5900. Fax: (208) 522-9696. Licensee: GAP Broadcasting Pocatello License LLC. Group owner: Clear Channel Communications (acq 2-13-2008; grpsl). Population served: 40,000 Natl. Network: CBS, . Natl. Rep: Target Broadcast Sales,. Drinker Biddle & Reath LLP. Format: News/talk. Target aud: 25-54; upscale decision-making professionals. Spec prog: Farm 18 hrs wkly. ◆Neica Kinney, gen mgr; Lisa Smith, gen sls mgr; Bill Hatch, news dir; Cami Chopski, traf mgr.

KID-FM— May 1, 1965: 96.1 mhz; 100 kw. Ant 1,500 ft TL: N43 29 51 W112 39 50. Stereo. Hrs open: 1406 Commerce Way, 83404. Phone: (208) 524-5900. Fax: (208) 522-9696. Licensee: GAP Broadcasting Pocatello License LLC. (acq 2-13-2008; grpsl). Format: Country.

KQEO(FM)— April 2003: 107.1 mhz; 82 kw. Ant 597 ft TL: N43 32 33 W111 53 04. Hrs open: 854 Lindsay Blvd., 83402. Secondary address: 854 Lindsay Blvd. 83402. Phone: (208) 522-1101. Fax: (208) 522-6110.E-mail: kupi@kupi.com Licensee: Sand Hill Media Corp. (group owner; acq 9-7-2001; $1.2 million with KSNA(FM) Rexburg plus 36-month employment agreement). Format: Classic Hits. ◆Jim Garshow, gen mgr.

KSPZ(AM)—(Ammon, Nov 9, 1957: 980 khz; 5 kw-D, 1 kw-N, DA-2. TL: N43 31 23 W112 00 36. Stereo. Hrs open: 854 Lindsay Blvd., Ammon, 83402. Phone: (208) 522-1101. Fax: (208) 522-6110. Licensee: Sandhill Media Group LLC. Group owner: Sand Hill Media Corp. (acq 2-27-2004; $2.65 million with co-located FM). Population served: 35,776 Natl. Rep: McGavren Guild,. Haley, Bader & Potts. Format: Rgnl Mexican. ◆James Garshow, exec VP, gen mgr; Ken Walker, gen sls mgr & natl sls mgr; Domingo Munoz, progmg dir.

KTHK(FM)— October 1993: 105.5 mhz; 100 kw. 659 ft TL: N43 21 06 W112 00 22. Stereo. Hrs open: 24 1190 Lincoln Rd., 83401. Phone: (208) 523-3722. Fax: (208) 525-2575. Web Site:www.1055thehawk.com Licensee: Riverbend Communications LLC. Group owner: Bonneville International Corp. (acq 4-17-2006; grpsl). Format: Country. ◆Delyn Hendricks, gen mgr; Sandie Fulks, gen mgr & sls.

KUPI-FM— Aug 16, 1975: 99.1 mhz; 100 kw. Ant 1,513 ft TL: N43 32 33 W111 53 04. Stereo. Hrs open: Prog sep from AM 854 Lindsay Blvd., Ammon, 83402. Phone: (208) 522-1101. Fax: (208) 522-6110. Format: Country.

Island Park

KWYS-FM— November 1998: 102.9 mhz; 46 kw. 2,732 ft TL: N44 33 41 W111 26 32. Stereo. Hrs open: 24 Box 2158, Ketchum, 83340. Phone: (208) 726-5324. Fax: (208) 726-5459. Licensee: Resurgence Development LLC Group owner: Chaparral Communications (acq 9-18-2007; with KEZQ(FM) West Yellowstone, MT). Population served: 100,000 Cohn & Marks. Format: Classic rock. News staff: 2; News: 10 hrs wkly. Target aud: 18-45; Adults. ◆Scott Anderson, gen mgr.

Jerome

KART(AM)— August 1956: 1400 khz; 1 kw-U. TL: N42 43 51 W114 32 17. Hrs open: Prog sep from FM 47 N. 100 W, 83338. Phone: (208) 324-8181. Fax: (208) 324-7124. Licensee: KART Broadcasting Co. (Acq 9-1-64). Population served: 75,000 Natl. Network: CBS, . Format: Real country. Target aud: 25 plus. ◆Lamont Summers, progmg dir; Tammy Davis, traf mgr.

KMVX(FM)— August 1970: 102.9 mhz; 100 kw. 760 ft TL: N42 43 54 W114 25 04. Stereo. Hrs open: 47 N. 100 West, 83338. Phone: (208) 324-8181. Fax: (208) 324-7124. Licensee: KART Broadcasting Co. Rgnl rep: Allied Radio Partners. Format: Adult contemp. Target aud: 25-54; general. ◆Kent Lee, gen mgr, gen sls mgr; Karla Cunha, news dir; Jerry Tharton, chief of engrg; Tammy Davis, traf mgr.

Kellogg

*KLGG(FM)—Not on air, target date: unknown: 89.3 mhz; 2 w horiz, 100 w vert. Ant 2,565 ft TL: N47 29 32 W116 08 33. Hrs open: Rebroadcasts KPBX-FM Spokane, WA 100%. 2319 N. Monroe St., Spokane, WA, 99205. Phone: (509) 328-5729. Fax: (509) 328-5764.E-mail: kpbx@kpbx.org Web Site:www.kpbx.org Licensee: Spokane Public Radio Inc. Natl. Network: NPR, PRI, . ◆Richard Kunkel, gen mgr.

Ketchum

KIKX(FM)— Dec 2, 1996: 104.7 mhz; 100 kw. 1,578 ft TL: N43 16 45 W114 09 14. Hrs open: 21361 Hwy. 30, Twin Falls, 83301. Phone: (208) 735-8300. Fax: (208) 733-4196.E-mail: lorproduction@gmail.com Web Site:kikx.com Licensee: Locally Owned Radio LLC. (group owner; acq 10-31-2003; grpsl). Format: Classic rock. ◆Larry Johnson, pres & gen mgr; Jerre Fender, opns dir, progmg dir; Deb Uvieu, gen sls mgr; Denis Jeffs, traf mgr.

Kootenai

KTPO(FM)— 2007: 106.7 mhz; 1.3 kw. Ant 1,158 ft TL: N48 13 45 W116 30 30. Hrs open: 327 S. Marion Ave., Sandpoint, 83864. Phone: (208) 263-2179. Fax: (208) 265-5440.E-mail: carolynp@953kpnd.com Web Site:www.1067thepoint.com Licensee: Hellroaring Communications L.L.C. Format: Classic rock. ◆Dylan L. Benefield, gen mgr; Mike Brown, news dir; John Goes, chief of engrg.

Kuna

*KARJ(FM)— 2005: 88.3 mhz; 23 kw vert. Ant 2,161 ft TL: N43 00 26 W116 42 23. Stereo. Hrs open: 24 Rebroadcasts KLRD(FM) Yucaipa, CA 100%. 2351 Sunset Blvd., Suite 170-218, Rocklin, CA, 95765. Phone: (916) 251-1600. Fax: (916) 251-1650.E-mail: info@air1.com Web Site:www.air1.com Licensee: Educational Media Foundation. Group owner: EMF Broadcasting. Natl. Network: Air 1, . Shaw Pittman. Format: Contemp Christian. News staff: 3. Target aud: 18-35; Judeo-Christian, female. ◆Richard Jenkins, pres; Mike Novak, VP; Lloyd Parker, gen mgr; Keith Whipple, dev dir; Eric Allen, natl sls mgr; Mke Novak, progmg dir; David Pierce, progmg mgr; Ed Lenane, news dir; Sam Wallington, engrg dir; Arthur Vassar, traf mgr.

Lapwai

KZBG(FM)— 2005: 97.7 mhz; 570 w. Ant 1,059 ft TL: N46 27 22 W117 02 56. Hrs open: 2470 Appleside Blvd., Suite B, Clarkston, WA, 99403. Phone: (509) 751-0976. Fax: (509) 751-0975.E-mail: bigcountryradio@clearwire.net Licensee: Xana Duke Radio Partners LLC (acq 7-30-2007; $310,000). Format: Country. ◆Thomas D. Hodgins, gen mgr.

Lewiston

KATW(FM)— Oct 2, 1986: 101.5 mhz; 100 kw. Ant 848 ft TL: N46 27 38 W117 01 00. Stereo. Hrs open: 24 403 Capital St., 83501. Phone: (208) 743-6564. Fax: (208) 798-0110.E-mail: markbolland@pacempire.com Web Site:www.catfm.com Licensee: Bolland Enterprises LLC. (group owner; acq 9-12-2008; grpsl). Population served: 50,000 Format: Hot adult contemp. Target aud: 18-49. ◆Leslie Gatherer, gen sls mgr, traf mgr; Evan Yeoman, progmg dir, progmg mgr.

KCLK-FM—See Clarkston, WA

*KLCZ(FM)— October 1967: 88.9 mhz; 230 w. Ant -840 ft TL: N46 24 45 W117 01 31. Hrs open: Attn: Radio, 500 Eighth Ave., 83501. Phone: (208) 792-2418. Fax: (208) 792-2568.E-mail: info@klczfm.com Web Site:www.lcsc.edu Licensee: Lewis-Clark State College (acq 3-23-2005; $5,000). Population served: 36,000 Format: Var/div. ◆Tate Smith, gen mgr.

KMOK(FM)— March 1983: 106.9 kw. 99 kw. 1,230 ft TL: N46 27 43 W117 02 18. Stereo. Hrs open: 24 805 Stewart Ave., 83501. Phone: (208) 743-1551. Fax: (208) 743-4440.E-mail: sales@idavend.com Licensee: Ida-Vend Co. Inc. Group owner: IdaVend Broadcasting Inc. Population served: 100,000 Natl. Network: AP Radio, . Wilkenson, Barkter & Knauer. Format: Country. News staff: one; News: 3 hrs wkly. Target aud: 25-49; female. ◆Robert Prasil, pres, gen mgr; Darin

Siebert, opns mgr; Ben Bonnfield, gen sls mgr; Jim Nelly, progmg dir; Steve Franco, mus dir, chief of engrg; John Thomas, news dir; Zoanne Byers, traf mgr.

KOZE(AM)— Oct 6, 1955: 950 khz; 5 kw-D, 1 kw-N, DA-2. TL: N46 23 32 W117 02 03. Stereo. Hrs open: 24 Box 936, 2560 Snake River Ave., 83501. Phone: (208) 743-2502. Fax: (208) 743-1995. Licensee: 4-K Radio Inc. (group owner; acq 6-1-71). Population served: 125,000 Rgnl rep: Tacher Company. Format: Talk. News staff: 2. Target aud: 25-54. Spec prog: Farm 2 hrs wkly. ♦Michael R. Ripley, pres; Chris Ripley, stn mgr, progmg VP; Lisa Jensen, gen sls mgr; Jason Ford, news dir; David Forsman, chief of engrg.

KOZE-FM— Jan 17, 1961: 96.5 mhz; 25 kw. 741 ft TL: N46 27 48 W117 00 01. Stereo. Hrs open: 24 Prog sep from AM Box 2560, 2560 Snake River Ave., 83501. Phone: (208) 743-2502. Fax: (208) 743-1995. Format: Adult rock. Target aud: 18-49. ♦Lee McVey, progmg dir.

KRLC(AM)— March 1935: 1350 khz; 5 kw-D, 1 kw-N, DA-N. TL: N46 23 39 W116 59 40. Hrs open: 24 805 Stewart Ave., 83501. Phone: (208) 743-1551. Fax: (208) 743-4440.E-mail: sales@idavend.com Licensee: Ida-Vend Inc. Group owner: IdaVend Broadcasting Inc. (acq 11-1-81). Population served: 100,000 Wilkenson, Barker & Knauer. Format: Country, news/talk, sports. News staff: one; News: 10 hrs wkly. Target aud: 25 plus; adults. Spec prog: Farm 5 hrs, radio auction one hr wkly. ♦Robert Prasil, pres, gen mgr; Melva Prasil, stn mgr; Ben Bonfield, gen sls mgr; John Thomas, news dir; ZoAnne Byers, traf mgr; Steve Franco, engr.

KVTY(FM)— July 20, 1998: 105.1 mhz; 500 w. 1,099 ft TL: N46 27 33 W117 02 18. Hrs open: 24 c/o KRLC(AM) and KMOK(FM), 805 Stewart Ave., 83501. Phone: (208) 743-1551. Fax: (208) 743-4440.E-mail: sales@idavend.com Licensee: IdaVend Co. Inc. Group owner: IdaVend Broadcasting Inc. Population served: 100,000 Natl. Network: AP Radio, . Wilkenson, Barker & Knauer. Format: CHR. News staff: one; News: 1 hr wkly. Target aud: 18-44. ♦Robert Prasil, pres, gen mgr; Melva Prasil, stn mgr; Darin Siebert, opns mgr; Ben Bonfield, gen sls mgr; Jeff Tuchscherer, progmg dir; John Thomas, news dir; Steve Franco, chief of engrg; Zoanne Byers, traf mgr.

Marsing

***KAWS(FM)**— 2007: 89.1 mhz; 8.75 kw vert. Ant 2,191 ft TL: N43 00 25 W116 42 13. Hrs open:
Rebroadcasts KAWZ(FM) Twin Falls 100%.
4002 N. 3300 E., Twin Falls, 83301-0354. Phone: (208) 733-3133. Fax: (208) 736-1958. Web Site:www.csnradio.com Licensee: Calvary Chapel of Twin Falls Inc. Format: Christian praise & worship, Bible teaching. ♦Mike Kestler, pres; Mike Stocklin, gen mgr.

McCall

***KBSK(FM)**— 2002: 89.9 mhz; 220 w. Ant 1,919 ft TL: N45 00 38 W116 07 53. Hrs open: Boise State Radio, 1910 University Dr., Boise, 83725-1915. Phone: (208) 426-3663. Fax: (208) 344-6631. Web Site:radio.boisestate.edu Licensee: Idaho State Board of Education. Format: Jazz. ♦John Hess, gen mgr; Brad Campell, opns mgr; Hy Kloc, dev dir; Ele Ellis, progmg dir; Sadie Babits, news dir; Tom Taylor, engrg dir.

***KBSM(FM)**— Jan 20, 1991: 91.7 mhz; 220 w. 1,912 ft TL: N45 00 38 W116 07 53. Stereo. Hrs open: 24 Boise State Radio, 1910 University Dr., Boise, 83725. Phone: (208) 426-3663. Fax: (208) 344-6631. Web Site:radio.boisestate.edu Licensee: Idaho State Board of Education. Natl. Network: PRI, NPR, . Dow, Lohnes & Albertson. Format: Class, news, new age. News: 15 hrs wkly. Target aud: General. Spec prog: Jazz. ♦John Hess, gen mgr; Brad Campbell, opns mgr; Hy Kloc, dev dir; Ele Ellis, progmg dir; Sadie Babits, news dir; Tom Taylor, engrg dir.

***KBSQ(FM)**—Not on air, target date: unknown: 90.7 mhz; 220 w. 1,919 ft Hrs open: Boise State Radio, 1910 University Dr., Boise, 83725. Phone: (208) 426-3663. Fax: (208) 344-6631. Web Site:radio.boisestate.edu Licensee: Idaho State Board of Education. Format: News, div. ♦John Hess, gen mgr; Brad Campbell, opns mgr; Hy Kloc, dev dir; Ele Ellis, progmg dir; Sadie Babits, news dir; Tom Taylor, engrg dir.

KDZY(FM)— 2001: 98.3 mhz; 500 w horiz. Ant 1,922 ft TL: N45 00 18 W116 08 01. Hrs open: 24 1440 S. Weideman Ave., Boise, 83709. Phone: (208) 377-3790. Phone: (208) 634-3781. Fax: (208) 377-3792. Licensee: KSPD Inc. (group owner; acq 4-15-02; $75,000). Natl. Network: AP Network News, . Format: Country. Target aud: 25 plus. ♦Lee Schafer, pres & gen mgr.

KMCL(AM)—(Donnelly, Oct 15, 1965: Stn currently dark. 1240 khz; 1 kw-U. TL: N44 46 52 W116 02 51. Hrs open: Box 813, 83638. Secondary address: 204 N. 3rd St. 83638. Licensee: Brundage Mountain Air Inc. Population served: 25,000 ♦David Eaton, gen mgr.

Meridian

KDJQ(AM)— May 1, 2005: 890 khz; 50 kw-D, 250 w-N, DA-N. TL: N43 27 36 W116 14 19. Hrs open: 1050 Clover Dr., Boise, 83703-0405. Phone: (208) 388-4502. Phone: (208) 424-3689. Fax: (208) 433-9318. Licensee: Robert E. Combs (acq 5-14-2004; $425,000 for CP). Format: Oldies. ♦Robert E. Combs, gen mgr.

Middleton

***KTYY(FM)**—Not on air, target date: unknown: 88.7 mhz; 5 kw. Ant 2,594 ft TL: N43 45 18 W116 05 52. Hrs open: 16115 S. Montana Ave., Caldwell, 83605. Phone: (209) 459-5879. Fax: (208) 459-3144.E-mail: fun@ktfy.org Licensee: Southern Idaho Corp. ♦Michael Agee, gen mgr.

Montpelier

KVSI(AM)— July 20, 1965: 1450 khz; 1 kw-U. TL: N42 18 54 W111 18 38. Hrs open: Box 340, 24681 US 89, 83254. Phone: (208) 847-1450. Fax: (208) 847-1451.E-mail: kvsi@dcdi.net Web Site:kvsi.com Licensee: Tri-States Broadcasting LLC (acq 11-1-68). Population served: 2,604 Format: Country. Spec prog: Farm 4 hrs, relg 2 hrs wkly. ♦Keith Martindale, gen mgr; Ada Jane Hillier, progmg dir.

Moscow

KQQQ(AM)—See Pullman, WA

***KRFA-FM**— Sept 1, 1963: 91.7 mhz; 1.45 kw. 1,009 ft TL: N46 40 54 W116 58 13. Stereo. Hrs open: 24 Box 642530, 382 Murrow Communications Ctr., Washington State Univ., Pullman, WA, 99164-2530. Phone: (509) 335-6500. Fax: (509) 335-6557.E-mail: nwpr@wsu.edu Web Site:www.nwpr.org Licensee: Washington State University. (acq 7-1-84). Population served: 190,000 Natl. Network: NPR, PRI, . Don, Lohnes & Albertson. Format: Class, news. News staff: one; News: 37 hrs wkly. Target aud: General. Spec prog: Folk, jazz. ♦Kerry Swanson, gen mgr, stn mgr; Gillian Coldsnow, opns mgr; Sarah McDaniel, dev dir; Dave Deeney, gen sls mgr; Robin Rilette, mus dir; Anna King, news rptr.

KRPL(AM)— May 20, 1947: 1400 khz; 1 kw-U. TL: N46 44 47 W117 01 06. Hrs open: 24 Box 8849, 1114 N. Almon, 83843. Phone: (208) 882-2551. Fax: (208) 883-3571. Licensee: KRPL Inc. (acq 1-27-2004; $1 million for two-thirds of the shares with co-located FM). Population served: 60,000 Natl. Rep: McGavren Guild,. Haley, Bader & Potts. Format: Oldies 50s, 60s & 70s. News staff: 4; News: 12 hrs wkly. Target aud: 25-54. Spec prog: Farm 4 hrs, relg 2 hrs wkly. ♦Gary Cummins, pres & gen mgr.

***KUOI-FM**— November 1945: 89.3 mhz; 400 w. -92 ft TL: N46 43 43 W117 00 11. Stereo. Hrs open: 24 Student Union Bldg., 3rd Fl., Univ. of Idaho, 83844-4272. Phone: (208) 885-2218. Fax: (208) 885-2222.E-mail: kuoi@uidaho.edu Web Site:www.kuoi.org Licensee: University of Idaho. Population served: 14,146 Format: Free-form, div. News staff: 3; News: 2 hrs wkly. Target aud: General; alternative mus listeners. Spec prog: Black 3 hrs, folk 3 hrs, jazz 4 hrs wkly. ♦Andy Jacobson, stn mgr; Richard Dana, progmg dir; Marcus Kellis, mus dir; Jeff Kimberling, chief of engrg.

KZFN(FM)— Feb 24, 1973: 106.1 mhz; 62 kw. Ant 921 ft TL: N46 40 51 W116 58 26. Stereo. Hrs open: 24 Prog sep from AM Box 8849, 83843. Phone: (208) 883-2551. Fax: (208) 883-3571. Web Site:www.zfun106.com Population served: 130,000 Format: CHR. News staff: 4; News: 5 hrs wkly. Target aud: 25-54. ♦Gary Cummings, progmg mgr.

Mountain Home

KMHI(AM)— Mar 20, 1962: 1240 khz; 1 kw-U. TL: N43 09 03 W115 42 26. Hrs open: 24 5660 E. Franklin Rd., Suite 200, Nampa, 83687. Phone: (208) 465-9966. Fax: (208) 465-2922.E-mail: barbara@impactradiogroup.com Web Site:www.impactradiogroup.com Licensee: FM Idaho Co. LLC. (group owner; acq 12-31-2006; grpsl). Population served: 20,000 Natl. Network: Westwood One, . Format: Classic hit country. News staff: one; News: 15 hrs wkly. Target aud: General. Spec prog: Sp 7 hrs wkly. ♦Larry Johnson, pres; Elliott Klein, sr VP, gen mgr; Darrell Calton, gen mgr; Mark Broz, gen sls mgr; Mikey Fuentes, progmg dir; Sarah McBride, traf mgr.

KQLZ(FM)— 1982: 99.1 mhz; 73 kw. Ant 2,191 ft TL: N43 14 43 W115 26 12. Stereo. Hrs open: 24 5660 E. Franklin Rd., Suite 200, Nampa, 83687. Phone: (208) 465-9966. Fax: (208) 465-2922. Licensee: FM Idaho Co. LLC. (group owner; (acq 12-31-2006; grpsl). Population served: 50,000 Format: Oldies. Target aud: 18-34. ♦Darrell Calton, gen mgr.

Nampa

KIDO(AM)— May 17, 1920: 580 khz; 5 kw-U, DA-N. TL: N43 33 35 W116 24 02. Hrs open: 24 827 E. Park Blvd., Suite 201, Boise, 83712. Phone: (208) 344-6363. Fax: (208) 344-1134. Web Site:www.kidoam.com Licensee: Peak Broadcasting of Boise Licenses LLC. Group owner: Clear Channel Communications Inc. (acq 6-28-2007; grpsl). Population served: 300,000 Format: News, talk. Target aud: 25-54. ♦Kevin Godwin, gen mgr; Dave Burnett, progmg dir, news dir.

KKGL(FM)— February 1977: 96.9 mhz; 44 kw. 2,520 ft TL: N43 45 19 W116 05 52. Stereo. Hrs open: 24 1419 W. Bannock St., Boise, 83702. Phone: (208) 336-3670. Fax: (208) 336-3734. Web Site:www.96-9meeagle.com Licensee: Citadel Broadcasting Co. Group owner: Citadel Broadcasting Corp. (acq 12-10-97; grpsl). Population served: 400,000 Natl. Rep: Katz Radio,. Format: Classic rock. Target aud: 25-44; upscale baby boomers who listen to primarily 70s based rock. ♦Kevin Godwin, gen mgr; Rich Summers, opns mgr; Rich Bryan, progmg dir; Bill Frahn, chief of engrg.

KRVB(FM)— Jan 10, 1975: 94.9 mhz; 49 kw. 2,692 ft TL: N43 45 18 W116 05 52. Stereo. Hrs open: 5257 W. Fairview Ave., Suite 260, Boise, 83706. Phone: (208) 344-3511. Fax: (208) 947-6765. Web Site:www.riverinteractive.com Licensee: Journal Broadcast Corp. Group owner: Journal Communications Inc. (acq 4-11-00). Natl. Rep: Katz Radio,. Format: AOR. Target aud: 18-64. ♦Bob Rosenthal, CFO, VP, gen mgr; Dan McColly, opns mgr, progmg dir; Kristine Simoni, prom mgr; Tim Johnstone, mus dir; Rich Kemp, engrg dir; Paula Jensen, traf mgr.

KSAS-FM—(Caldwell, Sept 28, 1982: 103.3 mhz; 54 kw. 2,578 ft TL: N43 45 18 W116 05 52. Stereo. Hrs open: 24 827 E. Park Blvd., Suite 201, Boise, 83712. Phone: (208) 344-6363. Fax: (208) 385-9064. Fax: (208) 344-1134. Web Site:www.1033kissfm.com Licensee: Peak Broadcasting of Boise Licenses LLC. Group owner: Clear Channel Communications Inc. (acq 6-28-2007; grpsl). Population served: 250000 Fletcher, Heald & Hildreth. Format: Top 40. News staff: one; News: one hr wkly. Target aud: 25-54; upscale, white collar. Spec prog: Class 2 hrs, jazz 4 hrs wkly. ♦Kevin Godwin, gen mgr; Steve Kicklighter, stn mgr, progmg dir; Mike Sutton, gen sls mgr, progmg dir; Crystal Struthers, prom dir; Dave Burnett, news dir, chief of engrg; Susan Green, traf mgr.

KTIK(AM)— Nov 1, 1962: 1350 khz; 5 kw-D, 600 w-N. TL: N43 32 58 W116 24 38. Hrs open: 24 Box 1280, 1419 W. Bannock St., Boise, 83702. Phone: (208) 336-3670. Fax: (208) 336-3736. Web Site:www.ktik.com Licensee: Citadel Broadcasting Co. Group owner: Citadel Broadcasting Corp. (acq 4-1-03; $750,000). Natl. Network: ESPN Radio, Westwood One, . Format: Sports, talk. News: one hr wkly. Target aud: 25-54; sports oriented men. ♦Don Morin, gen mgr, mktg mgr; Tom Newman, gen sls mgr; Andrew Paul, progmg dir.

New Plymouth

KZMG(FM)—Licensed to New Plymouth. See Boise

Orofino

KLER(AM)— Oct 15, 1958: 1300 khz; 5 kw-D, 1 kw-U, DA-N. TL: N46 28 41 W116 14 34. Hrs open: Box 32, 3110 Upper Fords Creek Rd., 83544. Phone: (208) 476-5702. Fax: (208) 476-5703.E-mail: kler@wildblue.net Licensee: Central Idaho Broadcasting. (acq 12-7-92; $75,000 with co-located FM; 1-4-93). Population served: 14,000 Natl. Network: ABC, Jones Radio Networks, . Format: Country. News staff: news progmg 8 hrs wkly News: 2;. Target aud: General; family or logging industry-federal employee workers. ♦Jeff Jones, gen mgr, gen sls mgr; Jason Ford, news dir; Ben Dickson, pub affrs dir; Jim Sheldon, chief of engrg.

KLER-FM— Sept 20, 1979: 95.1 mhz; 2.3 kw. Ant 676 ft TL: N46 28 09 W116 16 40. Stereo. Hrs open: 24 Prog sep from AM Box 3110, Upper Fords Creek Rd., 83544. Phone: (208) 476-5702. Fax: (208) 476-5703.E-mail: kler@wildblue.net Population served: 4,000 Natl. Network: Jones Radio Networks, . Format: Adult contemp. News staff: 2; News: 8 hrs wkly. ♦Jeff Jones, gen mgr, gen sls mgr; Jason Ford, news dir; Ben Dickson, pub affrs dir; Jim Sheldon, chief of engrg.

KZID(FM)— 2003: 98.5 mhz; 1.65 kw. Ant 630 ft TL: N46 28 09 W116 16 40. Hrs open: Torro Broadcasting, 2307 Princess Anne St., Greensboro, NC, 27408. Phone: (336) 286-2087. Licensee: Torro Broadcasting.

Parma

KWYD(FM)— Oct 22, 1990: 101.1 mhz; 96 kw. Ant 1,000 ft TL: N43 24 09 W116 54 09. Stereo. Hrs open: 24 5660 E. Franklin Rd., Suite 200, Nampa, 83687-5133. Phone: (208) 465-9966. Fax: (208) 465-2922. Web Site:www.wild101fm.com Licensee: FM Idaho Co. LLC. (acq 9-14-2007; $900,000). Natl. Network: ABC, . Natl. Rep: Target Broadcast Sales,. Format: Adult contemp. News staff: one; News: 5 hrs wkly. Target aud: 25-54; women. Spec prog: Sports, entertainment, business one hr, relg one hr wkly. ♦Darrell Calton, gen mgr & prom dir.

Payette

KIOV(AM)— Dec 20, 1957: 1450 khz; 1 kw-U. TL: N44 03 47 W116 54 27. Hrs open: 24 1406 N. Main St., Suite 107, Meridian, 83642-1798. Phone: (208) 267-5234. Fax: (208) 888-9647.E-mail: sports@kiov.com Web Site:www.kiov.com Licensee: Media Enterprises LLC. (Acq 8-00). Population served: 125,000 Rgnl rep: Tacher. Format: Sports. Target aud: 18-54; 65% male. ♦David Combes, gen mgr; Marshall Sage, opns mgr.

KQXR(FM)— Dec 1, 1978: 100.3 mhz; 98 kw. 708 ft TL: N43 49 31 W116 30 29. Stereo. Hrs open: 24 5257 W. Fairview Ave., Suite 260, Boise, 83706. Phone: (208) 344-3511. Fax: (208) 947-6765. Web Site:www.xrock.com Licensee: Journal Broadcast Corp. Group owner: Journal Broadcast Group Inc. (acq 5-13-98; grpsl). Population served: 293,600 Natl. Rep: Katz Radio,. Format: Rock, alternative. Target aud: 18-49. ♦Bob Rosenthal, VP, gen mgr; Dan McColly, opns mgr; Kristine Simoni, prom mgr; Jeremy Nicolato, progmg dir; Jeremi Smith, mus dir; Rick Kemp, engrg dir; Paula Jensen, traf mgr.

Plummer

***KWIS(FM)**—Not on air, target date: unknown: 88.3 mhz; 2.4 kw vert. Ant 945 ft TL: N47 19 37 W116 42 55. Hrs open: Box 408, 83851. Phone: (208) 686-5059. Fax: (208) 686-1182. Web Site:www.cdatribe.com Licensee: Coeur d'Alene Tribe. ♦Chief Allan, chmn.

Pocatello

KEGE(FM)— July 23, 2007: 92.1 mhz; 12 kw. Ant 987 ft TL: N42 52 26 W112 30 47. Hrs open: Box 998, 83204. Phone: (208) 233-1133. Fax: (208) 232-1240.E-mail: kellymartinez@gapbroadcasting.com Web Site:www.theedge921.com Licensee: GAP Broadcasting Pocatello License LLC. (acq 9-3-2008; $1.09 million). Format: Alternative. ♦Neica Kinney, gen mgr.

***KISU-FM**— Apr 15, 1998: 91.1 mhz; 4.5 kw. 1,043 ft TL: N42 51 46 W112 31 03. Stereo. Hrs open: 24 921 S. 8th Ave., Mail stop 8014, Idaho State University, 83209. Phone: (208) 282-3691. Fax: (208) 282-4600.E-mail: milljerr@isu.edu Web Site:www.kisu.org Licensee: Idaho State University. Population served: 100,000 Natl. Network: NPR, PRI, . Dow, Lohnes, Albertson. Format: Jazz, AAA, news, talk, entertainment. News: 60+. ♦Jerry Miller, gen mgr.

KLLP(FM)—See Chubbuck

KMGI(FM)— Apr 1, 1978: 102.5 mhz; 100 kw. Ant 1,023 ft TL: N42 51 57 W112 30 46. Stereo. Hrs open: 24 Prog sep from AM 544 N. Arthur, 83204. Phone: (208) 233-2121. Fax: (208) 234-7682. Web Site:www.classicrock102.fm Natl. Network: Westwood One, . Format: Classic rock. ♦C.J. Morrison, progmg mgr.

KOUU(AM)— Dec 20, 1956: 1290 khz; 50 kw-D, 24 w-N, DA-D. TL: N42 57 27 W112 25 46 (day), N42 57 28 W112 25 46 (night). Stereo. Hrs open: 24 Box 97, 436 N. Main, 83204. Phone: (208) 234-1290. Fax: (208) 234-9451. Licensee: Idaho Wireless Corp. (group owner; (acq 3-86; with co-located FM;12-9-85). Population served: 250,000 Natl. Network: ABC, . Format: Traditional country. Target aud: 35-64; adults. ♦Paul Anderson, gen mgr; Harry Newhardt, gen sls mgr.

KPKY(FM)— Aug 18, 1975: 94.9 mhz; 100 kw. Ant 1,004 ft TL: N42 52 26 W112 30 47. Stereo. Hrs open: Prog sep from AM Box 998, 259 E. Center St., 83201. Phone: (208) 233-1133. Fax: (208) 232-1240.E-mail: kellymartinez@gapbroadcasting.com Web Site:www.kpky.com Licensee: GAP Broadcasting Pocatello License LLC. (acq 2-13-2008; grpsl). Population served: 39,000 Format: Classic rock. ♦Marie Mccallister, progmg dir; Mike Hudson, min affrs dir; J.D. Kelly, spec ev coord.

KPTO(AM)— Dec 1, 2005: 1440 khz; 2.5 kw-D, 350 w-N, DA-2. TL: N42 56 30 W112 27 17. Hrs open: 24 Box 1450, St. George, UT, 84771-1450. Secondary address: 210 North 1000 East, St. George, UT 84770-3155. Phone: (208) 234-7000. Phone: (435) 628-1000. Fax: (208) 232-1440. Fax: (435) 628-6636.E-mail: legacy1@infowest.com Licensee: AM Radio 1440 Inc. Group owner: Diamond Broadcasting Corp. (acq 12-6-2004). Natl. Network: CNN Radio, Westwood One, . Dan J. Alpert. Format: Adult standards. News: On-The-Hour. Target aud: 25-64. ♦E. Morgan Skinner Jr., CEO & pres.

KRTK(AM)—See Chubbuck

KSEI(AM)— Sept 23, 1926: 930 khz; 5 kw-U, DA-N. TL: N42 57 44 W112 29 50. Hrs open: 24 Box 40, 83204. Secondary address: 544 N. Arthur St. 83204. Phone: (208) 233-2121. Fax: (208) 234-7682.E-mail: neilmab@pacempire.com Licensee: Pacific Empire Radio Corp. (group owner; acq 8-28-97; $1.2 million with co-located FM). Population served: 56,185 Natl. Rep: Katz Radio,. Format: Sporting news. Target aud: General. ♦Mark Bolland, pres, gen mgr; Neil Mayberry, gen mgr & gen sls mgr; Jim Christopher, news dir; Bill Trowe, chief of engrg.

KWIK(AM)— September 1946: 1240 khz; 1 kw-U. TL: N42 55 14 W112 27 17. Stereo. Hrs open: 24 Box 998, 259 E. Center St., 83201. Phone: (208) 233-1133. Phone: (800) 582-1240. Fax: (208) 232-1240.E-mail: kellymartinez@gapbroadcasting.com Web Site:www.newsradio1240.com Licensee: GAP Broadcasting Pocatello License LLC. Group owner: Clear Channel Communications Inc. (acq 2-13-2008; grpsl). Population served: 57,550 Rgnl rep: Art Moore. Drinker Biddle & Reath LLP. Format: Sports, news/talk. News staff: 3; News: 15 hrs wkly. Target aud: 45 plus. Spec prog: Farm 3 hrs, gospel 2 hrs, relg one hr, American Indian one hr wkly. ♦Tim Murphy, gen mgr; Jodie Bates, gen sls mgr; Neal Larson, news dir; Rhett Downing, chief of engrg.

KZBQ(FM)— Dec 27, 1969: 93.7 mhz; 100 kw. Ant 984 ft TL: N42 51 57 W112 30 46. Stereo. Hrs open: 24 Box 97, 436 N. Main, 83204. Phone: (208) 234-1290. Fax: (208) 234-9451.E-mail: paul@kzbq.com Population served: 250,000 Natl. Network: ABC, . Format: Country. Target aud: 25-54; adults. ♦Paul Anderson, stn mgr.

***KZJB(FM)**— 2006: 90.3 mhz; 910 w vert. Ant 1,031 ft TL: N42 51 46 W112 31 03. Hrs open: 4250 S. 25th East, Idaho Falls, 83404. Phone: (208) 524-1503. Fax: (208) 524-0697.E-mail: breinisch@ccifi.org Licensee: CSN International (group owner). Format: Christian relg. ♦James Knudsen, stn mgr.

Post Falls

KCDA(FM)—Licensed to Post Falls. See Spokane WA

Preston

KACH(AM)— Sept 4, 1948: 1340 khz; 1 kw-U. TL: N42 07 45 W111 51 00. (Simulcast on FM Translator K288 AG Preston 100%.). Hrs open: 24 1133 E. Glendale Rd., 83263. Phone: (208) 852-1340. Fax: (208) 852-1342.E-mail: kach@plmw.com Web Site:www.kachradio.com Licensee: Alan J. White, Nelada G. White. (acq 5-13-98). Population served: 10,500 Natl. Network: ABC, . Natl. Rep: Interep,. Wire Svc: AP Format: Adult standards. News: 12 hrs wkly. Target aud: 18-54; general. Spec prog: Farm. ♦Alan White, gen mgr.

KKEX(FM)— Dec 9, 1993: 96.7 mhz; 105 w. 226 ft TL: N47 07 45 W111 51 00. Hrs open: 24 Box 3369, Radio Stn. KKEX(FM), Logan, UT, 84323-3369. Secondary address: 810 W. 200 N., Logan, UT 84321. Phone: (435) 752-1390. Phone: (435) 753-9607. Fax: (435) 752-1392.E-mail: kkex@vradio.com Web Site:www.kix96.fm Licensee: Sun Valley Radio Inc. (group owner; acq 1994). Population served: 130,000 Format: Country. ♦M. Kent Frandsen, pres; Jay Eubanks, gen mgr; Lynn Simmons, progmg dir, progmg mgr; Dan Baker, chief of engrg.

Rathdrum

***KYMS(FM)**— June 2006: 89.9 mhz; 1.1 kw vert. Ant 1,965 ft TL: N48 05 38 W116 33 12. Hrs open: 24 Box 1208, Airway Heights, WA, 99001. Phone: (509) 244-5577. Fax: (509) 244-2232. Web Site:www.csnradio.com Licensee: Calvary Radio Network Inc. (group owner). Format: Relg.

Rexburg

***KBYI(FM)**— Nov 13, 1972: 100.5 mhz; 100 kw. 692 ft TL: N43 45 44 W111 57 30. Stereo. Hrs open: 24 102 RGS Bldg., BYU Idaho, 83460-1700. Phone: (208) 496-2907. Fax: (208) 496-2912.E-mail: clarkjim@byui.edu Web Site:www.kbyu.edu/kbyi Licensee: Brigham Young University-Idaho. Population served: 200,000 Natl. Network: NPR, PRI, . Format: Class, news. News staff: one; News: 33 hrs wkly. Target aud: General. ♦Jim Clark, gen mgr; Mark Bailey, gen sls mgr, news dir, traf mgr; Michelle Snyder, mktg.

***KBYR-FM**— 1993: 91.5 mhz; 100 w. -39 ft TL: N43 49 09 W111 46 51. Hrs open: 24 Ricks College, Spori Bldg., 83460-0105. Phone: (208) 496-2907. Fax: (208) 496-2912. Web Site:www.byui.edu/kbyr Licensee: Ricks College Corp. Population served: 30,000 Format: Mormon contemp. Target aud: General. ♦Jim Clark, gen mgr.

KGTM(FM)— Jan 17, 1986: 98.1 mhz; 3 kw. 299 ft TL: N43 48 55 W111 46 09. (CP: 25 kw, ant 276 ft.). Stereo. Hrs open: 24 1327 E. 17th St., Idaho Falls, 83404. Phone: (208) 529-6926. Fax: (208) 529-6927.E-mail: ricmason@pacempire.com Web Site:www.KGTM.com Licensee: Pacific Empire Radio Corp. (group owner; acq 7-25-2000; $495,000 with KRXK(FM) Rexburg). Population served: 60,000 Fletcher, Heald & Hildreth. Format: Classic hits. Target aud: 35 plus. ♦Phil Jimenez, gen mgr; Rick Mason, progmg dir.

KMRR(FM)—Not on air, target date: unknown: 89.9 mhz; 11 kw vert. Ant 1,056 ft TL: N43 49 06 W111 20 25. Hrs open: 219 Dodd Rd., Ringgold, GA, 30736-2958. Phone: (706) 965-2355. Fax: (706) 965-3755. Licensee: Victor Broadcasting Inc. ♦James E. Price III, pres.

KRXK(AM)— January 1951: 1230 khz; 1 kw-U. TL: N43 50 50 W111 47 03. Hrs open:
Simulcast with KSEI (AM) Pocotello.
1327 E. 17th St., Idaho Falls, 83404. Phone: (208) 529-6926. Fax: (208) 529-6927.E-mail: philjimenez@pacempire.com Licensee: Pacific Empire Radio Corp. (group owner; (acq 7-25-2000; $495,000 with KGTM(FM) Rexburg). Population served: 16,000 Rgnl. Network: Intermountain Farm/Ranch Network. Natl. Rep: Target Broadcast Sales,. Format: ESPN. Target aud: 25-54; male. ♦Phil Jimenez, gen mgr; Sean Green, progmg dir.

KSNA(FM)— Aug 18, 1975: 94.3 mhz; 43 kw. Ant 522 ft TL: N43 45 20 W111 57 56. Stereo. Hrs open: 24 854 Lindsay Blvd., Idaho Falls, 83402. Phone: (208) 522-1101. Fax: (208) 522-6110. Web Site:www.sunny943.com Licensee: Sand Hill Media Corp. (group owner; acq 9-7-2001; $1.2 million with KQEO(FM) Idaho Falls plus 36-month employment agreement). Population served: 50,000 Natl. Network: Jones Radio Networks, USA, . Natl. Rep: Tacher,. Format: Modern rock. ♦Keith Walker, gen mgr; Mike Steele, opns mgr & progmg dir; John Balginy, news dir.

Rigby

***KLRI(FM)**— 2005: 89.5 mhz; 78 kw vert. Ant 1,527 ft TL: N43 30 04 W112 39 44. Stereo. Hrs open: 24
Rebroadcasts KLVR(FM) Santa Rosa, CA 100%.
2351 Sunset Blvd., Suite 170-218, Rocklin, CA, 95765. Phone: (916) 251-1600. Fax: (916) 251-1650.E-mail: klove@klove.com Web Site:www.klove.com Licensee: Educational Media Foundation. Group owner: EMF Broadcasting. Natl. Network: K-Love, . Shaw Pittman. Format: Contemp Christian. News staff: 3. Target aud: 25-44; Judeo Christian, female. ♦Richard Jenkins, pres; Mike Novak, VP; Keith Whipple, dev dir; David Pierce, progmg mgr; Ed Lenane, news dir; Sam Wallington, engrg dir; Karen Johnson, news rptr.

Ririe

***KSQS(FM)**— 2006: 91.7 mhz; 250 w. Ant 532 ft TL: N43 32 37 W111 53 07. Hrs open: 2201 S. 6th St., Las Vegas, NV, 89104. Phone: (702) 731-5452. Fax: (702) 731-1992.E-mail: info@sosradio.net Web Site:www.sosradio.net Licensee: Faith Communications Corp. Format: Adult contemp Christian. ♦Brad Staley, gen mgr.

Rupert

KFTA(AM)— Oct 12, 1955: 970 khz; 2.5 kw-D. TL: N42 37 08 W113 39 31. (CP: 900 w-N, DA-N. TL: N42 36 10 W113 43 21). Hrs open: 24 120 S. 300 W., 83350. Phone: (208) 436-4757. Fax: (208) 436-3050.E-mail: lafantastica970@quepasa.com Licensee: Tri-Market Radio Broadcasters Inc. Group owner: Tri-Market Radio Broadcasters Inc. & Eagle Rock Broadcasting Inc. (acq 9-24-93; $700,000 with co-located FM; 10-11-93). Population served: 50000 Format: Sp. News staff: one. ♦Kim Lee, gen mgr & gen sls mgr; Ben Reed, progmg dir, news dir; Jerry Thaxton, chief of engrg.

KKMV(FM)— Dec 5, 1978: 106.1 mhz; 25 kw. Ant 2,496 ft TL: N42 20 06 W113 36 15. Stereo. Hrs open: 120 S. 300 W., 83350. Phone: (208) 436-4757. Fax: (208) 436-3050. Licensee: Tri-Market Radio

Broadcasters Inc. Population served: 125,000 Format: Hot country. News staff: one. Target aud: Adults: 25-54. ♦Kim Lee, pres.

Saint Anthony

KIGO(AM)— July 10, 1966: 1420 khz; 32 kw-D, 12 w-N. TL: N43 40 02 W111 52 14. Hrs open: 24 1447 Winter Lane, Jerome, 83338. Phone: (208) 280-1962. Licensee: Albino Ortega & Maria Juarez (acq 5-1-2005; $85,000). Population served: 265,000 Format: Rgnl Mexican. Target aud: 25-44; adults. ♦Albino Ortega, gen mgr.

Saint Maries

KOFE(AM)— Mar 1, 1970: 1240 khz; 1 kw-D, 500 w-N. TL: N47 19 14 W116 32 50. Hrs open: 24 Box 278, 201 N. 8th, 83861. Phone: (208) 245-1240. Fax: (208) 245-6525.E-mail: KOFE@sm-email.com Licensee: Campbell River Holding Co. L.L.C. (acq 5-3-01; $1,000 for 70%). Population served: 8,000 Natl. Network: Fox News Radio, . Format: Classic Hits. News staff: 2; News: 9 hrs wkly. Target aud: 25-55. ♦Theresa Plank, gen mgr; Phil Plank, chief of engrg, engr.

KXJO(FM)—Not on air, target date: unknown: 92.1 mhz; 25 kw horiz. Ant 328 ft TL: N47 18 15 W116 36 01. Hrs open: 980 N. Michigan Ave., Suite 1880, Chicago, IL, 60611. Phone: (312) 204-9900. Licensee: College Creek Media LLC. ♦Neal J. Robinson, pres.

Salmon

KSRA(AM)— Mar 1, 1959: 960 khz; 1 kw-D. TL: N45 11 02 W113 52 12. Hrs open: 315 Riverfront Dr., 83467. Phone: (208) 756-2218. Fax: (208) 756-2098.E-mail: ksraradio@ksrafm.com Licensee: Salmon River Communications Inc. (acq 6-19-00; $345,000 with co-located FM). Population served: 7,500 Natl. Network: ABC, . Format: Country, adult contemp. News: 4. Spec prog: Farm 4 hrs, class one hr wkly. ♦Jim Hone, pres; Rick Sessions, gen mgr; Leo Marshall, gen sls mgr; Todd Skeen, progmg dir; Rockwell Smith, engrg VP, chief of engrg.

KSRA-FM— September 1979: 92.7 mhz; 1.5 kw. -880 ft TL: N45 11 02 W113 52 12. Stereo. Hrs open: 6 AM-10 PM Dups AM 100% 315 Riverfront Dr., 83467. Phone: (208) 756-2218. Fax: (208) 756-2098.E-mail: ksraradio@ksrafm.com Population served: 10,000 Natl. Network: ABC, . ♦Rick Sessions, gen mgr; Todd Skeen, prom dir.

KXML(FM)—Not on air, target date: unknown: 99.9 mhz; 200 w. Ant -1,312 ft TL: N45 10 02 W113 52 14. Hrs open: Box 36148, Tucson, AZ, 85740. Phone: (520) 797-4434. Licensee: SkyWest Media L.L.C. ♦Ted Tucker, gen mgr.

Sandpoint

KIBR(FM)— 1994: 102.5 mhz; 3 kw. 177 ft TL: N48 15 22 W116 30 46. Stereo. Hrs open: 24
Rebroadcasts KICR(FM) Coeur d'Alene 100%.
327 Marion Ave., 83864. Phone: (208) 263-2179. Fax: (208) 265-5440.E-mail: carolynp@953kpnd.com Licensee: Benefield Broadcasting Inc. (acq 3-31-95; $250,000;5-22-95). Population served: 60,000 Natl. Network: ABC, . Format: Classic country. News staff: one. Target aud: 25-54. ♦Dylan Benefield, gen mgr, opns mgr, gen sls mgr; Jimmy Silver, progmg dir, progmg mgr; Mike Brown, news dir.

KPND(FM)— May 19, 1980: 95.3 mhz; 9.8 kw. Ant 2,368 ft TL: N48 22 40 W116 37 05. Stereo. Hrs open: 24 327 Marion Ave., 83864. Phone: (208) 263-2179. Fax: (208) 265-5440.E-mail: carolynp@953kpnd.com Population served: 80,000 Format: AAA. ♦Jim Tomchek, traf mgr.

KSPT(AM)— Mar 23, 1949: 1400 khz; 1 kw-U. TL: N48 18 16 W116 32 32. Hrs open: 24
Rebroadcasts KBFI(AM) Bonners Ferry 100%.
327 Marion Ave., 83864. Phone: (208) 263-2179. Fax: (208) 265-5440.E-mail: carolynp@953kpnd.com Licensee: Blue Sky Broadcasting Inc. (acq 5-4-83; $250,000;5-30-85). Population served: 37,000 Natl. Network: ABC, USA, . Natl. Rep: Tacher,. Smith & Belendiuk. Format: News/talk, sports. Target aud: 25 plus. Spec prog: Relg 2 hrs wkly. ♦Dylan Benefield, gen mgr, progmg dir; Mike Davis, news dir; Conrad Agtee, chief of engrg; Jim Tomchek, traf mgr.

Shelley

KBJX(FM)— October 1999: 106.3 mhz; 100 kw. 636 ft TL: N43 06 45 W112 29 34. Stereo. Hrs open: 24/7 1327 E. 17th St., Idaho Falls, 83404. Phone: (208) 529-6926. Fax: (208) 529-6927.E-mail: JJ@b106.FM Web Site:www.B106.FM Licensee: Pacific Empire Radio Corp. (group owner; acq 10-6-98; $788,500 with KATW(FM) Lewiston). Population served: 80,000 Format: Hot AC. Target aud: 25-54; adults. ♦Phil Jimenez, CEO & gen mgr; JJ Jeffrey, progmg dir.

Soda Springs

KBRV(AM)— Sept 22, 1957: 790 khz; 5 kw-D, 29 w-N. TL: N42 38 39 W111 36 41. Hrs open: 421 W. 2nd S., 83276. Phone: (208) 547-2400. Fax: (208) 547-4593. Fax: (208) 547-2401. Licensee: Caribou Broadcasting Inc. (acq 1-8-2001). Population served: 100,000 Format: Country. ♦Tom Mathis, gen mgr.

***KHCX(FM)**—Not on air, target date: unknown: 88.9 mhz; 100 w. Ant 243 ft TL: N42 38 39 W111 36 41. Hrs open: Houston Christian Broadcasters Inc., 2424 South Blvd., Houston, TX, 77098. Phone: (713) 520-5200.E-mail: email@khcb.org Web Site:www.khcb.org Licensee: Houston Christian Broadcasters Inc. (acq 1-15-2009). ♦Bruce Munsterman, pres & gen mgr.

KITT(FM)— Oct 17, 1983: 100.1 mhz; 3 kw horiz. Ant -276 ft TL: N42 38 30 W111 36 40. (CP: COL Wilson, WY. 11 kw, ant 1,050 ft. TL: N43 27 39 W110 45 09). Stereo. Hrs open: 24 Box 101, 213 East 2nd S., 83276. Secondary address: Box 1450, 210 North 1000 East, St. George, UT 84771. Phone: (208) 547-2500. Fax: (208) 547-4593.E-mail: legacy1@infowest.com Licensee: Tri-State Media Corp. Group owner: Legacy Communications Corp. (acq 7-8-2004; $234,000). Population served: 20,000 Dan J. Alpert. Format: Main country. News staff: 2. ♦E. Morgan Skinner, Jr., pres.

Sun Valley

***KBSS(FM)**— August 2004: 91.1 mhz; 700 w. Ant 1,870 ft TL: N43 38 36 W114 23 49. Hrs open: Boise State Radio, 1910 University Dr., Boise, 83725-1915. Phone: (208) 426-3663. Fax: (208) 344-6631.E-mail: radio@boisestate.edu Web Site:radio.boisestate.edu Licensee: Idaho State Board of Education. Natl. Network: NPR, . Format: News, info. ♦John Hess, gen mgr; Brad Campbell, opns mgr; Hy Kloc, dev dir; Ele Ellis, progmg dir; Sadie Babits, news dir; Tom Taylor, engrg dir.

KECH-FM— Nov 21, 1988: 95.3 mhz; 100 w. Ant 2,168 ft TL: N43 39 42 W114 24 07. (CP: 16 kw, ant 1,909 ft. TL: N43 38 36 W114 23 49). Hrs open: 24 220 Northwood Way, Ketchum, 83340. Phone: (208) 726-5324. Fax: (208) 726-5459. Web Site:www.kech95.com Licensee: Chaparral Broadcasting Inc. Group owner: Chaparral Communications acq 7-30-2004; grpsl). Cohn & Marks. Format: Classic rock. News staff: one; News: 6 hrs wkly. Target aud: 25-54; upscale adults. Spec prog: Alternative 5 hrs, blues 8 hrs, jazz 6 hrs wkly. ♦Scott Anderson, gen mgr; Cathy Nikolaisons, gen sls mgr; Bob Thompson, progmg dir; Sue Bailey, news dir.

KSKI-FM— Aug 3, 1977: 103.7 mhz; 53 kw. 1,905 ft TL: N43 38 36 W114 23 49. Stereo. Hrs open: 24 Box 2750, Hailey, 83333. Phone: (208) 726-5324. Fax: (208) 726-5459. Web Site:www.ketsvidaho.net Licensee: Chaparral Broadcasting Inc. Group owner: Chaparral Communications (acq 7-30-2004; grpsl). Population served: 100,000 Chon & Marks. Format: Alt rock. News staff: one; News: 2 hrs wkly. Target aud: 18-49; affluent, upscale consumers. ♦Scott Anderson, gen mgr; Cathy Nikolaisons, gen sls mgr, sls; Bob Thompson, progmg dir; Sue Bailey, news dir.

***KWRV(FM)**— July 29, 1993: 91.9 mhz; 100 w. Ant 2,154 ft TL: N43 39 41 W114 24 08. Hrs open: Box 67, MN, 83353. Phone: (651) 290-1500. Fax: (651) 290-1224.E-mail: molson@mpr.org Web Site:www.mpr.org Licensee: Minnesota Public Radio. Natl. Network: PRI, . Rgnl. Network: Minn. Pub. Minn. Pub. Radio Format: Class. ♦William Kling, pres.

KYZK(FM)—Not on air, target date: unknown: 107.5 mhz; 100 kw. 1,734 ft TL: N43 16 50 W114 09 08. Hrs open: 24 220 Northwood Way, Ketchum, 83340. Phone: (208) 726-5324. Fax: (208) 726-5459. Licensee: Chaparral Broadcasting Inc. Group owner: Chaparral Communications (acq 7-30-2004; grpsl). Population served: 15,000 Natl. Network: ABC, . Rgnl rep: Allied Radio Cohn & Marks. Format: Jazz. ♦Scott Anderson, gen mgr; Cathy Nikolaisons, gen sls mgr; Bob Thompson, progmg dir; Sue Bailey, news dir; Don Mussell, engrg dir.

Troy

KQZB(FM)— 2008: 100.5 mhz; 900 w. Ant 1,597 ft TL: N46 48 42 W116 54 59. Hrs open: 403 Capital St., Lewiston, 83501. Phone: (208) 743-4560. Fax: (208) 798-0110. Licensee: Pacific Empire Radio Corp. Format: Smooth Jazz. ♦Mark Bolland, pres.

Twin Falls

KART(AM)—See Jerome

***KAWZ(FM)**— Apr 13, 1988: 89.9 mhz; 33 kw horiz, 100 kw vert. Ant 991 ft TL: N42 43 47 W114 24 52. Stereo. Hrs open: 24 Box 391, 83303. Secondary address: 4002 N. 3300 E. 83301. Phone: (208) 734-6633. Fax: (208) 736-1958.E-mail: csn@csnradio.com Web Site:www.csnradio.com Licensee: Calvary Chapel of Twin Falls Inc. Population served: 125,000 Boothe, Ferert, and Tepper. Format: Christian praise & worship, Bible teaching. News: 2 hrs wkly. Target aud: General; 18-80. ♦Mike Kestler, pres, dev VP; Mike Stocklin, gen mgr; Don Mills, opns dir, opns mgr, progmg dir.

***KBSW(FM)**— May 15, 1989: 91.7 mhz; 4.5 kw. Ant 492 ft TL: N42 43 48 W114 25 06. Stereo. Hrs open: 24 Boise State Univ., 1910 University Dr., Boise, 83725. Phone: (208) 426-3663. Fax: (208) 344-6631. Web Site:radio.boisestate.edu Licensee: Idaho State Board of Education. Natl. Network: PRI, NPR, . Dow, Lohnes & Albertson. Format: Talk, class. News staff: 2; News: 15 hrs wkly. Target aud: General. ♦John Hess, gen mgr, stn mgr; Brad Campbell, opns mgr; Hy Kloc, dev dir; Ele Ellis, progmg dir; Sadie Babits, news dir; Tom Taylor, engrg dir & engrg mgr.

***KCIR(FM)**— Dec 12, 1982: 90.7 mhz; 20 kw. 2,519 ft TL: N42 20 07 W113 36 17. Stereo. Hrs open: 24
Rebroadcasts KILA(FM) Las Vegas 97%.
1446 Filer Ave. E., 83301. Phone: (208) 734-5777. Fax: (208) 734-0331.E-mail: info@kcirfm.com Web Site:www.sosradio.net Licensee: Faith Communications Corp. (acq 9-29-82). Population served: 300,000 Natl. Network: USA, . Format: Christian, educ. News: 5 hrs wkly. Target aud: 25-49; adults with families. Spec prog: Children 2 hrs wkly. ♦Jack French, pres, gen mgr; Brad Staley, gen mgr; Duane Luchsinger, stn mgr; Mike Mead, mus dir.

***KEFX(FM)**— 1996: 88.9 mhz; 3 kw. 20 ft TL: N42 33 25 W114 28 18. Hrs open: Box 271, 83303. Phone: (208) 734-6633. Fax: (208) 736-1958.E-mail: effectradio@effectradio.com Web Site:www.effectiveradio.com Licensee: Calvary Chapel of Twin Falls Inc. Group owner: CSN International Population served: 40,000 Format: Christian, relg, bible teaching. ♦Mike Kestler, pres, gen mgr; Matt McNeilly, stn mgr; Brian Harman, progmg dir; Ray Gorney, chief of engrg.

***KEZJ(AM)**— 1946: 1450 khz; 1 kw-U. TL: N42 32 36 W114 28 14. Hrs open:
Rebroadcasts KBSU(AM) Boise.
Box 1238, College of Southern Idaho, 83303-1238. Phone: (208) 736-3046. Fax: (208) 736-2188. Web Site:www.radio.boisestate.edu Licensee: College of Southern Idaho. Format: News/talk, jazz. ♦Don Wimberly, gen mgr.

KEZJ-FM— Mar 15, 1977: 95.7 mhz; 100 kw. Ant 620 ft TL: N42 43 42 W114 24 48. Stereo. Hrs open: Box 1259, 83301. Secondary address: 415 Park Ave. 83301. Phone: (208) 733-7512. Fax: (208) 733-7525.E-mail: bradweiser@clearchannel.com Web Site:www.957kezj.com Licensee: GAP Broadcasting Twin Falls License LLC. Group owner: Clear Channel Communications Inc. (acq 2-13-2008; grpsl). Population served: 140,000 Natl. Network: ABC, . Natl. Rep: Clear Channel,. Wire Svc: ABC Wire Svc: AP Format: Country. Target aud: 25-54. ♦Janice Degner, VP, gen mgr; Brad Weiser, opns dir, progmg VP; James Tidmarsh, news dir; Kelly Klaas, chief of engrg.

KIRQ(FM)— 2007: 102.1 mhz; 5.2 kw. Ant 722 ft TL: N42 43 54 W114 25 04. Hrs open: 21361 Hwy. 30, 83301-0197. Phone: (208) 735-8300. Fax: (208) 733-4196. Licensee: Locally Owned Radio LLC. (acq 9-8-2006; $2,911,000 with KTPZ(FM) Hazelton). Format: Rock. ♦Larry Johnson, pres & gen mgr; Jerre Fender, opns dir, progmg dir; Deb Uvieu, gen sls mgr; Denis Jeffs, traf mgr.

KLIX(AM)— Dec 12, 1946: 1310 khz; 5 kw-D, 2.5 kw-N, DA-N. TL: N42 33 30 W114 26 40. Hrs open: 24 Box 1259, 415 Park Ave., 83303. Phone: (208) 733-1310. Fax: (208) 733-7525. Web Site:www.newsradio1310.com Licensee: GAP Broadcasting Twin Falls License LLC. Group owner: Clear Channel Communications Inc. (acq 2-13-2008; grpsl). Population served: 26,209 Natl. Network: ABC, . Format: News/talk. News staff: one; News: 12 hrs wkly. Target aud: 35-54. Spec prog: Farm 2 hrs wkly. ♦Chris Muldaney, gen mgr, gen sls mgr; Brad Weiser, opns mgr, progmg dir; Suzanne Jusst, news dir; Kelly Klaas, chief of engrg, farm dir.

KLIX-FM— June 15, 1974: 96.5 mhz; 100 kw. Ant 130 ft TL: N42 33 05 W114 30 59. Stereo. Hrs open: Box 1259, 415 Park Ave., 83303. Phone: (208) 733-1310. Fax: (208) 733-7525. Web Site:www.coololdies965.com Licensee: GAP Broadcasting Twin Falls License LLC. (acq 2-13-2008; grpsl). Population served: 140,000 Format: Oldies. Target aud: 18-49. ♦Brad Hollstrom, opns mgr, progmg dir; Janice Degner, sls dir; Kelly Klaas, farm dir.

KMVX(FM)—See Jerome

KSNQ(FM)— September 2004: 98.3 mhz; 100 kw. Ant 620 ft TL: N42 43 42 W114 24 48. Hrs open: 415 Park Ave., 83301. Phone: (208) 733-7512. Fax: (208) 733-7525.E-mail: swfradio@aol.com Licensee: Intermart Broadcasting Twin Falls Inc. Format: Classic rock. ◆Patricia Woods, VP & gen mgr.

KTFI(AM)— October 1928: 1270 khz; 5 kw-D, 1 kw-N. TL: N42 33 30 W114 32 00. Hrs open: Secondary address: 21361 Hwy 30 83301. Phone: (208) 735-8300. Fax: (208) 733-4196. Web Site:www.ktfi.com Licensee: Locally Owned Radio LLC. (group owner; (acq 10-31-2003; grpsl). Population served: 150,000 Format: Oldies. Target aud: 35 plus. Spec prog: Farm 3 hrs, relg 5 hrs, sports 3 hrs wkly. ◆Larry Johnson, pres & gen mgr; Jerre Fender, opns dir; Deb Uvieu, gen sls mgr; Denis Jeffs, traf mgr, women's int ed.

Victor

KRVQ(FM)— May 2005: 92.3 mhz; 800 w hoirz. Ant 1,086 ft TL: N43 29 27 W110 57 16. Hrs open: Box 10219, Jackson, WY, 83002. Phone: (307) 732-0384.E-mail: info@923theriver.com Web Site:www.923theriver.com Licensee: Jackson Radio Group Inc. (acq 3-31-2006; $900,000 with KVRG(FM) Victor). Format: Classic rock. ◆Steven A. Silberberg, pres; Bruce Pollock, gen mgr.

KVRG(FM)— May 2005: 103.7 mhz; 800 w horiz. Ant 1,086 ft TL: N43 29 27 W110 57 16. Hrs open: Box 10219, Jackson, WY, 83002. Phone: (307) 732-0384.E-mail: info@1037therange.com Web Site:www.1037therange.com Licensee: Jackson Radio Group Inc. (acq 3-31-2006; $900,000 with KRVQ(FM) Victor). Format: Country. ◆Steven A. Silberberg, pres; Bruce Pollock, gen mgr, progmg dir.

Wallace

*KTWD(FM)— December 2000: 97.5 mhz; 1.6 kw. Ant -2212 ft TL: N47 33 49 W115 50 01. Stereo. Hrs open: 24 Box 1208, Airway Heights, WA, 99001. Phone: (509) 244-5577. Fax: (509) 244-2232.E-mail: ktwd@csnradio.com Licensee: CSN International (group owner; (acq 2-24-2000; $50,000 for CP). Format: Relg. ◆Barney Dasovich, gen mgr.

KWAL(AM)— May 1938: 620 khz; 1 kw-U, DA-N. TL: N47 30 29 W116 00 17. Stereo. Hrs open: 24 Box 828, 120 First St., Osburn, 83849. Phone: (208) 752-1141. Phone: (208) 752-1142. Fax: (208) 753-5111.E-mail: kwalradio@usamedia.tv Licensee: Silver Valley Broadcasters Inc. (acq 1-1-73). Population served: 30,000 Natl. Network: Jones Radio Networks, . Format: C&W. ◆Paul Robinson, pres; Paul Robinson, gen mgr; George White, gen sls mgr; John Davis, progmg dir, disc jockey, prom.

Weiser

KWEI(AM)— December 1947: 1260 khz; 1 kw-D, 60 w-N. TL: N44 14 00 W116 57 18. Hrs open: Sunrise-sunset Box 45234, Boise, 83704. Phone: (208) 367-1859. Fax: (208) 383-9170. Web Site:kweispanishradio.com Licensee: Treasure Valley Broadcasting Co. (Acq 1996). Population served: 475,000 Format: Sp news/talk personality. News staff: one. Target aud: 35-65; mass appeal.

KWEI-FM—(Fruitland, March 1984: 99.5 mhz; 8 kw. 2,634 ft TL: N44 00 58 W116 24 15. Stereo. Hrs open: 24 Box 45234, Boise, 83704. Phone: (208) 367-1859. Fax: (208) 383-9170.E-mail: kwei@cableone.net Web Site:kweispanishradio.com Licensee: Treasure Valley Broadcasting Co. (acq 1987). Population served: 475,000 Format: Mexican rgnl. News: 15 hrs wkly. Target aud: 25-54; mass appeal. ◆Connie Weisgerber, gen sls mgr; Melvin Albeniz, progmg dir; Melvin Albenez, news dir; Rockwell Smith, chief of engrg; Steve Ramirez, traf mgr & disc jockey.

Weston

KLZX(FM)— 2001: 95.9 mhz; 25 kw. Ant 216 ft TL: N41 52 18 W111 48 31. Stereo. Hrs open: Box 267, Logan, UT, 84323. Phone: (435) 792-0095. Fax: (435) 753-5555. Web Site:www.klzxfm.com Licensee: Sun Valley Radio Inc. (group owner). Format: Classic rock. ◆Lynn Simmons, gen mgr; Will Wheelwright, progmg dir.

Illinois

Albion

*WBJW(FM)— December 1997: 91.7 mhz; 6 kw. 328 ft TL: N38 26 51 W88 05 07. (CP: 1.7 kw, ant 499 ft. TL: 38 19 14 W88 02 37). Hrs open:
Rebroadcasts WBGW(FM) Fort Branch, IN 100%.
Box 4164, Evansville, IN, 47724. Phone: (812) 386-3342. Fax: (812) 768-5552.E-mail: mail@thyword.org Web Site:www.thyword.org Licensee: Music Ministries Inc. Format: Relg. ◆Floyd E. Turner, gen mgr.

Aledo

WRMJ(FM)— June 12, 1979: 102.3 mhz; 3 kw. 300 ft TL: N41 12 29 W90 46 10. Stereo. Hrs open: 24 Box 187, 2104 S.E. 3rd St., 61231. Phone: (309) 582-5666. Fax: (309) 582-5667.E-mail: contactus@wrmj.com Web Site:wrmj.com Licensee: Western Illinois Broadcasting Co. (acq 8-83; $200,000; 8-1-83). Population served: 20,000 Rgnl. Network: Brownfield. Brownfield Koerner & Olender. Format: Country, news. News staff: one; News: 20 hrs wkly. Target aud: 25-54. Spec prog: Relg 3 hrs wkly. ◆John Hoscheidt, gen mgr; Judy Bedford, gen sls mgr; Terry Tracy, progmg dir; Jim Taylor, news dir.

Alton

KATZ-FM— September 1961: 100.3 mhz; 50 kw. 482 ft TL: N38 55 44 W90 13 03. (CP: 50 kw). Stereo. Hrs open: 24 1001 Highlands Plaza Dr. W., Saint Louis, MO, 63110. Phone: (314) 333-8000. Fax: (314) 333-8300. Licensee: Citicasters Licenses L.P. Group owner: Clear Channel Communications Inc. (acq 5-4-99; grpsl). Population served: 2,700,000 Format: Rhythm & blues, hip hop. News staff: 2; News: 7 hrs wkly. Target aud: 18-34; adults. Spec prog: Black, relg 2 hrs wkly. ◆Dennis Lamme, gen mgr; Tommy Austin, opns mgr; Beth Davis, sls dir; Dan Sullivan, gen sls mgr; John Helmkamp, mktg dir.

WBGZ(AM)— 1948: 1570 khz; 1 kw-D, 74 w-N. TL: N38 55 44 W90 13 03. Hrs open: 24 Box 615, 227 Market St., 62002. Phone: (618) 465-3535. Fax: (618) 465-3546.E-mail: wbgz@wbgzradio.com Web Site:www.wbgzradio.com Licensee: Metroplex Communications Inc. (acq 12-6-2004; $70,000 for 39% of stock). Population served: 100,000 Natl. Network: USA, . Format: News/talk. News staff: 2; News: 20 hrs wkly. Target aud: General. Spec prog: Gospel 4 hrs, relg 3 hrs wkly. ◆Sam Stemm, gen mgr; Nancy Birens, gen sls mgr; Mark Ellebracht, news dir.

Anna

WIBH(AM)— Jan 10, 1957: 1440 khz; 500 w-D, 109 w-N. TL: N37 26 45 W89 15 00. Hrs open: 24 330 S. Main St., 62906. Phone: (618) 833-9424. Fax: (618) 833-9091.E-mail: wibh@ajinternet.net Web Site:www.wibhradio.com Licensee: WIBH Inc. (acq 3-2-98; $315,000). Population served: 110,000 Wire Svc: UPI Format: Classic country. News staff: one; News: 3 hrs wkly. Target aud: 25-69. ◆Maury Bass, VP; Ronald Ellis, pres & gen mgr; Maurice Bass, progmg dir.

WKIB(FM)— Jan 13, 1958: 96.5 mhz; 22.5 kw. Ant 745 ft TL: N37 22 16 W89 31 52. Stereo. Hrs open: 24 901 S. Kingshighway, Cape Girardeau, MO, 63703. Phone: (573) 339-7000 (business). Fax: (573) 651-4100. Licensee: W. Russell Withers Jr. Group owner: Withers Broadcasting Co. (acq 10-22-2001; $2 million). Population served: 200,000 Natl. Rep: Katz Radio,. Format: Pop contemp hit radio. News staff: one; News: 10 hrs wkly. Target aud: 18-45. ◆Rick Lambert, gen mgr; Steve Thomas, progmg dir.

Arcola

WUIL(FM)— Dec 19, 1974: 107.9 mhz; 3.6 kw horiz, 3 kw vert. Ant 426 ft TL: N39 52 43 W88 11 51. Stereo. Hrs open: 24 401 Lakeland Blvd., Mattoon, 61938. Phone: (217) 258-6060. Fax: (217) 258-6077. Licensee: Champaign Partners LLC (acq 5-10-2007; $500,000). Population served: 50,000 Format: Rhythmic CHR. News staff: one; News: 10 hrs wkly. Target aud: 25-54. ◆Shirley Browning, gen mgr.

Arlington Heights

*WCLR(FM)— Nov 1, 2003: 88.3 mhz; 1 w horiz, 1 kw vert. Ant 59 ft TL: N42 06 45 W87 58 58. Hrs open: 24 2351 Sunset Blvd., Suite 170-218, Rocklin, CA, 95765. Phone: (916) 251-1600. Phone: (888) 937-2471. Fax: (916) 251-1650.E-mail: info@air1.com Web Site:www.air1.com Licensee: Educational Media Foundation. Group owner: EMF Broadcasting (acq 8-13-03). Natl. Network: Air 1, . Shaw Pittman LLP. Format: Contemp Christian. News staff: 3. Target aud: 18-35; Judeo Christian, female. ◆Richard Jenkins, pres; Mike Novak, VP; Keith Whipple, dev dir; Ed Lenane, news dir; Sam Wallington, engrg dir; Karen Johnson, news rptr.

WCPT-FM—Licensed to Arlington Heights. See Chicago

Atlanta

WLCN(FM)— Apr 13, 2001: 96.3 mhz; 5.4 kw. Ant 266 ft TL: N40 14 39 W89 15 51. Stereo. Hrs open: 24 1779 2250th St., 61723. Phone: (217) 648-5510; (847) 674-0864. Fax: (217) 648-2499; (847) 674-9188. Web Site:www.wmnw.net Licensee: KM Radio of Atlanta L.L.C. Group owner: KM Communications Inc. (acq 5-3-99). Natl. Network: ABC, . Wire Svc: AP Wire Svc: Metro Weather Service Inc. Format: Country. Target aud: 25-54. ◆Jim Ash, gen mgr; Jeff Benjamin, traf mgr; Tamera Turner, sls.

Auburn

WCVS-FM—See Springfield

Aurora

WAUR(AM)—(Sandwich, May 1986: 930 khz; 2.5 kw-D, 4.2 kw-N, DA-2. TL: N41 36 26 W88 27 11. Hrs open: 24 130 S. Jefferson, Ste 200, Chicago, 60661. Phone: (312) 461-8540 or (219) 309-9327. Fax: (312) 588-0168.E-mail: aciabattari@relevantradio.com Web Site:www.waur-.relevantradio.com Licensee: Starboard Media Foundation Inc. Group owner: Relevant Radio (acq 5-4-2004; $3.5 million). Population served: 3,000,000 Format: Catholic/talk. Target aud: 25-54. Spec prog: Farm 15 hrs wkly. ◆Armand Ciabattari, gen mgr.

WBIG(AM)— Dec 13, 1938: 1280 khz; 1 kw-D, 500 w-N, DA-2. TL: N41 46 10 W88 14 44. Hrs open: 24 620 Eola Rd., 60504. Phone: (630) 851-5200. Fax: (630) 851-5286. Web Site:wbig1280.com Licensee: Big Broadcasting Co. Group owner: McNaughton-Jakle Stations (acq 1-94; $550,000). Population served: 600,000 Natl. Network: Fox Sports, . Leonard S. Joyce. Format: News/talk, sports. News staff: one; News: 10 hrs wkly. Target aud: 25-54; professional, upscale, suburbanites with children. Spec prog: Relg 6 hrs wkly. ◆Rick Jakle, pres; Steve Marten, exec VP & gen mgr; Jack Davis, opns mgr; Jim Sauers, gen sls mgr; Brian Felsten, progmg dir; Brien Prenevost, chief of engrg.

WERV-FM— Feb 12, 1961: 95.9 mhz; 3 kw. 338 ft TL: N41 26 12 W88 16 03. Stereo. Hrs open: 1884 Plain Ave., 60504. Phone: (630) 898-1580. Fax: (630) 898-2463. Web Site:www.959theriver.fm Licensee: NM Licensing LLC. Group owner: NextMedia Group L.L.C. (acq 11-26-2001; grpsl). Population served: 2,000,000 Natl. Rep: McGavren Guild,. Leibowitz & Associates. Format: Classic hits. News staff: one; News: 5 hrs wkly. Target aud: 25-54; suburban Chicago adults. ◆Brian Foster, gen mgr.

WLEY-FM— 1965: 107.9 mhz; 21 kw. 761 ft TL: N41 56 01 W88 04 23. Stereo. Hrs open: 24 150 N. Michigan Ave., Suite 1040, Chicago, 60601. Phone: (312) 920-9500. Fax: (312) 920-9516.E-mail: info@laley1079.com Web Site:www.laley1079.com Licensee: WLEY Licensing Inc. Group owner: Spanish Broadcasting System Inc. (acq 12-26-96; $33 million). Population served: 2,200,000 Format: Rgnl Mexican. News staff: one. Target aud: 25-54. ◆Jeff Schrinsky, gen mgr, natl sls mgr; Joe McKay, gen sls mgr, natl sls mgr, mktg dir; Leticia Aguilera, prom dir; Marylu Ramos, progmg dir; Sam Palerno, chief of engrg.

Ava

WXAN(FM)— Jan 11, 1982: 103.9 mhz; 2.9 kw horiz, 2.9 kw vert. 469 ft TL: N37 51 19 W89 28 06. Stereo. Hrs open: 24 9077 Ava Rd., 62907. Phone: (618) 426-3308. Phone: (618) 426-3309. Fax: (618) 426-3310.E-mail: wsstephens@wxan.net Web Site:www.wxan.net Licensee: Southern Gospetality LLC. Natl. Network: Salem Radio Network, . Format: Relg, southern gospel. News: 10 hrs wkly. Target aud: 30-55; Christians & family-oriented listeners. ◆Harold Lawder, pres; Will Stephens, gen mgr.

Bartonville

WWCT(FM)— February 1997: 99.9 mhz; 1.5 kw. Ant 584 ft TL: N40 36 23 W89 32 20. Hrs open: 24 4234 N. Brandywine Dr., Suite D, Peoria, 61614. Phone: (309) 686-0101. Fax: (309) 686-0111.E-mail: Studio@TheBuzzPeoria.com Web Site:www.thebuzzpeoria.com Licensee: IM IL Licenses LLC. Group owner: Regent Communications Inc. (acq

9-19-2006; grpsl). Population served: 350,000 Pepper & Corazzini. Format: Rock. ◆David Manning, gen mgr; Jason Stuckwisch, gen sls mgr; Gabe Reynolds, progmg dir.

Beardstown

WRMS(AM)— Nov 1, 1959: 790 khz; 500 w-D, 59 w-N, DA-2. TL: N40 00 11 W90 23 51. Hrs open: 4424 Hampton Ave., Saint Louis, MO, 63109. Phone: (314) 752-7000.E-mail: covenantnetwork@juno.com Licensee: Covenant Network. (acq 7-28-2004). Population served: 6,222 Format: Christian, relg, inspirational. ◆Tony Holman, pres & gen mgr; Jim Schaper, progmg dir.

WRMS-FM— 1976: 94.3 mhz; 6 kw. Ant 298 ft TL: N40 04 45 W90 25 58. Hrs open: 108 E. Main St., 62618. Phone: (217) 323-1790. Fax: (217) 323-1705.E-mail: wrmsfm@casscomm.com Licensee: Conner Family Broadcasting Inc. (acq 3-87). Format: Country. ◆John Conner, gen mgr, gen sls mgr & progmg dir; Glen Hopkins, chief of engrg.

Belleville

WSDZ(AM)— July 13, 1947: 1260 khz; 5 kw-U, DA-2. TL: N38 27 28 W89 57 43. Hrs open: 24 638 Westport Plaza, St. Louis, MO, 63146. Phone: (314) 682-1260. Fax: (314) 682-1190.E-mail: ted.m.zimmerman@abc.com Web Site:www.radiodisney.com/wsdzam1260 Licensee: Radio Disney Group LLC. Group owner: ABC Inc. (acq 9-22-98; $2.5 million). Population served: 2,500,000 Natl. Network: ABC, . Format: Family hits. Target aud: 25-54 plus; 6-14; affluent, well-educated, business & professional.children Spec prog: Caring is Cool 30 min wkly. ◆Ted Zimmerman, stn mgr; Nicole Polley, prom mgr.

WXOS(FM)—See East St. Louis

Belvidere

WXRX(FM)— Feb 27, 1971: 104.9 mhz; 4 kw. 333 ft TL: N42 19 21 W88 57 15. Stereo. Hrs open: 2830 Sandy Hollow Rd., Rockford, 61109. Phone: (815) 874-7861. Fax: (815) 874-2202. Web Site:www.wxrx.com Licensee: Maverick Media of Rockford License LLC. Group owner: RadioWorks Inc. (acq 4-27-2005; grpsl). Population served: 247,400 Shaw, Pittman. Format: Rock/AOR. Target aud: 18-49. ◆Gary Rozynek, pres; Jay Chapman, gen mgr; Jim Stone, progmg dir.

Benton

WQRL(FM)— Oct 1, 1973: 106.3 mhz; 12.5 kw. 328 ft TL: N37 55 51 W88 40 52. (CP: Ant 459 ft.). Stereo. Hrs open: 24 Box 818, 303 N. Main, 62812. Secondary address: 303 N. Main St. 62812. Phone: (618) 435-8100. Fax: (618) 435-8102.E-mail: wwqrlfm@shawneelink.net Licensee: Dana Communications Corp. (acq 4-28-92; $250,000; 5-18-92). Population served: 250,000 Format: Oldies. News staff: 2; News: 15 hrs wkly. Target aud: 25-49; adults & young adults preferring new country. Spec prog: Farm 3 hrs wkly. ◆Dana Withers, CEO, pres, gen mgr; Bleu Withers, exec VP; Gloria Holland, stn mgr; Jeff Oestreich, chief of engrg.

Berwyn

WVON(AM)— Oct 7, 2003: 1690 khz; 10 kw-D, 1 kw-N. TL: N41 44 14 W87 42 04. Hrs open: 1000 E. 87th St., Chicago, 60619. Phone: (773) 247-6200. Fax: (773) 247-5336. Licensee: CC Licenses LLC. Group owner: Clear Channel Communications Inc. (acq 1-18-2001). Natl. Network: ABC, . Format: Talk. Target aud: 25-54; urban talk listeners. ◆Melody Spann-Cooper, gen mgr.

Bethalto

WFUN-FM— April 1991: 95.5 mhz; 6 kw. 328 ft TL: N38 49 39 W90 00 53. Stereo. Hrs open: 24 9666 Olive Blvd., Suite 610, St. Louis, MO, 63132. Phone: (314) 989-9550. Fax: (314) 989-9551.E-mail: info@foxy995.net Web Site:www.foxy995.net Licensee: Radio One Licenses LLC. Group owner: Radio One Inc. (acq 11-8-01; grpsl). Population served: 2,500,000 Brown, Nietert & Kaufman. Format: Rhythm and blues, classic soul. News: 2 hrs wkly. Target aud: General; families. ◆Alfred Liggins, pres; Michael Douglass, gen mgr; Laura Steele, gen sls mgr; Gary Bennett, engrg VP, chief of engrg; Melissa Wakefields, traf mgr, min affrs dir.

Bloomington

WBNQ(FM)— 1947: 101.5 mhz; 50 kw. Ant 460 ft TL: N40 27 32 W89 00 38. Stereo. Hrs open: 236 Greenwood Ave., 61704. Phone: (309) 829-1221. Fax: (309) 827-8071. Web Site:www.wbnq.com Licensee: Regent Licensee of Erie Inc. Format: CHR. Spec prog: Farm one hr wkly. ◆Dan Westhoff, stn mgr; Tony Travatto, gen sls mgr; Dave Adams, progmg mgr; Russell Rush, mus dir.

WBWN(FM)—See Le Roy

*WESN(FM)— 1972: 88.1 mhz; 120 w. 98 ft TL: N40 29 28 W88 59 37. Stereo. Hrs open: Box 2900, 61701. Phone: (309) 556-2638. Fax: (309) 556-2949.E-mail: wesn@iwu.edu Web Site:www.wesn.org Licensee: Illinois Wesleyan University. Natl. Network: PRI, . Format: Div. Spec prog: Black 18 hrs, class 6 hrs, jazz 6 hrs wkly. ◆Ed Price, stn mgr; Nathan Breitling, progmg dir.

WIHN(FM)—See Normal

WJBC(AM)— 1925: 1230 khz; 1 kw-U. TL: N40 27 32 W89 00 38. Hrs open: 236 Greenwood Ave., 61704. Phone: (309) 829-1221. Fax: (309) 827-8071. Web Site:www.wjbc.com Licensee: Regent Broadcasting of Bloomington Inc. Group owner: Regent Communications Inc. (acq 5-12-2004; grpsl). Population served: 125,000 Natl. Rep: McGavren Guild,. Reddy, Begley & McCormick. Format: Full service. Spec prog: Farm 13 hrs wkly. ◆Red Pitcher, gen mgr; R.C. McBride, opns mgr, progmg dir; Julie Penn, gen sls mgr, natl sls mgr; Colleen Reynolds, news dir; Ron Schott, chief of engrg.

*WJWR(FM)—Not on air, target date: unknown: 90.3 mhz; 10 kw. Ant 328 ft TL: N40 41 23 W88 50 39. Hrs open: 16410 N. 800 East Rd., 61704-6801. Phone: (309) 963-4932. Licensee: Bloomington Normal Broadcasting Corp. ◆Jacqueline A. Dearing, pres.

Bluford

*WVYN(FM)— June 21, 2009: 90.9 mhz; 4.5 kw. Ant 148 ft TL: N38 20 05 W88 35 33. Hrs open: Box 248, Wayne City, 62895. Phone: (618) 895-3030. Web Site:thevine@wvyn.org Licensee: Real Life Radio Foundation Inc. Format: Christian. ◆Randall Lee Olson, pres.

Breese

WDLJ(FM)— 2003: 97.5 mhz; 2.5 kw. Ant 512 ft TL: N38 36 33 W89 23 35. Hrs open: KM Radio of Breese L.L.C., 3654 W. Jarvis Ave., Skokie, 60076. Phone: (847) 674-0864. Fax: (847) 674-9188. Web Site:www.wdlj.net Licensee: KM Radio of Breese L.L.C. Format: Classic rock. ◆Kevin Bae, gen mgr.

Brookport

WTHQ(AM)— October 1987: 750 khz; 500 w-D. TL: N37 08 31 W88 38 58. Hrs open: 6120 Waldo Church Rd., Metropolis, 62960-4903. Fax: (618) 564-3202. Licensee: Daniel S. Stratemeyer (acq 9-20-2002). Format: Talk. ◆Samuel Stratemeyer, gen mgr.

Bushnell

WLMD(FM)— August 1992: 104.7 mhz; 3 kw. Ant 328 ft TL: N40 32 52 W90 26 25. Stereo. Hrs open: 24 119 W. Carroll, Macomb, 61455. Phone: (309) 833-5561. Fax: (309) 833-3460.E-mail: wlmd@macomb.com Web Site:www.radiomacomb.com Licensee: WPW Broadcasting Inc. (group owner; (acq 12-27-99; grpsl). Population served: 22,300 Natl. Network: ABC, Jones Radio Networks, . Rgnl. Network: Ill Radio Net., Brownfield. Ill. Radio Net. Format: Country. News staff: one; News: 2 hrs wkly. Target aud: 25-54; general. Spec prog: Farm 3 hrs wkly. ◆Vanessa Wetterling, stn mgr; Mike Weaver, progmg dir, news dir.

Cairo

*WBEL(FM)— 2002: 88.5 mhz; 64 kw vert. Ant 558 ft TL: N36 59 32 W88 59 19. Hrs open: Box 3206, American Family Radio, Tupelo, MS, 38803. Phone: (662) 844-8888. Fax: (662) 842-6791. Web Site:www.afr.net Licensee: American Family Association. Group owner: American Family Radio Format: Christian. ◆Marvin Sanders, gen mgr.

WKRO(AM)— Jan 8, 1942: 1490 khz; 1 kw-U. TL: N37 02 36 W89 11 02. Hrs open: 24 Box 311, 62914. Phone: (618) 734-1490. Fax: (618) 734-0884.E-mail: djman75@hotmail.com Licensee: Alexander Broadcasting Corp. (acq 3-22-01; $20,500). Population served: 122,000 Natl. Network: ABC, . Format: Urban adult contemp. News staff: one; News:

12 hrs wkly. Target aud: 25-54; general. Spec prog: Gospel 12 hrs, farm 12 hrs wkly. ◆Danny McDonald, gen mgr, opns mgr; Marti Nicholson, gen sls mgr & adv dir.

Cambridge

WYEC(FM)— May 20, 1966: 93.9 mhz; 4.2 kw. Ant 394 ft TL: N41 22 56 W90 10 47. Stereo. Hrs open: 24 Box 266, Kewanee, 61443. Phone: (309) 853-4471. Fax: (309) 853-4474.E-mail: regionalradio@verizon.net Web Site:www.randyradio.com Licensee: Virden Broadcasting Corp. Natl. Network: CNN Radio, . Format: Soft adult contemp. Target aud: 35-64. ◆Randal J. Miller, pres & disc jockey.

Canton

WBYS(AM)— Oct 5, 1947: 1560 khz; 250 w-D. TL: N40 32 43 W90 01 08. Hrs open: 6 AM-sunset 1000 E. Linn St., 61520. Phone: (309) 647-1560. Fax: (309) 647-1563.E-mail: bj.stone@prairiecommunications.net Web Site:www.wbysradio.com Licensee: WPW Broadcasting Inc. (group owner; (acq 1999; $210,000 for stock with co-located FM). Population served: 44,000 Natl. Network: ABC, . Rgnl. Network: Tribune, Ill. Radio Net. Richard F. Swift. Format: News/talk/sports. News staff: one; News: 25 hrs wkly. Target aud: 30 plus; community-oriented with above average income. Spec prog: Farm 10 hrs wkly. ◆Don Davis, CEO & pres; BJ Stone, gen mgr, stn mgr.

WCDD(FM)— Oct 7, 1968: 107.9 mhz; 25 kw. Ant 265 ft TL: N40 32 43 W90 01 08. Stereo. Hrs open: 24 1000 E. Linn St., 61520. Phone: (309) 647-1560. Fax: (309) 647-1563.E-mail: bj.stone@prairiecommunications.net Web Site:www.cd1079.com Population served: 425,000 Natl. Network: ABC, . Format: Classic hits. News staff: one; News: 10 hrs wkly. Target aud: 35-54; males. Spec prog: High School Sports. ◆Don Davis, CEO, pres; BJ Stone, gen mgr; Wayne R. Miller, chief of engrg.

Carbondale

WCIL(AM)— Nov 14, 1946: 1020 khz; 1 kw-D. TL: N37 43 31 W89 15 25. Hrs open: Sunrise-sunset
Rebroadcasts WJPF(AM) Herrin 100%.
1431 Country Aire Dr., Carterville, 62918. Phone: (618) 985-4843. Fax: (618) 985-6529.E-mail: mail@wjpf.com Web Site:www.wjpf.com Licensee: MRR License LLC. Group owner: MAX Media L.L.C. (acq 3-29-2004; grpsl). Population served: 856,500 Natl. Rep: Christal,. Format: Sports, news/talk. News staff: 2; News: 10 hrs wkly. Target aud: 35 plus. Spec prog: Farm one hr wkly. ◆Steve J. Schimmel, gen mgr; Kim DeBose, gen sls mgr; Dave McKenzie, prom mgr; Ryan Patrick, adv mgr; Richard Cason, news dir, news rptr; Jon Brookmyer, chief of engrg; Felicia Dick, traf mgr; Dee James, news rptr; Tom Miller, opns dir, opns mgr, progmg dir & farm dir.

WCIL-FM— July 1968: 101.5 mhz; 50 kw. 430 ft TL: N37 43 31 W89 15 25. Stereo. Hrs open: 24 Prog sep from AM 1431 Country Aire Dr., Carterville, 62918. Phone: (618) 985-4843. Fax: (618) 985-6529. Web Site:www.cilfm.com Population served: 830,000 Natl. Rep: Christal,. Format: Top 40 hit music. Target aud: 18-34; adult females. ◆Steve J. Falat, gen mgr; Tom Miller, opns mgr; Kim DeBose, gen sls mgr; Jon E. Quest, progmg dir; Jon Brookmyer, chief of engrg; Felicia Dick, traf mgr.

*WDBX(FM)— February 1996: 91.1 mhz; 3 kw. Ant 131 ft TL: N37 43 43 W89 12 57. Stereo. Hrs open: 7 AM-4 AM 224 N. Washington St., 62901. Phone: (618) 457-3691. Phone: (618) 529-5900.E-mail: wdbx@globaleyes.net Web Site:www.wdbx.org Licensee: Heterodyne Broadcasting Co. Population served: 80,000 Format: Div. News: 2.5 hrs wkly. ◆Francis Murphy, pres; Brian R. Powell, stn mgr.

*WSIU(FM)— Sept 15, 1958: 91.9 mhz; 50 kw. 299 ft TL: N37 42 29 W89 14 05. Stereo. Hrs open: 24
Rebroadcasts WUSI(FM) Olney 100%, WVSI(FM) Mt. Venon 100%.
1003 Communications Bldg., 1100 Lincoln Dr., 62901. Phone: (618) 453-4343. Fax: (618) 453-6186.E-mail: jeff.williams@wsiu.org Web Site:wsiu.org Licensee: Board of Trustees Southern Illinois University. Population served: 106,000 Natl. Network: NPR, PRI, . Ill. Radio Net. Cohn & Marks. Wire Svc: AP Format: Class, news. News staff: 3; News: 36 hrs wkly. Target aud: 35-64; highly educated, upper income, socially conscious. Spec prog: New age 4 hrs, big band 4 hrs, folk 3 hrs wkly. ◆Greg Petrowich, CEO; Delores Kerstein, CFO; Jeff Williams, gen mgr, local news ed; Mike Zelten, opns mgr, progmg dir; Renee Dillard, dev dir, spec ev coord; Terry Harvey, chief of engrg. Co-owned TV: *WSIU-TV affil

WVZA(FM)—(Murphysboro, August 1972: 105.1 mhz; 25 kw. 308 ft TL: N37 45 15 W89 19 14. Stereo. Hrs open: 24 Box 127, 1822 N. Court St., Marion, 62959. Phone: (618) 997-8123. Fax: (618) 993-2319.

Web Site:www.105tao.com Licensee: Withers Broadcasting of Southern Illinois LLC. Group owner: Clear Channel Communications Inc. (acq 3-17-2008; grpsl). Population served: 135,000 Format: Rock/active rock. Target aud: M18-49. ♦Jerry Crouse, gen mgr; Paxton Guy, opns mgr; Mett Mellen, progmg dir; Tim Deterding, chief of engrg.

Carlinville

***WIBI(FM)**— Sept 30, 1975: 91.1 mhz; 50 kw. 476 ft TL: N39 20 58 W89 48 16. Stereo. Hrs open: 24 Box 140, 62626. Phone: (217) 854-4800. Phone: (800) 707-9191. Fax: (217) 854-4810.E-mail: wibi@wibi.org Web Site:www.wibi.org Licensee: Illinois Bible Institute Inc. (group owner) Population served: 2,000,000 Gammon & Grange. Format: Adult contemp Christian. Target aud: 25-49. ♦Barry Copeland, gen mgr, sls dir; Jeremiah Beck, stn mgr, opns mgr; Jessica Barton, prom dir; Rob Regal, progmg dir; Joe Buchanan, mus dir; Sally Braundmeier, traf mgr.

***WOLG(FM)**— Dec 8, 1990: 95.9 mhz; 6 kw. 325 ft TL: N39 14 25 W89 54 26. Stereo. Hrs open: 24 4424 Hampton Ave., Saint Louis, MO, 63109. Phone: (314) 752-7000.E-mail: covenantnetwork@juno.com Licensee: Covenant Network. (acq 8-10-98; $300,000). Population served: 50,000 Format: Relg. ♦Tony Holman, gen mgr; Jim Schaper, progmg dir.

***WTSG(FM)**— Aug 11, 1997: 90.1 mhz; 3 kw. 295 ft TL: N39 20 58 W89 48 16. Hrs open: 24 Box 140, 62626-0140. Phone: (217) 854-4851. Fax: (217) 854-4810.E-mail: wibi@wibi.org Web Site:www.wtsg.org Licensee: Illinois Bible Institute Inc. (group owner) Population served: 60,000 Gammon & Grange. Format: Southern gospel mus, relg. Target aud: 25-44. ♦Barry Copeland, gen mgr; Jeremiah Beck, stn mgr, opns mgr; Jessica Barton, prom dir; Rob Regal, progmg dir; Joe Buchanan, mus dir; Sally Braundmeier, traf mgr.

Carlyle

WCXO(FM)— 1999: 96.7 mhz; 2.1 kw. Ant 518 ft TL: N38 38 24 W89 22 40. Hrs open: 1611 County Farm Rd., 62231. Phone: (618) 594-2490. Fax: (618) 594-2826. Web Site:www.wcxo967.com Licensee: Clinton County Broadcasting Inc. Format: Adult hits. ♦John A. Perrine, pres; Scott Patric, stn mgr.

Carmi

WROY(AM)— Dec 13, 1948: 1460 khz; 1 kw-D, 85 w-N. TL: N38 04 54 W88 12 04. Hrs open: 24 Prog sep from FM Box 400, 101 N. Church St., 62821. Phone: (618) 382-4161. Fax: (618) 382-4162.E-mail: wroy1460@verizon.net Web Site:www.wrul.com Licensee: W. Russell Withers Jr. Population served: 100,000 Format: Hits of the 50s, 60s, 70s & 80s. News staff: 2; News: 25 hrs wkly. Target aud: 35 plus; general. Spec prog: Farm 6 hrs wkly.

WRUL(FM)— 1951: 97.3 mhz; 50 kw. 496 ft TL: N38 04 54 W88 12 04. Stereo. Hrs open: 24 Box 400, 101 N. Church St., 62821. Phone: (618) 382-4161. Phone: (618) 382-2345. Fax: (618) 382-4162.E-mail: wrul973@verizon.net Web Site:www.wrul.com Licensee: W. Russell Withers Jr. (acq 5-1-2006; $1.1 million with co-located AM). Population served: 500,000 Natl. Network: ABC, . Format: Country. News staff: one; News: 8 hrs wkly. Target aud: 25-55. ♦Russell Withers, pres, gen mgr & gen mgr; J.C. Tinsley, gen sls mgr; Irma O'Dell, progmg dir; Bob Miller, news dir.

***WYER(FM)**—Not on air, target date: unknown: 90.5 mhz; 2.5 kw vert. Ant 93 ft TL: N38 04 28.6 W88 12 31.9. Hrs open: 134 Huston St., Connersville, IN, 47331-1442. Phone: (765) 821-2180. Licensee: Connersville Apostolic Lighthouse Inc.

Carpentersville

***WWTG(FM)**—Not on air, target date: unknown: 88.1 mhz; 2 kw vert. Ant 108 ft TL: N42 06 21 W88 22 38. Stereo. Hrs open: Box 3006, Collegedale, TN, 37315. Phone: (615) 469-5122. Fax: (615) 216-7266.E-mail: office@lifetalk.net Web Site:www.lifetalk.net Licensee: LifeTalk Radio Inc. ♦Kalvin Follett, progmg dir.

Carrier Mills

***WBVN(FM)**— Jan 8, 1990: 104.5 mhz; 6 kw. 328 ft TL: N37 46 25 W88 44 20. Stereo. Hrs open: 24 Box 1126, Marion, 62959. Phone: (618) 252-2999. Fax: (618) 997-3194.E-mail: wbvn@shawneeclink.net Web Site:www.wbvn.org Licensee: Kenneth W. and Jane A. Anderson (acq 2-28-00). Population served: 165,000 Format: Contemp Christian. News staff: 3. Target aud: 18-45; general. ♦Ken Anderson, pres & gen mgr.

Carterville

WUEZ(FM)— Apr 2, 1992: 95.1 mhz; 17.6 kw. Ant 390 ft TL: N37 43 31 W89 15 25. Hrs open: 24 1431 Country Arc Dr., 62918. Phone: (618) 985-4843. Fax: (618) 985-6529.E-mail: mail@magic951.com Web Site:www.magic951.com Licensee: MRR License LLC. Group owner: MAX Media L.L.C. (acq 6-2-2004; grpsl). Population served: 250,000 Natl. Rep: Christal,. Format: Adult contemp. News staff: 2; News: 18 hrs wkly. Target aud: 25-49; 60% women, 40% men, good spendable income; mgrs, supvrs, professionals. ♦Mike Smith, gen mgr; Tom Miller, opns mgr; Kim DeBose, gen sls mgr; Amanda "Ivy" Graskewicz, progmg dir; Jon Brookmyer, chief of engrg; Felicia Dick, traf mgr, disc jockey.

Carthage

WCAZ(AM)— 1922: 990 khz; 1 kw-D, 9 w-N. TL: N40 24 30 W88 12 04. Hrs open: Box 498, 62321. Secondary address: 86 S. Madison 62321. Phone: (217) 357-3128. Fax: (217) 357-2014.E-mail: wcazam@adamas.net Web Site:www.wcazam990.com Licensee: Ralla Broadcasting Co. Inc. (acq 1993). Population served: 3,351 Format: Talk. ♦Rob Dunham, gen mgr; Chuck Porter, progmg dir.

WCEZ(FM)— 2001: 93.9 mhz; 6 kw. Ant 328 ft TL: N40 24 54 W91 15 11. Stereo. Hrs open: 24 108 Washington St., P.O. Box 427, Keokuk, IA, 52632. Secondary address: 303 N. Main 62812. Phone: (217) 357-9800.E-mail: krng963@imchsi.com Licensee: Dana R. Withers. Gary M. Follou, (319) 524-5410 Format: Adult contemp. News staff: one; News: 8 hrs wkly. Target aud: 18-45; 60% female, 40% male. ♦Dana Withers, pres; Gary M. Folluo, gen mgr; Dan Workman, progmg dir; Jim Worrell, news dir.

WQKQ(FM)— Nov 1, 1978: 92.1 mhz; 25 kw. Ant 328 ft TL: N40 35 37 W91 06 48. Stereo. Hrs open: 24 610 N. 4th St., Suite 300, Burlington, IA, 52601. Phone: (319) 752-5402. Fax: (319) 752-4715.E-mail: johnp@burlingtonradio.com Web Site:www.KQ92rocks.com Licensee: Pritchard Broadcasting Corp. (acq 12-1-99). Population served: 142,100 Natl. Rep: Katz Radio,. Format: Rock. News staff: 2; News: 2 hrs wkly. Target aud: 25-54. ♦John T. Pritchard, pres, VP, gen mgr; Joe Bates, opns mgr; Chet Young, gen sls mgr; Mike Savage, progmg dir.

Casey

WCBH(FM)— Sept 19, 1988: 104.3 mhz; 11.2 kw. 495 ft TL: N39 16 24 W87 55 39. Hrs open: 24 405 S. Banker, Suite 201, Effington, 62401. Phone: (217) 342-4141. Phone: (217) 342-4142. Fax: (217) 342-4143.E-mail: wcrc@wcrc975.com Licensee: Two Petaz Inc. Group owner: The Cromwell Group Inc. (acq 1-9-02; grpsl). Format: Christian. ♦Bud Walters, CEO; Marvin Phillips, gen mgr; Marvin Phillips, gen sls mgr; David Wilson, chief of engrg.

WKZI(AM)— Dec 14, 1963: 800 khz; 250 w-U. TL: N39 18 14 W87 58 15. Hrs open: 24 18889 N. 23rd 50th St., Dennison, 62423. Phone: (217) 826-9673.E-mail: wkzi@rr1.net Web Site:wordpower.us Licensee: Word Power Inc. (acq 5-4-93; $152,400;5-24-93). Population served: 358,500 Natl. Network: Moody, . Shook, Hardy & Bacon. Format: Christian. News: 17 hrs wkly. Target aud: General; 12 plus. ♦Eleanor Jean Ford, progmg dir, disc jockey; Mark Stephen Ford, engrg dir; Paul Dean Ford, pres, gen mgr, news dir, chief of engrg & disc jockey.

***WLHW(FM)**— 2006: 91.5 mhz; 6 kw. Ant 197 ft TL: N39 18 14 W87 58 15. Hrs open: 24 18889 N. 23rd 50th St., Dennison, 62423. Phone: (217) 826-9673.E-mail: wkzi@rrl.net Population served: 14,217 ♦Eleanor Jean Ford, disc jockey.

Centralia

WILY(AM)— Aug 15, 1946: 1210 khz; 10 kw-D, 3 w-N, 1.1 kw-CH, DA-2. TL: N38 28 55 W89 08 56 (day), N38 31 28 W89 08 03 (night). Hrs open: Sunrise-sunset Box 528, 62801. Secondary address: 302 S. Poplar 62801. Phone: (618) 533-5700. Fax: (618) 533-5737.E-mail: wrxx@mvn.net Licensee: Withers Broadcasting Co. of West Virginia. Group owner: Withers Broadcasting Co. (acq 11-4-97; $527,500 with co-located FM). Population served: 120,000 Rgnl. Network: Brownfield. Brownfield Dennis Kelly. Wire Svc: AP Format: Oldies. News staff: 2; News: 60 hrs wkly. Target aud: 25-54. Spec prog: Business news. ♦Russ Withers, pres; Dana Withers, gen mgr, progmg dir; Brenda Robinson, opns mgr.

WRXX(FM)— Dec 24, 1964: 95.3 mhz; 3 kw. Ant 217 ft TL: N38 34 44 W89 06 46. Stereo. Hrs open: 24 Box 528, 62801. Secondary address: 302 S. Poplar 62801. Phone: (618) 533-5700 . Fax: (618) 533-5737.E-mail: wrxx@mvn.net Licensee: Withers Broadcasting Co. of West Virginia. Population served: 50,000 Natl. Network: ABC, . Format: Rock. News staff: 2; News: 2 hrs wkly. Target aud: 18-49.

Champaign

WBCP(AM)—See Urbana

***WBGL(FM)**— Oct 31, 1982: 91.7 mhz; 20 kw. Ant 459 ft TL: N40 09 12 W88 06 56. Stereo. Hrs open: 24 2108 W. Springfield Ave., 61821. Phone: (217) 359-8232. Fax: (217) 359-7374.E-mail: wbgl@wbgl.org Web Site:www.wbgl.org Licensee: Illinois Bible Institute Inc. (group owner) Natl. Network: USA, . Format: Educ, relg. News staff: one. Target aud: 25-44. ♦Jeff Scott, stn mgr; Jennifer Briski, prom dir; Ryan Springer, progmg dir; Joe Buchanan, mus dir; John Symonds, chief of engrg, engr.

WCFF(FM)—See Urbana

WDWS(AM)— Jan 24, 1937: 1400 khz; 1 kw-U. TL: N40 05 04 W88 14 53. Stereo. Hrs open: 24 Box 3939, 61826. Phone: (217) 351-5300. Fax: (217) 351-5385.E-mail: talk@wdws.com Web Site:www.wdws.com Licensee: D.W.S. Inc. Population served: 170,000 Natl. Network: ABC, . Rgnl. Network: Ill. Radio Net. Natl. Rep: Christal,. Ill. Radio Net. Wire Svc: AP Format: News/talk, sports. News staff: 6; News: 26 hrs wkly. Target aud: 35-64; adults. Spec prog: Farm 10 hrs, relg 4 hrs wkly. ♦Mike Haile, VP; Mike Halle, gen mgr; Jim Lewis, opns mgr; Dave Burns, gen sls mgr; Carol Vorel, news dir.

WEBX(FM)—(Tuscola, Sept 30, 1970: 93.5 mhz; 6 kw. 308 ft TL: N39 54 24 W88 16 35. Stereo. Hrs open: 4108 Fieldstone Rd., Suite C, 61822. Phone: (217) 367-1195. Fax: (217) 367-3291. Web Site:www.935thesource.com Licensee: RadioStar Inc. Group owner: AAA Entertainment L.L.C. (acq 5-23-2006; grpsl). Natl. Rep: McGavren Guild,. Kaye, Scholer, Fierman, Hays & Handler. Format: Classic alternative rock. Target aud: 18-49; adult professionals & college students. ♦Jim Glassman, pres; Corey Berkemann, sls dir; Roxanne Charles, gen mgr & prom dir; Jon Mayotte, progmg dir, disc jockey; Jon Hail, engr.

***WEFT(FM)**— Sept 21, 1981: 90.1 mhz; 10 kw. 135 ft TL: N40 10 51 W88 19 04. Stereo. Hrs open: 6 AM-2 AM 113 N. Market St., 61820-4004. Phone: (217) 359-9338.E-mail: weft@weftfm.org Web Site:www.weftfm.org Licensee: Prairie Air Inc. Natl. Network: NPR, PRI, . Haley, Bader & Potts. Format: Var/div. News: 10 hrs wkly. Target aud: General. Spec prog: Black 8 hrs, blues 10 hrs, folk 10 hrs, pub affrs 5 hrs, Sp 3 hrs wkly. ♦Mick Woolf, gen mgr & stn mgr; Darren Martin, chief of engrg.

WHMS-FM— 1948: 97.5 mhz; 50 kw. 358 ft TL: N40 05 04 W88 14 53. Stereo. Hrs open: 24 Box 3939, 61826. Secondary address: 2301 S. Neil 61820. Phone: (217) 351-5300. Fax: (217) 351-5385.E-mail: literock@whms.com Web Site:www.whms.com Population served: 310,000 Wire Svc: AP Format: Soft adult contemp. News staff: 4; News: 10 hrs wkly. Target aud: 25-54; adults. ♦Mike Haile, gen mgr; Ryan Aurthur, progmg dir.

WILL(AM)—See Urbana

WILL-FM—See Urbana

WIXY(FM)— June 1, 1992: 100.3 mhz; 13 kw. Ant 453 ft TL: N40 00 45 W88 08 29. Hrs open: 2603 W. Bradley Ave., 61821. Phone: (217) 355-4141. Fax: (217) 352-1256.E-mail: info@wixy.com Web Site:www.wixy.com Licensee: Saga Communications of Illinois LLC. Group owner: Saga Communications Inc. (acq 11-4-92; $250,000;11-30-92). Population served: 469,000 Natl. Rep: Katz Radio,. Format: Country. News: 5 hrs wkly. Target aud: 25 plus. ♦Ed Christian, CEO, chmn; Steve Goldstein, exec VP; Alan Beck, gen mgr.

WKJR(AM)—(Rantoul, Feb 1, 1963: 1460 khz; 500 w-D, 65 w-N, DA-1. TL: N40 18 37 W88 12 54. Hrs open: 24 129 N. Garrard, Rantoul, 61866. Phone: (217) 893-1460. Fax: (217) 893-0884.E-mail: fanmail@1460sports.com Web Site:www.1460sports.com Licensee: Ruben's Productions Inc. (acq 9-19-2006; $215,000). Population served: 200,000 Natl. Network: ESPN Radio, . Format: Sports. Target aud: General. ♦Rueben Acevero, gen mgr; Armando Martinez, progmg dir; Scott Hudson, sports cmtr.

WLFH(FM)—(Rantoul, Mar 15, 1972: 95.3 mhz; 3 kw. Ant 425 ft TL: N40 13 05 W88 06 55. Stereo. Hrs open: 24 4108 Fieldstone Rd., Suite C, 61822. Phone: (217) 367-1195. Fax: (217) 367-3291. Web Site:www.wmye.com Licensee: RadioStar Inc. Group owner: AAA

Entertainment L.L.C. (acq 5-23-2006; grpsl). Population served: 175,000 Natl. Rep: McGavren Guild,. Format: Country. News staff: one. Target aud: 18-49. ♦Jim Glassman, pres; Roxanne Charles, gen mgr; Corey Berkemann, gen sls mgr; Joe McIntyre, progmg dir; Jon Hall, engr.

WLRW(FM)— January 1963: 94.5 mhz; 50 kw. Ant 453 ft TL: N40 07 35 W88 17 25. Stereo. Hrs open: 24 2603 W. Bradley, 61821. Phone: (217) 352-4141. Fax: (217) 352-1256.E-mail: info@mix945.com Web Site:www.mix945.com Licensee: Saga Communications of Illinois LLC. Group owner: Saga Communications Inc. (acq 10-86; grpsl;7-7-86). Population served: 469,000 Format: Hot adult contemp. Target aud: 18-49. ♦Alan Beck, gen mgr; Jonathan Drake, progmg dir.

***WPCD(FM)**— January 1978: 88.7 mhz; 10.5 kw. Ant 338 ft TL: N40 08 14 W88 17 10. Stereo. Hrs open: Parkland College, 2400 W. Bradley Ave., 61821. Phone: (217) 351-2450. Fax: (217) 351-2581.E-mail: wpcdradio@parkland.edu Web Site:www.parkland.edu/wpcd/ Licensee: Parkland College Community College District No. 505. Population served: 250,000 Natl. Network: AP Radio, . Format: Adult urban comtemp, alternative. News: 8 hrs wkly. Target aud: General. Spec prog: News 8 hrs, spanish 4 hrs wkly. ♦Dan Hughes, gen mgr.

WPGU(FM)—See Urbana

WQQB(FM)—See Urbana

Charleston

WEIC(AM)— Dec 10, 1954: 1270 khz; 1 kw-D, 500 w-N, DA-3. TL: N39 30 18 W88 12 54. Hrs open: 24/7 2560 W. State St., 61920. Phone: (217) 345-2148. Fax: (217) 348-7036.E-mail: info@weic.com Licensee: Eastern Illinois Christian Broadcasting Inc. (acq 9-9-03). Population served: 30,000 Format: Southern gospel. Spec prog: Farm 8 hrs wkly. ♦Brad Lee, gen mgr; Steve Hamm, chief of engrg.

***WEIU(FM)**— July 1, 1985: 88.9 mhz; 4 kw. 166 ft TL: N39 28 43 W88 10 21. Stereo. Hrs open: 24 600 Lincoln Ave., 61920. Phone: (217) 581-5956. Fax: (217) 581-6650.E-mail: hitmix@weiu.net Web Site:www.weiuhitmix.net Licensee: Eastern Illinois University. Population served: 72,000 Cohn & Marks. Format: mix/var. News staff: one; News: 3 hrs wkly. Target aud: 12 plus; 25-55 women. Spec prog: Folks 4 hrs, jazz 4 hrs wkly. ♦Denis Roche, gen mgr; Jeff Owens, stn mgr, dev dir; Linda Kingery, progmg dir; Kelly Runyon, news dir. Co-owned TV: *WEIU-TV affil

WWGO(FM)— Oct 1, 1965: 92.1 mhz; 6 kw. 140 ft TL: N39 30 18 W88 12 54. Stereo. Hrs open: 24 209 Lakeland Blvd., Mattoon, 61938. Phone: (217) 348-9292. Phone: (217) 235-5624. Fax: (217) 235-6624.E-mail: bub@radiomattoon.com Licensee: The Cromwell Group Inc. of Illinois. Group owner: The Cromwell Group Inc. (acq 1993). Population served: 100,000 Natl. Network: ABC, . Pepper & Corazzini. Format: Rock. News staff: one; News: 20 hrs wkly. Target aud: 25-54; upscale, educated adults. ♦Bud Walters, pres; Carol Floyd, gen mgr, gen sls mgr, news dir; Bub McCullough, progmg dir; Josh Jamison, chief of engrg; Kathie St. Clair, traf mgr.

***WZGL(FM)**— 2008: 88.1 mhz; 2.1 kw. Ant 229 ft TL: N39 28 38 W88 08 25. Hrs open:
Rebroadcasts WBGL(FM) Champaign 100%.
2108 W. Springfield Ave., Champaign, 61821. Phone: (217) 359-8232. Fax: (217) 359-7374. Web Site:www.wbgl.org Licensee: Illinois Bible Institute Inc. Format: Educ, relg. ♦Jeff Scott, stn mgr.

Chester

KPNT(FM)—See Sainte Genevieve, MO

KSGM(AM)— July 5, 1947: 980 khz; 1 kw-D, 500 w-N, DA-N. TL: N37 51 24 W89 49 44. Hrs open: 24
Rebroadcasts KBDZ(FM) Perryville, MO.
Box 428, St. Genevieve, MO, 63670. Phone: (573) 883-2980 618-826-2980. Phone: 573-547-6780. Fax: (573) 883-2866.E-mail: suntimesnews@brick.net Web Site:www.suntimesnews.com Licensee: Donze Communications Inc. (acq 6-20-89; $200,000; 7-10-89). Population served: 60,000 Reddy, Begley & McCormick. Format: Country, news/talk. News staff: 2; News: 14 hrs wkly. Target aud: General; adults. Spec prog: Farm 2 hrs, relg 6 hrs wkly. ♦Don Pritchard, gen mgr & news dir.

Chicago

WBBM(AM)— Nov 14, 1923: 780 khz; 50 kw-U. TL: N41 59 32 W88 01 36. Hrs open: 180 N. Stetson Ave., Suite 1100, 60601. Phone: (312) 297-7800. Fax: (312) 297-1720. Web Site:www.wbbm780.com Licensee: CBS Radio East Inc. Group owner: Infinity Broadcasting Corp. (acq 1931). Population served: 800,000 Natl. Network: CBS, CNN Radio, AP Network News, . Format: News. ♦Rod Zimmerman, VP, gen mgr; Drew Hayes, opns dir; Mark Day, gen sls mgr; Ron Gleason, progmg dir & news dir; Dan Coleman, chief of engrg.

WBBM-FM— Dec 7, 1941: 96.3 mhz; 4.2 kw. Ant 1,555 ft TL: N41 52 44 W87 38 08. Stereo. Hrs open: 180 N. Atetson Ave., 60601. Phone: (312) 729-3870. Fax: (312) 729-3887. Web Site:www.b96.com Licensee: CBS Radio East Inc. Natl. Network: CBS, . Natl. Rep: CBS Radio,. Format: CHR. ♦Dave Robbins, VP; Paul Agase, gen sls mgr; Thad Gentry, rgnl sls mgr; Michael Biemolt, mktg dir, prom mgr; Todd Cavanah, progmg dir; Eric Bradley, mus dir; Louis Segura, news dir; Tony Kelly, chief of engrg.

***WBEZ(FM)**— 1942: 91.5 mhz; 8.3 kw. Ant 1,180 ft TL: N41 53 56 W87 37 23. Stereo. Hrs open: 24 Navy Pier, 848 E. Grand Ave., 60611-3509. Phone: (312) 948-4600. Fax: (312) 832-3100.E-mail: questions@wbez.org Web Site:www.chicagopublicradio.org Licensee: The WBEZ Alliance Inc. (acq 9-7-90; 10-1-90). Population served: 1,336,695 Natl. Network: NPR, PRI, . Format: Jazz, pub affrs, news. News staff: 5; News: 45 hrs wkly. Target aud: General; people who want to know about the world around them. ♦Merrill Smith, chmn; Donna Moore, CFO; Torey Malatia, chmn, pres & gen mgr.

WBGX(AM)—See Harvey

WCFJ(AM)—See Chicago Heights

WCFS-FM—See Elmwood Park

WCPT(AM)—(Willow Springs, 1941: 820 khz; 5 kw-D. TL: N41 56 18 W87 45 05. Stereo. Hrs open: Daylight 6012 S. Pulaski Rd., 60629. Phone: (773) 767-1000. Fax: (773) 767-1100.E-mail: info@wcpt820.com Web Site:www.chicagoprogressivetalk.com Licensee: WYPA Inc. Group owner: Newsweb Corp. (acq 2-15-2001; $10.5 million). Natl. Network: CNN Radio, . Format: Progressive talk. Target aud: 25-64; adults. ♦Harvey Wells, gen mgr; Jeff Chardell, sls dir; Gavin Carroll, progmg mgr.

WCPT-FM—(Arlington Heights, Mar 10, 1960: 92.7 mhz; 3 kw. Ant 299 ft TL: N42 07 50 W87 58 59. Stereo. Hrs open: 24 6012 S. Pulaski Rd., 60629. Phone: (773) 767-1000. Fax: (773) 767-1100.E-mail: info@wcpt820.com Web Site:www.chicagoprogressivetalk.com Licensee: WKIE Inc. Group owner: Spanish Broadcasting System Inc. (acq 11-15-2004; grpsl). Population served: 16,861 Natl. Network: CNN Radio, . Format: Progressive talk. ♦Harvey Wells, gen mgr; Bill Cavanaugh, gen sls mgr; Mike McCarthy, chief of engrg; Roan Davis, traf mgr.

***WCRX(FM)**— July 29, 1975: 88.1 mhz; 100 w. 150 ft TL: N41 52 22 W87 38 52. Hrs open: 24 600 S. Michigan Ave., 60605. Phone: (312) 344-8155. Fax: (312) 663-5204. Web Site:wcrx.net Licensee: Columbia College. (acq 10-5-82). Natl. Network: AP Radio, . Dow, Lohnes & Albertson. Wire Svc: AP Format: Sports, news. News staff: 2; News: 20 hrs wkly. Target aud: 18-24; Men. ♦Cheryl Langston, gen mgr; Tony Kwiecinski, stn mgr; Dave Dennis, chief of engrg.

WDRV(FM)— July 9, 1955: 97.1 mhz; 8.4 kw. 1,196 ft TL: N41 53 08 W87 37 15. Stereo. Hrs open: 24 875 N. Michigan, Suite 1510, 60611. Phone: (312) 274-9710. Fax: (312) 274-1304. Web Site:www.wdrv.com Licensee: Bonneville Holding Co. Group owner: Bonneville International Corp. (acq 1-25-01; $165 million with WWDV(FM) Zion). Population served: 7,000,000 Natl. Rep: Katz Radio,. Format: Classic timeless rock. ♦Jerry Schnacke, VP, gen mgr; Greg Solk, opns VP; Chris Winston, gen sls mgr; Patty Martin, progmg dir.

WFMT(FM)— Dec 13, 1951: 98.7 mhz; 16 kw. 1,170 ft TL: N41 53 56 W87 37 23. Stereo. Hrs open: 24 5400 N. St. Louis Ave., 60625-4698. Phone: (773) 279-2000. Fax: (773) 279-2199.E-mail: finearts@wfmt.com Web Site:www.networkchicago.com Licensee: Window to the World Communications Inc. (acq 3-5-70). Population served: 8,000,000 Schwartz, Woods & Miller. Format: Class. News: 7 hrs wkly. Target aud: 25-54; upscale, professional, college educated, upper income adults. Spec prog: Folk 4 hrs, jazz 5 hrs wkly. ♦Dan Schmidt, CEO, pres; Steve Robinson, sr VP & gen mgr; Paul Ansell, gen sls mgr; Gordon Carter, engrg dir, chief of engrg. Co-owned TV: WTTW(TV) affil

WGCI-FM— Dec 11, 1958: 107.5 mhz; 33 kw. 600 ft TL: N41 52 57 W87 38 15. Stereo. Hrs open: Prog sep from AM 233 N. Michigan Ave., Suite 2800, 60601. Phone: (312) 540-2000. Fax: (312) 938-4477. Web Site:www.wgci.com Format: R&B hip hop. ♦Elroy Smith, progmg dir.

WGN(AM)— June 1, 1924: 720 khz; 50 kw-U. TL: N42 00 42 W88 02 07. Hrs open: 435 N. Michigan Ave., 60611. Phone: (312) 222-4700. Fax: (312) 222-5165.E-mail: info@wgnradio.com Web Site:www.wgnradio.com Licensee: WGN Continental Broadcasting Co., debtor-in-possession Group owner: Tribune Broadcasting Co. (acq 12-20-2007; grpsl). Natl. Network: ABC, . Natl. Rep: Christal,. Wire Svc: AP Format: News/talk, sports. Target aud: 35-64. Spec prog: Cubs, Northwestern play-by-play. ♦Tom Langmyer, VP, gen mgr, gen mgr; Wendi Power, sls dir; Lori Brayer, prom dir; Bob Shomper, progmg dir; Wes Bleed, news dir; Jim Carollo, engrg dir, chief of engrg. Co-owned TV: WGN-TV affil

WGRB(AM)— 1924: 1390 khz; 5 kw-U, DA-2. TL: N41 44 13 W87 42 00. Hrs open: 233 N. Michigan Ave., Suite 2800, 60601. Phone: (312) 540-2000. Fax: (312) 938-4477. Web Site:www.wgci.com Licensee: AMFM Broadcasting Licenses LLC. Group owner: Clear Channel Communications Inc. (acq 8-30-2000; grpsl). Population served: 300,000 Natl. Rep: Christal,. Format: Gospel. ♦Marv Dyson, pres; Sandra Robinson, progmg dir.

***WHPK-FM**— Mar 15, 1968: 88.5 mhz; 100 w. 121 ft TL: N41 47 40 W87 35 55. Stereo. Hrs open: 24 5706 S. University Ave., 60637. Phone: (773) 702-8289. Fax: (773) 702-7718.E-mail: whpk@uchicago.edu Web Site:whpk.uchicago.edu Licensee: The University of Chicago. Population served: 50,000 Format: Div, educ, jazz. News: 5 hrs wkly. Spec prog: Class 10 hrs, African one hr, Haitian 3 hrs, Israeli one hr, Irish one hrs wkly. ♦Naiara Testai, stn mgr; Eric Hanss, progmg dir.

***WIIT(FM)**— June 1974: 88.9 mhz; 17 w. 90 ft TL: N41 50 04 W87 37 43. Stereo. Hrs open: 24 3300 S. Federal St., 60616. Phone: (312) 567-3087. Phone: (312) 567-3088. Fax: (312) 567-7042.E-mail: wiit@iit.edu Licensee: Illinois Institute of Technology. Crowell & Moring. Format: Var/div. News: 5 hrs wkly. Target aud: 15-35; college & young urban community. Spec prog: Jazz 9 hrs, Ger 3 hrs, relg 2 hrs, Sp 5 hrs wkly. ♦Patrick Schneider, stn mgr.

WILV(FM)— 1947: 100.3 mhz; 5.7 kw. Ant 1,394 ft TL: N41 53 56 W87 37 23. Stereo. Hrs open: One Prudential Plaza, Suite 2780, 130 E. Randolph, 60601. Phone: (312) 297-5100. Fax: (312) 297-5111.E-mail: davidj@lovefm.fm Web Site:www.wnnd.com Licensee: Bonneville Holding Co. Group owner: Bonneville International Corp. (acq 6-13-97; $75 million). Population served: 6,000,000 Format: Adult contemp. Target aud: 25-49; women. ♦Barry James, exec VP, VP, gen mgr, progmg dir; Sue Werley, gen sls mgr; Mandy Irwin, prom dir; Keith Warner, chief of engrg.

WIND(AM)— 1927: 560 khz; 5 kw-U, DA-2. TL: N41 33 54 W87 25 11. Hrs open: 25 Northwest Point Blvd., Suite 400, Elk Grove Village, 60007. Phone: (847) 437-5200. Fax: (847) 956-5040. Web Site:www.560wind.com Licensee: Salem Media of Illinois LLC. Group owner: Univision Radio (acq 1-7-2005; with KNIT(AM) Dallas and KKHT-FM Winnie, both TX, in exchange for WPPN(FM) Des Plaines, IL). Population served: 336,695 Format: Conservative news/talk. ♦David Santrella, gen mgr; Eric Thomas, opns dir.

WJMK(FM)— Jan 2, 1961: 104.3 mhz; 4.1 kw. 1,575 ft TL: N41 52 44 W87 38 10. Stereo. Hrs open: Two Prudential Plaza, Suite 900, 60601. Phone: (312) 729-3870. Fax: (312) 729-3887.E-mail: wjmk@wjmk.com Web Site:www.wjmk.com Licensee: Infinity Broadcasting Corp. of Illinois. Population served: 762,800 Natl. Network: Westwood One, . Format: Oldies. Target aud: 25-54. ♦Dave Robbins, VP, gen mgr; Terry Hardin, natl sls mgr; Lisa Piovosi, mktg dir; Charlie Lake, progmg dir; John Galenta, chief of engrg.

***WKKC(FM)**— 1975: 89.3 mhz; 280 w horiz, 250 w vert. Ant 111 ft TL: N41 46 48 W87 38 38. Stereo. Hrs open: Kennedy-King College, 6800 S. Wentworth Ave., 60621. Phone: (773) 602-5540. Fax: (773) 602-5532.E-mail: mdyson@ccc.edu Web Site:www.ccc.edu Licensee: District 508 City College of Chicago. Population served: 250,000 Format: Urban contemp, educ, var/div. Target aud: 15-50. ♦Kevin Brown, gen mgr.

WKQX(FM)— 1948: 101.1 mhz; 8.3 kw. 1,710 ft TL: N41 53 56 W87 37 23. Hrs open: 24 Box 3404, 60654. Secondary address: 230 Merchandise Mart Plaza 60654. Phone: (312) 527-8348. Fax: (312) 527-3620.E-mail: info@q101.com Web Site:www.q101.com Licensee: Emmis Radio License LLC. Group owner: Emmis Communications Corp. Population served: 700,000 Natl. Rep: D & R Radio,. Format: Alternative rock. Target aud: 18-34. ♦Marv Nyren, VP, gen mgr; Lance Richard, gen sls mgr; Mike Stern, progmg dir; Patrick Berger, chief of engrg; Jennifer Welch, traf mgr.

WKSC-FM— November 1957: 103.5 mhz; 4.3 kw. Ant 1,548 ft TL: N41 52 44 W87 38 10. Stereo. Hrs open: 24 233 N. Michigan, Suite 2800, 60601. Phone: (312) 540-2000. Fax: (312) 938-0712. Web Site:www.kisschicago.com Licensee: AMFM Broadcasting Licenses LLC. Group owner: Clear Channel Communications Inc. (acq 8-30-2000; grpsl). Population served: 8,000,000 Format: CHR. News staff: one; News: 15 hrs wkly. Target aud: 18-34; upscale. ♦Dave Scharf, gen sls mgr; Bob Fukuda, chief of engrg; Lynn Clymer, traf mgr.

WLIT-FM— Apr 7, 1958: 93.9 mhz; 4 kw. 1,581 ft TL: N41 52 44 W87 38 10. Stereo. Hrs open: 24 233 N. Michigan Ave., Suite 2800, 60601. Phone: (312) 540-2000. Fax: (312) 938-0111.E-mail: info@wlit.com Web Site:www.wlit.com Licensee: AMFM Broadcasting Licenses LLC. Group owner: Clear Channel Communications Inc. (acq 8-30-2000; grpsl). Population served: 650,000 Natl. Network: Premiere Radio Networks, . Natl. Rep: Clear Channel,. Wire Svc: AP Format: Adult contemp. News staff: one; News: one hr wkly. Target aud: 25-54; affluent adults. ♦Earl Jones, VP; Ken Denton, gen sls mgr, rgnl sls mgr; Darren Davis, natl sls mgr, progmg dir; Eric Richeke, mus dir, news dir; Rick Zurick, news dir; Bob Fukuda, chief of engrg; Ella Hammitte, traf mgr.

WLS(AM)— Apr 12, 1924: 890 khz; 50 kw-U. TL: N41 33 21 W87 50 54. Stereo. Hrs open: 190 N. State St., 60601. Phone: (312) 984-0890. Fax: (312) 984-5305.E-mail: info@wlsam.com Web Site:www.wlsam.com Licensee: Radio License Holding XI LLC. Group owner: ABC Inc. (acq 6-12-2007; grpsl). Format: News/talk. Target aud: 35-64; listeners involved in Chicago news & community affairs. ♦Zemira Jones, pres & gen mgr; Bill Gamble, progmg dir; Carol O'Keefe, pub affrs dir.

WLS-FM— Apr 1, 1949: 94.7 mhz; 4.4 kw. Ant 1,535 ft TL: N41 53 56 W87 37 23. Stereo. Hrs open: Phone: (312) 984-9923. Fax: (312) 984-5357. Web Site:www.947zone.com Licensee: Radio License Holding V LLC. (acq 6-12-2007; grpsl). Population served: 900,000 Format: Oldies. ♦Jim Pastor, pres & gen mgr.

WLUP-FM— 1942: 97.9 mhz; 4 kw. Ant 1,394 ft TL: N41 53 56 W87 37 23. Stereo. Hrs open: 24 222 Merchandise Mart Plz Ste 230, 60654-1008. Phone: (312) 440-5270. Fax: (312) 440-9377.E-mail: info@wlup.com Web Site:www.wlup.com Licensee: Emmis Radio License LLC. Group owner: Bonneville International Corp. (acq 12-15-2004; swap for KMVP(AM) and KTAR(AM)-KKLT(FM) Phoenix, AZ). Population served: 2,800,000 Natl. Rep: D & R Radio,. Format: Rock. Target aud: 18-49. ♦Marv Nyren, gen mgr.

***WLUW(FM)—** Sept 19, 1978: 88.7 mhz; 100 w. 230 ft TL: N42 00 04 W87 39 36. Stereo. Hrs open: 24 6525 N. Sheridan Rd., 60626. Phone: (773) 508-8080. Fax: (773) 508-8082.E-mail: wluwradio@wluw.org Web Site:www.wluw.org Licensee: Loyola University, Chicago. Population served: 60,000 Wire Svc: Pacifica Network News Format: Var. Target aud: General. ♦Craig Kois, gen mgr; Sean Campbell, progmg dir; Matt Malooly, news dir.

***WMBI(AM)—** July 28, 1926: 1110 khz; 5 kw-D (L-WBT Charlotte, NC; KFAB Omaha). TL: N41 55 35 W88 00 22. Hrs open: Sunrise-sunset 820 N. LaSalle Blvd., 60610. Phone: (312) 329-4300. Fax: (312) 329-4468.E-mail: mbn@moody.edu Licensee: The Moody Bible Institute of Chicago Population served: 7,400,000 Natl. Network: Moody, . Southmayd & Miller. Wire Svc: AP Format: Urban contemp. Target aud: 35-54; Hispanic Christians, children, English-speaking. Spec prog: Sp 12 hrs wkly. ♦John Hayden, opns mgr; Collin Lambert, progmg mgr.

***WMBI-FM—** July 25, 1960: 90.1 mhz; 100 kw. 440 ft TL: N41 55 35 W88 00 22. Stereo. Hrs open: 24 820 N. LaSalle Blvd., 60610. Phone: (312) 329-4300. Fax: (312) 329-4468.E-mail: wmbi@moody.edu Web Site:www.wmbi.org Licensee: The Moody Bible Institute of Chicago (group owner) Population served: 7,400,000 Natl. Network: Moody, . Southmayd & Miller. Wire Svc: AP Format: Relg, educ, Christian. News staff: 2. Target aud: 35-54; Christian. ♦Paul Nyquist, pres; John Hayden, opns mgr; Collin Lambert, progmg mgr.

WMVP(AM)— June 25, 1926: 1000 khz; 50 kw-U, DA-2. TL: N41 49 05 W87 59 18. Hrs open: 24 190 N. State St., 7th Fl., 60601. Phone: (312) 980-1000. Fax: (312) 980-1020.E-mail: jeff.s.schwartz@abc.com Web Site:www.espnradio.com Licensee: Sports Radio Chicago LLC. Group owner: ABC Inc. (acq 4-1-99; $21 million). Population served: 394,110 Natl. Network: ESPN Radio, . Natl. Rep: ABC Radio Sales,. Latham & Watkins. Format: Sports, comedy, talk. Target aud: 25-54. ♦Jon Paul Rexing, CEO, rgnl sls mgr; James Pastor, gen mgr; Jeff Schwartz, opns dir; John Craveno, sls dir; Justin Craig, progmg dir; John Hurni, chief of engrg.

WNTD(AM)— May 1922: 950 khz; 1 kw-D, 5 kw-N, DA-N. TL: N41 38 29 W87 33 14. Hrs open: 541 N. Fairbanks Ct., Suite 1260, 60611. Phone: (312) 467-9755. Fax: (312) 467-9603.E-mail: WNTD@relevantradio.com Web Site:www.relevantradio.com Licensee: Sovereign City Radio Services LLC Group owner: Multicultural Radio Broadcasting Inc. (acq 10-18-2007; $15 million). Population served: 336,695 Format: Relg. Target aud: 25-54. ♦Scott Wert, gen mgr.

WNUA(FM)— Mar 9, 1959: 95.5 mhz; 8.3 kw. Ant 1,174 ft TL: N41 53 56 W87 37 23. Stereo. Hrs open: 233 N. Michigan Ave., Suites 2700 & 2800, 60601. Phone: (312) 540-2000. Fax: (312) 938-0712. Web Site:www.mega955.com Licensee: AMFM Broadcasting Licenses LLC. Group owner: Clear Channel Communications Inc. (acq 8-30-2000; grpsl). Population served: 534,000 Wire Svc: UPI Format: Sp. Target aud: 25-54. ♦Patrick Kelly, gen mgr.

WOJO(FM)—See Evanston

***WRTE(FM)—** Dec 1, 1969: 90.5 mhz; 8 w. 56 ft TL: N41 20 26 W87 43 05. (CP: 17 w, ant 85 ft.). Hrs open: 18 1401 W. 18th St., 60608. Secondary address: c/o Mexican Fine Arts Ctr. Museum, 1852 W. 19th St. 60608-2706. Phone: (312) 455-9455. Phone: (312) 738-1503. Fax: (312) 455-9755.E-mail: wrte@radioarte.org Web Site:www.radioarte.org Licensee: Mexican Fine Arts Center Museum. Population served: 50,000 Shaw Pittman. Format: Var/div. Target aud: 15-35. ♦Silvia Rivera, gen mgr; Carlos Mendez, progmg dir.

WRTO(AM)— December 1988: 1200 khz; 10 kw-D, 1 kw-N, DA-2. TL: N41 42 14 W87 35 47. Stereo. Hrs open: 24 625 N. Michigan Ave., 3rd Fl., 60611. Phone: (312) 981-1800. Fax: (312) 981-1806. Web Site:http://www.univision.com/content /channels.jhtml?chid=9627&schid=16219 Licensee: WLXX-AM License Corp. Group owner: Univision Radio (acq 9-22-2003; grpsl). Natl. Rep: McGavren Guild,. Shaw Pittman. Format: SPANISH NEWS/TALK. News staff: 4; News: 10 hrs wkly. Target aud: Urban Spanish. ♦Jerry Ryan, gen mgr; Cesar Canales, opns mgr; Alicia Chavarria, prom dir; Joshua Sigstad, engrg mgr.

WSBC(AM)— 1925: 1240 khz; 1 kw-U. TL: N41 56 18 W87 45 05. Hrs open: 24 5625 N. Milwaukee Ave., 60646. Phone: (773) 792-1121. Fax: (773) 792-2904.E-mail: wsbc@wsbcradio.com Licensee: WSBC Inc. (acq 2-23-98). Format: time brokered. Target aud: General. ♦Harvey Wells, VP; Mark Pinski, gen mgr; Jorge Murillo, opns mgr; Mike McCarthy, progmg dir & chief of engrg.

WSCR(AM)— April 1922: 670 khz; 50 kw-U. TL: N41 56 01 W88 04 23. Stereo. Hrs open: 24 NBC Tower, 455 N. City Front Plaza, 60611. Phone: (312) 644-6767. Fax: (312) 245-6143.E-mail: info@wscr670am.com Web Site:www.wscr670am.com Licensee: Infinity Broadcasting East Inc. Group owner: Infinity Broadcasting Corp. (acq 11-13-98; grpsl). Population served: 800000 Natl. Network: Westwood One, . Rgnl. Network: Ill. Radio Net. Ill. Radio Net. Format: Sports. Target aud: 25-54. ♦Rod Zimmerman, VP & gen mgr; Drew Hayes, opns dir, opns mgr; Paul Agase, gen sls mgr; Mary Lou Compton, natl sls mgr; Cher Ames, mktg dir, prom dir, prom mgr; Matt Fishman, progmg dir; George Offman, news dir; Jesse Rogers, pub affrs dir; Greg Davis, chief of engrg.

***WSSD(FM)—** Sept 15, 1987: 88.1 mhz; 10 w. 100 ft TL: N41 52 22 W87 38 52. Stereo. Hrs open: 515 W. 111th St., 60628-4019. Phone: (773) 928-8800. Fax: (773) 928-9009. Licensee: Lakeside Communications Inc. Lauren A. Colby. Format: Blues, gospel, talk. Target aud: 25 plus; Black. Spec prog: Gospel, jazz, talk. ♦Huey Williams, pres, gen mgr, progmg dir, progmg mgr; Steven McKinney, stn mgr & gen sls mgr.

WUSN(FM)— 1940: 99.5 mhz; 8.3 kw. 1,174 ft TL: N41 53 56 W87 37 23. Stereo. Hrs open: 2 Prudential Plaza, Suite 1000, 60601. Phone: (312) 649-0099. Fax: (312) 856-9586. Web Site:www.us99.com Licensee: Infinity Broadcasting Corp. of Chicago. Group owner: CBS Radio (acq 1996; grpsl). Format: Country. Target aud: 25-54. ♦Dave Robbins, gen mgr & stn mgr.

WXRT-FM— 1959: 93.1 mhz; 6.7 kw. Ant 1,309 ft TL: N41 53 56 W87 37 23. Stereo. Hrs open: 4949 W. Belmont Ave., 60641. Phone: (773) 777-1700. Fax: (773) 777-5031. Web Site:www.93xrt.com Licensee: CBS Radio East Inc. Group owner: Infinity Broadcasting Corp. (acq 11-13-98; grpsl). Population served: 600000 Natl. Rep: CBS Radio,. Format: Rock/AOR, alternative. News staff: one. Target aud: 25-54; upscale adults. ♦Michael Damsky, VP, gen mgr, gen sls mgr; John Farneda, opns mgr, mktg dir; Adrienne Szarmack, rgnl sls mgr; Brad Auerbach, mktg dir; Norm Winer, progmg VP & progmg dir; Mark Nielson, chief of engrg.

WYLL(AM)— Oct 13, 1924: 1160 khz; 50 kw-U, DA-2. TL: N42 02 30 W87 51 57 (day), N41 34 23 W87 59 37 (night). Hrs open: 24 25 North West Point Blvd., Suite 400, Elk Grove Village, 60007. Phone: (847) 956-5030. Fax: (847) 956-5040. Web Site:www.wyll.com Licensee: Salem Media Group LLC. Group owner: Salem Communications Corp. (acq 12-20-2000; $29 million). Population served: 477,700 Format: Relg. Target aud: 25-54; Upscale income adults. ♦David Santrella, gen mgr.

***WZRD(FM)—** July 8, 1974: 88.3 mhz; 100 w. 76 ft TL: N41 58 56 W87 43 07. Stereo. Hrs open: 11 AM-midnight 5500 N. St. Louis Ave., 60625. Phone: (773) 583-4050. Fax: (773) 442-4900. Web Site:www.wzrdchicago.com Licensee: Northeastern Illinois University. Population served: 336,695 Format: Div, educ. News staff: 29; News: 12 hrs wkly. Target aud: General. ♦Dennis Sagel, stn mgr.

Chicago Heights

WCFJ(AM)— Aug 15, 1963: 1470 khz; 1 kw-U, DA-2. TL: N41 25 29 W87 38 27. Hrs open: 24 5625 N. Milwaukee Ave., Chicago, 60646. Phone: (773) 792-1121. Fax: (773) 792-2904.E-mail: mp@wsbcradio.com Licensee: WCFJ Inc. (acq 2-23-98). Format: Var/div, time brokered. General. ♦Harvey Wells, VP; Mark Pinski, gen mgr; Jorge Murillo, opns mgr; Mike McCarthy, progmg dir & chief of engrg.

WYCA(FM)—See Crete

Chillicothe

WPMJ(FM)— May 16, 1977: Stn currently dark. 94.3 mhz; 6 kw. Ant 300 ft TL: N40 49 48 W89 29 54. Stereo. Hrs open: 24 3641 Meadowbrook Rd., Peoria, 61604. Phone: (309) 685-5975. Fax: (309) 685-9095. Licensee: Kelly Communications Inc. (acq 1-2-2003; $1.5 million value part of cash/swap for WXCL(FM) Pekin) Population served: 350,000 ♦Bob Kelly, CEO, chmn, pres, CFO & gen mgr.

Christopher

WXLT(FM)— Dec 25, 1990: 103.5 mhz; 6 kw. Ant 328 ft TL: N37 55 55 W88 57 28. Hrs open: 24 1431 Country Aire Dr., Carterville, 62918. Phone: (618) 985-4843. Fax: (618) 985-6529.E-mail: mail@wxlt.com Web Site:www.wxlt.com Licensee: MRR License LLC. Group owner: MAX Media L.L.C. (acq 6-2-2004; grpsl). Natl. Network: ESPN Radio, . Natl. Rep: Christal,. Format: Sports. ♦Steve J. Falat, gen mgr; Kim DeBose, gen sls mgr; Tom Miller, opns mgr & progmg dir; Jon Brookmyer, chief of engrg; Felicia Dick, traf mgr.

Cicero

WCEV(AM)— Oct 1, 1979: 1450 khz; 1 kw-U (ST: WVON[\][\]]). TL: N41 49 57 W87 42 40. Hrs open: 1-10 PM (M-F); 1-8:30 PM (S); 5 AM-10 PM (Su) 5356 W. Belmont Ave., Chicago, 60641-4192. Phone: (773) 282-6700. Phone: (773) 777-1450. Fax: (773) 282-0123.E-mail: wcev@wcev1450.com Web Site:www.wcev1450.com Licensee: Migala Communications Corp. Wire Svc: AP Format: Multi Ethnic. News: 7 hrs wkly. Target aud: Adult ethnic Americans. ♦Estelle Migala, pres; George Migala, stn mgr; Lucyna Migala, progmg dir; Sam Palermo, chief of engrg.

WLUP-FM—See Chicago

WRLL(AM)— 1979: 1450 khz; 1 kw-U (ST: WCEV[\][\]]). TL: N41 49 57 W87 42 20. Hrs open: Midnight-1 PM 1000 E. 87th St., Chicago, 60619. Phone: (773) 247-6200. Fax: (773) 247-5336. Licensee: Midway Broadcasting Corp. Population served: 200,000 Format: Sp. ♦Pervis Spann, CEO; Melody Spann-Cooper, pres, gen mgr; Gustavo Rios, stn mgr; Juanita Maze, gen sls mgr; Coz Carson, progmg dir; Denise King, traf mgr.

Clinton

WEZC(FM)— Dec 15, 1975: 95.9 mhz; 6 kw. Ant 308 ft TL: N40 05 43 W88 57 51. Hrs open: 24 R.R. 2, Box 117M, 61727. Phone: (217) 935-9590. Fax: (217) 935-9909. Web Site:www.dewittdailynews.com Licensee: Kaskaskia Broadcasting Inc. (acq 1-4-2008; $400,000 with co-located AM). Population served: 400,000 Natl. Network: CNN Radio, . Natl. Rep: Commercial Media Sales,. Format: Soft adult contemp. News staff: one; News: 4 hrs news programing wkly. Target aud: 35+. ♦Jared White, progmg dir.

WHOW(AM)— Aug 1, 1947: 1520 khz; 5 kw-D, 1 kw-CH. TL: N40 05 43 W88 57 51. Hrs open: Sunrise-sunset R.R. 2, Box 117M, 61727. Phone: (217) 935-9590. Fax: (217) 935-9909. Web Site:www.dewittdailynews.com Licensee: Kaskaskia Broadcasting Inc. (acq 1-4-2008; $400,000 with co-located FM). Population served: 1,000,000 Natl. Network: CNN Radio, . Natl. Rep: Commercial Media Sales,. Format: news/talk/agriculture. News staff: one; News: 20 hrs wkly. Target aud: 35+. ♦Jared White, progmg dir.

Coal City

WRXQ(FM)— Feb 8, 1991: 100.7 mhz; 1.4 kw. 482 ft TL: N41 17 39 W88 10 15. Stereo. Hrs open: 24 2410-B Caton Farm Rd., Crest Hill, 60435. Phone: (815) 556-0100. Fax: (815) 577-9231. Licensee: NM Licensing LLC. Group owner: NextMedia Group L.L.C. (acq 11-26-01; grpsl). Population served: 80,000 Natl. Rep: Christal,. Format: Classic rock. News: 5 hrs wkly. Target aud: 35-50; adults. ♦Todd Elbrink, gen mgr; Ryan Snow, opns dir, progmg dir; Roger Piper, gen sls mgr; Dan Waddick, prom dir.

Colchester

WGNX(FM)— 2007: 96.7 mhz; 1.8 kw. Ant 328 ft TL: N40 23 54 W90 43 55. Hrs open: 8834 Mill Creek Rd., Bloomington, 61704. Phone: (386) 690-2200. Licensee: Patricia Van Zandt. ♦Patricia E. Van Zandt, gen mgr.

WMQZ(FM)— 1999: 104.1 mhz; 6 kw. Ant 328 ft TL: N40 32 01 W90 51 45. Hrs open: 31 East Side Sq., Macomb, 61455. Phone: (309) 833-2121. Fax: (309) 836-3291.E-mail: wjeq@macomb.com Web Site:www.wmqz.com Licensee: Colchester Radio Inc. Format: Oldies. ♦Bruce Foster, pres, chief of engrg; Nancy Foster, gen mgr; Mike Grillette, news dir; Shana Drake, traf mgr.

Colfax

WRPW(FM)— 1997: 92.9 mhz; 6 kw. Ant 328 ft TL: N40 29 28 W88 43 14. Stereo. Hrs open: 108 Boeykens Pl., Normal, 61761. Phone: (309) 888-4496. Fax: (309) 452-9677. Web Site:www.power929fm.com Licensee: Pilot Media LLC. Group owner: AAA Entertainment L.L.C. (acq 6-19-2007; grpsl). Population served: 125,000 Format: CHR/rhythmic. ♦Patti Donsbach, gen mgr; Kevin Trueblood, opns mgr; Amber Goodwin, prom dir; Don Black, progmg dir.

Columbia

KMJM-FM— Feb 15, 1964: 104.9 mhz; 11.5 kw. 480 ft TL: N38 34 24 W90 19 30. Stereo. Hrs open: 24 1001 Highland Plaza Dr. W., St. Louis, MO, 63110. Phone: (314) 333-8000. Web Site:www.kmjm.com Licensee: Citicasters Licenses L.P. Group owner: Clear Channel Communications Inc. (acq 5-4-99; grpsl). Population served: 2,700,000 Format: Urban adult contemp. Target aud: 25-54; adults. ♦Dennis Lamme, gen mgr; Tommy Austin, opns mgr; Beth Davis, sls dir; Kevin Joyce, gen sls mgr; John Helmkamp, mktg dir.

Crest Hill

WCCQ(FM)—Licensed to Crest Hill. See Joliet

Crete

***WBMF(FM)**— 2002: 88.1 mhz; 90 w. Ant 374 ft TL: N41 25 17 W87 38 39. Hrs open: Box 3206, American Family Radio, Tupelo, MS, 38803. Phone: (662) 844-8888. Fax: (662) 842-6791. Web Site:www.afr.net Licensee: American Family Association. Group owner: American Family Radio Format: Christian. News: 2 hrs wkly.

WYCA(FM)— Sept 5, 1965: 102.3 mhz; 1 kw. 299 ft TL: N41 18 53 W87 37 11. Stereo. Hrs open: 6336 Calumet Ave., Hammond, IN, 46324. Phone: (773) 734-4455. Fax: (219) 933-0323.E-mail: wybainfo@crawfordbroadcasting.com Web Site:www.wyca1023.com Licensee: Dontron Inc. Group owner: Crawford Broadcasting Co. (acq 8-26-97; $1.8 million). Population served: 40,900 Format: Christian talk. Target aud: 35 plus; adult, African-Americans. ♦Donald B. Crawford, CEO; Taft Harris, gen mgr.

Crystal Lake

WAIT(AM)— Oct 1, 1965: 850 khz; 2.5 kw-D, DA. TL: N42 15 30 W88 21 48. Stereo. Hrs open: Sunrise-sunset 5625 N. Milwaukee Ave., Chicago, 60646. Phone: (773) 792-1121. Fax: (773) 792-2904. Web Site:www.thepromise850.com Licensee: Chicago Newsweb Corp. Group owner: Newsweb Corp. (acq 9-16-2003; $8.25 million). Population served: 6,000,000 Holland & Knight. Format: Christian in English and Spanish. ♦Mark Pinski, gen mgr; Jorge Murillo, opns mgr; Sally Gaigalas, gen sls mgr; Mike McCarthy, chief of engrg.

WZSR(FM)—See Woodstock

Danville

KUUL(FM)—See East Moline

WDAN(AM)— October 1938: 1490 khz; 1 kw-U. TL: N40 08 58 W87 37 35. Hrs open: 1501 N. Washington Ave., 61832. Phone: (217) 442-1700. Fax: (217) 431-1489. Web Site:www.1490wdan.com Licensee: Neuhoff Family L.P. (group owner; acq 11-5-03; grpsl). Population served: 80,000 Natl. Network: ESPN Radio, Fox News Radio, . Natl. Rep: McGavren Guild,. Format: News/talk, sports. News staff: one; News: 20 hrs wkly. Target aud: 25-54. Spec prog: Farm 20 hrs wkly. ♦Roger Neuhoff, pres; Geoffery Neuhoff, exec VP; Michael Hulvey, VP, gen mgr; Michelle Campbell, sls dir, adv mgr; Tom Barnes, opns mgr, prom mgr & progmg dir; Bill Pickett, news dir; Don Russel, chief of engrg.

WDNL(FM)— May 1967: 102.1 mhz; 50 kw. 380 ft TL: N40 08 58 W87 37 35. Stereo. Hrs open: 24 Prog sep from AM 1501 N. Washington Ave., 61832. Phone: (217) 442-1700. Fax: (217) 431-1489. Web Site:www.d102.com Licensee: Neuhoff Family L.P. Population served: 120,000 Format: Adult contemp. News: 2 hrs wkly. Target aud: 18-49. ♦Michael Hulvey, opns VP; Tom Barnes, progmg mgr; Carole Wade, mus dir.

WITY(AM)— Nov 24, 1953: 980 khz; 1 kw-U, DA-1. TL: N40 04 41 W87 38 20. Hrs open: 24 Box 142, 61834. Secondary address: 399 Spelter Ave., Tilton 61833. Phone: (217) 446-1312. Fax: (217) 446-1314.E-mail: wityradio@att.net Licensee: Vermilion Broadcasting Corporation. (acq 1981). Population served: 400,000 Natl. Network: Westwood One, . Format: Adult standards, info. Target aud: 35 plus; general. Spec prog: Relg 6 hrs, farm 12 hrs wkly. ♦Donald E. Ward, pres; David W. Brown, VP, gen mgr; David Brown, gen sls mgr; Lora Jacobson, news dir; Gale Cunningham, pub affrs dir, farm dir; George Dudich, chief of engrg.

WRHK(FM)— November 1992: 94.9 mhz; 6 kw. 328 ft TL: N40 10 40 W87 28 55. Hrs open: 24 1501 N. Washington Ave., 61832. Phone: (217) 442-1700. Fax: (217) 431-1489.E-mail: info@949rock.com Web Site:www.949krock.com Licensee: Neuhoff Family L.P. (group owner; acq 11-5-03; grpsl). Natl. Network: Motor Racing Net, Premiere Radio Networks, . Natl. Rep: McGavren Guild,. Schwartz, Wood & Miller. Format: Classic rock. News: 5 hrs wkly. Target aud: 18-49. ♦Roger Neuhoff, chmn; Pat Odea, CFO; Geoffery Neuhoff, exec VP; Michael Hulvey, gen mgr, opns VP; Michelle Campbell, gen sls mgr; Tom Barnes, progmg dir; Don Russell, chief of engrg.

WXTT(FM)— Mar 2, 1970: 99.1 mhz; 50 kw. Ant 500 ft TL: N40 08 52 W87 46 20. Hrs open: 2603 W. Bradley Ave., Champaign, 61821. Phone: (217) 352-4141. Fax: (217) 352-1256. Licensee: Saga Communications of Illinois LLC. Group owner: Saga Communications Inc. (acq 6-30-2004; $3.25 million). Population served: 469,000 Natl. Rep: D & R Radio,. Format: Classic rock. ♦Alan Beck, gen mgr; Bill Cain, progmg dir.

De Kalb

WCPY(FM)— Dec 17, 1961: 92.5 mhz; 20 kw. Ant 495 ft TL: N41 52 33 W88 45 16. Stereo. Hrs open: 24 6012 S. Pulaski Rd., Chicago, 60629. Phone: (773) 767-1000. Fax: (773) 767-1100.E-mail: info@wcpt820.com Web Site:www.chicagoprogressivetalk.com Licensee: WDEK Inc. Group owner: Spanish Broadcasting System Inc. (acq 11-15-2004; grpsl). Population served: 645,000 Natl. Network: CNN Radio, . Format: Progressive talk. ♦Harvey Wells, gen mgr; Bill Cavanaugh, gen sls mgr; Mike McCarthy, chief of engrg.

WDKB(FM)— Aug 13, 1990: 94.9 mhz; 3 kw. 328 ft TL: N41 56 58 W88 53 33. Hrs open: 24 2201 N. 1st St., Suite 95, 60115. Phone: (815) 758-0950. Phone: (815) 758-4926. Fax: (815) 758-6226. Web Site:www.b95fm.com Licensee: De Kalb County Radio Ltd. Shaw Pittman. Wire Svc: AP Format: Adult contemp. News staff: one; News: 3hrs wkly. Target aud: 25-54; adults with moderate to upper incomes. Spec prog: Relg one hr wkly. ♦Tana S. Knetsch, pres & gen mgr; Dave Bavido, gen sls mgr.

WLBK(AM)— Dec 7, 1947: 1360 khz; 1 kw-D. TL: N41 56 18 W88 45 03. Hrs open: 24 Box 448, 60115. Secondary address: 2410 Sycamore Rd. Suite C 60115. Phone: (815) 758-8686. Fax: (815) 756-9723.E-mail: sales@1360wlbk.com Licensee: WPW Broadcasting Inc. (group owner; (acq 4-12-2000). Population served: 100,000 Dow, Lohnes & Albertson. Format: News/talk. News staff: one; News: 21 hrs wkly. Target aud: General. Spec prog: Farm 12 hrs wkly. ♦Larry Timpe, gen mgr, gen sls mgr; Ryan Snow, opns dir; Scott Zak, news dir.

***WNIJ(FM)**— October 1954: 89.5 mhz; 50 kw. 421 ft TL: N42 00 55 W89 00 07. Stereo. Hrs open: 24 NIU Broadcast Ctr., 801 N. First St., DeKalb, 60115. Phone: (815) 753-9000. Fax: (815) 753-9938.E-mail: npr@niu.edu Web Site:www.northernpublicradio.org Licensee: Northern Illinois University. Population served: 500,000 Natl. Network: PRI, NPR, . Arter & Hadden. Format: News, jazz. News staff: 2; News: one hr wkly. Target aud: General. Spec prog: Folk 4 hrs wkly. ♦Tim Emmons, gen mgr; Jan Kilgard, dev dir; Bill Drake, progmg dir.

WNIU(FM)—See Rockford

Decatur

WDZ(AM)— Mar 17, 1921: 1050 khz; 1 kw-U. TL: N39 48 54 W89 00 05. Hrs open: 250 N. Water St., Suite 100, 62523. Phone: (217) 423-9744. Fax: (217) 423-9764.E-mail: info@magic1050am.com Licensee: Neuhoff Family L.P. Group owner: NextMedia Group L.L.C. (acq 2-23-2009; grpsl). Population served: 125,000 Natl. Network: Fox Sports, . Format: Sports. ♦Mark Hanson, gen mgr; Tricia LeVeck, progmg dir.

WDZQ(FM)— Nov 1, 1976: 95.1 mhz; 50 kw. Ant 500 ft TL: N39 37 36 W89 04 49. Stereo. Hrs open: 250 N. Water St., Suite 100, 62523. Phone: (217) 423-9744. Fax: (217) 423-9764. Web Site:www.95q.com Licensee: Neuhoff Family L.P. (acq 2-23-2009; grpsl). Population served: 1,000,000 Format: Country. ♦Mark Hanson, gen mgr; Brad Wells, progmg dir.

***WJMU(FM)**— Mar 10, 1971: 89.5 mhz; 1 kw. 95 ft TL: N39 50 30 W88 58 29. (CP: 1.66 kw). Stereo. Hrs open: 7 AM-1 AM 1184 W. Main St., 62522. Phone: (217) 424-6377. Fax: (217) 424-3993.E-mail: wjmu@mail.millikin.edu Licensee: Millikin University. Population served: 100,000 Format: Progsv. News: 8 hrs wkly. Target aud: 20 plus; students, surrounding community. ♦Dove Zemke, pres; Matt Tucker, gen mgr; Dan Bleyle, prom dir; Keith Chandler, progmg dir.

WSOY(AM)— 1925: 1340 khz; 1 kw-U. TL: N39 48 54 W89 00 08. Hrs open: 24 250 N. Water St., Suite 100, 62523. Phone: (217) 877-5371. Fax: (217) 877-8777. Web Site:www.wsoy.com Licensee: Neuhoff Family L.P. (acq 2-23-2009; grpsl). Format: News/talk, sports. News staff: 3; News: 13 hrs wkly. Target aud: 25 plus. ♦Mark Hanson, gen mgr; Ryan Forden, progmg dir & farm dir.

WSOY-FM— November 1946: 102.9 mhz; 54 kw. Ant 495 ft TL: N39 52 40 W88 56 30. Stereo. Hrs open: 24 250 N. Water St., Suite 100, 62523. Phone: (217) 877-5371. Fax: (217) 877-8777.E-mail: info@wsoyfm.com Web Site:www.wsoy.com Licensee: Neuhoff Family L.P. Group owner: NextMedia Group L.L.C. (acq 2-23-2009; grpsl). Population served: 130,000 Natl. Network: CBS, . Rgnl. Network: Ill. Radio Net. Ill. Radio Net. Schwartz, Woods & Miller. Format: CHR. News staff: 3; News: 3 hrs wkly. Target aud: 25-54. ♦Mark Hanson, gen mgr; Roy Jaynes, progmg dir.

WYDS(FM)— 1993: 93.1 mhz; 6 kw. 328 ft TL: N39 48 35 W88 59 31. Hrs open: 24 410 N. Water St., Suite C, 62523. Phone: (217) 428-4487. Fax: (217) 428-4501.E-mail: cbullock@cromwellradio.com Licensee: WEJT Inc. (acq 4-9-93; $750,000; 5-3-93). Population served: 200,000 Format: Top-40 contemporary Hit. News staff: one. Target aud: 18-49; females average age of 26. ♦Chris Bullock, gen mgr; Wayne Robbins, opns mgr; Jerry Scott, gen sls mgr, chief of engrg; Scott Lithgow, progmg dir.

Deerfield

WEEF(AM)—See Highland Park

WVIV-FM—See Highland Park

Des Plaines

WPPN(FM)— Dec 3, 1971: 106.7 mhz; 50 kw. Ant 423 ft TL: N42 08 10 W87 58 55. Stereo. Hrs open: 24 625 N. Michigan Ave. 3rd Fl., Chicago, 60611. Phone: (312) 981-1800. Fax: (312) 981-1806. Web Site:http://www.univision.com/content/channel.jhtml?chid=9627&schid=9828 Licensee: Univision Radio License Corp. Group owner: Salem Communications Corp. (acq 12-21-2004; asset exchange agreement). Format: SPANISH OLDIES. ♦Jerry Ryan, gen mgr; Cesar Canales, opns mgr; Victor Cerdo, progmg dir; Joshua Sigstad, engrg mgr.

Dixon

WIXN(AM)— July 1961: 1460 khz; 1 kw-D, DA. TL: N41 49 38 W89 29 11. Hrs open: 19 1460 S. College Ave., 61021. Phone: (815) 288-3341. Phone: (815) 626-3091. Fax: (815) 284-1017.E-mail: info@wixn.com Web Site:www.wixn.com Licensee: NRG License Sub. LLC. (group owner; (acq 10-31-2005; grpsl). Population served: 17,600 Miller & Fields, P.C. Format: News, oldies. News staff: 2; News: 14 hrs wkly. Target aud: 25-54. Spec prog: Farm 11 hrs wkly. ♦Al Knickrehm, gen mgr & stn mgr.

WRCV(FM)— Sept 1, 1965: 101.7 mhz; 6 kw. Ant 300 ft TL: N41 49 29 W89 29 51. Stereo. Hrs open: 24 1460 S. College Ave., 61021. Phone: (815) 288-3341. Phone: (815) 626-3091. Fax: (815) 284-1017.E-mail: info@wixn.com Web Site:www.wixn.com Licensee: NRG License Sub. LLC. Population served: 18,147 Rgnl. Network: Goetz Group. Format: Country. News staff: 2; News: 10 hrs wkly. ♦Steve Marco, progmg dir.

Dorsey

*WARW(FM)— 2006: 89.5 mhz; 30 w. Ant 279 ft TL: N38 59 04 W89 59 20. Hrs open:
Rebroadcasts KLRD(FM) Yucaipa, CA 100%.
2351 Sunset Blvd., Suite 170-218, Rocklin, CA, 95765. Phone: (916) 251-1600. Fax: (916) 251-1650. Web Site:www.air1.com Licensee: Educational Media Foundation. (acq 9-22-2005; $30,000 for CP). Natl. Network: Air 1, . Format: Christian. ◆Mike Novak, pres.

Downers Grove

*WDGC-FM— Feb 28, 1969: 88.3 mhz; 250 w. 130 ft TL: N41 48 16 W88 00 44. Stereo. Hrs open: 8 AM-10 PM (M-S) 4436 Main St., 60515. Phone: (630) 795-8490. Phone: (630) 795-8400. Fax: (630) 795-8499.E-mail: wdgcfm@hotmail.com Web Site:www.csd99.k12.il.us/wdgc Licensee: High School District No. 99 Dupage County. Population served: 40,400 Format: Div. News: 5 hrs wkly. Target aud: General; all age groups. Spec prog: Community affrs 6 hrs wkly. ◆John Waite, gen mgr & opns mgr.

Du Quoin

WDQN(AM)— 1951: 1580 khz; 170 w-D, 7 w-N. TL: N38 01 56 W89 14 30. Hrs open: 5:30 AM-11 PM Box 190, 62832. Secondary address: 2337 US Rt. 51 62832. Phone: (618) 542-3894. Fax: (618) 542-4514.E-mail: wdqnradio@onecliq.net Licensee: Du Quoin Broadcasting Co. Population served: 25,000 Natl. Network: ABC, Motor Racing Net, . Brownfield Wire Svc: AP Format: Adult contemp, country. Target aud: 25-64; male & female. Spec prog: Farm 3 hrs, relg 5 hrs wkly. ◆Greg Showalter, gen mgr; Michelle Klein, sls dir; Gordon Showalter, progmg dir.

WDQN-FM— Sept 1, 1969: 95.9 mhz; 6 kw. Ant 328 ft TL: N38 01 56 W89 14 30. Hrs open: 6 AM-11 PM Box 220, West Frankfort, 62896. Secondary address: 3391 Charley Good Rd., West Frankfort 62896. Phone: (618) 627-4651. Fax: (618) 627-2726.E-mail: info@wdqn.com Web Site:www.3abn.org Licensee: Three Angels Broadcasting Network Inc. (acq 7-16-2003; $600,000). Format: Christian. ◆Danny Shelton, pres; Mollie Steenson, gen mgr; Jim Morris, gen sls mgr; Sandra Juarez, progmg dir; Moses Primo, chief of engrg.

Dundee

WWYW(FM)— June 8, 1967: 103.9 mhz; 2.55 kw. Ant 321 ft TL: N42 06 21 W88 22 37. Stereo. Hrs open: 24 8800 Rt. 14, Crystal Lake, 60012. Phone: (815) 459-7000. Fax: (815) 459-7027. Web Site:www.y1039.com Licensee: NM Licensing LLC. Group owner: NextMedia Group L.L.C. (acq 5-19-2004; $5 million). Population served: 2,000,000 Leibowitz & Associates. Format: Oldies. ◆Doug Boyd, gen sls mgr; Stew Cohen, news dir.

Dwight

WJEZ(FM)— June 9, 1997: 98.9 mhz; 1.3 kw. Ant 489 ft TL: N41 02 06 W88 26 11. Hrs open: 315 N. Mill St., Pontiac, 61764. Phone: (815) 844-6101. Fax: (815) 844-7235. Web Site:www.wjez.com Licensee: Livingston County Broadcasters Inc. Group owner: Regent Communications Inc. (acq 5-12-2004; grpsl). Format: Adult contemp. Target aud: 18-49; general. ◆Red Pitcher, gen mgr; Julie Penn, sls dir; Shelley Grove, prom mgr; Kent Kasson, progmg dir, news dir; Lane Lindstrom, chief of engrg.

Earlville

WMKB(FM)— Feb 3, 2003: 102.9 mhz; 2.15 kw. Ant 558 ft TL: N41 37 16 W89 05 20. Stereo. Hrs open: 24 4756 E. 4th Rd., Mendota, 61342. Phone: (815) 538-7500. Fax: (866) 816-0064.E-mail: info@wmkbradio.com Web Site:www.wmkbradio.com Licensee: KM Radio of Earlville L.L.C. Group owner: KM Communications Inc. Natl. Network: ABC, . Format: Class rock. News: 2 hrs wkly. Target aud: 25-54. Spec prog: Blues 5 hrs wkly. ◆Anne Schenck, gen mgr.

East Moline

KUUL(FM)— Feb 23, 1976: 101.3 mhz; 50 kw. 500 ft TL: N41 37 10 W90 17 41. Stereo. Hrs open: 3535 E. Kimberly Rd., Davenport, IA, 52807. Phone: (563) 344-7000. Fax: (563) 359-8524. Web Site:www.kuul.com Licensee: Citicasters Licenses L.P. Group owner: Clear Channel Communications Inc. (acq 11-15-00; grpsl). Population served: 350,000 Natl. Rep: Katz Radio,. Format: Classic rock, hits of the 60s & 70s. Target aud: 25-54; contemp, upscale adults. Spec prog:

Pub affrs 6 hrs, farm one hr wkly. ◆Larry R. Rosmilso, VP, mktg VP; Jeff Ashcraft, sls mgr; Mike Hamann, gen sls mgr; Kevin Allensworth, chief of engrg.

*WDLM(AM)— Apr 3, 1960: 960 khz; 1 kw-D, 102 w-N, DA-2. TL: N41 24 57 W90 23 54. Hrs open: Box 149, 61244. Phone: (309) 234-5111. Fax: (309) 234-5114.E-mail: wdlm@moody.edu Web Site:www.mbn.org Licensee: Moody Bible Institute of Chicago. (group owner) Format: Relg. ◆Lane D. Morgan, gen mgr.

*WDLM-FM— Jan 20, 1980: 89.3 mhz; 100 kw. 500 ft TL: N41 32 52 W90 28 30. Hrs open: Dups AM 75% Box 149, 61244. Phone: (309) 234-5111. Fax: (309) 234-5114. Web Site:www.mbn.com Population served: 450,000 ◆Dave Jolly, stn mgr; Ken Brooks, progmg dir.

East St. Louis

*WCBW-FM— 2001: 89.7 mhz; 250 w. Ant 187 ft TL: N38 37 53 W90 12 09. Hrs open: New Life Evangelistic Center Inc., 1411 Locust St., St. Louis, MO, 63103. Phone: (314) 421-3020. Fax: (314) 436-2434.E-mail: larryr@hereshelpnet.org Web Site:www.hereshelpnet.org Licensee: New Life Evangelistic Center Inc. Format: Relg. ◆Larry Rice, gen mgr.

WFFX(AM)— Aug 1, 1934: 1490 khz; 1 kw-U, DA-2. TL: N38 37 16 W90 09 36. Stereo. Hrs open: 149 S. 8th St., 62201. Phone: (618) 271-7687. Fax: (618) 875-4315. Licensee: Simmons Austin, LS LLC. (acq 3-31-2005; $1.15 million). Population served: 622,236 Natl. Network: American Urban, . Natl. Rep: Katz Radio,. Format: Gospel, rhythm & blues. Target aud: 23-55. ◆Dave Greene, gen mgr.

WXOS(FM)— June 6, 1965: 101.1 mhz; 44 kw. Ant 525 ft TL: N38 45 11 W90 07 09. Stereo. Hrs open: 11647 Olive Blvd., St. Louis, MO, 63141. Phone: (314) 983-6000. Fax: (314) 994-9447. Web Site:www.toastedrav.com/section/wxos Licensee: Bonneville Holding Co. Group owner: Bonneville International Corp. (acq 9-26-2000; grpsl). Natl. Network: ESPN Radio, . Natl. Rep: McGavren Guild,. Format: Sports talk. Target aud: 25-49. ◆Bruce Reese, CEO, pres; Bob Johnson, CFO; John Kijowski, VP, gen mgr; Emily Bushman, gen sls mgr; Trish Gazzal, news dir; Marshall Rice, chief of engrg.

Edwardsville

*WRYT(AM)— Nov 20, 1987: 1080 khz; 500 w-D, DA. TL: N38 47 58 W89 57 45. (CP: 250 w-N, DA-2, TL: N38 38 30 W89 57 45). Hrs open: 4424 Hampton Ave., St. Louis, MO, 63109. E-mail: covenantnetwork@juno.com Licensee: Covenant Network. (acq 10-2-97). Population served: 200,000 Format: Catholic, relg. Target aud: General. ◆John A. Holman, pres; Tony Holman, gen mgr.

*WSIE(FM)— Sept 4, 1970: 88.7 mhz; 37 kw. 567 ft TL: N38 47 06 W89 59 10. Stereo. Hrs open: 24 Box 1773, So. Illinois Univ. at Edwardsville, 62026. Phone: (618) 650-2228. Fax: (618) 650-2233. Web Site:www.siue.edu.wsie Licensee: Board of Trustees, Southern Illinois University. Population served: 2,000,000 Natl. Network: NPR, PRI, . Rgnl. Network: Ill. Radio Net. Dow, Lohnes & Albertson. Format: Jazz. News staff: one; News: 20 hrs wkly. Target aud: 25-49; adults seeking a sophisticated alternative. Spec prog: New age 10 hrs wkly. ◆Frank Akers, gen mgr; Tom Dehner, news dir; David Caires, chief of engrg.

Effingham

WCRA(AM)— June 8, 1947: 1090 khz; 1 kw-D. TL: N39 06 26 W88 33 44. Hrs open: 405 S. Banker St., Suite 201, 62401. Phone: (217) 342-4141. Fax: (217) 342-4143. Licensee: Two Petaz Inc. Group owner: The Cromwell Group Inc. (acq 1-9-02; grpsl). Population served: 11,200 Natl. Network: CBS, . Format: News/talk. Target aud: 25-54. ◆Marv Phillips, gen mgr.

WCRC(FM)— June 14, 1963: 95.7 mhz; 50 kw. Ant 480 ft TL: N39 06 26 W88 33 44. Stereo. Hrs open: 24 405 S. Banker St., Suite 201, 62401. Phone: (217) 342-4141. Fax: (217) 342- 4143. Web Site:www.wcrc957.com Licensee: Two Petaz Inc. Population served: 50,000 Format: Country.

*WEFI(FM)— 2006: 89.5 mhz; 400 w. Ant 164 ft TL: N39 08 30 W88 33 36. Hrs open:
Rebroadcasts WAFR(FM) Tupelo, MS 100%.
Box 2440, Tupelo, MS, 38803-2440. Phone: (662) 844-8888. Fax: (662) 842-6791. Web Site:www.afr.net Licensee: American Family Association. Format: Christian. ◆Marvin Sanders, gen mgr.

*WGMR(FM)—Not on air, target date: unknown: 91.3 mhz; 3.4 kw vert. Ant 167 ft TL: N39 13 18.9 W88 30 36.8. Hrs open: 14319 E.

Southwind, 62401-4752. Phone: (217) 536-9278. Licensee: Brindisi Consortium. Natl. Network: EWTN Radio, . ◆William Bence, pres.

WXEF(FM)— Oct 4, 1982: 97.9 mhz; 6 kw. 300 ft TL: N39 07 25 W88 38 28. Stereo. Hrs open: 24 Box 988, 206 S. Willow, 62401. Phone: (217) 347-5518. Fax: (217) 347-5519.E-mail: info@thexradio.com Web Site:www.thexradio.com Licensee: Premier Broadcasting Inc. (acq 11-3-93; $380,000; 11-22-93). Population served: 50,000 Natl. Network: Fox News Radio, . Format: Adult contemp. News staff: 2; News: 15 hrs wkly. Target aud: General. Spec prog: High school sports. ◆Greg Sapp, stn mgr, opns dir, news dir; Tonya Siner, opns VP; George Flexter, opns mgr.

Eldorado

WEBQ-FM— April 1972: 102.3 mhz; 3 kw. 296 ft TL: N37 49 14 W88 27 11. Stereo. Hrs open: 24 701 S. Commercial, Harrisburg, 62946. Phone: (618) 252-6307. Fax: (618) 252-2366.E-mail: webq@yourclearwave.com Licensee: W. Russell Withers Jr. Group owner: Withers Broadcasting Co. (acq 7-28-2004; $450,000 with WEBQ(AM) Harrisburg). Population served: 9,535 Natl. Network: ABC, . Ill. Radio Net. Format: Adult contemp. News staff: one; News: 6 hrs wkly. Target aud: 25-45; young middle class adults. ◆Cathy Horton, gen mgr, stn mgr, progmg dir; Sonny Dotson, gen sls mgr; Wyatt Drake, news dir; Bob Romonosky, chief of engrg; Shelly Reeder, traf mgr.

Elgin

*WEPS(FM)— 1950: 88.9 mhz; 740 w. Ant 100 ft TL: N42 02 17 W88 16 15. Hrs open: 6 355 E. Chicago St., 60120. Phone: (847) 888-5000. Fax: (847) 888-0272.E-mail: jackieolsonkold@u-46.org Licensee: Board of Education, Union School District 46. Population served: 80,000 Format: Div, educ. Target aud: Parents of students. Spec prog: Class 5 hrs, jazz 6 hrs, community affrs 3 hrs, educ 13 hrs wkly. ◆Jackie Olson Kold, stn mgr.

WRMN(AM)— 1949: 1410 khz; 1 kw-D, 500 w-N, DA-N. TL: N42 20 21 W88 17 55. Hrs open: 14 Douglas Ave., 60120. Phone: (847) 741-7700. Fax: (847) 888-4227.E-mail: mail@wrmn1410.com Web Site:www.radioshoppingshow.com Licensee: Elgin Broadcasting Co. Group owner: McNaughton-Jakle Stations (acq 1952). Population served: 650,000 Blair, Joyce & Silva. Format: News/talk. News staff: news progmg 5 hrs wkly News: one;. Target aud: General. Spec prog: Sp 10 hrs wkly. ◆Richard Jakle, CEO, chmn, pres & gen mgr; Jack Davis, stn mgr; Chuck France, gen sls mgr.

Ellsworth

*WSPI(FM)—Not on air, target date: unknown: 89.5 mhz; 325 w. Ant 441 ft TL: N40 28 38 W88 33 14. Hrs open: 2820 Communications Inc., 11650 N. 2600 E. Rd., 61737. Phone: (309) 807-0100. Fax: (570) 644-2232 . Licensee: 2820 Communications Inc. ◆Morgan Grammer, gen mgr.

Elmhurst

WJJG(AM)— Oct 10, 1974: 1530 khz; 500 w-D, DA. TL: N41 52 03 W87 55 07. (CP: 760 w). Stereo. Hrs open: 5629 St. Charles Rd., Suite 208, Berkeley, 60163. Phone: (708) 493-1530. Fax: (708) 493-1537. Web Site:www.wjjg@15gmail.com Licensee: Joseph J. Gentile Inc. (acq 7-6-94; $700,000). Population served: 5,000,000 Format: News/talk. Target aud: 45 plus; affluent adults. ◆Joseph Gentile, pres; Mike Baker, opns mgr.

*WRSE(FM)— Dec 7, 1962: 88.7 mhz; 100 w. 95 ft TL: N41 53 46 W87 56 45. Stereo. Hrs open: 24 190 Prospect Ave., 60126-3296. Phone: (630) 617-3729. Fax: (630) 617-3313. Web Site:www.wrse.com Licensee: Board of Trustees Elmhurst College. Population served: 150,000 Booth, Frerat, Imlay & Tepper, P.C. Wire Svc: AP Format: Alternative, rock, oldies. News: one hr wkly. Target aud: 17-40; college & general. Spec prog: Metal 3 hrs, hip hop 6 hrs wkly. ◆Jon Morgan, gen mgr.

Elmwood

WFYR(FM)— Aug 2, 1993: 97.3 mhz; 23.5 kw. 338 ft TL: N40 46 22 W89 44 50. Stereo. Hrs open: 24 120 Eaton St., Peoria, 61603. Phone: (309) 676-5000. Fax: (309) 676-2600.E-mail: jgreeley@regentcomm.com Web Site:www.973rivercountry.com Licensee: Regent Broadcasting of Peoria Inc. Group owner: Regent Communications Inc. (acq 7-6-01; grpsl). Population served: 500,000 Natl. Rep: Katz Radio,. Reddy, Begley & McCormick. Format: Country. News: one hr

wkly. Target aud: 25-54; adults, family oriented & skewing female. ♦J.R. Greeley, gen mgr; Ric Morgan, opns mgr.

Elmwood Park

WCFS-FM— 1947: 105.9 mhz; 4.2 kw. Ant 1,575 ft TL: N41 52 44 W87 38 10. Stereo. Hrs open: 24 2 Prudential Plaza, Suite 1059, Chicago, 60601. Phone: (312) 240-7900. Fax: (312) 565-3181. Web Site:fresh1059.com Licensee: CBS Radio Holdings Corp. of Orlando. Group owner: CBS Radio (acq 1996). Natl. Network: Westwood One, . Format: Adult contemp. News staff: one; News: one hr wkly. Target aud: 25-54. ♦Rob Zimmerman, gen mgr.

Eureka

WPIA(FM)— 1989: 98.5 mhz; 3 kw. Ant 328 ft TL: N40 44 20 W89 16 13. Stereo. Hrs open: 24
Simulcast with WWCT(FM) Farmington 100%.
4234 N. Brandywine Dr., Suite D, Peoria, 61614. Phone: (309) 686-0101. Fax: (309) 686-0111. Licensee: IM IL Licenses LLC. Group owner: Regent Communications Inc. (acq 9-19-2006; grpsl). Population served: 400,000 Format: Top-40. ♦Michael Rea, gen mgr; Don Black, progmg dir, news dir.

Evanston

WCGO(AM)— 1947: 1590 khz; 3.5 kw-D, 2.5 kw-N, DA-2. TL: N42 01 20 W87 42 43. Hrs open: 24 2100 Lee St., 60202. Phone: (847) 475-1590. Fax: (847) 475-1590. Licensee: Kovas Communications Inc. (acq 12-1-75). Population served: 80,113 Format: Ethnic, Sp. News: 8 hrs wkly. Target aud: General. Spec prog: Greek 2 hrs, Indian 8 hrs, Assyrian 15 hrs, Haitian 5 hrs, Lithuanian one hr, Korean 20 hrs wkly. ♦Connie Walburn, gen mgr; Bob Richards, opns mgr.

WKTA(AM)— 1953: 1330 khz; 5 kw-D, 17 w-N, DA-1. TL: N42 08 23 W87 53 09. Hrs open: 24 4320 Dundee Rd., Northbrook, 60062. Phone: (847) 498-3350. Fax: (847) 498-5743.E-mail: wkta@inc-us.com Web Site:www.pclradio.com Licensee: Polnet Communications Ltd. (group owner; (acq 5-5-86; $1.66 million;2-17-86). Population served: 10,500,000 Wiley, Rein and Fielding. Format: AOR/rock, Russian, Korean. News: 5 hrs wkly. Target aud: 18-54; Russian, Korean and German speaking audience. Spec prog: Ger 5 hrs wkly. ♦Walter K. Kotaba, pres; Sara Vargas, gen mgr; Scott Davidson, opns mgr, progmg dir.

***WNUR-FM—** May 8, 1950: 89.3 mhz; 7.2 kw. 100 ft TL: N42 03 12 W87 40 33. Stereo. Hrs open: 24 1920 Campus Dr., 60208-2280. Phone: (847) 491-7101. Phone: (847) 491-2234. Fax: (847) 467-2058.E-mail: gm@wnur.org Web Site:www.wnur.org Licensee: Northwestern University. Population served: 4,000,000 Format: Progsv, jazz, new mus. News: 3 hrs wkly. Target aud: 18-34; general. Spec prog: Folk 3 hrs, world mus 10 hrs, reggae 4 hrs wkly. ♦Henry Bienen, pres; Mike Corsa, gen mgr; Ashley Ayarza, prom dir, news dir; Alex Freedman, progmg dir, pub affrs dir.

WOJO(FM)— 1946: 105.1 mhz; 5.7 kw. Ant 1,394 ft TL: N41 53 56 W87 37 23. (CP: 5.7 kw, ant 1,394 ft). Stereo. Hrs open: 24 625 N. Michigan Ave., Suite 300, Chicago, 60611-3110. Phone: (312) 981-1800. Fax: (312) 981-1806. Web Site:http://www.univison.com/content /channel.jhtml?chid=9627&schid=9638 Licensee: Tichenor License Corp. Group owner: Univision Radio (acq 9-22-2003; grpsl). Population served: 6,805,900 Natl. Rep: Katz Radio,. Format: REGIONAL MEXICAN. News staff: one. Target aud: 18-35; regional/Mexican. ♦Jerry Ryan, gen mgr; Cesar Canales, progmg dir; Joshua Sigstad, engrg mgr.

Fairbury

WYST(FM)— Aug 8, 2000: 107.7 mhz; 22.5 kw. Ant 351 ft TL: N40 37 45 W88 46 52. Stereo. Hrs open: 24 108 Boeykens Pl., Normal, 61761. Phone: (309) 888-4496. Fax: (309) 452-9677.E-mail: star1077@aaabloomington.com Web Site:www.star1077.net Licensee: Pilot Media LLC. Group owner: AAA Entertainment L.L.C. (acq 6-19-2007; grpsl). Population served: 125,000 Natl. Network: AP Radio, . Wire Svc: AP Format: Adult contemp. News: 2 hrs wkly. Target aud: 25+; women. ♦Patti Donsbach, gen mgr; Kevin Trueblood, opns mgr, progmg dir.

Fairfield

WFIW(AM)— Aug 21, 1953: 1390 khz; 710 w-D, 58 w-N. TL: N38 22 46 W88 19 33. Hrs open: 24 Box 310, Hwy. 15 E., 62837. Phone: (618) 842-2159. Fax: (618) 847-5907.E-mail: wfiwwokz@fairfieldwireless.net Web Site:www.wfiwradio.com Licensee: Wayne County Broadcasting Co. (group owner) Population served: 150,000 Natl. Network: ABC, . Format: News/talk. News staff: one; News: 22 hrs wkly. Target aud: 45 plus; small town rural, business, farm, older adults. Spec prog: Farm 16 hrs wkly. ♦Thomas S. Land, chmn, farm dir; David H. Land, pres, gen mgr, gen sls mgr, progmg dir; Len Wells, news dir; Kirk Wallace, chief of engrg, disc jockey; Deron Caudle, news rptr; Stan David, sports cmtr, disc jockey; Jessica James, disc jockey.

WFIW-FM— 1965: 104.9 mhz; 4.9 kw. 364 ft TL: N38 22 46 W88 19 33. Stereo. Hrs open: 24 Dups AM 20% Box 310, Hwy. 15 E., 62837. Phone: (618) 842-2159. Fax: (618) 847-5907. Web Site:www.wfiwradio.com Population served: 150,000 Format: Variety hits. News staff: one; News: 16 hrs wkly. Target aud: 25-49; small town rural, young, middle age, business, farm. Spec prog: Farm 12 hrs wkly. ♦David H. Land, opns VP, sls dir; Deron Caudle, disc jockey.

WOKZ(FM)— September 1996: 105.9 mhz; 6 kw. 328 ft TL: N38 22 46 W88 19 33. Stereo. Hrs open: 24 Box 310, Hwy. 15 E., 62837. Phone: (618) 842-2159. Fax: (618) 847-5907.E-mail: wfiwwokz@fairfieldwireless.net Web Site:www.wfiwradio.com Licensee: Wayne County Broadcasting Co., Inc. (group owner) Population served: 150,000 Natl. Network: Fox News Radio, . Format: Country. News staff: one; News: 20 hrs wkly. Target aud: 25-54; small town rural, business, farm. ♦Thomas S. Land, chmn; David H. Land, pres, gen mgr.

Farmer City

WWHP(FM)— Oct 1, 1983: 98.3 mhz; 6 kw. 300 ft TL: N40 16 54 W88 32 00. Stereo. Hrs open: 24 407 N. Main, 61842. Phone: (309) 928-9876. Fax: (309) 928-3708.E-mail: wwhp@farmwagon.com Web Site:www.wwhp.com Licensee: WMS1 Inc. Population served: 300,000 Format: Americana. Target aud: 18-65; reach city, suburbs & rural listeners in east central Illinois. Spec prog: Gospel 3 hrs, comedy 1 hr, Celtic 2 hrs wkly. ♦Larry Williams, gen mgr; Lori Allen, gen sls mgr.

Farmington

WZPN(FM)— 1997: 96.5 mhz; 4.3 kw. Ant 377 ft TL: N40 40 10 W89 53 31. Hrs open: 4234 N. Brandywine, Suite D, Peoria, 61614. Phone: (309) 282-7625. Phone: (309) 686-0101. Fax: (309) 686-0111. Licensee: IM IL Licenses LLC. Group owner: AAA Entertainment L.L.C. (acq 3-30-2007; $600,000). Natl. Network: ESPN Radio, . Format: Sports talk. ♦Michael Rea, gen mgr.

Fisher

***WGNN(FM)—** Apr 7, 1996: 102.5 mhz; 6 kw. 328 ft TL: N40 20 21 W88 24 18. Stereo. Hrs open: 24 Box 550, 61843. Secondary address: 2421 N. 1450 E. Rd., White Heath 61884. Phone: (217) 897-6333.E-mail: staff@greatnewsradio.org Web Site:www.greatnewsradio.org Licensee: Good News Radio Inc. (acq 4-7-96; $225,000). Population served: 300,000 Natl. Network: Moody, USA, Salem Radio Network, . Format: Educ, relg, news/talk. Target aud: 35 plus; general. ♦David B. Herriott, chmn; Mark Burns, pres & gen mgr; Carrie Burns, opns dir.

Flora

WNOI(FM)— May 21, 1971: 103.9 mhz; 3.3 kw. 300 ft TL: N38 40 42 W88 29 14. Stereo. Hrs open: 24 Box 368, 1001 N. Olive Rd., 62839. Phone: (618) 662-8331. Fax: (618) 662-2407.E-mail: info@wnoi.com Web Site:www.wnoi.com Licensee: H&R Communications Inc. (acq 10-16-88). Population served: 30,000 Natl. Network: Jones Radio Networks, . Format: Adult contemp. News staff: one; News: 12 hrs wkly. Target aud: General. ♦Steven S. Lovellette, pres; Randy Poole, gen mgr; Patrick Garret, opns dir; Brenda Miller, gen sls mgr; Patrick Garrett, progmg dir; Kirk Wallace, chief of engrg.

Flossmoor

***WHFH(FM)—** January 1965: 88.5 mhz; 1.5 kw. 92 ft TL: N41 32 43 W87 41 30. Stereo. Hrs open: 14 999 Kedzie Ave., 60422. Phone: (708) 798-9434. Fax: (708) 799-3142.E-mail: WHFH@HFHIGHSCHOOL.ORG Web Site:www.whfh.org Licensee: Community High School District No. 233. Population served: 7,845 Format: Rock. News: 4 hrs wkly. Target aud: Teens-Adult. Spec prog: News/talk one hr, sports talk one hr, live sports 4 hrs wkly. ♦John Henry, gen mgr, stn mgr.

Freeport

WFPS(FM)— Nov 1, 1970: 92.1 mhz; 3.6 kw. Ant 423 ft TL: N42 19 41 W89 43 30. Stereo. Hrs open: 24 Box 807, 834 N. Tower Rd., 61032. Phone: (815) 235-7191. Fax: (815) 235-4318. Licensee: Green County Broadcasting Group owner: RadioWorks Inc. (acq 3-29-2006; $1.48 million with co-located AM). Population served: 295,000 Format: New country. News staff: 4; News: 15 hrs wkly. Target aud: 25-49. ♦Kent McConnell, opns mgr; Wyatt Herrmann, progmg dir; Brad Hart, news dir; Todd Hausser, chief of engrg; Becky Koester, traf mgr.

WFRL(AM)— Oct 28, 1947: 1570 khz; 5 kw-D, 500 w-N, DA-2. TL: N42 18 45 W89 35 38. Hrs open: 24 Box 807, 834 N. Tower Rd., 61032. Phone: (815) 235-7191. Fax: (815) 235-4318. Licensee: Green County Broadcasting Population served: 50,000 Natl. Network: ABC, . Rgnl. Network: Tribune, Ill. Radio Net. Format: Adult standards. News staff: 4; News: 24 hrs wkly. Target aud: 35 plus. ♦Kent McConnell, opns mgr; Wyatt Herrmann, progmg dir; Brad Hart, news dir; Todd Hausser, chief of engrg; Becky Koester, traf mgr.

***WNIE(FM)—** 1999: 89.1 mhz; 6 kw. Ant 361 ft TL: N42 18 45 W89 35 38. Stereo. Hrs open: 24
Rebroadcasts WNIJ(FM) De Kalb & WNIU(FM) Rockford 50%.
NIU Broadcast Ctr., 801 N. First St., De Kalb, 60115. Phone: (815) 753-9000. Fax: (815) 753-9938.E-mail: npr@niu.edu Web Site:www.northernpublicradio.org Licensee: Northern Illinois University. Population served: 50,000 Natl. Network: PRI, NPR, . Arter & Hadden. Format: News, class. News staff: 2. Target aud: General. ♦Tim Emmons, gen mgr; Jan Kilgard, dev VP; Bill Drake, progmg dir; Susan Stephens, news dir; Jeff Glass, chief of engrg.

WXXQ(FM)— Apr 11, 1965: 98.5 mhz; 50 kw. 450 ft TL: N42 18 45 W89 35 38. Stereo. Hrs open: 24 3901 Brendenwood Rd., Rockford, 61107-2246. Phone: (815) 399-2233. Fax: (815) 484-2432. Web Site:www.wxxq.com Licensee: Cumulus Licensing Corp. Group owner: Cumulus Media Inc. (acq 3-15-00; grpsl). Population served: 500,000 Format: Contemp country. News staff: one. Target aud: 25-54. ♦Greg Sher, gen mgr; Dawn Plock, prom dir; Steve Summers, progmg dir.

Galatia

WISH-FM— 2001: 98.9 mhz; 4.1 kw. Ant 400 ft TL: N37 55 52 W88 40 50. Hrs open: R.R. 1 Box 46 A, Mc Leansboro, 62859. Phone: (618) 643-2311. Fax: (618) 643-3299. Licensee: W. Russell Withers Jr. Group owner: Withers Broadcasting Co. Format: CHR, adult contemp. ♦Dana Withers, gen mgr; Gloria Holland, opns mgr.

Galena

WDBQ-FM— February 1989: 107.5 mhz; 6 kw. Ant 328 ft TL: N42 24 02 W90 23 55. Stereo. Hrs open: 24 5490 Saratoga Rd., Dubuque, IA, 52002. Phone: (563) 557-1040. Fax: (563) 583-4535.E-mail: info@wbdq.com Licensee: Cumulus Licensing Corp. Group owner: Cumulus Media Inc. (acq 12-17-98; grpsl). Format: Classic hits. News staff: one. Target aud: 25-54. ♦Scott Lindahl, mktg mgr.

Galesburg

WAAG(FM)— Dec 15, 1966: 94.9 mhz; 50 kw. Ant 492 ft TL: N40 56 34 W90 20 39. Stereo. Hrs open: 24 Prog sep from AM Box 1227, 61402. Secondary address: 154 E. Simmons 61401. Phone: (309) 342-5131. Phone: (309) 342-0840.E-mail: brianp@fm95online.com Web Site:www.fm95online.com Population served: 77,000 Wire Svc: AP Format: Country. News staff: 4; News: 2 hrs wkly. Target aud: 25-54. ♦Brian Prescott, mus dir; Jim Lee, farm dir; Mike Perry, sports cmtr.

WAIK(AM)— 1957: 1590 khz; 5 kw-D, 50 w-N, DA-3. TL: N40 57 43 W90 18 30. Hrs open: 24 Box 885, Monmouth, 61462-0885. Phone: (309) 342-3161. Fax: (309) 342-0199.E-mail: wmoi@maplecity.com Licensee: WPW Broadcasting Inc. (group owner; acq 7-9-98; $439,500). Population served: 36,290 Natl. Network: ABC, . Fisher, Wayland, Cooper, Leader & Zaragoza L.L.P. Format: MOR, big band, nostalgia. News staff: 3; News: 24 hrs wkly. Target aud: 25 plus. Spec prog: Talk 10 hrs, loc sports 10 hrs, relg 6 hrs wkly. ♦Don Davis, CEO, news dir; David Klockenga, gen mgr; Heidi Aycock, opns dir; Greg Ford, progmg dir; Kris Kinney, traf mgr.

WGIL(AM)— June 12, 1938: 1400 khz; 740 w-U. TL: N40 56 34 W90 20 39. Hrs open: 24 Box 1227, 61402-1227. Secondary address: 154 E. Simmons 61401. Phone: (309) 342-5131. Fax: (309) 342-0840.E-mail: wgil@wgil.com Web Site:www.wgil.com Licensee: Galesburg Broadcasting Co. (group owner). Population served: 55,000 Natl. Network: Westwood One, . Rgnl. Network: Ill. Radio Net. Natl. Rep: Interep,. Ill. Radio Net. Cohn & Marks. Wire Svc: AP Format: News/talk, sports. News staff: 4;

News: 20 hrs wkly. Target aud: 25-54. Spec prog: Farm 10 hrs, relg 4 hrs, sports 15 hrs wkly. ◆John T. Pritchard, pres; Roger Lundeen, gen mgr.

WLSR(FM)— Jan 17, 1979: 92.7 mhz; 4.2 kw. Ant 390 ft TL: N40 56 34 W90 20 39. Stereo. Hrs open: 24 Box 1227, 154 E. Simmons St., 61401. Phone: (309) 342-5131. Fax: (309) 342-0840.E-mail: kfm@1053kfm.com Web Site:www.thelaseronline.com Licensee: Galesburg Broadcasting Co. (group owner; (acq 7-3-97). Population served: 55,000 Cohn & Marks, LLP. Wire Svc: AP Format: Rock/AOR. News staff: 4; News: one hr wkly. Target aud: 18-34. Spec prog: 24 Religious; 2 hrs. wkly. ◆John T. Pritchard, pres; Roger Lundeen, gen mgr; Chris Postin, sls dir; Brian Prescott, prom dir, opns; Chris Lagrow, progmg dir.

*WVKC(FM)— Apr 12, 1961: 90.7 mhz; 1 kw. 98 ft TL: N40 56 46 W90 22 11. Hrs open: Knox College, Box K 254, 2 E. South St., 61401-4999. Phone: (309) 341-7266 (staff). Phone: (309) 341-7000 (switchboard). Fax: (309) 341-7090.E-mail: wvkc@knox.edu Web Site:www.knox.edu/wvkc.xml Licensee: Knox College. Population served: 65,000 Format: Var/div. Spec prog: Black 6 hrs, jazz 15 hrs, class 18 hrs wkly. ◆Roger Moore, pres; Mark Iellski, gen mgr.

Galva

WGEN(AM)—(Geneseo, 1964: 1500 khz; 250 w-D, 1 w-N. TL: N41 26 23 W90 09 18. Hrs open: 24 Box 266, Kewanee, 61443-0266. Secondary address: 133 E. Division St., Kewanee 61443. Phone: (309) 944-1500. Fax: (309) 853-4474. Web Site:www.randyradio.com Licensee: Virden Broadcasting Corp. Population served: 58,000 Format: News/talk. News staff: one; News: 13 hrs wkly. Target aud: 25 plus; community oriented adults.

WJRE(FM)— Oct 15, 1995: 102.5 mhz; 6 kw. Ant 293 ft TL: N41 13 37 W89 56 08. Stereo. Hrs open: 24 Box 266, Kewanee, 61443-0266. Secondary address: 133 E. Division St., Kewanee 61443. Phone: (309) 853-4471. Fax: (309) 853-4474.E-mail: regionalradio@verizon.net Web Site:www.1025wjre.com Licensee: Virden Broadcasting Corp. Group owner: Miller Media Group (acq 3-31-2003; $475,000 with WGEN(AM) Geneseo). Population served: 125,000 Natl. Rep: Commercial Media Sales,. Womble, Carlyle, Sandridge & Rice. Format: Country. News staff: one. Spec prog: Southern gospel one hr wkly. ◆Randal Miller, pres; Kris Wexell, progmg dir.

Geneseo

*WAXR(FM)— 2001: 88.1 mhz; 3 kw vert. Ant 321 ft TL: N41 28 47 W90 16 08. Hrs open: 3316 Avenue of the Cities, Moline, 61265. Phone: (309) 736-9297. Fax: (309) 277-3122.E-mail: @waxr.org Web Site:www.waxr.org Licensee: American Family Association. Group owner: American Family Radio Format: Inspirational Christian. ◆Ron Cook, gen mgr.

WGEN(AM)—Licensed to Geneseo. See Galva

Geneva

WSPY(AM)— Nov 11, 1961: 1480 khz; 1 kw-D, 500 w-N, DA-2. TL: N41 54 25 W88 17 43. Hrs open: 24 1 Broadcast Center, Plano, 60545. Phone: (630) 552-1000. Fax: (630) 552-9300.E-mail: wspy@nelsonmultimedia.net Licensee: Nelson Multi Media Inc. (acq 9-30-01). Population served: 1,400,000 Miller and Miller. Format: Adult Standards. News staff: one; News: 2 hrs wkly. Target aud: 35-65; baby boomers. ◆Larry Nelson, pres, gen mgr; Chris Schwemlein, opns mgr; Beth Perrie, gen sls mgr; Jenny Beckman, mus dir, traf mgr; Lane Lindstrom, chief of engrg.

Genoa

WYRB(FM)— 2001: 106.3 mhz; 6 kw. Ant 213 ft TL: N42 04 28 W88 49 24. Hrs open:
Rebroadcasts WSRB(FM) Lansing 100%.
6336 Calumet Ave., Hammond, IN, 46324. Phone: (773) 734-4455. Fax: (219) 933-0323.E-mail: wycainfo@crawfordbroadcsting.com Web Site:www.soul1063radio.com Licensee: Dontron Inc. Group owner: Crawford Broadcasting Co. (acq 9-28-01; $1.5 million). Format: Soul, rhythm and blues. Target aud: 25-54; adult urban. ◆Donald Crawford, CEO; Taft Harris, gen mgr.

Gibson City

WGCY(FM)— Nov 28, 1983: 106.3 mhz; 6 kw. 292 ft TL: N40 34 01 W88 20 41. (CP: Ant 321 ft.). Stereo. Hrs open: 6 AM-midnight Box

192, 607 S. Sangamon Ave., 60936. Phone: (217) 784-8661. Fax: (217) 784-8677. Licensee: F & G Broadcasting Inc. (acq 12-30-86; $225,000; 11-24-86). Natl. Network: USA, . Format: Easy lstng. News staff: one. Target aud: 35 plus. ◆Fred McCullough; pres; Gary McCullough, gen mgr.

Gilman

WFAV(FM)— 2007: Stn currently dark. 103.7 mhz; 6 kw. Ant 328 ft TL: N40 43 04 W87 51 36. Stereo. Hrs open: 292 N. Convent, Bourbonnais, 60914. Phone: (815) 933-9287. Fax: (815) 933-8696. Licensee: Milner Broadcasting Co. ◆Tim Milner, pres & gen mgr.

Girard

WCVS-FM—See Springfield

Glasford

WHPI(FM)— 2000: 101.1 mhz; 3.3 kw. Ant 449 ft TL: N40 39 00 W89 46 46. Stereo. Hrs open: 24 4234 N. Brandywine Dr., Peoria, 61615. Phone: (309) 686-0101. Fax: (309) 686-0111.E-mail: info@myhippie.com Web Site:www.myhippie.com Licensee: IM IL Licenses LLC. Group owner: Regent Communications Inc. (acq 9-19-2006; grpsl). Population served: 350,000 Format: Oldies. ◆Becky Riojas, gen mgr.

Glen Ellyn

*WDCB(FM)— July 5, 1977: 90.9 mhz; 5 kw. 300 ft TL: N41 50 36 W88 05 00. Stereo. Hrs open: 24 College of DuPage, 425 Fawell Blvd., 60137. Phone: (630) 942-4200. Phone: (630) 942-3708. Fax: (630) 942-2788.E-mail: wdcbmktg@cdnet.cod.edu Web Site:www.wdcb.org Licensee: College of DuPage. Natl. Network: PRI, . Cohn & Marks. Format: Jazz, news, blues. News staff: 3; News: 13 hrs wkly. Target aud: General. Spec prog: College classes 12 hrs, folk 12 hrs, gospel 2 hrs, var music 7 hrs wkly. ◆Scott Wager, stn mgr; Jim Barker, sls dir, gen sls mgr; Ken Scott, mktg dir; Mary Pat LaRue, progmg dir; Paul Abella, mus dir; Brian O'Keefe, news dir.

Glendale Heights

WJKL(FM)— September 1960: 94.3 mhz; 6 kw. Ant 328 ft TL: N41 59 54 W88 14 33. Stereo. Hrs open: 24
Rebroadcasts KLVR(FM) Santa Rosa, CA 100%.
2351 Sunset Blvd., Suite 170-218, Rocklin, CA, 95765. Phone: (916) 251-1600. Fax: (916) 251-1650. Web Site:www.klove.com Licensee: Educational Media Foundation. (acq 4-10-2007; $17 million). Population served: 350,000 Natl. Network: K-Love, . Format: Contemp Christian. ◆Mike Novak, sr VP.

Glenview

*WGBK(FM)— Jan 13, 1979: 88.5 mhz; 185 w. 100 ft TL: N42 04 30 W87 49 23. Stereo. Hrs open: 6:30 AM-10 PM (M-F) 3 PM-10 PM (M-F) c/o Glenbrook S. High School, 4000 W. Lake Ave., 60025. Phone: (847) 486-4487. Phone: (847) 486-4573. Fax: (847) 486-4439.E-mail: wgbk@glenbrook.k12.il.us Licensee: Glenbrook High School District 225. (acq 1996; $110,000). Population served: 750,000 Format: Alternative, educ, sports. News: 1 hr wkly. Target aud: General; teens & adults. Spec prog: Sports talk 5 hrs, live sports 4 hrs. ◆Dr. Daniel Oswald, gen mgr.

Godfrey

*WLCA(FM)— 1974: 89.9 mhz; 1.5 kw. Ant 394 ft TL: N38 56 57 W90 11 47. Hrs open: 18 5800 Godfrey Rd., 62035. Phone: (618) 466-8936. Fax: (618) 466-7458. Licensee: Lewis and Clark Community College. Population served: 100,000 Natl. Network: USA, . Format: Progsv, AOR, alt rock. ◆Mike Lemons, gen mgr.

Golconda

WKYX-FM— Nov 22, 1990: 94.3 mhz; 3.1 kw. Ant 449 ft TL: N37 14 04 W88 29 48. Stereo. Hrs open: 24
Simulcast with WKYX(AM) Paducah, KY 100%.
Box 2397, Paducah, KY, 42002-2397. Phone: (270) 554-8255. Fax: (270) 554-4613.E-mail: info@wkyx.com Web Site:www.wkyx.com Licensee: Bristol Broadcasting Co. Inc. (group owner; (acq 2-20-2004; grpsl). Format: News/talk. Target aud: 25-54. Spec prog: Relg one hr wkly. ◆Pete Ninninger, pres; Gary Morse, gen mgr.

Granite City

WARH(FM)—Licensed to Granite City. See Saint Louis MO

WGNU(AM)—Licensed to Granite City. See Saint Louis MO

Greenville

WGEL(FM)— Dec 20, 1984: 101.7 mhz; 3 kw. 300 ft TL: N38 48 11 W89 20 56. Stereo. Hrs open: 24 Box 277, 309 W. Main, 62246. Phone: (618) 664-3300. Fax: (618) 664-3318.E-mail: john@wgel.com Web Site:www.wgel.com Licensee: Bond Broadcasting. (acq 6-1-85; $170,000; 6-10-85). Natl. Network: USA, . Format: Country. News staff: 2. Target aud: 25-64. Spec prog: Farm 19 hrs wkly. ◆John Kennedy, pres, gen mgr; Brad Rogers, progmg dir; Tom Kennedy, news dir; Joe Doll, farm dir.

Harrisburg

WEBQ(AM)— September 1923: 1240 khz; 1 kw-U. TL: N37 43 03 W88 32 37. Hrs open: 701 S. Commercial St., 62946. Phone: (618) 253-7282. Fax: (618) 252-2366.E-mail: webq@yourclearwave.com Licensee: W. Russell Withers Jr. Group owner: Withers Broadcasting Co. (acq 7-28-2004; $450,000 with WEBQ-FM Eldorado). Population served: 25,000 Natl. Network: ABC, . Brownfield Format: Country. News staff: one; News: 6 hrs wkly. Target aud: Older area residents. Spec prog: Farm 6 hrs wkly. ◆Cathy Horton, gen mgr, progmg dir; Bob Romonosky, chief of engrg; Shelly Reeder, traf mgr; Sonny Dotson, sls.

WOOZ-FM— September 1947: 99.9 mhz; 32 kw. 650 ft TL: N37 36 45 W88 52 03. Stereo. Hrs open: 1431 Countryaire Dr., Carterville, 62918. Phone: (618) 985-4843. Phone: (800) 455-3243. Fax: (618) 985-6529.E-mail: mail@z100fm.com Web Site:www.z100fm.com Licensee: MRR License LLC. Group owner: MAX Media L.L.C. (acq 3-29-2004; grpsl). Natl. Rep: Christal,. Fletcher, Heald & Hildreth. Format: Country. Target aud: 18-49. ◆Steve J. Falat, gen mgr; Tom Miller, opns mgr; Kim DeBose, gen sls mgr; Tracy McSherry-McKown, progmg dir; Jon Brookmyer, chief of engrg; Felicia Dick, traf mgr.

Harvard

WMCW(AM)— 1955: Stn currently dark. 1600 khz; 500 w-D, 19 w-N. TL: N42 26 07 W88 36 39. Hrs open: Box 786, 60033. Phone: (815) 943-7426. Fax: (815) 943-5120. Licensee: Kovas Communications of Indiana Inc. (group owner; (acq 1-23-2004; $650,000). Population served: 440,000 Natl. Network: CNN Radio, . Spec prog: . ◆Constance Kovas, pres.

Harvey

WBGX(AM)— 1955: 1570 khz; 1.1 kw-D, 500 w-N, DA-2. TL: N41 36 14 W87 40 45. Hrs open: 24 Great Lakes Radio-Chicago, 5956 S. Michigan Ave., Chicago, 60637. Phone: (773) 752-1570. Fax: (773) 752-2242.E-mail: gospel1570@aol.com Web Site:www.GOSPEL1570.com Licensee: Great Lakes Radio-Chicago LLC (acq 10-7-03; $1.78 million). Population served: 3,900,000 Hogan & Hartsen. Format: Gospel. Target aud: 18-64; African Americans. ◆Tim Gallagher, pres.

Havana

WDUK(FM)— Feb 27, 1970: 99.3 mhz; 3 kw. 300 ft TL: N40 18 43 W90 03 19. Hrs open: 901 N. Promenade, 62644. Phone: (309) 543-3331.E-mail: info@wduk.com Licensee: Illinois Valley Radio. (acq 3-5-73). Population served: 16,000 Rgnl. Network: Brownfield. Brownfield Rgnl rep: Brownfield. Format: C&W, div. Target aud: General. Spec prog: Farm 8 hrs wkly. ◆Edwin Stimpson, pres.

Henry

WRVY-FM— July 30, 1990: 100.5 mhz; 3 kw. Ant 328 ft TL: N41 14 32 W89 21 10. Stereo. Hrs open: 24 Box 69, Princeton, 61356. Phone: (815) 875-8014. Phone: (309) 364-4411. Fax: (815) 872-0308. Web Site:www.wrvy.com Licensee: WZOE Inc. (group owner; (acq 5-8-98). Natl. Network: CBS, CNN Radio, . Ill. Radio Net. Shaw Pittman. Format: Contemp country. News staff: 3; News: 3 hrs wkly. Target aud: 25-45. Spec prog: Farm 4 hrs wkly. ◆Steve Samet, gen mgr; Mary Harmon, opns dir.

Herrin

WDDD(AM)—See Johnston City

WJPF(AM)— Aug 28, 1940: 1340 khz; 1 kw-U. TL: N37 50 03 W89 01 37. (CP: 770 w-U). Hrs open: 24 1431 Countryaire Dr., Carterville, 62918. Phone: (618) 985-4843. Phone: (800) 455-3243. Fax: (618) 985-6529.E-mail: mail@wjpf.com Web Site:www.wjpf.com Licensee: MRR License LLC. Group owner: MAX Media L.L.C. (acq 6-2-2004; grpsl). Population served: 250,000 Natl. Network: Westwood One, . Rgnl. Network: Ill. Radio Net. Natl. Rep: Christal,. Ill. Radio Net. Format: News/talk, Sports. News staff: 3; News: 10 hrs wkly. Target aud: 35 plus; mature, middle-income wage earners. ♦Steve Falat, gen mgr, sls dir; Kim DeBose, gen sls mgr; Tom Miller, opns mgr & progmg dir; Jon Brookmyer, chief of engrg; Felicia Dick, traf mgr, disc jockey; Dee James, news rptr.

WTAO-FM— March 1994: 92.7 mhz; 3.3 kw. Ant 433 ft TL: N37 45 15 W88 56 05. Hrs open: 24 Box 127, 1822 N. Court St., Marion, 62959-0127. Phone: (618) 997-8123. Fax: (618) 993-2319. Licensee: Withers Broadcasting of Southern Illinois LLC. Group owner: Clear Channel Communications Inc. (acq 3-17-2008; grpsl). Population served: 250,000 Format: Hot adult contemp. Target aud: W18-49, 25-54. ♦Janet Jensen, gen mgr; Paxton Guy, opns dir; Gina Heern, gen sls mgr, natl sls mgr; April Bennett, news dir; Tim Deterding, chief of engrg.

Heyworth

WBBE(FM)— June 6, 2005: 97.9 mhz; 5.4 kw. Ant 344 ft TL: N40 27 08 W88 57 48. Hrs open: 520 N. Center St., Bloomington, 61701-2902. Phone: (309) 834-1100. Fax: (309) 834-4390. Web Site:www.bob979.com Licensee: Connoisseur Media LLC. Natl. Rep: Christal,. Shaw Pittman LLP. Format: Adult hits. Target aud: 18-54; Adults. ♦Jack Swart, gen mgr; Grant Thompson, gen sls mgr; Adam Chandler, progmg dir; Mark Hill, chief of engrg.

Highland

WIJR(AM)— Dec 2, 1963: 880 khz; 1.7 kw-D, 160 w-N, DA-1. TL: N38 45 23 W89 39 18. Hrs open: 24 Box 473, Saint Louis, MO, 63166. Secondary address: 13063 Winu Dr. 62249. Phone: (314) 351-7390.E-mail: hhnjim@hereshelpnet.org Licensee: Birach Broadcasting Corp. (acq 8-15-2006; $1 million). Population served: 135,000 Rgnl. Network: Brownfield. Brownfield Format: Christian. News staff: one; News: 18 hrs wkly. Target aud: General; mature adults. Spec prog: Farm 3 hrs, Ger one hr wkly. ♦Sima Birach, pres; Larry Rice, gen mgr; Bernard Turner, opns dir.

WXOZ(AM)— 2000: 1510 khz; 1 kw-D, DA. TL: N38 44 56 W89 34 10. Hrs open: c/o Dennis J. Watkins, 100 W. Main St., Belleville, 62220. Phone: (618) 394-9969. Licensee: Entertainment Media Trust, Dennis J. Watkins, Trustee (acq 5-11-2006; $450,000). Format: Country. ♦Greg Benfield, gen mgr.

Highland Park

WEEF(AM)— Aug 15, 1963: 1430 khz; 1 kw-D, 29 w-N, DA. TL: N42 10 53 W87 57 05. Hrs open: 4320 Dundee Rd., Northbrook, 60062. Phone: (847) 498-3350. Fax: (847) 498-5743.E-mail: info@plcradio.com Web Site:www.plcradio.com/1430_weef Licensee: Polnet Communications Ltd. (group owner; (acq 5-20-2003; $1 million). Dow, Lohnes & Albertson. Format: Ethnic. Target aud: General; ethnic. ♦Sara Vargas, gen mgr.

WVIV-FM— Aug 15, 1963: 103.1 mhz; 3 kw. Ant 241 ft TL: N42 09 24 W87 48 20. Stereo. Hrs open: 24 625 N. Michigan Ave., Suite 300, Chicago, 60611. Phone: (312) 981-1800. Fax: (312) 981-1806. Web Site:http://www.univision.com/content /channel.jhtml?chid=9627&schid=9808 Licensee: HBC License Corp. Group owner: Univision Radio (acq 9-22-2003; grpsl). Format: SPANISH CONTEMPORARY. Target aud: 25-54. ♦Jerry Ryan, gen mgr; Cesar Canales, opns mgr; Armando Reyes, progmg dir; Joshua Sigstad, engrg mgr.

Hillsboro

WXAJ(FM)— Sept 1, 2000: 99.7 mhz; 50 kw. 492 ft TL: N39 20 14 W89 32 04. Hrs open: 24 3055 S. 4th St., Springfield, 62703. Phone: (217) 528-3033. Fax: (217) 528-5348. Web Site:www.997kissfm.com Licensee: Neuhoff Family L.P. Group owner: Clear Channel Communications Inc. (acq 8-1-2007; grpsl). Population served: 350,000 Natl. Rep: Christal,. Wiley, Rein & Fielding, LLP. Format: CHR. Target aud: Adults; 18-49. ♦Kevin O'Dea, gen mgr; Danielle Outlaw, sls dir; Michelle Mitchell, prom dir; Jeremy Anderson, progmg dir; Jeff Hofmann, news dir; Frank Konwinski, chief of engrg.

Hinsdale

***WHSD(FM)**— Dec 6, 1970: 88.5 mhz; 200 w. 131 ft TL: N41 47 25 W87 55 11. Stereo. Hrs open: 3 PM-10 PM Hinsdale Central High School, 55th & Grant St., 60521. Phone: (630) 570-8463. Fax: (630) 887-1362. Licensee: Hinsdale Twsp. High School District 86. Population served: 16,631 Format: Var. Target aud: General.

Hoopeston

WHPO(FM)— May 29, 1979: 100.9 mhz; 3 kw. 280 ft TL: N40 28 36 W87 41 36. Stereo. Hrs open: 24 912 S. Dixie Hwy., 60942. Phone: (217) 283-7744. Fax: (217) 283-6090.E-mail: whporadio@whporadio.com Web Site:www.whporadio.com Licensee: Market Street Broadcasting LLC (acq 12-27-00; $900,000). Population served: 110,000 Format: Country. News staff: one; News: 6 hrs wkly. Target aud: 25 plus; rural middle class. Spec prog: Southern gospel 7 hrs, big band 2 hrs wkly. ♦Blanche Voss, gen mgr & opns mgr; Becky Voss, progmg dir.

Jacksonville

WJIL(AM)— November 1961: 1550 khz; 1 kw-D, 10 w-N, DA-2. TL: N39 43 20 W90 11 43. Hrs open: 24 Box 1055, Rt. 4, E. Morton Rd., 62651. Phone: (217) 245-5119. Fax: (217) 245-1596. Licensee: Morgan County Broadcasting Co. Inc. (acq 5-1-93; with co-located FM). Population served: 125,000 Natl. Network: Westwood One, . Natl. Rep: Roslin,. Fisher, Wayland, Cooper, Leader & Zaragoza L.L.P. Format: News/talk, btfl music. News staff: one; News: 9 hrs wkly. Target aud: 35-64. Spec prog: Farm 8 hrs wkly. ♦Sarah Hautala, gen mgr; Diana McCutcheon, sls dir; Matt Lakis, progmg dir; Julie Ann Cambridge, mus dir; Mike Kaiser, news dir; Glen Hopkiins, chief of engrg.

WJVO(FM)—(South Jacksonville, Sept 1, 1986: 105.5 mhz; 6 kw. Ant 340 ft TL: N39 43 20 W90 11 43. Stereo. Hrs open: 24 1251 E. Morton Ave., 62651. Phone: (217) 245-5119. Fax: (217) 245-1596. Licensee: Morgan County Broadcasting Co. Inc. Natl. Network: Westwood One, ABC, . Format: Country. News staff: one; News: 4 hrs wkly. Target aud: 25-54. ♦Sarah Hautala, gen mgr.

WLDS(AM)— Dec 9, 1941: 1180 khz; 1 kw-D. TL: N39 44 06 W90 11 50. Hrs open: Sunrise-sunset Box 1180, 2161 Old State Rd., 62651. Phone: (217) 245-7171. Fax: (217) 245-6711.E-mail: wlds@wlds.com Web Site:www.wlds.com Licensee: Jacksonville Area Radio Broadcasters Inc. (acq 7-1-2008; $2 million with WEAI(FM) Lynnville). Population served: 100,000 Natl. Network: CBS, . Rgnl. Network: Ill. Radio Net. Natl. Rep: Katz Radio,. Ill. Radio Net. Kaye Scholer LLP. Wire Svc: AP Format: Adult contemp, news/talk. News staff: 3; News: 23 hrs wkly. Target aud: 35 plus; business & professional people, farmers & housewives. Spec prog: Farm 20 hrs wkly. ♦Gary Scott, gen mgr; Mark Whalen, gen sls mgr; Bob Thomas, progmg dir; Gary Ballard, mus dir; Kevin Baxter, news dir; John Coe, engr.

WYMG(FM)—Licensed to Jacksonville. See Springfield

Jerseyville

WHHL(FM)— Oct 10, 1967: 104.1 mhz; 50 kw. Ant 500 ft TL: N38 51 36 W90 18 38. Stereo. Hrs open: 24 800 St. Louis Union Station, The Power House, St. Louis, MO, 63013. Phone: (314) 621-0400. Fax: (314) 621-3000.E-mail: stl.ms@emies.com Web Site:www.red1041.com Licensee: Radio One Licenses LLC. Group owner: Emmis Communications Corp. (acq 12-19-2005; $20 million). Population served: 2,500,000 Format: New American Standards. News staff: one; News: 2 hrs wkly. Target aud: 25-54; families with children, singles. Spec prog: Heartland issues one hr, today's issues one hr, pub agenda one hr wkly. ♦John Beck, VP; Lisa Sesti, stn mgr & gen sls mgr.

WJBM(AM)— Oct 11, 1959: 1480 khz; 500 w-D, 32 w-N, DA-2. TL: N39 06 46 W90 18 43. Hrs open: 1010 Shipman Rd., 62052. Phone: (618) 498-8265. Fax: (618) 498-9830.E-mail: wjbm@wjbmradio.com Web Site:www.wjbmradio.com Licensee: DJ Two Rivers Radio Inc. (acq 1-9-2004; $320,000 with WBBA-FM Pittsfield). Population served: 53,000 Rgnl. Network: Brownfield. Brownfield Format: Oldies. Target aud: 25 plus; general market through retirement. Spec prog: Farm 18 hrs, sports 13 hrs, relg 3 hrs wkly.

Johnston City

WDDD(AM)— July 1, 1979: 810 khz; 250 w-U, DA-N. TL: N37 51 14 W88 52 12. (CP: 300 w-U, DA-N). Hrs open: 24 Box 127, Marion, 62959. Secondary address: 1822 N. Court, Marion 62959. Phone: (618) 997-8123. Fax: (618) 993-2319. Web Site:www.foxsports810.com Licensee: CC Licenses LLC. Group owner: Clear Channel Communications Inc. (acq 12-19-2000; grpsl). Natl. Network: Fox Sports, . Format: talk, sports. News: 2 hrs wkly. Target aud: 18-49; Adults. ♦Janet Jensen, gen mgr; Paxton Guy, opns mgr; Gina Heern, gen sls mgr; April Bennett, news dir; Tim Deterding, chief of engrg.

WDDD-FM— Nov 22, 1970: 107.3 mhz; 50 kw. Ant 492 ft TL: N37 45 15 W88 56 05. Stereo. Hrs open: 24 1822 N. Court St, Marion, 62959. Phone: (618) 997-8123. Fax: (618) 993-2319. Web Site:www.w3dcountry.com Licensee: Withers Broadcasting of Southern Illinois LLC. Group owner: Clear Channel Communications Inc. (acq 3-17-2008; grpsl). Population served: 250,000 Format: Country. News staff: 2; News: 5 hrs wkly. Target aud: P25-54. ♦Janet Jensen, gen mgr; Paxton Guy, opns mgr, gen sls mgr; Tim Deterding, chief of engrg.

Joliet

WCCQ(FM)—(Crest Hill, Jan 28, 1976: 98.3 mhz; 3 kw. 300 ft TL: N41 27 55 W88 07 33. Hrs open: 24 2410-B Canton Farm Rd., Crest Hill, 60435. Phone: (815) 556-0100. Fax: (815) 577-9231.E-mail: info@wccq.com Web Site:www.wccq.com Licensee: NM Licensing LLC. Group owner: Three Eagles Communications (acq 2-1-2004; $14 million). Population served: 2,600,000 Natl. Network: ABC, . Natl. Rep: Christal,. Leibowitz & Associates PA. Wire Svc: UPI Format: Country. Target aud: 25-54; general. ♦Todd Elbrink, gen mgr; Ryan Snow, opns dir; Roger Piper, gen sls mgr; Dan Waddick, prom dir; Roy Gregory, progmg dir.

***WCSF(FM)**— Sept 5, 1988: 88.7 mhz; 100 w. 108 ft TL: N41 31 58 W88 05 54. Stereo. Hrs open: 7 AM-2 AM (M-F) 500 N. Wilcox St., 60435. Phone: (815) 740-3425. Phone: (815) 740-3214. Fax: (815) 740-3697.E-mail: webmaster@st.francis.edu Web Site:www.stfrancis.edu Licensee: University of St. Francis. Format: AOR. Target aud: 18-45; males. Spec prog: Black 2 hrs, jazz 2 hrs, talk 4 hrs, requests 4 hrs, classic rock 4 hrs wkly. ♦Don Burke, pres; Rick Lawrence, gen mgr.

***WJCH(FM)**— Apr 25, 1986: 91.9 mhz; 50 kw. 460 ft TL: N41 24 55 W88 16 19. Stereo. Hrs open: 24 13 Fairlane Dr., 60435. Phone: (815) 725-1331. Licensee: Family Stations Inc. (group owner) Format: Relg. Spec prog: Class 2 hrs wkly. ♦Harold Camping, pres, gen mgr; Virginia Beehn, opns mgr.

WJOL(AM)— 1924: 1340 khz; 1 kw-U. TL: N41 32 10 W88 03 15. Hrs open: 24 2410-B Caton Farm Rd., Crest Hill, 60435. Phone: (815) 556-0100. Fax: (815) 577-9231. Web Site:www.wjol.com Licensee: NM Licensing LLC. Group owner: NextMedia Group L.L.C. (acq 11-26-2001; grpsl). Population served: 150,000 Natl. Rep: Christal,. Rgnl rep: Ill. Radio Net. Format: Talk. News staff: 2; News: 40 hrs wkly. Target aud: 35 plus. Spec prog: Farm 3 hrs, gospel one hr, Pol one hr wkly. ♦Roger Piper, gen mgr, gen sls mgr; Ryan Snow, opns dir; Dan Waddick, prom dir; Scott Slocum, progmg dir.

WSSR(FM)— Feb 6, 1960: 96.7 mhz; 3.1 kw. Ant 466 ft TL: N41 36 01 W87 58 44. Stereo. Hrs open: 24 2410-B Caton Farm Rd., Crest Hill, 60435. Phone: (815) 556-0100. Fax: (815) 577-9231.E-mail: info@star967.net Web Site:www.star967.net Licensee: NM Licensing LLC. Population served: 220,000 Natl. Rep: Christal,. Format: Adult contemp. News staff: one. Target aud: 25-54; Adults. ♦Todd Elbrink, gen mgr; Roger Piper, gen sls mgr; Dan Waddick, prom dir; Ryan Snow, progmg dir.

WVIX(FM)— Apr 17, 1960: 93.5 mhz; 6 kw. Ant 328 ft TL: N41 36 39 W88 00 33. Stereo. Hrs open: 24
Simulcast with WVIV-FM Highland Park.
625 N. Michigan Ave., Suite 300, Chicago, 60611. Phone: (312) 981-1800. Fax: (312) 981-1806. Web Site:http://www.univision.com /content/channel.jhtml?chid=9627&schid=9808 Licensee: HBC License Corp. Group owner: Univision Radio (acq 9-22-2003; grpsl). Population served: 289,000 Format: Sp contemp. News staff: one; News: one. ♦Jerry Ryan, gen mgr; Cesar Canales, opns mgr; Armando Reyes, progmg dir; Joshua Sigstad, engrg mgr.

WWHN(AM)— Apr 10, 1964: 1510 khz; 1 kw-D. TL: N41 30 50 W88 03 10. Stereo. Hrs open: 10321 S. Halsted, Chicago, 60628. Phone: (773) 239-2300. Fax: (773) 239-9921.E-mail: wwhn@aol.com Licensee: Hawkins Broadcasting Co. (acq 12-89; $250,000; 12-4-89). Population served: 80,378 Format: Gospel. Target aud: 18-54; affluent adults. Spec prog: Sp one hr wkly. ♦Raymond E. Hawkins, pres; Toni Hawkins, gen mgr.

Kankakee

***WAWF(FM)**— 2000: 88.3 mhz; 1.25 kw. Ant 285 ft TL: N41 04 39 W87 45 22. Hrs open: Box 3206., American Family Radio, Tupelo, MS, 38803. Phone: (662) 844-8888. Fax: (662) 842-6791. Web Site:www.afr.net Licensee: American Family Radio. (group owner) Format: Inspirational Christian. ♦Marvin Sanders, gen mgr.

***WEGN(FM)**—Not on air, target date: unknown: 88.7 mhz; 3 kw. Ant 164 ft TL: N41 10 07 W87 58 27. Hrs open: 600 W. Mason St., Springfield, 62702. Phone: (217) 899-7190. Fax: (217) 528-2400. Licensee: Cornerstone Community Radio Inc. ♦Richard L. Van Zandt, pres & gen mgr.

WKAN(AM)— June 1, 1947: 1320 khz; 1 kw-D, 500 w-N, DA-N. TL: N41 08 08 W87 49 10. Hrs open: 24 329 Maine St, Quicy, 62301. Phone: (815) 935-9555. Fax: (815) 935-9593.E-mail: wkan@starradio.com Web Site:www.wkan.com Licensee: STARadio Corp. (acq 2-7-94; $1.31 million with co-located FM; 3-28-94). Population served: 325,000 Pepper & Corazzini. Wire Svc: UPI Format: Talk. News staff: one; News: 20 hrs wkly. Target aud: 25-54. Spec prog: Farm 10 hrs wkly. ♦Robert L. Kersmarki, pres & gen mgr; Brendan Michaels, opns mgr, progmg dir; Larry Regnier, gen sls mgr.

***WKCC(FM)**— June 1, 1992: 91.1 mhz; 2.6 kw. Ant 254 ft TL: N41 09 38.9 W87 52 29.8. Hrs open: 24 Box 888, 60901. Phone: (815) 802-8100. Fax: (815) 935-5169. Licensee: Kankakee Community College. Population served: 100,000 Format: Educ, tourism. Target aud: General; travelers in northern IL. ♦William Yohnka, gen mgr.

WKIF(FM)— Sept 21, 1986: 92.7 mhz; 3 kw. Ant 300 ft TL: N41 07 22 W87 53 35. Stereo. Hrs open: 24 6012 S. Pulaski Rd., Chicago, 60629. Phone: (773) 767-1000. Fax: (773) 767-1100.E-mail: info@weplayanything.com Licensee: WKIF Inc. Group owner: Spanish Broadcasting System Inc. (acq 11-15-2004; grpsl). Population served: 150,000 Natl. Network: CNN Radio, . Format: News. ♦Harvey Wells, gen mgr; Gary Wright, progmg dir.

***WONU(FM)**— 1966: 89.7 mhz; 35 kw. 421 ft TL: N41 09 24 W87 52 16. Stereo. Hrs open: 24 One University Ave., Bourbannais, 60914. Phone: (815) 939-5330. Fax: (815) 939-5087.E-mail: shinefm@wonu.fm Web Site:www.shine.fm Licensee: Olivet Nazarene University. Population served: 6,000,000 Miller & Miller. Format: Christian Pop. Target aud: 25-49; female, predominantly conservative. ♦Justin Knight, gen mgr; Johnathon Eltrevoog, prom dir, progmg dir; Don Johnson, chief of engrg, rsch dir.

WVLI(FM)— Oct 22, 1992: 95.1 mhz; 3 kw. 328 ft TL: N41 04 39 W87 45 22. Stereo. Hrs open: 24 Box 758, Bourbonnais, 60914-0756. Secondary address: 292 N. Convent, Bourbonnais 60914. Phone: (815) 933-9287. Fax: (815) 933-8696.E-mail: wvlifm@comcast.net Licensee: Milner Broadcasting Co. (acq 3-17-95; $400,000). Population served: 105,000 Natl. Network: AP Network News, . Womble, Carlyle, Sandridge & Rice. Wire Svc: AP Format: Greatest hits & artists. News staff: one; News: 20 hrs wkly. Target aud: 25 plus. ♦Tim Milner, pres, gen mgr & stn mgr; Jim Brandt, opns mgr.

Kewanee

WKEI(AM)— Sept 11, 1952: 1450 khz; 500 w-D, 1 kw-N. TL: N41 13 37 W89 56 08. Hrs open: 24 Box 266, 61443-0266. Secondary address: 133 E. Division St. 61443. Phone: (309) 853-4471. Fax: (309) 853-4474.E-mail: regionalradio@verizon.net Web Site:www.randyradio.com Licensee: Virden Broadcasting Corp. Group owner: Miller Media Group (acq 11-8-94; $400,000 with co-located FM;1-2-95). Population served: 92,000 Natl. Network: CBS Radio, . Natl. Rep: Commercial Media Sales,. Womble Carlyle. Format: News/talk. News staff: one. Spec prog: Farm 20 hrs, relg 6 hrs wkly. ♦Randal J. Miller, pres, sls dir; Kris Wexell, progmg dir, pub affrs dir; Will Stevenson, adv mgr & news dir; Wayne R. Miller, chief of engrg; Jennie Holtschult, traf mgr.

Kincaid

***WHJH(FM)**—Not on air, target date: unknown: 89.1 mhz; 45 kw. Ant 394 ft TL: N39 16 05 W89 16 07. Hrs open: 365 Walnut Glen Dr., Springfield, 62707. Phone: (217) 741-8224. Licensee: Saving Children Inc. ♦Eric A. Hansen, gen mgr.

Knoxville

WKAY(FM)— Dec 13, 2001: 105.3 mhz; 3.7 kw. Ant 423 ft TL: N40 56 34 W90 20 39. Hrs open: 24 154 E. Simmons, Galesburg, 61401. Phone: (309) 342-5131. Fax: (309) 342-0840.E-mail: kfm@1053kfm.com Web Site:www.1053kfm.com Licensee: Galesburg Broadcasting Co. Group owner: Galesburg Broadcasting Co. (acq 4-1-99). Population served: 55,000 Cohn & Marks, LLP. Wire Svc: AP Format: Adult contemp. News staff: 4; News: one hr wkly. Target aud: 25-54; adults. ♦John Pritchard, pres; Roger Lundeen, gen mgr; Brian Prescott, opns dir; Chris Postin, sls VP; Shannon Anderson, news dir; Rick Heath, engrg dir.

La Grange

***WLTL(FM)**— Jan 5, 1968: 88.1 mhz; 180 w. 138 ft TL: N41 48 45 W87 52 51. Stereo. Hrs open: 24 100 S. Brainard Ave., 60525. Phone: (708) 482-9585. Fax: (708) 482-7051.E-mail: cthomas@wltl.net Web Site:www.wltl.net Licensee: Lyons Township High School. Population served: 117,814 Format: Var, rock. News: 10 hrs wkly. Target aud: 14-35; young adults. Spec prog: Sports 5 hrs, news & views 10 hrs wkly. ♦Chris Thomas, gen mgr; Tim McLaughlin, progmg dir; Mike Dorris, chief of engrg.

WRDZ(AM)— October 1950: 1300 khz; 5 kw-D, 500 w-N, DA-2. (CP: 4 kw-N. TL: N41 40 29 W87 45 45). Hrs open: 190 N. State St., Chicago, 60601. Phone: (312) 683-1300. Fax: (312) 577-5994. Licensee: Radio Disney Chicago LLC. Group owner: ABC Inc. (acq 5-12-99; with WPJX(AM) Zion). Population served: 17,814 Natl. Network: ABC, . Wire Svc: City News Bureau Format: Children. Children, mom's & dad's. ♦Karyn Esken, stn mgr.

La Salle

WAJK(FM)— Dec 4, 1964: 99.3 mhz; 11 kw. 500 ft TL: N41 18 15 W89 05 46. Stereo. Hrs open: Prog sep from AM 1 Broadcast Ln., Oglesby, 61348. Phone: (815) 223-3100. Fax: (815) 223-3095. Web Site:wajk.com Licensee: La Salle County Broadcasting Corp. Format: Hot adult contemp. Target aud: 25-49. ♦Peter Miller, pres; John Spencer, progmg dir; Jennifer Nagle, news dir; Steve Vogler, engr.

WLPO(AM)— Nov 16, 1947: 1220 khz; 1 kw-D, 500 w-N, DA-2. TL: N41 18 14 W89 05 44. Hrs open: 24 1 Broadcast Ln., Oglesby, 61348. Phone: (815) 223-3100. Fax: (815) 223-3095. Web Site:wlpo.net Licensee: La Salle County Broadcasting Corp. (group owner; (acq 8-1-49). Population served: 60,000 Format: News/talk, sports. News staff: 3; News: 35 hrs wkly. Target aud: 30 plus. ♦Peter Miler, pres; Joyce McCullough, VP, gen mgr; Mark Lippert, gen sls mgr; John Spencer, progmg dir; Jennifer Nagle, news dir; Steve Vogler, engr.

***WNIW(FM)**— November 1998: 91.3 mhz; 8 kw. 331 ft TL: N41 26 44 W89 00 42. Stereo. Hrs open: 24
Rebroadcasts WNIJ(FM) De Kalb & WNIU(FM) Rockford 50%.
NIU Broadcast Ctr., 801 N. First St., DeKalb, 60115. Phone: (815) 753-9000. Fax: (815) 753-9938.E-mail: npr@niu.edu Web Site:www.northernpublicradio.org Licensee: Northern Illinois University. Population served: 100,000 Natl. Network: PRI, NPR, . Arter & Hadden. Format: News, classical. News staff: 2. Target aud: General. ♦Tim Emmons, gen mgr; Jan Kilgard, dev dir; Bill Drake, progmg dir.

Lake Forest

***WMXM(FM)**— Sept 10, 1973: 88.9 mhz; 300 w. 100 ft TL: N42 15 00 W87 49 45. Stereo. Hrs open: 18 555 N. Sheridan Rd., 60045. Phone: (847) 735-5220 (office). Phone: (847) 735-6038 (studio). Fax: (847) 735-6291. Web Site:www.lfcradio.com Licensee: Lake Forest College. Population served: 500,000 Format: Div, classic rock, progsv. News staff: 2; News: 5 hrs wkly. Target aud: 18-25; students. Spec prog: Black 6 hrs, class 3 hrs, gospel 3 hrs, jazz 6 hrs wkly. ♦Ethan Helm, gen mgr.

Lansing

WSRB(FM)— Aug 28, 1961: 106.3 mhz; 2 kw. Ant 397 ft TL: N41 34 44 W87 32 46. Hrs open: 24 6336 Calumet Ave., Hammond, IN, 46324. Phone: (773) 734-4455. Fax: (219) 933-0323.E-mail: wycainfo@crawfordbroadcasting.com Web Site:www.soul1063radio.com Licensee: Dontron Inc. Group owner: Crawford Broadcasting Co. (acq 4-10-97; $14.8 million). Population served: 25,805 Natl. Network: ABC, . Format: Soul, rhythm and blues. Target aud: 25-54; urban, adult, African-American. ♦Donald B. Crawford, CEO; Taft Harris, gen mgr.

Lawrenceville

WAKO(AM)— June 9, 1959: 910 khz; 500 w-D, 59 w-N, DA-2. TL: N38 43 23 W87 39 13. Hrs open: 5 AM-midnight Box 210, 62439. Phone: (618) 943-3354. Fax: (618) 943-4173.E-mail: wakoradio@yahoo.com Licensee: Lawrenceville Broadcasting Co. Inc. (acq 5-31-73). Population served: 489,200 Natl. Network: Westwood One, . Wire Svc: AP Format: Adult contemp, country. News staff: one; News: 12 hrs wkly. Target aud: 20-65+. ♦Stuart Kent Lankford, pres & stn mgr.

WAKO-FM— March 1965: 103.1 mhz; 6 kw. 328 ft TL: N38 43 23 W87 39 13. Stereo. Hrs open: 19 Dups AM 95% Box 210, 62439. Phone: (618) 943-3354. Fax: (618) 943-4173.E-mail: wakoradio@yahoo.com Population served: 250,000 Wire Svc: CNN Wire Svc: AP ♦Steve Anderson, news dir, local news ed; Stuart Kent Lankford, gen mgr & traf mgr.

Le Roy

WBWN(FM)— Oct 15, 1979: 104.1 mhz; 25 kw. 328 ft TL: N40 25 25 W88 51 28. (CP: .80 kw, ant 413 ft. TL: N40 27 01 W89 00 42). Stereo. Hrs open: 24 236 Greenwood Ave., Bloomington, 61704. Phone: (309) 829-1221. Fax: (309) 662-8598.E-mail: newroom@wjbc.com Web Site:www.wbwn.com Licensee: Regent Broadcasting of Bloomington Inc. Group owner: Regent Communications Inc. (acq 5-12-2004; grpsl). Population served: 300,000 Natl. Rep: McGavren Guild,. Format: Country. Target aud: 25-45. ♦Red Pitcher, stn mgr; Dan Westhoff, progmg dir.

Lena

WQLF(FM)— Aug 2, 2002: 102.1 mhz; 5.2 kw. Ant 351 ft TL: N42 20 31 W89 48 21. Stereo. Hrs open: 24 P.O. Box 807, Freeport, 61032. Phone: (815) 235-7191. Fax: (815) 235-4318. Web Site:www.bigradio.fm Licensee: Lena Radio Broadcasting (acq 2-26-2002). Format: Classic hits. News staff: 4; News: 3 hrs wkly. Target aud: 20-49. ♦Kent McConnell, opns mgr; Wyatt Herrmann, progmg dir; Todd Hauser, chief of engrg; Becky Koester, traf mgr.

Lexington

WDQZ(FM)— 2004: 99.5 mhz; 6 kw. Ant 328 ft TL: N40 34 30 W88 50 15. Stereo. Hrs open: 24 108 Boeykens Place, Normal, 61761. Phone: (309) 888-4496. Fax: (309) 452-9677. Web Site:www.eagleclassicrock.com Licensee: Pilot Media LLC. Group owner: AAA Entertainment L.L.C. (acq 6-19-2007; grpsl). Population served: 127,000 Wire Svc: NBC Format: Classic Rock. News: 2 hrs wkly. Target aud: 25-54. ♦Patti Donsbach, gen mgr.

Lincoln

WLLM(AM)— April 1951: 1370 khz; 1 kw-D, 35 w-N. TL: N40 08 24 W89 23 10. Hrs open: 24 800 S. Postville Dr., 62656. Phone: (217) 735-9735. Fax: (217) 735-9736. Web Site:www.wllmradio.com Licensee: Cornerstone Community Radio Inc. (acq 4-7-03; $275,000). Population served: 100,000 Natl. Network: USA, . Format: Easy listening, Christian music & talk. ♦Richard Van Zandt, gen mgr; William Dolan, stn mgr; Beverly Tibbs, opns mgr.

***WLNX(FM)**— Jan 28, 1974: 88.9 mhz; 225 w. Ant 68 ft TL: N40 09 23 W89 21 40. Stereo. Hrs open: 24 300 Keokuk St., 62656. Phone: (217) 732-3155. Fax: (217) 732-3715.E-mail: info@wlnxradio.com Web Site:www.wlnxradio.com Licensee: Lincoln University. Population served: 15,000 Womble, Carlyle, Sandridge & Rice. Format: Rock. Target aud: 18-34; adults. ♦John Malone, gen mgr.

Lincolnshire

***WAES(FM)**— 2002: 88.1 mhz; 150 w. Ant 49 ft TL: N42 11 59 W87 56 49. Hrs open: Adlai E. Stevenson High School, Two Stevenson Dr., 60069. Phone: (847) 634-4000 ext. 1710. Fax: (847) 634-0983. Licensee: Adlai E. Stevenson High School District No. 125. Format: Var. ♦Greg Sherwin, gen mgr.

Litchfield

WSMI(AM)— Nov 2, 1950: 1540 khz; 1 kw-D. TL: N39 10 21 W89 34 14. Hrs open: Box 10, WSMI Bldg, E. Rt. 16, 62056. Secondary address: 6308 IL Rt. 16, Hillsboro 62049. Phone: (217) 324-5921. Fax: (217) 532-2431.E-mail: wsmi@wsmiradio.com Web Site:wsmiradio.com Licensee: Talley Broadcasting Corp. Group owner: Talley Radio Stations Population served: 400,000 Natl. Network: CNN Radio, . Natl. Rep: Christal,. Wire Svc: AP Format: Farm, country, news/talk. News staff: 3; News: 15 hrs wkly. Target aud: General. Spec prog: Farm 18 hrs wkly. ♦Brian C. Talley, chmn, sr VP, opns mgr; Hayward L. Talley, gen mgr; Michael Niehaus, rgnl sls mgr; Kevin Talley, prom mgr.

WSMI-FM— Mar 5, 1960: 106.1 mhz; 50 kw. 500 ft TL: N39 15 21 W89 36 48. Stereo. Hrs open: 4:30 AM-midnight Dups AM 15% Box

10, WSMI Bldg, 62056. Secondary address: 6308 IL Rt. 16, Hillsboro 62049. Phone: (217) 324-5921. Fax: (217) 532-2431. Population served: 600,000 Natl. Network: CNN Radio, . Natl. Rep: Katz Radio,. Wire Svc: AP Format: News, farm, sports, country. News staff: 3. Spec prog: Farm. ♦Haywrd L. Talley, pres; Brian C. Talley, opns mgr; Terry Todt, progmg dir; Rick Davis, local news ed.

Lockport

***WLRA(FM)**— November 1972: 88.1 mhz; 140 w. Ant 131 ft TL: N41 36 10 W88 04 49. Stereo. Hrs open: 24 Lewis University, One University Pkwy. MS#528, Romeoville, 60446. Phone: (815) 838-0500 ext. 5214. Fax: (815) 838-9149.E-mail: wlraradio@lewisu.edu Web Site:www.lewisu.edu/wlra Licensee: Lewis University. Population served: 100,000 Natl. Network: AP Network News, . Wire Svc: AP Format: Educ, div. News: 6 hrs wkly. Target aud: 13-30; college bound or post-college. Spec prog: Black 15 hrs, class 6 hrs, jazz 15 hrs, sports 15 hrs, talk 15 hrs wkly. ♦John Carey, gen mgr.

Loves Park

***WGSL(FM)**— Mar 28, 1988: 91.1 mhz; 7 kw. Ant 528 ft TL: N42 19 20 W89 00 41. Stereo. Hrs open: Box 2730, Rockford, 61132-2730. Secondary address: 5375 Pebble Creek Tr. 61111. Phone: (815) 654-1200. Fax: (815) 282-7779.E-mail: home@radio91.com Web Site:www.radio91.com Licensee: Educational Media Foundation. (acq 8-19-2009; $2 million with WQFL(FM) Rockford). Natl. Network: USA, . Davis Wright Tremaine LLP. Format: Relg, contemp praise. Target aud: 35-50; older families. ♦Ralph Trendadue, gen mgr; Ron Tietsort, opns mgr.

WKGL-FM— Mar 25, 1964: 96.7 mhz; 3 kw. Ant 300 ft TL: N42 19 48 W89 04 58. Stereo. Hrs open: 3901 Brendenwood Rd., Rockford, 61107. Phone: (815) 399-2233. Fax: (815) 484-2432. Web Site:www.cumulus.com Licensee: Cumulus Licensing Corp. Group owner: Cumulus Media Inc. (acq 3-12-2001). Population served: 230,000 Format: Classic rock. ♦Greg Sher, gen mgr; Allisia Bri-Asperson, prom dir; John Brizolla, progmg dir; Paul Hannigan, news dir; John Huntley, chief of engrg; Jan Thorp, traf mgr.

WLUV(AM)— Sept 29, 1962: 1520 khz; 500 w-D. TL: N42 19 48 W89 04 58. (CP: 12.5 w). Hrs open: Box 2616, 61132. Secondary address: 2272 Elmwood Rd., Rockford 61103. Phone: (815) 877-9588. Fax: (815) 877-9649. Licensee: Loves Park Broadcasting Co. Population served: 230,000 Format: Classic country, sports. Target aud: 25-60; blue collar workers. Spec prog: Farm 6 hrs, polka 6 hrs wkly. ♦Joe Salvi, gen mgr.

Lynnville

WEAI(FM)— Nov 15, 1989: 107.1 mhz; 6 kw. 328 ft TL: N39 37 16 W90 15 28. Stereo. Hrs open: 5 AM-midnight Box 1180, Jacksonville, 62651. Secondary address: 2161 Old State Rd., Jacksonville 62651. Phone: (217) 243-2800. Fax: (217) 245-6711.E-mail: weai@weai.com Web Site:www.weai.com Licensee: Jacksonville Area Radio Broadcasters Inc. (acq 7-1-2008; $2 million with WLDS(AM) Jacksonville). Population served: 50,000 Natl. Network: NBC Radio, . Natl. Rep: Katz Radio,. Ill. Radio Net. Kaye Scholer LLP. Wire Svc: AP Format: Contemp hit, oldies. News staff: 3; News: 6 hrs wkly. Target aud: 20-40; active young adults. ♦Gary Scott, gen mgr; Mark Whalen, gen sls mgr; Perry Brown, progmg dir; Troy Armstrong, mus dir; Kevin Baxter, news dir; John Coe, chief of engrg; Marty Megginson, traf mgr.

Macomb

***WIUM(FM)**— May 23, 1956: 91.3 mhz; 50 kw. 485 ft TL: N40 25 40 W90 40 58. Stereo. Hrs open: 24 515 Univ. Svcs. Bldg., Western Illinois Univ., 61455. Phone: (309) 298-2424. Phone: (309) 298-1873. Fax: (309) 298-2133.E-mail: publicradio@wiu.edu Web Site:www.tristatesradio.com Licensee: Western Illinois University. Population served: 77,162 Natl. Network: NPR, PRI, . Cohn & Marks. Format: Class, news. News staff: 2; News: 58 hrs wkly. Target aud: General. Spec prog: Folk/blues 7 hrs, jazz 5 hrs wkly. ♦Dorothy Vallillo, gen mgr, progmg dir, news rptr; Ken Thermon, opns dir; Sharon Faust, dev dir; Rich Egger, news dir; Mark Garrett, chief of engrg.

***WIUS(FM)**— Feb 1, 1982: 88.3 mhz; 120 w. 83 ft TL: N40 27 47 W90 41 00. Stereo. Hrs open: Sallee Hall, One University Cir., Western Ill. Univ., 61455-1390. Phone: (309) 298-3217 (request). Fax: (309) 298-2133. Web Site:www.wiu.edu/the dog/ Licensee: Western Illinois University. Cohn & Marks. Format: Progsv new mus, urban contemp, alternative. Target aud: 18-30. Spec prog: Jazz 2 hrs, Sp 3 hrs, blues 4 hrs wkly. ♦Patrick Stout, stn mgr & progmg dir.

WJEQ(FM)— February 1983: 102.7 mhz; 25 kw. 269 ft TL: N40 29 00 W90 38 19. Stereo. Hrs open: 24 31 E. Side Sq., 61455-2248. Phone: (309) 833-2121. Fax: (309) 836-3291.E-mail: wjeq@macomb.com Web Site:www.wjeq.com Licensee: Central Illinois Broadcasting. (acq 6-14-89). Format: Classic rock. News staff: one; News: 10 hrs wkly. Target aud: 18-49. Spec prog: Farm one hr wkly. ♦Bruce Foster, pres, chief of engrg; Nancy Foster, gen mgr; Mike Grillette, progmg dir; Mick Wilkens, news dir; Shana Drake, traf mgr & disc jockey.

WKAI(FM)— June 6, 1966: 100.1 mhz; 3.08 kw. Ant 463 ft TL: N40 26 57 W90 42 22. Stereo. Hrs open: 24 Box 250, 119 W. Carroll, 61455. Phone: (309) 833-5561. Fax: (309) 833-3460.E-mail: wkai@macomb.com Web Site:www.radiomacomb.com Licensee: WPW Broadcasting Inc. Rgnl. Network: Ill. Radio Net. Format: Adult contemp. News staff: one; News: 5 hrs wkly. Target aud: 35 plus.

WLRB(AM)— July 4, 1947: 1510 khz; 1 kw-D. TL: N40 29 50 W90 40 30. Hrs open: Sunrise-sunset Box 250, 119 W. Carroll, 61455. Phone: (309) 833-5561. Fax: (309) 833-3460.E-mail: wlrb@macomb.com Web Site:www.radiomacomb.com Licensee: WPW Broadcasting Inc. (group owner; (acq 12-27-99; grpsl). Population served: 22,300 Natl. Network: Westwood One, Jones Radio Networks, . Rgnl. Network: Brownfield. Brownfield Format: Music of Your Life. News staff: one; News: 6 hrs wkly. Target aud: 45 plus. Spec prog: Farm 1.25 hrs wkly. ♦Don Davis, pres; Mike Weaver, opns mgr; Vanessa Wetterling, gen mgr & gen sls mgr; Mike Weave, progmg dir.

***WLWM(FM)**—Not on air, target date: unknown: 89.7 mhz; 4 kw. Ant 174 ft TL: N40 26 58 W90 42 25. Hrs open:
Rebroadcasts WLUJ(FM) Springfield 100%.
600 W. Mason St., Springfield, 62702. Phone: (217) 528-2300. Fax: (217) 528-2400.E-mail: wluj897@ameritech.net Web Site:www.wluj.org Licensee: Cornerstone Community Radio Inc. (acq 2-27-2009). Natl. Network: Moody, . ♦Richard Van Zandt, pres & gen mgr.

WNLF(FM)— 2003: 95.9 mhz; 6 kw. 328 ft TL: N40 25 03 W90 36 51. Hrs open: c/o WJEQ Radio, 31 E Side Sq., 61455. Phone: (309) 833-2121. Fax: (309) 836-3291.E-mail: wjeq@macomb.com Web Site:www.modernrock959.com Licensee: Nancy L. Foster. Format: Modern rock. ♦Bruce Foster, pres, chief of engrg; Nancy Foster, gen mgr; Mike Grillette, progmg dir; Mick Wilkens, news dir; Shana Drake, traf mgr.

Macon

WZUS(FM)— May 5, 1977: 100.9 mhz; 6 kw. Ant 328 ft TL: N39 47 11 W88 59 29. Stereo. Hrs open: 24 410 N. Water St., Suite B, Decatur, 62523. Phone: (217) 428-4487. Fax: (217) 428-4501.E-mail: cbullock@cromwellradio.com Web Site:www.us101decatur.com Licensee: The Cromwell Group Inc. of Illinois. Group owner: The Cromwell Group Inc. (acq 4-16-02; $900,000). Population served: 80,000 Natl. Network: Jones Radio Networks, . Natl. Rep: Eastman Radio,. Pepper & Corazzini. Format: Country. Target aud: General. Spec prog: Farm 5 hrs wkly. ♦Chris Bullock, gen mgr; Tara Nickerson, opns mgr & progmg dir; Larry Timmons, chief of engrg.

Mahomet

WGKC(FM)— Dec 15, 1990: 105.9 mhz; 1.25 kw. 512 ft TL: N40 13 27 W88 17 56. Hrs open: 24 4108 Fieldstone Rd., Suite C, Champaign, 61822. Phone: (217) 367-1195. Fax: (217) 367-3291. Web Site:www.wgkc.net Licensee: RadioStar Inc. Group owner: AAA Entertainment L.L.C. (acq 5-23-2006; grpsl). Population served: 175,000 Natl. Rep: McGavren Guild,. Format: Classic rock. News staff: one. Target aud: 25-54; adult men. ♦Ji m Glassman, pres; Roxanne Charles, gen mgr; Jon Mayotte, progmg dir; Jon Hall, chief of engrg.

Marion

***WAWJ(FM)**— 2001: 90.1 mhz; 3 kw vert. Ant 344 ft TL: N37 51 23 W89 08 22. Hrs open: Drawer 3206, Tupelo, MS, 38803. Phone: (662) 844-8888. Fax: (662) 842-6791. Web Site:www.afr.net Licensee: American Family Association. Group owner: American Family Radio Format: Inspirational Christian. ♦Marvin Sanders, gen mgr.

WDDD(AM)—See Johnston City

WGGH(AM)— Sept 24, 1949: 1150 khz; 5 kw-D, 44 w-N DA-1. TL: N37 43 47 W88 53 44. Hrs open: 24 hrs Box 340, 1801 E. Main St., 62959. Phone: (618) 993-8102. Phone: (618) 997-2305. Fax: (618) 997-2307.E-mail: wggh@shawneelink.net Web Site:www.wggh.net Licensee: Vine Broadcasting Inc. (acq 4-7-92; 6-9-92). Population served: 7,600,925 Natl. Network: Salem Radio Network, . Rgnl. Network: Ill. Radio Net. Ill. Radio Net. Format: News/talk, country. News: Hourly. Target aud: 18 plus; general. ♦Elaine Gomez, gen mgr, sls; Mat Canon, progmg dir; Johnny Gomez, chief of engrg; Brenda Bender, traf mgr.

Maroa

WDKR(FM)— May 1996: 107.3 mhz; 3 kw. 456 ft TL: N39 57 56 W89 03 27. Stereo. Hrs open: 24 120 Wildwood Dr., Mt. Zion, 62549. Phone: (217) 864-4141. Fax: (217) 864-4727.E-mail: wxfmwdkr@comcast.net Licensee: WDKR Inc. (acq 3-6-02). Population served: 3,00,000 Format: Oldies. Target aud: 25-54; general. ♦Mary Ellen Burns, gen mgr.

Marseilles

WKOT(FM)— March 1992: 96.5 mhz; 3 kw. 328 ft TL: N41 18 40 W88 49 07. Stereo. Hrs open: 24 1 Broadcast Ln., Oglesby, 61348. Phone: (815) 233-3100. Fax: (815) 223-3095.E-mail: john@wajk.com Web Site:www.wkot.com Licensee: La Salle County Broadcasting Corp. (group owner; acq 6-99 $550,000 Natl. Network: Jones Radio Networks, . Format: Classic Hits. News staff: one; News: 8 hrs wkly. Target aud: 35-54. ♦Peter Miller III, pres; Joyce McCullough, VP, gen mgr; John Spencer, opns dir, progmg dir; Jennifer Nagle, news dir.

Marshall

WMMC(FM)— Oct 2, 1989: 105.9 mhz; 2.3 kw. Ant 528 ft TL: N39 21 09 W87 49 19. Stereo. Hrs open: 24 Box 158, 62441. Secondary address: 627 1/2 Archer Ave. 62441. Phone: (217) 826-8017. Fax: (217) 826-8519. Licensee: JDL Broadcasting Inc. (acq 9-10-98; $300,000). Natl. Network: ABC, . Format: Adult contemp. News: 8 hrs wkly. Target aud: 25-54; career-oriented men and women. ♦J. D. Spangler, pres, gen mgr; Lori Spangler, opns mgr.

Mattoon

WLBH(AM)— Nov 26, 1946: 1170 khz; 5 kw-D, DA. TL: N39 31 05 W88 22 15. Hrs open: 6 AM-7 PM PO Box 1848, N. Rt. 45 (2 mi), 61938-1848. Phone: (217) 234-6464. Fax: (217) 234-6019. Licensee: Mattoon Broadcasting Co. Group owner: J.R. Livesay Group Population served: 500,000 Format: Farm, news/talk, MOR. News staff: 3; News: 20 hrs wkly. Target aud: 25 plus. Spec prog: Relg 5 hrs wkly. ♦J.R. Livesay II, chmn, gen mgr, CEO, pres; S.L. Herrington, CFO; Adam Kennedy, news dir; Chase Arnold, political ed.

WLBH-FM— August 1949: 96.9 mhz; 50 kw. Ant 500 ft TL: N39 31 02 W88 22 13. Stereo. Hrs open: 24 Box 1848, N. Rt. 45 (2 mi), 61938-1848. Phone: (217) 234-6464. Fax: (217) 234-6019. Licensee: Mattoon Broadcasting Co. Population served: 2,000,000 Format: Adult contemp. News staff: 3; News: 18 hrs wkly. Target aud: 25 plus. ♦S.L. Herrington, CFO; Adam Kennedy, news dir; J.R. Livesay, local news ed; Chase Arnold, political ed.

***WLKL(FM)**— Jan 20, 1975: 89.9 mhz; 1.3 kw. 203 ft TL: N39 25 07 W88 22 55. Stereo. Hrs open: 24 5001 Lakeland Blvd., 61938. Phone: (217) 234-5373. Fax: (217) 234-5506.E-mail: gpowers@lakeland.cc.il.us Licensee: Community College District 517 Lake Land College. Population served: 60,000 Format: CHR, AOR. News staff: one; News: 6 hrs wkly. Target aud: 18-34; general. ♦Greg Powers, gen mgr & gen sls mgr.

WMCI(FM)— Aug 24, 1989: 101.3 mhz; 14.5 kw. 433 ft TL: N39 31 39 W88 21 23. Stereo. Hrs open: 24 209 Lakeland Blvd., 61938. Phone: (217) 235-5624. Phone: (217) 348-9292. Fax: (217) 235-6624.E-mail: info@radiomattoon.com Web Site:www.radiomattoon.com Licensee: The Cromwell Group Inc. of Illinois. Group owner: The Cromwell Group Inc. Population served: 100,000 Rgnl rep: Katz Format: Country. News staff: one; News: 10 hrs wkly. Target aud: 25-54. Spec prog: Farm 5 hrs wkly. ♦Bud Walters, pres; Bub McCullough, opns mgr, progmg dir, sports cmtr; Carol Floyd, gen mgr, stn mgr & gen sls mgr.

McLeansboro

WMCL(AM)— Jan 26, 1968: 1060 khz; 2.5 kw-D, DA. TL: N38 06 16 W88 33 48. Hrs open: 24 Box 46 A R.R. 1, 62859. Phone: (618) 643-2311. Fax: (618) 643-3299. Licensee: Dana Communications Corp. (acq 7-23-98; $245,000). Population served: 100,000 Natl. Network: CNN Radio, . Bryan Cave. Format: Country, agriculture news. Target aud: 25-65; agricultural community. ♦Dana Withers, pres, gen mgr; Gloria Holland, opns mgr.

Mendota

WGLC-FM— Sept 1, 1965: 100.1 mhz; 6 kw. 328 ft TL: N41 32 16 W89 06 25. Stereo. Hrs open: 4162 E. 3rd Rd., 61342. Secondary address: 3905 Progress Blvd., Peru 61354. Phone: (815) 224-2100. Fax: (815) 225-2066.E-mail: wglc@theradiogroup.net Web Site:wglc.net Licensee: Mendota Broadcasting Inc. Group owner: Studstill Broadcasting (acq 4-8-88). Population served: 130,000 Natl. Network: ABC, . Natl. Rep: Rgnl Reps,. Booth, Freret, Imlay & Tepper. Wire Svc: AP Format: Country. Target aud: 35 plus. ♦Lee Studstill, CEO, gen mgr; Owen L. Studstill, pres; Cole Studstill, VP; Stuart Hall, opns dir; Chris Turnow, opns mgr.

Metropolis

WMOK(AM)— Feb 4, 1951: 920 khz; 1 kw-D, 750 w-N, DA-N. TL: N37 09 12 W88 42 33 (day), N37 08 56 W88 38 10 (night). Stereo. Hrs open: 24 Box 720, 339 Fairgrounds Rd., 62960. Phone: (618) 524-4400. Fax: (618) 524-3133.E-mail: 920wmok@hcis.net Licensee: Withers Broadcasting Co. of Paducah LLC. Group owner: Withers Broadcasting Co. (acq 9-11-97; grpsl). Population served: 150,000 Format: Country. News staff: one. Target aud: General. Spec prog: Relg 5 hrs wkly. ♦Rick Lambert, gen mgr; Kathy Duncan, gen sls mgr, rgnl sls mgr; Smokey King, chief of engrg; Steve Bunyard, progmg dir, local news ed & local news ed.

WREZ(FM)— Dec 12, 1988: 105.5 mhz; 6 kw. 328 ft TL: N37 10 25 W88 42 29. Stereo. Hrs open: 24 Prog sep from AM Box 7501, Paducah, KY, 42002. Phone: (270) 538-5251. Fax: (270) 415-0599. Licensee: Withers Broadcasting Co. of Paducah LLC Population served: 165,000 Format: Adult contemp. ♦Steve Thompson, progmg dir.

WRIK-FM— July 11, 1984: 98.3 mhz; 100 kw. 699 ft TL: N36 45 09 W88 29 58. Stereo. Hrs open: 6120 Waldo Church Rd., 62960-4903. Fax: (618) 564-3202.E-mail: K98@hitsandfavs.com Licensee: Sun Media Inc. Population served: 325,000 Format: Adult contemp. ♦Samuel K. Stratemeyer, pres, gen mgr; Willie Kerns, opns mgr & progmg dir.

Milford

***WJCZ(FM)—** 2005: 91.3 mhz; 25 kw. Ant 89 ft TL: N40 35 07 W87 57 47. Hrs open: CSN International, 4002N. 3300E., Twin Falls, ID, 83301. Phone: (208) 734-6633. Fax: (208) 736-1958.E-mail: csn@csnradio.com Web Site:www.csnradio.com Licensee: CSN International (group owner). Format: Christian. ♦Mike Kestler, pres; Mike Stockland, gen mgr; Don Mills, progmg dir.

Moline

WFXN(AM)— 1946: 1230 khz; 1 kw-U. TL: N41 28 54 W90 31 49. Hrs open: 24 3535 E. Kimberly Rd., Davenport, IA, 52807. Phone: (563) 344-7000. Fax: (563) 359-8524. Licensee: Citicasters Licenses L.P. Group owner: Clear Channel Communications Inc. (acq 11-15-00; grpsl). Population served: 50,000 Format: Country. News staff: one; News: 6 hrs wkly. Target aud: 25-54; upscale/contemp. Spec prog: Sports 8 hrs, pub affrs 4 hrs, farm one hr wkly. ♦John Laton, VP, mktg VP; Jeff Ashcraft, sls dir; Gordon Ehler, gen sls mgr, progmg dir; Ron Evans, gen mgr & progmg dir; Kevin Allensworth, chief of engrg.

WXLP(FM)— Nov 22, 1970: 96.9 mhz; 50 kw. Ant 499 ft TL: N41 20 16 W90 22 46. Stereo. Hrs open: 1229 Brady St., Davenport, IA, 52803. Phone: (563) 326-2541. Fax: (563) 326-1819. Fax: (319) 326-0844. Licensee: Cumulus Licensing Corp. Group owner: Cumulus Media Inc. (acq 3-15-2000; grpsl). Natl. Network: Westwood One, . Putbrese, Hunsaker & Trent. Format: Classic rock. Target aud: 25-54. ♦Julie Derrer, pres, gen sls mgr; Jack Swart, gen mgr; Dave Levora, progmg dir; Andy Andresen, chief of engrg; Tracey Hall, traf mgr.

Monee

***WOTW(FM)—** Nov 1, 1995: 88.9 mhz; 100 w vert. Ant 82 ft TL: N41 27 58 W87 47 35. Hrs open: 14820 Sherman Way, Van Nuys, CA, 91405. Phone: (312) 329-4300. Fax: (312) 329-4339. Web Site:www.worshipontheway.net Licensee: Life on the Way Communications Inc. (group owner) (acq 2-15-2007; $5,000). Population served: 1,000,000 Southmayd & Miller. Format: Christian, relg. Target aud: General. ♦Gary Curtis, VP & gen mgr.

Monmouth

WMOI(FM)— Dec 6, 1967: 97.7 mhz; 3.36 kw. Ant 439 ft TL: N40 53 25 W90 36 31. Stereo. Hrs open: 24 Prog sep from AM Box 885, 55 Public Sq., 61462. Phone: (309) 734-9452. Fax: (309) 734-3276. Population served: 100,000 Rgnl. Network: Tribune. Tribune Radio Networks Format: Adult contemp. News staff: 3; News: 40 hrs wkly. Target aud: General.

WRAM(AM)— May 1957: 1330 khz; 1 kw-D, 50 w-N, DA-2. TL: N40 56 59 W90 34 19. Hrs open: 6 AM-6 PM Box 885, 55 Public Sq., 61462. Phone: (309) 734-9452. Fax: (309) 734-3276. Web Site:www.977wmoi.com Licensee: WPW Broadcasting Inc. (group owner; (acq 12-24-97; $1.7 million with co-located FM). Population served: 85,000 Natl. Network: ABC, . Rgnl. Network: Tribune, Ill. Radio Net. Tribune Radio Networks Format: Country. News staff: 3; News: 20 hrs wkly. Target aud: General; adult, mature. Spec prog: Farm 18 hrs, relg 3 hrs wkly. ♦David Klockenga, gen mgr.

Monticello

WCZQ(FM)— Jan 18, 1972: 105.5 mhz; 3 kw. Ant 300 ft TL: N40 02 52 W88 34 22. Stereo. Hrs open: 24 250 N. Water St., Suite 100, Decatur, 62523. Phone: (217) 429-9595. Fax: (217) 423-9764.E-mail: wczq@piatt.com Web Site:www.wczq.piatt.com Licensee: Neuhoff Family L.P. Group owner: NextMedia Group L.L.C. (acq 2-23-2009; grpsl). Population served: 84,000 Natl. Network: ABC, . Format: Urban contemp. News: 5 hrs wkly. Target aud: 25-65; upscale suburban & prosperous farm. Spec prog: Farm 11 hrs wkly. ♦Mark Hanson, gen mgr, stn mgr; Wendy Tohill, gen sls mgr; Jamie Pendleton, progmg dir; Frank Konwinski, chief of engrg; Cindy Hansen, traf mgr.

Morris

***WBEQ(FM)—** November 2003: 90.7 mhz; 1.45 kw. Ant 468 ft TL: N41 17 09 W88 25 49. Hrs open:
Rebroadcasts WBEZ(FM) Chicago 100%.
848 E. Grand Ave., Navy Pier, Chicago, 60611. Phone: (312) 948-4600. Fax: (312) 832 3100.E-mail: questions@webq.org Web Site:www.chicagopublicradio.org Licensee: The WBEZ Alliance Inc. Natl. Network: NPR, . Format: Jazz, news/talk. ♦Merrill Smith, chmn; Donna Moore, CFO; Torey Malatia, pres & gen mgr; Greg Salustro, dev dir.

***WCFL(FM)—** 1962: 104.7 mhz; 50 kw. 496 ft TL: N41 21 17 W88 29 55. Stereo. Hrs open: 24
Rebroadcasts WBGL(FM) Champaign 100%.
1802 N. Division, Suite 403, 60450. Phone: (815) 942-4400. Fax: (815) 942-4401.E-mail: wbgl@wbgl.org Web Site:www.wbgl.org Licensee: Illinois District Council of Assembly. (acq 4-16-94). Population served: 1,500,000 Natl. Network: USA, . Gammon & Grange. Format: Adult contemp, Christian. Target aud: 24-39. ♦Jeff Scott, gen mgr & progmg dir.

WCSJ(AM)— Jan 15, 1964: Stn currently dark. 1550 khz; 250 w-D, 6 w-N. TL: N41 20 20 W88 25 20. Hrs open: 24 219 W. Washington St., 60450. Phone: (815) 941-1000. Fax: (815) 941-9300. Licensee: Grundy County Broadcasters Inc. (acq 7-22-97; $425,000). Population served: 49,000 Rgnl. Network: Tribune. Format: MOR, news/talk. Target aud: 35 plus. ♦Larry Nelson, pres; Jack Daly, gen mgr; Susan Pellegrini, gen sls mgr.

WCSJ-FM— 1993: 103.1 mhz; 6 kw. Ant 328 ft TL: N41 17 35 W88 20 04. Hrs open: 24 219 W. Washington St., 60450. Phone: (815) 941-1000. Fax: (815) 941-9300. Licensee: Grundy County Broadcasters Inc. (acq 11-5-2003; $426,000). Population served: 49,000 Natl. Network: ABC, . Format: MOR, news/talk. News staff: one; News: 20 hrs wkly. Target aud: 25 plus; community oriented. Spec prog: Farm 10 hrs wkly. ♦Larry Nelson, pres; Jack Daly, gen mgr; Kevin Schramm, opns mgr.

Morrison

WZZT(FM)— Apr 10, 1991: 102.7 mhz; 6 kw. Ant 328 ft TL: N41 50 16 W89 55 29. Hrs open: 3101 Freeport Rd., Sterling, 61081-8612. Phone: (815) 625-3400. Fax: (815) 625-6940.E-mail: wsdr1240@theramp.net Licensee: Withers Broadcasting Co. of Rock River LLC. Group owner: Withers Broadcasting Co. (acq 1-21-98; grpsl). Natl. Network: ABC, . Rgnl. Network: Ill. Radio Net. Natl. Rep: Christal,. Ill. Radio Net. Format: Classic rock, sports. Target aud: 25-54; adults/men. ♦Brian Zschiesche, gen mgr, gen sls mgr; Kathy Wagner, progmg dir, mus dir; Mary Carlson, news dir; Sherry Smith, traf mgr.

Morton

WDQX(FM)— Nov 28, 1976: 102.3 mhz; 6 kw. Ant 300 ft TL: N40 38 27 W89 24 33. Hrs open: 24 331 Fulton St., Suite 1200, Peoria, 61602. Phone: (309) 637-3700. Fax: (309) 272-1476. Web Site:www.1023maxfm.com Licensee: Monterey Licenses LLC. Group owner: AAA Entertainment L.L.C. (acq 4-21-2006; $5.2 million with WXCL(FM) Pekin). Population served: 350,000 Natl. Network: Westwood One, CBS, . Rgnl. Network: Ill. Radio Net. Ill. Radio Net. Format: Classic hits. News staff: one; News: 10 hrs wkly. Target aud: 25 plus; active, affluent males. Spec prog: Relg one hr wkly. ♦Mike Wild, gen mgr; Joey Davidson, progmg dir; Shawn Newell, mus dir.

Mount Carmel

***WVJC(FM)—** July 23, 1973: 89.1 mhz; 50 kw. 331 ft TL: N38 26 29 W87 45 26. Stereo. Hrs open: 24 2200 College Dr., 62863. Phone: (618) 262-8641, ext. 3575. Fax: (618) 262-8989.E-mail: peachk@iecc.edu Web Site:www.bashradio.com Licensee: Illinois Eastern Community Colleges. Population served: 544,000 Fletcher, Heald & Hildreth. Format: Educational, Alternative. Target aud: 12-24; general. ♦Kyle J. Peach, gen mgr.

WVMC(AM)— Dec 1, 1948: 1360 khz; 500 w-D, 20 w-N. TL: N38 26 58 W87 46 12. Hrs open: 24 328 Market St., 62863. Phone: (618) 262-4102. Fax: (618) 262-4103.E-mail: wsjd@midwest.net Licensee: Wabash Communications Inc. (acq 12-5-01; $85,000). Population served: 47,200 Natl. Network: Sporting News Radio Network, . Ill. Radio Net. Format: Sports. News staff: 1. Target aud: General; Men 18 yrs plus. Spec prog: Farm 5 hrs wkly. ♦Kevin Williams, pres.

WYNG(FM)— Nov 28, 1960: 94.9 mhz; 50 kw. Ant 425 ft TL: N38 23 57 W87 47 18. Stereo. Hrs open: 24 127 W. Third St, 62863. Phone: (618) 263-3500.E-mail: wyng@wyng949.com Licensee: W. Russell Withers Jr. Group owner: Regent Communications Inc. (acq 12-22-2006; $1.5 million). Population served: 531,300 Format: Soft adult contemp. ♦Scott Allen, gen mgr, news dir; Josh Howard, progmg dir.

Mount Sterling

WPWQ(FM)— September 1995: 106.7 mhz; 25 kw. Ant 328 ft TL: N39 56 33 W90 57 44. Hrs open: Quincy Regional Airport, 1645 Hwy. 104, Suite G, Quincy, 62305. Phone: (217) 224-4653. Fax: (217) 885-3233.E-mail: wpwq106@adams.net Web Site:www.oldies1067.com Licensee: WPW Broadcasting Inc. (group owner; (acq 12-6-99; $550,000 with WKXQ(FM) Rushville). Format: Oldies. ♦Don Davis, pres; Phil Alexander, gen mgr & gen sls mgr; Brian Myles, progmg dir, news dir.

Mount Vernon

***WAPO(FM)—** 1997: 90.5 mhz; 500 w. Ant 203 ft TL: N38 18 39 W88 56 11. (CP: 1.25 kw). Hrs open: Box 3206, American Family Radio, Tupelo, MS, 38803. Phone: (662) 844-8888. Fax: (662) 842-6791. Web Site:www.afr.net Licensee: American Family Association. Group owner: American Family Radio Format: Inspirational Christian. ♦Marvin Sanders, gen mgr; John Riley, progmg mgr.

***WBMV(FM)—** Sept 30, 1997: 89.7 mhz; 6.2 kw. 492 ft TL: N38 22 15 W88 55 20. Hrs open: 24
Rebroadcasts WIBI(FM) Carlinville 100%.
Box 140, Carlinville, 62626. Phone: (217) 854-4800. Fax: (217) 854-4810.E-mail: wibi@wibi.org Licensee: Illinois Bible Institute Inc. (group owner) Format: Adult contemp, Christian mus. Target aud: 29-45. ♦Barry Copeland, gen mgr; Jeremiah Beck, stn mgr, opns dir, sls dir; Jessica Barton, opns dir, prom dir; Rob Regal, progmg dir; Joe Buchanan, mus dir; Sally Braundmeier, traf mgr.

WIBV(FM)— 2001: 102.1 mhz; 10.5 kw. Ant 508 ft TL: N38 24 07 W89 08 09. Hrs open: 24 6120 Waldo Church Rd., Metropolis, 62960. Phone: (618) 564-9836. Fax: (618) 564-3202.E-mail: K98@hitsandfavs.com Web Site:www.wibv102.com Licensee: Benjamin Stratemeyer (acq 4-26-2002; $1.25 million). Population served: 100,000 Format: Country. Target aud: 18-54. ♦Samuel Stratemeyer, gen mgr.

WMIX(AM)— 1947: 940 khz; 5 kw-D, 1.5 kw-N, DA-2. TL: N38 21 15 W89 00 29. Hrs open: 24 Box 1508, 62864. Secondary address: 3501 Broadway 62864. Phone: (618) 242-3500. Fax: (618) 242-4444. Fax: (618) 242-2490.E-mail: wmix@mvn.net Licensee: Withers Broadcasting Co. of Illinois LLC. Group owner: Withers Broadcasting Co. (acq 5-30-73). Population served: 38,000 Natl. Network: Westwood One, . Dennis Kelly. Wire Svc: AP Format: Talk, great memories. News staff: 2; News: 15 hrs wkly. Target aud: 25 plus. Spec prog: Farm 18 hrs wkly. ♦W. Russell Withers Jr., pres; Dana Withers, gen mgr; Scott Smalls, sls dir; Nicholas Lemay, news dir.

WMIX-FM— 1946: 94.1 mhz; 50 kw. 550 ft TL: N38 22 14 W88 55 20. Stereo. Hrs open: 24 Prog sep from AM 3501 Broadway, 62864. Phone: (618) 242-3500. Fax: (618) 242-4444. E-mail: wmix@mvn.net Licensee: Withers Broadcasting Co. of Illinois LLC Format: C&W. ◆Russell Withers, CEO; Craig Warner, news dir; D.T. Brown, disc jockey.

*WVSI(FM)— 2003: 88.9 mhz; 1.9 kw horiz, 4 kw vert. Ant 338 ft TL: N38 21 13 W88 56 32. Stereo. Hrs open: 24 Rebroadcasts WSIU(FM) Carbondale. 1003 Communications Bldg, 1100 Lincoln Dr., Southern Illinois University, Carbondale, 62901. Phone: (618) 453-4343. Fax: (618) 453-6186. E-mail: jeff.williams@wsiu.org Web Site:wsiu.org Licensee: The Board of Trustees of Southern Illinois University. Population served: 34,700 Natl. Network: NPR, PRI, . Ill. Radio Net. Wire Svc: AP Format: Class, news. News staff: 3; News: 36 hrs wkly. ◆Greg Petrowich, CEO; Jeff Williams, stn mgr; Mike Zelten, opns mgr; Renee Dillard, dev dir.

Mount Zion

WXFM(FM)— October 1984: 99.3 mhz; 1.15 kw. 495 ft TL: N39 48 35 W88 59 31. Stereo. Hrs open: 24 120 Wildwood Dr., 62549. Phone: (217) 864-4141. Fax: (217) 864-4727. Licensee: Technicom Inc. Population served: 300,000 Natl. Network: CNN Radio, . Brownfield Format: Adult contemp. News: 5 hrs wkly. Target aud: Free spending, affluent adults. ◆Mary Ellen Burns, pres & gen mgr.

Murphysboro

WINI(AM)— Sept 15, 1954: 1420 khz; 420w-D, 500 w-N, DA-N. TL: N37 45 30 W89 14 02. Hrs open: 24 1677 Business Hwy. 13, 62966. Phone: (618) 684-2128. Fax: (618) 687-4318. E-mail: wini@intrnet.net Web Site:www.winiradio.com Licensee: Radio Station WINI. (acq 7-28-00). Population served: 10,200 Eugene T. Smith. Format: News/talk. News: 22 hrs wkly. Target aud: 25-59. Spec prog: Relg 6 hrs wkly. ◆Dale Adkins, gen mgr, gen sls mgr, chief of engrg; Nancy Engel, opns mgr.

WVZA(FM)—Licensed to Murphysboro. See Carbondale

Naperville

WBIG(AM)—See Aurora

WERV-FM—See Aurora

*WONC(FM)— July 1, 1968: 89.1 mhz; 1.5 w. 163 ft TL: N41 46 45 W88 08 25. Stereo. Hrs open: 24 30 N. Brainard St., 60566. Phone: (630) 637-8989. Fax: (630) 637-5900. E-mail: jvmadormo@noctrl.edu Web Site:www.wonc.org Licensee: North Central College. Population served: 3,500,000 Wire Svc: AP Format: Rock/AOR. News: 5 hrs/week. Target aud: 18-44. Spec prog: Relg 4 hrs, alternative 10 hrs wkly. ◆John Madormo, gen mgr.

Nashville

WNSV(FM)— July 10, 1994: 104.7 mhz; 3 kw. 328 ft TL: N38 20 38 W89 20 59. Hrs open: 24 168 E. St. Louis St., 62263. Phone: (618) 327-4444. Fax: (618) 327-3716. E-mail: wnsvfm@charter.net Licensee: Dana K. Withers. (acq 1-16-92; $60,000; 2-10-92). Population served: 1,950,000 Format: Adult contemp. Target aud: 30 plus. ◆Dana Withers, pres, gen mgr; Gloria Holland, opns mgr.

Neoga

WHQQ(FM)— September 1996: 98.9 mhz; 2.9 kw. Ant 482 ft TL: N39 14 59 W88 22 48. Stereo. Hrs open: 24 Box 150846, The Cromwell Group Inc., Nashville, TN, 37215. Secondary address: 405 S. Banker St., #201, Effingham 62401. Phone: (615) 361-7560. Phone: (217) 235-5624 (stn). Fax: (615) 366-4313. Fax: (217) 235-6624 (stn). E-mail: mphillips@cromwellradio.co Web Site:www.effinghamradio.com Westwood One Oldies Licensee: WSHY Inc. Group owner: The Cromwell Group Inc. Population served: 120,000 Natl. Network: Jones Radio Networks, . Womble Carlyle. Format: Oldies. News: 14 hrs wkly. Target aud: 25-54; adults. Spec prog: Farm 7 hrs wkly. ◆Bayard Walters, chmn, pres; Tommy Crocker, CFO; Marv Phillips, gen mgr; Woody Bushue, opns mgr.

Newton

WIKK(FM)— May 4, 1992: 103.5 mhz; 25 kw. Ant 328 ft TL: N38 59 23 W88 11 19. Stereo. Hrs open: 24 4667 Radio Tower Ln., Olney, 62450. Phone: (618) 783-8000. Phone: (618) 392-2156. Fax: (618) 783-4040. E-mail: wikk1035@psbnewton.com Web Site:www.929thelegend.com Licensee: V.L.N. Broadcasting Inc. Group owner: Key Broadcasting Inc. (acq 6-25-2002; $600,000). Natl. Network: CNN Radio, . Format: Classic rock (66). News staff: one; News: 8 hrs wkly. Target aud: 25-49. ◆Mike Shipman, opns VP, progmg dir & mus dir; Mark Weiler, news dir.

Normal

WBNQ(FM)—See Bloomington

*WGLT(FM)— Feb 4, 1966: 89.1 mhz; 25 kw. 377 ft TL: N40 28 46 W89 03 12. Stereo. Hrs open: 24 Box 8910, Illinois State Univ., 61790-8910. Phone: (309) 438-2255. Fax: (309) 438-7870. E-mail: wglt@ilstu.edu Web Site:www.wglt.org Licensee: Illinois State University. Population served: 150,000 Natl. Network: NPR, PRI, AP Radio, . Rgnl. Network: Illinois Public Radio. Ill. Radio Net. Dow, Lohnes & Albertson. Wire Svc: AP Format: Jazz, blues, pub affrs. News staff: 3; News: 40 hrs wkly. Target aud: 35-54. Spec prog: Folk 4 hrs, musical theater 2 hrs wkly. ◆Bruce Bergethon, gen mgr; Aaron Wissmiller, dev dir; Mike McCurdy, progmg dir; Jon Norton, mus dir; Willis Kern, news dir; Mark Hill, chief of engrg.

WIHN(FM)— Dec 21, 1973: 96.7 mhz; 3.9 kw. Ant 410 ft TL: N40 28 34 W89 02 02. Stereo. Hrs open: 24 520 N. Center St., Bloomington, 61701. Phone: (309) 834-1100. Fax: (309) 834-4390. Web Site:www.967irock.com Licensee: Connoisseur Media of Bloomington LLC. Group owner: AAA Entertainment L.L.C. (acq 11-2-2006; $4 million). Population served: 127,000 Natl. Network: ABC, . Natl. Rep: Christal,. Davis Wright Tremaine LLP. Format: Rock. News staff: one; News: 9 hrs wkly. Target aud: 18-44. ◆Jack Swart, gen mgr; Grant Thompson, gen sls mgr; Adam Chandler, progmg dir; Mark Hill, chief of engrg.

WVMG(FM)— Aug 12, 2005: 100.7 mhz; 4.2 kw. Ant 344 ft TL: N40 27 08 W88 57 48. Hrs open: 520 N. Center St., Bloomington, 61701-2902. Phone: (309) 834-1100. Fax: (309) 834-4390. Web Site:www.magic1007.fm Licensee: Connoisseur Media LLC. Natl. Rep: Christal,. Shaw Pittman LLP. Format: Adult contemp. Target aud: 25-54; adult. ◆Jack Swart, gen mgr; Grant Thompson, gen sls mgr; Chad Fasig, progmg dir; Mark Hill, chief of engrg.

Oak Lawn

WNWI(AM)— Dec 31, 1965: 1080 khz; 1.9 kw-D. TL: N41 38 36 W87 38 45. Hrs open: 24 934 W. 138th St., Riverdale, 60827. Phone: (708) 201-9600. Fax: (248) 557-2950. E-mail: infomacja@wietrzneradio.com Licensee: Birach Broadcasting Corp. (group owner; (acq 6-30-95; $375,000). Population served: 88,000 Format: Foreign language, Pol. ◆Sima Birach, pres & gen mgr.

Oak Park

WPNA(AM)— Oct 7, 1950: 1490 khz; 1 kw-U. TL: N41 52 52 W87 47 38. Hrs open: 24 408 S. Oak Park Ave., 60302. Phone: (708) 848-8980. Fax: (708) 848-9220. E-mail: email@wpna1490am.com Web Site:www.wpna1490am.com Licensee: Alliance Communications Inc. (acq 5-1-87). Wire Svc: AP Format: Ethnic, Polish. News: 7 hrs wkly. Target aud: General. Spec prog: Polka 15 hrs, gospel 2 hrs, relg 4 hrs, Irish 4 hrs, Ukranian 2 hrs wkly. ◆Frank Spula, pres; Emily Leszczynski, gen mgr; Alan Kearns, chief of opns; Jerry Obrecki, gen sls mgr, progmg mgr & news dir.

WVAZ(FM)— Oct 17, 1950: 102.7 mhz; 6 kw. 1,170 ft TL: N41 53 56 W87 37 23. (CP: 9 kw). Stereo. Hrs open: 24 233 N. Michigan Ave., 28th Fl., Chicago, 60601. Phone: (312) 540-2000. Fax: (312) 938-4404. E-mail: info@wvaz.com Web Site:www.wvaz.com Licensee: AMFM Broadcasting Licenses LLC. Group owner: Clear Channel Communications Inc. (acq 8-30-2000; grpsl). Population served: 9,119,500 Format: Black adult contemp. News staff: 2; News: one hr wkly. Target aud: 25-54; Black adults. Spec prog: Gospel 4 hrs, pub affrs 2 hrs wkly. ◆Elroy Smith, opns mgr; Anita Genes, gen sls mgr, natl sls mgr; Angela Ingram, prom dir; Armando Rivera, mus dir; Tim Wright, chief of engrg; Jodie Craigen, traf mgr; Wanda Wells, news dir, pub affrs dir & local news ed; Herb Kent, disc jockey.

Oglesby

WALS(FM)— February 1993: 102.1 mhz; 2.25 kw. 446 ft TL: N41 18 05 W88 57 11. Hrs open: 24 3905 Progress Blvd., Peru, 61354.

Phone: (815) 224-2100. Fax: (815) 224-2066. E-mail: walls102@theradiogroup.net Licensee: Laco Radio Inc. Group owner: Studstill Broadcasting Population served: 125,000 Booth, Freret, Imlay & Tepper. Format: Country. News staff: 2; News: 2 hrs wkly. Target aud: 25-55. ◆Cole C. Studstill, CFO; Doris A. Studstill, gen mgr; Lamar Studstill, chmn & stn mgr.

Olney

*WPTH(FM)— July 1992: 88.1 mhz; 133 w. 203 ft TL: N38 41 50 W88 02 15. (CP: 720 w). Hrs open: 817 Orchard Dr., 62450. Phone: (618) 863-2765. Fax: (618) 395-7064. Licensee: Olney Voice of Christian Faith Inc. Format: Christian, talk. ◆Dr. Thomas E. Benson, pres, gen mgr; Ron James, VP.

WSEI(FM)— 1953: 92.9 mhz; 50 kw. Ant 552 ft TL: N38 42 00 W88 04 49. Stereo. Hrs open: Box L , 62450. Secondary address: 4667 E. Radio Tower Ln. 62450. Phone: (618) 393-2156. Fax: (618) 392-4536. E-mail: 929thelegend@forchtbroadcasting.com Web Site:www.freedom929.com Licensee: V.L.N. Broadcasting Inc. (acq 7-21-87; $1.12 million with co-located AM; 6-8-87). Population served: 138,000 Format: Country.

*WUSI(FM)— Nov 1, 1992: 90.3 mhz; 25 kw. Ant 472 ft TL: N38 50 18 W88 07 46. Stereo. Hrs open: 24 Rebroadcasts WSIU(FM) Carbondale 100%. Rm. 1003, Communications Bldg., 1100 Lincoln Dr., Carbondale, 62901-6602. Phone: (618) 453-4343. Fax: (618) 453-6186. E-mail: wsiuradio@wsiu.org Web Site:www.wsiu.org Licensee: Southern Illinois University. (group owner) Population served: 21,759 Natl. Network: NPR, PRI, . Ill. Radio Net. Cohn & Marks. Wire Svc: AP Format: Class, news. News staff: 3; News: 36 hrs wkly. Target aud: 35-64; highly educated, upper income, socially conscious. ◆Greg Petrowich, CEO; Jeff Williams, stn mgr, news dir, chief of engrg; Mike Zelten, opns mgr. Co-owned TV: WUSI-TV affil

WVLN(AM)— Nov 11, 1947: 740 khz; 250 w-D, 7 w-N. TL: N38 42 00 W88 04 53. Hrs open: Box L, 62450. Secondary address: 4667 E. Radio Tower Ln. 62450. Phone: (618) 393-2156. Fax: (618) 392-4536. E-mail: 929thelegend@forchtbroadcasting.com Licensee: V.L.N. Broadcasting Inc. Group owner: Key Broadcasting Inc. (acq 7-21-87; $1.12 million with co-located FM; 6-8-87). Population served: 130,000 Natl. Network: ESPN Radio, . Format: Sports. ◆Terry E. Forcht, pres.

Oregon

WSEY(FM)— Dec 27, 1999: 95.7 mhz; 3.2 kw. Ant 358 ft TL: N42 04 19 W89 25 08. Hrs open: c/o WIXN-AM-FM, 1460 S. College Ave., Dixon, 61021. Phone: (815) 288-3341. Fax: (815) 284-1017. E-mail: wixnstaff@wixn.com Licensee: NRG License Sub. LLC. (group owner; (acq 10-31-2005; grpsl). Format: Oldies. ◆Allan Knickrehm, gen mgr, gen sls mgr; Steve Marco, progmg dir; Danette Dallgas-Frey, news dir; Mark Baker, chief of engrg.

Ottawa

WCMY(AM)— Mar 5, 1952: 1430 khz; 500 w-D, 38 w-N. TL: N41 20 53 W88 48 15. Hrs open: 24 216 W. Lafayette, 61350. Phone: (815) 434-6050. Fax: (815) 434-5311. E-mail: info@wcmy1430.com Licensee: NRG License Sub. LLC. (group owner; (acq 10-31-2005; grpsl). Population served: 135,000 Natl. Network: CBS Radio, Westwood One, . Natl. Rep: Interep,. Brownfield Wire Svc: AP Format: Adult contemp, news/talk. News staff: 2; News: 35 hrs wkly. Target aud: 25 plus. Spec prog: Farm 9 hrs wkly. ◆Bill Jankowski, gen mgr; Jay Le Seuve, opns mgr, progmg dir; Jill Williams, prom dir; Rick Koshko, news dir.

WRKX(FM)— Sept 1, 1964: 95.3 mhz; 4.3 kw. Ant 200 ft TL: N41 23 00 W88 51 16. Stereo. Hrs open: 216 W. Lafayette, 61350. Phone: (815) 434-6050. Fax: (815) 434-5311. Population served: 135,000 Wire Svc: AP Format: Modern adult contemp. ◆Bill Jankowski, gen mgr; Jay LeSeure, opns mgr; Rick Koshko, news dir.

*WWGN(FM)— Sept 24, 1994: 88.9 mhz; 1.5 w. 646 ft TL: N41 16 51 W88 56 13. Stereo. Hrs open: 24 Box 3206, Tupelo, MS, 38803. Phone: (662) 844-8888. E-mail: wwgn@afo.net Web Site:www.afr.net Licensee: American Family Association Group owner: American Family Radio (acq 1-4-99; $250,000). Population served: 885,00 Format: Relg, educ. News staff: 2; News: 14 hrs wkly. Target aud: General. ◆Tim Wildmon, pres; Marvin Sanders, gen mgr.

Palatine

*WHCM(FM)— 2003: 88.3 mhz; 100 w. Ant 56 ft TL: N42 04 54 W88 04 23. Hrs open: William Rainey Harper College, 1200 W. Algonquin

Rd., 60067. Phone: (847) 925-6000. Phone: (847) 925-6488. Web Site:www.harpercollege.edu Licensee: William Rainey Harper College. Format: College, div. ♦Dave Dluger, gen mgr.

Pana

WMKR(FM)— July 12, 1996: 94.3 mhz; 5.6 kw. Ant 341 ft TL: N39 27 08 W89 17 10. Stereo. Hrs open: 24 Box 169, 918 E. Park St., Taylorville, 62568-0169. Phone: (217) 824-3395. Fax: (217) 824-3301. Web Site:www.randyradio.com Licensee: Miller Communications Inc. Group owner: Miller Media Group Population served: 197,000 Natl. Network: CNN Radio, . Natl. Rep: Commercial Media Sales,. Womble, Carlyle, Sandridge & Rice. Format: Country. Target aud: 25-54. ♦Randal J. Miller, pres; Kami Payne, gen mgr; Brandon Fellows, progmg dir; Steve Butera, news rptr.

***WZRS(FM)**—Not on air, target date: unknown: 89.3 mhz; 500 w. Ant 233 ft TL: N39 22 19 W89 04 51. Hrs open: Drawer 3206, Tupelo, MS, 38803. Phone: (662) 844-8888. Fax: (662) 842-6791. Web Site:www.afr.net Licensee: American Family Association. Group owner: American Family Radio. Format: Inspirational Christian.

Paris

WIBQ(FM)— 1952: 98.5 mhz; 50 kw. 500 ft TL: N39 36 21 W87 43 35. Stereo. Hrs open: Prog sep from AM Rt. 133 W., IN, 61944. Secondary address: 824 S. 3rd St. 61944. Phone: (217) 465-6336. Fax: (217) 466-1408. Licensee: Midwest Communications Inc. Population served: 100,000 Format: Modern country. Target aud: 18 plus. ♦Al Larcher, progmg dir.

WPRS(AM)— 1951: 1440 khz; 1 kw-D, 250 w-N. TL: N39 36 21 W87 43 35. Stereo. Hrs open: 24 824 S. 3rd St., Terre Haute, IN, 47807. Secondary address: 12861 Illinos Hwy. 133 61944. Phone: (217) 465-6336. Fax: (217) 466-1408.E-mail: wacf@comwares.net Licensee: Midwest Communications Inc. Group owner: Key Broadcasting Inc. (acq 12-15-2005; $2.55 million with co-located FM). Population served: 50,000 Format: Talk, sports, news. News staff: one. Target aud: General. ♦Duke E. Wright, pres; Karl Wertzler, gen mgr; Doug Boyd, gen sls mgr; Steve Hall, opns mgr & progmg dir; B.J. Fessant, news dir.

Park Forest

WCPQ(FM)— Jan 5, 1962: 99.9 mhz; 50 kw. Ant 492 ft TL: N41 18 04 W87 49 35. Stereo. Hrs open: 24 6012 S. Pulaski Rd, Chicago, 60629. Phone: (773) 767-1000. Fax: (773) 767-1100.E-mail: info@wcpt820.com Web Site:www.chicagoprogressivetalk.com Licensee: WCLR Inc. Group owner: Newsweb Corp. (acq 3-16-2004; $24 million with WNDZ(AM) Portage, IN). Population served: 2,000,000 Natl. Network: CNN Radio, . Format: Progressive talk. ♦Harvey Wells, gen mgr; Jeff Chardell, sls dir.

Park Ridge

***WMTH(FM)**— May 22, 1960: 90.5 mhz; 100 w. 103 ft TL: N42 02 14 W87 51 30. Hrs open: 2601 W. Dempster St., 60068. Phone: (847) 692-8495. Fax: (847) 692-8499. Licensee: Board of Education, Maine Twp. #207. Population served: 42,466 Format: Var. ♦Jim Wunderlich, gen mgr.

Paxton

WPXN(FM)— Oct 1, 1984: 104.9 mhz; 3 kw. 298 ft TL: N40 27 11 W88 06 11. Hrs open: 24 361 N. Railroad Ave., 60957. Phone: (217) 379-4333. Phone: (217) 892-9796. Fax: (217) 379-4334.E-mail: wpxn@wpxnradio.com Web Site:wpxnradio.com Licensee: Paxton Broadcasting Corp. (acq 7-84). Population served: 100,000 Natl. Network: CNN Radio, . Rgnl. Network: Brownfield. Brownfield Borsari & Paxson. Wire Svc: AP Format: Oldies. News staff: 2; News: 8 hrs wkly. Target aud: 25-54. Spec prog: Farm 10 hrs wkly. ♦Dan Daugherity, pres, gen mgr, gen sls mgr; Joel Cluver, stn mgr & progmg VP.

Pekin

***WBNH(FM)**— Dec. 1988: 88.5 mhz; 48,000 kw. 495 ft TL: N40 38 34 W89 32 38. Stereo. Hrs open: Box 1132, 61555. Phone: (309) 347-8850. Fax: (309) 353-8850.E-mail: wbnh@wbnh.org Web Site:www.wbnh.org Licensee: Central Illinois Radio Fellowship Inc. Natl. Network: Moody, . Southmayd & Miller. Format: Relg. Target aud: General. ♦Don Rice, pres; Jim Huber, stn mgr.

***WCIC(FM)**— Nov 2, 1983: 91.5 mhz; 35 kw. 338 ft TL: N40 33 24 W89 34 04. Stereo. Hrs open: 24 3902 W. Baring Trace, Peoria, 61615. Phone: (309) 282-9191. Fax: (309) 282-9192.E-mail: wcic@wcicfm.com Web Site:www.wcicfm.org Licensee: Illinois Bible Institute. (group owner) Format: Relg, adult contemp, Christian. News: 2 hrs wkly. Target aud: 25-49. ♦Dave Brooks, gen mgr.

WGLO(FM)— Nov 18, 1971: 95.5 mhz; 25 kw. 620 ft TL: N40 36 23 W89 32 20. Stereo. Hrs open: Prog sep from AM 120 Eaton St., Peoria, 61603. Phone: (309) 676-5000. Fax: (309) 676-2600. Web Site:www.955glo.com Population served: 350,000 Natl. Rep: D & R Radio,. Format: Classic rock. Target aud: 18-49. ♦Matt Bahan, progmg dir.

WVEL(AM)— Apr 21, 1948: 1140 khz; 5 kw-D, 3.2 kw-CH. TL: N40 36 08 W89 37 32. Hrs open: 120 Eaton St., Peoria, 61603. Phone: (309) 676-5000. Fax: (309) 676-2600.E-mail: jgreeley@regentcomm.com Web Site:www.wvel.com Licensee: Regent Broadcasting of Peoria Inc. Group owner: Regent Communications Inc. (acq 7-6-01; grpsl). Population served: 1,000,000 Format: Gospel. Target aud: General. ♦J.R. Greeley, gen mgr; Robert Caruth, sls VP & progmg dir.

WXCL(FM)— 1973: 104.9 mhz; 6 kw. Ant 328 ft TL: N40 38 34 W89 32 38. Stereo. Hrs open: 24 331 Fulton St., Suite 1200, Peoria, 61602. Phone: (309) 637-3700. Fax: (309) 272-1476.E-mail: info@1049.com Web Site:www.1049thewolf.com Licensee: Monterey Licenses LLC. Group owner: AAA Entertainment L.L.C. (acq 4-21-2006; $5.2 million with WDQX(FM) Morton). Population served: 350,000 Format: Country. News staff: 2. Target aud: 25-54; affluent adults. ♦Mike Wild, gen mgr; chris michaels, progmg dir.

Peoria

***WAZU(FM)**—Not on air, target date: unknown: 90.7 mhz; 1.3 kw. Ant 230 ft TL: N40 46 22 W89 44 50. Hrs open: 2122 W. Kellogg Ave., West Peoria, 61604. Phone: (309) 253-1951. Licensee: Sirius Syncope Inc. ♦Jeremy Styninger, pres.

***WCBU(FM)**— January 1970: 89.9 mhz; 26.5 kw. Ant 647 ft TL: N40 37 44 W89 34 12. Stereo. Hrs open: 1501 W. Bradley Ave., 61625. Phone: (309) 677-3690. Fax: (309) 677-3462.E-mail: wcbu@bradley.edu Web Site:www.wcbufm.org Licensee: Bradley University. Population served: 300,000 Natl. Network: NPR, . Dow Lohnes. Wire Svc: AP Format: Class, news. ♦Thomas Hunt, gen mgr; Daryl Scott, opns mgr; Cindy Dermody, gen sls mgr; Nathan Irwin, progmg dir; Jonathan Ahl, news dir; William Porter, chief of engrg.

WGLO(FM)—See Pekin

WIRL(AM)— 1947: 1290 khz; 5 kw-U, DA-2. TL: N40 37 24 W89 35 27. Stereo. Hrs open: 331 Fulton St., Suite 1200, 61602. Phone: (309) 637-3700. Fax: (309) 673-9562. Web Site:www.1290wirl.com Licensee: Monterey Licenses LLC. Group owner: JMP Media LLC (acq 3-25-2003; grpsl). Population served: 374,000 Natl. Rep: Christal,. Format: Classic country. Target aud: 25-54; men. ♦David J. Benjamin III, pres; Mike Wild, gen mgr; Mark Bretsck, sls dir, prom mgr; Brian Rowell, gen sls mgr; John Malone, progmg dir; Dave Dahl, news dir; Wayne Miller, chief of engrg; Brenda Rundle, traf mgr.

WIXO(FM)— May 14, 1972: 105.7 mhz; 32 kw. Ant 555 ft TL: N40 43 25 W89 29 04. Stereo. Hrs open: 4234 Brandywine Dr., Suite D, 61614. Phone: (309) 686-0101. Fax: (309) 686-0111.E-mail: studio@mix1057.com Web Site:www.mix1057.com Licensee: Regent Broadcasting of Peoria Inc. Group owner: AAA Entertainment L.L.L. (acq 9-19-2006; $11.75 million with WZPW(FM) Peoria). Population served: 126,963 Natl. Rep: Christal,. Format: Modern rock. ♦Michael Rea, gen mgr; Marta Poznaska, prom dir; Scott Seipel, progmg dir & news dir; Brett Ring, chief of engrg; Becky Riojas, sls.

WMBD(AM)— 1927: 1470 khz; 5 kw-U, DA-2. TL: N40 34 22 W89 32 00. Stereo. Hrs open: 24 331 Fulton St., Suite 1200, 61602. Phone: (309) 637-3700. Fax: (309) 673-9562. Web Site:www.1470wmbd.com Licensee: Monterey Licenses LLC. Group owner: JMP Media LLC (acq 3-25-2003; grpsl). Natl. Network: Premiere Radio Networks, Westwood One, . Natl. Rep: Christal,. Shaw Pittman. Wire Svc: U.S. Weather Service Format: News/talk. News staff: 5; News: 40 hrs wkly. Target aud: 35-64; upscale, well educated, professional. Spec prog: Farm 15 hrs wkly. ♦David J. Benjamin III, pres; Mike Wild, gen mgr & stn mgr.

WOAM(AM)— Feb 8, 1960: Stn currently dark. 1350 khz; 1 kw-U, DA-2. TL: N40 35 41 W89 35 40. Hrs open: 24 Kelly Communications, 3641 Meadowbrook Rd., 61604. Phone: (309) 685-0977. Fax: (309) 685-7150. Licensee: Kelly Communications Inc. (acq 12-1-86; $500,000; 9-29-86). Population served: 350,000 ♦Bob Kelly, stn mgr & news dir.

WPBG(FM)— 1947: 93.3 mhz; 41 kw. Ant 548 ft TL: N40 38 07 W89 32 19. Stereo. Hrs open: 24 Prog sep from AM 331 Fulton St., Suite 1200, 61602. Fax: (309) 686-8659. Web Site:www.933thedrive.com Licensee: Monterey Licenses LLC Format: Classic hits. Target aud: 25-54; baby boomers.

WPEO(AM)— 1946: 1020 khz; 1 kw-D. TL: N40 41 53 W89 31 31. Hrs open: 1708 Highview Rd., East Peoria, 61611. Secondary address: Box 1 61650. Phone: (309) 698-9736. Fax: (309) 698-9740.E-mail: wpeo@wpeo.com Web Site:www.wpeo.com Licensee: Pinebrook Foundation Inc. (acq 1-6-70). Population served: 500,000 Wood, Maines & Brown. Format: Relg, talk. Target aud: 35 plus. ♦Richard T. Crawford, pres; Robert Ulrich, gen mgr; Roger Bennington, gen sls mgr; Nelson Hostetler, progmg dir; Denise Feller, traf mgr.

WPMJ(FM)—See Chillicothe

WSWT(FM)— 1964: 106.9 mhz; 50 kw. Ant 479 ft TL: N40 43 22 W89 30 40. Stereo. Hrs open: 24 331 Fulton St., 12th Fl., 61602. Phone: (309) 637-3700. Fax: (309) 686-8659. Web Site:www.literock107.com Licensee: Monterey Licenses LLC. Population served: 500,000 Natl. Rep: Christal,. Wire Svc: AP Format: Adult contemp. News: 2.5 hrs wkly. Target aud: 25-54. ♦Randy Rundle, opns mgr; Dirk Clemens, prom mgr; Wayne R. Miller, progmg dir & chief of engrg.

WVEL(AM)—See Pekin

WXCL(FM)—See Pekin

WZPW(FM)— November 1992: 92.3 mhz; 19.2 kw. Ant 374 ft TL: N40 47 10 W89 47 01. Hrs open: 120 Eaton, 61603. Phone: (309) 676-5000.E-mail: studio@power92.net Web Site:www.power92.net Licensee: B&G Broadcasting Inc. Group owner: AAA Entertainment L.L.C. (acq 9-19-2006; $11.75 million with WIXO(FM) Peoria). Format: Top 40, CHR. ♦J.R. Greeley, gen mgr; Quinton Hafron, progmg dir.

Peru

WBZG(FM)— Mar 15, 1970: 100.9 mhz; 3 kw. 328 ft TL: N41 18 09 W89 14 11. Stereo. Hrs open: 24 3905 Progress Blvd., 61354. Phone: (815) 224-2100. Fax: (815) 224-2066.E-mail: wbzg@theradiogroup.net Web Site:wbzg.net Licensee: Mendota Broadcasting Inc. Group owner: Studstill Broadcasting (acq 7-17-97; $700,000 with WIVQ(FM) Spring Valley). Population served: 130,300 Natl. Rep: Rgnl Reps,. Booth, Freret, Imlay & Tepper. Wire Svc: AP Format: Classic rock. News staff: 2. Target aud: Men 18-54. ♦Lamar Studstill, chmn; Cole Charles Studstill, CFO, VP; Owen L. Studstill, CEO, pres & gen mgr; Cole Studstill, opns mgr.

WXAN(FM)—See Ava

Petersburg

WLCE(FM)— March 1987: 97.7 mhz; 6 kw. Ant 328 ft TL: N40 00 05 W89 41 49. (CP: N39 54 35 W89 43 01). Stereo. Hrs open: 24 Box 460, Springfield, 62705. Phone: (217) 629-7077. Fax: (217) 629-7952.E-mail: alice@alice.fm Web Site:www.alice.fm Licensee: Long-Nine Inc. Group owner: The Mid-West Family Broadcast Group (acq 7-27-2001; $3 million). Shaw Pittman. Wire Svc: AP Format: CHR. Target aud: 18-34; female. Spec prog: Relg 5 hrs wkly. ♦Kevin Kavanaugh, gen mgr; Dave Duetsch, gen sls mgr; Valerie Knight, progmg dir; Jim Leach, news dir; Greg Stephens, chief of engrg; Quinn Fagg, traf mgr.

***WLWJ(FM)**— Oct 7, 2001: 88.1 mhz; 6 kw. 328 ft TL: N40 00 05 W89 41 49. Stereo. Hrs open: 600 W. Mason St., Springfield, 62702. Phone: (217) 528-2300. Fax: (217) 528-2400. Web Site:www.wluj.org Licensee: Cornerstone Community Radio Inc. Natl. Network: USA, . Format: Christian talk, inspirational music. ♦Richard Van Zandt, gen mgr; John McBride, stn mgr; Howard Fouks, opns mgr; Richard Beaman, gen sls mgr.

Pittsfield

WBBA-FM— Aug 1, 1966: 97.5 mhz; 10 kw. Ant 300 ft TL: N39 34 53 W90 47 52. Stereo. Hrs open: 24 Box 312, 62363. Phone: (217) 285-5975. Fax: (217) 285-5977. Web Site:www.wbbaradio.com Licensee: DJ Two Rivers Radio Inc. (acq 1-9-2004; $320,000 with WJBM(AM) Jerseyville). Population served: 225,000 Format: Country. Target aud: General. ♦David Fuhler, gen mgr.

***WIPA(FM)**— Jan 4 1993: 89.3 mhz; 50 kw. 492 ft TL: N39 43 25 W90 41 09. Stereo. Hrs open: 24
Rebroadcasts WUIS(FM) Springfield 100%.
1 Universiity Plaza, WUIS 130, Springfield, 62703-5407. Phone: (217)

206-6516. Fax: (217) 206-6527.E-mail: wuis@uis.org Web Site:www.wuis.org Licensee: University of Illinois at Springfield. Natl. Network: NPR, PRI, . Rgnl. Network: Ill. Radio Net. Dow, Lohnes & Albertson. Format: News, class, jazz. News staff: 4; News: 45 hrs wkly. Target aud: 25-54. ♦Bill Wheelhouse, gen mgr; Lisa Clemmons-Stott, dev dir; Sinta Seiber, opns mgr & prom dir; Rick Bradley, news dir; Greg Manfroi, engrg mgr, chief of engrg.

Plano

WSPY-FM— Jan 19, 1974: 107.1 mhz; 1.5 kw. 466 ft TL: N41 39 55 W88 34 34. Stereo. Hrs open: 24 One Broadcast Ctr., 60545. Phone: (630) 552-1000. Fax: (630) 552-9300.E-mail: wspy@nelsonmultimedia.net Licensee: Nelson Enterprises Inc. Population served: 750,000 Natl. Network: ABC, . Format: Full service. News: 12 hrs wkly. Target aud: 25-54. Spec prog: Farm 18 hrs wkly. ♦Larry Nelson, pres; Liz Clark, CFO; Beth Pierre, gen mgr, gen sls mgr; Chris Schwemlein, opns mgr, progmg dir; Vori Dhabolt, gen sls mgr; Lane Lindstrom, chief of engrg; Jeni Beckman, traf mgr.

Polo

WLLT(FM)— Dec 12, 1989: 107.7 mhz; 3 kw. Ant 476 ft TL: N41 53 51.9 W89 36 19.6. Stereo. Hrs open: 24 260 Illinois Rt. 2, Dixon, 61021. Phone: (815) 284-1077.E-mail: wllt@comcast.net Licensee: Sauk Valley Broadcasting Co. Population served: 75,000 Format: Soft adult contemp. ♦Bob Burns, gen mgr.

Pontiac

***WPJC(FM)**— 2003: 88.3 mhz; 500 w. Ant 207 ft TL: N40 56 42 W88 38 46. Hrs open: 150 Lincoln Way, Suite 2001, Valparaiso, IN, 46383. Phone: (219) 548-8956. Fax: (219) 548-5808.E-mail: wpjc@csnradio.com Licensee: CSN International (group owner; acq 12-31-2001; $25,000 for CP). Format: Christian talk. ♦Jim Motshagen, gen mgr.

WTRX-FM— July 1969: 93.7 mhz; 12 kw. Ant 472 ft TL: N40 45 27 W88 37 40. Stereo. Hrs open: 24 315 N. Mill St., 61764. Phone: (815) 844-6101. Fax: (815) 844-7235. Web Site:www.wtrxoldieschannel.com Licensee: Livingston County Broadcasters Inc. Group owner: Regent Communications Inc. (acq 5-12-2004; grpsl). Population served: 175,000 Format: Oldies. News staff: one. Target aud: 25-54. ♦Red Pitcher, gen mgr, gen sls mgr; Ron Ross, progmg dir.

Princeton

***WPRC(FM)**—Not on air, target date: unknown: 88.3 mhz; 150 w vert. Ant 315 ft TL: N41 16 53 W89 35 12. Hrs open: c/o WCIC, 3902 S. Baring Trace, Peoria, 61615. Phone: (309) 282-9191. Fax: (309) 282-9192.E-mail: wcic@wcicfm.org Licensee: Illinois Bible Institute Inc. (group owner). Format: Christian talk. ♦Dave Brooks, gen mgr; Tracey Moushon, prom dir.

WZOE(AM)— Oct 25, 1961: 1490 khz; 1 kw-U. TL: N41 21 08 W89 28 05. Hrs open: 24 Box 69, Broadcast Ctr., 61356. Secondary address: S. Main St. 61356. Phone: (815) 875-8014.E-mail: info@wzoeradio.com Web Site:www.wzoeradio.com Licensee: WZOE Inc. (group owner; acq 11-1-73). Population served: 63,000 Natl. Network: CBS, . Shaw Pittman. Wire Svc: Metro Weather Service Inc. Format: News/talk, sports. News staff: 3; News: 84 hrs wkly. Spec prog: Farm 15 hrs wkly. ♦Steve Samet, pres, gen mgr; Paul Bomleny, opns dir; Chris Compton, sls dir; Tommy Rose, progmg dir; Scott Mighle, news dir; Nedda Simon, pub affrs dir, women's int ed; Greg Stephens, chief of engrg; Mary Harmon, traf mgr.

WZOE-FM— July 1, 1980: 98.1 mhz; 6 kw. Ant 300 ft TL: N41 21 49 W89 23 36. Stereo. Hrs open: 24 Prog sep from AM Box 69 Broadcast Ctr., S. Main St., 61356. Phone: (815) 875-8014.E-mail: info@wzoeradio.com Web Site:www.wzoeradio.com Licensee: WZOE Inc. Population served: 70,700 Natl. Network: CNN Radio, . Wire Svc: Metro Weather Service Inc. Format: Classic hits. News staff: 3; News: 8 hrs wkly. ♦Mary Harmon, traf mgr; Nedda Simon, women's int ed.

Quincy

KGRC(FM)—See Hannibal, MO

WCOY(FM)— 1948: 99.5 mhz; 100 kw. Ant 489 ft TL: N39 56 30 W91 35 03. Hrs open: 24 Prog sep from AM Lincoln-Douglas, 329 Maine St., 62306. Phone: (217) 224-4102. Fax: (217) 224-4133. Population served: 80000 Natl. Network: CBS, . Format: Hot country classics. ♦Mike Moyers, progmg dir.

***WGCA-FM**— Sept 20, 1987: 88.5 mhz; 40 kw. 449 ft TL: N39 58 18 W91 19 42. Stereo. Hrs open: 535 Maine St., Suite 10, 62301. Phone: (217) 224-9422. Fax: (217) 228-0504.E-mail: themix@wgca.org Web Site:www.wgca.org Licensee: Great Commission Broadcasting Corp. Natl. Network: USA, . Format: Christian contemp. Target aud: 25-45. ♦Bruce Rice, gen mgr, progmg dir; Jim Taylor, progmg dir; Jim Wilson, chief of engrg.

WGEM(AM)— Jan 1, 1948: 1440 khz; 5 kw-D, 1 kw-N, DA-2. TL: N39 58 47 W91 19 27. Stereo. Hrs open: Box 80, 62306. Secondary address: 513 Hampshire 62301. Phone: (217) 228-6600. Fax: (217) 228-6670.E-mail: aelkins@wgem.com Web Site:wgem.com Licensee: Quincy Broadcasting Co. Group owner: Quincy Newspapers Inc. Population served: 150,000 Natl. Network: ESPN Radio, . Rgnl. Network: Tribune. Natl. Rep: Christal,. Wilkinson, Barker & Knauer. Format: Sports. Target aud: 25-54; general. ♦Ralph M. Oakley, pres, opns dir; Thomas Oakley, gen mgr.

WGEM-FM— 1947: 105.1 mhz; 27.5 kw. 500 ft TL: N39 57 03 W91 19 54. Stereo. Hrs open: 24 Box 80, 62306. Secondary address: 513 Hampshire 62301. Phone: (217) 228-6600. Fax: (217) 228-6670.E-mail: aelkins@wgem.com Web Site:www.wgem.com Population served: 300,000 Rgnl. Network: Miss. Net. Natl. Rep: Christal,. Miss. News Net. Wilkinson, Barker, Knauer & Quinn. Wire Svc: AP Format: News/talk. News: 110 hrs wkly. Target aud: 25-54. ♦Ralph Oakley, pres; Carlos Fernandez, gen mgr.

WLIQ(AM)— Dec 13, 1966: 1530 khz; 1.4 kw-D, 290 w-CH. TL: N39 55 51 W91 25 46. Stereo. Hrs open: Sunrise-sunset Box 711, Hannibal, MO, 63401. Phone: (573) 221-3450. Fax: (573) 221-5331.E-mail: hsmith@qraido.com Licensee: Bick Broadcasting Co. (group owner; (acq 10-14-2003). Population served: 103,010 Rgnl. Network: Brownfield. Format: Soft adult contemp. ♦Ed Foxall, gen mgr; Jeff Dorsey, progmg dir; John Hanvelt, news dir; Gary Glaenzer, chief of engrg.

WQCY(FM)— May 8, 1989: 103.9 mhz; 1.8 kw. Ant 436 ft TL: N39 56 30 W91 35 03. Hrs open: 329 Maine St., 62301. Phone: (217) 224-4102. Fax: (217) 224-4133.E-mail: wqcy@staradio.com Web Site:www.1039thefox.com Licensee: STARadio Corp. (group owner; acq 8-13-98; grpsl). Natl. Network: CBS, . Format: Hot 80s. Target aud: 18-44; general. ♦Michael J. Moyers, gen mgr; Brenda Park, gen sls mgr; Sean Secrease, progmg dir; Mary Griffith, mus dir, news dir; Phillip Reilly, chief of engrg; Jerry Shoup, traf mgr, disc jockey.

***WQUB(FM)**— April 1974: 90.3 mhz; 28 kw. 417 ft TL: N39 57 22 W91 23 22. Stereo. Hrs open: 24 1800 College Ave., 62301. Phone: (217) 228-5410. Fax: (217) 228-5616.E-mail: info@wqub.org Web Site:www.wqub.org Licensee: Quincy University Corp. Population served: 240,000 Natl. Network: NPR, AP Radio, . Wilkinson Barker Knauer. Format: Class, news, jazz. News staff: 2; News: 31 hrs wkly. Target aud: 25-64; male & female. Spec prog: Folk 2 hrs, blues 2 hrs, alternative rock 12 hrs, hip hop 2 hrs, oldies 2 hrs wkly. ♦Patrick Mays, dev dir; Jim Lenz, pub affrs dir; Jim Cate, engrg mgr, chief of engrg.

WTAD(AM)— July 25, 1925: 930 khz; 5 kw-D, 1 kw-N, DA-N. TL: N39 53 31 W91 25 25. Hrs open: 24 Lincoln-Douglas, 329 Maine St., 62306. Phone: (217) 224-4102. Fax: (217) 224-4133.E-mail: info@wtad.com Web Site:www.wtad.com Licensee: STARadio Corp. (group owner; (acq 8-13-98; grpsl). Population served: 80,000 Natl. Network: CBS, . Natl. Rep: McGavren Guild,. Format: News/talk. News staff: one; News: 22 hrs wkly. Target aud: 35 plus; general. ♦Brenda Parks, gen mgr.

Ramsey

***WJLY(FM)**— 1999: 88.3 mhz; 25 kw. Ant 502 ft TL: N39 08 06 W89 06 02. Hrs open: 24 Box 456, 62080. Secondary address: R.R. 2 Box 51A Phone: (618) 423-2082. Fax: (618) 423-2394.E-mail: wjly@frontiernet.net Licensee: Countryside Broadcasting. Population served: 73,184 Natl. Network: Moody, . Format: Christian. News: 14 hrs wkly. Target aud: 35 plus. ♦Richard Wheeler, gen mgr; John Stanley, gen sls mgr; Dave Carruthers, progmg dir; Henry Voss, chief of engrg.

WTRH(FM)— Nov 21, 1990: 93.3 mhz; 3 kw. Ant 466 ft TL: N39 08 06 W89 06 02. Stereo. Hrs open: 24 Box 456, 62080. Phone: (618) 423-2082. Fax: (618) 423-2394.E-mail: wtrh@frontiernet.net Licensee: Countryside Broadcasting Inc. Population served: 31,000 Format: Oldies, talk. News: 14 hrs wkly. Target aud: 35 plus; men & women who love old radio prgms & mus. ♦Richard Wheeler, gen mgr & opns mgr; Henry Voss, chief of engrg.

Rantoul

WKJR(AM)—Licensed to Rantoul. See Champaign

WLFH(FM)—Licensed to Rantoul. See Champaign

WQQB(FM)—Licensed to Rantoul. See Urbana

River Grove

***WRRG(FM)**— Mar 10, 1975: 88.9 mhz; 100 w. 128 ft TL: N41 54 56 W87 50 12. Stereo. Hrs open: 9 AM-midnight (M-F); 10 AM-midnight (S, Su) 2000 N. 5th Ave., R113, 60171. Phone: (708) 583-3110.E-mail: info@wrrg.org Web Site:www.wrrg.org Licensee: Triton College. Population served: 500,000 Format: CHR, alternative. Target aud: 14-40. Spec prog: Jazz 5 hrs, loc 4 hrs, metal 4 hrs, world mus 3 hrs, oldies 11 hrs, classic rock 2 hrs wkly. ♦Kelli A. Lynch, gen mgr, stn mgr & progmg mgr.

Robinson

WTAY(AM)— Jan 9, 1956: 1570 khz; 250 w-D. TL: N39 00 29 W87 46 41. Hrs open: 24 Box 245, Rt. 33 W., 62454. Phone: (618) 544-2191. Fax: (618) 544-3621.E-mail: wtaywtye@yahoo.com Licensee: Ann Broadcasting Corp. (acq 1994). Natl. Network: ABC, . Format: Adult contemp. News staff: one; News: 15 hrs wkly. Spec prog: C&W 12 hrs, farm 3 hrs, polka 3 hrs, big band 10 hrs wkly. ♦Jerry F. Tye, pres, gen mgr; Roy Rice, gen sls mgr; Tony Collins, progmg dir; Chris Forde, news dir.

WTYE(FM)— Jan 4, 1963: 101.7 mhz; 1.45 kw. 449 ft TL: N39 00 29 W87 46 41. Stereo. Hrs open: Dups AM 100% Box 245, Rt. 33 W., 62454. Phone: (618) 544-2191. Fax: (618) 544-3621.E-mail: wtaywtye@yahoo.com Population served: 35,000 Natl. Network: ABC, . ♦Jerry Tye, pres, gen mgr; Roy Rice, gen sls mgr; Tony Collins, progmg dir; Chris Forde, news dir.

Rochelle

WRHL(AM)— Sept 16, 1966: 1060 khz; 250 w-D, DA. TL: N41 55 24 W89 03 30. Hrs open: 24 Box 177, 61068. Secondary address: 400 May Mart Dr. 61068. Phone: (815) 562-7001. Fax: (815) 562-7002.E-mail: wrhlamfm@rochelle.net Web Site:www.wrhl.net Licensee: Rochelle Broadcasting Co. Inc. (acq 10-11-70). Population served: 45,000 Natl. Network: AP Network News, . Rgnl. Network: Ill. Radio Net., Tribune. Tribune Radio Networks Wire Svc: AP Format: News/talk. News staff: 2; News: 140 hrs wkly. Target aud: 25-75. ♦David Van Drew, gen mgr; Penny Helm, gen sls mgr; Greg Saunders, progmg dir; Jeffrey Leon, news dir; Doug White, chief of engrg; Becky Leininger, traf mgr, women's int ed.

WRHL-FM— Oct 5, 1973: 102.3 mhz; 4.6 kw. 180 ft TL: N41 55 24 W89 03 30. Stereo. Hrs open: 24 Box 177, 61068. Secondary address: 400 May Mart Dr. 61068. Phone: (815) 562-7001. Fax: (815) 562-7002.E-mail: jb@wrhl.net Web Site:www.hitsandfavorites.com Population served: 45,000 Natl. Network: ABC, . Format: Adult contemp. News: one hr wkly. Target aud: 25-54; female. ♦Becky Leininger, traf mgr & women's int ed.

Rock Falls

WSDR(AM)—See Sterling

Rock Island

WKBF(AM)— Feb 16, 1925: 1270 khz; 5 kw-U, DA-N. TL: N41 29 40 W90 28 00. Hrs open: 24 4020 N. 128th St., Brookfield, WI, 53005. Phone: (888) 321-1270.E-mail: info@truth1270.com Web Site:www.truth1270.com Licensee: Quad Cities Media LLC (group owner; (acq 12-4-2006; $150,000). Population served: 350,000 Format: Rgnl Mexican. ♦Randall R. Melchert, pres.

WLKU(FM)— October 1947: 98.9 mhz; 39 kw. Ant 900 ft TL: N41 19 40 W90 22 47. Stereo. Hrs open: 24 2351 Sunset Blvd., Suite 170-218, Rocklin, CA, 95765. Phone: (916) 251-1600. Fax: (916) 251-1650. Web Site:www.klove.com Licensee: Educational Media Foundation. (acq 2-3-2006; $3.5 million). Natl. Network: K-Love, . Format: Contemp Christian. ♦Richard Jenkins, pres; Mike Novak, VP; Keith Whipple, dev dir; David Pierce, progmg mgr; Ed Lenane, news dir; Sam Wallington, engrg dir; Karen Johnson, news rptr.

***WVIK(FM)**— Feb 25, 1963: 90.3 mhz; 31 kw. 1,096 ft TL: N41 32 52 W90 28 29. Stereo. Hrs open: 24 Augustana College, 639 38th St., 61201. Phone: (309) 794-7500. Fax: (309) 794-1236.E-mail: info@wvik.org Web Site:www.wvik.org Licensee: Augustana College. Population served: 780,000 Natl. Network: NPR, . Dow, Lohnes & Albertson. Wire Svc: AP Format: Class, news. News staff: 2; News: 35 hrs wkly. Target

aud: General. Spec prog: Jazz 9 hrs wkly. ◆Lowell Dorman, gen mgr; David Garner, opns dir; Sonita Oldfield-Carlson, dev dir; Mindy Heusel, gen sls mgr, mus dir; Herb Trix, news dir.

Rockford

*WFEN(FM)— Aug 25, 1991: 88.3 mhz; 8.5 kw. 575 ft TL: N42 21 51 W89 08 15. Hrs open: 4701 S. Main St., 61102. Phone: (815) 964-9336. Fax: (815) 964-9318.E-mail: fred@wfen.org Web Site:www.wfen.org Licensee: Faith Center (acq 10-2-91;10-28-91). Format: Contemp Christian, praise & worship. Target aud: 35-54. Spec prog: Sp one hr wkly. ◆Fred Tscholl, gen mgr.

WGFB(FM)—See Rockton

WLUV(AM)—See Loves Park

WNIJ(FM)—See De Kalb

*WNIU(FM)— Apr 28, 1991: 90.5 mhz; 50 kw. 367 ft TL: N42 00 55 W89 00 07. Stereo. Hrs open: 24 NIU Broadcast Ctr., 801 N. First St., DeKalb, 60115. Phone: (815) 753-9000. Phone: 641-8000. Fax: (815) 753-9938.E-mail: npr@niu.edu Web Site:www.northernpublicradio.org Licensee: Northern Illinois University. Population served: 500,000 Natl. Network: PRI, NPR, . Arter & Hadden. Format: Classical. News staff: 2; News: 52 hrs wkly. Target aud: General. Spec prog: New age 2 hrs, blues 4 hrs wkly. ◆Tim Emmons, gen mgr; Jan Kilgard, dev dir; Bill Drake, progmg dir; Susan Stephens, news dir; Jeff Glass, chief of engrg.

WNTA(AM)— Dec 24, 1953: 1330 khz; 1 kw-D, 91 w-N, DA-2. TL: N42 13 32 W89 02 47. Hrs open: 24 2830 Sandy Hollow Rd., 61109. Secondary address: 2830 Sandy Hollow Rd. 61109. Phone: (815) 874-7861. Fax: (815) 874-2202.E-mail: wnta@wnta.com Web Site:www.wnta.com Licensee: Maverick Media of Rockford License LLC. Group owner: RadioWorks Inc. (acq 4-27-2005; grpsl). Population served: 280,000 Shaw Pittman. Format: MOR, news, talk. News staff: 2; News: 2 hrs wkly. Target aud: 35 plus. Spec prog: Gospel 20 hrs wkly. ◆Gary Rozynek, pres; Jay Chapman, gen mgr; Ken DeCoster, progmg dir, news dir & chief of engrg.

WQFL(FM)— May 2, 1974: 100.9 mhz; 2.7 kw. Ant 489 ft TL: N42 19 20 W89 00 41. Stereo. Hrs open: 24 Box 2730, 61132-2730. Secondary address: 5375 Pebble Creek Tr., Loves Park 61111. Phone: (815) 654-1200. Fax: (815) 282-7779.E-mail: positive@101qfl.com Web Site:www.101qfl.com Licensee: Educational Media Foundation. (acq 8-19-2009; $2 million with WGSL(FM) Loves Park). Population served: 200,000 Davis Wright Tremaine LLP. Format: Christian pop. News staff: one; News: one hr wkly. Target aud: 25-44; female dominant, educated, upscale & middle class. ◆Ralph Trentadue, gen mgr; Rick Hall, progmg dir.

WROK(AM)— 1923: 1440 khz; 5 kw-D, 270 w-N, DA-D. TL: N42 16 50 W89 02 16. Stereo. Hrs open: 3901 Brendenwood Rd., 61107. Phone: (815) 399-2233. Fax: (815) 399-8148. Web Site:www.cumulus.com Licensee: Cumulus Licensing Corp. Group owner: Cumulus Media Inc. (acq 10-2-00; grpsl). Population served: 150,000 Natl. Rep: McGavren Guild,. Wiley, Rein & Fielding. Format: News/talk. Target aud: 35 plus. ◆Mary Gerard, rgnl sls mgr; Erika Mohr, prom dir; Jesse Garcia, progmg dir; Kelly Dukes, chief of engrg; Jan Thorpe, traf mgr.

WRTB(FM)—See Winnebago

WXRX(FM)—See Belvidere

WZOK(FM)— 1949: 97.5 mhz; 50 kw. 235 ft TL: N42 16 50 W89 02 16. (CP: Ant 429 ft.). Stereo. Hrs open: Prog sep from AM 3901 Brendenwood Rd., 61107. Phone: (815) 399-2233. Fax: (815) 399-8148. Web Site:www.97zok.com Format: CHR. Target aud: 25-34. ◆J.J. Morgan, progmg dir.

Rockton

WGFB(FM)— March 1963: 103.1 mhz; 1.2 kw. 525 ft TL: N42 22 02 W89 05 13. Stereo. Hrs open: 24 2830 Sandy Hollow Rd., Rockford, 61109. Phone: (815) 874-7861. Fax: (815) 874-2202. Web Site:www.B103fm.com Licensee: Maverick Media of Rockford License LLC. Group owner: RadioWorks Inc. (acq 4-27-2005; grpsl). Population served: 400000 Natl. Rep: Katz Radio,. Shaw Pittman. Format: Adult contemp. Target aud: 25-54; adult women. ◆Gary Rozynek, pres; Jay Chapman, gen mgr; Michelle Markhan, prom dir; Jim Stone, progmg dir; Ken DeCoster, news dir; Chuck Ingle, chief of engrg.

Rosemont

*WTZI(FM)—Not on air, target date: unknown: 88.1 mhz; 295 w. Ant 112 ft TL: N41 57 20 W87 52 02. Hrs open: 1039 Mohegan Ln., Schaumburg, 60193. Phone: (847) 524-4619.E-mail: ccelkgrove@yahoo.com Licensee: Calvary Chapel of Elk Grove Village. ◆Philipp F. Ballmaier, pres.

Rushville

WKXQ(FM)— May 1, 1985: 92.5 mhz; 6 kw. Ant 328 ft TL: N40 08 20 W90 39 26. Stereo. Hrs open: 5 AM-midnight 119 W. Carroll St., Macomb, 61455. Phone: (815) 758-8686. Fax: (309) 833-3460.E-mail: wkxq92@frontiernet.net Web Site:www.radiomacomb.com Licensee: WPW Broadcasting Inc. (group owner; (acq 12-6-99; $550,000 with WPWQ(FM) Mount Sterling). Population served: 50,000 Natl. Network: CNN Radio, . Reddy, Begley & McCormick. Format: Oldies. News staff: one; News: 12 hrs wkly. Target aud: 18-54. Spec prog: Relg 6 hrs, farm 6 hrs wkly. ◆Don Davis, pres; Vanessa Wetterling, gen mgr; Michael Weaver, progmg dir.

Saint Anne

WXNU(FM)— 2006: 106.5 mhz; 1.95 kw. Ant 462 ft TL: N41 00 20 W87 41 42. Hrs open: 329 Maine St, Quincy, 62301. Phone: (815) 935-9555. Fax: (815) 935-9593.E-mail: wlan@starradio.com Web Site:www.wxnu.com Licensee: STARadio Corp. Format: Country. ◆Bob Kersmarki, gen mgr; Brendan Michaels, opns mgr; Larry Regnier, gen sls mgr; Phil Reilly, chief of engrg.

Saint Joseph

*WGNJ(FM)— 1999: 89.3 mhz; 50 kw. Ant 351 ft TL: N40 05 16 W87 53 42. Stereo. Hrs open: 24 Box 550, Fisher, 61843. Secondary address: 2421 N. 1450 E. Rd., White Heath 61884. Phone: (217)897-6333.E-mail: staff@greatnewsradio.org Web Site:www.greatnewsradio.org Licensee: Good News Radio Inc. Population served: 1,000,000 Natl. Network: Salem Radio Network, . Format: Christian, religious, talk. Target aud: 35 plus; general. ◆David Herriott, chmn; Mark Burns, pres & gen mgr; Carrie Burns, opns dir.

Salem

WJBD(AM)— Dec 16, 1956: 1350 khz; 430 w-D, 60 w-N. TL: N38 37 56 W88 55 02. Hrs open: 24 Box 70, 310 W. McMackin St., 62881. Secondary address: 221 E. Broadway, Suite 107, Centralia 62801. Phone: (618) 548-2000. Phone: (618) 532-9600. Fax: (618) 548-2079.E-mail: wjbd@accessus.net Licensee: NRG License Sub. LLC. (group owner; (acq 10-31-2005; grpsl). Population served: 24,000 Format: Country. News staff: 3; News: 30 hrs wkly. Target aud: General. Spec prog: Farm 4 hrs, relg 6 hrs wkly. ◆Bruce Kropp, gen mgr, opns VP, sls VP, progmg dir & news dir.

WJBD-FM— June 1, 1972: 100.1 mhz; 1.5 kw. Ant 450 ft TL: N38 33 45 W88 59 57. Stereo. Hrs open: 24 Box 70, 62881. Secondary address: 310 W. McMackin St. 62881. Phone: (618) 548-2000. Phone: (618) 532-9600. Fax: (618) 548-2079.E-mail: wjbd@accessus.net Licensee: NRG License Sub. LLC. Format: Adult contemp, news. ◆Matt Tackett, opns mgr.

*WSLE(FM)— 2005: 91.3 mhz; 900 w. Ant 154 ft TL: N38 37 34 W88 56 41. Hrs open: Drawer 3206, Tupelo, MS, 38803. Phone: (662) 844-8888. Fax: (662) 842-6791. Licensee: American Family Association. Group owner: American Family Radio. Format: Christian. ◆Marvin Sanders, gen mgr; John Riley, progmg dir.

Sandwich

WAUR(AM)—Licensed to Sandwich. See Aurora

Savanna

WCCI(FM)— Nov 7, 1971: 100.3 mhz; 25 kw. 450 ft TL: N42 07 49 W90 08 24. Stereo. Hrs open: 24 Box 310, 316 Main, 61074. Phone: (815) 273-7757. Fax: (815) 273-2760.E-mail: radio@wccilive.com Web Site:www.wcciradio.com Licensee: Carroll County Communications Inc. (acq 9-1-76). Population served: 188,700 Natl. Network: Fox News Radio, . Rgnl. Network: Brownfield. Brownfield Lauren A. Colby. Format: New hit country, news. News staff: one; News: 35 hrs wkly. Target aud: 25-54. ◆John L. Miller, pres, gen mgr; Edward F. Bock, VP; Brian Reusch, stn mgr; Leslie Smith, progmg dir; Mark Schoening, news dir.

Seneca

WJDK-FM— 1993: 95.7 mhz; 3 kw. 328 ft TL: N41 13 12 W88 32 27. Stereo. Hrs open: 219 W. Washington St., Morris, 60450. Phone: (815) 941-1000. Fax: (815) 941-9300. Licensee: Grundy County Broadcasters Inc. (acq 4-20-98). Population served: 49,000 Natl. Network: ABC, . Format: Adult contemp. News staff: one; News: 14 hrs wkly. Target aud: 25-49. ◆Larry Nelson, pres; Jack Daly, gen mgr; Mike Williams, opns mgr.

Shelbyville

WEJT(FM)— Dec 31, 1969: 105.1 mhz; 13 kw. 459 ft TL: N39 35 39 W88 50 44. Stereo. Hrs open: 410 N. Water, Suite C, Decatur, 62523. Phone: (217) 428-4487. Fax: (217) 428-4501.E-mail: cbullock@cromwellradio.com Web Site:www.wejt.com Licensee: Cromwell Group Inc. of Illinois. Group owner: The Cromwell Group Inc. (acq 8-1-89; $320,000 with co-located AM; 7-31-89). Population served: 250,000 Pepper & Corazzini. Format: Classic hits. Target aud: 25-54; baby boomers. ◆Chris Bullock, gen mgr; Wayne Robbins, opns mgr; Tara Nickerson, progmg dir; Jerry Scott, chief of engrg.

WINU(AM)— Nov 24, 1972: 870 khz; 500 w-D, DA. TL: N39 29 14 W88 57 31. Hrs open: 4:30 AM-7:30 PM 126 W. Main St., 62565. Phone: (217) 774-5277. Fax: (217) 774-5280. Web Site:www.hereshelpnet.org Licensee: New Life Evangelistic Center Inc. (acq 7-31-98; $75,000). Population served: 60,000 Format: Christian. Target aud: 25-54. ◆Gary Scott, gen mgr.

Sherman

WABZ(FM)— May 10, 1971: 93.9 mhz; 15 kw. Ant 430 ft TL: N39 59 25 W89 30 46. Hrs open: 3501 E. Sangamon Ave., Springfield, 62707. Phone: (217) 753-5400 (business). Fax: (217) 753-7902.E-mail: info@wabz.com Licensee: Saga Communications of Illinois LLC. Group owner: Saga Communications Inc. (acq 7-96; grpsl). Population served: 15,000 Format: Continuous soft favorities. Target aud: 25-54. ◆Leanne Arndt, gen mgr; Brandy Moore, prom dir; Bob Parrish, progmg dir; Michelle Eecles, news dir.

Skokie

WTMX(FM)— Aug 18, 1961: 101.9 mhz; 4.2 kw. 1,561 ft TL: N41 52 44 W87 38 10. Stereo. Hrs open: 24 One Prudential Plaza, Suite 2700, Chicago, 60601. Phone: (312) 946-1019. Fax: (312) 946-4747.E-mail: info@wtmx.com Web Site:www.wtmx.com Licensee: Bonneville International Corp. (group owner; (acq 8-70). Population served: 600,000 Natl. Rep: Katz Radio,. Format: Adult contemp. News staff: one. ◆Drew Horowitz, pres, gen mgr; Barry James, stn mgr; Jessy Ferdman, prom dir; Mary Ellen Kachinske, progmg VP & progmg dir; Barry Keefe, news dir, pub affrs dir; Kent Lewin, chief of engrg.

Smithboro

*WTMH(FM)—Not on air, target date: unknown: 89.9 mhz; 10 kw. Ant 164 ft TL: N38 56 09 W89 13 56. Hrs open: 5210 S.E. Washington Blvd., Bartlesville, OK, 74006. Phone: (918) 333-8700. Fax: (918) 333-3526. Licensee: Pearl Communications Group. ◆Danny Hester, pres.

South Beloit

WTJK(AM)—Licensed to South Beloit. See Beloit WI

South Elgin

*WSEH(FM)—Not on air, target date: unknown: 88.5 mhz; 670 w. Ant 148 ft TL: N41 57 55 W88 22 58. Hrs open: 335 Locust St., Elgin, 60123. Phone: (847) 741-7535. Fax: (847) 695-4682. Licensee: St. Edward Central Catholic High School. Natl. Network: EWTN Radio, . ◆Thomas Doran, pres.

South Jacksonville

WJVO(FM)—Licensed to South Jacksonville. See Jacksonville

Sparta

WHCO(AM)— February 1955: 1230 khz; 1 kw-U. TL: N38 07 25 W89 43 20. Hrs open: 24 Box 255, 1230 W. Broadway, 62286. Secondary

address: 47 W. Maine, Mascoutah 62258. Phone: (618) 443-2121. Fax: (618) 443-2800.E-mail: Hoefft@Egyptian.Net Licensee: Hirsch Communication Engineering Co. Population served: 150,000 Natl. Network: CBS, Westwood One, . Rgnl. Network: Brownfield. Ill. Radio Net. Format: News/talk, sports. News staff: 2; News: 10 hrs wkly. Target aud: 25-65. Spec prog: Pol 2 hrs, farm 20 hrs, relg 10 hrs wkly. ♦Jack L. Scheper Sr., pres, gen mgr; Mike Hoeft, news dir.

Spring Valley

WIVQ(FM)— December 1993: 103.3 mhz; 4.9 kw. 361 ft TL: N41 18 09 W89 14 11. Hrs open: 24
Rebroadcasts WSTQ 100%.
3905 Progress Blvd., Peru, 61354. Phone: (815) 224-2100. Fax: (815) 224-2066.E-mail: q@theradiogroup.net Web Site:qhitmusic.com Licensee: Mendota Broadcasting Inc. Group owner: Studstill Broadcasting (acq 7-17-97; $700,000 with WBZG(FM) Peru). Population served: 130,000 Natl. Rep: Rgnl Reps,. Booth, Freret, Imlay & Tepper. Wire Svc: AP Format: Top-40, adult contemp. News staff: 2. Target aud: 18-44. ♦Lamar Studstill, chmn; Cole Charles Studstill, CFO; Owen L. Studstill, CEO, pres & gen mgr; Cole Studstill, stn mgr, opns mgr.

***WSOG(FM)**— 12/2002: 88.1 mhz; 4 kw vert. Ant 262 ft TL: N41 17 32 W89 07 59. Hrs open: 24 Box 34, 61362. Phone: (815) 220-1929. Fax: (815) 220-1929.E-mail: wsog881@hotmail.com Licensee: Spirit Education Association Inc. ♦Louis J. Perona, pres.

Springfield

WCVS-FM—(Virden, May 10, 1982: 96.7 mhz; 6 kw. Ant 328 ft TL: N39 38 26 W89 39 24. Stereo. Hrs open: 24 3055 S. 4th St., 62703. Phone: (217) 528-3033. Fax: (217) 528-5348.E-mail: wcvs@wcvs.com Web Site:www.wcvs.com Licensee: Neuhoff Family L.P. Group owner: Clear Channel Communications Inc. (acq 8-1-2007; grpsl). Population served: 400,000 Natl. Rep: Christal,. Wiley, Rein & Fielding LLP. Format: Modern rock. News staff: one. Target aud: 18-49; m/p. ♦Danielle Outlaw, sls dir; Kevin O'Dea, gen sls mgr; Michelle Mitchell, prom dir; Jeremy Anderson, progmg dir; Jeff Hofmann, news dir; Frank Konwinski, chief of engrg.

WDBR(FM)— April 1948: 103.7 mhz; 50 kw. 320 ft TL: N39 47 36 W89 36 18. (CP: 20 kw, ant 768 ft.). Hrs open: Prog sep from AM 3501 E. Sangamon Ave., 62707. Phone: (217) 753-5400. Fax: (217) 753-7902.E-mail: info@wdbr.com Web Site:www.wdbr.com Population served: 301,500 Wire Svc: UPI Format: CHR. Target aud: 18-49; general.

WFMB(AM)— 1922: 1450 khz; 1 kw-U. TL: N39 45 36 W89 39 05. Hrs open: 24 3055 S. 4th St., 62703. Phone: (217) 528-3033. Phone: (217) 544-9855. Fax: (217) 528-5348.E-mail: sportsradio1450@sportsradio1450.com Web Site:www.sportsradio1450.com Licensee: Neuhoff Family L.P. Group owner: Clear Channel Communications Inc. (acq 8-1-2007; grpsl). Population served: 161,000 Natl. Network: ABC, ESPN Radio, . Natl. Rep: Christal,. Brownfield Format: Sports/personality. News staff: 2; News: 5 hrs wkly. Target aud: 25-54; upscale professionals. ♦Kevin O'Dea, gen mgr; Danielle Outlaw, sls dir; John Price, progmg dir; Jeff Hofmann, news dir; Frank Konwinski, chief of engrg.

WFMB-FM— July 1965: 104.5 mhz; 43 kw. 465 ft TL: N39 45 36 W89 39 05. Stereo. Hrs open: 24 3055 S. 4th St., 62703. Phone: (217) 528-3033. Phone: (217) 544-9855. Fax: (217) 528-5348.E-mail: wfmb@wfmb.com Web Site:www.wfmb.com Population served: 300,000 Natl. Network: Motor Racing Net, . Natl. Rep: Christal,. Format: Country. News staff: one. Target aud: A 25-54. ♦Kevin O'Dea, VP; Danielle Outlaw, sls dir; Michele Mitchell, prom dir; Dave Marsh, progmg dir; John Spalding, mus dir; Frank Konwinski, chief of engrg.

***WLUJ(FM)**— May 24, 1995: 89.7 mhz; 20 kw. 328 ft TL: N39 48 30 W89 37 30. (CP: 10 kw). Stereo. Hrs open: 600 W. Mason St., 62702. Phone: (217) 528-2300. Fax: (217) 528-2400.E-mail: wluj897@ameritech.net Web Site:www.wluj.org Licensee: Cornerstone Community Radio Inc. Population served: 300,000 Natl. Network: Moody, . Format: Christian talk. Target aud: General. ♦Arthur Gregg, sr VP; Dick Reed, VP; Richard Van Zandt, pres & gen mgr; John McBride, stn mgr; Howard Fouks, opns mgr; Richard Beaman, gen sls mgr.

WMAY(AM)— Oct 15, 1950: 970 khz; 1 kw-D, 500 w-N, DA-2. TL: N39 51 42 W89 32 32. Stereo. Hrs open: Box 460, 62705. Secondary address: 1510 N. Third, Riverton 62561. Phone: (217) 629-7077. Fax: (217) 629-7952.E-mail: wmay@wmay.com Web Site:www.wmay.com Licensee: Long Nine Inc. Group owner: The Mid-West Family Broadcast Group (acq 12-7-76). Population served: 350,000 Natl. Rep: D & R Radio,. Fisher, Wayland, Cooper, Leader & Zaragoza. Format: News/talk. Target aud: 25-64. Spec prog: Big band 5 hrs wkly. ♦Kevan Kavanough, gen mgr; Dave Doetsch, sls VP; Amanda Johnson, prom dir; Robb Rose, progmg dir; Jim Leach, news dir; Greg Stephens, chief of engrg.

WNNS(FM)— Nov 1, 1980: 98.7 mhz; 50 kw. 500 ft TL: N39 41 59 W89 46 55. Stereo. Hrs open: Prog sep from AM 1510 N. third, Riverton, 62561. Phone: (217) 629-7077. Fax: (217) 629-7952.E-mail: wnns@wnns.com Web Site:www.wnns.com Licensee: Long Nine Inc. Population served: 300,000 Format: Adult contemp. Spec prog: Jazz 6 hrs wkly. ♦Kavan Kavanough, gen mgr, progmg dir; Kellie Michaels, pub affrs dir; Greg Stephens, engrg dir.

***WQNA(FM)**— Aug 31, 1979: 88.3 mhz; 250 w. Ant 256 ft TL: N39 44 03 W89 38 18. Stereo. Hrs open: 24 Capital Area Career Ctr., 2201 Toronto Rd., 62712. Phone: (217) 529-5431. Fax: (217) 529-7861.E-mail: info@wqna.org Web Site:www.wqna.org Licensee: Capital Area Career Center. Population served: 300,000 Rgnl rep: Illinois Student News Network Shaw Pittman. Format: Div. News staff: one; News: 6 hrs wkly. Target aud: 13-24; student, community, high school & college students. Spec prog: Varied. ♦Jim Grimes, gen mgr, news dir; Jim Pemberton, progmg dir; Kerri Donovan, engr.

WQQL(FM)— Nov 15, 1993: 101.9 mhz; 50 kw. 300 ft TL: N39 42 39 W89 38 42. Stereo. Hrs open: 24 3501 E. Sangamon Ave., 62707. Phone: (217) 753-5400. Fax: (217) 753-7902.E-mail: info@cool1019.com Web Site:www.cool1019.com Licensee: Saga Communications of Illinois LLC. Group owner: Saga Communications Inc. (acq 9-10-93; $1.44 million;10-4-93). Population served: 2,000,000 Natl. Rep: Katz Radio,. Smithwick & Belendiuk. Format: Oldies. News: 2 hrs wkly. Target aud: 25 plus; upscale educated adults. ♦Leanne Arndt, gen mgr; Kevin Anfield, gen sls mgr, prom dir.

***WSCT(FM)**— November 1993: 90.5 mhz; 3.8 kw. Ant 410 ft TL: N39 38 38 W89 30 51. Stereo. Hrs open: 24
Rebroadcasts WIBI(FM) Carlinville 100%.
Box 140, Carlinville, 62626. Phone: (217) 854-4800. Fax: (217) 854-4810.E-mail: wibi@wibi.org Web Site:www.wibi.org Licensee: Illinois Bible Institute. Population served: 150,000 Format: Christian. News: 5 hrs wkly. Target aud: 25-44; Christian & seeking non-Christians. ♦Reverend Larry Griswold, pres; Barry Copeland, gen mgr; Jeremiah Beck, stn mgr, opns dir; Jessica Barton, mktg dir, prom dir; Joe Buchanan, mus dir; Sally Braundmeier, chief of engrg & traf mgr.

WTAX(AM)— 1930: 1240 khz; 1 kw-U. TL: N39 47 36 W89 36 18. Hrs open: 3501 E. Sangamon Ave., 62707. Phone: (217) 753-5400. Fax: (217) 753-7902.E-mail: info@wtax.com Web Site:www.wtax.com Licensee: Saga Communications of Illinois LLC. Group owner: Saga Communications Inc. (acq 1996). Population served: 91,753 Natl. Network: Moody, CBS, . Natl. Rep: Christal,. Wire Svc: UPI Format: News/talk, sports. News staff: 3; News: 20, hrs wkly. Target aud: 30 plus. Spec prog: Farm 16 hrs wkly. ♦Leanne Arndt, gen mgr; Michelle Eccles, news dir.

***WUIS(FM)**— Jan 3, 1975: 91.9 mhz; 50 kw. 524 ft TL: N39 47 00 W89 26 46. Stereo. Hrs open: 24
Rebroadcasts WIPA(FM) Pittsfield 100%.
Box 19243, CBM-130, Univ. of Illinois at Springfield, 62794-9243. Secondary address: One University Plaza, MS CBM-130 62703. Phone: (217) 206-6516. Fax: (217) 206-6527.E-mail: wuis@uis.edu Web Site:www.wuis.org Licensee: University of Illinois at Springfield. Population served: 149,600 Natl. Network: NPR, PRI, . Rgnl. Network: Ill. Radio Net. Dow, Lohnes & Albertson. Format: News, class, jazz. News staff: 4; News: 45 hrs wkly. Target aud: 25-54. Spec prog: NPR entertainment 15 hrs, bluegrass 2 hrs, Singer/Songwriter 2 hrs, ambient 2 hrs wkly. ♦Bill Wheelhouse, gen mgr; Sinta Seiber, opns mgr; Lisa Clemmons-Stott, dev dir; Karl Scroggin, mus dir.

WYMG(FM)—(Jacksonville, March 1948: 100.5 mhz; 50 kw. 500 ft TL: N39 39 40 W89 55 18. Stereo. Hrs open: 3501 E. Sangamon Ave., 62707. Phone: (217) 753-5400. Fax: (217) 753-7902.E-mail: wymg@wymg.com Web Site:www.wymg.com Licensee: Saga Communications of Illinois LLC. Group owner: Saga Communications Inc. (acq 10-1-86). Population served: 500,000 Format: Classic rock. Target aud: 18-49. Spec prog: Jazz 2 hrs, comedy one hr wkly. ♦Leanne Arndt, gen mgr; Jane Cochran, progmg.

Staunton

WAOX(FM)— December 1, 1999: 105.3 mhz; 6 kw. Ant 285 ft TL: N39 02 37 W89 44 56. Stereo. Hrs open: 24 Box 10, Litchfield, 62056. Phone: (217) 532-2085. Fax: (217) 532-2431.E-mail: waox@theox1053.com Web Site:www.waox.com Licensee: Talley Broadcasting Corp. Group owner: Talley Radio Stations Natl. Network: ABC, . Natl. Rep: Christal,. Rgnl rep: Regional Reps Wire Svc: AP Format: Adult contemp. News staff: 2. Target aud: 18-54. ♦Hayward L. Talley, pres & gen mgr; Brian Talley, opns VP; Beth Niehaus, traf mgr.

Sterling

***WNIQ(FM)**— unknown: 91.5 mhz; 2.1 kw. 331 ft TL: N41 53 12 W89 35 43. Stereo. Hrs open: 24
Rebroadcasts WNIJ(FM) De Kalb & WNIU(FM) Rockford 50%.
NIU Broadcast Ctr., 801 N. First St., DeKalb, 60115. Phone: (815) 753-9000. Fax: (815) 753-9938.E-mail: npr@niu.edu Web Site:www.northernpublicradio.org Licensee: Northern Illinois University. Population served: 70,000 Natl. Network: PRI, NPR, . Arter & Hadden. Format: News/talk, class. News: 2 hrs wkly. Target aud: General. ♦Tim Emmons, gen mgr; Jan Kilgard, dev dir; Bill Drake, progmg dir.

WSDR(AM)— Aug 21, 1949: 1240 khz; 500 w-D, 1 kw-N. TL: N41 48 59 W89 40 13. Hrs open: 24 3101 Freeport Rd., 61081. Phone: (815) 625-3400. Fax: (815) 625-6940.E-mail: wsdr1240@theramp.net Licensee: Withers Broadcasting Co. of Rock River LLC. Group owner: Withers Broadcasting Co. (acq 1-21-98; grpsl). Population served: 165,000 Natl. Network: CBS, ABC, . Rgnl. Network: Ill. Radio Net. Natl. Rep: Christal,. Ill. Radio Net. Format: News, sports, talk. News staff: 2; News: 10 hrs wkly. Target aud: 25 plus. Spec prog: Farm 16 hrs, Sp 4 hrs wkly. ♦Brian Zschiesche, gen mgr; Sherry Smith, gen sls mgr; Lisa Taylor, progmg dir.

WSSQ(FM)— August 1966: 94.3 mhz; 6 kw. 309 ft TL: N41 51 06 W89 42 38. Stereo. Hrs open: Prog sep from AM 3101 Freeport Rd., 61081. Phone: (815) 625-3400. Fax: (815) 625-6940.E-mail: wsdr1240@theramp.net Population served: 190,000 Natl. Network: Westwood One, ABC, . Natl. Rep: Christal,. Format: Adult contemp. Target aud: 25-54; women.

Streator

WSPL(AM)— Sept 26, 1953: 1250 khz; 500 w-D, 100 w-N, DA-D. TL: N41 09 30 W88 50 13. Hrs open: 24 3905 Progress Blvd., Peru, 61354. Phone: (815) 672-2947. Fax: (815) 673-1833.E-mail: wspl@theradiogroup.net Web Site:am1250wspl.com Licensee: Mendota Broadcasting Inc. Group owner: Studstill Broadcasting (acq 5-30-2000; grpsl). Population served: 110,000 Format: News/talk, sports. News staff: 3; News: 25 hrs wkly. Target aud: 35 plus. ♦Lamar Studstill, chmn; Owen L. Studstill, pres; Cole Studstill, VP, opns mgr; Lee Studstill, gen mgr; Cheryl Knirlberger, sls dir; Dave Noesen, news dir; Mark Baker, chief of engrg.

WSTQ(FM)— Sept 15, 1964: 97.7 mhz; 6 kw. Ant 328 ft TL: N41 10 49 W88 52 06. Stereo. Hrs open: 24 Prog sep from AM 3905 Progress Blvd., Peru, 61354. Phone: (815) 224-2100. Fax: (815) 224-2066.E-mail: q@theradiogroup.net Web Site:qhitmusic.com Population served: 130,000 Format: CHR. Target aud: 18-44. ♦Cole Studstill, progmg dir.

WYYS(FM)— 1995: 106.1 mhz; 6 kw. Ant 292 ft TL: N41 10 49 W88 52 06. (CP: 2.45 kw, ant 520 ft. TL: N41 16 30 W88 57 56). Hrs open: 24 3905 Progess Blvd., Peru, 61354. Phone: (815) 224-2100. Fax: (815) 224-2066.E-mail: wyys@theradiogroup.net Licensee: Mendota Broadcasting Inc. Group owner: Studstill Broadcasting (acq 3-8-2000; grpsl). Population served: 130,000 Natl. Network: ABC, . Format: Oldies. News staff: 2. Target aud: 35 plus. ♦Lamar Studstill, chmn; Cole Studstill, CFO; Lee Studstill, pres & gen mgr.

Sugar Grove

***WSRI(FM)**— 2005: 88.7 mhz; 600 w. Ant 338 ft TL: N41 42 16 W88 26 02. Hrs open: 24
Rebroadcasts KLRD(FM) Yucaipa, CA 100%.
2351 Sunset Blvd., Suite170-218, Rocklin, CA, 95765. Phone: (916) 251-1600. Fax: (916) 251-1650. Web Site:www.air1.com Licensee: Educational Media Foundation. Group owner: EMF Broadcasting. Population served: 176,000 Natl. Network: Air 1, . Shaw Pittman. Format: Christian. Target aud: 25-44; female-Judeo/ Christian. ♦Richard Jenkins, pres; Mike Novak, VP; Lloyd Parker, gen mgr; Ed Lenane, opns dir, news dir; Keith Whipple, dev dir; David Pierce, progmg mgr; Sam Wallington, engrg dir; Karen Johnson, news rptr.

Sullivan

WZNX(FM)— April 1992: 106.7 mhz; 9.5 kw. 550 ft TL: N39 36 38 W88 41 32. Stereo. Hrs open: 24 410 N. Water St., Suite B, Decatur, 62523. Phone: (217) 428-4487. Fax: (217) 428-4501.E-mail: cbullock@cromwellradio.com Web Site:www.1067thefox.com Licensee: WSHY Inc. Group owner: The Cromwell Group Inc. (acq 2-14-97; $750,000). Population served: 300000 Natl. Rep: Eastman Radio,. Format: Classic rock. News staff: one; News: 24/7. Target aud: 25-54; strong men. ♦Chris Bullock, gen mgr, opns dir; Tara Nickerson, opns dir; Storm, progmg dir.

Summit

***WARG(FM)**— January 1976: 88.9 mhz; 500 w. 98 ft TL: N41 46 36 W87 48 17. Stereo. Hrs open: 8 AM-10 PM 7329 W. 63rd St., 60501. Phone: (708) 728-8368. Fax: (708) 728-3155.E-mail: info@warg.com

Licensee: Community High School District No. 217. Format: Alternative, rock. Target aud: High School Students; alternative subculture.

Sycamore

WCPY(FM)—See De Kalb

WLBK(AM)—See De Kalb

WSQR(AM)— June 11, 1981: 1180 khz; 900 w-D, 1 w-N. TL: N42 00 24 W88 40 40. Hrs open: 1 Broadcast Center, Plano, 60545. Phone: (630) 552-1000. Fax: (630) 552-9300.E-mail: wspy-news@nelsonmultimedia.net Licensee: De kalb County Broadcasters Inc. (acq 9-94). Natl. Network: ABC, . Format: Adult Standards. Target aud: 35-55. Spec prog: Farm 6 hrs wkly. ♦Larry Nelson, pres; Pam Nelson, CFO, gen mgr; Beth Pierre, gen mgr, sls VP; Vori Dhabolt, gen sls mgr.

Taylorville

***WIHM(AM)**— 1952: 1410 khz; 1 kw-D, 63 w-N, DA-1. TL: N39 32 38 W89 16 36. Hrs open: 3515 Hampton Ave., St. Louis, MO, 63139. Phone: (314) 752-7000.E-mail: office@covenantnet.net Web Site:www.covenantnet.net Licensee: Covenant Network (acq 7-31-98; $60,000). Population served: 30,000 Format: Christian; Religious; inspirtional. ♦Tony Holman, pres & gen mgr.

WQLZ(FM)— December 1967: 92.7 mhz; 11.5 kw. 482 ft TL: N39 38 38 W89 30 51. Stereo. Hrs open: 24 Box 460, Springfield, 62705. Secondary address: 1510 N. Third, Riverton 62561. Phone: (217) 629-7077. Fax: (217) 629-7952.E-mail: wqlz@wqlz.com Web Site:www.wqlz.com Licensee: Long Nine Inc. Group owner: Mid-West Family Stations (acq 2-3-93; $1 million; 2-22-93). Population served: 30,000 Davis Wright Tremaine LLP. Format: AOR. News staff: 4; News: 3 hrs wkly. Target aud: 18-34. ♦Kevan Kavanaugh, gen mgr; Dave Duetsch, gen sls mgr; Susan Groves, progmg dir; Jim Leach, news dir; Greg Stephens, chief of engrg; Quinn Fagg, traf mgr.

WTIM-FM— Nov 13, 1997: 97.3 mhz; 4.6 kw. Ant 374 ft TL: N39 27 08 W89 17 10. Hrs open: 24 Box 169, 62568-0169. Secondary address: 918 E. Park St. 62568. Phone: (217) 824-3395. Fax: (217) 824-3301. Web Site:www.randyradio.com Licensee: Miller Communications Inc. Group owner: Miller Media Group Population served: 197,000 Natl. Network: CNN Radio, . Natl. Rep: Commercial Media Sales,. Womble, Carlyle, Sandridge & Rice. Format: News/talk. News staff: one; News: 25 hrs wkly. Target aud: 25 plus. Spec prog: Farm 20 hrs, relg 4 hrs wkly. ♦Randal J. Miller, pres; Kami Payne, gen mgr; Brandon Fellows, progmg dir; Steve Butera, news rptr.

Teutopolis

WKJT(FM)— 1994: 102.3 mhz; 6 kw. 328 ft TL: N39 08 30 W88 33 36. Hrs open: 24 206 S. Willow, Effingham, 62401. Phone: (217) 347-5518. Fax: (217) 347-5519.E-mail: info@kjcountry.com Web Site:www.kjcountry.com Licensee: Kirby Broadcasting Inc. Natl. Network: Fox News Radio, . Format: Country. ♦John W. Kirby, pres; Greg Sapp, stn mgr, news dir; Tonya Siner, opns VP; George Flexter, progmg dir.

Tower Hill

WRAN(FM)— Nov 25, 1997: 98.3 mhz; 3.7 kw. 420 ft TL: N39 16 48 W88 58 22. Stereo. Hrs open: 24 918 E. Park, Box 169, Taylorville, 62568. Phone: (217) 824-3395. Fax: (217) 824-3301. Web Site:www. randyradio.com Licensee: Kaskaskia Broadcasting Inc. Group owner: Miller Media Group Population served: 197,000 Natl. Network: CBS, . Natl. Rep: Commercial Media Sales,. Womble, Carlyle, Sandridge & Rice. Format: Soft adult contemp music. News staff: one; News: 25 hrs wkly. Target aud: 35—64. Spec prog: Farm 6 hrs, relg 3 hrs wkly. ♦Randal J. Miller, pres; Kami Payne, gen mgr; Brandon Fellows, progmg dir; Steve Butera, news rptr.

Tuscola

WEBX(FM)—Licensed to Tuscola. See Champaign

Urbana

WBCP(AM)— 1948: 1580 khz; 250 w-D, 10 w-N. TL: N40 07 32 W88 17 29. Hrs open: 904 N. 4th St., Ste D, Champaign, 61820. Phone: (217) 359-1580. Fax: (217) 359-1583.E-mail: wbcpradio@sbcglobal.net Licensee: WBCP Inc. (acq 12-89; $135,000; 12-4-89). Natl. Network: American Urban, ABC, . Format: Gospel, rhythm and blues, smooth jazz. Spec prog: "". ♦Lonnie Clark, pres; J.W. Pirtle, VP, gen mgr; Sam Britten, opns VP; Lynn Randall, progmg dir; Steve Hamm, chief of engrg.

WCFF(FM)— Dec 4, 1967: 92.5 mhz; 11.5 kw. 485 ft TL: N40 01 29 W88 08 28. Stereo. Hrs open: 24 2603 W, Bradley Ave., Champaign, 61821. Phone: (217) 352-4141. Fax: (217) 352-1256.E-mail: studio@wkio.com Web Site:www.925thechief.com Licensee: Saga Communications of Illinois LLC. Group owner: Saga Communications Inc. (acq 2000; $7 million). Population served: 469,000 Natl. Rep: Katz Radio,. Format: Oldies. Target aud: 35-64. ♦Ed Christian, CEO, chmn; Steve Goldstein, exec VP; Alan Beck, gen mgr; Jonathan Drake, opns mgr; Gary Saladino, mktg dir; Ryan Leskis, prom dir; Mike Cation, news dir; Mark Spalding, chief of engrg.

***WILL(AM)**— Mar 28, 1922: 580 khz; 5 kw-D, DA-D. TL: N40 04 53 W88 14 18. Hrs open: 24 Campbell Hall for Public Telecommunications, 300 N. Goodwin Ave., 61801-2316. Phone: (217) 333-0850. Fax: (217) 244-9586. Fax: (217) 333-7151.E-mail: willamfm@uiuc.edu Web Site:www.will.uiuc.edu Licensee: University of Illinois Board of Trustees. Population served: 158,700 Natl. Network: NPR, PRI, . Dow, Lohnes & Albertson. Wire Svc: AP Format: News/talk, div. News staff: 3; News: 115 hrs wkly. Target aud: 25-60; educated, upper middle income, professionals. Spec prog: Farm 7 hrs wkly. ♦Mark Leonard, gen mgr; Jay H. Pearce, stn mgr, progmg dir; Mike Pritchard, opns dir, dev dir; Kate Dobrovolny, prom dir; Rick Finnie, chief of engrg; Denise Perry, traf mgr; Tom Rogers, news dir & local news ed.

***WILL-FM**— Sept 1, 1941: 90.9 mhz; 105 kw. Ant 850 ft TL: N40 06 52 W88 13 27. Stereo. Hrs open: 24 Campbell Hall for Public Telecommunications, 300 N. Goodwin Ave., 61801-2316. Phone: (217) 333-0850. Fax: (217) 244-9586. Fax: (217) 333-7151. Licensee: University of Illinois Board of Trustees. Population served: 158,700 Wire Svc: AP Format: Class, var. News: 2 hrs wkly. Target aud: 35-70. ♦Jake Schumacher, progmg dir. Co-owned TV: *WILL-TV affil

WLRW(FM)—See Champaign

WPGU(FM)— Apr 17, 1967: 107.1 mhz; 3 kw. 235 ft TL: N40 06 34 W88 14 06. Stereo. Hrs open: 24 512 E. Green St., Champaign, 61820. Phone: (217) 337-3100. Fax: (217) 337-3162.E-mail: wpgu@wpgu.com Web Site:www.wpgu.com Licensee: Illini Media Co. Population served: 233,800 Fisher, Wayland, Cooper, Leader & Zaragoza. Format: Alternative Rock. News: 7 hrs wkly. Target aud: 18-34. ♦Mary Cory, gen mgr; Beth Rehn, prom dir; Becky Brothman, progmg dir; Jon Hansen, news dir; Scott S. Downs, sls dir & chief of engrg; Melissa Pasco, traf mgr.

WQQB(FM)—(Rantoul, January 1993: 96.1 mhz; 3.8 kw. 403 ft TL: N40 12 27 W88 17 56. Stereo. Hrs open: 24 4108 Fieldstone Rd., Suite C, Champaign, 61822. Phone: (217) 367-1195. Fax: (217) 367-3291. Web Site:www.wqqb.com Licensee: RadioStar Inc. Group owner: AAA Entertainment LLC (acq 5-23-2006; grpsl). Population served: 175,000 Natl. Rep: McGavren Guild,. Format: CHR. Target aud: 18-34; female. ♦Jim Glassman, CEO, pres; Roxanne Charles, gen mgr; Corey Berkemann, gen sls mgr, rgnl sls mgr; Joe McIntyre, progmg dir.

Vandalia

WKRV(FM)— May 28, 1974: 107.1 mhz; 6 kw. Ant 164 ft TL: N38 57 30 W89 07 27. Stereo. Hrs open: 24 Dups AM 5% Box 100, 62471. Secondary address: 232 S. 4th St. 62471. Phone: (618) 283-2325. Phone: (618) 283-2355. Fax: (618) 283-1503.E-mail: wkrv@sbcglobal.net Licensee: Two Petaz Inc. Wire Svc: Metro Weather Service Inc. Format: CHR, adult contemp. News staff: one; News: 10 hrs wkly. Target aud: 20-45. ♦Dan Michael, progmg dir.

WPMB(AM)— Dec 9, 1963: 1500 khz; 250 w-D. TL: N38 57 30 W89 07 27. Hrs open: 6 AM-sunset Box 100, 62471. Secondary address: 232 S. 4th St. 62471. Phone: (618) 283-2325. Phone: (618) 283-2355. Fax: (618) 283-1503.E-mail: wkrv@sbcglobal.net Licensee: Two Petaz Inc. (acq 2-3-2005; $350,000 with co-located FM). Population served: 6,300 Rgnl. Network: Tribune, Ill. Radio Net. Wire Svc: Metro Weather Service Inc. Format: Big band, adult standards. News staff: 2; News: 8-10 hrs wkly. Target aud: General. Spec prog: Farm 4 hrs, gospel 3 hrs wkly. ♦Bayard H. Walters, pres; John D. Harris, gen mgr; John Harris, gen sls mgr; Todd Stapleton, opns mgr, progmg dir & news dir.

***WVNL(FM)**— 10/7/2002: 91.7 mhz; 100 w. 164 ft Hrs open: 24 hrs WIBI, Carlinville,IL, 100%.
Box 140, Carlinville, 62626. Phone: (217) 854-4800. Fax: (217) 854-4810.E-mail: wibi@wibi.org Web Site:www.wibi.org Licensee: Illinois Bible Institute Inc. ♦Barry Copeland, gen mgr; Jeremiah Beck, stn mgr, opns dir; Jessica Barton, prom dir; Rob Regal, progmg dir; Joe Buchanan, mus dir; Sally Braundmeier, traf mgr.

Vernon Hills

WNVR(AM)— Mar 1, 1988: 1030 khz; 5 kw-D, 120 w-N, DA-N. TL: N42 15 10 W88 23 45. Hrs open: 24 3656 W. Belmont, Chicago, 60618. Phone: (773) 588-6300. Fax: (773) 267-4913.E-mail: polskieradio @polskieradio.com Web Site:www.polskieradio.com Licensee: Polnet Communications Ltd. (group owner; acq 3-15-91; $495,000;1-25-93). Population served: 10,000,000 Wiley, Rein and Fielding. Wire Svc: AP Format: Pol language. News staff: 7; News: 20 hrs wkly. Target aud: 18-54; Polish speaking audience. ♦Walter Kotaba, pres; Kamilla Dworska, gen mgr.

Virden

WCVS-FM—Licensed to Virden. See Springfield

Virginia

WVIL(FM)— February 1998: 101.3 mhz; 4 kw. 390 ft TL: N40 00 52 W90 19 55. Stereo. Hrs open: 24 Box 101, Jacksonville, 62651. Secondary address: #7 Dunlap Ct., Jacksonville 62650. Phone: (217) 245-5700. Fax: (217) 245-5701.E-mail: lbostwick@mchsi.com Web Site:www.wvilfm.com Licensee: LB Sports Productions LLC (acq 2-6-2009; $180,000). Population served: 65,000 Natl. Network: Fox Sports, . Ill. Radio Net. Wiley Rein LLP. Format: All sports. News staff: one; News: one hr wkly. Target aud: 18-65; general. ♦Larry Bostwick, gen mgr.

Warsaw

***WIUW(FM)**— May 17, 1995: 89.5 mhz; 10 kw. 449 ft TL: N40 20 44 W91 24 11. Hrs open: 24
Rebroadcasts WIUM(FM) Macomb 100%.
515 Univ. Svcs. Bldg., Western Illinois Univ., Macomb, 61455. Phone: (309) 298-2424. Phone: (309) 298-1873. Fax: (309) 298-2133.E-mail: publicradio@wiu.edu Web Site:www.tristatesradio.com Licensee: Western Illinois University. Population served: 57,326 Cohn & Marks. Format: Class, news. News staff: 2; News: 58 hrs wkly. Target aud: General. ♦Dorothy Vallillo, gen mgr; Ken Thermon, opns dir; Sharon Faust, dev dir; Rich Egger, news dir.

Watseka

WGFA(AM)— Sept 1, 1960: 1360 khz; 1 kw-D, DA. TL: N40 47 48 W87 45 11. Stereo. Hrs open: 6 AM-6 PM 1973 E. 1950 North Rd., 60970. Phone: (815) 432-4955. Fax: (815) 432-4957. Web Site:www.wgfaradio.com Licensee: Iroquois County Broadcasting Co. Population served: 60,000 Natl. Network: Salem Radio Network, . Ill. Radio Net. Format: Talk. News staff: 2; News: 14 hrs wkly. Target aud: 30-65; upscale. ♦Margaret Martin, gen mgr, mktg dir; Justin Kaiser, opns mgr, progmg VP; Stacey Smith, stn mgr & adv dir.

WGFA-FM— Mar 2, 1961: 94.1 mhz; 50 kw. Ant 364 ft TL: N40 47 37 W87 45 17. Stereo. Hrs open: 24 1973 E. 1950 North Rd., 60970. Phone: (815) 432-4955. Fax: (815) 432-4957.E-mail: 941fm@wgfaradio.com Web Site:www.wgfaradio.com Licensee: Iroquois County Broadcasting Co. Population served: 150,000 Natl. Network: ABC, . Natl. Rep: Farmakis, Katz Radio,. Borsari & Paxson. Format: Adult contemp lite music. News staff: 2; News: 12 hrs wkly. Target aud: 25-54. Spec prog: Farm 18 hrs, business 2 hrs, sports 18 hrs wkly. ♦Margaret Martin, gen mgr, dev dir, prom mgr; Justin Kaiser, opns dir, progmg dir, progmg dir, sports cmtr; M'Lissa Long, rgnl sls mgr, pub affrs dir; Carl Gerdovich, news dir; Del Dayton, chief of engrg; Stacey Smith, stn mgr, gen sls mgr, natl sls mgr & spec ev coord.

WMLF(FM)—Not on air, target date: unknown: 95.9 mhz; 6 kw. Ant 234 ft TL: N40 46 17 W87 46 13. Hrs open: 1717 Dixie Hwy., Suite 650, Fort Wright, KY, 41011. Phone: (859) 331-9100. Licensee: Radioactive LLC. ♦Benjamin L. Homel, pres.

Waukegan

WKRS(AM)— Sept 25, 1949: 1220 khz; 1 kw-D, DA. TL: N42 20 59 W87 52 53. (CP: 99 w-N). Hrs open: 24 3250 Belvidere Rd., 60085. Phone: (847) 336-7900. Fax: (847) 336-1523. Web Site:www.wkrs.com Licensee: NM Licensing LLC. Group owner: NextMedia Group LLC (acq 11-26-01; grpsl). Population served: 900,000 Format: News/talk. News staff: 4; News: 40 hrs wkly. Target aud: 25 plus. ♦Kira La Fond, gen mgr; Libby Collins, progmg dir.

WXLC(FM)— May 1963: 102.3 mhz; 3 kw. 322 ft TL: N42 20 59 W87 52 53. Stereo. Hrs open: Prog sep from AM 3250 Belvidere Rd., 60085. Phone: (847) 336-7900. Fax: (847) 336-1523. Web

Site:www.1023xlc.com Format: Adult contemp. Target aud: 25-44. ◆Rory Fraley, gen mgr; Mike Peof, gen sls mgr; Haynes Johns, progmg dir.

West Frankfort

WFRX(AM)— May 2, 1951: 1300 khz; 1 kw-D. TL: N37 53 04 W88 55 44. Hrs open: Box 127, 1822 N. Court St., Marion, 62959. Phone: (618) 997-8123. Phone: (618) 932-8121. Fax: (618) 993-2319. Web Site:www.wfrx.com Licensee: Withers Broadcasting of Southern Illinois LLC. Group owner: Clear Channel Communications Inc. (acq 3-17-2008; grpsl). Population served: 8,836 Natl. Network: Jones Radio Networks, . Format: News, big band. News staff: 2; News: 20 hrs wkly. Target aud: P45+. ◆Janet Jensen, gen mgr; Paxton Guy, opns mgr, news dir; Gina Heern, gen sls mgr; Stavey Malick, prom dir; Tim Deterding, chief of engrg.

WHET(FM)— Mar 14, 1972: 97.7 mhz; 3.5 kw. 433 ft TL: N37 45 15 W88 56 05. Hrs open: 6 AM-10 PM Box 127, 1822 N. Court St., Marion, 62959. Phone: (618) 997-8123. Phone: (618) 932-8121. Fax: (6180 993-2319. Licensee: Withers Broadcasting of Southern Illinois LLC. (acq 3-17-2008; grpsl). Population served: 8,836 Format: Pure classic rock. News: 2 hrs wkly. Target aud: 25-54; adult. ◆Matt Mellen, progmg dir.

Wheaton

*WETN(FM)— Feb 27, 1962: 88.1 mhz; 250 w. 140 ft TL: N41 52 09 W88 05 56. Stereo. Hrs open: 24 Wheaton College, 60187. Phone: (630) 752-5074. Fax: (630) 752-5286.E-mail: wetn@wheaton.edu Web Site:www.wetn.org Licensee: Trustees of Wheaton College. Population served: 300,000 Format: Christian , classical. News: 2 hrs wkly. Target aud: 18-49. Spec prog: Live sports 5 hrs, live church svcs 3 hrs, live concerts 2 hrs wkly. ◆Dr. A. Duane Litfin, pres; John Rorvik, gen mgr; Mark Bartlebaugh, stn mgr.

Willow Springs

WCPT(AM)—Licensed to Willow Springs. See Chicago

Wilmington

WYKT(FM)— Sept 29, 1980: 105.5 mhz; 1.3 kw. 482 ft TL: N41 17 11 W88 14 23. Stereo. Hrs open: 329 Maine St, Quincy, 62301. Phone: (815) 935-9555. Fax: (815) 935-9593.E-mail: wkan@starradio.com Web Site:www.1055thepickle.com Licensee: STARadio Corp. (group owner; acq 7-6-98). Population served: 2,250,000 Format: Hits of the 60s & 70s. News staff: one; News: 4 hrs wkly. Target aud: 25-54. Spec prog: Gospel 4 hrs, pub svc 4 hrs, sports 12 hrs wkly. ◆Brendan Michaels, opns mgr, progmg dir; Larry Regnier, gen sls mgr, chief of engrg; Robert Kersmarki, VP, gen mgr & mktg VP.

Winnebago

WRTB(FM)— 1971: 95.3 mhz; 1.25 kw. Ant 512 ft TL: N42 17 26 W89 09 51. Stereo. Hrs open: 24 2830 Sandy Hollow Rd., Rockford, 61109. Phone: (815) 874-7861. Fax: (815) 874-2202. Web Site:www.953bobfm.com Licensee: Maverick Media of Rockford License LLC. Group owner: RadioWorks Inc. (acq 4-27-2005; grpsl). Population served: 247,400 Natl. Rep: Katz Radio,. Shaw Pittman. Format: Classic hits. Target aud: 25-54. ◆Gary Rozynek, pres; Jay Chapman, gen mgr; Tim Krull, progmg dir.

Winnetka

*WNTH(FM)— Dec 10, 1960: 88.1 mhz; 100 w. 105 ft TL: N42 05 40 W87 43 07. Stereo. Hrs open: 385 Winnetka Ave., 60093. Phone: (847) 784-2330. Fax: (847) 501-6400. Web Site:www.newtrier.kiz.il.us Licensee: New Trier Township Board of Education. (acq 1960). Population served: 60,000 Format: Div. ◆Nina Lynn, stn mgr.

Wood River

KFNS(AM)— Oct 5, 1961: 590 khz; 1 kw-D, DA-2. TL: N38 55 43 W90 05 08. Hrs open: 8045 Big Bend Blvd., Webster Groves, MO, 63119. Phone: (314) 962-0590. Fax: (314) 962-7576. Web Site:www.kfns.com Licensee: Big Stick One LLC. Group owner: Big League Broadcasting LLC (acq 7-31-2004; grpsl). Natl. Rep: Interep,. Format: Sports. Target aud: 25-54; men. ◆Dave Greene, gen mgr; James Oelklaus, gen sls mgr.

Woodlawn

WDML(FM)— Nov 5, 1993: 106.9 mhz; 3 kw. 328 ft TL: N38 21 29 W89 05 56. Stereo. Hrs open: 24 Box 1591, 3501 Broadway, Mount Vernon, 62864. Phone: (618) 242-3333. Fax: (618) 242-3334.E-mail: wdml@mvn.net Web Site:www.wdml.com Licensee: Volunteer Broadcasting of Illinois Inc. Population served: 100,000 Natl. Network: Westwood One, . Dennis Kelly. Format: Adult rock. News staff: one; News: everyday 5 3 minute segments. Target aud: 30 plus; male. Spec prog: Christian rock 3 hrs wkly, House of Blues Radio Hour. ◆David M. Lister, CEO, pres, gen mgr; Ryan Roddy, COO & stn mgr.

Woodstock

*WZKL(FM)—Not on air, target date: unknown: 91.7 mhz; 5 kw vert. Ant 328 ft TL: N42 17 37 W88 35 13. Hrs open: 2351 Sunset Blvd., Suite 170-218, Rocklin, CA, 95765. Phone: (916) 251-1600. Fax: (916) 251-1650. Licensee: Educational Media Foundation. (acq 5-22-2008; $32,000 for CP). ◆Mike Novak, pres.

WZSR(FM)— May 24, 1974: 105.5 mhz; 3 kw. 429 ft TL: N42 15 30 W88 21 48. (CP: 1.95 kw, ant 567 ft. TL: N42 15 34 W88 21 45). Stereo. Hrs open: 8800 Rt. 14, Crystal Lake, 60012. Phone: (815) 459-7000. Fax: (815) 459-7027. Web Site:www.star105.com Licensee: NM Licensing LLC. Group owner: NextMedia Group L.L.C. (acq 11-26-01; grpsl). Population served: 200,000 Wire Svc: UPI Format: Adult contemp. Target aud: 25-54; female. Spec prog: Relg one hr wkly. ◆Floyd Evans, gen mgr; Doug Boyd, gen sls mgr; Erica Lorenz, prom dir; Steve Cherry, progmg dir; Stew Cohen, news dir & chief of engrg.

Zion

WPJX(AM)— Sept 19, 1967: 1500 khz; 250 w-D, DA. TL: N42 27 18 W87 54 01. Hrs open:
Simulcast with WEEF(AM) Highland Park 100%.
4320 Dundee Rd., Northbrook, 60062. Phone: (847) 498-3350. Fax: (847) 498-5743. Licensee: Polnet Communications Ltd. (group owner; acq 5-15-2006; $230,000). Format: Ethnic. ◆Sara Vargas, gen mgr.

WWDV(FM)— 1962: 96.9 mhz; 50 kw. 500 ft TL: N42 30 36 W87 53 11. Stereo. Hrs open: 875 N. Michigan Ave., Suite 1510, Chicago, 60611. Phone: (312) 274-9710. Fax: (312) 274-1304. Web Site:www.wdrv.com Licensee: Bonneville Holding Co. Group owner: Bonneville International Corp. (acq 1-25-01; $165 million with WDRV(FM) Chicago). Population served: 18,500 Format: Classic rock. ◆Jerry Schnacke, pres, VP & gen mgr; Greg Solk, opns VP.

Indiana

Alexandria

WMQX(FM)— Sept 3, 1980: 96.7 mhz; 2.5 kw. Ant 351 ft TL: N40 10 38 W85 40 23. Stereo. Hrs open: 24 800 E. 29th St., Muncie, 47302. Phone: (765) 288-4403. Fax: (765) 378-2091.E-mail: maxstudio@maxrocks.net Web Site:www.maxrocks.net Licensee: Backyard Broadcasting Indiana License LLC. Group owner: Backyard Broadcasting LLC (acq 12-1-2002; grpsl). Population served: 300,000 Natl. Network: Motor Racing Net, . Format: Classic rock. News staff: one; News: 2 hrs wkly. Target aud: 25-54. ◆Brian Thomas, prom mgr, progmg dir; Sean Mattingly, chief of engrg.

Anderson

*WBSB(FM)— December 1996: 89.5 mhz; 400 w. 364 ft TL: N40 10 38 W85 40 23. Hrs open:
Rebroadcasts WBST(FM) Muncie 100%.
c/o WBST(FM), Ball State Univ., Muncie, 47306-0550. Phone: (765) 285-5888. Fax: (765) 285-8937.E-mail: info@bsu.edu/ipr Web Site:www.bsu.edu/ipr Licensee: Ball State University. Format: Class, news. News staff: one. ◆Marcus Jackman, gen mgr; Pam Coletti, gen sls mgr; Carol Trimmer, prom mgr; Steven Turpin, progmg dir; Robert Mittendorf, chief of engrg; Dorothy Marvell, traf mgr; Brian Beaver, news rptr.

*WGNR(AM)— 1946: 1470 khz; 1 kw-D, 35 w-N. TL: N40 03 43 W85 42 37. Hrs open: 12 hrs 2000 W. 53rd St., 46013. Phone: (765) 642-2750. Fax: (765) 642-4033.E-mail: wgnr@moody.com Web Site:www.wgnr.org Licensee: Moody Bible Institute of Chicago Format: Christian talk. Target aud: 35-54. ◆Ray Hashley, gen mgr.

*WGNR-FM— Sept 11, 1973: 97.9 mhz; 50 kw. 489 ft TL: N40 03 43 W85 42 34. Stereo. Hrs open: 24 2000 W. 53rd St., 46013. Phone: (765) 642-2750. Fax: (765) 642-4033.E-mail: wgnr@moody.edu Web Site:www.wgnr.org Licensee: Moody Bible Institute of Chicago Group owner: The Moody Bible Institute of Chicago (acq 12-17-97; $5.5 million with co-located AM). Population served: 70,787 Format: Inspirational, Christian. News staff: one. Target aud: 35-54. ◆Dr. Joe Stowell, pres; Ray Hashley, gen mgr, stn mgr; Tom Winn, progmg dir & progmg mgr; Sam Sundin, news dir; Jim Wagner, chief of engrg.

WHBU(AM)— April 1923: 1240 khz; 1 kw-U. TL: N40 06 17 W85 40 45. Hrs open: 24 800 E. 29th St., Muncie, 47302. Phone: (765) 288-4403. Fax: (765) 288-0429. Web Site:www.1240whbu.com Licensee: Indiana Sabrecom Inc. Group owner: Backyard Broadcasting LLC (acq 12-1-02; grpsl). Population served: 164,000 Format: News/talk info. News staff: one; News: 40 hrs wkly. Target aud: 25-54. ◆Steve Lindell, VP, gen mgr & stn mgr; Brett Beshore, mktg VP.

WQME(FM)— Nov 29 1990: 98.7 mhz; 4.5 kw. 400 ft TL: N39 58 59 W85 42 41. Stereo. Hrs open: 24 hours 1100 E. 5th St., 46012-3495. Phone: (765) 641-4349. Fax: (765) 641-3825.E-mail: email@wqme.com Web Site:www.wqme.com Licensee: Anderson University Inc. Population served: 2,368,000 Natl. Network: CNN Radio, . Fletcher, Heald & Hildreth. Wire Svc: AP Format: Adult contemp. News: 8 hrs wkly. Target aud: 25-54. Spec prog: Relg 9 hrs wkly. ◆Donald Boggs, gen mgr; Gerald Longenbaugh, gen sls mgr; Matt Rust, progmg dir; Jerry Morton, chief of engrg, engr; Norma Armogum, traf mgr; Jill O'Malia, mktg.

Angola

*WEAX(FM)— September 1979: 88.3 mhz; 920 w. Ant 151 ft TL: N41 37 53 W85 00 37. Stereo. Hrs open: 24 1 University Ave, 46703-1750. Phone: (260) 665-4288.E-mail: weaxfm@tristate.edu Web Site:www.88xradio.com Licensee: Tri-State University. Natl. Network: CNN Radio, . Reddy, Begley & McCormick. Format: Alt/college. News: one hrs wkly. Target aud: 18-44. ◆Josh Hornbacker, gen mgr & opns mgr.

WLKI(FM)— July 15, 1974: 100.3 mhz; 4 kw. Ant 393 ft TL: N41 40 51 W85 00 05. Stereo. Hrs open: 24 Box 999, 46703. Secondary address: 2655 State Rd. 127N 46703. Phone: (260) 665-9554. Fax: (260) 665-9064.E-mail: wlki@wlki.com Web Site:www.wlki.com Licensee: Lake Cities Broadcasting Corp. Population served: 25,000 Format: Hot adult contemp. Target aud: 25-49; adults with youthful outlook, skews female. ◆Bill Kerner, VP; Thomas R. Andrews, pres & gen mgr; Andy St. John, progmg dir; Jim Measel, news dir; Greg Case, chief of engrg.

Attica

*WFWR(FM)— 2002: 91.5 mhz; 160 w. Ant 171 ft TL: N40 16 47 W87 14 50. Hrs open: 909 S. McDonald St., 47918. Phone: (765) 764-1934.E-mail: info@atticaonline.com/wfwr.htm Web Site:www.atticaonline.com/wfwr.htm Licensee: Fountain Warren Community Radio Corp. Format: Var. ◆Larry Grant, gen mgr.

WSHP(FM)— April 1990: 95.7 mhz; 3.1 kw. Ant 433 ft TL: N40 23 02 W87 07 55. Stereo. Hrs open: 3824 S. 18th St., Lafayette, 47909. Phone: (765) 474-1410. Fax: (765) 474-3442. Licensee: Artistic Media Partners L.P. Group owner: Artistic Media Partners Inc. (acq 10-3-94; $410,000;10-17-94). Natl. Rep: Christal,. Rosenman & Colin. Format: Classic rock. Target aud: 25-54. ◆Arthur Angotti, pres, exec VP, gen mgr; Bob Henning, gen sls mgr, chief of engrg; Steve Clark, progmg dir.

Auburn

WGBJ(FM)— Apr 10, 1967: 102.3 mhz; 3 kw. Ant 300 ft TL: N41 20 01 W85 03 08. Stereo. Hrs open: 24 4534 Parnell Ave., Fort Wayne, 46825. Phone: (260) 482-4444. Fax: (260) 482-4410.E-mail: kfoate@summitcityradio.com Licensee: Three Amigo's Broadcasting Inc. Group owner: Summit City Radio Group (acq 11-30-2006; $1.35 million). Natl. Rep: McGavren Guild,. Format: Rgnl Mexician. ◆Robert J. Britt, VP; Angie Phillips, gen mgr.

WGLL(AM)— Sept 3, 1968: 1570 khz; 500 w-D, 151 w-N, DA-2. TL: N41 20 01 W85 03 08. Hrs open: 17
Rebroadcasts WGL(AM) Fort Wayne 100%.
5446 C. R. 29, Fort Wayne, 46706. Phone: (260) 925-4300. Fax: (260) 432-0986. Licensee: Kovas Communications of Indiana Inc. (acq 11-9-07; grpsl). Population served: 33,500 Natl. Network: CBS, . Rgnl. Network: Network Indiana. Natl. Rep: Rgnl Reps,. Network Indiana Lauren A. Colby. Format: Relg progmg. Target aud: 25-54. ◆Raymond Alexander, pres & gen mgr.

Aurora

WSCH(FM)— Oct 29, 1970: 99.3 mhz; 1.15 kw. 525 ft TL: N38 57 55 W84 56 51. Stereo. Hrs open: 24 20 E. High St., Lawrenceburg, 47025-1820. Phone: (812) 537-0944. Fax: (812) 537-5735.E-mail: production@eaglecountryonline.com Web Site:www.eaglecountryonline.com Licensee: Wagon Wheel Broadcasting LLC. (acq 2-1-2008; grpsl). Population served: 60,234 Natl. Network: ABC, Motor Racing Net, . Brownfield Format: Hot country. News staff: one; News: 12 one-minute newscasts each weekday. Target aud: 25-plus. Spec prog: Indiana University Basketball/Football, High School Basketball/Football, NASCAR, IndyCar. ♦Marty Pieratt, gen mgr; Chelsie Shinkle, progmg dir, mus dir; Mike Perleberg, news dir; Ted Ryan, chief of engrg.

Austin

WJAA(FM)— 1991: 96.3 mhz; 3 kw. 328 ft TL: N38 50 39 W85 49 26. Hrs open: 1531 W. Tipton St., Seymour, 47274. Phone: (812) 523-3343. Fax: (812) 523-5116.E-mail: coolbus@wjaa.net Web Site:www.wjaa.net Licensee: Midland Media Inc. (acq 6-28-91; $15,000; 7-22-91). Natl. Network: ABC, Westwood One, . Format: AOR, classic rock. News staff: News progmg 5 hrs wkly Target aud: 25-54; men & women. ♦Robert Becker, gen mgr; Tony Starkey, gen sls mgr; Shannon Pyle, progmg dir.

WXKU-FM— December 1993: 92.7 mhz; 2 kw. Ant 400 ft TL: N38 49 23 W85 47 24. Stereo. Hrs open: 24 2470 N. Hwy. 7, North Vernon, 47265. Phone: (812) 346-1927. Fax: (812) 346-9722. Licensee: BK Media LLC (acq 7-31-2006; $850,000). Population served: 300,000 Natl. Network: USA, . Format: Country. News staff: one; News: 21 hrs wkly. Target aud: 25-65. ♦Marty Pieratt, gen mgr.

Batesville

WRBI(FM)— May 14, 1977: 103.9 mhz; 1.95 kw. Ant 360 ft TL: N39 13 22 W85 15 28. Stereo. Hrs open: 24 133 S. Main St., 47006. Phone: (812) 934-5111. Fax: (812) 934-2765.E-mail: wrbi@wrbiradio.com Web Site:www.wrbiradio.com Licensee: White River Broadcasting Co. Inc. Group owner: The Findlay Publishing Co. (acq 7-31-97; grpsl). Population served: 102,000 Natl. Rep: Rgnl Reps,. Format: Country. News staff: one; News: 10 hrs wkly. Target aud: General. Spec prog: Farm 5 hrs wkly. ♦David Glass, VP; Ronald E. Green, gen mgr; Caz Burdetter, progmg dir; Mary Mattingly, news dir.

Battle Ground

WASK-FM— Mar 11, 1993: 98.7 mhz; 4.4 kw. Ant 384 ft TL: N40 29 57 W86 52 25. Stereo. Hrs open: 24 Box 7880, Lafayette, 47903-7880. Secondary address: 3575 McCarty Ln., Lafayette 47905. Phone: (765) 447-2186. Fax: (765) 448-4452. Web Site:www.wask.com Licensee: WASK Inc. Group owner: Schurz Communications Inc. (acq 3-6-95; $860,000; 6-26-95). Population served: 238,000 Natl. Rep: Christal,. Rgnl rep: Rgnl Reps. Hogan & Hartson. Wire Svc: AP Format: Oldies. News staff: 4; News: 20 hrs wkly. Target aud: 35 plus; general. ♦John A. Trent, pres, gen mgr, gen sls mgr; Mark Allen, opns mgr; Brian Green, gen sls mgr; Bryan McGarvey, progmg dir, progmg mgr; Steve Truex, chief of engrg.

Bedford

WBIW(AM)— October 1948: 1340 khz; 1 kw-U. TL: N38 52 23 W86 28 34. Hrs open: 24 424 Heltonville Rd., 47421. Phone: (812) 275-7555. Fax: (812) 279-8046.E-mail: wbiw1340am@yahoo.com Web Site:www.wbiw.com Licensee: Ad-Venture Media Inc. (acq 1-30-89; $1 million with co-located FM; 1-30-89). Population served: 13,087 Natl. Network: Westwood One, USA, . Rgnl. Network: Network Indiana. Natl. Rep: Rgnl Reps,. Brownfield Reed, Smith, Shaw & McClay. Format: Sports, news, talk. News staff: one; News: 28 hrs wkly. Target aud: 25 plus; general. Spec prog: Sports, weather, farm 3 hrs wkly. ♦Dean Spencer, pres & gen mgr.

WQRK(FM)— Oct 1, 1975: 105.5 mhz; 2 kw. 400 ft TL: N38 54 29 W86 28 28. Stereo. Hrs open: 24 424 Heltonville Rd., 47421. Phone: (812) 275-7555. Fax: (812) 279-8046.E-mail: oldies105@hpcisp.com Web Site:www.superoldies.net Population served: 123,000 Natl. Network: ABC, . Format: Oldies. News staff: one; News: 8 hrs wkly. Target aud: 35-55; upscale adults.

Beech Grove

WNTS(AM)— Dec 10, 1956: 1590 khz; 5 kw-D, 500 w-N, DA-3. TL: N39 44 21 W86 05 29. Hrs open: 24 Box 2368, Davidson, NC, 28036-5368. Phone: (317) 359-5591. Fax: (317) 359-3885. Web Site:www.lapoderosa1590am.com Licensee: Davidson Media Station WNTS Licensee LLC. (acq 9-28-2005; $2 million). Population served: 744,624 Fletcher, Heald & Hildreth. Format: Rgnl Mexican. ♦Steve Stiegelmeyer, gen mgr; Mayra Elisa Arroyo, progmg dir.

Berne

WZBD(FM)— Aug 27, 1993: 92.7 mhz; 4.1 kw. 394 ft TL: N40 46 15 W85 56 05. Hrs open: 5 AM-10 PM 1891 W. State Rd. 97, Portland, 47371. Secondary address: 955 US 27 N. 46711. Phone: (260) 726-8729. Fax: (260) 726-4311.E-mail: wpgw@jayco.net Licensee: Adams County Radio Inc. (acq 3-11-99). Population served: 150,000 Format: Adult contemp, local news. Target aud: General. ♦Rob Weaver, pres, gen mgr; Tony Giltner, opns mgr.

Bicknell

WUZR(FM)—Licensed to Bicknell. See Vincennes

Bloomington

WBWB(FM)— July 17, 1978: 96.7 mhz; 1.65 kw. 439 ft TL: N39 09 46 W86 28 21. Stereo. Hrs open: 24 Box 7797, 47407. Secondary address: 304 State Rd. 446 47401. Phone: (812) 336-8000. Fax: (812) 336-7000.E-mail: wbwb@wbwb.com Web Site:www.wbwb.com Licensee: Artistic Media Partners L.P. Group owner: Artistic Media Partners Inc. (acq 1-89; grpsl; 1-23-89). Population served: 230,000 Natl. Rep: McGavren Guild,. Rgnl rep: Rgnl Reps. Haley, Bader & Potts. Format: CHR. News staff: one. Target aud: 18-49. ♦Art Angotti, pres; Sandy Zehr, gen mgr; Dale Clark, gen sls mgr, progmg dir; Bob Henning, chief of engrg.

***WFHB(FM)—** December 1992: 91.3 mhz; 2.5 kw horiz, 2.45 kw vert. 266 ft TL: N39 01 55 W86 36 33. Hrs open: 24 Box 1973, 47402. Secondary address: 108 W. 4th St. 47404. Phone: (812) 323-1200. Fax: (812) 323-0320.E-mail: volunteer@wfhb.org Web Site:www.wfhb.org Licensee: Bloomington Community Radio Inc. Format: Div, news, pub affrs. News staff: one; News: 5 hrs wkly. Target aud: General. Spec prog: Folk 10 hrs, Latin 3 hrs, Finnish 3 hrs wkly. ♦Markus Lowe, gen mgr & progmg dir; Jim Manion, mus dir; Chad Carrothers, news dir, pub affrs dir.

***WFIU(FM)—** Sept 30, 1950: 103.7 mhz; 29 kw. Ant 646 ft TL: N39 08 31 W86 29 43. Stereo. Hrs open: 24 Radio-TV Ctr., Indiana Univ., 1229 E. 7th St, 47405. Phone: (812) 855-1357. Fax: (812) 855-5600.E-mail: wfiu@indiana.edu Web Site:www.indiana.edu/-wfiu Licensee: Trustees of Indiana University. Population served: 200,000 Natl. Network: NPR, . Crowell & Moring. Format: Class, jazz, news. News staff: one; News: 7 hrs wkly. Target aud: General. ♦Christina Kuzmych, stn mgr, prom dir; Will Murphy, news dir; Bradley Howard, chief of engrg. Co-owned TV: *WTIU(TV) affil.

WGCL(AM)— Mar 11, 1949: 1370 khz; 5 kw-D, 500 w-N, DA-2. TL: N39 11 25 W86 38 02. Stereo. Hrs open: 24 400 One City Ctr., 47404. Phone: (812) 332-3366. Fax: (812) 331-4570.E-mail: info@am1370wgll.com Web Site:www.am1370wgll.com Licensee: Sarkes Tarzian Inc. (group owner) Population served: 120,000 Natl. Network: ABC, ESPN Radio, . Natl. Rep: Christal,. Leventhal, Senter & Leman. Format: News/talk. News staff: 2; News: 5 hrs wkly. Target aud: 30 plus. ♦Ron Tarsi, gen mgr; Ducan Myers, gen sls mgr; Don Pratt, progmg dir; Marc Antonetti, chief of engrg.

WTTS(FM)— Jan 7, 1960: 92.3 mhz; 37 kw. 1,090 ft TL: N39 24 27 W86 08 52. Stereo. Hrs open: 24 407 N. Fulton St. Suite 92, Indianapolis, 46202. Phone: (317) 972-9887. Fax: (317) 972-9886. Web Site:www.wttsfm.com Population served: 2,600,000 Natl. Rep: Christal,. Format: AAA. News staff: one. Target aud: 25-54. Spec prog: Blues 2 hrs, acoustic show 4 hrs wkly. ♦Daryl McIntire, gen sls mgr, prom dir; Brad Holtz, progmg dir; Laura Duncan, news dir.

Bluffton

WNUY(FM)— Dec 10, 1963: 100.1 mhz; 6 kw. Ant 298 ft TL: N40 52 10 W85 10 20. Stereo. Hrs open: 24 4714 Parnell, Fort Wayne, 46825. Phone: (260) 824-2804. Fax: (260) 824-2805.E-mail: wnuy@wnuy.com Web Site:www.FM100Talks.com Licensee: IM IN Licenses LLC. (acq 3-21-2006; $1 million). Population served: 425,000 Natl. Network: Fox Sports, CNN Radio, Motor Racing Net, Westwood One, . Format: Talk & Sports. News staff: one; News: 2 hrs wkly. Target aud: 25-54; professional women. Spec prog: Relg 4 hrs wkly. ♦Dayle Mentzer, gen mgr, gen sls mgr; Pete LaFaucia, prom dir, progmg dir, sls; Rob Caylor, news dir; Zach Morton, chief of engrg; Diane Current, traf mgr, prom; Dick Stimpson, sls.

Boonville

WBNL(AM)— Sept 10, 1950: 1540 khz; 250 w-D. TL: N38 03 58 W87 16 27. Hrs open: 24 Box 270, 47601. Secondary address: 2177 N. Hwy. 61, 47601. Phone: (812) 897-2080. Fax: (812) 897-2130.E-mail: rturpen@1540.net Web Site:www.radio1540.net Licensee: Turpen Communications LLC (acq 8-22-01). Population served: 71,000 Natl. Network: USA, . Rgnl. Network: Network Indiana. Network Indiana Format: MOR, adult contemp. News staff: one; News: 14 hrs wkly. Target aud: 25-54; Women 25-54. Spec prog: Gospel 5 hrs wkly. ♦Ralph E. Turpen, pres & gen mgr.

WEJK(FM)— Dec 19, 1967: 107.1 mhz; 3 kw. 185 ft TL: N38 03 58 W87 16 27. Hrs open: 24 Box 3848, Evansville, 47736. Secondary address: 1162 Mt. Auburn Rd., Evansville 47720. Phone: (812) 424-8284. Fax: (812) 426-7928.E-mail: tim@sccradio.com Licensee: Boonville Broadcasting Co. Inc. Group owner: South Central Communications Corp. (acq 8-14-2000; $400,000 for stock with co-located AM). Population served: 200,000 Format: Jack FM. ♦John P. Engelbrecht, CEO; Tim Huelsing, VP & gen mgr; Rsuty James, progmg dir; Chris Myers, chief of engrg.

Brazil

WSDM-FM— Nov 13, 1973: 92.7 mhz; 6 kw. Ant 298 ft TL: N39 30 44 W87 08 18. Stereo. Hrs open: 24 1301 Ohio St., Terre Haute, 47807. Phone: (812) 234-9770. Fax: (812) 238-1576.E-mail: mike@radioworksforme.com Web Site:www.crock927.com Licensee: Crossroads Investments LLC (acq 8-1-90; with co-located AM). Population served: 100,000 Natl. Rep: Roslin,. Rgnl rep: Regional Reps Booth, Freret, Imlay & Tepper. Format: Country, rock. News staff: one; News: 2 hrs wkly. ♦Michael Petersen, gen mgr; Marty Combs, progmg dir.

WSDX(AM)— 1959: 1130 khz; 500 w-D, 20 w-N. TL: N39 30 44 W87 08 18. Hrs open: 6 AM-2 hrs past sunset Prog sep from FM Rebroadcasts WBOW(AM) Terre Haute 95%.
1301 Ohio St., Terre Haute, 47807. Phone: (812) 234-9770. Fax: (812) 238-1576.E-mail: hfarmer@radioworksforme.com Web Site:espnsportsradio.com Licensee: Crossroads Investments LLC Group owner: Crossroads Communications Inc. Population served: 25,000 Rgnl. Network: Network Indiana, AgriAmerica. Natl. Rep: Roslin,. Network Indiana Rgnl rep: Rgnl Reps. Booth, Freret, Imlay & Tepper. Format: Sports. News staff: one. Target aud: General; sports fans.

Bremen

WHPZ(FM)— Mar 1, 1993: 96.9 mhz; 2.99 kw. Ant 462 ft TL: N41 26 37 W86 01 18. Hrs open: 61300 S. Ironwood Rd., South Bend, 46614. Phone: (574) 291-8200. Fax: (574) 291-9043.E-mail: info@whpz.com Web Site:www.pulsefm.com Licensee: Le Sea Broadcasting Corp. Group owner: Le Sea Broadcasting Corp. (acq 1-4-2000; $280,296). Format: Contemp Christian. ♦Tony Hale, CFO; Anna Riblet, stn mgr, gen sls mgr; Wes Hylton, chief of engrg.

Brookston

WBPE(FM)— Apr 16, 1967: 95.3 mhz; 2.3 kw. Ant 505 ft TL: N40 32 48 W86 50 59. Stereo. Hrs open: 24 3824 S. 18th St., Lafayette, 47909-9102. Phone: (765) 474-1410. Fax: (765) 474-3442. Web Site:www.wbpefm.com Licensee: Artistic Media Partners Inc. (group owner; (acq 9-1-98; $1.8 million). Population served: 100,000 Rosenman & Colin. Format: Adult hits. News staff: one; News: 14 hrs wkly. Target aud: 35 plus; affluent, educated & upscale. ♦Ernie Caldemone, gen mgr; Kit Osborne, gen sls mgr; Jimmy Knight, progmg dir; Bob Henning, chief of engrg.

Brownsburg

WKLU(FM)— Mar 23, 1992: 101.9 mhz; 4 kw. Ant 361 ft TL: N39 47 13 W86 17 57. Stereo. Hrs open: 24 8120 Knue Rd., Indianapolis, 46250. Phone: (317) 841-1019. Fax: (317) 841-5167.E-mail: bart@wklu.net Web Site:www.wklu.net Licensee: Indy Radio LLC (acq 10-18-2004; $6.2 million). Population served: 950,000 Rgnl. Network: Metronews Radio Net. Format: Oldies. News staff: 2. Target aud: 25-54. Spec prog: Beetles brunch. ♦Bart Johnson, gen mgr; Monica Lephart, prom dir; Libby Zabriskie-Farr, progmg dir; Aimee McGrath, traf mgr.

Carmel

***WHJE(FM)—** September 1963: 91.3 mhz; 400 w. 100 ft TL: N39 58 45 W86 07 10. Stereo. Hrs open: 24 520 E. Main St., 46032. Phone: (317) 571-4055. Phone: (317) 846-7721. Fax: (317) 571-4066. Web Site:www.whje.com Licensee: Carmel Clay Schools. Population served:

30,000 Rgnl. Network: Network Indiana. Network Indiana Wire Svc: UPI Format: Classic rock, alternative. Target aud: 12 plus. ◆Tom Schoeller, gen mgr.

Centerville

WHON(AM)—Licensed to Centerville. See Richmond

Chandler

WLFW(FM)— Apr 2, 1994: 93.5 mhz; 3.2 kw. Ant 446 ft TL: N38 01 27 W87 21 43. Hrs open: 24 Box 3848, Evansville, 47736. Secondary address: 1162 Mt. Auburn Rd., Evansville 47720. Phone: (812) 424-8284. Fax: (812) 426-7928.E-mail: info@935thewolf.com Web Site:www.935thewolf.com Licensee: South Central Communications Corp. (group owner; (acq 1996; $860,000). Population served: 625,000 Natl. Network: Westwood One, . Format: Country. News staff: 3. Target aud: 35-49. ◆John D. Englebrecht, CEO, chmn; Craig Jacobus, pres; Paul Brayfield, gen mgr, gen sls mgr; James Ashley, prom dir; Rusty James, progmg dir.

Charlestown

WAYI(FM)— Apr 7, 1998: 104.3 mhz; 3 kw. Ant 328 ft TL: N38 28 55 W85 37 33. Stereo. Hrs open: 24 Box 1043, New Albany, 47151. Phone: (812) 945-1043. Fax: (812) 945-0317.E-mail: wayi@wayfm.com Web Site:wayi.wayfm.com Licensee: WAY-FM Media Group Inc. Group owner: Radio One Inc. (acq 11-20-2007; $1 million). ◆Robert D. Augsburg, pres; Matt Hahn, gen mgr.

Chesterton

*WBEW(FM)— 2001: 89.5 mhz; 7 kw. Ant 216 ft TL: N41 42 58 W86 51 47. (CP: 23 kw, ant 187 ft.). Hrs open: 848 E. Grand Ave., Navy Pier, Chicago, IL, 60611-3462. Phone: (312) 948-4600. Fax: (312) 948-4837.E-mail: tmalatia@chicagopublicradio.org Web Site:www.chicagopublicradio.org Licensee: The WBEZ Alliance Inc. (acq 10-4-02; $550,000). Format: News, talk, jazz. ◆Torey Malatia, pres & gen mgr; Greg Salustro, dev VP.

*WDSO(FM)— November 1976: 88.3 mhz; 400 w. 135 ft TL: N41 36 29 W87 03 37. Stereo. Hrs open: 6 AM Monday through 5 PM Friday Chesterton High School, 2125 S. 11th St., 46304. Phone: (219) 983-3777. Fax: (219) 983-3775. Web Site:www.wdso.org Licensee: Duneland School Corp. Population served: 149,200 Network Indiana Format: Rock. News: 6 hrs wkly. Target aud: General. Spec prog: Class one hr, specialty rock 8 hrs wkly. ◆Matthew Waters, stn mgr, chief of engrg; Michele Stipanovich, opns mgr.

Churubusco

WNHT(FM)— August 1994: 96.3 mhz; 6.7 kw. Ant 554 ft TL: N41 06 13 W85 10 44. Hrs open: 24 2000 Lower Huntington Rd., Fort Wayne, 46819. Phone: (260) 747-1511. Fax: (260) 747-3999. Web Site:wild963.com Licensee: Summit City License Sub, LLC. Group owner: Summit City Radio Group (acq 11-6-2006; grpsl). Natl. Rep: Eastman Radio,. Format: Rhythmic CHR. Target aud: 18-34; women. ◆J.J. Fabini, gen mgr; Shady Spencer, progmg dir.

Cicero

*WJCY(FM)— 2005: 91.5 mhz; 475 w vert. Ant 193 ft TL: N40 11 53 W86 07 44. Hrs open: CSN International, 4002N. 3300E., Twin Falls, ID, 83301. Phone: (208) 734-6633. Fax: (208) 736-1958. Licensee: CSN International. (group owner). ◆Mike Kestler, pres; Mike Stockland, gen mgr; Don Mills, progmg dir.

Clarksville

WTFX-FM— 1998: 93.1 mhz; 4.1 kw. Ant 374 ft TL: N38 17 02 W85 54 17. Stereo. Hrs open: 24 4000 Radio Drive, Louisville, KY, 40218. Phone: (502) 479-2308. Fax: (502) 479-2223. Web Site:www.foxrocks.com Licensee: CC Licenses LLC. Group owner: Clear Channel Communications Inc. Population served: 942,300 Format: Active rock. ◆Bill Gentry, mktg mgr; Charlie Steele, progmg dir.

Clifford

*WISG(FM)—Not on air, target date: unknown: 89.9 mhz; 1 w horiz, 100 w vert. Ant 82 ft TL: N39 18 27.1 W85 52 11.6. Hrs open: 3437

Kensington Ct., Columbus, 47203. Phone: (812) 376-8525. Licensee: Linda Jerome Foundation. ◆Linda Jerome, pres.

Clinton

WAXI(FM)—See Rockville

*WPFR-FM— 1998: 93.9 mhz; 2.3 kw. 531 ft TL: N39 33 18 W87 28 40. Stereo. Hrs open: 24 18889 N. 2350th St., Dennison, IL, 62423. Phone: (217) 826-9673.E-mail: wpfr@joink.com Licensee: Word Power Inc. Population served: 146,605 Natl. Network: Moody, . Format: Christian. News: 17 hrs wkly. Target aud: 12 plus. ◆Paul Dean Ford, pres & gen mgr; Mark S. Ford, opns dir; Dan Watson, chief of opns.

Cloverdale

*WSPM(FM)— 2003: 89.1 mhz; 25 w horiz, 49 kw vert. Ant 298 ft TL: N39 41 19 W86 42 03. Hrs open: 24 3500 DePauw Blvd., Suite 2085, Indianapolis, 46268. Phone: (317) 870-8400 ext 21. Fax: (317) 870-8404.E-mail: jim@catholicradioindy.org Web Site:www.catholicradioindy.org Licensee: Hoosier Broadcasting Corp. Format: Relg-Catholic. ◆Chuck Cunningham, gen mgr; Ed Roehling, gen sls mgr; Bill Shirk, progmg dir; Jim Ganley, news dir; Marty Hensley, chief of engrg.

Cole

*WVXI(FM)—Not on air, target date: unknown: 88.1 mhz; 100 w vert. Ant 121 ft TL: N40 27 37.5 W85 46 29.4. Hrs open: 15 Wood St., Greenfield, 46140. Phone: (317) 467-1602. Licensee: Electronic Applications Radio Service Inc. ◆Patrick Diemer, pres & gen mgr.

Columbia City

*WJHS(FM)— Aug 12, 1985: 91.5 mhz; 2.65 kw. 219 ft TL: N41 10 04 W85 29 41. Stereo. Hrs open: 24 600 N. Whitley St., 46725. Phone: (260) 248-8915. Phone: (260) 244-6136. Fax: (260) 244-5610.E-mail: wallsll@wjhs915.org Web Site:www.wjhs915.org Licensee: Whitley County Consolidated Schools Board of Control. Population served: 26,000 Format: Adult alternative. Target aud: Men 25-54; general. ◆Krystal Walker Zoltek, stn mgr; Laurie Walls, mus dir.

WVBB(FM)— Oct 13, 1968: 106.3 mhz; 5.6 kw. Ant 339 ft TL: N41 12 49 W85 12 04. Stereo. Hrs open: 2100 Goshen Rd., Suite 332, Fort Wayne, 46808. Phone: (260) 482-9288. Fax: (260) 482-8655.E-mail: info@wvbbfm.com Web Site:www.1063joefm.com Licensee: Oasis Radio 2 Corp. (group owner; (acq 10-19-2007; $3.8 million with WBTU(FM) Kendallville). Tieerney & Swift. Format: Adult hits. ◆Roger Diehm, gen mgr; Phil Becker, progmg dir.

Columbus

WCSI(AM)— 1950: 1010 khz; 500 w-D, 19 w-N. TL: N39 11 05 W85 57 17. Stereo. Hrs open: 24 Box 1789, 47202-1789. Secondary address: 3212 Washington St. 47203. Phone: (812) 372-4448. Fax: (812) 372-1061.E-mail: news@csiradio.com Licensee: White River Broadcasting Co. Group owner: The Findlay Publishing Co. (acq 11-1-57). Population served: 100,000 Rgnl. Network: AgriAmerica. Rgnl rep: Rgnl Reps. Wire Svc: CBS Format: News/talk, weather, sports. News staff: 3. Target aud: 35 plus. ◆John Foster, opns mgr, progmg dir, pub affrs dir; Tasha Mann, gen mgr & gen sls mgr; Kevin Keith, news dir; Chuck Weber, chief of engrg.

WINN(FM)— Jan 30, 1975: 104.9 mhz; 6 kw. Ant 300 ft TL: N39 11 09 W85 57 37. Stereo. Hrs open: 24 Box 1789, 47202-1789. Secondary address: 3212 Washington St. 47203. Phone: (812) 372-4448.E-mail: studio@1049theriver.fm Web Site:www.1049theriver.fm Licensee: White River Broadcasting Co. Inc. Group owner: The Findlay Publishing Co. (acq 1-8-2002). Population served: 100,000 Format: Classic hits. Target aud: 35-54. ◆Kurt Kah, pres; David Glass, VP; Tasha Mann, gen mgr; John Foster, opns mgr; Rich Anthony, progmg dir; Kevin Keith, news dir; Chuck Weber, engr.

*WKJD(FM)—Not on air, target date: unknown: 90.3 mhz; 1.5 kw vert. Ant 138 ft TL: N39 12 27 W86 01 27. Hrs open: 1680 Hwy. 62 N.E., Corydon, 47112. Phone: (812) 738-3482. Fax: (812) 375-2555. Licensee: Good Samaritan Educational Radio Inc. ◆Keith Reising, CEO.

WKKG(FM)— 1958: 101.5 mhz; 50 kw. Ant 492 ft TL: N39 11 05 W85 57 17. Stereo. Hrs open: 24 Prog sep from AM Box 1789, 47202. Secondary address: 3212 Washington St. 47203. Phone: (812) 372-4448. Fax: (812) 372-1061.E-mail: wkkg@wkkg.com Web

Site:wkkg.com Population served: 300,000 Format: Country. Target aud: 25-54. ◆Scott Michaels, progmg dir; Judy Watkins, traf mgr; Sam Simmermaker, sports cmtr.

WRZQ-FM—See Greensburg

WYGS(FM)— Feb 27, 2003: 91.1 mhz; 380 w vert. Ant 328 ft TL: N39 13 35 W85 44 47. Hrs open: 24 Box 2626, 47202. Secondary address: 825 Washington St. 47201. Phone: (812) 738-3482. Fax: (812) 375-2555.E-mail: info@wygs.org Web Site:www.wygs.org Licensee: Good Shepherd Radio Inc. Format: Southern gospel. ◆Keith Reising, CEO.

Connersville

WIFE(AM)— Apr 5, 1948: 1580 khz; 250 w-D, 5 w-N. TL: N39 38 18 W85 08 54. Hrs open: 24 Box 619, 47331. Secondary address: 406 Central Ave. Phone: (765) 825-6411. Phone: (765) 825-8561. Fax: (765) 825-2411.E-mail: info@wife.com Web Site:www.wifefm.com Licensee: Rodgers Broadcasting Corp. (group owner; (acq 8-88; grpsl; 8-29-88). Population served: 17,604 Rgnl rep: Rgnl Reps. Format: Oldies. News staff: 2; News: 3 hrs wkly. Target aud: 25-54; affluent, middle-aged country listeners. Spec prog: Relg 12 hrs wkly. ◆David A. Rodgers, pres; John Trine, gen mgr; Jeri L. Pruet, stn mgr; Bob Wills, progmg dir; Barry Welsh, mus dir; Brett Briscoe, news dir; Mike Peacock, engrg mgr; Bob Hawkins, chief of engrg; Becky Hymer, traf mgr; Kristin Dewert, local news ed.

WMOJ-FM— Feb 27, 1948: 100.3 mhz; 28 kw. Ant 215 ft TL: N39 38 15 W85 08 45. (CP: COL Norwood, OH. 3.6 kw, ant 426 ft. TL: N39 07 19 W84 32 52). Stereo. Hrs open: 24 1 Centennial Plaza, 705 Central Ave., Suite 200, Cincinnati, OH, 45202. Phone: (513) 679-6000. Fax: (513) 679-6014.E-mail: info@wmoj.com Licensee: Blue Chip Broadcasting Licenses Ltd. (acq 9-21-2006; $18 million). Population served: 85,000 Rgnl. Network: Network Indiana. Format: Urban adult contemp. ◆Lisa Thal, gen mgr.

Corydon

WOCC(AM)— May 22, 1964: 1550 khz; 250 w-D. TL: N38 11 26 W86 08 00. Hrs open: 24 Box 838, 47112. Secondary address: 211 N. Capitol Ave 47112. Phone: (812) 738-9622. Fax: (812) 738-1676.E-mail: wocc1550@cs.com Web Site:www.woccam1550.com Licensee: Richard Lee Brabandt. (acq 4-15-97). Natl. Network: USA, . Natl. Rep: Rgnl Reps,. Network Indiana Format: Classic oldies. News staff: one; News: 18 hrs wkly. Target aud: 34-55; baby boomers. ◆Richard Lee Brabandt, pres; MaryAnn Brabandt, gen mgr, progmg dir; Dave Riddle, chief of engrg.

WSFR(FM)— 1994: 107.7 mhz; 8.2 kw. 567 ft TL: N38 10 25 W85 54 50. (CP: 36 kw). Stereo. Hrs open: 24 612 4th Ave., Suite 100, Louisville, KY, 40202. Phone: (502) 589-4800. Fax: (502) 583-4820. Web Site:www.1077sfr.com Licensee: Cox Radio Inc. Group owner: Cox Broadcasting (acq 5-99). Population served: 976,800 Dow, Lohnes & Albertson. Format: Classic rock. Target aud: 25-54. ◆Todd Schumacher, VP; Don Nordin, gen mgr, progmg dir; Amy Torres, gen sls mgr.

Covington

*WFOF(FM)— June 17, 1984: 90.3 mhz; 19 kw. 265 ft TL: N40 09 08 W87 27 58. Stereo. Hrs open: 24 1920 W. 53rd St., Anderson, 46013. Phone: (765) 642-2750. Fax: (765) 642-4033.E-mail: wfof@wfof.org Web Site:www.wfof.org Licensee: Doxa Inc. Format: Relg. ◆Ray McDaniel, pres; Ray Hashley, gen mgr.

WKZS(FM)— June 1, 1982: 103.1 mhz; 3 kw. 300 ft TL: N40 08 46 W87 27 15. Stereo. Hrs open: 24 Box 67, Danville, IL, 61834. Secondary address: P.O. Box 67 47932. Phone: (217) 443-4004. Phone: (765) 793-4823. Fax: (765) 793-4644.E-mail: info@kisscountryradio.com Web Site:www.kisscountryradio.com Licensee: Benton-Weatherford Broadcasting Inc. of Indiana. (acq 7-12-85; 6-3-85). Population served: 100,000 Natl. Network: Jones Radio Networks, . Borsari & Paxson. Wire Svc: AP Format: Country. News staff: one; News: 10 hrs wkly. Target aud: 18-49. ◆Larry Weatherford, pres, opns dir; Rhea Benton-Weatherford, gen mgr; Greg Green, stn mgr; Tara Duncan, prom mgr.

Crawfordsville

WCDQ(FM)— Aug 13, 1953: 106.3 mhz; 3.4 kw. 440 ft TL: N40 03 19 W86 55 57. Stereo. Hrs open: 24 Box 603, 47933. Secondary address: 1800 N. 175 W. 47933. Phone: (765) 362-8200. Phone: (765) 364-1063. Fax: (765) 364-1550.E-mail: cd1063@keybroadcasting.net Licensee: C.V.L. Broadcasting Inc. Group owner: Key Broadcasting

Inc. (acq 12-13-99; $400,000). Population served: 50,000 Rgnl. Network: Ohio Radio Net. Arter & Hadden. Format: Hot adult contemp. News staff: 2; News: 48 hrs wkly. Target aud: 25-49; middle & upper class, educated, socially aware. ♦Sherry Moodie, gen mgr.

WCVL(AM)— Dec 12, 1964: 1550 khz; 250 w-U, DA-N. TL: N40 03 54 W86 56 00. Hrs open: Box 603, 47933-0603. Phone: (765) 362-8200. Fax: (765) 364-1550.E-mail: info@crawfordsvilleradio.com Web Site:www.crawfordsvilleradio.com Licensee: C.V.L. Broadcasting Inc. Group owner: Key Broadcasting Inc. (acq 1986). Population served: 50,000 Natl. Rep: Rgnl Reps,. Format: Oldies. News staff: one; News: 3 hrs/day. Target aud: 45 plus. ♦Dave Peach, gen mgr; Mark Webber, progmg dir.

WIMC(FM)— June 1, 1974: 103.9 mhz; 1.35 kw. 500 ft TL: N40 08 05 W86 54 12. Stereo. Hrs open: Prog sep from AM Box 603, 47933. Phone: (765) 362-8200. Fax: (765) 364-1550. Population served: 50,000 Format: Classic hits. Target aud: 25-49.

***WNDY(FM)**— 1997: 91.3 mhz; 2.2 kw. 194 ft TL: N40 03 19 W86 55 57. Hrs open: Box 352, 47933. Secondary address: 301 W. Wabash 47933. Phone: (765) 361-6240. Phone: (765) 361-6038. Fax: (765) 361-6437. Web Site:www.wabash.edu Licensee: Wabash College Radio Inc. Format: College eclectic. ♦Kevin Kilgore, gen mgr.

Crothersville

***WOJC(FM)**— 2005: 89.9 mhz; 300 w vert. Ant 244 ft TL: N38 50 39 W85 49 26. Hrs open: CSN International, 4002N. 3300E., Twin Falls, ID, 83301. Phone: (208) 734-6633. Licensee: CSN International. (group owner). ♦Mike Kestler, pres; Mike Stockland, gen mgr; Don Mills, progmg dir.

Crown Point

***WRTW(FM)**—Not on air, target date: unknown: 90.5 mhz; 10 kw. Ant 226 ft TL: N41 27 56 W87 24 29. Hrs open: 8400 Burr St., 46307. Phone: (219) 932-0711. Fax: (219) 365-2029. Licensee: Hyles-Anderson College. ♦Jack Schaap, gen mgr.

WXRD(FM)— Nov 10, 1972: 103.9 mhz; 3 kw. 330 ft TL: N41 19 24 W87 21 22. Stereo. Hrs open: 24 2755 Sager Rd., Valpraiso, 46383. Phone: (219) 462-6111. Fax: (219) 462-4880.E-mail: donclark@radiooneindiana.com Web Site:www.xrock1039.com Licensee: Porter County Broadcasting Holding Corporation, LLC. Group owner: Porter County Broadcasting Corp. (acq 2-6-2004; $4.9 million with WZVN(FM) Lowell). Population served: 200,000 Natl. Network: ABC, . Rgnl. Network: Network Indiana. Network Indiana Reddy, Begley & McCormick. Format: Classic rock. News staff: one; News: 12 hrs wkly. Target aud: 25-54; women. ♦Leigh Ellis, pres & gen mgr.

Danville

***WDVL(FM)**—Not on air, target date: unknown: 88.1 mhz; 10 kw vert. Ant 410 ft TL: N39 47 44 W86 48 04. Hrs open: 5331 Mount Alifan Dr., San Diego, CA, 92111-2622. Phone: (858) 277-4991. Fax: (858) 277-1365. Licensee: Horizon Christian Fellowship. ♦Michael MacIntosh, pres.

WEDJ(FM)— Jan 10, 1975: 107.1 mhz; 1.8 kw. Ant 604 ft TL: N39 48 06 W86 34 24. Stereo. Hrs open: 24 1800 N. Meridian, Suite 605, Indianapolis, 46202. Phone: (317) 924-1071. Fax: (317) 924-7766.E-mail: info@wedjfm.com Web Site:www.wedjfm.com Licensee: Continental Broadcast Group Inc. (acq 12-30-93; grpsl; 1-24-94). Population served: 744600 Natl. Rep: Univision Radio National Sales,. Pillsbury, Winthrop & Shaw Pittman. Format: Hispanic. Target aud: 18-54; hispanic adults. ♦Russ Dodge, gen mgr; Stephanie Tatay-Myers, mktg mgr; Manuel Sepulveda, progmg dir; Phil Alexander, chief of engrg.

Decatur

WADM(AM)— May 22, 1964: 1540 khz; 250 w-D. TL: N40 49 14 W84 55 12. Hrs open: 6:00 am-8:45 pm Box 530, 46733-0530. Secondary address: 133 West Main Street, Peru 46970. Phone: (260) 724-7161. Fax: (260) 724-8719.E-mail: jay@wadm.com Web Site:wadm.com Licensee: Lewis Broadcasting LLC (acq 12-14-2007). Population served: 33,625 Natl. Network: USA, . Rgnl. Network: AgriAmerica. Network Indiana Rgnl rep: Indiana Broadcasters Assn Pillsbury, Winthrop, Shaw, Pittman. Format: Country classics. Target aud: 30 plus. ♦Jay Lewis, gen mgr.

WQHK-FM— Nov 8, 1966: 105.1 mhz; 2 kw. 397 ft TL: N40 49 14 W84 55 12. (CP: 13.4 kw, ant 449 ft.). Stereo. Hrs open: 2915 Maples Rd., Fort Wayne, 46816. Phone: (260) 447-5511. Fax: (260) 447-7546.E-mail: info@k105fm.com Web Site:www.k105fm.com Licensee: Jam Communications Inc. Group owner: Federated Media. Population served: 100,000 Format: Country. ♦Mark DePrez, gen mgr; Rob Kelley, opns mgr & progmg dir; Mogan David, chief of engrg.

Delphi

WXXB(FM)— May 24, 1989: 102.9 mhz; 2.2 kw. 420 ft TL: N40 34 57 W86 38 26. Stereo. Hrs open: 24 Box 7093, Lafayette, 47903. Secondary address: 3575 McCarty Ln., Lafayette 47905. Phone: (765) 448-1566. Fax: (765) 448-1348.E-mail: trent@wask.com Web Site:www.b1029.com Licensee: WASK, Inc. Group owner: RadioWorks Inc. (acq 10-00; $1 million). Population served: 292,700 Format: CHR/Top 40. News staff: one. Target aud: 18-49. ♦Robert Rhea, pres; Ernie Caldemone, VP; John Trent, gen mgr; John Schurz, rgnl sls mgr; Anthony Bannon, progmg dir.

Earl Park

WIBN(FM)— Oct 15, 1983: 98.1 mhz; 25 kw. 328 ft TL: N40 34 22 W87 27 42. Stereo. Hrs open: Box 25, Oxford, 47971. Phone: (765) 385-2373. Fax: (765) 385-2374.E-mail: wibn@981wibn.com Web Site:www.981wibn.com Licensee: Brothers Broadcasting Corp. (group owner; acq 8-95; $100,000). Format: Oldies. ♦John Balvich, pres, gen mgr, gen sls mgr; Dan McKay, progmg dir; Ken Stapleton, news dir; Don Kerawac, chief of engrg.

Edinburgh

WYGB(FM)— Aug 24, 2000: 100.3 mhz; 6 kw. Ant 318 ft TL: N39 11 10 W85 57 29. Hrs open: 24 Edinburgh Radio, 825 Washington St., Columbus, 47201. Phone: (812) 348-1029. Fax: (812) 375-2555.E-mail: korncountry@korncountry.com Web Site:www.korncountry.com Licensee: Edinburgh Radio. Format: Country. Target aud: 25-54; Bartholomew & Johnson county folks. ♦Keith Reising Jr., CEO.

Elkhart

WAUS(FM)—See South Bend

WBYT(FM)— Apr 1, 1947: 100.7 mhz; 15 kw. 910 ft TL: N41 36 58 W86 11 38. Stereo. Hrs open: 237 Edison Rd., Mishawaka, 46545. Phone: (574) 258-5483. Fax: (574) 258-0930. Web Site:www.b100.com Population served: 41,305 Natl. Rep: Christal,. Format: Country. Target aud: 25-54. Spec prog: Relg 2 hrs wkly. ♦Brad Williams, gen mgr; Barb Deniston, gen sls mgr; Clint Marsh, progmg dir; Greg Trobridge, chief of engrg.

WCMR(AM)— Mar 16, 1956: 1270 khz; 5 kw-D, 1 kw-N, DA-2. TL: N41 37 16 W85 57 40. Hrs open: 24 Box 307, 46517. Secondary address: 25802 County Rd. 26 46515. Phone: (574) 875-5166. Fax: (574) 875-6662. Web Site:www.wfrn.com Licensee: Progressive Broadcasting System Inc. Population served: 200,000 Format: Christian relg, talk. Target aud: 30 plus. ♦Ed Moore, gen mgr; Doug Moore, progmg dir, news rptr.

WFRN-FM— June 10, 1963: 104.7 mhz; 50 kw. 488 ft TL: N41 37 18 W85 57 37. Stereo. Hrs open: 24 Box 307, 46517. Secondary address: 25802 County Rd. 26 46515. Phone: (574) 875-5166. Fax: (574) 875-6662.E-mail: moore@wfrn.com Web Site:www.wfrn.com Licensee: Progressive Broadcasting System Inc. (group owner). Population served: 1,150,000 Natl. Network: USA, . Rgnl. Network: Network Indiana. Network Indiana Reddy, Begley & McCormick. Format: Contemp Christian. News staff: one. Target aud: 25-54; families-primarily women. ♦Edwin Moore, pres, gen mgr; Joanne Matthews, prom dir & traf mgr; Don Wagner, news rptr.

WTRC(AM)— Nov 18, 1931: 1340 khz; 1 kw-U. TL: N41 40 28 W85 56 51. Hrs open: 24 421 S. 2nd St., Suite 100, 46516-3230. Phone: (574) 389-5100. Fax: (574) 389-5101.E-mail: info@am1340.com Web Site:www.hippieradio1340.com Licensee: Pathfinder Communications Corp. Group owner: Federated Media Population served: 139,000 Natl. Network: ABC, . Natl. Rep: Christal,. Format: Oldies. Target aud: 35-64; Elkhart County residents. ♦Kathy Uebler, gen mgr & gen sls mgr; Allan Strike, progmg dir; Gary Sieber, news dir.

***WVPE(FM)**— May 1972: 88.1 mhz; 10 kw. 400 ft TL: N41 36 20 W86 12 46. (CP: 10.5 w, ant 554 ft. TL: N41 36 59 W86 11 43). Stereo. Hrs open: 24 EACC, 2424 California Rd., 46514. Phone: (574) 262-5660. Phone: (574) 674-9873. Fax: (574) 262-5520.E-mail: wvpe@wvpe.org Web Site:www.wvpe.org Licensee: Elkhart Community Schools Corp. Population served: 43,152 Natl. Network: PRI, NPR, . Wire Svc: UPI Format: Jazz, news/talk. News staff: one; News: 13 hrs wkly. Target aud: 25-55. Spec prog: Blues 15 hrs, folk 9 hrs wkly. ♦Anthony Hupp, gen mgr & stn mgr.

WZOW(FM)—See Goshen

Ellettsville

WHCC(FM)— 1992: 105.1 mhz; 6 kw. 328 ft TL: N39 11 32 W86 41 46. Hrs open: 24 Box 7797, Bloomington, 47407. Secondary address: 304 State Rd. 446, Bloomington 47401. Phone: (812) 336-8000. Phone: (812) 335-1051. Fax: (812) 336-7000. Web Site:www.whcc105.com Licensee: Artistic Media Partners L.P. Group owner: Artistic Media Partners Inc. (acq 7-96; $675,000). Population served: 230,000 Natl. Network: Jones Radio Networks, . Rgnl rep: Russ Dodge Haley, Bader & Potts. Format: Country. News staff: 2. Target aud: 25-54. ♦Art Angotti, pres; Sandy Zehr, stn mgr; Rick Evans, opns dir; Deborah Green, gen sls mgr; Bob Henning, chief of engrg.

***WOMB(FM)**—Not on air, target date: unknown: 89.9 mhz; 1.25 kw vert. Ant 447 ft TL: N39 11 32 W86 41 46. Hrs open: 8220 W. State Rd. 48, Bloomington, 47404. Phone: (813) 825-3031. Licensee: Mary's Children Inc. ♦William Dunfee, VP.

Elwood

WURK(FM)— July 1964: 101.7 mhz; 6 kw. Ant 328 ft TL: N40 16 33 W85 51 44. Hrs open: 24
Simulcasts WERK(FM) Muncie 80%.
800 E. 29th St., Muncie, 47302. Secondary address: 9821 S. 800 W., Daleville 47334. Phone: (765) 288-4403. Fax: (765) 378-2091. Web Site:www.werkradio.com Licensee: Indiana Sabrecom Inc. Group owner: Backyard Broadcasting LLC (acq 12-1-02; grpsl). Population served: 37,100 Natl. Network: ABC, . Rgnl. Network: Network Indiana, AgriAmerica, ABC. Network Indiana Format: Oldies. News staff: one; News: 2 hrs wkly. Target aud: 25-54; adult buying public. Spec prog: Gospel 4 hrs wkly. ♦Steve Lindell, opns dir; Jay Garrison, progmg dir; Sean Mattingly, chief of engrg.

Evansville

WABX(FM)— 1997: 107.5 mhz; 2.35 kw. 518 ft TL: N37 59 21 W87 35 48. Hrs open: 24 Box 3848, 47736. Secondary address: 1162 Mount Auburn 47720. Phone: (812) 424-8284. Fax: (812) 426-7928.E-mail: info@wabx.net Web Site:www.wabx.net Licensee: South Central Communications Corp. (group owner) Natl. Rep: Katz Radio,. Format: Classic rock. Target aud: 25-49; men. ♦John P. Engelbrecht, CEO; Craig Jacobus, pres; Tim Huelsing, gen mgr; Krista Seaton, prom dir; Jason Mack, progmg dir; Randy Wheeler, news dir.

WEOA(AM)— 1935: 1400 khz; 1 kw-U. TL: N37 56 17 W87 31 51. Stereo. Hrs open: 24 915 Main St, Suite 001, 47708. Phone: (812) 424-8864. Fax: (812) 424-9946.E-mail: info@weoa.com Licensee: South Central Communications Corp. (group owner; acq 11-81). Population served: 138,764 Natl. Network: ABC, . Bryan Cave. Format: Urban adult contemp. News staff: 2; News: hourly. Target aud: 25-49; general. ♦Ed Lander, pres, gen sls mgr, progmg dir; Regina Lander, gen sls mgr; Larry Switzer, news dir.

WGBF(AM)— Nov 22, 1923: 1280 khz; 5 kw-D, 1 kw-N, DA-N. TL: N37 59 53 W87 28 33. Stereo. Hrs open: 24 117 SE 5th St, 47708. Phone: (812) 425-4226. Fax: (812) 421-0005.E-mail: info@iuhoosiers.com Web Site:iuhoosiers.com/iuradionetwork.html Licensee: Regent Broadcasting of Evansville/Owensboro Inc. Group owner: Regent Communications Inc. (acq 12-3-2003; grpsl). Population served: 565,400 Natl. Network: CNN Radio, Westwood One, . Natl. Rep: Katz Radio,. Format: News/talk. News staff: one; News: 10 hrs wkly. Target aud: 25-54; affluent, mature. ♦Mark Thomas, gen mgr.

WGBF-FM—See Henderson, KY

WIKY-FM— Aug 28, 1948: 104.1 mhz; 39 kw. 571 ft TL: N37 59 21 W87 35 48. Stereo. Hrs open: 1162 Mt. Auburn Rd., 47720. Phone: (812) 424-8284. Fax: (812) 426-7928.E-mail: info@wiky.com Web Site:www.wiky.com (Acq 1948). Format: Adult contemp. Target aud: 25-54; females, workplace. Spec prog: Farm 17 hrs wkly. ♦John P. Engelbrecht, CEO; Tim Huelsing, VP, gen mgr; Paul Broyfield, gen sls mgr; Nora Mitz, mktg dir; Stephanie Todich, prom mgr; Mark Baker, progmg dir, disc jockey; Randy Wheeler, news dir; Chris Myers, chief of engrg; Erin Johnson, traf mgr; Dave Lyons, news rptr; Charles Blake, farm dir; Joe Blair, disc jockey.

WJLT(FM)— Dec 22, 1964: 105.3 mhz; 50 kw. Ant 480 ft TL: N38 04 47 W87 36 36. Stereo. Hrs open: 24 117 S.E. 5th St, 47708. Phone: (812) 425-4226. Fax: (812) 421-0005.E-mail: info@lite1053.com Web

Site:www.lite1053.com Licensee: Regent Broadcasting of Evansville/Owensboro Inc. Group owner: Regent Communications Inc. (acq 12-3-2003; grpsl). Population served: 138,764 Natl. Network: ABC, . Format: Oldies. Target aud: 25-54. ♦Mike Sanders, CFO, opns mgr; Mark Thomas, gen mgr; Kris Mattingly, prom dir, news dir; Cindy Patrick, progmg dir; Rick Crago, gen mgr & chief of engrg.

***WNIN-FM—** Feb 1, 1982: 88.3 mhz; 17 kw. Ant 840 ft TL: N37 59 01 W87 16 13. Stereo. Hrs open: 24 405 Carpenter St., 47708. Phone: (812) 423-2973. Fax: (812) 428-7548.E-mail: wnin@wnin.org Web Site:www.wnin.org Licensee: Tri-State Public Teleplex Inc. Population served: 750,000 Natl. Network: PRI, NPR, . Dow, Lohnes & Albertson. Format: Class, news. News: 20 hrs wkly. Target aud: General. ♦David L. Dial, pres, gen mgr; Jean Noyes, stn mgr; Daniel Moore, progmg dir.

***WPSR(FM)—** September 1957: 90.7 mhz; 14 kw. 130 ft TL: N38 01 45 W87 34 42. Stereo. Hrs open: 6:45 AM-2:45 PM 5400 First Ave., 47710. Phone: (812) 435-8241. Fax: (812) 435-8241.E-mail: wpsr@907wpsr.com Licensee: Evansville Vanderburg School Corp. (acq 9-57). Population served: 150,000 Natl. Network Indiana Format: Div, educ, var music. News: 3 hrs wkly. Target aud: General. ♦Michael H. Reininga, gen mgr & dev dir.

***WSWI(AM)—** Aug 6, 1947: 820 khz; 250 w-D. TL: N37 57 53 W87 40 06. Hrs open: Liberal Arts Bldg., 8600 University Blvd., 47712. Phone: (812) 465-1665. Fax: (812) 461-5261.E-mail: wswi@usi.edu Web Site:www.usi.edu/wswi Licensee: University of Southern Indiana. (acq 11-3-81). Population served: 150,000 Format: College alternative. News staff: News progmg 3 hrs wkly Target aud: 18-54; students, faculty & community members. ♦John Morris, gen mgr.

***WUEV(FM)—** Apr 1, 1951: 91.5 mhz; 6.1 kw. 150 ft TL: N37 58 24 W87 31 48. Stereo. Hrs open: 24 1800 Lincoln Ave., 47722. Phone: (812) 479-2022. Fax: (812) 479-2320.E-mail: wuev@evansville.edu Web Site:wuev.evansville.edu Licensee: University of Evansville. Population served: 250,000 Rgnl. Network: Network Indiana. Network Indiana Wire Svc: UPI Format: Div, jazz. News staff: 3; News: 10 hrs wkly. Spec prog: Children 5 hrs, American Indian one hr wkly. ♦Mike Crowley, gen mgr, opns mgr; Phil Bailey, chief of engrg.

WVHI(AM)— Oct 31, 1948: 1330 khz; 5 kw-D, 1 kw-N, DA-N. TL: N38 03 12 W87 35 40. Hrs open: Box 3636, 47735. Phone: (812) 425-2221. Fax: (812) 425-2078. Web Site:www.wvhi.com Licensee: Word Broadcasting Network. (acq 3-17-99). Population served: 138,764 Format: Relg, adult contemp. Target aud: General. ♦Krista Denton, gen mgr & gen sls mgr.

WYNG(FM)—See Mount Carmel, IL

Fairland

***WABT(FM)—**Not on air, target date: unknown: 90.9 mhz; 110 w vert. Ant 97 ft TL: N39 35 37.2 W85 55 44.2. Hrs open: 15 Wood St., Greenfield, 46140. Phone: (317) 467-1064. Licensee: Hoosier Public Radio Corp. ♦Martin L. Hensley, pres.

Ferdinand

WQKZ(FM)— Nov 1, 1997: 98.5 mhz; 6 kw. 328 ft TL: N38 10 02 W86 49 49. Hrs open: Box 167, Jasper, 47547-0167. Phone: (812) 482-2131. Fax: (812) 482-9609.E-mail: wqkz@psci.net Licensee: Gem Communications L.L.P. (acq 4-17-98). Natl. Network: Jones Radio Networks, . Format: Country. ♦G. Earl Metzger, pres; Gene Kuntz, gen mgr; Gary Hoffman, progmg dir, progmg mgr; Chris James, news dir; Frank Hertel, chief of engrg.

Fort Branch

***WBGW(FM)—** July 20, 1990: 101.5 mhz; 1 kw. 561 ft TL: N38 10 45 W87 29 13. Stereo. Hrs open: 24 Box 4164, Evansville, 47724. Secondary address: Box 4463 E. 1200 F, R.R. 2, County Rd.1200 S., Haubstadt 47629. Phone: (812) 386-3342. Fax: (812) 768-5552.E-mail: mail@thyword.org Web Site:www.thyword.org Licensee: Music Ministries Inc. Natl. Network: Moody, USA, . Format: Relg. News: 12 hrs wkly. Target aud: 35-54. ♦Floyd E. Turner, gen mgr; Susan Turner, prom dir.

Fort Wayne

WAJI(FM)— August 1959: 95.1 mhz; 39 kw. 680 ft TL: N41 06 13 W85 11 28. Stereo. Hrs open: 24 347 W. Berry, Suite 600, 46802. Phone: (260) 423-3676. Fax: (260) 422-5266. Licensee: Sarkes Tarzian Inc. (group owner) Population served: 416,800 Natl. Rep: Katz Radio,. Leventhal, Senter & Lerman. Wire Svc: AP Format: Adult contemp. News staff: one. Target aud: 25-54; women. ♦Thomas Tarzian, CEO; Robert Davis, CFO; Darlene Lee, gen mgr; Lee Tobin, opns mgr; Shelly Steckler, sls dir, gen sls mgr; Barb Richards, progmg dir; Amy Collins, news dir, traf mgr; Geary Morrill, chief of engrg.

***WBCL(FM)—** Jan 8, 1976: 90.3 mhz; 26 kw. Ant 692 ft TL: N41 06 13 W85 11 46. Stereo. Hrs open: 24 1025 W. Rudisill Blvd., 46807. Phone: (260) 745-0576. Fax: (260) 456-2913.E-mail: wbcl@wbcl.org Web Site:www.wbcl.org Licensee: Taylor University Broadcasting Inc. (acq 6-24-92;7-20-92). Population served: 800,000 Format: Contemp Christian. ♦Marsha Bunker, gen mgr; Scott Tsuleff, progmg dir; Craig Albrecht, chief of engrg.

***WBOI(FM)—** June 15, 1978: 89.1 mhz; 34 kw. Ant 604 ft TL: N41 06 13 W85 10 44. Stereo. Hrs open: 24 Box 8459, 46898-8459. Secondary address: 3204 Clairmont Ct. 46808. Phone: (260) 452-1189. Fax: (260) 452-1188.E-mail: jbrown@nipr.fm Web Site:www.nipr.fm Licensee: Northeast Indiana Public Radio Inc. (acq 1-15-82). Population served: 500,000 Natl. Network: PRI, NPR, AP Radio, . Rgnl. Network: Network Indiana. Network Indiana Dow, Lohnes & Albertson. Format: News/talk, jazz. Target aud: 25 plus. ♦Bruce Haines, gen mgr; Colleen Condron, opns dir, opns mgr, progmg dir; Karen Fraser, dev dir & prom dir; Jeanette Dillon, progmg dir, news dir.

WBTU(FM)—(Kendallville, Dec 16, 1964: 93.3 mhz; 50 kw. Ant 450 ft TL: N41 23 55 W85 15 08. Stereo. Hrs open: 24 2100 Goshen Rd., Suite 232, 46808. Phone: (260) 482-9288. Fax: (260) 482-8655.E-mail: pd@wbtu.fm Web Site:www.us933.us Licensee: Oasis Radio 1 Corp. (acq 10-19-2007; $3.8 million with WVBB(FM) Columbia City). Population served: 900,000 Format: Country. Target aud: 18-54; upscale, young audience. ♦Roger Diehm, gen mgr; Dave Turpchinoff, gen sls mgr; Scott Roddy, progmg dir; Shelley Hall, traf mgr; Tami Gatchell, traf mgr & disc jockey.

WFCV(AM)— June 17, 1968: 1090 khz; 2.5 kw-D, 1 kw-CH, DA-2. TL: N41 05 01 W85 04 32. Hrs open: Sunrise-sunset 3737 Lake Ave., 46805. Phone: (260) 423-2337. Fax: (260) 423-6355. Web Site:www.bottradionetwork.com Licensee: Bott Broadcasting. (group owner; acq 5-1-80). Population served: 850,000 Natl. Network: USA, . Format: Christian info. Target aud: 25-54; family oriented. ♦Richard P. Bott, pres; Richard Bott II, VP; Dale Gerke, stn mgr; Kathy McClish, opns mgr.

WFWI(FM)— Mar 4, 1993: 92.3 mhz; 2.2 kw. Ant 544 ft TL: N41 06 39 W85 11 44. Hrs open: 24 1005 Production Rd., 46808. Phone: (260) 471-5100. Fax: (260) 471-5224.E-mail: info@wfwi.com Web Site:www.923thefort.com Licensee: Pathfinder Communications Corp. Group owner: Federated Media (acq 3-1-97). Population served: 380,000 Natl. Network: ABC, . Format: Classic rock. News staff: one; News: 6 hrs wkly. Target aud: 25-54; men and adults. ♦John Dille, pres; Jim Allgeier, gen mgr; Sonya Maldeney, mktg dir; Billy Elvis, progmg dir; Jack Didier, chief of engrg.

WGL(AM)— Jan 24, 1924: 1250 khz; 2.5 kw-D, 1.4 kw-N, DA-2. TL: N41 01 16 W85 09 46. Hrs open: 24 2000 Lower Huntington Rd., 46819. Phone: (260) 747-1511. Fax: (260) 747-3999. Web Site:1250theriver.com Licensee: Summit City License Sub, LLC. Group owner: Summit City Radio Group (acq 11-6-2006;. grpsl). Population served: 177,671 Natl. Network: CBS, . Format: Adult standards. News: 2 hrs wkly. ♦J.J. Fabini, progmg dir.

WKJG(AM)— November 1947: 1380 khz; 5 kw-U, DA-2. TL: N41 00 15 W85 05 57. Stereo. Hrs open: 2915 Maples Rd., 46816. Phone: (260) 447-5511. Fax: (260) 447-7546.E-mail: info@wise33.com Web Site:www.wise33.com Licensee: Pathfinder Communications Corp. Group owner: Federated Media. Population served: 102,500 Natl. Network: ABC, . Natl. Rep: Christal,. Format: All sports. ♦Mark DePrez, gen mgr, gen sls mgr; Jim Tighe, sls dir; Jon Zimney, progmg dir, news dir, news dir; Jack Didion, engrg VP; Mogan David, chief of engrg; Eileen Strickland, traf mgr.

***WLAB(FM)—** Aug 23, 1976: 88.3 mhz; 3.2 kw. Ant 607 ft TL: N41 06 13 W85 11 28. Stereo. Hrs open: 24 6600 N. Clinton St., 8 Martin Luther Dr., 46825. Phone: (260) 483-8236. Fax: (260) 482-7707.E-mail: don@star883.com Web Site:www.star883.com Licensee: STAR Educational Media Network (pending) Population served: 416,800 Shaw Pittman. Format: Adult contemp Christian. Target aud: 25-44; Christian. ♦Melissa Montana, gen mgr; Don Buettner, progmg dir.

WLDE(FM)— Aug 24, 1970: 101.7 mhz; 3 kw. 328 ft TL: N41 04 58 W85 04 22. Stereo. Hrs open: 24 347 W. Berry, Suite 600, 46802. Phone: (260) 423-3676. Fax: (260) 422-5266. Licensee: Sarkes Tarzian Inc. (group owner; acq 2-16-93; 3-8-93). Population served: 380,900 Natl. Network: CNN Radio, . Natl. Rep: Katz Radio,. Leventhal,Senter & Lerman. Wire Svc: AP Format: Classic Hits. News staff: one. Target aud: Adults 25-54. ♦Thomas Tarzian, CEO; R. Geoffrey Vargo, pres; Robert Davis, CFO; Chris Didier, gen mgr, progmg dir; Shelly Steckler, sls dir, gen sls mgr; Geary Morrill, chief of engrg; Aimee Collins, traf mgr.

WLYV(AM)— Mar 28, 1948: 1450 khz; 1 kw-U. TL: N41 04 14 W85 07 10. Stereo. Hrs open: 24 4705 Illinois Rd., Suite 104, 46804. Phone: (260) 436-9598. Fax: (260) 432-6179.E-mail: Info@redeemerradio.com Licensee: Fort Wayne Catholic Radio Group Inc. (group owner; (acq 12-1-2005; $700,000). Population served: 177,671 Natl. Network: USA, . Format: Christian, relg. Target aud: 25-54; Christian adults. Spec prog: Spanish one hr wkly. ♦Chris Langford, CEO, pres; Jason Garrett, gen mgr; Patty Becker, progmg dir.

WMEE(FM)— Feb 5, 1965: 97.3 mhz; 26 kw. 689 ft TL: N41 06 42 W85 11 43. Stereo. Hrs open: 24 2915 Maples Rd., 46816. Phone: (260) 447-5511. Fax: (260) 447-7546.E-mail: info@wmee.com Web Site:www.wmee.com Licensee: Pathfinder Communications Corp. Population served: 218,400 Format: Hot adult contemp. News: one hr wkly. Target aud: 25-54. ♦John Dille, pres; Bob Watson, CFO; Mark Evans, opns mgr; Joel Pyle, gen sls mgr; Rob Kiley, progmg dir; Chris Cage, mus dir; Jack Didier, engrg dir.

WOWO(AM)— Mar 31, 1925: 1190 khz; 50 kw-U, DA-N. TL: N40 59 47 W85 21 06. (CP: 9.8 kw-N). Stereo. Hrs open: 24 2915 Maples Rd., 46816. Phone: (260) 447-5511. Fax: (260) 447-7546.E-mail: info@wowo.com Web Site:www.wowo.com Licensee: Pathfinder Communications Corp. Group owner: Federated Media Natl. Network: CBS, . Natl. Rep: Christal,. Format: News/talk, sports. News staff: 5. Target aud: 25-54. ♦Tony Richards, COO; John Dille, pres; Bob Watson, CFO; Mark DePrez, gen mgr; Jon Zimney, opns mgr, prom mgr, progmg mgr; Jim Tighe, gen sls mgr, progmg dir; Andy Ober, news dir; Mogan David, chief of engrg.

WXKE(FM)— May 6, 1976: 103.9 mhz; 3 kw. Ant 380 ft TL: N41 06 31 W85 09 56. Stereo. Hrs open: 24 2000 Lower Huntington Rd., 46819. Phone: (260) 747-1511. Fax: (260) 747-3999. Web Site:www.rock104radio.com Licensee: Summit City License Sub, LLC. Group owner: Summit City Radio Group (acq 11-6-2006; grpsl). Population served: 417,300 Natl. Rep: Eastman Radio,. Format: Classic rock / Mainstream Rock. News staff: one. ♦Doc West, progmg dir.

Frankfort

WILO(AM)— Nov 23, 1953: 1570 khz; 250 w-U. TL: N40 16 40 W86 29 07. Hrs open: 5 AM-11 PM Box 545, 46041. Secondary address: 1401 Barner St. 46041-1506. Phone: (765) 659-3338. Fax: (765) 659-3338. Web Site:www.wilo.net Licensee: Kaspar Broadcasting Co. Inc. Group owner: Kaspar Broadcasting Group (acq 10-1-59). Population served: 14,956 Natl. Rep: Rgnl Reps,. Format: Community svc, nostalgia. Spec prog: Farm 12 hrs wkly. ♦Russ Kaspar, gen mgr, stn mgr; Randy Lawson, progmg dir.

WSHW(FM)— Sept 14, 1962: 99.7 mhz; 50 kw. Ant 460 ft TL: N40 25 14 W86 24 47. Stereo. Hrs open: Box 545, 46041. Secondary address: 1401 Barner St. 46041-1506. Phone: (800) 447-4463. Fax: (765) 452-0299. Fax: (765) 452-0399. Web Site:www.shine99.com Licensee: Kaspar Broadcasting Co. Inc. Format: Adult contemp. Spec prog: Farm 8 hrs wkly. ♦Russ Kaspar, gen sls mgr; Randy Lawson, progmg dir.

Franklin

***WFCI(FM)—** Oct 15, 1960: 89.5 mhz; 1.15 kw. Ant 140 ft TL: N39 24 29 W86 08 52. Stereo. Hrs open: 8 AM-2 AM Franklin College, 101 Branigan Blvd., 46131. Phone: (317) 738-8205. Phone: (317) 738-8204. Fax: (317) 738-8233.E-mail: info@franklincollege.edu Web Site:www.franklincollege.edu Licensee: Franklin College of Indiana. Population served: 14,956 Format: CHR. Target aud: 12-24; college & high school students.

WFDM(FM)— Dec 15, 1961: 95.9 mhz; 3 kw. Ant 300 ft TL: N39 30 49 W86 04 07. Stereo. Hrs open: 645 Industrial Dr., 46131. Phone: (317) 736-4040. Fax: (317) 736-4781. Web Site:www.freedom959.com Licensee: Pilgrim Communications LLC. (acq 7-2-99). Population served: 110,000 Natl. Rep: Rgnl Reps,. Format: Talk. ♦Randy Tipmore, VP, gen mgr & progmg dir.

French Lick

WFLQ(FM)— Apr 12, 1983: 100.1 mhz; 6 kw. 300 ft TL: N38 35 41 W86 36 48. Stereo. Hrs open: 24 Box 100, 47432. Phone: (812) 936-9100. Fax: (812) 936-9495.E-mail: wflqfm@smithville.net Web Site:www.wflq.com Licensee: W.G. Willis dba Willtronics Broadcasting.

Population served: 30,000 Natl. Network: ABC, . Rgnl. Network: Brownfield; AgriAmerica. Format: Modern country. News staff: one; News: 11 hrs wkly. Target aud: 25 plus. Spec prog: Farm 3 hrs, relg 6 hrs, Gospel 4 hrs wkly. ◆Bill Willis, gen sls mgr, chief of engrg; Randall Hamm, progmg dir & mus dir; Joe Randolph, news dir.

Gary

*WGVE(FM)— January 1954: 88.7 mhz; 2.1 kw. 91 ft TL: N41 33 15 W87 19 05. Stereo. Hrs open: 1800 E. 35th Ave., 46409. Phone: (219) 962-9483. Fax: (219) 962-3726.E-mail: wgve887fm@yahoo.com Licensee: Gary Community School Corp. Population served: 336,695 Format: Educ, talk, music. Northwest Indiana. ◆Sarita Stevens, gen mgr; Elizabeth Garcia, progmg dir, progmg.

WLTH(AM)— Nov 5, 1950: 1370 khz; 1 kw-D, 500 w-N, DA-N. TL: N41 34 17 W87 19 02. Hrs open: 1563 E. 85th Ave., Merrillville, 46410. Phone: (219) 794-1370. Fax: (219) 794-1377.E-mail: info@wlth.com Licensee: WLTH Radio Inc. (acq 4-21-98; $750,000). Population served: 350,000 Natl. Network: CNN Radio, . Format: News/talk, sports. ◆Pluria Marshall Jr., gen mgr.

WWCA(AM)— Dec 7, 1949: 1270 khz; 1 kw-U, DA-1. TL: N41 31 38 W87 22 36. Hrs open: Box10745, Meriville, 46411-0745. Phone: (219) 309-9327. Web Site:www.ca@revelantradio.com Licensee: Starboard Media Foundation Inc. Group owner: Relevant Radio (acq 7-1-2004; $1.5 million). Population served: 155,700 Format: Talk radio. ◆Armand Ciabattari, stn mgr.

Goshen

*WGCS(FM)— Oct 2, 1958: 91.1 mhz; 6 kw. 220 ft TL: N41 33 29 W85 51 06. Stereo. Hrs open: 24 1700 S. Main, 46526. Phone: (574) 535-7488. Phone: (574) 535-7688. Fax: (574) 535-7293.E-mail: globe@goshen.edu Web Site:globeradio.org Licensee: Goshen College Broadcasting Corp. Natl. Network: PRI, . Reddy, Bagley, McCormick. Format: Folk. News: 8 hrs wkly. Target aud: Adults 25-49. Spec prog: Sp 8 hrs, news 8 hrs, sports 10 hrs wkly. ◆Jason Samuel, gen mgr.

WKAM(AM)— 1954: 1460 khz; 2.5 kw-D, 500 w-N, DA-N. TL: N41 35 24 W85 48 56. Hrs open: 24 930 E. Lincoln Ave., 46528. Phone: (574) 533-1460. Fax: (574) 534-3698. Web Site:www.wkam1460.com Licensee: Fulmer Communications LLC (acq 5-16-02; $100,000). Population served: 156,198 Natl. Network: USA, . Rgnl. Network: Network Indiana. Natl. Rep: Katz Radio, Rgnl Reps,. Network Indiana Format: Adult contemp, Latin. News staff: one; News: 20 hrs wkly. Target aud: 30-65; mature, family oriented, goal oriented. Spec prog: Southern gospel 6 hrs wkly. ◆Kent Fulmer, gen mgr.

WZOW(FM)— Jan 17, 1977: 97.7 mhz; 3 kw. Ant 482 ft TL: N41 36 04 W85 55 41. Stereo. Hrs open: 24 3371 Cleveland Rd., Suite 300, South Bend, 46628. Phone: (574) 273-9300. Fax: (574) 273-9090.E-mail: michael@wzow.com Web Site:www.wzow.com Licensee: Artistic Media Partners Inc. (group owner; (acq 4-1-2002; $925,000). Format: Classic rock. Target aud: 25-54. ◆Jack Swart, gen mgr; Carrie Jones, natl sls mgr; Teresa Holden, prom dir; Chili Walker, progmg dir; Bob Henning, chief of engrg; Rita Kinzie, traf mgr.

Granger

WRBR-FM—See South Bend

Greencastle

*WGRE(FM)— Apr 25, 1949: 91.5 mhz; 1 kw. 160 ft TL: N39 39 16 W86 51 40. Stereo. Hrs open: 24 Ctr. for Contemporary Media, 609 S. Locust, 46135. Phone: (765) 658-4642. Phone: (765) 658-4637. Fax: (765) 658-4693.E-mail: newton@depauw.edu Web Site:www.wgre.org Licensee: DePauw University. Population served: 45,000 Natl. Network: AP Radio, . Wire Svc: AP Format: Alternative. News: 12 hrs wkly. Target aud: 18-25; college campus & loc community. Spec prog: Jazz 3 hrs, Intl 2 hrs, regl 2 hrs wkly. ◆Jeff McCall, pres & gen mgr; Chris Newton, opns mgr; Greg Stephan, chief of engrg.

*WIKL(FM)— 2005: 90.5 mhz; 15 kw vert. Ant 436 ft TL: N39 41 19 W86 42 03. Hrs open:
Rebroadcasts KLVR(FM) Middleton, CA 100%.
Box 779002, Rocklin, CA, 95677-9972. Phone: (916) 251-1600. Fax: (916) 251-1650. Web Site:www.klove.com Licensee: Educational Media Foundation. (acq 11-1-2006; $2 million). Natl. Network: K-Love, . Format: Contemp Christian. ◆Mike Novak, sr VP.

WREB(FM)— May 16, 1966: 94.3 mhz; 3 kw. 165 ft TL: N39 39 38 W86 53 34. Stereo. Hrs open: 24 2468 W. County Rd. 25 N., 46135.

Phone: (765) 653-9717. Fax: (765) 653-6677. Web Site:www.wrebfm.com Licensee: The Original Co. Group owner: The Original Co. Inc. (acq 6-22-94; $200,000; 7-11-94). Population served: 30,000 Rgnl. Network: Network Indiana, Brownfield. Brownfield Format: Country, loc news, sports. News staff: one; News: 37 hrs wkly. Target aud: General. Spec prog: Farm 5 hrs wkly. ◆Mark Lange, gen mgr; Tonya Sanders, progmg dir.

Greenfield

*WRGF(FM)— 2001: 89.7 mhz; 750 w horiz, 2 kw vert. Ant 164 ft TL: N39 44 55 W85 40 50. Hrs open: 110 W. North St., Greenfield Central Comm. School Corp., 46140. Secondary address: 810 N. Broadway 46140. Phone: (317) 462-9211. Fax: (317) 467-6755.E-mail: wrgf@insight66.com Web Site:gcsc.k12.in.us Licensee: Greenfield Central Community School Corp. Format: Old & new rock. ◆Tim Renshaw, gen mgr.

WZPL(FM)— June 1, 1962: 99.5 mhz; 12.5 kw. 991 ft TL: N39 46 03 W86 00 12. Stereo. Hrs open: 9245 N. Meridian, Suite 300, Indianapolis, 46260. Phone: (317) 816-4000. Fax: (317) 816-4080.E-mail: info@wzpl.com Web Site:www.wzpl.com Licensee: Entercom Indianapolis License LLC. (acq 8-26-2004; grpsl). Population served: 443,600 Natl. Rep: McGavren Guild,. Format: Modern adult contemp. Target aud: 18-49; women. ◆Phil Hoover, CFO, VP, gen mgr; Steve Hartley, gen sls mgr; Toni Williams, prom dir; Scott Sands, progmg dir; Gary Hunvnel, news dir; Mike Rabey, chief of engrg.

Greensburg

*WAUZ(FM)— Sept 1, 1998: 89.1 mhz; 1.2 kw vert. 420 ft TL: N39 14 13 W85 34 00. Hrs open: 24 c/o WYGS(FM), 825 Washington St., Columbus, 47201. Secondary address: Box 487 47201. Phone: (812) 738-3482. Fax: (812) 375-2555.E-mail: ygs@wygs.org Web Site:www.wygs.org Licensee: Good Shepherd Radio Inc. Population served: 70,000 Format: Christian/ southern Gospel. Target aud: 25-40. ◆Keith Reising, CEO & pres.

WRZQ-FM— December 1962: 107.3 mhz; 41.8 kw. 531 ft TL: N39 14 13 W85 34 00. Stereo. Hrs open: 24 Radio Bldg., 825 Washington St., Columbus, 47201. Phone: (812) 379-1077. Fax: (812) 375-2555.E-mail: qmix@qmix.com Web Site:www.qmix.com Population served: 445,000 Format: Adult contemp. News staff: one; News: 4 hrs wkly. Target aud: 18-49. ◆Keith Reising Jr., pres; Mike King, gen mgr; Dave Wineland, opns dir; Dale Marks, sls dir; Sara Beth Clark, mktg dir; Matt Joyce, prom dir; C.J. Miller, progmg dir; Keith Maddox, news dir; Jim Burgan, engrg dir; Mark Gravely, disc jockey.

WTRE(AM)— July 1, 1968: 1330 khz; 500 w-D, 41 w-N, DA-2. TL: N39 19 41 W85 30 06. Hrs open: 18 Box 487, 1217 W. Park Rd., 47240. Phone: (812) 663-3000. Fax: (812) 663-8355.E-mail: wtre@hsonline.net Web Site:www.treecountry.com Licensee: WTRE Inc. (acq 8-13-99; with co-located WTRE). Population served: 10,000 Rgnl. Network: Network Indiana. Network Indiana Format: Country, div, news/talk. News staff: one; News: 24 hrs wkly. Target aud: 25 plus. Spec prog: Farm 10 hrs, relg 3 hrs wkly. ◆Keith Reising Jr., pres; Dave Peach, sls dir; Robert Hawkins, chief of engrg; Mark Gravely, disc jockey.

Greenwood

WTLC-FM— 1994: 106.7 mhz; 3 kw. 328 ft TL: N39 42 42 W86 08 45. Hrs open: 21 E. Saint Joseph St., Indianapolis, 46204. Phone: (317) 266-9600. Fax: (317) 328-3870. Web Site:www.wtlc.com Licensee: Radio One of Indiana LLC. Group owner: Radio One Inc. (acq 2-15-01; grpsl). Format: Oldies, rhythm and blues. ◆Charles T. Williams, VP, gen mgr; Kay Feenye-Caito, prom dir; Brian Wallace, progmg dir; Terri Durrett, news dir; Don Payne, chief of engrg.

Hagerstown

*WBSH(FM)— December 1996: 91.1 mhz; 300 w. 216 ft TL: N39 56 31 W85 11 41. Hrs open:
Rebroadcasts WBST(FM) Muncie 100%.
c/o WBST(FM), Ball State Univ., Muncie, 47306. Phone: (765) 285-5888. Fax: (765) 285-8937.E-mail: info@bsu.edu/ipr Web Site:www.bsu.edu/ipr Licensee: Ball State University. Format: Class, news. News staff: one; News: 33 hrs wkly. Target aud: General. ◆Marcus Jackman, gen mgr; Pam Coletti, gen sls mgr; Carol Trimmer, prom mgr; Steven Turpin, progmg dir & mus dir; Robert Mittendorf, chief of engrg; Dorothy Marvell, traf mgr; Brian Beaver, news rptr.

Hammond

WJOB(AM)— 1928: 1230 khz; 1 kw-U. TL: N41 35 46 W87 28 42. Hrs open: 24 6405 Olcott, 46320. Phone: (219) 989-8502. Fax: (219) 844-6190. Web Site:www.heyregion.com Licensee: Vazquez Development LLC (acq 12-4-2003; $1.2 million with WIMS(AM) Michigan City). Population served: 450,000 Martin & McCormick. Format: News/talk. News staff: 10; News: 17 hrs wkly. Target aud: 25-49; general. Spec prog: Sports, Pol 2 hrs, relg 2 hrs, Greek one hr wkly. ◆Jim Dedelow, gen mgr; Michael Stewart, progmg dir; Ron Perzo, news dir.

WPWX(FM)— Sept 14, 1959: 92.3 mhz; 50 kw horiz, 44 kw vert. 492 ft TL: N41 37 50 W87 31 40. Stereo. Hrs open: 24 6336 Calumet Ave., 46324. Phone: (773) 734-4455. Fax: (219) 933-0323.E-mail: wpwxinfo@crawfordbroadcasting.com Web Site:www.power92chicago.com Licensee: Dontron Inc. Group owner: Crawford Broadcasting Co. (acq 9-14-59). Population served: 250,000 Format: Urban hip hop. Target aud: 18-34; urban. ◆Donald Crawford, pres; Taft Harris, gen mgr & stn mgr; Jay Allen, progmg dir.

Hanna

*WHLP(FM)— 2001: 89.9 mhz; 8 kw. Ant 505 ft TL: N41 26 09 W86 50 48. Hrs open: 150 Lincoln Way, Suite 2001, Valparaiso, 46383. Phone: (219) 548-8956. Fax: (219) 548-5808.E-mail: whlp@csnradio.com Web Site:csnradio.com Licensee: CSN International (group owner). Format: Relg. ◆Jim Motshagen, gen mgr; Kathy Motshagen, progmg dir.

Hardinsburg

WKLO(FM)— 2002: 96.9 mhz; 3.5 kw. Ant 433 ft TL: N38 28 21 W86 24 39. Hrs open: 514 N. JFK Ave., Loogootee, 47553. Phone: (812) 295-9480. Fax: (812) 295-4455. Licensee: Hembree Communications Inc. (acq 12-17-2003; $350,000). Format: Hot adult contemp. ◆Larry Hembree, gen mgr; Kim Lozano, gen sls mgr.

Hartford City

*WHCI(FM)— 2003: 88.1 mhz; 100 w. 72 ft Hrs open: 7:30 AM-4 PM 2392 N. State Rd. 3, Blackford County School Corp., 47348. Phone: (765) 348-7560. Fax: (765) 348-7568. Web Site:www.bcs.k12.in.us Licensee: Blackford County School Corp. Format: Var. ◆Harry Anderson, gen mgr.

WMXQ(FM)— Feb 26, 1965: 93.5 mhz; 3.04 kw. 456 ft TL: N40 25 16 W85 25 40. Hrs open: 24 800 E. 29th St., Muncie, 47302. Phone: (765) 288-4403. Fax: (765) 378-2091.E-mail: maxstudio@maxrocks.com Web Site:www.maxrocks.net Licensee: Backyard Broadcasting Indiana Licensee LLC. Group owner: Backyard Broadcasting LLC (acq 12-1-2002; grpsl). Population served: 150,000 Natl. Network: Westwood One, . Natl. Rep: Rgnl Reps,. Wire Svc: UPI Format: Classic rock. News staff: one; News: one hr wkly. Target aud: 25-54. ◆Steve Lindell, gen mgr & opns mgr.

Hope

WXCH(FM)— Nov 15, 1984: 102.9 mhz; 500 w horiz. Ant 46 ft TL: N39 18 41 W85 47 07. Stereo. Hrs open:
Rebroadcasts WSCH(FM) Aurora 98%.
20 E. High St., Lawrenceburg, 47025-1820. Phone: (812) 438-2777. Fax: (812) 537-5735.E-mail: wsch@one.net Licensee: Wagon Wheel Broadcasting LLC. (acq 11-15-2007; grpsl). Population served: 24,360 Format: Country. ◆Marty Pieratt, gen mgr; Dennis Drees, opns VP; Bob Shannon, news dir.

Howe

*WHWE(FM)— May 1, 1970: 89.7 mhz; 100 w. 68 ft TL: N41 43 32 W85 25 30. Stereo. Hrs open: 7 AM-4 PM Box 240, Howe Military School, 46746. Phone: (219) 562-2131. Fax: (219) 562-3678. Licensee: Howe Military School. Population served: 10,000 Format: Educ, CHR, div. Target aud: 7-20; high school. ◆Steve Clark, stn mgr.

*WQKO(FM)— 1994: 91.9 mhz; 3 kw. Ant 298 ft TL: N41 38 59 W85 21 12. Hrs open: 150 Lincolnway, Suite 2001, Valparaiso, 46383. Phone: (219) 548-5800. Fax: (219) 548-5808.E-mail: info@CalvaryRadioNetwork.com Web Site:www.calvaryradionetwork.com Licensee: CSN International (group owner; (acq 7-13-98; $80,000). Format: Christian praise & worship, teaching. ◆Jim Motshag, gen mgr; Judy Puente, progmg dir.

Huntingburg

WBDC(FM)—Licensed to Huntingburg. See Jasper

Huntington

WBZQ(AM)— May 25, 1957: 1300 khz; 500 w-D, DA. TL: N40 52 31 W85 28 27. Hrs open: 24 Box 5570, Fort Wayne, 46895. Phone: (260) 482-8500. Licensee: Larko Communications Inc. (acq 8-31-00; $16,500). Population served: 50,000 Format: Oldies. Target aud: 25-65. ♦Chris Larko, gen mgr.

WGL-FM— Sept 1, 1965: 102.9 mhz; 4.7 kw. Ant 298 ft TL: N40 55 33 W85 23 15. Stereo. Hrs open: 24 2000 Lower Huntington Rd., Ft. Wayne, 46819. Phone: (260) 747-1511. Fax: (260) 747-3999. Web Site:www.1029theriver.com Licensee: Summit City License Sub, LLC. Group owner: Summit City Radio Group (acq 11-6-2006; grpsl). Population served: 417,300 Natl. Network: CBS, . Natl. Rep: Eastman Radio,. Format: Adult standards. News staff: one. Target aud: 25-54. ♦J.J Fabini, progmg dir.

***WVSH(FM)**— Jan 1, 1950: 91.9 mhz; 920 w. 110 ft TL: N40 53 32 W85 30 38. Stereo. Hrs open: 450 MacGahan St., 46750. Phone: (260) 356-2019. Fax: (260) 358-2210.E-mail: bwalker@hccsc.k12in.us Licensee: Huntington County Community School Corp. Population served: 18,000 Rgnl. Network: Network Indiana. Network Indiana Format: CHR. ♦Bill Walker, gen mgr; George Castle, engr.

Indianapolis

***WBDG(FM)**— Sept 13, 1965: 90.9 mhz; 400 w. 78 ft TL: N39 47 05 W86 17 27. Stereo. Hrs open: 24 1200 N. Girls School Rd., 46214. Phone: (317) 244-9234. Fax: (317) 243-5506.E-mail: jon.easter @wayne.k12.in.us Web Site:www.wayne.k12.in.us/bdwbdg Licensee: Metropolitan School District of Wayne Township. Population served: 3,000 Wire Svc: Reuters Format: Contemp hit, rock/AOR, urban contemp. News: 10 hrs wkly. Target aud: 12-49. ♦Jon Easter, gen mgr; Matt Reedy, progmg dir; Paul McDonald, news dir; Kevin Van Wyk, chief of engrg, chief of engrg.

WBRI(AM)— Mar 10, 1964: 1500 khz; 5 kw-D, DA. TL: N39 52 14 W86 05 17. Hrs open: 6 AM-7 PM 4802 E. 62nd St., 46220. Phone: (317) 255-5484. Fax: (317) 255-8592.E-mail: wbri@wilkinsradio.com Licensee: Heritage Christian Radio Inc. (acq 7-1-2003; $1.5 million). Population served: 1,800,000 Natl. Network: Salem Radio Network, . Womble, Carlyle, Sandridge & Rice. Format: Christian teaching/talk. Target aud: 35 plus. ♦Bob Wilkins, pres; LuAnn Wilkins, exec VP; Mitchell Mathis, VP; Keith Smiley, stn mgr; Greg Garrett, opns mgr, progmg mgr; Phil Alexander, engr.

***WEDM(FM)**— Sept 14, 1970: 91.1 mhz; 180 w vert. Ant 216 ft TL: N39 47 29 W85 59 53. Stereo. Hrs open: 24 c/o Walker Career Ctr., 9651 E. 21st St., 46229. Phone: (317) 532-6301. Fax: (317) 532-6199. Licensee: Metropolitan School District of Warren Township. Population served: 30,000 Rgnl. Network: Network Indiana. Format: CHR. News: 3 hrs wkly. Target aud: General; Warren Township residents. ♦Daniel J. Henn, stn mgr.

WFBQ(FM)— Nov 26, 1959: 94.7 mhz; 58 kw. Ant 804 ft TL: N39 53 43 W86 12 04. Hrs open: 24 Prog sep from AM 6161 Fall Creek Rd., 46220. Phone: (317) 257-7565. Fax: (317) 253-6501.E-mail: info@wfbq.com Web Site:www.wfbq.com Licensee: Capstar TX LP Natl. Network: AP Radio, . Format: Classic rock. ♦Jim Kendall, prom dir; Drew Carey, progmg dir.

WFMS(FM)— Mar 17, 1957: 95.5 mhz; 13 kw. Ant 1,000 ft TL: N39 46 03 W86 00 12. Stereo. Hrs open: 24 6810 N. Shadeland Ave., 46220. Phone: (317) 842-9550. Fax: (317) 577-3361. Web Site:www.wfms.com Licensee: WFMS Lico Inc. Group owner: Susquehanna Radio Corp. (acq 11-20-72). Population served: 275,000 Format: Modern country. ♦Christopher J. Wheat, VP; Christopher J. Wheat, gen mgr, gen sls mgr; Bob Richards, opns dir, progmg dir; Robby Greene, gen sls mgr; Lisa Jullerst, prom dir; Jack Robinson, chief of engrg.

WFNI(AM)— 1938: 1070 khz; 50 kw-D, 10 kw-N, DA-2. TL: N39 57 21 W86 21 30. Stereo. Hrs open: 24 40 Monument Cir., Suite 600, 46204. Phone: (317) 266-9422. Fax: (317) 684-2021. Web Site:www.emmis.com Licensee: Emmis Radio License LLC. Group owner: Emmis Communications Corp. (acq 6-9-94; $26 million with co-located FM). Population served: 1,175,000 Natl. Network: ESPN Radio, . Rgnl. Network: Agri-America. Natl. Rep: D & R Radio,. Format: Sports. ♦Jeff Smulyan, CEO; Tom Severino, VP & gen mgr; Mike Cortese, sls dir; Patty England, gen sls mgr, natl sls mgr; Susan Wells, prom dir; Kent Sterling, progmg dir; Jeff Dinsmore, chief of engrg.

***WFYI-FM**— Oct 1, 1954: 90.1 mhz; 10 kw. Ant 560 ft TL: N39 53 59 W86 12 01. Stereo. Hrs open: 24 1630 N. Meridian St., 46202-2389. Phone: (317) 636-2020. Fax: (317) 397-2976.E-mail: webmaster@wfyi.org Web Site:www.wfyi.org Licensee: Metropolitan Indianapolis Public Broadcasting Inc. (acq 12-1-86). Population served: 1,314,960 Natl. Network: PRI, NPR, . Rgnl rep: Indiana Public Broadcasting Stations Wire Svc: AP Format: Class, news/talk. News: 41 hrs wkly. Target aud: 25-64; general. Spec prog: Black 5 hrs, blues 4 hrs wkly. ♦Lloyd Wright, pres; Anthony Lorenz, CFO; Alan Cloe, exec VP, sr VP; Theresa Tetrault, dev dir; Rena Barraclough, prom VP; Lori Plummer, prom mgr; Michael Toulouse, mus dir; Steve Jensen, engrg VP. Co-owned TV: *WFYI-TV affil.

WHHH(FM)— Oct 28, 1991: 96.3 mhz; 3.3 kw. 285 ft TL: N39 46 32 W86 09 10. Stereo. Hrs open: 24 21 E. St. Joseph, 46204. Phone: (317) 266-9600. Fax: (317) 328-3870. Web Site:www.hot963.com Licensee: Radio One of Indiana LLC. Group owner: Radio One Inc. (acq 11-8-01; grpsl). Natl. Network: CNN Radio, . Format: Urban hip hop, rhythm and blues. Target aud: 18-49. ♦Alfred Liggins, CEO, pres; Charles Williams, VP, gen sls mgr; Charles T. Williams, gen mgr; Anna Fraser, prom dir; Brian Wallace, progmg dir; Don Payne, chief of engrg.

WIBC(FM)— Dec 5, 1960: 93.1 mhz; 13.5 kw. Ant 991 ft TL: N39 46 03 W86 00 12. Stereo. Hrs open: Prog sep from AM 40 Monument Cir., Suite 400, 46204. Phone: (317) 266-9422. Fax: (317) 684-2021. Web Site:www.emmis.com Licensee: Emmis Radio License LLC. (acq 6-9-94; $26 million with co-located AM). Population served: 744,624 Format: News/talk. News staff: 12. Target aud: 25-54; white collar, above average income & education. ♦Jeff Smulyan, pres, stn mgr; Tom Severino, VP, gen mgr; Jon Quick, opns dir, progmg dir; Mike Cortese, sls dir; Jessica Butcher, prom dir; Sherry Fisher, news dir; David Hood, chief of engrg; Trish Boone, traf mgr.

***WICR(FM)**— Aug 20, 1962: 88.7 mhz; 5 kw. 1,000 ft TL: N39 53 59 W86 12 02. Stereo. Hrs open: 24 1400 E. Hanna Ave., 46227. Phone: (317) 788-3280. Fax: (317) 788-3490.E-mail: wicr@uindy.edu Web Site:wicr.uindy.edu Licensee: University of Indianapolis. Population served: 1,500,000 Natl. Network: PRI, . Rgnl. Network: Network Indiana. John D. Pellegrin. Format: Class, jazz. News: 5 hrs wkly. Target aud: 35 plus; Educated, Affluent, Older. ♦Beverley Pitts, pres; Scott Uecker, gen mgr; Russell Maloney, chief of engrg.

***WJEL(FM)**— Sept 3, 1975: 89.3 mhz; 1 kw. 115 ft TL: N39 54 34 W86 07 39. Stereo. Hrs open: 24 1901 E. 86th St., 46240. Phone: (317) 259-5278. Fax: (317) 259-5298. Web Site:www.geocities.com/wjelpower Licensee: Metropolitan School District of Washington Township. Population served: 1,100,000 Format: Var. ♦John R. King, gen mgr; Robert L. Hendrix, progmg dir; Tyler Hindman, pub affrs dir; Mike Rabey, chief of engrg.

WJJK(FM)—(Noblesville, Sep 25, 1950: 104.5 mhz; 50 kw. Ant 492 ft TL: N39 50 25 W86 10 34. Stereo. Hrs open: 24 6810 N. Shadeland Ave., 46220. Phone: (317) 842-9550. Fax: (317) 577-3361. Web Site:www.1045wjjk.com Licensee: Indy Lico Inc. Group owner: Susquehanna Radio Corp. (acq 5-5-2006; grpsl). Population served: 1,133,200 Haley, Bader & Potts. Format: Oldies. News staff: one. Target aud: 25-54. ♦Christopher J. Wheat, VP; Christopher J. Wheat, gen mgr, gen sls mgr; Michele Kiefer, gen sls mgr; Anna Fraser, prom dir; Steve Cannon, progmg dir; Jake Robinson, chief of engrg.

WNDE(AM)— Oct 23, 1924: 1260 khz; 5 kw-U, DA-N. TL: N39 51 54 W86 03 43. Hrs open: 24 6161 Fall Creek Rd., 46220. Phone: (317) 257-7565. Fax: (317) 253-6501.E-mail: info@wnde.com Web Site:www.wnde.com Licensee: Capstar TX L.P. Group owner: Clear Channel Communications Inc. (acq 8-30-00; grpsl). Population served: 744,624 Natl. Network: AP Radio, ESPN Radio, . Natl. Rep: Clear Channel,. Format: Sports, talk. Target aud: 25-54. Spec prog: 0. ♦Rick Green, gen mgr; Marty Bender, opns mgr; Lee Anne Brooks, gen sls mgr; Dan Anderson, prom dir; Drew Carey, progmg dir; Dan Mettler, engrg mgr; Scott Fenstermaker, chief of engrg; Debbie Tunny, traf mgr; Mark Patrick, sports cmtr.

WNOU(FM)—(Speedway, May 28, 1967: 100.9 mhz; 6 kw. Ant 328 ft TL: N39 48 01 W86 04 39. Hrs open: 24 21 E. St. Joseph, 46204. Phone: (317) 266-9600. Fax: (317) 328-3870. Web Site:www.wyjzradio.com Licensee: Radio One of Indiana LLC. Group owner: Radio One Inc. (acq 11-8-2001; grpsl). Population served: 151,000 Natl. Network: ABC, . Rgnl. Network: Agri-Net, Brownfield. Natl. Rep: Katz Radio,. Format: CHR. News staff: 2; News: 12 hrs wkly. Target aud: 25-54. ♦Alfred Liggins, pres; Brian Harrington, gen sls mgr; Carl Frye, progmg dir.

WNTR(FM)— Oct 15, 1984: 107.9 mhz; 22 kw. Ant 762 ft TL: N39 53 43 W86 12 04. Stereo. Hrs open: 24 9245 N. Meridian St., Suite 300, 46260. Phone: (317) 816-4000. Fax: (317) 816-4050.E-mail: info@wntr.com Web Site:www.1079thetrack.com Licensee: Entercom Indianapolis License LLC (group owner; (acq 8-26-2004; grpsl). Population served: 1,500,000 Natl. Rep: Christal,. Fletcher, Heald & Heldreth. Format: Adult contemp. News staff: 3. Target aud: 25-54. Spec prog: Jazz 6 hrs wkly. ♦Phil Hoover, VP, gen mgr; Alex Keddie, opns VP; Amy Dillon, gen sls mgr, pub affrs dir; Toni Williams, prom dir; Gary Hummel, progmg VP, news dir; Tom Watson, progmg dir, asst music dir.

***WRFT(FM)**— June 6, 1978: 91.5 mhz; 130 w. 180 ft TL: N39 40 39 W86 00 58. Stereo. Hrs open: 6215 S. Franklin Rd., 46259. Phone: (317) 803-5552. Fax: (317) 862-7262. Licensee: Franklin Township Community School Corp. Format: Educ, div. Target aud: General. ♦Steve George, gen mgr; Abby Wheeling, progmg dir.

WRZX(FM)— May 15, 1964: 103.3 mhz; 18 kw. 850 ft TL: N39 53 43 W86 12 04. Stereo. Hrs open: 6161 Fall Creek Rd., 46220. Phone: (317) 257-7565. Fax: (317) 254-9619. Web Site:www.x103.com Licensee: Capstar TX L.P. Group owner: Clear Channel Communications Inc. (acq 8-30-00; grpsl). Format: Modern rock. ♦Rick Green, VP, gen mgr; Marty Bender, opns mgr; Lee Anne Brooks, gen sls mgr; Scott Jameson, prom mgr & progmg dir; Scott Fenstermaker, chief of engrg.

WSYW(AM)— May 15, 1963: 810 khz; 250 w-D. TL: N39 43 32 W86 11 08. Hrs open: Sunrise-sunset 1800 N. Meridian St., Suite 603, 46202-1433. Phone: (317) 924-1071. Fax: (317) 924-7766.E-mail: steph@wedjfm.com Licensee: Continental Broadcast Group Inc. (acq 12-30-93; grpsl; 1-24-94). Population served: 1,000,000 Natl. Rep: Univision Radio National Sales,. Pillsbury, Winthrop, Shaw, Pittman. Format: Hispanic. Target aud: 18+; Hispanic Adults. ♦Russ Dodge, gen mgr; Stephanie Tatay-Myers, mktg mgr; Manuel Sepulveda, progmg dir; Phil Alexander, chief of engrg.

WTLC(AM)— July 27, 1941: 1310 khz; 5 kw-D, 1 kw-N, DA-N. TL: N39 43 08 W86 10 33. Stereo. Hrs open: 24 21 E. Saint Joseph St., 46204. Phone: (317) 266-9600. Fax: (317) 261-4664.E-mail: info@1310thelight.com Web Site:www.1310thelight.com Licensee: Radio One of Indiana LLC. Group owner: Radio One Inc. (acq 11-8-01; grpsl). Population served: 744,624 Natl. Network: ABC, . Rgnl. Network: Network Indiana. Natl. Rep: Katz Radio,. Network Indiana Format: Gospel, talk, Ammos Brown Show. News: one hr wkly. Target aud: 35 plus; black females. ♦Charles Williams, VP, gen mgr; Ian Banks, gen sls mgr; Paul Robinson, progmg dir; Don Payne, chief of engrg.

WXLW(AM)— August 1948: 950 khz; 5 kw-D, 117 w-N, DA-2. TL: N39 51 05 W86 14 39. Hrs open: 24 Box 47307, 46247. Phone: (317) 736-4040. Fax: (317) 736-4781.E-mail: dave@XL950.com Web Site:www.xl950.com Licensee: Raven Broadcasting Inc. (acq 5-10-2005; $3 million). Natl. Network: ABC, ESPN Radio, . Format: Sports talk. News: 7 hrs wkly. Target aud: 25-54; men, secondary women. Spec prog: Gospel 5 hrs wkly. ♦Randy Tipmore, gen mgr & news dir.

WXNT(AM)— 1923: 1430 khz; 5 kw-U, DA-N. TL: N39 50 17 W86 11 53. Stereo. Hrs open: 24 9245 N. Meridian St., Suite 300, 46260. Phone: (317) 816-4000. Fax: (317) 816-4050.E-mail: info@wxnt.com Web Site:newstalk1430.com Licensee: Entercom Indianapolis License LLC Format: News/talk. News staff: one; News: 18 hrs wkly. Target aud: 35-64. Spec prog: Big band 2 hrs wkly. ♦Steve Hartley, sls dir & gen sls mgr; Gary Havens, progmg dir.

WYXB(FM)— Jan 22, 1968: 105.7 mhz; 50 kw. 445 ft TL: N39 48 01 W86 04 39. Stereo. Hrs open: 24 One Emmis Plaza, 40 Monument Cir., 46204. Phone: (317) 684-1057. Fax: (317) 684-2021. Web Site:www.emmis.com Licensee: Emmis Radio License LLC. Group owner: Emmis Communications Corp. (acq 9-8-97; with co-located AM). Natl. Rep: D & R Radio,. Format: Soft Rock. News staff: one; News: 3 hrs wkly. Target aud: 25-34; adults, (secondary is 25-54). Spec prog: Gospel 10 hrs wkly. ♦Tom Severino, gen mgr; David Edgar, opns mgr; Mike Cortese, sls dir; Jenni Gray, rgnl sls mgr; Mary Young, mktg dir; Scott Wheeler, progmg dir; Dave Hood, chief of engrg.

WZPL(FM)—See Greenfield

Jasper

WBDC(FM)—(Huntingburg, Dec 22, 1975: 100.9 mhz; 11 kw. 500 ft TL: N38 12 31 W86 54 00. Stereo. Hrs open: 24 Box 1009, 511 Newton St., 2nd Fl., 47547-1009. Secondary address: Box 330, 501 Old State Rd., Huntingburg 47542-0330. Phone: (812) 683-4144. Phone: (812) 634-9232. Fax: (812) 683-5891.E-mail: wbdc@psci.net Web Site:www.dcbroadcasting.com JRN Licensee: Dubois County Broadcasting Inc. Group owner: DCBroadcasting Inc. Population served: 125,000 Natl. Network: CNN Radio, Jones Radio Networks, . Rgnl. Network: Brownfield Brownfield Miller & Miller. Wire Svc: AP Format: Country. News staff: 2; News: 10 hrs wkly. Target aud: 18-54. Spec prog: Farm 5 hrs, relg 5 hrs, sports 6 hrs, Sp .5 hr wkly. ♦Paul Knies, pres; Bill Potter, gen mgr; Ron Spaulding, sls dir & gen sls mgr; Joe Lacay, progmg dir; Dave Ferguson, chief of engrg; Janice Potter, traf mgr.

WITZ(AM)— July 4, 1948: 990 khz; 1 kw-D. TL: N38 21 02 W86 56 26. Stereo. Hrs open: Sunrise/Sunset Dups FM 100% Box 167, 47547-0167. Secondary address: 1978 South WITZ Road 47546. Phone: (812) 482-2131. Fax: (812) 482-9609.E-mail: witzamfm@psci.net Web Site:www.witzamfm.com Licensee: Jasper On The Air Inc. Population served: 37,000 ♦Jeri Weisheit, traf mgr.

WITZ-FM— Nov 1, 1954: 104.7 mhz; 50 kw. 490 ft TL: N38 21 02 W86 56 26. Stereo. Hrs open: Box 167, 1978 S. WITZ Rd., 47546. Phone: (812) 482-2131. Fax: (812) 482-9609.E-mail: witzamfm@psci.net Web Site:www.witzamfm.com Licensee: Jasper On The Air Inc. Population served: 37,000 Rgnl. Network: AgriAmerica, Network Indiana. Natl. Rep: Rgnl Reps,. Network Indiana Format: Adult contemp. Target aud: 18-54. Spec prog: Paul Harvey 3 hrs wkly. ♦Earl Metzger, gen mgr; Bob Boyles, gen sls mgr; Walt Ferber, progmg dir; Reed Parker, news dir; Jeri Weisheit, chief of engrg, traf mgr.

***WJPR(FM)**— 2006: 91.7 mhz; 2.6 kw. Ant 276 ft TL: N38 25 23 W86 49 47. Hrs open: 514 N. JFK Ave., Loogootee, 47553. Phone: (812) 295-9480. Fax: (812) 295-3295. Licensee: Jasper Public Radio Inc. (acq 12-4-2006). Format: Oldies. ♦Larry Hembree, gen mgr.

Jeffersonville

WQKC(AM)— June 26, 1961: 1450 khz; 1 kw-U. TL: N38 17 41 W85 45 07. Hrs open: 24 Box 726, 47131-0726. Phone: (812) 283-3577. Fax: (812) 285-5060. Web Site:1450theticket.com Licensee: Sunnyside Communications Inc. Group owner: Susquehanna Radio Corp. (acq 3-30-2001; grpsl). Population served: 50,034 Natl. Network: ESPN Radio, . Rgnl rep: Rgnl Reps. Dow, Lohnes & Albertson. Format: Sports. ♦Blair W. Trask, pres, stn mgr; Kelly Anderson, mktg dir, rsch dir; Kelly Trask, gen mgr & prom dir; Blair Trask, progmg dir, traf mgr; Gil Daugherty, news dir, news rptr; Bob Hawkins, chief of engrg.

WQMF(FM)— Apr 25, 1974: 95.7 mhz; 28.5 kw. 643 ft TL: N38 08 06 W85 56 05. Stereo. Hrs open: 4000 Radio Dr., Suite 1, Louisville, KY, 40218. Phone: (502) 479-2222. Fax: (502) 479-2227. Web Site:www.wqmf.com Licensee: CC Licenses LLC. Group owner: Clear Channel Communications Inc. (acq 1-23-97; $13.5 million). Population served: 361,472 Format: Classic Rock. Target aud: 35-54; men. ♦Kevin Hughes, VP, stn mgr, sls dir; Kim Combest, gen sls mgr; Bill Gentry, mktg mgr.

Kendallville

WAWK(AM)— Nov 9, 1955: 1140 khz; 250 w-D. TL: N41 27 16 W85 15 48. Hrs open: 931 East Ave., 46755. Phone: (260) 347-2400. Phone: (260) 347-2401. Fax: (260) 347-2524.E-mail: wawk@locl.net Web Site:www.wawk.com Licensee: Northeast Indiana Broadcasting Inc. Population served: 10,000 Natl. Network: USA, . Rgnl. Network: Brownfield. Network Indiana Irwin, Campbell. Format: Var, hits of the 50s to present. News: 7 hrs wkly. Target aud: 25-54. Spec prog: Big Band 2 hrs, bluegrass 2 hrs, Farm one hr wkly. ♦Don Moore, pres, VP, gen mgr, gen sls mgr; Scott Paul, progmg dir; Mike Shultz, news dir; Greg Case, chief of engrg.

WBTU(FM)—Licensed to Kendallville. See Fort Wayne

Kentland

WIVR(FM)— 2000: 101.7 mhz; 3.2 kw. Ant 453 ft TL: N40 51 52 W87 35 14. Stereo. Hrs open: 24 202 E. Walnut, Watseka, IL, 60970. Phone: (815) 432-0700. Phone: (815) 933-9287. Fax: (815) 432-6112.E-mail: wvliradio@comcast.net Licensee: Milner Broadcasting Enterprises LLC (acq 12-11-2000). Population served: 48,000 Natl. Network: AP Network News, . Womble, Carlyle, Sandridge & Rice. Wire Svc: AP Format: Traditional country. News staff: 2; News: 168 bcsts wkly. Target aud: 12 plus; anthology country with current & recurrent hits. ♦Jim Brandt, gen mgr, opns mgr; Chris Swain, gen sls mgr; Mickey Milner, progmg dir; Ken Zyre, news dir; Don Kerouac, chief of engrg; Jody Woloszyn, traf mgr.

Knightstown

***WKPW(FM)**— Sept 7, 1993: 90.7 mhz; 4.4 kw. TL: N39 46 08 W85 31 05. Hrs open: 10892 N. State Rd., 140, 46148. Phone: (765) 345-9070. Fax: (765) 345-7039.E-mail: wkpw@knightstown.net Web Site:www.wkpw.net Licensee: IN Soldiers' & Sailors' Childrens' HME. Booth, Freret, Imlay & Tepper. Wire Svc: AP Format: Country. Target aud: General. Spec prog: Gospel. ♦Dr. John Wittkamper, pres; Mike York, gen mgr & progmg dir; Bob Hawkins, chief of engrg.

Knox

WKVI(AM)— June 30, 1969: 1520 khz; 250 w-D. TL: N41 19 20 W86 36 17. (CP: 1.8 kw-D). Hrs open: Box 10, 400 W. Culver Rd., 46534. Phone: (574) 772-6241. Fax: (574) 772-5920.E-mail: info@spots.com Web Site:www.wkvi.com Licensee: Kankakee Valley Broadcasting Co. Inc. Population served: 10,000 Format: Adult contemp. ♦Ted Hayes, gen mgr; Lo Ann McDaniel, progmg dir; Anita Goodan, news dir.

WKVI-FM— July 21, 1969: 99.3 mhz; 3 kw. 303 ft TL: N41 19 20 W86 36 17. Stereo. Hrs open: Dups AM 50% Box 10, 400 W. Culver Rd., 46534. Phone: (574) 772-6241. Fax: (574) 772-5920.E-mail: info@spots.com Web Site:www.wkvi.com Population served: 10,000

Kokomo

WIOU(AM)— July 16, 1948: 1350 khz; 5 kw-D, 1 kw-N, DA-2. TL: N40 25 00 W86 06 49. Hrs open: 24 Box 2208, 46904-2208. Secondary address: 671 E. 400 S. 46902. Phone: (765) 453-1212. Fax: (765) 455-3882.E-mail: newsroom.wzwz.wiou@sbcglobal.net Licensee: Mid-America Radio Group Inc. (group owner; (acq 3-24-93; $1.21 million with co-located FM; 4-12-93). Population served: 100,000 Natl. Network: CBS, . Format: Sports, news/talk. News staff: 2; News: 9 hrs wkly. Target aud: 25-54. ♦Steve La Mar, gen mgr; Lora Lacy, gen sls mgr; Allan James, progmg dir.

***WIWC(FM)**— September 1993: 91.7 mhz; 2.1 kw. 299 ft TL: N40 36 00 W86 18 08. Hrs open: c/o WGNR, 2000 W. 53rd St., Anderson, 46013. Phone: (765) 642-2750. Fax: (765) 642-4033.E-mail: wiwc@moody.edu Web Site:wiwc.mbn.org Licensee: The Moody Bible Institute of Chicago. (group owner) Format: Relg. Target aud: 34-55; general. ♦Ray Hashley, gen mgr; Tom Winn, progmg dir; Sam Sundin, news dir; Jim Wagner, chief of engrg.

WWKI(FM)— Oct 21, 1962: 100.5 mhz; 50 kw. 480 ft TL: N40 27 04 W86 02 12. Stereo. Hrs open: 24 519 N. Main St., 46901-4661. Phone: (765) 459-4191. Fax: (765) 456-1111. Fax: (765) 456-1112.E-mail: info@wwki.com Licensee: Citadel Broadcasting Co. Group owner: Citadel Broadcasting Corp. (acq 6-30-99; grpsl). Population served: 132,000 Natl. Network: AP Radio, . Rgnl. Network: AgriAmerica. Natl. Rep: Katz Radio,. Rgnl rep: Rgnl Reps. Leventhal, Senter & Lehrman. Wire Svc: AP Format: Country. News staff: 2; News: 13 hrs wkly. Target aud: 25-54. ♦Mike Christopher, gen mgr; James Stonecipher, gen sls mgr; Dave Broman, progmg dir; Robert Longshore, chief of engrg.

WZWZ(FM)— Nov 20, 1964: 92.5 mhz; 6 kw. Ant 324 ft TL: N40 28 18 W86 09 52. Stereo. Hrs open: 24 Box 2208, 46904-2208. Secondary address: 671 E. 400 S. 46902. Phone: (765) 453-1212. Fax: (765) 455-3882.E-mail: wzwz-wiou-wmyk@sbcglobal.net Licensee: Mid-America Radio Group of Kokomo Inc. Population served: 80,000 Format: Modern adult contemp. News: 4 hrs wkly. Target aud: 18-49. ♦Steven La Mar, gen mgr; Allan James, progmg dir.

La Porte

WCOE(FM)— Jan 23, 1964: 96.7 mhz; 3 kw. 265 ft TL: N40 37 55 W86 45 43. Stereo. Hrs open: 24 Prog sep from AM 1700 Lincolnway Pl., Suite 8, 46350. Phone: (219) 362-5290. Fax: (219) 324-7418. Web Site:www.eaglewcoe.com Licensee: La Porte County Broadcasting Company Inc. Population served: 228,300 Format: Hot country. News staff: 2; News: 19 hrs wkly. Target aud: 35-54; upper income, middle aged. ♦Norma Sabie, adv dir; Kenneth S. Coe, adv mgr; Dennis Sidall, mus dir; Donna Eichelberg, pub affrs dir; Carl Fletcher, engrg dir; Bob Costigan, local news ed, news rptr; Chip Jones, sports cmtr; Bobby Rivers, disc jockey.

WLOI(AM)— 1948: 1540 khz; 250 w-D. TL: N41 37 55 W86 45 43. Hrs open: Sunrise-sunset 1700 Lincolnway Pl., Suite 8, 46350. Phone: (219) 362-6144. Phone: (219) 872-8986. Fax: (219) 324-7418.E-mail: wcoe@csinet.net Licensee: La Porte County Broadcasting Company Inc. (acq 1955). Population served: 115,000 Natl. Network: ABC, Westwood One, . Rgnl. Network: Network Indiana, Tribune. Natl. Rep: Rgnl Reps,. Va. News Net. Wiley, Rein & Fielding. Format: Adult standards, MOR. News staff: 2; News: 26 hrs wkly. Target aud: 35 plus. Spec prog: Farm 8 hrs wkly. ♦Kenneth S. Coe, pres, gen mgr, gen sls mgr; Norma Sabie, sls dir & prom mgr; Dennis Siddall, progmg dir, disc jockey; Kate O'Malley, disc jockey.

Ladoga

***WJCJ(FM)**—Not on air, target date: unknown: 88.9 mhz; 50 kw. Ant 207 ft TL: N40 31 19 W87 30 58. Hrs open: CSN International, 4002N. 3300E., Twin Falls, ID, 83301. Phone: (208) 734-6633. Fax: (208) 736-1958. Web Site:www.csnradio.com Licensee: CSN International (group owner; ♦Mike Kestler, pres; Mike Stockland, gen mgr; Don Mills, progmg dir.

Lafayette

WASK(AM)— 1942: 1450 khz; 1 kw-U. TL: N40 24 08 W86 50 59. Hrs open: 24 Box 7880, 47903. Secondary address: 3575 McCarty Ln. 47903. Phone: (765) 447-2186. Fax: (765) 448-4452.E-mail: info@wask.com Web Site:www.wask.com Licensee: WASK Inc. Group owner: Schurz Communications Inc. (acq 1-28-91; $8.25 million with co-located FM;1-28-91). Population served: 44,955 Natl. Network: ESPN Radio, . Natl. Rep: Christal,. Hogan & Hartson. Format: Sports. News staff: 6; News: 15 hrs wkly. Spec prog: Farm 2 hrs wkly. ♦John Trent, pres, gen mgr; Brian Green, gen sls mgr; Randy Jones, progmg dir; Steve Truex, news dir & chief of engrg; Bryan McGarvey, disc jockey.

WAZY-FM— March 1965: 96.5 mhz; 50 kw. 500 ft TL: N40 23 02 W87 07 55. Stereo. Hrs open: 24 3824 S. 18th St., 47909. Phone: (765) 474-1410. Fax: (765) 474-3442.E-mail: info@wazy.com Web Site:www.wazy.com Licensee: Artistic Media Partners L.P. Group owner: Artistic Media Partners Inc. (acq 10-86; $2 million; 9-22-86). Population served: 301,100 Natl. Network: ABC, . Rgnl. Network: Network Indiana. Natl. Rep: Christal,. Network Indiana Rosenman & Colin L.L.P. Format: Top-40, CHR. News staff: one; News: 4 hrs wkly. Target aud: 18-34. ♦Arthur Angotti, pres, gen mgr; Jack Swart, gen mgr; Kit Osborne, pres & sls dir; Chris Green, gen sls mgr, prom dir, progmg dir; Bob Henning, chief of engrg; Bitsy Matatall, traf mgr.

***WJEF(FM)**— Feb 7, 1972: 91.9 mhz; 250 w. 100 ft TL: N40 23 52 W86 52 26. Stereo. Hrs open: 24 1801 S. 18th St., 47905. Secondary address: 2300 Cason St. 47904. Phone: (765) 772-4700.E-mail: rbrist@lsc.k12.in.us Web Site:www.jeff92.org Licensee: Lafayette School Corp. Population served: 149,000 Format: Oldies. News: 6 hrs wkly. Target aud: General. ♦Randall J. Brist, gen mgr.

WKHY(FM)— Jan 1, 1970: 93.5 mhz; 6 kw. 311 ft TL: N40 23 13 W86 58 10. Stereo. Hrs open: 24 Box 7093, 47903. Secondary address: 711 N. Earl Ave. 47904. Phone: (765) 448-1566. Fax: (765) 448-1348. Web Site:www.wkhy.com Licensee: Stay Tuned Broadcasting Corp. Group owner: RadioWorks Inc. (acq 5-12-99; grpsl). Population served: 292,700 Natl. Network: AP Radio, . Natl. Rep: Katz Radio,. Shaw Pittman. Format: Classic rock/AOR. News staff: one. Target aud: 25-54; adults that are active, mobile & moderately affluent. ♦John Trent, gen mgr; John Schurz, gen sls mgr; Liz Hahn, prom dir; Jeff Strange, progmg dir; Eric Burch, news dir; Steve Truex, chief of engrg.

WKOA(FM)— Sept 28, 1964: 105.3 mhz; 50 kw. 375 ft TL: N40 24 08 W86 50 59. Stereo. Hrs open: 24 Prog sep from AM Box 7880, 47903. Secondary address: 3575 McCarty Ln. 47903. Phone: (765) 447-2186. Fax: (765) 448-4452.E-mail: info@wkoa.com Web Site:www.wkoa.com Group owner: Lafayette Broadcasting Inc. Format: Country. News staff: 3; News: 12 hrs wkly. Target aud: 25-54. Spec prog: Farm 3 hrs wkly. ♦Lindsay Reinert, mktg dir, prom dir; Mark Allen, progmg dir; Skip Davis, farm dir; Bob Vizza, disc jockey.

***WQSG(FM)**— 2005: 90.7 mhz; 17 kw vert. Ant 328 ft TL: N40 22 13 W86 30 06. Hrs open:
Rebroadcasts WAFR(FM) Tupelo, MS 100%.
Drawer 2440, Tupelo, MS, 38803. Phone: (662) 844-8888. Fax: (662) 842-6791. Web Site:www.afr.net Licensee: American Family Association. Group owner: American Family Radio (acq 7-29-2003). Format: Christian. ♦Marvin Sanders, gen mgr.

WSHY(AM)— Nov 28, 1959: 1410 khz; 1 kw-D, 65 w-N, DA-1. TL: N40 21 38 W86 52 38. Hrs open: 24 839 Main St., 47901. Phone: (765) 429-1100. Fax: (765) 428-8247. Web Site:www.wshy1410.com Licensee: Artistic Media Partners Inc. (acq 9-30-98; $275,000). Natl. Network: Fox News Radio, Fox Sports, . Format: News/talk. Target aud: 25-49. ♦Jeff Holmes, gen mgr; Brian Vice, gen sls mgr.

Lafayette Township

***WCYT(FM)**— 1995: 91.1 mhz; 200 w. 213 ft TL: N40 58 58 W85 17 42. Stereo. Hrs open: 24 Homestead High School, 4310 Homestead Rd., Fort Wayne, 46814. Phone: (260) 431-2299. Phone: (260) 431-2911. Fax: (260) 431-2330.E-mail: INFO@wcyt.com Web Site:www.wcyt.org Licensee: Southwest Allen County Schools. Format: Modern rock, alternative, contemp hit. Target aud: General. Spec prog: Oldies 2 hrs, blues 2 hrs wkly. ♦Adam Schenkel, stn mgr; Joe Asher, progmg dir; Julian Shine, mus dir.

Lagrange

WTHD(FM)— Sept 2, 1994: 105.5 mhz; 2.4 kw. Ant 522 ft TL: N41 37 24 W85 20 49. Hrs open: 24 206 S. High St., 46761. Phone: (260) 463-8500. Phone: (800) 856-1055. Fax: (260) 463-8580.E-mail: wthd@wthd.net Web Site:www.wthd.net Licensee: Lake Cities Broadcasting Corp. (acq 7-14-93; 8-9-93). Natl. Network: ABC, . Format: Country. News staff: one; News: 2 hrs wkly. Target aud: 25-54. ♦Penny Mitchell, opns mgr; Tim Murray, gen mgr & news dir; Thomas Andrews, chief of engrg.

Lanesville

WGZB-FM— June 20, 1988: 96.5 mhz; 1.6 kw. Ant 638 ft TL: N38 10 25 W85 54 50. Stereo. Hrs open: 520 S. 4th St., Suite 200, Louisville, KY, 40202. Phone: (502) 625-1220. Fax: (502) 625-1257. Web Site:www.b96jams.com Licensee: MLB-Louisville IV LLC. Group owner: Radio One Inc. (acq 9-12-2007; grpsl). Format: Urban contemp. ♦Dale Schafer, gen mgr.

Lawrence

WRWM(FM)— February 1993: 93.9 mhz; 6.9 kw. Ant 480 ft TL: N39 49 39 W85 58 51. Hrs open: 24 6810 N. Shadeland Ave., Indianapolis, 46220. Phone: (317) 842-9550. Fax: (317) 577-3361. Web Site:94hits.com Licensee: Indy Lico Inc. Group owner: Susquehanna Radio Corp. (acq 5-5-2006; grpsl). Population served: 1,500,000 McFadden, Evans & Sill. Format: Soft adult contemp. Spec prog: Hymns of praise 3 hrs, family values one hr wkly. ♦Christopher J. Wheat, VP; Christopher J. Wheat, gen mgr, gen sls mgr; Bob Richards, opns dir; John Trout, progmg dir; Jake Robinson, chief of engrg.

Lebanon

***WCNB(FM)**—Not on air, target date: unknown: 91.5 mhz; 900 w vert. Ant 246 ft TL: N40 16 51 W86 31 39. Hrs open: 3500 DePauw Blvd., Suite 2085, Indianapolis, 46268-6103. Phone: (317) 870-8400. Fax: (317) 870-8404. Licensee: Hoosier Broadcasting Corp. ♦William S. Poorman, pres.

***WIRE(FM)**— 2001: 91.1 mhz; 3.2 kw vert. Ant 220 ft TL: N40 03 48 W86 26 36. Stereo. Hrs open: 24 3500 DePauw Blvd., Suite 2085, Indianapolis, 46268-6103. Phone: (317) 870-8400. Fax: (317) 870-8404. Web Site:www.radiomom.fm Licensee: Hoosier Broadcasting Corp. Format: Adult contemp. Target aud: 25-54; adults. ♦William Shirk Poorman, pres; Annie Martin, CFO; Chuck Cunningham, VP, gen mgr.

***WWDL(FM)**—Not on air, target date: unknown: 91.5 mhz; 130 w vert. Ant 144 ft TL: N39 46 30 W86 25 44. Hrs open: 5331 Mt. Alifan Dr., San Diego, CA, 92111. Phone: (858) 277-4991. Fax: (858) 277-1365. Licensee: Horizon Christian Fellowship. (acq 3-6-2006). ♦Mike MacIntosh, pres.

Lewisport

WLME(FM)— July 1990: 102.9 mhz; 12.5 kw. 466 ft TL: N37 46 57 W86 36 26. Stereo. Hrs open: 24 1115 Tamarock Rd., Suite 500, Owensboro, KY, 42301. Phone: (270) 683-5200. Fax: (270) 688-0108.E-mail: spots@wrioradio.com Licensee: WLME Inc. Group owner: The Cromwell Group Inc. Population served: 47,200 Natl. Network: Jones Radio Networks, . Natl. Rep: Rgnl Reps,. Pepper & Corazzini. Format: Hot AC. News staff: one; News: 3 hrs wkly. Target aud: 25-54; general. Spec prog: Sports 6 hrs wkly. ♦Bayard H. Walters, pres; Kevin Riecke, gen mgr.

Liberty

***WKWH(FM)**—Not on air, target date: unknown: 89.7 mhz; 300 w vert. Ant 115 ft TL: N39 39 46.2 W84 55 38. Hrs open: 134 Huston St., Connersville, 47331. Phone: (765) 821-2180. Licensee: Connersville Apostolic Lighthouse Inc. ♦Ira Sult III, CEO & pres.

Ligonier

WLEG(FM)—Licensed to Ligonier. See Warsaw

Linton

***KXJH(FM)**—Not on air, target date: unknown: 90.1 mhz; 400 w. Ant 141 ft TL: N39 02 22 W87 07 33. Hrs open: American Family Radio, Box 3206, Tupelo, MS, 38803. Phone: (662) 844-8888. Fax: (662) 842-6791. Web Site:www.afr.net Licensee: American Family Association. Group owner: American Family Radio. Format: Inspirational Christian. ♦Marvin Sanders, gen mgr.

WBTO(AM)— Oct 10, 1953: 1600 khz; 500 w-D, 32 w-N. TL: N39 03 57 W87 11 19. Hrs open: 6 AM-6 PM
Rebroadcasts WQTY(FM) Linton.
Box 242, Vincennes, 47591. Phone: (812) 254-4300. Fax: (812) 254-4361.E-mail: info@bl.com Web Site:www.wqtyfm.com Licensee: The Original Co. Inc. (group owner; (acq 6-11-99; $350,000 with co-located FM). Population served: 33,000 Natl. Network: Moody, . Rgnl. Network: Tribune. Natl. Rep: Rgnl Reps,. Tribune Radio Networks Format: Country. ♦Mark Lange, pres, gen mgr; Kim Boothe, opns mgr; Michelle York, sls dir.

WQTY(FM)— Sept 14, 1970: 93.3 mhz; 12 kw. Ant 475 ft TL: N39 00 46 W87 22 23. Stereo. Hrs open: Prog sep from AM Box 242, 47591. Phone: (812) 254-4300. Fax: (812) 254-4361.E-mail: info@bl.com Web Site:www.wqtyfm.com Population served: 230,000 Format: Oldies.

***WYTJ(FM)**—Not on air, target date: Aug 2003: 89.3 mhz; 1 kw. Ant 292 ft TL: N39 05 59 W87 10 59. Hrs open: R.R. 3, Box 1034, 47441. Phone: (812) 847-7222. Licensee: Bethel Baptist Church. Format: Relg. ♦Doug Cassel, gen mgr; Harold Smith, stn mgr.

Logansport

WSAL(AM)— Feb 24, 1949: 1230 khz; 1 kw-U. TL: N40 45 16 W86 18 40. Hrs open: 24 Box 719, 46947. Phone: (574) 722-4000. Fax: (574) 722-4010. Web Site:www.wsal.com Licensee: Logansport Radio Corp. (acq 12-11-85; $850,000; 11-4-85). Population served: 150,000 Rgnl. Network: AgriAmerica. Natl. Rep: Rgnl Reps,. Format: Adult contemp, news/talk. News staff: 2; News: 14 hrs wkly. Target aud: General. Spec prog: Farm 10 hrs wkly. ♦John P. Jenkins, CEO, pres; Andy Eubank, gen mgr; Lynne Ness, gen sls mgr; Eric Pfeiffer, news dir; Jeff Smith, chief of engrg.

***WWTS(FM)**—Not on air, target date: unknown: 89.5 mhz; 5 w horiz, 24 kw vert. Ant 400 ft TL: N40 40 08 W86 41 44. Hrs open: CSN International, 4002N. 3300E., Twin Falls, ID, 83301. Phone: (208) 734-6633. Fax: (208) 736-1958. Licensee: CSN International (group owner). ♦Mike Kestler, pres.

Loogootee

***WBHW(FM)**— September 1995: 88.7 mhz; 1.7 kw. 761 ft TL: N38 38 30 W86 59 57. Hrs open:
Rebroadcasts WBGW(FM) Fort Branch 100%.
Box 4164, Evansville, 47724. Phone: (812) 386-3342. Fax: (812) 768-5552.E-mail: mail@thyword.org Web Site:www.thyword.org Licensee: Music Ministries Inc. Format: Relg. ♦Floyd E. Turner, gen mgr.

WRZR(FM)— Dec 6, 1984: 94.5 mhz; 1.8 kw. Ant 426 ft TL: N38 37 09 W86 58 27. Stereo. Hrs open: 24 Box 1009, Jasper, 47547. Secondary address: 514 JFK Ave. 47553. Phone: (812) 634-9232. Fax: (812) 482-3696.E-mail: mailbox@wrzr.us Web Site:dcbroadcasting.com (LMA) Licensee: Hembree Communications Inc. Group owner: DCBroadcasting Inc. (acq 8-97). Rgnl. Network: Network Indiana Network Indiana Rgnl rep: Ron Spaulding Miller & Miller. Wire Svc: AP Format: Classic rock. News staff: one; News: 2 hrs wkly. Target aud: 24-45. Spec prog: Farm 2 hrs wkly. ♦Paul Knies, pres; Bill Potter, gen mgr, opns mgr; Ron Spaulding, gen mgr & gen sls mgr; Alan Williams, progmg dir; Mike Carie, news dir; David Ferguson, chief of engrg.

Lowell

***WLPR-FM**— 2006: 89.1 mhz; 2.4 kw. Ant 253 ft TL: N41 19 24 W87 21 22. Hrs open: Lakeshore Public Radio, 8625 Indiana Pl., Merrillville, 46410-6352. Phone: (219) 756-5656. Fax: (219) 755-4312. Web Site:www.afr.net Licensee: Northwest Indiana Public Broadcasting Inc. (acq 1-16-2009; $1.05 million). Natl. Network: NPR, . Format: News/talk, var. ♦Thomas E. Carroll, CEO & pres; Len Clark, progmg dir.

***WTMK(FM)**— 2005: 88.5 mhz; 1.5 kw. Ant 167 ft TL: N41 04 59 W87 10 47. Hrs open: 150 Lincolnway, Suite 2001, Valparaiso, 46383-5556. Phone: (219) 548-5800. Fax: (219) 548-5808. Web Site:www.csnmidwest.com Licensee: CSN International (group owner). Format: Relg. ♦Jim Motshagen, gen mgr; Kathy Motshagen, progmg dir.

WZVN(FM)— Nov 24, 1972: 107.1 mhz; 1.29 kw. 499 ft TL: N41 21 09 W87 24 12. Hrs open: 2755 Sager Rd., Valparaiso, 46383. Phone: (219) 462-6111. Fax: (219) 462-4880.E-mail: donclark@radiooneindiana.com Web Site:www.z1071.com Licensee: Porter County Broadcasting Holding Corp. LLC. Group owner: Porter County Broadcasting Corp. (acq 2-6-2004; $4.9 million with WXRD(FM) Crown Point). Population served: 650,000 Natl. Network: ABC, . Wilmer, Cutler & Pickering. Format: Adult contemp. Target aud: 25-54. ♦Leigh Ellis, pres, pres, gen mgr; O.J. Jackson, gen sls mgr; Scott Wagner, progmg dir; Laura Waluszko, news dir; Carl Fletcher, chief of engrg.

Madison

***WHMO(FM)**—Not on air, target date: unknown: 91.1 mhz; 300 w. Ant 246 ft TL: N38 40 50 W85 19 45. Hrs open: 1680 Hwy. 62 N.E., Corydon, 47112. Phone: (812) 738-3482. Fax: (812) 375-2555. Licensee: Good Samaritan Educational Radio Inc. ♦Keith Reising, gen mgr.

WIKI(FM)—See Carrollton, KY

WORX-FM— March 1950: 96.7 mhz; 1.05 kw. Ant 551 ft TL: N38 44 32 W85 21 43. Stereo. Hrs open: 24 Box 95, 47250. Secondary address: 1224 E. Telegraph Hill Rd. 47250. Phone: (812) 265-3322. Fax: (812) 273-5509.E-mail: manager@worxradio.com Web Site:www.worxradio.com Licensee: Dubois County Broadcasting Inc. Population served: 50,000 Natl. Network: Jones Radio Networks, . Network Indiana Wire Svc: AP Format: Adult contemp. News staff: one; News: 20 hrs wkly. Spec prog: Agriculture business 3 hrs wkly. ♦Paul Knies, pres; Bill Potter, gen mgr.

WXGO(AM)— March 1956: 1270 khz; 1 kw-D, 58 w-N, DA-2. TL: N38 44 28 W85 21 41. (CP: COL Aurora. 330 w-D, DA. TL: N39 02 30 W84 56 28). Hrs open: 24 Dups FM 50% Box 95, 47250. Secondary address: 1224 E. Telegraph Hill Rd. 47520. Phone: (812) 265-3322. Fax: (812) 273-5509.E-mail: manager@worxradio.com Web Site:www.worxradio.com Licensee: Dubois County Broadcasting Inc. Group owner: DCBroadcasting Inc. Population served: 35,000 Natl. Network: USA, . Natl. Rep: Rgnl Reps,. Format: News, oldies. Target aud: General. Spec prog: Farm 3 hrs, relg 6 hrs wkly. ♦Paul E. Knies, pres; William C. Potter, gen mgr.

Marengo

***WBRO(FM)**— 2000: 89.9 mhz; 1 kw. Ant 279 ft TL: N38 21 49 W86 25 13. Hrs open: Box 181, 47140. Phone: (812) 365-9276. Fax: (812) 365-2127.E-mail: wbrofm@aol.com Web Site:www.wbro.org Licensee: Crawford County Community Radio Inc. (acq 6-25-01). Format: Var. ♦Shawn Scott, gen mgr.

Marion

WBAT(AM)— June 7, 1947: 1400 khz; 1 kw-U. TL: N40 33 40 W85 41 30. Hrs open: 24 Box 839, 46952. Secondary address: 820 Pennsylvania St. 46953. Phone: (765) 664-6239. Fax: (765) 662-0730.E-mail: wbat@comteck.com Web Site:www.wbat.com Licensee: Mid-America Radio Group. Group owner: Mid-America Radio Group Inc. (acq 12-88; grpsl; 12-19-88). Population served: 100,000 Natl. Network: CBS, ESPN Radio, . Rgnl rep: Regional Reps Format: Sports, oldies. News staff: one; News: 7 hrs wkly. Target aud: 25-54. ♦David Keister, pres; David Poehler, exec VP; Carolyn Bush, gen mgr; James F. Brunner, gen sls mgr; Tim George, progmg dir; Mike Jenkins, news dir; Warren Arnett, chief of engrg.

***WBSW(FM)**— 1997: 90.9 mhz; 1 kw horiz, 2.4 kw vert. 308 ft TL: N40 40 01 W85 37 50. Hrs open:
Rebroadcasts WBST(FM) Muncie 100%.
c/o WBST(FM), Ball State Univ., Muncie, 47306-0550. Phone: (765) 285-5888. Fax: (765) 285-8937.E-mail: info@bsu.edu/ipr Web Site:www.bsu.edu/ipr Licensee: Ball State University. Format: Class, news. News staff: one; News: 33 hrs wkly. Target aud: General. ♦Marcus Jackman, gen mgr; Pam Coletti, gen sls mgr; Carol Trimmer, prom mgr; Steven Turpin, progmg dir & mus dir; Robert Mittendorf, chief of engrg; Dorothy Marvell, traf mgr; Brian Beaver, news rptr.

WCJC(FM)—(Van Buren, Aug 28, 1989: 99.3 mhz; 3 kw. 328 ft TL: N40 40 01 W85 37 50. Stereo. Hrs open: 24 Box 839, 820 S. Pennsylvania, 46952. Phone: (765) 664-6239. Fax: (765) 662-0730.E-mail: wcjc@comteck.com Web Site:www.wcjc.com Licensee: Mid-America Radio Group Inc. (group owner; acq 12-19-88; grpsl;12-19-88). Natl. Network: ABC, . Rgnl rep: Regional Reps Format: Country. News staff: 2; News: 25 hrs wkly. Target aud: 25-54; consumer-oriented modern country fans. Spec prog: Relg 3 hrs wkly. ♦David Keister, pres; David Poehler, VP, stn mgr; Carolyn Bush, gen mgr; Tim George, opns mgr, progmg dir; James F. Brunner, gen sls mgr; Warren Arnett, chief of engrg.

WMRI(AM)— May 11, 1955: 860 khz; 1 kw-D, 500 w-N, DA-2. TL: N40 33 12 W85 38 45. Hrs open: 24 Box 1538, 46952. Secondary address: 820 S. Pennsylvania St. 46953. Phone: (765) 664-7396. Phone: (765)

664-9466. Fax: (765) 668-6767. Web Site:wmri.com Licensee: Mid-America Radio of Indiana Inc. Group owner: Mid-America Radio Group Inc. (acq 5-12-2003; with co-located FM). Population served: 40,253 Natl. Network: Music of Your Life, . Rgnl. Network: Network Indiana. Network Indiana Format: Nostalgia. Target aud: 35-70. ♦David Poehler, pres, VP; Carolyn Bush, gen mgr, chief of engrg; Vanessa Miller, opns mgr; Gloria Millspaugh, gen sls mgr; Mike Jenkins, news dir, pub affrs dir.

WXXC(FM)— Dec 19, 1948: 106.9 mhz; 50 kw. Ant 499 ft TL: N40 35 52 W85 39 21. Stereo. Hrs open: 24 Prog sep from AM Box 1538, 46952. Phone: (765) 664-7396. Fax: (765) 668-6767.E-mail: studio@1069wxxc.com Web Site:www.1069wxxc.com Licensee: Mid-America Radio of Indiana Inc. Population served: 500,000 Natl. Network: CNN Radio, . Rgnl. Network: Network Indiana. Network Indiana Format: Classic hits. Target aud: 25-54.

Martinsville

WCBK-FM— Oct 15, 1968: 102.3 mhz; 6 kw. 308 ft TL: N39 26 18 W86 27 58. Stereo. Hrs open: Dups AM 95% Box 1577, 46151-3004. Phone: (765) 342-3394. Fax: (765) 342-5020. Web Site:www.wcbk.com Licensee: Mid-America Radio Group Inc. ♦Ruth Ann Arney, gen sls mgr; John Taylor, progmg dir.

WMYJ(AM)— Apr 18, 1967: 1540 khz; 500 w-D. TL: N39 24 31 W86 25 10. Hrs open: Box 1577, 46151. Secondary address: 1639 Burton Ln. 46151-3004. Phone: (765) 342-3394. Fax: (765) 342-5020. Licensee: Mid-America Radio Group Inc. (group owner; (acq 8-4-97; with co-located FM). Population served: 100,000 Natl. Network: USA, . Rgnl. Network: Network Indiana, Tribune. Format: Gospel. Target aud: 25-54. Spec prog: Farm one hr wkly. ♦David Keister, gen mgr.

Michigan City

WEFM(FM)— Sept 15, 1966: 95.9 mhz; 3 kw. Ant 230 ft TL: N41 42 58 W86 51 47. Stereo. Hrs open: 24 1903 Springland Ave., 46360. Phone: (219) 879-8201. Fax: (219) 879-8202.E-mail: wefm@yahoo.com Licensee: Michigan City FM Broadcasters Inc. Natl. Network: Westwood One, NBC Radio, . Rgnl. Network: Network Indiana. Network Indiana Format: Adult contemp, oldies. News staff: one. Target aud: General. Spec prog: Farm, relg 4 hrs wkly. ♦Thomas Burns, pres; Ronald Miller, stn mgr; Jim Spevak, gen sls mgr; Tod Allen, progmg dir & progmg mgr; Tim Volckmann, chief of engrg.

WIMS(AM)— Aug 10, 1947: 1420 khz; 5 kw-U, DA-2. TL: N41 40 26 W86 55 58. Hrs open: 24 720 Franklin St., 46360. Phone: (219) 879-9810. Fax: (219) 879-9813. Web Site:www.wimsradio.com Licensee: Gerard Media LLC (acq 2-20-2007; $335,000). Population served: 39,369 Format: Talk. Target aud: 30 plus; general. Spec prog: Pol 3 hrs wkly. ♦Ric Federighi, gen mgr; Johnny Rush, progmg dir.

Mitchell

***WMBL(FM)**—Not on air, target date: unknown: 88.1 mhz; 1 kw. Ant 400 ft TL: N38 45 50 W86 31 15. Hrs open: 820 N. LaSalle Blvd., Chicago, IL, 60610. Phone: (312) 329-4438. Phone: (800) 246-0691. Web Site:www.mbn.org Licensee: The Moody Bible Institute of Chicago. Format: Relg. ♦Allen Henderson, gen mgr.

WPHZ(FM)— Aug 17, 1991: 102.5 mhz; 6 kw. Ant 282 ft TL: N38 38 16 W86 27 11. Hrs open: 24 Box 1307, Bedford, 47421. Phone: (812) 275-7555. Fax: (812) 279-8046.E-mail: info@wphz.com Web Site:www.wphz.com Licensee: Mitchell Community Broadcast Co. (acq 2-26-92; $8,000 for CP; 3-16-92). Natl. Network: ABC, Jones Radio Networks, . Natl. Rep: Rgnl Reps,. Reed, Smith, Shaw & McClay. Format: Adult Contemp. News staff: one; News: 2 hrs wkly. Target aud: General. ♦Holly Lindsey, gen mgr.

Monticello

WMRS(FM)— March 1989: 107.7 mhz; 4.4 kw. 500 ft TL: N40 45 03 W86 48 17. Stereo. Hrs open: 24 132 N. Main, 47960. Phone: (574) 583-8121. Phone: (574) 583-8933. Fax: (574) 583-8933.E-mail: kevinp@wmrsradio.com Web Site:www.wmrsradio.com Licensee: Monticello Community Radio Inc. (acq 1-15-91;2-11-91). Natl. Network: USA, Jones Radio Networks, . Format: Adult contemp, div, talk. News staff: 2; News: 20 hrs wkly. Target aud: 25-60; motivated, intelligent, diverse. Spec prog: Gospel 5 hrs, bluegrass 2 hrs wkly. ♦Kevin Page, gen mgr.

WXXB(FM)—See Delphi

Montpelier

***WJCO(FM)**—Not on air, target date: unknown: 91.3 mhz; 350 w vert. Ant 196 ft TL: N40 33 21 W85 17 39. Hrs open: CSN International, 4002N. 3300E., Twin Falls, ID, 83301. Phone: (208) 734-6633. Fax: (208) 736-1958. Licensee: CSN International (group owner). ♦Mike Kestler, pres; Mike Stockland, gen mgr; Don Mills, progmg dir.

Morgantown

***WCJL(FM)**— 2005: 90.9 mhz; 1 kw horiz, 13.5 kw vert. Ant 213 ft TL: N39 19 17 W86 31 08. Hrs open: 4002 N. 3300 E., Twin Falls, ID, 83301. Fax: (208) 734-6633. Fax: (208) 736-1958. Web Site:www.csnradio.com Licensee: CSN International. (group owner). ♦Mike Kestler, pres.

Morristown

***WJCF-FM**— 2000: 88.1 mhz; 2.7 kw vert. Ant 151 ft TL: N39 45 01 W85 33 19. Hrs open: Box 846, Greenfield, 46140. Secondary address: 15 Wood St., Greenfield 46140-2162. Phone: (317) 467-1064. Fax: (317) 467-1065. Web Site:www.wjcfradio.com Licensee: Indiana Community Radio Corp. Format: Contemp Christian. ♦Jennifer Cox-Hensley, gen mgr; Marty Hensley, progmg dir.

Mount Vernon

WRCY(AM)— Aug 21, 1955: 1590 khz; 500 w-D, 35 w-N. TL: N37 56 03 W87 55 42. Hrs open: 7109 Upton Rd., 47620-9483. Phone: (812) 838-4484. Fax: (812) 838-6434.E-mail: espn1067@gmail.com Web Site:www.wyfx.com Licensee: The Original Co. Inc. (group owner; (acq 1999; $360,000 with co-located FM). Population served: 7200 Format: Real country. Target aud: 25 plus; loc county. Spec prog: Farm 5 hrs wkly. ♦Mark Lange, pres; Sean Dulaney, gen mgr; Frank Hertel, chief of engrg.

WYFX(FM)— August 1992: 106.7 mhz; 3 kw. Ant 295 ft TL: N37 56 03 W87 55 35. Hrs open: 7109 Upton Rd., 47620. Phone: (812) 838-4484. Fax: (812) 838-6434.E-mail: espn1067@gmail.com Natl. Network: ESPN Radio, . Format: Sports/talk.

Muncie

***WBST(FM)**— Sept 12, 1960: 92.1 mhz; 3 kw. 300 ft TL: N40 12 48 W85 27 36. Stereo. Hrs open: 24 Ball State Univ., 47306-0550. Phone: (765) 285-5888. Fax: (765) 285-8937.E-mail: info@bsu.edu/ipr Web Site:www.bsu.edu/ipr Licensee: Ball State University. Population served: 1,500,000 Natl. Network: PRI, NPR, . Format: Classical, news. News staff: one; News: 33 hrs wkly. Target aud: General. ♦Marcus Jackman, gen mgr; Pam Coletti, sls dir, gen sls mgr; Carol Trimmer, prom mgr; Steven Turpin, progmg dir & mus dir; Robert Mittendorf, chief of engrg; Dorothy Marvell, traf mgr; Brian Beaver, news rptr.

WERK(FM)— Jan 16, 1986: 104.9 mhz; 3 kw. 328 ft TL: N40 09 19 W85 25 48. Stereo. Hrs open: 24
Simulcasts WURK(FM) Elwood 80%.
800 E. 29th St., 47302. Phone: (765) 288-4403. Fax: (765) 378-2091.E-mail: werkstudio@werkradio.com Web Site:www.werkradio.com Licensee: Indiana Sabrecom Inc. Group owner: Backyard Broadcasting LLC (acq 12-1-02; grpsl). Population served: 300,000 Format: Oldies. ♦Steve Lindell, gen mgr; Jay Garrison, progmg dir, news dir.

***WKMV(FM)**—Not on air, target date: unknown: 88.3 mhz; 200 w vert. Ant 295 ft TL: N40 05 06 W85 23 52. Hrs open: 5700 West Oaks Blvd., Rocklin, CA, 95765. Phone: (916) 251-1600. Fax: (916) 251-1650. Licensee: Educational Media Foundation. (acq 3-23-2007; grpsl). ♦Richard Jenkins, pres.

WLBC-FM— October 1947: 104.1 mhz; 50 kw. 420 ft TL: N40 09 38 W85 22 42. Stereo. Hrs open: 800 E. 29th St., 47302. E-mail: steve@wlbc.com Web Site:www.wlbc.com Licensee: Indiana Sabrecom Inc. Population served: 80,093 Wire Svc: AP Format: News. News staff: one; News: 19 hrs wkly. Target aud: 18-49; female. ♦Joanna Black, traf mgr; Dave Stout, news rptr; Steve Lindell, progmg VP, farm dir & mus critic.

WMDH-FM—See New Castle

WRFM(AM)— Feb 14, 1965: 990 khz; 250 w-D, 2 w-N, DA-1. TL: N40 06 54 W85 22 02. Stereo. Hrs open: 3611 S. Post Rd., 47302. Phone: (765) 747-6970. Fax: (765) 747-5054.E-mail: wlhn990@yahoo.com Web Site:wlhnradio.com Licensee: Electronic Applications Radio Service Inc. (acq 3-16-99). Population served: 300,000 Natl. Rep: Roslin, Rgnl Reps,. Harris, Beach & Wilcox. Format: Southern gospel. Target aud: 25-54; upscale adults & families, professional & blue collar. ♦Steven Dugger, gen mgr.

***WWDS(FM)**— 1978: 90.5 mhz; 100 w. Ant 174 ft TL: N40 16 42 W85 20 52. Stereo. Hrs open: 3400 E. State Rd. 28, 47303. Phone: (765) 288-5597. Fax: (765) 288-8498.E-mail: fclark@delcomschools.org Licensee: Delaware Community School Corp. Format: Adult contemp. ♦Ford Clark, stn mgr.

***WWHI(FM)**— 1950: 91.3 mhz; 310 w. 79 ft TL: N40 09 45 W85 22 45. Hrs open: 1601 E. 26th St., 47302. Phone: (765) 747-5339. Fax: (765) 747-5325. Licensee: Ball State University (acq 2-13-2004). Format: Educ. ♦Ken Wickliffe, gen mgr.

WXFN(AM)— November 1926: 1340 khz; 1 kw-U. TL: N40 09 42 W85 22 41. Hrs open: 800 E. 29th St., 47302. Phone: (765) 288-4403. Fax: (765) 288-0429. Licensee: Indiana Sabrecom Inc. Group owner: Backyard Broadcasting LLC (acq 12-1-2002; grpsl). Population served: 80,093 Natl. Network: ABC, ESPN Radio, Sporting News Radio Network, . Network Indiana Wire Svc: AP Format: Sports. News staff: 2; News: 12 hrs wkly. Target aud: 25-54. Spec prog: Black 3 hrs wkly. ♦Barry Drake, CEO; Robin Smith, CFO; Sean Mattingly, chief of engrg; Joanna Black, traf mgr; Steve Lindell, VP, gen mgr & mus critic; Jay Garreson, sports cmtr.

Nappanee

WYPW(FM)— Dec 16, 1991: 95.7 mhz; 1.4 kw. 500 ft TL: N41 24 43 W86 01 51. Stereo. Hrs open: 24 237 W. Edison Rd., Mishawaka, 46545. Phone: (574) 258-5483. Phone: (888) 737-6244.E-mail: wypw@power957.com Web Site:www.power957.com Licensee: Talking Stick Communications LLC. (group owner; (acq 8-25-2000). Population served: 600,000 Natl. Network: ABC, CBS, . Format: Adult contemp. News: 10 hrs wkly. Target aud: 35-70; secretaries, bankers. ♦Emily Wideman, exec VP, gen sls mgr; Abe Thompson, gen mgr; Alec Dille, stn mgr; Gene Walker, opns mgr; Chuck Wright, progmg dir; Greg Trobridge, chief of engrg.

Nashville

WVNI(FM)— August 1997: 95.1 mhz; 1.6 kw. 636 ft TL: N39 13 39 W86 25 05. (CP: 2.3 kw, ant 472 ft.). Hrs open: 24 Box 1628, Bloomington, 47402. Secondary address: 4317 E.3rd St., Bloomington 47401. Phone: (812) 335-9500. Fax: (812) 335-8880.E-mail: spitit95@spirit95fm.com Web Site:www.sprint95fm.com Licensee: Brown County Broadcasters Inc. Group owner: Mid-America Radio Group Inc. (acq 10-29-97; $20,000 for 51% of stock). Natl. Network: Salem Radio Network, . Format: Contemp Christian. Target aud: 25-54. ♦Diana Nuchols, gen mgr; Denise Ray, opns dir.

New Albany

WFIA-FM— Jan 1, 1996: 94.7 mhz; 6 kw. 328 ft TL: N38 17 02 W85 54 17. Stereo. Hrs open: 24 9960 Corporate Campus Dr., Suite 3600, Louisville, KY, 40223. Phone: (502) 339-9470. Fax: (502) 423-3139. Web Site:www.salemradiogroup.com Licensee: Salem Media of Kentucky Inc. Group owner: Salem Communications Corp. (acq 1999; $5 million with WRVI(FM) Valley Station, KY). Natl. Network: Salem Radio Network, . Natl. Rep: Salem,. Format: Talk, teaching, Southern gospel, Christian. Target aud: 30 plus. ♦Tom Hartlage, gen mgr.

***WNAS(FM)**— May 28, 1949: 88.1 mhz; 2.85 kw. 3 ft TL: N38 17 56 W85 48 45. Hrs open: 1020 Vincennes St., 47150. Phone: (812) 949-4272. Fax: (812) 949-6926. Web Site:www.wnas.org Licensee: New Albany-Floyd County Consolidated School Corp. Population served: 1,000,000 Format: Educ, Top-40. ♦Lee Kelly, gen mgr.

WNDA(AM)— June 15, 1949: 1570 khz; 1.5 kw-D, 233 w-N. TL: N38 19 40 W85 46 56. Hrs open: 24 Box 2623, Clarksville, KY, 47131. Phone: (812) 949-1570. Fax: (812) 949-9623. Web Site:www.kool1570.com Licensee: New Albany Broadcasting Co. Inc. Group owner: Mortenson Broadcasting Co. (acq 2-2-2005; $1 million). Population served: 1,000,000 Format: Oldies. ♦David Smith, gen mgr.

New Carlisle

WSMM(FM)— July 2, 1991: 102.3 mhz; 2 kw. Ant 397 ft TL: N41 43 38 W86 24 30. Stereo. Hrs open: 24 3371 Cleveland Rd., Suite 300, South Bend, 46628. Phone: (574) 273-9300. Fax: (574) 273-9090.E-mail: michael@wzow.com Web Site:www.wzow.com Licensee: Artistic Media Partners Inc. (group owner; (acq 3-22-2002; $1.5 million). Format:

Classic rock. ◆Jack Swart, gen mgr; Carrie Jones, natl sls mgr; Teresa Holden, prom dir; Chili Walker, progmg dir; Bob Henning, chief of engrg; Rita Kinzie, traf mgr.

New Castle

WMDH(AM)— Nov 14, 1960: 1550 khz; 250 w-U, DA-2. TL: N39 55 59 W85 24 26. Hrs open: Box 690, 1134 W. State Rd. 38, 47362. Phone: (765) 529-2600. Fax: (765) 529-1688. Web Site:www.wmdh.com Licensee: Citadel Broadcasting Co. Group owner: Citadel Broadcasting Corp. (acq 7-1-99; grpsl). Population served: 24,000 Rgnl. Network: Network Indiana. Natl. Rep: Katz Radio,. Network Indiana Leventhal Senter & Lerman. Format: Adult standards. Target aud: 49 plus. Spec prog: Farm 2 hrs, relg 2 hrs wkly. ◆Pam Price, gen sls mgr; Jon Sipes, progmg dir.

WMDH-FM— Aug 6, 1976: 102.5 mhz; 50 kw. 500 ft TL: N40 03 18 W85 23 05. Stereo. Hrs open: 24 Prog sep from AM Box 690, 1134 W. State Rd. 38, 47362. Phone: (765) 529-2600. Fax: (765) 529-1688. Web Site:www.wmdh.com Licensee: Citadel Broadcasting Co. Population served: 240,000 Format: Country. News staff: one; News: 2 hrs wkly. Target aud: 25-54. Spec prog: Farm one hr wkly.

New Haven

WJFX(FM)— April 1990: 107.9 mhz; 3.2 kw. Ant 453 ft TL: N41 01 26 W85 03 51. Stereo. Hrs open: 24 2100 Goshen Rd., Fort Wayne, 46808. Phone: (260) 493-9539. Fax: (260) 749-5151. Web Site:www.hot1079online.com Licensee: Fort Wayne Radio Corp. (acq 12-1-98; $1.3 million). Population served: 424,900 Natl. Rep: Interep,. Wiley, Rein & Fielding. Format: CHR. Target aud: 18-49; adults. ◆Russ Oasis, pres; Roger Diehm, VP, gen mgr; Beth Thornton, gen sls mgr; Phil Becker, progmg dir.

New Paris

WZRP(FM)—See Richmond

New Washington

*WARA(FM)— 1994: 88.3 mhz; 950 w. Ant 300 ft TL: N38 35 40 W85 28 06. Stereo. Hrs open: 24 Rebroadcasts KLRD(FM) Yucaipa, CA 100%. 2351 Sunset Blvd., Suite 170-218, Rocklin, CA, 95765. Phone: (916) 251-1600. Fax: (916) 251-1650.E-mail: info@air1.com Web Site:www.air1.com Licensee: Educational Media Foundation. Group owner: EMF Broadcasting (acq 10-2-2003; grpsl). Natl. Network: Air 1, . Davis Wright Tremaine LLP. Format: Christian. News staff: 3. Target aud: 18-35; Judeo Christian, female. ◆Mike Novak, pres.

New Whiteland

*WHZN(FM)— 2009: 88.3 mhz; 1 w horiz, 7.8 kw vert. Ant 725 ft TL: N39 24 14 W86 08 41. Hrs open: 7702 Indian Lake Rd., Indianapolis, 46236. Phone: (317) 826-9255. Fax: (317) 823-2396.E-mail: info@883thewalk.org Web Site:www.883thewalk.org Licensee: Horizon Christian Fellowship of Indianapolis Inc. (acq 2-2-2009). Format: Contemp Christian. ◆Bill Goodrich, gen mgr.

Newburgh

WDKS(FM)— Feb 11, 1991: 106.1 mhz; 6 kw. 328 ft TL: N37 57 16 W87 25 07. Stereo. Hrs open: 24 17 South East 5 St, Evansville, 47708. Phone: (812) 425-4226. Fax: (812) 428-5895.E-mail: mthomas@regentcomm.com Web Site:www.kissevansville.com Licensee: Regent Broadcasting of Evansville/Owensboro Inc. Group owner: Regent Communications Inc. (acq 12-3-2003; grpsl). Natl. Network: ABC, Westwood One, . Format: Top 40. News staff: one. Target aud: 18-34; women. ◆Mark Thomas, gen mgr; Max Powers, prom dir; Cat Michaels, progmg dir; Gene Stewart, news dir; Rick Crazo, chief of engrg.

WGAB(AM)— Mar 5, 1984: 1180 khz; 670 w-D. TL: N37 57 16 W87 25 07. Hrs open: 24 hrs 2601 South Boeke Rd., Evansville, 47714. Phone: (812) 853-9422. Fax: (812) 474-4483.E-mail: faithmusicbb@aol.com Licensee: Faith Broadcasting LLC (acq 12-1-2004; $300,000). Population served: 232,000 Natl. Network: ABC, Jones Radio Networks, Salem Radio Network, Westwood One, . Format: Christian progmg. Target aud: 18-54; men & women. ◆Gayle Russ, gen mgr, opns VP & opns mgr.

Noblesville

WJJK(FM)—Licensed to Noblesville. See Indianapolis

North Judson

*WTMW(FM)—Not on air, target date: unknown: 91.3 mhz; 50 kw. Ant 269 ft TL: N41 02 21 W86 30 55. Hrs open: 125 S. Main St., Bishop, CA, 93514-3414. Phone: (760) 954-6655. Fax: (760) 872-4155. Licensee: Living Proof Inc. Fletcher, Heald & Hildreth. ◆Daniel McClenaghan, pres & gen mgr.

North Manchester

*WBKE-FM— May 1967: 89.5 mhz; 3 kw. 80 ft TL: N41 00 40 W85 45 45. Stereo. Hrs open: 24 Rebroadcasts WBNI-FM Ft. Wayne 50%. Box 19, Manchester College, 604 E. College Ave., 46962. Phone: (260) 982-5272. Fax: (260) 982-5043.E-mail: wbke@manchester.edu Web Site:www.wbke.manchester.edu Licensee: Manchester College. Population served: 6,800 Format: Div, free form. News staff: one; News: 10 hrs wkly. Target aud: General. Spec prog: Class 10 hrs, Sp one hr, classic rock 6 hrs, AOR 6 hrs, Top 40/rap 10 hrs, alternative 7 hrs wkly. ◆Dan Daggett, gen mgr; Alicia Smith, stn mgr.

North Vernon

WJCP(AM)— Jan 8, 1955: 1460 khz; 1 kw-D, 92 w-N. TL: N38 59 46 W85 39 02. Stereo. Hrs open: 2470 N. State Hwy. 7, 47265-7184. Phone: (812) 346-1927. Fax: (812) 346-9722. Licensee: Columbus Radio Inc. (acq 11-20-2001; swap for WWWY(FM) Columbus plus $1.2 million). Population served: 25,000 Format: Sports. ◆Marty Pieratt, gen mgr.

WWWY(FM)— Mar 19, 1963: 106.1 mhz; 50 kw. 486 ft TL: N39 04 02 W85 42 10. Stereo. Hrs open: 24 Box 1789, Columbus, 47202-1789. Secondary address: 3212 Washington St., Columbus 47203. Phone: (812) 372-4448.E-mail: rockme@y106.com Web Site:www.y106.com Licensee: White River Broadcasting Co. Inc. Group owner: The Findlay Publishing Co. (acq 8-1-97; grpsl). Format: Rock. Target aud: 25-44. ◆Kurt Kah, pres; David Glass, VP; Tasha Mann, gen mgr; John Foster, opns mgr; Scott Michaels, progmg dir; Kevin Keith, news dir; Chuck Weber, engr.

Notre Dame

*WSND-FM— Sept 17, 1962: 88.9 mhz; 3.4 kw. Ant 361 ft TL: N41 36 20 W86 12 46. Stereo. Hrs open: 7am to 2am M-F; 9am to 2am Sa/Su 315 LaFortune Student Ctr., 46556. Phone: Studio (574) 631-7342 / Office (574) 631-4069. Fax: (574) 631-3653.E-mail: wsnd@nd.edu Web Site:www.nd.edu/~wsnd Licensee: Voice of the Fighting Irish Inc. Population served: 7,700 Wire Svc: UPI Format: Classical Music. News: 10. Target aud: General public radio. Spec prog: Jazz, Reggae, Celtic, Blues. ◆Laurie McFadden, gen mgr; Ed Jaroszewski, progmg dir.

Oolitic

*WMYJ-FM— 2005: 88.9 mhz; 5.2 kw vert. Ant 256 ft TL: N38 59 14 W86 27 31. Hrs open: Box 1970, Martinsville, 46151. Phone: (765) 349-1485. Fax: (765) 342-3569. Licensee: Spirit Educational Radio Inc. (acq 6-30-2005; $45,000 for CP). Population served: 136,000 Format: Southern gospel. ◆David Keister, chmn; Diana Nuchols, gen mgr.

Orland

*WCKZ(FM)— Feb 2, 2002: 91.3 mhz; 2 kw. Ant 298 ft TL: N41 44 36 W85 05 48. Stereo. Hrs open: 24 Box 8459, Fort Wayne, 46898. Phone: (260) 452-1189. Fax: (260) 452-1188.E-mail: jbrown@nipr.fm Web Site:www.nipr.fm Licensee: Northeast Indiana Public Radio Inc. Natl. Network: NPR, . Dow, Lohnes & Albertson, PLLC. Format: Classical. ◆Bruce Haines, gen mgr, prom dir; Colleen Condron, opns dir, progmg dir; Karen Fraser, dev dir; Janice Furtner, mus dir; Jeanette Dillon, news dir; Jackie Didier, traf mgr.

Paoli

WSEZ(AM)— Nov 7, 1963: 1560 khz; 250 w-D. TL: N38 32 25 W86 28 42. Hrs open: 6 AM-6 PM Box 26, 192 S. Court St., 47454. Phone: (812) 723-4484. Fax: (812) 723-4966.E-mail: wume@blueriver.net Web Site:hitsandfavorites.com Licensee: Ironic Broadcasting Inc. (acq

3-21-97; with co-located FM). Population served: 20,000 Rgnl. Network: Network Indiana. Natl. Rep: Rgnl Reps,. Network Indiana Haley, Bader & Potts. Format: Oldies. News staff: one; News: 7 hrs wkly. Target aud: General. Spec prog: Farm 7 hrs wkly. ◆Jerry Wall, gen mgr, gen sls mgr; Jason Archer, progmg mgr, pub affrs dir; Dave Dedrick, news dir; Todd Edwards, chief of engrg.

WUME-FM— September 1972: 95.3 mhz; 3 kw. 300 ft TL: N38 32 25 W86 28 42. Stereo. Hrs open: 24 Prog sep from AM Box 690, 192 S. Court St., 47454. Phone: (812) 723-4484. Fax: (812) 723-4966. Web Site:hitsandfavorites.com Population served: 20,000 Natl. Network: ABC, . Rgnl rep: Rgnl Reps Format: Comtemp hit. News staff: one; News: 9 hrs wkly. Target aud: General. ◆Jason Archer, traf mgr; Dave Dedrick, news rptr, farm dir, sports cmtr.

Pendleton

*WEEM-FM— Nov 1, 1971: 91.7 mhz; 1.2 kw. Ant 198 ft TL: N39 59 52 W85 44 07. Stereo. Hrs open: 24 One Arabian Dr., 46064. Phone: (765) 778-2161, EXT. 236. Fax: (765) 778-0605.E-mail: jpetrey@smadison.k12.in.us Web Site:www.917weem.org Licensee: South Madison Community School Corp. Population served: 250,000 Network Indiana Pillsbury Winthrop Shaw Pittman LLP. Format: Triple A. Target aud: Adults 18-45, students 13-18. Spec prog: High school sports 10 hrs, acoustic cafe 2 hrs, educ progmg 4 hrs wkly. ◆Jered Petrey, gen mgr; Steve Longenecker, chief of engrg.

Peru

WARU(AM)— Sept 12, 1954: 1600 khz; 1 kw-D. TL: N40 45 53 W86 02 26. Hrs open: 24 Box 1010, 46970. Secondary address: 1711 E. Wabash Rd. 46970. Phone: (765) 473-4448. Fax: (765) 473-4449.E-mail: waru@sbcglobal.net Web Site:www.warufm.com Licensee: Miami County Broadcasting Inc. Group owner: Mid-America Radio Group Inc. Population served: 14,139 Natl. Network: AP Radio, . Rgnl. Network: Tribune, Agri-Net. Natl. Rep: Rgnl Reps,. Format: Real country. News staff: one; News: 20 hrs wkly. Target aud: 25-54. ◆David Keister, pres; David Poehler, VP; Dan Keister, gen mgr, stn mgr; Steve Morris, progmg dir.

WARU-FM—(Roann, 2001: 101.9 mhz; 3.6 kw. Ant 423 ft TL: N40 48 30 W85 56 07. Stereo. Hrs open: 24 Dups AM 100% 1711 E. Wabash Rd., 46970. Phone: (765) 473-4448. Fax: (765) 473-4449. Web Site:www.warufm.com Licensee: Mid-America Radio Group Inc. Population served: 30,000 News staff: one; News: 4 hrs wkly.

WMYK(FM)— Apr 5, 1965: 98.5 mhz; 6 kw. Ant 328 ft TL: N40 37 46 W86 02 28. Stereo. Hrs open: 24 Box 2208, Kokomo, 46904-2208. Secondary address: 400 S., Kokomo 46902. Phone: (765)455-9850. Fax: (765) 455-3882.E-mail: classicrock985@sbcglobal.net Licensee: Hoosier AM/FM LLC Group owner: Mid-America Radio Group Inc. (acq 2-9-2009; grpsl). Population served: 14,139 Natl. Network: ABC, . Format: Classic rock. News staff: 2. Target aud: 25-54. ◆Steve LaMar, gen mgr; Allan James, opns mgr; Mike Turner, progmg dir; Elise Schrock, news dir; Steve Ross, chief of engrg.

Petersburg

WBTO-FM— Oct 8, 1984: 102.3 mhz; 3 kw. 321 ft TL: N38 30 33 W87 17 28. Stereo. Hrs open: 24 Box 616, Washington, 47501. Secondary address: Box 242, Vincennes 47591. Phone: (812) 254-4300. Phone: (812) 882-6060. Fax: (812) 254-4361. Fax: (812) 885-2604.E-mail: info@bl.com Web Site:www.wbtofm.com Licensee: The Original Co. Inc. (group owner; acq 11-24-99; $400,000). Natl. Rep: Rgnl Reps,. Format: Classic rock. News: 9 hrs wkly. Target aud: General. ◆Mark Lange, pres.

Plainfield

WRDZ-FM— July 1, 2003: 98.3 mhz; 3 kw. 300 ft TL: N39 45 33 W86 22 30. Stereo. Hrs open: 24 630 W. Carmel Dr., Indianapolis, 46032. Phone: (317) 574-2000. Fax: (317) 581-1985.E-mail: jim.mcconville@radiodisney.com Web Site:www.radiodisney.com Licensee: Radio Disney Group LLC. Group owner: ABC Inc. (acq 7-1-03; $5.6 million). Population served: 1,750,000 Natl. Network: Radio Disney, . Natl. Rep: McGavren Guild,. Format: Pop/CHR. Target aud: W25-44, Kids 4-12. ◆Jim McConville, gen mgr; Laura Sanchez, prom mgr & chief of engrg.

Plymouth

*WIKV(FM)— 2005: 89.3 mhz; 400 w. Ant 249 ft TL: N41 20 51 W86 20 23. Hrs open: 5700 West Oaks Blvd., Rocklin, CA, 95765. Phone: (916) 251-1600. Fax: (916) 251-1650. Web Site:www.klove.com

Licensee: Educational Media Foundation. Group owner: American Family Radio. (acq 3-23-2007; grpsl). Natl. Network: K-Love, . Format: Contemp Christian. ♦Richard Jenkins, pres.

WTCA(AM)— Aug 18, 1964: 1050 khz; 250 w-U, DA-2. TL: N41 19 06 W86 18 41. Hrs open: 24 112 W. Washington St., 46563. Phone: (574) 936-4096. Fax: (574) 936-6776. Licensee: Community Service Broadcasters Inc. (acq 11-27-98). Population served: 100,000 Natl. Network: Jones Radio Networks, . Brownfield Reddy, Begley & McCormick. Format: Classic Hits. Target aud: 25-65. Spec prog: Farm 3 hrs wkly religious 4 hrs wkly. ♦Kathryn E. Bottorff, stn mgr; Jim Bottorff, gen sls mgr; Tony Ross, progmg dir; Kathy Bottorff, news dir; James Kunze, chief of engrg.

WZOC(FM)— July 20, 1966: 94.3 mhz; 11.5 kw. 492 ft TL: N41 31 41 W86 15 53. Stereo. Hrs open: 112 W. Washington St., 46563. Phone: (574) 936-4096. Fax: (574) 936-6776. Licensee: Plymouth Broadcasting Inc. (acq 9-12-96; $575,000). Format: Oldies. ♦James Kunze, stn mgr.

Portage

WNDZ(AM)— May 13, 1987: 750 khz; 5 kw-D, DA. TL: N41 33 49 W87 09 18. (CP: 15 kw-D, DA). Hrs open: 5625 n. milwaukee ave., Chicago, IL, 60646. Phone: (773) 792-1121. Fax: (773) 792-2904.E-mail: mp@wsbcradio.com Licensee: WNDZ Inc. Group owner: Newsweb Corp. (acq 3-16-2004; $24 million with WCPQ(FM) Park Forest, IL). Format: time-brokered. Target aud: General. ♦Harvey Wells, VP; Mark Pinski, gen mgr; Mike McCarthy, engrg dir.

Portland

***WBSJ(FM)**— December 1996: 91.7 mhz; 2.1 kw. 210 ft TL: N40 24 26 W85 02 15. Hrs open:
Rebroadcasts WBST(FM) Muncie 100%.
c/o WBST(FM), Ball State Univ., Muncie, 47306-0550. Phone: (765) 285-5888. Fax: (765) 285-8937.E-mail: info@bsu.edu/ipr Web Site:www.bsu.edu/ipr Licensee: Ball State University. Format: Class, news. News staff: one; News: 33 hrs wkly. Target aud: General. ♦Marcus Jackman, gen mgr; Pam Coletti, gen sls mgr; Carol Trimmer, prom mgr; Steven Turpin, progmg dir; Robert Mittendorf, chief of engrg; Dorothy Marvell, traf mgr; Brian Beaver, news rptr.

WPGW(AM)— Jan 14, 1951: 1440 khz; 500 w-D, 35 w-N, DA-1. TL: N40 26 10 W85 00 56. Hrs open: 1891 W. State Rd 67, 47371. Phone: (260) 726-8729. Fax: (260) 726-4311.E-mail: wpgw@jayco.net Licensee: WPGW Inc. (acq 8-1-74). Population served: 25,000 Rgnl. Network: AgriAmerica. Natl. Rep: Rgnl Reps,. Format: Adult contemp. Target aud: General. ♦Robert A. Weaver, pres & gen mgr.

WPGW-FM— May 19, 1975: 100.9 mhz; 4.6 kw. 180 ft TL: N40 26 10 W85 00 54. Stereo. Hrs open: Dups AM 18% 1891 W State Rd 67, 47371. Phone: (260) 726-8729. Fax: (260) 726-4311.E-mail: wpgw@jayco.net Licensee: WPGW Inc. Population served: 25,000 Format: Country. Target aud: General. ♦Jeff Overholser, disc jockey.

Princeton

WRAY(AM)— Dec 16, 1950: 1250 khz; 1 kw-D, 59 w-N. TL: N38 21 25 W87 35 25. Stereo. Hrs open: 24 Box 8, 1900 W. Broadway, 47670-0008. Phone: (812) 386-1250. Fax: (812) 386-6249.E-mail: wray@wrayradio.com Web Site:www.wrayradio.com Licensee: Princeton Broadcasting Co. Inc. Population served: 250,000 Format: News, talk. News staff: 3. Target aud: 25-54. ♦Richard Langford, pres; Lynn Roach, gen sls mgr, prom mgr, spec ev coord; Stephen R. Langford, gen mgr, opns mgr & progmg dir; Cliff Ingram, news dir; Floyd Turner, chief of engrg; Dave Kunkel, disc jockey.

WRAY-FM— May 15, 1960: 98.1 mhz; 50 kw. 420 ft TL: N38 21 25 W87 35 25. Stereo. Hrs open: 24 Prog sep from AM Box 8 , 1900 W. Broadway, 47670. Phone: (812) 386-1250. Fax: (812) 386-6249. Web Site:www.wrayradio.com Format: Country. ♦Dave Kunkel, progmg dir, disc jockey; Charlene K. Garrison, traf mgr; Paul Viton, disc jockey.

WSJD(FM)— Oct 1, 1994: 100.5 mhz; 6 kw horiz, 5.5 kw vert. Ant 328 ft TL: N38 23 24 W87 34 23. Stereo. Hrs open: 24 606 Market St., Mount Carmel, IL, 62863. Phone: (618) 262-4102. Fax: (618) 262-4103.E-mail: wsjd@midwest.net Licensee: WSJD Inc. Group owner: Southern Wabash Communications Corp. (acq 8-3-01). Population served: 650,000 Format: Oldies. News staff: one; News: 20 hrs wkly. Target aud: 25 plus. ♦Randolph V. Bell, pres; Sally Dorgan Potts, exec VP; Kevin Madden, gen mgr.

Rensselaer

WLQI(FM)— 1973: 97.7 mhz; 3.3 kw. 300 ft TL: N40 58 14 W87 09 10. Stereo. Hrs open: 24 Prog sep from AM Box D , 47978. Secondary address: 560 W. Amster Rd. 47978. Phone: (219) 866-5105. Fax: (219) 866-4104. Fax: (219) 866-5106. Web Site:www.1560wrin.com Population served: 100,000 Natl. Network: Jones Radio Networks, . Rgnl. Network: Tribune. Tribune Radio Networks Cohn & Marks. Format: Classic hits. News staff: one; News: ndws progmg 10 hrs wkly. Target aud: 25 plus.

***WPUM(FM)**— Sept 6, 1977: 90.5 mhz; 10 w. 190 ft TL: N40 55 12 W87 09 27. Stereo. Hrs open: 24 Box 651, St. Joseph's College, 47978. Phone: (219) 866-6000.E-mail: wpum@saintjoe.edu Licensee: St. Joseph's College. (acq 8-1-76). Population served: 5,000 Natl. Network: Superadio, . Format: Rock. News staff: one; News: 10 hrs wkly. Target aud: 18-34; general. Spec prog: Country 3 hrs, classical 3 hrs, blues 3 hrs, talk one hr wkly. ♦Sally Nesselroad, stn mgr.

WRIN(AM)— Sept 14, 1963: 1560 khz; 1 kw-D, 500 w-CH. TL: N40 57 41 W87 09 07. Hrs open: Box D, 47978. Secondary address: 560 W. Amster Rd. Phone: (219) 866-5105. Fax: (219) 866-4104. Fax: (219) 866-5106. Web Site:www.1560wrin.com Licensee: Brothers Broadcasting Corp. (acq 6-18-86). Population served: 50,000 Rgnl. Network: AgriAmerica. Natl. Rep: Rgnl Reps,. Leventhal, Senter & Lerman. Format: Adult standards. News staff: one; News: 10 hrs wkly. Target aud: 30+. Spec prog: Farm 12 hrs, gospel 2 hrs, relg 10 hrs wkly. ♦John Balvich, pres & gen mgr; Connie Graham Luthi, sls dir; Bob Burt, progmg dir; Bob Kurtz, news dir.

Richmond

***WECI(FM)**— September 1964: 91.5 mhz; 400 w. 106 ft TL: N39 49 22 W84 54 39. Stereo. Hrs open: 6 AM-3 AM 801 National Rd. W., Drawer 45, 47374. Phone: (765) 983-1246. Fax: (765) 983-1641.E-mail: hennja@earlham.edu Web Site:www.earlham.edu/~weci Licensee: Earlham College. Population served: 70,000 Format: Class, country, var/div. Spec prog: Bluegrass/folk 19 hrs, classic rock 16 hrs, progsv 18 hrs wkly. ♦Alice Edgerton, stn mgr; Kate Galligan, progmg dir; Sam Robinson, news dir.

WFMG(FM)— Dec 17, 1960: 101.3 mhz; 50 kw. 280 ft TL: N39 49 30 W84 55 50. Stereo. Hrs open: 24 Prog sep from AM 2301 W. Main St., 47374. Phone: (765) 962-6533. Fax: (765) 966-1499.E-mail: info@g1013.com Web Site:www.g1013.com Licensee: Rodgers Broadcasting Corp. Population served: 500,000 Format: Hot adult contemp. News staff: 2; News: 2 hrs wkly. Target aud: 18-44. Spec prog: Miami University Sports 8 hrs wkly. ♦Rick Duncan, opns mgr.

WHON(AM)—(Centerville, Feb 17, 1964: 930 khz; 500 w-D, 114 w-N, DA-2. TL: N39 53 33 W84 56 09. Hrs open: 24 Box 1647, 47375. Phone: (765) 962-1595. Fax: (765) 966-4824. Web Site:www.whon930.com Licensee: Brewer Broadcasting Corp. (group owner; (acq 11-20-97). Population served: 43,999 Natl. Rep: Rgnl Reps,. Format: News/talk. News staff: one. Target aud: 35 plus. ♦Dave Strycker, gen mgr; Troy Derengowski, progmg dir.

WKBV(AM)— Sept 27, 1926: 1490 khz; 1 kw-U. TL: N39 49 30 W84 55 50. (CP: N39 49 41 W84 55 57). Hrs open: 24 Box 1646, 2301 W. Main St., 47374. Phone: (765) 962-6533. Fax: (765) 966-1499. Licensee: Rodgers Broadcasting Corp. (group owner; (acq 8-4-97; with co-located FM). Population served: 500,000 Natl. Network: ABC, ESPN Radio, . Network Indiana Format: News/talk. News staff: 2; News: 10 hrs wkly. Target aud: 25-54. Spec prog: Farm 4 hrs wkly. ♦David Rodgers, pres; Steve Frey, stn mgr & sls dir; Rick Duncan, progmg dir, local news ed; Bob Phillips, local news ed.

WQLK(FM)— Oct 15, 1973: 96.1 mhz; 50 kw. Ant 350 ft TL: N39 53 33 W84 56 09. Stereo. Hrs open: 24 Box 1647, 47375. Phone: (765) 962-1595. Fax: (765) 966-4824. Web Site:www.kicks96.com Licensee: Brewer Broadcasting Corp. Format: Hot country. News staff: one. Target aud: 25-54. ♦Steve Baker, progmg dir.

***WZRP(FM)**— Dec 24, 1988: 89.3 mhz; 4.2 kw. Ant 187 ft TL: N39 52 08 W84 47 47. Stereo. Hrs open: 24
Simulcasts WZCP(FM) Chillicothe, OH 100%.
Box 783, East Johnstown Rd., Gahanna, OH, 43230. Phone: 614-289-5700. Fax: (614) 289-5793.E-mail: thepromise @promiseradionetwork.com Web Site:www.promiseradionetwork.com Licensee: Christian Voice of Central Ohio Inc. (acq 5-15-2007; grpsl). Rgnl. Network: Ohio Radio Net. Format: Christian talk, educ, Muisc. ♦Dan Baughman, gen mgr; Scott Saunders, progmg dir.

Rising Sun

WSCH(FM)—See Aurora

Roann

WARU-FM—Licensed to Roann. See Peru

Roanoke

***WBNI-FM**— 1991: 94.1 mhz; 6 kw. Ant 328 ft TL: N40 58 51 W85 16 48. Hrs open: 24
Simulcast with WCKZ(FM) Orland 100%.
Box 8459, Fort Wayne, 46898-8459. Phone: (260) 452-1189. Fax: (260) 452-1188.E-mail: jbrown@nipr.fm Web Site:www.nipr.fm Licensee: Northeast Indiana Public Radio Inc. Group owner: Summit City Radio Group (acq 4-9-2007; $1.75 million). Natl. Network: NPR, . Dow, Lohnes & Albertson, PLLC. Format: Classical. ♦Bruce Haines, gen mgr; Karen Fraser, dev dir; Colleen Condron, progmg dir; Jeanette Dillon, news dir.

Rochester

***WQKV(FM)**— 2006: 88.5 mhz; 250 w. Ant 171 ft TL: N41 03 14 W86 16 12. Hrs open: 5700 West Oaks Blvd., Rocklin, CA, 95765. Phone: (916) 251-1600. Fax: (916) 251-1650. Licensee: Educational Media Foundation. Group owner: American Family Radio. (acq 3-23-2007; grpsl). Format: Christian. ♦Richard Jenkins, pres.

WROI(FM)— Aug 29, 1971: 92.1 mhz; 4.2 kw. 240 ft TL: N41 03 02 W86 15 39. Stereo. Hrs open: 24 110 E. 8th St., 46975. Phone: (574) 223-6059. Fax: (574) 223-2238.E-mail: wroi@rtcol.com Web Site:www.wroifm.com Licensee: Bair Communications Inc. (acq 10-21-92; 10-19-92). Population served: 65,000 Rgnl. Network: Brownfield, Network Indiana Natl. Rep: Rgnl Reps,. Network Indiana Format: Oldies. News staff: one; News: 20 hrs wkly. Target aud: General. Spec prog: Farm 10 hrs, relg 6 hrs wkly. ♦Tom Bair, pres & gen mgr; Sue Bair, gen sls mgr; Matt Bair, progmg dir; Baron Imhoof, news dir.

Rockville

WAXI(FM)— August 1977: 104.9 mhz; 3 kw. Ant 400 ft TL: N39 43 44 W87 17 56. Stereo. Hrs open: 24 1301 Ohio St., Terre Haute, 47807. Phone: (812) 234-9770. Fax: (812) 238-1576.E-mail: hfarmer@radioworksforme.com Web Site:www.waxifm.com Licensee: Crossroads Investments LLC. Group owner: Crossroads Communications Inc. (acq 4-20-98; $485,000). Population served: 100,000 Natl. Network: ABC, . Rgnl. Network: AgriAmerica, Network Indiana. Natl. Rep: Rgnl Reps,. Network Indiana Booth, Freret, Imlay & Tepper. Format: Oldies. News staff: one; News: 10 hrs wkly. Target aud: 35 plus; local to Parke, Vermillion counties, affluent boomers & seniors in Terre haute market. Spec prog: Gospel 2 hrs wkly. ♦Mike Petersen, pres; Doug Edge, gen mgr, prom dir; Brad Simon, prom dir; John Sigman, progmg dir; Tom Mulvihill, chief of engrg.

Royal Center

WHZR(FM)— Oct 16, 1989: 103.7 mhz; 6 kw. 328 ft TL: N40 48 43 W86 21 56. Stereo. Hrs open: 24 425 Second St., Logansport, 46947. Phone: (574) 732-1037. Fax: (574) 739-1037.E-mail: whzr@verizon.net Licensee: Mid-America Radio Group of Logansport-Peru Inc. Group owner: Mid-America Radio Group Inc. (acq 5-1-95; $450,000;6-5-95). Format: Country. News staff: one; News: 6 hrs wkly. Target aud: 18-49; mass appeal. ♦David Keister, pres; Dan Keister, gen mgr, news dir.

Rushville

WIFE-FM— Aug 5, 1971: 94.3 mhz; 1.05 kw. 561 ft TL: N39 42 22 W85 29 41. Stereo. Hrs open: 102 N. Perkins St., 46173. Phone: (765) 932-3983. Phone: (765) 932-3409. Fax: (765) 938-1916. Licensee: Rodgers Broadcasting Corp. (acq 7-5-2007; $1.5 million). Population served: 50,000 Rgnl. Network: Brownfield. Natl. Rep: Christal, Rgnl Reps,. Format: Country. Target aud: 35 plus. Spec prog: Farm 18 hrs wkly. ♦David Rodgers, pres; Scott Huber, gen mgr; Kevin Stone, gen sls mgr; Doug Raab, progmg dir, engrg mgr, chief of engrg; Martha Swain, chief of engrg, traf mgr.

***WMUI(FM)**—Not on air, target date: unknown: 91.9 mhz; 225 w. Ant 263 ft TL: N39 37 10.8 W85 24 24. Hrs open: 1223 Central Pkwy., Cincinnati, OH, 45214. Phone: (513) 352-9170. Fax: (513) 241-8456.E-mail: WMUB@WMUB.org Web Site:www.wmub.org Licensee: The President & Trustees of Miami University. ♦Richard Eiswerth, gen mgr.

Salem

WSLM(AM)— Feb 14, 1953: 1220 khz; 5 kw-D, 384 w-N, DA-2. TL: N38 36 55 W86 05 10. Hrs open: 18 Box 385, 47167. Secondary

address: 1308 Hwy 56 East 47167. Phone: (812) 883-5750. Fax: (812) 883-2797.E-mail: wslm@blueriver.net Licensee: Don H. Martin. Population served: 24,000 Rgnl. Network: AgriAmerica, Network Indiana, Tribune. Natl. Rep: Rgnl Reps,. Tribune Radio Networks Baraff, Koerner & Olender. Format: Farm, C&W, gospel. News staff: 5; News: 12 hrs wkly. Target aud: 21-70. ♦Don H. Martin, pres, gen mgr, gen sls mgr; J.R. Martin, stn mgr, prom mgr, chief of engrg; Becky L. White, adv dir; Rebecca White, progmg mgr & mus dir; Don Martin, progmg.

WSLM-FM— 1992: 97.9 mhz; 3 kw. 220 ft TL: N38 38 07 W86 10 37. Stereo. Hrs open: 18 Dups AM 50% Box 385, 47167. Secondary address: 1308 Hwy 56 East 47167. Phone: (812) 883-5750. Fax: (812) 883-2797.E-mail: wslm@blueriver.net Licensee: Rebecca L. White. Population served: 100,000 Format: News, talk shows. News staff: 2; News: 3. Target aud: 18-65. ♦Don H. Martin, adv mgr, progmg mgr; Rebecca White, progmg dir.

WZKF(FM)— 1962: 98.9 mhz; 50 kw. 300 ft TL: N38 35 59 W86 05 17. (CP: Ant 492 ft. TL: N38 21 56 W85 58 55). Stereo. Hrs open: 24 4000 Radio Drive, Louisville, KY, 40218-4568. Phone: (502) 479-2222. Fax: (502) 479-2308. Web Site:www.kisslouisville.com Licensee: CC Licenses LLC. Group owner: Clear Channel Communications Inc. (acq 12-31-96). Population served: 942,300 Natl. Rep: Clear Channel,. Format: CHR. Target aud: 18-54; country music listeners. ♦Bill Gentry, mktg mgr; Matt Ryan, progmg dir.

Santa Claus

WAXL(FM)— July 30, 1996: 103.3 mhz; 6 kw. 462 ft TL: N38 12 31 W86 54 00. Stereo. Hrs open: 24 Box 1009, Jasper, 47547. Secondary address: 501 Old State Rd., Huntingburg 47542. Phone: (812) 683-1215. Phone: (800) 522-1033. Fax: (812) 683-5891.E-mail: mailbox@waxl.us Web Site:www.dcbroadcasting.com ABC Licensee: Dubois County Broadcasting Inc. Group owner: DCBroadcasting Inc. (acq 7-25-97). Natl. Network: ABC, . Rgnl. Network: Network Indiana, Brownfield Brownfield Miller & Miller, P.C. Wire Svc: AP Format: Adult contemp. News staff: one; News: 3 hrs wkly. Target aud: 24-49. Spec prog: Agriculture 3 hrs wkly. ♦Paul Knies, pres; Bill Potter, gen mgr; Ron Spaulding, sls dir & gen sls mgr; Joe Lacay, progmg VP, progmg dir.

Scottsburg

WMPI(FM)— Dec 16, 1966: 105.3 mhz; 2.2 kw. 511 ft TL: N38 37 12 W85 45 15. Stereo. Hrs open: 24 Box 270, 22 E. McClain Ave., 47170. Phone: (812) 752-5612. Fax: (812) 752-2345.E-mail: i@1053online.com Web Site:www.i1053.com Licensee: D. R. Rice Broadcasting Inc. (acq. 1987). Population served: 50,000 Natl. Rep: Rgnl Reps,. Format: C&W. News staff: one; News: 5 hrs wkly. Target aud: 25-54. ♦Donald R. Rice, pres; Raymond Rice, gen mgr; Tom Cull, stn mgr; John Ross, progmg dir, news dir; Steve Woodruff, chief of engrg.

Seelyville

WWSY(FM)— Sept 12, 1996: 95.9 mhz; 4.1 kw. Ant 397 ft TL: N39 34 29 W87 24 06. Hrs open: 824 S. 3rd St., Terre Haute, 47807. Phone: (812) 232-4161. Fax: (812) 234-9999. Web Site:www.y959thevalley.com Licensee: Midwest Communications Inc. (acq 6-13-2005; $3.39 million with WMGI(FM) Terre Haute). Natl. Network: Jones Radio Networks, . Rgnl. Network: Jones Satellite Audio. Natl. Rep: Christal,. Format: Var rock. Target aud: 35-54. ♦Kathleen Walker, sls VP & gen sls mgr; Karl Wertzler, mktg mgr; Chad Edwards, progmg dir; Jerry Arnold, chief of engrg.

Sellersville

WLCL(FM)— Feb 23, 1961: 93.9 mhz; 2.65 kw. Ant 499 ft TL: N38 15 21.7 W85 45 29.1. Stereo. Hrs open: 24 9900 Corporate Campus Way, Louisville, KY, 40223. Phone: (502) 992-0939. Web Site:www.classichits939.com Licensee: S.C.I. Broadcasting Inc. (acq 5-25-2001; grpsl). Population served: 500,000 Format: Classic hits. Target aud: General. ♦Dugan Ryan, gen mgr.

Seymour

***WJLR(FM)—** August 1995: 91.5 mhz; 5.6 kw. Ant 351 ft TL: N38 49 23 W85 47 24. Stereo. Hrs open: 24 2351 Sunset Blvd., Suite 170-218, Rocklin, CA, 95765. Phone: (916) 251-1600. Fax: (916) 251-1650. Licensee: Educational Media Foundation. (acq 11-9-2004; $150,000). Natl. Network: K-Love, . Shaw Pittman LLP. Format: Christian info & educ. Target aud: 30-80; family oriented. ♦Richard Jenkins, pres; Keith Whipple, dev dir; Eric Allen, natl sls mgr; David Pierce, progmg mgr; Ed Lenane, news dir; Sam Wallington, engrg dir; Karen Johnson, news rptr.

WZZB(AM)— Nov 4, 1949: 1390 khz; 1 kw-D, 74 w-N. TL: N38 58 23 W85 53 20. Hrs open: 24 Box 806, 47274. Secondary address: 1534 Ewing St. 47274. Phone: (812) 522-1390. Fax: (812) 522-9541.E-mail: wzzb@comcast.net Licensee: Midnight Hour Broadcasting LLC. Group owner: Susquehanna Radio Corp. (acq 1-3-2008; $300,000). Population served: 97,000 Natl. Network: USA, Jones Radio Networks, . Rgnl. Network: AgriAmerica, Network Indiana. Network Indiana Rgnl rep: Rgnl Reps. Dow, Lohnes & Albertson. Format: Full service, news, sports, adult contemp, oldies. News staff: 2; News: 17 hrs wkly. Target aud: 25 plus; community oriented. Spec prog: Farm 2 hrs, relg 6 hrs wkly. ♦Blair W. Trask, pres, gen mgr, gen sls mgr; Bud Shippee, opns dir, progmg dir & news dir; Bob Hawkins, chief of engrg.

Shelbyville

WLHK(FM)— Nov 6, 1964: 97.1 mhz; 23 kw. 739 ft TL: N39 40 02 W86 01 51. Stereo. Hrs open: 24 One Emmis Plaza, 40 Monument Cir., Suite 600, Indianapolis, 46204. Phone: (317) 266-9700. Fax: (317) 684-2021. Web Site:www.emmis.com Licensee: Emmis Radio License LLC. Group owner: Emmis Communications Corp. (acq 6-81). Population served: 1,100,000 Natl. Rep: D & R Radio,. Gardner, Carton & Douglas. Format: Country. News staff: one. Target aud: 25-54; female. ♦Tom Severino, gen mgr; David Edgar, opns dir, progmg dir, news dir; Mike Cortese, gen sls mgr; Dave Hood, chief of engrg; Shelly Grimes, traf mgr.

WSVX(AM)— Jan 14, 1961: 1520 khz; 1 kw-D, 250 w-N, DA-2. TL: N39 33 29 W85 46 13. Hrs open: 24 2356 N. Morristown Rd., 46176. Phone: (317) 398-2200. Fax: (317) 392-3292.E-mail: info@wsvx.com Web Site:www.wsvx.com Licensee: RSE Broadcasting LLC. (acq 11-4-99). Population served: 300,000 Brownfield Format: Top-40. News staff: one; News: 3 hrs wkly. Target aud: Shelby County. ♦John Schoentrup, adv mgr; Douglas Raab, progmg dir, chief of engrg; Johnny McCrory, news dir.

South Bend

***WAUS(FM)—**(Berrien Springs, MI) 1971: 90.7 mhz; 50 kw. 492 ft TL: N41 57 42 W86 21 02. Stereo. Hrs open: 24 WAUS, Berrien Springs, MI, 49104-0240. Phone: (269) 471-3400. Fax: (269) 471-3804.E-mail: waus@andrews.edu Web Site:www.waus.org Licensee: Andrews Broadcasting Corp. Population served: 200,000 Natl. Network: PRI, . Donald E. Martin. Format: Class. News: 3 hrs wkly. Target aud: 35 plus; listeners with interest in classical music. Spec prog: Relg 10 hrs wkly. ♦Niels-Erik Andreasen, chmn; Sharon Dudgeon, gen mgr; Bill Brent, opns dir.

WBYT(FM)—See Elkhart

WDND(AM)— Nov 6, 1998: 1620 khz; 10 kw-D, 1 kw-N. TL: N41 38 11 W86 17 06. Hrs open: 3371 Cleveland Rd., Suite 310, 46628. Phone: (574) 273-9300. Fax: (574) 273-9090.E-mail: u93@u93.com Licensee: Artistic Media Partners Inc. (acq 3-31-2000; with WHLY(AM) South Bend). Format: Sports. Target aud: 25-54. ♦Jack Swart, gen mgr; Greg DeRue, stn mgr; Carrie Jones, natl sls mgr; Teresa Holden, prom dir; Chili Walker, progmg dir; Bob Henning, chief of engrg; Rita Kinzie, traf mgr.

***WETL(FM)—** Nov 17, 1958: 91.7 mhz; 3 kw. 200 ft TL: N41 37 24 W86 14 15. Stereo. Hrs open: 1902 S. Fellows, 46613. Phone: (574) 283-8432. Fax: (574) 283-8405.E-mail: jovermyer@sbcsc.k12.in.us Licensee: South Bend Community School Corp. (acq 11-17-58). Population served: 135,000 Format: Educ, instructional. Target aud: General; student in the South Bend community school and community. ♦Anita Brown, gen mgr; John Overmyer, progmg dir; Allen Wujcik, chief of engrg.

WHLY(AM)— Dec 22, 1947: 1580 khz; 10 kw-D, 500 w-N, DA-N. TL: N41 41 09 W86 09 53. Hrs open: 24 Box 1322, Elkhart, 46515. Phone: (574) 361-4618. Licensee: Times Communications Inc. Population served: 250,000 Natl. Network: EWTN Radio, . Format: Catholic.

WHME(FM)— January 1968: 103.1 mhz; 3 kw. 300 ft TL: N41 36 11 W86 12 51. Hrs open: 24 61300 Ironwood Rd., 46614. Phone: (574) 291-8200. Fax: (574) 291-9043.E-mail: info@whme.com Web Site:www.lesea.com Licensee: Le Sea Broadcasting Corp. Group owner: Le Sea Broadcasting Population served: 302,000 Gardner, Carton & Douglas. Format: Adult contemp Christian. News: 3 hrs wkly. Target aud: 24-36; general. ♦Tony Hale, CFO; Anna Riblet, stn mgr, gen sls mgr, natl sls mgr; Wes Hylton, chief of engrg & disc jockey. Co-owned TV: WHME-TV affil.

WNDV-FM— 1962: 92.9 mhz; 12.5 kw. 800 ft TL: N41 36 20 W86 12 45. Stereo. Hrs open: 24 3371 Cleveland Rd., Suite 310, 46628. Phone: (574) 273-9300. Fax: (574) 273-9090. Web Site:www.u93.com Population served: 255,800 Format: CHR. Target aud: 25-44; women. ♦Karen Rite, progmg dir.

WNSN(FM)— Aug 1, 1962: 101.5 mhz; 13 kw. 970 ft TL: N41 37 00 W86 13 01. Stereo. Hrs open: Prog sep from AM 300 W. Jefferson Blvd., 46601. Phone: (574) 233-3241. Fax: (574) 289-7382. Web Site:www.sunny1015.com Population served: 816,000 Format: Adult contemp. News staff: one; News: 2 hrs wkly. Target aud: 25-54; adults. ♦Brad King, mktg dir; Jim Roberts, opns mgr & progmg dir. Co-owned TV: WSBT-TV affil

WPNT(AM)— 1944: Stn currently dark. 1490 khz; 1 kw-U. TL: N41 41 38 W86 13 50. Hrs open: 3371 Cleveland Rd., Suite 310, 46628. Phone: (574) 273-9300. Fax: (574) 273-9090. Web Site:www.artisticradio.com/wdnd.htm Licensee: Artistic Media Partners Inc. (group owner; (acq 10-22-98; $6,123,180 with co-located FM). Population served: 238,000 ♦Arthur A. Angotti, pres; Jack Swart, gen mgr; Mike Sullivan, stn mgr.

WRBR-FM— 1965: 103.9 mhz; 3 kw. 328 ft TL: N41 41 53 W86 09 20. Stereo. Hrs open: 237 W. Edison Rd., Suite 200, Mishawaka, 46545. Phone: (574) 258-5483. Fax: (574) 258-0930. Web Site:www.wrbr.com Licensee: Talking Stick Communications L.L.C (acq 6-26-2002; $840,879). Natl. Rep: Christal,. Format: Active rock. Target aud: 25-54; affluent, older people. ♦Kathy Uebler, gen mgr; Tommy Carroll, progmg dir; Greg Trobridge, chief of engrg.

WSBT(AM)— April 1922: 960 khz; 5 kw-U, DA-2. TL: N41 37 00 W86 13 01. Hrs open: 24 300 W. Jefferson Blvd., 46601. Phone: (574) 233-3141. Fax: (574) 289-7382. Web Site:www.wsbtradio.com Licensee: WSBT Inc. Group owner: Schurz Communications Inc. Population served: 211,500 Natl. Network: Fox News Radio, . Natl. Rep: Katz Radio,. Format: News/talk, sports. News staff: 3; News: 10 hrs wkly. Target aud: 25-54. Spec prog: Relg 2 hrs wkly. ♦Sally Brown, VP & gen mgr; Jim Roberts, opns mgr; Bob Montgomery, progmg dir, news dir. Co-owned TV: WSBT-TV affil

***WUBS(FM)—** 1993: 89.7 mhz; 1.5 kw. 79 ft TL: N41 40 51 W86 15 34. Hrs open: Box 3931, 46619. Phone: (574) 287-4700. Fax: (574) 287-2478.E-mail: broshane@wubs.org Licensee: Interfaith Christian Union Inc. Format: Inspirational. ♦Rev. Sylvester Williams Jr., gen mgr; Shane R. Williams, progmg dir; Brian Hoover, chief of engrg.

WUBU(FM)— October 1992: 106.3 mhz; 3 kw. Ant 292 ft TL: N41 44 11 W86 17 19. Hrs open: 24 237 Edison Rd., Suite 200, Mishawaka, 46545. Phone: (574) 258-5483. Fax: (574) 258-0930. Web Site:www.wubufm.com Licensee: Partnership Radio LLC (acq 7-15-99). Natl. Network: Jones Radio Networks, . Natl. Rep: Interep, McGavren Guild,. Wiley, Rein & Fielding. Format: Urban adult contemp. Target aud: 35-64; adults. ♦Gene Walker, gen mgr, opns mgr; Greg Trobridge, chief of engrg.

WZOW(FM)—See Goshen

South Whitley

WMYQ(FM)— Dec 2, 1992: 101.1 mhz; 6 kw. Ant 328 ft TL: N41 04 42 W85 31 20. Stereo. Hrs open: 24 Box 5570, Ft. Wayne, 46895. Phone: (260) 482-8500.E-mail: q101@wlzq.com Licensee: Larko Communications Inc. Population served: 130,000 Natl. Network: ABC, . Format: Hot adult contemp. Target aud: 25-44. ♦Chris Larko, CEO & gen mgr.

Speedway

WNOU(FM)—Licensed to Speedway. See Indianapolis

Spencer

WCLS(FM)— Sept 15, 1983: 97.7 mhz; 6 kw. Ant 328 ft TL: N39 13 22 W86 38 40. Stereo. Hrs open: 201 N. VanDalia Ave., 47460. Phone: (812) 829-9393. Fax: (812) 829-9747. Licensee: Mid-America Radio of Indiana Inc. Group owner: Mid-America Radio Group Inc. (acq 11-13-2002; $321,100). Natl. Network: Westwood One, . Format: Mainstream country. Spec prog: Relg 6 hrs wkly. ♦Ruth Ann Arney, stn mgr; Tony Kale, opns mgr; Johnnie Robbins, gen sls mgr, mktg; Monica Witt, progmg dir, traf mgr; Steve Vail, news dir; Steve Ross, chief of engrg.

Sullivan

WNDI(AM)— Oct 7, 1963: 1550 khz; 250 w-D. TL: N39 04 32 W87 23 57. Hrs open: 556 E. State Rd. 54, 47882. Phone: (812) 268-6322. Fax: (812) 268-6652. Licensee: JTM Broadcasting Corp. (acq 7-13-94; $237,000 with co-located FM; 8-1-94). Population served: 200,000 Format: Country. Target aud: 24-54. Spec prog: Farm 6 hrs wkly. ♦John Montgomery, gen mgr.

WNDI-FM— Aug 10, 1982: 95.3 mhz; 6 kw. Ant 328 ft TL: N39 09 36 W87 32 32. Hrs open: Dups AM 100% 556 E. State Rd. 54, 47882. Phone: (812) 268-6322. Fax: (812) 268-6652. Licensee: JTM Broadcasting Corp. Population served: 4,683

Syracuse

WAWC(FM)— May 31, 1991: 103.5 mhz; 3 kw. 328 ft TL: N41 22 57 W85 41 35. Stereo. Hrs open: 24 216 W. Market St., Suite 1, Warsaw, 46580. Phone: (574) 457-8181. Phone: (800) 779-1094. Fax: (574) 457-4488.E-mail: bill@hoosier1035.com Licensee: Talking Stick Communications LLC. (acq 11-1-2006; $600,000). Population served: 120,000 Natl. Network: CBS, . Rgnl. Network: Network Indiana. Network Indiana Format: Adult contemp. News staff: one; News: 7 hrs wkly. Target aud: 25-54; people in Kosciusko, Elkhart & Noble counties. Spec prog: Relg 4 hrs wkly. ♦Patrick Brown, gen mgr; Jay Michaels, progmg dir; Bill Dixon, news dir; Brent Randall, pub affrs dir, sports cmtr; Greg Stoddard, chief of engrg.

Tell City

WTCJ(AM)— Feb 1, 1948: 1230 khz; 1 kw-U. TL: N37 56 16 W86 45 28. Hrs open: 24 1115 Tamarack Rd., Suite 500, Owensboro, KY, 42301. Phone: (270) 683-5200. Fax: (270) 688-0108.E-mail: spots@wbioradio.com Web Site:www.tellcityradio.com Licensee: Hancock Communications Inc. Group owner: The Cromwell Group Inc. (acq 12-20-99; $25,000). Population served: 47,200 Natl. Network: ABC, . Natl. Rep: Rgnl Reps,. Format: Timeless classics. News staff: one. Target aud: 25-54; community-oriented listeners. Spec prog: Gospel 6 hrs wkly. ♦Bayard Walters, pres; Kevin Riecke, gen mgr & gen sls mgr; Jeff Morgan, progmg dir, news dir.

WTCJ-FM— May 2001: 105.7 mhz; 4.8 kw. Ant 364 ft TL: N37 55 33 W86 43 19. Hrs open: 24 1115 Tamarack Rd., Suite 500, Owensboro, 42301. Phone: (270) 683-5200. Fax: (270) 688-0108.E-mail: sports@wrioradio.com Population served: 47,200 Format: Classic rock.

Terre Haute

WBOW(AM)— May 23, 1958: 1300 khz; 500 w-D, 75 w-N. TL: N39 28 01 W87 25 34. Hrs open: 24
Rebroadcasts WSDX(AM) Brazil.
1301 Ohio St., 47807. Phone: (812) 234-9770. Fax: (812) 238-1576.E-mail: mike@radioworksforme.com Web Site:www.espnsportsradio.com Licensee: Crossroads Investments LLC. Group owner: Crossroads Communications Inc. (acq 9-10-97; $57,500 assumption of debt). Population served: 70,286 Natl. Network: ESPN Radio, . Natl. Rep: Roslin,. Rgnl rep: Rgnl Reps. Booth, Freret, Imlay & Tepper. Format: All sports. News: 5 hrs wkly. Target aud: 25-64; Sports Fans. ♦Mike Petersen, gen mgr; Bill Cook, progmg dir, news dir; Kevin Berlen, chief of engrg.

WBOW-FM— Sept 11, 1962: 102.7 mhz; 28 kw. 659 ft TL: N39 20 13 W87 28 00. Stereo. Hrs open: 24 1301 Ohio St., 47807. Phone: (812) 234-9770. Fax: (812) 238-1576.E-mail: hfarmer@radioworksforme.com Web Site:www.literock1027.com Licensee: Crossroads Investments LLC (acq 5-12-2003; $2.09 million). Natl. Rep: Roslin,. Rgnl rep: Rgnl Reps Booth, Freret, Imlay & Tepper. Format: Soft adult contemp. News: 2 hrs wkly. Target aud: Adults 25-54. ♦Mike Petersen, pres; Doug Edge, gen mgr; Brad Simon, prom dir; Chris Carter, progmg dir; Tom Mulvihill, chief of engrg.

***WCRT-FM**— January 1992: 88.5 mhz; 550 w. 308 ft TL: N39 30 14 W87 26 37. Hrs open: 2108 W. Springfield, Champaign, IL, 61821. Phone: (217) 359-8232. Fax: (217) 359-7374.E-mail: wbgl@wbgl.org Web Site:www.wbgl.org Licensee: Illinois Bible Institute. Format: Adult contemp Christian. ♦Jeff Scott, stn mgr; Jennifer Briski, prom dir; Ryan Springer, progmg dir; Joe Buchanan, mus dir.

***WHOJ(FM)**— 1997: 91.9 mhz; 1 kw. Ant 95 ft TL: N39 28 06 W87 23 56. Hrs open: Covenant Network, 4424 Hampton Ave., St. Louis, MO, 63109. Phone: (314) 752-7000. Web Site:www.covenantnet.net Licensee: Covenant Network. (acq 3-30-2004; $112,500 with KBKC(FM) Moberly, MO). Format: Christian, relg, talk. ♦Tony Holman, gen mgr.

***WISU(FM)**— Sept 13, 1964: 89.7 mhz; 13.5 kw. 512 ft TL: N39 30 26 W87 31 50. Stereo. Hrs open: 11 AM-2 AM Rm. 217, 217 N. 6th St., 47809. Phone: (812) 237-3248. Phone: (812) 237-3252. Fax: (812) 237-8970. Fax: (812) 237-3241.E-mail: cmwisufm@ruby.indstate.edu Web Site:wisu.indstate.edu Licensee: Indiana State University Board of Trustees. Population served: 200,000 Crowell & Moring. Format: Urban contemp, AOR. News: 4 hrs wkly. Target aud: 18-25; young professionals, students. ♦Joe Tenerelli, gen mgr; David Sabaini, progmg dir; Dan Watson, chief of engrg.

WMGI(FM)— June 13, 1960: 100.7 mhz; 50 kw. 500 ft TL: N30 27 22 W87 28 50. Stereo. Hrs open: 824 S. 3rd St., 47807. Phone: (812) 232-4161. Fax: (812) 234-9999.E-mail: chad@1007mixfm.com Web Site:www.1007mixfm.com Licensee: Midwest Communications Inc. (acq 6-13-2005; $3.39 million with WWSY(FM) Seelyville). Population served: 70,286 Natl. Network: Westwood One, . Natl. Rep: Christal,. Format: CHR. Target aud: 18-34. ♦Karl Wertzler, gen mgr, mktg mgr; Kathleen Walker, gen sls mgr; Chad Edwards, progmg dir; Jerry Arnold, chief of engrg.

***WMHD-FM**— 1981: 90.7 mhz; 160 w. 79 ft TL: N39 28 57 W87 19 33. Stereo. Hrs open: 8 AM-2 AM 5500 Wabash Ave., 47803. Phone: (812) 872-6923. Fax: (812) 872-6926.E-mail: wmhd@wmhd.rose-hulman.edu Web Site:wmhd.rose-hulman.edu Licensee: Rose Hulman Institute of Technology. Population served: 2,000 Format: Educ, AOR, progsv. News: 2 hrs wkly. Loc & college audience. Spec prog: Classical 4 hrs, bluegrass one hr, Jazz 2 hrs, contemp Christian 2 hrs wkly. ♦Brandon Inzego, gen mgr; Brooks Borchers, opns dir; Ben Braun, progmg dir.

WPFR(AM)— Jan 6, 1948: 1480 khz; 5 kw-D, 1 kw-N, DA-2. TL: N39 30 02 W87 23 10. Hrs open: 24 18889 N. 23 50th St., Dennison, IL, 62423. Phone: (217) 826-9673.E-mail: wpfr@joink.com Licensee: Word Power Inc. (acq 1-1-00; $350,000 donation). Population served: 70286 Natl. Network: Moody, . Format: Christian. Target aud: 12 plus. ♦Paul Dean Ford, gen mgr; Mark S. Ford, opns VP; Dan Watson, chief of opns.

WTHI-FM— October 1948: 99.9 mhz; 50 kw. 494 ft TL: N39 27 57 W87 24 12. Hrs open: 24 Prog sep from AM Box 1486, 47808. Secondary address: 918 Ohio St. 47808. Phone: (812) 232-9481. Fax: (812) 234-0089.E-mail: jconner@wthi.emmis.com Web Site:www.hi99.com Licensee: Emmis Radio License LLC. Group owner: Emmis Communications Corp. (acq 1998 grpsl). Population served: 390,000 Natl. Network: ABC, . Natl. Rep: Interep, D & R Radio,. Format: Country. ♦James Conner, stn mgr; Barry Kent, opns mgr; Robert Rhodes, sls dir & gen sls mgr; Chris Perrot, prom dir, progmg mgr.

WWVR(FM)—See West Terre Haute

Union City

***WJYW(FM)**— 6/1/1999: 88.9 mhz; 4.1 kw. Ant 285 ft TL: N40 11 32 W84 47 58. Hrs open: 24
94.5-Richmond, IN, 97.7-News Paris, OH.
Box 445, 47390. Secondary address: 505 S. Division St., OH 45390. Phone: (937) 968-5633. Fax: (937) 968-3320.E-mail: office@899joyfm.com Web Site:www.889joyfm.com Licensee: Positive Alternative Radio Inc. Natl. Network: Salem Radio Network, . Booth, Freret, Imlay & Tepper. Format: Contemp Christian music. Target aud: 25-54; Women. ♦Vernon H. Baker, CEO; Dan Franks, gen mgr.

Upland

***WTUR(FM)**— Sept 4, 1995: 89.7 mhz; 150 w. 112 ft TL: N40 25 02 W85 29 31. Hrs open: 236 W. Reade Ave., 46989-1001. Phone: (765) 998-5263. Phone: (765) 998-2751. Fax: (765) 998-4810.E-mail: info@tayloru.edu Web Site:www.tayloru.edu/wtur Licensee: Taylor University. Format: Contemp Christian music. Target aud: College age. ♦Kevin Gehrett, stn mgr; Lauren Matters, mus dir.

Valparaiso

WAKE(AM)— Nov 4, 1964: 1500 khz; 1 kw-D, 25 w-N, DA-2. TL: N41 26 36 W87 02 54. Hrs open: 24 2755 Sager Rd., 46383. Phone: (219) 462-6111. Fax: (219) 462-4880.E-mail: donclark@radiooneindiana.com Web Site:www.wakeradio.com Licensee: Porter County Broadcasting Holding Corp. LLC. Group owner: Porter County Broadcasting Corp. Population served: 500,000 Natl. Network: CNN Radio, . Miller & Fields, P.C. Format: All news. Target aud: 30 plus; community oriented, middle to middle-upper class. ♦Leigh Ellis, chmn, pres, gen mgr; O.J. Jackson, gen sls mgr; Don Clark, progmg dir; Laura Waluszko, news dir; Carl Fletcher, chief of engrg; Jennifer Malmquist, traf mgr.

WLJE(FM)— Oct 6, 1967: 105.5 mhz; 1.25 kw. 513 ft TL: N41 31 28 W87 01 08. Stereo. Hrs open: 2755 Sager Rd., 46383. Phone: (219) 462-8125. Fax: (219) 462-4880.E-mail: donclark@radiooneindiana.com Web Site:www.indiana105.com Population served: 800,000 Format: Country. Target aud: 25-55; family, middle income.

***WVUR-FM**— Sept 25, 1966: 95.1 mhz; 36 w. 125 ft TL: N41 27 57 W87 02 29. Stereo. Hrs open: 24 1809 Chapel Dr., 46383. Phone: (219) 464-5383. Fax: (219) 464-6742.E-mail: wvur@valpo.edu Web Site:www.valpo.edu/wvur Licensee: The Lutheran University Association Inc. Population served: 350,000 Format: Free-form. News staff: 2; News: 8 hrs wkly. Target aud: 18-34. Spec prog: Class 3 hrs, jazz 3 hrs, urban contemp 3 hrs, metal 3 hrs, classic rock 3 hrs wkly. ♦Ken LaVicka, gen mgr; Lauren LaVicka, gen sls mgr; Rachel Cooper, progmg dir; Ben Hampton, news dir; Rich Robertson, chief of engrg.

Van Buren

WCJC(FM)—Licensed to Van Buren. See Marion

Veedersburg

WSKL(FM)— July 15, 1999: 92.9 mhz; 4.5 kw. 269 ft TL: N40 08 46 W87 27 15. Stereo. Hrs open: 24 Box 67, Danville, IL, 61834. Phone: (765) 793-5665. Fax: (765) 793-4644.E-mail: fmkool929@aol.com Web Site:www.koololdies.net Licensee: Zona Communications Inc. (acq 10-29-99). Population served: 110,000 Natl. Network: AP Radio, Jones Radio Networks, . Wire Svc: AP Format: Oldies. News staff: one; News: 5 hrs wkly. Target aud: 35-65. ♦Rhea Benton-Weatherford, gen mgr; Greg Green, stn mgr; J.J. McKay, progmg dir; Tara Duncan, traf mgr.

Versailles

***WCIX(FM)**—Not on air, target date: unknown: 89.5 mhz; 700 w. Ant 220 ft TL: N39 10 38 W85 17 00. Hrs open: 5114 Princeton-Glendale Rd., Hamilton, OH, 45011-2415. Phone: (513) 898-1574. Fax: (513) 795-0724. Licensee: Spryex Communications Inc. ♦William Spry, pres.

***WKRY(FM)**— Apr 11, 2003: 88.1 mhz; 600 w. Ant 233 ft TL: N39 03 55 W85 19 00. Hrs open: 24 825 Washington St., Columbus, 47201. Phone: (812) 738-3482. Fax: (812) 375-2555. Licensee: Good Shepherd Radio Inc. Format: Relg. ♦Keith Reising, CEO & gen mgr.

Vevay

WKID(FM)— Sept 6, 1974: 95.9 mhz; 2.7 kw. 308 ft TL: N38 50 12 W85 01 48. Stereo. Hrs open: 24 118 W. Main St., 47043. Phone: (812) 427-9590. Fax: (812) 427-2492.E-mail: info@k959froggy.com Web Site:www.k959froggy.com Licensee: Dial Broadcasting Inc. (acq 1996). Natl. Network: Jones Radio Networks, . Network Indiana Rgnl rep: Regl Reps Kaye, Scholer, Fierman, Hays & Handler. Wire Svc: AP Format: Country. News: 7 hrs wkly. Target aud: 25-49; middle-income families. ♦Ken Trimble, gen mgr.

Vincennes

WAOV(AM)— Oct 22, 1940: 1450 khz; 1 kw-U. TL: N38 42 26 W87 29 42. Hrs open: 24 Box 242, 47591-0242. Phone: (812) 882-6060. Fax: (812) 885-2604.E-mail: waov@originalcompany.com Web Site:www.waovam.com Licensee: Old Northwest Broadcasting Inc. Group owner: The Original Co. Inc. (acq 9-28-93; $250,000 with WWBL(FM) Washington; 10-18-93). Population served: 40,000 Natl. Rep: Rgnl Reps,. Format: News/talk, sports. News staff: 2; News: 56 hrs wkly. Target aud: 25 plus. ♦Mark R. Lange, pres, gen mgr & progmg dir; Jim Evans, news dir, chief of engrg.

***WATI(FM)**— 2002: 89.9 mhz; 500 w. Ant 157 ft TL: N38 41 47 W87 26 27. Hrs open: Box 3206, American Family Radio, Tupelo, MS, 38803. Phone: (662) 844-8888. Fax: (662) 842-6791. Web Site:www.afr.net Licensee: American Family Association. Group owner: American Family Radio Format: Relg (Christian), inspirational. ♦Marvin Sanders, gen mgr.

WFML(FM)— May 16, 1965: 96.7 mhz; 3 kw. 377 ft TL: N38 42 26 W87 29 42. Stereo. Hrs open: 24 1002 N. First St., 47591. Phone: (812) 888-5830. Fax: (812) 882-2237.E-mail: kdoades@hot96wfml.com Web Site:hot96wfml.com Licensee: The Vincennes University Foundation (acq 8-29-86). Population served: 113,000 Natl. Network: Fox News Radio, . Rgnl. Network: Network Indiana, AgriAmerica. Network Indiana Rgnl rep: Rgnl Reps Wire Svc: AP Format: Contemp country. News staff: 2; News: 2 hrs wkly. Target aud: 18-54. ♦Phil Smith, stn mgr; Kim Donaldson, sls dir; Keith Doades, gen sls mgr; Dave Folly, prom dir; Kevin Watson, progmg dir; John Szink, news dir; Steve McClure, chief of engrg.

WUZR(FM)—(Bicknell, June 4, 1991: 105.7 mhz; 1.8 kw. Ant 426 ft TL: N38 43 47 W87 24 44. Stereo. Hrs open: 24 Box 242, Historic Brevoort House, 522 Busseron St., 47591. Phone: (812) 882-6060. Fax: (812) 885-2604.E-mail: wuzr@originalcompany.com Web Site:www.wuzr.com Licensee: The Original Co. Inc. (group owner; (acq 4-20-98; $682,000). Format: Country. News staff: one; News: 7 hrs wkly. Target aud: 25-54. Spec prog: Loc news, high school sports,

Univ. of Evansville basketball. ◆Mark Lange, pres, gen mgr; Brad Deetz, opns dir; Michelle York, gen sls mgr; Dave Young, progmg dir.

*WVUB(FM)— Dec 7, 1970: 91.1 mhz; 50 kw. Ant 500 ft TL: N38 39 06 W87 28 37. Stereo. Hrs open: 1002 N. First St., 47591. Phone: (812) 888-5830. Phone: (812) 888-5354. Fax: (574) 882-2237.E-mail: blazerwvub@hotmail.com Licensee: Board of Trustees for Vincennes University. Natl. Network: PRI, . Rgnl. Network: Network Indiana. Format: Hot adult contemp/CHR. Spec prog: Class 6 hrs wkly. ◆Phil Smith, stn mgr & gen sls mgr; Michael Woods, progmg dir; John Szink, news dir; Michael Murphy, chief of engrg. Co-owned TV: WVUT(TV) affil

WZDM(FM)— September 1988: 92.1 mhz; 4.1 kw. 400 ft TL: N38 43 18 W87 33 37. Stereo. Hrs open: 24 Box 242, Historic Brevoort House, 522 Busseron St., 47591. Phone: (812) 882-6060. Fax: (812) 885-2604.E-mail: wzdm@originalcompany.com Web Site:www.wzdm.com Licensee: The Original Co. Inc. (group owner) Format: Adult contemp. News staff: 2; News: 10 hrs wkly. Target aud: 25-54; upscale. ◆Mark R. Lange, pres, gen mgr; Michelle York, gen sls mgr; Dave Young, progmg dir.

Wabash

WJOT(AM)— November 1971: 1510 khz; 250 w-D. TL: N40 47 11 W85 49 19. Hrs open: 1360 S. Wabash St. , 46992. Phone: (260) 563-1161. Fax: (260) 563-0883.E-mail: wjot@comtek.com Licensee: Mid-America Radio of Wabash Inc. Population served: 13,379 Natl. Network: Westwood One, . ◆Wade Weaver, prom mgr & progmg dir.

WJOT-FM— July 1, 1993: 105.9 mhz; 3 kw. 318 ft TL: N40 47 11 W85 49 19. Hrs open: 1360 S. Wabash St., 46992. Phone: (260) 563-1161. Fax: (260) 563-0883.E-mail: wjot@comtek.com Licensee: Mid-America Radio of Wabash Inc. Group owner: Mid-America Radio Group Inc. (acq 7-1-98; $190,000 with co-located AM). Natl. Network: Westwood One, . Rgnl rep: Rgnl Reps. Fletcher, Heald & Hildreth. Format: Oldies. Target aud: 25-64. ◆Bill Barrows, opns dir, opns mgr, news dir; Wade Weaver, gen mgr, gen sls mgr & progmg dir; Deb Dale, pub affrs dir, traf mgr; Jack Elmore, chief of engrg.

WKUZ(FM)— Apr 1, 1965: 95.9 mhz; 4.2 kw. Ant 394 ft TL: N40 41 54 W85 45 03. Stereo. Hrs open: 24 Box 342, 1864 S. Wabash St., 46992. Phone: (260) 563-4111. Fax: (260) 563-4425.E-mail: wkuz@kconline.com Web Site:www.wkuz.com Licensee: Upper Wabash Broadcasting Corp. Population served: 500,000 Natl. Network: USA, . Rgnl. Network: Brownfield. Brownfield Format: Adult contemp. News staff: one; News: 10 hrs wkly. Target aud: General. Spec prog: Farm 5 hrs wkly. ◆Charles Adams, gen mgr; Paul Adams, chief of engrg; Toni Adams, pres & disc jockey.

Wadesville

*WENS(FM)— 2005: 90.1 mhz; 6 kw vert. Ant 285 ft TL: N37 56 03 W87 55 35. Hrs open: Box 846, Greenfield, 46140. Secondary address: 15 Wood St., Greenfield 46140-2162. Phone: (317) 467-1064. Fax: (317) 467-1065. Licensee: Indiana Community Radio Corp. Format: Contemp Christian. ◆Jennifer Cox-Hensley, pres & gen mgr.

Wakarusa

*WYBV(FM)— 2006: 89.9 mhz; 1.75 kw. Ant 328 ft TL: N41 27 50 W85 49 22. Hrs open: Bible Broadcasting Network Inc., 11530 Carmel Commons Blvd., Charlotte, NC, 28226-3976. Phone: (704) 523-5555. Fax: (704) 522-1967. Web Site:www.bbnradio.org Licensee: Bible Broadcasting Network Inc.

Walton

WFRR(FM)— 1995: 93.7 mhz; 6 kw. 328 ft TL: N40 43 30 W86 10 30. Stereo. Hrs open: 24 Rebroadcasts WFRN-FM Elkhart 85%. c/o WFRN Box 307, Elkhart, 46515. Secondary address: 25802 CR 26, Elkhart 46517. Phone: (574) 875-5166. Phone: (574) 674-6626. Fax: (574) 875-6662.E-mail: moore@wfrn.com Web Site:www.wfrn.com Licensee: Christian Friends Broadcasting Inc. Population served: 185,000 Natl. Network: USA, . Natl. Rep: Salem.; Network Indiana Reddy, Begley & McCormick. Format: Contemp Christian. News staff: one. Target aud: 25-54; general. ◆Edwin Moore, pres & gen mgr; James Carter, progmg dir; Don Wagner, news dir.

Warsaw

WLEG(FM)— (Ligonier, June 10, 1991: 102.7 mhz; 2 kw. Ant 394 ft TL: N41 27 52 W85 44 40. Stereo. Hrs open: 24 Box 699, Elkhart, 46515. Secondary address: 421 S. 2nd St., Elkhart 46516. Phone: (574) 389-5100. Fax: (574) 389-5101.E-mail: bwilliams@federatedmedia.com Web Site:www.ilovemyfroggy.com Licensee: Pathfinder Communications Corp. Group owner: Federated Media (acq 9-26-2002; $550,000). Format: Hot adult contemp. ◆Kathy Uebler, gen mgr; Jeff Deweese, progmg dir; George Trobridge, chief of engrg.

WRSW(AM)— 1951: 1480 khz; 1 kw-D, 500 w-N. TL: N41 13 21 W85 50 17. Stereo. Hrs open: 24 216 W. Market St., 46580. Phone: (574) 372-3064. Fax: (574) 267-2230. Web Site:www.1480sportsbug.com Licensee: Talking Stick Communications LLC. (group owner; (acq 12-19-2003; $1.2 million with co-located FM). Population served: 60,000 Natl. Network: Westwood One, . Rgnl. Network: Tribune, Network Indiana. Network Indiana Format: All sports. News staff: one; News: 18 hrs wkly. Target aud: General. ◆Patrick Brown, gen mgr.

WRSW-FM— 1948: 107.3 mhz; 50 kw. 293 ft TL: N41 13 21 W85 50 17. Stereo. Hrs open: 216 W. Market St., 46580. Phone: (574) 372-3064. Fax: (574) 267-2230. Web Site:www.wrsw.net Population served: 90,000 Natl. Network: Westwood One, . Rgnl. Network: Network Indiana. Natl. Rep: Rgnl Reps,. Network Indiana Rgnl rep: Rgnl Reps Format: Classic hits. Target aud: General; affluent adults. ◆Patrick Brown, gen mgr.

Washington

WAMW(AM)— January 1955: 1580 khz; 500 w-D, DA-D. TL: N38 39 04 W87 09 55. Hrs open: 800 W. National Hwy., 47501. Phone: (812) 254-6761. Fax: (812) 254-3940.E-mail: wamw@rtccom.net Web Site:www.wamwamfm.com Licensee: Greene Electronics. Population served: 100,000 Natl. Network: ABC, . Brownfield Wire Svc: AP Format: Adult contemp. News staff: one. Target aud: 45 plus. ◆Dave Crooks, gen mgr; Andy Morrison, opns mgr, news dir; Macy Kalb, gen sls mgr; Taylor Brown, news dir.

WAMW-FM— Nov 20, 1989: 107.9 mhz; 3 kw. 328 ft TL: N38 38 47 W87 16 47. Stereo. Hrs open: 24 800 W. National Hwy., 47501. Phone: (812) 254-6761. Fax: (812) 254-3940. Web Site:www.wamwamfm.com Population served: 100,000 Natl. Network: ABC, . Rgnl. Network: AgriAmerica, Network Indiana. Brownfield Wire Svc: AP Format: Soft adult contemp. News staff: one. Target aud: 25+; soft adult contemporary.

WWBL(FM)— February 1948: 106.5 mhz; 50 kw. 340 ft TL: N38 39 04 W87 09 55. Stereo. Hrs open: Box 616, 47501-0616. Secondary address: Box 242, Vincennes 47591-0242. Phone: (812) 254-4300. Phone: (812) 882-6060. Fax: (812) 254-4361. Fax: (812) 885-2604.E-mail: info@bl.com Web Site:www.wwbl.com Licensee: Old Northwest Broadcasting Inc. Group owner: The Original Co. Inc. (acq 10-93; $250,000 with WAOV(AM) Vincennes; 10-18-93). Population served: 200,000 Natl. Network: ABC, . Natl. Rep: Rgnl Reps,. Format: Country. News staff: one; News: 15 hrs wkly. Target aud: 18 plus. Spec prog: Farm 15 hrs wkly. ◆Mark Lange, pres; Ken Booth, opns mgr.

West Lafayette

*WBAA(AM)— Apr 4, 1922: 920 khz; 5 kw-D, 1 kw-N, DA-N. TL: N40 20 29 W86 53 01. Hrs open: Purdue University, 712 3rd St., 47907. Phone: (765) 494-5920. Fax: (765) 496-1542.E-mail: wbaa@wbaa.org Web Site:www.wbaa.org Licensee: Purdue University. Natl. Network: NPR, PRI, . Wiley & Rein. Format: Jazz, news/talk. News staff: 3; News: 20 hrs wkly. ◆Tim Singleton, gen mgr; Bette Carson, opns mgr; David Bunte, progmg dir; Maurie Mogridge, chief of engrg.

*WBAA-FM— February 1993: 101.3 mhz; 5 kw. Ant 358 ft TL: N40 17 50 W86 54 05. Stereo. Hrs open: Purdue University, 712 3rd St., 47907. Phone: (765) 494-5920. Fax: (765) 496-1542. Natl. Network: NPR, PRI, . Format: Classical, news. News staff: 3; News: 20 hrs wkly. ◆Tim Singleton, gen mgr; Bette Carson, opns mgr; David Bunte, progmg dir.

WBPE(FM)— See Brookston

*WHPL(FM)— Sept 10, 1993: 89.9 mhz; 2 kw. 328 ft TL: N40 17 50 W86 54 05. Hrs open: 24 1920 W. 53rd St., Anderson, 46013. Phone: (765) 449-0899. Fax: (765) 449-3025.E-mail: WGNR@MOODY.EDU Licensee: The Moody Bible Institute of Chicago. (group owner; acq 6-20-97). Population served: 100,000 Natl. Network: Moody, . Southmayd & Miller. Format: Relg. News: 14 hrs wkly. Target aud: 35 plus; relg. ◆Ray Hashley, gen mgr.

*WKHL(FM)— June 15, 1992: 106.7 mhz; 6 kw. Ant 328 ft TL: N40 31 20 W86 58 57. Hrs open: 24 2351 Sunset Blvd., Suite 170-218, Rocklin, CA, 95765. Phone: (916) 251-1600. Fax: (916) 251-1650. Web Site:www.klove.com Licensee: Educational Media Foundation. (acq 4-17-2008); $1.2 million). Natl. Network: K-Love, . Format: Contemp Christian. ◆Mke Novak, pres.

West Terre Haute

WWVR(FM)— Jan 20, 1967: 105.5 mhz; 3.3 kw. Ant 314 ft TL: N39 27 15 W87 28 18. Hrs open: 6 AM-2 AM Box 1486, Terre Haute, 47808. Secondary address: St., Terre Haute 47808. Phone: (812) 232-9481. Fax: (812) 234-0089.E-mail: jconner@wthi.emmis.com Web Site:www.1055theriver.net Licensee: Emmis Radio License LLC. Group owner: Emmis Communications Corp. Population served: 500,000 Format: Classic rock. News: 6 hrs wkly. Target aud: 35-64. Spec prog: Gospel, news/talk, Black 6 hrs wkly. ◆James Conner, stn mgr, gen sls mgr; Chris Perrot, prom dir, prom mgr; Barry Kent, progmg dir; Jeff Tucker, chief of engrg.

Wilkinson

*WSMJ(FM)— 2008: 89.1 mhz; 150 w vert. Ant 102 ft TL: N39 52 46.4 W85 38 10.9. Hrs open: 15 Wood St., Greenfield, 46140. Phone: (317) 467-1064. Licensee: Hoosier Public Radio Corp. ◆Martin Hensley, pres.

Winamac

WFRI(FM)— 1998: 100.1 mhz; 6 kw. 328 ft TL: N41 02 21 W86 30 55. Stereo. Hrs open: 24 Rebroadcasts WFRN-FM Elkhart 80%. Box 307, Elkhart, 46515. Phone: (800) 522-9376. Fax: (219) 875-6662.E-mail: comments@wfrn.com Web Site:www.wfrn.com Licensee: Progressive Broadcasting System Inc. (group owner). Natl. Network: USA, . Network Indiana Format: Contemp Christian. Target aud: 25-54. ◆Edwin Moore, pres & gen mgr.

Winchester

WZZY(FM)— May 1967: 98.3 mhz; 3 kw. 300 ft TL: N40 05 23 W84 56 13. Stereo. Hrs open: 24 2301 W. Main St., Richmond, 47374. Phone: (765) 966-6533. Fax: (765) 966-1499.E-mail: promotions @todaysmusicmix.com Web Site:www.todaysmusicmix.com Licensee: Rodgers Broadcasting Corp. (group owner; acq 1-1-00). Population served: 300,000 Natl. Rep: Rgnl Reps. Format: Full service, adult contemp. News staff: 2; News: 10 hrs wkly. Target aud: 25-54; general. ◆David Rodgers, pres; Steve Frey, gen mgr; Rick Duncan, opns dir, progmg dir; Bob Phillips, news dir; Keith Wade, disc jockey.

Zionsville

*WITT(FM)— 2009: 91.9 mhz; 6 kw. Ant 297 ft TL: N40 00 14 W86 28 14. Hrs open: 6218 Kingsley Dr., Indianapolis, 46220. Phone: (317) 251-3851.E-mail: radio@919witt.org Web Site:www.919witt.org Licensee: Kids First Inc. Format: Var. ◆James E. Walsh, pres.

Iowa

Adel

*KIHS(FM)— 2004: 88.9 mhz; 10 kw. Ant 154 ft TL: N41 36 12 W94 02 53. Hrs open: CSN International, 4002N. 3300E., Twin Falls, ID, 83301. Phone: (208) 734-6633. Fax: (208) 736-1958.E-mail: csn@csnradio.com Web Site:www.csnradio.com Licensee: CSN International (group owner). Format: Christian. ◆Ray Garney, gen mgr.

Albia

KIIC(FM)— June 15, 1995: 96.7 mhz; 10 kw. Ant 508 ft TL: N41 01 47 W92 47 12. Stereo. Hrs open: 7 Benton Ave East, Suite 1, 52531. Phone: (641) 932-2112. Fax: (641) 932-2113. Licensee: Waveguide Communications Inc. (acq 8-7-2007; $160,000). Population served: 120 Natl. Network: AP Network News, Jones Radio Networks, . Brownfield Format: Classic hit country. News staff: one; News: news prgmg 10 hrs wkly. Target aud: 25-54. ◆Joe Milledge, pres.

Algona

KLGA(AM)— 1956: 1600 khz; 5 kw-D, 500 w-N, DA-2. TL: N43 03 52 W94 18 13. Hrs open: 24 Box 160, 50511. Secondary address: 2102 80th Ave. 50511. Phone: (515) 295-2475. Fax: (515) 295-3851.E-mail: info@waittmedia.com Web Site:www.waittmedia.com Licensee: NRG License Sub. LLC. Group owner: Waitt Broadcasting Inc. (acq 10-31-2005; grpsl). Natl. Network: ABC, . Rgnl. Network: Radio Iowa. Radio Iowa Bryan Cave. Format: Adult contemp. News staff: one; News: 44 hrs wkly. Target aud: 25-54. Spec prog: Farm, news, weather. ◆Bob Ketchum, gen mgr; Dana Myee, progmg dir.

KLGA-FM— Aug 17, 1970: 92.7 mhz; 3.5 kw. 449 ft TL: N43 04 05 W94 12 08. Stereo. Hrs open: 6 AM-10:30 PM Dups AM 100% Box 160, 50511. Secondary address: 2102 80th Ave. 50511. Phone: (515) 295- 2475. Fax: (515) 295-3851. Web Site:www.waittmedia.com

Alta

KBVU-FM— 1999: 97.5 mhz; 6 kw. Ant 315 ft TL: N42 38 05 W95 10 10. Hrs open: Buena Vista University, 610 W. 4th St., Storm Lake, 50588. Phone: (712) 749-1234. Fax: (712) 749-1211. Web Site:edge.bvu.edu Licensee: Buena Vista University. Format: Alternative rock. Target aud: 18-25; college students. ◆Bruce Ellingson, gen mgr.

Alton

***KRGO-FM**—Not on air, target date: unknown: 91.5 mhz; 1.3 kw. Ant 69 ft TL: N42 54 11 W96 04 29. Hrs open: 4604 Airpark Blvd., Duluth, MN, 55811-5751. Phone: (218) 722-3017. Fax: (218) 722-1650.E-mail: airstaff@refugeradio.com Web Site:www.refugeradio.com Licensee: Refuge Media Group. ◆Keith A. Johnson, pres.

Ames

KASI(AM)— 1948: 1430 khz; 1 kw-D, 32 w-N. TL: N42 02 15 W93 41 21. Hrs open: 5 AM-midnight 415 Main St., 50010. Phone: (515) 232-1430. Fax: (515) 232-1439.E-mail: info@1430kasi.com Web Site:www.1430kasi.com Licensee: Citicasters Licenses L.P. Group owner: Clear Channel Communications Inc. (acq 8-24-99; with co-located FM). Population served: 100,000 Natl. Network: ABC, . Format: Oldies, news/talk. News staff: 2; News: 25 hrs wkly. Target aud: 25 plus. ◆Joel McCrea, gen mgr; Tony Calumet, gen sls mgr; Linda Thede, progmg dir, traf mgr; Trent Rice, news dir; Mike Stover, chief of engrg; B.J. Schaben, sports cmtr.

KCCQ(FM)— June 20, 1968: 105.1 mhz; 25 kw. Ant 328 ft TL: N42 04 33 W93 38 54. Stereo. Hrs open: 24 415 Main St., 50010. Phone: (515) 232-1430. Fax: (515) 232-1439.E-mail: info@1430kasi.com Web Site:1051channelq.com Licensee: Citicasters Licenses L.P. Population served: 100,000 Format: CHR. Target aud: 18-40. ◆Joel McCrea, gen mgr; Linda Thede, opns dir & traf mgr; B.J. Schaben, sports cmtr.

KLTI-FM— June 2, 1967: 104.1 mhz; 100 kw. Ant 1,010 ft TL: N41 54 09 W93 54 15. Stereo. Hrs open: 24 1416 Locust St., Des Moines, 50309. Phone: (515) 280-1350. Fax: (515) 280-3011.E-mail: sallen@desmoinesradiogroup.com Web Site:www.lite1041.com Licensee: Saga Communications of Iowa LLC. Group owner: Saga Communications Inc. (acq 1-1-97; $3.2 million). Population served: 600,000 Natl. Rep: Katz Radio,. Smithwick & Belendiuk. Wire Svc: AP Format: Soft adult contemp. Target aud: Women; 25-54. ◆Ed Christian, CEO; Jeff Delvaux, gen mgr; Scott Allen, opns dir; Pam Washington, sls dir; Celia Rodine, natl sls mgr; Chris Beck, prom dir; Sarah LeVere, adv mgr.

***KURE(FM)**— Apr 17, 1970: 88.5 mhz; 250 w. 100 ft TL: N42 01 24 W93 39 00. Stereo. Hrs open: 24 1199 Friley Hall, Iowa State Univ., 50012. Phone: (515) 294-4332. Phone: (515) 294-9292. Fax: (515) 294-8093.E-mail: generalmanager@kure885.org Web Site:www.kure885.org Licensee: Residence Associations Broadcasting Service Inc. Population served: 60,000 Format: Var/div. News: 10 hrs wkly. Target aud: 18-25; Iowa State Univ students & Ames community. ◆Rob McMahon, gen mgr; Rezza Rahmoni, opns dir; Katherine Beaver, mktg dir; James Bishop, progmg dir.

***WOI(AM)**— 1922: 640 khz; 5 kw-D, 1 kw-N, DA-N. TL: N41 59 34 W93 41 27. Hrs open: 24 2022 Communicatons Bldg., Iowa State Univ., 50011. Phone: (515) 294-2025. Fax: (515) 294-1544. Web Site:www.woi.org Licensee: Iowa State University. Population served: 3,000,000 Natl. Network: NPR, PRI, . Dow, Lohnes & Albertson. Wire Svc: AP Format: News/talk. News staff: 3; News: 40 hrs wkly. Target aud: General. ◆Steve Carignan, pres; Donald Wirth, gen mgr; David Knippel, chief of engrg.

***WOI-FM**— July 1, 1949: 90.1 mhz; 100 kw. 1,490 ft TL: N41 48 33 W93 36 53. Stereo. Hrs open: 24 2022 Communicationa Bldg., Iowa State Univ., 50011. Phone: (515) 294-2025. Fax: (515) 294-1544. Web Site:www.woi.org Licensee: Iowa State University. Population served: 340,000 Format: Class, jazz. News staff: 3; News: 12 hrs wkly. Target aud: General.

Anamosa

KKSY(FM)— Feb 14, 2008: 95.7 mhz; 6 kw. Ant 328 ft TL: N42 08 19 W91 27 38. Hrs open: 600 Old Marion Rd. N.E., Cedar Rapids, 52402-2152. Phone: (319) 395-0530. Fax: (319) 393-9600. Licensee: Citicasters Licenses L.P. Format: Country. ◆John Laton, gen mgr.

Ankeny

KPTL(FM)— July 1, 1991: 106.3 mhz; 25 kw. Ant 328 ft TL: N41 40 45 W93 35 46. Hrs open: 24 2141 Grand Ave., Des Moines, 50312. Phone: (515) 245-8900.E-mail: GregChance@clearchannel.com Web Site:www.capital1063.com Licensee: Citicasters Licenses L.P. Group owner: Clear Channel Communications Inc. (acq 5-4-99; grpsl). Population served: 503,000 Natl. Rep: Clear Channel,. Wire Svc: AP Format: AAA. Target aud: 25-54. ◆Joel McCrea, VP, mktg mgr; Matt Gillon, sls dir; Molly Pins, prom mgr; Greg Chance, progmg dir; Jim Boyd, news dir; Raleigh Rubenking, chief of engrg.

Asbury

WJOD(FM)— Mar 31, 1994: 103.3 mhz; 6.6 kw. 643 ft TL: N42 34 19 W90 30 55. Stereo. Hrs open: 24 5490 Saratoga Rd., Dubuque, 52002-2593. Phone: (563) 557-1040. Fax: (563) 583-4535.E-mail: info@wjod.com Web Site:www.103wjod.com Licensee: Cumulus Licensing Corp. Group owner: Cumulus Media Inc. (acq 2-6-98). Population served: 120,000 Natl. Network: Jones Radio Networks, . Wiley, Rein & Fielding. Format: Country. Target aud: 18-49. ◆Scott Lindahl, gen mgr; Ken Peiffer, opns mgr, progmg VP.

Atlantic

KJAN(AM)— September 1950: 1220 khz; 250 w-D, 86 w-N. TL: N41 25 02 W95 00 15. Stereo. Hrs open: 24 Box 389, N. Olive St., 50022. Phone: (712) 243-3920. Fax: (712) 243-3937.E-mail: kjan@metc.net Web Site:www.kjan.com Licensee: Wireless Communications Corp. (acq 1-13-88; 11-16-87). Population served: 100,000 Natl. Network: Fox News Radio, . Rgnl. Network: Radio Iowa, Brownfield Natl. Rep: Commercial Media Sales,. Brownfield Wire Svc: AP Format: Adult contemp, MOR, news. News staff: 1; News: 40 hrs wkly. Target aud: 25 plus; general. Spec prog: Farm 12 hrs wkly. ◆J.C. Van Ginkel, chmn; Merlyn Christensen, pres; James M. Field, gen mgr.

KSWI(FM)— July 2000: 95.7 mhz; 20 kw. Ant 358 ft. TL: N41 26 07 W94 50 00. Stereo. Hrs open: 24 413 Chestnut St., 50022. Phone: (712) 243-6885. Fax: (712) 243-1691.E-mail: ksom@mchsi.com Web Site:www.iowasuperstation.com Licensee: Meredith Communications L.C. Population served: 30,000 Natl. Network: ABC, . Rgnl. Network: Iowa Radio Net. Format: Classic Hits. ◆Stephen O. Meredith, pres; Bill Saluk, gen mgr; Jill Christensen, progmg dir.

Audubon

KSOM(FM)— August 1995: 96.5 mhz; 100 kw. 528 ft TL: N41 26 07 W94 50 00. Stereo. Hrs open: 24 413 Chestnut St., Atlantic, 50022. Phone: (712) 243-6885. Fax: (712) 243-1691.E-mail: ksom@mchsi.com Web Site:www.iowasuperstation.com Licensee: Meredith Communications L.C. Population served: 180,000 Natl. Network: ABC, Motor Racing Net, Premiere Radio Networks, . Rgnl. Network: Iowa Radio Net. Format: Country. News staff: 2; News: 6 hrs wkly. Target aud: General; upscale & farmers. ◆Bill Saluk, gen mgr; Jill Christensen, opns mgr & progmg dir.

Belle Plaine

KZAT-FM— May 30, 1997: Stn currently dark. 95.5 mhz; 4.4 kw. Ant 384 ft TL: N41 56 35 W92 23 51. Stereo. Hrs open: 24 205 W. 3rd St., Tama, 52339. Phone: (641) 484-5958. Fax: (641) 484-5962.E-mail: ccamp@kzat.com Web Site:www.kzat.com Licensee: Camrory Broadcasting Inc. (acq 8-27-2004). Population served: 25,000 Natl. Network: CBS, Westwood One, ABC, . Katten Muchin Zavis Rosenman. Wire Svc: AP Format: Classic hits. News staff: one; News: 6 hrs wkly. Target aud: 25-54; listeners who are professionals, laborers, commuters, tourists & truckers. Spec prog: Polka 2 hrs Sun am. ◆Catherine A. Campbell Currier, pres & gen mgr.

Bettendorf

KQCS(FM)— July 7, 1984: 93.5 mhz; 6 kw. 300 ft TL: N41 35 59 W90 24 33. Stereo. Hrs open: 24 1229 Brady St., Davenport, 52803. Phone: (563) 326-2541. Fax: (563) 326-0844.E-mail: quadcities.prod@cumulus.com Web Site:www.93rock.net Licensee: Cumulus Licensing Corp. Group owner: Cumulus Media Inc. (acq 3-15-00; grpsl). Population served: 295,000 Putbrese, Hunsaker & Trent. Format: Active rock. Target aud: 18-34. ◆Jack Swart, gen mgr; Julie Derrer, gen sls mgr; Jeff James, progmg dir; Andy Andresen, chief of engrg; Tracy Hall, traf mgr.

***KWNJ(FM)**—Not on air, target date: unknown: 91.1 mhz; 20 kw vert. Ant 617 ft TL: N41 18 44 W90 22 46. Hrs open: University of Northern Iowa, 324 Communications Arts Center, Cedar Falls, 50614-0359. Phone: (319) 273-6325. Licensee: University of Northern Iowa. ◆Wayne Jarvis, gen mgr.

Bloomfield

KOJY(FM)— June 26, 1982: 106.9 mhz; 14 kw. Ant 367 ft TL: N40 46 39 W92 23 54. Stereo. Hrs open: 24 Box 186, 52537. Secondary address: 22620 195th St. 52537. Phone: (641) 664-3721. Fax: (641) 664-3738.E-mail: mmcvey@kmemfm.com Licensee: Bloomfield Broadcasting Co. Inc. (acq 1-16-2006; $460,000). Natl. Network: AP Radio, Jones Radio Networks, . Rgnl. Network: Brownfield. Radio Iowa Rgnl rep: Judy Shepherd Miller & Neely. Format: Oldies. Target aud: 25-54 yrs; 50/50 male/female split. ◆Douglas J. Neatrour, pres, gen mgr; Lana Norfleet, gen mgr, traf mgr; Mark Denney, progmg dir.

Boone

KFFF(AM)— 1927: 1260 khz; 5 kw-D, 33 w-N, DA-D. TL: N42 02 55 W93 53 54. Hrs open: 900 8th St., 50036. Phone: (515) 432-5014. Fax: (515) 432-2092.E-mail: mail@iowanewstalk.com Licensee: Boone Biblical Ministries Inc. Format: Conservative talk. ◆Robert Stumbo, pres; Jamie Johnson, gen mgr, progmg dir; Bob Pink, chief of engrg.

KFFF-FM— 1950: 99.3 mhz; 5.2 kw. Ant 351 ft TL: N42 02 55 W93 53 54. Hrs open: 900 8th St., 50036. Phone: (515) 432-5014. Fax: (515) 432-2092.E-mail: mail@iowanewstalk.com Licensee: Boone Biblical Ministries Inc. Format: Relg. ◆Jamie Johnson, progmg dir.

KWBG(AM)— Jan 15, 1950: 1590 khz; 1 kw-D, 500 w-N, DA-N. TL: N42 01 22 W93 52 36. Hrs open: 6 AM-11 PM 724 Story St., 50036. Phone: (515) 432-2046. Fax: (515) 432-1448.E-mail: ckuster@nrgmedia.com Web Site:www.kwbg.com Licensee: NRG License Sub. LLC. Group owner: Waitt Broadcasting Inc. (acq 10-31-2005; grpsl). Population served: 30,000 Natl. Network: ABC, ESPN Radio, . Brownfield Format: News/talk. News staff: one; News: 36 hrs wkly. Target aud: 35 plus; Boone County, Iowa residents. Spec prog: Farm 15 hrs wkly. ◆Carol Kuster, gen mgr; Jim Turbes, news dir; Ben Parsons, sls.

KWQW(FM)— May 15, 1975: 98.3 mhz; 41 kw. 541 ft TL: N41 49 51 W93 43 54. Stereo. Hrs open: 24 4143 109th St., Urbandale, 50322. Phone: (515) 331-9200. Fax: (515) 331-9292. Web Site:www.983wowfm.com Licensee: Citadel Broadcasting Co. Group owner: Citadel Broadcasting Corp. (acq 8-29-2003; grpsl). Natl. Rep: Christal,. Format: Talk. News: 15 hrs wkly. Target aud: 25-54. ◆Jack O'Brien, opns mgr; Doug Wood, sls dir; Terry Peters, gen mgr & mktg VP.

Britt

KHAM(FM)— 2006: 99.5 mhz; 200 w. Ant 52 ft TL: N43 05 47 W93 48 05. Hrs open: Box 308, Forest City, 50436. Phone: (641) 585-1073. Fax: (641) 585-2990. Licensee: Coloff Media LLC. (acq 7-31-2007; $10,000). ◆Tony Coloff, gen mgr.

Brooklyn

KSKB(FM)— Mar 1, 1988: 99.1 mhz; 50 kw. Ant 175 ft TL: N41 42 36 W92 27 54. Stereo. Hrs open: Box 440, 52211. Secondary address: 505 Josephine St., Titusville, FL 32796. Phone: (641) 522-7202. Fax: (641) 522-7239.E-mail: wpio@gate.net Web Site:noncomradio.net Licensee: Florida Public Radio Inc. (acq 1-8-90). Format: Adult contemp Christian mus. Target aud: General. Spec prog: Ger one hr, Pol one hr wkly. ◆Bill Korns, gen mgr.

Burlington

***KAYP(FM)**— Nov 1, 2000: 89.9 mhz; 9 kw vert. Ant 440 ft TL: N40 47 59 W91 32 35. Hrs open: 14267 Washington Rd., West Burlington, 52655. Phone: (319) 758-6911. Fax: (319) 758-6922.E-mail:

kayp@mchsi.com Web Site:www.kayp.afr.net Licensee: American Family Association. Group owner: American Family Radio Format: Christian adult contemp. ♦Marvin Sanders, gen mgr.

KBUR(AM)— July 1941: 1490 khz; 1 kw-U. TL: N40 49 26 W91 08 33. Stereo. Hrs open: 24 1411 N. Roosevelt Ave., 52601. Phone: (319) 752-2701. Fax: (319) 752-5287.E-mail: info@kbur.com Web Site:www.kbur.com Licensee: Pritchard Broadcasting Corp. Group owner: Clear Channel Communications Inc. (acq 6-6-2008; with KBKB(AM) Fort Madison). Population served: 275,000 Rgnl. Network: Radio Iowa. Radio Iowa Format: Adult contemp, MOR, news/talk. News staff: 3; News: 28 hrs wkly. Target aud: 25 plus; general. Spec prog: Farm 19 hrs wkly. ♦John Pritchard, gen mgr; Faith Krause, sls dir.

KCPS(AM)— July 30, 1965: 1150 khz; 500 w-D, 67 w-N, DA-1. TL: N40 51 11 W91 08 10. Hrs open: 24 Box 100, West Burlington, 52655. Secondary address: 205 S. Gear Aave., West Burlington 52655. Phone: (319) 754-6698. Fax: (319) 754-8899.E-mail: kcps@aol.com Web Site:www.kcpsradio.com Licensee: John Giannettino. (acq 1-88). Population served: 100,000 Natl. Network: CBS, Westwood One, ABC, Premiere Radio Networks, . Natl. Rep: Katz Radio,. Shaw Pittman. Format: Talk. News staff: one; News: 7 hrs wkly. Target aud: 25-54; middle-aged, upscale & well-informed adults. Spec prog: Agriculture-business 10 hrs, pro sports 10 hrs wkly. ♦John Giannettino, gen mgr.

KDMG(FM)— July 19, 1993: 103.1 mhz; 12 kw. 445 ft TL: N40 44 04 W91 15 16. Stereo. Hrs open: #112, 610 N. 4th Street, Suite 300, 52601. Phone: (319) 752-5402. Fax: (319) 752-4715.E-mail: traffic@burlingtonradio.com Licensee: Pritchard Broadcasting Corp. Population served: 109,600 Natl. Rep: Katz Radio,. Format: Country. News staff: one; News: 2 hrs wkly. Target aud: 25-54. ♦John T. Pritchard, pres & gen mgr; Joe Bates, opns mgr, progmg dir; Chet Young, gen sls mgr.

KGRS(FM)— Nov 27, 1968: 107.3 mhz; 100 kw. Ant 429 ft TL: N40 49 26 W91 08 33. Stereo. Hrs open: 24 Box 70, 52601. Secondary address: 1411 N. Roosevelt Ave. 52601. Phone: (319) 752-2701. Fax: (319) 752-5287.E-mail: info@kgrsfm.com Web Site:www.kgrsfm.com Licensee: GAP Broadcasting Burlington License LLC. (acq 2-13-2008; grpsl). Population served: 256,500 Format: Adult contemp. News staff: 3; News: 15 hrs wkly. Target aud: 25-45. ♦Cosmo Leone, progmg dir; Mark Hempen, traf mgr; J.K. Martin, local news ed.

KKMI(FM)— Oct 22, 1981: 93.5 mhz; 6.0 kw. 305 ft TL: N40 49 11 W91 07 02. Stereo. Hrs open: 24 610 N. 4th St., Suite 300, 2850 Mt. Pleasant St., 52601. Phone: (319) 752-5402. Fax: (319) 752-4715.E-mail: johnp@burlingtonradio.com Web Site:935kkmi.com Licensee: Pritchard Broadcasting Corp. (acq 8-5-91). Population served: 90,000 Natl. Rep: Katz Radio,. Format: Adult contemp. News staff: 2; News: 2 hrs wkly. Target aud: 25-55; upscale. ♦John T. Pritchard, pres, gen mgr; Scott Michael, opns mgr; Chet Young, gen sls mgr.

Carroll

KCIM(AM)— June 8, 1950: 1380 khz; 1 kw-U, DA-2. TL: N42 02 29 W94 53 06. Hrs open: 1119 E. Plaza Dr., 51401. Phone: (712) 792-4321. Fax: (712) 792-6667.E-mail: kcimkkrl@win-4-u.net Web Site:carrollbroadcasting.com Licensee: Carroll Broadcasting Co. (group owner; acq 8-1-85; $1.5 million with co-located FM; 5-20-85). Population served: 200,000 Natl. Network: CBS, . Natl. Rep: Katz Radio,. Womble, Carlyle, Sandridge & Rice. Format: Classic hits of the 50s, 60s & 70s. ♦Mary Collison, CEO; Kim Hackett, gen mgr, natl sls mgr; John Ryan, progmg mgr; Bob Grote, chief of engrg.

KKRL(FM)— Jan 18, 1967: 93.7 mhz; 100 kw. 300 ft TL: N42 03 14 W94 53 06. Stereo. Hrs open: 24 1119 E. Plaza Dr., 51401. Phone: (712) 792-4321. Fax: (712) 792-6667.E-mail: kcimkkrl@win-4-u.net Web Site:carrollbroadcasting.com Licensee: Carroll Broadcasting Co. Natl. Rep: Katz Radio,. Womble, Carlyle, Sandridge & Rice. Format: Hot AC 70s, 80s, 90s & today. News staff: one. Target aud: 18 plus. ♦John Ryan, progmg dir.

***KWOI(FM)**— 2004: 90.7 mhz; 10 kw. Ant 289 ft TL: N42 07 14 W94 48 49. Stereo. Hrs open: 24 2022 Communications Bldg. ISU, WOI Radio Group, Ames, 50011-3241. Phone: (515) 294-2025. Fax: (515) 294-1544.E-mail: woi@iastate.edu Web Site:www.woi.org Licensee: Iowa State University of Science and Technology. Natl. Network: NPR, PRI, . Format: Class, news. News: 40 hrs wkly. Target aud: General; educated.

Cascade

***KDSO(FM)**—Not on air, target date: unknown: 88.9 mhz; 2.25 kw vert. Ant 338 ft TL: N42 30 34 W90 56 25. Hrs open: N6554 Stenulson Rd., Black River Falls, WI, 54615. Phone: (308) 340-9741. Licensee: Cascade Community Radio Inc. ♦David M. Stout, gen mgr.

Castana

***KILV(FM)**— 2001: 107.5 mhz; 25 kw. Ant 328 ft TL: N42 12 26 W96 07 26. Stereo. Hrs open: 24 2351 Sunset Blvd., Suite 170-218, Rocklin, CA, 95765. Phone: (916) 251-1600. Fax: (916) 251-1650.E-mail: klove@klove.com Web Site:www.klove.com Licensee: Educational Media Foundation. Group owner: EMF Broadcasting (acq 10-26-01). Population served: 5,500 Natl. Network: K-Love, . Shaw Pittman. Format: Contemp Christian. News staff: 3. Target aud: 25-44; female-Judeo/Christian. ♦Richard Jenkins, pres; Mike Novak, VP, progmg dir; Keith Whipple, dev dir; David Pierce, progmg mgr; Sam Wallington, engrg dir; Karen Johnson, news rptr.

Cedar Falls

KCNZ(AM)— September 1998: 1650 khz; 10 kw-D, 1 kw-N. TL: N42 24 47 W92 26 15. Stereo. Hrs open: 24 Box 248, 50613. Phone: (319) 277-1918. Fax: (319) 277-5202.E-mail: radio@1650thefan.com Web Site:www.1650thefan.com Licensee: Fife Communications Co. LLC. Population served: 120,000 Natl. Network: CBS, . Format: Sports/talk. News staff: 2; News: 25 hrs wkly. Target aud: 25-54; eastern Iowa adults. Spec prog: Farm 6 hrs. ♦John Coloff, pres; Jim Coloff, gen mgr; Doug Petersen, progmg dir.

KDNZ(AM)— Feb 2, 1958: 1250 khz; 500 w-U, DA-2. TL: N42 32 41 W92 29 16. Hrs open: 24 Box 248, 721 Shirley St., 50613. Phone: (319) 277-1918. Fax: (319) 277-5202.E-mail: radio@1650.com Licensee: Fife Communications L.C. (acq 1995; $90,000). Population served: 120,000 Format: Sp. ♦Jim Coloff, pres, gen mgr; Tony Coloff, VP; Jeff Ryant, stn mgr; Sue Coloff, opns VP.

***KHKE(FM)**— Apr 1, 1974: 89.5 mhz; 10 kw. 410 ft TL: N42 23 58 W92 19 15. (CP: Ant 417 ft. TL: N42 23 55 W92 19 34). Stereo. Hrs open: 6 AM-2 AM 324 Communications Arts Center, Univ. of Northern Iowa, 50614-0359. Phone: (319) 273-6400. Fax: (319) 273-7911.E-mail: kuni@uni.edu Web Site:www.khke.org Licensee: University of Northern Iowa. Population served: 29,517 Format: Class. News staff: 3; News: 5 hrs wkly. Target aud: General. ♦Scott Vezdos, mktg mgr; Wayne Jarvis, gen mgr, gen mgr & progmg dir; Al Schares, mus dir; Greg Shanley, news dir; Steve Schoon, chief of engrg.

KOEL-FM— Jan 7, 1994: 98.5 mhz; 25 kw. 328 ft TL: N42 28 09 W92 29 05. Hrs open: 24 501 Sycamore St., Suite 300, Blacks Bldg., Waterloo, 50703. Phone: (319) 833-4800. Phone: (319) 833-4985 (Contest line). Fax: (319) 833-4866. Web Site:www.k985.com Licensee: Cumulus Licensing Corp. Group owner: Cumulus Media Inc. (acq 3-15-00; grpsl). Population served: 230,000 Format: Country. News staff: one; News: one hr wkly. Target aud: 18-49; general. ♦Lew Dickey, pres; William Hathaway, gen mgr.

***KUNI(FM)**— Sept 15, 1960: 90.9 mhz; 100 kw. 1,782 ft TL: N42 18 59 W91 51 31. Stereo. Hrs open: 24 324 Communications Art Center, Univ. of Northern Iowa, 50614-0359. Phone: (319) 273-6400. Fax: (319) 273-7911.E-mail: info@iowapublicradio.org Web Site:www.iowapublicradio.org Licensee: University of Northern Iowa. Natl. Network: NPR, PRI, . Format: News and Information, Triple A. News staff: 3; News: 74 hrs wkly. Target aud: General. Spec prog: Folk 4 hrs, rhythm and blues 2 hrs wkly. ♦Mary Grace Herrington, CEO; Al Shares, mus dir.

Cedar Rapids

***KCCK-FM**— Sept 5, 1972: 88.3 mhz; 10 kw. 420 ft TL: N41 54 33 W91 39 17. Stereo. Hrs open: 24 Box 2068, 214 Linn Hall, 6301 Kirkwood Blvd. S.W., 52406. Phone: (319) 398-5446. Fax: (319) 398-5492.E-mail: studio@kcck.org Web Site:www.kcck.org Licensee: Kirkwood Community College. Population served: 109,642 Natl. Network: NPR, . Wilkinson, Barker & Knauer. Wire Svc: AP Format: Jazz. News staff: one; News: 2 hrs wkly. Target aud: 25-54; educated, affluent, active in community. Spec prog: Blues 12 hrs, new age 7 hrs wkly. ♦Kathy Hall, exec VP; Dennis Green, gen mgr; George Dorman, opns dir, news dir; Lisa Baum, dev dir; Bob Stewart, progmg dir; Dave Maley, chief of engrg.

KDAT(FM)— May 1971: 104.5 mhz; 100 kw. 500 ft TL: N42 04 51 W91 41 45. Stereo. Hrs open: 24 4th Fl., 425 Second St. S.E., 52401. Phone: (319) 365-9431. Fax: (319) 363-8062.E-mail: kdat@kdat.com Web Site:www.kdat.com Licensee: Cumulus Licensing Corp. Group owner: Cumulus Media Inc. (acq 8-7-00; grpsl). Latham & Watkins. Format: Light rock. Target aud: 25-54. ♦Jim Worthington, gen mgr; Dick Stadler, progmg dir.

KFMW(FM)—See Waterloo

KGYM(AM)— Dec 20, 1947: 1600 khz; 5 kw-U, DA-N. TL: N41 58 15 W91 32 01. Hrs open: 24 1110 26th Ave. S.W., 52404-3430. Phone: (319) 363-2061. Fax: (319) 363-2948.E-mail: info@1600espn.com Web Site:www.1600espn.com Licensee: KZIA Inc. (acq 10-30-2006; $775,000). Population served: 315,000 Natl. Network: ESPN Radio, . Rgnl. Network: Radio Iowa Natl. Rep: D & R Radio,. Dow, Lohnes & Albertson. Wire Svc: AP Format: Sports. News: one hr wkly. Target aud: 18-49. ♦Eliot Keller, pres, gen mgr; Robert Norton Jr., exec VP, opns mgr; Julie Hein, sls dir; Kellie Lala, gen sls mgr; Jamie Burgin, prom dir; Scott Unash, progmg dir; Dorothy Roach, traf mgr.

KHAK(FM)— July 1, 1961: 98.1 mhz; 100 kw. 485 ft TL: N41 55 28 W91 36 55. Stereo. Hrs open: 24 425 Second St. S.E., 4th Fl., 52401. Phone: (319) 365-9431. Phone: (319) 365-3698. Fax: (319) 363-8062.E-mail: khak@khak.com Web Site:www.khak.com Licensee: Cumulus Licensing Corp. Group owner: Cumulus Media Inc. (acq 8-7-00; grpsl). Population served: 202,800 Rgnl. Network: Brownfield. Natl. Rep: Christal,. Brownfield Latham & Watkins. Format: Modern Country. Target aud: 25-54; general. ♦Greg Sher, gen mgr & mktg mgr; Bob James, progmg dir.

KMJM(AM)— July 1, 1961: 1360 khz; 1 kw-D, 124 w-N, DA-1. TL: N41 55 28 W91 36 55. Hrs open: 24 600 Old Marion Rd. N.E., 52402. Phone: (319) 395-0530. Fax: (319) 393-9600. Licensee: Capstar TX L.P. Group owner: Clear Channel Communications Inc. (acq 8-30-2000; grpsl). Population served: 142,000 Format: Sports. ♦John Laton, gen mgr.

KMRY(AM)— August 1949: 1450 khz; 1 kw-U. TL: N42 00 25 W91 42 29. (In-band On-channel). Hrs open: 24 1957 Blairsferry Rd. N.E., 52402. Phone: (319) 393-1450. Fax: (319) 393-1407.E-mail: kmry@kmryradio.com Web Site:www.kmryradio.com Licensee: Sellers Broadcasting Inc. (acq 3-5-98; $475,000). Population served: 200,000 Natl. Network: CBS, . Katten, Muchin, Rosenman, LLP. Wire Svc: AP Format: Adult standards. News staff: one; News: 20 hrs wkly. Target aud: 40 plus; affluent, upscale adults with large disposable income. Spec prog: 50's oldies 3 hrs, polka 3 hrs, big band 2 hrs weekly. ♦Rick Sellers, pres; Kevin Alexander, VP; Rick Sampson, opns mgr; Eric Christopher, progmg dir, progmg mgr; Jim Davies, chief of engrg.

KZIA(FM)— Apr 29, 1975: 102.9 mhz; 100 kw. Ant 853 ft TL: N42 03 25 W91 41 42. Stereo. Hrs open: 24 1110 26th Ave. S.W., 52404-3430. Phone: (319) 363-2061. Fax: (319) 363-2948.E-mail: kzia@kzia.com Web Site:www.kzia.com Licensee: KZIA Inc. (acq 5-13-94; $2 million; 2-25-85). Population served: 315,000 Natl. Rep: D & R Radio,. Dow, Lohnes & Albertson. Wire Svc: AP Format: CHR. News staff: one; News: one hr wkly. Target aud: 18-49. ♦Eliot Keller, pres, gen mgr; Robert Norton Jr., exec VP, opns mgr; Julie Hein, sls dir; Kellie Lala, gen sls mgr; Jamie Burgin, prom dir; Greg Runyon, progmg dir; Ric Swann, mus dir; Scott Schulte, news dir; Dorothy Roach, traf mgr.

WMT(AM)— 1922: 600 khz; 5 kw-U, DA-N. TL: N42 03 40 W91 32 44. Stereo. Hrs open: 24 600 Old Marion Rd. N.E., 52402-2152. Phone: (319) 395-0530. Fax: (319) 393-0918. Web Site:www.wmtradio.com Licensee: Citicasters Licenses L.P. Group owner: Clear Channel Communications Inc. (acq 5-4-99; grpsl). Population served: 170,000 Natl. Network: CBS, . Format: Full svc, news/talk. Target aud: 35 plus. Spec prog: Farm 19 hrs wkly. ♦John Laton, gen mgr; Andy Roat, gen sls mgr; Lisa Pucelik, mktg dir; Randy Lee, progmg mgr; Jeff Schmidt, news dir; Tom Spaight, chief of engrg.

WMT-FM— Feb 16, 1963: 96.5 mhz; 100 kw. 540 ft TL: N42 01 43 W91 38 27. Stereo. Hrs open: Prog sep from AM 600 Old Marion Rd. N.E., 52402-2152. Phone: (319) 395-0530. Fax: (319) 393-0918. Web Site:www.mix965.com Licensee: Citicasters Licenses L.P. Natl. Network: CBS, . Format: Adult contemp. Target aud: 25-49. ♦Randy Lee, progmg dir.

Centerville

KCOG(AM)— Mar 1, 1949: 1400 khz; 500 w-D, 1 kw-N. TL: N40 44 40 W92 54 32. Hrs open: 5 AM-midnight 402 N. 12th St., 52544. Phone: (641) 437-4242.E-mail: kcogam@lisco.net Web Site:www.kmgo.com Licensee: KCOG Inc. (acq 6-1-84; $406,000; 4-16-84). Population served: 6,531 Natl. Network: USA, . Rgnl. Network: Brownfield. Brownfield Format: Contemp Christian. ♦Fred Jenkins, gen mgr & progmg dir.

KMGO(FM)— Oct 1, 1974: 98.7 mhz; 100 kw. 500 ft TL: N40 47 34 W92 52 47. Stereo. Hrs open: 24 402 N. 12th St., 52544. Phone: (641) 856-3996. Fax: (641) 856-3337.E-mail: kmgofm@lisco.net Web Site:www.kmgo.com Licensee: KMGO Inc. (acq 6-5-85). Natl. Network: USA, . Format: Country. ♦Larry Stout, progmg dir.

Chariton

KEDB(FM)— Nov 15, 1979: 105.3 mhz; 34 kw. Ant 597 ft TL: N40 53 23 W93 01 29. Stereo. Hrs open: 24 215 N. Main St., 50049. Phone: (641) 774-8494. Fax: (641) 774-8495.E-mail: KELR@lisco.com Licensee: Honey Creek Broadcasting LLC (acq 3-3-2009; $349,000). Population served: 70,000 Format: Oldies. News staff: one; News: 30 hrs wkly. Target aud: 28 plus. Spec prog: Gosp 5 hrs wkly. ♦Cindy Spidle, adv mgr; Nick Hoffman, progmg VP & asst music dir; Fred Jenkins, engrg VP; Jill Schull, traf mgr, local news ed.

Charles City

KCHA(AM)— November 1949: 1580 khz; 500 w-D, 10 w-N. TL: N43 03 05 W92 40 00. Hrs open: 24 207 N. Main St., 50616. Phone: (641) 228-1000. Fax: (641) 228-1200.E-mail: A chrisberg@northiowabroadcasting.com Web Site:www.kchafm.com Licensee: Coloff Media LLC. Group owner: Clear Channel Communications Inc. (acq 9-1-2007; grpsl). Population served: 200,000 Natl. Rep: Farmakis,. Format: Adult standards. News staff: news progmg 7 hrs wkly News: one;. Target aud: 35 plus. ♦Hal Hoffman, gen mgr; Mike Watson, progmg dir.

KCHA-FM— October 1971: 95.9 mhz; 6 kw. 300 ft TL: N43 03 05 W92 40 00. Stereo. Hrs open: 24 207 N. Main St., 50616. Phone: (641) 228-1000. Fax: (641) 228-1200.E-mail: A chrisberg@northiowabroadcasting.com Web Site:www.kchafm.com Licensee: Coloff Media LLC. (acq 9-1-2007; grpsl). Population served: 245,000 Format: Adult contemp. News staff: one; News: 7 hrs wkly. Target aud: 25-54; adults.

Cherokee

KCHE(AM)— January 1953: 1440 khz; 500 w-D. TL: N42 47 21 W95 33 06. Hrs open: Box 1440, 201 S. 5th, 51012. Phone: (712) 225-2511. Fax: (712) 225-2513.E-mail: kche1@ncn.net Web Site:www.kcheradio.com Licensee: J & J Radio Corp. (acq 11-14-03; $600,000 with co-located FM). Population served: 25,000 Natl. Network: ABC, . Radio Iowa Format: Oldies. News staff: 2; News: 14 hrs wkly. Target aud: 45-80; general. Spec prog: Farm 12 hrs, Sp one hr wkly. ♦Jeff Fuller, pres, gen mgr, gen sls mgr; Curt Carlson, VP, gen mgr, sls VP; Dick Keane, chief of opns, chief of engrg; Bill Bezoni, progmg dir; Nikki Thunder, news dir; Hallie Dessell, traf mgr.

KCHE-FM— Dec 9, 1976: 92.1 mhz; 6 kw. 210 ft TL: N42 47 21 W95 33 08. Stereo. Hrs open: 24 Box 1440, 51012. Phone: (712) 225-2511. Fax: (712) 225-2513. Web Site:www.kcheradio.com Licensee: J & J Radio Corp. Population served: 17,000 Natl. Network: ABC, . Rgnl. Network: Radio Iowa. Natl. Rep: Farmakis,. Radio Iowa Format: Adult contemp. News staff: 2; News: 28 hrs wkly. ♦Hallie Dessell, traf mgr.

Clarinda

KMA-FM— Sept 25, 1990: 99.3 mhz; 50 kw. 492 ft TL: N40 33 12 W95 07 18. Stereo. Hrs open: 24 Box 960, 209 N. Elm, Shenandoah, 51601. Phone: (712) 246-5270. Fax: (712) 246-5275.E-mail: kmaradio@kmaland.com Web Site:www.kmaland.com Licensee: KMA Broadcasting L.P. Natl. Network: Westwood One, CNN Radio, . Duane Morris. Wire Svc: AP Format: Adult Contemp. News staff: 2; News: 5 hrs wkly. Target aud: 25-44. ♦Edward W. May, pres; Mark Eno, gen mgr; Don Hansen, stn mgr; Chuck Morris, opns mgr.

Clarion

KIAQ(FM)— May 18, 1964: 96.9 mhz; 100 kw. 578 ft TL: N42 40 18 W94 09 11. Stereo. Hrs open: 200 North 10th St., Fort Dodge, 50501. Phone: (515) 955-5656. Fax: (515) 955-5844.E-mail: gbuchanan@threeeagles.com Web Site:www.kiaqfm.com Licensee: Three Eagles of Ft. Dodge Inc. Group owner: Three Eagles Communications (acq 4-22-97; $1,244,117). Population served: 304,000 Format: Country. Target aud: 25-54. ♦Gary Buchanan, pres, traf mgr; Patrick Kolar, gen mgr; Gregg Ellendson, opns mgr; Travis Reeves, sls VP; Michael Moody, news dir; Barb Dennis, traf mgr.

Clear Lake

KLKK(FM)— Feb 16, 1978: 103.7 mhz; 25 kw. Ant 328 ft TL: N43 07 15 W93 11 36. Stereo. Hrs open: 24 341 Yorktown Pike, Mason City, 50401. Phone: (641) 423-1300. Fax: (641) 423-2906. Web Site:www.klkkfm.com Licensee: Coloff Media LLC. Group owner: Clear Channel Communications Inc. (acq 9-1-2007; grpsl). Population served: 100,000 Natl. Rep: Clear Channel,. Format: Classic rock. News staff: one; News: 42 hrs wkly. Target aud: 25-54. ♦Hal Hofman, gen mgr, gen sls mgr; Drew Kelly, progmg dir; Laurie Gansen, traf mgr.

Clinton

KCLN(AM)— Dec 21, 1956: 1390 khz; 1 kw-D, 91 w-N, DA-2. TL: N41 54 32 W90 13 16. Hrs open: 24 1853 442nd Ave., 52732. Phone: (563) 243-1390. Fax: (563) 242-4567.E-mail: kcln@kcln.com Web Site:www.kcln.com Licensee: WPW Broadcasting Inc. (group owner; (acq 4-29-99; $800,000 with co-located FM). Population served: 150,000 Rgnl. Network: Tribune. Brownfield Miller & Fields. Format: Music of the 40s, 50s & 60s, big band. News staff: one; News: 2 hrs wkly. Target aud: 40 plus. Spec prog: Farm 10 hrs wkly. ♦Don Davis, pres; Larry Timpe, gen mgr; Chris Streets, progmg dir; Brad Seward, news dir; Aaron Winski, chief of engrg; Tracie Morgan, traf mgr.

KMCN(FM)— Dec 7, 1970: 94.7 mhz; 3 kw. Ant 300 ft TL: N41 54 32 W90 13 20. Stereo. Hrs open: 24 Prog sep from AM 1853 442nd Ave., 52732. Phone: (563) 243-5256. Fax: (563) 242-4567.E-mail: kcln@kcln.com Web Site:kcln.com Licensee: WPW Broadcasting Inc. Population served: 150,000 Format: Adult hits. News staff: one; News: one hr wkly. Target aud: 25-54.

KMXG(FM)— July 1974: 96.1 mhz; 100 kw. 980 ft TL: N41 37 58 W90 24 38. Stereo. Hrs open: 24 3535 E. Kimberly Rd., Davenport, 52807. Phone: (563) 344-7000. Fax: (563) 344-7006. Web Site:www.kmxg.com Licensee: Citicasters Licenses L.P. Group owner: Clear Channel Communications Inc. (acq 11-15-00; grpsl). Population served: 350,000 Natl. Rep: Christal,. Format: Hot adult contemp. News staff: one; News: 3 hrs wkly. Target aud: 25-54; yuppies, baby boomers, upscale professional females. Spec prog: Jazz 3 hrs wkly. ♦Larry Rosmilso, VP & gen mgr; Jim O'Hara, opns mgr, progmg dir; Kevin Allensworth, chief of engrg.

KROS(AM)— Sept 28, 1941: 1340 khz; 1 kw-U. TL: N41 51 36 W90 12 18. Stereo. Hrs open: 5:30 AM-midnight Box 0518, William Scott Broadcast Ctr., 870 13th Ave. N., 52733-0518. Phone: (563) 242-1252. Fax: (563) 242-4825.E-mail: kros@clinton.net Web Site:www.krosradio.com Licensee: KROS Broadcasting Inc. (acq 7-28-98; $23,000 for 28). Population served: 34,719 Natl. Network: CNN Radio, . Rgnl. Network: Radio Iowa. Radio Iowa Format: Full service. News staff: one; News: 38 hrs wkly. Target aud: General; loc audience. Spec prog: Folk 2 hrs, jazz one hr, blues one hr, gospel one hr, women 5 hrs. ♦Brad Parker, pres; Dave Vickers, gen mgr.

Coggon

***KUBU(FM)**—Not on air, target date: unknown: 88.7 mhz; 5 kw. Ant 216 ft TL: N42 27 26 W91 34 49. Hrs open: 1029 Third St. S.E., Cedar Rapids, 52401-2303. Phone: (319) 363-1774. Licensee: New Bohemia Group Inc. ♦Michael Richards, gen mgr.

Council Bluffs

***KIWR(FM)**— Nov 23, 1981: 89.7 mhz; 100 kw. 1,100 ft TL: N41 18 40 W96 01 37. Stereo. Hrs open: 24 2700 College Rd., 51503. Phone: (712) 325-3254. Fax: (712) 325-3391.E-mail: sjohn@iwcc.edu Web Site:www.897theriver.com Licensee: Iowa Western Community College. Population served: 1,000,000 Format: Progsv. News: 5 hrs wkly. Target aud: 18-34; well-educated, upper & middle-upper income. Spec prog: Var/div 16 hrs wkly. ♦Dan Kinney, pres; Tom Johnson, CFO; Sophia John, gen mgr.

KLNG(AM)— 1947: 1560 khz; 1 kw-D. TL: N41 12 28 W95 54 04. Hrs open: 6 AM-sunset 120 S. 35th St., Suite 2, 51501. Phone: (712) 323-0100. Fax: (712) 323-0022.E-mail: klgn@wilkinsradio.com Web Site:www.wilkinsradio.com Licensee: Wilkins Communications Network Inc. (group owner; (acq 4-89; $250,000). Population served: 1,500,000 Natl. Network: Salem Radio Network, . Womble, Carlyle, Sandridge & Rice. Format: Christian teaching/talk. Target aud: 35 plus. Spec prog: Sp 10 hrs, Black 6 hrs wkly. ♦Bob Wilkins, pres; LuAnn Wilkins, exec VP; Mitchell Mathis, VP; Charles Yates, stn mgr; Greg Garrett, opns mgr; John Bible, engr.

KOTK(AM)—See Omaha, NE

KQKQ-FM— 1969: 98.5 mhz; 100 kw. Ant 1,102 ft TL: N41 18 25 W96 01 37. Stereo. Hrs open: 5011 Capitol Ave., Omaha, NE, 68132. Phone: (402) 342-2000. Fax: (402) 346-5748.E-mail: info@q985fm.com Web Site:www.q985fm.com Licensee: Waitt Omaha LLC. (group owner; (acq 1-7-2002; grpsl). Population served: 134,800 Format: Modern adult contemp. Target aud: 18-44. ♦Mary Quass, CEO, pres, sr VP; Chuck DuCoty, COO, mus dir; Rhonda Gerrard, gen mgr, chief of engrg; Sam Coughlin, sls dir; Brandon Pappas, prom dir; Nevin Dane, progmg dir; Lori Storz, traf mgr.

KSRZ(FM)—See Omaha, NE

Cresco

KCZQ(FM)— Apr 1, 1991: 102.3 mhz; 3 kw. Ant 328 ft TL: N43 25 47 W92 09 49. Stereo. Hrs open: 116 First Ave. W., 52136-1514. Phone: (563) 547-1000. Phone: (563) 547-3366. Fax: (563) 547-2200.E-mail: superc@iowatelecom.net Licensee: Mega Media Ltd. Population served: 250,000 Natl. Rep: Farmakis,. Radio Iowa Wire Svc: Agence France-Presse (AFP) Format: Adult contemp. Target aud: General. Spec prog: Farm 12 hrs wkly. ♦James B. Hebel, pres, gen mgr, gen sls mgr; Debra Lowe, opns mgr; Jim Bernard, progmg dir; Stan McHenry, mus dir.

Creston

***KLOX(FM)**— 2005: 90.9 mhz; 100 kw vert. Ant 335 ft TL: N41 04 29 W94 22 35. Hrs open: 505 Josephine St., Titusville, FL, 32796. Phone: (321) 267-3000. Fax: (321) 264-9370.E-mail: wpio@gate.net Web Site:noncomradio.net Licensee: Florida Public Radio Inc. Format: Adult contemp Christian. ♦Archie Shetler, exec VP; Randy Henry, pres & gen mgr.

KSIB(AM)— Dec 7, 1946: 1520 khz; 1 kw-D. TL: N41 02 16 W94 23 38. Hrs open: Box 426, 50801. Phone: (641) 782-2155. Fax: (641) 782-6963. Licensee: G.O. Radio Ltd. (acq 2-82; grpsl;2-22-82). Population served: 68,234 Natl. Network: ABC, . Rgnl. Network: Iowa Radio Net. Brownfield Format: C&W. Target aud: General. ♦Dave Rieck, pres, gen mgr; Chad Riek, gen sls mgr; Ben Walter, progmg dir; Mark Saylor, news dir; Charlie Maley, chief of engrg.

KSIB-FM— March 1966: 101.3 mhz; 19 kw. 364 ft TL: N41 05 41 W94 22 30. Stereo. Hrs open: 24 Dups AM 95% Box 426, 50801. Phone: (641) 782-2155. Fax: (641) 782-6963. Population served: 68,234 Rgnl. Network: Brownfield. Brownfield Format: C&W. Target aud: General.

Davenport

***KALA(FM)**— Nov 4, 1967: 88.5 mhz; 100 w. 110 ft TL: N41 32 28 W90 34 57. Stereo. Hrs open: 24 518 W. Locust St., 52803. Phone: (563) 333-6219. Fax: (563) 333-6218.E-mail: kala@sau.edu Web Site:www.sau.edu/kala Licensee: St. Ambrose University. (acq 11-4-67). Population served: 100,000 Format: Jazz, progsv, urban contemp. News staff: one; News: 34.5 hrs wkly. Target aud: General. Spec prog: Sp 15 hrs, gospel 13 hrs wkly. ♦David Baker, gen mgr & opns mgr.

KBEA-FM—(Muscatine, February 1949: 99.7 mhz; 100 kw. 895 ft TL: N41 26 43 W91 04 36. Stereo. Hrs open: 24 1229 Brady St., 52803. Phone: (563) 326-2541. Fax: (563) 326-1819. Licensee: Cumulus Licensing Corp. Group owner: Cumulus Media Inc. (acq 3-15-00; grpsl). Population served: 600000 Putbrese, Hunsaker & Trent. Format: Top 40. News staff: one. Target aud: 25-54. ♦Jack Swart, pres, gen mgr; Julie Derrer, gen sls mgr; Steve Fuller, progmg dir; Andy Andresen, chief of engrg; Tracy Hall, traf mgr.

KCQQ(FM)— Sept 1, 1996: 106.5 mhz; 100 kw. 210 ft TL: N41 32 14 W90 34 30. Stereo. Hrs open: 24 3535 E. Kimberly Rd., 52807. Phone: (563) 344-7000. Fax: (563) 359-8524.E-mail: bospates@clearchannel.com Web Site:www.kcqq106.com Licensee: Citicasters Licenses L.P. Group owner: Clear Channel Communications Inc. (acq 11-15-00; grpsl). Population served: 200,000 Format: Classic rock. News staff: one; News: 2 hrs wkly. Target aud: 25-54. Spec prog: Relg one hr wkly. ♦Jeff Ashcraft, sls dir, gen sls mgr; Mike Hamann, gen sls mgr; John Laton, mktg VP; Bo Spates, progmg dir; Kevin Allensworth, chief of engrg.

KJOC(AM)— 1947: 1170 khz; 1 kw-U, DA-2. TL: N41 23 22 W90 31 08. Hrs open: 24 1229 Brady St., 52803. Phone: (563) 326-2541. Fax: (563) 326-1819. Web Site:www.kjoc.com Licensee: Cumulus Licensing Corp. Group owner: Cumulus Media Inc. (acq 3-15-2000; grpsl). Population served: 49,900 Natl. Network: CBS, . Putbrese, Hunsaker & Trent, P. Format: Oldies. Target aud: 18-49. ♦Jack Swart, gen mgr.

WFXN(AM)—See Moline, IL

WLLR-FM— October 1948: 103.7 mhz; 100 kw. 1,191 ft TL: N41 32 49 W90 28 35. Stereo. Hrs open: 24 3535 E. Kimberly Rd. , 52807. Phone: (563) 359-9557. Fax: (563) 344-7016.E-mail: jimohara@clearchannel.com Web Site:www.wllr.com Licensee: Citicasters Licenses L.P. Population served: 200,000 Format: Country. News: 2 hrs wkly. Target aud: 25-54. ♦Mike Weindruch, gen sls mgr; Carrie Clearman, prom dir; Jim O'Hara, progmg dir; Kevin Allensworth, engrg dir; Lorraine Meier, traf mgr.

WOC(AM)— February 1922: 1420 khz; 5 kw-U, DA-2. TL: N41 33 00 W90 28 37. Hrs open: 24 3535 E. Kimberly Rd., 52807. Phone: (563) 344-7000. Fax: (563) 344-7065.E-mail: dankennedy@clearchannel.com

Web Site:www.woc1420.com Licensee: Citicasters Licenses L.P. Group owner: Clear Channel Communications Inc. (acq 11-15-2000; grpsl). Population served: 50,000 Rgnl. Network: Ill. Radio Net, Radio Iowa. Natl. Rep: Christal,. Radio Iowa Baker & Hostetler. Format: News/talk, info. News staff: 5. Target aud: 35-64; info-oriented adults. Spec prog: Farm 10 hrs wkly. ♦Larry Rosmilso, gen mgr; Scott Bitting, gen sls mgr; Caressa Clearman, prom dir; Dan Kennedy, progmg dir; Kevin Allensworth, chief of engrg.

De Witt

KBOB-FM— Jan 12, 1977: 104.9 mhz; 12.5 kw. Ant 469 ft TL: N41 43 11 W90 34 13. Stereo. Hrs open: 24 1229 Brady St., Davenport, 52803. Phone: (563) 326-2541. Fax: (563) 326-1819. Web Site:www.97rock.net Licensee: Cumulus Licensing Corp. Group owner: Cumulus Media Inc. (acq 10-2-2000; grpsl). Format: Active rock. ♦Jack Swart, gen mgr; Julie Derrer, gen sls mgr; Ryan Chase, progmg dir; Andy Andresen, chief of engrg; Deanna Flynn, traf mgr.

Decorah

KDEC(AM)— May 1947: 1240 khz; 1 kw-U. TL: N43 19 26 W91 47 04. Hrs open: 5 AM-10 PM (M-F) Prog sep from FM Box 27, 52101. Secondary address: 110 Highland Dr. 52101. Phone: (563) 382-4251. Fax: (563) 382-9540.E-mail: kdec@kdecradio.com Web Site:www.kdecradio.com Licensee: Decorah Broadcasting Inc. Population served: 40,000 Natl. Network: Westwood One, . Rgnl. Network: Tribune. Natl. Rep: Farmakis,. Format: MOR. News staff: 2; News: 12 hrs wkly. Target aud: 35 plus.

KDEC-FM— Sept 2, 1986: 100.5 mhz; 30 kw. Ant 420 ft TL: N43 19 26 W91 47 04. Stereo. Hrs open: 24 Box 27, 52101. Secondary address: 110 Highland Dr. 52101. Phone: (563) 382-4251. Fax: (563) 382-9540.E-mail: kdec@kdecradio.com Web Site:www.kdecradio.com Licensee: Decorah Broadcasting Inc. (acq 3-1-96; $696,500). Population served: 100,000 Reddy, Begley & McCormick. Format: AAA. News staff: 2; News: 3 hrs wkly. Target aud: 18-54. ♦Bob Holtan, pres, gen mgr; Colleen Holtan, VP; Jennifer Grouws, stn mgr.

***KLCD(FM)—** July 15, 1977: 89.5 mhz; 100 w. 140 ft TL: N43 18 56 W91 47 18. Stereo. Hrs open: 206 S. Broadway, Suite 735, Rochester, MN, 55904. Phone: (507) 282-0910. Fax: (507) 282-2107.E-mail: mail@mpr.org Web Site:www.mpr.org Licensee: Minnesota Public Radio Inc. Natl. Network: NPR, PRI, . Format: Class. News staff: one. ♦Chris Cross, gen mgr; Mary Stapek, dev dir; Sea Stachura, news rptr.

***KLNI(FM)—** 1993: 88.7 mhz; 100 w. -36 ft TL: N43 18 35 W91 48 30. Hrs open: 24 206 S. Broadway, Suite 735, Rochester, MN, 55904. Phone: (507) 282-0910. Fax: (507) 282-2107.E-mail: mail@mpr.org Web Site:www.mpr.org Licensee: Minnesota Public Radio (group owner; (acq 6-10-92). Population served: 10,000 Natl. Network: NPR, . Format: News & info. News staff: one. ♦Chris Cross, gen mgr; Mary Stapek, dev dir; Sea Stachura, news rptr.

***KWLC(AM)—** December 1926: 1240 khz; 1 kw-U. TL: N43 18 38 W91 48 41. Hrs open: 700 College Dr., 52101. Phone: (563) 387-1240. Fax: (563) 387-1489.E-mail: info@kwlc.com Web Site:kwlc.luther.edu Licensee: Luther College. Population served: 30,000 Format: Var/div, progsv. Target aud: General.

Denison

KDSN(AM)— Apr 11, 1956: 1530 khz; 500 w-D, 13 w-N. TL: N42 02 10 W95 19 44. Hrs open: 6 am-10pm Box 670, 51442. Secondary address: 1530 Ridge Rd. 51442. Phone: (712) 263-3141. Fax: (712) 263-2088.E-mail: info@kdsnradio.com Web Site:www.kdsnradio.com Licensee: M & J Radio Corp. (acq 8-3-93; $450,000 with co-located FM; 8-23-93). Population served: 90,000 Natl. Network: ABC, . Rgnl. Network: Agri-Net, Radio Iowa. Natl. Rep: Farmakis,. Radio Iowa Format: Country, adult contemp, farm markets. News staff: one; News: 8 rs wkly. Target aud: General. Spec prog: Farm 12 hrs, polka 4 hrs, Sp 3 hrs wkly. ♦Michael Dudding, pres, exec VP, gen mgr; Phyllis Rohlin, exec VP & gen mgr.

KDSN-FM— Aug 1, 1968: 107.1 mhz; 6 kw. 300 ft TL: N42 02 11 W95 19 50. Stereo. Hrs open: 24 Prog sep from AM Box 670, 51442. Secondary address: 1530 Ridge Rd. 51442. Phone: (712) 263-3141. Fax: (712) 263-2088.E-mail: info@kdsnradio.com Web Site:www.kdsnradio.com Licensee: M & J Radio Corp. Population served: 90,000 Natl. Network: ABC, . Rgnl. Network: Radio Iowa. Natl. Rep: Farmakis,. Format: Adult contemp. News staff: one; News: 8 hrs wkly. Target aud: 21-65. ♦Michael Dudding, adv dir; Michael Earl, news dir; Dick Keane, engrg dir; Kathy Dudding, traf mgr; Brian Schmid, farm dir; Randy Grossman, sports cmtr; Deb Nelson, women's int ed, prom; Tom Hamilton, progmg dir & disc jockey.

Des Moines

KBGG(AM)— 1998: 1700 khz; 10 kw-D, 1 kw-N. TL: N41 35 30 W93 31 43. Hrs open: 24 4143 109th St., Urbandale, 50322. Phone: (515) 331-9200. Fax: (515) 331-9292. Fax: (515) 254-1037 . Web Site:www.1700thechamp.com Licensee: Citadel Broadcasting Co. Group owner: Citadel Broadcasting Corp. (acq 8-29-2003; grpsl). Natl. Network: ESPN Radio, . Natl. Rep: Christal,. Wire Svc: UPI Format: Sports. ♦Jack O'Brien, opns mgr; Doug Wood, sls dir; Terry Peters, VP & mktg mgr.

***KDFR(FM)—** Mar 24, 1989: 91.3 mhz; 32 kw. 446 ft TL: N41 36 59 W93 31 36. Stereo. Hrs open: 24 Box 57023, 50317. Secondary address: 2350 N.E. 44th Ct. 50317. Phone: (515) 262-0449.E-mail: kdfr@familyradio.org Web Site:www.familyradio.com Licensee: Family Stations Inc. (group owner) Population served: 600,000 Format: Relg, inspirational. News staff: one; News: 6 hrs wkly. Target aud: 25 plus; general. Spec prog: Class 2 hrs wkly. ♦Harold Camping, pres; Larry Vavroch, opns mgr.

KDRB(FM)— Feb 1, 1948: 100.3 mhz; 100 kw. Ant 1,814 ft. TL: N41 48 33 W93 36 53. Stereo. Hrs open: 24 2141 Grand Ave., 50312. Phone: (515) 245-8900. Fax: (515) 245-8902.E-mail: johnmckeighan @clearchannel.com Web Site:www.thebusfm.com Licensee: Citicasters Licenses L.P. Population served: 111,300 Natl. Rep: Clear Channel,. Wire Svc: AP Format: Var. Target aud: 25-54. ♦Joel McCrea, VP; Matt Gillon, sls dir; Joel Mcrea, mktg mgr; John McKeighan, progmg dir; Jim Boyd, news dir.

KGGO(FM)— May 31, 1964: 94.9 mhz; 100 kw. 1,066 ft TL: N41 37 55 W93 27 27. Stereo. Hrs open: 24 4143 109th St., Urbandale, 50322. Phone: (515) 331-9200. Fax: (515) 312-9292.E-mail: louspolt@ctcomm.com Web Site:www.kggo.com Licensee: Citadel Broadcasting Co. Group owner: Citadel Broadcasting Corp. (acq 8-29-03; grpsl). Natl. Rep: Christal,. Format: Classic Rock. ♦Jack O'Brien, gen mgr, opns mgr; Doug Wood, sls dir; Terry Peters, mktg VP.

KHKI(FM)— July 4, 1964: 97.3 mhz; 105 kw. Ant 469 ft TL: N41 39 46 W93 45 24. Stereo. Hrs open: 24 4143 109th St., Urbandale, 50322. Phone: (515) 331-9200. Fax: (515) 331-9292. Web Site:973thehawk.com Licensee: Citadel Broadcasting Co. Group owner: Citadel Broadcasting Corp. (acq 8-29-03; grpsl). Population served: 400,000 Natl. Rep: Christal,. Format: Country. Target aud: 18-49. ♦Jack O'Brien, opns VP, progmg dir; Doug Wood, sls dir; Terry Peters, gen mgr & mktg VP.

KIOA(FM)— Sept 18, 1964: 93.3 mhz; 100 kw. 1,063 ft TL: N41 37 54 W93 27 24. Stereo. Hrs open: 24 1416 Locust St., 50309. Phone: (515) 280-1350. Fax: (515) 280-3011. Web Site:www.kioa.com Licensee: Saga Communications of Iowa LLC Group owner: Saga Communications Inc. (acq 4-19-93; $2.7 million with co-located AM;5-3-93). Population served: 410,000 Smithwick & Belendiuk. Format: Oldies. Target aud: 25-54. ♦Jeff Delvaux, gen mgr; Pam Washington, sls dir; Lindsay Reinert, prom mgr; Sarah Levere, adv mgr; Tim Fox, progmg dir; Jay Wells, news dir; Joe Farrington, chief of engrg; Lee Ann Rose, traf mgr.

KJJY(FM)—(West Des Moines, Feb 4, 1978: 92.5 mhz; 41 kw. Ant 541 ft TL: N41 39 53 W93 45 25. Stereo. Hrs open: 24 4143 109th St., Urbandale, 50322. Phone: (515) 331-9200. Fax: (515) 331-9292. Web Site:www.kjjy.com Licensee: Citadel Broadcasting Co. Group owner: Citadel Broadcasting Corp. (acq 8-29-03; grpsl). Population served: 758,000 Natl. Rep: Christal,. Format: Country. Target aud: 25-54; general. ♦Jack O'Brien, opns mgr; Doug Wood, sls dir, mktg dir; Terry Peters, gen mgr & mktg VP.

***KJMC(FM)—** May 1999: 89.3 mhz; 7.1 kw. Ant 200 ft TL: N41 39 21 W93 35 51. Stereo. Hrs open: 24 1169 25th St., 50311. Phone: (515) 279-1811. Fax: (515) 279-1802.E-mail: io@kjmcfm.com Licensee: Minority Communications Inc. Population served: 400,000 Natl. Network: ABC, . Format: Urban contemp, jazz, oldies. ♦Larry Rollins, gen mgr; Larry Neville, opns VP; John Farington, chief of opns.

KKDM(FM)— Aug 22, 1995: 107.5 mhz; 100 kw. 705 ft TL: N41 38 36 W93 17 21. Hrs open: 24 2141 Grand Ave., 50312. Phone: (515) 245-8900. Fax: (515) 245-8906.E-mail: kxno@clearchannel.com Web Site:www.kkdm.com Licensee: Clear Channel Broadcasting Licenses Inc. Group owner: Clear Channel Communications Inc. (acq 9-1-99; $7.35 million). Natl. Rep: Clear Channel,. Format: CHR. Target aud: 18-49. ♦Joel McCrea, gen mgr; Matt Gillon, sls dir; Greg Chance, progmg dir; Sean Cage, mus dir.

KPSZ(AM)— April 1947: 940 khz; 100 kw,. TL: N41 48 01 W93 36 27. Stereo. Hrs open: 24 1416 Locust St., 50309. Phone: (515) 280-1350. Fax: (515) 280-3011.E-mail: jbrown@desmoinesradiogroup.com Web Site:www.praise940.com Licensee: Saga Communications of Iowa LLC Population served: 456,400 Natl. Network: Salem Radio Network, . Natl. Rep: Katz Radio,. Wire Svc: AP Format: Christian. Target aud: Adult; adult christian, music and program format. ♦Jeff Delvaux, gen mgr, progmg mgr; Pam Washington, sls dir; Jim Brown, progmg mgr.

KRNT(AM)— Mar 17, 1935: 1350 khz; 5 kw-U, DA-N. TL: N41 33 34 W93 34 40. Hrs open: 24 Prog sep from FM 1416 Locust St., 50309. Phone: (515) 280-1350. Fax: (515) 280-3011.E-mail: jbrown@desmoinesradiogroup.com Web Site:www.1350kmt.com Licensee: Saga Communications of Iowa LLC Natl. Network: CBS, . Natl. Rep: Katz Radio,. Smithwick & Belendiuk. Wire Svc: AP Format: MOR. Target aud: 50 plus. ♦Jeff Delvaux, gen mgr; Marianne Coppock, mktg dir; Sarah LeVere, adv dir; Jim Brown, progmg dir.

KSTZ(FM)— 1970: 102.5 mhz; 100 kw. 1,248 ft TL: N41 48 01 W93 36 27. Stereo. Hrs open: 24 1416 Locust St., 50309. Phone: (515) 280-1350. Fax: (515) 280-3011.E-mail: sallen@desmoinesradiogroup.com Web Site:www.star1025.com Licensee: Saga Communications of Iowa LLC Group owner: Saga Communications Inc. (acq 8-88; $3.2 million with co-located AM; 8-1-88). Population served: 456,400 Natl. Network: CNN Radio, . Natl. Rep: Katz Radio,. Smithwick & Belendiuk. Wire Svc: AP Format: Hot adult contemp. Target aud: 25-54; emphasis on upscale women. ♦Jeff Delvaux, gen mgr; Pam Washington, sls dir; Marianne Coppock, mktg dir; Dan Abbuehl, adv mgr; Scott Allen, opns mgr & progmg dir.

KWKY(AM)— Feb 2, 1948: 1150 khz; 1 kw-U, DA-2, 2.5 kw-N. TL: N41 27 07 W93 40 44. Hrs open: 24 Secondary address: 6626 Dubuque Trail, Norwalk 50211. Phone: (515) 223-1150. Fax: (515) 981-0840.E-mail: info@kwky.com Web Site:www.kwky.com Licensee: Putbrese Communications Ltd. (acq 10-3-2006; $2.04 million). Population served: 400,000 Natl. Network: EWTN Radio, . Format: Catholic radio, talk, sports. ♦John Putbrese, pres; Charles E. Putbrese, gen mgr; Matthew Phelps, opns mgr; Dennis Ray, mus dir; Jon Farrington, chief of engrg.

KXNO(AM)— July 21, 1921: 1460 khz; 5 kw-U, DA-N. TL: N41 38 45 W93 32 12. Stereo. Hrs open: 24 2141 Grand Ave., 50312. Phone: (515) 245-8900. Fax: (515) 245-8906.E-mail: kxno@clearchannel.com Web Site:www.kxno.com Licensee: Capstar TX L.P. Group owner: Clear Channel Communications Inc. (acq 8-30-2000; grpsl). Population served: 350,000 Natl. Network: Fox Sports, . Format: Sports. Target aud: 35 plus; 25-54 Male. ♦Joel McCrea, gen mgr; Geoff Conn, opns mgr; Matt Gillon, sls dir, gen sls mgr; Van Harden, progmg dir; Jim Boyd, news dir; Raleigh Rubenking, chief of engrg; Julie Traver, traf mgr; Molly Pins, spec ev coord.

WHO(AM)— Apr 10, 1924: 1040 khz; 50 kw-U. TL: N41 39 10 W93 21 01. Hrs open: 24 2141 Grand Ave., 50312. Phone: (515) 245-8900. Web Site:www.whoradio.com Licensee: Citicasters Licenses L.P. Group owner: Clear Channel Communications Inc. (acq 5-4-99; grpsl). Population served: 419,000 Natl. Network: Fox News Radio, . Rgnl. Network: Iowa Radio Net. Natl. Rep: Clear Channel,. Wire Svc: AP Format: News/talk. News staff: 7. Target aud: 25-54; Adults. Spec prog: Farm 15 hrs wkly. ♦Joel McCrea, VP; Matt Gillon, sls dir; Molly Pins, prom dir; Cheryl Pannier, progmg dir; Jim Boyd, news dir; Bonnie Lucas, pub affrs dir; Raleigh RubenKing, chief of engrg; Julie Traver, traf mgr.

Dubuque

KATF(FM)— June 25, 1967: 92.9 mhz; 89.7 kw. Ant 1,014 ft TL: N42 31 44 W90 36 58. Stereo. Hrs open: 24 Prog sep from AM Box 659, 52004-0659. Secondary address: 346 W. 8th St. 52001. Phone: (563) 690-0800. Licensee: Radio Dubuque Inc. Wire Svc: NWS (National Weather Service) Format: Adult contemp. News: 3 hrs wkly. Target aud: 25-54; adults establishing families, careers & households. ♦Thomas Parsley, gen mgr.

KDTH(AM)— May 4, 1941: 1370 khz; 5 kw-U, DA-N. TL: N42 29 06 W90 38 39. Hrs open: 24 Box 659, 52004-0659. Secondary address: 346 W. 8th St. 52001. Phone: (563) 690-0800. Fax: (563) 588-5688.E-mail: kdth@kdth.com Web Site:www.kdth.com Licensee: Radio Dubuque Inc. (group owner; (acq 7-1-2000; $3.68 million with co-located FM). Population served: 129,800 Natl. Network: CBS, . Natl. Rep: Katz Radio,. Pepper & Corazzini. Wire Svc: NWS (National Weather Service) Format: Full service. News staff: 3; News: 25 hrs wkly. Target aud: 35 plus; responsible adults with established careers & households. Spec prog: Farm 17 hrs wkly. ♦Thomas Parsley, stn mgr; Perry Mason, gen sls mgr, natl sls mgr; Michael Kaye, progmg dir; Ed Anderson, news dir.

***KDUB(FM)—** 2005: 89.7 mhz; 530 w horiz, 2.6 kw vert. Ant 646 ft TL: N42 36 18 W90 47 57. Hrs open:
Rebroadcasts KUNI(FM) Cedar Falls 100%.
324 Communications Arts Center, Univ. of Northern Iowa, Cedar Falls, 50614. Phone: (319) 273-6400. Fax: (319) 273-2682.E-mail: kuni@uni.edu Web Site:www.kuniradio.org Licensee: University of Northern Iowa. Format: News/talk. News staff: 3; News: 77 hours. Spec prog: Blues

5 hrs, folk 4 hrs wkly. ♦Scott Vezdos, mktg dir; Wayne Jarvis, gen mgr & progmg dir; Al Shares, mus dir; Greg Shanley, news dir; Steve Schoon, chief of engrg.

*KIAD(FM)— 2006: 88.5 mhz; 750 w vert. Ant 518 ft TL: N42 24 16 W90 34 12. Hrs open:
Rebroadcasts WAFR(FM) Tupelo, MS 100%.
Drawer 2440, Tupelo, MS, 38803. Phone: (662) 844-8888. Fax: (662) 842-6791. Web Site:www.afr.net Licensee: American Family Association. Format: Christian. ♦Marvin Sanders, gen mgr.

KLYV(FM)— Sept 1, 1965: 105.3 mhz; 50 kw. 330 ft TL: N42 30 10 W90 42 11. Stereo. Hrs open: 5490 Saratoga Rd., 52002. Phone: (563) 557-1040. Fax: (319) 583-4535. Web Site:www.y105online.com Population served: 130,000 Format: CHR. Target aud: 18-49. ♦Scott Thomas, progmg dir.

KXGE(FM)— Mar 8, 1980: 102.3 mhz; 2.4 kw. 410 ft TL: N42 32 28 W90 36 46. Stereo. Hrs open: 24 5490 Saratoga Rd., 52002. Phone: (563) 557-1040. Fax: (563) 583-4535.E-mail: info@kxge.com Web Site:www.eagle102online.com Licensee: Cumulus Licensing Corp. Group owner: Cumulus Media Inc. (acq 12-17-98; grpsl). Population served: 246,290 Natl. Network: ABC, . Format: Classic rock. News staff: one; News: 2 hrs wkly. Target aud: 18-49; in high school or college in the 60s & 70s. ♦Dan Sullivan, gen mgr; Doris Garius, gen sls mgr; Scott Thomas, progmg dir; Tom Berryman, news dir.

WDBQ(AM)— Oct 30, 1933: 1490 khz; 1 kw-U. TL: N42 30 10 W90 42 24. Stereo. Hrs open: 5490 Saratoga Rd., 52002. Phone: (319) 583-6471. Fax: (319) 583-4535. Web Site:www.cumulus.com Licensee: Cumulus Licensing Corp. Group owner: Cumulus Media Inc. (acq 12-17-98; grpsl). Population served: 64,000 Natl. Network: ABC, Westwood One, . C. Reynolds. Format: News, talk, sports. ♦Jack Kilcoyne, progmg dir, news dir, sports cmtr; Alan Williams, traf mgr; Mike Field, disc jockey.

Dunkerton

KCOO(FM)—Not on air, target date: unknown: 103.9 mhz; 6 kw. Ant 312 ft TL: N42 42 23.9 W92 13 03.7. Hrs open: 2801 Via Fortuna Dr., Suite 675, Austin, TX, 78746. Phone: (512) 329-5843. Fax: (512) 329-5847. Web Site:www.matineemedia.com Licensee: Ace Radio Corp. ♦Stephen Hackerman, pres.

Dyersville

KDST(FM)— Aug 25, 1985: 99.3 mhz; 3 kw. 298 ft TL: N42 25 43 W91 12 50. Stereo. Hrs open: 24 1931 20th Ave. S.E., 52040. Phone: (563) 875-8193. Fax: (563) 875-6001.E-mail: kdst993@iowatelecom.net Web Site:www.realcountryonline.com Licensee: Design Homes Inc. (acq 12-88; $22,079; 12-26-88). Natl. Network: ABC, . Rgnl. Network: Brownfield. Brownfield Miller & Miller. Format: Country. News staff: one. Target aud: 45-60. Spec prog: Farm. ♦Randy Weeks, CEO; Franklin Weeks, pres; Doug Langston, stn mgr, opns mgr.

Eagle Grove

*KJYL(FM)— Feb 20, 1994: 100.7 mhz; 25 kw. 328 ft TL: N42 40 18 W94 09 11. Hrs open: 24 Box 325, 103 W. Broadway, 50533. Phone: (515) 448-4588. Fax: (515) 448-5267.E-mail: kjyl@kjyl.org Web Site:www.kjyl.org Licensee: Minn-Iowa Christian Broadcasting Inc. (group owner). Population served: 200,000 Format: Christian. News staff: one. Target aud: 30-55. ♦Jay Rudolph, opns mgr.

Eddyville

KKSI(FM)— July 30, 1990: 101.5 mhz; 49 kw. 498 ft TL: N41 07 57 W92 42 12. Stereo. Hrs open: 24 416 E. Main St., Ottumwa, 52501. Phone: (641) 684-5563. Fax: (641) 684-5832.E-mail: mail@ottumwaradio.com Web Site:www.ottumwaradio.com Licensee: "O"-Town Communications Inc. (acq 12-10-99; $162,400). Miller & Neely, P.C. Format: Classic Rock. News staff: 2; News: 4 hrs wkly. Target aud: 25-54. ♦Greg H. List, pres; Bruce Linder, VP; Jeff Downing, opns dir; Mike Buchanan, news dir.

Eldon

KRKN(FM)— 1996: 104.3 mhz; 23.5 kw. Ant 341 ft TL: N40 52 06 W92 18 20. Stereo. Hrs open: 24 416 E. Main St., Ottumwa, 52501. Phone: (641) 684-5563. Fax: (641) 684-5832.E-mail: mail@ottumwaradio.com Web Site:www.ottumwaradio.com Licensee: O-Town Communications Inc. (acq 12-10-99; $162,400). Miller & Neely, P.C. Format: New country. News staff: 2; News: 4 hrs wkly.

Target aud: 18-54. ♦Greg H. List, pres, stn mgr; Bruce Linder, VP; Jeff Downing, opns mgr; Mike Buchanan, news dir.

Eldora

KDAO-FM— June 1, 1992: 99.5 mhz; 3 kw. 328 ft TL: N42 15 49 W93 03 57. Stereo. Hrs open: 24 Box 538, Marshalltown, 50158. Secondary address: 1930 N. Center St., Marshalltown 50158. Phone: (641) 752-4122. Fax: (641) 752-5121.E-mail: kdao@kdao.com Licensee: Eldora Broadcasting Co. Inc. (acq 12-18-91; $15,000 for CP; 1-13-92). Natl. Network: Fox News Radio, . Format: Adult contemp. Target aud: 25-54. ♦Mark Osmundson, gen mgr.

Elkader

KADR(AM)— May 15, 1983: 1400 khz; 1 kw-U. TL: N42 50 57 W91 24 43. Hrs open: Box 990, 52043. Phone: (563) 245-1400. Fax: (563) 245-1402.E-mail: info@hitsandfavorites.com   Web Site:www.hitsandfavorites.com Licensee: KADR-AM 14, div of Design Homes Inc. (acq 3-20-85). Natl. Rep: Farmakis,. Format: Adult contemp. ♦Dan Berns, gen mgr; Troy Thein, chief of opns.

KCTN(FM)—See Garnavillo

Emmetsburg

KUYY(FM)— Jan 10, 1977: 100.1 mhz; 16 kw. Ant 300 ft TL: N43 01 20 W94 41 59. Stereo. Hrs open: 24 2303 W. 18th St., Spencer, 51301. Phone: (712) 264-1074. Fax: (712) 264-1077.E-mail: mspies@nrgmedia.com Licensee: Jim Dandy Broadcasting Inc. (acq 1-13-2003; $2.5 million with KKIA(FM) Ida Grove). Population served: 12,000 Rgnl. Network: Iowa Radio Network. Format: Active adult contemp. Target aud: 25-54. ♦Marty Spies, gen mgr; Stan Calvert, opns mgr, progmg dir; Stephanie Haviland, gen sls mgr; Steve Heaton, chief of engrg.

Epworth

KGRR(FM)— Dec 10, 1994: 97.3 mhz; 19 kw. 380 ft TL: N42 26 13 W90 50 43. Hrs open: 24 Box 659, Dubuque, 52004. Secondary address: 346 W. 8th St., Dubuque 52004. Phone: (563) 690-0800. Fax: (563) 588-5688.E-mail: kgrr@kgrr.com Web Site:kgrr.com Licensee: Radio Dubuque Inc. (group owner; acq 7-1-00; $1.5 million). Population served: 150,000 Natl. Rep: Katz Radio,. Format: Classic hits, classic rock. News staff: one; News: 2 hrs wkly. Target aud: 25-54; families. ♦Don Rabbitt, CEO; Paul Hemmer, VP; Thomas Parsley, pres, gen mgr & progmg dir.

Estherville

KILR(AM)— Dec 23, 1967: 1070 khz; 250 w-D, 48 w-N, DA-2. TL: N43 25 45 W94 49 23. Hrs open: 6 AM-2 hrs past sunset Box 453, 51334. Secondary address: 3875 150th St. 51334. Phone: (712) 362-2644. Fax: (712) 362-5951.E-mail: ubcbroadcast@netins.net Licensee: Jacobson Broadcasting Co. Inc. (acq 7-1-82; $610,000 with co-located FM; 7-5-82). Population served: 40,000 Natl. Network: ABC, . Natl. Rep: Farmakis,. Lauren A. Colby. Format: News/talk. News staff: one; News: 24 hrs wkly. Target aud: 29-65; loc baby boomers. Spec prog: Farm 9 hrs, relg 11 hrs wkly. ♦Barbara J. Jacobson, CFO; Peggy Zahrt, opns mgr; Ed Funston, news dir; Roger J. Jacobson, pres, gen mgr, gen sls mgr, prom dir, progmg dir & chief of engrg.

KILR-FM— Oct 17, 1969: 95.9 mhz; 20 kw. Ant 325 ft TL: N43 25 45 W94 49 23. Stereo. Hrs open: 3875 150th St., 51334. Phone: (712) 362-2644. Fax: (712) 362-5951.E-mail: kilrprod@netins.net Licensee: Jacobson Broadcasting Co. Inc. Natl. Rep: Salem,. Format: Country, sports. Target aud: 25-54.

Fairfield

*KHOE(FM)— 1994: 90.5 mhz; 100 w. 98 ft TL: N41 00 59 W91 58 09. Stereo. Hrs open: 24 Box 1017, 1000 N. 4th St., 52557. Phone: (641) 469-5463.E-mail: khoe@mum.edu Licensee: Fairfield Educational Radio Station. Population served: 14,000 Format: World music, class, educ. News: 2 hrs wkly. Target aud: 18-35; University & college audience. Spec prog: Children 3 hrs, folk 6 hrs, gospel 3 hrs, jazz 2 hrs, Sp 2 hrs wkly. ♦Bill Goldstein, CEO; Jeffrey Hedquist, pres; Stan Stansberry, gen mgr.

KKFD-FM— 1977: 95.9 mhz; 4.1 kw. Ant 400 ft TL: N40 58 47 W92 05 45. Stereo. Hrs open: 24 Prog sep from AM Box 648, 57 S. Court St., 52556. Phone: (641) 472-4191. Fax: (641) 472-2071.E-mail:

info@fairfieldiowaradio.com Web Site:www.fairfieldiowaradio.com Population served: 70,000 Natl. Network: ABC, . Format: Adult contemp. News staff: one; News: 12 hrs wkly. Target aud: 25-54.

KMCD(AM)— Mar 3, 1958: 1570 khz; 250 w-D, 108 w-N. TL: N41 00 25 W92 00 50. Hrs open: 24 Box 648, 57 S. Court St., 52556. Phone: (641) 472-4191. Fax: (641) 472-2071. Web Site:www.fairfieldiowaradio.com Licensee: Fairfield License Co. LLC. (group owner; (acq 6-1-2007; $750,000 with co-located FM). Population served: 30,000 Natl. Network: ABC, Jones Radio Networks, . Radio Iowa Format: News/talk. News staff: one; News: 22 hrs wkly. Target aud: 30 plus; community leaders & Jefferson County. ♦Jay Mitchell, gen mgr; Bob Harvey, gen sls mgr; Steve Smith, progmg dir; Emily Humble, news dir; E. Marie Kiefer, traf mgr.

*KUNJ(FM)—Not on air, target date: unknown: 88.1 mhz; 250 w. Ant 325 ft TL: N41 05 21 W91 58 05. Hrs open: University of Northern Iowa, 324 Communications Arts Center, Cedar Falls, 50614-0359. Licensee: University of Northern Iowa. ♦Wayne Jarvis, gen mgr.

Forest City

KIOW(FM)— Nov 8, 1978: 107.3 mhz; 25 kw. Ant 328 ft TL: N43 17 02 W93 37 50. Stereo. Hrs open: 24 Box 308, 50436. Secondary address: 18643 360th St. 50436. Phone: (641) 585-1073. Fax: (641) 585-2990.E-mail: kiow@kiow.com Web Site:www.kiow.com Licensee: Pilot Knob Broadcasting Inc. Population served: 150,000 Natl. Network: CNN Radio, . Rgnl. Network: Radio Iowa. Natl. Rep: Farmakis,. Radio Iowa Wire Svc: AP Format: Country, adult contemp, news. News staff: one; News: 15 hrs wkly. Target aud: General; Adults 25 +. Spec prog: Farm 15 hrs, contemp hits 19 hrs wkly. ♦Susan I. Coloff, CFO; Tony Coloff, pres & gen mgr.

Fort Dodge

*KEGR(FM)— 2005: 89.5 mhz; 17 kw vert. Ant 364 ft TL: N42 40 18 W94 09 11. Hrs open: Box 286, Shenandoah, 51601. Secondary address: 4136 Northgate Blvd., Suite 1, Sacramento 95834. Phone: (515) 545-4841. Web Site:www.familyradio.com Licensee: Family Stations Inc. (group owner). Natl. Network: Family Radio, . Format: Relg.

*KICB(FM)— September 1971: 88.1 mhz; 200 w. 130 ft TL: N42 29 27 W94 12 01. Stereo. Hrs open: 330 Ave. M, 50501. Phone: (515) 576-6049. Fax: (515) 576-5656. Licensee: Iowa Central Community College. Population served: 31,263 Format: Alternative. Target aud: 13-34; young men & women with progsv tastes. ♦Robert Paxton, pres; Brian Blessman, gen mgr; Jeff Nelsen, mus dir, chief of engrg.

KKEZ(FM)— 1966: 94.5 mhz; 100 kw. 640 ft TL: N42 29 43 W94 12 33. Stereo. Hrs open: 24 Prog sep from AM 540 A St., 50501. Phone: (515) 576-7333. Fax: (515) 955-4250.E-mail: kkez@clearchannel.com Web Site:www.kkez.com Population served: 31,623 Format: Adult contemp. News staff: 3; News: 5 hrs wkly. Target aud: 18-49.

*KTPR(FM)— Sept 15, 1980: 91.1 mhz; 100 kw. Ant 1,052 ft TL: N42 49 03 W94 24 41. Stereo. Hrs open: 24 WOI Radio Group, 2022 Communications Bldg., Ames, 50011-3241. Phone: (515) 294-2025.E-mail: woi@iastate.edu Web Site:www.woi.org Licensee: Iowa State University of Science and Technology. Population served: 17,000 Natl. Network: NPR, PRI, . Format: Class, jazz, news. News staff: one; News: 41 hrs wkly. Target aud: General; educated. ♦Don Wirth, opns mgr.

KUEL(FM)— July 28, 1975: 92.1 mhz; 6 kw. Ant 321 ft TL: N42 28 44 W94 12 10. Stereo. Hrs open: Box Y, 200 N. 10th St., 50501. Phone: (515) 955-5656. Fax: (515) 955-5844. Licensee: Three Eagles of Joliet Inc. (acq 7-1-2004; grpsl). Population served: 58,000 Format: Rock. ♦Rolland C. Johnson, chmn; Jay Alexander, progmg dir; Mike Laughter, engrg dir.

KVFD(AM)— Dec 24, 1939: 1400 khz; 1 kw-U. TL: N42 28 44 W94 12 10. Hrs open: 24 Box Y, 200 N. 10th St., 50501. Phone: (515) 955-1400. Fax: (515) 955-5844. Licensee: Three Eagles of Joliet Inc. Group owner: Three Eagles Communications (acq 7-1-2004; grpsl). Population served: 135,000 Natl. Network: ABC, . Wire Svc: AP Format: Sports, news, oldies. ♦Gary Buchanan, pres; Dennis Martin, gen mgr; Jay Alexander, opns mgr; Mike Laughter, engrg VP.

KWMT(AM)— April 1956: 540 khz; 5 kw-D, 200 w-N, DA-2. TL: N42 22 94 W94 12 27. Hrs open: 540 A St., 50501. Phone: (515) 576-7333. Fax: (515) 955-4250.E-mail: info@kwmt.com Web Site:www.kwmt.com Licensee: Three Eagles of Lincoln Inc. Group owner: Clear Channel Communications Inc. (acq 9-1-2007; grpsl). Population served: 68,000 Natl. Rep: McGavren Guild,. Reddy, Begley & McCormick. Format: Country. Target aud: General. Spec prog: Farm. ♦Ron Revere, gen mgr.

Fort Madison

KBKB(AM)— Feb 6, 1948: 1360 khz; 1 kw-D, 35 w-N. TL: N40 39 30 W91 16 20. Hrs open: 18 1411 N. Roosevelt Ave., Burlington, 52601. Phone: (319) 752-2701. Fax: (319) 752-5287.E-mail: info@1360kbkb.com Web Site:www.1360kbkb.com Licensee: Pritchard Broadcasting Corp. Group owner: Clear Channel Communications Inc. (acq 6-6-2008; with KBUR(AM) Burlington). Population served: 125,000 Format: Classic country. ♦John Pritchard, gen mgr; Faith Krause, sls dir.

KBKB-FM— June 1, 1973: 101.7 mhz; 50 kw. Ant 466 ft TL: N40 43 25 W91 13 49. Stereo. Hrs open: 24 Box 70, Burlington, 52601. Secondary address: 1411 N. Roosevelt Ave., Burlington 52601. Phone: (319) 752-2701. Fax: (319) 752-5287.E-mail: info@1017thebull.com Web Site:www.1017thebull.com Licensee: GAP Broadcasting Burlington License LLC. (acq 2-13-2008; grpsl). Population served: 187,000 Natl. Network: ABC, . Format: Country. News staff: 2; News: 7 hrs wkly. ♦Kosmo Leone, progmg dir; J.K. Martin, local news ed.

Garnavillo

KCTN(FM)— Dec 6, 1982: 100.1 mhz; 3 kw. 300 ft TL: N42 53 06 W91 19 11. Stereo. Hrs open: 24 Box 990, Elkader, 52043. Phone: (563) 245-1400. Fax: (563) 245-1402.E-mail: kctn@alpinecom.net Web Site:kctn.com Licensee: KCTN-FM 100 div of Design Homes Inc. Rgnl. Network: Brownfield. Natl. Rep: Farmakis,. Brownfield Format: Country. News staff: one. Target aud: 24-55; farmers & rural communities. ♦Randy Weeks, CEO; Dan Berns, gen mgr, opns mgr; Troy Thein, chief of opns.

Glenwood

KXKT(FM)— Apr 8, 1966: 103.7 mhz; 100 kw. Ant 1,086 ft TL: N41 18 32 W96 01 33. Stereo. Hrs open: 24 5010 Underwood Ave., Omaha, NE, 68132. Phone: (402) 561-2000. Phone: (402) 962-1037. Fax: (402) 551-4315.E-mail: request@thekat.com Web Site:www.thekat.com Licensee: Capstar TX L.P. Group owner: Clear Channel Communications Inc. (acq 8-30-2000; grpsl). Population served: 1250000 Haley, Bader & Potts. Format: Country. News staff: one. Target aud: 18-54; general. ♦Donna Baker, gen mgr; Mitch Baker, opns mgr; Bill Ryan, gen sls mgr; Brandon Howell, mktg dir, prom dir; Tom Goodwin, progmg dir; Greg Gade, chief of engrg.

Grinnell

KGRN(AM)— Nov 15, 1957: 1410 khz; 500 w-D, 47 w-N. TL: N41 44 44 W92 42 36. (CP: 300 w-D, 33 w-N. TL: N41 46 35 W92 38 56). Hrs open: Box 660, 50112. Phone: (641) 236-1410. Fax: (641) 236-8896.E-mail: kgrn@iowatelecom.net Web Site:www.kgrn1410.com Licensee: Grinnell License Co. LLC. (acq 5-2-2007; $2.25 million). Population served: 55,000 Rgnl. Network: Iowa Radio Net. Natl. Rep: Farmakis,. Format: Adult Contemp. Spec prog: Farm 12 hrs, C&W 12 hrs wkly. ♦Dean Goodman, pres; Ron McCarthy, gen mgr.

KRTI(FM)— May 1993: 106.7 mhz; 50 kw. 492 ft TL: N41 48 16 W92 40 09. Hrs open: 24 Box 306, 50112. Secondary address: 1801 N. 13th Ave. E., Newton 50208. Phone: (641) 792-5262. Fax: (641) 792-8403.E-mail: info@kcobradio.com Web Site:www.energy1067.com Licensee: Newton License Co. LLC. (acq 5-1-2007; grpsl). Population served: 200,000 Format: CHR mainstream. ♦Ron McCarthy, gen mgr; Tim Graves, opns dir.

Grundy Center

KCRR(FM)— Oct 8, 1983: 97.7 mhz; 16 kw. 407 ft TL: N42 23 28 W92 13 57. Stereo. Hrs open: 24 501 Sycamore St., Suite 300 Black's Bldg., Waterloo, 50703. Phone: (319) 833-4800. Fax: (319) 833-4866.E-mail: kcrr@kcrr.com Web Site:www.kcrr.com Licensee: Cumulus Licensing Corp. Group owner: Cumulus Media Inc. (acq 3-15-00; grpsl). Population served: 168,000 Format: Classic rock. News staff: 2; News: 3 hrs wkly. Target aud: 25-54. ♦Lew Dickey, CEO; Greg Sher, gen mgr; Dick Stadlen, opns mgr.

Hampton

KLMJ(FM)— May 16, 1983: 104.9 mhz; 6 kw. 255 ft TL: N42 49 45 W93 11 10. Stereo. Hrs open: 24 Box 495, 50441. Secondary address: 1509 4th St. N.E. 50441. Phone: (641) 456-5656. Fax: (641) 456-5655.E-mail: klmj@klmj.com Web Site:www.klmj.com Licensee: C.D. Broadcasting Inc. (acq 10-93; $60,000; 10-11-93). Population served: 100,000 Natl. Network: ABC, . Rgnl. Network: Radio Iowa, Brownfield. Natl. Rep: Farmakis,. Brownfield Fletcher, Heald & Hildreth, P.L.C. Format: Adult contemp,country, oldies. News staff: 2; News: 14 hrs wkly. Target aud: 25 plus; general. Spec prog: Iowa State & Univ. of Northern Iowa, farm 8 hrs wkly. ♦Craig Donnelly, gen mgr; Marlin Burrier, opns dir.

Harlan

KNOD(FM)— Nov 12, 1979: 105.3 mhz; 25 kw. 300 ft TL: N41 37 00 W95 16 10. Stereo. Hrs open: 24 Box 723, 51537. Phone: (712) 755-3883. Fax: (712) 755-7511.E-mail: knodnews@harlannet.com Web Site:knodfm.com Licensee: Wireless Broadcasting L.L.C. (acq 5-23-02). Population served: 22,500 Rgnl. Network: Brownfield. Brownfield Format: Oldies. News staff: one; News: 5 hrs wkly. Target aud: 25-50. Spec prog: Farm 3 hrs, relg 2 hrs wkly. ♦Judy Storm, gen mgr, gen sls mgr; Richard Keane, chief of opns; Jason Dinesen, news dir.

Hiawatha

***KXGM-FM**— 2002: 89.1 mhz; 400 w vert. Ant 400 ft TL: N42 03 13 W91 44 35. Hrs open: 1450 Boyson Rd, Bldg C 3-2, 52233. Phone: (319) 378-8600. Phone: (319) 236-5700. Fax: (319) 236-8777.E-mail: studio@891thespirit.com Web Site:www.891thespirit.com Licensee: Extreme Grace Media Inc. (acq 7-18-2008; $160,000 with KXGM(AM) Waterloo). Format: Christian hit radio. ♦Michael James, stn mgr.

Hudson

KCVM(FM)— Aug 27, 1997: 96.1 mhz; 6 kw. 312 ft TL: N42 23 33 W92 30 44. Stereo. Hrs open: 24 Box 248, 721 Shirley St., Cedar Falls, 50613. Phone: (319) 277-1918. Phone: (319) 266-6499. Fax: (319) 277-5202.E-mail: radio@1650thefan.com Web Site:www.mix96.net Licensee: Fife Communications Co. L.C. Population served: 120,000 Format: Adult contemp. News staff: one; News: 2 hrs wkly. Target aud: 25-54; eastern Iowa adult females. ♦Jim Coloff, pres, gen mgr, opns VP, opns mgr; Tony Coloff, VP; Jay Rhymer, prom dir; Teri Lynn, progmg dir.

Humboldt

KHBT(FM)— Aug 5, 1970: 97.7 mhz; 5.8 kw. 275 ft TL: N42 43 57 W94 12 23. Stereo. Hrs open: 24 Box 217, 50548. Secondary address: 2196 Montana Ave. 50548. Phone: (515) 332-4100. Fax: (515) 332-2723.E-mail: thebolt@waittradio.com Licensee: NRG License Sub. LLC. (group owner; (acq 10-31-2005; grpsl). Population served: 44,500 Pepper & Corazzini. Wire Svc: AP Format: Adult contemp. News staff: one; News: 30 hrs wkly. Target aud: 30-65; general. Spec prog: Farm 10 hrs wkly. ♦Bob Ketchum, gen mgr.

Ida Grove

KKIA(FM)— September 1981: 92.9 mhz; 25 kw. Ant 328 ft TL: N42 29 23 W95 17 40. Stereo. Hrs open: 24 606 1/2 Lake Ave., Storm Lake, 50588. Secondary address: P.O. Box 108, Storm Lake 50588. Phone: (712) 732-3520. Fax: (712) 732-1746.E-mail: info@stormlakeradio.com Web Site:www.stormlakeradio.com Licensee: Jim Dandy Broadcasting Inc. (acq 1-13-2003; $2.5 million with KUYY(FM) Emmetsburg). Population served: 50,000 Natl. Network: Fox News Radio, . Natl. Rep: Farmakis,. Format: Hot country. News staff: one; News: 5 hrs wkly. Target aud: 18-54. Spec prog: Farm 10 hrs wkly. ♦Mary Quass, CEO; Chuck DuCoty, COO; Buzz Paterson, stn mgr.

Independence

KQMG(AM)— Dec 10, 1959: 1220 khz; 250 w-D, 166 w-N. TL: N42 28 34 W91 52 31. Hrs open: 1812 Third Ave. S.E., 50644. Phone: (319) 334-3300. Fax: (319) 334-6158.E-mail: vrite@indytel.com Web Site:www.lite953.com Licensee: KM Radio of Independence L.L.C. Group owner: KM Communications Inc. (acq 10-9-03; $500,000 with co-located FM). Population served: 20,000 Natl. Network: ABC, . Format: Adult contemp. ♦Noel Showers, mus dir; Rick Peters, chief of engrg.

KQMG-FM— Jan 1, 1972: 95.3 mhz; 2.9 kw. 410 ft TL: N42 28 34 W91 52 31. Stereo. Hrs open: Dups AM 90% 1812 Third Ave. S.E., 50644. Phone: (319) 334-3300. Fax: (319) 334-6158. Population served: 20,000 ♦Noel Showers, progmg dir.

Indianola

***KSTM(FM)**— Apr 15, 1994: 88.9 mhz; 100 w. 124 ft TL: N41 22 00 W93 33 57. Hrs open: Simpson College, 701 N. C St., 50125. Phone: (515) 961-1747. Phone: (515) 961-1803. Fax: (515) 961-1674.E-mail: KSTM@storm.simpson.edu Licensee: Simpson College. Format: Alt. ♦Rich Ramos, gen mgr.

KXLQ(AM)— July 22, 1963: 1490 khz; 500 w-D, 1 kw-N. TL: N41 21 24 W93 35 16. Hrs open: 21700 Northwestern Hwy., Tower 14, Suite 1190, Southfield, 48075. Phone: (248) 557-3500. Licensee: Birach Broadcasting Corp. (acq 8-1-2007; $800,000 with WCXN(AM) Claremont, NC). Rgnl. Network: Brownfield. ♦Joe Milledge, chief of engrg.

Iowa City

KCJJ(AM)— Oct 14, 1998: 1630 khz; 10 kw-D, 1 kw-N. TL: N41 36 03 W91 30 04. Stereo. Hrs open: 24 Box 2118, 52244-2118. Phone: (319) 354-1242. Fax: (319) 354-1921.E-mail: kcjjam@aol.com Web Site:www.1630kcjj.com Licensee: River City Radio Inc. (acq 9-1-94; $650,000). Population served: 125,000 Natl. Network: ABC, CBS, . Wire Svc: AP Format: Hot talk, hot hits. News staff: 4. Target aud: 25-54. ♦Tom Suter, gen mgr.

KKRQ(FM)— May 1, 1966: 100.7 mhz; 100 kw. 981 ft TL: N41 45 26 W91 31 31. Stereo. Hrs open: Prog sep from AM 3365 Dubuque St. N.E., 52240. Phone: (329) 354-9500. Fax: (319) 354-9504. Web Site:www.thesox.com Population served: 185,000 Format: Classic rock.

KRNA(FM)— Oct 4, 1974: 94.1 mhz; 100 kw. 981 ft TL: N41 45 00 W91 50 16. Stereo. Hrs open: 24 4th Floor, 425 2nd St. S.E., Cedar Rapids, 52401-1819. Phone: (319) 365-9431. Fax: (319) 363-8062.E-mail: krna@krna.com Web Site:www.krna.com Licensee: Cumulus Licensing Corp. Group owner: Cumulus Media Inc. (acq 2000; grpsl). Population served: 202,800 Natl. Rep: Christal,. Dow, Lohnes & Albertson. Format: Active Rock. Target aud: 18-49. ♦Greg Sher, gen mgr, mktg mgr; Gregg Scharnau, progmg dir.

***KRUI-FM**— Mar 28, 1984: 89.7 mhz; 100 w. 90 ft TL: N41 39 29 W91 32 40. Stereo. Hrs open: 24 379 Iowa Memorial Union, 52242. Phone: (319) 335-9525. Fax: (319) 335-9526.E-mail: krui@uiowa.edu Web Site:www.uiowa.edu/~krui Licensee: Student Broadcasters Inc. Population served: 60,000 Format: Div, educ, progsv. News: 7 hrs wkly. Target aud: 18-34; Univ. ♦Brian Anstey, prom dir; Nate George, progmg dir; Bill Penisten, news dir; Aaron Roemig, pub affrs dir; Adam Erickson, chief of engrg; Rick Oswavay, news rptr; Ryal Brier, sports cmtr.

***KSUI(FM)**— 1948: 91.7 mhz; 100 kw. 1,292 ft TL: N41 43 15 W91 20 30. Hrs open: 710 S. Clinton St. Bldg., Univ . of Iowa, 52242. Phone: (319) 335-5730. Fax: (319) 335-6116. Web Site:ksui.uiowa.edu Format: Fine arts, class. ♦Joan Kjaer, progmg dir; Jim Davies, engrg dir, disc jockey.

KXIC(AM)— June 7, 1948: 800 khz; 1 kw-D, 199 w-N, DA-2. TL: N41 41 15 W91 32 39. Hrs open: 3365 Dubuque St. N.E., 52240-7970. Phone: (319) 354-9500. Fax: (319) 354-9504. Web Site:www.kxic.com Licensee: Citicasters Licenses L.P. Group owner: Clear Channel Communications Inc. (acq 5-4-99; grpsl). Population served: 81,000 Format: News & info. ♦John Laton, gen mgr; Roy Justis, news dir.

***WSUI(AM)**— 1919: 910 khz; 5 kw-U, DA-N. TL: N41 39 45 W91 34 30. Hrs open: 710 S. Clinton St. Bldg., Univ. of Iowa, 52242-1030. Phone: (319) 335-5730. Fax: (319) 335-6116.E-mail: wsui@uiowa.edu Web Site:wsui.uiowa.edu Licensee: The University of Iowa. Population served: 46,850 Natl. Network: NPR, . Format: News/talk. ♦John Monick, gen mgr; Dennis Reese, progmg dir; Jim Davis, chief of engrg.

Iowa Falls

KIFG(AM)— July 22, 1962: 1510 khz; 1 kw-D, 500 w-CH. TL: N42 30 49 W93 12 57. Hrs open: 406 Stevens St., 50126. Phone: (641) 648-4281. Phone: (641) 648-4282. Fax: (641) 648-4606.E-mail: kifg@iafalls.com Web Site:www.kifgradio.com Licensee: Times-Citizen Communications Inc. (acq 9-99; $320,000 with co-located FM). Population served: 40,000 Natl. Network: CNN Radio, Westwood One, . Rgnl. Network: Westwood One, CNN. Natl. Rep: Keystone (unwired net),. Reddy, Begley & McCormick. Format: Adult contemp. News staff: one. Target aud: 25 plus. Spec prog: Farm 5 hrs wkly. ♦T.J. Norman, gen mgr & progmg dir.

KIFG-FM— Oct 1, 1965: 95.3 mhz; 6 kw. Ant 194 ft TL: N42 30 49 W93 12 57. Stereo. Hrs open: 24 406 Stevens St., 50126. Phone: (641) 648-4281. Phone: (641) 648-4282. Fax: (641) 648-4606.E-mail: kifg@iafalls.com Web Site:www.kifgradio.com Licensee: Times-Citizen Communications Inc. Format: Sports, news, weather. News staff: one. ♦Ann Denholm, prom dir, prom mgr; Pat Dunn, disc jockey.

Jefferson

KGRA(FM)— Oct 1, 1981: 98.9 mhz; 11 kw. Ant 499 ft TL: N42 00 59 W94 22 26. Stereo. Hrs open: 24 2260 141st St., Perry, 50220-0022. Phone: (515) 465-5357. Fax: (515) 465-3952.E-mail: kg98@netins.net Licensee: Coon Valley Communications (acq 1-19-94; 3-28-94). Natl. Network: ABC, . Format: Classic Rock. News staff: one; News: 9 hrs wkly. Target aud: 25-49; Adults. ♦Patrick Delaney, pres, CFO, sls dir, chief of engrg; Sue Thomsen, stn mgr; Linda Hass, opns mgr.

Keokuk

***KMDY(FM)**— 2001: 90.9 mhz; 7.7 kw. Ant 197 ft TL: N40 30 41 W91 19 50. Hrs open: 521 Main St, Carthage, IL, 62321. Phone: (217) 357-3000. Fax: (217) 357-3001.E-mail: info@kmdyfm.com Licensee: Cornerstone Community Radio Inc. (group owner) (acq 2-23-2006). Natl. Network: Moody, . Format: Christian. ♦Robert Neff, VP.

KOKX(AM)— Oct 19, 1947: 1310 khz; 1 kw-D, 500 w-N, DA-N. TL: N40 22 50 W91 21 09. Hrs open: 24 Box 427, 108 Washington St., 52632. Phone: (319) 524-5410. Fax: (319) 524-7275.E-mail: krnq963@imchsi.com Licensee: Withers Broadcasting of Iowa. Group owner: Withers Broadcasting Co. (acq 7-15-81; $900,000 with co-located FM; 7-13-81). Population served: 100,000 Format: Adult standards, news/talk, sports. News staff: 2; News: 25 hrs wkly. Target aud: 25-54. Spec prog: Farm 6 hrs wkly. ♦W. Russell Withers Jr., pres; Gary M. Folluo, gen mgr, opns mgr, adv mgr; Dan Workman, progmg dir; Preston Hamtpon, news dir; Bill Reed, sports cmtr.

KOKX-FM— Jan 30, 1973: 95.3 mhz; 100 kw. Ant 804 ft TL: N40 24 01 W91 35 09. Stereo. Hrs open: 24 Box108, 52632. Secondary address: 108 Washington St. 52632. Phone: (319) 524-5410. Fax: (319) 524-7275.E-mail: krnq963@mchfi.com Population served: 190,000 Natl. Network: ABC, . Format: Var/div. News staff: 2; News: 4 hrs wkly. Target aud: 25-54; women 50% men 50%. ♦Jim Worrell, news dir, news rptr; Judy Hall, traf mgr; Robert Bertram, sports cmtr.

KRNQ(FM)— 1999: 96.3 mhz; 19 kw. Ant 804 ft TL: N40 24 01 W91 35 09. Stereo. Hrs open: 24/7 108 Washington St., P.O. Box 427, 52632. Phone: (319) 524-1111. Fax: (319) 524-7275.E-mail: krnq963@imchsi.com Web Site:keokukradio.com Licensee: David M. Lister. Gary M. Folluo, (319) 524-5410; gmkokx@mchsi.com Population served: 100,000 Format: Classic rock. Target aud: 18-45; 50/50 male, female. Spec prog: Local Sports. ♦Gary M. Folluo, gen mgr; Dan Workman, opns dir, progmg dir; Gary Folluo, gen sls mgr; Preston Hampton, news dir.

Knoxville

KNIA(AM)— Aug 30, 1960: 1320 khz; 500 w-D, 222 w-N. TL: N41 19 40 W93 06 34. Hrs open: 24 Box 31, 50138. Secondary address: 1610 N. Lincoln 50138. Phone: (641) 842-3161. Fax: (641) 842-5606.E-mail: kniaakrls@kniakrls.com Web Site:www.kniakrls.com Licensee: M & H Broadcasting Inc. (acq 2-23-93; $768,000 with co-located FM; 3-15-93). Population served: 7,755 Radio Iowa Format: Real country. News staff: 3; News: 25 hrs wkly. Target aud: 25-54; female. Spec prog: Relg 18 hrs wkly. ♦Jim Butler, gen mgr.

KRLS(FM)— July 16, 1973: 92.1 mhz; 15 kw. 300 ft TL: N41 21 40 W93 00 15. (CP: 15.5 kw, ant 308 ft.). Stereo. Hrs open: 24 Box 31, 50138. Secondary address: 1610 N. Lincoln 50138. Phone: (641) 842-3161. Fax: (641) 842-5606. Web Site:kniakrls.com Population served: 38,800 Wire Svc: AP Format: Adult contemp. News staff: 3; News: 25 hrs wkly. Target aud: 25-54; primarily female.

Lake City

KIKD(FM)— 1997: 106.7 mhz; 25 kw. 328 ft TL: N42 07 14 W94 48 49. Hrs open: 24 Box 886, Carroll, 51401-0886. Secondary address: 1119 East Plaza Dr., Carroll 51401. Phone: (712) 792-4321. Fax: (712) 792-6667.E-mail: kikd@carrollbroadcasting.com Web Site:carrollbroadcasting.com Licensee: Carroll Broadcasting Co. (group owner; acq 1999; $975,000). Population served: 85,000 Natl. Rep: Katz Radio,. Womble, Carlyle, Sandridge & Rice. Format: Country. News: 2. Target aud: 18-49; contemp country with strong families. Spec prog: Sports. ♦Mary Collison, pres; Kim Hackett, gen mgr; John Ryan, opns mgr; Lynda Dukes-Francy, gen sls mgr.

Lamoni

***KOWI(FM)**— 2000: 97.9 mhz; 50 kw. Ant 492 ft TL: N40 48 52 W93 50 15. Stereo. Hrs open: 24
WOI-AM.
WOI Radio Group, 2022 Communications Bldg., Iowa State University, Ames, 50011-3241. Phone: (515) 294-2025. Fax: (515) 294-1544.E-mail: woi@iastate.edu Web Site:www.woi.org Licensee: Iowa State University of Science and Technology (acq 7-30-2004; $450,000). Natl. Network: NPR, PRI, . Format: Class, news. News: 40 hrs wkly. Target aud: General; Educated.

Le Mars

KKMA(FM)— Jan 1, 1967: 99.5 mhz; 100 kw. 790 ft TL: N42 28 56 W96 15 30. Stereo. Hrs open: Prog sep from AM 2000 Indian Hills Dr., Sioux City, 51104. Phone: (712) 239-2100. Fax: (712) 239-3346. Web Site:www.kool995.com Population served: 285,000 Format: Oldies, classic hits. ♦Dennis Bullock, gen mgr, rgnl sls mgr; Kelli Erickson, gen sls mgr; Scott McKenzie, progmg dir; Stan Culley, chief of engrg; Christi Rush, traf mgr; Justin Barker, disc jockey.

KLEM(AM)— Oct 12, 1954: 1410 khz; 1 kw-D, 63 w-N. TL: N42 49 05 W96 10 00. Hrs open: 24 37 2nd Ave. N.W., 51031. Phone: (712) 546-4121. Fax: (712) 546-9672.E-mail: klem@lemarscomm.net Web Site:www.klem1410.com Licensee: Powell Broadcasting Co Inc. (acq 7-6-99; with co-located FM). Population served: 15,000 Format: Adult contemp, news, sports. News staff: 2. Spec prog: Farm 18 hrs wkly. ♦Tom Spies, pres; Dennis Bullock, gen mgr; Dave Grosenheider, stn mgr, gen sls mgr; Dave Ruden, progmg dir, women's int ed, disc jockey; Larry Schmitz, news dir, farm dir; Stan Culley, chief of engrg; Christi Rush, traf mgr; Joanne Glamm, reporter; Corey Pithan, disc jockey.

Madrid

KNWM(FM)— Aug. 21, 1997: 96.1 mhz; 2.5 kw. Ant 515 ft TL: N41 58 49 W93 44 23. Hrs open: 24 3737 Woodland Ave., Suite 111, Des Moines, 50366. Phone: (515) 327-1071. Fax: (515) 327-1073.E-mail: knwi@desmoines.fm Web Site:www.desmoines.fm Licensee: Northwestern College. Group owner: Northwestern College & Radio (acq 12-30-2003; $1.8 million with KNWI(FM) Osceola). Population served: 257,000 Format: Christian. ♦Richard Whitworth, gen mgr; Dave St. John, progmg dir.

Manchester

KMCH(FM)— Dec 5, 1991: 94.7 mhz; 6 kw. Ant 328 ft TL: N42 31 42 W91 22 53. Stereo. Hrs open: 24 Box 497, 212 E. Main St., 52057. Phone: (563) 927-6249. Fax: (563) 927-4372.E-mail: kmchradio@iowatelecom.net Web Site:www.kmch.com Licensee: Coloff Media LLC. Population served: 65,580 Natl. Network: CBS, . Format: Adult contemp, C&W. News staff: one; News: 20 hrs wkly. Target aud: 25-64; northeast Iowa adults & farm population. Spec prog: Farm 7 hrs, sports 7 hrs, relg 4 hrs wkly. ♦Anthony G. Coloff, pres; James A. Coloff, VP, gen mgr; Jackie Coates, stn mgr; Mike Johnson, opns mgr.

Manson

KXFT(FM)— 2007: 99.7 mhz; 25 kw. Ant 285 ft TL: N42 31 03 W94 20 43. Hrs open: 540 A St., Fort Dodge, 50501. Phone: (515) 576-7333. Fax: (515) 955-4250.E-mail: kkez@clearchannel.com Licensee: Three Eagles of Lincoln Inc. (acq 9-1-2007; grpsl). Format: CHR. ♦Tracey Williams, gen mgr.

Maquoketa

KMAQ(AM)— Aug 26, 1958: 1320 khz; 500 w-U. TL: N42 05 26 W90 37 43. Hrs open: 6 AM-10 PM Box 940, 129 N. Main St., 52060. Phone: (563) 652-2426. Fax: (563) 652-6210. Web Site:www.kmaq.com Licensee: Maquoketa Broadcasting Co. (acq 1965). Population served: 40,000 Natl. Network: CNN Radio, . Rgnl. Network: Brownfield, Radio Iowa. Natl. Rep: Farmakis,. Radio Iowa Miller & Fields, P.C. Format: C&W. News staff: one; News: 28 hrs wkly. Target aud: General; adults, high percentage of farmers. Spec prog: Farm 10 hrs, polka 3 hrs wkly. ♦Dennis W. Voy, pres, gen mgr, progmg dir; Leighton Hepker, opns dir, sls dir; Tom Messerli, chief of engrg.

KMAQ-FM— Sept 1, 1967: 95.1 mhz; 6 kw. 328 ft TL: N42 05 26 W90 37 43. Stereo. Hrs open: Prog sep from AM Box 940, 129 N. Main St., 52060. Phone: (563) 652-2426. Fax: (563) 652-6210. Web Site:www.kmaq.com Population served: 45,000 Natl. Network: CNN Radio, . Radio Iowa Wire Svc: AP Format: Adult Comt. News staff: one; News: 28 hrs wkly. ♦Dennis Voy, gen mgr; Leighton Hepker, stn mgr, gen sls mgr; Tom Messerli, chief of engrg.

Marion

***KZNJ(FM)**—Not on air, target date: unknown: 89.9 mhz; 1.1 kw. Ant 216 ft TL: N42 06 24 W91 42 05. Hrs open: University of Northern Iowa, 324 Communications Arts Center, Cedar Falls, 50614-0359. Phone: (319) 273-6400. Fax: (319) 273-2682. Licensee: University of Northern Iowa. ♦Wayne Jarvis, gen mgr.

Marshalltown

KDAO(AM)— Dec 16, 1978: 1190 khz; 250 w-D, 20 w-N. TL: N42 04 17 W92 55 19. Hrs open: 24 P.O. Box 538, 1930 N. Center St., 50158. Phone: (641) 752-4122. Fax: (641) 752-5121.E-mail: kdao@kdao.com Web Site:www.kdao.com Licensee: MTN Broadcasting Inc. Format: Adult standards. Target aud: 25-54. ♦Mark K. Osmundson, gen mgr. Co-owned TV: KDAO-TV affil

KFJB(AM)— June 1923: 1230 khz; 1 kw-U. TL: N42 04 01 W92 58 10. Hrs open: 24 Box 698, 123 W. Main St., 50158. Phone: (641) 753-3361. Fax: (641) 752-7201.E-mail: office@marshalltownbroadcasting.com Web Site:www.1230kfjb.com Licensee: Marshalltown Broadcasting Inc. (acq 12-29-86). Population served: 120,000 Natl. Network: ABC, . Rgnl. Network: Brownfield. Natl. Rep: Katz Radio,. Brownfield Wire Svc: AP Format: News/talk. News staff: 2; News: 12 hrs wkly. Target aud: 35-64. ♦David L. Nelson, pres; Clark L. Wideman, gen mgr; Kyle Martin, progmg dir.

***KRFH(FM)**—Not on air, target date: unknown: 88.7 mhz; 8.3 kw. Ant 95 ft TL: N42 04 17 W92 55 19. Hrs open: Box 538, 50158. Phone: (641) 752-4122. Licensee: Marshalltown Education Plus Inc.

KXIA(FM)— January 1968: 101.1 mhz; 100 kw. Ant 649 ft TL: N42 00 19 W92 55 45. Stereo. Hrs open: 24 Box 698, 50158. Secondary address: 123 W. Main St. 50158. Phone: (641) 753-3361. Fax: (641) 752-7201.E-mail: office@marshalltownbroadcasting.com Web Site:www.kixweb.com Licensee: Marshalltown Broadcasting Inc. Population served: 700,000 Natl. Network: ABC, . Rgnl. Network: Brownfield. Natl. Rep: Katz Radio,. Brownfield Wire Svc: AP Format: Country. News staff: 2; News: 6 hrs wkly. Target aud: 25-54. ♦Todd Collins, progmg dir.

Mason City

***KBDC(FM)**— 2001: 88.5 mhz; 1.8 kw vert. Ant 230 ft TL: N43 03 35 W93 22 47. Hrs open: Box 3206, American Family Radio, Tupelo, MS, 38803. Phone: (662) 844-8888, EXT. 204. Fax: (662) 842-6791. Licensee: American Family Association. Group owner: American Family Radio Format: Adult contemp. ♦Marvin Sanders, gen mgr.

***KCMR(FM)**— May 3, 1979: 97.9 mhz; 6 kw. 300 ft TL: N43 07 18 W93 11 32. (CP: Ant 315 ft.). Stereo. Hrs open: 24 Box 979, 50402-0979. Secondary address: 600 First St. N.W. 50401. Phone: (641) 424-9300. Fax: (641) 423-2221.E-mail: kcmr@kcmronline.org Licensee: TLC Broadcasting Corp. (acq 5-24-2004). Population served: 35,000 Format: Easy lstng, inspirational. Target aud: Over 30. Spec prog: Class 5 hrs, nostalgia 10 hrs wkly. ♦Bill Schickel, gen mgr; Bob Miller, dev dir.

***KDVO(FM)**—Not on air, target date: unknown: 90.7 mhz; 650 w horiz, 14 kw vert. Ant 294 ft TL: N43 09 17 W93 30 23. Hrs open: 324 Communications Arts Center, University of Northern Iowa, Cedar Falls, 50614-0359. Phone: (319) 273-6400. Fax: (319) 273-2682. Web Site:www.khke.org Licensee: University of Northern Iowa. ♦Wayne Jarvis, gen mgr.

KGLO(AM)— Jan 17, 1937: 1300 khz; 5 kw-U, DA-2. TL: N43 03 15 W93 12 17. Hrs open: Box 1300, 341 Yorktown Pike, 50401. Phone: (641) 423-1300. Fax: (641) 423-2906.E-mail: tfleming@kglo.theeeagles.com Web Site:www.kgloam.com Licensee: Three Eagles of Lincoln Inc. Group owner: Clear Channel Communications Inc. (acq 9-1-2007; grpsl). Population served: 110,000 Natl. Network: CBS, . Format: Talk. News staff: 3. Target aud: 25-35; adults. Spec prog: Farm 15 hrs wkly. ♦Tim Fleming, opns dir & progmg dir; Mark Dorenkamp, farm dir.

KIAI(FM)— November 1985: 93.9 mhz; 100 kw. Ant 790 ft TL: N43 10 04 W93 06 05. Stereo. Hrs open: Box 1300, 50401. Secondary address: 341 Yorktown Pike 50401. Phone: (641) 423-1300. Fax: (641) 423-2906.E-mail: wbowers@masoncity.threeeagles.com Web Site:www.kiaifm.com Licensee: Three Eagles of Lincoln Inc. Format: Country. News: 2 hrs wkly. Target aud: 24-54. ♦Walt Bowers, progmg dir & mus dir.

KLSS-FM— Nov 1, 1967: 106.1 mhz; 100 kw. Ant 315 ft TL: N43 08 31 W93 06 40. Stereo. Hrs open: 341 S Yorktown Pike, 50401. Phone: (641) 423-8634. Fax: (641) 423-8206.E-mail: klss@klssradio.com

Web Site:www.klssradio.com Licensee: Three Eagles of Mason City Inc. Population served: 240,000 Natl. Network: ABC, . Format: Adult contemp. Target aud: 18-54. ♦John Swinton, opns mgr, disc jockey; Pam Dzick, gen sls mgr; Harry O'Neil, mus dir, disc jockey; Brenda McWhorter, traf mgr; Brian Wilson, news rptr; Colleen Devine, disc jockey.

KRIB(AM)— April 1948: 1490 khz; 1 kw-U. TL: N43 08 05 W93 12 30. Stereo. Hrs open: 24 341 S Yorktown Pike, 50401. Phone: (641) 423-8634. Fax: (641) 423-8206.E-mail: klss@klssradio.com Web Site:www.kribradio.com Licensee: Three Eagles of Mason City Inc. Group owner: Three Eagles Communications (acq 5-2-97; $3.596 million with co-located FM). Population served: 150,000 Rgnl. Network: Iowa Radio Net. Natl. Rep: McGavren Guild,. Format: Adult standards, oldies. News staff: 2; News: 25 hrs wkly. Target aud: 35 plus; married up-scale adults, financially secure with two incomes or retired. Spec prog: Relg 5 hrs wkly. ♦Gary Buchanan, pres; Dalena Barz, gen mgr, natl sls mgr; John Swinton, progmg dir; Bob Fisher, news dir; Christi Lyman, pub affrs dir; Ron Schacts, chief of engrg.

***KRNI(AM)—** Mar 1, 1948: 1010 khz; 1 kw-D, 16 w-N. TL: N43 08 31 W93 06 40. Hrs open: Sunrise-sunset
Rebroadcasts KUNI(FM) Cedar Falls 100%.
c/o KUNI-FM, Univ. of Northern Iowa, Cedar Falls, 50614-0359. Phone: (319) 273-6400. Fax: (319) 273-2682.E-mail: kuni@uni.edu Web Site:www.kuniradio.org Licensee: University of Northern Iowa. (acq 10-30-98; grpsl). Population served: 40,000 Natl. Network: PRI, NPR, . Format: News & info, AAA. News staff: 3; News: 77 hrs wkly. Target aud: General. Spec prog: Folk 4 hrs, blues 5 hrs wkly. ♦Scott Vezdan, mktg dir; Wayne Jarvis, gen mgr & progmg dir; Al Schares, mus dir, disc jockey; Greg Shanley, news dir, news rptr; Steve Schoon, engrg dir; Tony Dehner, traf mgr; Jeneane Beck, local news ed; Pat Blank, reporter; Bob Dorr, disc jockey.

***KUNY(FM)—** Dec 15, 1987: 91.5 mhz; 8 kw vert. 371 ft TL: N43 09 27 W93 08 11. Stereo. Hrs open: 24 Dups AM 100%
Rebroadcast KUNI (FM) Cedar Falls 100%.
c/o KUNI-FM, Univ. of Northern Iowa, Cedar Falls, 50614. Phone: (319) 273-6400. Fax: (319) 273-2682.E-mail: kuni@uni.edu Web Site:www.kuniradio.org Natl. Network: PRI, NPR, . News staff: 3; News: 77 hrs wkly.

Milford

KUQQ(FM)—Licensed to Milford. See Spirit Lake

Mitchellville

***KDMR(FM)—**Not on air, target date: unknown: 88.9 mhz; 1 kw. Ant 236 ft TL: N41 40 05 W93 19 43. Hrs open:
KUNI-FM,Cedar Falls, IA.
University of Northern Iowa, 324 Communications Arts Center, Cedar Falls, 50614. Phone: (319) 273-6400. Fax: (319) 273-2682.E-mail: kuni@uni.edu Web Site:www.kuniradio.org Licensee: University of Northern Iowa. Format: News and Information, Triple A. News staff: 3; News: 77 hrs. Spec prog: Folk 4hrs, Blues 5 hrs. ♦Scott Vezdos, mktg mgr; Wayne Jarvis, gen mgr & progmg dir; Al Schares, mus dir; Greg Shanley, news dir; Steve Schoon, chief of engrg.

Montezuma

***KRNF(FM)—**Not on air, target date: unknown: 89.7 mhz; 2.35 kw. Ant 371 ft TL: N41 43 55 W92 34 01. Hrs open: 812 1/2 Main St., Pella, 50219. Phone: (641) 780-0017. Licensee: American Radio Missions Foundation. ♦Doug Smiley, gen mgr.

Mount Pleasant

KILJ(AM)— December 1974: 1130 khz; 250 w-D. TL: N40 57 32 W91 35 01. Hrs open: 24 2411 Radio Dr., 52641. Phone: (319) 385-8728. Fax: (319) 385-4517.E-mail: kilj@iowatelecom.net Web Site:www.kilj.com Licensee: KILJ Inc. (acq 10-29-2003; $1.01 million with co-located FM). Population served: 60,000 Natl. Network: ABC, . Radio Iowa Format: Country. News staff: one. ♦John R. Kuhens, gen mgr, stn mgr, sls dir, progmg dir; Paul Dennison, gen sls mgr; Bob Maltocks, news dir; Leo Septen, chief of engrg; Lora Roth, traf mgr.

KILJ-FM— October 1970: 105.5 mhz; 24 kw. Ant 338 ft TL: N40 56 55 W91 33 55. Stereo. Hrs open: 24 2411 Radio Dr., 52641. Phone: (319) 385-8728. Fax: (319) 385-4517. Web Site:www.kilj.com Licensee: KILJ Inc. Rgnl. Network: Brownfield, Radio Iowa. Radio Iowa Format: Smooth sounds. News staff: one. Target aud: 25-54. ♦John Kuhens, gen mgr, disc jockey; Lori Roth, traf mgr & disc jockey.

Mount Vernon

***KRNL-FM—** Apr 1, 1948: 89.7 mhz; 36 w. 167 ft TL: N41 55 24 W91 25 18. Stereo. Hrs open: Midnight-noon 810 Commons Cir., 52314. Phone: (319) 895-4431. Phone: (319) 895-5765.E-mail: krnl@cornellcollege.edu Web Site:www.cornellcollege.edu/krnl Licensee: Cornell College. Population served: 100,000 Natl. Network: USA, . Format: Free-form, progsv. Target aud: 18-25; collegians & those seeking an alternative to coml radio. Spec prog: Folk 2 hrs, Ger 2 hrs, jazz 2 hrs, Sp one hr wkly. ♦Sarah Altmann, gen mgr; Robin Schwab, stn mgr.

Muscatine

KBEA-FM—Licensed to Muscatine. See Davenport

KMCS(FM)— June 16, 1996: 93.1 mhz; 4.4 kw. Ant 384 ft TL: N41 26 34 W91 04 33. Stereo. Hrs open: 24 Prog sep from AM 3218 Mulberry Ave., 52761. Phone: (563) 263-2442. Fax: (563) 263-9206.E-mail: mail@voiceofmuscatine.com Natl. Network: USA, AP Radio, . Format: Country. News: 6 hrs wkly. Target aud: 25-54.

KWPC(AM)— Jan 5, 1947: 860 khz; 250 w-D, 8 w-N. TL: N41 26 43 W91 04 36. Stereo. Hrs open: 24 3218 Mulberry Ave., 52761. Phone: (563) 263-2442. Fax: (563) 263-9206.E-mail: mail@voiceofmuscatine.com Web Site:www.voiceofmuscatine.com Licensee: WPW Broadcasting Inc. (group owner; (acq 11-5-99; $2.2 million with co-located FM). Population served: 63,405 Natl. Network: USA, . Fletcher, Heald & Hildreth. Format: Oldies. News staff: 2; News: 20 hrs wkly. Target aud: 25-54. ♦Don Davis, pres, mus dir; Terri Forbes, CFO; DeWayne Hopkins, gen mgr.

New Hampton

KCZE(FM)— Dec 1, 1992: 95.1 mhz; 5.5 kw. 328 ft TL: N43 02 46 W92 18 09. Stereo. Hrs open: 207 N. Main St., Charles City, 50616. Phone: (641) 228-1000. Fax: (641) 228-1200.E-mail: A chrisberg@northiowabroadcasting.com Web Site:www.951thebull.com Licensee: Coloff Media LLC. Group owner: Clear Channel Communications Inc. (acq 9-1-2007; grpsl). Population served: 200,000 Natl. Rep: Farmakis,. Format: Country. Target aud: General. Spec prog: Farm 12 hrs wkly. ♦Hal Hofman, gen mgr; J. Brooks, opns mgr, progmg dir; Tami Ramon, mktg dir; Patrick Gwin, chief of engrg.

New London

KHDK(FM)— Oct 5, 2001: 97.3 mhz; 3.8 kw. Ant 410 ft TL: N40 47 53 W91 26 22. Stereo. Hrs open: 24 610 N. 4th St., Suite 300, Burlington, 52601. Phone: (319) 752-5402. Fax: (319) 752-4715.E-mail: johnp@burlingtonradio.com Web Site:hot973online.com Licensee: Pritchard Broadcasting Corp. (acq 12-27-99; $25,000 for CP). Population served: 147,800 Natl. Rep: Katz Radio,. Format: Top 40. News staff: one; News: 1 hrs wkly. Target aud: 25-54. ♦John T. Pritchard, pres, gen mgr; Joe Bates, opns mgr; Chet Young, gen sls mgr; Tim Bayless, progmg dir.

New Sharon

KCWN(FM)— Oct 16, 1995: 99.9 mhz; 25 kw. 297 ft Hrs open: 6 AM-11 PM Box 999, Pella, 50219. Secondary address: 304 Oskaloosa St., Pella 50219. Phone: (641) 628-9999. Phone: (888) 506-4562. Fax: (641) 628-9229.E-mail: kcwnfm@lisco.com Web Site:www.kcwnfm.org Licensee: Crown Broadcasting Co. Format: Adult contemp Christian. ♦Marion L. Vink, CEO, pres & gen mgr; Beverly DeVries, stn mgr.

Newell

KWDN(FM)—Not on air, target date: unknown: 100.9 mhz; 6 kw. Ant 292 ft TL: N42 38 43 W95 10 33. Hrs open: 5331 Mt. Alifan Dr., San Diego, CA, 92111. Phone: (858) 277-4991. Fax: (858) 277-1365. Licensee: Horizon Christian Fellowship. (acq 2-9-2006; grpsl). ♦Mike MacIntosh, pres.

Newton

KCOB(AM)— Sept 15, 1955: 1280 khz; 1 kw-D, 500 w-N. TL: N40 44 11 W93 01 12. Hrs open: Box 66, 1801 N. 13th Ave. E., 50208. Phone: (641) 792-5262. Fax: (641) 792-8403.E-mail: info@kcobradio.com Web Site:kcobradio.com Licensee: Newton License Co. LLC. (acq 5-1-2007; grpsl). Population served: 15,619 Format: Country, news. Target aud: 25-50. Spec prog: Farm 2 hrs wkly. ♦Dean Goodman, CEO, pres; Ron McCarthy, gen mgr, gen sls mgr; Terry Walter, progmg dir; Randy Van, news dir; Phil Benjamin, chief of engrg.

KCOB-FM— Jan 3, 1969: 95.9 mhz; 5.1 kw. Ant 354 ft TL: N41 44 11 W93 01 12. Stereo. Hrs open: 18 Dups AM 100% Box 66, 50208. Phone: (641) 792-5262. Fax: (641) 792-8403.E-mail: info@kcobradio.com Web Site:kcobradio.com Licensee: Newton License Co. LLC. Population served: 15,619

***KKLG(FM)—** 2005: 88.3 mhz; 400 w. Ant 218 ft TL: N41 41 33 W93 00 37. Hrs open:
Rebroadcasts KLVR(FM) Santa Rosa, CA 100%.
2351 Sunset Blvd., Suite 170-218, Rocklin, CA, 95765. Phone: (916) 251-1600. Fax: (916) 251-1650. Web Site:www.klove.com Licensee: Educational Media Foundation. (acq 9-22-2005; $20,000 for CP). Natl. Network: K-Love, . Format: Contemp Christian. ♦Richard Jenkins, pres; Mike Novak, VP; Keith Whipple, dev dir; David Pierce, progmg mgr; Ed Lenane, news dir; Sam Wallington, engrg dir; Karen Johnson, news rptr.

Northwood

KYTC(FM)— Oct 15, 1990: 102.7 mhz; 25 kw. Ant 318 ft TL: N43 29 18 W93 14 12. Stereo. Hrs open: 24 341 S Yorktown Pike, Mason City, 50401. Phone: (800) 598-2858. Phone: (641) 423-8634. Fax: (641) 423-8206.E-mail: klss@klssradio.com Web Site:www.kytcradio.com Licensee: Three Eagles of Mason City Inc. Group owner: Three Eagles Communications (acq 5-21-99). Population served: 75,000 Rgnl. Network: Tribune. Tribune Radio Networks Format: Rock. News staff: one; News: 6 hrs wkly. Target aud: 25-64; primary audience men & women 35+. Spec prog: Gospel one hr, relg 2 hrs wkly. ♦Rolland Johnson, CEO; Gary Buchanan, pres; Dalena Barz, gen mgr, stn mgr; Henry O'Neil, chief of opns.

Oelwein

KKHQ-FM— Dec 29, 1971: 92.3 mhz; 100 kw. 1,000 ft TL: N42 40 53 W91 52 52. (CP: 95.3 mhz, ant 991 ft.). Stereo. Hrs open: 24 Prog sep from AM Box 720, Blacks Bldg., 501 Sycamore St., Waterloo, 50703. Phone: (319) 833-4800. Phone: (800) 923-5635. Fax: (319) 833-4866. Population served: 150,000 Format: Country. News staff: one; News: 2 hrs wkly. Target aud: 35 plus. ♦Mark Anderson, gen sls mgr; April Walker, prom dir, mus dir; Bill Knight, progmg mgr; Elwin Huffman, news dir; Wes Davis, chief of engrg.

KOEL(AM)— July 23, 1950: 950 khz; 5 kw-D, 500 w-N, DA-2. TL: N42 39 26 W91 54 02. Hrs open: 24 2502 S. Frederick, 50662. Phone: (319) 283-1234. Fax: (319) 283-3615.E-mail: koelam@koel.com Licensee: Cumulus Licensing Corp. Group owner: Cumulus Media Inc. (acq 3-15-00; grpsl). Population served: 180,000 Format: News/talk, sports. News staff: 2; News: 30 hrs wkly. Target aud: 35 plus. Spec prog: Farm 16 hrs wkly.Jeffrey D. Warshaw, pres; Jeff Dientz, VP; Rob Murthum, gen mgr, mktg mgr; Dick Stadlen, opns mgr; Craig Friedrich, gen sls mgr; Bob Fisher, natl sls mgr; April Walker, prom mgr; Rich Calvert, progmg dir, progmg mgr, disc jockey; Matt Kelly, mus dir; Roger King, news dir, pub affrs dir, disc jockey; Arnold Zaruba, chief of engrg; Traci Berry, traf mgr; Mark Barber, farm dir, disc jockey

Okoboji

***KOJI(FM)—** 2002: 90.7 mhz; 4.5 kw. Ant 371 ft TL: N43 09 53 W95 19 29. Hrs open: 24
Rebroadcasts KWIT(FM) Sioux City 100%.
4647 Stone Ave., Sioux City, 51106-1997. Phone: (712) 274-6406. Fax: (712) 274-6411.E-mail: gondekg@witcc.edu Web Site:www.kwit-koji.org Licensee: Western Iowa Tech Community College. Natl. Network: NPR, PRI, . Wire Svc: AP Format: Class, news/talk, Sp. News staff: one; News: 36 hrs wkly. Spec prog: Triple A 18 hrs, blues 4 hrs, jazz 17 hrs wkly. ♦Gretchen Gondek, gen mgr; Steve Smith, opns mgr.

Onawa

KZSR(FM)— Nov 6, 1995: 102.3 mhz; 100 kw. Ant 643 ft TL: N42 10 29 W96 23 13. Hrs open: 24 2000 Indian Hills Dr., Sioux City, 51104. Phone: (712) 239-2100. Fax: (712) 239-3346. Web Site:www.jackfm1023.com Licensee: Powell Broadcasting Co. Inc. (acq 5-1-2007; $4.2 million with KKYY(FM) Whiting). Population served: 200,000 Format: Var. News: One. Target aud: 25-54. ♦Dennis Bullock, gen mgr.

Osage

KSMA-FM— July 9, 1980: 98.7 mhz; 25 kw. Ant 328 ft TL: N43 21 53 W93 02 53. Stereo. Hrs open: 341 Yorktown Pike, Mason City, 50401. Phone: (641) 423-1300. Fax: (641) 423-2906. Web Site:www.kiss987.com Licensee: Coloff Media LLC Group owner: Clear Channel Communications Inc. (acq 9-1-2007; grpsl). Population served: 190,000 Natl. Rep: Farmakis,. Format: Adult contemp, CHR. Target aud: General; 12-25.

◆Hal Hofman, gen mgr, gen sls mgr; Tim Fleming, opns dir; Tami Ramon, mktg dir; Dan Maynard, progmg dir; Laurie Gansen, traf mgr.

Osceola

*KNWI(FM)— Oct 4, 1982: 107.1 mhz; 27 kw. Ant 649 ft TL: N41 01 34 W93 51 43. Stereo. Hrs open: 24 3737 Woodland Ave., Suite 111, West Des Moines, 50266. Phone: (515) 327-1071. Fax: (515) 327-1073.E-mail: knwi@desmoines.fm Web Site:www.desmoines.fm Licensee: Northwestern College. Group owner: Northwestern College & Radio. (acq 12-30-2003; $1.8 million with KNWM(FM) Madrid). Format: Christian. Target aud: 18-44; women. ◆Richard Whitworth, gen mgr; Dave St. John, progmg dir.

Oskaloosa

KBOE(AM)— Nov 15, 1950: 740 khz; 250 w-D, 12 w-N. TL: N41 19 15 W92 38 44. Hrs open: 24 Box 380, 52577. Phone: (515) 673-3493. Fax: (515) 673-3495.E-mail: kboe@kboeradio.com Web Site:www.kboeradio.com Licensee: Jomast Corp. Population served: 72,000 Rgnl. Network: Brownfield, Radio Iowa. Radio Iowa Format: Country. News staff: one; News: 15 hrs wkly. Target aud: 25-50. Spec prog: Gospel 9 hrs wkly. ◆Brad Muhl, pres; Glenda Lind-Booy, gen mgr; Gary Wilson, chief of engrg.

KBOE-FM— Feb 7, 1964: 104.9 mhz; 50 kw. 492 ft TL: N41 19 15 W92 38 44. Stereo. Hrs open: 24 Box 380, 52577. Phone: (641) 673-3493. Fax: (641) 673-3495. Web Site:www.kboeradio.com Licensee: Jomast Corp. Natl. Network: ABC, . Format: Country. ◆Glenda Booy, gen mgr.

*KCNJ(FM)—Not on air, target date: unknown: 89.5 mhz; 420 w. Ant 308 ft TL: N41 19 15 W92 38 44. Hrs open: University of Northern Iowa, 324 Communications Arts Center, Cedar Falls, 50614-0359. Phone: (319) 273-6400. Fax: (319) 273-2682.E-mail: kuni@uni.edu Licensee: University of Northern Iowa. ◆Wayne Jarvis, gen mgr.

*KIGC(FM)— 1975: 88.7 mhz; 230 w. 93 ft TL: N41 18 37 W92 38 49. (CP: Ant 123 ft.). Stereo. Hrs open: 24 William Penn University, 201 Trueblood Ave., 52577. Phone: (641) 673-1095. Fax: (641) 673-1396. Licensee: William Penn University Population served: 15,000 Format: Oldies, alternative, Black. News: one hr wkly. Target aud: 13-25. Spec prog: Jazz 12 hrs, gospel 12 hrs wkly. ◆James Roberts, progmg dir; Larz G. Roberts, gen mgr & mus critic.

*KOSK(FM)—Not on air, target date: unknown: 90.5 mhz; 1.5 kw. Ant 292 ft TL: N41 19 15 W92 38 44. Hrs open: 204A Communications Bldg., Ames, 50011. Phone: (515) 294-9478. Fax: (515) 294-1544. Licensee: Iowa State University of Science and Technology. ◆Warren R. Madden, VP.

Ottumwa

KBIZ(AM)— 1941: 1240 khz; 1 kw-U. TL: N41 00 00 W92 23 23. Hrs open: 416 E. Main St., 52501. Phone: (641) 684-5563. Fax: (641) 684-5832. Licensee: O-Town Communications Inc. (group owner; (acq 10-20-2005; $890,000 with co-located FM). Population served: 301,700 Natl. Network: CBS, . Format: News/talk info. Target aud: 25-54. ◆Greg List, gen mgr, opns mgr; Phil Benjamin, chief of engrg.

*KDWI(FM)— 2009: 89.1 mhz; 13.5 kw. Ant 449 ft TL: N40 57 41 W92 22 13. Hrs open: 2022 Communications Bldg., Iowa State University, Ames, 50011. Phone: (515) 294-2025. Fax: (515) 294-1544. Web Site:iowapublicradio.org Licensee: Iowa State University of Science and Technology. Natl. Network: NPR, . Format: News and info, triple A. ◆Mary Grace Herrington, CEO.

KLEE(AM)— Aug 1, 1954: 1480 khz; 500 w-D, 33 w-N. TL: N41 01 27 W92 28 56. Stereo. Hrs open: 24 601 W. 2nd St., 52501. Phone: (641) 682-8711. Phone: (641) 682-8712. Fax: (641) 682-8482.E-mail: traffic@kotm.com Licensee: FMC Broadcasting Inc. (acq 1-16-92; $400,000 with co-located FM; 2-10-92). Population served: 203,000 Natl. Network: Westwood One, . Rgnl. Network: Iowa Radio Net, Brownfield. Brownfield Format: Country, news/talk. News staff: one; News: 28 hrs wkly. Target aud: General; people on the move. Spec prog: Gospel 6 hrs, polka one hr wkly. ◆Thomas A. Palen, pres, gen mgr & gen sls mgr; Marcia Wagner, prom dir; Dave Michaels, progmg dir; Mike Dixon, news dir; Fred Jenkins, chief of engrg.

KOTM-FM— Mar 22, 1976: 97.7 mhz; 6 kw. 200 ft TL: N41 01 27 W92 28 56. Stereo. Hrs open: Prog sep from AM 601 W. 2nd St., 52501. Phone: (641) 682-8711. Phone: (641) 682-8712. Fax: (641) 682-8482.E-mail: traffic@kotm.com Web Site:www.kotm.com Natl. Network: Westwood One, . Format: CHR. Target aud: Teens-50.

KTWA(FM)— December 1984: 92.7 mhz; 50 kw. 318 ft TL: N41 01 29 W92 28 09. Hrs open: 24 416 E. Main St., 52501. Phone: (641) 684-5563. Fax: (641) 684-5832. Licensee: O-Town Communications Inc. Format: Adult contemp. ◆Greg List, gen mgr; Phil Benjamin, chief of engrg.

*KUNE(FM)—Not on air, target date: unknown: 88.3 mhz; 500 w. Ant 350 ft TL: N40 57 41 W92 22 13. Hrs open: University of Northern Iowa, 324 Communications Arts Center, Cedar Falls, 50614-0359. Phone: (319) 273-6325. Licensee: University of Northern Iowa. ◆Wayne Jarvis, gen mgr.

*KUNZ(FM)— Mar 21, 2008: 91.1 mhz; 1.8 kw. Ant 400 ft TL: N40 57 41 W92 22 13. Hrs open:
Rebroadcasts KHKE(FM) Cedar Falls 100%.
University of Northern Iowa, 324 Communications Arts Center, Cedar Falls, 50614-0359. Phone: (319) 273-6325. Fax: (319) 273-2682.E-mail: kuni@uni.edu Web Site:www.khke.org Licensee: University of Northern Iowa. Format: Classical. ◆Wayne Jarvis, gen mgr; Scott Verdos, mktg dir; Al Schares, mus dir; Greg Shanley, news dir; Steve Schoon, chief of engrg.

Pacific Junction

KGGG(FM)—Not on air, target date: unknown: 107.7 mhz; 50 kw. Ant 423 ft TL: N41 04 55 W95 46 24. Hrs open: 136 Main St., Suite 202, Westport, CT, 06880-3304. Phone: (203) 227-1978. Licensee: Connoisseur Media LLC. ◆Michael O. Driscoll, gen mgr.

Parkersburg

KQCR-FM— Oct 18, 2000: 98.9 mhz; 6 kw. 328 ft TL: N42 33 48 W92 57 22. Stereo. Hrs open: 24 Box 495, Hampton, 50441-0495. Secondary address: 1509 4th St NE, Hampton 50441-1106. Phone: (641) 456-5656. Fax: (641) 456-5655.E-mail: kqcr@kqcr.fm Web Site:www.kqcr.fm Licensee: CD Broadcasting Inc. Population served: 100,000 Fletcher, Heald & Hildreth, P.L.C. Format: Adult contemp. News staff: 2; News: 12 hrs wkly. Target aud: 25-45; Light, Soft AC 70's, 80's, 90's. ◆Craig Donnelly, gen mgr; Marlin Burrier, opns dir.

Patterson

KZWF(FM)— Mar 12, 2008: 105.9 mhz; 900 w. Ant 39 ft TL: N41 18 50 W93 50 15. Hrs open: 1513 N. 1st St., Indianola, 50125. Phone: (515) 961-3338. Fax: (515) 961-3338. Licensee: Connoisseur Media LLC. Format: Classic country. ◆Rebecca Orr, gen mgr.

Pella

KAZR(FM)— Aug 1, 1976: 103.3 mhz; 100 kw. Ant 745 ft TL: N41 32 18 W93 17 58. Stereo. Hrs open: 24 1416 Locust St., Des Moines, 50309. Phone: (515) 280-1350. Fax: (515) 280-3011. Web Site:www.lazer1033.com Licensee: Saga Communications of Iowa LLC. Group owner: Saga Communications Inc. (acq 9-17-96; $2.7 million). Population served: 1,033,400 Natl. Rep: Katz Radio,. Smithwick & Belendiuk. Wire Svc: AP Format: Active rock. News: 4 hrs wkly. Target aud: 25-44. ◆Jeff Delvaux, gen mgr; Scott Allen, opns mgr; Pam Washington, sls dir; Celia Rodine, natl sls mgr; Marianne Coppock, mktg mgr; Dan Abbuehl, adv mgr; Ryan Patrick, progmg dir.

KNIA(AM)—See Knoxville

Perry

KDLS(AM)— May 10, 1961: 1310 khz; 500 w-D, 300 w-N, DA-2. TL: N41 49 58 W94 02 15. Hrs open: 6 AM-10 PM Box 548, 50220. Secondary address: 2260 141st Dr. 50220. Phone: (515) 465-5357. Fax: (515) 465-3952.E-mail: kdls@prairieinet.net Licensee: Coon Valley Communications Inc. (acq 2-15-2006; $300,000). Population served: 7,073 Natl. Network: Westwood One, CNN Radio, . Natl. Rep: Farmakis,. Wire Svc: AP Format: Var. News staff: one; News: 25 hrs wkly. Target aud: General. ◆Patrick Delaney, pres; Tom Quinlan, VP, farm dir; Patrick Graney, gen mgr, gen sls mgr; John Patrick, opns dir, progmg dir, news dir, local news ed; Bob Pink, chief of engrg; Marcia Murphy, traf mgr; Jerry Roberts, disc jockey.

KDLS-FM— Feb 26, 1971: 105.5 mhz; 6 kw. Ant 305 ft TL: N41 50 03 W94 02 12. Stereo. Hrs open: 6 AM-midnight 301 Ashworth Rd., West Des Moines, 50265. Phone: (515) 278-4117. Fax: (515) 254-1037.E-mail: info@kdlsfm.com Licensee: Perry Broadcasting Co. (acq 2-1-2006; with co-located AM). Format: Sp. ◆Joel Garcia, gen mgr.

*KDWT(FM)—Not on air, target date: unknown: 91.7 mhz; 23.5 kw. Ant 364 ft TL: N41 52 06 W94 04 54. Hrs open: 2022 Communications Bldg., Iowa State University, Ames, 50011. Phone: (515) 294-9478. Fax: (515) 294-1544. Web Site:www.woi.org Licensee: Iowa State University of Science and Technology. ◆Don Wirth, gen mgr.

Pleasantville

KZWU(FM)— Mar 12, 2008: 96.3 mhz; 500 w. Ant 255 ft TL: N41 21 04 W93 13 58. Hrs open: 1513 N. 1st St., Indianola, 50125. Phone: (515) 961-3338. Fax: (515) 961-3338. Licensee: Connoisseur Media LLC. Format: Classic country.

Postville

*KPVL(FM)— 2003: 89.1 mhz; 250 w. Ant 246 ft TL: N43 05 20 W91 33 54. (CP: 3 kw). Hrs open: Box 875, 52162. Phone: (563) 864-7945. Fax: (563) 864-7940.E-mail: info@kpvlradio.com Web Site:www.kpvlradio.com Licensee: Postville Chamber of Commerce. Format: Alternative. ◆Randy L. Frank, gen mgr.

Red Oak

KCSI(FM)— September 1979: 95.3 mhz; 20.5 kw. Ant 364 ft TL: N41 01 00 W95 12 46. Hrs open: 24 Box 465, 1991 Ironwood, 51566. Phone: (712) 623-2584. Fax: (712) 623-2583.E-mail: kcsi@kcsifm.com Web Site:www.kcsifm.com Licensee: Hawkeye Communications Inc. (acq 1994). Natl. Network: ABC, . Radio Iowa Wire Svc: AP Format: Contemporary country. ◆Melanie L. West, gen sls mgr; Marilyn J. Dietz, traf mgr.

KOAK(AM)— Aug 16, 1968: 1080 khz; 250 w-D. TL: N41 01 00 W95 12 46. Hrs open: Sunrise-sunset Box 465, 1991 Ironwood, 51566. Phone: (712) 623-2584. Fax: (712) 623-2583.E-mail: kcsi@kcsifm.com Web Site:kcsifm.com Licensee: Hawkeye Communications Inc. (acq 7-1-94). Population served: 7,000 Natl. Network: ABC, . Radio Iowa Wire Svc: AP Format: Contemp country. ◆Jerry V. Dietz, pres, gen mgr; Melanie L. West, gen sls mgr; Marilyn Dietz, traf mgr.

Rock Valley

KIHK(FM)— 1998: 106.9 mhz; 25 kw. 328 ft TL: N43 20 28 W96 19 03. Hrs open: 6 AM-6 AM Box 298, Sioux Center, 51250. Phone: (712) 722-1090. Fax: (712) 722-1102.E-mail: ksou@waittradio.com Web Site:www.ksoufm.com Licensee: Sorenson Broadcasting Corp. (group owner; (acq 7-1-2004; grpsl). Format: Country. Spec prog: Gospel bluegrass 3 hrs wkly. ◆Craig Aukes, gen mgr; Dan Bonnema, gen sls mgr; Doug Brock, news dir.

Rockford

KYME(FM)— 2008: 92.9 mhz; 375 w. Ant 33 ft TL: N43 03 12 W92 57 15. Hrs open: 1717 Dixie Hwy., Suite 650, Fort Wright, KY, 41011. Phone: (859) 331-9100. Licensee: Radioactive LLC. ◆Benjamin L. Homel, pres.

Sac City

KJLN(FM)—Not on air, target date: unknown: 104.7 mhz; 6 kw. Ant 159 ft TL: N42 24 40 W95 00 17. Hrs open: 1717 Dixie Hwy., Suite 650, Fort Wright, KY, 41011. Phone: (859) 331-9100. Licensee: Radioactive LLC. ◆Benjamin L. Homel, pres.

Sageville

KIYX(FM)— 1999: 106.1 mhz; 4.1 kw. 397 ft TL: N42 41 27 W90 37 26. Stereo. Hrs open: 24 51 Means Dr., Platteville, WI, 53818. Phone: (608) 349-2000. Fax: (608) 349-2002.E-mail: info@kyix.com Licensee: Queen B Radio Wisconsin Inc. (acq 6-8-99). Natl. Network: Westwood One, . Format: Top 40 hits of the 70s 80s. News staff: one. ◆Dan Sullivan, gen mgr.

Saint Ansgar

KJCY(FM)— September 2001: 95.5 mhz; 6 kw. Ant 328 ft TL: N43 21 12 W93 02 48. Hrs open: 24 Box 1069, Mason City, 50401. Phone: (641) 424-5529. Fax: (641) 424-5597.E-mail: kjcy@kjcy.com Web Site:www.kjcy.com Licensee: Minn-Iowa Christian Broadcasting Inc. (group owner; acq 3-20-01; $200,000). Format: Christian. ◆Matt Dorfner, exec VP; Matt Donfner, gen mgr.

Sheldon

KIWA(AM)— Oct. 27, 1961: 1550 khz; 283 w-D, 6 w-N. TL: N43 10 53 W95 51 56. Hrs open: 24 411 9th St., 51201. Phone: (712) 324-2597. Fax: (712) 324-2340.E-mail: newtips@kiwaradio.com Web Site:www.kiwaradio.com Licensee: Sheldon Broadcasting Co. Inc. (acq 10-27-61). Population served: 140,000 Natl. Network: ABC, . Rgnl. Network: Radio Iowa. Natl. Rep: Farmakis,. Radio Iowa Format: News/talk. News staff: 2; News: 15 hrs wkly. Target aud: General; adult. ♦Tim Torkildson, gen mgr, news dir; Wayne Barahona, progmg dir & chief of engrg; Jessica DeBoer, traf mgr; Larry Ahrens, sports cmtr.

KIWA-FM— Oct 1, 1971: 105.3 mhz; 50 kw. Ant 292 ft TL: N43 11 00 W95 52 05. Stereo. Hrs open: 24 411 9th St., 51201. Phone: (712) 324-2597. Fax: (712) 324-2340.E-mail: walt@kiwaradio.com Web Site:www.kiwaradio.com Licensee: Sheldon Broadcasting Co. Inc. Population served: 140,000 Natl. Rep: Farmakis,. Format: Classic hits. News staff: 2; News: 15 hrs wkly. Target aud: General.

Shenandoah

KMA(AM)— Aug 12, 1925: 960 khz; 5 kw-U, DA-N. TL: N40 46 48 W95 21 23. Hrs open: 24 Box 960, 209 N. Elm, 51601. Phone: (712) 246-5270. Fax: (712) 246-5275.E-mail: kmaradio@kmaland.com Web Site:www.kmaland.com Licensee: May Broadcasting Co. Population served: 5,968 Natl. Network: ABC, . Rgnl. Network: Radio Iowa. Duane Morris. Format: News/talk. News staff: 2; News: 15 hrs wkly. Target aud: 35-54. Spec prog: Farm. ♦Edward W. May, pres; Mark Eno, gen mgr; Don Hansen, stn mgr.

***KYFR(AM)**— 1977: 920 khz; 5 kw-D, 2.5 w-N, DA-2. TL: N40 37 22 W95 14 42. Hrs open: 24 112 N. Elm St., 51601. Secondary address: 700 W. Sheridan Ave. 51601. Phone: (712) 246-5151.E-mail: kyfr@familyradio.org Web Site:www.shenessex.heartland.net/kyfr Licensee: Family Stations Inc. (group owner; (acq 1976). Population served: 3,200,000 Natl. Network: Family Radio, . Format: Christian. ♦Harold Camping, pres; Mike DeStefano, stn mgr.

Sibley

KUSQ(FM)— 2008: 104.3 mhz; 3.4 kw. Ant 440 ft TL: N43 32 30 W95 45 05. Hrs open: 25138 C-60, Hinton, 51024. Phone: (712) 253-1807. Fax: (712) 947-4121. Licensee: Absolute Communications L.L.C. (acq 6-20-2008). ♦John D. Daniels, gen mgr.

Sioux Center

***KDCR(FM)**— Aug 16, 1968: 88.5 mhz; 100 kw. 320 ft TL: N43 05 00 W96 09 50. Stereo. Hrs open: Dordt College Campus, 498 4th Ave. N.E., 51250. Phone: (712) 722-0885. Fax: (712) 722-6244.E-mail: kdcr@dordt.edu Web Site:www.kdcrdordt.edu Licensee: Dordt College Inc. (acq 1-19-90). Natl. Network: USA, . Format: Relg. Spec prog: Farm 2 hrs, Dutch one hr wkly. ♦Dennis DeWaard, gen mgr; Jim Bolkema, mus dir; John Slezers, news dir; Ralph Goemaat, chief of engrg.

KSOU(AM)— Nov 17, 1969: 1090 khz; 500 w-D, DA. TL: N43 03 22 W96 10 17. Hrs open: Sunrise-sunset Box 298, 128 20th St. S.E., 51250. Phone: (712) 722-1090. Phone: (712) 722-1091. Fax: (712) 722-1102. Web Site:www.ksoufm.com Licensee: Sorenson Broadcasting Corp. (group owner; (acq 7-1-2004; grpsl). Population served: 80,000 Natl. Rep: Farmakis,. Format: Contempory Christian. News staff: one; News: 17 hrs wkly. Target aud: General. ♦Craig Aukes, gen mgr; Dan Bonnema, gen sls mgr; James DeBoer, progmg dir; Doug Broek, news dir, local news ed, sports cmtr; Steve Heaton, chief of engrg; Shirley Wierda, spec ev coord, women's int ed.

KSOU-FM— Oct 17, 1974: 93.9 mhz; 3 kw. 300 ft TL: N43 03 22 W96 10 17. (CP: 50 kw, ant 492 ft.). Stereo. Hrs open: 24 Dups AM 20% Box 298, 128 20th St. S.E., 51250. Phone: (712) 722-1090. Fax: (712) 722-1102. Population served: 82,000 Natl. Network: ABC, . Format: Adult contemp. ♦Scott France, progmg VP, progmg dir; Steve Heaton, chief of opns & engrg VP; Shirley Wierda, women's int ed.

Sioux City

KGLI(FM)— Mar 11, 1974: 95.5 mhz; 100 kw. Ant 900 ft TL: N42 30 53 W96 18 13. Stereo. Hrs open: 24 Box 3009, 51102. Secondary address: 1113 Nebraska St. 51105. Phone: (712) 258-5595. Fax: (712) 252-2430. Web Site:www.kg95.com Format: Adult contemp. Target aud: 18-49. ♦Rob Powers, opns mgr; Mike Newhouse, natl sls mgr; Laura Schiltz, mktg mgr; Rhonda Johnson, prom mgr; Ryan Reid, progmg dir; Stan Culley, chief of engrg; Monica Mattoon, traf mgr.

KKYY(FM)—See Whiting

KMNS(AM)— May 1, 1949: 620 khz; 1 kw-U, DA-2. TL: N42 22 15 W96 27 00. Hrs open: 24 Box 3009, 51102. Secondary address: 1113 Nebraska St. 51102. Phone: (712) 258-0628. Fax: (712) 252-2430. Web Site:www.620kmns.com Licensee: AMFM Radio Licenses LLC. Group owner: Clear Channel Communications Inc. (acq 10-1-2002; grpsl). Population served: 970,000 Rgnl. Network: Linder Farm. Natl. Rep: Katz Radio,. Format: Fox Sports Radio. Target aud: 18-54. ♦Rob Powers, opns mgr, sls dir; Rhonda Johnson, gen sls mgr, prom mgr; Laura Schiltz, mktg mgr; Curtis Anderson, progmg dir; Stan Culley, chief of engrg; Monica Mattoon, traf mgr.

***KMSC(FM)**— April 1978: 88.3 mhz; 10 w. 105 ft TL: N42 28 28 W96 21 34. Stereo. Hrs open: Library Bldg., 1501 Morningside Ave., 51106. Phone: (712) 274-5665. Phone: (712) 274-5299. Fax: (712) 274-5664.E-mail: fusion@morningside.edu Web Site:webs.morningside.edu/kmsc Licensee: Morningside College Board of Directors. Format: Alternative. News: 2 hrs wkly. Target aud: General; high school, college students & young professionals. Spec prog: Womens mus 5 hrs, techno 4 hrs, rock/AOR 4 hrs, urban contemp 4 hrs wkly. ♦John Reinders, pres; Ron Jorgensen, CFO; Bill Deeds, exec VP; Dr. Mark J. Heistad, gen mgr.

KSCJ(AM)— 1927: 1360 khz; 5 kw-D, 1 kw-N, DA-N. TL: N42 33 24 W96 20 12. Hrs open: 24 2000 Indian Hills Dr., 51104. Phone: (712) 239-2100. Fax: (712) 239-3346. Web Site:www.kscj.com Licensee: Powell Broadcasting Co. (acq 1996; $3.8 million with KSUX(FM) Winnebago, NE). Population served: 283,400 Natl. Network: ABC, . Rgnl. Network: Iowa Radio Net. Format: News/talk, sports. News staff: 2; News: 42 hrs wkly. Target aud: 35-64; educated, higher income, issues-oriented. ♦Dennis J. Bullock, gen mgr; Dave Grossenherder, sls dir, gen sls mgr; Steve Arthur, progmg dir; Randy Renshaw, news dir.

KSEZ(FM)— Feb 6, 1960: 97.9 mhz; 100 kw. Ant 643 ft TL: N42 29 48 W96 18 55. Stereo. Hrs open: 24 Box 3009, 51102. Secondary address: 1113 Nebraska St. 51105. Phone: (712) 258-5595. Fax: (712) 252-2430. Web Site:www.z98rocks.com Population served: 84,000 Natl. Network: ABC, . Natl. Rep: Katz Radio,. Leventhal, Senter & Lerman. Format: Classic rock. Target aud: 18-49. ♦Rob Powers, opns mgr; Rhonda Johnson, sls dir; Mike Newhouse, natl sls mgr; Laura Schiltz, mktg mgr, chief of engrg; Scott Miller, progmg dir; Stan Culley, chief of engrg; Monica Mattoon, traf mgr.

KTFC(FM)— July 1, 1965: 103.3 mhz; 100 kw. Ant 669 ft TL: N42 29 26 W96 18 21. Stereo. Hrs open: 24 1534 Buchanan Ave., 51106. Phone: (712) 252-4621.E-mail: kcotter@bottradionetwork.com Licensee: Community Broadcasting Inc. (acq 12-13-2007; $650,000 with KTFG(FM) Sioux Rapids). Natl. Network: USA, . Format: Gospel, all Bible. Spec prog: Farm one hr, news 10 hrs, children 5 hrs wkly. ♦Richard P. Bott, pres; Donald A. Swanson, gen mgr.

***KWIT(FM)**— Jan 31, 1978: 90.3 mhz; 100 kw. Ant 910 ft TL: N42 28 56 W96 15 30. Stereo. Hrs open: 24 4647 Stone Ave., 51106-1997. Phone: (712) 274-6406. Fax: (712) 274-6411.E-mail: gondekg@witcc.edu Web Site:www.kwit-koji.org Licensee: Western Iowa Tech Community College. Population served: 325,000 Natl. Network: PRI, NPR, . Format: Class, news/talk, Sp. News staff: one; News: 36 hrs wkly. Target aud: 25-54. Spec prog: Blues 2 hrs, Triple A 12 hrs, Sp 20 hrs wkly. ♦Gretchen Gondek, gen mgr; Steve Smith, opns mgr.

KWSL(AM)— April 1938: 1470 khz; 5 kw-U, DA-2. TL: N42 24 42 W96 25 30. Hrs open: Box 3009, 51102. Secondary address: 1113 Nebraska St. 51105. Phone: (712) 255-1470. Fax: (712) 252-2430. Licensee: AMFM Radio Licenses LLC. Group owner: Clear Channel Communications Inc. (acq 10-1-2002; grpsl). Population served: 272,300 Natl. Rep: Katz Radio,. Leventhal, Senter & Lerman. Format: Oldies. Target aud: 25 plus. ♦Rob Powers, opns mgr; Mike Newhouse, natl sls mgr; Laura Schiltz, mktg mgr; Rhonda Johnson, prom mgr; Curtis Anderson, progmg dir; Stan Culley, chief of engrg; Monica Mattoon, traf mgr.

Sioux Rapids

KTFG(FM)— 1991: 102.9 mhz; 50 kw. Ant 479 ft TL: N42 54 34 W95 09 35. Hrs open:
Rebroadcasts KTFC(FM) Sioux City 100%.
1534 Buchanan Ave., Sioux City, 51106. Phone: (712) 252-0327.E-mail: kcotter@bottradionetwork.com Licensee: Community Broadcasting Inc. (acq 12-13-2007; $650,000 with KTFC(FM) Sioux City). Natl. Network: USA, . Format: Gospel. Spec prog: Children 5 hrs wkly. ♦Donald A. Swanson, gen mgr.

Spencer

KICD(AM)— December 1942: 1240 khz; 1 kw-U. TL: N43 10 00 W95 08 45. Hrs open: 24 Box 260, 51301. Secondary address: 2600 N. Hwy. Blvd. 51301. Phone: (712) 262-1240. Fax: (712) 262-2076.E-mail: kicdott@fair.net Web Site:www.kicdam.com Licensee: Saga Communications of Iowa LLC. Group owner: Saga Communications Inc. (acq 11-22-99; grpsl). Population served: 124,000 Natl. Network: CBS, . Format: Talk. News staff: one; News: 26 hrs wkly. Target aud: 35 plus. ♦David Putnam, gen mgr, gen sls mgr; Bill Campbell, opns mgr, progmg dir; Brent Palm, news dir; Dave Inqualson, pub affrs dir; Joseph Schloss, chief of engrg.

KICD-FM— Sept 17, 1965: 107.7 mhz; 100 kw. Ant 310 ft TL: N43 10 00 W95 08 45. Stereo. Hrs open: 24 Box 260, 51301. Secondary address: 2600 N. Hwy. Blvd. 51301. Phone: (712) 262-1240. Fax: (712) 262-2076.E-mail: kicdott@fair.net Web Site:www.cd1077fm.com Licensee: Saga Communications of Iowa LLC. Natl. Network: CBS, . Format: Country. News staff: one. Target aud: 25 plus. ♦David Putman, gen sls mgr; Rhoda Wedeking, progmg dir.

KLLT(FM)— February 1979: 104.9 mhz; 25 kw. 279 ft TL: N43 17 13 W95 08 34. Stereo. Hrs open: 24 Box 260, 2600 N. Hwy. Blvd., 51301. Phone: (712) 262-1240. Fax: (712) 262-2076. Fax: (712) 262-5821.E-mail: kicdott@fair.net Web Site:www.lite1049.com Licensee: Saga Communications of Iowa LLC. Group owner: Saga Communications Inc. (acq 11-22-99; grpsl). Population served: 80000 Natl. Rep: Katz Radio,. Format: Light Rock. News: one hr wkly. Target aud: 25-54. ♦Edward Christian, CEO, pres; Dave Putnam, gen mgr; Bill Campbell, opns dir, opns mgr; Darby Bishop, prom dir; Kevin Tlam, progmg dir; Brent Palm, news dir.

Spirit Lake

***KJIA(FM)**— 2002: 88.9 mhz; 50 kw. Ant 272 ft TL: N43 20 34 W95 12 24. Hrs open: Box 738, Okoboji, 51355. Secondary address: 7 S. Highway 71, Arnolds Park 51331. Phone: (712) 332-7184. Fax: (712) 332-2428.E-mail: kjia@kjiaradio.com Web Site:www.kjiaradio.com Licensee: Minn-Iowa Christian Broadcasting Inc. (group owner). Format: Christian. ♦Matt Dorfner, gen mgr & progmg dir; Mark Groom, chief of engrg.

KUOO(FM)— Apr 1, 1985: 103.9 mhz; 50 kw. 492 ft TL: N43 20 34 W93 12 24. Stereo. Hrs open: 24 Box 528, 3200 18th St., 51360. Phone: (712) 336-5800. Fax: (712) 336-1634. Web Site:www.kuooradio.com Licensee: Sorenson Broadcasting Corp. (group owner; (acq 7-1-2004; grpsl). Natl. Network: Fox News Radio, . Format: Adult contemp. News staff: 2; News: 16 hrs wkly. Target aud: 25-54. ♦Dean Sorenson, pres; Marty Spies, gen mgr; Chad Taylor, opns mgr, prom dir.

KUQQ(FM)—(Milford, Oct 1, 1996: 102.1 mhz; 50 kw. 420 ft TL: N43 20 34 W93 12 24. Stereo. Hrs open: Box 528, 3200 18th St., 51360. Phone: (712) 336-5877. Fax: (712) 336-1634. Web Site:www.kuqqfm.com Licensee: Sorenson Broadcasting Corp. (group owner; (acq 7-1-2004; grpsl). Format: Classic rock. Target aud: 18-44. ♦Dean Sorenson, pres; Marty Spies, gen mgr; Chad Taylor, opns mgr, prom dir.

State Center

***KTDV(FM)**— Jan 9, 2009: 91.9 mhz; 22 kw. Ant 307 ft TL: N42 15 49 W93 03 57. Hrs open: Box 538, Marshalltown, 50158. Phone: (641) 752-4122. Fax: (641) 752-5121.E-mail: info@ktdvradio.com Web Site:ktdvradio.com Licensee: Marshalltown Education Plus Inc. Format: Adult contemp Christian. ♦Mark Osmundson, gen mgr.

Storm Lake

KAYL(AM)— November 1948: 990 khz; 250 w-D, 6 w-N. TL: N42 38 05 W95 10 10. Hrs open: Box 1037, 50588. Secondary address: 606 1/2 Lake Ave. 50588. Phone: (712) 732-3520. Fax: (712) 732-1746.E-mail: info@stormlakeradio.com Web Site:www.stormlakeradio.com Licensee: Sorenson Broadcasting Corp. (group owner; (acq 7-1-2004; grpsl). Population served: 14,200 Natl. Network: La Gran D, . Format: Sp. ♦Mary Quass, CEO; Chuck DuCoty, COO; Buzz Paterson, gen mgr.

KAYL-FM— February 1949: 101.7 mhz; 50 kw. 400 ft TL: N42 38 05 W95 10 10. Stereo. Hrs open: Box 1037, 50588. Phone: (712) 732-3520. Fax: (712) 732-1746.E-mail: info@stormlakeradio.com Web Site:www.stormlakeradio.com Licensee: Sorenson Broadcasting Corp. Population served: 23,400 Waitt Farm Net. Format: Hot adult contemp. News staff: one; News: 15 hrs wkly. Target aud: 25-54; male & female. ♦Mary Quass, CEO; Chuck DuCoty, COO; Buzz Paterson, gen mgr.

***KOIA(FM)**—Not on air, target date: unknown: 88.1 mhz; 1.4 kw. Ant 466 ft TL: N42 40 50 W95 11 22. Hrs open: 282 Country Estate Dr., Springer, OK, 73458. Phone: (580) 653-2777. Licensee: Ron Elmore Ministries Inc. ♦Ron Elmore, pres.

Story City

*KHOI(FM)—Not on air, target date: unknown: 88.3 mhz; 1.9 kw. Ant 230 ft TL: N42 13 30 W93 33 40. Hrs open: 1015 N. Hyland Ave., Ames, 50014-4005. Phone: (515) 292-5960. Licensee: Unitarian Universalist Fellowship of Ames. ◆Janet E. Klaas, pres.

Stuart

KKRF(FM)— Aug 11, 1993: 107.9 mhz; 12.kw. Ant 472 ft TL: N41 30 25 W94 18 06. Stereo. Hrs open: 204 S. Division St., 50250. Secondary address: 204 S. Division St. 50250-5021. Phone: (515) 465-5357. Fax: (515) 465-3952.E-mail: kkrf1079@aol.com Web Site:RealCountryOnline.Com Licensee: Coon Valley Communications Inc. Population served: 60,100 Natl. Network: ABC, . Format: Country. News staff: one; News: 10 hrs wkly. Target aud: 25-64; general. Spec prog: Farm 5 hrs wkly. ◆Pat Delaney, pres, CFO; Sue Thomsen, gen mgr; John France, opns mgr, progmg dir.

Twin Lakes

KTLB(FM)— Oct 5, 1975: 105.9 mhz; 25 kw. 328 ft TL: N42 32 09 W94 40 48. Stereo. Hrs open: 18 1014 Central Ave., Fort Dodge, 50501. Phone: (515) 573-5748. Fax: (515) 573-3376. Licensee: Three Eagles of Ft. Dodge Inc. Group owner: Three Eagles Communications (acq 4-22-97; $248,883). Population served: 25,000 Format: Oldies. News staff: one; News: 15 hrs wkly. Target aud: 35-54; baby boomers. Spec prog: Farm 15 hrs, gospel 2 hrs, relg 2 hrs wkly. ◆Gary Buchanan, pres; Pat Kolar, gen mgr, gen sls mgr; Greg Allenson, opns mgr, gen sls mgr.

Vinton

KRQN(FM)— 2005: 107.1 mhz; 4.7 kw. Ant 371 ft TL: N42 08 56 W91 52 50. Hrs open: 425 2nd St. S.E., 4th Fl., Cedar Rapids, 52401. Phone: (319) 365-9431. Fax: (319) 363-8062.E-mail: bob@khah.com Licensee: George S. Flinn Jr. Format: Rock and roll hits of the 60s & 70s. ◆Jim Worthington, gen mgr, opns mgr; Terry Weinacht, gen sls mgr; Bill Hahn, progmg dir; Ryan Brainard, news dir; Scott Wilcox, chief of engrg; Mike Meilly, traf mgr.

Wapello

*KAIP(FM)— 2005: 88.9 mhz; 1 w hoirz, 13.5 kw vert. Ant 494 ft vert TL: N41 04 59 W91 10 18. Hrs open: 2351 Sunset Blvd., Suite 170-218, Rocklin, CA, 95765. Phone: (916) 251-1600. Fax: (916) 251-1650.Web Site:www.air1.com Licensee: Educational Media Foundation. Group owner: EMF Broadcasting. Population served: 104,000 Natl. Network: Air 1, . Shaw Pittman. Format: Christian. News staff: 3. Target aud: 25-44; Judeo Christian, female. ◆Richard Jenkins, pres; Mike Novak, VP; Keith Whipple, dev dir; David Pierce, progmg mgr; Ed Lenane, news dir; Sam Wallington, engrg dir; Karen Johnson, news rptr.

Washington

KCII(AM)— Nov 12, 1961: 1380 khz; 500 w-D. TL: N41 18 18 W91 42 36. Hrs open: 5 AM-11 PM Box 524, 110 E. Main St., 52353. Phone: (319) 653-2113. Fax: (319) 653-3500.E-mail: kcii@kciiradio.com Web Site:kciiradio.com Licensee: Home Broadcasting Inc. (acq 9-3-96; $800,000 with co-located FM). Population served: 140,000 Natl. Network: AP Radio, . Shaw Pittman. Format: News, adult contemp. News staff: one; News: 14 hrs wkly. Target aud: 25-54; females. ◆Michael Suhr, gen mgr; Joe Nichols, gen sls mgr; Nic Sabatke, progmg dir; Ben Stanton, news dir; Becky Helmick, traf mgr.

KCII-FM— 1975: 106.1 mhz; 3 kw. Ant 300 ft TL: N41 18 18 W91 42 36. Stereo. Hrs open: 5 AM-11 PM Box 524, 110 E. Main St., 52353. Phone: (319) 653-2113. Fax: (319) 653-3500. E-mail: kcii@kciiradio.com Web Site:kciiradio.com Licensee: Home Broadcasting Inc. Format: News, oldies. ◆Nic Sabatke, spec ev coord; Ben Stanton, news rptr; Dagan Miller, sports cmtr.

Waterloo

*KBBG(FM)— July 26, 1978: 88.1 mhz; 9.5 kw. 150 ft TL: N42 30 35 W92 19 35. Stereo. Hrs open: 19 918 Newell St., 50703-2720. Phone: (319) 234-1441. Phone: (319) 235-1515. Fax: (319) 234-6182.E-mail: lou@kbbg.org Web Site:www.kbbgfm.org Licensee: Afro-American Community Broadcasting Inc. Natl. Network: American Urban, . Format: Educ, gospel, rhythmn and blues, jazz. Target aud: General. ◆Jimmie Porter, CEO; Lou Porter, pres; Beverly Douglas, stn mgr; Lou Lou Porter, dev dir, news dir.

KFMW(FM)— November 1968: 107.9 mhz; 100 kw. 1,850 ft TL: N42 24 04 W91 50 43. Stereo. Hrs open: 24 Prog sep from AM Box 1540, 50704. Secondary address: 514 Jefferson St. 56201. Phone: (319) 234-2200. Fax: (319) 234-0149.E-mail: info@rock108.com Web Site:www.rock108.com Format: Rock. Target aud: 18-34; men. ◆Michael Cross, opns mgr; Mark Chapman, progmg dir; Dolly Fortier, pub affrs dir.

*KNWS(AM)— 1953: 1090 khz; 1 kw-D. TL: N42 26 38 W92 17 58. Hrs open: Sunrise-sunset 4880 Texas, 50702. Phone: (319) 296-1975. Fax: (319) 296-1977.E-mail: info@life1019.com Web Site:www.knws.org Licensee: Northwestern College. Group owner: Northwestern College & Radio (acq 4-2-53). Rgnl. Network: Skylight. Format: Relg, Christian, talk. Target aud: 35 plus. ◆Paul Virts, exec VP; Doug Smith, gen mgr, stn mgr; Dan Raymond, progmg dir, asst music dir; David Dobes, chief of engrg.

*KNWS-FM— 1965: 101.9 mhz; 100 kw. 1,571 ft TL: N42 24 02 W91 50 36. Stereo. Hrs open: 24 4880 Texas, 50702. Phone: (319) 296-1975. Fax: (319) 296-1977. Web Site:www.knws.org (acq 1965). Population served: 350,000 Natl. Network: AP Radio, . Format: Adult contemp Christian music, relg. Target aud: 30-50; women. ◆Brent Manion, disc jockey.

KOKZ(FM)— Nov 21, 1962: 105.7 mhz; 100 kw. 1,403 ft TL: N42 24 35 W92 05 10. Stereo. Hrs open: 24 Box 1540, 514 Jefferson St., 50701. Phone: (319) 234-2200. Fax: (319) 234-0149.E-mail: info@cool1057.com Web Site:www.cool1057.com Format: Oldies. Target aud: 25-54. ◆Dolly Fortier, pub affrs dir.

KWLO(AM)— November 1947: 1330 khz; 5 kw-U, DA-2. TL: N42 28 56 W92 16 16. Stereo. Hrs open: 24 Box 1540, 50704. Secondary address: 514 Jefferson St. 50704. Phone: (319) 234-2200. Fax: (319) 234-0149. Web Site:www.star1330.com Licensee: KXEL Broadcasting Co. Inc. Group owner: Bahakel Communications (acq 8-16-96; grpsl). Natl. Network: ABC, . Natl. Rep: Katz Radio,. Brooks, Pierce, McLendon, Humphrey & Leonard. Format: Nostalgia. Target aud: 35 plus. ◆Beverly Poston, pres; Rhonda Benson Leach, gen mgr; Dennis Lowe, opns dir; Mark Schumacher, chief of engrg; Amy Mollus, traf mgr.

KXEL(AM)— July 14, 1942: 1540 khz; 50 kw-U, DA-N. TL: N42 10 47 W92 18 38. Stereo. Hrs open: 24 Box 1540, 514 Jefferson St., 50701. Phone: (319) 234-2200. Fax: (319) 234-0149. Web Site:www.kxel.com Licensee: KXEL Broadcasting Co. Inc. Group owner: Bahakel Communications (acq 1-11-58). Natl. Network: ABC, . Natl. Rep: Katz Radio,. Format: News/talk. News staff: 2; News: 28 hrs wkly. Target aud: 45-65. Spec prog: Relg 20 hrs wkly. ◆Beverly Poston, pres; Tim Mathews, gen mgr; Dennis Lowe, opns dir; Mark Schumacher, chief of engrg.

KXGM(AM)— Oct 31, 1972: 850 khz; 500 w-D, DA. TL: N42 28 56 W92 16 16. Hrs open: 3232 Osage Rd., 50703. Phone: (319) 319-236-5700. Fax: (319) 236-8777.E-mail: theprodigal @theprodigalradio.com Web Site:www.theprodigalradio.com Licensee: Extreme Grace Media Inc. (acq 7-18-2008; $160,000 with KXGM-FM Hiawatha). Format: Classic Christian rock. Target aud: 34-55; Christian, interdenominational. ◆Michael James, gen mgr.

Waukon

KHPP(AM)— July 1, 1967: 1160 khz; 880 w-D, 26 w-N. TL: N43 17 13 W91 28 06. Hrs open: 14 W. Main St., 52172. Phone: (563) 568-3477. Fax: (563) 568-3391.E-mail: knei@kneiradio.com Licensee: Wennes Communications Stations Inc. Format: Oldies.

KNEI-FM— Sept 1, 1968: 103.5 mhz; 37 kw. Ant 574 ft TL: N43 18 28 W91 27 18. Stereo. Hrs open: 14 W. Main St., 52172. Phone: (563) 568-3476. Phone: (563) 568-3477. Fax: (563) 568-3391 .E-mail: knei@kneiradio.com Licensee: Wennes Communications Stations Inc. (acq 4-5-2002; grpsl). Population served: 3,639 Natl. Network: CBS Radio, . Brownfield Sam Miller. Format: Real country. News: one hr wkly. Target aud: 25-45. ◆Greg Wennes, CEO; Chuck Bloxham, gen mgr, opns dir, gen sls mgr.

Waverly

*KWAR(FM)— 2008: 89.9 mhz; 100 w. Ant 52 ft TL: N42 43 38 W92 28 51. Hrs open: 24 Wartburg College, 100 Wartburg Blvd., 50677. Phone: (319) 352-8209. Phone: (319) 352-8306. Fax: (319) 352-8610.E-mail: yoursound.kwar@gmail.com Web Site:www.kwar.org Licensee: Wartburg College. Format: Educ, div. Target aud: General. ◆Andrew Nostvick, stn mgr; Anna Hauskins, progmg dir; Vince Abrahamson, mus dir.

KWAY(AM)— May 6, 1958: 1470 khz; 1 kw-D, 61 w-N, DA-2. TL: N42 42 13 W92 28 21. Hrs open: Box 307, 50677. Phone: (319) 352-3550.

Fax: (319) 352-3601.E-mail: kwayradio@kwayradio.com Licensee: Ael Suhr Enterprises Inc. Population served: 25,000 Format: Classic country. ◆Al Suhr, pres, gen mgr, chief of engrg; Steven Hatter, opns mgr.

KWAY-FM— Dec 21, 1971: 99.3 mhz; 4.6 kw. Ant 180 ft TL: N42 42 13 W92 28 21. Hrs open: Box 307, 50677. Phone: (319) 352-3550. Fax: (319) 352-3601. Web Site:www.kwayradio.com Licensee: Ael Suhr Enterprises Inc. Population served: 135,000 Format: Adult contemp.

*KWVI(FM)— 2006: 88.9 mhz; 20 kw vert. Ant 274 ft TL: N42 47 21 W92 14 22. Hrs open: Rebroadcasts WAFR(FM) Tupelo, MS 100%. Drawer 2440, Tupelo, MS, 38801. Phone: (662) 844-8888. Fax: (662) 842-6791. Web Site:www.afr.net Licensee: American Family Association. Format: Christian. ◆Marvin Sanders, gen mgr.

Webster City

KQWC(AM)— Feb 5, 1950: 1570 khz; 250 w-D, 132 w-N. TL: N42 27 45 W93 48 05. (CP: 147 w). Hrs open: Box 550, 50595. Phone: (515) 832-1570. Fax: (515) 832-2079. Licensee: NRG License Sub. LLC. Group owner: Waitt Broadcasting Inc. (acq 10-31-2005; grpsl). Population served: 50,000 Format: Btfl mus, big band. News staff: one; News: 45 hrs wkly. Target aud: 50 plus; affluent with max spendable income. Spec prog: Farm 8 hrs wkly. ◆Mary Harris, gen mgr; Darren Helton, progmg dir; Pat Powers, news dir; Chris Lockwood, disc jockey.

KQWC-FM— 1969: 95.7 mhz; 25 kw. 328 ft TL: N42 28 04 W93 47 48. Stereo. Hrs open: Prog sep from AM P.O. Box 550, 50595. Phone: (515) 832-1570. Fax: (515) 832-2079.E-mail: mharris@nrgmedia.com Web Site:www.kqradio.com Natl. Network: ABC, . Format: Adult Contemp. News staff: one; News: 35 hrs wkly. ◆Mary Harris, gen mgr; Darren Helton, progmg dir; Pat Powers, news dir; Chris Lockwood, disc jockey.

West Des Moines

KJJY(FM)—Licensed to West Des Moines. See Des Moines

*KWDM(FM)— March 1976: 88.7 mhz; 100 w. 170 ft TL: N41 35 25 W93 45 10. Stereo. Hrs open: 14 1140 35th St., 50266. Phone: (515) 226-2660. Phone: (515) 226-2600. Fax: (515) 226-2609.E-mail: kwdmfm@hotmail.com Web Site:www.wdm.k12.ia.us/kwdm Licensee: West Des Moines Community School District. Population served: 300,000 Reddy, Begley & McCormick. Format: Alternative. News: 3 hrs wkly. Target aud: 12-25; educ facility-var progmg. Spec prog: Sports 3 hrs wkly. ◆Mack Wzie Carey, stn mgr; Marianne Coppock, dev dir; Nicole Faust, mktg dir & progmg dir.

Whiting

KKYY(FM)— Dec 11, 1979: 101.3 mhz; 50 kw. Ant 492 ft TL: N42 21 25 W96 08 02. Stereo. Hrs open: 24 522 14th St., Sioux City, 51105. Phone: (712) 258-5655. Fax: (712) 258-1511. Web Site:www.y1013.net Licensee: Powell Broadcasting Co. Inc. Group owner: Waitt Broadcasting Inc. (acq 5-1-2007; $4.2 million with KZSR(FM) Onawa). Population served: 200,000 Natl. Network: Motor Racing Net, Westwood One, ABC, . Format: Country. News staff: one; News: 20 hrs wkly. Target aud: 18-54; adult men & women. ◆Jerry Haack, gen mgr; Kelli Erickson, gen sls mgr; Tim Guentz, progmg dir; Pam Guntz, chief of engrg.

Winterset

KPUL(FM)— March 1994: 99.5 mhz; 6 kw. 328 ft TL: N41 24 02 W93 54 58. Stereo. Hrs open: 24 3317 335th St., Waukee, 50263. Phone: (515) 987-9995. Fax: (515) 987-9808.E-mail: info@pulse995.com Web Site:www.kzzq.com Licensee: Positive Impact Media Inc. (acq 1-11-94; $600,000; 1-31-94). Format: Contemp Christian mus. Target aud: Families. ◆David Nadler Jr., gen mgr; David St. John, progmg dir.

Kansas

Abilene

KABI(AM)— Apr 8, 1963: 1560 khz; 250 w-D, 58 w-N. TL: N38 55 46 W97 14 46. Hrs open: 24 Secondary address: Box 80, Salina 67402.

Phone: (785) 823-1111. Fax: (785) 823-2034. Web Site:www.ksallink.com Licensee: MCC Radio LLC. Group owner: Morris Radio LLC (acq 1-30-2004; grpsl). Population served: 18,000 Natl. Network: ABC, . Kan. Agriculture Format: Adult standards. News staff: one; News: 2 hrs wkly. Target aud: 35 plus; loc residents of Dickinson County. Spec prog: Relg 4 hrs wkly. ◆Robert Protzman, VP & gen mgr; Clarke Sanders, opns mgr, prom mgr; Richie Allen, progmg dir; John Anderson, news dir; Mark Beaver, traf mgr.

KSAJ-FM— Dec 10, 1968: 98.5 mhz; 100 kw. 443 ft TL: N38 47 50 W97 13 01. Stereo. Hrs open: 24 Box 80, Salina, 67402. Secondary address: 131 N. Santa Fe, Salina 67401. Phone: (785) 823-1111. Fax: (785) 823-2034. Web Site:www.ksallink.com Licensee: MCC Radio LLC Population served: 311,000 Natl. Network: ABC, . Natl. Rep: Katz Radio,. Kan. Info. Format: Oldies. News staff: one; News: 3 hrs wkly. Target aud: 35-64; baby boomers. ◆Clarke Sanders, gen mgr, prom mgr; John Anderson, progmg dir; Mark Beaver, engrg mgr, traf mgr.

Andover

KDGS(FM)— Nov 1, 1993: 93.9 mhz; 25 kw. 328 ft TL: N37 37 00 W97 20 11. Hrs open: 2120 N. Woodlawn, Suite 352, Wichita, 67206. Phone: (316) 685-2121. Fax: (316) 685-3408.E-mail: info@power939.com Web Site:www.power939.com Licensee: Entercom Wichita License LLC. Group owner: Entercom Communications Corp. (acq 4-21-00; $3.15 million). Format: CHR. Target aud: 18-34. ◆Jackie Wise, gen mgr; Greg Williams, progmg dir.

Arkansas City

KACY(FM)— February 1999: 102.5 mhz; 6 kw. 328 ft TL: N37 05 01 W96 55 46. Hrs open: 24 106 N. Summitt, 67005. Phone: (620) 442-1102. Fax: (620) 442-8102. Licensee: Third Coast Broadcasting. Format: AAA, AOR. ◆Marshall Ice, gen mgr.

*KAXR(FM)— 2001: 91.3 mhz; 13.5 kw. Ant 321 ft TL: N36 55 32 W97 01 34. Hrs open: Box 3206, American Family Radio, Tupelo, MS, 38803. Phone: (662) 844-8888. Fax: (662) 842-6791.E-mail: comments@afr.net Web Site:www.afr.net Licensee: American Family Association. Group owner: American Family Radio. Format: Inspirational Christian. ◆Marvin Sanders, gen mgr.

KSOK(AM)— Jan 1, 1947: 1280 khz; 1 kw-D, 100 w-N. TL: N37 05 19 W97 01 56. Hrs open: 24 334 E. Radio Ln., 67005. Phone: (620) 442-5400. Fax: (620) 442-5401.E-mail: ksok@ksokradio.com Web Site:www.ksokradio.com Licensee: Cowley County Broadcasting Inc. (acq 9-3-2002; with KSOK-FM Winfield). Natl. Network: ABC, . Kan. Agriculture Format: Country classics. News staff: one. Target aud: 22-55; blue collar, middle America, people who have children, are still working, & have mortgages. ◆Marty Mutti, gen mgr; Brian Cunningham, opns mgr; Christy Bursack, chief of opns; Shawn Wheat, news dir.

KYQQ(FM)— Nov 1, 1979: 106.5 mhz; 100 kw. Ant 1,278 ft TL: N37 21 24 W96 57 55. Stereo. Hrs open: Box 1402, Wichita, 67201. Phone: (316) 838-9141. Fax: (316) 838-3607. Licensee: Journal Broadcast Corp. Group owner: Journal Broadcast Group Inc. (acq 6-11-99; grpsl). Population served: 720,000 Share Pittman. Format: Mexican. Target aud: 18-49; Hispanic. ◆Rob Burton, VP & gen mgr; Eric McCart, gen sls mgr; Manny Cowzinski, prom dir; Beverlee Brannigan, progmg dir.

Arlington

KNZS(FM)— Sept 15, 1989: 100.3 mhz; 14.5 kw. Ant 443 ft TL: N37 55 41 W98 17 58. Stereo. Hrs open: 24 106 N. Main St., Hutchinson, 67501-5219. Phone: (620) 665-5758. Fax: (620) 665-6655.E-mail: production@adastra.kscoxmail.com Licensee: Ad Astra Per Aspera Broadcasting Inc. (acq 12-13-2007; exchange for KIBB(FM) Haven). Natl. Network: Jones Radio Networks, . Format: Classic rock. News staff: 1; News: news prgmg 2 hrs wkly. Target aud: Adults 25-64. ◆Cliff C. Shank, pres; Cliff C. Shank, gen mgr; Aaron West, opns mgr; Mike Hill, VP & gen sls mgr.

Atchison

KAIR(AM)— July 28, 1939: 1470 khz; 1 kw-U, DA-1. TL: N39 37 09 W94 59 27. Hrs open: 5 AM-midnight Box G, 200 N. 5th St., 66002. Phone: (913) 367-1470. Fax: (913) 367-7021.E-mail: kair@lunworth.com Licensee: KNZA Inc. (group owner; (acq 8-13-2007 with KAIR-FM Horton). Population served: 256,500 Natl. Network: EWTN Radio, . Format: Catholic. Target aud: General; 25-65. Spec prog: Farm 7 hrs wkly. ◆Greg Buser, pres; Mark Oppold, gen mgr.

Augusta

KFXJ(FM)— Apr 1, 1992: 104.5 mhz; 45 kw. Ant 515 ft TL: N37 48 15 W97 15 56. Stereo. Hrs open: 24 Box 1402, Wichita, 67219. Secondary address: 4200 N. Old Lawrence Rd., Wichita 67219. Phone: (316) 838-9141. Fax: (316) 838-3607.E-mail: info@104thefox.com Web Site:www.1045thefox.com Licensee: Journal Broadcast Corp. Group owner: Journal Broadcast Group Inc. (acq 6-11-99; grpsl). Population served: 500,000 Format: Classic rock hits. Target aud: 25-54. ◆Rob Burton, VP & gen mgr; Ray Eric Michaels, opns mgr; Eric McCart, gen sls mgr; Jason Wituk, rgnl sls mgr; Manny Cowzinski, prom dir.

KVWF(FM)— 2006: 100.5 mhz; 25 kw. Ant 276 ft TL: N37 44 13 W97 09 25. Hrs open: Two Brittany Place, 1938 N. Woodlawn, Suite 150, Wichita, 67208. Phone: (316) 558-8800. Fax: (316) 558-8802.E-mail: kvwf@1005thewolf.com Licensee: Connoisseur Media LLC. Format: Country. ◆Doug Downs, gen mgr; Ron Allen, progmg dir.

Baldwin City

*KNBU(FM)— Nov 29, 1965: 89.7 mhz; 100 w. 118 ft TL: N38 46 45 W95 11 15. Hrs open: Box 65, 66006. Phone: (785) 594-6451, EXT. 300. Phone: (785) 594-8300. Fax: (785) 594-3570.E-mail: info@knbu.com Licensee: Baker University. Population served: 2,520 Spec prog: Jazz 15 hrs wkly. ◆Tom Hedrick, gen mgr.

Baxter Springs

KCAR-FM— June 29, 2000: 104.3 mhz; 6 kw. Ant 298 ft TL: N37 07 34 W94 42 12. Hrs open: 2510 W. 20th St., Joplin, MO, 64804. Phone: (417) 781-1313. Fax: (417) 781-1316. Licensee: American Media Investments Inc. Group owner: Petracom Media L.L.C. (acq 2-17-2009; grpsl). Format: Classic rock, oldies. ◆Dave Clemons, gen mgr, gen sls mgr; Bubba Fontaine, progmg dir; Kathleen Pike, traf mgr.

Belle Plaine

KANR(FM)— Mar 4, 1996: 92.7 mhz; 12 kw. Ant 469 ft TL: N37 20 15 W97 27 56. Hrs open: 24 2120 N. Woodlawn, Wichita, 67208. Phone: (316) 652-9275. Fax: (316) 683-0818.E-mail: fiesta927@gmail.com Web Site:www.fiesta927.com Licensee: Daniel D. Smith (acq 2-16-93; $10,700;3-8-93). Population served: 180,000 Format: Rgnl Mexican. ◆Daniel D. Smith, pres; Daniel Smith, gen mgr; Joe Roach, progmg dir; Bruce Adamek, traf mgr.

Belleville

KREP(FM)— June 26, 1984: 92.1 mhz; 14.5 kw. 276 ft TL: N39 45 00 W97 36 48. Stereo. Hrs open: 24 2307 US Hwy. 81, 66935. Phone: (785) 527-2266. Phone: (785) 527-2267. Fax: (785) 527-5919.E-mail: kr-92@nckcn.com Licensee: First Republic Broadcasting Corp. (acq 6-84; 1-84). Natl. Network: ABC, . Format: Country. News staff: one; News: 20 hrs wkly. Target aud: 25-55. ◆Deborah Sasser, pres, gen mgr, progmg dir, news dir; Christine Strutt, gen sls mgr, mktg dir; Marvin Hoffman, chief of engrg; Eric Allgood, sports cmtr.

Beloit

KVSV(AM)— Nov 21, 1979: 1190 khz; 2.3 kw-D, 90 w-N, DA. TL: N39 26 53 W98 04 45. Hrs open: 6 AM-9 PM Box 7, A. Hwy. 24, 67420. Phone: (785) 738-2206. Fax: (785) 738-2208. Web Site:www.kvsvradio.com Licensee: McGrath Publishing Co. (acq 11-1-99; $500,000 with co-located FM). Population served: 51,200 Rgnl. Network: Kan. Agri. Kan. Agriculture Format: Adult contemp. News staff: one; News: 11 hrs wkly. Target aud: General. Spec prog: Farm 9 hrs wkly. ◆John Swanson, gen mgr & progmg dir.

KVSV-FM— Nov 11, 1980: 105.5 mhz; 50 kw. 443 ft TL: N39 28 09 W98 05 37. Stereo. Hrs open: 24 Box 7, E. Hwy. 24, 67420. Phone: (785) 738-2206. Fax: (785) 738-2208.E-mail: info@kvsv.com Web Site:www.kvsvradio.com Format: Btfl music, easy lstng. ◆John Swanson, progmg mgr.

Bronson

*KBJQ(FM)— 2002: 88.3 mhz; 99 kw. Ant 380 ft TL: N37 53 56 W95 00 09. Hrs open: Drawer 3206, Tupelo, MS, 38803. Phone: (662) 844-8888 ext. 204. Fax: (662) 842-6791. Licensee: American Family Association. Group owner: American Family Radio Population served: 127,972 Format: Relg. ◆Marvin Sanders, gen mgr.

Burdett

KKDT(FM)—Not on air, target date: unknown: 93.5 mhz; 100 kw. Ant 974 ft TL: N38 36 32 W99 42 11. Hrs open: 980 N. Michigan Ave., Suite 1880, Chicago, IL, 60611. Phone: (312) 204-9900. Licensee: College Creek Media LLC. ◆Christopher F. Devine, gen mgr.

Burlington

KSNP(FM)— June 14, 1990: 97.7 mhz; 17.2 kw. Ant 584 ft TL: N38 09 57 W95 32 19. Hrs open: 6 AM-11 PM Box 233, 1910 S. 6th, 66839. Phone: (620) 364-8807. Fax: (620) 364-2047.E-mail: ksnp@kans.com Licensee: My Town Media Inc. (group owner; (acq 1999; $230,000). Rgnl. Network: Mid-American Ag. Mid-America Ag Format: Hot country. News staff: one; News: 5 hrs wkly. Target aud: 25-45; industrial employees. Spec prog: Farm 8 hrs, relg 3 hrs wkly. ◆Peg Downard, stn mgr, sls dir & gen sls mgr; Mindy Ryan, progmg dir.

Caney

KEOJ(FM)— Oct 15, 1992: 101.1 mhz; 3 kw. 328 ft TL: N36 58 19 W95 53 47. Stereo. Hrs open: 24 City Plex Towers, Ste 5500, 2448 E. 81 St., Tulsa, OK, 74137. Phone: (918) 492-2660. Fax: (918) 492-8840.E-mail: kxoj@kxoj.com Web Site:www.kxoj.com Licensee: KXOJ Inc. Group owner: Adonai Radio Group (acq 4-29-92; grpsl). Format: Contemp Christian. Target aud: 18-35; young married Christians. ◆Mike Stephens, pres; Joy Stephens, VP; David Stephens, gen mgr, stn mgr; Bob Thornton, sls dir, progmg dir; Joe Hancock, chief of engrg; Darcy Kimble, traf mgr.

Cawker City

KZDY(FM)— 1999: 96.3 mhz; 13 kw. Ant 230 ft TL: N39 30 29 W98 18 57. Stereo. Hrs open: 24 Box 88, Glen Elder, 67446. Phone: (785) 545-3220. Fax: (785) 545-3220.E-mail: info@kzdy.com Licensee: Dierking Communications Inc. Group owner: Hoeflicker Stns. (acq 7-27-2006). Natl. Network: Jones Radio Networks, AP Radio, . Kenkel & Associates. Format: Adult contemp. News staff: one; News: 6 hrs wkly. Target aud: 18-60. ◆Wade Gerstner, gen mgr.

Chanute

*KJVL(FM)—Not on air, target date: unknown: 90.3 mhz; 17 kw. Ant 528 ft TL: N37 35 59 W95 39 10. Hrs open: Box 14, Abilene, 67410. Phone: (785) 263-7200. Fax: (785) 263-3876.E-mail: radioforlife@kjill.com Web Site:www.kjill057.com Licensee: Great Plains Christian Radio Inc. ◆Robert D. Hughes, CEO.

KKOY(AM)— Nov 17, 1952: 1460 khz; 1 kw-D, 57 w-N. TL: N37 41 18 W95 28 12. Hrs open: 24 Box 788, 66720-0788. Secondary address: 702 N. Plummer Sts. 66720. Phone: (620) 431-3700. Fax: (620) 431-4643.E-mail: info@kkoy.com Web Site:www.tallgrassnation.com /1460KKOY/index.php Licensee: My Town Media Inc. (group owner; (acq 5-21-97; $464,447 with co-located FM). Population served: 53,000 Natl. Network: ESPN Radio, . Rgnl. Network: Kan. Info., Kan. Agri, Mid-American Ag. Format: Sports. Target aud: 25-54. ◆Bill Wachter, gen mgr; Heather Lee, progmg dir; Rob Strand, news dir.

KKOY-FM— Jan 1, 1971: 105.5 mhz; 8 kw. Ant 584 ft TL: N37 35 59 W95 39 10. Stereo. Hrs open: 24 Prog sep from AM Box 788 , 66720. Secondary address: 702 N. Plummer Sts. 66720. Phone: (620) 431-3700. Fax: (620) 431-4643.E-mail: sales@kkoy.com Web Site:www.kkoy.com Licensee: My Town Media Inc. Natl. Network: ABC, . Format: Hot adult contemp.

Cimarron

KMML(FM)— February 2008: 92.9 mhz; 7.1 kw. Ant 610 ft TL: N37 56 29.6 W100 18 44.3. Hrs open:
Rebroadcasts KSMM-FM Liberal 100%.
150 Plaza Dr., Liberal, 67901. Phone: (620) 624-8156. Fax: (620) 624-4606. Licensee: Radioactive LLC. Format: Rgnl Mexican. ◆Benjamin L. Homel, pres; Enrique Franz, gen mgr.

Clay Center

KCLY(FM)— Jan 6, 1978: 100.9 mhz; 35.5 kw. Ant 581 ft TL: N39 28 03 W97 03 45. Stereo. Hrs open: 1815 Meadowlark Rd., 67432. Phone: (785) 632-5661. Fax: (785) 632-5662. Web Site:www.kclyradio.com Licensee: Taylor Communications. (acq 8-94; 1-78). Population served: 150,000 Natl. Network: AP Network News, . Wire Svc: AP Format: Radio for grownups. Target aud: 24-55; general. ◆Kyle Bauer, gen

mgr; Rocky Downing, stn mgr, sports cmtr; Joyce Beck, gen sls mgr; Jamie Bloom, progmg dir; Rod Keen, engrg mgr; Joe Woodward, traf mgr.

Clearwater

KFH-FM—Licensed to Clearwater. See Wichita

Coffeyville

KGGF(AM)— 1930: 690 khz; 10 kw-D, 5 kw-N, DA-2. TL: N37 08 58 W95 28 27. Hrs open: Box 1087, 306 W. 8th St., 67337. Phone: (620) 251-3800. Fax: (620) 251-9210.E-mail: radioresultsgroup1@sbcglobal.net Web Site:radioresultsgoup.com Licensee: KGGF-KUSN Inc. Group owner: Mahaffey Enterprises Inc. (acq 12-26-90; $750,000 with co-located FM; 1-14-91). Population served: 100,000 Natl. Network: ABC, . Rgnl. Network: Kan. Agri. Kan. Agriculture Format: News/Talk/Sports. News staff: one; News: 5 hrs wkly. Target aud: 35 plus. ♦Robert Mahaffey, pres & gen mgr.

KKRK(FM)— Sept 1, 1983: 98.9 mhz; 6 kw. Ant 305 ft TL: N37 06 28 W95 43 22. Stereo. Hrs open: 24 Box 1087, 67337. Secondary address: 306 W. 8th St. 67337. Phone: (620) 251-3800. Fax: (620) 251-9210.E-mail: radioresultsgroup@sbcglobal.net Web Site:radioresultsgroup.com Licensee: KGGF-KUSN, Inc. Population served: 65,000. Format: Classic rock. News staff: one. Target aud: 35-54. ♦Rober Mahaffey, pres; Ron Lee, progmg dir; Lance Allred, news dir.

Colby

KRDQ(FM)— September 1971: 100.3 mhz; 100 kw. Ant 610 ft TL: N39 28 50 W100 54 34. Stereo. Hrs open: 24 1065 S. Range, 67701. Phone: (785) 462-3305. Fax: (785) 462-3307. Licensee: Rocking M Radio Inc. Population served: 55,000 Natl. Network: ABC, . Rgnl. Network: Mid America AG Network. Mid-America Ag Format: Hot adult contemp. Target aud: 18-49; general. ♦Mike Fell, gen mgr & farm dir.

***KTCC(FM)**— May 1974: 91.9 mhz; 3 kw. 199 ft TL: N39 22 34 W101 03 08. Stereo. Hrs open: 24 1255 S. Range, 67701. Phone: (785) 462-3984, EXT. 309. Fax: (785) 462-4600. Web Site:www.colbycc.edu Licensee: Colby Community College. Population served: 25,000 Format: CHR. News staff: one; News: 14 hrs wkly. Target aud: 18-25; young adults. Spec prog: Sports 3 hrs, classic rock 3 hrs, hard rock 7 hrs, hip hop 4 hrs wkly. ♦Corey Sorenson, stn mgr.

KWGB(FM)— Sept 1, 1998: 97.9 mhz; 100 kw. Ant 712 ft TL: N39 23 19 W101 33 34. Hrs open: 24 3023 W. 31st St., Goodland, 67765. Phone: (785) 899-2309. Fax: (785) 899-3062. Licensee: Melia Communications Inc. (group owner) Population served: 50,000 Format: Country. ♦Martin K. Melia, pres & gen mgr; Martin Melia, gen sls mgr; Curtis Duncan, progmg dir.

KXXX(AM)— August 1947: 790 khz; 5 kw-D. TL: N39 23 35 W101 00 06. Hrs open: 24 1065 S. Range, 67701. Phone: (785) 462-3305. Fax: (785) 462-3307. Licensee: Rocking M Radio Inc. Group owner: Waitt Broadcasting Inc. (acq 8-31-2007; grpsl). Population served: 55,000 Natl. Network: Westwood One, . Rgnl. Network: Mid-American Ag. Mid-America Ag Format: Country. News staff: one; News: 5 hrs wkly. Target aud: 35-55; male, female, city & rural. ♦Mike Fell, gen mgr & stn mgr; Joe Vyzourek, progmg dir.

Coldwater

***KNJT(FM)**—Not on air, target date: unknown: 90.3 mhz; 1 kw. Ant 128 ft TL: N37 16 06 W99 19 33. Hrs open: 505 Josephine St., Titusville, FL, 32796. Phone: (321) 267-3000. Fax: (321) 264-9370.E-mail: wpio@gate.net Licensee: Florida Public Radio Inc. ♦Randy Henry, pres.

Columbus

KBZI(FM)— Feb 1, 1980: 107.1 mhz; 11.7 kw. Ant 489 ft TL: N37 14 15 W94 44 15. Stereo. Hrs open: 2510 W. 20th St., Joplin, MO, 64804. Phone: (417) 781-1313. Fax: (417) 781-1316.E-mail: info@rock105kjml.com Licensee: American Media Investments Inc. (acq 2-17-2009; grpsl). Natl. Network: ABC, . Format: Modern rock. News staff: one; News: 2 hrs wkly. Target aud: 18-49; growing families with needs for a wide range of goods & svcs. ♦Dave Clemons, gen sls mgr; Bubba Fontaine, progmg dir; Kathleen Pike, gen mgr & traf mgr.

KMOQ(FM)— Dec 25, 1982: 105.3 mhz; 12.5 kw. Ant 289 ft TL: N37 07 58 W94 41 38. Stereo. Hrs open: 24 2510 W. 20th St., Joplin, MO, 64804. Phone: (417) 781-1313. Fax: (417) 781-1316.E-mail: info@kmoq10.com Web Site:www.kmoq107.com Licensee: American Media Investments Inc. Group owner: Petracom Media L.L.C. (acq 2-17-2009; grpsl). Population served: 325,000 Natl. Network: ABC, . Format: CHR. Target aud: 25-54. ♦Dave Clemons, CFO, gen sls mgr; Chris Stevens, progmg dir; Kathleen Pike, VP & traf mgr.

Concordia

KCKS(FM)— Sept 1, 1978: 94.9 mhz; 100 kw. Ant 528 ft TL: N39 26 19 W97 42 16. Stereo. Hrs open: 24 Box 629, 66901. Secondary address: Rt. 1 W. 11th St. 66901. Phone: (789) 243-1414. Fax: (785) 243-1391. Licensee: KNCK, Inc. Population served: 7,852 Wire Svc: National Weather Network Format: Hot adult contemp. ♦Joe Jindra, pres.

KNCK(AM)— Feb 6, 1954: 1390 khz; 500 w-D, 54 w-N. TL: N39 33 58 W97 41 04. Hrs open: 24 Box 629, Rt. 1 W. 11th St., 66901. Phone: (785) 243-1414. Fax: (785) 243-1391. Licensee: KNCK Inc. (acq 10-18-89; $190,000 with co-located FM; 11-6-89). Population served: 196,000 Rgnl. Network: Kan. Agri., Kan. Info. Format: Country. News staff: news progmg 7 hrs wkly News: one;. Target aud: 45 plus. Spec prog: Public affrs 2 hrs wkly. ♦Joe Jindra, pres, gen mgr; Marvin Hoffman, chief of engrg.

***KVCO(FM)**— May 1, 1977: 88.3 mhz; 127 w. 77 ft TL: N39 33 17 W97 39 48. Stereo. Hrs open: Box 1002, 2221 Campus Dr., 66901. Phone: (785) 243-1435. Phone: (785) 243-4444. Fax: (785) 243-1043.E-mail: info@kvco.com Licensee: Cloud County Community College. Population served: 8,000 Natl. Network: CNN Radio, . Format: Div/var. Target aud: 16-30 plus; students & young adults. ♦John Chapin, gen mgr.

Copeland

***KHYM(FM)**— Dec 23, 1997: 103.9 mhz; 100 kw. 702 ft TL: N37 28 35 W100 35 59. Stereo. Hrs open: 24 Box 991, 909 W. Carthage, Mead, 67864-0991. Phone: (620) 873-2991. Fax: (620) 873-2755.E-mail: khym@khym.com Web Site:www.khym.org Licensee: Great Plains Christian Radio Inc. Format: Relg, Christian. News staff: one. Target aud: 25-54. ♦Don Hughes, pres, gen mgr; Glenn Hascoll, stn mgr; Steve Larsen, chief of engrg.

***KJIL(FM)**— Sept 5, 1992: 99.1 mhz; 100 kw. Ant 935 ft TL: N37 23 35 W100 35 59. Stereo. Hrs open: 24 Box 991, 909 W. Carthage, Meade, 67864-0991. Phone: (620) 873-2991. Fax: (620) 873-2755.E-mail: kjil@kjil.com Web Site:www.kjil.com Licensee: Great Plains Christian Radio Inc. Population served: 368,164 Natl. Network: Moody, USA, . Format: Contemp Christian, relg. Target aud: 25-60; Evangelical Christians. ♦Don Hughes, pres, gen mgr; Michael Luskey, opns dir; Delvin Kinser, news dir; Steve Larson, chief of engrg; Polly Hughes, traf mgr.

KSKZ(FM)— May 1, 1994: 98.1 mhz; 100 kw. Ant 666 ft TL: N37 30 00 W100 40 00. Hrs open: 24 Box 759, 1402 E. Kansas Ave., Garden City, 67846. Phone: (620) 276-2366. Fax: (620) 276-3568.E-mail: info@wksradio.com Web Site:www.wksradio.com Licensee: Ingstad Broadcasting Inc. Group owner: Robert Ingstad Broadcast Properties (acq 1-27-95;3-20-95). Population served: 135,000 Format: Hot adult contemp. Target aud: 25-54. ♦Gil Wohler, gen mgr, gen sls mgr; James Janda, progmg dir; Andrew Mahoney, news dir; Tom Dial, chief of engrg; Rachel Wheet, traf mgr.

Dearing

KUSN(FM)— Oct 1, 1999: 98.1 mhz; 9.7 kw. 495 ft TL: N37 06 28 W95 43 22. Stereo. Hrs open: 24 hours daily Box 4584, Springfield, MO, 65808. Secondary address: 306 W. 8th St., Coffeyville 67337. Phone: (417) 883-9180. Fax: (417) 883-9096. Licensee: KGGF-KUSN Inc. Group owner: Mahaffey Enterprises Inc. Format: Country. Target aud: 18-49. ♦Robert B. Mahaffey, pres; John Leonard, gen mgr.

Derby

KZCH(FM)— 1978: 96.3 mhz; 50 kw. 492 ft TL: N37 37 03 W97 20 11. Stereo. Hrs open: 24 9323 E. 37th St. N., Wichita, 67226. Phone: (316) 494-6600. Fax: (316) 494-6730.E-mail: info@channel963.com Web Site:www.channel963.com Licensee: Clear Channel Broadcasting Licenses Inc. Group owner: Clear Channel Communications Inc. (acq 8-30-2000; grpsl). Population served: 276,554 Natl. Rep: Clear Channel,. Format: Chr. Target aud: 18-34; women.

Dodge City

KAHE(FM)— May 1966: 95.5 mhz; 100 kw. Ant 577 ft TL: N37 38 28 W100 20 40. Stereo. Hrs open: 24 2601 Central Ave., Suite C, 67801. Secondary address: 106 W Frontview 67801. Phone: (620) 225-8080. Fax: (620) 225-6655.E-mail: rockswks@global.net Web Site:www.rockingmradio.com Licensee: Rocking M Radio Inc. Population served: 130,000 Natl. Network: Fox Sports, . Format: contemporary oldies. News: 5 hrs wkly. Target aud: 25-49. ♦Brian Nugen, gen mgr; Peggy Burdick, sls dir.

***KAIG(FM)**— 2008: 89.9 mhz; 100 kw vert. Ant 695 ft TL: N37 55 56 W100 19 02. Hrs open:
Rebroadcasts KLRD(FM) Yucaipa, CA 100%.
2351 Sunset Blvd., Suite 170-218, Rocklin, CA, 95765. Phone: (916) 251-1600. Fax: (916) 251-1650. Web Site:www.air1.com Licensee: Educational Media Foundation. Natl. Network: Air 1, . Format: Christian. ♦Mike Novak, pres; Keith Whipple, dev dir; David Pierce, progmg mgr; Ed Lenane, news dir; Sam Wallington, engrg dir; Marya Morgan, news rptr.

KDCC(AM)— 1992: 1550 khz; 1 kw-D, 90 w-N, DA-2. TL: N37 47 14 W100 01 55. Hrs open: 7 AM-10 PM 3004 N. 14th, 67801-2007. Phone: (620) 225-6783. Phone: (620) 225-6720. Fax: (620) 225-0918. Licensee: Dodge City Community College (acq 6-7-92; $11,400; 7-27-92). Population served: 30,000 Natl. Network: Sporting News Radio Network, . Format: Sports. Target aud: 18 plus. ♦John Ewy, gen mgr & sls dir.

KGNO(AM)— June 30, 1930: 1370 khz; 5 kw-D, 230 w-N. TL: N37 45 36 W100 05 53. Hrs open: 2601 Central Ave., Suite C, Village Plaza, 67801. Secondary address: 106 W Frontview 67801. Phone: (620) 225-8080. Fax: (620) 225-6655.E-mail: rockswks@sbcgobal.net Web Site:www.rockingmradio.com Licensee: Rocking M Radio Inc. Group owner: Waitt Broadcasting Inc. (acq 8-31-2007; grpsl). Population served: 85,000 Natl. Network: ESPN Radio, Fox News Radio, . Rgnl. Network: Mid-American Ag. Mid-America Ag Format: News, sports, talk radio. Target aud: 25-54. Spec prog: Farm 15 hrs wkly. ♦Mark Hinca, gen mgr; Brian Nugen, opns mgr; Peggy Burdick, rgnl sls mgr.

***KONQ(FM)**— Apr 26, 1978: 91.9 mhz; 2.6 kw. 123 ft TL: N37 46 33 W100 02 12. Hrs open: 3004 N. 14th, 67801-2007. Phone: (620) 225-6783. Phone: (620) 225-6720. Fax: (620) 225-0918. Web Site:www.dodgecitycommunitycollege.com Licensee: Dodge City Community College. Population served: 25,000 Format: Var/div, educ, MOR. News: 7 hrs wkly. Spec prog: Black 10 hrs, sports 5 hrs wkly. ♦John Ewy, gen mgr.

***KVDC(FM)**—Not on air, target date: unknown: 88.7 mhz; 45 kw vertr. Ant 348 ft TL: N37 55 37 W99 55 07. Hrs open: 219 Dodd Rd., Ringgold, GA, 30736-2958. Phone: (706) 965-2355. Licensee: Victor Broadcasting Inc. (acq 2-5-2009). ♦James E. Price III, pres.

KZRD(FM)— December 1997: 93.9 mhz; 100 kw. 511 ft TL: N38 00 07 W101 14 45. Hrs open: 2601 Central Ave., Village Plaza Suite C, 67801. Secondary address: 106 W Frontview 67801. Phone: (620) 225-8080. Fax: (620) 225-6655.E-mail: rockswks@sbcglobal.net Web Site:www.rockingmradio.com Licensee: Rocking M Radio Inc. Group owner: Waitt Broadcasting Inc. (acq 8-31-2007; grpsl). Format: Classic rock. ♦Mark Hinca, gen mgr; Brian Nugen, opns mgr.

Downs

KDNS(FM)— Apr 11, 1994: 94.1 mhz; 28 kw. Ant 292 ft TL: N39 30 29 W98 18 57. Stereo. Hrs open: 5 AM-1 AM Box 88, West Hwy. 24, Glen Elder, 67446. Phone: (785) 545-3220.E-mail: info@kdnsfm.com Licensee: Dierking Communications Inc. (acq 7-27-2006; $276,000). Natl. Network: Jones Radio Networks, . Rgnl. Network: Brownfield. Brownfield Format: Country. News staff: one; News: 4 hrs wkly. Target aud: 25-54. Spec prog: Farm 6 hrs, gospel 5 hrs wkly. ♦Wade Gerstner, gen mgr.

Effingham

KDVB(FM)— Mar 12, 2008: 96.9 mhz; 120 w. Ant 227 ft TL: N39 33 07 W95 25 23. Hrs open: 825 S. Kansas Ave., Suite 100, Topeka, 66612. Phone: (785) 272-2122. Fax: (785) 272-6219. Licensee: Cumulus Licensing LLC. ♦Spike Santee, gen mgr.

El Dorado

KAHS(AM)— Nov 16, 1953: 1360 khz; 1 kw-D. TL: N37 48 47 W96 48 44. Hrs open: 24 201 N. Industrial Park Rd., Excelsior Springs, MO, 64024. Phone: (316) 320-1360.E-mail: 1360kahs@gmail.com Web Site:www.1360kahs.com Licensee: Catholic Radio Network Inc. (group

owner; (acq 12-12-2005; $525,000). Population served: 500,000 Natl. Network: CNN Radio, Westwood One, . Format: Relg. Target aud: 35-69. Spec prog: . Jazz 2 hrs wkly ♦James E. O'Laughlin, pres.

***KBTL(FM)**— March 1998: 88.1 mhz; 400 w. 92 ft TL: N37 48 16 W96 53 02. Stereo. Hrs open: Butler County Community College, 901 S. Haverhill Rd., 67042. Phone: (316) 321-2222. Licensee: Butler County Community College. Format: Div. ♦Lance D. Hayes, gen mgr.

***KTLI(FM)**— Feb 15, 1972: 99.1 mhz; 100 kw. Ant 617 ft TL: N37 56 22 W96 59 20. Stereo. Hrs open: 125 N. Market, Suite 1900, Wichita, 67202. Phone: (316) 303-9999. Fax: (316) 303-9900.E-mail: info@ktli.com Web Site:k-love.com Licensee: El Dorado Licenses Inc. Group owner: KXOJ Inc. (acq 12-3-2004; $2.95 million). Population served: 500,000 Format: Adult contemp, Christian. News: 25 hrs wkly. Target aud: 25-54; women. ♦Crystal Wojtecko, gen mgr & rgnl sls mgr.

Emporia

***KANH(FM)**— 2002: 89.7 mhz; 3 kw. Ant 262 ft TL: N38 21 45 W96 07 00. Hrs open: 1120 W. 11th St., Lawrence, 66044. Phone: (785) 864-4530. Fax: (785) 864-5278.E-mail: kpr@ku.edu Web Site:www.kpr.ku.edu Licensee: University of Kansas. Natl. Network: NPR, . Format: Class, jazz. ♦Janet Campbell, gen mgr.

KANS(FM)— April 1998: 96.1 mhz; 6 kw. 318 ft TL: N38 24 21 W96 14 13. Hrs open: 1811 W. 6th Ave., 66801. Phone: (620) 343-9393. Fax: (620) 342-7617.E-mail: kans@ksradio.com Licensee: C&C Consulting Inc. (acq 11-14-97; $10,000 for CP). Format: Soft hits. ♦Brook Reed, pres, traf mgr; Marty Hill, gen mgr, opns mgr & dev dir; Angie Boden, progmg dir.

KFFX(FM)— June 15, 1966: 104.9 mhz; 3 kw. Ant 279 ft TL: N38 23 10 W96 10 36. Stereo. Hrs open: 24 Prog sep from AM Box 968, 1420 C of E Dr., 66801. Phone: (620) 342-1400. Fax: (620) 342-0804. Format: Hot adult contemp. News: 4 hrs wkly. Target aud: 20-40.

***KNGM(FM)**— Jan 11, 1987: 91.9 mhz; 3 kw. Ant 263 ft TL: N38 24 35 W96 13 30. Stereo. Hrs open: 24 Box 506, 815 Graham St., 66801. Phone: (620) 343-9292.E-mail: kngm@osprey.net Licensee: Great Plains Christian Radio Inc. (acq 12-1-2007; $32,000). Population served: 60,000 Format: Contemp Christian. News staff: one. Target aud: Young families and adults. ♦Robert D. Hughes, CEO.

***KPOR(FM)**— June 19, 2002: 90.7 mhz; 2 kw. Ant 328 ft TL: N38 26 50 W96 07 42. Hrs open: 24 Box 286, Shenandoah, IA, 51501. Phone: (620) 342-1474. Web Site:www.familyradio.com Licensee: Family Stations Inc. (group owner) Format: Relg. ♦Harold Camping, gen mgr.

KVOE(AM)— Jan 21, 1939: 1400 khz; 1 kw-U. TL: N38 23 10 W96 10 36. Hrs open: Box 968, 1420 C of E Dr., 66801. Phone: (620) 342-1400. Fax: (620) 342-0804.E-mail: kvoe@kvoe.com Web Site:www.kvoe.com Licensee: Emporia Radio Stations Inc. Group owner: Emporia's Radio Stations Inc. (acq 1-7-87). Population served: 37,500 Irwin, Campbell & Tannenwald. Format: Adult contemp, oldies, news. Target aud: 35-54. Spec prog: Sp 3 hrs wkly. ♦Lee Schroeder, gen mgr, gen sls mgr; Ron Thomas, progmg dir; Jeff O'Dell, news dir; Charlie Allen, chief of engrg.

KVOE-FM— Jan 16, 1985: 101.7 mhz; 3.2 kw. Ant 298 ft TL: N38 21 45 W96 07 00. Stereo. Hrs open: 24 1420 C of E Dr., 66801. Phone: (620) 342-1400. Fax: (620) 342-0804.E-mail: kvoe@kvoe.com Licensee: Emporia Radio Stations Inc. Group owner: Emporia's Radio Stations Inc. (acq 1994). Rgnl. Network: Kan. Agri. Irwin, Campbell & Tannenwald. Format: Country. News staff: 2; News: 7 hrs wkly. Target aud: 25-54. ♦Erren Harter, pres, prom mgr; Steve Sauder, CEO, pres & gen sls mgr; Jef O'Dell, news dir, chief of engrg; Greg Rahe, sports cmtr.

Enterprise

***KBMP(FM)**— Mar 6, 2002: 90.5 mhz; 19 kw. Ant 384 ft TL: N39 07 53.9 W97 19 58.8. Hrs open: 24
Rebroadcasts KSIV-FM Saint Louis, MO 100%.
209 N. Meridian Rd., Newton, 67114. Phone: (316) 283-4592. Fax: (316) 283-3177.E-mail: comments@bottradionetwork.com Web Site:www.bottradionetwork.com Licensee: Community Broadcasting Inc. Group owner: American Family Radio (acq 1-26-2006; $30,000 with KARF(FM) Independence). Format: Christian teaching and talk. Target aud: 25-54; adults. ♦Dan Snell, gen mgr.

Eureka

KOTE(FM)— October 1988: 93.5 mhz; 3 kw. 321 ft TL: N37 47 29 W96 17 25. Stereo. Hrs open: 24 Box 350, 67045. Secondary address: 1275 P. Rd. 67045. Phone: (620) 583-7414. Fax: (620) 583-7233.E-mail: steve@kotefm.com Web Site:www.koteinfo.com Licensee: Niemeyer Communications LLC (acq 8-15-2005; $125,000). Population served: 15,000 Rgnl. Network: Kan. Info. Format: Classic rock, country. News staff: one. Target aud: General. ♦Steve Niemeyer, gen mgr.

Fairway

KCNW(AM)— Apr 16, 1953: 1380 khz; 2.5 kw-D, 29 w-N. TL: N39 04 19 W94 40 58. Hrs open: 24 4535 Metropolitan Ave., Kansas City, 66106. Phone: (913) 384-1380. Fax: (913) 236-9470.E-mail: kcnw@wilkinsradio.com Web Site:www.wilkinsradio.com Licensee: Kansas City Radio Inc. Group owner: Wilkins Communications Network Inc. (acq 1-17-2001; $725,000). Population served: 2,000,000 Natl. Network: Westwood One, . Womble, Carlyle, Sandridge & Rice. Format: Christian teaching, talk. News staff: one. Target aud: 35 plus; adults involved in community & family. ♦Bob Wilkins, pres; LuAnn Wilkins, exec VP; Mitchell Mathis, VP; Kevin Fears, gen mgr, stn mgr; Greg Garrett, opns mgr; Kirk Chestnut, engr.

Fort Scott

KMDO(AM)— Oct 8, 1954: 1600 khz; 770 w-D, 35 w-N. TL: N37 47 01 W94 42 00. Hrs open: Box 72, 2 N. National, 66701. Secondary address: 2 North National Ave 66701. Phone: (620) 223-4500. Phone: (620) 223-4501. Fax: (620) 223-5662.E-mail: kmdo@kombfm.com Web Site:www.kombfm.com Licensee: Fort Scott Broadcasting Co. (acq 2-1-60). Population served: 25,000 Natl. Network: CNN Radio, . Format: Oldies, rock. Target aud: General; 30 plus. ♦Tim McKenney, pres.

KOMB(FM)— Jan 23, 1981: 103.9 mhz; 25 kw. Ant 328 ft TL: N37 54 30 W94 45 58. Stereo. Hrs open: Box 72, 2 N. National, 66701. Secondary address: 2 North Naitonal Ave. 66701. Phone: (620) 223-4500. Phone: (620) 223-4501. Fax: (620) 223-5662.E-mail: komb@kombfm.com Web Site:kombfm.com Natl. Network: CNN Radio, . Format: Classic Hits. ♦Timothy McKenney, pres; Don Pollnow, gen mgr; Sibyl Overstreet, gen sls mgr; Kent Jones, progmg mgr; Stephen Bennett, news dir; Lisa Sykes, prom.

***KVCY(FM)**— November 1983: 104.7 mhz; 16 kw. 410 ft TL: N37 47 47 W94 42 20. Stereo. Hrs open: 24 3434 W. Kilbourn Ave., Milwaukee, WI, 53208. Phone: (414) 935-3000. Fax: (414) 935-3015.E-mail: kvcy@vcyamerica.org Web Site:www.vcyamerica.org Licensee: VCY America Inc. (group owner) Natl. Network: USA, Moody, . Format: Relg, Christian. ♦Vic Eliason, VP & gen mgr; Jim Schneider, progmg dir.

Fredonia

KGGF-FM— July 14, 1997: 104.1 mhz; 6 kw. 328 ft TL: N37 31 36 W95 49 39. Hrs open: 24 Box 1087, Coffeyville, 67337. Phone: (620) 251-3800. Fax: (620) 251-9210. Licensee: KGGF-KUSN Inc. Group owner: Mahaffey Enterprises Inc. Format: Oldies 60s & 70s. ♦Paul Cooper, gen mgr.

Galena

KQYX(AM)— 1927: 1450 khz; 940 w-U. TL: N37 04 10 W94 32 49. Hrs open: 24 2510 W. 20th St., Joplin, MO, 64804-0216. Phone: (417) 781-1313. Fax: (417) 781-1316. Licensee: American Media Investments Inc. Group owner: Petracom Media L.L.C. (acq 2-17-2009; grpsl). Population served: 240,000 Wiley Rein LLP. Format: News/talk. Target aud: 18-39. ♦Dave Clemons, gen sls mgr; Matt Kruger, progmg dir; Kathleen Pike, traf mgr.

Garden City

***KANZ(FM)**— June 29, 1980: 91.1 mhz; 100 kw. Ant 958 ft TL: N37 46 43 W100 53 43.4. Stereo. Hrs open: 5 AM-midnight
Rebroadcasts KZNA(FM) Hill City 100%.
210 N. 7th St., 67846-5519. Phone: (620) 275-7444. Phone: (800) 678-7444. Web Site:www.hppr.org Licensee: KANZA Society Inc. (acq 11-77; 7-80). Population served: 270,000 Natl. Network: PRI, NPR, . Format: Div, educ, class. News: 39 hrs wkly. Target aud: General. Spec prog: Jazz 15 hrs, folk 6 hrs, Sp 6 hrs wkly. ♦Richard Hicks, gen mgr; Robert Kirby, progmg dir.

KBUF(AM)—(Holcomb, 1948: 1030 khz; 2.5 kw-D, 1.2 kw-N, DA-N. TL: N38 00 01 W100 53 54. Hrs open: 24 Box 759, 1402 E. Kansas, 67846. Phone: (620) 276-2366. Fax: (620) 276-3568. Licensee: KBUF Partnership. Group owner: Robert Ingstad Broadcast Properties (acq 11-1-79). Population served: 30000 Rgnl. Network: Mid-American Ag. Mid-America Ag Fisher, Wayland, Cooper, Leader & Zaragoza L.L.P. Wire Svc: NWS (National Weather Service) Wire Svc: UPI Format: C&W, talk. News staff: one. Target aud: 25-54; people interested in class country & info progmg. Spec prog: Farm 15 hrs wkly. ♦Gill Wohler, gen mgr; James Janda, progmg mgr.

KGGS(AM)—Not on air, target date: unknown: 1340 khz; 1 kw-D, 880 w-N. TL: N37 58 08 W100 55 56. Hrs open: 609 E. Kansas Plaza, 67846. Phone: (620) 276-3251. Fax: (620) 276-3649. Licensee: Steckline Communications Inc. (acq 6-17-2009; $60,000 for CP). ♦Gregory R. Steckline, pres.

KIUL(AM)— May 20, 1935: 1240 khz; 1 kw-U. TL: N37 59 52 W100 54 25. Hrs open: 609 E. Kansas Plaza, 67846. Phone: (620) 276-3251. Fax: (620) 276-3649. Web Site:www.kiulradio.com Licensee: Steckline Communications Inc. (group owner; (acq 11-28-2006; $550,000 with KYUL(AM) Scott City). Population served: 50,000 Natl. Network: CBS, Westwood One, . Rgnl. Network: Mid-American Ag. Dow, Lohnes & Albertson. Format: Sports, news/talk. News staff: 2; News: 20 hrs wkly. Target aud: 45 plus; upscale adults. Spec prog: Farm 5 hrs wkly. ♦Rick Thomeczek, gen mgr; Danny Havel, opns mgr.

KKJQ(FM)— Nov 20, 1962: 97.3 mhz; 100 kw. 850 ft TL: N37 46 48 W100 27 36. Stereo. Hrs open: 24 Prog sep from AM Box 759, 67846. Phone: (620) 276-2366. Fax: (620) 276-3568. Licensee: KBUF Partnership Population served: 75,000 Natl. Network: ABC, . Format: Country, adult contemp. Target aud: 18-49.

KWKR(FM)—See Leoti

Girard

***KFKB(FM)**—Not on air, target date: unknown: 91.9 mhz; 50 kw. Ant 305 ft TL: N37 36 15.8 W95 16 30. Hrs open: 4703 Orkney Dr., Missouri City, TX, 77459. Phone: (281) 923-7100. Licensee: Grace Public Radio. ♦Fred R. Morton, gen mgr.

KSEK-FM— Sept 1, 1988: 99.1 mhz; 6 kw. Ant 325 ft TL: N37 29 02 W94 51 08. Hrs open: 202 E. Centenial Dr., Suite 2B, Pittsburg, 66762. Phone: (620) 232-9912. Fax: (620) 232-9915.E-mail: lynnm@skilonline.com Licensee: Southeast Kansas Independent Living Resource Center Inc. (group owner; (acq 11-30-2004; $700,000 with KSEK(AM) Pittsburg). Natl. Network: AP Network News, . Format: Classic rock. News: 10 hrs wkly. Target aud: 25-54; resident adults & univ. students. ♦Lynn Meredith, pres & gen mgr.

Goodland

***KDOO(FM)**—Not on air, target date: unknown: 88.3 mhz; 3.3 kw. Ant 285 ft TL: N39 18 30 W101 44 35. Hrs open: 151 Morgan St., Cranston, RI, 02920. Phone: (401) 578-7919. Licensee: The Marconi Broadcasting Foundation. ♦Michael Cardillo, pres.

***KGCR(FM)**— Mar 1, 1988: 107.7 mhz; 100 kw. 446 ft TL: N39 22 03 W101 26 44. Stereo. Hrs open: 24 Box 9, Brewster, 67732. Secondary address: 3410 Rd. 66, Brewster 67732. Phone: (785) 694-2877. Fax: (785) 694-2875.E-mail: info@kgcr.com Licensee: The Praise Network Inc. (acq 7-2-98). Population served: 40,000 Natl. Network: Moody, USA, . Format: Relg. News staff: one; News: 30 hrs wkly. Target aud: 25-54; Christian families. Spec prog: Farm 2 hrs wkly. ♦Lloyd Mintzmyer, CEO & pres; James Claasson, gen mgr.

KKCI(FM)— Sept 15, 1990: 102.5 mhz; 100 kw. 712 ft TL: N39 23 19 W101 33 34. Stereo. Hrs open: 24 Box 569 , 3023 W. 31st St., 67735. Phone: (785) 899-2309. Fax: (785) 899-3062. (Acq 4-90; $40,000; 5-21-90). Natl. Network: Jones Radio Networks, . Format: Adult contemp, sports, jazz. Target aud: 25-55.

KLOE(AM)— 1947: 730 khz; 1 kw-D, 20 w-N. TL: N39 20 04 W101 45 28. Hrs open: 24 Box 569, 3023 W. 31st St., 67735-0569. Phone: (785) 899-2309. Fax: (785) 899-3062.E-mail: info@kloe.com Web Site:www.kloe.com Licensee: Melia Communications Inc. (group owner; acq 1-26-96; $990,000 with co-located FM). Population served: 100,000 Natl. Network: CBS, . Rgnl. Network: Kan. Agri. Kan. Agriculture Format: News/talk, country, farm. Target aud: General. ♦Martin K. Melia, pres & gen mgr; Curtis Duncan, progmg dir.

Great Bend

*KBDA(FM)— 1999: 89.7 mhz; 1.4 kw. Ant 112 ft TL: N38 20 16 W98 45 48. Hrs open: American Family Radio Assoc., Box 3206, Tupelo, MS, 38803. Phone: (662) 844-8888, Ext 204. Fax: (662) 842-6791. Web Site:www.afr.net Licensee: American Family Radio Format: Inspirational Christian. ◆Marvin Sanders, gen mgr.

*KHCT(FM)— Aug 3, 1992: 90.9 mhz; 50 kw. 781 ft TL: N38 37 04 W98 56 32. Hrs open: 815 N. Walnut St., Suite 300, Hutchinson, 67501. Phone: (620) 662-6646.E-mail: rfragoza@radiokansas.org Web Site:radiokansas.org Licensee: Hutchinson Community College. Natl. Network: NPR, . Format: Class, new age, news. ◆David Horning, gen mgr; Geralyn Smith, opns dir; Sharon Webb, dev dir; Ken Baker, progmg dir; Frederic Jung, engrg dir.

KHOK(FM)—(Hoisington, 1978: 100.7 mhz; 100 kw. 430 ft TL: N38 32 49 W98 45 59. Stereo. Hrs open: 24 Box 609, 1200 Baker St., 67530. Phone: (620) 792-3647. Fax: (620) 792-3649.E-mail: info@eagleradio.net Web Site:www.eagleradio.net Licensee: Eagle Communications Inc. Group owner: Eagle Communications Group (acq 9-1-86; grpsl;4-8-91). Population served: 50,000 Format: Country. News staff: one. Target aud: 18-44. Spec prog: Relg 2 hrs wkly. ◆Gary Shorman, pres; Rick Nulton, gen mgr.

*KRTT(FM)—Not on air, target date: unknown: 88.1 mhz; 900 w vert. Ant 128 ft TL: N38 21 46 W98 45 50. Hrs open: 505 Josephine St., Titusville, FL, 32796. Phone: (321) 267-3000. Fax: (321) 264-9370.E-mail: wpio@gate.net Licensee: Florida Public Radio Inc. ◆Randy Henry, pres.

KVGB(AM)— Mar 10, 1937: 1590 khz; 5 kw-U, DA-N. TL: N38 18 50 W98 47 35. Hrs open: Box 609, 1200 Baker St., 67530. Phone: (620) 792-4637. Fax: (620) 792-3649.E-mail: info@eagleradio.net Web Site:eagleradio.net Licensee: Eagle Communications Inc. Group owner: Eagle Communications Group (acq 4-95). Population served: 25,000 Natl. Network: ABC, . Format: News, talk, sports. Target aud: 28 plus. Spec prog: Farm 7 hrs, relg 2 hrs wkly. ◆Rick Nulton, gen mgr; Randy Goering, sls dir.

KVGB-FM— Jan 17, 1977: 104.3 mhz; 96 kw. 810 ft TL: N38 25 54 W98 46 18. Stereo. Hrs open: Dups AM 50% Box 609 , 1200 Baker St., 67530. Phone: (620) 792-4637. Fax: (620) 792-3649.E-mail: info@eagleradio.net Web Site:eagleradio.net Natl. Network: ABC, . Format: Classic rock. ◆Randy Goering, sls VP.

*KWBI(FM)— Oct 10, 2001: 91.9 mhz; 1.8 kw. Ant 259 ft TL: N38 20 16 W98 45 48. Stereo. Hrs open: 24 2351 Sunset Blvd., Suite 170-218, Rocklin, CA, 95765. Phone: (916) 251-1600. Fax: (916) 251-1650.E-mail: klove@klove.com Web Site:www.klove.com Licensee: Educational Media Foundation. Group owner: EMF Broadcasting. Population served: 27,000 Natl. Network: K-Love, . Shaw Pittman. Format: Contemp Christian. News staff: 3. Target aud: 25-44; Judeo Christian, female. ◆Richard Jenkins, pres; Mike Novak, VP; Keith Whipple, dev dir; Eric Allen, natl sls mgr; David Pierce, progmg mgr; Ed Lenane, news dir; Sam Wallington, engrg dir; Karen Johnson, news rptr.

KZRS(FM)— Feb 3, 1986: 107.9 mhz; 100 kw. Ant 886 ft TL: N38 46 16 W98 44 17. Stereo. Hrs open: 24 5501 10th St., 67530. Phone: (620) 792-7108. Fax: (620) 792-7051.E-mail: kzls@waittradio.com Licensee: Rocking M Radio Inc. Group owner: Waitt Broadcasting Inc. (acq 8-31-2007; grpsl). Rgnl. Network: Mid-American Ag. Mid-America Ag Blooston, Mordkofsky, Jackson & Dickens. Format: Adult contemp. News staff: one; News: 5 hrs wkly. Target aud: 25-54. ◆Ken Schwamborn, gen mgr; Chris Elson, opns dir, progmg dir; Rod Rogers, chief of engrg.

Haven

KIBB(FM)— 1998: 97.1 mhz; 18.5 kw. Ant 823 ft TL: N37 48 00.7 W97 31 29. Hrs open: Two Brittany Place, 1938 N. Woodlawn, Suite 150, Wichita, 67208. Phone: (316) 558-8800. Fax: (316) 558-8802.E-mail: kibb@971bobfm.com Web Site:www.971bobfm.com Licensee: Connoisseur Media of Wichita LLC. (group owner; (acq 12-13-2007; exchange for KNZS(FM) Kingman). Format: Adult hits. ◆Doug Downs, gen mgr; Kim Kretchmar, rgnl sls mgr; Ron Allen, progmg dir.

Hays

KAYS(AM)— Oct 15, 1948: 1400 khz; 1 kw-U. TL: N38 53 29 W99 22 03. Stereo. Hrs open: 24 Prog sep from FM Box 817, 2300 Hall St., 67601. Secondary address: 2300 Hall St. 67601. Phone: (785) 625-2578. Fax: (785) 625-3632. Licensee: Eagle Communications Inc.

(Acq 3-20-91; grpsl; 4-8-91). Population served: 15,396 Format: Oldies. News staff: one; News: 6 hrs wkly. Target aud: Adults. ◆Mike Cooper, progmg dir.

KHAZ(FM)— May 1, 1985: 99.5 mhz; 100 kw. 515 ft TL: N38 56 29 W99 21 22. Stereo. Hrs open: 24 Box 6, 67601. Secondary address: 2300 Hall St. 67601. Phone: (785) 625-2578. Fax: (785) 625-3632. Licensee: Eagle Communications Inc. Group owner: Eagle Communications Group Natl. Network: ABC, . Format: Country. News staff: 2; News: 4 hrs wkly. Target aud: 25-54. Spec prog: Farm 10 hrs, gospel 3 hrs wkly. ◆Todd Nelson, gen mgr; Dwayne Detter, gen sls mgr; Theresa Trapp, progmg dir; Callie Kolacney, news dir; Mark Goff, chief of engrg.

KHYS(FM)— 2009: 89.7 mhz; 250 w. Ant 292 ft TL: N38 51 16 W99 22 55. Hrs open:
Rebroadcasts WAFR(FM) Tupelo, MS 100%.
Drawer 2440, Tupelo, MS, 38803. Phone: (662) 844-8888. Fax: (662) 842-6791. Web Site:www.afr.net Licensee: American Family Association. (acq 6-9-2006). Natl. Network: American Family Radio, . Format: Christian. ◆Donald E. Wildmon, chmn.

KJLS(FM)— June 27, 1974: 103.3 mhz; 100 kw. 994 ft TL: N39 01 15 W99 28 12. Stereo. Hrs open: 24 Box 6, 2300 Hall St., 67601. Phone: (785) 625-2578. Fax: (785) 625-3632. Licensee: Eagle Communications Inc. Group owner: Eagle Communications Group (acq 9-12-00; with KKQY(FM) Hill City). Population served: 110,000 Format: Adult contemp. News staff: one; News: 8 hrs wkly. Target aud: 25-49; 60% female, 40% male. ◆Todd Nelson, VP & gen mgr.

*KPRD(FM)— 1994: 88.9 mhz; 83 kw. 636 ft TL: N38 46 16 W98 44 17. Hrs open: 205 E. 7th St., Suite 218, 67601. Phone: (785) 628-6300. Fax: (785) 628-6389.E-mail: kprd@kprd.org Web Site:www.kprd.org Licensee: The Praise Network Inc. Population served: 75,000 Format: Relg. Target aud: 20-48. ◆Lloyd Mintzmyer, CEO; David Breedon, stn mgr.

KRMR(FM)— June 16, 2008: 105.7 mhz; 20.5 kw. Ant 495 ft TL: N38 55 59 W99 19 51. Hrs open: 207 E. 7th St., Suite 102, 67601. Phone: (785) 628-6108. Fax: (785) 628-1055. Licensee: Radioactive LLC. Natl. Network: Fox News Radio, . Format: Talk. ◆Benjamin L. Homel, pres; Corey Sorenson, gen mgr.

*KZAN(FM)—Not on air, target date: unknown: 91.7 mhz; 1.25 kw. Ant 246 ft TL: N38 56 28 W99 21 20. Hrs open: 24
Rebroadcast KANZ(FM) Garden City 100%.
Kanza Society Inc., 210 N. 7th St., Garden City, 67846. Phone: (620) 274-7444. Fax: (620) 275-7496. Web Site:www.hppr.org Licensee: Kanza Society Inc. Natl. Network: NPR, PRI, AP Radio, . Format: Educ, class, news/talk. Target aud: 25-80; educated. ◆Richard Hicks, gen mgr; Diana Gonzales, dev dir; Debra Stout, prom dir; Bob Kirby, progmg dir; Chuck Springer, chief of engrg.

Haysville

KFBZ(FM)— Aug 25, 1985: 105.3 mhz; 100 kw. 1,000 ft TL: N37 46 40 W97 30 37. Stereo. Hrs open: 2120 N. Woodlawn, Suite 352, Wichita, 67208-1847. Phone: (316) 685-2121. Fax: (316) 685-3408.E-mail: info@1053thebuzz.com Web Site:www.1053thebuzz.com Licensee: Entercom Wichita License LLC. Group owner: Entercom Communications Corp. (acq 2000; grpsl). Format: Hot AC. News: 2 hrs wkly. Target aud: 25-54. Spec prog: Relg 2 hrs wkly. ◆Jackie Wise, gen mgr.

Herington

*KJRL(FM)— Sept 6, 1997: 105.7 mhz; 12.5 kw. 500 ft TL: N38 37 01 W96 59 09. Stereo. Hrs open: 24 Box 14, 805 S. Buckeye Avenue, Abilene, 67410. Phone: (785) 263-7200. Fax: (785) 263-3876.E-mail: radioforlife@kjil.com Web Site:www.kjil1057.com Licensee: Great Plains Christian Radio Inc. (acq 9-5-01). Population served: 320,000 Natl. Network: Salem Radio Network, Moody, . Rgnl. Network: Kan. Info. Wire Svc: AP Format: Adult Contemp Christian. News staff: one; News: 16 hrs wkly. Target aud: 18-54; farmers, railroad & transportation workers, military & professional. ◆Don Hughes, CEO, gen mgr; Frank York, chmn; Mark Hinca, stn mgr; Gabriel Peter, opns dir; Delvin Kinser, news dir.

Hiawatha

KNZA(FM)— Aug 18, 1977: 103.9 mhz; 50 kw. 492 ft TL: N39 34 41 W95 33 46. Stereo. Hrs open: 24 Box 104, 66434-0104. Secondary address: 1828 Hwy. 73 66434-0104. Phone: (785) 547-3461. Fax: (785) 547-9900.E-mail: knza@rainbowtel.net Web Site:knzafm.com Licensee: KNZA Inc. (group owner; acq 6-83; 6-20-83). Population served: 84,000 Natl. Network: ABC, . Brownfield Wire Svc: AP Format:

Country. News staff: one; News: 10 hrs wkly. Target aud: 18-54; general. Spec prog: Farm 14 hrs wkly. ◆Greg Buser, gen mgr; Robert Hilton, opns mgr.

Hill City

KKQY(FM)— Aug 29, 1997: 101.9 mhz; 97 kw. 994 ft TL: N39 01 15 W99 28 13. Stereo. Hrs open: 24 Box 6, Hays, 67601. Phone: (785) 625-2578. Fax: (785) 625-3632. Licensee: Eagle Communications Inc. Group owner: Eagle Communications Group (acq 9-12-00; with KJLS(FM) Hays). Population served: 110,000 Format: Country. News: 5 hrs wkly. Target aud: 25-54. ◆Todd Nelson, gen mgr; Todd Lynn, gen sls mgr; Craig Taylor, progmg dir.

*KZNA(FM)— 1986: 90.5 mhz; 100 kw. 600 ft TL: N39 15 56 W99 49 48. Stereo. Hrs open: 24
Rebroadcasts KANZ(FM) Garden City 100%.
210 N. 7th St., Garden City, 67846. Phone: (620) 275-7444. Fax: (620) 275-7496.E-mail: hppr@hppr.org Web Site:www.hppr.org Licensee: Kanza Society Inc. (acq 11-77; 7-80). Population served: 200,000 Natl. Network: PRI, NPR, AP Radio, . Format: Educ, class, news/talk. News: 39 hrs wkly. Target aud: 25-80; educated. Spec prog: Jazz 15 hrs, folk 6 hrs, Sp 6 hrs wkly. ◆Richard Hicks, gen mgr; Bob Kirby, progmg dir; Chuck Springer, chief of engrg.

Hoisington

KHOK(FM)—Licensed to Hoisington. See Great Bend

Holcomb

KBUF(AM)—Licensed to Holcomb. See Garden City

Horton

KAIR-FM— Jan 25, 1995: 93.7 mhz; 25 kw. Ant 328 ft TL: N39 37 43 W95 18 53. Stereo. Hrs open: 24 Box G, Atchison, 66002. Secondary address: 200 N. 5th St., Atchinson 66002. Phone: (913) 367-1470. Fax: (913) 367-7021.E-mail: thewakeupcrew@hotmail.com Web Site:www.kairfm.com Licensee: KNZA Inc. (group owner; (acq 8-13-2007; with KAIR(AM) Atchison). Natl. Network: AP Radio, . Wire Svc: AP Format: Country. News staff: 4; News: 133 hrs wkly. Target aud: 25-54. ◆Greg Buser, pres; Mark Oppold, gen mgr.

Hugoton

KFXX-FM— Sept 16, 1983: 106.7 mhz; 35 kw. Ant 259 ft TL: N37 19 03 W101 20 16. Stereo. Hrs open: 24 1402 E. Kansas Ave, Garden City, 67846. Phone: (620) 276-2366. Fax: (620) 356-3635. Licensee: KBUF Partnership. Group owner: Robert Ingstad Broadcast Properties. Population served: 18,000 Rgnl. Network: Kan. Info., Kan. Agri. Baraff, Koerner & Olender. Format: Rgnl Mexican. ◆Gil Wohler, gen mgr.

Humboldt

KINZ(FM)— September 1998: 95.3 mhz; 24 kw. Ant 335 ft TL: N37 44 52 W95 33 39. Stereo. Hrs open: 24 702 N. Plummer Ave., Chanute, 66720. Phone: (620) 431-1333. Fax: (620) 431-4643.E-mail: mike@kinz.biz Web Site:www.kinz.biz Licensee: My Town Media Inc. (acq 3-2-2009; $330,000). Natl. Network: CNN Radio, . Format: Classic rock. Target aud: 25-55. Spec prog: Gospel 3 hrs wkly. ◆William B. Wachter, pres; Mike Sutcliffe, gen mgr; Rob Olson, progmg dir.

Hutchinson

*KHCC-FM— Sept 11, 1972: 90.1 mhz; 100 kw. 1,080 ft TL: N38 23 40 W97 45 49. Hrs open: 24 815 N. Walnut, Suite 300, 67501-6217. Phone: (620) 662-6646.E-mail: rfragoza@radiokansas.org Web Site:www.radiokansas.org Licensee: Hutchinson Community College. Population served: 1,000,000 Natl. Network: NPR, . Format: Class, new age, news. News: 27 hrs wkly. ◆David M. Horning, gen mgr; Geralyn Smith, opns dir; Sharon Webb, dev dir; Melody Fisher, prom dir; Ken Baker, progmg dir; Frederic Jung, engrg dir.

KHUT(FM)— Mar 15, 1972: 102.9 mhz; 28.5 kw. 496 ft TL: N38 02 36 W98 00 53. (CP: TL: N38 02 39 W98 00 56). Hrs open: 825 N. Main St., 67501. Phone: (620) 662-4486. Fax: (620) 662-5357.E-mail: info@khutfm.com Web Site:www.khutfm.com Format: C&W. ◆Terry Drowhard, gen sls mgr; Jason Younger, progmg dir; Fred Gough, news dir; Mark Trotman, financial ed.

KWBW(AM)— May 28, 1935: 1450 khz; 1 kw-U. TL: N38 04 02 W97 57 53. Hrs open: 825 N. Main St., 67501. Phone: (620) 662-4486. Fax: (620) 662-5357.E-mail: info@khutfm.com Web Site:www.khutfm.com Licensee: Eagle Communications Inc. Group owner: Eagle Communications Group (acq 11-4-91; with co-located FM). Population served: 65,000 Format: Talk, new/sports. Spec prog: Black 2 hrs, gospel 11 hrs wkly. ♦Dan Deming, gen mgr, progmg dir; John Brennan, gen sls mgr; Rod Zook, news dir.

KWHK(FM)— 2007: 95.9 mhz; 2.85 kw. Ant 489 ft TL: N38 02 57 W98 00 44. Stereo. Hrs open: 24 106 N. Main St., 67501-5219. Phone: (620) 665-5758. Fax: (620) 665-6655.E-mail: production @adastra.kscoxmail.com Licensee: Ad Astra Per Aspera Broadcasting Inc. Population served: 75,000 Natl. Network: ABC, . Kan. Info. Format: Oldies. News staff: one; News: 2 hrs wkly. ♦Aaron West, opns mgr.

KZSN(FM)— Oct 7, 1968: 102.1 mhz; 100 kw. Ant 1,027 ft TL: N37 46 40 W97 30 37. Stereo. Hrs open: 24 9323 E. 37th St. N., Wichita, 67226. Phone: (316) 494-6600. Fax: (316) 494-6730.E-mail: info@kzsn.com Web Site:www.kzsn.com Licensee: Clear Channel Broadcasting Licenses, Inc. Group owner: Clear Channel Communications Inc. (acq 8-30-00; grpsl). Population served: 276,554 Natl. Rep: Clear Channel,. Format: Country. News staff: one. Target aud: 25-54; Adults.

Independence

***KARF(FM)—** 1997: 91.9 mhz; 250 w. Ant 180 ft TL: N37 15 54 W95 39 26. Hrs open: 10550 Barkley St., Suite 100, Overland Park, 66212-1824. Phone: (913) 642-7770. Fax: (913) 642-1319.E-mail: comments@bottradionetwork.com Web Site:www.bottradionetwork.com Licensee: Community Broadcasting Inc. Group owner: American Family Radio (acq 1-26-2006; $30,000 with KBMP(FM) Enterprise). Natl. Network: USA, . Format: Christian Talk. ♦Richard P. Bott II, VP; Pat Rulon, natl sls mgr; Rachel Moser, mktg mgr; Jason Potocnik, traf mgr.

***KBQC(FM)—** 2002: 88.5 mhz; 20 kw vert. Ant 476 ft TL: N37 03 11 W96 06 07. Hrs open: Drawer 2440, Tupelo, MS, 38801. Phone: (662) 844-8888. Fax: (662) 842-6791. Licensee: American Family Association. Group owner: American Family Radio (acq 12-18-00; buyer paid construction & bcst costs of CP). Format: Christian. ♦Marvin Sanders, gen mgr.

KIND(AM)— Dec 8, 1947: 1010 khz; 250 w-D, 32 w-N. TL: N37 13 07 W95 43 30. Hrs open: 24 122 W. Myrtle, 67301. Phone: (620) 331-3000. Fax: (620) 331-8008.E-mail: a.bradshaw@tallgrassnation.com Licensee: Tallgrass Broadcasting Inc. (acq 10-25-2006; $306,000 with co-located FM). Population served: 12,100 Natl. Network: Westwood One, . Wire Svc: AP Format: Adult Standards. Target aud: 35-65; baby boomers. Spec prog: Big band 2 hrs, class 3 hrs wkly. ♦Joseph E. Walker, pres; Mark Wilson, gen mgr.

KIND-FM— May 10, 1969: 102.9 mhz; 25 kw. Ant 272 ft TL: N37 15 42 W95 45 59. Hrs open: 24 122 W. Myrtle, 67301. Phone: (620) 331-3000. Fax: (620) 331-8008.E-mail: a.bradshaw@tallgrassnation.com Licensee: Tallgrass Broadcasting Inc. Population served: 65,000 Natl. Network: CNN Radio, . Wire Svc: AP Format: Hot adult contemp. Target aud: 22-44. Spec prog: Alternative 4 hrs, Christian hot adult contemp 2 hrs wkly.

Ingalls

KERP(FM)— Jan 1, 2001: 96.3 mhz; 100 kw. Ant 659 ft TL: N37 38 28 W100 20 40. Stereo. Hrs open: 24 Secondary address: 106 W Frontview, Dodge City 67801. Phone: (620) 225-8080. Fax: (620) 225-6655.E-mail: rockswks@sbcglobal.net Web Site:www.rockingmradio.com Licensee: Rocking M Radio Inc. (group owner; (acq 8-31-2007; grpsl). Natl. Network: Fox News Radio, . Format: Country. ♦Mark Hinca, gen mgr; Brian Nugen, opns mgr; Peggy Burdick, sls dir; Candace Thomas, traf mgr.

KSSA(FM)— July 1, 1999: 105.9 mhz; 100 kw. Ant 666 ft TL: N37 46 48 W100 27 36. Hrs open: 24 1402 E. Kansas Ave., Garden City, 67846. Phone: (620) 276-3251. Fax: (620) 276-3568.E-mail: kssa@wksradio.com Licensee: KBUF Partnership. Group owner: Robert Ingstad Broadcast Properties (acq 1999; $250,000). Shaw Pittman. Format: Sp. ♦G.L. Wohler, gen mgr; Rachel Wheet, traf mgr.

Iola

KIKS-FM— June 9, 1977: 101.5 mhz; 11.5 kw. Ant 289 ft TL: N37 54 04 W95 24 04. Stereo. Hrs open: 24 Prog sep from AM Box 710, S. Hwy. 169, 66749. Phone: (620) 365-3151. Fax: (620) 365-5431.E-mail: radiostation@iolaradio.com Licensee: Iola Broadcasting Inc. Format: Adult contemp.

KIOL(AM)— July 25, 1961: 1370 khz; 500 w-D, 62 w-N, DA. TL: N37 54 07 W95 24 26. Hrs open: 24 Box 710, S. Hwy. 169, 66749. Phone: (620) 365-3151. Fax: (620) 365-5431. Web Site:www.iolaradio.com Licensee: Iola Broadcasting Inc. (acq 9-1-73). Population served: 14,125 Kan. Info. Format: Talk. ♦Tom Norris, gen mgr, stn mgr & progmg dir.

Junction City

KJCK(AM)— May 15, 1949: 1420 khz; 1 kw-D, 500 w-N, DA-N. TL: N39 01 33 W96 48 36. Hrs open: 24 Box 789, 1030 Southwind Dr., 66441. Phone: (785) 762-5525. Fax: (785) 762-5387.E-mail: platinum@kjck.com Web Site:www.kjck.com Licensee: Platinum Broadcasting Inc. (group owner; (acq 9-4-86). Population served: 25,000 Natl. Network: ABC, Fox News Radio, Sporting News Radio Network, . Wire Svc: AP Format: News/talk. News staff: 2; News: 75 hrs wkly. Target aud: 35-54. ♦Mark Ediger, gen mgr, opns dir; Ed Klimek, gen sls mgr; Jerry Brecheisen, progmg dir; Dewey Terrill, news dir; Randy Stewart, chief of engrg; Jacqueline Petty, news rptr.

KJCK-FM— July 22, 1965: 97.5 mhz; 100 kw. Ant 630 ft TL: N39 00 53 W96 52 15. Stereo. Hrs open: 24 Box 789, 66441. Secondary address: 1030 Southwind Dr. 66441. Phone: (785) 762-5525. Fax: (785) 762-5387.E-mail: platinum@kjck.com Web Site:www.kjck.com Licensee: Platinum Broadcasting Inc. Population served: 690,000 Wire Svc: AP Format: Top-40. News staff: 2; News: one hr wkly. Target aud: 18-34; young adults. ♦Ed Klimek, VP; Robert Elfman, progmg dir; Dewey Terrill, news dir; Erin Voirol, traf mgr; Matt McBain, disc jockey.

Kansas City

KDTD(AM)— 1925: 1340 khz; 1 kw-U. TL: N39 06 50 W94 40 05. Hrs open: 24 1701 S. 55th St., 66106-2241. Phone: (913) 287-1480. Fax: (913) 287-5881. Licensee: Davidson Media Station KCKN Licensee LLC. (acq 10-11-2005; $1.9 million). Population served: 1,500,000 Format: Rgnl Mexican. News staff: 2. ♦Dan Perez, gen mgr; Carlos Mercado, opns dir.

KFKF-FM— May 28, 1963: 94.1 mhz; 100 kw. 994 ft TL: N39 00 57 W94 30 24. Stereo. Hrs open: 4717 Grand Ave., Suite 600, MO, 64112. Phone: (816) 753-4000. Fax: (816) 753-4045.E-mail: info@kfkf.com Web Site:www.kfkf.com Licensee: Wilks License Co.-Kansas City LLC. Group owner: Infinity Broadcasting Corp. (acq 1-10-2007; grpsl). Population served: 280,000 Format: Contemp country. ♦Mike Rowen, gen mgr; Dale Carter, progmg dir; Jillian Gregg, news dir; Ben Weiss, chief of engrg.

KUDL(FM)— Oct 9, 1959: 98.1 mhz; 100 kw. 994 ft TL: N39 04 23 W94 29 06. Stereo. Hrs open: 24 7000 Squibb Rd, Mission, 66202. Phone: (913) 744-3600. Fax: (913) 677-8061.E-mail: info@kudl.com Web Site:www.kudl.com Licensee: Entercom Kansas City License L.L.C. Group owner: Entercom Communications Corp. (acq 10-17-97; grpsl). Population served: 1,500,000 Format: Adult contemp. News staff: one. Target aud: 25-44; women. ♦Dave Alpert, gen mgr; Dan Prendiville, gen sls mgr; Marcy Caldwell, prom dir; Tom McGinty, opns mgr & progmg dir; Darcie Blake, news dir.

KXTR(AM)— 2001: 1660 khz; 10 kw-D, 1 kw-N. TL: N39 06 50 W94 40 45. Hrs open: 24 7000 Squibb Rd, Mission, 66202. Phone: (913) 677-8998. Fax: (913) 677-8061.E-mail: info@1065thewolf.com Web Site:www.kxtr.com Licensee: Entercom Kansas City License LLC. Group owner: Entercom Communications Corp. Format: Classical. ♦Dave Alpert, gen mgr; John Verlin, sls dir; Patrick Nease, progmg dir.

KYYS(AM)— 1926: 1250 khz; 25 kw-D, 3.7 kw-N, DA-N. TL: N39 11 06 W94 27 28. Hrs open: 6220 Kansas Ave., 66611. Phone: (913) 788-1255. Fax: (913) 788-1254.E-mail: lasuperx1250@lasuperx1250.com Web Site:www.lasuperx1250.com Licensee: Entercom Kansas City License LLC. Group owner: Entercom Communications Corp. (acq 3-3-99; $2.75 million). Format: Mexican rgnl. ♦Juan C. Ramirez, gen mgr.

Kingman

KCVW(FM)— December 1997: 94.3 mhz; 50 kw. 492 ft TL: N37 48 03 W97 56 49. Hrs open: 24 Mezzanine, 100 N. Main, Hutchinson, 67501. Phone: (620) 663-0943. Fax: (620) 663-0913.E-mail: kcvw@bottradionetwork.com Web Site:www.bottradionetwork.com Licensee: Bott Communications Inc. Group owner: Bott Radio Network Natl. Network: USA, . Format: Christian talk. Target aud: 25-55. ♦Richard P. Bott II, exec VP; Jason Potoenik, traf mgr.

Kiowa

KQZQ(FM)— 2008: 98.3 mhz; 100 kw. Ant 279 ft TL: N37 00 52 W98 28 37. Hrs open: 506 N. Pine, Pittsburg, 66762. Phone: (620) 231-5620. Licensee: Troy Unruh. ♦Troy Unruh, gen mgr.

Larned

KBGL(FM)— 2001: 106.9 mhz; 100 kw. Ant 485 ft TL: N38 27 06 W99 10 03. Hrs open: 1200 Baker St., Great Bend, 67530. Phone: (620) 792-3647. Fax: (620) 792-3649.E-mail: info@eagleradio.net Web Site:www.eagleradio.net Licensee: Hull Broadcasting Inc. (acq 9-12-00; with KFIX(FM) Plainville). Format: Oldies. ♦Rick Nulton, gen mgr; Phil Grossardt, opns mgr; Mike Durler, sls dir.

KNNS(AM)— Nov 4, 1963: 1510 khz; 1 kw-D. TL: N38 09 54 W99 06 05. Hrs open: 5501 W. 10 St., Great Bend, 67530. Phone: (620) 792-7108. Fax: (620) 792-7051.E-mail: kzls@nrgmedia.com Licensee: Rocking M Radio Inc. Group owner: Waitt Broadcasting Inc. (acq 8-31-2007; grpsl). Population served: 30,000 Rgnl. Network: Kan. Info., Kan. Agri. Kan. Agriculture Format: ESPN sports. Target aud: General; people looking for loc info. Spec prog: Farm 10 hrs, gospel 6 hrs, relg 5 hrs wkly. ♦Jen Schwamborn, gen mgr; Chris Elsen, progmg dir.

KSOB(FM)— Nov 1, 1965: 96.7 mhz; 3 kw. 290 ft TL: N38 09 54 W99 06 05. (CP: Ant 265 ft.). Stereo. Hrs open: Prog sep from AM 5501 W. 10 St., Great Bend, 67530. Phone: (620) 792-7108. Fax: (620) 792-7051.E-mail: info@ksob.com Format: Oldies. Target aud: 30-60; baby boomers with disposable income. ♦Dan Cormack, local news ed.

Lawrence

***KANU(FM)—** Sept 15, 1952: 91.5 mhz; 100 kw. 698 ft TL: N38 57 18 W95 15 57. Stereo. Hrs open: 24 1120 W. 11th St., 66044. Phone: (785) 864-4530. Fax: (785) 864-5278.E-mail: kpr@ku.edu Web Site:www.kpr.ku.edu Licensee: University of Kansas. Population served: 85,000 Natl. Network: PRI, NPR, . Rgnl. Network: Kan. Pub. Arter & Hadden. Format: Class, jazz. News staff: 3; News: 35 hrs wkly. Target aud: 25-49; upscale. Spec prog: Bluegrass 4 hrs, Celtic 2 hrs, blues 4 hrs wkly. ♦Janet Campbell, gen mgr.

***KJHK(FM)—** 1975: 90.7 mhz; 2.9 kw. Ant 163 ft TL: N38 57 30 W95 15 00. Stereo. Hrs open: 24 2051 A. Dole Ctr., 66045. Phone: (785) 864-4745. Fax: (785) 864-5173.E-mail: kjhk@mail.ku.edu Web Site:www.kjhk.org Licensee: University of Kansas. Population served: 75,000 Format: Rock, jazz. News: 15 hrs wkly. Target aud: 18-34; Univ & community population. Spec prog: Reggae 3 hrs, blues 2 hrs wkly. ♦Tom Johnson, gen mgr; Danielle Basci, stn mgr; Joe Noh, prom dir; Tom Kimmel, progmg dir.

KLWN(AM)— Feb 22, 1951: 1320 khz; 500 w-D, 250 w-N. TL: N38 56 05 W95 17 12. Hrs open: 24 3125 W. 6th St., 66049-3101. Phone: (785) 843-1320. Fax: (785) 841-5924. Fax: (785) 843-4585.E-mail: mail@lazer.com Web Site:www.klwn.com Licensee: Great Plains Media Inc. Group owner: Zimmer Radio Group (acq 6-30-2006; with co-located FM). Population served: 100,000 Fletcher, Heald & Hildreth. Format: News/talk, sports. News staff: 2; News: 10 hrs wkly. Target aud: 25-59; adults. Spec prog: Relg 4 hrs wkly. ♦John Flood, progmg dir.

KLZR(FM)— Aug 20, 1963: 105.9 mhz; 100 kw. 771 ft TL: N39 02 21 W95 26 59. Stereo. Hrs open: 24 Prog sep from AM 3125 W. 6th St., 66049. Phone: (785) 843-1320. Fax: (785) 841-5924. Fax: (785) 843-4585.E-mail: info@lazer.com Web Site:www.lazer.com Population served: 100,000 Format: CHR, top 40. News staff: 2; News: one hr wkly. Target aud: 18-34; young adults.

Leavenworth

KKLO(AM)— 1946: 1410 khz; 5 kw-D, 500 w-N, DA-2. TL: N39 16 24 W94 54 27. Hrs open: 481 Muncie Rd., 66048. Phone: (913) 351-1410. Fax: (913) 351-1410.E-mail: info@kkloam.com Web Site:www.hereshelpnet.org Licensee: New Life Evangelistic Center Inc. (acq 10-29-99). Population served: 41,100 Format: Christian. Target aud: 25-49; upscale, educated, loyal Christian listeners. ♦Larry Rice, CEO, chmn, pres, gen mgr, progmg dir; Saint Johns, gen mgr & opns mgr.

KQRC-FM—Licensed to Leavenworth. See Kansas City MO

Leoti

KWKR(FM)— Nov 1, 1983: 99.9 mhz; 100 kw. Ant 395 ft TL: N38 16 39 W101 17 50. Stereo. Hrs open: Box 759, Garden City, 67846. Secondary address: 1402 E. Kansas, Garden City 67846. Phone: (620) 276-3251. Fax: (620) 276-3568.E-mail: info@wksradio.com Web Site:www.wksradio.com Licensee: KBUF Partnership. Group owner: Robert Ingstad Broadcast Properties (acq 12-1-97; $841,170). Population served: 70,000 Natl. Network: Westwood One, . Dow, Lohnes & Albertson. Format: Classic rock. Target aud: 25-44. Spec prog: Sp 3 hrs wkly. ♦Gil Wohler, gen mgr; James Janda, VP & progmg dir.

Liberal

KLDG(FM)— October 1994: 102.7 mhz; 100 kw. 466 ft TL: N37 02 45 W101 06 11. Hrs open: 24 1410 Northwestern Ave., 67901. Phone: (620) 624-3891. Fax: (620) 624-7885.E-mail: info@kldgfm.com Web Site:www.kscb.net Licensee: Seward County Broadcasting Co. Inc. (group owner) Population served: 85,000 Natl. Network: Jones Radio Networks, . Natl. Rep: Roslin,. Shaw Pittman. Format: Country. News staff: 2; News: 2 hrs wkly. Target aud: 18-49; young, mobile & impulsive consumers. ♦John Landon, chmn; Don Ford, pres; Bob Larrabee, VP; Stuart Melchert, gen mgr; Terry Miller, opns mgr; John Mulhern, chief of engrg; Mikki Hofferber, traf mgr.

KSCB(AM)— July 25, 1948: 1270 khz; 1 kw-D, 30 w-N. TL: N37 03 15 W100 53 39. Hrs open: 24 1410 N. Western Ave., 67901. Phone: (620) 624-3891. Fax: (620) 624-9472.E-mail: kscb@kscb.net Web Site:www.kscb.net Licensee: Seward County Broadcasting Co. Population served: 13,471 Natl. Network: ABC, Westwood One, . Rgnl. Network: Kan. Info. Natl. Rep: Roslin,. Kan. Info. Wiley, Rein & Felding. Format: News/talk. News staff: 3. Target aud: 35 plus. Spec prog: Farm 6 hrs wkly. ♦Stuart Melchert, gen mgr; Cheryl Collins, gen sls mgr; Terry Miller, VP, opns mgr & progmg dir; Brock Kappelmann, news dir; John Mulhurn, engrg dir, chief of engrg; Mikki Hofferber, traf mgr.

KSCB-FM— July 10, 1978: 107.5 mhz; 100 kw. 511 ft TL: N37 02 45 W101 06 11. Stereo. Hrs open: 24 Prog sep from AM 1410 N. Western Ave., 67901. Phone: (620) 624-3891. Fax: (620) 624-9472.E-mail: kscb@kscb.net Web Site:www.kscb.net Licensee: Seward County Broadcasting Co. Population served: 50,000 Natl. Network: Jones Radio Networks, . Rgnl. Network: Kan. Info. Natl. Rep: Roslin,. Kan. Info. Format: Adult contemp. News staff: 2; News: 7 hrs wkly. Target aud: 25-49; young adults. ♦Mikki Hofferber, traf mgr.

KSMM(AM)— Sept 15, 1960: 1470 khz; 1 kw-D, 125 w-N. TL: N37 03 17 W100 53 06. Hrs open: 150 Plaza Dr., 67901. Phone: (620) 624-8156. Fax: (620) 624-4606. Licensee: Rocking M Radio Inc. Group owner: Waitt Broadcasting Inc. (acq 8-31-2007; grpsl). Population served: 16,500 Rgnl. Network: Mid-American Ag. Natl. Rep: McGavren Guild,. Mid-America Ag Format: Sp. News: one hr wkly. Target aud: 25-54; Spanish speaking. ♦Steve Schiffner, gen mgr; Matt Younkin, progmg dir.

KSMM-FM— July 1978: 101.5 mhz; 100 kw. Ant 550 ft TL: N37 03 20 W100 48 40. Stereo. Hrs open: 150 Plaza Dr., 67901. Phone: (620) 624-8156. Fax: (620) 624-4606. Licensee: Rocking M Radio Inc. (acq 8-31-2007; grpsl). Format: Rgnl Mexican. ♦Enrique Franz, gen mgr.

KZQD(FM)— October 1997: 105.1 mhz; 50 kw. 492 ft TL: N37 17 39 W100 51 38. (CP: Ant 387 ft. TL: N37 02 53 W100 54 34). Hrs open: Box 2636, 67905. Phone: (620) 626-8282.E-mail: radiolibertat@sbglobal.net Licensee: Mario Loredo. (acq 3-8-94; 5-9-94). Format: Christian. ♦Mario Loredo, gen mgr & progmg dir.

Lindsborg

KDJM(FM)— 2008: 101.7 mhz; 16 kw. Ant 410 ft TL: N38 40 00 W97 41 30. Hrs open: 641 W. Cloud, Salina, 67401. Phone: (785) 827-2100. Fax: (785) 827-3503. Licensee: Radioactive LLC. Format: Classic country. ♦Benjamin L. Homel, pres; Pat Foster, gen mgr.

KVOB(FM)— Oct 8, 1985: 95.5 mhz; 15.5 kw. Ant 417 ft TL: N38 40 00 W97 41 30. Stereo. Hrs open: 24 641 W. Cloud, Salina, 67401. Phone: (785) 827-2100. Fax: (785) 827-3503. Licensee: Rocking M Radio Inc. (acq 8-31-2007; grpsl). Population served: 325,000 Format: Adult contemp. News: 2 hrs wkly. Target aud: 25-49. ♦Pat Foster, gen mgr.

Lyons

KXKU(FM)— Apr 10, 1970: 106.1 mhz; 100 kw. Ant 659 ft TL: N38 16 33 W98 12 11. Stereo. Hrs open: 24 106 N. Main St., Hutchinson, 67501-5219. Phone: (620) 665-5758. Fax: (620) 665-6655.E-mail: production@adastra.kscoxmail.com Licensee: Ad Astra Per Aspera Broadcasting Inc. (group owner; (acq 9-17-86; $366,816; 6-9-86). Population served: 150,000 Natl. Network: Jones Radio Networks, . Kan. Info. Format: Country. News staff: one; News: 2 hrs wkly. Target aud: 25-64; listeners throughout central KS. ♦Cliff C. Shank, pres; Mike Hill, VP; Aaron West, stn mgr, opns mgr; Lucky Kidd, sls VP; Susie Deines, rgnl sls mgr.

Manhattan

***KGLV(FM)**— 2008: 88.9 mhz; 11 kw. Ant 1,046 ft TL: N39 00 22 W96 02 57. Hrs open:
Rebroadcasts KLVR(FM) Middletown, CA 100%.
2351 Sunset Blvd., Suite 170-218, Rocklin, CA, 95765. Phone: (916) 251-1600. Fax: (916) 251-1650. Web Site:www.klove.com Licensee: Educational Media Foundation. (acq 10-27-2006; $325,000 for CP). Natl. Network: K-Love, . Format: Contemp Christian. ♦Mike Novak, pres.

KJCK-FM—See Junction City

KMAN(AM)— June 1950: 1350 khz; 500 w-D, 40 w-N. TL: N39 13 00 W96 33 30. Stereo. Hrs open: 24 Box 1350, 66502. Secondary address: 2414 Casement Rd. 66502. Phone: (785) 776-1350. Fax: (785) 539-1000. Web Site:www.1350kman.com Licensee: Manhattan Broadcasting Co. Group owner: Seaton Stations Population served: 110,000 Natl. Network: CBS, ESPN Radio, Westwood One, . Rgnl. Network: Kan. Info. Kan. Info. Shaw Pittman. Format: News/talk, sports. News staff: one; News: 60 hrs wkly. Target aud: 30 plus. ♦Richard Seaton, chmn; Richard T. Wartell, pres & gen mgr; Kevin Block, chief of engrg.

KMKF(FM)— Sept 1, 1972: 101.5 mhz; 39 kw. 577 ft TL: N39 15 55 W96 27 56. Stereo. Hrs open: 24 Box 1350, 66502. Secondary address: 2414 Casement Rd. 66502. Phone: (785) 776-1350. Fax: (785) 539-1000. Web Site:www.purerock.com Population served: 400,000 Format: Rock/AOR. News staff: one; News: 2 hrs wkly. Target aud: 18-35. ♦Richard Wartell, gen mgr; Corey Dean, progmg dir, disc jockey; Kevin Block, engrg dir.

KQLA(FM)—(Ogden, Feb 14, 1986: 103.5 mhz; 41 kw. Ant 312 ft TL: N39 09 21 W96 36 44. Stereo. Hrs open: 24 Box 104, 66505. Secondary address: 122 S. 4th, Suite A 66502. Phone: (785) 587-0103. Phone: (785) 323-9797. Fax: (785) 776-0110.E-mail: platinum@kqck.com Web Site:www.kqla.com Licensee: Platinum Broadcasting Co. (group owner; (acq 9-24-97; $650,000). Population served: 110,000 Natl. Network: ABC, . Rgnl rep: Regional Rep Corp Format: Adult contemp. News staff: one; News: 10 hrs wkly. Target aud: 18-44; mobile, educated persons with quality income. ♦Ed Klimek, exec VP; Mark Ediger, gen mgr.

***KSDB-FM**— 1949: 91.9 mhz; 1.4 kw. Ant 290 ft TL: N39 09 49 W96 31 54. Stereo. Hrs open: 24 A.Q. Miller School of Journalism, Rm. 105, Kedzie Hall, 66506. Phone: (785) 532-2971. Fax: (785) 532-5484.E-mail: radio@ksu.edu Web Site:www.wildcat919.com Licensee: Kansas State University. Population served: 150,000 Format: Progsv, rock, urban contemp. News staff: one; News: 12 hrs wkly. Target aud: 18-34; young adults. Spec prog: Black 4 hrs, gospel 3 hrs, jazz 3 hrs wkly. ♦Steve Smethers, COO & pres; Kristen Russell, stn mgr.

KXBZ(FM)— September 1994: 104.7 mhz; 20 kw. 502 ft TL: N39 15 55 W96 27 56. Hrs open: 2414 Casement Rd., 66502. Phone: (785) 776-1350. Fax: (785) 539-1000.E-mail: dubs@purerock.com Web Site:www.b1047.com Licensee: Manhattan Broadcasting Co. Inc. Group owner: Seaton Stations (acq 3-2-99). Natl. Network: Westwood One, . Format: Hot country. Target aud: 18-35; men & women. ♦Richard T. Wartell, pres & gen mgr.

***KYAH(FM)**—Not on air, target date: unknown: 89.9 mhz; 11 kw. Ant 230 ft TL: N39 24 04 W96 25 29. Hrs open: 102 Red Branch Ln., Simpsonville, SC, 29681. Phone: (864) 297-0216. Fax: (864) 297-0344.E-mail: info@networkofglory.org Web Site:networkofglory.com Licensee: Network of Glory Inc. ♦Lola Richey, pres.

Marysville

***KMLL(FM)**—Not on air, target date: unknown: 91.7 mhz; 600 w. Ant 285 ft TL: N39 52 12 W96 44 45. Hrs open: Box 2440, Tupelo, MS, 38803-2440. Phone: (662) 844-8888. Fax: (662) 842-6791. Web Site:www.afr.net Licensee: American Family Association. ♦Donald E. Wildmon, chmn.

KNDY(AM)— July 10, 1956: 1570 khz; 250 w-D. TL: N39 51 02 W96 38 52. Hrs open: 24 937 Jayhawk Rd., 66508. Phone: (785) 562-2361. Fax: (785) 562-2188. Licensee: Dierking Communications Inc. (group owner; (acq 9-6-88). Population served: 40,000 Natl. Network: ABC, . Rgnl. Network: Mid-American Ag. Mid-America Ag Format: Farm, C&W. News: 24 hrs wkly. Target aud: General. ♦Bruce Dierking, pres, gen mgr, gen sls mgr & progmg dir.

KNDY-FM— July 23, 1974: 95.5 mhz; 25 kw. Ant 328 ft TL: N39 57 36 W96 44 05. Stereo. Hrs open: 24 Dups AM 10% 937 Jayhawk Rd., 66508. Phone: (785) 562-2361. Fax: (785) 562-2188. Natl. Network: ABC, . Mid-America Ag Format: C&W. ♦Myron Nolind, chief of engrg; Larry Steckline, farm dir.

McPherson

KBBE(FM)— Jan 12, 1974: 96.7 mhz; 6 kw. 245 ft TL: N38 20 30 W97 40 12. Stereo. Hrs open: Box 1069, 67460. Phone: (620) 241-1504. Fax: (620) 241-3196.E-mail: oldies96.7@midkansasradio.com Web Site:midkansasradio.com Population served: 50,000 Natl. Network: ABC, . Format: Oldies. News staff: one. ♦Joe Johnston, gen mgr & disc jockey.

KNGL(AM)— Jan 4, 1949: 1540 khz; 250 w-D. TL: N38 20 30 W97 40 12. Hrs open: Box 1069, 67460. Phone: (620) 241-1504. Fax: (620) 241-3196.E-mail: talkradio1540@midkansasradio.com Web Site:midkansasradio.com Licensee: Davies Communications Inc. (acq 10-1-85; $589,000 with co-located FM; 8-19-85). Population served: 140,000 Natl. Network: ABC, . Kan. Agriculture Format: Talk. News staff: 1. Target aud: 25-54. Spec prog: Relg 5 hrs wkly. ♦Jerry Davies, pres; Diane Davies, exec VP, progmg dir; Joe Johnston, gen mgr; Mark Ekeland, opns mgr; Scott Seirer, gen sls mgr, local news ed; Nick Gosnell, news dir; Shawn White, engrg dir; Kelsey Walker, traf mgr.

Medicine Lodge

KREJ(FM)— January 1990: 101.7 mhz; 50 kw. 492 ft TL: N37 13 58 W98 39 43. Hrs open: 24 301 S. Main St., 67104-1513. Phone: (620) 886-3537. Fax: (321) 264-9370. Licensee: Florida Public Radio Inc. (acq 5-90; 6-11-90). Natl. Network: Moody, . Format: Relg. Target aud: General. ♦Mike Henry, gen mgr; Randy Henry, chief of engrg.

***KSNS(FM)**— April 1999: 91.5 mhz; 48 kw. Ant 462 ft TL: N37 14 02 W98 39 55. Hrs open: 301 S. Main, 67104-1513. Secondary address: 505 Josephine St., Titusville, FL 32796. Phone: (620) 886-3537. Licensee: Florida Public Radio Inc. Format: Contemp Christian music. ♦Mike Henry, gen mgr.

Minneapolis

KZUH(FM)— Feb 24, 1993: 92.7 mhz; 50 kw. 492 ft TL: N39 00 52 W97 37 42. Hrs open: 24 641 W. Cloud, Salina, 67401. Phone: (785) 827-2100. Fax: (785) 827-3503. Licensee: Rocking M Radio Inc. Group owner: Waitt Broadcasting Inc. (acq 8-31-2007; grpsl). Population served: 150,000 Format: Classic rock. Target aud: 18-54. ♦Pat Foster, gen mgr.

Mission

KCNW(AM)—See Fairway

KCZZ(AM)— October 1957: 1480 khz; 1 kw-D, 500 w-N, DA-2. TL: N39 04 05 W94 42 09. Hrs open: 24 1701 S. 55th St., Kansas City, 66106. Phone: (913) 287-1480. Fax: (913) 287-5881. Licensee: Davidson Media Station KCZZ Licensee LLC. (acq 1-28-2005; $3.9 million with KAKS(FM) Huntsville, AR). Population served: 1,500,000 Natl. Rep: Lotus Entravision Reps LLC,. Format: Sp. Target aud: 18-49; adults. ♦Dan Perez, gen mgr; Carlos Mercado, opns dir.

KRBZ(FM)—See Kansas City, MO

Ness City

KXNC(FM)—Not on air, target date: unknown: 104.7 mhz; 100 kw. Ant 974 ft TL: N38 36 31.9 W99 42 11. Hrs open: 980 N. Michigan Ave., Suite 1880, Chicago, IL, 60611. Phone: (312) 204-9900. Licensee: College Creek Media LLC. ♦Christopher F. Devine, gen mgr.

Newton

KFTI-FM— 1959: 92.3 mhz; 100 kw. Ant 640 ft TL: N38 01 09 W97 23 01. Stereo. Hrs open: 24 Box 1402, Wichita, 67201. Secondary address: 4200 N. Old Lawrence Rd., Wichita 67219. Phone: (316) 838-9141. Fax: (316) 838-3607.E-mail: info@classiccountry923.com Web Site:www.classiccountry923.com Licensee: Journal Broadcast

Corp. Group owner: Journal Communications Inc. (acq 3-20-2000; $4.25 million). Population served: 720,000 Format: Classic country. ♦Rob Burton, VP & gen mgr; Eric McCart, gen sls mgr; Manny Cowzinski, prom dir; Ray Micheals, progmg dir.

KJRG(AM)— May 24, 1953: 950 khz; 500 w-D, 147 w-N. TL: N38 02 45 W97 22 24. Hrs open: 209 N. Meridian Rd., 67114. Phone: (620) 663-0943. Fax: (620) 663-0913.E-mail: kjrg@bottradionetwork.com Web Site:www.bottradionetwork.com Licensee: Community Broadcasting Inc. (acq 6-20-2006; $650,000). Population served: 15,439 Natl. Network: USA, . Format: Christian Talk. Target aud: 25-54. ♦Richard P. Bott, gen mgr; Eben Fowler, opns dir; Candy Green, progmg dir; Jason Potocnik, traf mgr.

North Fort Riley

KBLS(FM)— Jan 1, 1993: 102.5 mhz; 100 kw. 492 ft TL: N38 57 05 W96 47 45. Stereo. Hrs open: 5008 Skyway Dr., Manhattan, 66503. Phone: (785) 537-3232. Fax: (785) 587-9495.E-mail: angie.reed@sunny1025.com Licensee: MCC Radio LLC. Group owner: Morris Radio LLC (acq 1-14-2004; grpsl). Population served: 125,000 Format: Adult contemp. News staff: 3; News: 2 hrs wkly. Target aud: 25-54; women. ♦William S. Morris IV, pres; Robert Protzman, gen mgr; Clarke Sanders, prom dir; John Anderson, progmg dir; Mark Beaver, traf mgr.

North Newton

*KBCU(FM)— Apr 6, 1989: 88.1 mhz; 149 w. 56 ft TL: N38 04 26 W97 20 35. Hrs open: 24 (T-Su); 8 AM-midnight (M) 300 E. 27th St., 67117. Phone: (316) 284-5228. Phone: (316) 284-5271. Fax: (316) 284-5286.E-mail: info@kbcufm.com Licensee: Bethel College. Population served: 16,000 Rgnl. Network: Kan. Info. Kan. Info. Format: Var/div. News: 5 hrs wkly. Target aud: General; college students & Harvey County. Spec prog: Sp 2 hrs wkly. ♦Christine Crouse-Dick, gen mgr & stn mgr.

Norton

KQNK(AM)— Oct 30, 1963: 1530 khz; 1 kw-D. TL: N38 35 04 W95 15 57. Hrs open: 1530 KQNK Road, 67654. Phone: (785) 877-3378. Fax: (785) 877-3379.E-mail: kqnk@ruraltel.net Web Site:www.kqnk.com Licensee: Dierking Communications Inc. (group owner; (acq 7-13-99; $165,000 with co-located FM). Population served: 3,976 Natl. Rep: Keystone (unwired net),. Format: Soft adult contemp. ♦Bruce Dierking, pres; Marvin Matchett, gen mgr; Mandi Fick, gen sls mgr, disc jockey; Deena Wente, progmg dir, news dir, chief of engrg, disc jockey.

KQNK-FM— Mar 1, 1993: 106.7 mhz; 51 kw. 92 ft TL: N39 49 37 W99 52 08. Hrs open: 1530 KQNK Road, 67654. Phone: (785) 877-3378. Fax: (785) 877-3379. Web Site:www.kqnk.com Format: Adult contemp.

*KSNB(FM)—Not on air, target date: unknown: 91.5 mhz; 6 kw. Ant 171 ft TL: N39 47 51 W99 53 29. Hrs open: Box 2440, Tupelo, MS, 38803-2440. Phone: (662) 844-8888. Fax: (662) 842-6791. Web Site:www.afr.net Licensee: American Family Association. ♦Donald E. Wildmon, chmn.

Oberlin

KFNF(FM)— July 1977: 101.1 mhz; 100 kw. 420 ft TL: N39 49 33 W100 39 09. Stereo. Hrs open: 24 499 Highway 36, 6 Miles W. of Oberlin, 67749. Phone: (785) 475-2225. Phone: (785) 475-2226. Fax: (785) 475-2510.E-mail: kfnf@highplainsradio.net Licensee: Armada Media - McCook Inc. (group owner; (acq 3-31-2007; grpsl). Population served: 60,000 Natl. Network: ABC, . Rgnl. Network: Mid-American Ag. Mid-America Ag Format: Country. Target aud: 25-65; farmers. Spec prog: Gospel 3 hrs wkly. ♦Bryan Loker, gen mgr; Adam Kadavy, chief of opns.

*KRLE(FM)— 2009: 91.3 mhz; 250 w. Ant 118 ft TL: N39 47 14 W100 31 54. Hrs open:
Rebroadcasts KLVR(FM) Middletown, CA 100%.
2351 Sunset Blvd., Suite 170-218, Rocklin, CA, 95765. Phone: (916) 251-1600. Fax: (916) 251-1650. Web Site:www.klove.com Licensee: Educational Media Foundation. (acq 3-23-2007; grpsl). Natl. Network: K-Love, . Format: Contemp Christian. ♦Mike Novak, pres.

Ogden

KQLA(FM)—Licensed to Ogden. See Manhattan

Oketo

*KOKN(FM)—Not on air, target date: unknown: 88.7 mhz; 17 kw. Ant 436 ft TL: N39 52 33 W96 38 05. Hrs open: 282 Country Estate Dr., Springer, OK, 73458. Phone: (580) 653-2777. Licensee: Ron Elmore Ministries Inc. ♦Ron Elmore, pres.

Olathe

KCCV-FM— Dec 1, 1993: 92.3 mhz; 8.3 kw. 564 ft TL: N38 56 10 W94 50 41. Stereo. Hrs open: 24 10550 Barkley, Suite 112, Overland Park, 66212. Phone: (913) 642-7600. Fax: (913) 642-2424.E-mail: kccv@bottradionetwork.com Web Site:www.bottradionetwork.com Licensee: Bott Broadcasting Co. (group owner; acq 7-1-92; $537,500; 8-3-92). Population served: 3,000,000 Natl. Network: USA, . Format: Christian talk. Target aud: 25-54; family oriented. ♦Trace Thurlby, COO; Richard P. Bott Sr., pres; Tom Holdeman, CFO; Richard P. Bott II, exec VP, VP; Pat Rulon, natl sls mgr; Rachel Moser, mktg mgr; Jason Potocnik, traf mgr.

Olpe

KEKS(FM)—Not on air, target date: unknown: 103.1 mhz; 2.45 kw. Ant 315 ft TL: N38 17 37 W96 13 03. Hrs open: 1711 N. Grand St., Pittsburg, 66762-3229. Phone: (620) 404-8108. Fax: (620) 343-6844.E-mail: info@keksfm.com Licensee: Andrew A. Wachter. ♦Andrew A. Wachter, gen mgr.

Olsburg

*KANV(FM)— 2003: 91.3 mhz; 6 kw. Ant 328 ft TL: N39 00 55 W96 53 55. Hrs open: 1120 W. 11th St., Lawrence, 66044. Phone: (785) 864-4530. Fax: (785) 864-5278.E-mail: kpr@ku.edu Web Site:www.kpr.ku.edu Licensee: The University of Kansas. Natl. Network: NPR, . Format: Class, jazz. ♦Janet Campbell, gen mgr; Cordelia Brown, opns mgr.

Osage City

KMXN(FM)— July 26, 1982: 92.9 mhz; 7.9 kw. Ant 538 ft TL: N38 48 21 W95 42 58. (CP: 36 kw, ant 564 ft. TL: N38 31 47 W96 05 09). Stereo. Hrs open: 24 3125 W. 6th St., Lawrence, 66049. Phone: (785) 843-1320. Fax: (785) 841-5924. Licensee: Great Plains Media Inc. (acq 6-30-2006). Rgnl. Network: Mid-American Ag. Format: Rhythmic CHR. ♦Ron Covert, gen mgr; Jon Thomas, progmg dir; Mike Mayfield, chief of engrg.

Ottawa

KCHZ(FM)— Mar 1, 1962: 95.7 mhz; 96 kw. Ant 981 ft TL: N39 00 45 W95 01 46. Hrs open: 5800 Foxridge Dr., Suite 600, Mission, 66202. Phone: (913) 514-3000. Fax: (913) 262-3946. Web Site:www.957thevibe.com Licensee: CMP KC Licensing LLC. Group owner: Cumulus Media Inc. (acq 5-3-2006; grpsl). Population served: 11,036 Format: Rhythmic top-40. ♦Tim Robisch, gen mgr; Maurice DeVoe, opns mgr, progmg dir; Pat Gibbs, gen sls mgr; Jamie Cox, prom mgr.

KOFO(AM)— Sept 24, 1949: 1220 khz; 250 w-D, 40 w-N. TL: N38 35 04 W95 15 57. Hrs open: 24 320 E. Radio Rd., Box 16, 66067. Phone: (785) 242-1220. Fax: (785) 242-1442.E-mail: kofo@kofo.com Web Site:www.kofo.com Licensee: Brandy Communications Inc. Population served: 55,000 Natl. Network: ABC, . Rgnl. Network: Kan. Agri. Kan. Agriculture Format: C&W. News staff: 1; News: 7 hrs wkly. Target aud: 25-54; Male & Female. Spec prog: Farm 2 hrs wkly. ♦Brad Howard, pres & gen mgr.

*KRBW(FM)— 1997: 90.5 mhz; 250 w. 187 ft TL: N38 35 04 W95 15 57. Hrs open: American family Radio, 320 E. Radio Rd., 66067. Phone: (785) 242-9050. Fax: (662) 842-6791. Web Site:www.afr.net Licensee: American Family Association Group owner: American Family Radio (acq 1-24-97). Format: Comtemp Christian. ♦Marvin Sanders, gen mgr.

*KTJO-FM— May 1951: 88.9 mhz; 145 w. 66 ft TL: N38 36 16 W95 15 49. Stereo. Hrs open: 7 AM-midnight Ottawa Univ., 1001 S. Cedar St., 66067. Phone: (785) 242-5200. Fax: (785) 242-7429.E-mail: info@ktjo.com Licensee: Ottawa University. Population served: 13,102 Format: Div, CHR, Contemp Christian. News: 5 hrs wkly. Target aud: General; Ottawa Univ community & City of Ottawa, KS. ♦Bradley A. Howard, CEO; Ben Weiss, engrg VP.

Overland Park

KCCV(AM)— 1962: 760 khz; 6 kw-D, 200 w-N, DA-2. TL: N39 02 26 W94 30 34. Hrs open: Sunrise-sunset 10550 Barkley, Suite 112, 66212. Phone: (913) 642-7600. Fax: (913) 642-2424.E-mail: kccv@bottradionetwork.com Web Site:www.bottradionetwork.com Licensee: Bott Broadcasting Co. Group owner: Bott Radio Network (acq 1962). Population served: 3,000,000 Natl. Network: USA, . Format: Christian talk, Christian, relg, news/talk. Target aud: 25-54; family-oriented. ♦Trace Thurlby, COO; Richard P Bolt, pres; Tom Holdeman, CFO; Richard P. Bott II, exec VP; Pat Rulon, natl sls mgr; Rachel Moser, mktg mgr; Jason Potocnik, traf mgr.

Paola

*KCPK(FM)—Not on air, target date: unknown: 89.7 mhz; 1.5 kw. Ant 292 ft TL: N38 28 32 W94 56 23. Hrs open: 1016 N. Pearl St., 66071. Phone: (913) 294-2429. Licensee: Paola Assembly of God. ♦Roy Rhodes, CEO.

Parsons

KLKC(AM)— 1948: 1540 khz; 250 w-D. TL: N37 20 35 W95 13 55. Hrs open: Box 853, 1812 Main St., 67357-0853. Phone: (620) 421-6400. Fax: (620) 421-5570.E-mail: lynnm@skilonline.com Web Site:klkc.com Licensee: Southeast Kansas Independent Living Resource Center Inc. (acq 12-6-2005; $334,932 with co-located FM). Population served: 113,015 Format: Talk, sports. News: 28 hrs wkly. Target aud: 12-60; general. Spec prog: Farm 2 hrs, relg 2 hrs, big band 3 hrs wkly. ♦Lynn Meredith, gen mgr; Colt Smith, gen sls mgr; Steve Lardy, progmg dir; Terry Blackburn, mus dir; Annette Tucker, news dir, chief of engrg.

KLKC-FM— October 1978: 93.5 mhz; 3 kw. Ant 267 ft TL: N37 20 35 W95 13 55. Hrs open: 6 AM-11 PM Box 853, 1812 Main St., 67357. Phone: (620) 421-6400. Fax: (620) 421-5570.E-mail: lynnm@skilonline.com Format: Oldies.

Phillipsburg

KKAN(AM)— Dec 31, 1959: 1490 khz; 1 kw-U. TL: N39 47 32 W99 19 55. Hrs open: Box 548, 67661. Phone: (785) 543-2151. Phone: (785) 543-6593. Fax: (785) 543-2152. Web Site:www.kkankqma.com Licensee: Walter C. Seidel. (acq 3-29-88). Population served: 120,000 Rgnl. Network: Kan. Info. Kan. Info. Format: Div, news. Target aud: General; rural population & small towns. Spec prog: Farm 10 hrs, gospel 12 hrs wkly. ♦Bob Yates, gen mgr, stn mgr, progmg dir; Tad Felts, news dir.

KQMA-FM— July 14, 1984: 92.5 mhz; 100 kw. 510 ft TL: N39 37 02 W99 17 55. Stereo. Hrs open: Dups AM 60% Box 548, 67661. Phone: (785)543-2151, (785)543-6593. Fax: (785) 543-2152. Licensee: Walter C. Seidel Population served: 80,000 Format: Var.

Pittsburg

KKOW(AM)— Oct 11, 1937: 860 khz; 10 kw-D, 5 kw-N, DA-N. TL: N37 24 46 W94 38 16. Hrs open: 24 1162 E. Hwy. 126, 66762. Phone: (620) 231-7200. Fax: (620) 231-3321.E-mail: kkow@kkowradio.com Web Site:www.kkowam.com Licensee: American Media Investment Inc. (acq 6-89; $400,000 with co-located FM; 6-26-89). Population served: 342,000 Natl. Network: CBS, . Natl. Rep: McGavren Guild,. Format: Classic country. News staff: 2; News: 5 hrs wkly. Target aud: General. ♦Chris Kelly, gen mgr & prom dir.

KKOW-FM— Apr 20, 1975: 96.9 mhz; 100 kw. 278 ft TL: N37 23 44 W94 40 42. Stereo. Hrs open: 1162 E. Hwy. 126, 66762. Phone: (620) 231-7200. Fax: (620) 231-3321.E-mail: kkow@kkowradio.com Web Site:www.kkowfm.com Licensee: American Media Investments Inc. Format: Contemp country. ♦Chris Kelly, gen mgr; Dave Fink, gen sls mgr.

*KRPS(FM)— Apr 29, 1988: 89.9 mhz; 100 kw. 1,000 ft TL: N37 18 44 W94 48 58. Stereo. Hrs open: 24 Box 899, 66762. Phone: (620) 235-4288. Fax: 620(235-4290).E-mail: krps@pittstate.edu Web Site:www.krps.org Licensee: Pittsburg State University. Natl. Network: NPR, PRI, . Format: Class, jazz, news. News: 39 hrs wkly. Spec prog: Folk 3 hrs. ♦Missi Kelly, gen mgr; Matt Larson, opns mgr; Vicki Pritchett, dev dir; Tim Metcalf, progmg dir.

KSEK(AM)— 1948: 1340 khz; 1 kw-U. TL: N37 23 44 W94 40 42. Hrs open: 202 E. Centenial Dr., Suite 2B, 66762. Phone: (620) 232-9912. Fax: (620) 232-9915.E-mail: lynnm@skilonline.com Licensee: Southeast Kansas Independent Living Resource Center Inc. (group owner; (acq

11-30-2004; $700,000 with KSEK-FM Girard). Natl. Network: ESPN Radio, AP Network News, . Format: Sports. News: 10 hrs wkly. Target aud: 25 plus. Spec prog: High school basketball & football. ♦Lynn Meredith, gen mgr.

Plainville

KFIX(FM)— May 11, 1998: 96.9 mhz; 10.5 kw. 876 ft TL: N39 01 15 W99 28 13. Stereo. Hrs open: 24 Box 6, Hays, 67601. Secondary address: 2300 Hall, Hays 67601. Phone: (785) 625-2578. Fax: (785) 625-3632.E-mail: studio@kfix.com Web Site:www.kfix.com Licensee: Hull Broadcasting Inc. (acq 9-12-00; with KBGL(FM) Larned). Population served: 65,000 Format: AOR. Target aud: 25-64. ♦Richard C. Hull, pres; Nancy E. Baumrucker, gen mgr; Cameron Perry, progmg dir; Callie Kolacny, news dir; Kristy Pfeifer, traf mgr.

Pleasanton

KPIO-FM—Not on air, target date: unknown: 93.7 mhz; 25 kw. Ant 328 ft TL: N38 14 23 W94 56 36. Hrs open: 201 N. Industrial Park Rd., Excelsior Springs, MO, 64024-1736. Phone: (816) 630-1090.E-mail: kccatholic@aol.com Web Site:www.thecatholicradionetwork.com Licensee: Kansas City Catholic Network Inc. ♦James E. O'Laughlin, pres & gen mgr.

Pratt

KHMY(FM)— July 1, 1965: 93.1 mhz; 100 kw. Ant 1,007 ft TL: N37 55 50 W98 19 04. Stereo. Hrs open: 24 Box 1036, Hutchinson, 67504-1030. Phone: (620) 662-5900. Fax: (620) 662-5797.E-mail: info@khmtfm.com Licensee: Eagle Communications Inc. Group owner: Eagle Communications Group (acq 3-17-03; swap for KSSH(FM) Ingalls). Population served: 100,000 Natl. Rep: McGavren Guild,. Format: Adult contemp. ♦Mark Trotman, gen mgr, sls dir; Jason Younger, opns mgr; Terry Drouhard, gen sls mgr; Fred Gough, news dir.

KMMM(AM)— Sept 19, 1963: 1290 khz; 5 kw-D, 500 w-N, DA-2. TL: N37 38 34 W98 40 39. Hrs open: 24 Box 486, 30129 E. Hwy. 54, 67124. Phone: (620) 672-5581. Fax: (620) 672-5583.E-mail: kwls@rocking.com Web Site:www.superhits129.com Licensee: Rocking M Radio Inc. Group owner: Waitt Broadcasting Inc. (acq 8-31-2007; grpsl). Population served: 22,000 Rgnl. Network: Mid-American Ag. Natl. Rep: McGavren Guild,. Mid-America Ag Shaw Pittman. Format: Oldies 60s & 70s. News staff: one; News: 3 hrs wkly. Target aud: 25 plus; rural. ♦Eric Strobel, gen mgr; Carl Raida, progmg dir.

Riley

KACZ(FM)— Sept 16, 2003: 96.3 mhz; 11.5 kw. Ant 479 ft TL: N39 13 34 W96 37 00. Hrs open: Box 1350, 2414 Casement Rd., Manhattan, 66502. Phone: (785) 776-1350. Fax: (785) 539-1000. Web Site:www.z963.com Licensee: Manhattan Broadcasting Co. Inc. Group owner: Seaton Stations. Wire Svc: AP Format: CHR. News staff: 3; News: 4 hrs wkly. Target aud: 18-59; woman. ♦Richard T. Wartell, pres & gen mgr.

***KONZ(FM)**—Not on air, target date: unknown: 90.9 mhz; 9.1 kw. Ant 305 ft TL: N39 14 38 W96 39 30. Hrs open: 1221 Thurston St., Manhattan, 66502. Phone: (785) 341-9459. Fax: (785) 539-9460. Licensee: UFM Community Learning Center. Format: Educ. ♦Linda Inlow Teener, pres.

Rozel

KKCV(FM)— 2007: 102.5 mhz; 100 kw. Ant 488 ft TL: N37 57 28 W99 25 45.2. Hrs open: 24 10550 Barkley, Suite 100, Overland Park, 66212. Phone: (913) 642-7770. Fax: (913) 642-1319. Web Site:www.bot-tradionetwork.com Licensee: Bott Communications Inc. Natl. Network: USA, . Format: Christian talk. Target aud: 25-55. ♦Trace Thurlby, COO; Richard P. Bott Sr., pres; Tom Holdeman, CFO; Richard P. Bott II, VP; Eben Fowler, opns dir; Pat Rulon, natl sls mgr; Rachel Moser, mktg mgr; Jason Potocnik, traf mgr.

Russell

KRSL(AM)— Jan 11, 1956: 990 khz; 250 w-D, 30 w-N. TL: N38 54 22 W98 51 39. Hrs open: Box 666, 1984 N. Main St., 67665. Phone: (785) 483-3121. Fax: (785) 483-6511.E-mail: larry@krsl.com Web Site:www.krsl.com Licensee: White Communications L.L.C. (acq 9-1-2006; $435,000 with co-located FM). Population served: 5,371 Format: Classic hits. Target aud: 24 plus; general. Spec prog: Polka 4 hrs, farm 2 hrs wkly. ♦Larry Calvery, gen mgr; Mike McKenna, stn mgr; Carol McKenna, news dir.

KRSL-FM— July 1, 1965: 95.9 mhz; 1.35 kw. Ant 487 ft TL: N38 54 22 W98 51 39. Stereo. Hrs open: Box 666, 1984 N. Main St., 67665. Phone: (785) 483-3121. Fax: (785) 483-6511.E-mail: larry@krsl.com Web Site:www.krsl.com Licensee: White Communications L.L.C. (acq 9-1-2006; $435,000 with co-located AM). Format: Classic hits. ♦Larry Calvery, gen mgr; Mike McKenna, stn mgr; Carol McKenna, news dir.

Saint Marys

KQTP(FM)— Dec 4, 1994: 102.9 mhz; 50 kw. 320 ft TL: N39 05 34 W95 47 05. Hrs open: 825 S. Kansas Ave., Topeka, 66603. Phone: (785) 272-2122. Fax: (785) 272-6219.E-mail: oldieskqtp@aol.com Web Site:www.cumulus.com Licensee: Cumulus Licensing Corp. Group owner: Cumulus Media Inc. (acq 4-13-01; with KWIC(FM) Topeka). Format: Classic country. Target aud: 35-54. ♦John Walker, gen mgr; Keith Liefmann, gen sls mgr; Carla Newman, prom dir; Rich Bowers, progmg dir; Mike Manns, news dir.

Salina

***KAKA(FM)**— 2002: 88.5 mhz; 46 kw. Ant 394 ft TL: N39 04 12 W97 51 14. Hrs open: American Family Radio, Box 2440, Tupelo, MS, 38803. Phone: (662) 844-8888. Fax: (662) 842-6791. Web Site:www.afr.net Licensee: American Family Association. Group owner: American Family Radio Format: Relg. ♦Marvin Sanders, stn mgr.

***KCVS(FM)**— 1994: 91.7 mhz; 11.5 kw. Ant 748 ft TL: N38 39 58 W97 41 30. Stereo. Hrs open: 24 3434 W. Kilbourn Ave., Milwaukee, WI, 53208. Phone: (414) 935-3000. Fax: (414) 935-3015.E-mail: kcvs@vcyamerica.org Web Site:www.vcyamerica.org Licensee: VCY/America Inc. (group owner; (acq 7-2-97). Natl. Network: Moody, USA, . Format: Christian. ♦Vic Eliason, VP & gen mgr; Jim Schneider, progmg dir.

KFRM(AM)— 1947: 550 khz; 5 kw-D, 110 w-N, DA-2. TL: N39 26 10 W97 39 40. Hrs open: sun up to sun down 1815 Meadowlark Rd., Clay Center, 67432. Phone: (785) 632-5661. Fax: (785) 632-5662.E-mail: kbauer@kfrm.com Web Site:kfrm.com Licensee: Taylor Communications Inc. (acq 9-12-96; $500,000). Population served: 1,800,000 Natl. Network: AP Network News, . Wire Svc: AP Format: Farm, talk. News staff: 2; News: 6 hrs wkly. Target aud: 25-55; agricultural. Spec prog: Gospel 5 hrs wkly. ♦Kyle Bauer, gen mgr, gen sls mgr, progmg dir; Rod Keen, opns mgr; Michelle Tessaro, news dir; Joe Woodward, traf mgr; Duane Toews, farm dir; Rocky Downing, sports cmtr.

***KHCD(FM)**— Jan 28, 1988: 89.5 mhz; 100 kw. 925 ft TL: N39 06 16 W97 23 15. Stereo. Hrs open: 24
Rebroadcasts KHCC-FM Hutchinson 100%.
815 N. Walnut, Suite 300, Hutchinson, 67501. Phone: (620) 662-6646.E-mail: rfragoza@radiokansas.org Web Site:radiokansas.org Licensee: Hutchinson Community College. Natl. Network: NPR, . Format: Class, new age, news. ♦David M. Horning, gen mgr; Geralyn Smith, opns dir; Sharon Webb, dev dir; Ken Baker, progmg dir; Frederic Jung, engrg dir.

KINA(AM)— Apr 20, 1964: 910 khz; 500 w-D, 29 w-N, DA-2. TL: N38 45 52 W97 32 30. Hrs open: 24 hrs 1825 S. Ohio St., 67401-0198. Phone: (785) 825-4631. Fax: (785) 825-4600. Web Site:www.910kina.com Licensee: Eagle Communications Inc. (Acq 11-1-95; $235,000). Population served: 142,000 Natl. Network: Fox News Radio, . Rgnl. Network: Kan. Info. Wire Svc: AP Format: News/talk, sports. Target aud: 45 plus; middle to upper income adults. ♦Jerry Hinrikus, gen mgr; Larry Avery, gen sls mgr; Scott Woodson, opns dir & progmg dir.

KSAL(AM)— May 18, 1937: 1150 khz; 5 kw-U, DA-N. TL: N38 53 08 W97 30 58. Hrs open: 24 Box 80, 67402. Secondary address: 131 N. Santa Fe 67401. Phone: (785) 823-1111. Fax: (785) 823-2034. Web Site:www.ksallink.com Licensee: MCC Radio LLC. Group owner: Morris Radio LLC (acq 1-30-2004; grpsl). Population served: 163,900 Natl. Network: ABC, . Natl. Rep: Katz Radio,. Kan. Info. Wire Svc: AP Format: News/talk. News staff: 3; News: 20 hrs wkly. Target aud: 35-64. Spec prog: Farm 3 hrs wkly. ♦Robert Protzman, gen mgr; Bill Ray, opns mgr, gen sls mgr; Clarke Sanders, prom mgr; Rich Alexander, progmg dir; Todd Pittenger, news dir.

KSAL-FM— October 1988: Stn currently dark. 104.9 mhz; 14 kw. 440 ft TL: N38 53 23 W97 38 46. Stereo. Hrs open: Box 80, 67402-0080. Secondary address: 131 N.Santa Fe 67401. Phone: (785) 823-1111. Fax: (785) 823-2034. Web Site:www.ksallink.com Licensee: MCC Radio LLC. Group owner: Morris Radio LLC (acq 1-14-2004; grpsl). Population served: 163,900 Natl. Rep: Katz Radio,. Format: Contemp classic hits. News staff: 3; News: 5 hrs wky. Target aud: 18-44. ♦Robert Protzman, gen mgr; Bill Ray, opns mgr; Mitch Drees, sls dir; Clarke Sanders, prom mgr; Kevin Taylor, progmg dir; Mark Beaver, traf mgr.

KSKG(FM)— 1961: 99.9 mhz; 100 kw. 570 ft TL: N38 47 36 W97 31 33. Hrs open: 24 1825 S. Ohio St., 67401-0198. Phone: (785) 825-4631. Fax: (785) 825-4600. Web Site:www.999kskg.com Licensee: Eagle Communications Inc. Group owner: Eagle Communications Group. Population served: 300,000 Format: Modern country. Target aud: 25-54; 51% female, 49% male (baby boomers). Spec prog: Gospel 3 hrs wkly. ♦Gary Shorman, pres; Jerry Hinrikus, gen mgr; Scott Carroll, opns mgr & progmg dir; Randy Picking, news dir; Mark Goff, chief of engrg; Cher Richards, traf mgr.

KYEZ(FM)— May 1, 1975: 93.7 mhz; 100 kw. 510 ft TL: N38 57 14 W97 36 29. Stereo. Hrs open: 24 Box 80 , 67401. Secondary address: 131 N. Santa Fe 67401. Phone: (785) 823-1111. Fax: (785) 823-2034. Web Site:www.y937.com Population served: 163,900 Natl. Rep: Katz Radio,. Format: Country. News staff: 3; News: 2 hrs wkly. Target aud: 25-54. ♦Robert Protzman, gen mgr; Bill Ray, opns mgr; Mitch Drees, sls dir; Clarke Sanders, prom dir; Chad Allen, progmg dir.

Scott City

***KJLJ(FM)**—Not on air, target date: unknown: 88.5 mhz; 25 kw. Ant 344 ft TL: N38 31 35 W100 54 42. Hrs open: Box 991, Meade, 67864. Phone: (620) 873-2991. Fax: (620) 873-2755.E-mail: kjil@kjil.com Web Site:www.kjil.com Licensee: Great Plains Christian Radio Inc. ♦Robert D. Hughes, CEO.

KSKL(FM)— Nov 9, 1964: 94.5 mhz; 100 kw. Ant 345 ft TL: N38 31 35 W100 34 42. Stereo. Hrs open: Box 246, 67871. Phone: (620) 872-5345. Fax: (620) 872-5422.E-mail: info@wksradio.com Web Site:www.wksradio.com Licensee: Western Kansas Wireless Inc. Group owner: Robert Ingstad Broadcast Properties (acq 3-26-93; $175,000 with co-located AM;4-12-93). Rgnl. Network: Kan. Info. Kan. Info. Format: Oldies. ♦Gil Wohler, gen mgr.

KYUL(AM)— Oct 13, 1962: 1310 khz; 500 w-D, 147 w-N. TL: N38 31 35 W100 54 42. Hrs open: Box 246, 67871. Phone: (620) 872-5345. Fax: (620) 872-5422. Licensee: Steckline Communications Inc. (group owner; (acq 11-28-2006; $550,000 with KIUL(AM) Garden City). Population served: 4,100 Rgnl. Network: Kan. Agri., Kan. Info. Kan. Agriculture Format: Relg. Spec prog: Farm 5 hrs wkly. ♦Gil Wohler, gen mgr.

Seneca

KMZA(FM)— Oct 15, 1992: 92.1 mhz; 4.5 kw. 377 ft TL: N39 49 50 W96 02 39. Stereo. Hrs open: 24
Rebroadcasts KNZA(FM) Hiawatha 90%.
28 S. 4th St., 66538. Phone: (785) 336-6166. Fax: (785) 336-3600.E-mail: kmzafm@bbwi.net Web Site:www.kmzafm.com Licensee: KNZA Inc. (group owner) Format: Country, loc news. News staff: one; News: 10 hrs wkly. Target aud: General. Spec prog: Farm 7 hrs wkly. ♦Greg Buser, pres, gen mgr; Robert Hilton, opns mgr; L.J. Trant, progmg dir; Heidi Wolfgang, news dir.

Silver Lake

KCVT(FM)— 1996: 92.5 mhz; 6.7 kw. 387 ft TL: N39 08 42 W95 55 37. Hrs open: 24 534 S. Kansas, Suite 930, Topeka, 66603. Phone: (785) 233-9250. Fax: (785) 233-9260.E-mail: kcvt@bottradionetwork.com Web Site:www.bottradionetwork.com Licensee: Richard P. Bott II. Group owner: Bott Radio Network Population served: 320,000 Natl. Network: USA, . Format: Christian talk. ♦Pat Rulon, gen mgr; Candy Green, progmg dir.

Sterling

KSKU(FM)— June 12, 1995: Stn currently dark. 94.7 mhz; 50 kw. Ant 485 ft TL: N38 13 50 W98 18 53. Hrs open: 24 106 N. Main St., Hutchinson, 67501-5219. Phone: (620) 665-5758. Fax: (620) 665-6655.E-mail: production@adastra.kscoxmail.com Licensee: Ad Astra Per Aspera Broadcasting Inc. (group owner) Population served: 100,000 Natl. Network: Jones Radio Networks, . Format: CHR. News staff: one; News: 2 hrs wkly. Target aud: 18-54; general. ♦Cliff C. Shank, pres, gen mgr; Aaron West, opns mgr; Mike Hill, VP, stn mgr & sls VP; Lucky Kidd, natl sls mgr, news dir.

Topeka

***KBUZ(FM)—** 1994: 90.3 mhz; 11 kw. 840 ft TL: N39 00 19 W96 02 58. Hrs open: Box 2240, Tupelo, MS, 38803. Phone: (662) 844-8888. Fax: (662) 842-6791. Web Site:www.afr.net Licensee: American Family Association. Group owner: American Family Radio (acq 12-30-94; 3-20-95). Format: Relg. ♦Bob Faulkner, stn mgr, sls VP, progmg VP; Jennie Crable, prom VP; George McGurk, chief of engrg.

KDVV(FM)— May 29, 1960: 100.3 mhz; 100 kw. Ant 984 ft TL: N38 57 15 W95 54 43. Stereo. Hrs open: 825 S. Kansas Ave., 66612. Phone: (785) 272-2122. Fax: (785) 272-6219.E-mail: info@v100rocks.com Web Site:www.v100rocks.com Licensee: Cumulus Licensing LLC. Population served: 125,011 Natl. Network: Westwood One, . Format: AOR. Target aud: 18-54.

***KJTY(FM)—** Aug 31, 1985: 88.1 mhz; 100 kw. Ant 426 ft TL: N39 11 25 W95 39 29. Stereo. Hrs open: 24 Box 35300, Tucson, AZ, 85740. Phone: (785) 357-8888. Fax: (785) 357-0100.E-mail: info@kjtyfm.com Web Site:www.myflr.org Licensee: Family Life Broadcasting Inc. (acq 5-23-2007; grpsl). Natl. Network: USA, . Format: Relg. News: 15 hrs wkly. Target aud: 25-49. Spec prog: Children 5 hrs wkly. ♦Randy L. Carlson, pres; Dawn Bumstead, progmg mgr.

KMAJ(AM)— July 1947: 1440 khz; 5 kw-D, 1 kw-N, DA-1. TL: N39 01 17 W95 34 15. Hrs open: 825 S. Kansas Ave., 66603. Phone: (785) 272-2122. Fax: (785) 272-6219.E-mail: info@kmaj.com Web Site:www.kmaj.com Licensee: Cumulus Licensing Corp. Group owner: Cumulus Media Inc. (acq 7-31-98; grpsl). Population served: 155,500 Natl. Network: ABC, ESPN Radio, Westwood One, . Format: News/talk, sports. Target aud: General. ♦John Walker, gen mgr; Keith Liefmann, gen sls mgr; Carla Newman, prom dir; Rose Diehl, progmg dir; Mike Manns, news dir.

KMAJ-FM— July 1, 1971: 107.7 mhz; 100 kw. Ant 1,214 ft TL: N39 01 34 W95 54 58. Stereo. Hrs open: 825 S. Kansas Ave., Suite 100, 66603. Phone: (785) 272-2122. Fax: (785) 272-6219.E-mail: info@kmaj.com Web Site:www.kmaj.com Licensee: Kansas City Trust LLC, Trustee (acq 3-3-2006). Population served: 200,000 Natl. Network: Westwood One, . Format: Adult contemp. ♦John Walker, gen mgr; Keith Liefmann, gen sls mgr; Carla Newman, prom dir; Rich Bowers, progmg dir; Mike Manns, news dir.

KTOP(AM)— July 1947: 1490 khz; 1 kw-U. TL: N39 04 39 W95 40 46. Hrs open: 825 S. Kansas Ave., 66612. Phone: (785) 272-2122. Fax: (785) 272-6219. Licensee: Cumulus Licensing Corp. Group owner: Cumulus Media Inc. (acq 7-31-98; grpsl). Population served: 125,011 Natl. Network: ESPN Radio, . Format: Sports. ♦Kevin Klein, gen mgr.

KTPK(FM)— Nov 25, 1974: 106.9 mhz; 100 kw. Ant 1,210 ft TL: N39 01 34 W95 55 01. Stereo. Hrs open: 24 2121 S.W. Chelsea, 66614. Phone: (785) 273-1069. Phone: (785) 297-1069. Fax: (785) 273-0123.E-mail: Jallangm@countrylegends1069.com Web Site:www.countrylegends1069.com Licensee: JMJ Broadcasting Co. Inc. (acq 11-24-2004; $5.7 million). Population served: 512,000 Natl. Rep: Katz Radio,. Format: Country. News staff: 2; News: 6 hrs wkly. Target aud: 25-64; mobile, family-oriented, high-income professional adults. ♦Herbert W. McCord, pres; Jim Allan, gen mgr; Bill Kentling, sls dir; Michael Newman, prom dir; Chris Fisher, adv VP, progmg dir; Trevor Kirkwood, mus dir; Megan Kirkwood, traf mgr; Roy Baum, engr.

KWIC(FM)— Oct 15, 1993: 99.3 mhz; 6 kw. 292 ft TL: N39 02 56 W95 40 32. Hrs open: 24 825 S. Kansas Ave., 66603. Phone: (785) 272-2122. Fax: (785) 272-6219.E-mail: info@eagle993.com Web Site:www.eagle993.com Licensee: Cumulus Licensing Corp. Group owner: Cumulus Media Inc. (acq 4-13-01; with KQTP(FM) Saint Marys). Format: Classic hits. ♦John Walker, gen mgr; Keith Liefmann, gen sls mgr; Carla Newman, prom dir; Les Glenn, progmg dir; Mike Manns, news dir.

WIBW(AM)— May 8, 1927: 580 khz; 5 kw-U, DA-N (ST-KKSU). TL: N39 05 05 W95 46 58. Hrs open: 24 1210 S.W. Executive Dr., 66615. Phone: (785) 272-3456. Fax: (785) 228-7282. Web Site:www.580radio.com Licensee: Morris Communications Corp. Group owner: Morris Communications Inc. (acq 12-22-97; grpsl). Population served: 485,700 Natl. Network: ABC, . Natl. Rep: Katz Radio,. Kan. Info. Wiley, Rein & Fielding. Wire Svc: AP Format: News/talk, sports. News staff: 4; News: 15 hrs wkly. Target aud: Adults 25+. ♦Michael Osterhaut, VP; Larry Riggins, gen mgr; Michelle Hay, gen sls mgr; Amber Rome, prom dir; Bruce Steinbrock, progmg dir; Jan Lundsford, news dir; Roy Baum, chief of engrg.

WIBW-FM— Sept 1, 1961: 94.5 mhz; 100 kw. Ant 1,161 ft TL: N39 01 34 W95 55 01. Stereo. Hrs open: 24 1210 S.W. Executive Dr., 66615. Phone: (785) 272-3456. Fax: (785) 228-7282. Web Site:www.94country.com Licensee: Morris Communications Corp. Natl. Rep: Katz Radio,. Kan. Agriculture Format: Country. News staff: 4; News: 4 hrs wkly. Target aud: Adults 25-54. ♦Michael Osterhout, VP, progmg dir; Larry Riggins, gen mgr, mus dir; Michelle Hay, gen sls mgr; Keith Montgomery, progmg dir; Stephanie Lynn, mus dir; Jan Lundsford, news dir; Roy Baum, chief of engrg.

Ulysses

KULY(AM)— Mar 1, 1965: 1420 khz; 1 kw-D, 500 w-N, DA-N. TL: N37 14 28 W101 21 49. Hrs open: 24 2917 S. Colorado, 67880. Phone: (620) 276-2366. Fax: (620) 356-3635. Licensee: KBUF Partnership. Group owner: Robert Ingstad Broadcast Properties. Population served: 5,779 Natl. Network: Westwood One, . Rgnl. Network: Kan. Info., Kan. Agri. Kan. Agriculture Fisher, Wayland, Cooper, Leader & Zaragoza. Format: Country. News staff: one; News: 24 hrs wkly. Target aud: 21-65; middle to upper class workers, farmers & housewives. Spec prog: Farm 12 hrs, Sp 3 hrs wkly. ♦Gil Wohler, gen mgr.

Wamego

KHCA(FM)— Mar 6, 1986: 95.3 mhz; 6 kw. 328 ft TL: N39 12 35 W96 21 05. Stereo. Hrs open: 24 Box 1471, Manhattan, 66505. Secondary address: 103 N. 3rd, Manhattan 66502. Phone: (785) 537-9595. Fax: (785) 537-2955.E-mail: angel95@kansas.net Web Site:www.angel95fm.com Licensee: KHCA Inc. (acq 9-18-91; $126,000; 10-7-91). Population served: 90,000 Natl. Network: Salem Radio Network, . Format: Christian, adult contemp, rock. News staff: one. ♦Jerry Hutchinson, pres & gen mgr.

Wellington

KLEY(AM)— Nov 19, 1966: 1130 khz; 250 w-D, 1 w-N. TL: N37 14 28 W97 24 04. Hrs open: 24 338 S. Kley Dr., 67152. Phone: (620) 326-3341. Fax: (620) 326-8512.E-mail: kley@sutv.com Licensee: Johnson Enterprises Inc. (acq 5-1-89; $575,000 with co-located FM; 3-27-89). Natl. Network: USA, . Rgnl. Network: Kan. Info., Kan. Agri. Kan. Agriculture Format: Talk, news. News staff: one; News: 20 hrs wkly. Target aud: General. Spec prog: Farm 10 hrs, relg 4 hrs wkly. ♦E. Gordon Johnson, pres, gen mgr, gen sls mgr; Travis Turner, opns mgr, prom mgr, progmg dir & news dir; Larry Waggoner, engrg dir, chief of engrg.

KWME(FM)— Aug 27, 1979: 93.5 mhz; 6 kw. 321 ft TL: N37 14 28 W97 24 04. Hrs open: 24 Dups AM 10% 338 S. Kley Dr., 67152. Phone: (620) 326-8512. Fax: (620) 326-8512. Natl. Network: USA, . Format: Oldies. News staff: one. Target aud: 35-64. ♦Travis Turner, progmg mgr.

Wichita

***KCFN(FM)—** Apr 23, 1978: 91.1 mhz; 100 kw. 345 ft TL: N37 48 01 W97 17 50. Stereo. Hrs open: 24 720 N. Murray, 67212. Phone: (316) 831-9111. Fax: (316) 831-9119.E-mail: INFO@AFR.NET Web Site:www.kcfn.net Licensee: American Family Association Group owner: American Family Radio (acq 5-94). Population served: 650,000 Format: Christian. News: 2 hrs wkly. Target aud: 35-65; general. Spec prog: Relg, news/talk. ♦Don Wildmon, chmn; Tim Widmon, pres; Cindy Kreyer, gen mgr, stn mgr, opns dir.

KEYN-FM— October 1968: 103.7 mhz; 95 kw. 859 ft TL: N37 46 37 W97 31 01. Stereo. Hrs open: 24 2120 N. Woodlawn, Suite 352, 67208. Phone: (316) 685-2121. Fax: (316) 685-3408.E-mail: info@keyn.com Web Site:www.keyn.com Licensee: Entercom Wichita License LLC. Group owner: Entercom Communications Corp. (acq 2000; grpsl). Population served: 420,000 Natl. Network: ABC, . Format: Oldies. News: 5 hrs wkly. Target aud: 25-54; baby boomers. Spec prog: Dr. Demento 2 hrs wkly. ♦Jackie Wise, gen mgr.

KFDI-FM— June 6, 1963: 101.3 mhz; 100 kw. Ant 1,139 ft TL: N37 47 47 W97 31 59. Stereo. Hrs open: Box 1402, 67201. Secondary address: 4200 N. Old Lawrence Rd. 67219. Phone: (316) 838-9141. Fax: (316) 838-3607. Licensee: Journal Broadcast Corp. Population served: 276,554 Format: Modern country. Target aud: 25-54; adults. ♦Dugg Collins, disc jockey.

KFH(AM)— Oct 28, 1947: 1240 khz; 637 w-U. TL: N37 43 06 W97 19 05. Hrs open: 2120 N. Woodlawn, Suite 352, 67208. Phone: (316) 685-2121. Fax: (316) 685-3408.E-mail: letters@kfhradio.com Web Site:www.kfhradio.com Licensee: Entercom Wichita License L.L.C. Group owner: Entercom Communications Corp. (acq 2000; grpsl). Natl. Network: CBS, . Natl. Rep: D & R Radio,. Format: Hot talk, sports. Target aud: 35 plus; professionals. ♦Jackie Wise, gen mgr.

KFH-FM—(Clearwater, July 4, 1995: 98.7 mhz; 50 kw. Ant 492 ft TL: N37 24 11 W97 35 22. Stereo. Hrs open: 24 2120 N. Woodlawn, Suite 352, 67208. Phone: (316) 685-2121. Fax: (316) 685-3408.E-mail: letters@kfhradio.com Web Site:www.kfhradio.com Licensee: Entercom Witicha License LLC. Group owner: Entercom Communications Corp. (acq 5-8-00; $2 million). Population served: 494,569 Format: Sports, talk. Target aud: 18-49; general. ♦Jackie Wise, gen mgr; Mark Yearout, gen sls mgr, mus dir; Tony Duesing, progmg VP & progmg dir; Jessie Hosning, pub affrs dir, traf mgr; Craig Maudlin, chief of engrg.

KFRM(AM)—See Salina

KFTI(AM)— September 1923: 1070 khz; 10 kw-D, 1 kw-N, DA-N. TL: N37 42 47 W97 19 59. Stereo. Hrs open: 24 Box 1402, 67201. Secondary address: 4200 N. Old Lawrence Rd. 67219. Phone: (316) 838-9141. Fax: (316) 838-3607.E-mail: info@kfdi.com Web Site:www.kfdi.com Licensee: Journal Broadcast Corp. Group owner: Journal Communications Inc. (acq 6-11-99; grpsl). Population served: 411,000 Natl. Network: ABC, . Dow, Lohnes & Albertson. Format: C&W, oldies. News staff: 7. Target aud: 25-54. ♦Beverlee Brannigan, progmg dir; Dan Dillon, news dir; Krysti Bradford, traf mgr; Dugg Collins, disc jockey.

KGSO(AM)— 1950: 1410 khz; 5 kw-D, 1 kw-N, DA-2. TL: N37 44 05 W97 21 06. Hrs open: 24 1632 S. Maize Rd., 67209. Phone: (316) 721-4407. Fax: (316) 721-8276. Web Site:www.kgso.com Licensee: Steckline Communications Inc. (acq 7-1-2005; $1.3 million). Population served: 400,000 Natl. Network: ESPN Radio, NBC Radio, USA, . Mid-America Ag Format: Sports. Target aud: Men 25-54. ♦Todd Johnson, gen mgr.

KICT-FM— Apr 28, 1972: 95.1 mhz; 100 kw. 1,026 ft TL: N37 47 58 W97 31 58. Stereo. Hrs open: 24 Box 1402, 67201. Phone: (316) 838-9141. Fax: (316) 838-3607.E-mail: info@t95.com Web Site:www.t95.com Licensee: Journal Broadcast Corp. Group owner: Journal Broadcast Group Inc. (acq 6-14-99; grpsl). Population served: 720,000 Format: Active rock. News staff: 2; News: 15 hrs wkly. Target aud: 18-44. ♦Rob Burton, gen mgr; Eric McCart, gen sls mgr; Jason Wituk, rgnl sls mgr; Manny Cowzinski, prom dir; Ray Michaels, progmg dir.

***KMUW(FM)—** Apr 26, 1949: 89.1 mhz; 100 kw. 450 ft TL: N37 45 01 W97 18 12. Stereo. Hrs open: 24 3317 E. 17th St., 67208. Phone: (316) 978-6789. Fax: (316) 978-3946.E-mail: info@kmuw.org Web Site:www.kmuw.org Licensee: Wichita State University. Population served: 517,000 Natl. Network: NPR, PRI, . Rgnl. Network: Kan. Info., Kan. Pub. Kan. Info. Schwartz, Woods & Miller. Wire Svc: AP Format: AAA, jazz, news. News staff: 2; News: 121 hrs wkly. Target aud: General. Spec prog: Gospel 2 hrs, jazz 14 hrs, folk/world 5 hrs, AAA 14 hrs wkly. ♦Mark McCain, gen mgr; Lu Stephens, prom dir; Jon Cyphers, engr.

KNSS(AM)— May 26, 1922: 1330 khz; 5 kw-U, DA-N. TL: N37 42 47 W97 14 51. Stereo. Hrs open: 24 2120 N. Woodlawn St., Suite 352, 67208-1847. Phone: (316) 685-2121. Fax: (316) 685-3408.E-mail: info@knssradio.com Web Site:www.knssradio.com Licensee: Entercom Wichita License LLC. Group owner: Entercom Communications Corp. (acq 2000; grpsl). Population served: 276,554 Natl. Network: CBS, . Wire Svc: Weather Wire Format: News/talk. Target aud: 25-54. ♦Jackie Wise, gen mgr.

KQAM(AM)— 1936: 1480 khz; 5 kw-D, 1 kw-N, DA-2. TL: N37 44 21 W97 16 14. Hrs open: 5610 E. 29th St. N., 67220. Phone: (316) 686-5726. Fax: (316) 686-5728.E-mail: bob.martin@disney.com Web Site:www.radiodisney.com/wichita Licensee: Radio Disney Group LLC. Group owner: ABC Inc. (acq 7-29-02; $2 million). Population served: 400,000 Natl. Network: Radio Disney, . Format: Children. ♦Bob Martin, gen mgr.

KRBB(FM)— Sept 19, 1948: 97.9 mhz; 100 kw. Ant 1,027 ft TL: N37 46 40 W97 30 37. Stereo. Hrs open: 24 9323 E. 37th St. N., 67226. Phone: (316) 494-6600. Fax: (316) 494-6730.E-mail: info@698fm.com Web Site:www.698fm.com Licensee: Capstar TX L.P. Group owner: Clear Channel Communications Inc. (acq 8-30-00; grpsl). Population served: 276,554 Natl. Rep: Clear Channel,. Format: Adult contemp. News staff: one. Target aud: W 25-54; a 25-54; working & family oriented. Spec prog: Jazz 2 hrs, Sp 3 hrs, love songs 18 hrs wkly.

KSGL(AM)— August 1957: 900 khz; 250 w-D, 28 w-N, DA-2. TL: N37 41 33 W97 22 54. Hrs open: 3337 W. Central, 67203. Phone: (316) 942-3231. Fax: (316) 942-9314.E-mail: info@ksgl.com Web Site:www.ksgl.com Licensee: Agape Communications Inc. (acq 1977). Population served: 500,000 Natl. Network: USA, . Format: Relg, adult standards. ♦Don Clifford, pres; Norbert Atherton, sr VP; Terry Atherton, gen mgr.

KTHR(FM)— Apr 17, 1967: 107.3 mhz; 100 kw. 884 ft TL: N37 46 37 W97 31 01. Stereo. Hrs open: 24 9323 E. 37th N., 67226. Phone: (316) 494-6600. Fax: (316) 494-6730.E-mail: info@1073theroad.com Web Site:www.1073theroad.com Licensee: Clear Channel Broadcasting Licenses, Inc. Group owner: Clear Channel Communications Inc. (acq

8-30-2000; grpsl). Population served: 276,554 Natl. Rep: Clear Channel,. Wire Svc: UPI Format: Classic rock. Target aud: 25-54; Males.

*KYFW(FM)— Sept 24, 1988: 88.3 mhz; 17 kw. 141 ft TL: N37 40 22 W97 20 08. Stereo. Hrs open: 24 11530 Carmel Commons Blvd., Charlotte, 28226-3976. Phone: (704) 523-5555. Fax: (316) 788-7883.E-mail: kyfw@bbnradio.org Web Site:www.bbnradio.org Licensee: Bible Broadcasting Network. (group owner; acq 6-26-89). Format: Christian mus & progmg. Target aud: General. ◆Lowell Davey, pres; Matt Johnson, gen mgr.

KYQQ(FM)—See Arkansas City

*KYWA(FM)— Mar 25, 1990: 90.7 mhz; 25 kw horiz, 23 kw vert. Ant 335 ft TL: N37 21 53 W97 20 30. Stereo. Hrs open: 24 110 S. Main St., Suite 1050, 67202-3732. Phone: (316) 831-0907. Fax: (316) 831-0910.E-mail: kywa@wayfm.com Web Site:www.wayfm.com Licensee: WAY-FM Media Group Inc. (group owner; (acq 4-12-2004; $485,000). Format: Christian CHR. Target aud: 25-44; females. ◆Dave Conour, stn mgr, opns dir.

KZCH(FM)—See Derby

Winfield

*KBDD(FM)— 2000: 91.9 mhz; 48 kw. Ant 492 ft TL: N37 22 56 W96 57 20. Hrs open: Box 262550, Baton Rouge, LA, 70826. Secondary address: 8919 World Ministry Ave., Baton Rouge, LA 70810. Phone: (225) 768-3688. Fax: (225) 768-3724.E-mail: kawikfish@yahoo.com Web Site:www.jsm.org Licensee: Family Worship Center Church Inc. (group owner; acq 6-10-2004; $1.15 million). Format: Christian. ◆David Whitelaw, COO; Jimmy Swaggart, pres; John Santiago, progmg dir.

KKLE(AM)— Aug 19, 1963: 1550 khz; 250 w-D, 52 w-N. TL: N37 14 21 W97 00 43. Hrs open:
Rebroadcasts KLEY(AM) Wellington 98%.
Box 249, Wellington, 67152. Phone: (620) 221-3341. Fax: (620) 326-8512. Web Site:www.kkle.com Licensee: Johnson Enterprises Inc. (group owner; (acq 1990). Population served: 35000 Natl. Network: ESPN Radio, USA,. Format: Sports. Target aud: General. ◆Gordon Johnson, pres & gen mgr.

KSOK-FM— 1996: 95.9 mhz; 15.2 kw. Ant 420 ft TL: N37 04 32 W96 56 13. Stereo. Hrs open: 24 334 E. Radio Ln., Arkansas City, 67005. Phone: (620) 442-5400. Fax: (620) 442-5401.E-mail: ksok@ksokradio.com Web Site:www.ksokradio.com Licensee: Cowley County Broadcasting Inc. (acq 9-3-02; with KSOK(AM) Arkansas City). Population served: 40,000 Natl. Network: ABC, . Kan. Agriculture Format: Today's best country. News staff: 1. Target aud: 22-55; blue collar, middle America, people who have children, are still working, & have mortgages. ◆Marty Mutti, gen mgr; Brian Cunningham, opns mgr; Christy Bursack, prom dir; Shawn Wheat, news dir.

*KSWC(FM)— November 1967: 100.3 mhz; 10 w. 70 ft TL: N37 14 42 W96 54 19. Hrs open: 100 College St., 67156. Phone: (620) 229-6263. Licensee: Southwestern College. Population served: 11,405 Format: College rock. Target aud: 21 & younger. ◆Tom Jacobs, gen mgr.

KWLS(FM)— 1980: 107.9 mhz; 50 kw. Ant 397 ft TL: N37 14 42 W96 54 19. Stereo. Hrs open: 24 7701 E. Kellogg, Suite 107, Wichita, 67207. Phone: (316) 776-9530. Fax: (316) 612-1077. Licensee: Mid-America Ag Network Inc. Group owner: Carter Broadcast Group Inc. (acq 12-31-2007; $600,000). . Population served: 228,519 Natl. Rep: McGavren Guild,. Fletcher, Heald & Hildreth. Format: Country. ◆Larry Steckline, pres, gen mgr; Chris Carter, VP; Denise Sherman, gen sls mgr; Michael Carter, prom dir.

Kentucky

Albany

WANY(AM)— Oct 25, 1958: 1390 khz; 1 kw-D. TL: N36 41 54 W85 09 00. Hrs open: Box 400, 42602. Phone: (606) 387-5186. Fax: (606) 387-6595.E-mail: mix1063@hotmail.com Licensee: Pamela Allred dba Albany Broadcasting Co. (acq 11-13-01; with co-located FM). Population served: 1,891 Rgnl. Network: Ky. Agri. Natl. Rep: Keystone (unwired net),. Format: Country. Spec prog: Farm 2 hrs, gospel 6 hrs wkly. ◆Randy Speck, gen mgr, prom mgr, progmg dir & news dir; Larry Nelson, chief of engrg.

WANY-FM— Apr 18, 1966: 106.3 mhz; 2.7 kw. 155 ft TL: N36 41 54 W85 09 00. Hrs open: Dups AM 75% Box 400, 42602. Phone: (606) 387-5186. Fax: (606) 387-6595. Population served: 1,891 Format: Country.

Allen

WMDJ-FM— Sept 1, 1984: 100.1 mhz; 1.3 kw. 492 ft TL: N37 35 12 W82 42 57. (CP: 2.6 kw). Stereo. Hrs open: Box 1530, Martin, 41649. Secondary address: Old Hwy. Rt. 80, Martin 41649. Phone: (606) 874-8005. Fax: (606) 874-0057.E-mail: fm100wmdj@mikrotec.com Licensee: Floyd County Broadcasting Co. Inc. (acq 12-84; grpsl;12-31-84). Population served: 40,000 Natl. Rep: Katz Radio,. Format: Country, oldies. Target aud: 25-65. ◆Dale McKinney, pres, gen mgr; Jamie Johnson, stn mgr, progmg dir; Mona Dingus, gen sls mgr.

Annville

WANV(FM)— 2006: 96.7 mhz; 1.85 kw. Ant 499 ft TL: N37 13 24 W84 02 01. Hrs open: Box 1227, Corbin, 40702-5656. Phone: (606) 528-8787. Fax: (606) 528-9824.E-mail: info@wanvfm.com Licensee: F.T.G. Broadcasting Inc. Format: Oldies. ◆Trevor Grigsby, gen mgr.

Ashland

WCMI(AM)— 1935: 1340 khz; 1 kw-U. TL: N38 28 02 W82 35 50. Hrs open: 24 401 11th St., Suite 200, Huntington, WV, 25701. Phone: (304) 523-8401. Fax: (304) 523-4848. Web Site:www.wcmi.am Licensee: Fifth Avenue Broadcasting Co. Inc. Group owner: Kindred Communications Inc. (acq 1-26-98; with WCMI-FM Catlettsburg). Population served: 24,000 Natl. Network: Air America, . Rgnl. Network: Ky. Net. Format: Progressive talk. ◆Mike Kirtner, pres & gen mgr; Cameron Smith, opns VP.

WCMI-FM—See Catlettsburg

WDGG(FM)— 1948: 93.7 mhz; 100 kw. 741 ft TL: N38 23 14 W82 39 45. Stereo. Hrs open: 24 401 11th St., Suite 200, Huntington, WV, 25701. Phone: (304) 523-8401. Fax: (304) 523-4848. Web Site:www.wdgg.fm Licensee: Fifth Avenue Broadcasting Co. Inc. Group owner: Kindred Communications Inc. (acq 1988). Population served: 30,700 Natl. Network: Jones Radio Networks, Motor Racing Net, . Natl. Rep: McGavren Guild,. W. Va. MetroNews Network Arent, Fox, Kintner, Plotkin & Kahn. Wire Svc: Accu-Weather Wire Svc: AP Format: Country. News staff: one; News: 2 hrs wkly. Target aud: 25-49; male. ◆Mike Kirtner, pres, gen mgr; Rae Ann Parsons, natl sls mgr; Cameron Smith, engrg dir.

*WKAO(FM)—Not on air, target date: unknown: 91.1 mhz; 7 kw. Ant 354 ft TL: N38 25 11 W82 24 06. Hrs open: Box 889, Blacksburg, VA, 24063. Phone: (540) 552-4282. Fax: (540) 951-5282. Web Site:www.parfm.com Licensee: Positive Alternative Radio Inc. ◆Edward A. Baker, pres.

WTCR-FM—See Huntington, WV

Auburn

*WAYD(FM)— 2005: 88.1 mhz; 1 kw. Ant 371 ft TL: N36 57 37 W86 32 49. Hrs open: WAY-FM, 1095 W. McEwen Dr., Franklin, TN, 37067. Phone: (615) 261-9293. Fax: (615) 261-3967.E-mail: waym@wayfm.com Web Site:www.wayfm.com Licensee: WAY-FM Media Group Inc. (group owner). Format: Christian. ◆Matt Austin, gen mgr; Teresa White, dev dir; Jeff Brown, progmg dir.

WBVR-FM— May 1965: 96.7 mhz; 45 kw. Ant 423 ft TL: N36 50 35 W86 15 30. Stereo. Hrs open: 24 1919 Scottsville Rd., Bowling Green, 42104. Phone: (270) 843-3333. Fax: (270) 843-0454.E-mail: mark@forevercomm.com Web Site:www.beaverfm.com Licensee: Forever Communications Inc. (group owner; (acq 1984). Population served: 280,000 Natl. Rep: Christal,. Kaye, Scholer, LLP. Format: Country. Target aud: 18-54. ◆Christine Hillard, pres, opns dir; Mark Mackey, gen mgr; Myla Thomas, progmg dir.

Barbourville

WKKQ(FM)— Oct 2, 1974: 96.1 mhz; 25 kw. 300 ft TL: N36 51 55 W83 53 55. Stereo. Hrs open: Prog sep from AM 222 Daniel Boone Dr., 40906. Fax: (606) 546-4138.E-mail: wkkqproduction@yahoo.com Licensee: Barbourville Commuity Broadcasting Co. Population served: 90,000 Format: Hot adult contemp. Target aud: 25-34. ◆Randy Brock, gen sls mgr; Sean Terrell, disc jockey.

WYWY(AM)— Dec 13, 1955: 950 khz; 1 kw-D. TL: N36 50 26 W83 52 16. Hrs open: 222 Daniel Boone Dr., 40906. Phone: (606) 546-4128. Fax: (606) 546-4138.E-mail: wkkqproduction@yahoo.com Licensee: Barbourville Community Broadcasting Co. (acq 11-66). Population served: 3,549 Format: Relg, southern gospel. ◆Mildred Engle, pres; Chad Engle, gen mgr; Pat Jordan, opns mgr, traf mgr; Orville Burnett, chief of engrg; Sherry Moore, sls.

Bardstown

WBRT(AM)— December 1954: 1320 khz; 1 kw-D. TL: N37 49 09 W85 29 10. Hrs open: 106 S. 3rd St., 40004. Phone: (502) 348-3943. Fax: (502) 348-4043.E-mail: wbrt@wbrtradio.com Licensee: Central Kentucky Broadcasting Inc. Group owner: Commonwealth Broadcasting Corp. (acq 7-17-2006; $240,000). Population served: 5,800 Rgnl. Network: Ky. Net. Natl. Rep: Rgnl Reps,. Format: C&W, info. Target aud: 20 plus. Spec prog: Farm 10 hrs wkly. ◆Kenny Fogle, gen mgr.

Beattyville

WLJC(FM)— May 12, 1965: 102.1 mhz; 1.2 kw. 520 ft TL: N37 36 23 W83 41 16. Hrs open: 219 Radio Stn. Loop, 41311. Phone: (606) 464-3600. Fax: (606) 464-5021.E-mail: wljc@wljc.com Web Site:www.wljc.com Licensee: Hour of Harvest Inc. Population served: 260,000 Natl. Rep: Rgnl Reps,. Format: Adult contemp. ◆Margaret Drake, pres; Jonathan Drake, gen mgr; Kim Mitchell, gen sls mgr, progmg; Alan Mulford, chief of engrg.

Beaver Dam

WAIA(AM)—Licensed to Beaver Dam. See Hartford

WXMZ(FM)—See Hartford

Benton

*WAAJ(FM)— 1996: 89.7 mhz; 6 kw vert. Ant 298 ft TL: N36 48 31 W88 13 26. Hrs open: Box 281, Hardin, 42048. Secondary address: 219 College St., Harding 42048. Phone: (270) 437-4095. Fax: (270) 437-4098.E-mail: info@hmiradio.com Web Site:www.hmiradio.com Licensee: Heartland Ministries. Format: Gospel and bluegrass. ◆Darrell Gibson, pres.

WCBL(AM)— Dec 13, 1954: 1290 khz; 5 kw-D. TL: N36 51 30 W88 20 13. Hrs open: 24 Box 387, 1039 Eggners Ferry Rd., 42025. Phone: (270) 527-3102. Fax: (270) 527-5606.E-mail: wcbl@bellsouth.net Licensee: Jim W. Freeland. (acq 11-17-98; with co-located FM). Population served: 25,000 Rgnl. Network: Ky. Net. Format: Talk/sports. News staff: one; News: 7 hrs wkly. Target aud: General. ◆Chris Freeland, gen mgr, gen sls mgr; Sherry Rickman, opns mgr; Gregg Leath, progmg dir; Sam Rickmon, news dir; Shane Freeland, disc jockey.

WCBL-FM— Mar 3, 1966: 99.1 mhz; 3 kw. 298 ft TL: N36 51 30 W88 20 13. (CP: 3.3 kw). Hrs open: Prog sep from AM Box 387, 1039 Eggners Ferry Rd., 42025. Phone: (270) 527-3102. Fax: (270) 527-5606. Format: Oldies. ◆Chad Winstead, disc jockey.

*WTRT(FM)— December 1998: 88.1 mhz; 600 w. 253 ft TL: N36 47 53 W88 20 50. Stereo. Hrs open: 24 Box 281, Hardin, 42048. Secondary address: 219 College St., Harding 42048. Phone: (270) 437-4095. Fax: (270) 437-4098.E-mail: info@hmiradio.com Web Site:www.hmiradio.com Licensee: Heartland Ministries Format: Christian adult contemp. ◆Darrell Gibson, pres; Jeremy Johnson, stn mgr & progmg dir; Eddie Sheriden, mus dir.

*WVHM(FM)— June 1989: 90.5 mhz; 8 kw. 351 ft TL: N36 48 31 W88 13 26. Hrs open: Box 281, Hardin, 42048. Secondary address: 219 College St., Hardin 42048. Phone: (270) 437-4095. Fax: (270) 437-4098.E-mail: info@hmiradio.com Web Site:www.hmiradio.com Licensee: Heartland Ministries. Natl. Network: USA, . Format: Southern gospel. Target aud: 18-49. ◆Darrell Gibson, pres; Jeremy Johnson, progmg dir; Eddie Sheridan, mus dir.

Berea

WKXO(AM)— July 18, 1971: 1500 khz; 250 w-D. TL: N37 35 12 W84 18 04. Hrs open: 6 AM-7 PM 128 Big Hill Ave., Richmond, 40475. Phone: (859) 623-1389. Fax: (859) 623-1341.E-mail: coyote@wcyofm.com Licensee: Wallingford Communications LLC. Group owner: Wallingford Broadcasting Co. (acq 1999; grpsl). Population served: 10,000 Natl. Network: Jones Radio Networks, . Rgnl. Network: Ky. Net. Format:

News/talk. News staff: one; News: 3 hrs wkly. Target aud: 21 plus. ◆ Kelly Wallingford, gen mgr, stn mgr; Ray White, progmg dir & edit dir.

WLFX(FM)— Sept 27, 1990: 106.7 mhz; 1.95 kw. 584 ft TL: N37 30 15 W84 12 58. Stereo. Hrs open: 24 Prog sep from AM 128 Big Hill Ave., Richmond, 40475. Phone: (859) 623- 1389. Fax: (859) 623-1341.E-mail: coyote@wcyofm.com Format: Classic rock. Spec prog: Gospel 12 hrs wkly.

Bowling Green

WBGN(AM)— Nov 24, 1959: 1340 khz; 1 kw-U. TL: N37 00 34 W86 27 09. Hrs open: 24 1919 Scottsville Rd., 42101. Phone: (270) 843-3333. Fax: (270) 783-0454.E-mail: mark@forevercomm.com Web Site:www.1340wbgn.com Licensee: Forever Communications Inc. (group owner; (acq 2001). Population served: 70,000 Natl. Network: ABC, ESPN Radio, . Rgnl. Network: Ky. Net. Natl. Rep: Christal,. Ky. News Net Kaye, Scholer, LLP. Format: Sports. Target aud: 35-54. ◆ Mark Mackey, gen mgr; Chris Idle, opns dir, progmg dir.

*WCVK(FM)— Apr 22, 1986: 90.7 mhz; 14 kw. 448 ft TL: N37 00 18 W86 31 19. Stereo. Hrs open: Box 539, 42102. Secondary address: 1407 Scottsville Rd. 42104. Phone: (270) 781-7326. Fax: (270) 781-8005.E-mail: mail@christianfamilyradio.com Web Site:www.christianfamilyradio.com Licensee: Bowling Green Community Broadcasting Inc. Natl. Network: Salem Radio Network, . Format: Christian Adult Contemporary. Target aud: 25-54; Christian men & women. Spec prog: Christian Rock 10 hrs weekly. ◆ Mike Wilson, gen mgr.

WDNS(FM)— Mar 12, 1973: 93.3 mhz; 12 kw. 472 ft TL: N36 56 39 W86 15 11. Stereo. Hrs open: 24 Box 930, 42102. Phone: (270) 781-2121. Fax: (270) 842-0232.E-mail: info@wdnsfm.com Web Site:www.wdnsfm.com Licensee: Daily News Broadcasting Co. Format: Classic Rock. News staff: one; News: 7 hrs wkly. Target aud: 18-54.

WGGC(FM)— June 23, 1961: 95.1 mhz; 100 kw. Ant 987 ft TL: N36 54 43 W86 11 21. Hrs open: 24 Box 70163, 42101. Phone: (270) 783-8730. Fax: (270) 783-8665.E-mail: darrin@wggc.com Web Site:www.wggc.com Licensee: Heritage Communications Inc. (acq 10-20-97; $400,000 for stock). Format: Country. ◆ Bill Evans, gen mgr; Darrin Evans, stn mgr.

WKCT(AM)— Nov 1, 1947: 930 khz; 5 kw-D, 500 w-N, DA-N. TL: N37 01 53 W86 26 18. Hrs open: 24 Box 930, 42102. Secondary address: 804 College St. 42101. Phone: (270) 781-2121. Fax: (270) 842-0232.E-mail: alan@wdnsfm.com Web Site:www.93wkct.com Licensee: Daily News Broadcasting Co. Population served: 221,000 Natl. Network: CBS, . Format: News/talk, info. News staff: one; News: 25 hrs wkly. Target aud: 25 plus. ◆ Alan Cooper, gen mgr; Chad Young, pres & progmg dir.

*WKYU-FM— November 1980: 88.9 mhz; 100 kw. 721 ft TL: N37 05 22 W86 38 05. Stereo. Hrs open: 24 Western Kentucky Univ., 1906 College Heights Blvd., # 11035, 42101. Phone: (270) 745-5489. Phone: (800) 599-9598. Fax: (270) 745-6272.E-mail: wkyufm@wku.edu Web Site:www.wkyu.org Licensee: Western Kentucky University. Natl. Network: NPR, PRI, . Rgnl. Network: Ky. Net. Leventhal, Senter & Lerman. Format: Class, news. News staff: 3; News: 35 hrs wkly. Target aud: General. ◆ Peter Bryant, gen mgr. Co-owned TV: *WKYU-TV affil

*WWHR(FM)— Aug 18, 1988: 91.7 mhz; 1.3 kw. 10 ft TL: N36 59 00 W86 27 24. Stereo. Hrs open: 24 1906 College Heights Blvd. #11070, 42101. Phone: (270) 745-5439. Phone: (270) 745-5350. Fax: (270) 745-5835.E-mail: gm@revolution.fm Web Site:www.revolution.fm Licensee: Western Kentucky University. Population served: 50,000 Format: College progsv. News staff: 2; News: 5 hrs wkly. Target aud: Adults 18-34. Spec prog: Soul 2 hrs, punk 2 hrs, gothic 2 hrs, loc 2 hrs, electronic 2 hrs, metal 2 hrs wkly. ◆ Dr. Marjorie Yambor, gen mgr; Max Meiners, stn mgr.

Brandenburg

WMMG(AM)— July 1984: 1140 khz; 250 w-D. TL: N37 59 05 W86 09 24. Hrs open: Box 505, 40108. Secondary address: 1715 Bypass Rd. 40108. Phone: (270) 422-3961. Fax: (270) 422-3464.E-mail: wmmg935@bbtel.com Web Site:www.wmmgradio.com Licensee: Meade County Communications Inc. Rgnl. Network: Ky. Net. Natl. Rep: Rgnl Reps,. Format: Country. Spec prog: Relg 8 hrs wkly. ◆ Gwen Blevins, gen mgr.

WMMG-FM— Aug 23, 1972: 93.5 mhz; 3.4 kw. 290 ft TL: N37 59 05 W86 09 24. Stereo. Hrs open: Dups AM 100% Box 505, 40108. Phone: (270) 422-3961. Fax: (270) 422-3464.E-mail: wmmg935@bbtel.com

Web Site:www.wmmgradio.com Licensee: Meade County Communications Inc. Population served: 500,000 Natl. Rep: Rgnl Reps,. Target aud: 18-65.

Brownsville

WKLX(FM)— 2000: 100.7 mhz; 8 kw. Ant 584 ft TL: N37 09 17 W86 19 33. Hrs open: Box 457, Glasgow, 42142. Phone: (270) 651-6050. Fax: (270) 651-7666. Licensee: Charles M. Anderson. Leventhal, Senter & Lerman. Format: Adult hits. ◆ Darron Steenbergen, gen mgr.

Buffalo

WXAM(AM)— Nov 26, 1974: 1430 khz; 1 kw-D. TL: N37 31 49 W85 42 49. Hrs open: 611 W. Poplar St., Suite C2, Elizabethtown, 42701-2483. Phone: (270) 763-0800. Fax: (270) 769-6349. Licensee: Mark Goodman Productions Inc. (acq 2-1-89; $99,292; 2-13-89). Natl. Network: ESPN Radio, . Format: ESPN radio. ◆ Roth Stratton, gen mgr & gen sls mgr.

Burgin

WKYB(FM)—Not on air, target date: unknown: 105.9 mhz; 1.1 kw. Ant 472 ft TL: N37 47 18 W84 42 50. Hrs open: 2351 Sunset Blvd., Suite 170-218, Rocklin, CA, 95765. Phone: (916) 251-1600. Fax: (916) 251-1650. Licensee: Educational Media Foundation. ◆ Mike Novak, sr VP.

Burkesville

WKYR-FM— October 1988: 107.9 mhz; 6 kw. Ant 312 ft TL: N36 47 26 W85 22 47. Stereo. Hrs open: 24 Box 340, 42717. Secondary address: Hwy. 90 E. 42717. Phone: (270) 433-7191. Fax: (270) 433-7195.E-mail: wkyr@mchsi.com Licensee: Cumberland Broadcasting LLC (acq 7-31-2007; $153,375). Natl. Network: ABC, Jones Radio Networks, . Rgnl. Network: Ky. News Net. Ky. News Net Format: Country. ◆ Jessie Crabtree, gen mgr & gen sls mgr.

Burnside

WSEK(FM)— Aug 17, 1985: 93.9 mhz; 50 kw. 492 ft TL: N37 09 15 W84 27 35. Stereo. Hrs open: Prog sep from AM Box 740, Somerset, 42502. Secondary address: 101 First Radio Ln. 42503. Phone: (606_ 678-5151. Fax: (606) 678-2026.E-mail: wsek@clearchannel.com Web Site:www.wsfeam.com Format: Country.

WSFE(AM)— Feb 28, 1984: 910 khz; 430 w-D, 115 w-N. TL: N37 01 46 W84 36 28. Hrs open: 24 Box 740, Somerset, 42502. Secondary address: 101 First Radio Ln., Somerset 42503. Phone: (606) 678-5151. Fax: (606) 678-2026. Web Site:www.wsfeam.com Licensee: Capstar TX L.P. Group owner: Clear Channel Communications Inc. (acq 12-8-2000; grpsl). Format: Talk. News staff: one; News: 5 hrs wkly. Target aud: 25-54. ◆ Richard Dills, gen mgr, stn mgr; Jo-Ella Shelly, gen sls mgr; Rod Zimmerman, progmg dir; Jim Mercer, chief of engrg.

Cadiz

WKDZ(AM)— Apr 8, 1966: 1110 khz; 1 kw-D. TL: N36 52 57 W87 50 44. Hrs open: 24 Box 1900, 42211-0316. Secondary address: 19 Wooldridge Ln. 42211-0316. Phone: (270) 522-3232. Fax: (270) 522-1110.E-mail: bmann@wkdzradio.com Web Site:www.oldies1480.com Licensee: Ham Broadcasting Co. Inc. (acq 1-22-91; $200,000 with co-located FM; 2-11-91). Population served: 100,000 Natl. Network: ABC, CNN Radio, Fox News Radio, . Format: Oldies. News staff: 3; News: 18 hrs wkly. Target aud: 25-54. Spec prog: Farm 2 hrs wkly. ◆ D.J. Everett III, pres; Beth A. Mann, gen mgr; Alan Watts, news dir.

WKDZ-FM— May 18, 1972: 106.5 mhz; 13.4 kw. 449 ft TL: N36 48 29 W87 38 09. Stereo. Hrs open: 24 Prog sep from AM Box 1900, 42211-0316. Phone: (270) 522-3232. Fax: (270) 522-1110.E-mail: wkdz@wkdzradio.com Web Site:www.wkdzradio.com Licensee: Ham Broadcasting Co. Inc. Population served: 225,000 Format: Real country. News staff: 2; News: 20 hrs wkly. Target aud: 35-64.

Calvert City

WCCK(FM)— 1993: 95.7 mhz; 3 kw. 505 ft TL: N37 04 21 W88 15 04. Hrs open: 24 Box 1116, 7 Aspen St., 42029. Phone: (270) 395-5133. Fax: (270) 395-5231.E-mail: wcck@freelandbroadcasting.com Licensee: Jim Freeland DBA Freeland Broadcasting. Population served: 175,000 Natl. Network: AP Radio, . Format: Classic Country. News: 10 hrs

wkly. Target aud: 30 plus; professionals and retired. ◆ Jim Freeland, CEO, gen mgr, gen sls mgr; Sherry Darnall, opns dir; Greg Leath, progmg dir; Brad Hosford, chief of engrg.

Campbellsville

*WAPD(FM)— 1996: 91.7 mhz; 2.323 kw vert. Ant 216 ft TL: N37 19 59 W85 19 53. Hrs open: Box 3206, Tupelo, 38803. Phone: (662) 844-8888. Phone: (662) 844-6191. Licensee: American Family Association. Group owner: American Family Radio Format: Christian. ◆ Linda Collins, gen mgr.

WCKQ(FM)— Dec 1, 1964: 104.1 mhz; 17 kw. 374 ft TL: N37 19 29 W85 18 36. Stereo. Hrs open: 24 50 Friendship Pike, 42718. Secondary address: Box 1053 42719. Phone: (270) 789-2401. Fax: (270) 789-1450.E-mail: wckq@commonwealthbroadcasting.com Web Site:www.myq104.com Licensee: CBC of Marion and Taylor Counties Inc. Group owner: Commonwealth Broadcasting Corp. (acq 6-30-97; $720,000 with co-located AM). Population served: 100,000 Natl. Network: ABC, Jones Radio Networks, . Natl. Rep: Rgnl Reps,. Womble, Carlyle, Sandridge & Rice, PLLC. Format: Hot adult contemp. News staff: one; News: 7 hrs wkly. Target aud: 18-44. ◆ Steve Newberry, pres; Barb Smith, gen mgr, stn mgr; Marty Bagby, opns mgr, news dir; Greg Gribbins, gen sls mgr; Rob Collins, prom mgr, progmg dir; Mike Graham, chief of engrg.

WGRK-FM—See Greensburg

*WLCU(FM)—Not on air, target date: unknown: 88.7 mhz; 800 w. Ant 207 ft TL: N37 20 39 W85 21 34. Hrs open: Campbellsville University, 1 University Dr., 42718. Phone: (270) 789-5008. Licensee: Campbellsville University. ◆ J. Alvin Hardy, gen mgr.

WTCO(AM)— March 1948: 1450 khz; 1 kw-U. TL: N37 20 07 W85 22 33. Hrs open: 24 Prog sep from FM 50 Friendship Pike, 42718. Secondary address: Box 1053 42718. Phone: (270) 469-9826. Licensee: CBC of Marion and Taylor Counties Inc. Population served: 23,000 Natl. Network: ESPN Radio, . Format: All sports. News staff: one. Target aud: 25-64.

Campton

WCBJ(FM)— 1999: 103.7 mhz; 6 kw. 328 ft TL: N37 44 23 W83 33 59. Hrs open: 129 College St., West Liberty, 41472. Phone: (606) 743-3145. Fax: (606) 743-9557. Licensee: Morgan County Industries Inc. (group owner) Format: Classic Rock. ◆ Tina Moore, gen mgr; Dewey Blevins, gen sls mgr; Paul Lyons, chief of engrg.

Cannonsburg

WYHY(AM)— December 1987: 1080 khz; 1.8 kw-D. TL: N38 23 10 W82 41 53. Hrs open: Sunrise-sunset
Simulcast with WOKU(AM) Hurricane, WV 100%.
3006 Mount Vernon Rd., Hurricane, WV, 25526. Phone: (304) 757-9661. Fax: (304) 757-9620.E-mail: info@i64country.com Web Site:i64country.com Licensee: Big River Radio Inc. Group owner: Baker Family Stations (Positive Radio Group) Population served: 340,000 Format: Country. Target aud: General. ◆ Jeremy Holbrook, stn mgr.

Carlisle

WBVX(FM)— December 1994: 92.1 mhz; 32 kw. Ant 610 ft TL: N38 11 19 W84 22 13. Stereo. Hrs open: 24 401 W. Main, Suite 301, Lexington, 40507. Phone: (859) 233-1515. Fax: (859) 233-1517. Web Site:www.b92fm.com Licensee: L.M. Communications of Kentucky LLC. Group owner: L.M. Communications Inc. (acq 8-17-01; $4.8 million). Population served: 41,000 Natl. Rep: Katz Radio,. Format: Classic hits. News: one hr wkly. Target aud: General. ◆ Lynn Martin, pres; James MacFarlane, gen mgr, mktg mgr.

Carrollton

WIKI(FM)— Apr 12, 1968: 95.3 mhz; 3 kw. 423 ft TL: N38 39 58 W85 16 51. Stereo. Hrs open: 24 2470 N. State Hwy. 7, North Vernon, IN, 47265. Phone: (812) 346-1927. Fax: (812) 346-9722. Licensee: Wagon Wheel Broadcastiing LLC. (acq 11-14-2007; grpsl). Population served: 400,000 Natl. Network: Jones Radio Networks, CNN Radio, . Natl. Rep: Rgnl Reps, Pepper & Corazzini. Format: Country. News: 10 hrs wkly. Target aud: 10-90; general. ◆ Marty Pieratt, gen mgr.

Catlettsburg

WCMI-FM— Jan 19, 1972: 92.7 mhz; 3 kw. 298 ft TL: N38 27 58 W82 35 27. Stereo. Hrs open: 24 401 11th St., Suite 200, Huntington, WV, 25701. Phone: (304) 523-8401. Fax: (304) 523-4848.E-mail: wrvc@wrvc.com Web Site:www.planet927.com Licensee: Fifth Avenue Broadcasting Co. Inc. Group owner: Kindred Communications Inc. (acq 7-7-98; with WCMI(AM) Ashland). Natl. Rep: McGavren Guild,. Ky. News Net Wire Svc: Accu-Weather Wire Svc: AP Format: Rock. News staff: one; News: news progrmg 5 hrs wkly. ◆Mike Kirtner, pres, pres, gen mgr; Rae Ann Parsons, natl sls mgr; Rich Mhyrwold, rgnl sls mgr; Cameron Smith, engrg dir.

Cave City

WPTQ(FM)— Sept 2, 1988: 103.7 mhz; 13.5 kw. 449 ft TL: N37 06 39 W85 58 41. Stereo. Hrs open: 24 Box 475, Glasgow, 42142. Secondary address: 113 W. Public Sq. , Suite 400, Glasgow 42141. Phone: (270) 651-6060. Fax: (270) 651-7666.E-mail: wptq@commonwealthbroadcasting.com Web Site:www.1037thepoint.net Licensee: Commonwealth Broadcasting Corp. (acq 11-25-97). Population served: 150,000 Natl. Network: Westwood One, . Pepper & Corazzini. Format: Classic rock & the best new rock. News staff: one; News: 7 hrs wkly. Target aud: 25-44. ◆Darren Steenbergen, gen mgr; Kellie Wood, opns mgr.

Central City

WMTA(AM)— Feb 19, 1955: 1380 khz; 500 w-D, 23 w-N. TL: N37 16 34 W87 08 39. Stereo. Hrs open: 24 2601 South Boeke Rd., Evansville, IN, 47714. Phone: (812) 479-5342. Fax: (812) 474-0483.E-mail: sales@faith1180.com Web Site:www.faith1180.com Licensee: Faith Broadcasting Company (acq 2-26-2004; $65,000). Population served: 30,000 Shaw Pittman. Format: Christian. News: 20 hrs wkly. Target aud: General. ◆Gayle Russ, CEO.

WNES(AM)— Jan 1, 1955: 1050 khz; 1 kw-D, 172 w-N. TL: N37 16 09 W87 08 32. Hrs open: Box 471, 42330. Phone: (270) 754-3000. Fax: (270) 754-9484. Licensee: Starlight Broadcasting. (acq 9-28-89). Population served: 33,400 Natl. Network: CBS, . Rgnl. Network: Ky. Net. Format: Sports, talk. Spec prog: Farm 7 hrs wkly. ◆Andy Anderson, pres; Jowanna Bandy, gen mgr; Stan Barnett, progmg mgr.

WQXQ(FM)— Dec 18, 1956: 101.9 mhz; 100 kw. 215 ft TL: N37 16 09 W87 08 32. (CP: Ant 676 ft.). Hrs open: Box 471, 42330. Phone: (270) 754-3000. Fax: (270) 754-9484.E-mail: wqxq@ocdirect.net Web Site:www.q1019.com Licensee: Starlight Broadcasting Population served: 200,000 Format: Hot adult contemp.

Clinton

WLLE(FM)— 1997: 102.1 mhz; 12.5 kw. Ant 476 ft TL: N36 44 22 W88 47 13. Hrs open: Box 2397, Paducah, 42002. Secondary address: 1176 State Rt. 45 N., Mayfield 42066. Phone: (270) 247-5122. Fax: (270) 554-5468. Web Site:www.wlle.com Licensee: Bristol Broadcasting Co. Inc. (group owner; acq 3-15-2004; grpsl). Format: Classic Country. News staff: one. ◆Gary Morse, gen mgr.

Coal Run

WPKE-FM— Sept 21, 1974: 103.1 mhz; 1.2 kw. Ant 741 ft TL: N37 27 57 W82 33 04. Stereo. Hrs open: 24 Box 2200, Pikeville, 41502. Secondary address: 1240 Radio Dr., Pikeville 41501. Phone: (606) 437-4051. Fax: (606) 432-2809.E-mail: wdhr@wdhr.com Web Site:www.ekbradio.com Licensee: East Kentucky Broadcasting Corp. (group owner; acq 6-94; $480,000 with WBPA(AM) Elkhorn City). Population served: 56,000 Natl. Network: ABC, . Rgnl rep: Rgnl Reps Womble, Carlyle, Sandridge & Rice. Format: Rock. News staff: one. Target aud: General. ◆Keith Casebolt, gen mgr.

Columbia

WAIN(AM)— Aug 1, 1951: 1270 khz; 1 kw-D, 68 w-N. TL: N37 06 26 W85 16 42. Hrs open: 24 Box 69, 42728. Secondary address: 1521 Liberty Rd. 42728. Phone: (270) 384-2134. Fax: (270) 384-6722.E-mail: wain@keybroadcasting.net Web Site:www.935wain.com Licensee: Tri-County Radio Broadcasting Corp. Group owner: Key Broadcasting Inc. Population served: 240,000 Natl. Rep: Rgnl Reps,. Ky. News Net Rgnl rep: Rgnl Reps Format: Oldies 50s, 60s & 70s. News staff: one; News: 8 hrs wkly. Target aud: 16-65. Spec prog: Farm 2 hrs. ◆Gary Phelps, gen mgr; Louise Wooten, gen mgr & gen sls mgr.

WAIN-FM— Mar 1, 1968: 93.5 mhz; 5.2 kw. 220 ft TL: N37 06 36 W85 16 42. Stereo. Hrs open: 24 Dups AM 100% Box 69, 42728. Secondary address: 1521 Liberty Rd. 42728. Phone: (270) 384-2134. Fax: (270) 384-6722.E-mail: wain@forchtboroadcasting.com Web Site:935wain.com Population served: 240,000 Natl. Network: ABC, . Rgnl. Network: Ky. Net. Format: Country. News staff: one. Target aud: 16-65. ◆Delno Salmon, disc jockey.

WHVE(FM)—See Russell Springs

Corbin

WCTT(AM)— May 9, 1947: 680 khz; 1 kw-U, DA-N. TL: N36 54 09 W84 04 50. Hrs open: 5 AM-midnight Box 742, 40702-0742. Secondary address: 821 Adams Rd. 40701. Phone: (606) 528-4717. Fax: (606) 528-4487. Licensee: Encore Communications Inc. (acq 5-95; with co-located FM; 6-22-81). Population served: 7,988 Natl. Network: ABC, . Rgnl. Network: Ky. Net. Natl. Rep: Rgnl Reps,. Shaw Pittman. Format: Oldies, news/talk, MOR. News staff: one. ◆Stephanie Mullins, gen mgr.

WCTT-FM— June 1, 1967: 107.3 mhz; 50 kw. 492 ft TL: N36 54 09 W84 04 55. Stereo. Hrs open: 24 Prog sep from AM Box 742, 40702. Secondary address: 821 Adams Rd. 40701. Phone: (606) 528-6617. Fax: (606) 528-4487. Natl. Rep: Rgnl Reps,. Format: Adult contemp. News: one hr wkly. Target aud: 18-54.

*WEKF(FM)— June 24, 2003: 88.5 mhz; 21 kw vert. Ant 499 ft TL: N37 01 13 W84 23 41. Stereo. Hrs open: 24 Rebroadcasts WEKU(FM) Richmond 100%. 102 Perkins Bldg., 521 Lancaster Ave., Richmond, 40475-3102. Phone: (859) 622-1660. Phone: (859) 622-1657. Fax: (859) 622-6276.E-mail: wekunews@eku.edu Web Site:www.weku.fm Licensee: Eastern Kentucky University. Natl. Network: NPR, PRI, . Hardy, Carey & Chautin. Wire Svc: AP Format: News, classical. News staff: 3; News: 35 hrs wkly. Target aud: General. ◆Tim Singleton, gen mgr; Mary Ellyn Cain, opns mgr; Carol Siler, dev dir; Laura Allen, progmg dir; Charles Compton, news dir; Bill Browning, chief of engrg.

WKDP(AM)— Nov 23, 1961: 1330 khz; 5 kw-D, DA. TL: N36 56 20 W84 04 44. Hrs open: Box 742, 40702. Secondary address: 821 Adams Rd. 40701. Phone: (606) 528-6617. Fax: (606) 528-4487.E-mail: swaggoner@wkdp.com Licensee: Eubanks Broadcasting Inc. (acq 12-28-89). Population served: 30,000 Natl. Rep: Rgnl Reps,. Format: Relg, news/talk. Target aud: 30-64. ◆Dallas R. Eubanks, pres; Stephanie Mullins, gen mgr; Derek Eubanks, chief of engrg.

WKDP-FM— 1967: 99.5 mhz; 50kw. 709 ft TL: N36 57 14 W84 58 41. Stereo. Hrs open: Prog sep from AM Box 742, 40702. Phone: (606) 528-6617. Fax: (606) 528-4487. Licensee: Eubanks Broadcasting Inc. Population served: 250,000 Natl. Network: ABC, . Fisher, Wayland, Cooper, Leader & Zaragoza. Format: Country. Target aud: General.

WKFO(AM)— Nov 1, 1961: 1600 khz; 2 kw-D, 27 w-N. TL: N37 01 06 W84 05 58. Stereo. Hrs open: Sunrise-sunset 1100 S. Main St., London, 40741-1529. Phone: (606) 878-1600. Fax: (606) 878-1116. Licensee: Lincoln-Garrard Broadcasting Co. Inc. (acq 2-11-2002; with co-located FM). Population served: 70,000 Format: Info. ◆Johnathan Smith, pres; Dave Colvin, gen mgr, opns mgr.

Covington

WCVG(AM)— Oct 29, 1965: 1320 khz; 500 w-D, 430 w-N, DA-2. TL: N39 02 44 W84 30 30. Hrs open: 24 Box 14425, Cincinnati, OH, 45250-0425. Phone: (859) 291-2255. Fax: (859) 655-4345.E-mail: info@wcvg.com Licensee: Davidson Media Station WCVG Licensee LLC. Group owner: Plessinger Radio Group (R.L. Plessinger Holding Co.) (acq 11-2-2006; $1.9 million). Population served: 1,500,000 Format: Gospel. ◆Simon Cipriano, gen mgr; Jeff Eldred, opns mgr; Avery Corbin, prom dir, prom mgr; John Jones, mus dir.

Crab Orchard

WPBK(FM)— 2008: 102.9 mhz; 2.75 kw. Ant 361 ft TL: N37 25 39 W84 39 21. Hrs open: 24 201-A East Main St., Stanford, 40484. Phone: (606) 365-2126.E-mail: renee@wpbkfm.com Web Site:www.wpbkfm.com Licensee: Radioactive LLC. ◆Renee Knies, stn mgr.

Crittenden

*WKCX(FM)—Not on air, target date: unknown: 89.1 mhz; 9.5 kw. Ant 283 ft TL: N38 49 47 W84 41 14. Hrs open: 9999 Haven Hill Dr., Florence, 41042. Phone: (859) 525-0959. Licensee: 24-7 Broadcasting Inc. ◆Deborah Ives, VP.

Cumberland

WCPM(AM)— October 1951: 1280 khl; 1 kw-D. TL: N36 58 25 W82 59 15. Hrs open: 24 hrs a day 101 Keller St., 40823. Phone: (606) 589-4623.E-mail: wcpmradio@windstream.net Web Site:www.wcpmradio.com Licensee: Cumberland City Broadcasting Inc. (acq 8-22-2003). Population served: 25,000 Natl. Network: Jones Radio Networks, AP Radio, . Format: Country; relg, news. News: 9 hrs wkly. Target aud: 18-49; general. Spec prog: Black one hr, farm one hr wkly. ◆Laura Hewitt, traf mgr; Susan Burton, gen mgr, sls & progmg.

Cynthiana

WCYN(AM)— Sept 1, 1956: 1400 khz; 500 w-D, 1 kw-N. TL: N38 24 20 W84 17 32. Hrs open: 111 Court St., 41031. Phone: (859) 234-1400. Fax: (859) 234-1425. Web Site:www.wcyn.com Licensee: WCYN Broadcasting Inc. (acq 12-29-2004; $122,000). Population served: 16,000 Rgnl. Network: Ky. Agri., Ky. Net. Natl. Rep: Keystone (unwired net), Rgnl Reps,. Format: Oldies. Target aud: General. ◆Chris Winkle, gen mgr.

WCYN-FM— June 1, 1970: 102.5 mhz; 3.4 kw. Ant 400 ft TL: N38 24 39 W84 19 07. Hrs open: Rebroadcasts WLXX(FM) Lexington 100%. 300 W, Vine St., Suite 3, Lexington, 40507. Phone: (859) 253-5900. Fax: (859) 253-5940. Web Site:www.wlxxthebear.com Licensee: Cumulus Licensing LLC. (acq 11-26-2002). Population served: 16,000 Format: Country. ◆Ken Fearnow, gen mgr.

Danville

*WDFB-FM— Sept 1992: 88.1 mhz; 170 w. 328 ft TL: N37 35 46 W84 50 19. Hrs open: 24 Box 106, 40423-0106. Secondary address: 3596 Alum Springs Rd. 40422. Phone: (859) 236-9333. Fax: (859) 236-3348.E-mail: wdfb@searnet.com Web Site:www.wdfb.com Licensee: Alum Springs Educational Corp. (acq 6-8-92). Natl. Network: USA, . Format: Educ, Christian. Target aud: General. ◆Donald A. Drake, pres; Jim Gaskin, gen sls mgr; Mildred Drake, exec VP, gen mgr & progmg dir; Cindy Pike, traf mgr.

WHIR(AM)— Oct 27, 1947: 1230 khz; 1 kw-U. TL: N37 40 28 W84 46 06. Hrs open: 24 2063 Shakertown Rd., 40422. Phone: (859) 236-2711. Fax: (859) 236-1461.E-mail: hometownradio@bellsouth.net Web Site:www.hometownlive.net Licensee: Hometown Broadcasting of Danville Inc. (acq 1995; $525,000 with co-located FM). Population served: 200,000 Natl. Network: Westwood One, Sporting News Radio Network, Talk Radio Network, Motor Racing Net, . Natl. Rep: Rgnl Reps,. Format: News/talk. News staff: one; News: 2 hrs wkly. Target aud: 25-54; business owners, sports fans, housewives. ◆Bruce Leslie, pres; Robert Wagner, gen mgr; Jim Parman, opns dir, progmg dir; Vicki Hyde, news dir.

*WLAI(FM)— Oct 27, 1969: 107.1 mhz; 4.9 kw. Ant 157 ft TL: N37 40 28 W84 46 06. (CP: 4.4 kw, ant 387 ft. TL: N37 45 40 W84 44 46). Stereo. Hrs open: 24 Rebroadcasts KLRD(FM) Yucaipa, CA 100%. 2351 Sunset Blvd., Suite 170-218, Rocklin, CA, 95765. Phone: (916) 251-1600. Fax: (916) 251-1650. Web Site:www.air1.com Licensee: Educational Media Foundation. (group owner; (acq 5-20-2005; $1 million). Population served: 200,000 Natl. Network: Air 1, . Format: Alternative, Christian. ◆Richard Jenkins, pres; Mike Novak, VP; Keith Whipple, dev dir; David Pierce, progmg mgr; Ed Lenane, news dir; Sam Wallington, engrg dir; Karen Johnson, news rptr.

Drakesboro

WNTC(FM)— 2001: 103.9 mhz; 1.95 kw. Ant 407 ft TL: N37 06 50 W87 03 52. Hrs open: 2514 Eugenia Ave., Nashville, TN, 37211. Phone: (615) 844-1039. Phone: (615) 251-1222. Fax: (615) 313-9933.E-mail: sabrosa810@aol.com Licensee: Nashville's SportsRadio Inc. Group owner: Southern Wabash Communications Corp. (acq 10-17-01). Population served: 150,000 Format: Mexican. ◆Randolph V. Bell, pres; Wayne DeSylvia, gen mgr & stn mgr.

Eddyville

WWLK(AM)— May 2, 1981: Stn currently dark. 900 khz; 1 kw-D, 120 w-N, DA-2. TL: N37 04 26 W88 04 48. Hrs open: Box 90, 42038. Licensee: Tilent Inc. (acq 7-20-89; $65,000;8-14-89). Format: Relg. ◆Jim Baggett, pres.

Edmonton

WHSX(FM)— Apr 5, 1990: 99.1 mhz; 3 kw. 328 ft TL: N37 01 33 W85 33 14. Stereo. Hrs open: 24 Box 85, Horse Cave, 42749. Phone: (270) 786-1000. Phone: (270) 432-7991. Fax: (270) 786-4402. Fax: (866) 999-hoss.E-mail: 991@scrtc.com Web Site:www.thehoss.com Licensee: Hart County Communications Inc. (acq 7-5-2001; $350,000). Population served: 50,000 Format: Country. News staff: one; News: 10 hrs wkly. Target aud: 25-54. Spec prog: Farm 15 hrs wkly. ◆Dewayne Forbis, gen mgr.

Elizabethtown

WIEL(AM)— Oct 1, 1950: 1400 khz; 1 kw-U. TL: N37 41 11 W85 52 19. Hrs open: 24 611 W. Poplar St., 42701. Phone: (270) 763-0800. Fax: (270) 769-6349. Licensee: Elizabethtown CBC Inc. Group owner: Commonwealth Broadcasting Corp. (acq 5-12-00; grpsl). Population served: 150,000 Natl. Network: ABC, . Natl. Rep: Rgnl Reps,. Wire Svc: AP Format: ESPN, sports. News staff: one; News: one hr wkly. Target aud: 24-54; upscale adult. ◆Roth Stratton, gen mgr; Holli Lee, traf mgr; Dan Michaels, opns.

*WKUE(FM)— Oct 15, 1990: 90.9 mhz; 5.2 kw. 633 ft TL: N37 44 46 W85 53 18. Stereo. Hrs open: 24 Rebroadcasts WKYU-FM Bowling Green 100%. Western Kentucky Univ., 1906 College Heights Blvd., Bowling Green, 42101. Phone: (270) 745-5489. Phone: (800) 599-9598. Fax: (270) 745-6272.E-mail: wkyufm@wku.edu Web Site:www.wkufm.org Licensee: Western Kentucky University. Natl. Network: NPR, PRI, . Rgnl. Network: Ky. Net. Leventhal, Senter & Lerman. Format: Class, news. News staff: 3; News: 30 hrs wkly. Target aud: General. Spec prog: Jazz 15 hrs, folk 5 hrs wkly. ◆Peter Bryant, gen mgr.

WQXE(FM)— Nov 24, 1969: 98.3 mhz; 8.5 kw. Ant 531 ft TL: N37 43 18 W86 02 10. Stereo. Hrs open: 233 W. Dixie Ave., 42701. Phone: (270) 737-8000. Fax: (270) 737-7229.E-mail: bill@wqxe.com Web Site:www.wqxe.com Licensee: Skytower Communications E'town Inc. Population served: 100,000 Natl. Network: Westwood One, . Format: Hot adult contemp. Target aud: 25-54; upscale, dual income families. ◆Bill Evans, pres & gen mgr.

WTHX(FM)—See Hodgenville

Elkhorn City

WEKB(AM)— Nov 24, 1979: 1460 khz; 5 kw-D, 114 w-N. TL: N37 18 25 W82 19 53. Hrs open: 24 Simulcast with WPKE(AM) Pikeville 100%. Box 2200, Pikeville, 41502. Secondary address: 1240 Radio Dr., Pikeville 41501. Phone: (606) 437-4051. Fax: (606) 432-2809.E-mail: wdhr@wdhr.com Web Site:www.ekbradio.com Licensee: East Kentucky Broadcasting Corp. (group owner; acq 6-94; $480,000 with co-located FM). Population served: 55,000 Natl. Network: ABC, . Rgnl. Network: Ky. Net. Rgnl rep: Rgnl Reps Womble, Carlyle, Sanridge & Rice. Format: Oldies. Target aud: 25-49. ◆Keith Casebolt, gen mgr.

Elkton

WEKT(AM)— July 21, 1977: 1070 khz; 500 w-D. TL: N36 48 33 W87 09 38. Hrs open: Box 577, 42220. Phone: (270) 265-5636. Fax: (270) 265-5637.E-mail: wektan1070@yahoo.com Licensee: M&R Broadcasting Inc. (acq 1-22-98; $55,000 for 50% of stock). Population served: 200,000 Natl. Network: USA, . Format: Southern gospel. ◆Marshall Sidebottom, gen mgr.

Eminence

WTSZ(AM)— June 1, 1956: 1600 khz; 500 w-D, 48 w-N. TL: N38 21 02 W85 11 11. Hrs open: 111 S. First St., La Grange, 40031. Phone: (502) 222-9171. Fax: (502) 222-9173. Web Site:www.latina1600.com Licensee: Metro East CBC Inc. Group owner: Commonwealth Broadcasting Corp. (acq 4-13-00; $600,000 with WTSZ-FM Eminence). Population served: 16,000 Rgnl. Network: Ky. News Net. Format: Sp var. Target aud: 25-54. ◆Dugan Ryan, gen mgr.

WTUV-FM— July 4, 1988: 105.7 mhz; 3 kw. Ant 325 ft TL: N38 21 09 W85 11 09. Hrs open: 4109 Bardstown Rd., Suite 104, Louisville, 40218. Phone: (502) 671-8407. Fax: (502) 671-8743.E-mail: info@lacalienteradio.com Web Site:www.lacalienteradio.com Licensee: Davidson Media Station WTSZ Licensee LLC. Group owner: Commonwealth Broadcasting Corp. (acq 5-3-2006; $500,000). Population served: 452,524 Format: Rgnl Mexican. ◆Dennis Mendez, progmg dir.

Erlanger

WIZF(FM)— Sept 22, 1965: 101.1 mhz; 2.5 kw. Ant 508 ft TL: N39 06 18 W84 33 25. Stereo. Hrs open: 705 Central Ave., Suite 200, Cincinnati, OH, 45202. Phone: (513) 679-6000. Fax: (513) 679-6014.E-mail: info@wizefm.com Web Site:www.wizefm.com Licensee: Blue Chip Broadcasting Licenses Ltd. Group owner: Radio One Inc. (acq 4-30-2001; grpsl). Population served: 10,000 Format: Urban mainstream. Target aud: 18-54. ◆Alfred Wiggins, CEO; Lisa Thal, gen mgr.

Falmouth

WIOK(FM)— June 1981: 107.5 mhz; 6 kw. 695 ft TL: N38 43 15 W84 22 27. Stereo. Hrs open: 24 Box 50, 41040. Phone: (859) 472-1075. Fax: (859) 472-2875.E-mail: wiok@fuse.net Web Site:www.wiok.com Licensee: Hammond Broadcasting Inc. (acq 1993). Population served: 3,100,000 Natl. Network: USA, . Natl. Rep: Rgnl Reps,. Format: Southern gospel. News: 12 hrs wkly. Target aud: 25-64; women. ◆Jan Hammond, VP; Jamie Porter, gen sls mgr.

Fearsville

*WYJZ(FM)—Not on air, target date: unknown: 91.7 mhz; 100 w vert. Ant 7 ft TL: N36 56 17.5 W87 19 38.8. Hrs open: 15 Wood St., Greenfield, IN, 46140. Phone: (317) 467-1062. Licensee: Electronic Applications Radio Service Inc. ◆Patrick Diemer, pres & gen mgr.

Flemingsburg

WFLE(AM)— November 1981: 1060 khz; 1 kw-D, DA. TL: N38 27 01 W83 44 06. Hrs open: 334 Recreation Park Rd., 41041. Phone: (606) 849-4433. Fax: (606) 845-9353. Licensee: DreamCatcher Communications Inc. (group owner; acq 5-23-02; $607,491 with co-located FM). Format: Gospel, country. Target aud: 25-54. ◆Don Bowles, pres; Carl Haight, gen mgr; Kim Hester, gen sls mgr; Eddie Plummer, prom mgr, progmg dir.

WFLE-FM— February 1993: 95.1 mhz; 1.61 kw. Ant 449 ft TL: N38 24 42 W83 34 41. Hrs open: 334 Recreation Park Rd., 41041. Phone: (606) 849-4433. Fax: (606) 845-9353. Format: Country. ◆Carl Haight, gen mgr.

Florence

WQRT(AM)— September 1984: 1160 khz; 5 kw-D, 990 w-N, DA-2. TL: N38 58 09 W84 40 56. Hrs open: 24 635 W. 7th St., Suite 400, Cincinnati, OH, 45203. Phone: (513) 533-2500. Fax: (513) 533-2527. Licensee: Christian Broadcasting System Ltd. Group owner: Salem Communications Corp. (acq 2-10-2006; swap of WQRT(AM) and WCVX(AM) Cincinnati, OH plus $6.75 million cash for WLQV(AM) Detroit, MI). Population served: 1,800,000 Format: Talk. News: 6 hrs wkly. Target aud: 25-54; 35-64; adults. ◆Jon R. Yinger, pres; Brian Kauffman, gen mgr; Rodger Kay, opns mgr; Michael Gavin, gen sls mgr; Dusty Rhodes, progmg mgr.

Fort Campbell

WCVQ(FM)— August 1969: 107.9 mhz; 100 kw. Ant 950 ft TL: N36 32 23 W87 39 45. Stereo. Hrs open: 24 1640 Old Russellville Pike, Clarksville, TN, 37043. Phone: (931) 648-7720. Fax: (931) 648-7769.E-mail: q108@q108.com Web Site:www.q108.com Licensee: Saga Communications of Tuckessee LLC. (acq 2-1-2001; grpsl). Population served: 198,000 Format: Adult contemp. News staff: one; News: 2 hrs wkly. Target aud: 25-40. ◆Katie Gambill, gen mgr; Scott Chase, opns dir & progmg dir.

WEGI(AM)— July 27, 1963: 1370 khz; 1 kw-D, 53 w-N. TL: N36 38 28 W87 26 04. Hrs open: 24 1640 Old Russellville Pike, Clarksville, TN, 37043. Phone: (931) 648-7720. Fax: (931) 648-7769. Licensee: Saga Communications of Tuckessee L.L.C. (acq 2-1-2001; grpsl). Population served: 180,000 Format: Southern gospel. News staff: one; News: 14 hrs wkly. Target aud: 18-34. ◆Scott Farkas, pres; Katie Gambill, gen mgr; Scott Chase, opns dir, progmg dir.

Fort Knox

WLVK(FM)— Oct 1, 1967: 105.5 mhz; 6 kw. 299 ft TL: N37 46 57 W85 54 38. Stereo. Hrs open: 24 Box 2087, Elizabethtown, 42702. Secondary address: 519 N. Miles St. , Elizabethtown 42702. Phone: (270) 766-1035. Fax: (270) 769-1052.E-mail: rbell@wase.org Web Site:www.bigcat1055.com Licensee: W & B Broadcasting Co. Inc. (acq 6-26-2000; $900,000). Population served: 120,000 Miller & Miller. Format: Country. News staff: 14; News: 4 hrs wkly. Target aud: 25-49; young & middle age country fans. Spec prog: Lou Helton Country Countdown. ◆Bill Walters, pres; Rene Bell, gen mgr; Cale Tharp, opns mgr, chief of engrg.

Fort Thomas

WYGY(FM)— Apr 18, 1994: 97.3 mhz; 2.55 kw. Ant 508 ft TL: N39 12 01 W84 31 22. Stereo. Hrs open: 24 2060 Reading Rd., Cincinnati, OH, 45202. Phone: (513) 699-5959. Fax: (513) 699-5000. Web Site:www.theworldwidewolf.com Licensee: Bonneville Holding Co. Group owner: Infinity Broadcasting Corp. (acq 3-14-2008; grpsl). Population served: 395,000 Tierney & Swift. Format: Country. News: 4 hrs wkly. ◆Jim Bryant, VP; Rory Flynn, gen sls mgr; Jay Kruz, prom dir, progmg dir.

Frankfort

WFKY(FM)— Jan 1, 1967: 104.9 mhz; 3 kw. 300 ft TL: N38 13 19 W84 54 55. Stereo. Hrs open: 24 115 W. Main St., 40601. Phone: (502) 875-1130. Fax: (502) 875-1225. Population served: 150,000 Format: Country. News staff: 2; News: 168 hrs wkly. Target aud: 25-54. ◆Brian Sands, gen mgr.

WKYW(AM)— February 1946: 1490 khz; 1 kw-U. TL: N38 12 46 W84 52 31. Hrs open: 24 115 W. Main St., 40601. Phone: (502) 875-1130. Fax: (502) 875-1225. Web Site:www.wfky.com Licensee: Forever South Licenses LLC. Group owner: Clear Channel Communications Inc. (acq 11-1-2007; grpsl). Population served: 75,000 Natl. Network: Westwood One, . Natl. Rep: Rgnl Reps,. Format: Oldies. News staff: 2; News: 12 hrs wkly. Target aud: 25-55. ◆Brian Sands, gen mgr.

WSTV-FM— Apr 15, 1991: 103.7 mhz; 2.5 kw. 350 ft TL: N38 13 17 W84 54 52. Stereo. Hrs open: 24 115 W. Main St., 40601-2807. Phone: (502) 875-1130. Fax: (502) 875-1225. Web Site:www.star1037.com Licensee: Forever South Licenses LLC. Group owner: Clear Channel Communications Inc. (acq 11-1-2007; grpsl). Population served: 42,000 Natl. Network: Westwood One, . Format: Adult contemp. News staff: 2; News: 4 hrs wkly. Target aud: 25-54. ◆Brian Sands, gen mgr.

Franklin

WFKN(AM)— Apr 25, 1954: 1220 khz; 250 w-D, 90 w-N. TL: N36 44 20 W86 34 42. Hrs open: 24 103 N. High St., 42135-0390. Phone: (270) 586-4481. Fax: (270) 586-6031.E-mail: wfkn@franklinfavorite.com Licensee: WFKN LLC (acq 11-27-01). Population served: 25,000 Rgnl. Network: Ky. Net. Natl. Rep: Rgnl Reps,. Format: Country. News staff: 2; News: 16 hrs wkly. Target aud: General. Spec prog: Relg, farm 6 hrs wkly. ◆Jamie Johnson, gen mgr; Shelly Jent, news dir.

Fredonia

*WPRZ-FM— 2008: 92.1 mhz; 4.6 kw. Ant 374 ft TL: N37 10 51 W88 00 04. Hrs open: Rebroadcasts KLVR(FM) Middletown, CA 100%. 2351 Sunset Blvd., Suite 170-218, Rocklin, CA, 95765. Phone: (916) 251-1600. Fax: (916) 251-1650. Web Site:www.klove.com Licensee: Educational Media Foundation. (acq 5-22-2008; $299,600 for CP). Natl. Network: K-Love, . Format: Contemp Christian. ◆Mike Novak, pres.

Fulton

WFUL(AM)— July 8, 1951: 1270 khz; 1 kw-D, 54 w-N. TL: N36 30 54 W88 54 16. Stereo. Hrs open: 8635 State Rt. 166 E., 42041. Phone: (270) 472-0405. Fax: (270) 472-1189. Licensee: River County Broadcasting Inc. (acq 8-23-2004; $350,000). Population served: 3,250 Format: Country, gospel. Target aud: 40 plus. ◆Max McDade, gen mgr.

*WKMT(FM)—Not on air, target date: unknown: 89.5 mhz; 25 w horiz, 5 kw vert. Ant 328 ft TL: N36 29 31 W88 50 44. Hrs open: c/o WKMS-FM, 2018 University Station, Murray, 42071. Phone: (270) 809-4745. Fax: (270) 809-4667. Licensee: Board of Regents, Murray State University. ◆Randy J. Dunn, pres; Kate Lochte, stn mgr.

WWKF(FM)— September 1954: 99.3 mhz; 3.3 kw. 337 ft TL: N36 27 59 W88 56 47. Stereo. Hrs open: 24 1729 Nailling Dr., Union City, TN, 38261. Phone: (731) 885-1240. Fax: (731) 885-3405. Web Site:www.kf99kq105.com Licensee: WENK of Union City Inc. Group owner: WENK Broadcast Group Inc. (acq 10-1-82; $473,131; 10-18-82). Population served: 73,500 Natl. Rep: Rgnl Reps,. Shainis & Peltzman. Format: CHR. News staff: one. Target aud: 18-34. ♦Terry L. Hailey, pres, gen mgr & prom mgr.

Garrison

WOKE(FM)— Sept 7, 1998: 98.3 mhz; 5.2 kw. Ant 351 ft TL: N38 36 26 W83 02 33. Hrs open: 492 Main St., South Shore, 41175. Phone: (606) 932-2223. Fax: (606) 932-6132.E-mail: info@wokejoyfm.org Web Site:www.wokejoyfm.org Licensee: Big River Radio Inc. (acq 10-25-94; 11-14-94). Booth, Freret, Imlay & Tepper. Format: Southern gospel. ♦Paul Hunt, gen mgr.

Georgetown

WGVN(AM)— Sept 6, 1957: 1580 khz; 10 kw-D, 45 w-N, DA-2. TL: N38 10 05 W84 35 37. Hrs open: 2601 Nicholasville Rd., Lexington, 40503. Phone: (859) 422-1000. Fax: (859) 422-1071.E-mail: mj@groovin1580.com Web Site:www.groovin1580.com Licensee: Citicasters Licenses L.P. Group owner: Clear Channel Communications Inc. (acq 6-30-97; grpsl). Population served: 300,000 Natl. Rep: Christal,. Format: Urban contemp. News: 2 hrs wkly. ♦Gene Guinn, gen mgr.

***WRVG(FM)**— Oct 1, 1963: 89.9 mhz; 50 kw. Ant 410 ft TL: N38 12 15 W84 32 51. Hrs open: 24 2351 Sunset Blvd., Suite 170-218, Rocklin, CA, 95765. Phone: (916) 251-1600. Fax: (916) 251-1650. Web Site:www.klove.com Licensee: Educational Media Foundation. Group owner: EMF Broadcasting (acq 3-12-2004; $1.7 million). Population served: 260,000 Format: Christian. ♦Richard Jenkins, pres, progmg dir; Mike Novak, VP; Keith Whipple, dev dir; David Pierce, progmg mgr; Ed Lenane, news dir; Sam Wallington, engrg dir; Arthur Vassar, traf mgr; Karen Johnson, news rptr.

WXZZ(FM)— Sept 10, 1973: 103.3 mhz; 1.8 kw. Ant 607 ft TL: N38 02 07 W84 27 02. Stereo. Hrs open: 300 W. Vine St., Suite 3, Lexington, 40507. Phone: (859) 253-5900. Fax: (859) 253-5940. Web Site:www.zrock103.com Licensee: Cumulus Licensing Corp. Group owner: Cumulus Media Inc. (acq 7-22-99; grpsl). Format: Rock. News staff: 3. Target aud: 18-34. ♦Andrea Ayers, gen mgr & prom dir.

Glasgow

WCDS(AM)— 2007: 1230 khz; 750 w-U. TL: N37 00 17 W85 56 27. Hrs open: PO Box 457, 42142. Secondary address: 113 W Public Sq., Suite 400 42141. Phone: (270) 651-6050. Fax: (270) 651-7666. Licensee: Anderson Communications LLC. Natl. Network: ESPN Radio, . Format: Sports. ♦Charles M. Anderson, gen mgr.

WCLU(AM)— Sept 25, 1946: 1490 khz; 1 kw-U. TL: N37 00 19 W85 54 42. Hrs open: Box 1628, 42142. Phone: (270) 651-9149. Fax: (270) 651-9222.E-mail: info@wcluradio.com Web Site:www.wcluradio.com Licensee: Royse Radio Inc. Natl. Network: CBS, . Format: Full service. Target aud: 30 plus; listeners with disposable income. ♦Henry Royse, pres & gen mgr.

WLYE-FM— 1997: 94.1 mhz; 4.5 kw. Ant 298 ft TL: N36 59 02 W85 52 20. Stereo. Hrs open: 24 1919 Scottsville Rd., Bowling Green, 42104-3303. Phone: (270) 843-3333. Fax: (270) 843-0454 .E-mail: mark@forevercom.com Licensee: Forever Communications Inc. (group owner; acq 9-3-03). Population served: 125,000 Natl. Rep: Christal,. Kaye, Scholer, LLP. Format: Classic Country. News staff: one; News: 6 hrs wkly. Target aud: 25-54; adults, serving southern central Kentucky. ♦Christine Hillard, pres; Mark Mackey, gen mgr.

WOVO(FM)— July 14, 1972: 105.3 mhz; 25 kw. Ant 318 ft TL: N36 54 50 W85 43 20. Stereo. Hrs open: Box 457, 42142-0457. Secondary address: 113 W. Public Sq., Suite 400 42141. Phone: (270) 651-6050. Fax: (270) 651-7666.E-mail: wovo@cbcradio.net Web Site:www.my1053.com Licensee: Newberry Broadcasting Inc. Group owner: Commonwealth Broadcasting Corp. (acq 11-25-97; grpsl). Population served: 500,000 Format: Oldies. ♦Derron Steenbergen, gen mgr, gen sls mgr; Kelly McKay, progmg dir & disc jockey.

***WSGP(FM)**— 2002: 88.3 mhz; 13 kw. Ant 298 ft TL: N36 49 05 W85 41 30. Hrs open: Secondary address: 93 Rainbow Terr., Somerset 42503. Phone: (606) 679-6300. Fax: (606) 679-1342.E-mail: dcradio@alltel.net Web Site:www.kingofkingsradio.net Licensee: Somerset Educational Broadcasting Foundation. Format: Conservative, traditional relg & edu. ♦David Carr, gen mgr; Carolyn Jones, progmg dir; Marvin Whitaker, chief of engrg.

WWKU(AM)— Oct 1, 1962: 1440 khz; 500 w-D, 30 w-N. TL: N37 00 17 W85 56 27. Hrs open: Box 457, 42142-0457. Secondary address: 113 W. Public Sq., Suite 400 42141. Phone: (270-651-6050. Fax: (270-651-7666. Licensee: Newberry Broadcasting Inc. Population served: 250,000 Format: Sports.

Grayson

WGOH(AM)— June 1, 1959: 1370 khz; 5 kw-D, 21 w-N. TL: N38 19 44 W82 58 33. Hrs open: 6 AM-2 hrs past sunset Box 487, 150 Radio Tower Dr., 41143. Phone: (606) 474-5144. Fax: (606) 474-7777.E-mail: mail @wgohwugo.com Web Site:www.wgohwugo.com Licensee: Carter County Broadcasting Co. Natl. Network: CBS, . Natl. Rep: Rgnl Reps,. Ky. News Net Booth, Freret, Imlay & Tepper. Wire Svc: AP Format: Classic country. News staff: one; News: 30 hrs wkly. Target aud: 35-65. Spec prog: Bluegrass. ♦Francis M. Nash, gen mgr; Jeff Roe, opns dir, opns mgr; Melodie Carter, progmg dir, traf mgr; Mike Phillips, mus dir; Jim Phillips, news dir; William H. Craig, chief of engrg & engr.

***WRYS(FM)**—Not on air, target date: unknown: 91.7 mhz; 425 w. Ant 281 ft TL: N38 20 50.8 W83 05 20.5. Hrs open: Box 1887, Westerville, OH, 43086. Phone: (614) 839-7137. Fax: (614) 839-1329. Licensee: Spirit Communications Inc. (acq 2-6-2009; $5,000 for CP). ♦John P. Shumate, pres; Michael Buckingham, gen mgr.

WUGO(FM)— February 1967: 102.3 mhz; 4.8 kw. 360 ft TL: N38 19 44 W82 58 33. Stereo. Hrs open: 24 Box 487, 150 Radio Tower Dr., 41143. Phone: (606) 474-5144. Fax: (606) 474-7777. Web Site:www.wgohwugo.com Licensee: Carter County Broadcasting Co. Inc. Natl. Rep: Rgnl Reps,. Wire Svc: AP Format: Adult contemp. News: 30 hrs wkly. Target aud: 25-54. ♦Francis Nash, gen mgr.

Greensburg

WGRK(AM)— Mar 15, 1972: 1540 khz; 1 kw-D. TL: N37 15 34 W85 30 57. Hrs open: Box 1053, Campbellsville, 42719. Secondary address: 50 Friendship Pike, Campbellsville 42719. Phone: (270) 932-7401. Phone: (270) 789-1464. Fax: (270) 789-1450.E-mail: wgrk@commonwealthbroadcasting.com Web Site:www.kcountry1057.com Licensee: Green County CBC Inc. (acq 10-30-97; $600,000 with co-located FM). Population served: 11,000 Natl. Network: ABC, Jones Radio Networks, . Natl. Rep: Rgnl Reps,. Format: Country. News staff: one; News: 7 hrs wkly. Target aud: 25-54. ♦Steve Newberry, pres; Barb Smith, gen mgr, stn mgr; Marty Bagby, opns mgr; Greg Gribbins, gen sls mgr; Trent Ford, progmg dir; Mike Graham, chief of engrg.

WGRK-FM— Dec 15, 1977: 103.1 mhz; 2.2 kw. 375 ft TL: N37 15 34 W85 30 57. (CP: 4.6 kw). Stereo. Hrs open: 24 Dups AM 50% Box 1053, Campbellsville, 42719. Secondary address: 50 Friendship Pike 42719. Phone: (270) 932-7401. Phone: (270) 789-1464. Fax: (270) 789-1450. Population served: 20,000 Womble, Carlyle, Sandridge & Rice, PLLC. Format: Mainstream country hits. News staff: one.

Greenup

WLGC(AM)— Apr 1, 1985: 1520 khz; 5 kw-D. TL: N38 35 44 W82 51 20. Stereo. Hrs open: Dups FM 50% 1401 Winchester Ave., Ashland, 41101. Phone: (606) 920-9565. Fax: (606) 920-9523. Licensee: Greenup County Broadcasting Inc. Natl. Network: Sporting News Radio Network, . Format: Sports/talk, gospel. News staff: one. ♦Bobby Hall, gen mgr.

WLGC-FM— Sept 1, 1982: 105.7 mhz; 12.5 kw. Ant 466 ft TL: N38 35 44 W82 51 22. Stereo. Hrs open: 1401 Winchester Ave., Ashland, 41101. Phone: (606) 920-9565. Fax: (606) 920-9523.E-mail: wlgc@inet99.net Licensee: Greenup County Broadcasting Inc. Rgnl. Network: Ky. Net. Ky. News Net Wire Svc: AP Format: Country. News staff: one; News: 3 hrs wkly. Target aud: 25-54; middle income listeners. ♦Bob Hall, gen mgr; Scott Martin, gen sls mgr; Mark Justice, progmg dir.

Greenville

WKYA(FM)— Dec 11, 1981: 105.5 mhz; 3 kw. 300 ft TL: N37 11 45 W87 12 38. Stereo. Hrs open: 464 St. Rt. 189 S., 42345. Phone: (270) 338-6655. Fax: (270) 338-7388. Licensee: Starlight Broadcasting Co. (group owner; acq 1996; grpsl). Rgnl. Network: Ky. Net. Format: Good time oldies. Target aud: 18-40. ♦Andy Anderson, gen mgr; Richard Neathamer, opns mgr.

Hardinsburg

WULF(FM)— July 9, 1970: 94.3 mhz; 43 kw. 290 ft TL: N37 45 40 W86 26 22. (CP: Ant 525 ft.). Stereo. Hrs open: 233 W. Dixie Ave., Elizabethtown, 42701. Phone: (270) 765-0943. Fax: (270) 737-7229.E-mail: jodie@wqxe.com Licensee: Skytower Communications - 94.3 LLC (acq 12-12-01; $1.15 million). Population served: 100,000 Format: Country. ♦Bill Evans, pres & gen mgr.

WXBC(FM)— Aug 15, 1992: 104.3 mhz; 3 kw. 328 ft TL: N37 45 12 W86 26 08. Stereo. Hrs open: 24 Box 104, 40143. Secondary address: 110 S. Main St. 40143. Phone: (270) 756-1043. Fax: (270) 756-1086.E-mail: wxbc@bbtel.com Web Site:wxbc1043.com Licensee: Breckinridge Broadcasting Co. Inc. Population served: 50,000 Natl. Network: Fox News Radio, . Rgnl. Network: Ky. Net. Booth, Freret, Imlay & Tepper. Format: Classic hit country & today's hits. News staff: one; News: 15 hrs wkly. Target aud: 25-55. ♦Jo Ann Keenan, CEO, pres, CFO & gen mgr; Dennis Day, chief of opns.

Harlan

WFSR(AM)— April 1976: 970 khz; 5 kw-D, 94 w-N. TL: N36 50 59 W83 23 41. Hrs open: Box 818, 40831-0818. Secondary address: 125 S. Main 40831. Phone: (606) 573-1470. Fax: (606) 573-1473.E-mail: wtuk-wfsr@harlanonline.net Licensee: Eastern Broadcasting Co. (acq 5-26-98; $400,000 with co-located FM). Population served: 18,000 Rgnl. Network: Ky. Net. Format: Southern gospel. Target aud: 25-54; adult purchasers. ♦Jeff Capps, gen mgr, gen sls mgr, chief of engrg & local news ed.

WHLN(AM)— May 30, 1941: 1410 khz; 5 kw-D, 94 w-N. TL: N36 52 02 W83 19 36. Hrs open: Box 898, 40831. Secondary address: 100 Eversole St., Suite 1 40831. Phone: (606) 573-2540. Fax: (606) 573-7557.E-mail: whln@harlanonline.net Licensee: Radio Harlan Inc. (acq 6-1-56). Population served: 200,000 Natl. Network: ABC, . Natl. Rep: Rgnl Reps,. Wire Svc: AP Format: Adult Contemp. Target aud: 25-54. ♦James T. Morgan, pres; James O. Morgan, VP, gen mgr.

WTUK(FM)— June 26, 1991: 105.1 mhz; 270 w. 1,037 ft TL: N36 54 09 W83 18 01. Hrs open: Box 818, 40831. Secondary address: 125 S. Main 40831. Phone: (606) 573-1470. Fax: (606) 573-1473.E-mail: wtuk-wfsr@harlanonline.net Format: Country.

Harold

WXLR(FM)— January 1994: 104.9 mhz; 370 w. 922 ft TL: N37 31 59 W82 29 40. Hrs open: Box 1049, 41635. Phone: (606) 478-1200. Fax: (606) 478-4202.E-mail: wifx@foxy943.com Web Site:www.thedoublex.com Licensee: Adam D. Gearheart. Format: New country. ♦Adam D. Gearheart, pres & gen mgr.

Harrodsburg

WHBN(AM)— June 25, 1955: 1420 khz; 1 kw-D, 46 w-N. TL: N37 44 03 W84 48 50. Hrs open: 24 2063 Shakertown Rd., Danville, 40422. Phone: (859) 236-2711. Fax: (859) 236-1461.E-mail: hometownradio@bellsouth.net Web Site:www.hometownlive.net Licensee: Hometown Broadcasting of Harrodsburg Inc. (acq 1-4-01). Population served: 200,000 Natl. Network: Jones Radio Networks, AP Radio, . Rgnl. Network: Ky. Net. Natl. Rep: Rgnl Reps,. Ky. News Net Rgnl rep: Rgnl Reps. Format: Country, gospel. News staff: one; News: 21 hrs wkly. Target aud: General; residents of Mercer county. ♦Robert Wagner, gen mgr, sls dir, prom mgr; Jim Parman, opns mgr, progmg dir; Vicki Hyde, news dir.

Hartford

WAIA(AM)—(Beaver Dam, June 21, 1969: 1600 khz; 1 kw-D. TL: N37 26 36 W86 53 57. Hrs open: 6 AM-sunset
Rebroadcasts WKYA(FM) Greenville 100%.
Box 106, 42347. Phone: (270) 298-3268. Phone: (270) 298-3269. Fax: (270) 298-9326. Licensee: Starlight Broadcasting Co. (group owner; acq 1996; grpsl). Population served: 20,000 Rgnl. Network: Ky. News Net. Natl. Rep: Rgnl Reps,. Ky. News Net Format: News/talk, sports. Target aud: General. ♦Andy Anderson, pres, gen mgr, opns mgr, gen sls mgr, progmg dir & chief of engrg.

WXMZ(FM)— May 18, 1972: 106.3 mhz; 3 kw. 280 ft TL: N37 26 36 W86 53 57. Stereo. Hrs open: 16
Rebroadcasts WKYA(FM) Greenville 100%.
Box 106, 42347. Phone: (270) 298-3268. Phone: (270) 298-3269. Fax: (270) 298-9326.E-mail: info@wxmzfm.com Web Site:www.wxmzfm.com Format: Oldies.

Hawesville

WKCM(AM)— Nov 7, 1972: 1160 khz; 2.5 kw-D, 1 kw-N, DA-N. TL: N37 54 20 W86 45 30. Stereo. Hrs open: 24 1115 Tamarack Rd., Suite 500, Owensboro, 42301. Phone: (270) 683-5200. Fax: (270) 688-0108.E-mail: dpowers@cromwellradio.com   Web Site:www.owensbororadio.com Licensee: Hancock Communications Inc. Group owner: The Cromwell Group Inc. Population served: 1,262 Rgnl. Network: Ky. Agri. Format: Real country. News staff: one; News: 10 hrs wkly. Target aud: 25-54; general. Spec prog: Farm 3 hrs, sports 6 hrs wkly. ◆Bayard H. Walters, pres; Dale Powers, gen mgr; Jeff Morgan, progmg dir; Amy Spalding, traf mgr; Jeff Nalley, farm dir.

WXCM(FM)—(Whitesville, May 1993): 97.1 mhz; 4 kw. Ant 403 ft TL: N37 41 50 W86 59 28. Hrs open: 1115 Tamarack Rd., Suite 500, Owensboro, 42301. Phone: (270) 683-5200. Fax: (270) 688-0108.E-mail: spots@wrioradio.com Web Site:www.owensbororadio.com Licensee: The Cromwell Group Inc. of Kentucky. (acq 1993; $170,000;9-6-93). Format: Rock. Target aud: Males in 30's. ◆Bayard H. Walters, CEO; Kevin Riecke, opns mgr; Amy Spalding, traf mgr; Jeff Nalley, farm dir.

Hazard

*WEKH(FM)— February 1985: 90.9 mhz; 33 kw. 1,004 ft TL: N37 11 34 W83 11 16. Stereo. Hrs open: 24
Rebroadcasts WEKU-FM Richmond 100%.
102 Perkins Bldg., 521 Lancaster Ave., Richmond, 40475-3102. Phone: (859) 622-1660. Fax: (859) 622-6276.E-mail: wekunews@eku.edu Web Site:www.weku.fm Licensee: Board of Regents, Eastern Kentucky University. Natl. Network: NPR, PRI, . Hardy, Carey & Chautin. Wire Svc: AP Format: Class, news magazine, info. News staff: 3; News: 35 hrs wkly. Target aud: General. ◆Tim Singleton, gen mgr & stn mgr; Mary Ellyn Cain, opns mgr; Carol Siler, dev dir; Laura Allen, progmg dir; Charles Compton, news dir; Bill Browning, chief of engrg.

WJMD(FM)— July 26, 1989: 104.7 mhz; 2.5 kw. 1,135 ft TL: N37 11 36 W83 11 04. Hrs open: 24 P.O. Box 7001, 41702. Secondary address: 516 Main Street 41701. Phone: (606) 439-3358. Fax: (606) 439-3371.E-mail: wjmd@windstream.net Licensee: Hazard Broadcasting Services (acq 4-13-01; $250 for 25%). Natl. Network: Salem Radio Network, . Format: Relg. News staff: 2; News: 7 hrs wkly. Target aud: General. ◆Michael R. Barnett, gen mgr.

WKIC(AM)— Nov 23, 1947: 1390 khz; 5 kw-D. TL: N37 14 19 W83 12 41. Stereo. Hrs open: Box 7428, 41702. Secondary address: 516 Main St. 41701. Phone: (606) 436-2121. Fax: (606) 436-4172.E-mail: wsgsfm@alltel.net Licensee: Mountain Broadcasting Service Inc. (acq 12-67). Population served: 5,459 Natl. Network: Westwood One, . Rgnl. Network: Ky. Net. Natl. Rep: Rgnl Reps,. Format: Adult standards. ◆Faron Sparkman, gen mgr, gen sls mgr & gen sls mgr.

WQXY(AM)— Mar 1, 1988: 1560 khz; 1 kw-D, 500 w-CH, DA. TL: N37 16 27 W83 11 29. Stereo. Hrs open: Box 864, Hindman, 41822. Phone: (606) 785-6129. Fax: (606) 785-0106.E-mail: info@wqmg.com Licensee: Black Gold Broadcasting. (acq 8-90; $97,500; 9-24-90). Natl. Network: Jones Radio Networks, AP Radio, CNN Radio, . Format: Oldies. Target aud: 25-54; educated, mobile, child-rearing couples in suburbs, blue collar workers. ◆Randy Thompson, gen mgr.

WSGS(FM)— Feb 3, 1959: 101.1 mhz; 100 kw. 1,463 ft TL: N37 11 38 W83 10 52. Stereo. Hrs open: Prog sep from AM Box 7428, 41702. Phone: (606) 436-2121. Fax: (606) 436-4172.E-mail: wsgsfm@alltel.net Web Site:www.wsgs.com Licensee: Mountain Broadcasting Service Inc. Population served: 1,000,000 Natl. Network: ABC, . Rgnl. Network: Ky. News Net. Ky. News Net Format: Country.

Henderson

WGBF-FM— Dec 1, 1971: 103.1 mhz; 6 kw. 460 ft TL: N37 46 54 W87 37 24. (CP: 3.16 kw, ant 453 ft.). Stereo. Hrs open: 24 117 SE 5th St, Evansville, IN, 47708. Phone: (812) 425-4226. Fax: (812) 421-0005.E-mail: info@103gbfrocks.com Web Site:www.103gbfrocks.com Licensee: Regent Broadcasting of Evansville/Owensboro Inc. Group owner: Regent Communications Inc. (acq 12-3-2003; grpsl). Population served: 185,000 Natl. Network: ABC, . Format: Rock/AOR. News staff: one. Target aud: 18-49. ◆Mark Thomas, gen mgr; Bobby Gates, prom dir; Mike Sanders, progmg dir.

WKDQ(FM)— 1947: 99.5 mhz; 100 kw. 944 ft TL: N37 49 36 W87 33 00. Stereo. Hrs open: 24 117 Southeast 5th St., Evansville, IN, 47708. Phone: (812) 425-4226.E-mail: info@wkdq.com Web Site:www.wkdq.com Licensee: Regent Broadcasting of Evansville/Owensboro Inc. Group owner: Regent Communications Inc. (acq 2-25-03; grpsl). Population served: 250,000 Natl. Rep: Christal,. Format: Country. News staff: 2. Target aud: 25-54. ◆Lori Tevault, prom dir; Jon Prell, progmg dir.

Highland Heights

*WNKU(FM)— Apr 29, 1985: 89.7 mhz; 12 kw. 318 ft TL: N39 02 21 W84 27 57. Stereo. Hrs open: 21 (M-F); 20 (S); 19 (Su) 301 Landrum Academic, 41099. Phone: (859) 572-6500. Fax: (859) 572-6604.E-mail: wnku@nku.edu Web Site:www.wnku.org Licensee: Northern Kentucky University. Natl. Network: PRI, NPR, . Arter & Hadden. Format: AAA, news. News staff: 2; News: 40 hrs wkly. Target aud: 35-49. ◆Aaron Sharpe, dev dir; Grady Kirkpatrick, progmg dir.

Hindman

WKCB(AM)— Jan 26, 1971: 1340 khz; 6 kw-U. TL: N37 19 45 W83 00 17. Hrs open: Box 864, 41822. Secondary address: 1517 Hwy. 550 W. 41822. Phone: (606) 785-3129. Fax: (606) 785-0106.E-mail: request@wkcb.com Web Site:www.wkcb.com Licensee: Hindman Broadcasting Corp. (acq 9-15-89; $100,000 with co-located FM; 10-23-89). Population served: 18,200 Natl. Network: Ky. Net. Natl. Rep: Rgnl Reps,. Format: Christian. ◆Randy Thompson, pres & gen mgr; Paul Hoskins, progmg mgr, news dir.

WKCB-FM— Dec 13, 1974: 107.1 mhz; 770 w. 650 ft TL: N37 19 56 W82 56 52. Stereo. Hrs open: Prog sep from AM Box 864, 41822. Phone: (606) 785-3129. Fax: (606) 785-0106.E-mail: request@wkcb.com Web Site:www.wkcb.com Licensee: Hindman Broadcasting Corp. Population served: 65,000 Format: Heart of rock.

Hodgenville

WTHX(FM)— March 1974: 107.3 mhz; 3.8 kw. Ant 420 ft TL: N37 40 21 W85 44 34. Stereo. Hrs open: 611 W. Poplar St., Suite C2, Elizabethtown, 42701. Phone: (270) 763-0800. Fax: (270) 769-6349.E-mail: info@etownstar.com Web Site:www.etownstar.com Licensee: Elizabethtown CBC Inc. Group owner: Commonwealth Broadcasting Corp. (acq 7-1-2000; grpsl). Population served: 98,000 Natl. Rep: Keystone (unwired net), Rgnl Reps,. Verner, Liipfert, Bernhard, McPherson & Hand. Format: CHR. Target aud: 18-44; females. Spec prog: Farm 2 hrs wkly. ◆Steve Newberry, pres; Dale Thornhill, VP; Roth Stratton, gen mgr.

WXAM(AM)—See Buffalo

Hopkinsville

WHOP(AM)— Jan 8, 1940: 1230 khz; 830 w-U. TL: N36 52 54 W87 30 44. Hrs open: 24 Box 709, 42241-0709. Secondary address: 220 Dink Embry's Buttermilk Rd. 42240-8802. Phone: (270) 885-5331. Fax: (270) 885-2688.E-mail: whopamfm@bellsouth.net Web Site:www.lite987whop.com Licensee: Hop Broadcasting Inc. (acq 10-28-99; with co-located FM). Population served: 190,000 Natl. Network: CBS, . Rgnl. Network: Ky. Net. Natl. Rep: Rgnl Reps,. Ky. News Net Format: News/talk. News staff: 2. Target aud: 30 plus. ◆Mike Chadwell, gen mgr.

WHOP-FM— May 1948: 98.7 mhz; 100 kw. Ant 620 ft TL: N36 55 41 W87 32 50. Stereo. Hrs open: 24 Box 709, 42241-0709. Secondary address: 220 Buttermilk Rd. 42240-8802. Phone: (270) 885-5331. Fax: (270) 885-2688. Web Site:www.lite987whop.com Licensee: Hop Broadcasting Inc. Population served: 300,000 Natl. Rep: Rgnl Reps,. Format: Adult contemp. News staff: 2; News: 15 hrs wkly. Target aud: 18-54. ◆Traci Mason, gen sls mgr.

WHVO(AM)— Sept 19, 1954: 1480 khz; 1 kw-D, 24 w-N. TL: N36 52 15 W87 30 43. Hrs open: 24 Oldies Radio, P.O. Box 1900, Cadiz,

42211-1900. Phone: (270) 886-1480. Fax: (270) 886-6286.E-mail: oldies@oldies1480.com Web Site:www.oldies1480.com Licensee: Ham Broadcasting Inc. (acq 10-95). Population served: 100,000 Natl. Network: AP Network News, Jones Radio Networks, Fox News Radio, . Natl. Rep: Rgnl Reps, Ky. News Net Format: Oldies. News staff: two; News: 3 hrs wkly. Target aud: 35-54; Upscale Baby-boomers. Spec prog: Relg 6 hrs, gospel 3 hrs wkly. ◆D.J. Everett, pres; Beth Mann, gen mgr; Bill Booth, opns mgr; Amy Berry, gen sls mgr; Alan Watts, news dir.

*WNKJ(FM)— Aug 3, 1981: 89.3 mhz; 12 kw. 330 ft TL: N36 48 34 W87 24 20. Stereo. Hrs open: 24 Box 1029, 42241-1029. Secondary address: 1100 E. 18th St. 42240. Phone: (270) 886-9655. Fax: (270) 885-7210.E-mail: wnkj@wnkj.org Web Site:www.wnkj.org Licensee: Pennyrile Christian Community Inc. Natl. Network: Moody, . Format: Christian. News: 12 hrs wkly. Target aud: General. Spec prog: Black 4.5 hrs, Korean 1/2 hr, Sp 3/4 hr wkly. ◆Jim Dozier Adams, gen mgr.

WVVR(FM)— July 1, 1960: 100.3 mhz; 100 kw. Ant 1,000 ft TL: N36 56 58 W87 40 18. Stereo. Hrs open: 24 1640 Old Russellville Pike, Clarksville, TN, 37043. Phone: (931) 648-7720. Fax: (931) 648-7769. Web Site:www.thebeaver.com Licensee: Saga Communications of Tuckessee LLC. Group owner: Saga Communications Inc. (acq 11-27-2000; $7 million). Population served: 1,100,000 Rgnl rep: Rgnl Reps. Format: Country. News staff: one; News: 7 hrs wkly. Target aud: 18-54; working class. ◆Katie Gambill, gen mgr.

WZZP(FM)— Feb 28, 2001: 97.5 mhz; 6 kw. Ant 328 ft TL: N36 45 47 W87 26 59. Hrs open: 1640 Old Russellville Pike, Clarksville, TN, 37043. Phone: (931) 648-7720. Fax: (931) 648-7769. Web Site:www.z975.com Licensee: Saga Communications of Tuckessee L.L.C. Group owner: Saga Communications Inc. (acq 2-1-01; grpsl). Format: Rock. ◆Katie Gambill, gen mgr; Scott Chase, opns dir; Jared Mims, progmg dir.

Horse Cave

WHHT(FM)— Sept 19, 1994: 106.7 mhz; 2.9 kw. Ant 476 ft TL: N37 13 57 W85 52 06. Hrs open: Box 457, Glasgow, 42142-0457. Secondary address: 113 W. Public Sq., Suite 400, Glasgow 42141. Phone: (270) 651-6050. Fax: (270) 651-7666. Licensee: Commonwealth Broadcasting Corp. (acq 11-25-97; grpsl). Natl. Network: Westwood One, . Format: Adult contemp. ◆Derron Steenbergen, gen mgr, stn mgr; Kellie Wood, opns mgr.

Hyden

WZQQ(FM)— Nov 7, 1988: 97.9 mhz; 1.75 kw. Ant 1,207 ft TL: N37 11 36 W83 11 04. Stereo. Hrs open: Box 7280, Hazard, 41702. Secondary address: 516 Main St., Hazard 41701. Phone: (606) 436-9898. Fax: (606) 436-4172.E-mail: wzqq@alltel.net Licensee: Leslie County Broadcasting Inc. (acq 4-3-2001; $50 for 50%). Natl. Network: ABC, . Format: Hot adult contemp, CHR. Target aud: General. ◆Stuart Shane Sparkman, CEO; Mike Reeves, gen mgr, gen sls mgr; Bob Hale, chief of engrg.

Inez

WBTH(AM)—See Williamson, WV

WXCC(FM)—See Williamson, WV

Irvine

WCYO(FM)— August 1991: 100.7 mhz; 9.2 kw. Ant 505 ft TL: N37 39 40 W84 08 55. Hrs open: 24 128 Big Hill Ave., Richmond, 40475. Phone: (859) 623-1386. Fax: (859) 623-1241. Licensee: Kentucky River Broadcasting Co. Inc. Population served: 200,000 Format: Country.

WIRV(AM)— July 2, 1960: 1550 khz; 1 kw-D. TL: N37 42 26 W83 58 15. (CP: TL: N37 42 57 W83 58 29). Hrs open: 128 Big Hill Ave., Richmond, 40475. Phone: (859) 623-1386. Fax: (859) 623-1241. Licensee: Kentucky River Broadcasting Co Inc. Population served: 100,000 Natl. Network: Ky. Net. Natl. Rep: Rgnl Reps,. Format: Oldies. ◆Kelly T. Wallingford, gen mgr; Ray White, gen sls mgr & progmg dir.

Jackson

WEKG(AM)— Mar 7, 1969: 810 khz; 5 kw-D. TL: N37 34 41 W83 24 19. Hrs open: 1501 Hargas Ln., 41339. Phone: (606) 666-7531. Fax: (606) 666-4946.E-mail: kdavidson@wjsn.com Licensee: Intermountain

Broadcasting Co. Population served: 100,000 Rgnl. Network: Ky. Net. Format: Gospel. ◆ Doug Neace, gen mgr, gen sls mgr.

WJSN-FM— Jan 1, 1979: 97.3 mhz; 19 kw. Ant 813 ft TL: N37 40 19 W83 04 21. Stereo. Hrs open: 1501 Hargas Ln., 41339. Phone: (606) 666-7531. Fax: (606) 666-4946. E-mail: kdavidson@wjsn.com Population served: 50,000 Format: Country.

*WYLC(FM)—Not on air, target date: unknown: 89.7 mhz; 400 w. Ant 348 ft TL: N37 34 08 W83 16 28. Hrs open: Box 427, 41339. Secondary address: 3019 Hwy. 30 W. 41339. Phone: (606) 295-3225. Licensee: Breathitt Listeners Choice Radio Inc. ◆ Earl Lovely, chmn.

Jamestown

WJKY(AM)— Sept 3, 1967: 1060 khz; 1 kw-D. TL: N37 01 31 W85 04 23. Hrs open: Box 800, 42629. Secondary address: 2804 South US Hwy 127 , Russell Springs 42642. Phone: (270) 866-3487. Phone: (270) 343-4444. Fax: (270) 866-2060. Web Site:www.lakercountry.com Licensee: Lake Cumberland Broadcasters (acq 7-1-70). Population served: 50,000 Format: Country. ◆ Mae Hoover, gen mgr & gen sls mgr.

WJRS(FM)— Sept 3, 1966: 104.9 mhz; 2 kw. Ant 360 ft TL: N37 01 31 W85 04 23. Hrs open: Box 800, 42629. Secondary address: 2804 South US Hwy 127, Russell Springs 42642. Phone: (270) 866-3487. Phone: (270) 343-4444. Fax: (270) 866-2060. Licensee: Lake Cumberland Broadcasters. Rgnl. Network: Ky. Agri. Wire Svc: NWS (National Weather Service) Format: Country.

Jeffersontown

WMJM(FM)— Dec 1, 1978: 101.3 mhz; 2 kw. 194 ft TL: N38 13 42 W85 38 22. Stereo. Hrs open: 520 S. 4th St., Suite 200, Louisville, 40202. Phone: (502) 625-1220. Fax: (502) 625-1259. Web Site:www.1013online.com Licensee: MLB-Louisville IV LLC. Group owner: Radio One Inc. (acq 9-12-2007; grpsl). Format: Urban adult contemp. ◆ Dale Schaefer, gen mgr.

Jenkins

WIFX-FM— May 10, 1975: 94.3 mhz; 4.2 kw. Ant 1,565 ft TL: N37 06 38 W82 44 18. Hrs open: 24 Box 1049, Harold, 41635. Phone: (606) 478-1200. Fax: (606) 478-4202. E-mail: wifx@foxy943.com Licensee: AJSPD LLC (acq 12-11-2006; $1.5 million). Population served: 250,000. Kilpatrick Stockton LLP. Format: Adult rock. News: 2 hrs wkly. Target aud: 25-45. ◆ Adam D. Gearheart, gen mgr.

WKVG(AM)— Feb 1, 1970: 1000 khz; 1 kw-D. TL: N37 09 59 W82 37 13. Hrs open: 7:30 AM- 6 PM Box 613, Pound, VA, 24279-0613. Secondary address: Box 1474 41537. Phone: (606) 832-4655. Fax: (606) 832-4656. Licensee: Martins and Assoc. Inc. (acq 6-15-92; $40,000; 6-7-92). Population served: 10,000 Format: Gospel, relg. News: 9 hrs wkly. Target aud: General. ◆ Emma Jean Martin, gen mgr.

Junction City

WDFB(AM)— May 20, 1985: 1170 khz; 1 kw-D, DA. TL: N37 35 46 W84 50 19. Hrs open: Sunrise-sunset 3596 Alumspring Road, Danville, 40422. Secondary address: 3596 Alum Springs Rd., Danville 40422. Phone: (859) 236-9333. Fax: (859) 236-3348. E-mail: wdfb@searnet.com Web Site:www.wdfb.com Licensee: Alum Springs Vision and Outreach Corp. Natl. Network: USA, . Format: Relg. Target aud: General. ◆ Donald A. Drake, pres; Mildred Drake, exec VP & gen mgr; Cindy Pike, traf mgr.

Keavy

*WVCT(FM)— January 1984: 91.5 mhz; 100 w. 341 ft TL: N36 58 21 W84 07 28. Stereo. Hrs open: 24 968 W. City Dam Rd., 40737. Phone: (606) 528-4671. Fax: (606) 526-0589. E-mail: csivley@bellsouth.net Licensee: Victory Training School Corp. Format: Gospel. ◆ Charles Sivley, gen mgr.

Keene

WJMM-FM— Dec 9, 1969: 99.1 mhz; 4.5 kw. Ant 384 ft TL: N37 57 37 W84 32 42. Stereo. Hrs open: 24 501 Darby Creek #62, Lexington, 40509. Phone: (859) 264-9700. Fax: (859) 264-9705. Web Site:www.wjmm.com Licensee: Christian Broadcasting System Ltd. (acq 7-1-2006; grpsl). Format: Christian teaching/inspirational. ◆ Benson Gregory, gen mgr & stn mgr.

La Center

WRJJ(FM)— 2008: 104.3 mhz; 4 kw. Ant 125 ft TL: N37 04 30 W88 58 22. Hrs open: 801 N. Garfield, Apt. B, Marion, IL, 62959. Phone: (618) 967-3704. Licensee: Janet Jensen. ◆ Janet Jensen, gen mgr.

Lancaster

WRNZ(FM)— Oct 1, 1988: 105.1 mhz; 3 kw. 325 ft TL: N37 36 06 W84 34 27. Stereo. Hrs open: 24 2063 Shakertown Rd., Danville, 40422. Phone: (859) 236-2711. Fax: (859) 236-1461. E-mail: hometownradio@bellsouth.net Web Site:www.hometownLIVE.net Licensee: Hometown Broadcasting of Lancaster Inc. Population served: 200,000 Natl. Rep: Rgnl Reps,. Rgnl rep: Rgnl Reps Format: Hot adult contemp. News staff: one; News: 2 hrs wkly. Target aud: 25-54; upscale, white collar, baby boomers, business owners. Spec prog: Relg 4 hrs wkly. ◆ Robert Wagner, gen mgr; Vicki Hyde, news dir.

Lawrenceburg

WKYL(FM)— May 11, 1993: 102.1 mhz; 6 kw. Ant 328 ft TL: N38 01 37 W84 52 59. Stereo. Hrs open: 24 1010 Industry Rd., 40342. Phone: (502) 839-1021. Licensee: Davenport Broadcasting Inc. (acq 1-16-97; $525,000). Population served: 150,000 Natl. Network: Jones Radio Networks, . Pepper & Corazzini. Format: Smooth jazz. Target aud: 30-50; higher income; especially at-work listeners. Spec prog: Relg 2 hrs wkly. ◆ C. Michael Davenport, CEO & gen mgr.

Lebanon

WLBN(AM)— October 1954: 1590 khz; 1 kw-D, 74 w-N, DA-1. TL: N37 35 55 W85 14 47. Hrs open: 24 253 W. Main St., 40033. Phone: (270) 692-3126. Fax: (270) 692-6003. Web Site:www.1590wlbn.com Licensee: CBC of Marion County Inc. Group owner: CBC of Marion and Taylor Counties Inc. (acq 7-3-97; $360,000 with co-located FM). Population served: 126,000 Natl. Network: Jones Radio Networks, . Natl. Rep: Rgnl Reps,. Leonard S. Joyce. Format: Oldies. News staff: one; News: 13 hrs wkly. Target aud: 35-64. Spec prog: Gospel 5 hrs, open mike 5 hrs wkly. ◆ Lisa Kearnes, gen mgr, gen mgr, gen sls mgr, gen sls mgr, rgnl sls mgr, prom mgr, adv dir; Andy Colley, opns mgr, progmg mgr, mus dir; Patty Brown, news dir; Mike Graham, chief of engrg.

WLSK(FM)— Oct 1, 1979: 100.9 mhz; 16.5 kw. Ant 410 ft TL: N37 41 43 W85 19 06. Stereo. Hrs open: 24 Prog sep from AM 253 W. Main St., 40033. Phone: (2700 692-3126. Fax: (270) 692-6003. E-mail: wlsk@commonwealthbroadcasting.com Web Site:www.lebanonmike.com Population served: 121,000 Rgnl. Network: Rgnl Reps. Format: Mike 80s & 90s—whatever. News staff: one; News: 9 hrs wkly. Target aud: 30-49. ◆ Lisa Kearnes, gen mgr, mktg dir, sls, prom; Andy Colley, opns mgr, disc jockey; Patty Brown, news dir & traf mgr.

Lebanon Junction

WKMO(FM)— October 1979: 99.3 mhz; 6 kw. Ant 312 ft TL: N37 44 26 W85 49 28. Stereo. Hrs open: 611 W. Poplar St., Suite C2, Elizabethtown, 42701. Phone: (270) 763-0800. Fax: (270) 769-6349. E-mail: info@1063thebear.com Web Site:www.myspace.com/kmocountry993 Licensee: Elizabethtown CBC Inc. Group owner: Commonwealth Broadcasting Corp. (acq 12-23-2002; $900,000). Natl. Rep: Rgnl Reps,. Format: Country. News staff: one; News: one hr wkly. ◆ Steve Newberry, CEO & chmn; Dale Thornhill, sr VP; Roth Stratton, gen mgr; Holli Lee, traf mgr; Dan Michaels, opns, progmg.

Ledbetter

*WHMR(FM)— 2004: 90.1 mhz; 1 kw vert. Ant 328 ft TL: N37 06 10 W88 24 15. Hrs open: Box 281, Hardin, 42048. Secondary address: 219 College St., Harding 42048. Phone: (270) 437-4095. Fax: (270) 437-4098. E-mail: info@hmiradio.com Web Site:www.hmiradio.com Licensee: Heartland Ministries Inc. Format: Traditional christian. ◆ Darrell Gibson, pres; Jeremy Johnson, progmg dir.

Leitchfield

WKHG(FM)— Oct 29, 1967: 104.9 mhz; 3.5 kw. 250 ft TL: N37 30 40 W86 17 15. Stereo. Hrs open: Prog sep from AM 2160 Brandenburg Rd., 42754. Phone: (270) 259-5692. Fax: (270) 259-5692. E-mail: news@k105.com Web Site:www.k105.com Licensee: Heritage Media of Kentucky Inc. Format: Adult contemp.

WMTL(AM)— Jan 17, 1959: 870 khz; 500 w-D. TL: N37 30 40 W86 17 15. Hrs open: 2160 Brandenburg Rd., 42754. Phone: (270) 259-3165. Fax: (270) 259-5693. E-mail: news@k105.com Licensee: Heritage Media of Kentucky Inc. (acq 1-26-95; $350,000 with co-located FM; 3-20-95). Format: Country. ◆ Mark Buckles, pres, gen mgr & gen sls mgr; Ed Thomas, chief of engrg.

Lerose

*WOCS(FM)— March 1999: 88.3 mhz; 1 kw. Ant 321 ft TL: N37 36 23 W83 41 16. Hrs open: 3 PM-9 PM (M-F) Owsley County High School, Hwy. 28/ E. Shepherd Ln., Booneville, 41314. Phone: (606) 593-5185. Fax: (606) 593-6312. E-mail: tburns@owsley.k12.ky.us Web Site:www.owsley.kyschools.us Licensee: Board of Regents - Morehead State University (acq 4-13-01; $15,000). Population served: 15,000 Format: Div. Target aud: 12-35; poor & uneducated in need of information. ◆ Diana Gross, chmn; Stephen F. Jackson, CEO & pres; Jerry McIntosh, CFO; Dan Conti, gen mgr; Bill Hodges, mus dir.

Lewisport

WKCM(AM)—See Hawesville

Lexington

WBUL-FM— July 15, 1969: 98.1 mhz; 100 kw. 561 ft TL: N38 02 07 W84 27 02. Stereo. Hrs open: 2601 Nicholasville Rd., 40503. Phone: (859) 422-1000. Fax: (859) 422-1038. E-mail: info@wbul.com Web Site:www.wbul.com Licensee: Citicasters Licenses L.P. Group owner: Clear Channel Communications Inc. (acq 5-4-99; grpsl). Population served: 120,000 Format: Country. Target aud: 25-49; baby boomers who grew up with Stones & Beatles. ◆ Gene Guinn, gen mgr.

WGKS(FM)—(Paris, June 5, 1968: 96.9 mhz; 50 kw. 492 ft TL: N38 07 32 W84 21 12. Stereo. Hrs open: Prog sep from AM 401 W. Main St., Suite 301, 40507. Phone: (859) 233-1515. Fax: (859) 233-1517. Web Site:www.969kissfm.com Licensee: L.M. Communications Inc. Natl. Network: ABC, . Natl. Rep: Katz Radio,. Format: Adult contemp. News staff: one; News: 10 hrs wkly. ◆ Lynn Martin, pres; James E. MacFarlane, gen mgr, mktg mgr, progmg dir.

WLAP(AM)— September 1922: 630 khz; 5 kw-D, 1 kw-N, DA-2. TL: N38 07 25 W84 26 45. Hrs open: 24 Prog sep from FM 2601 Nicholasville Rd., 40503. Phone: (859) 422- 1000. Fax: (859) 422-1038. E-mail: info@wlap.com Web Site:www.wlap.com Licensee: Citicasters Licenses L.P. Population served: 1,951,000 Natl. Network: CBS, . Natl. Rep: Christal,. Format: News. News staff: one. Target aud: 18-49; men. ◆ Kevin Bell, progmg dir.

WLXG(AM)— 1946: 1300 khz; 2.5 kw-D, 1 kw-N, DA-N. TL: N38 05 50 W84 31 45. Hrs open: 401 W. Main St., Suite 301, 40507. Phone: (859) 233-1515. Fax: (859) 233-1517. E-mail: jmac@lmcomm.com Web Site:www.wlxg.com Licensee: L.M. Communications Inc. (group owner; acq 7-1-84). Population served: 190,000 Natl. Network: ESPN Radio, . Natl. Rep: Katz Radio,. Format: Sports radio/ESPN. News: 5 hrs wkly. Target aud: 25-54; adults. ◆ Lynn Martin, pres; James MacFarlane, gen mgr, mktg mgr.

WLXX(FM)— February 1962: 92.9 mhz; 100 kw. Ant 854 ft TL: N38 02 22 W84 24 11. Stereo. Hrs open: 24 Prog sep from AM 300 W. Vine St., Suite 3, 40507. Phone: (859) 253-5900. Fax: (859) 253-5940. Web Site:www.wlxxthebear.com Format: Country. ◆ Marshall Stewark, progmg dir.

WMXL(FM)— 1940: 94.5 mhz; 100 kw. Ant 640 ft TL: N38 07 25 W84 22 45. Stereo. Hrs open: 24 2601 Nicholasville Rd., 40503. Phone: (859) 422-1000. Fax: (859) 422-1038. E-mail: info@wmxl.com Web Site:www.wmxl.com Licensee: Citicasters Licenses L.P. Group owner: Clear Channel Communications Inc. (acq 5-4-99; grpsl). Population served: 195,100 Format: Adult contemp. News: 3 hrs wkly. Target aud: 25-54; women. ◆ Gene Guinn, gen mgr; Barry Fox, opns mgr; Dale O'Brien, progmg dir; Gerry Westerberg, mus dir, chief of engrg; Karyn Czar, news dir; Michael Jordan, mktg dir, traf mgr & disc jockey.

*WRFL(FM)— Mar 3, 1988: 88.1 mhz; 250 w. 289 ft TL: N38 02 19 W84 30 16. Hrs open: Box 777, University Stn., Music Director, 40506. Phone: (859) 257-4636. Phone: (859) 257-9735. Fax: (859) 323-1030. E-mail: gm@wrfl881.org Licensee: Radio Free Lexington Inc. Format: Var. ◆ John Clark, gen mgr.

*WUKY(FM)— Mar 13, 1941: 91.3 mhz; 100 kw. 750 ft TL: N37 52 45 W84 19 33. Stereo. Hrs open: 24 Univ. of Kentucky, 340 McVey, 40506-0045. Phone: (859) 257-3221. Fax: (859) 257-6291. E-mail: npr.rocks@email.uky.edu Web Site:www.wuky.org Licensee: University of Kentucky. Population served: 50,000 Natl. Network: NPR, PRI, .

Sanchez Law Firm. Wire Svc: AP Format: News, AAA music. News staff: 2.5; News: 62 hrs wkly. Target aud: 25-54. ♦Tom Godell, gen mgr; John Lumagui, opns mgr; Gail Bennett, mktg mgr, mus dir.

WVLK(AM)— October 1947: 590 khz; 5 kw-D, 1 kw-N, DA-2. TL: N38 06 42 W84 34 36. (CP: 1.6 kw-N). Stereo. Hrs open: 24 300 W. Vine St., Suite 3, 40507. Phone: (859) 253-5900. Fax: (859) 253-5940. Web Site:www.wvlkam.com Licensee: Cumulus Licensing Corp. Group owner: Cumulus Media Inc. (acq 7-22-99; grpsl). Population served: 275,400 Natl. Network: CBS, . Rgnl. Network: Ky. Net. Latham & Watkins. Format: News/talk, sports. News staff: 5. Target aud: 25-54. ♦Ken Fearnow, gen mgr; Robert Lindsey, opns mgr & progmg dir.

Lexington-Fayette

WLKT(FM)— July 30, 1992: 104.5 mhz; 50 kw. 492 ft TL: N38 05 54 W84 18 38. Hrs open: 2601 Nicholasville Rd., Lexington, 40503. Phone: (859) 422-1000. Fax: (859) 422-1038.E-mail: info@wlkt.com Web Site:www.wlkt.com Licensee: Citicasters Licenses L.P. Group owner: Clear Channel Communications Inc. (acq 5-4-99; grpsl). Format: Contemp hit. ♦Gene Guinn, gen mgr.

Liberty

WKDO(AM)— November 1963: 1560 khz; 1 kw-D. TL: N37 18 22 W84 55 02. Hrs open: Box 990, 42539. Secondary address: 988 Dry Ridge Rd. 42539. Phone: (606) 787-7331. Fax: (606) 787-2166. Licensee: Radio Station WKDO. (acq 11-27-75). Population served: 2,500 Natl. Network: USA, . Format: Country. Target aud: 18-49. ♦Carlos Wesley, pres, gen mgr, gen sls mgr; David Smith, chief of engrg.

WKDO-FM— January 1977: 98.7 mhz; 25 kw. 239 ft TL: N37 18 22 W84 55 02. Stereo. Hrs open: 16 Dups AM 50% Box 990, 42539. Phone: (606) 787-7331. Fax: (606) 787-2166. Licensee: Radio Station WKDO. Population served: 15,500 News staff: 3; News: 21 hrs wkly. Target aud: 15-35.

London

WFTG(AM)— Sept 1, 1955: 1400 khz; 1 kw-U. TL: N37 08 28 W84 04 45. Hrs open: 24 Box 1988, 40743-0647. Secondary address: 534 Tobacco Rd. 40741. Phone: (606) 864-2148. Fax: (606) 864-0645.E-mail: trgrigsby@broadcasting.net Licensee: F.T.G. Broadcasting Inc. Group owner: Key Broadcasting Inc. (acq 8-5-92; $410,000; 8-24-92). Population served: 43,537 Rgnl. Network: Ky. News Net. Ky. News Net Format: Classic Country. News staff: one. Target aud: 40 plus. ♦Mike Tarter, pres; Trever Grigsby, gen mgr; Travis Stevens, progmg dir; Phillip Fraley, chief of engrg.

WGWM(AM)— Aug 8, 1981: 980 khz; 900 w-D, 109 w-N. TL: N37 10 16 W84 06 39. Hrs open: 24 948 Moriah Church Rd., 40741-7635. Phone: (606) 878-0980. Fax: (606) 878-0980. Licensee: WGWM Broadcasting Inc. (acq 1996; $35,000). Format: Southern gospel. News: 5 hrs wkly. Target aud: 25-54; male/female. ♦Elmer Oakley, gen mgr.

WWEL(FM)— Sept 15, 1970: 103.9 mhz; 3 kw. 190 ft TL: N37 08 28 W84 04 45. Stereo. Hrs open: 24 Box 1988, 40743-1988. Secondary address: 534 Tobacco Rd. 40741. Phone: (606) 864-2148. Fax: (606) 864-0645. Web Site:www.sam1039.com Natl. Network: NBC Radio, . Rgnl. Network: Ky. News Net. Ky. News Net Format: Hot Adult Contemp. News staff: one; News: 21 hrs wkly. Target aud: 18-40. ♦Mike Tarter, pres; Travis Stevens, gen mgr.

WYGE(FM)— 1994: 92.3 mhz; 23.5 kw. Ant 722 ft TL: N37 09 01 W83 59 32. Hrs open: 24 201 E. 2nd St., 40741. Phone: (606) 877-1326. Fax: (606) 864-3702.E-mail: wygeradio@yahoo.com Web Site:www.good-news-outreach.org Licensee: Ethel Huff Broadcasting LLC. Population served: 200,000 Natl. Network: Salem Radio Network, USA, . Format: Relg. ♦Ethel Huff, chmn; Gene Huff, gen mgr.

Louisa

WBTH(AM)—See Williamson WV

WXCC(FM)—See Williamson WV

WZAQ(FM)— May 17, 1991: 92.3 mhz; 4.48 kw. 377 ft TL: N38 10 33 W82 37 39. Hrs open: 112 Madison St., 41230. Phone: (606) 638-9203. Fax: (606) 638-9210. Licensee: Louisa Communications Inc. Format: Country. ♦Harold Britton, pres; Marti Fairchild, gen mgr.

Louisville

WAMZ(FM)— September 1966: 97.5 mhz; 100 kw. Ant 672 ft TL: N38 03 49 W85 43 52. Stereo. Hrs open: 24 4000 #1 Radio Dr., 40218. Phone: (502) 479-2222. Fax: (502) 479-2308.E-mail: info@wamz.com Web Site:www.wamz.com Licensee: CC Licenses LLC. Population served: 1,300,000 Format: Country. ♦Coyote Calhoun, progmg dir.

WDJX(FM)— Aug 1, 1963: 99.7 mhz; 24 kw. 720 ft TL: N38 21 53 W85 50 18. Stereo. Hrs open: 520 S. 4th, Suite 200, 40202. Phone: (502) 625-1220. Fax: (502) 625-1256. Web Site:www.wdjx.com Licensee: MLB-Louisville IV LLC. Group owner: Radio One Inc. (acq 9-12-2007; grpsl). Format: Adult CHR.

WFIA(AM)— March 1947: 900 khz; 1 kw-U. TL: N38 16 12 W85 42 25. Stereo. Hrs open: 24 9960 Corporate Campus Dr., Suite 3600, 40223. Phone: (502) 339-9470. Fax: (502) 423-3139. Web Site:www.salemradiogroup.com Licensee: Salem Media Group LLC. Group owner: Salem Communications Corp. (acq 1-24-2001; $1.75 million). Population served: 1,000,000 Natl. Rep: Salem,. Format: Christian teaching, talk. News: 2 hrs wkly. Target aud: 30 plus; general. ♦Tim Hartlage, gen mgr.

***WFPK(FM)**— Oct 4, 1954: 91.9 mhz; 100 kw. 236 ft TL: N38 14 40 W85 45 27. Stereo. Hrs open: 24 619 S. 4th St., 40202. Phone: (502) 814-6500. Fax: (502) 814-6599.E-mail: dreynolds@louisvillepublicmedia.org Web Site:www.wfpk.org Licensee: Kentucky Public Radio Inc. Population served: 1,300,000 Natl. Network: PRI, NPR, . Format: Alternative. Target aud: 25 plus. ♦Donovan Reynolds, gen mgr, gen sls mgr; Stacy Owen, progmg dir & mus dir.

***WFPL(FM)**— Feb 20, 1950: 89.3 mhz; 21 kw. 774 ft TL: N38 21 55 W85 50 24. Stereo. Hrs open: 24 619 S. 4th St., 40202. Phone: (502) 814-6500. Fax: (502) 814-6599.E-mail: tmundt@louisvillepublicmedia.org Web Site:www.wfpl.org Licensee: Kentucky Public Radio Inc. Population served: 1,300,000 Natl. Network: NPR, PRI, . Format: News/talk. News staff: 3; News: 124 hrs wkly. Target aud: General. ♦Donovan Reynolds, gen mgr; Rick Howlett, progmg dir.

WGTK(AM)— Dec 30, 1933: 970 khz; 5 kw-U, DA-2. TL: N38 19 05 W85 44 39. Stereo. Hrs open: 24 9960 Campus Dr., Suite 3600, 40223. Phone: (502) 339-9470. Fax: (502) 423-3139. Web Site:www.970wgtk.com Licensee: Salem Media of Kentucky Inc. (group owner; (acq 10-4-2000). Population served: 900000 Brooks, Pierce, McLendon, Humphrey & Leonard. Format: News/talk. News staff: one; News: 21 hrs wkly. Target aud: 35 plus; people with most discretionary incomes. ♦Tim Hartlage, gen mgr; CC Matthews, opns mgr.

WHAS(AM)— July 18, 1922: 840 khz; 50 kw-U. TL: N38 15 40 W85 25 43. Stereo. Hrs open: 24 4000 #1 Radio Dr., 40218. Phone: (502) 479-2222. Fax: (502) 479-2308.E-mail: info@whas.com Web Site:www.whas.com Licensee: CC Licenses LLC. (acq 8-86; with co-located FM). Population served: 1,300,000 Natl. Rep: Clear Channel,. Cohn & Marks. Format: News/talk. News staff: 12; News: 14 hrs wkly. Target aud: 25-54. ♦Kevin Hughes, gen mgr; Doug Wethington, stn mgr, gen sls mgr; Kelly Carls, progmg dir; Kirk Wesley, chief of engrg.

WKJK(AM)— November 1948: 1080 khz; 10 kw-D, 1 kw-N, DA-2. TL: N38 18 29 W85 49 45. Hrs open: 24 4000 Radio Drive, 40218. Phone: (502) 479-2222. Fax: (502) 479-2308. Web Site:www.talkradio1080.com Licensee: CC Licenses LLC. Group owner: Clear Channel Communications Inc. (acq 9-13-96; $1 million with intellectual property of WSFR(FM) Corydon, IN) Population served: 942,300 Natl. Network: CBS Radio, . Natl. Rep: Clear Channel,. Format: Talk. Target aud: 35-64; men. ♦Bill Gentry, gen mgr, mktg mgr; Jim Fenn, progmg dir.

WKRD(AM)— 1936: 790 khz; 5 kw-D, 1 kw-N, DA-2. TL: N38 11 34 W85 31 14. Hrs open: 24
Simulcast with WKRD-FM Shelbyville 100%.
4000 #1 Radio Dr., 40218. Phone: (502) 479-2222. Fax: (502) 479-2308.E-mail: jimfenn@clearchannel.com Web Site:www.790wkrd.com Licensee: Clear Channel Broadcasting Licenses Inc. (acq 1996). Natl. Network: Fox Sports, Premiere Radio Networks, . Natl. Rep: Clear Channel,. Format: Sports. News: 2 hrs wkly. Target aud: 25-54. ♦Kevin Hughes, stn mgr & gen sls mgr; Jim Fenn, progmg dir.

WLLV(AM)— June 1940: 1240 khz; 1 kw-U. TL: N38 14 49 W85 42 19. Hrs open: 2001 W. Broadway, 40203. Phone: (502) 776-1240. Fax: (502) 776-1250.E-mail: wlouwllv@aol.com Licensee: Davidson Media Station WLLV Licensee LLC. Group owner: Mortenson Broadcasting Co. (acq 4-12-2006; $2.65 million with WLOU(AM) Louisville). Population served: 361,472 Format: Black gospel. ♦Vivien Ogburn, gen mgr & stn mgr.

WLOU(AM)— 1948: 1350 khz; 5 kw-U, DA-N. TL: N38 13 45 W85 46 47. (CP: 2.2 kw). Hrs open: 2001 W. Broadway, Ste 13, 40203. Phone: (502) 776-1240. Fax: (502) 776-1250.E-mail: wlouwllv@aol.com Licensee: Davidson Media Station WLOU Licensee LLC. Group owner: Mortenson Broadcasting Co. (acq 4-12-2006; $2.65 million with WLLV(AM) Louisville). Population served: 361,472 Natl. Network: American Urban, . Format: Gospel. Target aud: 25-54; mature adults. ♦Vivien Ogburn, stn mgr.

WLUE(FM)— June 7, 1993: 100.5 mhz; 37.4 kw. Ant 554 ft TL: N38 03 49 W85 43 52. Hrs open: 24 4000 #1 Radio Dr., 40218. Phone: (502) 479-2222. Fax: (502) 479-2308.E-mail: louie@louieonline.com Web Site:www.louieonline.com Licensee: Clear Channel Broadcasting Licenses Inc. Group owner: Clear Channel Communications Inc. (acq 9-13-96; $6.9 million with co-located AM). Natl. Rep: Clear Channel,. Format: Adult hits. News: 3 hrs wkly. Target aud: 18-49; general. ♦Bill Gentry, gen mgr & gen sls mgr.

WMJM(FM)—See Jeffersontown

WNDA(AM)—See New Albany, IN

WQKC(AM)—See Jeffersonville, IN

WQMF(FM)—See Jeffersonville, IN

WRKA(FM)— 1974: 103.9 mhz; 1.35 kw. Ant 490 ft TL: N38 15 20 W85 45 28. Stereo. Hrs open: 24 612 4th Street, Suite 100, 40202. Phone: (502) 589-4800. Web Site:www.countrylegends1039.com Licensee: Cox Radio Inc. Group owner: Cox Broadcasting (acq 8-26-99; $1.77 million). Population served: 1,000,000 Natl. Rep: Christal,. Dow, Lohnes & Albertson. Wire Svc: AP Format: Country. News: one hr wkly. Target aud: 25-54; emphasis on 25-44. ♦Todd Schumacher, VP; Amy Torres, gen mgr; Kitty Malone, natl sls mgr; Matt Killion, progmg dir.

WTUV(AM)— Aug 20, 1958: 620 khz; 500 w-U, DA-2. TL: N38 18 59 W85 42 08. Hrs open: 24 4109 Bardstown Rd., 40218. Phone: (502) 583-6200. Phone: (502) 671-8407 . Fax: (502) 473-7500.E-mail: info@bcalienteradio.com Web Site:www.lacalienteradio.com Licensee: Davidson Media Station WTMT Licensee LLC. (acq 6-30-2006; $1 million). Population served: 361,472 Format: Rgnl Mexican. ♦Paul Dendy, gen mgr; Dennis Mendez, progmg dir.

***WUOL(FM)**— Dec 20, 1976: 90.5 mhz; 21 kw. Ant 774 ft TL: N38 21 55 W85 50 24. Stereo. Hrs open: 24 619 S. 4th St., 40202. Phone: (502) 814-6500. Fax: (502) 814-6599.E-mail: dgilliam@louisvillepublicmedia.org Web Site:www.wuol.org Licensee: Kentucky Public Radio Inc. Population served: 2,000,000 Rgnl. Network: Ky. Pub. Format: Class. News: 2 hrs wkly. Target aud: General; those interested in quality music & info. ♦Donovan Reynolds, gen mgr; Daniel Gilliam, progmg dir.

WVEZ(FM)— Apr 1, 1967: 106.9 mhz; 24.5 kw. 670 ft TL: N38 22 20 W85 49 32. Stereo. Hrs open: 612 4th Ave., Suite 100, 40202. Phone: (502) 589-4800. Fax: (502) 583-4820.E-mail: info@lite1069.com Web Site:www.lite1069.com Licensee: Cox Radio Inc. Group owner: Cox Broadcasting (acq 5-99). Population served: 976,800 Dow, Lohnes & Albertson. Format: Adult contemp. Target aud: 24-54; upper-scale, working women. Spec prog: Delilah. ♦Todd Schumacher, VP & gen mgr; Kitty Malone, gen sls mgr; Don Nordin, progmg dir.

WXMA(FM)— October 1964: 102.3 mhz; 3 kw. 300 ft TL: N38 14 37 W85 45 34. Hrs open: 24 520 S. 4th Ave., Suite 200, 40202-2532. Phone: (502) 625-1220. Fax: (502) 625-1258.E-mail: info@wxma.com Web Site:www.themaxfm.com Licensee: MLB-Louisville IV LLC. Group owner: Radio One Inc. (acq 9-12-2007; grpsl). Population served: 361,472 Format: Hot adult contemp. Target aud: 25-49; young adults who enjoy modern/alternative rock. ♦Dale Schaefer, gen mgr.

Lyndon

WQNU(FM)— Oct 19, 1964: 103.1 mhz; 23 kw. Ant 554 ft TL: N38 19 28 W85 33 00. Stereo. Hrs open: 24 612 4th Street, Suite 100, Louisville, 40202. Phone: (502) 589-4800. Web Site:newcountryq1031.com Licensee: Cox Radio Inc. Group owner: Cox Broadcasting Population served: 976,800 Natl. Rep: Christal,. Dow, Lohnes & Albertson. Wire Svc: AP Format: Country. Target aud: 35-54. ♦Matt Killion, progmg dir.

Madisonville

WFMW(AM)— January 1947: 730 khz; 500 w-D, 215 w-N. TL: N37 21 03 W87 29 25. Stereo. Hrs open: 24 Box 338, 42431. Secondary address: 2380 N. Main St. 42431. Phone: (270) 821-4096. Fax: (270) 821-5954.E-mail: wfmw@wfmw.net Web Site:www.wfmw.net Licensee:

Sound Broadcasters Inc. Population served: 50,000 Natl. Network: CNN Radio, . Natl. Rep: Rgnl Reps,. Wire Svc: AP Format: C&W. News staff: one; News: 13 hrs wkly. Target aud: 18 plus. ♦Robert T. Kelley, pres, gen mgr; Danny Koeber, progmg dir, farm dir, women's int ed, disc jockey; Chris Gardener, news dir; Chris Meyers, chief of engrg; Erin Grant, disc jockey.

***WKMD(FM)**—Not on air, target date: unknown: 90.9 mhz; 25 kw. Ant 403 ft TL: N37 21 47 W87 30 56. Hrs open: Box 2018, University Station, Murray, 42071. Phone: (270) 809-4359. Fax: (270) 809-4667. Web Site:www.wkms.org Licensee: Board of Regents, Murray State University. ♦Kate Lochte, stn mgr.

WKTG(FM)— Apr 19, 1949: 93.9 mhz; 50 kw. 584 ft TL: N37 21 05 W87 29 25. Stereo. Hrs open: 24 Prog sep from AM Box 338, 42431. Secondary address: 2380 N. Main St. 42431. Phone: (270) 821-1156.E-mail: wktg@wktg.com Web Site:www.wktg.com Population served: 500,000 Natl. Network: USA, . Pepper & Corazzini. Format: Rock/AOR. News staff: one; News: 3 hrs wkly. Target aud: 20-45. ♦Robert T. Kelley, stn mgr; Bill McClone, progmg dir; Erin Grant, disc jockey.

***WSOF-FM**— February 1977: 89.9 mhz; 39.4 kw. 282 ft TL: N37 19 11 W87 30 57. Stereo. Hrs open: Box 1246, 1415 Island Ford Rd., 42431. Phone: (270) 825-3004.E-mail: comments@wsof.org Web Site:www.wsof.org Licensee: Temple Broadcasting Co. Natl. Network: USA, . Format: Christian educ. Target aud: General; Christian. ♦Gary Hall, gen mgr.

WTTL(AM)— Sept 16, 1956: 1310 khz; 1.5 kw-D, 500 w-N, DA-N. TL: N37 20 12 W87 32 41. Hrs open: 24 Box 1310, 42431. Secondary address: 265 S. Main St. 42431. Phone: (270) 821-1310. Fax: (270) 825-3260. Licensee: Madisonville CBC Inc. Group owner: Commonwealth Broadcasting Corp. (acq 2-8-2000; $1.31 million with co-located FM). Population served: 80,000 Format: News, talk, sports. Target aud: 25-54. ♦Lee Ann Oliver, gen sls mgr; Tom Rogers, gen mgr & progmg dir; Stephanie Vandygraiff, traf mgr.

WYMV(FM)— Sept 7, 1992: 106.9 mhz; 2 kw. 528 ft TL: N37 22 51 W87 28 04. Stereo. Hrs open: 24 Box 1310, 42431. Secondary address: 265 S. Main St. 42431. Phone: (270) 825-1079. Fax: (270) 825-3260. Natl. Network: ABC, Jones Radio Networks, . Format: Adult contemp. Target aud: 25-34.

Manchester

WKLB(AM)— Sept 26, 1981: 1290 khz; 50 kw-U. TL: N37 09 29 W83 47 06. Stereo. Hrs open: 24 Box 448, 40962. Secondary address: 106 Richmond Rd. 40962. Phone: (606) 598-2445. Fax: (606) 598-2653.E-mail: wklb1stchoice@yahoo.com Licensee: Barker Broadcasting Co. Group owner: Larry Barker (acq 1981). Population served: 500,000 Rgnl. Network: Ky. Net. Natl. Rep: Rgnl Reps,. Rgnl rep: Barker Broadcasting Robert Olender. Format: Country. News staff: one; News: 8 hrs wkly. Target aud: 24-65; working people. ♦Larry Barker, pres & gen mgr.

WTBK(FM)— October 1989: 105.7 mhz; 7.5 kw. 462 ft TL: N37 08 57 W83 45 09. Stereo. Hrs open: 19 Box 453, 40962. Secondary address: 107 Dickerson St. 40962. Phone: (606) 598-7588. Fax: (606) 598-7598.E-mail: wtbkradio@yahoo.com Licensee: Manchester Communications Inc. (acq 3-24-89). Natl. Network: Westwood One, ABC, . Format: Classic rock. News staff: one; News: 10 hrs wkly. Target aud: General; 18 plus in the morning, 16-45 at night. Spec prog: Talk 8 hrs wkly. ♦Tim Finley, gen mgr.

WWLT(FM)— Aug 9, 1967: 103.1 mhz; 2.25 kw. Ant 538 ft TL: N37 04 30 W83 49 14. Stereo. Hrs open: 24 8686 Michael Ln., Fairfield, OH, 45014. Phone: (513) 829-7700. Web Site:www.klove.com Licensee: Wilderness Hills Broadcasting Co. Group owner: Vernon R. Baldwin Inc. (acq 1956). Population served: 100,000 Natl. Network: K-Love, . Format: Contemp Christian. ♦Vernon R. Baldwin, pres.

WWXL(AM)— 1956: 1450 khz; 1 kw-U. TL: N37 09 04 W83 45 45. Hrs open: 24 Hours 103 Third St., 40962. Phone: (606) 598-9995. Fax: (606) 598-9995. Licensee: Juanita H. Nolan (acq 1-3-2004). Population served: 18,600 Format: Oldies. News staff: one; News: 3 hrs wkly. Target aud: 35-54; programmed for adults 35-54. ♦Jonathan Dobson, gen mgr.

Mannsville

WVLC(FM)— Dec 31, 1994: 99.9 mhz; 11 kw. 492 ft TL: N37 10 04 W85 11 26. Stereo. Hrs open: 24 Box 4190, Campbellsville, 42719. Secondary address: 101 East Main St., Campbellsville 42719. Phone: (270) 789-4998. Fax: (270) 789-4584.E-mail: bigdawg@wvlc.com Web Site:www.wvlc.com Licensee: Patricia Rodgers. Natl. Network: CNN Radio, . Ky. News Net Format: Country. News staff: one. Target aud: General. ♦Jan Royse, gen mgr.

Marion

WMJL(AM)— July 10, 1968: 1500 khz; 250 w-D. TL: N37 20 11 W88 04 12. Stereo. Hrs open: 6 AM-sunset Box 68, 42064. Secondary address: 251 Club Dr. 42064. Phone: (270) 965-2271. Licensee: Joe Myers Production Inc. Population served: 20,000 Rgnl. Network: Ky. Net. Natl. Rep: Rgnl Reps,. News staff: one; News: 12 hrs wkly. Target aud: General. ♦Joe Myers, pres, gen mgr, gen sls mgr, progmg dir & chief of engrg.

WMJL-FM— June 1993: 102.7 mhz; 6 kw. 328 ft TL: N37 20 16 W88 04 03. Stereo. Hrs open: 24 Dups AM 50% Box 68, 42064. Phone: (270) 965-2271. Licensee: Joe Myers Production Inc. (Acq 3-12-91; 4-1-91). Format: Oldies.

Mayfield

WNGO(AM)— Jan 7, 1947: 1320 khz; 1 kw-D, 97 w-N. TL: N36 45 37 W88 38 20. Hrs open: 5 AM-10 PM
Rebroadcasts WKYX(AM) Paducah 90%.
Box 2397, Paducah, 42002. Secondary address: 6000 Bristol Dr., Paducah 42003. Phone: (270) 554-8255. Fax: (270) 554-5468. Web Site:www.wkyx.com Licensee: Bristol Broadcasting Co. Inc. (group owner; acq 2-20-2004; grpsl). Population served: 33,000 Rgnl. Network: Ky. Agri. Mullin, Rhyne, Emmons & Topel. Format: News/talk. News staff: one; News: 12 hrs wkly. Target aud: 24-54. ♦Gary Morse, gen mgr; Jamie Futrell, gen sls mgr & prom dir; Greg Dunker, progmg dir; Greg Walker, chief of engrg.

WQQR(FM)— Nov 2, 1955: 94.7 mhz; 32 kw. Ant 443 ft TL: N36 45 58 W88 38 50. (CP: COL Clinton. 50 kw, ant 472 ft. TL: N36 45 19 W88 39 36.6). Stereo. Hrs open: 24 P.O. Box 2397, Paducah, 42002. Secondary address: 6000 Bristol Drive, Paducah 42003. Phone: (270) 554-8255. Fax: (270) 554-5468. Web Site:www.wqqr.com Licensee: Bristol Broadcasting Co. Inc. Rgnl rep: Rgnl Reps. Format: Classic rock. News staff: one. Target aud: 25 plus. ♦Nick Black, progmg dir.

WYMC(AM)— Oct 18, 1976: 1430 khz; 1 kw-U, DA-N. TL: N36 47 12 W88 39 16. Hrs open: 24 Box V, 42066. Secondary address: 197 WYMC Rd. 42066. Phone: (270) 247-1430. Fax: (270) 247-1825.E-mail: radio@wymcradio.com Licensee: JDM Communications Inc. (acq 12-31-90; $277,649; 1-21-91). Population served: 38,000 Wiley, Rein & Fielding. Format: MOR. News staff: one. Target aud: 35-64; affluent, business oriented. ♦Jim Moore, gen mgr.

Maysville

WFTM(AM)— Jan 1, 1948: 1240 khz; 1 kw-U. TL: N38 38 10 W83 45 38. Hrs open: 6 AM-11 PM Box 100, 41056. Phone: (606) 564-3361. Fax: (606) 564-4291.E-mail: wftmnews@maysvilleky.net Licensee: Standard Tobacco Co. Population served: 100,000 Natl. Rep: Keystone (unwired net), Rgnl Reps,. Format: Music of Your Life. News staff: one; News: 10 hrs wkly. Target aud: 50-70. Spec prog: Farm 6 hrs, gospel 5 hrs, relg 5 hrs wkly. ♦J.A. Finch, pres; Jeff Cracraft, VP; Doug McGill, gen mgr, gen sls mgr, chief of engrg; Dave Gray, news dir.

WFTM-FM— Oct 26, 1965: 95.9 mhz; 3 kw. 207 ft TL: N38 38 04 W83 46 48. Stereo. Hrs open: 24 Dups AM 30% Box 100, 41056. Phone: (606) 564-3361. Fax: (606) 564-4291.E-mail: wftmsales@maysvilleky.net Web Site:soft96.com Population served: 165,000 Natl. Network: AP Radio, . Format: Soft hits. News staff: one. Target aud: 18-55. ♦Danny Weddle, sls dir; Philip Hay, mus dir & sls.

McDaniels

***WBFI(FM)**— Sept 7, 1987: 91.5 mhz; 5 kw. Ant 328 ft TL: N37 36 06 W86 22 13. Stereo. Hrs open: 24 Box 2, 40152. Phone: (270) 257-2689. Phone: (888) 333-9234. Fax: (270) 257-8344. Web Site:www.wbfiradio.com Licensee: Bethel Fellowship Inc. Population served: 20,000 Natl. Network: USA, . Reddy, Begley & McCormick. Format: Relg, educ, news/talk. News staff: 20 hrs wkly. Target aud: General; Christians. ♦Ronald W. Miller, pres; Roger Goostree, gen mgr, opns mgr; Daryl Cook, progmg dir.

McKee

WWAG(FM)— Nov 1, 1990: 107.9 mhz; 3.9 kw. 400 ft TL: N37 23 39 W83 54 32. Hrs open: 24 1680 State Rd. 1071, Tyner, 40486-9543. Phone: (606) 287-9924. Licensee: Dandy Broadcasting Inc. (acq 1994). Population served: 2000 Natl. Network: ABC, . Natl. Rep: Rgnl Reps,. Lauren A. Colby. Format: Country. News staff: one; News: 10 hrs wkly. Target aud: General. Spec prog: Bluegrass 9 hrs wkly. ♦Dan Brockman, pres; Sherry Brockman, gen mgr.

Middlesboro

WFXY(AM)— Mar 1, 1969: 1490 khz; 1 kw-U. TL: N36 36 47 W83 42 34. Stereo. Hrs open: 24 Box 999, 40965. Secondary address: 2118 Cumberland Ave. 40965. Phone: (606) 248-1550. Fax: (606) 248-6397.E-mail: brian@1490wfxy.com Web Site:1490wfxy.com Licensee: Country-Wide Broadcasters Inc. (acq 4-18-2006; with WANO(AM) Pineville). Population served: 120,000 Natl. Network: Jones Radio Networks, . Rgnl. Network: Ky. Net., Tenn. Radio Net. Natl. Rep: Rgnl Reps,. Tenn. Radio Net. Bechtel & Cole. Format: Hot adult contemp. News staff: 2; News: 20 hrs wkly. Target aud: 25-54; community-oriented. Spec prog: Black 2 hrs, gospel 3 hrs, relg 3 hrs wkly. ♦Brian O'Brien, gen mgr.

WMIK(AM)— Nov 15, 1948: 560 khz; 500 w-D, 88 w-N. TL: N36 37 38 W83 42 52. (CP: 2.5 kw-D). Hrs open: Box 608, 40965. Secondary address: N. 19th St. 40965. Phone: (606) 248-5842. Fax: (606) 248-7660.E-mail: radiog2@bellsouth.net Licensee: Gateway Broadcasting Inc. Population served: 11,844 Format: Southern gospel. Spec prog: Farm one hr, gospel 2 hrs wkly. ♦Roy Shotten, gen mgr & progmg dir; Chuck Owens, chief of engrg.

WMIK-FM— June 4, 1971: 92.7 mhz; 130 w. 1,438 ft TL: N36 35 50 W83 47 49. Stereo. Hrs open: Prog sep from AM Box 608, 40965. Phone: (606) 248-5842. Fax: (606) 248-7660.E-mail: radiog2@bellsouth.net Licensee: Gateway Broadcasting Inc. Population served: 11,844 Rgnl. Network: Tenn. Radio Net., Ky. Net. Tenn. Radio Net. Format: Christian.

Midway

WBTF(FM)— 1998: 107.9 mhz; 6 kw. 328 ft TL: N38 11 41 W84 38 25. Stereo. Hrs open: 401 W. Main, Suite 301, Lexington, 40507. Phone: (859) 233-1515. Fax: (859) 233-1517. Web Site:www.1079thebeat.com Licensee: L.M. Communications of Kentucky L.L.C. Group owner: L.M. Communications Inc. (acq 4-10-01). Natl. Rep: Katz Radio,. Format: Urban contemp, CHR. News: 24 hrs wkly. Target aud: 18-49; adults. ♦Lynn Martin, pres; James MacFarlane, gen mgr; James McFarlane, mktg mgr.

Monticello

WFLW(AM)— May 19, 1955: 1360 khz; 1 kw-D. TL: N36 49 30 W84 51 20. Hrs open: 6 AM-6 PM Box 696, 150 Worsham Ln., 42633. Phone: (606) 348-8427. Phone: (606) 348-7083.E-mail: stephen@wkym.com Web Site:wflw.com Licensee: Stephen Staples Jr. (acq 11-9-94; with co-located FM; 1-2-95). Population served: 20,000 Rgnl. Network: Ky. Net. Natl. Rep: Rgnl Reps,. Format: Gospel. News staff: one. Target aud: General. Spec prog: Farm 5 hrs, news/talk 10 hrs wkly. ♦Stephen Staples Jr., gen mgr; Debbie Brown, mus dir; Bruce Correll, chief of engrg.

WKYM(FM)— Dec 19, 1965: 101.7 mhz; 1.75 kw. 617 ft TL: N36 48 08 W84 50 51. Stereo. Hrs open: 24 Prog sep from AM Box696, 150 Worsham Ln., 42633. Phone: (606) 348-8427. Phone: (606) 348-7083.E-mail: wkymmail@wkym.com Web Site:www.wkym.com Population served: 80,000 Natl. Rep: Rgnl Reps,. Format: Classic rock. Target aud: 18-50; baby boomers. ♦Stephen Staples Jr., progmg dir.

WMKZ(FM)— June 1, 1990: 93.1 mhz; 2.15 kw. 558 ft TL: N36 48 29 W84 50 46. Stereo. Hrs open: 24 183 Old Hwy. 90, 42633. Phone: (606) 348-3393. Fax: (606) 348-3330.E-mail: studio@z93cantry.com Web Site:www.wmkz.com Licensee: Monticello-Wayne County Media Inc. Natl. Network: USA, . Format: Country. News: 9 hrs wkly. Target aud: 24-55; general. ♦Joel Catron, gen mgr.

Morehead

***WBMK(FM)**— 2002: 88.5 mhz; 600 w. Ant 522 ft TL: N38 10 38 W83 24 24. Hrs open: Box 3206, Tupelo, MS, 38803. Phone: (662) 844-8888. Fax: (666) 842-6791.E-mail: info@afr.net Web Site:www.afr.net Licensee: American Family Association. Group owner: American Family Radio (acq 11-26-99). Format: Christian. ♦Marvin Sanders, gen mgr.

WIVY(FM)— July 1, 1994: 96.3 mhz; 2.15 kw. Ant 518 ft TL: N38 10 33 W83 24 28. Stereo. Hrs open: 24 Box 963, 40351. Secondary address: 123 East First St. 40351. Phone: (606) 784-9966. Fax: (606) 674-6700.E-mail: feedback@wivyradio.com Web Site:www.wivyradio.com Licensee: Gateway Radio Works Inc. (group owner). Population served: 150,000 Natl. Network: ABC, . William Silva. Format: Unforgettable favorites. News staff: 2. Target aud: 25 plus; affluent, well educ, mature adult, higher spendable income. ♦Hays McMakin, pres; Jeff Ray, gen mgr, stn mgr; Tom McMakin, opns mgr; Carol Lynn, prom dir; Becky Black, progmg dir; Doug Walker, chief of engrg.

WKYN(FM)—See Owingsville

*WMKY(FM)— June 1965: 90.3 mhz; 37 kw. Ant 895 ft TL: N38 10 38 W83 24 18. Stereo. Hrs open: 24 150 University Blvd., Morehead State Univ., 40351. Phone: (606) 783-2001. Fax: (606) 783-2335.E-mail: wmky@moreheadstate.edu Web Site:www.msuradio.com Licensee: Morehead State University. Population served: 155,317 Natl. Network: PRI, NPR, . Rgnl. Network: Ky. News Net, Ky. Pub. Ky. News Net Wire Svc: AP Format: Var. News staff: 10. Target aud: 25-54. ◆Paul W. Hitchcock, gen mgr & stn mgr; Greg Jenkins, opns dir; Chuck Mraz, news dir.

WMOR(AM)— Feb 18, 1955: 1330 khz; 570 w-D. TL: N38 10 56 W83 26 56. Hrs open: Box 338, 129 College St., West Liberty, 41472. Phone: (606) 743-3145. Fax: (606) 743-9557. Licensee: Morgan County Industries Inc. (group owner; acq 3-16-99; $300,000 with co-located FM). Population served: 15,000 Natl. Network: Moody, . Format: Country. ◆C.C. Smith, pres, pres & gen mgr.

WMOR-FM— June 15, 1965: 106.1 mhz; 8 kw. 348 ft TL: N38 10 56 W83 26 56. Hrs open: Prog sep from AM Box 338, 129 College St., West Liberty, 41472. Phone: (606) 743-3145. Fax: (606) 743-9557. Licensee: Morgan County Industries Inc. Population served: 20,000 Format: Adult contemp.

Morganfield

*WBOO(FM)—Not on air, target date: unknown: 90.3 mhz; 1 kw vert. Ant 108 ft TL: N37 36 41.8 W87 57 19.1. Hrs open: 15 Wood St., Greenfield, IN, 46140. Phone: (317) 467-1062. Licensee: Electronic Applications Radio Service Inc. ◆Patrick Diemer, pres.

*WEUC(FM)— Dec 29, 2008: 88.7 mhz; 2.2 kw vert. Ant 269 ft TL: N37 44 09 W87 59 45. Hrs open: 218 Jim Veatch Rd., 42437. Phone: (270) 389-4281. Fax: (270) 389-3581. Licensee: Saint Ann Radio Group Inc. (acq 7-25-2008; $16,000 for CP). Natl. Network: EWTN Radio, . Format: Catholic. ◆Gerald H. Baker, pres.

*WKVN(FM)— Aug 8, 1967: 95.3 mhz; 25 kw. Ant 269 ft TL: N37 46 38 W87 37 26. Hrs open: 2351 Sunset Blvd., Suite 170-218, Rocklin, CA, 95765. Phone: (916) 251-1600. Fax: (916) 251-1650. Web Site:www.klove.com Jones Licensee: Educational Media Foundation. (acq 1-21-2009). Population served: 50,000 Natl. Network: K-Love, . Rgnl. Network: Ky. News Net. Davis Wright Tremaine LLP. Format: Contemp Christian. Target aud: 25-64; general. ◆Mike Novak, CEO.

WMSK(AM)— Nov 21, 1960: 1550 khz; 250 w-D. TL: N37 40 00 W87 55 40. Hrs open: 24 Box 369, 42437. Secondary address: 1339 US 60 W. 42437. Phone: (270) 389-1550. Fax: (270) 389-1553.E-mail: wmsk@bellsouth.net Jones U.S. Country Licensee: Henson Media Inc. (acq 9-13-2007; $145,000). Population served: 50000 Natl. Network: Jones Radio Networks, . Natl. Rep: Rgnl Reps,. Ky. News Net Womble, Carlyle, Sandridge & Rice. Wire Svc: AP Format: Relg, country. News: 20 hrs wkly. Target aud: General; adults 25-64. ◆Edward Henson, pres; John Robinson, gen mgr, gen sls mgr, adv VP, progmg dir; Don Sheridan, sls VP, news dir; Rhonda Gibson, traf mgr; Bob Hite, edit mgr.

Morgantown

WLBQ(AM)— 1976: 1570 khz; 1 kw-D, 150 w-N. TL: N37 14 10 W86 42 29. (CP: TL: N37 13 09 W86 41 21). Hrs open: 6 AM-10 PM Box 130, 42261. Phone: (270) 526-3321. Fax: (270) 526-5393.E-mail: info@wlbqam.com Web Site:www.wlbqam.com Licensee: Butler County Broadcasting Co. Population served: 11,000 Natl. Network: ABC, . Rgnl. Network: Ky. Net. Format: Country. News staff: one; News: 8 hrs wkly. Target aud: General; residents of Morgantown & Butler County, KY. ◆Charles Black, pres; Jan Embry, VP; Howard Phelps, stn mgr.

WWKN(FM)—Not on air, target date: unknown: 99.1 mhz; 6 kw. Ant 184 ft TL: N37 17 38 W86 44 30. Hrs open: 8226 Douglas Ave., Suite 627, Dallas, TX, 75225. Phone: (469) 619-1001. Licensee: Independence Media Holdings LLC. ◆David Jacobs, CEO.

Mt. Sterling

*WAXG(FM)— 1998: 88.1 mhz; 300 w. 174 ft TL: N38 03 39 W83 57 20. Hrs open: Box 2440, American Family Radio, Tupelo, MS, 38803. Phone: (662) 844-8888. Fax: (662) 842-6791. Web Site:www.afr.net Licensee: American Family Association. Group owner: American Family Radio Format: Relg. ◆Marvin Sanders, gen mgr.

WKYN(FM)—See Owingsville

WMKJ(FM)— May 28, 1968: 105.5 mhz; 3 kw. 300 ft TL: N38 05 36 W83 56 39. Stereo. Hrs open: 2601 Nicholasville Rd., Lexington, 40503-3307. Phone: (859) 422-1000. Fax: (859) 422-1038.E-mail: info@wmkj.com Web Site:www.wmkj.com Licensee: Aloha Station Trust LLC Group owner: Clear Channel Communications Inc. (acq 7-30-2008; grpsl). Population served: 28,000 Format: Oldies. ◆Gene Guinn, gen mgr.

WMST(AM)— Oct 17, 1957: 1150 khz; 2.5 kw-D, 53 w-N. TL: N38 02 41 W83 54 05. Hrs open: 24 22 West Main, 40353. Phone: (859) 498-5608. Fax: (859) 498-7930.E-mail: feedback@wmstradio.com Web Site:www.wmstradio.com Licensee: Gateway Radio Works Inc. (group owner; acq 1-1-00). Population served: 165,000 Natl. Network: CBS Radio, . Rgnl. Network: Ky. Net. Natl. Rep: Rgnl Reps,. William Silva. Format: Timeless favorites, news/talk. News staff: one; News: 37 hrs wkly. Target aud: 25 plus; affluent, mature adult, high spendalbe income, well educated. Spec prog: Farm 2 hrs wkly. ◆Hays McMakin, pres, chief of engrg; Jeff Ray, VP; Vernice Taylor, stn mgr; Frances Denny, opns mgr; Tom Byron, prom dir; Dan Manley, news dir.

Mt. Vernon

WRVK(AM)— April 30, 1957: 1460 khz; 500 w-D. TL: N37 23 49 W84 19 45. Hrs open: 6 AM-9 PM Box 7, Renfro Valley, 40473. Phone: (606) 256-2146. Fax: (606) 256-9146.E-mail: manager@wrvk1460.com Web Site:www.wrvk1460.com Licensee: Saylor Broadcasting Inc. (acq 2-1-02). Population served: 35,000 Format: Classic country, country gospel. Target aud: General. ◆Charles W. Saylor, pres; Charles Saylor, gen mgr; Charles Napier, sls VP, gen sls mgr.

Mt. Washington

WLCR(AM)— Oct 29, 1955: 1040 khz; 1.5 kw-D. TL: N38 00 11 W85 40 51. Stereo. Hrs open: 3600 Goldsmith Ln., Louisville, 40220. Phone: (502) 451-9527. Fax: (502) 451-9527.E-mail: wlcr@wlcr.net Web Site:www.wlcr.net Licensee: LCR Partners L.P. (acq 1999; $162,500). Population served: 1,000,000 Format: Relg. Target aud: General; Those interested in the existance of God. ◆Vince Heuser, gen mgr.

Munfordville

WCLU-FM— Aug 1, 1964: 102.3 mhz; 3 kw. 99 ft TL: N37 16 30 W85 55 00. Hrs open: Box 1628, Glasgow, 42142. Phone: (270) 651-9149. Fax: (270) 651-9222.E-mail: info@wcluradio.co Web Site:www.wcluradio.com Licensee: Royse Radio Inc. (acq 3-9-98; $225,000 with co-located AM). Format: Adult contemp. ◆Henry Royse, pres & gen mgr.

WLOC(AM)— February 1993: 1150 khz; 1 kw-D, 61 w-N. TL: N37 16 30 W85 55 00. Hrs open: 24 P.O. Box 98, Horse Cave, 42749. Secondary address: 1130 South Dixie , Horse Cave 42749. Phone: (270) 786-4400. Fax: (270) 786-4402.E-mail: wloc@scrtc.com Web Site:www.wloconline.com Licensee: Forbis Communications Inc. (acq 12-5-2003; $120,000). Population served: 6,000 Format: Country, gospel. Target aud: 25 plus; serve entire area. ◆DeWayne Forbis, pres; Dewayne Forbis, gen mgr, gen sls mgr; Chris Jessie, progmg dir; Joe Berry, news dir.

Murray

WFGS(FM)— June 23, 1967: 103.7 mhz; 100 kw. 659 ft TL: N36 32 58 W88 19 52. Stereo. Hrs open: 24 Prog sep from AM 1500 Diuguid Dr., 42071. Phone: (270) 753-2400. Fax: (270) 753-9434. Web Site:www.froggy103.com Licensee: Forever Communications Inc. Population served: 800,000 Natl. Network: Westwood One, . Format: Country. News staff: one; News: 4 hrs wkly. Target aud: 18-45. ◆Jay Crockett, stn mgr & progmg dir.

*WKMS-FM— May 11, 1970: 91.3 mhz; 100 kw. 602 ft TL: N36 55 18 W88 05 50. Stereo. Hrs open: 24 Box 2018, University Stn., 42071. Phone: (800) 599-4737. Phone: (270) 809-4359. Fax: (270) 809-4667.E-mail: wkms@murraystate.edu Web Site:www.wkms.org Licensee: Board of Regents, Murray State University. Population served: 110,250 Natl. Network: NPR, PRI, . Don Martin. Wire Svc: AP Format: News, div. News staff: 2; News: 82 hrs wkly. Target aud: 35 plus; life long learners. Spec prog: Class 15 hrs; folk & bluegrass 3 hrs, AAA 3 hrs, urban contemp 3 hrs wkly. ◆Kate Lochte, stn mgr; Tracy Ross, opns mgr; Ronda Gibson, dev dir, dev mgr; Allen Fowler, prom mgr, chief of engrg; Mark Welch, progmg dir, mus dir; Chad Lampe, news dir.

WNBS(AM)— July 1948: 1340 khz; 1 kw-U. TL: N36 37 42 W88 18 04. Hrs open: 24 1500 Diuguid Dr., 42071-1669. Phone: (270) 753-2400. Fax: (270) 753-9434. Licensee: Forever Communications Inc. (group owner; acq 12-31-02; grpsl). Population served: 35,000 Natl. Network: ESPN Radio, CBS Radio, . Ky. News Net Rgnl rep:

Rgnl Reps. Format: News, talk, sports. News staff: one; News: 10 hrs wkly. Target aud: 25-55. ◆Debbie Howard, gen mgr; Candi Freeland, news dir; Neal Bradley, progmg dir & sports cmtr.

WOFC(AM)— Sept 12, 1978: 1130 khz; 1.5 kw-D. TL: N36 38 08 W88 19 10. Hrs open: 24 1500 Diuguid Dr., 42071. Phone: (270) 753-2400. Fax: (270) 753-9434. Web Site:www.1130theoffice.com Licensee: Forever Communications Inc. (group owner; (acq 12-31-2002; grpsl). Population served: 200,000 Natl. Network: ESPN Radio, . Rgnl. Network: Ky. Net., Ky. Agri. Rgnl rep: Rgnl reps. Format: Sports. ◆Scott Swalls, gen mgr; Mary Ellen Smith, gen sls mgr; Neal Bradley, progmg dir; Adam Bittel, chief of engrg.

Neon

WGCK(AM)— Aug 31, 1956: 1480 khz; 5 kw-D. TL: N37 11 54 W82 42 42. Hrs open: 12 486 Lakeside Dr., Jenkins, 41537. Phone: (606) 634-9430. Licensee: Letcher County Broadcasting Inc. (acq 2-7-2007; $30,000). Population served: 150,000 Format: Relg. Target aud: 24-60; general. ◆Ernestine Kincer, pres; G.C. Kincer, gen mgr.

Newburg

WDRD(AM)— 1992: 680 khz; 1.3 kw-D, 450 w-N, DA-2. TL: N38 05 31 W85 40 56. Hrs open: 24 11700 Commonwealth Dr., Suite 800, Louisville, 40299. Phone: (502) 240-0602. Fax: (502) 240-0940.E-mail: john.salzman@disney.com Web Site:www.radiodisney.com Licensee: Radio Disney Group LLC. Group owner: ABC Inc. (acq 2-14-02; $1.92 million). Format: Family hits. Target aud: Age 25-44 mothers of children; Mothers of children younger than 15. ◆John Salzman, gen mgr & stn mgr.

Newport

WNOP(AM)— Aug 21, 1948: 740 khz; 2.5 kw-D, 30 w-N, DA-2. TL: N39 05 41 W84 34 59. Stereo. Hrs open: 24 5440 Moeller Ave., Norwood, OH, 45212. Phone: (513) 731-7740. Fax: (513) 731-6465.E-mail: info@sacredheartradio.com Web Site:www.sacredheartradio.com Licensee: Sacred Heart Radio, Inc. (acq 9-10-01). Format: Catholic talk. ◆Bill Levitt, stn mgr.

Nicholasville

WCGW(AM)— Sept 15, 1986: 770 khz; 1 kw-D. TL: N37 53 07 W84 31 46. Stereo. Hrs open: 501 Darby Creek #62, Lexington, 40509. Phone: (859) 264-9700. Fax: (859) 264-9705. Web Site:www.wcgwam.com Licensee: Christian Broadcasting System Ltd. (group owner) (acq 7-1-2006; grpsl). Population served: 988,000 Natl. Network: USA, . Format: Southern gospel. Target aud: 25-54; above average in educ, family size, income. ◆Benson Gregory, gen mgr & stn mgr.

WLRT(AM)— December 1962: 1250 khz; 500 w-D, 59 w-N. TL: N37 54 18 W84 33 25. Hrs open: 24 501 Darby Creek #62, Lexington, 40509. Phone: (859) 264-9700. Fax: (859) 264-9705. Licensee: Christian Broadcasting System Ltd. Group owner: Mortenson Broadcasting Co. (acq 7-1-2006; grpsl). Population served: 350,000 Format: News/talk. ◆Jonathon R. Yinger, pres; Benson Gregory, gen mgr.

WLTO(FM)— Aug 29, 1988: 102.5 mhz; 2 kw. Ant 400 ft TL: N37 49 52 W84 30 18. Stereo. Hrs open: 24 300 W. Vine St., Suite 3, Lexington, 40507. Phone: (859) 253-5900. Fax: (859) 253-5940. Licensee: Cumulus Licensing Corp. Group owner: Cumulus Media Inc. (acq 7-22-99; grpsl). Format: Top-40. ◆Ken Fearnow, gen mgr.

North Corbin

WKFC(FM)— 2008: 101.9 mhz; 6 kw. Ant 328 ft TL: N37 02 09 W84 05 05. Hrs open: 1100 S. Main St., London, 40741-1529. Phone: (606) 878-1600. Fax: (606) 878-1116. Web Site:www.wkfcradio.com Licensee: Radioactive LLC. Format: Var. ◆Benjamin L. Homel, pres; Dave Colvin, gen mgr & opns mgr.

Oak Grove

WEGI-FM— Aug 31, 1964: 94.3 mhz; 6 kw. Ant 256 ft TL: N36 38 28 W87 26 01. Stereo. Hrs open: 24 1640 Old Russellville Pike, Clarksburg, TN, 37043. Phone: (931) 648-7720. Fax: (931) 648-7769. Web Site:eagle943.com Licensee: Saga Communications of Tuckessee LLC. Group owner: Saga Communications Inc. (acq 10-4-2002; $1.5 million with co-located AM). Population served: 85,000 Format: Classic hits. News staff: one; News: 5 hrs wkly. Target aud: 25-54. ◆Katie Gambill, gen mgr; Scott Chase, opns dir; J.T. Daniels, progmg dir.

Okolona

***WJIE-FM**— Jan 1, 1988: 88.5 mhz; 24.5 kw. 623 ft TL: N38 01 59 W85 45 16. Stereo. Hrs open: 24 Box 197309, Louisville, 40259. Secondary address: 5400 Minors Ln. , Louisville 40219. Phone: (502) 968-1220. Fax: (502) 962-3143. Web Site:www.wjie.org Licensee: Evangel Schools Inc. Population served: 900000 Natl. Network: Moody, . Pepper & Corazzini. Format: Contemp christian music. News: 7 hrs wkly. Target aud: 25-49; Christian adults. ♦Jim Fraser, gen mgr.

Owensboro

WBKR(FM)— 1948: 92.5 mhz; 91 kw. 1,049 ft TL: N37 36 29 W87 03 15. (CP: 96 kw, ant 1,000 ft. TL: N37 46 20 W87 21 27). Stereo. Hrs open: 24 Prog sep from AM 3301 Frederica St., Owensboro, 42301-6082. Phone: (270) 683-1558. Fax: (270) 683-2128.E-mail: info@wbkr.com Web Site:wbkr.com Licensee: Regent Broadcasting of Evansville/Owensboro Inc. Population served: 250,000 Format: Country. News staff: 2. Target aud: 25-54. Spec prog: Farm 2 hrs wkly. ♦Moon Mullins, progmg dir; Dave Spenser, mus dir; Cathy Carton, news dir; Rick Crago, engrg mgr; Michael Owns, traf mgr.

***WJVK(FM)**— 2004: 91.7 mhz; 100 w. Ant 174 ft TL: N37 44 48 W87 06 58. Stereo. Hrs open:
WCVK (FM).
Box 539, Bowling Green, 42102. Secondary address: 1407 Scottsville Rd., Bowling Green 42104. Phone: (270) 781-7326. Fax: (270) 781-8005.E-mail: mail@christianfamilyradio.com Web Site:www.christianfamilyradio.com Licensee: Bowling Green Community Broadcasting Inc. Format: Christian. ♦Mike Wilson, gen mgr.

***WKWC(FM)**— Jan 21, 1983: 90.3 mhz; 5 kw. 100 ft TL: N37 44 37 W87 07 12. Stereo. Hrs open: 24 3000 Frederica St., 42301. Phone: (270) 852-3601. Phone: (270) 852-3603. Fax: (270) 852-3599.E-mail: patherradio@kwc.edu Licensee: Kentucky Wesleyan College. Format: Triple AAA. News: 2 hrs wkly. Target aud: 12 plus. ♦Derik Wayne Hancock, gen mgr & progmg dir.

WOMI(AM)— Mar 7, 1938: 1490 khz; 830 w-U. TL: N37 44 29 W87 06 58. Hrs open: 24 3301 Frederica St., 42301.6082. Phone: (270) 683-1558. Fax: (270) 683-2128.E-mail: lcraig@wbkr.com Web Site:www.wbkr.com Licensee: Regent Broadcasting of Evansville/Owensboro Inc. Group owner: Regent Communications Inc. (acq 2-25-03; with co-located FM). Population served: 54,000 Rgnl. Network: Ky. Net. Natl. Rep: Christal,. Format: News/talk. News staff: 2. Target aud: 35-64. ♦Bill Stakelin, CEO; Mark Thomas, pres, gen mgr; Joe O'Neal, gen mgr, gen sls mgr; Chad Benefield, prom dir; Rick Crago, engrg dir.

WSTO(FM)— June 7, 1948: 96.1 mhz; 100 kw. 1,000 ft TL: N37 46 20 W87 21 27. Stereo. Hrs open: 24 Box 3848, Evansville, IN, 47736. Secondary address: 1162 Mt. Auburn Rd., Evansville 47720. Phone: (812) 424-8284. Fax: (812) 463-7911. Web Site:www.hot96.com Licensee: South Central Communications Corp. (group owner; (acq 12-30-2003; $13 million). Population served: 187,600 Format: CHR. News staff: 4; News: one hr wkly. Target aud: 18-34. ♦Robert Shirel, CFO; Tim Huelsing, VP & gen mgr; Falen Bonsett, prom dir; Jason Addams, progmg dir.

WVJS(AM)— Nov 26, 1947: 1420 khz; 5 kw-D, 1 kw-N, DA-2. TL: N37 46 32 W87 09 31. Stereo. Hrs open: 24 1115 Tamarack Rd., Suite 500, 42301. Phone: (270) 683-5200. Fax: (270) 688-0108.E-mail: spots@wrioradio.com Licensee: Cromwell Group Inc. of Kentucky. Group owner: The Cromwell Group Inc. (acq 11-20-02; $300,000). Population served: 150,000 Natl. Network: ABC, . Natl. Rep: Rgnl Reps,. Pepper & Corazzini. Format: Timeless Classics. News: One. Target aud: 35-54. Spec prog: Farm one hr wkly. ♦Bayard Walters, pres; Kevin Riecke, gen mgr.

Owingsville

WKYN(FM)— Dec 1, 1983: 107.7 mhz; 6 kw. Ant 328 ft TL: N38 06 08 W83 50 12. Stereo. Hrs open: 24 22 W. Main St., Mount Sterling, 40353. Phone: (859) 498-1077. Fax: (859) 498-7930.E-mail: feedback@wkynradio.com Web Site:www.wkynradio.com Licensee: Gateway Radio Works Inc. (group owner). Natl. Network: NBC Radio, . Rgnl. Network: Ky. Agri., Ky. News Net. William Silva. Wire Svc: NWS (National Weather Service) Format: Classic hit country. News staff: 2; News: 10 hrs wkly. ♦Hays McMakin, pres; Jeff Ray, gen mgr; Tom McMakin, opns mgr; Doug Walker, chief of engrg; Frances Denney, traf mgr; Tom Byron, prom.

Paducah

WDDJ(FM)— Nov 26, 1946: 96.9 mhz; 100 kw. 340 ft TL: N37 05 55 W88 37 19. (CP: Ant 777 ft. TL: N37 02 56 W88 36 52). Stereo. Hrs open: 24 Box 2397, 42002. Secondary address: 6000 Bristol Dr. 42003. Phone: (270) 534-9690. Fax: (270) 554-4613.E-mail: pd@electric969.com Web Site:www.electric969.com Licensee: Bristol Broadcasting Co. Inc. Group owner: Nininger Stations (acq 6-24-97; $2.7 million with co-located AM). Population served: 250,000 Format: Adult top 40. News staff: 2; News: 2 hrs wkly. Target aud: 18-49; active, white & blue collar adults. ♦Gary Morse, gen mgr; Jamie Futrell, gen sls mgr, rgnl sls mgr; Mark Summer, progmg dir; Greg Walker, chief of engrg.

WDXR(AM)— Dec 24, 1957: 1450 khz; 1 kw-U. TL: N37 05 55 W88 37 19. Hrs open: 24 Secondary address: 1176 Stat Rt. 45 N., Mayfield 42066. Phone: (270) 247-5122. Fax: (270) 554-5468. Licensee: Bristol Broadcasting Co. Inc. (group owner; (acq 3-15-2004; grpsl). Population served: 250,000 Natl. Network: ABC, . Rosenman & Colin L.L.P. Format: Urban contemp. News staff: one; News: 5 hrs wkly. Target aud: 30-65. ♦Gary Morse, gen mgr & stn mgr.

***WGCF(FM)**— December 1996: 89.3 mhz; 12 kw. 492 ft TL: N37 11 31 W88 58 41. Hrs open: 24 1112 E. Kentucky Ave., Kevil, 42053. Phone: (270) 462-3020. Fax: (270) 462-3024.E-mail: info@wgcf.org Web Site:www.wgcf.org Licensee: American Family Association. Group owner: American Family Radio (acq 11-25-2003; $200,000). Population served: 250,000 Format: Adult contemp, CHR, contemp Christian. ♦Bill Hughes, chmn & gen mgr.

WKYQ(FM)— 1947: 93.3 mhz; 100 kw. 915 ft TL: N37 00 53 W88 36 46. Stereo. Hrs open: 24 Prog sep from AM Box 2397, 42002. Secondary address: 6000 Bristol Drive 42003. Phone: (270) 554-8255. Fax: (270) 554-5468.E-mail: production@wkyq.com Web Site:www.wkyq.com Population served: 450,000 Format: Country. News staff: 3. Target aud: 25-54. ♦Gary Morse, gen mgr; Bobby Cook, opns mgr; Jamie Futrell, gen sls mgr; Jeff Lawrence, progmg dir; Donna Groves, news dir; Greg Walker, engr.

WKYX(AM)— 1946: 570 khz; 1 kw-D, 500 w-N, DA-2. TL: N37 00 53 W88 36 46. Hrs open: 24
Simulcast with WKYX-FM Golconda, IL 100%.
Box 2397, 42002. Secondary address: 6000 Bristol Dr. 42003. Phone: (270) 554-8255. Fax: (270) 554-5468. Web Site:www.wkyx.com Licensee: Bristol Broadcasting Co. Inc. Group owner: Nininger Stations (acq 11-23-71). Population served: 250,000 Natl. Rep: Christal,. Fisher, Wayland, Cooper, Leader & Zaragoza L.L.P. Format: News/talk. News staff: 3; News: 20 hrs wkly. Target aud: 25-54; middle to upper income. ♦Gary Morse, gen mgr; Jamie Futrell, gen sls mgr; Greg Dunker, progmg dir; Donna Groves, news dir.

***WNFC(FM)**—Not on air, target date: unknown: 91.7 mhz; 12.5 kw. Ant 288 ft TL: N37 03 37 W88 50 32. Hrs open: Box 91, Upton, 42784-0091. Phone: (270) 369-8614. Fax: (270) 369-7402. Licensee: FM 90.1 Inc. ♦Don Powell, gen mgr.

WPAD(AM)— Aug 23, 1930: 1560 khz; 10 kw-D, 5 kw-N, DA-3. TL: N37 03 08 W88 36 03. Hrs open: 24 Prog sep from FM Box 2397, 42002. Secondary address: 6000 Bristol Dr. 42003. Phone: (270) 534-9690. Fax: (270) 554-4613.E-mail: info@electric969.com Web Site:www.electric969.com Licensee: Bristol Broadcasting Co. Inc. Population served: 100,000 Natl. Network: Westwood One, . Format: Sports. News staff: 2; News: 22 hrs wkly. Target aud: 35-64; upscale, white-collar.

WREZ(FM)—See Metropolis, IL

WRIK-FM—See Metropolis, IL

WZZL(FM)—See Reidland

Paintsville

WKLW-FM— June 18, 1993: 94.7 mhz; 4.9 kw. 731 ft TL: N37 42 42 W82 48 03. Stereo. Hrs open: 24 Box 1407, 41240. Secondary address: 865 S. Mayo Tr. 41240. Phone: (606) 789-6664. Fax: (606) 789-6669.E-mail: wklwfm@belsouth.net Web Site:www.wklw.com Licensee: B & G Broadcasting Inc. Format: Hot adult contemp. ♦Alan Burton, gen mgr & stn mgr.

WKYH(AM)— Mar 18, 1985: 600 khz; 5 kw-D, 43 w-N. TL: N37 47 19 W82 47 07. Stereo. Hrs open: 330 2nd St, 41240. Phone: (606) 789-3333. Fax: (859) 402-0260.E-mail: ckbelhasen@belsouth.net Web Site:www.wkyh.com Licensee: Highlands Broadcasting Corp. (acq 11-30-99). Natl. Network: Westwood One, . Midlen & Guillot. Format: News/talk/sports info. Target aud: 25-49; middle to upper class adults. ♦Charles K. Belhasen, gen mgr, pres, opns mgr, gen sls mgr, progmg dir, news dir & chief of engrg.

WSIP(AM)— April 24, 1949: 1490 khz; 1 kw-U. TL: N37 48 21 W82 46 01. Hrs open: Box 597, 41240. Secondary address: 127 Main St. 41240. Phone: (606) 789-5311. Fax: (606) 789-7200.E-mail: wsipradio@bellsouth.net Licensee: S.I.P. Broadcasting Inc. Group owner: Key Broadcasting Inc. (acq 2-84). Population served: 66,300 Rgnl. Network: Ky. Net. Natl. Rep: Rgnl Reps,. Format: Oldies. Target aud: General. ♦Spike Berkhimer, gen mgr, gen sls mgr & sports cmtr.

WSIP-FM— Jan 12, 1965: 98.9 mhz; 94 kw. Ant 600 ft TL: N37 47 45 W82 48 04. Stereo. Hrs open: 24 Box 597, 41240. Secondary address: 127 Main St. 41240. Phone: (606) 789-5311. Fax: (606) 789-7200.E-mail: wsipradio@bellsouth.net Web Site:www.wsipfm.com Population served: 579,000 Format: New country.

Paris

WGKS(FM)—Licensed to Paris. See Lexington

***WPTJ(FM)**— August 2003: 90.7 mhz; 10 kw. Ant 314 ft TL: N38 19 40 W84 07 44. Hrs open: 24 1811 Cynthiana Millersburg Rd., 40361. Secondary address: Lay Witness Broadcasting, Box 7 40362-0007. Phone: (859) 484-9691.E-mail: jsmith@wptj.org Web Site:www.wptj.org Licensee: Lay Witness Outreach Inc. Population served: 225,000 Format: Relg. ♦John Smith, gen mgr; John Wesley Brett, progmg dir.

WYGH(AM)— January 1993: 1440 khz; 1 kw-D, 25 w-N. TL: N38 13 30 W84 14 59. Hrs open: 24 Box 50, Falmouth, 41040. Phone: (859) 472-1075. Fax: (859) 472-2875.E-mail: wiok@fuse.net Web Site:www.wygh.com Licensee: Hammond Broadcasting Inc. Population served: 500,000 Format: Southern gospel. ♦Jan Hammond, gen mgr.

Philpot

WBIO(FM)— Nov 18, 1993: 94.7 mhz; 3 kw. 328 ft TL: N37 41 51 W86 59 26. Stereo. Hrs open: 24 1115 Tamarack Rd., Suite 500, Owensboro, 42301. Phone: (270) 683-5200. Fax: (270) 688-0108.E-mail: spots@wbioradio.com Web Site:www.wbio.com Licensee: Hancock Communications Inc. Group owner: The Cromwell Group Inc. (acq 6-17-93; $90,565; 7-5-93). Population served: 70,000 Natl. Network: ABC, . Natl. Rep: Rgnl Reps,. Pepper & Corazzini. Format: True country. News staff: one; News: 4 hrs wkly. Target aud: 25-54. ♦Bayard Walters, CEO; Kevin Riecke, gen mgr.

Pikeville

WBTH(AM)—Williamson WV

WDHR(FM)— Mar 25, 1966: 93.1 mhz; 22 kw. Ant 758 ft TL: N37 27 57 W82 33 04. Stereo. Hrs open: 24 Prog sep from AM Box2200 , 41501. Phone: (606) 437-4051. Fax: (606) 432-2809.E-mail: wdhr@wdhr.com Web Site:www.wdhr.com Licensee: East Kentucky Broadcasting Corp. Population served: 600,000 Natl. Network: ABC, . Format: Country. News staff: 2.

***WJSO(FM)**— Apr 1989: 90.1 mhz; 3.8 kw. 455 ft TL: N37 27 52 W82 32 45. Hrs open: 24 Box 3237, 41502. Phone: (606) 432-0351. Fax: (312) 329-8980.E-mail: wjso@moody.edu Web Site:wjso.mbn.org Licensee: Moody Bible Institute of Chicago. (group owner; acq 12-18-91; donation; 1-13-92). Natl. Network: Moody, . Format: Relg. News: 15 hrs wkly. Target aud: 35-55. ♦Scott Keegan, gen mgr.

WLSI(AM)— Jan 20, 1949: 900 khz; 5 kw-D. TL: N37 29 06 W82 32 44. Hrs open: 24
Simulcast with WPRT(AM) Prestonburg 100%.
Box 2200, 41502. Secondary address: 1240 Radio Dr. 41501. Phone: (606) 437-4051. Fax: (606) 432-2809.E-mail: wdhr@wdhr.com Web Site:www.ekbradio.com Licensee: East Kentucky Broadcasting Corp. (acq 5-14-2003; $531,273 with WZLK(FM) Virgie). Population served: 50,000 Natl. Network: CNN Radio, NBC Radio, Sporting News Radio Network, . Format: Talk. News staff: one; News: 21 hrs wkly. Target aud: 25-49. ♦Keith Casebolt, gen mgr.

WPKE(AM)— July 31, 1949: 1240 khz; 1 kw-U. TL: N37 28 53 W82 31 27. Stereo. Hrs open: 24
Rebroadcasts WBPA(AM) Elkhorn City 100%.
Box 2200, 41502. Secondary address: 1240 Radio Dr. 41501. Phone: (606) 437-4051. Fax: (606) 432-2809.E-mail: wdhr@wdhr.com Web Site:www.wdhr.com Licensee: East Kentucky Broadcasting Corp. (group owner; acq 1962). Population served: 35,000 Natl. Rep: Rgnl Reps,. Rgnl rep: Rgnl Reps Womble, Carlylee, Sandridge & Rice. Format: Oldies. News staff: one; News: 5 hrs wkly. Target aud: General. ♦Keith Casebolt, gen mgr; Randy Jones, progmg dir; Walter Dingus, chief of engrg.

WXCC(FM)—Williamson WV

Pineville

WANO(AM)— Mar 16, 1957: 1230 khz; 1 kw-U. TL: N36 46 07 W83 42 59. Hrs open: Box 999, Middlesboro, 40965. Phone: (606) 248-1560. Fax: (606) 248-6397.E-mail: brian@1490wfxy.com Web Site:1490wfxy.com Licensee: Cumberland Media Group Inc. (acq 4-18-2006; grpsl). Population served: 12,000 Format: Oldies. ♦Brian O'Brien, opns mgr.

WRIL(FM)— Feb 24, 1973: 106.3 mhz; 1.05 kw. Ant 768 ft TL: N36 45 15 W83 42 23. Hrs open: Box 693, 40977. Secondary address: 25 E. Log Mountain 40977. Phone: (606) 337-5202. Fax: (606) 337-8020.E-mail: wrilcountry@yahoo.com Licensee: Pine Hills Broadcasting Inc. (acq 2-22-84; $300,000; 3-5-84). Population served: 100,000 Format: Country. ♦Gayle McPherson, gen mgr.

Pippa Passes

***WWJD(FM)**— Nov 1, 1986: 91.7 mhz; 7.3 kw. 544 ft TL: N37 19 45 W82 52 30. Stereo. Hrs open: 24 Alice Lloyd College, 100 Purpose Rd., 41844. Phone: (606) 368-6131. Fax: (606) 368-6017.E-mail: wwjd@alc.edu Licensee: Alice Lloyd College. Population served: 500,000 Format: Adult contemp, Christian. Target aud: 13-25. ♦Jason Stowers, gen mgr.

Prestonsburg

WDOC(AM)— November 1957: 1310 khz; 5 kw-D, 25 w-N. TL: N37 41 45 W82 45 24. Hrs open: Sunrise-sunset Box 345, 95 Jackson, 41653. Phone: (606) 886-2338. Phone: (606) 886-8409. Fax: (606) 886-1026.E-mail: q95prod@bellsouth.net Licensee: WDOC Inc. Population served: 135,000 Natl. Rep: Rgnl Reps,. Format: Solid Gospel. Target aud: 25-64. ♦Gormon Collins Jr., pres, gen mgr; Samantha Osborne, gen sls mgr.

WPRT(AM)— Dec 5, 1952: 960 khz; 5 kw-D. TL: N37 40 14 W82 45 14. Hrs open:
Simulcast with WLSI(AM) Pikeville 100%.
Box 2200, Pikeville, 41502. Secondary address: 1240 Radio Dr., Pikesville 41501. Phone: (606) 437-4051. Fax: (606) 432-2809.E-mail: wdhr@wdhrcom Web Site:www.900wlsi.com Licensee: East Kentucky Radio Network Inc. (group owner; (acq 10-26-2001). Population served: 5,000 Natl. Network: CNN Radio, NBC Radio, Sporting News Radio Network, . Format: Talk. ♦Keith Casebolt, gen mgr.

WQHY(FM)— Feb 11, 1968: 95.5 mhz; 100 kw. 1,000 ft TL: N37 41 45 W82 45 24. Stereo. Hrs open: 24 Prog sep from AM Box 345, 95 Jackson, 41653. Phone: (606) 886-2338. Phone: (606) 886-8409. Fax: (606) 886-1026.E-mail: q95prod@bellsouth.net Web Site:www.q95fm.net Licensee: WDOC, Inc. Population served: 900,000 Natl. Network: ABC, . Natl. Rep: Rgnl Reps,. Format: CHR. News staff: one; News: 2 hrs wkly. Target aud: 18-34. ♦Gormon Collins, Jr., gen mgr; Russ Lafforty, chief of engrg; Carla Hughes, traf mgr.

WXKZ-FM— Feb 10, 1967: 105.3 mhz; 4.7 kw. Ant 371 ft TL: N37 39 24 W82 45 58. Stereo. Hrs open: Box 1049, Harold, 41635. Phone: (606) 478-1200. Fax: (606) 478-4202.E-mail: wifx@foxy943.com Web Site:www.thedoublex.com Licensee: Adam Gearheart dba WXLR-FM (acq 1-17-97; with co-located AM). Population served: 5,000 Format: Oldies. ♦Barry Boyd, gen mgr, gen sls mgr; Mel Stevens, progmg dir.

Princeton

WAVJ(FM)— Apr 1, 1969: 104.9 mhz; 3 kw. 187 ft TL: N37 07 14 W83 51 31. Stereo. Hrs open: 24 Dups AM 99% Box 270, 42445. Secondary address: 108 W. Main St. 42445. Phone: (270) 365-2072. Fax: (270) 365-2073.E-mail: wavj@commonwealthbroadcasting.com Web Site:www.literock1049.com Licensee: Caldwell County CBC Inc. Population served: 40,000 Format: Lite rock AC.

WPKY(AM)— Mar 15, 1950: 1580 khz; 250 w-D. TL: N37 07 14 W87 51 31. Hrs open: 24 Box 270, 42445. Secondary address: 108 W. Main St. 42445. Phone: (270) 365-2072. Fax: (270) 365-2073.E-mail: wavj@commonwealthbroadcasting.com Licensee: Caldwell County CBC Inc. (acq 6-25-98; $362,000 with co-located FM). Population served: 25,000 Natl. Network: ESPN Radio, . Format: Sports. News staff: one; News: 11 hrs wkly. Target aud: General. ♦LeeAnn Oliver, gen sls mgr, progmg dir; Tom Rogers, gen mgr, opns mgr & progmg dir; Ed Thomas, news dir, chief of engrg.

Providence

WWKY(FM)— Apr 9, 1976: 97.7 mhz; 6 kw. 328 ft TL: N37 24 52 W87 34 23. Stereo. Hrs open: 24 Box 1310, Madisonville, 42431. Secondary address: 265 S. Main St. , Madisonville 42431. Phone: (270) 825-9779. Fax: (270) 825-3260.E-mail: wwky@commonwealthbroadcasting.com Licensee: Hopkins-Webster CBC Inc. Group owner: Commonwealth Broadcasting Corp. (acq 5-21-98; $425,000). Population served: 152,752 Natl. Network: CNN Radio, . Rgnl. Network: Ky. Net. Ky. News Net Leonard S. Joyce. Format: Oldies. News staff: 2; News: 21 hrs wkly. Target aud: 25-54. ♦Lee Ann Oliver, gen sls mgr; Tom Rogers, gen mgr & progmg dir; Stephanie Vandygraiff, traf mgr.

Radcliff

WAKY(FM)— July 25, 1995: 103.5 mhz; 3.5 kw. Ant 761 ft TL: N37 52 45 W85 43 03. Stereo. Hrs open: 24 Box 2087, Elizabethtown, 42702. Secondary address: 519 N. Miles, Elizabethtown 42701. Phone: (270) 766-1035. Fax: (270) 769-1052. Web Site:www.waky1035.com Licensee: W & B Broadcasting Inc. Population served: 513,878 Natl. Network: ABC, . Miller & Miller. Format: Oldies. News staff: 14; News: 4 hrs wkly. Target aud: 25-54; baby boomers. ♦Bill Walters, pres; Rene Bell, gen mgr; Cale Tharp, opns mgr, chief of engrg.

Reidland

WZZL(FM)— October 1992: 106.7 mhz; 1.35 kw. 492 ft TL: N37 03 23 W88 27 22. Hrs open: 24 Box 7501, Paducah, 42002-8123. Phone: (270) 538-5251. Fax: (270) 415-0599. Web Site:www.wzzl.com Licensee: Withers Broadcasting Co. of Paducah LLC. Group owner: Withers Broadcasting Co. (acq 9-11-97; grpsl). Population served: 162,000 Format: Rock/AOR. Target aud: 18-49. ♦Rick Lambert, gen mgr.

Richmond

WCBR(AM)— March 1969: 1110 khz; 250 w-D. TL: N37 44 09 W84 16 05. Hrs open: Sunrise-sunset Box 570, 40476-0570. Secondary address: 509 Leighway Dr. 40475. Phone: (859) 623-1235. Fax: (859) 623-7094.E-mail: wcbrradio@bellsouth.net Web Site:wcbr1110.com Licensee: WCBR Inc. (acq 2-4-2009; $50,000 for stock). Population served: 21,141 Natl. Network: USA, . Format: Southern gospel. News: 5 hrs wkly. Target aud: 35 plus; older adult listener. Spec prog: Loc talk shows, news, sports & relg talk 35 hrs wkly. ♦Bill Robbins, pres; David L. Humes, exec VP, gen mgr; Malissa Blair, traf mgr.

***WEKU(FM)**— September 1968: 88.9 mhz; 50 kw. 720 ft TL: N37 52 45 W84 19 33. Stereo. Hrs open: 24 102 Perkins Bldg., 521 Lancaster Ave., 40475-3102. Phone: (859) 622-1660. Fax: (859) 622-6276.E-mail: wekunews@eku.edu Web Site:www.weku.fm Licensee: Board of Regents, Eastern Kentucky University. Population served: 700,000 Natl. Network: NPR, PRI, . Hardy, Carey & Chautin. Wire Svc: AP Format: Class, news. News staff: 3; News: 35 hrs wkly. Target aud: General. ♦Tim Singleton, gen mgr & stn mgr; Mary Ellyn Cain, opns mgr; Carol Siler, dev dir; Laura Allen, progmg dir; Charles Compton, news dir; Bill Browning, chief of engrg.

WEKY(AM)— Oct 17, 1953: 1340 khz; 1 kw-U. TL: N37 43 00 W84 18 25. Hrs open: 24 128 Big Hill Ave., 40475. Phone: (859) 623-1386. Fax: (859) 623-1341.E-mail: coyote@wcyofm.com Web Site:www.wekyam.com Licensee: Wallingford Communications Inc. Group owner: Wallingford Broadcasting Co. (acq 1999; grpsl). Population served: 16,861 Rgnl. Network: Ky. News Net. Natl. Rep: Rgnl Reps,. Ky. News Net Format: News/talk, info. News staff: one; News: 3 hrs wkly. Target aud: 25-54. Spec prog: Black 12 hrs, relg 6 hrs wkly. ♦Kelly Wallingford, gen mgr; Ray White, opns mgr & progmg dir.

WVLK-FM— May 12, 1972: 101.5 mhz; 7.2 kw. Ant 541 ft TL: N37 52 45 W84 19 33. Stereo. Hrs open: 24 300 W. Vine St., Suite 3, Lexington, 40507. Phone: (859) 253-5900. Fax: (859) 253-5940. Licensee: Cumulus Licensing Corp. Group owner: Cumulus Media Inc. (acq 10-5-99; grpsl). Format: Sports talk. News staff: one; News: 6 hrs wkly. ♦Anread Ayers, gen mgr.

Russell Springs

WHVE(FM)— 1993: 92.7 mhz; 6 kw. 328 ft TL: N37 00 31 W85 12 14. Hrs open: Box 927, Columbia, 42728. Secondary address: 7955 Russell Springs Rd. 42642. Phone: (270) 384-7979. Fax: (270) 384-6244.E-mail: thewave@ridingthewave.com Web Site:www.ridingthewave.com Licensee: Shoreline Communications Inc. (group owner; (acq 5-2002; $525,000). Format: Adult contemp. ♦Alan W. Reed, gen mgr; Don Salmon, opns mgr.

WIDS(AM)— Oct 14, 1982: 570 khz; 500 w-D. TL: N37 05 42 W85 05 05. Hrs open: 24 Box 50, Falmouth, 41040. Phone: (859) 472-1075. Fax: (859) 472-2875.E-mail: wiok@fuse.net Web Site:www.tri-stategospel.org Licensee: Hammond Broadcasting Inc. (acq 8-16-94; 8-29-94). Format: Southern gospel. ♦Jan Hammond, gen mgr.

WJKY(AM)—See Jamestown

WJRS(FM)—See Jamestown

Russellville

WRUS(AM)— Aug 28, 1953: 610 khz; 2.5 kw-D, 73 w-N. TL: N36 48 51 W86 52 50. (CP: 500 w-N, TL: N36 52 29 W86 52 56 (night)). Hrs open: 24 Box 1740, 42276. Phone: (270) 726-2471. Fax: (270) 726-3095.E-mail: wrus@bellsouth.net Web Site:www.wrusam.com Licensee: Logan Radio Inc. (acq 10-24-02). Population served: 300,000 Format: Variety. ♦Chris McGinnis, gen mgr & gen sls mgr.

WUBT(FM)— Mar 28, 1965: 101.1 mhz; 47 kw. 1,289 ft TL: N36 31 36 W86 41 14. Stereo. Hrs open: 24 55 Music Sq. W., Nashville, TN, 37203. Phone: (615) 664-2400. Fax: (615) 664-2457.E-mail: info@101thebeat.com Web Site:www.101thebeat.com Licensee: Capstar TX L.P. Group owner: Clear Channel Communications Inc. (acq 8-30-00; grpsl). Format: Urban contemp. ♦David Alpert, gen mgr; Bill Reed, sls dir; Keith Kaufman, mktg dir.

Salt Lick

WKCA(FM)— Apr 19, 1976: 97.7 mhz; 3 kw. Ant 469 ft TL: N38 10 33 W83 24 28. Stereo. Hrs open: 24 Box 970, Morehead, 40351. Secondary address: 123 East First St., Morehead 40351. Phone: (606) 674-2266. Fax: (606) 674-6700.E-mail: feedback@wkcaradio.com Web Site:wkcaradio.com Licensee: Gateway Radio Works Inc. Group owner: First Broadcasting Investment Partners LLC (acq 9-7-2007). Natl. Network: CBS Radio, . Rgnl. Network: Ohio Radio Net., Agri Bcstg. Format: Real country. News staff: 2; News: 35 hrs wkly. Spec prog: Farm 10 hrs wkly. ♦Jeff Ray, gen mgr; Tom McMakin, opns mgr; Carol Lynn, prom dir; Becky Black, progmg dir; Doug Walker, chief of engrg.

Salyersville

WRLV(AM)— September 1979: 1140 khz; 1 kw-D. TL: N37 44 58 W83 05 19. Hrs open: 12 Box 550, 41465. Secondary address: 225 S. Church St. 41465. Phone: (606) 349-6125. Phone: (606) 349-6126. Fax: (606) 349-6129.E-mail: coyote2@foothills.net Web Site:www.wrlvradio.com Licensee: Morgan County Industires Inc. (acq 7-5-2007; $460,000 with co-located FM). Population served: 65,000 Natl. Rep: Rgnl Reps,. Format: Country. News staff: 2; News: 5 hrs wkly. Target aud: 35-65; middle age to elderly. ♦C.C. Smith, pres; Kathy Puckett, gen mgr, gen sls mgr, mktg VP, prom mgr, adv VP; Bryan Russell, prom dir, news dir, mus critic; Teresa Witten, progmg dir, progmg dir, traf mgr; Sanford Baca, local news ed; Terry Lykins, relg ed; Scott Ratliff, disc jockey.

WRLV-FM— Aug 25, 1989: 106.5 mhz; 5.9 kw. Ant 331 ft TL: N37 45 27 W83 03 50. Stereo. Hrs open: 24 Box 550, 414645. Secondary address: 225 S. Church St. 41465. Phone: (606) 349-6125. Fax: (606) 349-6129. Web Site:www.wrlvradio.com Population served: 100,000 Natl. Rep: Rgnl Reps,. Format: Country. News staff: 2; News: 5 hrs wkly. Target aud: 18-80; young to elderly. ♦Kathy Puckett, sls VP, adv dir, spec ev coord; Bryan Russell, mus dir, mus critic; Teresa Witten, traf mgr; Sanford Baca, local news ed; Hershall Wright, relg ed; Scott Ratliff, sports cmtr.

Science Hill

WYKY(FM)— 2008: 106.1 mhz; 1.95 kw. Ant 584 ft TL: N37 07 53 W84 32 21. Hrs open: Box 1480, Somerset, 42502. Phone: (606) 678-8151. Fax: (606) 678-8152. Web Site:www.somerset106.com Licensee: F.T.G. Broadcasting Inc. Format: Adult hits. ♦Terry E. Forcht, pres; Bryan McFarland, gen mgr; Trevor Grigsby, progmg dir.

Scottsville

WLCK(AM)— Feb 27, 1958: 1250 khz; 1 kw-D. TL: N36 44 24 W86 10 20. Hrs open: 6 AM-9 PM Box 158, 42164. Secondary address: 104 1/2 Public Sq. 42164. Phone: (270) 237-3148. Fax: (270) 237-3533.E-mail: wlckwvle@nctc.com Web Site:www.wvleradio.com Licensee: Skytower Communications Group LLC (acq 5-30-2007; $800,000 with co-located FM). Population served: 20,000 Natl. Network: USA, . Hardy & Carey. Format: Relg. News staff: one; News: 12 hrs wkly. Target aud: General. ♦Darrin Evans, pres, gen sls mgr, progmg dir, mus dir; Chris Nelson, gen mgr, news dir; Max Murphy, chief of engrg.

WVLE(FM)— Feb 26, 1967: 99.3 mhz; 6 kw. Ant 328 ft TL: N36 44 25 W86 10 31. Stereo. Hrs open: Prog sep from AM Box 158, 42164.

Secondary address: 104 1/2 Public Sq. 42164. Phone: (270) 237-3148. Fax: (270) 237-3533. Web Site:www.wvleradio.com Population served: 25,000 Format: Lite rock.

Shelbyville

WCND(AM)— June 3, 1964: 940 khz; 250 w-D. TL: N38 13 00 W85 09 45. Hrs open: Licensee: Birach Broadcasting Corp. Group owner: Clear Channel Communications Inc. Population served: 401,112 Rgnl. Network: Ky. Net. Format: Oldies. News staff: one; News: one hr wkly. Target aud: 35-64; upscale, white collar.

WKRD-FM— Sept 30, 1989: 101.7 mhz; 6 kw. Ant 328 ft TL: N38 12 48 W85 10 16. Hrs open: 24
Simulcasts WKRD(AM) Louisville 100%.
4000 Radio Drive, Louisville, 40218. Phone: (502) 479-2222. Fax: (502) 479-2308. Web Site:www.790wkrd.com Licensee: CC Licenses LLC. (acq 2-1-2002; with co-located AM). Population served: 750,000 Natl. Network: Fox Sports, . Format: Sports. ♦Bill Gentry, mktg mgr; Jim Fenn, progmg dir.

Shepherdsville

WLRS(FM)— 1993: 105.1 mhz; 2.2 kw. Ant 446 ft TL: N38 02 54 W85 46 04. Hrs open: 520 S. 4th Ave., Suite 200, Louisville, 40202. Phone: (502) 625-1220. Fax: (502) 584-1051.E-mail: info@wlrs.com Web Site:www.1051fmtalk.com Licensee: MLB-Louisville IV LLC. Group owner: Radio One Inc. (acq 9-12-2007; grpsl). Population served: 1000000 Format: Talk. ♦Dale Schaeffer, gen mgr.

Smiths Grove

WUHU(FM)— Dec 1, 1986: 107.1 mhz; 50 kw. Ant 492 ft TL: N36 50 35 W86 15 30. Stereo. Hrs open: 24 1919 Scottsville Rd., Bowling Green, 42104. Phone: (270) 843-3333. Fax: (270) 843-0454.E-mail: mark@forevercomm.com Web Site:www.allhitwuhu107.com Licensee: Forever Communications Inc. (group owner; (acq 2001). Population served: 280,000 Natl. Rep: Christal,. Kaye, Scholer, LLP. Format: Hot adult contemp. Target aud: 18-49. ♦Christine Hillard, pres; Brooke Summers, opns dir, progmg dir.

Somerset

***WDCL-FM**— July 1985: 89.7 mhz; 100 kw. 570 ft TL: N37 09 29 W85 09 50. Stereo. Hrs open: 24
Rebroadcasts WKYU-FM Bowling Green 100%.
Western Kentucky Univ., 1906 College Heights Blvd., Bowling Green, 42101. Phone: (270) 745-5489. Phone: (800) 599-9598. Fax: (270) 745-6272.E-mail: wkyufm@wku.edu Web Site:www.wkyufm.org Licensee: Western Kentucky University. Natl. Network: PRI, NPR, . Rgnl. Network: Ky. Net. Leventhal, Senter & Lerman. Format: Class, news. News staff: 3; News: 35 hrs wkly. Target aud: General. Spec prog: Folk 5 hrs, jazz 15 hrs wkly. ♦Peter Bryant, gen mgr.

WKEQ(FM)— Sept 1, 1964: 97.1 mhz; 27.5 kw. 659 ft TL: N36 57 40 W84 34 07. Stereo. Hrs open: Prog sep from AM Box 740, 42502. Secondary address: 101 First Radio Ln. 42503. Phone: (606) 678-5151. Fax: (606) 678-2026. Web Site:www.wsfcam.com Population served: 85,000 Wire Svc: NOAA Weather Format: Classic hits.

***WKVY(FM)**— 2004: 88.1 mhz; 4 kw vert. Ant 526 ft TL: N37 04 36 W84 48 39. Stereo. Hrs open: 24 2351 Sunset Blvd., Suite 170-218, Rocklin, CA, 95765. Phone: (916) 251-1600. Fax: (916) 251-1650.E-mail: klove@klove.com Web Site:www.klove.com Licensee: Educational Media Foundation. Group owner: EMF Broadcasting. Natl. Network: K-Love, . Shaw Pittman. Format: Contemp Christian. News staff: 3. Target aud: 25-44; Judeo Christian, female. ♦Richard Jenkins, pres; Mike Novak, VP; Keith Whipple, dev dir; David Pierce, progmg mgr; Ed Lenane, news dir; Sam Wallington, engrg dir; Karen Johnson, news rptr.

WLLK-FM— Aug 14, 1989: 102.3 mhz; 6 kw. 328 ft TL: N37 04 41 W84 40 39. Hrs open: 24 Box 740, 42502. Secondary address: 101 First Radio Ln. 42503. Phone: (606) 678-5151. Fax: (606) 678-2026.E-mail: wsek@clearchannel.com Web Site:www.somersetradio.com Licensee: Capstar TX L.P. Group owner: Clear Channel Communications Inc. (acq 12-8-2000; grpsl). Population served: 100,000 Format: Hot adult contemp. News staff: one; News: 6 hrs wkly. Target aud: 25-54. ♦Richard Dills, gen mgr.

WSFC(AM)— Dec 14, 1947: 1240 khz; 790 w-U. TL: N37 07 06 W84 36 44. Stereo. Hrs open: 24 Box 740, 42502. Secondary address: 101 First Radio Ln. 42503. Phone: (606) 678-5151. Fax: (606) 678-2026. Web Site:www.wsfcam.com Licensee: Capstar TX L.P. Group owner: Clear Channel Communications Inc. (acq 12-8-2000; grpsl). Population served: 50,000 Natl. Rep: Rgnl Reps,. Latham & Watkins. Wire Svc: NOAA Weather Format: Talk. News staff: one; News: 15 hrs wkly. Target aud: General. ♦Richard Dills, gen mgr, stn mgr, sls dir, gen sls mgr; Rod Zimmerman, progmg dir & traf mgr.

***WTHL(FM)**— July 16, 1987: 90.5 mhz; 50 kw. 590 ft TL: N37 07 52 W84 33 15. Stereo. Hrs open: Box 1423, 42502. Secondary address: 93 Rainbow Terr. 42503. Phone: (606) 679-6300. Fax: (606) 679-1342.E-mail: dcradio@alltel.net Web Site:www.kingofkingsradio.net Licensee: Somerset Educational Broadcasting Foundation. Natl. Network: Moody, . Format: Conservative, traditional relg, educ. Target aud: 40 plus; people with conservative, traditional & relg values & interests. ♦David Carr, gen mgr; Carolyn Jones, progmg dir; Marvin Whitaker, gen sls mgr & chief of engrg.

WTLO(AM)— Nov 1, 1958: 1480 khz; 1 kw-D. TL: N37 05 15 W84 38 14. Stereo. Hrs open: Box 1480, 42502. Secondary address: 290 WTLO Rd. 42503. Phone: (606) 678-8151. Fax: (606) 678-8152.E-mail: wtlo@usa.com Web Site:www.wtloradio.com Licensee: F.T.G. Broadcasting Inc. (acq 2-4-2008; $300,000). Population served: 67,800 Natl. Network: ABC, . Format: Timeless favorites. Target aud: 45 plus; upscale & highly mobile. Spec prog: Farm one hr, relg 4 hrs wkly. ♦Roy Taylor, gen mgr & opns mgr; John Maggard, gen sls mgr.

Springfield

WYSB(FM)— Feb 17, 1989: 102.7 mhz; 4 kw. Ant 354 ft TL: N37 41 43 W85 19 06. Hrs open: 24 Box 190, Bardstown, 40004. Phone: (502) 350-4482. Fax: (502) 350-4483.E-mail: lkearnes@commonwealthbroadcashieg.com Licensee: Washington County CBC Inc. Group owner: Commonwealth Broadcasting Corp. (acq 10-30-97; $350,000). Population served: 50,000 Natl. Network: ABC, . Rgnl. Network: Ky. Net. Ky. News Net Format: Adult contemp. News staff: one; News: 20 hrs wkly. Target aud: 25-55. Spec prog: Sports 12 hrs, farm 10 hrs wkly. ♦Lisa Kearnes, gen mgr, gen sls mgr; Kenny Fogle, adv dir; Tom Redmon, news dir; Jim Parker, opns.

Stamping Ground

WLXO(FM)— Dec 15, 1994: 96.1 mhz; 6 kw. Ant 328 ft TL: N38 12 15 W84 32 51. Stereo. Hrs open: 401 W. Main, Suite 301, Lexington, 40507. Phone: (859) 233-1515. Fax: (859) 233-1517. Web Site:www.supertalk961.com Licensee: Clarity Communications Inc. (acq 8-7-01; $400,000). Natl. Network: Talk Radio Network, . Natl. Rep: Katz Radio,. Format: Talk. News: 20 hrs wkly. ♦Charlie Cohn, pres; James MacFarlane, gen mgr & sls dir.

Stanford

WXKY-FM— May 22, 1967: 96.3 mhz; 12.5 kw. Ant 472 ft TL: N37 31 27 W84 52 12. Hrs open: 2351 Sunset Blvd., Suite 170-218, Rocklin, CA, 95765. Phone: (916) 251-1600. Fax: (916) 251-1650. Web Site:www.klove.com Licensee: Educational Media Foundation. (acq 10-20-2004; $800,000). Population served: 100,000 Natl. Network: K-Love, . Shaw Pittman LLP. Format: Christian music. ♦Richard Jenkins, pres; Mike Novak, VP; Keith Whipple, dev dir; David Pierce, progmg mgr; Ed Lenane, news dir; Sam Wallington, engrg dir; Karen Johnson, news rptr.

Stanton

WBFC(AM)— June 21, 1975: 1470 khz; 2.5 kw-D, 25 w-N. TL: N37 52 58 W83 52 56. Hrs open: Box 577, 40380. Secondary address: 2401 Paint Creek Rd. 40380. Phone: (606) 663-6631. Fax: (606) 663-2267.E-mail: beverly@wbfcam.com Web Site:www.wbfcam.com Licensee: Combs Broadcasting Inc. (acq 10-13-98; $70,000). Population served: 150,000 Format: Southern gospel. ♦James Harold Combs, pres; Beverly Combs, gen mgr.

WSKV(FM)— Aug 10, 1974: 104.9 mhz; 440 w. 680 ft TL: N37 45 43 W83 50 36. Stereo. Hrs open: 24 Box 610, 40380. Secondary address: 28 W. Hall's Rd. 40380. Phone: (606) 663-2811. Fax: (606) 663-2895. Web Site:www.wskvfm.com Licensee: Moore Country 104 LLC (acq 12-16-2004; $650,000). Population served: 50,000 Rgnl. Network: Ky. Net. Format: Classic Country, Bluegrass. Target aud: General. ♦A.C. Moore, gen mgr.

Sturgis

WMSK-FM— Nov 9, 2006: 101.3 mhz; 6 kw. Ant 276 ft TL: N37 40 00 W87 55 40. Stereo. Hrs open: 24 P O Box 369, Morganfield, 42437. Secondary address: 1339 U.S. Highway 60, Morganfield 42437. Phone: (270) 389-1550. Fax: (270) 389-1553.E-mail: wmsk@bellsouth.net Licensee: Henson Media Inc. Natl. Network: Jones Radio Networks, . Rgnl rep: Regional Reps Wire Svc: AP Format: Country, local news, sports, information. News: 20 hrs wkly. Target aud: 25-64; adults. ♦Ed Henson, pres; Rhonda Gibson, opns mgr.

Tompkinsville

WKWY(FM)— 2003: 102.7 mhz; 6 kw. Ant 315 ft TL: N36 43 27 W85 40 53. Hrs open: 24 341 Radio Station Rd., 42167. Phone: (270) 487-6119. Fax: (270) 487-8462.E-mail: wtky@alltel.net Licensee: Paul Burrow, Executor (acq 11-30-2007). Population served: 329,321 Natl. Network: USA, . Natl. Rep: Rgnl Reps,. Format: Country. News staff: 2; News: 2 wkly. ♦Tina Norris, gen mgr; Jeff Wix, gen sls mgr.

WTKY(AM)— May 28, 1960: 1370 khz; 2.1 kw-D. TL: N36 43 27 W85 40 53. Stereo. Hrs open: daytimer 341 Radio Station Rd., 42167. Phone: (270) 487-6119. Fax: (270) 487-8462.E-mail: kixcountry@scrtc.com Licensee: Whittimore Enterprises Inc. (acq 8-10-2006). Population served: 329,321 Natl. Network: USA, . Natl. Rep: Rgnl Reps,. Format: Classic Country. News staff: 2; News: progmg 4 hrs wkly. Target aud: 55+. Spec prog: gospel/religious & bluegrass. ♦Rebecca Brown, gen mgr, gen mgr, gen sls mgr & progmg dir.

WTKY-FM— Jan 20, 1972: 92.1 mhz; 5.3 kw. Ant 351 ft TL: N36 49 07 W85 39 32. Stereo. Hrs open: 6AM-11PM 341 Radio Station Rd., 42167. Phone: (270) 487-6119. Fax: (270) 487-8462.E-mail: kixcountry@scrtc.com Licensee: Whittimore Enterprises Inc. Population served: 329,321 Natl. Network: USA, . Natl. Rep: Rgnl Reps,. Format: Country. News staff: 2; News: 2 hrs wkly. Target aud: Female 18-45. ♦Rebecca Brown, gen mgr, gen sls mgr & progmg dir.

Upton

***WJCR-FM**— February 1990: 90.1 mhz; 100 kw. Ant 383 ft TL: N37 25 57 W86 01 50. Stereo. Hrs open: 24 Box 91, 42784-0091. Secondary address: 13101 Raider Hollow Rd. 42784. Phone: (270) 369-8614. Fax: (270) 369-7402.E-mail: wjcrfm@yahoo.com Web Site:www.wjcr.org Licensee: FM 90.1 Inc. Reddy, Begley & McCormick. Format: Southern gospel. Target aud: General. Spec prog: 5 hrs live prayline wkly. ♦Don Powell, pres, gen mgr; Lauree K. Powell, CFO & VP; Gary Richardson, stn mgr, progmg dir; Larry Baysinger, engrg dir, chief of engrg.

Valley Station

WRVI(FM)— 1982: 105.9 mhz; 1.9 kw. 413 ft TL: N38 08 16 W85 56 06. Hrs open: 9960 Corporate Campus Dr., Suite 3600, Louisville, 40223. Phone: (502) 339-9470. Fax: (502) 423-3139. Web Site:www.salemradiogroup.com Licensee: WAY-FM Media Group Inc. Group owner: Salem Communications Corp. (acq 10-2-2008; $3 million). Natl. Network: Salem Radio Network, . Natl. Rep: Salem,. Format: Christian contemp music. ♦Tim Hartlage, gen mgr; CC Matthews, opns dir, progmg dir.

Vanceburg

WKKS(AM)— June 1, 1958: 1570 khz; 1 kw-D. TL: N38 35 50 W83 20 50. Hrs open: 1074 Fairlane Dr., 41179. Phone: (606) 796-3031. Fax: (606) 796-6186. Licensee: Brown Communications Inc. (acq 1984). Population served: 1,773 Format: Classic country. ♦Dennis Brown, pres, gen mgr, gen sls mgr & progmg dir.

WKKS-FM— 1983: 104.9 mhz; 3 kw. 298 ft TL: N38 36 19 W83 19 57. Hrs open: Dups AM 95% 1074 Fairlane Dr., 41179. Phone: (606) 796-3031. Fax: (606) 796-6186. Licensee: Brown Communications Inc. Format: Top-40.

Vancleve

WMTC(AM)— June 1948: 730 khz; 5 kw-D, DA. TL: N37 36 12 W83 26 39. Hrs open: 6 AM-sunset 1036 Hwy. 541, Jackson, 41339. Phone: (606) 666-5006. Phone: (606) 666-9512. Fax: (606) 666-7534.E-mail: studio@mountaingospel.org Web Site:www.mountaingospel.org Licensee: Kentucky Mountain Holiness Assn. Population served: 2,000,000 Natl. Network: Salem Radio Network, . Womble, Carlyle, Sandridge & Rice. Format: Relg, Christian. News: 14 hrs wkly. Spec prog: Farm one hr wkly. ♦Philip Speas, pres; Jennifer Cox, gen mgr, mus dir; Anna Marshall, progmg dir; Kenneth Amspaugh, chief of engrg.

WMTC-FM— Jan 1, 1991: 99.9 mhz; 6 kw. Ant 328 ft TL: N37 36 23 W83 26 48. Stereo. Hrs open: 24 1036 Hwy. 541, Jackson, 41339. Phone: (606) 666-5006. Fax: (606) 666-7534.E-mail: studio@mountaingospel.org Licensee: Kentucky Mountain Holiness

Assn. Population served: 2,000,000 Format: Christian, relg. Spec prog: Farm one hr wkly. ◆Seldon Short, VP; Seldon Short, gen mgr; sls dir, edit dir, farm dir; Jennifer Cox, progmg dir; Gordon Sampsel, mus dir; Theresa Kerley, disc jockey.

Versailles

WCDA(FM)— July 16, 1973: 106.3 mhz; 3 kw. Ant 316 ft TL: N38 02 44 W84 39 29. Stereo. Hrs open: 24 401 W. Main, Suite 301, Lexington, 40507. Phone: (859) 233-1515. Fax: (859) 233-1517. Web Site:www.your1063.com Licensee: L.M. Communications Inc. (group owner; acq 9-3-98). Population served: 400,000 Natl. Rep: Katz Radio,. Format: Hot adult contemp. News staff: one; News: 2 hrs wkly. Target aud: 25-49; female. ◆Lynn Martin, pres; James MacFarlane, gen mgr; James McFarlane, mktg mgr.

Vine Grove

WRZI(FM)— Oct 5, 1993: 101.5 mhz; 6 kw. Ant 328 ft TL: N37 35 07 W85 50 20. Stereo. Hrs open: 24 611 W. Poplar St., Suite C2, Elizabethtown, 42701-2483. Phone: (270) 763-0800. Fax: (270) 769-6349.E-mail: info@etownpoint.com Web Site:etownpoint.com Licensee: Elizabethtown CBC Inc. Group owner: Commonwealth Broadcasting Corp. (acq 7-1-00; grpsl). Population served: 200,000 Rgnl rep: Rgnl Reps. Verner, Liipfert, Bernhard, McPherson & Hand. Format: Rock. News staff: one; News: 3 hrs wkly. Target aud: 25-45; males. ◆Steve Newberry, pres; Roth Stratton, gen mgr, sls VP; Dan Diaz, opns VP, opns dir; Misty Russell, progmg dir; Mike Graham, engrg dir; Holli Lee, traf mgr.

Virgie

WZLK(FM)— Nov 15, 1992: 107.5 mhz; 580 w. TL: N37 22 47 W82 34 11. (CP: 1.12 kw). Hrs open: Box 2200, Pikesville, 41502. Secondary address: 1240 Radio Dr., Pikesville 41502. Phone: (606) 437-4051. Fax: (606) 432-2809.E-mail: wdhr@wdhr.com Web Site:www.ekbradio.com Licensee: East Kentucky Broadcasting Corp. (acq 5-14-2003; $531,273 with WLSI(AM) Pikeville). Format: CHR, rock. ◆Keith Casebolt, gen mgr.

Warfield

***WNON(FM)—**Not on air, target date: unknown: 91.3 mhz; 7 kw. Ant 16 ft TL: N37 50 37 W82 25 51. Hrs open: Box 369, Lovely, 41231. Phone: (606) 395-6831. Licensee: Calvery Temple Community Church. ABN Radio ◆Arnold Damron, pres.

Warsaw

WKID(FM)—See Vevay, IN

West Liberty

WLKS(AM)— July 25, 1965: 1450 khz; 1 kw-U. TL: N37 55 36 W83 16 41. Stereo. Hrs open: 24 Box 338, 129 College St., 41472. Phone: (606) 743-3145. Fax: (606) 743-9557. Licensee: Morgan County Industries Inc. (group owner) Population served: 83,920 Natl. Rep: Rgnl Reps,. Format: Oldies. News staff: one; News: 35 hrs wkly. Target aud: General. Spec prog: Farm 5 hrs wkly. ◆Paul Lyons, gen mgr.

WLKS-FM— Jan 1, 1994: 102.9 mhz; 6 kw. Ant 328 ft TL: N37 55 36 W83 16 41. Hrs open: 24 129 College St., 41472. Phone: (606) 743-1029. Fax: (606) 743-9557. Licensee: Morgan County Industries Inc. Format: Country.

Whitesburg

***WMMT(FM)—** Nov 1, 1985: 88.7 mhz; 1 kw horiz 15 kw vert. 1,469 ft TL: N37 06 38 W82 44 15. Stereo. Hrs open: 24 91 Madison Ave., 41858. Phone: (606) 633-0108. Fax: (606) 633-1009.E-mail: wmmtfm@appalshop.org Web Site:www.appalshop.org Licensee: Appalshop Inc. Rgnl. Network: Ky. Pub. Kentucky Educational Television Format: Variety. Target aud: General. ◆Cheryl Marshall, gen mgr & dev dir.

WTCW(AM)— Feb 19, 1953: 920 khz; 4.2 kw-D, 43 w-N. TL: N37 08 46 W82 46 01. Hrs open: Box 288, Mayking, 41837. Phone: (606) 633-4434. Fax: (606) 633-4445.E-mail: wxkq@yahoo.com Web Site:www.1039thebulldog.com Licensee: T.C.W. Broadcasting Co. Inc. Group owner: Key Broadcasting Inc. (acq 1-1-86; $765,000 with co-located FM; 10-7-85). Population served:

80,000 Natl. Network: CBS, . Rgnl. Network: Ky. Net. Natl. Rep: Rgnl Reps,. Format: Classic country. Target aud: 30 plus. ◆Kevin Day, gen mgr.

WXKQ-FM— Nov 25, 1964: 103.9 mhz; 280 w. Ant 1,500 ft TL: N37 06 38 W82 44 15. Stereo. Hrs open: Dups AM 40% Box 288, 41837. Phone: (606) 633-4434. Phone: (606) 633-2711. Fax: (606) 633-4445. Web Site:www.1039thebulldog.com Format: Classic hits.

Whitesville

WXCM(FM)—Licensed to Whitesville. See Hawesville

Whitley City

WHAY(FM)— Dec 1, 1990: 98.3 mhz; 5.1 kw. Ant 354 ft TL: N36 39 40 W84 26 53. Hrs open: 24 Box 69, 42653. Phone: (606) 376-2218. Fax: (606) 376-5146.E-mail: whayradio@highland.net Web Site:www.hay98.com Licensee: Tim Lavender. Population served: 18,000 Format: Americana. News: 5 hrs wkly. Target aud: 30 plus. ◆Dave Shelley, gen mgr.

Wickliffe

WBCE(AM)— Jan 4, 1981: 1200 khz; 1 kw-D. TL: N36 58 54 W89 04 39. Hrs open: Box 128, 42087. Secondary address: 1136 Barlow Rd. 42087. Phone: (270) 335-5171. Fax: (270) 335-5172.E-mail: wbce@brtc.net Licensee: WBCE Inc. Format: Relg. Target aud: General. ◆Faye Crews, gen mgr.

WGKY(FM)— January 1987: 95.9 mhz; 3 kw. Ant 759 ft TL: N36 56 24 W88 57 59. Stereo. Hrs open: 24 930 Wickliffe Rd., 42087. Phone: (270) 335-3696. Fax: (270) 335-3698.E-mail: wgky@brtc.net Web Site:www.959wgky.com Licensee: W. Russell Withers Jr. (acq 2-21-2006; $400,000). Population served: 250,000 Natl. Network: Jones Radio Networks, . Rgnl. Network: Ky. News Net., Brownfield. Brownfield Rgnl rep: Rgnl Reps. Miller & Miller. Format: Oldies. News: 5 hrs wkly. Target aud: 24-54; rural homeowners, farmers. ◆Rick Lambert, gen mgr; Kathy Duncan, stn mgr; Clay Reed, opns mgr.

Williamsburg

***WCWC(AM)—** Mar 7, 1959: 1440 khz; 2.5 kw-D, 500 w-N, DA-1. TL: N36 43 48 W84 09 04. Hrs open: Daylight Whitley County Board of Education, 300 Main St., 40769-1124. Phone: (606) 549-8722. Fax: (606) 549-7045.E-mail: radiocwc@bellsouth.net Licensee: Whitley County Board of Education (group owner; (acq 8-28-2007; donation). Population served: 20,000 Rgnl. Network: Ky. Net. ◆Lonnie Anderson, gen mgr; Jill Roaden, stn mgr.

WEKC(AM)— Sept 21, 1981: 710 khz; 4.2 kw-D. TL: N36 46 28 W84 10 05. Stereo. Hrs open: Box 419, 40769. Secondary address: 402 Main St. 40769. Phone: (606) 549-3000. Fax: (606) 539-0916.E-mail: wekc@wekc.net Web Site:www.wekc.net Licensee: Gerald Parks (acq 6-21-00). Natl. Network: USA, . Format: Relg teaching, gospel. News: 5 hrs wkly. Target aud: General; young adults, All ages, race & creed. ◆Kay Parks, gen mgr & stn mgr.

WEZJ-FM— November 1990: 104.3 mhz; 1.4 kw. Ant 656 ft TL: N36 44 43 W84 11 24. Hrs open: 522 Main St., 40769. Phone: (606) 549-2285. Fax: (606) 549-5565. Licensee: Whitley Broadcasting Co. Inc. (acq 5-31-2002; grpsl). Natl. Rep: Rgnl Reps,. Format: Country. ◆David Estes, gen mgr; Rick Campbell, progmg mgr; Frank Folson, chief of engrg.

Williamstown

WNKR(FM)— Apr 1, 1992: 106.7 mhz; 1.8 kw. Ant 607 ft TL: N38 41 19 W84 35 07. Stereo. Hrs open: 24 Box 182, 118 S. Main St., Dry Ridge, 41035. Phone: (859) 824-9106. Phone: (800) 925-1220. Fax: (859) 824-9835.E-mail: wnkrproduction@fuse.net Web Site:www.1067wnkr.com Licensee: Grant County Broadcasters Inc. (acq 1992). Population served: 600,000 Rgnl. Network: Ky. Net. Natl. Rep: Rgnl Reps,. Ky. News Net Koerner & Olender. Format: Classic country. News staff: one; News 6 hrs wkly. Target aud: 35-54; adults. ◆Robert Wallace, pres; Jeffrey K. Ziesmann, gen mgr; Jay Anthony, opns mgr; Laura Ziesmann, sls dir, gen sls mgr; Katherine Marshall, pub affrs dir, traf mgr; Jim Stitt, chief of engrg.

Wilmore

WVRB(FM)— Sept 18, 1995: 95.3 mhz; 4.1 kw. Ant 397 ft TL: N37 57 37 W84 32 42. Hrs open: 24 5700 W. Oaks Blvd., Rocklin, CA, 95765. Phone: (707) 528-9236. Web Site:www.air1.com Licensee: Vernon R. Baldwin Inc. (group owner; acq 7-26-94;8-8-94). Population served: 500,000 Natl. Network: Air 1, . Format: Contemp Christian. Target aud: 20-45; Christians baby boomers. ◆Keith Whipple, gen mgr & stn mgr.

Winchester

WKQQ(FM)— 1974: 100.1 mhz; 32 kw. 490 ft TL: N38 07 25 W84 26 45. Stereo. Hrs open: 24 2601 Nicholasville Rd., Lexington, 40503. Phone: (859) 422-1000. Fax: (859) 422-1038.E-mail: info@wkqq.com Web Site:www.wkqq.com Licensee: Citicasters Licenses L.P. Group owner: Clear Channel Communications Inc. (acq 5-4-99; grpsl). Population served: 70,000 Format: Classic rock. News staff: one; News: 3 hrs wkly. Target aud: 18-49; women. ◆Gene Guinn, gen mgr & prom dir.

WMJR(AM)— Oct 19, 1954: 1380 khz; 2.5 kw-D, 40 w-N. TL: N38 00 46 W84 09 38. (CP: COL Nicholasville. 5 kw-D, 38 w-N. TL: N37 54 27 W84 28 42). Hrs open: 24 195 Moore Dr., Lexington, 40503. Phone: (859) 278-0894. Fax: (859) 278-0426.E-mail: info@wmjr.net Web Site:www.wmjr.net Licensee: Thy Kingdom Come Network Inc. (acq 1999; $583,000). Population served: 28,000 Rgnl. Network: Ky. Net. Pepper & Corazzini. Format: Christian. Target aud: 35-64. ◆Leo Brown, pres, gen mgr & progmg dir.

Louisiana

Abbeville

KPEL-FM— June 1, 1974: 105.1 mhz; 25 kw. 300 ft TL: N30 00 40 W92 07 21. (CP: Ant 292 ft.). Stereo. Hrs open: 24 1749 Bertrand Dr., Lafayette, 70506. Phone: (337) 233-6000. Fax: (337) 234-7360.E-mail: info@kpel1051news.com Web Site:www.kpel1051news.com Format: News/talk. ◆Bernadette Lee, progmg dir.

KROF(AM)— July 9, 1948: 960 khz; 1 kw-D, 95 w-N. TL: N30 00 40 W92 07 21. Hrs open: 24 1749 Bertrand Dr., Lafayette, 70506. Phone: (337) 233-6000. Fax: (337) 234-7360.E-mail: info@960thegator.com Web Site:www.960thegator.com Licensee: Regent Broadcasting of Lafayette LLC. Group owner: Regent Communications Inc. (acq 12-7-2001; grpsl). Format: Cajun. ◆Mike Grimsley, gen mgr; Chuck Wood, gen sls mgr; Camey Doucet, progmg dir; Kyle Vidrine, chief of engrg.

Alexandria

***KAPM(FM)—** June 1998: 91.7 mhz; 1 kw. 128 ft TL: N31 16 04 W92 26 24. Hrs open: Box 3206, American Family Radio, Tupelo, MS, 38803. Phone: (662) 844-8888. Fax: (662) 842-6791. Web Site:www.afr.net Licensee: American Family Association. Group owner: American Family Radio Format: Inspirational Christian. ◆Marvin Sanders, gen mgr.

KBCE(FM)—(Boyce, Mar 29, 1982: 102.3 mhz; 21 kw. Ant 289 ft TL: N31 22 21 W92 38 09. Hrs open: 1605 Murray St., Suite 111, 71301. Phone: (318) 445-0800. Fax: (318) 445-1445. Licensee: Trinity Broadcasting Corp. (acq 7-2-98; $26,248). Population served: 50,000 Natl. Network: American Urban, . Natl. Rep: D & R Radio,. Format: Urban contemp. News staff: 2. Target aud: General. ◆Kevin Wagner, pres; Bruce Pattani, sls dir; Cheron Holland, traf mgr.

KDBS(AM)— December 1953: 1410 khz; 1 kw-D, 30 w-N. TL: N31 16 25 W92 25 43. Hrs open: 24 1115 JTexas Ave., 71301. Phone: (318) 443-7454. Phone: (318) 445-1234. Fax: (318) 473-1960.E-mail: daveg@kswl.com Web Site:www.kdixie.com Licensee: Cenla Broadcasting Licensing Co. LLC. Group owner: Clear Channel Communications Inc. (acq 11-13-2006; grpsl). Population served: 140,000 Natl. Network: ESPN Radio, . Pepper & Corazzini. Format: Sports. ◆Taylor Thompson, gen mgr; Charlie Sopraz, opns mgr; Tish Robertson, gen sls mgr; Dave Grachien, progmg dir; Linnie Dupree, chief of engrg; Sybil Ford, traf mgr.

KEDG(FM)— 2001: 106.9 mhz; 6 kw. Ant 328 ft TL: N31 25 35 W92 24 25. Hrs open: 92 W. Shamrock St., Pineville, 71360. Secondary address: 1115 Texas Ave 71301. Phone: (318) 445-1234. Phone: (318) 487-1035. Fax: (318) 473-1960. Licensee: Flinn Broadcasting Corp. Format: Urban contemp. ◆Taylor Thompson, gen mgr.

KEZP(FM)—(Bunkie, 1993: 104.3 mhz; 19.2 kw. Ant 374 ft TL: N31 05 14 W92 21 34. Hrs open: 24 92 W. Shamrock Ave., Pineville, 71360-6414. Phone: (318) 487-1035. Fax: (318) 487-1045.E-mail: info@kezp.com Web Site:www.red1043.com Licensee: Opus Broadcasting Alexandria LLC. Group owner: Opus Media Partners LLC (acq 9-30-2004; $1.83 million). Population served: 250,000 Natl. Network: Westwood One, . Format: Modern rock. News staff: one. Target aud: 35-64. ♦Mark Jones, gen mgr.

KJMJ(AM)— Sept 21, 1935: 580 khz; 5 kw-D, 1 kw-N, DA-N. TL: N31 18 25 W92 25 00. Hrs open: 24 601 Washington St., 71301. Phone: (318) 561-6145. Fax: (318) 449-9954.E-mail: info.usa@radiomaria.org Web Site:www.radiomaria.us Licensee: Radio Maria Inc. (group owner; acq 9-20-99). Population served: 502010 Putbrese, Hunsaker & Trent, P.C. Format: Christian, relg, talk. News: 8 hrs wkly. Homebound, prisoners & sick. ♦Dale DePerrodill, gen sls mgr; Duane Stenzel, progmg dir; Danny Brou, chief of engrg.

KLAA-FM—(Tioga, May 25, 1984: 103.5 mhz; 50 kw. 476 ft TL: N31 25 39 W92 24 18. Stereo. Hrs open: 24 92 W. Shamrock, Pineville, 71360. Phone: (318) 487-1035. Fax: (318) 487-4419. Web Site:www.la103.com Licensee: Opus Broadcasting Alexandria LLC. Group owner: Opus Media Partners LLC (acq 9-30-2004; $3.38 million with KBKK(FM) Ball). Population served: 200,000 Natl. Rep: Christal,. Dow, Lohnes & Albertson. Wire Svc: AP Format: Country. News staff: one; News: 4 hrs wkly. Target aud: 25-54; working people, upscale professionals. ♦Kim Jones, pres & gen mgr.

***KLSA(FM)**— 1987: 90.7 mhz; 100 kw. Ant 1,243 ft TL: N31 33 56 W92 32 50. Hrs open: 24
Rebroadcasts KDAQ(FM) Shreveport 100%.
Box 5250, Shreveport, 71135. Phone: (318) 797-5150. Phone: (800) 552-8502. Fax: (318) 797-5265.E-mail: listenermail@redriverradio.com Web Site:www.redriverradio.org Licensee: Board of Supervisors Louisiana State University & Agricultural Mechanical College. Natl. Network: NPR, PRI, . Format: Classical, news, jazz. News: Nws progmg 40 hrs wkly. ♦Kermit Poling, gen mgr; Rick Shelton, opns mgr.

***KLXA-FM**— November 1998: 89.9 mhz; 3 kw. Ant 328 ft TL: N31 22 40 W92 28 27. Hrs open: 24 2351 Sunset Blvd., Suite 170-218, Rocklin, CA, 95765. Phone: (916) 251-1600. Fax: (916) 251-1650.E-mail: klov@klove.com Web Site:www.klove.com Licensee: Educational Media Foundation. Group owner: EMF Broadcasting (acq 12-1-03; $125,000). Natl. Network: K-Love, . Shaw Pittman. Format: Contemp Christian. News staff: 3. Target aud: 25-44; Judeo Christian, female. ♦Richard Jenkins, pres; Mike Novak, VP; Lloyd Parker, gen mgr; Ed Lenane, opns dir, news dir; Keith Whipple, dev dir; David Pierce, progmg mgr; Sam Wallington, engrg dir; Arthur Vassar, traf mgr; Karen Johnson, news rptr.

KMXH(FM)— February 1993: 93.9 mhz; 6 kw. Ant 328 ft TL: N31 16 04 W92 26 24. Hrs open: 1605 Murray St., Suite 111, 71301. Phone: (318) 445-0800. Fax: (318) 445-1445. Licensee: FM Broadcasting Corp. (acq 7-1-2005; $1.2 million). Population served: 50,000 Format: Urban Contemp. ♦Kevin Wagner, pres; Bruce Pattani, sls dir; Cheron Holland, traf mgr.

KQID(FM)— Sept 17, 1978: 93.1 mhz; 100 kw. 1,700 ft TL: N31 38 20 W92 12 18. Stereo. Hrs open: Box 7057, 71301. Secondary address: 1115 Texas Ave. 71306. Phone: (318) 445-1234. Fax: (318) 473-1960.E-mail: info@q93fm.com Web Site:www.q93fm.com Population served: 750,000 Format: Top-40.

KRRV-FM— May 11, 1969: 100.3 mhz; 100 kw. Ant 1,055 ft TL: N31 01 59 W92 30 08. Stereo. Hrs open: 24 1115 JTexas Ave., 71301. Phone: (318) 443-7454. Phone: (318) 445-1234. Fax: (318) 473-1960.E-mail: hollywood@cenlabroadcasting.com Web Site:www.krrv-fm.com Licensee: Cenla Broadcasting Licensing Co. LLC. Population served: 210,000 Format: Country. ♦Hollywood Harrison, progmg dir.

KSYL(AM)— Apr 1, 1947: 970 khz; 1 kw-U, DA-N. TL: N31 19 33 W92 29 17. Stereo. Hrs open: Box 7057, 71306. Secondary address: 1115 Texas Ave. 71301. Phone: (318) 445-1234. Fax: (318) 473-1960.E-mail: info@ksyl.com Web Site:www.ksyl.com Licensee: Cenla Broadcasting Inc. (acq 8-1-80). Population served: 41,557 Format: Talk. ♦Taylor Thompson, pres & gen mgr.

KTTP(AM)—(Pineville, Sept 13, 1974: 1110 khz; 2 kw-D. TL: N31 21 52 W92 27 15. Stereo. Hrs open: 3419 Hyson St., 71303. Phone: (318) 473-4388. Fax: (318) 449-1779.E-mail: kttpam1110@aol.com Licensee: Benjamin-Dane LLC (acq 4-7-2005; $175,000). Format: Gospel. Target aud: 25-70. ♦Ronald Reeves, pres; Carolyn Frazier, gen mgr, stn mgr; Dave Grayso, gen sls mgr, engr.

KWDF(AM)—(Ball, 1986: 840 khz; 10 kw-D. TL: N31 22 41 W92 28 27. Hrs open: 3735 Rigolette Rd., Pineville, 71360. Phone: (318) 640-4373. Fax: (318) 640-5971. Licensee: Capital City Radio Corp. Group owner: EMF Broadcasting (acq 8-29-2008; $122,000). Natl. Network: USA, . Format: Southern gospel. ♦Robert L. Wilkins, pres; Sharon Thorne, gen mgr; Jimmy Bryant, opns dir; Jimmy Bryant, progmg mgr; Tommy Moore, chief of engrg.

KZMZ(FM)— 1947: 96.9 mhz; 98 kw. Ant 1,053 ft TL: N31 01 59 W92 30 08. Stereo. Hrs open: 24 1115 Texas Ave, 71301. Phone: (318) 445-1234. Fax: (318) 445-7231.E-mail: chad@cenlabroadcasting.com Licensee: Cenla Broadcasting Licensing Co. LLC. Group owner: Clear Channel Communications Inc. (acq 11-13-2006; grpsl). Population served: 475,000 Pepper & Corazzini. Format: Classic rock. News staff: one; News: 2 hrs wkly. Target aud: 18-49; baby boomers. ♦Taylor Thompson, gen mgr.

Amite

WABL(AM)— January 1956: 1570 khz; 500 w-D. TL: N30 42 31 W90 31 31. Hrs open: 12 Box 787, 70422. Secondary address: 12515 Bankston Rd. 70422. Phone: (985) 748-8385. Fax: (985) 748-3918.E-mail: wabl1570@hotmail.com Licensee: Spotlight Broadcasting LLC (group owner; acq 6-8-01; $70,000). Population served: 200,000 Format: News/talk, country. Target aud: 20-64. ♦Patrick Andras, gen mgr.

WTGG(FM)— Mar 3, 1997: 96.5 mhz; 6 kw. 328 ft TL: N30 41 39 W90 26 41. Hrs open: 24 200 E. Thomas St., Hammond, 70401. Phone: (985) 345-0060. Fax: (985) 542-9377. Licensee: Southwest Broadcasting Inc. (group owner; acq 4-8-98; $650,000). Population served: 80,000 Natl. Network: Westwood One, . Rgnl. Network: La. Net. La. Net. Format: 50s, 60s & 70s oldies. News staff: one; News: one hr wkly. Target aud: 25-54; women. ♦Charles Dowdy, CEO; Eloise Dowdy, gen mgr & gen sls mgr; Ben Bickham, chief of engrg.

Angola

***KLSP(FM)**— Aug 12, 1986: 91.7 mhz; 100 w. 90 ft TL: N30 57 17 W91 35 45. Hrs open: Louisiana State Penitentiary, Hwy. 66, 70712. Phone: (225) 655-2001. Fax: (225) 655-2790.E-mail: info@klspfm.com Web Site:www.corrections.state.la.us/lsp/klsp.htm Licensee: Angola Educational Foundation Inc. Format: Div. Target aud: General. Spec prog: Black 10 hrs, C&W 6 hrs, jazz 7 hrs, poets corner one hr, legal wave 3 hrs wkly. ♦Burl Cain, gen mgr; Cheryl M. Ranatza, stn mgr.

Arcadia

***KHCL(FM)**— Jan 20, 2001: 92.5 mhz; 6 kw. Ant 328 ft TL: N32 27 27 W92 59 38. Hrs open: 24
Rebroadcasts KHCB-FM Houston, TX 95%.
Houston Christian Broadcasters Inc., 2424 South Blvd., Houston, TX, 77098. Phone: (713) 520-5200. Web Site:www.khcb.org Licensee: Houston Christian Broadcasters Inc. (group owner) Natl. Network: Moody, . Format: Christian. ♦Bruce Munsterman, gen mgr; Dan Wales, chief of engrg.

Atlanta

KCIJ(FM)— January 2002: 106.5 mhz; 25 kw. Ant 328 ft TL: N31 48 29 W92 48 22. Stereo. Hrs open: 24 213 Renee St., Natchitoches, 71457. Phone: (318) 354-4000. Fax: (318) 352-9598. Licensee: North Face Broadcasting L.L.C. (acq 5-9-2003; $348,000 with KNOC(AM) Natchitoches). Population served: 150,000 Format: Classic Hits. Target aud: 25-54; general. ♦Bill Vance, stn mgr; John Brewer, opns dir; Shane Evath, news dir.

Baker

WTGE(FM)— June 16, 1994: 107.3 mhz; 4.6 kw. 328 ft TL: N30 37 24 W91 09 50. Stereo. Hrs open: 24 Box 2231, Baton Rouge, 70821. Secondary address: 929-B Government St., Baton Rouge 70802. Phone: (225) 388-9898. Fax: (225) 383-3700.E-mail: owen.weber@gbcradio.com Web Site:www.countrylegends1073.com Licensee: Guaranty Broadcasting Co. of Baton Rouge LLC. Group owner: Guaranty Broadcasting Co. (acq 2-5-97). Population served: 750,000 Wiley, Rein & Fielding. Format: Classic Country. Target aud: 25-54; Adults. Spec prog: LSU Women's Basketball. ♦George A. Foster Jr., chmn; Bridger Eglin, pres, gen mgr; Owen Weber, VP; Dave Dunaway, opns mgr.

Ball

KBKK(FM)— September 1998: 105.5 mhz; 6 kw. 318 ft TL: N31 25 39 W92 24 18. Stereo. Hrs open: 24 92 W. Shamrock, Pineville, 71360. Phone: (318) 487-1035. Fax: (318) 487-4419. Web Site:www.1055kbuck.com Licensee: Opus Broadcasting Alexandria LLC. Group owner: Opus Media Partners LLC (acq 9-30-2004; $3.38 million with KLAA-FM Tioga). Population served: 150,000 Natl. Rep: Christal,. Wire Svc: AP Format: Classic country. Target aud: 50 plus. Spec prog: Nascar. ♦Kim Jones, pres & gen mgr.

KWDF(AM)—Licensed to Ball. See Alexandria

Basile

KQIS(FM)— May 4, 1990: 102.1 mhz; 3 kw. Ant 328 ft TL: N30 28 52 W92 35 50. Hrs open: 24 Box 60571, Lafeyette, 70596. Phone: (337) 783-2521. Fax: (337) 783-5744. Web Site:www.kqis.com Licensee: Third Partner Broadcasting Inc. (acq 3-21-94; $380,000; 5-30-94). Natl. Network: ABC, . Format: Todays hits & yesterdays favorites. News: 3 hrs wkly. Target aud: 25-55; middle-income. ♦Phil Lizotte, gen mgr; Jimmy Cole, gen sls mgr; Hans Nelson, progmg dir.

Bastrop

***KAXV(FM)**— 2000: 91.9 mhz; 12 kw. Ant 456 ft TL: N32 49 22 W92 07 28. Hrs open: Box 3206, American Family Radio, Tupelo, MS, 38803. Phone: (662) 844-8888. Fax: (662) 842-6791.E-mail: comments@afr.net Web Site:www.afr.net Licensee: American Family Radio. (group owner) Format: Inspirational Christian. ♦Marvin Sanders, gen mgr.

KJMG(FM)— 1996: 97.3 mhz; 6 kw. 328 ft TL: N32 45 46 W91 57 35. Stereo. Hrs open: 24 1109 Hudson Ln., Monroe, 71201. Secondary address: Box 4808, Monroe 71211. Phone: (318) 388-2323. Fax: (318) 388-0569. Web Site:www.majic97.com Licensee: Holladay Broadcasting of Louisiana LLC (group owner; acq 9-30-98; $700,000). Natl. Network: ABC, . Natl. Rep: McGavren Guild,. Latham & Watkins. Format: Urban adult contemp. Target aud: 25-54. Spec prog: Blues 12 hrs wkly. ♦Bob Holladay, pres.

KRVV(FM)— 1977: 100.1 mhz; 50 kw. 490 ft TL: N32 40 20 W91 55 06. Stereo. Hrs open: 24 Box 4808, Monroe, 71211. Secondary address: 1109 Hudson Ln., Monroe 71201. Phone: (318) 388-2323. Fax: (318) 388-0569.E-mail: krvv@bayou.com Web Site:www.thebeat.net Licensee: Holladay Broadcasting of Louisiana LLC (group owner; acq 10-15-91; $1 million;11-4-91). Population served: 254,000 Natl. Network: ABC, . Natl. Rep: McGavren Guild,. Latham & Watkins. Format: Urban. Target aud: 18-49. Spec prog: Gospel 4 hrs wkly. ♦Bob Holladay, pres & gen mgr.

Baton Rouge

KBRH(AM)— 1953: 1260 khz; 5 kw-D, 127 w-N. TL: N30 27 38 W91 14 37. Hrs open: 24 2825 Government St., 70806. Phone: (225) 383-3243. Fax: (225) 379-7685. Licensee: East Baton Rouge Parish School Board (Acq 7-7-93; 8-2-93). Format: Classic rhythm and blues. Target aud: 35 plus.

***KLSU(FM)**— October 1981: 91.1 mhz; 5 kw. 159 ft TL: N30 24 37 W91 10 37. Stereo. Hrs open: 24 B-39 Hodges Hall, Louisiana State Univ., 70803. Phone: (225) 578-8688. Fax: (225) 388-1698. Fax: (225) 578-0579.E-mail: info@klsufm.com Web Site:www.klsu.fm Licensee: Louisiana State University. Population served: 325,000 Natl. Rep: Rgnl Reps,. Format: Var. News: one hr wkly. Target aud: 18-25; university students & college age listeners. ♦Peyton Juneau, stn mgr.

***WBRH(FM)**— September 1977: 90.3 mhz; 21 kw. Ant 197 ft TL: N30 26 42 W91 09 33. Stereo. Hrs open: 24 2825 Government St., 70806. Phone: (225) 383-3243. Fax: (225) 379-7685. Licensee: East Baton Rouge Parish School Board Population served: 460,000 Natl. Network: NPR, . Format: Jazz. Target aud: 25-54; men. ♦Larry Davis, gen mgr, stn mgr; Lyn Kenyon, sls dir; Rob Payer, mus dir.

WCDV(FM)—See Hammond

WDGL(FM)— Oct 1, 1968: 98.1 mhz; 100 kw. 1,550 ft TL: N30 21 58 W91 12 47. Stereo. Hrs open: 24 Box 2231, 70821. Secondary address: 929-B Government St. 70802. Phone: (225) 388-9898. Fax: (225) 383-3700.E-mail: owen.weber@gbcradio.com Web Site:www.eagle981.com Licensee: Guaranty Broadcasting Co. of Baton Rouge LLC. Group owner: Guaranty Broadcasting Co. Population served: 750,000 Wiley, Rein & Fielding. Wire Svc: AP Format: Classic rock. Target aud: 25-54; Adult. Spec prog: LSU Football and Baseball, Play by Play broadcasts; Don Dubuc Fishing. ♦George A. Foster Jr., chmn; Bridger Eglin, pres, VP; Owen Weber, VP & gen mgr; Dave Dunaway, opns mgr.

WDVW(FM)—See La Place

WFMF(FM)— 1941: 102.5 mhz; 85 kw. Ant 1,260 ft TL: N30 17 49 W91 11 40. Stereo. Hrs open: 5555 Hilton Ave., Suite 500, 70808. Phone: (225) 231-1860. Fax: (225) 231-1873.E-mail: info@wfmw.com Web Site:www.wfmf.com Licensee: Capstar TX L.P. Format: CHR. Target aud: 18-34; female.

WIBR(AM)— July 18, 1948: 1300 khz; 5 kw-D, 1 kw-N, DA-2. TL: N30 28 25 W91 13 34. Hrs open: 650 Wooddale Blvd., 70806. Phone: (225) 926-1106. Fax: (225) 928-1606. Web Site:1300espn.com Licensee: Citadel Broadcasting Co. Group owner: Citadel Broadcasting Corp. (acq 1999; grpsl). Population served: 245,752 Natl. Network: ABC, . Rgnl. Network: La. Net. Natl. Rep: McGavren Guild,. La. Net. Wire Svc: UPI Format: Sports. Target aud: 25-50. ◆Greg Benefield, gen mgr.

WJBO(AM)— Dec 11, 1934: 1150 khz; 5 kw-U, DA-1. TL: N30 27 47 W91 16 10. Hrs open: 5555 Hilton Ave., Suite 500, 70808. Phone: (225) 231-1860. Fax: (225) 231-1873.E-mail: info@wjbo.com Web Site:www.wjbo.com Licensee: Capstar TX L.P. Group owner: Clear Channel Communications Inc. (acq 8-30-2000; grpsl). Population served: 525,700 Natl. Network: CBS, Westwood One, . Format: Talk, news, sports. Target aud: 20 plus. ◆Donnie Picou, VP & gen mgr.

*WJFM(FM)— June 1995: 88.5 mhz; 25.5 kw. Ant 269 ft TL: N30 23 06 W91 05 28. Stereo. Hrs open: 24 Box 262550, 70826-2550. Secondary address: 8919 World Ministry Ave. 70810. Phone: (225) 768-3688. Phone: (225) 768-8300. Fax: (225) 768-3729.E-mail: kawikfish@yahoo.com Web Site:www.jsm.org Licensee: Family Worship Center Church Inc. (group owner; acq 12-15-99). Population served: 150,000 Format: Christian. News staff: one; News: 2 hrs wkly. Target aud: 25-54; full gospel Christians & anyone searching for hope. ◆David Whitelaw, COO; Jimmy Swaggart, pres; stn mgr; John Santiago, dev dir & progmg dir.

WPFC(AM)—(Port Allen, 1963: 1550 khz; 5 kw-D. TL: N30 30 07 W91 12 39. Hrs open: Sunrise-sunset 6943 Titian Ave., 70806. Phone: (225) 926-1506. Fax: (225) 590-3238. Web Site:www.1550wpfc.com Licensee: Victory and Power Ministries Inc. (acq 11-15-94; $450,000; 12-12-94). Population served: 500,000 Natl. Network: USA, . Latham & Watkins. Format: Relg, gospel music. News staff: 2; News: 3 hrs wkly. Target aud: 35-59; middle-class female. ◆Pastor Ralph Moore, CEO & gen mgr; Keith Richard, stn mgr.

WPYR(AM)— 1956: 1380 khz; 5 kw-D, DA. TL: N30 27 39 W91 13 23. Hrs open: 5555 Hilton Ave., Suite 500, 70808. Phone: (225) 231-1860. Fax: (226) 231-1879.E-mail: info@talkradio1380.com Web Site:www.talkradio1380.com Licensee: Davidson Media Station WPYR Licensee LLC. Group owner: Clear Channel Communications Inc. (acq 9-16-2008; exchange for WBZK(AM) York, SC). Population served: 550,000 Format: Talk. ◆Mark Kennedy, progmg dir.

*WRKF(FM)— Jan 18, 1980: 89.3 mhz; 28 kw. 935 ft TL: N30 22 22 W91 12 16. Stereo. Hrs open: 24 3050 Valley Creek, 70808. Phone: (225) 926-3050. Fax: (225) 926-3105. Web Site:www.wrkf.org Licensee: Public Radio Inc. Natl. Network: NPR, PRI, . Format: Class, news/talk. News staff: one; News: 35 hrs wkly. Target aud: General. ◆Blythe Earl, gen mgr, opns dir; Malcolm Robinson, pres & dev mgr.

WUBR(AM)— Nov 1, 1946: Stn currently dark. 910 khz; 1 kw-U, DA-1. TL: N30 34 48 W91 07 50. Hrs open: 1111 Michigan Ave., East Lansing, MI, 48823. Phone: (517) 351-3333. Licensee: Communications Capital Co. III LLC. (acq 2-17-2006; $75,000). Target aud: 18-59. ◆Michael H. Oesterle, CEO; Sandra Pate, gen mgr.

WXOK(AM)— February 1953: 1460 khz; 5 kw-D, 1 kw-N, DA-3. TL: N30 28 08 W91 12 24. Hrs open: 24 650 Wooddale Blvd., 70806. Phone: (225) 926-1106. Fax: (225) 928-1606.E-mail: wxok.am@citcomm.com Web Site:www.heaven1460.com Licensee: Citadel Broadcasting Co. Group owner: Citadel Broadcasting Corp. (acq 1-14-99). Population served: 180,000 Natl. Network: ABC, . Format: Urban gospel. Target aud: 18 plus. ◆Greg Benefield, gen mgr.

WYNK-FM— Dec 7, 1968: 101.5 mhz; 97 kw. Ant 1,499 ft TL: N30 19 34 W91 16 36. Stereo. Hrs open: 24 5555 Hilton Ave., Suite 500, 70808. Phone: (225) 231-1860. Fax: (225) 231-1873.E-mail @wynk.com Web Site:www.wynk.com Licensee: Capstar TX L.P. Group owner: Clear Channel Communications Inc. (acq 8-30-2000; grpsl). Format: Country. News staff: 2. Target aud: 18-54. ◆Donnie Picou, gen mgr; Bob Murphy, progmg dir.

WYPY(FM)— Sept 10, 1966: 100.7 mhz; 97 kw. 1,499 ft TL: N30 19 35 W91 16 36. Stereo. Hrs open: 24 Box 2231, 70821. Secondary address: 929-B Government St. 70802. Phone: (225) 388-9898. Fax: (225) 383-3700.E-mail:owen.weber@gbcradio.com Web Site:www.newcountry1007.com Licensee: Guaranty Broadcasting Co. of Baton Rouge LLC. Group owner: Guaranty Broadcasting Co. (acq 1996; $5.5 million). Population served: 750,000 Natl. Rep: D & R

Radio,. Wiley, Rein & Fielding. Format: New Country. Target aud: 25-54; Adults. Spec prog: New Orleans Saints Football Play by Play and LSU Men's Basketball. ◆George A. Foster Jr., chmn, VP; Bridger Eglin, pres; Owen Weber, VP; Dave Dunaway, opns mgr, progmg dir.

Bayou Vista

KQKI(FM)— Dec 31, 1976: 95.3 mhz; 16.5 kw. 400 ft TL: N29 29 38 W91 17 41. Hrs open: 128 Pluto St., 70381. Phone: (985) 395-2853. Fax: (985) 395-5094.E-mail: kqki@cajun.net Web Site:www.kqki.com Licensee: Teche Broadcasting Corp. Population served: 59,000 Natl. Network: ABC, . Rgnl. Network: La. Net. La. Net. Format: Country. News staff: one; News: 17 hrs wkly. Target aud: 30 plus; general. ◆Paul J. Cook, pres & gen mgr; Ernest Dean Polk, stn mgr, news dir; Julie Boyne, gen sls mgr, progmg dir.

Belle Chasse

KKND(FM)— March 1990: 102.9 mhz; 4.7 kw. Ant 604 ft TL: N29 57 14 W89 56 58. Hrs open: 201 St. Charles Ave., Suite 201, New Orleans, 70170. Phone: (504) 581-7002. Fax: (504) 566-4857.E-mail: lbj.kmez@citcomm.com Web Site:www.power1029.com Licensee: Citadel Broadcasting Co. Group owner: Citadel Broadcasting Corp. (acq 8-29-2003; grpsl). Population served: 2,965,100 Dow, Lohnes & Albertson. Format: Rhythm & blues. Target aud: 35-54; female. ◆Dave Siebert, gen mgr, mktg dir; LeBron Joseph, progmg dir.

Benton

KSYR(FM)— 1981: 92.1 mhz; 3 kw. 299 ft TL: N32 39 19 W93 41 38. Stereo. Hrs open: 24 208 N. Thomas Dr., Shreveport, 71107. Phone: (318) 222-3122. Fax: (318) 459-1493. Licensee: Access. 1 Louisiana Holding Co. LLC. Group owner: Access.1 Communications Corp. (acq 5-5-00; grpsl). Natl. Network: ABC, . Format: Rgnl Mexican. News staff: one. Target aud: 35 plus; upper income, upwardly mobile. ◆Cary D. Camp, pres, gen mgr, stn mgr; Don Zimmerman, gen sls mgr.

Berwick

KBZE(FM)— July 4, 1990: 105.9 mhz; 3.2 kw. Ant 403 ft TL: N29 45 27 W91 10 25. Stereo. Hrs open: Box 1560, Morgan City, 70381. Secondary address: 1320 Victor II Blvd., Morgan City 70380. Phone: (985) 385-6266. Fax: (985) 385-6268.E-mail: kbze@petronet.net Web Site:ww.kbze.com Licensee: HubCast Broadcasting Inc. (acq 6-6-94; $105,500). Population served: 75,000 Natl. Network: ABC, . Format: Urban adult contemp, relg, sports. News staff: one; News: 10 hrs wkly. Target aud: 24-54; middle to upper income. ◆Howard Castay Jr., pres & gen mgr; Darlene Castay, opns VP.

Blanchard

KDKS-FM— Oct 19, 1998: 102.1 mhz; 14 kw. 440 ft TL: N32 35 57 W93 54 01. Hrs open: 24 208 N. Thomas Dr., Shreveport, 71107. Phone: (318) 222-3122. Fax: (318) 459-1493.E-mail: info@kdks.fm Web Site:www.kdks.fm Licensee: Access. 1 Louisiana Holding Co. LLC. Group owner: Access.1 Communications Corp. (acq 6-30-00; $7.9 million with KLKL(FM) Minden). Format: Urban adult contemp. News staff: one. Target aud: 25-54. ◆Cary Camp, gen mgr; Quinn Echols, progmg dir.

*KFLO-FM— 2006: 89.1 mhz; 20 kw vert. Ant 406 ft TL: N32 18 28 W93 58 34. Hrs open: Box 7277, Shreveport, 71137. Secondary address: 2097 N. Hearne Ave., Shreveport 71107. Phone: (318) 550-2000. Fax: 318-550-2002.E-mail: info@miracle891.org Web Site:miracle891.org Licensee: Family Life Educational Foundation (acq 10-7-2005; $97,000 for CP). Format: Inspirational music. ◆A.T. Moore, pres; Donna Cole, gen mgr; Dan Perkins, opns mgr; Joe Miot, progmg dir.

Bogalusa

WBOX(AM)— Mar 1, 1954: 920 khz; 1 kw, DA-N. TL: N30 50 29 W89 50 06. Hrs open: Box 280, 70429. Secondary address: 22037 Hwy. 436 70427. Phone: (985) 732-4288. Phone: (985) 732-4288.E-mail: info@wbox(am/fm).com Licensee: Best Country Broadcasting LLC (acq 9-6-2002; $150,000 with WBOX-FM Varnado). Population served: 18,412 Format: Country. ◆Ben R. Strickland, pres & gen mgr.

WBOX-FM—See Varnado

WIKC(AM)— May 15, 1947: 1490 khz; 1 kw-U. TL: N30 47 30 W89 52 47. Hrs open: 24 Box 638, 70429. Secondary address: 607 Rio

Grande St. 70429. Phone: (985) 732-4190. Fax: (985) 732-7594.E-mail: timberlands@bellsouth.net Licensee: Timberlands Broadcasting Corp. (acq 6-29-82). Population served: 65,000 Natl. Network: Salem Radio Network, . Format: Relg, gospel, news/talk. News: 30 hrs wkly. Target aud: General. ◆G.S. Adams Jr., pres; Gardner Adams, gen mgr.

Bossier

KRMD(AM)—See Shreveport

KRMD-FM—See Shreveport

Bossier City

KBCL(AM)— September 1957: 1070 khz; 250 w-D. TL: N32 32 14 W93 43 28. Hrs open: 316 Gregg St., Shreveport, 71104. Phone: (318) 861-1070.E-mail: kbcl_radio@bellsouth.net Web Site:www.praise1070.org Licensee: Barnabas Center Ministries (acq 8-26-02; donation). Population served: 182,064 Format: Christian, talk shows. ◆Leon McKee, gen mgr; Jean McKee, progmg dir.

Boyce

KBCE(FM)—Licensed to Boyce. See Alexandria

Breaux Bridge

KFTE(FM)— May 1, 1993: 96.5 mhz; 22.5 kw. 328 ft TL: N30 06 09 W91 59 30. Stereo. Hrs open: 24 1749 Bertrand Dr., Lafayette, 70506-2054. Phone: (337) 233-6000. Fax: (337) 234-7360.E-mail: info@planet965.com Web Site:www.planet965.com Licensee: Regent Broadcasting of Lafayette LLC. Group owner: Regent Communications Inc. (acq 12-7-2001; grpsl). Wiley, Rein & Fielding. Format: Modern rock. ◆Mike Grimsley, gen mgr; Scott Pessin, progmg dir.

Broussard

*WHFG(FM)— 2008: 91.3 mhz; 6 kw. Ant 367 ft TL: N29 58 04 W91 55 31. Hrs open: 1115 Honeysuckle Dr., Keene, TX, 76059. Phone: (817) 641-3495. Licensee: Mary V. Harris Foundation. ◆Linda De Romanett, pres.

Brusly

KRVE(FM)— Sept 9, 1989: 96.1 mhz; 43 kw. 449 ft TL: N30 29 34 W91 00 15. Stereo. Hrs open: 24 5555 Hilton Ave., Suite 500, Baton Rouge, 70808. Phone: (225) 231-1860. Fax: (225) 231-1869.E-mail: info@murphysamandjodi.com Web Site:www.961theriver.com Licensee: Capstar TX L.P. Group owner: Clear Channel Communications Inc. (acq 8-30-00; grpsl). Format: Lite adult contemp. News staff: 3. Target aud: 25-54; women. ◆Dick Lewis, gen mgr; Bob Murphy, progmg dir; Libby Davis, prom dir & pub affrs dir.

Bunkie

KEZP(FM)—Licensed to Bunkie. See Alexandria

Buras

*KMRL(FM)— Apr 22, 1995: Stn currently dark. 91.9 mhz; 3 kw. Ant 164 ft TL: N29 20 15 W89 28 46. Hrs open: 3600 Manhattan Blvd., Harvey, 70058. Phone: (504) 362-3379. Licensee: New Orleans Quality Radio Inc. (acq 11-9-2007; $70,000). Population served: 25,000 Target aud: General. ◆W. Christopher Beary, pres.

Church Point

*KCKR(FM)— 2007: 91.9 mhz; 12.5 kw. Ant 465 ft TL: N30 19 47 W92 05 06. Hrs open: 24 Box 262550, 70826-2550. Secondary address: 8919 World Ministry Ave., Baton Rouge 70810. Phone: (225) 768-3102. Web Site:www.jsm.org Licensee: Family Worship Center Church Inc. (acq 10-22-2007; $3.6 million). Format: Relg. ◆Jimmy Swaggart, pres.

Clinton

*WBKL(FM)— Sept 23, 1981: 92.7 mhz; 32 kw. Ant 604 ft TL: N30 51 03 W91 04 31. Stereo. Hrs open: 24
Rebroadcasts KLVR(FM) Santa Rosa, CA 100%.
2351 Sunset Blvd., Suite 170-218, Rocklin, CA, 95765. Phone: (916) 251-1600. Fax: (916) 251-1650. Web Site:www.klove.com Licensee: Educational Media Foundation. (acq 7-1-2005; $3.2 million). Natl. Network: K-Love,. Format: Contemp Christian. ◆Richard Jenkins, pres; Mike Novak, VP; Keith Whipple, dev dir; David Pierce, progmg mgr; Ed Lenane, news dir; Sam Wallington, engrg dir; Karen Johnson, news rptr.

*WWRA(FM)— 2008: 91.9 mhz; 5 kw. Ant 269 ft TL: N30 49 00 W90 48 42. Hrs open: 3953 N. Flannery Rd., Baton Rouge, 70814. Phone: (225) 791-1429. Web Site:www.amorradio.org Licensee: Victory Harvest Church. Population served: 50,000 Format: Sp relg. ◆Dulio F. Canossa, gen mgr.

Columbia

KQLQ(FM)— Jan 21, 1980: 103.1 mhz; 25 kw. 348 ft TL: N32 09 25 W92 10 58. Stereo. Hrs open: 24 1200 N. 18th St., Suite D, Monroe, 71201. Phone: (318) 387-3922. Fax: (318) 322-4585. Web Site:1031theparty.com Licensee: Opus Broadcasting Monroe L.L.C. Group owner: Opus Media Partners LLC (acq 7-19-2004; grpsl). Format: Hip hop. ◆Chris Zimmerman, gen mgr.

Cotton Valley

*KLHV(FM)—Not on air, target date: unknown: 88.5 mhz; 32 kw vert. Ant 443 ft TL: N32 42 19 W93 38 24. Hrs open: Box 8525, Tyler, TX, 75711. Phone: (903) 593-5863. Licensee: Educational Radio Foundation of East Texas Inc. ◆Troy Kriechbaum, pres.

Coushatta

KRRP(AM)— May 1981: 950 khz; 500 w-D, 209 w-N, DA-2. TL: N31 56 49 W93 21 13. Stereo. Hrs open: 24 Rt. 4 Box 197, Jordan Ferry Rd., 71019. Phone: (318) 932-6704. Phone: (800) 374-0323. Fax: (318) 932-9700.E-mail: krrp@cp-tel.net Licensee: Roberto Feliz (acq 12-1-2003; $350,000). Population served: 950000 Natl. Network: ESPN Radio,. Cohn & Marks. Format: Sports. News staff: one; News: 20 hrs wkly. Target aud: 35 plus; mature, educated, affluent listeners. ◆Chris Boyd, gen mgr, gen sls mgr; George Moore, progmg dir; Robert Abrahams, chief of engrg.

KSBH(FM)— Nov 15, 1992: 94.9 mhz; 25 kw. 328 ft TL: N31 51 34 W93 13 00. Stereo. Hrs open: 24 213 Renee St., Natchitoches, 71457. Phone: (318) 354-4000. Fax: (318) 352-9598. Licensee: KSBH L.L.C. (acq 6-3-98; $350,000). Population served: 150,000 Format: Country. Target aud: 18-54. ◆Bill Vance, stn mgr; John Brewer, opns mgr; Shane Evath, news dir.

Covington

WASO(AM)— November 1953: 730 khz; 250 w-D, 25 w-N. TL: N30 29 37 W90 08 37. Hrs open: 3313 Kingmen St., Metairie, 70006. Phone: (504) 888-8255. Fax: (504) 888-8329.E-mail: info@hottalkradio.com Web Site:www.hottalkradio.com Licensee: MCDJ LLC (acq 8-30-2007; $578,100). Population served: 75,000 Format: News/talk. Target aud: 25 plus. ◆Robert Namer, gen mgr.

Crowley

KAJN-FM— Oct 1, 1977: 102.9 mhz; 95 kw. 1,499 ft TL: N30 02 19 W92 22 15. Stereo. Hrs open: 24 Box 1469, 70527-1469. Secondary address: 110 W. 3rd St. 70526. Phone: (337) 783-1560. Fax: (337) 783-1674. Web Site:www.kajn.com Licensee: Agape Broadcasters Inc. Population served: 1,500,000 Natl. Network: USA,. Shaw Pittman. Wire Svc: AP Format: Relg. News staff: one; News: 3 hrs wkly. Target aud: 25-44; female, family oriented. Spec prog: Black 2 hrs wkly. ◆Barry D. Thompson, CEO, pres, gen mgr; Annette G. Thompson, VP; Craig Thompson, progmg dir.

KSIG(AM)— May 1947: 1450 khz; 1 kw-U. TL: N30 13 50 W92 21 45. Hrs open: Box 228, 70527. Secondary address: 320 N. Parkerson Ave. 70527. Phone: (337) 783-2520. Fax: (337) 783-5744. Licensee: Acadia Broadcast Partners Inc. (acq 12-7-92; $350,000; 1-4-93). Population served: 16,104 Format: Oldies. Spec prog: Fr 18 hrs, farm 5 hrs wkly. ◆Phil Lizotte, pres, gen mgr, stn mgr; Jimmy Cole, gen sls mgr; Hans Nelson, progmg dir; Tony Evans, chief of engrg.

De Quincy

KTSR(FM)— Nov 1, 1985: 92.1 mhz; 13.5 kw. Ant 448 ft TL: N30 13 24 W93 18 36. Stereo. Hrs open: 24 900 N. Lakeshore Dr., Lake Charles, 70601. Phone: (337) 433-1641. Fax: (337) 433-2999. Web Site:www.kissfm921.com Licensee: GAP Broadcasting Lake Charles License LLC. (group owner; (acq 2-6-2008; grpsl). Format: Adult top-40. ◆Sara Cormier, gen mgr; Aaron Turner, gen sls mgr; Eric Scott, progmg dir; Dave Chimeno, chief of engrg.

De Ridder

*KBAN(FM)— 2001: 91.5 mhz; 20.5 kw. Ant 361 ft TL: N30 38 10 W93 02 33. Hrs open: American Family Radio, Box 3206, Tupelo, MS, 38803. Secondary address: Quicken Ministries %AFR, 1411 Parish Rd., Lake Charles 70611. Phone: (662) 844-8888. Phone: (337) 217-0252. Fax: (662) 842-6791. Fax: (337) 217-0253.E-mail: comments@myafr.com Web Site:www.afr.net Licensee: American Family Association. Group owner: American Family Radio Format: Inspirational Christian. ◆Marvin Sanders, gen mgr; Elizabeth Arrington, stn mgr.

KDLA(AM)— Nov 11, 1950: 1010 khz; 1 kw-D, 40 w-N. TL: N30 52 43 W93 17 25. Hrs open: Sunrise-sunset 645 Church St., Suite 400, Norfolk, 23510. Phone: (757) 622-4600. Licensee: Christian Broadcasting of De Ridder Inc. (group owner; (acq 2-18-98; $150,000). Population served: 150,000 Natl. Network: Reach Satellite,. Format: Gospel. Target aud: 18-54.

KQLK(FM)— Sept 6, 1991: 97.9 mhz; 50 kw. Ant 492 ft TL: N30 36 57 W93 13 31. Stereo. Hrs open: 24 425 Broad St., Lake Charles, 70601. Phone: (337) 439-3300. Fax: (337) 433-7278.E-mail: info@kqlk.com Web Site:www.kqlk.com Licensee: Cumulus Licensing LLC. (group owner; (acq 12-6-2004; $3 million with KAOK(AM) Lake Charles). Format: Adult contemp. ◆Crash Kelley, progmg dir; Richard Rhodes, chief of engrg.

Delhi

KGGM(FM)— September 1991: 93.5 mhz; 3 kw. 328 ft TL: N32 37 45 W91 33 13. Hrs open: 1204 Hwy. 80, 71232. Phone: (318) 878-8255. Licensee: Kenneth W. Diebel (acq 9-10-2003; $120,000). Format: Southern gospel. ◆Ken Diebel, pres & gen mgr.

Denham Springs

WSKR(AM)— Apr 15, 1959: 1210 khz; 10 kw-D, 1 kw-N, DA-N. TL: N30 31 20 W90 58 15. Stereo. Hrs open: 18 5555 Hilton Ave., Suite 500, Baton Rouge, 70808. Phone: (225) 231-1860. Fax: (225) 231-1869. Web Site:www.thescore1210.com Licensee: Capstar TX L.P. Group owner: Clear Channel Communications Inc. (acq 8-30-00; grpsl). Population served: 750,000 Natl. Network: Westwood One,. Format: Sports. News staff: 2. Target aud: 25-54. ◆Dick Lewis, gen mgr; Mike Scott, gen sls mgr; Bob Murphy, opns; Libby Davis, prom.

Donaldsonville

KNXX(FM)— 1972: 104.9 mhz; 6 kw. Ant 299 ft TL: N30 05 57 W91 00 13. Hrs open: 24
Rebroadcasts WNXX(FM) Jackson 100%.
Box 2231, Baton Rouge, 70821-2231. Secondary address: 929 B Government St., Baton Rouge 70802-6033. Phone: (225) 388-9898 ext 148. Fax: (225) 499-9800.E-mail: owen.weber@9bcradio.com Web Site:www.104thex.com Licensee: Guaranty Broadcasting Co. of Baton Rouge LLC. Group owner: Guaranty Broadcasting Co. (acq 2-18-2000; $1.2 million). Population served: 150,000 Natl. Rep: McGavren Guild,. Wiley, Rein & Fielding. Format: Alternative, new rock. News: 2 hrs wkly. Target aud: 18-34. ◆George Foster Jr., chmn; Bridger Eglin, pres; Owen Weber, VP; Dave Dunaway, opns mgr.

Dry Prong

*KVDP(FM)— Aug 13, 1985: 89.1 mhz; 4.5 kw. 295 ft TL: N31 35 20 W92 30 59. Stereo. Hrs open: Box 249, 71423. Secondary address: 160 Bud Walker Rd. 71423. Phone: (318) 899-5837. Fax: (318) 899-7624. Licensee: Dry Prong Educational Broadcasting Foundation Inc. (acq 11-24-92; 12-21-92). Natl. Network: USA,. Format: Relg, educ, Christian. ◆Donna Clina, gen mgr; Darris Cline, mus dir, chief of engrg.

Dubach

KNBB(FM)— June 4, 1984: 97.7 mhz; 50 kw. Ant 464 ft TL: N32 40 09 W92 37 58. Stereo. Hrs open: 5 AM-11 PM Box 430, Ruston, 71273. Secondary address: 500 N. Monroe St., Ruston 71270. Phone: (318) 255-5000. Fax: (318) 255-5084.E-mail: seanfox@espn977.com Web Site:www.espn977.com Licensee: Communications Capital Co. II of Louisiana LLC. Group owner: Communications Capital Managers LLC (acq 5-27-2003; $1.5 million). Population served: 250,000 Natl. Network: ESPN Radio,. Format: Sports talk. Target aud: 25-44; men. ◆Gary McKenney, gen mgr; Sean Fox, progmg dir.

Empire

KNOU(FM)— June 2001: Stn currently dark. 104.5 mhz; 7.8 kw. Ant 850 ft TL: N29 33 45 W89 49 46. Hrs open: c/o Hartman Leito & Bolt LLP, 6100 Southwest Blvd., Suite 500, Fort Worth, TX, 76109. Phone: (817) 738-2400. Licensee: On Top Communications of Louisiana LLC, Debtor-in-Possession Group owner: On Top Communications Inc. (acq 1-13-2006). Format: Urban contemp. ◆Bryan C. Rice, gen mgr.

Erath

KRKA(FM)— April 1992: 107.9 mhz; 25 kw. 328 ft TL: N30 02 54 W91 59 49. (CP: 10 kw, ant 469 ft.). Stereo. Hrs open: 24 1749 Bertrand Dr., Lafayette, 70506-2054. Phone: (337) 233-6000. Fax: (337) 234-7360.E-mail: info@1079ishot.com Web Site:www.1079ishot.com Licensee: Regent Broadcasting of Lafayette LLC. Group owner: Regent Communications Inc. (acq 12-7-2001; grpsl). Population served: 300000 Rgnl. Network: La. Net. Natl. Rep: Katz Radio,. La. Net. Format: Rhythmic CHR. News: 25 hrs wkly. Target aud: 12-34. ◆Mike Grimsley, gen mgr; Chris Logan, progmg dir.

Erwinville

*KPAE(FM)— Sept 30, 1985: 91.5 mhz; 5 kw. 167 ft TL: N30 32 09 W91 14 52. Stereo. Hrs open: 24
Rebroadcasts WPAE (FM) Centreville, MS 75%.
Box 1390, Centreville, MS, 39631. Secondary address: 122 E. Main St., Centreville, MS 39631. Phone: (601) 645-6515. Fax: (225) 627-4970. Fax: (601) 645-9122.E-mail: wpaefm@telepak.net Web Site:www.soundradio.org Licensee: Port Allen Educational Broadcasting Foundation. Natl. Network: Moody,. Format: Relg teaching. Target aud: General. ◆Willie F. Kennedy, pres.

Eunice

KEUN(AM)— October 1952: 1490 khz; 1 kw-U. TL: N30 28 17 W92 24 51. Hrs open: 24 Box 105-5, 70535. Phone: (337) 457-3041. Fax: (337) 457-3081.E-mail: spots@keunworldwide.com Web Site:www.keunworldwide.com Licensee: Tri-Parish Broadcasting Co. Inc. (acq 5-12-2003; with co-located FM). Population served: 25,000 Natl. Network: Radio America,. La. Net. Format: News/talk. News staff: one; News: 3 min every hr. Target aud: 25 plus. Spec prog: Cajun one hr wkly. ◆Rick Nesbitt, gen mgr, progmg dir, news dir; Tony Evans, chief of engrg.

KEUN-FM— Oct 22, 1981: 105.5 mhz; 1 kw. Ant 485 ft TL: N30 26 16 W92 26 49. Stereo. Hrs open: 24 P.O. Box 105-5, 70535. Phone: (337) 457-3041. Fax: (337) 457-3081.E-mail: spots@keunworldwide.com Web Site:www.keunworldwide.com Licensee: Tri-Parish Broadcasting Co. Inc. Natl. Network: ABC,. Format: Contemp country. News staff: one; News: local one hr wkly. Target aud: P 25-54. Spec prog: Cajun music 12 hrs wkly. ◆Rick Nesbitt, gen mgr & progmg dir.

Farmerville

KBYO-FM— Apr 19, 1979: 92.7 mhz; 6 kw. Ant 328 ft TL: N32 40 31 W92 19 10. Stereo. Hrs open: 24 321 N. 2nd St., Monroe, 71203. Phone: (318) 323-2700. Fax: (318) 323-3719. Web Site:www.fox927.com Licensee: Union Broadcasting Co. Inc. Natl. Network: Fox Sports,. Rgnl. Network: La. Net. Format: Talk, sports. Target aud: 24-65; adult audience with incomes to buy. ◆Lee Fletcher, gen mgr.

Ferriday

KFNV-FM— October 1971: 107.1 mhz; 18.5 kw. Ant 233 ft TL: N31 36 08 W91 32 27. Stereo. Hrs open: Box 1510, 71334. Secondary address: 917 S. EE Wallace Blvd. 71334. Phone: (318) 757-4200. Fax: (318) 757-7689.E-mail: kfnv@bellsouth.net Web Site:www.kfnvfm.com Licensee: Tom D. Gay Group owner: The Radio Group Population served: 30,000 Format: Classic hits. News: 2 hrs wkly. Target aud:

25-55; baby boomers. ◆Desiree Smith, gen mgr; Mike Smith, gen sls mgr; Eddie Ray, progmg dir; Selena Book, traf mgr.

Folsom

WJSH(FM)— March 1996: 104.7 mhz; 6 kw. Ant 328 ft TL: N30 39 55 W90 04 49. Hrs open: 24 200 E. Thomas St., Hammond, 70401. Phone: (985) 542-0060. Fax: (985) 542-9377. Licensee: Southwest Broadcasting. (acq 11-17-2000). Population served: 250000 Format: Smooth jazz. ◆Charles Dowdy, gen mgr; Eloise Dowdy, gen mgr & gen sls mgr; Ben Bickham, chief of engrg.

Franklin

KDDK(FM)— May 9, 1975: 105.5 mhz; 3 kw. Ant 300 ft TL: N29 50 14 W91 32 22. (CP: COL Addis. 6 kw, ant 328 ft. TL: N30 19 25 W91 16 52). Stereo. Hrs open:
Rebroadcasts KJCB(AM) Lafayette 100%.
5047 Hwy. 1148, Plaquemine, 70764-52227. Phone: (225) 687-2882.E-mail: kddk@bellsouth.net Web Site:www.kddkfm.com Licensee: Radio & Investments Inc. Population served: 100,000 James Cooke. Format: Adult standards. ◆Ken Noble, gen mgr, gen sls mgr & progmg dir.

KFRA(AM)— June 4, 1961: 1390 khz; 500 w-D. TL: N29 50 14 W91 32 22. Stereo. Hrs open: Stn currently dark 5047 Hwy. 87, 70538. Phone: (337) 924-7100. Licensee: Castay Media Inc. (acq 9-7-2007; $125,000). Population served: 150,000 ◆Howard Castay, pres.

Franklinton

WOMN(AM)— Dec 5, 1966: 1110 khz; 1 kw-D. TL: N30 51 34 W90 09 57. Hrs open: Sunrise-sunset 3015 E. Causeway Approach, Mandeville, 70448. Phone: (985) 624-9452. Fax: (985) 624-9559.E-mail: mpittman@pittmanbroadcasting.com Licensee: Pittman Broadcasting Services LLC. (group owner; (acq 6-4-2002; with co-located FM). Population served: 10,000 Format: Country. Target aud: General. ◆Mike Mitchell, gen sls mgr; Tony Evans, chief of engrg.

WUUU(FM)— Mar 3, 1997: 98.9 mhz; 6 kw. 108 ft TL: N30 51 34 W90 09 57. Hrs open: 24 3015 E. Causeway Approach, Mandeville, 70448. Phone: (985) 624-9452. Fax: (985) 624-9559.E-mail: mpittman@pittmanbroadcasting.com Licensee: Pittman Broadcasting Services LLC.

Galliano

WTIX-FM—Licensed to Galliano. See Golden Meadow

Garyville

*WCKW(AM)— Dec 22, 1970: 1010 khz; 500 w-D, 42 w-N. TL: N30 04 35 W90 37 17. Stereo. Hrs open: 24 4424 Hampton Ave., St. Louis, MO, 63109. Phone: (314) 752-7000. Fax: (314) 752-7702. Web Site:www.covenantnet.net Licensee: Covenant Network (acq 10-17-2006). Population served: 96,000 Format: Relg. Target aud: 18-54. ◆John Anthony Holman, pres.

Gibsland

KBEF(FM)— May 23, 2001: 104.5 mhz; 6 kw. Ant 328 ft TL: N32 31 59 W93 11 34. Hrs open: 410 Lakeshore Dr., Minden, 71055. Phone: (318) 377-1240. Fax: (318) 377-4619.E-mail: kaso1240@yahoo.com Web Site:www.kbef.com Licensee: Amistad Communications Inc. (acq 7-12-2000; $375,000 for CP with KASO(AM) Minden). Format: Contemp Christian. ◆Mike Griffith, gen mgr.

Golden Meadow

KLEB(AM)— May 13, 1963: 1600 khz; 5 kw-D, 250 w-N. TL: N29 22 41 W90 15 50. Hrs open: 24 Drawer 1350, 11603 Hwy. 308, Larose, 70373. Phone: (985) 798-7792. Fax: (985) 798-7793.E-mail: klrz@mobiletel.com Web Site:www.klrzfm.com Licensee: Coastal Broadcasting of Larose Inc. (acq 1999; $250,000). Format: C&W, Fr, Oldies. Target aud: 25 plus; general. ◆Jerry J. Gisclair, pres & gen mgr; Andrea Galjour, opns mgr.

*KUHN(FM)—Not on air, target date: unknown: 89.3 mhz; 11 kw. Ant 161 ft TL: N29 13 02 W90 13 11. Hrs open: 20986 Hwy. 1, 70357. Phone: (985) 475-6640. Fax: (985) 475-7109. Web Site:www.unitedhoumanation.org Licensee: United Houma Nation Inc. ◆Brenda Dardar Robichaux, gen mgr.

WTIX-FM—(Galliano, Nov 16, 1975: 94.3 mhz; 100 kw. 982 ft TL: N29 33 46 W89 49 46. Hrs open: 24 4539 I-10 Service Rd., 3rd Fl., Metairie, 70006. Phone: (504) 454-9000. Fax: (504) 454-9002.E-mail: info@wtixfm.com Web Site:wtixfm.com Licensee: Fleur de Lis Broadcasting Inc. (acq 6-8-95; $600,000). Population served: 1250000 Natl. Network: ABC, . Reddy, Begley & McCormick. Format: Oldies. News: 4 hrs wkly. Target aud: 25-54. ◆George Buck, pres; Michael Costello, gen mgr.

Grambling

*KGRM(FM)— January 1974: 91.5 mhz; 50,000 watt. 492 ft TL: N32 30 56 W92 43 27. Stereo. Hrs open: 24 Box 4254, Grambling State Univ., 71245. Secondary address: Washington Johnson Complex 2nd Fl., 403 Main St. 71245. Phone: (318) 274-6343. Fax: (318) 274-3245.E-mail: evansjb@gram.edu Web Site:www.gram.edu/kgrm Licensee: Grambling State University. Format: Gospel, urban contemp. Target aud: Black community. ◆Joyce Evans, gen mgr.

Gretna

KGLA(AM)— Jan 6, 1969: 1540 khz; 1 kw-D. TL: N29 53 27 W90 05 05. Hrs open: 3850 N. Causeway Blvd., Metairie, 70072. Phone: (504) 799-4242. Fax: (504) 799-3434.E-mail: mailto:info@kgla.tv Web Site:www.tropical1540.com Licensee: Crocodile Broadcasting Corp. (acq 6-30-2007; $245,000). Population served: 1,500,000 Format: Sp contemp. ◆Ernesto Schweikert, gen mgr.

KKNO(AM)— Sept 10, 1989: 750 khz; 250 w-D, DA. TL: N29 53 15 W90 05 03. Hrs open: Sunrise-sunset 980 Avenue A, Marrero, 70072. Phone: (504) 347-7775. Fax: (504) 347-7440.E-mail:kkno750am@aol.com Licensee: Robert C. Blakes Enterprises Inc. (acq 6-24-93; $275,000; 7-12-93). Format: Christian gospel, relg. News: 10 hrs wkly. Target aud: General. ◆Robert C. Blakes Sr., pres; Lois R. Blakes, gen mgr; Stacey Blakes, opns mgr, gen sls mgr & progmg dir.

Hammond

*KSLU(FM)— Nov 11, 1974: 90.9 mhz; 3 kw. Ant 141 ft TL: N30 30 53 W90 27 59. Stereo. Hrs open: 24 D. Vickers Hall Rm 112, SLU 10783, 70402. Phone: (985) 549-2330. Fax: (985) 549-3960.E-mail: kslu@selu.edu Web Site:www.kslu.org Licensee: Southeastern Louisiana University. Population served: 150,000 Natl. Network: PRI, . Format: Alternative. News staff: one; News: 30 hrs wkly. Target aud: General. ◆Todd Delaney, gen mgr; Steve Portier, chief of engrg.

WCDV(FM)— Apr 3, 1965: 103.3 mhz; 100 kw. Ant 1,004 ft TL: N30 24 06 W90 50 43. Stereo. Hrs open: 24 650 Wooddale Blvd., Baton Rouge, 70806-2930. Phone: (225) 926-1106. Fax: (225) 928-1606.E-mail: wcdv.fm@citcomm.com Web Site:www.sunny1033.com Licensee: Citadel Broadcasting Co. Group owner: Citadel Broadcasting Corp. (acq 1999; grpsl). Natl. Network: ABC, . Rgnl. Network: La. Net. Natl. Rep: McGavren Guild,. La. Net. Format: Soft rock. News staff: one; News: 3 hrs wkly. Target aud: 25-54. ◆Greg Benefield, gen mgr & sls dir.

WDVW(FM)—La Place

WFPR(AM)— Nov 15, 1947: 1400 khz; 1 kw-U. TL: N30 30 31 W90 30 18. Hrs open: 24 200 E. Thomas, 70401. Phone: (985) 345-0060. Fax: (985) 542-9377.E-mail: swapshop@nsbradiobroadcasting.com Licensee: North Shore Broadcasting Co. Inc. (acq 12-4-2003; $1.85 million with co-located FM). Population served: 80,000 Natl. Network: CBS, . Format: Country. News staff: one; News: 7 hrs wkly. Target aud: 35-64. Spec prog: Farm one hr, gospel 12 hrs wkly. ◆Wayne Dowdy, pres; Eloise Dowdy, gen mgr, gen sls mgr; Ben Bickham, progmg dir, chief of engrg, disc jockey.

WHMD(FM)— Aug 26, 1974: 107.1 mhz; 6 kw. Ant 328 ft TL: N30 25 32 W90 17 01. Stereo. Hrs open: Dups AM 50% 200 E. Thomas, 70401. Phone: (985) 345-0060. Fax: (985) 542-9377. Format: New country.

Haughton

KBTT(FM)— 1993: 103.7 mhz; 6 kw. 328 ft TL: N32 31 20 W93 30 05. Hrs open: 24 208 N. Thomas Dr., Shreveport, 71107. Phone: (318) 222-3122. Fax: (318) 459-1493. Web Site:www.1037thabeat.fm Licensee: Access. 1 Louisiana Holding Co. LLC. Group owner: Access.1 Communications Corp. (acq 5-10-00; grpsl). Format: Urban contemp. News staff: 1. Target aud: 18-34. ◆Cary D. Camp, gen mgr.

Hodge

KRLQ(FM)— Aug 15, 2007: 94.1 mhz; 35 kw. Ant 507 ft TL: N32 24 35 W92 53 49. Hrs open: Box 2941, Ruston, 71273. Secondary address: 1319 N. Vienna , Ruston 71270. Phone: (318) 255-7941. Fax: (318) 255-8211.E-mail: krlq941fm@bellsouth.net Web Site:krlq941.com Licensee: William W. Brown. Format: Country, sports, talk. ◆William W. Brown, gen mgr.

Homer

KYLA(FM)— March 1998: 106.7 mhz; 50 kw. Ant 492 ft TL: N32 37 03 W93 14 36. Hrs open: 2351 Sunset Blvd., Suite 170-218, Rocklin, CA, 95765. Phone: (916) 251-1600. Fax: (916) 251-1650. Web Site:www.klove.com Licensee: Educational Media Foundation. (acq 5-30-2006). Natl. Network: K-Love, . Format: Christian. ◆Richard Jenkins, pres; Mike Novak, VP; Keith Whipple, dev dir; David Pierce, progmg mgr; Ed Lenane, news dir; Sam Wallington, engrg dir; Karen Johnson, news rptr.

Houma

KCIL(FM)— Dec 31, 1965: 107.5 mhz; 69 kw. Ant 650 ft TL: N29 26 48 W90 44 34. Stereo. Hrs open: Box 2068, 70361. Secondary address: 120 Prevost Dr. 70364. Phone: (985) 851-1020. Fax: (985) 872-4403.E-mail: info@1075kcil.net Web Site:www.1075kcil.net Licensee: Sunburst Media-Louisiana LLC. Population served: 250,000 Format: Country. News staff: one; News: 2 hrs wkly. Target aud: Adults; 25-54.

KJIN(AM)— Apr 1, 1946: 1490 khz; 1 kw-U. TL: N29 34 14 W90 43 42. Hrs open: 24 Box 2068, 70361. Secondary address: 120 Prevost Dr. 70364. Phone: (985) 851-1020. Fax: (985) 872-4403.E-mail: info@mix967.net Licensee: Sunburst Media-Louisiana LLC. (acq 1-23-2007; grpsl). Population served: 125,000 Natl. Network: ABC, . Natl. Rep: Roslin,. Wiley, Rein & Fielding. Format: Sports. News staff: one; News: 3 hrs wkly. Target aud: 35 plus. ◆Danny Fletcher, gen mgr, gen sls mgr; John Delise, opns mgr; Cade Voison, progmg dir; Bo Hoover, chief of engrg.

KYRK(FM)— Nov 15, 1968: 104.1 mhz; 100 kw. Ant 1,945 ft TL: N29 57 13 W90 43 25. Stereo. Hrs open: 24 929 Howard Ave., New Orleans, 70113. Phone: (504) 679-7300. Fax: (504) 679-7358.E-mail: info@kyrk.com Web Site:www.kissneworleans.com Licensee: Clear Channel Broadcasting Licenses Inc. Group owner: Clear Channel Communications Inc. (acq 1-27-2009; with WJRR(FM) Cocoa Beach, FL). Population served: 2,500,000 Natl. Rep: Clear Channel,. Format: New rock. News staff: one; News: 2 hrs wkly. Target aud: 25-54. ◆Dick Lewis, pres, gen mgr; Michael Scott, gen sls mgr; Mike Kramer, progmg dir; Tom Courtney, chief of engrg.

Iota

*KITA(FM)— 2008: 89.5 mhz; 19 kw vert. Ant 433 ft TL: N30 11 17 W92 37 55. Hrs open:
Rebroadcasts KLRD(FM) Yucaipa, CA 100%.
2351 Sunset Blvd., Suite 170-218, Rocklin, CA, 95765. Phone: (916) 251-1600. Fax: (916) 251-1650. Web Site:www.air1.com Licensee: Educational Media Foundation. (acq 11-1-2006; grpsl). Natl. Network: Air 1, . Format: Alternative rock, Christian music, div. ◆Mike Novak, pres.

Jackson

WNXX(FM)— Oct 17, 2001: 104.5 mhz; 3 kw. Ant 472 ft TL: N30 44 44 W91 07 32. Stereo. Hrs open: 24
Rebroadcasts KNXX(FM) Donaldsonville 100%.
Box 2231, Baton Rouge, 70821. Secondary address: 929-B Government St., Baton Rouge 70802. Phone: (225) 388-9898. Fax: (225) 344-3077.E-mail: owen.weber@gbcradio.com Web Site:www.104thex.com Licensee: Guaranty Broadcasting Co. of Baton Rouge LLC. Group owner: Guaranty Broadcasting Co. (acq 10-5-2000; $1.044 million). Natl. Rep: McGavren Guild,. Wiley, Rein & Fielding. Format: Alternative new rock. Target aud: 18-34. ◆George A. Foster Jr., chmn; Bridger Eglin, pres, gen mgr; Owen Weber, VP; Dave Dunaway, opns mgr.

Jena

*KAYT(FM)— Jan 1, 2001: 88.1 mhz; 15.5 kw horiz, 70 kw vert. 1,007 ft TL: N31 33 54 W92 33 00. Hrs open: 5003 Masonic Dr., Suite 113, Alexandria, 71301. Phone: (318) 484-2500. Fax: (318) 487-0909.E-mail: kayt88@suddenlink.mail.com Licensee: Black Media Works Inc. (group owner). Format: Relg. ◆Raymond Kassis, gen mgr; Jocelyn Jacob, stn mgr.

KJNA-FM— November 1976: 102.7 mhz; 6 kw. 298 ft TL: N31 41 51 W92 05 43. Stereo. Hrs open: 24 Box 2750, 71342. Secondary address: 1791 N. 2nd St. 71342. Phone: (318) 992-4155. Fax: (318) 992-4479.E-mail: kjnafm@hotmail.com Licensee: Little River Radio Co. Population served: 75,000 Format: Country. News staff: one; News: 20 hrs wkly. Target aud: 25-54. ♦Larry Evans, gen mgr.

Jennings

KHLA(FM)— January 1963: 92.9 mhz; 33 kw. Ant 600 ft TL: N30 00 31 W92 46 47. Stereo. Hrs open: 24 900 N. Lakeshore Dr., Lake Charles, 70601. Phone: (337) 433-1641. Fax: (337) 433-2999. Web Site:www.929thelake.com Licensee: GAP Broadcasting Lake Charles License LLC. (acq 2-6-2008; grpsl). Population served: 500,000 Format: Classic hits. ♦Aaron Turner, gen sls mgr, min affrs dir; Gary Shannon, progmg dir; Sara Cormier, stn mgr & political ed.

KJEF(AM)— November 1950: 1290 khz; 1 kw-U. TL: N30 12 38 W92 39 55. Stereo. Hrs open: 24 900 N. Lakeshore Dr., Lake Charles, 70601. Phone: (337) 433-1641. Fax: (337) 433-2999. Web Site:www.cajunradio.net Licensee: GAP Broadcasting Lake Charles License LLC. (group owner; (acq 2-6-2008; grpsl). Population served: 11,783 Rgnl. Network: La. Net. La. Net. Format: Cajun. Target aud: General. ♦Sara Cormier, gen mgr; Aaron Turner, gen sls mgr; Mike Soileau, progmg dir; Dave Chimeno, chief of engrg.

Jonesboro

***KTOC-FM—** Oct 1, 1967: 104.9 mhz; 25 kw. Ant 236 ft TL: N32 13 28 W92 43 27. Stereo. Hrs open: Box 262550, Baton Rouge, 70826. Secondary address: 8919 World Ministry Ave., Baton Rouge 70810. Phone: (225) 768-3688. Phone: (225) 768-8300. Fax: (225) 768-3729.E-mail: kawikfish@yahoo.com Web Site:www.jsm.org Licensee: Family Worship Center Church Inc. (acq 9-25-2002; $200,000 with co-located AM). Population served: 8,000 Format: Christian. ♦David Whitelaw, COO; Jimmy Swaggart, pres; John Santiago, progmg dir.

Jonesville

KTGV(FM)— 2001: 105.1 mhz; 6 kw. Ant 315 ft TL: N31 36 21 W91 50 06. Hrs open: Box 768, Natchez, MS, 39121. Secondary address: 2 Oferrall St., Natchez 39120-3000. Phone: (601) 442-4895. Fax: (601) 446-8260. Licensee: First Natchez Corp. Group owner: First Natchez Radio Group (acq 8-30-99; $150,000). Format: Urban contemp. ♦Margaret Perkins, gen mgr; Mickey Alexander, progmg dir; Keith Sanders, chief of engrg; Brenda Green, traf mgr.

Kaplan

KMDL(FM)— Aug 1, 1981: 97.3 mhz; 42 kw. 535 ft TL: N30 02 54 W91 59 49. Stereo. Hrs open: 24 1749 Bertrand Dr., Lafayette, 70506-2054. Phone: (337) 233-6000. Fax: (337) 234-7360.E-mail: info@973thedawg.com Web Site:www.973thedawg.com Licensee: Regent Broadcasting of Lafayette LLC. Group owner: Regent Communications Inc. (acq 12-7-2001; grpsl). Natl. Network: AP Radio, . Wiley, Rein & Fielding. Format: Classic country. News: 7 hrs wkly. Target aud: 25-54. ♦Mike Grimsley, gen mgr; Scott Bryant, progmg dir.

Kenner

WWL-FM— Sept 8, 1970: 105.3 mhz; 96 kw. Ant 1,004 ft TL: N29 58 57 W89 57 09. Stereo. Hrs open: 400 Poydras, Suite 500, New Orleans, 70112. Phone: (504) 593-6376. Fax: (504) 593-2285.E-mail: info@wwl.com Web Site:www.wwl.com Licensee: Entercom New Orleans License LLC. Group owner: Entercom Communications Corp. (acq 12-13-99; grpsl). Format: News, talk. ♦Ken Beck, gen mgr; Patrick Galloway, sls dir; Mark Broudreaux, gen sls mgr; Diane Newman, progmg dir, chief of engrg; Joe Pollet, chief of engrg.

Kentwood

WEMX(FM)— Dec 14, 1967: 94.1 mhz; 100 kw. 981 ft TL: N30 51 18 W90 39 59. Stereo. Hrs open: 24 650 Wooddale Blvd., Baton Rouge, 70806. Phone: (225) 926-1106. Fax: (225) 928-1606.E-mail: wemx.fm@citcomm.com Web Site:www.max94one.com Licensee: Citadel Broadcasting Co. Group owner: Citadel Broadcasting Corp. (acq 1-14-99; grpsl). Population served: 500,000 Format: Hip hop, rhythm and blues. ♦Greg Benefield, gen mgr.

***WPEF(FM)—**Not on air, target date: unknown: 91.5 mhz; 6 kw. Ant 295 ft TL: N31 02 02 W90 25 27. Hrs open: 3939 Gentilly Blvd., New Orleans, 70126. Phone: (504) 816-8000. Fax: (504) 816-8580. Licensee: Providence Educational Foundation Inc. ♦Clay Corvin, gen mgr.

La Place

WDVW(FM)— Jan 10, 1966: 92.3 mhz; 100 kw. Ant 1,945 ft TL: N29 57 10 W90 43 26. Stereo. Hrs open: 24 201 St. Charles Ave., Suite 201, New Orleans, 70170. Phone: (504) 581-7002. Fax: (504) 566-4857. Web Site:www.diva923.com Licensee: Citadel Broadcasting Co. Group owner: Citadel Broadcasting Corp. (acq 1-30-2004; $14.25 million). Population served: 2,068,800 Natl. Rep: Christal,. Rgnl rep: Christal Radio Format: Hot adult contemp. ♦Dave Siebert, gen mgr; John McQueen, progmg dir.

Lacombe

WYLK(FM)— March 1996: 94.7 mhz; 5.3 kw horiz, 5.2 kw vert. Ant 348 ft TL: N30 15 08 W89 45 46. Hrs open: 24 324 Lockwood St., Covington, 70433. Phone: (985) 867-5990. Fax: (985) 867-9530. Licensee: North Shore Broadcasting Inc. (group owner; (acq 7-6-2005; $4.5 million with WPRF(FM) Reserve). Population served: 256,000 Format: Hot CHR. News staff: one; News: 2 hrs wkly. Target aud: 25-54; general. ♦Vicki Hays, gen mgr & sls dir.

Lafayette

KFXZ(AM)— Nov 15, 1960: 1520 khz; 10 kw-D, 500 w-N, DA-N. TL: N30 16 51 W92 00 53. Stereo. Hrs open: 24 3225 Ambassador Caffery Pkwy., 70506. Phone: (337) 993-5500. Fax: (337) 993-5510.E-mail: info@fsr1520.com Web Site:fsr1520.com Licensee: Pittman Broadcasting Services LLC (group owner; (acq 1-28-2004; grpsl). Population served: 176,000 Format: Sports, talk. ♦Charles Sagona, gen mgr.

***KIKL(FM)—** Feb 7, 1988: 90.9 mhz; 6 kw. Ant 476 ft TL: N30 17 08 W92 04 03. Stereo. Hrs open: 24 2351 Sunset Blvd., Suite 170-218, Rocklin, CA, 95765. Phone: (916) 251-1600. Fax: (916) 251-1650. Licensee: Educational Media Foundation. Group owner: EMF Broadcasting (acq 4-25-2005; $1.5 million). Population served: 350,000 Shaw Pittman LLP. Format: Christian. ♦Richard Jenkins, pres; Mike Novak, VP; Keith Whipple, dev dir; David Pierce, progmg mgr; Ed Lenane, news dir; Sam Wallington, engrg dir; Karen Johnson, news rptr.

KJCB(AM)— Apr 9, 1982: 770 khz; 1 kw-D, 500 w-N, DA-N. TL: N30 17 55 W91 59 30. Stereo. Hrs open: 604 St. John St., 70501. Phone: (337) 233-4262. Fax: (337) 235-9681. Web Site:www.blackaction.net Licensee: R & M Broadcasting Inc. (acq 11-16-92; $100,000; 12-14-92). Format: Urban contemp, gospel. Target aud: 25-54. Spec prog: . ♦Jenelle Schargios, gen mgr.

KPEL(AM)— Jan 2, 1950: 1420 khz; 1 kw-D, 750 w-N, DA-N. TL: N30 16 38 W92 03 51. Hrs open: KPEL AM FM, 1749 Bertrand Dr., 70506. Phone: (337) 233-6000. Fax: (337) 234-7360.E-mail: info@espn1420.com Web Site:www.espn1420.com Licensee: Regent Broadcasting of Lafayette LLC. Group owner: Regent Communications Inc. (acq 12-7-2001; grpsl). Population served: 250,000 Rgnl. Network: La. Net. Natl. Rep: Christal,. La. Net. Format: Sports. Target aud: 35-54; male. ♦Mike Grimsley, gen mgr; Chuck Wood, gen sls mgr; Kyle Vidrine, chief of engrg.

KRRQ(FM)— 1996: 95.5 mhz; 50 kw. 443 ft TL: N30 21 08 W92 10 51. Hrs open: 202 Galbert Rd., 70506. Phone: (337) 232-1311. Fax: (337) 233-3779.E-mail: krrq@krrq.com Web Site:www.krrq.com Licensee: Citadel Broadcasting Co. Group owner: Citadel Broadcasting Corp. (acq 1-14-99; grpsl). Format: Urban contemp/hip hop. ♦Jim Beard, gen mgr.

***KRVS(FM)—** 1962: 88.7 mhz; 100 kw. 449 ft TL: N30 15 25 W92 09 38. Stereo. Hrs open: Box 42171, 70504. Secondary address: 231 Hebrard Blvd. 70503. Phone: (337) 482-5787. Fax: (337) 482-6101.E-mail: krvs@louisiana.edu Web Site:www.krvs.org Licensee: University of Southwestern Louisiana. Population served: 300,000 Natl. Network: NPR, . Format: Var, Eclectic (cajun, zydeco, blues, jazz). Target aud: General. ♦Dave Spizale, gen mgr; James Hebert, opns mgr; Judith Meriwether, dev dir, prom mgr; Kim Neustrom Richard, mktg dir; Karl Fontenot, chief of engrg.

KSMB(FM)— 1964: 94.5 mhz; 100 kw. Ant 1,079 ft TL: N30 21 44 W92 12 53. Stereo. Hrs open: 202 Galbert Rd., 70506. Phone: (337) 232-1311. Fax: (337) 233-3779. Web Site:www.ksmb.com Licensee: Citadel Broadcasting Co. Group owner: Citadel Broadcasting Corp. (acq 4-26-01; grpsl). Population served: 414,800 Format: CHR/Top-40. Target aud: 18-49; active on-the-go adults.

KTDY(FM)— Sept 15, 1966: 99.9 mhz; 100 kw. 984 ft TL: N30 12 04 W91 46 33. Stereo. Hrs open: 1749 Bertrand Dr., 70506. Phone: (337) 233-6000. Fax: (337) 234-7360.E-mail: info@999ktdy.com Web Site:www.999ktdy.com Population served: 750,000 Format: Adult contemp. Target aud: 25-54; female. ♦C.J. Clements, gen sls mgr & progmg dir.

KVOL(AM)— May 18, 1935: 1330 khz; 5 kw-D, 1 kw-N, DA-2. TL: N30 14 29 W92 03 31. Hrs open: 3225 Ambassador Caffery Pkwy., 70506. Phone: (337) 993-5500. Fax: (337) 993-5510.E-mail: kvol@pittmanbroadcasting.com Web Site:www.kvol1330.com Licensee: Pittman Broadcasting Services LLC (group owner; acq 1-28-2004; grpsl). Natl. Network: Westwood One, . Format: News talk. Target aud: 25-54; middle & upper income. ♦Charles Sagona, gen mgr.

KXKC(FM)—See New Iberia

Lake Arthur

KJMH(FM)— Aug 1, 1998: 107.5 mhz; 50 kw. Ant 462 ft TL: N30 12 07 W92 56 47. Hrs open: 24 900 N. Lakeshore Dr., Lake Charles, 70601. Phone: (337) 433-1641. Fax: (337) 433-2999. Web Site:www.107jamz.com Licensee: GAP Broadcasting Lake Charles License LLC. (group owner; (acq 2-6-2008; grpsl). Natl. Rep: Christal,. Format: Hip Hop, rhythm and blues. News staff: one. Target aud: 25-54. ♦Sara Cormier, gen mgr; Aaron Turner, gen sls mgr; Erik Johnson, progmg dir; Dave Chimeno, chief of engrg.

Lake Charles

KAOK(AM)— May 10, 1947: 1400 khz; 1 kw-U. TL: N30 12 35 W93 12 43. Hrs open: 24 425 Broad St., 70601. Phone: (337) 439-3300. Fax: (337) 433-7278.E-mail: info@kaok.com Web Site:www.kaok.com Licensee: Cumulus Licensing LLC. Group owner: Pittman Broadcasting Services LLC (acq 12-6-2004; $3 million with KQLK(FM) De Ridder). Population served: 167,000 Natl. Network: CBS, . Rgnl. Network: La. Net. La. Net. Format: News/talk, info. News staff: one; News: 168 hrs wkly. Target aud: 24 plus; baby boomers. ♦Lewis W. Dickey Jr., pres; Larry LeBlanc, stn mgr, gen sls mgr; Eric Nielson, progmg dir; Richard Rhodes, chief of engrg.

KBIU(FM)— Dec 1, 1976: 103.3 mhz; 35 kw. Ant 479 ft TL: N30 14 41 W93 20 37. Stereo. Hrs open: 24 425 Broad St., 70601. Phone: (337) 439-3300. Fax: (337) 433-7701.E-mail: cj.jones@cumulus.com Web Site:www.kbiu.com Licensee: Cumulus Licensing Corp. Group owner: Cumulus Media Inc. (acq 12-17-98; grpsl). Population served: 270,000 Natl. Rep: Katz Radio,. Bryan Cave. Format: Adult contemp. Target aud: 25-54; adult. ♦Eric Nielson, opns mgr; C.C. Jones, gen sls mgr, mktg mgr; Richard Rhodes, chief of engrg; Holly Fontenot, traf mgr.

KEZM(AM)—See Sulphur

KKGB(FM)—See Sulphur

KLCL(AM)— May 12, 1935: 1470 khz; 5 kw-D, 500 w-N. TL: N30 15 31 W93 16 07. Hrs open: 900 N. Lake Shore Dr., 70601. Phone: (337) 433-1641. Fax: (337) 433-2999. Web Site:www.cajunradio.net Licensee: GAP Broadcasting Lake Charles License LLC (acq 2-6-2008; grpsl). Population served: 175,000 Rgnl. Network: La. Net. La. Net. Format: Cajun. Target aud: 18-64. ♦Sara Cormier, gen mgr; Mike Soileau, progmg dir.

KNGT(FM)— Nov 8, 1965: 99.5 mhz; 100 kw. 984 ft TL: N30 23 59 W93 00 10. Stereo. Hrs open: 900 N. Lake Shore Dr., 70601. Phone: (337) 433-1641. Fax: (337) 433-2999. Web Site:www.gator995.com Licensee: GAP Broadcasting Lake Charles License LLC (group owner; (acq 2-6-2008; grpsl). Population served: 175,000 Natl. Rep: Christal,. Format: Country. Target aud: 25-54. ♦Sara Cormier, pres, gen mgr; Aaron Turner, gen sls mgr; Todd Stone, progmg dir; Dave Chimeno, chief of engrg.

***KOJO(FM)—** 1990: 91.1 mhz; 4 kw horiz, 14 kw vert. Ant 387 ft TL: N30 12 07 W92 56 47. Hrs open: 24
Rebroadcasts KJMJ(AM) Alexandria.
601 Washington St., Alexandria, 71301. Phone: (318) 561-6145. Fax: (318) 449-9954.E-mail: info.usa@radiomaria.org Web Site:www.radiomaria.us Licensee: Radio Maria Inc. (group owner; acq 10-13-99). Format: Christian, relg, talk. Target aud: General; Christians seeking training & encouragement through Bible teaching programs. ♦Dale DePerrodell, gen sls mgr; Duane Stenzel, gen mgr & progmg dir; Danny Brou, chief of engrg.

KXZZ(AM)— 1947: 1580 khz; 1 kw-U, DA-N. TL: N30 15 28 W93 11 55. Stereo. Hrs open: 24 Prog sep from FM 425 Broad St., 70601. Phone: (337) 439-3300. Fax: (337) 433-7701. Web

Site:www.kxzz1580am.com Licensee: Cumulus Licensing Corp. Population served: 100,000 Natl. Network: American Urban, . Natl. Rep: Katz Radio,. Format: Classic soul. Target aud: 25-54; adult. ♦CJ Jones, gen mgr.

KYKZ(FM)— January 1976: 96.1 mhz; 97 kw. 1,204 ft TL: N30 17 26 W93 34 35. Stereo. Hrs open: 24 425 Broad St., 70601. Phone: (337) 439-3300. Fax: (337) 436-7278.E-mail: info@kykz.com Web Site:www.kykz.com Licensee: Cumulus Licensing Corp. Group owner: Cumulus Media Inc. (acq 12-17-98; grpsl). Population served: 150,000 Format: Country. News staff: 3; News: 8 hrs wkly. Target aud: General. ♦Eric Nielson, progmg dir; Richard Rhodes, gen mgr & chief of engrg.

***KYLC(FM)**— 2001: 90.3 mhz; 80 kw vert. 469 ft TL: N30 38 10 W93 02 33. Hrs open: American Family Radio, Box 3206, Tupelo, MS, 38803. Phone: (662) 844-8888. Fax: (662) 842-6791.E-mail: comments@afr.net Web Site:www.afr.net Licensee: American Family Association. Group owner: American Family Radio (acq 3-14-01). Format: Inspirational Christian. ♦Marvin Sanders, gen mgr.

Lake Providence

KLPL(AM)— June 27, 1957: Stn currently dark. 1050 khz; 250 w-D, 22 w-N. TL: N32 48 59 W91 12 22. Hrs open: Willis Broadcasting Corp., 645 Church St., Suite 400, Norfolk, VA, 23510. Phone: (757) 622-4600. Fax: (757) 624-6515. Licensee: Willis Broadcasting Corp. (group owner; acq 4-21-98; $120,000 with co-located FM). Population served: 10,300 Rgnl. Network: Prog Farm. Target aud: General.

KLPL-FM— Jan 28, 1975: Stn currently dark. 92.7 mhz; 3 kw. Ant 154 ft TL: N32 48 59 W91 12 22. Stereo. Hrs open: Willis Broadcasting Corp., 645 Church St., Norfolk, 23510. Phone: (757) 622-4600. Fax: (757) 624-6515. Population served: 10,300

Larose

KLRZ(FM)— Mar 29, 1993: 100.3 mhz; 89 kw. Ant 586 ft TL: N29 33 01 W90 21 04. Hrs open: 24 11603 Hwy. 308, Drawer 1350, 70373. Phone: (985) 798-7792. Fax: (985) 798-7793.E-mail: klrz@mobilete.com Web Site:www.klrzfm.com Licensee: Coastal Broadcasting of Larose Inc. Natl. Network: Westwood One, . Format: All Louisiana all the time. News staff: one; News: 22 hrs wkly. Target aud: 25-54; professionals. ♦Andrea Galjour, opns mgr; Jerry Gisclair, gen mgr & chief of engrg.

Leesville

KBDV(FM)— 2008: 92.7 mhz; 6 kw. Ant 328 ft TL: N31 07 07 W93 11 12. Hrs open: 24 605 San Antonio Ave., Many, 71449. Phone: (318) 256-5924. Fax: (318) 256-0950.E-mail: eagles92.7@suddenlinkmail.com Web Site:www.bdcradio.com Licensee: Baldridge-Dumas Communications Inc. Format: A/C Soft Hits. ♦Tedd W. Dumas, VP; Rhonda Leach, gen mgr; Cindy Ezernack, stn mgr.

KJAE(FM)— October 1979: 93.5 mhz; 7.5 kw. 328 ft TL: N31 08 28 W93 17 44. Stereo. Hrs open: Prog sep from AM Box 1323, 71446. Secondary address: 101 Lees Ln. 71446. Phone: (337) 239-3402. Fax: (337) 238-9283.E-mail: info@kjae935.com Web Site:www.kjae935.com Format: Country.

KLLA(AM)— September 1956: 1570 khz; 1 kw-D. TL: N31 06 24 W93 17 38. Hrs open: Box 1323, 71446. Secondary address: 101 Lees Ln. 71446. Phone: (337) 239-3402. Fax: (337) 238-9283.E-mail: info@kjae935.com Web Site:www.kjae935.com Licensee: Pene Broadcasting Co. (acq 12-1-76). Population served: 60,000 Format: Oldies. ♦Penny Scogin, pres, gen mgr; Peggy Merritt, gen sls mgr; Tony Evans, chief of engrg.

KVVP(FM)— Jan 20, 1977: 105.7 mhz; 25 kw. 400 ft TL: N31 00 17 W93 16 40. Stereo. Hrs open: 24 168 KVVP Dr., 71446. Phone: (337) 537-5887. Fax: (337) 537-4152.E-mail: kvvp@kvvp.com Web Site:www.kvvp.com Licensee: Stannard Broadcasting Co. Inc. James Popham. Format: New country. News staff: one; News: 15 hrs wkly. Target aud: 18-54; adults with spending power. Spec prog: Relg 9 hrs wkly. ♦Alan Taylor, CFO, political ed; Doug Stannard, pres, gen mgr & progmg dir.

Mamou

KBON(FM)— June 1997: 101.1 mhz; 25 kw. Ant 328 ft TL: N30 39 33 W92 19 00. Hrs open: 24 109 S. 2nd St., Eunice, 70535. Phone: (337) 546-0007. Fax: (337) 546-0097.E-mail: 101.1@kbon.com Web Site:www.kbon.com Licensee: Rose Ann Marx. (acq 9-8-98; $70,000). Format: Var, country. ♦Paul Marx, gen mgr.

Mansfield

***KHMD(FM)**— May 1994: 104.7 mhz; 25 kw. Ant 328 ft TL: N31 57 49 W93 53 58. Hrs open: 24 Houston Christian Broadcasters Inc., 2424 South Blvd., Houston, TX, 77098. Phone: (713) 520-5200. Web Site:www.khcb.org Licensee: Houston Christian Broadcasters Inc. (group owner; (acq 12-30-2008; $150,000). Population served: 250,000 Format: Christian. ♦Bruce Munsterman, gen mgr.

KJVC(FM)— September 1976: 92.7 mhz; 3 kw. 299 ft TL: N32 01 18 W93 44 18. Stereo. Hrs open: 24 Box 700, Logansport, 71049. Phone: (318) 697-4000. Fax: (318) 697-4004. Licensee: Metropolitan Radio Group Inc. (group owner; acq 10-97; $85,000). Population served: 320,000 Format: Country. ♦David Grahams, gen mgr.

***KMSL(FM)**— 2006: 91.7 mhz; 12 kw vert. Ant 339 ft TL: N32 10 39 W93 55 02. Hrs open:
Rebroadcasts WAFR(FM) Tupelo, MS 100%.
Box 2440, Tupelo, MS, 38803-2440. Phone: (662) 844-8888. Fax: (662) 842-6791. Web Site:www.afr.net Licensee: American Family Association. (acq 5-13-2005; $10 for CP). Natl. Network: American Family Radio, . Format: Christian. ♦Marvin Sanders, gen mgr.

Mansura

KZLG(FM)— July 2000: 95.9 mhz; 6 kw. 328 ft Stereo. Hrs open: 24 Box 516, Moreauville, 71355. Secondary address: 10586 Hwy. 1, Moreauville 71355. Phone: (318) 985-3070. Fax: (318) 985-2995.E-mail: kzlg@kricket.net Licensee: Amy M. Coco. Population served: 50,000 Natl. Network: AP Radio, . La. Net. Format: Adult Contemporary. News: 3 hrs. Target aud: 25 plus. ♦Louis Coco, Jr., gen mgr.

Many

***KAVK(FM)**— June 1998: 89.7 mhz; 1 kw. 430 ft TL: N31 32 06 W93 25 21. Hrs open: Box 3206, American Family Radio, Tupelo, MS, 38803. Phone: (662) 844-8888. Fax: (662) 842-6791.E-mail: comments@afr.net Web Site:www.afr.net Licensee: American Family Association. Group owner: American Family Radio Format: Inspirational Christian. ♦Marvin Sanders, gen mgr.

KWLA(AM)— August 1962: Stn currently dark. 1400 khz; 1 kw-U. TL: N31 34 30 W93 29 47. Stereo. Hrs open: 24 605 San Antonio, 71449. Phone: (318) 256-5177. Fax: (318) 256-0950.E-mail: kthp@sabinenet.com Licensee: Baldridge-Dumas Communications Inc. (group owner; acq 1-10-2000; with co-located FM). Population served: 7,500 Rgnl. Network: La. Net. ♦Cindy Ezemack, gen sls mgr, adv VP; Rhonda Benson-Leach, gen mgr, sls VP & progmg dir; Kenny Carter, chief of engrg.

KWLV(FM)— Nov 12, 1977: 107.1 mhz; 25 kw. 253 ft TL: N31 36 27 W93 24 05. Hrs open: 605 San Antonio, 71449. Phone: (318) 256-5177. Fax: (318) 256-0950.E-mail: kwlv@bellsouth.net Web Site:www.bdcradio.com Format: Country. Target aud: 20 plus. ♦Cindy Ezernack, stn mgr.

Marksville

KAPB-FM— Aug 14, 1971: 97.7 mhz; 6 kw. 328 ft TL: N31 07 27 W92 04 40. Stereo. Hrs open: Box 7, 71351. Secondary address: 520 Chester 71351. Phone: (318) 253-5272. Fax: (318) 253-5262.E-mail: kapbfm@yahoo.com Licensee: Three Rivers Radio Co. Group owner: The Radio Group Population served: 100,000 Rgnl. Network: Prog Farm. Format: Classic hit country. ♦Pamela Couvillion, gen mgr; Larry Young, news dir, chief of engrg.

Maurice

KYMK-FM— June 13, 1985: 106.3 mhz; 1.3 kw. Ant 495 ft TL: N30 04 16 W92 11 53. Stereo. Hrs open: 3225 Ambassador Caffery Pkwy., Lafayette, 70506. Phone: (337) 993-5500. Fax: (337) 993-5510. Licensee: Pittman Broadcasting Services LLC. (group owner; (acq 1-28-2004; grpsl). Format: Hot adult contemp. ♦Charles Sagona, gen mgr.

Minden

KASO(AM)— Apr 1, 1952: 1240 khz; 1 kw-U. TL: N32 37 50 W93 16 56. Hrs open: 24 410 Lakeshore Dr., 71055. Phone: (318) 377-1240. Fax: (318) 377-4619.E-mail: kaso1240@yahoo.com Web Site:www.kbef.com Licensee: Amistad Communications Inc. (acq 10-2000; $375,000 with CP for KBEF(FM) Gibsland). Population served: 15,500 Natl. Network: Jones Radio Networks, . Rgnl. Network: La. Net. La. Net. Format: Adult standards. News: 102 hrs wkly. Target aud: 35-64; male & female. ♦Fred Caldwell Sr., pres; Mike Griffith, gen mgr; Mark Cheesne, opns mgr, progmg dir.

KLKL(FM)—Licensed to Minden. See Shreveport

Monroe

***KBMQ(FM)**— Aug. 15, 1999: 88.7 mhz; 25 kw horiz, 24.5 kw vert. Ant 458 ft TL: N32 24 15 W92 02 07. Stereo. Hrs open: 24 Box 3265, 71201. Phone: (318) 387-1230. Fax: (318) 387-8856.E-mail: info@887fm.org Web Site:www.887fm.org Licensee: Media Ministries Inc. Population served: 135,000 Format: Christian. News: one hr wkly. Target aud: 25-54; women. ♦Phillip Brooks, progmg dir.

***KEDM(FM)**— Apr 23, 1991: 90.3 mhz; 87.1 kw. 863 ft TL: N32 39 38 W91 59 28. Stereo. Hrs open: 24 ULM, 225 Stubbs Hall, 71209-6805. Phone: (318) 342-5556. Fax: (318) 342-5570.E-mail: kedm@ulm.edu Web Site:www.kedm.org Licensee: University of Louisiana at Monroe. Natl. Network: NPR, PRI, . Rgnl. Network: La. Net. La. Net. Dow, Lohnes & Albertson. Wire Svc: AP Format: Var. News staff: one; News: 40 hrs wkly. Target aud: 35 plus; involved, upscale, educated, movers & shakers. ♦Ray Davidson, opns mgr.

KJLO-FM— July 1946: 104.1 mhz; 100 kw. Ant 1,017 ft TL: N32 39 36 W92 05 15. Stereo. Hrs open: 24 Box 4808, 71211. Secondary address: 1109 Hudson Ln. 71201. Phone: (318) 388-2323. Fax: (318) 388-0569. Web Site:www.kjlo.com Licensee: Holladay Broadcasting of Louisiana LLC. (group owner; (acq 10-1-2006; $500,000). Population served: 397,000 Natl. Rep: McGavren Guild,. Latham & Watkins. Format: Country. News staff: one. Target aud: 25-54. Spec prog: Gospel 4 hrs wkly. ♦Robert H. Holladay, pres.

KLIC(AM)— 1950: 1230 khz; 1 kw-U. TL: N32 29 16 W92 05 25. Stereo. Hrs open: 24 130 N 2nd St. Ste C, 71201. Phone: (318) 387-1230. Fax: (318) 387-8856.E-mail: phillip@887fm.org Web Site:www.am1230thesource.com Licensee: Media Ministries Inc. (acq 10-28-92; $165,000; 11-23-92). Population served: 150,000 Natl. Network: Salem Radio Network, . Format: Christian, talk. News: 14 hrs wkly. Target aud: 25-54; Adults 35 +. ♦Tony Davis, pres; Mike Downhour, gen mgr, progmg dir; Diane Osborne, sls dir, mktg dir; Naomi Thompson, news dir, pub affrs dir; Ernie Sandidge, engrg dir; Mark Kemp, traf mgr.

KLIP(FM)— April 1993: 105.3 mhz; 50 kw. 433 ft TL: N32 33 08 W92 08 33. Stereo. Hrs open: 24 Box 4808, 71211. Secondary address: 1109 Hudson Ln. 71201. Phone: (318) 388-2323. Fax: (318) 388-0569.E-mail: la105@bayou.com Web Site:www.la105.com Licensee: Holladay Broadcasting of Louisiana LLC (group owner; acq 11-21-2003; grpsl). Natl. Network: ABC, . Natl. Rep: McGavren Guild,. Latham & Watkins. Format: Classic hits. News: 2 hrs wkly. Target aud: 25-54. ♦Bob Holladay, pres & gen mgr.

KMLB(AM)— Oct 4, 1944: 540 khz; 5 kw-D, 1 kw-N, DA-2. TL: N32 32 36 W92 10 45. Hrs open: Box 4808, 71211. Secondary address: 1109 Hudson Ln. 71201. Phone: (318) 388-2323. Fax: (318) 388-0569.E-mail: talk540@bayou.com Web Site:www.kmlb.com Licensee: Holliday Broadcasting of Louisiana LLC. (acq 3-4-2008; $150,000). Population served: 130,000 Natl. Network: ABC, . Natl. Rep: McGavren Guild,. Latham & Watkins. Format: Talk/news. Target aud: 25 plus. ♦Bob Holladay, gen mgr; Cory Crowe, progmg dir.

KNOE-FM— Jan 29, 1967: 101.9 mhz; 97 kw horiz, 96 kw vert. Ant 1,670 ft TL: N32 11 45 W92 04 10. Stereo. Hrs open: 1107 Hudson Ln., Ste. C, 71201. Phone: (318) 807-3285. Fax: (318) 325-9466. Web Site:www.starradiomonroe.com Licensee: Radio Monroe LLC (acq 5-13-2008; $900,000). Population served: 300,000 Format: CHR. ♦Bobby Richards, progmg dir & mus dir.

KRJO(AM)— May 2001: 1680 khz; 10 kw-D, 1 kw-N. TL: N32 27 24 W92 01 06. Stereo. Hrs open: 24 Box 4808, 71211. Secondary address: 1109 Hudson Ln. 71201. Phone: (318) 338-2323. Fax: (318) 388-0569.E-mail: olskool@bayou.com Web Site:www.olskool.com Licensee: Holladay Broadcasting of Louisiana LLC (group owner; acq 11-21-2003; grpsl). Rgnl. Network: ABC. Natl. Rep: McGavren Guild,. Latham & Watkins. Format: Gospel. ♦Bob Holladay, gen mgr.

KRVV(FM)—See Bastrop

KXRR(FM)— Nov 15, 1965: 106.1 mhz; 97 kw. Ant 1,017 ft TL: N32 39 36 W92 05 15. Stereo. Hrs open: 1200 N. 18th St., Suite D, 71201. Phone: (318) 387-3922. Fax: (318) 322-4585. Web Site:rock106kxrr.com Licensee: Opus Broadcasting Monroe L.L.C. Group owner: Opus Media Partners LLC (acq 7-19-2004; grpsl). Population served: 85,000 Natl. Rep: Christal,. Format: Rock. Target aud: 25-49. ♦Chris Zimmerman, gen mgr & stn mgr.

***KXUL(FM)—** May 9, 1973: 91.1 mhz; 8.5 kw. 716 ft TL: N32 39 38 W91 59 28. Stereo. Hrs open: 24 130 Stubbs Hall, 401 Bayou Drive, 71209. Phone: (318) 342-5985. Web Site:www.kxul.com Licensee: University of Lousiana at Monroe. Population served: 215000 Dow, Lohnes & Albertson. Format: Alternative, rock. Target aud: 12-34. ♦Joel Willer, gen mgr.

***KYFL(FM)—** Oct 8, 1992: 89.5 mhz; 25 kw. Ant 377 ft TL: N32 33 08 W92 08 33. Stereo. Hrs open: 24 Box 7300, Charlotte, NC, 28241. Phone: (704) 523-5555.E-mail: bbn@bbnradio.org Web Site:www.bbnradio.org Licensee: Bible Broadcasting Network Inc. Group owner: Bible Broadcasting Network. Format: Conservative Christian. News: 3 hrs wkly. Target aud: General. ♦Michael Thomson, gen mgr.

Moreauville

KLIL(FM)— July 25, 1980: 92.1 mhz; 6 kw. 300 ft TL: N31 02 53 W91 59 47. Stereo. Hrs open: Box 365, 71355. Secondary address: 10586 Hwy. 1 71355. Phone: (318) 985-2929. Fax: (318) 985-2995.E-mail: klil@kricket.net Licensee: Cajun Broadcasting Inc. Population served: 50,000 Natl. Network: AP Radio, . La. Net. Format: Oldies. Target aud: 20 plus; working adults. ♦Louis B. Coco Jr., pres & gen mgr.

Morgan City

KMRC(AM)— April 1954: 1430 khz; 500 w-D, 100 w-N. TL: N29 45 03 W91 10 24. Hrs open: 24 409 Duke St., 70381. Phone: (985) 384-1430. Fax: (985) 384-2351.E-mail: kmrc@kmrc1430.com Web Site:www.kmrc1430.com Licensee: Spotlight Broadcasting L.L.C. (group owner; acq 2-1-00; $109,000). Population served: 60,000 Format: Swamp pop. News staff: one; News: 5 hrs wkly. Target aud: 25-54; middle to upper income. ♦John Stork, gen mgr & news dir.

KMYO-FM— Aug 1, 1967: 96.7 mhz; 12 kw. Ant 476 ft TL: N29 41 39 W90 59 58. Stereo. Hrs open: 24 Box 2068, Houma, 70361. Secondary address: 120 Prevost Dr., Houma 70364. Phone: (985) 851-1020. Fax: (985) 872-4403.E-mail: info@mix967.net Web Site:www.mix967.net Licensee: Sunburst Media-Louisiana LLC. (acq 1-23-2007; grpsl). Natl. Network: Jones Radio Networks, . Format: Oldies. News: 2 hrs wkly. Target aud: 18-34; majority women. ♦Danny Fletcher, gen mgr; John Delise, opns mgr & progmg dir.

Moss Bluff

KZWA(FM)— Aug 12, 1994: 104.9 mhz; 25 kw. Ant 328 ft TL: N30 27 15 W93 08 20. Hrs open: 305 Enterprise Blvd., Lake Charles, 70601. Phone: (337) 491-9955. Fax: (337) 433-8097.E-mail: info@kzwa.com Web Site:www.kzwa.com Licensee: B & C Broadcasting Inc. Format: Urban contemp mainstream. Target aud: 18-34. ♦Faye Brown-Blackwell, CEO & gen mgr.

Natchitoches

***KBIO(FM)—** July 2, 2002: 89.7 mhz; 100 w. Ant 295 ft TL: N31 47 13 W93 07 52. Hrs open:
Rebroadcasts KJMJ(AM) Alexandria.
601 Washington St., Alexandria, 71301. Phone: (318) 561-6145. Fax: (318) 449-9954.E-mail: info.usa@radiomaria.org Web Site:www.radiomaria.us Licensee: Radio Maria Inc. (group owner; (acq 9-6-2001). Format: Christian, relg, talk. ♦Dale DePerrodil, gen sls mgr; Duane Stenzel, gen mgr & progmg dir; Danny Brou, chief of engrg.

KDBH(FM)— July 1, 1965: 97.3 mhz; 25 kw. Ant 220 ft TL: N31 48 17 W93 01 27. Stereo. Hrs open: 605 San Antonio Ave., Many, 71449. Phone: (318) 352-9696. Fax: (318) 357-9595.E-mail: kdbh@suddenlinkmail.com Licensee: Baldridge-Dumas Communications Inc. (group owner; acq 5-14-01; $340,000 with co-located AM including two-year noncompete agreement). Population served: 80,000 Natl. Network: Jones Radio Networks, . Rgnl. Network: La. Net. La. Net. Kaye, Scholer, Fierman, Hays & Handler. Format: Country. ♦Rhonda Benson, gen mgr & stn mgr; Gordon Rivet, news dir; Kenny Carter, chief of engrg.

KNOC(AM)— May 1, 1947: 1450 khz; 1 kw-U. TL: N31 45 47 W93 03 47. Hrs open: 24 213 Renee St., 71457. Phone: (318) 354-4000. Fax: (318) 352-9598. Licensee: North Face Broadcasting L.L.C. (acq 5-9-2003; $348,000 with KCIJ(FM) Atlanta). Population served: 150,000 Natl. Network: ABC, . Format: News/talk. News staff: one; News: 20 hrs wkly. Target aud: 35 plus; upper-middle class. ♦Bill Vance, stn mgr; John Brewer, opns dir; Shane Erath, news dir.

***KNWD(FM)—** September 1975: 91.7 mhz; 255 w horiz. 164 ft TL: N31 44 51 W93 05 47. Stereo. Hrs open: 24 109 Kyser Hall, 165 Sam Sibley Dr., 71497. Phone: (318) 357-4180. Fax: (318) 357-4398.E-mail: knwd917@yahoo.com Web Site:www.nsula.edu/thedemon Licensee: Northwestern State University of Louisiana. Population served: 35,000 Format: Var. News staff: one; News: 3 hrs wkly. Target aud: 18-25. ♦Elliot Westphal, gen mgr & stn mgr.

KZBL(FM)— Oct 8, 1985: 100.7 mhz; 3 kw. 299 ft TL: N31 48 18 W93 01 29. Stereo. Hrs open: 24 605 San Antonio Ave., Many, 71449. Phone: (318) 352-4363. Fax: (318) 357-9595.E-mail: kzbl@suddenlinkmail.com Licensee: Baldridge-Dumas Communications Inc. (group owner; acq 6-21-99; $400,000). Natl. Network: Jones Radio Networks, . Format: Oldies. News: 10 hrs wkly. Target aud: 25-50. ♦Rhonda Benson, gen mgr & stn mgr.

New Iberia

KANE(AM)— August 1946: 1240 khz; 1 kw-U. TL: N30 01 03 W91 50 10. Stereo. Hrs open: 24 145 B. West, 70560. Phone: (337) 365-3434. Fax: (337) 365-9117.E-mail: kane@kane1240.com Web Site:www.kane1240.com Licensee: Coastal Broadcasting of Lafourche L.L.C. (acq 12-31-01). Population served: 250,000 Rgnl. Network: La. Net. La. Net. Format: Cajun. News: 30 hrs wkly. Target aud: 25-54. ♦Jerry Gisclair, gen mgr.

KNIR(AM)— June 1, 1951: 1360 khz; 1 kw-D, 209 w-N. TL: N30 01 32 W91 49 20. Hrs open: 24 Radio Maria Inc., 601 Washington St., Alexandria, 71301. Phone: (318) 561-6145. Fax: (318) 449-9954.E-mail: info.usa@radiomaria.org Web Site:www.radiomaria.us Licensee: Radio Maria Inc. (group owner; (acq 6-10-2003; $45,000). Population served: 50,000 Format: Catholic prgmg. ♦Father Duane Stenzel, gen mgr.

KRDJ(FM)— 1991: 93.7 mhz; 100 kw. Ant 971 ft TL: N30 20 19 W91 31 23. Hrs open: 24 20 Galbert Rd., Lafayette, 70506. Phone: (337) 232-1311.E-mail: krdj.fm@citcomm.com Web Site:www.red937.com Licensee: Citadel Broadcasting Co. Group owner: Citadel Broadcasting Corp. (acq 10-8-99; $9.5 million). Population served: 500,000 Format: Classic rock. Target aud: 18-44; men. ♦Mary Galyean, gen mgr.

KXKC(FM)— January 1969: 99.1 mhz; 100 kw. 1,039 ft TL: N30 12 06 W91 46 37. Stereo. Hrs open: 24 202 Galbert Rd., Lafayette, 70506. Phone: (337) 232-1311. E-mail: info@kxkc.com Web Site:www.kxkc.com Licensee: Citadel Broadcasting Co. Group owner: Citadel Broadcasting Corp. (acq 12-5-2003; $7.6 million). Population served: 500,000 Format: New country. Target aud: 18-49. ♦Mary Galyean, gen mgr.

New Orleans

KGLA(AM)—See Gretna

WBOK(AM)— February 1951: 1230 khz; 1 kw-U. TL: N29 59 18 W90 02 45. Hrs open: Bakewell Media of Louisiana LLC, 3800 Crenshaw Blvd., Los Angeles, CA, 90008. Phone: (323) 291-6803. Fax: (291) 291-6804.E-mail: info@wbok.com Licensee: Bakewell Media of Louisiana LLC. Group owner: Willis Broadcasting Corp. (acq 4-27-2007; $550,000). Population served: 593,471 Format: Gospel. Target aud: 25 plus. ♦Danny J. Bakewell Sr., gen mgr.

***WBSN-FM—** Feb 5, 1979: 89.1 mhz; 8.5 kw. Ant 623 ft TL: N29 56 59 W89 57 27. Stereo. Hrs open: 24 3939 Gentilly Blvd., 70126. Phone: (504) 816-8000. Fax: (504) 816-8580.E-mail: onair@lifesongs.com Web Site:www.lifesongs.com Licensee: Providence Educational Foundation. Population served: 1,200,000 Format: Contemp Christian. Target aud: 25-49; active, Christian oriented families. ♦Stan Watts, gen mgr.

WBYU(AM)— 1950: 1450 khz; 1 kw-U. TL: N29 57 27 W90 09 47. Hrs open: 3330 W. Esplanade Ave., Suite 605, Metairie, 70002. Phone: (504) 841-2800. Fax: (504) 841-2805.E-mail: info@wbyu.com Web Site:www.radiodisney.com Licensee: Radio Disney Group LLC. Group owner: ABC Inc. (acq 2-5-2003; $1.5 million). Natl. Network: ABC, . Natl. Rep: Roslin,. Format: Children. ♦Steve Finney, stn mgr.

WDVW(FM)—See La Place

WEZB(FM)— Sept 1, 1945: 97.1 mhz; 100 kw. 984 ft TL: N29 55 11 W90 01 29. Stereo. Hrs open: 400 Poydras St., Suite 800, 70130. Phone: (504) 593-6376. Fax: (504) 593-2205.E-mail: ino@b97.com Web Site:www.b97.com Licensee: Entercom New Orleans License LLC. Group owner: Entercom Communications Corp. (acq 12-13-99; grpsl). Population served: 593,471 Format: CHR/top-40. Target aud: 18-34; females. ♦Ken Beck, gen mgr; Patrick Galloway, sls dir & gen sls mgr; Mike Kaplan, progmg dir; Joe Pollet, chief of engrg.

WGSO(AM)— Jan 27, 1946: 990 khz; 1 kw-D, 400 w-N. TL: N29 57 24 W90 04 34. Hrs open: 24 2250 Gause Blvd. E., Suite 205, Slidell, 70461-4235. Phone: (985) 639-3820. Fax: (985) 639-3869.E-mail: info@wgso.com Web Site:wgso.com Licensee: Northshore Radio LLC (acq 5-30-2007; $1.01 million). Format: News/talk. ♦Mike Starr, gen mgr.

WIST(AM)— 1948: 690 khz; 10 kw-D, 5 kw-N, DA-2. TL: N29 57 53 W89 57 31. Hrs open: 24 1218 B Decatur St., 70116. Phone: (504) 552-2412. Fax: (504) 552-2430.E-mail: feedback@wistradio.com Web Site:www.wistradio.com Licensee: WTIX Inc. Group owner: GHB Radio Group (acq 2-12-92; $800,000; 3-16-92). Population served: 914,700 Cohn & Marks. Format: Talk, oldies. News: 30 hrs wkly. Target aud: 25 plus; affluent, educated, professional. ♦Daniel Frazier, gen mgr.

WKBU(FM)— February 1953: 95.7 mhz; 100 kw. 984 ft TL: N29 55 11 W90 01 29. Stereo. Hrs open: 1450 Poydras, Suite 500, 70112. Phone: (504) 593-6376. Fax: (504) 593-1850.E-mail: mail@entercom.com Web Site:bayou957.com Licensee: Entercom New Orleans License LLC. Group owner: Entercom Communications Corp. (acq 12-13-99; grpsl). Latham & Watkins. Format: Classic Rock. Target aud: 25-54. ♦Patrick Galloway, gen sls mgr; Mike Kaplan, progmg dir; Dave Cohen, news dir; Joe Pollet, chief of engrg.

WLMG(FM)— Mar 15, 1970: 101.9 mhz; 100 kw. 984 ft TL: N29 55 11 W90 01 29. Stereo. Hrs open: 24 Prog sep from AM 1450 Poydras, Suite 500, 70112. Phone: (504) 593-6376. Fax: (504) 593-1850.E-mail: info@magic1019.com Web Site:www.magic1019.com Population served: 1,022,800 Format: Adult contemp. ♦Patrick Galloway, gen sls mgr; Andy Holt, progmg dir, mus dir.

WLNO(AM)— 1925: 1060 khz; 50 kw-D, 5 kw-N, DA-2. TL: N29 52 46 W89 59 51. Stereo. Hrs open: 24 401 Whitney Ave., #160, Gretna, 70056. Phone: (504) 362-9800. Fax: (504) 362-5541.E-mail: wlno@i-55.com Web Site:www.wlno.com Licensee: Communicom Co. of Louisiana L.P. (acq 1-25-95; $700,000; 3-20-95). Population served: 1,100,000 Format: Christian, relg. Target aud: General. ♦Carl DiMaria, CEO, gen mgr & opns dir.

WNOE-FM— Sept 15, 1968: 101.1 mhz; 100 kw. 1,004 ft TL: N29 58 57 W89 57 09. Stereo. Hrs open: 24 929 Howard Ave., 70113. Phone: (504) 679-7300. Fax: (504) 679-7345.E-mail: webmaster@wnoe.com Web Site:www.wnoe.com Licensee: Clear Channel Communications Inc. (group owner: Clear Channel Communiaction Inc. acq 1996; grpsl). Natl. Network: ABC, Westwood One, . Natl. Rep: Clear Channel,. Verner, Liipfert, Bernhard, McPherson & Hand. Format: Country. News staff: one. Target aud: 25-54. ♦Dick Lewis, gen mgr; Mike Scott, gen sls mgr; Sam McGuire, progmg dir; Richard Atwood, chief of engrg.

WODT(AM)— July 23, 1923: 1280 khz; 5 kw-U, DA-1. TL: N29 53 43 W90 00 16. Stereo. Hrs open: 24 929 Howard Ave., 70113. Phone: (504) 679-7300. Fax: (504) 679-7345.E-mail: darnettamahaffy@clearchannel.com Licensee: Clear Channel Radio Licenses Inc. Group owner: Clear Channel Communications Inc. (acq 7-24-92). Population served: 1,000,000 Natl. Rep: Clear Channel,. Riley & Fielding. Format: Urban Gospel. News: one hr wkly. Target aud: 35 plus; general. ♦Dick Lewis, gen mgr; Mike Scott, sls dir; Derrick Corbett, progmg dir; Richard Atwood, chief of engrg.

WQUE-FM— Jan 1, 1949: 93.3 mhz; 93 kw. 459 ft TL: N29 57 24 W90 04 31. (CP: 100 kw, ant 984 ft. TL: N29 55 11 W90 01 29). Stereo. Hrs open: 24 Dups AM 100% 929 Howard Ave., 70113. Phone: (504) 679-7300. Fax: (504) 679-7345.E-mail: webmaster@Q93.com Web Site:www.Q93.com Licensee: Clear Channel Radio Licenses Inc. Natl. Network: Premiere Radio Networks, . Natl. Rep: Clear Channel,. Format: Urban contemp. News staff: one; News: news prgmg 2 hrs/week. ♦Mike Scott, sls dir; Derrick Corbett, gen sls mgr, progmg dir; Richard Atwood, chief of engrg.

***WRBH(FM)—** 1980: 88.3 mhz; 54 kw. 600 ft TL: N29 57 01 W89 57 29. Hrs open: 24 3606 Magazine St., 70115. Phone: (504) 899-1144. Fax: (504) 899-1165.E-mail: Natalia@WRBH.ORG Web Site:www.wrbh.org Licensee: Radio for the Blind and Print Handicapped Inc. Format: Radio reading svc, news. News: 28 hrs wkly. Target aud: Blind & print handicapped. ♦Natalia Gonzales, gen mgr; Jackie Bullock, progmg dir; Ernie Kain, chief of engrg.

WRNO-FM— Oct 17, 1967: 99.5 mhz; 100 kw. Ant 1,004 ft TL: N29 58 57 W89 57 09. Stereo. Hrs open: 929 Howard Ave., 70113. Phone: (504) 679-7300. Fax: (504) 679-7345. Web Site:www.wrno.com Licensee: Clear Channel Broadcasting Licenses Inc. Group owner: Clear Channel Communications Inc. (acq 8-8-2002; swap for KKND(FM) Port Sulphur). Population served: 593,471 Natl. Network: ABC, Fox News Radio, Premiere Radio Networks, Westwood One, . Dow, Lohnes & Albertson. Format: News/talk. News staff: 3. ♦Mike Scott, opns mgr, gen sls mgr; Jim Fisher, progmg dir; Bob Christopher, news dir; Richard Atwood, chief of engrg.

WSHO(AM)— 1926: 800 khz; 1 kw-D, 233 w-N, DA-1. TL: N29 50 42 W90 06 39. Hrs open: 365 Canal St., Suite 1175, 70130. Phone: (504) 527-0800. Fax: (504) 527-0881.E-mail: whso@wsho.com Web Site:www.wsho.com Licensee: Shadowlands Communications L.L.C. (acq 1996). Population served: 593,471 Natl. Network: Salem Radio Network, . Format: Christian music & talk. Target aud: 25-54. ◆William Ainsworth, pres, gen mgr & opns mgr; Mike Patton, chief of engrg.

WSLA(AM)—See Slidell

*WTUL(FM)— Nov 14, 1974: 91.5 mhz; 1.5 kw. 161 ft TL: N29 56 18 W90 07 07. Stereo. Hrs open: 24 Tulane Univ. Ctr., 70118. Phone: (504) 865-5887.E-mail: wtul@wtul.fm Web Site:www.wtul.fm Licensee: Tulane Educational Fund. Format: Progsv. News: 3 hrs wkly. Target aud: General. ◆Li Yaffe, gen mgr.

WVOG(AM)— Apr 23, 1964: 600 khz; 1 kw-D. TL: N29 57 25 W90 09 33. Hrs open: 5:30 AM-8:30 PM 2730 Loumour Ave., Metairie, 70001. Phone: (504) 831-6941.E-mail: wvog@gellsouth Web Site:www.wwcr.com Licensee: F.W. Robbert Broadcasting Co. Inc. (group owner; acq 6-28-74). Population served: 593,471 Format: Christian talk. News: 2 hrs wkly. Target aud: 30 plus. ◆Fred P. Westenberger, pres; Eric Westenberger, gen mgr.

WWL(AM)— Mar 31, 1922: 870 khz; 50 kw-U, DA-1. TL: N29 50 14 W90 07 55. Hrs open: 24 1450 Poydras, Suite 500, 70112. Phone: (504) 593-6376. Fax: (504) 593-1850.E-mail: info@wwl.com Web Site:www.wwl.com Licensee: Entercom New Orleans License LLC. Group owner: Entercom Communications Corp. (acq 12-13-99; grpsl). Population served: 1,022,800 Natl. Network: CBS, . Natl. Rep: D & R Radio,. Format: News/talk, sports. ◆Ken Beck, gen mgr, opns mgr; Malcolm Pelham, sls dir, prom dir; Diane Newman, progmg dir, progmg mgr; Mark Broudreaux, gen sls mgr & news dir; Joe Pollet, chief of engrg.

*WWNO(FM)— Feb 20, 1972: 89.9 mhz; 85 kw vert. Ant 748 ft TL: N29 55 11 W90 01 29. Stereo. Hrs open: 24 Univ. of New Orleans, 2000 Lakeshore, Dr., 70148. Phone: (504) 280-7000. Fax: (504) 280-6061.E-mail: info@wwno.org Web Site:www.wwno.org Licensee: Louisiana State University. Population served: 1,300,000 Natl. Network: PRI, NPR, . Wire Svc: AP Format: Class, news jazz. News: 39 hrs wkly. Target aud: 35 plus; well-educated professionals, mgrs, artists & art patrons. ◆Chuck Miller, gen mgr; Ron C. Curtis, opns dir; Karen Anklam, dev dir, prom mgr; Fred Kasten, progmg dir.

*WWOZ(FM)— Dec 6, 1980: 90.7 mhz; 19 w. 279 ft TL: N29 57 01 W90 09 16. (CP: 4 kw, ant 508 ft. TL: N29 57 24 W90 04 31). Stereo. Hrs open: 24 Box 51840, 70151. Secondary address: 1008 N. Peters 70116. Phone: (504) 568-1239. Fax: (504) 558-9332.E-mail: wwoz@wwoz.org Web Site:www.wwoz.org Licensee: Friends of WWOZ Inc. (acq 10-14-86). Garvey, Schubert & Barer. Format: Jazz, rhythm and blues. News: 7 hrs wkly. Target aud: 35-55; upscale & educated males. ◆David Freedman, gen mgr; Dwayne Breashears, progmg dir.

WWWL(AM)— Apr 21, 1925: 1350 khz; 5 kw-U, DA-2. TL: N29 55 27 W90 02 04. Hrs open: 24 1450 Poydras, Suite 500, 70112. Phone: (504) 593-6376. Fax: (504) 593-1850. Web Site:www.1350espn.com Licensee: Entercom New Orleans License LLC. Group owner: Entercom Communications Corp. (acq 12-13-99; grpsl). Population served: 593,471 Natl. Network: ESPN Radio, . Format: Sports. ◆Ken Beck, gen mgr; Mark Broudreaux, gen sls mgr; Diane Newman, progmg dir; Joe Pollet, chief of engrg.

WYLD(AM)— 1949: 940 khz; 10 kw-D, 500 w-N, DA-2. TL: N29 54 00 W90 00 17. Hrs open: 24 929 Howard Ave., 70113. Phone: (504) 679-7300. Fax: (504) 679-7343.E-mail: info@am940.com Web Site:www.am940.com Licensee: Clear Channel Radio Licenses Inc. Group owner: Clear Channel Communications Inc. (acq 3-25-93; 3-20-95). Population served: 593,471 Natl. Network: ABC, Westwood One, . Natl. Rep: Clear Channel,. Wiley, Rein & Fielding. Format: Gospel. Target aud: 25-54. ◆Dick Lewis, gen mgr.

WYLD-FM— 1971: 98.5 mhz; 100 kw. 984 ft TL: N29 55 11 W90 01 29. (CP: ant 902 ft.). Stereo. Hrs open: 24 Prog sep from AM 929 Howard Ave., 70113. Web Site:www.wyldfm.com Licensee: Clear Channel Radio Licenses Inc. Population served: 1,000,000 Format: Urban adult contemp. News staff: 2; News: 5 hrs wkly.

New Roads

KCLF(AM)— Aug 19, 1964: 1500 khz; 1 kw-D. TL: N30 44 08 W91 24 58. Hrs open: 803 Parent St., 70760. Phone: (225) 638-6821. Fax: (225) 638-6882. Web Site:www.kclf1500am.com Licensee: New World Broadcasting Co. Inc. (acq 7-21-89; $230,000; 7-3-89). Format: Urban contemp. ◆Roosevelt Gremillion, gen mgr.

*KPCP(FM)—Not on air, target date: unknown: 88.3 mhz; 1 kw. Ant 98 ft TL: N30 44 08 W91 24 58. Hrs open: 8677 St. Joseph St., 70760. Phone: (225) 638-6821. Licensee: Stop the Violence/Save the Children Inc. ◆Roosevelt Gremillion, pres.

KQXL-FM— Oct 1, 1979: 106.5 mhz; 50 kw. Ant 485 ft TL: N30 37 24 W91 09 50. Stereo. Hrs open: 24 650 Wooddale Blvd., Baton Rouge, 70806. Phone: (225) 926-1106. Fax: (225) 928-1606.E-mail: kqxl.fm@citcom.com Web Site:www.q106dot5.com Licensee: Citadel Broadcasting Co. Group owner: Citadel Broadcasting Corp. (acq 1-14-99; grpsl). Population served: 600,000 Natl. Network: CBS, . Format: Urban contemp. News staff: one. Target aud: 18-54; Black adults. ◆Greg Benefield, gen mgr.

Norco

WFNO(AM)— 1987: 830 khz; 5 kw-D, 750 w-N, DA-2. TL: N30 03 00 W90 22 41. Hrs open: 3841 Veterans Memorial Blvd., Suite 201, Metairie, 70002. Phone: (504) 260-9366. Fax: (504) 830-7200. Licensee: Davidson Media Station WFNO Licensee LLC. (acq 1-11-2007; $2 million). Wire Svc: AP Format: Sp contemp. News staff: 2; News: 12 hrs wkly. Target aud: 18-44. ◆Yadira Hernandez, gen mgr; Jose Hidalgo, progmg dir.

*WNKV(FM)— 2007: 91.1 mhz; 4.7 kw vert. Ant 230 ft TL: N29 48 34 W90 25 17. Hrs open:
Rebroadcasts KLVR(FM) Middletown, CA 100%.
2351 Sunset Blvd., Suite 170-218, Rocklin, CA, 95765. Phone: (916) 251-1600. Fax: (916) 251-1650. Web Site:www.klove.com Licensee: Educational Media Foundation. (acq 11-1-2006; grpsl). Natl. Network: K-Love, . Format: Contemp Christian. ◆Richard Jenkins, pres.

North Fort Polk

KUMX(FM)— May 10, 1995: 106.7 mhz; 6 kw. 328 ft TL: N31 03 46 W93 16 11. Stereo. Hrs open: 24 168 KWP Dr., Leesville, 71446. Phone: (337) 537-9000. Fax: (337) 537-4152. Licensee: West Central Broadcasting Co. Inc. (acq 3-8-02; $208,000). Natl. Network: ABC, . Format: R & B. News staff: 12; News: 12pm-5pm. Target aud: 22-42. Spec prog: Tom Joiner. ◆Alan Taylor, CFO; Doug Stannard, pres & gen mgr.

Oak Grove

KWCL-FM— Jan 30, 1973: 96.7 mhz; 23 kw. Ant 341 ft TL: N32 51 32 W91 21 22. Stereo. Hrs open: 24 Box 260, 71263. Secondary address: 230 E. Main St. 71263. Phone: (318) 428-9670. Fax: (318) 428-2476.E-mail: kwcl@bellsouth.net Licensee: KWCL-FM Broadcasting Co. Inc. (acq 12-10-90). Population served: 52,000 Natl. Network: ABC, Jones Radio Networks, . Miller & Miller. Format: Good time oldies. News staff: one; News: 17 hrs wkly. Target aud: General. ◆Irene Robinson, pres, gen mgr; Kelley Lovell, progmg dir & disc jockey.

Oakdale

KKST(FM)— 1972: 98.7 mhz; 48 kw. Ant 1,053 ft TL: N31 01 59 W92 30 08. Stereo. Hrs open: 24 1515 Texas Ave., Alexandria, 71301. Phone: (318) 445-1234. Fax: (318) 445-7231.E-mail: chad@cenlabroadcasting.com Web Site:www.cenlabroadcasting.com Licensee: Cenla Broadcasting Licensing Co. LLC. Group owner: Clear Channel Communications Inc. (acq 11-13-2006; grpsl). Population served: 150,000 Format: Urban hip hop. News staff: one; News: 20 hrs wkly. Target aud: 18-49; women. ◆Taylor Thompson, gen mgr.

Opelousas

KFXZ-FM— Aug 3, 1989: 105.9 mhz; 3.4 kw. Ant 433 ft TL: N30 27 53 W92 04 31. Hrs open: 3225 Ambassador Caffery Pkwy., Lafayette, 70506. Phone: (337) 993-5500. Fax: (337) 993-5510.E-mail: kfxz@pittmanbroadcasting.com Web Site:www.z1059.com Licensee: Pittman Broadcasting Services LLC (group owner; (acq 1-28-2004; grpsl). Format: Urban contemp. ◆Charles Sagona, gen mgr.

KOGM(FM)— June 18, 1965: 107.1 mhz; 3 kw. Ant 205 ft TL: N30 31 31 W92 06 17. Stereo. Hrs open: 24 Box 1150, 70571. Secondary address: 216 N. Court St. 70570. Phone: (337) 942-2633. Fax: (337) 942-2635.E-mail: kslokogm@bellsouth.net Licensee: KSLO Broadcasting Company Natl. Network: ABC, . La. Net. Format: Adult contemp. News staff: one; News: one hr wkly. Target aud: 25 plus. ◆Chris Lamke, gen mgr, gen sls mgr; Missy Benoit, progmg dir; Jay Miller, traf mgr; Kyle Vidrine, engr, engr.

KSLO(AM)— September 1947: 1230 khz; 1 kw-U. TL: N30 31 31 W92 06 17. Hrs open: 24 Box 1150, 70571-1150. Secondary address: 216 N. Court St. 70570. Phone: (337) 942-2633. Fax: (337) 942-2635.E-mail: kslokogm@bellsouth.net Licensee: KSLO Broadcasting Co. Inc. Population served: 75,000 Natl. Network: ABC, . La. Net. Format: Country/News. News staff: one; News: 10 hrs. per week. ◆Penny A. Smith, pres; Chris Lamke, gen mgr, gen sls mgr; Missy B. Benoit, progmg dir; Justin Duren, mus dir; Kyle Vidrine, engr.

Pineville

KTTP(AM)—Licensed to Pineville. See Alexandria

Plaquemine

*KPAQ(FM)—Not on air, target date: unknown: 88.1 mhz; 2.9 kw vert. Ant 308 ft TL: N30 15 41 W91 18 40. Hrs open: Drawer 2440, Tupelo, MS, 38803. Phone: (662) 844-8888. Fax: (662) 842-6791. Licensee: American Family Association. ◆Marvin Sanders, gen mgr.

Port Allen

WPFC(AM)—Licensed to Port Allen. See Baton Rouge

Port Sulphur

KAGY(AM)— Aug 17, 1966: 1510 khz; 1 kw-D. TL: N29 29 03 W89 42 15. Hrs open: 6 AM-6 PM 409 Duke St., Morgan City, 70380. Phone: (985) 384-1430. Fax: (985) 384-2351.E-mail: kmrc@kmrc1430.com Web Site:www.kmrcradio.com Licensee: Spotlight Broadcasting of New Orleans LLC Group owner: Spotlight Broadcasting LLC (acq 12-30-2002; $250,000). Population served: 750,000 Format: Swamp pop. Target aud: 24-54; general. ◆John Stork, gen mgr.

KMEZ(FM)— July 4, 1989: 106.7 mhz; 100 kw. Ant 981 ft TL: N29 48 30 W89 45 42. Hrs open: 24 201 St. Charles Ave., Suite 201, New Orleans, 70170. Phone: (504) 581-7002. Fax: (504) 566-4857.E-mail: trapper.john@citcom.com Web Site:www.oldschool1067.com Licensee: Citadel Broadcasting Co. Group owner: Citadel Broadcasting Corp. (acq 8-29-2003; grpsl). Natl. Rep: Clear Channel,. Format: Urban contemp. News staff: one. Target aud: 25-54. ◆Dave Siebert, VP, gen mgr; Trapper John, progmg dir.

*KSUL(FM)—Not on air, target date: unknown: 91.5 mhz; 100 w. Ant 184 ft TL: N29 30 52 W89 43 48. Hrs open: Drawer 2440, Tupelo, MS, 38803. Phone: (662) 844-8888. Fax: (662) 842-6791. Web Site:www.afr.com Licensee: American Family Association. Group owner: American Family Radio. Format: Christian. ◆Marvin Sanders, chmn.

Rayne

KKOO(FM)— 1993: 106.7 mhz; 3 kw. Ant 328 ft TL: N30 18 17 W92 20 47. Hrs open: Box 228, Crowley, 70527. Secondary address: 320 N. Parkerson Ave., Crowley 70526. Phone: (337) 783-2520. Fax: (337) 783-5744. Web Site:www.countrylegends1067.com Licensee: Broadcast Partners Inc. (acq 12-18-92; $60,000; 1-11-93). Format: Classic country. ◆Phil Lizotte, pres, gen mgr; Jimmy Cole, gen sls mgr; Hans Nelson, progmg dir; Tony Evans, chief of engrg.

Rayville

KMYY(FM)— September 1984: 92.3 mhz; 26 kw. 492 ft TL: N32 27 51 W91 39 10. Stereo. Hrs open: 16 1200 N. 18th St., Suite D, Monroe, 71201. Phone: (318) 322-4585. Web Site:www.realcountry923.com Licensee: Opus Broadcasting Monroe L.L.C. Group owner: Opus Media Partners LLC (acq 7-19-2004; grpsl). Format: Real country. ◆Chris Zimmerman, gen mgr.

Reserve

WPRF(FM)— August 1991: 94.9 mhz; 50 kw. Ant 482 ft TL: N29 43 48 W90 43 37. Stereo. Hrs open: 24 3500 N. Causeway Blvd., Suite 400, Metairie, 70002. Phone: (504) 834-7005. Fax: (504) 834-7096.E-mail: praise@praisefm949.com Licensee: Southeastern Broadcasting Inc. Group owner: Citadel Broadcasting Corp. (acq 7-6-2005; $4.5 million with WOPR(FM) Lacombe). Population served: 1,000,000 Format: Gospel. News: 2 hrs wkly. Target aud: 25-54; general.

Richwood

KHLL(FM)— March 1995: 100.9 mhz; 6 kw. 328 ft TL: N32 24 25 W92 04 13. Hrs open: 704-C Trenton St., West Monroe, 71291. Phone: (318) 323-5994. Fax: (318) 323-6680.E-mail: hillradio@centurytel.net Web Site:www.hillradio.com Licensee: Dan Gilliland. (acq 3-95). Format: Christian hit radio. ◆Rick Godley, gen mgr.

Ruston

*KAPI(FM)— February 1998: 88.3 mhz; 300 w. Ant 197 ft TL: N32 33 08 W92 39 21. Hrs open: Box 3206, American Family Radio, Tupelo, MS, 38803. Phone: (662) 844-8888. Fax: (662) 842-6791.E-mail: comments@afr.net Web Site:www.afr.net Licensee: American Family Association. Group owner: American Family Radio Format: Inspirational Christian. ◆Marvin Sanders, gen mgr.

*KLPI-FM— 1973: 89.1 mhz; 4 kw. 285 ft TL: N32 31 09 W92 39 02. (CP: 20 kw). Stereo. Hrs open: Box 8638, 71272. Secondary address: Union Bldg., 101 Wysteria St. 71272. Phone: (318) 257-4851. Fax: (318) 257-5073.E-mail: general@891klpi.org Web Site:www.891klpi.org Licensee: Louisiana Tech University. Population served: 35,000 Format: Alternative. News staff: 2. Target aud: 18-24; college students. ◆Angela Carter, gen mgr; Chris Hertlein, progmg dir & spec ev coord.

KPCH(FM)— 1999: 99.3 mhz; 15.5 kw. Ant 328 ft TL: N32 28 53 W92 40 37. Hrs open: 24 Box 430, 71270. Secondary address: 500 N. Monroe St. 71270. Phone: (318) 255-6993. Fax: (318) 255-5084.E-mail: thepeach@bayou.com Licensee: Communications Capital Co. II of Louisiana LLC. Group owner: Communications Capital Managers LLC (acq 3-4-2002; grpsl). La. Net. Format: Oldies. ◆Gary McKenney, gen mgr, progmg dir; Tommy Gray, chief of engrg.

KRUS(AM)— Nov 7, 1947: 1490 khz; 1 kw-U. TL: N32 30 48 W92 39 56. Hrs open: Box 430, 71273. Secondary address: 500 N. Monroe St. 71270. Phone: (318) 255-5000.E-mail: z1075fm@bayou.com Licensee: Communications Capital Co. II of Louisiana LLC. Group owner: Communications Capital Managers LLC (acq 3-4-2002; grpsl). Population served: 47,000 Format: Black gospel. Target aud: 25-55; Black. ◆Gary McKenney, gen mgr, stn mgr, gen sls mgr; James Cooper, opns dir, progmg dir; Tommy Gray, mus dir & chief of engrg.

KXKZ(FM)— June 29, 1966: 107.5 mhz; 98 kw. 1,066 ft TL: N32 26 38 W92 42 42. Stereo. Hrs open: 24 Prog sep from AM Box 430, 71273. Secondary address: 500 N. Monroe St. 71270. Phone: (318) 255-5000. Web Site:www.z1075fm.com Population served: 650,000 Natl. Network: ABC, . Wire Svc: ESSA Weather Service Format: Country. News staff: one; News: 7 hrs wkly. Target aud: 25-54. ◆Matt McKenney, progmg dir.

Saint Martinville

*KSJY(FM)— 2005: 89.9 mhz; 30 kw. Ant 466 ft TL: N30 08 03 W91 51 46. Hrs open: Box 3206, American Family Radio, Tupelo, MS, 38803. Phone: (662) 844-8888. Fax: (662) 842-6791.E-mail: comments@afr.net Web Site:www.afr.net Licensee: American Family Association. Group owner: American Family Radio. Format: Inspirational Christian. ◆Marvin Sanders, gen mgr.

Shreveport

*KDAQ(FM)— Dec 21, 1984: 89.9 mhz; 100 kw. 932 ft TL: N32 40 41 W93 55 35. Stereo. Hrs open: 24 Box 5250, 71135. Secondary address: One University Pl. 71115. Phone: (318) 797-5150. Phone: (800) 552-8502. Fax: (318) 797-5265.E-mail: listenermail@redriverradio.com Web Site:www.redriverradio.org Licensee: Louisiana State University Board of Supervisors. Natl. Network: NPR, PRI, . Format: Classical, news, jazz. News: 40 hrs wkly. Target aud: General. ◆Kermit Poling, gen mgr; Rick Shelton, opns mgr.

KEEL(AM)— 1922: 710 khz; 50 kw-D, 5 kw-N, DA-2. TL: N32 40 35 W93 51 35. Hrs open: 24 6341 Westport Ave., 71129. Phone: (318) 688-1130. Fax: (318) 687-8574.E-mail: info@710keel.com Web Site:www.710keel.com Licensee: GAP Broadcasting Shreveport License LLC. Group owner: Clear Channel Communications Inc. (acq 8-3-2007; grpsl). Population served: 896,600 Rgnl. Network: La. Net. Natl. Rep: D & R Radio,. La. Net. Format: News, talk. News staff: 5; News: 6 hrs wkly. Target aud: 25-54; men. ◆Charlie Thomas, gen mgr, opns dir; Lisa Janes, gen sls mgr; Erin McCarty, progmg dir; Craig Westbrook, chief of engrg, local news ed.

KIOU(AM)— 1950: 1480 khz; 1 kw-D. TL: N32 31 30 W93 48 30. Hrs open: 6 AM-6 PM 4149 George Rd., 71107. Phone: (318) 222-0272. Fax: (318) 222-0271. Licensee: Capital City Radio Corp. (group

owner; (acq 12-10-2008; $150,000). Population served: 182,064 Format: Gospel. Target aud: General. ◆Ernest Pickens, gen mgr.

KLKL(FM)— (Minden, July 1, 1978: 95.7 mhz; 50 kw. 469 ft TL: N32 33 24 W93 31 45. Stereo. Hrs open: 24 208 N. Thomas Dr., 71107. Phone: (318) 222-3122. Fax: (318) 459-1493.E-mail: info@oldies957.fm Web Site:www.oldies957.fm Licensee: Access. 1 Louisiana Holding Co. LLC. Group owner: Access.1 Communications Corp. (acq 6-30-00; $7.9 million with KDKS-FM Blanchard). Format: Oldies. News staff: 1. Target aud: 25-54. ◆Cary D. Camp, gen mgr.

KMJJ-FM— Dec 5, 1976: 99.7 mhz; 50 kw. 462 ft TL: N32 30 24 W93 45 13. Hrs open: Box 5459, Bossier City, 71171. Phone: (318) 549-8500. Fax: (318) 549-8505.E-mail: cumulus.shreveport@cumulus.com Web Site:www.997kmjj.com Licensee: Cumulus Licensing Corp. Group owner: Cumulus Media Inc. (acq 8-7-00; grpsl). Format: Urban contemp. News: one hr wkly. Target aud: 18-49; African American & general. ◆Gary Robinson, prom dir; Mychael Maguire, progmg dir; Jasen Bragg, chief of engrg.

KOKA(AM)— Aug 1, 1954: 980 khz; 5 kw-D. TL: N32 34 18 W93 44 39. Hrs open: 24 208 N. Thomas Dr., 71107. Phone: (318) 222-3122. Fax: (318) 459-1493.E-mail: info@koka.am Web Site:www.koka.am Licensee: Access. 1 Louisiana Holding Co. LLC. Group owner: Access.1 Communications Corp. (acq 12-20-02; grpsl). Natl. Rep: D & R Radio,. Format: Gospel. News staff: 1. Target aud: 25-64; middle-aged, middle class, Black adults. ◆Cary D. Camp, gen mgr; Don Zimmerman, gen sls mgr; Eddie Giles, progmg dir.

KRMD(AM)— June 1928: 1340 khz; 1 kw-U. TL: N32 29 36 W93 45 55. Stereo. Hrs open: 24 Box 5459, 270 Plaza Loop, Bossier City, 71111. Phone: (318) 549-8500. Fax: (318) 549-8505.E-mail: cumulus.shreveport@cumulus.com Web Site:www.supertalk1340.com Licensee: Cumulus Licensing Corp. Format: Sports, news, talk. ◆John Sherman, progmg dir.

KRMD-FM— August 1948: 101.1 mhz; 98 kw. Ant 1,119 ft TL: N32 41 08 W93 56 00. (CP: 100 kw, ant 1,627 ft). Stereo. Hrs open: Box 5459, 270 Plaza Loop, Bossier City, 71111. Phone: (318) 549-8500. Fax: (318) 549-8505.E-mail: cumulus.shreveport@cumulus.com Web Site:www.krmd.com Licensee: Cumulus Licensing Corp. Group owner: Cumulus Media Inc. (acq 8-7-2000; grpsl). Population served: 369,800 Natl. Rep: Christal,. Format: Contemp country. News staff: 2. Target aud: 25-54. ◆Gary Robinson, prom dir, disc jockey; Jasen Bragg, engrg dir, disc jockey; Todd Nixon, progmg dir & disc jockey.

KRUF(FM)— Nov 5, 1948: 94.5 mhz; 100 kw. Ant 1,096 ft TL: N32 40 13 W93 55 59. (CP: Ant 1,666 ft. TL: N32 39 57 W93 55 58). Stereo. Hrs open: 24 6341 Westport Ave., 71129. Phone: (318) 688-1130. Fax: (318) 687-8574.E-mail: info@k945.com Web Site:www.k945.com Population served: 896,600 Format: CHR. ◆Erin Bristol, progmg dir.

*KSCL(FM)— Mar 11, 1976: 91.3 mhz; 2.6 kw. Ant 184 ft TL: N32 28 51.4 W93 43 51.1. Stereo. Hrs open: 24 2911 Centenary Blvd., 71104. Phone: (318) 869-5296. Fax: (318) 869-5294.E-mail: kscl@centenary.edu Web Site:www.centenary.edu Licensee: Centenary College of Louisiana. Population served: 250,000 Format: Alternative music. News staff: one; News: 4 hrs wkly. Target aud: General; college students & adults interested in div music. ◆John Schleass, stn mgr; Alyson Escude, progmg dir, progmg dir; Tyler Davis, mus dir.

KSYB(AM)— July 10, 1975: 1300 khz; 5 kw-D. TL: N32 31 48 W93 48 16. Hrs open: 24 Box 7685, 71137. Secondary address: 1526 Corporate Dr. 71107. Phone: (318) 222-2744. Fax: (318) 425-7507.E-mail: ksyb@amistadradiogroup.com Licensee: Amistad Communications Inc. (acq 10-26-2000; $900,000). Population served: 182,064 Format: Christian, gospel. ◆Fred Caldwell, CEO, chief of engrg; Rhonda Sanders, stn mgr; Steve Anderson, mus dir.

KTUX(FM)— (Carthage, TX) Apr 1, 1985: 98.9 mhz; 100 kw. 1,049 ft TL: N32 23 19 W94 01 10. Stereo. Hrs open: 24 6341 Westport Ave., 71129. Phone: (318) 688-1130. Fax: (318) 688-9839. Web Site:www.therockstation99x.com Licensee: GAP Broadcasting Shreveport License LLC. Group owner: Clear Channel Communications Inc. (acq 8-3-2007; grpsl). Format: New rock. Target aud: 18-49; super-active adults. ◆Charlie Thomas, gen mgr.

KVKI-FM— May 1959: 96.5 mhz; 95 kw. 797 ft TL: N32 35 38 W93 51 39. Stereo. Hrs open: 24 6341 Westport Ave., 71129. Phone: (318) 688-1130. Fax: (318) 688-9839. Web Site:www.965kvki.com Licensee: GAP Broadcasting Shreveport License LLC. Group owner: Clear Channel Communications Inc. (acq 8-3-2007; grpsl). Population served: 328,000 Natl. Rep: D & R Radio,. Format: Adult contemp. News staff: one. Target aud: 25-54; female. ◆Charlie Thomas, gen mgr.

KVMA-FM— 2001: 102.9 mhz; 42 kw. Ant 535 ft TL: N32 29 36 W93 45 55. Hrs open: 24 Box 5459, Bossier City, 71171. Phone: (318) 549-8500. Fax: (318) 549-8505.E-mail: cumulus.shreveport@cumulus.com Web Site:magic1029fm.com Licensee: Cumulus Licensing Corp. Group owner: Cumulus Media Inc. (acq 10-23-2000). Wire Svc: AP Format: Urban contemp. ◆Mychael Maguire, progmg dir; Jasen Bragg, chief of engrg.

KWKH(AM)— September 1925: 1130 khz; 50 kw-U, DA-N. TL: N32 42 15 W93 52 52. Hrs open: 24 6341 Westport Ave., 71129. Phone: (318) 688-1130. Fax: (318) 687-8574.E-mail: info@kwkhonline.com Web Site:www.kwkhonline.com Licensee: GAP Broadcasting Shreveport License LLC. Group owner: Clear Channel Communications Inc. (acq 8-3-2007; grpsl). Population served: 896,600 Natl. Rep: D & R Radio,. Format: Country. News staff: 4; News: 18 hrs wkly. Target aud: Male 25-54. ◆Charlie Thomas, gen mgr; Lisa Janes, gen sls mgr; Barney Cannon, progmg dir; Craig Westbrook, chief of engrg, farm dir.

KXKS-FM— May 17, 1968: 93.7 mhz; 95 kw. 1,010 ft TL: N32 40 39 W93 55 41. Stereo. Hrs open: Prog sep from AM 6341 Westport Ave., 71129. Phone: (318) 688-1130. Fax: (318) 687-8574.E-mail: info@kisscountry937.com Web Site:www.kisscountry937.com Licensee: GAP Broadcasting Shreveport License LLC. Population served: 896,600 Format: Country. Target aud: 25-54; 30 yr old female. ◆Chris Evans, progmg dir & disc jockey.

Simmesport

KXKW(FM)— 2008: 105.3 mhz; 190 w. Ant 205 ft TL: N30 59 32 W91 50 53. Hrs open: 3501 Northwest Evangeline Thruway, Carencro, 70520. Phone: (337) 896-1600. Fax: (337) 896-2695. Licensee: Delta Media Corp. ◆Eddie Blanchard, gen mgr.

Slidell

WSLA(AM)— Dec 5, 1963: 1560 khz; 1 kw-U, DA-N. TL: N30 15 08 W89 45 46. Stereo. Hrs open: Daytime Box 1175, 70459. Secondary address: 38230 Coast Blvd. 70458. Phone: (985) 643-1560. Fax: (985) 649-9822.E-mail: 1560@bellsouth.net Licensee: MAPA Broadcasting L.L.C. (acq 7-2-93; 8-2-93). Population served: 1,200,000 Natl. Network: USA, . Rgnl. Network: La. Net. La. Net. Format: ESPN & loc sports. Target aud: 25 plus; news intensive audience & sports fans. ◆George Mayoral, gen mgr; Jim Sommers, opns mgr & progmg dir.

South Fort Polk

KROK(FM)— Feb 22, 2003: 95.7 mhz; 6 kw. Ant 289 ft TL: N31 03 05 W93 16 41. Hrs open: 168 KVVP Dr., Leesville, 71446. Phone: (337) 537-5887. Fax: (337) 537-4152. Web Site:www.krok.com Licensee: West Central Broadcasting Co. Inc. (acq 1-25-02). Format: Adult album alternative. Target aud: 18-54. ◆Alan Taylor, CFO; Doug Stannard, pres & gen mgr.

Springhill

KBSF(AM)— June 30, 1954: Stn currently dark. 1460 khz; 1 kw-D, 220 w-N. TL: N33 00 02 W93 28 43. Hrs open: Sunrise-sunset 541 S. Main St., 71075. Phone: (318) 539-4616. Fax: (318) 539-2356. Licensee: The RAFTT Corp. (acq 4-6-2009; $55,000). Population served: 25,000 ◆Earnest Pickens, gen mgr.

KTKC(FM)— Sept 5, 1975: 92.9 mhz; 40 kw. 548 ft TL: N33 00 30 W93 28 38. Stereo. Hrs open: 24 541 S. Main St., 71075. Phone: (318) 539-4616. Fax: (318) 539-2356. Licensee: Metropolitan Radio Group Inc. (group owner; acq 6-97; with co-located AM). Population served: 100,000 Natl. Network: ABC, . Format: Black gospel. Target aud: 35-54. ◆Earnest Pickens, gen mgr; Rudy Johnson, chief of engrg.

Sulphur

KEZM(AM)— 1955: 1310 khz; 500 w-D, 50 w-N, DA-1. TL: N30 13 27 W93 22 44. Hrs open: 24 113 E. Napoleon St., 70663-3313. Phone: (337) 527-3611. Fax: (337) 527-0213. Licensee: Merchant Broadcasting Inc. (acq 1-30-98; $75,000). Population served: 185,000 Natl. Network: Sporting News Radio Network, . Cohn & Marks. Format: Sports. News staff: one; News: 5 hrs wkly. Target aud: 18-63; upscale baby-boomers. ◆Bruce L. Merchant, pres; Bruce Merchant, gen mgr; Kathy Soileau, sls dir & gen sls mgr.

KKGB(FM)— Dec 17, 1977: 101.3 mhz; 12 kw. Ant 479 ft TL: N30 14 41 W93 20 37. Stereo. Hrs open: 24 425 Broad St., Lake Charles, 70601-4225. Phone: (337) 439-3300. Fax: (337) 436-7278.E-mail:

info@kkgb.com Web Site:www.kkgb.com Licensee: Cumulus Licensing Corp. Group owner: Cumulus Media Inc. (acq 12-17-98; grpsl). Population served: 230,000 Natl. Rep: Christal,. Kaye, Scholer, Fierman, Hays & Handler. Format: Classic rock. News staff: one. Target aud: General; baby boomers. ◆Eric Nielson, opns mgr; Jim Vidler, mktg mgr.

*KRLR(FM)— 2007: 89.1 mhz; 1 w horiz, 16 kw vert. Ant 394 ft TL: N30 21 06 W93 23 49. Hrs open: Rebroadcasts KLVR(FM) Santa Rosa, CA 100%. 2351 Sunset Blvd., Suite 170-218, Rocklin, CA, 95765. Phone: (916) 251-1600. Fax: (916) 251-1650. Web Site:www.klove.com Licensee: Educational Media Foundation. (acq 11-1-2006; grpsl). Natl. Network: K-Love, . Format: Contemp Christian. ◆Richard Jenkins, pres.

KYKZ(FM)—See Lake Charles

Tallulah

KBYO(AM)— Sept 4, 1954: 1360 khz; 500 w-D. TL: N32 25 37 W91 13 15. Hrs open: Box 88, 71284. Phone: (318) 574-3119. Fax: (318) 574-3150. Licensee: First United Methodist Church of Tallulah, Louisiana (acq 9-22-2008; donation). Population served: 9,634

KLSM(FM)— Apr 29, 1983: 104.5 mhz; 3 kw. Ant 320 ft TL: N29 45 35 W90 49 30. (CP: 7 kw, ant 196 ft). Stereo. Hrs open: 1601 N. Frontage Rd., Suite E, Vicksburg, MS, 39180. Phone: (601) 636-2340. Fax: (601) 638-0869.E-mail: spots@river101.com Licensee: Holladay Broadcasting of Louisiana LLC. Latham & Watkins. Format: Hot A/C. Target aud: 25-54. ◆Bob Holladay, gen mgr.

KTJZ(FM)— 2008: 97.5 mhz; 6 kw. Ant 302 ft TL: N32 25 42 W91 18 47. Hrs open: 3313 Government St., Baton Rouge, 70806-5629. Phone: (225) 334-7490. Fax: (225) 334-7491.E-mail: lanaapc1@juno.com Licensee: Mid South Communications Co. Inc. Format: Gospel, rhythm and blues. ◆Ernest L. Johnson, chmn & pres.

Thibodaux

*KNSU(FM)— Feb 15, 1972: 91.5 mhz; 250 w vert. 148 ft TL: N29 47 29 W90 48 07. (CP: 91.3 mhz, 3 kw, ant 285 ft. TL: N29 45 35 W90 49 30). Hrs open: 10 AM-2 AM (M-F); noon-2 AM (S, Su) po Box 2031, Nicholls State Univ., 70310. Phone: (985) 448-4586. Fax: (985) 449-7106.E-mail: lance.arnold@nicholls.edu Web Site:www.nicholls.edu/knsu Licensee: Board of Trustees, Nicholls State University. Population served: 14,925 Format: Alternative. News: 10 hrs wkly. Target aud: 18 plus. ◆Katie Kingdon, stn mgr; Jonathan DeSilvie, progmg dir.

KTIB(AM)— Dec 24, 1953: 640 khz; 5 kw-D, 1 kw-N, DA-2. TL: N29 50 05 W90 54 48. Stereo. Hrs open: 24 108 Green Street, 70301. Phone: (985) 447-6404. Fax: (985) 447-6464.E-mail: ktib@charter.net Web Site:www.ktib640.com Licensee: Gap Broadcasting LLC (acq 2-5-2007; $650,000). Population served: 2,963,913 Natl. Network: Jones Radio Networks, Premiere Radio Networks, Talk Radio Network, . Natl. Rep: Commercial Media Sales,. La. Net. ◆Linda Bellanger, gen mgr.

*KTLN(FM)— May 1995: 90.5 mhz; 200 w. 357 ft TL: N29 43 18 W90 46 33. Stereo. Hrs open: 24 Rebroadcasts WWNO(FM) New Orleans 100%. Univ. of New Orleans, New Orleans, 70148. Phone: (504) 280-7000. Fax: (504) 280-6061.E-mail: info@wwno.org Web Site:www.wwno.org Licensee: Board of Supervisors of Louisiana State University and Agricultural and Mechanical College, University of New Orleans. Population served: 100,000 Natl. Network: NPR, PRI, . Format: Class, news, jazz. News: 39 hrs wkly. Target aud: 35-70; well educated professionals, managers, artists & arts patrons. ◆Chuck Miller, gen mgr; Ronald C. Curtis, opns dir; Karen Anklam, dev dir; Fred Kasten, prom mgr, progmg dir.

KXOR-FM— May 1, 1966: 106.3 mhz; 25 kw. Ant 328 ft TL: N29 38 52 W90 41 34. Stereo. Hrs open: 24 Box 2068, Houma, 70361. Secondary address: 120 Prevost Dr., Houma 70364. Phone: (985) 851-1020. Fax: (985) 872-4403.E-mail: info@rock1063.net Web Site:www.rock1063.net Licensee: Sunburst Media-Louisiana LLC. (acq 1-23-2007; grpsl). Population served: 75,000 Rgnl. Network: La. Agri-News. La. Agri-News Format: Rock. News: 20 hrs wkly. Target aud: 18-54. ◆Danny Fletcher, gen mgr; John Delise, opns mgr & progmg dir.

Tioga

KLAA-FM—Licensed to Tioga. See Alexandria

Varnado

WBOX-FM— November 1985: 92.9 mhz; 3 kw. 321 ft TL: N30 54 10 W89 57 36. Stereo. Hrs open: Box 280, Bogalusa, 70429. Secondary address: 22037 Hwy. 436, Bogalusa 70427. Phone: (985) 732-4288. Fax: (985) 732-4288. Licensee: Best Country Broadcasting LLC (acq 9-6-2002; $150,000 with WBOX(AM) Bogalusa). Population served: 70,000 Format: Contemp country. ◆Ben R. Strickland, pres.

Vidalia

KWTG(FM)— 1994: 104.7 mhz; 3 kw. Ant 266 ft TL: N31 35 05 W91 23 18. Hrs open: Box 1510, Ferriday, 71334. Secondary address: 917 S.E.E. Wallace Blvd., Ferriday 71334. Phone: (318) 757-4200. Fax: (318) 757-7689. Web Site:www.kwtgfm.com Licensee: Tom D. Gay. Format: Classic country. ◆Desiree Smith, gen mgr; Mike Smith, gen sls mgr; Eddie Ray, progmg dir; Selena Book, traf mgr.

WQNZ(FM)—See Natchez, MS

Ville Platte

KVPI(AM)— November 1953: 1050 khz; 250 w-D, 10 w-N. TL: N30 41 39 W92 18 46. Hrs open: 6 AM-midnight Box J, 70586. Secondary address: 809 W. LaSalle St. 70586.E-mail: kvpiamfm@gmail.com Licensee: Ville Platte Broadcsting Co. Population served: 79,692 Rgnl. Network: La. Net. La. Net. Format: Classic country. News staff: one; News: 12 hrs wkly. Target aud: 32-65. Spec prog: Cajun 12 hrs wkly.

KVPI-FM— Feb 26, 1967: 92.5 mhz; 3.9 kw horiz. Ant 220 ft TL: N30 41 39 W92 18 46. Stereo. Hrs open: 24 Box J, 70586. Secondary address: 809 W. LaSalle St. 70586. Phone: (337) 363-2124. Fax: (337) 363-3574.E-mail: kvpiamfm@gmail.com Web Site:www.oldies925.com Licensee: Ville Platte Broadcasting Co. (acq 11-7-2005; with co-located AM). Population served: 72,940 Natl. Network: NBC Radio, . Wire Svc: AP Format: Oldies/Classic Hits. News staff: one; News: 12 hrs wkly. Target aud: 32-65. Spec prog: Cajun French 6 hrs wkly. ◆Rhonda Pucheu, pres; Mark Layne, gen mgr; Danny Poullard, progmg dir; Cheryl DeBallion, traf mgr; Randy Guillory, sports cmtr.

Vivian

KNCB(AM)— Apr 9, 1966: 1320 khz; 5 kw-D. TL: N32 54 08 W93 58 59. Hrs open: Sunrise-sunset Box 1072, 71082. Secondary address: 17525 Hwy. 1 N. 71082. Phone: (318) 375-3278. Fax: (318) 375-3329.E-mail: rjc1072@cs.com Licensee: North Caddo Broadcasting Co. (acq 4-9-66). Population served: 90,000 Format: Country, gospel, news/talk. Target aud: General. ◆Ruby J. Collins, gen mgr; Ruby Collins, gen sls mgr; Rudy Johnson, chief of engrg.

KNCB-FM— Sept 28, 1996: 105.3 mhz; 3.2 kw. 449 ft TL: N32 55 54 W93 54 22. Stereo. Hrs open: 24 Dups AM 50% Box 1072, 71082. Secondary address: 17525 Hwy. 1 N. 71082. Phone: (318) 375-3278. Fax: (318) 375-3329.E-mail: rjc1072@cs.com (Acq 9-27-96.). Natl. Network: ABC, . Format: Real country.

Washington

KNEK(AM)— Aug 18, 1980: 1190 khz; 250 w-D. TL: N30 35 09 W92 04 00. Hrs open: 202 Galbert Rd., Lafayette, 70506-1806. Phone: (337) 232-1311. Fax: (337) 233-3779. Web Site:www.knek.com Licensee: Citadel Broadcasting Co. Group owner: Citadel Broadcasting Corp. (acq 1-14-99; grpsl). Rgnl. Network: La. Net. La. Net. Format: Urban contemp. Target aud: 25-54.

KNEK-FM— 1989: 104.7 mhz; 25 kw. Ant 328 ft TL: N30 25 17 W92 06 50. Stereo. Hrs open: 24 202 Galbert Rd., Lafayette, 70506-1806. Phone: (337) 232-1311. Fax: (337) 233-3779. Web Site:www.knek.com Licensee: The Last Bastion Station Trust LLC, as Trustee (acq 6-12-2007; grpsl). Format: Adult contemp. ◆Dave Kubicki, gen sls mgr; Deidre Williams, progmg dir; Doug Allen, chief of engrg.

West Monroe

KMBS(AM)— August 1956: 1310 khz; 5 kw-D, 49 w-N. TL: N32 29 02 W92 09 10. Hrs open: 613 N. 5th St., 1133 Hwy. 15, 71291. Phone: (318) 323-1310. Licensee: Red Bear Broadcasting (acq 6-10-93; $200,000;6-28-93). Population served: 260,000 Natl. Network: ABC, . Format: Sports. ◆Chuck Redden, gen mgr.

KZRZ(FM)— Aug 1, 1967: 98.3 mhz; 50 kw. 492 ft TL: N32 39 38 W91 59 28. Stereo. Hrs open: 24 1200 N. 18th St., Suite D, Monroe, 71201.

Phone: (318) 387-3922. Fax: (318) 322-4585.E-mail: sunny983@comcast.net Web Site:www.sunny983.com Licensee: Opus Broadcasting Monroe L.L.C. Group owner: Opus Media Partners LLC (acq 7-19-2004; grpsl). Population served: 30286 Format: Adult contemp. Target aud: 18-54; mid to upper income. ◆Chris Zimmerman, gen mgr; Mike Dawnhour, gen sls mgr.

White Castle

KKAY(AM)— November 1976: 1590 khz; 1 kw-D. TL: N30 11 01 W91 06 27. Hrs open: 24 706 Railroad Ave., Donaldsonville, 70346. Phone: (225) 473-6397. Fax: (225) 473-5764.E-mail: dave@kkay1590.com Web Site:www.kkay1590.com Licensee: Cactus Communications LLC. Format: Full service. ◆David Dawson, gen mgr.

Winnfield

KVCL(AM)— Dec 17, 1955: 1270 khz; 820 w-D. TL: N31 56 54 W92 37 37. Stereo. Hrs open: 24 304 KVCL Rd., 71483. Phone: (318) 628-5822. Fax: (318) 628-7355. Licensee: Baldridge-Dumas Communications Inc. (acq 12-28-2006; $300,000 with co-located FM). Population served: 150,000 Natl. Network: CNN Radio, Jones Radio Networks, . Rgnl. Network: La. Net. La. Net. Format: News/talk info. News staff: 2; News: 21 hrs wkly. Target aud: General; financially able persons, blacks and professionals. ◆Michael Parker, opns mgr, adv mgr; Kresi Parker, gen sls mgr; Rhonda Leach, gen mgr & natl sls mgr.

KVCL-FM— Nov 3, 1966: 92.1 mhz; 6 kw. Ant 210 ft TL: N31 56 54 W92 37 37. Stereo. Hrs open: 24 304 KVCL Rd., 71483. Phone: (318) 628-5822. Fax: (318) 628-7355. Licensee: Baldridge-Dumas Communications Inc. (acq 12-28-2006; $300,000 with co-located AM). Population served: 275,000 Format: Country. News staff: 2; News: 22 hrs wkly. ◆Ted Dumas, gen mgr.

Winnsboro

KMAR-FM— August 1969: 95.9 mhz; 6 kw. Ant 178 ft TL: N32 11 02 W91 44 51. Stereo. Hrs open: 24 Box 312, 71295. Secondary address: 1823 Hwy. 618 71295. Phone: (318) 435-5141. Fax: (318) 435-5749.E-mail: kmarfm@bellsouth.net Web Site:www.kmarfm.com Licensee: Boeuf River Broadcasting Co. Group owner: The Radio Group (acq 11-89; $200,000 with co-located AM; 11-6-89). Population served: 65,000 Natl. Network: ABC, . Wire Svc: UPI Format: Country. News staff: one; News: 20 hrs wkly. Target aud: 30-60; adults. ◆Rene Johnston, gen mgr.

Zwolle

KTEZ(FM)— July 4, 2002: 99.9 mhz; 6 kw. Ant 328 ft TL: N31 39 17 W93 29 04. Hrs open: 24 605 San Antonio Ave., Many, 71449. Phone: (318) 256-5924. Fax: (318) 256-0950.E-mail: kwlv@bellsouth.net Web Site:www.bdcradio.com Licensee: Baldridge-Dumas Communications Inc. (group owner; (acq 2-25-2002). Format: Adult contemp. ◆Tedd W. Dumas, VP; Rhonda Leach, gen mgr; Cindy Ezernack, stn mgr.

Maine

Auburn

WFNK(FM)—See Portland

WLAM(AM)—See Lewiston

WTHT(FM)— February 1977: 99.9 mhz; 50 kw. 492 ft TL: N43 57 07 W70 17 46. Stereo. Hrs open: 24 477 Congress St., Suite 3 A, 3rd Fl. Annex, Portland, 04101. Phone: (207) 797-0780. Fax: (207) 797-0368.E-mail: info@999thewolf.com Web Site:www.999thewolf.com Licensee: Nassau Broadcasting III L.L.C. Group owner: Nassau Broadcasting Partners L.P. (acq 4-6-2004; grpsl). Population served: 750,800 Format: Country. Target aud: Women 18-34, women 25-54; Maine's kiss 99.9. ◆Pat Collins, gen mgr; Stan Manning, opns dir, progmg dir; Tim Gatz, gen sls mgr; Bill Ryall, chief of engrg.

Augusta

WABK-FM—See Gardiner

WFAU(AM)—See Gardiner

WJZN(AM)— Feb 23, 1932: 1400 khz; 1 kw-U. TL: N44 17 30 W69 46 27. Hrs open: 24
Rebroadcasts WTVL(AM) Waterville 100%.
Box 5070, 52 Western Ave., 04330. Phone: (207) 623-4735. Fax: (207) 626-5948.E-mail: augusta@catomm.com Web Site:www.1400and1490.com Licensee: Citadel Broadcasting Co. Group owner: Citadel Broadcasting Corp. (acq 4-26-2001; grpsl). Population served: 100,000 Natl. Rep: D & R Radio,. Format: Oldies. News staff: one. Target aud: 20-40; young adults. ♦Al Perry, gen mgr; Julie Beaulieu, gen sls mgr; Renee Nelson, news dir; Bob Perry, chief of engrg.

***WMDR(AM)**— Oct 2, 1946: 1340 khz; 1 kw-U. TL: N44 19 43 W69 45 53. Hrs open: 24 160 Riverside Dr, 04330. Phone: (207) 622-1340. Fax: (207) 623-2874.E-mail: denise@worshipradionetwork.org Web Site:www.worshipradionetwork.org Licensee: Light of Life Ministries Inc. (acq 12-94; 2-13-95). Population served: 100,000 Format: Conservative talk. News: 5 hrs wkly. Target aud: General. Spec prog: stories. ♦Denise LaFountain, gen mgr; Frank Speed, progmg dir.

WMME-FM— Jan 14, 1981: 92.3 mhz; 50 kw. Ant 500 ft TL: N44 20 07 W69 41 01. Stereo. Hrs open: Prog sep from AM Box 5070, 52 Western Ave., 31707. Phone: (229) 439-9704. Fax: (229) 439-1509. Web Site:www.92moose.fm Population served: 310,000 Format: CHR.

WVQM(FM)— July 1961: 101.3 mhz; 50 kw. Ant 321 ft TL: N44 18 51 W69 50 03. Hrs open:
Simulcast with WVOM(FM) Howland 100%.
150 Whitten Rd., 04330. Phone: (207) 623-9000. Fax: (207) 623-9007.E-mail: kellyslater@clearchannel.com Web Site:www.wvomfm.com Licensee: Blueberry Broadcasting LLC. Group owner: Clear Channel Communications Inc. (acq 7-29-2008; grpsl). Format: News/talk. ♦Kelly Slater, gen mgr; Steve Smith, opns dir; Rick Dugal, gen sls mgr.

***WWTP(FM)**—Not on air, target date: unknown: 89.5 mhz; 410 w vert. Ant 329 ft TL: N44 21 06.6 W69 39 30.3. Hrs open: 103 Spring St., Gardiner, 04345. Licensee: Columbus Home Association. ♦Phillip Theriault, pres.

Bangor

WAEI(AM)— 1924: 910 khz; 5 kw-U, DA-N. TL: N44 46 44 W68 44 22. Hrs open: 18 184 Target Industrial Cir., 04410-5718. Phone: (207) 947-9100. Fax: (207) 942-8039. Web Site:www.weei.com Licensee: Blueberry Broadcasting LLC. Group owner: Clear Channel Communications Inc. (acq 7-29-2008; grpsl). Population served: 33,168 Cohn & Marks LLP. Format: Sports. ♦Jon Shields, opns dir; Josh Scroggins, gen mgr & gen sls mgr.

WAEI-FM— Mar 15, 1961: 97.1 mhz; 5 kw. Ant 1,230 ft TL: N44 42 13 W69 04 07. Stereo. Hrs open: 24 184 Target Industrial Cir., 04410. Phone: (207) 947-9100. Fax: (207) 942-8039. Web Site:www.weei.com Licensee: Blueberry Broadcasting LLC. (acq 7-29-2008; grpsl). Population served: 200,000 Format: Sports. Target aud: General. ♦Holly Rae, progmg dir.

WBFB(FM)—See Belfast

WEZQ(FM)— June 9, 1976: 92.9 mhz; 20 kw. 787 ft TL: N44 45 35 W68 33 55. Stereo. Hrs open: 24 Box 100, Brewer, 04412. Phone: (207) 989-5631. Fax: (207) 989-5685.E-mail: info@wezq-fm.com Web Site:www.wezq-fm.com Licensee: Cumulus Licensing Corp. Group owner: Cumulus Media Inc. (acq 3-1-99; grpsl). Population served: 50,000 Natl. Rep: D & R Radio,. Fisher, Wayland, Cooper, Leader & Zaragoza. Format: Easy lstng. News staff: one. Target aud: 25-54. ♦Tom Preble, gen mgr; Paul Dupuis, opns VP, opns mgr; Dorian Daniels, progmg dir.

***WHCF(FM)**— Aug 10, 1981: 88.5 mhz; 100 kw. 1,604 ft TL: N45 07 46 W68 21 28. (CP: 35 kw, ant 1,620 ft.). Stereo. Hrs open: 24 Box 5000, 04402-5000. Secondary address: 1476 Broadway 04401. Phone: (207) 947-2751. Fax: (207) 947-0010.E-mail: whcf@whcf.cc Web Site:whcf.cc Licensee: Bangor Baptist Church. Population served: 450,000 Natl. Network: Salem Radio Network, . Fletcher, Heald & Hildreth. Format: Inspirational Christian, gospel. News: 7 hrs wkly. Target aud: 35-55; Adults. Spec prog: Childdren 5 1/2 hrs wkly. ♦Scott Stewart, chmn; Jerry Mick, pres; Pencil Boone, gen mgr; Tina Collins, opns mgr; Ed Paradis, chief of opns; Hal Welch, chief of engrg.

***WHSN(FM)**— September 1974: 89.3 mhz; 3 kw. Ant 85 ft TL: N44 49 46 W68 47 39. Stereo. Hrs open: 24 One College Cir., 04401. Phone: (207) 941-7116. Phone: (207) 973-1011. Fax: (207) 947-3987.E-mail: whsn@nescom.edu Web Site:www.whsn-fm.com Licensee: Husson University Board of Trustees. Population served: 5,000 Wire Svc: AP Format: Alternative. News staff: one; News: 7 hrs wkly. Target aud: 12-25; high school & college students. ♦Ben Haskell, gen mgr; Mark Nason, progmg VP, progmg dir; Susan Patten, news dir & chief of engrg; David MacLaughlin, engr.

WKIT-FM—See Brewer

***WMEH(FM)**— Sept 14, 1970: 90.9 mhz; 13.5 kw. 850 ft TL: N44 45 36 W68 33 59. Stereo. Hrs open: 24 63 Texas Ave., 04401. Secondary address: 1450 Lisbon St., Lewiston 04240. Phone: (207) 783-9101. Fax: (207) 942-2857.E-mail: cbeck@mpbn.net Web Site:www.mpbn.net Licensee: Maine Public Broadcasting Corp. (acq 6-23-92; 7-13-92). Population served: 35,000 Natl. Network: NPR, PRI, . Dow, Lohnes & Albertson. Format: Class, pub affrs, news, jazz, folk. ♦Alexander G. Maxwell, Jr., COO, stn mgr; P. James Dowe, Jr., CEO & pres; Christopher F. Amann, CFO; Alexander G. Maxwell, sr VP; Mary Mayo, dev VP; Charles Beck, progmg VP.

WWMJ(FM)—See Ellsworth

WZON(AM)— December 1926: 620 khz; 5 kw-U, DA-N. TL: N44 49 44 W68 47 08. Hrs open: 24 Box 1929, 04402. Phone: (207) 990-2800. Fax: (207) 990-2444.E-mail: wzon@zoneradio.com Web Site:www.zoneradio.com Licensee: The Zone Corp. (group owner; acq 9-1-93; $236,200; 9-27-93). Format: Sports, talk. News staff: one; News: 18 hrs wkly. Target aud: General; info & entertainment seekers. ♦Stephen King, pres; Bobby Russell, gen mgr, stn mgr; Ken Wood, sls dir, gen sls mgr; Dale Duff, progmg dir.

Bar Harbor

WBQI(FM)— May 6, 1995: 107.7 mhz; 11.5 kw. 489 ft TL: N44 33 13 W68 05 40. Stereo. Hrs open: 24
Rebroadcasts WBQQ (FM) Kennebunk 90%.
169 Port Rd., Kennebunk, 04043. Phone: (207) 797-0780. Fax: (207) 967-8671. Web Site:www.wbachradio.com Licensee: Nassau Broadcasting III L.L.C. Group owner: Nassau Broadcasting Partners L.P. (acq 4-6-2004; grpsl). Natl. Network: CBS, Westwood One, . Format: Class. News staff: one; News: 6 hrs wkly. Target aud: 25-54; baby boomers. Spec prog: Blues 15 hrs wkly. ♦Pat Collins, gen mgr.

WLKE(FM)— June 1, 1992: 99.1 mhz; 45 kw. 400 ft TL: N44 32 53 W68 18 53. Stereo. Hrs open: 24 184 Target Cir., Bangor, 04401-5718. Phone: (207) 947-9100. Fax: (207) 942-8039. Licensee: Blueberry Broadcasting LLC. Group owner: Clear Channel Communications Inc. (acq 7-29-2008; grpsl). Population served: 75,000 Natl. Network: ABC, . Natl. Rep: Christal,. Cohn & Marks LLP. Format: Country. News staff: one. Target aud: General. ♦Jon Shields, opns dir, gen sls mgr, mus dir; Josh Scroggins, gen mgr & gen sls mgr.

Bath

WBCI(FM)— June 1971: 105.9 mhz; 50 kw. 499 ft TL: N44 04 09 W69 55 28. Stereo. Hrs open: Box 359, Topsham, 04086. Secondary address: 122 Main St., Topsham 04086. Phone: (207) 725-9224. Fax: (207) 725-2686.E-mail: info@wbci.net Web Site:www.wbci.fm Licensee: Blount Communications Inc. Group owner: Blount Communications Group (acq 4-20-95; $375,000). Population served: 750,000 Natl. Network: Salem Radio Network, . Natl. Rep: Salem,. Format: Talk, Christian. Target aud: 25-54; 60% men, 40% women. ♦Bill Blount, pres; Deborah Blount, exec VP; David Young, sr VP; Lee Pelletier, stn mgr.

WJTO(AM)— Sept 30, 1957: 730 khz; 1 kw-D, 29 w-N. TL: N43 52 39 W69 50 49. Hrs open: 24 Box 308, 04530. Phone: (207) 443-6671. Web Site:www.wjto.com Licensee: Blue Jey Broadcasting Co. Group owner: Bob Bittner Broadcasting Inc. (acq 2-28-97; $150,000). Population served: 880,000 Format: Adult Standards. News: 2 hrs wkly. Target aud: 35 plus; adults along the Maine coastline. ♦Bob Bittner, gen mgr.

***WTBP(FM)**—Not on air, target date: unknown: 89.7 mhz; 1 w horiz, 14 kw vert. Ant 197 ft TL: N43 54 50.8 W69 36 50. Hrs open: Box 358, 04530. Secondary address: 807 Middle St. 04530. Phone: (207) 443-9801. Licensee: Knights of Columbus Inc. Natl. Network: EWTN Radio, . ♦Michael Page, pres.

WTQX(FM)—See Boothbay Harbor

Belfast

WBFB(FM)— Mar 7, 1986: 104.7 mhz; 10 kw. 1,099 ft TL: N44 34 51 W68 53 51. Stereo. Hrs open: 24 184 Target Industrial Circle, Bangor, 04401-5718. Phone: (207) 947-9100. Fax: (207) 942-8039.E-mail: info@1074the bear.com Web Site:www.1047the bear.com Licensee: Blueberry Broadcasting LLC. Group owner: Clear Channel Communications Inc. (acq 7-29-2008; grpsl). Population served: 300,000 Cohn & Marks LLP. Format: Country. News staff: 2. Target aud: 18-49. ♦Josh Scroggins, gen mgr.

***WJVH(FM)**—Not on air, target date: unknown: 91.5 mhz; 50 kw. Ant 282 ft TL: N44 18 58 W68 58 12. Hrs open: 160 Bangor St., Augusta, 04330. Phone: (207) 622-1340. Fax: (207) 623-2874. Web Site:worshipradionetwork.lightoflife.info Licensee: Light of Life Ministries Inc. Format: Christian Adult Contemp. ♦Ray Bouchard, gen mgr.

Benedicta

***WRPB(FM)**—Not on air, target date: unknown: 89.3 mhz; 13 kw. Ant 225 ft TL: N45 47 11 W68 24 44. Hrs open: 160 Bangor St., Augusta, 04330. Phone: (207) 622-1340. Fax: (207) 623-2874. Web Site:www.worshipradionetwork.org Licensee: Light of Life Ministries Inc. Format: Southern Gospel, Christian Country. ♦Denise La Fountain, gen mgr.

Biddeford

WCYY(FM)— August 1972: 94.3 mhz; 12 kw. 472 ft TL: N43 32 34 W70 24 12. Stereo. Hrs open: 24 One City Ctr., Portland, 04101. Phone: (207) 774-6364. Fax: (207) 774-8707. Web Site:www.wcyy.com Licensee: Citadel Broadcasting Co. Group owner: Citadel Broadcasting Corp. (acq 7-7-99; grpsl). Population served: 137,900 Natl. Rep: Christal,. Format: Modern rock. News staff: one. Target aud: 25-44; educated, affluent. ♦Michael Sambrook, gen mgr; Herb Ivy, opns VP, progmg dir; Mike Marcello, prom dir & adv.

WVAE(AM)— 1948: 1400 khz; 1 kw-U. TL: N43 28 52 W70 29 08. Hrs open: 24 420 Western Ave., South Portland, 04106. Phone: (207) 774-4561. Fax: (207) 774-3788.E-mail: info@ilovethebay.com Web Site:www.ilovethebay.com Licensee: Saga Communications of New England LLC. Group owner: Saga Communications Inc. (acq 11-17-03; $350,000). Population served: 177,976 Natl. Network: Jones Radio Networks, . Format: Adult standards. News staff: one. Target aud: 35 plus; upscale professional. Spec prog: Relg 2 hrs wkly. ♦Harry Nelson, stn mgr.

Blue Hill

***WERU-FM**— June 1, 1988: 89.9 mhz; 15 kw. 899 ft TL: N44 26 04 W68 35 25. Stereo. Hrs open: 6 AM-1 AM Box 170, East Orland, 04431-0170. Secondary address: 1186 Acadia Hwy., East Orland 04431. Phone: (207) 469-6600. Fax: (207) 469-8961.E-mail: info@weru.org Web Site:www.weru.org Licensee: Salt Pond Community Broadcasting Co. Population served: 150,000 Format: Div, educ. Target aud: General. ♦Matt Murphy, gen mgr.

Boothbay Harbor

WTQX(FM)— Apr 1, 1984: 96.7 mhz; 25 kw. Ant 449 ft TL: N44 01 31 W69 34 17. Stereo. Hrs open: 24
Simulcast with WTOS-FM Skowhegan 100%.
150 Whitten Rd., Agusta, GA, 04330. Phone: (207) 623-9000. Fax: (207) 623-9007.E-mail: donaldshieldsjr@clearchannel.com Web Site:www.wtosfm.com Licensee: Blueberry Broadcasting LLC. Group owner: Clear Channel Communications Inc. (acq 7-29-2008; grpsl). Cohn & Marks LLP. Format: Rock. Target aud: 25-49. ♦Kelly Slater, gen mgr; Don Shields, opns dir; Rick Dougal, gen sls mgr, chief of engrg; Steve Smith, progmg dir.

Brewer

WKIT-FM— Feb 14, 1979: 100.3 mhz; 50 kw. 850 ft TL: N44 40 39 W68 45 15. Stereo. Hrs open: 24 Box 1929, Bangor, 04402. Phone: (207) 990-2800. Fax: (207) 990-2444.E-mail: wkit@zoneradio.com Web Site:www.zoneradio.com Licensee: The Zone Corp. (group owner; acq 9-95; $800,000 with co-located AM). Fisher, Wayland, Cooper, Leader & Zaragoza. Format: Classic Rock. News staff: 2. Target aud: 18-49. ♦Stephen King, CEO; Bobby Russell, gen mgr, progmg dir; Ken Wood, gen sls mgr.

WQCB(FM)— Jan 20, 1986: 106.5 mhz; 98 kw. 1,079 ft TL: N45 03 26 W69 11 27. Stereo. Hrs open: 24 Box 100, 04412. Secondary address: 49 Acme Rd. 04412. Phone: (207) 989-5631. Fax: (207) 989-5685.E-mail: q1065@midmaine.com Web Site:www.wqcb-fm.com Licensee: Cumulus Licensing Corp. Group owner: Cumulus Media LLC (acq 2-20-98; $6.4 million with WBZN(FM) Old Town). Natl. Rep: McGavren Guild,. Format: Country. News staff: 2; News: 4 hrs wkly. Target aud: 25-54; general. ♦Tom Preble, gen mgr; Paul Dupuis, opns mgr; Darin Ingersoll, progmg dir.

Brunswick

WBCI(FM)—See Bath

*WBOR(FM)— April 1957: 91.1 mhz; 300 w. 154 ft TL: N43 54 34 W69 57 43. Stereo. Hrs open: 7 AM-2 AM WBOR 91.1 FM, 3400 College Stn., Bowdoin College, 04011-8462. Phone: (207) 725-3210. Phone: (207) 725-3250. Fax: (207) 725-3510.E-mail: wbor@bowdoin.edu Web Site:www.wbor.org Licensee: Trustees of Bowdoin College. Population served: 35,000 Format: Div. Target aud: General. ◆Adam Paltrineri, stn mgr.

WCLZ(FM)— Apr 11, 1965: 98.9 mhz; 48 kw. Ant 400 ft TL: N43 55 40 W69 59 43. Stereo. Hrs open: One City Ctr., Portland, 04101. Phone: (207) 774-6364. Fax: (207) 774-8707.E-mail: wclz@989wclz.com Web Site:www.989wclz.com Licensee: Saga Communications of New England LLC. Group owner: Citadel Broadcasting Corp. (acq 10-15-2007; $3.5 million). Natl. Rep: Christal,. Format: AAA. ◆Michael Sambrook, gen mgr.

WCME(AM)— December 1955: 900 khz; 1 kw-D, 66 w-N. TL: N43 55 40 W69 59 43. Hrs open: 24
Simulcasts WJAE(AM) Westbrook.
Atlantic Coast Radio, 779 Warren Ave., Portland, 04103-1007. Phone: (207) 773-9695. Fax: (207) 761-4406.E-mail: shoe@thebigjab.com Web Site:www.thebigjab.com Licensee: James B. Bleikamp (group owner; (acq 5-18-2009; $35,000). Population served: 35,000 Natl. Rep: McGavren Guild,. Format: Sports, talk. News staff: 2; News: 4 hrs wkly. Target aud: 25-54. ◆Jon Van Hoogenstyn, gen mgr; David Shumacher, progmg dir.

Calais

*WMED(FM)— November 1983: 89.7 mhz; 30 kw. 525 ft TL: N45 01 44 W67 19 25. Hrs open:
Rebroadcasts WMEH(FM) Bangor 100%.
63 Texas Ave., Bangor, 04401. Secondary address: 1450 Lisbon St., Lewiston 04240. Phone: (207) 783-9101. Fax: (207) 942-2857.E-mail: cbeck@mpbn.net Web Site:www.mpbn.net Licensee: Maine Public Broadcasting Corp. (acq 6-23-92). Natl. Network: NPR, PRI, . Dow, Lohnes & Albertson. Format: Class, pub affrs, news, jazz, folk. ◆Alexander G. Maxwell, Jr., COO, sr VP, stn mgr; Charles Beck, pres, progmg VP; Christopher Amann, CFO; Mary Mayo, dev VP.

WQDY-FM— Jan 14, 1976: 92.7 mhz; 3 kw. Ant 299 ft TL: N45 10 02 W67 16 38. Stereo. Hrs open: 24 637 Main St., 04619. Phone: (207) 454-7545. Fax: (207) 454-3062.E-mail: wqdy@wqdy.fm Web Site:www.wqdy.fm Licensee: WQDY Inc. (acq 11-26-96; for stock). Natl. Network: Jones Radio Networks, ABC, . Fletcher, Heald & Hildreth. Wire Svc: AP Format: Classic rock. News staff: one. ◆Bill McVicar, pres; Roger Holst, chief of engrg.

Camden

*WMEP(FM)— Oct 2002: 90.5 mhz; 2 kw vert. 1,178 ft TL: N44 12 40 W69 09 06. Hrs open:
Rebroadcasts WMEH(FM) Bangor 100%.
63 Texas Ave., Bangor, 04401. Secondary address: 1450 Lisbon St., Lewiston 04240. Phone: (207) 783-9101. Fax: (207) 942-2857.E-mail: cbeck@mpbn.net Web Site:www.mpbn.net Licensee: Maine Public Broadcasting Corp. Natl. Network: NPR, PRI, . Dow, Lohnes & Albertson. Format: Class, pub affrs, news, jazz, folk. ◆Alexander G. Maxwell, Jr., COO, sr VP; P. James Dowe, Jr., CEO & pres; Christopher Amann, CFO; Mary Mayo, dev VP; Charles Beck, progmg VP.

WQSS(FM)— May 1988: 102.5 mhz; 7.9 kw. Ant 1,201 ft TL: N44 12 40 W69 09 06. Stereo. Hrs open: 24 150 Whitten Rd., Augusta, 04330. Phone: (207) 623-9000. Fax: (207) 623-9007. Licensee: Blueberry Broadcasting LLC. Group owner: Clear Channel Communications Inc. (acq 7-29-2008; grpsl). Format: Adult contemp. ◆Bruce Biette, VP.

Caribou

WBPW(FM)—See Presque Isle

WCXU(FM)— Nov 15, 1986: 97.7 mhz; 20 kw. Ant 328 ft TL: N46 47 26 W67 55 07. Stereo. Hrs open: 24 152 E. Green Ridge Rd., 04736-3737. Phone: (207) 473-7513. Fax: (207) 472-3221.E-mail: channelxradio@yahoo.com Web Site:www.channelxradio.com Licensee: The Canxus Broadcasting Corp. (group owner) Population served: 150,000 Rgnl rep: Cyr Associates. Koteen & Naftalin. Format: Adult contemp, news, oldies. News staff: one; News: 21 hrs wkly. Target

aud: 25-54; educated, div occupations, affluent. ◆Dennis H. Curley, CEO, chmn, pres, CFO; Richard Chandler, gen mgr & opns mgr; Phil Shaw, progmg dir.

*WFST(AM)— July 15, 1956: 600 khz; 5 kw-D, 127 w-N. TL: N46 53 12 W68 02 44. (CP: TL: N46 45 52 W67 59 23). Hrs open: 24 Box 600, 04736-0600. Secondary address: 670 Sweden Rd. 04736. Phone: (207) 492-6000. Fax: (207) 493-3268.E-mail: wfst@maine.rr.com Web Site:www.wfst.net Licensee: Northern Broadcast Ministries Inc. (acq 6-8-93; $54,000; 6-28-93). Population served: 75,000 Natl. Network: Moody, Salem Radio Network, . Format: Christian, gospel, relg. Target aud: General. ◆Donald Flewelling, pres; Tom Hale, VP; John Stephenson, gen mgr; Dick Waugh, progmg mgr.

Dennysville

WCRQ(FM)— May 1998: 102.9 mhz; 100 kw. 456 ft TL: N45 01 44 W67 19 25. Stereo. Hrs open: 24 637 Main St., Calais, 04619. Phone: (207) 454-7545. Fax: (207) 454-3062.E-mail: wcrq@wcrqfm.com Web Site:www.wcrqfm.com Licensee: WQDY Inc. (acq 5-30-03; $195,000). Population served: 300,000 Fletcher, Heald & Hildreth. Format: Hot adult contemp. News: 6 hrs wkly. Target aud: 18-49; mass appeal. ◆Bill McVicar, pres; Bill Conley, mus dir.

Dexter

*WKVZ(FM)— 1993: 102.1 mhz; 50 kw. Ant 672 ft TL: N45 02 40 W69 15 01. Stereo. Hrs open: 24 2351 Sunset Blvd., Suite 170-218, Rocklin, CA, 95765. Phone: (916) 251-1600. Fax: (916) 251-1650. Web Site:www.klove.com Licensee: Educational Media Foundation. Group owner: Clear Channel Communications Inc. (acq 4-6-2009; $550,000 with WKVV(FM) Searsport). Population served: 165,000 Natl. Network: K-Love, . Format: Contemp Christian. ◆Mike Novak, pres.

Dover Foxcroft

WDME-FM— November 1980: 103.1 mhz; 4.8 kw. 385 ft TL: N45 12 58 W69 14 34. Stereo. Hrs open: 24 Box 1929, Bangor, 04402. Phone: (207) 990-2800. Fax: (207) 990-2444.E-mail: wdme@zoneradio.com Web Site:www.zoneradio.com Licensee: The Zone Corp. (group owner; acq 2-16-01; $175,100). Population served: 100,000 Natl. Network: ABC, . Verner, Liipfert, Bernhard, McPherson & Hand. Format: Adult contemp. News staff: one. Target aud: General. ◆Stephen King, pres; Bobby Russell, VP, gen mgr, progmg dir; Ken Wood, gen sls mgr, pub affrs dir; Howard Soule, chief of engrg.

Eastport

*WSHD(FM)— April 1984: 91.7 mhz; 12 w. Ant 115 ft TL: N44 54 30 W66 59 24. Stereo. Hrs open: Shead High School, 89 High St., 04631. Phone: (207) 853-6254. Fax: (207) 853-2919. Web Site:www.shead.org Licensee: Shead High School. Population served: 3,500 Format: Div. Target aud: General. ◆Rafi Hopkins, chief of engrg.

Ellsworth

WDEA(AM)— Dec 13, 1958: 1370 khz; 5 kw-U, DA-2. TL: N44 28 00 W68 28 11. Hrs open: Box 100, Brewer, 04412. Secondary address: 49 Acme Rd., Brewer 04412. Phone: (207) 989-5631. Fax: (207) 989-5685.E-mail: q1065@midmaine.com Licensee: Cumulus Licensing Corp. Group owner: Cumulus Media Inc. (acq 1999; grpsl). Population served: 40,000 Natl. Network: CBS, . Natl. Rep: D & R Radio,. Shaw Pittman. Format: Nostalgia. Target aud: 35 plus. ◆Tom Preble, gen mgr & gen sls mgr; Michael O'Hara, prom dir; Fred Miller, progmg dir; Jodi Hersey, news dir; Richard Hyatt, chief of engrg.

WKSQ(FM)— May 27, 1982: 94.5 mhz; 11.5 kw. 1,027 ft TL: N44 39 31 W68 36 17. Stereo. Hrs open: 24 184 Target Cir., Bangor, 04401-5718. Phone: (207) 947-9100. Fax: (207) 942-8039.E-mail: info@kiss945.com Web Site:www.kiss945.com Licensee: Blueberry Broadcasting LLC. Group owner: Clear Channel Communications Inc. (acq 7-29-2008; grpsl). Population served: 250,000 Natl. Rep: Christal,. Cohn & Marks LLP. Format: Adult contemp. News staff: 3; News: 7 hrs wkly. Target aud: 25-54. ◆Jon Shields, opns dir; Josh Scroggins, gen sls mgr & natl sls mgr.

*WRNM(FM)—Not on air, target date: unknown: 91.7 mhz; 2 kw. Ant 191 ft TL: N44 32 31 W68 25 58. Hrs open: 160 Bangor St., Augusta, 04330. Phone: (207) 622-1340. Fax: (207) 623-2874. Web Site:www.worshipradionetwork.org Licensee: Light of Life Ministries Inc. ◆Denise Lafountain, gen mgr.

WWMJ(FM)— Dec 27, 1965: 95.7 mhz; 11.5 kw. Ant 1,029 ft TL: N44 39 31 W68 36 20. Stereo. Hrs open: Prog sep from AM Box 100, Brewer, 04412. Secondary address: 49 Acme Rd. 04412. Phone: (207) 989-5631. Fax: (207) 989-5685.E-mail: q1065@midmaine.com Web Site:www.wwmj-fm.com Population served: 300,000 Format: Classic hits. Target aud: 25-54.

Fairfield

WCTB(FM)— November 1993: 93.5 mhz; 10.5 kw. Ant 499 ft TL: N44 44 42 W69 41 32. Stereo. Hrs open: Box 159, Skowhegan, 04976. Phone: (207) 474-5171. Fax: (207) 474-3299. Licensee: Mountain Wireless Inc. (group owner; acq 4-20-94; $60,000 7-4-94). Schwartz, Woods & Miller. Format: Classic rock. ◆Jay Hanson, gen mgr.

Farmington

WKTJ-FM— Aug 21, 1973: 99.3 mhz; 3 kw. 400 ft TL: N44 39 22 W70 11 48. Stereo. Hrs open: 24 Box 590, 04938. Phone: (207) 778-3400. Fax: (207) 778-3000.E-mail: wktj@wktj.com Web Site:www.wktj.com Licensee: Franklin Broadcasting Corp. 12/1/05 Population served: 25,000 Format: Classic hits of the 60s, 70s & 80s. News: 12 hrs wkly. Target aud: 25-54. ◆Rick Davis, gen mgr; Steve Bull, gen sls mgr & mus dir; Kathy Shrewsbury, chief of engrg, traf mgr.

*WUMF-FM— February 1972: 100.1 mhz; 13 w. Ant -190 ft TL: N44 40 09 W70 09 00. Stereo. Hrs open: 111 South St., 04938. Phone: (207) 778-7352. Fax: (207) 778-7113.E-mail: wumf@umf.maine.edu Web Site:http://wumf.umf.maine.edu Licensee: University of Maine System. Population served: 3,096 Format: AOR, progsv, div. Target aud: 18-45; college students & local residents. Spec prog: Jazz 15 hrs, tech/industrial 15 hrs wkly. ◆Derek Gilbert, gen mgr, stn mgr; Bill Moss, progmg dir; Shawn Rogers, mus dir.

Fort Kent

*WMEF(FM)— March 1994: 106.5 mhz; 25 kw. 302 ft TL: N47 15 30 W68 33 30. Hrs open:
Rebroadcasts WMEH(FM) Bangor 100%.
63 Texas Ave., Bangor, 04401. Secondary address: 1450 Lisbon St., Lewiston 04240. Phone: (207) 783-9101. Fax: (207) 942-2857.E-mail: cbeck@mpbn.net Web Site:www.mpbn.net Licensee: Maine Public Broadcasting Corp. Natl. Network: PRI, NPR, . Dow, Lohnes & Albertson. Format: Class, pub affrs, news, jazz, folk. ◆Alexander G. Maxwell Jr., COO, sr VP; P. James Dowe Jr., CEO & pres; Charles Beck, CFO, progmg VP; Mary Mayo, dev VP.

Freeport

*WMSJ(FM)— Dec 1, 1997: 89.3 mhz; 7.5 kw vert. 394 ft TL: N43 45 45 W70 19 30. Hrs open: Box 287, 04032. Phone: (207) 865-3448. Fax: (207) 865-1763.E-mail: info@positive.fm Web Site:www.positive.fm Licensee: The Positive Radio Network. Format: Contemp Christian music. Target aud: 25-48. ◆John A. Libby, chmn, pres; Chris Scotland, stn mgr, prom; Paula K, gen mgr & progmg dir.

Fryeburg

*WFYB(FM)—Not on air, target date: unknown: 91.5 mhz; 430 w. Ant 1,269 ft TL: N44 02 51 W70 49 19. Hrs open: 160 Bangor St., Augusta, 04330. Phone: (207) 622-1340. Fax: (207) 623-2874. Web Site:www.worshipradionetwork.org Licensee: Light of Life Ministries Inc. ◆Denise Lafountain, gen mgr.

Gardiner

WABK-FM— Apr 1, 1974: 104.3 mhz; 50 kw. 492 ft TL: N44 18 36 W69 49 51. Stereo. Hrs open: 150 Whitten Rd., Augusta, 04330. Phone: (207) 623-9000. Fax: (207) 623-9007. Web Site:www.104wabk.com Licensee: Blueberry Broadcasting LLC. (acq 7-29-2008; grpsl). Format: Oldies. ◆Mark Jackson, progmg dir.

WFAU(AM)— Sept 23, 1968: 1280 khz; 5 kw-U, DA-N. TL: N44 14 53 W69 48 51. Stereo. Hrs open: 24
Simulcasts with WRKD(AM) Rockland 100%.
150 Whitten Rd., Augusta, 04330. Phone: (207) 623-9000. Fax: (207) 623-9007. Web Site:www.foxsportsmaine.com Licensee: Blueberry Broadcasting LLC. Group owner: Clear Channel Communications Inc. (acq 7-29-2008; grpsl). Population served: 200,000 Cohn & Marks LLP. Format: Sports. News staff: one; News: 34 hrs wkly. Target aud: 25-54. ◆Kelly Slater, gen mgr; Sharon Griffith, traf mgr.

Gary

WJJB-FM— Nov 15, 1975: 96.3 mhz; 40 kw. Ant 1,410 ft TL: N44 15 03 W70 25 16. Stereo. Hrs open: 779 Warren Ave., Portland, 04103. Phone: (207) 773-9695. Fax: (207) 761-4406.E-mail: shoe@thebigjab.com Web Site:www.thebigjab.com Licensee: Atlantic Coast Radio L.L.C. (group owner; (acq 9-8-2000; grpsl). Population served: 950,000 Natl. Network: Sporting News Radio Network, . Natl. Rep: McGavren Guild,. Format: Sports talk. ◆Jon Van Hoogenstyn, gen mgr.

Gorham

WLVP(AM)— Mar 3, 1980: 870 khz; 10 kw-D, 1 kw-N. TL: N43 41 19 W70 30 34. Hrs open:
Simulcasts WLAM(AM) Lewiston 100%.
477 Congress St., Suite 3A, 3rd Fl. Annex, Portland, 04101. Phone: (207) 797-0780. Fax: (207) 797-0368. Licensee: Nassau Broadcasting III L.L.C. Group owner: Nassau Broadcasting Partners L.P. (acq 4-6-2004; grpsl). Format: Oldies. ◆Patrick Collins, gen mgr; Stan Manning, opns dir; Tim Gatz, gen sls mgr; Sean Baker, progmg mgr, news dir; Bill Ryall, chief of engrg.

*WMPG(FM)— Sept 1, 1973: 90.9 mhz; 110 w horiz, 1 kw vert. 233 ft TL: N43 40 50 W70 26 59. Stereo. Hrs open: 24 Box 9300, 96 Falmouth St., Portland, 04104-9300. Phone: (207) 780-4943. Fax: (207) 780-4590.E-mail: stationmanager@wmpg.org Web Site:www.wmpg.org Licensee: Trustees University of Maine. Population served: 10,000 Format: Div, community. News: 10 hrs wkly. Target aud: General; any group currently underserved by other loc stns. Spec prog: Sp 4 hrs, Balkan 2 hrs, Cambodian 2 hrs, African 4 hrs, Irish 2 hrs wkly, Vietnamese 2 hrs, Middle Eastern 2 hrs. ◆James Rand, stn mgr; Dave Bunker, progmg dir; Ron Raymond, mus dir; Brian Dyer, chief of engrg.

Gouldsboro

WLEK(FM)— May 2009: 101.1 mhz; 17 kw. Ant 397 ft TL: N44 26 41 W68 01 22. Hrs open: Box 2600, Kennebunkport, 04046. Phone: (207) 967-8094. Licensee: Blueberry Broadcasting LLC. ◆Louis Vitali, CEO & pres.

Greene

*WFGP(FM)—Not on air, target date: unknown: 91.1 mhz; 450 w vert. Ant 164 ft TL: N44 10 12 W70 10 19.1. Hrs open: 150 East Ave., Lewiston, 04240. Phone: (207) 782-9265. Web Site:www.kofcmaine.com Licensee: Andy Valley Knights of Columbus Home Inc. Natl. Network: EWTN Radio, . ◆Norman Gray, pres.

Hampden

WRME(AM)—Not on air, target date: unknown: 750 khz; 50 kw-D, 10 kw-N, DA-N. TL: N44 51 27 W68 49 36. Hrs open: 16 Doe Run, Pittstown, NJ, 08867. Phone: (908) 730-7959. Licensee: Charles A. Hecht and Alfredo Alonso. ◆Charles A. Hecht, gen mgr.

Harpswell

*WYFP(FM)— July 8, 1993: 91.9 mhz; 6 kw. 144 ft TL: N43 44 14 W69 59 39. Hrs open: 24 11530 Carmel Commons Blvd., Charlotte, NC, 28226. Phone: (704) 523-5555. Fax: (704) 522-1967.E-mail: bbn@bbnradio.org Web Site:www.bbnradio.org Licensee: Bible Broadcasting Network Inc. (group owner; acq 9-30-97; $150,000). Population served: 350,000 Natl. Network: USA, . Format: Bible teaching, religious. Target aud: 25-49. Spec prog: Christian rock 4 hrs, praise & worship 3 hrs wkly. ◆T. A. Smith, gen mgr; Dennis Gast, opns mgr; Teddi Wilson, disc jockey.

Houlton

WHOU-FM— Jan 13, 1976: 100.1 mhz; 9.6 kw. 525 ft TL: N46 08 35 W68 06 50. Hrs open: 24 Box 40, 04730. Secondary address: 39 Court St., Suite 215 04730. Phone: (207) 532-3600. Fax: (207) 521-0056.E-mail: sales@whoufm.com Web Site:www.whoufm.com Licensee: County Communications Inc. (acq 4-96; $350,000). Population served: 240,000 Natl. Network: ABC, . Crowell & Moring. Format: Adult contemp. News: 8 hrs wkly. Target aud: 25-54. Spec prog: Sacred one hr wkly. ◆David Moore, pres, gen mgr; JoLene Ledger, stn mgr; Jacqueline Spencer, opns mgr; George Kelley, progmg dir; Barrett Quinn, chief of engrg.

Howland

WVOM(FM)— June 1993: 103.9 mhz; 54 kw. 1,509 ft TL: N45 07 46 W68 21 28. Hrs open:
Rebroadcasts WBYA(FM) Searsport 80%.
184 Target Industrial Cir., Bangor, 04401. Phone: (207) 947-9100. Fax: (207) 942-8039.E-mail: info@thevoicemaine.com Web Site:www.thevoicemaine.com Licensee: Blueberry Broadcasting LLC. (acq 7-29-2008; grpsl). Natl. Network: CBS, Westwood One, . Format: News/talk. Target aud: 25-64; upper income, professional, managerial. ◆Jon Shields, CEO, opns dir, news dir; Josh Scroggins, gen mgr; Katrina Walls, progmg dir.

Islesboro

WBYA(FM)— 1999: 105.5 mhz; 20 kw. Ant 305 ft TL: N44 18 58 W68 58 12. Hrs open: 119 Tillson Ave., Rockland, 04841. Phone: (207) 594-9283. Fax: (207) 594-1620.E-mail: pcollins@nassaubroadcasting.com Web Site:www.frank1055fm.com Licensee: Nassau Broadcasting III L.L.C. Group owner: Nassau Broadcasting Partners L.P. (acq 4-6-2004; grpsl). Format: Classic hits. News staff: one; News: 7 hrs wkly. Target aud: 50 plus. ◆Pat Collins, gen mgr; Stan Manning, opns dir.

Kennebunk

WBQQ(FM)— November 1991: 99.3 mhz; 3 kw. Ant 324 ft TL: N43 24 16 W70 26 15. Hrs open: 24 169 Port Rd., 04043. Phone: (207) 797-0780. Fax: (207) 967-8671. Web Site:www.wbachradio.com Licensee: Nassau Broadcasting III L.L.C. Group owner: Nassau Broadcasting Partners L.P. (acq 4-6-2004; grpsl). Natl. Network: ABC, . Format: Class. Target aud: 35-64; upscale. ◆Pat Collins, pres, sr VP, gen mgr; Stan Manning, opns dir & opns mgr; Scott Hooper, progmg dir.

Kennebunkport

WBQW(FM)— Dec 1, 1994: 104.7 mhz; 6 kw. Ant 292 ft TL: N43 26 36 W70 26 38. Hrs open:
Rebroadcasts WBQQ(FM) Kennebunk 90%.
169 Port Rd., Kennebunk, 04043. Phone: (207) 797-0780. Fax: (207) 967-8671. Web Site:www.wbachradio.com Licensee: Nassau Broadcasting III L.L.C. Group owner: Nassau Broadcasting Partners L.P. (acq 4-6-2004; grpsl). Natl. Network: AP Radio, . Format: Classical. Target aud: 25-54; upscale, affluent, management, professionals. Spec prog: Jazz 5 hrs wkly. ◆Pat Collins, sr VP, gen mgr; Scott Hooper, progmg dir; Stan Manning, opns dir & chief of engrg.

*WMTP(FM)—Not on air, target date: unknown: 88.3 mhz; 250 w. Ant 138 ft TL: N43 24 16 W70 26 15. Hrs open: 17 Varney St., Lebanon, 04027. Phone: (603) 767-5994. Licensee: New Life Media. ◆Ford Bishop, pres.

Kittery

WSHK(FM)— October 1992: 105.3 mhz; 2.2 kw. 371 ft TL: N43 10 28 W70 46 50. Stereo. Hrs open: 24
Rebroadcasts WSAK(FM) Hampton, NH 100%.
Box 576, Dover, NH, 03821-0576. Secondary address: 292 Middle Rd., Dover, NH 03820-4901. Phone: (603) 749-9750. Phone: (603) 749-2776. Fax: (603) 749-1459.E-mail: info@wokq.com Web Site:www.shark1053.com Licensee: Citadel Broadcasting Co. Group owner: Citadel Broadcasting Corp. (acq 7-7-99; grpsl). Population served: 500000 Natl. Network: CNN Radio, . Natl. Rep: Christal,. Wiley, Rein & Fielding. Wire Svc: AP Format: Classic rock. News staff: 2. Target aud: 25-54. ◆Farid Suleman, CEO; Judy Ellis, pres; Marty Lessard, gen mgr; Mark Ericson, opns mgr; Jonathan Smith, progmg dir.

Lewiston

*WARX(FM)— Feb 29, 1948: 93.9 mhz; 27.5 kw. Ant 633 ft TL: N44 08 40 W70 01 22. Hrs open: 24 2351 Sunset Blvd., Suite 170-218, Rocklin, CA, 95765. Phone: (916) 251-1600. Fax: (916) 251-1650. Web Site:www.air1.com Licensee: Educational Media Foundation. Group owner: Citadel Broadcasting Corp. (acq 6-5-2008; $1 million). Population served: 600,000 Natl. Network: Air 1, . Format: Christian. ◆Mike Novak, pres.

WEZR(AM)— Aug 21, 1938: 1240 khz; 1 kw-U. TL: N44 06 55 W70 14 56. Hrs open: 24 555 Center St., Auburn, 04210. Phone: (207) 784-5868. Fax: (207) 784-4700.E-mail: dick@ezr.com Web Site:www.ez1240.com Licensee: Mountain Valley Broadcasting Inc. Group owner: Gleason Radio Group (acq 11-28-90). Population served: 100,000 Natl. Network: USA, . Natl. Rep: CYR Associates,. Rgnl rep: Cyr Associates Womble, Carlyle, Sandridge & Rice, PLLC.

Howland *(right column)*

Format: EZ oldies. News staff: 3; News: top & bottom of each hour. Target aud: General. ◆Richard D. Gleason, pres, gen mgr; Scott Garrett, news dir.

WFNK(FM)—Licensed to Lewiston. See Portland

WLAM(AM)— Sept 4, 1947: 1470 khz; 5 kw-U, DA-1. TL: N44 03 47 W70 15 00. Hrs open: 477 Congress St., 3rd Fl. Annex, Suite 3A, Portland, 04101. Phone: (207) 797-0780. Fax: (207) 797-0368. Licensee: Nassau Broadcasting III L.L.C. Group owner: Nassau Broadcasting Partners L.P. (acq 4-6-2004; grpsl). Population served: 75,000 Natl. Rep: D & R Radio,. Format: Oldies. ◆Pat Collins, sr VP, gen mgr; Stan Manning, opns dir; Tim Gatz, gen sls mgr.

*WRBC(FM)— Oct 6, 1958: 91.5 mhz; 150 w. 16 ft TL: N44 06 18 W70 12 32. Stereo. Hrs open: 24 31 Frye St., 04240. Phone: (207) 777-7532. Fax: (207) 795-8793.E-mail: mgraham3@bates.edu Web Site:www.bates.edu/wrbc Licensee: President and Trustees of Bates College. Population served: 180,000 Format: Rhythmic/CHR. Target aud: General; anyone searching for something different. ◆Ky Windborn, gen mgr.

Lincoln

*WHMX(FM)— Apr 1, 1975: 105.7 mhz; 50 kw. 413 ft TL: N45 20 34 W68 30 25. Stereo. Hrs open: 24 Box 5000, Bangor, 04402-5000. Secondary address: 1476 Broadway, Bangor 04401. Phone: (207) 262-1057.E-mail: contact@solutionfm.com Web Site:www.solutionfm.com Licensee: Bangor Baptist Church. (acq 12-31-96; $80,000 with co-located AM). Population served: 200,000 Fletcher, Heald & Hildreth. Format: Contemp Christian. Target aud: 18-35. ◆Pencil Boone, gen mgr; Jolie Littlefield, prom dir, chief of engrg; Tim Collins, progmg dir; Morgan Smith, mus dir.

*WMWR(FM)—Not on air, target date: unknown: 89.5 mhz; 330 w. Ant 558 ft TL: N45 13 10.8 W68 30 47.9. Hrs open: 4 Shep Rd., Springfield, 04487. Phone: (207) 738-2143. Licensee: Sonlight Inc. Natl. Network: EWTN Radio, . ◆Selby Beebe-Lawson, pres.

WSYY(AM)—See Millinocket

*WWLN(FM)—Not on air, target date: unknown: 90.5 mhz; 65 w. Ant 476 ft TL: N45 20 46 W68 30 24. Hrs open: 160 Bangor St., Augusta, 04330. Phone: (207) 622-1340. Fax: (207) 623-2874. Web Site:worshipradionetwork.lightoflife.info Licensee: Light of Life Ministries Inc. Format: Adult Contemp. Christian. ◆Raymond Bouchard, gen mgr.

Machias

WALZ-FM— Nov 25, 1978: 95.3 mhz; 3 kw. 220 ft TL: N44 44 08 W67 30 11. Stereo. Hrs open: 24
Rebroadcasts WQDY-FM Calais 100%.
637 Main St., Calais, 04619. Phone: (207) 454-7545. Fax: (207) 454-3062.E-mail: wqdy@wqdy.fm Web Site:www.wqdy.fm Licensee: William McVicar & Roger Holst, general partnership (acq 10-26-01). Natl. Network: ABC, Jones Radio Networks, . Wire Svc: AP Format: Classic Hits. News staff: one. ◆William McVicar, gen mgr; Roger Holst, opns dir.

*WUMM(FM)— 2008: 91.7 mhz; 100 w. Ant 72 ft TL: N44 42 33 W67 27 29. Hrs open: University of Maine, 9 O'Brien Ave., 04654. Phone: (207) 255-1371.E-mail: wumm@maine.edu Web Site:www.umm.maine.edu/wumm Licensee: University of Maine System. Format: Var. ◆Daniel Swain, gen mgr.

Madawaska

WCXX(FM)— Jan 30, 1988: 102.3 mhz; 1.75 kw. 384 ft TL: N47 19 54 W68 20 31. Stereo. Hrs open: 24
Rebroadcasts WCXU(FM) Caribou 50%.
152 E. Green Ridge Rd., Caribou, 04736. Phone: (207) 473-7513. Fax: (207) 472-3221.E-mail: channelxradio@yahoo.com Web Site:www.channelxradio.com Licensee: Canxus Broadcasting Corp. Population served: 30,000 Natl. Network: CNN Radio, . Rgnl rep: Cyr Associates. Koteen & Naftalin. Format: Adult contemp, news, oldies. News staff: one; News: 16 hrs wkly. Target aud: 18-54. ◆Dennis H. Curley, pres; Richard Chandler, gen mgr & opns mgr.

Madison

WIGY(FM)— 1995: 97.5 mhz; 6 kw. 328 ft TL: N44 47 32 W69 58 10. Stereo. Hrs open: 24 150 Whitten Rd., Augusta, 04330. Phone: (207)

623-9000. Fax: (207) 623-9007.E-mail: donaldshields@clearchannel.com Web Site:www.foxsportsmaine.com Licensee: Blueberry Broadcasting LLC. Group owner: Clear Channel Communications Inc. (acq 7-29-2008; grpsl). Population served: 68,000 Rgnl rep: Cyr Associates. Cohn & Marks LLP. Format: Sports. Target aud: 25-54. ◆ Kelly Slater, gen mgr, progmg mgr; Rick Dugal, gen sls mgr; Donald Shield, progmg dir.

Mexico

WTBM(FM)— Sept 15, 1988: 100.7 mhz; 850 w. Ant 1,273 ft TL: N44 34 56 W70 37 59. Stereo. Hrs open: 24
Simulcast with WOXO-FM Norway 99%.
PO Box 72, 243 Main St., Norway, 04268. Phone: (207) 743-5911. Fax: (207) 743-5913.E-mail: info@woxo.com Web Site:www.woxo.com Licensee: Mountain Valley Broadcasting Inc. Group owner: Gleason Radio Group (acq 12-90;10-22-90). Population served: 150,000 Natl. Network: USA, . Natl. Rep: CYR Associates,. Womble, Carlyle, Sandridge & Rice ,PLLC. Format: Country, sports. News staff: 2; News: 12 hrs wkly. Target aud: General. ◆ Richard Gleason, pres, gen mgr; Vic Hodgkins, stn mgr; Jeremy Rush, opns mgr, progmg mgr.

Milbridge

WRMO(FM)— 2005: 93.7 mhz; 130 w. Ant 7 ft TL: N44 32 19 W67 52 58. Hrs open: 24 Box 241, 04658. Phone: (207) 546-7510.E-mail: info@937wrmo.com Licensee: Steven A. Roy, Personal Representative, Estate of Lyle Evans (acq 6-27-2006; with KHAM(FM) Britt, IA). Natl. Rep: Rgnl Reps,. Format: Adult standards. News: 5am, 6am, 7am, 8am, 9am, 12pm, 5pm. Target aud: 35+. ◆ Mike McSorley, gen mgr.

Millinocket

WSYY(AM)— Dec 7, 1963: 1240 khz; 1 kw-U. TL: N45 40 24 W68 43 07. Hrs open: 24 Box 1240, 04462. Phone: (207) 723-9657. Fax: (207) 723-5900.E-mail: calendar@themountain949.com Web Site:www.themountain949.com Licensee: Katahdin Communications Inc. (acq 12-29-86; $295,000 with co-located FM; 11-10-86). Population served: 20,000 Natl. Network: ESPN Radio, . Rgnl rep: Cyr Associates. Format: All sports. Target aud: General. ◆ James Talbot, pres & gen mgr; Dave Keys, chief of engrg, traf mgr.

WSYY-FM— Apr 12, 1978: 94.9 mhz; 23.5 kw. 692 ft TL: N45 52 58 W68 47 54. Stereo. Hrs open: 24 Prog sep from AM Box 1240, 04462. Phone: (207) 723-9657. Fax: (207) 723-5900. Web Site:www.themountain949.com Population served: 150,000 Natl. Network: CBS Radio, . Format: Var. Target aud: 20-45.

Monticello

WBCQ-FM— September 2008: 94.7 mhz; 6 kw. Ant 312 ft TL: N46 20 30 W67 49 04. Hrs open: 39 Court St., Suite 215, Houlton, 04730. Phone: (207) 532-3600. Fax: (207) 521-0056. Licensee: Allan H. Weiner & Barbara A. Weiner dba WBCQ Radio. Format: Classic country. ◆ David Moore, gen mgr.

WXME(AM)— Sept 2, 1981: 780 khz; 5 kw-D, 60 w-N. TL: N46 20 30 W67 49 04. Hrs open: 274 Britton Rd., 04760-3110. Phone: (207) 538-9180. Fax: (207) 538-9180. Licensee: Allan H. Weiner (acq 2-12-2002). Population served: 50,000 Format: Talk. ◆ Allan H. Weiner, pres & gen mgr.

Newport

WGUY(AM)—Not on air, target date: unknown: 1230 khz; 1 kw-D, 690 w-N. TL: N44 52 14 W69 16 20. Hrs open: 453 Riverside Dr., Eddington, 04428. Phone: (207) 949-1902. Licensee: Wireless Fidelity of North America Inc. (acq 6-11-2009; $44,000 for CP and CP for New AM Ellsworth on 1240 khz) ◆ Gary A. Fogg, pres.

North Windham

WHXR(FM)— 1996: 106.7 mhz; 810 w. Ant 623 ft TL: N43 51 06 W70 19 40. Stereo. Hrs open: 24 477 Congress St., 3rd Fl. Annex, Suite 3A, Portland, 04101. Secondary address: 99 Danville Corner Rd. 04210. Phone: (207) 797-0780. Fax: (207) 797-0368.E-mail: info@boneradio.com Web Site:www.boneradio.com Licensee: Nassau Broadcasting III L.L.C. Group owner: Nassau Broadcasting Partners L.P. (acq 4-6-2004; grpsl). Natl. Network: AP Radio, . Format: Classic rock. Target aud: 35 plus; general. ◆ Patrick Collins, gen mgr; Tim Gatz, gen sls mgr; Sean Baker, progmg mgr, news dir; Bill Ryall, chief of engrg; Jennifer Bachelder, traf mgr.

Norway

WOXO-FM— Dec 12, 1970: 92.7 mhz; 2 kw. 360 ft TL: N44 12 24 W70 33 18. Stereo. Hrs open: 24
Rebroadcasts WTBM(FM) Mexico 99%.
PO Box 72, 243 Main St., 04268. Phone: (207) 743-5911. Fax: (207) 743-5913.E-mail: info@woxo.com Web Site:www.woxo.com Licensee: Mountain Valley Broadcasting Inc. Group owner: Gleason Radio Group (acq 12-12-75). Population served: 150,000 Natl. Network: USA, . Natl. Rep: CYR Associates,. Womble, Carlyle, Sandridge & Rice, PLLC. Format: Country, sports. News staff: 2; News: 12 hrs wkly. Target aud: General. ◆ Richard D. Gleason, pres, gen mgr; Vic Hodgkins, stn mgr; Jeremy Rush, opns mgr; Jay Philips, progmg dir, chief of engrg.

Oakland

*WMDR-FM— 2006: 88.9 mhz; 600 w vert. Ant 574 ft TL: N44 42 48 W69 43 39. Hrs open: 24 160 Bangor St., Augusta, 04330. Phone: (207) 622-1340. Fax: (207) 623-2874.E-mail: denise@lworshipradionetwork.org Web Site:www.worshipradionetwork.org Licensee: Light of Life Ministries Inc. Population served: 300,000 Format: Christian country. News: one hr wkly. ◆ Denise Lafountain, gen mgr; Randy Todd, progmg dir.

Old Town

WBZN(FM)— Jan 1, 1995: 107.3 mhz; 50 kw. 308 ft TL: N45 02 06 W68 40 57. Hrs open: Box 100, Brewer, 04412. Secondary address: 49 Acme Rd., Brewer 04412. Phone: (207) 989-5631. Fax: (207) 989-5685.E-mail: z1073@midmaine.com Web Site:www.wbzn-fm.com Licensee: Cumulus Licensing Corp. Group owner: Cumulus Media Inc. (acq 2-20-98; $6.4 million with WQCB(FM) Brewer). Format: CHR. ◆ Tom Preble, gen mgr; Paul Dupuis, opns dir; Dick Hyatt, chief of engrg.

Orono

WFGO(AM)—Not on air, target date: unknown: 1530 khz; 50 kw-D, 270 w-N, 9 kw-CH, DA-3. TL: N44 51 48 W68 40 06. Hrs open: 6930 Cahaba Valley Rd., Suite 202, Birmingham, AL, 35242. Phone: (205) 618-2020. Fax: (205) 618-2029. Licensee: Brantley Broadcast Assoiates LLC. (acq 5-8-2007; $100 for CP). ◆ Paul Reynolds, gen mgr.

*WMEB-FM— Apr 1, 1963: 91.9 mhz; 600 w. 150 ft TL: N44 55 08 W68 39 58. Stereo. Hrs open: 24 5748 Memorial Union, 04469. Phone: (207) 581-4340. Phone: (207) 581-2333. Fax: (207) 581-4343.E-mail: wmeb919@hotmail.com Web Site:www.umaine.edu/wmeb Licensee: Board of Trustees, University of Maine. Population served: 70,000 Format: Progsv, rock, div. Target aud: General. ◆ Thomas Grucza, stn mgr.

Pittsfield

WJCX(FM)— December 1993: 99.5 mhz; 6 kw. 328 ft TL: N44 48 11 W69 10 06. Hrs open: 2881 Ohio St., Suite 8, Bangor, 04401. Phone: (207) 884-6052. Fax: (207) 884-6052.E-mail: wjcx@calvarychapel.com Licensee: CSN International. (acq 1996; $87,500.) Format: Contemp Christian, news/talk, relg. Target aud: 18-34; young adults. ◆ Mike Archer, gen mgr, stn mgr, progmg dir & mus dir.

Pittston Farm

*WHPF(FM)—Not on air, target date: unknown: 88.1 mhz; 250 w. Ant -239 ft TL: N45 53 38 W69 57 54. Hrs open: 160 Bangor St., Augusta, 04330. Phone: (207) 622-1340. Fax: (207) 623-2874. Web Site:www.worshipradionetwork.org Licensee: Light of Life Ministries Inc. Format: Christian Country, Southern Gospel. ◆ Denise LaFountain, gen mgr.

Portland

WBAE(AM)— March 1946: 1490 khz; 1 kw-U. TL: N43 39 48 W70 16 16. Hrs open: 24 420 Western Avenue, 04106. Phone: (207) 774-4561. Fax: (207) 774-3788.E-mail: feedback@ilovethebay.com Web Site:www.ilovethebay.com Licensee: Saga Communications of New England LLC. Group owner: Saga Communications Inc. (acq 1996; $10 million with co-located FM). Population served: 150,000 Natl. Network: CNN Radio, . Format: Music of Your Life. News staff: 5. Target aud: 25-54; general. ◆ Cary Pahigian, pres & gen mgr.

WPOR(FM)— Oct 31, 1967: 101.9 mhz; Oct 31, 1967. Oct 31, 1967 TL: Oct 31, 1967. Oct 31, 1967. Stereo. 24 Prog sep from AM 420 Western Avenue, 04106. Phone: (207) 774-4561. Fax: (207) 774-3788.E-mail: wpor@wpor.com Web Site:www.wpor.com Format: Country.

WBLM(FM)— February 1966: 102.9 mhz; 100 kw. 1,460 ft TL: N43 55 28 W70 29 28. Stereo. Hrs open: One City Ctr., 04101. Phone: (207) 774-6364. Fax: (207) 774-8707.E-mail: wblm@wblm.com Web Site:www.wblm.com Licensee: Citadel Broadcasting Co. Group owner: Citadel Broadcasting Corp. (acq 7-7-99; grpsl). Population served: 220,000 Natl. Rep: Christal,. Format: Classic rock. Target aud: 25-54; active, involved, fun-loving. ◆ Michael Sambrook, gen mgr; Mike Marcello, adv.

WFNK(FM)— (Lewiston, Mar 1, 1973: 107.5 mhz; 100 kw. Ant 928 ft TL: N44 00 12 W70 25 24. Stereo. Hrs open: 477 Congress St., Ste. 3A, 04101. Phone: (207) 797-0780. Fax: (207) 797-0368.E-mail: info@1075frank.com Web Site:www.1075frank.com Licensee: Nassau Broadcasting III L.L.C. Group owner: Nassau Broadcasting Partners L.P. (acq 4-6-2004; grpsl). Population served: 150,000 Natl. Rep: D & R Radio,. Format: Classic rock. ◆ Pat Collins, sr VP, gen mgr; Stan Manning, opns dir; Tim Gatz, gen sls mgr.

WGAN(AM)— Aug 3, 1938: 560 khz; 5 kw-U, DA-2. TL: N43 41 22 W70 19 00. (CP: 4.8 kw-U, DA-1). Hrs open: 420 Western Ave., South Portland, 04106. Phone: (207) 774-4561. Fax: (207) 774-3788.E-mail: wgan@560wgan.com Web Site:www.560wgan.com Licensee: Saga Communications of New England LLC. Group owner: Saga Communications Inc. (acq 6-2-92; grpsl, including co-located FM). Natl. Network: CNN Radio, . Format: News/talk. ◆ Cary Pahigian, CEO, pres, VP & gen mgr.

WHOM(FM)—See Mt. Washington, NH

WJBQ(FM)— June 1, 1960: 97.9 mhz; 16 kw. 889 ft TL: N43 51 06 W70 19 40. (CP: 37.5 kw, ant 567 ft. TL: N43 45 32 W70 19 14). Stereo. Hrs open: One City Center, 04101. Phone: (207) 774-6364. Fax: (207) 774-8087.E-mail: wjbq@wjbq.com Web Site:www.wjbq.com Licensee: Citadel Broadcasting Co. Group owner: Citadel Broadcasting Corp. (acq 7-7-99; grpsl). Population served: 150,000 Natl. Rep: Christal,. Format: CHR. Target aud: 25-44; female listeners. ◆ Michael Sambrook, gen mgr; Tim Moore, progmg dir.

WLOB(AM)— Feb 2, 1957: 1310 khz; 5 kw-U, DA-2. TL: N43 41 22 W70 20 06. Hrs open: 24
Simulcast with WLOB-FM Topsham 100%.
779 Warren Ave., 04103-1007. Phone: (207) 773-9695. Fax: (207) 761-4406.E-mail: newstalkWLOB@yahoo.com Licensee: Atlantic Coast Radio L.L.C. (group owner; acq 9-8-00; grpsl). Population served: 250,000 Natl. Network: Fox News Radio, . Natl. Rep: McGavren Guild,. Format: News/talk. News: 17 hrs wkly. Target aud: General. ◆ J.J. Jeffrey, pres, opns mgr, progmg dir; Jon VanHoogenstyn, gen mgr.

*WMEA(FM)— April 1974: 90.1 mhz; 49 kw. Ant 1,919 ft TL: N43 51 33 W70 42 43. Stereo. Hrs open: 24
Rebroadcasts WMEH(FM) Bangor 100%.
63 Texas Ave., Bangor, 04401. Secondary address: 1450 Lisbon St., Lewiston 04240. Phone: (207) 783-9101. Fax: (207) 942-2857.E-mail: cbeck@mpbn.net Web Site:www.mpbn.net Licensee: Maine Public Broadcasting Corp. (acq 6-23-92). Population served: 60,000 Natl. Network: NPR, PRI, . Dow, Lohnes & Albertson. Format: Class, pub affrs, news, jazz, folk. News staff: 8; News: 20 hrs wkly. Target aud: 25-64. ◆ Alexander G. Maxwell, Jr., COO, sr VP, gen mgr, mktg dir; P. James Dowe, Jr., pres; Christopher Amann, CFO; Charles Beck, stn mgr, progmg VP; Mary Mayo, dev VP, dev dir.

WMGX(FM)— June 10, 1977: 93.1 mhz; 50 kw. Ant 443 ft TL: N43 41 17 W70 15 27. Stereo. Hrs open: Prog sep from AM 420 Western Ave., South Portland, 04106. Phone: (207) 774-4561. Fax: (207) 774-3788.E-mail: info@coast931.com Web Site:www.coast931.com Format: Adult contemp.

WPKQ(FM)—See North Conway, NH

WPOR(FM)— Oct 31, 1967: 101.9 mhz; 32.5 kw. 606 ft TL: N43 45 45 W70 19 30. Stereo. Hrs open: 24 Prog sep from AM 420 Western Avenue, 04106. Phone: (207) 774-4561. Fax: (207) 774-3788.E-mail: wpor@wpor.com Web Site:www.wpor.com Format: Country.

WTHT(FM)—See Auburn

WYNZ(FM)—See Westbrook

WZAN(AM)— July 13, 1925: 970 khz; 5 kw-U, DA-N. TL: N43 36 19 W70 19 18. Hrs open: 420 Western Ave., S. Portland, 04106. Phone:

(207) 774-4561. Fax: (207) 774-3788.E-mail: feedback@970wzan.com Web Site:www.970wzan.com Licensee: Saga Communications of New England LLC. Group owner: Saga Communications Inc. (acq 6-23-93; $350,000 with WYNZ-FM Westbrook;7-12-93). Natl. Network: CBS, CNN Radio, . Natl. Rep: Katz Radio,. Format: Talk. Target aud: 25-54 Males. ◆Cary Pahigian, pres, gen mgr; Chris McGorrill, opns.

Presque Isle

WBPW(FM)— September 1973: 96.9 mhz; 100 kw. 440 ft TL: N46 45 52 W67 59 23. Hrs open: 24 551 Main St., 04769. Phone: (207) 769-6600. Fax: (207) 764-5274.E-mail: wbpw.radio@citcomm.com Web Site:www.BigCountry97.com Licensee: Citadel Broadcasting Co. Group owner: Citadel Broadcasting Corp. (acq 4-26-00; grpsl). Population served: 150,000 Natl. Network: ABC, . Natl. Rep: Katz Radio,. Format: Country. News staff: 1; News: 2 hrs wkly. Target aud: 25-54. Spec prog: NASCAR, American Country Countdown. ◆Lisa Miles, gen mgr, gen sls mgr; Mark Shaw, news dir.

WEGP(AM)— June 24, 1960: 1390 khz; 25 kw-D, 10 kw-N, DA-N. TL: N46 39 15 W68 03 00. Hrs open: 24 Box 4088, 04769. Phone: (207) 762-6700. Fax: (207) 762-3319.E-mail: wegp@mfx.net Web Site:www.wegp.net Licensee: Decelles/Smith Media Inc. (acq 9-18-2000). Population served: 100,000 Natl. Network: Fox News Radio, Premiere Radio Networks, Talk Radio Network, Westwood One, . Format: Talk, news. Target aud: Adults; mature listeners over age 29. ◆Paul Decelles, pres; Patrick Patterson, gen mgr, opns mgr, progmg dir; Bonnie Pack, disc jockey.

*WMEM(FM)— 1975: 106.1 mhz; 99 kw. 1,079 ft TL: N46 33 06 W67 48 38. Hrs open:
Rebroadcasts WMEH(FM) Bangor 100%.
63 Texas Ave., Bangor, 04401. Secondary address: 1450 Lisbon St., Lewiston 04240. Phone: (207) 783-9101. Fax: (207) 942-2857.E-mail: cbeck@mpbn.net Web Site:www.mpbn.net Licensee: Maine Public Broadcasting Corp. (acq 6-23-92). Natl. Network: NPR, PRI, . Dow, Lohnes & Albertson. Format: Class, pub affrs, news, jazz, folk. ◆Alexander G. Maxwell, Jr., COO, sr VP; P. James Dowe, Jr., CEO & pres; Christopher Amann, CFO; Charles Beck, stn mgr, progmg VP; Mary Mayo, dev VP.

WOZI(FM)— Feb 2, 1981: 101.9 mhz; 7.9 kw. Ant 1,207 ft TL: N46 32 51 W67 48 35. Stereo. Hrs open: 24 551 Main St., 04769. Phone: (207) 769-6600. Fax: (207) 764-5274.E-mail: wozi.radio@citcomm.com Web Site:www.102therock.com Licensee: Citadel Broadcasting Co. Group owner: Citadel Broadcasting Corp. (acq 4-26-01; grpsl). Population served: 150,000 Natl. Rep: Katz Radio,. Format: Classic rock. News staff: one; News: one hr wkly. Target aud: 25-54. ◆Lisa Miles, gen mgr; Chris O' Brien, progmg dir.

WQHR(FM)— 1981: 96.1 mhz; 95 kw. 1,309 ft TL: N46 32 55 W67 48 35. Stereo. Hrs open: 24 551 Main St., 04769. Phone: (207) 769-6600. Fax: (207) 764-5274.E-mail: wqhr.radio@citcomm.com Web Site:www.HitMusicQ96.com Licensee: Citadel Broadcasting Co. Group owner: Citadel Broadcasting Corp. (acq 4-26-01; grpsl). Population served: 250,000 Natl. Network: ABC, . Natl. Rep: Katz Radio,. Format: Hot adult contemp. News staff: one; News: 2 hrs wkly. Target aud: 18-49. ◆Lisa Miles, gen mgr; Mark Shaw, progmg dir.

*WUPI(FM)— July 26, 1973: 92.1 mhz; 17 w. -39 ft TL: N46 40 15 W68 01 00. Hrs open: 24 181 Main St., 04769. Phone: (207) 768-9741. Phone: (207) 768-9711. Fax: (207) 768-9742.E-mail: meg@wupifm.com Web Site:www.umpi.maine.edu Licensee: University of Maine Trustees. Population served: 5,000 Format: Div. News staff: 2; News: 5 hrs wkly. Target aud: 16-35. ◆Dr. Don Zillman, pres; Marjorie McNamara, gen mgr; Larry French, stn mgr; Laura Mooney, adv mgr; Meg Medlinskas, mus dir; Jeffery Carmicheal, engr.

Rangeley

*WRGY(FM)—Not on air, target date: unknown: 90.5 mhz; 50 w. Ant 2,116 ft TL: N44 56 06 W70 30 35. Hrs open: Box 340, 04970. Phone: (207) 864-3400. Licensee: Tranet. ◆Gary Patnode, pres.

Richmond

WZME(AM)—Not on air, target date: unknown: 1120 khz; 1 kw-D, 600 w-N, DA-2. TL: N44 05 20 W69 50 08. Hrs open: 2505 Thontosassa Rd., Plant City, FL, 33563. Phone: (808) 753-5111. Licensee: Acme Broadcasting II Inc. (acq 5-7-2009; $13,500 for CP). ◆Ira Littman, pres.

Rockland

WMCM(FM)— Apr 16, 1968: 103.3 mhz; 20.5 kw. Ant 771 ft TL: N44 07 35 W69 08 18. Stereo. Hrs open: 24 150 Whitten Rd., Augusta, 04330. Phone: (207) 623-9000. Fax: (207) 623-9007. Web Site:www.realcountry1033.com Licensee: Blueberry Broadcasting LLC. (acq 7-29-2008; grpsl). Population served: 100,000 Format: Country. News staff: one. Target aud: General. ◆Sharon Griffith, traf mgr; Matt Thompson, local news ed; Don Shields, political ed, sports cmtr.

WRKD(AM)— Oct 1, 1952: 1450 khz; 1 kw-U. TL: N44 06 22 W69 06 31. Stereo. Hrs open: 24 150 Whitten Rd., Augusta, 04330. Phone: (207) 623-9000. Fax: (207) 623-9007. Web Site:www.foxsportsmaine.com Licensee: Blueberry Broadcasting LLC. Group owner: Clear Channel Communications Inc. (acq 7-29-2008; grpsl). Population served: 30,600 Natl. Network: Westwood One, . Natl. Rep: CYR Associates, Cohn & Marks LLP. Format: Sports. News staff: one; News: 11 hrs wkly. Target aud: 35 plus. ◆Kelly Slater, gen mgr; Rick Dugal, gen sls mgr; Don Shields, progmg dir.

Rumford

WTME(AM)— Aug 21, 1953: 780 khz; 10 kw-D, 18 w-N. TL: N44 30 53 W70 31 01. Hrs open:
Simulcast with WKTQ(AM) South Paris 100%.
PO Box 72, 243 Main St., Norway, 04268. Phone: (207) 743-5911. Fax: (207) 743-5913.E-mail: info@woxo.com Web Site:www.wtme.com Licensee: Mountain Valley Broadcasting Inc. Group owner: Gleason Radio Group (acq 11-2-2000; $50,000). Population served: 100,000 Natl. Network: USA, . Natl. Rep: CYR Associates,. Womble Carlyle. Format: Talk & religion. News staff: one; News: top of each hour. Target aud: General. ◆Richard Gleason, pres & gen mgr; Jeremy Rush, opns mgr, progmg dir.

Saco

WCYY(FM)—See Biddeford

WPEI(FM)— July 18, 1982: 95.9 mhz; 4.1 kw. Ant 397 ft TL: N43 32 33 W70 24 17. Stereo. Hrs open: 24 779 Warren Ave., Portland, 04103. Phone: (207) 773-9695. Fax: (207) 761-4406. Web Site:www.weei.com Licensee: Atlantic Coast Radio L.L.C. (group owner; acq 7-12-99; $1.15 million). Natl. Network: Westwood One, . Natl. Rep: McGavren Guild,. Rick Hayes. Wire Svc: AP Format: Sports. Target aud: 18-34. ◆J.J. Jeffrey, pres; Lisa Menconi, CFO; Jon Van Hoogenstyn, gen mgr; Buzz Bradley, stn mgr, opns VP; Gene Terwilliger, chief of engrg; Morgan Grumbach, sls.

WVAE(AM)—See Biddeford

Sanford

WPHX(AM)— Nov 9, 1957: 1220 khz; 1 kw-D, 234 w-N. TL: N43 25 53 W70 45 44. Hrs open: 24 One Washington St., Dover, NH, 03820. Phone: (603) 749-5900. Fax: (603) 749-0088.E-mail: info@fnxradio.com Web Site:fnxradio.com Licensee: FNX Broadcasting LLC. Group owner: Phoenix Media Communications Group (acq 5-17-99; $1.025 million with co-located FM). Population served: 20000 Format: Sports. ◆Sam Pseifle, gen mgr.

WPHX-FM— Oct 10, 1975: 92.1 mhz; 1.2 kw. 525 ft TL: N43 35 24 W70 22 20. Stereo. Hrs open: 24 One Washington St., Dover, NH, 03820. Phone: (603) 749-5900. Fax: (603) 749-0088.E-mail: info@fnxradio.com Web Site:www.fnxradio.com Licensee: FNX Broadcasting LLC. Natl. Rep: McGavren Guild,. Format: Alternative. News staff: one. Target aud: General. Spec prog: Jazz 6 hrs, talk 2 hrs wkly. ◆Gary Kurtz, gen mgr; Michael Snow, mktg dir; Keith Dakin, prom dir, progmg dir; Chris Hall, engrg mgr, chief of engrg.

*WSEW(FM)— Mar 2, 1992: 88.5 mhz; 100 w. 387 ft TL: N43 25 11 W70 48 09. Stereo. Hrs open: Box 398, New Durham, NH, 03855. Phone: (603) 859-9170. Fax: (603) 859-8172.E-mail: wsew@wsew.org Web Site:www.wsew.org Licensee: Word-Radio Educational Foundation. Natl. Network: Moody, . Format: Relg. ◆Ronald Malone, gen mgr; Sharon Malone, opns mgr.

Scarborough

WHXQ(FM)— 1960: 106.3 mhz; 3 kw. Ant 299 ft TL: N43 35 24 W70 22 20. Stereo. Hrs open: 477 Congress St., Suite 3 A, 3rd Fl. Annex, Portland, 04101. Phone: (207) 797-0780. Fax: (207) 797-0368.E-mail: info@boneradio.com Web Site:www.boneradio.com Licensee: Nassau Broadcasting III L.L.C. Group owner: Nassau Broadcasting Partners

L.P. (acq 4-6-2004; grpsl). Population served: 200,000 Format: Classic rock. ◆Pat Collins, pres, sr VP, gen mgr; Stan Manning, opns dir.

Searsport

*WKVV(FM)— Oct 10, 1994: 101.7 mhz; 2.65 kw. Ant 1,004 ft TL: N44 34 51 W68 53 47. Hrs open: 6 AM-midnight 2351 Sunset Blvd., Suite 170-218, Rocklin, CA, 95765. Phone: (916) 251-1600. Fax: (916) 251-1650. Web Site:www.klove.com Licensee: Educational Media Foundation. (group owner; acq 4-6-2009; $550,000 with WKVZ(FM) Dexter). Natl. Network: K-Love, . Format: Contemp Christian. ◆Mike Novak, pres.

Skowhegan

WFMX(FM)— September 1989: 107.9 mhz; 6 kw. Ant 666 ft TL: N44 42 46 W69 43 36. Stereo. Hrs open: Box 159, 04976. Phone: (207) 474-5171. Fax: (207) 474-3299.E-mail: maine.radio@verizon.net Web Site:www.mixmaine.com Licensee: Mountain Wireless Inc. (group owner; (acq 11-20-97; $222,355). Format: Adult contemp. Target aud: 25-54; baby boomers who grew up with Top-40 radio. ◆Jay Hanson, gen mgr & opns mgr.

WSKW(AM)— 1956: 1160 khz; 10 kw-D, 1 kw-N. TL: N44 44 43 W69 41 36. Hrs open: Box 159, 04976. Secondary address: 208 Middle Rd. 04976. Phone: (207) 474-5171. Fax: (207) 474-3299.E-mail: maine.radio@verizon.net Licensee: Mountain Wireless Inc. (group owner; (acq 1999; $1.6 million with WCTB(FM) Fairfield). Population served: 70,000 Natl. Network: ESPN Radio, . Format: Sports. Target aud: 12 plus; loc sports fans. ◆Jay Hanson, gen mgr & opns mgr.

WTOS-FM— Nov 13, 1969: 105.1 mhz; 50 kw. Ant 2,431 ft TL: N45 01 54 W70 18 50. Stereo. Hrs open: 24 150 Whitten Rd., Augusta, 04330. Phone: (207) 623-9000. Fax: (207) 623-9007.E-mail: reverend@clearchannel.com Web Site:www.wtosfm.com Licensee: Blueberry Broadcasting LLC. Group owner: Clear Channel Communications Inc. (acq 7-29-2008; grpsl). Format: Active Rock. News staff: one; News: 3 hrs wkly. Target aud: 18-49. ◆Kelly Slater, gen mgr; Steve Smith, progmg dir.

South Paris

WKTQ(AM)— Oct 28, 1955: 1450 khz; 1 kw-U. TL: N44 13 16 W70 31 43. Hrs open: 24
Simulcast with WTME(AM) Rumford 100%.
PO Box 72, 243 Main St., Norway, 04268. Phone: (207) 743-5911. Fax: (207) 743-5913.E-mail: dick@gleasonmedia.com Web Site:www.wtme.com Licensee: Mountain Valley Broadcasting Inc. Group owner: Gleason Radio Group (acq 7-27-76). Population served: 20,000 Natl. Network: USA, . Natl. Rep: CYR Associates,. Womble, Carlyle, Sandridge & Rice, PLLC. Format: Talk & religion. News staff: one; News: top of each hour. Target aud: General. ◆Richard D. Gleason, pres, gen mgr; Victor Hodgkins, stn mgr; Jeremy Rush, opns dir.

WOXO-FM—See Norway

Thomaston

WBQX(FM)— May 29, 1992: 106.9 mhz; 29.5 kw. 633 ft TL: N44 06 30 W69 09 28. Stereo. Hrs open: 24
Rebroadcasts WBQQ(FM) Kennebunk 100%.
119 Tillson Ave., Rockland, 04841. Phone: (207) 594-9283. Fax: (207) 594-1620.E-mail: pcollins@nassaubroadcasting.com Web Site:www.wbachradio.com Licensee: Nassau Broadcasting III L.L.C. Group owner: Nassau Broadcasting Partners L.P. (acq 4-6-2004; grpsl). Population served: 170,000 Rgnl rep: Kettell-Carter. Smithwick & Belendiuk. Format: Class. News: 4 hrs wkly. Target aud: 35 plus; affluent, upscale adults. Spec prog: Jazz 2 hrs, children one hr wkly. ◆Louis F. Mercantanti, CEO, pres; Pat Collins, sr VP, gen mgr; Scott Hooper, progmg dir & mus dir.

Topsham

WLOB-FM— 1993: 95.5 mhz; 6 kw. Ant 456 ft TL: N43 54 12 W70 02 13. Hrs open: 24
Simulcasts with WEEI(AM) Boston, MA.
779 Warren Ave., Portland, 04103. Phone: (207) 773-9695. Fax: (207) 761-4406. Web Site:www.wlobradio.com Licensee: Atlantic Coast Radio L.L.C. (group owner; acq 9-30-99). Population served: 700,000 Natl. Network: Fox News Radio, . Natl. Rep: McGavren Guild,. Arter & Hadden. Format: Talk. Target aud: 25-49; middle class, active lifestyle with discretionary income. ◆J.J. Jeffrey, pres; Jon Van

Hoogenstyn, gen mgr; David Schumacher, opns mgr, progmg mgr; Gene Terwilliger, engrg dir, chief of engrg.

Van Buren

WCXV(FM)—Not on air, target date: 2006: 98.1 mhz; 6 kw. Ant 89 ft TL: N47 10 04 W67 57 43. Hrs open:
Rebroadcasts WCXU (FM) Caribou 100%.
152 E. Green Ridge Rd., Caribou, 04736-3737. Phone: (207) 473-7513. Fax: (207) 472-3221.E-mail: channelxradio@yahoo.com Web Site:www.channelxradio.com Licensee: Canxus Broadcasting Corp. Format: Adult contemp, news, oldies. ♦Dennis Curley, pres.

Veazie

WNZS(AM)— August 2002: 1340 khz; 1 kw-D, 630 w-N. TL: N44 51 10 W68 40 44. Hrs open: 24 Box 8526, Bangor, 04402. Secondary address: 379 Riverside Dr, Eddington 04428. Phone: (207) 947-9697. Fax: (207) 989-5251. Licensee: Waterfront Communications Inc. Group owner: Daniel F. Priestley Stns. Population served: 150,000 Natl. Network: Salem Radio Network, Talk Radio Network, ABC, . Natl. Rep: Commercial Media Sales,. Rgnl rep: Cyr Association Fletcher, Healld & Hildreth. Format: News/talk. News staff: 2; News: 15 hrs wkly. Target aud: 25-54; 35-64; adults in metro Banger area. ♦Jocelynn Priestley, stn mgr.

WWNZ(AM)— August 2004: 1400 khz; 1 kw-D, 810 w-N. TL: N44 50 50 W68 40 48. Hrs open: 24 Box 8526, Bangor, 04402-8526. Secondary address: 379 Riverside Dr., Eddington 04428. Phone: (207) 947-9697. Fax: (207) 989-5251.E-mail: wnzproduction@aol.com Licensee: Waterfront Communications Inc. Group owner: Daniel F. Priestley Stns. Population served: 150,000 Natl. Network: USA, Fox News Radio, Wall Street, . Natl. Rep: Commercial Media Sales,. Rgnl rep: Cyr Associates Fletcher, Heald & Hildreth. Format: News/talk. Target aud: 25-54; 35-64; Banger metro area adults 25 plus. ♦Daniel F. Priestley, pres; Jocelynn Priestley, stn mgr.

Waterville

WEBB(FM)— Mar 26, 1968: 98.5 mhz; 50 kw. 305 ft TL: N44 33 52 W69 36 39. Stereo. Hrs open: 24 Dups AM 50% Box 5070, Augusta, 04330. Secondary address: 56 Western Ave. Suite 13, Augusta 04330. Phone: (207) 623-4735. Fax: (207) 626-5948. Web Site:www.b985.fm Population served: 400,000 Fisher, Wayland, Cooper, Leader & Zaragoza. Format: Country. News staff: one.

***WMEW(FM)**— November 1983: 91.3 mhz; 3 kw. 299 ft TL: N44 29 23 W69 39 05. Stereo. Hrs open: 24
Rebroadcasts WMEH(FM) Bangor 100%.
63 Texas Ave., Bangor, 04401. Secondary address: 1450 Lisbon St., Lewiston 04240. Phone: (207) 783-9101. Fax: (207) 942-2857.E-mail: cbeck@mpbn.net Web Site:www.mpbn.net Licensee: Maine Public Broadcasting Corp. (acq 6-23-92; 7-13-92). Natl. Network: NPR, PRI, . Dow, Lohnes & Albertson. Format: Class, pub affrs, news, jazz, folk. News staff: 8; News: 20 hrs wkly. Target aud: 25-64. ♦Alexander G. Maxwell, Jr., COO, sr VP; Christopher Amann, CFO, mktg dir; Mary Mayo, dev VP, dev dir; Charles Beck, progmg dir.

***WMHB(FM)**— Oct 1, 1974: 89.7 mhz; 110 w. 98 ft TL: N44 33 57 W69 39 49. Stereo. Hrs open: 6 AM-12 AM Colby College, 4000 Mayflower Hill Dr., 04901-8840. Phone: (207) 859-5454. Phone: (207) 859-5451.E-mail: info@wmhb.org Web Site:www.wmhb.org Licensee: Mayflower Hill Broadcasting Corp. Population served: 40,000 Format: Div. News: 2.5 hrs wkly. Target aud: 5-100; we cater to everyone. Spec prog: Indie, Folk, Hip-hop, Jazz, World, Rock, Loud Rock, Blues. ♦Kathleen Fallon, gen mgr; Benjamin Ogden, opns dir; Jeffrey Oakes, progmg dir; Chris Scharff, mus dir.

WTVL(AM)— June 19, 1946: 1490 khz; 1 kw-U. TL: N44 33 52 W69 36 39. Hrs open: Box 5070, Augusta, 04330. Secondary address: 52 Western Ave., Augusta 04330. Phone: (207) 623-4735. Fax: (207) 626-5948. Web Site:www.1400and1490.com Licensee: Citadel Broadcasting Co. Group owner: Citadel Broadcasting Corp. (acq 4-26-2001; grpsl). Population served: 18,192 Format: Oldies. Target aud: 25-54. ♦Farid Suleman, CEO; Bob Proffitt, pres; Julie Beaulieu, gen sls mgr; Al Perry, rgnl sls mgr; Mac Dickson, prom dir; Renee Nelson, news dir & pub affrs dir; Bob Perry, chief of engrg.

Westbrook

WHXQ(FM)—See Scarborough

WRED(AM)— Nov 8, 1959: 1440 khz; 5 kw-D, 1 kw-N, DA-1. TL: N43 40 50 W70 22 47. Hrs open: 779 Warren Ave., Portland, 04103. Phone: (207) 773-9695. Fax: (207) 761-4406.E-mail: shoe@thebigjab.com Web Site:www.thebigjab.com Licensee: Atlantic Coast Radio L.L.C. (group owner; (acq 9-99). Population served: 150,000 Natl. Network: Sporting News Radio Network, . Natl. Rep: McGavren Guild,. Format: Sports talk. Target aud: General; male. ♦Jon Van Hoogenstyn, gen mgr; Dave Schumacher, opns mgr.

***WRKJ(FM)**—Not on air, target date: unknown: 88.5 mhz; 415 w. Ant 10 ft TL: N43 38 31 W70 19 51. Hrs open: 677 Main St., 04092. Phone: (207) 854-4062. Licensee: Calvary Chapel of Portland. ♦Vincent M. Magowan, CEO & pres.

WYNZ(FM)— February 1976: 100.9 mhz; 25 kw. Ant 305 ft TL: N43 41 26 W70 19 05. Stereo. Hrs open: 420 Western Ave., South Portland, 04106. Phone: (207) 774-4561. Fax: (207) 774-3788.E-mail: bighits@y1009.com Web Site:www.y1009.com Licensee: Saga Communications of New England LLC. Group owner: Saga Communications Inc. (acq 6-23-93; $350,000 with WYNZ(AM) Portland; 7-12-93). Natl. Network: CNN Radio, . Natl. Rep: Katz Radio,. Format: Oldies. Target aud: 25-54. ♦Cary Pahigian, pres, gen mgr; Chris McGorrill, opns mgr, mktg VP, prom mgr; Tina Segerstrom, sls VP; Tina Seuerstrom, gen sls mgr; Randi Kirshbaun, progmg dir; Jeffrey Wade, news dir; Andy Armstrong, engrg VP; Michael Bray, traf mgr.

Winslow

***WWWA(FM)**— Apr 23, 1999: 95.3 mhz; 12 kw. Ant 672 ft TL: N44 42 48 W69 43 39. Stereo. Hrs open: 24 160 Bangor St., Augusta, 04330. Phone: (207) 622-1340. Fax: (207) 623-2874.E-mail: denise@worshipradionetwork.org Web Site:www.worshipradionetwork.org Licensee: Light of Life Ministries Inc. Population served: 130,000 Format: Christian Adult Contemp. ♦Denise LaFountain, stn mgr; Ryan Gagne, gen mgr & progmg dir.

Winter Harbor

WNSX(FM)— 1999: 97.7 mhz; 50 kw. Ant 489 ft TL: N44 33 13 W68 05 40. Stereo. Hrs open: Box 1171, Ellsworth, 04605. Phone: (207) 667-0002. Fax: (207) 667-0627. Licensee: Stony Creek Broadcasting LLC Group owner: Clear Channel Communications Inc. (acq 9-30-2005; $800,000). Wire Svc: AP Format: Soft classic rock. News staff: one; News: 4 hrs wkly. Target aud: Adults; 25+. ♦Mark Osborne, gen mgr; Bill Da Butler, opns mgr; Irene Hafford, gen sls mgr; Bill Ducharme, chief of engrg; Natalie Knox, sls.

Yarmouth

***WYAR(FM)**— Nov 16, 1998: 88.3 mhz; 1 kw horiz. Ant 79 ft TL: N43 45 56 W70 08 27. Hrs open: 24 Box 219, Heritage Radio Society Inc., Cousins St., 04096. Phone: (207) 847-3169.E-mail: wyar@maine.rr.com Web Site:www.wyar.org Licensee: Heritage Radio Society Inc. Population served: 250,000 Format: Btfl music, big band, oldies, class, educ. Target aud: General; senior citizens & young people. ♦Gary D. King Sr., CEO, pres, opns dir, pub affrs dir, chief of engrg; James Brown, VP & gen mgr.

York Center

WSKX(FM)— June 1987: 95.3 mhz; 1.4 kw. Ant 682 ft TL: N43 13 24 W70 41 35. Stereo. Hrs open: 24 815 Lafayette Rd., Portsmouth, NH, 03801. Phone: (603) 436-7300. Fax: (603) 430-9415.E-mail: ianhorne@clearchannel.com Web Site:www.wubbfm.com Licensee: Capstar TX L.P. Group owner: Clear Channel Communications Inc. (acq 8-30-2000; grpsl). Natl. Rep: Katz Radio,. Format: Top-40. News staff: one; News: 7 hrs wkly. Target aud: 25-54. ♦Jeffery Pierce, opns mgr; Ian Horne, progmg dir.

Maryland

Aberdeen

WAMD(AM)— May 1, 1957: 970 khz; 300 w-D, 500 w-N, DA-2. TL: N39 30 35 W76 11 38. Hrs open: 24 400 Hiob Ln., 21001. Phone: (410) 272-4400. Fax: (410) 575-6890. Licensee: Salem Media of New York LLC. (group owner; (acq 3-31-2009; $3 million). Population served: 30,000 Format: Christian talk. Target aud: 35+; primarily female. ♦David Ruleman, gen mgr.

Annapolis

WBIS(AM)— Jan 10, 1947: 1190 khz; 10 kw-D, DA. TL: N38 56 32 W76 28 54. (CP: COL Garrison. 5 kw-D, 7 kw-N, DA-2. TL: N39 24 29 W76 46 32). Stereo. Hrs open: 1610 West St., Suite 209, 21401. Phone: (410) 269-0700.E-mail: wbis@businessradio.net Web Site:www.wbis1190.com Licensee: Nations Radio L.L.C. (acq 3-31-98; $400,000). Population served: 6,000,000 Reynolds & Manning. Format: Business talk. ♦Alan Pendleton, gen mgr.

***WFSI(FM)**— May 16, 1960: 107.9 mhz; 50 kw. Ant 500 ft TL: N38 59 45 W76 39 27. Stereo. Hrs open: 24 918 Chesapeake Ave., 21403. Phone: (410) 268-6200. Fax: (410) 268-0931. Web Site:www.familyradio.com Licensee: Family Stations Inc. (group owner; (acq 1-7-72). Natl. Network: Family Radio, . Format: Relg, educ. ♦Harold Camping, gen mgr & stn mgr.

WLZL(FM)— 1947: 99.1 mhz; 50 kw. Ant 459 ft TL: N38 59 46 W76 39 26. Stereo. Hrs open: 24 4200 Parliament Pl., Suite 300, Lanham, 20706. Phone: (301) 306-0991. Fax: (301) 731-0431. Web Site:www.elzolradio.com Licensee: CBS Radio East Inc. Group owner: Infinity Broadcasting Corp. (acq 11-13-98; grpsl). Population served: 5,000,000 Natl. Rep: CBS Radio,. Leventhal, Senter & Lerman. Format: Sp. News staff: one; News: 5 hrs wkly. Target aud: Adults 18-49; upscale professionals. ♦Michael Hughes, gen mgr; Areacely Rivera, progmg dir.

WNAV(AM)— 1949: 1430 khz; 5 kw-D, 1 kw-N, DA-N. TL: N38 59 00 W76 31 21. Hrs open: Box 6726, 21401. Phone: (410) 263-1430. Fax: (410) 268-5360.E-mail: stevehopp@wnav.com Web Site:www.wnav.com Licensee: Sajak Broadcasting Corp. (acq 5-26-98; $2.2 million). Population served: 500,000 Natl. Network: CBS Radio, Westwood One, . Format: Adult contemp, full service. News staff: 2. Target aud: 35 plus. Spec prog: Baltimore Orioles baseball, Naval Academy sports. ♦Patrick L. Sajak, pres; Steve Hopp, VP & gen mgr; Bill Lusby, progmg dir, mus dir.

WRNR-FM—(Grasonville, Apr 1, 1980: 103.1 mhz; 6 kw. 328 ft TL: N38 56 37 W76 10 43. Stereo. Hrs open: 112 Main St., 21401. Phone: (410) 626-0103. Fax: (410) 267-7634.E-mail: info@wrnr.com Web Site:www.wrnr.com Licensee: Empire Broadcasting System Inc. (acq 6-17-97; $2.15 million). Population served: 2,000,000 Natl. Network: CBS Radio, . Leventhal, Senter & Lerman. Format: Progressive /diversified. News staff: one; News: 2 hrs wkly. Target aud: 25-54; adults. ♦Bob Waugh, opns mgr, mus dir; Judy Buddensick, gen sls mgr.

WYRE(AM)— 1946: 810 khz; 250 w-D. TL: N38 58 13 W76 30 28. Hrs open: Sunrise-Sunset 9B Crain Hwy. N., Glen Burnie, 21061. Phone: (410) 760-5111. Fax: (410) 766-2877. Licensee: Bay Broadcasting Corp. (acq 2-28-2002). Population served: 400,000 Baraff, Koerner & Olender. Format: Sp. ♦Richard Dent, pres; Raul Lopez Bastidas, gen mgr.

Baltimore

WBAL(AM)— Nov 2, 1925: 1090 khz; 50 kw-U, DA-N. TL: N39 22 33 W76 46 21. Hrs open: 24 3800 Hooper Ave., 21211. Phone: (410) 467-3000. Fax: (410) 338-6483.E-mail: news@wbal.com Web Site:www.wbal.com Licensee: WBAL Div., The Hearst Corp. (acq 1-14-35). Population served: 2,100,000 Natl. Network: CBS Radio, . Natl. Rep: D & R Radio,. Brooks, Pierce, McLendon, Humphrey & Leonard. Format: News/talk, sports. Target aud: 25-54. ♦Bob Cecil, VP, sls dir; Edward C. Kiernan, gen mgr; Jeffrey Beauchamp, stn mgr; Kerry Plackmeyer, opns mgr; Steve Hartman, natl sls mgr; Arthur Hawkins, rgnl sls mgr; Alison Jessie, prom mgr; Mark Miller, news dir; Jeff Halapin, chief of engrg; Donna Valentine, traf mgr.

WBGR(AM)— July 27, 1955: 860 khz; 2.5 kw-D, 66 w-N, DA-2. TL: N39 18 43 W76 29 26. Hrs open: 600 Washington Ave., Towson, 21204. Phone: (410) 825-7700.E-mail: info@familyradio.com Web Site:www.familyradio.com Licensee: Family Stations Inc. Group owner: Infinity Broadcasting Corp. (acq 3-2-2005; $7.5 million with WBMD(AM) Baltimore). Population served: 905,759 Format: Relg, foreign. Target aud: 18-49. ♦Harold Camping, gen mgr; Bill Sadlier, rgnl sls mgr.

WBIS(AM)—See Annapolis

***WBJC(FM)**— Apr 6, 1951: 91.5 mhz; 50 kw. 500 ft TL: N39 23 11 W76 43 52. Stereo. Hrs open: 6776 Riesterstown Rd., Suite 202, 21215. Phone: (410) 462-8444. Fax: (410) 333-7016.E-mail: wbjcinformation@wbjc.com Web Site:www.wbjc.com Licensee: Baltimore City Community College. (acq 4-22-91). Population served: 200,000 Natl. Network: PRI, . Format: Class. ♦Cary Smith, gen mgr; Kati Harrison, opns dir & opns mgr; Jim Ward, dev dir; Jonathan Palevsky, progmg dir.

WBMD(AM)— Dec 7, 1947: 750 khz; 1 kw-D. TL: N39 19 26 W76 32 56. Hrs open: Sunrise-sunset 918 Chesapeake Ave., Annapolis, 21203. Phone: (410) 821-9000. Fax: (410) 268-0931. Web Site:www.familyradio.com Licensee: Family Stations Inc. Group owner: Infinity Broadcasting Corp. (acq 3-2-2005; $7.5 million with WBGR(AM) Baltimore). Format: Relg. Target aud: 12 plus. ♦Harold Camping, gen mgr; Bill Sadlier, rgnl sls mgr.

WCAO(AM)— May 8, 1922: 600 khz; 5 kw-U, DA-1. TL: N39 25 47 W76 45 42. Hrs open: 711 W. 40th St., Suite 350, 21211. Phone: (410) 366-7600. Fax: (410) 467-0011.E-mail: yourvoice@heaven600.com Web Site:www.heaven600.com Licensee: Citicasters Licenses L.P. Group owner: Clear Channel Communications Inc. (acq 5-99; grpsl). Population served: 2,000,000 Format: Contemporary Black gospel. ♦Kevin Friedman, gen mgr; Bill Hopkinson, sls dir, gen sls mgr; Lee Michaels, progmg dir.

WCBM(AM)— 1924: 680 khz; 10 kw-D, 5 kw-N, DA-2. TL: N39 24 30 W76 46 34. Hrs open: 24 Hilton Plaza, 1726 Reisterstown Rd., Suite 117, 21208. Phone: (410) 580-6800. Fax: (410) 580-6810.E-mail: bcarl@wcbm.com Web Site:www.wcbm.com Licensee: M-10 Broadcasting (acq 9-5-95). Population served: 1,500,000 Natl. Network: CBS, . Fisher, Wayland, Cooper, Leader & Zaragoza L.L.P. Format: Talk. News staff: 3; News: 11 hrs wkly. Target aud: 25-54; informed adults with major purchasing power. ♦Nick Mangione Jr., sr VP; Bob Pettit, gen mgr; Marc Beavin, gen sls mgr; Sean Casey, progmg dir; Eddie Applefeld, prom.

WCHH(FM)— 1949: 104.3 mhz; 13 kw. Ant 964 ft TL: N39 20 10 W76 38 59. Stereo. Hrs open: 711 W. 40th St., Suite 350, 21211. Phone: (410) 366-7600. Fax: (410) 467-0011. Web Site:www.channel1043.com Licensee: Citicasters Licenses L.P. Group owner: Clear Channel Communications Inc. (acq 5-4-99; grpsl). Population served: 1,200,000 Natl. Rep: Katz Radio,. Format: Modern rock. Target aud: 25-44. ♦Kevin Friedman, gen mgr.

***WEAA(FM)**— Jan 10, 1977: 88.9 mhz; 12.5 kw. Ant 220 ft TL: N39 20 31 W76 35 13. Stereo. Hrs open: 24 1700 East Coldspring Ln., 21251. Phone: (443) 885-3564. Fax: (443) 885-8206.E-mail: weaa@moac.morgan.edu Web Site:www.weaa.org Licensee: Morgan State University. Population served: 1,100,000 Natl. Network: NPR, . Schwartz, Woods & Miller. Wire Svc: AP Format: Jazz, news/talk. News staff: one; News: 10 hrs wkly. Target aud: 25-49; 85% Black. Spec prog: Urban oldies 5 hrs, Caribbean 7 hrs, Africian world 4 hrs, gospel 13 hrs, hip hop 5 hrs wkly. ♦LaFontaine Oliver, gen mgr; Sandi Mallony, progmg dir & progmg mgr.

WERQ-FM— 1960: 92.3 mhz; 37 kw. 571 ft TL: N39 20 20 W76 40 02. Stereo. Hrs open: 24 1705 Whitehead Rd., 21207. Phone: (410) 332-8200. Fax: (410) 944-7182.E-mail: info@werq.com Web Site:www.92qjams.com Licensee: Radio One Licenses LLC Group owner: Radio One Inc. (acq 6-21-93; $9 million with co-located AM;7-19-93). Population served: 325,000 Arent, Fox, Kintner, Plotkin & Kahn. Format: Urban contemp. Target aud: 18-34; young adults. ♦Alfred Liggins, CEO, prom dir; Howard Mazer, gen mgr; Jonell White, gen sls mgr; Karl Goehring, chief of engrg; Neke Howse, progmg dir & traf mgr.

WIYY(FM)— Dec 7, 1958: 97.9 mhz; 13.5 kw. 945 ft TL: N39 20 05 W76 39 03. Stereo. Hrs open: Prog sep from AM 3800 Hooper Ave., 21211. Phone: (410) 467-3000. Fax: (410) 338-6483.E-mail: info@98online.com Web Site:www.98online.com Format: AOR. Target aud: 18-49. ♦Hugues Jean, gen sls mgr; Steve Hartman, rgnl sls mgr; Lori Smyth, prom mgr; Dave Hill, progmg dir.

WJZ(AM)— June 8, 1922: 1300 khz; 5 kw-U, DA-2. TL: N39 20 00 W76 46 13. Hrs open: 24
Rebroadcasts WJFK-FM Manassas, VA 77%.
1423 Clarkview Rd., 21209. Phone: (410) 825-1000. Fax: (410) 821-5482. Web Site:www.espn1300.com Licensee: CBS Radio WLIF-AM Inc. (group owner; Infinity Broadcasting Corp. (acq 5-29-89; $32 million with co-located FM; 4-24-89). Population served: 460,000 Natl. Network: ESPN Radio, . Natl. Rep: CBS Radio,. Leventhal, Senter & Lerman. Format: Talk, sports. Target aud: 18-49; men. ♦Dan Mason, pres; Bob Philips, opns mgr.

WJZ-FM—See Catonsville

WLIF(FM)— Dec 24, 1970: 101.9 mhz; 13.5 kw. Ant 960 ft TL: N39 25 02 W76 33 23. Stereo. Hrs open: 1423 Clarkview Rd., 21209. Phone: (410) 825-1000. Fax: (410) 296-9543.E-mail: info@1019litefm.com Web Site:www.1019litefm.com Licensee: CBS Radio WLIF-AM Inc. Population served: 905,759 Format: Lite adult contemp. Spec prog: Jazz 8 hrs wkly.

WNST(AM)—See Towson

WOLB(AM)— Nov 25, 1947: 1010 khz; 250 w-D, 30 w-N. TL: N39 18 06 W76 34 09. Hrs open: 24 1705 Whitehead Rd., 21207. Phone: (410) 332-8200. Fax: (410) 944-1047. Web Site:www.wolb1010.com Licensee: Radio One Licenses LLC Population served: 21,000 Natl. Rep: Katz Radio,. Format: News/talk. News: 5 hrs wkly. Target aud: 35 plus; African American adults. Spec prog: Relg 2 hrs, Sp 2 hrs wkly. ♦Howard Mazer, gen mgr; Al Payne, opns mgr; Jonell White, gen sls mgr, traf mgr; Karl Goehring, engr.

WPOC(FM)— 1959: 93.1 mhz; 16 kw. Ant 860 ft TL: N39 17 13 W76 45 16. Stereo. Hrs open: 711 W. 40th St., Suite 350, 21211. Phone: (410) 366-7600. Fax: (410) 235-3899.E-mail: megstevens@wpoc.com Web Site:www.wpoc.com Licensee: Citicasters Licenses L.P. Group owner: Clear Channel Communications Inc. (acq 4-29-99; grpsl). Population served: 2,075,600 Format: Country. ♦Kevin Friedman, gen mgr, gen sls mgr, natl sls mgr, mktg dir; Meg Stevens, progmg dir.

WQSR(FM)— Dec 15, 1947: 102.7 mhz; 50 kw. 436 ft TL: N39 23 11 W76 43 52. Stereo. Hrs open: 711 W. 40th St., 21211. Phone: (410) 366-7600. Fax: (240) 747-3747.E-mail: info@wqsr.com Web Site:www.1027jackfm.com Licensee: Citicasters Licenses Inc. Group owner: Infinity Broadcasting Corp. (acq 4-1-2009; grpsl). Format: Mixed/automated. ♦Hartley Adkins, gen mgr; Jason Kidd, progmg dir.

WRBS(AM)— Mar 1, 1941: 1230 khz; 1 kw-U. TL: N39 18 58 W76 36 03. Stereo. Hrs open: 24 3600 Georgetown Rd., 21227. Phone: (410) 247-4100. Fax: (410) 247-4533.E-mail: info@wrbs.com Web Site:www.wrbsam.com Licensee: WRBS-AM LLC Group owner: Salem Communications Corp. (acq 12-22-2006; $3.25 million). Population served: 8,000,000 Davis Wright Tremaine LLP. Format: Christian. ♦Joe Norris, opns mgr.

WRBS-FM— Aug 1, 1964: 95.1 mhz; 50 kw. 499 ft TL: N39 15 21 W76 40 29. Stereo. Hrs open: 24 3600 Georgetown Rd., 21227. Phone: (410) 247-4100. Fax: (410) 247-4533.E-mail: info@wrbs.com Web Site:www.wrbs.com Licensee: Peter and John Radio Fellowship Inc. (acq 9-64). Population served: 2,00,000 Format: Contemp Christian. News staff: one; News: 6 hrs wkly. ♦Steven D. Lawhon, gen mgr; David Paul, progmg dir.

WWIN(AM)— 1951: 1400 khz; 1 kw-U. TL: N39 19 21 W76 36 33. Stereo. Hrs open: 24 1705 Whitehead Rd., 21207. Phone: (410) 332-8200. Fax: (410) 944-1047. Web Site:www.spirit1400.com Licensee: Radio One Licenses LLC. Group owner: Radio One Inc. (acq 1-23-92; $7.5 million with WWIN-FM Glen Burnie). Population served: 905,759 Natl. Rep: Katz Radio,. Verner, Liipfert, Bernhard, McPherson & Hand. Format: Gospel. News staff: one; News: one hr wkly. Target aud: 25-54; Black, relg. ♦Howard Mazer, gen mgr; Al Payne, opns mgr; Dave Willner, sls dir; Jack McCarty, gen sls mgr.

WWIN-FM—See Glen Burnie

WWMX(FM)— 1960: 106.5 mhz; 7.4 kw. 1,217 ft TL: N39 20 10 W76 38 59. Stereo. Hrs open: 24 1423 Clarkview Rd., Suite 100, 21209. Phone: (410) 825-1065. Fax: (410) 321-4548.E-mail: dave.labrozzi @infinitybroadcasting.com Web Site:www.mix1065.fm Licensee: CBS Radio Stations Inc. Group owner: Infinity Broadcasting Corp. Population served: 905,759 Format: Adult contemp. Target aud: 25-54. ♦Tracy Brandys, gen mgr; Dave Labrozzi, progmg dir. Co-owned TV: WJZ-TV

***WYPR(FM)**— May 23, 1979: 88.1 mhz; 10 kw. Ant 360 ft TL: N39 19 53 W76 39 28. Stereo. Hrs open: 2216 N. Charles St., 21218. Phone: (410) 235-1660. Fax: (410) 235-1161.E-mail: tbrandon@wypr.org Web Site:www.wypr.org Licensee: WYPR License Holding LLC (acq 1-16-2002). Natl. Network: NPR, PRI, . Format: Jazz, news/talk. ♦Anthony Brandon, pres & gen mgr; Andy Bienstock, progmg dir.

Bel Air

***WHFC(FM)**— 1972: 91.1 mhz; 1.10 kw. 226 ft TL: N39 33 22 W76 16 48. Stereo. Hrs open: 24 Harford Community College, 401 Thomas Run Rd., 21015-1698. Phone: (410) 836-4151. Fax: (410) 836-4180.E-mail: whfc@harford.edu Web Site:www.whfc911.org Licensee: Harford Community College. Population served: 250,000 Format: Var. Target aud: 24-42; upwardly mobile professionals. Spec prog: AAA 15 hrs, class 18 hr, jazz 18 hrs, Christian 6 hrs, Americain Indian 3 hrs wkly. ♦Gary Helton, gen mgr.

Berlin

WOCQ(FM)— June 25, 1981: 103.9 mhz; 3 kw. 328 ft TL: N38 22 58 W75 18 58. Stereo. Hrs open: 24 20200 DuPont Blvd., Georgetown, 19947. Fax: (302) 856-7633. Web Site:www.oc104.com Licensee: Great Scott Broadcasting. (group owner; acq 11-7-97; $2.775 million). Population served: 228,000 Format: Rhythmic/CHR. News staff: one; News: 4 hrs wkly. Target aud: 18-49. ♦Sue Timmons, gen mgr.

Bethesda

WMMJ(FM)— Nov 12, 1961: 102.3 mhz; 2.9 kw. 480 ft TL: N38 56 09 W77 05 33. Stereo. Hrs open: 5900 Princess Garden Pkwy., 8th Floor, Lanham, 20706. Phone: (301) 306-1111. Fax: (301) 306-9510.E-mail: info@magic1023.com Web Site:www.magic1023.com Licensee: Radio One Licenses LLC. Group owner: Radio One Inc. (acq 11-8-01; grpsl). Population served: 3,500,000 Format: Adult contemp. ♦Alfred Liggins, CEO, pres; Catherine Hughes, chmn; Scott Royster, CFO; Michele Williams, gen mgr.

WTGB-FM— October 1959: 94.7 mhz; 20.5 kw. Ant 771 ft TL: N38 57 49 W77 06 18. Stereo. Hrs open: 24 8403 Colesville Rd., Ste. 1500, Silver Spring, 20910-3474. Phone: (301) 683-0947. Fax: (301) 881-8746. Web Site:www.947freshfm.com Licensee: CBS Radio East Inc. Group owner: Infinity Broadcasting Corp. (acq 8-1-85; grpsl; 6-10-85). Natl. Network: CNN Radio, . Natl. Rep: CBS Radio,. Format: Adult contemp. Target aud: 25-49. ♦Michael Hughes, gen mgr; Greg Dunkin, progmg dir.

WTNT(AM)— Jan 2, 1946: 570 khz; 5 kw-D, 1 kw-N, DA-2. TL: N39 02 07 W77 10 11. Hrs open: 24 1801 Rockville Pike, Rockville, 20852. Phone: (301) 231-7798. Fax: (301) 881-8030.E-mail: redzebra@broadcasting.com Web Site:www.wtntam570.com Licensee: Red Zebra Broadcasting Licensee LLC. Group owner: Clear Channel Communications Inc. (acq 7-29-2008; grpsl). Natl. Rep: Clear Channel,. Format: Talk. Target aud: 25-54. ♦Kaiya Ramsey, gen sls mgr; Kevin Cannady, prom dir & prom mgr.

WTOP-FM—See Washington, DC

WUST(AM)—See Washington, DC

Braddock Heights

WTLP(FM)— Apr 8, 1972: 103.9 mhz; 350 w. Ant 958 ft TL: N39 27 50 W77 29 44. Stereo. Hrs open: 24
Rebroadcasts WTOP-FM Washington, DC 100%.
3400 Idaho Ave. N.W., Washington, DC, 20016. Phone: (202) 895-5000. Fax: (202) 895-5103.E-mail: newsroom@wtopnews.com Web Site:www.wtopnews.com Licensee: Bonneville Holding Co. Group owner: Bonneville International Corp. (acq 1996; grpsl). Population served: 125,000 Natl. Network: CBS Radio, . Natl. Rep: Katz Radio,. Format: News. Target aud: General. ♦Joel Oxley, gen mgr.

Brunswick

WTRI(AM)— Oct 2, 1966: 1520 khz; 9.3 kw-D, 14 kw-CH. TL: N39 18 45 W77 36 31. Stereo. Hrs open: 214 13th Ave., 21716. Phone: (301) 834-9000. Fax: (301) 834-6944.E-mail: earl@radioearl.com Web Site:www.radioearl.com Licensee: WTRI Holding LLC (acq 10-20-2004; $1.6 million). Population served: 500,000 Format: Country. ♦Fred Rohner, gen mgr, news dir; Buddy Rizer, progmg dir.

California

WKIK-FM— December 1994: 102.9 mhz; 4 kw. Ant 394 ft TL: N38 22 03 W76 36 55. Stereo. Hrs open: 24
Simulcast with WKIK(AM) La Plata 100%.
Box 2908, La Plata, 20646. Phone: (301) 870-5550.E-mail: wsmdfm@aol.com Licensee: Somar Communications Inc. (group owner; acq 1993; $130,000;5-24-93). Format: Country. Target aud: 25-54. ♦Roy Robertson, pres, gen mgr; Terrell Soellner, opns mgr; Sharon Robertson, gen sls mgr.

Cambridge

WCEM(AM)— 1947: 1240 khz; 1 kw-U. TL: N38 35 02 W76 04 56. Stereo. Hrs open: 24 Box 237, 21613. Phone: (410) 228-4800. Fax: (410) 228-0130.E-mail: espn@intercom.net Web Site:www.mtslive.com Licensee: MTS Broadcasting L.C. Group owner: MTS Broadcasting (acq 6-20-93; $1.8 million with co-located FM; 8-9-93). Population served: 11,595 Natl. Network: Westwood One, ESPN Radio, . Format: Sports. News staff: one. Target aud: 25-54. Spec prog: Relg 5 hrs wkly. ♦Troy D. Hill, gen mgr; Shane Walker, opns mgr; Shan Shariff, progmg dir; Mike Detmer, news dir; Bryan Harz, engrg dir; Dwight Cromwell, reporter; Bob Kinnamon, sports cmtr.

WCEM-FM— Jan 29, 1968: 106.3 mhz; 6 kw. Ant 325 ft TL: N38 35 03 W76 04 54. Stereo. Hrs open: 2 Bay Street, 21613. Secondary address: Box 237 21613. Phone: (410) 228-4800. Fax: (410) 228-0130.E-mail: theheat@intercom.net Web Site:www.mtslive.com

(Acq 1993; 8-23-93). Population served: 60,000 Format: Hot adult contemp. Target aud: 18-49. ♦Mike Detmer, news rptr; Shan Shariff, sports cmtr.

Catonsville

WJZ-FM— Nov 22, 1963: 105.7 mhz; 50 kw. Ant 492 ft TL: N39 19 26 W76 32 56. Stereo. Hrs open: 24 1423 Clarkview Rd., Towson, 21209. Phone: (410) 825-1000. Fax: (410) 821-8256. Web Site:www.1057thefan.com Licensee: CBS Radio Stations Inc. Group owner: Infinity Broadcasting Corp. (acq 11-13-98; grpsl). Population served: 905,759 Natl. Rep: Christal,. Format: Sports. News staff: one. Target aud: 25-54. ♦Robert Philips, VP, gen mgr & stn mgr.

Chestertown

WCTR(AM)— June 16, 1963: 1530 khz; 1 kw-D, 270 w-CH. TL: N39 13 35 W76 05 20. Hrs open: Box 700, 21620. Secondary address: 231 Flatland Rd. 21620. Phone: (410) 778-1530. Fax: (410) 778-4800.E-mail: wctr@wctr.com Web Site:www.wctr.com Licensee: WCTR Broadcasting LLC (acq 5-12-2004; $340,000). Population served: 50,000 Natl. Network: ABC, . Rgnl rep: Rgnl Reps Format: Oldies. News: 10 hrs wkly. Target aud: 35 plus. ♦Richard Gelfman, pres; Ken Collins, gen mgr; Keith Thompson, opns mgr; Sean Hall, progmg dir & news dir.

College Park

***WMUC-FM—** Sept 10, 1979: 88.1 mhz; 10 w. 3 ft TL: N38 58 59 W76 56 37. Stereo. Hrs open: 24 Box 99, 3130 S. Campus Dining Hall, 20742-8431. Phone: (301) 314-7865. Phone: (301) 314 7868. Fax: (301) 314-7879. Web Site:wmuc.umd.edu Licensee: University of Maryland. Population served: 50,000 Format: Var/div. Target aud: College students. ♦Steve Gnadt, gen mgr & opns mgr.

Crisfield

WBEY-FM— July 1995: 97.9 mhz; 4.3 kw. Ant 379 ft TL: N38 01 45 W75 45 05. Hrs open: Box 69, 21817. Secondary address: 1637 Dunn Swamp Rd., Pocomoke City 21851. Phone: (410) 957-6081. Fax: (410) 957-6080.E-mail: bay979@gmail.com Web Site:www.easternshoreradio.com Licensee: Bay Broadcasting. Format: Adult country. ♦Michael Powell, gen mgr, opns mgr & gen sls mgr; Adam Riggin, progmg dir.

Cumberland

WCBC(AM)— June 24, 1953: 1270 khz; 5 kw-D, 1 kw-N, DA-2. TL: N39 40 28 W78 46 48. Hrs open: Box 1290, 21501. Phone: (301) 724-5000. Fax: (301) 722-8336.E-mail: dnorman@wcbc1270am.com Web Site:www.wcbc1270am.com Licensee: Cumberland Broadcasting Co. Inc. (acq 4-8-76). Population served: 30,000 Natl. Network: ABC, Westwood One, . Format: News/talk. News staff: 2; News: 3 hrs wkly. Target aud: 25 plus. ♦David N. Aydelotte Sr., pres; Jim Robey, gen mgr, stn mgr.

WCMD(AM)— 1948: 1230 khz; 1 kw-U. TL: N39 38 36 W78 44 35. Hrs open: 24 516 White Ave., 21502. Phone: (301) 777-5400. Fax: (301) 777-5404.E-mail: info@wrogfm.com Licensee: Broadcast Communications Inc. Population served: 65,000 Shaonis & Peltzman. Format: Oldies, adult standards. News staff: 2; News: 20 hrs wkly. Target aud: 25-54.

WKGO(FM)— April 1962: 106.1 mhz; 5.4 kw. Ant 1,410 ft TL: N39 34 54 W78 53 58. Stereo. Hrs open: 24 Box 1644, 21501. Secondary address: 350 Byrd Ave. 21502. Phone: (301) 722-6666. Fax: (301) 722-0945.E-mail: go106@go106.com Web Site:www.go106.com Licensee: WTBO-WKGO Corp. L.L.C. Population served: 2,000,000 Natl. Network: Westwood One, . Format: Classic rock, new rock. News staff: one; News: one hr wkly. Target aud: 25-54. ♦Richard Cornwell, adv mgr; Jim Van, local news ed; Mark St. John, disc jockey.

WROG(FM)— 1948: 102.9 mhz; 3.5 kw. Ant 1,437 ft TL: N39 34 56 W78 53 53. (CP: COL Chambersburg. 93.3 mhz; 350 w, ant 1,351 ft. TL: N40 02 54 W77 45 02). Stereo. Hrs open: 24 516 White Ave., 21502. Phone: (301) 777-5400. Fax: (301) 777-5404.E-mail: mail@wrogfm.com Web Site:www.wrogfm.com Licensee: Broadcast Communications Inc. (group owner; (acq 1-8-2004; $2 million with co-located AM). Population served: 350,000 Shaonis & Peltzman. Format: Country. News staff: 2; News: 20 hrs wkly. Target aud: 25-49. ♦Eva Mace, gen mgr, gen sls mgr; Grant Garland, progmg dir & news dir.

WTBO(AM)— Dec 13, 1928: 1450 khz; 1 kw-U. TL: N39 38 43 W78 45 05. Stereo. Hrs open: 24 Box 1644, 21501-1644. Secondary address: 350 Byrd Ave. 21502. Phone: (301) 722-6666. Fax: (301) 722-0945. Web Site:www.am1450.com Licensee: WTBO-WKGO Corp. LLC. Group owner: Dix Communications (acq 11-1-77). Population served: 2,500,000 Natl. Network: CSN, . Baker & Hostetler. Format: Nostalgia, adult standards. News staff: one; News: 20 hrs wkly. Target aud: 40 plus. ♦G. Charles Dix II, pres; Richard L. Cornwell, gen mgr, gen sls mgr; Tim Martin, prom dir & progmg dir; Jim Van, news dir; Mark Workman, chief of engrg; R. DiBuono, traf mgr; Linda Ward, spec ev coord.

Denton

WKDI(AM)— Dec 27, 1988: 840 khz; 1 kw-D, DA. TL: N38 53 53 W75 51 10. Stereo. Hrs open: Sunrise-sunset Box 309, 21629. Secondary address: 24580 Station Rd. 21629. Phone: (410) 479-2288. Fax: (410) 479-5188.E-mail: wkdi@broadcast.net Licensee: Bayshore Communications Inc. Format: Christian/talk. News: 12 hrs wkly. Target aud: 25-49; middle-income Christians. ♦Edward Baker, CEO; Michael A. McCoy, gen mgr & progmg dir.

Easton

WCEI-FM— May 14, 1975: 96.7 mhz; 25 kw. 245 ft TL: N38 46 13 W76 04 55. Stereo. Hrs open: 24 Prog sep from AM 306 Port St., 21601. Phone: (410) 822-3301. Fax: (410) 822-0576. Web Site:www.wceiradio.com Population served: 120,000 Format: Adult contemp. News staff: one. Target aud: 25-54. ♦Alex Kolbieski, CEO; Stacie Monz, gen mgr & sls dir; Julie Johnson, traf mgr; Don Bumpus, local news ed.

WEMD(AM)— Sept 29, 1960: 1460 khz; 1 kw-D, 500 w-N, DA-2. TL: N38 46 13 W76 04 55. Hrs open: 306 Port St., 21601. Phone: (410) 822-3301. Fax: (410) 822-0576.E-mail: stacie@wceiradio.com Licensee: First Media Radio L.L.C. (group owner; (acq 11-30-99; $4 million with co-located FM). Population served: 70,000 Natl. Network: Jones Radio Networks, . Dow, Lohnes & Albertson. Format: Music of Your Life. Target aud: 45 plus; mature adults. ♦Matt Spence, progmg dir.

Elkton

***WOEL-FM—** September 1978: 89.9 mhz; 3 kw. 259 ft TL: N39 35 35 W75 51 49. Hrs open: Box 246, 21922. Secondary address: 3141 Old Elk Neck Rd. 21922. Phone: (410) 398-3764. Fax: (410) 392-3229.E-mail: apd.saved@juno.com Web Site:www.mbcmin.org Licensee: Maryland Baptist Bible College. Population served: 200,000 Natl. Network: USA, . Format: Relg-Educ. ♦Ray Linzy, gen mgr.

WSRY(AM)— Aug 22, 1963: 1550 khz; 1 kw-D, 10 w-N, DA-2. TL: N39 35 45 W75 47 50. Hrs open: Box 372, Wilmington, DE, 19899. Phone: (302) 731-7270. Fax: (302) 738-3090. Licensee: Priority Radio Inc. (group owner; (acq 12-10-99). Population served: 70,000 Natl. Network: ESPN Radio, . Format: Sports, sports talk. Target aud: 25-64. Spec prog: Relg 3 hrs, farm one hr wkly. ♦Dan Edwards, gen mgr.

Emmittsburg

***WMTB-FM—** Oct 1, 1977: 89.9 mhz; 100 w. 144 ft TL: N39 41 02 W77 21 25. Hrs open: Noon-3 PM Mt. Saint Mary's College, 16300 Old Emmittsburg Rd., 21727. Phone: (301) 447-5240. Web Site:www.msmary.edu/wmtb Licensee: Mount Saint Mary's College. Format: Classic rock, new age, alternative. News: 2 hrs wkly. Target aud: General; college & community. Spec prog: Folk one hr, gospel one hr, relg 4 hrs wkly. ♦Randy Gray, gen mgr.

Federalsburg

WTDK(FM)— Dec 2, 1978: 107.1 mhz; 3.9 kw. 408 ft TL: N38 46 02 W75 44 46. Hrs open: 24 Box 237, Cambridge, 21613. Phone: (410) 288-4800. Fax: (410) 228-0130.E-mail: theduck@mtslive.com Web Site:www.mtslive.com Licensee: MTS Broadcasting. (group owner; acq 1-30-97). Natl. Network: USA, Westwood One, . Format: Hits of the 50s 60s & 70s. News: 4 hrs wkly. Target aud: 25-54; affluent listeners. ♦Thomas Mulitz, pres; Troy Hill, gen mgr; Shane Walker, opns mgr; Al Ackerman, progmg dir.

Frederick

WFMD(AM)— Jan 1, 1936: 930 khz; 5 kw-D, 2.5 kw-N, DA-2. TL: N39 24 55 W77 27 41. Hrs open: 24 Prog sep from FM 5966 Grove Hill Rd., 21703-6012. Phone: (301) 663-4181. Fax: (301) 682-8018.E-mail: info@wfmd.com Web Site:www.wfmd.com Licensee: Aloha Station Trust LLC Group owner: Clear Channel Communications Inc. (acq 7-30-2008; grpsl). Population served: 200,000 Natl. Network: ABC, . Wire Svc: AP Format: News/talk, sports. News staff: 3. Target aud: 35-64. ♦Frank Mitchell, opns mgr, prom dir & progmg dir; Dianah Gibson, news dir.

WFRE(FM)— Feb 19, 1961: 99.9 mhz; 7.6 kw. Ant 1,164 ft TL: N39 30 00 W77 29 58. Stereo. Hrs open: 24 5966 Grove Hill Rd., 21703. Phone: (301) 663-4181. Fax: (301) 682-8018. Web Site:www.wfre.com Licensee: Aloha Station Trust LLC (acq 7-30-2008; grpsl). Population served: 500,000 Natl. Rep: Clear Channel,. Wire Svc: AP Format: Country. News staff: 3; News: one hr wkly. Target aud: 25-54. ♦Doug Hillard, gen mgr; Troy Skinner, gen sls mgr.

WWEG(FM)—See Hagerstown

WWFD(AM)— Dec 15, 1960: 820 khz; 4.3 kw-D, 430 w-N, DA-N. TL: N39 24 42 W77 28 20. Hrs open: 24
Rebroadcasts WFED(AM) Washington, DC 100%.
6633 Mt. Phillip Rd., 21703. Phone: (202) 895-5000. Fax: (202) 895-5144. Web Site:www.federalnewsradio.com Licensee: Bonneville Holding Co. Group owner: Bonneville International Corp. (acq 1996; grpsl). Population served: 125,000 Natl. Rep: Katz Radio,. Format: Federal news. Target aud: General. ♦Joel Oxley, gen mgr; Lisa Wolfe, progmg dir.

***WYPF(FM)—** May 1991: 88.1 mhz; 4 kw. Ant 554 ft TL: N39 25 05 W77 30 03. Stereo. Hrs open: 24 2216 N. Charles St., Baltimore, 21218. Phone: (410) 235-1660. Fax: (410) 235-1161. Web Site:www.wypr.org Licensee: Your Public Radio Corp. (acq 11-24-2004; $1.2 million). Natl. Network: NPR, PRI, . Format: News/talk info. Target aud: General. ♦Anthony S. Brandon, pres; Anthony Brandon, gen mgr.

Frostburg

WFRB(AM)— Dec 20, 1958: 560 khz; 5 kw-D. TL: N39 41 02 W78 57 57. Hrs open: 24 242 Finzel Rd., Frostberg, 21532. Phone: (301) 689-8871. Phone: (301) 722-6666. Fax: (301) 689-8880.E-mail: wfrb@wfrb.com Web Site:www.talkradio560.com Licensee: WTBO-WKGO Corp. L.L.C. Group owner: Dix Communications (acq 6-1-97; $3.5 million with co-located FM). Population served: 2,500,000 Format: Talk radio. News staff: one; News: 10 hrs wkly. Target aud: 40 plus; those gainfully employed in the market for goods & svcs. ♦G. Charles Dix II, pres; Richard Cornwell, gen mgr, gen sls mgr; Hannah Ford, prom dir, disc jockey; Carson Yoder, progmg mgr; Jim Van, news dir, pub affrs dir, local news ed; Mark Workman, engrg mgr; Chris Bagley, traf mgr; Chris Williams, disc jockey.

WFRB-FM— Oct 1, 1965: 105.3 mhz; 16.5 kw. 960 ft TL: N39 41 02 W78 57 57. Stereo. Hrs open: 24 242 Finzel Rd., 21532. Phone: (301) 689-8871. Phone: (301) 722-6666. Fax: (301) 689-8880. Web Site:www.wfrb.com Population served: 2,000,000 Format: Country. News staff: 2; News: 5 hrs wkly.

***WFWM(FM)—** April 1986: 91.9 mhz; 255 w horiz, 1.3 kw vert. Ant 1,424 ft TL: N39 34 54 W78 53 53. Stereo. Hrs open: 24 Stangle Bldg., Frostburg State Univ., 21532. Phone: (301) 687-4143. Fax: (301) 687-7040.E-mail: wfwm@frostburg.edu Web Site:www.wfwm.org Licensee: Frostburg State University. Natl. Network: NPR, . Wire Svc: AP Format: Classical, jazz, roots music. News staff: one; News: 2 hrs wkly. Target aud: General. Spec prog: Educ 11 hrs wkly. ♦Chuck Dicken, gen mgr, progmg mgr; Jeff Rosedale, news dir.

***WLIC(FM)—** October 1989: 97.1 mhz; 3 kw. 1,401 ft TL: N39 34 56 W78 53 53. (CP: 150 w, ant 1,355 ft.). Stereo. Hrs open: 24
Rebroadcasts WAIJ(FM) Grantsville 100%.
Box 540, Grantsville, 21536-0540. Secondary address: He's Alive Corp. Offices, 34 Springs Rd., Grantsville 21536. Phone: (301) 895-3292. Fax: (301) 895-3293.E-mail: hesalive@hesalive.net Web Site:www.hesalive.net Licensee: He's Alive Inc. (group owner) Population served: 250,000 Natl. Network: USA, . Format: Gospel, Christian, adult contemp, relg. Target aud: 18-35. ♦Sharon Johnson, pres.

Fruitland

WKHI(FM)— 1972: 107.7 mhz; 6 kw. Ant 236 ft TL: N38 23 00 W75 24 53. (CP: 5.3 kw, ant 348 ft). Stereo. Hrs open: 24 20200 Dupont Blvd, Georgetown, DE, 19947. Phone: (302) 856-2567. Fax: (302) 856-7633.E-mail: sue@greatscottbroadcasting.com Web Site:www.1077joefm.com Licensee: Great Scott Broadcasting. (group owner; (acq 7-16-99; $700,000 with WXSH(FM) Pocomoke City, MD). Natl. Network: NBC, . Cohn & Marks. Format: Hot country. Target aud: 25-54. Spec prog: Black 5 hrs, gospel 5 hrs wkly. ♦Faye Scott, pres; Sue Timmons, gen mgr; Adam Davis, progmg dir; Tracy Baker, traf mgr.

Gaithersburg

WMET(AM)— Jan 31, 1983: 1160 khz; 50 kw-D, 1.5 kw-N, DA-2. TL: N39 11 16 W77 12 56. Hrs open: 24 8121 Georgia Ave., Suite 806, Silver Spring, 20910. Phone: (202) 969-9884. Fax: (202) 969-9900.E-mail: ylevin@wmet1160.com Web Site:www.wmet1160.com Licensee: Beltway Acquisition Corp. (acq 7-24-2002; $7.03 million). Population served: 1,000,000 Natl. Network: NBC Radio, . Format: Var-paid prgmg. Target aud: 25 plus. ◆Yube Levin, gen mgr.

Glen Burnie

WFBR(AM)— May 15, 1963: 1590 khz; 1 kw-U, DA-2. TL: N39 10 36 W76 37 20. Hrs open: 159 8th Ave. N.W., 21061. Phone: (410) 761-1590. Fax: (410) 761-9220. Licensee: Way Broadcasting Licensee LLC (group owner; (acq 8-1-2005; exchange for WKDV(AM) Manassas, VA). Population served: 1,300,000 ◆Arthur S. Liu, pres; Libby Parris, gen mgr.

WWIN-FM— Sept 15, 1964: 95.9 mhz; 3 kw horiz, 3 kw vert. 299 ft TL: N39 12 16 W76 34 07. Hrs open: 24 1705 Whitehead Rd., Baltimore, 21207. Phone: (410) 332-8200. Fax: (410) 944-1282. Web Site:www.magic959.com Licensee: Radio One Licenses LLC. Group owner: Radio One Inc. (acq 1-23-92; $7.5 million with WWIN(AM) Baltimore). Population served: 915,800 Natl. Network: ABC, . Natl. Rep: Christal,. Verner, Liipfert, Bernhard, McPherson & Hand. Format: Urban contemp. News staff: one; News: one hr wkly. Target aud: 35-54; Black adult. ◆Howard Mazer, gen mgr, natl sls mgr; Al Payne, opns mgr; Jack McCarty, gen sls mgr.

Grantsville

***WAIJ(FM)**— October 1984: 90.3 mhz; 10 kw. Ant 561 ft TL: N39 42 14 W79 05 31. Stereo. Hrs open: 19 Box 540, 21536-0540. Secondary address: He's Alive Corp. Offices, 34 Springs Rd. 21536. Phone: (301) 895-3292. Fax: (301) 895-3293.E-mail: hesalive@hesalive.net Web Site:www.hesalive.net Licensee: He's Alive Inc. (group owner) Population served: 1,000,000 Natl. Network: USA, . Format: Gospel, Christian. Target aud: 18-35. ◆Sharon Johnson, pres; Tim Eutin, progmg dir & relg ed.

Grasonville

WRNR-FM—Licensed to Grasonville. See Annapolis

Hagerstown

WARK(AM)— July 20, 1947: 1490 khz; 925 w-U. TL: N39 37 36 W77 42 40. Hrs open: 24
Rebroadcasts WAFY(FM) Middletown 20-30%.
880 Commonwealth Ave., 21740. Phone: (301) 733-4500. Fax: (301) 733-0040.E-mail: webmaster@wark.am Licensee: Nassau Broadcasting III L.L.C. (acq 2-25-2005; $18 million with co-located FM). Population served: 35,862 Shaw Pittman. Format: Talk. News staff: 2; News: 8 hrs wkly. Target aud: 25-54. Spec prog: Jazz 2 hrs wkly. ◆Rick Mussleman, gen mgr; Marcia Cason, gen sls mgr; Bill McCarrey, engrg dir; Caroline Henneberger, traf mgr.

WAYZ(FM)— 1946: 104.7 mhz; 8.3 kw, 1,379 ft TL: N39 41 47 W77 30 47. Stereo. Hrs open: 24 Box 788, Greencastle, PA, 17225. Phone: (717) 597-9200. Fax: (717) 597-9210.E-mail: info@wayz.com Web Site:www.wayz.com Licensee: H.J.V. L.P. (acq 8-28-2000; $2.5 million and WWMD(FM) Waynesboro, PA). Population served: 200,000 Wire Svc: UPI Format: Country. Target aud: 25-54. Spec prog: Relg 3 hrs wkly. ◆Blake Truman, stn mgr, pub affrs dir; Chris Maestle, progmg dir, local news ed; Toni Anderson, mus dir.

WDLD(FM)—(Halfway, January 1965: 96.7 mhz; 4.8 kw. 164 ft TL: N39 37 03 W77 44 17. Hrs open: Prog sep from AM 1250 Maryland Ave., 21740. Phone: (301) 797-7300. Fax: (301) 797-2659.E-mail: info@wild967.fm.com Web Site:www.wild967.fm Population served: 351,000 Natl. Network: ABC, . Format: New & classic rock, AOR. Target aud: 18-54; adults, young families.

***WGMS(FM)**— June 15, 1993: 89.1 mhz; 900 w. Ant 1,338 ft TL: N39 41 39 W77 30 50. Hrs open: 24
Rebroadcasts WETA-FM Washington 100%.
2775 S. Quincy, Arlington, VA, 22206-2304. Phone: (703) 998-2600. Fax: (703) 824-7288. Web Site:www.weta.org/fm Licensee: Greater Washington Education Telecommunication Association. Population served: 250,000 Natl. Network: NPR, PRI, . Format: Class. Target aud: General; educated adults. ◆Dan De Vany, gen mgr; Mike Byrnes, chief of engrg.

WHAG(AM)—(Halfway, June 9, 1962: 1410 khz; 1 kw-D, 99 w-N, DA-2. TL: N39 37 03 W77 44 17. Hrs open: 6 AM-7 PM 1250 Maryland Ave., 21740. Phone: (301) 797-7300. Fax: (301) 797-2659. Licensee: MLB-Hagerstown-Chambersburg IV LLC. (group owner; (acq 7-20-2005; grpsl). Population served: 250,000 Format: News/talk. News staff: 2; News: 7 hrs wkly. Target aud: 25-64. ◆Rich Bateman, gen mgr.

WICL(FM)—See Williamsport

WJEJ(AM)— October 1932: 1240 khz; 1 kw-U. TL: N39 40 00 W77 43 30. Hrs open: 24 1135 Haven Rd., 21742. Phone: (301) 739-2323. Fax: (301) 797-7408.E-mail: wjej@myactv.net Web Site:www.wjejradio.com Licensee: Hagerstown Broadcasting Co. Inc. (acq 12-21-72). Population served: 35,862 Natl. Network: CBS, . Rgnl. Network: Metro. Koerner & Olender, P.C. Wire Svc: Metro Weather Service Inc. Format: Easy lstng/pop standards. News staff: one; News: 24 hrs wkly. Target aud: 35 plus. ◆John T. Staub, pres, gen mgr, gen sls mgr, rgnl sls mgr; Joanna C. Staub, opns dir; Louis J. Scally, progmg dir, chief of engrg; Tom Bradley, news dir; Jackie Hall, traf mgr.

WWEG(FM)— March 1957: 106.9 mhz; 15.5 kw. Ant 853 ft TL: N39 29 57 W77 36 42. Stereo. Hrs open: 24 880 Commonwealth Ave., 21740. Phone: (301) 733-4500. Fax: (301) 733-0040.E-mail: info@1069theeagle.com Web Site:www.1069theeagle.com Population served: 250,000 Natl. Network: Westwood One, . Format: Classic hits. News staff: 2.

***WZXH(FM)**— 2009: 91.7 mhz; 900 w. Ant 423 ft TL: N39 27 39 W77 41 58. Hrs open:
Rebroadcasts WBYO(FM) Sellersville, PA 100%.
Box 186, Sellersville, PA, 18960. Phone: (215) 721-2141. Fax: (215) 721-9811. Web Site:www.wordfm.org Licensee: Four Rivers Community Broadcasting Corp. Format: Christian. ◆Charles W. Loughery, pres & gen mgr.

Halfway

WDLD(FM)—Licensed to Halfway. See Hagerstown

WHAG(AM)—Licensed to Halfway. See Hagerstown

Havre de Grace

WJSS(AM)— May 15, 1948: 1330 khz; 5 kw-D, 500 w-N, DA-N. TL: N39 33 55 W76 07 08. Hrs open: 24 1605 Level Rd., 21078. Phone: (410) 939-0800. Fax: (410) 939-2156.E-mail: info@wjss.com Web Site:www.wjss1330.com Licensee: Benjamin-Dane LLC (acq 5-12-2004; $350,000). Population served: 2,000,000 Format: News/talk. Target aud: General. ◆Ronald Reeves, pres & gen mgr.

WXCY(FM)— June 19, 1960: 103.7 mhz; 50 kw. 341 ft TL: N39 33 55 W76 07 08. Stereo. Hrs open: 24 Box 269, 707 Revolution St., 21078. Phone: (410) 939-1100. Fax: (410) 939-1104.E-mail: wxcy@wxcyfm.com Web Site:www.wxcyfm.com Licensee: Delmarva Broadcasting Co. (group owner) Wire Svc: Metro Weather Service Inc. Format: Modern country. News staff: 2. Target aud: 25-54. Spec prog: Relg 2 hrs, NASCAR info updates on race day 6 hrs wkly. ◆Pete Booker, CEO, pres; Willis Schenk, chmn; Bob Bloom, gen mgr; Bob Mercer, opns dir.

Hurlock

WAAI(FM)— June 1, 1989: 100.9 mhz; 1.3 kw. 502 ft TL: N38 37 28 W75 53 20. Stereo. Hrs open: 24 Box 237, Cambridge, 21613. Secondary address: 2 Bay St., Cambridge 21613. Phone: (410) 228-4800. Fax: (410) 228-0130.E-mail: waai@mtslive.com Web Site:www.mtslive.com Licensee: MTS Broadcasting. (group owner; acq 1-30-97). Population served: 30,000 Natl. Network: USA, . Format: Country. News staff: one; News: 6 hrs wkly. Target aud: 25-54; general. Spec prog: Gospel 3 hrs wkly. ◆Thomas Mulitz, pres; Troy Hill, gen mgr; Shane Walker, opns mgr, progmg dir; Thomas Latimer, sls dir; Bryan Harz, chief of engrg.

Indian Head

WWGB(AM)— June 1986: 1030 khz; 50 kw-D, DA. TL: N38 33 53 W76 49 01. Stereo. Hrs open: Sunrise-sunset 5210 Auth Rd., Suite 500, Suitland, 20746. Phone: (301) 899-1444. Fax: (301) 899-7244.E-mail: radio@wwgb.com Web Site:www.wwgb.com Licensee: Good Body Media LLC. (acq 7-15-2002). Population served: 100,000 Roy F. Perkins. Format: Sp, Christian. ◆Ruth Salmeron, stn mgr.

La Plata

WKIK(AM)— October 1965: 1560 khz; 1 kw-D. TL: N38 32 36 W76 59 37. Hrs open: 12 Box 2908, 20646. Phone: (301) 870-5550.E-mail: wsmdfm@aol.com Licensee: Somar Communications Inc. (group owner; acq 4-12-91; $65,000; 5-6-91). Natl. Network: ABC, . Format: Country. News: 5 hrs wkly. Target aud: 25-54. Spec prog: Local news, Baltimore Ravens football. ◆Roy Robertson, gen mgr; Terrell Soellner, opns mgr.

Laurel

WILC(AM)— Dec 23, 1965: 900 khz; 1.9 kw-D, 500 w-N. TL: N39 04 57 W76 50 19. Hrs open: 5 AM-4 AM 13499 Baltimore Ave., Suite 200, 20707. Phone: (301) 419-2122. Fax: (301) 419-2409.E-mail: viva900@tvcontacto.net Web Site:www.radiovivc900.com Licensee: ZGS Radio Inc. (acq 2-11-02; $5.5 million). Population served: 200,000 Natl. Network: CNN Radio, . Natl. Rep: Univision Radio National Sales,. Format: Sp, adult contemp. News: 10 hrs wkly. Target aud: General. ◆Patricia Omana, gen mgr; Sergio Uriola, mus dir.

Lexington Park

WMDM(FM)— Dec 16, 1976: 97.7 mhz; 6 kw. Ant 328 ft TL: N38 16 58 W76 33 39. Stereo. Hrs open: 28095 Three Notch Rd., Suite 2-B, Mechanicsville, 20659. Phone: (301) 870-5550. Web Site:www.977therocket.com Licensee: Somar Communications Inc. (group owner; (acq 2-12-2001; $2.25 million with WPTX(AM) Lexington Park including three-year, $100,000 noncompete agreement) Population served: 100,000 Format: Rock. Target aud: 25-54. ◆Roy Robertson, gen mgr, progmg dir; Sharon Robertson, sr VP & gen sls mgr; Patrick Wood, traf mgr.

WPTX(AM)— July 1998: 1690 khz; 10 kw-D, 1 kw-N. TL: N38 16 57 W76 33 35. Hrs open: Box 2908, La Plata, 20646. Phone: (301) 870-5550.E-mail: wsmdfm@aol.com Licensee: Somar Communications Inc. (group owner; (acq 2-12-2001; $2.25 million with WMDM(FM) Lexington Park including three-year, $100,000 noncompete agreement) Format: News/talk. ◆Roy Robertson, gen mgr, progmg dir; Terrell Soellner, opns mgr; Sharon Robertson, gen sls mgr.

Mechanicsville

WSMD-FM— Sept 1, 1988: 98.3 mhz; 3 kw. Ant 328 ft TL: N38 24 49 W76 46 31. Stereo. Hrs open: 24 Box 2908, La Plata, 20646. Phone: (301) 870-5550.E-mail: wsmdfm@aol.com Licensee: Somar Communications Inc. (group owner). Natl. Network: ABC, . Format: 80s, 90s and today. News staff: one; News: 6 hrs wkly. Target aud: 25-54. Spec prog: Local news. ◆Roy Robertson, pres, gen mgr, progmg dir; Terrell Soellner, opns mgr; Sharon Robertson, gen sls mgr.

Middletown

WAFY(FM)— May 7, 1990: 103.1 mhz; 1 kw. Ant 571 ft TL: N39 25 05 W77 30 03. Stereo. Hrs open: 24 5742 Industry Ln., Frederick, 21704. Phone: (301) 620-7700. Fax: (301) 620-1031. Fax: (301) 696-0509. Web Site:www.key103radio.com Licensee: Nassau Broadcasting III L.L.C. (acq 2-14-2005; $15.7 million). Natl. Rep: Katz Radio,. Dickstein Shapiro Morin & Oshinsky. Format: Adult contemp. News staff: 2. Target aud: 25-54; upscale, well-educated, great radio commitment. ◆Rick Musselman, COO, exec VP, gen mgr; Larry Veihmeyer, sls dir; Mick Rapeer, chief of engrg; Dan Stevens, disc jockey.

Midland

WVMD(FM)— 2008: 99.5 mhz; 1.05 kw. Ant 787 ft TL: N39 40 29.5 W78 57 43.3. Hrs open: 15 Industrial Blvd., Cumberland, 21502. Phone: (301) 759-1005. Fax: (301) 759-3124. Licensee: West Virginia Radio Corp. of the Alleghenies. (acq 1-18-2007; $375,000 for CP). Format: Country. ◆Dale B. Miller, pres; Brian Mo, progmg dir; Jerry Hannahs, sls.

***WYUR(FM)**—Not on air, target date: unknown: 88.3 mhz; 2 w vert. Ant 1,351 ft TL: N39 34 51 W78 54 01. Hrs open: 4271 Muncy-Exchange Rd., Turbotville, PA, 17772. Phone: (570) 412-6295. Licensee: Muncy Hills Broadcasting Inc. ◆Van A. Michael, pres.

Morningside

WHFS(AM)— October 1954: 1580 khz; 50 kw-D, 250 w-N, DA. TL: N38 52 07 W76 53 48. Hrs open: 24 4200 Parliament Place, Suite

300, Lanham, 20706. Phone: (301) 918-0955. Fax: (301) 459-9509. Web Site:www.bigtalker1580.com Licensee: CBS Radio WPGC(AM) Inc. (group owner; (acq 1994; with co-located FM). Population served: 756,510 Leventhal, Senter & Lerman. Format: Conservative talk. Target aud: 18-54. ◆Sam Rogers, gen mgr.

WPGC-FM— February 1959: 95.5 mhz; 50 kw. Ant 500 ft TL: N38 51 48 W76 54 38. Stereo. Hrs open: 24 4200 Parliament Place, Suite 300, Lanham, 20706. Phone: (301) 918-0955. Fax: (301) 459-9509. Web Site:www.wpgc955.com Licensee: CBS Radio Inc. of Maryland. Format: CHR. Target aud: 18-54.

Mountain Lake Park

WKHJ(FM)— July 9, 1990: 104.5 mhz; 1.5 kw. 663 ft TL: N39 24 37 W79 17 15. Stereo. Hrs open: 24 Box 2337, 21550. Phone: (301) 334-4272. Fax: (301) 334-2152.E-mail: wkhj@verizon.net Licensee: Southern Highlands Inc. (acq 11-14-2005). Population served: 100,000 Natl. Network: CNN Radio, . Format: Hot adult contemp. News staff: one; News: 12 hrs wkly. Target aud: 18-49. ◆Pam Trickett, prom mgr; Terry King, gen mgr, opns mgr, gen sls mgr & mus dir; James Shaffer, news dir; Paul Mullan, chief of engrg.

Oakland

WKHJ(FM)—See Mountain Lake Park

WMSG(AM)— May 19, 1963: 1050 khz; 1 kw-D, 75 w-N. TL: N39 25 15 W79 25 00. Hrs open: Box 449, 21550. Phone: (301) 334-3800. Fax: (301) 334-2152. Licensee: Oakland Media Group Inc. (acq 11-14-2005; with co-located FM). Population served: 1,786 Natl. Network: CBS, . Format: Adult standard. Target aud: General. ◆Paul Mullan, gen mgr & opns mgr.

WWHC(FM)— 1966: 92.3 mhz; 1.4 w. 689 ft TL: N39 26 41 W79 31 42. Stereo. Hrs open: Prog sep from AM Box 449, 21550. Phone: (301) 334-3800. Fax: (301) 334-2152. Licensee: Oakland Media Group Population served: 2,500 Natl. Network: ABC, . Format: Country. ◆Paul Mullen, gen mgr; Paul Mullen, opns mgr.

Ocean City

WKHZ(AM)— July 1, 1960: 1590 khz; 1 kw-D, 500 w-N, DA-2. TL: N38 24 16 W75 07 37. Hrs open: 24 11500 Coastal Hwy., Sea Watch Suite #1, 21842. Secondary address: 12216 Parklawn Dr., Suite 203, Rockville 20852. Phone: (410) 723-9100.E-mail: wkhz1590@aol.com Web Site:khzradio.com Licensee: Radio Broadcast Communications Inc. (acq 2-2001). Population served: 550,000 Format: Top 40. News: 2 hrs wkly. Target aud: 25-54; active, thinking, responsive, affluent adults, with high disposable income. ◆Bill Parris, pres & gen mgr.

WOCQ(FM)—See Berlin

WOSC(FM)—See Bethany Beach, DE

*WRAU(FM)—Not on air, target date: unknown: 88.3 mhz; 50 kw. Ant 492 kw TL: N38 23 12 W75 17 27. Hrs open: c/o WAMU(FM) - Brandywine Bldg., 4400 Massachusetts Ave. N.W., Washington, DC, 20016-8082. Phone: (202) 885-1200. Fax: (202) 885-1269. Licensee: Exec. Comm. of Bd. of Trustees of American University. ◆Caryn Mathes, gen mgr.

*WSDL(FM)— Feb 13, 1998: 90.7 mhz; 15 kw. Ant 331 ft TL: N38 30 06 W75 10 07. Stereo. Hrs open: 24 Box 2596, Salisbury, 21802. Phone: (410) 543-6895. Fax: (410) 548-3000.E-mail: prd@salisbury.edu Web Site:www.wscl.org Licensee: Salisbury State University Foundation Inc. Natl. Network: NPR, PRI, . Format: News/talk. News staff: one; News: 24 hrs wkly. Target aud: General. ◆Gerry Weston, gen mgr.

WWFG(FM)— June 30, 1978: 99.9 mhz; 38 kw. Ant 469 ft TL: N38 25 20 W75 08 23. Hrs open: Gateway Crossing, 351 Tilghman Rd., Salisbury, 21804. Phone: (410) 742-1923. Fax: (410) 742-2329.E-mail: froggyemail@yahoo.com Web Site:www.froggy999 .com Licensee: Capstar TX L.P. Group owner: Clear Channel Communications Inc. (acq 8-7-00; grpsl). Natl. Rep: Clear Channel,. Format: Country. Target aud: 25-54; affluent, upwardly mobile. ◆Frank Hamilton, gen mgr; Brian Cleary, opns mgr; Dixie Penner, prom dir; Marie Merrill, traf mgr.

*WYPO(FM)— Apr 15, 1994: 106.9 mhz; 4.5 kw. Ant 384 ft TL: N38 19 39 W75 11 50. Stereo. Hrs open: 2216 N. Charles St., Baltimore, 21218. Phone: (410) 235-1660. Fax: (410) 235-1161. Web Site:www.wypr.org Licensee: WYPR License Holding LLC (acq 11-27-2007; $1.08 million). Natl. Network: NPR, PRI, . Format: News/talk, jazz. ◆Anthony Brandon, gen mgr.

Ocean City-Salisbury

WQHQ(FM)—Licensed to Ocean City-Salisbury. See Salisbury

Ocean Pines

WQJZ(FM)— March 1994: 97.1 mhz; 4.6 kw. 374 ft TL: N38 22 75 W75 10 32. Stereo. Hrs open: 24 Box 909, Salisbury, 21803. Secondary address: 919 Ellegood St., Salisbury 21801. Phone: (410) 219-3500. Fax: (410) 548-1543.E-mail: wqjz@radiocenter.com Web Site:www.wqjz.com Licensee: Delmarva Broadcasting Co. (group owner; acq 6-26-97; grpsl). Natl. Rep: Katz Radio,. Wire Svc: AP Format: Smooth jazz. News staff: 3. Target aud: 30-60. ◆Joe Beail, gen mgr, gen sls mgr; Joe Edwards, opns mgr.

Owings Mills

WCBM(AM)—See Baltimore

Pikesville

WVIE(AM)— Apr 5, 1955: 1370 khz; 50 kw-D, 7.7 kw-N, DA-2. TL: N39 26 23 W76 21 20. Hrs open: Hilton Plaza, 1726 Reisterstown, Suite 117, Baltimore, 21208. Phone: (410) 580-6800. Fax: (410) 580-6810.E-mail: bcarl@wcbm.com Web Site:www.v1370.com Licensee: M-10 Broadcasting Inc. (acq 6-12-98; $1.1 million with WJSS(AM) Havre de Grace). Population served: 2,500,000 Natl. Network: Fox Sports, . Format: Sports. ◆Nick Mangione Jr., sr VP, opns mgr; Bob Pettit, gen mgr; Terry Trouyet, opns dir; Marc Beavin, gen sls mgr; Eddie Applefeld, prom.

Pocomoke City

WCRW(AM)—Not on air, target date: unknown: 1070 khz; 500 w-D, 250 w-N, DA-2. TL: N38 04 45 W75 34 34. Hrs open: 1637 Dunn Swamp Rd., 21851-3300. Phone: (410) 957-6081. Fax: (410) 957-6080. Licensee: Bay Broadcasting Inc. ◆Michael Powell, gen mgr.

WGOP(AM)— Aug 1, 1955: 540 khz; 500 w-D, 243 w-N. TL: N38 03 11 W75 34 11. (CP: COL: Damascus, 1 kw-U, DA-2. TL: N39 17 46 W77 13 12). Hrs open: 1637 Dunn Swamp Rd., 21851. Phone: (410) 957-6081. Fax: (410) 957-6080.E-mail: bay979@gmail.com Web Site:www.easternshoreradio.com Licensee: Birach Broadcasting Corp. (group owner; acq 11-25-92; $127,500;12-14-92). Population served: 80,000 Pepper & Corazzini. Format: Adult standards. ◆Michael Powell, gen mgr; Choppy Layton, opns dir, mus dir, farm dir.

WICO-FM— October 2000: 92.5 mhz; 2.95 kw. Ant 472 ft TL: N38 08 35 W75 39 53. Hrs open: Box 909, Salisbury, 21803. Phone: (410) 219-3500. Fax: (410) 548-1543.E-mail: max925@radiocenter.com Web Site:www.wicotalk.com Licensee: Delmarva Broadcasting Co. (group owner; acq 7-10-2000; $425,000). Natl. Rep: Katz Radio,. Hogan & Hartson. Wire Svc: AP Format: Talk. News staff: one; News: 2 hrs wkly. Target aud: Adults 35-54; baby boomers. ◆Joe Beail, gen mgr; Joe Edwards, opns mgr & progmg mgr; Bill Reddish, news dir; Jeff Twilley, chief of engrg.

WXSH(FM)— May 1, 1992: 106.1 mhz; 4 kw. Ant 341 ft TL: N38 04 36 W75 32 18. Hrs open: 1637 Dunn Swamp Rd., 21851. Phone: (410) 957-6081. Fax: (410) 957-6080.E-mail: bay979@gmail.com Licensee: Great Scott Broadcasting. (group owner; (acq 7-16-99; $700,000 with WKHI(FM) Fruitland). Cohn & Marks. ◆Michael Powell, gen mgr.

Potomac-Cabin John

WCTN(AM)— 1965: 950 khz; 2.5 kw-D, 47 w-N, DA-2. TL: N39 02 12 W77 12 09. Hrs open: 24 7825 Tucker Ln., Suite 217, Potomac, 20854. Phone: (301) 424-9292. Fax: (301) 879-2562. Licensee: Win Radio Broadcasting Corp. (acq 1-15-2004; $2.2 million). Population served: 2,500,000 Fisher, Wayland, Cooper, Leader & Zaragoza L.L.P. Format: Oldies. ◆Richard S. Yoon, pres; Mauricio Rosales, gen mgr.

Prince Frederick

WWXT(FM)— August 1971: 92.7 mhz; 2.85 kw. Ant 476 ft TL: N38 40 26 W76 35 40. Stereo. Hrs open: 24 8121 Georgia Ave., Suite 1050, Silver Spring, 20910. Phone: (301) 562-5800. Fax: (301) 562-5850. Web Site:www.espn980.com Licensee: Red Zebra Broadcasting Licensee LLC. Group owner: Mega Communications Inc. (acq 5-9-2006; grpsl). Population served: 500,000 Natl. Network: ESPN Radio, . Format: Sports. ◆Bruce Gilbert, CEO.

Princess Anne

*WESM(FM)— Mar 29, 1987: 91.3 mhz; 50 kw. 347 ft TL: N38 12 37 W75 40 56. Stereo. Hrs open: 24 Univ. of Maryland Eastern Shore, Backbone Rd., 21853. Phone: (410) 651-8001. Fax: (410) 651-8005.E-mail: wesm913@umes.edu Web Site:www.wesm913.org Licensee: University of Maryland Eastern Shore. Population served: 150,000 Natl. Network: NPR, PRI, . Format: Jazz, blues, NPR. News staff: one; News: 15 hrs wkly. Target aud: General. Spec prog: Blues 5 hrs, reggae 2 hrs, big band 10 hrs, gospel 20 hrs wkly. ◆Dr. Thelma B. Thompson, pres; Marva Lovett, gen mgr, mktg dir; Angel Resto Jr., opns VP; Brian Daniels, mktg mgr, progmg; Yancy Carrigan, mus dir.

WOLC(FM)— Dec 24, 1976: 102.5 mhz; 50 kw. Ant 500 ft TL: N38 06 43 W75 39 14. Stereo. Hrs open: 24 Box 130, 21853. Phone: (410) 543-9652. Fax: (410) 651-9652.E-mail: wolc@wolc.org Web Site:www.wolc.org Licensee: Maranatha Inc. Population served: 200,000 Shainis - Peltzman. Format: Relg. Target aud: 25-64. ◆Robert L. Shores, pres; Deborah G. Byrd, gen mgr; Jack Tucker, gen sls mgr; Rodney Baylous, progmg dir; Mark Bohnett, chief of engrg.

Rockville

WLXE(AM)— November 1951: 1600 khz; 1 kw-D, 500 w-N, DA-N. TL: N39 05 51 W77 09 07. Hrs open: 24 13321 New Hampshire Ave, Suite 207, Silver Spring, 20904. Phone: (301) 424-9292. Fax: (301) 424-8266. Licensee: Multicultural Radio Broadcasting Licensee LLC. Group owner: Multicultural Radio Broadcasting Inc. (acq 7-31-01; $800,000). Population served: 4,000,000 Format: Sp. ◆Bill Parris, gen mgr.

Saint Mary's City

*WGWS(FM)—Not on air, target date: unknown: 88.1 mhz; 1.9 kw vert. Ant 177 ft TL: N38 09 06 W76 22 41. Hrs open: 46376 Pegg Ln., Lexington Park, 20653. Phone: (301) 862-4435. Licensee: Calvary Baptist Church of Lexington Park Inc. ◆William B. Ruckman, chmn & pres.

Saint Michaels

WINX-FM— 2000: 94.3 mhz; 4.6 kw. Ant 361 ft TL: N38 37 49 W76 03 25. Stereo. Hrs open: 8903 Glebe Park Dr., Easton, 21601. Phone: (410) 770-3939. Fax: (410) 770-5855.E-mail: info@winxfm.com Web Site:www.winxfm.com Licensee: First Media Radio LLC (acq 4-2-2009; $2 million). Format: Country. ◆Steve Kingston, gen mgr; Bill Parris, stn mgr; Cheryl Baynard, gen sls mgr; Don O'Brien, progmg dir.

Salisbury

*WDIH(FM)— June 1990: 90.3 mhz; 378 w. 180 ft TL: N38 24 28 W75 36 16. Hrs open: Box 186, 21801. Phone: (410) 860-5000. Fax: (410) 713-4371.E-mail: biscope@acninc.net Licensee: Salisbury Educational Broadcasting Foundation. Format: Christian preaching & mus, info progmg. ◆Bishop Dr. George Copeland, gen mgr.

WDKZ(FM)— July 25, 1982: 105.5 mhz; 2.1 kw. Ant 384 ft TL: N38 24 26 W75 35 57. Stereo. Hrs open: Gateway Crossing, 351 Tilghman Rd., 21804. Phone: (410) 742-1923. Fax: (410) 742-2329.E-mail: kissfm@kiss1055.com Web Site:www.kiss1055.com Licensee: Aloha Station Trust LLC Group owner: Clear Channel Communications Inc. (acq 7-30-2008; grpsl). Natl. Rep: Clear Channel,. Format: Top-40. News staff: one. Target aud: 18-44. ◆Frank Hamilton, gen mgr; Brian Cleary, opns mgr; Dixie Penner, prom dir; Marie Merrill, traf mgr.

WGOP(AM)—See Pocomoke City

WICO(AM)— September 1957: 1320 khz; 1 kw-D, 36 w-N. TL: N38 21 39 W75 37 00. Hrs open: 24 Box 909, 21803. Secondary address: 919 Ellegood St., Salisbury 21801. Phone: (410) 219-3500. Fax: (410) 548-1543.E-mail: wico@radiocenter.com Web Site:www.wicoam.com Licensee: Delmarva Broadcasting Co. (group owner; acq 6-26-97; grpsl). Population served: 100,000 Natl. . Natl. Rep: Katz Radio,. Hogan & Hartson. Wire Svc: ABC Wire Svc: AP Format: News/talk, sports. News staff: 2; News: 18 hrs wkly. Target aud: 35-64. Spec prog: Farm one hr wkly. ◆Joe Beail, gen mgr, gen sls mgr; Joe Edwards, opns mgr & progmg mgr; Bill Reddish, news dir, pub affrs dir; Jeff Twilley, chief of engrg.

WJDY(AM)— Mar 14, 1958: 1470 khz; 5 kw-D, 500 w-N, DA-D. TL: N38 23 30 W75 38 48. Hrs open: 6 AM-midnight Gateway Crossing, 351 Tilghman Rd., 21804. Phone: (410) 742-1923. Fax: (410)

742-2329.E-mail: billbaker@clearchannel.com Web Site:www.wjdy.com Licensee: Capstar TX L.P. Format: News/talk. ◆John Thomas-Mason, traf mgr.

WKTT(FM)— Sept 3, 1969: 97.5 mhz; 4.5 kw. Ant 299 ft TL: N38 21 39 W75 37 00. Stereo. Hrs open: 24 Rebroadcasts WXJN(FM) Lewes, DE 100%. Box 909, 21803. Secondary address: 919 Ellegood St. 21801. Phone: (410) 219-3500. Fax: (410) 548-1543.E-mail: catcountry@radiocenter.com Web Site:www.catcountryradio.com Licensee: Delmarva Broadcasting Co. Population served: 250,000 Wire Svc: AP Format: Country. News staff: one; News: 3 hrs wkly. Target aud: 25-54. ◆Joe Edwards, chief of opns; E.J. Foxx, mus dir; Brian K. Hall, disc jockey.

WQHQ(FM)—(Ocean City-Salisbury, July 31, 1965: 104.7 mhz; 33 kw. 610 ft TL: N38 23 15 W75 17 30. Stereo. Hrs open: Prog sep from AM 351 Tilghman Rd., 21804. Phone: (410) 742-1923. Fax: (410) 742-2329. Web Site:www.q105fm.com Arent, Fox, Kintner, Plotkin & Kahn. Format: Adult contemp. Target aud: 25-54.

WSBY-FM— Dec 13, 1989: 98.9 mhz; 6 kw. 328 ft TL: N38 18 00 W75 37 41. Hrs open: 24 Gateway Crossing, 351 Tilghman Rd., 21804. Phone: (410) 742-1923. Fax: (410) 742-2329.E-mail: billbaker@clearchannel.com Web Site:www.wsby.com Licensee: Capstar TX L.P. Group owner: Clear Channel Communications Inc. (acq 8-7-00; grpsl). Population served: 250,000 Mullin, Rhyne, Emmons & Topel. Format: Urban contemp. News staff: one. Target aud: 25-54. ◆Frank Hamilton, gen mgr; Brian Cleary, opns mgr, news dir; Ed Fennessy, gen sls mgr; Bill Baker, progmg dir; Kenny Love, chief of engrg; Marie Merrill, traf mgr.

*WSCL(FM)— May 29, 1987: 89.5 mhz; 33 kw. 600 ft TL: N38 39 15 W75 36 42. Stereo. Hrs open: 24 Box 2596, 21802. Secondary address: S. Salisbury Blvd. 21802. Phone: (410) 543-6895. Fax: (410) 548-3000.E-mail: prd@salisbury.edu Web Site:www.wscl.org Licensee: Salisbury State University Foundation Inc. Population served: 415,800 Natl. Network: NPR, PRI, AP Radio, . Format: Class, news. News staff: one; News: 29 hrs wkly. Target aud: General. ◆Gerry Weston, gen mgr; Pamela Andrews, progmg dir; Bill Bukowski, opns.

WTGM(AM)— Sept 13, 1940: 960 khz; 5 kw-U, DA-2. TL: N38 25 44 W75 37 26. Stereo. Hrs open: 24 351 Tilghman Rd., 21804-1891. Phone: (410) 742-1923. Fax: (410) 742-2329. Web Site:www.sportstalk960.com Licensee: Capstar TX L.P. Group owner: Clear Channel Communications Inc. (acq 8-7-00; grpsl). Population served: 250,000 Format: Sports. News staff: one. Target aud: 25-64. ◆Frank Hamilton, gen mgr; John Thomas-Mason, traf mgr.

WWFG(FM)—See Ocean City

Silver Spring

WIHT(FM)—See Washington, DC

WWRC(AM)—See Washington, DC

WZAA(AM)—Licensed to Silver Spring. See Washington DC

Snow Hill

WQMR(FM)— February 2004: 101.1 mhz; 1.2 kw. Ant 489 ft TL: N38 12 57 W75 19 21. Stereo. Hrs open: 24 Snow Hill Broadcasting L.L.C., 7200 Coastal Hwy., Suite 101, Ocean City, 21843. Phone: (410) 524-6862. Fax: (410) 524-6808.E-mail: kevin@wqmr.com Web Site:www.wqmr.com Licensee: Snow Hill Broadcasting L.L.C. (acq 5-21-2004; $200,000). Population served: 296,100 Format: News/talk, sports. Target aud: 18-64 Persons. Spec prog: Power Talk(local) Travel Show/Car Doc/Garison Show/ Tasting Room/ Satellite Sisters. ◆Jack Gillen, pres, gen mgr; Kevin Brenahan, VP; Corey Duices, progmg dir; Heather Renee Shingleton, news dir.

Takoma Park

*WGTS(FM)— May 8, 1957: 91.9 mhz; 23.5 kw. Ant 610 ft TL: N38 53 30 W77 07 55. Stereo. Hrs open: 24 7600 Flower Ave., 20912. Phone: (301) 891-4200. Fax: (301) 270-9191.E-mail: wgts@wgts919.com Web Site:www.wgts919.com Licensee: Columbia Union College Broadcasting Inc. Format: Educ, relg. Target aud: General. ◆Gerry Fuller, chmn; John Konrad, gen mgr; Becky Wilson Ali Gray, progmg dir.

Thurmont

WTHU(AM)— June 12, 1967: 1450 khz; 500 w-D, 400 w-N. TL: N39 37 37 W77 24 11. Hrs open: 24 10 Radio Ln., 21788. Phone: (310) 271-2188. Licensee: Christian Radio Coalition Inc. (acq 6-9-2008; $150,000). Format: Christian. ◆Michael Betteridge, pres.

Towson

WLIF(FM)—See Baltimore

WNST(AM)— Oct 27, 1955: 1570 khz; 5 kw-D, 236 w-N. TL: N39 25 04 W76 33 23. Hrs open: 1550 Hart Rd., Baltimore, 21286. Phone: (410) 821-9678. Fax: (410) 828-4698.E-mail: nasty@wnst.net Web Site:www.wnst.net Licensee: Nasty 1570 Sports LLC. (acq 1-11-01; $1 million). Population served: 200,000 Format: Sports. ◆Paul Kopelke, gen mgr; Steve Hennessey, gen sls mgr.

*WTMD(FM)— Feb 12, 1976: 89.7 mhz; 10.16 kw. 236 ft TL: N39 23 45 W76 36 29. Stereo. Hrs open: 24 8000 York Rd., 21252. Phone: (410) 704-8938. Fax: (410) 704-2609.E-mail: wtmd@towson.edu Web Site:www.wtmd.org Licensee: Towson University. Population served: 2,088,400 Format: AAA. News: 6 hrs wkly. Target aud: 25-64. ◆Stephen Yasko, gen mgr; Mike Vasilikos, progmg dir; Mike Matthews, mus dir.

Waldorf

WPRS-FM— February 1965: 104.1 mhz; 20 kw. Ant 800 ft TL: N38 37 07 W76 50 42. Stereo. Hrs open: 24 5900 Princess Garden Pkwy., 8th Fl., Lanhan, 20706. Phone: (301) 306-1111.E-mail: info@praise1041.com Web Site:www.praise1041.com Licensee: Radio One Licenses LLC. Group owner: Bonneville International Corp. (acq 9-5-2007). Population served: 2,800,000 Format: Black gospel. ◆Michele Williams, gen mgr.

Walkersville

WDMV(AM)— December 1994: Stn currently dark. 700 khz; 5 kw-D, DA. TL: N39 27 27 W77 19 27. Hrs open: 3975 Fair Ridge Dr., Suite 200, Fairfax, VA, 22033. Phone: (703) 272-7600. Fax: (703) 272-7604.E-mail: sima@dcradio.com Web Site:www.birach.com Licensee: Birach Broadcasting Corp. (group owner; acq 9-95). ◆Sima Birach, pres & gen mgr.

Westernport

WWPN(FM)— Oct 1, 1993: 101.1 mhz; 6 kw. -541 ft TL: N39 29 14 W79 03 13. Stereo. Hrs open: Box 3382, Lavale, 21502. Phone: (301) 463-5100. Licensee: Ernest F. Santmyire. Population served: 2,000,000 Format: Relg, contemp Christian. Target aud: 18-45; working class. ◆Ernest F. Santmyire, CEO & gen mgr.

Westminster

WTTR(AM)— July 1953: 1470 khz; 1 kw-U, DA-N. TL: N39 34 37 W77 01 21. Hrs open: 24 101 WTTR Ln., 21158. Phone: (410) 876-1515. Fax: (410) 876-5095.E-mail: info@wttr.com Web Site:www.wttr.com Licensee: Sajak Broadcasting Corp. (acq 12-20-2004; $540,000). Population served: 160,000 Format: Classic Hits (Kool Gold). News staff: one; News: 12 hrs wkly. Target aud: 35-64. Spec prog: Farm 4 hrs wkly. ◆Pat Sajak, CEO; Steve Hopp, gen mgr; Dwight Dingle, stn mgr, mus dir; Mark Woodworth, news dir, pub affrs dir.

WZBA(FM)— Nov 1, 1959: 100.7 mhz; 27 kw. Ant 660 ft TL: N39 27 01 W76 46 37. Stereo. Hrs open: 24 11350 McCormick Rd., Executive Plaza 3, Suite 701, Hunt Valley, 21031. Phone: (410) 771-8484. Fax: (410) 771-1616.E-mail: jlaird@thebayonline.com Web Site:www.thebayonline.com Licensee: Shamrock Communications Inc. (group owner; acq 4-7-81; $1.74 million with co-located AM;5-4-81). Population served: 1000000 Format: Classic rock. News: one hr wkly. Target aud: 25-49; men & women active in the country life group. ◆Jeff Laird, gen mgr; Lynn Pollvoy, gen sls mgr; Jon McGann, progmg dir; Dave Schmidt, chief of engrg; Laura Sigler, traf mgr.

Wheaton

WACA(AM)— 1954: 1540 khz; 5 kw-D. TL: N39 00 50 W77 01 46. Hrs open: 11141 Georgia Ave., Suite 310, 20902. Phone: (301) 942-3500. Fax: (301) 942-7798.E-mail: news@radioamerica.net Web Site:www.radioamerica.net Licensee: Entravision Holdings LLC. Group owner: Entravision Communications Corp. (acq 3-14-00; grpsl). Leventhal, Senter & Lerman. Format: Sp. Target aud: General; Hispanic, Central & Latin American, Caribbean listeners. ◆Alejandro Carrasco, gen mgr.

WASH(FM)—See Washington, DC

Williamsport

*WCRH(FM)— July 24, 1976: 90.5 mhz; 10 kw. Ant 884 ft TL: N39 39 34 W77 57 56. Stereo. Hrs open: 24 Box 439, 21795. Secondary address: 12146 Cedar Ridge Rd. 21795. Phone: (301) 582-0285. Fax: (301) 582-2707.E-mail: wcrh@wcrh.org Web Site:www.wcrh.org Licensee: Cedar Ridge Children's Home and School Inc. Population served: 1,000,000 Natl. Network: Moody, . Hardy, Carey & Chautin, L.L.P. Format: Relg. News staff: one; News: 9 hrs wkly. Target aud: 25-45. ◆David Swacina, CEO; Jeff Ward, opns mgr.

WICL(FM)— Nov 15, 1972: 95.9 mhz; 3 kw. 300 ft TL: N39 36 17 W77 46 49. Stereo. Hrs open: 24 1606 W. King St., Martinsburg, WV, 25401. Phone: (304) 263-8868. Fax: (304) 263-8906. Web Site:www.cool959.com Licensee: Prettyman Broadcasting Co. (group owner; acq 3-10-98; $1.05 million). Population served: 500,000 Dow, Lohnes, & Albertson, PLLC. Format: True Oldies. News: 15 hrs wkly. Target aud: 35-64. ◆Norm Slemenda, gen mgr.

Worton

*WKHS(FM)— Mar 28, 1974: 90.5 mhz; 17.5 kw. 215 ft TL: N39 16 55 W76 05 26. Stereo. Hrs open: Box 905, 21678. Secondary address: Rts. 297 & 298 21678. Phone: (410) 778-4249. Fax: (410) 778-3802.E-mail: wkhs@kent.k12.md.us Licensee: Board of Education of Kent County. Population served: 20,000 Format: Div. Target aud: 12 plus. Spec prog: Oldies 6 hrs, children 5 hrs, country 2 hrs, big band 2 hrs, rhythm and blues 2 hrs, jazz 2 hrs wkly. ◆Steve Kramarck, gen mgr.

Massachusetts

Acton

*WHAB(FM)— Aug 1, 1979: 89.1 mhz; 9.1 w. 53 ft TL: N42 28 48 W71 27 28. Hrs open: 10 AM-5:30 PM (M-F) Acton Boxboro Regional High School, 36 Charter Rd., 01720. Phone: (978) 264-4700, EXT. 3470. Web Site:www.quadphonic.com Licensee: Acton-Boxborough Regional School District. Format: Div, news. ◆Dan Drinkwater, gen mgr.

Allston

WGBH(FM)—See Boston

Amherst

*WAMH(FM)— 1955: 89.3 mhz; 150 w. 718 ft TL: N42 21 51 W72 25 24. Stereo. Hrs open: 24 AC# 1907Campus Center, 2171 Amherst College, 01002-5000. Phone: (413) 542-2224. Phone: (413) 542-2288.E-mail: wamh@amherst.edu Web Site:www.amherst.edu/~wamh Licensee: Trustees of Amherst College. Population served: 17,926 Format: Var/div. News: 2 hrs wkly. Target aud: 16-32; youth of today. ◆Claire Kiechel, gen mgr.

*WFCR(FM)— May 6, 1961: 88.5 mhz; 13 kw. Ant 895 ft TL: N42 21 49 W72 25 24. Stereo. Hrs open: 24 131 County Circle, Hampshire House, Univ. of Mass., 01003-9257. Phone: (413) 545-0100. Fax: (413) 545-2546.E-mail: radio@wfcr.org Web Site:www.wfcr.org Licensee: University of Massachusetts. Population served: 1,183,119 Natl. Network: PRI, NPR, . Wiley, Rein & Fielding. Wire Svc: AP Format: News, classical, jazz. News staff: 6; News: 40 hrs wkly. Target aud: General. Spec prog: Sp 2 hrs wkly. ◆Martin Miller, gen mgr.

*WMUA(FM)— 1949: 91.1 mhz; 1 kw. 26 ft TL: N42 23 31 W72 31 13. Stereo. Hrs open: 24 Univ. of Massachusetts, 105 Campus Ctr., 01003. Phone: (413) 545-2876. Fax: (413) 545-0682.E-mail: adviser@wmua.org Web Site:www.wmua.org Licensee: Board of Trustees of University of Massachusetts. Population served: 1,000,000 Format: Var/div. News: 3 hrs wkly. Target aud: General; Univ. ◆Zach Claudio, gen mgr; Leila Denna, progmg dir; Corey Charron, mus dir; Dan Ferreira, chief of engrg.

WPNI(AM)— Apr 2, 1963: 1430 khz; 5 kw-D, DA. TL: N42 21 25 W72 29 13. Hrs open: 6 AM-midnight 1331 Main St., Suite 4, Springfield, 01103. Phone: (413) 536-1105. Fax: (413) 536-1153. Web Site:www.wpni.org Licensee: 6 Johnson Road Licenses Inc. Group owner: Pamal Broadcasting Ltd. (acq 5-29-2003; $8 million with co-located FM). Population served: 17926 Ginsburg, Feldman & Bress. Format: News/talk info.

WRNX(FM)— Nov 12, 1990: 100.9 mhz; 1.35 kw. Ant 692 ft TL: N42 18 24 W72 31 59. Hrs open: 1331 Main St., 4th Fl., Springfield, 01103. Phone: (413) 781-1011. Fax: (413) 734-4434. Web Site:www.wrnx.com Licensee: CC Licenses LLC. (acq 4-1-2007; grpsl). Format: AAA. ♦Sean Davey, gen mgr.

Andover

WXRV(FM)— June 1959: 92.5 mhz; 25 kw. Ant 712 ft TL: N42 46 23 W71 06 01. Stereo. Hrs open: 24 30 How St., Haverhill, 01830. Phone: (978) 374-4733. Fax: (978) 373-8023.E-mail: info@wxrv.com Web Site:www.wxrv.com Licensee: Beanpot License Corp. Group owner: Northeast Broadcasting Co. Inc. (acq 1981). Population served: 2,000,000 Format: AAA, adult contemp. Target aud: 25-54. ♦Terry Lieberman, gen mgr; Steve Young, gen sls mgr, chief of engrg; Ron Bowen, progmg dir, mus dir.

Ashland

WSRO(AM)— May 1967: 650 khz; 250 w-D. TL: N42 17 17 W71 25 53. Hrs open: 100 Mt. Wayte Ave., Framingham, 01702. Phone: (508) 424-2568. Fax: (508) 820-2473.E-mail: wsroam650@yahoo.com Web Site:www.wsro.com Licensee: Langer Broadcasting Group L.L.C. (group owner; acq 1996; $10,000). Format: Talk, relg. Target aud: 20-80; general. ♦Carl Abrams, gen mgr.

Athol

WJOE(AM)—See Orange-Athol

WXRG(FM)— Dec 4, 1989: 99.9 mhz; 1.85 kw. Ant 407 ft TL: N42 35 39 W72 12 02. Stereo. Hrs open: 24 362 Green St., Gardner, 01440. Phone: (978) 630-3473. Fax: (978) 630-3011.E-mail: info@theeagle.com Web Site:www.theeagle999.com Licensee: County Broadcasting Co. LLC. Group owner: Northeast Broadcasting Company Inc. (acq 10-6-2003; $650,000 with WJOE(AM) Orange-Athol). Population served: 50,000 Natl. Network: ABC, . Format: Classic rock. ♦Glenn Cardinal, gen mgr; Spencer Marshall, progmg dir.

Attleboro

WARL(AM)— Oct 8, 1950: 1320 khz; 5 kw-U, DA-2. TL: N41 57 33 W71 19 37. Hrs open: 127 Dorrance St., 5th Fl., Providence, RI, 02903. Phone: (508) 989-5013. Fax: (401) 521-5878.E-mail: scott@spojo.com Web Site:www.1320thedrive.com Licensee: The ADD Radio Group Inc. (acq 6-1-98; $600,000). Population served: 800,000 Arent, Fox, Kintner, Plotkin & Kahn. Format: News/talk, sports radio. Target aud: 18 plus; middle to upper middle class. ♦Scott MacPherson, gen mgr.

Baptist Village

***WJCI(FM)**—Not on air, target date: unknown: 89.5 mhz; 40 w horiz, 35 w vert. Ant 384 ft TL: N42 05 01 W72 24 51. Hrs open: 52 New Hartford Rd., Barkhamsted, CT, 06063. Phone: (860) 379-3365. Fax: (860) 828-6109. Web Site:www.junctionradio.org Licensee: Morgan Brook Chirstian Radio Inc. Format: Contemp Christian music. ♦G. Thomas Palmer, pres.

Barnstable

WQRC(FM)— July 20, 1970: 99.9 mhz; 50 kw. 378 ft TL: N41 41 19 W70 20 49. Stereo. Hrs open: 24 737 W. Main St., Hyannis, 02601. Phone: (508) 771-1224. Fax: (508) 775-2605.E-mail: @wqrc.com Web Site:www.wqrc.com Licensee: Sandab Communications Limited Partnership II (group owner; acq 4-16-92; grpsl; 1-13-92). Population served: 225,000 Natl. Network: AP Radio, . Natl. Rep: Clear Channel,. Covington & Burling. Wire Svc: AP Format: Adult contemp. News staff: 4; News: 32 hrs wkly. Target aud: Adults/women; 25-54. ♦Gregory D. Bone, gen mgr; Wayne W. White, opns mgr; Stephen M. Colella, sls dir; Michelle Lorraine, prom mgr; Donna C. Credit, traf mgr.

Bayview

***WPMW(FM)**—Not on air, target date: unknown: 88.5 mhz; 880 w. Ant 164 ft TL: N41 34 50 W71 00 20. Hrs open: 600 Pleasant St., New Bedford, 02740. Phone: (508) 996-8274. Fax: (508) 996-8296. Licensee: Academy of the Immaculate Inc. Natl. Network: EWTN Radio, . ♦Rev. Angelo Geiger, gen mgr.

Beverly

WNSH(AM)— Dec 23, 1963: 1570 khz; 500 w-D, 85 w-N, DA-D. TL: N42 33 22 W70 50 13. (CP: 30 kw-D, 85 w-N). Hrs open: 24 31 Woodbury St., South Hamilton, 01982. Phone: (978) 921-1570. Fax: (978) 468-1954.E-mail: jackwhite@wnsh.com Web Site:www.wnsh.com Licensee: Willow Farm Inc. (acq 9-24-97; $50,000). Population served: 150,000 Format: Women's talk. News staff: 2; News: 15 hrs wkly. Target aud: 35 plus. ♦Jack White, gen mgr.

Boston

WBMX(FM)— May 1968: 104.1 mhz; 20.9 kw. Ant 771 ft TL: N42 20 50 W71 04 59. Stereo. Hrs open: 83 Leo M Birmingham Pkwy., Brighton, 02135. Phone: (617) 746-1400. Fax: (617) 746-1408. Web Site:www.mix1041.com Licensee: Hemisphere Broadcasting Corp. Group owner: Infinity Broadcasting Corp. (acq 11-13-98; grpsl). Population served: 650,000 Natl. Network: CBS, . Format: Hot adult contemp. ♦Mel Karmazin, pres; Tony Berardini, gen mgr.

WBOS(FM)—See Brookline

***WBUR-FM**— March 1950: 90.9 mhz; 7.2 kw. Ant 1,046 ft TL: N42 18 27 W71 13 27. Stereo. Hrs open: 24 890 Commonwealth Ave., 3rd Fl., 02215. Phone: (617) 353-0909. Fax: (617) 353-4747.E-mail: info@wbur.bu.edu Web Site:www.wbur.org Licensee: The Executive Committee of Trustees of The Boston University. Population served: 3,100,000 Natl. Network: NPR, PRI, . Format: News, talk. Target aud: 25-54; intelligent adults interested in news natl, internatl & local. ♦Paul LaCamera, gen mgr, progmg dir; Corey Lewis, stn mgr; Sam Fleming, progmg dir; John Davidow, news dir; Jeff Hutton, engrg dir.

WBZ(AM)— Sept 19, 1921: 1030 khz; 50 kw-U, DA-1. TL: N42 16 44 W70 52 34. Stereo. Hrs open: 24 1170 Soldiers Field Rd., 02134. Phone: (617) 787-7000. Fax: (617) 787-5969. Web Site:www.wbz1030.com Licensee: CBS Radio East Inc. Group owner: Infinity Broadcasting Corp. Population served: 641,071 Natl. Network: ABC, CBS, . Natl. Rep: CBS Radio,. Format: News/talk. Target aud: 25-54. ♦Ted Jordan, gen mgr; Peter Casey, progmg dir, news dir.

WBZ-FM— 1948: 98.5 mhz; 9 kw. Ant 1,145 ft TL: N42 18 27 W71 13 27. Stereo. Hrs open: 24 83 Leo M. Birmingham Pkwy., 02135. Phone: (617) 746-1400. Fax: (617) 779-2002. Web Site:www.cbssports.com/local/boston Licensee: CBS Radio Stations Inc. Group owner: Infinity Broadcasting Corp. (acq 6-5-98; grpsl). Natl. Rep: Christal,. Format: Sports. ♦Mark Hannon, gen mgr; Chris Hill, gen sls mgr; Caroline Murtagh, natl sls mgr; Cha-Chi Loprete, mktg dir; Chris Rucker, prom mgr; Mike Thomas, progmg dir.

WCRB(FM)—See Lowell

WEEI(AM)— Dec 1, 1926: 850 khz; 50 kw-U, DA-2. TL: N42 16 41 W71 16 02. Hrs open: 24 20 Guest St., 3rd Flr., Brighton, 02135-2040. Phone: (617) 779-3500. Fax: (617) 779-3557.E-mail: info@weei.com Web Site:www.weei.com Licensee: Entercom Boston License L.L.C. Group owner: Entercom Communications Corp. (acq 10-15-98; $82 million with WRKO(AM) Boston). Population served: 3,300,000 Natl. Network: CBS, . Format: Sports talk. News staff: 6. Target aud: 25-54. ♦Jason Wolfe, progmg dir, progmg; Julie Kahn, gen mgr & engrg dir; Jim Rushton, chief of engrg, adv.

***WERS(FM)**— Nov 14, 1949: 88.9 mhz; 4 kw. 614 ft TL: N42 21 08 W71 03 25. Stereo. Hrs open: 24 c/o Emerson College, 120 Boylston St., 02116. Phone: (617) 824-8891. Fax: (617) 824-8804.E-mail: howard_simpson@emerson.edu Web Site:www.wers.org Licensee: Emerson College. Population served: 3,000,000 Wire Svc: AP Format: Var. News staff: 6; News: 3.5 hrs wkly. ♦Dr. Jack Casey, gen mgr; Howard D. Simpson, opns mgr; R.J. Perkins, engr.

WEZE(AM)— Sept 29, 1924: 590 khz; 5 kw-U, DA-1. TL: N42 24 24 W71 05 14. Hrs open: 24 308 Victory Rd., North Quincy Phone: (617) 328-0880. Fax: (617) 328-0375.E-mail: A ScottC@salemradioboston.com Web Site:www.wezeradio.com Licensee: Pennsylvania Media Associates Inc. Group owner: Salem Communications Corp. (acq 1-31-97; $6 million). Population served: 5,000,000 Natl. Network: ABC, . Irwin, Campbell, Crowe & Tannenwald. Format: Relg, talk. News: 5 hrs wkly. Target aud: 25 plus. ♦Edward G. Atsinger III, pres; Scott Cohagan, gen mgr.

***WGBH(FM)**— Oct 6, 1951: 89.7 mhz; 98 kw. 650 ft TL: N42 12 42 W71 06 51. Stereo. Hrs open: 24 1 Gwert St., Brighton, 02135. Phone: (617) 300-2000. Fax: (617) 300-1026.E-mail: wgbh@wgbh.org Web Site:www.wgbh.org Licensee: WGBH Educational Foundation. Population served: 330,000 Natl. Network: PRI, NPR, . Format: Class, jazz, news. News: 22 hrs wkly. Target aud: General. Spec prog: Folk 10 hrs, blues 8 hrs, Irish 2 hrs, cultural 3 hrs wkly. ♦John Abbott, pres; Marita Rivero, gen mgr. Co-owned TV: *WGBH-TV, *WGBX-TV affils

WHRB(FM)—See Cambridge

WILD(AM)— 1946: 1090 khz; 5 kw-D. TL: N42 24 40 W71 04 28. Hrs open: 500 Victory Rd., Quincy, 02179. Phone: (617) 471-0618. Fax: (617) 471-4289.E-mail: randerson@radio-one.com Licensee: Radio One of Boston Licenses LLC. Group owner: Radio One Inc. (acq 12-20-2000; $5 million in cash & stock merger). Population served: 2,805,911 Natl. Network: ABC, . Natl. Rep: Roslin,. Format: News/talk. Target aud: General. ♦Rick Anderson, pres & progmg dir.

WJIB(AM)—(Cambridge, 1948: 740 khz; 250 w-D, 5 w-N. TL: N42 23 13 W71 08 21. Stereo. Hrs open: 24 443 Concord Ave., Cambridge, 02138. Phone: (617) 868-7400. Licensee: Bob Bittner Broadcasting Inc. (group owner; acq 9-12-91). Population served: 3,200,000 Format: Adult Standards. News: 3 hrs wkly. Target aud: 40-75; locally-programmed for those enjoying good adult mus. Spec prog: French 10 hrs, gospel 4 hrs wkly. ♦Bob Bittner, pres & gen mgr.

WJMN(FM)— Mar 31, 1948: 94.5 mhz; 11.5 kw. 1,053 ft TL: N42 18 27 W71 13 27. Stereo. Hrs open: 10 Cabot Rd., Suite 302, Medford, 02155. Phone: (781) 663-2500. Fax: (781) 290-0722.E-mail: management@jamn945.com Web Site:www.jamn945.com Licensee: AMFM Radio Licenses L.L.C. Group owner: Clear Channel Communications Inc. (acq 8-30-00; grpsl). Population served: 3,672,000 Natl. Rep: Katz Radio,. Latham & Watkins. Format: Top-40. Target aud: 12-44. ♦Tom McConnell, gen mgr.

WKLB-FM—See Waltham

WMJX(FM)— Jan 6, 1982: 106.7 mhz; 21.5 kw. 750 ft TL: N42 20 50 W71 04 59. Stereo. Hrs open: 55 Morrissey Blvd., 02125. Phone: (617) 822-9600. Fax: (617) 822-6571.E-mail: dkelley@magic1067.com Licensee: Greater Boston Radio Inc. Group owner: Greater Media Inc. (acq 2-85). Population served: 3,300,000 Natl. Rep: Katz Radio,. Format: Adult contemp, soft rock. ♦Phil Redo, gen mgr; Jackie Laudry, gen sls mgr; Don Kelley, progmg dir.

WMKI(AM)— 1922: 1260 khz; 5 kw-U, DA-N. TL: N42 16 30 W71 02 31. Hrs open: 226 Lincoln St., Allston, 02134. Phone: (617) 787-0146. Fax: (617) 787-1236. Web Site:www.disney.com Licensee: Radio Disney Group LLC. Group owner: ABC Inc. (acq 8-22-00; grpsl). Population served: 3000000 Natl. Network: USA, . Format: Family. Target aud: 6-14. ♦Michael Kellogg, gen mgr & stn mgr.

WMKK(FM)—(Lawrence, April 1960: 93.7 mhz; 50 kw. 430 ft TL: N42 40 26 W71 11 26. (CP: 29.5 kw, ant 640 ft. TL: N42 35 42 W71 02 18). Stereo. Hrs open: 24 Entercom Boston, 20 Guest St., 3rd Fl., Brighton, 02135. Phone: (617) 779-5300. Fax: (617) 931-7827.E-mail: info@937mikefm.com Web Site:www.937mikefm.com Licensee: Entercom Boston II License L.L.C. Group owner: Entercom Communications Corp. (acq 10-15-98; grpsl). Population served: 300,000 Format: Var. Target aud: 25-54. ♦Julie Kahn, gen mgr; Christina Anders, prom dir.

WNTN(AM)—See Newton

WODS(FM)— 1948: 103.3 mhz; 16.5 kw. 938 ft TL: N42 18 27 W71 13 27. Stereo. Hrs open: 24 83 Leo Birmingham Pkwy., 02135. Phone: (617) 787-7500. Fax: (617) 787-7523.E-mail: murley.tina@cbsradio.com Web Site:www.oldies1033.com Licensee: CBS Radio East Inc. Group owner: Infinity Broadcasting Corp. (acq 11-13-98; grpsl). Natl. Rep: CBS Radio,. Format: Oldies. ♦Ted Jordan, gen mgr; Tina Murley, gen sls mgr; Tanya Frazier, mktg dir; Courtney Conners, prom mgr; Pete Falconi, progmg dir; Don Albanese, chief of engrg.

***WRBB(FM)**— October 1970: 104.9 mhz; 10.9 w. 89 ft TL: N42 20 19 W71 05 28. Hrs open: 24 #174 Curry Student Ctr., 360 Huntington Ave., 02115. Phone: (617) 373-4338. Fax: (617) 373-5095. Web Site:www.wrbbradio.org Licensee: Northeastern University. Population served: 900,000 Format: Var/div. News staff: one; News: 2 hrs wkly. Target aud: 12-35; college, urban. ♦Emily Rodrigues, gen mgr; Michelle Bablo, progmg; Ryan Scianino, engr.

WRKO(AM)— 1922: 680 khz; 50 kw-U, DA-2. TL: N42 29 25 W71 13 05. Hrs open: 20 Guest St., 3rd Fl., Brighton, 02135. Phone: (617) 779-3400. Fax: (617) 779-3467. Web Site:www.wrko.com Licensee: Entercom Boston License L.L.C. Group owner: Entercom Communications Corp. (acq 10-15-98; $82 million with WEEI(AM) Boston). Population served: 641,071 Natl. Network: ABC, . Format: Talk. Target aud: 25-54. ♦Julie Kahn, gen mgr; Christina Andres, prom mgr; Jim Rushton, adv.

WROL(AM)— Oct 8, 1950: 950 khz; 5 kw-D, 500 w-N. TL: N42 26 15 W70 59 40. Hrs open: 24 500 Victory Road, Quincy, 02171. Phone: (617) 328-0880. Fax: (617) 328-0375.E-mail: PatR@SalemRadioBoston.com Web Site:www.wrolboston.com Licensee: Salem Media Group LLC. Group owner: Salem Communications Corp. (acq 3-2-2001; $11

million). Population served: 3,000,000 Format: Christian. Target aud: Adults. Spec prog: Irish music programming; Car Doctor. ◆Patricia Ryan, gen mgr & gen sls mgr.

WROR-FM—See Framingham

WTKK(FM)— 1945: 96.9 mhz; 12.5 kw. 1,010 ft TL: N42 18 12 W71 13 08. (CP: 22.5 kw, ant 735 ft.). Stereo. Hrs open: 55 Morrissey Blvd., 02125. Phone: (617) 822-9600. Fax: (617) 822-6871. Web Site:www.wtkk.com Licensee: Greater Boston Radio Inc. Group owner: Greater Media Inc. (acq 3-31-93; $11.65 million; 4-19-93). Population served: 641071 Natl. Rep: Katz Radio,. Format: Talk. ◆Chris Paquin, gen mgr, gen sls mgr; Paula O'Connor, progmg dir.

*WUMB-FM— Sept 19, 1982: 91.9 mhz; 320 w. 207 ft TL: N42 15 27 W71 01 44. Stereo. Hrs open: 24 Univ. of Massachusetts Boston, 100 Morrissey Blvd., 02125-3393. Phone: (617) 287-6900. Fax: (617) 287-6916.E-mail: wumb@umb.edu Web Site:www.wumb.org Licensee: The University of Massachusetts. (group owner) Population served: 2,500,000 Natl. Network: PRI, NPR, . Format: Folk. News: 5 hrs wkly. Target aud: 25-40. ◆Patricia A. Monteith, gen mgr; Brian Quinn, progmg dir.

WUNR(AM)—(Brookline, 1947: 1600 khz; 5 kw-U, DA-1. TL: N42 17 20 W71 11 22. Hrs open: 160 N. Washington St., 02114. Phone: (617) 367-9003. Fax: (617) 367-2265.E-mail: e@wunr.com Web Site:wunr.com Licensee: Champion Broadcasting System Inc. Population served: 641,071 Format: Ethnic, Sp. ◆Steve Lalli, gen mgr; Velma May, progmg dir & pub affrs dir.

WWDJ(AM)— Jan 1, 1979: 1150 khz; 5 kw-U, DA-2. TL: N42 24 48 W71 12 40. Stereo. Hrs open: 500 Victory Rd/, N. Quincy, 02171. Phone: (617) 328-0880. Fax: (617) 328-0375. Web Site:www.talk1150.com Licensee: Pennsylvania Media Associates Inc. Group owner: Salem Communications Corp. (acq 10-31-2003; $8.6 million). Population served: 1,000,000 Format: Sp contemp Christian. ◆Scott Cohagan, gen mgr.

WWZN(AM)— 1934: 1510 khz; 50 kw-U, DA-2. TL: N42 23 10 W71 12 01. Stereo. Hrs open: 1 Van De Graaff Dr., Suite 300, Burlington, 01803-5171. Phone: (781) 221-7878. Fax: (781) 221-7877.E-mail: wwzn@1510thezone.com Web Site:www.1510thezone.com Licensee: Rose City Radio Corp. (group owner; acq 3-23-01; grpsl). Population served: 535,000 Natl. Network: Sporting News Radio Network, . Haley, Bader & Potts. Format: Sports. Target aud: 25-54. ◆Anthony Pepe, gen mgr; Jon Anik, progmg dir; Brad Parsons, chief of engrg.

WXKS-FM—See Medford

WZLX(FM)— Jan 1, 1979: 100.7 mhz; 21.5 kw. Ant 777 ft TL: N42 20 50 W71 04 59. Stereo. Hrs open: 83 Leo M. Birmingham Pkwy., Brighton, 02135. Phone: (617) 746-5100. Fax: (617) 746-5105.E-mail: info@wzlx.com Web Site:www.wzlx.com Licensee: CBS Radio Inc. of Boston. Group owner: Infinity Broadcasting Corp. (acq 11-13-98; grpsl). Population served: 641,071 Natl. Network: CBS, . Natl. Rep: CBS Radio,. Format: Classic rock. Target aud: 25-54; males. ◆Mark Hannon, gen mgr; Joe Soucise, chief of engrg.

Boxford

*WBMT(FM)— Jan 30, 1978: 88.3 mhz; 710 w. 17 ft TL: N42 37 39 W70 58 21. Hrs open: 2:30 PM-9 PM(M-F); 10 AM-6 PM(S,Su) 20 Endicott Rd., Topsfield, 01983. Phone: (978) 887-8830.E-mail: wbmtradio@masconomet.org Web Site:www.masconomet.org Licensee: Masconomet Regional High School System. Population served: 35,000 Format: AOR. ◆Joseph Czarnecki, gen mgr.

Brewster

WZAI(FM)— 2006: 94.3 mhz; 4.7 kw. Ant 372 ft TL: N41 46 36 W70 00 40. Hrs open:
Rebroadcasts WCAI-FM Woods Hole 100%.
Box 82, Woods Hole, 02543. Secondary address: 3 Water St, Woods Hole 02543. Phone: (508) 548-9600. Fax: (508) 548-5517.E-mail: cainan@wgbh.org Web Site:www.capeandislands.org Licensee: WGBH Educational Foundation. Natl. Network: NPR, . Format: News/talk. ◆John Voci, stn mgr.

Bridgewater

*WBIM-FM— November 1972: 91.5 mhz; 180 w. Ant 71 ft TL: N41 59 15 W70 58 21. Stereo. Hrs open: 24 Campus Ctr. 109, Bridgewater State College, 02325. Phone: (508) 531-1303. Phone: (508) 531-1366. Fax: (508) 531-1786.E-mail: wbim@bridgew.edu Web

Site:www.bridgew.edu/wbim Licensee: Bridgewater State College. Population served: 20,000 Format: Var. News staff: one; News: 14 hrs wkly. Target aud: 18-35; college students & loc residents. ◆Mark C. Lilly, gen mgr & stn mgr; Kevin Kennedy, progmg dir.

Brockton

WKAF(FM)— July 21, 1948: 97.7 mhz; 1.7 kw. Ant 567 ft TL: N42 12 42 W71 06 51. Hrs open:
simulcasts WAAF (FM) Westborough 100%.
20 Guest St, 3rd floor, Boston, 02135. Phone: (617) 779-5400. Web Site:www.waaf.com Licensee: Entercom Boston License L.L.C. Group owner: Radio One Inc. (acq 12-27-2006; $30 million). Population served: 1,500,000 Format: Active Rock. ◆Julie Kahn, gen mgr.

WMSX(AM)— July 17, 1961: 1410 khz; 1 kw-D, DA. TL: N42 03 30 W71 02 40. Hrs open: 758 Crescent St., 02302-3343. Phone: (508) 584-7400. Fax: (508) 584-7403.E-mail: info@kingdomchurch.net Licensee: Kingdom Church (acq 2-5-2009; $540,000). Population served: 400,000 Format: Contemp Christian. ◆Alex Hurt, pres.

WXBR(AM)— Nov 27, 1946: 1460 khz; 5 kw-D, 1 kw-N, DA-N. TL: N42 04 23 W71 02 39. Hrs open: 60 Main St., 02301. Phone: (508) 587-2400. Fax: (508) 587-4786. Web Site:www.1460wxbr.com Licensee: BTR Boston Inc. (acq 11-13-2006; $1 million). Population served: 250,000 Format: News/talk, sports. Target aud: 35 plus; general. ◆Richard Muserlian, gen mgr.

Brookline

WBOS(FM)— 1955: 92.9 mhz; 8.8 kw. 1,100 ft TL: N42 18 27 W71 13 27. Stereo. Hrs open: 24 55 Morrissey Blvd., Boston, 02125. Phone: (617) 822-9600. Fax: (617) 822-6771.E-mail: romotion@baston92.9.com Web Site:www.wbos.com Licensee: Greater Los Angeles Radio Inc. Group owner: Greater Media Inc. (acq 7-23-97). Population served: 400,000 Natl. Rep: Katz Radio,. Format: AAA. News staff: one; News: 3 hrs wkly. Target aud: 25-49; baby boomers seeking diverse quality music. ◆Phil Redo, gen mgr; David Straws, gen sls mgr; David Ginsburg, progmg dir.

WUNR(AM)—Licensed to Brookline. See Boston

Cambridge

WHRB(FM)— May 1957: 95.3 mhz; 3 kw. 110 ft TL: N42 22 20 W71 07 09. (CP: 1.55 kw, ant 508 ft.). Stereo. Hrs open: 24 389 Harvard St., 02138. Phone: (617) 495-8138. Fax: (617) 496-3990.E-mail: mail@whrb.org Web Site:www.whrb.org Licensee: Harvard Radio Broadcasting Co. Inc. Population served: 3,000,000 Format: Class, jazz, AOR. News: 4 hrs wkly. ◆Stanley Chang, pres & gen mgr.

WJIB(AM)—Licensed to Cambridge. See Boston

*WMBR(FM)— Apr 10, 1961: 88.1 mhz; 360 w. 285 ft TL: N42 21 42 W71 05 03. Stereo. Hrs open: 6 AM-2 AM 3 Ames St., 02142. Phone: (617) 253-4000. Fax: (617) 232-1384.E-mail: info@wmbr.mit.edu Web Site:www.wmbr.mit.edu Licensee: Technology Broadcasting Corporation. Population served: 600,000 Format: Var/div. Target aud: General. ◆Dugan Hayes, gen mgr; Christopher Bobko, stn mgr.

WTKK(FM)—See Boston

Charlton

*WYCM(FM)— 1976: 90.1 mhz; 100 w. Ant 390 ft TL: N42 08 01 W71 57 26. Stereo. Hrs open: 24 Box 573, 01507. Phone: (508) 248-0049. Fax: (508) 248-4518.E-mail: stationmanager@wycm.com Web Site:www.wycm.com Licensee: Christian Mix Radio Inc. (acq 3-17-2004; $200,000). Population served: 750,000 Format: Christian music. ◆Stephen Binley, stn mgr; Judy Pelletier, prom.

Chatham

WFCC-FM— Mar 24, 1987: 107.5 mhz; 50 kw. 341 ft TL: N41 44 14 W70 00 40. Stereo. Hrs open: 24 737 W. Main St., Hyannis, 02601. Phone: (508) 771-1224. Fax: (508)775-2065.E-mail: info@capecodbroadcasting.com Web Site:www.wfcc.com Licensee: Cape Cod Broadcasting License I LLC (acq 7-10-2007; $7.5 million with WOCN-FM Orleans). Population served: 225,000 Format: Classical. News staff: 2; News: 2 hrs wkly. Target aud: 25 plus; upscale, affluent, educated adults. ◆Greg Bone, gen mgr; Wayne White, opns mgr.

Chicopee

WACE(AM)— Dec 1, 1946: 730 khz; 5 kw-U. TL: N42 10 01 W72 37 31. Hrs open: 24 Box 1, Springfield, 01101. Secondary address: 326 Chicopee St. 01013. Phone: (413) 594-6654.E-mail: wace730@wmconnect.com Licensee: Carter Broadcasting Corp. (acq 12-24-86). Population served: 3,000,000 Format: Relg, talk. Spec prog: Pol one hr, Irish 2 hrs, Por one hr wkly. ◆Ken Carter, pres, gen mgr; Michael Durocher, opns mgr; Cal McLain, progmg dir.

Concord

WBNW(AM)— Aug 28, 1989: 1120 khz; 5 kw-D, 1 kw-N, DA-2. TL: N42 26 54 W71 25 39. Hrs open: 5 AM-10 PM 144 Gould St. Suite 155, Needham, 02494. Phone: (781) 433-0001. Fax: (781) 433-0002.E-mail: info@wbnw.com Web Site:www.moneymattersradio.net Licensee: Money Matters Radio Inc. (acq 6-17-98; $550,000). Population served: 8,000 Rgnl rep: New England. Format: Business, personal finance. News: 17 hrs wkly. Target aud: 35 plus; upscale, suburban families. ◆Barry Armstrong, pres; Scott McCall, gen mgr.

*WIQH(FM)— December 1971: 88.3 mhz; 100 w. 30 ft TL: N42 26 48 W71 20 49. Stereo. Hrs open: 1-9:30 PM (M-F); 10 AM-10 PM (S) 500 Walden St., 01742. Phone: (978) 318-1400 ext. 7185. Phone: (978) 369-2440.E-mail: wiqh@colonial.net Web Site:www.wiqh.org Licensee: Concord-Carlisle Regional School District. Population served: 17,500 Format: AOR, progsv. Target aud: 12-21; teenagers. ◆Ned Roos, gen mgr & stn mgr.

Dalton

*WJNF(FM)—Not on air, target date: unknown: 91.7 mhz; 175 w. Ant 948 ft TL: N42 26 12 W73 03 13. Hrs open: 178 Harryel St., Pittsfield, 01201. Phone: (413) 499-4115.E-mail: calvaryotb@aol.com Licensee: Calvary Chapel of the Berkshires. ◆Donald Roach, pres.

Danvers

WNSH(AM)—See Beverly

Dedham

WAMG(AM)— June 2005: 890 khz; 25 kw-D, 3.4 kw-N, DA-2. TL: N42 14 49 W71 25 30. Hrs open: 24 529 Main St., Suite 200, Charlestown, 02129-1119. Phone: (617) 830-1000.E-mail: laura.wareck@espnboston.com Web Site:www.890espn.com Licensee: J Sports Licensee LLC Group owner: Mega Communications Inc. (acq 6-22-2005; $9 million with WLLH(AM) Lowell). Population served: 2,900,000 Natl. Network: ESPN Radio, . Natl. Rep: McGavren Guild,. Davis, Wright, Tremaine. Format: Sports. Target aud: 18 plus; males. ◆Jessamy Tang, gen mgr; Neil Kelleter, sls dir; Kara Lachance, prom mgr; Len Weiner, progmg dir.

Deerfield

*WGAJ(FM)— May 1982: 91.7 mhz; 100 w. 314 ft TL: N42 32 05 W72 35 32. Stereo. Hrs open: 7 AM-8 PM (M-F); 4 AM-11 PM (S); 7 AM-11 PM (Su) Deerfield Academy, 01342. Phone: (413) 774-1539. Fax: (413) 772-1100. Licensee: Trustees of Deerfield Academy. Population served: 150,000 Format: Var. Target aud: 10-20; teens, young adults, pre-teens. ◆Christopher Stacy, gen mgr & stn mgr.

Dennis

WEII(FM)— June 15, 1981: 96.3 mhz; 25 kw. Ant 297 ft TL: N41 43 44 W70 10 02. Stereo. Hrs open: 24 154 Barnstable Rd., Hyannis, 02601. Phone: (508) 778-2888. Fax: (508) 778-9651. Web Site:www.963weei.com Licensee: Qantum of Cape Cod License Co. LLC. Group owner: Qantum Communications Corp. (acq 6-11-2003; grpsl). Natl. Rep: Eastman Radio,. Format: Sports. Target aud: 18-49. ◆Allison Makkay, gen mgr; Steve McVie Solomon, opns dir.

Dudley

*WXRB(FM)— 1975: 95.1 mhz; 14 w. Ant 125 ft TL: N42 02 40 W71 55 52. Stereo. Hrs open: 24 48 Homeland Dr., Whitman, 02382. Phone: (508) 213-2138.E-mail: wxrbfm@yahoo.com Web Site:wxrbfm.bravehost.com Licensee: WXRB-FM Educational Broadcasting Inc. (acq 5-17-2006; $1,000). Population served: 5,000 Format: Golden oldies, educ, old time radio. Target aud: 18 plus. Spec prog: Nichols College sports. ◆Peter Q. George, stn mgr & chief of engrg.

East Longmeadow

WHNP(AM)— 1947: 1600 khz; 5 kw-D, 2.5 kw-N, DA-2. TL: N42 04 30 W72 31 40. Hrs open: 24
simulcast of WHMP (AM) Northampton.
15 Hampton Ave., Northampton, 01060. Phone: (413) 586-7400. Fax: (413) 585-0927. Web Site:www.whmp.com Licensee: Saga Communications of New England LLC. Group owner: Saga Communications Inc. (acq 6-2-92; grpsl). Format: News/talk, info. Target aud: 18-49; upscale young adults. ◆Sean O'Mealy, gen mgr; Dave Musante, gen sls mgr; Chris Collins, progmg dir.

Easthampton

WVEI-FM— October 1967: 105.5 mhz; 720 w horiz, 706 w vert. Ant 918 ft TL: N42 14 29 W72 38 57. Stereo. Hrs open: 24
Simulcast with WEEI (AM) Boston 100%.
Secondary address: 1350 Main St., Suite 1206 01103. Phone: (413) 594-6585. Fax: (413) 592-1891. Web Site:www.wveifm.com Licensee: Entercom Springfield License LLC. (acq 9-5-2007; $5.75 million). Population served: 139,000 Natl. Network: Fox Sports, Westwood One, . Natl. Rep: D & R Radio, Interep,. Format: Sports. Target aud: 25-54; men; adults. ◆Julie Kahn, VP, mktg mgr; Stephen Paul Garsh, gen mgr.

Easton

*WSHL-FM— Jan 1, 1973: 91.3 mhz; 100 w. 66 ft TL: N42 03 27 W71 04 47. Stereo. Hrs open: 24 Stonehill College, 320 Washington St., North Easton, 02357. Phone: (508) 565-1000. Phone: (508) 565-1919. Fax: (508) 565-1974.E-mail: wshl@stonehill.edu Web Site:www.stonehill.edu/wshl Licensee: Stonehill College. Population served: 10,000 Wire Svc: UPI Format: Div. Target aud: 19-30. ◆Ryan Delehunt, gen mgr; Peter Q. George, chief of engrg.

Edgartown

*WMEX(FM)—Not on air, target date: unknown: 88.1 mhz; 150 w vert. Ant 89 ft TL: N41 23 03 W70 31 30. Hrs open: 19 Boas Ln., Wilton, CT, 06897-1301. Phone: (203) 762-9425. Licensee: Foothills Public Radio Inc. ◆Dennis Jackson, gen mgr.

Everett

WXKS(AM)—Licensed to Everett. See Medford

Fairhaven

WFHN(FM)— Mar 1, 1989: 107.1 mhz; 6 kw. 325 ft TL: N41 37 43 W71 00 24. Stereo. Hrs open: 24 22 Sconticutneck Rd., 02719. Phone: (508) 999-6690. Fax: (508) 999-1420.E-mail: petebraley@wbsm.com Web Site:www.fun107.com Licensee: Citadel Broadcasting Co. Group owner: Citadel Broadcasting Corp. (acq 2-23-00; grpsl). Population served: 800,000 Natl. Rep: McGavren Guild,. Format: CHR. Target aud: 18-49. ◆Wayne Leland, exec VP; Gail Leblanc, gen mgr.

Fall River

WCTK(FM)—See Providence, RI

WHTB(AM)— May 13, 1948: 1400 khz; 1 kw-U. TL: N41 41 23 W71 08 43. Hrs open: 5 AM-11 PM 1 Home St., Somerset, 02725. Phone: (508) 678-9727. Fax: (508) 673-0310. Licensee: SNE Broadcasting Ltd. (acq 5-8-89; $650,000; 5-29-89). Natl. Rep: McGavren Guild,. Format: Ethnic talk. Target aud: 25-64; Portuguese (ethnic). Spec prog: English 10 hrs, Pol one hr, Cambodian one hr, Fr one hr wkly. ◆Robert S. Karam, pres; Hector Gauthier, stn mgr, chief of opns.

WSAR(AM)— 1921: 1480 khz; 5 kw-U, DA-1. TL: N41 43 26 W71 11 21. Hrs open: One Home St., Somerset, 02725. Phone: (508) 678-9727. Fax: (508) 673-0310.E-mail: hector@wsar.com Web Site:www.wsar.com Licensee: Bristol County Broadcasting Inc. (acq 1992;11-23-92). Population served: 96,898 Format: News/talk, sports. Target aud: 25 plus. Spec prog: Por 3 hrs wkly. ◆Hector A. Gauthier Jr., gen mgr; Keri Rodrigues, opns mgr & progmg dir.

Falmouth

WCIB(FM)— 1970: 101.9 mhz; 50 kw. 479 ft TL: N41 33 31 W70 35 46. Stereo. Hrs open: 154 Barnstable Rd., Hyannis, 02601. Phone: (508) 778-2888. Fax: (508) 778-9651.E-mail: info@cool102.com Web

Site:www.cool102.com Licensee: Qantum of Cape Cod License Co. LLC. Group owner: Qantum Communications Corp. (acq 6-11-03; grpsl). Population served: 200,000 Natl. Rep: Eastman Radio,. Format: Classic hits. Target aud: 25-54. ◆Allison Makkay, gen mgr; Steve McVie Solomon, opns dir.

*WFPB-FM— 1996: 91.9 mhz; 300 w. 177 ft TL: N41 36 50 W70 35 56. Hrs open:
Rebroadcasts WUMB-FM Boston 100%.
Univ. of Massachusetts, 100 Morrissey Blvd., Boston, 02125-3393. Phone: (617) 287-6900. Fax: (617) 287-6916.E-mail: wumb@umb.edu Web Site:www.wumb.org Licensee: University of Massachusetts. Natl. Network: NPR, . Format: Folk. ◆Patricia A. Monteith, gen mgr; Danielle Knight, dev dir; Brian Quinn, progmg dir.

Fitchburg

WFGL(AM)— February 1950: 960 khz; 2.5 kw-D, 1 kw-N, DA-2. TL: N42 35 24 W71 49 41. Hrs open: 24
Rebroadcasts KAWZ(FM) Twin Falls, ID 50%.
356 Broad St., 01420-3030. Phone: (978) 342-5025.E-mail: mail@wfgl.org Web Site:www.wfgl.org Licensee: CSN International. (group owner; acq 1993). Population served: 250,000 Format: Christian. Target aud: 25-54; college & career age, young families. ◆Jim Mottshager, gen mgr; Pete Cesnoia, stn mgr.

WPKZ(AM)— Oct 6, 1941: 1280 khz; 5 kw-D, 1 kw-N, DA-1. TL: N42 35 40 W71 50 12. Hrs open: 24 762 Water St., 01420. Phone: (978) 343-3766. Fax: (978) 345-6397.E-mail: radio@i1280.com Web Site:www.i1280.com Licensee: Central Broadcasting Co. LLC (acq 11-1-2005; $795,000). Population served: 500,000 Natl. Network: ABC, . Format: Talk, sports (Red Sox & Patriots—high school & college). News staff: 2; News: 10 hrs wkly. Target aud: 28 plus; loc listeners in the heart of New England. ◆William J. Macek, gen mgr; Ben Parker, stn mgr; Anne Bisbee, opns mgr; John Speeney, gen sls mgr; Ray C, pub svc dir.

WXLO(FM)—Licensed to Fitchburg. See Worcester

*WXPL(FM)— August 1985: 91.3 mhz; 100 w. 134 ft TL: N42 35 18 W71 47 26. Stereo. Hrs open: 24 Fitchburg State College, 160 Pearl St., 01420. Phone: (978) 665-3163. Fax: (978) 665-3693.E-mail: wxpl@fsc.edu Web Site:falcon.fsc.edu/~wxpl Licensee: Fitchburg State College. Format: Var. Target aud: 16-25. ◆Sherry Horeanopoulos, gen mgr & stn mgr.

Framingham

WBIX(AM)—See Natick

*WDJM-FM— 1973: 91.3 mhz; 100 w. 89 ft TL: N42 17 44 W71 26 18. Stereo. Hrs open: Framingham State College, 100 State St., 01701. Phone: (508) 626-4622. Fax: (508) 626-4939. Licensee: Framingham State College. Format: Alternative. Target aud: 15-35; college, surrounding community & commuters. ◆Jason Harrington, gen mgr.

WKOX(AM)— April 1947: 1200 khz; 10 kw-D, 1 kw-N, DA-N. TL: N42 17 17 W71 25 53. (CP: COL Newton. 50 kw-D, DA-2. TL: N42 17 20 W71 11 21). Hrs open: 24 99 Revase Beach Pkwy., Medford, 02155. Phone: (781) 396-1430. Fax: (781) 391-3064. Web Site:www.1200rumba.com Licensee: Capstar TX L.P. Group owner: Clear Channel Communications Inc. (acq 2-15-2001; $10 million). Population served: 1,700,000 Haley, Bader & Potts. Format: Sp. ◆Tom McConnell, VP & gen mgr.

WROR-FM— 1959: 105.7 mhz; 23 kw. Ant 735 ft TL: N42 20 50 W71 04 59. Stereo. Hrs open: 55 Morrissey Blvd., Boston, 02125. Phone: (617) 822-9600. Fax: (617) 822-6471. Web Site:www.wror.com Licensee: Greater Boston Radio Inc. Group owner: Greater Media Inc. (acq 10-11-96). Population served: 3,200,000 Format: Classic hits. Target aud: 25-54. ◆Phil Redo, gen mgr; Chris Paquin, gen sls mgr, news dir.

Franklin

*WGAO(FM)— 1975: 88.3 mhz; 125 w. 174 ft TL: N42 05 08 W71 23 54. Stereo. Hrs open: Dean College, 99 Main St., 02038. Phone: (508) 528-4210. Fax: (508) 528-7846. Licensee: Dean College. Population served: 100,000 Natl. Network: AP Radio, . Format: Classic rock, CHR. Target aud: 15-25. Spec prog: Relg 8 hrs wkly. ◆Vic Michaels, gen mgr, opns dir & progmg dir.

Gardner

WGAW(AM)— 1946: 1340 khz; 1 kw-U. TL: N42 35 33 W71 59 20. Hrs open: 362 Green St., ME, 01440. Phone: (978) 630-8700. Fax: (978) 632-1332. Fax: (603) 577-8682. Web Site:www.wgaw1340.com Licensee: County Broadcasting Co. LLC. Group owner: Northeast Broadcasting Company Inc. (acq 12-2-2003; $235,000). Population served: 30,000 Natl. Network: ABC, . Format: News/talk. ◆Chris Thompson, gen mgr; William B. Curtis, opns dir; Chuck Wright, progmg dir, chief of engrg; Kevin Kistler, traf mgr.

*WJWT(FM)— 2006: 91.7 mhz; 850 w. Ant 276 ft TL: N42 33 29 W72 03 06. Hrs open: CSN International, 3232 W. MacArthur Blvd., Santa Ana, CA, 92704. Phone: (714) 825-9663. Fax: (714) 825-9661. Licensee: CSN International (group owner). Format: Relg. ◆Patrick Lannoye, gen mgr & opns mgr.

Gloucester

WBOQ(FM)— Sept 14, 1964: 104.9 mhz; 3.2 kw. 446 ft TL: N42 35 36 W70 43 28. Stereo. Hrs open: 24 8 Enon St., North Beverly, 01915. Phone: (978) 927-1049. Fax: (978) 921-2635.E-mail: info@wboq.com Web Site:www.wboq.com Licensee: Westport Communications L.P. Population served: 650,000 Akin, Gump, Strauss, Hauer & Feld. Format: Classic hits. News: 3 hrs wkly. Target aud: 25-54; mass appeal classical favorites. ◆Todd Tanger, gen mgr; Charlie Curtis, opns mgr, progmg dir.

Great Barrington

*WAMQ(FM)— November 1988: 105.1 mhz; 730 w. 918 ft TL: N42 09 36 W73 28 48. Stereo. Hrs open: 24
Rebroadcasts WAMC-FM Albany, N.Y. 100%.
318 Central Ave., Box 66600, Albany, NY, 12206-6600. Phone: (518) 465-5233. Fax: (518) 432-6974.E-mail: mail@wamc.org Web Site:www.wamc.org Licensee: WAMC. Group owner: WAMC/Northeast Public Radio (acq 3-5-93; $325,000; 3-29-93). Natl. Network: NPR, PRI, . Dow, Lohnes & Albertson. Wire Svc: AP Format: News/talk. Target aud: General. Spec prog: Folk 7 hrs, jazz 13 wkly. ◆Alan Chartock, CEO; David Galletly, VP, progmg dir; Dona Frank, dev dir.

WSBS(AM)— December 1956: 860 khz; 2.7 kw-D. TL: N42 12 52 W73 20 45. Hrs open: 24 425 Stockbridge Rd., 01230. Phone: (413) 528-0860. Fax: (413) 528-2162.E-mail: fun@wsbs.com Web Site:www.wsbs.com Licensee: Vox Communications Group LLC. Group owner: Vox Radio Group L.P. (acq 5-10-2004; grpsl). Population served: 188,594 Natl. Rep: D & R Radio,. Wilkinson Barker Knauer. Wire Svc: AP Format: Adult contemp,. News staff: 3; News: 10 hrs wkly. Target aud: 25 plus; general. ◆David Isby, gen mgr.

Greenfield

WHAI(FM)— May 15, 1948: 98.3 mhz; 2 kw. Ant 403 ft TL: N42 34 15 W72 38 42. Stereo. Hrs open: 24 81 Woodard Rd., 01301. Phone: (413) 774-4301. Fax: (413) 773-5637.E-mail: info@whai.com Web Site:whai.com Licensee: Saga Communications of New England LLC. Population served: 100,000 Format: Adult contemp. News staff: one. Target aud: 25-54. ◆Dan Guin, gen mgr; Nick Danjer, progmg dir & disc jockey.

WHMQ(AM)— May 15, 1938: 1240 khz; 1 kw-U. TL: N42 35 21 W72 37 08. Hrs open: 24
Rebroadcasts WHMP(AM) Northampton 98%.
15 Hampton Ave., Northampton, 01060. Phone: (413) 586-7400. Fax: (413) 585-0927. Web Site:www.whmp.com Licensee: Saga Communications of New England LLC. Group owner: Saga Communications Inc. (acq 4-1-2001; $2.2 million with co-located FM). Population served: 65,000 Natl. Network: CBS, . Wiley, Rein & Fielding. Format: News info. News staff: 2; News: 20 hrs wkly. Target aud: 35 plus. ◆Sean O'Mealy, gen mgr; Dave Musante, gen sls mgr, news dir; Chris Collins, progmg dir, news dir; Barbara Kuschka, traf mgr.

WINQ(FM)—See Winchester NH

WIZZ(AM)— Aug 26, 1980: 1520 khz; 10 kw-D, DA. TL: N42 36 12 W72 36 21. Hrs open: Box 983, 01302. Secondary address: 369 S. Shelburne Rd. 01370. Phone: (413) 774-5757. Fax: (413) 625-8274.E-mail: phild@wizzradio.com Web Site:www.wizzradio.com Licensee: P. & M. Radio LLC (acq 1-31-03; $150,000). Natl. Network: AP Network News, . Format: Nostalgia. ◆Phillip G. Drumheller, pres & gen mgr.

WPVQ(FM)— July 26, 1981: 95.3 mhz; 320 w. 780 ft TL: N42 41 50 W72 36 20. Hrs open: 24 81 Woodard Rd., 01301. Phone: (413) 774-4301. Fax: (413) 773-5637.E-mail: info@whai.com Web

Site:www.bear953.com Licensee: Saga Communications of New England LLC. Group owner: Saga Communications Inc. (acq 2-13-2004; grpsl). Format: Country. Target aud: 18-45. ◆Dan Guin, gen mgr & gen sls mgr.

Harwich

*WCCT-FM— May 1988: 90.3 mhz; 160 w horiz, 640 w vert. 125 ft TL: N41 42 40 W70 04 34. Hrs open: 24
Rebroadcasts WBUR(FM) Boston 90%.
Cape Cod Tech., 351 Pleasant Lake Ave., 02645. Phone: (508) 432-4500. Fax: (508) 432-7916.E-mail: jganss@capetech.us Web Site:www.wbur.org Licensee: Cape Cod Regional Technical High School. (acq 11-11-87). Natl. Network: NPR, . Format: Music & talk. News: 30 hrs wkly. Target aud: 20-65; educated adults. ◆John Ganss, gen mgr.

Harwich Port

WFQR(FM)— May 11, 1989: 93.5 mhz; 3 kw. Ant 328 ft TL: N41 44 19 W70 00 40. Stereo. Hrs open: 24
Rebroadcasts WFRQ(FM) Mashpee.
278 S. Sea Ave., W. Yarmouth, 02673. Phone: (508) 775-5678. Fax: (508) 862-6329. Web Site:www.weplayitall.com Licensee: Nassau Broadcasting III L.L.C. Group owner: Boch Broadcasting (acq 11-7-2005; grpsl). Natl. Network: Westwood One, . Natl. Rep: Katz Radio,. Format: Adult hits. Target aud: 35-64. ◆Jake Demmin, gen mgr.

Haverhill

WCEC(AM)— 1947: 1490 khz; 1 kw-U. TL: N42 46 22 W71 06 01. Hrs open: 24 462 Merrimac St., Methuen, 01844. Phone: (978) 683-7171. Phone: (978) 686-9966. Fax: (978) 687-1180.E-mail: traffic@1110wccmam.com Web Site:www.1490wcec.com Licensee: Costa-Eagle Radio Ventures L.P. (group owner; (acq 1998). Population served: 249,700 Natl. Rep: Roslin,. Bryan Cave. Format: Sp talk and info. Target aud: Sp speaking. ◆Patrick J. Costa, gen mgr; Luis Reyes, opns mgr.

Holliston

*WHHB(FM)— Apr 17, 1979: 99.9 mhz; 10 w. 52 ft TL: N42 12 29 W71 26 19. (CP: 170 w, ant 203 ft.). Hrs open: Holliston High School, 370 Hollis St., 01746. Phone: (508) 429-0677. Fax: (508) 429-8225.E-mail: requests@whhbfm.com Licensee: Holliston High School. Format: Var. ◆Christopher Murphy, gen mgr & stn mgr.

Holyoke

*WCCH(FM)— 1977: 103.5 mhz; 10 w. 258 ft TL: N42 11 55 W72 38 27. Hrs open: 6 AM-11 PM Holyoke Community College, 303 Homestead Ave., 01040. Phone: (413) 552-2488. Phone: (413) 538-7060.E-mail: wcchradio@hotmail.com Licensee: Holyoke Community College. Format: Var. ◆Joanne Kostides, gen mgr.

Hyannis

WCOD-FM— June 2, 1967: 106.1 mhz; 50 kw. 450 ft TL: N41 43 46 W70 10 01. Stereo. Hrs open: 24 154 Barnstable Rd., 02601-2930. Phone: (508) 778-2888. Fax: (508) 778-9651.E-mail: info@106wcod.com Web Site:www.106wcod.com Licensee: Qantum of Cape Cod License Co. LLC. Group owner: Boch Broadcasting (acq 4-11-2005; grpsl). Natl. Rep: Eastman Radio,. Format: Hot adult contemp. News staff: 2. Target aud: 25-54. ◆Allison Makkay, gen mgr; Kevin Matthews, progmg dir.

WPXC(FM)— Jan 9, 1987: 102.9 mhz; 6 kw. 325 ft TL: N41 41 19 W70 20 49. Stereo. Hrs open: 24 278 S. Sea Ave., West Yarmouth, 02673. Phone: (508) 775-5678. Fax: (508) 862-6329.E-mail: info@pixy103.com Web Site:www.pixy103.com Licensee: Nassau Broadcasting III L.L.C. Group owner: Qantum Communications Corp. (acq 11-8-2005; grpsl). Population served: 200,000 Natl. Rep: McGavren Guild,. Format: Rock. News staff: 3; News: 4 hrs wkly. Target aud: General. ◆Jake Demmin, gen mgr; Suzanne Tonaire, progmg dir.

WQRC(FM)—See Barnstable

Lawrence

WLLH(AM)—See Lowell

WMKK(FM)—Licensed to Lawrence. See Boston

WNNW(AM)— August 1947: 800 khz; 1 kw-D, 250 w-N. TL: N42 40 26 W71 11 26. Hrs open: 24 462 Merrimack St., Methuen, 01844. Phone: (978) 686-9966. Fax: (978) 687-1180.E-mail: traffic@1110wccmam.com Web Site:www.power800am.com Licensee: Costa-Eagle Radio Ventures L.P. (group owner; acq 3-27-98; $405,000). Population served: 525,000 Natl. Network: CNN Radio, . Rgnl. Network: Metronews Radio Net. Natl. Rep: Lotus Entravision Reps LLC,. Bryan Cave. Wire Svc: AP Format: Sp. News staff: 2; News: 10 hrs wkly. Target aud: 35-64; general. ◆Patrick Costa, gen mgr; Johnny McKenzie, opns mgr, progmg dir.

Leicester

WVNE(AM)— June 19, 1991: 760 khz; 25 kw-D. TL: N42 14 57 W72 04 41. Hrs open: Sunrise-sunset 70 James St., Suite 201, Worcester, 01603. Phone: (508) 831-9863. Fax: (508) 831-7964.E-mail: info@wvne.net Web Site:www.wvne.net Licensee: Blount Masscom Inc. Group owner: Blount Communications Group (acq 5-15-90; 6-4-90). Population served: 3,000,000 Natl. Network: Salem Radio Network, . Format: Religious. Target aud: 25-54. ◆William A. Blount, pres; Deborah Blount, exec VP; David O. Young, VP; Emanuel DaCunha, stn mgr.

Leominster

WCMX(AM)— Nov 13, 1967: 1000 khz; 1 kw-D. TL: N42 31 25 W71 44 07. Hrs open: 6 AM-2 hrs past sundown 194 Electric Ave., Lunenburg, 01462. Phone: (978) 582-4901. Fax: (978) 582-4978.E-mail: nate@hope1000.com Web Site:hope1000.net Licensee: Twin City Baptist Temple Inc. (acq 1-95). Population served: 1,500,000 Natl. Network: Salem Radio Network, . Format: Christian music, praise & worship. News: 7 hrs wkly. Target aud: 35-54 women. ◆Pastor Erven Burke, gen mgr; Nathan Burke, stn mgr, stn mgr, progmg dir.

WPKZ(AM)—See Fitchburg

Lowell

WCAP(AM)— June 10, 1951: 980 khz; 5 kw-U, DA-2. TL: N42 39 16 W01 21 43. Hrs open: 24 243 Central St., 01852. Phone: (978) 454-0404. Fax: (978) 458-9124.E-mail: clark@980wcap.com Web Site:www.980wcap.com Licensee: Merrimack Valley Radio LLC (acq 9-25-2007; $2.66 million). Population served: 2,500,000 Natl. Network: ABC, . Rgnl rep: LOCAL Garvey, Schubert & Barer. Wire Svc: AP Format: Talk/news, Full Service. News: 20 hrs wkly. Target aud: 25 plus; business people, professionals, factory workers, housewives. ◆Ryan Johnston, opns dir; Dean Johnson, progmg dir; Bernice Corpuz, news dir; Clark Smidt, sls.

WCRB(FM)— 1947: 99.5 mhz; 27 kw. Ant 653 ft TL: N42 39 14 W71 13 02. Stereo. Hrs open: 750 South St., Waltham, 02453-1496. Phone: (781) 893-7080. Fax: (781) 893-0038.E-mail: wcrb@wcrb.com Web Site:www.wcrb.com Licensee: Nassau Broadcasting II L.L.C. Group owner: Greater Media Inc. (acq 11-15-2006; exchange for WNUW(FM) Burlington, NJ). Population served: 535,000 Format: Classical. Target aud: 30-64; adults. ◆Nancy Dieterich, gen mgr; Tim Neill, mktg dir & prom dir; Mark Edwards, progmg dir.

WLLH(AM)— June 2005: 1400 khz; 1 kw-U. TL: N42 39 29 W71 19 04. Hrs open: 24 529 Main St., Suite 200, Charlestown, 02129-1119. Phone: (617) 830-1000.E-mail: laura.wareck@espnboston.com Web Site:www.890espn.com Licensee: J Sports Licensee LLC Group owner: Mega Communications Inc. (acq 6-22-2005; $9 million with WAMG(AM) Dedham). Population served: 94,239 Natl. Network: ESPN Radio, . Natl. Rep: McGavren Guild,. Davis, Wright, Tremaine. Format: Sports. Target aud: Males 18+. ◆Jessamy Tang, gen mgr; Neil Kelleher, sls dir; Kara Lachance, progmg dir.

*WUML(FM)— Nov 6, 1967: 91.5 mhz; 1.4 kw. 207 ft TL: N42 39 07 W71 19 15. Stereo. Hrs open: 18 One University Ave., 01854. Phone: (978) 934-4975 . Fax: (978) 934-3031.E-mail: wuml@wuml.org Web Site:www.wuml.org Licensee: University of Massachusetts-Lowell Board of Trustees. Population served: 3,000,000 Format: Div, progsv rock. Target aud: 16-25. ◆Nate Osit, gen mgr; Joe Keefe, progmg dir.

Lynn

WFNX(FM)— Aug 5, 1963: 101.7 mhz; 1.7 kw. 626 ft TL: N42 21 08 W71 03 25. Stereo. Hrs open: 24 25 Exchange St., 01901. Phone: (781) 595-6200. Fax: (781) 595-3810.E-mail: fnxradio@fnxradio.com Web Site:www.fnxradio.com Licensee: MCC Broadcasting Inc. Group owner: Phoenix Media Communications Group (acq 11-10-82;11-29-82). Population served: 3,880,000 Natl. Rep: McGavren Guild,. Rubin,

Winston, Diercks, Harris & Cooke. Wire Svc: AP Format: Alternative rock. News staff: one; News: 2 hrs wkly. Target aud: 18-49; well-educated, affluent & socially active trend setters. Spec prog: Jazz 8 hrs, loc music 2 hrs wkly. ◆Stephen Mindich, CEO; Brad Mindich, chmn; Rick Gallagher, CFO; Gary Kurtz, gen mgr, news dir; Jordi Chapdelaine, gen sls mgr; Keith Dakin, progmg dir, chief of engrg; Christopher Hall, chief of engrg.

WLYN(AM)— November 1947: 1360 khz; 700 w-D, 76 w-N. TL: N42 27 17 W70 58 44. Stereo. Hrs open: 24 500 W. Cummings Park, Suite 2600, Woburn, 01801. Phone: (781) 938-0869. Fax: (781) 938-0933.E-mail: jeffk@mrbi.net Web Site:www.mrbi.net Licensee: Multicultural Radio Broadcasting Licensee LLC. Group owner: Multicultural Radio Broadcasting Inc. (acq 8-7-2002; $1.78 million). Population served: 3,000,000 Format: Ethnic - leased time. Hispanic (Spanish & Portuguese). Spec prog: Greek 2 hrs wkly. ◆Jeff Kline, gen mgr.

Marion

*WWTA(FM)— 1996: 88.5 mhz; 19 w horiz, 100 w vert. 53 ft TL: N41 42 32 W70 45 57. Hrs open: 85 Spring St., 02738. Phone: (508) 748-2000. Fax: (508) 291-6666.E-mail: kkistler@taboracademy.org Web Site:www.taboracademy.org Licensee: Tabor Academy. Format: Var. ◆Karl Kistler, gen mgr.

Marshfield

WATD-FM— Dec 5, 1977: 95.9 mhz; 2.8 kw. 350 ft TL: N42 06 40 W70 42 14. Stereo. Hrs open: 24 130 Enterprise Dr., 02050. Phone: (781) 837-1166. Fax: (781) 837-1978.E-mail: news@959watd.com Web Site:www.959watd.com Licensee: Marshfield Broadcasting Co. Population served: 500,000 Format: Adult contemp, blues, oldies. News staff: 2; News: 10 hrs wkly. Target aud: 25-64; South Shore residents. ◆Edward Perry, Jr., pres & gen mgr.

Mashpee

WFRQ(FM)— Feb 12, 1987: 101.1 mhz; 3.7 kw. Ant 253 ft TL: N41 36 50 W70 35 56. Stereo. Hrs open: 24
Rebroadcasts WFQR(FM) Harwich Port 100%.
278 South Sea Ave., West Yarmouth, 02673. Phone: (508) 775-5678. Fax: (508) 862-6329. Web Site:www.weplayitall.com Licensee: Nassau Broadcasting III L.L.C. Group owner: Boch Broadcasting (acq 11-7-2005; grpsl). Natl. Network: Westwood One, . Natl. Rep: Katz Radio,. Format: Adult hits. News staff: one. Target aud: 35-64. ◆Jake Demmin, gen mgr.

Maynard

*WAVM(FM)— April 1973: 91.7 mhz; 16 w. -7 ft TL: N42 25 18 W71 27 02. Stereo. Hrs open: 24 Maynard High School, One Tiger Dr., 01754. Phone: (978) 897-5179. Fax: (978) 897-6089.E-mail: studio@wavm.org Web Site:www.wavm.org Licensee: Maynard Public Schools. Format: Var. Target aud: General. ◆Mark Minasian, gen mgr & stn mgr.

Medford

*WMFO(FM)— March 1971: 91.5 mhz; 125 w. 135 ft TL: N42 24 27 W71 07 15. Stereo. Hrs open: Box 65, 02155. Secondary address: 474 Boston Ave. 02155. Phone: (617) 625-0800. Fax: (617) 625-6072.E-mail: wmfo@wmfo.org Web Site:www.wmfo.org Licensee: Tufts University. Population served: 74,397 Format: Var/div. ◆Annie Ross, gen mgr.

WXKS(AM)—(Everett, Jan 20, 1952: 1430 khz; 5 kw-D, 1 kw-N, DA-N. TL: N42 24 11 W71 04 29. Hrs open: 24 99 Revere Beach Pkwy., 02155. Phone: (781) 396-1430. Fax: (781) 391-3064. Web Site:www.1200rumba.com Licensee: AMFM Radio Licenses L.L.C. Group owner: Clear Channel Communications Inc. (acq 8-30-2000; grpsl). Population served: 743,900 Format: Sp. ◆Jake Karger, gen mgr.

WXKS-FM— Sept 1, 1960: 107.9 mhz; 20.5 kw. Ant 771 ft TL: N42 20 50 W71 04 59. Stereo. Hrs open: 24 10 Cabot Rd., Suite 302, 02155. Phone: (781) 663-2500. Fax: (781) 290-0722. Web Site:www.kiss108.com Licensee: AMFM Radio Licenses L.L.C. Format: Adult CHR. Target aud: 18-34. ◆Tom McConnell, gen mgr.

Middleborough Center

WVBF(AM)— 1993: 1530 khz; 2.2 kw-D, 2 w-N, 940 w-CH. TL: N41 55 26 W70 56 07. Hrs open: 24 Box 329, 02346. Secondary address:

130 Enterprise Dr., Marshfield 02050. Phone: (781) 834-4400. Phone: (800) 696-9505. Fax: (781) 834-7716. Licensee: Steven J. Callahan. Natl. Network: Westwood One, NBC Radio, . Format: Info. ◆Steven Callahan, gen mgr; John Zeiler, gen sls mgr; Don Schaeffer, progmg dir; Dianna Monk, news dir; Al Pynenburg, chief of engrg; Roxanne Davison, traf mgr.

Milford

WMRC(AM)— Oct 6, 1956: 1490 khz; 1 kw-U. TL: N42 08 12 W71 30 50. Hrs open: 24 Box 421, 01757. Secondary address: 258 Main St. 01757. Phone: (508) 473-1490. Fax: (508) 478-2200. Licensee: First Class Radio Corp. (acq 12-4-2006). Population served: 250,000 Format: Adult contemp, var radio. News staff: 2; News: 32 hrs wkly. Target aud: 25-54. ◆Thomas M. McAuliffe Sr., pres; Thomas M. McAuliffe II, gen mgr.

Milton

*WMLN-FM— Apr 1, 1975: 91.5 mhz; 170 w. 98 ft TL: N42 14 27 W71 06 52. Hrs open: 24 1071 Blue Hill Ave., 02186. Phone: (617) 333-0311.E-mail: afrank@curry.edu Web Site:www.curry.edu Licensee: Curry College. Population served: 200,000 Natl. Network: CNN Radio, . Wire Svc: AP Format: News/talk, adult contemp, div. News: 15 hrs wkly. Target aud: General. ◆Alan H. Frank, gen mgr.

Nantucket

*WNAN(FM)— Mar. 15, 2000: 91.1 mhz; 2 kw. 72 ft TL: N41 18 22 W70 00 28. Hrs open:
Rebroadcasts WCAI-FM Woods Hole 100%.
Box 82, Woods Hole, 02543. Secondary address: 3 Water St., Woods Hole 02543. Phone: (508) 548-9600. Fax: (508) 548-5517.E-mail: cainan@wgbh.org Web Site:www.capeandislands.org Licensee: WGBH Educational Foundation. (acq 12-31-97; $25,000 with WCAI-FM Woods Hole). Natl. Network: NPR, . Format: News/talk. ◆John Voci, gen mgr & stn mgr.

*WNCK(FM)— June 28, 2002: 89.5 mhz; 78 w horiz, 500 w vert. Ant 118 ft TL: N41 17 06 W70 08 39. Hrs open: 24
Rebroadcasts WGBH(FM) Boston 100%.
C/O WGBH, One Guest St., Boston, 02135. Phone: (617) 300-2300. Fax: (617) 300-1025. Web Site:www.wgbh.org Licensee: Nantucket Public Radio Inc. Format: Var. Target aud: 40 plus. ◆Robert Shapiro, gen mgr.

Natick

WBIX(AM)— November 1972: 1060 khz; 40 kw-D, 2.5 kw-N, 22 kw-CH, DA-3. TL: N42 17 17 W71 25 55. Hrs open: 24 100 Mount Wayte St., 100 Summer St., Framingham, 01702. Phone: (508) 820-2430.E-mail: alex@wbix.com Web Site:www.wbix.com Licensee: WBIX Corp. Group owner: Langer Broadcasting Group L.L.C. (acq 11-29-2005). Population served: 2,900,000 Format: News/talk/business. ◆Alex Langer, gen mgr; Jim Harris, gen sls mgr.

New Bedford

WBSM(AM)— July 17, 1949: 1420 khz; 5 kw-D, 1 kw-N, DA-2. TL: N41 39 02 W70 54 58. Hrs open: 22 Sconticut Neck Rd., Fairhaven, 02719. Phone: (508) 993-1767. Fax: (508) 999-1420.E-mail: petebraley@wbsm.com Web Site:www.wbsm.com Licensee: Citadel Broadcasting Co. Group owner: Citadel Broadcasting Corp. (acq 4-26-2001; grpsl). Population served: 800,000 Natl. Rep: Christal,. Format: News/talk, sports. ◆Gail Le Blanc, gen mgr; Deborah Aguiar, prom dir; Pete Braley, progmg dir.

WCTK(FM)—Licensed to New Bedford. See Providence RI

*WFHL(FM)— 2003: 88.1 mhz; 300 w vert. Ant 134 ft TL: N41 38 15 W70 52 19. Stereo. Hrs open: Box 3025, 02741. Secondary address: 71 William 02740. Phone: (508) 991-7600.E-mail: radio@radiowfhl.com Web Site:www.radiowfhl.com Licensee: New Bedford Christian Radio Inc. Format: Sp, English, Portugese. ◆Manuel Pereira, gen mgr.

WJFD-FM— Feb 22, 1949: 97.3 mhz; 50 kw. 500 ft TL: N41 38 20 W70 52 27. Stereo. Hrs open: 24 270 Union St., 02740. Phone: (508) 997-2929. Fax: (508) 990-3893.E-mail: jorge@wjfd.com Web Site:www.wjfd.com Licensee: Edmund Dinis, trustee (acq 12-18-2001). Population served: 250,000 Format: Ethnic. Target aud: General; Portuguese-speaking community. ◆Edmund Dinis, pres.

WNBH(AM)—Licensed to New Bedford. See Providence RI

Newburyport

WNBP(AM)— Mar 10, 1957: 1450 khz; 1 kw-U. TL: N42 49 23 W70 51 42. Hrs open: 24 8 Enon St, North Beverly, 01915. Phone: (978) 927-1049. Fax: (978) 921-2635.E-mail: info@wnbp.com Web Site:www.wnbp.com Licensee: Port Broadcasting LLC (acq 3-5-2009; $425,000). Population served: 42,000 Natl. Network: AP Radio, . Wire Svc: AP Format: Adults Standards. News staff: one; News: 5 hrs wkly. Target aud: 25-54. Spec prog: Irish 4 hrs wkly. ◆Charlie Curtis, progmg dir; Win Damon, sls dir, news dir, sports cmtr & disc jockey.

*WNEF(FM)— 91.7 mhz; 400 w vert. 354 ft TL: N42 51 56 W70 56 18. Hrs open:
Rebroadcasts WUMB-FM Boston 100%.
Univ. of Massachusetts, 100 Morrissey Blvd., Boston, 02125-3393. Phone: (617) 287-6900. Fax: (617) 287-6916.E-mail: wumb@umb.edu Web Site:www.wumb.org Licensee: University of Massachusetts. Format: Folk. ◆Patricia Monteith, gen mgr; Danielle Knight, dev dir; Brian Quinn, progmg dir.

Newton

WNTN(AM)— Apr 1, 1968: 1550 khz; 10 kw-D. TL: N42 21 27 W71 14 30. Hrs open: 143 Rumford Ave., 02466. Phone: (617) 969-1550. Web Site:www.wntn.com Licensee: Colt Communications LLC. (acq 12-23-98; $602,800). Population served: 2,500,000 Format: Var, Greek, Haitian. Target aud: 40 plus. Spec prog: Irish 6 hrs, Indian 2 hrs wkly. ◆Rob Rudnick, gen mgr; Paul Roberts, opns dir; Leo Sullivan, chief of engrg.

*WZBC(FM)— April 1974: 90.3 mhz; 1 kw. 220 ft TL: N42 20 05 W71 10 31. Stereo. Hrs open: 24 Boston College, McElroy Commons 107, Chestnut Hill, 02467. Phone: (617) 552-3511. Fax: (617) 552-1738.E-mail: info@wzbc.org Web Site:www.wzbc.org Licensee: Trustees of Boston College. Population served: 7,500 Format: Alternative. Target aud: 18-34. ◆Maddie Hall, gen mgr.

Norfolk

WDIS(AM)— Mar 20, 1978: 1170 khz; 1 kw-D, DA. TL: N42 05 32 W71 18 13. Hrs open: Day Time 100 Pond St., 02056. Phone: (508) 384-8255. Fax: (508) 384-1530.E-mail: wdismgmt@aol.com Web Site:www.wdis.com Licensee: Discussion Radio Inc. (acq 8-12-92; $65,000; 9-7-92). Population served: 250,000 Natl. Network: Salem Radio Network, . Format: News/talk. News staff: one; News: 6 hrs wkly. Target aud: 35-64. ◆Corine Slade, gen mgr; Dan Collier, progmg dir.

North Adams

*WJJW(FM)— Sept 5, 1973: 91.1 mhz; 423 w. -830 ft TL: N42 41 27 W73 06 16. Stereo. Hrs open: North Adam State College, 01247. Phone: (413) 662-5405.E-mail: webmaster@mcla.edu Web Site:www.mcla.edu Licensee: Massachusetts College of Liberal Arts. Population served: 20,000 ◆Harris Elder, gen mgr; Nick Strassel, progmg dir; Paul Wiley, chief of engrg.

WNAW(AM)— Nov 23, 1947: 1230 khz; 1 kw-U. TL: N42 41 03 W73 06 23. Hrs open: Box 707, 466 Curran Hwy., 01247-0707. Phone: (413) 663-6567. Fax: (413) 662-2143.E-mail: wnaw@wnaw.com Web Site:www.wnaw.com Licensee: Vox Communications Group LLC. Group owner: Vox Radio Group L.P. (acq 5-10-2004; grpsl). Population served: 45,000 Natl. Rep: McGavren Guild,. Wilkinson Barker Knauer. Format: Full service, adult contemp. News staff: 2. Target aud: Adults. ◆Earl Ingalls, gen mgr, gen sls mgr; Peter Barry, mktg mgr & progmg mgr; Ken Jones, chief of engrg.

WUPE-FM— July 12, 1964: 100.1 mhz; 1.3 kw. Ant 502 ft TL: N42 41 51 W73 03 52. Stereo. Hrs open: Prog sep from AM Box 707, 466 Curran Hwy., 01247-0707. Phone: (413) 663-6567. Fax: (413) 662-2143.E-mail: info@wupe.com Web Site:www.wupe.com Licensee: Vox Communications Group LLC Population served: 150,000 Format: Oldies. Target aud: 35 plus. ◆Dick Savage, gen sls mgr.

North Dartmouth

*WTKL(FM)— September 1973: 91.1 mhz; 1.2 kw. Ant 300 ft TL: N41 37 43 W71 00 24. Stereo. Hrs open: 2351 Sunset Blvd., Suite 170-218, Rocklin, CA, 95765. Phone: (916) 251-1600. Fax: (916) 251-1650. Web Site:www.klove.com Licensee: Educational Media Foundation. (acq 6-30-2006; $725,000). Population served: 200,000 Natl. Network: K-Love, . Format: Contemp Christian. ◆Richard Jenkins, pres.

*WUMD(FM)— June 10, 2006: 89.3 mhz; 96 w horiz, 9.6 kw vert. Ant 305 ft TL: N41 37 43 W71 00 24. Hrs open: 24 285 Old Westport Rd., Dartmouth, 02747. Phone: (508) 999-8149. Fax: (508) 999-8173.E-mail: wumd@umassd.edu Web Site:www.893wumd.org Licensee: University of Massachusetts. Format: Progsv, alternative rock, jazz, free form. Target aud: 13-60; general, high school, college, community. ◆Jennifer Mulcare-Sullivan, stn mgr.

Northampton

WEIB(FM)— 2001: 106.3 mhz; 3 kw. Ant 289 ft TL: N42 22 25 W72 40 26. Stereo. Hrs open: 24 8 North King St., 01060. Phone: (413) 585-1112. Fax: (413) 585-9138.E-mail: weibfm@aol.com Web Site:www.weibfm.com Licensee: Cutting Edge Broadcasting Inc. Format: Smooth jazz. ◆Carol Moore Cutting, pres, gen mgr; Drew Dawson, progmg dir.

WHMP(AM)— December 1950: 1400 khz; 1 kw-U. TL: N42 19 36 W72 39 28. Hrs open: 15 Hampton Ave., 01060-3809. Phone: (413) 586-7400. Fax: (413) 585-0927. Web Site:www.whmp.com Licensee: Saga Communications of New England LLC. Group owner: Saga Communications Inc. (acq 2000; $12 million with co-located FM). Population served: 100,000 Natl. Network: CBS Radio, CNN Radio, . Natl. Rep: Katz Radio,. Wire Svc: AP Format: news/talk, info. News staff: 4; News: 40 hrs wkly. Target aud: 35 plus; upscale, well educated. Spec prog: Pol 3 hrs wkly. ◆Sean O'Mealy, gen mgr.

WLZX(FM)— Nov 1, 1956: 99.3 mhz; 3 kw. 321 ft TL: N42 22 29 W72 40 24. (CP: 6 kw). Stereo. Hrs open: 24 45 Fisher Ave, East Longmeadow, 01028. Phone: (413) 525-4141. Fax: (413) 525-4334.E-mail: info@lazer993.com Web Site:www.lazer993.com Licensee: Saga Communications of New England LLC. Group owner: Saga Communications Inc. (acq 2000; $12 million with co-located AM). Population served: 200,000 Format: Rock/Active. News staff: 2. Target aud: 18-34; male. ◆Gary Zenobi, gen mgr; Bill Buller, gen sls mgr; Courtney Quinn, progmg dir; Kristin McCauley, traf mgr.

*WOZQ(FM)— 1981: 91.9 mhz; 200 w. 115 ft TL: N42 19 13 W72 38 14. Stereo. Hrs open: 6 AM-2 AM Smith College, Campus Ctr 106, North Hampton, 01063. Phone: (413) 585-4956. Phone: (413) 585-4977. Fax: (413) 585-4166.E-mail: wozq@email.smith.edu Web Site:www.smith.edu/wozq Licensee: Trustees of Smith College. Format: Educ, var/div, urban contemp. Target aud: 15 plus; college students & area businesses. ◆Dana Feldesman, stn mgr; Carolyn Cunha, mus dir; Matthea Doughtry, news dir; Elizabeth Willis, chief of engrg; Patrick Connelly, adv.

Northfield

*WNMH(FM)— Sept 10, 1984: 91.5 mhz; 235 w. 308 ft TL: N42 42 52 W72 26 38. Stereo. Hrs open: Northfield Mt. Hermon School, 206 Main St., 01360. Phone: (413) 498-3603. Licensee: Northfield Mount Hermon School. Format: Div. Target aud: Student body & surrounding communities. ◆Bill Hattendorf, gen mgr & opns VP.

Orange

WJDF(FM)— 1995: 97.3 mhz; 3 kw. Ant 328 ft TL: N42 37 19 W72 21 58. (CP: 5.8 kw, ant 82 ft.). Stereo. Hrs open: Box 973, 01364. Phone: (978) 544-5335. Phone: (978) 544-0957. Fax: (978) 544-2131.E-mail: info@wjdf.com Web Site:www.wjdf.com Licensee: Deane Brothers Broadcasting Corp. Format: Adult contemp. ◆Donn Deane, gen mgr; Chad Songer, gen sls mgr; Jay Deane, progmg dir.

Orange-Athol

WJOE(AM)— May 13, 1956: 700 khz; 2.5 kw-D. TL: N42 35 06 W72 16 56. Hrs open: Sunrise-sunset 362 Green St., Gardner, 01440. Secondary address: 660 E. Main St., Orange 01364. Phone: (978) 544-2321. Fax: (978) 544-6977. Licensee: County Broadcasting Co. LLC. Group owner: Northeast Broadcasting Company Inc. (acq 10-6-2003; $650,000 with WXRG(FM) Athol). Population served: 50,000 Format: Oldies. Target aud: 45 plus. ◆Chris Thompson, gen mgr; Billy Curtis, progmg dir.

Orleans

*WFMR(FM)—Not on air, target date: unknown: 91.3 mhz; 750 w vert. Ant 367 ft TL: N41 46 36 W70 00 40. Hrs open: 14 Center St., Provincetown, 02657. Phone: (508) 487-2619. Fax: (508) 487-5524. Licensee: Lower Cape Communications Inc. ◆Tina Lynde, pres.

WFPB(AM)— Apr 10, 1970: 1170 khz; 1 kw-D, DA. TL: N41 46 48 W70 00 36. Hrs open: 24
Rebroadcasts WUMB-FM Boston 100%.
Univ. of Massachusetts, 100 Morrissey Blvd., Boston, 02125-3393. Phone: (617) 287-6900. Fax: (617) 287-6916.E-mail: wumb@umb.edu Web Site:www.wumb.org Licensee: University of Massachusetts. (acq 10-30-98). Population served: 185,000 Format: Folk. ♦Patricia Monteith, gen mgr; Danielle Knight, dev dir; Brian Quinn, progmg dir.

WOCN-FM— July 25, 1974: 104.7 mhz; 50 kw. Ant 504 ft TL: N41 46 48 W70 00 36. Stereo. Hrs open: 24 737 W. Main St., Hyannis, 02601. Phone: (508) 771-1224. Fax: (508) 775-2605.E-mail: wocn@ocean1047.com Web Site:www.ocean1047.com Licensee: Cape Cod Broadcasting License II LLC. (acq 7-10-2007; $7.5 million with WFCC-FM Chatham). Population served: 225,000 Natl. Network: AP Radio, . Natl. Rep: Clear Channel,. Covington & Burling. Wire Svc: AP Format: Full service, soft rock. News staff: 4; News: 32 hrs wkly. Target aud: Adults 25-64. ♦Gregory D. Bone, gen mgr; Wayne W. White, opns mgr; Stephen M. Colella, sls dir; Michelle Lorraine, prom mgr; Donna C. Credit, traf mgr.

Petersham

***WNGB(FM)—**Not on air, target date: unknown: 91.3 mhz; 600 w. Ant -174 ft TL: N42 31 30 W72 16 42. Hrs open: 65 King Rd., Buskirk, NY, 12028-0036. Phone: (518) 686-0975. Fax: (518) 686-0975.E-mail: wngn@wngn.org Web Site:www.wngn.org Licensee: Northeast Gospel Broadcasting Inc. ♦Brian A. Larson, pres & gen mgr.

Pittsfield

WBEC(AM)— March 1947: 1420 khz; 1 kw-U, DA-N. TL: N42 26 40 W73 16 43. Hrs open: 24 211 Jason St., 01201-5907. Phone: (413) 499-3333. Fax: (413) 442-1590.E-mail: info@live959.com Web Site:www.live959.com Licensee: Vox Communications Group LLC. Group owner: Vox Radio Group L.P. (acq 9-13-2002; grpsl). Population served: 80,000 Smithwick & Belendiuk. Format: News/talk, sports. News staff: 2; News: 15 hrs wkly. Target aud: 25-55; 60% male, 40% female. Spec prog: Relg 3 hrs wkly. ♦Peter Barry, gen mgr; Mike Patrick, opns mgr.

WBEC-FM— 1975: 95.9 mhz; 1 kw. Ant 560 ft TL: N42 24 44 W73 17 05. Stereo. Hrs open: 24 Prog sep from AM 211 Jason St., 01201. Phone: (413) 499-3333. Fax: (413) 442-1590.E-mail: info@959.com Web Site:live959.com Population served: 150,000 Natl. Network: Westwood One, . Format: Hot adult contemp. News staff: one; News: 28 hrs wkly. Target aud: 25-54; young adults with families. ♦Tom Conklin, news dir.

WBRK(AM)— Feb 20, 1938: 1340 khz; 1 kw-U. TL: N42 27 00 W73 12 55. Hrs open: 24 100 North St., 01201. Phone: (413) 442-1553. Fax: (413) 445-5294.E-mail: wbrk1340@aol.com Web Site:www.wbrk.com Licensee: WBRK Inc. (acq 6-30-84). Population served: 57,020 Natl. Network: CBS, Westwood One, ABC, . Rgnl rep: interep loca focus Drinker, Biddle & Reath. Format: Full service. News staff: 2. Target aud: 35 plus. Spec prog: Pol 2 hrs, Irish one hr, relg 2 hrs wkly. ♦Willard H. Hodgkins III, CEO & pres; John Campoli, exec VP; Michael J. Bunn, opns VP, opns mgr; Cheryl Tripp, prom dir; Rick Beltaire, progmg VP, progmg dir.

WBRK-FM— Oct 10, 1970: 101.7 mhz; 3 kw. 145 ft TL: N42 28 31 W73 16 07. Stereo. Hrs open: 24 Prog sep from AM 100 North St., 01201. Phone: (413) 442-1553. Fax: (413) 445-5294. Web Site:www.wbrk.com Population served: 65,000 Natl. Network: ABC, . Format: Adult contemp. Target aud: 25-54. ♦Willard Hodgkins III, pres; John Campoli, exec VP; Michael Bunn, opns mgr; Cheryl Tripp, prom dir; Rick Beltaire, progmg dir.

WUPE(AM)— Sept 9, 1971: 1110 khz; 5 kw-D, DA. TL: N42 26 22 W73 17 30. Hrs open: 24 211 Jason St., ., 01201. Phone: (413) 499-3333. Fax: (413) 442-1590.E-mail: wupe@wupe.com Web Site:www.wupe.com Licensee: Vox Communications Group LLC. (acq 12-8-2003; $2.83 million with co-located FM). Population served: 250,000 Natl. Network: ABC, . Natl. Rep: D & R Radio,. Pepper & Corazzini. Format: Oldies. News staff: one; News: 14 hrs wkly. Target aud: 25-54; baby boomers. ♦Peter Barry, gen mgr; Mike Patrick, opns mgr; Dick Savage, sls dir; Larry Kratka, news dir, news rptr; Ken Jones, chief of engrg; Bob Heck, traf mgr.

Plymouth

WPLM(AM)— Aug 8, 1955: 1390 khz; 5 kw-U, DA-2. TL: N41 58 05 W70 42 06. Hrs open: 17 Columbus Rd., 02360. Phone: (508) 746-1390. Fax: (508) 830-1128.E-mail: alana@991.com Licensee: Plymouth Rock Broadcasting Co. Inc. Population served: 85,000 Natl. Rep: Roslin,. Arent, Fox, Kintner, Plotkin & Kahn. Format: Soft adult contemp, business talk. ♦Dr. Laurie Campbell, pres; Alan Anderson, gen mgr, gen sls mgr; Pat Carroll, chief of opns, pub svc dir; Sean Casey, prom dir & progmg dir; Chip Morgan, chief of engrg.

WPLM-FM— June 25, 1961: 99.1 mhz; 50 kw. 430 ft TL: N41 58 02 W70 42 04. Hrs open: Dups AM 100% 17 Columbus Rd., 02360. Phone: (508) 746-1390. Fax: (508) 830-1128.E-mail: alana@991.com Licensee: Plymouth Rock Broadcasting Co. Inc. Format: Adult contemp.

Provincetown

***WOMR(FM)—** Mar 21, 1982: 92.1 mhz; 6 kw. Ant 161 ft TL: N42 03 54 W70 09 31. Stereo. Hrs open: 24 Box 975, 494 Commercial St., 02657. Phone: (508) 487-2106. Fax: (508) 487-5524.E-mail: info@womr.org Web Site:www.womr.org Licensee: Lower Cape Communications Inc. Garvey, Schubert, Baker. Format: Eclectric. News: 5.5 hrs wkly. Target aud: General; div. Spec prog: Black 6 hrs, class 16 hrs, educ 10 hrs, folk 19 hrs, oldies 9 hrs wkly. ♦Tina Lynde, pres; Dave Willard, VP; John Braden, opns mgr.

Quincy

WJDA(AM)— Sept 13, 1947: 1300 khz; 1 kw-D, 72 w-N. TL: N42 15 35 W70 58 36. Hrs open: 24 90 Everett Ave, Chelsea, 02150. Phone: (617) 884-4500. Fax: (617) 884-4515.E-mail: info@wjda1300am.com Web Site:www.wjda1300am.com Licensee: South Shore Broadcasting Co. Population served: 125,000 Natl. Network: ABC, . Format: Ethnic. News staff: 2; News: 10 hrs wkly. Target aud: 35 plus. Spec prog: Cantonese 3 hrs wkly. ♦Charles W. Banta, pres, progmg dir; Mike Logan, news dir.

Rockland

***WRPS(FM)—** Feb 8, 1974: 88.3 mhz; 100 w. 120 ft TL: N42 07 43 W70 55 01. Stereo. Hrs open: 24 34 MacKinlay Way, 02370. Phone: (781) 871-0724. Fax: (781) 982-1483.E-mail: wrps883@yahoo.com Licensee: Rockland Public Schools. Population served: 50,000 Format: Public service, educ, adult contemp. Target aud: General. ♦David J. Cable-Murphy, gen mgr; Robert Mulligan, chief of engrg.

Rockport

***WWRN(FM)—**Not on air, target date: unknown: 91.5 mhz; 800 w. Ant 285 ft TL: N42 37 28 W70 39 15. Hrs open: 160 Bangor St., Augusta, ME, 04330. Phone: (207) 622-1340. Fax: (207) 623-2874. Web Site:www.worshipradionetwork.org Licensee: Light of Life Ministries Inc. ♦Denise Lafountain, gen mgr.

Salem

WESX(AM)— Jan 1, 1939: 1230 khz; 1 kw-U. TL: N42 31 06 W70 51 41. Hrs open: 90 Everett Ave, Chelsea, 02150. Phone: (617) 884-4500. Fax: (617) 884-4515.E-mail: info@wesx1230am.com Web Site:www.wesx1230am.com Licensee: North Shore Broadcasting Corp. (acq 4-1-50). Population served: 550,000 Natl. Network: ABC, Westwood One, . Wire Svc: AP Format: Ethnic. News staff: 2; News: 25 hrs wkly. Target aud: 35 plus; general. Spec prog: Auto repair 2 hrs, gardening 2 hrs, home improvement 2 hrs, restaurant/dining 2 hrs, Pol 2 hrs wkly. ♦Charles Banta, gen mgr & news dir.

***WMWM(FM)—** 1976: 91.7 mhz; 130 w. Ant 132 ft TL: N42 30 14 W70 53 26. Stereo. Hrs open: 7 AM-midnight Campus Ctr., 352 Lafayette St., 01970-5353. Phone: (978) 745-9401. Fax: (978) 542-8127.E-mail: eboard@wmwm.com Web Site:www.wmwmsalem.com Licensee: Salem State College. Population served: 40,000 Format: Var. Target aud: General. ♦Bruce Perry, gen mgr; Paul Collins, chief of engrg; Richard Tucker, progmg dir & disc jockey.

Sandwich

***WSDH(FM)—** 1976: 91.5 mhz; 310 w. 150 ft TL: N41 44 06 W70 27 35. Hrs open: 10 AM-4 PM (M-F) Stn currently dark Sandwich High School, 365 Quaker Meetinghouse Rd., East Sandwich, 02563. Phone: (508) 888-0420. Phone: (508) 888-4900. Fax: (508) 833-8392. Licensee: Sandwich Public Schools. Format: CHR, classic rock, educ. News: 4 hrs wkly. Target aud: 12-40. ♦Chip Hill, gen mgr.

Scituate

***WSMA(FM)—** May 2006: 90.5 mhz; 5 w horiz, 7.7 kw vert. Ant 492 ft TL: N41 56 02 W70 35 10. Hrs open: 400 A. Franklin St., Braintree, 02184. Phone: (781) 848-0500. Fax: (978) 343-0665.E-mail: doug@blesseddesigns.com Licensee: CSN International. (group owner). Format: Relg.

Sheffield

***WBSL-FM—** September 1973: 91.7 mhz; 250 w. 50 ft TL: N42 06 57 W73 25 00. Hrs open: Berkshire School, 245 N. Undermountain Rd., 01257-9672. Phone: (413) 229-8511. Phone: (413) 229-1927. Fax: (413) 229-1229.E-mail: jharris@berkshireschool.org Web Site:www.berkshireschool.org Licensee: Berkshire School Inc. Population served: 10,000 Format: Div. Target aud: General. Spec prog: Jazz 15 hrs, Black 2 hrs, folk 2 hrs, Sp 2 hrs, Pol one hr wkly. ♦James Harris, gen mgr; John Weinner, stn mgr; Thomas Jaworski, engr.

South Hadley

***WMHC(FM)—** May 14, 1957: 91.5 mhz; 100 w. Ant -18 ft TL: N42 15 12 W72 34 40. Stereo. Hrs open: Box 9010, Mt. Holyoke College, 01075. Phone: (413) 538-2044. Phone: (413) 538-2019. Fax: (413) 538-2431.E-mail: amlewis@mtholyoke.edu Web Site:www.mtholyoke.edu/org/wmhc Licensee: President & Trustees of Mount Holyoke College. Population served: 50,000 Natl. Network: AP Radio, . Format: Rock, urban contemp, var/div. Target aud: General; Mount Holyoke College Community. ♦Catherine Moldonado, progmg dir.

South Yarmouth

WKPE-FM— August 1994: 103.9 mhz; 5.5 kw. Ant 341 ft TL: N41 41 30 W70 08 43. Stereo. Hrs open: 24 737 W Main St., Hyamis, 02601. Phone: (508) 771-1224. Fax: (508) 775-2605.E-mail: wkpe@capecountry104.com Web Site:www.capecountry104.com Licensee: Sandab Communications L.P. II. (group owner; acq 6-19-98; $1.2 million). Population served: 225,000 Natl. Rep: Clear Channel,. Garvey, Schubert & Barer. Format: Country. Target aud: 18 - 49; males. Spec prog: American Top 40. ♦Gregory D. Bone, gen mgr; Wayne W. White, opns mgr; Stephen M. Colella, sls dir; Michelle Lorraine, prom dir.

Southbridge

WESO(AM)— Mar 20, 1955: 970 khz; 1 kw-D, 21 w-N. TL: N42 03 59 W71 59 28. Hrs open: 24 100 Foster St., 01550. Phone: (508) 909-0970. Fax: (508) 764-2682. Web Site:thespirit970.com Licensee: Money Matters Inc. (acq 4-11-01; $250,000). Population served: 60,000 Format: Pop country, loc news/talk, sports. News staff: 2; News: 30 hrs wkly. Target aud: 34-59. Spec prog: Pol 3 hrs. ♦Dick Vaughan, COO, pres; Lia Zaido, opns mgr; J.P. Ellery, news dir.

WWFX(FM)— Nov 1, 1968: 100.1 mhz; 2.85 kw. 295 ft (CP: 1.74 kw, ant 590 ft.). Hrs open: 24 250 Commercial St., Worcester, 01608. Secondary address: WBA Inc., 295 Bridle Trail Rd, Needham 02192. Phone: (508) 752-1045. Fax: (508) 793-0824. Web Site:www.thefoxfm.com Licensee: Citadel Broadcasting Co. Group owner: Citadel Broadcasting Corp. (acq 4-26-01; grpsl). Population served: 400,000 Natl. Network: Jones Radio Networks, . Natl. Rep: D & R Radio,. Format: Main Stream Rock. News staff: 2; News: 10 hrs wkly. Target aud: 25-54. ♦Bonnie Gomes, gen mgr; JayBeau Jones, opns mgr; Tim Brennan, prom dir.

Springfield

WACE(AM)—See Chicopee

WACM(AM)—See West Springfield

***WAIC(FM)—** February 1967: 91.9 mhz; 230 w. 66 ft TL: N42 06 44 W72 33 29. Stereo. Hrs open: 1000 State St., 01109. Phone: (413) 205-3941. Fax: (413) 205-3943.E-mail: proswhughes@msn.com Licensee: American International College. Population served: 163,905 Format: Div. Target aud: 16-40. Spec prog: Gospel. ♦Will Hughes, CEO, chmn & pres; Doc Holiday, gen mgr; Jean Paul, opns dir.

WAQY(FM)— Dec 17, 1966: 102.1 mhz; 50 kw. 780 ft TL: N42 05 00 W72 42 16. Stereo. Hrs open: 24 45 Fisher Ave., East Longmeadow, 01028. Phone: (413) 525-4141. Fax: (413) 525-4334.E-mail: gzenobi@springfieldrock.com Web Site:www.rock102.com Licensee: Saga Communications of New England LLC. Group owner: Saga Communications Inc. (acq 6-2-92; grpsl). Natl. Rep: Katz Radio,. Smithwick & Belendiuk. Format: Classic rock. Target aud: General; upscale young adults with high income. ♦Gary Zenobi, gen mgr; Dave Cooper, gen sls mgr, progmg dir; Kristin McCauley, traf mgr.

WHLL(AM)— Sept 1, 1932: 1450 khz; 1 kw-U. TL: N42 06 32 W72 36 44. Stereo. Hrs open: Box 9500, 01102. Secondary address: 101 West St. 01104. Phone: (413) 737-1414. Fax: (413) 737-1488.E-mail: info@947wmas.com Web Site:www.947wmas.com Licensee: Citadel Broadcasting Co. Group owner: Citadel Broadcasting Corp. (acq 6-3-2004; $22 million with co-located FM). Population served: 493,000 Natl. Network: ESPN Radio, . Format: Sports. Spec prog: Black one hr, relg 2 hrs wkly. ◆Susan Van Stone, VP & gen mgr; Craig Swim, gen sls mgr; Lucie Grondin, prom dir, prom mgr; Frank Connolly, progmg dir, news dir; Richard Kenadek, chief of engrg.

WHYN(AM)— 1941: 560 khz; 5 kw-D, 1 kw-N, DA-2. TL: N42 11 37 W72 41 02. Stereo. Hrs open: 24 1331 Main St., 01103-. Phone: (413) 781-1011. Fax: (413) 734-4434. Web Site:www.whynam560.com Licensee: CC Licenses LLC. Group owner: Clear Channel Communications Inc. (acq 1996; grpsl). Population served: 163,905 Haley, Bader & Potts. Format: News/talk. News staff: 6. Target aud: General. ◆Sean Davey, gen mgr; Pat McKay, opns mgr.

WHYN-FM— 1946: 93.1 mhz; 8.9 kw. Ant 1,000 ft TL: N42 14 28 W72 38 56. Stereo. Hrs open: 1331 Main St., 01103. Phone: (413) 781-1011. Fax: (413) 734-4434.E-mail: fm@mix931.com Web Site:www.mix931.com Licensee: CC Licenses LLC. Format: Adult contemp. Target aud: 25-54.

WMAS-FM— Dec 1, 1947: 94.7 mhz; 50 kw. 194 ft TL: N42 06 32 W72 36 44. Stereo. Hrs open: Prog sep from AM Box 9500, 01102. Phone: (413) 737-1414. Fax: (413) 737-1488.E-mail: info@947wmas.com Web Site:www.947wmas.com Licensee: Citadel Broadcasting Co. Population served: 163,905 Format: Adult contemp. ◆Paul Cannon, progmg dir.

*WNEK-FM— Feb 17, 1976: 105.1 mhz; 13 w. -23 ft TL: N42 06 55 W72 31 05. Stereo. Hrs open: Western New England College, 1215 Wilbraham Rd., 01119-2684. Phone: (413) 782-1582. Licensee: Trustees of Western New England College. Population served: 250,000 Format: Var. Target aud: 15-35; college community, greater Springfield area. ◆Ian Martin, gen mgr & opns dir.

WNNZ(AM)—(Westfield, July 8, 1987: 640 khz; 50 kw-D, 1 kw-N, DA-2. TL: N42 10 46 W72 45 05. Stereo. Hrs open: 24 1331 Main St., 01103. Phone: (413) 781-1011. Fax: (413) 734-4434. Web Site:www.wnnz.com Licensee: CC Licenses LLC. Group owner: Clear Channel Communications Inc. (acq 11-24-98; $1.2 million). Population served: 1,500,000 Natl. Network: NPR, . Akin, Gump, Strauss, Hauer & Feld. Format: News, public radio. Target aud: 25-54; upscale adults. ◆Sean Davey, gen mgr.

*WSCB(FM)— Mar 1, 1958: 89.9 mhz; 100 w. 35 ft TL: N42 05 59 W72 33 30. Hrs open: 263 Alden St., 01109. Phone: (413) 748-3722. Phone: (413) 748-3712. Fax: (413) 748-3153. Licensee: President & Trustees of Springfield College. Population served: 200,000 Format: Div. ◆Shazz Wilson, stn mgr; Hunter Golden, progmg dir; Greg Antonelli, news dir.

WSPR(AM)— June 1936: 1270 khz; 5 kw-D, 1 kw-N, DA-2. TL: N42 05 24 W72 36 11. Hrs open: 34 Sylvan St., West Springfield, 01089. Phone: (413) 781-5200. Fax: (413) 734-2240.E-mail: msanchez@davidsonmediagroup.com Web Site:www.wspr1270.com Licensee: Davidson Media Station WSPR Licensee LLC. (acq 5-16-2005; $6.8 million with WACM(AM) West Springfield). Format: Sp, tropical. ◆Paul Gois, gen mgr & opns dir.

*WTCC(FM)— Aug 19, 1971: 90.7 mhz; 4 kw. 92 ft TL: N42 06 32 W72 34 45. Stereo. Hrs open: Box 9000, 01103. Secondary address: One Armory Sq. 01105. Phone: (413) 746-9822. Fax: (413) 781-3747. Fax: (413) 755-6305.E-mail: managerwtcc@stcc.edu Web Site:www.wtccfm.org Licensee: Springfield Technical Community College. Population served: 200,000 Format: Var. Target aud: General. ◆Denise Stewart, gen mgr, stn mgr; Mark Leak, progmg dir; Beverly Showell, news dir; Fred Krampito, chief of engrg.

Stockbridge

*WDMY(FM)—Not on air, target date: unknown: 91.9 mhz; 1.7 kw. Ant -56 ft TL: N42 17 55 W73 17 28. Hrs open: Box 486, 01262. Phone: (703) 465-2361. Web Site:www.mercysong.com Licensee: MercySong Inc. ◆Vincent J. Flynn, pres.

Sudbury

*WYAJ(FM)— September 1980: 97.7 mhz; 4 w. 220 ft TL: N42 22 30 W71 24 28. Hrs open: 390 Lincoln Rd., 01776. Phone: (978) 443-9961. Fax: (978) 443-8824.E-mail: paul_sarapas@lsrhs.net Web Site:www.lsrhs.net Licensee: Lincoln-Sudbury Regional School District. Population served: 2,000 Format: CHR, new age, classic rock. Target

aud: General. Spec prog: Black 6 hrs, class 3 hrs, jazz 5 hrs, loc rock artists 3 hrs wkly. ◆Paul Sarapas, gen mgr.

Taunton

WSNE-FM— Jan 26, 1966: 93.3 mhz; 30 kw. 620 ft TL: N41 51 56 W71 17 22. Stereo. Hrs open: 75 Oxford St., Suite 302, Providence, 02905. Phone: (401) 781-9979. Phone: (401) 224-1933. Fax: (401) 781-9329.E-mail: feedback@933coastfm.com Web Site:www.933coastfm.com Licensee: Capstar TX L.P. Group owner: Clear Channel Communications Inc. (acq 8-30-00; grpsl). Population served: 2,100,200 Natl. Network: AP Radio, Premiere Radio Networks, . Natl. Rep: Clear Channel,. Format: Adult contemp. Target aud: 25-54; mostly women. Spec prog: Pub affrs 4 hrs wkly. ◆James Corwin, gen mgr; Mark Coffey, sls dir; Melissa Bowler, prom mgr; Rick Everett, progmg VP & progmg dir.

Tisbury

WMVY(FM)— June 1, 1981: 92.7 mhz; 3 kw. 300 ft TL: N41 26 17 W70 36 47. (CP: Ant 328 ft.). Stereo. Hrs open: 21 Box 1148, Vineyard Haven, 02568. Secondary address: 57 Carrolls Way, Vineyard Haven 02568. Phone: (508) 693-5000. Fax: (508) 693-8211.E-mail: pj@mvyradio.com Web Site:www.mvyradio.com Licensee: Aritaur Communications Inc. (acq 6-17-98; $1 million). Population served: 180,000 Natl. Network: Moody, AP Radio, . Natl. Rep: McGavren Guild,. Format: Album-Oriented Rock. News staff: one. Target aud: 25-49; upper income, active consumer group. Spec prog: Class 4 hrs, jazz 4 hrs wkly. ◆Greg Orcutt, gen mgr; Nick Ward, gen sls mgr, prom dir; P.J. Finn, progmg dir.

Truro

WGTX(FM)— 2000: 102.3 mhz; 340 w. Ant 98 ft TL: N42 01 03 W70 04 23. Hrs open: 300 Western Ave., Allsston, 02134. Phone: (617) 254-6333. Fax: (617) 254-2234.E-mail: karl@karlnurse.com Licensee: Dunes 102FM LLC (acq 6-5-2007; $550,000). Format: News/talk. ◆Karl Nurse, gen mgr.

Turners Falls

WRSI(FM)— July 1994: 93.9 mhz; 3 kw. Ant 328 ft TL: N42 32 01 W72 35 34. Stereo. Hrs open: 24 15 Hampton Ave, Northampton, 01060-3809. Phone: (413) 586-7400. Fax: (413) 585-0927. Web Site:www.wrsi.com Licensee: Saga Communications of New England LLC. Group owner: Saga Communications Inc. (acq 2-13-2004; grpsl). Population served: 180,000 Natl. Network: ABC, . Format: AAA. News: 9 hrs wkly. Target aud: 18-54; young, educated, spend money. ◆Sean O'Mealy, gen mgr.

Waltham

*WBRS(FM)— Feb 5, 1968: 100.1 mhz; 25 w. 151 ft TL: N42 22 09 W71 15 28. Stereo. Hrs open: 24 Brandeis Univ., 415 South St., 02453-2728. Phone: (781) 736-5277.E-mail: info@wbrs.org Web Site:www.wbrs.org Licensee: Brandeis University. Population served: 300,000 Wire Svc: UPI Format: Div. News: 5 hrs wkly. Target aud: General. ◆Jonathan Lehrfeld, gen mgr; Anton Kovalski, progmg dir; Joanna Simon, news dir.

WKLB-FM— 1948: 102.5 mhz; 8.1 kw. Ant 1,151 ft TL: N42 18 27 W71 13 27. Stereo. Hrs open: 24 55 William T Morrissey Blvd., Dorchester, 02125-3315. Phone: (617) 822-9600. Fax: (617) 822-6671.E-mail: info@wklb.com Web Site:www.wklb.com Licensee: Charles River Broadcasting WCRB License Corp. (acq 11-15-2006). Population served: 535,000 Natl. Rep: Katz Radio,. Format: Country. Target aud: 25-54. ◆Phil Redo, gen mgr & sls VP; Cathy Cram, gen sls mgr; Mike Brophey, progmg dir.

WRCA(AM)— 1948: 1330 khz; 5 kw-U, DA-2. TL: N42 21 16 W71 15 44. (CP: COL Watertown. 25 kw-D, 17 kw-N, DA-2). Stereo. Hrs open: 24 552 Massachusetts Ave., Suite 201, Cambridge, 02139. Phone: (617) 492-3330. Fax: (617) 492-2800. Web Site:1330wrca.com Licensee: WAEC License LP. Group owner: Beasley Broadcast Group Inc. (acq 5-2000; $6 million). Format: Sp/ethnic. News: 10 hrs wkly. Target aud: General. ◆Stu Fink, gen mgr, opns mgr & progmg dir.

Ware

WARE(AM)— July 11, 1948: 1250 khz; 5 kw-D, 2.5 kw-N, DA-2. TL: N42 14 41 W72 12 30. Hrs open: 3 Converse St., Palmer, 01069. Phone: (413) 289-2300. Fax: (413) 289-2323.E-mail: info@realoldies1250.com Web Site:www.realoldies1250.net Licensee:

Success Signal Broadcasting Inc. (acq 12-3-02; $250,000). Population served: 500,000 Natl. Network: Fox News Radio, . Natl. Rep: Rgnl Reps,. Cohn & Marks. Format: Oldies 50s, 60s & 70s. News staff: 3. Target aud: 30 plus. Spec prog: Pol 4 hrs wkly. ◆Marshall Sanft, pres, exec VP & gen mgr.

Watertown

WAZN(AM)— January 1958: 1470 khz; 1.4 kw-D, 3.4 kw-N, DA-2. TL: N42 24 49 W71 12 40. Hrs open: 24 Rebroadcasts WLYN(AM) Lynn (partial schedule). 500 W. Cummings Park, Suite 2600, Woburn, 01801. Phone: (781) 938-0869. Fax: (781) 938-0933.E-mail: Jeffk@mrbi.net Web Site:www.mrbi.net Licensee: Multicultural Radio Broadcasting Licensee LLC. Group owner: Multicultural Radio Broadcasting Inc. (acq 12-11-2002; $1.8 million). Population served: 2,000,000 Format: Russian, leased time-ethnic. Russian, Hispanic (Sp & Portuguese). ◆Jeff Kline, gen mgr.

Webster

WGFP(AM)— Apr 1, 1980: 940 khz; 1 kw-D. TL: N42 03 17 W71 50 00. Hrs open: 24 27 Douglas Rd., 01570. Phone: (508) 943-9400. Fax: (508) 943-0405.E-mail: barry@coolcountry940.com Web Site:www.coolcountry940.com Licensee: Just Because Inc. (acq 6-12-2003). Population served: 250,000 Format: Country. News: 25 hrs wkly. Target aud: 25-54. Spec prog: live high school sports. ◆Barry Sims, CEO.

WORC-FM— Apr 8, 1994: 98.9 mhz; 3 kw. 410 ft TL: N42 02 30 W71 59 18. Stereo. Hrs open: 24 Dups AM 100% 250 Commercial St., Suite 530, Worcester, 01608. Phone: (508) 752-1045. Fax: (508) 793-0824.E-mail: jaybeau.jones@citcomm.com Web Site:www.oldies989.com Licensee: Citadel Broadcasting Co. Group owner: Citadel Broadcasting Corp. (acq 6-8-99; $3.5 million). Population served: 500,000 Natl. Network: Westwood One, ABC, . Format: Oldies. News: 8 hrs wkly. Target aud: 25-49. Spec prog: Sp one hr wkly. ◆Bonnie Gomes, gen mgr; Tim Brennan, prom dir; JayBeau Jones, progmg dir, progmg mgr.

Wellesley

*WZLY(FM)— Sept 20, 1976: 91.5 mhz; 10 w. 164 ft TL: N42 17 35 W71 18 21. Stereo. Hrs open: Schneider Ctr., 106 Central St., 02181. Phone: (781) 283-2690.E-mail: info@wzly.net Web Site:www.wzly.net Licensee: Wellesley College. Population served: 2,000 Format: Var. Target aud: General; Wellesley town and college community. ◆Julia Luechtefeld, gen mgr.

Wellfleet

*WRYP(FM)— 2006: 90.1 mhz; 2.5 kw vert. Ant 80 ft TL: N42 01 53 W70 05 26. Hrs open: 356 Broad St., Fitchburg, 01420-3030. Phone: (888) 310-7729. Web Site:www.renewfm.com Licensee: Horizon Christian Fellowship (acq 3-24-2006; $150,000 for CP). Format: Christian. ◆George Small, gen mgr.

West Barnstable

*WKKL(FM)— Sept 19, 1977: 90.7 mhz; 205 w. 71 ft TL: N41 41 31 W70 20 16. Hrs open: 24 Cape Cod Community College, Rt. 132, 02668. Phone: (508) 375-4030. Phone: (508) 362-2131, EXT. 4684. Fax: (508) 375-4020.E-mail: wkkl247@yahoo.com Web Site:www.geocities.com/wkkl247 Licensee: Board of Trustees Cape Cod Community Colleges. Population served: 40,000 Format: Alternative. ◆Lisa Zinsius, gen mgr.

West Springfield

WACM(AM)— Aug 28, 1949: 1490 khz; 1 kw-U. TL: N42 06 06 W72 37 22. Hrs open: 34 Sylvan St., 01089. Phone: (413) 781-5200. Fax: (413) 734-2240.E-mail: msanchez@davidsonmediagroup.com Web Site:www.wacm1490.com Licensee: Davidson Media Station WACM Licensee LLC. (acq 5-16-2005; $6.8 million with WSPR(AM) Springfield). Population served: 1,200,000 Format: Sp. ◆Paul Gois, gen mgr.

West Yarmouth

*WBUR(AM)— October 1940: 1240 khz; 1 kw-U. TL: N41 38 07 W70 14 06. Hrs open: 24 Rebroadcasts WBUR-FM Boston 98%. 890 Commonwealth Ave., Boston, 02215. Phone: (617) 353-0909.

Fax: (617) 353-4747.E-mail: info@wbur.bu.edu Web Site:www.wbur.org Licensee: The Executive Committee of Trustees of The Boston University Group owner: WBUR Group (acq 12-17-96). Format: News/talk. News: 78 hrs wkly. Target aud: 25-54; intelligent adults interested in news & politics. Spec prog: Sp 5 hrs wkly. ♦Paul LaCamera, gen mgr; Corey Lewis, stn mgr; Sam Fleming, progmg dir; John Davidson, news dir; Jeffrey Hutton, engrg dir.

WXTK(FM)— Dec 30, 1948: 95.1 mhz; 50 kw. 246 ft TL: N41 38 08 W70 14 06. Stereo. Hrs open: 154 Barnstable Rd., Hyannis, 02601-2930. Phone: (508) 778-2888. Fax: (508) 778-9651.E-mail: info@95wxtk.com Web Site:www.95wxtk.com Licensee: Qantum of Cape Cod License Co. LLC. Group owner: Boch Broadcasting (acq 2005; grpsl). Natl. Network: ABC, . Natl. Rep: Eastman Radio,. Format: News/talk, sports. Target aud: 25 plus. ♦Allison Makkay, VP, gen mgr; Steve McVie Solomon, progmg dir.

Westborough

WAAF(FM)—Licensed to Westborough. See Worcester

Westfield

WNNZ(AM)—Licensed to Westfield. See Springfield

***WSKB(FM)**— October 1974: 89.5 mhz; 100 w. 130 ft TL: N42 07 55 W72 47 51. Stereo. Hrs open: Westfield State College, Ely Campus, 01086. Phone: (413) 572-5579. Fax: (413) 572-5625. Web Site:www.wsc.ma.edu/wskb Licensee: Westfield State College. Population served: 250,000 Format: Talk, alternative, div. Target aud: General. ♦Barbara Hand, opns mgr; Dave Kowalski, progmg dir.

Williamstown

***WCFM(FM)**— Sept 8, 1958: 91.9 mhz; 440 w. Ant -836 ft TL: N42 42 38 W73 12 06. Hrs open: The Paresky Ctr., Williams College, 01267. Phone: (413) 597-3265. Fax: (413) 597-2259.E-mail: wcfmbd@wso.williams.edu Web Site:wcfm.williams.edu Licensee: The President & Trustees of Williams College. ♦Adam Ain, gen mgr.

Winchendon

***WKMY(FM)**— 2006: 91.1 mhz; 60 w. Ant 450 ft TL: N42 42 09 W72 02 18. Hrs open:
Rebroadcasts KLVR(FM) Middletown, CA 100%.
2351 Sunset Blvd., Suite 170-218, Rocklin, CA, 95765. Phone: (916) 251-1600. Fax: (916) 251-1650. Web Site:www.klove.com Licensee: Educational Media Foundation. (acq 6-30-2005; $15,000 for CP). Natl. Network: K-Love, . Format: Contemp Christian. ♦Mike Novak, pres.

Woods Hole

***WCAI(FM)**— Sept. 25, 2000: 90.1 mhz; 6.5 kw. 298 ft TL: N41 25 26 W70 40 20. Hrs open: Box 82, 02543. Secondary address: 3 Water St. 02543. Phone: (508) 548-9600. Fax: (508) 548-5517.E-mail: cainan@wgbh.org Web Site:www.capeandislands.org Licensee: WGBH Educational Foundation (acq 12-31-97; $25,000 with WNAN(FM) Nantucket). Natl. Network: NPR, . Format: News/talk. ♦John Voci, gen mgr, stn mgr; Susan Loucks, pres & dev dir; Steve Young, progmg dir.

Worcester

WAAF(FM)—(Westborough, June 15, 1961: 107.3 mhz; 20 kw. Ant 784 ft TL: N42 18 11 W71 53 52. Stereo. Hrs open: 20 Guest St., 3rd Fl., Boston, 02135. Phone: (617) 779-5400. Fax: (617) 779-5484.E-mail: info@waaf.com Web Site:www.waaf.com Population served: 542,000 Format: Active rock. Target aud: 25-54. ♦Julie Kahn, gen mgr & gen sls mgr.

***WBPR(FM)**— 1994: 91.9 mhz; 1 kw. 469 ft TL: N42 15 11 W71 57 41. Hrs open:
Rebroadcasts WUMB-FM Boston 100%.
Univ. of Massachutts, 100 Morrissey Blvd., Boston, 02125-3393. Phone: (617) 287-6900. Fax: (617) 287-6916.E-mail: wumb@umb.edu Web Site:www.wumb.org Licensee: University of Massachusetts. Format: Folk. Target aud: 25-45. ♦Patricia A. Monteith, gen mgr; Danielle Knight, dev dir; Brian Quinn, progmg dir.

***WCHC(FM)**— Sept 12, 1977: 88.1 mhz; 100 w. -656 ft TL: N42 14 15 W71 48 31. Hrs open: 7 AM-2 AM Box G, Holy Cross College, One College St., 01610. Phone: (508) 793-2475. Fax: (508) 793-2471.E-mail: info@wchc.com Web Site:www.college.holycross.edu/wchc Licensee: Trustees of the College of the Holy Cross. Population served: 5,000 Winston & Strawn. Format: Alternative. News: 5 hrs wkly. Target aud: 12-35; adventurous. Spec prog: Black 8 hrs, class 6 hrs, jazz 6 hrs, metal 6 hrs, funk 3 hrs wkly. ♦Andrew Rhoades, gen mgr.

WCRN(AM)— Dec 5, 1994: 830 khz; 7 kw-D, 5 kw-N, DA-2. TL: N42 14 47 W71 55 51. Hrs open: 82 Franklin, 01608. Phone: (508) 792-5803. Fax: (508) 770-0659.E-mail: studio@wcrnradio.com Web Site:www.wcrnradio.com Licensee: Carter Broadcasting Corp. (acq 1-16-90). Format: True Talk. Target aud: 25-54. ♦Ken Carter, pres; Kurt Carberry, gen mgr; Art Dufault, stn mgr; Chris Thompson, sls dir.

***WCUW(FM)**— Dec 4, 1973: 91.3 mhz; 630 w. 145 ft TL: N42 15 46 W71 47 59. Stereo. Hrs open: 24 910 Main St., 01610. Phone: (508) 753-1012.E-mail: wcuw@wcuw.org Web Site:www.wcuw.com Licensee: WCUW Inc. Population served: 500,000 Format: Div. News: one hr wkly. Target aud: General. Spec prog: Fr 2 hrs, Sp 19 hrs, Ger 2 hrs, Pol 6 hrs, ethnic 10 hrs wkly. ♦Joe Cutroni, gen mgr.

***WICN(FM)**— Nov 21, 1969: 90.5 mhz; 8.1 kw horiz, 7.2 kw vert. Ant 371 ft TL: N42 20 07 W71 42 54. (CP: N42 20 09 W71 42 57). Stereo. Hrs open: 24 50 Portland St., 01608. Phone: (508) 752-0700. Fax: (508) 752-7518.E-mail: webmaster@wicn.org Web Site:www.wicn.org Licensee: WICN Public Radio Inc. Population served: 500,000 Natl. Network: NPR, . Shaw Pittman. Format: Jazz, big band, folk. News: 12 hrs wkly. Target aud: 35 plus; high education, high income. ♦Mike Gorman, pres; Thomas Kenney, VP, mktg mgr; Brian Barlow, gen mgr; Kyle Warren, opns dir, opns mgr; Tyra Penn, dev dir.

WNEB(AM)— Dec 18, 1946: 1230 khz; 1 kw-U. TL: N42 16 23 W71 49 23. Hrs open: 24 70 James St., Suite 201, 01603. Phone: (508) 831-9863. Fax: (508) 831-7964.E-mail: info@wvne.net Web Site:www.wneb.net Licensee: Blount Masscom Inc. Group owner: Blount Communications Group Population served: 500,000 Format: Spanish. Target aud: 25-54. ♦William A. Blount, pres; David Young, VP; Emanuel DaCunha, stn mgr; Randolph Berkson, opns mgr.

WORC(AM)— February 1925: 1310 khz; 5 kw-D, 1 kw-N, DA-2. TL: N42 13 19 W71 49 02. Stereo. Hrs open: 24 122 Green St., Ste 2R, 01604-4138. Phone: (508) 791-2111, x203. Fax: (508) 752-6897.E-mail: info@power1310.com Web Site:www.power1310.com Licensee: Antonio F. Gois. (acq 1-7-2005; $950,000). Population served: 600,000 Natl. Network: Westwood One, . Format: Tropical. News staff: one. Target aud: 29-54; Latinos. Spec prog: Sports 6 hrs, Pol 4 hrs wkly, Sp one hr wkly. ♦Ivon Gois, gen mgr.

WSRS(FM)— June 17, 1940: 96.1 mhz; 14 kw. 863 ft TL: N42 18 34 W71 54 10. Stereo. Hrs open: 24 Prog sep from AM 98 Stereo Ln., Paxton, 01612. Phone: (508) 757-9696. Fax: (508) 757-1779.E-mail: info@wsrs.com Web Site:www.wsrs.com Population served: 744,800 Natl. Network: ABC, . Format: Adult contemp. News staff: one; News: 5 hrs wkly. Target aud: 25-54. ♦Bruce Palmer, prom dir; Tom Holt, progmg dir & mus dir; George Brown, news dir; Lanie Brown, traf mgr.

WTAG(AM)— May 1, 1924: 580 khz; 5 kw-U, DA-2. TL: N42 20 13 W71 49 15. Stereo. Hrs open: 24 98 Stereo Ln., Paxton, 01612. Phone: (508) 795-0580. Phone: (508) 757-9696. Fax: (508) 757-1779.E-mail: info@wsrs.com Web Site:www.wtag.com Licensee: Capstar TX L.P. Group owner: Clear Channel Communications Inc. (acq 8-30-2000; grpsl). Population served: 620,000 Natl. Network: CBS, . Format: News/talk. News staff: 6; News: 40 hrs wkly. Target aud: 25-54. Spec prog: Sports. ♦Michael Schaus, gen mgr; Susan Remkiewicz, natl sls mgr; Bruce Palmer, prom dir, prom mgr; George Brown, progmg dir, news dir; Greg Byrne, pub affrs dir; Dan Kelleher, chief of engrg.

WVEI(AM)— 1926: 1440 khz; 5 kw-U, DA-N. TL: N42 20 13 W71 49 15. Hrs open: 24
Simulcast with WEEI(AM) Boston 100%.
181 Moreland St., 01609-1049. Phone: (508) 752-5611. Fax: (508) 752-1006.E-mail: jsheridan@entercom.com Licensee: Entercom Boston II License LLC. Group owner: Entercom Communications Corp. (acq 10-15-98; grpsl). Population served: 43600 Natl. Rep: CBS Radio,. Format: Sports. ♦Julie Kahn, gen mgr & stn mgr; Jack Sheridan, sls dir, natl sls mgr; Eric Fitch, chief of engrg.

WVNE(AM)—See Leicester

WXLO(FM)—(Fitchburg, August 1960: 104.5 mhz; 37 kw. 563 ft TL: N42 30 27 W71 49 37. Stereo. Hrs open: 24 250 Commercial St., Suite 530, 01608. Phone: (508) 752-1045. Fax: (508) 793-0824. Web Site:www.wxlo.com Licensee: Citadel Broadcasting Co. Group owner: Citadel Broadcasting Corp. Population served: 1,000,000 Natl. Rep: McGavren Guild,. Kaye, Scholer, Fierman, Hays & Handler. Format: Hot A/C. News: 5 hrs wkly. Target aud: 25-54. Spec prog: 70s mus 5 hrs wkly. ♦Bonnie Gomes, gen mgr; JayBeau Jones, progmg dir.

Michigan

Ada

WPRR(AM)— 1998: 1680 khz; 10 kw-D, 680 w-N. TL: N42 56 09 W85 27 26. Stereo. Hrs open: 24 3777 44th St. S.E., Kentwood, 49512. Phone: (616) 554-5958. Fax: (616) 656-9326.E-mail: ggoodrich@gqti.com Licensee: Goodrich Radio L.L.C. Population served: 650,000 Format: Talk. News staff: one. ♦Robert Goodrich, chmn; Ross Pettinga, gen mgr & stn mgr.

Adrian

WABJ(AM)— Nov 13, 1946: 1490 khz; 1 kw-U. TL: N41 54 02 W84 00 51. Hrs open: 24 121 W. Maumee St., 49221. Phone: (517) 265-1500. Fax: (517) 263-4525.E-mail: friends@tc3net.com Licensee: Friends Communications of Michigan Inc. Group owner: Friends Communications Inc. (acq 10-1-90; grpsl; 10-29-90). Population served: 92,000 Rgnl. Network: Mich. Farm. Mich. Farm Rgnl rep: Michigan. Fletcher, Heald & Hildreth. Format: News/talk. News staff: 2; News: 9 hrs wkly. Target aud: General. Spec prog: Farm 7 hrs, relg 3 hrs wkly. ♦Bob Elliot, chmn & gen mgr.

WLEN(FM)— June 9, 1965: 103.9 mhz; 3 kw. 299 ft TL: N41 54 11 W83 59 13. Stereo. Hrs open: 24 Box 687, 49221. Secondary address: 242 W. Maumee St. 49221. Phone: (517) 263-1039. Fax: (517) 265-5362. Web Site:www.wlen.com Licensee: Lenawee Broadcasting Co. Natl. Network: CNN Radio, . Format: Adult contemp. News staff: one. Target aud: 25-54. Spec prog: Sp 4 hrs wkly. ♦Julie M. Koehn, pres & gen mgr.

WQTE(FM)— Sept 1, 1976: 95.3 mhz; 3 kw. Ant 299 ft TL: N41 48 15 W84 05 25. Stereo. Hrs open: 24 121 W. Maumee St., 49221. Phone: (517) 265-1500. Fax: (517) 263-4525.E-mail: friends@tc3net.com Licensee: Friends Communications of Michigan Inc. (acq 10-1-90; grpsl; 10-29-90). Population served: 150,000 Format: Country. News: 2 hrs wkly. Target aud: 25-54.

***WVAC-FM**— Feb 13, 1967: 107.9 mhz; 13 w horiz. 79 ft TL: N41 53 55 W84 03 33. Hrs open: Adrian College, 110 S. Madison St., 49221. Phone: (517) 265-5161, Ext 4154. Phone: (517) 264-3141. Fax: (517) 264-3331. Licensee: Adrian College Board of Trustees. Population served: 15,000 Format: Div. Target aud: 18-23; those affiliated to the college lifestyle. ♦Steven Shehan, gen mgr.

Albion

WBXX(FM)—(Marshall, Oct 1, 1968: 104.9 mhz; 6 kw. Ant 328 ft TL: N42 18 47 W84 55 46. Hrs open: 390 Golden Ave., Battle Creek, 49015. Phone: (269) 963-5555. Fax: (269) 963-5185.E-mail: info@battlecreekradio.com Web Site:www.battlecreekradio.com Licensee: Capstar TX L.P. Group owner: Clear Channel Communications Inc. Population served: 168,840 Format: Adult contemp. Target aud: 18-49. ♦Steve Stoimenoff, gen mgr; Jeff Cassidy, progmg dir.

***WUFN(FM)**— April 1971: 96.7 mhz; 3.2 kw. Ant 456 ft TL: N42 15 56 W84 38 43. Stereo. Hrs open: 24 7355 N. Oracle Rd., Suite 200, Tucson, 85704. Phone: (520) 742-6976. Fax: (520) 469-7312.E-mail: dphelps@flc.org Web Site:www.967flr.org Licensee: Family Life Broadcasting System. (group owner) Population served: 150,000 Natl. Network: USA, AP Radio, . Format: Inspirational, Christian. News: 1.5 hrs wkly. Target aud: 25-54; Christian families. ♦Randy Carlson, pres; Dawn Bumstead, gen mgr, dev VP.

Allegan

WZUU(FM)— April 1991: 92.3 mhz; 860 w. 600 ft TL: N42 34 52 W85 45 17. Stereo. Hrs open: 24 Box 80, 706 E. Allegan St., Otsego, 49078. Phone: (269) 343-1717. Fax: (269) 692-6861.E-mail: tflynn@wqxc.com Web Site:www.wzuu.com Licensee: Forum Communications Inc. (acq 6-1-97). Population served: 500,000 Natl. Rep: Roslin,. Rgnl rep: Michigan. Richard Hayes. Format: Classic rock. News staff: one; News: 2 hrs wkly. Target aud: 25-54; professionals. ♦Robert Brink, pres; Tom Flynn, gen mgr; Tim Bontrager, gen sls mgr; Bill Mitchell, progmg dir.

Allendale

***WGVU-FM**— July 15, 1983: 88.5 mhz; 3 kw. 311 ft TL: N43 03 24 W85 57 31. Stereo. Hrs open: 24 Grand Valley State Univ., 301 W. Fulton, Grand Rapids, 49504-6492. Phone: (616) 331-6666. Fax: (616) 331-6625.E-mail: wgvu@gvsu.edu Web Site:www.wgvu.org Licensee:

Board of Control of Grand Valley State University. Population served: 700,000 Natl. Network: NPR, AP Radio, . Rgnl. Network: Mich. Pub. Format: Jazz, news. News staff: 5; News: 26 hrs wkly. Target aud: 25 plus; mid to upper educ & income levels. ♦Michael T. Walenta, gen mgr; Ken Kolbe, opns mgr; Pamela Holtz, prom mgr; Fred Martino, news dir.

Alma

WFYC(AM)— Aug 17, 1948: 1280 khz; 1 kw-D, 45 w-N. TL: N43 22 08 W84 36 19. Hrs open: 24 Box 665, 48801. Phone: (989) 463-3175. Fax: (989) 463-6674. Web Site:www.wqbxradio.com Licensee: Jacom Inc. (acq 1996). Population served: 100,000 Format: Sports. Target aud: 25-50. Spec prog: Farm 4 hrs wkly. ♦James Sommerville, pres, gen mgr, progmg dir; Susan Sommerville, prom mgr.

WMLM(AM)—See Saint Louis

***WQAC-FM**— Mar 27, 1993: 90.9 mhz; 100 w. 66 ft TL: N43 22 50 W84 40 14. Hrs open: 7 AM-2 AM (M-F); noon-2 AM (S, Su) Alma College, 614 W. Superior St., 48801. Phone: (989) 463-7095. Fax: (989) 463-7277.E-mail: wqaccharts@blazemail.com Web Site:students.alma.edu/organizations/wqac Licensee: Alma College. Population served: 15,000 Format: Adult alternative. Target aud: 13-24; high school & college students. ♦Steven Best, gen mgr.

WQBX(FM)— November 1964: 104.9 mhz; 6 kw. Ant 328 ft TL: N43 22 08 W84 36 19. Stereo. Hrs open: 24 Box 665, 48801. Phone: (989) 463-3175. Fax: (989) 463-6674. Web Site:www.wqbxradio.com Population served: 250,000 Natl. Network: ABC, . Format: Adult contemp.

Alpena

WATZ(AM)— 1946: 1450 khz; 1 kw-U. TL: N45 03 58 W83 29 06. Hrs open: 20 Box 536, 49707. Secondary address: 123 Prentiss 49707. Phone: (989) 354-8400. Fax: (989) 354-3436.E-mail: watz@watz.com Web Site:www.watz.com Licensee: WATZ Radio Inc. Group owner: Midwestern Broadcasting Co. Population served: 17,500 Rgnl. Network: Mich. Farm. Mich. Farm Format: Talk. News staff: 2; News: 31 hrs wkly. Target aud: 35-64. Spec prog: Farm 3 hrs, Ger 2 hrs, Pol 2 hrs, relg 2 hrs wkly. ♦Mike Centala, gen mgr; Steve Wright, opns mgr; Bruce Johnson, news dir.

WATZ-FM— 1967: 99.3 mhz; 17 kw. Ant 843 ft TL: N44 51 25 W83 32 34. Stereo. Hrs open: 20 Box 536, 49707. Secondary address: 123 Prentiss 49707. Phone: (989) 354-8400. Fax: (989) 354-3436. Web Site:www.watz.com Population served: 130,000 Format: Country. Target aud: 25-54. ♦Suzie Martin, mus dir.

***WCML-FM**— Apr 24, 1978: 91.7 mhz; 100 kw. 1,171 ft TL: N45 08 17 W84 09 44. Stereo. Hrs open: 24
Rebroadcasts WCMU-FM Mount Pleasant 100%.
Public Broadcasting Ctr., Central Michigan Univ., Mount Pleasant, 48859. Phone: (989) 774-3105. Fax: (989) 774-4427.E-mail: cmuradio@cmich.edu Web Site:www.wcmu.org Licensee: Central Michigan University. Population served: 30,000 Natl. Network: NPR, PRI, . Rgnl. Network: Mich. Pub. Dow, Lohnes & Albertson. Wire Svc: AP Format: Jazz, class, news & info. News staff: 2; News: 45 hrs wkly. Target aud: General. ♦Edward Grant, gen mgr & rgnl sls mgr. Co-owned TV: *WCML(TV) affil

WHSB(FM)— May 1965: 107.7 mhz; 99 kw. 760 ft TL: N45 03 40 W83 43 05. Stereo. Hrs open: 1491 M-32 W., Apena, 49707. Phone: (989) 354-4611. Fax: (989) 354-4014.E-mail: tnrn@charterinternet.com Web Site:www.1077thebay.com Licensee: Edwards Communications LC. Group owner: Northern Radio Network (acq 12-21-2004; grpsl). Population served: 58,300 Natl. Rep: Michigan Spot Sales,. Wire Svc: UPI Format: Adult contemp. Target aud: 25-54. ♦Jerry Edwards, pres; Darrel Kelly, progmg dir, chief of engrg.

WKJZ(FM)—(Hillman, December 1993: 94.9 mhz; 50 kw. 492 ft TL: N45 01 33 W83 54 52. Hrs open:
Rebroadcasts WQLB(FM) Tawas City 85%.
Box 549, Tawas City, 48764. Phone: (989) 362-3417. Fax: (989) 362-4544.E-mail: wkjc@wkjc.com Web Site:www.wkjc.com Licensee: Carroll Enterprises Inc. (group owner; acq 6-29-92; 7-27-92). Format: Classic rock. ♦John Carroll Jr., gen mgr.

Ann Arbor

WAAM(AM)— October 1947: 1600 khz; 5 kw-U, DA-2. TL: N42 11 32 W83 41 09. Stereo. Hrs open: 24 4230 Packard Rd., 48108. Phone: (734) 971-1600. Fax: (734) 973-2916.E-mail: alan.black@waamradio.com Web Site:www.talkradio1600.com Licensee: Ann Arbor First Ventures L.P. (group owner; (acq 12-26-2007). Population served: 250,000 Natl. Network: Westwood One, . Bryan Cave. Format: MOR, news/talk. News staff: 4; News: 20 hrs wkly. Target aud: 35 plus; home owners & professionals. Spec prog: Relg 4 hrs, old time radio 6 hrs wkly. ♦David Drolshagen, gen mgr & gen sls mgr.

***WCBN-FM**— Jan 23, 1972: 88.3 mhz; 200 w. 177 ft TL: N42 16 37 W83 44 07. Stereo. Hrs open: 24 530 Student Activities Bldg., 48109-1285. Phone: (734) 647-4122. Phone: (734) 763-3535.E-mail: fm@wcbn.org Web Site:www.wcbn.org Licensee: Regents of the University of Michigan. Population served: 99,797 Format: Var. Target aud: 18-49. ♦Brendt Rioux, gen mgr; Rachel Silveri, gen mgr & progmg dir; Alex Sergay, chief of engrg.

WDEO(AM)—(Ypsilanti, Nov 16, 1962: 990 khz; 9.2 kw-D, 250 w-N. TL: N42 15 53 W83 36 47 (D), N42 15 55 W83 36 42 (N). Stereo. Hrs open: 24 Box 504, One Ave Maria Dr., 48106. Phone: (734) 930-5200. Fax: (734) 930-3179.E-mail: hroot@wdeo.net Web Site:www.wdeo.net Licensee: Word Broadcasters Inc. 990 Investors LLC (acq 9-8-99; $2.5 million). Population served: 4,600,000 Dennis Kelly Law Offices. Format: Christian, talk. News: 9 hrs wkly. Target aud: 21 plus; adult Christian. ♦Al Kresta, CEO; Michael Jones, gen mgr; Steve Clarke, opns mgr.

WQKL(FM)— Feb 14, 1967: 107.1 mhz; 3 kw. 289 ft TL: N42 16 41 W83 44 32. Stereo. Hrs open: Prog sep from AM 1100 Victors Way, Suite 100, 48108. Phone: (734) 302-8100. Fax: (734) 213-7508. Web Site:www.annarbors107one.com Population served: 130,000 Natl. Rep: Cumulus Radio Sales,. Format: AAA. News staff: one; News: 4 hrs wkly. Target aud: 25-50; women. ♦Chris Ammel, progmg dir; Brian Larsen, news dir; Chris Wachner, prom.

WSDS(AM)—(Salem Township, 1962: 1480 khz; 750 w-D, 5 kw-N, DA-2. TL: N42 15 42 W83 37 10. Hrs open: 24 580 W. Clark Rd., Ypsilanti, 48198. Phone: (734) 484-0078. Fax: (734) 484-5313.E-mail: wsds@wsds1480.com Web Site:www.explosiva1480.com Licensee: Birach Broadcasting Corp. (acq 1-25-2005; $1.5 million). Population served: 2,050,000 Format: Spanish variety. News staff: one; News: top at hour 8am-8pm. Target aud: 25 plus. Spec prog: Mexican Regional Music and Latin. ♦Jose Vazquez, pres; Alex Resendez, gen mgr; Ivonne Machado, opns mgr, prom; Miguel A. Vega, sls dir, disc jockey; Francisco Urrutia, prom mgr, sls; Carmen Perez, progmg mgr; Ralph Hines, chief of engrg.

WTKA(AM)— Apr 26, 1945: 1050 khz; 10 kw-D, 500 w-N, DA-2. TL: N42 08 46 W83 39 36. Hrs open: 1100 Victors Way, Suite 100, 48108. Phone: (734) 302-8100. Fax: (734) 213-7508. Web Site:www.wtka.com Licensee: Capstar TX L.P. Group owner: Clear Channel Communications Inc. (acq 8-7-00; grpsl). Population served: 99,797 Natl. Network: ESPN Radio, . Natl. Rep: Cumulus Radio Sales,. Format: Sports. News staff: one. Target aud: 18-34; male. ♦Brian Cowan, progmg dir; Brian Laren, news dir.

***WUOM(FM)**— 1948: 91.7 mhz; 93 kw. 780 ft TL: N42 24 24 W83 54 54. Stereo. Hrs open: 24 535 W. William St., Suite 110, 48103. Phone: (734) 764-9210. Fax: (734) 647-3488.E-mail: michigan.radio@umich.edu Web Site:www.michiganradio.org Licensee: The Regents of University of Michigan. Population served: 130,000 Natl. Network: NPR, PRI, . Rgnl. Network: Mich. Pub. Dow, Lohnes & Albertson. Wire Svc: AP Format: News/talk. News staff: 7; News: 140 hrs wkly. ♦Peggy J. Watson, opns mgr.

WWWW-FM— March 1962: 102.9 mhz; 49 kw horiz, 42 kw vert. 499 ft TL: N42 15 04 W83 48 28. Stereo. Hrs open: 24 1100 Victors Way, Suite 100, 48108. Phone: (734) 302-8100. Fax: (734) 213-7508.E-mail: programming@w4country.com Web Site:www.w4country.com Licensee: Capstar TX L.P. Group owner: Clear Channel Communications Inc. (acq 8-7-2000; grpsl). Population served: 200,000 Natl. Rep: Cumulus Radio Sales,. Format: Country. ♦Bob Bolak, gen mgr; Brent Dingman, gen sls mgr; Brian Cowan, progmg dir.

Ashley

WJSZ(FM)— Mar 14, 1994: 92.5 mhz; 2 kw. 400 ft TL: N43 10 55 W84 26 58. Hrs open: 24 103 N. Washington, Owosso, 48867. Phone: (989) 725-1925. Fax: (989) 725-7925.E-mail: rodk@voyager.net Web Site:www.z925.com Licensee: Krol Communications Inc. (acq 12-29-2005; $650,000). Mich. Farm Miller & Neely. Format: Adult contemp. News: 90 mins wkly. Target aud: 25-54; general. ♦Rob Krol, pres & opns dir; Angie Bucsf, local news ed.

Atlanta

WFDX(FM)—Licensed to Atlanta. See Petoskey

Auburn Hills

***WAHS(FM)**— 1975: 89.5 mhz; 100 w. 141 ft TL: N42 37 42 W83 13 56. Hrs open: 2800 Waukegan St., 48326. Phone: (248) 852-9247. Fax: (248) 852-0595. Licensee: Avondale School District. Population served: 3,000 Format: CHR. ♦Rick Kreinbring, gen mgr.

WXOU(FM)—Licensed to Auburn Hills. See Rochester

Bad Axe

WLEW(AM)— 1950: 1340 khz; 1 kw-U, DA-D. TL: N43 47 56 W83 01 21. Hrs open: 24 Prog sep from FM 935 S. Van Dyke Rd, 48413. Phone: (989) 269-9931. Fax: (989) 269-7702. Licensee: Thumb Broadcasting Inc. Population served: 80,000 Format: Country. News staff: 2; News: 19 hrs wkly. Target aud: 18-50. ♦Richard Aymen, gen mgr.

WLEW-FM— 1956: 102.1 mhz; 50 kw. Ant 492 ft TL: N43 53 28 W83 07 26. Stereo. Hrs open: 24 935 S. Van Dyke Rd., 48413. Phone: (989) 269-9931. Fax: (989) 269-7702. Licensee: Thumb Broadcasting Inc. (acq 9-15-93; with co-located AM; 10-11-93). Population served: 620,000 Format: Adult contemp, classic rock. Target aud: 25-50. ♦Richard Aymen, CEO, VP, gen mgr, progmg dir; Matthew Aymen, VP, sls VP; Craig Routzhan, gen mgr, news dir, pub affrs dir; Jerry Stocker, sls VP, chief of engrg; Tina Hind, traf mgr & farm dir.

Baraga

***WVCN(FM)**— 1998: 104.3 mhz; 100 kw. Ant 859 ft TL: N46 39 50 W88 23 06. Stereo. Hrs open: 24 3434 W. Kilbourn Ave., Milwaukee, WI, 53208. Phone: (414) 935-3000. Fax: (414) 935-3015.E-mail: wvcn@vcyamerica.org Web Site:www.vcyamerica.org Licensee: Keweenaw Bay Broadcasting Inc. Group owner: VCY/America Inc. (acq 7-8-99). Format: Christian. ♦Dr. Randall Melchert, pres; Vic Eliason, VP & gen mgr; Jim Schneider, progmg dir, pub affrs dir; Tom Schlueter, mus dir; Gordon Morris, news dir; Andy Eliason, chief of engrg.

Battle Creek

WBCK(AM)— July 9, 1948: 930 khz; 5 kw-D, 1 kw-N, DA-2. TL: N42 17 40 W85 11 00. Hrs open: 390 Golden Ave., 49015. Phone: (269) 963-5555. Fax: (269) 963-5185. Licensee: Stratus Radio LLC Group owner: Clear Channel Communications Inc. (acq 12-20-2007). Population served: 170,000 Format: News/talk. ♦Steve Gaines, gen mgr.

WBCK-FM— Feb 28, 1975: 95.3 mhz; 3 kw. Ant 269 ft TL: N42 17 17 W85 09 54. Stereo. Hrs open: 390 Golden Ave., 49015. Phone: (269) 963-5555. Fax: (269) 963-5185.E-mail: info@battlecreekradio.com Web Site:www.battlecreekradio.com Licensee: Capstar TX L.P. (acq 8-30-2000; grpsl). Population served: 170,000 Format: News/talk. Target aud: 25-54. ♦Steve Stoimenoff, gen mgr; Tim Collins, prom mgr, progmg dir; Walker Sisson, chief of engrg.

WBFN(AM)— July 1, 1993: 1400 khz; 1 kw-U. TL: N42 18 15 W85 11 31. Hrs open: 7355 N. Oracle Rd., Tucson, AZ, 85704. Phone: (520) 742-6976. Fax: (520) 742-6979. Web Site:www.flc.org Licensee: Aloha Station Trust LLC Group owner: Clear Channel Communications Inc. (acq 7-30-2008; grpsl). Population served: 168,840 Format: Christian. ♦Randy L. Carlson, pres.

WKFR-FM— June 11, 1963: 103.3 mhz; 50 kw. 500 ft TL: N42 21 19 W85 20 28. Stereo. Hrs open: 24 4154 Jennings Dr., Kalamazoo, 49048. Phone: (269) 344-0111. Fax: (269) 344-4223.E-mail: radio@wkfr.com Web Site:www.wkfr.com Licensee: Cumulus Licensing Corp. Group owner: Cumulus Media Inc. (acq 5-26-98; grpsl). Population served: 700,000 Format: CHR. News staff: one; News: 3 hrs wkly. Target aud: 25-54. ♦Lew Dickey, CEO, pres; John Pinch, COO; Martin Gausvik, CFO; Mike McKelly, opns mgr; Ken Evans, progmg dir.

Bay City

***WCHW-FM**— Sept 1, 1973: 91.3 mhz; 110 w. 125 ft TL: N43 35 19 W83 52 28. Hrs open: 1624 Columbus Ave., 48708. Phone: (989) 892-1741. Phone: (989) 892-5533. Fax: (989) 892-7946.E-mail: wchwonline@fnmail.com Web Site:www.wchwonline.freewebspace.com Licensee: School District Bay City. Population served: 49,449 Format: AOR. ♦Jeremy Powers, gen mgr & progmg dir.

WHNN(FM)— 1947: 96.1 mhz; 100 kw. 1,020 ft TL: N43 33 10 W83 41 24. Stereo. Hrs open: 24 1740 Champagne Dr. N., Saginaw, 48604. Phone: (989) 298-9466. Fax: (989) 754-9600. Web Site:www.whnn.com Licensee: Citadel Broadcasting Co. Group owner:

Citadel Broadcasting Corp. (acq 4-26-01; grpsl). Population served: 1,000,000 Format: Oldies. News staff: one; News: 6 hrs wkly. Target aud: 25-54. ◆Scott Meier, gen mgr; Scott Stein, progmg dir.

WIOG(FM)— September 1969: 102.5 mhz; 86 kw. 860 ft TL: N43 28 24 W83 50 40. Stereo. Hrs open: 24 1740 N. Champagne Dr., Saginaw, 48604. Phone: (989) 776-2100. Fax: (989) 754-5990.E-mail: info@wiog.com Web Site:www.wiog.com Licensee: Citadel Broadcasting Co. Group owner: Citadel Broadcasting Corp. (acq 2-8-99; grpsl). Population served: 500,000 Natl. Network: ABC, . Natl. Rep: McGavren Guild,. Format: Adult contemp. News staff: one; News: 5 hrs wkly. Target aud: 25-54. ◆Chris Monk, gen mgr; Matt Bing, gen sls mgr; Jerry Noble, progmg dir.

*WLKB(FM)— July 25, 1993: 89.1 mhz; 50 kw vert. Ant 371 ft TL: N43 33 42 W83 58 52. Stereo. Hrs open: 24
Rebroadcasts KLVR(FM) Santa Rosa, CA 100%.
2351 Sunset Blvd., Suite 170-218, Rocklin, CA, 95765. Phone: (916) 251-1600. Fax: (916) 251-1650. Web Site:www.klove.com Licensee: Educational Media Foundation. (acq 8-8-2006; $800,000). Natl. Network: K-Love, . Format: Contemp Christian. ◆Richard Jenkins, pres.

WMAX(AM)—Licensed to Bay City. See Saginaw

WSGW(AM)—See Saginaw

*WUCX-FM— September 1989: 90.1 mhz; 30 kw. 479 ft TL: N43 33 10 W83 41 24. Stereo. Hrs open: 1961 Delta Rd., Univ. Ctr., 48710. Phone: (989) 686-9292. Fax: (989) 686-0155.E-mail: wucx@delta.edu Web Site:www.delta.edu/broadcasting Licensee: Central Michigan University. Natl. Network: NPR, PRI, . Rgnl. Network: Mich. Pub. Radio, Lohnes & Albertson. Format: Jazz, blues, news. Target aud: General. ◆Barry Baker, gen mgr; Howard Sharper, progmg mgr, news dir, chief of engrg; Tom Garnett, chief of engrg.

Bear Creek Township

*WTLI(FM)— Sept 16, 1998: 89.3 mhz; 6 kw vert. 1,023 ft TL: N45 10 12 W84 45 04. Hrs open:
rebroadcast of WLGH(FM) Leroy Township.
Box 388, Williamston, 48895. Phone: (517) 381-0573. Fax: (877) 850-0881.E-mail: info@positivehits.net Web Site:www.positivehits.net Licensee: Superior Communications. Format: Adult Christian hit. ◆Jenn Czelada, gen mgr; Ed Czelada, progmg dir.

Bear Lake

WCUZ(FM)— Nov 2, 1987: 100.1 mhz; 3 kw. Ant 328 ft TL: N44 25 18 W86 07 17. Hrs open:
Simulcasts WLDR-FM Traverse City 100%.
13999 S. West Bay Shore Dr., Traverse City, 49684-6206. Secondary address: 1532 Forrester Rd, Frankfort 49635. Phone: (231) 947-3220. Fax: (231) 947-7201. Web Site:www.wldr.com Licensee: Roy E. Henderson. (group owner; (acq 9-27-2000; $590,000 with WBNZ(FM) Beulah). Population served: 35,000 Baraff, Koerner & Olender. Format: Country. ◆Roy Henderson, pres & gen mgr.

Beaverton

WMRX-FM— Sept 15, 1980: 97.7 mhz; 4.1 kw. Ant 400 ft TL: N43 53 16 W84 31 45. Stereo. Hrs open:
Rebroadcasts WMPX(FM) Midland 100%.
Box 1689, Midland, 48641-1689. Secondary address: 1510 Bayliss St., Midland 48640. Phone: (989) 631-1490. Fax: (989) 631-6357.E-mail: requests@wmpxwmrx.com Web Site: www.wmpxwmrx.com Licensee: Steel Broadcasting Inc. (acq 1990). Natl. Network: ABC, . Format: Adult standards, big band, classic. News: 8 hrs wkly. Target aud: General; 35+. Spec prog: Sounds of Sinatra 2 hrs wkly. ◆Thomas Steel, pres & gen mgr; Aaron Whiting, gen sls mgr.

Belding

*WSLI(FM)— 2009: 90.9 mhz; 2.9 kw vert. Ant 98 ft TL: N43 05 12 W85 18 59. Hrs open:
Rebroadcasts WLGH(FM) Leroy Township 100%.
148 E Grand River Rd, Williamstown, 48895. Phone: (517) 381-0573. Web Site:www.smile.fm Licensee: Smile FM. Format: Contemp Chirstian. ◆Edward Czelada, pres; Jenn Czelada, gen mgr.

Benton Harbor

*WAYO-FM—Not on air, target date: unknown: 89.9 mhz; 250 w. Ant 335 ft TL: N42 04 19 W86 22 14. Hrs open: 1159 E. Beltline Ave. N.E., Grand Rapids, 49525. Phone: (616) 942-1500. Fax: (616) 942-7078. Web Site:www.way.fm Licensee: Cornerstone University. Target aud: Teens, young adults. ◆Rich Anderson, gen mgr.

WHFB-FM—Licensed to Benton Harbor. See Benton Harbor-St. Joseph

WSJM-FM— June 15, 1998: 94.9 mhz; 2.2 kw. Ant 380 ft TL: N42 04 19 W86 22 14. Hrs open: 24 Box 107, St. Joseph, 49085. Secondary address: 580 E. Napier Ave. 49022. Phone: (269) 925-1111. Fax: (269) 925-1011.E-mail: info@wsjm.com Web Site:www.wsjm.com Licensee: WSJM Inc. Group owner: The Mid-West Family Broadcast Group Rgnl rep: Michigan Spot Sales Format: News/talk. ◆Joe Daguanno, VP, sls dir; Gayle Olson, gen mgr; Jim Gifford, opns dir; Sue Patzen, prom dir.

Benton Harbor-St. Joseph

WHFB(AM)— Sept 22, 1947: 1060 khz; 5 kw-D, 2.5 kw-CH. TL: N42 04 44 W86 28 00. Hrs open: 2100 Fairplain Ave., Benton Harbor, 49022. Phone: (269) 925-9300. Fax: (269) 925-0065.E-mail: whfbam@whfbam.com Licensee: WHFB Broadcast Associates L.P. Group owner: WinCom Communications Group Inc. (acq 8-85). Population served: 180,000 Natl. Network: Mich. Farm. Mich. Farm Format: News/talk. News staff: one. Target aud: General. ◆Bill Stanley, gen mgr, progmg dir; Jill Ferraro, rgnl sls mgr.

WHFB-FM—(Benton Harbor, Oct 10, 1947: 99.9 mhz; 50 kw. Ant 497 ft TL: N42 03 17 W86 27 31. Stereo. Hrs open: 2100 Fairplain Ave., Benton Harbor, 49022. Phone: (269) 925-9300. Fax: (269) 925-0065.E-mail: info@catcountry999.com Web Site:www.catcountry999.com Licensee: WHFB Broadcast Associates L.P. Format: Country. Target aud: 25-54. ◆Mike Sullivan, gen sls mgr; Jim Roberts, progmg dir.

WIRX(FM)—(Saint Joseph, June 20, 1966: 107.1 mhz; 1.2 kw. 498 ft TL: N42 04 19 W86 22 14. Stereo. Hrs open: 24 Prog sep from AM Box 107, St. Joseph, 49085. Secondary address: 580 E. Napier, Saint Joseph 49022. Phone: (269) 925-1111. Phone: (269) 925-9756. Fax: (269) 925-1011.E-mail: info@wirx.com Web Site:wirx.com Population served: 293,000 Davis Wright Tremaine. Wire Svc: AP Format: Rock. Target aud: 18-49. ◆Bob Bucholtz, gen sls mgr.

WSJM(AM)—(Saint Joseph, Nov 18, 1956: 1400 khz; 880 w-U. TL: N42 05 12 W86 26 40. Hrs open: 24 Box 107, St. Joseph, 49085. Secondary address: 580 E. Napier, Benton Harbor 49022. Phone: (269) 925-1111. Phone: (269) 925-9756. Fax: (269) 925-1011.E-mail: info@wsjm.com Web Site:www.wsjm.com Licensee: WSJM Inc. Group owner: The Mid-West Family Broadcast Group (acq 1-1-59). Population served: 170,000 Natl. Network: ABC, . Mich. Talk Davis Wright Tremaine. Wire Svc: AP Format: Full service, news/talk, sports. News staff: 4; News: 30 hrs wkly. Target aud: 35 plus. Spec prog: Black 5 hrs wkly. ◆Gayle Olson, pres, gen mgr; Jim Gifford, opns dir; Joe Daguanno, VP & sls dir; Annette Weston, news dir; Bob Bucholtz, sls.

Berrien Springs

WAUS(FM)—Licensed to Berrien Springs. See South Bend IN

Beulah

WBNZ(FM)— January 1998: 92.3 mhz; 50 kw. Ant 446 ft TL: N44 36 38 W86 09 38. Stereo. Hrs open: 13999 S.W. Bayshore Dr., Traverse City, TX, 49684. Phone: (231) 947-3220. Fax: (231) 947-7201. Licensee: Roy E. Henderson. (group owner; acq 9-27-2000; $590,000 with WCUZ(FM) Bear Lake). Format: Country. Target aud: 18-54; male. ◆Roy Henderson, gen mgr.

Big Rapids

WBRN(AM)— Jan 6, 1953: 1460 khz; 5 kw-D, 2.5 kw-N, DA-N. TL: N43 39 49 W85 28 54. Stereo. Hrs open: 24 18720 16 Mile Rd., 49307. Phone: (231) 796-7000. Fax: (231) 796-7951.E-mail: wbrnfm@wbrn.com Web Site:www.wbrn.com Licensee: Mentor Partners Inc. (acq 6-21-2005; $850,000 with co-located FM). Population served: 110,900 Natl. Network: ESPN Radio, . Natl. Rep: Michigan Spot Sales,. Minn. News Net. Format: News/talk, sports. News staff: one; News: 12 hrs wkly. Target aud: 35 plus; adults. ◆Jeffrey Scarpelli, pres; Brian Goodenow, opns dir; George Keen, chief of engrg.

WWBR(FM)— September 1964: 100.9 mhz; 6 kw. 318 ft TL: N43 39 49 W85 28 54. Stereo. Hrs open: 24 Prog sep from AM 18720 16 Mile Rd., 49307. Phone: (231) 796-7000. Fax: (231) 796-7951. Web Site:www.wwbr.com Mich. Radio Wire Svc: AP Format: Country. News staff: one; News: 10 hrs wkly. Target aud: 25-54. ◆Jeff Scarpelli, pres; Marc Pittman, opns dir; George Keen, chief of engrg.

WYBR(FM)— June 30, 1982: 102.3 mhz; 10.5 kw. 436 ft TL: N43 41 01 W85 34 56. Stereo. Hrs open: 24 18720 16 Mile Rd., 49307. Phone: (231) 796-7000. Fax: (231) 796-7951.E-mail: DIANE@WYBR.COM Web Site:www.wybr.com Licensee: Mentor Partners Inc. (acq 8-10-98). Population served: 175,000 Format: Hot AC. News staff: 2; News: 8 hrs wkly. Target aud: 25-49. Spec prog: Relg one hr wkly. ◆Jeffrey J. Scarpelli, pres; Marc Pittman, gen mgr & opns dir; George Keen, chief of engrg.

Birmingham

WCSX(FM)— Mar 14, 1987: 94.7 mhz; 13.5 kw. 945 ft TL: N42 27 13 W83 09 50. Stereo. Hrs open: 24 One Radio Plaza, Ferndale, 48220. Phone: (248) 398-9470. Fax: (248) 541-9279.E-mail: info@wcsx.com Web Site:www.wcsx.com Licensee: Greater Michigan Radio Inc. Group owner: Greater Media Inc. (acq 7-3-73). Population served: 443,800 Natl. Rep: McGavren Guild,. Format: Classic rock. Target aud: 25-54; males. ◆Tom Bender, VP & gen mgr.

Bloomfield Hills

*WBFH(FM)— Oct 1, 1976: 88.1 mhz; 360 w. 100 ft TL: N42 34 42 W83 17 10. Stereo. Hrs open: 24 4200 Andover Rd., 48302. Phone: (248) 341-5690. Fax: (248) 341-5679.E-mail: thebiff@Radio.fm Web Site:www.wbfh.fm Licensee: Board of Education of Bloomfield Hills School District. Population served: 250,000 Putbrese, Hunsaker & Trent, P.C. Format: Div, CHR, educ. Target aud: 12-34. Spec prog: Prep sports 6 hrs wkly. ◆Pete Bowers, gen mgr; Randy Carr, stn mgr; Ron Wittebols, progmg.

Boyne City

WBCM(FM)— Apr 10, 1978: 93.5 mhz; 14.1 kw. 928 ft TL: N45 10 44 W85 05 42. Stereo. Hrs open: 24
Simulcast of WTCM-FM Traverse City.
314 E. Front St., Traverse City, 49684. Phone: (231) 947-7675. Fax: (231) 929-3988.E-mail: country@wtcmradio.com Web Site:www.wtcmi.com Licensee: Biederman Investments Inc. (acq 9-6-90; $250,000; 10-1-90). Natl. Rep: Katz Radio,. Cordon & Kelly. Format: Modern country. News staff: 4; News: 25 hrs wkly. Target aud: 25-54. Spec prog: Farm one hr wkly. ◆Ross Biederman, pres; Chris Warren, gen mgr; Jack O'Malley, stn mgr, opns dir, progmg dir; Joel Frank, news dir; Eric Send, chief of engrg; Barbara Kanarek, traf mgr.

Bridgeport

WNEM(AM)— Nov 26, 1956: 1250 khz; 5 kw-D, 1.1 kw-N, DA-2. TL: N43 20 31 W83 53 57. Hrs open: 24 Box 531, Saginaw, 48606. Secondary address: 107 N. Franklin St., Saginaw 48607. Phone: (989) 755-8191. Fax: (989) 758-2110.E-mail: wnem@wnem.com Web Site:www.wnem.com Licensee: Meredith Corp. Group owner: Meredith Broadcasting Group, Meredith Corp. (acq 5-18-2004; $1.1 million). Format: Local news & info. ◆Al Blinke, gen mgr; Jeff Guilbert, gen sls mgr; Karen Frey, progmg dir; Ian Rubin, news dir; Mike Tamme, chief of engrg.

Bridgman

WYTZ(FM)— March 1993: 97.5 mhz; 3.8 kw. 413 ft TL: N41 59 19 W86 31 46. Stereo. Hrs open: 24 580 E. Napier, Benton Harbor, 48022. Phone: (269) 925-1111. Fax: (269) 925-1011.E-mail: robb@975country.com Web Site:www.975country.com Licensee: WSJM Inc. Group owner: The Mid-West Family Broadcasting Group (acq 1996; grpsl). Natl. Rep: Christal,. Shaw Pittman. Format: Country. News staff: 5. Target aud: 25-54. ◆Joe Daguanno, VP, chief of engrg; Gayle Olson, gen mgr; Jim Gifford, opns mgr; Bob Bucholtz, gen sls mgr; Sue Patzer, prom dir; Robb Rose, progmg dir.

Bronson

*WCVM(FM)— 1998: 94.7 mhz; 4 kw. 403 ft TL: N41 44 32 W85 14 34. Hrs open: 24 150 W Lincolnway, Ste 2001, Valparaiso, IN, 46383. Phone: (219) 548-5800. Fax: (219) 548-5808.E-mail: wqko@wqko.com Licensee: CSN International. (group owner; acq 12-1-98; $80,000). Format: Cutting edge Christian music & teaching. Target aud: Teen-young adult. ◆Jim Motshagen, gen mgr.

Brooklyn

WKHM-FM— January 1994: 105.3 mhz; 2.2 kw. 377 ft TL: N42 06 29 W84 22 46. Hrs open: 24 1700 Glenshire Dr., Jackson, 49201. Phone: (517) 787-9546. Fax: (517) 787-7517.E-mail: mdaly@wkhm.com Web Site:www.k1053.com Licensee: Jackson Radio Works Inc. (group owner; (acq 12-8-97; grpsl). Population served: 175,000 Rgnl rep: Michigan Spot Sls Format: Adult contemp. News staff: 2. Target aud: 18-49. ◆Bruce I. Goldsen, pres, gen mgr; Sue Goldsen, VP; Jamie McKibbin, stn mgr, progmg dir; Michael Bradford, chief of engrg.

Buchanan

WSMK(FM)— 1991: 99.1 mhz; 3 kw. 328 ft TL: N41 52 51 W86 18 13. Hrs open: 24 925 N. 5th St., Niles, 49120. Phone: (269) 683-4343. Fax: (269) 683-7759.E-mail: sales@wsmkradio.com Web Site:www.wsmkradio.com Licensee: Marion R. Williams. Population served: 800,000 Format: Rhythmic AC. Target aud: 25 - 44; females. ◆Marion R. Williams, gen mgr.

Burton

*WTAC(FM)— 2002: 89.7 mhz; 1 kw vert. Ant 187 ft TL: N43 05 07 W83 40 19. Hrs open:
simulcasts WLGH (FM) Leroy Township 100%.
148 E Grand River Rd, Williamston, 48895. Phone: (810) 724-2638. Fax: (877) 850-0881.E-mail: 411@smile.fm Web Site:www.smile.fm Licensee: Superior Communications. Format: Christian Contemp. ◆Edward Czelada, pres.

Cadillac

WATT(AM)— September 1945: 1240 khz; 1 kw-U. TL: N44 13 27 W85 24 06. Hrs open: 24 Box 520, 49601. Secondary address: 7825 S. Mackinaw Tr. 49601. Phone: (231) 775-1263. Fax: (231) 779-2844. Web Site:www.watt1240.com Licensee: MacDonald Garber Broadcasting Inc. (group owner; (acq 11-17-98; grpsl). Population served: 11,500 Natl. Network: Fox News Radio, Radio America, Premiere Radio Networks, Westwood One, . Natl. Rep: McGavren Guild,. Rgnl rep: McGavren Guild. Format: News/talk. Target aud: General. ◆Trish Garber, pres & gen mgr; Greg Marshall, progmg dir.

WCKC(FM)— Sept 15, 1985: 107.1 mhz; 2.75 kw. 482 ft TL: N44 10 16 W85 20 13. Stereo. Hrs open:
WGFM-FM Cheboygan 100%.
1356 Mackinaw Ave., Cheboygan, 49721. Phone: (231) 627-2341. Fax: (231) 627-7000.E-mail: info@classicrockthebear.com Web Site:www.classicrockthebear.com Licensee: Northern Star Broadcasting L.L.C. (group owner; (acq 9-11-98; grpsl). Format: Classic rock. Target aud: 25-54. ◆Palmer Pyle, pres; April Hurley-Rose, opns dir.

*WGCP(FM)—Not on air, target date: unknown: 91.9 mhz; 2.1 kw. Ant 144 ft TL: N44 17 08 W85 29 20. Hrs open: 14625 Twenty Mile Rd., Tustin, 49688. Phone: (217) 763-5671. Licensee: West Central Michigan Media Ministries. ◆David Bolduc, pres.

WJZQ(FM)— Oct 15, 1961: 92.9 mhz; 100 kw. Ant 912 ft TL: N44 35 41 W85 11 53. Stereo. Hrs open: 24 314 E. Front St., Traverse City, 49684. Phone: (231) 947-7675. Fax: (231) 929-3988.E-mail: wjzq@929thebreeze.com Web Site:www.929thebreeze.com Licensee: WKJF Radio Inc. Group owner: Midwestern Broadcasting Co. (acq 10-29-2001; with co-located AM). Population served: 275,000 Natl. Rep: Katz Radio,. Format: Smooth jazz. News staff: one; News: 2 hrs wkly. Target aud: 35-64; affluent adults. ◆John Dew, gen mgr; Joel Franck, news dir; Eric Send, chief of engrg; Barbara Kanarek, traf mgr.

WLJW(AM)— Mar 15, 2004: 1370 khz; 5 kw-D, 1 kw-N, DA-N. TL: N44 13 54 W85 24 45. Stereo. Hrs open: 24
Simulcast with WLJN(AM) Elmwood Township.
Box 1400, Traverse City, 49685. Phone: (231) 946-1400. Fax: (231) 946-3959.E-mail: info@wljn.com Web Site:www.wljn.com Licensee: Good News Media Inc. (group owner; acq 3-5-2004; $85,001). Population served: 45,000 Natl. Network: Moody, Salem Radio Network,. Natl. Rep: Katz Radio,. Southmayd & Miller. Wire Svc: AP Format: Christian talk, relg. Target aud: General. ◆Brian Harcey, pres, gen mgr; Pete Lathrop, progmg dir & news dir.

WLXV(FM)— July 7, 1974: 96.7 mhz; 1.7 kw. 443 ft TL: N44 14 56 W85 18 48. Hrs open: Box 520, 49601. Secondary address: 7825 S. Mackinaw Tr. 49601. Phone: (231) 775-1263. Fax: (231) 779-2844. Web Site:www.mix96cadillac.com Population served: 30,000 Format: Adult contemp. News staff: one; News: one hr wkly. ◆Trish MacDonald Garber, CEO; Rich Spicer, progmg dir.

*WOLW(FM)— May 26, 1988: 91.1 mhz; 50 kw horiz, 28 kw vert. 700 ft TL: N44 16 33 W85 42 49. Stereo. Hrs open: 24
Rebroadcasts WPHN(FM) Gaylord 100%.
PO Box 695, Gaylord, 49734-0695. Secondary address: 1511 M-32 E., Gaylord 49735. Phone: (989) 732-6274. Fax: (989) 732-8171.E-mail: ncr@ncradio.org Web Site:www.ncradio.org Licensee: Northern Christian Radio Inc. (group owner). Population served: 150,000 Natl. Network: Moody, . Southmayd & Miller. Format: Religious, Christian. News: 10 hrs wkly. Target aud: 35-54. ◆George A. Lake Jr., CEO, gen mgr, chief of engrg; Joe Sereno, chmn.

Carney

WMUP(FM)— 2008: 99.9 mhz; 200 w. Ant 56 ft TL: N45 35 11 W87 33 13. Hrs open: Box 13213, Green Bay, WI, 54307-3213. Phone: (888) 233-3021. Fax: (920) 469-3023. Licensee: Starboard Media Foundation Inc. ◆Mark C. Follett, chmn.

Caro

WIDL(FM)— Oct 16, 1974: 92.1 mhz; 6 kw. Ant 318 ft TL: N43 28 51 W83 20 31. Stereo. Hrs open: Prog sep from AM 1521 W. Caro Rd, 48723. Phone: (989) 672-1360. Fax: (989) 673-0256. Population served: 550,000 Format: Adult contemp.

WKYO(AM)— May 19, 1962: 1360 khz; 1 kw-U, DA-2. TL: N43 27 32 W83 23 39. Hrs open: 1521 W. Caro Rd, 48723-9260. Phone: (989) 672-1360. Fax: (989) 673-0256. Licensee: Edwards Communications L.C. (group owner; (acq 2-25-98; with co-located FM). Population served: 500,000 Natl. Network: Jones Radio Networks, . Rgnl. Network: Mich. Farm. Mich. Farm Format: Classic country. Spec prog: Farm 18 hrs wkly. ◆Tim Murphy, gen mgr; Brad Morgan, progmg dir.

Carrollton

WSGW-FM—Licensed to Carrollton. See Saginaw

Cassopolis

WGTO(AM)— August 1988: 910 khz; 1 kw-D, 35 w-N, DA-1. TL: N41 57 14 W86 00 59. Stereo. Hrs open: 24 26914 Marcellus Hwy, Dowagiac, 49047. Secondary address: 58176 O'Keefe Rd 49031. Phone: (269) 782-9010. Fax: (269) 782-5107. Web Site:www.wgtoradio.com Licensee: Larry Langford Jr. Population served: 450,000 Lauren A. Colby. Format: Golden oldies. Target aud: 25-49; middle class Black adults. Spec prog: Blues 4 hrs, gospel 10 hrs wkly. ◆Larry Langford, pres; Chris Cole, gen mgr, stn mgr.

Charlevoix

WCZW(FM)— Jan 31, 2003: 107.9 mhz; 5 kw. Ant 164 ft TL: N45 20 00 W85 14 47. Hrs open: 24
Rebroadcasts WCCW-FM Traverse City 100%.
300 E. Front St., suite 450, Traverse City, 49684. Phone: (231) 946-6211. Fax: (231) 946-1914 . Web Site:www.wccwi.com Licensee: WCCW Radio Inc. Group owner: Midwestern Broadcasting Co. Natl. Network: ABC, . Natl. Rep: Katz Radio,. Format: Oldies. Target aud: 35 plus; baby boomers. ◆Hal Payne, gen mgr, sls dir; Brian Hale, opns mgr; Dave Gauthier, mus dir; Eric Send, chief of engrg; Wendy Sobeck, traf mgr.

WKHQ-FM— May 16, 1980: 105.9 mhz; 100 kw. Ant 892 ft TL: N45 10 49 W85 05 50. Stereo. Hrs open: 24 Box 286, Petoskey, 49770. Secondary address: 2095 U.S. 131 S., Petoskey 49770. Phone: (231) 347-8713. Fax: (231) 347-8782.E-mail: info@106khq.com Web Site:www.106khq.com Licensee: MacDonald Garber Broadcasting Co. (group owner); acq 11-17-98; grpsl). Population served: 200,000 Natl. Network: ABC, . Natl. Rep: McGavren Guild,. Koteen & Naftalin. Format: Top 40. News staff: one. Target aud: 18-34. ◆Trish MacDonald-Garder, gen mgr; Tom Clemens, gen sls mgr; Luke Spencer, progmg dir, progmg; Bob White, engrg dir, chief of engrg; Bob Sheen, traf mgr.

WMKT(AM)— July 20, 1974: 1270 khz; 5 kw-U, DA-N. TL: N45 16 22 W85 15 08. Hrs open: 24 Prog sep from FM Box 286, Petoskey, 49770. Secondary address: 2095 U.S. 131 S., Petoskey 49770. Web Site:www.wmktthetalkstation.com Licensee: MacDonald Garber Broadcasting Co. Population served: 72,600 Format: News/talk. Target aud: 35 plus; listeners with spendable income. ◆Eric Michaels, progmg dir.

*WTCK(FM)— 2006: 90.9 mhz; 1 w horiz, 1.1 kw vert. Ant 659 ft TL: N45 10 49 W85 05 50. Hrs open: 24 Box 1109, Indian River, 49749. Phone: (231) 238-0811. Fax: (231) 238-0803.E-mail:

baragabroadcasting@utmi.net Web Site:www.baragabroadcasting.com Licensee: Baraga Broadcasting Inc. (acq 11-8-2006; $130,000). Format: Catholic. ◆Harry Speckman, opns mgr.

Charlotte

WJZL(FM)— Dec 29, 1965: 92.7 mhz; 1.5 kw. Ant 466 ft TL: N42 38 31 W84 47 55. Stereo. Hrs open: 24 2495 N. Cedar, Suite 106, Holt, 48842. Phone: (517) 699-0111. Fax: (517) 699-1880.E-mail: djohnson@mmrglansing.com Licensee: Rubber City Radio Group. Group owner: Rubber City Radio Group Inc. (acq 2-15-2001; $600,000). Population served: 397,000 Natl. Network: Jones Radio Networks, . Baraff, Koerner & Olender. Wire Svc: AP Format: Smooth jazz. News: 3 hrs wkly. ◆Dave Johnson, pres, gen mgr; Paul Cashin, opns dir & progmg mgr.

Cheboygan

WCBY(AM)— Oct 28, 1954: 1240 khz; 1 kw-U. TL: N45 39 38 W84 29 26. Hrs open: 1356 Mackinaw Ave., 49721. Phone: (231) 627-2341. Fax: (231) 627-7000.E-mail: info@classicrockthebear.com Licensee: Northern Star Broadcasting L.L.C. (group owner; (acq 12-12-2005; grpsl). Natl. Rep: Michigan Spot Sales,. Format: Nostalgia, big band. Target aud: 35-64. ◆Palmer Pyle, pres; April Hurley-Rose, gen mgr, opns dir; Mark Belanger, gen sls mgr.

WGFM(FM)— Aug 15, 1968: 105.1 mhz; 100 kw. Ant 610 ft TL: N45 26 50 W84 28 30. Stereo. Hrs open: 1356 Mackinaw Ave., 49721. Phone: (231) 627-2341. Fax: (231) 627-7000.E-mail: info@classicrockthebear.com Web Site:www.classicrockthebear.com Format: Classic rock.

Clare

WCFX(FM)— June 28, 1967: 95.3 mhz; 6 kw. 328 ft TL: N43 44 41 W84 48 09. Stereo. Hrs open: 24 5847 Venture Way, Mount Pleasant, 48858. Phone: (989) 772-4173. Fax: (989) 773-1236.E-mail: kent@wcfx.com Web Site:www.wcfx.com Licensee: Grenax Broadcasting LLC (acq 2-5-2004). Population served: 165,000 Format: Adult/CHR. Target aud: 18-49. ◆Greg Dinetz, pres; Jim Spangenberg, gen mgr; Kent Bergstrom, opns mgr; Rob Ryan, prom dir & progmg dir.

Clyde Township

*WXPZ(FM)—Not on air, target date: unknown: 90.1 mhz; 1.5 kw. Ant 243 ft TL: N42 33 57 W86 12 26. Hrs open: 2286 Ball N.E., Grand Rapids, 49505. Phone: (616) 726-0193. Licensee: Tim Woodson Ministries Inc. (acq 4-7-2008; $50,000 for CP). ◆Timothy Woodson, chmn & pres.

Coldwater

*WCWB(FM)— July 15, 2008: 90.1 mhz; 250 w vert. Ant 62 ft TL: N41 56 24 W85 02 47. Hrs open: Box 220, 49036. Secondary address: 385 Airport Dr. 49036. Phone: (517) 278-7339. Fax: (517) 278-6973.E-mail: bbn@bbnradio.org Web Site:www.bbnradio.org Licensee: Michiana Christian Broadcasters Inc. Natl. Network: Bible Bcstg Net, . Format: Christian. ◆Wayne Reese, pres & gen mgr.

WNWN-FM—Licensed to Coldwater. See Kalamazoo

WTVB(AM)— Aug 7, 1949: 1590 khz; 5 kw-D, 1 kw-N, DA-N. TL: N41 54 34 W85 00 21. Hrs open: 24 182 N. Angola Rd., 49036. Phone: (517) 279-1590. Fax: (517) 279-4695.E-mail: wtvb@wtvbam.com Web Site:www.oldiesradioonline.com Licensee: Midwest Communications Inc. (group owner; acq 6-1-95; grpsl). Population served: 44,000 Natl. Rep: Christal,. Wire Svc: NOAA Weather Format: Oldies, full service. News staff: 2; News: 10 hrs wkly. Spec prog: Farm 6 hrs wkly. ◆D.E. Wright, pres; Peter Tanz, gen mgr; Ken Delaney, stn mgr.

Coleman

*WPRJ(FM)— Dec 7, 1992: 101.7 mhz; 4.6 kw. Ant 374 ft TL: N43 48 39 W84 27 50. Stereo. Hrs open: 24 Box 236, 227 Jackson St., 48618. Phone: (989) 465-9775. Fax: (989) 465-1060.E-mail: 1017thefuse @1017thefuse.com Web Site:www.wprj.org Licensee: Come Together Ministries Inc. (acq 11-9-89; $8,000; 11-27-89). Reddy, Begley & McCormick. Format: Full-time Christian adult contemp, CHR. Target aud: 18 plus; youth, young singles & married. ◆Gary H. Bugh, pres & gen mgr; Connie Wieber, stn mgr, opns mgr.

Coopersville

WHTS(FM)— Sept 14, 1983: 105.3 mhz; 20 kw. Ant 794 ft TL: N43 18 35 W85 54 45. Stereo. Hrs open: 60 Monroe Ctr. N.W., 3rd Floor, Grand Rapids, 49503. Phone: (616) 774-8461. Fax: (616) 774-2491.E-mail: info@1053hotfm.com Web Site:1053hotfm.com Licensee: Citadel Broadcasting Co. (acq 11-29-2005; $4.1 million). Format: Top 40. Target aud: 25-54; adult women. ♦Matt Hanlon, gen mgr; Kate Conley, stn mgr, gen sls mgr; Brent Alberts, opns mgr.

Crystal Falls

WOBE(FM)— June 2000: 100.7 mhz; 100 kw. Ant 653 ft TL: N45 49 15 W88 02 38. Stereo. Hrs open: 24 212 W. J St., Iron Mountain, 49801. Phone: (906) 774-5731. Fax: (906) 774-4542.E-mail: peterson.trisha@gmail.com Web Site:www.classichitsb100fm.com Licensee: Results Broadcasting of Iron Mountain Inc. Group owner: Results Broadcasting (acq 11-1-2001; $800,000). Natl. Network: ABC, . Format: Classic hits. News staff: one. Target aud: 25-65. ♦Bruce Grassman, pres; Trisha Peterson, VP & gen mgr; Keith Huotari, opns mgr.

WUPZ(FM)— 2008: 94.9 mhz; 6.2 kw. Ant 157 ft TL: N46 09 49 W88 22 50. Hrs open: 1717 Dixie Hwy., Suite 650, Fort Wright, KY, 41011. Licensee: Radioactive LLC. ♦Benjamin L. Homel, pres.

Dearborn

WDTW(AM)— Dec 29, 1946: 1310 khz; 5 kw-U, DA-2. TL: N42 15 50 W83 15 14. Hrs open: 24 27675 Halsted Rd., Farmington Hills, 48331. Phone: (248) 324-5800. Fax: (248) 848-0396.E-mail: elliotlerner @clearchannel.com Web Site:www.1310wdtw.com Licensee: AMFM Radio Licenses L.L.C. Group owner: Clear Channel Communications Inc. (acq 8-30-2000; grpsl). Population served: 125,000 Natl. Network: Westwood One, . Format: Progressive talk. News staff: 4; News: 27 hrs wkly. Target aud: 25-54; men 25-54. ♦Til Levesque, gen mgr; Dom Theodore, opns mgr.

***WHFR(FM)**— Dec 20, 1985: 89.3 mhz; 270 w. 98 ft TL: N42 19 26 W83 14 09. Stereo. Hrs open: 24 Henry Ford Community College, 5101 Evergreen Rd., 48128. Phone: (313) 845-9676. Phone: (313) 845-9842. Fax: (313) 317-4034.E-mail: whfr@hfcc.edu Web Site:www.whfr.fm Licensee: Henry Ford Community College. Population served: 800,000 Natl. Network: PRI, . Format: Var, alternative. News: one hr wkly. Target aud: General. Spec prog: Jazz 10 hrs, world mus 2 hrs, big band 6 hrs, blues 12 hrs wkly. ♦Susan McGraw, gen mgr; Lara Hrycaj, opns mgr.

WNIC(FM)—Licensed to Dearborn. See Detroit

Dearborn Heights

WNZK(AM)—Licensed to Dearborn Heights. See Detroit

Detroit

WCAR(AM)—See Livonia

***WDET-FM**— Feb 13, 1949: 101.9 mhz; 48 kw. Ant 554 ft TL: N42 21 06 W83 03 48. Stereo. Hrs open: 24 4600 Cass Ave., 48201. Phone: (313) 577-4146. Fax: (313) 577-1300.E-mail: wdetfm@wdetfm.org Web Site:www.wdetfm.org Licensee: Wayne State University. (acq 5-52). Population served: 4,541,696 Natl. Network: NPR, . Rgnl. Network: Mich. Pub. Paul, Weiss, Rifkind, Wharton & Garrison. Format: News, Information. News staff: 6; News: 118 hrs wkly. Target aud: 35-64; public radio & news consumers. Spec prog: Jazz 15 hrs, folk 3 hrs, bluegrass 2 hrs, gospel 2 hrs, blues 3 hrs, reggae 2 hrs wkly. ♦Allen Mazeruk, gen mgr; Tim Hygh, stn mgr, prom mgr; Jerome Vaughn, progmg dir; Yolanda Dunn, chief of engrg.

WDFN(AM)— Dec 17, 1939: 1130 khz; 50 kw-D, 10 kw-N, DA-2. TL: N42 06 39 W83 11 52. Hrs open: 27675 Halsted Rd., Farmington Hills, 48331. Phone: (248) 324-5800. Fax: (248) 848-0396. Web Site:www.wdfn.com Licensee: AMFM Radio Licenses L.L.C. Group owner: Clear Channel Communications Inc. (acq 8-30-2000; grpsl). Population served: 3,900,000 Natl. Network: Westwood One, . Format: Sports talk. Target aud: 25-54. ♦Til Levesque, gen mgr; Elliot Lerner, gen sls mgr.

WDMK(FM)— May 26, 1960: 105.9 mhz; 20 kw. 725 ft TL: N42 28 16 W83 12 03. Stereo. Hrs open: 3250 Franklin St., 48207. Phone: (313) 259-2000. Fax: (313) 259-7011.E-mail: kyoung@radio-one.com Web Site:www.kissdetroit.com Licensee: Radio One of Detroit LLC. Group owner: Radio One Inc. (acq 11-8-2001; grpsl). Population served: 4,000,000 Format: Hip hop, Rhythm and Blues. Target aud: 25-49. Spec prog: Sports 2 hrs, entertainment guide 2 hrs wkly. ♦Alfred Liggins, pres; Carol Lawrence-Dobrusin, gen mgr; Benita Gray, mus dir.

WDRQ(FM)— July 9, 1947: 93.1 mhz; 26.5 kw. 669 ft TL: N42 28 16 W83 12 03. Stereo. Hrs open: 24 3011 W. Grand Blvd. Fisher Building, Suite 800, 311 West Grand Blvd., 48202-9816. Phone: (313) 871-9300. Fax: (313) 872-0190.E-mail: info@931dougfm.com Web Site:www.931dougfm.com Licensee: Radio License Holding I LLC. Group owner: ABC Inc. (acq 6-12-2007; grpsl). Population served: 3,800,000 Natl. Rep: ABC Radio Sales,. Wire Svc: AP Format: Adult Hits. News staff: one; News: news prgmg 3 hrs/day. Target aud: Persons 25-54. ♦Matt Spatafora, sls dir; Kevin Hawley, chief of engrg.

WDTK(AM)— 1926: 1400 khz; 1 kw-U. TL: N42 24 22 W83 06 44. Hrs open: 2 Radio Pl St., Ferndale, 48220. Phone: (248) 581-1234. Fax: (248) 581-1231.E-mail: zaron@wdtkam.com Web Site:www.wdtkam.com Licensee: Pennsylvania Media Associates Inc. Group owner: Salem Communications Corp. (acq 9-30-2004; $4.75 million). Natl. Rep: Salem,. Format: News/talk. ♦Christian D. MacCourtney, gen mgr; Steve Dealy, opns mgr.

WDTW(AM)—See Dearborn

WDTW-FM— Oct 16, 1960: 106.7 mhz; 61 kw. Ant 508 ft TL: N42 19 55 W83 02 42. Hrs open: 27675 Halsted Rd., Farmington Hills, 48331. Phone: (248) 324-5800. Fax: (248) 848-0396. Web Site:www.foxspacelive.com Licensee: AMFM Radio Licenses L.L.C. Format: Country. ♦Til Levesque, gen mgr; David Crumb, sls dir.

WDVD(FM)— June 1, 1948: 96.3 mhz; 20 kw. Ant 787 ft TL: N42 27 13 W83 09 50. Stereo. Hrs open: 3011 W. Grand Blvd., Fisher Bldg., Suite 800, 48202. Phone: (313) 871-3030. Fax: (313) 875-9636. Web Site:www.963wdvd.com Licensee: Radio License Holding I LLC. Population served: 280,000 Format: Modern adult contemp. ♦Steve Kosbau, pres & gen mgr; Ron Harrell, progmg dir; Lisa Jesswein, news dir.

WGPR(FM)— 1961: 107.5 mhz; 50 kw. Ant 405 ft TL: N42 21 28 W83 03 55. Stereo. Hrs open: 24 3146 Jefferson E., 48207. Phone: (313) 259-8862. Fax: (313) 259-6662.E-mail: wgprvp@aol.com Web Site:www.wgprdetroit.com Licensee: WGPR Inc. (acq 7-64). Population served: 151,148 Hogan & Hartson. Format: Urban adult contemp. Target aud: 18-49. ♦George Mathews, CEO, pres, gen mgr; James O. Dogan, VP, stn mgr; Stefanie Grimes, gen sls mgr; Carolyn James, progmg dir. Co-owned TV: WGPR-TV affil

WJLB(FM)— 1926: 97.9 mhz; 50 kw. 489 ft TL: N42 24 22 W83 06 44. Stereo. Hrs open: 645 Griswold, Suite 633, 48226. Phone: (313) 965-2000. Fax: (313) 965-3965.E-mail: brianboettcher@clearchannel.com Web Site:www.fm98wjlb.com Licensee: AMFM Radio Licenses L.L.C. Group owner: Clear Channel Communications Inc. (acq 8-30-00; grpsl). Population served: 580,000 Format: Urban contemp. Target aud: 18-49; Black adults. ♦Til Levesque, gen mgr; David Crumb, sls dir; Brian Boettcher, gen sls mgr; K. J. Holiday, progmg dir, traf mgr; Cheron Mans, mus dir; Charles Pugh, news dir; Thomas Christie, engrg mgr, chief of engrg.

WJR(AM)— May 4, 1922: 760 khz; 50 kw-U. TL: N42 10 07 W83 13 00. Hrs open: 3011 W. Grand Blvd., Fisher Bldg., Suite 800, 48202. Phone: (313) 875-4440. Fax: (313) 875-9022.E-mail: info@wjr.net Web Site:www.wjr.net Licensee: Radio License Holding I LLC. Group owner: ABC Inc. (acq 6-12-2007; grpsl). Population served: 300,000 Natl. Rep: ABC Radio Sales,. Format: News/talk. Target aud: 12 plus. ♦Mike Fezzey, pres, gen mgr; Tom O'Brien, gen sls mgr & progmg dir; Dick Haefner, news dir.

WKQI(FM)— Feb 12, 1949: 95.5 mhz; 100 kw. 437 ft TL: N42 28 22 W83 11 59. Stereo. Hrs open: 24 27675 Halsted, Farmington Hill, 48331. Phone: (248) 324-5800. Fax: (248) 848-0272.E-mail: programing@channel955.com Web Site:www.channel955.com Licensee: AMFM Radio Licenses L.L.C. Group owner: Clear Channel Communications Inc. (acq 8-30-00; grpsl). Population served: 3,692,300 Natl. Network: Premiere Radio Networks, . Latham & Watkins. Format: Top 40. Target aud: 18-49; active, upscale women. ♦Til Levesque, VP & gen mgr; Rebecca Falk, mktg dir, prom dir; Beau Daniels, prom dir, mus dir; Dom Theodore, progmg VP, progmg dir.

WLQV(AM)— 1925: 1500 khz; 50 kw-D, 10 kw-N, DA-2. TL: N42 13 52 W83 11 58. Hrs open: 24 Two Radio Plaza, Ferndale, 48220. Phone: (248) 581-1234. Fax: (248) 581-1231. Web Site:www.am1500wlqv.net Licensee: Caron Broadcasting Inc. (group owner; (acq 2-10-2006; swap for WQRT(AM) Florence, KY and WCVX(AM) Cincinnati, OH plus $6.75 million cash) Natl. Network: Salem Radio Network, . Format: Relg/teach talk. News staff: one; News: 2 hrs wkly. Target aud: 25-65 plus; middle class. ♦Chris MacCourtney, VP, gen mgr; Steve Dealy, opns mgr.

WMGC-FM— Mar 6, 1960: 105.1 mhz; 20 kw. 784 ft TL: N42 28 16 W83 12 03. Stereo. Hrs open: One Radio Plaza, Ferndale, 48220-2140. Phone: (248) 414-5600. Fax: (248) 542-7700.E-mail: info@detroitmagic.com Web Site:www.detroitmagic.com Licensee: Greater Boston Radio Inc. Group owner: Greater Media Inc. (acq 12-5-96). Population served: 4,300,000 Format: Adult contemp. Target aud: General; professional, upscale, educated. ♦Peter Smyth, pres; Tom Bender, gen mgr.

WMUZ(FM)— Nov 11, 1958: 103.5 mhz; 50 kw. 500 ft TL: N42 22 40 W83 14 32. Hrs open: 12300 Radio Pl., 48228. Phone: (313) 272-3434.E-mail: station@wumz.com Web Site:www.wmuz.com Licensee: WMUZ Radio Inc. Group owner: Crawford Broadcasting Co. Population served: 300,000 Format: Contemp Christian Music. ♦Donald B. Crawford, pres; Frank Franciosi, gen mgr; Rich Hanovich, opns mgr.

WMXD(FM)— Dec 8, 1964: 92.3 mhz; 50 kw. 479 ft TL: N42 19 55 W83 02 42. Stereo. Hrs open: 645 Griswold, Suite 633, 48226. Phone: (313) 965-2000. Fax: (313) 965-3965. Web Site:www.mix923fm.com Licensee: AMFM Radio Licenses L.L.C. Group owner: Clear Channel Communications Inc. (acq 8-30-00; grpsl). Format: Urban adult contemp. ♦Til Levesque, gen mgr; Jeff Luckoff, gen sls mgr; Jamillah Muhammad, progmg dir; Randy Auerbach, engrg mgr, chief of engrg.

WNIC(FM)—(Dearborn, December 1946: 100.3 mhz; 32 kw. 600 ft TL: N42 23 22 W83 08 53. Stereo. Hrs open: 24 27675 Halstead, Farmington Hills, 48331. Phone: (248) 324-5800. Fax: (248) 848-0396. Web Site:www.wnic.com Licensee: AMFM Radio Licenses L.L.C. Group owner: Clear Channel Communications Inc. (acq 8-30-00; grpsl). Population served: 498,700 Latham & Watkins. Format: Lite adult contemp. News staff: one; News: 2 hrs wkly. Target aud: 25-54; female. ♦Liz Walterhouse, gen sls mgr; Rebecca Falk, prom mgr; Don Gosselin, progmg dir.

WNZK(AM)—(Dearborn Heights, Oct 12, 1985: 690 khz-D; 2.5 kw-U, DA-2. TL: N42 05 55 W83 19 48. (Note: Stn operates on 680 khz-N). Hrs open: 21700 Northwestern Hwy., Suite 1190, Southfield, 48075. Phone: (248) 557-3500. Fax: (248) 557-2950.E-mail: sima@birach.com Web Site:www.birach.com Licensee: Birach Broadcasting Corp. (acq 1984). Format: Talk, news, ethnic. Target aud: General. ♦Sima Birach, gen mgr.

WOMC(FM)— Mar 5, 1948: 104.3 mhz; 190 kw. 361 ft TL: N42 28 25 W83 06 56. Stereo. Hrs open: 24 2201 Woodward Heights Blvd., Ferndale, 48220. Phone: (248) 546-9600. Fax: (248) 546-5446.E-mail: kpmurphy@cbs.com Web Site:www.womc.com Licensee: CBS Radio Inc. of Michigan. Group owner: Infinity Broadcasting Corp. (acq 4-28-88). Population served: 3,826,700 Natl. Network: Westwood One, . Format: Oldies. News staff: one; News: 4 hrs wkly. Target aud: 25-54; upscale. ♦Dan Mason, pres; Walter Berger, CFO; Don Bouloukos, sr VP; Kevin Murphy, gen mgr; Lynn Montemayor, gen sls mgr; Scott Walker, progmg dir; Hal Buttermore, chief of engrg.

***WRCJ-FM**— Feb 5, 1948: 90.9 mhz; 42 kw horiz, 38 kw vert. 437 ft TL: N42 22 25 W83 06 50. Stereo. Hrs open: Midnight-noon 123 Selden Ave., Suite 250, 48201. Phone: (313)494-6400. Fax: (313) 494-6087. Web Site:www.wrcj909fm.org Licensee: Board of Education, City of Detroit. Population served: 1,000,000 Format: Class, jazz. News staff: 15. Target aud: General; intergenerational-urban/suburban. ♦Robert Scott, gen mgr; Donald Walker, opns dir; Dave Wagner, progmg dir, pub affrs dir; Steve Johnson, chief of engrg.

WRIF(FM)— Jan 1, 1948: 101.1 mhz; 27.2 kw. 879 ft TL: N42 28 15 W83 15 00. Stereo. Hrs open: 24 One Radio Plaza St., Ferndale, 48220-2140. Phone: (248) 547-0101. Fax: (248) 542-8800. Web Site:wrif.com Licensee: Greater Media Inc. (group owner; acq 12-15-87). Population served: 3,860,000 Natl. Rep: Katz Radio,. Format: Active rock. Target aud: 18-49; men. ♦Tom Bender, gen mgr.

WVMV(FM)— 1961: 98.7 mhz; 50 kw. 462 ft TL: N42 23 42 W83 08 58. Stereo. Hrs open: 26495 American Dr., Southfield, 48034. Phone: (248) 455-7350. Fax: (248) 855-1302. Web Site:www.wvmv.com Licensee: CBS Radio East Inc. Group owner: Infinity Broadcasting Corp. (acq 12-89; grpsl; 12-11-89). Population served: 3,500,000 Format: Smooth Jazz. ♦Debbie Kenyon, VP, gen mgr; Sheryl Coyne, gen sls mgr; Tom Sleeker, opns mgr & progmg dir.

WWJ(AM)— Aug 20, 1920: 950 khz; 5 kw-U, DA-N. TL: N42 26 47 W83 10 23. Hrs open: 24 26495 American Dr., Southfield, 48034. Phone: (248) 455-7200. Fax: (248) 304-4970.E-mail: wwjnewsroom@cbsradio.com Web Site:www.wwj.com Licensee: CBS Radio East Inc. Group owner: Infinity Broadcasting Corp. (acq 3-9-89; 2-27-89). Population served: 3,660,200 Natl. Network: CBS, . Format: News. News staff: 32. Target aud: General. ♦Kevin Murphy, gen mgr; Rob Davidek, opns mgr, progmg dir, news dir, local news ed; Pete Kowalski, gen sls mgr; Debbie Spatafora, prom mgr; Ralph Hunt, chief of engrg; Florence Walton, news rptr; Tim Skubick, political ed; Larry Henry, sports cmtr. Co-owned TV: WWJ-TV affil

WXYT(AM)— Oct 10, 1925: 1270 khz; 5 kw-U, DA-N. TL: N42 27 58 W83 15 00. Hrs open: 24 Dups FM 100% 26495 American Rd., Southfield, 48034. Secondary address: 31555. 14 Mille Rd., Farminhtion Hill 48334. Phone: (248) 855-5100. Fax: (248) 455-7369.E-mail: 971@theticket.com Web Site:www.1270sports.com Licensee: CBS Radio Inc. of Detroit Group owner: Infinity Broadcasting Corp. (acq 11-13-98; grpsl). Population served: 3,660,200 Target aud: 25-54. ♦Kevin Murphy, gen mgr; Steve Wright, stn mgr; Greg Smith, gen sls mgr; Dan Zampillo, progmg dir.

WXYT-FM— May 9, 1941: 97.1 mhz; 15 kw. Ant 890 ft TL: N42 28 59 W83 12 20. Stereo. Hrs open: 26495 American Rd., Southfield, 48034. Secondary address: 31555.14 Mile Rd Farnubgtion Hill 48334. Phone: (248) 855-5100. Fax: (248) 455-7369.E-mail: wxyt@wxyt.com Web Site:www.1270sports.com Licensee: CBS Radio East Inc. (acq 3-9-89; 2-27-89). Natl. Network: ESPN Radio, Westwood One, . Covington & Burling. Format: Sports. News staff: 3. ♦Kevin Murphy, VP & gen mgr; Dan Zampillo, progmg dir.

WYCD(FM)— May 4, 1960: 99.5 mhz; 21 kw horiz, 19 kw vert. 755 ft TL: N42 28 16 W83 12 03. Stereo. Hrs open: 26555 Evergreen, Suite 675, Southfield, 48076. Phone: (248) 799-0600. Fax: (248) 358-9216.E-mail: stephen.schram@infinitybroadcasting.com Web Site:www.wycd.com Licensee: CBS Radio Inc. of Michigan. Group owner: CBS Radio (acq 1-96; grpsl). Population served: 3,500,000 Shaw Pittman. Format: Country. Target aud: 12-34. ♦Debbie Kenyon, gen mgr; Jay Jennings, gen sls mgr & natl sls mgr.

Dewitt

WQHH(FM)— 1991: 96.5 mhz; 3 kw. Ant 328 ft TL: N42 51 06 W84 40 06. Hrs open: 600 W. Cavanaugh, Lansing, 48910. Phone: (517) 393-1320. Fax: (517) 393-0882. Web Site:www.power965fm.com Licensee: The MacDonald Broadcasting Co. (acq 10-3-2006; $3.65 million with WXLA(AM) Dimondale). Natl. Rep: D & R Radio,. Format: Urban contemp. Target aud: 18-49. ♦Kenneth H. MacDonald Jr., CEO; Cindy Tuck, gen mgr; Sharon Crane, gen sls mgr.

Dimondale

WXLA(AM)— Sept 20, 1982: 1180 khz; 1 kw-D, DA. TL: N42 39 01 W84 34 49. Hrs open: 12 600 W. Cavanaugh, Lansing, 48910. Phone: (517) 393-1320. Fax: (517) 393-0882. Licensee: The MacDonald Broadcasting Co. (acq 10-3-2006; $3.65 million). Natl. Rep: D & R Radio,. Format: Timeless classics. ♦Kenneth H. MacDonald Jr., CEO; Cindy Tuck, gen mgr; Sharon Crane, gen sls mgr.

Dowagiac

WAUS(FM)—South Bend IN

WDOW(AM)— September 1960: 1440 khz; 1 kw-D, 89 w-N. TL: N41 59 35 W86 05 10. Hrs open: 24 26914 Marcellus Hwy., 49047. Phone: (269) 782-5106. Fax: (269) 782-5107. Licensee: Langford Broadcasting LLC (acq 5-12-2007). Population served: 150,000 Natl. Network: Fox Sports, . Format: Sports. News staff: one. Target aud: 25-49. ♦Larry Langford, pres; Chris Cole, stn mgr.

WHPD(FM)— January 1971: 92.1 mhz; 3.3 kw. Ant 299 ft TL: N41 59 52 W86 03 14. Stereo. Hrs open: 24
Simulcast with WHPZ(FM) Bremen, IN 100%.
61300 S. Ironwood Rd., South Bend, IN, 46614. Secondary address: 26914 Marcellus Hwy. 49047. Phone: (574) 291-8200. Fax: (574) 291-9043.E-mail: info@whpd.com Web Site:www.pulsefm.com Licensee: LeSea Broadcasting Corp. (acq 4-12-2005; $950,000 with co-located AM). Population served: 250,000 Natl. Rep: Michigan Spot Sales,. Keorner & Olender. Format: Contemp Christian. Target aud: 25-64. ♦Pete Sumrall, gen mgr; Tom Scott, progmg dir.

Eagle

***WJOM(FM)**— 2006: 88.5 mhz; 4.3 kw vert. Ant 131 ft TL: N42 48 25 W84 47 18. Hrs open: Michigan Community Radio, 148 E Grand River Rd, Williamston, 48895. Phone: (517) 381-0573. Web Site:www.smile.fm Licensee: Michigan Community Radio. ♦Ed Czelada, pres.

East Jordan

***WICV(FM)**— June 25, 1989: 100.9 mhz; 2.8 kw. 489 ft TL: N45 10 40 W85 05 57. Stereo. Hrs open: 24
Rebroadcasts WIAA(FM) Interlochen 100%.
Box 199, Interlochen, 49643. Phone: (231) 276-4400. Fax: (231) 276-4417.E-mail: ipr@interlochen.org Web Site:www.interlochen.org/ipr Licensee: Interlochen Center for the Arts (acq 5-23-90). Population served: 60,000 Natl. Network: NPR, PRI, ABC, . Rgnl. Network: Mich. Pub. Mich. Radio Haley, Bader & Potts. Format: Classical, news. Target aud: 35-80; upper income, arts-oriented, civic-minded professionals. ♦Thom Paulson, VP & gen mgr.

East Lansing

***WDBM(FM)**— Feb 24, 1989: 88.9 mhz; 2 kw. 279 ft TL: N42 42 20 W84 28 30. Stereo. Hrs open: 24 G-4 Holden Hall, Michigan State Univ. Campus, 48825-1206. Phone: (517) 353-4414.E-mail: gm@impact89fm.org Web Site:www.impact89fm.org Licensee: Board of Trustees of Michigan State University. Format: Alternative rock. News: 10 hrs wkly. Target aud: 18-34; students of MSU. Spec prog: Blues 4 hrs, jazz 5 hrs, heavy metal 4 hrs, progsv country 4 hrs, Christian rock 4 hrs wkly. ♦Gary Reid, gen mgr.

WFMK(FM)— July 16, 1959: 99.1 mhz; 28 kw. 600 ft TL: N42 40 33 W84 30 00. Stereo. Hrs open: 24 Secondary address: 3420 Pine Tree Rd., Lansing 48911. Phone: (517) 394-3999. Fax: (517) 394-3391.E-mail: wfmk@acd.net Web Site:www.99wfmk.com Licensee: Citadel Broadcasting Co. Group owner: Citadel Broadcasting Corp. (acq 2000; grpsl). Population served: 379,500 Natl. Rep: Christal,. Leventhal, Senter & Lerman. Format: Adult contemp. News staff: one; News: 2 hrs wkly. Target aud: 25-54. ♦Matt Hanlon, gen mgr; Brent Alberts, opns mgr, mus dir.

WJZL(FM)—See Charlotte

***WKAR(AM)**— Aug 18, 1922: 870 khz; 10 kw-D, DA. TL: N42 42 19 W84 28 30. Hrs open: 283 Communication Arts Bldg., Michigan State Univ., 48824-1212. Phone: (517) 432-9527. Fax: (517) 353-7124.E-mail: mail@wkar.org Web Site:wkar.org Licensee: Board of Trustees of Michigan State University. Population served: 410,000 Natl. Network: NPR, PRI, . Rgnl. Network: Mich. Pub. Schwartz, Woods & Miller. Format: News/talk. News staff: 5; News: 25 hrs wkly. Spec prog: Sp 3 hrs wkly. ♦DeAnne Hamilton, gen mgr; Gene Purdum, opns mgr; Cindy Herfindahl, dev dir; Diane Hutchens, prom dir; Curt Gilleo, progmg dir; Kevin Laveny, news dir; Gary Blievernicht, engrg dir, engrg mgr.

***WKAR-FM**— Oct 10, 1948: 90.5 mhz; 86 kw horiz, 57 kw vert. 895 ft TL: N42 42 08 W84 24 51. Hrs open: Prog sep from AM 1111 Virginia St. E., Charleston, WV, 25301. Phone: (517) 432-9527. Fax: (517) 353-7124.E-mail: mail@wkar.org Web Site:wkar.org Licensee: Board of Trustees of Michigan State University. Population served: 400,000 Format: Class, news. Spec prog: Jazz 7 hrs wkly. Co-owned TV: *WKAR-TV affil

WMMQ(FM)— Nov 16, 1963: 94.9 mhz; 49 kw. 499 ft TL: N42 38 44 W84 33 38. Stereo. Hrs open: 3420 Pine Tree Rd., Lansing, 48911. Phone: (517) 394-7272. Fax: (517) 394-3391.E-mail: brent.alberts@citcomm.com Web Site:www.wmmq.com Population served: 379,500 Natl. Network: CNN Radio, . Format: Classic rock. News staff: one. Target aud: 25-54; baby boomers who grew up listening to the Beatles, the Who & the Stones. ♦Farid Suleman, chmn; Brent Alberts, progmg dir; Deb Hart, news dir.

WVFN(AM)— September 1964: 730 khz; 500 w-D, 17.5 w-N, DA-2. TL: N42 38 45 W84 33 39. Hrs open: 24 3420 Pine Tree Rd., Lansing, 48911. Phone: (517) 394-7272. Fax: (517) 394-3391.E-mail: info@thegame730am.com Web Site:www.thegame730am.com Licensee: Citadel Broadcasting Co. Group owner: Citadel Broadcasting Corp. (acq 2000; grpsl). Population served: 379,500 Natl. Network: ESPN Radio, . Natl. Rep: Christal,. Leventhal, Senter & Leman. Format: All sports, talk. Target aud: 25-54. ♦Farid Suleman, CEO, chmn; Matt Hanlon, gen mgr; Brent Alberts, opns mgr; Steve Goupil, traf mgr; Tim Staudt, sports cmtr.

East Tawas

***WRQC(FM)**— 2008: 91.3 mhz; 20 kw vert. Ant 269 ft TL: N44 16 25 W83 39 48. Hrs open:
Rebroadcasts WPHN(FM) Gaylord 100%.
Box 695, Gaylord, 49734-0695. Phone: (989) 732-6274. Fax: (989) 732-8171.E-mail: ncr@ncradio.org Web Site:www.ncradio.org Licensee: Northern Christian Radio Inc. Format: Relg, Christian. ♦George A. Lake Jr., gen mgr.

Elkton

***WJCE(FM)**—Not on air, target date: unknown: 88.9 mhz; 50 kw. Ant 262 ft TL: N43 16 25 W82 35 16. Hrs open: CSN International, 4002 N. 3300 E., Twin Falls, ID, 83301. Phone: (208) 734-6633. Fax: (208) 736-1958. Web Site:www.csnradio.com Licensee: CSN International. ♦Mike Kestler, pres; Mike Stockland, gen mgr; Don Mills, progmg dir.

Elmwood Township

***WLJN(AM)**— Dec 23, 1982: 1400 khz; 640 w-U. TL: N44 46 36 W85 39 43. Hrs open: 24
Simulcast with WLJW(AM) Cadillac.
Box 1400, Traverse City, 49685. Secondary address: 1101 Cass St., Traverse City 49684. Phone: (231) 946-1400. Fax: (231) 946-3959.E-mail: info@wljn.com Web Site:www.wljn.com Licensee: Good News Media Inc. (group owner). Format: Relg, contemp, talk. News: 4 hrs wkly. Target aud: General. ♦Brian Harcey, gen mgr; Pete Lathrop, progmg dir & news dir.

Elsie

WOES(FM)—See Ovid-Elsie

Escanaba

WCHT(AM)— Dec 1, 1958: 600 khz; 1 kw-D, 191 w-N, DA-2. TL: N42 40 28 W87 08 41. Hrs open: 24 524 Ludington St., Suite 300, 49829. Phone: (906) 789-9700. Fax: (906) 789-9700.E-mail: rick@radioresultsnetwork.com Web Site:www.radioresultsnetwork.com Licensee: Lakes Radio Inc. (group owner) Population served: 38,000 Natl. Network: CBS Radio, . Natl. Rep: Christal,. Format: News/talk. News: 4. Target aud: 25-54. Spec prog: Farm one hr, forestry one hr wkly. ♦Rick Duerson, gen mgr & opns dir.

WDBC(AM)— Sept 4, 1941: 680 khz; 10 kw-D, 1 kw-N, DA-2. TL: N45 45 53 W87 05 48. Hrs open: 24 604 Ludington St., 49829. Phone: (906) 786-6144. Phone: (906) 786-1104. Fax: (906) 789-9959.E-mail: wdbcam@charteinternet.com Web Site:www.mywdbc.com Licensee: KMB Broadcasting Co. Inc. (acq 12-31-88). Population served: 90,000 Natl. Network: AP Radio, . Natl. Rep: Katz Radio,. Mich. Radio Wire Svc: AP Format: Full service, nostalgia. News staff: one; News: 12 hrs wkly. Target aud: 25-54. Spec prog: Relg 4 hrs, children one hr wkly. ♦Betsy Cooke, pres; Alice Sabuco, gen mgr; Kim Rabitoy, gen sls mgr; Erik Adams, news dir.

WGLQ(FM)— Sept 11, 1976: 97.1 mhz; 100 kw. 1,070 ft TL: N46 08 04 W85 56 02. Stereo. Hrs open: 524 Ludington St., Suite 300, 49829. Phone: (906) 228-9700. Fax: (906) 789-9700.E-mail: info@radioresultsnetwork.com Web Site:www.radioresultsnetwork.com Population served: 50,000 Format: Adult contemp.

WYKX(FM)— Dec 22, 1977: 104.7 mhz; 100 kw. 351 ft TL: N45 55 41 W87 16 00. (CP: Ant 1,000 ft. TL: N45 52 40 W87 28 00). Stereo. Hrs open: 24 Prog sep from AM 604 Ludington St., 49829. Phone: (906) 786-3800. Fax: (906) 789-9959.E-mail: wdbcam@charterinternet.com Web Site:www.kxcountry.net Population served: 110,000 Natl. Network: ABC, Jones Radio Networks, . Waitt Farm Net. Wire Svc: AP Format: Country. News staff: one; News: 4 hrs wkly. Target aud: General; 25-54. ♦Alice Sabuco, gen mgr; Kim Rabitoy, gen sls mgr; Allen Gibbs, progmg dir; Wayne Nault, mus dir; Erik Adams, news dir.

Essexville

WMJO(FM)— Jan 1, 1992: 97.3 mhz; 3 kw. 328 ft TL: N43 36 48 W83 45 51. Hrs open: 24 Box 1776, Saginaw, 48605. Secondary address: 2000 Whittier St., Saginaw 48601. Phone: (989) 752-8161. Fax: (989) 752-8102. Web Site:www.973joefm.com Licensee: The MacDonald Broadcasting Co. Group owner: MacDonald Broadcasting Co. (acq 12-20-2001; grpsl). Population served: 340,800 Rgnl rep: Interep. Fisher, Wayland, Cooper, Leader & Zaragoza. Format: Adult Hits. News staff: one; News: 3 hrs wkly. Target aud: 25-54; Women with families. ♦Kenneth H. MacDonald Jr., CEO, pres; Duane Alverson, pres; Jim Kramer, opns mgr; Mary Yearham, gen sls mgr.

Farmington Hills

WFDF(AM)— May 25, 1922: 910 khz; 50 kw-D, 19 kw-N, DA-2. TL: N42 03 57 W83 23 39. Stereo. Hrs open: 24 3011 W. Grand Blvd., Detroit, 48202. Phone: (248) 304-4381. Fax: (248) 304-4391. Web Site:www.radiodisney.com/detroit Licensee: Radio Disney Group LLC. Group owner: ABC Inc. (acq 8-15-2002; $3 million). Population served: 4,474,614 Natl. Network: Radio Disney, . Natl. Rep: Interep,. Format: Family hits. ♦Rich Padgen, gen mgr; Brian Christy, prom mgr.

Fenton

WCXI(AM)— Nov 15, 1985: 1160 khz; 1 kw-U, DA-1. TL: N42 38 30 W83 43 50. Hrs open: 15130 North Rd., 48430. Phone: (810) 750-1911. Phone: (248) 557-3500. Fax: (810) 750-9028.E-mail: sima@birach.com Web Site:www.birach.com Licensee: Birach Broadcasting Corp. (group owner; acq 9-13-99; $708,000). Natl. Network: American

Urban, . Format: Traditional country. Target aud: General; average age 35, primarily female, average income $35,000. ◆Sima Birach, CEO; Brenda Charette, opns mgr; John Morris, progmg dir, mus dir.

Flint

*WAKL(FM)— September 1997: 88.9 mhz; 380 w. Ant 263 ft TL: N42 58 49 W83 34 40. Stereo. Hrs open: 24 2351 Sunset Blvd., Suite 170-218, Rocklin, CA, 95765. Phone: (916) 251-1600. Fax: (916) 251-1650.E-mail: klove@klove.com Web Site:www.klove.com Licensee: Educational Media Foundation. Group owner: EMF Broadcasting (acq 11-19-01; $450,000). Population served: 279,000 Natl. Network: K-Love, . Shaw Pittman. Format: Contemp Christian. News staff: 3. Target aud: 25-44; female-Judeo Christian. ◆Richard Jenkins, pres; Mike Novak, VP; Keith Whipple, dev dir; David Pierce, progmg dir; Ed Lenane, news dir; Sam Wallington, engrg dir; Karen Johnson, news rptr.

WCRZ(FM)— Nov 4, 1961: 107.9 mhz; 50 kw. 331 ft TL: N42 58 49 W83 34 40. Stereo. Hrs open: Prog sep from AM 3338 E. Bristol Rd., Burton, 48529. Phone: (810) 743-1080. Fax: (810) 742-5170.E-mail: info@wcrz.com Web Site:www.wcrz.com Format: Adult contemp. ◆Kelly Quinn, gen sls mgr.

WDZZ-FM— Sept 29, 1979: 92.7 mhz; 3 kw. Ant 260 ft TL: N43 00 57 W83 41 24. Stereo. Hrs open: 6317 Taylor Dr., 48507. Phone: (810) 238-7300. Fax: (810) 743-2500.E-mail: jeff.wade@cumulus.com Web Site:www.wdzz.com Licensee: Cumulus Licensing Corp. Group owner: Cumulus Media Inc. (acq 3-15-00; grpsl). Population served: 424,902 Format: Urban adult. Target aud: Adults. Spec prog: Gospel 8 hrs, teen talk one hr, concerned pastors one hr wkly. ◆Scott Meier, gen mgr; Jeff Wade, opns mgr, progmg dir.

WFBE(FM)— Oct 5, 1953: 95.1 mhz; 50 kw. 243 ft TL: N43 01 13 W83 40 40. Stereo. Hrs open: 5 AM-1 AM G 4511 Miller Rd., 48507. Phone: (810) 720-9510. Fax: (810) 720-9513.E-mail: chris.monk@citcomm.com Web Site:www.b95.fm Licensee: Citadel Broadcasting Co. Group owner: Citadel Broadcasting Corp. (acq 4-26-01; grpsl). Population served: 15,000 Natl. Network: PRI, . Format: Country. News: 3 hrs wkly. Target aud: General; country music listeners. ◆Chris Monk, gen mgr; Greg Bryant, gen sls mgr; April Hurley Rose, progmg dir.

WFLT(AM)— Dec 5, 1955: 1420 khz; 500 w-D, 142 w-N, DA-2. TL: N43 01 19 W83 38 35. Hrs open: 317 S. Averill, 48506. Phone: (810) 239-5733. Fax: (810) 239-7134.E-mail: wflt1420am@aol.com Licensee: Metropolitan Missionary Baptist Church (acq 7-2-90; $225,000;7-23-90). Natl. Rep: Michigan Spot Sales,. Format: Black gospel. ◆Sammie Jordan, gen mgr.

WFNT(AM)— Apr 10, 1953: 1470 khz; 5 kw-D, 1 kw-N, DA-2. TL: N42 58 22 W83 38 24. Hrs open: 24 3338 E. Bristol Rd., Burton, 48529. Phone: (810) 742-1470. Fax: (810) 742-5170.E-mail: info@wfnt.com Web Site:www.wfnt.com Licensee: Regent Broadcasting of Flint Inc. Group owner: Regent Communications Inc. (acq 8-13-98; grpsl). Population served: 430,000 Haley, Bader & Potts. Format: Nostalgia. News staff: 3. ◆Zoe Burdine-Fly, gen mgr; Carolyn Gerace, prom dir; Chris Pavelich, news dir; Mike Hutchens, chief of engrg.

*WFUM-FM— Aug 23, 1985: 91.1 mhz; 18 kw. 489 ft TL: N42 53 57 W83 27 42. Stereo. Hrs open: 24
Rebroadcasts WUOM(FM) Ann Arbor 100%.
535 W. William St., Suite 110, Ann Arbor, 48103. Phone: (734) 764-9210. Fax: (734) 647-3488.E-mail: michigan.radio@umich.edu Web Site:michiganradio.org Licensee: Regents of the University of Michigan. Natl. Network: NPR, . Format: News/talk. ◆Peggy Watson, opns mgr; Michael Leland, dev dir, news dir. Co-owned TV: *WFUM-TV affil

WSNL(AM)— Apr 26, 1946: 600 khz; 440 w-D, 250 w-N, DA-2. TL: N42 54 27 W83 50 07. Hrs open: 24 5210 S. Saginaw St., 48507. Phone: (810) 694-4146. Fax: (810) 694-0661. Web Site:www.cbsl.biz Licensee: Christian Broadcasting System Ltd. (group owner; (acq 1-22-93; $400,000;2-8-93). Population served: 500,000 Format: Christian, teaching, talk. Target aud: 25-54; 35+. ◆Jon Yinger, pres; Evelyn Shaw, VP, gen mgr; Graham Parker, opns mgr, rgnl sls mgr.

WTRX(AM)— Oct 1, 1947: 1330 khz; 5 kw-D, 1 kw-N, DA-2. TL: N42 58 24 W83 39 02. Stereo. Hrs open: G 4511 Miller Rd., 48507. Phone: (810) 720-9510. Fax: (810) 720-9513. Web Site:www.wtrxsports.com Licensee: Citadel Broadcasting Co. Group owner: Citadel Broadcasting Corp. (acq 10-6-00; $180,000). Format: Sports, talk. 18-49 Males. ◆Chris Monk, gen mgr; Greg Bryant, gen sls mgr; Doug Fisher, progmg dir.

WWCK(AM)— Nov 11, 1946: 1570 khz; 1 kw-D, 238 w-N. TL: N43 00 38 W83 39 09. Hrs open: 6317 Taylor, 48507. Phone: (810) 238-7300. Fax: (810) 238-7310.E-mail: info@1570supertalk.com Web Site:www.1570supertalk.com Licensee: Cumulus Licensing Corp. Group owner: Cumulus Media Inc. (acq 3-15-00; grpsl). Population served: 193,317 Natl. Network: Westwood One, . Format: News/talk. Target aud: 18-34. ◆Scott Meier, gen mgr; Les Root, news dir; Dan Greer, chief of engrg.

WWCK-FM— September 1964: 105.5 mhz; 25 kw. 328 ft TL: N43 00 39 W83 39 04. Stereo. Hrs open: Dups AM 50% 6317 Taylor Dr., 48507. Phone: (810) 238-7300. Fax: (810) 238-7310.E-mail: info@wwck.com Web Site:www.wwck.com Population served: 193,317 Format: CHR.

Frankenmuth

WRCL(FM)— 2001: 93.7 mhz; 3.5 kw. 436 ft TL: N43 18 16 W83 33 07. Stereo. Hrs open: 24 3338 E. Bristol Rd., Burton, 48529. Phone: (810) 742-1470. Fax: (810) 742-5170.E-mail: info@club937.com Web Site:www.club937.com Licensee: Regent Broadcasting of Flint Inc. Group owner: Regent Communications Inc. (acq 11-9-01; $7 million with WFGR(FM) Grand Rapids). Natl. Network: CNN Radio, Westwood One, . Format: Rhythmic CHR. Target aud: 12-34; children & adults. ◆Zoe Burdine-Fly, gen mgr; J. Patrick, gen mgr; Nathan Reed, progmg dir; Clay Church, mus dir.

Frankfort

WOUF(FM)— Oct 2, 1978: 99.3 mhz; 50 kw. Ant 410 ft TL: N44 36 38 W86 09 38. Stereo. Hrs open: 24 13999 Bayshore Dr, Traverse City, 49684. Secondary address: 1532 Forrester Rd 49635. Phone: (231) 352-6374. Fax: (231) 352-4335. Licensee: Roy E. Henderson. (group owner; (acq 8-7-2001). Population served: 25,000 Natl. Rep: Patt,. Format: Soft rock. News staff: one; News: 3 hrs wkly. Target aud: 25-54. Spec prog: Folk 2 hrs, big band 2 hrs wkly. ◆Roy Henderson, gen mgr.

Frederic

WGRL(FM)—Not on air, target date: unknown: 95.3 mhz; 3.3 kw. Ant 447 ft TL: N44 52 43 W84 40 50. Hrs open: Box 1766, Gaylord, 49734. Phone: (989) 732-2341. Fax: (989) 732-6202. Licensee: Darby Advertising Inc. ◆Kent D. Smith, pres & gen mgr.

Freeland

*WTRK(FM)— 2005: 90.9 mhz; 430 w. Ant 324 ft TL: N43 33 42 W83 58 52. Hrs open:
Rebroadcasts KLVR(FM) Santa Rosa, CA 100%.
2351 Sunset Blvd., Suite 170-218, Rocklin, CA, 95765. Phone: (916) 251-1600. Fax: (916) 251-1650. Web Site:www.klove.com Licensee: Educational Media Foundation. Group owner: American Family Radio. (acq 6-29-2005; $75,000). Natl. Network: K-Love, . Format: Contemp Christian. ◆Richard Jenkins, pres; Mike Novak, VP; Keith Whipple, dev dir; David Pierce, progmg dir; Ed Lenane, news dir; Sam Wallington, engrg dir; Arthur Vassar, traf mgr; Karen Johnson, news rptr.

Fremont

WSHN(AM)— May 23, 1961: 1550 khz; 1 kw-D. TL: N43 28 15 W85 56 25. Hrs open: Box 190, 49412. Phone: (231) 924-4700. Fax: (231) 924-9746. Licensee: WSHN Inc. (acq 3-11-97; grpsl). Population served: 200,000 Natl. Network: ESPN Radio, . Natl. Rep: Patt,. Format: Espn Sports. ◆John Russell, news dir.

Gagetown

*WCTP(FM)— 2006: 88.5 mhz; 6 kw. Ant 328 ft TL: N43 45 36 W83 05 45. Stereo. Hrs open: 24 4330 Farver Rd., 48735. Phone: (989) 872-3525. Phone: (989) 872-3700. Fax: (989) 872-3525.E-mail: dplonta@hotmail.com Licensee: Plonta Broadcasting Inc. Format: Southern gospel. News staff: 3. ◆Duane Plonta, pres.

Gaylord

*WBLW(FM)— 2000: 88.1 mhz; 3 kw vert. Ant 200 ft TL: N45 01 28 W84 43 44. Stereo. Hrs open: 24 hours Box 177, 49734. Secondary address: 232 S. Townline Rd. 49735. Phone: (989) 705-7464. Fax: (989) 731-1122.E-mail: info@wblwradio.com Web Site:www.wblwradio.com Licensee: Gaylord Baptist Christian School. Population served: 4,000 Natl. Network: USA, . Format: Christian. ◆Jay Towne, gen mgr; Tim Ramsey, progmg dir.

WMJZ-FM— 1984: 101.5 mhz; 50 kw. Ant 492 ft TL: N45 01 10 W84 24 28. Stereo. Hrs open: Box 1766, 49734. Secondary address: 3687 Old US Hwy. 27 S. 49735. Phone: (989) 732-2341. Fax: (989) 732-6202. Web Site:www.radioeaglegaylord.com Licensee: Darby Advertising Inc. (acq 1-1-98; with co-located AM). Population served: 45,000 Natl. Network: Motor Racing Net, . Irwin Campbell & Tanneweld. Format: News, sports, adult hits. Target aud: 25-54. ◆Kent D. Smith, pres, gen mgr; Mike Reling, opns mgr; Rob Weaver, progmg dir.

*WPHN(FM)— Apr 7, 1985: 90.5 mhz; 100 kw. Ant 1,000 ft TL: N45 08 17 W84 09 44. Stereo. Hrs open: 24 PO Box 695, 49734-0695. Secondary address: 1511 M-32 E. 49735. Phone: (989) 732-6274. Fax: (989) 732-8171.E-mail: ncr@ncradio.org Web Site:www.ncradio.org Licensee: Northern Christian Radio Inc. (group owner). Population served: 150,000 Natl. Network: Moody, USA, . Southmayd & Miller. Format: Religious, Christian. News: 10 hrs wkly. Target aud: 25-55. ◆George A. Lake Jr., CEO, gen mgr; Joe Sereno, chmn & pres.

WSRT(FM)— Nov 18, 1972: 106.7 mhz; 100 kw. 580 ft TL: N45 02 42 W84 50 44. Stereo. Hrs open: 24 1020 Hastings St., Traverse City, 49686. Phone: (231) 947-0003. Fax: (231) 947-7002. Web Site:www.1067wsrt.com Licensee: Northern Radio of Gaylord Inc. (acq 9-23-96; $1.4 million with WMLQ(FM) Rogers City). Population served: 3,012 Natl. Rep: Christal,. Format: Hot adult contemp. Target aud: 18-49; rgnl orientation including Traverse City, Petoskey, Cheboygan-active life style. ◆Charlie Ferguson, gen mgr; Greg Marsh, gen sls mgr, natl sls mgr; Dennis Winslow, progmg dir; Dennis Murray, chief of engrg; Kristal Flateau, traf mgr.

Gladstone

WGKL(FM)— Feb 15, 1999: 105.5 mhz; 4.6 kw. 377 ft TL: N45 48 17 W87 10 15. Hrs open: 524 Ludington St, Suite 300, Escanaba, 49829. Phone: (906) 228-9700. Fax: (906) 789-9700.E-mail: kool105fm@chartermi.net Web Site:www.radioresultsnetwork.com Licensee: Lakes Radio Inc. (group owner) Format: Oldies. ◆Rick Duerson, gen mgr.

Gladwin

WGDN(AM)— Dec 7, 1974: 1350 khz; 1 kw-D, DA. TL: N43 57 03 W84 30 34. Hrs open: 3601 W. Woods Rd., 48624. Phone: (989) 426-1031.E-mail: steve@103country.com Web Site:www.103country.com Licensee: Apple Broadcasting Co. Inc. (acq 3-87; with co-located FM; 12-22-86). Population served: 56,000 Format: Relg. Target aud: 35 plus. ◆Steve Coston, gen mgr.

WGDN-FM— Feb 7, 1978: 103.1 mhz; 11.5 kw. 453 ft TL: N43 57 03 W84 30 34. Stereo. Hrs open: Prog sep from AM 3601 W. Woods Rd., 48624. Phone: (989) 426-1031.E-mail: steve@103country.com Population served: 185,000 Natl. Network: Westwood One, . Format: Country.

Glen Arbor

WGFN(FM)— February 1991: 98.1 mhz; 21 kw. Ant 738 ft TL: N44 49 16 W85 59 47. Stereo. Hrs open: 24
WGFN-FM Cheboygan 100%.
1356 Mackinaw Ave., Cheboygan, 49721. Phone: (231) 627-2341. Fax: (231) 627-7000.E-mail: info@classicrockthebear.com Web Site:www.classicrockthebear.com Licensee: Northern Star Broadcasting L.L.C. (group owner; (acq 12-12-2005); grpsl). Format: Classic rock. News staff: one. ◆Palmer Pyle, pres; April Hurley-Rose, gen mgr, opns dir.

WJZJ(FM)— Sept 1, 1997: 95.5 mhz; 21 kw. 738 ft TL: N44 49 16 W85 59 47. Stereo. Hrs open: 24 1356 Mackinaw Ave., Cheboygan, 49721. Phone: (231) 627-2341. Fax: (231) 627-7000.E-mail: info@modernrockthezone.com Web Site:www.modernrockthezone.com Licensee: Northern Star Broadcasting L.L.C. (group owner; (acq 12-12-2005); grpsl). Format: Modern rock. ◆Palmer Pyle, pres; April Hurley-Rose, gen mgr.

Good Hart

*WJOG(FM)— 2006: 91.3 mhz; 600 w vert. Ant 623 ft TL: N45 30 33 W85 02 11. Hrs open:
simulcasts WJOM (FM) Eagle 100%.
Michigan Community Radio, 148 E Grand River Rd., Williamston, 48895. Phone: (517) 381-0573. Web Site:www.smile.fm Licensee: Michigan Community Radio. ◆Ed Czelada, pres.

Goodland Township

***WHYT(FM)**— 2004: 88.1 mhz; 400 w vert. Ant 581 ft TL: N43 10 30 W83 04 02. Hrs open: Box 388, 148 E. Grand River Rd., Williamston, 48895. Phone: (517) 381-0573. Fax: (877) 850-0881.E-mail: 411@smile.fm Web Site:www.smile.fm Licensee: Smile FM. ♦Jenn Czelada, gen mgr; Ed Czelada, progmg dir.

Grand Haven

WGHN(AM)— July 16, 1956: 1370 khz; 500 w-D, 22 w-N. TL: N43 02 17 W86 13 46. Hrs open: 24 Box 330, One S. Harbor, 49417. Phone: (616) 842-8110. Fax: (616) 842-4350. Web Site:www.sportsradio1370.com Licensee: WGHN Inc. (acq 8-9-2007; $1.65 million with co-located FM). Population served: 120,000 Natl. Network: ESPN Radio, . Rgnl. Network: Mich. Farm. Natl. Rep: Patt,. Rothman, Gordon, Foreman & Groudine. Format: Sports. ♦Will Tieman, pres; Eric Kaelin, gen mgr.

WGHN-FM— Jan 28, 1969: 92.1 mhz; 3 kw. Ant 246 ft TL: N43 03 23 W86 14 27. Stereo. Hrs open: 24 Box 330, One S. Harbor, 49417. Phone: (616) 842-8110. Fax: (616) 842-4350. Web Site:www.wghn.com Natl. Network: CBS Radio, . Mich. Farm Format: Adult contemp. News staff: 2; News: 30 hrs wkly. Target aud: 25-54. Spec prog: Farm 5 hrs wkly. ♦Jesse Bruce, progmg dir; Walt Zerlaut, news dir.

Grand Marais

***WQMI(FM)**—Not on air, target date: unknown: 91.7 mhz; 30 kw. Ant 403 ft TL: N46 38 29.1 W85 59 35.4. Hrs open: Box 97, Charlevoix, 49720. Phone: (231) 420-1325. Licensee: Korkee Inc. ♦Robert A. Naismith, CEO.

Grand Rapids

***WAYG(FM)**— May 18, 1978: 89.9 mhz; 4.9 w. Ant 207 ft TL: N42 58 40 W85 35 44. Stereo. Hrs open: 24
Rebroadcasts WAYK(FM) Kalamazoo 75%.
1159 E. Beltline Ave. N.E., 49525. Phone: (616) 942-1500. Fax: (616) 942-7078. Web Site:www.way.fm Licensee: Cornerstone University (acq 1-21-98; $200,000). Population served: 700,000 Format: Christian hits. News: one hr wkly. Target aud: Teens/ Young Adults. ♦Dr. Joseph Stowell, pres; Lee Geysbeek, VP; Rich Anderson, gen mgr.

WBBL-FM—(Greenville, October 1989: 107.3 mhz; 50 kw. Ant 492 ft TL: N43 01 10 W85 20 58. Stereo. Hrs open: 24 60 Monroe Ctr. N.W., 3rd Fl., 49503. Phone: (616) 774-8461. Fax: (616) 774-2491.E-mail: info@wbbl.com Web Site:www.wbbl.com Licensee: Citadel Broadcasting Co. Group owner: Citadel Broadcasting Corp. (acq 5-30-2000; grpsl). Population served: 600,000 Natl. Network: Fox Sports, . Natl. Rep: D & R Radio,. Format: Sports. News staff: one. Target aud: 18-49; men. ♦Matt Hanlon, gen mgr; Russ Hines, gen sls mgr; Bret Bakita, progmg dir.

WBCT(FM)— October 1951: 93.7 mhz; 320 kw. 781 ft TL: N42 37 56 W85 32 16. Stereo. Hrs open: 24 77 Monroe Center, Suite 1000, 49503. Phone: (616) 459-1919. Fax: (616) 242-9373. Web Site:www.b93.com Licensee: CC Licenses LLC. Group owner: Clear Channel Communications Inc. (acq 1996; grpsl). Natl. Rep: Clear Channel,. Format: Country. News staff: one; News: 3 hrs wkly. Target aud: 25-49. ♦Skip Essick, VP & gen mgr; Rich Berry, gen sls mgr; Andrea Sipka, natl sls mgr.

WBFX(FM)— 1965: 101.3 mhz; 50 kw. Ant 420 ft TL: N43 02 28 W85 28 23. Stereo. Hrs open: 24 Dups AM 50% 77 Monroe Ctr., Suite 1000, 49503. Phone: (616) 459-1919. Fax: (616) 242-6599.E-mail: info@101thefoxrocks.com Web Site:www.101thefoxrocks.com Population served: 197,649 Format: Classic rock. ♦Rich Berry, gen sls mgr; Doug Montgomery, progmg dir.

***WBLU-FM**— Aug 18, 1979: 88.9 mhz; 650 w. 400 ft TL: N42 59 15 W85 37 26. Stereo. Hrs open:
Rebroadcasts WBLV(FM) Twin Lake 100%.
Blue Lake Fine Arts Camp, Twin Lake, 49457. Phone: (231) 894-2616. Phone: (231) 458-9258. Fax: (231) 893-2457.E-mail: radio@bluelake.org Web Site:www.bluelake.org Licensee: Blue Lake Fine Arts Camp. (acq 3-1-93; $200,000; 3-15-93). Natl. Network: PRI, NPR, . Rgnl. Network: Mich. Pub. Format: Class, jazz, news. Target aud: Adults. Spec prog: Folk 5 hrs wkly. ♦Dave Myers, gen mgr; Gordon Christensen, opns dir; Steve Albert, progmg dir; Bonnie Bierma, mus dir; Don Hoogeboom, chief of engrg.

***WCSG(FM)**— June 9, 1973: 91.3 mhz; 37 kw. 570 ft TL: N42 47 46 W85 38 58. Stereo. Hrs open: 1159 E. Beltline Ave. N.E., 49525. Phone: (616) 942-1500. Fax: (616) 942-7078. E-mail: wcsg@wcsg.org Web Site:www.wcsg.org Licensee: Cornerstone University. Population served: 1,300,000 Natl. Network: AP Radio, . Format: Christian, AC. News staff: 2; News: 2 hrs wkly. Target aud: 35-49. ♦Dr. Joseph Stowell, pres; Lee Geysbeek, VP; Chris Lemke, gen mgr, progmg dir; Patty Riva, prom dir; Tom Bosscher, chief of engrg.

WFGR(FM)— Aug 9, 1992: 98.7 mhz; 2.75 kw. Ant 492 ft TL: N43 01 57 W85 41 47. Hrs open: 50 Monroe N.W., Suite 500, 49503. Phone: (616) 451-4855. Fax: (616) 451-4225.E-mail: info@wfgr.com Web Site:www.wfgr.com Licensee: Regent Broadcasting of Grand Rapids Inc. Group owner: Regent Communications Inc. (acq 6-1-2002; $3.9 million for stock). Format: Classic hits. Target aud: 25 plus; affluent, well-educated professionals. ♦Terry Jacobs, pres; Phil Catlett, gen mgr; Paul Boscarino, sls dir.

WFUR(AM)— November 1947: 1570 khz; 1 kw-D, 306 w-N. TL: N42 57 14 W85 41 52. Hrs open: 24 Box 1808, 49501. Secondary address: 399 Garfield Ave. S.W. 49504. Phone: (616) 451-9387. Fax: (616) 451-8460.E-mail: wfuramfm@cbcglobal.net Web Site:www.wfuramfm.com Licensee: Furniture City Broadcasting Corp. Group owner: Kuiper Stations (acq 3-10-50). Population served: 500,000 Natl. Network: USA, . Format: Relg. News: 5 hrs wkly. Target aud: 35 plus; 60% female, 30% male. ♦William E. Kuiper Sr., pres & gen mgr; Steven Kuiper, opns mgr, mus dir; Dave Kuiper, news dir, local news ed, farm dir, relg ed, disc jockey; Pat Deja, pub affrs dir; Bill Kuiper Jr., chief of engrg.

WFUR-FM— September 1960: 102.9 mhz; 50 kw. 492 ft TL: N42 57 13 W85 41 55. Stereo. Hrs open: 24 Prog sep from AM Box 1808, 49501. Secondary address: 399 Garfield Ave. S.W. 49504. Phone: (616) 451-9387. Fax: (616) 451-8460. Population served: 1,000,000 Natl. Network: USA, . Format: Relg music. News: 5 hrs wkly. Target aud: 35-64; Christian family music listeners & homeowners. ♦Doug Wentworth, sports cmtr; Dave Kuiper, disc jockey.

WGRD-FM— Aug 1, 1962: 97.9 mhz; 13 kw. 590 ft TL: N42 47 46 W85 38 58. Stereo. Hrs open: 24 50 Monroe N.W., Suite 500, Grands Rapids, 49503. Phone: (616) 451-4800. Fax: (616) 451-0113. Web Site:www.wgrd.com Licensee: Regent Broadcasting of Grand Rapids Inc. Group owner: Regent Communications Inc. (acq 8-7-00; grpsl). Natl. Rep: Katz Radio,. Format: Modern rock, alternative. News staff: one; News: 3 hrs wkly. Target aud: 18-49. ♦Phil Catlett, gen mgr; Paul Boscarino, sls dir.

***WGVU(AM)**—(Kentwood, Dec 25, 1954: 1480 khz; 2 kw-D, 5 kw-N. TL: N42 57 13 W85 41 36. Hrs open: 24 301 W. Fulton, Grand Valley State University, 49504-6492. Phone: (616) 331-6666. Fax: (616) 331-6625.E-mail: wgvu@gvsu.edu Web Site:www.wgvu.org Licensee: Grand Valley State Univ. (acq 4-7-92; $240,000 part sale & part gift; 4-27-92). Population served: 400,000 Natl. Network: NPR, PRI, . Format: News, info. News staff: 3; News: 89 hrs wkly. Target aud: 35-44; college-educated men with average income. ♦Michael T. Walenta, gen mgr; Ken Kolbe, opns mgr; Pamela Holtz, mktg mgr & prom mgr; Fred Martino, news dir; Bob Lumbert, chief of engrg; Ed Spier, traf mgr; Jim Rademaker, spec ev coord.

WGVU-FM—See Allendale

WJNZ(AM)—See Kentwood

WJRW(AM)— Sept 18, 1940: 1340 khz; 1 kw-U. TL: N42 57 02 W85 41 55. Hrs open: 24 60 Monroe Ctr. N.W., 3rd Fl., 49503. Phone: (616) 774-8461. Fax: (616) 774-2491.E-mail: info@wbbl.com Web Site:www.wbbl.com Licensee: Citadel Broadcasting Co. Natl. Network: ABC, . Format: Talk. Target aud: 18-49. ♦Bret Bakita, progmg dir.

WLAV-FM— January 1947: 96.9 mhz; 50 kw. 499 ft TL: N43 02 01 W85 31 15. Stereo. Hrs open: 24 60 Monroe Ctr. N.W., 3rd Fl., 49503. Phone: (616) 774-8461. Fax: (616) 774-2491.E-mail: info@wlav.com Web Site:www.wlav.com Licensee: Citadel Broadcasting Co. Group owner: Citadel Broadcasting Corp. (acq 5-30-00; grpsl). Population served: 194,649 Natl. Network: ABC, . Reddy, Begley & McCormick. Format: Classic rock. Target aud: 25-49. ♦Matthew R. Hanlon, pres; Matt Hanlon, gen mgr; Brent Alberts, opns mgr; Kim Lozano, gen sls mgr; Rob Brant, progmg dir; John Alan, chief of engrg; Melissa Bosvich, traf mgr.

WLHT-FM— Feb 28, 1962: 95.7 mhz; 40 kw. 551 ft TL: N43 01 57 W85 41 47. Stereo. Hrs open: 50 Monroe N.W., Suite 500, 49503. Phone: (616) 451-4855. Fax: (616) 451-9595.E-mail: billb@wlht.com Web Site:www.wlht.com Licensee: Regent Broadcasting of Grand Rapids Inc. Population served: 584,400 Dow, Lohnes & Albertson. Format: Adult contemp. Target aud: 25-54. ♦Terry Jacobs, pres & gen sls mgr; Bill Bailey, progmg dir.

WMJH(AM)—See Rockford

WNWZ(AM)— Nov 1, 1947: 1410 khz; 1 kw-D, 48 w-N. TL: N42 59 14 W85 37 76. Stereo. Hrs open: 50 Monroe N.W., Suite 500, 49503. Phone: (616) 459-4111. Fax: (616) 451-9595.E-mail: billb@wlht.com Web Site:www.1401lamaquina.com Licensee: Regent Broadcasting of Grand Rapids Inc. Group owner: Regent Communications Inc. (acq 8-7-00; grpsl). Population served: 197,649 Natl. Network: Jones Radio Networks, . Format: Latin mix /Sp language. Target aud: 35 plus; professionals. ♦Phil Catlett, gen mgr.

WOOD(AM)— 1924: 1300 khz; 20 kw-U, DA-2. TL: N42 45 22 W85 39 24. Stereo. Hrs open: 24 77 Monroe Ctr., Suite 1000, 49503. Phone: (616) 459-1919. Fax: (616) 242-6599.E-mail: info@woodradio.com Web Site:www.woodradio.com Licensee: CC Licenses LLC. Group owner: Clear Channel Communications Inc. (acq 5-10-96; grpsl). Population served: 680,000 Natl. Network: ABC, . Natl. Rep: Clear Channel,. Format: News/talk. News staff: 6; News: 24 hrs wkly. Target aud: 35-54. ♦Skip Essick, VP & gen mgr; Phil Tower, opns dir, progmg dir; Henry Capogna, gen sls mgr, rgnl sls mgr; Andrea Sipka, natl sls mgr; Glenn Del Vecchio, mktg dir, prom dir; Kristen Everhart, prom dir; Rob St. Mary, news dir; Don Missad, chief of engrg; Kay Jaarsma, traf mgr.

WOOD-FM— 1962: 105.7 mhz; 265 kw. Ant 810 ft TL: N42 41 13 W85 30 35. Stereo. Hrs open: 24 77 Monroe Cir., Suite 1000, 49503. Phone: (616) 459-1919. Fax: (616) 242-6599.E-mail: info@woodfm.com Web Site:www.woodfm.com Licensee: CC Licenses LLC. Format: Adult contemp. News: 10 hrs wkly. ♦Doug Montgomery, opns mgr; Glenn Del Vecchio, prom mgr; Tim Kiesling, progmg dir; David Messner, traf mgr.

WTKG(AM)— February 1945: 1230 khz; 1 kw-U. TL: N42 59 42 W85 40 36. Stereo. Hrs open: 24 77 Monroe Ctr., Suite 1000, 49503. Phone: (616) 459-1919. Fax: (616) 242-6599.E-mail: info@wtkg.com Web Site:www.wtkg.com Licensee: CC Licenses LLC. Group owner: Clear Channel Communications Inc. (acq 1996; grpsl). Population served: 224,700 Natl. Rep: Clear Channel,. Format: Talk. News staff: 2; News: 7 hrs wkly. Target aud: 25-54; conservative. ♦Skip Essick, VP & gen mgr; Phil Tower, opns dir, progmg dir; Henry Capogna, gen sls mgr; Andrea Sipka, natl sls mgr; Kristen Everhart, prom mgr; Rob St. Mary, news dir; Don Missad, chief of engrg; Kay Jaarsma, traf mgr.

WTNR(FM)—See Holland

***WVGR(FM)**— Dec 7, 1961: 104.1 mhz; 108 kw. 600 ft TL: N42 41 13 W85 30 35. Stereo. Hrs open: 24
Rebroadcasts WUOM(FM) Ann Arbor 100%.
535 W. William St., Suite 110, Ann Arbor, 48103. Phone: (734) 764-9210. Fax: (734) 647-3488.E-mail: michigan.radio@umich.edu Web Site:www.michiganradio.org Licensee: Regents of the University of Michigan. Population served: 720,000 Natl. Network: NPR, PRI, . Rgnl. Network: Mich. Pub. Dow, Lohnes & Albertson. Format: News/talk. News staff: 7; News: 140 hrs wkly. ♦Bob Skon, stn mgr, chief of engrg; Peggy Watson, opns mgr, dev dir; Vincent Duffey, news dir.

Grayling

WGRY(AM)— Aug 1, 1970: 1230 khz; 750 w-U. TL: N44 39 05 W84 44 18. Hrs open: 24 6514 Old Lake Rd., 49738. Phone: (989) 348-6171. Fax: (989) 348-6181.E-mail: radio@i2k.net Web Site:www.gannonbroadcasting.com Licensee: Gannon Broadcasting. Population served: 50,000 Natl. Rep: Michigan Spot Sales,. Format: Music of Your Life. News staff: one; News: 16 hrs wkly. Target aud: 25 plus. ♦William S. Gannon, pres & gen mgr; Pete Michaels, opns mgr.

WGRY-FM— June 16, 1977: 100.3 mhz; 50 kw. 436 ft TL: N44 36 50 W84 41 05. Stereo. Hrs open: 6514 Old Lake Rd., 49738. Phone: (989) 348-6171. Fax: (989) 348-6181.E-mail: radio@i2k.net Web Site:www.gannonbroadcasting.com Licensee: Gannon Broadcasting Systems Inc. Population served: 23,000 Natl. Network: ABC, . Natl. Rep: Patt,. Format: Country. Target aud: 25-54. ♦William Gannon, pres & gen mgr; Pete Michaels, opns mgr.

Greenville

WBBL-FM—Licensed to Greenville. See Grand Rapids

***WDPW(FM)**—Not on air, target date: unknown: 91.9 mhz; 6 kw vert. Ant 157 ft TL: N43 05 27 W85 16 27. Hrs open: 6808 Hanna Lake S.E., Caledonia, 49316. Phone: (616) 698-1831. Licensee: Larlen Communications Inc.

WGLM(AM)— May 19, 1960: 1380 khz; 1 kw-D, 500 w-N, DA-N. TL: N43 09 18 W85 15 25. Hrs open: Box 578, 48838. Secondary address: 9181 S. Greenville Rd. Phone: (616) 754-3656. Fax: (616) 754-2390.E-mail: wscgradio@chartermi.net Licensee: Packer Radio

Greenville Inc. (acq 12-19-2008; $195,000 with WGLM-FM Lakeview). Population served: 9,500 Format: News, talk, sports. ◆Chris Loiselle, CFO; Bruce Bentley, gen mgr, opns mgr, progmg dir; Ralph Haines, chief of engrg.

Gulliver

WCMM(FM)— 1982: 102.5 mhz; 100 kw. 813 ft TL: N45 58 01 W86 29 18. Stereo. Hrs open: 524 Ludington, Suite 300, Escanaba, 49829. Phone: (906) 789-9700. Fax: (906) 789-9700.E-mail: rick@radioresultsnetwork.com Web Site:www.radioresultsnetwork.com Licensee: Lakes Radio Inc. (group owner; acq 11-30-99; grpsl). Population served: 200,000 Natl. Network: ABC, . Natl. Rep: Christal,. Format: Country. News staff: 4. Target aud: 18-54; younger, contemp, mobile adult workers. ◆Rick Duerson, gen mgr.

Gwinn

WUPT(FM)— 2008: Stn currently dark. 100.3 mhz; 66 kw. Ant 456 ft TL: N46 30 52.2 W87 28 36.5. Hrs open: 1717 Dixie Hwy., Suite 650, Fort Wright, KY, 41011. Phone: (859) 331-9100. Licensee: Radioactive LLC. ◆Benjamin L. Homel, pres.

Hancock

WGLI(FM)— Feb 11, 2003: 98.7 mhz; 100 kw. Ant 522 ft TL: N47 06 13 W88 34 04. Hrs open: 24 805-B U.S. 41 S., Baraga, 49908. Phone: (906) 353-9287. Fax: (906) 353-9200.E-mail: cupadmin@up.net Web Site:www.keepitintheup.com Licensee: Keweenaw Bay Indian Community (acq 2-13-03). Population served: 50,000 Natl. Network: Jones Radio Networks, . Format: Classic rock. Spec prog: Loc talk 5 hrs wkly. ◆Ed Janisse, gen mgr; John Preston, gen sls mgr; Todd VanDyke, progmg dir.

WKMJ-FM— 1968: 93.5 mhz; 13.5 kw. Ant 456 ft TL: N47 06 06 W88 34 11. Hrs open: Prog sep from AM Box 547, 49930. Phone: (906) 482-3700. Fax: (906) 482-1540.E-mail: wmpl@chartermi.net Licensee: J & J Broadcasting Inc. Population served: 4,820 Natl. Network: Jones Radio Networks, . Booth, Freret, Imlay & Tepper. Format: Hot adult contemp, sports. News staff: one. Target aud: 18-45.

WMPL(AM)— Mar 2, 1957: 920 khz; 1 kw-D, 206 w-N. TL: N47 06 05 W88 35 26. Hrs open: Box 547, 49930. Phone: (906) 482-3700. Fax: (906) 482-1540.E-mail: wmpl@chartermi.net Licensee: J & J Broadcasting Inc. (acq 8-5-2006; $775,000 with co-located FM). Population served: 4,820 Natl. Network: USA, . Natl. Rep: Michigan Spot Sales,. Format: Talk/news, info, sports. News staff: one; News: 15 hrs wkly. Target aud: General. ◆Jerry Hackman, pres; Jay Nix, VP; Ken Waldrop, gen mgr; Mariann Schulze, gen sls mgr; Josh Ylitalo, progmg dir, traf mgr; Mitchell Lake, news dir; Ted Franz, chief of engrg.

Hanover

*WJKZ(FM)—Not on air, target date: unknown: 90.9 mhz; 500 w. Ant 161 ft TL: N42 04 25 W84 35 38. Hrs open: Box 4872, East Lansing, 48826. Phone: (517) 999-3737. Web Site:www.foundationradio.org Licensee: Saidnewsfoundation. ◆David C. Schaberg, gen mgr.

Harbor Beach

WCZE(FM)— 2005: 103.7 mhz; 50 kw. Ant 440 ft TL: N43 41 25 W82 56 27. Hrs open: Box 388, Williamston, 48895. Phone: (810) 721-0891.E-mail: jennc@smile.FM Web Site:www.smile.fm Licensee: Jennifer & Edward Czelada. Format: Christian. ◆Jenn Czelada, gen mgr; Ed Czelada, progmg dir.

Harbor Springs

*WCMW-FM— Aug 15, 1988: 103.9 mhz; 28 kw. 663 ft TL: N45 29 02 W84 58 00. Stereo. Hrs open: 24
Rebroadcasts WCMU-FM Mount Pleasant 100%.
Public Broadcasting Ctr., Central Michigan Univ., Mount Pleasant, 48859. Phone: (989) 774-3105. Fax: (989) 774-4427.E-mail: cmuradio@cmich.edu Web Site:www.wcmu.org Licensee: Central Michigan University. (acq 7-21-93; $325,000; 8-23-93). Natl. Network: NPR, PRI, . Rgnl. Network: Mich. Pub. Dow, Lohnes & Albertson. Wire Svc: AP Format: Class jazz, news, info. News staff: 2; News: 45 hrs wkly. ◆Ed Grant, gen mgr & rgnl sls mgr.

*WHBP(FM)—Not on air, target date: unknown: 90.1 mhz; 1.2 kw. Ant 1,004 ft TL: N45 30 08 W85 01 44. Hrs open: Box 199, Interlochen,

49643-0199. Phone: (231) 276-4400. Fax: (231) 276-4417. Web Site:www.interlochen.org/ipr Licensee: Interlochen Center for the Arts. ◆Thom Paulson, gen mgr.

Harrietta

WKAD(FM)— 2003: 93.7 mhz; 4.3 kw. Ant 390 ft TL: N44 16 41 W85 35 28. Hrs open: Box 520, Cadillac, 49601. Secondary address: 7825 S. Mackinaw Trail, Cadillac 49601. Phone: (231) 775-1263. Fax: (231) 779-2844. Web Site:www.cadillacoldies.com Licensee: Cadillac Broadcasting LLC (acq 1-4-02). Population served: 20,000 Format: Oldies. ◆Trish Garber, CEO; Rich Spicer, progmg dir.

Harrison

*WKKM(FM)—Not on air, target date: unknown: 90.7 mhz; 100 w. Ant 98 ft TL: N44 01 02 W84 47 56. Hrs open: Box 549, 48625-0549. Phone: (989) 539-7105. Licensee: The Country King Inc. Format: Classic country. ◆David A. Carmine, pres.

WTWS(FM)— Mar 26, 1975: 92.1 mhz; 6 kw. Ant 298 ft TL: N43 59 38 W84 50 13. Hrs open: 24 Box 468, Prudenville, 48651. Phone: (989) 366-5364. Fax: (989) 366-6200. Web Site:www.921thetwister.com Population served: 300,000 Format: Country. ◆Michael Jay, pres; Sindy Fuller, sr VP & opns mgr.

Harrisville

*WJOJ(FM)— December 2001: 89.7 mhz; 31 kw. Ant 469 ft TL: N44 42 12 W83 31 27. Hrs open: Box 388, Williamston, 48895. Phone: (810) 721-0891.E-mail: info@smile.fm Web Site:www.joyfm.net Licensee: Northland Community Broadcasters. Format: Contemporary Christian. ◆Jenn Czelada, gen mgr; Ed Czelada, progmg dir.

Hart

WWKR(FM)— July 1, 1995: 94.1 mhz; 13 kw. Ant 462 ft TL: N43 51 33 W86 18 25. Stereo. Hrs open: 24 PO Box 855, Ludington, 49431. Phone: (231) 843-0941. Fax: (231) 843-9411. Web Site:www.94k-rock.com Licensee: Synergy Media Inc. (acq 4-10-98; $250,000). Population served: 350,000 Natl. Network: AP Network News, . Rgnl. Network: Michigan Sport Sales. Natl. Rep: Michigan Spot Sales,. Rgnl rep: Michigan Spot Sales Drinker, Biddle & Reath. Format: Classic rock. News staff: one; News: 2 hrs wkly. Target aud: 25-54; baby boomers. Spec prog: Relg 3 hrs wkly. ◆Todd A. Mohr, pres, gen mgr; Mary Mohr, opns mgr; Melissa Reed, gen sls mgr; Tom Green, chief of engrg.

Hartford

WCXT(FM)— Oct 31, 1981: 98.3 mhz; 3.7 kw. Ant 426 ft TL: N42 15 14 W86 20 09. Stereo. Hrs open: Box 107, St. Joseph, 49085. Secondary address: 580 E. Napier Ave., Benton Harbor 49022. Phone: (269) 925-1111. Fax: (269) 925-1011. Web Site:www.thecoast.fm Licensee: WSJM Inc. (acq 10-95; with WCSY(AM) South Haven). Format: Adult contemp, hits of the 80s & 90s. ◆Gayle Olson, gen mgr, gen sls mgr; Jim Gifford, opns mgr; Sue Patzer, prom dir; Mark Durocher, progmg dir.

Hastings

WBCH(AM)— November 1957: 1220 khz; 250 w-D, 48 w-N. TL: N42 37 36 W85 16 39. Hrs open: 24 Box 88, 49058. Secondary address: 119 W. State St. 49058. Phone: (269) 945-3414. Fax: (269) 945-3470.E-mail: wbch@wbch.com Web Site:www.wbch.com Licensee: Barry Broadcasting Co. (acq 8-17-58). Population served: 50,000 Rgnl. Network: Mich. Farm. Mich. Farm Rgnl rep: Patt. Wire Svc: NOAA Weather Format: Country, news/talk. News staff: one; News: 16 hrs wkly. Target aud: 25-54. ◆Kenneth Radant, gen mgr; Steven K. Radant, stn mgr.

WBCH-FM— December 1967: 100.1 mhz; 3 kw. 295 ft TL: N42 37 36 W85 16 39. Stereo. Hrs open: 24 Prog sep from AM Box 88, 49058. Phone: (269) 945-3414. Fax: (269) 945-3470. Web Site:www.wbch.com Population served: 806,500 Natl. Network: ABC, . Wire Svc: NOAA Weather Format: Hit country. ◆Dave McIntyre, local news ed, news rptr, farm dir; Sue Radant, women's int ed.

Hemlock

WCEN-FM— Aug 8, 1963: 94.5 mhz; 100 kw. Ant 981 ft TL: N43 43 36 W84 36 16. Stereo. Hrs open: 1795 Tittabawassee Rd., Saginaw, 48604-9431. Phone: (989) 752-3456. Fax: (989) 754-5046.E-mail: info@945themoose.com Web Site:www.945themoose.com Licensee: NM Licensing LLC. Group owner: NextMedia Group L.L.C. (acq 12-30-02; grpsl). Population served: 1,000,000 Shaw Pittman. Wire Svc: Metro Weather Service Inc. Format: Hot country. Target aud: 25-54; medium income, rural & urban. ◆Joby Phyllips, progmg dir.

Highland Park

*WHPR(FM)— May 21, 1954: 88.1 mhz; 11 w. Ant 105 ft TL: N42 24 50 W83 05 48. Hrs open: 24 15851 Woodward, 48203. Phone: (313) 868-6612. Fax: (313) 868-8725.E-mail: tv68whpr@aol.com Licensee: R.J.s Late Night Entertainment Corp. Population served: 900,000 Format: Talk, CHR, oldies. Target aud: 21 & over; African Americans 40 plus politically aware & motivated. ◆Henry Tyler, VP, stn mgr; R. J. Watkins, sr VP & gen mgr.

Hillman

WKJZ(FM)—Licensed to Hillman. See Alpena

Hillsdale

WCSR(AM)— May 21, 1959: 1340 khz; 500 w-D, 1 kw-N. TL: N41 55 41 W84 38 10. Hrs open:
Simulcast with WCSR-FM Hillsdale 98%.
Box 273, 49242. Secondary address: 170 N. West St. 49242. Phone: (517) 437-4444. Fax: (517) 437-7461.E-mail: wcsrinc@comcast.net Web Site:www.radiohillsdale.com Licensee: WCSR Inc. (acq 11-15-61). Rgnl. Network: Mich. Farm. Mich. Farm Format: Adult contemp. Target aud: 25 plus; county-wide. Spec prog: Farm 3 hrs, relg 10 hrs wkly. ◆Anthony Flynn, pres; Michael Flynn, gen mgr.

WCSR-FM— May 19, 1973: 92.1 mhz; 6 kw. 243 ft TL: N41 55 41 W84 38 10. Stereo. Hrs open: Dup AM 75% Box 273, 49242. Secondary address: 170 N. West St. 49242. Phone: (517) 437-4444. Fax: 517) 437-7461.E-mail: wcsrinc@comcast.net Web Site:www.radiohillsdale.com Population served: 50,000

Holland

WHTC(AM)— July 31,1948: 1450 khz; 1 kw-U. TL: N42 47 41 W86 06 22. Hrs open: 24 87 Central Ave., 49423. Phone: (616) 392-3121. Fax: (616) 392-8066.E-mail: whtc@whtc.com Web Site:www.whtc.com Licensee: Midwest Communications Inc. (group owner; acq 8-1-00; grpsl). Population served: 120,000 Natl. Network: CBS, . Natl. Rep: Christal,. Format: News/talk, full service. News staff: one; News: 15 hrs wkly. Target aud: 35 plus. Spec prog: Sp 3 hrs wkly. ◆Duke Wright, pres; Peter Tanz, gen mgr; Kevin Oswald, gen sls mgr; Brent Alan, progmg mgr; Gary Stevens, news dir.

WJQK(FM)—(Zeeland, Aug 23, 1971: 99.3 mhz; 4.7 kw. 371 ft TL: N42 48 59 W85 57 24. Stereo. Hrs open: 24 425 Centerstone Ct., Zeeland, 49464. Phone: (616) 931-9930. Phone: (888) 993-1260. Fax: (616) 931-1280.E-mail: traffic@jq99.com Web Site:www.jq99.com Licensee: Lanser Broadcasting Corp. (acq 1-1-87). Population served: 1,200,000 Natl. Network: Fox News Radio, . Natl. Rep: Salem,. Rgnl rep: Mich Spot Sales Wire Svc: Metro Weather Service Format: Contemp Christian. News: 7 hrs wkly. Target aud: 25-49. ◆Les Lanser, pres; Brad Lanser, VP, gen mgr; Troy West, stn mgr.

WMAX-FM— September 1962: 96.1 mhz; 50 kw horiz, 45 kw vert. Ant 492 ft TL: N42 49 10 W85 52 09. Stereo. Hrs open: 24 77 Monroe Ctr., Suite 1000, Grand Rapids, 49503. Phone: (616) 459-1919. Fax: (616) 235-9600. Web Site:www.961espn.com Licensee: CC Licenses LLC. Group owner: Clear Channel Communications Inc. (acq 1-27-2009). Natl. Network: ESPN Radio, . Natl. Rep: Clear Channel,. Format: Sports. ◆Skip Essick, VP & gen mgr.

*WTHS(FM)— Oct 15, 1984: 89.9 mhz; 1 kw. 154 ft TL: N42 47 16 W86 06 02. Stereo. Hrs open: 24 Box 9000, Hope College, 49423. Phone: (616) 395-7878. Phone: (616) 395-7880. Fax: (616) 395-7958.E-mail: wths@hope.edu Web Site:http://wths.hope.edu Licensee: Hope College Board of Trustees. Lauren A. Colby. Format: Alternative. News: 7 hrs wkly. Target aud: 15-30; students & adults. Spec prog: Jazz 6 hrs, relg 14 hrs, Sp 8 hrs wkly. ◆Jason Cash, gen mgr; Gerry Ruffino, progmg dir.

WTNR(FM)— Mar 21, 1961: 94.5 mhz; 50 kw. Ant 499 ft TL: N42 51 20 W85 57 45. Stereo. Hrs open: 24 60 Monroe Ctr. N.W., 3rd Fl.,

Grand Rapids, 49503. Phone: (616) 774-8461. Fax: (616) 774-2491.E-mail: info@thunder945.com Web Site:www.thunder945.com Licensee: Citadel Broadcasting Co. Group owner: Citadel Broadcasting Corp. (acq 4-26-2001; grpsl). Population served: 194,649 Natl. Network: ABC, . Natl. Rep: Katz Radio,. Fletcher, Heald & Hildreth. Format: Country. Target aud: 18-34; men. ♦Matt Hanlon, gen mgr; Jeff Morton, sls dir, rgnl sls mgr; Kate Conley, gen sls mgr.

Holt

WLCM(AM)— Aug 25, 1956: 1390 khz; 970 w-D, 4.5 kw-N, DA-D. TL: N42 34 02 W84 51 58 (day), N42 33 07 W84 33 05 (night). Hrs open: 6 AM-sunset Box 338, Charlotte, 48813. Secondary address: 1613 W. Lawrence, Charlotte 48813. Phone: (517) 543-8200. Fax: (517) 543-7779.E-mail: jeff@wlcmradio.com Web Site:www.wlcmradio.com Licensee: Christian Broadcasting System Ltd. (group owner; (acq 1-5-93; assumption of land contract; 1-25-93). Population served: 700,000 Format: Relg, Christian progmg. News: 2 hrs wkly. Target aud: 25-55; general. Spec prog: Gospel 3 hrs wkly. ♦Jon R. Yinger, CEO & pres; Evelyn Shaw, VP; Jeff Frank, gen mgr, stn mgr, opns dir.

Holton

WVIB(FM)— 1971: 100.1 mhz; 3 kw. Ant 302 ft TL: N43 28 17 W85 56 19. Stereo. Hrs open: 3375 Merriam St., Muskegon, 49444. Phone: (231) 830-0176. Fax: (231) 830-0194. Licensee: Citadel Broadcasting Co. (acq 1-19-2006). Format: Urban contemp. ♦Jeff Morton, gen mgr.

Honor

WSRJ(FM)— 2002: 100.7 mhz; 4.7 kw. Ant 367 ft TL: N44 39 41 W85 48 53. Hrs open:
Rebroadcasts WSRT(FM) Gaylord 75%.
1020 Hastins St, Suite 102, Traverse City, 49686. Phone: (231) 947-0003. Fax: (231) 947-7002.E-mail: programming@1067wsrt.com Web Site:www.1067wsrt.com Licensee: Northern Radio of Michigan Inc. Format: soft rock. ♦Charlie Ferguson, gen mgr.

Houghton

WCCY(AM)— 1929: 1400 khz; 1 kw-U. TL: N47 08 06 W88 33 53. Hrs open: 24 313 Montezuma Ave., 49931. Phone: (906) 482-7700. Fax: (906) 482-7751. Web Site:www.wccy.com Licensee: Heartland Comm. Houghton License LLC. (acq 1-6-2005; grpsl). Population served: 20,000 Natl. Network: ABC, ESPN Radio, Jones Radio Networks, . Natl. Rep: Michigan Spot Sales,. Mich. Radio Format: Adult standards. sports. News staff: one; News: 18 hrs wkly. Target aud: 35+. Spec prog: Relg one hr, pub affrs one hr wkly. ♦Chuck Sebastian, opns mgr, progmg dir; John Speeney, gen mgr & gen sls mgr.

***WGGL-FM**— February 1982: 91.1 mhz; 100 kw. 809 ft TL: N47 02 08 W88 41 43. Stereo. Hrs open: 24 480 Cedar St., St. Paul, MN, 55101. Phone: (651) 290-1500. Fax: (651) 290-1224.E-mail: info@mpr.org Web Site:www.mpr.org Licensee: Minnesota Public Radio Inc. Natl. Network: PRI, NPR, . Rgnl. Network: Minn. Pub. Minn. Pub. Radio Format: Class, news. News staff: one. Target aud: General. ♦William H. Kling, pres; Erik Nycklemoe, gen mgr, opns mgr, progmg dir, chief of engrg.

WHKB(FM)— Sept 1, 1989: 102.3 mhz; 1.05 kw. 554 ft TL: N47 06 13 W88 34 04. (CP: 35.5 kw, ant 492 ft.). Stereo. Hrs open: 313 E. Montezuma Ave., 49931. Phone: (906) 482-7700. Fax: (906) 482-7751. Web Site:www.kbear102.com Licensee: Heartland Comm. Houghton License LLC. (acq 1-6-2005; grpsl). Population served: 50,000 Natl. Network: ABC, Jones Radio Networks, . Natl. Rep: Michigan Spot Sales,. Mich. Radio Format: Country. News staff: one; News: news prgmg 18 hrs/week. Target aud: 25-54. ♦Betsy Ely, opns dir, news dir; Chuck Sebastian, opns mgr, progmg VP; John Speeney, gen mgr & chief of engrg.

***WMTU-FM**— Jan 26, 1994: 91.9 mhz; 4.4 kw vert. Ant 479 ft TL: N47 08 27 W88 32 26. Hrs open: West Wadsworth Hall, MTUniversity G03, 49931. Phone: (906) 487-2333. Fax: (906) 487-3016.E-mail: wmtu@mtu.edu Web Site:www.wmtu.mtu.edu Licensee: Michigan Technological University. Format: Var. ♦Lindsay Worden, gen mgr & stn mgr.

WOLV(FM)— Mar 7, 1980: 97.7 mhz; 875 w. 508 ft TL: N47 08 27 W88 32 26. Stereo. Hrs open: Prog sep from AM 313 Montezuma Ave., 49931. Phone: (906) 482-7700. Fax: (906) 482-7751. Web Site:www.thewolf.com Population served: 43,000 Natl. Network: ABC, Jones Radio Networks, . Natl. Rep: Michigan Spot Sales,. Mich. Radio Format: Classic Hits. News staff: news prgmg 18 hrs/week News: one;. Target aud: 25-54. ♦John Speeney, gen mgr; Chuck Sebastian, opns mgr.

Houghton Lake

WUPS(FM)— July 1, 1961: 98.5 mhz; 100 kw. Ant 981 ft TL: N44 17 18 W84 44 30. Stereo. Hrs open: 24 Box 468, Prudenville, 48651. Phone: (989) 366-5364. Fax: (989) 366-6200.E-mail: wupsfm@yahoo.com Web Site:www.wups.com Licensee: Coltrace Communications Inc. (acq 3-15-88; $900,000). Population served: 200,000 Natl. Network: ABC, . Natl. Rep: Rgnl Reps,. Drinker, Biddle & Reath, LLP. Format: Classic hits. News staff: one; News: 6 hrs wkly. Target aud: 25-54; general. ♦John M. Salov, pres; Sindy Fuller, sr VP & opns mgr.

Howell

WHMI-FM— Sept 1, 1977: 93.5 mhz; 5.2 kw. 354 ft TL: N42 39 47 W83 56 23. Stereo. Hrs open: 24 Box 935, 48844. Secondary address: 1277 Parkway Dr. 48843. Phone: (517) 546-0860. Fax: (517) 546-1758.E-mail: whmi@whmi.com Web Site:www.whmi.com Licensee: The Livingston Radio Co. (acq 3-3-89). Population served: 400,000 Natl. Network: CNN Radio, . Natl. Rep: Michigan Spot Sales,. Irwin, Campbell & Tannenwald. Format: Classic hits. News staff: 3; News: 10 hrs wkly. Target aud: 25-64. ♦Greg Jablonski, pres; Reed Kittredge, opns mgr.

Hudson

WBZV(FM)— Mar 1, 1995: 102.5 mhz; 6 kw. 328 ft TL: N41 53 03 W84 31 24. Hrs open: 24 121 W. Maumee St., Adrian, 49221-2019. Phone: (517) 448-8988. Fax: (517) 263-4525.E-mail: friends@tc3net.com Licensee: Friends Communications of Hudson Inc. Group owner: Friends Communications Inc. Population served: 150,000 Natl. Network: ABC, . Natl. Rep: Michigan Spot Sales,. Fletcher, Heald & Hildreth. Format: Classic Rock. News staff: one; News: 6 hrs wkly. Target aud: 25-54. ♦Bob Elliot, chmn, pres & gen mgr.

Imlay City

***WWKM(FM)**— December 2000: 89.1 mhz; 1.5 kw. Ant 171 ft TL: N43 03 42 W83 05 44. Hrs open: Michigan Community Radio, Box 388, Williamston, 48896. Phone: (810) 721-0891. Fax: (413) 410-9708.E-mail: info@joyfm.net Web Site:www.positivehits.com Licensee: Michigan Community Radio. Format: Contemporary Christian. ♦Jenn Czelada, gen mgr; Ed Czelada, progmg dir.

Inkster

WDMK(FM)—See Detroit

WDRJ(AM)— November 1956: 1440 khz; 1 kw-U, DA-2. TL: N42 15 22 W83 21 48. Hrs open: 24 2994 E. Grand Blvd., Detroit, 48202. Phone: (313) 871-1440. Fax: (313) 871-6088.E-mail: 1440@communicom.com Web Site:www.1440wdrj.com Licensee: Davidson Media Station WMKM Licensee LLC. Group owner: Davidson Media Group LLC (acq 5-28-2004; $5.75 million). Format: Gospel. Target aud: 35 plus; adult Black church audience. ♦Rich Kylberg, pres; Raymond Burkhart, gen mgr.

Interlochen

***WIAA(FM)**— July 22, 1963: 88.7 mhz; 100 kw. Ant 1,033 ft TL: N44 16 33 W85 42 49. Stereo. Hrs open: 24 Box 199, 49643. Secondary address: One Lyon St. 49643. Phone: (231) 276-4400. Fax: (231) 276-4417.E-mail: ipr@interlochen.org Web Site:www.interlochen.org/ipr Licensee: Interlochen Center for the Arts. Population served: 290,100 Natl. Network: NPR, PRI, . Rgnl. Network: Mich. Pub. Format: Classical, news. Target aud: 35-80; professional, arts-oriented, upper-income. ♦Thom Paulson, CFO, VP & gen mgr.

Ionia

WION(AM)— Feb 1, 1953: 1430 khz; 5 kw-D, 330 w-N, DA-2. TL: N43 00 16 W85 05 09. pending for non directional signal. Hrs open: 24 1150 Haynor Rd., 48846-8532. Phone: (616) 527-9466. Fax: (616) 775-5908.E-mail: office@i1430.com Web Site:www.i1430.com Licensee: Packer Radio WION LLC (acq 12-14-2004; $127,000). Population served: 77,294 Natl. Network: Fox News Radio, Sporting News Radio Network, . Rgnl. Network: Mich. Farm. Mich. Radio Dykema Gossett PLLC. Format: Full service. News staff: one. ♦Peter Jeff, gen mgr & rgnl sls mgr.

Iron Mountain

WHTO(FM)— 2003: 106.7 mhz; 6.1 kw. Ant 676 ft TL: N45 49 16 W88 02 34. Hrs open: 212 W. J St., 49801. Phone: (906) 774-5731. Fax: (906) 774-4542.E-mail: peterson.trisha@gmail.com Web Site:www.1067themountain.com Licensee: Results Broadcasting of Iron Mountain Inc. (acq 6-29-2005; $650,000). Natl. Network: ABC, . Format: Oldies. ♦Trisha Peterson, gen mgr.

WIMK(FM)— Dec 27, 1981: 93.1 mhz; 100 kw. 590 ft TL: N45 49 16 W88 02 28. Stereo. Hrs open: 24
Rebroadcasts WUPK-FM Marquette 100%.
101 E. Kent St., 49801. Phone: (906) 774-4321. Fax: (906) 774-7799.E-mail: thebear@uplogon.com Web Site:rockthebear.com Licensee: Northern Star Broadcasting L.L.C. (group owner; acq 11-5-01; grpsl). Population served: 300,000 Reddy, Begley & McCormick. Format: Classic rock, AOR. News staff: one. Target aud: 25-54. ♦Veronica Roberts, gen mgr; Steve Ponchaud, opns mgr; Tom Hill, news dir; Coral Howe, chief of engrg; Michelle Ellsworth, traf mgr.

WJNR-FM— Aug 17, 1972: 101.5 mhz; 100 w. 620 ft TL: N45 49 15 W88 02 38. (CP: 100 kw, ant 613 ft.). Stereo. Hrs open: 212 W. J St., 49801. Phone: (906) 774-5731. Fax: (906) 774-4542.E-mail: peterson.trisha@gmail.com Web Site:www.frogcountry.com Licensee: Results Broadcasting of Michigan Inc. Group owner: Results Broadcasting (acq 6-5-97). Population served: 14,450 Natl. Network: ABC, . Format: New Hit country. Target aud: 25-54. ♦Bruce Grassman, pres; Trisha Peterson, gen mgr; Keith Huotari, opns mgr; Aaron Harper, news dir; Walt Baldwin, engrg VP & chief of engrg.

WMIQ(AM)— January 1947: 1450 khz; 1 kw-U. TL: N45 49 16 W88 03 16. Hrs open: 24 101 E. Kent St., 49801. Phone: (906) 774-4321. Fax: (906) 774-7799.E-mail: talk1450wmiq@uplogon.con Web Site:talk1450.tripod.com Licensee: Northern Star Broadcasting L.L.C. Population served: 25,600 Natl. Network: USA, . Natl. Rep: Patt,. Format: News/talk, sports. News staff: one; News: 24 hrs wkly. Target aud: 35-64; educated, middle to upper income listeners. ♦Kevin Richtig, progmg dir.

***WVCM(FM)**—Not on air, target date: unknown: 91.5 mhz; 500 w. 600 ft TL: N45 49 15 W88 02 25. Stereo. Hrs open: 24 3434 W. Kilbourn Ave., Milwaukee, WI, 53208. Phone: (414) 935-3000. Fax: (414) 935-3015.E-mail: wvcm@vcyamerica.org Web Site:www.vcyamerica.org Licensee: VCY America Inc. Group owner: VCY/America Inc. Format: Christian. ♦Randall Melchert, pres; Vic Eliason, VP & gen mgr; Jim Schneider, progmg dir.

Iron River

WIKB(AM)— Nov 18, 1949: 1230 khz; 1 kw-U. TL: N46 03 55 W88 38 17. Hrs open: 5 AM-11 PM Box AC, 809 W. Genesee St., 49935. Phone: (906) 265-5104. Fax: (906) 265-3486.E-mail: wikb@sbcglobal.net Licensee: Heartland Communications License LLC. (group owner; (acq 5-10-2004; $1.25 million with co-located FM). Population served: 20,000 Natl. Rep: Roslin,. Format: Adult standards. News staff: one; News: 15 hrs wkly. Target aud: General. ♦Jay Barry, gen mgr; Margaret Henschel, gen sls mgr; Jeff Bonno, chief of engrg.

WIKB-FM— Sept 25, 1981: 99.1 mhz; 50 kw. Ant 492 ft TL: N46 06 03 W88 32 23. Stereo. Hrs open: 5 AM-11 PM Box AC, 49935. Secondary address: 809 W. Genesee St. 49935. Phone: (906) 265-5104. Fax: (906) 265-3486. Licensee: Heartland Communications License LLC. Format: Adult contemp.

Ironwood

WIMI(FM)— March 1976: 99.7 mhz; 100 kw. Ant 561 ft TL: N46 25 25 W90 14 53. Stereo. Hrs open: 222 S. Lawrence St., 49938. Phone: (906) 932-2411. Fax: (906) 932-2485.E-mail: wimi@broadcast.net Web Site:www.wimifm.com Licensee: Magellan Broadcasting LLC. Format: Adult contemp.

WJMS(AM)— Nov 3, 1931: 590 khz; 5 kw-D, 1 kw-N, DA-N. TL: N46 25 25 W90 12 30. Hrs open: 24 222 S. Lawrence St., 49938. Phone: (906) 932-2411. Fax: (906) 932-2485.E-mail: wimi@broadcast.net Web Site:www.wjmsam.com Licensee: Magellan Broadcasting LLC. Group owner: Badger Communications L.L.C. Natl. Network: CBS, . Natl. Rep: D & R Radio,. Format: Country, talk. News staff: one. Target aud: 25 plus. ♦David Winters, pres; Frede Falls, progmg dir.

***WLVM(FM)**— 2008: 88.3 mhz; 300 w vert. Ant 515 ft TL: N46 26 28 W90 11 26. Hrs open:
Rebroadcasts KLVR(FM) Middletown, CA 100%.
2351 Sunset Blvd., Suite 170-218, Rocklin, CA, 95765. Phone: (916) 251-1600. Fax: (916) 251-1650. Web Site:www.klove.com Licensee:

Educational Media Foundation. (acq 7-23-2007; grpsl). Natl. Network: K-Love, . Format: Contemp Christian. ♦Mike Novak, pres.

WUPM(FM)— Oct 17, 1977: 106.9 mhz; 53 kw. 495 ft TL: N46 28 18 W90 00 43. Hrs open: 209 Harrison, 49938. Phone: (906) 932-5234. Fax: (906) 932-1548. Licensee: Big G Little O Inc. Population served: 25,000 Natl. Network: ABC, . Format: Adult contemp. ♦Charles H. Gervasio, pres, gen mgr; Laura Keller, progmg VP & progmg dir.

Ishpeming

WIAN(AM)— 1947: 1240 khz; 1 kw-U. TL: N46 30 16 W87 40 46. Hrs open: 1009 W. Ridge St., Marquette, 49855. Phone: (906) 225-1313. Fax: (906) 225-1324.E-mail: info@wjpd.com Licensee: Northern Star Broadcasting L.L.C. (group owner; (acq 11-5-2001; grpsl). Format: News/talk. ♦Tammy Johnson, gen mgr & rgnl sls mgr; Ariane Kachmarsky, progmg dir; John Focke, news dir; Coral Howe, chief of engrg.

WJPD(FM)— May 15, 1975: 92.3 mhz; 100 kw. Ant 508 ft TL: N46 30 51 W87 28 58. Stereo. Hrs open: 1009 W. Ridge St., Marquette, 49855. Phone: (906) 225-1313. Fax: (906) 225-1324.E-mail: info@wjpd.com Web Site:www.wjpd.com Licensee: Northern Star Broadcasting L.L.C. Population served: 300,000 Wire Svc: UPI Format: Country.

WMQT(FM)— Jan 26, 1974: 107.7 mhz; 98 kw. Ant 639 ft TL: N46 30 08 W87 38 52. Stereo. Hrs open: 24 121 N. Front St., Suite A, Marquette, 49855. Phone: (906) 225-9100. Fax: (906) 225-5577.E-mail: tom@wmqt.com Web Site:www.wmqt.com Licensee: Taconite Broadcasting Inc. Population served: 250,000 Format: Hot adult contemp. News staff: one. Target aud: 18-49. ♦Tom Mogush, gen mgr & gen sls mgr; Carol Keast, traf mgr; Casey Ford, sports cmtr.

WZAM(AM)— June 26, 1959: 970 khz; 5 kw-D, 62 w-N. TL: N46 30 20 W87 32 24. Hrs open: 24 121 N. Front St., Suite A, Marquette, 49855. Phone: (906) 225-9100. Fax: (906) 225-5577.E-mail: tom@wmqt.com Web Site:www.espn970.com Licensee: Taconite Broadcasting Inc. (acq 7-25-2005; $827,300 with co-located FM). Population served: 100,000 Natl. Network: ESPN Radio, . Format: Sports talk. News staff: one. Target aud: 25-54. ♦Tom Mogush, gen mgr & sls dir; Jim Koski, progmg dir.

Jackson

WIBM(AM)— 1925: 1450 khz; 1 kw-U. TL: N42 13 16 W84 26 03. Hrs open: 24 1700 Glenshire Dr., 49201. Phone: (517) 787-9546. Fax: (517) 787-7517.E-mail: mdaly@wkhm.com Web Site:www.espnradio1450.com Licensee: Jackson Radio Works Inc. (group owner; acq 11-14-97; grpsl). Population served: 175,000 Natl. Network: ESPN Radio, . Rgnl rep: Michigan Spot Sales Davis, Wright , Tremain, LLP. Format: Sports. News staff: 2; News: one hr wkly. Target aud: 18-49; sports enthusiasts. Spec prog: Polish, Spanish. ♦Bruce I. Goldsen, pres; Jamie McKibbin, stn mgr; Sue Goldsen, VP, sls VP & mktg VP; Marc Daly, progmg dir, progmg mgr; Michael Bradford, chief of engrg.

***WJKN(AM)**— January 1962: Stn currently dark. 1510 khz; 5 kw-D, DA. TL: N42 11 10 W84 22 39. (CP: TL: N42 10 08 W84 23 30). Stereo. Hrs open: Spring Arbor University, 106 E. Main St., Spring Arbor, 49283. Phone: (517) 750-9723. Fax: (517) 750-6619.E-mail: info@home.fm Licensee: Spring Arbor University (acq 1-12-01). Population served: 45,484 Natl. Network: CBS, Westwood One, . Natl. Rep: Patt,. Format: Inspirational. ♦Carl Fletcher, gen mgr; Dave Benson, chief of engrg.

***WJKQ(FM)**— 2004: 88.5 mhz; 100 w vert. Ant 112 ft TL: N42 16 22 W84 21 27. Hrs open: 901 Elizabeth Ct., Mount Pleasant, 48858. Phone: (989) 779-9178. Fax: (989) 779-1558. Web Site:www.foundationradio.org Licensee: Great Lakes Community Broadcasting Inc. Format: Oldies. ♦James McCluskey, gen mgr.

WJXQ(FM)— May 30, 1976: 106.1 mhz; 50 kw. 489 ft TL: N42 23 28 W84 37 22. Stereo. Hrs open: 24 2495 N. Cedar, Suite 106, Holt, 48842. Phone: (517) 699-0111. Fax: (517) 699-1880. Web Site:www.q106fm.com Licensee: Rubber City Radio Group. Group owner: Rubber City Radio Group Inc. (acq 7-12-00; grpsl). Population served: 500,000 Natl. Network: Jones Radio Networks, . Natl. Rep: Katz Radio,. Wire Svc: AP Format: AOR. News staff: one; News: one hr wkly. Target aud: 25-44; baby boomers with an inclination for rock and roll. ♦Dave Johnson, gen mgr; Paul Cashin, opns mgr, mus dir; Scott Truman, gen sls mgr; Sheri Vegas, progmg dir.

WKHM(AM)— Dec. 7, 1951: 970 khz; 1 kw-U, DA-2. TL: N42 11 39 W84 25 50. Hrs open: 24 1700 Glenshire Dr., 49201. Phone: (517) 787-9546. Phone: (517) 787-3397. Fax: (517) 787-7517.E-mail: mdaly@wkhm.com Web Site:www.wkhm.com Licensee: Jackson Radio Works Inc. (group owner; acq 12-8-97; grpsl). Population served: 175,000 Natl. Network: ABC, . Rgnl. Network: Mich. Farm. Mich. Radio Rgnl rep: Mich. Spot Sales Davis, Wright, Tremaine, LLP. Format: News/talk. News staff: one; News: 15 hrs wkly. Target aud: 25-64. ♦Bruce I. Goldsen, pres; Jamie McKibbin, stn mgr; Deanna Stocker, sls dir; Sue Goldsen, VP, sls VP & mktg VP; Marc Daly, progmg dir; Michael Bradford, chief of engrg; Kathy Beauchamp, traf mgr, local news ed.

WVIC(FM)— 1955: 94.1 mhz; 40 kw. Ant 551 ft TL: N42 23 32 W84 40 00. Stereo. Hrs open: 2495 N. Cedar, Holt, 48842. Phone: (517) 699-0111. Fax: (517) 699-1880. Web Site:www.wvic.net Licensee: Rubber City Radio Group. Group owner: Rubber City Radio Group Inc. (acq 7-12-2000; grpsl). Population served: 864,300 Natl. Rep: Katz Radio,. Wire Svc: AP Format: Soft rock. News staff: one; News: 17.5 hrs wkly. Target aud: 25-54; female 25-49. ♦Dave Johnson, gen mgr; Paul Cashin, opns mgr, progmg dir; Scott Truman, gen sls mgr.

Kalamazoo

***WAYK(FM)**— Feb 3, 1997: 88.3 mhz; 10 kw. Ant 397 ft TL: N42 18 23 W85 39 25. Hrs open: 24 161 E. Michigan Ave., Suite 600, 49007. Phone: (269) 383-0600. Fax: (269) 381-0239.E-mail: way@way.fm Web Site:www.way.fm Licensee: Cornerstone University. Population served: 300,000 Format: Christian hit radio. ♦Rich Anderson, gen mgr; Tom Bos, rgnl sls mgr; Terri Brogan, prom dir; Mike Couchman, progmg dir.

***WIDR(FM)**— July 7, 1975: 89.1 mhz; 100 w. 158 ft TL: N42 16 55 W85 37 05. Stereo. Hrs open: 24 Western Michigan Univ., 1501 Faunce Student Ser. Bldg., 49008-5350. Phone: (269) 387-6301. Phone: (269) 387-2251. Fax: (269) 387-2839.E-mail: info@widr.org Web Site:www.widr.org Licensee: Western Michigan University Board of Trustees. Population served: 120,000 Format: Var/div, educ, progsv. News: 7 hrs wkly. Target aud: 18-25; college students. ♦Andrew Grabowski, gen mgr; Mallory Dowd, progmg dir.

***WKDS(FM)**— October 1982: 89.9 mhz; 100 w. 150 ft TL: N42 14 36 W85 34 19. Stereo. Hrs open: 24 359 S Kalamazoo Mall #300, 49007. Phone: (269) 343-2211. Fax: (269) 343-3710.E-mail: operations@cactv.org Licensee: Kalamazoo Board of Education. Arent, Fox, Kintner, Plotkin & Kahn. Format: Div, educ. News: 3 hrs wkly. Target aud: High school & college students. ♦Mark Monk, opns mgr.

WKFR-FM—See Battle Creek

WKMI(AM)— August 1947: 1360 khz; 5 kw-D, 1 kw-N, DA-2. TL: N42 19 36 W85 31 39. Hrs open: 24 4154 Jennings Dr., 49048. Phone: (269) 344-0111. Fax: (269) 344-4223.E-mail: radio@wkmi.com Web Site:www.wkmi.com Licensee: Cumulus Licensing Corp. Group owner: Cumulus Media Inc. (acq 5-26-98; grpsl). Population served: 400,000 Format: News/talk. News staff: one; News: 30 hrs wkly. Target aud: 25 plus. Spec prog: Sports. ♦Lew Dickey, CEO, pres; Jon Pinch, COO; Martin Gausvik, CFO; Rob Wagley, gen mgr; Mike McKelly, opns mgr; Bill Anthony, progmg dir.

WKPR(AM)— Oct 20, 1960: 1420 khz; 1 kw-D, DA. TL: N42 18 46 W85 37 06. Hrs open: 6 AM-sunset 2244 Ravine Rd., 49004. Phone: (269) 381-1420. Licensee: Kalamazoo Broadcasting Co. Group owner: Kuiper Stations Population served: 150,000 Natl. Network: USA, . Format: Relg. Target aud: 25 plus. ♦William E. Kuiper Sr., pres; Stan Gebben, stn mgr; William E. Kuiper Jr., chief of engrg.

WKZO(AM)— Sept 10, 1931: 590 khz; 5 kw-U, DA-N. TL: N42 21 00 W85 33 43. Hrs open: 24 4200 W. Main St., 49006. Phone: (269) 345-7121. Fax: (269) 345-1436. Web Site:www.wkzo.com Licensee: Midwest Communications Inc. (acq 5-1-2006; grpsl). Natl. Network: CBS, . Rgnl. Network: Mich. Farm. Natl. Rep: Christal,. Format: News/talk. News staff: 5. Target aud: 25 plus; upscale, 60% male, 40% female. Spec prog: Farm 10 hrs, relg 5 hrs wkly. ♦Duey Wright, pres; Peter Tanz, gen mgr; Michael Klein, opns dir, sls VP; Jay Morris, progmg mgr; Walker Sisson, chief of engrg.

***WMUK(FM)**— Jan 8, 1951: 102.1 mhz; 50 kw. 490 ft TL: N42 25 03 W85 31 55. Stereo. Hrs open: 24 1903 W. Michigan Ave., 49008-5351. Phone: (269) 387-5715. Fax: (269) 387-4630.E-mail: wmukfm@wmich.edu Web Site:www.wmuk.org Licensee: Western Michigan University Board of Trustees. Population served: 85,555 Natl. Network: NPR, PRI, . Rgnl. Network: Mich. Pub. Minn. Pub. Radio Gammon & Grange. Format: Class, jazz, news. News staff: 3; News: 38 hrs wkly. Target aud: General; educated adults. Spec prog: Bluegrass 4 hrs wkly. ♦Floyd Pientka, gen mgr; Gordon Bolar, dev dir; Michael Hahn, adv mgr; Klayton Woodworth, progmg dir; Andy Robins, news dir.

WNWN(AM)—See Portage

WNWN-FM—(Coldwater, Nov 11, 1950: 98.5 mhz; 50 kw. 500 ft TL: N42 03 28 W84 59 51. Stereo. Hrs open: 24 25 W. Michigan Ave., Battle Creek, 49017. Phone: (269) 968-1991. Fax: (269) 968-1881. Web Site:www.wincountry.com Licensee: Midwest Communications Inc. (group owner; acq 6-1-95; grpsl). Population served: 300,000 Natl. Rep: Christal,. Wire Svc: Accu-Weather Format: Contemp country. News staff: 3; News: 5 hrs wkly. Target aud: 25-54. ♦D.E. Wright, pres; Peter Tanz, gen mgr; Dennis Martin, gen sls mgr; Bridgett Bowman, traf mgr; Woody Houston, progmg dir & progmg.

WQLR(AM)— Sept 24, 1998: 1660 khz; 10 kw-D, 1 kw-N. TL: N42 14 11 W85 34 37. Hrs open: 4200 W. Main St., 49006. Phone: (269) 345-7121. Fax: (269) 345-1436. Web Site:www.espn1660.com Licensee: Midwest Communications Inc. (acq 5-1-2006; grpsl). Natl. Network: ESPN Radio, . Natl. Rep: Christal,. Format: Sports. News staff: 4. ♦D. E. Wright, pres; Mike Klein, exec VP, sls dir; Peter Tanz, gen mgr, mktg mgr; Brian Hayes, opns mgr; Walker Sisson, opns dir & engrg dir.

WRKR(FM)—(Portage, Oct 13, 1988: 107.7 mhz; 50 kw. 500 ft TL: N42 07 43 W85 20 16. Stereo. Hrs open: 24 4154 Jennings Dr., 49001-1087. Phone: (269) 344-0111. Fax: (269) 344-4223.E-mail: radio@wrkr.com Web Site:www.wrkr.com Licensee: Cumulus Licensing Corp. Group owner: Cumulus Media Inc. (acq 5-26-98; grpsl). Population served: 700,000 Format: Classic rock, AOR. News staff: 2; News: 4 hrs wkly. Target aud: 25-54. Spec prog: Blues 5 hrs, jazz 4 hrs wkly. ♦Lew Dickey, CEO, pres; John Pinch, COO; Martin Gausvik, CFO; Mike McKelly, opns mgr; Jay Deacon, progmg dir, disc jockey; Dale Schiesser, chief of engrg.

WVFM(FM)— June 19, 1964: 106.5 mhz; 33 kw. Ant 600 ft TL: N42 28 32 W85 29 22. Stereo. Hrs open: 4200 W. Main St., 49006. Phone: (269) 345-7121. Fax: (269) 345-1436. Web Site:www.wvfm.com Licensee: Midwest Communications Inc. (acq 5-1-2006; grpsl). Natl. Rep: Christal,. Format: Adult contemp. News staff: 4. Target aud: 25-54; women. ♦D. E. Wright, pres; Mike Klein, sls dir; Peter Tanz, mktg mgr; Ken Lanphear, progmg dir; John McNeill, news dir; Walker Sisson, engrg dir.

Kalkaska

WKLT(FM)— Apr 8, 1979: 97.5 mhz; 32 kw. 670 ft TL: N44 47 29 W85 14 20. Stereo. Hrs open: 24 1020 Hastings St., Traverse City, 49686. Phone: (231) 947-0003. Fax: (231) 947-7002. Web Site:www.wklt.com Licensee: Northern Radio of Michigan (acq 1-82; $320,000;1-18-82). Natl. Rep: Christal,. Fletcher, Heald & Hildreth. Format: Classic AOR. News: 2 hrs wkly. Target aud: 25-54; baby boomers & young adults. Spec prog: Sunday night classics, blues 2 hrs wkly. ♦Charlie Ferguson, pres, gen mgr; Greg Marsh, natl sls mgr; Terri Ray, progmg dir; Dennis Murray, chief of engrg; Kristal Flateau, traf mgr.

Kentwood

WGVU(AM)—Licensed to Kentwood. See Grand Rapids

WJNZ(AM)— Sept 18, 1978: 1140 khz; 5 kw-D, DA. TL: N42 56 13 W85 27 20. Hrs open: 15 hrs 1919 Eastern Ave. S.E., Grand Rapids, 49507. Phone: (616) 475-4299 Ext. 11. Fax: (616) 475-4335.E-mail: mjs@wjnz.com Web Site:www.wjnz.com Licensee: WJNZ Radio L.L.C. (acq 9-22-2003; $360,000). Population served: 703,400 Natl. Network: ABC, Premiere Radio Networks, . Koerner, & Olender. Format: Urban, rhythm and blues. News: Top of the hour 6a-7p. Target aud: 25-54; Baby Boomers. Spec prog: Jazz 6 hrs, gospel 4 hrs. ♦Mike St. Cyr, pres & gen mgr.

Kingsford

***WEUL(FM)**— Feb 11, 1990: 98.1 mhz; 240 w. 482 ft TL: N45 49 58 W88 04 57. Hrs open:
Simulcast with WHWL(FM) Marquette, WHWG(FM) Trout Lake.
130 Carmen Dr., Marquette, 49855. Phone: (906) 249-1423. Fax: (906) 249-4042.E-mail: whwl@whwl.net Web Site:www.gospelopportunities.com Licensee: Gospel Opportunities Inc. Population served: 50,000 Format: Relg. News staff: 3. ♦W. Curtis Marker, gen mgr & progmg dir.

Kingsley

WJNL(AM)— Apr 17, 1947: 1210 khz; 50 kw-D, 2.5 kw-CH. TL: N44 33 34 W85 35 37. Hrs open: 2175 Click Rd., Petoskey, 49770-8818. Secondary address: 310 West Front St., Traverse City 49684. Phone: (231) 947-1210.E-mail: talk@wjml.com Web Site:www.wjml.com Licensee: Stone Communications Inc. (group owner; (acq 4-25-2007; . swap with WARD(AM) Petoskey). Population served: 510,000 Natl. Network:

CBS Radio, . Mich. Talk Format: Talk, sports, news. News: 72 hrs wkly. Target aud: 25 plus. ◆Philip Clever, stn mgr; Richard Stone, pres, gen mgr & gen sls mgr.

Lake City

*WAIR(FM)—Not on air, target date: Fall 2003: 104.9 mhz; 1.6 kw. Ant 489 ft TL: N44 14 56 W85 18 48. Hrs open: Box 388, Williamston, 48895. Phone: (517) 381-0573. Fax: (877) 850-0881.E-mail: info@positivehits.com Web Site:www.positivehits.com Licensee: Superior Communications. ◆Jenn Czelada, gen mgr; Ed Czelada, progmg dir.

Lakeview

WGLM-FM— November 1989: 106.3 mhz; 3 kw. 328 ft TL: N43 24 33 W85 15 53. Stereo. Hrs open: Box 578, Greenville, 48838. Secondary address: 9181 S. Greenville Rd., Greenville 48838. Phone: (616) 754-3656. Fax: (616) 754-2390.E-mail: wscgradio@chartermi.net Licensee: Packer Radio Greenville Inc. (acq 12-19-2008; $195,000 with WGLM(AM) Greenville). Format: True Country. ◆Bruce Bentley, gen mgr, opns mgr.

L'Anse

WCUP(FM)— Jan 1, 1998: 105.7 mhz; 50 kw. 492 ft TL: N46 46 48 W88 32 06. Stereo. Hrs open: 24 805-B U.S. 41 S, Baraga, 49908. Phone: (906) 353-9287. Fax: (906) 353-9200.E-mail: cupadmin@up.net Web Site:www.keepitintheup.com Licensee: Keweenaw Bay Indian Community (acq 5-31-01; $176,000 for debt for 70%). Population served: 50,000 Natl. Network: ABC, . Format: Country. News: News progrmg one hr wkly. Target aud: 18 plus. Spec prog: American Indian 2 hrs; polka 2 hrs wkly. ◆Ed Janisse, gen mgr; Jacki Marinich, sls dir; Todd VanDyke, progmg mgr.

Lansing

WHZZ(FM)— January 1967: 101.7 mhz; 4 kw. Ant 400 ft TL: N42 43 42 W84 30 54. Stereo. Hrs open: 24 600 W. Cavanaugh, 48910. Phone: (517) 393-1320. Fax: (517) 393-0882. Web Site:www.1017fm.com Licensee: MacDonald Broadcasting Co. Population served: 350,000 Natl. Rep: D & R Radio,. Wire Svc: AP Format: Adult hits. Target aud: 25-54; upscale adults. ◆Sharon Crane, gen sls mgr; Gary Harding, engrg dir, chief of engrg; Shane Pitman, traf mgr.

WILS(AM)— July 17, 1947: 1320 khz; 25 kw-D, 1.9 kw-N, DA-2. TL: N42 37 19 W84 38 38. Hrs open: 600 W. Cavanaugh Rd., 48910. Phone: (517) 393-1320. Fax: (517) 393-0882. Web Site:www.1320wils.com Licensee: MacDonald Broadcasting Co. (group owner; (acq 12-20-2001; grpsl). Population served: 131,456 Natl. Network: Fox News Radio, . Natl. Rep: D & R Radio,. Format: News/talk. ◆Cindy Tuck, gen mgr, gen sls mgr; Sharon Crane, gen sls mgr.

WITL-FM— Apr 15, 1964: 100.7 mhz; 26.5 kw. 640 ft TL: N42 40 33 W84 30 00. Stereo. Hrs open: 3200 Pine Tree Rd., 48911. Phone: (517) 393-1010. Fax: (517) 394-3391. Web Site:www.witl.com Licensee: Citadel Broadcasting Co. Group owner: Citadel Broadcasting Corp. (acq 2000; grpsl). Population served: 379,500 Natl. Rep: Christal,. Leventhal,Senter& Lerman. Format: Country. News staff: one. Target aud: 25-54. ◆Farid Suleman, chmn; Matt Hanlon, gen mgr; Brent Alberts, opns mgr; Kelly Norton, sls dir; Chris Potter, rgnl sls mgr; Jordan Lee, prom mgr; Chris Tyler, progmg mgr; Rick Housley, chief of engrg; Steve Goupil, traf mgr.

WJIM(AM)— 1934: 1240 khz; 1 kw-U. TL: N42 44 22 W84 30 39. (CP: 890 w). Hrs open: 24 3420 Pine Tree Rd., 48911. Phone: (517) 394-7272. Fax: (517) 394-3391.E-mail: tim.nester@citcomm.net Web Site:www.wjimam.com Licensee: Citadel Broadcasting Co. Group owner: Citadel Broadcasting Corp. (acq 2000; grpsl). Population served: 379,500 Natl. Network: Westwood One, ABC, . Natl. Rep: Christal,. Leventhal, Senter & Lerman. Format: News, info, talk. News staff: one; News: 4 hrs wkly. Target aud: 25-54. ◆Farid Suleman, CEO, chmn; Matt Hanlon, gen mgr; Brent Alberts, opns mgr; Steve Goupil, traf mgr.

WJIM-FM— June 1960: 97.5 mhz; 45 kw. Ant 512 ft TL: N42 40 33 W84 30 00. Stereo. Hrs open: 24 3420 Pine Tree Rd., 48911. Phone: (517) 394-7272. Fax: (517) 394-3391.E-mail: info@new975.com Web Site:www.new975.com Licensee: Citadel Broadcasting Co. Population served: 500,000 Format: CHR. News staff: one; News: 2 hrs wkly. ◆Farid Suleman, chmn; Matt Hanlon, gen mgr; Brent Alberts, opns mgr; Josh Strickland, progmg dir.

WJXQ(FM)—See Jackson

WJZL(FM)—See Charlotte

*WLNZ(FM)— Feb 11, 1994: 89.7 mhz; 100 w. 98 ft TL: N42 44 16 W84 33 09. Hrs open: Lansing Community College, 400 N. Capitol Ave., Suite 001, 48933. Phone: (517) 483-1710. Fax: (517) 483-1894.E-mail: info@wlnz.org Web Site:www.wlnz.org Licensee: Lansing Community College. Population served: 500,000 Natl. Network: PRI, NPR, . Format: Jazz, blues, AAA. Spec prog: Reggae 4 hrs, big band 3 hrs, folk 3 hrs, Sp 4 hrs wkly. ◆Dave Downing, gen mgr; Lyn Peraino, progmg dir; Dae Lowry, mus dir; Lyle Laylin, chief of engrg.

WMMQ(FM)—See East Lansing

WQTX(FM)—See Saint Johns

WVFN(AM)—See East Lansing

WWSJ(AM)—See Saint Johns

Lapeer

WLCO(AM)— Nov 16, 1962: 1530 khz; 5 kw-D, DA-D. TL: N43 01 35 W83 17 12. Hrs open: 3338 E. Bristol Rd., Burton, 48529. Phone: (810) 743-1080. Fax: (810) 742-5170.E-mail: info@wlco.com Web Site:www.wlco.com Licensee: Regent Broadcasting of Flint Inc. Group owner: Regent Communications Inc. (acq 7-18-2002; $1.3 million with co-located FM). Population served: 10,000 Natl. Network: ABC, . Natl. Rep: Patt,. Earl Stanley. Format: Country. Target aud: 35 plus. ◆Zoe Burdine-Fly, gen mgr.

*WMPC(AM)— Dec 6, 1926: 1230 khz; 1 kw-U. TL: N43 04 46 W83 18 35. Hrs open: 24 Box 104, 1800 N. Lapeer Rd., 48446. Phone: (810) 664-6211. Fax: (810) 664-5361.E-mail: wmpc@chartermi.net Web Site:http://lapeer.org/ServiceOrg/WMPC Licensee: The Calvary Bible Church of Lapeer Inc. Population served: 200,000 Natl. Network: Moody, . Wire Svc: AP Format: Relg. News staff: one; News: 24 hrs wkly. Target aud: General. ◆Bob Baldwin, gen mgr & opns dir.

WQUS(FM)— Feb 6, 1968: 103.1 mhz; 3 kw. 299 ft TL: N43 04 49 W83 11 30. Stereo. Hrs open: 3338 E. Bristol Rd., Burton, 48529. Phone: (810) 743-1080. Fax: (810) 742-5170.E-mail: info@us103.com Web Site:www.us103.com Format: Adult rock. Target aud: 25-40; college educated men & women. Spec prog: AOR, gospel, blues. ◆David Corley, sls dir; Mr. Brian Beddow, progmg dir; Tony LaBrie, mus dir.

Leland

WFCX(FM)— Aug 9, 1991: 94.3 mhz; 3.6 kw. 426 ft TL: N44 54 48 W85 49 18. (CP: 14.88 kw). Stereo. Hrs open: 24 Rebroadcasts WFDX(FM) Atlanta 100%. 1020 Hastings St., Traverse City, 49686. Phone: (231) 947-0003. Fax: (231) 947-7002. Licensee: Northern Michigan Radio Inc. (acq 12-23-93; $1.1 million with WFDX(FM) Atlanta, MI;1-17-94). Natl. Rep: Christal,. Fletcher, Heald & Hildreth. Format: Classic Hits. News staff: one; News: 7 hrs wkly. Target aud: 25-54. Spec prog: Relg one hr wkly. ◆Charlie Ferguson, gen mgr; Dennis Winslow, progmg dir.

Leroy Township

*WLGH(FM)— December 1996: 88.1 mhz; 2.5 kw. Ant 328 ft TL: N42 42 20 W84 21 25. Hrs open: Box 388, Williamston, 48895. Phone: (517) 381-0573. Fax: (877) 850-0881.E-mail: info@positivehits.com Web Site:www.positivehits.com Licensee: Superior Communications. Format: Adult, Christian hit radio. ◆Jenn Czelada, gen mgr; Ed Czelada, progmg dir.

Lexington

WBTI(FM)—Licensed to Lexington. See Port Huron

Linwood

WSAG(FM)— Nov 1, 2002: 104.1 mhz; 4.6 kw. Ant 325 ft TL: N43 43 30 W83 56 50. Hrs open: 2000 Whittier St., Saginaw, 48601. Phone: (989) 752-8161. Fax: 989-752-8102. Web Site:thebay104fm.com Licensee: MacDonald Broadcasting Co. (acq 6-30-2005). Format: Soft rock. ◆Duane Alverson, pres, gen mgr; Mike Skot, progmg dir; Gary Harding, chief of engrg.

Livonia

WCAR(AM)— Oct 23, 1963: 1090 khz; 250 w-D, 500 w-N, DA-2. TL: N42 19 46 W83 21 43. Hrs open: 32500 Park Ln., Garden City, 48135. Phone: (734) 525-1111. Fax: (734) 525-3608. Web Site:www.michigancatholicradio.org Licensee: 1090 Investments L.L.C. (acq 7-6-98; $2 million). Population served: 500,000 Format: Catholic. Target aud: 25 plus. Spec prog: Ethnic. ◆John F.X. Browne, pres.

Ludington

WKLA(AM)— Oct 9, 1944: 1450 khz; 1 kw-U. TL: N43 57 05 W86 25 28. Hrs open: 24 5941 W. U.S. 10, 49431. Phone: (231) 843-3438. Fax: (231) 843-1886. Web Site:www.wkla.com Licensee: Lake Michigan Broadcasting Inc. (group owner; (acq 9-20-96; grpsl). Population served: 28,000 Format: News/talk. News staff: one; News: 4 hrs wkly. Target aud: 40 plus; mature adults. ◆Lynn Baerwolf, gen mgr, prom mgr; Jason Wilder, opns mgr, mus dir; Alan Neushwander, news dir, chief of engrg; Richard Young, sls dir & mus critic.

WKLA-FM— May 1971: 106.3 mhz; 6 kw. 400 ft TL: N43 03 30 W86 24 59. Stereo. Hrs open: Prog sep from AM 5941 W. U.S. 10, 49431. Phone: (231) 843-3438. Fax: (231) 843-1886. Web Site:www.wkla.com Licensee: Lake Michigan Broadcasting Inc. Population served: 70,000 Natl. Network: ABC, . Rgnl rep: Patt Media Shaw Pittman. Format: Adult contemp. News staff: 2; News: 3 hrs wkly. Target aud: 25-50. ◆Richard Young, mktg dir, local news ed; Rod Beckman, sports cmtr.

WKZC(FM)—See Scottville

*WXYP(FM)—Not on air, target date: unknown: 91.5 mhz; 610 w. Ant 328 ft TL: N43 55 01 W86 26 12. Hrs open: 803 E. Dowland St., 49431-2316. Phone: (231) 845-2000. Licensee: Sandy Shores Arts Society. ◆Judy L. Lavaute, pres & gen mgr.

Luna Pier

WTWR-FM— July 16, 1967: 98.3 mhz; 3.4 kw. Ant 443 ft TL: N41 40 05 W83 27 11. Stereo. Hrs open: 24 14930 Laplaisance Rd. Suite 113, Monroe, 48161. Phone: (734) 242-6600. Fax: (734) 242-6599.E-mail: info@tower983.com Web Site:www.tower983.com Licensee: Cumulus Licensing Corp Group owner: Cumulus Media L.L.C. (acq 7-98; $2.8 million). Population served: 300,000 Natl. Rep: Michigan Spot Sales,. Crowell & Moring. Format: CHR. News staff: one; News: 3 hrs wkly. Target aud: 25-54. Spec prog: Relg 3 hrs wkly. ◆Skip Schmidt, gen mgr; Sherri Borer, gen sls mgr; Steve Marshall, progmg dir; London Mitchell, news dir.

Mackinaw City

*WIAB(FM)— Oct 1, 2000: 88.5 mhz; 20 kw. Ant 430 ft TL: N45 40 00 W84 38 05. Hrs open: Simulcast with WIAA(FM) Interlochen 100%. Box 199, Interlochen, 49643. Phone: (231) 276-4400. Fax: (231) 276-4417.E-mail: ipr@interlochen.org Web Site:www.interlochen.org/ipr Licensee: Interlochen Center for the Arts (acq 3-14-2005; $580,000). Format: Classical, news. ◆Thom Paulson, stn mgr.

WLJZ(FM)— Sept 6, 1989: 94.5 mhz; 40 kw. Ant 380 ft TL: N45 40 00 W84 38 05. Stereo. Hrs open: 1356 Mackinaw Ave., Cheboygan, 49721. Phone: (231) 627-2341. Fax: (231) 627-7000.E-mail: info@nsbroadcasting.com Web Site:www.nsbroadcasting.com Licensee: Northern Star Broadcasting L.L.C. (group owner; (acq 12-12-2005; grpsl). Format: Classic country. ◆Palmer Pyle, pres; April Hurley-Rose, opns dir.

Manistee

*WLMN(FM)—Not on air, target date: unknown: 89.7 mhz; 15 kw. Ant 282 ft TL: N44 06 18 W86 15 01. Hrs open: Box 199, Interlochen, 49643-0199. Phone: (231) 276-4400. Fax: (231) 276-4417. Web Site:www.interlochen.org/ipr Licensee: Interlochen Center for the Arts. ◆Thom Paulson, gen mgr.

WMLQ(FM)— Aug 1, 1970: 97.7 mhz; 2.5 kw. Ant 515 ft TL: N44 12 40 W86 17 53. Stereo. Hrs open: 24 Box 855, Ludington, 49431. Fax: (231) 843-9411. Web Site:www.977coastfm.com Licensee: Synergy Media Inc. (acq 6-1-2006; $380,000). Population served: 40,000 Rgnl. Network: Ohio Radio Net. Natl. Rep: Michigan Spot Sales,. Mich. Farm Rgnl rep: Michigan Spot Sales Drinker, Biddle & Reath. Format: Soft adult contemp/Gold. Target aud: 35-64; Adults. ◆Todd Mohr, gen mgr; Stacy Johnson, opns mgr; Tom Green, chief of engrg.

WMTE(AM)— June 7, 1951: 1340 khz; 1 kw-U. TL: N44 14 07 W86 19 05. Hrs open: 24 52 Greenbush St., 49660. Phone: (231) 723-9906. Fax: (231) 723-9908. Licensee: Lake Michigan Broadcasting Inc. (group owner; (acq 9-20-96; grpsl). Population served: 40,000 Natl. Network: ABC, . Natl. Rep: Michigan Spot Sales,. Format: News/talk. News staff: one. Target aud: General. ◆Judith Ouvry, stn mgr; Jason Wilder, opns mgr; Richard Young, gen sls mgr; Ben Failor, rgnl sls mgr; Alan Neushwander, news dir; Mike Baerwolf, chief of engrg.

WMTE-FM— June 22, 1994: 101.5 mhz; 3 kw. 115 ft TL: N44 12 18 W86 17 22. Stereo. Hrs open: 24 52 Greenbush, 49660. Phone: (231) 723-9906. Fax: (231) 723-9908.E-mail: judy@wkla.com Web Site:www.oldies1015.com Licensee: Lake Michigan Broadcasting Inc. (group owner; (acq 2000; $300,000). Population served: 14056 Rgnl rep: Patt Media Format: Oldies. News staff: one. Spec prog: Pol 6 hrs, relg 2 hrs wkly. ◆Judith Ouvry, stn mgr, opns dir, progmg dir; Jason Wilder, opns mgr; Richard Young, gen sls mgr; Ben Failor, rgnl sls mgr; Mike Baerwolf, progmg dir, chief of engrg; Alan Neushwander, news dir.

Manistique

WPIQ(FM)— 2005: 99.9 mhz; 6 kw. Ant 151 ft TL: N45 58 13 W86 11 06. Hrs open: 2025 U.S. Hwy. 41 W., Marquette, 49855. Phone: (201) 221-4251. Fax: (906) 228-8128.E-mail: toddn@greatlakesradio.org Web Site:www.wpiqradio.com Licensee: Todd Stuart Noordyk. Group owner: Great Lakes Radio Inc. Natl. Network: Premiere Radio Networks, ABC, . Format: News/talk. News staff: 2. ◆Todd Noordyk, gen mgr; Devin Lawrence, stn mgr; Walt Lindala, news dir; Staci Zanetti, traf mgr.

WTIQ(AM)— Feb 11, 1968: 1490 khz; 1 kw-U. TL: N45 57 51 W86 16 37. Stereo. Hrs open: 7876W County Rd. 442, 49854-9000. Phone: (906) 341-1490. Fax: (906) 341-6222.E-mail: wtiq@chartermi.net Web Site:www.radioresultsnetwork.com Licensee: Lakes Radio Inc. (group owner; acq 11-30-99; grpsl). Population served: 38,000 Rgnl. Network: MNN. MNN Meyer, Faller, Weisman & Rosenberg, P.C. Format: Oldies. Target aud: 25-54; blue & white collar. ◆Rick Duerson, gen mgr; L. David Vaughan, stn mgr.

Marine City

WHLX(AM)—Licensed to Marine City. See Port Huron

Marlette

WBGV(FM)— July 25, 1999: 92.5 mhz; 3 kw. TL: N43 17 10 W82 58 17. Stereo. Hrs open: 24 1260 Yosemite Blvd., Birmingham, 48009. Secondary address: 19 S. Elk St., Sandusky 48422. Phone: (810) 648-2700. Phone: (248) 540-3380. Fax: (248) 540-3379.E-mail: gebv@aol.com Licensee: GB Broadcasting Co.(acq 6-5-92). Population served: 35,000 Natl. Network: ABC, . Format: Country. News staff: one; News: 2 hrs wkly. Target aud: General. ◆George Benko V, pres; Robert Armstrong, gen mgr & opns mgr; George Benko, reporter.

*WMSQ(FM)— 2004: Stn currently dark. 89.3 mhz; 100 w. Ant 98 ft TL: N43 22 06 W83 07 00. Hrs open: 901 Elizabeth Ct., Mount Pleasant, 48858. Phone: (517) 779-9178. Licensee: Great Lakes Community Broadcasting Inc. Format: Oldies. ◆James McClusky, gen mgr.

Marquette

WDMJ(AM)— July 1, 1931: 1320 khz; 5 kw-D, 1 kw-N, DA-N. TL: N46 32 40 W87 26 42. Hrs open: 1009 W. Ridge St., Suite A, 49855-3963. Phone: (906) 225-1313. Fax: (906) 225-1324.E-mail: info@wjpd.com Web Site:www.wjpd.com Licensee: Northern Star Broadcasting L.L.C. (group owner; acq 11-5-01; grpsl). Population served: 75,000 Natl. Rep: Michigan Spot Sales,. Format: News/talk. Target aud: 25-54. ◆Tammy Johnson, gen mgr.

WFXD(FM)— Apr 6, 1974: 103.3 mhz; 100 kw. Ant 938 ft TL: N46 36 14 W87 37 15. Stereo. Hrs open: 24 2025 US 41 W., 49855. Phone: (906) 228-6800. Fax: (906) 228-8128.E-mail: toddn@greatlakesradio.org Web Site:www.wfxd.com Licensee: Great Lakes Radio Inc. (group owner; (acq 11-30-99; grpsl). Format: Hot country hits. Target aud: 25-54. ◆Todd Noordyk, gen mgr; Walt Lindala, news dir; Staci Zanetti, traf mgr.

*WHWL(FM)— Dec 16, 1965: 95.7 mhz; 100 kw. Ant 531 ft TL: N46 29 52 W87 24 59. Stereo. Hrs open: 130 Carmen Dr., 49855. Phone: (906) 249-1423. Fax: (906) 249-4042.E-mail: whwl@whwl.net Web Site:www.whwl.net Licensee: Gospel Opportunities Inc. (acq 4-19-76). Population served: 150,000 Format: Relg. ◆W. Curtis Marker, gen mgr & progmg dir.

WIAN(AM)—See Ishpeming

*WNMU-FM— August 1963: 90.1 mhz; 100 kw. 930 ft TL: N46 21 09 W87 51 32. Stereo. Hrs open: 24 Learning Resources Ctr., Northern Michigan Univ., 1401 Presque Isle Ave., 49855. Phone: (906) 227-2600. Fax: (906) 227-2905. Web Site:www.nmu.edu/wnmufm Licensee: Board of Trustees of Northern Michigan University. Population served: 250,000 Natl. Network: NPR, PRI, . Rgnl. Network: Mich. Pub. Cohn & Marks. Wire Svc: AP Format: Class, jazz, news. News: 31 hrs wkly. Spec prog: Educ. ◆Eric Smith, gen mgr; Evelyn Massaro, stn mgr. Co-owned TV: *WNMU-TV affil

WUPK(FM)— May 1, 1992: 94.1 mhz; 4.4 kw. Ant 380 ft TL: N46 30 51 W87 28 58. Hrs open: 24
Rebroadcasts WIMK(FM) Iron Mountain 100%.
1009 W. Ridge St., Suite A, 49855-3963. Phone: (906) 225-1313. Fax: (906) 225-1324.E-mail: info@wjpd.com Licensee: Northern Star Broadcasting L.L.C. (group owner; acq 11-5-01; grpsl). Natl. Rep: Patt,. Reddy, Begley & McCormick. Format: Classic rock, AOR. News staff: one; News: 3 hrs wkly. Target aud: 25-54; baby boomers. ◆Chris Monk, VP; Tammy Johnson, gen mgr.

*WUPX(FM)— 1994: 91.5 mhz; 200 w. 138 ft TL: N46 34 44 W87 23 42. Hrs open: 24 Northern Michigan Univ., 1204 University Ctr., 49855. Phone: (906) 227-2348. Phone: (906) 227-1844. Fax: (906) 227-2344.E-mail: wupx@nmu.edu Web Site:www.wupx.com Licensee: Board of Control of Northern Michigan University. Format: Alternative. Target aud: College. Spec prog: Black 6 hrs, jazz 2 hrs wkly. ◆Troy Hanson, gen mgr; Anne Bradley, prom dir; Jeffrey Matthias, progmg dir. Co-owned TV: *WNMU-TV affil

Marshall

WBXX(FM)—Licensed to Marshall. See Albion

Mason

*WUNN(AM)— May 11, 1967: 1110 khz; 1 kw-D, DA. TL: N42 33 04 W84 24 15. Hrs open: Sunrise-sunset 7355 N. Oracle Rd., Suite 200, Tucson, 85704. Phone: (800) 776-1070. Phone: (520) 742-6976. Fax: (520) 469-7312.E-mail: wunn@flc.org Web Site:www.967flr.org Licensee: Family Life Broadcasting System. (group owner; (acq 1-1-69). Population served: 250,000 Format: Southern gospel. News: 1.5 hrs wkly. Target aud: 25-54; Christian families. ◆Randy Carlson, pres; Dawn Bumstead, gen mgr, dev dir; Bob Wolfe, chief of engrg.

McMillan

WMJT(FM)— 2006: 96.7 mhz; 50 kw. Ant 413 ft TL: N46 32 02 W85 35 24. Hrs open: Box 486, Newberry, 49868-0486. Secondary address: 210 W. John St., Newberry 49868-1125. Phone: (906) 293-1400. Fax: (906) 293-5161.E-mail: kent@radioeagle.com Web Site:www.radioeagle.com Licensee: David L. Smith. Format: Adult hits. ◆Kent Smith, gen mgr; Mike Reling, opns mgr; Vern Cavitch, natl sls mgr; Rob Weaver, progmg dir; Teri Petrie, traf mgr.

Menominee

WAGN(AM)— Nov 14, 1952: 1340 khz; 1 kw-U. TL: N45 06 27 W87 36 25. Hrs open: 24 413 10th Ave., 49858. Phone: (906) 863-5551. Fax: (906) 863-5679. Web Site:baycitiesradio.net Licensee: Armada Media - Menominee Inc. (group owner; (acq 12-19-2006); grpsl). Population served: 55,000 Natl. Network: ABC, . Wisconsin Radio Net. McCabe & Allen. Wire Svc: AP Format: Oldies. News staff: one; News: 15 hrs wkly. Target aud: 30 plus; older, affluent adults. ◆Joan Jensen, gen sls mgr.

WHYB(FM)— Oct 24, 1984: 103.7 mhz; 7 kw. Ant 298 ft TL: N45 04 00 W87 39 55. Stereo. Hrs open: 24 413 10th Ave., 49858. Phone: (906) 863-5551. Fax: (906) 863-5679. Licensee: Armada Media-Menominee Inc. Wire Svc: AP Format: Oldies. News staff: one; News: 5 hrs wkly. Target aud: 25-49; females. ◆Joan Jensen, gen sls mgr.

WMAM(AM)—See Marinette, WI

Michigamme

*WKPK(FM)— 2009: 88.3 mhz; 15 kw vert. Ant 827 ft TL: N46 36 14 W87 37 15. Hrs open: 148 E Grand River Rd, Williamston, 48895. Phone: (517) 381-0573. Web Site:www.smile.fm Licensee: Northland Community Broadcasters. Format: Contemp Chirstian. ◆Edward T. Czelada, pres; Jennifer Czelada, gen mgr.

Midland

WKQZ(FM)— Dec 14, 1976: 93.3 mhz; 39.2 kw. 554 ft TL: N43 50 46 W84 05 32. Stereo. Hrs open: 1740 Champagne Dr., Saginaw, 48604. Phone: (989) 776-2100. Fax: (989) 754-5990.E-mail: info@z93kqz.fm Web Site:www.z93kqz.fm Licensee: Citadel Broadcasting Co. Group owner: Citadel Broadcasting Corp. (acq 2-8-99; grpsl). Natl. Rep: McGavren Guild,. Reddy, Begley & McCormick. Format: Rock. Target aud: 25-44; males. ◆Chris Monk, pres, gen mgr; Tom Clark, sls dir & gen sls mgr; Stan Parman, progmg dir; Hal Maas, news dir; Bob Friedle, chief of engrg.

WMPX(AM)— Sept 11, 1948: 1490 khz; 1 kw-U, DA-2. TL: N43 36 48 W84 13 17. Hrs open: 24 Box 1689, 48641. Secondary address: 1510 Bayliss St. 48640. Phone: (989) 631-1490.E-mail: wmpx@journey.com Web Site:www.wmpxwmrx.com Licensee: Steel Broadcasting Inc. (acq 8-19-81; $900,000; 8-24-81). Population served: 38,500 Natl. Network: ABC, . Natl. Rep: Patt,. Format: Adult standards, Oldies. News staff: one; News: 9 hrs wkly. Target aud: General. Spec prog: Sounds of Sinatra 2 hrs wkly, relg 3 hrs wkly. ◆Thomas Steel, pres & gen mgr; Jon Walding, gen sls mgr.

*WUGN(FM)— Dec 2, 1973: 99.7 mhz; 100 kw. 997 ft TL: N43 30 56 W84 32 49. Stereo. Hrs open: 510 E. Isabella Rd., 48640. Phone: (989) 631-7060. Fax: (989) 631-4825.E-mail: 997@997.org Web Site:www.997.org Licensee: Family Life Communications System. (acq 1996). Population served: 1,000,000 Natl. Network: Salem Radio Network, . Format: Contemp Christian. News: 8 hrs wkly. Target aud: 35-54; female with young children. ◆Peter Brooks, gen mgr.

Mio

WAVC(FM)— Oct 1, 1994: 93.9 mhz; 50 kw. 433 ft TL: N44 43 40 W84 21 35. Stereo. Hrs open:
Rebroadcasts WMKC(FM) Saint Ignace 100%.
1356 Mackinaw Ave., Cheboygan, 49721. Phone: (231) 627-2341. Fax: (231) 627-7000.E-mail: info@1029bigcountry.com Web Site:www.1029bigcountry.com Licensee: Northern Star Broadcasting L.L.C. (group owner; (acq 9-11-98; grpsl). Format: Country. ◆Palmer Pyle, pres; April Hurley-Rose, gen mgr, opns dir.

Monroe

WCSX(FM)—See Birmingham

*WDTR(FM)— 2003: 88.1 mhz; 910 w. Ant 144 ft TL: N41 55 08 W83 22 34. Hrs open:
rebroadcast of WHYT(FM) Imlay city 100%.
Box 388, Williamston, 48895. Phone: (810) 721-0891. Fax: (413) 410-9708.E-mail: info@joyfm.net Web Site:www.joyfm.net Licensee: Northland Community Broadcasters. Format: Contemporary Christian. ◆Jenn Czelada, gen mgr.

WRDT(AM)— July 12, 1956: 560 khz; 500 w-D, 27 w-N. TL: N41 53 28 W83 25 39. (CP: 14 w-N). Hrs open: 24 12300 Radio Pl., Detroit, 48228. Phone: (313) 272-3434.E-mail: station@wmuz.com Web Site:www.wrdt560.com Licensee: WMUZ Radio Inc. Group owner: Crawford Broadcasting Co. (acq 6-16-97; $3.15 million). Population served: 100,000 Natl. Rep: McGavren Guild,. Format: Bible teaching. ◆Frank Franciosi, gen mgr, gen sls mgr; Rich Hanovich, opns mgr.

*WYDM(FM)— November 1978: 97.5 mhz; 8 w. Ant 135 ft TL: N41 55 07 W83 26 12. Hrs open: Monroe High School, 901 Herr Rd., 48161. Phone: (734) 265-3550.E-mail: mbeaudr@monroeccc.edu Web Site:www.monroeccc.edu Licensee: Monroe Public Schools (acq 8-77). Format: Var/div. Target aud: 15-24.

Mount Clemens

WHTD(FM)— Nov 6, 1960: 102.7 mhz; 50 kw. 499 ft TL: N42 32 39 W82 54 09. Stereo. Hrs open: 24 3250 Franklin, Detroit, 48207. Phone:(313) 259-2000. Fax:(313) 259-7011. Web Site:www.kissdetroit.com Licensee: Radio One of Detroit LLC. Group owner: Radio One Inc. (acq 1999; $27 million). Natl. Network: ABC, . Natl. Rep: D & R Radio,. Format: Urban / AC. Target aud: 25-49; rock and rollers of all ages. ◆Carol Lawrence-Dobrusin, gen mgr.

Mount Pleasant

WCFX(FM)—See Clare

*WCMU-FM— Apr 6, 1964: 89.5 mhz; 100 kw. 423 ft TL: N43 34 24 W84 46 21. Stereo. Hrs open: 24 Public Broadcasting Ctr., 1999 E. Campus Dr., 48859. Phone: (989) 774-3105. Fax: (989) 774-4427.E-mail: cmuradio@radio.cmich.edu Web Site:www.wcmu.org Licensee: Central Michigan University. Population served: 45,000 Natl. Network: NPR, PRI, . Rgnl. Network: Mich. Pub. Dow, Lohnes & Albertson. Format: Class, jazz, news & info. News staff: 2; News: 30 hrs wkly. Target aud: General. ◆ Ed Grant, gen mgr. Co-owned TV: *WCMU-TV affil

WCZY-FM— Aug 20, 1991: 104.3 mhz; 3 kw. 328 ft TL: N43 35 39 W84 49 26. Stereo. Hrs open: 24 4065 E. Wing Rd., 48858. Phone: (989) 772-9664. Fax: (989) 773-5000.E-mail: wczy@wczy.net Web Site:www.wczy.net Licensee: Central Michigan Communications Inc. Natl. Network: Jones Radio Networks, . Natl. Rep: Michigan Spot Sales,. Rgnl rep: Patt. Reddy, Begley & McCormick. Format: Easy lstng, adult contemp. News staff: one; News: 6 hrs wkly. Target aud: 25-54. ◆ Mike Carey, pres, gen mgr; Bob Peters, gen sls mgr; Tina Sawyer, progmg dir & news dir; Lisa Johnson, traf mgr.

*WMHW-FM— Nov 20, 1972: 91.5 mhz; 13 kw vert. Ant 459 ft TL: N43 34 33 W84 46 29. Stereo. Hrs open: 24 180 Moore Hall, Central Michigan Univ., 48859. Phone: (989) 774-7287. Phone: (989) 774-3851. Fax: (989) 774-2426.E-mail: wmhw@mail.cmich.edu Web Site:www.bca.cmich.edu Licensee: Board of Trustees, Central Michigan University. Population served: 188,800 Mich. Radio Irwin, Campbell & Tannenwald. Format: Alternative rock. News: 10 wkly. Target aud: 12-34. ◆ Peter B. Orlik, gen mgr; Heather Polinsky, opns mgr; Randy Kapenga, chief of engrg.

Munising

WQXO(AM)— Sept 20, 1955: 1400 khz; 1 kw-U. TL: N46 24 30 W86 38 22. Hrs open: 24 2025 US Hwy. 41 W., Marquette, 49855. Phone: (906) 228-6800. Fax: (906) 228-8128.E-mail: toddn@greatlakesradio.org Web Site:www.wqxo.com Licensee: Great Lakes Radio Inc. (group owner; (acq 11-30-99; grpsl). Population served: 3,677 Natl. Rep: Patt,. Haley, Bader & Potts. Format: Good time oldies. Target aud: 25-54. ◆ Todd Noordyk, gen mgr; Bill Tibor, gen sls mgr; Joel Polkinghorne, progmg dir; Walt Lindala, news dir.

WRUP(FM)— June 21, 1974: 98.3 mhz; 32 kw. Ant 357 ft TL: N46 24 53 W86 40 27. Stereo. Hrs open: 24 Prog sep from AM 2025 US Hwy. 41 W., Marquette, 49855. Phone: (906) 228-6800. Fax: (906) 228-8128.E-mail: toddn@greatlakesradio.org Web Site:wrup.com Population served: 67,000 Natl. Network: Westwood One, . Natl. Rep: Patt,. Format: Classic rock. Target aud: 18-54.

Muskegon

WGVS(AM)— 1926: 850 khz; 1 kw-U, DA-1. TL: N43 08 05 W86 15 14. Hrs open: 24
Rebroadcasts WGVU(AM) Kentwood 100%.
c/o WGVU, 301 W. Fulton, Grand Rapids, 49504-6492. Phone: (616) 331-6666. Fax: (616) 331-6625.E-mail: wgvu@gvsu.edu Web Site:www.wgvu.org Licensee: Grand Valley State University. (acq 4-9-99; with WGVS-FM Whitehall). Population served: 100,000 Natl. Network: NPR, PRI, . Cohn & Marks. Format: News, info. ◆ Michael T. Walenta, gen mgr; Ken Kolbe, opns mgr; Gary Hunt, gen sls mgr; Pamela Holtz, mktg mgr, prom mgr; Scott Vander Werf, mus dir; Fred Martino, news dir, pub affrs dir; Bob Lumbert, engrg dir; Ed Spier, traf mgr.

WGVS-FM—(Whitehall, 1975: 95.3 mhz; 2 kw. 360 ft TL: N43 21 14 W86 19 38. Stereo. Hrs open:
Rebroadcasts WGVU-FM Allendale 100%.
c/o WGVU, 301 W. Fulton, Grand Rapids, 49504. Phone: (616) 331-6666. Fax: (616) 331-6625.E-mail: wgva@gvsu.edu Web Site:www.wgvu.edu Format: Jazz, news. ◆ Ed Spier, traf mgr.

WKBZ(AM)— June 15, 1947: 1090 khz; 1 kw-D. TL: N43 16 35 W86 15 10. Hrs open: 6 AM-2 hrs past sunset 3565 Green St., 49444. Phone: (231) 733-2600. Fax: (231) 733-7461.E-mail: info@talkmuskegon.com Web Site:www.talkmuskegon.com Licensee: CC Licenses LLC. Group owner: Clear Channel Communications Inc. (acq 1-17-2001; grpsl). Population served: 44,631 Natl. Rep: D & R Radio,. John Garziglia. Format: Talk, news. News staff: one. Target aud: 25-54 primary; 35-64 secondary. ◆ Bart Brandmiller, gen mgr; John Bouwhuis, gen sls mgr; Don Beno, progmg dir; Christy Mack, prom.

*WMCQ(FM)— Mar 31, 2005: 91.7 mhz; 6 kw. Ant 328 ft TL: N43 18 37 W85 54 44. Hrs open: Drawer 2440, Tupelo, MS, 38801. Phone:

(662) 844-8888. Fax: (662) 842-6791. Licensee: American Family Association. (acq 12-20-2002). Format: Chirstian. ◆ Marvin Sanders, gen mgr.

WMUS(FM)— 1962: 106.9 mhz; 50 kw. Ant 479 ft TL: N43 13 48 W86 05 03. Stereo. Hrs open: 24 Dups AM 100% 3565 Green St., 49444. Phone: (231) 733-2600. Fax: (231) 733-7461. Web Site:www.107mus.com Licensee: CC Licenses LLC. Population served: 160,000 ◆ Mark Dixon, progmg dir.

WSHZ(FM)— February 1990: 107.9 mhz; 15 kw. 348 ft TL: N43 17 41 W86 13 12. Hrs open: 24 3565 Green St., 49444. Phone: (231) 733-2600. Fax: (231) 739-9037. Fax: (213) 733-7461. Web Site:www.star108.com Licensee: CC Licenses LLC. Group owner: Clear Channel Communications Inc. (acq 1-17-2001; grpsl). Population served: 350,000 Format: Adult contemp. Target aud: 18-49. ◆ Bart Brandmiller, gen mgr; David Taff, opns mgr, chief of engrg; John Bouwhuis, gen sls mgr; Christy Mack, prom dir; Don Beno, progmg dir.

WSNX-FM— Nov 18, 1971: 104.5 mhz; 50 kw. 361 ft TL: N43 12 13 W86 01 49. (CP: 32 kw, ant 620 ft. TL: N43 12 16 W86 01 35). Stereo. Hrs open: 24 77 Monroe Dr., Suite 1000, Grand Rapids, 49503. Phone: (616) 459-1919. Fax: (616) 235-9104.E-mail: info@wsnx.com Web Site:www.wsnx.com Licensee: CC Licenses LLC. Group owner: Clear Channel Communications Inc. (acq 9-30-99). Population served: 125,000 Natl. Network: ABC, . Natl. Rep: Clear Channel,. Format: CHR, urban contemp. News staff: one; News: news progmg one hr wkly. Target aud: 18-34; women. ◆ Skip Essick, VP & gen mgr.

Muskegon Heights

WMRR(FM)— Mar 29, 1974: 101.7 mhz; 15 kw. 305 ft TL: N43 16 38 W86 20 05. Stereo. Hrs open: 24 3565 Green St., Muskegon, 49444. Phone: (231) 733-2600. Fax: (231) 739-9037. Web Site:www.wmrr.com Licensee: CC Licenses LLC. Group owner: Clear Channel Communications Inc. (acq 1-17-2001; grpsl). Population served: 350,000 Natl. Network: Westwood One, . Wire Svc: UPI Format: Classic rock. Target aud: 25-54; male. ◆ Tim Feagan, gen mgr; David Talt, opns mgr; John Bouwhuis, gen sls mgr; Emily Harger, prom dir; Andy O'Riley, progmg dir.

Negaunee

WKQS-FM— Jan 5, 1998: 101.9 mhz; 12 kw. Ant 1,007 ft TL: N46 36 14 W87 37 15. Stereo. Hrs open: 2025 U.S. 41 W., Marquette, 49855. Phone: (906) 228-6800. Fax: (906) 228-8128.E-mail: toddn@greatlakesradio.org Web Site:www.wkqsfm.com Licensee: Great Lakes Radio Inc. (group owner) Booth, Freret, Imlay & Tepper. Format: Today's hits, yesterday's favorites. ◆ Todd Noordyk, gen mgr; Walt Lindala, news dir; Staci Zanetti, traf mgr.

WNGE(FM)— 2001: 99.5 mhz; 3.6 kw. Ant 430 ft TL: N46 30 51 W87 28 58. Hrs open: 1009 W. Ridge St., Suite A, Marquette, 49855-3963. Phone: (906) 225-1313. Fax: (906) 225-1324.E-mail: info@wjpd.com Licensee: Northern Star Broadcasting L.L.C. (group owner; acq 11-5-01; grpsl). Format: Oldies. ◆ Tammy Johnson, gen mgr.

Newaygo

WLAW(FM)— Aug 15, 2005: 92.5 mhz; 2.25 kw. Ant 543 ft TL: N43 18 37 W85 54 44. Hrs open: 60 Monroe Ctr. N.W., 3rd Fl., Grand Rapids, 49503. Phone: (616) 774-8461. Fax: (616) 774-2491.E-mail: info@924fmtheoutlaw.com Web Site:www.925fmtheoutlaw.com Licensee: Citadel Broadcasting Co. (acq 7-8-2005). Format: Classic country. ◆ Matt Hanlon, gen mgr.

Newberry

WIHC(FM)— Apr 24, 1989: 97.9 mhz; 50 kw. 352 ft TL: N46 18 53 W85 33 45. Stereo. Hrs open: 24
WGFM-FM Cheboygan 75%.
1356 Mackinaw Ave., Cheboygan, 49721. Phone: (231) 627-2341. Fax: (231) 627-7000.E-mail: info@classicrockthebear.com Web Site:www.classicrockthebear.com Licensee: Northern Star Broadcasting L.L.C. (group owner; (acq 9-11-98; grpsl). Population served: 183,000 Format: Classic rock. Target aud: 18-44. ◆ Palmer Pyle, pres; April Hurley-Rose, gen mgr, opns dir.

WNBY(AM)— May 16, 1966: 1450 khz; 1 kw-U. TL: N46 18 48 W85 30 38. Hrs open: Box 501, 49868. Secondary address: Hwy. S. M-123 49868. Phone: (906) 293-3221. Fax: (906) 293-8275.E-mail: wnby@up.net Licensee: Sovereign Communications LLC (acq 8-21-2003; $400,000 with co-located FM). Population served: 20,000 Natl. Rep: Patt,.

Format: Country Gold. Target aud: 35 plus. Spec prog: Polka 2 hrs wkly. ◆ Travis Freeman, gen mgr; Linda Peters, gen sls mgr; Sarah Price, progmg dir.

WNBY-FM— 1977: 93.9 mhz; 50 kw. Ant 443 ft TL: N46 26 58 W85 06 04. Stereo. Hrs open: Box 501, 49868. Phone: (906) 293-3221. Fax: (906) 293-8275. Licensee: Sovereign Communications LLC Population served: 25,000 Format: Oldies. Target aud: 25-45.

*WUMI(FM)—Not on air, target date: unknown: 90.3 mhz; 70 kw. Ant 203 ft TL: N46 18 48 W85 30 38. Hrs open: Box 97, Charlevoix, 49720. Phone: (231) 420-1325. Licensee: Korkee Inc. ◆ Robert A. Naismith, gen mgr.

Niles

WAOR(FM)— Sept 13, 1968: 95.3 mhz; 3.3 kw. 298 ft TL: N41 49 22 W86 17 03. Stereo. Hrs open: 24 237 Edison Rd., Mishawaka, IN, 46545. Phone: (574) 258-5483. Fax: (574) 258-0930.E-mail: waor@waor.com Web Site:www.waor.com Licensee: Pathfinder Communications Corp. Population served: 500,000 Natl. Rep: Christal,. Format: Classic rock. News: 5 hrs wkly. Target aud: 25-54; predominantly male, socially active, economically secure. ◆ Brad Williams, gen mgr, disc jockey; Mike Ragozino, prom dir.

WAUS(FM)—See South Bend, IN

WNIL(AM)— Dec 6, 1956: 1290 khz; 500 w-D, 44 w-N. TL: N41 49 22 W86 17 03. Hrs open: 24 237 Edison Rd., Mishawaka, IN, 46545. Phone: (574) 258-5483. Fax: (574) 258-0930.E-mail: cmarsh@b100.com Web Site:www.mighty1290.com Licensee: Pathfinder Communications Corp. Group owner: Federated Media (acq 7-21-99; $2 million with co-located FM). Population served: 50,000 Natl. Network: Salem Radio Network, . Wilkinson Barker Knauer. Format: Inspirational talk. News: 5 hrs wkly. Target aud: 35-54; adult, pro-active, community-involved people. Spec prog: Relg 6 hrs wkly. ◆ Brad Williams, gen mgr; Clint Marsh, opns mgr & progmg dir.

North Muskegon

*WHEY(FM)—Not on air, target date: unknown: 88.9 mhz; 1 kw. Ant 157 ft TL: N43 16 47 W86 20 28. Hrs open: Box 1511, Muskegon, 49443-1511. Phone: (231) 744-6940. Licensee: Muskegon Community Radio Broadcast Co. ◆ William J. Erickson, pres.

WLCS(FM)— November 1983: 98.3 mhz; 1.6 kw. Ant 456 ft TL: N43 18 50 W86 09 17. Stereo. Hrs open: 24 3375 Merriam St., Muskegon, 49444. Phone: (231) 830-0176. Fax: (231) 830-0194. Licensee: Citadel Broadcasting Co. (group owner; (acq 1-19-2006; grpsl). Rgnl. Network: Patt. Format: Oldies. News: one hr wkly. Target aud: 35-54; general. ◆ Jeff Morton, gen mgr; John Russell, opns mgr; Renee Dudek, gen sls mgr.

Norway

WZNL(FM)— Mar 15, 1990: 94.3 mhz; 2.4 kw. 649 ft TL: N45 49 15 W88 02 25. Hrs open: 101 E. Kent St., Iron Mountain, 49801-8110. Phone: (906) 774-4321. Fax: (906) 774-7799.E-mail: star943@uplogon.com Web Site:www.wznl.tripod.com Licensee: Northern Star Broadcasting L.L.C. (group owner; acq 11-5-01; grpsl). Natl. Network: Westwood One, . Format: Adult contemp. Target aud: 18-54. ◆ Veronica Roberts, gen mgr; Tom Hill, opns mgr.

Novi

*WOVI(FM)— Sept 4, 1978: 89.5 mhz; 100 w. 67 ft TL: N42 27 49 W83 29 28. Stereo. Hrs open: 24 Novi High School, 24062 Taft Rd., 48375. Phone: (248) 449-1526. Fax: (248) 449-1519. Licensee: Board of Education Novi School District. (acq 3-8-76). Population served: 77,000 Format: Alternative, classic rock. Target aud: General. ◆ Dave Legg, gen mgr.

Olivet

*WOCR(FM)— Apr 22, 1975: 89.7 mhz; 110 w. 75 ft TL: N42 26 31 W84 55 30. Stereo. Hrs open: 16 Kirk Ctr., Olivet College, 320 S. Main St., 49076. Phone: (269) 749-7598. Fax: (269) 749-7695.E-mail: wocr@olivetcollege.edu Licensee: Olivet College. Population served: 25,000 Format: CHR. News: one hr wkly. Target aud: College; high school and college-age, variety. ◆ Jim Collins, gen mgr; Karolyn Batt, stn mgr; Garth Sims, opns mgr, chief of engrg.

Onsted

*WAQQ(FM)— 2001: 88.3 mhz; 250 w vert. Ant 77 ft TL: N42 03 33 W84 12 54. Hrs open: 901 Elizabeth Ct., Mount Pleasant, 48858. Phone: (517) 779-9178. Fax: (989) 779-1558. Web Site:www.foundationradio.org Licensee: Great Lakes Community Broadcasting Inc. Format: Oldies. ◆James J. McCluskey, gen mgr.

Ontonagon

*WOAS(FM)— Nov 15, 1978: 88.5 mhz; 10 w. 124 ft TL: N46 52 30 W89 18 00. Hrs open: 8 AM-10 PM (M-F) 701 Parker, 49953. Phone: (906) 884-4433. Fax: (906) 884-2742.E-mail: ken@oasd.k12.mi.us Web Site:www.woas-fm.org Licensee: Ontonagon Area School District. Population served: 1,000 Format: Var/div. Target aud: General; local residents of the area. ◆Ken Raisanen, gen mgr.

WUPY(FM)— 1987: 101.1 mhz; 30 kw. 620 ft TL: N46 44 49 W89 11 27. Stereo. Hrs open: 24 Box 265, 49953. Phone: (906) 884-9668. Fax: (906) 884-4985.E-mail: wupy@jamadots.com Web Site:www.wupy101.com Licensee: SNRN Broadcasting Inc. (acq 7-90). Natl. Network: ABC, . Format: Country. News staff: 2; News: 13 hrs wkly. Target aud: 25 plus. Spec prog: relg 3 hrs, polka 1 hr wkly. ◆Ken Waldrop, gen mgr; Jackie Dobbins, opns mgr, progmg dir; Jay Nix, gen sls mgr.

Orchard Lake

*WBLD(FM)— May 28, 1974: 89.3 mhz; 10 w. 110 ft TL: N42 33 56 W83 21 32. Stereo. Hrs open: 2 4925 Orchard Lake Rd., West Bloomfield, 48323. Phone: (248) 865-6754. Fax: (248) 865-6756.E-mail: wbld@hotmail.com Web Site:wbld893.tripod.com Licensee: West Bloomfield Board of Education. Format: Div, rock. ◆Paul S. Townley, stn mgr; Randy G. Long, chief of engrg.

Oscoda

*WCMB-FM— June 1998: 95.7 mhz; 25 kw. 699 ft TL: N44 40 30 W83 31 06. Hrs open: 24
Rebroadcasts WCMU-FM Mount Pleasant 100%.
Central Michigan Univ., 1999 E. Campus Dr., Mount Pleasant, 48859. Phone: (989) 774-3105. Fax: (989) 774-4427.E-mail: cmuradio@mail.cmich.edu Web Site:www.wcmu.org Licensee: Central Michigan University. Natl. Network: NPR, PRI, . Mich. Radio Wire Svc: AP Format: Class, jazz, News. News staff: 2; News: 45 hrs wkly. ◆Edward Grant, gen mgr; Kim Walters, dev dir, prom mgr; Art Curtis, rgnl sls mgr, mktg dir; Ray Ford, progmg dir; David Nicholas, news dir; Randy Kapenga, chief of engrg.

WWTH(FM)— Aug 29, 1992: 100.7 mhz; 20.5 kw. 360 ft TL: N44 34 42 W83 22 40. Stereo. Hrs open: 24 1491 M32, Alpena, 49707. Phone: (989) 354-4611. Fax: (989) 354-4014.E-mail: tnrn@charterinternet.com Licensee: Edwards Communications LC. Group owner: Northern Radio Network (acq 12-21-2004; grpsl). Population served: 150,000 Natl. Rep: Roslin,. Rgnl rep: Michigan. Carter, Ledyard & Milburn. Format: Soft adult contemp. News staff: one; News: 4 hrs wkly. Target aud: 25-54. ◆Tony Calumet, gen mgr; Darrel Kelly, gen sls mgr, progmg dir.

Otsego

WAKV(AM)— 1958: 980 khz; 1 kw-D. TL: N42 27 33 W85 43 58. Hrs open: 24 213 Gilkey St., Plainwell, 49080. Phone: (269) 685-2438.E-mail: 980am@net-link.net Licensee: Vintage Radio Enterprises L.L.C. (acq 7-17-98; $17,500). Population served: 300,000 Wire Svc: AP Format: MOR oldies, adult standards. Target aud: 50 plus; adults. ◆Jim Higgs, gen mgr & progmg dir.

WQXC-FM— Apr 17, 1981: 100.9 mhz; 3 kw. 299 ft TL: N42 30 31 W85 46 08. Stereo. Hrs open: Box 80, 49078. Secondary address: 706 E. Allegan St. 49078. Phone: (269) 692-6851. Fax: (269) 692-6861.E-mail: tflynn@wqxc.com Web Site:www.wqxc.com Licensee: Forum Communications Inc. Population served: 300,000 Format: Oldies. ◆Robert Brink, pres; Deb Whiteman, CFO; Tom Flynn, gen mgr; Tim Bontrager, gen sls mgr; Bill Mitchell, progmg dir; Todd Overhuel, mus dir; Jim McKinney, news dir, pub affrs dir.

Ovid-Elsie

*WOES(FM)— Mar 21, 1978: 91.3 mhz; 553 w. 140 ft TL: N43 02 44 W84 23 14. Stereo. Hrs open: 24 8989 Colony Rd., Elsie, 48831. Phone: (989) 834-2271. Fax: (989) 862-4463. Licensee: Ovid-Elsie

Area Schools. (acq 1978). Population served: 3,000 Format: Polka. ◆George Bishop, gen mgr; Kevin Somers, opns mgr & progmg dir.

Owosso

WOAP(AM)— Jan 1, 1948: Stn currently dark. 1080 khz; 1 kw-D. TL: N43 01 51 W84 10 41. (CP: COL Waverly. 50 kw-D, DA. TL: N42 37 10 W84 34 31). Hrs open: 32500 Parklane St., Garden City, 48135-1527. Phone: (989) 725-8196. Fax: (734) 525-3608. Licensee: 1090 Investments L.L.C. (acq 2-18-2000). Population served: 73,000 Rgnl. Network: Mich. Farm, Mich. Pub.

WRSR(FM)— Dec 2, 1965: 103.9 mhz; 2.85 kw. 482 ft TL: N42 59 44 W83 59 33. Stereo. Hrs open: 6317 Taylor Dr., Flint, 48507. Phone: (810) 238-7300. Fax: (810) 238-7310.E-mail: info@classicfox.com Web Site:www.classicfox.com Licensee: Cumulus Licensing Corp. Group owner: Cumulus Media Inc. (acq 3-15-00; grpsl). Population served: 75,000 Format: Classic Rock. Target aud: 25-54. Spec prog: Class one hr, relg one hr, sports 4 hrs wkly. ◆Scott Meier, gen mgr; Jeff Wade, progmg dir; Les Root, news dir; Dan Greer, chief of engrg.

Paradise

WUPN(FM)—Not on air, target date: unknown: 94.7 mhz; 25 kw. Ant 7 ft TL: N46 40 38 W85 01 55. Hrs open: Box 1766, Gaylord, 49734. Phone: (989) 732-2341. Fax: (989) 732-6202. Licensee: Darby Advertising Inc. ◆Kent D. Smith, pres & gen mgr.

Pentwater

WMOM(FM)— Sept 26, 1999: 102.7 mhz; 6 kw. Ant 328 ft TL: N43 52 10 W86 21 32. Hrs open: 206 E. Ludington Ave., Ludington, 49431. Phone: (231) 845-9666. Fax: (231) 845-9322.E-mail: news@wmom.fm Web Site:www.wmom.fm Licensee: Bay View Broadcasting Inc. Format: Hot adult contemp. ◆Patrick Lopeman, pres & gen mgr; Brian Renchler, news dir.

Petoskey

WARD(AM)— June 16, 2000: 750 khz; 1 kw-D, 330 w-N, DA-2. TL: N45 20 05 W84 55 34. Hrs open: 24
Rebroadcasts WLDR-FM Traverse City 100%.
13999 S. West Bay Shore Dr., Traverse City, 49684-6206. Phone: (231) 947-3220. Fax: (231) 947-7201. Web Site:www.wldr.com Licensee: Roy E. Henderson. (acq 4-25-2007; swap with WJNL(AM) Kingsley). Population served: 198,000 Format: Country. ◆Roy Henderson, gen mgr.

WFDX(FM)—(Atlanta, Oct 20, 1988: 92.5 mhz; 100 kw. 868 ft TL: N45 01 00 W84 21 10. Stereo. Hrs open: 24 1020 Hastings St., Traverse City, 49686. Phone: (231) 947-0003. Fax: (231) 947-7002.E-mail: markelliot@classichitsthefox.com Web Site:www.943thefoxfm.com Licensee: Northern Michigan Radio Inc. (acq 12-23-93; $1.165 million with WFCX(FM) Leland;1-17-94). Population served: 374,600 Natl. Rep: Christal,. Format: Classic hits. News staff: one. Target aud: 25-54. ◆Charlie Ferguson, gen mgr; Greg Marsh, natl sls mgr; Dennis Winslow, progmg dir; Kristal Flateau, traf mgr.

WJML(AM)— Dec 6, 1966: 1110 khz; 10 kw-D, DA. TL: N45 20 05 W84 55 34. Hrs open: 24 2175 Click Rd., 49770. Phone: (231) 348-5000.E-mail: talk@wjml.com Web Site:www.wjml.com Licensee: Stone Communications Inc. (acq 10-8-91; $24,000; 1-6-92). Population served: 415,627 Natl. Network: CBS, . Mich. Talk Reddy, Begley & McCormick. Format: News/talk. News staff: one; News: 72 hrs wkly. Target aud: 25 plus. Spec prog: Loc professional and college sports, relg 4 hrs wkly. ◆Richard D. Stone, pres & gen mgr; Philip Clever, stn mgr.

WKHQ-FM—See Charlevoix

WKLZ-FM— Dec 7, 1965: 98.9 mhz; 50 kw. 800 ft TL: N45 28 40 W84 57 04. Stereo. Hrs open: 24
Rebroadcasts WKLT(FM) Kalkaska 85%.
1020 Hastings St., Traverse City, 49686. Phone: (231 947-0003. Fax: (231) 947-7002. Web Site:www.wklt.com Licensee: Northern Radio of Petoskey Inc. (acq 8-15-91; $800,000). Population served: 415,627 Natl. Network: ABC, . Natl. Rep: Christal,. Fletcher, Heald & Hildreth. Format: Classic, AOR. News: 2 hrs wkly. Target aud: 18-49; baby boomers. ◆Charlie Ferguson, gen mgr; Greg Marsh, natl sls mgr; Terri Ray, progmg dir; Dennis Murray, chief of engrg; Kristal Flateau, traf mgr.

WLXT(FM)— Jan 1, 1967: 96.3 mhz; 100 kw. 981 ft TL: N45 19 17 W84 52 33. Stereo. Hrs open: Box 286, 49770. Phone: (231)

347-8713. Fax: (231) 347-9920.E-mail: info@lite96.com Web Site:www.lite96.com Licensee: MacDonald Garber Broadcasting Inc Population served: 300,000 Format: Gold Based AC. News staff: 4. ◆Heather Leigh, progmg dir.

WMBN(AM)— May 1946: 1340 khz; 1 kw-U. TL: N45 20 50 W84 58 01. Hrs open: 24 Box 286, 49770. Secondary address: 2095 U.S. 131 S. 49770. Phone: (231) 347-8713. Fax: (231) 347-9920. Licensee: MacDonald Garber Broadcasting Inc. (group owner; acq 11-17-98; grpsl). Population served: 40,000 Natl. Rep: D & R Radio,. Format: Adult Standards. News staff: 2; News: 2 hrs wkly. Target aud: 35 plus. ◆Trish MacDonald-Garber, gen mgr; Kerry Davis, gen sls mgr; Greg Marshall, progmg dir; Bob White, news dir; Brian Brachel, chief of engrg.

Pickford

WMKD(FM)— Dec 22, 2000: 105.5 mhz; 55 kw. Ant 108 ft TL: N46 17 24 W84 18 53. Hrs open: 3183 Logan Valley Rd., Traverse City, 49684. Phone: (800) 968-0981. Web Site:www.nsbroadcasting.com Licensee: Northern Star Broadcasting LLC. (acq 10-21-2005; $900,000). Format: Relg. ◆Palmer Pyle, gen mgr.

Pinconning

WLUN(FM)— Nov 15, 1983: 100.9 mhz; 2.6 kw. Ant 495 ft TL: N43 50 46 W84 05 32. Stereo. Hrs open: 24 Box 365, Midland, 48640. Phone: (989) 837-6126. Fax: (989) 837-8780. Licensee: The Last Bastion Station Trust LLC, as Trustee Group owner: Citadel Broadcasting Corp. (acq 6-12-2007; grpsl). Natl. Network: ESPN Radio, . Format: Sports talk. Target aud: 25-54; general. ◆Paul Barbeau, gen mgr; Brad Golder, progmg dir.

Pittsford

*WPCJ(FM)— Oct 23, 1985: 91.1 mhz; 270 w. Ant 184 ft TL: N41 53 04 W84 28 15. Hrs open: 16 9400 Beecher Rd., 49271. Phone: (517) 523-3427. Fax: (517) 523-3427.E-mail: wpcj@freedomfarm.info Web Site:www.freedomfarm.info Licensee: Pittsford Educational Broadcasting Foundation. Natl. Network: Moody, . Format: Educ, relg, Christian. News: 10 hrs wkly. Target aud: General; rural. ◆Tim Neinas, stn mgr; Ed Trombley, chief of engrg.

Plymouth

*WSDP(FM)— Feb 14, 1972: 88.1 mhz; 200 w. 110 ft TL: N42 20 50 W83 29 51. Stereo. Hrs open: 24 46181 Joy Rd., Canton, 48187. Phone: (734) 416-7732. Phone: (734) 416-7745. Fax: (734) 416-7732.E-mail: keithb@pccs.klz.mi.us Web Site:www.881theescape.com Licensee: Plymouth Canton Community Schools. Population served: 1,000,000 Format: New music. News: 2 hrs wkly. Target aud: General. ◆Bill Keith, gen mgr & stn mgr.

Port Huron

WBTI(FM)—(Lexington, July 13, 1991: 96.9 mhz; 3 kw. 380 ft TL: N43 12 34 W82 32 10. Stereo. Hrs open: 24 Box 807, 48061-0807. Phone: (810) 987-9380. Web Site:www.wbti.net Licensee: Liggett Communications L.L.C Population served: 200,000 Natl. Rep: Michigan Spot Sales,. Format: Adult contemp. Target aud: 18-34. ◆Ben Coburn, progmg mgr.

WGRT(FM)— December 1991: 102.3 mhz; 3 kw. 318 ft TL: N43 04 08 W82 28 48. Hrs open: 24 624 Grand River Ave., 48060. Phone: (810) 987-3200. Fax: (810) 987-3325.E-mail: wgrtoffice@sbcglobal.net Web Site:www.wgrt.com Licensee: Port Huron Family Radio Inc. (acq 11-10-2004; $100,000). Population served: 200,000 Natl. Network: ABC, . David Oxenford. Format: Adult contemp. News staff: one. Target aud: General. ◆Martin Doorn, gen mgr; Cathie Martin, news dir.

WHLS(AM)— Aug 8, 1938: 1450 khz; 1 kw-U. TL: N42 58 37 W82 27 52. Hrs open: 24 Box 807, 48061-0807. Secondary address: 808 Huron Ave. 48060. Phone: (810) 982-9000. Fax: (810) 987-9380.E-mail: info@whls.net Web Site:www.whls.net Licensee: Liggett Communications L.L.C. (acq 1-1-56). Population served: 250,000 Natl. Rep: Michigan Spot Sales,. Format: Oldies. Target aud: 18-50; middle class. Spec prog: Black one hr, Sp one hr wkly. ◆Robert Liggett, chmn; James A. Jensen, pres; Lawrence C. Smith, gen mgr; Kristine Sikkema, sls dir, gen sls mgr; Jim McKenzie, progmg dir; Bill Gilmer, news dir; Craig Bowman, chief of engrg; Staci O'Brien, traf mgr; Dennis Stuckey, sports cmtr.

WHLX(AM)—(Marine City, Dec 10, 1951: 1590 khz; 1 kw-D, 102 w-N, DA-1. TL: N42 43 42 W82 31 15. Hrs open: 24 Rebroadcasts WHLS (AM) Port Huron 100%.
808 Huron Ave., 48060. Phone: (810) 982-9000. Fax: (810) 987-9380. Licensee: Liggett Communications LLC. Group owner: Liqgctt Communications (acq 5-1-2000). Population served: 300,000 Natl. Network: ABC, . Format: Adult contemp, oldies. Target aud: 25-54. ◆Robert Liggett, chmn; James A. Jenson, pres; Lawrence Smith, VP; Lawrence C. Smith, gen mgr.

*****WNFA(FM)**— May 15, 1986: 88.3 mhz; 1.3 kw. 227 ft TL: N42 59 36 W82 28 06. Stereo. Hrs open: 24
Rebroadcasts WNFR(FM) Sandusky 100%.
2865 Maywood Dr., 48060. Phone: (810) 985-3260. Fax: (810) 985-7712.E-mail: lori@wnradio.com Web Site:www.wnradio.com Licensee: Ross Bible Church. Population served: 150,000 Natl. Network: Moody, USA, . Southmayd & Miller. Format: Relg, inspirational. News: 14 hrs wkly. Target aud: 25-44; females. ◆Brian Smith, progmg dir; Ellyn Davey, mus dir, news dir; Lori McNaughton, opns mgr & pub affrs dir.

*****WORW(FM)**— May 31, 1973: 91.9 mhz; 188 w. 78 ft TL: N43 01 30 W82 26 10. (CP: 180 w). Hrs open: 24 1799 Krafft Rd., 48060. Phone: (810) 984-2675, Ext. 363. Fax: (810) 984-2747. Licensee: Port Huron Area School District. Population served: 200 Format: Top-40. ◆Carrie Meggs, gen mgr.

WPHM(AM)— Dec 6, 1947: 1380 khz; 5 kw-U, DA-2. TL: N42 51 50 W82 29 40. Hrs open: 24 808 Huron St., 48060. Phone: (810) 982-9000. Fax: (810) 987-9380.E-mail: info@wphmam.net Web Site:www.wphm.net Licensee: Liggett Communications L.L.C. (group owner; acq 5-1-2000; grpsl). Population served: 300,000 Natl. Rep: Michigan Spot Sales,. Wire Svc: NWS (National Weather Service) Format: News/talk. News: 40 hrs wkly. Target aud: 25-54. ◆Robert Liggett, chmn; James A. Jwesen, pres; Lawrence C. Smith, gen mgr; Kristine Sikkema, sls dir, gen sls mgr; Paul Miller, progmg dir; Craig Bowman, engrg VP.

WSAQ(FM)— Aug 7, 1964: 107.1 mhz; 6 kw. Ant 298 ft TL: N42 58 37 W82 27 52. Stereo. Hrs open: 24 Box 807, 48061-0807. Secondary address: 808 Huron Ave. 48060. Phone: (810) 982-9000. Fax: (810) 987-9380. Web Site:www.wsaq.net Licensee: Liggett Communications L.L.C. Population served: 550,000 Format: Country. Target aud: 25-55.

*****WSGR-FM**— October 1971: 91.3 mhz; 100 w. 87 ft TL: N42 58 43 W82 25 45. Stereo. Hrs open: Box 5015, 323 Erie St., 48061-5015. Phone: (810) 989-5564. Fax: (810) 984-8991. Web Site:www.stclair.cc.mi.us Licensee: St. Clair County Community College. Population served: 180,000 Format: Pop jazz. Target aud: General; all age groups. Spec prog: Metal-hard rock 12 hrs, urban 6 hrs wkly. ◆John Hill, gen mgr.

Portage

WNWN(AM)— July 25, 1986: 1560 khz; 4.1 kw-D, DA. TL: N42 10 59 W85 35 30. Hrs open: Sunrise-sunset 4200 W. Main St., Kalamazoo, 49006. Phone: (269) 345-7121. Fax: (269) 345-1436. Web Site:www.1560radio.com Licensee: Midwest Communications Inc. (group owner; acq 1995; grpsl). Population served: 300,000 Natl. Rep: Christal,. Format: Urban contemp. News staff: 2; News: 5 hrs wkly. Target aud: 25-54; emphasis on 35-50 age group. Spec prog: Blues 3 hrs wkly. ◆D.E. Wright, pres; Peter Tanz, gen mgr; Michael Klein, gen sls mgr; John McNeill, news dir; Walker Sisson, chief of engrg.

WRKR(FM)—Licensed to Portage. See Kalamazoo

WYZO(FM)— June 1992: 96.5 mhz; 3 kw. Ant 321 ft TL: N42 12 55 W85 36 37. Hrs open: 4200 W. Main St., Kalamazoo, 49006. Phone: (269) 345-7121. Fax: (269) 345-1436. Web Site:www.y965country.com Licensee: Midwest Communications Inc. Natl. Rep: Christal,. Format: Country. News staff: 4. Target aud: 25-49. ◆D.J. Wright, pres; Mike Klein, sls dir; Peter Tanz, mktg mgr; P.J. Lacey, progmg dir; Walker Sisson, engrg dir.

Powers

WUPF(FM)— 2008: Stn currently dark. 107.3 mhz; 25 kw. Ant 318 ft TL: N45 42 39 W87 20 49. Hrs open: 1317 Ludington St., Suite 3, Escanaba, 49829. Phone: (906) 233-0279. Fax: (906) 233-0282. Licensee: Radioactive LLC. Format: Classic rock. ◆Benjamin L. Homel, pres; Tommy Kareckas, gen mgr.

Raco

*****WJOH(FM)**— 2006: 91.5 mhz; 5.5 kw. Ant 328 ft TL: N46 23 28 W84 27 52. Hrs open:
simulcasts WJOM (FM) Eagle 100%.

Michigan Community Radio, 148 E Grand River Rd, Williamston, 48895. Phone: (517) 381-0573. Web Site:www.smile.fm Licensee: Michigan Community Radio. ◆Ed Czelada, pres.

Reed City

WDEE-FM— Aug 16, 1997: 97.3 mhz; 2.85 kw. Ant 479 ft TL: N43 46 53 W85 36 58. Hrs open: Box 722, Big Rapids, 49307. Phone: (231)796-9730. Fax: (231) 796-9738.E-mail: sunny@sunny973.com Web Site:www.sunny973.com Licensee: Steven V. Beilfuss. Format: Classic hits, oldies. Target aud: 35 plus; anyone who likes oldies. ◆Steven V. Beilfuss, gen mgr.

*****WZMI(FM)**—Not on air, target date: unknown: 91.9 mhz; 2.4 kw. Ant 226 ft TL: N43 53 14 W85 35 37. Hrs open: Box 4872, East Lansing, 48826. Phone: (517) 999-3737. Web Site:www.foundationradio.org Licensee: Saidnewsfoundation. ◆Scott Boehme, CEO.

Republic

WUPG(FM)— 2008: 96.7 mhz; 25 kw. Ant 172 ft TL: N46 32 23.6 W88 03 17.9. Hrs open: 1717 Dixie Hwy., Suite 650, Fort Wright, KY, 41011. Licensee: Radioactive LLC. ◆Benjamin L. Homel, pres.

Richland

*****WTNP(FM)**— 2008: 91.9 mhz; 6 kw vert. Ant 221 ft TL: N42 27 13 W85 20 39. Hrs open: 5331 Mt. Alifan Dr., San Diego, CA, 92111. Phone: (858) 277-4991. Fax: (858) 277-1365. Web Site:www.ksrdradio.com Licensee: Horizon Christian Fellowship. (acq 2-3-2006; $250,000 for CP). ◆Mike MacIntosh, pres; Brian KC Jones, gen mgr.

Riverside

*****WSIS(FM)**— 2008: 88.7 mhz; 6 kw. Ant 384 ft TL: N42 15 14 W86 20 09. Hrs open:
Rebroadcasts WHYT(FM) Goodland Township 100%.
Box 388, Williamston, 48895. Phone: (517) 381-0573. Fax: (877) 850-0881.E-mail: 411@smile.fm Web Site:www.smile.fm Licensee: Smile FM. ◆Jenn Czelada, gen mgr.

Rochester

*****WXOU(FM)**—(Auburn Hills, August 1995: 88.3 mhz; 110 w. 256 ft TL: N42 42 35 W83 13 50. Stereo. Hrs open: 24 69 Oakland Ctr., 48309. Phone: (248) 370-4273. Fax: (248) 370-2846.E-mail: wxou@wxou.org Web Site:www.wxou.org Licensee: Oakland University. Format: Educ. News staff: 5; News: 8 hrs wkly. Target aud: General; univ & loc community not serviced by coml media. ◆Erik Anderson, gen mgr; Justin Rumenampp, progmg dir; Christine Stover, adv.

Rockford

WMJH(AM)— 1965: 810 khz; 3.6 kw-D. TL: N43 07 03 W85 34 06. Stereo. Hrs open: 574 S Division, Suite 22, Second Floor, Grand Rapids, 49503. Phone: (616) 451-0551. Fax: (616) 451-0565.E-mail: elprimo_e@yahoo.com Licensee: Birach Broadcasting Corp. (group owner; acq 11-6-2001; $1.9 million with WMFN(AM) Zeeland). Population served: 1,000,000 Natl. Network: CBS, Westwood One, . Format: Rgnl Mexican. Target aud: 30 plus. ◆Efraim Cano, gen mgr.

Rogers City

WHAK(AM)— May 1949: 960 khz; 5 kw-D. TL: N45 23 53 W83 55 19. Hrs open: 1491 M-32 W., Alpena , 49707. Phone: (989) 354-4611. Fax: (989) 354-4014.E-mail: tnrn@charterinternet.com Web Site:www.1007theundercountry.com Licensee: Edwards Communications LC Natl. Rep: Michigan Spot Sales,. Format: Country. Target aud: 18-75. ◆Darrell Kelly, progmg dir; Mary Garrow, natl sls mgr & traf mgr.

WHAK-FM— April 1994: 99.9 mhz; 50 kw. 476 ft TL: N45 23 53 W83 55 19. Hrs open: 1491 M-32 W., Alpena, 49707. Phone: (989) 354-4611. Fax: (989) 354-4014.E-mail: tnrn@charterinternet.com Web Site:www.999thewave.com Licensee: Edwards Communications LC Group owner: Northern Radio Network (acq 12-21-2004; grpsl). Format: Oldies. ◆Tony Calumet, gen mgr & gen sls mgr; Danny Stann, progmg dir; Phil Heimerl, news dir; Darrel Kelly, chief of engrg; Mary Garrow, traf mgr.

WRGZ(FM)— June 16, 1984: 96.7 mhz; 42 kw. Ant 531 ft TL: N45 21 02 W83 46 59. Stereo. Hrs open:
Simulcast with WATZ-FM Alpena 100%.
Box 536, Alpena, 49707. Secondary address: 123 Prentiss St., Alpena 49707. Phone: (989) 354-8400. Fax: (989) 354-3436.E-mail: watz@watz.com Web Site:www.watz.com Licensee: WATZ Radio Inc. (acq 5-26-2006; $411,000). Format: Country. ◆Mike Centala, gen mgr.

Roscommon

WQON(FM)— March 1990: 101.1 mhz; 3.4 kw. Ant 444 ft TL: N44 34 31 W84 42 19. Stereo. Hrs open: 24 6514 Old Lake Rd., Grayling, 49738. Phone: (989) 348-6171. Fax: (989) 348-6181.E-mail: radio@i2k.net Web Site:www.gannonbroadcasting.com Licensee: Gannon Broadcasting Systems Inc. (acq 9-88). Population served: 50,000 Natl. Rep: Michigan Spot Sales,. Format: Adult contemp. News staff: one; News: 16 hrs wkly. Target aud: 25 plus. ◆William Gannon, gen mgr; Pete Michaels, opns mgr.

Rose Township

*****WMSD(FM)**— Aug 11, 2000: 90.9 mhz; 5 kw vert. Ant 69 ft TL: N44 25 58 W84 00 33. Stereo. Hrs open: 24 2906 E Heath Rd., Lupton, 48635. Phone: (989) 473-4616.E-mail: wmsd@M33access.com Web Site:bbc.northern-michigan.net Licensee: Bible Baptist Church. Population served: 90,000 Format: Relg. ◆Paul E. Heaton, pres & stn mgr; Paul Heaton, progmg mgr.

Royal Oak

WEXL(AM)— October 1923: 1340 khz; 1 kw-U, DA-D. TL: N42 28 25 W83 06 56. Hrs open: 24 12300 Radio Pl., Detroit, 48228. Phone: (313) 272-3434.E-mail: station@wmuz.com Web Site:www.wexl1340.com Licensee: WMUZ Radio Inc. Group owner: Crawford Broadcasting Co. (acq 4-18-97; $3.5 million). Population served: 3,500,000 Format: Gospel. Target aud: General. ◆Frank Franciosi, gen mgr; Rich Hanovich, opns mgr.

Rust Township

*****WSFP(FM)**— 2006: 88.5 mhz; 480 w. Ant 472 ft TL: N45 03 50 W83 42 57. Hrs open:
Simulcasts WJOM(FM) Eagle 100%.
Michigan Community Radio, 148 E Grand River Rd, Williamston, 48895. Phone: (517) 381-0573.E-mail: info@wkkmfm.com Web Site:www.smile.fm Licensee: Michigan Community Radio. Format: Contemp Christian. ◆Edward Czelada, pres.

Saginaw

WGER(FM)— Feb 19, 1969: 106.3 mhz; 4.4 kw. Ant 380 ft TL: N43 28 36 W83 57 06. Hrs open: 1795 Tittabawassee, 48604. Phone: (989) 752-3456. Fax: (989_754-5046. Web Site:www.mix1063fm.com Population served: 750,000 Format: Adult Contemporary. Target aud: 25-54; upscale, mid/high level income. ◆Brian "Fig" Figula, progmg dir.

WHNN(FM)—See Bay City

WILZ(FM)— 1992: 104.5 mhz; 2.9 kw. Ant 413 ft TL: N43 23 34 W83 55 37. Hrs open: 1740 Champagne Dr. N., 48604. Phone: (989) 776-2100. Fax: (989) 754-5990.E-mail: info@wheelz.fm Web Site:www.wheelz.fm Licensee: Citadel Broadcasting Co. Group owner: Citadel Broadcasting Corp. (acq 2-8-99). Natl. Rep: McGavren Guild,. Reddy, Begley & McCormick. Format: Classic rock. Target aud: 35-54; adults. ◆Scott Meier, VP, gen mgr; Stan Parman, progmg dir; Hal Maas, mus dir; Bob Friedle, chief of engrg.

WIOG(FM)—See Bay City

WKCQ(FM)— 1947: 98.1 mhz; 50 kw. 500 ft TL: N43 25 04 W83 58 06. Stereo. Hrs open: Prog sep from AM Box 1776, 48601. Phone: (989) 752-8161. Fax: (989) 752-8102. Web Site:www.98fmkcq.com Population served: 91,849 Format: Country. Spec prog: Ger 3 hrs wkly. ◆Duane Alverson, pres; Mike Skot, opns mgr; Mary Yearham, gen sls mgr, traf mgr.

WMAX(AM)—(Bay City, June 5, 1925: 1440 khz; 5 kw-D, 2.5 kw-N, DA-2. TL: N43 31 27 W83 57 58. Hrs open: 24
WDEO(AM) Ypsilanti 97%.
1 Ave. Maria Drive, Box 504, Ann Arbor, 48106-0504. Phone: (734) 930-5200. Fax: (989) 930-3101.E-mail: mjones@avemariaradio.net Web Site:www.avemariaradio.net Licensee: 990 Investors L.L.C. (acq

6-01; $650,000). Population served: 1,500,000 Natl. Network: EWTN Radio, . Format: Catholic, talk. News staff: 2; News: 14 hrs wkly. Target aud: 25-54; adult Christian. ◆Al Kresta, CEO; Michael P. Jones, exec VP & gen mgr.

WSAM(AM)— 1940: 1400 khz; 1 kw-U. TL: N43 25 00 W83 55 05. Hrs open: Box 1776, 48601. Phone: (989) 752-8161. Fax: (989) 752-8102. Web Site:thebay104fm.com Licensee: MacDonald Broadcasting Co. (group owner; acq 12-20-2001; grpsl). Population served: 400,000 Natl. Rep: D & R Radio,. Fletcher, Heald & Hildreth. Format: Soft rock. Target aud: 25 plus. ◆Kenneth MacDonald Jr., CEO; Duane Alverson, pres, gen mgr; Jocelyn Hall, VP, news rptr; Mary Yearham, gen sls mgr; Jim Kramer, progmg dir; Gary Harding, chief of engrg.

WSGW(AM)— Aug 11, 1950: 790 khz; 5 kw-D, 1 kw-N, DA-2. TL: N43 27 40 W83 48 48. Hrs open: 24 1795 Tittabawassee, 48604. Phone: (989) 752-3456. Fax: (989) 754-5046.E-mail: info@wsgw.com Web Site:www.wsgw.com Licensee: NM Licensing LLC. Group owner: NextMedia Group L.L.C. (acq 12-30-2002; grpsl). Population served: 91,849 Natl. Network: CBS, . Rgnl. Network: Mich. Farm. Mich. Farm Format: News/talk. News staff: 5; News: 40 hrs wkly. Target aud: 35-54; general. Spec prog: Farm 10 hrs wkly. ◆Shannone Dunlap, gen mgr; Dave Maurer, opns dir, progmg dir, news dir; Doug Brinks, chief of engrg; Terry Henne, farm dir.

WSGW-FM—(Carrollton, Mar 11, 1991): 100.5 mhz; 3 kw. Ant 328 ft TL: N43 33 43 W85 58 54. Stereo. Hrs open: 24 1795 Tittabauassee Rd., 48604. Phone: (989) 752-3456. Fax: (989) 754-5046.E-mail: info@fmtalk1005.com Web Site:www.fmtalk1005.com Licensee: NM Licensing LLC. Group owner: NextMedia Group L.L.C. (acq 12-30-2002; grpsl). Population served: 1,047,321 Wire Svc: Metro Weather Service Inc. Format: Talk. News staff: one. Target aud: 18-49; women & teens. ◆Shannone Dunlap, gen mgr; David Mauer, opns mgr, progmg dir, news dir.

WTLZ(FM)— Nov 15, 1968: 107.1 mhz; 4.9 kw. 400 ft TL: N43 21 14 W83 55 06. Stereo. Hrs open: 24 1795 Tittabawassee Rd., 48604. Phone: (989) 752-3456. Fax: (989) 754-5046. Web Site:www.hotwtlz.com Licensee: NM Licensing LLC. Group owner: NextMedia Group L.L.C. (acq 12-30-02). Population served: 234,000 Natl. Network: American Urban, . Pepper & Corazzini. Format: Rhythm and blues. News: 6 hrs wkly. Target aud: 18-49; upscale, Blacks, women. Spec prog: Gospel 6 hrs wkly. ◆Shannone Dunlap, gen mgr; Yvonne Daniels, progmg dir.

Saint Ignace

WIDG(AM)— June 7, 1966: 940 khz; 5 kw-D. TL: N45 52 04 W84 47 09. Hrs open: Sunrise-sunset Box 1109, Indian River, 49749. Phone: (231) 238-0811. Fax: (231) 238-0803. Web Site:www.baragabroadcasting.com Licensee: Baraga Broadcasting Inc. (group owner; acq 11-26-2008; $100,000). Population served: 3,130 Format: Catholic. ◆Harry Speckman, gen mgr.

WMKC(FM)— Feb 8, 1982: 102.9 mhz; 100 kw. Ant 374 ft TL: N45 52 07 W84 47 09. Stereo. Hrs open: Web Site:www.countrydj.com Population served: 351,000 Format: Country. ◆Chris Monk, VP.

Saint Johns

WQTX(FM)— July 15, 1972: 92.1 mhz; 6 kw. Ant 400 ft TL: N42 53 29 W84 34 27. Stereo. Hrs open: 24 2495 N. Cedar, Holt, 48842. Phone: (517) 699-0111. Fax: (517) 699-1880.E-mail: wqtx@wqtx.net Web Site:www.wqtx.net Licensee: Rubber City Radio Group. Group owner: Rubber City Radio Group Inc. (acq 7-12-2000; grpsl). Population served: 397,000 Natl. Network: Jones Radio Networks, . Natl. Rep: Katz Radio,. Wire Svc: AP Format: Classic hits. News staff: one; News: 8 hrs wkly. Target aud: 35 plus. ◆Thomas Mandel, pres; Mark Biviano, exec VP; Dave Johnson, gen mgr; Drew Henderson, progmg dir.

WWSJ(AM)— Sept 23, 1959: 1580 khz; 1 kw-D, DA. TL: N42 58 14 W84 32 59. Hrs open: 24 Box 451, 1363 W. Parks Rd., St. John, 48879. Phone: (989) 224-7911. Fax: (989) 224-4683.E-mail: info@wwsj.com Web Site:www.wwsj.com Licensee: L. Harp, H. Harp, W. Hill, Elmira Hill. (acq 1-97; $160,000; 3-20-95). Natl. Network: American Urban, . Format: Urban gospel. ◆Larry Harp, pres; Danielle Beckley, prom VP; Helen Harp, progmg dir; Dione Harp, mus dir; Ed Czelada, chief of engrg.

Saint Joseph

WHFB(AM)—See Benton Harbor-St. Joseph

WHFB-FM—See Benton Harbor-St. Joseph

WIRX(FM)—Licensed to Saint Joseph. See Benton Harbor-St. Joseph

WSJM(AM)—Licensed to Saint Joseph. See Benton Harbor-St. Joseph

Saint Louis

WFYC(AM)—See Alma

WMLM(AM)— Dec 15, 1977: 1520 khz; 1 kw-U, DA-2. TL: N43 21 08 W84 36 15. Hrs open: 24 Box 17, 48880. Secondary address: 4170 N. State Rd., Alma 48801. Phone: (989) 463-4013. Fax: (989) 463-4014.E-mail: wmlm@cmsinter.net Web Site:www.wmlm.com Licensee: Siefker Broadcasting Corp. Population served: 150,000 Natl. Network: ABC, . Format: Country. Target aud: 35 plus. Spec prog: Farm 5 hrs, gospel 2 hrs wkly. ◆Gregory Siefker, pres & gen mgr.

WQBX(FM)—See Alma

Salem Township

WSDS(AM)—Licensed to Salem Township. See Ann Arbor

Saline

WLBY(AM)— 1958: 1290 khz; 500 w-D, DA. TL: N42 12 17 W83 47 19. Hrs open: Sunrise-sunset 1100 Victors Way, Suite 100, Ann Arbor, 48108. Phone: (734) 302-8100. Fax: (734) 213-7508. Web Site:www.1290wlby.com Licensee: Capstar TX L.P. Group owner: Clear Channel Communications Inc. (acq 8-7-2000; grpsl). Population served: 231,600 Natl. Rep: Cumulus Radio Sales,. Wire Svc: AP Format: Business talk. News staff: one; News: 15 hrs wkly. ◆Scott Meier, gen mgr; Brent Dingman, gen sls mgr.

Sandusky

WMIC(AM)— June 27, 1968: 660 khz; 1 kw-D, DA. TL: N43 23 34 W82 49 57. Hrs open: 19 S. Elk St., 48471. Phone: (810) 648-2700. Fax: (810) 648-3242.E-mail: wmic@avc1.net Licensee: Sanilac Broadcasting Co. Population served: 1,000,000 Rgnl. Network: Mich. Farm. Mich. Farm Format: Country, news/talk. News staff: 2; News: 20 hrs wkly. Target aud: 25 plus; general. Spec prog: Farm 12 hrs, Pol 5 wkly. ◆George E. Benko, pres; Robert Benko, VP; Bob Armstrong, gen mgr, gen sls mgr; Stan Grabitz, mus dir; Renae Davis, news dir; Kevin Larke, chief of engrg.

*WNFR(FM)— Feb 14, 1994: 90.7 mhz; 18 kw. 328 ft TL: N43 27 32 W82 57 42. Stereo. Hrs open:
Rebroadcasts WNFA(FM) Port Huron 100%.
Wonderful News Radio, 2865 Maywood Dr., Port Huron, 48060. Phone: (810) 985-3260. Fax: (810) 985-7712. Web Site:www.wnradio.com Licensee: Ross Bible Church. Population served: 100,000 Natl. Network: Moody, USA, . Southmayd & Miller. Format: Relg, inspirational. Target aud: 25-44; females. ◆Lori McNaughton, opns mgr; Ellyn Davey, mus dir, news dir; Ed Czelada, chief of engrg.

WTGV-FM— Aug 16, 1971: 97.7 mhz; 3 kw. 325 ft TL: N43 23 33 W82 49 56. Stereo. Hrs open: 24 Prog sep from AM 19 S. Elk St., 48471. Phone: (810) 648-2700. Fax: (810) 648-3242.E-mail: renaed@sanilacbroadcasting.com Licensee: Sanilac Broadcasting Co Population served: 50,000 Format: Adult contemp.

Saugatuck

WYVN(FM)— July 4, 1987: 92.7 mhz; 2.15 kw. 387 ft TL: N42 41 10 W86 10 05. Stereo. Hrs open: 24 87 Central Ave., Holland, 49423. Phone: (616) 392-3121. Fax: (616) 392-8066.E-mail: advertising@thevan.fm Web Site:www.thevan.fm Licensee: Midwest Communications Inc. (group owner; acq 9-5-2001). Natl. Rep: Christal,. Format: Classic hits. News staff: one; News: one hr wkly. Target aud: 25-54. ◆D.E. Wright, pres; Peter Tanz, mktg mgr; Brent Alan, progmg dir; Gary Stevens, news dir, sls.

Sault Ste. Marie

*WCMZ-FM— July 13, 1990: 98.3 mhz; 25 kw. 328 ft TL: N46 29 10 W84 13 49. Stereo. Hrs open: 24
Rebroadcasts WCMU-FM Mount Pleasant 100%.
Central Michigan Univ., 1999 E. Campus Dr., Mount Pleasant, 48859. Phone: (989) 774-3105. Fax: (989) 774-4427.E-mail: cmuradio@radio.cmich.edu Web Site:www.wcmu.org Licensee: Central Michigan University. Natl. Network: NPR, PRI, . Rgnl. Network: Mich. Pub. Mich. Radio Dow, Lohnes & Albertson. Wire Svc: AP Format: Class, jazz, news. News staff: 3; News: 45 hrs wkly. Target aud: General. ◆Ed Grant, gen mgr; Ann Blatte, dev dir, prom mgr; Art Curtis, rgnl sls mgr, mktg dir; Ray Ford, progmg dir; Randy Kapenga, chief of engrg.

WKNW(AM)— Aug 25, 1990: 1400 khz; 250 w-U. TL: N46 29 18 W84 19 45. Stereo. Hrs open: 24 Prog sep from FM 1402 Ashmun St., 49783. Phone: (906) 635-0995. Fax: (906) 635-1216. Web Site:www.talkradio1400.com Licensee: Northern Star Broadcasting L.L.C. Format: Sports, news/talk. ◆Paul Van Wagner, progmg dir.

*WLSO(FM)— 1995: 90.1 mhz; 100 w. 98 ft TL: N46 29 31 W84 21 48. Hrs open: 680 W. Easterday Ave., 49783. Phone: (906) 635-2107. Fax: (906) 635-2111.E-mail: wlso@gw.lssu.edu Web Site:www.lssu.edu/wlso Licensee: Lake Superior State University. Format: Var. ◆Scott Korb, stn mgr.

WSOO(AM)— June 1, 1940: 1230 khz; 1 kw-U. TL: N46 26 16 W84 22 42. Hrs open: Box 1230, 49783. Phone: (906) 632-2231. Fax: (906) 632-4411. Licensee: Sovereign Communications LLC (acq 12-18-03; $2.6 million with co-located FM). Population served: 15,136 Natl. Network: ABC, ESPN Radio, . Natl. Rep: Michigan Spot Sales,. Format: Adult contemp. ◆Tom Ewing, gen mgr; Linda Peters, gen sls mgr; Mark Sanangelo, progmg dir; John Bell, news dir.

WSUE(FM)— 1978: 101.3 mhz; 100 kw. 978 ft TL: N46 26 16 W84 22 42. Hrs open: Prog sep from AM Box 1230, 49783. Phone: (906) 632-2231. Fax: (906) 632-4411. Format: Classic rock.

*WTHN(FM)— Jan 29, 2005: 102.3 mhz; 22.5 kw. Ant 344 ft TL: N46 29 08 W84 13 49. Hrs open: 24
WPHN (FM) Gaylord 100%.
PO Box 695, Gaylord, 49734. Phone: (989) 732-6274. Fax: (989) 732-8171.E-mail: ncr@ncradio.org Web Site:www.ncradio.org Licensee: Northern Christian Radio Inc. (group owner). Format: Religious, Christian. ◆George A. Lake Jr., CEO & gen mgr.

WYSS(FM)— July 12, 1972: 99.5 mhz; 26.5 kw. 275 ft TL: N46 23 48 W84 23 52. (CP: 100 kw). Stereo. Hrs open: 1402 Ashmun St., 49783. Phone: (906) 635-0995. Fax: (906) 635-1216. Web Site:www.995yesfm.com Licensee: Northern Star Broadcasting L.L.C. (group owner; acq 11-5-01; grpsl). Population served: 13,000 Natl. Network: Westwood One, . Cohn & Marks. Format: CHR. Target aud: 18-49. ◆Keith Yes, gen mgr, gen sls mgr, gen sls mgr; Brian Larson, news dir, disc jockey; Carol Howe, chief of engrg; Renee Peterson, traf mgr, disc jockey; Tim Ellis, progmg dir & disc jockey.

Schoolcraft

*WOFR(FM)— May 2003: 89.5 mhz; 10 kw. Ant 138 ft TL: N42 06 38 W85 37 57. Hrs open: 24 Family Stations Inc., 4135 Northgate Blvd., Suite 1, Sacramento, CA, 95834. Phone: (916) 641-8191. Fax: (916) 641-8238. Web Site:www.familyradio.com Licensee: Family Stations Inc. (group owner). Format: Relg. ◆Harold Camping, gen mgr; Craig Hulsebos, progmg dir; Rick Prime, chief of engrg.

Scottville

WKZC(FM)— Feb 16, 1983: 94.9 mhz; 17 kw. 400 ft TL: N44 03 27 W86 24 58. Stereo. Hrs open: 24 5941 W. U.S. 10, Ludington, 49431. Phone: (231) 843-3438. Fax: (231) 843-1886.E-mail: mike@wkla.com Licensee: Lake Michigan Broadcasting Inc. (group owner; acq 9-20-96; grpsl). Population served: 70,000 Natl. Network: ABC, . Natl. Rep: Patt,. Shaw Pittman. Format: Country. News staff: one; News: 5 hrs wkly. Target aud: 25-54. ◆Lynn Baerwolf, pres & gen mgr; Jason Wilder, opns mgr, prom VP.

Shepherd

WMMI(AM)— Feb 2, 1987: 830 khz; 1 kw-D. TL: N43 33 42 W84 45 00. Stereo. Hrs open: Daytime 4065 E. Wing Rd., Mount Pleasant, 48858. Phone: (989) 772-9664. Fax: (989) 773-5000.E-mail: wczy@wczy.net Web Site:www.wczy.net Licensee: Central Michigan Communications Inc. (acq 8-15-88). Natl. Rep: Michigan Spot Sales,. Mich. Talk Rgnl rep: Patt. Reddy, Begley & McCormick. Wire Svc: AP Format: Talk. News staff: one; News: 6 hrs wkly. Target aud: 25-54; general. ◆Mike Carey, pres; John Sebastian, progmg dir; Tina Sawyer, news dir; Lisa Johnson, traf mgr.

South Haven

WCSY(AM)— 1961: 940 khz; 1 kw-D, 5 w-N, DA-2. TL: N42 24 34 W86 16 01. (CP: COL Hudsonville. 300 w-D, DA. TL: N42 47 38 W85 52 24). Hrs open: 602 Broadway, 49090. Phone: (269) 637-6397. Fax: (269) 637-2675. Licensee: WSJM Inc. (group owner; (acq 10-95; with WCXT(FM) South Haven). Population served: 300,000 Rgnl. Network: Mich. Farm. Mich. Farm Format: Nostalgia. Target aud: 35-45; females. Spec prog: Farm 3 hrs wkly. ◆Gayle Olson, pres, gen mgr; Joe Jason, stn mgr; Sue Patzer, prom dir; Joe Daguanno, adv mgr; Annette Weston, news dir.

WCSY-FM— March 1996: 103.7 mhz; 3 kw. Ant 328 ft TL: N42 18 02 W86 15 03. Stereo. Hrs open: 24 602 Broadway, 49090. Phone: (269) 637-6397. Phone: (269) 934-9830. Fax: (269) 637-2675.E-mail: info@cosy.fm Web Site:www.cosy.fm Licensee: WSJM Inc. Group owner: The Mid-West Family Broadcast Group (acq 4-96; grpsl). Natl. Network: ABC, . Natl. Rep: Rgnl Reps,. Davis Wright Tremaine. Wire Svc: AP Format: Super hits of the 60s & 70s. ◆Gayle Olson, gen mgr; Joe Jason, stn mgr; Joe Daguanno, sls dir; Sue Patzen, prom dir; Annette Weston, news dir; Terry Green, engrg dir & chief of engrg.

Southfield

*WSHJ(FM)— Feb 28, 1967: 88.3 mhz; 105 w. Ant 69 ft TL: N42 28 12 W83 15 51. Stereo. Hrs open: 7:30 AM-10 PM Southfield High School, 24675 Lasher Rd., 48034. Phone: (248) 746-8630. Phone: (248) 746-8631. Web Site:www.southfield.l12.mi.us/itc Licensee: Board of Education Southfield Public Schools. Population served: 69,285 Format: Oldies, hip-hop. Target aud: General; students & families. ◆Jamie Rudolph, gen mgr.

Spring Arbor

*KTGG(AM)— Aug 15, 1985: 1540 khz; 450 w-D. TL: N42 09 13 W84 32 58. Hrs open: Sunrise-sunset Spring Arbor Univ., 106 E. Main St., 49283. Phone: (517) 750-6540. Fax: (517) 750-6619.E-mail: info@home.fm Web Site:www.home.fm Licensee: Spring Arbor University. Lauren A. Colby. Format: Inspirational, relg. Target aud: 18-49; rural to urban. ◆Hal Munn, pres; Carl Fletcher, gen mgr, stn mgr; Rachel Buchanan, progmg dir & pub affrs dir.

*WJKN-FM— 2005: 89.3 mhz; 2.5 kw vert. Ant 272 ft TL: N42 09 13 W84 32 57. Hrs open: Spring Arbor Univ., 106 E. Main St., 49283. Phone: (517) 750-6540. Fax: (517) 750-6619.E-mail: info@893themessage.com Web Site:www.893themessage.com Licensee: Spring Arbor University. Format: Christian. ◆Malachi Crane, gen mgr; Rachel Ryder, mus dir; Dave Benson, chief of engrg.

WSAE(FM)—Listing follows KTGG(AM).

Springfield

*WCFG(FM)—Not on air, target date: 2008: 90.9 mhz; 700 w vert. Ant 351 ft TL: N42 21 20 W85 20 28. Hrs open: 24 1159 E. Beltline Ave. N.E., Grand Rapids, 49525-5805. Phone: (616) 942-1500. Fax: (616) 942-7078.E-mail: wcsg@wcsg.org Web Site:www.wcsg.org Licensee: Cornerstone University. Format: Christian, adult contemp. Target aud: 35-49. ◆Chris Lemke, gen mgr.

Standish

WWCM(FM)— January 1990: 96.9 mhz; 3 kw. Ant 328 ft TL: N44 02 08 W84 00 31. Stereo. Hrs open: 24
Rebroadcasts WCMU-FM Mount Pleasant 100%.
Public Broadcasting Ctr., 1999 E. Campus Dr., Mount Pleasant, 48859. Phone: (989) 774-3105. Fax: (989) 774-4427.E-mail: cmuradio@radio.cmich.edu Web Site:www.wcmu.org Licensee: Central Michigan University (acq 9-14-00). Format: Class, jazz, news & info. Target aud: General. ◆Ed Grant, gen mgr.

Stephenson

WMXG(FM)— 1999: 106.3 mhz; 50 kw. Ant 492 ft TL: N45 38 36 W87 22 37. Hrs open: 1101 A Ludington St., Escanaba, 49829. Phone: (906) 786-0060. Fax: (906) 786-2990.E-mail: mix106@chartermi.net Web Site:www.wmxg.com Licensee: Pacer Radio of the Near-North. Format: Classic Hits, Todays Hits. ◆Mike DuBord, gen mgr.

Sterling Heights

*WUFL(AM)— Oct 26, 1988: 1030 khz; 5 kw-D, DA. TL: N42 36 19 W82 54 37. Hrs open: Daytime Box 1030, 48311. Secondary address: 42669 Garfield Rd. , Suite 328 , Clinton Township 48038 . Phone: (586) 263-1030. Fax: (586) 228-1030.E-mail: wufl@flc.org Web Site:wufl.org Licensee: Family Life Broadcasting System. (group owner; acq 10-25-88). Natl. Network: USA, . Format: Relg, Christian. News: 45 min wkly. Target aud: 35-54; Women. ◆Donald D. Aupperle, stn mgr.

Sturgis

WMSH(AM)— 1951: 1230 khz; 1 kw-U, DA-1. TL: N41 46 11 W85 25 09. (CP: 2.16 kw). Hrs open: Box 7080, 49091. Secondary address: 70808 S. Nottawa Rd. 49091. Phone: (269) 651-2383. Phone: (269) 651-2384. Fax: (269) 659-1111.E-mail: wmsh@wmshradio.com Web Site:www.wmshradio.com Licensee: Lake Cities Broadcasting Corp. (group owner; acq 1-12-98; $600,000 with co-located FM). Population served: 100,000 Natl. Network: ABC, ESPN Radio, . Natl. Rep: Michigan Spot Sales,. Format: All sports. Target aud: 25-54. ◆Carter Snider, gen mgr, sls VP, gen sls mgr, progmg dir; Mike Stiles, news dir.

WMSH-FM— 1951: 99.3 mhz; 2.15 kw. Ant 390 ft TL: N41 46 11 W85 25 09. Stereo. Hrs open: Box 7080, 49091. Phone: (269) 651-2383. Fax: (269) 659-1111. Web Site:www.wmshradio.com Licensee: Lake Cities Broadcasting Corp. Format: Oldies.

Tawas City

*WGJU(FM)—Not on air, target date: unknown: 88.9 mhz; 3.4 kw vert. Ant 302 ft TL: N44 24 47.9 W83 37 14. Hrs open: 411 N. Wilkinson, East Tawas, 48730. Phone: (989) 362-5651. Licensee: Holy Family School. Natl. Network: EWTN Radio, . ◆Linda D. Howe, chmn.

*WHST(FM)— Nov 1, 1972: 106.1 mhz; 6 kw. 280 ft TL: N44 16 27 W83 39 42. Stereo. Hrs open: 24
Rebroadcasts WPHN(FM) Gaylord 100%.
Box 695, Gaylord, 49734. Phone: (989) 732-6274. Fax: (989) 732-8171.E-mail: ncr@ncradio.org Web Site:www.ncradio.org Licensee: Northern Christian Radio Inc. (group owner; acq 7-19-01). Population served: 75,000 Format: Religious, Christian. Target aud: 25-54. ◆George A. Lake Jr., gen mgr.

WIOS(AM)— Sept 27, 1958: 1480 khz; 1 kw-D, DA. TL: N44 15 48 W83 32 42. Hrs open: Box 549, 48764. Secondary address: 523 Meadow Rd. 48763. Phone: (989) 362-3417. Fax: (989) 362-4544.E-mail: wkjc@wkjc.com Licensee: Carroll Enterprises Inc. (group owner; (acq 5-1-69). Population served: 50,000 Rgnl. Network: Mich. Farm. Natl. Rep: Michigan Spot Sales,. Mich. Farm Booth, Freret, Imlay & Tepper P. Format: Easy Istng, talk. Target aud: 25 plus; general. Spec prog: Big band 6 hrs wkly. ◆John Carroll Jr., CEO, pres, gen mgr; John Carroll Sr., chmn; Tim Carroll, gen sls mgr.

WKJC(FM)— October 1979: 104.7 mhz; 50 kw. Ant 492 ft TL: N44 24 43 W83 37 17. Stereo. Hrs open: Box 549, 48764. Secondary address: 523 Meadow Rd. 48763. Phone: (989) 362-3417. Fax: (989) 362-4544.E-mail: wkjc@wkjc.com Web Site:www.wkjc.com Licensee: Carroll Enterprises Inc. Population served: 750,000 Format: Modern C&W.

WQLB(FM)— July 1997: 103.3 mhz; 25 kw. 328 ft TL: N44 21 06 W83 31 39. Hrs open: Box 549, 48764. Phone: (989) 362-3417. Fax: (989) 362-4544.E-mail: wkjc@wkjc.com Web Site:www.wkjc.com Licensee: Carroll Broadcasting Inc. (acq 12-1-97). Minn. News Net. Booth, Freret, Imlay & Tepper. Format: Classic rock. ◆John Carroll Jr., gen mgr; Tim Carroll, gen sls mgr; Deb Michaels, progmg dir; Marvin Walther, chief of engrg; Mary Hill, traf mgr.

Taylor

WCHB(AM)— 1990: 1200 khz; 25 kw-D, 15 kw-N, DA-2. TL: N42 09 24 W83 19 56. Hrs open: 3250 Franklin St., Detroit, 48207. Phone: (313) 259-2000. Fax: (313) 259-7011. Web Site:www.wchb1200.com Licensee: Radio One of Detroit LLC. Group owner: Radio One Inc. (acq 6-19-98; $34.2 million with WDTJ(FM) Detroit). Population served: 151,148 Format: Gospel. Target aud: Adults 25-54. ◆Alfred Liggins, pres; Dr. Wendell Cox, VP; Carol Lawrence-Dobrusin, gen mgr.

Three Rivers

WLKM-FM— March 1975: 95.9 mhz; 3 kw. Ant 315 ft TL: N41 55 43 W85 38 15. Stereo. Hrs open: 24 59750 Constantine Rd., 49093-9394. Phone: (269) 278-1815. Fax: (269) 273-7975.E-mail: info@wlkm.com

Web Site:www.wlkm.com Licensee: Impact Radio LLC Population served: 50,000 Natl. Network: CNN Radio, . Rgnl rep: Patt Media Sales Wire Svc: AP Format: Classic hits. News staff: one; News: 2 hrs wkly. Target aud: 25-54. ◆Kathy Loker, gen sls mgr; Walker Sisson, chief of engrg.

WRCI(AM)— May 3, 1962: 1520 khz; 430 w-D, 8 w-N. TL: N41 55 43 W85 38 15. Hrs open: 24 59750 Constantine Rd., 49093-9394. Phone: (269) 278-1815. Fax: (269) 273-7975.E-mail: info@wlkm.com Web Site:www.wlkm.com Licensee: Impact Radio LLC (group owner; acq 8-1-2002; grpsl). Population served: 30,000 Natl. Network: AP Radio, Jones Radio Networks, . Rgnl. Network: Mich. Farm. Mich. Radio Rgnl rep: Patt Media Sales Irwin, Campbell & Tannenwald. Format: Classic country. News staff: one; News: 14 hrs wkly. Target aud: General. ◆Dennis Rumsey, pres; Kathy Loker, gen sls mgr; Walker Sisson, gen mgr & chief of engrg.

Traverse City

WCCW(AM)— July 15, 1960: 1310 khz; 15 kw-D, 7.5 kw-N, DA-2. TL: N44 40 38 W85 39 56. Hrs open: 300 E. Front, Suite 450, 49684. Phone: (231) 946-6211. Fax: (231) 946-1914. Web Site:www.wccwi.com Licensee: Midwestern Broadcasting Co. (group owner; (acq 9-16-96; $2.2 million with co-located FM). Population served: 18,048 Natl. Rep: Michigan Spot Sales, Katz Radio,. Format: Sports. ◆Hal Payne, sls mgr; John Patrick, natl sls mgr; Dave Gauthier, progmg dir.

WCCW-FM— Nov 8, 1967: 107.5 mhz; 50 kw. 518 ft TL: N44 46 11 W85 41 22. (CP: 660 w, ant 702 ft. TL: N44 46 02 W85 41 26). Stereo. Hrs open: Prog sep from AM 300 E. Front, Suite 450, 49684. Phone: (231) 946-6211. Fax: (231) 946-1914. Web Site:www.wccwi.com Format: Oldies.

*WICA(FM)— Sept 13, 2000: 91.5 mhz; 4 kw. Ant 748 ft TL: N44 45 22 W85 40 42. Stereo. Hrs open: 24 Box 199, Interlochen, 49643. Phone: (231) 276-4400. Fax: (231) 276-4417.E-mail: ipr@interlochen.org Web Site:www.interlochen.org/ipr Licensee: Interlochen Center for the Arts. Population served: 81,000 Wire Svc: AP Format: News, talk. News staff: 4; News: 168 hrs wkly. Target aud: 25-80. ◆Thom Paulson, VP & stn mgr.

WLDR-FM— July 17, 1966: 101.9 mhz; 100 kw. Ant 538 ft TL: N44 46 13 W85 41 43. (CP: Ant 630 ft.). Stereo. Hrs open: 24 13999 S. W. Bay Shore Dr., 49684. Phone: (231) 352-9603. Fax: (231) 352-7877.E-mail: wldr@wldr.com Web Site:www.wldr.com Licensee: Great Northern Broadcasting System Inc. Group owner: Fort Bend Broadcasting Co. (acq 4-10-2001; $3.6 million for stock). Population served: 250,000 Format: Country. News staff: one. Target aud: 25-54. ◆Roy Henderson, CEO, gen mgr; Steve Smith, CFO.

*WLJN-FM— Oct 1, 1989: 89.9 mhz; 39 kw vert. Ant 554 ft TL: N44 46 36 W85 39 43. Stereo. Hrs open: 24 Box 1400, 49685. Secondary address: 1101 Cass St., Traverse 49684. Phone: (231) 946-1400. Fax: (231) 946-3959.E-mail: info@wljn.com Web Site:www.wljn.com Licensee: Good News Media Inc. (group owner). Format: Relg, Christian music. News: 4 hrs wkly. Target aud: General. ◆Brian Harcey, gen mgr; Pete Lathrop, progmg dir & news dir.

WLXT(FM)—See Petoskey

*WNMC-FM— October 1967: 90.7 mhz; 600 w. 538 ft TL: N44 46 36 W85 41 02. Stereo. Hrs open: 8 AM-2 AM 1701 E. Front St., 49686. Phone: (231) 995-2562. Phone: (231) 883-4753. Fax: (231) 922-8963. Web Site:www.wnmc.org Licensee: Northwestern Michigan College. Population served: 25,000 Format: Div, jazz, rock,blues. Spec prog: American Indian one hr, Black 20 hrs, folk 11 hrs, Sp 2 hrs wkly. ◆Eric Hines, gen mgr.

WTCM(AM)— 1941: 580 khz; 50 kw-D, 1.1 kw-N, DA-2. TL: N44 43 18 W85 42 18. Stereo. Hrs open: 24 314 E. Front St., 49684. Phone: (231) 947-7675. Fax: (231) 929-3988. Web Site:www.wtcmi.com Licensee: WTCM Radio Inc. Group owner: Midwestern Broadcasting Co. Population served: 500,000 Cordon & Kelly. Format: News/talk. News staff: 4; News: 12 hrs wkly. Target aud: 25-54. Spec prog: Farm 5 hrs wkly. ◆Ross Biederman, pres; Chris Warren, gen mgr; Paul Binsfeld, gen sls mgr; David Barr, prom dir; Jack O'Malley, progmg dir; Joel Frank, news dir.

WTCM-FM— Dec 13, 1965: 103.5 mhz; 100 kw. 989 ft TL: N44 27 31 W85 42 02. Stereo. Hrs open: 24 Prog sep from AM 314 E. Front St., 49684. Phone: (231) 947-7675. Fax: (231) 929-3988. Web Site:www.wtcmi.com Population served: 500,000 Format: Country. Target aud: 25-54.

Trout Lake

*WHWG(FM)— 1999: 89.9 mhz; 500 w. Ant 390 ft TL: N46 11 17 W84 56 46. Hrs open:
Rebroadcasts WHWL(FM) Marquette 100%.
130 Carmen Dr., Marquette, 49855. Phone: (906) 249-1423. Fax: (906) 249-4042.E-mail: whwl@whwl.net Web Site:www.gospelopportunities.com Licensee: Gospel Opportunities Inc. Format: Relg. ◆W. Curtis Marker, gen mgr & progmg dir.

Tuscola

WWBN(FM)— Sept 14, 1987: 101.5 mhz; 1.8 kw. Ant 489 ft TL: N43 12 00 W83 33 30. Stereo. Hrs open: 24 3338 E. Bristol Rd., Burton, 48529. Phone: (810) 742-1470. Fax: (810) 742-5170.E-mail: info@banana1015.com Web Site:www.banana1015.com Licensee: Regent Broadcasting of Flint Inc. Group owner: Regent Communications Inc. (acq 12-19-97; grpsl). Natl. Rep: Katz Radio,. Format: Rock/AOR. News staff: one; News: 20 hrs wkly. Target aud: 18-49; men. ◆Bill Stakelin, pres; Fred Murr, sr VP; J. Patrick, opns VP & opns mgr; Brian Beddow, progmg dir.

Twin Lake

*WBLV(FM)— July 3, 1982: 90.3 mhz; 100 kw. Ant 649 ft TL: N43 33 00 W86 02 34. Stereo. Hrs open: 24
Rebroadcasts WBLU-FM Grand Rapids 100%.
Blue Lake Fine Arts Camp, 300 East Crystal Lake Rd., 49457-9592. Phone: (231) 894-2616. Fax: (231) 893-2457.E-mail: radio@bluelake.org Web Site:www.bluelake/radio.html Licensee: Blue Lake Fine Arts Camp. Natl. Network: PRI, NPR, . Rgnl. Network: Mich. Pub. Minn. Pub. Radio Booth, Freret, Imlay & Tepper. Format: Class, jazz, news. News: 20 hrs wkly. Target aud: Adult. Spec prog: Folk 5 hrs wkly. ◆Dave Myers, gen mgr; Steve Albert, progmg dir.

Vassar

WOWE(FM)— July 1, 1990: 98.9 mhz; 3 kw. 328 ft TL: N43 17 56 W83 30 34. Hrs open: 126 W. Kearsley St., Flint, 48502. Phone: (810) 234-4335. Fax: (810) 234-7286.E-mail: wowe@sbcglobal.net Licensee: Praestantia Broadcasting Inc. Format: Urban contemp. ◆Michael Shumpert, pres, gen mgr, progmg dir & chief of engrg.

Walhalla

WRAX(FM)—Not on air, target date: unknown: 98.9 mhz; 6 kw. Ant 328 ft TL: N43 52 51 W86 13 04. Hrs open: 1717 Dixie Hwy., Suite 650, Fort Wright, KY, 41011. Phone: (859) 331-9100. Licensee: Radioactive LLC. ◆Benjamin L. Homel, pres.

Walker

WTRV(FM)— June 15, 1993: 100.5 mhz; 3 kw. Ant 328 ft TL: N43 00 59 W85 44 24. Hrs open: 24 50 Monroe N.W., Suite 500, Grand Rapids, 49503. Phone: (616) 451-4800. Fax: (616) 451-0113. Web Site:www.theriver-fm.com Licensee: Regent Broadcasting of Grand Rapids Inc. Group owner: Regent Communications Inc. (acq 8-7-00; grpsl). Natl. Rep: Katz Radio,. Format: Soft adult contemp. Target aud: 35-64. ◆Phil Catlett, gen mgr; Paul Boscarino, sls dir; Mark Renzenbrink, gen sls mgr; Nikki Havener, prom dir; Gene Parker, mus dir; Chuck Latour, news dir; Mike Maciejewski, engrg dir; Kathie Bogerd, traf mgr.

Walled Lake

WPON(AM)— December 1954: 1460 khz; 1 kw-D, 760 w-N, DA-2. TL: N42 32 38 W83 29 58. Hrs open: 24 21700 Northwestern Hwy., Suite 1190, Southfield, 48075. Phone: (248) 557-3500. Fax: (248) 557-4321.E-mail: wpon@wpon.com Web Site:www.wpon.com Licensee: Birach Broadcasting Corp. (group owner; acq 5-25-2004; $800,000). Population served: 3,750,000 Format: Oldies, talk. News staff: . Target aud: 35-65; 35 and above. ◆Sima Birach, gen mgr; Jimmie James, stn mgr, opns mgr.

Warren

*WPHS(FM)— Mar 20, 1964: 89.1 mhz; 100 w. Ant 98 ft TL: N42 31 00 W83 00 36. Stereo. Hrs open: 6:30 AM-8:30 PM P.K. Cousino High School, 30333 Hoover Rd., 48093. Secondary address: Warren Consolidated Schools, 31300 Anita 48093. Phone: (586) 698-4501.E-mail: wphs@wphs.com Web Site:www.wphs.com Licensee: Warren Consolidated Schools. (acq 1963). Population served: 2,000,000 Format: Techno. News staff: 2; News: 10 hrs wkly. Target aud: 12-27; males. Spec prog: Blues 3 hrs, Pol 2 hrs, news 5 hrs, country 4 hrs, Christian rock 4 hrs wkly. ◆Jenny S. Stanczyk, gen mgr.

West Branch

WBMI(FM)— Nov 7, 1977: 105.5 mhz; 6 kw. Ant 298 ft TL: N44 17 57 W84 15 54. Stereo. Hrs open: Box 807, 48661. Phone: (989) 345-4269. Fax: (989) 345-3996. Licensee: Peggy R. Warner (acq 4-14-2008). Population served: 11,000 Natl. Network: Jones Radio Networks, . Format: Oldies. Target aud: 25-54. Spec prog: Pol 6 hrs wkly. ◆Charlie Cobb, gen mgr, opns mgr; Mike McCall, progmg dir.

White Star

*WEJC(FM)— July 2001: 88.3 mhz; 30 kw vert. 472 ft TL: N43 57 18 W84 32 57. Hrs open: Superior Communications, Box 388, Williamson, 48895. Phone: (517) 381-0573. Fax: (877) 850-0881.E-mail: info@positivehits.com Web Site:www.positivehits.com Licensee: Superior Communications. Format: Contemporary Christian. ◆Jenn Czelada, gen mgr; Ed Czelada, progmg dir.

Whitehall

WEFG-FM— Apr 1, 1991: 97.5 mhz; 1.7 kw. Ant 426 ft TL: N43 23 04 W86 19 30. Stereo. Hrs open: 24 3375 Merriam St, Suite 201, Muskegon Heights, MS, 49444. Phone: (616) 774-8461. Fax: (616) 774-2491.E-mail: info@975thechamp.com Web Site:www.975thechamp.com Licensee: Unity Broadcasting Inc. (acq 12-16-2002; grpsl). Natl. Network: Westwood One, . Format: Sports talk. News: one hr wkly. Target aud: 25-49; male and female. ◆Jeff Morton, gen mgr; Jon Russell, opns mgr, engrg VP; John Alan, chief of engrg; Renee Dudek, gen sls mgr & traf mgr.

WGVS-FM—Licensed to Whitehall. See Muskegon

WKLQ(AM)— Oct 21, 1959: 1490 khz; 1 kw-U. TL: N43 23 04 W86 19 30. Stereo. Hrs open: 24 3375 Merriam St., Muskegon, 49444. Phone: (231) 830-0176. Fax: (231) 830-0194. Licensee: Citadel Broadcasting Co. (group owner; acq 1-19-2006; grpsl). Population served: 300,000 Format: Talk. ◆Jeff Morton, gen mgr.

Wixom

*WSHM(FM)—Not on air, target date: unknown: 88.3 mhz; 100 w vert. Ant 121 ft TL: N42 30 14 W83 34 07. Hrs open: 44764 Fenwick Dr., Canton, 48188. Phone: (313) 755-5163. Licensee: By Grace Through Faith. ◆Mark S. Ramseyer, gen mgr.

Wyoming

*WYCE(FM)— Nov 1, 1983: 88.1 mhz; 7 kw. 167 ft TL: N42 54 43 W85 41 00. Stereo. Hrs open: 24 711 Bridge St. NW, Grand Rapids, 49504. Phone: (616) 459-4788. Fax: (616) 742-0599.E-mail: comment@wyce.org Web Site:www.wyce.org Licensee: Grand Rapids Cable Access Center Inc. (acq 5-31-89; $30,616; 6-19-89). Population served: 600,000 Format: Alternative, eclectic. Target aud: 25-54; general. Spec prog: Folk one hr, Sp 10 hrs. ◆Kevin Murphy, stn mgr; Pete Bruinsma, mus dir.

WYGR(AM)— Nov 14, 1964: 1530 khz; 500 w-D. TL: N42 55 38 W85 44 50. Hrs open: Box 9591, 49509. Phone: (616) 452-8589. Phone: (616) 248-9947. Fax: (616) 248-0176. Web Site:www.wygr.net Licensee: WYGR Broadcasting. (acq 3-18-89). Natl. Rep: Patt,. Meyer, Faller, Weisman & Rosenberg. Format: Sp var. Target aud: Sp speaking Hispanics. Spec prog: Polka pops 3 hrs wkly. ◆Roland Rusticus, gen mgr, stn mgr, gen sls mgr, prom mgr, spanish dir; Scott Richards, progmg mgr, news dir & pub affrs dir; Robert Van Prooyen, chief of engrg.

Ypsilanti

WDEO(AM)—Licensed to Ypsilanti. See Ann Arbor

*WEMU(FM)— Dec 8, 1965: 89.1 mhz; 15.5 kw. Ant 289 ft TL: N42 15 48 W83 37 34. Stereo. Hrs open: 24 Box 980350, 48198-0350. Secondary address: Eastern Michigan Univ., 426 King Hall 48197. Phone: (734) 487-2229. Phone: (734) 487-8936. Fax: (734) 487-1015.E-mail: wemu@emich.edu Web Site:www.wemu.org Licensee: Eastern Michigan University. Population served: 295,000 Natl. Network: NPR, . Rgnl. Network: Mich. Pub. Cohn & Marks. Wire Svc: AP Format: News, jazz, blues. News staff: 4; News: 39 hrs wkly. Target aud: General. ◆Arthur Timko, gen mgr; Michael Jewett, opns mgr; Mary Motherwell, dev dir; Clark Smith, progmg dir, progmg mgr, news dir; Linda Yohn, mus dir; Ray Cryderman, chief of engrg.

Zeeland

*WGNB(FM)— Jan 21, 1989: 89.3 mhz; 30 kw. 499 ft TL: N42 50 14 W85 59 17. Stereo. Hrs open: 24 Box 40, 3764 84th Ave., 49464. Phone: (616) 772-7300. Fax: (616) 772-9663.E-mail: wgnb@moody.edu Web Site:www.wgnb.fm Licensee: The Moody Bible Institute of Chicago Inc. (group owner; acq 2-5-91; 2-25-91). Natl. Network: Salem Radio Network, Moody, . Southmayd & Miller. Format: Relg. News: 15 hrs wkly. Target aud: 35-54; Evangelical Christians. ◆Dr. Paul Nyquist, pres, VP; Jack Haveman, stn mgr; Scott Curtis, opns dir, opns mgr; Tom Bosscher, chief of engrg.

WJQK(FM)—Licensed to Zeeland. See Holland

WMFN(AM)— February 1990: 640 khz; 1 kw-D, 250 w-N. TL: N42 48 59 W85 57 24. Stereo. Hrs open: 24 2422 Burton S.E., Grand Rapids, 49546. Phone: (616) 949-8585. Fax: (616) 949-9262.E-mail: production@hottalk640.com Web Site:www.black-perspective.com Licensee: Birach Broadcasting Corp. (group owner; acq 11-6-01; $1.9 million with WMJH(AM) Rockford). Population served: 500,000 Natl. Network: CBS, . Format: Urban adult contemp, smooth jazz. Target aud: 25-54. ◆Tyrone Bynum, gen mgr & opns mgr.

WPNW(AM)— Nov 2, 1956: 1260 khz; 10 kw-D, 1 kw-N, DA-2. TL: N42 43 56 W86 06 06. Hrs open: 24 425 Centerstone Ct., Suite 1, 49464. Phone: (616) 931-6620. Fax: (616) 931-1280.E-mail: traffic@jq99.com Web Site:www.1260thepledge.com Licensee: Lanser Broadcasting Corp. (acq 11-1-83; $950,000; 10-3-83). Population served: 750,000 Natl. Network: CNN Radio, . Natl. Rep: Salem,. Reddy, Begley & McCormick. Format: News, talk. News staff: one; News: 9 hrs wkly. Target aud: 35 plus; mature adults. Spec prog: Sp 2 hrs, farm one hr wkly. ◆Leslie J. Lanser, pres; Bradley Lanser, exec VP; Troy West, stn mgr; Chad Millard, gen sls mgr, rgnl sls mgr; Jason Cramer, progmg dir.

Minnesota

Ada

KRJB(FM)— Sept 1, 1985: 106.3 mhz; 3 kw. 276 ft TL: N47 18 41 W96 31 13. Stereo. Hrs open: 312 W. Main St., 56510. Phone: (218) 784-2844. Fax: (218) 784-3749.E-mail: krjbada@loretel.net Web Site:www.krjbradio.com Licensee: R & J Broadcasting. (acq 10-1-87). Population served: 326,000 Rgnl. Network: MNN. MNN Format: Country. ◆Jim Birkemeyer, gen mgr, gen sls mgr, mktg VP; Woody Roux, progmg dir & news dir; Heather Krogstadt, traf mgr.

Aitkin

KKIN(AM)— June 1, 1961: 930 khz; 2.5 kw-D, 400 w-N. TL: N46 32 26 W93 39 22. Stereo. Hrs open: 24 Box 140, 56431. Secondary address: 37208 U.S. Hwy. 169 56431. Phone: (218) 927-2344. Fax: (218) 927-4090.E-mail: kkin@mlecmn.net Web Site:www.kkinradio.com Licensee: Red Rock Radio Corp. (group owner; acq 9-1-2006; grpsl). Population served: 120,000 Natl. Network: Jones Radio Networks, . Timothy K. Brady. Format: Music of Your Life. News staff: one. Target aud: General. ◆Ro Grignon, pres; Terry Dee, gen mgr.

KKIN-FM— Jan 3, 1972: 94.3 mhz; 14 kw. Ant 436 ft TL: N46 41 18 W93 35 58. Stereo. Hrs open: 24 Box 140, 56431. Secondary address: 37208 U.S. Hwy. 169 56431. Phone: (218) 927-2344. Fax: (218) 927-4090.E-mail: kkinradio@embarqmail.com Web Site:www.kkinradio.com Licensee: Red Rock Radio Corp. Population served: 120,000 Format: Classic country. News staff: one; News: 5 hrs wkly. Target aud: 35 plus.

Albany

KASM(AM)— Nov 20, 1950: 1150 khz; 2.5 kw-D, 23 w-N. TL: N45 37 59 W94 36 00. (CP: 2.1 kw. TL: N45 37 53 W94 36 00). Hrs open: Box 390, 56307. Secondary address: 35223 238th Ave. Phone: (320) 845-2184. Fax: (320) 845-2187.E-mail: kasm1150am@albanytel.com Licensee: Starcom LLC (acq 1997; $1.25 million with co-located FM). Population served: 223,900 Rgnl. Network: MAGNET. Rgnl rep: Hyett/Ramsland. Baker & Hostetler. Format: Country, news, polka. News staff: one; News: 2 hrs wkly. Target aud: 36 plus. Spec prog: Oldies, Ger mus 2 hrs, farm 6 hrs wkly. ◆Randy Rothstein, gen mgr; Mark Sprint, progmg dir.

KDDG(FM)— October 1993: 105.5 mhz; 6 kw. Ant 328 ft TL: N45 37 53 W94 36 00. Hrs open: Box 390 Phone: (320) 845-2184. Fax: (320) 845-2187.E-mail: kddg1150fm@albanytel.com Licensee: Starcom LLC Format: Adult contemp.

Albert Lea

KATE(AM)— October 1937: 1450 khz; 1 kw-U. TL: N43 38 00 W93 22 15. Stereo. Hrs open: 24 1633 W. Main, 56007. Phone: (507) 373-2338. Fax: (507) 373-4736.E-mail: copy@albertlearadio.com Licensee: Three Eagles of Luverne Inc. Group owner: Three Eagles Communications (acq 5-21-99; with co-located FM). Population served: 100,000 Natl. Rep: McGavren Guild,. Minn. Farm Rgnl rep: Midwest Radio. Reynolds & Manning. Wire Svc: AP Format: News/talk, MOR. News staff: 3; News: 30 hrs wkly. Target aud: 12 plus; general. Spec prog: Farm 18 hrs, Sp 2 hrs wkly. ♦Gary Buchanan, pres; Bob Mithuen, gen mgr, opns mgr; Courtnay Doyle, gen sls mgr, farm dir; Steve Oman, news dir.

KCPI(FM)— July 1974: 94.9 mhz; 5 kw. Ant 295 ft TL: N43 38 00 W93 22 15. Stereo. Hrs open: 24 Prog sep from AM 1633 W. Main, 56007. Phone: (507) 373-2338. Fax: (507) 373-4736.E-mail: copy@albertlearadio.com Licensee: Three Eagles of Luverne Inc. (Acq 8-1-99). Population served: 121,000 Natl. Network: ABC, . Format: Adult contemp. News staff: one; News: 12 hrs wkly. Target aud: 25-54.

KQPR-FM— Aug 14, 1990: 96.1 mhz; 25 kw. 328 ft TL: N43 34 54 W93 23 42. Stereo. Hrs open: 24 Box 1106, 56007-1106. Phone: (507) 373-9600. Fax: (507) 373-9045.E-mail: kqpr@power96rocker.com Web Site:www.power96rocker.com Licensee: Hometown Broadcasting Inc. (acq 11-21-01; grpsl). Natl. Network: Jones Radio Networks, . Natl. Rep: Hyett/Ramsland,. Linder Farm Format: Classic rock. News staff: one. Target aud: General. ♦Greg Jensen, CEO, CFO; Anna Rahn, gen mgr, gen sls mgr; Ron Hunter, progmg dir; Jim Pilgrim, news dir; Marv Olson, chief of engrg; Kristi Swalve, traf mgr.

Alexandria

***KBHG(FM)**—Not on air, target date: unknown: 89.5 mhz; 7.2 kw. 321 ft TL: N45 55 55 W95 26 41. Hrs open: 515 E. Pike St., 56360. Phone: (320) 859-3000. Fax: (320) 859-3010.E-mail: david@praisefm.org Licensee: Christian Heritage Broadcasting Inc. Format: Christian. ♦David McIver, gen mgr.

KULO(FM)— 1976: 94.3 mhz; 12 kw. Ant 466 ft TL: N45 56 25 W95 28 03. Stereo. Hrs open: 24 Box 1024, 56308-1024. Secondary address: 604 Third Ave. W. 56308. Phone: (320) 762-2154. Fax: (320) 762-2156.E-mail: 100.7@kikvfm.com Web Site:cool943.com Licensee: BDI Broadcasting Inc. Group owner: Omni Broadcasting Co. (acq 12-31-2001; $700,000). Population served: 198,000 Natl. Network: ABC, . Rgnl. Network: MNN. Garvey, Schubert & Barer. Format: Oldies. News staff: one; News: 12 hrs wkly. Target aud: 35-64; adults. ♦Lou Buron, CEO, pres; Mary Campbell, CFO, VP; Dave Vagle, gen mgr; Trudy Blanshan, gen sls mgr & prom dir; Johnny Rocket, progmg dir, mus dir; Jim Rohn, news dir; Paul Sorum, pub affrs dir; Dave Cox, engrg dir, chief of engrg.

KXRA(AM)— July 27, 1949: 1490 khz; 1 kw-U. TL: N45 52 05 W95 21 47. Hrs open: 24 Box 69, 1312 Broadway, 56308. Phone: (320) 763-3131. Fax: (320) 763-5641.E-mail: thefolks@kxra.com Web Site:www.kxra.com Licensee: Paradis Broadcasting of Alexandria Inc. (group owner; (acq 10-1-88). Population served: 40,000 Natl. Network: CNN Radio, . Rgnl. Network: MNN. MNN Rgnl rep: Midwest Radio. Fletcher, Heald & Hildreth. Format: News/talk. News staff: one; News: 25 hrs wkly. Target aud: 35-64. Spec prog: Farm 5 hrs, relg 2 hrs wkly. ♦Mel Paradis, chmn; Brett Paradis, pres, gen mgr.

KXRA-FM— May 1, 1968: 92.3 mhz; 13.5 kw. 446 ft TL: N45 52 30 W95 21 30. Stereo. Hrs open: 24 Box 69, 1312 Broadway, 56308. Phone: (320) 763-3131. Fax: (320) 763-5641. Web Site:www.kxra.com Population served: 50,000 Format: Classic rock. News staff: one; News: 5 hrs wkly. Target aud: 25-45; young adults, dual income households.

KXRZ(FM)— Apr 2, 1984: 99.3 mhz; 6 kw. Ant 285 ft TL: N45 52 47 W95 18 35. Stereo. Hrs open: 24 1312 Broadway, 56308. Secondary address: Box 69 56308. Phone: (320) 763-3131. Fax: (320) 763-5641.E-mail: thefolks@kxra.com Web Site:www.z99radio.com Licensee: Paradis Broadcasting of Alexandria Inc. (group owner; acq 5-1-00; $900,000). Population served: 40,000 Natl. Network: Jones Radio Networks, . Rgnl rep: Midwest Radio. Fletcher, Heald & Hildreth. Format: 80s, 90s & today. News staff: one; News: 5 hrs wkly. Target aud: 18-40; young adults. Spec prog: Relg 3 hrs wkly. ♦Brett Paradis, pres & gen mgr.

Anoka

KMNQ(AM)—(Brooklyn Park, Apr 15, 1956: 1470 khz; 5 kw-U, DA-2. TL: N45 05 17 W93 22 59. Hrs open: 24 1516 E Lake St, Suite 200, Minneapolis, 55407. Phone: (612) 729-5900. Fax: (612) 729-5999.E-mail: lainvasora1400@lainvasora1400.com Web Site:www.lainvasora1400.com Licensee: Davidson Media Station KLBP Licensee LLC. (acq 9-7-2005; $5.2 million with KMNV(AM) Saint Paul). Population served: 100,000 Natl. Network: Westwood One, . Rgnl. Network: MNN. MNN Format: Sp. ♦Marian Sanchez, gen mgr.

KQQL(FM)— Aug 1, 1968: 107.9 mhz; 96 kw. Ant 1,092 ft TL: N45 20 20 W93 23 27. Stereo. Hrs open: 1600 Utica Ave. S., Suite 400, Minneapolis, 55416. Phone: (952) 417-3000. Fax: (952) 417-3001.E-mail: info@kqql.com Web Site:www.kqql.com Licensee: AMFM Broadcasting Licenses LLC. Group owner: Clear Channel Communications Inc. (acq 8-30-2000; grpsl). Population served: 2,600,000 Natl. Rep: Clear Channel,. Wiley, Rein & Fielding. Format: Super hits. Target aud: 25-54.

Appleton

***KNCM(FM)**— February 1997: 88.5 mhz; 100 kw. 984 ft TL: N45 10 03 W96 00 02. Hrs open: Saint Johns University, Box 7711, Collegeville, 56321. Phone: (320) 363-7702, (651) 290-1500. Fax: (320) 363-4948.E-mail: kncm@mpr.org Licensee: Minnesota Public Radio. Format: News & info. ♦William H. Kling, CEO & pres; Mark Alfuth, CFO; Thomas Kigin, exec VP; Steve Griffith, opns mgr; Jon Gossett, dev VP; Deborah Brown, dev dir; Eric Nycklemoe, progmg dir; Bill Wareham, news dir; Doug Thompson, chief of engrg.

***KRSU(FM)**— Oct 25, 1989: 91.3 mhz; 75 kw. 1,158 ft TL: N45 10 03 W96 00 02. Stereo. Hrs open: 24
Rebroadcast of KSJN(FM) Minneapolis-St. Paul.
480 Cedar St., St. Paul, 55101. Phone: (800) 228-7123. Phone: (651) 290-1500. Fax: (651) 290-1224.E-mail: info@mpr.org Web Site:www.mpr.org Licensee: Minnesota Public Radio Inc. Natl. Network: NPR, PRI, . Rgnl. Network: Minn. Pub. Minn. Pub. Radio Format: Class. ♦William H. Kling, pres & gen mgr.

Atwater

KKLN(FM)—Licensed to Atwater. See Litchfield

Austin

KAUS(AM)— May 30, 1948: 1480 khz; 1 kw-U, DA-2. TL: N43 37 20 W92 59 26. Hrs open: 24 18431 State Hwy. 105, 55912. Phone: (507) 437-7666. Phone: (507) 437-1480. Fax: (507) 437-7669.E-mail: kaus@kaus.com Web Site:www.kaus.com Licensee: Three Eagles of Luverne Inc. Group owner: Three Eagles Communications (acq 4-1-00; grpsl). Population served: 65,000 Natl. Network: NBC, . Rgnl. Network: MNN. MNN Wiley, Rein & Fielding. Format: Oldies, adult contemp, news/talk. News staff: 2; News: 20 hrs wkly. Target aud: 25-54. ♦Rolland Johnson, chmn; Gary Buchanan, pres; Bob Mithuen, gen mgr; Joyce Marshall, gen sls mgr; John Schramek, progmg dir, news dir; Ron Schat, engrg VP.

KAUS-FM— 1963: 99.9 mhz; 100 kw. 928 ft TL: N43 37 42 W93 09 12. Stereo. Hrs open: 24 Prog sep from AM 18431 State Hwy. 105, 55912. Phone: (507) 437-7666. Fax: (507) 437-7669.E-mail: kaus@kaus.com Web Site:www.kaus.com Licensee: Three Eagles of Luverne Inc. Population served: 400,000 Format: Country. News staff: 2; News: 12 hrs wkly. Target aud: 25-54. ♦Scott Soderberg, progmg dir; Tim Allen, prom mgr & progmg mgr.

***KMSK(FM)**— Jan 12, 1981: 91.3 mhz; 135 w. 221 ft TL: N43 40 39 W93 00 04. Stereo. Hrs open: 24
Rebroadcasts KMSU(FM) Mankato 100%.
205 AFC, Mankato State University, 1536 Warren St., Mankato, 56001. Phone: (507) 389-5678. Fax: (507) 389-1705.E-mail: info@kmsu.org Web Site:www.kmsu.org Licensee: Mankato State University. (acq 12-23-91). Population served: 25,000 Natl. Network: NPR, . Cohn & Marks. Format: Pub affrs, educ, mus. News staff: one; News: 50 hrs wkly. Target aud: General; upscale, educated. Spec prog: Drama 3 hrs, folk/ethnic 5 hrs, new age 5 hrs wkly. ♦Jim Gullickson, gen mgr; Karen Wright, opns dir.

***KNSE(FM)**— 90.1 mhz; 6 kw. Ant 318 ft TL: N43 38 27 W93 08 51. Hrs open: summer 2003 Minnesota Public Radio, 480 Cedar St., Saint Paul, 55101. Phone: (651) 290-1500. Fax: (651) 290-1224.E-mail: mail@mpr.org Web Site:www.mpr.org Licensee: Minnesota Public Radio. Format: News. ♦William H. Kling, pres & gen mgr; Jon Gossett, dev dir; Erik Nycklemoe, progmg dir; Bill Wareham, news dir.

KQAQ(AM)— Apr 16, 1960: 970 khz; 5 kw-D, 500 w-N, DA-2. TL: N43 42 27 W92 56 45. Hrs open: 5 AM-midnight Box 1106, Albert Lea, 56007. Phone: (507) 373-9600. Fax: (507) 373-9045.E-mail: kqar@classiccountrylegends.com Web Site:www.classiccountrylegends.com Licensee: Hometown Broadcasting Inc. Group owner: Clear Channel Communications Inc. (acq 5-29-2008; $250,000). Population served: 210,000 Natl. Network: Fox News Radio, Motor Racing Net, Jones Radio Networks, . Rgnl. Network: Linder Farm, Tribune. Linder Farm Format: Classic Country. ♦Anna Rahn, gen mgr.

Babbitt

KAOD(FM)— 1999: 106.7 mhz; 19.8 kw. 790 ft TL: N47 41 18 W91 54 15. Hrs open:
Rebroadcast of KQDS-FM Duluth 100%.
501 Lake Ave. S., Suite 200A, Duluth, 55802. Phone: (218) 722-0921. Fax: (218) 723-1499. Licensee: Red Rock Radio Corp. (group owner; acq 1-10-00; grpsl). Format: Classic new rock. ♦Shawn Skramstad, gen mgr; Jim Payne, gen sls mgr; Bill Jones, progmg dir; Jason Manning, news dir.

Bagley

***KBXE(FM)**—Not on air, target date: unknown: 90.5 mhz; 100 kw. Ant 413 ft TL: N47 36 04 W95 25 03. Hrs open: 260 N.E. 2nd St., Grand Rapids, 55744. Phone: (218) 326-1234. Fax: (218) 326-1235. Licensee: Northern Community Radio Inc. (acq 8-5-2009; $30,000 for CP). ♦Sandy Roggenkamp, pres; Maggie Montgomery, gen mgr.

KKCQ-FM— October 1997: 96.7 mhz; 25 kw. 328 ft TL: N47 36 08 W95 32 18. Hrs open: 24 Box 606, Fosston, 56542. Phone: (218) 435-1071. Fax: (218) 435-1480.E-mail: info@q107fm.com Web Site:www.q107fm.com Licensee: Pine to Prairie Broadcasting Inc. (acq 6-16-97; $5,553 for CP). Population served: 40,000 Natl. Network: ABC, . Format: Country. News staff: one. Spec prog: Farm 10 hrs, relg 9 hrs wkly. ♦Phil Ehlke, gen mgr; Karen Bingham, progmg dir, traf mgr.

Barnesville

KBVB(FM)— Jan 2, 1976: 95.1 mhz; 98 kw. Ant 991 ft TL: N46 40 29 W96 13 40. Stereo. Hrs open: 24 1020 25th St. S., Fargo, ND, 58103. Secondary address: Box 10097, Fargo, ND 58106. Phone: (701) 237-5346. Fax: (701) 237-0980.E-mail: studio@bob95fm.com Web Site:www.bob95fm.com Licensee: Radio Fargo-Moorhead Inc. Group owner: Clear Channel Communications Inc. (acq 1-19-2007; grpsl). Natl. Rep: Eastman Radio,. Format: Country. Target aud: Adults 18-54. ♦Nancy Odney, COO & gen mgr; John Austin, opns mgr, progmg dir.

Baxter

WWWI(AM)— Aug 29, 1987: 1270 khz; 5 kw-U, DA-N. TL: N46 17 55 W94 16 42. Hrs open: 24 Box 783, 305 W. Washington St., Brainerd, 56401. Phone: (218) 828-9994. Fax: (218) 828-8327.E-mail: wwwi@brainerd.net Web Site:www.3wiradio.com Licensee: Tower Broadcasting Corp. Natl. Network: CBS, . Format: News/talk. Target aud: 25 plus. ♦James R. Pryor, pres, gen mgr, gen sls mgr, chief of engrg; Lon Schmidt, news dir; Mary Pryor, VP & pub affrs dir.

Bemidji

KBHP(FM)— Aug 3, 1972: 101.1 mhz; 100 kw. Ant 522 ft TL: N47 22 12 W94 52 54. Stereo. Hrs open: 24 Prog sep from AM Box 1656, 56619-1656. Phone: (218) 444-1500. Fax: (218) 759-0345.E-mail: phanson@pbbroadcasting.com Licensee: Paul Bunyan Broadcasting Co. Population served: 75,000 Natl. Network: ABC, . MNN Format: Country, mainstream. News staff: one; News: 12 hrs wkly. Target aud: 25-54. ♦Peggy Hanson, gen sls mgr; Todd Haugen, opns mgr, progmg dir & mus dir; Mark Anderson, chief of engrg.

***KBSB(FM)**— Jan 19, 1970: 89.7 mhz; 115 w. 126 ft TL: N47 29 00 W94 52 27. Hrs open: 24 FM 90 KBSB, Bemidji State Univ., 1500 Birchmont Avenue NE, Deputy Hall # 215, 56601. Phone: (218) 755-4120. Fax: (218) 755-4119. Web Site:www.fm90.org Licensee: Bemidji State University. Population served: 11,490 Format: CHR. Target aud: 12-28; teens to young adults. Spec prog: American Indian 3 hrs, folk 3 hrs wkly. ♦Nick Stroltman, stn mgr.

KBUN(AM)— 1946: 1450 khz; 1 kw-U, DA-1. TL: N47 27 56 W94 54 37. Hrs open: 24 Box 1656, 56619-1656. Secondary address: 502 Beltrami Ave. N.W. 56601. Phone: (218) 444-1500. Fax: (218) 751-8091.E-mail: phanson@pbbroadcasting.com Licensee: Paul Bunyan Broadcasting Co. Group owner: Omni Broadcasting Co. (acq 6-22-89;6-26-89). Population served: 45,000 Natl. Network: ESPN

Radio, Westwood One, . Rgnl. Network: MNN. MNN Garvey, Schubert & Barer. Format: Sports talk. News staff: one; News: 12 hrs wkly. Target aud: 18-54. ♦Lou Buron, CEO, pres, gen mgr; Mary Campbell, CFO, VP; Kevin Jackson, opns dir, opns mgr, progmg dir; Peggy Hanson, gen sls mgr; Mardy Karger, news dir, pub affrs dir; Mark Anderson, engrg dir, chief of engrg.

***KCRB-FM—** Dec 22, 1982: 88.5 mhz; 95 kw. 994 ft TL: N47 42 03 W94 29 15. Hrs open: 24
Rebroadcast of KSJN(FM) Minneapolis-St. Paul.
480 Cedar St., St. Paul, 55101. Phone: (651) 290-1500. Fax: (651) 290-1224.E-mail: info@mpr.org Web Site:www.mpr.org Licensee: Minnesota Public Radio Inc. Natl. Network: PRI, NPR, . Rgnl. Network: Minn. Pub. Minn. Pub. Radio Format: Class. News staff: one; News: 25 hrs wkly. ♦William H. Kling, gen mgr & stn mgr.

KKBJ(AM)— Oct 31, 1977: 1360 khz; 5 kw-D, 2.5 kw-N, DA-N. TL: N47 26 32 W94 55 07. Hrs open: 24 2115 Washington Ave. S., 56601. Phone: (218) 751-7777. Fax: (218) 759-0658.E-mail: info@kkbj.com Web Site:www.kkbj.com Licensee: R.P. Broadcasting Corp. (acq 4-1-95). Population served: 70,000 Natl. Network: AP Radio, . Bechtel & Cole. Wire Svc: AP Format: Talk. News staff: one; News: 15 hrs wkly. Target aud: 25-54. ♦Daniel J. Voss, gen mgr, gen sls mgr; Chuck Sebastian, progmg dir; Roger Paskvan, pres & engrg VP; Rocky Coffin, relg ed.

KKBJ-FM— Aug 8, 1983: 103.7 mhz; 100 kw. 460 ft TL: N47 33 19 W94 47 59. Stereo. Hrs open: 24 Prog sep from AM 2115 Washington Ave. S., 56601. Phone: (218)751-7777. Fax: (218) 759-0658. Licensee: R.P. Broadcasting Corp. Population served: 75,000 Wire Svc: AP Format: Hot adult contemp. News staff: one; News: 20 hrs wkly. Target aud: 18-49; 40% male & 60% female. ♦Tracy Bailey, prom dir; Daniel Voss, adv mgr.

KKZY(FM)— May 7, 1999: 95.5 mhz; 100 kw. Ant 423 ft TL: N47 22 12 W94 52 54. Stereo. Hrs open: 24 Box 1656, 56619-1656. Secondary address: 502 Beltrami Ave. N.W. 56601. Phone: (218) 444-1500. Fax: (218) 751-8091.E-mail: phanson@pbbroadcasting.com Licensee: BG Broadcasting Inc. Group owner: Omni Broadcasting Co. (acq 6-22-98). Population served: 75,000 Natl. Network: ABC, . Garvey, Schubert & Barer. Format: Adult contemp. News staff: one; News: 12 hrs wkly. Target aud: 25-54; adults. ♦Lou Buron, CEO, pres, gen mgr; Mary Campbell, CFO, VP; Peggy Hanson, gen sls mgr; Kevin Jackson, progmg dir; Mardy Karger, news dir, pub affrs dir; Mark Anderson, chief of engrg.

***KNBJ(FM)—** July 1, 1994: 91.3 mhz; 60 kw. 974 ft Hrs open: 24
Rebroadcasts KNOW-FM Minneapolis-St. Paul 90%.
480 Cedar St., St. Paul, 55101. Phone: (651) 290-1500. Fax: (651) 290-1224. Web Site:www.mpr.org Licensee: Minnesota Public Radio. Natl. Network: PRI, NPR, . Rgnl. Network: Minn. Pub. Minn. Pub. Radio Format: News. ♦William H. Kling, gen mgr & stn mgr.

Benson

KBMO(AM)— December 1956: 1290 khz; 500 w-D. TL: N45 19 06 W95 33 48. Hrs open: 24 105 13th St. N., 56215. Phone: (320) 843-3290. Fax: (320) 843-3955.E-mail: kscr@info-link.net Licensee: Quest Broadcasting Inc. (acq 5-2-94; $390,000 with co-located FM). Population served: 60687 Rgnl. Network: MNN. MNN Shainis & Peltzman. Format: Adult standards. News staff: one; News: 25 hrs wkly. Target aud: 40 plus. Spec prog: Farm 10 hrs wkly. ♦Paul Estenson, pres & gen mgr; Marilyn Lee, gen sls mgr; Jason Brandt, progmg dir, news dir; Maynard Meyer, chief of engrg; Jolene Moreland, traf mgr.

KSCR-FM— Apr 26, 1968: 93.5 mhz; 25 kw. Ant 328 ft TL: N45 19 06 W95 33 48. Stereo. Hrs open: 24 105 13th St. N., 56215. Phone: (320) 843-3290. Fax: (320) 843-3955.E-mail: KSCR@info-link.net Licensee: Quest Broadcasting Inc. Population served: 113,291 Natl. Network: AP Network News, . MNN Format: Classic hits. Target aud: 18-54. ♦Paul Estenson, gen mgr; Maynard Meyer, chief of engrg; Jolene Moreland, traf mgr.

Blackduck

WBJI(FM)— 1991: 98.3 mhz; 50 kw. 456 ft TL: N47 33 19 W94 47 59. Stereo. Hrs open: 24 2115 Washington Ave. S.E., Bemidji, 56601-8942. Phone: (218) 751-7777. Fax: (218) 759-0658.E-mail: wbji@paulbunyon.net Web Site:www.wbji.com Licensee: R.P. Broadcasting Inc. Population served: 50,000 Natl. Network: ABC, . Bechtel & Cole. Format: Real country. News staff: one; News: 8 hrs wkly. Target aud: 35-64; adults with above average income. Spec prog: NASCAR 4 hrs wkly. ♦Roger Paskvan, CEO; Marla Weckman, exec VP; Dan Voss, gen mgr; Chuck Sebastian, progmg dir; Brian Schultz, news dir; Tracy Bailey, traf mgr.

WMIS-FM— 2007: 92.1 mhz; 36 kw. Ant 577 ft TL: N47 33 26 W94 48 04. Hrs open: 1410 30th St. N.W., Suite 115, Bemidji, 56601. Phone: (218) 766-7970. Web Site:www.wmisfm.com Licensee: Paskvan Media Inc. ♦Troy Paskvan, pres & gen mgr.

WQXJ(FM)— 2008: 104.5 mhz; 8.5 kw. Ant 485 ft TL: N47 33 26 W94 48 04. Hrs open: Box 1656, Bemidji, 56619-1656. Phone: (218) 444-1500. Fax: (218) 751-8091.E-mail: phanson@pbbroadcasting.com Licensee: BG Broadcasting Inc. Natl. Network: ABC, . Format: Oldies. ♦Lou Buron, gen mgr; Kev Jackson, opns mgr, progmg dir; Peggy Hanson, gen sls mgr; Mark Anderson, chief of engrg.

***WYNJ(FM)—** 2009: 89.5 mhz; 800 w. Ant 328 ft TL: N47 44 21 W94 41 10. Hrs open: Box 481, Park Rapids, 56470. Phone: (218) 237-4673. Licensee: We Have This Hope Christian Radio Inc. ♦Vern Erickson, pres.

Blooming Prairie

KOWZ-FM— September 1995: 100.9 mhz; 100 kw. 620 ft TL: N44 02 46 W93 23 03. Hrs open: 255 Cedardale Dr. S.E., Owatonna, 55060. Phone: (507) 444-9224. Fax: (507) 444-9080. Licensee: Blooming Prairie Farm Radio Inc. Group owner: Linder Broadcasting Group. Format: Adult contemp. ♦Jeff Seaton, gen mgr.

Blue Earth

KBEW(AM)— Aug 29, 1963: 1560 khz; 1 kw-D. TL: N43 38 48 W95 33 48. Hrs open: Box 278, 56013. Phone: (507) 526-2181. Fax: (507) 526-7468.E-mail: kbew@bevcomm.net Licensee: KBEW Radio Inc. Group owner: Result Radio Group (acq 2-1-81). Population served: 50,000 Natl. Network: ABC, . Rgnl. Network: Linder Farm. Natl. Rep: Katz Radio,. Linder Farm Wire Svc: AP Format: Oldies, news/talk. News staff: one; News: 17 hrs wkly. Target aud: Farming community. Spec prog: Farm 15 hrs wkly. ♦Jerry Papenfuss, pres; Kevin Benson, stn mgr, gen sls mgr; Randy Allen, progmg dir; Norm Hall, news dir; Jeff Vriesen, chief of engrg.

KBEW-FM— 1993: 98.1 mhz; 25 kw. 328 ft TL: N43 38 44 W94 05 33. Stereo. Hrs open: 24 Box 278, 56013. Phone: (507) 526-2181. Fax: (507) 526-7468.E-mail: kbew@bevcomm.net Licensee: KBEW Radio Inc. Population served: 50,000 Rgnl. Network: Linder Farm. Linder Farm Wire Svc: AP Format: Country. News staff: one; News: 3 hrs wkly. Target aud: 18-54. ♦Kevin Benson, gen mgr & mktg mgr.

KJLY(FM)— Nov 1, 1983: 104.5 mhz; 50 kw. 453 ft TL: N43 39 41 W94 06 29. Stereo. Hrs open: Box 72, 56013. Secondary address: 12089 380th Ave. 56013. Phone: (507) 526-3233. Fax: (507) 526-3235.E-mail: kjly@kjly.com Web Site:www.kjly.com Licensee: Minn-Iowa Christian Broadcasting Inc. (group owner). Natl. Network: Moody, Salem Radio Network, . Format: Inspirational relg. News: 21 hrs wkly. Target aud: 45-65. Spec prog: Farm 5 hrs, children 4 hrs wkly. ♦Maurice Schwen, pres; Eugene Stallkang, VP; Matt Dorfner, gen mgr; Steve Ware, progmg dir; Mark Croom, chief of engrg.

Brainerd

***KBPN(FM)—** July 2003: 88.3 mhz; 5 kw. Ant 669 ft TL: N46 25 21 W94 27 41. Hrs open: 24 Box 578, Bemidji, 56619. Secondary address: Minnesota Public Radio, 45 E. 7th St., Saint Paul 55101. Phone: (218) 829-1072. Fax: (218) 751-8640.E-mail: info@mpr.org Web Site:www.mpr.org Licensee: Minnesota Public Radio. Format: News. ♦Kristi Booth, stn mgr; Tim Post, local news ed; Barb Treat, sls.

KBPR(FM)—Licensed to Brainerd. See Collegeville

KLIZ(AM)— Aug 6, 1946: 1380 khz; 5 kw-U, DA-N. TL: N46 19 56 W94 10 26. Hrs open: 24 Box 746, 56401-0746. Secondary address: 13225 Dogwood Dr., Baxter 56425-8613. Phone: (218) 828-1244. Fax: (218) 828-1119.E-mail: production@brainerd.net Web Site:brainerdradio.net Licensee: BL Broadcasting Inc. Group owner: Omni Broadcasting Co. (acq 4-1-2004; grpsl). Population served: 70,000 Natl. Network: Sporting News Radio Network, . Rgnl. Network: MNN. Garvey, Schubert & Barer. Format: Sports talk. News staff: one; News: 12 hrs wkly. Target aud: 25-64; adults. ♦Lou Buron, CEO, pres; Mary Campbell, CFO, VP; G. Michael Boen, gen mgr; Danny Wild, opns dir, progmg dir, pub affrs dir; Jeff Hilborn, gen sls mgr; Tess Taylor, news dir; Dave Cox, chief of engrg.

KLIZ-FM— May 23, 1960: 107.5 mhz; 100 kw. Ant 350 ft TL: N46 19 56 W94 10 26. Stereo. Hrs open: Prog sep from AM Box 746, 56401. Secondary address: 13225 Dogwood Dr., Baxter 56425. Phone: (218) 828-1244. Fax: (218) 828-1119.E-mail: production@branerd.net Population served: 200,000 Natl. Network: ABC, . Minn. News Net. Format: Classic rock. News staff: one; News: 12 hrs wkly. Target aud: 18-54; adults.

KUAL-FM— June 3, 1994: 103.5 mhz; 20 kw. Ant 279 ft TL: N46 20 55 W94 13 29. Hrs open: Box 746, 56401. Phone: (218) 828-1244. Fax: (218) 828-1119.E-mail: production@branerd.net Natl. Network: ABC, . Format: Oldies. News staff: one; News: 12 hrs wkly. Target aud: 25-54; adults. ♦Billy Holiday, progmg dir; Tess Taylor, pub affrs dir.

KVBR(AM)— May 16, 1964: 1340 khz; 1 kw-U. TL: N46 20 51 W94 10 52. Hrs open: 24 Box 746, 56401-0746. Secondary address: 13225 Dogwood Dr., Baxter 56425-8613. Phone: (218) 828-1244. Fax: (218) 828-1119.E-mail: production@brainerd.net Web Site:brainerdradio.net Licensee: BL Broadcasting Inc. Group owner: Omni Broadcasting Co. (acq 4-1-2004; grpsl). Population served: 44,000 Natl. Network: ABC, USA, Westwood One, . Rgnl. Network: MNN. MNN Garvey, Schubert & Barer. Format: All sports. News staff: one; News: 12 hrs wkly. Target aud: 25-54; adults. ♦Lou Buron, CEO, pres; Mary Campbell, CFO, VP; G. Michael Boen, gen mgr; Danny Wild, opns dir, progmg dir, pub affrs dir; Jeff Hilborn, gen sls mgr; Tess Taylor, news dir; Dave Cox, engrg dir, chief of engrg.

WJJY-FM— July 21, 1978: 106.7 mhz; 100 kw. Ant 448 ft TL: N46 26 36 W94 22 58. Stereo. Hrs open: 24 Box 746, 56401-0746. Secondary address: 13225 Dogwood Dr., Baxter 56425-8613. Phone: (218) 828-1244. Fax: (218) 828-1119.E-mail: production@brainerd.net Web Site:brainerdradio.net Licensee: BL Broadcasting Inc. Group owner: Omni Broadcasting Co. (acq 3-2-94; $900,000;5-2-94). Population served: 200,000 Natl. Network: ABC, . Garvey, Schubert & Barer. Format: Full service adult contemp. News staff: one; News: 20 hrs wkly. Target aud: 25-54; adults. ♦Lou Buron, CEO, pres; Mary Campbell, CFO, VP; G. Michael Boen, gen mgr; Mark Hegstrom, opns mgr, progmg dir; Jeff Hillborn, gen sls mgr; Tess Taylor, news dir & pub affrs dir; David Cox, chief of engrg.

Breckenridge

KBMW(AM)—Licensed to Breckenridge. See Wahpeton ND

KLTA(FM)— Feb 17, 1970: 105.1 mhz; 100 kw. 713 ft TL: N46 32 41 W96 37 33. Stereo. Hrs open: 24 Box 9919, Fargo, ND, 58106. Secondary address: 2720 7th Ave. S., Fargo, ND 58103. Phone: (701) 237-4500. Fax: (701) 235-9082.E-mail: info@fm.105.net Web Site:www.fm1051.net Licensee: Monterey Licenses LLC. Group owner: Triad Broadcasting Co. LLC (acq 10-99; grpsl). Population served: 194,800 Natl. Rep: Christal,. Shaw Pittman. Wire Svc: AP Format: Adult contemp. Target aud: 25-54; skews female. ♦Tom Douglas, CEO; David Benjamin, pres; Nancy Odney, gen mgr.

Breezy Point

KLKS(FM)— June 14, 1984: 104.3 mhz; 50 kw. 492 ft TL: N46 36 13 W94 15 04. Stereo. Hrs open: 24 Box 300, 56472. Secondary address: 7170 Ski Chatet Dr. 56472. Phone: (218) 562-4884. Phone: (218) 829-2997. Fax: (218) 562-4058. Fax: (218) 829-9341.E-mail: klakes@uslink.net Web Site:www.klks.com Licensee: Lakes Broadcasting Group Inc. Hogan & Hartson. Format: Adult standards, btfl mus, big band. News staff: 2; News: 25 hrs wkly. Target aud: 40 plus. ♦Bob Bundgaard, CEO, pres; Allen Gray, chmn; Diane Anderson, CFO, opns VP; Marj Bundgaard, gen mgr; Thomas Kenow, sls VP; David Pundt, news dir; Carol Bundgaard, traf mgr.

Brooklyn Park

KMNQ(AM)—Licensed to Brooklyn Park. See Anoka

Browerville

KXDL(FM)—Licensed to Browerville. See Long Prairie

Buffalo

KRWC(AM)— Nov 16, 1971: 1360 khz; 500 w-D. TL: N45 10 00 W93 55 11. Hrs open: 24 Box 267, 55313. Secondary address: 1472 10th St. N.W. 55313. Phone: (763) 682-4444. Fax: (763) 682-3542.E-mail: info@krwc1360.com Web Site:www.krwc1360.com Licensee: Donnell Inc. (acq 6-15-98; $460,000). Population served: 150,000 Natl. Network: CNN Radio, . Rgnl. Network: MNN. MNN Format: Country, oldies, adult contemp, news/talk. News staff: one; News: 16 hrs wkly. Target aud: 25 plus. ♦Joe Carlson, pres, gen mgr, gen sls mgr; Tim Matthews, opns dir, progmg dir & news dir; John George, chief of engrg.

Buhl

*WIRN(FM)— 1997: 92.5 mhz; 39 kw. 558 ft TL: N47 29 46 W92 47 05. Hrs open: 480 Cedar St., Saint Paul, 55101. Phone: (651) 291-1500. Fax: (651) 222-7795.E-mail: info@mpr.org Web Site:www.mpr.org Licensee: Minnesota Public Radio. Minn. Pub. Radio Format: News & info. ◆ William Kling, pres; Kat Eldred, gen mgr; Doug Thompson, engrg dir; Bob Kelleher, local news ed.

Caledonia

KCLH(FM)— Nov 14, 1994: 94.7 mhz; 1.9 kw. Ant 584 ft TL: N43 41 24 W91 30 09. Stereo. Hrs open: 24 201 State St., La Crosse, WI, 54602. Phone: (608) 782-1230. Fax: (608) 782-1170. Web Site:www.classichits947.com Licensee: Family Radio Inc. Group owner: The Mid-West Family Broadcast Group (acq 7-19-01; grpsl). Population served: 300,000 Shaw Pittman. Wire Svc: AP Format: Classic hits. News staff: 4; News: one hr wkly. Target aud: General; 25-54. ◆ Dick Record, pres; Brian Michaels, opns mgr, progmg dir; Samantha Strong, progmg dir; Stephanie Paige, prom.

Cambridge

WGVY(FM)— May 5, 1973: 105.3 mhz; 25 kw. Ant 298 ft TL: N45 31 17 W93 10 27. Stereo. Hrs open: 24 Rebroadcasts WGVX(FM) Lakeville. 2000 S.E. Elm St., Minneapolis, 55414. Phone: (612) 617-4000. Fax: (612) 676-8292.E-mail: email@love105.fm Web Site:www.love105.fm Licensee: Radio License Holding III LLC. Group owner: ABC Inc. (acq 6-12-2007; grpsl). Population served: 500,000 Natl. Network: ABC, . Natl. Rep: Interep,. Haley, Bader & Potts. Format: Love songs of the 60s, 70s and 80s. Spec prog: Farm 8 hrs wkly. ◆ Marc Kalman, pres, stn mgr; Dave Hamilton, opns mgr; Pete Frisch, sls dir; Susan Larkin, gen sls mgr; Leslie Heinemann, natl sls mgr; Brook Johnson, mktg dir; Shelley Miller, prom dir, prom mgr; Chris Rahn, progmg dir; Ben Gnam, mus dir; Christopher Taykalo, pub affrs dir; Dave Szaflarski, chief of engrg.

Cass Lake

*KOJB(FM)—Not on air, target date: unknown: 90.1 mhz; 45 kw. Ant 302 ft TL: N47 20 01 W94 12 35. Hrs open: 115 Sixth St. N.W., Suite E, 56633. Phone: (218) 335-3750. Fax: (218) 335-3731. Licensee: Leech Lake Band of Ojibwe. Natl. Network: NPR, . ◆ Arthur D. La Rose, chmn.

Cloquet

*WGZS(FM)—Not on air, target date: unknown: 89.1 mhz; 5.37 kw hoirz, 25 kw vert. Ant 439 ft TL: N46 50 10.7 W92 42 08.1. Hrs open: 1720 Big Lake Rd., 55720. Phone: (218) 878-2625. Licensee: Fond du Lac Band of Lake Superior Chippewa. ◆ Karen R. Diver, gen mgr.

WKLK(AM)— Jan 31, 1950: 1230 khz; 1 kw-U, DA-1. TL: N46 44 58 W92 25 17. Hrs open: 24 1104 Cloquet Ave., 55720-1613. Phone: (218) 879-4534. Fax: (218) 879-1962.E-mail: info@wklkradio.com Web Site:www.wklkradio.com Licensee: QB Broadcasting Ltd. (acq 5-12-92; $200,000 with co-located FM;6-1-92). Population served: 150,000 Format: Music of Your Life. News staff: one; News: 16 hrs wkly. Target aud: Community oriented. ◆ Mark Senarighi, gen mgr; Jake Kachinske, progmg dir, news dir; Bill Meyes, chief of engrg.

WKLK-FM— Apr 30, 1992: 96.5 mhz; 6 kw. 315 ft TL: N46 44 58 W92 25 17. Hrs open: 24 1104 Cloquet Ave., 55720-1613. Phone: (218) 879-4534. Fax: (218) 879-1962.E-mail: info@wklkradio.com Web Site:www.wklkradio.com Licensee: QB Broadcasting Ltd. Format: Adult hit.

*WSCN(FM)— Nov 17, 1975: 100.5 mhz; 100 kw. 875 ft TL: N46 47 21 W92 06 51. Stereo. Hrs open: 24 207 W Superior St, Suite 224, Duluth, 55802. Phone: (218) 722-9411. Fax: (218) 720-4900.E-mail: info@minnesotapublicradio.org Web Site:www.minnesotapublicradio.org Licensee: Minnesota Public Radio. (acq 12-88; $200,000; 12-19-88). Natl. Network: PRI, NPR, . Rgnl. Network: Minn. Pub. Minn. Pub. Radio Format: News. ◆ William H. Kling, pres; Kat Eldred, gen mgr.

Cold Spring

KMXK(FM)— Aug 30, 1968: 94.9 mhz; 50 kw. 492 ft TL: N45 23 53 W94 25 15. Stereo. Hrs open: 24 640 Lincoln Ave. S.E., St. Cloud, 56304. Phone: (320) 251-4422. Fax: (320) 251-1855.E-mail: studio@kiss96.com Web Site:www.mix949.com Licensee: Regent of St. Cloud Inc. Group owner: Regent Communications Inc. (acq 5-1-99;

grpsl). Format: Hot adult contemp. Target aud: 35-54. ◆ Terry Jacobs, CEO; Bill Stakelin, pres; Fred Murr, sr VP; David Engberg, gen mgr; John Schroeder, gen sls mgr; Mike Dylan, progmg dir, mus dir; Lee Voss, news dir; Mark Young, chief of engrg; Don Burggraff, traf mgr.

Coleraine

KGPZ(FM)— July 1, 1995: 96.1 mhz; 100 kw. 577 ft TL: N47 19 31 W93 16 18. Hrs open: 24 Box 447, Grand Rapids, 55744-0447. Phone: (218) 327-3339. Fax: (218) 327-3425.E-mail: kgpz@paulbunyan.net Web Site:www.kgpzfm.com Licensee: Latto Northland Broadcasting Inc. Group owner: Lew Latto Group of Northland Radio Stations Natl. Network: ABC, . Pepper & Corazzini. Format: Real country. Target aud: 35-64. ◆ Lew Latto, pres; Dennis Yourczek, VP, gen mgr, opns dir.

Collegeville

*KBPR(FM)—(Brainerd, February 1988: 90.7 mhz; 34.2 kw. 679 ft TL: N46 25 21 W94 27 41. Stereo. Hrs open: 24 Rebroadcast of KSJN(FM) Minneapolis-St. Paul. 480 Cedar St., St. Paul, 55101. Phone: (651) 290-1500. Fax: (651) 290-1224.E-mail: info@mpr.org Web Site:www.mpr.org Licensee: Minnesota Public Radio. Natl. Network: PRI, NPR, . Rgnl. Network: Minn. Pub. Minn. Pub. Radio Format: Class. News staff: 2. Target aud: General. ◆ William H. Kling, pres & gen mgr; Erik Nycklemoe, opns mgr, dev VP.

*KNSR(FM)— Aug 29, 1988: 88.9 mhz; 100 kw. 728 ft TL: N45 29 52 W94 32 14. Stereo. Hrs open: 24 Box 7711, St. John's Univ., 56321. Phone: (320) 363-7702. Fax: (320) 363-4948.E-mail: knsr@mpr.org Web Site:www.minnesotapublicradio.org Licensee: Minnesota Public Radio. Natl. Network: PRI, NPR, . Rgnl. Network: Minn. Pub. Minn. Pub. Radio Format: News. News staff: 2. Target aud: General. ◆ William H. Kling, pres; Kat Eldred, gen mgr.

*KSJR-FM— Jan 21, 1967: 90.1 mhz; 100 kw. 700 ft TL: N45 29 52 W94 32 14. Stereo. Hrs open: 24 Rebroadcast of KSJN(FM) Minneapolis. 480 Cedar St., St. Paul, 55101. Phone: (651) 290-1500. Fax: (651) 290-1224.E-mail: info@mpr.org Web Site:www.mpr.org Licensee: Minnesota Public Radio. Population served: 20,000 Natl. Network: PRI, . Rgnl. Network: Minn. Pub. Minn. Pub. Radio Format: Class. News staff: 2. Target aud: General. ◆ William H. Kling, pres, gen mgr & stn mgr.

Cook

*WQRN(FM)—Not on air, target date: unknown: 88.3 mhz; 1 kw. Ant 230 ft TL: N47 53 09 W92 39 47. Hrs open: 3434 W. Kilbourn Ave., Milwaukee, WI, 53208-3313. Phone: (414) 935-3000. Fax: (414) 935-3015. Web Site:www.vcyamerica.org Licensee: VCY America Inc. ◆ Vic Eliason, gen mgr.

Coon Rapids

WFMP(FM)—Licensed to Coon Rapids. See Minneapolis-St. Paul

Crookston

KQHT(FM)—Licensed to Crookston. See Grand Forks ND

KROX(AM)— April 1948: 1260 khz; 1 kw-D, 500 w-N, DA-N. TL: N47 47 20 W96 35 40. Hrs open: 208 S. Main St., Box 620, 56716-0620. Phone: (218) 281-1140. Fax: (218) 281-5036.E-mail: krox@rrv.net Web Site:www.kroxam.com Licensee: Gopher Communications Co. (acq 5-11-87). Natl. Network: CNN Radio, . Rgnl. Network: MNN MNN Wire Svc: AP Format: Soft adult contemp, country, MOR, talk. News staff: one. Target aud: 35 plus; general. Spec prog: Farm 10 hrs wkly. ◆ Frank Fee, pres, gen mgr, sls; Jeanette Fee, VP; Chris Fee, progmg dir; Jacob Fee, mus dir; Maryann Simmons, news dir.

KYCK(FM)— Mar 4, 1980: 97.1 mhz; 100 kw. 360 ft TL: N47 49 17 W96 49 03. Stereo. Hrs open: 24 Box 13638, Grand Forks, ND, 58208. Phone: (701) 775-4611. Fax: (701) 772-0540.E-mail: morningkyck@97kyck.com Web Site:www.97kyck.com Licensee: Leighton Enterprises Inc. (group owner). Population served: 175,000 News staff: 2. ◆ Jarrod Thomas, pres, opns mgr; Jack Hansen, VP, gen mgr; Phil O'Reilley, progmg dir.

Crosby

KFGI(FM)— Oct 10, 1990: 101.5 mhz; 25 kw. Ant 328 ft TL: N46 33 52 W93 57 03. Hrs open: Box 140, Aitkin, 56431. Phone: (218) 927-2100. Fax: (218) 927-4090. Web Site:kkinradio.com Licensee: Red Rock Radio Corp. (group owner; acq 9-1-2006; grpsl). Natl. Network: Jones Radio Networks, . Format: Classic rock. ◆ Terry Dee, gen mgr; Rick Skog, progmg dir; Tom Martin, news dir; Marcy Daun, traf mgr.

Dassel

KARP-FM—Licensed to Dassel. See Hutchinson

Deer River

KBAJ(FM)— 2000: 105.5 mhz; 100 kw. 508 ft TL: N47 20 22 W93 23 48. Hrs open: Rebroadcasts KQDS-FM Duluth 100%. 501 Lake Ave. S., Suite 200, Duluth, 55802. Phone: (218) 722-0921. Fax: (218) 723-1499. Licensee: Red Rock Radio Corp. (group owner; acq 1-10-00; grpsl). Format: Classic new rock. ◆ Shawn Skramstad, gen mgr; Jim Payne, gen sls mgr; Bill Jones, progmg dir; Jason Manning, news dir.

Detroit Lakes

KDLM(AM)— October 1951: 1340 khz; 1 kw-U. TL: N46 50 14 W95 50 17. Hrs open: 24 Box 746, 56502-0746. Phone: (218) 847-5624. Fax: (218) 847-7657.E-mail: kdlmkbot@lakesnet.net Web Site:www.1340kdlm.com Licensee: Leighton Enterprises Inc. (group owner) Population served: 30,000 Natl. Network: CBS, . Rgnl. Network: MNN. MNN Wire Svc: AP Format: Sports, news/talk, adult contemp. News staff: one; News: 10 hrs wkly. Target aud: 30 plus. Spec prog: Farm one hr, relg 8 hrs wkly. ◆ Alver Leighton, chmn; John Sowada, pres; Denny Niess, VP; Jeff Leighton, gen mgr; Andy Lia, opns mgr.

KRCQ(FM)— July 4, 1994: 102.3 mhz; 50 kw. 492 ft TL: N46 48 24 W95 46 23. Stereo. Hrs open: 24 Box 556, 1119 Jackson Ave., 56502. Phone: (218) 847-2001. Fax: (218) 847-2271.E-mail: krcq@lakesnet.net Licensee: Detroit Lakes Broadcasting Co. Inc. (acq 7-8-97; $1.2 million). Population served: 300,000 Miller & Miller. Wire Svc: AP Format: Real country. News staff: one; News: 10 hrs wkly. Target aud: General. ◆ Robert D. Spilman, gen mgr.

Dilworth

WZFG(AM)— 2007: 1100 khz; 50 kw-D, 440 w-N, 5 kw-CH. TL: N46 45 44 W96 40 19 (day), N46 45 43 W96 40 18 (night). Hrs open: Box 9556, Fargo, ND, 58106. Secondary address: 64 Broadway, Fargo, ND 58102. Phone: (701) 356-1156. Fax: (701) 356-1155. Web Site:www.am1100.tv/ Licensee: SMAHH Communications Inc. (acq 4-11-2008; $720,000). Format: Talk. ◆J. Scott Hennen, pres, gen mgr; Jill Renee Helm, opns mgr; Greg Burd, gen sls mgr; Dustin Moore, progmg dir.

Duluth

KDAL(AM)— Nov 26, 1936: 610 khz; 5 kw-U, DA-N. TL: N46 43 13 W92 10 34. Hrs open: 715 E. Central Entrance, 55811. Phone: (218) 722-4321. Fax: (218) 722-5423.E-mail: info@kdal.com Web Site:http://www.kdal.am Licensee: Midwest Communications Inc. (group owner; (acq 8-1-2001; grpsl). Population served: 100,578 Natl. Network: CBS, Westwood One, Jones Radio Networks, . Rgnl. Network: MNN, Midwest Radio. MNN Rgnl rep: Hyett/Ramsland. Rosenman & Colin. Wire Svc: AP Format: Div, news/talk. News staff: 3. Target aud: 35-64. ◆ Duke Wright, CEO, pres; Jack Lawson, opns mgr; Mike Rasmusson, sls dir; John Talcott, engrg mgr, chief of engrg.

KDAL-FM— July 1985: 95.7 mhz; 100 kw. Ant 725 ft TL: N46 47 15 W92 07 21. Stereo. Hrs open: Prog sep from AM 715 E. Central Entrance, 55811. Phone: (218) 722-4321. Fax: (218) 722-5423.E-mail: tr@957thebridge.com Licensee: Midwest Communications Inc. Wire Svc: AP Format: Adult album alternative. Target aud: 25-49. ◆ Duke Wright, CEO; Jack Lawson, opns mgr; Mike Rasmusson, sls dir; John Talcott, chief of engrg.

KDNI(FM)—Licensed to Duluth. See Roseville

*KDNW(FM)— December 1993: 97.3 mhz; 40 kw. 548 ft TL: N46 47 20 W92 07 04. Stereo. Hrs open: 24 1101 E. Central Entrance, 55811.

Phone: (218) 722-6700. Fax: (218) 722-1092.E-mail: kdnw@kdnw.fm Web Site:www.kdnw.fm Licensee: Northwestern College. Group owner: Northwestern College & Radio (acq 12-4-91; $20,000;1-6-92). Natl. Network: AP Radio, . Bryan Cave. Wire Svc: AP Format: Contemp Christian music. Target aud: 25-54. ♦Paul Virts, sr VP; Paul Harkness, stn mgr.

KKCB(FM)— 1966: 105.1 mhz; 100 kw. Ant 789 ft TL: N46 47 21 W92 06 51. Stereo. Hrs open: 14 E. Central Entrance, 55811-5508. Phone: (218) 727-4500. Fax: (218) 727-9356. Web Site:www.kkcb.com Licensee: GAP Broadcasting Duluth License LLC. (acq 2-13-2008; grpsl). Format: Country. Target aud: General. ♦Merry Wallin, VP & gen mgr; David Drew, progmg dir.

KLDJ(FM)— Jan 1, 1994: 101.7 mhz; 18.5 kw. Ant 823 ft TL: N46 47 13 W92 07 17. Hrs open: 24 14 E. Central Entrance, 55811. Phone: (218) 727-4500. Fax: (218) 727-9356. Web Site:www.kool1017.com Licensee: GAP Broadcasting Duluth License LLC. Group owner: Clear Channel Communications Inc. (acq 2-13-2008; grpsl). Natl. Rep: Christal,. Format: Oldies. Target aud: 25-54; general. ♦Merry Wallin, VP & gen mgr; David Drew, opns mgr; Debbi Passo, gen sls mgr; Karina Bite, prom dir; Mark Marette, sports cmtr.

KQDS(AM)— Mar 11, 1963: 1490 khz; 1 kw-U. TL: N46 47 42 W92 07 08. Hrs open: 24 501 Lake Ave. S., Suite 200, 55802. Phone: (218) 728-9500. Fax: (218) 723-1499.E-mail: production@redrockradio.org Licensee: Red Rock Radio Corp. Natl. Network: Fox Sports, . Format: Sports.

KQDS-FM— Apr 1, 1976: 94.9 mhz; 100 kw. Ant 730 ft TL: N46 47 41 W92 07 05. Stereo. Hrs open: 24 501 Lake Ave S., Suite 200, 55802. Phone: (218) 728-9500. Fax: (218) 723-1499.E-mail: production @redrockradio.org Licensee: Red Rock Radio Corp. (group owner; (acq 1-10-2000; grpsl). Population served: 377,300 Natl. Rep: McGavren Guild,. Rgnl rep: O'Malley. Format: Classic rock, AOR. Target aud: 25-54. ♦Shawn Skramstad, gen mgr; Jim Payne, gen sls mgr; Bill Jones, progmg dir, news dir; Carlene Burstad, traf mgr.

KTCO(FM)— June 14, 1972: 98.9 mhz; 100 kw. 600 ft TL: N46 47 30 W92 06 59. Stereo. Hrs open: 24 715 E. Central Entrance, 55811. Phone: (218) 722-4321. Fax: (218) 722-5423.E-mail: david@ktco.fm.net Web Site:www.ktco.fm Licensee: Midwest Communications Inc. (group owner; acq 8-1-01; grpsl). Population served: 200,000 Rgnl rep: Hyett/Ramsland. Rosenman & Colin. Format: Country hits. Target aud: 25-49. ♦Duke Wright, pres; Jack Lawson, opns mgr; Jayson McQueary, progmg dir, disc jockey; John Talcott, chief of engrg, disc jockey.

***KUMD-FM**— May 26, 1971: 103.3 mhz; 95 kw. 820 ft TL: N46 47 31 W92 07 21. Stereo. Hrs open: 5 AM-3 AM (M-F); 6 AM-11 PM (Su) 130 Humanities Bldg., University of Minnesota, 55812. Phone: (218) 726-7181. Fax: (218) 726-6571.E-mail: kumd@kumd.org Web Site:www.kumd.org Licensee: Board of Regents of University of Minnesota. (acq 8-75). Population served: 100,600 Natl. Network: PRI, . Dow, Lohnes & Albertson. Format: Triple A. News: 12 hrs wkly. Target aud: 25-45. ♦Paul Damberg, dev dir; John Ziegler, progmg dir.

WDSM(AM)—See Superior, WI

WEBC(AM)— June 1924: 560 khz; 5 kw-U, DA-2. TL: N46 38 37 W91 59 09. Hrs open: 14 E. Central Entrance, 55811-5508. Phone: (218) 727-4500. Fax: (218) 727-9356. Web Site:www.560webc.com Licensee: GAP Broadcasting Duluth License LLC. Group owner: Clear Channel Communications Inc. (acq 2-13-2008; grpsl). Population served: 422,000 Natl. Network: ESPN Radio, . Natl. Rep: Christal,. Format: News/talk, sports. ♦Erik Hellum, pres; Merry Wallin, VP, gen mgr; David Drew, opns mgr; Debbie Paaso, gen sls mgr; Corey Carter, progmg dir; Randy Wabik, chief of engrg.

WGEE(AM)—See Superior, WI

***WIRR(FM)**—(Virginia-Hibbing, December 1985: 90.9 mhz; 21 kw. 552 ft TL: N47 29 46 W92 47 05. Stereo. Hrs open: 24 207 W Superior St, Suite 224, 55802. Phone: (218) 722-9411. Fax: (218) 720-4900.E-mail: info@mpr.org Web Site:www.mpr.org Licensee: Minnesota Public Radio Inc. Natl. Network: PRI, NPR, . Rgnl. Network: Minn. Pub. Minn. Pub. Radio Format: Class. News staff: 3. Target aud: General. ♦William H. Kling, pres; Kat Eldred, gen mgr.

***WJRF(FM)**— Nov 1, 1982: 89.5 mhz; 2.85 kw vert. Ant 512 ft TL: N46 47 21 W92 07 09. Stereo. Hrs open: 24 4604 Airpark Blvd., 55811. Phone: (218) 722-3017. Fax: (218) 722-1650.E-mail: airstaff@refugeradio.com Web Site:www.refugeradio.com Licensee: Refuge Media Group. Population served: 180,000 Format: Contemp Christian. News: 5 hrs wkly. Target aud: 18-34; female. ♦Brett M. Gibson, CEO, gen mgr; Paul Hitchcock, pres; Keith Johnson, VP.

***WSCD-FM**— 1975: 92.9 mhz; 70 kw. 614 ft TL: N46 47 20 W92 07 04. Stereo. Hrs open: 207 W Superior St, Suite 224, 55802. Phone: (218) 722-9411. Fax: (218) 720-4900.E-mail: info@mpr.org Web Site:www.mpr.org Licensee: Minnesota Public Radio. Population served: 22,000 Minn. Pub. Radio Format: Classical music. ♦William Kling, pres; Kat Eldred, gen mgr.

WWJC(AM)— Apr 26, 1963: 850 khz; 10 kw-D. TL: N46 39 19 W92 12 40. Hrs open: 1120 E. McCuen St., 55808. Phone: (218) 626-2738. Fax: (603) 907-7881.E-mail: radio@wwjc.com Web Site:www.wwjc.com Licensee: WWJC Inc. Population served: 225,000 Natl. Network: USA, . Format: Solid gospel / talk. ♦Ted Elm, gen mgr.

Eagan

KKMS(AM)—See Minneapolis-St. Paul

Eagle Lake

KXLP(FM)— 2007: 94.1 mhz; 3.8 kw. Ant 417 ft TL: N44 10 20 W94 02 23. Hrs open: 59346 Madison Ave., Mankato, 56001. Phone: (507) 345-4537. Fax: (507) 345-5364. Web Site:www.94kxlp.com Licensee: Radioactive LLC. Format: Classic rock and roll. Target aud: 25-54. Spec prog: Oldies 15 hrs wkly. ♦Benjamin L. Homel, pres; Jo Guck Bailey, VP & gen mgr.

East Grand Forks

KCNN(AM)— Aug 14, 1959: 1590 khz; 5 kw-D, 1 kw-N, DA-2. TL: N47 52 41 W97 00 24. Hrs open: 24 Box 13638, Grand Forks, ND, 58208. Secondary address: 1185 9th St. N.E., Thompson, ND 58278. Phone: (701) 772-2204. Fax: (701) 772-0540.E-mail: general@kcnn.com Web Site:www.leightonbroadcasting.com Licensee: Leighton Enterprises Inc. (group owner; (acq 11-14-2003;. $2.5 million). Population served: 100,000 Natl. Network: Fox Sports, . Wire Svc: AP Format: Sports. Target aud: 25-60. Spec prog: Farm 6 hrs wkly. ♦Jeff Hoberg, gen mgr; Jarrod Thomas, opns mgr; Linn Hodgson, gen sls mgr; Doug Barrett, news dir.

KSNR(FM)—(Thief River Falls, May 1976: 100.3 mhz; 100 kw. Ant 620 ft TL: N47 58 38 W96 36 42. Stereo. Hrs open: 24 505 University Ave., Grand Forks, ND, 58203. Phone: (701) 746-1417. Fax: (701) 746-1410.E-mail: patmclean@clearchannel.com Web Site:www.ksnrfm100.com Licensee: Citicasters Licenses L.P. Group owner: Clear Channel Communications Inc. (acq 10-26-99; grpsl). Population served: 200,000 Haley, Bader & Potts. Format: Country. News staff: one; News: 10 hrs wkly. Target aud: 25-54; boomers & kids. Spec prog: Farm one hr wkly. ♦Pat McLean, gen mgr, gen sls mgr; Susie Johnson, prom mgr; David Andrews, progmg dir; Ken Morgan, pub affrs dir; Dave Schroeder, engrg mgr, chief of engrg; Shannon Stone, local news ed; Josh Jones, disc jockey.

KZLT-FM— Apr 1, 1975: 104.3 mhz; 100 kw. 550 ft TL: N47 48 37 W96 55 46. Hrs open: Prog sep from AM Box 13638, Grand Forks, ND, 58208. Phone: (701) 772-2204. Fax: (701) 772-0540.E-mail: general@kcnn.com Web Site:www.1043moremusic.com Licensee: Leighton Enterprises Inc. Population served: 100,000 Format: Adult contemp. ♦Matt Opsahl, progmg dir.

Eden Prairie

WGVZ(FM)— March 1993: 105.7 mhz; 950 w. Ant 833 ft TL: N44 58 34 W93 16 20. Hrs open: 24
Rebroadcasts WGVX(FM) Lakeville.
2000 S. Elm St., Minneapolis, 55414. Phone: (612) 617-4000. Fax: (612) 676-8292. Web Site:www.love105.fm Licensee: Radio License Holding III LLC. Group owner: ABC Inc. (acq 6-12-2007; grpsl). Population served: 500,000 Natl. Network: ABC, . Natl. Rep: Katz Radio,. Format: Love songs of the 60s, 70s and 80s. ♦Marc Kalman, pres, gen mgr; Dave Hamilton, opns mgr; Pete Frisch, sls dir; Shelley Malecha Wilkes, gen sls mgr; Leslie Heinemann, natl sls mgr; Brook Johnson, mktg dir; Joni Schmidt, prom mgr; Chris Rahn, progmg dir; Jeremy Stone, mus dir, pub affrs dir; Ranee Hanson, pub affrs dir; Dave Szaflarski, chief of engrg.

Elk River

KLCI(FM)—Licensed to Elk River. See Princeton

Ely

WELY(AM)— Oct 2, 1954: 1450 khz; 1 kw-U, DA-N. TL: N47 53 37 W91 51 59. (CP: TL: N47 53 40 W91 51 50). Hrs open: 133 E. Chapman St., 55731-1229. Phone: (218) 365-4444. Fax: (218) 365-3657.E-mail: wely@spacestar.net Web Site:www.wely.com Licensee: Bois Forte Tribal Council (acq 6-1-2005; $445,000 with co-located FM). Population served: 20,000 Rini & Coran. Format: Var/div. Target aud: General; senior citizens. ♦Bill Roloff, gen mgr; Brett Ross, progmg dir; Joany Haag, traf mgr.

WELY-FM— July 25, 1992: 94.5 mhz; 6 kw. Ant 328 ft TL: N47 53 40 W91 51 50. (CP: 14.5 kw, ant 338 ft). Stereo. Hrs open: 133 E. Chapman St., 55731. Phone: (218) 365-4444. Fax: (218) 365-3657.E-mail: welydj@wely.com Web Site:www.wely.com

***WIRC(FM)**—Not on air, target date: unknown: 89.3 mhz; 19 kw. Ant 336 ft TL: N47 53 39.9 W91 51 50. Hrs open: Minnesota Public Radio, 480 Cedar St., St. Paul, 55101. Phone: (651) 290-1500. Fax: (651) 290-1243.E-mail: info@mpr.org Web Site:www.mpr.org Licensee: Minnesota Public Radio. ♦William H. Kling, gen mgr.

Eveleth

KRBT(AM)— December 1948: 1340 khz; 1 kw-U. TL: N47 28 40 W92 32 00. Hrs open: 24 Box 650, 906 Old Hwy. 53, 55734. Phone: (218) 741-5922. Fax: (218) 741-7302.E-mail: weve@spacestar.net Licensee: Iron Range Broadcasting Inc. Group owner: Lew Latto Group of Northland Radio Stations (acq 5-1-78). Population served: 30,000 Format: News/talk. Target aud: 25-54. Spec prog: Finnish one hr, polka 3 hrs wkly. ♦Dennis Jerrold, gen mgr; Ken Daniels, progmg dir; Steve Carlson, news dir.

WEVE-FM— June 26, 1978: 97.9 mhz; 71 kw. 555 ft TL: N47 35 53 W92 13 26. Stereo. Hrs open: 24 Dups AM 90% Box 650, 906 Old Hwy. 53, 55734. Phone: (218) 741-5922. Fax: (218) 741-7302. Population served: 75,000 Format: Adult contemp. News staff: one; News: one hr wkly. ♦Annie Wargowski, stn mgr & traf mgr.

Eyota

KLCX(FM)— 2008: 103.9 mhz; 1.3 kw. Ant 566 ft TL: N44 02 25 W92 13 05. Hrs open: 122 4th St. S.W., Rochester, 55902. Phone: (507) 286-1010. Fax: (507) 286-9370.E-mail: info@klcxfm.com Web Site:www.klcxfm.com Licensee: Cumulus Licensing LLC. Natl. Network: Westwood One, . Natl. Rep: Christal,. Wire Svc: AP Format: Classic hits. News staff: one; News: 2 hrs wkly. Target aud: 25-49. ♦Shannon Knoepke, gen mgr; Terry Lee, gen sls mgr; Jeff Cecil, progmg dir; Kim David, news dir; Bill Davis, chief of engrg.

Fairmont

KFMC(FM)— July 31, 1978: 106.5 mhz; 100 kw. 400 ft TL: N43 37 45 W94 29 00. Stereo. Hrs open: 24 Prog sep from AM Box 491, 56031. Secondary address: 1371 W. Lair Rd. 56031. Phone: (507) 235-5595. Fax: (507) 235-5973.E-mail: classic@kfmc.com Web Site:www.ksum.com Population served: 113,530 Format: Classic rock. Target aud: 25-54.

KSUM(AM)— Jan 1, 1949: 1370 khz; 1 kw-U, DA-2. TL: N43 37 45 W94 29 00. Stereo. Hrs open: Box 491, 56031. Secondary address: 1371 W. Lair Rd. 56031. Phone: (507) 235-5595. Fax: (507) 235-5973.E-mail: classics@kfmc.com Web Site:www.ksum.com Licensee: Woodward Broadcasting Inc. (acq 11-1-62). Population served: 20,200 Natl. Rep: Hyett/Ramsland,. Booth, Freret, Imlay & Tepper. Format: News. sports, agriculture info. Target aud: General. ♦Charles Woodward, gen mgr; Stan Brookens, progmg dir; Rod Halverson, news dir.

Faribault

KBGY(FM)— October 2001: 107.5 mhz; 48 kw. 394 ft TL: N44 12 42 W93 20 18. Stereo. Hrs open: 24 14589 Grand Ave. S., Burnsville, 55306. Phone: (952) 435-5777. Fax: (952) 435-3181.E-mail: info@spirit.fm Web Site:www.spirit.fm Licensee: Milestone Radio II LLC (acq 10-3-01; $2.2 million). Format: Christian music. News staff: one; News: 10 hrs wkly. Target aud: General; 25-54. ♦Tom Payne, gen mgr.

KDHL(AM)— Jan 10, 1948: 920 khz; 5 kw-U, DA-2. TL: N44 15 47 W93 16 29. Hrs open: 24 601 Central Ave., 55021. Phone: (507) 334-0061. Fax: (507) 334-7057.E-mail: info@kdhlradio.com Web Site:www.kdhlradio.com Licensee: Cumulus Licensing Corp. Group owner: Cumulus Media Inc. (acq 7-21-98; grpsl). Population served: 250,000 Rgnl. Network: MNN. MNN Format: News, sports, farm. News staff: one; News: 8 hrs wkly. Target aud: 35 plus. ♦Gary Foss, gen mgr; Bob Buck, progmg dir; Gordon Kosfeld, news dir.

KQCL(FM)— Jan 10, 1968: 95.9 mhz; 3 kw. 328 ft TL: N44 21 25 W93 11 31. Stereo. Hrs open: 601 Central Ave., 55021. Phone: (507) 334-0061. Fax: (507) 334-7057.E-mail: info@kdhlradio.com Web

Site:www.cumulus.com Licensee: Cumulus Licensing Corp. Population served: 200,000 Format: Class rock. Target aud: 18-49. ◆Mike Eiler, progmg dir.

Fergus Falls

KBRF(AM)— Oct 20, 1926: 1250 khz; 5 kw-D, 2.2 kw-N, DA-N. TL: N46 16 22 W96 02 41. Hrs open: 24 Box 495, 56538. Secondary address: 728 Western Ave. N. 56537. Phone: (218) 736-7596. Fax: (218) 736-2836.E-mail: lakesradio@lakesradio.net Web Site:www.lakesradio.net Licensee: Result Radio Inc. Group owner: The Result Radio Group (acq 1-30-78). Population served: 400,000 Natl. Network: Westwood One, . Rgnl. Network: MNN. Natl. Rep: Hyett/Ramsland,. Wire Svc: AP Format: News/talk/information. News staff: 2; News: 20 hrs wkly. Target aud: Adults 35+. Spec prog: Farm 15 hrs, relg 5 hrs wkly. ◆Greg Brady, pres, opns mgr; Doug Gray, gen mgr, gen sls mgr; Jerry Papenfuss, CEO, pres & opns mgr; Brian Lokken, news dir.

*KCMF(FM)— June 6, 2003: 89.7 mhz; 2.7 kw. Ant 216 ft TL: N46 19 12 W96 05 32. Hrs open:
Rebroadcasts KSJN(FM) Minneapolis.
Minnesota Public Radio, 480 Cedar St., St. Paul, 55101. Phone: (651) 290-1500. Fax: (651) 290-1224.E-mail: info@mpr.org Web Site:www.mpr.org Licensee: Minnesota Public Radio. Format: Class. ◆William H. Kling, gen mgr.

KJJK(AM)— Dec 1, 1986: 1020 khz; 2 kw-D, 370 kw-N. TL: N46 14 43 W95 58 46. Hrs open: 24 Box 495, 56538. Secondary address: 728 Western Ave. N. 56537. Phone: (218) 736-7596. Fax: (218) 736-2836.E-mail: lakesradio@lakesradio.net Web Site:www.lakesradio.net Licensee: Result Radio Inc. Group owner: The Result Radio Group (acq 3-27-97; $1.1 million with co-located FM). Population served: 54,000 Natl. Network: ABC, Westwood One, . Natl. Rep: Hyett/Ramsland,. Pepper & Corazzini. Format: Oldies. News staff: 2; News: one hr wkly. Target aud: 35 plus; family, home owners, execs, mgrs, dual house income. Spec prog: Relg 3 hrs wkly. ◆Jerry Papenfuss, CEO & pres; Doug Gray, gen mgr, gen sls mgr, gen sls mgr; Greg Brady, opns mgr; Jeff Swedberg, progmg dir; Brian Lokken, news dir.

KJJK-FM— Oct 14, 1981: 96.5 mhz; 100 kw. Ant 480 ft TL: N46 14 43 W95 58 46. Stereo. Hrs open: 24 Box 495, 56538. Secondary address: 728 Western Ave. N. 56537. Phone: (218) 736-7596. Fax: (218) 736-2836.E-mail: lakesradio@lakesradio.net Web Site:www.lakesradio.net Licensee: Result Radio Inc. Population served: 400,000 Natl. Network: ABC, . Natl. Rep: Hyett/Ramsland,. Format: Country. News staff: 2; News: 3 hrs wkly. Target aud: 21-54; today's country music fans. ◆Doug Gray, gen mgr; Greg Brady, opns mgr; Jeff Swedberg, progmg dir.

*KNWF(FM)— April 2003: 91.5 mhz; 100 w. 226 ft Hrs open:
Rebroadcast of KNOW-FM Minneapolis-St. Paul.
480 Cedar St., St. Paul, 55101. Phone: (651) 290-1500. Fax: (651) 290-1224.E-mail: info@mpr.org Web Site:www.mpr.org Licensee: Minnesota Public Radio. Format: News. ◆William H. Kling, gen mgr.

KZCR(FM)— Jan 19, 1968: 103.3 mhz; 100 kw. Ant 649 ft TL: N46 28 06 W96 11 54. Stereo. Hrs open: 24 Box 495, 56538. Secondary address: 728 Western Ave. 56537. Phone: (218) 736-7596. Fax: (218) 736-2836.E-mail: lakesradio@lakesradio.net Web Site:www.lakesradio.net Licensee: Result Radio Inc. Population served: 400,000 Natl. Rep: Hyett/Ramsland,. Rgnl rep: Hyett/Ramsland Format: Rock. News staff: 2; News: 10 hrs wkly. Target aud: Adults 25-49. ◆Doug Gray, gen mgr; Greg Brady, progmg dir; Susan Kay, pub affrs dir.

Forest Lake

WLKX-FM— Oct 28, 1978: 95.9 mhz; 3 kw. 300 ft TL: N45 17 40 W93 04 22. Stereo. Hrs open: 24 15226 W. Freeway Dr., 55025. Phone: (651) 464-6796. Fax: (651) 464-3638.E-mail: tom@spirit.net Web Site:www.spirit.net Licensee: Lakes Broadcasting Co. Inc. Population served: 50,000 Format: Adult contemp Christian. News staff: one; News: 20 hrs wkly. Target aud: 25-54; general. Spec prog: Auction show 9 hrs, relg 6 hrs wkly. ◆Gary Kastner, gen mgr.

Fosston

KKCQ(AM)— Dec 12, 1966: 1480 khz; 5 kw-D, 90 w-N. TL: N47 33 51 W95 43 27. Hrs open: 24 Box 606, 56542. Secondary address: 35006 Hwy. 2 E. 56542. Phone: (218) 435-1919. Fax: (218) 435-1480.E-mail: info@q107fm.com Web Site:www.q107fm.com Licensee: Pine to Prairie Broadcasting Inc. (acq 2-1-92; $335,000 with co-located FM; 2-10-92). Population served: 1,684 Rgnl. Network: MNN. MNN Eugene T. Smith. Format: Talk, oldies. News staff: one; News: 4 hrs wkly. Target aud: 25-54; family-oriented adults. Spec prog: Farm 5 hrs, relg 4 hrs wkly. ◆Bob Overmoe, pres; Phil Ehlke, gen mgr, gen sls

mgr; Tom Lano, progmg dir; Jamie Nesvold, mus dir; Laura Hamilton, news dir; Jim Offerdahl, chief of engrg.

Glencoe

KTTB(FM)— Sept 23, 1993: 96.3 mhz; 100 kw. Ant 577 ft TL: N44 56 25 W93 55 43. Hrs open: 24 5300 Edina Industrial Blvd., Suite 200, Edina, 55439. Phone: (952) 842-7200. Fax: (952) 842-1048.E-mail: info@kttbfm.com Web Site:www.b96online.com Licensee: Northern Lights Broadcasting LLC Group owner: Radio One Inc. (acq 8-31-2007; $28 million). Rgnl. Network: Linder Farm. Format: Rhythmic CHR. News staff: one. Target aud: 18-34; adults. ◆John McMonagle, gen sls mgr; Steve Woodbury, VP, gen mgr & engrg VP.

Glenwood

KMGK(FM)— Mar 11, 1983: 107.1 mhz; 3 kw. 300 ft TL: N45 36 53 W95 23 28. Stereo. Hrs open: 24 Box 241, 56334. Phone: (320) 634-5358. Fax: (320) 634-5359.E-mail: traffic@kmgk1071.com Web Site:www.kmgk1071.com Licensee: Branstock Communications Inc. Minn. News Net. Format: Soft Gold. News staff: one; News: 13 wkly. Target aud: 25-54. ◆Steven R. Nestor, CEO; Steven Nestor, gen mgr; Paul Rykhus, gen sls mgr; Rockland DeBoer, traf mgr.

*KRFG(FM)— Not on air, target date: unknown: 90.5 mhz; 10.5 kw. Ant 216 ft TL: N45 39 10 W95 29 38. Hrs open: 4604 Airpark Blvd., Duluth, 55811-5751. Phone: (218) 722-3017. Fax: (218) 722-1650.E-mail: airstaff@refugeradio.com Web Site:www.refugeradio.com Licensee: Refuge Media Group. ◆Brett M. Gibson, gen mgr.

Golden Valley

KDIZ(AM)— May 13, 1948: 1440 khz; 5 kw-D, 500 w-N, DA-N. TL: N44 59 20 W93 21 06. Hrs open: 24 2000 Elm St. S.E., Minneapolis, 55414. Phone: (612) 617-4000. Fax: (612) 676-8292. Web Site:www.disney.com Licensee: RD Minneapolis Assets LLC. (Acq 6-30-86). Population served: 659,300 Natl. Rep: ABC Radio Sales,. Format: Children. News staff: one; News: 5 hrs wkly. Target aud: 18-49; baby boomers/Generation X. ◆Kevin McCarthy, prom dir; Beth Muschel, progmg dir.

KQRS-FM— Sept 1, 1963: 92.5 mhz; 100 kw. 900 ft TL: N44 59 20 W93 21 06. (CP: Ant 1,033 ft.). Stereo. Hrs open: 24 2000 Elm St. S.E., Minneapolis, 55414. Phone: (612) 617-4000. Fax: (612) 676-8292.E-mail: mail@92kqrs.com Web Site:www.92kqrs.com Licensee: Radio License Holding III LLC. Group owner: ABC Inc. (acq 6-12-2007; grpsl). Population served: 2,400,000 Natl. Network: ABC, . Natl. Rep: ABC Radio Sales,. Format: Classic rock. ◆Marc Kalman, pres, gen mgr; Pete Frisch, sls dir; Brent Wilcox, prom dir; Dave Hamilton, progmg dir; Reed Endersbe, mus dir; David Szaflarski, chief of engrg; Carolyn Kuhrke, rsch dir, traf mgr.

KYCR(AM)— Licensed to Golden Valley. See Minneapolis-St. Paul

Grand Marais

*WLSN(FM)— 2005: 89.7 mhz; 6 kw. Ant 636 ft TL: N47 46 04 W90 20 47. Hrs open: 207 W Superior St, Suite 224, Duluth, 55802. Phone: (218) 722-9411. Fax: (218) 720-4900.E-mail: info@mpr.org Web Site:www.mpr.org Licensee: Minnesota Public Radio. Minn. Pub. Radio Format: News & info. ◆William H. Kling, pres; Kat Eldred, gen mgr.

*WMLS(FM)— Not on air, target date: unknown: 88.7 mhz; 6 kw. 613 ft Hrs open: 207 W Superior St, Suite 224, Duluth, 55802. Phone: (218) 722-9411. Fax: (218) 720-4900.E-mail: info@mpr.org Web Site:www.mpr.org Licensee: Minnesota Public Radio. Minn. Pub. Radio Format: Classical. ◆William Kling, pres; Kat Eldred, gen mgr; Doug Thompson, engrg dir.

*WTIP(FM)— July 1, 1998: 90.7 mhz; 25 kw. Ant 584 ft TL: N47 46 09 W90 20 49. Hrs open: 5 AM-3 AM
Rebroadcasts KUMD-FM Duluth 70%.
Box 1005, 55604. Secondary address: 55 W. 5th St. 55604. Phone: (218) 387-1070. Fax: (218) 387-1120.E-mail: info@wtip.org Web Site:www.wtip.org Licensee: Cook County Community Radio Corp. Population served: 150,000 Format: AAA, var, adult contemp. News: 15 hrs wkly. Target aud: General. Spec prog: Blues 15 hrs, AOR 15 hrs, progsv rock 15 hrs wkly. ◆Ann Possis, pres; Mike Raymond, exec VP & VP; Deb Benedict, stn mgr; Melanie Steele, dev dir; Kristy Johnson, progmg dir; Cathy Quinn, mus dir; Barbara Jean Meyers, news dir, pub affrs dir; Jeff Nemitz, engrg dir.

WXXZ(FM)— 1999: 95.3 mhz; 100 kw. 699 ft TL: N47 39 55 W90 42 22. Hrs open:
Rebroadcasts KQDS-FM Duluth 100%.
501 Lake Ave. S., Suite 200A, Duluth, 55802. Phone: (218) 722-0921. Fax: (218) 723-1499. Licensee: Red Rock Radio Corp. (group owner; acq 1-10-00; grpsl). Format: Classic rock. ◆Shawn Skramstad, gen mgr; Jim Payne, gen sls mgr; Bill Jones, progmg dir; Jason Manning, news dir.

Grand Portage

*WGPO(FM)— Not on air, target date: unknown: 90.1 mhz; 1 kw. Ant 230 ft TL: N47 58 40 W89 41 05. Hrs open: Box 1005, Grand Marais, 55604. Phone: (218) 387-1070. Fax: (218) 387-1120.E-mail: wtip@boreal.org Web Site:www.wtip.org Licensee: Cook County Community Radio Corp. ◆Ann Possis, pres; Deb Benedict, stn mgr.

Grand Rapids

*KAXE(FM)— Apr 23, 1976: 91.7 mhz; 100 kw. 460 ft TL: N47 15 17 W93 26 03. Stereo. Hrs open: 260 NE 2nd St., 55744. Phone: (218) 326-1234. Fax: (218) 326-1235.E-mail: kaxe@kaxe.org Web Site:www.kaxe.org Licensee: Northern Community Radio Inc. Population served: 220,000 Natl. Network: NPR, PRI, . Format: Var/div. Target aud: General. ◆Maggie Montgomery, gen mgr; John Bauer, dev dir; Dan Houg, progmg dir, engrg dir.

KMFY(FM)— Dec 5, 1975: 96.9 mhz; 100 kw. 450 ft TL: N47 15 17 W93 26 03. Stereo. Hrs open: 24 Prog sep from AM Box 597, 55744. Secondary address: 507 11th St. S.E. 55744. Phone: (218) 999-5639. Fax: (218) 990-5609. Population served: 43,000 Format: Adult contemp. News staff: one. Target aud: 35-54.

KOZY(AM)— Jan 29, 1948: 1320 khz; 5 kw-U, DA-2. TL: N47 10 22 W93 27 10. Hrs open: 24 Box 597, 55744. Secondary address: 507 11th St. S.E. 55744. Phone: (218) 999-5699. Fax: (218) 990-5609.E-mail: kozykmfy@mchsi.com Licensee: Itasca Broadcasting Inc. (acq 4-15-02; with co-located FM). Population served: 44,000 Natl. Network: ABC, . Rgnl. Network: MNN. MNN Format: Gold classics. News staff: one. ◆Mike Iaizzo, pres & gen mgr.

*WRFR(FM)— Not on air, target date: unknown: 88.1 mhz; 6 kw vert. Ant 341 ft TL: N47 15 17 W93 26 03. Hrs open: 4604 Airpark Blvd., Duluth, 55811-5751. Phone: (218) 722-3017. Fax: (218) 279-5010. Web Site:www.refugeradio.com Licensee: Refuge Media Group. ◆Mike Marrone, pres; Paulette Kutzler, gen mgr.

Granite Falls

KKRC(FM)— Oct 5, 1993: 93.9 mhz; 6 kw. 262 ft TL: N44 54 06 W95 32 53. Hrs open: 24 Box 513, Montevideo, 56001. Phone: (320) 269-8815. Fax: (320) 269-8449. Licensee: Iowa City Broadcasting Co. Group owner: Tom Ingstad Broadcasting Group Natl. Network: ABC, . Natl. Rep: Katz Radio,. Minn. News Net. Format: Oldies. ◆Dwight Mulder, opns mgr, progmg dir; Roger Hill, gen sls mgr.

KMGM(FM)— See Montevideo

Hastings

KDWA(AM)— Oct 24, 1963: 1460 khz; 1 kw-D, 45 w-N. TL: N44 42 49 W92 50 30. Hrs open: 24 514 Vermillion St., 55033. Phone: (651) 437-1460. Fax: (651) 438-3042.E-mail: dan@kdwa.com Web Site:www.kdwa.com Licensee: K & M Broadcasting Inc. (acq 6-30-92; $161,000; 7-20-92). Population served: 250000 Natl. Network: CNN Radio, . Rgnl. Network: MNN. MNN Format: Loc news, sports, talk. News staff: 1.5; News: 18 hrs wkly. Target aud: 25-65; general. ◆Dan Massman, gen mgr.

Hermantown

WWAX(FM)— June 17, 1996: 92.1 mhz; 780 w. 905 ft TL: N46 47 13 W92 07 17. Hrs open: 501 Lake Ave. S., Suite 200A, Duluth, 55802. Phone: (218) 722-0921. Fax: (218) 723-1499. Licensee: Red Rock Radio Corp. (group owner; acq 1-10-00; grpsl). Format: Adult contemp. Target aud: 18-35; general. ◆Shawn Skramstad, gen mgr; Jim Payne, gen sls mgr; Bill Jones, progmg dir; Jason Manning, news dir.

Hibbing

***KADU(FM)—** July 18, 1994: 90.1 mhz; 100 w. Ant 220 ft TL: N47 23 59 W92 57 47. (CP: 2.2 kw horiz, 22 kw vert, ant 371 ft. TL: N47 24 34 W92 57 02). Hrs open:
Simulcast with KBHW(FM) International Falls 100%.
Box 433, 55746. Phone: (218) 285-7398. Licensee: Heartland Christian Broadcasters Inc. (acq 4-22-2005; $30,000). Format: Christian. ♦Bruce Christopherson, stn mgr; Gene Gee, progmg dir.

KMFY(FM)—See Grand Rapids

WIRR(FM)—See Duluth

WMFG(AM)— 1935: 1240 khz; 1 kw-U. TL: N47 24 30 W92 57 04. Hrs open: 24 807 W. 37th St., 55746. Phone: (218) 263-7531. Fax: (218) 263-6112.E-mail: lindas@mwcradio.com Licensee: Midwest Communications Inc. (group owner; (acq 5-10-2004; grpsl). Population served: 70,000 Rgnl. Network: MNN. MNN Format: Sports, talk. News staff: 2; News: 13 hrs wkly. Target aud: 25-55; men. Spec prog: Folk, relg 4 hrs, polka 4 hrs wkly. ♦Kristi Garrity, gen mgr, gen sls mgr, mktg dir, prom dir & adv dir; Doug Diedrich, progmg dir; Craig Holgate, news dir; Dan Klaysmat, engrg dir.

WMFG-FM— 1971: 106.3 mhz; 25 kw. 253 ft TL: N47 24 30 W92 57 04. (CP: 25 kw, ant 259 ft.). Stereo. Hrs open: 24 807 W. 37th St., 55746. Phone: (218) 263-7531. Fax: (218) 263-6112.E-mail: lindas@mwcradio.com Licensee: Midwest Communications Inc. Rgnl. Network: Hyett/Ramsland. Format: Oldies. Target aud: 25-54.

WNMT(AM)—(Nashwauk, June 2, 1975: 650 khz; 10 kw-D, 500 w-N, DA-N. TL: N47 22 31 W93 00 56. (CP: 10 kw-D, 1 kw-N). Hrs open: 807 W. 37th St., 55746. Phone: (218) 263-7531. Fax: (218) 263-6112.E-mail: lindas@mwcradio.com Web Site:www.wnmtradio.com Licensee: Midwest Communications Inc. (group owner; acq 5-10-2004; grpsl). Population served: 356,000 Format: News/talk. Target aud: 35 plus. Spec prog: Pol 2 hrs wkly. ♦Kristi Garrity, gen mgr; Craig Holgate, progmg dir, news dir, farm dir; Danny Klaysmat, chief of engrg.

WTBX(FM)— Dec 31, 1980: 93.9 mhz; 100 kw. Ant 531 ft TL: N47 22 24 W93 00 48. Stereo. Hrs open: Prog sep from AM 807 W. 37th St., 55746. Phone: (218) 263-7531. Fax: (218) 263-6112.E-mail: lindas@mwcradio.com Web Site:www.wtbx.com Licensee: Midwest Communications Inc. Format: CHR. Target aud: 18-40.

Hinckley

WGRH(FM)—Not on air, target date: unknown: 88.5 mhz; 5.3 kw. Ant 349 ft TL: N46 01 39.2 W93 01 20.3. Hrs open: Minnesota Public Radio, 480 Cedar St., 55101. Phone: (651) 290-1500. Fax: (651) 290-1243.E-mail: info@mpr.org Web Site:www.mpr.org Licensee: Minnesota Public Radio. ♦William H. Kling, gen mgr.

Hutchinson

KARP-FM—(Dassel, June 6, 1968: 106.9 mhz; 7 kw. 554 ft TL: N45 02 43 W94 33 32. Stereo. Hrs open: 24 20132 Hwy. 15 N., 55350-5643. Phone: (320) 587-2140. Fax: (320) 587-5158.E-mail: info@karpfmradio.com Web Site:www.karpradio.com Licensee: Iowa City Broadcasting Co. Inc. Population served: 80,400 Wire Svc: AP Format: Country. News staff: 2; News: 3 hrs wkly. Target aud: 18 plus.

KDUZ(AM)— Sept 16, 1953: 1260 khz; 1 kw-D, 64 w-N. TL: N44 54 24 W94 21 59. Hrs open: 24 20132 Hwy. 15 N., 55350-5643. Phone: (320) 587-2140. Fax: (320) 587-5158.E-mail: kduz@hutchtel.net Web Site:www.kduz.com Licensee: Iowa City Broadcasting Co. Inc. Group owner: Tom Ingstad Broadcasting Group (acq 4-1-2000; grpsl). Population served: 50,000 Minn. Farm Rgnl rep: Hyett/Ramsland. Wire Svc: AP Format: Oldies, news, sports. News staff: 2; News: 21 hrs wkly. Target aud: 30 plus; general. Spec prog: Farm 18 hrs, gospel 3 hrs, polka 8 hrs, Sp one hr wkly. ♦Tom Ingstag, chmn; Dale Koktan, gen mgr, gen sls mgr; John Mons, opns mgr, disc jockey; Jim Ohnstad, progmg dir, pub affrs dir, disc jockey; Mark Wodarczyk, news dir, farm dir; Duane Wawyrzniak, chief of engrg; Joel Niemeyer, sports cmtr; Joel Neimeyer, disc jockey.

International Falls

***KBHW(FM)—** Jan 4, 1983: 99.5 mhz; 100 kw. Ant 580 ft TL: N48 33 45 W93 49 22. Stereo. Hrs open: 24 Box 433, 56649. Secondary address: 4090 Hwy.11 56649. Phone: (218) 285-7398. Fax: (218) 285-7419.E-mail: studio@psalm995.org Web Site:www.psalm995.org Licensee: Heartland Christian Broadcasters. (acq 7-23-99; $1 with KXBR(FM) International Falls). Natl. Network: USA, Moody, . Format: Christian. News: 15 hrs wkly. Target aud: General. ♦Bruce Christopherson, gen mgr, chief of engrg; Gene Gee, opns mgr.

KGHS(AM)— Sept 1, 1959: 1230 khz; 500 w-D, 250 w-N. TL: N48 35 29 W93 22 54. Hrs open: 24 519 3rd St., 56649. Phone: (218) 283-3481. Fax: (218) 283-3087.E-mail: kghsksdm@northwinds.net Web Site:www.ksdmradio.com Licensee: Red Rock Radio Corp. (group owner; (acq 9-1-2006; grpsl). Population served: 8,500 Natl. Network: Jones Radio Networks, . Rgnl. Network: MNN. MNN Format: Oldies. News staff: one; News: 10 hrs wkly. ♦Ro Grignon, pres; Dennis Martin, gen mgr; Jerry Franzen, progmg dir, news dir; Bill Meys, chief of engrg.

***KITF(FM)**—Not on air, target date: unknown: 88.3 mhz; 5.75 kw. Ant 154 ft TL: N48 28 24 W93 20 00. Hrs open: 480 Cedar St., Saint Paul, 55101-2217. Phone: (651) 290-1259. Web Site:www.mpr.org Licensee: Minnesota Public Radio. Minn. Pub. Radio Format: News and info. ♦Thomas J. Kigin, exec VP.

KSDM(FM)— Mar 17, 1979: 104.1 mhz; 8.5 kw. Ant 200 ft TL: N48 35 39 W93 22 56. Stereo. Hrs open: 24 519 3rd St., 56649. Phone: (218) 283-2622. Fax: (218) 283-3087. Web Site:www.ksdmradio.com Licensee: Red Rock Radio Corp. Population served: 30,000 Natl. Network: ABC, . Format: Country. News staff: one; News: 20 hrs wkly.

***KXBR(FM)—** June, 2000: 91.9 mhz; 1.5 kw. 128 ft TL: N48 34 15 W93 26 19. Hrs open: Box 433, 4090 Hwy. 11, 56649. Phone: (218) 285-9190. Fax: (218) 285-7419.E-mail: dj@edge919.com Web Site:www.edge919.com Licensee: Heartland Christian Broadcasters. (acq 7-23-99; $1 with KBHW(FM) International Falls). Format: Christian rock. ♦Bruce Christopherson, gen mgr, chief of engrg; Gene Gee, opns mgr.

Jackson

KKOJ(AM)— July 10, 1980: 1190 khz; 5 kw-D, DA. TL: N43 31 45 W95 00 02. Hrs open: Sunrise-sunset Box 29, 56143. Secondary address: 71991 US Hwy. 71 56143. Phone: (507) 847-5400. Fax: (507) 847-5745.E-mail: kkoj@rconnect.com Web Site:www.kkoj.com Licensee: Kleven Broadcasting Co. of Minnesota. Population served: 275,000 Rgnl. Network: Linder Farm. Linder Farm Wire Svc: AP Format: Modern country. News staff: one; News: 20 hrs wkly. Target aud: General. Spec prog: Farm 15 hrs wkly. ♦Doug Johnson, pres, gen mgr, gen sls mgr; Dave Maschoff, news dir; Jerrie Johnson, chief of engrg, traf mgr; Lee Larson, sports cmtr.

KRAQ(FM)— Apr 25, 1994: 105.7 mhz; 25 kw. 328 ft TL: N43 36 54 W94 57 48. Stereo. Hrs open: 24 Box 29, 56143. Secondary address: 71991 US Hwy. 71 56143. Phone: (507) 847-5400. Fax: (507) 847-5745.E-mail: kkoj@rconnect.com Web Site:www.kkoj.com Licensee: Kleven Broadcasting Co. of Minnesota. (acq 2-27-98). Population served: 150,000 Natl. Network: AP Radio, . Baraff, Koerner & Olender. Wire Svc: AP Format: Oldies, classic Rock. News staff: one; News: new progmg 18 hrs wkly. ♦Doug Johnson, pres, gen mgr, gen sls mgr; Dave Maschoff, news dir; Jerrie Johnson, traf mgr & sports cmtr.

Kelliher

KKWB(FM)— 2008: 102.5 mhz; 50 kw. Ant 472 ft TL: N47 44 21 W94 41 10. Hrs open: Box 1021, Bemidji, 56619. Secondary address: 324 Beltrami Ave. N.W., Bemidji 56601-3105. Phone: (218) 444-1025. Licensee: Bemidji Radio Inc. Format: Country. ♦Edward P. De La Hunt, gen mgr.

La Crescent

KQEG(FM)—Licensed to La Crescent. See La Crosse WI

***KXLC(FM)—** Nov 24, 1991: 91.1 mhz; 230 w. 843 ft TL: N43 48 16 W91 22 18. Stereo. Hrs open: 24 206 S. Broadway, Suite 735, Rochester, 55904. Phone: (507) 282-0910. Fax: (507) 282-2107. Web Site:www.mpr.org Licensee: Minnesota Public Radio. (acq 4-9-90). Natl. Network: NPR, PRI, . Rgnl. Network: Minn. Pub. Minn. Pub. Radio Format: News. News staff: one; News: 24 hrs wkly. Target aud: General. ♦Chris Cross, gen mgr; Mary Stapek, dev dir; Sea Stachura, news rptr.

Lake City

KLCH(FM)— December 2001: 94.9 mhz; 6 kw. Ant 328 ft TL: N44 22 56 W92 22 05. Hrs open: 24 474 Guernsey Ln., Red Wing, 55066. Phone: (651) 388-7151. Fax: (651) 388-7153.E-mail: news@kwng.com Web Site:www.lakehits95.com Licensee: Q Media Group LLC (group owner; (acq 11-21-2007; $150,000). Population served: 35,000 Format: Adult contemp. News staff: 2. Target aud: 25-54. ♦Don Kliewer, gen mgr; Tom Hughes, opns dir.

KMFX-FM— Feb 14, 1991: 102.5 mhz; 9.4 kw. 528 ft TL: N44 16 45 W92 23 38. Hrs open: 1530 Greenview Dr. S.W., Suite 200, Rochester, 55902. Phone: (507) 288-3888. Fax: (507) 288-7815. Licensee: CC Licenses LLC. Group owner: Clear Channel Communications Inc. (acq 10-2000; grpsl). Natl. Rep: D & R Radio,. Format: Country. ♦Bob Fox, gen mgr.

Lake Crystal

KQYK(FM)— 2005: 95.7 mhz; 6 kw. Ant 328 ft TL: N44 03 06 W94 17 59. Hrs open: 54934 210th Ln., Mankato, 56001. Phone: (507) 345-4646. Fax: (507) 345-3299. Licensee: Three Eagles of Luverne Inc. (acq 9-12-2005; $620,000 for CP). Format: Rock. ♦Ron Gates, gen mgr; e Schoen, opns mgr; Miles Riker, progmg dir; Natalie Janssen, traf mgr.

Lakeville

WGVX(FM)— February 1993: 105.1 mhz; 2.6 kw. Ant 499 ft TL: N44 42 05 W93 09 02. Hrs open: 24 2000 S. E. Elm Street, Minneapolis, 55414. Phone: (612) 617-4000. Fax: (612) 676-8293.E-mail: email@love105.fm Web Site:www.love105.fm Licensee: Radio License Holdiing III LLC. Group owner: ABC Inc. (acq 6-12-2007; grpsl). Population served: 500,000 Natl. Network: ABC, . Natl. Rep: Interep,. Format: Love songs of the 60s, 70s and 80s. ♦Marc Kalman, pres, stn mgr; Dave Hamilton, opns mgr; Pete Frisch, sls dir; Susan Larkin, gen sls mgr; Leslie Heinemann, natl sls mgr; Brook Johnson, mktg dir; Joni Schmidt, prom dir; Chris Rahn, progmg dir; Ben Gnam, mus dir; Christopher Taykalo, pub affrs dir; Dave Szaflarski, chief of engrg.

Litchfield

KKLN(FM)—(Atwater, Nov 26, 1988: 94.1 mhz; 6 kw. Ant 328 ft TL: N45 04 24 W94 45 19. Stereo. Hrs open: 24 Kandi Mall, 1605 S. 1st St., Willmar, 56201-4234. Phone: (320) 235-1194. Fax: (320) 235-6894.E-mail: info@kkln.com Web Site:www.kkln.com Licensee: Flagship Broadcasting. (acq 1999). Format: Classic rock. Target aud: General. ♦Rick Anderson, pres; Justin Klinghagen, gen mgr, gen sls mgr; Nate Thomas, opns mgr, progmg dir; Melanie Echart, news dir.

KLFD(AM)— Jan 2, 1959: 1410 khz; 500 w-D, 47 w-N. TL: N45 07 02 W94 33 13. Hrs open: 24 234 N. Sibley Ave., 55355. Phone: (320) 693-3281. Fax: (320) 693-3283.E-mail: info@klfd1410.com Web Site:www.klfd1410.com Licensee: Mid-Minnesota Broadcasting Co. (acq 11-26-91; 12-16-91). Population served: 22,000 Leventhal, Senter & Lerman. Format: Full service. News staff: one; News: 10 hrs wkly. Target aud: 25-54. Spec prog: Farm 20 hrs, relg 3 hrs wkly. ♦Steve Gretsch, pres, gen mgr, opns VP; Jennifer Flynn, gen sls mgr; Aaron Imholte, progmg dir; Tim Bergstrom, news dir.

Little Falls

KFML(FM)— November 1988: 94.1 mhz; 6 kw. Ant 275 ft TL: N46 00 16 W94 19 42. Stereo. Hrs open: 24 16405 Haven Rd., 56345. Phone: (320) 632-2992. Fax: (320) 632-2571.E-mail: acls@fallsradio.com Web Site:www.fallsradio.com Licensee: Little Falls Radio Corp. (acq 6-28-2004). Natl. Network: CNN Radio, . Minn. News Net. Format: Adult contemp. News staff: one; News: 3 hrs wkly. Target aud: 25-54. Spec prog: Relg 6 hrs wkly. ♦Rob Grams, progmg dir.

KLTF(AM)— October 1950: 960 khz; 5 kw-D, 35 w-N. TL: N46 00 16 W94 19 42. Hrs open: 24 16405 Haven Rd., 56345. Phone: (320) 632-2992. Fax: (320) 632-2571.E-mail: ads@fallsradio.com Web Site:www.fallsradio.com Licensee: Little Falls Radio Corp. (group owner; acq 6-28-2004; grpsl). Population served: 100,000 Natl. Network: Fox News Radio, ABC, Fox Sports, Westwood One, . Rgnl. Network: MNN. Linder Farm Format: News/talk. News staff: one; News: 24 hrs wkly. Target aud: 35-65; loc audience who listen for news & info. Spec prog: Farm 8 hrs, relg 4 hrs, polka 2 hrs, party line 5 hrs wkly. ♦Chris Grams, gen mgr, stn mgr; Melanie Lintner, gen sls mgr; Rod Grams, pres & progmg dir; Lacey Welle, traf mgr; Al Windsperger, sports cmtr.

WYRQ(FM)— May 19, 1980: 92.1 mhz; 3 kw. 299 ft TL: N45 56 57 W94 17 48. Stereo. Hrs open: 24 16405 Haven Rd., 56345. Phone: (320) 632-2992. Fax: (320) 632-2571. Web Site:www.fallsradio.com Licensee: Little Falls Radio Corp. (group owner; acq 6-28-2004; grpsl). Population served: 50,000 Natl. Network: CNN Radio, . Rgnl. Network: MNN. Minn. Farm Wire Svc: UPI Format: Agriculture, country, news/talk. News staff: one; News: 20 hrs wkly. Target aud: 25-54;

farmers & working people. ◆Chris Grams, gen mgr; Rod Grams, pres & prom mgr; Al Windsperger, progmg dir; Mark Persons, chief of engrg.

Long Prairie

KEYL(AM)— Sept 15, 1959: 1400 khz; 1 kw-U. TL: N45 57 45 W94 52 09. Hrs open: 24 Box 187, 221 Central Ave., 56347. Phone: (320) 732-2164. Fax: (320) 732-2284.E-mail: keyl@keylrealcountry.com Licensee: Prairie Broadcasting Co. (acq 10-28-98; $375,000 for stock with KXDL(FM) Browerville). Population served: 28,000 Natl. Network: ABC, . Miller & Miller, P.C. Format: Country. News: 15 hrs wkly. Target aud: 25 plus. Spec prog: Farm 5 hrs, sports 10 hrs, relg 4 hrs wkly. ◆Gene Sullivan, pres, gen mgr; Todd Jensen, gen sls mgr.

KXDL(FM)—(Browerville, May 15, 1992: 99.7 mhz; 6 kw. 328 ft TL: N46 03 15 W94 50 50. Hrs open: 24 Box 187, 56347. Phone: (320) 732-2164. Fax: (320) 732-2284. Web Site:kxdlhotrodradio.com Licensee: Prairie Broadcasting Co. (acq 10-28-98; $375,000 for stock with KEYL(AM) Long Prairie). Population served: 27,000 Rgnl rep: O'Malley. Miller & Miller. Format: Adult contemp. News: 4 hrs wkly. Target aud: 18-44; female. Spec prog: Sports 2 hrs wkly. ◆Gene Sullivan, pres, gen mgr; Clif Cline, opns mgr, progmg dir; Todd Jensen, gen sls mgr.

Luverne

KLQL(FM)— Nov 24, 1971: 101.1 mhz; 100 kw. 530 ft TL: N43 48 24 W96 12 23. Stereo. Hrs open: 24 Prog sep from AM Box 599, County Rd. 4 E., 56156. Phone: (507) 283-4444. Fax: (507) 283-4445. Web Site:www.kqad.net Population served: 350,000 Format: C&W. News: 4 hrs wkly. Target aud: 25-54. Spec prog: Farm 10 hrs, gospel 4 hrs wkly. ◆Bruce Thalhuber, progmg dir; Matt Crosby, farm dir.

KQAD(AM)— Mar 1, 1971: 800 khz; 500 w-D, 80 w-N, DA-2. TL: N43 39 01 W96 10 19. Stereo. Hrs open: 24 1140 150th Ave., 56156. Phone: (507) 283-4444. Fax: (507) 283-4445.E-mail: sg@kqad.threeeagles.com Web Site:www.kqad.net Licensee: Three Eagles Communications, Luverne. Group owner: Three Eagles Communications (acq 1996; grpsl). Population served: 30,000 Natl. Rep: Hyett/Ramsland,. Format: Soft adult contemp. News staff: one; News: 5 hrs wkly. Target aud: 50 plus. Spec prog: Relg 5 hrs wkly. ◆Steve Graphenteen, gen mgr.

Madison

KLQP(FM)— Jan 31, 1983: 92.1 mhz; 25 kw. 300 ft TL: N45 01 37 W96 11 15. Stereo. Hrs open: 24 Box 70, 623 W. 3rd St., 56256. Phone: (320) 598-7301. Fax: (320) 598-7955.E-mail: klqpfm@farmerstel.net Web Site:www.klqpfm.com Licensee: Lac Qui Parle Broadcasting Co. Inc. Population served: 40,000 Network: CNN Radio, . Minn. News Net. Format: Country, oldies. News: 18 hrs wkly. Target aud: General. Spec prog: Farm 5 hrs wkly. ◆Maynard R. Meyer, CEO, pres & gen mgr; Kris Kuechenmeister, opns mgr.

Mahnomen

KRJM(FM)— Aug 27, 2001: 101.5 mhz; 25 kw. 328 ft TL: N47 27 23 W96 07 57. Hrs open: 24 213 N. Main St., 56510. Phone: (218) 935-5355. Fax: (218) 935-9020.E-mail: info@krjmradio.com Web Site:www.krjmradio.com Licensee: R & J Broadcasting. (acq. 9-1-01; Format: Oldies. ◆Jim Birkemeyer, gen mgr.

Mankato

KATO-FM—(New Ulm, Nov 21, 1966: 93.1 mhz; 100 kw. Ant 489 ft TL: N44 07 44 W94 11 15. Stereo. Hrs open: 24 59346 Madison Ave., 56001. Phone: (507) 345-4537. Fax: (507) 345-5364. Licensee: Minnesota Valley Broadcasting Co. Group owner: Clear Channel Communications Inc. (acq 9-1-2007; $3.13 million). Population served: 100,000 Format: Country. ◆Jo Guck Bailey, VP & gen mgr.

KDOG(FM)—(North Mankato, Apr 1, 1985: 96.7 mhz; 18 kw. Ant 390 ft TL: N44 13 20 W94 07 03. Stereo. Hrs open: 24 59346 Madison Ave., 56001. Phone: (507) 345-4537. Fax: (507) 345-5364. Web Site:www.katoinfo.com Licensee: Minnesota Valley Broadcasting Co. Format: Adult contemp. News staff: one; News: 4 hrs wkly. ◆Jo Guck Bailey, VP & gen mgr.

KEEZ-FM— Apr 1, 1968: 99.1 mhz; 100 kw. 864 ft TL: N43 56 14 W94 24 41. Stereo. Hrs open: 24 54934 210 Ln., 56001. Phone: (507) 345-4646. Fax: (507) 345-3299.E-mail: zdesk@keez.com Web Site:www.keez.com Licensee: Three Eagles of Luverne Inc. Group owner: Three Eagles Communications (acq 6-19-00; grpsl). Population

served: 350,000 Natl. Network: Westwood One, . Rgnl rep: O'Malley. Format: Hot adult contemp. News staff: one. Target aud: 25-54. ◆Ron Gates, gen mgr; Mike Schoen, opns mgr; Miles Riker, progmg dir; Natalie Janssen, traf mgr.

KGAC(FM)—See Saint Peter

*KMSU(FM)— Jan 7, 1963: 89.7 mhz; 20 kw. 400 ft TL: N44 08 34 W94 00 08. Stereo. Hrs open: 24 AF 205 Mankato State Univ., 1536 Warren St., 56001. Phone: (507) 389-5678. Fax: (507) 389-1705.E-mail: info@kmsu.org Web Site:www.kmsu.org Licensee: Mankato State University. Population served: 140,000 Natl. Network: PRI, . Cohn & Marks. Format: Pub affrs, educ, music. News staff: one; News: 50 hrs wkly. Target aud; General; upscale, educated. Spec prog: Drama 3 hrs, folk/ethnic 5 hrs, new age 5 hrs wkly. ◆Jim Gullickson, gen mgr; Karen Wright, opns dir.

KNGA(FM)—See Saint Peter

KTOE(AM)— 1950: 1420 khz; 5 kw-U, DA-N. TL: N44 10 06 W93 54 37. Hrs open: 24 59346 Madison Ave., 56001. Phone: (507) 345-4537. Fax: (507) 345-5364.E-mail: info@ktoe.com Web Site:www.katoinfo.com Licensee: Minnesota Valley Broadcasting Co. Group owner: Linder Broadcasting Group Population served: 200,000 Format: News/talk info. News staff: 3; News: 21 hrs wkly. Target aud: 25-54. ◆John Linder, CEO; Jo Guck Bailey, VP, gen mgr.

KYSM(AM)—Licensed to Mankato. See North Mankato

KYSM-FM—Licensed to Mankato. See North Mankato

Maplewood

WCTS(AM)—Licensed to Maplewood. See Minneapolis-St. Paul

Marshall

KARZ(FM)— July 7, 1985: 107.5 mhz; 25 kw. 300 ft TL: N44 24 37 W95 51 43. (CP: 15 kw, ant 430 ft. TL: N44 19 32 W95 52 19). Stereo. Hrs open: Box 61, 56258. Secondary address: 1414 E. College Dr. 56258. Phone: (507) 537-0566. Fax: (507) 532-3739. Web Site:www.marshallradio.net Licensee: KMHL Broadcasting Co. Inc. Group owner: Linder Broadcasting Group (acq 5-6-97; $450,000). Format: Classic rock. Target aud: 25-54. ◆Brad Strootman, gen mgr, sls VP; Keith Petermeier, chief of opns; Scott Schmeling, chief of engrg.

KKCK(FM)— Dec 13, 1967: 99.7 mhz; 100 kw. 925 ft TL: N44 26 55 W95 45 27. Stereo. Hrs open: 24 Prog sep from AM Box 61, 1414 E. College Dr., 56258. Phone: (507) 532-2282. Fax: (507) 532-3739. Web Site:marshallradio.net Population served: 65,000 Format: Hot adult contemp, rock. News staff: one; News: 8 hrs wkly. Target aud: 21-39. ◆Brad Stoutman, exec VP, adv VP; Keith Petermierer, prom mgr; Russ Berreth, mus dir, mus critic; Val Braun, traf mgr; Aaron Ziemer, local news ed.

KMHL(AM)— Nov 30, 1946: 1400 khz; 1 kw-U. TL: N44 26 55 W95 45 27. (CP: TL: N44 26 59 W95 45 43). Hrs open: 24 Box 61, 1414 E. College Dr., 56258. Phone: (507) 532-2282. Fax: (507) 532-3739. Web Site:www.marshallradio.net Licensee: KMHL Broadcasting Co. Group owner: Linder Broadcasting Group Population served: 155,000 Natl. Network: ABC, . Rgnl. Network: Linder Radio. Natl. Rep: Lack Radio,. MNN Format: Farm, news/talk. News staff: one; News: 20 hrs wkly. Target aud: 27 plus. Spec prog: Relg 7 hrs wkly. ◆Donald Linder, pres, sports cmtr; John Linder, VP; Brad Strootman, gen mgr, sls dir; Keith Petermeier, chief of opns; Justin Thordsen, progmg dir; Aaron Ziemer, pub affrs dir; Scott Schmelling, chief of engrg; Val Braun, traf mgr; Lynn Kettelson, farm dir.

*KOMH(FM)—Not on air, target date: unknown: 90.7 mhz; 2.5 kw. Ant 211 ft TL: N44 28 47.8 W96 02 07.1. Hrs open: 1460 Old Ocean Hwy., Bolivia, NC, 28422. Phone: (910) 368-1581. Licensee: Shining Light Ministries. ◆Joshua Hawkins, pres.

*KRGM(FM)—Not on air, target date: unknown: 89.9 mhz; 4 kw. Ant 535 ft TL: N44 29 03 W95 29 27. Hrs open: 4604 Airpark Blvd., Duluth, 55811-5751. Phone: (218) 722-3017. Fax: (218) 279-5010. Web Site:www.refugeradio.com Licensee: Refuge Media Group. ◆Mike Marrone, pres; Paulette Kutzler, gen mgr.

Minneapolis

KBEM-FM—Licensed to Minneapolis. See Minneapolis-St. Paul

KFAI(FM)—Licensed to Minneapolis. See Minneapolis-St. Paul

KFAN(AM)—Licensed to Minneapolis. See Minneapolis-St. Paul

KFXN(AM)—Licensed to Minneapolis. See Minneapolis-St. Paul

KMOJ(FM)—Licensed to Minneapolis. See Minneapolis-St. Paul

KSJN(FM)—Licensed to Minneapolis. See Minneapolis-St. Paul

KTCZ-FM—Licensed to Minneapolis. See Minneapolis-St. Paul

KTIS(AM)—Licensed to Minneapolis. See Roseville

KTIS-FM—Licensed to Minneapolis. See Minneapolis-St. Paul

KTLK-FM—Licensed to Minneapolis. See Minneapolis-St. Paul

KUOM(AM)—Licensed to Minneapolis. See Minneapolis-St. Paul

KXXR(FM)—Licensed to Minneapolis. See Minneapolis-St. Paul

WCCO(AM)—Licensed to Minneapolis. See Minneapolis-St. Paul

WLOL(AM)—Licensed to Minneapolis. See Minneapolis-St. Paul

WLTE(FM)—Licensed to Minneapolis. See Minneapolis-St. Paul

WWTC(AM)—Licensed to Minneapolis. See Minneapolis-St. Paul

Minneapolis-St. Paul

*KBEM-FM—(Minneapolis, Oct 4, 1970: 88.5 mhz; 2.15 kw. 370 ft TL: N44 58 38 W93 15 55. Stereo. Hrs open: 24 1555 James Ave. N., Minneapolis, 55411. Phone: (612) 668-1735. Phone: (612) 529-5236. Fax: (612) 668-1766.E-mail: studio@jazz88fm.com Web Site:jazz88.mpls.k12.mn.us Licensee: Special School District No. 1, Board of Education. Population served: 2,000,000 Natl. Network: PRI, . Format: Jazz. News staff: one; News: 14 hrs wkly. Target aud: 35 plus; jazz/progsv adults, club/audiophiles. Spec prog: Bluegrass 4 hrs, Sp 4 hrs wkly. ◆Michele McKenzie, gen mgr, stn mgr; Ted Allison, dev dir; Kevin O'Connor, mus dir; Ed Jones, news dir.

KDIZ(AM)—See Golden Valley

KDWB-FM—(Richfield, 1969: 101.3 mhz; 100 kw. Ant 1,033 ft TL: N45 03 30 W93 07 27. Hrs open: 24 1600 Utica Ave. S., Suite 400, Minneapolis, 55416. Phone: (952) 417-3000. Fax: (952) 417-3001.E-mail: info@kdwb.com Web Site:www.kdwb.com Licensee: AMFM Radio Licenses LLC. Group owner: Clear Channel Communications Inc. (acq 8-30-00; grpsl). Population served: 3,127,100 Natl. Rep: Clear Channel,. Wiley Rein LLP. Format: CHR. News staff: one. Target aud: 18-34; women. ◆Mick Anselmo, pres & gen mgr.

KEEY-FM—(Saint Paul, June 1, 1969: 102.1 mhz; 100 kw. Ant 1,033 ft TL: N45 03 30 W93 07 27. Stereo. Hrs open: 24 1600 Utica Ave. S., Suite 400, Minneapolis, 55416. Phone: (952) 417-3000. Fax: (612) 417-3001.E-mail: info@keey.com Web Site:www.k102.com Licensee: AMFM Broadcasting Licenses LLC. Population served: 309,866 Natl. Rep: Clear Channel,. Format: Country. News staff: 40; News: 2 hrs wkly. Target aud: 25-54; women. ◆Mike Anselmo, pres; Rob Berrell, gen sls mgr; Matt Tell, prom dir; Gregg Swedberg, progmg dir; Mary Gallas, mus dir; Cathy Maness, traf mgr.

*KFAI(FM)—(Minneapolis, May 1, 1978: 90.3 mhz; 125 w. 440 ft TL: N44 58 29 W93 16 17. Stereo. Hrs open: 24 1808 Riverside Ave., Minneapolis, 55454-1035. Phone: (612) 341-3144. Fax: (612) 341-4281.E-mail: janislaneewart@kfai.org Web Site:www.kfai.org Licensee: Fresh Air Inc. Population served: 200,000 Format: Div. News staff: one; News: 7 hrs wkly. Target aud: General; underserved, under-represented communities. Spec prog: Black 10 hrs, folk 6 hrs, Fr 2 hrs, jazz 12 hrs, Sp 8 hrs wkly. ◆Janis Lane-Ewart, gen mgr; Diane Wanner, dev dir; Jackson Buck, mktg dir; Dan Richmond, progmg dir; Lauretta Dawolo, news dir; Dan Zimmerman, chief of engrg.

KFAN(AM)—(Minneapolis, 1923: 1130 khz; 50 kw-D, 25 kw-N, DA-2. TL: N44 38 48 W93 23 31. Hrs open: 24 1600 Utica Ave. S., Suite 400, Minneapolis, 55416. Phone: (952) 417-3000. Fax: (612) 417-3001.E-mail: info@k102.com Web Site:www.kfan.com Licensee: AMFM Broadcasting Licenses LLC. Group owner: Clear Channel Communications Inc. (acq 8-30-2000; grpsl). Natl. Rep: Clear Channel,. Format: Sports talk. News staff: 40; News: 20 hrs wkly. Target aud: 25-54; males. ◆Mick Anselmo, VP; Todd Kalman, gen sls mgr; Jeff Framke, natl sls mgr;

Matt Tell, mktg dir; Lisa Sanderson, prom dir; Chad Abbott, progmg dir, progmg mgr; John Jansen, pub affrs dir; Dan Motler, engrg VP; Jess Meyer, engrg dir, chief of engrg; Cathy Maness, traf mgr.

KFXN(AM)—(Minneapolis, Apr 5, 1962: 690 khz; 500 w-D, DA. TL: N45 01 25 W93 22 58. (CP: 1.5 kw-D, 500 w-N. TL: N44 44 58 W92 59 35). Stereo. Hrs open: 1600 Utica Ave. S., Suite 400, Minneapolis, 55416. Phone: (952) 417-3000. Fax: (952) 417-3001.E-mail: info@kdwb.com Web Site:www.thescore690.com Licensee: AMFM Broadcasting Licenses LLC. Group owner: Clear Channel Communications Inc. (acq 8-30-2000; grpsl). Population served: 434,400 Wiley, Rein & Fielding. Format: Syndicated sports, talk. Target aud: 25-54. ♦Mick Anselmo, pres, opns dir, mktg mgr; Todd Kalman, gen sls mgr; Chad Abbott, progmg dir; Jess Meyer, chief of engrg.

KKMS(AM)—(Richfield, Oct 18, 1949: 980 khz; 5 kw-U, DA-1. TL: N44 47 18 W93 12 54. Stereo. Hrs open: 24 2110 Cliff Rd., Eagan, 55122. Phone: (651) 405-8800. Fax: (651) 405-8222. Web Site:www.kkms.com Licensee: Common Ground Broadcasting Inc. Group owner: Salem Communications Corp. (acq 9-27-96; $3 million). Population served: 1,961,380 Format: Christian, talk. Target aud: 18-50. ♦Ron Stone, gen mgr; Lee Michaels, opns mgr; Brian Acker, gen sls mgr; Kate Fisher, mktg dir; Nick Novak, progmg dir; Scott Todd, chief of engrg.

KMNV(AM)—(Saint Paul, 1936: 1400 khz; 1 kw-U. TL: N44 57 28 W93 12 23. Hrs open: 24 1516 E. Lake St., Suite 200, Minneapolis, 55435. Phone: (612) 729-5900. Fax: (612) 729-5999.E-mail: info@kmnvam.com Licensee: Davidson Media Station KLBB Licensee LLC. (acq 9-7-2005; $5.2 million with KMNQ(AM) Brooklyn Park). Population served: 309,866 Rgnl. Network: MNN. ABN Radio Format: Rgnl Mexican. ♦Tim Dennis, gen mgr & opns mgr.

***KMOJ(FM)**—(Minneapolis, Sept 15, 1978: 89.9 mhz; 1 kw. 600 ft TL: N44 59 00 W93 17 22. Stereo. Hrs open: 24 555 Girard Terr., Suite 130, Minneapolis, 55405. Phone: (612) 377-0594. Fax: (612) 377-3990.E-mail: in fo@kmojfm.com Licensee: Center for Communication & Development. (acq 1975). Population served: 1,200,000 Format: Urban contemp. News staff: 2; News: 4 hrs wkly. Target aud: General. ♦Kelvin Quarles, gen mgr.

KNOF(FM)—(Saint Paul, Apr 10, 1960: 95.3 mhz; 3 kw. 200 ft TL: N44 56 48 W93 09 26. Stereo. Hrs open: 6 AM-10 PM 1347 Selby Ave., St. Paul, 55104. Phone: (651) 645-8271. Fax: (651) 645-4593. Licensee: Selby Gospel Broadcasting Co. Natl. Network: Salem Radio Network, . Format: Gospel. News: 2 hrs wkly. Target aud: All ages. Spec prog: Black 5 hrs, Sp one hr, Russian one hr wkly. ♦Paul Freitag, pres, gen mgr; Phil Mullen, opns mgr.

***KNOW-FM**— July 1, 1967: 91.1 mhz; 100 kw. Ant 1,310 ft TL: N45 03 44 W93 08 21. Stereo. Hrs open: 480 Cedar St., St. Paul, 55101. Phone: (651) 290-1500. Fax: (651) 290-1224.E-mail: info@mpr.org Web Site:www.mpr.org Licensee: Minnesota Public Radio. Wire Svc: Reuters Format: News. ♦William H. Kling, pres & gen mgr; Erik Nycklemoe, opns dir.

KQRS-FM—See Golden Valley

***KSJN(FM)**—(Minneapolis, 1956: 99.5 mhz; 100 kw. Ant 1,033 ft TL: N44 03 30 W93 07 27. Stereo. Hrs open: 480 Cedar St., St. Paul, 55101. Phone: (651) 290-1500. Fax: (651) 290-1224.E-mail: info@mpr.org Web Site:www.mpr.org Licensee: Minnesota Public Radio Inc. Population served: 2,500,000 Wire Svc: Reuters Format: Class. ♦William H. Kling, pres & gen mgr; Erik Nycklemoe, opns dir, progmg dir; Jon Gossett, dev dir; Mary Pat Ladner, mktg dir; Bill Wareham, news dir.

KSTP(AM)—(Saint Paul, April 1924: 1500 khz; 50 kw-U, DA-N. TL: N45 01 32 W93 03 06. Hrs open: 3415 University Ave., Minneapolis, 55414. Phone: (651) 647-1500. Fax: (651) 649-1515.E-mail: info@kstp.com Web Site:www.am1500.com Licensee: KSTP-AM L.L.C., a Delaware L.L.C. Group owner: Hubbard Broadcasting Inc. Population served: 300,000 Natl. Rep: Christal,. Holland & Knight. Wire Svc: AP Format: Talk. News staff: 3; News: 5 hrs wkly. Target aud: 25-54; adults. ♦Stanley S. Hubbard, CEO; Virginia H. Morris, pres; Todd Fisher, VP, gen mgr; Dave Munson, gen sls mgr; Steve Conrad, progmg dir. Co-owned TV: KSTP-TV affil.

KSTP-FM—(Saint Paul, Nov 1, 1965: 94.5 mhz; 100 kw. 1,225 ft TL: N45 03 45 W93 08 22. Stereo. Hrs open: Prog sep from AM 3415 University Ave., Minneapolis, 55414. Phone: (651) 642-4141. Fax: (651) 642-4239.E-mail: info@kstp.com Web Site:www.ks95.com Licensee: KSTP-FM L.L.C. a Delaware L.L.C. Population served: 500,000 Natl. Network: ABC, . Natl. Rep: Christal,. Wire Svc: AP Format: Adult contemp. News staff: one. Target aud: 25-54; female. ♦Dave Bestler, VP, gen mgr; John Gonzales, gen sls mgr; Leighton Peck, progmg dir. Co-owned TV: KSTP-TV affil

KTCZ-FM—(Minneapolis, 1956: 97.1 mhz; 100 kw. Ant 1,033 ft TL: N45 03 30 W93 07 27. Stereo. Hrs open: 24 1600 Utica Ave. S., Suite 400, Minneapolis, 55416. Phone: (952) 417-3000. Fax: (952) 417-3001.E-mail: info@cities97.com Web Site:cities97.com Licensee: AMFM Broadcasting Licenses LLC. Wiley, Rein & Fielding. Format: Adult contemp. ♦Mick Anselmo, pres; Erik Christopherson, gen sls mgr; Dave Sheets, prom dir; Lauren MacLeash, progmg dir.

***KTIS-FM**—(Minneapolis, May 1949: 98.5 mhz; 100 kw. 1,033 ft TL: N45 03 30 W93 07 27. Stereo. Hrs open: 24 3003 Snelling Ave. N., St. Paul, 55113-1598. Phone: (651) 631-5000. Fax: (651) 631-5084.E-mail: info@ktis.fm Web Site:www.ktis.fm Licensee: Northwestern College. Group owner: Northwestern College & Radio. Population served: 2,000,000 Natl. Network: AP Network News, . Bryan Cave. Format: Inspirational. News staff: one; News: 20 hrs wkly. Target aud: 25-45. ♦Alan Cureton, pres; Dr. Paul Virts, exec VP; Harv Hendrickson, VP; David Fitts, stn mgr.

KTLK-FM—(Minneapolis, June 26, 1965: 100.3 mhz; 97 kw. 905 ft TL: N45 20 12 W93 23 28. (CP: Ant 922 ft.). Stereo. Hrs open: 24 1600 Utica Ave. S., Suite 400, Minneapolis, 55416. Phone: (952) 417-3000. Fax: (952) 417-3001.E-mail: info@kjzi.com Web Site:www.kjzi.com Licensee: AMFM Broadcasting Licenses LLC. Group owner: Clear Channel Communications Inc. (acq 8-30-2000; grpsl). Population served: 2,500,000 Natl. Network: Fox News Radio, . Natl. Rep: Clear Channel,. Wiley, Rein & Fielding. Format: Adult contemp, smooth jazz, news/talk. News staff: 3. Target aud: Adults 25-54; adults. ♦Mick Anselmo, pres, gen mgr & mktg mgr.

KTNF(AM)—See Saint Louis Park

***KUOM(AM)**—(Minneapolis, Jan 13, 1922: 770 khz; 5 kw-D. TL: N44 59 54 W93 11 18. Hrs open: Sunrise-sunset Univ. of Minn., 330 21st Ave. S., Suite 610, Minneapolis, 55455-0415. Phone: (612) 625-3500. Fax: (612) 625-2112.E-mail: radiok@umn.edu Web Site:www.radiok.org Licensee: University of Minnesota. Population served: 2,500,000 Dow, Lohnes & Albertson. Wire Svc: AP Format: Alternative. News: 5 hrs wkly. Target aud: 18-34. ♦Andrew Marlow, stn mgr; Stuart Sanders, dev dir; Amy Daml, progmg dir; Larry Oberg, chief of engrg.

KXXR(FM)—(Minneapolis, Jan 6, 1961: 93.7 mhz; 100 kw. 1,033 ft TL: N45 03 30 W93 07 27. Hrs open: 24 2000 S. E. Elm Street, Minneapolis, 55414. Phone: (612) 617-4000. Fax: (612) 676-8293.E-mail: mail@93x.com Web Site:www.93x.com Licensee: Radio License Holding III LLC. Group owner: ABC Inc. (acq 6-12-2007; grpsl). Population served: 2,500,000 Natl. Rep: Interep,. Format: Active rock. Target aud: 18-54. ♦Marc Kalman, stn mgr; Shelly M. Wilkes, sls dir, gen sls mgr; Wendy Ellis, mktg mgr; Wade Linder, progmg dir.

KYCR(AM)—(Golden Valley, Oct 27, 1961: 1570 khz; 2.5 kw-D, 237 w-N. TL: N44 57 39 W93 21 25. Hrs open: 24 2110 Cliff Rd., Eagan, 55122. Phone: (651) 405-8800. Fax: (651) 405-8222.E-mail: info@kycr.com Web Site:www.business1570.com Licensee: Common Ground Broadcasting Co. Inc. Group owner: Salem Communications Corp. (acq 7-2-98; $2.7 million with KTEK(AM) Alvin, TX). Population served: 2,400,000 Putbrese, Hunsaker & Trent, P.C. Format: Business talk. News: 6 hrs wkly. Target aud: 25-49. Spec prog: Sp 14 hrs wkly. ♦Ron Stone, gen mgr; Lee Michaels, opns mgr; Brian Acker, gen sls mgr; Kate Fisher, mktg dir; Nick Novak, progmg dir; Scott Todd, chief of engrg.

WCCO(AM)—(Minneapolis, Oct 2, 1924: 830 khz; 50 kw-U. TL: N45 10 40 W93 20 55. (CP: 46 kw-N. TL: N45 05 06 W93 31 06). Hrs open: 24 625 2nd Ave. S., Minneapolis, 55402. Phone: (612) 370-0611. Fax: (612) 370-0159.E-mail: admin@wccoradio.cbs.com Web Site:www.wccoradio.com Licensee: Infinity Media Corp. Group owner: Infinity Broadcasting Corp. (acq 11-13-98; grpsl). Population served: 2,000,000 Natl. Network: CBS, . Natl. Rep: Interep,. Format: News/talk. News staff: 7; News: 25 hrs wkly. Target aud: General. ♦Mary Niemeyer, gen sls mgr; Sue Hemmeke, natl sls mgr; Amy Mauzy, prom dir; Wendy Paulson, opns mgr & progmg mgr; Craig Walters, chief of engrg.

WCTS(AM)—(Maplewood, August 1964: 1030 khz; 50 kw-D, 1 kw-N, DA-2. TL: N44 52 01 W92 54 02. Hrs open: 24 900 Forestview Ln. N., Plymouth, 55441-5934. Phone: (763) 417-8270. Fax: (763) 417-8278. Web Site:www.wctsradio.com Licensee: Central Baptist Theological Seminary of Plymouth. (acq 1-30-93; $1.5 million; 11-23-92). Population served: 2,915,523 Natl. Network: Moody, . Wire Svc: AP Format: Christian, relg. News: 3 hrs wkly. Target aud: 30 plus; Christian. ♦Kimball Cummings Jr., gen mgr.

WFMP(FM)—(Coon Rapids, Sept 1, 1968: 107.1 mhz; 22 kw. Ant 587 ft TL: N45 03 45 W93 08 21. Stereo. Hrs open: 24 3415 University Ave., Minneapolis, 55414. Phone: (651) 642-4107. Fax: (651) 647-2932.E-mail: info@fm107.fm Web Site:www.fm107.fm Licensee: WFMP-FM LLC. (acq 12-21-2000; $27 million). Natl. Rep: Christal,. Wire Svc: Wheeler News Service Format: Talk. ♦Dan Seeman, gen mgr.

WIXK(AM)—(New Richmond, WI) Sept 29, 1960: 1590 khz; 5 kw-D, 200 w/95w-N. TL: N45 05 10 W92 34 19. Hrs open: 24 Box 8, New Richmond, WI, 54017. Secondary address: 125 East 3rd St., New Richmond, WI Phone: (715) 246-2254. Fax: (715) 246-7090.E-mail: jpetersen@hbi.com Web Site:wixk.com Licensee: WIXK-AM LLC. Group owner: Hubbard Broadcasting Inc. (acq 5-18-2000; with co-located FM). Population served: 323,000 Natl. Network: ABC, . Wisconsin Radio Net. Miller & Miller. Format: Country. News staff: one; News: 9 hrs wkly. Target aud: 25-54. ♦Stanley S. Hubbard, CEO; Virginia H. Morris, pres; Todd Fisher, gen mgr.

WLOL(AM)—(Minneapolis, 1939: 1330 khz; 9.7 kw-D, 5.1 kw-N, DA-2. TL: N44 47 02 W93 20 38. Hrs open: 24 919 Lilac Dr. N., Golden Valley, 55422. Phone: (612)643-4119. Fax: (763)546-4444.E-mail: wlol@relevantradio.com Licensee: Starboard Media Foundation Inc. Group owner: Relevant Radio (acq 3-16-2004; $6.75 million). Population served: 2,300,000 Rgnl. Network: MNN. Format: Catholic. News: 3 hrs wkly. ♦Trish Leurck, CEO; Paul Sadek, stn mgr.

WLTE(FM)—(Minneapolis, Aug 27, 1973: 102.9 mhz; 100 kw. 1,033 ft TL: N45 03 30 W93 07 27. Stereo. Hrs open: 24 625 2nd Ave. S., Minneapolis, 55402. Phone: (612) 339-1029. Phone: (612) 339-1083. Fax: (612) 339-5653.E-mail: info@wlte.com Web Site:www.wlte.com Format: Soft adult contemp. News: 5 hrs wkly. Target aud: 25-54. ♦Chris Kalis, prom dir.

***WMCN(FM)**—(Saint Paul, Sept 15, 1979: 91.7 mhz; 10 w. 1,004 ft TL: N44 36 22 W93 10 04. Stereo. Hrs open: 8 AM-4 AM (M-F); 11 AM-4 AM (S, Su) 1600 Grand Ave., St. Paul, 55105. Phone: (651) 696-6082. Phone: (651) 696-6000. Fax: (651) 696-6689.E-mail: wmcn@macalester.edu Web Site:www.macalester.edu/~wmcn Licensee: Macalester College. Population served: 2,000,000 Format: New rock. Target aud: All ages. Spec prog: Country 2 hrs, Latin 6 hrs, multicultural 10 hrs, class 4 hrs, folk 2 hrs, jazz 4 hrs, punk 4 hrs wkly. ♦Patrick McGrath, gen mgr; Ethan Torrey, chief of engrg.

WREY(AM)—(Hudson, WI) Sept 19, 1959: 630 khz; 1 kw-D, 2.5 kw-N, DA-2. TL: N44 52 01 W92 54 02. Hrs open: 2619 E. Lake St., Minneapolis, 55406. Phone: (612) 729-3776. Fax: (612) 724-0437.E-mail: radiorey630am@yahoo.com Web Site:www.radiorey630am.com Licensee: 630 Radio Inc. Population served: 1,200,000 Format: Sp music. ♦Guadalupe Gonzales, pres; Manuel Robles, gen mgr.

WWTC(AM)—(Minneapolis, Aug 10, 1925: 1280 khz; 5 kw-U, DA-N. TL: N44 57 41 W93 21 24. Hrs open: 2110 Cliff Rd., Egan, 55122. Phone: (651) 405-8800. Fax: (651) 405-8222. Web Site:www.am1280thepatriot.com Licensee: Salem Media Group LLC. Group owner: Salem Communications Corp. (acq 12-18-2000; $7 million with WAUK(AM) Jackson, WI). Population served: 2,000,000 Format: News/talk. Target aud: 18-54. ♦Ron Stone, gen mgr; Lee Michaels, opns dir; Brian Acker, gen sls mgr; Kate Fisher, mktg dir; Nick Novak, progmg dir; Scott Todd, chief of engrg.

Montevideo

***KBPG(FM)**— July, 2002: 89.5 mhz; 500 w. 151 ft TL: N44 54 50 W95 44 10. Hrs open: American Family Radio, Box 3206, Tupelo, MS, 38803. Phone: (662) 844-8888. Fax: (662) 842-6791. Web Site:www.afr.net Licensee: American Family Association. Group owner: American Family Radio (acq 11-26-99). Natl. Network: USA, . Format: Inspirational. ♦Don Wildman, gen mgr.

KDMA(AM)— Dec 21, 1951: 1460 khz; 1 kw-U, DA-N. TL: N44 56 05 W95 44 50. Hrs open: 24 Box 513, 4454 Hwy. 212 W., 56265. Phone: (320) 269-8815. Phone: (320) 269-5131. Fax: (320) 269-8449.E-mail: kdmaprod@charterinternet.com Licensee: Iowa City Broadcasting Co. Group owner: Tom Ingstad Broadcasting Group (acq 10-21-97; grpsl). Population served: 110,000 Natl. Network: ABC, . Rgnl. Network: Linder Farm. Linder Farm Rgnl rep: O'Malley. Wire Svc: Weather Wire Format: Country. News staff: one. Spec prog: Farm 7 hrs wkly. ♦Dwight Mulder, opns dir; Roger Hill, gen mgr & gen sls mgr.

KMGM(FM)— Oct 1, 1982: 105.5 mhz; 3 kw. 300 ft TL: N44 51 24 W95 37 46. Stereo. Hrs open: 24 Prog sep from AM Box 513, 56265. Phone: (320) 269-8815. Phone: (320) 269-5131. Fax: (320) 269-8449. Licensee: Iowa City Broadcasting Co. Wire Svc: Weather Wire Format: Classic Rock. Target aud: 25-54. ♦Roger Hill, gen mgr.

Moorhead

***KCCD(FM)**— June 1, 1992: 90.3 mhz; 100 kw. 495 ft TL: N46 45 35 W96 36 26. Hrs open: 24 901 S. 8th St., 56562. Phone: (218) 299-3666. Fax: (218) 299-3418. Web Site:www.mpr.org Licensee: Minnesota Public Radio. Population served: 460,000 Natl. Network: NPR, PRI, . Rgnl. Network: Minn. Pub. Minn. Pub. Radio Format:

News. News staff: 2. Target aud: General. ◆William Kling, pres; Vern Goodin, gen mgr; Julia Beaton, dev dir.

*KCCM-FM— Oct 23, 1971: 91.1 mhz; 67 kw. 656 ft TL: N46 45 35 W96 36 26. Stereo. Hrs open: 24 Concordia College, 901 8th St. S., 56562. Phone: (218) 299-3666. Fax: (218) 299-3418. Web Site:www.mpr.org Licensee: Minnesota Public Radio Inc. Population served: 460,000 Natl. Network: NPR, PRI, . Rgnl. Network: Minn. Pub. Minn. Pub. Radio Format: Class mus, cultural progmg. News staff: 2; News: one hr wkly. Target aud: General. ◆William H. Kling, pres; Vern Goodin, gen mgr; Julia Beaton, dev dir.

KLTA(FM)—See Breckenridge

KQWB-FM—Licensed to Moorhead. See Fargo ND

KRWK(FM)—See Fargo, ND

KVOX-FM— Nov 30, 1966: 99.9 mhz; 100 kw. 444 ft TL: N46 49 09 W96 45 56. Stereo. Hrs open: 24 Box 9919, Fargo, ND, 58106. Secondary address: 2720 7th Ave. St., Fargo, ND 58103. Phone: (701) 237-4500. Fax: (701) 235-9082.E-mail: studio@froggyweb.com Web Site:www.froggyweb.com Licensee: Monterey Licenses L.L.C. Group owner: Triad Broadcasting Co. LLC. Population served: 194,800 Natl. Rep: Christal,. Wire Svc: AP Format: Country. News: 7 hrs wkly. Target aud: 25-54; female skew. ◆David Benjamin, pres; Nancy Odney, gen mgr.

KVXR(AM)— Nov 30, 1937: 1280 khz; 5 kw-D, 1 kw-N, DA-2. TL: N46 49 10 W96 45 56. Hrs open: 24 PO Box 99, Moorhead, ND, 56561. Phone: (701) 866-2606.E-mail: bob@am1280thevoice.com Licensee: Voice of Reason Radio Group owner: Clear Channel Communications Inc. (acq 10-4-2007). Population served: 70,000 Format: Catholic. ◆Robert A. Schumacher, pres.

Moose Lake

WMOZ(FM)— 2001: 106.9 mhz; 6 kw. Ant 118 ft TL: N46 30 20 W92 41 10. Hrs open: Agate Broadcasting Inc., 1104 Cloquet Ave., Cloquet, 55720. Phone: (218) 879-4534. Fax: (218) 879-1962. Licensee: QB Broadcasting Ltd. Format: Oldies. ◆Mark Senarighi, gen mgr.

Mora

KBEK(FM)— May 12, 1995: 95.5 mhz; 25 kw. 328 ft TL: N45 44 33 W93 22 48. Stereo. Hrs open: 24 Box 136, 1947 Dennis Rd., 55051. Phone: (320) 679-6955. Phone: (763) 689-5500. Fax: (320) 679-2348.E-mail: kbek@besttimes.com Web Site:www.besttimes.com Licensee: Colleen McKinney, personal representative (acq 11-5-2004). Format: Lite rock, golden oldies. News: 8 hrs wkly. Target aud: General. ◆Colleen McKinney, gen mgr, opns mgr, gen sls mgr; Scott McKenney, progmg dir, mus dir; Ty Laugerman, sports cmtr.

Morris

KKOK(FM)— Sept 16, 1976: 95.7 mhz; 100 kw. 474 ft TL: N45 36 11 W95 53 14. Stereo. Hrs open: Dups AM 15% Box 533, 56267. Phone: (320) 589-3131. Fax: (320) 589-2715.E-mail: kmrskkok@fedtel.net Format: Country. ◆Deb Mattheis, gen mgr; Bill Eckersen, progmg dir; Katie McKenzie, news dir.

KMRS(AM)— Sept 16, 1956: 1230 khz; 1 kw-U. TL: N45 36 11 W95 53 14. Hrs open: 19 Box 533, 56267. Phone: (320) 589-3131. Fax: (320) 589-2715.E-mail: kmrskkok@fedtel.net Web Site:www.kmrskkok.com Licensee: Iowa City Broadcasting Co. Group owner: Tom Ingstad Broadcasting Group (acq 1-11-2000; with co-located FM). Population served: 60,000 Natl. Rep: McGavren Guild,. Format: News/talk, MOR. News staff: one; News: 80 hrs wkly. Target aud: 35-64; farmers & agri-business people. ◆Deb Mattheis, gen mgr; Deb Mattheis, gen sls mgr; Bill Eckersen, progmg dir; Katie McKenzie, news dir; Ken Bartz, chief of engrg.

*KUMM(FM)— Sept 17, 1970: 89.7 mhz; 225 w. Ant 56 ft TL: N45 35 20 W95 54 22. Stereo. Hrs open: 24 KUMM, 600 E. 4th St., 56267. Phone: (320) 589-6076. Fax: (320) 589-6084.E-mail: kumm@kumm.org Web Site:www.kumm.org Licensee: University of Minnesota. Population served: 7,000 Dow, Lohnes & Albertson. Wire Svc: AP Format: Adult alternative. News: 3 hrs wkly. Target aud: 18-30; primarily college students. ◆Mike Doucette, gen mgr.

Nashwauk

KMFG(FM)— October 1997: 102.9 mhz; 25 kw. 253 ft TL: N47 24 30 W92 57 05. Hrs open: 807 W. 37th St., Hibbing, 55746. Phone: (218) 263-7531. Fax: (218) 263-6112.E-mail: info@kmfgfm.com Web Site:www.kmfgfm.com Licensee: Midwest Communications Inc. (group owner: acq 5-10-2004; grpsl). Natl. Network: ABC, . Format: Classic rock. Target aud: 24-55. ◆Kristi Garrity, gen mgr; Doug Diedrich, progmg dir.

WMFG(AM)—See Hibbing

WNMT(AM)—Licensed to Nashwauk. See Hibbing

New Prague

KCHK(AM)— Sept 22, 1969: 1350 khz; 500 w-D, 70 w-N, DA-2. TL: N44 34 39 W93 30 16. Hrs open: 24 Box 251, 56071. Secondary address: 25821 Langford Ave. 56071. Phone: (952) 758-2571. Phone: (952) 758-2572. Fax: (952) 758-3170. Licensee: Ingstad Brothers Broadcasting LLC (group owner; acq 5-1-2004; grpsl). Population served: 4,000 Natl. Network: ABC, . Rgnl. Network: MNN. MNN Rosenman & Colin L.L.P. Wire Svc: NWS (National Weather Service) Format: News/talk. News: 50 hrs wkly. Target aud: 35-59. Spec prog: Sp. 6 hrs, Pol, Czch, Ger 40 hrs wkly. ◆Ned Newberg, gen mgr; Dave Douglas, engrg mgr.

KRDS-FM— Dec 1, 1990: 95.5 mhz; 6 kw. 328 ft TL: N44 27 41 W93 35 21. Stereo. Hrs open: 24 Dups AM 50% Box 251, 56071. Phone: (952) 758-2571. Fax: (952) 758-3170.E-mail: kchkamfm@beucomm.net Licensee: Ingstad Brothers Broadcasting LLC Population served: 140,000 Wire Svc: NWS (National Weather Service) Format: Oldies. News staff: 3; News: 7 hrs wkly. Target aud: 25-64; general.

New Ulm

KATO-FM—Licensed to New Ulm. See Mankato

KNUJ(AM)— May 1949: 860 khz; 1 kw-U. TL: N44 17 10 W94 25 50. Hrs open: 24 Box 368, Grand Hotel Bldg., 56073. Secondary address: 317 North Minn St. 56073. Phone: (507) 359-2921. Fax: (507) 359-4520.E-mail: knuj@knuj.net Web Site:www.knuj.net Licensee: Ingstad Brothers Broadcasting LLC (group owner; acq 5-1-2004; grpsl). Population served: 43,000 Format: Country. News staff: 2; News: 30 hrs wkly. Spec prog: 30 plus. Spec prog: Old-time 8 hrs wkly. ◆Jim Bartels, sr VP; Janine Enter, gen sls mgr; Brian Filzen, progmg dir; Greg Brandt, chief of engrg.

Nisswa

KBLB(FM)— 2002: 93.3 mhz; 100 kw. Ant 558 ft TL: N46 26 34 W94 22 55. Stereo. Hrs open: 24 Box 746, Brainerd, 56401-0746. Secondary address: 13225 Dogwood Dr., Baxter 56425-8613. Phone: (218) 828-1244. Fax: (218) 828-1119.E-mail: production@brainerd.net Web Site:brainerdradio.net Licensee: BL Broadcasting Inc. Group owner: Omni Broadcasting Co. (acq 12-11-2000). Population served: 200,000 Natl. Network: ABC, . Minn. News Net. Garvey, Schubert & Barer. Format: Country, mainstream. News staff: one; News: 12 hrs wkly. Target aud: 25-54; adults. ◆Lou Buron, CEO, pres; Mary Campbell, CFO, VP; G. Michael Boen, gen mgr; Al Davison, progmg dir; Tess Taylor, news dir & pub affrs dir; David Cox, chief of engrg.

North Branch

*KMKL(FM)— Oct 6, 2001: 90.3 mhz; 15 kw vert. Ant 397 ft TL: N45 32 36 W92 58 24. Stereo. Hrs open: 24 Rebroadcasts KLVR(FM) Middletown, CA 100%. 2351 Sunset Blvd., Suite 170-218, Rocklin, CA, 95765. Phone: (916) 251-1600. Fax: (916) 251-1650.E-mail: klove@klove.com Web Site:www.klove.com Licensee: Educational Media Foundation. Group owner: EMF Broadcasting. Population served: 52,400 Natl. Network: K-Love, . Shaw Pittman. Format: Contemp Christian. News staff: 3. Target aud: 25-44; Judeo Christian, female. ◆Mike Novak, pres.

North Mankato

KDOG(FM)—Licensed to North Mankato. See Mankato

KYSM(AM)—(Mankato, July 25, 1938: 1230 khz; 1 kw-U. TL: N44 10 20 W94 02 23. Stereo. Hrs open: 24 59346 Madison Ave., Mankato, 56001. Phone: (507) 345-4537. Fax: (507) 345-5364. Licensee: Minnesota Valley Broadcasting Co. Group owner: Clear Channel Communications Inc. (acq 12-31-2007; $700,000). Population served: 150,000 Rgnl. Network: MNN. Format: Sports talk. ◆Jo Guck Bailey, VP & gen mgr.

KYSM-FM—(Mankato, April 1948: 103.5 mhz; 100 kw. Ant 541 ft TL: N44 10 20 W94 02 23. Stereo. Hrs open: 24 1807 Lee Blvd., 56003. Phone: (507) 388-2900. Fax: (507) 345-4675.E-mail: jobailey@clearchannel.com Web Site:country103.com Licensee: Three Eagles of Lincoln Inc. (acq 6-8-2007; grpsl). Natl. Rep: Katz Radio,. Wire Svc: AP Format: New country. News staff: one; News: one hr wkly. Target aud: 25-54. Spec prog: Sp one hr wkly. ◆Jo Guck Bailey, gen mgr; Chris Painter, gen sls mgr; Kaaren Kohene, prom dir; Terry Cooley, progmg dir; Randall Harter, news dir.

Northfield

*KCMP(FM)— Apr 4, 1968: 89.3 mhz; 97.6 kw. Ant 768 ft TL: N44 41 21 W93 04 21. Stereo. Hrs open: 24 480 Cedar St., Saint Paul, 55101. Phone: (651) 290-1500. Fax: (651) 290-1295. Web Site:www.mpr.org/thecurrent Licensee: Minnesota Public Radio (acq 11-15-2004; $10.5 million with KMSE(FM) Rochester). Population served: 2,500,000 Format: AAA. ◆William Kling, pres & gen mgr; Jon Gossett, dev dir; Bill Wareham, news dir.

*KRLX(FM)— Jan 25, 1975: 88.1 mhz; 100 w. 16 ft TL: N44 27 39 W93 09 21. Stereo. Hrs open: Carleton College, 300 N. College St., 55057. Phone: (507) 646-4102. Web Site:krlxweb.carleton.edu Licensee: Carleton College. Cohn & Marks. Format: Eclectic. Target aud: General; college-associated people and rural. ◆Mary Henke-Haney, stn mgr; Ben Blink, progmg dir; Brandon Walker, news dir.

KYMN(AM)— Sept 27, 1968: 1080 khz; 1 kw-D. TL: N44 29 12 W93 06 20. Stereo. Hrs open: 24 Box 201, 55057. Phone: (507) 645-5695. Fax: (507) 645-9768.E-mail: kymn@qwestoffice.net Licensee: Ingstad Brothers Broadcasting LLC (group owner; acq 5-1-2004; grpsl). Population served: 100,000 Natl. Network: Motor Racing Net, Westwood One, . Rgnl. Network: Linder Farm. Linder Farm Rgnl rep: O'Malley. Pepper & Corazzini. Format: Adult contemp. News staff: 1; News: 72 hrs wkly. Target aud: 35-54; parents with school-age children, well-educated. Spec prog: Big band 3 hrs, farm 6 hrs, relg 2 hrs, Latin/Hispanic 2 hrs wkly. ◆James Ingstad, CEO, pres; Ned Newberg, gen mgr & gen sls mgr; Jeff Johnson, progmg dir.

Olivia

KOLV(FM)— June 27, 1983: 100.1 mhz; 6 kw. 285 ft TL: N44 45 51 W94 55 45. Stereo. Hrs open: Box 6, 56277. Phone: (320) 523-1017. Fax: (320) 523-1018.E-mail: askusa@kwlm.com Web Site:www.k100realcountry.com Licensee: Bold Radio Inc. Group owner: Linder Broadcasting Group (acq 3-18-98; $335,000). Rgnl. Network: Linder Farm, AgriAmerica. Natl. Rep: Keystone (unwired net),. Linder Farm Format: Country, farm, div. Spec prog: Big band, adult contemp, oldies, Top-40. ◆Steve Linder, pres; Doug Loy, gen mgr, stn mgr, gen sls mgr; Maryelin Macht, progmg dir.

Ortonville

KCGN-FM—Licensed to Ortonville. See Milbank SD

KDIO(AM)— July 23, 1956: 1350 khz; 670 w-D, 38 w-N. TL: N45 20 59 W96 27 08. Hrs open: 47 N.W. Second St., 56278. Phone: (320) 839-2581. Fax: (320) 839-2571.E-mail: kdio@bigstonelake.net Web Site:bigstoneradio.com Licensee: Armada Media-Watertown Inc. Group owner: Robert Ingstad Broadcast Properties (acq 8-3-2007; grpsl). Population served: 115,000 Natl. Network: ABC, . Rgnl. Network: Linder Farm. Minn. News Net. Richard Hayes. Format: Real country. Spec prog: Farm 18 hrs, relg 5 hrs wkly. ◆Jeff Kurtz, pres, gen mgr; Joan Lien, gen sls mgr; Julie Anne French, progmg dir.

KPHR(FM)— 1996: 106.3 mhz; 100 kw. Ant 954 ft TL: N45 06 17 W96 59 17. Hrs open: 508 10th Ave. S.E., Watertown, SD, 57201. Phone: (605) 884-3548. Fax: (605) 884-3549.E-mail: power106@iw.net Licensee: Armada Media-Watertown Inc. Format: Classic rock. ◆Jeff Kurtz, opns mgr, gen sls mgr, progmg dir; Kim Krause, traf mgr.

Osakis

KBHL(FM)— Mar 11, 1985: 103.9 mhz; 3 kw. 341 ft TL: N45 50 24 W95 05 56. (CP: 6 kw, ant 328 ft.). Hrs open: Box 247, 56360. Phone: (320) 859-3000. Fax: (320) 859-3010.E-mail: mail@praisefm.org Web Site:www.praisefm.org Licensee: Christian Heritage Broadcasting Inc. (acq 3-85; $14,127; 3-4-85). Natl. Network: Moody, . Format: Christian. ◆David McIver, gen mgr.

Owatonna

KRFO(AM)— 1950: 1390 khz; 500 w-D, 100 w-N. TL: N44 04 29 W93 10 46. Hrs open: 5 AM-midnight 245 18th St. S.E., 55060. Phone: (507) 451-2250. Fax: (507) 451-8837. Web Site:www.krforadio.com Licensee: Cumulus Licensing Corp. Group owner: Cumulus Media Inc. (acq 7-21-98; grpsl). Population served: 40,000 Format: Oldies. News staff: one; News: 18 hrs wkly. Target aud: 35 plus. Spec prog: Sp 2 hrs wkly. ◆ Gary Foss, gen mgr; John Connor, gen sls mgr; Loren Hart, progmg dir; Bill Dahlstrom, chief of engrg.

KRFO-FM— Dec 29, 1966: 104.9 mhz; 4.7 kw. 200 ft TL: N44 04 29 W93 10 46. Stereo. Hrs open: 18 Prog sep from AM 245 18th St. S.E., 55060. Phone: (507) 451-2250. Fax: (507) 451-8837.E-mail: info@krfonews.com Population served: 45,000 Format: Country. News staff: one; News: 12 hrs wkly. Target aud: 25-54.

Park Rapids

KDKK-FM— December 1967: 97.5 mhz; 100 kw. 636 ft TL: N46 55 51 W95 00 27. Stereo. Hrs open: Prog sep from AM Box 49 , Hwy. 34 E., 56470. Phone: (218) 732-3306. Population served: 100,000 Wire Svc: Weather Wire Format: Music of Your Life. Target aud: 40 plus. ◆E.P. De La Hunt, gen mgr, progmg dir & farm dir; Bernie Schumacher, women's int ed.

KPRM(AM)— Dec 1, 1962: 870 khz; 25 kw-D, 1 kw-N, DA-N. TL: N46 55 42 W95 00 22. Stereo. Hrs open: Box 49, Hwy. 34 E., 56470. Phone: (218) 732-3306. Licensee: De La Hunt Broadcasting Corp. Population served: 150,000 Natl. Network: CBS, . Format: Country. Target aud: 25 plus. ◆ Bernie Schumacher, pres, gen sls mgr, progmg dir; Ed DeLa Hunt, gen mgr; David De La Hunt, chief of engrg.

KXKK(FM)— 1998: 92.5 mhz; 25 kw. 328 ft TL: N46 55 42 W95 00 22. Hrs open: Box 49, 56470. Phone: (218) 732-3306. Fax: (218) 732-3307. Licensee: Bernadine A. Schumacher. Format: Hot country. ◆Bernadine A. Schumacher, gen mgr.

Paynesville

KZPK(FM)— Dec 1, 1995: 98.9 mhz; 50 kw. 492 ft TL: N45 23 15 W94 24 47. Hrs open: 24 Box 1458, St. Cloud, 56302. Phone: (320) 251-1450. Fax: (320) 251-8952.E-mail: info@wildcountry989.com Web Site:www.wildcountry989.com Licensee: Leighton Enterprises Inc. (group owner; acq 4-15-97; $1 million). Format: Country. ◆Al Leighton, CEO; John Sowada, gen mgr; Denny Niess, sls VP; Denise Prozinski, gen sls mgr; Matt Senne, progmg dir; Cassie Hart, news dir; Dale Daley, chief of engrg; Cindy Niess, traf mgr.

Pelican Rapids

KBOT(FM)— June 1994: 104.1 mhz; 50 kw. Ant 492 ft TL: N46 29 57 W96 05 10. Stereo. Hrs open: 24 Box 746, Detroit Lakes, 56502-0746. Secondary address: 128 Junius Ave. W., Fergus Falls 56537. Phone: (218) 847-5624. Fax: (218) 847-7657.E-mail: kdlmkbot@lakesnet.net Web Site:www.wild1041.com Licensee: Leighton Enterprises Inc. (group owner; (acq 9-24-96; $700,000). Population served: 150,000 Rgnl rep: O'Malley. Format: Hot country. News staff: one; News: one hr wkly. Target aud: 25-54; Fargo-Moorhead, metro & TSA listeners. ◆Alver Leighton, CEO; John Sowada, pres; Denny Niess, VP; Jeff Leighton, gen mgr; Andy Lia, opns mgr; Kevin Flynn, progmg dir.

Pequot Lakes

KTIG(FM)— Apr 30, 1978: 102.7 mhz; 40 kw. 541 ft TL: N46 40 48 W94 25 02. Stereo. Hrs open: 24 Box 409, 56472. Phone: (218) 568-4422. Fax: (320) 568-5950. Licensee: Minnesota Christian Broadcasters Inc. Population served: 100,000 Natl. Network: Moody, USA, . Reddy, Begley & McCormick. Format: Relg. Target aud: 35-55; general. ◆Mike Heuberger, gen mgr; Jim Park, progmg dir; Randy Kennedy, news dir; Dwayne Walker, chief of engrg.

WZFJ(FM)— 2002: 100.1 mhz; 3.9 kw. Ant 407 ft TL: N46 40 48 W94 25 02. Hrs open: Box 409, 56472. Phone: (866) 568-4422. Fax: (218) 568-5950. Licensee: Minnesota Christian Broadcasters Inc. Natl. Network: Moody, USA, . Format: Contemp Christian. ◆Mike Heuberger, gen mgr; Jim Park, progmg dir; Randy Kennedy, news dir; Dwayne Walker, chief of engrg.

Perham

KPRW(FM)— Aug 26, 1996: 99.5 mhz; 6 kw. 328 ft TL: N46 33 16 W95 27 12. Hrs open: 24 Box 363, 235 West Main, 56573. Phone:

(218) 346-7596. Fax: (218) 346-7595.E-mail: lakesradio@lakesradio.net Web Site:www.lakes995.com Licensee: Jerry Papenfuss. Group owner: The Result Radio Group Population served: 150,000 Natl. Rep: Hyett/Ramsland,. Format: Adult hit radio. News staff: one; News: 10 hrs wkly. Target aud: 25-54. ◆Doug Gray, gen mgr; David Howey, progmg dir.

Pillager

WWWI-FM— 2000: 95.9 mhz; 6 kw. Ant 239 ft TL: N46 15 03 W94 19 30. Hrs open: 305 W. Washington St., Brainard, 56401. Phone: (218) 828-9994. Fax: (218) 828-8327. Licensee: Tower Broadcasting Corp. (acq 5-28-2004; $360,000). Format: News/talk. ◆James Pryor, gen mgr, progmg dir; Lon Schmidt, news dir.

Pine City

WCMP(AM)— June 13, 1957: 1350 khz; 1 kw-D. TL: N45 49 10 W92 59 45. Hrs open: 24 15429 Pokegama Lake Rd., 55063. Phone: (320) 629-7575. Fax: (320) 629-3933.E-mail: pinemill@ecenet.net Web Site:www.radiowcmp.net Licensee: Quarnstrom Media Group LLC (group owner; acq 9-22-03). Population served: 127,500 Rgnl. Network: MNN. MNN Blair, Joyce & Silva. Format: News, info, music of your life. News: 25 hrs wkly. Target aud: 30 plus; farmers, commuters, homemakers. Spec prog: Farm 6 hrs wkly. ◆ Al Quarstrom, pres; Mike Hughes, gen mgr, opns mgr; Matt Born, progmg dir; Bill Mayes, chief of engrg; Paula Butterfield, traf mgr.

WCMP-FM— Oct 15, 1977: 100.9 mhz; 25 kw. Ant 300 ft TL: N45 54 07 W92 57 25. Stereo. Hrs open: 24 15429 Pokegama Lake Rd., 55063. Phone: (320) 629-7575. Fax: (320) 629-3933.E-mail: pinemill@ecenet.com Web Site:www.radiowcmp.com Licensee: Quarnstrom Media Group LLC (group owner; acq 8-23-01; $1.2 million with co-located AM including five-year noncompete agreement). Population served: 127,500 Format: Contemp country, sports, news. Target aud: 18 plus; commuters, working adults with families. ◆ Mike Hughes, gen mgr & gen sls mgr.

Pipestone

KISD(FM)— Nov 20, 1968: 98.7 mhz; 100 kw. 1,014 ft TL: N43 53 52 W95 56 50. Stereo. Hrs open: 24 Prog sep from AM Secondary address: 608 W. Hwy. 30 56164. Phone: (507) 825-4282. Fax: (507) 825-3364.E-mail: kloh@klohradio.com Web Site:kisdradio.com Population served: 600,000 Natl. Network: ABC, . Wire Svc: AP Format: Oldies. Target aud: 18-65.

KLOH(AM)— June 1955: 1050 khz; 9 kw-D, 400 w-N. TL: N43 59 32 W96 20 37. Stereo. Hrs open: 24 Box 456, 56164. Secondary address: 608 W. Hwy. 30 56164. Phone: (507) 825-4282. Fax: (507) 825-3364.E-mail: kloh@klohradio.com Web Site:www.klohradio.com Licensee: Wallace Christensen. (acq 8-1-76). Population served: 750,000 Natl. Network: ABC, . Rgnl. Network: Linder Farm. Linder Farm Wire Svc: AP Format: Talk, news, C&W, farm. Spec prog: Relg 5 hrs, Sp 2 hrs wkly. ◆Collin Christensen, gen mgr, natl sls mgr, chief of engrg; Carmen Christensen, gen sls mgr, farm dir; Mylan Ray, mus dir; Bernie Wieme, news dir; Diane Carlson, pub affrs dir, local news ed; Honee Lee Longstreet, traf mgr; Joel Herrig, sports cmtr.

Preston

KFIL(AM)— May 21, 1966: 1060 khz; 1 kw-D. TL: N43 40 48 W92 08 27. Hrs open: Box 370, 300 St. Paul St. S.W., 55965. Phone: (507) 765-3856. Fax: (507) 765-2738. Licensee: KFIL Inc. Group owner: Cumulus Media Inc. (acq 3-30-2004; grpsl). Population served: 1,413 Rgnl. Network: MNN. MNN Format: C&W. ◆ Bruce Fishbaugher, gen mgr; Bruce Fishbaugher, gen sls mgr; John Milne, progmg dir; John Milne, news dir; Bill Davis, chief of engrg.

KFIL-FM— Sept 1, 1970: 103.1 mhz; 6 kw. 270 ft TL: N43 40 48 W92 08 27. Stereo. Hrs open: Dups AM 80% Box 370, 55965. Secondary address: 300 St. Paul St. S.W. 55965. Phone: (507) 765-3856. Fax: (507) 765-2738. Licensee: KFIL Inc. Format: Country.

Princeton

KLCI(FM)—(Elk River, Dec 1, 1974: 106.1 mhz; 9.1 kw. Ant 538 ft TL: N45 14 20 W93 41 14. Stereo. Hrs open: 24 Box 106, 55271. Secondary address: 32215 124th St., Elk River 55271. Phone: (763) 389-1300. Fax: (763) 389-1359. Population served: 1,500,000 Format: Country. News: 7 hrs wkly.

*KPCS(FM)—Not on air, target date: unknown: 89.7 mhz; 50 kw vert. Ant 105 ft TL: N45 35 54 W93 33 18. Hrs open: Box 18000, Pensacola, FL, 32523. Phone: (850) 479-6570 . Fax: (850) 969-1638. Web Site:www.rejoice.org Licensee: Pensacola Christian College Inc. ◆Arlin Horton, pres & gen mgr.

WQPM(AM)— Feb 1, 1967: 1300 khz; 1 kw-D, 83 w-N. TL: N45 32 54 W93 34 52. Hrs open: 24 Box 106, 55371. Secondary address: 32215 124th St. 55271. Phone: (763) 389-1300. Fax: (763) 389-1359. Web Site:www.bob106radio.com Licensee: Milestone Radio L.L.C. (acq 9-30-98; $1 million with co-located FM). Population served: 50,000 Natl. Network: ABC, . Rgnl. Network: Minn. Pub. Minn. Pub. Radio Mullin, Rhyne, Emmons & Topel. Format: Contemp country. News staff: one; News: 20 hrs wkly. Target aud: 25-54. Spec prog: Farm 2 hrs wkly. ◆ Dennis Carpenter, pres; Neil Freeman, gen mgr; Howard Johnson, gen sls mgr; Neil Freedman, progmg dir.

Proctor

KBMX(FM)— 1994: 107.7 mhz; 7.7 kw. Ant 912 ft TL: N46 47 13 W92 07 17. Hrs open: 24 14 E. Central Entrance, Duluth, 55811. Phone: (218) 727-4500. Fax: (218) 727-9356. Web Site:www.mix108.com Licensee: GAP Broadcasting Duluth License LLC. Group owner: Clear Channel Communications Inc. (acq 2-13-2008; grpsl). Population served: 375,000 Format: Adult Contemp. News: one hr wkly. Target aud: 25-54; working adults & families. ◆Merry Wallin, VP, gen mgr; Kariana Bite, gen mgr, prom dir; David Drew, opns mgr; Corey Carter, progmg mgr, disc jockey; Randy Wabik, chief of engrg.

Red Wing

KCUE(AM)— Jan 29, 1949: 1250 khz; 1 kw-D, 110 w-N. TL: N44 32 20 W92 31 25. Hrs open: 24 474 Guernsey Ln., 55066. Phone: (651) 388-7151. Fax: (651) 388-7153.E-mail: news@kwng.com Web Site:www.1250kcue.com Licensee: Sorenson Broadcasting Corp. (group owner; (acq 6-81; $1.1 million with co-located FM; 6-22-81). Population served: 30,000 Rgnl. Network: MNN. MNN Format: News/talk, farm, relg. News staff: 2; News: 7 hrs wkly. Target aud: 35 plus; information consumer. ◆Don Kliewer, gen mgr, gen sls mgr; Tom Hughes, opns mgr; Desi Foy, progmg dir; Jim Alan, news dir; Jack Calwell, sports cmtr.

KWNG(FM)— Aug 26, 1965: 105.9 mhz; 20 kw. 300 ft TL: N44 29 15 W92 13 56. Stereo. Hrs open: 24 Prog sep from AM 474 Guernsey Ln., 55066. Phone: (651) 388-7151. Fax: (651) 388-7153.E-mail: news@kwng.com Web Site:www.1250kcue.com Licensee: Sorenson Broadcasting Corp. Population served: 39,000 Format: Rock classics of the 60s, 70s & 80s. News staff: 2; News: one hr wkly. Target aud: 25-44; family & yuppie.

Redwood Falls

KLGR(AM)— November 1954: 1490 khz; 1 kw-U. TL: N44 32 33 W95 07 57. (CP: 470 w. TL: N44 32 35 W95 07 57). Hrs open: 639 W. Bridge, 56283. Phone: (507) 637-2989. Fax: (507) 637-5347.E-mail: klgr@mchsi.com Web Site:www.klgram.com Licensee: Three Eagles of Luverne Inc. Group owner: Three Eagles Communications (acq 12-13-99; with co-located FM). Population served: 50,000 Rgnl. Network: MNN. MNN Format: Country. Target aud: General. ◆Joel Koetke, gen mgr; Laura Olson, progmg dir & news dir.

KLGR-FM— June 3, 1974: 97.7 mhz; 3 kw. Ant 298 ft TL: N44 32 33 W95 07 57. Stereo. Hrs open: 639 W. Bridge, 56283. Phone: (507) 637-2989. Fax: (507) 637-5347. Web Site:www.klgram.com Licensee: Three Eagles of Luverne Inc. Format: Oldies.

*KRFI(FM)—Not on air, target date: unknown: 88.1 mhz; 2.1 kw. Ant 265 ft TL: N44 32 35.2 W95 07 57. Hrs open: 480 Cedar St., Saint Paul, 55101. Phone: (651) 290-1259. Web Site:www.mpr.org Licensee: Minnesota Public Radio. Minn. Pub. Radio Format: News and info. ◆Thomas J. Kigin, exec VP.

Richfield

KDWB-FM—Licensed to Richfield. See Minneapolis-St. Paul

KKMS(AM)—Licensed to Richfield. See Minneapolis-St. Paul

Rochester

*KFSI(FM)— Apr 28, 1981: 92.9 mhz; 6 kw. Ant 318 ft TL: N44 01 21 W92 32 36. Stereo. Hrs open: 4016 28th St. S.E., 55904. Phone: (507) 289-8585. Fax: (507) 529-4017.E-mail: shine@kfsi.org Web

Site:www.kfsi.org Licensee: Faith Sound Inc. Natl. Network: Moody, . Format: Adult contemp Christian. ♦Ray Logan, pres, gen mgr; Paul Logan, VP, progmg dir; Mike Anderson, mus dir, news dir; Steve Schuh, engrg VP.

***KLSE-FM**— Dec 17, 1974: 91.7 mhz; 100 kw. Ant 953 ft TL: N44 02 26 W92 20 28. Stereo. Hrs open: 24 206 S. Broadway, Suite 735, 55904. Phone: (507) 282-0910. Fax: (507) 282-2107. Web Site:www.mpr.org Licensee: Minnesota Public Radio Inc. Population served: 463,000 Natl. Network: NPR, PRI, . Rgnl. Network: Minn. Pub. Minn. Pub. Radio Format: Class. News staff: one. ♦Chris Cross, stn mgr; Mary Stapek, dev dir; Sea Stachura, news rptr.

***KMSE(FM)**— Aug 1, 1998: 88.7 mhz; 250 w. Ant 531 ft TL: N44 02 32 W92 20 26. Hrs open: 24 206 S. Broadway, Suite 735, 55904. Phone: (507) 282-0910. Fax: (507) 282-2107. Web Site:www.mpr.org Licensee: Minnesota Public Radio (acq 11-15-2004; $10.5 million with WCAL(FM) Northfield). Population served: 125,000 Format: AAA. News staff: one. ♦Chris Cross, gen mgr; Mary Stapek, dev dir; Steve Nelson, progmg dir.

KNXR(FM)— Dec 24, 1965: 97.5 mhz; 100 kw. 1,040 ft TL: N44 02 28 W92 20 25. Stereo. Hrs open: 1620 Greenview Dr. S.W., 55902-1034. Phone: (507) 288-7700. Fax: (507) 288-4531. Web Site:www.knxr.com Licensee: United Audio Corp. Population served: 225,000 Natl. Network: CBS, Wall Street, . Natl. Rep: McGavren Guild,. Miller & Neely. Wire Svc: AP Format: Adult traditional. Target aud: 35 plus. Spec prog: Class 4 hrs, talk 2 hrs wkly. ♦Thomas H. Jones, pres & gen mgr.

KOLM(AM)— November 1963: 1520 khz; 10 kw-D, 800 w-N. TL: N43 59 13 W92 25 05. Hrs open: 24 122 4th St. S.W., 55902. Phone: (507) 286-1010. Fax: (507) 286-9370.E-mail: info@1520theticket.com Web Site:www.1520theticket.com Licensee: Cumulus Licensing LLC. Group owner: Cumulus Media Inc. (acq 3-31-2004; grpsl). Population served: 250,000 Natl. Network: Westwood One, . Rgnl. Network: Linder Farm. Natl. Rep: Christal,. Linder Farm Smithwick & Belendiuk. Format: Sports. News staff: 2; News: 3 hrs wkly. Target aud: 35-64; male 55%, female 45%. ♦Shannon Knoepke, gen mgr; Terry Lee, gen sls mgr; Brent Ackerman, progmg dir; Kim David, news dir; Bill Davis, chief of engrg.

KRCH(FM)— 1972: 101.7 mhz; 39.1 kw. 554 ft TL: N44 06 59 W92 41 22. Stereo. Hrs open: 24 1530 Greenview Dr. S.W., Suite 200, 55902. Phone: (507) 288-3888. Fax: (507) 288-7815.E-mail: info@laser1017.net Web Site:www.laser1017.net Format: Classic rock. Target aud: 25-54. ♦Bob Fox, gen mgr.

KROC(AM)— October 1935: 1340 khz; 1 kw-U. TL: N44 01 47 W92 29 31. Hrs open: 24 122 4th St. S.W., 55902. Phone: (507) 286-1010. Fax: (507) 280-0000.E-mail: brent@kroc.com Web Site:www.kroc.com Licensee: Cumulus Licensing LLC. Group owner: Cumulus Media Inc. (acq 3-29-2004; grpsl). Population served: 95,000 Natl. Rep: Hyett/Ramsland,. Format: News/talk. News staff: 3; News: 42 hrs wkly. Target aud: 30-64. Spec prog: Farm 12 hrs wkly. ♦Perry Lee, gen sls mgr; Brent Ackerman, progmg dir; Bill Davis, chief of engrg; Kim David, news cmtr.

KROC-FM— July 1, 1965: 106.9 mhz; 100 kw. 1,110 ft TL: N43 34 15 W92 25 37. Hrs open: 122 4th Ave. S.W., 55902. Phone: (507) 286-1010. Fax: (507) 280-0000.E-mail: brent@kroc.com Web Site:www.kroc.com Population served: 300,000 Format: CHR. Target aud: 18-54.

***KRPR(FM)**— 1976: 89.9 mhz; 3.2 kw. Ant 590 ft TL: N44 02 28 W92 20 25. Stereo. Hrs open: 24 Rochester Public Radio, 1620 Greenview Dr. S.W., 55902-1034. Phone: (507) 288-2376. Fax: (507) 288-4531. Web Site:www.krpr.org Licensee: Rochester Public Radio (acq 5-13-99). Population served: 100,000 Natl. Network: USA, . Miller & Neely. Format: Classic rock. Target aud: General. ♦Thomas H. Jones, pres; Todd D. Brakke, gen mgr & stn mgr.

KWEB(AM)— Nov 27, 1957: 1270 khz; 5 kw-D, 1 kw-N, DA-2. TL: N43 58 47 W92 26 51. Hrs open: 1530 Greenview Dr. S.W., Suite 200, 55902. Phone: (507) 288-3888. Fax: (507) 288-7815.E-mail: info@laser1017.net Web Site:www.laser1017.net Licensee: CC Licenses LLC. Group owner: Clear Channel Communications Inc. (acq 9-25-2000; grpsl). Population served: 75,000 Natl. Network: CBS, . Rgnl. Network: MNN. Natl. Rep: D & R Radio,. MNN Format: Sports, talk. Target aud: Men. ♦Bob Fox, gen mgr, opns mgr; Mary Anne Nonn, gen sls mgr; Mark Clark, prom dir, progmg dir; Craig Erpestad, chief of engrg.

KWWK(FM)— July 4, 1967: 96.5 mhz; 43 kw. 528 ft TL: N44 01 59 W92 36 10. Stereo. Hrs open: 24 Prog sep from AM 122 4th St. S.W., 55902. Phone: (507) 286-1010. Fax: (507) 286-9370.E-mail: info@quickcountry.com Web Site:www.quickcountry.com Rgnl. Network: McGavren Guild. Natl. Rep: Christal,. Format: Country. News: 2 hrs wkly. Target aud: 25-54; male & female 18-49, 25-54, 35-54. ♦Shannon Knoepke, gen mgr; Brent Ackerman, progmg dir; Bill Davis, chief of engrg.

***KZSE(FM)**— February 1989: 90.7 mhz; 1.38 kw. Ant 259 ft TL: N44 02 26 W92 20 28. Hrs open: 24 206 S. Broadway, Suite 735, 55904. Phone: (507) 282-0910. Fax: (507) 282-2107. Web Site:www.mpr.org Licensee: Minnesota Public Radio Inc. Natl. Network: NPR, PRI, . Rgnl. Network: Minn. Pub. Minn. Pub. Radio Format: News & info. News staff: one. ♦Chris Cross, gen mgr; Mary Stapek, dev dir; Sea Stachura, news rptr.

Rockville

KYES(AM)— 2009: 1180 khz; 50 kw-D, 5 kw-N, 8 kw-CH, DA-3. TL: N45 21 43 W94 17 57. Hrs open: Box 547, Sauk Rapids, 56379-0547. Secondary address: 1310 2nd St. N., Sauk Rapids 56379-2532. Phone: (320) 257-9669.E-mail: David@KYESRadio.com Web Site:www.kyesradio.com Licensee: Throw Fire Project. Format: Catholic. ♦Andrew W. Hilger, pres.

Roseau

KCAJ-FM— June 1996: 102.1 mhz; 50 kw. Ant 285 ft TL: N48 38 50 W95 44 10. Hrs open: 24 107 Center Street West, 56751. Phone: (218) 463-3360. Fax: (218) 463-1977.E-mail: info@kcatam.com Web Site:wild102fm.com Licensee: Jack J. Swanson. Population served: 25,000 Natl. Network: CNN Radio, . Minn. News Net. Format: Top-40. News staff: one; News: 10 hrs wkly. Target aud: General. ♦Jack Swanson, gen mgr, opns VP; Jack McDonald, gen sls mgr; Justin Gallo, prom dir.

KRWB(AM)— Apr 5, 1963: 1410 khz; 1 kw-U, DA-N. TL: N48 50 43 W95 43 34. Hrs open: 24 Box 69, Warroad, 56763. Phone: (218) 463-1410. Fax: (218) 463-3778.E-mail: agency@kq92.com Web Site:www.1410krwb.com Licensee: Border Broadcasting L.P. (acq 10-1-00; $62,000). Population served: 2,552 Natl. Network: ABC, . Format: Classic Rock. News staff: one. Target aud: 25-54; general. ♦Mike Pederson, gen mgr.

***KRXW(FM)**— 2008: 103.5 mhz; 48 kw. Ant 493 ft TL: N48 54 10 W95 22 38.1. Hrs open: 480 Cedar St., St. Paul, 55101. Phone: (651) 290-1500. Fax: (651) 290-1224. Web Site:www.mpr.org Licensee: Minnesota Public Radio. Format: News/talk. ♦William H. Kling, gen mgr.

Roseville

***KDNI(FM)**—(Duluth, Apr 16, 1983: 90.5 mhz; 2 kw. 728 ft TL: N46 47 21 W92 06 51. Stereo. Hrs open: 24 1101 E. Central Entrance, Duluth, 55811. Secondary address: Northwestern College, 3003 N. Snelling Ave. N. 55811. Phone: (218) 722-6700. Fax: (218) 722-1092.E-mail: kdnw@kdnw.fm.org Web Site:www.kdnw.fm Licensee: Northwestern College Radio Network. Group owner: Northwestern College & Radio (acq 12-18-92). Population served: 200,000 Natl. Network: AP Radio, . Bryan Cave. Wire Svc: AP Format: Talk, classic praise music. News: 5 hrs wkly. Target aud: 25-54; baby boomers. ♦Paul Virts, sr VP & VP; Paul Harkness, stn mgr.

***KTIS(AM)**—(Minneapolis, Feb 7, 1949: 900 khz; 50 kw-D, 500 w-N, DA-2. TL: N44 59 24 W92 58 52. Hrs open: 24 3003 Snelling Ave. N., St. Paul, 55113. Phone: (651) 631-5000. Fax: (651) 631-5084.E-mail: info@ktis.fm Web Site:www.ktis.fm Licensee: Northwestern College. Group owner: Northwestern College & Radio. Population served: 2,000,000 Format: Relg, Christian, news. News staff: 2; News: 20 hrs wkly. Target aud: 35-45. ♦Paul Virts, exec VP; David Fitts, stn mgr; Marilyn Ryan, opns dir.

Rushford

KWNO-FM— Dec 18, 1991: 99.3 mhz; 11 kw. 495 ft TL: N43 56 32 W91 45 30. Hrs open: 24 Box 767, Winona, 55987. Secondary address: 752 Bluffview Cir., Winona 55987. Phone: (507) 452-4154. Fax: (507) 452-9494.E-mail: jpapenfuss@winonaradio.com Web Site:winonaradio.com Licensee: KAGE Inc. Group owner: The Result Radio Group (acq 6-19-95; $1 million with KWNO(AM) Winona). Population served: 70,000 Wiley, Rein & Fielding. Wire Svc: AP Format: Hot country. News staff: one; News: one hr wkly. Target aud: 18-49; active young students & working persons. ♦Jerry Papenfuss, CEO, gen mgr, mktg VP; Les Guderian, sls dir; Pat Papenfuss, pres, exec VP, opns mgr & prom VP; Aaron Taylor, progmg dir; Darryl Smelser, news dir; Bob Sebo, pub affrs dir.

Saint Charles

KDZZ(FM)— Apr 18, 1998: 107.7 mhz; 1.95 kw. Ant 571 ft TL: N44 02 25 W92 13 05. Hrs open: 24 122 4th St. S.W., Rochester, 55902. Phone: (507) 286-1010. Fax: (507) 286-9370. Licensee: Cumulus Licensing LLC. Group owner: Cumulus Media Inc. (acq 3-31-2004; grpsl). Population served: 200,000 Smithwick & Belenduik. Format: Rock. ♦Rosanne Rybak, gen mgr.

Saint Cloud

***KCFB(FM)**— Nov 17, 1986: 91.5 mhz; 15 kw. 348 ft TL: N45 30 02 W94 14 31. Stereo. Hrs open: 24
Rebroadcasts KTIG(FM) Pequot Lakes 100%.
Box 409, Pequot Lakes, 56472. Phone: (320) 252-4214. Fax: (218) 568-5950. Licensee: Minnesota Christian Broadcasters Inc. (acq 9-4-97; $250,000). Natl. Network: Moody, . Reddy, Begley & McCormick. Wire Svc: AP Format: Relg. News staff: one; News: 14 hrs wkly. Target aud: General. ♦Mike Heuberger, gen mgr; Jim Park, progmg dir.

KCLD-FM— May 1, 1948: 104.7 mhz; 100 kw. 984 ft TL: N45 34 03 W94 30 43. Stereo. Hrs open: Prog sep from AM Box 1458, 56302. Secondary address: 619 W. St. Germain St. 56302.E-mail: info@1047kcld.com Web Site:www.1047kcld.com Licensee: Leighton Enterprises Inc. Population served: 200,000 Format: CHR. ♦J.J. Holiday, progmg dir.

KNSI(AM)— June 1938: 1450 khz; 1 kw-U. TL: N45 32 21 W94 10 05. Stereo. Hrs open: Box 1458, 56302. Secondary address: 619 W. St. Germain St. 56302. Phone: (320) 251-1450. Fax: (320) 251-8952.E-mail: info@1450knsi.com Web Site:www.1450knsi.com Licensee: Leighton Enterprises Inc. (group owner; acq 9-15-75). Rgnl rep: O'Malley. Format: News/talk. Target aud: 35 plus; males. ♦John J. Sowada, pres, VP, gen mgr; Denny Niess, sls VP; Denise Prozinski, sls dir; Matt Senne, progmg dir; Dale Daley, chief of engrg; Kathy Carton, traf mgr.

***KVSC(FM)**— May 10, 1967: 88.1 mhz; 16.5 kw. Ant 446 ft TL: N45 31 00 W94 13 52. Stereo. Hrs open: 20-24 St. Cloud State Univ., 27 Stewart Hall, 56301-4498. Phone: (320) 308-3066. Fax: (320) 308-5337.E-mail: info@kvsc.org Web Site:www.kvsc.org Licensee: St. Cloud State University. Population served: 210,000 Natl. Network: PRI, . Wire Svc: AP Format: educ., alternative. News staff: 2.5; News: 12 hrs wkly. Target aud: 17-60; educated, progsv. Spec prog: jazz, indie, folk, americana, MN music. ♦Roya Majid, gen mgr; Jo McMullen-Boyer, stn mgr; Jim Gray, opns dir.

KXSS(AM)—See Waite Park

KZRV(FM)—(Sartell, Aug 26, 1988: 96.7 mhz; 50 kw. Ant 453 ft TL: N45 46 03 W94 08 04. Stereo. Hrs open: 24 640 S.E. Lincoln Ave., St. Cloud, 56304. Phone: (320) 251-4422. Fax: (320) 251-1855.E-mail: studio@kiss96.com Web Site:www.kiss96.com Licensee: Regent Licensee of St. Cloud Inc. Group owner: Regent Communications Inc. (acq 5-8-2001; grpsl). Wiley, Rein & Fielding. Format: Modern rock. News staff: one. ♦Dave Engberg, gen mgr; Lee Voss, news dir; Mark Young, chief of engrg.

WJON(AM)— September 1950: 1240 khz; 1 kw-U. TL: N45 33 36 W94 08 20. Hrs open: 24 640 Southeast Lincoln Ave., 56304. Phone: (320) 251-4422.E-mail: info@wjon.com Web Site:www.wjon.com Licensee: Regent Licensee of St. Cloud Inc. Group owner: Regent Communications Inc. (acq 5-1-99; grpsl). Population served: 100,000 Natl. Network: CBS, . Rgnl. Network: MNN. MNN Pepper & Corazzini. Format: News/talk, full service. News staff: 3; News: 30 hrs wkly. Target aud: 25 plus. ♦Dave Engberg, gen mgr, sls dir; Mike Dylan, opns mgr; Bob Hughes, progmg dir; Lee Voss, news dir; Mark Young, chief of engrg.

WWJO(FM)— 1975: 98.1 mhz; 97 kw. Ant 1,000 ft TL: N45 48 52 W94 01 38. Stereo. Hrs open: 640 Southeast Lincoln Ave., 56304. Phone: (320) 251-4422. Web Site:www.98country.com Licensee: Regent Licensee of St. Cloud Inc. Format: Country. Target aud: 18 plus. ♦Terry Jacobs, CEO; Bill Stakelin, pres; Fred Murr, sr VP; Lynn Larson, mktg VP, chief of engrg; Bill Fink, progmg dir; Sandi Davis, asst music dir.

Saint James

KRRW(FM)— July 24, 1983: 101.5 mhz; 14 kw. Ant 446 ft TL: N43 52 29 W94 36 04. Stereo. Hrs open: 24 59346 Madison Ave., Mankato, 56001. Phone: (507) 345-4537. Fax: (507) 345-5364.E-mail: krrw@linderradio.com Licensee: Minnesota Valley Broadcasting Co. Group owner: Linder Broadcasting Group (acq 1996; $800,000 with KXAC(FM) St). Rgnl. Network: Linder Farm. Linder Farm Miller & Miller. Format: Modern country. News staff: one; News: 16 hrs wkly. Target aud: 25-54. Spec prog: Sp one hr wkly. ♦Jo Guck Bailey, VP & gen mgr.

KXAC(FM)— Nov. 1, 1992: 100.5 mhz; 34 kw. Ant 590 ft TL: N43 57 03 W94 23 25. Hrs open: 24 59346 Madison Ave., Mankato, 56001. Phone: (507) 345-4537. Fax: (507) 345-5364.E-mail: kxac@linderradio.com Licensee: Minnesota Valley Broadcasting Co. Group owner: Linder Broadcasting Group (acq 1996; $800,000 with KXAX(FM) St). Rgnl. Network: MNN. MNN Miller & Miller. Format: Oldies. Target aud: 25-58. ◆Jo Guck Bailey, VP & gen mgr.

Saint Joseph

KCML(FM)— 1998: 99.9 mhz; 6 kw. 328 ft TL: N45 32 21 W94 10 05. Hrs open: Box 1458, St. Cloud, 56302. Secondary address: 619 W. Saint Germain, St. Cloud 56301. Phone: (320) 251-1450. Fax: (320) 251-8952.E-mail: info@lite999.com Web Site:www.lite999.com Licensee: Leighton Enterprises Inc. (group owner) Format: Contemp lite. ◆Al Leighton, CEO; John Sowada, gen mgr; Denny Niess, sls VP; Denise Prozinski, gen sls mgr; Ron Linder, progmg dir; Dale Daley, chief of engrg; Cindy Niess, traf mgr.

KKJM(FM)— May 7, 1996: 92.9 mhz; 25 kw. 328 ft TL: N45 38 19 W94 22 23. Stereo. Hrs open: 24 1310 Second St. N., Sauk Rapids, 56379. Phone: (320) 251-1780. Fax: (320) 257-1624.E-mail: friends@spirit929.com Web Site:www.spirit929.com Licensee: Gabriel Communications Co., St. Cloud. (acq 11-30-99). Population served: 150,000 Wire Svc: AP Format: Christian adult contemp. News: 5 hrs wkly. Target aud: 25-54; females. ◆Deb Huschle, gen mgr; Diana Madsen, progmg dir; Michelle Crabb, traf mgr.

Saint Louis Park

*KDXL(FM)— Mar 17, 1977: 106.5 mhz; 10 w (ST: KUOM-FM). Ant 85 ft TL: N44 56 36 W93 21 39. Stereo. Hrs open: 7:30 AM-10 PM (M-F) Independent School District #283, 6425 W. 33rd St., 55426. Phone: (952) 928-6000. Fax: (952) 928-6208. Licensee: Independent School District 283. Format: AOR, classic rock, progsv. Target aud: 15-30; high school students & loc residents. ◆Charlie Fiss, stn mgr.

KTNF(AM)— May 13, 1958: 950 khz; 1 kw-U, DA-2. TL: N44 52 08 W93 25 11. Hrs open: 24 11320 Valley View Rd., Eden Praire, 55344. Phone: (952) 946-8885. Fax: (952) 946-0888.E-mail: am950ktnf@am950ktnf.com Web Site:www.am950ktnf.com Licensee: JR Broadcasting LLC Group owner: Infinity Broadcasting Corp. (acq 10-21-2004; $3 million). Population served: 6,938 Natl. Network: Air America, CNN Radio, Jones Radio Networks, . Wire Svc: AP Format: Talk. Target aud: 35+. ◆Janet Robert, pres & gen mgr.

*KUOM-FM— Feb 17, 2003: 106.5 mhz; 8 w (ST: KDXL(FM)). Ant 253 ft TL: N44 56 46 W93 19 27. Stereo. Hrs open: 4:30 PM-8 AM M-F; 24 S-S
Rebroadcasts KUOM(AM) Minneapolis 100%.
University of Minnesota, 330 21st Ave. S, 610 Rarig Ctr, Minneapolis, 55455-0415. Phone: (612) 625-3500. Fax: (612) 625-2112.E-mail: radiok@umn.edu Web Site:www.radiok.org Licensee: Regents of the University of Minnesota. Population served: 200,000 Dow, Lohnes & Albertson. Wire Svc: AP Format: Indie. Target aud: 18-34. ◆Sara Milller, stn mgr; Larry Oberg, chief of opns; Stuart Sanders, dev dir.

KZJK(FM)— July 1, 1962: 104.1 mhz; 89 kw. Ant 1,033 ft TL: N45 03 30 W93 07 27. Stereo. Hrs open: 625 2nd Ave. S., Suite 200, Minneapolis, 55402-1908. Phone: (612) 370-0611. Web Site:www.1041jackfm.com Licensee: The Audio House Inc. Format: Hits of the 80s. ◆Mary Neimeyer, sr VP; Mary Niemeyer, gen mgr; Patrick Stelzner, gen sls mgr; Chris Kalis, prom dir; John Lassman, progmg dir.

Saint Paul

KEEY-FM—Licensed to Saint Paul. See Minneapolis-St. Paul

KMNV(AM)—Licensed to Saint Paul. See Minneapolis-St. Paul

KNOF(FM)—Licensed to Saint Paul. See Minneapolis-St. Paul

KSTP(AM)—Licensed to Saint Paul. See Minneapolis-St. Paul

KSTP-FM—Licensed to Saint Paul. See Minneapolis-St. Paul

WMCN(FM)—Licensed to Saint Paul. See Minneapolis-St. Paul

Saint Peter

*KGAC(FM)— Mar 29, 1985: 90.5 mhz; 75 kw. 708 ft TL: N44 13 20 W94 07 03. Stereo. Hrs open: 24 Stn currently dark Minnesota Public

Radio Inc., 480 Cedar St., St. Paul, 55101. Phone: (651) 290-1500. Fax: (651) 290-1224.E-mail: mail@mpr.org Web Site:www.mpr.org Licensee: Minnesota Public Radio Inc. Population served: 200,000 Natl. Network: PRI, . Rgnl. Network: Minn. Pub. Minn. Pub. Radio Format: Class, arts. News staff: 2. Target aud: General. Spec prog: Folk var 17 hrs wkly. ◆William H. Kling, pres & gen mgr.

KGLB(AM)— Aug 5, 1957: Stn currently dark. 1310 khz; 1 kw-D, 343 w-N, DA-1. TL: N44 19 51 W93 58 19. Hrs open: 24 5300 Edina Industrial Blvd., Suite 200, Edina, 55439. Phone: (952) 842-7200. Fax: (952) 842-1048. Licensee: Northern Lights Broadcasting LLC. Group owner: Three Eagles Communications (acq 7-28-2008; $350,000). Population served: 71,000 Rgnl. Network: Linder Farm. Womble Carlyle Sandridge & Rice PLLC. ◆Steve Woodbury, gen mgr.

*KNGA(FM)— Mar 1, 1992: 91.5 mhz; 8.5 kw. 600 ft TL: N44 13 20 W94 07 03. Hrs open: 24
Rebroadcasts KNOW-FM Minneapolis-St. Paul.
Minnesota Public Radio, 480 Cedar St., Saint Paul, 55101. Phone: (800) 228-7123. Fax: (507) 651-1295.E-mail: mail@mpr.org Web Site:www.mpr.org Licensee: Minnesota Public Radio. Population served: 150,000 Natl. Network: NPR, PRI, . Rgnl. Network: Minn. Pub. Minn. Pub. Radio Format: News, info. News staff: 2. Target aud: General. ◆William H. Kling, gen mgr; Jon Gossett, dev dir; Mary Pat Ladner, mktg dir; Erik Nycklemoe, progmg dir; Bill Wareham, news dir.

KRBI-FM— Sept 1, 1966: 105.5 mhz; 25.kw. Ant 200 ft TL: N44 19 42 W93 58 16. Stereo. Hrs open: 24 1807 Lee Blvd., North Mankato, 56003. Phone: (507) 345-4646. Fax: (507) 345-3299. Web Site:www.buzzard105.com Licensee: Three Eagles Communications LLC. (acq 7-16-2003; $3.2 million with co-located AM). Population served: 75,000 Format: Classic hits. News staff: one; News: one hr wkly. Target aud: 25-54; people liking classic hits, 70s-90s & small amounts of news, weather, & sports. ◆Dave Sturgeos, gen mgr.

Sartell

KZRV(FM)—Licensed to Sartell. See Saint Cloud

Sauk Centre

KIKV-FM— Dec 25, 1970: 100.7 mhz; 100 kw. Ant 790 ft TL: N45 41 10 W95 08 03. Stereo. Hrs open: 24 Box 1024, Alexandria, 56308-1024. Secondary address: 604 Third Ave. W., Alexandria 56308. Phone: (320) 762-2154. Fax: (320) 762-2156.E-mail: 100.7@kikvfm.com Web Site:kikvradio.com Licensee: BDI Broadcasting Inc. Group owner: Omni Broadcasting Co. (acq 9-25-89; $855,000; 10-16-89). Population served: 500,000 Natl. Network: ABC, AP Radio, . Rgnl. Network: Linder Farm. Linder Farm Garvey, Schubert & Barer. Format: Country. News staff: one; News: 12 hrs wkly. Target aud: 25-54; adults. Spec prog: Farm 20 hrs wkly. ◆Lou Buron, CEO, pres; Mary Campbell, CFO, VP; Dave Vagle, gen mgr; Trudy Blanshan, gen sls mgr & prom mgr; Rick Blanshan, progmg dir; Paul Sorum, mus dir, pub affrs dir; Jim Rohn, news dir; Dave Cox, engrg dir, chief of engrg.

Sauk Rapids

WBHR(AM)— Aug 3, 1963: 660 khz; 10 kw-D, 250 w-N, DA-2. TL: N45 36 18 W94 08 21. Hrs open: 24 1010 2nd St. N., 56379. Phone: (320) 252-6200. Fax: (320) 252-9367. Web Site:www.660wbhr.com Licensee: Tri-County Broadcasting Inc. Population served: 1,752,103 Natl. Network: Radio Disney, . Format: Sports. ◆Herb M. Hoppe, pres & gen mgr; Gary E. Hoppe, opns mgr, chief of engrg; Doug Kurtz, gen sls mgr; Gary Hoppe, progmg dir.

WHMH-FM— Oct 31, 1975: 101.7 mhz; 50 kw. 423 ft TL: N45 35 48 W94 09 25. Stereo. Hrs open: 24 Dups AM 98% 1010 2nd St. N, 56379. Phone: (320) 252-6200. Fax: (320) 252-9367. Web Site:www.rockin101.com Population served: 163,000 Format: Rock.

WMIN(AM)— 2008: 1010 khz; 1.7 kw-D, 240 w-N, DA-2. TL: N45 36 18 W94 08 21. Hrs open: 1010 2nd St. N., 56379. Phone: (320) 252-6200. Fax: (320) 252-9367. Web Site:www.wmin1010.com Licensee: Herbert M. Hoppe. Format: Adult standards. ◆Herb M. Hoppe, gen mgr; Doug Kertz, gen sls mgr; Gary Tyler Moore, progmg dir.

WPPI(AM)—Not on air, target date: unknown: 540 khz; 250 w-U, DA-2. TL: N45 36 18 W94 08 21. Hrs open: Box 366, 56379-0366. Phone: (320) 252-6200. Fax: (320) 252-9367. Licensee: Herbert M. Hoppe. ◆Herbert M. Hoppe, gen mgr.

WVAL(AM)— Mar 1, 1999: 800 khz; 2.6 kw-D, 850 w-N, DA-2. TL: N45 36 18 W94 08 21. Hrs open: Box 366, 56379. Secondary address: 1010 2nd St. N. 56379. Phone: (320) 252-6200. Fax: (320) 252-9367.E-mail: original@800wval.com Web Site:www.800wval.com

Licensee: Tri-County Broadcasting Inc. Format: Classical country. ◆Herb M. Hoppe, gen mgr; Doug Kertz, gen sls mgr; Kevin Lange, progmg dir.

Sebeka

*KOPJ(FM)— Nov 5, 2005: 89.3 mhz; 99.23 kw. Ant 469 ft TL: N46 33 08 W94 39 03. Hrs open: 200 S. Main Ave., Park Rapids, 56470. Phone: (218) 237-4673. Web Site:www.kopj.org Licensee: LifeTalk Radio Inc. Natl. Network: Life Talk, . Format: Christian. ◆James Gilley, pres; Sharon Erickson, stn mgr.

Shakopee

KQSP(AM)— Oct 6, 1963: 1530 khz; 8.6 kw-D, 10 w-N, DA-2. TL: N44 48 26 W93 33 25. Hrs open: 24 2519 Osage Dr., Glenview, IL, 60026. Phone: (847) 687-6550. Licensee: Broadcast One Inc. Group owner: Relevant Radio (acq 9-8-2006; $1.2 million). Population served: 2,300,000 ◆Yong W. Kim, pres.

Slayton

KJOE(FM)— 1993: 106.1 mhz; 13 kw. 971 ft TL: N43 53 52 W95 56 50. Hrs open: 24 2660 Broadway Ave., 56172. Phone: (507) 836-6125. Phone: (507) 836-6126. Fax: (507) 836-6537.E-mail: kjoe@kjoeradio.com Web Site:www.kjoeradio.com Licensee: Wallace Christensen. Format: Country. ◆Wallace Christensen, pres; Collin Christensen, gen mgr; Carmen Christensen, gen sls mgr; Bernard Wieme, prom dir; Mylan Ray, mus dir; Joel Herrig, news dir; Diane Marie, pub affrs dir; Honee Lee Longstreet, traf mgr.

Sleepy Eye

KNUJ-FM— June 1, 1995: 107.3 mhz; 1.9 kw. 400 ft TL: N44 19 38 W94 43 42. Stereo. Hrs open: 24
Rebroadcasts KNUJ(AM) New Ulm 70%.
Box 368, New Ulm, 56073. Secondary address: 317 North Minn St., New Ulm 56073. Phone: (507) 359-2921. Fax: (507) 359-4520.E-mail: knuj@knuj.net Web Site:www.knuj.net Licensee: Ingstad Brothers Broadcasting LLC (group owner; acq 5-1-2004; grpsl). Population served: 50,000 Format: Adult contemp. News staff: one; News: 20 hrs wkly. Target aud: 18-49; slightly more females than males. ◆Jim Bartels, VP, gen mgr; Janine Enter, gen sls mgr; Brian Filzen, progmg dir; Mike Lemmer, news dir; Greg Brandt, chief of engrg.

Spring Grove

KQYB(FM)— Aug 2, 1980: 98.3 mhz; 33 kw. 607 ft TL: N43 40 53 W91 45 28. Stereo. Hrs open: 24 PO Box 99, 201 State St., Lacrosse, WI, 54602. Phone: (507) 498-5720. Fax: (507) 498-5766.E-mail: email@kq98.com Web Site:www.kq98.com Licensee: Family Radio Inc. Group owner: The Mid-West Family Broadcast Group (acq 7-19-01; grpsl). Population served: 209,000 Shaw Pittman. Wire Svc: AP Format: Hot country. News staff: one; News: one hr wkly. Target aud: General. ◆Dick Record, CEO, CEO & gen mgr.

Spring Valley

*KVCS(FM)—Not on air, target date: unknown: 89.1 mhz; 3.5 kw vert. Ant 266 ft TL: N43 42 14 W92 22 48. Hrs open: 3434 W. Kilbourn Ave., Milwaukee, WI, 53208-3313. Phone: (414) 935-3000. Fax: (414) 935-3015. Web Site:www.vcyamerica.org Licensee: VCY America Inc. ◆Vic Eliason, VP & gen mgr.

KVGO(FM)— 1993: 104.3 mhz; 2.8 kw. 472 ft TL: N43 33 46 W92 25 29. Hrs open: Box 370, Preston, 55965. Phone: (507) 765-3856. Fax: (507) 765-2738. Licensee: KVGO Inc. Group owner: Cumulus Media Inc. (acq 3-30-2004; grpsl). Natl. Rep: D & R Radio,. Format: Oldies. ◆Bruce Fishbaugher, gen mgr, stn mgr, gen sls mgr; John Milne, progmg dir & news dir.

Springfield

KNSG(FM)— 1995: 94.7 mhz; 50 kw. Ant 472 ft TL: N44 21 54 W95 19 27. Stereo. Hrs open: 24 1414 E. College Dr., Marshall, 56258. Phone: (507) 532-2282. Fax: (507) 532-3739.E-mail: info@marshallradio.net Web Site:marshallradio.net Licensee: Springfield Radio Inc. Group owner: Linder Broadcasting Group (acq 6-11-2007; $500,000). Natl. Network: Westwood One, . Natl. Rep: Katz Radio,. Minn. News Net. Wire Svc: AP Format: Adult contemp. Target aud: 30 plus; women. Spec prog: Farm 15 hrs, women 3 hrs wkly. ◆Brad Strootman, gen mgr; Heath Radke, chief of opns.

Staples

KNSP(AM)— June 3, 1982: 1430 khz; 1 kw-D, 199 w-N. TL: N46 21 34 W94 46 55. Hrs open: 24 Box 551, Wadena, 56482-0551. Secondary address: 201 1/2 Jefferson St. S., Wadena 56482. Phone: (218) 631-1803. Fax: (218) 631-4557.E-mail: kwadkkws@arvig.net Web Site:kwadknsp.net Licensee: BL Broadcasting Inc. Group owner: Omni Broadcasting Co. (acq 4-1-2004; grpsl). Population served: 20,000 Natl. Network: ABC, . Minn. News Net. Garvey, Schubert & Barer. Format: Country, mainstream. News staff: one; News: 20 hrs wkly. Target aud: 25-54; adults. Spec prog: Farm 10 hrs wkly. ♦Lou Buron, CEO, pres; Mary Campbell, CFO, VP; Rick Youngbauer, gen mgr, gen sls mgr, news dir; Sherry Linnes, prom dir; Kyle Gylsen, progmg dir, pub affrs dir; Dave Cox, engrg dir, chief of engrg; Tammy Waln, traf mgr.

KSKK(FM)— Aug 1, 1994: 94.7 mhz; 50 kw. 469 ft TL: N46 33 08 W94 39 03. Stereo. Hrs open: 24 11 S.E. Bryant Ave., Wadena, 56482. Phone: (218) 631-3441. Fax: (218) 631-3414.E-mail: kskk@eot.com Licensee: NorMin Broadcasting Co. Natl. Network: CBS, . Rgnl. Network: Linder Farm. Format: Soft hits. News: 20 hrs wkly. Target aud: 30 plus. ♦David J. De LaHunt, CEO, pres, CFO; Gene Marie Kanten, gen mgr; Joleen De LaHunt, VP & stn mgr; Heidi Hutson, gen sls mgr.

Starbuck

KRVY-FM— 2001: 97.3 mhz; 50 kw. Ant 492 ft TL: N45 31 42 W95 32 52. Hrs open: 24 Box 380, Willmar, 56201. Secondary address: 730 N.E. Hwy. 71, Willmar 56201. Phone: (320) 231-1600. Fax: (320) 235-7010. Web Site:www.k-musicradio.com Licensee: Iowa City Broadcasting Co. Group owner: Tom Ingstad Broadcasting Group (acq 7-19-99; $200,000 for stock). Wire Svc: UPI Format: Adult contemp, light rock. News staff: one; News: 8 hrs wkly. Target aud: 25-54; male & female. ♦Doug Hanson, gen mgr, gen sls mgr; Rob Ryan, progmg dir; Beverly Ahlquist, news dir.

Stewartville

KYBA(FM)— Feb 1, 1993: 105.3 mhz; 50 kw. 492 ft TL: N43 40 23 W92 41 54. Hrs open: 122 4th St. S.W., Rochester, 55902-3320. Phone: (507) 286-1010. Fax: (507) 286-9370.E-mail: info@y105fm.com Web Site:www.y105fm.com Licensee: Cumulus Licensing LLC Group owner: Cumulus Media Inc. (acq 3-29-2004; grpsl). Natl. Network: ABC, . Natl. Rep: Christal,. Rgnl rep: Christal Radio Format: Adult contemp. Target aud: 25-54. ♦Shannon Knoepke, gen mgr; Terry Lee, gen sls mgr; Tom Garrett, progmg dir; Kim David, news dir; Bill Davis, chief of engrg.

Stillwater

KLBB(AM)— Mar 13, 1949: 1220 khz; 5 kw-D, 254 w-N. TL: N45 03 15 W92 49 42. Hrs open: 24 c/o Endurance Broadcasting LLC, 104 N. Main St., 55082. Phone: (651) 439-5006. Fax: (651) 439-5015.E-mail: dan@mighty1220.com Web Site:www.mighty1220.com Licensee: Endurance Broadcasting LLC (acq 7-5-2001). Population served: 2,200,000 Natl. Network: ABC, Westwood One, . Minn. News Net. Miller & Miller, P.C. Format: Adult standards. News staff: one. Target aud: 35-64. ♦Daniel Smith, CEO, pres; Scott Murray, VP & gen mgr; Reed Hagen, progmg dir.

Sunburg

KLFN(FM)— 2003: 106.5 mhz; 2.3 kw. Ant 525 ft TL: N45 22 25 W95 08 23. Hrs open: Box 838, Willmar, 56201. Phone: (320) 235-3535. Fax: (320) 235-9111. Web Site:www.kwlm.com Licensee: Lakeland Broadcasting Co. (acq 10-5-01). Format: Classic rock. ♦Doug Loy, gen mgr, gen sls mgr; Maryelin Macht, progmg dir; J.P. Cola, news dir.

Thief River Falls

KKAQ(AM)— Nov 2, 1979: 1460 khz; 2.5 kw-U. TL: N48 07 21 W96 08 24. Hrs open: 24 Box 40, 56701. Phone: (218) 681-4900. Fax: (218) 681-3717.E-mail: info@trradio.com Web Site:www.trfradio.com Licensee: Iowa City Broadcasting Co. Inc. Group owner: Tom Ingstad Broadcasting Group (acq 11-19-99; $620,000 with co-located FM). Population served: 30,000 Eugene T. Smith. Format: Country. News staff: one; News: 4 hrs wkly. Target aud: 25-54. Spec prog: Oldies 6 hrs wkly. ♦John Praska, gen mgr; Mark Stromstodt, progmg dir; Key Teeters, news dir; Stan Mueller, chief of engrg; Sheila Strange, traf mgr.

KKDQ(FM)— Nov 1, 1989: 99.3 mhz; 6.5 kw. 167 ft TL: N48 07 25 W96 08 31. Stereo. Hrs open: 24 Dups AM 100% Box 40 , 56701. Phone: (218) 681-4900. Fax: (218) 681-3717.E-mail: info@trradio.com Web Site:www.trfradio.com Licensee: Iowa City Broadcasting Co. Inc.

***KNTN(FM)**— Dec 13, 1991: 102.7 mhz; 100 kw. 538 ft TL: N47 58 38 W96 36 32. Stereo. Hrs open: 24 c/o KCCM, 901 S. 8th St., Moorhead, 56562. Phone: (218) 299-3666. Fax: (218) 299-3418. Web Site:www.mpr.org Licensee: Minnesota Public Radio Inc. Natl. Network: NPR, PRI, . Rgnl. Network: Minn. Pub. Minn. Pub. Radio Format: News. News staff: 2. Target aud: General. ♦William H. Kling, pres; Vern Goodin, gen mgr; Julia Beaton, dev dir.

***KQMN(FM)**— Nov 26, 1990: 91.5 mhz; 100 kw. 449 ft TL: N47 58 38 W96 36 32. Stereo. Hrs open: 24 901 S. 8th St., Concordia College, Moorhead, 56562. Phone: (218) 299-3666. Fax: (218) 299-3418. Web Site:www.mpr.org Licensee: Minnesota Public Radio. Natl. Network: NPR, PRI, . Format: Class music,cultural progmg. News staff: 2. ♦William H. Kling, pres; Vern Goodin, gen mgr.

KSNR(FM)—Licensed to Thief River Falls. See East Grand Forks

***KSRQ(FM)**— Nov 15, 1971: 90.1 mhz; 24 kw. 338 ft TL: N48 01 19 W96 22 12. Stereo. Hrs open: 24 1101 Hwy 1 E, 56701. Phone: (218) 681-0791. Phone: (800) 959-6282. Fax: (218) 681-0774.E-mail: travis.ryder@northlandcollege.edu Web Site:www.pioneer90.org Licensee: Northland Community & Technical College (acq 5-29-92). Population served: 140,000 Rgnl rep: Jim Lowe, Independent Community Media Wire Svc: AP Format: Alternative, AAA. News: 10 hrs wkly. Target aud: 18-54; professionals. Spec prog: Sp one hr, adult standards 5 hrs wkly. ♦Anne Temte, pres; Ben Kosharek, gen mgr, opns dir; Travis Ryder, gen mgr & dev dir; Stan Mueller, chief of engrg.

KTRF(AM)— Jan 30, 1947: 1230 khz; 1 kw-U. TL: N48 07 47 W96 11 11. Hrs open: 24 Box 40, 56701. Phone: (218) 681-4900. Fax: (218) 681-3717.E-mail: ktrf@mncable.net Web Site:www.trfradio.com Licensee: Iowa City Broadcasting Co. (acq 9-30-97; with KSNR(FM) Thief River Falls). Population served: 45,000 Natl. Network: CBS, . Rgnl. Network: MNN. MNN Haley, Bader & Potts. Format: MOR, news. News staff: 2; News: 35 hrs wkly. Target aud: General; 25 plus. Spec prog: Farm 12 hrs wkly. ♦Jon Praska, gen mgr; Mark Allen, progmg dir; Key Teters, news dir.

Tracy

KARL(FM)— July 19, 1994: 105.1 mhz; 45 kw. 390 ft TL: N44 19 32 W95 52 19. Stereo. Hrs open: 24 Box 61, KMHL Broadcasting Co., Marshall, 56258. Secondary address: 1414 E. College Dr., Marshall 56258. Phone: (507) 629-3355. Phone: (507) 532-2282. Fax: (507) 532-3739. Web Site:www.marshallradio.net Licensee: KMHL Broadcasting Co. Group owner: Linder Broadcasting Group (acq 12-17-92; $22,100; 1-11-93). Natl. Network: ABC, . Rgnl. Network: Linder Farm. Linder Farm Format: Hot country. News: 3 hrs wkly. Target aud: General. Spec prog: Farm 15 hrs wkly. ♦Donald Linder, pres; John Linder, VP; Brad Strootman, gen mgr; Justin Thordson, opns mgr.

Two Harbors

KZIO(FM)— September 1995: 104.3 mhz; 50 kw. 233 ft TL: N46 55 48 W91 53 01. Stereo. Hrs open: 501 Lake Ave. S., Suite 200A, Duluth, 55802. Phone: (218) 722-0921. Fax: (218) 723-1499. Licensee: Red Rock Radio Corp. (group owner; acq 1-10-00; grpsl). Format: Active rock. ♦Sean Skramstad, gen mgr; Jim Payne, gen sls mgr; Bill Jones, progmg dir; Jason Manning, news dir.

Verndale

KVKK(AM)— 2005: 1070 khz; 10 kw-D, 5 kw-N, DA-N. TL: N46 23 43 W94 57 54 (D), N46 23 45 W94 57 52 (N). Hrs open: Box 49, Park Rapids, 56470. Phone: (218) 732-3306. Fax: (218) 732-3307. Licensee: DJ Broadcasting Corp. Format: Country. ♦Edward P. DeLaHunt Sr., gen mgr.

Virginia

WUSZ(FM)— June 2, 1971: 99.9 mhz; 100 kw. Ant 567 ft TL: N47 22 52 W92 57 18. Stereo. Hrs open: 24 807 W. 37th St., Hibbing, 55746. Phone: (218) 262-4545. Fax: (218) 263-6112.E-mail: kristi@mwcradio.com Web Site:www.radiousa.com Licensee: Midwest Communications Inc. (group owner; acq 5-10-2004; grpsl). Population served: 330,000 Natl. Network: USA, . Rgnl. Network: MNN. MNN Format: Contemp country. News: one hr wkly. Target aud: 25-49; blue and white collar workers and families. ♦Kristi Garrity, gen mgr & sls VP.

Virginia-Hibbing

WIRR(FM)—Licensed to Virginia-Hibbing. See Duluth

Wabasha

KMFX(AM)— April 1976: 1190 khz; 1 kw-D. TL: N44 20 44 W91 58 28. Hrs open: 6 AM-sunset
Rebroadcasts KMFX-FM Lake City 90%.
1530 Greenview Dr. S.W., Rochester, 55902. Phone: (507) 288-3888. Fax: (507) 288-7815. Web Site:www.1025thefox.com Licensee: CC Licenses LLC. Group owner: Clear Channel Communications Inc. (acq 9-25-2000; grpsl). Rgnl. Network: MNN. MNN Format: Hot Country. Target aud: 18-54. ♦Bob Fox, gen mgr; Craig Erpestad, opns dir, progmg dir, news dir; Mary Anne Nons, gen sls mgr.

Wadena

KKWS(FM)— Sept 23, 1968: 105.9 mhz; 100 kw. Ant 564 ft TL: N46 36 00 W94 54 03. Stereo. Hrs open: 24 Box 551, 56482. Secondary address: 201 1/2 Jefferson St. S. 56482. Phone: (218) 631-1803. Fax: (218) 631-4557.E-mail: info@superstationk106.com Web Site:www.superstationk106.com Population served: 65,000 Natl. Network: ABC, . Rgnl. Network: Red River Farm Net. Format: Country, mainstream. News staff: one; News: 12 hrs wkly. Target aud: 25-54; adults. ♦Mike Danvers, progmg dir, mus dir & pub affrs dir.

KWAD(AM)— Apr 24, 1948: 920 khz; 1 kw-U, DA-N. TL: N46 22 15 W95 08 58. Hrs open: 24 Box 551, 56482-0551. Secondary address: 201 1/2 Jefferson St. S. 56482. Phone: (218) 631-1803. Fax: (218) 631-4557.E-mail: kwadkkws@arvig.net Web Site:www.superstation106.com Licensee: BL Broadcasting Inc. Group owner: Omni Broadcasting Co. (acq 4-1-2004; grpsl). Population served: 24,800 Natl. Network: ABC, . Rgnl. Network: MN News Net., MN Farm Net. Minn. News Net. Garvey, Schubert & Barer. Format: C&W. News staff: one; News: 20 hrs wkly. Target aud: 25-54; adults. Spec prog: Farm 10 hrs wkly. ♦Lou Buron, CEO, pres; Mary Campbell, CFO, VP; Rick Youngbauer, gen mgr, gen sls mgr, news dir; Sherry Linnes, prom dir; Kyle Gylsen, progmg dir, mus dir, pub affrs dir; Dave Cox, engrg dir, chief of engrg.

Waite Park

KLZZ(FM)— July 1989: 103.7 mhz; 3 kw. 328 ft TL: N45 32 35 W94 15 41. (CP: 25 kw. TL: N45 29 02 W94 08 12). Hrs open: 640 S.E. Lincoln Ave., St. Cloud, 56304. Phone: (320) 251-4422. Fax: (320) 251-1855. Web Site:www.1037theloon.com Format: Classic rock. ♦Don Monson, progmg dir & traf mgr.

KXSS(AM)— Jan 1, 1981: 1390 khz; 2.5 kw-D, 1 kw-N, DA-2. TL: N45 32 31 W94 15 41. Stereo. Hrs open: 640 S.E. Lincoln Ave., St. Cloud, 56304. Phone: (320) 251-4422. Fax: (320) 251-1855.E-mail: studio@kiss96.com Web Site:www.1390thefan.com Licensee: Regent Licensee of St. Cloud Inc. Group owner: Regent Communications Inc. (acq 5-8-2001; grpsl). Format: Sports. Target aud: 18-49. ♦William Stakelin, pres; David Engberg, gen mgr, gen sls mgr; Dick Nelson, progmg dir; Lee Voss, news dir; Mark Young, chief of engrg.

Walker

KAKK(AM)— July 11, 1970: 1570 khz; 9.5 kw-D, 250 w-N. TL: N47 04 44 W94 35 25. Hrs open: 24 Box 1022, 56484. Phone: (218) 732-3306. Fax: (218) 547-4001. Licensee: Edward De La Hunt (acq 12-26-00). Population served: 25,000 Rgnl. Network: MNN. MNN Format: Oldies. Target aud: General. ♦Brad Walhof, gen mgr, gen sls mgr; Marcus Mitchell, news dir.

KLLZ-FM— May 6, 1984: 99.1 mhz; 100 kw. Ant 505 ft TL: N47 12 52 W94 55 18. Stereo. Hrs open: 24 Box 1656, Bemidji, 56619-1656. Secondary address: 502 Beltrami Ave. N.W., Bemidji 56601. Phone: (218) 444-1500. Fax: (218) 751-8091.E-mail: phanson@pbbroadcasting.com Licensee: BG Broadcasting Inc. Group owner: Omni Broadcasting Co. (acq 10-24-2000). Population served: 75,000 Natl. Network: ABC, . Garvey, Schubert & Barer. Format: Classic rock. News staff: one; News: 12 hrs wkly. Target aud: 25-54; adults. ♦Lou Buron, CEO, pres, gen mgr; Mary Campbell, CFO, VP; Jack Hicks, opns mgr, progmg dir, mus dir; Peggy Hanson, gen sls mgr; Mardy Karger, news dir, pub affrs dir; Mark Anderson, chief of engrg.

KQKK(FM)— May 1, 1999: 101.9 mhz; 50 kw. 328 ft TL: N47 03 03 W94 28 12. Stereo. Hrs open: 5:30 AM-Midday Box 1022, Hwy. 34 W., 56484. Phone: (218) 732-3306. Fax: (218) 547-4001.E-mail: kqkkkakk@eot.com Web Site:www.dbcradionet.com/kqkk Licensee: CJ Broadcasting. Population served: 30,000 Natl. Network: CBS Radio, . Wire Svc: AP Format: Adult contemp. ♦Bradley J. Walhof, gen mgr; Marcu Mitchell, news dir.

Warroad

KKWQ(FM)— August 1989: 92.5 mhz; 100 kw. 472 ft TL: N48 49 41 W92 23 16. Stereo. Hrs open: 24 113A Lake St. Ctr., Box 69, 56763. Phone: (218) 386-3024. Fax: (218) 386-3090.E-mail: info@kkwqfm.com Web Site:www.kq92.com Licensee: Border Broadcasting LP (acq 1996). Natl. Network: ABC, Jones Radio Networks, . Minn. News Net. Wombie, Carlyle. Format: Country. Target aud: 25-54. ♦Mike Pederson, pres & gen mgr.

***KOLJ-FM**—Not on air, target date: unknown: 91.7 mhz; 45 kw. Ant 239 ft TL: N48 49 41 W95 23 16. Hrs open: Box 481, Park Rapids, 56470. Phone: (218) 237-4673. Licensee: We Have This Hope Christian Radio Inc. ♦Vern Erickson, pres.

Waseca

KOWZ(AM)— Dec 22, 1971: 1170 khz; 2.5 kw-D, 60 w-N, 1 kw-CH. TL: N44 02 45 W93 23 08 (D), N44 04 45 W93 30 24 (N). Hrs open: 24 255 Cedarale Dr. S.E., Owatonna, 55060. Phone: (507) 444-9224. Fax: (507) 444-9080. Licensee: Main Street Broadcasting Inc. Group owner: Linder Broadcasting Group (acq 12-26-01; with co-located FM). Population served: 65,000 Rgnl. Network: MNN, Midwest Radio. MNN Miller & Miller. Format: News, talk. News staff: 2; News: 12 hrs wkly. Target aud: 30-65; general, farm. ♦Jeff Seaton, gen mgr.

KRUE(FM)— June 1972: 92.1 mhz; 25 kw. 286 ft TL: N44 02 45 W93 23 08. Stereo. Hrs open: 24 Phone: (507) 444-9224. Fax: (507) 444-9080. Web Site:www.star92radio.com Natl. Network: ABC, . Format: Classic hits. News staff: one; News: 4 hrs wkly. Target aud: 25-54. ♦Jeff Seaton, gen mgr.

Watertown

KPNP(AM)— May 16, 1996: 1600 khz; 5 kw-U, DA-1. TL: N44 55 23 W93 46 56. Hrs open: 24 6500 Brooklyn Blvd., Suite 206, Brooklyn Center, 55429. Phone: (763) 585-1600.E-mail: info@kpnp1600.com Web Site:www.radiohmong.net Licensee: Self Retire Inc. (acq 9-1-2006; $670,000). Format: Ethnic. ♦Peter Phia Xiong, gen mgr.

Willmar

***KBHZ(FM)**— Feb 16, 1996: 91.9 mhz; 25 kw. 328 ft TL: N45 00 40 W94 53 56. Hrs open: Box 247, Osakis, 56360. Phone: (320) 859-3000. Fax: (320) 859-3010.E-mail: mail@praisefm.org Web Site:www.praisefm.org Licensee: Christian Heritage Broadcasting Inc. Format: Worship mus. ♦David McIver, gen mgr.

KDJS(AM)— Mar 2, 1981: 1590 khz; 1 kw-D, 89 w-N, DA-2. TL: N45 05 07 W95 00 19. Hrs open: 24 Box 380, 56201. Secondary address: 730 N.E. Hwy. 71 56201. Phone: (320) 231-1600. Fax: (320) 235-7010.E-mail: spots@k-musicradio.com Web Site:www.k-musicradio.com Licensee: Iowa City Broadcasting Inc. (acq 4-1-2000; with co-located FM). Population served: 100,000 Format: Oldies. News staff: one. Target aud: 25-54. Spec prog: Farm 5 hrs wkly. ♦Doug Hanson, gen mgr, gen sls mgr; Rob Ryan, progmg dir; Bev Ahlquist, news dir; Steve Youngberg, chief of engrg; Pam Tanner, traf mgr.

KDJS-FM— May 17, 1993: 95.3 mhz; 50 kw. 436 ft TL: N45 01 23 W95 15 57. Stereo. Hrs open: 24 Box 380, 56201. Secondary address: 730 N.E. Hwy. 71 56201. Phone: (320) 231-1600. Fax: (320) 235-7010.E-mail: spots@k-musicradio.com Web Site:www.k-musicradio.com Licensee: Iowa City Broadcasting Inc. Population served: 100,000 Rgnl rep: Hyett/Ramsland Format: Country. News staff: one. ♦Doug Hanson, gen mgr; Bob Ryan, progmg dir; Steve Youngberg, engrg mgr; Brenda Schmitz, traf mgr.

***KKLW(FM)**— Jan 29, 2004: 90.9 mhz; 400 w. Ant 423 ft TL: N45 11 52 W94 56 58. Stereo. Hrs open: 24 2351 Sunset Blvd., Suite 170-218, Rocklin, CA, 95765. Phone: (916) 251-1600. Fax: (916) 251-1650.E-mail: klove@klove.com Web Site:www.klove.com Licensee: Educational Media Foundation. Group owner: EMF Broadcasting. Natl. Network: K-Love, . Shaw Pittman. Format: Contemp Christian. News staff: 3. Target aud: 25-44; Judeo Christian, female. ♦Richard Jenkins, pres; Mike Novak, VP; Keith Whipple, dev dir; David Pierce, progmg mgr; Ed Lenane, news dir; Sam Wallington, engrg dir; Marya Morgan, news rptr.

KQIC(FM)— July 1, 1965: 102.5 mhz; 100 kw. 830 ft TL: N45 11 40 W95 05 01. Stereo. Hrs open: Prog sep from AM Box 838, 56201. Secondary address: 1340 N. 7th St. 56201. Phone: (320) 235-3535. Fax: (320) 235-9111. Web Site:www.1025fm.com Population served: 120,000 Format: Adult contemp. Target aud: 18-49. ♦MaryElin Macht, mus dir.

KWLM(AM)— 1940: 1340 khz; 1 kw-U. TL: N45 08 00 W95 02 35. Hrs open: 24 Box 838, 56201. Secondary address: 1340 N. 7th St. 56201. Phone: (320) 235-1340. Fax: (320) 235-9111. Web Site:www.kwlm.com Licensee: Steven W. Linder. (acq 4-5-91; $691,937 with co-located FM; 4-22-91). Population served: 50,000 Rgnl. Network: Linder Farm. Linder Farm Format: News/talk. News staff: 3; News: 30 hrs wkly. Target aud: General. Spec prog: Farm 8 hrs wkly. ♦J.P. Cola, gen mgr, news dir; Doug Loy, gen sls mgr; Pete Hoagland, chief of engrg; Mary Overman, traf mgr.

Wilton

WBKK(AM)—Not on air, target date: unknown: 820 khz; 15 kw-D, 750 w-N, DA-2. TL: N47 23 29 W95 04 40. Hrs open: Box 49, Park Rapids, 56470. Phone: (218) 732-3306. Licensee: Edward De La Hunt Sr. ♦Edward De La Hunt Sr., gen mgr.

Windom

KDOM(AM)— Dec 28, 1958: 1580 khz; 1 kw-D, 2 w-N, DA-2. TL: N43 51 41 W95 05 50. Hrs open: 24 Box 218, 56101. Phone: (507) 831-3908. Fax: (507) 831-3913.E-mail: kdomnew@windomnet.com Web Site:www.kdomradio.com Licensee: Windom Radio Inc. (acq 4-89; with co-located FM; 4-14-80). Population served: 165,500 Rgnl. Network: MNN. MNN Format: Country, news/talk, sports. News staff: one; News: 21 hrs wkly. Target aud: General; farm audience, housewives, business owners & laborers. ♦Dave Cory, gen mgr; Dirk Abraham, news dir.

KDOM-FM— Dec 8, 1976: 94.3 mhz; 5.7 kw. Ant 335 ft TL: N43 53 06 W95 10 53. Stereo. Hrs open: 6 AM-midnight Box 218, 56101. Phone: (507) 831-3908. Fax: (507) 831-3913.E-mail: kdomnew@windomnet.com Web Site:www.kdomradio.com Licensee: Windom Radio Inc. Format: Country, news/talk, sports.

***KJWR(FM)**— 2008: 90.9 mhz; 25 kw. Ant 328 ft TL: N44 00 22 W95 12 09. Hrs open: 24
Rebroadcasts KJIA(FM) Spirit Lake, IA 100%.
Box 125, 56101-0125. Phone: (712) 332-7184. Fax: (712) 332-2428.E-mail: kjwr@kjwrradio.com Web Site:www.kjwrradio.com Licensee: Minn-Iowa Christian Broadcasting Inc. Format: Christian. ♦Matt Dorfner, gen mgr.

KQRB(FM)— February 2003: 89.9 mhz; 250 w. Ant 171 ft TL: N43 51 15 W95 07 30. Hrs open: Box 3206, American Family Radio, Tupelo, MS, 38803. Phone: (662) 844-8888. Fax: (662) 842-6791. Web Site:www.afr.net Licensee: American Family Association. Group owner: American Family Radio. Natl. Network: USA, . Format: Christian. ♦Roy Willoff, gen mgr.

***KRLP(FM)**— 2008: 88.1 mhz; 40 w. Ant 387 ft TL: N43 53 03 W95 10 56. Hrs open:
Rebroadcasts KLVR(FM) Middletown, CA 100%.
5700 West Oaks Blvd., Rocklin, CA, 95765. Phone: (916) 251-1600. Fax: (916) 251-1650. Web Site:www.klove.com Licensee: Educational Media Foundation. (acq 3-23-2007; grpsl). Natl. Network: K-Love, . Format: Contemp Christian. ♦Mike Novak, pres.

Winona

KAGE(AM)— Feb 17, 1957: 1380 khz; 2.2 kw-D, 28 w-N. TL: N44 02 01 W91 36 18. Hrs open: Sunrise-sunset Box 767, 752 Bluffview Cir., 55987-0767. Phone: (507) 452-4000. Phone: (507) 452-2867. Fax: (507) 452-9494.E-mail: jpapenfuss@winonradio.com Web Site:www.winonaradio.com Licensee: KAGE Inc. Group owner: The Result Radio Group (acq 1-73). Population served: 90,420 Wiley, Rein & Fielding. Wire Svc: AP Format: C&W. News staff: one; News: 7 hrs wkly. Target aud: 35 plus; general. Spec prog: Farm, relg. ♦Pat Papenfuss, pres, opns mgr, progmg dir; Jerry Papenfuss, gen mgr; Les Guderian, sls dir, gen sls mgr; Darryl Smelser, news dir; Steve Schuh, chief of engrg; Paul Van Beck, sports cmtr.

KAGE-FM— Aug 14, 1971: 95.3 mhz; 11 kw. 495 ft TL: N44 02 31 W91 40 47. Stereo. Hrs open: 24 Prog sep from AM Box 767, 752 Bluffview Cir., 55987-0767. Phone: (507) 452-4000. Fax: (507) 452-9494. Web Site:www.winonaradio.com Licensee: KAGE Inc. Wire Svc: AP Format: Adult contemp. News staff: one; News: 14 hrs wkly. Target aud: 25-54. ♦Jerry Papenfuss, CEO; Aaron Taylor, progmg dir.

KHME(FM)— June 4, 1992: 101.1 mhz; 25 kw. 741 ft TL: N44 04 26 W91 34 38. Stereo. Hrs open: 24 Box 767, 55987. Secondary address: 752 Bluffview Cir. 55987. Phone: (507) 452-4000. Fax: (507) 452-9494.E-mail: softrock@winonaradio.com Web Site:www.winonaradio.com Licensee: KAGE Inc. Group owner: The Result Radio Group (acq 10-19-01; $1 million). Population served: 143,000 Wire Svc: AP Format: Soft rock. News staff: 2; News: 21 hrs wkly. Target aud: 25-54; women. ♦Jerry Papenfuss, gen mgr; Les Guderian, gen sls mgr; Pat Papenfuss, opns mgr & chief of engrg.

***KQAL(FM)**— Dec 12, 1975: 89.5 mhz; 1.8 kw. 628 ft TL: N44 02 52 W91 38 40. 2.5 kw. Stereo. Hrs open: 24 Box 5838, 55987-0838. Secondary address: 175 W. Mark St. 55987. Phone: (507) 453-2222. Fax: (507) 457-5226. Web Site:www.kqal.org Licensee: Winona State University. Population served: 75,000 Natl. Network: AP Radio, . Wire Svc: AP Format: Aor/Jazz. News: 5 hrs wkly. Target aud: General. Spec prog: Class 14 hrs, pub affrs 10 hrs wkly. ♦Mike Martin, gen mgr.

***KSMR(FM)**— Nov 1, 1978: 92.5 mhz; 4 w. -141 ft TL: N42 02 47 W91 41 43. Stereo. Hrs open: St. Mary's Univ., #29, 700 Terrace Heights, 55987-1399. Phone: (507) 457-1613. Fax: (507) 457-1439.E-mail: info@ksmr.com Web Site:www.smumn.edu Licensee: St. Mary's University Population served: 35,000 Format: AOR, hip hop, varied. Target aud: 18-24. ♦Dean Beckman, gen mgr.

KWNO(AM)— January 1938: 1230 khz; 1 kw-U. TL: N44 01 52 W91 38 31. Hrs open: 24 752 Bluffview Cir., 55987-0767. Phone: (507) 452-4154. Fax: (507) 452-9494.E-mail: jristow@winonaradio.com Web Site:www.winonaradio.com Licensee: KAGE Inc. Group owner: The Result Radio Group (acq 6-19-95; $1 million with KWNO-FM Rushford). Population served: 38,000 Rgnl. Network: MNN. MNN Wiley, Rein & Fielding. Wire Svc: AP Format: Oldies, news/talk, sports. News staff: one; News: 21 hrs wkly. Target aud: 35 plus; Sports fans. Spec prog: Polka 5 hrs wkly. ♦Jerry Papenfuss, CEO, gen mgr; Pat Papenfuss, chmn, exec VP, opns VP & opns mgr.

Winthrop

KHRS(FM)— July 1, 2008: 105.9 mhz; 23 kw. Ant 344 ft TL: N44 28 25 W94 28 15. Hrs open:
Simulcast with KXLP(FM) Eagle Lake 100%.
511 3rd St. N., New Ulm, 56073-1704. Phone: (507) 345-4537. Fax: (507) 345-5364. Licensee: Ketelsen Radio Inc. Format: Classic rock. ♦Jo Guck Bailey, VP & gen mgr.

Worthington

***KBOJ(FM)**— 2002: 88.1 mhz; 250 w. Ant 144 ft TL: N43 35 53 W95 37 30. Hrs open: Box 3206, American Family Radio, Tupelo, MS, 38803. Phone: (662) 844-8888. Fax: (662) 842-6791. Web Site:www.afr.net Licensee: American Family Association. Group owner: American Family Radio Natl. Network: USA, . Format: Christian. ♦Marvin Sanders, gen mgr.

KITN(FM)— November 1994: 93.5 mhz; 50 kw. Ant 466 ft TL: N43 31 31 W95 24 47. Hrs open: 24 28779 County Hwy. 35, 56187. Phone: (507) 376-6165. Fax: (507) 376-5071.E-mail: contactus@935thebreeze.com Web Site:www.935thebreeze.com Licensee: Three Eagles of Luverne Inc. Group owner: Three Eagles Communications (acq 12-23-99; grpsl). Population served: 121,300 Rgnl. Network: MNN. MNN Format: Adult contemp. ♦Gary Buchanan, CFO, prom dir; Tom Mulso, gen mgr & gen sls mgr; Jerry Mason, progmg dir, farm dir; Darrell Stitt, news dir; Bob Cook, chief of engrg.

***KRSW(FM)**— December 1973: 89.3 mhz; 100 kw. Ant 554 ft TL: N43 53 01 W95 55 44. Stereo. Hrs open: 480 Cedar St., St. Paul, 55101. Phone: (605) 335-6666. Phone: (651) 290-1259. Fax: (605) 335-1259. Licensee: Minnesota Public Radio Inc. Population served: 20,000 Natl. Network: PRI, NPR, . Format: Class. ♦William H. Kling, pres & gen mgr.

KWOA(AM)— Oct 11, 1947: 730 khz; 1 kw-U, 159 w-N. TL: N43 37 48 W95 40 32. Hrs open: 24 28779 County Hwy. 35, 56187. Phone: (507) 376-6165. Fax: (507) 376-5071.E-mail: contactus@935thebreeze.com Web Site:www.kwoa.com Licensee: Three Eagles of Luverne Inc. Group owner: Three Eagles Communications (acq 12-23-99; grpsl). Population served: 100,000 Natl. Network: CBS, Fox Sports, . Natl. Rep: Hyett/Ramsland,. Rgnl rep: Midwest Radio. Pepper & Corazzini. Format: News/talk. News staff: 2; News: 18 hrs wkly. Target aud: 35 plus. Spec prog: Farm. ♦Tom Mulso, gen mgr; Jerry Mason, opns mgr; Tony Winter, progmg dir; Darrell Stitt, news dir.

KWOA-FM— May 3, 1961: 95.1 mhz; 100 kw. Ant 660 ft TL: N43 37 48 W95 40 32. Stereo. Hrs open: 20 Prog sep from AM 28779 County Hwy. 35, 56187. Phone: (507) 376-6165. Fax: (507) 376-5071.E-mail: contactus@935thebreeze.com Web Site:951theeagle.com Population served: 103,500 Format: Classic hits. News staff: one; News: 10 hrs wkly. ♦Jay Kelly, progmg dir; Tony Winter, progmg dir & mus dir.

Worthington-Marshall

*KNSW(FM)— 1979: 91.7 mhz; 99 kw. Ant 797 ft TL: N43 53 01 W95 55 44. Hrs open: Minnesota Public Radio, Saint Paul, 55101-2202. Phone: (651) 290-1500. Fax: (651) 290-1224.E-mail: info@mpr.org Web Site:www.mpr.org Licensee: Minnesota Public Radio. Format: News/talk. ◆William H. Kling, gen mgr.

Mississippi

Aberdeen

WWZQ(AM)— February 1952: 1240 khz; 1 kw-U. TL: N33 48 32 W88 32 33. Hrs open: Box 458, Amory, 38821. Phone: (662) 256-9726. Fax: (662) 256-9725.E-mail: fm95@fm95radio.com Web Site:www.fm95radio.com Licensee: Stanford Communications Inc. (group owner; acq 12-2-99; $51,000). Population served: 11,600 Natl. Network: USA, . Format: talk, news, sports. Spec prog: Gospel 8 hrs wkly. ◆Ed Stanford, gen mgr.

Ackerman

WFCA(FM)— 1986: 107.9 mhz; 100 kw. 1,007 ft TL: N33 25 25 W89 24 13. Stereo. Hrs open: 24 40 Mecklin Ave., 155 Mecklin, French Camp, 39745. Phone: (662) 547-6414. Fax: (662) 547-9451.E-mail: sales@wfcafm108.com Web Site:www.wfcafm108.com Licensee: French Camp Radio Inc. Rgnl. Network: Miss. Net. Miss. News Net. Format: Southern gospel. Target aud: General. ◆Charles S. Carroll, stn mgr.

Amory

WAFM(FM)— 1974: 95.3 mhz; 6 kw. 272 ft TL: N33 58 33 W88 29 29. Stereo. Hrs open: 24 Prog sep from AM Box 458, 38821. Secondary address: 521 Hwy.278 W. 38821. Phone: (662) 256-9726. Fax: (662) 256-9725.E-mail: fm95@fm95radio.com Web Site: www.fm95radio.com Natl. Network: ABC, . Format: Oldies. Spec prog: Relg 2 hrs wkly. ◆Ken Wardlaw, mus dir, disc jockey; Clara Kennedy, traf mgr; Olen Booth, engrg VP & women's int ed.

WAMY(AM)— Oct 23, 1955: 1580 khz; 1 kw-D. TL: N33 58 33 W88 29 29. Hrs open: 6 AM-10PM Rebroadcasts WWZQ(AM) Aberdeen 75%. Box 458, 38821. Secondary address: 521 Hwy.278 W. 38821. Phone: (662) 256-9726. Fax: (662) 256-9725.E-mail: fm95radio@fm95radio.com Web Site:fm95radio.com Licensee: Stanford Communications Inc. (group owner; acq 9-21-92; $85,000 with co-located FM; 11-9-92). Population served: 45,000 Natl. Network: USA, . Rgnl. Network: Miss. Net. Format: Sports, talk/news. News staff: one. Target aud: Genral. Spec prog: Relg 6 hrs, Gospel 6 hrs wkly. ◆Ed Stanford, CEO, gen mgr, sls VP, news dir; Teresa Stanford, VP; Ken Wardlaw, opns mgr, progmg mgr, mus dir, disc jockey; Olen Booth, chief of engrg; Clara Kennedy, traf mgr, women's int ed.

Artesia

WSMS(FM)— 1985: 99.9 mhz; 6 kw. Ant 328 ft TL: N33 39 14 W88 37 15. Hrs open: 24 200 6th St. N., Suite 205, Columbus, 39701. Phone: (662) 327-1183. Fax: (662) 328-1122.E-mail: info@999thefoxrocks.com Web Site:www.999thefoxrocks.com Licensee: Cumulus Licensing Corp. Group owner: Cumulus Media Inc. (acq 9-99; grpsl). Population served: 150,000 Format: Album Rock. Target aud: 18-49. ◆Cole Evans, gen sls mgr; C. S. Jones, mktg mgr.

Baldwyn

WESE(FM)— Oct 1, 1980: 92.5 mhz; 12 kw. Ant 472 ft TL: N34 21 46 W88 35 28. Hrs open: 24 Box 3300, Tupelo, 38803. Secondary address: 5026 Cliff Gookin Blvd., Tupelo 38801. Phone: (662) 842-1067. Fax: (662) 842-0725. Web Site:www.925jamz.com Licensee: Clear Channel Broadcasting Licenses Inc. Group owner: Clear Channel Communications Inc. (acq 12-19-2000; grpsl). Population served: 174,600 Natl. Network: ABC, . Natl. Rep: Interep,. Format: Urban contemp. Target aud: 18-54. Spec prog: Gospel 6 hrs, Blues 6 hrs wkly. ◆Mark Maharrey, gen mgr; Rick Stevens, opns VP.

Batesville

WBLE(FM)— Aug 1, 1978: 100.5 mhz; 50 kw. Ant 492 ft TL: N34 18 13 W89 58 59. Stereo. Hrs open: Box 1528, 38606. Phone: (662) 563-4664. Fax: (662) 563-9002. Licensee: Batesville Broadcasting Co. Inc. Population served: 225,000 Format: Country. Target aud: 25 plus. ◆J. Boyd Ingram, gen mgr.

WJBI(AM)— June 19, 1953: 1290 khz; 730 w-D, 91 w-N. TL: N31 18 13 W89 58 59. Hrs open: Box 1528, 38606. Phone: (662) 563-1290. Fax: (662) 563-9002. Licensee: Batesville Broadcasting Co. Inc. (acq 4-1-78). Population served: 24,700 Format: Adult standards. Target aud: 30 plus. ◆J. Boyd Ingram, pres & gen mgr.

Bay Springs

WIZK(AM)— 1570 khz; 3.2 kw-D. TL: N31 57 56 W89 18 03. Hrs open: 12 Box 548, 150 Bay Ave., 39422. Phone: (601) 764-9888. Fax: (601) 764-9887.E-mail: mitchhughey@hughes.net Licensee: M. Jerome Hughey (Acq 3-15-02.). Population served: 200,000 Format: Traditional Country, Southern gospel, oldies. Target aud: 25-54; baby boomers & older consumers. ◆Mitchell Jerome Hughey, CEO, pres, gen mgr; Mitchell ODell Hughey, opns VP; Tom Diaz, stn mgr & chief of engrg.

WKZW(FM)— July 7, 1975: 94.3 mhz; 3 kw. 328 ft TL: N31 59 00 W89 13 50. (CP: 50 kw, ant 531 ft.). Stereo. Hrs open: Box 6408, Laurel, 39441. Secondary address: Box 16596, Hattiesburg 39404. Phone: (601) 649-0095. Fax: (601) 649-8199.E-mail: kz94@kz94.com Web Site:www.kz94.c0m Licensee: Blakeney Communications Inc. (group owner; acq 3-25-98; $553,000 for stock). Format: Hot adult contemp. Target aud: 18-60; average working people. ◆Larry Blakeney, pres; Randy Blakeney, gen mgr, engrg dir; Stephen St. James, progmg dir.

Bay St. Louis

WJZD(AM)— March 1974: 1190 khz; 5 kw-D. TL: N30 19 25 W89 21 03. Hrs open: 13 1190 Hollywood Blvd., 39520. Phone: (228) 467-1190. Phone: (228) 467-7009. Fax: (228) 467-5295.E-mail: ihatchatt@billsouth.nett Licensee: Hancock Broadcasting Corp. Population served: 15,000 Format: Blues/talk. News staff: one; News: 6 hrs wkly. Target aud: Men 25-54; sports enthusiasts. Spec prog: Gospel 13 hrs wkly. ◆Ira Hatchett, CEO; Benni Hatchett, pres; Barry Hatchett, exec VP; Delores Hatchett, VP.

WZKX(FM)—Licensed to Bay St. Louis. See Poplarville

Belzoni

WBYP(FM)— 1986: 107.1 mhz; 9.4 kw. Ant 531 ft TL: N33 03 04 W90 37 51. Stereo. Hrs open: 24 Box 130, Yazoo City, 39194. Secondary address: 611 Center Park Ln., Yazoo City Phone: (662) 746-7676. Fax: (662) 746-1525.E-mail: power107@power107.org Web Site:www.power107.org Licensee: Zoo-Bel Broadcasting LLC. Natl. Network: ABC, . Natl. Rep: Rgnl Reps,. Miss. News Net. Format: Country, southern gospel. News staff: 3; News: 18 hrs wkly. Target aud: 18-65; Adults. ◆Colon Johnston, gen mgr, sls dir, progmg dir & chief of engrg; Brenda Johnston, traf mgr.

WELZ(AM)— 1959: 1460 khz; 1 kw-D. TL: N33 10 24 W90 28 51. Hrs open: Box 299, 39038. Secondary address: 204 Church St. 39038. Phone: (662) 746-7676. Fax: (662) 746-1525.E-mail: colon@power107.org Web Site:www.power107.org Licensee: Zoo-Bel Broadcasting LLC. (acq 6-9-98; $200,000). Population served: 10,000 Rgnl. Network: Miss. Net. Miss. News Net. Format: Black Gospel & Blues. News staff: one; News: news prgmg 5 hrs/week. Target aud: 25-65; general. ◆Colon Johnston, gen mgr.

Benton

*WYAD(FM)—Not on air, target date: unknown: 88.3 mhz; 2.2 kw horiz, 7.8 kw vert. Ant 262 ft TL: N32 52 11 W90 06 04. Hrs open: Box 524, Yazoo City, 39071. Phone: (662) 571-2987. Licensee: Bountiful Blessings Broadcasting Inc. ◆Joseph C. Thomas, gen mgr.

Biloxi

*WMAH-FM— December 1983: 90.3 mhz; 100 kw. 1,410 ft TL: N30 45 14 W88 56 44. Stereo. Hrs open: 24 3825 Ridgewood Rd., Jackson, 39211. Phone: (601) 432-6565. Fax: (601) 432-6806. Web Site:www.mpbonline.org Licensee: Mississippi Authority for Educational Television. Natl. Network: PRI, NPR, . Schwartz, Woods & Miller. Wire Svc: AP Format: News and info, music. News staff: 7; News: 10 hrs wkly. Target aud: General. ◆Jay Woods, gen mgr; Jason Klein, opns mgr, progmg mgr; Ty Warren, dev mgr; Beverly Belding, rgnl sls mgr; Mari Irby, prom mgr; Karen Hearn, mus dir; Teresa Colier, news dir; Bob Buie, engrg dir; LaSharne Patton, traf mgr.

WMJY(FM)— July 11, 1966: 93.7 mhz; 100 kw. 1,012 ft TL: N30 29 09 W88 42 53. Stereo. Hrs open: 24 286 Debuys Rd., 39531. Phone: (228) 388-2323. Fax: (228) 388-2362.E-mail: reggiebates@clearchannel.com Web Site:www.magic937.com Licensee: Clear Channel Communications Inc. (acq 2-2-2004; grpsl). Population served: 350,000 Natl. Rep: Clear Channel,. Wire Svc: AP Format: Adult contemp. News staff: one; News: 5 hrs wkly. Target aud: 25-54. ◆Reggie Bates, gen mgr.

WTNI(AM)— 2003: 1640 khz; 10 kw-D, 1 kw-N. TL: N30 28 27 W88 51 23. Hrs open: 1909 E. Pass Rd., Suite D-11, Gulfport, 39507. Phone: (228) 388-2001. Fax: (228) 896-9736. Web Site:www.1640wtni.com Licensee: Monterey Licenses LLC. Group owner: Triad Broadcasting Co. LLC (acq 5-16-00). Natl. Network: ABC, . Wire Svc: AP Format: News/talk, info.

WXBD(AM)— May 1948: 1490 khz; 1 kw-U. TL: N30 23 38 W88 59 58. Hrs open: 24 1909 E. Pass Rd., Suite D-11, Gulfport, 39507. Phone: (228) 388-2001. Fax: (228) 896-9736. Fax: (228) 896-9114.E-mail: wxbd@sportsradiowxbd.com Web Site:www.sportsradiowxbd.com Licensee: Monterey Licenses LLC. Group owner: Triad Broadcasting Co. LLC (acq 6-30-99; grpsl). Shaw Pittman. Format: ESPN sports. ◆Jay Taylor, opns mgr.

Booneville

WBIP(AM)— Sept 1, 1950: 1400 khz; 1 kw-U. TL: N34 38 21 W88 34 33. Hrs open: 24 Box 356, 38829-0356. Secondary address: 1100 So. Second St. 38829-2572. Phone: (662) 728-0200. Fax: (662) 728-2572.E-mail: WBIPAM@YAHOO.COM Licensee: Community Broadcasting Services of Mississippi Inc. (acq 8-31-98; $1,000 for 50% of stock with co-located FM). Population served: 50,000 Miss. News Net. Format: Classic country. News: 7 hrs wkly. Target aud: 24-54. ◆Larry Melton, pres; Jerry Thornton, VP; Larry Hill, gen mgr; Marty Williams, stn mgr, opns mgr, gen sls mgr & progmg dir.

*WMAE-FM— December 1983: 89.5 mhz; 85 kw. Ant 660 ft TL: N34 40 00 W88 45 05. Stereo. Hrs open: 24 3825 Ridgewood Rd., Jackson, 39211. Phone: (601) 432-6565. Fax: (601) 432-6806. Web Site:www.mpbonline.org Licensee: Mississippi Authority for Educational Television. Natl. Network: PRI, NPR, . Schwartz, Woods & Miller. Wire Svc: AP Format: News and info, music. News staff: 7; News: 100 hrs wkly. Target aud: General. ◆Jay Woods, gen mgr; Jason Klein, opns mgr.

Brandon

WJFN(AM)— June 1967: 970 khz; 1 kw-D, DA. TL: N32 17 20 W89 59 50. Hrs open: 209 Commerce Dr., Suite D, 39042. Phone: (601) 825-2970. Fax: (601) 825-0339. Web Site:www.thefan970.com Licensee: Jackson Radio LLC (acq 6-21-2005). Population served: 500,000 Format: Sports. ◆Max Howell, gen mgr.

WRBJ-FM— Dec 1, 1974: 97.7 mhz; 6 kw. Ant 328 ft TL: N32 10 31 W89 56 10. Stereo. Hrs open: 24 745 N. State St., Jackson, 39202. Phone: (601) 974-5700. Fax: (601) 974-5711. Web Site:www.cw34jackson.com/997fm Licensee: Roberts Radio Broadcasting LLC Group owner: On Top Communications Inc. (acq 9-29-2006;. $1.95 million). Format: Urban contemp. Target aud: 18-34. ◆Keith Smith, gen mgr.

Brookhaven

WBKN(FM)— July 29, 1976: 92.1 mhz; 5.2 kw. 351 ft TL: N31 36 00 W90 27 09. Stereo. Hrs open: 24 225 S. Church, 39601. Secondary address: 911 Hwy. 550 39602. Phone: (601) 833-9210. Fax: (601) 833-6221.E-mail: brookhavenbroadcast@yahoo.com Licensee: Brookhaven Broadcasting Inc. (acq 2-27-2007; $1.4 million with WMJU(FM) Bude). Population served: 100,000 Rgnl. Network: Miss. Net. Miss. News Net. Fletcher, Heald & Hildreth. Format: Country. News: 5 hrs wkly. Target aud: 25-54. Spec prog: Gospel 3 hrs wkly. ◆C. Wayne Dowdy, pres; Ken Hollingsworth, gen mgr, traf mgr, local news ed, news rptr, edit dir, outdoor ed; Robbie Hamilton, sls dir, prom mgr; Gaye Laird, progmg dir; Jamey Lambert, min affrs dir, farm dir; Tyler Bridge, spec ev coord & mus critic.

WCHJ(AM)— Aug 15, 1955: 1470 khz; 1 kw-D, 66 w-N. TL: N31 33 46 W90 26 51. Hrs open: 24 hrs Box 177, 39602. Secondary address: 983 Sawmill Ln. 39601. Phone: (601) 823-9006. Fax: (601) 823-0503.E-mail: wchjgospel@netsouth.com Licensee: Tillman Broadcasting Network Inc. (acq 4-9-99; $150,000). Population served: 100,000 Natl. Network: USA, . Rgnl. Network: Miss. Net. Format: Black, gospel. News: one hr wkly. Target aud: 25-54. ◆Charles Tillman, CEO, gen mgr & opns mgr.

Brooksville

WAJV(FM)— August 1995: 98.9 mhz; 5.8 kw. 676 ft TL: N33 20 40 W88 32 47. Hrs open: 24 608 Yellow Jacket Dr., Starkville, 39759. Phone: (662) 338-5424. Fax: (662) 338-5436.E-mail: wmsuproduction@urbanradio.fm Web Site:www.joy989.com Licensee: Urban Radio Licenses LLC (acq 4-20-2001). Format: Urban contemp, gospel. News: 14 hrs wkly. Target aud: General. ♦Kevin Wagner, pres, gen mgr; James Alexander, opns mgr; Ron Davis, progmg dir.

Bruce

WCMR-FM— 1995: 94.5 mhz; 5.1 kw. Ant 358 ft TL: N34 04 15 W89 13 29. Hrs open:
Rebroadcasts KSRD(FM) Saint Joseph, MO 100%.
KSRD Radio, 1212 Faraon St., St. Joseph, MO, 64501. Phone: (816) 233-5773. Fax: (816) 233-5777.E-mail: info@ksrdradio.com Web Site:www.ksrdradio.com Licensee: Horizon Christian Fellowship. (acq 11-17-2006; $250,000). Format: Christian. ♦Michael MacIntosh, pres; Brian K.C. Jones, gen mgr.

Bude

***WMAU-FM**— December 1983: 88.9 mhz; 100 kw. 960 ft TL: N31 22 19 W90 45 05. Stereo. Hrs open: 24 3825 Ridgewood Rd., Jackson, 39211. Phone: (601) 432-6565. Fax: (601) 432-6806. Web Site:www.mpbonline.org Licensee: Mississippi Authority for Educational Television. Natl. Network: NPR, PRI, . Schwartz, Woods & Miller. Wire Svc: AP Format: News and info, music. News staff: 7; News: 100 hrs wkly. Target aud: General. ♦Jay Woods, gen mgr; Jason Klein, opns mgr.

WMJU(FM)— Aug 30, 1999: 104.3 mhz; 25 kw. Ant 328 ft TL: N31 33 33 W90 40 26. Stereo. Hrs open: 24 225 S. Church, Brookhaven, 39601. Secondary address: 911 Hwy. 550, Brookhaven 39601. Phone: (601) 833-9210. Fax: (601) 833-6221.E-mail: brookhavenbroadcast@yahoo.com Jonos Licensee: Brookhaven Broadcasting Inc. (group owner) (acq 2-27-2007; $1.4 million with WBKN(FM) Brookhaven). Population served: 100,000 Format: Adult contemp. News staff: one; News: 10 hrs wkly. Target aud: 25-49; adults who are middle income & above. ♦C. Wayne Dowdy, pres; Ken Hollingsworth, gen mgr; Robbie Hamilton, sls dir & prom dir; Gaye Laird, progmg dir.

Burnsville

***WOWL(FM)**— 2000: 91.9 mhz; 18 kw. Ant 548 ft TL: N34 55 47 W88 24 37. Stereo. Hrs open: 121 Front St., Iuka, 38852. Phone: (662) 423-9919. Fax: (662) 423-9333. Licensee: Southern Community Services Inc. Population served: 500,000 Natl. Rep: Rgnl Reps,. Garvey, Schubert & Barer. Format: Adult contemp. ♦Derrick Robinson, gen mgr.

Byhalia

***WKVF(FM)**— November 1994: 94.9 mhz; 6 kw. 403 ft TL: N34 55 30 W89 40 57. Stereo. Hrs open: 24 2351 Sunset Blvd., Suite 170-218, Rocklin, CA, 95765. Phone: (916) 251-1600. Fax: (916) 251-1650.E-mail: klove@klove.com Web Site:www.klove.com Licensee: Educational Media Foundation. Group owner: EMF Broadcasting (acq 2-1-00; $1.4 million). Population served: 750,000 Natl. Network: K-Love, . Shaw Pittman. Format: Contemp, Christian. News staff: 3. Target aud: 25-44; Judeo Christian, female. ♦Richard Jenkins, pres; Mike Novak, VP, progmg dir; Lloyd Parker, gen mgr; Ed Lenane, opns dir; Keith Whipple, dev dir; Eric Allen, natl sls mgr; David Pierce, progmg mgr; Jon Rivers, mus dir; Sam Wallington, engrg dir; Arthur Vassar, traf mgr; Karen Johnson, news rptr.

Canton

WMGO(AM)— Dec 9, 1954: 1370 khz; 1 kw-D, 280 w-N. TL: N32 37 36 W90 01 47. Hrs open: 24 107 W. Peace St., 39046. Phone: (601) 859-2373. Phone: (601) 859-2374. Fax: (601) 859-2664.E-mail: info@wmgo.com Licensee: WMGO Broadcasting Corp. Inc. (acq 5-3-93; $100,000; 5-24-93). Population served: 95,000 Rgnl. Network: Miss. Net. Miss. News Net. Format: Adult contemp, urban contemp, gospel. News staff: one; News: 12 hrs wkly. Target aud: 25-54; upscale & involved adults. ♦Jerry Lousteau, pres, gen mgr, progmg VP; John Woods, disc jockey.

WONG(AM)— April 1989: 1150 khz; 500 w-D. TL: N32 32 35 W90 03 36. Hrs open: 24 126 E. Sowell Rd., 39046. Phone: (601) 855-2035. Fax: (601) 855-2094.E-mail: wong1150am@cs.com Licensee: Marion R. Williams. (acq 7-26-99; $50,000). Natl. Network: American Urban, . Format: Gospel, blues. Target aud: 25 plus. ♦Marion Williams, pres; Kaple Hill, gen mgr.

Carthage

WCKK(FM)— April 1979: 98.3 mhz; 20 kw. Ant 328 ft TL: N32 43 29 W89 32 44. Hrs open: Box 1700, Kosciusko, 39090. Secondary address: 1 Golf Course Rd., Kosciusko 39039. Phone: (662) 289-1340. Fax: (662) 289-7907.E-mail: info@kicks98.com Web Site:www.kicks98.com Licensee: Johnny Boswell Radio LLC (acq 8-15-2003; $450,000). Natl. Network: USA, . Wire Svc: NOAA Weather Format: C&W. ♦Eric Matthews, opns mgr.

Centreville

WKJN(FM)— Nov 21, 1977: 104.9 mhz; 3 kw. Ant 298 ft TL: N31 06 07 W91 02 27. Hrs open: Box 1649, McComb, 39649. Phone: (601) 684-4116. Fax: (601) 684-4654. Licensee: Southwest Broadcasting. Format: Classic country. ♦Charles Dowdy, gen mgr.

***WPAE(FM)**— 1997: 89.7 mhz; 70 kw. 298 ft TL: N31 05 56 W91 02 27. Hrs open: 24
Rebroadcasts KPAE(FM) Erwinville, LA 100%.
Box 1390, 39631. Secondary address: 122 E. Main St. 39631. Phone: (601) 645-6515. Fax: (601) 645-9122.E-mail: wpaefm@telepak.net Web Site:www.soundradio.org Licensee: Port Allen Educational Broadcasting Foundation. Population served: 1,000,000 Natl. Network: Moody, . Format: Relg, educ. Spec prog: Children 5 hrs, Gospel 15 hrs wkly. ♦Willie F. Kennedy, gen mgr.

Charleston

WTGY(FM)— Apr 1, 1986: 95.7 mhz; 6 kw. Ant 328 ft TL: N33 53 28 W90 03 09. Stereo. Hrs open: 18 Box 262550, Baton Rouge, LA, 70826. Phone: (225) 768-8300. Phone: (225) 768-3688. Fax: (225) 768-3729.E-mail: kawikfish@yahoo.com Web Site:jsm.org Licensee: Family Worship Center Church Inc. (group owner; acq 7-15-02; $300,000). Format: Relg. ♦David Whitelaw, COO; Jimmy Swaggart, pres; John Santiago, gen mgr & progmg dir.

Clarksdale

WAID(FM)— July 1, 1978: 106.5 mhz; 30 kw. 296 ft TL: N34 09 22 W90 37 52. Stereo. Hrs open: 24 Box 668, 38614. Phone: (662) 627-2281. Fax: (662) 624-2900. Web Site:www.missradio.com Licensee: Radio Cleveland Inc. (group owner; acq 8-2-83; $185,000; 8-1-83). Population served: 100,000 Natl. Network: USA, . Format: Urban contemp. News staff: one; News: 2 hrs wkly. Target aud: General. ♦Clint Webster, gen mgr; Greg Shurden, gen sls mgr; Jim Thomas, progmg dir; Houston McDavid, chief of engrg.

WKDJ-FM— Nov 1, 1988: 96.5 mhz; 6 kw. 180 ft TL: N34 09 22 W90 37 52. Stereo. Hrs open: Box 668, 38614. Phone: (662) 627-2281. Fax: (662) 624-2900. Web Site:www.missradio.com Licensee: Clint Webster. (acq 12-3-93). Format: Country. Target aud: 25-55. ♦Clint Webster, gen mgr; Greg Shurden, stn mgr; Jim Thomas, progmg dir.

WROX(AM)— 1944: 1450 khz; 1 kw-U. TL: N34 12 40 W90 34 42. Hrs open: 24 330 Sunflower, 38614. Phone: (662) 627-1450. Fax: (662) 621-1176. Licensee: Delta Radio LLC. Group owner: Contemporary Communications (acq 12-18-98; $54,000 with WQMA(AM) Marks). Population served: 65,000 Rgnl. Network: Mississippi Network Wood, Maines & Brown. Format: Rhythm and Blues. News staff: one; News: 3 hrs wkly. Target aud: General. ♦George Hinds, gen mgr; Bill Perry Sr., stn mgr.

Cleveland

WCLD(AM)— 1949: 1490 khz; 1 kw-U. TL: N33 44 01 W90 42 50. Hrs open: 24 Hwy. 61 S., 38732. Secondary address: Drawer 780 Phone: (662) 843-4091. Fax: (662) 843-9805.E-mail: wcld@tecinfo.com Web Site:www.missradio.com Licensee: Radio Cleveland Inc. (group owner; acq 1957). Population served: 175,000 Format: Black gospel. Target aud: 18 plus. ♦Clint L. Webster, gen mgr; Jim Thomas, opns mgr, progmg dir, news dir; Kevin Cox, gen sls mgr; Houston McDavitt, chief of engrg; Vicky Lowry, traf mgr.

WCLD-FM— 1972: 103.9 mhz; 24.5 kw. 300 ft TL: N33 44 01 W90 42 50. Stereo. Hrs open: 24 Prog sep from AM Hwy. 61 S., 38732. Secondary address: Drawer 780 38732. Phone: (662) 843-4091. Fax: (662) 843-9805. Web Site:www.missradio.com Population served: 200,000 Fletcher, Heald & Hildreth. Format: Urban contemp. Target aud: 18 plus. ♦Vicky Lowry, traf mgr.

WDFX(FM)— 1993: 98.3 mhz; 25 kw. 328 ft TL: N33 52 44 W90 43 04. Hrs open: Box 3206, American Family Radio, Tupelo, 38803. Phone: (662) 844-8888. Fax: (662) 842-6791. Web Site:www.afr.net Licensee: American Family Association Inc. (acq 5-3-93; $6,150; 5-24-93). Natl. Network: USA, . Format: Christian. ♦Don Wildman, gen mgr.

WDSK(AM)— June 25, 1958: 1410 khz; 920 w-D, 23 w-N. TL: N33 45 56 W90 42 41. Stereo. Hrs open: 24 Box 1438, 309 N. Chrisman Ave., 38732. Phone: (662) 846-0929. Fax: (662) 843-1410. Licensee: M.R.S. Ventures Inc. Population served: 130,000 Natl. Network: CBS Radio, . Rgnl. Network: Miss. Net. Miss. News Net. Format: News/talk. Target aud: 35 plus; male & female.

WDTL-FM— May 22, 1970: 92.9 mhz; 50 kw. 492 ft TL: N33 44 17 W90 39 29. Stereo. Hrs open: 24 Box 1438, 309 N. Chrisman Ave., 38732. Phone: (662) 271-9111. Fax: (662) 843-1410. Licensee: M.R.S. Ventures Inc. (group owner; acq 11-1-2003; grpsl). Population served: 130,000 Rgnl. Network: Miss. Net. Miss. News Net. Wood, Maines & Brown. Format: Sports. News staff: one; News: 3 hrs wkly. Target aud: 25-54. ♦Wash Sellers Jr., opns VP, opns dir, progmg dir; Wendy Hodges, gen mgr, gen mgr, gen sls mgr, engrg dir & traf mgr.

WMJW(FM)— 1993: 107.5 mhz; 25 kw. 328 ft TL: N33 43 36 W90 43 53. Stereo. Hrs open: 24 Box 780, 38732. Phone: (662) 843-4091. Fax: (662) 843-9805. Web Site:www.missradio.com Licensee: Radio Cleveland Inc. (group owner; acq 7-18-95). Fletcher, Heald & Hildreth. Format: Country. News: 8 hrs wkly. Target aud: 25-54; adults. ♦Clint L. Webster, pres, gen mgr; Kevin W. Cox, VP, sls dir, gen sls mgr, prom dir; Jim Thomas, opns mgr; Jim Gregory, pub affrs dir; Vickie Lowery, traf mgr.

WRKG(FM)—(Drew, June 1, 1971: 95.3 mhz; 2.65 kw. Ant 492 ft TL: N33 44 17 W90 39 29. Stereo. Hrs open: 24 Box 1438, 309 N. Chrisman Ave., 38732. Phone: (662) 721-9111. Fax: (662) 843-1410. Licensee: M.R.S. Ventures Inc. (group owner; (acq 11-1-2003; grpsl). Population served: 85,000 Natl. Network: Jones Radio Networks, . Wood, Maines & Brown. Format: Classic rock. News staff: one; News: 2 hrs wkly. Target aud: General. ♦Andy Hodges, gen mgr.

WZYQ(FM)—(Mound Bayou, Oct 10, 1997: 101.9 mhz; 6 kw. Ant 328 ft TL: N33 52 49 W90 42 24. Stereo. Hrs open: 24 Box 1438, 309 N. Chrisman Ave., 38732. Phone: (662) 846-0929. Fax: (662) 843-1410.E-mail: mrsviradio@aol.com Licensee: M.R.S. Ventures Inc. (group owner; (acq 11-1-2003; grpsl). Population served: 85,000 Natl. Network: Jones Radio Networks, . Wood, Maines & Brown. Format: Pop contemporary hits. Target aud: General. ♦Wendy Hodges, gen mgr.

Clinton

WHJT(FM)— 1974: 93.5 mhz; 6 kw. 328 ft TL: N32 20 15 W90 19 47. Stereo. Hrs open: 24 Box 4048, 39058. Secondary address: 100 S. Jefferson 39058. Phone: (601) 925-3458. Fax: (601) 925-3337.E-mail: Sales@Star93FM.com Web Site:www.star93fm.com Licensee: Mississippi College. Population served: 400,000 Smithwick & Belendiuk. Wire Svc: NOAA Weather Format: CHR Christian. News: 7 hrs wkly. Target aud: 18-54; upper & middle class Christian listeners. Spec prog: Relg 6 hrs wkly. ♦Billy Lytal, pres; Russ Robinson, gen mgr & stn mgr.

WTWZ(AM)— Oct 10, 1982: 1120 khz; 10.0 kw-D (2.5 kw-CH). TL: N32 21 03 W90 20 22. Hrs open: Sunrise-sunset 4611 Terry Rd., Suite C, Jackson, 39212-5646. Phone: (601) 346-0074. Fax: (601) 346-0896.E-mail: am1120@wtwzradio.com Licensee: Terry E. Wood. Population served: 500,000 Natl. Network: USA, . Miss. News Net. Format: Bluegrass. News: 7 hrs wkly. Target aud: 18-50; 50% men & 50% women. ♦Terry Wood, pres & gen mgr.

Coldwater

WVIM-FM— 1976: 95.3 mhz; 3.6 kw. Ant 423 ft TL: N34 46 45 W89 58 01. Stereo. Hrs open: 24 230 Goodman Rd., Bldg. 2, Suite 202, Southaven, 38671. Phone: (662) 349-9953. Fax: (662) 349-9255.E-mail: ppesce@comcast.net Web Site:www.953rebelcountry.com Licensee: Memphis First Ventures L.P. (group owner; (acq 12-26-2007). Population served: 80,300 Format: Country. Target aud: 25-54. ♦Chip Miller, pres, progmg dir; Paul Pesce, pres & stn mgr.

Collins

***WLVZ(FM)**— Aug 15, 1978: 107.1 mhz; 2.25 kw. Ant 541 ft TL: N31 31 49 W89 30 29. Stereo. Hrs open: 24
Rebroadcasts KLVR(FM) Middletown, CA 100%.

2351 Sunset Blvd., Suite 170-218, Rocklin, CA, 95765. Phone: (916) 251-1600. Fax: (916) 251-1650. Web Site:www.klove.com Licensee: Educational Media Foundation. (acq 7-15-2005; $700,000). Population served: 200,000 Natl. Network: K-Love, . Format: Contemp Christian. ◆Mike Novak, pres.

Columbia

WCJU(AM)— Dec 20, 1946: 1450 khz; 1 kw-U. TL: N31 14 14 W89 50 24. Stereo. Hrs open: 24 Box 472, 39429. Phone: (601) 736-2616. Fax: (601) 736-2617.E-mail: wcju@wcjufm.com Licensee: WCJU Inc. (acq 6-69). Population served: 45,000 Natl. Network: ABC, . Natl. Rep: Keystone (unwired net),. Format: News/talk, sports. News staff: 2; News: 30 hrs wkly. Target aud: 18-54. Spec prog: Gospel 4 hrs wkly. ◆Steve Mercier, opns dir, opns mgr; T. McDaniel, pres & gen sls mgr; Pam Ball, rgnl sls mgr; John Pittman Jr., mus dir.

WFFF(AM)— Apr 14, 1961: 1360 khz; 1 kw-D, 159 w-N. TL: N31 15 44 W89 50 41. Hrs open: 24 Box 550, 11 Gardner Shopping Ctr., 39429. Phone: (601) 736-1360. Fax: (601) 736-1361.E-mail: wfffradio@zzip.cc Licensee: Haddox Enterprises Inc. (acq 10-9-91; $250,000 with co-located FM; 11-4-91). Population served: 50,000 Natl. Network: ABC, . Rgnl. Network: Miss. Net. Miss. News Net. Format: C&W, gospel. News staff: 4; News: 8 hrs wkly. Target aud: General. ◆Ronnie Geiger, pres, gen mgr, gen sls mgr, gen sls mgr, progmg dir, news dir, chief of engrg, local news ed, sports cmtr; Terri Geiger, VP & traf mgr.

WFFF-FM— October 1966: 96.7 mhz; 3 kw. 400 ft TL: N31 15 44 W89 50 41. Stereo. Hrs open: 24 Dups AM 10% Box 550, 11 Gardner Shopping Ctr., 39429. Phone:(601) 736-1360. Fax: (601) 736-1361.E-mail: wfffradio@zzip.cc Population served: 60,000 Rgnl. Network: Miss. Net. Miss. News Net. Format: Adult contemp. News staff: 4; News: 8 hrs wkly. Target aud: 25-54. ◆Ronnie Geiger, opns VP, engrg dir, local news ed, sports cmtr; Terri Geiger, traf mgr.

*WPRG(FM)—Not on air, target date: unknown: 89.5 mhz; 250 w. 177 ft TL: N31 16 50 W89 51 12. Hrs open: American Family Radio, Box 3206, Tupelo, 38803. Phone: (662) 844-8888. Fax: (662) 842-6791. Web Site:www.afr.net Licensee: American Family Association. Group owner: American Family Radio (acq 10-1-01). Natl. Network: USA, . Format: Christian. ◆Marvin Sanders, gen mgr.

Columbus

*WCSO(FM)—** 2006: 90.5 mhz; 10 kw vert. Ant 530 ft TL: N33 20 44 W88 14 06. Hrs open:
Rebroadcasts WAFR(FM) Tupelo 100%.
Drawer 3206, Tupelo, 38803. Phone: (662) 844-8888. Fax: (662) 842-6791. Web Site:www.afr.net Licensee: American Family Association. Format: Christian. ◆Marvin Sanders, gen mgr.

WJWF(AM)— Nov 1, 1969: 1400 khz; 1 kw-U. TL: N33 29 30 W88 24 14. Hrs open: 200 6th St. N., Suite 205, 39701. Phone: (662) 327-1183. Fax: (662) 328-1122. Licensee: Cumulus Licensing Corp. Group owner: Cumulus Media Inc. (acq 2-14-2002; with co-located FM). Natl. Network: ESPN Radio, . Format: Sports. ◆C.J. Jones, VP, mktg mgr & progmg dir.

WKOR-FM— Dec 16, 1992: 94.9 mhz; 29.5 kw. 492 ft TL: N33 28 38 W88 16 25. Stereo. Hrs open: 24 200 6th St. N., Suite 205, 39701. Phone: (662) 327-1183. Fax: (662) 328-1122.E-mail: info@k949.net Web Site:www.k949.net Licensee: Cumulus Licensing Corp. Group owner: Cumulus Media Inc. (acq 2-14-02; grpsl). Natl. Network: ABC, . Format: Hot country. Target aud: 18-54. ◆Cole Evans, gen sls mgr; C. J. Jones, mktg mgr.

*WMUW(FM)—** Feb 22, 2008: 88.5 mhz; 980 w. Ant 89 ft TL: N33 29 23 W88 25 18. Stereo. Hrs open: 6 AM-midnight Mississippi University for Women, 1100 College St. - MUW - 1619, 39701-5800. Phone: (662) 329-7255. Fax: (662) 329-7250.E-mail: wmuw@muw.edu Web Site:www.muw.edu/wmuw Licensee: Mississippi University for Women. Population served: 30,000 Format: Eclectic (college radio). News: 5 hrs wkly. College students and those that like music. ◆Eric Harlan, gen mgr; Sarah Reeder, opns mgr; Dale Jones, mus dir.

WNMQ(FM)— Nov 1, 1969: 103.1 mhz; 22 kw. Ant 754 ft TL: N33 29 30 W88 24 14. Stereo. Hrs open: 200 6th St. N., Court Square Towers, 39701. Phone: (662) 327-1183.E-mail: davis.hawkins@cumulus.com Licensee: Cumulus Licensing LLC. Population served: 130,000 Format: Hot adult contemp.

WTWG(AM)— 1950: 1050 khz; 1 kw-D, 48 w-N, DA. TL: N33 30 36 W88 24 46. Hrs open: Box 1078, 39703. Secondary address: 1910 14th Ave. N. 39703. Phone: (662) 328-1050. Fax: (662) 328-1054.E-mail: wtwg1050@yahoo.com Licensee: T & W Communications Inc. (acq

1997; $110,000 with co-located FM;9-13-93). Population served: 25,795 Format: Gospel. Target aud: 25-54; general. ◆Edna Turner, gen mgr, gen sls mgr, traf mgr; J. Michael Bailey, progmg dir; Lloyd Mitchell, chief of engrg.

WWKZ(FM)— Dec 15, 1978: 103.9 mhz; 50 kw. Ant 492 ft TL: N33 24 27 W88 08 27. (CP: COL Okolona. Ant 394 ft. TL: N34 12 18 W88 41 49). Stereo. Hrs open: 24 Box 3300, Tupelo, 38803. Phone: (662) 842-1067. Fax: (662) 842-0725. Licensee: Citicasters Licenses L.P. (acq 7-13-2005; $2.2 million). Population served: 182,000 Natl. Network: American Urban, . Format: Urban contemp. News: 6 hrs wkly. ◆Mark Maharrey, gen mgr.

Columbus AFB

WACR-FM— June 1, 1975: 105.3 mhz; 50 kw. Ant 352 ft TL: N33 40 09 W88 40 08. Stereo. Hrs open: 608 Yellow Jacket Dr., Starkville, 39759-3736. Phone: (662) 338-5424. Fax: (662) 338-5436.E-mail: wmsuproduction@urbanradio.fm Web Site:www.wacrfm.com Licensee: Urban Radio Licenses LLC. (acq 7-13-2005; $1.1 million). Population served: 485,700 Format: Blues-based urban adult contemp. ◆Pamela Hancock, gen mgr.

Como

WRBO(FM)— Sept 28, 1966: 103.5 mhz; 100 kw. Ant 587 ft TL: N34 51 44 W89 52 42. Stereo. Hrs open: 24 5629 Murray Rd., Memphis, TN, 38119. Phone: (901) 682-1106. Web Site:www.soulclassics.com Licensee: Citadel Broadcasting Co. Group owner: Citadel Broadcasting Corp. (acq 3-23-2004; grpsl). Population served: 463,800 Natl. Network: ABC, Westwood One, . Natl. Rep: Katz Radio,. Format: Soul classics. Target aud: 25-54. ◆Sherri Sawyer, gen mgr; Amy Goodman, gen sls mgr; Henry Nelson, progmg dir; Marvin Emilien, prom.

Corinth

WADI(FM)— Oct 26, 1968: 95.3 mhz; 2.6 kw. 472 ft TL: N34 55 47 W88 24 37. Stereo. Hrs open: 121 Front St., Iuka, 38852. Phone: (662) 423-9533. Fax: (662) 423-9333.E-mail: biddleandsons @crossroadsisp.com Licensee: Power Valley Communications Inc. Population served: 30,000 Format: Country. ◆Frederick A. Biddle, pres, CFO; Rick Biddle, gen mgr; Brian Biddle, stn mgr; Mike Cannon, opns dir.

WKCU(AM)— Oct 24, 1965: 1350 khz; 900 w-D, 44 w-N. TL: N34 54 29 W88 30 06. Hrs open: 24 1608 S. Johns St., 38834. Phone: (662) 286-8451. Fax: (662) 286-8452.E-mail: wxrz@earthlink.net Licensee: TeleSouth Communications Inc. (group owner; acq 12-20-02; $350,000 with co-located FM). Population served: 100,000 Rgnl. Network: Miss. Net. Miss. News Net. Wire Svc: NWS (National Weather Service) Format: Today's Christian music. News: 12 hrs wkly. Target aud: 25-54; female. Spec prog: Black 2 hrs wkly. ◆James H. Anderson, gen mgr.

WTKN(AM)— Mar 1, 1946: Stn currently dark. 1230 khz; 1 kw-U. TL: N34 52 07 W88 31 17. Hrs open: 121 Front St., Iuka, 38852. Phone: (662) 423-9533. Fax: (662) 423-9333. Licensee: Perihelion Global Inc. (acq 12-14-2004; $45,000). Population served: 30,000 ◆Rick Biddle, gen mgr.

WXRZ(FM)— January 1967: 94.3 mhz; 25 kw. 328 ft TL: N34 48 36 W88 34 45. Stereo. Hrs open: 24 Prog sep from AM 1608 S. Johns St., 38834. Phone: (662) 286-8451. Fax: (662) 286-8452.E-mail: wxrz@earthlink.net Licensee: TeleSouth Communications Inc. Population served: 200,000 Wire Svc: NWS (National Weather Service) Format: Super talk Mississippi. ◆James H. Anderson, stn mgr.

Crenshaw

WHKL(FM)— Mar 1, 1997: 106.9 mhz; 6 kw. 328 ft TL: N34 26 51 W90 06 25. Hrs open: Box 1528, Batesville, 38606. Phone: (662) 563-4664. Fax: (662) 563-9008.E-mail: country101radio@yahoo.com Licensee: Batesville Broadcasting Co. Inc. Format: Oldies. ◆John Ingram, gen mgr & stn mgr.

De Kalb

WJXM(FM)— 1999: 105.7 mhz; 50 kw. Ant 384 ft TL: N32 38 37 W88 40 29. Hrs open: Box 5797, Meridian, 39302. Phone: (601) 693-2661. Fax: (601) 483-0826.E-mail: wjxm@wokk.com Licensee: Mississippi Broadcasters L.L.C. (group owner). Format: Urban contemp. ◆Clay Holladay, gen mgr; Scott Stevens, opns mgr.

Decatur

WZKR(FM)— 2001: 103.3 mhz; 4.8 kw. Ant 590 ft TL: N32 21 46 W88 54 48. Hrs open: 24 1106 18th Ave., Meridian, 39301. Phone: (601) 693-1103. Fax: (601) 693-9949.E-mail: B103@comcast.net Licensee: Morning Star Media LLC (acq 9-28-2007; $850,000). Population served: 300,000 Natl. Rep: Salem,. Fletcher, Heald & Hildreth. Format: Country. Target aud: 25-54. ◆Ron Harper, gen mgr.

D'Iberville

WCPR-FM— December 1992: 97.9 mhz; 50 kw. 466 ft TL: N30 36 59 W89 08 03. Hrs open: 24 1909 E. Pass Rd., Suite D-11, Gulfport, 39507. Phone: (228) 388-2001. Phone: (228) 388-2771 (request line). Fax: (228) 896-9736.E-mail: wcpr@wcprfm.com Web Site:www.wcprfm.com Licensee: Monterey Licenses LLC. Group owner: Triad Broadcasting Co. LLC (acq 7-14-99; grpsl). Natl. Network: ABC, . Format: Active Rock/alternative. ◆Buddy Burch, VP; Jay Taylor, opns dir.

Drew

WRKG(FM)—Licensed to Drew. See Cleveland

Duck Hill

*WAUM(FM)—** 1998: 91.9 mhz; 3 kw. Ant 466 ft TL: N33 38 34 W89 29 59. Hrs open: Box 3206, American Family Radio, Tupelo, 38803. Phone: (662) 844-8888. Fax: (662) 842-6791. Web Site:www.afr.net Licensee: American Family Association. Group owner: American Family Radio Natl. Network: USA, . Format: Classic gospel. ◆Marvin Sanders, gen mgr.

Durant

WLIN-FM— 1997: 101.1 mhz; 4.8 kw. 371 ft TL: N33 03 51 W89 36 12. Hrs open: Box1700, Kosciusko, 39090. Phone: (662) 289-1050. Fax: (662) 289-7907.E-mail: breezy@boswellmedia.net Web Site:www.breezynews.com Licensee: Boswell Radio LLC. Format: Adult contemp. ◆Johnny Boswell, gen mgr; Ann Steen, stn mgr; Jerry Price, gen sls mgr; Eric Matthews, progmg dir.

Ellisville

WJKX(FM)— Oct 5, 1973: 102.5 mhz; 50 kw. 492 ft TL: N31 46 05 W89 10 12. Stereo. Hrs open: 24 6555 Highway 98 W., Suite 8, Hattiesburg, 39402. Phone: (601) 296-9800. Fax: (601) 296-9838.E-mail: mailto:contact@102jkx.com Web Site:www.102jkx.com Licensee: CC Licenses LLC. Group owner: Clear Channel Communications Inc. (acq 12-19-2000; grpsl). Population served: 250,000 Format: Urban. ◆Mike Comfort, gen mgr.

Eupora

WLZA(FM)—Licensed to Eupora. See Starkville

Fayette

WTYJ(FM)— Oct 17, 1983: 97.7 mhz; 6 kw. 500 ft TL: N31 40 32 W91 06 18. (CP: 6 kw, 328 ft.). Stereo. Hrs open: 20 E. Franklin St., Natchez, 39120. Phone: (601) 442-2522. Fax: (601) 446-9918.E-mail: wmiswtyj@bellsouth.net Licensee: Natchez Broadcasting Inc. (acq 4-86; $200,000; 4-14-86). Population served: 100,000 Natl. Network: American Urban, . Miss. News Net. Format: Gospel, blues, black. Target aud: Black. ◆James B. Nutter, pres; Diana E. Nutter, VP; Calvin Butler, gen mgr, opns mgr; LlJuna Grennell Weir, stn mgr.

Flora

WFMN(FM)— July 7, 1997: 97.3 mhz; 19.5 kw. 367 ft TL: N32 27 21 W90 15 32. Hrs open: 24 TeleSouth Communications Inc., 6311 Ridgewood Rd., Jackson, 39211. Phone: (601) 957-1700. Fax: (601) 956-5228.E-mail: apeterson@telesouth.com Web Site:www.supertalkms.com Licensee: TeleSouth Communications Inc. (group owner; acq 9-8-97; $700,000). Population served: 500,000 Natl. Network: ABC, . Format: Talk. ◆Steve Davenport, pres; Paul Gallo, gen mgr; John Winfield, opns mgr.

WYAB(FM)— August 1997: 103.9 mhz; 6 kw. Ant 289 ft TL: N32 31 24 W90 15 52. Hrs open: 24 740 Hwy. 49, Suite R, 39071. Phone: (601) 879-0093. Fax: (601) 427-8800.E-mail: matt@wyab.com Web

Site:www.wyab.com Licensee: SSR Communications Inc. (acq 4-1-2003; $207,500). Population served: 270,000 Format: Talk. News staff: one. Target aud: 25-64. ◆Matthew Wesolowski, CEO & engrg dir.

Flowood

WPBQ(AM)— January 1995: 1240 khz; 880 w-U. TL: N32 18 03 W90 08 12. Hrs open: 24 1985 Lakeland Dr., Suite 108, Jackson, 39216. Phone: (601) 982-3210. Fax: (601) 982-3220. Web Site:www.espnradio1240.com Licensee: PDB Corp. (acq 2-10-92; $4,000; 3-2-92). Population served: 300,000 Haley, Bader & Potts. Format: All sports. Target aud: 25-54. ◆Derrel Palmer, gen mgr & engrg dir.

Forest

*****WMBU(FM)**— Oct 3, 1997: 89.1 mhz; 10 kw horiz, 100 kw vert. 640 ft TL: N32 18 54 W89 21 12. Stereo. Hrs open: 24
Rebroadcasts WMBV(FM) Dixon's Mills, AL 95%.
Box 400, Lake, 39092. Secondary address: Box 91, Dixons Mills, AL 36736. Phone: (601) 775-3100. Fax: (601) 775-3400.E-mail: wmbu@radiosouth.edu Web Site:www.wmbu.org Licensee: The Moody Bible Institute of Chicago. (group owner) Population served: 600,000 Natl. Network: Moody, . Southmayd & Miller. Wire Svc: AP Format: Christian. Target aud: 35-54. Spec prog: Children 2 hrs wkly. ◆Rob Moore, gen mgr; John Roger, progmg dir.

WQST(AM)— September 1955: 850 khz; 500w-D, DA. TL: N32 21 46 W89 25 09. Hrs open: Daylight
website streaming audio @ www. 850amwqst.com.
Box 1040, 39074. Phone: (601) 469-1960. Fax: (601) 469-1366.E-mail: wqstgospel@aol.com Web Site:www.850amwqst.com Licensee: Ace Broadcasting Inc. (acq 1999; $45,000). Population served: 500,000 Miss. News Net. Garvey, Schubert & Barer. Format: Southern Gospel. News: 12 hrs per day. Target aud: 35+; Adults. ◆Frank Edmondson, gen mgr; Dan Davis, progmg dir.

WQST-FM— September 1962: 92.5 mhz; 100 kw. 1,040 ft TL: N32 21 48 W89 25 29. Stereo. Hrs open: 1329 Deerfield Ln., Jackson, 39211. Phone: (601) 362-4277. Fax: (601) 362-1994.E-mail: info@afr.net Web Site:www.afr.net Licensee: American Family Association Inc. Group owner: American Family Radio Population served: 1,000,000 Natl. Network: USA, . Format: Christian. ◆Jim Thorn, gen mgr & stn mgr.

*****WQVI(FM)**— July 20, 2004: 90.5 mhz; 60 kw vert. Ant 430 ft TL: N32 42 51 W89 49 19. Hrs open: Box 3206, Tupelo, 38803. Phone: (662) 844-8888. Fax: (662) 842-6791. Web Site:www.afr.net Licensee: American Family Association. Group owner: American Family Radio. Population served: 310,000 Natl. Network: USA, . Format: Christian classics. ◆Marvin Sanders, gen mgr.

*****WSQH(FM)**— 2005: 91.7 mhz; 15 kw. Ant 474 ft TL: N32 23 57 W89 05 02. Hrs open: Box 3206, Tupelo, 38803-3206. Phone: (662) 844-8888. Fax: (662) 842-6791. Web Site:www.afr.net Licensee: Salt & Light Communications Inc. Natl. Network: USA, . Format: Christian. ◆Marvin Sanders, gen mgr.

Friar's Point

WNEV(FM)—Not on air, target date: unknown: 98.7 mhz; 6 kw. Ant 328 ft TL: N34 21 56 W90 38 14. Hrs open: Box 2870, West Helena, AR, 72390. Phone: (870) 572-7000. Fax: (870) 572-1845.E-mail: force2@sbcglobal.net Licensee: L.T. Simes II & Raymond Simes. ◆Raymond Simes, gen mgr.

WWUN-FM— 1973: 101.5 mhz; 14 kw. Ant 395 ft TL: N34 34 02 W90 37 37. Stereo. Hrs open: Box 2981, West Helena, 72390. Phone: (870) 572-3677.E-mail: wwun@csnradio.com Licensee: CSN International. (group owner; (acq 8-27-2001). Population served: 750,000 Format: Relg, Christian. ◆Charles W. Smith, pres; Jeffrey W. Smith, VP & gen mgr; Clayton Collier, stn mgr.

Fulton

WFTA(FM)—Licensed to Fulton. See Tupelo

Gluckstadt

WYOY(FM)— Jan 7, 1976: 101.7 mhz; 50 kw. 300 ft TL: N32 30 03 W90 02 28. Stereo. Hrs open: 24 265 High Point Dr., Ridgeland, 39157. Phone: (601) 956-0102. Fax: (601) 978-3980.E-mail: frontdesk@us963.com Web Site:www.y101.com Licensee: New South

Radio Inc. Group owner: New South Communications Inc. (acq 11-10-94; $750,000 with WLRM(AM) Ridgeland; 12-12-94). Natl. Rep: McGavren Guild,. Format: CHR. Target aud: 18-49. ◆Gwen Rakestraw, gen mgr.

Greenville

WBAD(FM)—See Leland

WBAQ(FM)— May 1, 1970: 97.9 mhz; 48 kw horiz. Ant 502 ft TL: N33 23 51 W91 00 35. Stereo. Hrs open: 5:30 AM-midnight Box 1816, 38702-1816. Secondary address: 800 Hwy 1 South, Delta Plaza, Ste #39 38701. Phone: (662) 378-2617. Fax: (662) 378-8341.E-mail: info@wbaq.com Licensee: Debut Broadcasting Mississippi Inc. Group owner: The River Group (acq 6-19-2007; grpsl). Population served: 75,000 Natl. Network: ABC, . Rgnl. Network: Prog Farm, Miss. Net. Miss. News Net. Format: Btfl music, easy lstng. News: 14 hrs wkly. Target aud: 25-54; quality-conscious adults with spendable income. Spec prog: Farm one hr, btfl sacred music 4 hrs wkly. ◆James P. Karr, gen mgr; Linda mcKee, opns mgr.

WDMS(FM)— December 1967: 100.7 mhz; 100 kw. 449 ft TL: N33 24 20 W91 01 41. Stereo. Hrs open: Prog sep from AM 1383 Pickett St., 38701. Phone: (662) 334-4559. Fax: (662) 332-1315.E-mail: wdms@bellsouth.net Web Site:www.wdmsradio.com Population served: 100,000 Rgnl. Network: Miss. Net. Miss. News Net. Format: Country. ◆Linda Tackett, traf mgr & disc jockey.

*****WDSV(FM)**—Not on air, target date: unknown: 91.9 mhz; 4.2 kw. Ant 138 ft TL: N33 21 57 W90 57 20. Hrs open: 819 Main St., 38701-4100. Phone: (662) 335-5291. Licensee: Delta Foundation Inc. ◆Cindy Ayers, CEO & pres.

WESY(AM)—See Leland

WGVM(AM)— 1948: 1260 khz; 5 kw-D, 32 w-N. TL: N33 25 20 W91 01 41. Hrs open: Box 1438, 38701. Secondary address: 1383 Pickett St. 38701. Phone: (662) 334-4550. Fax: (662) 332-1315.E-mail: wdms@bellsouth.net Licensee: WDMS Inc. (acq 11-9-2006; $780,000 with co-located FM). Population served: 100,000 Rgnl. Network: Miss. Net. Target aud: General.

WIQQ(FM)—See Leland

WJIW(FM)—Not on air, target date: unknown: 104.7 mhz; 31 kw. Ant 620 ft TL: N33 28 10 W90 50 30. Hrs open: 830 Main St., 38701. Phone: (662) 332-5701. Fax: (870) 338-3166. Licensee: Mondy-Burke Broadcasting Network. Format: Gospel. ◆Elijah Mondy, gen mgr; Belinda Mondy, gen sls mgr; April Mondy, mus dir.

*****WLRK(FM)**— 2006: 91.5 mhz; 50 kw vert. Ant 321 ft TL: N33 32 25 W91 22 39. Hrs open: 2351 Sunset Blvd., Suite 170-218, Rocklin, CA, 95765. Phone: (601) 992-6988. Fax: (916) 251-1650. Web Site:www.klove.com Licensee: Educational Media Foundation. (acq 1-23-2008; $320,000 with KAKV(FM) El Dorado, AR). Natl. Network: K-Love, . Format: Contemp Chirstian. ◆Phillip O'Bryan, gen mgr.

WNIX(AM)— August 1937: 1330 khz; 1 kw-D, 500 w-N, DA-N. TL: N33 24 36 W91 01 03. Hrs open: 24 Box 1816, 38702-1816. Secondary address: Unit 39 Delta Plaza Mall, 800 Hwy. 1 S. 38701. Phone: (662) 378-2617. Fax: (662) 378-8341.E-mail: lindamckee @debutbroadcasting.com Licensee: Debut Broadcasting Mississippi Inc. Group owner: The River Group (acq 6-19-2007; grpsl). Population served: 250,000 Rgnl. Network: Ark. Radio Net. Stephen R. Ross. Format: Oldies. ◆James P. Karr Jr., gen mgr.

Greenwood

WABG(AM)— February 1950: 960 khz; 1 kw-D, 500 w-N, DA-N. TL: N33 33 45 W90 12 38. Hrs open: 6 AM-1 PM 2001 Garrard Ave., 38930. Secondary address: Box 408 38935-0408. Phone: (662) 453-7822. Fax: (662) 455-3311. Licensee: SPB LLC Group owner: Bahakel Communications (acq 1-8-2008; $12,000). Population served: 26,000 Format: Country, talk. News: 11 hrs wkly. Target aud: 35 plus. Spec prog: Black 4 hrs wkly. ◆Sherry Nelson, gen mgr.

WBLZ(FM)—Not on air, target date: unknown: 103.3 mhz; 6 kw. Ant 328 ft TL: N33 32 21 W90 02 08. Hrs open: Box 1686, 38935-1686. Phone: (662) 453-2174. Fax: (662) 455-5733. Licensee: TeleSouth Communications Inc. ◆Charlotte Michael, gen mgr.

WGNL(FM)— Dec 1, 1989: 104.3 mhz; 50 kw. 360 ft TL: N33 31 30 W90 09 52. (CP: TL: N33 21 56 W90 14 59). Stereo. Hrs open: 24 Box 1801, 38930. Secondary address: 503 Ione St. 38930. Phone: (662)

453-1646. Fax: (662) 453-7002.E-mail: wgnlbooth@bellsouth.net Web Site:www.broadcasturban.net Licensee: Team Broadcasting Co. Inc. Natl. Rep: Dora-Clayton,. Mullin, Rhyne, Emmons & Topel. Format: Adult contemp. News staff: one; News: 12 hrs wkly. Target aud: 18 plus. Spec prog: Jazz 6 hrs wkly. ◆Maxine Hughes, opns mgr; Ruben C. Hughes, gen mgr & gen sls mgr.

WGRM(AM)— 1937: 1240 khz; 1 kw-U. TL: N33 31 55 W90 11 38. (CP: 730 w). Hrs open: 1110 Wright St., 38930. Phone: (662) 453-1240. Fax: (662) 453-1241.E-mail: wgrmradiostation@bellsouth.net Licensee: Christian Broadcasting of Greenwood Inc. (group owner; (acq 2-22-99; $500,000 with co-located FM). Population served: 180,000 Format: Gospel. Target aud: 25-45. Spec prog: Black 2 hrs wkly. ◆Gwen Riley, mus dir, news dir; Lee Hall, gen mgr, gen sls mgr, progmg dir & chief of engrg; Gwen Rilley, traf mgr.

WGRM-FM— July 17, 1989: 93.9 mhz; 3 kw. 328 ft TL: N33 32 02 W90 11 42. (CP: 25 kw). Hrs open: 24 1110 Wright St., 38930. Phone: (662) 453-1240. Fax: (662) 453-1241.E-mail: wgrmradiostation@bellsouth.net Population served: 180,000

WKXG(AM)— Jan 1, 1987: Stn currently dark. 1540 khz; 1 kw-D. TL: N33 31 12 W90 08 28. Hrs open: 6 AM-10 PM Box 1686, 38935-1686. Secondary address: 3192 Browning Rd. 38935. Phone: (662) 453-2174. Fax: (662) 455-5733. Licensee: TeleSouth Communications Inc. (group owner; (acq 8-1-88). Rgnl. Network: Miss. Net. ◆Charlotte Michael, gen mgr.

*****WMAO-FM**— December 1983: 90.9 mhz; 100 kw. 880 ft TL: N33 22 34 W90 32 32. Stereo. Hrs open: 24 3825 Ridgewood Rd., Jackson, 39211. Phone: (601) 432-6565. Fax: (601) 432-6806. Web Site:www.mpbonline.org Licensee: Mississippi Authority for Educational Television. Natl. Network: PRI, NPR, . Schwartz, Woods & Miller. Wire Svc: AP Format: News and info, music. News staff: 7; News: 100 hrs wkly. Target aud: General. ◆Jay Woods, gen mgr; Jason Klein, opns mgr, progmg dir; Ty Warren, dev mgr; Bill Ellison, rgnl sls mgr; Mari Irby, prom dir; Karen Hearn, mus dir; Teresa Collier, news dir; Bob Buie, engrg dir; LaSharne Patton, traf mgr.

WTCD(FM)—(Indianola, May 1990): 96.9 mhz; 12.5 kw. 469 ft TL: N33 35 35 W90 32 30. Stereo. Hrs open: 24 Box 1686, 38935. Phone: (662) 453-2174. Fax: (662) 455-5733. Web Site:www.supertalkms.com Licensee: TeleSouth Communications Inc. (group owner; acq 5-28-97; $325,000). Population served: 250,000 Natl. Network: USA, . Rgnl. Network: Miss. Net. Miss. News Net. Emmerson & Belendiuk. Format: News/talk. News staff: one; News: 20 hrs wkly. Target aud: 35-64; strong family orientation, middle to upper incomes. Spec prog: Farm 5 hrs, relg 11 hrs, talk 10 hrs wkly. ◆Charlotte Michael, gen mgr.

WYMX(FM)— June 15, 1965: 99.1 mhz; 100 kw. Ant 1,029 ft TL: N33 31 12 W90 08 28. Stereo. Hrs open: Box 1686, 38935. Phone: (662) 453-2174. Fax: (662) 455-5733. Licensee: TeleSouth Communications Inc. Population served: 315,000 Format: Adult hits. ◆Rea Edwards, traf mgr.

Grenada

WMUT(FM)— 2004: 101.3 mhz; 6 kw. Ant 328 ft TL: N33 49 20 W89 55 40. Hrs open: Box 2266, 38902. Secondary address: 157 Dowdle Rd. 38901. Phone: (662) 226-3133. Fax: (662) 226-3233.E-mail: rock101@cableone.net Licensee: George S. Flinn Jr. Natl. Network: CNN Radio, Westwood One, . Format: Classic rock. Target aud: 18-54. ◆Will Stammerjohan, gen mgr; Connie Stammerjohan, gen sls mgr.

WOHT(FM)— 2003: 92.3 mhz; 4.1 kw. Ant 397 ft TL: N33 51 33 W89 55 13. Hrs open: Box 2266, 38902. Phone: (662) 226-3133. Fax: (662) 226-3233.E-mail: star92@star92fm.com Licensee: Century Broadcasting L.L.C. (acq 4-18-03). Format: Oldies. ◆Will Stammerjohan, gen mgr.

WQXB(FM)— Oct 16, 1970: 100.1 mhz; 3 kw. 300 ft TL: N33 46 36 W89 49 23. Stereo. Hrs open: 1348 Sunset Dr., 38901. Licensee: Chatterbox Inc. (Acq 2-24-78). Population served: 9,944 Format: Hot country.

WTGY(FM)—See Charleston

WYKC(AM)— February 1949: 1400 khz; 1 kw-U. TL: N33 46 48 W89 48 09. Hrs open: 1348 Sunset Dr., 38901. Phone: (662) 226-1400. Fax: (662) 226-1464.E-mail: b100@bellsouth.net Licensee: Chatterbox Inc. (acq 1-16-81). Population served: 9,944 Rgnl. Network: Prog Farm. Format: Country. ◆Bob Evans Jr., pres & gen mgr.

Gulfport

***WAOY(FM)—** 1999: 91.7 mhz; 78 kw. 1,089 ft TL: N30 42 29 W89 05 06. Hrs open:
Rebroadcasts WAFR(FM) Tupelo 80%.
Box 3206, American Family Radio, Tupelo, 38803. Phone: (601) 844-8888. Fax: (601) 842-6791. Web Site:www.afr.net Licensee: American Family Association Inc. Group owner: American Family Radio Natl. Network: USA, . Format: Christian. Target aud: General. ♦Marvin Sanders, pres & gen mgr.

WGCM(AM)— 1928: 1240 khz; 1 kw-U. TL: N30 22 38 W89 04 45. Hrs open: 24 10250 Lorrian, 39503. Phone: (228) 896-5500. Fax: (228) 896-0458. Licensee: JMD Inc. (acq 11-15-94; $950,000 with co-located FM;12-12-94). Format: Country. Target aud: 35 plus. ♦Morgan Dowdy, pres, gen mgr; Buddy Baylor, opns mgr; Steve Spillman, gen sls mgr; Brian Rhodes, progmg dir; Gwen Wilson, news dir; Dave Melton, chief of engrg.

WGCM-FM— Nov 14, 1969: 102.3 mhz; 25 kw. 299 ft TL: N30 22 28 W89 04 45. (CP: 16 kw, ant 358 ft.). Stereo. Hrs open: 24 10250 Lorrian, 39503. Phone: (228) 896-5500. Fax: (228) 896-0458. Format: Easy listening. Target aud: 25-54. ♦Buddy Baylor, gen sls mgr; Pat McGowan, progmg dir.

WQFX(AM)— May 7, 1975: 1130 khz; 500 w-D. TL: N30 23 21 W89 06 23. Hrs open: 336 Rodenberg Ave., Biloxi, 39531-3444. Phone: (228) 374-9739. Fax: (228) 374-9739.E-mail: wqfxradio@aol.com Web Site:www.wqfx.net Licensee: Walking by Faith Ministries Inc. (acq 1994). Population served: 58,000 Format: Power gospel. ♦James Black, gen mgr.

WROA(AM)— Feb 27, 1955: 1390 khz; 5 kw-U, DA-2. TL: N30 27 30 W89 04 45. Hrs open: Box 2639, 39505. Phone: (228) 896-5500. Fax: (228) 896-0458.E-mail: www.morgan@kiker108.com Licensee: Dowdy & Dowdy Partnership. (acq 12-19-86). Population served: 100,000 Format: Music of your life. Spec prog: Farm one hr wkly. ♦Charles W. Dowdy, pres; Morgan Dowdy, gen mgr.

WUJM(FM)— July 13, 1977: 96.7 mhz; 3 kw. 245 ft TL: N30 23 21 W89 06 23. Stereo. Hrs open: 24 1909 E. Pass Rd., Suite D11, 39507. Phone: (228) 388-2001. Fax: (228) 896-9736.E-mail: molly967@molly967.com Web Site:www.molly967.com Licensee: Monterey Licenses LLC. Group owner: Triad Broadcasting Co. LLC (acq 7-14-99; grpsl). Population served: 200000 Format: Hot adult contemp. ♦Buddy Burch, VP; Jay Taylor, opns dir & opns mgr.

WXYK(FM)— 1964: 107.1 mhz; 1.85 kw. 394 ft TL: N30 27 32 W89 04 45. (CP: 2.8 kw, ant 400 ft.). Stereo. Hrs open: 24 1909 E. Pass Rd., Suite D-11, 39507. Phone: (228) 388-2001. Fax: (228) 896-9736.E-mail: wxyk@monkeyradio.com Web Site:www.monkeyradio.com Licensee: Monterey Licenses LLC. Group owner: Triad Broadcasting Co. LLC (acq 7-14-99; grpsl). Population served: 200,000 Natl. Network: ABC, . Format: Top-40/CHR. ♦Jay Taylor, opns dir & opns mgr.

WZKX(FM)—See Poplarville

Guntown

WBVV(FM)— Jan 15, 1976: 99.3 mhz; 15.5 kw. Ant 420 ft TL: N34 21 46 W88 35 28. Hrs open: 24 Box 3300, Tupelo, 38803. Licensee: CC Licenses LLC. Group owner: Clear Channel Communications Inc. (acq 9-27-2001; $700,000 including 5-year noncompete agreement). Natl. Network: USA, Reach Satellite, . Rgnl. Network: Miss. Net. Miss. News Net. Format: Contemp inspirational. ♦Mark Maharrey, gen mgr.

Hattiesburg

***WAII(FM)—** 1998: 89.3 mhz; 1 kw. 220 ft TL: N31 16 59 W89 21 01. Hrs open: American Family Radio, Box 3206, Tupelo, 38803. Phone: (662) 844-8888. Fax: (662) 842-6791. Web Site:www.afr.net Licensee: American Family Association. Group owner: American Family Radio Natl. Network: USA, . Format: Relg. ♦Marvin Sanders, gen mgr.

WFOR(AM)— May 1924: 1400 khz; 1 kw-U. TL: N31 20 03 W89 19 08. Hrs open: 24 6555 US Hwy. 98 W., Suite 8, 39402. Phone: (601) 296-9800. Fax: (601) 296-9838. Licensee: CC Licenses LLC. Group owner: Clear Channel Communications Inc. (acq 12-19-2000; grpsl). Population served: 38,277 Format: Sports. Target aud: 35 plus. ♦Mike Comfort, gen mgr; Jackson Walker, progmg dir; Glen Musgrove, chief of engrg.

WHSY(AM)— Sept 1, 1954: Stn currently dark. 950 khz; 5 kw-D, 64 w-N. TL: N31 22 33 W89 19 49. Hrs open: 24 63 Braswell Rd., 39401. Phone: (601) 582-7078. Fax: (601) 582-7122.E-mail: whsy950@yahoo.com Web Site:www.whsy950.com Licensee: Gulf South Communications LLC (acq 9-5-2004). Population served: 304,475 Natl. Network: CBS Radio, . Format: News, talk, sport. ♦Charlie W. Holt, pres; Charlie Holt, gen mgr.

WJMG(FM)— May 10, 1982: 92.1 mhz; 6 kw. 300 ft TL: N31 20 33 W89 17 53. Stereo. Hrs open: 24 1204 Kinnard St., Hattiesbug, 39401. Phone: (601) 544-1941. Fax: (601) 544-1947. Licensee: Vernon C. Floyd dba Circuit Broadcasting of Hattiesburg Population served: 66,277 Format: Urban contemp. ♦Vernon Floyd, gen mgr.

WORV(AM)— June 7, 1969: 1580 khz; 1 kw-D, 88 w-N. TL: N31 20 33 W89 17 53. Hrs open: 1204 Graveline St., 39401. Phone: (601) 544-1941. Fax: (601) 544-1947. Licensee: Vernon C. Floyd dba Circuit Broadcasting of Hattiesburg. Population served: 66,000 Natl. Network: American Urban, . Natl. Rep: Dora-Clayton,. Format: Gospel. ♦Vernon C. Floyd, pres & gen mgr.

***WUSM-FM—** May 10, 1973: 88.5 mhz; 3 kw. 282 ft TL: N31 21 02 W89 22 12. Stereo. Hrs open: USM-118 College Dr., #10045, 39406-0045. Phone: (601) 266-4287. Phone: (601) 266-5649. Fax: (601) 266-4288.E-mail: wusmmik@yahoo.com Web Site:www.wusm.usm.edu Licensee: University of Southern Mississippi. Population served: 250,000 Natl. Network: AP Radio, . Format: Class, var/div, AAA. News staff: 4; News: 22 hrs wkly. Target aud: General; college students & upper income univ & community listeners. ♦Shelby Thames, pres; Dennis Webster, exec VP; Michael Davis, gen mgr.

WUSW(FM)— July 1, 1966: 103.7 mhz; 100 kw. Ant 1,056 ft TL: N31 31 37 W89 08 07. Stereo. Hrs open: 24 6555 Hwy. 98 W., Suite 8, 39402. Phone: (601) 296-9800. Fax: (601) 296-9838. Web Site:www.thefoxrocks1037.com Licensee: CC Licenses LLC. Population served: 500,000 Format: Rock. Target aud: 25-54. ♦Mike Comfort, gen mgr.

WXRR(FM)— July 1, 1967: 104.5 mhz; 100 kw. 984 ft TL: N31 25 50 W89 08 51. (CP: TL: N31 25 52 W89 08 51). Stereo. Hrs open: 24 Box 16596, 39404. Phone: (601) 544-0095. Fax: (601) 649-8199.E-mail: rock104fm@rock104fm.com Web Site:www.rock104fm.com Licensee: Blakeney Communications Inc. (group owner; acq 8-30-94; $450,000 with co-located AM; 10-24-94). Population served: 100,000 Format: Classic rock. Target aud: General. ♦Larry Blakeney, pres & gen mgr.

WZLD(FM)—See Petal

Hazlehurst

WDXO(FM)— Dec 24, 1970: 92.9 mhz; 6 kw. 295 ft TL: N31 53 34 W90 24 08. Stereo. Hrs open: 24 110 W. Monticello St., Brookhaven, 39601. Phone: (601) 587-9363. Fax: (601) 587-5005. Licensee: TeleSouth Communications Inc. Population served: 200,000 Natl. Network: ABC, . Format: All sports. Target aud: 18-50. ♦Rusty O'Neal, gen mgr.

WOEG(AM)— June 1, 1953: 1220 khz; 250 w-D, 46 w-N. TL: N31 53 34 W90 24 08. Hrs open: 6 AM-6 PM Box 2016, Monticello, 39654. Phone: (601) 587-9363. Phone: (601) 587-7625. Fax: (601) 587-9401. Licensee: TeleSouth Communications Inc. (group owner; (acq 6-20-2006; grpsl). Population served: 36,000 Booth, Freret, Imlay & Tepper. Format: Urban gospel. Target aud: General; Black. ♦Heather Thurgood, opns mgr, progmg dir, traf mgr; Robert Byrd, gen sls mgr; Randy Bullock, prom dir; Rusty O'Neal, stn mgr, news dir & chief of engrg.

Heidelberg

WHER(FM)— May 1, 1980: 99.3 mhz; 50 kw. 492 ft TL: N31 49 17 W89 18 37. Stereo. Hrs open: 24 6555 Hwy. 98 W., Suite 8, Hattiesburg, 39402. Phone: (601) 296-9800. Fax: (601) 296-9838.E-mail: contact@eagle99.com Web Site:www.eagle99.com Licensee: CC Licenses LLC. Group owner: Clear Channel Communications Inc. (acq 12-19-2000; grpsl). Population served: 350,000 Rgnl. Network: Miss. Net. Miss. News Net. Format: Classic country. Target aud: General. ♦Mike Comfort, gen mgr; Jackson Walker, opns mgr; Glenn Musgrove, chief of engrg.

Holly Springs

WKRA(AM)— Sept 2, 1966: 1110 khz; 1 kw-D. TL: N34 47 11 W89 25 00. Hrs open: Sunrise-sunset Box 398, 38635. Secondary address: 1400 Hwy 4 E, Ste C, MO 38635. Phone: (662) 252-1110. Fax: (662) 252-2739.E-mail: wkraradio@gmail.com Licensee: Bill Autrey. (acq 8-10-94; $250,000 with co-located FM; 9-5-94). Population served: 100,000 Rgnl. Network: Miss. Net. Miss. News Net. Format: Ethnic. News staff: one; News: 9 hrs wkly. Target aud: 25-55. Spec prog: Gospel 12 hrs wkly. ♦Pamela Rideout, gen mgr & stn mgr.

WKRA-FM— June 30, 1976: 92.7 mhz; 3 kw. 299 ft TL: N34 47 11 W89 25 00. Hrs open: 24 Box 398, 38635. Secondary address: 1400 Hwy 4 E, Ste C, MO 58635. Phone: (662) 252-1110. Fax: (662) 252-2739.E-mail: power927@gmail.com Web Site:power927fm.com Format: Hip hop, rhythm and blues, Gospel at night. News staff: one. Target aud: General; Black community. ♦Ricky Williams, opns mgr.

***WURC(FM)—** Oct 14, 1988: 88.1 mhz; 3 kw. 328 ft TL: N34 46 53 W89 26 49. Hrs open: WURC Rust College, 150 Rust Ave., 38635. Phone: (662) 252-5881. Fax: (662) 252-8869. Licensee: Rust College Inc. Natl. Network: NPR, . Format: Jazz, News/talk, Gospel, Blues. Target aud: General; alternative seekers and minority listeners. ♦David L. Beckley, pres; Debayo R. Moyo, gen mgr.

Horn Lake

WHAL-FM— July 26, 1994: 95.7 mhz; 6 kw. Ant 289 ft TL: N35 08 09 W89 58 17. Hrs open: 24 2650 Thousand Oaks Blvd., Suite 4100, Memphis, TN, 38118. Phone: (901) 259-1300. Fax: (901) 259-6451.E-mail: info@halleujahfm.com Web Site:www.hallelujahfm.com Licensee: CC Licenses LLC. Group owner: Clear Channel Communications Inc. (acq 1996; grpsl). Natl. Rep: Clear Channel,. Format: Gospel. News: 3 hrs wkly. Target aud: 35-54; baby boomers. ♦Tim Davies, gen mgr; Ralph Salierno, sls dir; Frank Gilbert, mktg dir; Eileen Collier, progmg dir.

Houston

WCPC(AM)— Oct 21, 1955: 940 khz; 50 kw-D, 250 w-N, DA-2. TL: N33 56 00 W89 00 33. Hrs open: 5 AM-9:15 PM 1189 N. Jackson St., 38851. Phone: (662) 456-3071. Fax: (662) 456-3072. Licensee: Cajun Radio Corp. (acq 6-1-2007; $200,000). Population served: 750,000 Natl. Network: USA, . Miss. News Net. Format: Christian, country, gospel, Black. News staff: one; News: 14 hrs wkly. Adults. ♦Robert L. Wilkins, pres; Robin H. Mathis, gen mgr; Melanie Mathis Munlin, opns dir, opns mgr, mus dir; Don Tallent, news dir.

WSYE(FM)— Sept 19, 1968: 93.3 mhz; 100 kw. 1,804 ft TL: N33 45 06 W88 52 40. Stereo. Hrs open: 24 Box 410, Tupelo, 38802. Secondary address: 2214 S. Gloster , Tupelo 38802. Phone: (662) 842-7658. Fax: (662) 842-0197. Web Site:www.sunny93fm.com Licensee: JMD Inc. (acq 9-28-99). Population served: 750,000 Natl. Rep: Christal,. Format: Adult contemp. News staff: one; News: 2 hrs wkly. Target aud: 25-54. ♦Scott Bebout, gen mgr, mktg mgr; Brenda Bebout, stn mgr; Steve Drunam, opns mgr.

Indianola

WNLA(AM)— May 1953: 1380 khz; 500 w-D, 44 w-N. TL: N33 27 32 W90 37 45. Hrs open: 12 Box 667, Hwy. 448, 38751. Phone: (662) 887-1380. Fax: (662) 887-1396.E-mail: wnlaamfm@bellsouth.net Licensee: Debut Broadcasting Mississippi Inc. (acq 6-7-2007; $300,000 with co-located FM). Population served: 36,000 Rgnl. Network: Miss. Net. Miss. News Net. Format: Black gospel. Target aud: 21-55; Black. ♦Robert Marquitz, pres; Erin Ely, gen mgr, progmg dir; Gerry Brophy, sls dir, engrg dir; Bob Taylor, chief of engrg.

WNLA-FM— Sept 1, 1969: 105.5 mhz; 4.4 kw. 200 ft TL: N33 28 41 W90 38 28. Stereo. Hrs open: 24 Prog sep from AM Box 667, Hwy. 448, 38751. Phone: (662) 887-1380. Fax: (662) 887-1396.E-mail: wnlaamfm@bellsouth.net Licensee: Debut Broadcasting Mississippi Inc. Format: Adult contemp. News: 21 hrs wkly. Target aud: 21-55.

WTCD(FM)—Licensed to Indianola. See Greenwood

***WYTF(FM)—** Aug 26, 2004: 88.7 mhz; 100 kw vert. Ant 636 ft TL: N33 35 03 W90 36 13. Hrs open: Drawer 3206, Tupelo, 38801. Phone: (662) 844-8888. Fax: (662) 842-6791. Web Site:www.afr.net Licensee: American Family Association. Group owner: American Family Radio. Natl. Network: USA, . Format: Christian. ♦Don Wildman, gen mgr.

Itta Bena

***WVSD(FM)—** June 23, 1991: 91.7 mhz; 3 kw. 292 ft TL: N33 31 05 W90 20 38. Hrs open: 6 AM-midnight 14000 Hwy. 82 W. MVSU, 38941. Phone: (662) 254-3612. Fax: (662) 254-3611. Licensee: Mississippi Valley State University. Format: Jazz, gospel, blues. Spec prog: Oldies 10 hrs, reggae/Latin 3 hrs, comedy 2 hrs wkly. ♦Dr. Lester Newman, pres; Larz G. Roberts, gen mgr & progmg dir; Debra Harmon, progmg mgr.

Iuka

WKZU(FM)— Nov 5, 1970: 104.9 mhz; 50 kw. Ant 443 ft TL: N34 46 35 W88 23 40. Hrs open: PO Box 572, Ripley, 38663. Phone: (662) 423-2369. Fax: (662) 423-6059.E-mail: classicradiofm@aol.com Web Site:www.kudzu102.com Licensee: Kudzu Communications Inc. (acq 1-8-2008; $365,000). Population served: 2,389 Format: Classic country. Target aud: 25-54; 50% men & 50% women. ♦Billy McLain, gen mgr, gen sls mgr & progmg dir.

Jackson

WHLH(FM)— Nov 19, 1973: 95.5 mhz; 100 kw. Ant 1,115 ft TL: N32 14 26 W90 24 15. Stereo. Hrs open: 1375 Beasley Rd., 39206. Phone: (601) 982-1062. Fax: (601) 362-1905.E-mail: info@hallelujah955.com Web Site:www.hallelujah955.com Licensee: Capstar TX L.P. Group owner: Clear Channel Communications Inc. (acq 8-30-00; grpsl). Natl. Network: CBS, . Natl. Rep: D & R Radio,. Cohn & Marks. Format: Gospel. Target aud: 18-34; female. ♦Jenell Roberts, gen mgr & progmg dir.

WJDX(AM)— 1929: 620 khz; 5 kw-D, 1 kw-N, DA-N. TL: N32 22 56 W90 11 26. Stereo. Hrs open: 24 Box 31999, 39286. Secondary address: 1375 Beasley Rd. 39206. Phone: (601) 982-1062. Fax: (601) 362-1905.E-mail: info@wjdx.com Web Site:www.wjdx.com Licensee: Capstar TX L.P. Group owner: Clear Channel Communications Inc. (acq 8-30-2000; grpsl). Population served: 153,968 Natl. Rep: McGavren Guild,. Format: Sports/talk. News staff: one; News: 10 hrs wkly. Target aud: 25-54; middle to upper income contemp adults. Spec prog: Farm 2 hrs wkly. ♦Kenneth E. Windham, gen mgr; Mary Ann Kirby, gen sls mgr; Randy Bell, progmg dir, news dir; Jason Black, chief of engrg; Theresa Banks, traf mgr.

WJFN(AM)—See Brandon

WJMI(FM)— 1967: 99.7 mhz; 100 kw. 1,060 ft TL: N32 16 39 W90 17 41. Stereo. Hrs open: 24 Prog sep from AM 731 S. Pear Orchard Rd., Suite 27, Ridgeland, 39157. Phone: (601) 957-1300. Fax: (601) 956-0516.E-mail: production@wjmi.com Web Site:www.wjmi.com Licensee: Urban Radio II L.L.C. Population served: 700,000 Format: Urban hip-hop. News staff: one. Target aud: 18-49. ♦Stan Branson, progmg dir.

WJQS(AM)— 1947: 1400 khz; 1 kw-U. TL: N32 19 12 W90 11 25. Hrs open: 24 840 E. River Pl. #503, 39202. Phone: (601) 965-2001. Fax: (601) 961-3042.E-mail: info@1400wjqs.com Web Site:www.1400wjqs.com Licensee: Urban Radio II L.L.C. Group owner: Inner City Broadcasting (acq 8-25-2000; grpsl). Population served: 300,000 Format: Business news. ♦Gary Michiels, gen mgr.

***WJSU(FM)**— August 1975: 88.5 mhz; 3 kw. 203 ft TL: N32 17 47 W90 12 23. Stereo. Hrs open: Box 18450, Jackson State Univ., 39217. Phone: (601) 979-2285. Fax: (601) 979-2878.E-mail: wjsufm@jsums.edu Web Site:www.wjsu.org Licensee: Jackson State University. Population served: 176,000 Natl. Network: NPR, AP Network News, PRI, . Format: Jazz, news. News staff: 2; News: news prgmg 36 hrs wkly. Target aud: 25-54; middle-class multiracial who prefer jazz. ♦Gina Carter-Simmers, gen mgr.

***WMPN-FM**— November 1984: 91.3 mhz; 100 kw. 760 ft TL: N32 16 53 W90 17 41. Stereo. Hrs open: 24 3825 Ridgewood Rd., 39211. Phone: (601) 432-6565. Fax: (601) 432-6806. Web Site:www.mpbonline.org Licensee: Mississippi Authority for Educational Television. Natl. Network: PRI, NPR, . Schwartz, Woods & Miller. Wire Svc: AP Format: News and info, music. News staff: 7; News: 100 hrs wkly. Target aud: General. ♦Jay Woods, gen mgr; Jason Holland, opns mgr; Mari Irby, prom dir.

***WMPR(FM)**— 1983: 90.1 mhz; 100 kw. 500 ft TL: N32 11 33 W90 05 28. Stereo. Hrs open: Box 9782, 39209. Phone: (601) 948-5835. Fax: (601) 948-6162.E-mail: wmpr@wmpr901.com Web Site:www.wmpr901.com Licensee: J.C. Maxwell Broadcasting Group Inc. Format: Blues, gospel, urban contemp. ♦Charles Evers, gen mgr.

WMSI(FM)— 1948: 102.9 mhz; 100 kw. Ant 1,800 ft TL: N32 12 46 W90 22 54. Stereo. Hrs open: 24 Box 31999, 39286. Secondary address: 1375 Beasley Rd. 39206. Phone: (601) 982-1062. Fax: (601) 362-1905.E-mail: info@miss103.com Web Site:www.miss103.com Licensee: Capstar TX L.P. Population served: 153,968 Format: C&W. News: 4 hrs wkly. Target aud: 25 plus. Spec prog: Farm one hr wkly. ♦Sam McLeod, gen sls mgr; Rick Adams, progmg dir; Marshall Stewart, mus dir, news dir; Diana Bass, traf mgr.

WOAD(AM)— 1929: 1300 khz; 5 kw-D, 1 kw-N. TL: N32 23 12 W90 09 47. Hrs open: 731 S. Pear Orchard Rd., Suite 27, Ridgeland, 39157. Phone: (601) 957-1300. Fax: (601) 956-0516.E-mail: production@wjmi.com Web Site:www.woad.com Licensee: Urban Radio II L.L.C. Group owner: Inner City Broadcasting (acq 8-25-2000; grpsl). Population served: 330,000 Natl. Network: American Urban, ABC, . Wire Svc: Weather Wire Format: Gospel. Target aud: 25-54. ♦Kevin Webb, gen mgr, gen sls mgr; Percy Davis, progmg dir; Emmett Rushing, chief of engrg; Kelly Greer, traf mgr.

WSFZ(AM)— September 1938: 930 khz; 5 kw-U, DA-N. TL: N32 23 42 W90 09 14. Hrs open: 24 571 Highway 51 North, Suite H, Ridgeland, 39157. Secondary address: 574 Highway 51 North, Suite F, Ridgeland, MA 39157. Phone: (601) 605-6656. Fax: (601) 605-6646.E-mail: eubie@supersport930.com Web Site:www.supersport930.com Licensee: Sportsrad Inc. (acq 12-20-01; $222,500). Population served: 153,968 Natl. Network: Westwood One, Sporting News Radio Network, . Format: Sports. ♦Bryan Eubank, gen mgr, stn mgr & opns dir; Bo Bounds, sls.

WSTZ-FM—(Vicksburg, June 1968): 106.7 mhz; 100 kw. 1,365 ft TL: N32 12 22 W90 24 50. (CP: Ant 1,059 ft. TL: N32 12 29 W90 24 50). Stereo. Hrs open: Box 31999, 39286. Secondary address: 1375 Beasley Rd. 39206. Phone: (601) 982-1062. Fax: (601) 362-1905.E-mail: dougjones@clearchannel.com Web Site:www.z106.com Licensee: Capstar TX L.P. Group owner: Clear Channel Communications Inc. (acq 8-30-00; grpsl). Population served: 25,478 Natl. Rep: D & R Radio,. Format: Classic rock. Target aud: 25-54. ♦Kenneth Windham, gen mgr.

WWJK(FM)— Aug 10, 1971: 94.7 mhz; 100 kw. 1,168 ft TL: N32 16 53 W90 17 41. Stereo. Hrs open: 24 222 Beasley Rd., 39206. Phone: (601) 957-3000. Fax: (601) 956-0370.E-mail: jack@947jackfm.com Web Site:www.947jackfm.com Licensee: Backyard Broadcasting Mississippi Licensee LLC Group owner: Backyard Broadcasting LLC (acq 5-31-2002; $4,830,000 with WRXW(FM) Pearl). Population served: 330,000 Natl. Rep: Christal,. Fletcher, Heald & Hildreth. Format: Adult Hits. News staff: one; News: one hr wkly. Target aud: 25-54. ♦Barry Drake, pres; Jason Williams, gen mgr; Don Wayne, progmg dir.

WYOY(FM)—See Gluckstadt

WZRX(AM)— Apr 8, 1965: 1590 khz; 5 kw-D, 1 kw-N, DA-N. TL: N32 22 01 W90 13 26. Stereo. Hrs open: 24 Box 9734, 39286. Secondary address: 2980 Forest Ave. Ext. 39286. Phone: (601) 981-9080. Fax: (601) 981-9093.E-mail: radioair@bellsouth.net Licensee: Capstar MS L.P. Group owner: Clear Channel Communications Inc. (acq 5-29-98; grpsl). Natl. Network: American Urban, . Format: Gospel. Target aud: 25 plus; general. ♦Carl Haynes, gen mgr, stn mgr; Emmitte Rushing, chief of engrg.

Kosciusko

WKOZ(AM)— Oct 31, 1947: 1340 khz; 1 kw-U. TL: N33 03 51 W89 36 12. Hrs open: 24 Box 1700, 39090-1700. Phone: (662) 289-1050. Fax: (662) 289-7907.E-mail: breezy@boswellmedia.net Web Site:www.breezynews.com Licensee: Boswell Radio LLC (acq 6-1-62). Population served: 10,000 William D. Silva. Format: News/talk. News staff: one. Target aud: 50 plus. ♦Johnny Boswell, gen mgr; Ann Steen, stn mgr; Eric Matthews, opns mgr.

WQJQ(FM)— June 25, 1965: 105.1 mhz; 100 kw. 981 ft TL: N32 41 25 W89 52 06. Stereo. Hrs open: 24 Box 31999, Jackson, 39268. Phone: (601) 982-1062. Fax: (601) 362-8270.E-mail: stancebinghan@clearchannel.com Web Site:www.q1051.com Licensee: Capstar TX L.P. Group owner: Clear Channel Communications Inc. (acq 8-30-00; grpsl). Population served: 450,000 Format: Motown & Jammin Oldies. Target aud: 35-64. ♦Kenneth Windham, gen mgr; Steve Kelly, opns mgr.

Laurel

WAML(AM)— Oct 20, 1932: 1340 khz; 1 kw-U. TL: N31 40 01 W89 08 59. Hrs open: 24 Box 6226, 1425 Ellisville Blvd., 39440. Phone: (601) 425-0011. Licensee: Walking by Faith Ministries Inc. (acq 10-1-99). Population served: 24,145 Format: Sports talk. Target aud: General. ♦James Black, gen mgr.

***WATP(FM)**— 1998: 90.7 mhz; 350 w. 489 ft TL: N31 46 54 W89 09 31. Hrs open: American Family Radio, Box 3206, Tupelo, 38803. Phone: (662) 844-8888. Fax: (662) 842-6791. Web Site:www.afr.net Licensee: American Family Association. Group owner: American Family Radio Natl. Network: USA, . Format: Relg. ♦Marvin Sanders, gen mgr.

WHJA(AM)— Feb 27, 1957: Stn currently dark. 890 khz; 10 kw-D. TL: N31 31 29 W89 14 31. Hrs open: Sunrise-sunset 6555 Highway 98 West, Suite 8, Hattiesburg, 39402. Phone: (601) 296-9800. Fax: (601) 296-9838. Licensee: CC Licenses LLC. Group owner: Clear Channel Communications Inc. (acq 12-19-2000; grpsl). Population served: 143,000 Format: Blues. News staff: one; News: 4 hrs wkly. Target aud: General. ♦Mike Comfort, gen mgr, sls dir; Jackson Walker, opns mgr; James Harris, gen sls mgr; Denise Brooks, progmg dir; Glen Musgrove, chief of engrg; Terri Hudson, traf mgr.

WIZK(AM)—See Bay Springs

WKZW(FM)—See Bay Springs

WMXI(FM)— April 1989: 98.1 mhz; 2.55 kw. Ant 512 ft TL: N31 33 22 W89 09 09. Hrs open: Box 15935, Hattiesburg, 39403. Secondary address: 7501 U.S. Hwy. 49, Hattiesburg 39403. Phone: (601) 261-0898. Fax: (601) 261-3798.E-mail: zoo107@bellsouth.net Web Site:www.wmxi.com Licensee: Rainey Broadcasting Inc. (acq 10-21-96; $75,000). Population served: 200,000 Format: News/talk. ♦Ted Tibbett, gen mgr.

WNSL(FM)— Mar 10, 1959: 100.3 mhz; 100 kw. 1,050 ft TL: N31 31 37 W89 08 07. Stereo. Hrs open: Prog sep from AM 6555 Highway 98 West, Suite 8, Hattiesburg, 39402. Phone: (601) 296-9800. Fax: (601) 296-9838. Web Site:www.sl100.com Population served: 278,000 Natl. Network: ABC, . Format: CHR. Target aud: 18-49. ♦Don King, progmg dir.

Leland

WBAD(FM)— 1973: 94.3 mhz; 50 kw. 300 ft TL: N33 24 55 W90 59 18. Stereo. Hrs open: 19 Prog sep from AM Box 5804, Greenville, 38704. Secondary address: 126 Seven Oaks Rd., Greenville 38701. Phone: (662) 335-9265. Fax: (662) 335-5538. Licensee: Interchange Communications Inc. (acq 5-12-73). Natl. Network: American Urban, . Format: Urban contemp.

WESY(AM)— Apr 8, 1957: 1580 khz; 1 kw-D, 48 w-N. TL: N33 22 46 W90 55 47. (CP: 1 kw-N, DA-N). Hrs open: 24 Box 5804, Greenville, 38704. Secondary address: 126 Seven Oaks Rd., Greenville 38701. Phone: (662) 335-9265. Fax: (662) 335-5538.E-mail: wbad@tecinfo.com Licensee: East Delta Communications Inc. (acq 1980). Population served: 400,000 Natl. Network: American Urban, . David Tillotson. Format: Blues, relg, gospel. Target aud: 18-54. ♦Stanley S. Sherman, exec VP, gen sls mgr; William D. Jackson, pres & gen mgr.

WIQQ(FM)— Sept 1, 1985: 102.3 mhz; 1.65 kw. Ant 446 ft TL: N33 23 51 W91 00 35. Stereo. Hrs open: 24 Box 1816, Greenville, 38702-1816. Secondary address: Unit 39, 800 Hwy. 1 S., Greenville 38702. Phone: (662) 378-2617. Fax: (662) 378-8341.E-mail: wiqq@sellsouth.net Licensee: Debut Broadcasting Mississippi Inc. Group owner: The River Group. (acq 6-19-2007; grpsl). Population served: 200,000 Natl. Network: USA, Jones Radio Networks, . Rgnl. Network: Ark. Radio Net. Natl. Rep: McGavren Guild,. Ark. Radio Net. Baraff, Koerner & Olender. Format: Adult contemp. News staff: one; News: 4 hrs wkly. Target aud: 18-49; multi-paycheck & spendable income. Spec prog: Farm 6 hrs, relg 6 hrs wkly. ♦Robert Marquitz, pres; James P. Karr Jr., VP, gen mgr; Linda McKee, opns mgr; Percy Kuhn, chief of engrg.

Lexington

WAGR-FM— June 1, 1990: 102.5 mhz; 6 kw. 328 ft TL: N33 09 06 W90 07 45. (CP: 12.5 kw, ant 459 ft.). Stereo. Hrs open: Box 369, 100 Radio Rd., 39095. Phone: (662) 834-1025. Phone: (662) 834-1254. Fax: (662) 834-1254.E-mail: class102@cablesouthmedia.net Licensee: Brad Maurice Cothran (acq 12-21-01). Format: Country, oldies. ♦Brad Maurice Cothran, gen mgr.

WXTN(AM)— Oct 23, 1959: 1000 khz; 5 kw-D. TL: N33 06 39 W90 02 21. (CP: COL Benton). Hrs open: Box 369, 39095. Phone: (662) 834-1025. Fax: (662) 834-1254.E-mail: class102@cablesouthmedia.net Licensee: Brad Maurice Cothran (acq 12-21-01). Population served: 500,000 Format: Gospel, Black. ♦Brad M. Cothran, gen mgr.

Liberty

WAZA(FM)— 1998: 107.7 mhz; 25 kw. Ant 328 ft TL: N31 17 12 W90 47 53. Hrs open: 215 E. Bay St., Magnolia, 39652. Phone: (601) 684-4116. Fax: (601) 684-4654.E-mail: sandow@telapak.net Licensee: Southwest Broadcasting Inc. Format: Oldies. Target aud: 18-30; adult contemp, retro 80s shows. ♦Charles Dowdy, gen mgr.

Long Beach

WJZD-FM— Mar 20, 1994: 94.5 mhz; 6 kw. 321 ft TL: N30 22 25 W89 06 38. Hrs open: 24 Box 6216, Gulfport, 39506. Secondary address:

10211 Southpark Dr., Gulfport 39503. Phone: (228) 896-5307. Fax: (228) 896-5703.E-mail: info@wjzd.com Web Site:www.wjzd.com Licensee: WJZD Inc. Population served: 300,000 Natl. Network: ABC, . Fletch, Heald & Hildreth. Wire Svc: AP Format: Urban adult contemp, news/talk. News staff: 2; News: 2 hrs wkly. Target aud: P 18-54. Spec prog: American Blues Network. ◆Rip Daniels, CEO & gen mgr; Danielle Jewett, opns dir.

Lorman

*WPRL(FM)— Oct 12, 1987: 91.7 mhz; 3 kw. 300 ft TL: N31 53 37 W91 08 54. Stereo. Hrs open: 6 AM-2 AM (M-F); 6 AM-midnight (S, Su) Box 269, 39096. Secondary address: Alcorn State Univ., 1000 Alcorn Dr. 39096. Phone: (601) 877-6290. Phone: (601) 877-6613. Fax: (601) 877-2213.E-mail: lljunag@hotmail.com Web Site:alconstateuniv.edu Licensee: Alcorn State University. Population served: 24,750 Natl. Network: PRI, NPR, AP Radio, . Format: Var/div. News staff: one; News: 23 hrs wkly. Target aud: General; African-American, rural, University faculty & students. ◆Lijuana Weir, opns mgr.

Louisville

*KOUI(FM)—Not on air, target date: unknown: 90.7 mhz; 6.3 kw vert. Ant 525 ft TL: N33 13 08 W89 08 51. Hrs open: 282 Country Estate Dr., Springer, OK, 73458. Phone: (580) 653-2777. Licensee: Ron Elmore Ministries Inc. ◆Ron Elmore, pres.

WLSM-FM— Apr 22, 1966: 107.1 mhz; 12.5 kw. Ant 466 ft TL: N33 07 20 W89 01 05. Stereo. Hrs open: 24 Box 279, 39339. Secondary address: 2142 Hwy. 14 E. 39339. Phone: (662) 773-3481. Fax: (662) 773-3482.E-mail: majic107@dixie-net.com Licensee: Harrison Communications Inc. Natl. Network: ABC, Jones Radio Networks, . Rgnl. Network: Miss. Net. Miss. News Net. Format: Adult contemp. Target aud: 18-54. ◆Phillip A. Harrison, pres, gen mgr, gen sls mgr; Stacy S. Harrison, stn mgr & progmg dir.

Lucedale

WRBE(AM)— Sept 3, 1960: 1440 khz; 5 kw-D. TL: N30 56 00 W88 36 20. (CP: TL: N30 55 58 W88 36 21). Hrs open: Box 827, 39452. Secondary address: 3276 Hwy. 198 W. 39452. Phone: (601) 947-8151. Fax: (601) 947-8152.E-mail: wrbe@mycallis.com Licensee: JDL Corp. (acq 2-24-98; $220,000 with co-located FM). Population served: 35,000 Natl. Rep: Dora-Clayton, Keystone (unwired net),. Format: Country. Target aud: General. ◆Larry Shirley, pres, gen mgr, progmg dir, news dir; Yvette Hillman, gen sls mgr; Bob Bonnell, farm dir.

WRBE-FM— April 1993: 106.9 mhz; 6 kw. Ant 258 ft TL: N30 55 58 W88 36 21. Hrs open: Box 827, 39452. Secondary address: 3276 Hwy. 198 W. 39452. Phone: (601) 947-8151. Fax: (601) 947-8152.E-mail: wbre@mycallis.com Web Site:www.wrbeamfm.com Licensee: JDL Corp. Natl. Network: Jones Radio Networks, Westwood One, . Miss. News Net. Format: Country. ◆Larry Shirley, gen mgr; Anthony Pugh, pub svc dir; Bob Bonnell, farm dir.

Lumberton

WZNF(FM)— Dec 10, 1983: 95.3 mhz; 50 kw. Ant 1,181 ft TL: N30 44 48 W89 03 30. Hrs open: 24 10250 Lorraine Rd., Gulfport, 39503. Phone: (228) 896-5500. Fax: (228) 896-0458.E-mail: patty@z95fm.com Web Site:www.z95fm.com Licensee: JMD Inc. (acq 1-11-00; $5 million). Format: Classic rock. ◆Morgan Dowdy, CEO, chmn & pres; Buddy Baylor, gen mgr.

Madison

WUSJ(FM)— Sept 16, 1966: 96.3 mhz; 100 kw. Ant 1,284 ft TL: N32 11 29 W90 24 22. Stereo. Hrs open: 265 High Point Rd., Ridgeland, 39157. Phone: (601) 956-0102. Fax: (601) 978-3890.E-mail: gwenr@radiopeople.net Web Site:www.us963.com Licensee: New South Communications Inc. (group owner; acq 8-24-99; $5 million). Format: Country. ◆Gwen Rakestraw, gen mgr.

Magee

WKXI-FM— Apr 11, 1970: 107.5 mhz; 98 kw. 952 ft TL: N32 15 28 W89 47 22. Stereo. Hrs open: 731 S. Pear Orchard Rd., Suite 27, Ridgeland, 39157. Phone: (601) 957-1300. Fax: (601) 956-0516.E-mail: production@wjmi.com Web Site:www.kixie107.com Licensee: Urban Radio II L.L.C. Group owner: Inner City Broadcasting (acq 8-25-2000; grpsl). Format: Urban contemp. Target aud: 25-54. ◆Kevin Webb, VP, gen mgr; Stan Branson, opns mgr.

WSJC(AM)— July 5, 1957: 810 khz; 50 kw-D, 500 w-N, DA-N. TL: N31 52 00 W89 41 35. Hrs open: 130 Radio Station Dr., 39111. Phone: (601) 849-5838. Fax: (601) 849-5838. Licensee: Witko Broadcasting L.L.C. (acq 12-3-98). Format: Christian. ◆Norm Wick, gen mgr.

Marietta

WXWX(FM)— 2008: 96.3 mhz; 3.9 kw. Ant 410 ft TL: N34 24 33 W88 32 24. Hrs open: 306 Troy St., Tupelo, 38804. Phone: (662) 680-1606. Licensee: George S. Flinn Jr. Natl. Network: ESPN Radio, . Format: Sports. ◆Russ Wilson, gen mgr.

Marion

WJDQ(FM)— Mar 15, 1990: 95.1 mhz; 50 kw. 606 ft TL: N32 26 08 W88 36 24. Stereo. Hrs open: 4307 Hwy. 39 N., Meridian, 39301. Phone: (601) 693-2381. Fax: (601) 485-2972. Licensee: CC Licenses LLC. Group owner: Clear Channel Communications Inc. (acq 3-16-2001; grpsl). Population served: 45,083 Format: Adult Contemporary. Target aud: 25-54. ◆Mark Maharrey, gen mgr; Ann Burton, sls dir.

McComb

WAKH(FM)— Oct 15, 1978: 105.7 mhz; 100 kw. 489 ft TL: N31 16 50 W90 27 05. Stereo. Hrs open: 24 Box 1649, 39649. Secondary address: 206 N. Front 39649. Phone: (601) 648-4116. Fax: (601) 684-4654. Format: Country. Target aud: General. ◆Charles Dowdy, gen mgr.

WAKK(AM)— Apr 18, 1948: 980 khz; 5 kw-D, 152 w-N. TL: N31 12 51 W90 27 42. Hrs open: 206 N. Front St., 39648. Secondary address: Drawer 1649 39648. Phone: (601) 684-4116. Fax: (601) 684-4654. Licensee: Southwest Broadcasting Inc. (group owner; (acq 9-86; $600,000 with co-located FM; 7-28-86). Population served: 22,000 Natl. Network: ABC, . Format: Gospel. Target aud: General. ◆Wayne Dowdy, pres; Charles Dowdy, gen mgr; David Hughes, progmg dir.

WAPF(AM)— Apr 25, 1975: 1140 khz; 1 kw-D. TL: N31 14 51 W90 25 14. Hrs open: Box 1649, 39649. Secondary address: 206 N. Front 39648. Phone: (601) 684-4116. Fax: (601) 684-4654. Licensee: Southwest Broadcasting Inc. (group owner; (acq 8-5-93; $600,000; 8-23-93). Population served: 11,969 Rgnl. Network: Miss. Net. Miss. News Net. Format: Sports. Target aud: General. ◆Charles Dowdy, gen mgr & gen sls mgr.

*WAQL(FM)— 1999: 90.5 mhz; 3.75 kw. 331 ft TL: N31 16 40 W90 26 56. Hrs open: American Family Radio, Box 3206, Tupelo, 38803. Phone: (662) 844-8888. Fax: (662) 842-6791. Web Site:www.afr.net Licensee: American Family Association. Group owner: American Family Radio Natl. Network: USA, . Format: Relg. ◆Marvin Sanders, gen mgr.

WHNY(AM)— 1939: 1250 khz; 5 kw-D, 1 kw-N, DA-N. TL: N31 16 07 W90 26 03. Hrs open: 24 1114 Hwy. 570 E., 39648. Phone: (601) 250-1250. Fax: (601) 250-1254.E-mail: whny@eaglepc.net Licensee: C.W.H. Broadcasting Inc. (acq 1952; $43,000). Natl. Network: ABC, . Format: News, talk, sports.

McLain

WXAB(FM)— January 1999: 96.9 mhz; 4 kw. Ant 400 ft TL: N31 06 56 W88 45 56. Stereo. Hrs open: Box 723, Wiggins, 39577. Licensee: Community Broadcasting Co. Inc. (acq 5-24-2006; $245,000 with WIGG(AM) Wiggins). Population served: 45,000 ◆Mike Self, gen mgr.

Meridian

WALT(AM)— 1946: 910 khz; 5 kw-D, 1 kw-N. TL: N32 23 37 W88 40 08. Stereo. Hrs open: 24 302 17th St., Suite C, 39302. Phone: (601) 693-3434. Fax: (601) 693-3439.E-mail: michelle@910talkradio.com Licensee: New South Communications Inc. (group owner; acq 4-1-57). Population served: 200,000 Natl. Rep: McGavren Guild,. Format: News/talk. Target aud: 35-64. ◆F.E. Holladay, pres; Paul Bucurel, gen mgr.

*WMAW-FM— December 1983: 88.1 mhz; 100 kw. 1,050 ft TL: N32 08 18 W89 05 36. Stereo. Hrs open: 24 3825 Ridgewood Rd., Jackson, 39211. Phone: (601) 432-6565. Fax: (601) 432-6806. Web Site:www.mpbonline.org Licensee: Mississippi Authority for Educational Television. Natl. Network: PRI, NPR, . Schwartz, Woods & Miller. Wire

Svc: AP Format: News and info, music. News staff: 7; News: 100 hrs wkly. Target aud: General. ◆Jay Woods, gen mgr; Jason Klein, opns mgr.

WMER(AM)— Oct 16, 1973: 1390 khz; 5 kw-D, 250 w-N. TL: N32 20 41 W88 41 32. Hrs open: 19 315 A St., 39301. Phone: (601) 693-9637. Fax: (601) 693-9637. Licensee: Michael H. Glass. (acq 1-9-98; $55,000). Population served: 279,000 Natl. Network: USA, . Format: Gospel, Christian. Target aud: 25-54; upscale, young families, non-working mothers.

WMOX(AM)— Dec 1, 1945: 1010 khz; 10 kw-D, 1 kw-N, DA-2. TL: N32 23 42 W88 39 28. Hrs open: 24 Box 5184, 39302. Phone: (601) 693-1891. Fax: (601) 693-1010. Fax: (601) 483-1010.E-mail: wmox@wmox.net Web Site:www.wmox.net Licensee: Magnolia State Broadcasting Inc. (acq 12-27-98; $125,000; 1-25-93). Population served: 45,083 Rgnl. Network: Miss. Net. Natl. Rep: Dora-Clayton,. Miss. News Net. Format: Talk/news, sports. News staff: one. Target aud: 25 plus; College educated with 30k plus annual income. Spec prog: Relg 8 hrs wkly. ◆Eddie Smith, pres, gen mgr; William T. Smith, VP & opns dir.

WMSO(FM)— February 1968: 101.3 mhz; 99 kw. Ant 581 ft TL: N32 18 43 W88 41 33. Stereo. Hrs open: 4307 Hwy. 39 N., 39301. Phone: (601) 693-2381. Fax: (601) 485-2972. Licensee: CC Licenses LLC. Group owner: Clear Channel Communications Inc. (acq 3-16-2001; grpsl). Population served: 101,300 Format: Country. ◆Mark Maharrey, gen mgr; Ann Burton, sls dir; Jack Edwards, progmg dir.

WNBN(AM)— Nov 1, 1987: 1290 khz; 2.5 kw-D, 90 w-N. TL: N32 21 42 W88 37 26. Hrs open: 18 266 23rd St., 39301. Phone: (601) 483-3401. Fax: (601) 483-3411. Licensee: Frank Rackley Jr. Population served: 45,000 Spec prog: Black, women's, business, inspirational. ◆Frank Rackley Jr., gen mgr & opns VP.

WOKK(FM)— August 1967: 97.1 mhz; 100 kw. 600 ft TL: N32 19 45 W88 41 26. Stereo. Hrs open: Prog sep from AM 302 17th St., Suite C , 39302. Phone: (601) 693-3434. Fax: (601) 693-3439.E-mail: michelle@910talkradio.com Web Site:www.wokk.com Population served: 300,000 Format: Country. Target aud: 25-54.

WUCL(FM)— 1994: 102.1 mhz; 800 w. Ant 610 ft TL: N32 21 51 W88 38 34. Hrs open: 3436 Hwy. 45 N., 39301. Phone: (601) 693-2661. Fax: (601) 483-0826.E-mail: wmmz@wokk.com Licensee: Mississippi Broadcasters L.L.C. (group owner; (acq 2-26-93; $243,500;3-22-93). Format: Classic country. ◆Clay Holladay, pres, gen mgr; Scott Stevens, opns mgr; Karen Bostick, sls dir; Scott Shepperd, chief of engrg.

WYHL(AM)— December 1957: 1450 khz; 1 kw-U. TL: N32 23 09 W88 41 36. Hrs open: 24/7 4307 Hwy. 39 N., 39301. Phone: (601) 693-2381. Fax: (601) 485-2972. Licensee: CC Licenses LLC. Group owner: Clear Channel Communications Inc. (acq 3-16-2001; grpsl). Population served: 45,083 Format: Urban Gospel. ◆Mark Maharrey, gen mgr; Ann Burton, sls dir; Sam Weaver, progmg dir.

Merigold

WKXY(FM)— 2003: 92.1 mhz; 6 kw. Ant 328 ft TL: N33 52 49 W90 42 24. Hrs open: 201 E. Sunflower Rd., Suite 5, Cleveland, 38732. Phone: (662) 843-3392. Fax: (662) 846-9002. Web Site:www.kix921.com Licensee: Delta Radio LLC. Format: Country. ◆Shawn McIntire, gen mgr; Dan Hawthorne, news dir.

Mississippi State

*WMAB-FM— December 1983: 89.9 mhz; 63 kw. 1,080 ft TL: N33 21 07 W89 08 56. Stereo. Hrs open: 24 3825 Ridgewood Rd., Jackson, 39211. Phone: (601) 432-6565. Fax: (601) 432-6806. Web Site:www.mpbonline.org Licensee: Mississippi Authority for Educational Television. Natl. Network: PRI, NPR, . Schwartz, Woods & Miller. Wire Svc: AP Format: News and info, music. News staff: 7; News: 100 hrs wkly. Target aud: General. ◆Marie Antoon, chmn; Jay Woods, gen mgr; Jason Klein, progmg mgr.

Monticello

WMLC(AM)— 1969: 1270 khz; 1 kw-D, 53 w-N. TL: N31 33 24 W90 08 06. Hrs open: 20 WMLC Rd., 39654. Phone: (601) 587-1270. Fax: (601) 587-2119.E-mail: wmlc@bellsouth.net Licensee: Walking by Faith Ministries Inc. (acq 6-28-2006; $50,000). Natl. Network: ESPN Radio, . Format: Sports. ◆Will Watson, gen mgr.

WRQO(FM)— Nov 19, 1990: 102.1 mhz; 50 kw. Ant 500 ft TL: N31 36 13 W90 12 26. Stereo. Hrs open: 24 Box 2016, Q102 Rd., 39654. Secondary address: Box 1084 39654. Phone: (601) 587-9363. Phone: (601) 587-7625. Fax: (601) 587-9401. Fax: (601) 835-5005.E-mail: country@wrqo-q102.com Licensee: TeleSouth Communications Inc. (group owner) (acq 6-20-2006; grpsl). Natl. Network: CBS, . Rgnl. Network: Miss. Net. Miss. News Net. Booth, Freret, Imlay & Tepper. Format: Talk. News: 15 hrs wkly. Target aud: 25-54. Spec prog: Farm one hr, relg 10 hrs wkly. ◆Stephen C. Davenport, pres; Marcus Rusty O'Neal, gen mgr; Randy Bullock, opns mgr.

Morton

WQST(AM)—See Forest

Moss Point

WBUV(FM)—Licensed to Moss Point. See Pascagoula-Moss Point

Mound Bayou

WZYQ(FM)—Licensed to Mound Bayou. See Cleveland

Natchez

*WASM(FM)— 2001: 91.1 mhz; 1 kw. Ant 482 ft TL: N31 29 10 W91 21 42. Hrs open: American Family Radio, Box 3206, Tupelo, 38803. Phone: (662) 844-8888. Fax: (662) 842-6791. Web Site:www.afr.net Licensee: American Family Association. Group owner: American Family Radio Natl. Network: USA, . Format: Relg. ◆Marvin Sanders, gen mgr.

WKSO(FM)— March 1993: 97.3 mhz; 1.45 kw. Ant 686 ft TL: N31 30 33 W91 24 19. Hrs open: Box 768, 39121. Secondary address: 2 O'Ferrall St. 39420. Phone: (601) 442-4895. Fax: (601) 446-8260. Licensee: Will Perk Broadcasting. Group owner: First Natchez Radio Group (acq 8-31-92; $36,000;9-21-92). Natl. Network: ABC, . Format: Adult contemp. ◆Margaret Perkins, gen mgr.

WMIS(AM)— May 18, 1941: 1240 khz; 1 kw-U. TL: N31 31 14 W91 23 09. Hrs open: 19 Box 1248, 39121. Secondary address: 20 E. Franklin St. 39120. Phone: (601) 442-2522. Fax: (601) 446-9918.E-mail: wmiswtyj@bellsouth.net Licensee: Natchez Broadcasting Co. Population served: 100,000 Natl. Network: American Urban, . Format: Black, gospel, blues. Target aud: General; Black. ◆Diana Ewing Nutter, pres; James B. Nutter, VP, gen mgr; Lijuna Weir, stn mgr.

WNAT(AM)— Dec 4, 1949: 1450 khz; 1 kw-U. TL: N31 33 24 W91 23 00. Stereo. Hrs open: 24 Box 768, 39121. Secondary address: 2 O'Ferral St. 39121. Phone: (601) 442-4895. Fax: (601) 446-8260. Web Site:www.wnat1450am.com Licensee: First Natchez Corp. Group owner: First Natchez Radio Group (acq 11-28-58). Population served: 48,000 Rgnl. Network: Miss. Net. Miss. News Net. Schwartz, Woods & Miller. Format: News/talk, sports. News staff: 2. Target aud: 25-54. Spec prog: Gospel 18 hrs wkly. ◆Marie Perkins, pres; Margaret Perkins, gen mgr, gen sls mgr, pub affrs dir; Mickey Alexander, progmg dir; Keith Sanders, news dir, chief of engrg; Brenda Green, traf mgr.

WQNZ(FM)— Mar 1, 1968: 95.1 mhz; 98 kw. 1,056 ft TL: N31 30 33 W91 24 19. (CP: ant 1,896 ft). Stereo. Hrs open: 24 Prog sep from AM Box 768, 39121. Phone: (601) 442-4895. Fax: (601) 446-8260. Web Site:www.wnat1450.com Licensee: First Natchez Corp. Population served: 150,000 Rgnl. Network: La. Net. La. Net. Format: Country. News staff: 2; News: 7 hrs wkly. Target aud: 25 plus.

WTYJ(FM)—See Fayette

New Albany

WNAU(AM)— Mar 27, 1955: 1470 khz; 500 w-U, DA-N. TL: N34 29 48 W89 00 52. Hrs open: Box 808, 38652. Phone: (662) 534-8133. Fax: (662) 538-4183. Licensee: MPM Investment Group (acq 11-9-2004). Population served: 10,000 Rgnl. Network: Miss. Net. Miss. News Net. Format: Oldies. Target aud: 25-54. Spec prog: Gospel. ◆Ricky McCollum, exec VP; Terry Cook, pres & gen mgr.

WTPO(FM)—Not on air, target date: unknown: 101.5 mhz; 6 kw. Ant 325 ft TL: N34 30 43 W89 03 02. Hrs open: 2801 Via Fortuna Dr., Suite 675, Austin, TX, 78746. Phone: (512) 329-5843. Web Site:www.matineemedia.com Licensee: Ace Radio Corp. ◆Stephen Hackerman, pres.

WWZD-FM— Mar 3, 1986: 106.7 mhz; 50 kw. 657 ft TL: N34 26 08 W88 57 35. Stereo. Hrs open: 24 Box 3300, Tupelo, 38803. Secondary address: 5026 Cliff Gookin Blvd., Tupelo, 38803. Phone: (662) 842-1067. Fax: (662) 842-0725.E-mail: rickstevens@clearchannel.com Licensee: Clear Channel Broadcasting Licenses Inc. Group owner: Clear Channel Communications Inc. (acq 12-19-00; grpsl). Population served: 174,600 Natl. Network: ABC, . Natl. Rep: Interep,. Format: Country. News staff: one. Target aud: 25-54. Spec prog: Southern gospel 4 hrs wkly. ◆Mark Maharrey, gen mgr; Rick Stevens, opns VP.

New Augusta

WZHL(FM)—Not on air, target date: unknown: 101.7 mhz; 5 kw. Ant 312 ft TL: N31 13 00.5 W89 10 56.8. Hrs open: 2801 Via Fortuna Dr., Suite 675, Austin, TX, 78746. Phone: (713) 528-2517. Licensee: Ace Radio Corp. ◆Stephen Hackerman, pres.

New Hebron

*WSMP(FM)—Not on air, target date: unknown: 91.9 mhz; 5 kw. Ant 269 ft TL: N31 37 24 W89 50 23. Hrs open: Box 768, Magee, 39111. Phone: (601) 849-9111. Fax: (601) 849-0582.E-mail: info@churchalive.net Licensee: Church Alive Inc. ◆Gene Amason II, gen mgr.

Newton

WHTU(FM)— Apr 17, 1975: 97.9 mhz; 11 kw. Ant 492 ft TL: N32 29 16 W89 01 23. Hrs open: 24 4307 Hwy. 39 N., Meridian, 39301-9704. Phone: (601) 693-2381. Fax: (601) 485-2972. Licensee: CC Licenses LLC. Group owner: Clear Channel Communications Inc. (acq 3-16-2001; grpsl). Format: Hip Hop & R&B. ◆Mark Maharrey, gen mgr; Ann Burton, sls dir; Sam Weaver, progmg dir.

Ocean Springs

WOSM(FM)— Feb 12, 1971: 103.1 mhz; 50 kw. Ant 459 ft TL: N30 24 34 W88 42 23. (CP: 100 kw, ant 679 ft. TL: N30 36 42 W88 39 17). Stereo. Hrs open: 24 4720 Radio Rd., 39564. Phone: (228) 875-9031. Fax: (228) 875-6461.E-mail: wosm@wosmradio.com Licensee: Charles H. Cooper. Population served: 300,000 Natl. Network: AP Radio, Salem Radio Network, . Wire Svc: AP Format: Southern gospel. News: 14 hrs wkly. Target aud: 18-54; family. ◆Charles H. Cooper, gen mgr; Phil Moss, opns dir & prom dir; Margaret Cooper, progmg dir.

WQYZ(FM)— Sept 1, 1992: 92.5 mhz; 6 kw. Ant 197 ft TL: N30 23 40 W88 53 41. Hrs open: 24 286 DeBuys Rd., Biloxi, 39531. Phone: (228) 388-2323. Fax: (228) 388-2362. Web Site:www.925fmthebeat.com Licensee: Capstar TX L.P. (acq 7-5-2005; $1,287,200). Natl. Rep: Clear Channel,. Wire Svc: AP Format: Rhythm and blues. News: one hr wkly. Target aud: 28-42; adult families/singles. ◆Reggie Bates, gen mgr; Walter Brown, opns mgr; Ron Hill, sls dir; Kelly Bennett, news dir; Sheila Taylor, traf mgr.

Olive Branch

KJMS(FM)— Mar 10, 1965: 101.1 mhz; 100 kw. Ant 561 ft TL: N35 13 22 W90 02 36. Stereo. Hrs open: 24 2650 Thousand Oaks Blvd., Suite 4100, Memphis, TN, 38118. Phone: (901) 259-1300. Fax: (901) 259-6449.E-mail: jeffreyjones@clearchannel.com Web Site:www.v10ll.com Licensee: CC Licenses LLC. Group owner: Clear Channel Communications Inc. Format: Urban contemp. Target aud: 18-49. ◆Tim Davies, VP; Ralph Salierno, sls dir; Franklin Gilbert Jr., mktg dir, mus dir; Eileen Collier, progmg dir; Alonzo Pendleton, chief of engrg.

Oxford

*WAVI(FM)— 2002: 91.5 mhz; 8.13 kw. Ant 574 ft TL: N34 11 57 W89 49 09. Hrs open: American Family Radio, Box 3206, Tupelo, 38803. Phone: (662) 844-8888. Fax: (662) 842-6791. Web Site:www.afr.net Licensee: American Family Association. Group owner: American Family Radio Natl. Network: USA, . Format: Christian. ◆Marvin Sanders, gen mgr.

*WMAV-FM— December 1983: 90.3 mhz; 100 kw. 1,240 ft TL: N34 17 26 W89 42 24. Stereo. Hrs open: 24 3825 Ridgewood Rd., Jackson, 39211. Phone: (601) 432-6565. Fax: (601) 432-6806. Web Site:www.mpbonile.org Licensee: Mississippi Authority for Educational Television. Natl. Network: PRI, NPR, . Schwartz, Woods & Miller. Wire Svc: AP Format: News and info, music. News staff: 7; News: 100 hrs wkly. Target aud: General. ◆Jay Woods, gen mgr; Jason Klein, opns mgr; Ty Warren, dev dir.

WOXD(FM)— October 1988: 95.5 mhz; 6 kw. 328 ft TL: N34 18 10 W89 31 25. Stereo. Hrs open: 24 302 Hwy 7 S., 38655-9799. Phone: (662) 533-4487. Phone: (662) 234-9631. Fax: (662) 236-5390.E-mail: production@bullseye955.com Web Site:www.bullseye955.com Licensee: Taylor Communications. (acq 1996). Population served: 35,000 Natl. Rep: Rgnl Reps,. Format: Classic Hits. Target aud: 25-54. Spec prog: Gospel 12 hrs wkly. ◆Jason T. Plunk, pres; Ron Cox, gen mgr.

WQLJ(FM)— Dec 31, 1984: 93.7 mhz; 25 kw. 328 ft TL: N34 20 05 W89 43 29. Stereo. Hrs open: 24 Box 1077, 38655-1077. Secondary address: 461 Hwy. 6 W. 38655. Phone: (662) 236-0093. Fax: (662) 234-5155.E-mail: q937@exceedtech.net Web Site:www.wqlj.com Licensee: TeleSouth Communications Inc. (group owner; acq 11-30-99; $1.4 million). Population served: 280,000 Rgnl. Network: Miss. Net. Miss. News Net. Fletcher, Heald & Hildreth. Format: Adult contemp. News staff: one; News: one hrs wkly. Target aud: 18-45. Spec prog: Contemp Christian 9 hrs wkly. ◆Steve Davenport, CEO & pres; Rick Mize, gen mgr; Jim Martin, opns dir; Judy McCormick, progmg dir, traf mgr; Bryan Hadley, news dir.

WWMS(FM)— Jan 1, 1969: 97.5 mhz; 100 kw. 1,000 ft TL: N34 10 05 W89 09 23. Stereo. Hrs open: Box 410, Tupelo, 38802. Secondary address: 2214 S. Gloster St., Tupelo 38801. Phone: (662) 842-7658. Fax: (662) 842-0197. Web Site:www.miss98.net Licensee: San-Dow Broadcasting Inc. (acq 5-10-85). Population served: 176,000 Format: Country. Target aud: General. Spec prog: Farm 2 hrs wkly. ◆Brenda Bebout, VP, gen mgr; Scott Bebout, stn mgr & mktg mgr.

Pascagoula

WHGO(FM)—Licensed to Pascagoula. See Pascagoula-Moss Point

WKNN-FM— December 1964: 99.1 mhz; 100 kw. 1,012 ft TL: N30 29 09 W88 42 53. Stereo. Hrs open: 24 286 Debuys, Biloxi, 39531. Phone: (228) 388-2323. Fax: (228) 388-2362. Web Site:www.k99fm.com Licensee: CC Licenses LLC. Group owner: Clear Channel Communications Inc. (acq 2-2-2004; grpsl). Population served: 300,000 Natl. Rep: Clear Channel,. Wire Svc: AP Format: Country. News staff: one; News: 6 hrs wkly. Target aud: 25-54. ◆Reggie Bates, gen mgr; Walter Brown, opns mgr; Ron Hill, sls dir; Kelly Bennett, news dir; Sheila Taylor, traf mgr.

*WPAS(FM)— Mar 25, 2004: 89.1 mhz; 60 kw. Ant 574 ft TL: N30 33 03 W88 27 06. Hrs open: American Family Radio, Box 3206, Tupelo, 33880. Phone: (662) 844-8888. Fax: (662) 842-6791. Web Site:www.afr.net Licensee: American Family Association. Group owner: American Family Radio. Population served: 585,000 Natl. Network: USA, . Format: Christian. ◆Marvin Sanders, gen mgr.

Pascagoula-Moss Point

WBUV(FM)—(Moss Point, June 1, 1964: 104.9 mhz; 33 kw. Ant 600 ft TL: N30 34 08 W88 22 48. Stereo. Hrs open: 24 286 Debuys Rd., Biloxi, 39531. Phone: (228) 388-2323. Fax: (228) 388-2362.E-mail: kippgreggory@clearchannel.com Web Site:www.newsradio1049fm.com Licensee: CC Licenses LLC. Group owner: Clear Channel Communications Inc. (acq 12-7-98; $1.4 million swap with WYOK(FM) Atmore, AL). Population served: 300,000 Natl. Network: Fox News Radio, Fox Sports, Premiere Radio Networks, . Natl. Rep: Clear Channel,. Cohn & Marks. Wire Svc: AP Format: News/talk. News staff: 4. Target aud: 25-54; men. ◆Reggie Bates, gen mgr; Ron Hill, sls dir; Kipp Greggory, progmg dir; Kelly Bennett, news dir; Sheila Taylor, traf mgr.

WHGO(FM)—(Pascagoula, June 1, 1976: 105.9 mhz; 25 kw. 312 ft TL: N30 22 05 W88 44 35. Stereo. Hrs open: 24 1909 E. Pass Rd., Suite D-11, Gulfport, 39507. Phone: (228) 388-2001. Fax: (228) 896-9736.E-mail: gofm@cableone.net Web Site:www.1059gofm.com Licensee: Monterey Licenses LLC. Group owner: Triad Broadcasting Co. LLC (acq 7-14-99; grpsl). Population served: 110,000 Natl. Network: ABC, . Natl. Rep: Katz Radio,. Format: Classic hits. Target aud: 25-54; male/female. ◆Buddy Birch, gen mgr; Jay Taylor, opns dir; Kenny Vest, opns mgr; Wayne Watkins, progmg dir.

WPMP(AM)— September 1951: 1580 khz; 5 kw-D, 51 w-N, DA-2. TL: N30 23 01 W88 32 07. Hrs open: 24 5115 Telephone Rd., Pascagoula, 39567. Phone: (228) 762-5683. Fax: (228) 762-1222. Licensee: Flagship Radio Group Inc. (acq 5-26-2005; $88,000). Format: Talk.

Pearl

WJNT(AM)— Oct 28, 1980: 1180 khz; 50 kw-D, 500 w-N. TL: N32 17 43 W90 06 54. Hrs open: 24 731 S. Pear Orchard Rd., Suite 27, Ridgeland, 39157. Phone: (601) 957-1300. Fax: (601) 956-0516.E-mail: contactus@wjnt.com Web Site:www.wjnt.com Licensee: Urban Radio

II L.L.C. (acq 10-23-2006; $1.65 million). Population served: 540,000 Natl. Network: ABC, Premiere Radio Networks, Talk Radio Network, . Natl. Rep: D & R Radio,. Latham & Watkins LLP. Format: News/talk. News staff: 0; News: 28 hrs wkly. Target aud: 35 plus; high income, college educated, home owners. ◆Charles M. Warfield, pres; Kevin Webb, gen mgr; Stan Carter, chief of opns.

WRXW(FM)— Nov 7, 1994: 93.9 mhz; 6 kw. 328 ft TL: N32 17 52 W89 59 56. Stereo. Hrs open: 24 222 Beasley Rd., Jackson, 39206. Phone: (601) 957-3000. Fax: (601) 956-0370.E-mail: brad.stevens@bybradio.com Web Site:www.rock939.com Licensee: Backyard Broadcasting Mississippi LLC Group owner: Backyard Broadcasting LLC (acq 5-31-2002; $4,830,000 with WWJK(FM) Jackson). Population served: 250,000 Natl. Network: ABC, Westwood One, . Rgnl rep: Christal. Fletcher, Heald & Hildreth. Format: Active Rock. News staff: one; News: one hr wkly. Target aud: 35 plus. ◆Barry Drake, pres, gen mgr; Jason Williams, gen mgr; Brad Stevens, progmg dir.

Petal

WZLD(FM)— January 1986: 106.3 mhz; 3 kw. Ant 400 ft TL: N31 23 02 W89 10 44. Stereo. Hrs open: 24 6555 Hwy. 98 W., Suite 8, Hattiesburg, 39402. Phone: (601) 296-9800. Fax: (601) 296-9838.E-mail: contact@wizldfm.com Web Site:www.wild1063.com Licensee: CC Licenses LLC. Group owner: Clear Channel Communications Inc. (acq 12-19-2000; grpsl). Natl. Network: CNN Radio, . Miss. News Net. Format: Hip hop, rhythm and blues. News: 4 hrs wkly. Target aud: 25-54; upscale, educated & professional. Spec prog: Sports 3 hrs wkly. ◆Michael Comfort, gen mgr; Jackson Walker, opns mgr.

Philadelphia

WHOC(AM)— July 31, 1948: 1490 khz; 1 kw-U. TL: N32 45 52 W89 07 48. Hrs open: Box 26, 1016 W. Beacon St., 39350. Phone: (601) 656-1490. Fax: (601) 656-1491.E-mail: wwslfm@yahoo.com Licensee: WHOC Inc. (acq 1-31-89; $300,000; 2-20-89). Population served: 6,274 Rgnl. Network: Miss. Net. Miss. News Net. Format: Adult standard, talk. Target aud: General. Spec prog: Farm 2 hrs wkly. ◆Leah Jarrell, gen mgr; Joe Vines, opns mgr, gen sls mgr, progmg dir, traf mgr; Rex Smith, chief of engrg.

WWSL(FM)— Jan 1, 1981: 102.3 mhz; 4.9 kw. Ant 364 ft TL: N32 43 35 W89 05 56. Stereo. Hrs open: Box 26, 39350. Secondary address: 1016 W. Beacon St. 39350. Phone: (601) 656-7102. Fax: (601) 656-1491. Licensee: H & GC Inc. Population served: 40,000 Natl. Network: Westwood One, . Rgnl. Network: Miss. Net. Miss. News Net. Format: Adult contemp.

Picayune

WMTI(FM)— November 1973: 106.1 mhz; 28 kw. Ant 659 ft TL: N30 31 17 W90 01 12. Stereo. Hrs open: 24 201 St. Charles, Suite 201, New Orleans, LA, 70170. Phone: (504) 581-7002. Fax: (504)-566-4857. Web Site:www.martini1061.com Licensee: Citadel Broadcasting Co. (acq 1-3-2006; $7 million). Population served: 1,000,000 Format: Oldies. News staff: 2; News: 2 hrs wkly. Target aud: 18-45; young professionals. ◆Dave Siebert, gen mgr; Steven Kline, gen sls mgr; Jim Hanzo, progmg dir; Bill Major, chief of engrg.

WRJW(AM)— October 1949: 1320 khz; 5 kw-D, 75 kw-N. TL: N30 31 06 W89 38 41. Hrs open: 5a-10p Box 907, 39466. Secondary address: 2438 Hwy. 43 S. 39466. Phone: (601) 798-4835. Fax: (601) 798-9755.E-mail: wrjw@charter.net Web Site:www.wrjwradio.com Licensee: Pearl River Communications Inc. (acq 8-2-91). Population served: 36,000 Natl. Network: ABC, . Rgnl. Network: Miss. Net., ABC. Miss. News Net. Format: Country/southern gospel. News staff: 2; News: 10 hrs wkly. Target aud: 18-54; contemp country listeners. Spec prog: Black 8 hrs, farm 6 hrs, relg 16 hrs, sports 4 hrs wkly. ◆Delores Wood, gen mgr; Denise Wilson, opns dir, prom mgr, traf mgr; Phil Moss, mus dir; Dusty Dearman, news dir.

Pickens

WZNO(FM)— July 20, 1980: 105.9 mhz; 23 kw. Ant 735 ft TL: N32 38 53 W89 59 20. Stereo. Hrs open: 731 S. Pear Orchard, Suite 27, Ridgeland, 39157. Phone: (601) 957-1300. Fax: (601) 956-0516.E-mail: production@wjmi.com Licensee: Urban Radio II L.L.C. Group owner: Inner City Broadcasting (acq 2000; grpsl). Natl. Network: ESPN Radio, . Format: Sports. ◆Kevin Webb, gen mgr; Bill Wilson, prom dir.

Pontotoc

WSEL(AM)— Nov 30, 1962: 1440 khz; 890 w-D, DA. TL: N34 15 10 W88 57 36. Stereo. Hrs open: Box 3788, Tupelo, 38803. Phone: (662)

489-0297. Fax: (662) 488-9735. Licensee: Ollie Collins Jr. (acq 5-5-92; $46,500 with co-located FM; 6-1-92). Format: Urban gospel. ◆Ollie Collins Jr., gen mgr, opns mgr & progmg dir; Jerry Campbell, chief of engrg.

WSEL-FM— Jan 1, 1966: 96.7 mhz; 3 kw. 299 ft TL: N34 15 10 W88 57 36. Stereo. Hrs open: Prog sep from AM Box 3788, 38803. Phone: (662) 489-0297. Fax: (662) 489-9735. Format: Urban gospel.

Poplarville

WRPM(AM)— 1963: Stn currently dark. 1530 khz; 10 kw-D, 1 kw. TL: N30 48 55 W89 30 24. Hrs open: 6 AM-6 PM Box 3788, 38803. Phone: (601) 795-4900. Fax: (601) 795-0277.E-mail: wrpm@wrpm.com Licensee: Dowdy & Dowdy Partnership (acq 3-87; $2.25 million with co-located FM; 12-15-86). Population served: 500,000 ◆Thomas Vaughn, gen mgr & chief of engrg.

WZKX(FM)—(Bay St. Louis, Feb 14, 1966: 107.9 mhz; 92 kw. 1,460 ft TL: N30 44 48 W89 03 30. Hrs open: Box 2639, Gulfport, 39505. Phone: (228) 896-5500. Fax: (228) 896-3724.E-mail: info@usasingles.com/wrpm.htm Web Site:www.usasingles.com/wrpm.htm Format: Country. ◆Morgan Dowdy, gen mgr.

Port Gibson

*WATU(FM)— 1999: 89.3 mhz; 40 kw vert. Ant 384 ft TL: N32 07 56 W90 45 29. Hrs open: Box 3206, American Family Radio, Tupelo, 38803. Phone: (662) 844-8888. Fax: (662) 842-6791. Web Site:www.afr.net Licensee: American Family Association. Group owner: American Family Radio Natl. Network: USA, . Format: Relg. ◆Marvin Sanders, gen mgr.

WRTM-FM— July 16, 1999: 100.5 mhz; 44 kw. Ant 492 ft. TL: N31 59 38 W90 58 15. Stereo. Hrs open: 24 Box 820583, Vicksburg, 39182. Secondary address: 1901 N. Frontage Rd. #8, Vicksburg 39180. Phone: (601) 636-7944. Fax: (601) 373-1343.E-mail: radioair@bellsouth.net Licensee: Commander Communications Corp. (acq 10-15-99). Format: Urban adult contemp. Target aud: 25-54. ◆Carl Haynes, gen mgr, gen sls mgr; Marty Hart, opns mgr.

Potts Camp

WCNA(FM)— Oct 1, 1995: 95.9 mhz; 14 kw. Ant 436 ft TL: N34 35 51 W89 06 12. Stereo. Hrs open: 24 Box 2116, Radio Bldg., 1241 Cliff Gookin Blvd., Tupelo, 38803. Phone: (662) 842-7625. Fax: (662) 842-9568. Licensee: Olvie E. Sisk. Group owner: Air South Radio Inc. Format: Classic rock. News: 14 hrs wkly. ◆Gene Sisk, pres; Fred Blalock, stn mgr; Ivous Sisk, opns VP.

Prentiss

WCJU-FM— 2002: 104.9 mhz; 2.8 kw. Ant 436 ft TL: N31 31 56 W89 56 17. Hrs open: Box 472, Columbia, 39429. Phone: (601) 736-8889. Fax: (601) 736-2617.E-mail: wcju@wcjufm.com Licensee: Sunbelt Broadcasting Corp. (group owner) Format: Classic Hits. ◆Tommy McDaniel, gen mgr; Steve Mercier, opns mgr.

WJDR(FM)— June 1, 1982: 98.3 mhz; 6 kw. 325 ft TL: N31 29 43 W89 53 33. Stereo. Hrs open: 24 Box 351, 37 S. High School Ave., Columbia, 39429. Phone: (601) 731-2298. Phone: (601) 792-2056. Fax: (601) 792-2057. Licensee: Sunbelt Broadcasting Corp. (group owner; acq 12-1-85). Population served: 75,000 Natl. Network: ABC, . Rgnl. Network: Miss. Net. Miss. News Net. Format: Hot country. News: 20 hrs wkly. Target aud: 25-54. Spec prog: Black 5 hrs wkly. ◆Thomas F. McDaniel, pres; Jody Fortenberry, stn mgr.

Quitman

*WLKO(FM)— July 31, 1981: 98.9 mhz; 25 kw. Ant 315 ft TL: N32 03 51 W88 43 27. Stereo. Hrs open: 24
Rebroadcasts KLVR(FM) Santa Rosa, CA 100%.
2351 Sunset Blvd., Suite 170-218, Rocklin, CA, 95765. Phone: (916) 251-1600. Fax: (916) 251-1650. Web Site:www.klove.com Licensee: Educational Media Foundation. (acq 4-29-2005; $500,000). Natl. Network: K-Love, . Format: Contemp Christian. ◆Richard Jenkins, pres; Mike Novak, VP; Keith Whipple, dev dir; David Pierce, progmg mgr; Ed Lenane, news dir; Sam Wallington, engrg dir; Karen Johnson, news rptr.

WQMS(AM)— Feb 2, 1968: Stn currently dark. 1500 khz; 1 kw-D. TL: N32 03 51 W88 43 27. Hrs open: 901 N.E. 173rd St., Miami, FL,

33162. Phone: (305) 770-1961. Licensee: Stephen C. Hellinger (acq 4-4-2006; $12,500). Population served: 2,702 Format: Sports. ◆Simcha Hellinger, gen mgr.

Redwood

WVBG-FM— 2005: 105.5 mhz; 1.95 kw. Ant 430 ft TL: N32 23 22 W90 48 34. Hrs open: 1102 Newitt Vick Dr., Vicksburg, 39183. Phone: (601) 883-0848. Licensee: Lendsi Radio LLC. Format: Oldies. ◆Lina H. Jones, gen mgr.

Richton

WXHB(FM)— 1995: 96.5 mhz; 6 kw. Ant 328 ft TL: N31 21 01 W88 59 11. Hrs open: Box 6408, Laurel, 39441. Phone: (601) 649-0095. Phone: (601) 544-0095. Fax: (601) 649-8199. Licensee: Blakeney Communications Inc. (group owner; acq 3-27-03; $650,000). Format: Solid gospel. ◆Larry Blakeney, gen mgr.

Ridgeland

WIIN(AM)— Dec 1, 1984: Stn currently dark. 780 khz; 5 kw-D. TL: N32 25 36 W90 12 19. Hrs open: Sunrise-sunset 265 Highpoint Dr., 39157. Phone: (601) 956-0102. Fax: (601) 978-3980.E-mail: frontdesk@us963.com Licensee: New South Radio Inc. Group owner: New South Communications Inc. (acq 11-10-94; $750,000 with WLIN(FM) Gluckstadt; 12-12-94). ◆Gwen Rakestraw, gen mgr.

Ripley

WCSA(AM)— 1995: Stn currently dark. 1260 khz; 500 w-D, 38 w-N. TL: N34 43 15 W88 56 40. Hrs open: 4598 Appleville St., Memphis, TN, 38109. Licensee: Keyboard Broadcasting Communication.

WSKK(FM)— June 1, 1979: 102.3 mhz; 3.5 kw. Ant 433 ft TL: N34 42 35 W88 50 36. Stereo. Hrs open: 24 Box 572, 107 E. Spring St., 38663. Phone: (662) 837-1023. Phone: (662) 837-2990. Fax: (662) 837-2994.E-mail: classicradiofm@aol.com Licensee: Kudzu Communications Inc. (acq 7-23-98). Population served: 125,000 Rgnl rep: Miss. Net. Format: Classic hits. News: 2 hrs wkly. Spec prog: Relg 2 hrs, gospel 6 hrs, bluegrass 2 hrs wkly. ◆Scott Peters, pres & gen mgr.

Saltillo

WWMR(FM)— 2008: 102.9 mhz; 12.5 kw. Ant 466 ft TL: N34 24 33 W88 32 24. Hrs open: 306 Troy St., Tupelo, 38804. Phone: (662) 680-1606. Web Site:www.supertalkms.com/stations/wwmr.php Licensee: George S. Flinn III. Format: Talk. ◆Russ Wilson, gen mgr.

Sardis

KBUD(FM)— 2005: 102.1 mhz; 4 kw. Ant 403 ft TL: N34 22 33 W89 45 52. Hrs open:
Simulcast with WHBQ-FM Germantown, TN 100%.
6080 Mt. Moriah Ext., Memphis, TN, 38115. Phone: (901) 375-9324. Fax: (901) 375-0041.E-mail: info@flinn.com Web Site:www.flinn.com Licensee: George S. Flinn Jr. Format: Top-40. ◆Keith Parnell, gen mgr; Edrick Kearney, stn mgr.

Senatobia

*WMSB(FM)— Jan 4, 1971: 88.9 mhz; 100 kw. Ant 380 ft TL: N34 37 39 W90 01 27. Stereo. Hrs open: 24 Drawer 2440, Tupelo, 38803. Phone: (662) 844-5036. Fax: (662) 842-7798.E-mail: info@afa.net Web Site:www.afr.net Licensee: American Family Association. (acq 4-13-2007; $2 million). Population served: 600,000 Natl. Network: American Family Radio, . Format: Christian. ◆Donald E. Wildmon, chmn.

WSAO(AM)— Aug 8, 1962: 1140 khz; 5 kw-D. TL: N34 36 56 W89 56 09. Hrs open: 5 AM-5 PM Box 190, 38668-0190. Secondary address: 15763 Hwy. 4 E. 38668. Phone: (662) 562-4445. Fax: (662) 562-4445. Licensee: Jesse C. Ross and Earnestine A. Ross. (acq 3-95). Population served: 25,000 Rgnl. Network: Miss. Net. Miss. News Net. Format: Christian, gospel, spiritual music. News staff: one. Target aud: General. ◆Jesse Ross, gen mgr & stn mgr.

Southaven

WAVN(AM)— June 4, 1990: 1240 khz; 580 w-U. TL: N34 58 57 W90 00 45. Hrs open: 24 1336 Brookhaven Dr., 38671. Phone: (662) 393-8056. Fax: (662) 393-8066. Licensee: Arlington Broadcasting Co. Inc. (acq 8-31-92; $115,000; 9-21-92). Rgnl. Network: Miss. Net. Miss. News Net. Format: Traditional gospel. News: 7 hrs wkly. Target aud: 20-50; general. ◆Walter Stevens, gen mgr & progmg dir.

Starkville

*****WJZB(FM)—** 1999: 88.7 mhz; 430 w. Ant 243 ft TL: N33 27 47 W88 49 01. Hrs open: American Family Radio, Box 3206, Tupelo, 38803. Phone: (662) 844-8888. Fax: (662) 842-6791. Web Site:www.afr.net Licensee: American Family Association Inc. Group owner: American Family Radio (acq 10-8-97). Natl. Network: USA, . Format: Relg. ◆Marvin Sanders, gen mgr.

WKOR(AM)— July 5, 1968: 980 khz; 1 kw-D. TL: N33 28 44 W88 44 40. Hrs open: 200 6th St. N., Suite 200, Columbus, 39701. Phone: (662) 327-1183. Fax: (662) 328-1122.E-mail: info@K949.net Web Site:k949.net Licensee: Cumulus Licensing Corp. Group owner: Cumulus Media Inc. (acq 2-14-02). Population served: 45,500 Format: ESPN/The Team. Target aud: General; business professionals. ◆Cole Evans, gen mgr & gen sls mgr; CJ Jones, mktg mgr.

WLZA(FM)— (Eupora, Sept 1, 1978: 96.1 mhz; 50 kw. 500 ft TL: N33 28 18 W89 13 36. Stereo. Hrs open: 24 Box 884, 1105 A Stark Rd, 39760. Phone: (662) 324-9601. Fax: (662) 324-7400.E-mail: wlza@961wlza.com Licensee: Metro Radio. Group owner: Air South Radio Inc. Format: Adult contemp. Target aud: General. ◆Olvie E. Sisk, pres; Carolyn Jackson, gen mgr.

WMSU(FM)— Sept 13, 1979: 92.1 mhz; 1.1 kw. 500 ft TL: N33 25 49 W88 45 17. Stereo. Hrs open: 608 Yellow Jacket Dr., 39759. Phone: (662) 338-5424. Fax: (662) 338-5436.E-mail: wmsuproduction@urbanradio.fm Web Site:www.power92fm.net Licensee: Urban Radio Licenses LLC. (acq 12-7-2000). Format: Mainstream urban. Target aud: 25-54. ◆James Alexander, opns mgr; Kevin Wagner, pres & progmg dir.

*****WMSV(FM)—** March 1994: 91.1 mhz; 14.1 kw. Ant 449 ft TL: N33 25 49 W88 45 17. Hrs open: Box 6210, Mississippi State University, 39762. Phone: (662) 325-8034. Fax: (662) 325-8037.E-mail: wmsv@msstate.edu Web Site:www.wmsv.msstate.edu Licensee: Mississippi State University. Format: Alternative. ◆Steve Ellis, gen mgr.

WMXU(FM)— July 15, 1968: 106.1 mhz; 40 kw. Ant 502 ft TL: N33 17 38 W88 39 27. Stereo. Hrs open: 24 Prog sep from AM 200 6th St. N., Suite 205, 39701. Phone: (662) 327-1183. Fax: (662) 328-1122.E-mail: info@mix1061.com Web Site:mix1061.com Population served: 120,000 Format: Adult urban. ◆Bobby Holiday, progmg dir.

WSSO(AM)— Nov 8, 1948: 1230 khz; 1 kw-U. TL: N33 27 09 W88 49 15. Hrs open: 200 6th St. N., Suite 205, Columbus, 39701. Phone: (662) 327-1183. Fax: (662) 328-1122. Licensee: Cumulus Licensing Corp. Group owner: Cumulus Media Inc. (acq 1998; grpsl). Population served: 120,000 Rgnl. Network: Miss. Net. Natl. Rep: Keystone (unwired net),. Miss. News Net. Rgnl rep: Allied Radio Partners. Format: Sports. Spec prog: Black 12 hrs wkly. ◆C.J. Jones, VP.

State College

WQJB(FM)— Not on air, target date: unknown: 104.5 mhz; 25 kw. Ant 328 ft TL: N33 24 14 W88 55 21. Hrs open: 6080 Mt. Moriah, Memphis, TN, 38115. Phone: (901) 375-9324. Fax: (901) 375-0041.E-mail: info@flinn.com Web Site:www.flinn.com Licensee: George S. Flinn Jr. Format: Classic country. ◆Melanie Henkin-Booth, gen mgr.

Stonewall

WKZB(FM)— 1998: 106.9 mhz; 2.55 kw. 508 ft TL: N32 10 48 W88 40 22. Hrs open: 24 Box 5797, Meridian, 39302. Phone: (601) 693-2661. Fax: (601) 483-0826.E-mail: wmlv@wokk.com Licensee: Mississippi Broadcasters L.L.C. (group owner). Latham & Watkins. Format: Adult contemp. Target aud: 25-54. ◆Clay Holladay, pres, gen mgr; Scott Stevens, opns mgr, progmg mgr; Karen Bostick, sls dir; Van Mac, news dir & pub affrs dir; Scott Shepperd, chief of engrg.

Sumrall

WFMM(FM)— 1998: 97.3 mhz; 1 kw. 200 ft TL: N31 21 18 W89 31 19. Hrs open:

Rebroadcasts WFMN(FM) Flora 100%.
611 Ridgewood Rd., Jackson, 39211. Phone: (601) 957-1700. Fax: (601) 956-5228.E-mail: apeterson@telesouth.com Web Site:www.supertalkms.com Licensee: TeleSouth Communications Inc. (group owner; acq 1999; $200,000). Format: News/talk info. ◆Paul Gallo, gen mgr.

WGDQ(FM)— 2005: 93.1 mhz; 25 kw. Ant 302 ft TL: N31 22 58 W89 23 43. Hrs open: 704 River St., Hattiesburg, 39401. Phone: (601) 544-1941. Fax: (601) 544-1947. Licensee: Unity Broadcasters. ◆Victor Floyd, gen mgr.

Taylorsville

WBBN(FM)— Mar 20, 1985: 95.9 mhz; 100 kw. Ant 731 ft TL: N31 38 03 W89 28 35. Stereo. Hrs open: Box 6408, Laurel, 39441. Phone: (601) 649-0095. Phone: (601) 544-0095. Fax: (601) 649-8199.E-mail: b95@b95country.com Web Site:www.b95country.com Licensee: Blakeney Communications Inc. (group owner) Format: Country. Target aud: 25-54. ◆Larry Blakeney, CEO, pres; Randall A. Blakeney, VP; David Blakeney, gen mgr; Debbie Blakeney, gen sls mgr.

Tchula

WGNG(FM)— 2001: 106.3 mhz; 7.1 kw. Ant 499 ft TL: N33 18 06 W90 07 31. Hrs open: 503 Ione St., Greenwood, 38930. Phone: (662) 453-1646. Fax: (662) 453-7002.E-mail: wgnlbooth@bellsouth.net Licensee: Team Broadcasting Co. Inc. Format: Urban contemporary. ◆Reuben C. Hughes, gen mgr.

Tunica

WIVG(FM)— 1998: 96.1 mhz; 4.1 kw. Ant 807 ft TL: N34 43 36 W90 09 43. Hrs open: 3654 Park Ave., Memphis, TN, 38111. Phone: (901) 454-9948. Fax: (901) 454-1027. Licensee: Flinn Broadcasting Corp. (acq 10-20-99). Format: Hispanic. ◆Carmen Reyes, gen mgr.

Tupelo

*****WAFR(FM)—** Aug 31, 1991: 88.3 mhz; 75 kw. Ant 492 ft TL: N34 28 28 W88 43 41. Stereo. Hrs open: 24 American Family Radio, Box 3206, 38803. Phone: (662) 844-8888. Phone: (662) 844-8893. Fax: (662) 842-6791. Web Site:www.afr.net Licensee: American Family Association. Population served: 250,000 Natl. Network: American Family Radio, . Format: Christian. News staff: one; News: 3 hrs wkly. Target aud: 30-60; conservative Christian. ◆Don Wildmon, gen mgr.

*****WAJS(FM)—** 1996: 91.7 mhz; 23 kw. Ant 505 ft TL: N33 55 35 W88 39 46. Hrs open: Box 3206, American Family Radio, 38803. Phone: (662) 844-8888. Fax: (662) 842-6791. Web Site:www.afr.net Licensee: American Family Association. Group owner: American Family Radio Natl. Network: USA, . Format: Christian. ◆Marvin Sanders, gen mgr.

*****WAQB(FM)—** 1997: 90.9 mhz; 9.5 kw. Ant 426 ft TL: N34 28 28 W88 43 41. Hrs open: American Family Radio, Box 3206, 38803. Phone: (662) 844-8888. Fax: (662) 842-6791. Web Site:www.afr.net Licensee: American Family Association. Group owner: American Family Radio Natl. Network: USA, . Format: Classic gospel. ◆Don Wildmon, gen mgr.

WELO(AM)— May 15, 1944: 580 khz; 1 kw-D, 500 w-N, DA-2. TL: N34 18 10 W88 42 17. Hrs open: 24 2214 S. Gloster Ave., 38802. Phone: (662) 842-7658. Fax: (662) 842-0197. Licensee: JMD Inc. Population served: 25,471 Format: Classic country. Target aud: 45 plus. ◆Brenda Bebout, gen mgr; Scott Bebout, mktg mgr; Jeff Covington, progmg mgr.

WFTA(FM)— (Fulton, Aug 19, 1976: 101.9 mhz; 100 kw. 560 ft TL: N34 15 46 W88 32 24. Stereo. Hrs open: 24 Box 2116, 38803. Secondary address: 1241 Cliff Gookin Blvd., Radio Bldg. 38801. Phone: (662) 842-7625. Fax: (662) 842-9568. Licensee: Air South Radio Inc. (group owner) Population served: 325,000 Format: Adult contemp. News: 4 hrs wkly. Target aud: 14-44. ◆Gene Sisk, pres; Olvie E. Sisk, gen mgr; Fred Blalock, stn mgr, gen sls mgr.

WKMQ(AM)— Aug 25, 1972: 1060 khz; 1 kw-D, 33 w-N. TL: N34 15 19 W88 41 46. Hrs open: 24 Box 3300, 38803. Secondary address: 5026 Cliff Gookin Blvd. 38801. Phone: (662) 842-1067. Fax: (662) 842-0725.E-mail: rickstevens@clearchannel.com Licensee: Capstar TX L.P. Group owner: Clear Channel Communications Inc. (acq 12-19-2000; grpsl). Population served: 62800 Format: Talk. Target aud: 35-54. ◆Mark Maharrey, gen mgr; Cynthia South, gen sls mgr; Rick Stevens, opns mgr & progmg dir; Jerry Mathis, chief of engrg.

WTUP(AM)— October 1953: 1490 khz; 1 kw-U. TL: N34 15 19 W88 41 46. Hrs open: 24 Box 3300, 38803. Secondary address: 5026 Cliff Gookin Blvd. 38801. Phone: (662) 842-1067. Fax: (662) 842-0725.E-mail: markmaharrey@clearchannel.com Web Site:www.wtup1490.com Licensee: Capstar TX L.P. Group owner: Clear Channel Communications Inc. (acq 12-19-2000; grpsl). Population served: 174,600 Rgnl. Network: Miss. Net. Natl. Rep: Interep,. Miss. News Net. Gurman, Blask & Freedman. Format: Sports. News staff: one; News: 12 hrs wkly. Target aud: 25-54; men. ◆Mark Maharrey, gen mgr; Rick Stevens, opns dir.

WZLQ(FM)— September 1968: 98.5 mhz; 100 kw. 951 ft TL: N34 10 05 W89 09 23. Stereo. Hrs open: Rock 2214 S. Gloster St., 38802. Phone: (662) 842-7658. Fax: (662) 842-0197. Web Site:www.z985.net Licensee: JMD Inc. Population served: 150,000 Format: Adult contemp. Target aud: 25-54. ◆Brenda Bebout, gen mgr; Scott Bebout, mktg mgr.

Tylertown

WFCG(FM)— 2005: 107.3 mhz; 3.2 kw. Ant 457 ft TL: N31 04 39 W90 04 46. (CP: 2.2 kw, ant 550 ft). Hrs open: Box 1649, McComb, 39648. Phone: (985) 839-3782. Fax: (985) 839-3783. Licensee: Southwest Broadcasting Inc. Format: Southern gospel. ◆C. Wayne Dowdy, pres; William Giles, gen mgr.

WTYL(AM)— Feb 8, 1969: 1290 khz; 1 kw-D. TL: N31 07 50 W90 08 13. Hrs open: 11 930 Union Rd., 39667. Phone: (601) 876-2105. Fax: (601) 876-9551. Licensee: Tylertown Broadcasting Co. Population served: 20,000 Format: Country. Spec prog: Farm 6 hrs wkly. ◆Carolyn Dillon, pres, gen mgr; Gail Ratcliff, progmg dir & traf mgr.

WTYL-FM— Apr 9, 1970: 97.7 mhz; 3 kw. 145 ft TL: N31 07 50 W90 08 13. Hrs open: 24 Dups AM 90% 930 Union Rd., 39667. Phone: (601) 876-2105. Fax: (601) 876-9551. ◆Gail Ratcliff, traf mgr.

Union

WZKS(FM)— October 1995: 104.1 mhz; 16 kw. 535 ft TL: N32 29 53 W88 53 20. (CP: 19 kw). Hrs open: 4307 Hwy. 39 N., Meridian, 39301. Phone: (601) 693-2381. Fax: (601) 485-2972. Licensee: CC Licenses LLC. Group owner: Clear Channel Communications Inc. (acq 3-16-2001; grpsl). Format: Urban contemp. ◆Ron Harper, gen mgr.

University

WUMS(FM)— Apr 10, 1989: 92.1 mhz; 2.9 kw. Ant 476 ft TL: N34 24 12 W89 24 13. Stereo. Hrs open: 24 201 Bishop Hall, Oxford, 38677. Phone: (662) 915-5503. Fax: (662) 915-5703.E-mail: manager@myrebelradio.com Web Site:http://www.myrebelradio.com/ Licensee: Student Media Center of the University of Mississippi. Natl. Network: Premiere Radio Networks, CNN Radio, . Wire Svc: AP Format: Alternative, hot adult contemp. News: 2 hrs wkly. Target aud: 18-24. Spec prog: International 2 hrs, women one hr, the 80s 2 hrs wkly. ◆Stephen Goforth, pres; Jason Caviness, stn mgr.

Utica

WJXN-FM— Aug 28, 1990: 100.9 mhz; 39 kw. Ant 551 ft TL: N32 03 13 W90 20 23. Stereo. Hrs open: 24 5700 W. Oaks Blvd., Rocklin, 95765. Phone: (800) 434-8400. Fax: (800) 372-0888. Web Site:www.klove.com Licensee: Flinn Broadcasting Corp. (acq 12-31-97). Natl. Network: USA, . Wire Svc: NWS (National Weather Service) Format: Contemp Christian. Target aud: 25 plus. ◆George S. Flinn, pres; Karen Porter, stn mgr; Steve Poston, stn mgr & progmg dir.

Vicksburg

WBBV(FM)— Aug 21, 1989: 101.3 mhz; 13 kw. Ant 394 ft TL: N32 20 42 W90 52 55. Stereo. Hrs open: 1601 E. North Frontage Rd., 39180. Phone: (601) 638-0101. Phone: (601) 636-2340 (business). Fax: (601) 638-0869.E-mail: spots@river101.com Licensee: Debut Broadcasting Mississippi Inc. Group owner: New South Communications Inc. (acq 8-27-2008; $900,000). Population served: 65,000 Format: Country. Target aud: 24-54. ◆Robert Marquitz, pres; Betsy McEachern, gen mgr; Ron Anderson, opns mgr; Deloris Dorbeck, gen sls mgr.

WJKK(FM)— Mar 19, 1966: 98.7 mhz; 100 kw. 950 ft TL: N32 12 29 W90 24 50. Stereo. Hrs open: 24 265 Highpoint Dr., Ridgeland, 39157. Phone: (601) 956-0102. Fax: (601) 978-3980.E-mail: frontdesk@us963.com Web Site:www.mix987.com Licensee: New South Radio Inc. Group owner: New South Communications Inc. (acq

1-89; $1.1 million; 1-23-89). Format: Soft adult contemp. News staff: one; News: one hr wkly. Target aud: 18-49; upper income & educ. ◆Gwen Rakestraw, gen mgr.

WQBC(AM)— 1931: 1420 khz; 5 kw-D, 500 w-N. TL: N32 19 56 W90 51 00. Hrs open: 24 3190 Porter's Chapel Rd., 39180. Secondary address: Box 820483 39182. Phone: (601) 636-1108. Fax: (601) 631-0087. Licensee: Grace Media International LLC (acq 3-20-2001; $100,000). Population served: 26,091 Natl. Network: ESPN Radio, . Format: Sports talk. ◆Jerry Rushins, gen mgr, gen sls mgr; Mike Corley, prs & opns dir.

WSTZ-FM—Licensed to Vicksburg. See Jackson

WVBG(AM)— 1948: 1490 khz; 1 kw-U. TL: N32 21 27 W90 51 29. Hrs open: 24 1102 Newitt Vick Dr., MA, 39183. Phone: (601) 883-0848. Licensee: Commander Communications Corp. (acq 5-11-99). Population served: 35,000 Format: News/talk. News: 168 hrs. wkly. Target aud: 25 plus. ◆Mark Jones, gen mgr.

Walnut

WLRC(AM)— June 21, 1982: 850 khz; 963 w-D. TL: N34 56 46 W88 52 44. Hrs open: Box 37, 38683. Secondary address: 7760 Hwy. 72 E. 38683. Phone: (662) 223-4071. Fax: (662) 223-4072. Web Site:www.wlrcradio.com Licensee: B.R. & Martha S. Clayton. (acq 11-83; $100,000; 11-28-83). Rgnl. Network: Miss. Net. Miss. News Net. Format: Christian. News: 14 hrs wkly. ◆Scotti Clayton, gen mgr; Robin Clayton, mus dir.

Water Valley

WTNM(FM)— Aug 1, 1996: 105.5 mhz; 4.7 kw. Ant 371 ft TL: N34 12 45 W89 44 49. Stereo. Hrs open: 24 Box 1077, Oxford, 38655. Secondary address: 461 Hwy. 6 W., Oxford 38655. Phone: (662) 236-0073. Fax: (662) 234-5155.E-mail: supertalk1055@exceedtech.net Web Site:www.supertalkms.com Licensee: TeleSouth Communications Inc. (group owner; acq 3-17-00). Population served: 89500 Miss. News Net. Format: Talk. News staff: one; News: 3 hrs wkly. Target aud: 25 plus. Spec prog: Christian, contemp 4 hrs wkly. ◆Rick Mize, gen mgr; Jim Martin, opns mgr; Steve Davenport, CEO & engrg VP.

Waynesboro

WABO(AM)— Sept 11, 1954: 990 khz; 1 kw-D. TL: N31 40 48 W88 40 34. Hrs open: Box 507, 39367. Secondary address: 6746 Hwy. 184 W. 39367. Phone: (601) 735-4331. Fax: (601) 735-4332.E-mail: waboradio@c-gate.net Web Site:www.wabo105.com Licensee: Martin Broadcasting Inc. (acq 12-18-61). Population served: 16,000 Format: Country, soul. ◆Jamie Heathcock, progmg dir; Lisa Singley, traf mgr; Nancy N. Martin, pres, gen mgr, gen sls mgr & women's int ed.

WABO-FM— June 13, 1973: 105.5 mhz; 3 kw. 145 ft TL: N31 40 48 W88 40 34. Stereo. Hrs open: Dups AM 50% Box 507, 39367. Secondary address: 6746 Hwy. 184 W. 39367. Phone: (601) 735-4331. Fax: (601) 735-4332.E-mail: waboradio@c-gate.net Web Site:www.wabo105.com Population served: 35,000 Format: Hot country.

*WZKM(FM)—Not on air, target date: unknown: 89.7 mhz; 67 kw. Ant 581 ft TL: N31 50 09 W88 52 21. Hrs open: Americian Family Radio, Box 3206, Tupelo, 38803. Phone: (662) 844-8888. Fax: (662) 842-6791. Web Site:www.afr.net Licensee: American Family Radio. Group owner: American Family Radio (acq 1-24-03). Natl. Network: USA, . Format: Relg. ◆Don Wildmon, gen mgr.

West Point

WKBB(FM)— Apr 14, 1974: 100.9 mhz; 10 kw. Ant 515 ft TL: N33 40 43 W88 48 18. Stereo. Hrs open: 413 N. Forest St., 39773. Phone: (662) 494-1450. Fax: (662) 494-9762.E-mail: wkbb@telesouth.com Web Site:www.supertalk.fm Population served: 150,000 Format: News/talk. Target aud: 35-54. ◆Debbie Smothers, gen mgr.

WROB(AM)— September 1947: 1450 khz; 1 kw-U. TL: N33 36 30 W88 39 15. Hrs open: 413 N. Forest St., 39773. Phone: (662) 494-1450. Fax: (662) 494-9762.E-mail: wkbb@telesouth.com Licensee: TeleSouth Communications Inc. (group owner; acq 12-5-2003; $900,000 with co-located FM). Population served: 20,000 Rgnl. Network: Miss. Net. Miss. News Net. Format: Oldies. Target aud: General. Spec prog: Gospel 2 hrs wkly. ◆Debbie Smothers, gen mgr.

Wiggins

WIGG(AM)— February 1968: 1420 khz; 5 kw-D. TL: N30 52 18 W89 09 00. Hrs open: 24 Box 723, 39577. Secondary address: 959 N. Magnolia Dr. 39577. Phone: (601) 928-7281. Fax: (601) 528-5011. Licensee: Community Broadcasting Co. Inc. (acq 5-24-2006; $245,000 with WXAB(FM) McLain). Population served: 6,000 Rgnl. Network: Miss. Net. Miss. News Net. Format: Country. News: 5 hrs wkly. Target aud: 25-54; general. Spec prog: Gospel, sports. ◆A.R. Byrd, gen mgr.

Winona

WONA(AM)— Oct 25, 1958: 1570 khz; 1 kw-D. TL: N33 27 52 W89 44 11. Hrs open: 1006 S. Applegate St., 38967. Phone: (662) 283-1570. Fax: (662) 283-1520.E-mail: hawg95@cablesouthmedia.net Licensee: Southern Electronics Co. Population served: 25,521 Format: Country. ◆Johnny Pettit, pres; Seth Kent, opns mgr, gen sls mgr, progmg dir, chief of engrg; Sharon Kent, VP, gen mgr, news dir & traf mgr.

WONA-FM— Jan 4, 1976: 95.1 mhz; 3 kw. 328 ft TL: N33 29 34 W89 45 17. Stereo. Hrs open: 1006 S. Applegate St., 38967. Phone: (662) 283-1570. Fax: (662) 283-1520.E-mail: hawg95@cablesouthmedia.net Licensee: Southern Electronics Co.

Yazoo City

WJNS-FM— Dec 13, 1968: 92.1 mhz; 20 kw. 300 ft TL: N32 50 48 W90 23 18. Stereo. Hrs open: 1405 Enchanted Dr., 39194. Phone: (662) 746-5921. Fax: (662) 746-5996. Licensee: Family Worship Center Church Inc. (group owner; acq 6-16-2004; $350,000). Population served: 84,355 Format: Relg. Target aud: 25-54. Spec prog: Farm 16 hrs, weather 16 hrs wkly.

*WYAZ(FM)— 2005: 89.5 mhz; 25 kw vert. Ant 518 ft TL: N32 48 04 W89 56 32. Hrs open: American Family Radio, Drawer 2440, Tupelo, 38801. Phone: (662) 844-8888. Fax: (662) 842-6791. Licensee: American Family Association. Group owner: American Family Radio (acq 5-13-2004). ◆Marvin Sanders, gen mgr.

Missouri

Albany

KAAN-FM—See Bethany

*KGTR(FM)—Not on air, target date: unknown: 89.9 mhz; 22 kw. Ant 423 ft TL: N40 06 26 W94 02 57. Hrs open: 282 Country Estate Dr., Springer, OK, 73458. Phone: (580) 653-2777. Licensee: Ron Elmore Ministries Inc. ◆Ron Elmore, pres & gen mgr.

Arcadia

KTNX(FM)— 2006: 103.9 mhz; 450 w. Ant 932 ft TL: N37 34 23 W90 41 35. Hrs open: PO Box 305, Farmington, 63640. Phone: (573) 701-9590. Fax: (573) 701-9696. Licensee: Southern Star Broadcasting of Missouri LLC. (acq 5-8-2008; grpsl). Format: CHR. ◆Chip Miller, pres; Joel Jordan, VP.

Arnold

*KGNA-FM— Mar 26, 1987: 89.9 mhz; 150 w horiz, 84 w vert. Ant 131 ft TL: N38 26 14 W90 23 24. Hrs open: 24 Rebroadcasts KGNV(FM) Washington 100%. Box 187, Washington, 63090. Phone: (636) 239-0400. Fax: (636) 239-4448.E-mail: info@goodnewsvoice.org Web Site:www.goodnewsvoice.org Licensee: Missouri River Christian Broadcasting Inc. (acq 10-5-99). Population served: 150,000 Natl. Network: Moody, Salem Radio Network, . Format: News/talk, Southern gospel, Inspirational. News: 14 hrs wkly. Target aud: 20-70:; inquisitive, conservative, liberal, philosophical. ◆James C. Goggan, pres.

Asbury

KWXD(FM)— October 1993: 103.5 mhz; 16 kw. Ant 413 ft TL: N37 23 44 W94 40 42. Hrs open: Box 383, 412 Locust St., Pittsburg, KS, 66762. Phone: (620) 232-5993. Fax: (620) 232-5550. Licensee: My Town Media Inc. (group owner) Lauren A. Colby. Format: New rock. ◆Lance Sayler, pres & gen mgr.

Ash Grove

KSGF-FM— Mar 1, 1994: 104.1 mhz; 21.5 kw. Ant 354 ft TL: N37 15 22 W93 41 14. Hrs open: 2330 W. Grand St., Springfield, 65781. Phone: (417) 865-6614. E-mail: ccannon@journalbroadcastgroup.com Web Site:www.ksgf.com Licensee: Journal Broadcast Corp. Group owner: Journal Communications Inc. (acq 11-26-2003; $5 million with KZRQ-FM Mount Vernon). Format: News, talk. ◆Rex Hansen, gen mgr; Chris Cannon, opns mgr.

Ashland

KQQL(FM)— October 1993: 106.1 mhz; 69 kw. Ant 958 ft TL: N38 45 01 W92 33 31. Stereo. Hrs open: 24 503 Old 63 N., Columbia, 65201. Phone: (573) 449-4141. Fax: (573) 449-7770.E-mail: info@q1061.com Web Site:www.q1061.com Licensee: Cumulus Licensing LLC. Group owner: Cumulus Media Inc. (acq 4-26-2004; grpsl). Population served: 260,000 Natl. Rep: Katz Radio,. Format: Top-40. ◆D. Larimer, VP & progmg dir.

Aurora

KSWF(FM)— Feb 19, 1968: 100.5 mhz; 33 kw. 600 ft TL: N37 05 39 W93 31 05. Stereo. Hrs open: 1856 S. Glenstone, Springfield, 65804. Phone: (417) 890-5555. Fax: (417) 890-5050.E-mail: studio@1005thewolf.com Web Site:www.1005thewolf.com Licensee: Clear Channel Broadcasting Licenses Inc. Group owner: Clear Channel Communications Inc. (acq 10-10-2000; grpsl). Population served: 5,359 Format: Country. Target aud: 18-54; general. ◆Paul Windisch, gen mgr; Paul Kelley, opns mgr.

KSWM(AM)— Oct 19, 1961: 940 khz; 1 kw-D, 30 w-N. TL: N36 59 39 W93 42 58. Hrs open: 24 126 S. Jefferson Ave., 65605. Phone: (417) 678-0416. Fax: (417) 678-4111.E-mail: kswm@radiotalon.com Web Site:www.talonbroadcasting.com Licensee: Falcon Broadcasting Inc. Group owner: Community Service Radio Group (acq 9-1-2005; $417,500). Population served: 250,000 Natl. Network: CNN Radio, USA, . Format: News/talk. News staff: 2; News: 168 hrs wkly. Target aud: General. ◆DeWayne Gandy, gen mgr, engrg mgr; Bill Lewis, opns mgr; Lance Matlock, gen sls mgr; Dan Kesterson, progmg dir.

Ava

KKOZ(AM)— 1968: 1430 khz; 500 w-U. TL: N36 55 48 W92 39 19. Hrs open: Dups FM 100% Box 386, 65608. Phone: (417) 683-4191.E-mail: news@kkoz.com Web Site:www.kkoz.com Licensee: Corum Industries Inc. (Acq 7-97; $11,200). Population served: 50,000

KKOZ-FM— 1990: 92.1 mhz; 4 kw. 380 ft TL: N36 55 48 W92 39 19. Hrs open: 6 AM-10 PM Box 386, 65608. Phone: (417) 683-4191.E-mail: news@kkoz.com Web Site:www.kkoz.com Licensee: Corum Industries Inc. Rgnl. Network: Missourinet. Missourinet Format: News/talk, farm. News: 15 hrs wkly. Target aud: 45 plus; farm oriented. ◆Joe Corum, pres, gen mgr; Art Corum, opns mgr, prom mgr, progmg dir; Vickie Corum, traf mgr.

Ballwin

*KYMC(FM)— February 1978: Stn currently dark. 89.7 mhz; 120 w. Ant 171 ft TL: N38 37 23 W90 32 01. Stereo. Hrs open: Box 4038, 16464 Burkhardt Pl., Chesterfield, 63006. Phone: (636) 532-6515. Phone: (636) 532-3100. Fax: (636) 530-7928.E-mail: nhall@ymcastlouis.org Web Site:ymcastlouis.org Licensee: YMCA of Greater St. Louis-W. County Branch. Womble, Carlyle, Sandridge & Rice.

Bethany

KAAN(AM)— Dec 3, 1983: 870 khz; 1 kw-D. TL: N40 15 23 W94 09 23. Hrs open: Sunrise-sunset Box 447, 1212 South 25th St., 64424. Phone: (660) 425-6380. Fax: (660) 425-8148.E-mail: stuartj@regionalradio.com Web Site:www.northwestmoinfo.com Licensee: Cameron/Bethany Radio Co. LLC. Group owner: Shepherd Group (acq 8-8-2007; grpsl). Rgnl. Network: Missourinet. Missourinet Format: Country, news. News staff: 3; News: 10 hrs wkly. Target aud: 25 plus. Spec prog: Farm 10 hrs, relg one hr wkly. ◆Doug Schmitz, gen mgr, sls dir; Denise Fritzel, gen sls mgr; Stuart Johnson, progmg dir; Stuart Johsnon, news dir; Gregg Richwine, chief of engrg.

KAAN-FM— Oct 27, 1978: 95.5 mhz; 50 kw. 360 ft TL: N40 15 23 W94 09 23. Hrs open: 19 Dups AM 90% Box 447, 1212 South 25th St., 64424. Phone: (660) 425-6380. Fax: (660) 425-8148.E-

stuartj@regionalradio.com Web Site:www.northwestmoinfo.com Licensee: Cameron/Bethany License Co. LLC News staff: 3. ♦Doug Schmitz, gen mgr.

Birch Tree

KBMV-FM— 1983: 107.1 mhz; 25 kw. Ant 328 ft TL: N36 56 03 W91 43 07. Stereo. Hrs open: 24 Box 107, West Plains, 65775. Phone: (417) 255-0427. Fax: (417) 255-2907.E-mail: info@todaysbesthits.com Web Site:www.todaysbesthits.com Licensee: Mountain Lakes Broadcasting Corp. (acq 9-8-2003; $175,000). Format: Hot adult contemp. ♦Connie P. Feifer, gen mgr.

Bismarck

KHCR(FM)— 2005: 99.5 mhz; 4.2 kw. Ant 798 ft TL: N37 38 52 W90 37 33. Hrs open: 627 State Hwy. 47, Bonne Terre, 63628. Phone: (573) 358-7700.E-mail: info@joyfmonline.org Licensee: Joseph W. & Donna M. Bollinger. ♦Joseph W. Bollinger, gen mgr.

Blue Springs

KCWJ(AM)— Feb 2, 1984: 1030 khz; 5 kw-D, 500 w-N, DA-2. TL: N39 02 44 W94 14 06. Hrs open: 24 4240 Blue Ridge Blvd., Suite 530, Kansas City, 64133. Phone: (816) 313-0049. Fax: (816) 313-1036.E-mail: info@kcwj.org Web Site:www.kcwj.org Licensee: KCWJ Inc./dba Christian Broadcasting Associates L.P. (acq 1-13-99; $750,000). Population served: 1,800.000 Natl. Network: Salem Radio Network, . Natl. Rep: Salem,. Rgnl rep: PioneerSports Sales Miller & Neely, P.C. Wire Svc: Metro Weather Service Inc. Format: Christian,traditional christian. News: 5 hrs wkly. Target aud: 18-49; family oriented Christian audience. ♦Ken Ball, gen mgr.

Bolivar

KYOO(AM)— November 1961: 1200 khz; 1 kw-D. TL: N37 41 50 W93 25 45. Hrs open:
Simulcast with KYOO-FM Halfway 100%.
205 N. Pike Ave., 65613-1550. Phone: (417) 326-5259. Phone: (417) 326-5257. Fax: (417) 326-5900.E-mail: contact@kyooradio.com Web Site:www.kyooradio.com Licensee: KYOO Communications KYOO Communications (acq 7-29-97; $52,000 assumption of note). Population served: 500,000 Rgnl. Network: Brownfield Wire Svc: NWS (National Weather Service) Format: Country. News staff: one; News: 12 hrs. wkly. Target aud: 10-72 yrs. Spec prog: Farm 3 hrs, gospel 2 hrs wkly. ♦Ann Paris, VP; Stephen Paris, pres, gen mgr, gen sls mgr & progmg dir.

Bonne Terre

KDBB(FM)— September 1989: 104.3 mhz; 790 w. 630 ft TL: N37 48 04 W90 33 44. Hrs open: 24 Box 36, Park Hills, 63601. Phone: (573) 431-1000. Fax: (573) 431-0850.E-mail: radio@b104fm.com Web Site:www.b104fm.com Licensee: MKS Broadcasting Inc. (acq 9-6-94; $315,753;10-17-94). Natl. Network: Westwood One, . Format: Rock. News staff: one; News: 20 hrs wkly. Target aud: 25-55. ♦M.L. Steinmetz, pres; Larry D. Joseph, gen mgr; Kelly Valle, gen sls mgr; Greg Camp, progmg mgr; Gib Collins Jr., news dir, pub affrs dir.

Boonville

KCLR-FM— Oct 1, 1974: 99.3 mhz; 33.2 kw. 590 ft TL: N38 46 34 W92 32 45. Stereo. Hrs open: 24 3215 Lemone Industrial Blvd., Suite 200, Columbia, 65201. Phone: (573) 875-1099. Fax: (573) 875-2439. Web Site:www.clear99.com Licensee: Zimmer Broadcasting Co. Format: Country. News staff: 3; News: 3 hrs wkly. Target aud: 25-54. ♦Carla Lieble, gen mgr; Cynthia Schreen, gen sls mgr; Olive Humphrey, prom dir; Teresa Davis, gen mgr & progmg dir; Shelley Tucker, news dir; Drew Haines, chief of engrg.

KWJK(FM)— Sept 15, 1999: 93.1 mhz; 7.2 kw. Ant 413 ft TL: N38 56 31 W92 34 32. Hrs open: 24 1600 Radio Hill Rd., 65233. Phone: (573) 441-9310.E-mail: kwrt@classicnet.net Web Site:www.931jack.fm Licensee: Bittersweet Broadcasting Inc. Population served: 150,000 Format: Adult hits.

KWRT(AM)— Aug 11, 1953: 1370 khz; 1 kw-D, 84 w-N. TL: N38 56 44 W92 34 30. Hrs open: 24 1600 Radio Hill Rd., 65233. Phone: (660) 882-6686. Fax: (660) 882-6688.E-mail: kwrt@classicnet.net Licensee: Big Country of Missouri Inc. Population served: 150000 Natl. Network: Jones Radio Networks, . Rgnl. Network: Missourinet. Missourinet Format: Country. News staff: one; News: 5 hrs wkly. Target aud: 35 plus; general. Spec prog: Farm 5 hrs wkly. ♦Dick Billings, pres; Matt Billings, gen mgr, gen sls mgr; Pat Billings, opns mgr; Ted Bleil, news dir; Mike Mcgowan, chief of engrg; Sharon Korte, sports cmtr.

Bowling Green

KPVR(FM)— Aug 1, 1975: 94.1 mhz; 7.5 kw. Ant 592 ft TL: N39 15 45 W91 04 09. Stereo. Hrs open: 24 13358 Manchester Rd., Suite 100, Des Peres, 63131. Phone: (314) 909-8569. Fax: (314) 835-9739.E-mail: info@joyfmonline.org Web Site:www.joyfmonline.org Licensee: Four Him Enterprises L.L.C. (acq 5-15-2001; $725,000 with co-located AM). Population served: 121,582 Format: Contemp Christian. ♦Sandi Brown, gen mgr; Greg Cassidy, progmg dir.

Branson

***KLFC(FM)—** July 1988: 88.1 mhz; 1.8 kw. Ant 390 ft TL: N36 33 06 W93 14 17. Stereo. Hrs open: 24 205 W. Atlantic, 65616-0921. Phone: (417) 334-5532. Fax: (417) 335-2437.E-mail: 881fm@klfcradio.com Web Site:www.klfcradio.com Licensee: Mountaintop Broadcasting Inc. (acq 6-1-01). Population served: 25,000 Natl. Network: USA, . Format: Christian (AC). News staff: one; News: 7 hrs wkly. Target aud: Adults 25-50. ♦Herb Smith, pres, gen mgr, stn mgr; Vicky Smith, opns dir; Darin Ahrends, news dir.

KOMC(AM)— Dec 21, 1956: 1220 khz; 1 kw-D, 53 w-N. TL: N36 37 12 W93 12 40. Hrs open: 24
Rebroadcasts KDMC-FM Kimberling City 95%.
202 Courtney St., 65616. Phone: (417) 334-6003. Phone: (417) 334-6012. Fax: (417) 334-7141.E-mail: krzk@krzk.com Web Site:www.hometownradioonline.com Licensee: KOMC-KRZX LLC. Group owner: Orr & Earls Broadcasting Inc. (acq 11-21-86; $335,000). Population served: 42,000 Natl. Network: CBS, . Rgnl. Network: Missourinet. Missourinet Format: Christian, relg, southern gospel. News staff: 3; News: 10 hrs wkly. Target aud: 40 plus. ♦Charles C. Earls, pres; Scottie Earls, gen mgr, stn mgr, opns mgr; Steve Willoughby, stn mgr & mktg mgr; Scott McCaulley, progmg dir; Morris James, news dir; Greg Pyron, chief of engrg.

***KOZO(FM)—** 1998: 89.7 mhz; 150 w horiz, 20 kw vert. Ant 426 ft TL: N36 33 04 W93 14 36. Stereo. Hrs open: 24 Box 1924, Tulsa, OK, 74101-1924. Phone: (918) 455-5693. Phone: (417) 339-3388. Fax: (417) 339-3410.E-mail: mail@oasisnetwork.org Web Site:www.oasisnetwork.org Licensee: Creative Educational Media Corp. Inc. Natl. Network: USA, . Rgnl rep: Rgnl Reps Format: Relg. Target aud: General. ♦David Ingles, pres & gen mgr.

KRZK(FM)— Mar 1, 1971: 106.3 mhz; 5.7 kw. 672 ft TL: N36 43 52 W93 10 03. (CP: 100 kw, ant 564 ft.). Stereo. Hrs open: 24 Prog sep from AM 202 Courtney St., 65616. Phone: (417) 334-6003. Phone: (417) 334-6012. Fax: (417) 334-7141.E-mail: krzk@krzk.com Web Site:hometowndailynews.com Natl. Network: ABC, . Format: Country. News staff: 3; News: 7 hrs wkly. Target aud: 25-54; Branson & loc tourists. ♦Charles C. Earles, CEO; Steve Willoughby, mktg dir; Scott Earls, engrg mgr, chief of engrg.

Brookfield

KFMZ(AM)— Feb 14, 1956: 1470 khz; 500 w-D, 20 w-N, DA. TL: N39 50 26 W93 04 52. Hrs open: 24
Rebroadcasts KZBK-FM Brookfield.
107 S. Main, 64628. Phone: (660) 258-3383. Fax: (660) 258-7307.E-mail: kzbk@kzbkradio.com Web Site:www.kzbkradio.com Licensee: Best Broadcasting Inc. Group owner: Best Broadcast Group (acq 6-14-93; $70,000 with co-located FM; 6-28-93). Population served: 54,910 Natl. Network: ABC, . Bryan Cave. Format: Hot adult contemp. News: 4 hrs wkly. Target aud: 18-49; men & women with spendable income. ♦Phillip A. Chirillo, pres; Dale A. Palmer, VP, gen mgr.

KZBK(FM)— September 1981: 96.9 mhz; 50 kw. Ant 492 ft TL: N39 54 32 W93 04 34. Stereo. Hrs open: 24 107 S. Main, 64628. Phone: (660) 258-3383. Fax: (660) 258-7307. Licensee: Best Broadcasting Inc. Population served: 70,000 Format: Hot adult contemp. ♦Phil Chirillo, pres; Dale A. Palmer, VP; Dale A. Palmer, gen mgr.

Brookline

KQRA(FM)— May 28, 2002: 102.1 mhz; 4.9 kw. Ant 361 ft TL: N37 12 39 W93 13 42. Stereo. Hrs open: 24 319 B E. Battlefield, Springfield, 65807. Phone: (417) 886-5677. Fax: (417) 886-2155.E-mail: info@q1021.fm Web Site:www.q1021.fm Licensee: MW SpringMo Inc. Group owner: The Mid-West Family Broadcast Group. Population served: 285,500 Natl. Rep: Eastman Radio,. Davis Wright Tremaine, LLP. Format: Rock. Target aud: 18-49; active adults. ♦Rick McCoy, pres, gen mgr; Mary Fleenor, opns mgr; Malcolm Hukriede, gen sls mgr; Keith Abercrombie, rgnl sls mgr; Kristen Bergman, progmg dir; Shadow Williams, mus dir; Nichole Buckner, traf mgr.

Buffalo

KBFL-FM— 1965: 99.9 mhz; 3.1 kw. Ant 476 ft TL: N37 31 14 W93 06 14. Stereo. Hrs open: 24 Box 1385, 65622. Secondary address: 304 S. Pine 65622. Phone: (417) 345-2412. Fax: (417) 345-2410.E-mail: info@kbfl.com Web Site:www.radiospringfield.com Licensee: Meyer-Baldridge Inc. Group owner: Meyer Communications Inc. (acq 6-1-2000; $550,000). Population served: 30,000 Natl. Network: NBC Radio, . Rgnl. Network: Missourinet. Missourinet Fletcher, Heald & Hildreth. Format: Nostalgia, news/talk, sports. News staff: one; News: 15 hrs wkly. Target aud: 34-54; male-female adults. Spec prog: Gospel 3 hrs wkly. ♦Kenneth E. Meyer, pres; Bill Jones, gen mgr, gen sls mgr; Rob Evans, progmg dir; R.J. McCalister, news dir; Dale Blankenship, chief of engrg.

Bunker

KHZA(FM)—Not on air, target date: unknown: 106.3 mhz; 25 kw. Ant 328 ft TL: N37 34 48 W91 19 38. Hrs open: 5331 Mt. Alifan Dr., San Diego, CA, 92111. Phone: (858) 277-4991. Fax: (858) 277-1365. Licensee: Horizon Christian Fellowship. (acq 2-9-2006; grpsl). ♦Mike MacIntosh, pres.

Butler

KMAM(AM)— May 11, 1962: 1530 khz; 500 w-D. TL: N38 14 56 W94 19 18. Hrs open: 16 800 E. Nursery St., 64730. Phone: (660) 679-4191. Fax: (660) 679-4193.E-mail: news@fm92radio.com Web Site:www.921kmoe.com Licensee: Bates County Broadcasting Co. Population served: 249,000 Natl. Network: ABC, . Rgnl. Network: Brownfield. Brownfield Format: Country. News staff: one; News: 15 hrs wkly. Target aud: General; family. Spec prog: Farm/Abc World News/Local News. ♦Melody A. Thornton, pres & gen mgr.

KMOE(FM)— Jan 15, 1975: 92.1 mhz; 4.7 kw. Ant 148 ft TL: N38 14 56 W94 19 18. Stereo. Hrs open: 16 Dups AM 100% 800 E. Nursery St., 64730. Phone: (660) 679-4191. Fax: (660) 679-4193. Web Site:www.921knoe.com

Cabool

***KCVY(FM)—** 2003: 89.9 mhz; 10.5 kw. Ant 495 ft TL: N37 05 32 W92 03 10. Stereo. Hrs open: 24
Rebroadcasts KCVO-FM Camdenton 100%.
c/o Spirit FM Radio, Box 800, Camdenton, 65020-0800. Phone: (573) 346-3200. Fax: (573) 346-1010. Web Site:www.spiritfm.org Licensee: Lake Area Educational Broadcasting Foundation. (acq 7-11-2006). Population served: 75,000 Natl. Network: Salem Radio Network, . Format: Comtemp Christian. News: one hr wkly. Target aud: 25-45. ♦James J. McDermott, pres & gen mgr.

KOZX(FM)— May 1978: 98.1 mhz; 3 kw. Ant 220 ft TL: N37 07 58 W92 08 04. Stereo. Hrs open: 800 N. Hubbard, Mountain Grove, 65711. Phone: (417) 926-4650. Fax: (417) 926-7604. Licensee: Ozark Media Inc. (group owner; (acq 5-1-2007; $625,000 with KELE-FM Mountain Grove). Population served: 87,000 Format: Classic hits. Spec prog: Farm 2 hrs wkly. ♦Tracy O'Quinn, gen mgr & gen sls mgr; Shawn Anthony, progmg dir; Jim Morris, news dir; Tonya Shannon, traf mgr.

***KZGM(FM)—** 2009: 88.1 mhz; 12.5 kw vert. Ant 443 ft TL: N37 07 15 W92 00 09. Hrs open: 1211 Ozark St., 65689. Phone: (417) 962-4888. Fax: (206) 202-1735.E-mail: staff@kz88.org Web Site:www.kz88.org Licensee: Real Community Radio Network Inc. Population served: 25,000 Format: Var. ♦Kazie Perkins, opns mgr; Gene Colliflower, news dir.

California

KATI(FM)— July 27, 1984: 94.3 mhz; 50 kw. 492 ft TL: N38 31 25 W92 24 25. Stereo. Hrs open: 19 3109 S. Ten Mile Dr., Jefferson City, 65109. Phone: (573) 893-5696. Fax: (573) 893-4137.E-mail: kati@zrgmail.com Web Site:www.kat943.com Licensee: Zimmer Radio of Mid-Missouri Inc. Group owner: Zimmer Radio Group (acq 11-19-99; grpsl). Format: Country. ♦Ron Covert, gen mgr.

KRLL(AM)— July 27, 1984: 1420 khz; 500 w-D, 225 w-N. TL: N38 38 12 W92 35 00. Hrs open: 18 100 A.E. Buchanan, 65018. Phone: (573) 796-3139. Fax: (573) 796-4131.E-mail: krll01@embarqmail.com Licensee: Moniteau Communications Inc. (acq 3-30-95; $50,000;6-19-95). Leibowitz & Spencer. Format: Country. News staff: one; News: 19 hrs wkly.

Target aud: 20 plus. Spec prog: Farm 5 hrs, gospel 3 hrs wkly. ◆Jeffrey G. Shackleford, pres & gen mgr; Jeffrey Shackleford, progmg dir.

Camdenton

*KCVO-FM— Sept 23, 1985: 91.7 mhz; 10 kw. 435 ft TL: N38 01 13 W92 45 27. Stereo. Hrs open: 24 Box 800, Lake Rd. 5-92, 65020. Phone: (573) 346-3200. Fax: (573) 346-1010. Licensee: Lake Area Educational Broadcasting Foundation. Population served: 250,000 Natl. Network: Salem Radio Network, . Format: Contemporary, Christian. News: one hr wkly. Target aud: 25-45. ◆Alice McDermott, CFO; James J. McDermott, pres & gen mgr; James McDermott, progmg dir.

Cameron

KKWK(FM)— Apr 5, 1995: 100.1 mhz; 50 kw. 492 ft TL: N39 57 28 W94 06 55. Stereo. Hrs open: 607 E. Platte Clay Way, P.O. Box 643, 64429. Phone: (816) 632-6661. Fax: (816) 632-1334. Web Site:www.northwestmoinfo.com Population served: 250000 Natl. Network: Fox News Radio, . Format: Classic Hits. News staff: 2. Target aud: 25-49. Spec prog: Community Affairs. ◆Doug Schmitz, gen mgr, gen sls mgr; Chris Ward, news dir, sports cmtr; Ruth Hammontree, traf mgr; Gregg Richwine, engr.

KMRN(AM)— February 1971: 1360 khz; 500 w-D, 25 w-N. TL: N39 41 05 W94 14 22. Hrs open: 5:30 AM-7 PM 607 E. Platte Clay Way, P.O. Box 643, 64429. Phone: (816) 632-6661. Fax: (816) 632-1334. Web Site:www.regionalradio.com Licensee: Cameron/Bethany License Co. LLC. Group owner: Shepherd Group (acq 8-8-2007; grpsl). Population served: 50,000 Rgnl. Network: Missourinet, Brownfield. Brownfield Format: News/talk. News staff: one; News: 40 hrs wkly. Target aud: General. Spec prog: Farm 12 hrs, relg 4 hrs wkly. ◆Doug Schmitz, gen mgr, gen sls mgr; Chris Ward, progmg dir; Gregg Richwine, chief of engrg; Ruth Hammontree, traf mgr.

*WJTJ(FM)—Not on air, target date: unknown: 91.7 mhz; 20 kw. Ant 321 ft TL: N39 52 42 W94 05 33. Hrs open: 219 Dodd Rd., Ringgold, GA, 30736-2958. Phone: (706) 965-2355. Fax: (706) 965-3755. Licensee: Victor Broadcasting Inc. ◆James E. Price III, pres.

Campbell

KFEB(FM)— October 1998: 107.5 mhz; 17.5 kw. 390 ft TL: N36 29 55 W89 51 16. Stereo. Hrs open: 932 CR Box 448, Poplar Bluff, 63901. Phone: (573) 686-3700. Fax: (573) 686-1713.E-mail: info@foxradionetwork.com Licensee: Eagle Bluff Enterprises. (group owner) Population served: 220,000 Format: Modern rock. ◆Steven C. Fuchs, gen mgr.

Canton

KRRY(FM)— May 4, 1971: 100.9 mhz; 28 kw. 656 ft TL: N40 07 33 W91 31 42. Stereo. Hrs open: 24 408 N. 24th St., Quincy, IL, 62301. Phone: (217) 223-5292. Fax: (217) 223-5299.E-mail: y101@hqradio.com Web Site:www.y101radio.com Licensee: Double O Radio of Missouri 9/01/2006 Population served: 150,000 Natl. Rep: McGavren Guild,. Format: Hot adult contemp. ◆Ed Foxall, pres; Jeff Dorsey, gen mgr; Jeff Asmussen, gen sls mgr; Dennis Oliver, progmg dir; Gary Glaenzer, chief of engrg.

Cape Girardeau

KAPE(AM)— 1951: 1550 khz; 5 kw-D, 50 w-N, DA-2. TL: N37 16 45 W89 33 28. Hrs open: Box 558, 63702. Secondary address: 901 S. Kings Hwy. 63703. Phone: (573) 339-7000. Fax: (573) 651-4100. Licensee: Withers Broadcasting Co. of Missouri LLC. Group owner: Withers Broadcasting Co. (acq 6-72). Population served: 275,000 Natl. Network: Westwood One, Fox Sports, Fox News Radio, . Natl. Rep: Katz Radio,. Wire Svc: AP Format: News, talk, sports. Target aud: 25-54; active, aware adults. ◆W. Russell Withers Jr., pres; Rick Lambert, gen mgr; Smokey King, chief of engrg.

KCGQ-FM—(Gordonville, 1978: 99.3 mhz; 5 kw. Ant 358 ft TL: N37 21 34 W89 37 16. Stereo. Hrs open: 24 324 Broadway, 63701. Phone: (573) 335-8291. Fax: (573) 335-4806. Web Site:www.realrock993.com Licensee: MRR License LLC. Format: Real rock. Target aud: 18-49; general. ◆Scott Hartline, progmg dir.

KEZS-FM— Dec 10, 1970: 102.9 mhz; 100 kw. 947 ft TL: N37 24 23 W89 33 44. Stereo. Hrs open: 24 324 Broadway, 63702. Phone: (573) 335-8291. Fax: (573) 335-4806.E-mail: k103@zrgmail.com Web

Site:www.k103fm.com Licensee: MRR License LLC Group owner: MAX Media L.L.C. (acq 6-2-2004; grpsl). Fletcher, Heald & Hildreth. Format: Country. News staff: one. Target aud: 25-54. ◆Whitney Thomas, progmg dir.

KGIR(AM)— June 10, 1966: 1220 khz; 250 w-D, 140 w-N. TL: N37 18 03 W89 29 27. Stereo. Hrs open: 24 324 Broadway, 63701. Phone: (573) 335-8291. Fax: (573) 335-4806.E-mail: kgir@kgir.com Web Site:www.espn1220.com Licensee: MRR License LLC. Group owner: MAX Media L.L.C. (acq 6-2-2004; grpsl). Population served: 200,000 Natl. Network: ESPN Radio, . Leventhal, Senter & Lerman. Format: Sports talk. Target aud: 18 plus; men. ◆Cristy Benton, gen mgr, sls dir; Meg Davis, gen sls mgr; Erik Sean, progmg dir; Faume Riggin, news dir; Sherry Crider, traf mgr.

KGMO(FM)— Mar 17, 1969: 100.7 mhz; 100 kw. 987 ft TL: N37 22 16 W89 31 52. Stereo. Hrs open: Prog sep from AM Box 558, 63703. Phone: (573) 339-7000. Phone: (573) 651-4100.E-mail: info@kgmofm.com Licensee: Withers Broadcasting Co. of Missouri LLC Population served: 800,000 Natl. Rep: Katz Radio,. Format: Classic rock. ◆Chris Cook, prom mgr.

*KRCU(FM)— Mar 3, 1976: 90.9 mhz; 6 kw. Ant 259 ft TL: N37 18 37 W89 31 57. Stereo. Hrs open: One University Plaza, 63701. Phone: (573) 651-5070. Fax (573) 651-5071.E-mail: info@southeastpublicradio.org Web Site:www.southeastpublicradio.org Licensee: Board of Regents of Southeast Missouri State University. Population served: 102,106 Natl. Network: NPR, PRI, . Dow, Lohnes & Albertson. Format: Jazz, news, classical. Target aud: General. ◆Dan Woods, gen mgr, opns dir; Jason Brown, opns dir; Amanda Lincoln, dev dir; Allen Lane, chief of engrg.

KREZ(FM)—(Chaffee, July 1, 1990: 104.7 mhz; 7.7 kw. Ant 585 ft TL: N37 09 46 W89 28 59. Stereo. Hrs open: 901 S. Kings Hwy., 63702-0558. Phone: (573) 339-7000. Fax: (573) 651-4100. Licensee: Dana R. Withers (acq 4-12-90; $33,587;5-7-90). Natl. Rep: Katz Radio,. Format: Adult contemp. Target aud: 18-49. ◆Rick Lambert, gen mgr.

KZIM(AM)— 1925: 960 khz; 5 kw-D, 500 w-N, DA-N. TL: N37 18 59 W89 29 06. Hrs open: 24 Prog sep from FM 324 Broadway, 63702. Phone: (573) 355-8291. Fax: (573) 355-4806.E-mail: kzim@zrgmail.com Web Site:www.960kzim.com Licensee: MRR License LLC Population served: 150,000 Natl. Network: CBS, . Format: News/talk. Target aud: 35-64. ◆Faume Riggin, progmg dir.

Carrollton

KAOL(AM)— Apr 18, 1959: 1430 khz; 500 w-U, 27 w-N. TL: N39 19 58 W93 32 15. Hrs open: 24 KMZU Bldg., 102 N. Mason, 64633. Phone: (660) 542-0404. Fax: (660) 542-0420.E-mail: kmzu@carolnet.com Web Site:www.kmzu.com Licensee: Kanza Inc. (acq 11-1-81; $665,000 with co-located FM; 11-23-81). Population served: 35,700 Natl. Rep: McGavren Guild,. Format: Country, farm. News staff: 2; News: 10 hrs wkly. Target aud: 25-54; farm families & those with agricultural backgrounds. Spec prog: Sp 3 hrs wkly. ◆Miles Carter, gen mgr; Rick Barton, gen sls mgr; Scott Powell, progmg dir; Jim Woods, mus dir; Chastity Anderson, news dir; Sue Lightfoot, traf mgr.

KMZU(FM)— July 13, 1962: 100.7 mhz; 98.6 kw. 990 ft TL: N39 22 05 W93 29 40. Stereo. Hrs open:
Rebroadcasts WHB(AM) Kansas City 95%.
KMZU Bldg., 102 N. Mason, 64633. Phone: (660) 542-0404. Fax: (660) 542-0420. Web Site:www.kmzu.com Licensee: Kanza Inc. Population served: 800,000 ◆Don Sibley, women's cmtr & disc jockey.

Carthage

KDMO(AM)— June 3, 1947: 1490 khz; 1 kw-U. TL: N37 10 58 W94 21 43. Hrs open: 24 Box 426, 221 E. 4th St., 64836. Phone: (417) 358-6054. Phone: (417) 358-2648. Fax: (417) 358-1278. Licensee: Ronald L. Petersen. (acq 1-23-90). Population served: 397,000 Natl. Network: CNN Radio, . Rgnl. Network: Missourinet, Brownfield. Format: Adult standards. News staff: one; News: 10 hrs wkly. Target aud: 55 plus. Spec prog: Sp 6 hrs wkly. ◆Ronald Petersen Sr., pres; Ronald Petersen Jr., gen mgr & stn mgr.

KMXL(FM)— Jan 10, 1972: 95.1 mhz; 50 kw. 472 ft TL: N37 10 58 W94 21 35. Stereo. Hrs open: 24 Prog sep from AM Box 426, 64836. Secondary address: 221 E. 4th St. 64836. Phone: (417) 358-6054. Phone: (417) 358-2648. Fax: (417) 358-1278.E-mail: traffic@cbciradio.com Web Site:www.951mikefm.com Licensee: Ronald L. Petersen. Population served: 775,000 Natl. Network: NBC Radio, . Format: Adult hits. News staff: one; News: one hr wkly. Target aud: 25-54; young adults & baby-boomers. ◆Ronald Petersen Sr., pres; Ronald Petersen Jr., stn mgr.

Carthage-

KKLL(AM)— Mar 10, 1984: 1100 khz; 5 kw-D. TL: N37 06 23 W94 16 50. Hrs open: 831 Moffitt, Joplin, 64801. Phone: (417) 781-1100. Fax: (417) 781-1100.E-mail: info@kkllam.com Licensee: New Life Evangelistic Center Inc. (acq 8-10-98; $730,000 with KWAS(AM) Joplin). Format: Christian. ◆Charlie Hale, opns dir.

Caruthersville

KCRV(AM)— Feb 22, 1950: 1370 khz; 1 kw-D, 63 w-N. TL: N36 12 50 W89 41 25. Hrs open: Box 509, Kennett, 63857-0509. Secondary address: 1303 Southwest Dr., Kennett 63857. Phone: (573) 888-4616. Fax: (573) 888-4991.E-mail: info@kcrvradio.com Web Site:www.kcrvradio.com Licensee: Pollack Broadcasting Co. (group owner; (acq 9-21-99; with co-located FM). Population served: 23,000 Natl. Network: Moody, . Rgnl. Network: Prog Farm, Brownfield. Brownfield Format: Country. Target aud: General; residents of Pemiscot county. Spec prog: Relg 20 hrs wkly.

KCRV-FM— Apr 28, 1975: 105.1 mhz; 3 kw. 200 ft TL: N36 12 50 W89 41 25. (CP: 6 kw, ant 328 ft.). Stereo. Hrs open: Prog sep from AM Box 509, Kennett, 63857-0509. Secondary address: 1303 Southwest Dr., Kennett 63857. Phone: (573) 888-4616. Fax: (573) 888-4991.E-mail: info@kcrvradio.com Licensee: Pollack Broadcasting Co. Population served: 23,000 Format: Oldies.

Cassville

KRMO(AM)—Licensed to Cassville. See Monett

Cedar Hill

*KNLH(FM)— October 1998: 89.5 mhz; 68 w. 699 ft TL: N38 21 40 W90 32 54. Hrs open: New Life Evangelistic Center Inc., 1411 Locust St., St. Louis, 63103. Phone: (314) 436-2424. Fax: (314) 436-2434.E-mail: larryr@hereshelpnet.org Web Site:www.hereshelpnet.org Licensee: New Life Evangelistic Center Inc. Format: Adult contemp, gospel, talk. ◆Victor Anderson, gen mgr.

Centralia

KMFC(FM)— Feb 3, 1986: 92.1 mhz; 1.85 kw. Ant 418 ft TL: N39 09 58 W92 09 52. Stereo. Hrs open: 24 1249 E. Hwy. 22, 65240. Phone: (573) 682-5525. Fax: (573) 682-2744.E-mail: info@kmfc.com Web Site:www.kmfc.com Licensee: Clair Broadcasting Co. Population served: 260,000 Natl. Network: USA, . Format: Relg, Christian contemp. Target aud: 25-50. Spec prog: Black 3 hrs, gospel 2 hrs, Sp one hr wkly. ◆Kevin Hilley, pres, progmg dir; Jerry D. Clair, gen mgr; John Benke, gen sls mgr; Sharon Dollens, stn mgr & traf mgr.

Chaffee

KREZ(FM)—Licensed to Chaffee. See Cape Girardeau

Charleston

KCHR(AM)— 1953: 1350 khz; 1 kw-D, 79 w-N. TL: N36 55 30 W89 17 45. Hrs open: 24 205 E. Commercial St., 63834. Phone: (573) 683-6044. Licensee: South Missouri Broadcasting Co. Inc. Population served: 5,200 Format: Talk, Oldies. News: 21 hr per day. Target aud: General. Spec prog: Oldies about 3 hrs. ◆James L. Byrd, III, pres; Danny Adams, gen mgr, gen sls mgr; Pam Haws, progmg dir; Charlie Lampe, chief of engrg.

KWKZ(FM)— February 1993: 106.1 mhz; 34 kw. 384 ft TL: N36 57 29 W89 23 38. Stereo. Hrs open: 24 753 Enterpirse, Cape Girardeau, 63703. Phone: (573) 334-7800. Fax: (573) 334-7440. Web Site:www.kwkz.com Licensee: Anderson Broadcasting Co. Inc. (acq 7-30-92). Format: Country. Target aud: 18-44; 35-55 male, 30-45 female. ◆Bill Anderson, CEO, gen mgr; Ann Anderson, chmn; Palmer Johnson, engrg dir, edit dir; Susan Bell, progmg dir & rsch dir.

Chillicothe

KCHI(AM)— Mar 3, 1950: 1010 khz; 250 w-D, 37 w-N. TL: N39 45 51 W93 33 21. Hrs open: 421 Washington St., 64601. Phone: (660) 646-4173. Fax: (660) 646-2868.E-mail: kchi@greenhills.net Web Site:www.kchi.com Licensee: Livingston Broadcasting Inc. (acq 7-1-84). Population served: 9,519 Rgnl. Network: Missourinet. Missourinet

Format: Todays news & yesterdays music. Target aud: 35-49. ♦Dan Leatherman, gen mgr; Randy Dean, progmg dir; Tom Tingerthal, news dir; Jessica Frizzell, traf mgr.

KCHI-FM— October 1976: 103.9 mhz; 4.1 kw. Ant 400 ft TL: N39 48 52 W93 35 20. Stereo. Hrs open: Dups AM 98% 421 Washington St., 64601. Phone: (660) 646-4173. Fax: (660) 646-2868.E-mail: kchi@greenhills.net Web Site:www.kchi.com Licensee: Livingston Broadcasting Inc.

***KCKE(FM)—**Not on air, target date: unknown: 90.3 mhz; 30 kw. Ant 344 ft TL: N39 54 35.23 W93 21 42.44. Hrs open: Box 800, Camdenton, 65020-0800. Phone: (573) 346-3200. Fax: (573) 346-1010. Licensee: Lake Area Educational Broadcasting Foundation (acq 5-14-2009; $50,000 for CP). ♦James J. McDermott, gen mgr.

***KRNW(FM)—** Aug 30, 1993: 88.9 mhz; 38 kw. 498 ft TL: N39 48 50 W93 35 20. Stereo. Hrs open: 24 Wells Hall, 800 University Dr., Maryville, 64468. Phone: (660) 562-1163. Phone: (660) 562-1164. Fax: (660) 562-1832.E-mail: kxcv@nwmissouri.edu Web Site:www.kxcv.org Licensee: Northwest Missouri State University. Population served: 64,000 Format: News, class, jazz. News staff: 2; News: 39 hrs wkly. Target aud: General. ♦John Jasinski, pres; Rodney Harris, gen mgr & stn mgr; Patty Andrews Holley, opns mgr.

Clayton

***KFUO(AM)—** Dec 14, 1924: 850 khz; 5 kw-D. TL: N38 38 20 W90 18 57. Hrs open: Sunrise-sunset Prog sep from FM 85 Founders Lane, St. Louis, 63105. Phone: (314) 725-3030. Fax: (314) 725-3801.E-mail: worldwide@kfuo.org Web Site:www.kfuo.org Licensee: Lutheran Church-Missouri Synod Natl. Network: AP Network News, . Format: Religious, talk. Target aud: General. ♦Dennis Stortz, gen mgr; Chuck Rathert, prom dir.

KFUO-FM— Jan 1, 1948: 99.1 mhz; 100 kw. 1,026 ft TL: N38 39 08 W90 17 03. Stereo. Hrs open: 24 85 Founders Ln., St. Louis, 63105. Phone: (314) 725-0099. Fax: (314) 725-3801.E-mail: dstortz@classic99.com Web Site:www.classic99.com Licensee: Lutheran Church-Missouri Synod Natl. Network: Wall Street, CNN Radio, . Natl. Rep: McGavren Guild,. Shaw Pittman. Format: Classical. Target aud: General; upscale, educated. Spec prog: Metrpolitan Opera. ♦Dennis Stortz, gen mgr, chief of engrg; Oliver Trittler, sls dir & gen sls mgr; Jim Connett, progmg dir.

KSIV(AM)— 1320 khz; 4.6 kw-D, 270 w-N, DA-N. TL: N38 36 26 W90 21 14. Hrs open: 24 1750 S. Brentwood Blvd., Suite 811, St. Louis, 63144. Phone: (314) 961-1320. Fax: (314) 961-7562.E-mail: info@bottradionetwork.com Web Site:www.bottradionetwork.com Licensee: Bott Broadcasting. (group owner; acq 2-25-82; 3-15-82). Population served: 3,000,000 Natl. Network: USA, . Format: Christian info. Target aud: 25-54; family-oriented. ♦Richard P. Bott, pres; Richard Bott II, VP; Michael McHardy, gen mgr; Joy Elder, sls dir, mktg dir.

***KWUR(FM)—** July 4, 1976: 90.3 mhz; 10 w. 136 ft TL: N38 38 45 W80 19 07. Stereo. Hrs open: 24 Washington Univ. Box 1205, One Brookings Dr., St. Louis, 63105. Phone: (314) 935-5952. Fax: (314) 935-8833. Web Site:www.kwur.com Licensee: Washington University. Format: Progressive/diversified. Target aud: 18 plus; those seeking alternative radio. ♦John Klacsmann, gen mgr.

Cleveland

KCTO(AM)— Nov 8, 2007: 1160 khz; 500 w-D, 230 w-N, DA-2. TL: N38 40 26 W94 36 28. Hrs open: 310 S. La Frenz Rd., Liberty, 64068. Phone: (816) 792-1140. Fax: (816) 792-8258.E-mail: kcxl1140@yahoo.com Licensee: Alpine Broadcasting Corp. Format: Talk. ♦Peter E. Schartel, pres & gen mgr; Jonne Santoli, adv mgr.

Clinton

KDKD(AM)— 1951: 1280 khz; 1 kw-D, 58 w-N. TL: N38 23 55 W93 46 19. Hrs open: 24 Box 448, 64735. Secondary address: 2201 N. Antioch Rd. 64735. Phone: (660) 885-6141. Fax: (660) 885-4801. Web Site:www.kdkd.net Licensee: Legend Communications of Missouri LLC. Group owner: Legend Communications L.L.C. (acq 10-7-2003; with co-located FM). Population served: 230,000 Rgnl. Network: Missourinet. Missourinet Format: Oldies. News staff: one; News: 10 hrs wkly. Target aud: 25-55. ♦Bob May, gen mgr; Ken Dillon, progmg dir; David Lee, news dir; Jennifer Schlagle, traf mgr.

KDKD-FM— 1975: 95.3 mhz; 14.5 kw. Ant 433 ft TL: N38 22 18 W93 55 06. Stereo. Hrs open: 24 Box 448, 64735. Secondary address: 2201 N. Antioch Rd. 64735. Phone: (660) 885-6141. Fax: (660) 885-4801.E-mail: bob@kdkd.com Web Site:www.kdkd.net Licensee: Legend Communications of Missouri LLC. (acq 5-28-1985). Population served: 250,000 Natl. Network: ABC, Motor Racing Net, . Rgnl. Network: Missourinet. Missourinet Format: Hot new country, news, sports. News staff: one. Target aud: 25-55.

***KLRQ(FM)—** Oct 5, 1990: 96.1 mhz; 100 kw. Ant 987 ft TL: N38 28 27 W93 30 28. Hrs open: 24
Rebroadcasts KLVR(FM) Santa Rosa, CA 100%.
2351 Sunset Blvd., Suite 170-218, Rocklin, CA, 95765. Phone: (916) 251-1600. Fax: (916) 251-1650. Web Site:www.klove.com Licensee: Educational Media Foundation. Group owner: EMF Broadcasting (acq 12-23-2003; $1.9 million). Population served: 920,000 Natl. Network: K-Love, . Format: Contemp Christian. ♦Richard Jenkins, pres; Mike Novak, VP, progmg dir; Lloyd Parker, gen mgr; Ed Lenane, opns dir, news dir; Keith Whipple, dev dir; Eric Allen, natl sls mgr; David Pierce, progmg mgr; Jon Rivers, mus dir; Sam Wallington, engrg dir; Arthur Vassar, traf mgr; Karen Johnson, news rptr.

Columbia

***KBIA(FM)—** 1972: 91.3 mhz; 100 kw. 610 ft TL: N38 53 16 W92 15 48. Stereo. Hrs open: 24 Univ. of Missouri, 409 Jesse Hall, 65211. Phone: (573) 882-3431. Fax: (573) 882-2636.E-mail: dunnm@missouri.edu Web Site:www.kbia.org Licensee: Board of Curators, University of Missouri. Group owner: The Curators of the University of Missouri Population served: 300,000 Natl. Network: NPR, PRI, . Fisher, Wayland, Cooper, Leader & Zaragoza. Format: News, class. News staff: 2; News: 55 hrs wkly. Target aud: 25-64. ♦Michael Dunn, gen mgr; Roger Karwoski, stn mgr; John Bailey, dev dir, progmg dir.

KBXR(FM)— Nov 11, 1994: 102.3 mhz; 88 kw. 420 ft TL: N38 57 21 W92 16 24. Stereo. Hrs open: 24 503 Old 63 N., 65201. Phone: (573) 449-4141. Fax: (573) 449-7770.E-mail: bxr@bxr.com Web Site:www.bxr.com Licensee: Cumulus Licensing LLC. Group owner: Cumulus Media Inc. (acq 4-26-2004; grpsl). Population served: 110,000 Natl. Rep: Katz Radio,. Format: Album adult alternative. News staff: 3; News: one hr wkly. Target aud: 29-59; educated professional/technical. ♦Greg DeRue, pres, gen mgr; Liz Mozzocco, gen mgr, progmg dir; Dan Claxton, news dir; Tom Holmes, chief of engrg; Mary Kelley, traf mgr.

KCMQ(FM)— Dec 3, 1967: 96.7 mhz; 18 kw. 344 ft TL: N38 41 30 W92 05 44. (CP: 98 kw, ant 912 ft. TL: N38 41 30 W92 05 44). Stereo. Hrs open: 24 3215 LeMone Industrial, Suite 200, 65201. Phone: (573) 875-1099. Fax: (573) 875-2439. Web Site:www.kcmq.com Licensee: Zimmer Radio of Mid-Missouri Inc. (acq 7-15-93; $625,000 with co-located AM; 8-9-93). Population served: 130,000 Format: AOR. News: one hr wkly. Target aud: 25-54; male. ♦John Zimmer, chmn; Carla Leible, gen mgr; Dave Wisniewski, sls dir; Nicci Garmon, progmg dir; Shelley Tucker, news dir; Drew Haigh, engrg mgr, chief of engrg.

***KCOU(FM)—** Oct 31, 1973: 88.1 mhz; 435 w. 110 ft TL: N38 56 23 W92 19 20. Stereo. Hrs open: 24 Univ. of Missouri, 101-F Pershing Hall, 65201. Phone: (573) 882-7820. Fax: (573) 882-6262.E-mail: kcou@mu.org Web Site:www.kcou.mu.org Licensee: The Curators of the University of Missouri. (acq 12-14-98; $80,000). Population served: 75,000 Format: Progsv, rock. Target aud: 18-22; students & community members. ♦Jon Wujcik, gen mgr.

KFRU(AM)— Oct 10, 1925: 1400 khz; 1 kw-U. TL: N38 57 52 W92 18 26. Hrs open: 24 503 Old Hwy., 63 N., 65201. Phone: (573) 449-4141. Fax: (573) 449-7770. Fax: (573) 499-1414.E-mail: news@kfru.com Web Site:www.kfru.com Licensee: Cumulus Licensing LLC. Group owner: Cumulus Media Inc. (acq 4-26-2004; grpsl). Population served: 110,000 Rgnl. Network: Missourinet. Missourinet Format: News/talk. News staff: 9; News: 40 hrs wkly. Target aud: General. ♦Brian Wilson, progmg dir.

***KOPN(FM)—** Mar 1, 1973: 89.5 mhz; 36 kw. 236 ft TL: N38 59 53 W92 11 48. (CP: 36.4 kw). Stereo. Hrs open: 24 915 E. Broadway, 65201-4857. Phone: (573) 874-1139. Fax: (573) 499-1662.E-mail: mail@kopn.org Web Site:www.kopn.org Licensee: New Wave Corp. Population served: 200,000 Natl. Network: NPR, PRI, . Haley, Bader & Potts. Format: News/talk, Americana. News staff: News progmg 40 hrs wkly Target aud: 25-54; well educated, upwardly mobile. Spec prog: Blues 13 hrs, Black 10 hrs, AAA 10 hrs, Grateful Dead 6 hrs, jazz 4 hrs, gospel 3 hrs, bluegrass 6 hrs, folk 2 hrs wkly. ♦David Owens, gen mgr; Julie Baka, dev dir; Steve Jerrett, mus dir; Rich Winkel, chief of engrg.

KPLA(FM)— Feb 23, 1983: 101.5 mhz; 100 kw. 1,062 ft TL: N39 00 52 W92 16 32. Stereo. Hrs open: 24 503 Old 63 N., 65201. Phone: (573) 449-4141. Fax: (573) 449-7770.E-mail: studio@kpla.com Web Site:www.kpla.com Licensee: Cumulus Licensing LLC. Group owner: Cumulus Media Inc. (acq 4-26-2004; grpsl). Population served: 500,000 Format: Adult contemp. News staff: 2; News: one hr wkly. Target aud: 25-54. ♦Chris Kellogg, progmg dir.

KTGR(AM)— 1955: 1580 khz; 214 w-D, 8 w-N. TL: N38 57 45 W92 18 14. Hrs open: 3215 LeMone Industrial, Suite 200, 65201. Phone: (573) 875-1099. Fax: (573) 875-2439. Web Site:ktgr.com Licensee: Zimmer Radio of Mid-Missouri Inc. Population served: 130,000 Natl. Network: ABC, ESPN Radio, . Format: Sports. Target aud: 18-34; male.

***KWWC-FM—** Feb 2, 1965: 90.5 mhz; 1.25 kw. 131 ft TL: N38 57 12 W92 19 05. Stereo. Hrs open: 24 Box 2114, Stephens College, 65215. Phone: (573) 876-7297. Phone: (573) 876-7272. Fax: (573) 876-2330.E-mail: jwise@stephens.edu Licensee: Stephens College. Population served: 655,000 Format: Jazz, 80s hits, oldies, eclectic. Target aud: 25-60; college educated, professional or retired with middle upper income. ♦Jonna Wiseman, gen mgr, mktg dir, progmg dir; Max Ornles, chief of engrg.

Concordia

***KYRV(FM)—** 1998: 88.1 mhz; 1 kw. Ant 213 ft TL: N38 52 10 W93 32 58. Hrs open: 712 Chaucer Ln., Warrensburg, 64093. Phone: (660) 747-4155. Fax: (660) 747-4155. Licensee: Full Smile Inc. Format: Southern gospel. ♦Jim McCollum, gen mgr.

Country Club

***KJCV(FM)—** 2005: 89.7 mhz; 3.9 kw. Ant 548 ft TL: N39 42 35 W95 02 33. Hrs open: Bott Radio Network, 10550 Barkley, Overland Park, KS, 66212. Phone: (913) 642-2424. Fax: (913) 642-1319. Web Site:www.bottradionetwork.com Licensee: Community Broadcasting Inc. Group owner: Bott Radio Network. Natl. Network: USA, . Format: Christian Talk. ♦Rich Bott, exec VP; Dan Snell, rgnl sls mgr; Rachel Moser, mktg mgr; Jason Potocnik, traf mgr.

Crestwood

KSHE(FM)— Feb 11, 1961: 94.7 mhz; 100 kw. 1,019 ft TL: N38 34 24 W90 19 30. Stereo. Hrs open: 24 The Powerhouse, 800 St. Louis Union Stn., St. Louis, 63103. Phone: (314) 621-0095. Fax: (314) 621-3428.E-mail: info@kshe95.com Web Site:www.kshe95.com Licensee: Emmis Radio License LLC. Group owner: Emmis Communications Corp. (acq 3-19-84; grpsl;1-30-84). Natl. Rep: D & R Radio,. Format: Classic rock, AOR. News staff: one; News: one hr wkly. Target aud: 18-40. ♦John R. Beck Jr., gen mgr.

Cuba

KESY(FM)— 2005: 107.3 mhz; 6.7 kw. Ant 626 ft TL: N37 55 17 W91 26 36. Hrs open: 3418 Douglas Rd., Florissant, 63034. Phone: (314) 921-9330.E-mail: X93@knsx.com Licensee: East Central Broadcasting LLC (acq 3-4-2008). Format: Country. ♦Ruth Choate, gen mgr, gen sls mgr & progmg dir; Randy Wachter, chief of engrg.

***KGNN-FM—** Jan 26, 1997: 90.3 mhz; 6.3 kw. Ant 325 ft TL: N38 05 11 W91 18 30. Hrs open: 24
Rebroadcasts KGNV(FM) Washington 100%.
Box 187, Washington, 63090-0187. Phone: (636) 239-0400. Fax: (636) 239-4448.E-mail: info@goodnewsvoice.org Web Site:goodnewsvoice.org Licensee: Missouri River Christian Broadcasting Inc. Population served: 20,000 Natl. Network: Moody, Salem Radio Network, . Format: News/talk, southern gospel, inspirational. News: 14 hrs wkly. Target aud: 20-70; inquisitive, conservative, philosophical, liberal. Spec prog: Children 7 hrs wkly. ♦James Goggan, pres.

***KNLQ(FM)—** 2004: 91.9 mhz; 5 kw. Ant 249 ft TL: N38 02 14 W91 23 04. Hrs open: New Life Evangelistic Center Inc., 1411 Locust St., St. Louis, 63103. Phone: (314) 421-3020. Fax: (314) 436-2434. Web Site:www.hereshelpnet.org Licensee: New Life Evangelistic Center Inc. Format: Gospel. ♦Rick Jesse, stn mgr.

De Soto

KDJR(FM)— Jan 29, 1991: 100.1 mhz; 2 kw. Ant 348 ft TL: N38 01 25 W90 34 02. Stereo. Hrs open: Box 262550, Baton Rouge, LA, 70826. Secondary address: 8919 World Ministry Ave., Baton Rouge, LA 70810. Phone: (225) 768-3688. Phone: (225) 766-8300. Fax: (225) 768-3729.E-mail: kawikfish@yahoo.com Web Site:www.jsm.org Licensee: Family Worship Center Church Inc. (acq 9-27-2005; $1.25 million). Format: Relg. ♦David Whitelaw, COO, gen mgr; Jimmy Swaggart, pres; John Santiago, progmg dir.

KRFT(AM)— Nov 1, 1968: 1190 khz; 10 kw-D, 22 w-N, DA-2. TL: N38 42 25 W90 03 10. (CP: COL University City. 10 kw-D, 6.5 kw-N, DA-2. TL: N38 42 25 W90 03 10 day, N 38 26 13 W90 16 45 night). Hrs

open: Sunrise-sunset 8045 Big Bend Blvd., St. Louis, 63119. Phone: (314) 962-0590. Fax: (314) 962-7576. Web Site:www.kfns.com Licensee: Big Stick Three LLC. Group owner: Big League Broadcasting LLC (acq 7-13-2004; grpsl). Natl. Network: ESPN Radio, . Format: Sports. Target aud: 25-64; sports fans, men 25-54. ◆Mike Phares, gen mgr.

Dexter

KDEX(AM)— Feb 1, 1956: 1590 khz; 620 w-D, 78 w-N. TL: N36 47 20 W89 54 28. Hrs open: 5 AM-midnight Dups FM 100% Box 249, 63841. Secondary address: 20487 State Hwy 114 63841. Phone: (573) 624-3545. Fax: (573) 624-9926.E-mail: kdex1@sbcglobal.net Population served: 75,000 Natl. Network: ABC, Jones Radio Networks, Premiere Radio Networks, . Yancey AG Network Format: Modern Country. ◆Walter F Turner, gen mgr; Joeli Barbour, stn mgr, natl sls mgr, traf mgr; Tony James, opns dir; Walt Turner, gen sls mgr; Dave Obergoenner, chief of engrg.

KDEX-FM— July 17, 1969: 102.3 mhz; 6 kw. 279 ft TL: N36 47 18 W89 54 22. Stereo. Hrs open: 24 Box 249, 20487 State Hwy. 114, 63841. Phone: (573) 624-3545. Fax: (573) 624-9926.E-mail: kdex1@sbcglobal.net Web Site:www.kdexfm.com Licensee: Dexter Broadcasting Inc. (acq 7-15-88). Natl. Network: ABC, Jones Radio Networks, Premiere Radio Networks, . Rgnl. Network: Prog Farm, Yancey Action. Yancey AG Network Shaw Pittman. Format: Modern country. News staff: 2; News: 5 hrs wkly. Target aud: 25-54. ◆Tony James, opns dir, progmg dir; Joeli Barbour, natl sls mgr, traf mgr; Walt Turner, gen mgr, gen sls mgr & rgnl sls mgr; Dave Obergoenner, chief of engrg.

Dixon

***KCVZ(FM)**— May 2003: 92.1 mhz; 6 kw. Ant 328 ft TL: N37 57 59 W92 10 03. Stereo. Hrs open: 24
Rebroadcasts KCVO-FM Camdenton 100%.
Box 800, Camdenton, 65020. Phone: (573) 346-3200. Fax: (573) 346-1010. Web Site:www.spiritfm.org Licensee: Lake Area Educational Broadcasting Foundation (acq 12-20-2001). Population served: 80,000 Natl. Network: Salem Radio Network, . Format: Contemp Christian. News: one hr wkly. Target aud: 25-45. ◆Alice McDermott, CFO; James McDermott, pres, gen mgr & progmg dir.

***KGNY(FM)**—Not on air, target date: unknown: 89.3 mhz; 220 w vert. Ant 312 ft TL: N37 59 42 W92 05 57. Hrs open: Box 187, Washington, 63090. Phone: (636) 239-0400. Fax: (636) 239-4448. Web Site:www.goodnewsvoice.org Licensee: Missouri River Christian Broadcasting Inc. ◆James Goggan, pres & gen mgr.

Doniphan

KDFN(AM)— Feb 4, 1963: 1500 khz; 2.5 kw-D, DA. TL: N36 36 53 W90 49 23. Hrs open: 932 Country Rd. 448, Poplar Bluff, 63901. Phone: (573) 686-3700. Fax: (573) 686-1713.E-mail: info@foxradionetwork.com Licensee: Eagle Bluff Enterprises. (group owner; (acq 9-8-99); grpsl). Population served: 10,000 Rgnl. Network: Missourinet. Missourinet Format: Oldies. Target aud: General. Spec prog: Farm 5 hrs wkly. ◆Steven Fuchs, gen mgr; Shelley Fuchs, progmg dir; Ken Hosler, news dir; Maria Tillman, traf mgr.

KOEA(FM)— Apr 11, 1975: 97.5 mhz; 50 kw. 577 ft TL: N36 35 20 W90 49 10. Stereo. Hrs open: 932 Country Rd. 448, Poplar Bluff, 63901. Phone: (573) 686-3700. Fax: (573) 686-1713.E-mail: info@foxradionetwork.com Licensee: Eagle Bluff Enterprises. Population served: 25,000 Format: Country. ◆Steven Fuchs, gen sls mgr; Tammy Jameson, mktg mgr; Skeet Collins, progmg dir.

Doolittle

KUMR(FM)—Not on air, target date: unknown: 104.5 mhz; 3.9 kw. Ant 407 ft TL: N37 56 21.3 W91 56 44.9. Hrs open: 1282 Smallwood Dr., Suite 372, Waldorf, MD, 20603. Phone: (202) 251-7589. Licensee: Alma Corp. ◆Dennis Wallace, pres.

East Prairie

KYMO(AM)— Nov 15, 1965: 1080 khz; 500 w-D. TL: N36 47 49 W89 21 19. Hrs open: Box 130, 63845. Secondary address: 390 S. Hwy. 102 63845. Phone: (573) 649-3597. Fax: (573) 649-3983.E-mail: kymo@bootheel.net Licensee: Usher Broadcasting Inc. (acq 6-1-69). Population served: 15,000 Format: Relg. ◆Barney L. Webster, pres, gen mgr, gen sls mgr; Michael Bennett, opns mgr; Reid Howell, progmg dir & news dir.

El Dorado Springs

KESM(AM)— July 18, 1961: 1580 khz; 500 w-D. TL: N37 51 51 W94 00 54. Stereo. Hrs open: 200 Radio Ln., 64744. Phone: (417) 876-2741. Fax: (417) 876-2743.E-mail: kesm@kesmradio.com Licensee: Wildwood Communications Inc. (acq 12-17-85). Population served: 44,500 Format: C&W, oldies. Target aud: General. ◆Donald Kohn, pres, gen mgr; Jena Worthington, stn mgr, gen sls mgr & progmg dir.

KESM-FM— June 1, 1965: 105.5 mhz; 6.0 kw. 187 ft TL: N37 51 51 W94 00 54. Stereo. Hrs open: Dups AM 100% 200 Radio Ln., 64744. Phone: (417) 876-2741. Fax: (417) 876-2743.E-mail: kesm@kesmradio.com Licensee: Wildwood Communications Inc. (acq 12-17-85; $200,000; 11-11-85).

Eldon

KLOZ(FM)— July 1, 1979: 92.7 mhz; 50 kw. Ant 620 ft TL: N38 20 27 W92 35 33. Stereo. Hrs open: 24 160 Hwy 42, Kaiser, 65047. Phone: (573) 348-1958. Fax: (573) 348-1923.E-mail: mike@mix927.com Web Site:www.todaysbesthits.com Licensee: Benne Broadcasting Co. L.L.C. Population served: 500,000 Natl. Network: ABC, . Format: Hot adult contemp. Target aud: 25-54; 70% female/30% male with average or above income. ◆Denny Benne, gen mgr; Greg Sullens, stn mgr, news dir; Mike Clayton, progmg dir; Dan Yeager, engrg mgr.

KZWV(FM)— 2006: 101.9 mhz; 42.7 kw. Ant 528 ft TL: N38 16 46 W92 35 06. Stereo. Hrs open: 24 1081 Osage Beach Rd., Osage Beach, 65065-2232. Phone: (573) 746-7873.E-mail: jcaran@1019thewave.com Web Site:www.1019thewave.com Licensee: Randall C. Wright. Format: Adult contemp w/ smooth jazz. Target aud: 25 plus; affluent adults. ◆John Caran, gen mgr, sls dir; Steve Richards, progmg dir; Stacy Johnson, news dir; Jessica Brink, traf mgr.

Ellington

KAUL(FM)— 1999: 106.7 mhz; 3 kw. 298 ft TL: N37 13 58 W90 51 08. Hrs open: 1411 Locust St., St. Louis, 63103. Phone: (314) 421-3020. Fax: (314) 436-2434.E-mail: larryr@hereshelpnet.org Web Site:www.hereshelpnet.org Licensee: New Life Evangelistic Center. Format: Adult contemp, gospel, pub affrs. ◆Larry Rice, gen mgr; Judy Redlich, sls dir.

Elsberry

KLPW-FM— Aug 1, 1966: 101.7 mhz; 3.1 kw. Ant 466 ft TL: N39 06 09 W90 49 23. Stereo. Hrs open: 24 Box 623, Washington, 63090. Secondary address: 6531 Hwy. BB, Washington 63090. Phone: (636) 583-5155. Phone: (636) 239-3355. Fax: (636) 583-1644. Licensee: Marathon Media Group L.L.C. (acq 1999; grpsl). Population served: 600,000 Format: Country. News staff: 2; News: 16.5 hrs wkly. Target aud: 18-49. ◆Tim McDonald; Steve Leslie, mus dir; Marcy Frankenberg, traf mgr; John Covington, local news ed, news rptr, sports cmtr.

Excelsior Springs

***KEXS(AM)**— August 1968: 1090 khz; 1 kw-D. TL: N39 20 25 W94 14 26. Hrs open: 201 N. Industrial Park Rd., 64024. Phone: (816) 630-1090.E-mail: kccatholic@aol.com Web Site:www.thecatholicradionetwork.com Licensee: Catholic Radio Network Inc. (acq 5-17-2004; $825,000). Population served: 500,000 Natl. Network: USA, . Format: Catholic radio. Target aud: 25-54. ◆James E. O'Laughlin, pres & gen mgr.

Farmington

KREI(AM)— Dec 7, 1947: 800 khz; 1 kw-D, 150 w-N. TL: N37 47 45 W90 24 30. Hrs open: 24 Box 461, 63640. Secondary address: 1401 KREI Blvd. 63640. Phone: (573) 756-6476. Fax: (573) 756-1110.E-mail: j98@j98.com Web Site:www.myMOinfo.com Licensee: Festus/Farmington License Co. LLC. Group owner: Shepherd Group (acq 8-8-2007; grpsl). Population served: 500,000 Natl. Network: ABC, Premiere Radio Networks, Talk Radio Network, Westwood One, NBC Radio, . Rgnl. Network: Missourinet. Missourinet Format: News/talk. News staff: 12; News: 40 hrs wkly. Target aud: General. ◆Dean Goodman, pres; Richard Womack, gen mgr; Kimberly Long, stn mgr; Scott Kubala, progmg dir; Kevin Brooks, chief of engrg.

***KSEF(FM)**— Sept 14, 2006: 88.9 mhz; 9.5 kw. Ant 640 ft TL: N37 47 57 W90 33 43. Stereo. Hrs open:
Rebroadcasts KRCU(FM) Cape Girardeau 100%.

Southeast Missouri State University, One University Plaza, Cape Girardeau, 63701. Phone: (573) 651-5070. Fax: (573) 651-5071.E-mail: comments@krcu.org Web Site:www.southeastpublicradio.org Licensee: Board of Regents, Southeast Missouri State University. Population served: 109,918 Natl. Network: NPR, PRI, . Dow, Lohres & Albertson. Format: Classical, jazz, news. ◆Dan Woods, gen mgr; Jason Brown, opns dir; Amanda Lincoln, dev dir; Allen Lane, chief of engrg.

KTJJ(FM)— June 5, 1977: 98.5 mhz; 100 kw. Ant 1,040 ft TL: N37 43 07 W90 33 01. Stereo. Hrs open: 24 Box 461, 63640. Secondary address: 1401 KREI Blvd. 63640. Phone: (573) 756-6476. Fax: (573) 756-1110.E-mail: j98@j98.com Web Site:www.myMOinfo.com Licensee: Festus/Farmington License Co. LLC. Population served: 750,000 Natl. Network: ABC, . Format: Country. News staff: 12; News: 16 hrs wkly. Target aud: General. ◆Dean Goodman, pres; Richard Womack, gen mgr; Kim Long, stn mgr; Scott Kubala, progmg dir; Kevin Brooks, chief of engrg.

Fayette

KSSZ(FM)— July 15, 1994: 93.9 mhz; 25 kw. 328 ft TL: N39 03 28 W92 28 49. Stereo. Hrs open: 24 3215 Lemone Industrial Blvd., Suite 200, Columbia, 65201. Phone: (573) 875-1099. Fax: (573) 875-2439.E-mail: eagle939@zrgmail.com Web Site:www.939theeagle.com Licensee: Zimmer Radio of Mid-Missouri Inc. (acq 9-27-96; $550,000). Population served: 250,000 Natl. Network: ABC, Jones Radio Networks, Westwood One, . Wire Svc: AP Format: News/talk. News staff: 2; News: 4 hrs wkly. Target aud: 25-54; adults. ◆Carla Lieble, gen mgr; Cynthia Schreen, gen sls mgr; Shelley Tucker, news dir; Drew Haines, chief of engrg.

Ferguson

***KCFV(FM)**— Apr 17, 1972: 89.5 mhz; 100 w. 159 ft TL: N38 46 07 W90 17 16. Stereo. Hrs open: 16 3400 Pershall Rd., St. Louis, 63135-1499. Phone: (314) 513-4472. Fax: (314) 513-4478. Fax: (314) 513-4217.E-mail: tgorry@stlcc.edu Web Site:www.stlcc.edu/fv/kcfv Licensee: St. Louis Community College District. Population served: 100,000 Dow, Lohnes & Albertson. Format: Hot ac, rhythmic. News: 2 hrs wkly. Target aud: General. Spec prog: Jazz 8 hrs, Black 4 hrs, hard rock 4 hrs wkly. ◆Dianna L. Kirby, gen mgr; Tim Croskey, chief of engrg.

Festus

KJFF(AM)— May 10, 1951: 1400 khz; 1 kw-U. TL: N38 13 56 W90 23 50. Hrs open: 24 Box 368, 63028. Phone: (636) 937-7642. Fax: (636) 937-3636.E-mail: kjff@k98.com Web Site:www.kjff.com Licensee: Festus/Farmington License Co. LLC. Group owner: Shepherd Group (acq 8-8-2007; grpsl). Population served: 250,000 Natl. Network: ABC, . Rgnl. Network: Missourinet. Missourinet Format: News/talk. News staff: 4; News: 30 hrs wkly. Target aud: General. ◆Dean Goodman, pres; Dick Womack, gen mgr; Kirk Mooney, stn mgr, sls dir; Matt West, progmg dir; Kevin Brooks, chief of engrg.

***KTBJ(FM)**— 1998: 89.3 mhz; 25 kw. Ant 371 ft TL: N38 09 16 W90 02 07. Stereo. Hrs open: 115 E. Main St., 63028. Phone: (636) 937-5222. Fax: (636) 937-5224.E-mail: info@ktbj.com Web Site:www.csnradio.com Licensee: CSN International (group owner; acq 6-17-98; $100,000). Population served: 42,000 Format: Christian talk/music. ◆Scott Parker, stn mgr.

Florissant

KFTK(FM)— Apr 15, 1977: 97.1 mhz; 100 kw. 560 ft TL: N38 46 45 W90 43 43. Stereo. Hrs open: 24 800 St. Louis Union St., The Powerhouse, St. Louis, 63103. Phone: (314) 231-9710. Fax: (314) 621-3000.E-mail: stl.ms@emies.com Licensee: Emmis Radio License LLC. Group owner: Emmis Communications Corp. (acq 9-26-2000; grpsl). Natl. Rep: McGavren Guild,. Format: Talk. ◆John Beck, sr VP, gen mgr & gen mgr.

Fredericktown

KYLS(AM)— June 29, 1963: 1450 khz; 1 kw-U. TL: N37 35 00 W90 17 31. Hrs open: 24 P.O. Box 305, Farmington, 63640. Secondary address: 900 East Karsch Blvd., Farmington Phone: (573) 701-9590. Fax: (573) 701-9696. Web Site:www.froggy96.com Licensee: Southern Star Broadcasting of Missouri LLC. (acq 5-8-2008; grpsl). Population served: 300,000 Natl. Network: ESPN Radio, . Format: Sports. Target aud: 24-55; Men. ◆Chip Miller, pres; Joel Jordan, VP & gen mgr.

Fulton

KFAL(AM)— Nov 14, 1950: 900 khz; 1 kw-D, 121 w-N. TL: N38 51 58 W91 57 15. Hrs open: 19 1805 Westminster, Jefferson City, 65251. Phone: (573) 642-3341. Phone: (573) 875-1099. Fax: (573) 642-3343. Licensee: Zimmer Radio of Mid-Missouri Inc. Group owner: Zimmer Radio Group (acq 11-19-99; grpsl). Population served: 439,000 Natl. Network: Motor Racing Net, . Missourinet Format: Traditional country. News staff: one; News: 3 hrs wkly. Target aud: 35 plus. Spec prog: Other 6 hrs wkly. ◆Jerry Zimmer, CEO; John Zimmer, chmn; Don Zimmer, pres; Jeremiah Washington, gen mgr, progmg dir; Steve Mallinkrott, gen sls mgr.

KKCA(FM)— 1970: 100.5 mhz; 6 kw. Ant 300 ft TL: N38 51 58 W91 57 15. Stereo. Hrs open: 24 1805 Westminster, Jefferson City, 65251. Phone: (573) 642-3341. Phone: (573) 875-1099. Fax: (573) 642-3343. Licensee: Zimmer Radio of Mid-Missouri Inc. Population served: 12,248 Natl. Network: ABC, Westwood One, Jones Radio Networks, . Format: Classic hits. News staff: one; News: 2 hrs wkly. Target aud: 25-54.

Gainesville

KMAC(FM)— Mar 17, 1994: 99.7 mhz; 50 kw. Ant 492 ft TL: N36 36 06 W92 25 48. Stereo. Hrs open: 24 100 Bluebird St., Harrison, AR, 72601. Phone: (870) 743-1157. Fax: (870) 743-1168.E-mail: kmac997@hotmail.com Licensee: Pearson Broadcasting of Gainesville Inc. Group owner: Pearson Broadcasting (acq 12-19-94; $150,000; 2-13-95). Format: Modern rock. Target aud: General. ◆David Fransen, gen mgr.

Gallatin

KGOZ(FM)— June 1994: 101.7 mhz; 25 kw. Ant 423 ft TL: N39 53 14 W93 43 24. Stereo. Hrs open: 24 Box 217, 804 Main, Trenton, 64683. Phone: (660) 359-2727. Fax: (660) 359-4126.E-mail: john@kttn.com Web Site:www.kgozfm.com Licensee: PAR Broadcasting Co. Inc. (acq 1-3-94; $11,571 for CP;1-24-94). Population served: 50,000 Natl. Network: Jones Radio Networks, . Natl. Rep: Rgnl Reps,. Reddy, Begley & McCormick. Format: Hot country. News: 2 hrs wkly. Target aud: 14-50. ◆John Ausberger, pres; John Anthony, gen mgr.

Garden City

KCJK(FM)— January 2001: 105.1 mhz; 69 kw. 1,145 ft TL: N39 05 26 W94 28 18. Stereo. Hrs open: 24 5800 Foxridge Dr., Suite 600, Mission, KS, 66202. Phone: (913) 514-3000. Fax: (913) 514-3002. Web Site:www.1051jackfm.com Licensee: CMP Houston-KC LLC. Group owner: Susquehanna Radio Corp. (acq 5-3-2006; grpsl). Population served: 1,475,000 Natl. Rep: Katz Radio,. Format: Adult hits. News: 10.5 hrs wkly. Target aud: 25-54. ◆Pat Gibbs, gen sls mgr; Bryan Truta, progmg dir.

Gideon

KGLU(FM)—Not on air, target date: unknown: 103.9 mhz; 6 kw. Ant 328 ft TL: N36 32 10 W89 49 18. Hrs open: 5525 Yates Cove, Memphis, TN, 38120. Phone: (901) 685-0882. Licensee: Pollack Steel Supply Inc. (acq 3-8-2007; $155,000 for CP). ◆Sydney Pollack, pres.

Gladstone

KGGN(AM)— Nov 18, 1996: 890 khz; 1 kw-D, DA. TL: N39 20 03 W94 34 01. (CP: 960 w-D, DA). Hrs open: 1734 E. 63rd St., Suite 600, Kansas City, 64110. Phone: (816) 333-0092. Fax: (816) 363-8120.E-mail: kggnproduction@aol.com Web Site:www.kggnam.com Licensee: Mortenson Broadcasting Co. (group owner; acq 12-24-96; $450,000). Format: Gospel. ◆Doris Newman, gen mgr; Reggie Brown, progmg dir.

Gordonville

KCGQ-FM—Licensed to Gordonville. See Cape Girardeau

Halfway

KYOO-FM— April 1995: 99.1 mhz; 25 kw. Ant 328 ft TL: N37 45 41 W93 15 42. Hrs open:
Simulcast with KYOO(AM) Bolivar 100%.
205 N. Pike Ave., Bolivar, 65613-1550. Phone: (417) 326-5259. Phone: (417) 326-5257. Fax: (417) 326-5900.E-mail: contact@kyooradio.com Web Site:www.kyooradio.com Licensee: KYOO Communications. Population served: 500,000 Format: Traditional Country, local news. News staff:

one; News: 5 hrs wkly. Target aud: 10-72. ◆Ann Paris, VP; Stephen Paris, pres, gen mgr, gen sls mgr & progmg dir.

Hannibal

KGRC(FM)— Nov 28, 1968: 92.9 mhz; 100 kw. 489 ft TL: N39 43 45 W91 24 15. (CP: Ant 502 ft. TL: N39 43 48 W91 24 19). Stereo. Hrs open: 329 Maine St., Lincoln Douglas Bldg., Quincy, IL, 62301. Phone: (217) 224-4102. Fax: (217) 224-4133.E-mail: jbates@staradio.com Web Site:www.real929.com Licensee: STARadio Corp. (group owner; acq 12-2-98; $2.1 million with KZZK(FM) New London). Population served: 250,000 Natl. Network: Westwood One, . Natl. Rep: Katz Radio,. Pepper & Corazzini. Format: Hot adult contemp. News staff: one; News: one hr wkly. Target aud: 18-49; women. ◆Howard Doss, pres; Michael J. Moyers, VP & gen mgr; Casey, progmg dir, chief of engrg.

KHMO(AM)— April 1941: 1070 khz; 5 kw-D, 1 kw-N, DA-2. TL: N39 37 46 W91 22 33. Hrs open: 24 Box 711, 63401. Phone: (573) 221-3450. Fax: (573) 221-5331.E-mail: hsmith@graido.com Licensee: Bick Broadcasting. (acq 8-1-85; $1.35 million; 6-17-85). Population served: 100,000 Natl. Rep: McGavren Guild,. Eugene T. Smith. Wire Svc: Weather Wire Format: News/talk, sports. News staff: 2; News: 22 hrs wkly. ◆Ed Foxall, gen mgr, gen sls mgr; Jeff Dorsey, progmg dir; John Hanvelt, news dir; Gary Glaenzer, chief of engrg.

*KJIR(FM)— April 2000: 91.7 mhz; 5.1 kw. Ant 554 ft TL: N39 43 48 W91 24 19. Stereo. Hrs open: 24 Believers Broadcasting Corp., 220 N. 6th St., Quincy, IL, 62301. Phone: (217) 221-9410. Fax: (217) 228-0966.E-mail: thecross@kjir.org Licensee: Believers Broadcasting Corp. Population served: 200,000 Format: Southern gospel. News: 7.5 hrs wkly. Target aud: Christian; 30-70. ◆I. Carl Geisendorfer, gen mgr; Michael Wartman, progmg dir.

Harrisonville

KCFX(FM)— July 19, 1974: 101.1 mhz; 97 kw. Ant 1,099 ft TL: N39 01 20 W94 30 49. Stereo. Hrs open: 6th Fl., 5800 Foxridge Dr., Mission, KS, 66202. Phone: (913) 514-3000. Fax: (913) 514-3001.E-mail: info@kcfxfm.com Web Site:www.101thefox.net Licensee: Susquehanna Kansas City Partnership. Group owner: Susquehanna Radio Corp. (acq 7-14-00; grpsl). Population served: 1,300,000 Natl. Rep: Katz Radio,. Format: Classic rock. Target aud: 25-54; baby boomers. ◆Dave Alpert, VP, gen mgr; Chris Hoffman, opns mgr, mktg mgr; Jeanna White, gen sls mgr.

Hayti

KCRV(AM)—See Caruthersville

KCRV-FM—See Caruthersville

*WGCQ(FM)— Jan 1, 1993: 94.9 mhz; 6 kw. Ant 220 ft TL: N36 19 06 W89 42 01. Hrs open: 2351 Sunset Blvd., Suite 170-218, Rocklin, CA, 95765. Phone: (916) 251-1600. Fax: (916) 251-1650. Web Site:www.godscountryradionetwork.com Licensee: Educational Media Foundation. Group owner: EMF Broadcasting (acq 1-25-2001; $450,000). Format: Country, gospel. Target aud: 18-50. ◆Mike Novak, pres.

Hermann

KQQX(FM)— September 1985: 93.3 mhz; 33 kw. Ant 594 ft TL: N38 48 17 W91 15 52. Hrs open: 3418 Douglas Rd., Florissant, 63034. Phone: (314) 921-9330.E-mail: 93x@knsx.com Web Site:www.knsx.com Licensee: Broadcast Communications Inc. Format: Alternative. ◆Ruth Choate, gen mgr.

High Point

*KMCV(FM)— 2001: 89.9 mhz; 18 kw vert. Ant 325 ft TL: N38 35 48 W92 32 17. Hrs open: 3732 W. Truman Blvd., Jefferson City, 65109. Phone: (573) 893-8990. Fax: (573) 893-8991.E-mail: kmcv@bottradionetwork.com Web Site:www.bottradionetwork.com Licensee: Community Broadcasting Inc. Group owner: Bott Radio Network (acq 2-7-01; $1.25 million with KSCV(FM) Springfield). Natl. Network: USA, . Format: Christian talk. ◆Richard Bott II, exec VP; Sue Stoltz, gen mgr; Pat Rulon, natl sls mgr; Rachel Moser, mktg mgr; Jason Potocnik, traf mgr.

Hollister

KBCV(AM)— 2004: 1570 khz; 5 kw-D, 3 kw-N, DA-2. TL: N36 36 52 W93 12 49 (D), N36 36 51 W93 12 50 (N). Hrs open: 500 West Main St., Ste. 103-A, Branson, 65616. Phone: (417) 336-1570. Fax: (417) 336-2097.E-mail: kbcv@bottradionetwork.com Web Site:www.bottradionetwork.com Licensee: Bott Communications Inc. Group owner: Bott Radio Network. Natl. Network: USA, . Format: Christian Talk. ◆Richard P Bott Sr., pres; Monna Stafford, gen mgr; Pat Rulon, natl sls mgr; Rachel Moser, mktg mgr; Jason Potocnik, traf mgr.

Houston

KBTC(AM)— June 28, 1962: 1250 khz; 1 kw-D, 51 w-N. TL: N37 19 45 W91 53 55. Hrs open: Box 230, 17647 Hwy. B, 65483. Phone: (417) 967-3353. Fax: (417) 967-2281. Licensee: Metropolitan Radio Group Inc. Population served: 42,178

KUNQ(FM)— May 1965: 99.3 mhz; 30 kw. Ant 604 ft TL: N37 05 32 W92 03 10. Stereo. Hrs open: 24 Box 230, 17647 Hwy. B, 65483. Phone: (417) 967-3353. Fax: (417) 967-2281.E-mail: kunq@kunq.net Web Site:www.bigcountry99.com Licensee: Metropolitan Radio Group Inc. (group owner; acq 6-22-2000; $150,000 with co-located AM). Population served: 900,000 Shaw Pittman. Format: Classic country. News staff: one; News: 12 hrs wkly. Target aud: 25-69; blue collar. Spec prog: Farm 2 hrs, gospel 10 hrs wkly. ◆Rick Vermillion, gen mgr; Shelly Adams, stn mgr; Marilou Candela, sls dir, gen sls mgr; Max Owens, gen sls mgr; Bob Moore, mus dir, chief of engrg; Cynthia Spratt, news dir.

Independence

KCTE(AM)— 1947: 1510 khz; 10 kw-D, DA. TL: N39 04 14 W94 26 58. Hrs open: Sunrise-sunset 6721 W. 121 St., Overland Park, 66209. Phone: (913) 344-1500. Fax: (913) 344-1599. Web Site:www.1510.com Licensee: Union Broadcasting Inc. (acq 8-19-98; $925,000). Natl. Network: CBS Radio, ESPN Radio, Sporting News Radio Network, . Format: Talk and sports. News staff: 2. Target aud: Adults. ◆Chad Boeger, gen mgr, progmg dir; Nick McCabe, opns dir; Gary Hailes, gen sls mgr; Dennis Rooney, news dir.

Ironton

KYLS-FM— Jan 6, 1984: 95.9 mhz; 3.2 kw. 922 ft TL: N37 34 23 W90 41 35. Stereo. Hrs open: 24 P.O. Box 305, Farmington, 63640. Phone: (573) 701-9590. Fax: (573) 701-9696.E-mail: joel.jordan @southernstarbroadcasting.com Web Site:www.froggy96.com Licensee: Southern Star Broadcasting of Missouri LLC. (acq 5-8-2008; grpsl). Format: Today's Country. Target aud: 18-54. ◆Chip Miller, pres; Joel Jordan, VP, opns mgr; Jeremy Martin, progmg dir; Wanda Emert, prom dir & traf mgr.

Jackson

KJXX(AM)— March 1972: 1170 khz; 250 w-D, 5 w-N. TL: N37 22 55 W89 39 12. Hrs open: 24 907 S. Kings Hwy., Cape Girardeau, 63702. Phone: (573) 339-7000. Fax: (573) 651-4100. Licensee: W. Russell Withers Jr. (acq 6-28-2005; $150,000). Natl. Network: Fox News Radio, . Format: Relg, adult standards. Target aud: General. Spec prog: Parenting and family talk. ◆Rick Lambert, gen mgr.

KYRX(FM)—(Marble Hill, December 1999: 97.3 mhz; 3.6 kw. Ant 426 ft TL: N37 22 49 W90 04 49. Hrs open: 901 S. Kings Hwy., Cape Girardean, 63702. Phone: (573) 339-7000. Fax: (573) 651-4100. Licensee: Dana R. Withers. Natl. Rep: Katz Radio,. Format: Classic Top 40. ◆Rick Lambert, gen mgr.

Jefferson City

KBBM(FM)— 1974: 100.1 mhz; 33 kw. 600 ft TL: N38 31 25 W92 24 25. Stereo. Hrs open: 24 Prog sep from AM 3605 Country Club Dr., 65109. Phone: (573) 893- 5100. Fax: (573) 893-8330.E-mail: buzz@buzz.fm Web Site:www.buzz.fm Population served: 200,000 Format: Active rock. News staff: 2. Target aud: 18-34.

*KJLU(FM)— August 1973: 88.9 mhz; 29.5 kw. 510 ft TL: N38 27 29 W92 13 32. Stereo. Hrs open: 6 AM-midnight 1004 E. Dunklin St., 65102-0029. Phone: (573) 681-5301. Phone: (573) 681-5296. Fax: (573) 681-5299.E-mail: info@kjlu.com Web Site:www.lincolnu.edu/~kjlu/ Licensee: Board of Curators of Lincoln University. Population served: 200,000 Format: Jazz. Target aud: 18-54. ◆Michael P. Downey, gen mgr; LaVaughn Wilson, prom dir; Dan Turner, progmg dir; Leslie Cross, news dir.

KLIK(AM)— January 1937: 1240 khz; 1 kw-U. TL: N38 33 50 W92 11 21. Hrs open: 24 3605 Country Club Dr., 65109. Phone: (573) 893-5100. Fax: (573) 893-8330.E-mail: info@klik1240.com Web Site:www.klik1240.com Licensee: Cumulus Licensing LLC. Group owner: Cumulus Media Inc. (acq 4-26-2004; grpsl). Population served: 68000 Format: News/talk. News staff: 4; News: 39 hrs wkly. Target aud: 35 plus; mid to upper income-well informed. ♦Lew Dickey, pres; Brian Wilson, gen mgr, progmg dir; Darryl Burnett, gen sls mgr; Dean Morgan, news dir.

KTXY(FM)— Dec 1, 1969: 106.9 mhz; 100 kw. 1,250 ft TL: N38 38 16 W92 29 34. Stereo. Hrs open: Prog sep from AM 3215 LeMone Industrial, Suite 200, Columbia, 65201. Phone: (573) 875-1099. Fax: (573) 875-2439.E-mail: y107@zrgmail.com Web Site:www.y107.com Population served: 250,000 Format: Hot adult contemp. ♦Dave Wisniewski, gen sls mgr.

KWOS(AM)— February 1954: 950 khz; 5 kw-D, 500 w-N, DA-N. TL: N38 31 13 W92 10 42. Hrs open: 3109 S. 10 Mile Dr., 65109. Phone: (573) 893-5696. Fax: (573) 893-4137.E-mail: kati@zrgmail.com Web Site:www.kwos.com Licensee: Zimmer Radio of Mid-Missouri Inc. Group owner: Zimmer Radio Group (acq 11-19-99; grpsl). Population served: 58000 Format: News/talk. Spec prog: Farm 12 hrs wkly. ♦John Zimmer, chmn; Carla Leible, gen mgr; Russ Davis, gen sls mgr; Warren Krech, progmg dir; John Marsh, news dir; Jeff Studley, chief of engrg.

KZJF(FM)— 2000: 104.1 mhz; 6 kw. Ant 312 ft TL: N38 34 45 W92 14 02. Hrs open: 24 3605 Country Club Dr., 65109. Phone: (573) 893-5100. Fax: (573) 893-8330.E-mail: buzz@buzz.fm Licensee: Cumulus Licensing LLC. Group owner: Cumulus Media Inc. (acq 4-26-2004; grpsl). Population served: 100,000 Natl. Rep: Katz Radio,. Format: Country. ♦Greg DeRue, gen mgr; Darryl Burnett, gen sls mgr; C.J. Engle, prom dir; Mike Alan, progmg dir; Dean Morgan, news dir.

Joplin

KIXQ(FM)— November 1974: 102.5 mhz; 100 kw. 410 ft TL: N37 04 43 W94 32 26. Stereo. Hrs open: 24 2702 E. 32nd, 64804. Phone: (417) 624-1025. Fax: (417) 781-6842. Web Site:www.kix1025.com Licensee: Zimco Inc. Group owner: Zimmer Radio Group (acq 6-30-97; grpsl). Format: Contemp country. News staff: one; News: 2 hrs wkly. Target aud: 25-54. Spec prog: Class 3 hrs wkly. ♦James Zimmer, pres; Chad Elliott, opns mgr; Jessica Leighman, prom dir; Cody Carlson, progmg dir; Tom Hoglen, news dir; Mel Williams, chief of engrg.

***KOBC(FM)—** Mar 17, 1969: 90.7 mhz; 60 kw. Ant 500 ft TL: N37 03 11 W94 23 17. Stereo. Hrs open: 18 2351 Sunset Blvd., Suite 170-218, Rocklin, CA, 95765. Phone: (916) 251-1600. Fax: (916) 251-1650. Licensee: Educational Media Foundation. (acq 10-1-2008; $1 million). Population served: 250,000 Format: Christian contemp. ♦Mike Novak, pres.

KSYN(FM)— Dec 19, 1960: 92.5 mhz; 100 kw. 430 ft TL: N37 04 10 W94 32 49. Stereo. Hrs open: 2702 E. 32nd, 64804. Phone: (417) 624-1025. Fax: (417) 781-6842. Web Site:www.ksyn925.com Licensee: Zimco Inc. Group owner: Zimmer Radio Group (acq 6-30-97; grpsl). Format: CHR. Target aud: 18-39. ♦Larry Boyd, gen mgr; Chad Elliott, opns mgr; Jessica Leighman, prom dir; Steve Kraus, progmg dir; Tom Hoglen, news dir; Mel Williams, chief of engrg.

***KXMS(FM)—** Apr 5, 1986: 88.7 mhz; 10 kw. 185 ft TL: N37 05 57 W94 27 46. Stereo. Hrs open: Missouri Southern State Univ., 3950 E. Newman, 64801-1595. Phone: (417) 625-9356. Fax: (417) 625-9742.E-mail: kxms@mssc.edu Web Site:www.kxms.org Licensee: Board of Governors—Missouri Southern State College Format: Joplin's fine art stn. Spec prog: Big band 2 hrs wkly. ♦Jeffrey Skibbe, gen mgr; Jeffrey Scibbe, progmg dir.

KZRG(AM)— Nov 21, 1948: 1310 khz; 5 kw-D, 1 kw-N, DA-2. TL: N37 07 03 W94 32 41. Hrs open: 24 2702 E. 32nd St., 64804. Phone: (417) 624-1025. Fax: (417) 781-6842.E-mail: chade@zrgmail.com Web Site:http://www.1310kzrg.com Licensee: Zimmer Radio Inc. (acq 11-15-2005; $350,100). Natl. Network: Fox News Radio, . Natl. Rep: Christal,. Wire Svc: AP Format: News/talk. News staff: 4; News: news prgmg 5 hrs wkly. ♦James Zimmer, pres; Larry Boyd, gen mgr; Chad Elliott, progmg dir; Kara Marxer, news dir; Mel Williams, chief of engrg.

KZYM(AM)— June 1, 1946: 1230 khz; 1 kw-U. TL: N37 04 48 W94 33 10. Hrs open: 24 2702 E. 32nd St., 64804. Phone: (417) 624-1025. Fax: (417) 626-7111.E-mail: info@kzym.com Web Site:www.1230thetalker.com Licensee: Zimmer Radio Inc. (acq 9-30-2005; $300,000). Population served: 115,000 Format: Talk. News staff: one; News: 2 hrs wkly. Target aud: General. ♦James Zimmer, pres.

WMBH(AM)— May 25, 1962: 1560 khz; 10 kw-D, DA. TL: N37 04 10 W94 32 49. Hrs open: 6 AM-9 PM 611 S. Main St., 64801. Phone: (417) 781-1313. Fax: (417) 781-1316. Licensee: Hardman Broadcasting Inc. Group owner: Petracom Media L.L.C. (acq 8-11-2005; $1). Population served: 360,000 Format: Hip hop, rhythm and blues hits. ♦Dave Clemons, gen sls mgr.

Kansas City

KBEQ-FM— November 1960: 104.3 mhz; 100 kw. 987 ft TL: N39 04 59 W94 28 49. Stereo. Hrs open: 24 508 Westport Rd., Suite 202, 64111. Phone: (816) 753-4000. Fax: (816) 753-8771. Web Site:info@q104kc.com Licensee: Wilks License Co.-Kansas City LLC. Group owner: Infinity Broadcasting Corp. (acq 1-10-2007; grpsl). Population served: 1,239,000 Koteen & Naftalin. Format: Country. News staff: one; News: 6 hrs wkly. Target aud: 18-54; women. ♦Mike Rowen, gen mgr; Ted Ivey, gen sls mgr; Mike Kennedy, progmg dir; Jillian Gregg, news dir; Ben Weiss, chief of engrg.

KCCV(AM)—See Overland Park, KS

KCFX(FM)—See Harrisonville

KCKC(FM)— Mar 5, 1961: 102.1 mhz; 100 kw. Ant 1,118 ft TL: N39 05 26 W94 28 18. Hrs open: CBS Radio, 508 Port Rd, Suite202, 64111. Phone: (816) 561-9102. Fax: (816) 531-6547.E-mail: info@ksrh.com Web Site:www.star102.com Licensee: Wilks License Co.-Kansas City LLC. Group owner: Infinity Broadcasting Corp. (acq 1-10-2007; grpsl). Population served: 402,600 Wire Svc: UPI Format: Hot adult contemp. ♦Mike Rowen, gen mgr; Tony DeMarco, gen sls mgr; Heather Fischer, prom dir.

KCMO(AM)— March 1922: 710 khz; 10 kw-D, 5 kw-N, DA-2. TL: N39 19 08 W94 29 48. Stereo. Hrs open: 24 5800 Foxridge Dr., Suite 600, Mission, KS, 66202. Phone: (913) 514-3000. Fax: (913) 514-3007. Web Site:www.710kcmo.com Licensee: Susquehanna Kansas City Partnership. Group owner: Susquehanna Radio Corp. (acq 7-14-2000; grpsl). Population served: 1,349,300 Natl. Rep: Katz Radio,. Cohn & Marks. Format: Talk. News staff: 3; News: 30 hrs wkly. Target aud: 35-64. Spec prog: Pub affrs one hrs wkly. ♦Dave Alpert, VP, mktg mgr; Jeanna White, gen sls mgr; Chris Hoffman, progmg dir.

KCMO-FM— May 4, 1948: 94.9 mhz; 100 kw. Ant 1,120 ft TL: N39 05 26 W94 28 18. Stereo. Hrs open: 24 Prog sep from AM 5800 Foxridge Dr., Suite 600, Mission, KS, 66202. Phone: (913) 514-3000. Fax: (913) 514-3003.E-mail: info@kcmofm.com Licensee: Susquehanna Kansas City Partnership. Natl. Rep: Katz Radio,. Format: Greatest Hits of the 60's & 70's. News staff: one; News: 2 hrs wkly. Target aud: 25-54. ♦Page Olson, gen sls mgr; Don Daniels, progmg dir.

KCNW(AM)—See Fairway, KS

KCSP(AM)— Feb 16, 1922: 610 khz; 5 kw-U. TL: N38 59 03 W94 37 40. Stereo. Hrs open: 24 7000 Squibb Rd, Mission, KS, 66202. Phone: (913) 744-3600. Fax: (913) 677-8061.E-mail: info@610sports.com Web Site:www.610sports.com Licensee: Entercom Kansas City License L.L.C. Group owner: Entercom Communications Corp. (acq 10-17-97; grpsl). Population served: 1,435,800 Natl. Network: Sporting News Radio Network, . Natl. Rep: D & R Radio,. Format: Country. News staff: News progmg 8 hrs wkly Target aud: 25-54; general. ♦Dave Alpert, gen mgr; Dustin Boehm, prom dir, rsch dir; Allan Davis, progmg dir; Wayne WalkerParks, gen sls mgr & news dir.

KCTE(AM)—See Independence

***KCUR-FM—** October 1957: 89.3 mhz; 100 kw. Ant 820 ft TL: N39 04 59 W94 28 49. Stereo. Hrs open: 24 4825 Troost, Suite 202, 64110. Phone: (816) 235-1551. Fax: (816) 235-2864.E-mail: kcur@umkc.edu Web Site:www.kcur.org Licensee: Curators of the University of Missouri. Group owner: The Curators of the University of Missouri Population served: 1,500,000 Natl. Network: NPR, PRI, . Format: Pub affrs, news. News staff: 3; News: 50 hrs wkly. Target aud: General; educated. Spec prog: Sp 2 hrs wkly. ♦Patricia Deal Cahill, gen mgr; Parker Van Hecke, dev dir; Bill Anderson, progmg VP; Robert Moore, mus dir; Frank Morris, news dir, news rptr; Robin Cross, engrg mgr, chief of engrg; Steve Bell, reporter.

KCZZ(AM)—See Mission, KS

KEXS(AM)—See Excelsior Springs

***KKFI(FM)—** Feb 28, 1988: 90.1 mhz; 100 kw. 503 ft TL: N39 05 05 W94 28 47. Stereo. Hrs open: 24 Box 32250, 64171-2250. Secondary address: 900 1/2 Westport Rd. 64111. Phone: (816) 931-3122. Phone: (816) 931-5534. Fax: (816) 931-7870.E-mail: info@kkfi.org Web Site:www.kkfi.org Licensee: Mid-Coast Radio Project Inc. Format: News/ talk. News: 10 hrs wkly. Target aud: General; women & minorities. Spec prog: Jazz 10 hrs, blues 9 hrs, Sp 16 hrs, folk 4 hrs, American Indian 2 hrs wkly. ♦Dorothy Hawkins, gen mgr.

KKSN(FM)— October 1962: 99.7 mhz; 100 kw. Ant 1,010 ft TL: N39 05 01 W94 30 57. Stereo. Hrs open: 7000 Squibb Rd., Mission, KS, 66202. Phone: (913) 744-3600.E-mail: gberg@enentercom.com Web Site:www.997theboulevard.com Licensee: Entercom Kansas City License L.L.C. Format: AAA. ♦Kevin Klein, gen sls mgr; Greg Bergen, progmg dir.

***KLJC(FM)—** Aug 9, 1970: 88.5 mhz; 100 kw. 745 ft TL: N39 04 24 W94 29 06. Stereo. Hrs open: 24 c/o Calvary Bible College, 15800 Calvary Rd., 64147-1341. Phone: (816) 331-8700. Fax: (816) 331-3497.E-mail: kljc@kljc.org Web Site:www.kljc.org Licensee: Calvary Bible College. Population served: 1,507,087 Natl. Network: Salem Radio Network, . Format: Christian contemp. News: 6 hrs wkly. Target aud: 25-54. ♦Wayne Geiger, gen mgr; Michael Griman, progmg dir; Glenn Williams, chief of engrg.

KMBZ(AM)— 1921: 980 khz; 5 kw-U, DA-N. TL: N39 02 17 W94 36 55. Hrs open: 7000 Squibb Rd., Mission, KS, 66202. Phone: (913) 677-8998. Fax: (913) 677-8901.E-mail: info@kmbzam.com Web Site:www.kmbz.com Licensee: Entercom Kansas City News License L.L.C. Group owner: Entercom Communications Corp. (acq 3-6-97; grpsl). Population served: 1,349,300 Format: News radio. ♦Rich Deutsch, gen sls mgr; Neil Larrimore, progmg dir; Nicole Teich, news dir; Mike Cooney, chief of engrg; Megan Wilson, traf mgr.

KMXV(FM)— Mar 3, 1958: 93.3 mhz; 100 kw. Ant 1,066 ft TL: N39 00 57 W94 30 57. Stereo. Hrs open: 24 4717 Grand Ave., Suite 600, 64112. Secondary address: 508 West Port Road, Suite 202 64111. Phone: (816) 756-5698. Fax: (816) 931-8540.E-mail: info@mix93.com Web Site:www.mix93.com Licensee: Wilks License Co.-Kansas City LLC. Group owner: Infinity Broadcasting Corp. (acq 1-10-2007; grpsl). Population served: 1,500,000 Format: CHR. News staff: one. Target aud: 18-49; women. ♦Mike Rowen, gen mgr; Mike Kennedy, opns mgr; Mark Herrell, gen sls mgr; Teresa Maxwell, news dir; Ben Weiss, chief of engrg.

KPHN(AM)— Sept 1, 1971: 1190 khz; 5 kw-D, 250 w-N, DA-2. TL: N39 03 49 W94 30 37. Stereo. Hrs open: 24 1212 Baltimore, 64105. Phone: (816) 421-1900. Fax: (816) 471-1320.E-mail: mark.t.ballard@abc.com Web Site:www.radiodisney.com Licensee: Radio Disney Group LLC. Group owner: ABC Inc. (acq 7-19-2002; $3.8 million). Population served: 2,165,000 Natl. Network: Radio Disney, . Format: Children. ♦Bob Martin, gen mgr; Robert Hill, prom mgr.

KPRS(FM)— 1963: 103.3 mhz; 100 kw. 994 ft TL: N39 00 57 W94 30 24. Stereo. Hrs open: 24 Prog sep from AM 11131 Colorado Ave., 64137. Phone: (816) 763-2040. Fax: (816) 966-1055.E-mail: 103@kprs.com Web Site:www.kprs.com Format: Urban contemp. News: one hr wkly. Target aud: 25-54; mid-upper income. ♦Rich McCauley, prom dir; Beth Baker, traf mgr.

KPRT(AM)— 1950: 1590 khz; 1 kw-D, 47 w-N. TL: N39 04 05 W94 32 10. Hrs open: 24 11131 Colorado Ave., 64137. Phone: (816) 763-2040. Fax: (816) 966-1055. Licensee: Carter Broadcast Group Inc. (group owner). Population served: 507,087 Natl. Rep: Eastman Radio,. Bryan Cave. Format: Gospel. Target aud: 25-54. ♦Beth Baker, chmn, traf mgr; Michael Carter, gen mgr; Audrey Herbert, natl sls mgr; Vic Dyson, sls dir & rgnl sls mgr; Andre Carson, progmg dir; Rich McCauley, news dir; Mark Leaver, chief of engrg.

KQRC-FM—(Leavenworth, KS) 1962: 98.9 mhz; 100 kw. 990 ft TL: N39 04 14 W94 54 39. Stereo. Hrs open: 7000 Squibb Rd., Mission, KS, 66202. Phone: (913) 744-3600. Fax: (913) 677-8061.E-mail: info@989therock.com Web Site:www.989therock.com Licensee: Entercom Kansas City License LLC. Group owner: Entercom Communications Corp. (acq 7-14-00; grpsl). Crowell & Moring. Format: AOR. Target aud: 18-34; above average education & income; upscale professionals. ♦Dave Alpert, gen mgr; Kevin Kline, sls dir; Jennifer Morton, prom dir; Bob Edwards, progmg dir.

KRBZ(FM)— Jan 1, 1959: 96.5 mhz; 99 kw. 984 ft TL: N39 00 57 W94 30 24. Stereo. Hrs open: 24 4935 Belinder Rd., West Wood, 66205. Phone: (913) 677-8998. Fax: (913) 677-7520.E-mail: bedwards@entercom.com Web Site:www.965thebuzz.com Licensee: Entercom Kansas City License L.L.C. Group owner: Entercom Communications Corp. (acq 7-14-00; grpsl). Population served: 1500000 Wiley, Rein & Fielding. Format: Rock/AOR. Target aud: 25 plus; adults with above-average disposable income. ♦Cindy Schloss, gen mgr.

KUDL(FM)—See Kansas City, KS

WHB(AM)— June 10, 1936: 810 khz; 50 kw-D, 5 kw-N, DA-N. TL: N39 18 21 W94 34 30. Hrs open: 24 6721 W. 121st St., Overland Park, KS, 66209. Phone: (913) 344-1500. Fax: (913) 344-1599. Web Site:www.810whb.com Licensee: Union Broadcasting Inc. (acq 11-23-99; $8 million). Natl. Network: ESPN Radio, Sporting News Radio Network, . Format: Sports talk. News staff: 2; News: 19 hrs wkly. Target aud: Males: 18 plus. Spec prog: Sp 2 hrs wkly. ♦Chad Boeger, gen mgr, progmg dir; Nick McCabe, opns dir; Gabe Boucher, prom dir; Ed Treese, chief of engrg.

Kennett

***KAUF(FM)**— June 1998: 89.9 mhz; 1 kw. 164 ft TL: N36 14 32 W90 03 54. Hrs open: Box 3206, American Family Radio, Tupelo, MS, 38803. Phone: (662) 844-8888. Fax: (662) 842-6791. Web Site:www.afr.net Licensee: American Family Association. Group owner: American Family Radio Format: Inspirational Christian. ♦Marvin Sanders, gen mgr.

KBOA(AM)— 1963: 1540 khz; 1 kw-D. TL: N36 15 11 W90 02 56. Hrs open: Box 509, 63857. Phone: (573) 888-4616. Fax: (573) 888-4890. Licensee: Pollack Broadcasting Co. (group owner; acq 9-25-98; $450,000 with KBOA-FM Piggott, AR). Population served: 50,000 Format: Music of Your Life. Spec prog: Farm 5 hrs wkly. ♦Perry Jones, gen mgr & gen sls mgr; Monte Lyons, progmg dir; Charles Isbell, news dir; Palmer Johnson, chief of engrg.

KOTC(AM)— July 19, 1947: 830 khz; 10 kw-D. TL: N36 13 29 W90 04 31. Hrs open: Sunrise-sunset Box 271, 63857. Secondary address: 700 N. Bypass 63857. Phone: (573) 686-3700. Fax: (573) 686-6116.E-mail: kotc@sheltonbbs.com Web Site:www.foxradionetwork.com Licensee: Eagle Bluff Enterprises (acq 9-18-96; $190,000). Population served: 20,000 Format: Talk. News staff: one. Target aud: 35-65; adults. ♦Steven Fuchs, pres, gen mgr & progmg dir; Charles Isabell, news dir; P.J. Johnson, chief of engrg.

KXOQ(FM)— Dec 13, 1995: 104.3 mhz; 6 kw. 328 ft TL: N36 21 01 W90 02 43. Hrs open: Box 271, 63857. Secondary address: 700 N. Bypass 63857. Phone: (573) 686-3700. Fax: (573) 686-6116.E-mail: kotc@sheltonbbs.com Web Site:www.foxradionetwork.com Format: Rock & oldies mix.

Kimberling City

KOMC-FM— 1992: 100.1 mhz; 36 kw. Ant 577 ft TL: N36 31 58 W93 19 43. Stereo. Hrs open: 24 202 Courtney St., Branson, 65616. Phone: (417) 334-6003. Fax: (417) 334-7141.E-mail: krzk@krzk.com Web Site:www.komc.com Licensee: KOMC-KRZK LLC. Group owner: Orr & Earls Broadcasting Inc. (acq 6-27-97; $1,064,919). Population served: 70,000 Natl. Network: ABC, CBS, . Format: Adult standards, big band. News staff: 2; News: 11 hrs wkly. Target aud: 45 plus; Branson & local tourists. ♦Charles Earls, pres; Scottie Earls, gen mgr, chief of opns; Steve Willoughby, stn mgr; Eric Marshall, progmg dir; Sally Kaucher, news dir.

Kirksville

***KCKV(FM)**—Not on air, target date: unknown: 91.9 mhz; 1 kw. Ant 308 ft TL: N40 13 46 W92 32 38. Hrs open: 535 Maine St., Suite 10, Quincy, IL, 62306. Phone: (573) 346-3200. Fax: (573) 346-1010. Licensee: Great Commission Broadcasting Corp. ♦Bruce Rice, gen mgr.

***KHGN(FM)**— Oct 6, 1997: 90.7 mhz; 32.5 kw. 325 ft TL: N40 13 46 W92 32 38. Stereo. Hrs open: 24 Box 500, 63501. Secondary address: RR5, Box 14AB 63501. Phone: (660) 665-0466. Fax: (660) 665-7304.E-mail: khgn@kvmo.net Web Site:www.khgn.org Licensee: Care Broadcasting Inc. Natl. Network: Moody, . Rgnl. Network: Moody. Format: Relg. Target aud: 30 plus; general. ♦Dennis Phelps, pres; Tom Lloyd, chief of engrg.

KIRX(AM)— Oct 17, 1947: 1450 khz; 1 kw-U. TL: N40 12 24 W92 34 31. Hrs open: 24 Box 130, 1308 N. Baltimore, 63501. Phone: (660) 665-3781. Fax: (660) 665-0711.E-mail: kirx@cableone.net Web Site:www.1450kirx.com Licensee: KIRX Inc. (acq 10-1-85; $1.3 million with co-located FM; 8-12-85). Population served: 25,000 Rgnl. Network: Brownfield. Brownfield Format: Oldies. News staff: 2; News: 40 hrs wkly. Target aud: 25-54; general. Spec prog: Farm 10 hrs wkly. ♦David L. Nelson, pres; Steven D. Lloyd, exec VP, gen mgr & gen sls mgr.

***KKTR(FM)**— 2002: 89.7 mhz; 3.5 kw. Ant 197 ft TL: N40 10 40 W92 34 40. Hrs open: 409 Jesse Hall, Columbia, 65211-1310. Phone: (573) 882-3431. Fax: (573) 882-2636. Web Site:www.kbia.org Licensee: Truman State University. Format: News, class, talk. ♦Mike Dunn, gen mgr; Robert Wells, gen sls mgr; John Bailey, progmg dir.

KLTE(FM)— May 20, 1991: 107.9 mhz; 100 kw. 715 ft TL: N39 57 23 W92 58 29. Hrs open: 24 3 Crown Dr., Suite 100, 63501. Phone: (660) 627-5583. Fax: (660) 665-8900.E-mail: klte@bottradionetwork.com Web Site:www.bottradionetwork.com Licensee: Bott Communications Inc. Group owner: Bott Radio Network Population served: 1,500,000 Natl. Network: USA, . Natl. Rep: Salem,. Format: Christian. News: 3 hrs wkly. Target aud: 35 plus. ♦Dick Bott Sr., CEO, pres; Trace Thurlby, COO; Richard Bott II, chmn; Tom Holdeman, CFO; Paul Shipman, gen sls mgr; Candy Green, progmg dir.

KRXL(FM)— September 1967: 94.5 mhz; 100 kw. Ant 1,010 ft TL: N40 14 34 W92 25 42. Stereo. Hrs open: 24 Box 130, 63501. Secondary address: 1308 N. Baltimore 63501. Phone: (660) 665-9828. Fax: (660) 665-0711.E-mail: krxl@cableone.net Web Site:www.945thex.com Licensee: KIRX Inc. Population served: 488,000 Natl. Network: ABC, . Format: Classic rock. News: 2 hrs wkly. Target aud: 25-54.

***KTRM(FM)**— Feb 10, 1998: 88.7 mhz; 1 kw. Ant 197 ft TL: N40 10 40 W92 34 40. Hrs open: 7 AM-2 AM SUB Truman State University, Div. Language & Literature, 63501. Phone: (660) 785-4000.E-mail: ktrmtheedge@hotmail.com Web Site:ktrm.truman.edu Licensee: Truman State University. Format: Alternative. News: 3 hrs wkly. ♦Clair Maronack, system mgr.

KTUF(FM)— Feb 14, 1983: 93.7 mhz; 50 kw. 492 ft TL: N40 13 38 W92 36 35. Stereo. Hrs open: 24 Box 130, 63501. Secondary address: 1308 N. Baltimore Rd. 63501. Phone: (660) 627-5883. Fax: (660) 665-0711.E-mail: ktuf@cableone.net Web Site:www.937ktuf.com Licensee: KIRX Inc. Natl. Network: ABC, . Format: Country. News staff: 2; News: 40 hrs wkly. Target aud: 18-44. ♦David L. Nelson, pres; Steven D. Lloyd, exec VP & gen mgr; Duncan Miller, opns mgr.

Knob Noster

***KCVQ(FM)**— July 1998: 89.7 mhz; 5 kw. 230 ft TL: N38 52 10 W93 32 58. Stereo. Hrs open: 24
Rebroadcasts KCVO-FM Camdenton 100%.
Box 800, c/o Spirit FM Radio, Camdenton, 65020. Phone: (573) 346-3200. Fax: (573) 346-1010.E-mail: email@spiritfm.org Web Site:www.spiritfm.org Licensee: Lake Area Educational Broadcasting Foundation. Population served: 120,000 Format: Contemporary Christian. News: One. Target aud: 25-45. ♦Alice McDermott, CFO; James J. McDermott, pres & gen mgr; James McDermott, progmg dir.

KXKX(FM)— June 24, 1983: 105.7 mhz; 40 kw. 502 ft TL: N38 46 28 W93 37 34. Stereo. Hrs open: 24 2209 S. Limit Ave., Sedalia, 65301. Phone: (660) 826-1050. Fax: (660) 827-5072.E-mail: info@kxkx.com Web Site:www.kxkx.com Licensee: Bick Broadcasting Co. (acq 7-19-89; $185,000; 8-7-89). Format: Hot Country. News staff: one; News: 5 hrs wkly. Target aud: 25-54. ♦Dennis Polk, gen mgr, gen sls mgr; Doug Sokolowski, progmg dir; Danny Hampton, news dir; Carl Zimmerschied, chief of engrg; Dee Johnson, traf mgr.

La Monte

KPOW-FM— Nov 18, 1998: 97.7 mhz; 100 kw. Ant 981 ft TL: N39 03 10 W93 16 01. Stereo. Hrs open: 24 301 S. Ohio Ave., Sedalia, 65301-4431. Phone: (660) 826-5005. Phone: (660) 829-9700. Fax: (660) 826-5557.E-mail: delliot@power977.com Web Site:www.power97.net Licensee: Sedalia Investment Group L.L.C. Population served: 232,000 Natl. Network: CNN Radio, . Format: Classic rock. News staff: one; News: 2 hrs wkly. Target aud: 25-54. Spec prog: Blues 6 hrs wkly. ♦Stu Steinmetz, gen mgr.

Lake Ozark

KQUL(FM)— May 9, 1994: 102.7 mhz; 6 kw. 328 ft TL: N38 02 06 W92 34 31. Stereo. Hrs open: 24 160 Hwy. 42, Kaiser, 65047. Phone: (573) 348-1958. Fax: (573) 348-1923.E-mail: mike@mix927.com Licensee: Benne Broadcasting of Lake Ozark Inc. (acq 5-20-98; $800,000). Format: Oldies. Target aud: 35-60. ♦Denny Benne, gen mgr; Greg Sullens, stn mgr; Mike Clayton, opns mgr & progmg dir.

Lamar

KHST(FM)— May 1, 1992: 101.7 mhz; 22 kw. Ant 328 ft TL: N37 25 27 W94 16 11. Stereo. Hrs open: Box 383, Pittsburg, KS, 66762. Secondary address: 412 Locust St., Pittsburg, KS 66762. Phone: (620) 232-5993. Fax: (620) 232-5550.E-mail: info@hometownstation.com Licensee: My Town Media Inc. (group owner; (acq 9-22-98; $330,000). Format: Country. Target aud: 25-54. ♦Lance Sayler, pres & gen mgr; Dave Lee, opns mgr.

Lebanon

KBNN(AM)— Oct 20, 1973: 750 khz; 5 kw-D. TL: N37 41 11 W92 41 35. Hrs open: 6 AM-sunset Box 1112, 18553 Gentry Rd., 65536. Phone: (417) 532-9111. Fax: (417) 532-3989.E-mail: kjel@regionalradio.com Web Site:www.regionalradio.com Licensee: Waynesville/Lebanon License Co. LLC. Group owner: Shepherd Group (acq 8-8-2007; grpsl). Population served: 208,000 Rgnl. Network: Agri-Net, Brownfield, Missourinet. Missourinet Format: Talk. News staff: 5; News: 35 hrs wkly. Target aud: 35-64; middle America. Spec prog: News, farm 8 hrs wkly. ♦Mike Edwards, gen mgr, gen sls mgr; Theresa Nixon, opns mgr; Marcy Todd, traf mgr.

KCLQ(FM)— May 18, 1979: 107.9 mhz; 19 kw. Ant 669 ft TL: N37 48 11 W92 33 01. Stereo. Hrs open: 24 Prog sep from AM 18785 Finch Rd., 65536. Phone: (417) 532-2962. Fax: (417) 532-5184.E-mail: kclq@kclq.com Web Site:www.kclq.com Population served: 350,000 Format: Country. News staff: 3; News: 3 hrs wkly. Target aud: 25-54; female.

KJEL(FM)— Oct 20, 1973: 103.7 mhz; 100 kw. Ant 984 ft TL: N37 49 10 W92 44 51. Stereo. Hrs open: 24 Box 1112, 18553 Gentry Rd., 65536. Phone: (417) 532-9111. Fax: (417) 532-3989. Web Site:www.regionalradio.com Licensee: Waynesville/Lebanon License Co. LLC. Population served: 804,000 Natl. Network: ABC, . Format: Country. News staff: 5; News: 45 hrs wkly. Target aud: 25-65; equal Male/Female. ♦Mike Edwards, gen mgr, gen sls mgr; Teresa Nixon, opns mgr; Bob Moore, chief of engrg; Mary Todd, traf mgr.

KLWT(AM)— July 4, 1948: 1230 khz; 1 kw-U. TL: N37 40 40 W92 41 16. Hrs open: 24 18785 Finch Rd., 65536. Phone: (417) 532-2962. Fax: (417) 532-5184.E-mail: klwt@klwt1230.com Web Site:www.klwt1230.com Licensee: Pearson Broadcasting of Lebanon Inc. Population served: 30,000 Format: Country, news/talk, sports. News staff: 3; News: 10 hrs wkly. Target aud: 30 plus; adults. ♦Jannise Restivo, pres, traf mgr; Dan Caldwell, gen mgr; Brian McClendon, rgnl sls mgr; Kit Caldwell, opns dir, progmg dir & news dir.

***KTTK(FM)**— 1992: 90.7 mhz; 11 kw. Ant 476 ft TL: N37 37 58 W92 45 22. Hrs open: 5 AM-midnight Box 1232, 65536. Phone: (417) 588-1435. Fax: (417) 532-3055. Licensee: Lebanon Educational Broadcasting Foundation. Natl. Network: USA, . Format: Christian. Spec prog: Gospel 7 hrs wkly. ♦Max Rhoades, gen mgr; Dave Hutton, progmg dir.

Lee's Summit

KLRX(FM)— 1998: 97.3 mhz; 55 kw. Ant 1,171 ft TL: N39 05 26 W94 28 18. Hrs open: 6721 W. 121st, Leawood, KS, 66209. Phone: (913) 344-1500. Fax: (913) 344-1599.E-mail: info@klove.com Web Site:www.klove.com Licensee: Union First Broadcasting LLC (acq 12-11-2003; $10 million). Natl. Network: K-Love, . Format: Contemp Christian. ♦Chad Boeger, gen mgr.

Lexington

KLEX(AM)— Apr 19, 1956: 1570 khz; 250 w-D, 58 w-N. TL: N39 11 14 W93 50 03. Hrs open: 24
Rebroadcasts KAYX(FM) Richmond 100%.
111 W. Main St., Richmond, 64085. Phone: (816) 470-9925. Fax: (816) 470-8925.E-mail: comments@bottradionetwork.com Web Site:www.bottradionetwork.com Licensee: Bott Communications Inc. Group owner: Bott Radio Network (acq 1994; with KAYX(FM) Richmond). Population served: 50,000 Natl. Network: USA, . Format: Christian talk. Target aud: 25-54. ♦Trace Thurlby, COO; Candy Green, pres; Tom Holdeman, CFO; Richard P. Bott II, exec VP; Eben Fowler, opns dir; Pat Rulon, natl sls mgr; Rachel Launius, mktg mgr; Jason Potochik, traf mgr.

KMJK(FM)— Sept 11, 1969: 107.3 mhz; 100 kw. 1,184 ft TL: N39 02 15 W93 55 48. Stereo. Hrs open: 24 5800 Foxridge Dr, Suite 600, Mission, KS, 66202. Phone: (913) 514-3000. Fax: (816) 353-2300.E-mail: magic@1073.com Licensee: CMP KC Licensing LLC. Group owner: Cumulus Media Inc. (acq 5-3-2006; grpsl). Population served: 2,000,000 Format: Urban. News staff: one; News: 5 hrs wkly. Target aud: 25-54. ♦Lewis W. Dickey Jr., CEO; Tim Robisch, gen mgr; Page Olson, sls dir; John Groves, prom dir; Jerold Jackson, progmg dir; Dennis Ebersoll, chief of engrg.

Liberty

KCXL(AM)— Feb 14, 1967: 1140 khz; 500 w-D, 5 w-N. TL: N39 14 18 W94 23 59. Hrs open: 310 S. La Frenz Rd., 64068. Phone: (816) 792-1140. Fax: (816) 792-8258.E-mail: kcxl11140@yahoo.com Web Site:www.kcxl.com Licensee: Alpine Broadcasting Corp.(4-2-84). Population served: 1,700,000 Natl. Network: Jones Radio Networks, AP Network News, . Reddy, Begley & McCormick. Format: Talk, variety, MOR. Target aud: 25-54; baby boomers. Spec prog: News 4 hrs, Sp 5 hrs, relg 3 hrs, health 17 hrs wkly. ◆David Brewer, opns mgr; Jonne Santoli, rgnl sls mgr; Peter E. Schartel, pres & progmg dir; Ed Treese, chief of engrg.

*KWJC(FM)— Apr 14, 1974: 91.9 mhz; 240 w. Ant 166 ft TL: N39 14 52 W94 24 47. Stereo. Hrs open: 24 500 College Hill, Box 1063, 64068. Phone: (816) 415-7594. Fax: (816) 415-5027. Licensee: William Jewell College. Population served: 100,000 Format: CHR, modern rock, class. News: 5 hrs wkly. Target aud: 12-34; men & women. Spec prog: Class 10 hrs, Christian 10 hrs wkly. ◆Paul Worstell, gen mgr.

WDAF-FM— Nov 9, 1979: 106.5 mhz; 100 kw. Ant 981 ft TL: N39 04 23 W94 29 06. Stereo. Hrs open: 7000 Squibb Rd, Mission, KS, 66202. Phone: (913) 677-8998. Fax: (913) 677-8061.E-mail: info@1065thewolf.com Web Site:www.1065thewolf.com Licensee: Entercom Kansas City License LLC. Group owner: Entercom Communications Corp. (acq 7-14-00; grpsl). Population served: 100,000 Natl. Rep: D & R Radio,. Format: Smooth jazz. Target aud: 18-34. ◆Dave Alpert, gen mgr, opns mgr; Dan Pendiville, gen sls mgr.

Licking

*KIKG(FM)— Not on air, target date: unknown: 91.1 mhz; 2 kw. Ant 358 ft TL: N37 37 06 W91 51 50. Hrs open: 282 Country Estate Dr., Springer, OK, 73458. Phone: (580) 653-2777. Licensee: Ron Elmore Ministries Inc. ◆Ron Elmore, pres.

Linn

KJMO(FM)— 2006: 97.5 mhz; 6 kw. Ant 328 ft TL: N38 29 56.9 W91 53 00.4. Hrs open: 3605 Country Club Dr., Jefferson City, 65109. Phone: (573) 893-5100. Fax: (573) 893-8330.E-mail: info@kjmo.com Web Site:www.kjmo.com Licensee: Cumulus Licensing LLC. Format: Oldies. ◆Darryl Burnett, gen sls mgr; Scott Boltz, progmg dir.

Louisiana

KJFM(FM)— Sept 4, 1984: 102.1 mhz; 1.85 kw. 387 ft TL: N39 26 29 W91 02 19. Stereo. Hrs open: Box 438, 63353. Secondary address: 615 Georgia St. 63353. Phone: (573) 754-5102. Fax: (573) 754-5544.E-mail: kjfmradio@yahoo.com Licensee: Foxfire Communications Inc. Natl. Network: CBS Radio, . Rgnl. Network: Missourinet. Missourinet Format: Country. News: 27 hrs wkly. Target aud: 25-54. ◆Thom T. Sanders, pres; Gordon Sanders, opns mgr, gen sls mgr; Mark Fronick, progmg dir; John Scheper, news dir.

Lutesville

KMHM(FM)— Aug 4, 1995: 104.1 mhz; 2.5 kw. 508 ft TL: N37 22 40 W89 56 04. Hrs open: 24 Box 266E, Hwy. B, Marble Hill, 63764. Phone: (573) 238-1041. Fax: (573) 238-0104.E-mail: kmhm1041@clas.net Web Site:www.kmhm.net Licensee: Southern Gospetality LLC. Natl. Network: Salem Radio Network, . Format: Southern gospel. News: 14 hrs wkly. Target aud: 30-55; Christians and family-oriented listeners. ◆Harold L. Lawder, CEO; Will Stephens, gen mgr; Glen Aulgur, stn mgr, gen sls mgr; Joy Duprey, progmg mgr; Sheila Kirkpatrick, mus dir; Tom Beattie, chief of engrg.

Macon

KIRK(FM)— 1998: 99.9 mhz; 12.5 kw. 462 ft TL: N39 36 02 W92 34 24. Hrs open: 24 Box 619, Moberly, 65270. Secondary address: 300 W. Reed St., Moberly 65270. Phone: (660) 263-6999. Fax: (660) 263-2300. Web Site:regionalradio.com Licensee: Moberly/Macon License Co. LLC. Group owner: Shepherd Group (acq 8-8-2007; grpsl). Format: HOT adult contemp. ◆Terry Strickland, gen mgr.

KLTI(AM)— Jan 30, 1966: 1560 khz; 1 kw-D. TL: N39 42 34 W92 27 50. (CP: COL Springfield. 660 khz; 1.5 kw-D, 44 w-N, DA-2. TL: N37 11 30 W93 32 22). Hrs open: 24 32968 US Hwy. 63 S., 63552. Phone: (660) 385-1560. Fax: (660) 385-7090.E-mail: klti@kltiradio.com Web

Site:www.kltiradio.com Licensee: Chirillo Electronics Inc. Group owner: Best Broadcast Group. Format: Country. Target aud: 25-44. ◆Dale A. Palmer, gen mgr.

Madison

KCDG(FM)— Not on air, target date: unknown: 97.3 mhz; 25 kw. Ant 328 ft TL: N39 28 52 W92 10 13. Hrs open: 525 S. Flagler Dr., # 21-A, West Palm Beach, FL, 33401. Phone: (561) 515-6142. Licensee: Christine Radio LLC. (acq 10-4-2007).

WGNU(AM)— See Saint Louis

Malden

KLSC(FM)— Nov 23, 1979: 92.9 mhz; 23.5 kw. 174 ft TL: N36 33 08 W89 58 42. Stereo. Hrs open: 6 AM-midnight Prog sep from AM 324 Broadway Cape, Girardeau, 63701. Phone: (573) 471-1400. Fax: (573) 471-1402. Format: Hot adult contemp. News staff: 2; News: 30 hrs wkly. Target aud: General. ◆Mike Renick, progmg dir.

KMAL(AM)— Sept 15, 1954: 1470 khz; 1 kw-D. TL: N36 33 08 W89 58 42. Hrs open: 6 AM-sunset
Simulcasts KSIM (Sikeston).
324 Broadway Cape, Girardeau, 63701. Phone: (573) 471-1400. Fax: (573) 471-1402. Web Site:www.1400ksim.com Licensee: MRR License LLC. Group owner: MAX Media L.L.C. (acq 6-2-2004; grpsl). Population served: 178000 Format: News/talk. News staff: 3. Target aud: 35 plus. ◆Christy Benton, gen mgr; Meg Davis, gen sls mgr; Tyler Morrison, progmg dir & news dir; Mike Coffey, chief of engrg; Sherry Crider, traf mgr.

Malta Bend

KRLI(FM)— Oct 28, 1996: 103.9 mhz; 3.4 kw. Ant 879 ft TL: N39 21 59 W93 24 12. Stereo. Hrs open: 24 102 N. Mason, Carrollton, 64633. Phone: (660) 542-0404. Fax: (660) 542-3152.E-mail: advertise@krli.net Web Site:www.krli.net Licensee: Kanza Inc. Format: Jazz, big band, oldies. News staff: 2; News: 6 hrs wkly. Target aud: 45 plus; baby boomers. ◆Miles Carter, CEO, pres & gen mgr.

Mansfield

KTRI-FM— 1978: 95.9 mhz; 6 kw. Ant 312 ft TL: N37 02 18 W92 40 29. Stereo. Hrs open: 24 1569 N. Central St., Monett, 65708. Phone: (417) 235-6041. Fax: (417) 235-6388. Licensee: Thirteen Forty Productions Inc. (group owner; (acq 1-8-2007; $200,000). Population served: 57,000 Format: Adult contemp. ◆Gary W. Snadon, pres.

Marble Hill

KYRX(FM)— Licensed to Marble Hill. See Jackson

Marshall

KMMO(AM)— May 29, 1949: 1300 khz; 1 kw-D, 68 w-N. TL: N39 08 03 W93 13 19. Hrs open: 24 Dups FM 80% Box 128, Hwy. 65 N, 65340. Phone: (660) 886-7422. Fax: (660) 886-6291. Web Site:www.kmmo.com Licensee: Missouri Valley Broadcasting Inc. Natl. Network: CBS Radio, . ◆John Wilson, gen mgr; Peter Hollabarch, gen sls mgr; Ken Lewellen, news dir.

KMMO-FM— December 1968: 102.9 mhz; 100 kw. 380 ft TL: N39 08 03 W93 13 19. Stereo. Hrs open: 24 Box 128, Hwy. 65 N., 65340. Phone: (660) 886-7422. Fax: (660) 886-6291. Web Site:www.kmmo.com Licensee: Missouri Valley Broadcasting Inc. (acq 11-19-84; with co-located AM; 12-10-84). Population served: 40,000 Natl. Network: CBS, . Target aud: General. ◆John Wilson, gen mgr, progmg dir; Peter Hollabaugh, gen sls mgr; Ken Lewellen, news dir.

*KMVC(FM)— Nov 1, 1968: 91.7 mhz; 100 w vert. 51 ft TL: N39 06 31 W93 11 29. (CP: 93.1 mhz, 16 w). Stereo. Hrs open: 7 AM-11 PM (M-F); 9 AM-11 PM (S); noon-8 PM (Su) Missouri Valley College, 500 E. College St., 65340. Phone: (660) 831-4193. Fax: (660) 886-9818.E-mail: kmvc@moval.edu Licensee: Missouri Valley College. Format: Alternative, rhythm and blues. News: 3 hrs wkly. Target aud: 17-26; pre-, current & post-college age. Spec prog: Black 10 hrs, progsv 10 hrs, relg 16 hrs, classic rock 4 hrs, hip hop 10 hrs, urban 10 hrs wkly. ◆Brent Foster, gen mgr; Josh Branch, stn mgr.

Marshfield

KKLH(FM)— June 1982: 104.7 mhz; 34 kw. Ant 594 ft TL: N37 12 21 W92 54 20. Stereo. Hrs open: 24 319 B-East Battlefield, Springfield, 65807. Phone: (417) 886-5677. Fax: (417) 886-2155.E-mail: info@1047thecave.com Web Site:www.1047thecave.com Licensee: MW SpringMo Inc. Group owner: The Mid-West Family Broadcast Group (acq 1996; $1.8 million). Population served: 295,300 Natl. Rep: Eastman Radio,. Davis Wright Tremaine, LLP. Format: Classic rock. Target aud: 35-54. ◆ Rick McCoy, pres & gen mgr; Mary Fleenor, opns mgr; Malcolm Hurriede, gen sls mgr; Keith Abercrombie, rgnl sls mgr; John Kimmons, progmg VP, progmg mgr.

KMRF(AM)— Nov 1, 1969: 1510 khz; 250 w-D. TL: N37 20 55 W92 54 28. (CP: 1 kw). Hrs open: Sunrise-sunset 3208 State Hwy. 00, 65706-2438. Phone: (417) 468-6188. Fax: (417) 859-2916. Licensee: New Life Evangelistic Center Inc. (acq 4-4-94). Population served: 50,000 Natl. Network: USA, . Rgnl. Network: Missourinet, Brownfield. Brownfield Format: Southern gospel. News staff: one; News: 6 hrs wkly. Target aud: General. ◆Larry Rice, pres; Ed Moore, opns mgr; Hank Zenicwicz, progmg dir.

*KNLM(FM)— Not on air, target date: unknown: 91.9 mhz; 3 kw. 210 ft TL: N37 19 09 W92 57 43. Hrs open:
Rebroadcasts KNLG(FM) New Bloomfield 100%.
3208 State Hwy. 00, 65706. Phone: (417) 468-6188. Fax: (417) 859-2916. Format: Contemp Christian. Target aud: General.

Maryville

KNIM(AM)— 1953: 1580 khz; 500 w-D, 7 w-N. TL: N40 23 31 W94 58 04. Hrs open: 24 Box 278, 64468. Secondary address: 1618 S. Main 64468. Phone: (660) 582-2151. Fax: (660) 582-3211.E-mail: knim@knimmaryville.com Web Site:knimmaryville.com Licensee: Nodaway Broadcasting Corp. (acq 5-14-2003; $50,000 for 10% of stock with co-located FM). Population served: 30,000 Natl. Network: CNN Radio, . Natl. Rep: Keystone (unwired net),. Format: News, sports. News staff: one. Target aud: 25-54. Spec prog: Farm 5 hrs wkly. ◆Joyce Cronin, pres; Jim Cronin, exec VP, gen mgr.

KNIM-FM— September 1972: 97.1 mhz; 21.5 kw. Ant 354 ft TL: N40 23 31 W94 58 04. Stereo. Hrs open: 24 Box 278, 64468. Secondary address: 1618 S. Main 64468. Phone: (660) 582-2151. Fax: (660) 582-3211. Web Site:www.knimmaryville.com Population served: 120,000 Wiley, Rein & Fielding. Wire Svc: AP Format: Rock. News staff: one; News: 25 hrs wkly.

*KXCV(FM)— 1971: 90.5 mhz; 100 kw. 500 ft TL: N40 21 36 W94 53 00. Stereo. Hrs open: 24 Wells Hall, 800 University Dr., 64468. Phone: (660) 562-1163. Phone: (660) 562-1164. Fax: (660) 562-1832.E-mail: kxcv@nwmissouri.edu Web Site:www.kxcv.org Licensee: Northwest Missouri State University. Population served: 138,000 Natl. Network: NPR, PRI, . Format: News, class, jazz. News staff: 2; News: 39 hrs wkly. Target aud: General. ◆Dean L. Hubbard, pres; Patty Andrews Holley, gen mgr, mus dir; Patty Holley, opns mgr; Gayle Hull, prom dir, progmg mgr, spec ev coord; Kirk Wayman, news dir; Darren Perkins, engrg dir, chief of engrg; Marcia Fish, traf mgr.

Memphis

KMEM-FM— Mar 29, 1982: 100.5 mhz; 25 kw. 298 ft TL: N40 29 59 W92 09 58. Stereo. Hrs open: 24 Box 121, 63555. Secondary address: 650 N. Clay 63555. Phone: (660) 465-7225. Fax: (660) 465-2626.E-mail: mdenney@kmemfm.com Web Site:www.kmemfm.com Licensee: Boyer Broadcasting Co. Inc. (acq 2-14-01; $202,000). Population served: 50,000 Rgnl. Network: Missourinet, Iowa Radio Net., Brownfield. Brownfield Format: Country. News staff: one; News: 15 hrs wkly. Target aud: General; adult audience 30+. Spec prog: Farm 8 hrs, relg 4 hrs wkly. ◆Mark McVey, pres; Karen McVey, VP, gen mgr; Mark Denney, gen mgr.

Mexico

*KAUD(FM)— Not on air, target date: unknown: 90.5 mhz; 450 w. Ant 158 ft TL: N39 10 36 W91 47 41.9. Hrs open: University of Missouri, 409 Jesse Hall, Columbia, 65211-1310. Phone: (573) 882-3431. Fax: (573) 882-2636. Web Site:www.kbia.org Licensee: The Curators of the University of Missouri. Natl. Network: NPR, PRI, . ◆Michael Dunn, gen mgr.

*KJAB-FM— Oct 9, 1985: 88.3 mhz; 4.8 kw. 272 ft TL: N39 06 13 W91 53 35. Stereo. Hrs open: 24 621 W. Monroe, 65265. Phone: (573) 581-8606. Fax: (573) 581-9655.E-mail: kjab@kjab.com Web Site:www.kjab.com Licensee: Mexico Educational Broadcasting Foundation. Population served: 250,000 Natl. Network: USA, . Format: Southern gospel. News staff: one; News: 2 hrs wkly. Target aud: General. Spec

prog: Gospel 20 hrs, relg 20 hrs wkly. ◆Kevin Weber, pres, gen mgr & opns mgr; Daniel Taylor, progmg dir.

KWWR(FM)— Dec 14, 1966: 95.7 mhz; 100 kw. Ant 1,181 ft TL: N39 15 49 W92 08 06. Stereo. Hrs open: 24 Box 475, 65265-0475. Secondary address: 1705 E. Liberty St. 65265-3537. Phone: (573) 581-5500. Fax: (573) 581-1801.E-mail: production@radiogetsresults.net Web Site:info.kwwr.com Licensee: KXEO Radio Inc. (acq 2-4-91; with co-located AM; 2-18-91). Population served: 638,605 Natl. Network: CNN Radio, Westwood One, . Wire Svc: NWS (National Weather Service) Wire Svc: AP Format: Country. News staff: 21. Target aud: 24-54. Spec prog: Farm, News, Sports. ◆Anne Johnson, pres; Gary Leonard, VP, gen mgr; Greg Holman, progmg dir; Chris Newbrough, news dir; Penny Daugherty, traf mgr.

KXEO(AM)— Dec 3, 1948: 1340 khz; 1 kw-U. TL: N39 10 01 W91 51 44. Hrs open: 24 Box 475, 65265-0475. Secondary address: 1705 E. Liberty St. 65265-0475. Phone: (573) 581-2340. Fax: (573) 581-1801.E-mail: kxeo@radiogetsresults.net Web Site:ino.kxeo.com Licensee: KXEO Radio Inc. Population served: 368,605 Natl. Network: CNN Radio, Westwood One, . Rgnl. Network: Missourinet, Brownfield. Brownfield Wire Svc: AP Format: Adult contemp/ News/ Sports. News: 4 hrs wkly. Target aud: 25-54. ◆Gary Leonard, gen mgr.

Miner

KBHI(FM)—Licensed to Miner. See Sikeston

Moberly

*KBKC(FM)— 2004: 90.1 mhz; 250 w. Ant 256 ft TL: N39 24 39 W92 26 46. Hrs open: 4424 Hampton Ave., Saint Louis, 63109. Phone: (314) 752-7000.E-mail: covenantnetwork@juno.com Web Site:www.covenantnet.net Licensee: Covenant Network. (acq 3-30-2004; $112,500 with WHOJ(FM) Terre Haute, IN). Format: Christian. ◆Tony Holman, gen mgr; Jim Schaper, progmg dir.

KRES(FM)— October 1966: 104.7 mhz; 100 kw. 1,025 ft TL: N39 27 53 W92 42 07. Stereo. Hrs open: Prog sep from AM Box 619, 65270. Secondary address: 300 West Reed 65270. Phone: (660) 263-1600. Fax: (660) 269-8811.E-mail: kresnews@regionalradio.com Web Site:www.centralmoinfo.com Population served: 250,000 Natl. Network: ABC, . Format: Country. ◆George Pelletier, COO; Dean Goodman, pres; Terry Strickland, gen mgr; Brad Boyer, progmg dir; Mike Lear, news dir.

*KSDQ(FM)—Not on air, target date: unknown: 88.7 mhz; 12 kw vert. Ant 200 ft TL: N39 15 11 W92 12 42. Hrs open: 7300 E. Hwy. 151, Centralia, 65240. Phone: (573) 682-5313. Licensee: Sunnydale Seventh-Day Adventist Church. ◆Erving Bales, gen mgr.

KWIX(AM)— June 1950: 1230 khz; 1 kw-U. TL: N39 24 11 W92 25 57. Hrs open: 24 Box 619, 65270. Secondary address: 300 West Reed 65270. Phone: (660) 263-1600. Fax: (660) 269-8811.E-mail: bignews@regionalradio.com Web Site:www.regionalradio.com Licensee: Moberly/Macon License Co. LLC. Group owner: Shepherd Group (acq 8-8-2007; grpsl). Population served: 212,000 Natl. Network: CBS, . Wire Svc: NOAA Weather Format: Talk. News staff: 4; News: 30 hrs wkly. Target aud: General. ◆George Pelletier, COO; Darrell Stuart, pres, gen sls mgr; Terry Strickland, gen mgr; Ken Kujawa, progmg dir; Stephanie Ross, mus dir; Brad Boyer, news dir; Lloyd Collins, chief of engrg.

KZZT(FM)— Apr 10, 1987: 105.5 mhz; 25 kw. 328 ft TL: N39 24 54 W92 24 36. (CP: 50 kw). Stereo. Hrs open: Box 128, 65270. Secondary address: 1037 County Rd. 65270. Phone: (660) 263-9390. Phone: (660) 263-5796. Fax: (660) 263-8800.E-mail: kzzt@bestbroadcastgroup.com Web Site:www.bestbroadcastgroup.com/kzzt.htm Licensee: FM 105 Inc. Group owner: Best Broadcast Group (acq 7-9-97; $200,000 for 43%). Natl. Network: ABC, . Bryan Cave. Format: Oldies. News: 5 hrs wkly. Target aud: 25-54; men & women with spendable income. ◆Phil Chirillo, pres; Dale Palmer, VP; Dale A. Palmer, gen mgr.

Monett

KKBL(FM)— December 1977: 95.9 mhz; 6 kw. 269 ft TL: N36 56 15 W93 55 30. Stereo. Hrs open: 24 Prog sep from AM 1569 N. Central, 65708. Phone: (417) 235-6041. Fax: (417) 235-6388.E-mail: info@buzz959.com Web Site:www.buzz959.com Population served: 65,000 Format: CHR. News staff: one; News: 4 hrs wkly. Target aud: General; young, adults, families. Spec prog: Children 2 hrs wkly.

KRMO(AM)—(Cassville, August 1950: 990 khz; 2.5 kw-D, 47 w-N. TL: N36 56 15 W93 55 30. Hrs open: 24 1569 N. Central, 65708. Phone:

(417) 235-6041. Fax: (417) 235-6388.E-mail: kkbl@talonbroadcasting.com Web Site:www.krmo.com Licensee: Eagle Broadcasting Inc. (acq 8-4-03; $650,000 with KKBL(FM) Monett). Population served: 6,500 Rgnl. Network: Brownfield, Missourinet. Missourinet Format: Country. News staff: one; News: 10 hrs wkly. Target aud: 35 plus; business professionals, farmers, elderly. ◆Duane Gandy, pres; Bill Lewis, VP; Janet Gandy, gen mgr, stn mgr; Dan Kesterson, gen sls mgr, progmg dir.

Monroe City

KWBZ(FM)— July 4, 1981: 107.5 mhz; 10 kw. Ant 328 ft TL: N39 35 12 W91 47 57. Stereo. Hrs open: 1645 Hwy 104, Suite G, Quincy, IL, 62305. Phone: (217) 885-3222. Phone: (217) 224-4653. Fax: (217) 885-3233.E-mail: wpwq106@adams.net Web Site:www.oldies-superstation.com Licensee: WPW Broadcasting Inc. (acq 8-17-2000). Format: Oldies. ◆Phil Alexander, gen mgr.

Montgomery City

KMCR(FM)— Aug 15, 1977: 103.9 mhz; 3 kw. 300 ft TL: N38 59 12 W91 30 48. Stereo. Hrs open: 24 205 E. Norman St., 63361. Phone: (573) 564-2275. Phone: (573) 258-3383. Fax: (573) 564-8036.E-mail: kmcr@socket.net Web Site:www.bestbroadcastgroup.com Licensee: Chirillo Electronics Inc. Group owner: Best Broadcast Group (acq 1994). Population served: 50,000 Rgnl. Network: Missourinet. Missourinet Format: Hot adult contemp. News staff: one; News: 3 hrs wkly. Target aud: 25-60; male/female. Spec prog: Farm 2 hrs, relg 2 hrs wkly. ◆Dale A. Palmer, VP & gen mgr.

Mount Vernon

KZRQ-FM— July 29, 1993: 106.7 mhz; 25 kw. 328 ft TL: N37 09 16 W93 36 58. Hrs open: 2330 W. Grand St., Springfield, 65781. Phone: (417) 865-6614. Fax: (417) 865-9643.E-mail: ccannon@journalbroadcastgroup.com Web Site:www.2rocks.com Licensee: Journal Broadcast Corp. Group owner: Journal Communications Inc. (acq 11-26-2003; $5 million with KSGF-FM Ash Grove). Format: Rock. ◆Rex Hansen, gen mgr; Chris Cannon, opns mgr; Janelle Carter, gen sls mgr.

Mountain Grove

KELE(AM)— Nov 16, 1954: 1360 khz; 1 kw-D, 60 w-N. TL: N37 08 07 W92 14 59. Hrs open: 24 800 N. Hubbard, 65711. Phone: (417) 926-4650. Fax: (417) 926-7604.E-mail: tonya@925thegrove.com Licensee: Ozark Media Inc. (group owner; (acq 4-15-2009; $15,000). Population served: 50,000 Natl. Network: USA, . Rgnl. Network: Brownfield. Brownfield ◆Tracy O'Quinn, gen mgr; Shaun Anthony, progmg dir; Jim Morris, news dir; Tonya Shannon, traf mgr.

KELE-FM— Jan 1, 1977: 92.5 mhz; 3 kw. Ant 299 ft TL: N37 08 07 W92 14 59. Stereo. Hrs open: 800 N. Hubbard, 65711. Phone: (417) 926-4650. Fax: (417) 926-7604.E-mail: tonya@925thegrove.com Licensee: Ozark Media Inc. (acq 5-1-2007; $625,000 with KOZX(FM) Cabool). Population served: 50,000 Format: Real country. News staff: one; News: 8 hrs wkly. Target aud: 24-59; general. Spec prog: Relg 3 hrs wkly. ◆Tracy O'Quinn, gen mgr; Shaun Anthony, progmg dir; Jim Morris, news dir; Tonya Shannon, traf mgr; Perry Dobson, sports cmtr.

Mountain View

KUPH(FM)— July 31, 1998: 96.9 mhz; 50 kw. 420 ft TL: N36 59 29 W91 47 41. Stereo. Hrs open: 24 6962 U.S. Hwy. 60 W., 65548. Phone: (417) 934-1000. Phone: (417) 934-0969. Fax: (417) 934-2565.E-mail: ed@thefox969.com Web Site:www.thefox969.com Licensee: Central Ozark Radio Network Inc. (acq 8-21-98; $196,500). Format: Hot adult contemp. News: 2 hrs wkly. Target aud: 25-54; upscale, mature individuals. ◆Tom Marhefka, CEO & pres; Bob Eckman, gen mgr, opns mgr; Gary Lee, opns mgr, progmg dir; Jonathon Bergman, gen sls mgr; Mike Robertson, news dir; Jim White, chief of engrg.

Naylor

KZMA(FM)— 2005: 99.9 mhz; 4.2 kw. Ant 387 ft TL: N36 39 43 W90 29 16. Hrs open: 1115 Nooney Dr., Poplar Bluff, 63901. Phone: (573) 778-1219. Fax: (573) 686-2377. Licensee: Daniel S. Stratemeyer (acq 6-1-2003; $30,000 for CP). Shaw Pittman LLP. Format: Adult contemp. ◆Jim Borders, gen mgr.

Neosho

KBTN(AM)— Feb 1, 1954: 1420 khz; 1 kw-D, 500 w-N, DA-N. TL: N36 50 52 W94 19 12. Hrs open: 5 AM-midnight Box 570, 64850. Secondary address: 216 W. Spring 64850. Phone: (417) 451-1420. Fax: (417) 451-2526. Licensee: American Media Investments Inc. Group owner: Petracom Media L.L.C. (acq 2-17-2009; grpsl). Population served: 40,000 Natl. Network: ABC, CNN Radio, . Rgnl. Network: Missourinet. Format: Country. News staff: 2; News: 14 hrs wkly. Target aud: 18-54. Spec prog: Farm 6 hrs wkly. ◆Gail Johnson, gen mgr, gen sls mgr; David Horvath, news dir; Art Morris, chief of engrg; Monica Blain, progmg dir, progmg mgr, traf mgr & farm dir.

KBTN-FM— 1995: 99.7 mhz; 4.2 kw. Ant 393 ft TL: N36 46 05 W94 19 52. Hrs open: 24 2510 W. 20th St, Joplin, 64804. Phone: (417) 781-1313. Fax: (417)781-1316.E-mail: info@997kbtn.com Web Site:www.997kbtn.com Licensee: American Media Investments Inc. (acq 2-17-2009; grpsl). Format: Country. News staff: 2; News: 9 hrs wkly. Target aud: 18 plus. ◆Jennifer Isom, gen mgr; Warren McDonald, opns mgr; Dave Clemons, gen sls mgr; Steve Smith, progmg dir.

*KNEO(FM)— October 1986: 91.7 mhz; 4.6 kw. 374 ft TL: N36 52 49 W94 26 59. Hrs open: 24 10827 E. Hwy. 86, 64850-7052. Phone: (417) 451-5636. Fax: (417) 451-1891.E-mail: kneo@kneo.org Web Site:www.kneo.org Licensee: Sky High Broadcasting Corp. (acq 6-19-00). Population served: 250,000 Natl. Network: USA, Moody, . Format: News/talk. News: 10 hrs wkly. Target aud: 30-65. ◆Mark Taylor, pres, gen mgr; Adam Winkler, opns dir; Roberta Foster, traf mgr.

Nevada

KNEM(AM)— 1949: 1240 khz; 500 w-U. TL: N37 51 37 W94 22 54. Hrs open: 24 Box 447, 414 E. Walnut., 64772. Phone: (417) 667-3113. Fax: (417) 667-9797.E-mail: mharbit@knemknmo.com Web Site:www.knemknmo.com Licensee: Harbit Communications Inc. (acq 12-5-97; $475,000 with co-located FM). Population served: 30,000 Rgnl. Network: Brownfield, Missourinet. Missourinet Format: Country. News staff: one; News: 30 hrs wkly. Target aud: General. Spec prog: Farm one hr, Christian 5 hrs wkly. ◆Mike Harbit, pres, gen mgr, gen sls mgr, progmg dir; Russ Warren, news dir; Daryl Nickolaus, chief of engrg.

KNMO(FM)— Sept 10, 1984: 97.5 mhz; 6 kw. Ant 281 ft TL: N37 52 45 W94 20 15. Stereo. Hrs open: 24 Dups AM 100% Box 447, 414 E. Walnut., 64772. Phone: (417) 667-3113. Fax: (417) 667-9797. Web Site:www.knemknmo.com Population served: 30,000

New Bloomfield

*KNLG(FM)— July 20, 1997: 90.3 mhz; 150 w. 216 ft TL: N38 42 16 W92 05 20. Stereo. Hrs open: 24 c/o KNLJ(TV) Box 2525, MT, 65063. Phone: (573) 896-5945. Fax: (573) 896-4376. Web Site:www.heresshelpnet.org Licensee: New Life Evangelistic Center Inc. Population served: 2,000 Format: Southern gospel. News: 9 hrs wkly. Target aud: General. ◆Rev. Larry Rice, pres & gen mgr; John Shepard, progmg dir.

New London

KZZK(FM)— April 1996: 105.9 mhz; 10 kw. 515 ft TL: N39 43 45 W91 24 15. Stereo. Hrs open: 24 329 Maine St., Quincy, IL, 62301. Phone: (217) 224-4102. Fax: (217) 224-4133.E-mail: kzzk@staradio.com Web Site:www.kzzk.com Licensee: STARadio Corp. (group owner; acq 12-2-98; $2.1 million with KGRC(FM) Hannibal). Population served: 200,000 Format: Adult alternative, classic rock. News: 2 hrs wkly. Target aud: 18-49; skews male. ◆Howard Doss, pres; Michael J. Moyers, gen mgr; "Quaid", progmg dir.

New Madrid

KTMO(FM)—Licensed to New Madrid. See Portageville

Nixa

KGBX-FM—Licensed to Nixa. See Springfield

North Kansas City

WDAF-FM—See Liberty

Oran

*KCGR(FM)— 2008: 90.5 mhz; 2.1 kw. Ant 241 ft TL: N36 59 52 W89 38 52. Hrs open:
Rebroadcasts KSIV-FM Saint Louis 100%.
1750 S. Brentwood Blvd., Suite 811, Saint Louis, 63144. Phone: (314) 961-1320. Fax: (314) 961-7562. Web Site:www.bottradionetwork.com Licensee: Community Broadcasting Inc. Format: Christian info, relg. ♦Michael McHardy, gen mgr.

Osage Beach

*KIRL(FM)—Not on air, target date: unknown: 89.3 mhz; 300 w vert. Ant 210 ft TL: N38 07 20 W92 40 42. Hrs open: 712 Chaucer Ln., Warrensburg, 64093. Phone: (660) 238-1024. Licensee: Full Smile Inc. ♦Joey Anderson, VP & gen mgr.

KMYK(FM)— Apr 12, 1964: 93.5 mhz; 39 kw. Ant 551 ft TL: N38 07 29 W92 40 39. Stereo. Hrs open: Prog sep from AM Box 225, Hwy 54, 65065. Phone: (573) 348-2772. Fax: (573) 348-2779.E-mail: info@1150kmrs.com Population served: 85,000 Format: AOR, classic rock.

KRMS(AM)— December 1952: 1150 khz; 1 kw-D, 55 w-N. TL: N38 07 29 W92 40 39. Hrs open: 24 Box 225, Hwy. 54, 65065. Phone: (573) 348-2772. Fax: (573) 348-2779.E-mail: info@1150kmrs.com Licensee: Viper Communications Inc. Group owner: Viper Communications Broadcast Group (acq 11-97; $500,000 with co-located FM). Population served: 75,000 Natl. Network: CBS, . Rgnl. Network: Missourinet. Missourinet Format: News/talk. ♦Ken Kuenzie, pres, chief of engrg; Dennis Klautzer, VP, sls dir, progmg dir; Paul Hannigan, news dir; Tammy Pitts, traf mgr.

Osceola

*KCVJ(FM)— June 29, 1990: 100.3 mhz; 6 kw. Ant 282 ft TL: N38 03 43 W93 33 24. Stereo. Hrs open: 24
Rebroadcasts KCVO-FM Camdenton 100%.
Box 800, c/o Spirit FM Radio, Camdenton, 65020. Phone: (573) 346-3200. Fax: (573) 346-1010. Web Site:www.spiritfm.org Licensee: Lake Area Educational Broadcasting Foundation (acq 1999; $70,000). Population served: 25,000 Natl. Network: Salem Radio Network, . Format: Contemporary, Christian. News: 1. Target aud: 25-45. ♦Alice McDermott, CFO; James McDermott, pres, gen mgr & progmg dir.

Otterville

*KCVK(FM)— 2001: 107.7 mhz; 2.5 kw horiz, 2.3 kw vert. Ant 499 ft TL: N38 39 21 W92 54 27. Stereo. Hrs open: 24
Rebroadcasts KCVO-FM Camdenton 100%.
Box 800, Camdenton, 65020. Phone: (573) 346-3200. Fax: (573) 346 1010. Web Site:www.spiritfm.org Licensee: Lake Area Educational Broadcasting Foundation (acq 8-15-2001). Population served: 100,000 Natl. Network: Salem Radio Network, . Format: Contemp Christian. News: one hr wkly. Target aud: 25-45. ♦James McDermott, pres, gen mgr; Alice McDermott, CFO; James McDermott, progmg dir.

Overland

*KRHS(FM)— Nov 7, 1977: 90.1 mhz; 10 w. 60 ft TL: N38 42 38 W90 21 22. Hrs open: 9100 St. Charles Rock Rd., St. Louis, 63114. Phone: (314) 429-7111. Fax: (314) 429-6725. Licensee: Ritenour Consolidated School District. Format: Educ. Target aud: General. ♦Jane Bannester, gen mgr.

Owensville

KXMO-FM— Jan 1, 2001: 95.3 mhz; 37 kw. 564 ft TL: N38 08 06 W91 23 59. Hrs open: 24 Box 4584, Springfield, 65808. Phone: (417) 883-9180. Fax: (417) 883-9096. Licensee: KTTR-KZNN Inc. (acq 8-23-2001). Format: Oldies. Target aud: 35-64; male & female. ♦John B. Mahaffey, chmn; Robert B. Mahaffey, pres.

Ozark

KOMG(FM)— 1995: 92.9 mhz; 50 kw. Ant 492 ft TL: N36 58 26 W93 25 37. Stereo. Hrs open: 24 319 E. Battlefield, Suite B, Springfield, 65807. Phone: (417) 886-5677. Fax: (417) 886-2155.E-mail: info@basscountry.fm Web Site:www.basscountry.fm Licensee: MW Springmo Inc. Group owner: The Mid-West Family Broadcast Group (acq 12-15-99). Population served: 295,300 Natl. Network: NBC Radio, . Natl. Rep: Eastman Radio,. Davis Wright Tremaine, LLP.

Format: Classic country. Target aud: 30-50. ♦Rick McCoy, pres & gen mgr; Mary Fleenor, opns mgr, progmg dir; Malcolm Hukriede, gen sls mgr; Keith Abercrombie, rgnl sls mgr; Charlie Mason, prom.

Palmyra

KICK-FM— Sept 1, 1981: 97.9 mhz; 50 kw. 348 ft TL: N39 45 25 W91 29 57. Stereo. Hrs open: 24 Box 711, Hannibal, 63401-0711. Phone: (573) 221-3450. Fax: (573) 221-5331.E-mail: hsmith@graido.com Web Site:www.979kickfm.com Licensee: Bick Broadcasting Co. Population served: 100,000 Natl. Rep: McGavren Guild,. Format: Country. News staff: 2. Target aud: 25-54; mainstream adults. ♦Ed Foxall, gen mgr; Jeff Dorsey, progmg dir; John Hanvelt, news dir; Gary Glaenzer, chief of engrg.

Park Hills

*KBGM(FM)— 2001: 91.1 mhz; 8 kw. Ant 620 ft TL: N37 48 04 W90 33 51. Hrs open: Box 3206, American Family Radio, Tupelo, MS, 38803. Phone: (662) 844-8888, EXT. 204. Fax: (662) 842-6791. Web Site:www.afr.net Licensee: American Family Association. Group owner: American Family Radio Format: Inspirational Christian. ♦Marvin Sanders, gen mgr.

KFMO(AM)— July 1947: 1240 khz; 1 kw-U. TL: N37 51 10 W90 31 13. Hrs open: Box 36, 63601. Secondary address: 804 St. Joe Dr. 63601. Phone: (573) 431-2000. Fax: (573) 431-0850.E-mail: radio@b104fm.com Web Site:www.kfmo.com Licensee: MKS Broadcasting Inc. (acq 3-16-92; 4-6-92). Population served: 74,000 Natl. Network: Westwood One, . Format: Sports, news/talk loc information. Target aud: 25-54; females. ♦M.L. Steinmetz, pres; Larry D. Joseph, VP, gen mgr; Kelly Valle, gen sls mgr; Greg Camp, progmg dir; Gib Collins, news dir.

Parkville

*KGSP(FM)— April 1972: 90.3 mhz; 100 w. 140 ft TL: N39 11 24 W94 40 49. Stereo. Hrs open: 6 AM-midnight (M-F); 9 AM-midnight (S, Su) Box 2, 8700 N.W. River Park Dr., 64152. Phone: (816) 741-2000 ext. 6325. Fax (816) 741-4911.E-mail: kgsp@park.edu Web Site:www.park.com Licensee: Board of Trustees of Park College. Population served: 57,000 Format: Alternative, var. News: 6 hrs wkly. Target aud: General; college students. Spec prog: Jazz 14 hrs, gospel 3 hrs, blues 12 hrs wkly. ♦Steve Youngblood, gen mgr.

Perryville

KBDZ(FM)— Jan 30, 1990: 93.1 mhz; 1.6 kw. ant 623 ft TL: N37 38 56 W89 56 21. Stereo. Hrs open: 24 Box 344, 122 Perry Plaza, 63775. Secondary address: Box 428, Radio Hill, St. Genevieve 63670. Phone: (573) 883- 2980 (618/826-2980[\]]. Fax: (573) 883-2866. Fax: (573) 547-8005.E-mail: news@suntimenews.com Web Site:www.suntimesnews.com Licensee: Donze Communications Inc. Format: Hot country, news. News staff: 3; News: 5 hrs wkly. Target aud: 25-54. Spec prog: Sports 5 hrs, relg 5 hrs, farm 2 hrs wkly. ♦Elmo L. Donze, pres, gen mgr, chief of engrg; Bob Scott, gen sls mgr, progmg dir; Don Pritchard, news dir, local news ed, edit dir, outdoor ed, women's cmtr; Brian Snider, reporter, mus critic; Michelle Hoog, women's int ed.

Piedmont

KPWB(AM)— May 16, 1966: 1140 khz; 1 kw-D. TL: N37 08 29 W90 42 11. Hrs open: 235 Business HH, 63957. Phone: (573) 223-4218. Fax: (573) 223-2351. Licensee: Southern Star Broadcasting of Missouri LLC. (acq 5-8-2008; grpsl). Population served: 5,000 Natl. Network: USA, . Rgnl. Network: Missourinet. Missourinet Format: Gospel. Target aud: 18 plus; Christians. ♦Wanda Emert, gen mgr, mktg dir, progmg dir & news dir.

KPWB-FM— Sept 5, 1985: 104.9 mhz; 3 kw. Ant 300 ft TL: N37 07 54 W90 41 28. Stereo. Hrs open: 235 Business HH, 63957. Phone: (573) 223-4218. Fax: (573) 223-2351. Licensee: Southern Star Broadcasting of Missouri LLC. (acq 5-8-2008; grpsl). Population served: 12,350 Natl. Network: USA, . Format: Country. Target aud: General. ♦Wanda Emert, opns mgr, gen sls mgr, mktg mgr, prom mgr & progmg mgr; Fred Dockins, chief of engrg.

Pleasant Hope

KTOZ-FM— May 1, 1993: 95.5 mhz; 50 kw. 497 ft TL: N37 25 32 W93 16 38. Hrs open: 1856 S. Glenstone, Springfield, 65804. Phone: (417) 890-5555. Fax: (417) 890-5050.E-mail: alice955@alice955.com Web Site:www.alice955.com Licensee: Clear Channel Broadcasting Licenses

Inc. Group owner: Clear Channel Communications Inc. (acq 10-10-00; grpsl). Format: Modern adult contemp. Target aud: 18-34; young adults, 60/40 female/male split. ♦Paul Windisch, gen mgr; Paul Kelley, opns dir.

Point Lookout

*KCOZ(FM)— January 1995: 91.7 mhz; 200 w. 151 ft TL: N36 36 40 W93 14 29. Stereo. Hrs open: College of the Ozarks, 65726. Phone: (417) 334-6411 ext. 4280. Fax: (417) 335-2618.E-mail: info@kcozfm.com Licensee: College of the Ozarks. Population served: 500,000 Natl. Network: PRI, NPR, . Format: News/talk, jazz, new age, blues. Target aud: Older & educated. Spec prog: Folk 10 hrs, new age 10 hrs wkly. ♦Jae Jones, gen mgr, progmg dir & chief of engrg.

*KSMS-FM— Feb 12, 1962: 90.5 mhz; 8.5 kw. 768 ft TL: N36 33 44 W93 15 35. Hrs open:
Rebroadcasts KSMU(FM) Springfield 100%.
Missouri State Univ., 901 S. National Ave., Springfield, 65897. Phone: (417) 836-5878. Fax: (417) 836-5889.E-mail: ksmu@missouristate Web Site:www.ksmu.org Licensee: Board of Governors, Southwest Missouri State University (acq 6-21-93; 7-19-93). Population served: 36,000 Dow, Lohnes & Albertson. Format: NPR News & Classical Music. Target aud: 25-54. ♦Tammy Wiley, gen mgr & stn mgr.

Poplar Bluff

KAHR(FM)— Mar 3, 1985: 96.7 mhz; 6 kw. Ant 328 ft TL: N36 45 59 W90 28 52. Stereo. Hrs open: 932 County Rd. 448, 63901. Phone: (573) 686-3700. Fax: (573) 686-1713.E-mail: info@faxradionetwork.com Web Site:www.foxradionetwork.com Licensee: Eagle Bluff Enterprises (acq 8-3-93; $350,000; 8-30-93). Format: Adult hits. Target aud: 18-54; listeners living in the middle-class strata. ♦Steven C. Fuchs, gen mgr.

KJEZ(FM)— Aug 20, 1977: 95.5 mhz; 100 kw. 860 ft TL: N36 50 50 W90 19 52. Stereo. Hrs open: 24 1015 West Pine St., 63901. Phone: (573) 785-0881. Fax: (573) 785-0646.E-mail: A johnr@riverradio.net Web Site:www.kjez.com Licensee: MRR License LLC. Group owner: MAX Media L.L.C. (acq 6-2-2004; grpsl). Population served: 125,000 Natl. Network: Westwood One, . Format: Classic rock and roll. News: 10 hrs wkly. Target aud: 18-49; general. ♦John Rice, gen mgr; Katie Wylie, gen sls mgr; Randy Bailey, progmg dir; Charlie Lampe, chief of engrg.

KKLR(FM)— 1952: 94.5 mhz; 100 kw. 807 ft TL: N36 43 18 W90 22 10. Stereo. Hrs open: Prog sep from AM Box 130, 63902. Phone: (573) 785-0881. Fax: (573) 785-0646.E-mail: A johnr@riverradio.net Web Site:www.kklr.com Population served: 90,000 Format: Country. Target aud: 18-49. ♦Galen Stevens, progmg dir & mus dir.

KLID(AM)— May 22, 1961: 1340 khz; 1 kw-U. TL: N36 46 03 W90 22 11. Hrs open: 24 KLID Bldg., 102 N. 11th St., 63901. Phone: (573) 686-1600. Fax: (573) 785-9844.E-mail: info@klidam.com Licensee: Browning Skidmore Broadcasting Inc. (acq 5-21-93; 6-14-93). Population served: 45,000 Format: Oldies, talk, sports. News: 15 hrs wkly. Target aud: 18-54; upper class, professionals. Spec prog: Relg 2 hrs, Black 2 hrs wkly. ♦Chris Browning, pres; Dolores Skidmore, gen mgr, dev mgr, progmg dir; Alverna Skidmore, sls dir, pub affrs dir, traf mgr; Palmer Johnson, chief of engrg; Nick Novak, sports cmtr; Dave Michaels, disc jockey.

KLUE(FM)— Jan 1, 1995: 103.5 mhz; 50 kw. 492 ft TL: N36 53 56 W90 18 27. Hrs open: 24 6120 Waldo Church Rd., Metropolis, IL, 62960. Phone: (618) 564-9836. Fax: (618) 564-3202. Licensee: Benjamin Stratemeyer (acq 5-1-02; $800,000). Shaw Pittman. Format: Div. ♦Samuel Stratemeyer, gen mgr; Willie Kerns, opns mgr & progmg dir.

*KLUH(FM)— Oct 8, 1988: 90.3 mhz; 25 kw. 300 ft TL: N36 43 07 W90 23 48. Hrs open: Box 1313, 63902-1313. Phone: (573) 686-1663. Fax: (573) 686-7703.E-mail: info@kluhfm.com Web Site:www.unity903.org Licensee: Word of Victory Outreach Center Inc. (acq 4-5-95; 7-10-95). Format: Relg. Target aud: General. ♦David Craig, gen mgr; John Armbruster, gen sls mgr; John Moore, progmg dir.

*KOKS(FM)— Oct 2, 1988: 89.5 mhz; 100 kw. 423 ft TL: N36 48 40 W90 27 50. Hrs open: 24 2773 Barron Road, 63901. Phone: (573) 686-5080. Fax: (573) 686-5544.E-mail: koksradio@mycitycable.com Licensee: Calvary Educational Broadcasting Network Population served: 1,000,000 Format: Christian. News: 14 hrs wkly. Target aud: General. ♦Nina Stewart, stn mgr & progmg dir; Ben Stewart, mus dir; Charley Lampe, chief of engrg.

KPPL(FM)— 2003: 92.5 mhz; 25 kw. Ant 328 ft TL: N36 50 59 W90 22 20. Stereo. Hrs open: 932 County Rd. 448, 63901. Phone: (573) 686-3700. Fax: (573) 686-1713.E-mail: info@foxradionetwork.com

Licensee: George S. Flinn Jr. Population served: 220,000 Format: Country. ♦Steven Fuchs, gen mgr & gen sls mgr; Shelly Fuchs, progmg dir; Palmer Johnson, chief of engrg.

KWOC(AM)— May 10, 1938: 930 khz; 5 kw-D, 500 w-N, DA-N. TL: N36 43 15 W90 22 04. Hrs open: 24 Box 130, 63902. Phone: (573) 785-0881. Fax: (573) 785-0646.E-mail: A john@riverradio.net Web Site:www.kwoc.com Licensee: MRR License LLC. Group owner: MAX Media L.L.C. (acq 6-2-2004; grpsl). Population served: 50,000 Rgnl. Network: Missourinet, Brownfield. Brownfield Format: News/talk. News staff: 2; News: 5 hrs wkly. Target aud: 25-54; adults with middle to upper income. ♦John Rice, gen mgr; Katie Wylie, sls dir, gen sls mgr; Rick Carl, progmg dir & news dir; Charlie Lampe, chief of engrg; Pam Gray, traf mgr.

Portageville

KMIS(AM)— Sept 1, 1960: 1050 khz; 1 kw-D, 87 w-N. TL: N36 25 30 W89 41 39. Hrs open: 24 Box 509, Kennett, 63857. Secondary address: 1303 Southwest Dr., Kennett 63857. Fax: (573) 888-4890.E-mail: ktme@il.net Licensee: Pollack Broadcasting Co. (group owner; (acq 5-7-2001; with KTMO(FM) New Madrid). Population served: 40,000 Rgnl. Network: missiourinet Missourinet Format: News, sports. News staff: one. Target aud: General. Spec prog: Relg gospel 5 hrs wkly. ♦Bill Pollack, pres; Monte Lyons, opns mgr, prom dir, progmg dir, traf mgr, sports cmtr; Perry Jones, gen mgr, sls dir & gen sls mgr; Charles Isabell, news dir; P.J. Johnson, chief of engrg.

KTMO(FM)—(New Madrid, Jan 31, 1976: 106.5 mhz; 50 kw. 469 ft TL: N36 25 30 W89 41 39. Stereo. Hrs open: 24 Box 509, Kennett, 63857. Secondary address: 12323 Jefferson Ave., New Madrid 63857. Fax: (573) 888-4890. Population served: 100,000 Natl. Network: ABC, . Format: Country. News staff: one. Target aud: 18-49 adults; males.

Potosi

KHZR(FM)— Apr 17, 1997: 97.7 mhz; 9.4 kw. Ant 528 ft TL: N37 52 51 W90 47 01. Hrs open: 24 13358 Manchester Rd., Suite 100, Des Peres, 63131. Phone: (314) 909-8569. Fax: (314) 835-9739.E-mail: info@joyfmonline.org Web Site:www.joyfmonline.org Licensee: Four Him Enterprises L.L.C. (acq 11-2-2000; $1.2 million). Format: Contemp Christian. ♦Sandi Brown, gen mgr.

***KNLP(FM)**— April 1998: 89.7 mhz; 2.3 kw. 262 ft TL: N37 55 42 W90 46 02. Hrs open: New Life Evangelistic Center, 1411 Locust St., St. Louis, 63103. Phone: (314) 436-2424. Phone: (573) 438-1473. Fax: (314) 436-2434.E-mail: larryr@hereshelpnet.org Web Site:www.hereshelpnet.org Licensee: New Life Evangelistic Center Inc. Format: Adult contemp, gospel, talk. ♦Larry Rice, gen mgr.

KYRO(AM)— Feb 22, 1959: Stn currently dark. 1280 khz; 500 w-D. TL: N37 58 28 W90 45 44. Stereo. Hrs open: 24 P.O. Box 280, 63664. E-mail: news@kyro.com Licensee: JLF Communications LLP. Population served: 30,000 Natl. Network: ABC, . Rgnl. Network: Missourinet Missourinet Format: New country, news. News staff: one; News: 12 hrs wkly. Target aud: 25 plus; general. ♦Debra S. Porter, VP; James T. Porter, pres & gen mgr.

Ravenwood

***KEXS-FM**— 2008: 106.1 mhz; 50 kw. Ant 423 ft TL: N40 25 15 W94 43 20. Hrs open: 201 N. Industrial Park Rd., Excelsior Springs, 64024-1736. Phone: (816) 630-1090.E-mail: catholicradionetwork@gmail.com Web Site:www.thecatholicradionetwork.com Licensee: Catholic Radio Network Inc. Format: Relg. ♦James E. O'Laughlin, gen mgr.

Republic

KADI-FM— June 18, 1990: 99.5 mhz; 6 kw. 328 ft TL: N37 09 54 W93 23 44. Stereo. Hrs open: 24 5431 W. Sunshine, Springfield, 65619. Phone: (417) 831-0995. Fax: (417) 831-4026.E-mail: info@99hitfm.com Web Site:www.kadi.com Licensee: Vision Communications Inc. (acq 7-10-2000; $550,000). Format: Adult contemp Christian mus. News: 8 hrs wkly. Target aud: General; adults in their mid 30s. ♦R.C. Amer, gen mgr; Mark Hill, gen sls mgr; Rod Kettleman, progmg dir.

Richmond

KAYX(FM)— Aug 1, 1990: 92.5 mhz; 6 kw. Ant 500 ft TL: N39 14 52 W93 58 16. Stereo. Hrs open:
Rebroadcasts KCCV(AM) Overland Park, KS 85%.
111 W. Main St., 64085. Phone: (816) 470-9925. Fax: (816) 470-8925.E-mail: kayx@bottradionetwork.com Web Site:www.bottradionetwork.com Licensee: Bott Communications, Inc. Group owner: Bott Radio Network (acq 1996). Natl. Network: USA, . Format: Christian talk & info. ♦Richard P. Bott Sr., pres; Richard P. Bott II, VP; Pat Rulon, natl sls mgr; Rachel Launius, mktg mgr; Jason Potocnik, traf mgr.

Rolla

KDAA(FM)— Nov 20, 1964: 103.1 mhz; 2.05 kw. Ant 571 ft TL: N37 52 39 W91 44 45. Stereo. Hrs open: 24 Box 727, 65402. Phone: (573) 364-2525. Fax: (573) 364-5161. Licensee: KDAA-KMOZ LLC. Group owner: Mahaffey Enterprises Inc. (acq 9-28-2001; $418,000 assumption of debt for 50% with co-located AM). Population served: 25,000 Format: Classic hits. Target aud: 18-44. ♦Mike Thompson, gen mgr; Steve Ryan, progmg dir; Tracy Weber, traf mgr.

***KMNR(FM)**— 1974: 89.7 mhz; 450 w. 230 ft TL: N37 57 12 W91 46 29. Hrs open: 218 Havener Ctr, University Dr., 65409. Phone: (573) 341-4272.E-mail: kmnr@mst.edu Web Site://kmnr.org Licensee: Curators of the University of Missouri. (group owner) Population served: 16,600 Natl. Network: AP Radio, . Format: Var, educ. Target aud: 18-25; college community. ♦Patrick Turley, gen mgr.

KMOZ(AM)— Aug 19, 1960: 1590 khz; 1 kw-D, 88 w-N. TL: N37 56 41 W91 48 40. Hrs open: 1701 N. Bishop, Suite 15, 65401. Phone: (573) 647-6285. Fax: (573) 426-4450.E-mail: comments@bottradionetwork.com Web Site:www.bottradionetwork.com Licensee: Community Broadcasting Inc. (acq 5-5-2006; $40,000). Natl. Network: USA, . Format: Country. Target aud: 50 plus; mature adults. ♦Trace Thurlby, COO; Tom Holdeman, CFO; Richard P. Bott II, VP; Pat Rulon, natl sls mgr; Rachel Moser, mktg mgr; Jason Potocnik, traf mgr.

***KMST(FM)**— January 1964: 88.5 mhz; 100 kw. Ant 480 ft TL: N37 47 56 W91 43 28. Stereo. Hrs open: 24 G-6 Library, 400 W. 14th St., 65409. Phone: (573) 341-4386. Fax: (573) 341-4889.E-mail: kmst@mst.edu Web Site:www.kmst.org Licensee: The Curators of the University of Missouri. (group owner) Population served: 200,000 Natl. Network: NPR, PRI, . Fisher, Wayland, Cooper, Leader & Zaragoza. Wire Svc: AP Format: Class, div, news. News: 35 hrs wkly. Target aud: General. Spec prog: Bluegrass 5 hrs, jazz 3 hrs, folk 5 hrs wkly. ♦Jim Sigler, gen mgr; Tricia Crout, mktg mgr; John Francis, progmg dir; Charles Knapp, chief of engrg. Co-owned TV: *KOMU-TV affil.

KTTR(AM)— Sept 30, 1947: 1490 khz; 1 kw-U. TL: N37 56 42 W91 44 46. Hrs open: 24 Box 727, 65402. Secondary address: 1505 Soest Rd. 65401. Phone: (573) 364-2525. Fax: (573) 364-5161. Licensee: KTTR-KZNN Inc. Group owner: Mahaffey Enterprises Inc. (acq 6-1-84; with co-located FM; 4-16-84). Population served: 19,800 Rgnl. Network: Missourinet. Missourinet Format: News/talk, sports. News staff: one. Target aud: General. ♦John Mahaffey, chmn, pres; Robert B. Mahaffey, pres, stn mgr; Mike Thompson, gen mgr; Steve Gidstad, progmg dir; Lee Buhr, news dir; Bob Moore, chief of engrg.

KZNN(FM)— Feb 12, 1973: 105.3 mhz; 100 kw. 631 ft TL: N37 52 39 W91 44 45. Stereo. Hrs open: Prog sep from AM Box 727, 65402. Secondary address: 1505 Soest Rd. 65401. Phone: (573) 364-2525. Fax: (573) 364-5161. Population served: 13,245 Natl. Network: ABC, . Rgnl. Network: Brownfield. Brownfield Format: Modern country.

Saint Charles

***KCLC(FM)**— October 1968: 89.1 mhz; 35 kw. 257 ft TL: N38 47 12 W90 29 49. Stereo. Hrs open: 24 209 S. Kings Hwy., 63301. Phone: (636) 949-4880. Fax: (636) 949-4111 .E-mail: fm891@lindenwood.edu Web Site:www.lindenwood.edu/kclc Licensee: Lindenwood University. Population served: 250,000 Format: AAA. Target aud: 18-34; young adults. ♦Mike Wall, gen mgr & opns mgr.

KFTK(FM)—See Florissant

KHOJ(AM)— Apr 13, 1958: 1460 khz; 5 kw-D, 85 w-N, DA-2. TL: N38 50 05 W90 28 08. Hrs open: 4424 Hampton Ave., Saint Louis, 63109. Phone: (314) 752-7000.E-mail: covenantnetwork@juno.com Web Site:www.covenantnet.net Licensee: Covenant Network. (acq 5-13-2005; $730,000). Population served: 2,500,000 ♦Tony Holman, gen mgr; Jim Schaper, progmg dir.

Saint James

KTTR-FM— 1994: 99.7 mhz; 12 kw. 472 ft TL: N37 56 41 W91 42 23. Stereo. Hrs open: 24
Rebroadcasts KTTR(AM) Rolla 90%.
Box 4584, Springfield, MT, 65808. Secondary address: 1505 Soest Rd., Rolla 65808. Phone: (573) 364-2525. Fax: (573) 364-5161. Licensee: KTTR-KZNN Inc. Group owner: Mahaffey Enterprises Inc. Rgnl. Network: Missourinet. Missourinet Format: News/talk. News staff: one; News: 20 hrs wkly. Target aud: 25-54. ♦John Mahaffey, chmn; Robert B. Mahaffey, pres.

Saint Joseph

KESJ(AM)— June 1, 1946: 1550 khz; 5 kw-U, DA-N. TL: N39 42 23 W94 44 36. Hrs open: 24 Box 8550, 64508. Secondary address: 4104 Country Ln. 64506. Phone: (816) 233-8881. Fax: (816) 279-8280. Web Site:www.stjoeradio.com Licensee: Eagle Communications Inc. Group owner: Eagle Communications Group (acq 3-1-99; $4 million with co-located FM). Population served: 150,000 Natl. Network: ESPN Radio, . Rgnl. Network: Missourinet. Wiley Rein LLP. Format: Sports. News: 5 hrs wkly. Target aud: 45-64. ♦Gary Shorman, CEO; Mark Vail, COO, gen mgr; Gary Exline, pres, gen mgr, sls dir, gen sls mgr; Kevin Wagner, opns dir, progmg dir; Teresa Hetz, prom mgr; Barry Birr, news dir; Ed Jurich, engrg dir, chief of engrg; Georgia Roades, traf mgr.

KFEQ(AM)— Feb 16, 1926: 680 khz; 5 kw-U, DA-2. TL: N39 49 43 W94 48 20. Hrs open: 24 Box 8550, 64508. Secondary address: 4104 Country Ln. 64506. Phone: (816) 233-8881. Fax: (816) 279-8280.E-mail: garyexline@eagleradio.net Web Site:www.stjoeradio.com Licensee: Eagle Communications Inc. Group owner: Eagle Communications Group (acq 3-20-69; grpsl;4-8-91). Population served: 250,000 Natl. Network: ABC, . Natl. Rep: Katz Radio,. Wiley, Rein & Fielding. Wire Svc: AP Format: News/talk, Sports. News staff: 4; News: 50 hrs wkly. Target aud: 18 plus; adults. Spec prog: Farm 20 hrs wkly. ♦Gary Shorman, CEO; Gary Exline, VP, gen mgr; Kevin Wagner, opns dir.

KGNM(AM)— November 1985: 1270 khz; 1 kw-D, DA. TL: N39 44 39 W94 47 16. Hrs open: 24 2414 S. Leonard Rd., 64503. Phone: (816) 233-2577. Fax: (816) 233-2374.E-mail: kgnm@stjoelive.com Web Site:kgnmradio.com Licensee: Orama Inc. (acq 6-80; $400,000; 6-30-80). Population served: 100,000 Natl. Network: USA, . Format: Adult contemp, Christian music. Target aud: 30-55; conservative. ♦Rory Pullen, pres; Greg Glauser, VP; Chris Meikel, gen mgr; Marci Meikel, progmg dir.

KKJO(FM)— Sept 1, 1962: 105.5 mhz; 100 kw. Ant 981 ft TL: N39 42 35 W95 02 33. Stereo. Hrs open: 24 Prog sep from AM 4104 Country Ln., 64508. Phone: (816) 233-8881. Fax: (816) 279-8280. Web Site:www.stjoeradio.com Format: Adult contemp. News staff: 2; News: 2 hrs wkly. Target aud: 18-49. ♦Greg Lynn, progmg dir.

***KSJI(FM)**—Not on air, target date: unknown: 91.1 mhz; 50 kw. Ant 492 ft TL: N39 40 51 W94 46 47. Hrs open: 2414 S. Leonard Rd., 64503. Phone: (816) 233-2577. Fax: (816) 233-2374. Licensee: Good News Ministries Inc. ♦Chris Meikel, gen mgr.

***KSRD(FM)**— 2004: 91.9 mhz; 10 kw. Ant 492 ft TL: N39 42 35 W95 02 33. Hrs open: 1212 Faraon St., 64501. Phone: (816) 233-5773. Fax: (816) 233-5777.E-mail: info@ksrdradio.com Web Site:www.ksrdradio.com Licensee: Horizon Christian Fellowship. (acq 8-26-2004; $10,600). Format: Christian. ♦Brian KC Jones, gen mgr; Brian Jones, gen sls mgr, progmg dir.

Saint Louis

KATZ(AM)— Jan 3, 1955: 1600 khz; 5 kw-U, DA-N. TL: N38 39 19 W90 07 53. Hrs open: 24 1001 Highlands Plaza Dr. W., Suite 100, 63110. Phone: (314) 333-8000. Fax: (314) 333-8311. Web Site:www.gospel1600.com Licensee: Citicasters Licenses L.P. Group owner: Clear Channel Communications Inc. (acq 5-4-99; grpsl). Population served: 2,700,000 Natl. Network: American Urban, . Format: Contemporary/Traditional Gospel. Target aud: 25-54; Adults. ♦Dennis Lamme, gen mgr; Tommy Austin, opns VP; Beth Davis, sls dir; Pierre Troupe, gen sls mgr.

***KDHX(FM)**— Oct 14, 1987: 88.1 mhz; 42.4 kw. 1,314 ft TL: N38 25 01 W90 25 59. Stereo. Hrs open: 24 3504 Magnolia, 63118. Phone: (314) 664-3955. Fax: (314) 664-1020.E-mail: ljweir@kdhx.org Web Site:www.kdhx.org Licensee: Double Helix Corp. Natl. Network: PRI, . Format: Div. Target aud: General. ♦Larry Weir, stn mgr & opns mgr.

KEZK-FM— September 1968: 102.5 mhz; 100 kw. 400 ft TL: N38 36 47 W90 20 09. Stereo. Hrs open: 24 3100 Market St., St. Louis, 63103. Phone: (314) 531-0000. Fax: (314) 969-7638.E-mail: info@kezk.com Web Site:www.kezk.com Licensee: CBS Radio Holdings Inc. Group owner: Infinity Broadcasting Corp. (acq 11-13-98; grpsl). Population served: 2,112,400 Format: Soft adult contemp. Target aud: 25-54; high average household income. ♦Beth Davis, gen mgr.

KFNS(AM)—See Wood River, IL

KFUO(AM)—See Clayton

KHOJ(AM)—See Saint Charles

KIHT(FM)— Dec 22, 1959: 96.3 mhz; 100 kw. 650 ft TL: N38 36 47 W90 20 09. (CP: 80 kw, ant 1,027 ft.). Stereo. Hrs open: 800 Saint Louis Union Stn., The Powerhouse, 63103. Phone: (314) 621-4106. Fax: (314) 621-3000.E-mail: stl.ms@emies.com Web Site:www.k-hits.com Licensee: Emmis Radio License LLC. Group owner: Emmis Communications Corp. (acq 9-26-2000; grpsl). Population served: 622,236 Format: Classic hits. Target aud: 25-54. ♦John Beck, sr VP; Lois Sampson-Hooker, gen mgr; Joe Rush, gen sls mgr; Jeff Allen, progmg dir.

KJFF(AM)—See Festus

KJSL(AM)— Sept 19, 1938: 630 khz; 5 kw-U, DA-2. TL: N38 40 18 W90 06 52. Hrs open: 24 KJSL(AM), 10845 Olive Blvd., Suite 160, 63141. Phone: (314) 878-3600. Fax: (314) 656-3608.E-mail: bethk@crawfordbroadcasting.com Web Site:www.kjslradio.net Licensee: WMUZ Radio Inc. Group owner: Crawford Broadcasting Co. (acq 1994; $1.57 million). Population served: 500,000 Format: Christian, talk. Target aud: 30-60. ♦Beth Kreminski, stn mgr, gen sls mgr & progmg dir.

KLOU(FM)— November 1962: 103.3 mhz; 100 kw. Ant 920 ft TL: N38 31 47 W90 17 58. Stereo. Hrs open: 24 10001 Highlands Dr. W., 63110. Phone: (314) 333-8000. Fax: (314) 333-8314. Web Site:www.playwhatiwant.com Licensee: Citicasters Licenses L.P. Group owner: Clear Channel Communications Inc. (acq 5-4-99; grpsl). Population served: 2,700,000 Format: Oldies. News staff: one. Target aud: 25-54. ♦Dennis Lamme, gen mgr; Tommy Austin, opns mgr; Beth Davis, sls dir; Al Fox, gen sls mgr; John Helmkamp, mktg dir.

KMOX(AM)— Dec 24, 1925: 1120 khz; 50 kw-U. TL: N38 43 20 W90 03 16. Stereo. Hrs open: 24 One Memorial Dr., St. Louis, 63102-2498. Phone: (314) 621-2345. Fax: (314) 444-1860 (SALES).E-mail: kmox@kmox.com Web Site:www.kmox.com Licensee: CBS Radio East Inc. Group owner: Infinity Broadcasting Corp. (acq 11-13-98; grpsl). Population served: 2,098,500 Natl. Network: CBS, . Leventhal, Senter & Lerman. Format: News/talk, info, sports. News staff: 16; News: 60 hrs wkly. Target aud: 25 plus. Spec prog: Jazz 4 hrs, relg one hr wkly.

KSD(FM)— November 1954: 93.7 mhz; 100 kw. 859 ft TL: N38 34 05 W90 19 55. Stereo. Hrs open: 24 10001 Highlands Dr. W., Suite 100, 63110. Phone: (314) 333-8000. Fax: (314) 333-8332. Web Site:thebullrocks.com Licensee: Citicasters Licenses L.P. Group owner: Clear Channel Communications Inc. (acq 5-4-99; grpsl). Population served: 2,700,000 Format: Country. News staff: one. Target aud: 18-34; adults. ♦Dennis Lamme, sr VP, gen mgr; Tommy Austin, opns mgr; Beth Davis, sls dir; Aaron Hyland, gen sls mgr; John Helmkamp, mktg dir.

KSHE(FM)—See Crestwood

KSIV(AM)—See Clayton

***KSIV-FM**— Apr 13, 1950: 91.5 mhz; 12.5 kw. Ant 400 ft TL: N38 37 10 W90 14 12. Hrs open: 1750 S. Brentwood Blvd., Suite 811, 63144. Phone: (314) 961-1320. Fax: (314) 961-7562.E-mail: info@bottradionework.com Web Site:www.bottradionetwork.com Licensee: Community Broadcasting Inc. Group owner: Bott Radio Network (acq 1996; $1.625 million). Format: Christian info, relg. ♦Richard P. Bott, pres & VP; Michael McHardy, gen mgr; Joy Elder, sls dir, mktg dir.

KSLG(AM)— 1927: 1380 khz; 5 kw-D, 1 kw-N, DA-3. TL: N38 31 27 W90 14 17. Hrs open: 24 22 Morgan St, 63102. Phone: (314) 969-1380. Phone: (314) 436-3283. Fax: (314) 367-8647. Web Site:www.1380espn.com Licensee: Simmons Austin, LS LLC. Group owner: Simmons Media Group (acq 7-29-2004; $2.05 million). Population served: 504000 Natl. Network: ESPN Radio, . Format: Sports. News: 168 hrs wkly. Target aud: 25-54; men and women. ♦John Helmkamp, gen mgr, gen sls mgr; Mike Brownsher, progmg dir.

KSLZ(FM)— Sept 28, 1972: 107.7 mhz; 100 kw. 1,027 ft TL: N38 34 24 W90 19 30. Stereo. Hrs open: 24 10001 Highlands Dr. W., Suite 100, 63110. Phone: (314) 333-8000. Fax: (314) 333-8312. Web Site:www.z1077.com Licensee: Citicasters Licenses L.P. Group owner: Clear Channel Communications Inc. (acq 5-4-99; grpsl). Population served: 2,700,000 Format: Contemp hit. Target aud: 18-34; adults. ♦Dennis Lamme, gen mgr; Tommy Austin, opns mgr; Beth Davis, sls dir; Scott Adamec, gen sls mgr; John Helmkamp, mktg dir.

KSTL(AM)— 1948: 690 khz; 1 kw-D, 18 w-N. TL: N38 37 01 W90 10 17. Hrs open: 24 10845 Olive Blvd., Suite 160, Creve Coeur, 63141. Phone: (314) 878-3600. Phone: (618) 874-5785. Fax: (314) 656-3608.E-mail: bethk@crawfordbroadcasting.com Licensee: WMUZ Radio Inc. Group owner: Crawford Broadcasting Co. (acq 1994). Population served: 3,000,000 Bryan Cave. Format: Gospel. ♦Donald Crawford, pres; Beth Kriminski, stn mgr, progmg dir.

KTRS(AM)— Feb 14, 1922: 550 khz; 5 kw-U, DA-N. TL: N38 39 45 W90 07 43. Stereo. Hrs open: 24 638 West Port Plaza, 63146. Phone: (314) 453-5500. Fax: (314) 453-9704.E-mail: info@ktrs.com Web Site:www.ktrs.com Licensee: KTRS-AM License L.L.C. (acq 1997). Population served: 622,236 Natl. Network: ABC, . Natl. Rep: Christal,. Bryan Cave. Wire Svc: AP Format: News/talk, sports. News staff: 40. Target aud: 35-64. ♦Tim Dorsey, pres & gen mgr; Geoff Witt, sls dir.

***KWMU(FM)**— June 2, 1972: 90.7 mhz; 97 kw. 981 ft TL: N38 34 50 W90 19 45. (CP: 100 kw, ant 1,000 ft.). Stereo. Hrs open: 8001 Natural Bridge Rd., 63121. Phone: (314) 516-5968. Fax: (314) 516-5993.E-mail: kwmu@kwmu.org Web Site:www.kwmu.org Licensee: The Curators of the University of Missouri. (group owner) Population served: 90,000 Natl. Network: NPR, PRI, . Shaw Pittman. Wire Svc: AP Format: News info. News staff: 5; News: 40 hrs wkly. Target aud: 27-45; upscale. ♦Patricia Wente, gen mgr; Shelly Kerley, stn mgr; Shelley Kerley, dev dir; Phil Donato, prom dir; Mike Schrand, progmg dir; Bill Raack, news dir.

KXEN(AM)— May 10, 1951: 1010 khz; 50 kw-D, 500 w-n, DA-2. TL: N38 45 46 W90 03 35. Hrs open: 24 Box 8085, Granite City, IL, 62040. Phone: (314) 436-6550. Fax: (618) 797-2293.E-mail: kxen@aol.com Web Site:www.kxen1010.com Licensee: BDJ Radio Enterprises LLC (acq 7-2-02). Population served: 3,000,000 Format: Relg. ♦Dirk L. Hallemeier, gen mgr; Jay Madas, progmg dir.

KYKY(FM)— 1960: 98.1 mhz; 90 kw. 1,027 ft TL: N38 34 24 W90 19 30. Stereo. Hrs open: 24 3100 Market St., St. Louis, 63103. Phone: (314) 531-0000. Fax: (314) 531-9855.E-mail: eeleavy@stl.cbs.com Web Site:www.y98.com Licensee: CBS Radio Holdings Inc. Group owner: Infinity Broadcasting Corp. (acq 11-13-98; grpsl). Population served: 1,981,700 Natl. Network: Westwood One, . Format: Hot adult contemp. Target aud: 25-54. ♦Beth Davis, gen mgr.

KZQZ(AM)— Feb 9, 1922: 1430 khz; 5 kw-U, DA-2. TL: N38 32 09 W90 11 26. Hrs open: 24 6500 W. Main St., Suite 315, Belleville, 62223. Phone: (314) 983-6000. Fax: (314) 994-9421. Web Site:kzqz1430am.com Licensee: Entertainment Media Trust, Dennis J. Watkins, trustee Group owner: Bonneville International Corp. (acq 3-5-2008; $1.2 million). Population served: 2,021,000 Natl. Network: Westwood One, . Format: Oldies. News staff: one. Target aud: 35 plus; affluent, mature baby boomers. ♦John Kijowski, gen mgr; Keith Kraus, gen sls mgr; Greg Mozingo, progmg dir; Marshall Rice, chief of engrg; Tom Ennis, traf mgr.

WARH(FM)—(Granite City, IL) Nov 24, 1965: 106.5 mhz; 90 kw. Ant 1,027 ft TL: N38 34 24 W90 19 30. Stereo. Hrs open: 11647 Olive Blvd., St. Louis, 63141. Phone: (314) 983-6000. Fax: (314) 994-9447.E-mail: info@wssm.com Web Site:www.wssm.com Licensee: Bonneville Holding Co. Group owner: Bonneville International Corp. (acq 9-26-2000; grpsl). Format: Smooth jazz. ♦Bruce Reese, CEO, pres; Bob Johnson, CFO; John Kijowski, VP, gen mgr; Mike Jennewein, sls dir; Ben Granger, gen sls mgr, natl sls mgr; Amanda Koeppe, pub affrs dir; Marshall Rice, chief of engrg.

WEW(AM)— Apr 26, 1921: 770 khz; 1 kw-D. TL: N38 37 17 W90 04 36. Hrs open: 2 hrs past sunset (pssa) 2740 Hampton Ave., 63139. Secondary address: 21700 Northwestern Hwy, Tower 14, Ste 1190, Southfield, MI 48075. Phone: (314) 781-9397. Phone: (314) 969-7700. Fax: (314) 781-8545.E-mail: wewradio@oal.com Web Site:www.wewradio.com Licensee: Birach Broadcasting Corp. (group owner; acq 1-6-2004; $1.35 million). Population served: 622,236 Natl. Network: CBS Radio, CNN Radio, . Format: Ethnic. Target aud: 35-64; Mature audience/older. Spec prog: Ger 2 hrs, Pol 2 hrs wkly. ♦Sima Birach, CEO, pres & gen mgr; Rich Vannoy, opns mgr.

WGNU(AM)—(Granite City, IL) Dec 1, 1961: 920 khz; 450 w-D, 500 w-N, DA-2. TL: N38 45 33 W90 03 00. Hrs open: 24 P.O. Box 8085, Mitchell, 62040. Phone: (618) 797-2299.E-mail: KXEN@AOL.COM Web Site:WGNU920AM.com Licensee: 920 AM LLC (acq 9-26-2007; $1.3 million). Population served: 2,300,000 Miller & Miller. Format: Contemp Christian music. ♦Dirk Hallemeier, gen mgr, gen sls mgr; Jay Madas, opns dir, progmg dir, news dir & edit dir.

WHHL(FM)—See Jerseyville, IL

WIL-FM— July 15, 1962: 92.3 mhz; 99 kw. Ant 984 ft TL: N38 28 56 W90 23 53. Stereo. Hrs open: 11647 Olive St., 63141. Phone: (314) 983-6000. Fax: (314) 994-9421.E-mail: info@wil92.com Web Site:www.wil92.com Licensee: Bonneville Holding Co. Format: Contemp country.

Saint Robert

KFLW(FM)— Mar 22, 1994: 98.9 mhz; 6.7 kw. Ant 626 ft TL: N37 52 42 W92 01 04. Hrs open: 24 555 Marshall Dr., St. Robert, 65584. Phone: (573) 336-5359. Fax: (573) 336-7619.E-mail: toquinn@kflw99.com Web Site:www.kflw989.com Licensee: Ozark Media Inc. (acq 2-21-2002; $575,000). Format: Solid rock. News: 3 hrs wkly. Target aud: 25-55. ♦Dalton Wright, pres; Tracey O'Quinn, gen mgr.

Sainte Genevieve

KPNT(FM)— March 1967: 105.7 mhz; 100 kw. Ant 1,374 ft TL: N38 13 10 W90 35 44. Stereo. Hrs open: 24 800 St. Louis Union Stn., The Power House, St. Louis, 63103. Phone: (314) 231-1057. Fax: (314) 621-3000.E-mail: stl.ms@emies.com Web Site:www.1057thepoint.com Licensee: Emmis Radio License LLC. Group owner: Emmis Communications Corp. Natl. Network: ABC, . Format: New rock alternative. Target aud: 18-34. ♦John Beck, gen mgr; Tommy Mathern, natl sls mgr & progmg dir; Sam Caputa, chief of engrg.

KSGM(AM)—See Chester, IL

Salem

***KCVX(FM)**— February 2004: 91.7 mhz; 40kw. Ant 210 ft TL: N37 39 53 W91 32 00. Stereo. Hrs open: 24
Rebroadcasts KCVO(FM) Campenton 100%.
Box 800, % Spirit FM Radio, Camdenton, 65020-0800. Phone: (573) 346-3200. Fax: (573) 346-1010. Web Site:www.spiritfm.org Licensee: Lake Area Educational Broadcasting Foundation (acq 12-20-2002). Population served: 60,000 Natl. Network: Salem Radio Network, . Format: contemp Christian. News: one hr wkly. Target aud: 25-45; primarily females, married with children. ♦James J. McDermott, pres; Alice McDermott, CFO; James McDermott, gen mgr, progmg dir.

KKID(FM)— January 1971: 92.9 mhz; 21 kw. Ant 361 ft TL: N37 43 45 W91 28 23. Stereo. Hrs open: 6 AM-midnight 1415 Forum Dr., Rolla, 65401-2508. Phone: (573) 364-4433. Fax: (573) 364-8385.E-mail: 929fm@kkid929fm.com Web Site:www.kkid929fm Licensee: Ultra-Sonic Broadcast Stations Inc. Population served: 250,000 Natl. Network: USA, . Format: Classic country. News staff: one; News: 20 hrs wkly. Target aud: 30-49. ♦David Wheeler, pres, gen mgr; Steve Wheeler, gen sls mgr; Al Martia, progmg dir.

KSMO(AM)— November 1953: 1340 khz; 1 kw-U. TL: N37 37 36 W91 32 09. Hrs open: 24 800 S. Main, P.O. Box 229, 65560. Phone: (573) 729-6117. Fax: (573) 729-7337.E-mail: ksl340@fidnet.com Web Site:www.ksmoradio.com Licensee: KSMO Enterprises. (acq 11-84). Population served: 25,000 Natl. Network: AP Network News, . Rgnl. Network: Missourinet, Brownfield. Natl. Rep: Commercial Media Sales,. Brownfield Booth, Freret, Imlay & Tepper. Wire Svc: The Sports Network Wire Svc: AP Format: Country, news/talk, sports. News staff: one; News: 40 hrs wkly. Target aud: General; middle class. Spec prog: Farm 18 hrs wkly. ♦Stanley M. Podorski, pres & gen mgr; Stanley Podorski, progmg dir; Stan Stevens, news dir.

Sarcoxie

***KITG(FM)**—Not on air, target date: unknown: 89.5 mhz; 31 kw. Ant 328 ft TL: N37 04 34 W93 55 27. Hrs open: 4899 E. 7th St., Joplin, 64801. Phone: (417) 782-2141. Fax: (417) 782-9141. Licensee: Calvary Chapel of Joplin. ♦Jeffery A. Kingery, pres.

Savannah

KSJQ(FM)— September 1991: 92.7 mhz; 50 kw. 492 ft TL: N39 58 34 W94 58 37. Stereo. Hrs open: 24 Box 8550, St. Joseph, 64508. Secondary address: 4104 Country Ln., St. Joseph 64506. Phone: (816) 233-8881. Fax: (816) 279-8280. Web Site:stjoeradio.com Licensee: Eagle Communications Inc. Group owner: Eagle Communications Group (acq 1993; $450,000;9-13-93). Population served: 200,000 Natl. Rep: Katz Radio,. Wiley, Rein & Fielding. Wire Svc: AP Format: Country. News staff: 2; News: 3 hrs wkly. ♦Gary Shorman, CEO, pres; Mark Vail, COO, VP; Gary Exline, VP, gen mgr; Kevin Wagner, opns dir; Teresa Hetz, prom mgr; Brent Harmon, progmg dir; Barry Birr, news dir; Shannon Diggs, traf mgr; Tom Brand, farm dir.

Scott City

KGKS(FM)— 1998: 93.9 mhz; 5.4 kw. 344 ft TL: N37 22 07 W89 35 34. Hrs open: 324 Broadway, Cape Girardeau, 63701. Phone: (573) 335-8291. Fax: (573) 335-4806.E-mail: kiss@riverradio.net Web Site:www.kiss939.com Licensee: MRR License LLC. Group owner: MAX Media L.L.C. (acq 6-2-2004; grpsl). Format: Adult contemp.

♦Christy Benton, gen mgr; Meg Davis, gen sls mgr; Nicole Arnzen, prom dir; Whitney Thomas, progmg dir; Mike Cossey, chief of engrg.

Sedalia

KDRO(AM)— Sept 13, 1939: 1490 khz; 1 kw-U. TL: N38 40 35 W93 15 18. Hrs open: 24 301 S. Ohio, 65301-4431. Phone: (660) 826-5005. Fax: (660) 826-5557.E-mail: 1490@kdro.com Web Site:www.kdro.com Licensee: Mathewson Broadcasting Co. (acq 4-16-90; $300,000; 5-7-90). Population served: 231,830 Natl. Network: CBS, . Rgnl. Network: Brownfield, Missourinet. Missourinet Format: Country. News staff: 2; News: 11 hrs wkly. Target aud: General. Spec prog: Farm 6 hrs, Black one hr, relg 3 hrs wkly. ♦Stu Steinmetz, gen mgr, gen sls mgr; Don Elliott, progmg dir; Jeff Spalding, news dir; Susan Daniels, traf mgr.

KSDL(FM)— May 11, 1964: 92.1 mhz; 3 kw. Ant 280 ft TL: N38 43 52 W93 13 32. Stereo. Hrs open: 24 Prog sep from AM 2209 S. Limit, 65301. Phone: (660) 826-1050. Fax: (660) 827-5072.E-mail: radio92@ksdl.com Web Site:www.ksdl.com Wire Svc: U.S. Weather Service Format: Adult contemp. News staff: 2. Target aud: 12-40; women.

KSIS(AM)— Feb 18, 1954: 1050 khz; 1 kw-D, 86 w-N. TL: N38 43 52 W93 13 32. Stereo. Hrs open: 24 2209 S. Limit, 65301. Phone: (660) 826-1050. Fax: (660) 827-5072.E-mail: ksis@bickbroadcasting.com Licensee: Bick Broadcasting Co. (acq 1-1-87). Population served: 33400 Wire Svc: U.S. Weather Service Format: News/talk. News staff: 2. Target aud: 25-54. ♦Dennis Polk, gen mgr.

Seligman

KIGL(FM)— Aug 1, 1986: 93.3 mhz; 100 kw. Ant 492 ft TL: N36 28 03 W94 10 25. Stereo. Hrs open: 24 Box 8190, Fayetteville, AR, 72703. Secondary address: 2049 E Joyce Blvd, Suite, Fayetteville, AR 72703. Phone: (479) 973-9339. Fax: (479) 582-5302. Web Site:www.933theeagle.com Licensee: Capstar TX L.P. Group owner: Clear Channel Communications Inc. (acq 8-30-00; grpsl). Population served: 250,000 Natl. Network: USA, . Format: Classic rock. News staff: one; News: 7 hrs wkly. Target aud: 35 plus; mature, upscale professionals. ♦Tony Beringer, gen mgr; Dave Ashcroft, progmg dir; Jess Smith, news dir.

Shell Knob

KQMO(FM)— July 16, 1999: 97.7 mhz; 2.1 kw. Ant 558 ft TL: N36 44 54 W93 39 32. Stereo. Hrs open: 24 126 S. Jefferson Ave., Aurora, 65605. Phone: (417) 678-0416. Fax: (417) 678-4111.E-mail: kqmo@radiotalon.com Web Site:www.talonbroadcasting.com Licensee: Falcon Broadcasting Inc. (acq 9-1-2005; $417,500). Population served: 150,000 Format: Sp. News staff: one; News: 21 hrs wkly. Target aud: Mexican-Hispanic. ♦Dewayne Gandy, gen mgr.

Sikeston

KBHI(FM)—(Miner, 2001: 107.1 mhz; 3.7 kw. Ant 420 ft TL: N36 56 33 W89 41 47. Hrs open: 125 S. Kingshighway, 63801. Phone: (573) 339-7000. Fax: (573) 471-8525. Licensee: Dana R. Withers. Natl. Rep: Katz Radio,. Format: Hits of the 80's. ♦Rick Lambert, gen mgr.

KBXB(FM)— Sept 12, 1968: 97.9 mhz; 50 kw. 469 ft TL: N36 59 52 W89 38 52. Stereo. Hrs open: 24 Dups AM 50% Box 907, 125 S. Kings Hwy., 63801. Phone: (573) 471-2000. Fax: (573) 471-8525. Population served: 200,000 Natl. Rep: Katz Radio,. Target aud: 18-49. ♦Hugh Robinson, farm dir.

KRHW(AM)— Mar 17, 1966: 1520 khz; 5 kw-D, 1.6 kw-N, DA-3. TL: N36 49 25 W89 35 45. Hrs open: Box 907, 125 S. Kings Hwy., 63801. Phone: (573) 471-2000. Fax: (573) 471-8525. Licensee: Withers Broadcasting Co. of Southeast Missouri LLC. Group owner: Withers Broadcasting Co. (acq 4-96; with co-located FM). Population served: 50,000 Format: Country, relg. Target aud: 45 plus. Spec prog: Farm 6 hrs wkly. ♦Rick Lambert, gen mgr; Joe Bill Davis, rgnl sls mgr; Kidd Manning, progmg dir; John Steeke, news dir; Smokey King, chief of engrg.

KSIM(AM)— July 17, 1948: 1400 khz; 1 kw-U. TL: N36 52 12 W89 36 32. Hrs open: 324 Broadway, Cape Girardeau, 63701. Phone: (573) 335-8291. Fax: (573) 335-4806.E-mail: Ksim@riverradio.net Web Site:www.1400ksim.com Licensee: MRR License LLC. Group owner: MAX Media L.L.C. (acq 6-2-2004; grpsl). Population served: 200,000 Natl. Rep: Christal,. Format: News/talk. News staff: 4. Target aud: 25-54. Spec prog: Loc sports, news, Paul Harvey, various features. ♦Steve Stephenson, gen mgr; Whitney Thomas, opns mgr; Meg Davis, gen sls mgr; Faune Riggin, news dir.

Sparta

KSPW(FM)— Mar 1, 1989: 96.5 mhz; 3.2 kw. 453 ft TL: N37 05 17 W93 10 34. (CP: 50 kw, ant 492 ft. TL: N35 56 23 W93 17 15). Stereo. Hrs open: 24 Box 2180, Springfield, 65801. Secondary address: 2330 W. Grand St., Springfield 65802. Phone: (417) 865-6614. Fax: (417) 865-9643. Web Site:www.power965jams.com Licensee: Journal Broadcast Corp. Group owner: Journal Communications Inc. (acq 6-11-99; grpsl). Natl. Rep: Christal,. Format: CHR. News staff: 6. Target aud: 18-34; young active adults. ♦Steven Smith, CEO & chmn; Doug Kiel, pres; Carl Gardner, exec VP; Rex Hansen, gen mgr, natl sls mgr; Chris Cannon, opns mgr, progmg dir; Janelle Carter, gen sls mgr.

Springfield

KADI(AM)— July 29, 1949: 1340 khz; 1 kw-U. TL: N37 12 30 W93 17 32. Hrs open: 5431 W. Sunshine St., Brookline Station, 65619. Phone: (417) 831-0995. Fax: (417) 831-4026.E-mail: info@1340kadi.com Web Site:www.kadi.com Licensee: Vision Communications Inc. (acq 5-26-2005; $375,000). Population served: 250,000 Format: Talk. ♦R.C. Amer, gen mgr; Mark Hill, gen sls mgr; Jason Worth, progmg dir.

KBFL(AM)— 1972: 1060 khz; 500 w-D. TL: N37 11 29 W93 19 45. Stereo. Hrs open: 6 AM-sunset + 2 hrs 610 W. College., 65806. Phone: (417) 862-3751. Fax: (417) 869-7675.E-mail: ktozam@pcis.net Web Site:www.ktozam.com Licensee: Meyer-Baldridge Inc. (acq 2-27-2006; $275,000). Population served: 500,000 Format: Big band, nostalgia, MOR. Target aud: General. Spec prog: Jazz 12 hrs, blues 4 hrs, 50s mus 4 hrs wkly. ♦Kenneth E. Meyer, pres; Kenneth Meyer, gen mgr; Bonnie Bell, gen sls mgr; Jamie Turner, progmg dir; R.J. McAlister, news dir.

KGBX-FM—(Nixa, December 1989: 105.9 mhz; 38 kw. 558 ft TL: N37 25 16 W93 24 06. Stereo. Hrs open: 24 1856 S. Glenstone, 65804. Phone: (417) 890-5555. Fax: (417) 890-5050.E-mail: studio@kgbx.com Web Site:www.kgbx.com Licensee: Clear Channel Broadcasting Licenses Inc. Population served: 220,000 Format: Adult contemp. News staff: one; News: 5 hrs wkly. Target aud: 25-54; educated, high income, women. ♦Brian Edwards, progmg dir.

KGMY(AM)— Oct 31, 1926: 1400 khz; 1 kw-U. TL: N37 11 46 W93 19 21. Stereo. Hrs open: 1856 S. Glenstone, 65804. Phone: (417) 890-5555. Fax: (417) 890-5050.E-mail: studio@espn1400.com Web Site:www.espn1400.com Licensee: Clear Channel Broadcasting Licenses Inc. Group owner: Clear Channel Communications Inc. (acq 10-10-2000; grpsl). Population served: 220,000 Format: Sports. Target aud: 35 plus; affluent, educated white-collar skewing 35 plus year olds. ♦Paul Windisch, gen mgr; Paul Kelley, opns mgr; Eldon Combs, gen sls mgr; Kelli Presley, natl sls mgr; Sarah Green, prom dir; Shawn Baker, chief of engrg; Mary Brown, traf mgr.

KLFJ(AM)— Nov 1, 1974: 1550 khz; 5 kw-D, 28 w-N. TL: N37 11 45 W93 19 07. Hrs open: 24 225 E. Primrose, 65807. Phone: (417) 831-1550.E-mail: sobrien@kgrandcrowneresorts.com Licensee: 127 Inc. (acq 6-99; $432,500). Population served: 250,000 Format: Info, news. ♦Kent Emmons, gen mgr; Patricia Pugh, mktg dir; Shelly O'Brien, gen mgr, stn mgr & progmg dir.

KLPW(AM)—See Union

***KSCV(FM)**— Apr 3, 2001: 90.1 mhz; 9 kw. Ant 492 ft TL: N37 17 41 W93 09 10. (CP: 9 kw, ant 492 ft. TL: N37 17 41 W93 09 10). Stereo. Hrs open: 24
Rebroadcasts KCCV(FM) Overland Park, KS 90%.
1111 S. Glenstone Ave., Suite 3-102, 65804. Phone: (417) 864-0901. Fax: (417) 862-7263.E-mail: pschneider@bottradionetwork.com Web Site:bottradionetwork.com Licensee: Community Broadcasting Inc. Group owner: Bott Radio Network (acq 2-7-01; 1.25 million with KMCV(FM) High Point). Population served: 350,000 Natl. Network: USA, . Format: Christian, talk. News: 4 hrs wkly. Target aud: 25-54 plus; women 60%, men 40%. ♦Paul Schneider, gen mgr & opns mgr; Monna Stafford, gen sls mgr.

KSGF(AM)— 1926: 1260 khz; 5 kw-U, DA-N. TL: N37 15 51 W93 19 04. Stereo. Hrs open: 24
Rebroadcast KSGF-FM Ash Grove.
Box 2180, 65801. Secondary address: 2330 W. Grand 65802. Phone: (417) 865-6614. Fax: (417) 865-9643. Web Site:www.ksgf.com Licensee: Journal Broadcast Corp. Group owner: Journal Communications Inc. (acq 6-11-99; grpsl). Population served: 400,000 Rgnl. Network: Missourinet. Natl. Rep: Christal,. Missourinet Format: News/talk. News staff: 4; News: 30 hrs wkly. Target aud: 35-54.Steven Smith, CEO & chmn; Doug Kiel, pres; Carl Gardner, exec VP; Rex Hansen, VP, gen mgr, gen sls mgr; Chris Cannon, opns mgr; Karen Campbell, natl sls mgr; Kris Addison, prom dir, mus dir; David Hayes, progmg dir; Don Louzader, news dir, local news ed; David Rahmoeller, chief of engrg; Cristie Cummings, traf mgr, edit mgr; Jason Rima, reporter, outdoor ed

***KSMU(FM)**— May 7, 1974: 91.1 mhz; 40 kw. Ant 403 ft TL: N37 10 14 W93 19 25. Stereo. Hrs open: 24 Missouri State Univ., 901 S. National Ave., 65897. Phone: (417) 836-5878. Fax: (417) 836-5889.E-mail: ksmu@missouristate Web Site:www.ksmu.org Licensee: Board of Governors, Southwest Missouri State University Population served: 360,000 Natl. Network: NPR, . Dow, Lohnes & Albertson. Format: News & classical music. News staff: one; News: 54 hrs wkly. Target aud: 25-54. Spec prog: Jazz 10 hrs wkly. ♦Tammy Wiley, gen mgr.

KTTS-FM— Aug1948: 94.7 mhz; 100 kw. Ant 1,125 ft TL: N37 13 26 W93 14 33. Stereo. Hrs open: 24 2330 W. Grand, 65802. Phone: (417) 865-6614. Fax: (417) 865-9643. Web Site:www.ktts.com Licensee: Journal Broadcast Corp. Population served: 675,800 Natl. Rep: Christal,. Dow, Lohnes & Albertson. Format: Country. News staff: 4; News: 5 hrs wkly. Target aud: 25-54; adults. ♦Rex Hansen, gen mgr; Chris Michaels, progmg dir.

KTXR(FM)— June 12, 1962: 101.3 mhz; 97.8 kw. Ant 1,488 ft TL: N37 11 41 W92 56 07. Stereo. Hrs open: 24 3000 E. Chestnut Expwy., 65802. Secondary address: Box 3925 65802. Phone: (417) 862-3751. Fax: (417) 869-7675.E-mail: manager@radiospringfield.com Web Site:www.radiospringfield.com Licensee: Stereo Broadcasting Inc. Group owner: Meyer Communications Inc. Population served: 1,000,000 Format: Contemp easy lstng. News staff: 2; News: 21. Target aud: 35 plus; female. Spec prog: MSU Bears sports, St. Louis Cardinals baseball. ♦Kenneth E. Meyer, pres, gen mgr; Bonnie Bell, gen sls mgr; Jamie Turner, progmg dir; Dale Blankenship, chief of engrg; Pat Willis, traf mgr.

***KWFC(FM)**— Apr 17, 1985: 89.1 mhz; 100 kw. 1,122 ft TL: N37 12 06 W92 56 33. Stereo. Hrs open: 24 Box 8900, 65801-8900. Secondary address: 2316 N. Benton 65801. Phone: (417) 869-0891. Fax: (417) 866-7525.E-mail: info@kwfc.org Web Site:www.kwfc.org Licensee: Baptist Bible College Inc. Population served: 151,000 Natl. Network: USA, . Wire Svc: AP Format: Relg, Christian. News staff: one; News: 17 hrs wkly. Target aud: General; conservative, church-oriented. ♦Gary Longstaff, gen mgr; Kyle Dowden, progmg dir; Brady Shoemaker, news dir; Vickie Hawkins, traf mgr.

***KWND(FM)**— July 12, 1993: 88.3 mhz; 12 kw. 328 ft TL: N37 10 30 W93 02 35. Stereo. Hrs open: 24 2550-100 S. Campbell, 65807. Phone: (417) 889-0883. Fax: (417) 886-8656.E-mail: 883@883thewind.com Web Site:www.88.3thewind.com Licensee: The Radio Training Network. (acq 7-95). Format: Adult contemp, Christian. Target aud: 25-49. Spec prog: Gospel 3 hrs wkly. ♦Ben Birdsong, gen mgr, gen sls mgr; Jeremy Morris, progmg dir.

KWTO(AM)— Dec 25, 1933: 560 khz; 5 kw-U, DA-N. TL: N37 08 08 W93 16 36. Hrs open: Box 3793, 65808. Secondary address: 3000 E. Chestnut Expwy. 65808. Phone: (417) 862-5600. Fax: (417) 869-7675.E-mail: manager@radiospringfield.com Web Site:www.radiospringfield.com Licensee: KWTO Inc. Group owner: Meyer Communications Inc. (acq 3-20-95; $1.88 million with co-located FM; 6-19-95). Population served: 1,500,000 Format: Sports, news/talk. News: one hr wkly. Target aud: 25-55; male. Spec prog: Farm 20 hrs, relg one hr wkly. ♦Kenneth E. Meyer, pres, gen mgr, gen sls mgr; Bonnie Bell, dev mgr, spec ev coord; Dan Vaughn, progmg dir; Dale Blankenship, chief of engrg; Susie Proffitt, traf mgr; R.J. McAllister, news rptr; Lewis Miller, farm dir.

KWTO-FM— Nov 23, 1967: 98.7 mhz; 100 kw. 600 ft TL: N37 04 06 W93 18 31. Stereo. Hrs open: 24 Prog sep from AM Box 3793, 65808. Secondary address: 3000 E. Chestnut Expwy. 65808. Phone: (417) 862-5600. Fax: (417) 869-7675. Web Site:www.radiospringfield.com Population served: 200,000 Format: Sports, talk. Target aud: 25-45; male dominant middle class. ♦Susie Proffitt, traf mgr; Bonnie Bell, spec ev coord; R.J. McAllister, reporter; Lewis Miller, farm dir.

KXUS(FM)— Apr 17, 1969: 97.3 mhz; 100 kw. 479 ft TL: N37 14 23 W93 17 05. (CP: Ant 987 ft. TL: N37 11 10 W93 01 23). Stereo. Hrs open: 24 1856 S. Glenstone Ave., 65804. Phone: (417) 890-5555. Fax: (417) 890-5050.E-mail: us97@us97.com Web Site:www.us97.com Licensee: Clear Channel Broadcasting Licenses Inc. Group owner: Clear Channel Communications Inc. (acq 10-10-00; grpsl). Format: Classic rock. News staff: one; News: 5 hrs wkly. Target aud: 25-54; males -75%. ♦Paul Windisch, gen mgr; Paul Kelley, opns dir; Dave Hines, progmg dir; Shawn Baker, chief of engrg; Mary Brown, traf mgr.

Stockton

KRWP(FM)— Jan 20, 1999: 107.7 mhz; 11.7 kw. Ant 479 ft TL: N37 31 24 W93 52 40. Stereo. Hrs open: 24 Box 1070, 1225 South St., Suite B, 65785. Phone: (417) 276-5253. Fax: (417) 276-2255. Licensee: Cumulus Licensing LLC. Group owner: Cumulus Media Inc.

(acq 4-27-2004); $825,000). Population served: 79,000 Natl. Network: Jones Radio Networks, . Rgnl. Network: Jones Satellite Audio, Missourinet. Missourinet Fletcher, Heald & Hildreth. Format: Classic country. News: 16 hrs wkly. Target aud: 25-54; male & female. Spec prog: Local news, weather, farm 8 hrs wkly. ◆Lance Beamer, gen mgr.

Sullivan

KTUI(AM)— Feb 14, 1966: 1560 khz; 1 kw-D. TL: N38 11 42 W91 11 12. Hrs open: 6 AM-sunset Box 99, 63080-0099. Phone: (573) 468-5101. Fax: (573) 468-5884.E-mail: info@ktui.com Web Site:www.ktui.com Licensee: Fidelity Broadcasting Inc. (acq 10-23-97; $497,000 with co-located FM). Population served: 100,000 Rgnl. Network: Missourinet. Missourinet Format: News/talk. News staff: one. Target aud: General. ◆John C. Rice, gen mgr, gen sls mgr; Sam Scott, progmg dir, news dir; Wilma Scott, traf mgr.

KTUI-FM— 1981: 102.1 mhz; 6 kw. Ant 276 ft TL: N38 11 42 W91 11 12. Stereo. Hrs open: Box 99, 63080. Phone: (573) 468-5101. Fax: (573) 468-5884.E-mail: info@ktui.com Web Site:www.ktui.com Licensee: Fidelity Broadcasting Inc. (acq 10-23-97; $497,000 with co-located AM). Population served: 210,000 Rgnl. Network: Missourinet. Missourinet Format: Country, sports. Target aud: General. ◆John Rice, opns dir.

Sunrise Beach

*KCRL(FM)— Sept 1, 1998: 90.3 mhz; 4.5 kw. 197 ft TL: N38 14 11 W92 46 03. Hrs open: 24 Community Broadcasting, 10550 Barkley St, Ste 100, Overland Park, KS, 66212. Secondary address: 30690 Gray Eagle Rd., Gravois Mills 65037. Phone: (573) 372-1903. Fax: (573) 372-3801.E-mail: kcrl@bottradionetwork.com Web Site:www.bot-tradionetwork.com Licensee: Community Broadcasting Inc. Group owner: Bott Radio Network Natl. Network: USA, . Format: Christian talk. Target aud: 25-55. ◆Trace Thurlby, COO; Richard P. Bott Sr., pres; Tom Holdeman, CFO; Richard P. Bott II, exec VP, gen mgr; Eben Fowler, opns dir, sls dir; Pat Rulon, natl sls mgr; Rachel Moser, mktg mgr; Jason Potocnik, traf mgr.

Tarkio

*KRSS(FM)— Aug 22, 1977: 93.5 mhz; 11 kw. 489 ft TL: N40 31 11 W95 11 03. Hrs open: 24 23979 Hwy. 136, 64491. Phone: (660) 736-4321. Fax: (660) 736-5789. Web Site:www.calvarychapel.com/krss Licensee: CSN International (group owner). Population served: 10,000 Format: Christian. Target aud: General. ◆Mick Miller, gen mgr.

Thayer

KALM(AM)— Dec 11, 1953: 1290 khz; 1 kw-D, 56 w-N. TL: N36 32 58 W91 33 05. Hrs open: 6 AM-sunset Box 15, N. Hwy. 63, 65791. Phone: (417) 264-7211. Phone: (417) 264-7063. Fax: (417) 264-7212.E-mail: radio@AM1290TheGift.com Web Site:www.AM1290TheGift.com Licensee: E-Communications LLC (acq 4-24-2008; $830,000 with KAMS(FM) Mammoth Spring, AR). Population served: 40,000 Rgnl. Network: Brownfield, Missourinet. Missourinet Rgnl rep: Regional Reps Greg Skall. Format: Southern Gospel/Contemporary Christian. News staff: one; News: 70 hrs wkly. Target aud: 18 plus; farmers, ranchers, rural families. ◆Robert Eckman, pres, gen mgr & progmg dir.

KAMS(FM)—See Mammoth Spring, AR

KSAR(FM)— 92.3 mhz; 50 kw. 426 ft TL: N36 21 58 W91 28 35. Hrs open: 24 Box 458, Salem, AR, 72576. Secondary address: 352 Hwy. 62/412, Salem, AR 72576. Phone: (870) 895-2665. Fax: (870) 895-4088.E-mail: hometownradio@centurytel.net Web Site:www.yourhometownstations.com Licensee: Bragg Broadcasting Corp. Population served: 75,000 Rgnl. Network: Ark. Radio Net. Ark. Radio Net. Format: Country, news, sports. Target aud: 25-54. Spec prog: Farm 4 hrs wkly. ◆James Bragg, gen mgr.

Trenton

KTTN(AM)— Apr 17, 1955: 1600 khz; 500 w-D, 35 w-N. TL: N40 05 00 W93 33 30. Stereo. Hrs open: 24 Box 307, 64683. Secondary address: 804 Main St. 64683. Phone: (660) 359-2261. Fax: (660) 359-4126. Web Site:www.kttn.com Licensee: Luehrs Broadcasting Co. Population served: 10,000 Natl. Network: AP Radio, Jones Radio Networks, . Reddy, Begley & McCormick. Format: Adult contemp. News: 8 hrs wkly. Target aud: 35 plus; general.

KTTN-FM— Sept 15, 1978: 92.3 mhz; 18.5 kw. Ant 380 ft TL: N40 05 00 W93 33 30. Stereo. Hrs open: 24 Box 307, 64683. Secondary address: 804 Main St. 64683. Phone: (660) 359-2261. Fax: (660)

359-4126.E-mail: kttnamfm@grm.net Web Site:www.kttn.com Licensee: Luehrs Broadcasting Co. (acq 8-1-92). Population served: 40,000 Natl. Network: AP Radio, . Missourinet Rgnl rep: Rgnl Reps Reddy, Begley & McCormick. Format: Country, news, sports. News staff: 2; News: 15 hrs wkly. Target aud: General. Spec prog: Gospel 6 hrs wkly. ◆John Ausberger, pres; John Anthony, gen mgr.

Troy

KFNS-FM— Nov 29, 1993: 100.7 mhz; 6 kw. Ant 328 ft TL: N39 03 13 W90 59 47. Hrs open: 8045 Big Bend Blvd., Suite 200, St. Louis, 63119. Phone: (314) 962-0590. Fax: (314) 962-7576.E-mail: kfns@kfns.com Web Site:www.westplexradio.com Licensee: Big Stick Two LLC. Group owner: Big League Broadcasting LLC (acq 7-31-2004; grpsl). Format: Classic hits. ◆Dave Greene, gen mgr; James Oelklaus, gen sls mgr.

Union

KLPW(AM)— Aug 18, 1954: 1220 khz; 1 kw-D, 126 w-N. TL: N38 28 57 W91 02 39. Hrs open: 24 6501 Hwy BB, Washington, 63090. Phone: (636) 239-3355. Fax: (636) 583-1644.E-mail: klpwam@klpw.com Web Site:www.klpwam.com Licensee: Broadcast Properties Inc. (acq 7-5-2007; $200,000 for 50% of stock). Population served: 600,000 Format: All talk. News staff: 2; News: 40 hrs wkly. Target aud: 25-54; male. Spec prog: Relg 6 hrs wkly. ◆ Tim McDonald, gen mgr, gen sls mgr; Ray Heller, opns dir, pub affrs dir; Dee Coppeans, sls dir; Diana Stanley, prom dir; Greg Marshall, progmg dir; John Covington, news dir, local news ed, news rptr, sports cmtr; Tom Lyons, chief of engrg; Marcy Frankenberg, traf mgr; Alex Pennock, reporter.

Van Buren

*KBIY(FM)— 2001: 91.3 mhz; 100 kw. Ant 492 ft TL: N37 06 25 W90 59 30. Hrs open: New Life Evangelistic Center Inc., 1411 Locust St., St. Louis, 63103. Phone: (314) 436-2424. Fax: (314) 436-2434.E-mail: larryr@hereshelpnet.org Web Site:www.hereshelpnet.org Licensee: New Life Evangelistic Center Inc. Format: Adult contemp, gospel, loc pub affrs-news. ◆Larry Rice, pres & gen mgr.

Vandalia

KKAC(FM)—Not on air, target date: unknown: 104.3 mhz; 6 kw. 292 ft TL: N39 19 00 W91 28 22. Hrs open: 400 S. Lindell St., 63382. Phone: (573) 594-6000. Fax: (314) 594-2100.E-mail: kkacfm@vandaliamo.net Web Site:www.actioncountry.com Licensee: Broadcast Associates Inc. Format: Country.

Versailles

KTKS(FM)— June 16, 1989: 95.1 mhz; 12.5 kw. Ant 462 ft TL: N38 24 32 W92 45 42. Stereo. Hrs open: 24 Box 409, 65084. Secondary address: 16875 Hwy 52, Barnett 65011. Phone: (573) 378-5669. Fax: (573) 378-6640.E-mail: jay@lakeradio.net Web Site:lakeradio.com Licensee: Twin Lakes Communications Inc. Population served: 100,000 Natl. Network: CNN Radio, . Fletcher, Heald & Hildreth. Wire Svc: AP Format: Country. News staff: one; News: 23 hrs wkly. Target aud: 25-54; loc rural audience & transient tourist population. Spec prog: Farm 2 hrs, relg 3 hrs wkly. ◆Douglas A. Fisher, chmn; James D. Fisher, pres, gen mgr; Sheryl Lehman, gen sls mgr; J.T. Gerlt, progmg dir.

Vienna

*KNLN(FM)—Not on air, target date: unknown: 90.9 mhz; 10 kw. 328 ft TL: N38 11 27 W92 07 22. Hrs open: New Life Evangelistic Center Inc., 1411 Locust St., St. Louis, 63103. Phone: (314) 421-3020. Fax: (314) 436-2434.E-mail: larryr@hereshelpnet.org Web Site:www.hereshelpnet.org Licensee: New Life Evangelistic Center Inc. Format: Relg. ◆Larry Rice, gen mgr.

Warrensburg

KOKO(AM)— December 1953: 1450 khz; 1 kw-U. TL: N38 46 32 W93 43 12. Hrs open: 24 Box 398, 64093. Phone: (660) 747-9191. Fax: (660) 747-5611. Web Site:www.warrensburgradio.com Licensee: D & H Media L.L.C. (acq 10-3-01; $435,000). Population served: 42,514 Natl. Network: ABC, . Rgnl. Network: Missourinet, Brownfield. Missourinet Format: Oldies, Sports. News staff: one; News: 20 hrs wkly. Target aud: 25-54; educated-mainly female & sports enthusiasts. ◆Vance Delozier, pres; Greg Hassler, gen mgr, opns mgr.

Warrenton

KFAV(FM)— November 1991: 99.9 mhz; 10.5 kw. 512 ft TL: N38 50 20 W91 02 40. Hrs open: 24 Box 220, 63383. Phone: (636) 456-3311. Fax:(636) 978-4710.E-mail: kwreksava@socket.net Web Site:www.kfav.com Format: Today's hot country. News staff: 3; News: 2 hrs wkly. Target aud: 20-49; general.

KWRE(AM)— Mar 9, 1949: 730 khz; 1 kw-D, 120 w-N. TL: N38 49 20 W91 08 15. Hrs open: 5 AM-11 PM Box 220, 63383. Phone: (636) 456-3311. Fax: (636) 456-8767.E-mail: kwrekfav@socket.net Web Site:www.kwre.com Licensee: Kaspar Broadcasting Co. Group owner: Kaspar Broadcasting Group. Population served: 500,000 Format: Traditional country. News staff: 3; News: 3 hrs wkly. Target aud: 35 plus. Spec prog: Farm one hr wkly. ◆Mike Thomas, opns dir, mus dir, news dir; Mark Becker, gen sls mgr; V.J. Kaspar, pres, gen mgr & chief of engrg.

Warsaw

KAYQ(FM)— Mar 10, 1980: 97.1 mhz; 6 kw. Ant 239 ft TL: N38 17 19 W93 18 32. Stereo. Hrs open: 24 Box 1420, 1649 Commercial, 65355. Secondary address: Truman Hills Mall, Suite 6 Phone: (660) 438-7343. Fax: (660) 438-7159.E-mail: kayqtraffic@embarqmail.com Web Site:na Licensee: Valkyrie Broadcasting Co. Inc. Population served: 30,000 Natl. Network: AP Radio, . Rgnl. Network: Missourinet. Format: Classic country. News staff: one; News: 5 hrs wkly. ◆Jim McCollum, pres; Joey Anderson, gen mgr & chief of opns; Glenna Thrasher, prom mgr, traf mgr.

Washington

*KGNV(FM)— Dec 25, 1990: 89.9 mhz; 1 kw. 213 ft TL: N38 35 49 W91 06 17. Hrs open: 24 Box 187, 63090. Phone: (636) 239-0400. Fax: (636) 293-4448. Web Site:goodnewsvoice.org Licensee: Missouri River Christian Broadcasting Inc. Population served: 60,000 Natl. Network: Moody, Salem Radio Network, . Format: News/talk, Southern gospel, inspirational. News: 14 hrs wkly. Target aud: 20-70; inquisitive, conservative, liberal, philosophical. Spec prog: Class 5 hrs, children 6 hrs, teen 5 hrs wkly. ◆James Goggan, pres & gen mgr; Charles Sachse, stn mgr.

KLPW-FM—See Elsberry

KSLQ-FM— Nov 21, 1989: 104.5 mhz; 3 kw. 328 ft TL: N38 36 03 W90 56 04. Stereo. Hrs open: 24 Dups AM 25% 511 W. 5th St., 63090. Phone: (636) 239-5432. Fax: (636) 239-0364. Licensee: Y2K Inc. (acq 6-24-98; $1.1 million). Natl. Network: USA, . Rgnl. Network: Missourinet. Missourinet Format: Hot adult contemp. Target aud: 25-54.

KWMO(AM)— Oct 19, 1985: 1350 khz; 500 w-D, 84 w-N, DA-1. TL: N38 34 44 W90 59 57. Hrs open: 511 W. 5th St., 63090. Phone: (636) 239-5432. Fax: (636) 239-0364. Web Site:www.themouth.info Licensee: Computraffic Inc. (acq 2-13-98; $200,000). Population served: 350,000 Natl. Network: USA, . Rgnl. Network: Missourinet. Missourinet Format: Talk. Target aud: 35-54. ◆Waldo Zimarskie, gen mgr, opns mgr, gen sls mgr, chief of engrg & chief of engrg; Chris Dieckhause, traf mgr.

Waynesville

KFBD-FM— Dec 9, 1964: 97.9 mhz; 3 kw. Ant 259 ft TL: N37 49 42 W92 10 27. Stereo. Hrs open: 5 AM-midnight 313 Old Rte. 66, 65584. Phone: (573) 336-4913. Fax: (573) 336-2222. Format: Adult contemp. ◆Mike Edwards, gen mgr & progmg dir.

KIIK-FM— May 2, 1968: 102.3 mhz; 2.65 kw. Ant 492 ft TL: N37 49 09 W92 09 06. Stereo. Hrs open: 19 Box D, 65583-0480. Phone: (573) 336-4913. Phone: (573) 336-4450. Fax: (573) 336-2222.E-mail: kjpw@regionalradio.com Licensee: Waynesville/Lebanon License Co. LLC. Population served: 60,000 Natl. Network: Fox News Radio, . Format: Country. News staff: one; News: 7 hrs wkly. Target aud: General. ◆Mike Edwards, gen mgr; Gary Knehans, opns mgr; Mke Edwards, gen sls mgr; Warren Goforth, news dir; Dan Boucher, engr.

KJPW(AM)— Apr 3, 1962: 1390 khz; 5 kw-D, 67 w-N. TL: N37 49 09 W92 09 06. Hrs open: 19 Box D, 65583-0480. Secondary address:

313 Old Rte 66, St. Robert 65583-0480. Phone: (573) 336-4913. Phone: (573) 336-4450. Fax: (573) 336-2222.E-mail: kjpw@regionalradio.com Licensee: Waynesville/Lebanon License Co. LLC. Group owner: Shepherd Group (acq 8-8-2007; grpsl). Population served: 60,000 Natl. Network: Fox News Radio, . Rgnl. Network: Missourinet. Missourinet Cohn & Marks. Format: Talk radio. News staff: one; News: 14 hrs wkly. Target aud: General. Spec prog: Relg 2 hrs wkly. ♦Mike Edwards, exec VP; gen mgr, gen sls mgr, traf mgr; Gary Knehans, stn mgr, prom mgr; Warren Goforth, news dir; Bob Moore, chief of engrg.

KOZQ(AM)— May 9, 1968: 1270 khz; 500 w-D. TL: N37 49 42 W92 10 27. Hrs open: Box D, 65583. Secondary address: 313 Old Rte. 66 65584. Phone: (573) 336-4913. Fax: (573) 336-2222. Licensee: Waynesville/Lebanon License Co. LLC. (acq 8-8-2007; grpsl). Population served: 100,000 Format: Adult contemp. Target aud: 40 plus. ♦Mike Edwards, gen mgr.

Webb City

KJMK(FM)— Sept 10, 1985: 93.9 mhz; 48 kw. 505 ft TL: N37 14 34 W94 30 21. Stereo. Hrs open: 24 2702 E. 32nd, Joplin, 64804. Phone: (417) 624-1025. Fax: (417) 781-6842.E-mail: chade@zrgmail.com Web Site:www.939literock.com Licensee: Zimmer Radio Inc. Group owner: Zimmer Radio Group (acq 6-17-97; grpsl). Natl. Rep: Christal,. Format: Adult contemporary. Target aud: 25-54. ♦James Zimmer, pres; Chad Elliott, opns mgr; Kara Marxer, news dir; Mel Williams, chief of engrg.

KXDG(FM)— Sept 1, 1988: 97.9 mhz; 6 kw. 400 ft TL: N37 06 11 W94 24 11. Stereo. Hrs open: 24 2702 E. 32nd St., Joplin, 64804. Phone: (417) 624-1025. Fax: (417) 781-6842. Web Site:www.bigdog979.com Licensee: Zimco Inc. Group owner: Zimmer Radio Group (acq 6-17-97; grpsl). Natl. Network: USA, . Format: Classic rock. Target aud: General. ♦Larry Boyd, gen mgr; Chad Elliott, opns mgr; Jessica Leighman, prom dir; Chris Hayes, progmg dir; Tom Hoglen, news dir; Mel Williams, chief of engrg.

West Plains

KKDY(FM)— Mar 31, 1984: 102.5 mhz; 50 kw. 485 ft TL: N36 41 22 W91 53 45. Stereo. Hrs open: 24 983 E. Hwy. 160, 65775. Phone: (417) 256-1025. Fax: (417) 256-2208.E-mail: hotcountrykdy@kkdy.com Web Site:www.kkdy.com Licensee: Central Ozark Radio Network Inc. (acq 8-1-94). Population served: 34,000 Natl. Network: CNN Radio, . Haley, Bader & Potts. Format: Hot country. News staff: 2; News: 10 hrs wkly. Target aud: 18-49. Spec prog: Contemp Christian 3 hrs wkly. ♦Tom Marhefka, pres & gen mgr; Bob Eckman, opns VP; Chuck Boone, opns dir, progmg dir; Jonathan Bergman, sls dir, gen sls mgr; Bobby Helm, news dir, news rptr; Bill Martin, chief of engrg; Crystal Cook, traf mgr.

*KSMW(FM)—Not on air, target date: unknown: 90.9 mhz; 350 w. Ant 387 ft TL: N36 45 00 W91 49 40. Hrs open: Missouri State Univ., 901 S. National Ave., Springfield, 65897. Phone: (417) 836-5878. Fax: (417) 836-5889.E-mail: ksmu@missouristate Web Site:www.ksmu.org Licensee: Board of Governors, Southwest Missouri State University. Format: Class, news. ♦Tammy Wiley, gen mgr.

KSPQ(FM)— 1951: 93.9 mhz; 100 kw. Ant 650 ft TL: N37 00 12 W91 54 24. Stereo. Hrs open: Prog sep from AM 983 U.S. Hwy. 160 E., 65775. Phone: (417) 256-2322. Fax: (417) 256-2208.E-mail: hotcountrykdy@kkdy.com Population served: 150,000 Format: Classic rock. Target aud: 45-65 plus. ♦Jonathan Bergman, natl sls mgr; Mike Crase, progmg dir.

KWPM(AM)— 1947: 1450 khz; 1 kw-U. TL: N36 44 28 W91 50 01. Hrs open: 24 983 U.S. Hwy. 160 E., 65775. Phone: (417) 256-3131. Phone: (417) 256-5976. Fax: (417) 256-2208.E-mail: hotcountrykdy@kkdy.com Web Site:www.ozarkradionetwork.com Licensee: Missouri Ozarks Radio Network. (acq 1996). Population served: 50,000 Rgnl. Network: Brownfield, Missourinet. Missourinet Format: News/talk. News staff: 4. Target aud: 25-54. ♦Gerry Elan, gen mgr, progmg dir; Tom Marheska, opns mgr; Jonathan Bergman, gen sls mgr; Bobby Helm, news dir; Bill Martin, chief of engrg; Crystal Cook, traf mgr.

Wheeling

KULH(FM)— May 3, 1999: 105.9 mhz; 6 kw. 328 ft TL: N39 54 25 W93 20 28. Hrs open: 24 802 Calhoun St., Chillicothe, 64601. Phone: (877) 639-1059. Fax: (660) 646-2242.E-mail: ean1059@sbcglobal.net Web Site:www.1059thewave.com Licensee: Resources Management Unlimited, Inc. (acq 3-28-01; $350,000). Population served: 70,000 Natl. Network: USA, . Reddy, Begley & McCormick. Format: Christian, adult contemp. Target aud: General. ♦Ean Leppin, gen mgr.

Willard

KOSP(FM)— Aug 15, 1992: 105.1 mhz; 50 kw. Ant 492 ft TL: N37 01 01 W93 30 31. Stereo. Hrs open: 319-B E. Battlefield, Springfield, 65807. Phone: (417) 886-5677. Fax: (417) 886-2155.E-mail: info@star1051.fm Web Site:www.star1051.fm Licensee: MW SpringMo Inc. Group owner: The Mid-West Family Broadcast Group Population served: 295,300 Natl. Network: NBC Radio, . Natl. Rep: Eastman Radio,. Davis Wright Tremaine, LLP. Format: Oldies. Target aud: 35-64. ♦Rick McCoy, pres, gen mgr; Mary Fleenor, opns mgr, progmg dir; Malcolm Hukriede, gen sls mgr; Keith Abercrombie, rgnl sls mgr; Summer Stevens, prom mgr.

Willow Springs

KUKU(AM)— Oct 1957: 1330 khz; 1 kw-D, 52 w-N. TL: N36 58 47 W91 59 29. Hrs open: Sunrise-sunset Rebroadcasts KWPM(AM) West Plains 100%. 6962 US Hwy. 60, Mountain View, 65548. Phone: (417) 469-2500. Fax: (417) 934-2565.E-mail: gto@kuku.com Web Site:kuku.com Licensee: Missouri Ozarks Radio Network. (acq 1996). Population served: 20,000 Natl. Network: ABC, . Format: News/talk.

KUKU-FM— June 15, 1985: 100.3 mhz; 50 kw. 492 ft TL: N37 03 49 W92 01 39. Stereo. Hrs open: 24 6962 US Hwy. 60, Mountain View, 65548. Phone: (417) 469-2500. Fax: (417) 934-2565. Web Site:kuku.com Population served: 100,000 Format: Oldies. News staff: 2; News: 27 hrs wkly. Target aud: 29 plus. ♦Gary Taylor, progmg dir, local news ed; Harlin Hutchinson, local news ed.

Windsor

KWKJ(FM)— Feb 21, 2002: 98.5 mhz; 2.3 kw. Ant 535 ft TL: N38 35 37 W93 31 26. Stereo. Hrs open: 24 Box 398, Warrensburg, 64093. Phone: (660) 747-9191. Phone: (660) 747-3883. Fax: (660) 747-5611. Web Site:www.warrensburgradio.com Licensee: D & H Media LLC (acq 7-26-00; $47,500 for CP). Wire Svc: AP Format: Country + more. News staff: one; News: 1 hr wkly. Target aud: Students; Central MO State Univ. Students and like age group. ♦Vance DeLozier, pres; Greg Hassler, VP, gen mgr.

Montana

Alberton

KERT(FM)—Not on air, target date: unknown: 105.5 mhz; 1.1 kw. Ant 787 ft TL: N47 02 05 W114 41 11. Hrs open: Box 4106, Missoula, 59806. Phone: (406) 728-5000. Fax: (406) 721-3020. Licensee: CCR-Missoula IV LLC. (acq 10-31-2006; grpsl). ♦Chad Parrish, gen mgr.

Anaconda

KANA(AM)— Aug 1947: 580 khz; 1 kw-D, 197 w-N. TL: N46 07 50 W112 55 07. Hrs open: 24 105 Main St., 59711. Phone: (406) 563-8011. Fax: (406) 563-8259.E-mail: mail@magic97.mobi Licensee: Butte Broadcasting Inc. Group owner: Jimmy Ray Carroll Stns (acq 12-31-2006; grpsl). Population served: 50,000 Natl. Network: ABC, . Format: Oldies. News: one hr wkly. Target aud: 40+. ♦Ron Davis, pres; Paula Carriger, gen mgr; Joe Frankland, opns mgr.

KGLM-FM— Jan 18, 1974: 97.7 mhz; 2.75 kw. Ant 984 ft TL: N46 06 04 W112 56 59. Stereo. Hrs open: 24 105 Main St., 59711. Phone: (406) 563-8011. Fax: (406) 563-8259.E-mail: mail@magic97.mobi Licensee: Butte Broadcasting Inc. Group owner: Jimmy Ray Carroll Stns (acq 12-31-2006; grpsl). Population served: 50,000 Format: Hot adult contemp. Target aud: 18 plus. ♦Ron Davis, pres; Paula Carriger, gen mgr; Joe Frankland, opns mgr, progmg dir.

Arlee

*KJFT(FM)— 2007: 90.3 mhz; 125 w. Ant 1,906 ft TL: N47 01 04 W114 00 49. Hrs open: 1501 S. Sixth St., Missoula, 59801. Phone: (406) 721-2780. Web Site:www.csnradio.com Licensee: CSN International (group owner). Format: Christian. ♦Jason Pace, gen mgr.

Baker

KATQ-FM—See Plentywood

KFLN(AM)— July 14, 1964: 960 khz; 5 kw-D, 91 w-N. TL: N46 22 31 W104 16 25. Hrs open: Box 790, 3600 Hwy. 7, 59313. Phone: (406) 778-3371. Fax: (406) 778-3373.E-mail: kfln@midrivers.com Licensee: Newell Broadcasting Corp. (acq 3-1-84; $870,000; 3-5-84). Population served: 2,584 Natl. Network: ABC, . Agrinet Wire Svc: AP Format: C&W. Spec prog: Farm 10 hrs wkly. ♦Russ Newell, pres, gen mgr, progmg dir; Devin Bannister, gen sls mgr; Tony Cuesta, chief of engrg; Alysia Putnam, traf mgr.

KJJM(FM)— May 26, 2001: 100.5 mhz; 6 kw. Ant 108 ft TL: N46 22 31 W104 16 25. Stereo. Hrs open: 24 Box 790, 59313. Secondary address: 3600 Hwy. 7 59313. Phone: (406) 778-3371. Fax: (406) 778-3373. Licensee: Newell Broadcasting Corp. Format: Classic rock. ♦Russ Newell, gen mgr; Vaughn Zenko, progmg dir.

Belgrade

KCMM(FM)— 2001: 99.1 mhz; 25 kw. Ant 203 ft TL: N45 46 15 W111 13 26. Hrs open: 2050 Amsterdam Rd., 59714. Phone: (406) 388-4281. Fax: (406) 388-1700.E-mail: info@kcmmtheone.com Web Site:www.kcmmtheone.com Licensee: Gallatin Valley Witness Inc. Format: Christian music. ♦Mark Brashear, gen mgr & gen sls mgr; Bob Sloan, progmg dir; Dale Heidner, chief of engrg.

*KGCM(FM)— 2006: 90.9 mhz; 5.5 kw vert. Ant 623 ft TL: N45 57 25 W111 22 11. Hrs open: Rebroadcasts KLVR(FM) Middletown, CA 100%. 2351 Sunset Blvd., Suite 170-218, Rocklin, CA, 95765. Phone: (916) 251-1600. Fax: (916) 251-1650. Web Site:www.klove.com Licensee: Educational Media Foundation. Natl. Network: K-Love, . Format: Contemp Christian. ♦Mike Novak, pres.

KGVW(AM)— Feb 1, 1959: 640 khz; 10 kw-D, 1 kw-N, DA-2. TL: N45 46 15 W111 13 26. Hrs open: 24 2050 Amsterdam Rd., 59714. Phone: (406) 388-4281. Fax: (406) 388-1700.E-mail: mwbrashear@yahoo.com Web Site:www.kcmmtheone.com Licensee: Gallatin Valley Witness Inc. (acq 1996). Population served: 76,000 Natl. Network: Salem Radio Network, Moody, . Format: Relg, news/talk. News staff: one; News: 16 hrs wkly. Target aud: 35-64; business people, farmers & housewives. ♦Mark Brashear, pres, gen mgr, gen sls mgr & adv VP; Bob Sloan, progmg dir; Dale Heidner, chief of engrg.

KISN(FM)— Nov 1, 1963: 96.7 mhz; 18.5 kw. Ant 813 ft TL: N45 40 24 W110 52 02. Hrs open: 125 W. Mendenhall, Suite 1, Bozeman, 59715. Phone: (406) 586-2343. Fax: (406) 587-2202. Web Site:www.bozemanskissfm.com Licensee: GAP Broadcasting Bozeman License LLC. Group owner: Clear Channel Communications Inc. (acq 2-13-2008; grpsl). Population served: 3,500 Format: CHR. Target aud: 25-54; women. ♦Sammy Suarez, progmg dir.

Belt

*KGFJ(FM)—Not on air, target date: unknown: 88.1 mhz; 1 kw. Ant 288 ft TL: N47 15 57 W111 08 39. Hrs open: Box 391, Twin Falls, ID, 83383. Phone: (208) 733-3133. Fax: (208) 736-1958. Web Site:www.csnradio.com Licensee: Calvary Chapel of Twin Falls Inc. ♦Michael Kestler, pres.

Big Sky

KBZM(FM)— July 31, 1998: 104.7 mhz; 5 kw. Ant 3,336 ft TL: N45 16 41 W111 26 57. Stereo. Hrs open: 24 Simulcast on KKQX(FM) Manhattan. 8274 Huffine, Bozeman, 59718-6860. Phone: (406) 582-1045. Fax: (406) 582-0388.E-mail: sbalding@kbzm.com Web Site:www.kbzm.com Licensee: Orion Media LLC. Natl. Rep: Interep,. Rgnl rep: Local Focus 310-441-8188 Format: Classic hits/classic rock. News staff: 2. Target aud: Adults; 25-54. Spec prog: 6a-10a; 3p-6p. ♦Jeff Balding, gen mgr; Susan Balding, gen sls mgr; Colter Langan, progmg dir.

Big Timber

*KYPB(FM)—Not on air, target date: unknown: 89.3 mhz; 890 w vert. Ant 502 ft TL: N45 53 40 W109 51 24. Hrs open: Yellowstone Public Radio, 1500 University Dr., Billings, 59101-0298. Phone: (406) 657-2941. Fax:(406) 657-2977. Web Site:www.yellowstonepublicradio.org Licensee: Montana State University - Billings. ♦Lois Bent, gen mgr.

Bigfork

KIBG(FM)— 2001: 100.7 mhz; 85 kw. Ant 2,119 ft TL: N47 46 25 W114 16 04. Hrs open: 581 N. Reservoir Rd., Polson, 59860. Phone: (406) 883-5255. Fax: (406) 883-4441.E-mail: info@750kerr.com Web

Site:www.thebig100.com Licensee: Anderson Radio Broadcasting Inc. (group owner; (acq 9-22-2003; grpsl). Population served: 100,000 ♦Dennis Anderson, gen mgr; Gary Meili, gen sls mgr; Dean August, progmg dir; Jeff Smith, news dir; Tony Mulligan, chief of engrg.

Billings

KBBB(FM)— Dec 6, 1987: 103.7 mhz; 100 kw. 480 ft TL: N45 46 00 W108 27 27. Stereo. Hrs open: 24 Box 1276, 59103. Phone: (406) 248-7827. Fax: (406) 252-9577. Web Site:www.bee104.com Licensee: GAP Broadcasting Billings License LLC. Group owner: Clear Channel Communications Inc. (acq 2-13-2008; grpsl). Natl. Rep: Tacher,. Reddy, Begley & McCormick. Format: Adult contemp. Target aud: 25-54; general. ♦Dennis Koffman, gen mgr; Roy Brown, opns dir & prom VP.

KBLG(AM)— Sept 25, 1955: 910 khz; 1 kw-D, 63 w-N. TL: N45 45 10 W108 30 57. Hrs open: 24 2075 Central Ave., 59102. Phone: (406) 652-8400. Fax: (406) 652-4899. Web Site:www.kblg.com Licensee: CCR-Billings IV LLC Population served: 120,000 Natl. Network: CBS, . Format: News/talk, sports. News staff: one; News: 46 hrs wkly. Target aud: 35-64; upscale executives.

***KBLW(FM)**— August 2002: 90.1 mhz; 250 w vert. Ant 331 ft TL: N45 45 51 W108 27 18. Stereo. Hrs open: 24
Rebroadcasts KXEI(FM) Havre 100%.
Box 2426, Havre, 59501. Secondary address: 317 First St., Havre 59501. Phone: (406) 265-5845. Fax: (406) 265-8860.E-mail: ynop@ynopradio.org Web Site:www.ynopradio.org Licensee: Hi-Line Radio Fellowship Inc. (acq 8-7-02). Natl. Network: Moody, Salem Radio Network, . Wire Svc: AP Format: Inspirational. Target aud: General; those looking for Christian inspirational music & progmg. ♦Brenda Boyum, stn mgr; Roger Lonnquist, dev dir; Brian Jackson, progmg dir.

KBUL(AM)— Mar 20, 1951: 970 khz; 5 kw-U, DA-N. TL: N45 44 35 W108 32 37. Stereo. Hrs open: 24 Box 1276, 59103. Secondary address: 27 N. 27th St., 23rd Fl. 59101. Phone: (406) 248-7827. Fax: (406) 252-9577. Web Site:www.newsradio970.com Licensee: GAP Broadcasting Billings License LLC. Group owner: Clear Channel Communications Inc. (acq 2-13-2008; grpsl). Population served: 120,000 Natl. Rep: Christal,. Format: News. News staff: one; News: 2 hrs wkly. Target aud: 25-54. ♦Dennis Coffman, pres, gen mgr; Roy Brown, sls dir, gen sls mgr; Tommy Braaten, progmg dir & mus dir; Dick Jones, chief of engrg; Stacy Ulstad, traf mgr.

KCTR-FM— Aug 14, 1979: 102.9 mhz; 100 kw. Ant 500 ft TL: N45 45 59 W108 27 19. Stereo. Hrs open: Box 1276, 59103. Secondary address: 27 N. 27th St., 23rd Fl. 59101. Phone: (406) 248-7827. Fax: (406) 252-9577. Web Site:www.kctr.com Licensee: GAP Broadcasting Billings License LLC. (acq 2-13-2008; grpsl). Format: Country. ♦Erik Bowen, progmg dir.

***KEMC(FM)**— Apr 25, 1973: 91.7 mhz; 100 kw. Ant 520 ft TL: N45 39 51 W108 34 14. Stereo. Hrs open: 24 1500 N. 30th St., 59101-0298. Phone: (406) 657-2941. Fax: (406) 657-2977.E-mail: mail@yellowstonepublicradio.org Web Site:www.yellowstonepublicradio.org Licensee: Montana State University/Billings. Population served: 100,000 Natl. Network: NPR, AP Radio, . Format: News, class, jazz. News staff: one; News: 24 hrs wkly. Target aud: General. Spec prog: Folk 5 hrs wkly. ♦Lois Bent, gen mgr.

KGHL(AM)— June 8, 1928: 790 khz; 5 kw-U, DA-N. TL: N45 43 34 W108 36 35. Stereo. Hrs open: 24 222 N. 32nd St., 59101. Phone: (406) 238-1000. Fax: (406) 238-1038.E-mail: kyle.mccoy@nnbradio.com Licensee: New Northwest Broadcasters LLC. (group owner; (acq 8-10-99; grpsl). Population served: 165,500 Natl. Network: CBS, . Dow, Lohnes & Albertson. Format: Classic country. News staff: one; News: 4 hrs wkly. Target aud: 25-54. ♦Pete Benedetti, CEO; Tommy Ehrman, gen mgr; Dave Tester, sls dir; Jeff Howell, progmg dir; Mike Powers, chief of engrg; Tracey McCarthy, traf mgr & farm dir.

KGHL-FM— August 1978: 98.5 mhz; 85 kw. Ant 370 ft TL: N45 45 51 W108 27 18. Stereo. Hrs open: 222 N. 32nd St., 59101. Phone: (406) 238-1000. Fax: (406) 238-1038.E-mail: kyle.mccoy@nnbradio.com Licensee: New Northwest Broadcasters LLC. Population served: 192800 Format: Continuous country. Target aud: 18-54. ♦Karen Gallagher, progmg dir.

KKBR(FM)— Dec 17, 1963: 97.1 mhz; 28 kw. 325 ft TL: N45 45 51 W108 27 18. Stereo. Hrs open: Box 1276, 59103. Phone: (406) 248-7827. Fax: (406) 252-9577. Web Site:www.kbear.com Licensee: GAP Broadcasting Billings License LLC. Group owner: Clear Channel Communications Inc. (acq 2-13-2008; grpsl). Format: Oldies. ♦Dennis Koffman, gen mgr; Keith Todd, progmg dir.

***KLMT(FM)**— Dec 18, 2002: 89.3 mhz; 1 kw vert. Ant 335 ft TL: N45 45 41 W108 27 19. Hrs open: 24 Western Inspirational Broadcasters Inc., 6363 Hwy. 50 E., Carson City, NV, 89701. Phone: (775) 883-5647. Licensee: Western Inspirational Broadcasters Inc. Natl. Network: AP Radio, . Wire Svc: AP Format: Contemp Christian. News: 16 hrs wkly. ♦Tom Hesse, gen mgr; Tim Weidemann, opns mgr; Bill Feltner, progmg dir; Patrick Herman, mus dir; Paul Lierman, chief of engrg.

***KLRV(FM)**— 2005: 90.9 mhz; 7.5 kw vert. Ant 593 ft TL: N45 45 54 W108 27 19. Hrs open:
Rebroadcasts KLVR(FM) Santa Rosa, CA).
2351 Sunset Blvd., Suite 170-218, Rocklin, CA, 95765. Phone: (916) 251-1600. Fax: (916) 251-1650. Web Site:www.klove.com Licensee: Educational Media Foundation. (acq 12-8-2004; $100,000 for CP with CP for KLWC(FM) Casper, WY). Natl. Network: K-Love, . Format: Christian. ♦Richard Jenkins, pres; Mike Novak, VP; Keith Whipple, dev dir; David Pierce, progmg mgr; Ed Lenane, news dir; Sam Wallington, engrg dir; Arthur Vassar, traf mgr; Karen Johnson, news rptr.

KMZK(AM)— Sept 8, 1946: 1240 khz; 1 kw-U. TL: N45 45 26 W108 32 08. Hrs open: 24 Box 31038, 636 Haugen St., 59102. Phone: (406) 245-3121. Fax: (406) 245-0822.E-mail: www.genmgr@kmzk.com Web Site:www.kmzk.com Licensee: Elenbaas Media Inc. (acq 1-8-98; $115,000). Population served: 87,500 Natl. Network: Salem Radio Network, . Wire Svc: AP Format: Today's Christian Music. Target aud: 18-44; young & energetic high school & college students & young adults. ♦Herm Elenbaas, pres; John Black, progmg dir; Holly Howard, pub affrs dir; Deb Padilla, traf mgr.

KQBL(FM)— December 1998: 105.1 mhz; 6 kw. Ant 233 ft TL: N45 45 57 W108 27 17. Stereo. Hrs open: 24 222 N. 32nd St., 10th Floor, 59101. Phone: (406) 238-1000. Fax: (406) 238-1038.E-mail: kyle.mccoy @benedettimedia.com Web Site:www.kqbl1051.com Licensee: New Northwest Broadcasters LLC. (group owner; (acq 10-26-99; grpsl). Natl. Network: ESPN Radio, . Format: Sports. Target aud: 25-54. ♦Pete Benedetti, CEO; Kyle McCoy, gen mgr, opns mgr.

KRKX(FM)— July 1989: 94.1 mhz; 100 kw. 590 ft TL: N45 32 25 W108 38 31. Stereo. Hrs open: 24 2075 Central Ave., 59102. Phone: (406) 652-8400. Fax: (406) 652-4899. Web Site:www.krkx.com Licensee: CCR-Billings IV LLC Group owner: Fisher Broadcasting Company (acq 10-31-2006; grpsl). Population served: 140,000 Format: Classic rock. Target aud: 25-54; affluent. ♦Debbie Sundberg, gen mgr; Terry Keys, opns mgr; Augie Aga, gen sls mgr.

KRPM(FM)— 2001: 107.5 mhz;; 100 kw. Ant 984 ft TL: N45 44 29 W108 08 19. Hrs open: 222 N. 32nd St., 59101. Phone: (406) 238-1000. Fax: (406) 238-1038.E-mail: kyle.mccoy@nnbradio.com Licensee: New Northwest Broadcasters LLC. (group owner; (acq 10-26-99). Format: Hot adult contemp. Target aud: 25-54. ♦Pete Benedetti, CEO; Dave Tester, gen mgr.

KRZN(FM)— 1998: 96.3 mhz; 100 kw. 695 ft TL: N45 45 37 W108 27 09. Hrs open: 2075 Central Ave., 59102. Phone: (406) 652-8400. Fax: (406) 652-4899. Web Site:www.thezone963.com Licensee: CCR-Billings IV LLC. Group owner: Fisher Broadcasting Company. (acq 10-31-2006; grpsl). Format: New rock. ♦Dan Reese, gen mgr & stn mgr.

KURL(AM)— Oct 15, 1959: 730 khz; 5 kw-D, 236 w-N. TL: N45 45 29 W108 29 53. Hrs open: 24 Box 31038, 59107. Secondary address: 636 Haugen 59107. Phone: (406) 245-3121. Fax: (406) 245-0822.E-mail: genmgr@kurlradio.com Web Site:www.kurlradio.com Licensee: Elenbaas Media Inc. (acq 11-14-94; $300,000; 1-2-95). Population served: 125,000 Natl. Network: USA, AP Radio, . Format: Relg, syndicated talk. Target aud: 35-64. ♦Herm Elenbaas, pres & gen mgr.

KYYA-FM— Apr 5, 1969: 93.3 mhz; 100 kw. 700 ft TL: N45 45 37 W108 27 09. Stereo. Hrs open: 24 2075 Central Ave., 59102. Phone: (406) 652-8400. Fax: (406) 652-4899.E-mail: y930@y93.com Web Site:www.y93.com Licensee: CCR-Billings IV LLC. Group owner: Fisher Broadcasting Company (acq 10-31-2006; grpsl). Population served: 102,000 Natl. Network: ABC, . Format: Lite rock. News staff: one; News: 2 hrs wkly. Target aud: 18-49; women. ♦Steve Aga, gen mgr, gen sls mgr, natl sls mgr & rgnl sls mgr; Dave Wood, progmg dir; Michael Lyon, news dir; Bruce Faulkner, chief of engrg.

Bozeman

***KBMC(FM)**— October 1991: 102.1 mhz; 20.5 kw. 728 ft TL: N45 38 18 W111 16 05. Stereo. Hrs open:
Rebroadcasts KEMC(FM) Billings 100%.
1500 University Dr., Billings, 59101-0298. Phone: (406) 657-2941. Fax: (406) 657-2977. Licensee: Montana State University/Billings. (acq 3-29-91; 4-15-91). Format: Class, jazz, news. ♦Lois Bent, gen mgr.

KBOZ(AM)— Dec 19, 1975: 1090 khz; 5 kw-U, DA-N. TL: N45 36 58 W111 05 16. Hrs open: Box 20, 59718. Secondary address: 5445 Johnson Rd. 59715. Phone: (406) 587-9999. Fax: (406) 587-5855.E-mail: less@kboz.com Licensee: Reier Broadcasting Co. Inc. (group owner; acq 10-18-96; grpsl). Population served: 60,000 Natl. Network: CBS, Jones Radio Networks, . Format: Talk. Target aud: 25-64. ♦Bill Reier, gen mgr, opns mgr; Eric Reier, gen sls mgr; Brian Bennett, progmg dir; Les Clay, news dir; Dick Jones, chief of engrg; Diane Stovall, traf mgr.

KBOZ-FM— 1983: 99.9 mhz; 100 kw. 338 ft TL: N45 41 34 W110 58 57. Hrs open: Box 20, 59718. Secondary address: 5445 Johnson Rd. 59718. Phone: (406) 587-9999. Fax: (406) 587-5855.E-mail: less@kboz.com Format: Hot country. ♦Terry Michaels, progmg dir; Diane Stovall, chief of engrg, traf mgr.

***KGLT(FM)**— December 1963: 91.9 mhz; 2 kw. 365 ft TL: N45 41 35 W110 59 00. Stereo. Hrs open: Montana State Univ., Rm. 324, 59717. Phone: (406) 994-3001. Fax: (406) 994-1987. Licensee: Montana State University. Population served: 67,000 Format: Div, educ, alternative. Target aud: General. Spec prog: Black 3 hrs, class 11 hrs, folk 12 hrs wkly. ♦Philip Charles, gen mgr; Jim Kehoe, mus dir; John Campbell, chief of engrg.

***KLBZ(FM)**— 2007: 89.3 mhz; 7 kw vert. Ant 679 ft TL: N45 57 25 W111 22 11. Hrs open:
Rebroadcasts KLVR(FM) Middletown, CA 100%.
2351 Sunset Blvd., Suite 170-218, Rocklin, CA, 95765. Phone: (916) 251-1600. Fax: (916) 251-1650. Web Site:www.klove.com Licensee: Educational Media Foundation. Natl. Network: K-Love, . Format: Contemp Christian. ♦Richard Jenkins, pres.

KMMS(AM)— Oct 15, 1939: 1450 khz; 1 kw-U. TL: N45 39 33 W111 03 22. Hrs open: 125 W. Mendenhall, 59715. Phone: (406) 586-2343. Fax: (406) 587-2202. Web Site:www.kmmsam.com Licensee: GAP Broadcasting Bozeman License LLC. Group owner: Clear Channel Communications Inc. (acq 2-13-2008; grpsl). Population served: 66,000 Natl. Network: ABC, . Natl. Rep: Clear Channel,. Drinker Biddle & Reath LLP. Format: News/talk, sports. News: one hr wkly. Target aud: 35-64. ♦Samuel L. Weller, pres; Sylvia Drain, gen mgr; Kay Ruh, natl sls mgr; Mary Atkins, prom dir, prom mgr; George Carter, progmg dir; John Russell, news dir; Dennis Mountford, chief of engrg; Lenny Jones, traf mgr.

KMMS-FM— Aug 14, 1986: 95.1 mhz; 94 kw. Ant 781 ft TL: N45 40 24 W110 52 02. Hrs open: 24 125 W. Mendenhall, 59715. Phone: (406) 586-2343. Fax: (406) 587-2202. Web Site:www.mooseradio.com Licensee: GAP Broadcasting Bozeman License LLC. (acq 2-13-2008; grpsl). Population served: 66,000 Format: AAA. ♦Michelle Wolfe, progmg dir.

KOBB(AM)— May 22, 1950: 1230 khz; 1 kw-U, DA-2. TL: N45 42 02 W111 02 49. Hrs open: 24 Box 20, 59718. Secondary address: 5445 Johnson Rd. 59718. Phone: (406) 587-9999. Fax: (406) 587-5855.E-mail: reier@bigsky.net Licensee: Reier Broadcasting Co. Inc. (group owner; (acq 2-19-93; $125,000;5-17-93). Population served: 50,000 Natl. Network: ABC, . Rgnl. Network: Agri-Net. Agrinet Rgnl rep: Tacher. Reddy, Begley & McCormick. Format: Adult Standards. News: 15 hrs wkly. Target aud: 30 plus; affluent adults. ♦William Reier Sr., pres & gen mgr; Eric Reier, gen sls mgr; Diane Stovall, progmg dir, traf mgr; Dick Jones, chief of engrg.

KOBB-FM— Nov 1, 1980: 93.7 mhz; 100 kw. 245 ft TL: N45 41 35 W110 58 50. Stereo. Hrs open: Prog sep from AM Box 20, 59718. Phone: (406) 587-9999. Fax: (406) 587-5855.E-mail: less@kboz.com Licensee: Reier Broadcasting Co. Inc. Population served: 45,000 Format: Oldies. Target aud: 25-54. ♦Tuck Reier, opns dir; Dave Visscher, progmg dir.

KOZB(FM)—See Livingston

KZMY(FM)— 2004: 103.5 mhz; 100 kw. Ant 948 ft TL: N45 57 25 W111 22 11. Hrs open: 24 125 W. Mendenhall St., Suite 102, 59715. Phone: (406) 556-0123. Fax: (406) 587-2202.E-mail: kzmy@hotmail.com Web Site:my1035.com Licensee: GAP Broadcasting Bozeman License LLC. Group owner: Clear Channel Communications Inc. (acq 2-13-2008; grpsl). Format: Adult contemp. ♦Nick Shannon, gen mgr & progmg dir.

Broadus

***KCBG(FM)**—Not on air, target date: unknown: 91.1 mhz; 1.35 kw. Ant 426 ft TL: N45 28 31 W105 29 54. Hrs open: Box 629, 59317-0629. Phone: (406) 853-7867. Licensee: School Community Development Council. ♦Christine Franklin, gen mgr.

Butte

KAAR(FM)— Nov 1, 1988: 92.5 mhz; 4.5 kw. 1,840 ft TL: N46 00 29 W112 26 30. Hrs open: 24 750 Dewey Blvd., Suite 1, 59701. Secondary address: Box 3788 59702. Phone: (406) 494-1030. Fax: (406) 494-6020.E-mail: jgray@cherrycreekradio.com Licensee: CCR-Butte IV LLC. Group owner: Fisher Broadcasting Company (acq 10-31-2006; grpsl). Natl. Rep: McGavren Guild,. Format: Country. News: 8 hrs wkly. Target aud: General. ◆Chris Ackerman, gen mgr; Jeff Gray, opns dir; Rene Wimberley, sls dir.

*KAPC(FM)— 1999: 91.3 mhz; 880 w. 1,893 ft TL: N46 00 29 W112 26 30. Hrs open: c/o KUFM(FM), Univ. of Montana, Missoula, 59812. Phone: (406) 243-4931. Fax: (406) 243-3299. Web Site:www.kufm.org Licensee: University of Montana. Natl. Network: NPR, . Wire Svc: AP Format: Jazz, classical, news. News: 2 hrs wkly. ◆William Marcus, gen mgr.

KBOW(AM)— Feb 14, 1947: 550 khz; 5 kw-D, 1 kw-N, DA-N. TL: N45 58 30 W112 34 18. Hrs open: Box 3389, 59702. Secondary address: 660 Dewey Blvd. 59702. Phone: (406) 494-7777. Fax: (406) 494-5534.E-mail: mail@kbow&kopr.com Licensee: Butte Broadcasting Inc. (acq 1-13-94; $550,000 with co-located FM; 1-31-94). Natl. Network: CBS, . Haley, Bader & Potts. Format: Sports. Target aud: 25 plus; general. Spec prog: Farm 5 hrs, relg 2 hrs wkly. ◆Fran Workman, opns mgr, progmg dir; Ron Davis, pres, gen mgr & gen sls mgr; Mike Beckworth, prom dir; Paul Panisko, progmg dir; Pat Schulte, news dir; Chuck Beardslee, engrg VP; Araka Williams, traf mgr.

*KFRD(FM)— 2006: 88.9 mhz; 2.8 kw vert. Ant 1,729 ft TL: N46 00 27 W112 26 30. Hrs open:
Rebroadcasts KUFR(FM) Salt Lake City, UT 100%.
c/o KUFR(FM), 136 E.S. Temple, Suite 1630, Salt Lake City, UT, 84111. Phone: (801) 359-3147. Fax: (801) 359-8112.E-mail: info@familyradio.com Web Site:www.familyradio.com Licensee: Family Stations Inc. Format: Christian relg. ◆Harold Camping, gen mgr.

*KFRT(FM)— 2003: Stn currently dark. 88.1 mhz; 850 w vert. Ant 1,729 ft TL: N46 00 27 W112 26 30. Hrs open:
Rebroadcasts KUFR(FM) Salt Lake City, UT 100%.
c/o Radio Station KUFR(FM), 136 E.S. Temple, Suite 1630, Salt Lake City, UT, 84111. Phone: (801) 359-3147. Fax: (801) 359-8112.E-mail: info@familyradio.com Web Site:www.familyradio.com Licensee: Family Stations Inc. (group owner). Natl. Network: Family Radio, . Format: Christian relg. ◆Harold Camping, gen mgr.

*KJLF(FM)— 2008: 90.5 mhz; 1 kw vert. Ant 1,738 ft TL: N46 00 22 W112 26 33. Hrs open:
Rebroadcasts KXEI(FM) Havre 100%.
Box 2426, Havre, 59501. Phone: (406) 265-5845. Fax: (406) 265-8860.E-mail: info@ynopradio.org Web Site:www.ynopradio.org Licensee: Hi-Line Radio Fellowship Inc. Natl. Network: Salem Radio Network, . Format: Christian inspirational. General; those looking for inspirational Christian music & programming. ◆Roger Lonnquist, gen mgr; Brenda Boyum, stn mgr; Brian Jackson, progmg mgr.

KMBR(FM)— Feb 7, 1980: 95.5 mhz; 50 kw. 1,820 ft TL: N46 00 29 W112 26 30. Stereo. Hrs open: Prog sep from AM Box 3788, 59702. Secondary address: 750 Dewey Blvd. 59702. Phone: (406) 494-5895. Fax: (406) 494-6020.E-mail: jgray@cherrycreekradio.com Web Site:www.955kmbr.com Population served: 50,000 Natl. Rep: McGavren Guild,. Format: Classic rock.

*KMSM-FM— 1975: 106.9 mhz; 500 w. 93 ft TL: N46 00 43 W112 33 23. Stereo. Hrs open: 24 Student Union Bldg, Montana Tech., 59701. Phone: (406) 496-4601.E-mail: kmsm@mtech.edu Web Site:www.mtech.edu/kmsm Licensee: Associated Students of Montana Tech. Population served: 3,000 Pepper & Corazzini. Format: Educ, div, alternative. News: 2 hrs wkly. Target aud: General; very diversified group. Spec prog: Jazz 5 hrs, relg 3 hrs, class 2 hrs wkly. ◆Wendy Dyer, gen mgr; Ben Carter, stn mgr.

KOPR(FM)— Oct 26, 1972: 94.1 mhz; 100 kw. 1,840 ft TL: N46 00 23 W112 26 28. (CP: 58.4 kw). Stereo. Hrs open: 24 Box 3389, 59702. Phone: (406) 494-7777. Fax: (406) 494-5534.E-mail: mail@kbow&kopr.com Licensee: Butte Broadcasting Inc. (Acq 4-1-94). Population served: 70,000 Rgnl. Network: Intermountain Farm/Ranch Network. Format: 80's & more. News staff: 2; News: 5 hrs wkly. Target aud: 25-45; women. ◆Fran Workman, pub affrs dir.

KXTL(AM)— 1927: 1370 khz; 5 kw-U. TL: N46 00 21 W112 37 54. Stereo. Hrs open: 24 Box 3788, 59702. Secondary address: 750 Dewey Blvd., Suite 1 59702. Phone: (406) 494-4442. Fax: (406) 494-6020.E-mail: jgray@cherrycreekradio.com Web Site:www.kxtl.com Licensee: CCR-Butte IV LLC. Group owner: Fisher Broadcasting Company (acq 10-31-2006; grpsl). Population served: 40,000 Natl. Rep: McGavren Guild,. Format: Hits of the 50s, 60s & 70s. News: 14 hrs wkly. Target aud: 25-54. Spec prog: Relg one hr wkly. ◆Chris

Ackerman, gen mgr, gen sls mgr; Jeff Gray, opns mgr, progmg dir; news dir; Roger Bennett, chief of engrg; Tammy Gordon, traf mgr.

Cascade

KIKF(FM)— January 2002: 104.9 mhz; 94 kw. Ant 2,037 ft TL: N47 09 34 W111 00 39. Hrs open: Box 3129, Great Falls, 59403. Phone: (406) 761-2800. Fax: (406) 727-7218.E-mail: tjlee@mykikfm.com Web Site:www.mykikfm.com Licensee: Fisher Radio Regional Group Inc. Group owner: Fisher Broadcasting Company (acq 3-12-01). Natl. Rep: McGavren Guild,. Format: Country. ◆Kieth Teski, gen mgr.

Chinook

KRYK(FM)—Licensed to Chinook. See Havre

Choteau

*KUDI(FM)—Not on air, target date: unknown: 88.7 mhz; 110 w. Ant -118 ft TL: N47 48 24 W112 10 43. Hrs open: Box 97, 59422. Secondary address: 414 S. Main St. 59422. Phone: (406) 467-2303. Licensee: New Life Assembly Church. ◆Mike Manuel, pres.

Circle

*KMGT(FM)—Not on air, target date: unknown: 90.3 mhz; 250 w. Ant 10 ft TL: N47 24 58 W105 35 45. Hrs open: Box 99, 59215. Secondary address: 1105 F Ave. 59215. Phone: (406) 696-8555. Fax: (406) 485-2332. Licensee: Circle Community Radio Association. ◆Jerrod Williams, gen mgr.

Colstrip

KMCJ(FM)— August 2001: 99.5 mhz; 100 kw. Ant 800 ft TL: N46 10 32 W106 24 21. Stereo. Hrs open: 24
Rebroadcasts KXEI(FM) Havre 100%.
Box 2426, Havre, 59501. Secondary address: 317 First St., Havre 59501. Phone: (406) 265-5845. Fax: (406) 265-8860.E-mail: ynop@ynopradio.org Web Site:www.ynopradio.org Licensee: Hi-Line Radio Fellowship Inc. (acq 4-13-01; $52,000 for CP). Population served: 4,000 Natl. Network: Salem Radio Network, . Wire Svc: AP Format: Christian Inspirational. Target aud: General:; those looking for inspirational Christian music & programming. ◆Roger Lonnquist, gen mgr; Brenda Boyum, stn mgr; Brian Jackson, progmg dir.

*KYPC(FM)—Not on air, target date: unknown: 89.9 mhz; 3.5 kw. Ant 1,210 ft TL: N45 50 17 W106 54 16. Hrs open: KEMC(FM), 1500 N. 30th St., Billings, 59103. Phone: (406) 657-2941. Fax: (406) 657-2977. Web Site:www.yellowstonepublicradio.org Licensee: Montana State University - Billings. ◆Lois Bent, gen mgr.

Columbia Falls

KHNK(FM)— Nov 17, 1998: 95.9 mhz; 55 kw horiz, 5.6 kw vert. Ant 2,286 ft TL: N48 30 42 W114 22 16. Hrs open: 24 2432 Hwy. 2 E., Kalispell, 59901. Phone: (406) 755-8700. Fax: (406) 755-8770.E-mail: kkmt@beebroadcasting.com Web Site:www.beebroadcasting.com Licensee: Bee Broadcasting Inc. (group owner; (acq 12-31-97; $337,500). Format: Country. ◆Mark Wagner, gen mgr.

KQDE(AM)—Not on air, target date: unknown: 1400 khz; 1 kw-D, 670 w-N. TL: N48 24 09 W114 11 47. Hrs open: Box 272, Green Bay, WI, 54307-0272. Phone: (920) 271-1000. Fax: (920) 271-1010. Licensee: Advance Acquisition Inc. ◆Joseph R. Giganti, pres.

KRVO(FM)— 2006: 103.1 mhz; 8 kw. Ant 2,362 ft TL: N48 30 43 W114 22 13. Hrs open: Box 5409, Kalispell, 59903. Phone: (406) 755-8700. Fax: (406) 755-8770.E-mail: kdbr@beebroadcasting.com Web Site:www.beebroadcasting.com Licensee: Cathleen R. Bee. Smithwick & Belendiuk. ◆Cathleen R. Bee, gen mgr.

Conrad

KTZZ(FM)— July 1, 1997: 93.7 mhz; 100 kw. 558 ft TL: N47 49 13 W111 47 56. Hrs open: 24 Box 1239, Great Falls, 59403. Secondary address: 3313 15th St. N.E., Black Eagle 59414. Phone: (406) 761-1310. Fax: (406) 454-3775. Licensee: Jeannine M. Mason. Population served: 85118 Natl. Network: ABC, . Format: Classic rock. News staff: one; News: 5 hrs wkly. Target aud: 25-54; general. ◆Steven Dow, pres; Laurie Vosberg, adv dir.

Darby

KHDV(FM)— 2007: 107.9 mhz; 14 kw. Ant 361 ft TL: N46 13 46 W114 14 01. Hrs open: Box 309, Missoula, 59806-0309. Phone: (406) 542-1025. Fax: (406) 721-1036. Licensee: Sheila Callahan and Friends Inc. ◆Sheila Callahan, gen mgr.

Deer Lodge

KBCK(AM)— 1963: 1400 khz; 1 kw-U. TL: N46 24 26 W112 43 08. Hrs open: Licensee: Robert Cummings Toole Group owner: Jimmy Ray Carroll Stns (acq 12-31-2006; grpsl). Population served: 30,000 Target aud: 18 plus. ◆Chuck Schwartz, gen mgr.

KQRV(FM)— July 4, 1997: 96.9 mhz; 20 kw. Ant 984 ft TL: N46 06 03 W112 57 00. Hrs open: 302 Missouri Ave., 59722. Phone: (406) 846-1100. Fax: (406) 846-1100.E-mail: riverradio@bresnan.net Licensee: Robert Cummings Toole. Format: Country, full service. ◆Robert Cummings Toole, gen mgr; Karen Toole, gen sls mgr.

Dillon

KBEV-FM— August 1972: 98.3 mhz; 10.5 kw. 495 ft TL: N45 14 22 W112 40 03. Stereo. Hrs open: Prog sep from AM 610 N. Montana St., 59725. Phone: (406) 683-2800. Phone: (406) 683-6171. Fax: (406) 683-9480.E-mail: deadair@kdbm-kbev.com Web Site:www.kdbm-kbev.com Licensee: Dead-Air Broadcasting Co. Inc. Natl. Network: ABC, . Format: Contemp hits, Adult Contemp. ◆Joann Juliano, pres; John B. Schuyler, VP; Kasey Briggs, gen sls mgr.

KDBM(AM)— Jan 1, 1957: 1490 khz; 1 kw-U. TL: N45 14 13 W112 38 32. Hrs open: 610 N. Montana St., 59725. Phone: (406) 683-2800. Phone: (406) 683-6171. Fax: (406) 683-9480.E-mail: deadair@kdbm-kbev.com Licensee: Dead-Air Broadcasting Co. Inc. (acq 3-6-98; $330,000 with co-located FM). Population served: 4,548 Natl. Network: ABC, . Format: Country. ◆Jo Ann Juliano, pres; Kathy Wise, gen mgr; Kasey Briggs, sls dir; John Schuyler, progmg dir, news dir; Ron Huckaby, chief of engrg.

KDIL(AM)—Not on air, target date: unknown: 940 khz; 10 kw-D, 350 w-N, DA-2. TL: N45 13 26 W112 35 58. Hrs open: 501 S. Lincoln Ave., Jerome, ID, 83338. Phone: (208) 324-9268. Licensee: Scott Powell. Shanis & Peltzman. ◆Amy Meredith, pres; Scott Powell, gen mgr.

*KDWG(FM)—Not on air, target date: unknown: 90.9 mhz; 850 w. -236 ft TL: N45 12 33 W112 38 14. Hrs open: 24 Univ. of Montana, Western, Campus Box 52, 710 S. Atlantic St., 59725. Phone: (406) 683-7156. Licensee: Western Montana College University of Montana. Format: Mainstream, educ, rock. ◆Cory Craden, mus dir.

Dutton

KVVR(FM)— Aug 7, 2001: 97.9 mhz; 100 kw. Ant 715 ft TL: N47 36 52 W111 20 51. Hrs open: Box 3309, Great Falls, 59403. Phone: (406) 761-7600. Fax: (406) 761-5511. Licensee: CCR-Great Falls IV LLC. Group owner: Cherry Creek Radio LLC (acq 12-19-2003; grpsl). Format: Adult contemp. ◆Ron Korb, gen mgr.

East Helena

KHKR-FM— Apr 13, 1989: 104.1 mhz; 5 kw. Ant 653 ft TL: N46 46 11 W112 01 25. Stereo. Hrs open: 110 Broadway St., Helena, 59601. Phone: (406) 442-4490. Fax: (406) 442-7356.E-mail: info@khkr.com Web Site:www.khkr.com Licensee: CCR-Helena IV LLC. Group owner: Cherry Creek Radio LLC (acq 2-3-2004; grpsl). Format: Hot country. Target aud: 25-54. ◆Dewey Bruce, gen mgr.

KKGR(AM)— May 26, 1988: 680 khz; 5 kw-D. TL: N46 33 58 W111 54 12. Hrs open: 1400 11th Ave., Helena, 59601. Phone: (406) 443-5237. Fax: (406) 442-7595.E-mail: info@kkgram.com Licensee: KKGR. (acq 3-16-99). Format: Oldies. ◆Jim Schaffer, gen mgr.

East Missoula

KMPT(AM)—Licensed to East Missoula. See Missoula

Eureka

KZXT(FM)—Not on air, target date: unknown: 93.5 mhz; 2.4 kw. Ant 1,817 ft TL: N48 38 35 W115 05 31. Hrs open: 581 N. Reservoir Rd., Polson, 59860. Phone: (406) 883-5255. Fax: (406) 883-4441. Licensee:

Anderson Radio Broadcasting Inc. (acq 6-6-2008; $140,406 for CP).
◆ Dennis L. Anderson, pres & gen mgr.

Evergreen

KQJZ(AM)— 2008: 1340 khz; 1 kw-D, 670 w-N. TL: N48 14 20 W114 15 09. Hrs open: 120 E. 3rd St., Kalispell, 59901. Phone: (406) 257-9430. Fax: (406) 752-0313. Web Site:www.smoothkqjz.com Licensee: Anderson Radio Broadcasting Inc. (acq 2-29-2008; $200,000). Format: Smooth jazz. ◆ Dennis L. Anderson, pres.

Fairfield

KEAU(FM)— 2008: Stn currently dark. 102.7 mhz; 100 kw. Ant 895 ft TL: N47 36 24 W111 21 31. Hrs open: 118 6th St. S., Great Falls, 59401-3625. Phone: (406) 761-8816. Fax: (406) 454-3484. Licensee: College Creek Media LLC. ◆ Neal J. Robinson, pres; Darnell Washington, gen mgr.

Florence

KDTR(FM)— 2005: 103.3 mhz; 1.95 kw. Ant 2,083 ft TL: N46 48 06 W113 58 22. Stereo. Hrs open: 2425 W. Central Ave., Suite 203, Missoula, 59801. Phone: (406) 721-6800. Fax: (406) 329-1850.E-mail: rharsell@simmonsmedia.com Web Site:www.trail1033.com Licensee: Spanish Peaks Broadcasting LLC. Population served: 150,000 Natl. Rep: Interep,. Format: Triple A. News staff: one. Target aud: 25-54; adults. ◆ Rod Harsell, gen mgr; Robert Chase, progmg dir.

Forsyth

KIKC(AM)— Oct 10, 1975: 1250 khz; 5 kw-D, 132 w-N. TL: N46 15 30 W106 41 21. Hrs open: 24 Box 1140, 59327. Secondary address: 210 W. Front St. 59327. Phone: *406) 346-2711. Fax (406) 346-2712.E-mail: kikc@rangeweb.net Web Site:kikcamfm.com Licensee: Mile City, Forsyth Broadcasting Inc. Population served: 60,000 Wire Svc: AP Format: CHR, oldies. Target aud: 18-35; general. ◆ Stephen Marks, pres.

KIKC-FM— September 1980: 101.3 mhz; 100 kw. Ant 1,010 ft TL: N46 10 32 W106 24 21. Stereo. Hrs open: 24 Box 1140, 59327. Secondary address: 210 W. Front St. 59327. Phone: (406) 346-2711. Fax: (406) 346-2712.E-mail: kikc@rangeweb.net Web Site:kikcamfm.com Licensee: Miles City, Forsyth Broadcasting Inc. (acq 1996; grpsl). Population served: 60,000 Natl. Network: CNN Radio, . Natl. Rep: Interep,. Rgnl rep: Allied Radio Partners Wire Svc: AP Format: Country. News: 4 hrs wkly. Target aud: 18 plus; general. ◆ Steve Marks, CEO; Dick Haugen, VP, gen mgr; Patti Haugen, opns mgr; Grant West, progmg dir, mus dir.

Fort Belknap Agency

*KGVA(FM)— October 1996: 88.1 mhz; 95 kw. 797 ft TL: N48 11 18 W108 42 36. Hrs open: Box 159, Harlem, 59526. Phone: (406) 353-4656. Fax: (406) 353-2898.E-mail: info@kgvafm.com Licensee: Fort Belknap College. Natl. Network: NPR, . Format: Eclectic, news/talk. Target aud: General. Spec prog: American Indian 15 hrs wkly. ◆ Will Gray Jr., gen mgr & spec ev coord.

Fort Benton

KJCD(FM)— 2008: 95.9 mhz; 100 w horiz. Ant 13 ft TL: N47 50 08 W110 39 10. Hrs open: Box 4218, Helena, 59604-4218. Phone: (406) 442-2655. Licensee: Montana Christian Radio Association (acq 11-6-2008). ◆ Roger Lonnquist, pres.

Four Corners

*KLSN(FM)—Not on air, target date: unknown: 90.3 mhz; 1 w horiz, 1 kw vert. Ant -187 ft TL: N45 37 49 W110 55 23. Hrs open: Box 125, Bozeman, 59771-0125. Phone: (406) 624-6762. Licensee: Gallatin Valley Community Radio. ◆ Susan M. Cole, chmn.

KSCY(FM)— Mar 1, 2008: 106.9 mhz; 4 kw. Ant 646 ft TL: N45 38 20 W111 15 56. Hrs open: 8274 Huffine Ln., Bozeman, 59718. Phone: (406) 582-1045. Fax: (406) 582-0388. Licensee: Radick Construction Inc. Format: Country. ◆ Jeff Balding, gen mgr.

Frenchtown

KVWE(FM)— 2007: 101.5 mhz; 3.4 kw. Ant 2,089 ft TL: N46 48 08 W113 58 21. Hrs open: 3250 S. Reserve St., Suite 200, Missoula, 59801-8236. Phone: (406) 728-9300. Fax: (406) 542-2329.E-mail: erik@1015theview.com Web Site:www.1015theview.com Licensee: GAP Broadcasting Missoula License LLC. (acq 2-13-2008; $500,000). Format: Soft rock. ◆ Dave Cowan, gen mgr; Kathy Anderson, gen sls mgr; Erik O'Connor, progmg dir.

Glasgow

KLAN(FM)— Mar 1, 1983: 93.5 mhz; 3 kw. 300 ft TL: N48 05 42 W106 37 08. Stereo. Hrs open: Box 671, 59230. Phone: (406) 228-9336. Fax: (406) 228-9338.E-mail: kltz@kltz.com Web Site:www.kltz.com Licensee: Glasgow Broadcasting Corp. Format: Adult contemp. ◆ Shirley Trang, gen mgr.

KLTZ(AM)— Aug 14, 1954: 1240 khz; 1 kw-U. TL: N48 13 09 W106 38 54. Hrs open: Box 671, 59230. Phone: (406) 228-9336. Fax: (406) 228-9338.E-mail: kltz@kltz.com Web Site:www.kltz.com Licensee: Glasgow Broadcasting Inc. Population served: 5,000 Rgnl. Network: Agri-Net. Agrinet Format: C&W. Target aud: 25 plus. ◆ Shirley Trang, gen mgr.

Glendive

KDZN(FM)— Dec 21, 1969: 96.5 mhz; 100 kw. 400 ft TL: N47 05 15 W104 48 04. Stereo. Hrs open: 24 210 S. Douglas St., 59330. Phone: (406) 377-3377. Fax: (406) 365-2181.E-mail: kxgnkdzn@midrivers.com Web Site:www.kxgn.com Licensee: Magic Air Communications Co. Natl. Network: CBS Radio, Westwood One, . Davis Wright Tremaine, LLP. Wire Svc: AP Format: Country. News: 4 hrs wkly. Target aud: 25-54. ◆ Steven Marks, pres; Paul Sturlaugson, gen mgr, sports cmtr; Marcy Copp, progmg dir; Ed Agre, news dir.

KGLE(AM)— Aug 22, 1962: 590 khz; 1 kw-D. TL: N47 05 50 W104 47 09. Hrs open: 24 Box 931, 86 Seven Mile Dr., 59330. Phone: (406) 377-3331. Fax: (406) 377-3332.E-mail: kgle@midrivers.com Web Site:www.kgle.org Licensee: Friends of Christian Radio Inc. (acq 1-12-93; $90,000; 2-1-93). Population served: 8,800 Natl. Network: Salem Radio Network, . Wire Svc: AP Format: Relg, farm. Target aud: 35-64; general. ◆ Tom Fatzinger, pres; Jim McBride, gen mgr.

KXGN(AM)— Sept 23, 1948: 1400 khz; 1 kw-U. TL: N47 05 40 W104 42 50. Hrs open: 24 210 S. Douglas, 59330. Phone: (406) 377-3377. Fax: (406) 365-2181.E-mail: kxgnkdzn@midrivers.com Web Site:www.glendivebroadcasting.com Licensee: Glendive Broadcasting Corp. Population served: 6,305 Natl. Network: ABC, . Davis Wright Tremaine. Wire Svc: NWS (National Weather Service) Format: Adult contemp, oldies. News staff: one; News: 6 hrs wkly. Spec prog: Derry Brownfield 5 hrs, farm 2 hrs wkly. ◆ Stephen Marks, pres; Paul Strulaugson, exec VP; Paul Sturlaugson, gen mgr. Co-owned TV: KXGN-TV affil

Great Falls

KAAK(FM)— June 19, 1972: 98.9 mhz; 100 kw. Ant 500 ft TL: N47 32 08 W111 17 02. Stereo. Hrs open: 24 Box 3309, 59403. Phone: (406) 761-7600. Fax: (406) 761-5511. Licensee: CCR-Great Falls IV LLC. (acq 5-31-2007; grpsl). Population served: 86,000 Format: Hot adult contemp. Target aud: 25-44. ◆ Ron Korb, gen mgr.

*KAFH(FM)— 2006: 91.5 mhz; 1 kw. Ant 297 ft TL: N47 31 57 W111 16 38. Hrs open:
Rebroadcasts WAFR(FM) Tupelo, MS 100%.
Drawer 2440, Tupelo, MS, 38803. Phone: (662) 844-8888. Fax: (662) 842-6791. Web Site:www.afr.net Licensee: American Family Association. Format: Christian. ◆ Marvin Sanders, gen mgr.

KEIN(AM)— July 1922: 1310 khz; 5 kw-D, 1 kw-N. TL: N47 31 20 W111 23 18. Hrs open: 24 Box 1239, 59403. Secondary address: 3313 15th St. N.E., Black Eagle 59414. Phone: (406) 761-1310. Fax: (406) 454-3775. Licensee: Munson Radio Inc. (acq 7-1-97). Population served: 135,000 Format: Adult standards. News staff: one; News: 5 hrs wkly. Target aud: 35 plus. ◆ Steven Dow, pres.

*KFRW(FM)— 2007: 91.9 mhz; 50 kw. Ant 466 ft TL: N47 49 13 W111 47 56. Hrs open:
Rebroadcasts KUFR(FM) Salt Lake City, UT 100%.
136 E.S. Temple, Suite 1630, Salt Lake City, UT, 84111. Phone: (801) 359-3147. Fax: (801) 359-8112.E-mail: info@familyradio.com Web Site:www.familyradio.com Licensee: Family Stations Inc. Format: Christian relg. ◆ Harold Camping, gen mgr.

*KGFA(FM)— 2006: 90.7 mhz; 1 kw. Ant 297 ft TL: N47 31 57 W111 16 38. Hrs open: 5700 West Oaks Blvd., Rocklin, CA, 95765. Phone: (916) 251-1600. Fax: (916) 251-1650. Web Site:www.air1.com Licensee: Educational Media Foundation. (acq 3-23-2007; grpsl). Natl. Network: Air 1, . Format: Christian. ◆ Richard Jenkins, pres.

*KGFC(FM)— 1996: 88.9 mhz; 6 kw. Ant 243 ft TL: N47 27 53 W111 21 24. Stereo. Hrs open: 24
Rebroadcasts KXEI(FM) Havre 100%.
Box 2426, Havre, 59501. Phone: (406) 265-5845. Fax: (406) 265-8860.E-mail: ynop@ynopradio.org Web Site:www.ynopradio.org Licensee: Hi-Line Radio Fellowship Inc. Wire Svc: AP Format: Christian Inspirational. Target aud: General; those looking for inspirational Christian music & progmg. ◆ Roger Lonnquist, gen mgr; Brenda Boyum, stn mgr; Brian Jackson, progmg dir.

*KGPR(FM)— April 1984: 89.9 mhz; 9.5 kw. 295 ft TL: N47 32 23 W111 17 06. Stereo. Hrs open: 24
Rebroadcasts KUFM(FM) Missoula 100%.
Box 3343, 59403. Secondary address: Box 6010, 2100 16th Ave. S. 59406-6010. Phone: (406) 268-3739. Fax: (406) 268-3736.E-mail: kgpr@msugf.edu Web Site:www.kgpr.msugf.edu Licensee: Great Falls Public Radio Association. Population served: 100,000 Natl. Network: PRI, NPR, . Format: Class, educ, news, world mus. News: 44 hrs wkly. Target aud: General. ◆ Joseph Duffy, pres; Bill Tacke, VP; Tom Halverson, stn mgr; Carol Spahr, dev dir.

KINX(FM)— Feb 4, 2002: 107.3 mhz; 94 kw. Ant 2,037 ft TL: N47 09 34 W111 00 39. Hrs open: Box 3129, 59403. Phone: (406) 761-2800. Fax: (406) 727-7218. Web Site:www.sam1073.com Licensee: Fisher Radio Regional Group Inc. Group owner: Fisher Broadcasting Company. Natl. Rep: McGavren Guild,. Format: Var. Target aud: 25-54. ◆ Keith Teski, gen mgr & gen mgr.

KLFM(FM)— Feb 14, 1982: 92.9 mhz; 98 kw. 410 ft TL: N47 32 19 W111 15 41. Hrs open: 24 Box 3309, 59403. Secondary address: 20 3rd St. N. 59403. Phone: (406) 761-7600. Fax: (406) 761-5511. Licensee: CCR-Great Falls IV LLC. Group owner: Cherry Creek Radio LLC (acq 12-19-2003; grpsl). Population served: 100,000 Format: Good time oldies. Target aud: 25-54. ◆ Ron Korb, gen mgr & gen sls mgr.

KLSK(FM)— 2003: 100.3 mhz; 100 kw. Ant 495 ft TL: N47 15 57 W111 08 39. Hrs open: 6080 Mt. Moriah, Memphis, TN, 38115. Phone: (901) 375-9324. Fax: (901) 375-0041.E-mail: mail@flinn.com Licensee: Flinn Broadcasting Corp. Format: Hip-hop-rap. ◆ Karen Wheatley, gen mgr.

KMON(AM)— May 30, 1947: 560 khz; 5 kw-U, DA-N. TL: N47 25 29 W111 17 20. Stereo. Hrs open: 24 Box 3309, 20 3rd St. N., Suite 231, 59401. Phone: (406) 761-7600. Fax: (406) 761-5511.E-mail: 560@kmon.com Web Site:www.kmon.com Licensee: CCR-Great Falls IV LLC. Group owner: Cherry Creek Radio LLC (acq 12-19-2003; grpsl). Population served: 210,000 Pepper & Corazzini. Format: Country, farm. News staff: one; News: 20 hrs wkly. Target aud: 35-64. Spec prog: Sports 5 hrs wkly. ◆ Ron Korb, gen mgr; Melissa Horton, gen sls mgr; Skip Walters, progmg dir & news dir; Ken Eklund, chief of engrg; Angie Depping, rsch dir.

KMON-FM— Oct 1, 1972: 94.5 mhz; 98 kw. 495 ft TL: N47 32 19 W111 15 41. Stereo. Hrs open: 24 Box 3309, 20 3rd St. N., 59401. Phone: (406) 761-7600. Fax: (406) 761-5511. Web Site:www.kmonfm.com Wire Svc: U.S. Weather Service Format: Hot country. News staff: one; News: 5 hrs wkly. Target aud: 25-54. ◆ Ron Korb, sls dir, gen sls mgr, spec ev coord; Scott Hershey, progmg dir.

KQDI(AM)— 1955: 1450 khz; 1 kw-U. TL: N47 31 26 W111 18 04. Hrs open: 1300 Central Ave. W., 59404. Phone: (406) 761-2800. Fax: (406) 727-7218. Licensee: Fisher Radio Regional Group Inc. Group owner: Fisher Broadcasting Company (acq 9-27-95; with co-located FM). Natl. Rep: Christal,. Format: News/talk. Target aud: 25-54. ◆ Keith Teski, gen mgr.

KQDI-FM— Dec 31, 1963: 106.1 mhz; 100 kw. 276 ft TL: N47 31 57 W111 16 41. Stereo. Hrs open: Prog sep from AM Box 3129 Phone: (406) 761-2800. Fax: (406) 727-7218. Population served: 65,000 Format: Classic rock, AOR. Target aud: 18-49.

KXGF(AM)— 1987: 1400 khz; 1 kw-U. TL: N47 27 56 W111 20 22. Hrs open: Box 3129, 59403. Secondary address: 1300 Central Ave. W. 59403. Phone: (406) 761-2800. Fax: (406) 727-7218. Licensee: Fisher Radio Regional Group Inc. Group owner: Fisher Broadcasting Company (acq 12-28-94; grpsl, including co-located FM; 2-20-95). Population served: 86,000 Natl. Rep: McGavren Guild,. Format: MOR. Target aud: 35-64. Spec prog: Farm 2 hrs wkly. ◆ Keith Teski, gen mgr.

Hamilton

KBAZ(FM)— Feb 11, 1969: 96.3 mhz; 50 kw. Ant 2,089 ft TL: N46 48 08 W113 58 21. Stereo. Hrs open: 24 Prog sep from AM 3250 South Reserve-Suite 200, Missoula, 59801. Phone: (406) 728-9300. Fax: (406) 542-2329. Web Site:www.963theblaze.com Licensee: GAP Broadcasting Missoula License LLC. (acq 2-13-2008; grpsl). Format: Alternative rock. ♦Angel Hughes, opns dir; Dave Cowan, gen mgr & gen sls mgr.

KLYQ(AM)— Feb 3, 1961: 1240 khz; 1 kw-U. TL: N46 15 22 W114 09 45. Hrs open: 5:30 AM-midnight Box 660, 217 N. 3rd St., Suite L, 59840. Phone: (406) 363-3010. Fax: (406) 363-6436.E-mail: contact@klyq.com Web Site:www.klyq.com Licensee: GAP Broadcasting Missoula License LLC. Group owner: Clear Channel Communications Inc. (acq 2-13-2008; grpsl). Population served: 35,250 Format: News/talk. News staff: one; News: 25 hrs wkly. Target aud: 25-54; adults. ♦Gene Peterson, gen mgr; Jim Coulter, sls dir; Steve Fullerton, opns dir, progmg dir & news dir; Mike Daniels, chief of engrg; Don Davis, sports cmtr.

***KMZO(FM)**—Not on air, target date: unknown: 90.3 mhz; 725 w. Ant 331 ft TL: N46 13 46 W114 14 01. Stereo. Hrs open: 24 Faith Communications Corp., 2201 S. 6th St., Las Vegas, NV, 89104. Phone: (702) 731-5452. Fax: (702) 731-1992.E-mail: info@sosradio.net Web Site:www.sosradio.net Licensee: Faith Communications Corp. Format: Contemp Christian. News: 5 hrs wkly. ♦Jack French, CEO; Brad Staley, gen mgr; Chris Staley, prom dir; Scott Herrold, progmg dir.

***KUFN(FM)**— October 1998: 91.9 mhz; 850 w. 499 ft TL: N46 13 46 W114 14 01. Hrs open: c/o KUFM(FM), Univ. of Montana, Missoula, 59812. Phone: (406) 243-4931. Fax: (406) 243-3299. Web Site:www.kurn.org Licensee: The University of Montana. Natl. Network: NPR, . Wire Svc: AP Format: Jazz, classical, news, eclectic. News: 2 hrs wkly. ♦William Marcus, gen mgr.

KXDR(FM)— July 16, 1999: 98.7 mhz; 100 kw. 417 ft TL: N46 30 36 W113 58 45. Hrs open: 24 1600 North Ave. W., Suite 101, Missoula, 59801. Phone: (406) 728-5000. Fax: (406) 721-3020. Web Site:www.starfm.net Licensee: CCR-Missoula IV LLC. Group owner: Fisher Broadcasting Company (acq 10-31-2006; grpsl). Natl. Rep: McGavren Guild,. Format: Contemp hits. ♦Chad Parrish, gen mgr; Scott Richards, opns mgr; Bill McPherson, gen sls mgr; Samantha Honold, traf mgr.

Hardin

KHDN(AM)— Dec 28, 1962: 1230 khz; 1 kw-U. TL: N45 42 55 W107 35 59. Hrs open: 24 Box 230, 59034. Phone: (406) 665-2828. Fax: (406) 665-2131.E-mail: rich@bigskyradio.net Web Site:www.bigskyradio.net Licensee: Sun Mountain Inc. (acq 11-30-2000). Population served: 15,000 Natl. Network: ABC, . Rgnl. Network: Intermountain Farm/Ranch Network. Format: Adult contemp/news. News: 24 hrs wkly. Target aud: 25-54. ♦Richard Solberg, pres & gen mgr.

KMHK(FM)— 1975: 95.5 mhz; 100 kw. 984 ft TL: N45 44 29 W108 08 19. Stereo. Hrs open: Box 1276, Billings, 59103. Phone: (406) 248-7827. Fax: (406) 252-9577. Web Site:www.kmhk.com Licensee: GAP Broadcasting Billings License LLC. Group owner: Clear Channel Communications Inc. (acq 2-13-2008; grpsl). Format: Rock. Target aud: 18-34; general. ♦Dennis Koffman, gen mgr; Jay Branden, mktg dir & progmg dir.

Havre

***KNMC(FM)**— February 1979: 90.1 mhz; 10 w. 56 ft TL: N48 32 30 W109 41 06. (CP: 375 w, ant -112 ft. TL: N48 32 31 W109 41 17). Stereo. Hrs open: c/o KEMC, 1500 University Dr., Billings, 59101-0298. Phone: (406) 657-2941. Fax: (406) 657-2977. Licensee: Montana State University-Northern. Format: Class, jazz. Spec prog: Class 10 hrs wkly. ♦Marvin Granger, gen mgr.

KOJM(AM)— Oct 31, 1947: 610 khz; 1 kw-U, DA-2. TL: N48 34 48 W109 38 54. Stereo. Hrs open: 5 a.m.-midnight 2210 31st St. N., 59501. Phone: (406) 265-7841. Fax: (406) 265-8855.E-mail: nmb@nmbi.com Web Site:www.kojm.com Licensee: New Media Broadcasters Inc. (group owner; (acq 12-30-2002; grpsl). Population served: 80,000 Natl. Network: ABC, . Cohn & Marks. Wire Svc: AP Format: Adult hits. News staff: 3; News: 20 wkly. Target aud: 30-64; boomer generation. Spec prog: Agriculture 4 hrs wkly. ♦C. David Leeds, pres, natl sls mgr; Kyle Leeds, prom dir; Geoff Cole, progmg dir; Justin Krezelak, news dir; Bruce Faulkner, chief of engrg.

KPQX(FM)— Mar 8, 1975: 92.5 mhz; 100 kw. Ant 1,788 ft TL: N48 10 55 W109 41 01. Stereo. Hrs open: 5 a.m.-midnight 2210 31st St. N., 59501. Phone: (406) 265-7841. Fax: (406) 265-8855.E-mail: nmb@nmbi.com Web Site:www.kpqx.com Licensee: New Media Broadcasters Inc. (acq 12-30-2002; grpsl). Population served: 80,000 Natl. Network: ABC, . Cohn & Marks. Wire Svc: AP Format: Country. News staff: 3; News: 20 hrs wkly. Target aud: 25-54. Spec prog: Farm 10 hrs wkly. ♦C. David Leeds, pres, natl sls mgr; Kyle Leeds, prom dir; Geoff Cole, progmg dir; Justin Krezelak, news dir; Bruce Faulkner, chief of engrg.

KRYK(FM)—(Chinook, Nov 19, 1983: 101.3 mhz; 100 kw. Ant 688 ft TL: N48 23 29 W109 17 50. Stereo. Hrs open: 5 a.m. - midnight 2210 31st St. N., 59501. Phone: (406) 265-7841. Fax: (406) 265-8855.E-mail: nmb@nmbi.com Web Site:www.kryk.com Licensee: New Media Broadcasters Inc. (group owner; (acq 12-30-2002). Population served: 80,000 Natl. Network: ABC, . Cohn & Marks. Format: Hot adult contemp. News staff: 3; News: 5 hrs wkly. Target aud: 18-49. ♦C. David Leeds, pres, natl sls mgr; Kyke Leeds, prom dir; Geoff Cole, progmg dir; Justin Krezelak, news dir; Bruce Faulkner, engrg dir.

***KXEI(FM)**— July 28, 1983: 95.1 mhz; 98 kw. Ant 1,699 ft TL: N48 10 42 W109 41 21. Stereo. Hrs open: 24 Box 2426, 59501. Secondary address: 317 First St. 59501. Phone: (406) 265-5845. Fax: (406) 265-8860.E-mail: ynop@ynopradio.org Web Site:www.ynopradio.org Licensee: Hi-Line Radio Fellowship Inc. Natl. Network: Moody, Salem Radio Network, . Cohn & Marks. Wire Svc: AP Format: Christian inspirational. Target aud: General; those looking for Christian inspirational music & progmg. Spec prog: C&W one hr, farm one hr wkly. ♦Roger Lonnquist, gen mgr; Brenda Boyum, stn mgr; Brian Jackson, progmg dir.

Helena

KBLL(AM)— September 1937: 1240 khz; 1 kw-U. TL: N46 35 24 W112 00 59. Hrs open: Box 4111, 59604. Secondary address: 110 E. Broadway St. 59601. Phone: (406) 442-4490. Fax: (406) 442-6161. Licensee: CCR-Helena IV LLC Group owner: Cherry Creek Radio LLC (acq 6-30-2004; $2.8 million with co-located FM). Population served: 40,000 Dow, Lohnes & Albertson. Format: News/talk. Target aud: 29-54; high buying power. ♦Dewey Bruce, gen mgr; Chris McCarthy, gen sls mgr; Stan Evans, progmg dir; Cato Butler, news dir; Ken Eklund, chief of engrg; Michele McAlister, traf mgr.

KBLL-FM— August 1979: 99.5 mhz; 30 kw. 790 ft TL: N46 46 12 W112 01 22. Stereo. Hrs open: Prog sep from AM Box 4111, 59601. Phone: (406) 442-4490. Fax: (406) 442-6161. Licensee: CCR-Helena IV LLC. Population served: 40,000 Format: Country. ♦Kurt Kittelson, progmg dir.

KCAP(AM)— October 1949: 1340 khz; 1 kw-U. TL: N46 36 43 W112 03 13. Hrs open: Box 4111, 59604. Secondary address: 110 E. Broadway St. 59601. Phone: (406) 442-4490. Fax: (406) 442-7356.E-mail: kbllfm@cherrycreekra.com Web Site:www.kcap.com Licensee: CCR-Helena IV LLC. Group owner: Cherry Creek Radio LLC (acq 2-3-2004; grpsl). Population served: 30,000 Natl. Network: CBS, Moody, Fox Sports, . Format: News/talk. Target aud: 25-54. ♦Dewey Bruce, gen mgr; Chris McCarthy, gen sls mgr; Stan Evans, progmg dir; Cato Butler, news dir; Ken Eklund, chief of engrg; Michele McAlister, traf mgr.

***KHLV(FM)**— 2005: 90.1 mhz; 1 w horiz, 3.5 kw vert. Ant 662 ft vert TL: N46 46 07 W112 01 21. Stereo. Hrs open: 24
Rebroadcasts KLVR(FM) Santa Rosa, CA 100%.
2351 Sunset Blvd., Suite 170-218, Rocklin, CA, 95765. Phone: (916) 251-1600. Fax: (916) 251-1650.E-mail: klove@klove.com Web Site:www.klove.com Licensee: Educational Media Foundation. Group owner: EMF Broadcasting. Natl. Network: K-Love, . Shaw Pittman. Format: Contemp Christian. News staff: 3. Target aud: 25-44; Judeo Christian, female. ♦Richard Jenkins, pres; Mike Novak, VP; Keith Whipple, dev dir; David Pierce, progmg dir; Ed Lenane, news dir; Sam Walington, engrg dir; Karen Johnson, news rptr.

KMTX(AM)— Nov 1, 1976: 950 khz; 5 kw-U, DA-N. TL: N46 40 28 W112 01 05. Stereo. Hrs open: 24/7 Box 1183, 59624. Secondary address: 516 Fuller 59601. Phone: (406) 442-0400. Fax: (406) 442-0491. Licensee: KMTX LLC. Population served: 40,000 Natl. Network: AP Radio, . Format: Oldies. ♦James O'Connell, pres; Kevin Skaalure, gen mgr.

KMTX-FM— Jan 19, 1985: 105.3 mhz; 86.9 kw. 1,878 ft TL: N46 44 52 W112 19 47. (CP: 100 kw, ant 1,954 ft.). Stereo. Hrs open: Prog sep from AM Box 1183, 59624. Secondary address: 516 Fuller 59601. Phone: (406) 443-1053. Natl. Network: ABC, . Format: Adult contemp. ♦Kevin Skaalure, gen mgr; Steve Phillips, prom dir; Shawn Ketchum, chief of engrg; Karen Feldner, traf mgr.

KUFM(FM)—See Missoula

***KUHM(FM)**— 2000: 91.7 mhz; 910 w. Ant 761 ft TL: N46 46 11 W112 01 22. Hrs open:
Rebroadcasts KUFM(FM) Missoula 100%.
PARTV Bldg., Univ. of Montana, Missoula, 59812. Phone: (406) 243-4931. Phone: (800) 325-1565. Fax: (406) 243-3299. Licensee: The University of Montana. Natl. Network: NPR, . Wire Svc: AP Format: Jazz, classical, news. News staff: 2. ♦William Marcus, gen mgr.

***KVCM(FM)**— Aug 2, 1993: 103.1 mhz; 30 kw. Ant 679 ft TL: N46 46 11 W112 01 25. Stereo. Hrs open: 24
Rebroadcasts KXEI(FM) Havre 100%.
Box 2426, 317 First St., Havre, 59501. Phone: (406) 265-5845. Fax: (406) 265-8860.E-mail: ynop@ynopradio.org Web Site:www.ynopradio.org Licensee: Hi-Line Radio Fellowship Inc. Natl. Network: Moody, Salem Radio Network, . Wire Svc: AP Format: Christian Inspirational. Target aud: General:; those looking for inspirational Christian music & progmg. ♦Brenda Boyum, stn mgr; Brian Jackson, progmg dir.

KZMT(FM)— 1975: 101.1 mhz; 95 kw. 1,899 ft TL: N46 44 52 W112 19 47. Stereo. Hrs open: Prog sep from AM Box 4111, 59604. Phone: (406) 442-4490. Fax: (406) 442-7356.E-mail: kbllfm@cherrycreekradio.com Web Site:www.kzmt.com Licensee: CCR-Helena IV LLC. Population served: 130,000 Format: Classic rock. Target aud: 18-54; upscale, entrepreneurial, adults. ♦Michele McAlister, traf mgr.

Highwood

KZUS(FM)— 2008: Stn currently dark. 101.7 mhz; 100 kw. Ant 895 ft TL: N47 36 24 W111 21 31. Hrs open: 118 6th St. S., Great Falls, 59401-3625. Phone: (406) 761-8816. Fax: (406) 454-3484. Licensee: College Creek Media LLC. ♦Neal J. Robinson, pres; Darnell Washington, gen mgr.

Joliet

KPBR(FM)— Mar 15, 2006: 105.9 mhz; 100 kw. Ant 440 ft TL: N45 39 31 W108 34 14. Stereo. Hrs open: 24 101 Grand Ave., Billings, 59101. Phone: (406) 248-7777. Fax: (406) 248-8577.E-mail: thebar@1059thebar.com Web Site:www.1059thebar.com Licensee: Connoisseur Media LLC. Format: Country. ♦Michael Schutta, gen mgr.

Kalispell

KALS(FM)— November 1974: 97.1 mhz; 26 kw. 2,488 ft TL: N48 00 48 W114 21 55. Stereo. Hrs open: Box 9710, 59904-2710. Phone: (406) 752-5257. Fax: (406) 752-3416.E-mail: info@kals.com Web Site:www.kals.com Licensee: Kalispell Christian Radio Fellowship Inc. (acq 11-26-01; $700,000). Population served: 14,000 Format: Christian, adult contemp. Spec prog: Class one hr wkly. ♦Brad Rauch, gen mgr.

KBBZ(FM)— Sept 12, 1983: 98.5 mhz; 58 kw. 2,378 ft TL: N48 30 42 W114 22 14. (CP: 60 kw, ant 2,313 ft.). Stereo. Hrs open: 2432 Hwy. 2 E., 59901. Phone: (406) 755-8700. Fax: (406) 755-8770.E-mail: kbbz@beebroadcasting.com Web Site:www.beebroadcasting.com Licensee: Bee Broadcasting Inc. (group owner; acq 6-12-83; $315,000; 9-26-83). Format: Adult classic, contemp rock. ♦Benny Bee, pres; Mark Wagner, gen mgr; Benny Bee Jr., opns mgr.

KDBR(FM)— November 1993: 106.3 mhz; 30 kw. 413 ft TL: N48 10 34 N114 20 53. Hrs open: Box 5409, 59903. Phone: (406) 257-5327. Phone: (406) 755-8700. Fax: (406) 755-8770.E-mail: kdbr@beebroadcasting.com Web Site:www.beebroadcasting.com Licensee: Bee Broadcasting Inc. (group owner) Format: Country. ♦Benny Bee, pres; Mark Wagner, gen mgr.

KGEZ(AM)— Mar 24, 1927: 600 khz; 5 kw-D, 1 kw-N, DA-2. TL: N48 09 40 W114 16 51. Hrs open: 24 Box 923, 59903. Phone: (406) 752-2600. Fax: (406) 257-0459.E-mail: traffic@z600.com Web Site:www.z600.com Licensee: Skyline Broadcasters Inc. (acq 12-2-99). Population served: 80,000 Natl. Network: USA, . Format: News/talk, sports. Target aud: 25-60. ♦John Stokes, gen mgr.

***KLKM(FM)**— 2006: 88.7 mhz; 8.5 kw vert. Ant 312 ft TL: N48 04 07 W114 02 20. Hrs open:
Rebroadcasts KLVR(FM) Santa Rosa, CA 100%.
2351 Sunset Blvd., Suite 170-218, Rocklin, CA, 95765. Phone: (916) 251-1600. Fax: (916) 251-1650. Web Site:www.klove.com Licensee: Educational Media Foundation. (acq 1-11-2005; $95,000 for CP). Natl. Network: K-Love, . Format: Contemp Christian. ♦Richard Jenkins, pres; Mike Novak, VP; Keith Whipple, dev dir; Eric Allen, natl sls mgr; David Pierce, progmg mgr; Ed Lenane, news dir; Sam Wallington, engrg dir; Karen Johnson, news rptr.

KOFI(AM)— Nov 11, 1955: 1180 khz; 50 kw-D, 10 kw-N, DA-N. TL: N48 11 52 W114 15 03. Stereo. Hrs open: 24 Box 608, 59903.

Secondary address: 317 First Ave. E. 59901. Phone: (406) 755-6690. Fax: (406) 752-5078.E-mail: kofi@kofi.radio.com Web Site:www.kofi.com Licensee: KOFI Inc. (acq 9-11-90; $750,000 with co-located FM;10-1-90). Population served: 105,000 Natl. Network: ABC, CNN Radio, . Reddy, Begley & McCormick. Format: CHR, oldies, news/talk. News staff: 2; News: 35 hrs wkly. Target aud: 25-54. ◆Dave Rae, gen mgr.

KQRK(FM)—See Ronan

*KSPL(FM)— February 1997: 90.9 mhz; 250 w. 2,529 ft TL: N48 30 22 W114 20 49. Hrs open:
Rebroadcasts KMBI-FM Spokane, WA 100%.
c/o KMBI-FM, 5408 S. Freya, Spokane, WA, 99223. Phone: (509) 448-2555. Fax: (509) 448-6855.E-mail: kmbi@moody.edu Web Site:www.moody.edu Licensee: Moody Bible Institute of Chicago. Group owner: The Moody Bible Institute of Chicago Format: Relg. Target aud: 35-54; Christian men & women. ◆Richard Monteith, gen mgr, progmg mgr; Scott Richardson, chief of engrg; Bret Bremberg, disc jockey.

*KUKL(FM)— October 1998: 89.9 mhz; 850 w. 443 ft TL: N48 10 34 W114 20 53. Hrs open: c/o KUFM(FM), Univ. of Montana, Missoula, 59812. Phone: (406) 243-4931. Fax: (406) 243-3299. Fax: (800) 325-1565. Web Site:mtpr.org Licensee: University of Montana. Natl. Network: NPR, . Wire Svc: AP Format: Jazz, classical, news, eclectic. News: 2 hrs wkly. ◆William Marcus, gen mgr.

KZMN(FM)— June 10, 1988: 103.9 mhz; 100 kw horiz, 55 kw vert. 571 ft TL: N48 05 39 W114 16 11. Stereo. Hrs open: 24 Box 608, 59903. Secondary address: 317 First Ave. E. 59901. Phone: (406) 755-6690. Phone: (406) 752-5078.E-mail: kofi@kofiradio.com Web Site:www.kzmn.com Natl. Network: CNN Radio, . Format: Classic rock. News: 3 hrs wkly. Target aud: 18-49. ◆Dave Rae, pres; Mike Jorgensen, VP.

Laurel

KBSR(AM)— September 1979: 1490 khz; 1 kw-U. TL: N45 39 11 W108 45 09. Hrs open: 24 Box 248, 59044. Phone: (406) 665-2828. Fax: (406) 665-2131.E-mail: rich@bigskyradio.net Web Site:www.bigskyradio.net Licensee: Sun Mountain Inc. (acq 11-30-2000). Natl. Network: ABC, . Format: News, talk, radio theatre. News: News prgmg 24 hrs wkly. Target aud: 35 plus; professional, business people. ◆Richard Solberg, pres.

KRSQ(FM)— June 9, 1994: 101.9 mhz; 100 kw. Ant 367 ft TL: N45 45 48 W108 27 20. Hrs open: 222 North 32nd St., 10th Floor, Billings, 59101. Phone: (406) 238-1000. Fax: (406) 238-1038.E-mail: kyle.mccoy@nnbradio.com Web Site:www.hot1019.com Licensee: New Northwest Broadcasters LLC (group owner; acq 8-10-99; grpsl). Natl. Network: ABC, . Dow, Lohnes & Albertson. Format: CHR. Target aud: 18-49. ◆Pete Benedetti, CEO; Tommy Ehrman, gen mgr; Tom Oakes, opns mgr.

Lewistown

KLCM(FM)— April 1975: 95.9 mhz; 3 kw. Ant -230 ft TL: N47 04 16 W109 24 32. Stereo. Hrs open: 620 N.E. Main St., 95457. Phone: (406) 707-5275. Fax: (406) 538-3495.E-mail: info@kxlo-klcm.com Web Site:www.kxlo-klcm.com Licensee: Montana Broadcast Communications Inc. Format: Classic hits. Target aud: 18-54.

*KLEU(FM)— Oct 21, 2003: 91.1 mhz; 4 kw. Ant 1,879 ft TL: N47 10 46 W109 32 05. Hrs open: 24
Rebroadcasts KXEI(FM) Havre 100%.
Box 2426, Havre, 59501-2426. Phone: (406) 265-5845. Fax: (406) 265-8860. Web Site:www.ynoradio.org Licensee: Hi-Line Radio Fellowship Inc. acq 12-10-2003; $20,000 for CP). Natl. Network: Moody, Salem Radio Network, . Wire Svc: AP Format: Christian Inspirational. ◆Roger Lonnquist, gen mgr; Brenda Boyum, stn mgr; Brian Jackson, progmg dir.

KXLO(AM)— 1947: 1230 khz; 1 kw-U. TL: N47 04 13 W109 24 26. Hrs open: 620 N.E. Main St., 95457. Phone: (406) 707-5275. Fax: (406) 538-3495.E-mail: kxlo@lewistown.net Web Site:www.kxlo-klcm.com Licensee: KXLO Broadcast Inc. (acq 4-16-73). Population served: 7,500 Natl. Network: CBS, . Rgnl. Network: Intermountain Farm/Ranch Network. Format: Country. Target aud: General. Spec prog: Farm. ◆Fred Lark, pres & gen mgr; Bethany Lark, progmg dir.

Libby

KLCB(AM)— Dec 23, 1950: 1230 khz; 1 kw-U. TL: N48 22 14 W115 32 19. Hrs open: 16 Box 730, 59923. Secondary address: 251 W. Cedar St. 59923. Phone: (406) 293-6234. Fax: (406) 293-6235.

Licensee: Lincoln County Broadcasters Inc. (acq 12-66). Population served: 14,000 Natl. Network: ABC, . Format: Country. News staff: one; News: 13 hrs wkly. Target aud: 25-54. ◆Duane J. Williams, VP & gen mgr.

KTNY(FM)— Apr 5, 1986: 101.7 mhz; 3 kw. Ant -1,029 ft TL: N48 22 14 W115 32 19. Stereo. Hrs open: 16 Box 730, 59923. Secondary address: 251 W. Cedar St. 59923. Phone: (406) 293-6234. Fax: (406) 293-6235. Licensee: Lincoln County Broadcasters Inc. Population served: 14,000 Natl. Network: ABC, . Format: Smooth Oldies Soft Gold. News staff: one; News: 16 hrs wkly. Target aud: 35-54.

*KUFL(FM)—Not on air, target date: unknown: 90.5 mhz; 1 kw. Ant 449 ft TL: N48 26 20 W115 31 37. Hrs open: The University of Montana, PARTV Bldg. Rm. 180, Missoula, 59812. Phone: (406) 243-4931. Fax: (406) 243-3299. Web Site:www.mtpr.org Licensee: The University of Montana. ◆William Marcus, gen mgr.

*KVRZ(FM)—Not on air, target date: unknown: 88.9 mhz; 400 w. Ant 1,246 ft TL: N48 29 13 W115 47 39. Hrs open: Box 762, Troy, 59935. Phone: (406) 295-2046. Licensee: Troy Fine Arts Council. ◆Tyann Hermes, pres.

Livingston

KOZB(FM)— December 1977: 97.5 mhz; 100 kw. 265 ft TL: N45 39 26 W110 48 22. (CP: Ant 790 ft.). Stereo. Hrs open: 24 Box 20, 5445 Johnson Rd., Bozeman, 59718. Phone: (406) 587-9999. Phone: (406) 586-5858. Fax: (406) 587-5855.E-mail: reier@bigsky.net Licensee: Reier Broadcasting Co. Inc. (group owner; acq 10-18-96; grpsl). Population served: 60,000 Format: Rock alternative. News staff: 2. Target aud: 18-44. ◆Bill Reier, gen mgr.

KPRK(AM)— Jan 10, 1947: 1340 khz; 1 kw-U. TL: N45 40 21 W110 32 21. Hrs open: 5:30 AM-midnight Box1340, Hwy. 10 E., 59047. Phone: (406) 222-2841. Phone: (406) 222-1340. Fax: (406) 222-1341.E-mail: kprkam@mooseradio.com Licensee: GAP Broadcasting Bozeman License LLC. Group owner: Clear Channel Communications Inc. (acq 2-13-2008; grpsl). Population served: 18,000 Natl. Network: AP Radio, . Rgnl. Network: AP. Format: Classic hits. News: 15 hrs wkly. Target aud: 25-64; general. Spec prog: Oldies 5 hrs, big band 4 hrs wkly. ◆Dave Cowan, gen mgr; Courtney Lehman, stn mgr; Kaye Rugh, gen sls mgr; Gary Weiss, news dir; Ron Huckeby, chief of engrg.

KXLB(FM)—Not on air, target date: unknown: 100.7 mhz; 94 kw. 813 ft TL: N45 40 24 W110 32 02. Hrs open: Box 1340 , Hwy. 10 E., 59047. Phone: (406) 222-2841, (406) 222-1340. Fax: (406) 222-1341.E-mail: kxlbam@mooseradio.com Licensee: GAP Broadcasting Bozeman License LLC. (acq 2-13-2008; grpsl). Format: Country.

*KYPM(FM)—Not on air, target date: unknown: 90.1 mhz; 2.1 kw. Ant 846 ft TL: N45 35 51 W110 32 45. Hrs open: Yellowstone Public Radio, 1500 University Dr., Billings, 59101. Phone: (406) 657-2941. Fax: (406) 657-2977. Web Site:www.yellowstonepublicradio.org Licensee: Montana State University -Billings. ◆Lois Bent, gen mgr.

Lockwood

KPLN(FM)— Mar 1, 2006: 106.7 mhz; 100 kw. Ant 512 ft TL: N45 45 54 W108 27 19. Hrs open: 101 Grand Ave., Billings, 59101. Phone: (406) 248-7777. Fax: (406) 248-8577. Licensee: Connoisseur Media LLC. Format: CHR. ◆Cam Maxwell, gen mgr.

KYLW(AM)— 2005: 1450 khz; 1 kw-U. TL: N45 48 37 W108 25 38. Hrs open: 24 9045 Hobble Creek, Billings, 59101. Phone: (406) 665-2828. Fax: (406) 665-2131.E-mail: rich@bigskyradio.net Web Site:www.bigskyradio.net Licensee: Sun Mountain Inc. (acq 7-7-2005; $26,000 for CP). Population served: 135,000 Natl. Network: ABC, . Target aud: General.

*KYWH(FM)— 2006: 88.9 mhz; 1.9 kw vert. Ant 452 ft TL: N45 51 12 W108 45 50. Hrs open: 2121 South 48th St. West, Billings, 59106. Phone: (406) 254-1944. Fax: (406) 294-1946. Web Site:www.calvarychapel.com/billings Licensee: CSN International (group owner). Format: Christian. ◆Wayne Hathaway, gen mgr.

Lolo

KDXT(FM)— 2008: 97.9 mhz; 10 kw. Ant 417 ft TL: N46 30 37 W113 58 48. Hrs open: 725 Strand Ave., Missoula, 59801. Phone: (406) 542-1025. Fax: (406) 721-1036. Licensee: Sheila Callahan and Friends Inc. ◆Sheila Callahan, gen mgr.

Malta

KLTZ(AM)—See Glasgow

KMMR(FM)— Sept 9, 1980: 100.1 mhz; 2.25 kw. 377 ft TL: N48 15 17 W107 49 18. Stereo. Hrs open: 6 AM-11 PM Box 1073, 140 S. 2nd Ave. E., 59538. Phone: (406) 654-2472. Fax: (406) 654-2506. Web Site:www.kmmrfm.com Licensee: KMMR Radio Inc. (acq 5-95; $160,000). Population served: 13,000 Natl. Network: Country, MOR. News staff: one; News: 3 hrs wkly. Target aud: 18-65; general, rural. ◆Gregory A. Kielb, pres, gen mgr, gen sls mgr; Claudette Kielb, opns VP; Joyce Robinson, opns dir; Valene Kielb, progmg dir.

Manhattan

KKQX(FM)— Nov 1, 2005: 105.7 mhz; 12.3 kw. Ant 682 ft TL: N45 38 16 W111 16 05. Hrs open: 24
Simulcast on KBZM (FM) Big Sky.
8274 Huffine, Bozeman, 59718. Phone: (406) 582-1045. Fax: (406) 582-0388.E-mail: sbalding@kbzm.com Web Site:www.kbzm.com Licensee: Radick Construction Inc. Rgnl rep: Local Focus 310-441-8188 Format: Classic hits, classic rock. News staff: 2. Target aud: 25-54. ◆John Radick, pres.

Miles City

KATL(AM)— Sept 4, 1941: 770 khz; 10 kw-D, 1 kw-N, DA-N. TL: N46 23 46 W105 46 44. Hrs open: 24 Box 700, 59301. Secondary address: 818 Main St. 59301. Phone: (406) 234-7700. Fax: (406) 234-7783.E-mail: katlradio@katlradio.com Web Site:www.katlradio.com Licensee: Star Printing Co. Population served: 28,700 Natl. Network: Westwood One, ABC, . Cohn & Marks. Wire Svc: AP Format: Adult contemp. News staff: 8; News: 17 hrs wkly. Target aud: 25-54; Adults. ◆John Sullivan, pres; Donald L. Richard, gen mgr, progmg dir, chief of engrg; Mark Waddington, gen sls mgr.

KIKC-FM—See Forsyth

KMTA(AM)— October 1986: 1050 khz; 10 kw-D, 136 w-N. TL: N46 24 04 W105 39 06. Hrs open: 24 Box 1426, 59301. Secondary address: 508 Main St., Rm. 200 59301. Phone: (406) 234-5626. Fax: (406) 874-7000. Licensee: Custer County Community Broadcasting Corp. Population served: 45,000 Format: Classic rock. News staff: one; News: 6 hrs wkly. Target aud: 25-54. ◆Kevin J. Senger, chmn.

*KYPR(FM)— Nov 17, 1988: 90.7 mhz; 500 w. 502 ft TL: N46 23 22 W105 45 22. Stereo. Hrs open: 24
Rebroadcasts KEMC(FM) Billings 100%.
M.S.U. Billings, 1500 University Dr., Billings, 59101-0298. Phone: (406) 657-2941. Fax: (406) 657-2977. Web Site:www.yellowstonepublicradio.org Licensee: Montana State University-Billings. Natl. Network: NPR, PRI, . Format: Div. News: 39 hrs wkly. Target aud: General. ◆Lois Bent, gen mgr.

KYUS-FM— Nov 8, 1984: 92.3 mhz; 100 kw. Ant 984 ft TL: N46 24 04 W105 39 06. Stereo. Hrs open: 24 Box 1426, 59301. Secondary address: 508 Main St. , Rm. 200 53901. Phone: (406) 234-5626. Fax: (406) 232-7000.E-mail: studiokyus@kmta.com Licensee: Custer County Community Broadcasting Corp. (acq 1-26-2007; $540,000 with co-located AM). Population served: 44,000 Format: Country. News staff: one; News: 3 hrs wkly. Target aud: 18-54; programmed for general audience appeal. Spec prog: Farm one hr wkly. ◆Kevin J. Senger, gen mgr; Kevin Senger, opns mgr, gen sls mgr; Karla Ellison, progmg dir, traf mgr; C.W. Wilcox, news dir, sports cmtr; Tony Questa, chief of engrg.

Missoula

*KBGA(FM)— Aug 24, 1996: 89.9 mhz; 1 kw. -262 ft TL: N46 52 56 W113 59 08. Hrs open: Univ. Center, Univ. of Montana, 59812. Phone: (406) 243-6758. Fax: (406) 243-6428.E-mail: kbga@selway.umt.edu Web Site:www.kbga.org Licensee: The University of Montana. Format: Alternative, rock and roll, educ. ◆Carly Dandrea, gen mgr.

KGGL(FM)— Apr 29, 1977: 93.3 mhz; 43 kw. Ant 2,440 ft TL: N47 02 24 W113 59 00. Stereo. Hrs open: Box 4106, 59806. Secondary address: 1600 N. Ave. W. 59801. Phone: (406) 728-9399. Fax: (406) 721-3020. Licensee: CCR-Missoula IV LLC. Natl. Rep: McGavren Guild,. Format: Country. Target aud: 25-54. ◆Chad Parrish, gen mgr; Scott Richards, opns mgr; Bill McPherson, gen sls mgr; Joe Bowers, chief of engrg; Samantha Honold, traf mgr.

KGRZ(AM)— 1947: 1450 khz; 1 kw-U. TL: N46 52 36 W114 00 47. (CP: TL: N46 52 39 W114 02 36). Hrs open: 24 Box 4106, 59806. Secondary address: 1600 N. Ave. W. 59801. Phone: (406) 728-1450.

Fax: (406) 721-3020. Licensee: CCR-Missoula IV LLC. Group owner: Fisher Broadcasting Company (acq 10-31-2006; grpsl). Population served: 70,000 Natl. Rep: McGavren Guild,. Fisher, Wayland, Cooper, Leader & Zaragoza L.L.P. Format: Sports, talk. Target aud: 25-54; male, sports orientated. ◆Chad Parrish, gen mgr; Scott Richards, opns mgr; Bill McPherson, gen sls mgr, rgnl sls mgr; Joe Bowers, chief of engrg; Samantha Honold, traf mgr.

KGVO(AM)— Jan 18, 1931: 1290 khz; 5 kw-U, DA-N. TL: N46 49 47 W114 04 45. Hrs open: 3250 S. Reserve St., Suite 200, 59801. Phone: (406) 728-9300. Fax: (406) 542-2329. Web Site:www.kgvo1290.com Licensee: GAP Broadcasting Missoula License LLC. Group owner: Clear Channel Communications Inc. (acq 2-13-2008; grpsl). Population served: 90,000 Natl. Network: Fox News Radio, . Format: News/talk. Target aud: General. ◆Dave Cowan, CEO, gen mgr; Kathy Anderson, gen sls mgr.

*KJCG(FM)—Not on air, target date: unknown: 88.3 mhz; 1 kw vert. Ant 2,086 ft TL: N46 48 09 W113 58 21. Hrs open: 820 N. LaSalle St., Chicago, IL, 60610-3214. Phone: (312) 329-4438. Fax: (312) 329-8980.E-mail: info@kjcg.com Web Site:www.mbn.org Licensee: The Moody Bible Institute of Chicago.

KMPT(AM)—(East Missoula, June 27, 1959: 930 khz; 5 kw-D, 1 kw-N, DA-N. TL: N46 51 57 W114 04 57. Hrs open: 24 3250 S. Reserve, Suite 200, 59801. Phone: (406) 728-9300. Fax: (406) 542-2329. Web Site:www.klcy930.com Licensee: GAP Broadcasting Missoula License LLC. Group owner: Clear Channel Communications Inc. (acq 2-13-2008; grpsl). Population served: 65,000 Drinker Biddle & Reath LLP. Format: Progressive talk. News: 14 hrs wkly. Target aud: 35-54; adult spenders. ◆Gene Peterson, gen mgr; Jim Colter, gen sls mgr; Kirk Patrick, progmg dir; Pete Denault, news dir; Todd Clark, chief of engrg.

KMSO(FM)— Feb 9, 1985: 102.5 mhz; 21 kw. Ant 1,748 ft TL: N46 48 30 W113 58 38. Stereo. Hrs open: 24 Box 309, 59806-0309. Secondary address: 725 Strand Ave. 59801. Phone: (406) 542-1025. Fax: (406) 721-1036.E-mail: info@kmso.com Web Site:www.moclub.com Licensee: Sheila Callahan & Friends Inc. Population served: 150,000 Natl. Network: AP Radio, . Rgnl rep: Tacher, Portland Keller & Heckman. Wire Svc: AP Format: Hot adult contemp. News: 6 hrs wkly. Target aud: 25-54; upscale professional, well-educated mgmt level. Spec prog: Relg one hr wkly. ◆Sheila Callahan, gen mgr; Diana Helms, gen sls mgr; Dale Desmond, progmg dir; Kris Hardy, traf mgr.

*KMZL(FM)— 1998: 91.1 mhz; 2.2 kw. Ant 2,053 ft TL: N46 48 09 W113 58 21. Stereo. Hrs open: 24 2201 S. 6th St., Las Vegas, NV, 89104. Phone: (800) 804-5452. Phone: (702) 731-5452.E-mail: info@sosradio.net Web Site:sosradio.net Licensee: Faith Communications Corp. Cohn & Marks. Format: Adult contemp Christian. News: 5 hrs wkly. Target aud: 25-44. ◆Jack French, CEO; Brad Staley, gen mgr, opns VP; Chris Staley, progmg mgr.

*KUFM(FM)— Jan 31, 1965: 89.1 mhz; 14.5 kw. Ant 2,473 ft TL: N47 01 58 W113 59 29. Hrs open: Univ. of Montana, 59812. Phone: (406) 243-4931. Fax: (406) 243-3299. Web Site:www.mtpr.org Licensee: University of Montana. Population served: 320,000 Natl. Network: NPR, . Wire Svc: AP Format: Class, jazz, pub radio. News staff: 2. ◆William Marcus, gen mgr.

KYJK(FM)— July 2005: 105.9 mhz; 1.84 kw. Ant 2,083 ft TL: N46 48 06 W113 58 22. Stereo. Hrs open: 24/7 2425 W. Central Ave., Suite 203, 59801. Phone: (406) 721-6800. Fax: (406) 329-1850.E-mail: rharsell@simmonsmedia.com Web Site:www.1059JackFM.net Licensee: Spanish Peaks Broadcasting Inc. Population served: 150,000 Natl. Rep: Interep,. Format: Adult Hits. Target aud: 25-54; adults. ◆Rod Harsell, gen mgr.

KYLT(AM)— July 15, 1955: 1340 khz; 1 kw-U. TL: N46 52 56 W113 59 08. Hrs open: 24 Box 4106, 59806-4106. Secondary address: 1600 North Ave. W., Suite 101 59801-5500. Phone: (406) 728-5000. Fax: (406) 721-3020.E-mail: kylt@1340kylt.com Web Site:www.1340kylt.com Licensee: CCR-Missoula IV LLC. Group owner: Fisher Broadcasting Company (acq 10-31-2006; grpsl). Population served: 47,538 Natl. Network: Fox Sports, . Natl. Rep: McGavren Guild,. Format: Sports. Target aud: 35-55. ◆Chad Parrish, gen mgr; Bill McPherson, gen sls mgr; Scott Richards, opns mgr & natl sls mgr; Joe Bowers, chief of engrg; Samantha Honold, traf mgr.

KYSS-FM— May 11, 1969: 94.9 mhz; 62 kw horiz, 12.5 kw vert. Ant 2,381 ft TL: N47 01 57 W113 59 30. Stereo. Hrs open: 24 3250 S. Reserve, Suite 200, 59801. Phone: (406) 728-9300. Fax: (406) 542-2329. Web Site:www.kyssfm.com Licensee: GAP Broadcasting Missoula License LLC. (acq 2-13-2008; grpsl). Population served: 120,000 Format: Country. News: 12 hrs wkly. Target aud: 25-54; adults. ◆Dave Cowan, gen mgr; Kathy Anderson, gen sls mgr; Craig Johnson, progmg dir.

KZOQ-FM— July 29, 1974: 100.1 mhz; 13.5 kw. Ant 2,102 ft TL: N46 48 09 W113 58 21. Stereo. Hrs open: 24 Box 4106, 1600 North Ave. W., 59806. Phone: (406) 728-5000. Fax: (406) 721-3020. Natl. Rep: McGavren Guild,. Format: Classic rock. Target aud: 25-54. ◆Lily Konda, gen mgr, progmg dir; Scott Richards, opns mgr; Bill McPherson, gen sls mgr; Joe Bowers, chief of engrg; Samantha Honold, traf mgr.

Montana City

KHLN(FM)— 2007: 98.5 mhz; 6 kw. Ant -108 ft TL: N46 33 25.8 W111 55 01.4. Hrs open: Box 4111, Helena, 59604. Phone: (406) 442-4490. Fax: (402) 442-7356. Licensee: Cherry Creek Radio LLC. ◆Dewey Bruce, gen mgr.

Pablo

KKMT(FM)— 2006: 99.7 mhz; 1.8 kw. Ant 2,112 ft TL: N47 46 25 W114 16 04. Hrs open: 36581 N. Reservoir Rd., Polson, 59860. Phone: (406) 883-5255. Fax: (406) 883-4411.E-mail: info@kkmtfm.com Web Site:www.star99hits.com Licensee: Anderson Radio Broadcasting Inc. ◆Dennis L. Anderson, pres.

Park City

*KBIL(FM)— 2006: 89.7 mhz; 2.7 kw vert. Ant 525 ft TL: N45 51 12 W108 45 50. Hrs open: 24
Rebroadcasts KLRD(FM) Yucaipa, CA 100%.
2351 Sunset Blvd., Suite 170-218, Rocklin, CA, 95765. Phone: (916) 251-1600. Fax: (916) 251-1650. Web Site:www.air1.com Licensee: Educational Media Foundation. Group owner: EMF Broadcasting (acq 10-2-2003; grpsl). Natl. Network: Air 1, . Shaw Pittman. Format: Christian. News staff: 3. Target aud: 25-44; Judeo Christian female. ◆Richard Jenkins, pres; Mike Novak, VP; Ed Lenane, opns dir, news dir; Keith Whipple, dev dir; David Pierce, progmg mgr; Sam Wallington, engrg dir; Karen Johnson, news rptr.

KWMY(FM)— Feb. 15, 2006: 92.5 mhz; 100 kw. Ant 620 ft TL: N45 45 54 W108 27 19. Stereo. Hrs open: 24 101 Grand Ave., Billings, 59101. Phone: (406) 248-7777. Fax: (406) 248-8577.E-mail: planet@planet1067.com Web Site:www.my925fm.com Licensee: Chaparral Broadcasting Inc. (acq 11-30-92; $215,000 with KPOW(AM) Powell, WY; 12-21-92). Format: Classic hits. ◆Cam Maxwell, gen mgr.

Pinesdale

KBQQ(FM)— 2003: 106.7 mhz; 13 kw. Ant 2,089 ft TL: N46 48 09 W113 58 19. Hrs open: Cherry Creek Radio, 1600 North Ave., Missoula, 59801. Phone: (406) 728-5000. Fax: (406) 721-3020. Licensee: CCR-Missoula IV LLC. Group owner: Fisher Broadcasting Company (acq 10-31-2006; grpsl). Natl. Rep: McGavren Guild,. Format: Oldies. ◆Chad Parrish, gen mgr; Scott Richards, opns mgr; Bill McPherson, gen sls mgr; Joe Bowers, chief of engrg; Samantha Honold, traf mgr.

Plains

*KPLG(FM)— 1998: 91.5 mhz; 470 w. 4,041 ft TL: N47 22 21 W114 51 31. Stereo. Hrs open: 24
Rebroadcasts KXEI(FM) Havre 100%.
Box 2426, Havre, 59501. Phone: (406) 265-5845. Fax: (406) 265-8860.E-mail: ynop@ynopradio.org Web Site:www.ynopradio.org Licensee: Hi Line Radio Fellowship Inc. Natl. Network: Moody, Salem Radio Network, . Wire Svc: AP Format: Religious. Target aud: General; those who are looking for Christian progmg. ◆Roger Lonnquist, gen mgr; Brenda Boyum, stn mgr; Brian Jackson, progmg dir.

Plentywood

KATQ(AM)— Sept 14, 1979: 1070 khz; 5 kw-D. TL: N48 46 03 W104 32 45. Hrs open: 6 AM-6 PM 112 E. 3rd Ave., 59254. Phone: (406) 765-1480. Fax: (406) 765-2357.E-mail: katq@nemont.net Licensee: Radio International-KATQ Broadcast Association Inc. (acq 1-13-92; $5,000 with co-located FM; 2-10-92). Population served: 400,000 Format: Country. Target aud: 18-54. Spec prog: Top-40, farm 5 hrs, relg 6 hrs wkly. ◆Myrna Kampen, pres; Casandra Syme, gen mgr, sls dir, gen sls mgr, traf mgr; Bruce Lapke, opns dir, mus dir, news dir, news rptr; Art Gehnert, chief of engrg.

KATQ-FM— June 1, 1962: 100.1 mhz; 3 kw. 34 ft TL: N48 47 06 W104 32 00. Stereo. Hrs open: 24 Dups AM 100% 112 E. 3rd Ave., 59254. Phone: (406) 765-1480. Fax: (406) 765-2357.E-mail:

katq@nemont.net Licensee: Radio International-KATQ Broadcast Association Inc. Population served: 6,000 Natl. Network: ABC, AP Radio, . ◆Grant Lindsey, sports cmtr.

Polson

KERR(AM)— Mar 22, 1976: 750 kw-D, 1 kw-N, DA-N. TL: N47 38 34 W114 07 25. Hrs open: 581 N. Reservoir Rd., 59860. Phone: (406) 883-5255. Fax: (406) 883-4441.E-mail: info@750kerr.com Web Site:www.750kerr.com Licensee: Anderson Radio Broadcasting Inc. (group owner; acq 9-22-2003; grpsl). Population served: 100,000 Format: Country. Target aud: General. ◆Dennis Anderson, pres & gen mgr.

*KMBM(FM)—Not on air, target date: unknown: 90.7 mhz; 2 kw. Ant 131 ft TL: N47 40 37 W114 08 33. Hrs open: 82 Devlin Ln., 59860. Phone: (406) 883-7252. Licensee: Divine Mercy Apostolate. Natl. Network: EWTN Radio, . ◆Jeffrey S. Devlin, pres.

*KPJH(FM)—Not on air, target date: unknown: 89.5 mhz; 780 w. Ant 1,883 ft TL: N47 46 25 W114 16 05. Hrs open: Broadcast Media Center, PARTV Bldg., Rm. 180, Missoula, 59812-8064. Phone: (406) 243-4931. Fax: (406) 243-3299. Web Site:www.mtpr.org Licensee: The University of Montana. Natl. Network: NPR, . ◆William Marcus, gen mgr.

Pryor

*KBWY(FM)—Not on air, target date: unknown: 90.5 mhz; 37 kw vert. Ant 1,187 ft TL: N45 11 40 W109 20 30. Hrs open: 116 Hillcrest Dr., Seminole, OK, 74868. Phone: (405) 380-3516.E-mail: info@bpba.us Web Site:www.bpba.us Licensee: Better Public Broadcasting Association. ◆Dennis Burton, gen mgr.

*KPGB(FM)—Not on air, target date: unknown: 88.3 mhz; Hrs open: Box 24, 59066. Phone: (406) 255-0935. Fax: (406) 255-8688. Licensee: Faith Baptist Church. Format: Relg. ◆Ronnie Henderson, gen mgr.

Red Lodge

KMXE-FM— Jan 24, 1994: 99.3 mhz; 30 kw. 1,210 ft TL: N45 11 15 W109 14 46. Stereo. Hrs open: 24 Box 1678, 59068. Phone: (406) 446-1199. Fax: (406) 446-9178.E-mail: fm99mtn@starband.net Licensee: Silver Rock Communications Inc. (acq 7-19-89; $30,000;8-7-89). Population served: 150,000 Format: Rockin' oldies. News staff: one; News: one hr wkly. Target aud: 25-49; upwardly mobile. ◆Jeffrey S. Oliphant, exec VP, opns mgr, news dir; Leslie Brent-Oliphant, pres & gen mgr.

Rocky Boy's Reservation

*KHEW(FM)—Not on air, target date: unknown: 88.5 mhz; 16 kw. Ant 1,578 ft TL: N48 10 42 W109 41 21. Hrs open: R.R. 1, Box 544, Box Elder, 59521. Phone: (406) 395-4396. Fax: (406) 395-4497. Web Site:www.rockyboy.org Licensee: Chippewa Cree Tribe of the Rocky Boy's Reservation. Format: Native American, Cree. ◆John "Chance" Houle, chmn.

Ronan

KQRK(FM)— Oct 4, 1981: 92.3 mhz; 60 kw. 3,500 ft TL: N47 46 25 W114 16 04. Stereo. Hrs open: 24 581 N. Reservoir Rd., 59860. Phone: (406) 883-5255. Fax: (406) 883-4441.E-mail: info@750kerr.com Web Site:www.750kerr.com Licensee: Anderson Radio Broadcasting Inc. (group owner; (acq 9-22-2003; grpsl). Population served: 40,000 Format: Adult contemp. Target aud: 25-49. ◆A.L. Anderson, pres; Dennis Anderson, gen mgr.

Roundup

*KLMB(FM)—Not on air, target date: unknown: 88.3 mhz; 250 w vert. Ant 79 ft TL: N46 27 58 W108 33 20. Hrs open: 515 9th Ave. W., 59072. Phone: (406) 323-1861. Licensee: Roundup Community Radio Association. ◆Bill Edwards, pres.

Saint Regis

KZJZ(FM)—Not on air, target date: unknown: 99.1 mhz; 850 w. Ant 2,758 ft TL: N47 22 22 W114 51 34. Hrs open: 581 N. Reservoir Rd.,

Polson, 59860. Phone: (406) 883-5255. Fax: (406) 883-4441. Licensee: Anderson Radio Broadcasting Inc. (acq 6-6-2008; $75,000 for CP). ◆Dennis L. Anderson, pres & gen mgr.

Scobey

KCGM(FM)— June 21, 1971: 95.7 mhz; 52 kw. Ant 660 ft TL: N48 48 03 W105 21 00. Stereo. Hrs open: 16 Box 220, 20 Main St., 59263. Phone: (406) 487-2293. Fax: (406) 487-5923.E-mail: kegm@nemont.net Licensee: Prairie Communications Inc. Population served: 11,570 Natl. Network: USA, . Rgnl rep: Taylor Brown Wire Svc: AP Format: Country. News staff: 2; News: 8 hrs wkly. Spec prog: Farm 6 hrs wkly. ◆Dixie Halverson, CEO & gen mgr.

Shelby

KSEN(AM)— Aug 11, 1947: 1150 khz; 5 kw-U, DA-2. TL: N48 28 54 W111 53 03. Hrs: 19 830 Oilfield Ave., 59474. Phone: (406) 434-5241. Fax: (406) 434-2122.E-mail: ksen@shelby.mt.us Licensee: Capstar TX L.P. Group owner: Clear Channel Communications Inc. (acq 2-21-01; grpsl). Population served: 58,750 Format: Golden oldies. News staff: one; News: 15 hrs wkly. Target aud: 25-59. Spec prog: Farm 8 hrs wkly. ◆Lowrey Maya, CEO, pres; Julie Martin, gen mgr, gen sls mgr, progmg dir; Jim Sargent, opns dir, opns mgr, progmg dir; Mark Daniels, news dir; Anne James, pub affrs dir; Tony Mulligan, chief of engrg; Jim Sargent, traf mgr.

KZIN-FM— Dec 9, 1978: 96.7 mhz; 100 kw. Ant 551 ft TL: N48 19 42 W112 02 03. Stereo. Hrs open: 24 Dups AM 13% 830 Oilfield Ave., 59474. Phone: (406) 434-5241. Fax: (406) 434-2122. Population served: 35,000 Format: C&W. News staff: one; News: 6 hrs wkly. Target aud: 18-49. ◆Anne Weins, progmg dir & traf mgr.

Sidney

KGCX(FM)— June 1, 2004: 93.1 mhz; 55 kw. Ant 499 ft TL: N47 45 02 W104 18 22. Stereo. Hrs open: 24 213 2nd Ave. S.W., 59270. Phone: (406) 433-5429. Fax: (406) 433-5430.E-mail: kgcxeagle@midrivers.com Web Site:www.kgcx.net Licensee: Sidney Community Broadcasting Corp. (acq 7-30-2002; $10,000 for CP). Natl. Network: Fox News Radio, . Format: Classic rock. News: 15 hrs wkly. ◆Stephen A. Marks, pres; Mitch Miller, gen mgr; Melissa Quilling, gen sls mgr.

KTHC(FM)— December 1996: 95.1 mhz; 100 kw. Ant 718 ft TL: N48 02 52 W103 59 01. Stereo. Hrs open: 120 E. Main, 59270. Secondary address: Box 2048, Williston, ND 58802. Phone: (406) 433-5090. Phone: (701) 572-5371. Fax: (406) 433-5095. Fax: (701) 572-7511.E-mail: power95@midrivers.com Licensee: CCR-Williston IV LLC. Group owner: Cherry Creek Radio LLC (acq 12-19-2003; grpsl). Format: Adult contemp. Target aud: General. ◆Larry Timpe, VP & gen mgr.

Somers

*KFLF(FM)—Not on air, target date: unknown: 91.3 mhz; 1 kw. Ant 203 ft TL: N48 04 05 W114 02 17. Hrs open: 111 Main St., Kalispell, 59901. Phone: (703) 812-0415. Licensee: Fresh Life Church Inc. ◆Levi Lusko, pres.

Stanford

*KYPF(FM)—Not on air, target date: unknown: 89.5 mhz; 4 kw. Ant 1,958 ft TL: N47 10 39 W109 32 06. Hrs open: KEMC(FM), 1500 N. 30th St., Billings, 59103. Phone: (406) 657-2941. Fax: (406) 657-2977. Web Site:www.yellowstonepublicradio.org Licensee: Montana State University - Billings. ◆Lois Bent, gen mgr.

Stevensville

KKVU(FM)— July 16, 2005: 104.5 mhz; 14.15 kw. Ant 2,083 ft TL: N46 48 06 W113 58 22. Hrs open: 2425 W. Central Ave., Suite 203, Missoula, 59801. Phone: (406) 721-6800. Fax: (406) 329-1850.E-mail: tanthony@simmonsmedia.com Web Site:www.fresh1045.com Licensee: Spanish Peaks Broadcasting Inc. Population served: 150,000 Natl. Rep: Interep,. Format: Adult contemp. News staff: one. Target aud: Adults 18-49. ◆Rod Harsell, gen mgr.

Superior

KENR(FM)— October 1999: 107.5 mhz; 100 kw horiz. Ant 945 ft TL: N47 01 45 W114 41 18. Stereo. Hrs open: 3250 Reserve St., Suite

200, Missoula, 59801. Phone: (406) 728-9300. Fax: (406) 542-2329. Web Site:www.energy1075.com Licensee: GAP Broadcasting Missoula License LLC. Group owner: Clear Channel Communications Inc. (acq 2-13-2008; grpsl). Format: Rhythmic adult contemp. ◆Dave Cowan, gen mgr; Kathy Anderson, gen sls mgr; Aaron Traylor, progmg dir.

Thompson Falls

*KBHK(FM)—Not on air, target date: unknown: 88.5 mhz; 200 w. Ant -1,407 ft TL: N47 35 50 W115 20 32. Hrs open: Box 129, 59873. Phone: (406) 827-3561. Fax: (406) 827-9463. Licensee: Thompson Falls School District 2. ◆Sandra Muster, chmn.

Three Forks

KMTZ(FM)—Not on air, target date: unknown: 107.7 mhz; 100 kw. Ant 823 ft TL: N45 38 16 W111 16 05. Hrs open: Box 309, Missoula, 59806-0309. Phone: (406) 542-1025. Fax: (406) 721-1036. Licensee: Sheila Callahan and Friends Inc. ◆M. Sheila Callahan Murphy, pres.

Valier

KWDV(FM)—Not on air, target date: unknown: 105.7 mhz; 100 kw. Ant 640 ft TL: N48 19 44 W112 02 03. Hrs open: 5331 Mt. Alifan Dr., San Diego, CA, 92111. Phone: (858) 277-4991. Fax: (858) 277-1365. Licensee: Horizon Christian Fellowship. (acq 2-9-2006; grpsl). ◆Mike MacIntosh, pres.

Vaughn

KUUS(FM)— 2008: Stn currently dark. 103.9 mhz; 3.5 kw. Ant 895 ft TL: N47 36 24 W111 21 31. Hrs open: 118 6th St. S., Great Falls, 59401-3625. Phone: (406) 761-8816. Fax: (406) 454-3484. Licensee: College Creek Media LLC. ◆Neal J. Robinson, pres; Darnell Washington, gen mgr.

West Yellowstone

KEZQ(FM)— June 1, 1996: Stn currently dark. 92.9 mhz; 46 kw. Ant 2,732 ft TL: N44 33 41 W111 26 32. Hrs open: 14 Cockenoe Dr., Westport, CT, 06880. Phone: (203) 912-3761. Licensee: Resurgence Development LLC Group owner: Chaparral Communications (acq 9-18-2007; with KWYS-FM Island Park, ID). Format: Soft adult contemp. ◆Scott Parker, gen mgr.

KWYS(AM)— Dec 20, 1967: 920 khz; 1 kw-D. TL: N44 38 56 W111 05 50. Hrs open: 603 N. Canyon, Box 9, 59758. Phone: (406) 646-7361. Licensee: Chaparral Broadcasting Inc. Population served: 1,500 Natl. Network: CNN Radio, . Format: Oldies. ◆Scott Anderson, gen mgr.

Whitefish

KJJR(AM)— Feb 14, 1979: 880 khz; 10 kw-D, 500 w-N. TL: N48 23 44 W114 19 11. Hrs open: Box 5409, Kalispell, 59903. Phone: (406) 755-8700. Fax: (406) 755-8770.E-mail: KJJR@beebroadcasting.com Web Site:www.beebroadcasting.com Licensee: Bee Broadcasting Inc. (group owner) Population served: 60,000 Format: News/talk. ◆Benny Bee, pres; Mark Wagner, gen mgr.

KSAM(AM)— 2006: 1240 khz; 400 w-U. TL: N48 23 44 W114 19 40. Hrs open: 2432 US Highway 2 E., Kalispell, 59901. Phone: (406) 755-8700. Fax: (406) 755-8770.E-mail: kdbr@beebroadcasting.com Web Site:www.beebroadcasting.com Licensee: Bee Broadcasting Inc. ◆Benny Bee, pres; Mark Wagner, gen mgr.

KWOL-FM— 2005: 105.1 mhz; 62 kw. Ant 2,404 ft TL: N48 30 43 W114 22 13. Hrs open: Box 5409, Kalispell, 59903. Phone: (406) 755-8700. Fax: (406) 755-8770.E-mail: info@1051cool.com Web Site:www.1051cool.com Licensee: Cathleen R. Bee dba Rose Communications. Format: Oldies. ◆Cassie Bee, gen mgr.

Whitehall

*KQLR(FM)— 2007: 89.7 mhz; 1.45 kw vert. Ant 1,794 ft TL: N46 00 22 W112 26 33. Hrs open:
Rebroadcasts KLVR(FM) Santa Rosa, CA 100%.
2351 Sunset Blvd., Suite 170-218, Rocklin, CA, 95765. Phone: (916) 251-1600. Fax: (916) 251-1650. Web Site:www.klove.com Licensee:

Educational Media Foundation. (acq 12-2-2005; $28,450 for CP). Natl. Network: K-Love, . Format: Contemp Christian. ◆Richard Jenkins, pres.

Wolf Point

KVCK(AM)— Sept 1, 1957: 1450 khz; 1 kw-U. TL: N48 05 18 W105 39 22. Hrs open: 24 324 Main St., 59201. Phone: (406) 653-1900. Fax: (406) 653-1909.E-mail: kvck@nemont.net Licensee: Wolf Town Wireless Inc. (acq 8-31-92; $120,000 with co-located FM; 11-16-92). Population served: 18,000 Natl. Network: ABC, . Format: Oldies. News: 15 hrs wkly. Target aud: General. Spec prog: Farm 6 hrs wkly. ◆Larry Corns, progmg dir.

KVCK-FM— Sept 1, 1981: 92.7 mhz; 11.5 kw. Ant 499 ft TL: N48 11 09 W105 40 08. Stereo. Hrs open: 24 Prog sep from AM 324 Main St., 59201. Phone: (406) 653-1900. Fax: (406) 653-1909.E-mail: kvck@nemont.net Format: Country. News: 15 hrs wkly. Spec prog: Farm 6 hrs wkly. ◆Susan Allmer, gen mgr.

*KYPW(FM)—Not on air, target date: unknown: 88.3 mhz; 500 w. Ant 10 ft TL: N48 06 08 W105 38 57. Hrs open: KEMC(FM), 1500 N. 30th St., Billings, 59103. Phone: (406) 657-2941. Fax: (406) 657-2977. Web Site:www.yellowstonepublicradio.org Licensee: Montana State University - Billings. ◆Lois Bent, gen mgr.

Wyola

*KZXZ(FM)—Not on air, target date: unknown: 90.9 mhz; 30 kw. Ant 180 ft TL: N44 55 16 W107 13 49. Hrs open: Box 217, Gainesville, TX, 76241. Phone: (940) 668-7971. Licensee: 1 A Chord Inc. ◆Mary Fay Jackson, pres.

Nebraska

Ainsworth

KBRB(AM)— Feb 6, 1968: 1400 khz; 1 kw-U. TL: N42 33 16 W99 49 52. Hrs open: 24 Box 285, 122 E. 2nd St., 69210. Phone: (402) 387-1400. Fax: (402) 387-2624.E-mail: kbrb@sscg.net Web Site:kbrbradio.com Licensee: K.B.R. Broadcasting Co. Population served: 2,073 Natl. Network: Brownfield. Brownfield Bryan Cave. Wire Svc: AP Format: C&W, MOR. News: 30 hrs wkly. Target aud: General. ◆Lorris C. Rice, pres, gen mgr; Angie Von Heeder, prom VP; Cody Goochey, progmg dir; Randy Brudigan, chief of engrg; Renee Adkisson, traf mgr.

KBRB-FM— May 30, 1983: 92.7 mhz; 4.5 kw. 331 ft TL: N42 33 16 W99 49 52. Hrs open: Box 285, 122 E. 2nd St., 69210. Phone: (402) 387-1400. Fax: (402) 387-2624. Licensee: K.B.R. Broadcasting Co. Natl. Network: ABC, . Rgnl. Network: Brownfield. Brownfield Wire Svc: AP Format: Adult contemp mix. ◆Renee Adkisson, traf mgr.

Albion

KUSO(FM)— May 10, 2000: 92.7 mhz; 50 kw. 492 ft TL: N41 49 50 W97 41 12. Hrs open: 24 Box 747, Norfolk, 68702-0747. Secondary address: 214 N. 7th St., Norfolk 68701. Phone: (402) 371-0100. Fax: (402) 371-0050.E-mail: us92@us92.com Web Site:www.us92.com Licensee: Flood Communications L.L.C. (acq 4-27-99; $50,000). Population served: 85,000 Reddy, Begley & McCormick. Format: Full service, country. News staff: one; News: 3 hrs wkly. Target aud: General. Spec prog: Farm 10 hrs wkly. ◆Michael J. Flood, pres, gen mgr; Dave Amick, opns dir; Angela Richard, gen sls mgr; Brian Masters, progmg dir; Tammy Partch, news dir; Ann Neilsen, traf mgr.

Allen

KHSK(FM)—Not on air, target date: unknown: 100.9 mhz; 5.6 kw. Ant 686 ft TL: N42 34 18 W96 48 09. Hrs open: 980 N. Michigan Ave., Suite 1880, Chicago, IL, 60611. Phone: (312) 204-9900. Licensee: College Creek Media LLC. ◆Neal J. Robinson, pres.

Alliance

KAAQ(FM)— Sept 30, 1985: 105.9 mhz; 100 kw. Ant 705 ft TL: N41 50 29 W103 05 07. Stereo. Hrs open: 24 Box 600, 69301. Secondary address: 1210 W. 10th 69301. Phone: (308) 762-1400. Fax: (308) 762-7804.E-mail: kcow@bbcw.net Web Site:www.doubleqcountry.com

Licensee: Eagle Communications Inc. Population served: 65,000 Natl. Network: ABC, . Natl. Rep: Interep,. Wire Svc: NWS (National Weather Service) Wire Svc: AP Format: Country. News staff: 2; News: 15 hrs wkly. Target aud: 18-54. Spec prog: Farm 4 hrs wkly. ♦Mark Vail, opns VP.

KCOW(AM)— Feb 15, 1949: 1400 khz; 1 kw-U. TL: N42 06 26 W102 53 15. Hrs open: 24 (M-S) Box 600, 69301. Secondary address: 1210 W. 10th 69301. Phone: (308) 762-1400. Fax: (308) 762-7804.E-mail: kcow@bbcw.net Web Site:www.doubleqcountry.com Licensee: Eagle Communications Inc. Group owner: Eagle Communications Group (acq 1965). Population served: 15,000 Natl. Network: ABC, . Natl. Rep: Interep,. Wire Svc: NWS (National Weather Service) Wire Svc: AP Format: Oldies, news/talk. News staff: 2; News: 22 hrs wkly. Target aud: 25-54. Spec prog: Farm 18 hrs wkly. ♦Gary Shorman, pres; Mark Vail, VP; Mike Garwood, gen mgr; John Jones, rgnl sls mgr; Jason Wentworth, progmg dir; Jennifer Schmid, traf mgr; Kevin Horn, news rptr; Mike Glesinger, sports cmtr.

KPNY(FM)— 1978: 102.1 mhz; 100 kw. Ant 521 ft TL: N42 07 01 W103 07 09. Stereo. Hrs open: 24 Box 30345, Lincoln, 68503-0345. Phone: (402) 845-6595. Phone: (402) 477-1090.E-mail: email@mybridgeradio.net Web Site:www.missionnebraska.org Licensee: Mission Nebraska Inc. (acq 2-5-2007; $360,000). Population served: 72,000 Format: Relg. Target aud: 18-35. ♦Stan Parker, gen mgr.

KQSK(FM)—(Chadron, June 1, 1983: 97.5 mhz; 100 kw. Ant 840 ft TL: N42 38 06 W103 06 12. Stereo. Hrs open: 24
Simulcast with KAAQ(FM) Alliance 95%.
1210 West 10th St., P.O. Box 600, 69301. Phone: (308) 762-1400. Fax: (308) 762-7804.E-mail: kcow@bbc.net Web Site:www.doubleqcountry.com Licensee: Eagle Communications Inc. Group owner: Eagle Communications Group (acq 6-13-91; $125,000; 7-1-91). Population served: 65,000 Natl. Network: ABC, . Natl. Rep: Interep,. Wire Svc: AP Wire Svc: NWS (National Weather Service) Format: Country. News staff: 2; News: 15 hrs wkly. Target aud: 18-54. Spec prog: Farm 4 hrs wkly. ♦Mike Fell, gen mgr; Michael Glesinger, opns mgr.

***KTNE-FM**— May 1990: 91.1 mhz; 92 kw. Ant 1,325 ft TL: N41 50 24 W103 03 18. Stereo. Hrs open: 24
Rebroadcasts KUCV(FM) Lincoln 100%.
Secondary address: 1800 N. 33rd St., Lincoln 68503. Phone: (402) 472-3611. Fax: (402) 472-2403.E-mail: radio@netnebraska.org Web Site:netnebraska.org/radio Licensee: Nebraska Educational Telecommunications Commission. Natl. Network: PRI, NPR, . Rgnl. Network: Neb. Pub. Nebraska Public Radio Dow, Lohnes & Albertson. Format: Classical, news. News staff: 3. Target aud: 35 plus; general. ♦Nancy Finken, gen mgr, progmg dir; William Stibor, mus dir; Jeff Smith, traf mgr.

Auburn

KNCY-FM— Sept 18, 1981: 103.1 mhz; 14 kw. Ant 436 ft TL: N40 27 57 W95 45 38. Hrs open: 24 Box 278, 814 Central Ave., Nebraska City, 68410. Phone: (402) 873-3348. Fax: (402) 873-7882.E-mail: kncy@kncycountry.com Web Site:kncycountry.com Licensee: Riverfront Broadcasting LLC (acq 8-31-2007; with KNCY(AM) Nebraska City). Natl. Network: ABC, . Rgnl. Network: Brownfield. Wire Svc: AP Format: Country, news. News staff: 2; News: 30 hrs wkly. ♦Scott Kooistra, VP & gen mgr; Chris Yates, gen sls mgr; Doug Jennings, progmg dir.

Aurora

KRGY(FM)— Mar 1, 1980: 97.3 mhz; 50 kw. Ant 348 ft TL: N40 52 44 W98 05 36. Stereo. Hrs open: 24 3205 W. North Front St., 68802. Secondary address: Box 4907 68802. Phone: (308) 381-1430. Fax: (308) 382-6701.E-mail: info@gifamilyradio.com Web Site:www.gifamilyradio.com/STAR/star.htm Licensee: Legacy Communications LLC (group owner; (acq 5-17-2004; grpsl). Natl. Network: ABC, . Format: Hot adult contemp. News staff: 2; News: 2 hrs wkly. Target aud: 18-49. ♦Lyle Nelson, gen mgr; Jim Davis, opns mgr.

KROA(FM)—See Grand Island

Bassett

***KMNE-FM**— June 1991: 90.3 mhz; 92.3 kw. 1,292 ft TL: N42 20 05 W99 29 01. Stereo. Hrs open: 24
Simulcasts KUCV(FM) Lincoln 100%.
1800 N. 33rd St., Lincoln, 68503-1409. Phone: (402) 472-3611. Fax: (402) 472-2403.E-mail: radio@netnebraska.org Web Site:netnebraska.org/radio Licensee: Nebraska Educational Telecommunications Commission. Natl. Network: NPR, PRI, . Format: Classical, news. News staff: 3; News: 38 hrs wkly. Target aud: General. ♦Nancy Finken, gen mgr, progmg dir; William Stibor, mus dir; Jeff Smith, traf mgr.

Beatrice

***KNBE(FM)**— 2008: 88.9 mhz; 7.5 kw vert. Ant 459 ft TL: N40 33 03 W96 38 45. Hrs open: Box 262550, Baton Rouge, LA, 20826. Phone: (225) 768-3102. Fax: (225) 768-3729.E-mail: kawikfish@yahoo.com Web Site:www.jsm.org Licensee: Family Worship Center Church Inc. (acq 10-12-2006; grpsl). Format: Relg, Christian. ♦David Whitelaw, COO.

KTGL(FM)—Licensed to Beatrice. See Lincoln

KWBE(AM)— June 12, 1949: 1450 khz; 1000 W. TL: N40 15 49 W96 46 27. Hrs open: 24 Box 10, 200 Sherman St., 68310. Phone: (402) 228-5923. Fax: (402) 228-3704.E-mail: kwbe@broadcasthouse.com Web Site:www.kwbe.com Licensee: NRG License Sub. LLC. Group owner: Triad Broadcasting Co. LLC (acq 12-28-2007; grpsl). Population served: 90,000 Natl. Network: CBS, Westwood One, . Rgnl rep: Howard Anderson. Format: Adult contemp, news/talk. News staff: one; News: 25 hrs wkly. Target aud: 24-54; mature, affluent adults. Spec prog: Farm 14 hrs wkly. ♦Charlie Brogan, gen mgr, gen sls mgr; Jay Stalder, gen mgr & progmg dir; Doug Kennedy, news dir; Dave Neidfeldt, pub affrs dir, news rptr.

Bellevue

KOIL(AM)— Mar 19, 1987: Stn currently dark. 1180 khz; 25 kw-D, 1 kw-N, DA-2. TL: N41 16 12 W95 47 10. Hrs open: 24 5011 Capitol Ave., Omaha, 68132. Phone: (402) 342-2000. Fax: (402) 346-5748.E-mail: info@1180labonita.com Web Site:1180labonita.com Licensee: Waitt Omaha LLC. (group owner; (acq 1-7-2002; grpsl). Population served: 350,000 Format: Spanish. Target aud: 18+; General. ♦Rhonda Gerrard, pres, gen mgr; Mark Todd, opns mgr; Sam Coughlin, sls dir; Neil Nelkin, progmg dir; Darwin Stinton, chief of engrg; Lyn Farhenbruch, traf mgr.

KOZN(AM)— June 1999: 1620 khz; 10 kw-D, 1 kw-N. TL: N41 16 12 W95 47 10. Hrs open: 24 5011 Capitol Ave., Omaha, 68132. Phone: (402) 342-2000. Fax: (402) 346-5748.E-mail: info@1620thezone.com Web Site:www.1620thezone.com Licensee: Waitt Omaha LLC. Group owner: Waitt Radio Inc. (acq 1-7-2002; grpsl). Natl. Network: ESPN Radio, Westwood One, . Natl. Rep: Katz Radio,. Pepper & Corazzini. Format: Sports. Target aud: 25-54; men. ♦Rhonda Gerrard, gen mgr; Mark Todd, opns mgr; Sam Coughlin, sls dir; Brandon Pappas, prom dir; Neil Nelkin, progmg dir; Lori Storz, traf mgr.

Bennington

KTWI(FM)— June 10, 1991: 93.3 mhz; 6 kw. Ant 350 ft TL: N41 22 57 W96 07 57. Stereo. Hrs open: 5010 Underwood Ave., Omaha, 68132. Phone: (402) 561-2000. Fax: (402) 556-8937. Fax: (402) 551-9333.E-mail: michellematthews@clearchannel.com Web Site:www.krrk.com Licensee: Capstar TX L.P. Group owner: Clear Channel Communications Inc. (acq 8-30-2000; grpsl). Format: Country, hard rock. ♦Jean St. James, gen sls mgr; Erik Johnson, progmg dir; Taylor Walet, gen mgr & engrg mgr.

Blair

KBLR-FM— Sept 10, 2002: 97.3 mhz; 25 kw. Ant 302 ft TL: N41 38 21 W96 12 31. Hrs open: 118 E. 5th St., Fremont, 68025. Phone: (402) 721-1340. Fax: (402) 721-5023.E-mail: kfmt@nrgmidia.com Licensee: Waitt Omaha LLC. (group owner; (acq 1-7-2002; grpsl). Format: Country. ♦Del Meyer, gen mgr; Chris Walz, opns mgr.

***KDCV-FM**— Oct 1, 1972: 91.1 mhz; 10 w. 60 ft TL: N41 33 07 W96 09 20. Stereo. Hrs open: 24 2848 College Dr., 68008. Phone: (402) 426-7322. Fax: (402) 426-7382.E-mail: kdcv@dana.edu Web Site:www.huntel.net/kdcv Licensee: Dana College. Population served: 8,000 Format: Var/div. Target aud: 25-54; community, 18-34 college community. ♦Vern Wirka, gen mgr.

Bridgeport

KOZY-FM— 2001: 101.3 mhz; 100 kw. Ant 1,112 ft TL: N41 50 23 W103 49 36. Hrs open: Box 1263, Scottsbluff, 69363-1263. Phone: (308) 632-5667. Fax: (308) 635-1905.E-mail: info@hometownfamilyradio.com Web Site:www.kozylightrock.com Licensee: Legacy Communications LLC. (group owner). (acq 12-13-2007; grpsl). Format: Soft rock. News staff: 2. Target aud: 25-54; general. ♦Julie Marshall, gen mgr, natl sls mgr; Jeff McKenzie, progmg dir; Pat Leach, engrg dir & chief of engrg.

Broken Bow

KBBN-FM— June 15, 1982: 98.3 mhz; 25 kw. Ant 312 ft TL: N41 23 49 W99 37 02. Stereo. Hrs open: 6 AM-11 PM Box 409, 68822. Phone: (308) 872-5881. Fax: (308) 872-3284.E-mail: info@sandhillexpress.com Licensee: Custer County Broadcasting Co. Format: Classic rock. News staff: one; News: 10 hrs wkly. Target aud: 24-45; baby boomers & on either edge of age breakdown.

KCNI(AM)— Sept 28, 1949: 1280 khz; 1 kw-D. TL: N41 24 31 W99 40 28. Hrs open: 6 AM-6 PM Box 409, W. Hwy., 2 Calaway Rd., 68822. Phone: (308) 872-5881. Fax: (308) 872-3284.E-mail: info@sandhillexpress.com Licensee: Custer County Broadcasting Co. Population served: 6,200 Format: C&W. News staff: one; News: 24 hrs wkly. Target aud: 25-65; focus on rural audience. ♦David Birnie, VP, gen mgr, opns dir, sls dir; Brent Apperson, progmg dir; Dale Sell, news dir, pub affrs dir; Val Lane, chief of engrg.

***KPSS(FM)**—Not on air, target date: unknown: 91.3 mhz; 40 kw vert. Ant 492 ft TL: N41 20 08 W100 14 12. Hrs open: 136 Wando Circle, Lexington, SC, 29073. Phone: (803) 359-3324. Licensee: Dayspring Ministries of Concord Baptist Church. ♦Frank Townsend, pres.

Central City

KZEN(FM)— July 22, 1985: 100.3 mhz; 100 kw. 1,854 ft TL: N41 32 28 W97 40 45. Stereo. Hrs open: 24 1418 25th St., Columbus, 68601. Phone: (402) 564-2866. Fax: (402) 564-2867. Licensee: Three Eagles of Columbus Inc. Group owner: Three Eagles Communications (acq 9-5-97; grpsl). Population served: 186,000 Natl. Network: ABC, AP Radio, . Natl. Rep: Interep,. Wire Svc: AP Format: Country. News staff: 2; News: 18 hrs wkly. Target aud: 25-54; rgnl, rural & small town audience. Spec prog: Relg 5 hrs, farm 20 hrs wkly. ♦Rolland Johnson, CEO; Gary Buchanan, pres; Cindy Harris, CFO; Greg Wells, gen mgr; Dean Johnson, opns dir, mus dir.

Chadron

KCNB(FM)— Feb 28, 2008: 94.7 mhz; 100 kw. Ant 843 ft TL: N42 38 06 W103 06 12. Stereo. Hrs open: 24 Box 1117, 69337. Secondary address: 331 Main St. 69337. Phone: (308) 432-2060. Fax: (308) 432-2059. Licensee: Eagle Communications Inc. Format: Adult contemp. News staff: one. Target aud: 18-54. ♦Mark Vail, VP; Mike Fell, gen mgr.

***KCNE-FM**— Aug 29, 1991: 91.9 mhz; 8.4 kw. 338 ft TL: N42 48 47 W103 00 22. Stereo. Hrs open: 24
Rebroadcasts KUCV(FM) Lincoln 100%.
Secondary address: 1800 N. 33rd St., Lincoln 68503. Phone: (402) 472-3611. Fax: (402) 472-2403.E-mail: radio@netnebraska.org Web Site:netnebraska.org/radio Licensee: Nebraska Educational Telecommunications Commission. Natl. Network: PRI, NPR, . Nebraska Public Radio Format: Classical, news. News staff: 3. Target aud: General. ♦Nancy Finken, gen mgr, progmg mgr; William Stibor, mus dir; Jeff Smith, traf mgr.

KCSR(AM)— May 9, 1954: 610 khz; 1 kw-D, 118 w-N. TL: N42 49 56 W103 01 00. Stereo. Hrs open: 24 226 Bordeaux, 69337. Phone: (308) 432-5545. Phone: (308) 432-2233. Fax: (308) 432-5601.E-mail: kcsr@chadrad.com Web Site:www.chadrad.com Licensee: Chadrad Communications Inc. (acq 8-30-91; $150,000). Population served: 75,000 Natl. Network: AP Radio, . Rgnl. Network: Mid-American Ag Brownfield Fletcher, Heald & Hildreth. Wire Svc: AP Format: Country, farm. News staff: 2; News: 20 hrs wkly. Target aud: 25-54; people in the ranch, farm & agricultural industry. Spec prog: Farm 6 hrs wkly. ♦Dennis A. Brown, pres; J.J. Archer, progmg dir; Joe Lowery, mus dir; Brian Taylor, asst music dir, chief of engrg; Chris Faukhauser, news dir; Duanne Ekwall, pub affrs dir; Kathi Brown, gen sls mgr & traf mgr; Greg Mahaco, sports cmtr.

KQSK(FM)—Licensed to Chadron. See Alliance

Columbus

KJSK(AM)— Apr 28, 1948: 900 khz; 1 kw-D, 66 w-N. TL: N41 26 12 W97 23 47. Hrs open: 24 1418 25th St., 68601. Phone: (402) 564-2866. Fax: (402) 564-1999.E-mail: kjsk@megavision.com Web Site:www.kjsk.com Licensee: Three Eagles of Columbus Inc. Group owner: Three Eagles Communications (acq 8-23-01; $2.7 million with co-located FM including five-year noncompete agreement). Population served: 25,000 Natl. Network: CBS Radio, . Rgnl. Network: Brownfield. Wire Svc: AP Format: News/talk, farm, sports. News staff: one; News:

news prgmg one hour/week. Target aud: General. Spec prog: Pol 4 hrs, Sp 6 hrs, relg 20 hrs wkly. ♦Steve Gossweiler, gen mgr; Tim Barrett, opns mgr; Lisa Cherry, gen sls mgr; Jamie Afrank, prom dir; James Nickel, progmg dir; Bob Cook, engrg dir, chief of engrg; Gina Jackson, traf mgr.

KKOT(FM)— Nov 25, 1969: 93.5 mhz; 100 kw. Ant 981 ft TL: N41 32 28 W97 40 45. Stereo. Hrs open: 24 1418 25th St., 68601. Phone: (402) 564-2866. Fax: (402) 564-2867. Licensee: Three Eagles of Columbus Inc. Population served: 450,000 Natl. Rep: McGavren Guild,. Format: Classic rock. News staff: 2; News: 15 hrs wkly. Target aud: 18-49; young families. Spec prog: Farm 8 hrs wkly. ♦Gary Buchanan, COO, opns dir; Dean Johnson, progmg dir; Bobbie Freeborn, traf mgr; Susan Littlefield, farm dir.

KLIR(FM)— August 1964: 101.1 mhz; 100 kw. 760 ft TL: N41 16 55 W97 24 30. Stereo. Hrs open: Prog sep from AM 1418 25th St., 68601. Phone: (402) 564-2866. Fax: (402) 564-1999.E-mail: klirnet@megavision.com Web Site:www.klir.net Licensee: Three Eagles of Columbus Inc. Population served: 25,000 Natl. Network: CNN Radio, . Wire Svc: AP Format: Adult contemp. News staff: one. Target aud: General. Spec prog: Oldies 12 hrs wkly. ♦Steve Gossweiler, gen mgr, opns mgr; Tim Barrett, opns mgr, sls dir; Lisa Cherry, gen sls mgr, progmg dir; Jamie Afrank, prom dir, news rptr; Gina Jackson, mus dir, traf mgr; Tony Correa, news dir & spec ev coord; Rob Hadland, local news ed.

***KTLX(FM)**— July 1974: 91.9 mhz; 100 w. 78 ft TL: N41 26 26 W97 21 14. Hrs open: c/o Trinity Lutheran Church, 2200 25th St., 68601. Phone: (402) 564-8548. Fax: (402) 562-6003.E-mail: ktlx@megavision.com Licensee: TLC Educational Corp. Format: Educ, relg. ♦Gary Spuit, pres; Russ Rote, gen mgr.

KTTT(AM)— Dec 2, 1962: 1510 khz; 500 w-D. TL: N41 27 14 W97 24 20. Hrs open: 1418 25th St., 68601. Phone: (402) 564-2866. Fax: (402) 564-2867. Licensee: Three Eagles Communications Inc. (group owner; acq 1996). Population served: 50,000 Natl. Rep: McGavren Guild,. Format: Talk. News staff: one; News: 10 hrs wkly. Target aud: 25-65. Spec prog: Polka, farm 5 hrs, Ger 5 hrs, Pol 5 hrs wkly. ♦Rolland Johnson, CEO; Gary Buchanan, pres; Cindy Harris, CFO; Greg Wells, gen mgr; Dean Johnson, opns dir; Melissa Sanford, sls dir; Jim Dolezel, progmg dir; Bob Cook, chief of engrg; Bobbie Freeborn, traf mgr; Susan Littlefield, farm dir.

Cozad

***KAMI(AM)**— November 1965: 1580 khz; 1 kw-D, 17 w-N. TL: N40 50 18 W99 56 20. Hrs open: 8 AM-5 PM Dups FM 100% 233 S. 13th St., Suite 1520, Lincoln, 68508. Phone: (402) 465-8850. Fax: (402) 465-8852. Licensee: Community Broadcasting Inc. Natl. Network: USA, . ♦Rich Bott, exec VP; Tom Millett, gen mgr; Pat Rulon, natl sls mgr; Jason Potocnik, traf mgr.

***KCVN(FM)**— Aug 4, 1983: 104.5 mhz; 100 kw. Ant 360 ft TL: N40 46 35 W100 01 47. Stereo. Hrs open: 24 233 S. 13th St., Suite 1520, Lincoln, 68508. Phone: (402) 465-8850. Fax: (402) 465-8852.E-mail: kcvn@bottradionetwork.com Web Site:www.bottradionetwork.com /station_cozad/cozad_home.asp Licensee: Community Broadcasting Inc. Group owner: Bott Radio Network (acq 7-9-2004; $365,000 with co-located AM). Natl. Network: USA, . Format: Christian talk. Target aud: 25-54; adults. ♦Tom Millett, gen mgr; Pat Rulon, natl sls mgr; Jason Potocnik, traf mgr.

Crawford

***KCFD(FM)**—Not on air, target date: unknown: 88.1 mhz; 500 w. Ant 328 ft TL: N42 39 25 W103 35 47. Hrs open: Box 563, Tanner, AL, 35671. Phone: (256) 497-4502.E-mail: southcultural@yahoo.com Licensee: Southern Cultural Foundation. ♦Richard W. Dabney, gen mgr.

Crete

***KDNE(FM)**— Aug 30, 1993: 91.9 mhz; 200 w. 66 ft TL: N40 37 16 W96 57 04. Stereo. Hrs open: 1014 Boswell Ave., 68333. Phone: (402) 826-8677. Fax: (402) 826-8634.E-mail: kdne@doane.edu Licensee: Doane College Board of Trustees. Population served: 7,500 Format: Progsv. Target aud: General; males & females between the ages of 12 to 34. ♦Jonathan Brand, pres; Lee Thomas, gen mgr; John Thayer, stn mgr; Corey Rotschafer, progmg dir.

KIBZ(FM)— Aug 20, 1976: 104.1 mhz; 50 kw. 613 ft TL: N40 31 06 W96 46 07. Stereo. Hrs open: 24 3800 Cornhusker Hwy., Lincoln, 68504. Phone: (402) 466-1234. Fax: (402) 467-4095. Web Site:www.kibz.com Licensee: Three Eagles of Lincoln Inc. Group owner: Clear Channel Communications Inc. (acq 4-10-2007; grpsl). Format: New rock. News staff: one. Target aud: 18-34. ♦James Keck, gen mgr.

Crookston

***KINI(FM)**— January 1978: 96.1 mhz; 90 kw. Ant 499 ft TL: N43 07 50 W100 54 02. Stereo. Hrs open: 24 Box 499, St. Francis, SD, 57572-0499. Phone: (605) 747-2291. Fax: (605) 747-5791.E-mail: kinifm@gwtc.net Web Site:www.gwtc.net/~kinifm Licensee: Rosebud Educational Society Inc. (acq 1-78). Wire Svc: AP Format: Adult contemp, rock, native American. News staff: one; News: 12 hrs wkly. Target aud: General; Indian & white. Spec prog: American Indian 15 hrs, gospel 6 hrs, relg 6 hrs wkly. ♦Fr. John Hatcher, pres; Marcy VanWinkle, exec VP; Richard K. Iyotte Jr., gen mgr & stn mgr.

Dakota City

KTFJ(AM)— 1991: 1250 khz; 500 w-D, 700 w-N, DA-2. TL: N42 26 33 W96 15 41. Hrs open: 24
Rebroadcasts KTFC(FM) Sioux City, IA.
1534 Buchanan Ave., Sioux City, IA, 51106. Phone: (712) 252-4621. Licensee: Donald A. Swanson. Natl. Network: USA, . Format: Gospel. ♦Kim Cotter, pres & gen mgr.

Fairbury

KGMT(AM)— June 13, 1960: 1310 khz; 500 w-D, 97 w-N. TL: N40 06 58 W97 09 05. Hrs open: 6 AM-6 PM 414 4th St., 68352. Phone: (402) 729-3382. Fax: (402) 729-3446.E-mail: kutt@diodecom.net Licensee: Siebert Communications Inc. (acq 8-1-84). Population served: 5,265 Natl. Rep: Farmakis,. Shaw Pittman. Format: Oldies, news. News: one. Target aud: 25-52. Spec prog: Farm 18 hrs wkly. ♦Rick Siebert, pres; Randy Bauer, gen mgr.

KUTT(FM)—Listing follows KGMT(AM).

Falls City

KLZA(FM)— July 7, 1998: 101.3 mhz; 25 kw. Ant 328 ft TL: N40 06 54 W95 39 06. Hrs open: Box 101, 68355. Phone: (402) 245-6010. Fax: (402) 245-6040.E-mail: sunny1013fm@hotmail.com Licensee: KNZA Inc. (group owner) Format: Soft rock. ♦Mike Gilmore, stn mgr; Robert Hilton, opns mgr; Mike Slocum, chief of engrg.

KTNC(AM)— Aug 3, 1957: 1230 khz; 500 w-D, 1 kw-N. TL: N40 03 57 W95 36 55. Hrs open: 24 1602 Stone St., 68355. Phone: (402) 245-2453. Fax: (402) 245-5862.E-mail: ktnc@sentco.net Web Site:www.ktncradio.com Licensee: KNZA Inc. (acq 9-7-2007; $330,000). Population served: 60,000 Natl. Network: ABC, . Rgnl. Network: Brownfield. Brownfield Format: Oldies. News staff: one; News: 23 hrs wkly. Target aud: 25 plus; farmers, businessmen, employees, retirees. Spec prog: Christian mus one hr wkly. ♦Gregory F. Buser, pres; Gregory Buser, gen mgr; Robert Hilton, opns mgr; Gerald Hopp, news dir; Jackie Johnson, traf mgr; Aaron Wisdom, pub svc dir.

Firth

KOLB(FM)—Not on air, target date: unknown: 93.7 mhz; 6 kw. Ant 226 ft TL: N40 34 57.4 W96 37 15.2. Hrs open: 5829 N. 60th St., Omaha, 68104. Phone: (402) 571-0200. Fax: (402) 571-0833. Licensee: VSS Catholic Communications Inc. ♦Jim Carroll, gen mgr.

Franklin

***KNEF(FM)**—Not on air, target date: unknown: 90.1 mhz; 40 kw. Ant 328 ft TL: N39 49 39 W98 48 22. Hrs open: Box 94, Stonewall, OK, 74872. Phone: (580) 265-9475. Licensee: Union Valley Baptist Church Inc. ♦Steve Vandegrift, gen mgr.

Fremont

KFMT-FM— July 1972: 105.5 mhz; 1.2 kw. Ant 450 ft TL: N41 24 40 W96 31 53. Stereo. Hrs open: 5 AM-midnight 118 E. Fifth St., 68025. Phone: (402) 721-1340. Fax: (402) 721-5023.E-mail: kfmt@midia.com Web Site:www.kfmt.com Licensee: NRG Media LLC. Format: Oldies, classic rock. Target aud: 25-54. ♦Chris Walz, traf mgr.

KHUB(AM)— December 1939: 1340 khz; 500 w-D, 1 kw-N. TL: N41 25 58 W96 27 16. Hrs open: 5 AM-midnight 118 E. Fifth St., 68025. Phone: (402) 721-1340. Fax: (402) 721-5023.E-mail: kfmt@nrgmidia.com Licensee: NRG Media LLC. Group owner: Waitt Radio Inc. (acq 10-31-2005; grpsl). Population served: 165,000 Format: News/talk. News staff: one; News: 25 hrs wkly. Target aud: 35 plus; mature adults. Spec prog: Farm 6 hrs wkly. ♦Del Meyer, gen mgr, dev dir, progmg dir; Chris Walz, opns mgr, progmg dir, chief of engrg, traf mgr; Barry Reker, gen sls mgr; Jessica Meistrell, news dir.

Gering

KMOR(FM)— August 1996: 93.3 mhz; 100 kw. Ant 1,020 ft TL: N41 50 23 W103 49 36. Hrs open: Box 1263, Scottsbluff, 69363-1263. Phone: (308) 632-5667. Fax: (308) 635-1905.E-mail: info@hometownfamilyradio.com Web Site:www.kmorfm.com Licensee: Legacy Communications LLC. (group owner). (acq 12-13-2007; grpsl). Population served: 125,000 Format: Classic rock, adult contemp. ♦Julie Marshal, gen mgr.

Gordon

KSDZ(FM)— May 19, 1979: 95.5 mhz; 60 kw. 310 ft TL: N42 47 56 W102 15 40. Stereo. Hrs open: 24 Box 390, W. Hwy. 20, 69343. Phone: (308) 282-2500. Fax: (308) 282-0061.E-mail: thetwister@ksdzfm.com Licensee: DJ Broadcasting Inc. (acq 12-26-91; 1-13-92). Population served: 35,000 Natl. Network: ABC, . Rgnl. Network: Mid-American Ag. Wire Svc: AP Format: C&W, oldies. Target aud: 25-54. ♦Jim Lambley, pres.

Grand Island

***KBTK(FM)**— 2009: 91.5 mhz; 1.5 kw. Ant 98 ft TL: N40 54 35 W98 23 00. Hrs open:
Rebroadcasts WLOG(FM) Markleysburg, PA 100%.
Box 5725, Twin Falls, ID, 83303. Phone: (208) 733-3551. Fax: (208) 734-0674.E-mail: connect@freedomradiofm.com Web Site:freedomradiofm.com Licensee: Edgewater Broadcasting Inc. (acq 12-5-2007; $45,000 for CP). ♦Clark Parrish, pres.

***KLNB(FM)**— 2005: 88.3 mhz; 1.7 kw. Ant 147 ft TL: N40 54 50 W98 23 52. Hrs open: 24 2351 Sunset Blvd., Suite 170-218, Rocklin, CA, 95765. Phone: (916) 251-1600. Fax: (916) 251-1650.E-mail: klove@klove.com Web Site:www.klove.com Licensee: Educational Media Foundation. Group owner: EMF Broadcasting (acq 3-11-2003; grpsl). Natl. Network: K-Love, . Shaw Pittman. Format: Contemp Christian. News staff: 3. Target aud: 25-44; Judeo Christian, female. ♦Richard Jenkins, pres; Mike Novak, VP; Keith Whipple, dev dir; David Pierce, progmg mgr; Ed Lenane, news dir; Sam Wallington, engrg dir; Karen Johnson, news rptr.

KMMJ(AM)— November 1925: 750 khz; 10 kw-U, DA-1. TL: N41 08 05 W97 59 38. Hrs open: Sunrise-sunset 3205 W. North Front St., 68802. Secondary address: Box 4907 68802. Phone: (308) 382-2800. Phone: (308) 381-1430. Fax: (308) 382-6701.E-mail: ausher@krgi.com Web Site:missionnebraska.org/thebridge/ Licensee: Mission Nebraska Inc. (group owner; (acq 5-1-2006; $825,000). Population served: 250,000 Format: Christian. ♦Alan Usher, VP, gen mgr; Jim Davis, progmg dir.

***KNFA(FM)**— 2008: 90.7 mhz; 250 w. Ant 161 ft TL: N40 54 50 W98 23 52. Hrs open: Box 262550, Baton Rouge, LA, 20826. Secondary address: 8919 World Ministry Ave., Baton Rouge 70810. Phone: (225) 768-3102. Fax: (225) 768-3729.E-mail: kawikfish@yahoo.com Web Site:www.jsm.org Licensee: Family Worship Center Church Inc. (acq 10-12-2006; grpsl). Format: Relg, Christian. ♦David Whitelaw, COO.

KRGI(AM)— Apr 1, 1953: 1430 khz; 5 kw-D, 1 kw-N, DA-N. TL: N40 62 26 W98 16 24. Hrs open: Box 4907, 68802-4907. Secondary address: 3205 W. N. Front St. 68803. Phone: (308) 381-1430. Fax: (308) 382-6701.E-mail: krgi@krgi.com Web Site:www.gifamilyradio.com/KRGI/krgi.htm Licensee: Legacy Communications LLC. (group owner; (acq 5-17-2004; grpsl). Population served: 135,000 Natl. Rep: Christal,. Fletcher, Heald & Hildreth. Format: Adult contemp, news/talk. Target aud: 25-54. ♦Alan Usher, gen mgr, gen sls mgr; Chris Loghry, opns dir, progmg dir; Rob Fossberg, news dir; Chuck Walker, chief of engrg; Alie Schlachter, traf mgr.

KRGI-FM— Oct 30, 1975: 96.5 mhz; 100 kw. 416 ft TL: N40 51 53 W98 23 47. Stereo. Hrs open: 24 Prog sep from AM Box 4907, 68802. Secondary address: 3205 W. N. Front St. 68803. Phone: (308) 381-1430. Fax: (308) 382-6701.E-mail: ausher@krgi.com Web Site:www.gifamilyradio.com/C96/C96.htm Natl. Network: ABC, . Format: Hot C&W. ♦Alie Schlachter, traf mgr.

***KROA(FM)**— Aug 11, 1967: 95.7 mhz; 100 kw. Ant 460 ft TL: N40 47 11 W98 22 00. Stereo. Hrs open: 24 Box 495, Doniphan, 68832.

Phone: (402) 845-6595. Fax: (402) 845-6597.E-mail: email@mybridgeradio.net Web Site:www.missionnebraska.org/thebridge Licensee: Mission Nebraska Inc. (acq 11-25-2003; $1.5 million). Population served: 250,000 Natl. Network: Moody, . Format: Adult contemp Christian. ♦Dr. James Eckman, pres; Gordon Wheeler, stn mgr; Taryn Julane, mus dir.

KSYZ-FM— November 1982: 107.7 mhz; 100 kw. 899 ft TL: N40 51 53 W98 23 47. (CP: TL: N40 42 07 W98 35 20). Stereo. Hrs open: 24 3532 W. Captial Ave., 68803. Secondary address: Box 5108 68802. Phone: (308) 381-1077. Fax: (308) 384-8900.E-mail: ksyzprod@nrgmedia.com Web Site:www.ksyz.com Licensee: NRG Media LLC. (acq 10-31-2005; $5.28 million). Format: Adult contemp. Target aud: 25-49; adults. ♦Tim Marshall, gen mgr; Jim Cartwright, opns mgr.

Hastings

***KCNT(FM)**— Feb 22, 1971: 88.1 mhz; 2 kw. 182 ft TL: N40 34 52 W98 19 58. Hrs open: 24 Box 1024, 68902. Phone: (402) 461-2580. Fax: (402) 461-2507.E-mail: jbrooks@cccneb.edu Web Site:www.cccneb.edu /programs/mart/kcnt/index.html Licensee: Central Community College. Population served: 23,580 Format: CHR, educ. ♦John L. Brooks, gen mgr.

***KFKX(FM)**—Not on air, target date: Sept 1, 2008: Stn currently dark. 90.1 mhz; Stereo. Hrs open: 710 Turner Hastings College, 68901. Phone: (402) 461-7367. Fax: (402) 461-7442.E-mail: kfkx@hastings.edu Licensee: Hastings College. Population served: 29,625 Booth, Freret, Imlay & Tepper. Wire Svc: AP Target aud: General. ♦Phillip Dudley, pres; Sharon Behl Brooks, gen mgr; Tyler Maffitt, stn mgr; Bart Jones, opns dir.

KHAS(AM)— Sept 30, 1940: 1230 khz; 1 kw-U. TL: N40 34 40 W98 24 17. Hrs open: 24 Box 726, 68902. Secondary address: 500 East J St. 68901. Phone: (402) 462-5101. Fax: (402) 461-3866.E-mail: khaskics@windstream.net Web Site:hastingslink.com Licensee: Platte River Radio Inc. (acq 2-1-2006; $560,000 with KICS(AM) Hastings). Population served: 130,000 Natl. Network: CBS, . Rgnl. Network: Brownfield. Brownfield Rgnl rep: Howard Anderson Miller & Neely. Wire Svc: AP Format: Adult contemp. News staff: one; News: 20 hrs wkly. Target aud: 35 plus; general. Spec prog: Farm 2 hrs, class 2 hrs wkly. ♦David Oldfather, pres; Wayne Specht, gen mgr; Jim Stevens, stn mgr, prom VP, progmg VP, progmg dir; Mike Smithson, news dir; Gwen Sheppard, traf mgr.

***KHNE-FM**— June 1990: 89.1 mhz; 64.3 kw. 328 ft TL: N40 46 17 W98 05 22. Stereo. Hrs open: 24
Rebroadcasts KUCV(FM) Lincoln 100%.
1800 N. 33rd St., Lincoln, 68503-1409. Phone: (402) 472-3611. Fax: (402) 472-2403.E-mail: radio@netnebraska.org Web Site:netnebraska.org/radio Licensee: Nebraska Educational Telecommunications Commission. Natl. Network: PRI, NPR, . Rgnl. Network: Neb. Pub. Nebraska Public Radio Format: Classical, news. News staff: 3; News: 38 hrs wkly. Target aud: General. ♦Nancy Finken, gen mgr, progmg dir; William Stibor, mus dir; Jeff Smith, traf mgr.

KICS(AM)— Apr 15, 1964: 1550 khz; 500 w-D. TL: N40 34 09 W98 21 57. Hrs open: 24 500 E. J St., 68901-7113. Phone: (402) 462-5101. Fax: (402) 461-3866.E-mail: khaskics@windstream.net Web Site:www.khasradio.com Licensee: Platte River Radio Inc. (acq 2-1-2006; $560,000 with KHAS(AM) Hastings). Population served: 23,580 Natl. Network: ESPN Radio, . Rgnl rep: Howard Anderson Miller & Miller. Format: Sports. News staff: one; News: 12 hrs wkly. Target aud: 18-54; males. ♦David Oldfather, pres; Wayne Specht, gen mgr; Jim Stevens, stn mgr.

KLIQ(FM)— 2001: 94.5 mhz; 97.7 kw. Ant 948 ft TL: N40 36 08 W98 50 21. Stereo. Hrs open: 24 PO Box 726, 68902. Phone: (402) 461-4922. Fax: (402) 461-3866.E-mail: thebreeze@kliqfm.com Web Site:www.kliqfm.com Licensee: Platte River Radio Inc. Group owner: Waitt Radio Inc. (acq 2-1-2006; $700,000). Population served: 100,000 Natl. Network: ABC, . Pepper & Corazzini. Wire Svc: AP Format: Adult contemp. News staff: one. Target aud: 25-54. Spec prog: News & special community interest. ♦Kevin Michaelson, news rptr; Jim Stevens, opns; Brad Beahm, progmg.

***KNHS(FM)**—Not on air, target date: unknown: 91.7 mhz; 1.3 kw. Ant 148 ft TL: N40 31 13 W98 22 10. Hrs open: Drawer 2440, Tupelo, MS, 38801. Phone: (662) 844-8888. Fax: (662) 842-6791. Web Site:www.afr.net Licensee: American Family Association. ♦Marvin Sanders, gen mgr.

KROR(FM)— February 1965: 101.5 mhz; 100 kw. Ant 1,004 ft TL: N40 39 28 W98 52 04. Stereo. Hrs open: 24 3532 W. Capital Ave., Grand Island, 68803. Phone: (308) 381-1077. Fax: (308) 384-8900.E-mail: ksyzprod@nrgmedia.com Web Site:www.rock1015.com Licensee: NRG License Sub LLC. (acq 1-31-2006; swap for KLIQ(FM) Hastings). Population served: 250,000 Format: Classic rock. Target aud: 25-54. ♦Tim Marshall, gen mgr; Jim Cartwright, opns mgr.

Hershey

KNPQ(FM)— 2008: 107.3 mhz; 25 kw. Ant 226 ft TL: N41 09 14 W100 46 22.4. Stereo. Hrs open: 24 Box 248, North Platte, 69103. Secondary address: 1301 E. 4th St., North Platte 69101. Phone: (308) 532-1120. Fax: (308) 532-0458.E-mail: chuck.schwartz@eagleradio.net Web Site:knpqcountry.com Licensee: Eagle Communications Inc. Population served: 40,000 Format: Country. News staff: one; News: news prgmg one hour wkly. Target aud: 18-44. ♦Gary Shorman, pres; Chuck Schwartz, gen mgr; Jerome Gilg, gen sls mgr; Kellie Vap, prom dir; David Fudge, progmg dir; Tony Cuesta, chief of engrg.

Holdrege

KMTY(FM)— October 1970: 97.7 mhz; 55 kw. Ant 253 ft TL: N40 26 26 W99 23 59. Stereo. Hrs open: 24 Box 465, 68949. Secondary address: 613 4th Ave. 68949. Phone: (308) 995-4020. Fax: (308) 995-2202. Web Site:kmtyfm.com Licensee: Armada Media-McCook Inc. (acq 5-16-2008; grpsl). Population served: 150,000 Natl. Network: ABC, . Format: Hot adult contemp. Target aud: 20-45. ♦Bryan Loker, gen mgr; Kris Shaver, gen sls mgr.

KUVR(AM)— Oct 20, 1956: 1380 khz; 500 w-D, 62 w-N. TL: N40 26 26 W99 24 00. Hrs open: Box 465, 68949. Secondary address: 613 4th Ave. 68949. Phone: (308) 995-4020. Fax: (308) 995-2202. Licensee: Armada Media-McCook Inc. (group owner; (acq 5-16-2008; grpsl). Population served: 5,635 Garvey Schubert Barer. Format: Oldies. Target aud: 35-54. Spec prog: Farm 5 hrs, big band 5 hrs, contemp gospel 5 hrs wkly. ♦John McDonald, gen mgr, progmg dir, news dir; Jim Conner, gen sls mgr; Randy Issler, mus dir, traf mgr; Val Lane, chief of engrg.

Hubbard

***KAYA(FM)**— 1998: 91.3 mhz; 5.1 kw. Ant 377 ft TL: N42 21 10 W96 31 32. Hrs open: Box 3206, Sioux City, MS, 38803. Secondary address: 1211 Tri-View, Sioux City, IA 51103. Phone: (662) 844-8888. Phone: (712) 255-9191. Fax: (662) 842-6791. Fax: (712) 255-3177.E-mail: comments@afr.net Web Site:www.afr.net Licensee: American Family Association. Group owner: American Family Radio Format: Christian inspirational, relg. ♦Marvin Sanders, gen mgr.

Humboldt

***KNHU(FM)**—Not on air, target date: unknown: 89.9 mhz; 6.3 kw. Ant 607 ft TL: N40 13 11 W95 39 55. Hrs open: Box 94, Stonewall, OK, 74872. Phone: (580) 265-9475. Licensee: Union Valley Baptist Church Inc. ♦Steve Vandegrift, gen mgr.

Hyannis

KNPE(FM)—Not on air, target date: unknown: 97.9 mhz; 100 kw. Ant 610 ft TL: N42 01 28 W102 00 22. Hrs open: 5833 Paradise Cir., Naples, FL, 34110. Licensee: In Phase Broadcasting Inc. ♦Peter L. Cea, pres.

Imperial

KADL(FM)— 2003: 102.9 mhz; 300 w. Ant 223 ft TL: N40 30 45 W101 38 39. Hrs open: Box 333, McCook, 69001. Secondary address: 824 Douglas St. 69033. Phone: (308) 345-5400. Phone: (308) 882-4209. Fax: (308) 345-4720. Fax: (308) 882-4319.E-mail: bryan@highplainsradio.net Web Site:www.kadlimperial.com Licensee: Armada Media - McCook Inc. (acq 1-17-2007; grpsl). Format: Oldies. ♦Bryan Loker, gen mgr.

Kearney

KGFW(AM)— 1927: 1340 khz; 1 kw-U. TL: N40 40 05 W99 04 52. Hrs open: 24 Box 666, 68848. Secondary address: 2223 Central Ave. 68847. Phone: (308) 698-2131. Fax: (308) 237-0312.E-mail: mail@kgfw.com Web Site:www.kgfw.com Licensee: NRG License Sub. LLC. Group owner: Waitt Radio Inc. (acq 10-31-2005; grpsl). Population served: 100,000 Natl. Network: Westwood One, . Rgnl. Network: Brownfield. Natl. Rep: Christal,. Brownfield Wire Svc: AP Format: News/talk. News staff: 2; News: 25 hrs wkly. Target aud: 25 plus; adults in central Nebraska. Spec prog: Farm 8 hrs, sports 10 hrs wkly. ♦Mary Quass, pres; John McDonald, gen mgr.

KKPR-FM— Nov 1, 1962: 98.9 mhz; 100 kw. Ant 700 ft TL: N40 48 53 W98 46 12. Stereo. Hrs open: 24 Prog sep from AM Box 130 , 68848. Phone: (308) 236-9900. Fax: (308) 234-6781.E-mail: generalmanager@kkpr.com Web Site:www.kkpr.com Format: Oldies. News staff: one; News: 3 hrs wkly. Target aud: 35-64. ♦Dan Beck, chief of opns; Johnnie McCann, gen sls mgr.

***KLPR(FM)**— Mar 8, 1968: 91.3 mhz; 1 kw. 100 ft TL: N40 42 30 W99 05 45. Stereo. Hrs open: 6 AM-midnight Univ. of Nebraska at Kearney, 905 West 25th Street, 68849. Phone: (308) 865-8217. Phone: (308) 865-8737. Web Site://klpr.unk.edu Licensee: University of Nebraska at Kearney. Population served: 30,000 Format: Jazz, new age, AOR. Spec prog: Class 18 hrs wkly. ♦Roy Hyatte, gen mgr.

KQKY(FM)— October 1979: 105.9 mhz; 97.6 kw. Ant 1,204 ft TL: N40 36 08 W98 50 21. Stereo. Hrs open: 24 Box 666, 68848. Secondary address: 2223 Central Ave. 68847. Phone: (308) 698-2100. Fax: (308) 237-0312. Web Site:www.kqky.com Licensee: NRG License Sub. LLC. Population served: 200,000 Natl. Network: Fox News Radio, Superadio, . Natl. Rep: Christal,. Wire Svc: AP Format: Top-40. Target aud: 18-49. ♦Mary Quass, pres; John McDonald, gen mgr.

KRNY(FM)— 1987: 102.3 mhz; 77.1 kw. Ant 1,086 ft TL: N40 36 08 W98 50 21. Stereo. Hrs open: 24 Box 666, 68848. Secondary address: 2223 Central Ave. 68847. Phone: (308) 698-2100. Fax: (308) 237-0312. Web Site:www.krny.com Licensee: NRG License Sub. LLC. Group owner: Waitt Radio Inc. (acq 10-31-2005; grpsl). Population served: 200,000 Natl. Network: Fox News Radio, Premiere Radio Networks, . Natl. Rep: Christal,. Haley, Bader & Potts. Wire Svc: AP Format: Hot country. News: 2 hrs wkly. Target aud: 25 plus. ♦Mary Quass, pres; John McDonald, gen mgr.

KXPN(AM)— Dec 5, 1956: 1460 khz; 5 kw-D, 56 w-N. TL: N40 42 45 W99 10 15. Hrs open: 24 Box 130, 68848. Secondary address: 403 E. 25th St. 68848. Phone: (308) 236-9900. Fax: (308) 234-6781.E-mail: espn1460@charter.net Web Site:www.espnsuperstation.com Licensee: Platte River Radio Inc. (acq 1-1-94; $750,000 with co-located FM;12-13-93). Natl. Network: ESPN Radio, . Format: Sports. News staff: one; News: 2 hrs wkly. Target aud: 25-54; men. ♦David Oldfather, pres; Craig Eckert, gen mgr; Dan Beck, opns mgr, progmg dir.

Kimball

***KGCQ(FM)**—Not on air, target date: unknown: 88.3 mhz; 510 w. Ant 282 ft TL: N41 11 36 W103 31 45. Hrs open: 6139 Franklin Park Rd., McLean, VA, 22101-4214. Phone: (703) 761-5013. Licensee: Ocean Side Broadcasting Inc. ♦A. Wray Fitch III, pres.

KIMB(AM)— 1958: Stn currently dark. 1260 khz; 1 kw-D, 112 w-N. TL: N41 15 42 W103 40 06. (CP: COL Ogallala. 50 kw-D, 110 w-N. TL: N41 04 30 W101 45 24). Hrs open: Box 472, Fort Morgan, CO, 80701. Phone: (970) 867-7271. Fax: (970) 867-2676. Licensee: Sterling Radio LLC. (group owner; (acq 8-29-2008; $50,000). Population served: 30,000 Target aud: General. ♦Alec C. Creighton, gen mgr.

KYOY(FM)— 1999: 100.1 mhz; 6 kw. Ant 328 ft TL: N41 11 36 W103 31 45. (CP: 26 kw horiz, ant 223 ft). Stereo. Hrs open: 24 Box 532, Scottsbluff, 69363-0532. Phone: (308) 632-5667. Fax: (308) 635-1905. Licensee: Kimball Radio LLC. (group owner). (acq 4-2-2007; $300,000 with KIMB(AM) Kimball). Population served: 125,000 Natl. Network: AP Radio, . Format: Oldies. News staff: 2. ♦Larry Swikard, gen mgr.

Lexington

***KLNE-FM**— May 4, 1990: 88.7 mhz; 43.8 kw. 938 ft TL: N40 23 05 W99 27 30. Stereo. Hrs open: 24
Rebroadcasts KUCV(FM) Lincoln 100%.
1800 N. 33rd St., Lincoln, 68503-1409. Phone: (402) 472-3611. Fax: (402) 472-2403.E-mail: radio@netnebraska.org Web Site:netnebraska.org/radio Licensee: Nebraska Educational Telecommunications Commission. Natl. Network: PRI, NPR, . Rgnl. Network: Neb. Pub. Nebraska Public Radio Format: Classical, news & info. News staff: 3; News: 38 hrs wkly. General. ♦Nancy Finken, gen mgr, progmg dir; William Stibor, mus dir; Jeff Smith, traf mgr.

KRVN(AM)— Feb 1, 1951: 880 khz; 50 kw-U, DA-N. TL: N40 31 03 W99 23 20. Hrs open: 24 Box 880, 1007 Plum Creek Pkwy., 68850-0880. Phone: (308) 324-2371. Fax: (308) 324-5786.E-mail: krvnam@krvn.com Web Site:www.krvn.com Licensee: Nebraska Rural Radio Assn. (group owner) (acq 2-1-51). Natl. Network: Fox News Radio, . Natl. Rep: Katz Radio,. Garvey Schubert & Barer. Wire Svc: AP Format: Country, news, farm. News staff: 4; News: 30 hrs wkly. Target aud: General; Nebraska farm/ranch families & consumers. Spec prog: Relg 12 hrs wkly. ♦Eric Brown, gen mgr; Ed Bennett, opns mgr; Dennis Waddle, gen sls mgr; Pam Snyder, prom dir, spec ev

coord; Stafford Thompson, progmg dir; Frank Snyder, news dir; Rod Zeigler, engrg dir; Mike LePorte, farm dir.

KRVN-FM— Nov 1, 1962: 93.1 mhz; 100 kw. 890 ft TL: N40 41 48 W99 47 18. Stereo. Hrs open: 24 Dups AM 50% Box 880, 1007 Plum Creek Pkwy., 68850. Phone: (308) 324-2371. Fax: (308) 324-5786. Web Site:www.krvnfm.com Population served: 125,000 Natl. Network: Fox News Radio, . Natl. Rep: Katz Radio,. Format: News, new country. News staff: one; News: 20 wkly. Contemp young adults. Spec prog: Farm 10 hrs wkly. ♦Eric Brown, gen mgr; Ed Bennett, opns mgr; Dennis Waddle, gen sls mgr; Pam Snyder, prom dir; Stafford Thompson, progmg dir; Frank Snyder, news dir; Rod Zeigler, engrg dir; Mike LePorte, farm dir.

Lincoln

KBBK(FM)— Sept 1, 1968: 107.3 mhz; 100 kw. Ant 551 ft TL: N40 43 38 W96 36 49. Stereo. Hrs open: 24 4343 O St., 68510. Phone: (402) 475-4567. Fax: (402) 479-1411.E-mail: news@broadcasthouse.com Web Site:www.b1073.com Licensee: NRG License Sub. LLC. (acq 12-28-2007; grpsl). Population served: 330000 Format: Adult contemp. Target aud: 25-54; middle-to-upper income, households, in-office & in-store lstng. ♦T. Pat Miller, progmg dir.

KFOR(AM)— Mar 4, 1924: 1240 khz; 1 kw-U. TL: N40 49 12 W96 39 29. Hrs open: 24 3800 Cornhusker Hwy., 68504-1533. Phone: (402) 466-1234. Fax: (402) 467-4095.E-mail: kfor@threeeagles.com Web Site:www.kfor1240.com Licensee: Coloff Broadcasting. (acq 1996; $5.3 million with co-located FM). Population served: 239,000 Format: News/talk. News staff: 6; News: 20 hrs wkly. Target aud: 25-54. ♦Roland Johnson, CEO; Gary Buchanan, COO; Cindy Harris, CFO; James Keck, stn mgr; Joy Patton, sls dir; Mark Taylor, progmg dir; Dale Johnson, news dir.

KFRX(FM)— Feb 23, 1973: 106.3 mhz; 100 kw. Ant 702 ft TL: N40 43 40 W96 36 50. Stereo. Hrs open: 24 3800 Cornhusker Hwy., 68504-1533. Phone: (402) 466-1234. Fax: (402) 467-4095. Web Site:www.kfrxfm.com Licensee: Three Eagles of Lincoln Inc. Group owner: Clear Channel Communications Inc. (acq 4-10-2007; grpsl). Population served: 172,400 Format: CHR. ♦James Keck, gen mgr.

***KLCV(FM)**— 1996: 88.5 mhz; 4.7 kw vert. Ant 315 ft TL: N40 55 49 W96 32 42. Hrs open: 8 AM-5 PM (M-F) 233 S. 13th St., Suite 1520, 68508. Phone: (402) 465-8850. Fax: (402) 465-8852.E-mail: klcv@bottradionetwork.com Licensee: Community Broadcasting Inc. Population served: 700,000 Natl. Network: USA, . Format: Christian talk. Target aud: 25 plus; Christian families. ♦Richard Bott Sr., pres; Tom Millett, gen mgr.

KLIN(AM)— August 1947: 1400 khz; 1 kw-U. TL: N40 50 54 W96 40 29. Hrs open: 24 4343 O St., 68510. Phone: (402) 475-4567. Fax: (402) 479-1411.E-mail: news@broadcasthouse.com Web Site:www.klin.com Licensee: NRG License Sub. LLC. Group owner: Triad Broadcasting Co. LLC (acq 12-28-2007; grpsl). Population served: 200,000 Natl. Network: Fox News Radio, . Format: News/talk. News staff: 4; News: 80 hrs wkly. Target aud: 35-64; upper income, business owner, educated with high disposable income. ♦Mark Halverson, gen mgr; John Bishop, progmg dir; Greg Jackson, news dir, pub affrs dir; Bill Frost, chief of engrg.

KLMS(AM)— October 1949: 1480 khz; 5 kw-D, 1 kw-N, DA-2. TL: N40 47 47 W96 34 56. Stereo. Hrs open: 3800 Cornhusker Hwy., 68504. Phone: (402) 466-1234. Fax: (402) 467-4095. Web Site:www.espn1480.com Licensee: Coloff Broadcasting. (acq 1996; grpsl). Population served: 222,900 Format: Sports. ♦Roland Johnson, CEO; Gary Buchanan, COO; Cindy Harris, CFO; Mark Taylor, opns mgr; Vicki Marker, prom dir; Bill Doleman, progmg dir; Bob Cook, chief of engrg; Terri Hutchinson, traf mgr; Dale Johnson, local news ed.

KLNC(FM)— 1992: 105.3 mhz; 3 kw. Ant 328 ft TL: N40 49 12 W96 39 29. Hrs open: 4343 O St., 68510. Phone: (402) 475-4567. Fax: (402) 479-1411.E-mail: news@broadcasthouse.com Web Site:1053wow.com Licensee: NRG License Sub. LLC. Group owner: Triad Broadcasting Co. LLC (acq 12-28-2007; grpsl). Format: Oldies. ♦Mark Halverson, VP, gen mgr; J. Pat Miller, opns mgr; Ami Graham, gen sls mgr; E.J. Marshall, progmg dir; Steve Looney, chief of engrg.

KOOO(FM)— June 22, 1958: 101.9 mhz; 100 kw. Ant 1,132 ft TL: N40 47 09 W96 23 07. Stereo. Hrs open: 24 5011 Capitol Ave., Omaha, 68132. Phone: (402) 342-2000. Fax: (402) 346-5748.E-mail: info@thebigo1019.com Web Site:thebigo1019.com Licensee: Waitt Omaha LLC. (group owner; (acq 1-7-2002; grpsl). Population served: 2,120,000 Natl. Rep: Katz Radio,. Format: Adult contemp. Target aud: 25-54; general. ♦Rhonda Gerrard, gen mgr; Mark Todd, opns mgr; Sam Coughlin, sls dir; Chris Pflaum, prom dir; Billy Shears, progmg dir; Cynthia Wallace, traf mgr.

***KRNU(FM)**— Feb 23, 1970: 90.3 mhz; 100 w. Ant 180 ft TL: N40 49 11 W96 42 11. Stereo. Hrs open: 24 147 Anderson Hall, Univ. of Nebraska, 68588-0466. Phone: (402) 472-3054. Fax: (402) 472-8403.E-mail: krnu@unl.edu Web Site:www.krnu.unl.edu Licensee: University of Nebraska. Population served: 200,000 Natl. Network: ABC, . Dow, Lohnes & Albertson. Format: Alternative. News: 5 hrs wkly. Spec prog: Hip-hop 2 hrs, electronic 4 hrs, gospel 2 hrs, jazz 2 hrs, sports-talk 4 hrs, A Capella 2 hrs wkly. ♦Rick Alloway, gen mgr, opns mgr, gen sls mgr, progmg dir; Barney McCoy, news dir; Vance Payne, chief of engrg. Co-owned TV: *KUON-TV affil.

KTGL(FM)—(Beatrice, Nov 26, 1962: 92.9 mhz; 100 kw. Ant 809 ft TL: N40 31 06 W96 46 07. Stereo. Hrs open: 24 3800 Cornhusker Hwy., 68504. Phone: (402) 466-1234. Fax: (402) 467-4095. Web Site:www.ktgl.com Licensee: Three Eagles of Lincoln Inc. Group owner: Clear Channel Communications Inc. (acq 4-10-2007; grpsl). Population served: 210,000 Format: Classic rock. News staff: one; News: 3 hrs wkly. Target aud: 18-49. ♦James Keck, gen mgr.

***KUCV(FM)**— Jan 1, 1968: 91.1 mhz; 19.5 kw horiz, 100 kw vert. Ant 689 ft TL: N40 31 06 W96 46 06. Stereo. Hrs open: 24 1800 N. 33rd St., 68503-1409. Phone: (402) 472-3611. Fax: (402) 472-2403.E-mail: radio@netnebraska.org Web Site:netnebraska.org/radio Licensee: Nebraska Educational Telecommunications Commission. (acq 8-88). Population served: 1,100,000 Natl. Network: NPR, PRI, . Rgnl. Network: Neb. Pub. Nebraska Public Radio Format: Classical, news. News staff: 3; News: 38 hrs wkly. Target aud: General. ♦Ray Dilley, gen mgr; Nancy Finken, progmg dir; Bill Stibor, mus dir; Jeff Smith, traf mgr.

KVSS(FM)— May 2, 1965: 102.7 mhz; 100 kw. Ant 430 ft TL: N40 49 12 W96 39 29. (CP: COL Papillion. 46.1 kw, ant 1,343 ft. TL: N41 04 15.9 W96 13 31.2). Stereo. Hrs open: 5829 N. 60th St., Omaha, 68104. Phone: (402) 571-0200. Fax: (402) 571-0833. Web Site:www.kvss.com Licensee: VSS Catholic Communications Inc. Group owner: Three Eagles Communications (acq 1-29-2009; $4.5 nillion). Population served: 239,000 Format: Catholic. ♦John Soukup, stn mgr.

KZKX(FM)—See Seward

***KZUM(FM)**— 1978: 89.3 mhz; 1.5 kw. 174 ft TL: N40 48 47 W96 42 24. Stereo. Hrs open: 6 AM-2 AM 941 O St., Suite 1025, 68508-3608. Phone: (402) 474-5086. Fax: (402) 474-5091.E-mail: kzumradio@aol.com Web Site:www.kzum.org Licensee: Sunrise Communications Inc. Format: Div, jazz, urban contemp. News: 11 hrs wkly. Target aud: General; the unserved & underserved population. Spec prog: Sp 4 hrs, rock/progsv 15 hrs, new age 8 hrs, blues 13 hrs, folk 8 hrs, gospel 3 hrs wkly. ♦Jayne Sebby, gen mgr; Jesse Starita, progmg dir.

Loup City

***KSRC(FM)**—Not on air, target date: unknown: 88.1 mhz; 40 kw vert. Ant 289 ft TL: N41 00 16 W99 14 19. Hrs open: 5210 S.E. Washington Blvd., Bartlesville, OK, 74006. Phone: (918) 333-8700. Licensee: Pearl Communications Group. ♦Danny Hester, pres.

Maxwell

KHAQ(FM)— 2000: 98.5 mhz; 85 kw. Ant 371 ft TL: N41 12 49 W100 43 49. Hrs open: 24 Box 333, McCook, 69001. Secondary address: 1811 W. O St., McCook 69001. Phone: (308) 345-5400. Fax: (308) 345-4720.E-mail: bryan@highplainsradio.net Web Site:www.kicx.net Licensee: Armada Media - McCook Inc. (group owner; (acq 3-31-2007; grpsl). Population served: 40,000 Format: Classic rock. Target aud: 18-54. ♦Bryan Loker, gen mgr, gen sls mgr; Clint Bradbury, opns mgr; Rich Barnett, news dir.

McCook

KBRL(AM)— Sept 26, 1947: 1300 khz; 5 kw-D, DA. TL: N40 11 31 W100 39 06. Hrs open: Box 333, 69001. Secondary address: 1811 W. O St. 699001. Phone: (308) 345-5400. Fax: (308) 345-4720.E-mail: bryan@highplainsradio.net Web Site:www.kicx.net Licensee: Armada Media - McCook Inc. (group owner; (acq 3-31-2007; grpsl). Population served: 40,000 Format: Oldies, full service. Target aud: 35-64. ♦Bryan Loker, gen mgr, gen sls mgr; Clint Bradbury, opns mgr, adv dir; Rich Barnett, news dir; Ron Fritz, chief of engrg.

KICX-FM— Jan 31, 1979: 96.1 mhz; 55 kw. Ant 318 ft TL: N40 10 19 W100 41 05. Stereo. Hrs open: 24 Box 333, 69001. Phone: (308) 345-5400. Fax: (308) 345-4720.E-mail: bryan@highplainsradio.net Web Site:www.kicx.net Licensee: Armada Media - McCook Inc. (acq 3-31-2007; grpsl). Population served: 40,000 Natl. Network: ABC, . Format: Adult contemp. News staff: one. Target aud: 25-64. ♦Bryan Loker, gen mgr, gen sls mgr; Clint Bradbury, opns mgr.

KIOD(FM)— May 1, 1981: 105.3 mhz; 100 kw. Ant 591 ft TL: N40 11 27 W100 48 29. Stereo. Hrs open: 24 Box 939, 69001. Secondary address: 106 W. 8th St. 69001. Phone: (308) 345-1981. Fax: (308) 345-7202.E-mail: info@hometownfamilyradio.com Web Site:mccookfamilyradio.gifamilyradio.com/Coyote_Country/coyote.htm Licensee: Legacy Communications LLC. (acq 10-13-2005; $1.3 million with KSWN(FM) McCook). Population served: 40,000 Rgnl. Network: Agri-Net. Larry D. Perry. Format: Hot country. News staff: one; News: 5 hrs wkly. Target aud: 25-54. Spec prog: Sports 10 hrs, farm 6 hrs wkly. ♦Alan Usher, gen mgr; Jesse Stevens, progmg dir & progmg mgr; Derek Beck, mus dir; Ann Doyle, traf mgr.

KNAX(AM)—Not on air, target date: unknown: 700 khz; 250 w-U, DA-N. TL: N40 16 00 W100 34 09. Hrs open: Box 333, 69001. Phone: (308) 345-5400. Fax: (308) 345-4720. Licensee: McCook Radio Group L.L.C. (group owner). ♦David Stout, gen mgr, opns mgr; Connie Stout, gen sls mgr; Rich Barnett, news dir.

***KNGN(AM)**— June 23, 1961: 1360 khz; 1 kw-D. TL: N40 11 45 W100 41 57. Hrs open: 6 AM-2 hrs past sunset 38005 Road 717, 69001-7217. Phone: (308) 345-2006. Fax: (308) 345-2052.E-mail: goodnews@mccooknet.com Web Site:www.kngn.org Licensee: Kansas Nebraska Good News Broadcasting Corp. (acq 9-5-01). Format: Relg. News: 7 hrs wkly. Target aud: 35 plus; family oriented. ♦Greg Stuekwiseh, pres; Mike Nielsen, gen mgr.

KQHK(FM)— 2008: 103.9 mhz; 50 kw. Ant 371 ft TL: N40 10 19 W100 41 05. Hrs open: Box 333, 69001. Phone: (308) 345-5400. Fax: (308) 345-4720. Web Site:www.kicx.net Licensee: Armada Media - McCook Inc. (acq 3-31-2007; grpsl). Format: Classic rock. ♦Bryan Loker, gen mgr.

KSWN(FM)— Sept 17, 1998: 93.9 mhz; 50 kw. Ant 492 ft TL: N40 11 27 W100 48 29. Stereo. Hrs open: 24 Box 939, 106 W. 8th St., 69001-0218. Phone: (308) 345-1100. Fax: (308) 345-7202.E-mail: jay@coyote105.com Web Site:mccookfamilyradio.gifamilyradio.com/us939.htm Licensee: Legacy Communications LLC. (acq 10-13-2005; $1.3 million with KIOD(FM) McCook). Population served: 72,000 Natl. Network: ESPN Radio, . Larry D. Perry. Format: Adult contemp, sports. Target aud: 25-54. ♦Jay D. Austin, gen mgr; Eileen G. Austin, opns VP; Jay Austin, gen sls mgr; Jesse Stevens, progmg mgr.

KZMC(FM)— Oct 25, 2006: 102.1 mhz; 100 kw. Ant 590 ft TL: N40 11 27 W100 48 29. Hrs open: Box 939, 69001-0939. Secondary address: 106 W. 8th St. 69001-3508. Phone: (308) 345-1981. Fax: (308) 345-7202.E-mail: info@hometownfamilyradio.com Web Site:www.hometownfamilyradio.com/Z/index.php Licensee: Legacy Communications LLC. Format: Rock. ♦Alan Usher, VP, gen mgr; Jesse Stevens, opns mgr.

Merriman

***KRNE-FM**— Aug 29, 1991: 91.5 mhz; 92 kw. 964 ft TL: N42 40 38 W101 42 36. Stereo. Hrs open: 24
Rebroadcasts KUCV(FM) Lincoln 100%.
1800 N. 33rd St., Lincoln, 68503-1409. Phone: (402) 472-3611. Fax: (402) 472-2403.E-mail: radio@netnebraska.org Web Site:netnebraska.org/radio Licensee: Nebraska Educational Telecommunications Commission. Natl. Network: NPR, PRI, . Format: Classical, news. News staff: 3; News: 38 hrs wkly. Target aud: General. ♦Nancy Finken, gen mgr & progmg dir; Bill Stibor, mus dir; Jeff Smith, traf mgr.

Milford

KFGE(FM)— 1996: 98.1 mhz; 100 kw. 981 ft TL: N40 51 52 W97 16 14. Hrs open: 4343 O St., Lincoln, 68510. Phone: (402) 475-4567. Fax: (402) 479-1411.E-mail: news@broadcasthouse.com Web Site:www.froggy981.com Licensee: NRG License Sub. LLC. Group owner: Triad Broadcasting Co. LLC (acq 12-28-2007; grpsl). Format: Country. ♦Mark Halverson, VP, gen mgr; J. Pat Miller, opns mgr; Ami Graham, gen sls mgr; Steve Albertson, progmg dir; Steve Looney, chief of engrg.

Minatare

KHYY(FM)— 2008: 106.9 mhz; 50 kw. Ant 474 ft TL: N41 54 28 W103 28 34. Hrs open: Box 1263, Scottsbluff, 69361-1263. Secondary address: 2002 Char Ave., Scottsbluff 69361. Phone: (308) 632-5667. Fax: (308) 635-1905. Licensee: Legacy Communications LLC. (acq 2-19-2008; $200,000 with KETT(FM) Mitchell). Format: Country. ♦Julie Marshall, gen mgr.

Mitchell

KETT(FM)— 2008: 99.3 mhz; 50 kw. Ant 474 ft TL: N41 54 28 W103 28 34. Hrs open: Box 1263, Scottsbluff, 69361-1263. Secondary address: 2002 Char Ave., Scottsbluff 69361. Phone: (308) 632-5667. Fax: (308) 635-1905. Licensee: Legacy Communications LLC. (acq 2-19-2008; $200,000 with KHYY(FM) Minatare). Format: Rock. ♦Julie Marshall, gen mgr.

Nebraska City

KBBX-FM— Feb 1, 1995: 97.7 mhz; 100 kw. 981 ft TL: N40 53 31 W96 09 10. Hrs open: 24 5030 N. 72nd St., Omaha, 68134. Phone: (402) 592-5300. Fax: (402) 592-6605.E-mail: info@z92.com Licensee: Connoisseur Media of Omaha LLC. Group owner: Journal Broadcast Group Inc. (acq 9-25-2006; $7.5 million). Population served: 942,906 Natl. Network: ABC, . Rgnl. Network: S.W. Agri-Radio. Southwest Agri-Radio Rosenman & Colin. Format: Sp. Target aud: 25-54. ♦Steve Wexler, gen mgr; Tom Land, opns dir; Jim Timm, gen sls mgr; RosAnna Salcido, mktg mgr; Kurt Owens, progmg dir; Bill Jensen, news dir.

KNCY(AM)— June 29, 1959: 1600 khz; 500 w-D, 31 w-N, DA-2. TL: N40 40 27 W95 53 08. Hrs open: 24 Box 278, 814 Central Ave., 68410. Phone: (402) 873-3348. Fax: (402) 873-7882.E-mail: kncy@kncycountry.com Web Site:www.kncycountry.com Licensee: Riverfront Broadcasting LLC (acq 8-31-2007; with KNCY-FM Auburn). Population served: 400,000 Natl. Network: ABC, . Format: Variety. News staff: 2; News: 21 hrs wkly. Target aud: 18-80; local residents, farmers, business owners, workers, students. Spec prog: Farm 3 hrs, sports 6 hrs wkly. ♦Chris Yates, gen sls mgr; Scott Kooistra, gen mgr & news dir.

Norfolk

KEXL(FM)— Aug 1, 1971: 106.7 mhz; 100 kw. Ant 1,027 ft TL: N41 55 59 W97 40 49. Stereo. Hrs open: 24 Box 789, 68702. Secondary address: 309 Braasch Ave. 68701. Phone: (402) 371-0780. Fax: (402) 371-6303.E-mail: bhughes@kexl.com Web Site:www.kexl.com Licensee: WJAG Inc. Population served: 100,000 Natl. Network: Fox News Radio, Westwood One, . Wire Svc: AP Format: Adult contemp. News staff: 2; News: 6 hrs wkly. Target aud: 18-49; full service FM adults. ♦Bradley Hughes, VP, gen mgr; Jeffrey Steffen, opns mgr; Sally Lewis, gen sls mgr; Michael Nissen, mus dir; Jim Curry, news dir; Denise Reikofski, traf mgr; Susan Risinger, farm dir; Joe Tjaden, sports cmtr.

KNEN(FM)— Apr 6, 1979: 94.7 mhz; 100 kw. Ant 539 ft TL: N41 55 28 W97 36 22. Stereo. Hrs open: 214 N. 7th St., 68701. Phone: (402) 371-0100. Fax: (402) 371-0050. Web Site:www.knenfm.com Licensee: Red Beacon Communications LLC. (acq 2-5-2008; grpsl). Population served: 150,000 Format: Classic rock. News staff: 2; News: 15 hrs wkly. Target aud: 25-54; young to middle-aged. Spec prog: Farm 10 hrs wkly. ♦Andy Stenger, gen mgr.

***KPNO(FM)**— Sept 23, 1992: 90.9 mhz; 50 kw. 351 ft TL: N42 06 16 W97 20 11. Stereo. Hrs open: 24 109 S. 2nd St., 68701-5327. Phone: (402) 379-3677. Fax: (402) 379-3662.E-mail: kpnofm@kpno.org Web Site:www.kpno.org Licensee: The Praise Network Inc. Population served: 200,000 Natl. Network: Moody, USA, . Format: Relg, inspirational. News: 14 hrs wkly. Target aud: 25-54; family-oriented adults. ♦Herb Roszhart Jr., CEO; Jon Shipman, gen mgr; Brian Gall, stn mgr.

***KSTJ(FM)**—Not on air, target date: unknown: 91.7 mhz; 8 kw. Ant 454 ft TL: N42 04 54 W97 48 55. Hrs open: Box 159, Rural Hall, NC, 27045. Phone: (605) 868-0525. Licensee: Church Planters of America. ♦Danny Hawkins, pres & gen mgr.

***KXNE-FM**— May 29, 1990: 89.3 mhz; 42.3 kw. 984 ft TL: N42 14 15 W97 16 41. Hrs open: 24
Rebroadcasts KUCV(FM) Lincoln 100%.
1800 N. 33rd St., Lincoln, 68503-1409. Phone: (402) 472-3611. Fax: (402) 472-2403.E-mail: radio@netnebraska.org Web Site:netnebraska.org/radio Licensee: Nebraska Educational Telecommunications Commission. Natl. Network: PRI, NPR, . Nebraska Public Radio Format: Classical, news. News staff: 3; News: 38 hrs wkly. Target aud: General. ♦Nancy Finken, gen mgr, progmg dir; William Stibor, mus dir; Jeff Smith, traf mgr.

WJAG(AM)— July 27, 1922: 780 khz; 1 kw-U (L-WBBM). TL: N42 01 54 W97 29 47. Stereo. Hrs open: Sunrise-sunset Box 789, 68702. Secondary address: 309 Braasch Ave. 68701. Phone: (402) 371-0780. Fax: (402) 371-6303.E-mail: bhughes@wjag.com Web Site:www.wjag.com Licensee: WJAG Inc. Population served: 40,000 Natl. Network: ABC, ESPN Radio, . Fletcher, Heald & Hildreth. Wire Svc: AP Format: News/talk/sports. News staff: 2; News: 10 hrs wkly. Target aud: 35-64; info-oriented. ♦Bradley Hughes, VP, gen mgr, sls dir, mktg dir; Jeffrey Steffen, opns mgr; Sally Lewis, gen sls mgr, progmg dir; Stephanie Hoff, prom dir; Michael Nissen, mus dir; Jim Curry, news dir; Susan Risinger, farm dir; Joe Tjaden, sports cmtr.

North Platte

KELN(FM)— February 1979: 97.1 mhz; 100 kw. 458 ft TL: N41 14 20 W100 41 43. Stereo. Hrs open: 24 Prog sep from AM Box 248, 69103. Secondary address: 1301 E. 4th St. 69103. Phone: (308) 532-1120. Fax: (308) 532-0458. Web Site:mix97one.com Licensee: Eagle Communications Inc. (acq 1982). Population served: 40,000 Wire Svc: AP Format: Adult contemp. News staff: one; News: one hr wkly. Target aud: 21-44; Young adults. ♦Gary Shorman, pres; Chuck Schwartz, gen mgr; Jerome Gilg, gen sls mgr; David Fudge, progmg dir; Tony Cuesta, engr.

***KJLT(AM)**— July 1, 1957: 970 khz; 5 kw-D, 55 w-N. TL: N41 09 30 W100 52 36. (CP: TL: N41 09 36 W100 52 42). Hrs open: Sunrise-sunset Box 709, 69103. Secondary address: 201 S. Bailey Ave. 69101. Phone: (308) 532-5515.E-mail: kjlt@kjlt.org Web Site:www.kjlt.org Licensee: Tri-State Broadcasting Assn. Inc. (acq 7-1-57). Population served: 100,000 Natl. Network: Moody, Salem Radio Network, . Wire Svc: NOAA Weather Wire Svc: AP Format: Christian educ. Target aud: General; families. Spec prog: Sp one hr wkly. ♦John L. Townsend, pres, gen mgr & progmg dir; Gary Hofer, chief of engrg.

***KJLT-FM**— Sept 24, 1979: 94.9 mhz; 100 kw. Ant 652 ft TL: N40 59 49 W100 52 47. Stereo. Hrs open: 24 Box 709, 69103. Secondary address: 201 S. Bailey Ave. 69101. Phone: (308) 532-5515. Web Site:www.kjlt.org Licensee: Tri-State Broadcasting Assn. Inc. (acq 3-22-90; $85,000; 4-16-90). Natl. Network: Moody, Salem Radio Network, . Wire Svc: AP Format: Inspirational, gospel, adult contemp. Target aud: General; young adults.

KODY(AM)— July 5, 1930: 1240 khz; 1 kw-U. TL: N41 09 14 W100 46 23. Hrs open: 305 E. Fourth St., 69101. Phone: (308) 532-3344. Fax: (308) 534-6651.E-mail: info@kodyradio.com Web Site:www.kodyradio.com Licensee: Armada Media-McCook Inc. Group owner: Waitt Radio Inc. (acq 5-16-2008; grpsl). Population served: 38,000 Natl. Network: CBS, Moody, Westwood One, . Natl. Rep: Katz Radio,. Format: News/talk. Target aud: 25 plus; middle to upper income. ♦Rob Mandeville, gen mgr; Rob Mandeville, gen sls mgr; George Keltz, news dir; Tony Lama, opns mgr, progmg dir & chief of engrg; Lisa Arent, traf mgr.

KOOQ(AM)— January 1966: 1410 khz; 5 kw-D, 1 kw-N, DA-N. TL: N41 10 30 W100 45 07. Hrs open: 24 Box 248, 69103. Secondary address: 1301 E. 4th St. 69103. Phone: (308) 532-1120. Fax: (308) 532-0458.E-mail: chuck.schwartz@eagleradio.net Web Site:1410amespn.com Licensee: Eagle Communications Inc. Group owner: Eagle Communications Group. Population served: 40,000 Natl. Network: ESPN Radio, . Format: Sports. News staff: one; News: news prmrg one hour/week. Target aud: 18-45; males. ♦Gary Shorman, pres, gen sls mgr; Chuck Schwartz, gen mgr; Jerome Gilg, gen sls mgr; Dianne Morales, prom dir; David Fudge, progmg dir; Tony Cuesta, chief of engrg.

***KPNE-FM**— July 1, 1991: 91.7 mhz; 16.5 kw horiz, 81 kw vert. 843 ft TL: N41 01 21 W101 09 13. Stereo. Hrs open: 24
Rebroadcasts KUCV(FM) Lincoln 100%.
1800 N. 33rd St., Lincoln, 68503-1409. Phone: (402) 472-3611. Fax: (402) 472-2403.E-mail: radio@netnebraska.org Web Site:netnebraska.org Licensee: Nebraska Educational Telecommunications Commission. Natl. Network: PRI, NPR, . Nebraska Public Radio Format: Classical, news. News staff: 3. ♦Nancy Finken, gen mgr, progmg dir; William Stibor, mus dir; Jeff Smith, traf mgr.

KXNP(FM)— June 7, 1982: 103.5 mhz; 100 kw. 479 ft TL: N41 12 49 W100 43 48. Stereo. Hrs open: 24 Prog sep from AM 305 E. Fourth St., 69101. Phone: (308) 532-3344. Fax: (308) 534-6651.E-mail: info@kodyradio.com Web Site:www.kx104.com Licensee: Armada Media-McCook Inc. (acq 5-16-2008; grpsl). Population served: 125,000 Natl. Network: Jones Radio Networks, . Format: Contemp country. ♦Lisa Arent, traf mgr.

Ogallala

KMCX(FM)— 1975: 106.5 mhz; 100 kw. 300 ft TL: N41 08 02 W101 41 42. Stereo. Hrs open: 24 Box 509, 113 W. 4th St., 69153. Phone: (308) 284-3633. Fax: (308) 284-3517. Web Site:www.4koga.com Licensee: Capstar TX L.P. Group owner: Clear Channel Communications Inc. (acq 8-30-2000; grpsl). Population served: 40,000 Format: Country. News staff: one; News: 10 hrs wkly. Target aud: 25-54; general. Spec prog: Farm 2 hrs wkly. ♦Katrina Twomey, gen mgr; Corey Andersen, opns dir; John Brandt, gen sls mgr; Dave Geho, chief of engrg; Susan Jones, traf mgr.

KOGA(AM)— Jan 23, 1955: 930 khz; 5 kw-U, DA-2. TL: N41 08 32 W101 42 48. Stereo. Hrs open: Box 509, 69153. Secondary address: 113 W. 4th St. 69153. Phone: (308) 284-3633. Fax: (308) 284-3517.E-mail: thelake@lakemac.net Web Site:www.4koga.com Licensee: Capstar TX L.P. Group owner: Clear Channel Communications Inc. (acq 8-30-00; grpsl). Population served: 85,000 Fletcher, Heald & Hildreth. Format: Oldies. Spec prog: Farm 10 hrs wkly. ♦Katrina Twomby, gen mgr; Corey Anderson, opns mgr; John Brandt, sls dir; Tracey Knapp, progmg dir; Greg Holl, news dir; Dave Geho, chief of engrg.

KOGA-FM— November 1978: 99.7 mhz; 100 kw. 805 ft TL: N41 03 50 W101 20 16. Stereo. Hrs open: 24 Prog sep from AM Box 509, 69153. Secondary address: 113 W. 4th St. 69153. Phone: (308) 284-3633. Fax: (308) 284-3517. Web Site:997thelake.com Population served: 100,000 Format: Adult rock. ♦Greg Hill, local news ed.

Omaha

KCRO(AM)— March 1922: 660 khz; 1 kw-D, 54 w-N. TL: N41 18 47 W96 00 36. Hrs open: 11717 Burt St, Suite 202, 68154. Phone: (402) 422-1600. Fax: (402) 422-1602. Web Site:www.kcro.com Licensee: Salem Media of Illinois LLC. (acq 9-1-2005; $3.1 million). Population served: 1,101,000 Natl. Network: Salem Radio Network, . Natl. Rep: Salem,. Format: Christian talk. ♦Greg Vogt, gen mgr; Mike Shane, opns mgr; Jim Leedham, chief of engrg.

KEZO-FM— May 15, 1961: 92.3 mhz; 100 kw. Ant 1,250 ft TL: N41 18 40 W96 01 37. Stereo. Hrs open: 5030 N. 72nd St., 68134-2363. Phone: (402) 592-5300. Fax: (402) 592-6605.E-mail: info@z92.com Web Site:www.z92.com Licensee: Journal Broadcast Corp. (acq 11-29-94; $9 million with co-located AM; 1-16-95). Population served: 347,328 Format: Rock/AOR. ♦Rob Burton, gen mgr; James Barton, prom dir; Jim Spector, progmg dir; Susie Copenhaver, traf mgr.

KFAB(AM)— 1924: 1110 khz; 50 kw-U, DA-N. TL: N41 07 11 W96 00 06. Stereo. Hrs open: 24 5010 Underwood Ave., 68132. Phone: (402) 561-2000. Fax: (402) 556-8937. Web Site:www.kfab.org Licensee: Capstar TX L.P. Group owner: Clear Channel Communications Inc. (acq 8-30-2000; grpsl). Population served: 347,328 Natl. Network: ABC, . Natl. Rep: Christal,. Format: News/talk. News staff: 3; News: 6 hrs wkly. Target aud: 35-64. Spec prog: Farm 5 hrs wkly. ♦Taylor Walet, gen mgr; Michelle Matthews, opns mgr; Marnie Simpson, gen sls mgr; Kevin Simonson, prom dir; Gary Sadlemyer, progmg dir; Tom Stanton, news dir; Greg Gade, chief of engrg; Sarah McCabe, traf mgr; Rich Denison, news rptr; Jim Rose, sports cmtr.

***KGBI-FM**— May 17, 1966: 100.7 mhz; 100 kw. Ant 1,014 ft TL: N41 18 40 W96 01 37. Stereo. Hrs open: 24 11717 Burt St., Suite 202, 68154-1500. Phone: (402) 422-1600. Fax: (402) 422-1602.E-mail: kgbi@kgbifm.com Web Site:www.kgbifm.com Licensee: Pennsylvania Media Associates Inc. (acq 1-31-2005; $8 million). Population served: 1,480,000 Natl. Rep: Salem,. Format: Contemp Christian. News staff: one; News: 28 hrs wkly. Target aud: 25-54; conservative, Evangelical. ♦Greg Vogt, gen mgr; Mike Shane, opns mgr; Jim Leedham, chief of engrg.

KGOR(FM)— 1959: 99.9 mhz; 110 kw. Ant 1,214 ft TL: N41 18 29 W96 01 36. Stereo. Hrs open: 24 5010 Underwood Ave., 68132. Phone: (402) 561-2000. Fax: (402) 556-8937. Web Site:www.kgor.com Licensee: Capstar TX L.P. Format: Super Hits. News staff: 1. Target aud: 35-54. ♦Marnie Simpson, gen sls mgr; Lester St. James, progmg dir; Kim Shotwell, traf mgr.

***KIOS-FM**— September 1969: 91.5 mhz; 55 kw. 554 ft TL: N41 17 15 W95 59 37. Stereo. Hrs open: 3230 Burt St., 68131. Phone: (402) 557-2777. Fax: (402) 557-2559.E-mail: edward.mcgrath@ops.org Web Site:www.kios.org Licensee: Douglas County School District 001. Population served: 347,328 Natl. Network: NPR, PRI, . Cohn & Marks. Wire Svc: AP Format: News & jazz. News staff: one. Spec prog: Local Jazz 15 hrs wkly. ♦Keith Neisler, stn mgr; Edward McGrath, dev dir; Molly Nicklin, sls dir; Bob Coate, progmg dir; Mike Jacobs, mus dir; Katie Knapp, news dir; Richard Dennis, chief of engrg.

KKAR(AM)— March 1925: 1290 khz; 5 kw-U, DA-N. TL: N41 11 20 W96 00 21. Hrs open: 24 5011 Capitol Ave., 68132. Phone: (402) 342-2000. Fax: (402) 346-5748.E-mail: info@1290kkar.com Web Site:www.1290kkar.com Licensee: Waitt Omaha LLC. (group owner; (acq 1-7-2002; grpsl). Population served: 346,929 Natl. Network: ABC, Fox News Radio, Jones Radio Networks, Premiere Radio Networks, Talk Radio Network, . Natl. Rep: Katz Radio,. Format: News/talk. Target aud: General. ♦Rhonda Gerrard, gen mgr; Mark Todd, opns mgr; Sam Coughlin, sls dir; Neil Nelkin, progmg dir; Terry Leahy, pres & news dir; Darwin Stinton, chief of engrg; Lori Storz, traf mgr.

KKCD(FM)— Aug 11, 1990: 105.9 mhz; 50 kw. 479 ft TL: N41 18 16 W96 01 41. Hrs open: 24 5030 N. 72nd St., 68134. Phone: (402) 592-5300. Fax: (402) 331-1348.E-mail: info@cd1059.com Web Site:www.cd1059.com Licensee: Journal Broadcast Corp. Group

owner: Journal Broadcast Group Inc. (acq 2-95; $3.55 million; 3-13-95). Population served: 800,000 Natl. Network: AP Network News, . Leventhal, Senter & Lerman. Format: Classic Rock. News staff: one; News: 10 hrs wkly. Target aud: 25-54. Spec prog: Jazz 4 hrs, blues one hr, reggae one hr wkly. ♦Steve F. Wexler, VP, gen mgr; Tom Land, opns dir; Mike Stodden, gen sls mgr; Kurt Owens, progmg dir; Bill Jensen, news dir, traf mgr; John Gaeta, chief of engrg.

KOMJ(AM)— March 1942: 1490 khz; 1 kw-U. TL: N41 14 06 W95 57 57. Stereo. Hrs open: 24 5030 N. 72nd St., 68134. Phone: (402) 592-5300. Phone: (402) 898-5300. Fax: (402) 592-9434. Fax: (402) 331-1348. Licensee: Cochise Broadcasting LLC. Group owner: Journal Broadcast Group Inc. (acq 3-27-2007; $500,000). Format: Adult standards. News staff: one. Target aud: 18-49. ♦Tom Land, opns dir & opns mgr; Kathy Hedstrom, gen sls mgr; Heath Hedstrom, prom dir, prom mgr; Kurt Owens, progmg dir; Bill Jensen, news dir; John Gaeta, chief of engrg; Cheryl Brye, traf mgr.

KOTK(AM)— Mar 2, 1957: 1420 khz; 1 kw-D, 330 w-N, DA-2. TL: N41 11 59 W95 54 34. Hrs open: 11717 Burt St., Suite 202, 68154-1500. Phone: (402) 422-1600. Fax: (402) 422-1602. Licensee: Pennsylvania Media Associates Inc. Group owner: Journal Broadcast Group Inc. (acq 12-7-2005; $900,000). Population served: 347,328 Natl. Rep: Salem,. Format: Sp relg. ♦Greg Vogt, gen mgr; Mike Shane, opns mgr; Jim Leedham, chief of engrg.

KQBW(FM)— Oct 21, 1983: 96.1 mhz; 100 kw. Ant 1,414 ft TL: N41 04 14 W96 13 33. Stereo. Hrs open: 24 5010 Underwood Avenue, 68132. Phone: (402) 561-2000. Fax: (402) 558-8937.E-mail: info@kqbw.com Web Site:www.961thebrew.com Licensee: Clear Channel Broadcasting Licenses Inc. (acq 10-9-2003; $10.5 million). Population served: 537,700 Format: Classic rock. News staff: one; News: one hr wkly. ♦Donna Baker, gen mgr; Jean St. James, gen sls mgr; Tom Stanton, prom dir; Greg Grade, chief of engrg.

KQCH(FM)— 1959: 94.1 mhz; 100 kw. 508 ft TL: N41 18 47 W96 00 36. Stereo. Hrs open: 24 5030 N. 72nd St., 68134. Phone: (402) 592-5300. Fax: (402) 331-1348. Population served: 574,100 Wire Svc: Weather Wire Wire Svc: Reuters Format: Rhythm-based contemp. Target aud: 25-54. ♦Larkin Cavanaugh, gen mgr, prom dir; Jill Butler, gen sls mgr; Erik Johnson, progmg dir; Kathi Knutson, traf mgr; Bill Jensen, news rptr; Peter Shinn, farm dir.

KSRZ(FM)— May 12, 1972: 104.5 mhz; 100 kw. 1,040 ft TL: N41 18 25 W96 01 37. Stereo. Hrs open: Dups AM 100% 5030 N. 72nd St., 68134. Phone: (402) 592-5300. Fax: (402) 592-6605.E-mail: info@104star.com Web Site:www.104star.com Licensee: Journal Broadcast Corp. (acq 1-98; $5.475 million with co-located AM). Population served: 500,000 Format: Hot adult contemp. ♦Steve Wexler, gen mgr; Jill Butler, stn mgr, gen sls mgr; Tom Land, opns dir; James Barton, prom dir; Darla Thomas, progmg dir; Dave Swan, mus dir; John Gaeta, chief of engrg; Kathi Knutson, traf mgr.

***KVNO(FM)—** Aug 27, 1972: 90.7 mhz; 8.9 kw. Ant 646 ft TL: N41 18 25 W96 01 37. Stereo. Hrs open: 24 CB200, 60th & Dodge, 68182. Phone: (402) 559-5866. Fax: (402) 554-2440.E-mail: info@kvno.com Web Site:www.kvno.org Licensee: University of Nebraska Board of Regents. Population served: 750,000 Format: Class. News staff: one; News: 2.5 hrs wkly. Target aud: General. ♦Robert Franklin, gen mgr; Dana Buckingham, opns mgr; Anne Hellbusch, mktg mgr; James Arey, mus dir; Frank Vacek, engrg mgr, chief of engrg.

KXSP(AM)— Apr 2, 1923: 590 khz; 5 kw-U. TL: N41 19 00 W95 59 52. Stereo. Hrs open: 24 5030 N. 72nd St., 68134. Phone: (402) 592-5300. Fax: (402) 331-1348.E-mail: info@bigsports590.com Web Site:www.bigsports590.com Licensee: Journal Broadcast Corp. Group owner: Journal Broadcast Group Inc. (acq 10-26-98 with co-located FM). Population served: 347,328 Format: Sports. News staff: 4. Target aud: General. ♦Steve Wexler, gen mgr; Jim Timm, gen sls mgr; Tom Land, opns mgr & progmg dir; Bill Jensen, news dir; John Gaeta, chief of engrg; Cheryl Brye, traf mgr.

***KYFG(FM)—** Jan 9, 1999: 88.9 mhz; 85 w horiz, 1.5 kw vert. Ant 482 ft TL: N41 18 47 W96 00 36. Hrs open: 24
Rebroadcasts WYFQ(AM) Charlotte, NC 100%.
Secondary address: Box 7300, Charlotte, NC 28241-7300. Phone: (704) 523-5555. Fax: (704) 291-7807.E-mail: bbn@bbnradio.org Web Site:www.bbnradio.org Licensee: Bible Broadcasting Network Inc. (acq 6-12-2009; $825,000). Natl. Network: Bible Bcstg Net, . Format: Christian. ♦Lowell L. Davey, pres; Rob Ferguson, gen mgr.

O'Neill

KBRX(AM)— November 1955: 1350 khz; 1 kw-D, 44 W-N. TL: N42 27 34 W98 39 23. Hrs open: 24 Box 150, 68763. Secondary address: 251 N. Jefferson St. Phone: (402) 336-1612. Fax: (402) 336-3585.E-mail: Gil@kbrx,com Web Site:www.kbrx.com Licensee: Ranchland Broadcasting Co. Inc. (acq 7-1-61). Population served: 45,000 Natl. Network: ABC, . Rgnl. Network: Brownfield. Brownfield Bryan Cave. Wire Svc: AP Format: Classic Rock. News staff: one; News: 25 hrs wkly. Target aud: 25-65. Spec prog: Farm 12 hrs, Ger 6 hrs wkly. ♦Gilbert L. Poese, pres; Scott Poese, gen mgr.

KBRX-FM— December 1973: 102.9 mhz; 100 kw. Ant 500 ft TL: N42 26 06 W98 33 39. Stereo. Hrs open: 24 Box 150, 251 N. Jefferson, 68763. Phone: (402) 336-1612. Fax: (402) 336-3585.E-mail: scott@kbrx.com Web Site:www.kbrx.com Licensee: Ranchland Broadcasting Co. Inc. Population served: 45,000 Natl. Network: ABC, . Rgnl. Network: Brownfield. Brownfield Bryan Cave . Wire Svc: AP Format: Country. News staff: one. Target aud: 25-60. ♦Gil Poese, pres, local news ed; Pat Poese, sls VP; Scott Poese, gen mgr & farm dir.

***KOEC(FM)—**Not on air, target date: unknown: 91.5 mhz; 3 kw. Ant 200 ft TL: N42 17 19.2 W98 39 24.4. Hrs open: Box 159, Rural Hall, NC, 27045. Phone: (605) 868-0525. Licensee: Church Planters of America. ♦Danny Hawkins, pres & gen mgr.

Orchard

***KGRD(FM)—** June 14, 1987: 105.3 mhz; 100 kw. 502 ft TL: N42 20 45 W98 25 05. Stereo. Hrs open: 24 128 S. 4th St., O'Neill, 68763-1814. Phone: (402) 336-3886.E-mail: kgrd@kgrd.org Web Site:www.kgrd.org Licensee: The Praise Network Inc. (acq 10-16-91). Population served: 50,000 Natl. Network: Salem Radio Network, . Wire Svc: AP Format: Christian, Inspirational. News: 10 hrs wkly. Target aud: 35-54. ♦Lloyd Mintzmeyer, pres; Todd Gunnarson, gen mgr & stn mgr; Bill Taylor, mus dir.

Ord

KNLV(AM)— July 15, 1965: 1060 khz; 650 w-D, 23 w-N. TL: N41 34 17 W98 55 21. Hrs open: 24 205 S. 16th St., 68862. Phone: (308) 728-3263. Fax: (308) 728-3264.E-mail: knlv@yahoo.com Licensee: Sandhills Advertising Corp. (acq 7-1-2000). Population served: 2,642 Natl. Network: ABC, . Rgnl. Network: Brownfield. Wire Svc: AP Format: Oldies. Target aud: 18-54. Spec prog: Farm 8 hrs, Pol/Czeck/Bohemian 4 hrs wkly. ♦Johnnie James, gen mgr, progmg dir; Gene McCoy, gen sls mgr; Johnnie James, news dir; Randy Faaborg, chief of engrg; Denise O'Neel, traf mgr; Jeannie Neidhardt, prom.

KNLV-FM— July 10, 1981: 103.9 mhz; 30 kw. Ant 638 ft TL: N41 34 17 W98 55 21. Stereo. Hrs open: 24 205 S. 16th St., 68862. Phone: (308) 728-3263. Fax: (308) 728-3264. Licensee: Sandhills Advertising Corp. (acq 7-1-2000). Population served: 7,200 Natl. Network: ABC, . Wire Svc: AP Format: Country. Target aud: 18-54. Spec prog: Farm 8 hours. ♦Gene McCoy, gen sls mgr; Jeannie Neidhardt, prom mgr; Denis O'Neal, traf mgr; Johnnie James, stn mgr, news dir & disc jockey.

Overton

KHZY(FM)— 2007: 99.3 mhz; 100 kw. Ant 751 ft TL: N40 41 49 W99 47 16. Hrs open:
Rebroadcasts KSRD(FM) Saint Joseph, MO 100%.
1212 Faraon St., Saint Joseph, MO, 64501. Phone: (816) 233-5773. Fax: (816) 233-5777. Web Site:www.ksrdradio.com Licensee: Horizon Christian Fellowship. (acq 2-9-2006; grpsl). Format: Christian. ♦Mike MacIntosh, pres; Brian KC Jones, gen mgr.

Paxton

KZTL(FM)— 2007: 93.5 mhz; 100 kw. Ant 753 ft TL: N41 03 50 W101 20 16. Hrs open: 400 N. Dewey St., North Platte, 69101. Phone: (308) 532-5767. Fax: (308) 535-9100. Licensee: Legacy Communications LLC. (acq 8-14-2007; $475,000 for CP with CP for KRNP(FM) Sutherland). Format: Country. ♦Alan Usher, gen mgr.

Plattsmouth

KMMQ(AM)— Oct 26, 1970: 1020 khz; 1 kw-D, 1400 kw-N. TL: N41 01 35 W95 54 00. Hrs open: Sunrise-sunset 5011 Capital Ave., Omaha, 68132. Phone: (402) 342-2000. Fax: (402) 342-6146. Web Site:www.1020kepadre.com Licensee: Waitt Omaha LLC. (group owner; (acq 1-17-2001; $750,000). Population served: 750,000 Rgnl. Network: Brownfield. Format: Rgnl Mexican. ♦Rhonda Gerrard, gen mgr; Sam Coughlin, sls dir.

KOPW(FM)— July 1993: 106.9 mhz; 25 kw. Ant 328 ft TL: N41 09 18 W95 45 42. Stereo. Hrs open: 24 5011 Capitol Ave., Omaha, 68132. Phone: (402) 342-2000. Fax: (402) 346-5748.E-mail: info@power1069fm.com Web Site:power1069fm.com Licensee: Platte Broadcasting Co. Inc. Population served: 450,000 Natl. Rep: Katz Radio,. Format: Contemp rhythm. Target aud: 18-34; gen. ♦Rhonda Gerrard, gen mgr; Mark Todd, opns mgr; Sam Coughlin, sls dir; Marcey Gibson, prom dir; Bryant McCain, progmg dir; Cynthia Wallace, traf mgr.

Ponca

***KFHC(FM)—** 2008: 88.1 mhz; 2.28 kw horiz, 8.8 kw vert. Ant 417 ft TL: N42 27 48 W96 37 01.9. Hrs open: 705 Douglas St., Suite 238, Sioux City, IA, 51101-1043. Phone: (712) 224-5342. Fax: (712) 224-5345. Licensee: St. Gabriel Communications Ltd. Natl. Network: EWTN Radio, . Format: Catholic radio.

Ralston

***KMLV(FM)—** July 21, 2001: 88.1 mhz; 3.7 kw vert. Ant 794 ft TL: N41 18 40 W96 01 37. Stereo. Hrs open: 24
Rebroadcasts KLVR(FM) Middletown, CA 100%.
2351 Sunset Blvd., Suite 170-218, Rocklin, CA, 95765. Phone: (916) 251-1600. Fax: (916) 251-1650.E-mail: klove@klove.com Web Site:www.klove.com Licensee: Educational Media Foundation. Group owner: EMF Broadcasting. Population served: 735,000 Natl. Network: K-Love, . Davis Wright Tremaine LLP. Format: Contemp Christian music. Target aud: 25-44; Judeo Christian, female. ♦Mike Novak, pres.

Ravenna

KKJK(FM)— June 1, 2006: 103.1 mhz; 100 kw. Ant 640 ft TL: N40 48 57 W98 46 18. Hrs open: Box 5853, Grand Island, 68802. Secondary address: 3205 W. North Front St., Grand Island 68803. Phone: (308) 381-1430. Fax: (308) 382-6701.E-mail: info@familyradio.com Web Site:www.thunder1031.com Licensee: Community Radio Inc. Format: Rock and roll. ♦Donald Wilks, pres; Alan Usher, gen mgr.

Sargent

KHZZ(FM)— 2008: 92.1 mhz; 110 w. Ant 52 ft TL: N41 38 29 W99 22 12. Hrs open: 5331 Mt. Alifan Dr., San Diego, CA, 92111. Phone: (858) 277-4991. Fax: (858) 277-1365. Licensee: Horizon Christian Fellowship. (acq 2-9-2006; grpsl). Format: Relg. ♦Mike MacIntosh, pres.

Scottsbluff

***KDAI(FM)—** 2008: 89.1 mhz; 1.4 kw. Ant 781 ft TL: N41 50 21 W103 49 53. Hrs open:
Rebroadcasts KLRD(FM) Yucaipa, CA 100%.
2351 Sunset Blvd., Suite 170-218, Rocklin, CA, 95765. Phone: (916) 251-1600. Fax: (916) 251-1650. Web Site:www.air1.com Licensee: Educational Media Foundation. (acq 7-23-2007; grpsl). Natl. Network: Air 1, . Format: Alternative rock, Christian music, div. ♦Mike Novak, pres.

***KLJV(FM)—** Feb 20, 2003: 88.3 mhz; 390 w. Ant 259 ft TL: N41 56 24 W103 39 20. Stereo. Hrs open: 24 2351 Sunset Blvd., Suite 170-218, Rocklin, CA, 95765. Phone: (916) 251-1600. Fax: (916) 251-1650.E-mail: klove@klove.com Web Site:www.klove.com Licensee: Educational Media Foundation. Group owner: EMF Broadcasting. Population served: 32,600 Natl. Network: K-Love, . Shaw Pittman. Format: Contemp Christian. News staff: 3. Target aud: 25-44. ♦Richard Jenkins, pres; Mike Novak, VP; Keith Whipple, dev dir; David Pierce, progmg mgr; Ed Lenane, news dir; Sam Wallington, engrg dir; Karen Johnson, news rptr.

KNEB(AM)— Jan 1, 1948: 960 khz; 5 kw-D, 350 w-N, DA-2. TL: N41 47 30 W103 38 29. Hrs open: 5 AM-1 AM Box 239, 1928 E. Portal Pl., 69363-0239. Phone: (308) 632-7121. Fax: (308) 635-1079.E-mail: kneb@actcom.net Web Site:www.kneb.com Licensee: Nebraska Rural Radio Association. Group owner: Nebraska Rural Radio Assn. (acq 8-1-84). Population served: 46,750 Format: C&W, news/talk. News staff: 2. Target aud: 18 plus. Spec prog: Farm 18 hrs, Sp 5 hrs wkly. ♦Larry Hudkins, pres; Craig Larson, stn mgr; Kendra Feather, gen sls mgr, natl sls mgr, rgnl sls mgr, news dir; Dennis Ernest, progmg dir.

KNEB-FM— Dec 25, 1960: 94.1 mhz; 100 kw. 680 ft TL: N41 42 04 W103 40 49. Stereo. Hrs open: 5 AM-1 AM Dups AM 10% Box 239, 1928 E. Portal Pl., 69363. Phone: (308) 632-7121. Fax: (308) 635-1079. Population served: 112,200 Format: Farm, C&W. ♦Craig Larson, stn mgr; Kendra Feather, natl sls mgr; Dennis Ernest, progmg dir.

KOAQ(AM)—See Terrytown

KOLT(AM)— Feb 15, 1930: 1320 khz; 5 kw-D, 1 kw-N, DA-N. TL: N41 51 37 W103 41 53. Hrs open: 24 Box 1263, 69361-1263. Secondary address: 2002 Char Ave. 69361. Phone: (308) 632-5667. Fax: (308) 635-1905.E-mail: info@hometownfamilyradio.com Web Site:www.koltam.com Licensee: Legacy Communications LLC. Group owner: Tracy Broadcasting Corp. (acq 12-13-2007; grpsl). Population served: 15,000 Natl. Network: ESPN Radio, . Fletcher, Heald & Hildreth. Format: News/talk, sports. ◆Julie Marshall, gen mgr & stn mgr.

Seward

KMHB(FM)—Not on air, target date: unknown: 89.5 mhz; 100 w. Ant 230 ft TL: N40 53 56 W97 00 39. Hrs open: Box 30345, Lincoln, 68503-0345. Phone: (402) 477-1090. Web Site:www.missionnebraska.org Licensee: Mission Nebraska Inc. ◆Stanley A. Parker, gen mgr.

KZKX(FM)— Nov 12, 1976: 96.9 mhz; 100 kw. 610 ft TL: N41 07 26 W96 50 03. Stereo. Hrs open: 3800 Cornhusker Hwy., Lincoln, 68504. Phone: (402) 466-1234. Fax: (402) 467-4095. Web Site:www.kzkx.com Licensee: Three Eagles of Lincoln Inc. Group owner: Clear Channel Communications Inc. (acq 4-10-2007; grpsl). Format: Country. Target aud: 25-54. ◆James Keck, gen mgr.

Shubert

KSSH(FM)—Not on air, target date: unknown: 91.3 mhz; 2 kw. Ant 607 ft TL: N40 13 11 W95 39 55. Hrs open: 282 Country Estate Dr., Springer, OK, 73458. Phone: (580) 653-2777. Licensee: Ron Elmore Ministries Inc. ◆Ron Elmore, pres.

Sidney

KSID(AM)— June 2, 1952: 1340 khz; 1 kw-U. TL: N41 07 50 W102 58 15. Hrs open: 24 Box 37, Legion Park, 69162. Phone: (308) 254-5803. Fax: (308) 254-5901. Licensee: KSID Radio Inc. (acq 1962). Population served: 128,500 Format: Country. Target aud: General. Spec prog: Farm 5 hrs wkly. ◆Elizabeth Young, pres; Lana Butts, opns mgr, gen sls mgr; Marge Elliott, progmg dir; Jason Lockwood, news dir; Dennis Brothers, engrg mgr, chief of engrg; Jean Spruckmeyer, traf mgr.

KSID-FM— Sept 13, 1974: 98.7 mhz; 62 kw. 368 ft TL: N41 11 03 W103 11 37. Stereo. Hrs open: Dups AM 30% Box 37, Legion Park, 69162. Phone: (308) 254-5803. Fax: (308) 254-5901. Population served: 134,493 Format: Adult contemp. ◆Susan Ernest, traf mgr.

South Sioux City

KSFT-FM— 1997: 107.1 mhz; 1.55 kw. 328 ft TL: N42 29 00 W96 35 34. Stereo. Hrs open: 24 Box 3009, Sioux City, IA, 51102. Secondary address: 1113 Nebraska St., Sioux City, IA 51102. Phone: (712) 258-6740. Fax: (712) 252-2430. Web Site:www.kiss107siouxcity.com Licensee: AMFM Radio Licenses LLC. Group owner: Clear Channel Communications Inc. (acq 10-1-2002; grpsl). Natl. Rep: Katz Radio,. Format: KISS. Target aud: 12-35. ◆Rob Powers, opns mgr, progmg dir; Laura Schiltz, gen sls mgr, mktg mgr; Mike Newhouse, natl sls mgr; Rhonda Johnson, prom mgr; Stan Culley, chief of engrg; Monica Mattoon, traf mgr.

Superior

KRFS(AM)— Mar 17, 1959: 1600 khz; 500 w-D. TL: N40 01 30 W98 04 38. Hrs open: 6 AM-sunset Rte. 2, Box 149, 68978. Phone: (402) 879-4741. Fax: (402) 879-4741.E-mail: krfsfm@yahoo.com Licensee: CK Broadcasting Inc. (acq 1-4-02; $150,000 with co-located FM). Population served: 100,000 Rgnl. Network: Brownfield. Brownfield Format: Adult standards. News: 11 hrs wkly. Target aud: 25-55; general. Spec prog: Farm 5 hrs, gospel 3 hrs, relg 3 hrs wkly. ◆Cory Kopsa, gen mgr, sls VP, gen sls mgr, prom mgr, progmg dir, news dir, traf mgr, sports cmtr; Marvin Hoffman, chief of engrg.

KRFS-FM— Feb 25, 1977: 103.9 mhz; 6 kw. 220 ft TL: N40 01 30 W98 04 38. (CP: TL: N40 06 20 W98 06 20). Stereo. Hrs open: 24 Dups AM 100% Rte. 2, Box 149, 68978. Phone: (402) 879-4741. Fax: (402) 879-4741.E-mail: krfs@yahoo.com Rgnl. Network: Brownfield. Brownfield Format: Country. ◆Cory Kopsa, traf mgr & sports cmtr.

Sutherland

KRNP(FM)— 2007: 100.7 mhz; 100 kw. Ant 753 ft TL: N41 03 50 W101 20 16. Hrs open: 400 N. Dewey St., North Platte, 69101. Phone: (308) 532-5767. Fax: (308) 535-9100. Licensee: Legacy Communications LLC. (acq 8-14-2007; $475,000 for CP with CP for KZTL(FM) Paxton). Format: Rock. ◆Alan Usher, gen mgr.

Tecumseh

KMBT(FM)—Not on air, target date: unknown: 91.7 mhz; 6 kw. Ant 308 ft TL: N40 16 31 W95 58 05. Hrs open: Box 30345, Lincoln, 68503-0345. Phone: (402) 477-1090.E-mail: email@mybridgeradio.net Web Site:www.mybridgeradio.net Licensee: Mission Nebraska Inc. ◆Stanley Parker, gen mgr.

Terrytown

KCMI(FM)— Mar 1, 1981: 96.9 mhz; 100 kw. 692 ft TL: N41 42 08 W103 41 00. Stereo. Hrs open: 24 Box 1888, 209 E. 15th, Scottsbluff, 69363-1888. Phone: (308) 632-5264. Fax: (308) 635-0104.E-mail: info@kcmifm.com Web Site:www.kcmi.cc Licensee: Christian Media Inc. Population served: 85,000 Natl. USA, . Rgnl. Network: Mid-American Ag. Brownfield Format: Relg. News: 12 hrs wkly. Target aud: 25 plus. Spec prog: Class 4 hrs wkly. ◆Glenn A. Hascall, gen mgr; Gary Almquist, gen sls mgr, progmg dir; Lorraine Brown, traf mgr.

KOAQ(AM)— June 15, 1961: 690 khz; 1 kw-D, 64 w-N, DA-1. TL: N41 50 02 W103 39 20. Stereo. Hrs open: 24 Box 1263, Scottsbluff, 69361-1263. Secondary address: 2002 Char Ave., Scottsbluff 69361. Phone: (308) 632-5667. Fax: (308) 635-1905.E-mail: info@hometownfamilyradio.com Web Site:www.koaqam.com Licensee: Legacy Communications LLC. (group owner; (acq 12-13-2007; grpsl). Population served: 45,000 Fletcher, Heald & Hildreth. Format: Oldies. Target aud: 25-54; Baby Boomers. ◆Julie Marshall, gen mgr; Mandi Adams, prom dir.

Utica

KUTN(FM)—Not on air, target date: unknown: 91.7 mhz; 3 kw. Ant 328 ft TL: N40 59 52 W97 16 02. Hrs open: 9705 Valley Lake Ct., Irving, TX, 75063. Phone: (972) 402-0290. Licensee: The Johnson Foundation. ◆I. Johnson, pres.

Valentine

KKNL(FM)—Not on air, target date: unknown: 89.3 mhz; 6 kw. Ant 184 ft TL: N42 53 22 W100 33 15. Hrs open: Drawer 2440, Tupelo, MS, 38803-2440. Phone: (662) 844-5036. Fax: (662) 842-7798.E-mail: info@afa.net Web Site:www.afr.net Licensee: American Family Association. ◆Donald E. Wildmon, chmn.

KMBV(FM)—Not on air, target date: unknown: 90.7 mhz; 100 kw. Ant 433 ft TL: N42 33 12 W100 32 01. Hrs open: Box 30345, Lincoln, 68503-0345. Phone: (402) 477-1090. Web Site:www.missionnebraska.org Licensee: Mission Nebraska Inc. ◆Stanley A. Parker, gen mgr.

KVSH(AM)— Mar 6, 1961: 940 khz; 5 kw-D, 20 w-N. TL: N42 51 54 W100 31 07. Hrs open: 16 126 W. 3rd St., 69201. Phone: (402) 376-2400. Fax: (402) 376-2402.E-mail: info@kvsh.com Licensee: Heart City Radio Corp. (acq 6-90; $235,000; 6-4-90). Population served: 2,880 Fletcher, Heald & Hildreth. Wire Svc: AP Format: Country. News staff: one; News: 24 hrs wkly. Target aud: 35-60; general. ◆Dave Otradovsky, pres; Mike Burge, progmg dir, news dir, chief of engrg; Zach Dean, gen sls mgr & disc jockey.

Valley

KRKR(FM)— Mar 6, 1975: 94.9 mhz; 6 kw. Ant 328 ft TL: N41 16 06 W96 11 39.9. Stereo. Hrs open: 24 3800 Cornhusker Hwy., Lincoln, 68504. Phone: (402) 466-1234. Fax: (402) 467-4095. Web Site:www.mybridgeradio.net Licensee: Chapin Enterprises LLC Group owner: Three Eagles Communications (acq 4-10-2007; with KBZR(FM) Lincoln). Fletcher, Heald & Hildreth. Format: Adult contemp Chirstian.

Wayne

KCTY(FM)— Oct 19, 1975: 104.9 mhz; 25,000 kw. Ant 300 ft TL: N42 14 03 W97 03 19. Hrs open: 24 Box 413 , W. Hwy. 35, 68787. Phone: (509) 783-0783. Fax: (509) 735-8627.E-mail: info@ktch.com Web Site:www.ktch.com Licensee: Wayne Radio Work LLC. (acq

5-30-2008; $450,000 with KTCH(AM) Wayne). Population served: 40,000 News staff: one. Target aud: General.

KTCH(AM)— Mar 18, 1968: 1590 khz; 2.5 kw-D, 33.4 w-N, DA-2. TL: N42 14 03 W97 03 19. Hrs open: 24 Box 413, W. Hwy. 35, 68787. Phone: (402) 375-3700. Fax: (402) 375-5402.E-mail: ktch@ktch.com Web Site:www.waynedailynews.com Licensee: Wayne Radio Works LLC. (group owner; (acq 5-30-2008; $450,000 with KCTY(FM) Wayne). Population served: 40,000 Natl. Network: Air 1, Motor Racing Net, USA, . Rgnl. Network: Brownfield. Brownfield Wire Svc: AP Format: Country. News staff: one; News: 15 hrs wkly. Target aud: 30-64. Spec prog: Farm 20 hrs wkly. ◆Mick Kemp, gen mgr, gen sls mgr; Dan Baddorf, progmg dir, news dir; Tony Wortman, chief of engrg.

KWSC(FM)— Oct 13, 1971: 91.9 mhz; 350 w. 96 ft TL: N42 14 30 W97 00 48. Hrs open: 1111 Main St., 68787. Phone: (402) 375-7536. Phone: (402) 375-7426.E-mail: k92radio@hotmail.com Web Site:www.wsc.edu/k92 Licensee: Wayne State College. Population served: 35,000 Natl. Network: Westwood One, . Format: AOR, alternative. Target aud: 18 plus. Spec prog: Black 4 hrs, jazz 2 hrs, heavy metal 2 hrs, blues 2 hrs wkly.

West Point

KTIC(AM)— Mar 17, 1985: 840 khz; 5 kw-D. TL: N41 47 06 W96 40 39. Hrs open: Sunrise-sunset Box 84, 1011 N. Lincoln St., 68788-0084. Phone: (402) 372-5423. Fax: (402) 372-5425.E-mail: dlane@kticradio.com Web Site:www.kticam.com Licensee: Nebraska Rural Radio Association. Group owner: Nebraska Rural Radio Association (acq 8-1-97; $1.5 million with co-located FM). Population served: 1,921,459 Natl. Network: ABC, . Natl. Rep: Katz Radio,. Nebraska Public Radio Rgnl rep: Neb. Pub. Wire Svc: AP Format: Farm market news, country. News staff: one; News: 20 hrs wkly. Target aud: General; farmers, ranchers, stockmen and all involved in agri-business. ◆Charlie Brogan, gen mgr, stn mgr, progmg dir; Denny Waddle, sls dir, gen sls mgr; Judy Mauch, gen sls mgr; Richard Sterling, mus dir; Bob Flittie, news dir; Vern Killion, chief of engrg; Tammie Harrington, traf mgr; Randy Koenen, farm dir; Tom McMahon, sports cmtr.

KTIC-FM— Aug 1, 1988: 107.9 mhz; 50 kw. Ant 318 ft TL: N41 47 06 W96 40 39. Stereo. Hrs open: 18 Box 84 , 1011 N. Lincoln St., 68788. Phone: (402) 372-5423. Fax: (402) 372-5425.E-mail: dlane@kticradio.com (Acq 1997). Population served: 888,400 Natl. Network: ABC, . Format: Country. News staff: one; News: 12 hrs wkly. Target aud: 25-49; general audience, adults. Spec prog: Farm 10 hrs wkly. ◆Richard Sterling, progmg dir; Karen Benne, traf mgr; Randy Koenen, news rptr, farm dir; Tom McMahon, sports cmtr.

Wilber

KFLV(FM)— Mar 1, 2001: 89.9 mhz; 8.8 kw. Ant 351 ft TL: N40 30 33 W96 50 41. Stereo. Hrs open: 24 2351 Sunset Blvd., Suite 170-218, Rocklin, CA, 95765. Phone: (916) 251-1600. Fax: (916) 251-1650.E-mail: klove@klove.com Web Site:www.klove.com Licensee: Educational Media Foundation. Group owner: EMF Broadcasting. Population served: 246,000 Natl. Network: K-Love, . Shaw Pittman. Format: Contemp Christian music. News staff: 3. Target aud: 25-44; Judeo-Christian, female. ◆Richard Jenkins, pres; Mike Novak, VP; Keith Whipple, dev dir; Eric Allen, natl sls mgr; David Pierce, progmg mgr, mus dir; Ed Lenane, news dir; Sam Wallington, engrg dir; Karen Johnson, news rptr.

Winnebago

KSUX(FM)— June 1, 1990: 105.7 mhz; 50 kw. 463 ft TL: N42 20 33 W96 31 13. Stereo. Hrs open: 24 2000 Indian Hills Dr., Sioux City, IA, 51104. Phone: (712) 239-2100. Fax: (712) 239-3346. Web Site:www.ksux.com Licensee: Powell Broadcasting Co. (acq 1996; $3.8 million with KSCJ(AM) Sioux City, IA). Population served: 283,400 Format: Country. News staff: 2. Target aud: 25-54; female average to above average income, suburban male. ◆Dennis Bullock, gen mgr; Dave Grosenheider, sls dir; Tony Michaels, progmg dir.

York

KAWL(AM)— September 1954: 1370 khz; 500 w-D, 176 w-N. TL: N40 50 30 W97 35 16. Hrs open: 24 1309 Rd. 11, 68467. Phone: (402) 362-4433. Fax: (402) 362-6501.E-mail: kawl@alltel.net Web Site:www.oldiesradioonline.com Licensee: MWB Broadcasting LLC (acq 12-3-2004; $1 million with co-located FM). Population served: 115,000 Natl. Network: ABC, . Rgnl. Network: Mid-American Ag. Natl. Rep: Interep,. Mid-America Ag Wire Svc: AP Format: Oldies, talk. News staff: one; News: 10 hrs wkly. Target aud: 20 plus; general. Spec prog: Farm 7 hrs, women 3 hrs wkly. ◆Mark Jensen, gen mgr; Brenda

Janzen, opns mgr, traf mgr; Bob Bedient, news dir; Linda Korbelik, chief of engrg, sls; Donna Panritz, sls.

*KEIS(FM)—Not on air, target date: unknown: 90.3 mhz; 8 kw. Ant 233 ft TL: N40 44 13 W97 39 19. Hrs open: 102 Red Branch Ln., Simpsonville, SC, 29681. Phone: (864) 297-0216. Fax: (864) 297-0344.E-mail: info@networkofglory.org Web Site:networkofglory.com Licensee: Network of Glory Inc. ♦Lola Richey, pres.

KTMX(FM)— Sept 1, 1970: 104.9 mhz; 25 kw. 974 ft TL: N40 45 07 W97 27 04. Stereo. Hrs open: 24 Prog sep from AM 1309 Rd. 11, 68467. Phone: (402) 362-4433. Fax: (402) 362-6501.E-mail: ktmx@alltel.net Web Site:hitsandfavorites.com Licensee: MWB Broadcasting LLC Population served: 390,000 Natl. Network: ABC, . Natl. Rep: McGavren Guild,. Format: Adult contemp. News staff: one; News: 3 hrs wkly. Target aud: 25-54; general.

Nevada

Alamo

*KQLN(FM)—Not on air, target date: unknown: 91.3 mhz; 6 kw vert. Ant -954 ft TL: N37 22 16 W115 10 18. Hrs open: Box 5303, Pahrump, 89041. Phone: (775) 751-2579. Licensee: Talk Radio of Pahrump Inc. ♦Geraldine Ahrens, pres.

Amargosa Valley

KPKK(FM)— 2003: 101.1 mhz; 51 kw horiz. Ant -49 ft TL: N36 38 33 W116 23 53. Hrs open: Sky Media L.L.C., 980 N. Michigan Ave., Suite 1880, Chicago, IL, 60611. Phone: (312) 204-9900. Fax: (312) 587-9466. Licensee: Sky Media L.L.C. (acq 11-20-2002; $5.1 million for CP). ♦Bruce Buzil, gen mgr.

Beatty

KDAN(AM)—Not on air, target date: unknown: 1240 khz; 1 kw-U. TL: N36 54 59 W116 45 47. Hrs open: 24 6854 Deer Mesa Cir., Herriman, UT, 84096. Phone: (801) 915-5281. Licensee: Intermountain Media LLC (acq 6-3-2009; $20,000 for CP). Population served: 3,946 ♦Jeffrey Bate, gen mgr.

*KWLH(FM)—Not on air, target date: unknown: 89.5 mhz; 58 kw vert. Ant 1,594 ft TL: N37 17 59 W117 15 39. Hrs open: 125 S. Main St., Bishop, CA, 93515. Phone: (760) 954-6655. Fax: (760) 872-4155. Licensee: Living Proof Inc. ♦Daniel McClenaghan, pres & gen mgr.

Boulder City

KCYE(FM)—Licensed to Boulder City. See Las Vegas

Cal-Nev-Ari

KVAL(FM)— 2008: 104.9 mhz; 100 w. Ant 2,371 ft TL: N35 15 08 W114 44 58. Hrs open: Number 10 Media Center Dr., Lake Havasu, AZ, 86403. Phone: (928) 855-1051. Fax: (928) 855-7996. Licensee: Smoke and Mirrors LLC. Format: Hot adult contemp. ♦Rick L. Murphy, gen mgr.

Carlin

KHIX(FM)— March 2001: 96.7 mhz; 33 kw. Ant 1,597 ft TL: N40 55 18 W115 50 58. Hrs open: 24 1750 Manzanita Drive, Suite 1, Elko, 89801. Phone: (775) 777-1196. Fax: (775) 777-9587.E-mail: ken@mix96.fm Web Site:www.mix96.fm Licensee: Ruby Radio Corp. (group owner; (acq 6-15-2003; $475,000 for CP). Population served: 25,000 David Tillotson. Format: Adult hit radio (contemp). ♦Alene Sutherland, VP; Ken Sutherland, progmg dir; Mike Allen, news dir.

Carson City

KBUL-FM— Nov 30, 1984: 98.1 mhz; 72.5 kw. 2,273 ft TL: N39 15 32 W119 42 06. (CP: Ant 2,286 ft.). Stereo. Hrs open: 24 595 E. Plumb Ln., Reno, 89502-3773. Phone: (775) 789-6700. Fax: (775) 789-6767. Web Site:www.kbul.com Licensee: Citadel Broadcasting Co. Group owner: Citadel Broadcasting Corp. (acq 5-29-92). Population served: 275,000 Format: C&W. News staff: one; News: 4 hrs wkly. Target aud:

25-54. ♦Andrew Perini, gen mgr; Jennifer Odom, gen sls mgr; Nick Elliott, progmg dir; Rick Worthington, news dir.

KCMY(AM)— May 14, 1955: 1300 khz; 5 kw-D, 500 w-N, DA-N. TL: N39 09 59 W119 43 37. Hrs open: 1960 Idaho, 89701. Phone: (775) 884-8000. Fax: (775) 882-3961. Licensee: The Evans Broadcast Co. Inc. (acq 5-17-2004; $700,000). Population served: 350,000 Natl. Network: Fox News Radio, . Shainis & Peltzman. Format: Classic Country. News staff: 2; News: 16 hrs wkly. Target aud: 35-54. ♦Jerry Evans, gen mgr, progmg dir & progmg.

*KNIS(FM)— Oct 15, 1989: 91.3 mhz; 67 kw. 2,165 ft TL: N39 15 30 W119 42 36. Stereo. Hrs open: 24 Western Inspirational Broadcasters, Inc., 6363 Hwy. 50 E., 89701. Phone: (775) 883-5647. Fax: 775-883-5704. Licensee: Western Inspirational Broadcasters Inc. (acq 10-15-89). Population served: 340,000 Natl. Network: AP Radio, . Wire Svc: AP Format: Contemp Christian, educ, talk. News: 16 hrs wkly. Target aud: 24-44. ♦Tom Hesse, gen mgr; Tim Weidemann, opns mgr; Bill Feltner, progmg dir; Patrick Herman, mus dir; Paul Lierman, chief of engrg.

KZTQ(FM)—Licensed to Carson City. See Reno

Crystal

KHWG-FM— 2009: 100.1 mhz; 1.2 kw horiz. Ant 761 ft TL: N36 27 45 W116 03 33. Hrs open: 250 W. Nopah Vista Ave., Pahrump, 89060. Licensee: Keily Miller. ♦Keily Miller, gen mgr.

Dayton

KTHX-FM—Licensed to Dayton. See Reno

Elko

KELK(AM)— Dec 7, 1948: 1240 khz; 1 kw-U. TL: N40 50 37 W115 44 58. Hrs open: 24 1800 Idaho St., 89802. Phone: (775) 738-1240. Fax: (775) 753-5556.E-mail: elko@elkoradio.com Web Site:elkoradio.com Licensee: Elko Broadcasting Co. (acq 11-1-74). Population served: 30,000 Format: Full service, adult contemp. News staff: one; News: 25 hrs wkly. Target aud: 25-54; upscale, family oriented, white collar workforce. ♦Paul G. Gardner, pres; Tyler Gunter, gen mgr.

KLKO(FM)— May 1982: 93.7 mhz; 4.5 kw. Ant 1,538 ft TL: N40 55 20 W115 50 56. Stereo. Hrs open: Prog sep from AM 1800 Idaho St., 89802. Phone: (775) 738-1240. Fax: (775) 753-5556. Web Site:elkoradio.com Licensee: Elko Broadcasting Co. Population served: 35,000 Format: Adult hits. News staff: one; News: 5 hrs wkly.

*KLKR(FM)—Not on air, target date: unknown: 89.3 mhz; 5 kw. Ant 777 ft TL: N40 54 35 W115 49 05. Hrs open: 1289 S. Torrey Pines Dr., Las Vegas, 89146. Phone: (702) 258-9895. Fax: (702) 258-5646.E-mail: info@knpr.org Web Site:www.knpr.org Licensee: Nevada Public Radio. Natl. Network: NPR, PRI, . ♦Florence Rogers, gen mgr.

*KNCC(FM)— 1992: 91.5 mhz; 50 w. 741 ft TL: N40 49 16 W115 42 04. Hrs open: 24
Rebroadcasts *KUNR(FM) Reno.
Great Basin College, 1500 College Pkwy., 89801. Phone: (775) 327-5867. Fax: (775) 738-8171. Fax: (775) 327-5386.E-mail: carl@gbcnv.edu Licensee: Great Basin College. Population served: 50,000 Format: Class, big band, educ, jazz, news. Spec prog: Public radio. ♦Carl Diekhans, gen mgr.

KOYT(FM)— 2005: 94.5 mhz; 36 kw. Ant 1,519 ft TL: N40 55 18 W115 50 58. Hrs open: 1750 Manzanita Drive, Suite 1, 89801. Phone: (775) 777-1196. Fax: (775) 777-9587. Licensee: Ruby Radio Corp. (acq 10-25-2005; exchange for KCLS(FM) Ruby). Format: Rock. ♦Alene Sutherland, VP; Mike Allen, progmg dir.

KPHD(FM)—Not on air, target date: unknown: 97.5 mhz; 90 kw. Ant 1,604 ft TL: N40 55 43 W115 50 33. Hrs open: College Creek Media LLC, 980 N. Michigan Ave., Suite 1880, Chicago, IL, 60611. Phone: (312) 204-9900. Licensee: College Creek Media LLC. ♦Neal J. Robinson, pres.

KRJC(FM)— October 1981: 95.3 mhz; 25 kw. Ant 774 ft TL: N40 54 35 W115 49 05. Stereo. Hrs open: 24 1250 Lamoille Hwy., Suite 1045, 89801-1626. Phone: (775) 738-9895. Fax: (775) 753-8085.E-mail: krjc@krjc.com Web Site:www.krjc.com Licensee: Holiday Broadcasting of Elko. Group owner: Carlson Communications International. Population served: 40,000 Natl. Network: AP Network News, . Wire Svc: AP Format: Country, news. News staff: one; News: 4 hrs wkly. Target aud: 25-54. ♦Ralph J. Carlson, pres; Jennifer Sprout, stn mgr; Kristi Agenbroad, gen sls mgr, rgnl sls mgr.

KTSN(AM)— November 1996: 1340 khz; 1 kw-D. TL: N40 52 08 W115 43 09. Hrs open: 1250 Lamoille Hwy., Suite 1045, 89801. Phone: (775) 738-9895. Fax: (775) 753-9895. Web Site:www.ktsn1340.com Licensee: Humboldt Broadcasting LLC. Group owner: Carlson Communications International. Format: Talk, sports, news. ♦Jennifer Sprout, stn mgr; Kristi Agenbroad, gen mgr & gen sls mgr.

Ely

KCLS(FM)— Nov 1, 1986: 101.7 mhz; 480 w. Ant 804 ft TL: N39 14 46 W114 55 39. Stereo. Hrs open: 24 College Creek Media LLC, 980 N. Michigan Ave., Suite 1880, Chicago, IL, 60611. Phone: (312) 204-9900. Licensee: College Creek Media LLC. (acq 10-25-2005; exchange for KOYT(FM) Elko). Format: Talk. ♦Neal J. Robinson, pres.

KDSS(FM)— Dec 22, 1984: 92.7 mhz; 14 kw. Ant 941 ft TL: N39 14 46 W114 55 39. Stereo. Hrs open: 24 501 Aultman St., Suite 208, 89301. Phone: (775) 289-6474. Fax: (775) 289-6531.E-mail: kdssfm@sbcglobal.net Licensee: Coates Broadcasting Inc. (acq 5-1-96; $180,000). Irwin, Campbell & Tannenwald, P.C. Format: C & W. News: 10 hrs wkly. Target aud: 18-64; older demographics, new & classic C&W listeners. ♦Karen Livingston, gen mgr, sls; Jim Liebsack, chief of engrg; Samantha Coates, pres, VP & sls.

KELY(AM)— July 8, 1950: 1230 khz; 1 kw-U. TL: N39 15 45 W114 51 46. Hrs open: 24 Box 151465, 89315. Phone: (775) 289-2077. Fax: (775) 289-6997. Web Site:www.elyradio.com Licensee: Ely Radio LLC. (group owner; (acq 3-21-2006; $140,000). Population served: 12,650 Format: Talk. News staff: one; News: 5. Target aud: 35 plus. Spec prog: Local High School Sports. ♦Wyatt Cox, gen mgr.

Fallon

KHWG(AM)— June 2005: 750 khz; 10 kw-D, 280 w-N, 10 kw-CH. TL: N39 28 57 W118 45 36. Hrs open: 1050 W. Williams Ave., 89406. Phone: (775) 428-1764. Fax: (775) 428-1765.E-mail: khwg@ccomm.net Web Site:www.khwgclassiccountry.com Licensee: Media Enterprises Inc. (acq 1-8-2003). Format: Classic country. ♦Keily Miller, pres; Dee Gregory, gen mgr.

*KQNV(FM)—Not on air, target date: unknown: 89.9 mhz; 25 kw. Ant 1,797 ft TL: N39 54 35 W118 55 15. Hrs open: 3185 S. Highland Dr., Suite 13, Las Vegas, 89109. Phone: (702) 731-5588. Fax: (702) 731-5851. Licensee: American Educational Broadcasting Inc. ♦Carl J. Auel, pres.

KRNG(FM)— July 4, 1997: 101.3 mhz; 1.65 kw. Ant 2,207 ft TL: N39 42 30 W119 10 16. Stereo. Hrs open: 1050 W. Wadsworth, 89442. Secondary address: 360 Pyramid St., Wadsworth 89442. Phone: (775) 575-7777. Fax: (775) 575-7737.E-mail: email@renegaderadio.org Web Site:www.renegaderadio.org Licensee: Sierra Nevada Christian Music Association Inc. Population served: 200,000 Natl. Rep: McGavren Guild,. Format: Christian rock. Target aud: 12-35; youth, young adults. ♦Rev. Karry Crites, pres, stn mgr; William E. Bauer PhD., opns VP.

KVLV(AM)— May 9, 1957: 980 khz; 5 kw-D. TL: N39 29 47 W118 48 50. Hrs open: 6 AM-sunset 1155 Gummow Dr., 89406. Phone: (775) 423-2243. Phone: (775) 423-5858. Fax: (775) 423-8889.E-mail: kvlv@phonewave.net Licensee: Lahontan Valley Broadcasting LLC. Population served: 60,000 Natl. Network: ABC, . Format: C&W. News: 10 hrs wkly. Target aud: 25 plus. ♦Mike McGinness, gen mgr.

KVLV-FM— Nov 26, 1966: 99.3 mhz; 3.7 kw. Ant 250 ft TL: N39 29 47 W118 48 50. Stereo. Hrs open: 24 1155 Gummow Dr., 89406. Phone: (775) 423-2243. Phone: 775-423-5858. Fax: (775) 423-8889. Licensee: Lahontan Valley Broadcasting LLC. Population served: 40,000 Natl. Network: AP Radio, . Format: Adult contemp. News: 10 hrs wkly. ♦Mike McGinness, gen mgr.

KZZD(FM)—Not on air, target date: unknown: 104.1 mhz; 100 kw horiz. Ant 1,968 ft TL: N39 54 46 W118 55 18. Hrs open: 149 Penn Ave., Scranton, PA, 18503. Phone: (570) 348-9103. Fax: (570) 348-9109. Licensee: Shamrock Communications Inc. ♦William R. Lynett, pres.

Fernley

KEHD(FM)—Not on air, target date: unknown: 107.3 mhz; 100 kw horiz. Ant 1,968 ft TL: N39 54 46 W118 55 18. Hrs open: 149 Penn Ave., Scranton, PA, 18503. Phone: (570) 348-9108. Fax: (570) 348-9109. Licensee: Shamrock Communications Inc. (acq 9-19-2007; $500,000 for CP). ♦William R. Lynett, pres.

Gardnerville-Minden

KKFT(FM)— Sept 19, 1985: 99.1 mhz; 410 w. Ant 2,006 ft TL: N39 15 34 W119 42 21. Stereo. Hrs open: 24 1960 Idaho St., Carson City, 89701. Phone: (775) 884-8000. Fax: (775) 882-3961.E-mail: jerry@991fmtalk.com Web Site:www.991fmtalk.com Licensee: Jerry Evans (acq 11-28-2003; $850,000). Population served: 600,000 Natl. Network: Fox News Radio, . Shainis & Peltzman. Format: News, talk. News staff: 2; News: 24 hrs wkly. Target aud: 25-54; btfl people. ♦Jerry Evans, CEO, gen mgr & stn mgr.

Gerlach

***KLAP(FM)**—Not on air, target date: unknown: 89.5 mhz; 130 w. Ant -325 ft TL: N40 39 06 W119 21 14. Hrs open: 42528 Rd. 1, Lake City, CA, 96115. Phone: (530) 279-6262.E-mail: info@openskyradio.org Web Site:openskyradio.org Licensee: OpenSkyRadio Corp. ♦Jeff Cotton, gen mgr.

Hawthorne

KAVB(FM)— December 2007: 98.7 mhz; 5.5 kw. Ant 3,139 ft TL: N38 27 28 W118 45 52. Hrs open: 24 Box 2434, La Puente, CA, 91746. Phone: (213) 627-8711. Fax: (213) 627-8712.E-mail: info@almavision.com Web Site:www.almavision.com Licensee: Alma Vision Hispanic Network Inc. Format: Sp Christian. ♦Juan Bruno Caamano, pres.

***KELC(FM)**—Not on air, target date: unknown: 91.9 mhz; 500 w. Ant -853 ft TL: N38 31 26.6 W118 37 18. Hrs open: 3185 S. Highland Dr., Suite 13, Las Vegas, 89109. Phone: (702) 731-5588. Fax: (702) 731-5851. Licensee: American Educational Broadcasting Inc. ♦Carl J. Auel, pres.

KIFO(AM)—Not on air, target date: unknown: 1450 khz; 1 kw-U. TL: N38 30 46 W118 37 58. Hrs open: Box 1450, St. George, UT, 84771-1450. Secondary address: 210 North 1000 East, St. George, UT 84770-3155. Phone: (435) 628-1000. Fax: (435) 628-6636. Licensee: Radio 1450 LLC. (acq 3-15-2006; $13,000 for CP). Population served: 3,946 Dan J. Alpert. ♦E. Morgan Skinner Jr., pres.

***KQMC(FM)**—Not on air, target date: unknown: 90.1 mhz; 1.3 kw. Ant 3,677 ft TL: N38 47 04 W118 49 59. Hrs open: American Educational Broadcasting Inc., 3185 S. Highland Dr. #13, Las Vegas, 89109. Phone: (702) 731-5588. Licensee: American Educational Broadcasting Inc. ♦Lee Amundsen, gen mgr.

Henderson

KDOX(AM)— May 1956: 1280 khz; 5 kw-D, 28 w-N. TL: N36 03 13 W114 58 30. Hrs open: 24 150 Spectrum Blvd., Las Vegas, 89101. Phone: (702) 258-0285. Fax: (702) 732-3060.E-mail: info@kdoxam.com Web Site:www.1280talk.com Licensee: S & R Broadcasting Inc. (acq 9-28-2005; $2 million). Population served: 160,000 Natl. Rep: Lotus Entravision Reps LLC,. Rosenman & Colin L.L.P. Format: Sp. Target aud: General; Hispanic, above-average income, high home ownership. ♦Paul Ruttan, pres; Scott Gentry, gen mgr; Ellen Walker, gen sls mgr; Roberto Ibarra, progmg dir; Warren Brown, chief of engrg.

KKJJ(FM)— Nov 28, 1982: 100.5 mhz; 100 kw. 1,105 ft TL: N36 00 28 W115 00 20. Stereo. Hrs open: 24 6655 W. Sahara Ave., Suite C 216, Las Vegas, 89146. Phone: (702) 889-5100. Fax: (702) 257-2936.E-mail: jack@jackbaby.com Web Site:www.jackbaby.com Licensee: Infinity Radio Inc. Group owner: Infinity Broadcasting Corp. (acq 11-13-98; grpsl). Natl. Network: CBS Radio, . Natl. Rep: Katz Radio,. Steven Lerman. Format: Adult hits. News: one hr wkly. Target aud: 25-54. ♦Joel Hollander, CEO; John Sykes, pres; Tom Humm, VP, gen mgr, gen sls mgr; Lorene Malis, natl sls mgr; Sam Ballenger, mktg dir, prom dir; Craig Powers, progmg dir; Herb Perry, pub affrs dir; Tracy Teagarden, chief of engrg; Stephanie Lindelow, traf mgr.

KMXB(FM)— Feb 10, 1970: 94.1 mhz; 100 kw. 1,210 ft TL: N36 00 26 W115 00 24. Stereo. Hrs open: 24 6655 W. Sahara Ave., Suite D-110, Las Vegas, 89146. Phone: (702) 889-5100. Fax: (702) 257-2936.E-mail: justin@mix941.fm Web Site:www.mix941.fm Licensee: CBS Radio Stations Inc. Group owner: Infinity Broadcasting Corp. (acq 11-13-98; grpsl). Population served: 1,500,000 Natl. Network: CBS Radio, . Leventhal, Senter & Lerman. Format: Modern adult contemp. News staff: one. Target aud: 18-49; female. ♦John Sykes, CEO, chmn; John Fullam, COO, pres; Jacques Tortoli, CFO; Tom Humm, VP, gen mgr; Lorene Malis, natl sls mgr; Lori Heeren, rgnl sls mgr; Jennifer DiFazio, mktg dir, progmg dir; Justin Chase, progmg dir; Tracy Teagarden, chief of engrg; Stephanie Lindelow, traf mgr.

KWNR(FM)— July 18, 1972: 95.5 mhz; 92 kw. 1,161 ft TL: N36 00 31 W115 00 22. Hrs open: 2880 Meade Ave., Suite 250, Las Vegas, 89102. Phone: (702) 238-7300. Fax: (702) 732-4890.E-mail: info@kwnr.com Web Site:www.kwnr.com Licensee: Citicasters Licenses L.P. Group owner: Clear Channel Communications Inc. (acq 1999; grpsl). Hogan & Hartson. Format: Country. Target aud: 18-54. ♦Brandy Newman, VP, gen mgr; Sean Cassidy, gen mgr & gen sls mgr; Bill Lubitz, prom dir; Brooks O'Brien, progmg dir; Mitch Kelly, news dir; Greg Benson, engrg dir, chief of engrg.

Incline Village

KRNO(FM)—Licensed to Incline Village. See Reno

Indian Springs

KRGT(FM)— Nov 22, 2002: 99.3 mhz; 31 kw. Ant 2,263 ft TL: N36 19 28 W115 33 58. Hrs open: 24 6767 W. Tropicana Ave., Suite 102, Las Vegas, 89103. Phone: (702) 284-6400. Fax: (702) 284-6403. Web Site:www.univision.com Licensee: Univision Radio License Corp. Group owner: Univision Radio (acq 9-22-2003; grpsl). Format: Sp. ♦Dana Demerjian, VP, gen mgr; Cristina Valarezo, gen sls mgr; Joe Reynolds, natl sls mgr; Zulema Santacruz, prom mgr; Rataël Miramontes, progmg dir; Manny Garcia, chief of engrg; Glocia Salvador, traf mgr.

Jackpot

***KBSJ(FM)**—Not on air, target date: unknown: 91.3 mhz; 3.7 kw. 2,463 ft Hrs open: Idaho State Board of Education, 1910 University Dr., Boise, ID, 83725. Phone: (208) 426-3663. Fax: (208) 344-6631. Licensee: Idaho State Board of Education. Format: Classical jazz. ♦John Hess, gen mgr; Brad Campbell, opns mgr; Hy Kloc, dev dir; Ele Ellis, progmg dir; Sadie Babits, news dir; Tom Taylor, engrg dir.

Las Vegas

KBAD(AM)— June 1953: 920 khz; 5 kw-D, 500 w-N, DA-2. TL: N36 11 25 W115 10 35. Hrs open: 8755 W. Flamingo Rd., 89147-8667. Phone: (702) 876-1460. Fax: (702) 876-6685. Web Site:www.wearelv.com Licensee: Lotus Broadcasting Corp. (acq 11-4-92; $1.42 million with co-located FM; 11-23-92). Population served: 500,000 Natl. Network: Fox Sports, . Natl. Rep: Interep,. Format: Sports. Target aud: 18 plus. ♦Tony Bonnici, gen mgr; Mitch Moss, progmg dir.

***KCEP(FM)**— October 1973: 88.1 mhz; 10,000 kw. -39 ft TL: N36 10 51 W115 08 43. (CP: 10 kw, ant 1,079 ft.). Stereo. Hrs open: 24 330 W. Washington St., 89106. Phone: (702) 648-0104. Fax: (702) 647-0803.E-mail: cknight@power881v.com Web Site:www.power881v.com Licensee: Economic Opportunity Board of Clark County. Population served: 1,500,000 Format: Black, urban contemp, rhythm & blues. News: 11 hrs wkly. Target aud: 12-55; African-Americans. Spec prog: Gospel 14 hrs, Jazz 12 hrs wkly. ♦Craig Knight, progmg dir & progmg mgr.

***KCNV(FM)**— Mar 24, 1980: 89.5 mhz; 98 kw. Ant 1,532 ft TL: N35 56 50 W115 03 01. Stereo. Hrs open: 24 1289 S. Torrey Pines, 89146. Phone: (702) 258-9895. Fax: (702) 258-5646.E-mail: info@knpr.org Web Site:www.knpr.org Licensee: Nevada Public Radio Corp. Population served: 1,200,000 Dow, Lohnes & Albertson. Format: Classical. Target aud: 35-54. ♦Florence Rogers, chmn, pres, gen mgr; Melanie Canon, CFO, dev dir; Phil Burger, opns dir; Jay Bartos, pub affrs dir; Warren Brown, chief of engrg.

KCYE(FM)—(Boulder City, Sept 1, 1982: 102.7 mhz; 96 kw. Ant 1,978 ft TL: N35 56 46 W115 02 34. Stereo. Hrs open: 24 1455 E. Tropicana Ave., Suite 800, 89119. Phone: (702) 730-0300. Fax: (702) 736-8447.E-mail: kfrhfm@kfrhfm.com Web Site:www.kcye.com Licensee: KJUL License LLC. Group owner: Beasley Broadcast Group Inc. (acq 9-6-2000; grpsl). Population served: 780,000 Format: Country. ♦Tom Davis, gen mgr; Mark Warlaumont, sls dir; Patti Mills, gen sls mgr; Courtney Smith, mktg dir, prom dir; Justin Chase, progmg dir.

KDOX(AM)—See Henderson

KDWN(AM)— Apr 7, 1975: 720 khz; 50 kw-U, DA-N. TL: N36 04 22 W114 58 20. Hrs open: 24 1455 E. Tropicana, .Suite 800, 89119. Phone: (702) 730-0300. Fax: (702) 736-8447.E-mail: kdwn@kdwn.com Web Site:www.kdwn.com Licensee: KDWN License L.P. (acq 8-7-2006; $17 million). Population served: 1,000,000 Natl. Network: Fox News Radio, . Format: News/talk. Target aud: 35-54. ♦Tom Davis, gen mgr; Mark Warlaumont, sls dir, sls dir; Al Mollet, gen sls mgr; Charlotte Burke, progmg dir; Brian Shapiro, news dir; Stephen Rutherford, chief of engrg. Co-owned TV: .

KEIP(AM)—Not on air, target date: unknown: 760 khz; 1 kw-D, 930 w-N, DA-2. TL: N36 03 30 W115 12 39. Hrs open: 3185 Highland Dr., Suite 13, 89109. Phone: (702) 731-5588. Fax: (702) 731-5851. Licensee: Las Vegas Broadcasters Partnership. Irwin, Campbell & Tannenwald. ♦Carl Auel, CEO, pres; Fred Hodges, gen mgr.

KENO(AM)— 1940: 1460 khz; 10 kw-D, 620 w-N, DA-2. TL: N36 11 25 W115 10 35. Hrs open: 8755 W. Flamingo Rd., 89147-8667. Phone: (702) 876-1460. Fax: (702) 876-6685. Licensee: Lotus Broadcasting Corp. (group owner; (acq 6-1-65). Population served: 850,000 Natl. Network: ESPN Deportes, . Natl. Rep: Interep,. Format: Sp sports. ♦Tony Bonnici, gen mgr; Alvaro Puentes, progmg dir.

KISF(FM)— March 1989: 103.5 mhz; 100 kw. Ant 1,158 ft TL: N36 00 29 W115 00 20. Hrs open: 6767 W. Tropicana Ave., Suite 102, 89103. Phone: (702) 284-6400. Fax: (702) 284-6403. Web Site:www.univision.com Licensee: HBC License Corp. Group owner: Univision Radio (acq 9-22-2003; grpsl). Format: Rgnl Mexican. ♦Dana Demerjian, VP, gen mgr; Cristina Valarelo, gen sls mgr; Joe Reynolds, natl sls mgr; Brent Berger, rgnl sls mgr; Zulema Santacruz, prom mgr; Roberto Warling, progmg dir; Manny Garcia, chief of engrg; Gloria Salvador, traf mgr.

KKLZ(FM)— Jan 26, 1984: 96.3 mhz; 100 kw. Ant 1,170 ft TL: N36 00 29 W115 00 20. Stereo. Hrs open: 24 1455 E. Tropican, Suite 800, 89119. Phone: (702) 739-9600. Fax: (702) 736-8447.E-mail: kklzfm@kklzfm.com Web Site:www.963kklz.com Licensee: Beasley Broadcasting of NV LLC. Group owner: Beasley Broadcast Group Inc. (acq 2-1-2001; grpsl). Population served: 850,000 Format: Classic hits. News staff: one. Target aud: 25-44; baby boomers. ♦Al Mollet, gen mgr, gen sls mgr; Mark Warlaumont, sls dir; Brian Shapiro, gen sls mgr, news dir; Dan Hallett, progmg dir; Dan Lea, mus dir; Dennis Mitchell, news dir; Stephen Rutherford, chief of engrg.

KKVV(AM)— May 1, 1990: 1060 khz; 5 kw-D, 43 w-N. TL: N36 09 22 W115 15 24. Hrs open: 24 3185 S. Highland Dr., Suite 13, 89109. Phone: (702) 731-5588. Phone: (702) 650-5588. Fax: (702) 731-5851.E-mail: kkvv@kkvv.com Web Site:www.kkvv.com Licensee: Las Vegas Broadcasters Inc. (acq 11-8-93; $17,000; 11-29-93). Population served: 1,700,000 Natl. Network: Salem Radio Network, . Natl. Rep: Salem,. Format: Relg, talk, adult contemp, christian, Sp. News staff: 2; News: 2 hrs wkly min. Target aud: General; General. Spec prog: Sp christian 20 hrs wkly. ♦Carl J. Auel, pres; Jane A. Filler, VP; Fred Hodges, gen mgr.

KLAV(AM)— June 1947: 1230 khz; 1 kw-U. TL: N36 11 20 W115 08 40. (CP: TL: N36 12 52 W115 09 18). Hrs open: 24 1130 East Desert Inn Rd., 89109. Phone: (702) 796-1230. Fax: (702) 853-2599.E-mail: patriceburker@broadcasting.com Web Site:www.klav1230am.com Licensee: Burken Broadcasting LLC (acq 8-6-2004; $3.2 million). Population served: 1,500,000 Haley, Bader & Potts. Format: Talk, info, sports. Target aud: 25-54. Spec prog: Relg 3 hrs, Indian one hr, Hawaiian 4 hrs, Arabic 7 hrs, Filipino 5 hrs, Hebrew one hr wkly. ♦Patrice Donley, VP, gen mgr; Peggy Merrill, stn mgr; Jon Lindquist, opns mgr.

KLSQ(AM)—See Whitney

KLUC-FM— 1956: 98.5 mhz; 100 kw. 1,191 ft TL: N36 00 29 W115 00 20. Stereo. Hrs open: 24 6655 W. Sahara Ave., Suite D208, 89146. Phone: (702) 253-9800. Fax: (702) 889-7373.E-mail: info@kluc.com Web Site:www.kluc.com Licensee: Infinity Radio Inc. Group owner: Infinity Broadcasting Corp. (acq 12-14-00; grpsl). Population served: 1,000,000 Format: CHR/top-40. News staff: one. Target aud: 18-34. ♦Marty Basch, gen mgr; Frank Feder, gen sls mgr; Cat Thomas, progmg dir; Tracy Teagarden, chief of engrg; Theresa Dunbar, traf mgr.

KMZQ(AM)— 2008: 670 khz; 30 kw-D, 600 w-N, DA-2. TL: N36 23 05 W115 21 05 (day), N36 23 03 W115 21 04 (night). Hrs open: 3800 Howard Hughes Pkwy., 17th Fl., 89169. Phone: (702) 385-6000. Fax: (702) 385-6001. Licensee: Kemp Communications Inc. Format: Classic hits. ♦Will Kemp, pres.

***KNPR(FM)**— Oct 31, 2003: 88.9 mhz; 24.5 kw. Ant 3,680 ft TL: N35 58 02 W115 30 06. (CP: 22 kw, ant 3,903 ft. TL: N35 57 55 W115 29 58.77). Stereo. Hrs open: 1289 S. Torrey Pines Dr., 89146. Phone: (702) 258-9895. Fax: (702) 258-5646.E-mail: info@knpr.org Web Site:www.knpr.org Licensee: Nevada Public Radio. Population served: 1,800,000 Natl. Network: NPR, PRI, . Format: All news and info. ♦Florence Rogers, pres & gen mgr.

KNUU(AM)—(Paradise, Feb 21, 1962: 970 khz; 5 kw-D, 500 w-N, DA-2. TL: N36 00 40 W115 14 28. Hrs open: 24 1455 E. Tropicana Ave., Suite 550, 89119. Phone: (702) 735-8644. Fax: (702) 734-4755. Web Site:www.knews970.com Licensee: BTR West Inc. (acq 11-13-2006; $3.9 million). Population served: 1,600,000 Natl. Network: Wall Street, ABC, CNN Radio, . Format: News/talk. News staff: 8; News: 154 hrs wkly. Target aud: 35 plus. ♦Michael Metter, pres; Jim Servino, gen mgr.

KOMP(FM)— Sept 1, 1966: 92.3 mhz; 100 kw. 1,520 ft TL: N35 56 50 W115 03 01. (CP: 22.9 kw, ant 3,844 ft.). Stereo. Hrs open: Prog sep from AM 8755 W. Flamingo Rd., 89147-8667. Phone: (702) 876-1460. Fax: (702) 876-6685. Web Site:www.wearelv.com Licensee: Lotus Broadcasting Corp. Population served: 500,000 Natl. Rep: Interep,. Wire Svc: UPI Format: AOR. ♦John Griffin, progmg dir.

KPLV(FM)— Sept 1, 1977: 93.1 mhz; 24 kw. Ant 3,742 ft TL: N35 58 02 W115 30 06. Stereo. Hrs open: 2880 Meade Ave., Suite 250, 89102. Phone: (702) 238-7300. Fax: (702) 732-4890.E-mail: info@931theparty.com Web Site:931theparty.com Licensee: Citicasters Licenses L.P. Group owner: Clear Channel Communications Inc. (acq 1999). Hogan & Hartson. Format: Rhythmic adult contemp. ♦Randy Newman, gen mgr; Aaron Crowley, gen sls mgr; Rik McNeil, progmg dir; Mitch Kelly, news dir; Greg Benson, chief of engrg; Tom Chase, opns dir & farm dir.

KQRT(FM)— 1993: 105.1 mhz; 50 kw. 1,614 ft TL: N36 19 46 W115 21 49. Stereo. Hrs open: 24 500 Pilot Rd., Suite D89119, 89119. Phone: (702) 434-0015. Phone: (323) 900-6100. Fax: (702) 507-1081. Licensee: Entravision Holdings LLC. Group owner: Entravision Communications Corp. (acq 3-14-2000; grpsl). Natl. Rep: Lotus Entravision Reps LLC,. Format: Sp, CHR. Target aud: Spanish; young. ♦Walter Ulloa, CEO & pres; Chris Roman, gen mgr; Jr Desamours, stn mgr, natl sls mgr; Gerry Fernandez, prom dir; Erin Thomas, traf mgr. Co-owned TV: KINC(TV)

KRLV(AM)— 1947: 1340 khz; 1 kw-U. TL: N36 09 22 W115 15 24. Hrs open: 24 1130 E. Desert Inn Rd., Suite 100, 89109. Phone: (702) 736-3145. Fax: (702) 740-8196.E-mail: generalmanager@krlv.net Web Site:www.krlv1340am.com Licensee: Burken Broadcasting LLC (acq 9-7-2007; $3.4 million). Cohn & Marks, LLP. Format: Sp, news, sports. News staff: 3; News: 12 hrs wkly. Target aud: 25-54. ♦Patrice Donley, gen mgr; Peggy Merrill, stn mgr; Bruce Garrett, sls dir, mktg dir; John Lindquist, progmg dir.

KSHP(AM)—(North Las Vegas, 1954: 1400 khz; 1 kw-U. TL: N36 12 52 W115 09 18. Stereo. Hrs open: 24 2400 S. Jones, Suite 3, 89146. Phone: (702) 221-1200. Fax: (702) 221-2285.E-mail: info@kshp.com Licensee: Las Vegas Radio Co. Group owner: McNaughton-Jakle Stations (acq 9-20-96; $600,000). Population served: 2,400,000 Format: Radio shopping, sports. ♦K. Richard Jakle, pres; Brett Grant, VP, gen mgr, gen sls mgr, progmg dir; Mark Blum, gen sls mgr; Joe Sands, chief of engrg.

KSNE-FM— Aug 18, 1987: 106.5 mhz; 100 kw. 1,155 ft TL: N36 00 30 W115 00 20. Stereo. Hrs open: 24 2880 Meade Ave., Suite 250, 89102. Phone: (702) 238-7300. Fax: (702) 732-4597. Licensee: Citicasters Licenses L.P. Group owner: Clear Channel Communications Inc. (acq 1999; grpsl). Hogan & Hartson. Format: Soft adult contemp. News: 4 hrs wkly. Target aud: 25-54; emphasis on women. Spec prog: Relg one hr, pub affrs one hr wkly. ♦Jamal Parker, gen sls mgr; Tom Chase, progmg dir; Mitch Kelly, news dir; Tree Lee, engrg dir & chief of engrg.

***KSOS(FM)**— July 18, 1972: 90.5 mhz; 100 kw. 1,269 ft TL: N36 00 29 W115 00 20. Stereo. Hrs open: 24 2201 S. 6th St., 89104. Phone: (702) 731-5452. Phone: (800) 804-5452. Fax: (702) 731-1992.E-mail: info@sosradio.net Web Site:www.sosradio.net Licensee: Faith Communications Corp. (acq 12-31-71). Population served: 1,900,000 Cohn & Marks. Format: Christian, adult contemp. News: 5 hrs wkly. Target aud: 25-44; young families. ♦Jack French, CEO & VP; Brad Staley, gen mgr; Chris Staley, opns mgr, progmg mgr.

***KUNV(FM)**— Apr 21, 1981: 91.5 mhz; 15 kw. 1,100 ft TL: N36 00 28 W115 00 20. Stereo. Hrs open: 24 4505 Maryland Parkway, Box 452010, 89154-2010. Phone: (702) 798-9169. Fax: (702) 736-0983. Web Site:www.kunv.org Licensee: University of Nevada Board of Regents. Population served: 1,700,000 Natl. Network: NPR, . Format: Jazz, multi-cultural. Target aud: General. Spec prog: Sp 5 hrs, electronic 2 hrs, community affrs 4 hrs, Ger one hr wkly. ♦David Reese, gen mgr; Frank Muller, opns mgr; Kim Lizny, progmg dir & mus dir; Joe Sands, chief of engrg.

***KVKL(FM)**— 2006: 91.1 mhz; 1.6 kw vert. Ant 994 ft TL: N35 37 37 W115 16 11. Hrs open: 3185 S. Highland Dr., Suite 13, 89108. Phone: (702) 731-5588. Licensee: Southern Nevada Educational Broadcasters. ♦Carl Auel, CEO; Carl J. Auel, pres; Fred Hodges, gen mgr.

KWID(FM)— Mar 22, 1963: 101.9 mhz; 100 kw. Ant 1,181 ft TL: N36 00 28 W115 00 20. Stereo. Hrs open: 2880-B Meade Ave., Suite 250, 89119. Phone: (702) 238-7300. Fax: (702) 792-9018.E-mail: info@kwidfm.com Licensee: Texas Lotus Corp. Group owner: Clear Channel Communications Inc. (acq 7-29-2008; with KVMX(FM) Bakersfield, CA in exchange for KZEP-FM San Antonio, TX). Population served: 750,000 Bryan Cave LLP. Format: Sp adult hits. Target aud: 25-49. ♦Brandy Newman, VP, gen mgr; Kelly Kibler, gen mgr; Sam Loya, gen sls mgr; Benjamin Acevedo, prom dir; Greg Benson, chief of engrg.

KWWN(AM)— 2007: 1100 khz; 20 kw-D, 2 kw-N, DA-2. TL: N36 12 45 W115 09 45. Hrs open: 8755 W. Flamingo Rd., 89147-8667. Phone: (702) 876-1460. Fax: (702) 876-6685.E-mail: info@espn1100.com Web Site:www.wearelv.com Licensee: Lotus Broadcasting Corp. Natl. Network: ESPN Radio, . Natl. Rep: Interep,. Format: Sports. ♦Tony Bonnici, gen mgr; Jessee Leeds, gen sls mgr; Mitch Moss, progmg dir; Andy Kaye, news dir.

KXPT(FM)— Nov 29, 1961: 97.1 mhz; 50 kw. 1,950 ft TL: N35 56 44 W115 02 31. (CP: 24 kw). Stereo. Hrs open: Prog sep from AM 8755 W. Flamingo Rd., 89147-8667. Phone: (702) 876-1460. Fax: (702) 876-6685.E-mail: info@point97.com Web Site:www.wearelv.com Licensee: Lotus Broadcasting Corp. Population served: 600,000 Natl. Rep: Interep,. Format: Classic hits. Target aud: 35-49. ♦John Griffin, opns mgr & progmg dir.

KYDZ(AM)—(North Las Vegas, 1956: 1140 khz; 10 kw-D, 2.5 kw-N, DA-N. TL: N36 16 05 W115 02 41. Hrs open: 24 hrs 6655 W. Sahara Ave., Suite D-110, 89146-0851. Phone: (702) 253-9800. Fax: (702) 889-7373. Web Site:www.kydzradiolv.com Licensee: CBS Radio Stations Inc. Format: Children. ♦Leah Hovig, VP, gen mgr; Bob Proffitt, sls dir; Lori Heeren, gen sls mgr; Monique Linder, progmg dir; Mike Weaver, chief of engrg.

Laughlin

KVGS(FM)— 1991: 107.9 mhz; 98 kw. Ant 1,984 ft TL: N35 39 07 W114 18 42. Hrs open: 24 2725 E. Desert Inn Rd, Suite 180, Las Vegas, 89121. Phone: (702) 784-4000. Fax: (702) 784-4040.E-mail: info@v108fm.com Web Site:www.v108fm.com Licensee: RBG Las Vegas Licenses LLC (acq 10-3-2005; $38 million with KOAS(FM) Dolan Springs, AZ). Natl. Network: ABC, . Format: Urban contemp. Target aud: 25-54; adults. ♦Dave Presher, gen mgr; Joshua Mednick, sls dir; Craig Knight, prom dir; Tony Rankin, progmg dir; Theresa Dunbar, mus dir, traf mgr; Ray Fodge, chief of engrg.

Logandale

KADD(FM)— September 1997: 93.5 mhz; 93 kw horiz. Ant 2,089 ft TL: N36 38 07 W114 07 18. Hrs open: 10 Media Center Dr., Havasu City, AZ, 86403. Phone: (928) 855-4560. Fax: (928) 855-7996.E-mail: epress@maddog.net Web Site:www.maddog.net Licensee: M&M Broadcasting LLC (acq 5-11-2001; $150,000). Format: Hot adult contemp. ♦Chris Rolando, gen mgr.

Lovelock

KZHD(FM)— 2008: 106.3 mhz; 3 kw horiz. Ant 2,106 ft TL: N40 07 05.2 W118 43 35.5. Hrs open: 149 Penn Ave., Scranton, PA, 18503. Phone: (570) 348-9103. Fax: (570) 348-9109. Licensee: Shamrock Communications Inc. (acq 9-19-2007; $500,000 for CP). ♦William R. Lynett, pres.

Lund

***KWPR(FM)**— September 2000: 88.7 mhz; 3 kw. Ant 2,201 ft TL: N39 18 54 W115 05 19. Stereo. Hrs open: 24
Rebroadcasts KNPR(FM) Las Vegas 100%.
Nevada Public Radio, 1289 S. Torrey Pines Dr., Las Vegas, 89146. Phone: (702) 258-9895. Fax: (702) 258-5646.E-mail: reception@knpr.org Web Site:www.nevadapublicradio.org Licensee: Nevada Public Radio. Population served: 4,000 Format: Div, news. ♦Florence Rogers, gen mgr.

Mesquite

***KAIZ(FM)**— 2005: 91.1 mhz; 400 w. Ant 827 ft TL: N36 53 51 W114 17 10. Stereo. Hrs open: 24
Rebroadcasts KLRD(FM) Yucaipa, CA 100%.
2351 Suinset Blvd., Suite 170-218, Rocklin, CA, 95765. Phone: (916) 251-1600. Fax: (916) 251-1650.E-mail: info@air1.com Web Site:www.air1.com Licensee: Educational Media Foundation. Group owner: EMF Broadcasting. Natl. Network: Air 1, . Shaw Pittman. Format: Contemp Christian. News staff: 3. Target aud: 18-35; Judeo-Christian, female. ♦Richard Jenkins, pres; Mike Novak, VP, progmg dir; Lloyd Parker, gen mgr; Keith Whipple, dev dir; Eric Allen, natl sls mgr; David Pierce, progmg mgr; Ed Lenane, news dir; Sam Wallington, engrg dir.

***KEKL(FM)**— 2005: 88.5 mhz; 20.5 kw. Ant 489 ft TL: N36 41 00 W114 30 48. Hrs open: Southern Nevada Educational Broadcasters, 3185 S. Highland Dr., Suite 13, Las Vegas, 89109-1029. Phone: (702) 731-5588. Licensee: Southern Nevada Educational Broadcasters. ♦Carl Auel, CEO; Carl J. Auel, pres; Fred Hodges, gen mgr.

KHIJ(FM)—Not on air, target date: unknown: 96.7 mhz; 100 kw horiz. Ant 1,886 ft TL: N36 49 53 W114 26 12. Hrs open: 980 N. Michigan Ave., Suite 1880, Chicago, IL, 60611. Phone: (312) 204-9900. Licensee: College Creek Media LLC. ♦Bruce Buzil, gen mgr.

KVEG(FM)— July 23, 2001: 97.5 mhz; 100 kw. Ant 981 ft TL: N36 34 52 W114 35 59. Hrs open: 24 3999 Las Vegas Blvd. S., Suite K, Las Vegas, 89119. Phone: (702) 736-6161. Fax: (702) 736-2986.E-mail: mail@kvegas.com Web Site:www.kvegas.com Licensee: Kemp Broadcasting Inc. Population served: 1,400,000 Koerner & Olender, P.C. Format: CHR/rhythmic. Target aud: 25-39. ♦Gary Cox, VP, gen mgr, gen sls mgr; Sherita Salisbury, progmg dir.

Moapa

KVBE(FM)— 2008: 94.5 mhz; 93 kw horiz. Ant 2,089 ft TL: N36 38 07 W114 07 18. Hrs open: 7251 W. Lake Mead Blvd., Suite 300, Las Vegas, 89128-8380. Phone: (702) 655-1249. Fax: (702) 655-6175. Web Site:www.vibevegas.com Licensee: Aurora Media LLC. ♦Scott G. Mahalick, gen mgr.

Moapa Valley

KJUL(FM)— July 1, 2001: 104.7 mhz; 100 kw. Ant 604 ft TL: N36 41 00 W114 30 48. Hrs open: 24 Summit Media Inc., 150 Spectrum Blvd., Las Vegas, 89101. Phone: (702) 258-0285. Fax: (702) 258-7570. Licensee: Summit American Inc. KMZ Rosenman. Wire Svc: AP Format: Adult contemp, country. Target aud: 25-54. ♦Scott Gentry, gen mgr.

North Las Vegas

KFRH(FM)— April 1989: 104.3 mhz; 24.5 kw. Ant 3,700 ft TL: N35 58 02 W115 30 06. Stereo. Hrs open: 24 1455 E. Tropicana Ave., Suite 800, Las Vegas, 89119. Phone: (702) 730-0300. Fax: (702) 736-8447.E-mail: kcyefm@kcyefm.com Web Site:www.1043now.com Licensee: KJUL License LLC. Group owner: Beasley Broadcast Group Inc. (acq 1-31-2001; grpsl). Format: Top-40. News: one hr wkly. Target aud: 35-64. ♦Al Mollet, CEO, gen sls mgr; R.W. Smith, gen mgr, progmg dir; Mark Warlaumont, sls dir; Tom Davis, sls dir & gen sls mgr; Patti Mills, natl sls mgr; Brian Shapiro, news dir; Stephen Rutherford, chief of engrg.

KSHP(AM)—Licensed to North Las Vegas. See Las Vegas

KXNT(AM)— 1986: 840 khz; 50 kw-D, 25 kw-N, DA-2. TL: N36 23 53 W114 54 57. Stereo. Hrs open: 24 6655 W. Sahara Ave., Suite D210, Las Vegas, 89146. Phone: (702) 364-8400. Fax: (702) 889-7384.E-mail: info@kxnt.com Web Site:www.kxnt.com Licensee: Infinity Radio Inc. Group owner: Infinity Broadcasting Corp. (acq 11-13-98; grpsl). Natl. Network: CBS Radio, . Baraff, Koerner & Olender. Format: News/talk. Target aud: 35-64; upscale adults. ♦Tom Humm, gen mgr; Dan Larson, gen sls mgr; Jack Landreth, progmg dir; Tracy Teagarden, engrg dir & chief of engrg.

KYDZ(AM)—Licensed to North Las Vegas. See Las Vegas

Overton

KONV(FM)—Not on air, target date: unknown: 106.9 mhz; 92 kw. Ant 2,043 ft TL: N36 50 55 W114 28 23. Hrs open: Wells Fargo Tower, 17th Fl., 3800 Howard Hughes Pkwy., Las Vegas, 89109. Fax: (702) 736-2986. Licensee: Kemp Communications Inc. ♦Will Kemp, pres.

Pahrump

KNYE(FM)— Nov 19, 2001: 95.1 mhz; 6 kw. Ant -92 ft TL: N36 11 52 W116 02 08. Hrs open: 24 1230 Dutch Ford Rd., 89048. Phone: (775) 751-6100. Fax: (775) 751-6193.E-mail: karen@knye.com Web Site:www.knye.com Licensee: Pahrump Radio Inc. (acq 2-14-01). Format: Oldies. ♦Karen Jackson, pres & gen mgr; Joe Sands, chief of engrg.

KXTE(FM)— 1989: 107.5 mhz; 24.5 kw. 3,715 ft TL: N35 58 02 W115 30 06. Stereo. Hrs open: 24 6655 W. Sahara Ave., Suite C-202, Las Vegas, 89146. Phone: (702) 257-1075. Fax: (702) 889-7575. Web Site:www.xtremeradio.fm Licensee: Infinity Radio Inc. Group owner: Infinity Broadcasting Corp. (acq 11-13-98; grpsl). Format: Talk, alternative. Target aud: 18-49. ♦Marty Basch, gen mgr; Frank Feder, gen sls mgr; Chris Ripley, progmg dir, mus dir; Tracy Teagarden, chief of engrg.

Panaca

***KLNR(FM)**— May 1989: 91.7 mhz; 1 kw. Ant 3,424 ft TL: N37 53 38 W114 34 40. Stereo. Hrs open: 24
Rebroadcasts KNPR(FM) Las Vegas 100%.
1289 S. Torrey Pines Dr., Las Vegas, 89146. Phone: (702) 258-9895. Fax: (702) 258-5646.E-mail: reception@knpr.org Licensee: Nevada Public Radio. Population served: 2,000 Natl. Network: NPR, . Dow, Lohnes & Albertson. Format: All news. ♦Florence Rogers, gen mgr.

Paradise

KNUU(AM)—Licensed to Paradise. See Las Vegas

Reno

KBZZ(AM)—See Sparks

KDOT(FM)— Oct 12, 1966: 104.5 mhz; 25 kw. 2,929 ft TL: N39 18 48 W119 52 59. Stereo. Hrs open: 24 Box 9870, 2900 Sutro St., 89512. Phone: (775) 329-9261. Fax: (775) 323-1450.E-mail: javet@kdot.com Web Site:www.kdot.com Licensee: Lotus Radio Corp. Group owner: Lotus Communications Corp. (acq 3-30-93; $600,000 with KIRS(AM) Sun Valley;4-19-93). Natl. Rep: D & R Radio,. Format: Active rock. News staff: one; News: 3 hrs wkly. Target aud: 18-49; young active adults that like today's lifestyle. ♦Dane Wilt, gen mgr; Marc Isquith, gen sls mgr; Derek Sante, prom dir; Jack Landreth, progmg dir; Joanne Silvernail, traf mgr.

KHIT(AM)— Jan 29, 1955: 1450 khz; 1 kw-U. TL: N39 33 26 W119 47 47. Hrs open: 24 Box 9870, 2900 Sutro St., 89512. Phone: (775) 329-9261. Fax: (775) 323-1450.E-mail: kena@kozzradio.com Licensee: Lotus Radio Corp. Group owner: Lotus Communications Corp. (acq 9-67). Population served: 225,000 Natl. Network: Fox Sports, . Natl. Rep: D & R Radio,. Format: Sports. Target aud: 25-49. ♦Dane Wilt, gen mgr; Jim McClain, opns mgr; Raina Weathers, gen sls mgr; Ken Allen, prom dir, progmg dir; Steve Diamond, news dir; Mike Weaver, chief of engrg; Dawn Keeble, traf mgr.

***KIHM(AM)**— Jan 1, 1984: 920 khz; 4.6 kw-D, 850 w-N. TL: N39 30 41 W119 42 51. Hrs open: 24 Immaculate Heart Radio, 7956 California Avenue, Fair Oaks, 95628. Phone: (916) 535-0500. Fax: (916) 535-0504. Web Site:www.ihradio.org Licensee: IHR Educational Broadcasting (group owner; acq 8-24-2000). Format: Catholic. ♦Doug Pearson, stn mgr.

KJFK(AM)— Oct 30, 1963: 1230 khz; 1 kw-U. TL: N39 30 42 W119 42 48. Hrs open: 24 Prog sep from FM 961 Matley Ln, Suite 120, 89502. Phone: (775) 829-1964. Fax: (775) 825-3183. Licensee: Americom Las Vegas L.P. Format: Progressive talk. Target aud: 35 plus. ♦Tom Quinn, pres; Daniel Cook, gen mgr, gen sls mgr; Dan Fritz, progmg dir; Steve Weber, chief of engrg.

***KJIV(FM)**—Not on air, target date: unknown: 89.5 mhz; 5 kw. Ant -3 ft TL: N39 34 20 W119 47 51. Hrs open: Truckee Meadows Community College, 7000 Dandini Blvd., 89512-3999. Phone: (775) 824-8611. Web Site:www.tmcc.edu Licensee: Board of Regents of the Nevada System of Higher Education. ♦Michael Rainey, gen mgr.

KKOH(AM)— Oct 13, 1970: 780 khz; 50 kw-U, DA-N. TL: N39 40 41 W119 48 06. Hrs open: 24 595 E. Plumb Ln., 89502. Phone: (775) 789-6700. Fax: (775) 789-6767.E-mail: dan.mason@citcomm.com Web Site:www.kkoh.com Licensee: Citadel Broadcasting Co. Group owner: Citadel Broadcasting Corp. (acq 5-18-92; $12.5 million; grpsl;6-8-92). Population served: 1,500,000 Natl. Rep: McGavren Guild,. Format: News/talk. News staff: 4; News: 28 hrs wkly. Target aud: 35-64. Spec prog: Sports, Sp 2 hrs wkly. ♦Andrew Perini, gen mgr, chief of engrg; Jerry Juskiw, gen mgr & gen sls mgr; Dan Mason, progmg dir.

KLCA(FM)—(Tahoe City, CA) Apr 5, 1985: 96.5 mhz; 4 kw. 2,965 ft TL: N39 18 47 W119 52 59. Stereo. Hrs open: 24 961 Matley Ln., Suite 120, 89502. Phone: (775) 829-1964. Fax: (775) 825-3183. Web Site:www.alice965.com Licensee: Americom Broadcasting. Group owner: Americom (acq 1996; $1.225 million). Format: Modern hits. News: 3 hrs wkly. Target aud: 18-34. Spec prog: Metal shop 2 hrs wkly. ♦Tom Quinn, pres; Daniel Cook, gen mgr; Carrie Carano, gen sls mgr; Beej ., progmg dir; Steve Weber, chief of engrg; Tina ., traf mgr.

KNEV(FM)— Dec 25, 1953: 95.5 mhz; 60 kw. 2,280 ft TL: N39 15 34 W119 42 16. Stereo. Hrs open: 595 E. Plumb, 89502. Phone: (775) 789-6700. Fax: (775) 789-6767. Web Site:www.magic95.com Licensee: Citadel Broadcasting Co. Group owner: Citadel Broadcasting Corp. (acq 4-13-93; $500,000;5-3-93). Population served: 450,000 Format: Hot adult contemp. Target aud: General. Spec prog: Jazz 2 hrs, relg one hr, pub affrs one hr wkly. ♦Andrew Perini, gen mgr; Kathy Williams, gen sls mgr; Nick Elliott, progmg dir; Rick Worthington, news dir; Martin Stabbert, chief of engrg.

KNIS(FM)—See Carson City

KODS(FM)—(Carnelian Bay, CA) 1970: 103.7 mhz; 6.3 kw. 2,985 ft TL: N39 18 16 W119 53 00. Stereo. Hrs open: 961 Matley Ln., Suite 120, 89502. Phone: (775) 829-1964. Fax: (775) 825-3183. Web Site:www.river1037.com Licensee: Americom, a Nevada L.P. (acq 1996). Population served: 442,800 Natl. Rep: CBS Radio,. Format: Hits of the 60s & 70s. ♦Tom Quinn, pres; Daniel Cook, gen mgr; Heather Forcier, gen sls mgr; Beej ., progmg dir; Steve Weber, chief of engrg; Sandy Vance, traf mgr, disc jockey.

KOZZ-FM— September 1969: 105.7 mhz; 75 kw. Ant 2,120 ft TL: N39 15 34 W119 42 21. Stereo. Hrs open: 24 Box 9870, 89512. Secondary address: 2900 Sutro St. 89512. Phone: (775) 329-9261. Fax: (775) 323-1450. Web Site:www.kozzradio.com Licensee: Lotus Radio Corp. (acq 1-1-78). Format: Classic rock. ♦Bill Shriftman, CFO; Dawn Keeble, gen sls mgr, traf mgr; Rick Carter, prom mgr & progmg dir.

KPLY(AM)— Oct 25, 1928: 630 khz; 5 kw-D, 1 kw-N, DA-N. TL: N39 34 25 W119 50 48. Hrs open: Box 9870, 2900 Sutro St., 89512. Phone: (775) 329-9261. Fax: (775) 323-1450.E-mail: espnradio630@aol.com Licensee: Lotus Radio Corp. (Acq 1995; $325,000). Population served: 200,000 Format: Sports. Target aud: 25-54. ♦Dane Wilt, VP; Ken Allen, progmg mgr.

KRNO(FM)—(Incline Village, July 1974: 106.9 mhz; 35 kw. Ant 2,988 ft TL: N39 18 38 W119 53 01. Stereo. Hrs open: 24 961 Matley Ln, Suite 120, 89502. Phone: (775) 829-1964. Fax: (775) 825-3183. Web Site:www.sunny1069.com Licensee: Americom Las Vegas L.P. Group owner: Americom (acq 4-16-98; grpsl). Population served: 332,457 Shaw Pittman. Format: Soft rock, soft adult contemp. News staff: one; News: 18 hrs wkly. Target aud: 25-54; women. ♦Tom Quinn, pres; Daniel Cook, gen mgr; Greg Cobb, gen sls mgr; Dan Fritz, progmg dir; Sandy Vance, news dir, traf mgr; Steve Weber, chief of engrg.

KRNV-FM— Aug 12, 1986: 102.1 mhz; 11 kw. Ant 492 ft TL: N39 35 03 W119 47 52. Hrs open: 24 300 S. Wells Ave., Suite 12, 89502. Phone: (775) 333-1017. Fax: (775) 333-9046. Web Site:www.entravision.com Network progmg Licensee: Entravision Holdings LLC. Group owner: Entravision Communications Corp. (acq 3-14-00; grpsl). Format: Sp. Target aud: 18-49; adults. ♦Walter F. Ulloa, chmn; Jeff Liberman, pres; Viola Cody, gen sls mgr; Julio Cisneros, progmg dir.

KRZQ-FM—See Sparks

KTHX-FM—(Dayton, June 10, 1983: 100.1 mhz; 12.2 kw. Ant 2,162 ft TL: N39 15 34 W119 42 21. Stereo. Hrs open: 24 300 E Second St., 14th Fl., 89501. Phone: (775) 333-0123. Fax: (775) 322-7361.E-mail: info@ktjxfm.com Web Site:www.kthxfm.com Licensee: Wilks License Co.-Reno LLC. Group owner: NextMedia Group L.L.C. (acq 9-29-2005; grpsl). Natl. Network: ABC, . Leventhal, Senter & Lerman. Format: AAA. News: 2 hrs wkly. Target aud: 18-49; upscale, high income & educated. ♦Mark Keefe, pres, progmg dir; Reina Malone, gen mgr; Jay Davis, news dir.

***KUNR(FM)**— Oct 7, 1963: 88.7 mhz; 20 kw. 2,169 ft TL: N39 15 34 W119 42 16. Stereo. Hrs open: Mail Stop 0294, Univ. of Nevada, 89557. Phone: (775) 327-5867. Fax: (775) 784-1381.E-mail: info@kunr.com Web Site:www.kunr.org Licensee: University of Nevada Board of Regents. Population served: 370,000 Natl. Network: NPR, PRI, . Format: News, jazz, class music. Target aud: General. Spec prog: Folk 2 hrs, ethnic 9 hrs wkly. ♦Steven Zink, exec VP; David Stipech, stn mgr; Terry Joy, opns dir; Shannon Graves, chief of engrg.

KURK(FM)— November 1994: 92.9 mhz; 48 kw. Ant 502 ft TL: N39 35 03 W119 48 06. Hrs open: 300 E. Second St., 89501. Phone: (775) 333-0123. Fax: (775) 322-7361.E-mail: info@kurkfm.com Web Site:www.kurkfm.com Licensee: Wilks License Co.-Reno LLC. Group owner: NextMedia Group L.L.C. (acq 9-29-2005; grpsl). Format: Classic rock and roll. ♦Raina Malone, gen mgr; Chuck Reeves, progmg dir; Jay Davis, news dir.

KXEQ(AM)— July 1946: 1340 khz; 1 kw-U. TL: N39 32 22 W119 46 53. Hrs open: 225 Linden St., 89502. Phone: (775) 827-1111. Phone: (775) 827-1313. Fax: (775) 827-2082.E-mail: kxeq@scbglobal.net Licensee: Azteca Broadcasting Corp. (group owner; acq 10-16-91; $30,000; 11-4-91). Population served: 250,000 Natl. Network: AP Radio, . Format: Sp. ♦Jose Mares, gen mgr; Jose Arriaga, progmg dir.

KXTO(AM)— 1991: 1550 khz; 2.5 kw-D, 94 w-N. TL: N39 34 39 W119 50 52. Hrs open: 24 2580 Wrondel Way, 89502. Phone: (775) 248-3257. Fax: (775) 284-3259.E-mail: radio@lavozcristiana.com Web Site:www.lavozcristiana.com Licensee: First Broadcasting of Nevada Inc. Population served: 500,000 Format: Sp, relg. News: 10 hrs wkly. Target aud: Hispanics. ♦Yolanda Amaya, gen mgr.

KZTQ(FM)—(Carson City, June 27, 1972: 97.3 mhz; 87 kw. 2,112 ft TL: N39 15 21 W119 42 37. Stereo. Hrs open: 24 961 Matley Ln., Suite 120, 89502. Phone: (775) 829-1964. Fax: (775) 825-3183. Web Site:www.973bobfm.com Licensee: Americom Las Vegas L.P. Group owner: Americom (acq 4-27-98; grpsl). Population served: 285,000 Format: CHR. News staff: one; News: 2 hrs wkly. Target aud: 18-34; women. ♦Tom Quinn, pres; Daniel Cook, gen mgr; Greg Cobb, gen sls mgr; Steve Webber, chief of engrg; Sandy Vance, traf mgr.

Smith

KSVL(FM)— 1999: 92.3 mhz; 490 w. Ant 2,073 ft TL: N38 41 06 W119 11 04. Hrs open: Box 123, 89430. Phone: (775) 465-2200. Licensee: Donegal Enterprises. Format: Class. ♦Wayne Donegal, gen mgr.

Sparks

KBDB(AM)— 2002: 1400 khz; 600 w-U. TL: N39 34 10 W119 45 03. Hrs open: 1085 E. 2nd St., Suite 1, Reno, 89502. Phone: (775) 348-5852. Fax: (775) 348-5865.E-mail: mega@lameganet.com Web Site:www.mega1400.com Licensee: George S. Flinn Jr. Format: Sp. ♦Nora Breton, gen sls mgr; Ruben Villalobos, gen mgr & progmg dir.

KBZZ(AM)— Aug 9, 1960: 1270 khz; 5 kw-U, DA-2. TL: N39 32 03 W119 39 44. Hrs open: 24 961 Matley Ln., Suite 120, Reno, 89502. Phone: (775) 829-1964. Fax: (775) 825-3183. Web Site:www.kbzz.com Licensee: Americom Las Vegas L.P. Group owner: Americom (acq 1996; grpsl). Population served: 300,000 Natl. Network: CBS, Westwood One, . Format: Sports & info, news/talk. Target aud: 25-54; primarily men who are interested in sports. ♦Tom Quinn, pres; Daniel Cook, gen mgr; Dan Fritz, gen sls mgr, progmg dir; Steve Webber, chief of engrg.

KFOY(AM)—Not on air, target date: unknown: 1060 khz; 15 kw-D, 370 w-N, DA-3. TL: N39 30 41 W119 42 51. Hrs open: Box 1254, Alameda, CA, 94501. Phone: (510) 769-5904. Licensee: Eastern Sierra Broadcasting. ♦Chris Kidd, pres.

KJZS(FM)— 1993: 92.1 mhz; 8.9 kw. Ant 502 ft TL: N39 35 03 W119 48 06. Hrs open: 24 300 E. Second St. 14 th Fl., Reno, 89501. Phone: (775) 333-0123.E-mail: info@smoothjazzreno.com Web Site:www.smoothjazzreno.com Licensee: Wilks License Co.-Reno LLC. Group owner: NextMedia Group L.L.C. (acq 9-29-2005; grpsl). Population served: 300000 Latham & Watkins. Format: Jazz, adult Contempo. ♦Jay Davis, progmg dir; Jay Davis, news dir.

***KLRH(FM)**—Not on air, target date: unknown: 88.3 mhz; 1.78 kw. Ant 2,886 ft TL: N39 45 38 W119 27 59. Hrs open: 2351 Sunset Blvd., Suite 170-218, Rocklin, CA, 95765. Phone: (916) 251-1600. Fax: (916) 251-1650.E-mail: klove@klove.com Web Site:www.klove.com Licensee: Educational Media Foundation. Group owner: EMF Broadcasting. Natl. Network: K-Love, . Shaw Pittman. Format: Contemp Christian. News staff: 3. Target aud: 25-44; Judeo Christian female. ♦Richard Jenkins, pres; Mike Novak, VP; Keith Whipple, dev dir; David Pierce, progmg mgr; Ed Lenane, news dir; Sam Wallington, engrg dir; Karen Johnson, news rptr.

KRZQ-FM— July 1, 1983: 100.9 mhz; 2.9 kw. 203 ft TL: N39 22 04 W119 47 07. Stereo. Hrs open: 24 300E. 2nd St. 14th Floor, Reno, 89015. Phone: (775) 333-0123. Fax: (775) 333-0110. Licensee: Wilks License Co.-Reno LLC. Group owner: NextMedia Group L.L.C. (acq 9-29-2005; grpsl). Natl. Network: ABC, . Leibowitz & Associates. Format: Alternative rock, talk. Target aud: 18-54; general. ♦Raina Malone, gen mgr; Jeremy Smith, progmg dir; Matt Bates, mus dir; Lori Quinn, traf mgr.

Spring Creek

KEBG(FM)— Nov 18, 2007: 103.9 mhz; 12.6 kw. Ant 1,597 ft TL: N40 55 18 W115 50 58. Hrs open: c/o Ruby Radio Corp., 1750 Manzanita, Suite 1, Elko, 89801. Phone: (775) 777-1196. Fax: (775) 777-9587. Licensee: Ruby Radio Corp. Population served: 25,000 Format: Mainstream country. Target aud: 18-54; men & women. ♦Alene Sutherland, VP; Mike Allen, news dir.

Sun Valley

KQLO(AM)— 1946: 1590 khz; 5 kw-D, 67 w-N. TL: N39 24 57 W119 42 51. Hrs open: 2450 Wrondel Way, Suite G, Reno, 89502. Phone: (775) 322-0847. Fax: ((775) 322-0927.E-mail: business@kqlo.com Web Site:www.kqlo.com Licensee: Universal Broadcasting Inc. (acq

11-4-2008). Population served: 186,500 Natl. Rep: Interep,. Format: Sp contemp. Target aud: General. ◆Lee Chavez, gen mgr, natl sls mgr; Sonya Saz, progmg dir.

KUUB(FM)— 1999: 94.5 mhz; 12 kw. Ant 459 ft TL: N39 35 02 W119 47 53. (CP: 50 kw). Hrs open: 2900 Sutro St., Reno, 89512. Phone: (775) 329-9261. Fax: (775) 323-1450. Web Site:www.945themountain.com Licensee: Lotus Radio Corp. Group owner: Lotus Communications Corp. Format: Country. ◆Dane Wilt, gen mgr; Chip Cooper, gen sls mgr; Chuck Short, news dir; Mike Weaver, chief of engrg.

KWNZ(FM)— 2002: 93.7 mhz; 3.6 kw. Ant 423 ft TL: N39 35 02 W119 47 54. Hrs open: 595 E. Plumb Ln., Reno, 89502. Phone: (775) 789-6700. Fax: (775) 789-6767.E-mail: angel.garcia@citcomm.com Web Site:wild937.com Licensee: Flinn Broadcasting Corp. Format: CHR. ◆Dana Johnson, gen mgr.

Tonopah

KHWK(FM)— July 29, 1982: Stn currently dark. 92.7 mhz; 290 w. Ant 971 ft TL: N38 04 22 W117 13 16. Stereo. Hrs open: Box 1669, 89049. Phone: (435) 628-1000. Fax: (435) 628-6636.E-mail: morgan@legacy.cc Licensee: Donald W. Kaminiski Jr. (acq 3-16-92; $240,000;4-6-92). ◆Don Kaminski, CEO & gen mgr.

KTNP(AM)—Not on air, target date: unknown: 1400 khz; 1 kw-D, 880 w-N. TL: N38 05 06 W117 13 18. Hrs open: Box 1450, 210 North 1000 East, St. George, UT, 84771. Phone: (435) 628-1000. Fax: (435) 628-6636. Licensee: Radio 1400 LLC. (acq 5-4-2007). Population served: 2,881 ◆E. Morgan Skinner Jr., pres & gen mgr.

*KTPH(FM)— October 1988: 91.7 mhz; 100 w. Ant 1,433 ft TL: N38 03 07 W117 13 30. Stereo. Hrs open: 24 Rebroadcasts KNPR(FM) Las Vegas 100%. 1289 S. Torrey Pines Dr., Las Vegas, 89146. Phone: (702) 258-9895. Fax: (702) 258-5646.E-mail: reception@knpr.org Licensee: Nevada Public Radio. Population served: 4,000 Natl. Network: NPR, . Format: Classical, news. ◆Florence Rogers, pres & gen mgr.

Wendover

KVUW(FM)— 2006: 102.3 mhz; 3 kw. Ant 26 ft TL: N40 44 30 W114 02 10. Hrs open: 479 E. Wendover Blvd., 84083. Phone: (435) 665-0600. Fax: (435) 665-0600. Licensee: Murray Grey Broadcasting Inc. (group owner). (acq 12-21-2005; $750,000 with KRQU(FM) Laramie, WY). ◆Steven A. Silberberg, pres.

Whitney

KLSQ(AM)— Aug 15, 1986: 870 khz; 5 kw-D, 430 w-N, DA-N. TL: N35 58 35 W114 57 03. Stereo. Hrs open: 24 6767 W. Tropicana, Ste. 102, Las Vegas, 89103. Phone: (702) 284-6400. Fax: (702) 284-6403. Web Site:www.univision.com Licensee: HBC-Las Vegas Inc. Group owner: Univision Radio (acq 9-22-2003; grpsl). Format: Sp. Target aud: 35 plus. ◆Dana Demerjiah, VP; Dana Demerjian, gen mgr; Cristina Valarezo, gen sls mgr; Jose Santos, progmg dir; Manny Garcia, chief of engrg; Gloria Salvador, traf mgr.

Winchester

KBET(AM)— May 22, 2006: Stn currently dark. 790 khz; 1 kw-D, 300 w-N, DA-2. TL: N36 05 27 W115 00 59. Hrs open: 1455 E. Tropicana, Suite 800, Las Vegas, 89119. Phone: (702) 730-0300. Fax: (702) 736-8477. Licensee: WAEC License L.P. Group owner: Diamond Broadcasting Corp. (acq 3-28-2007; $2.5 million for CP). Format: Country legends. ◆R.W. Smith, progmg dir; Stephen Rutherford, chief of engrg.

Winnemucca

*KDNV(FM)—Not on air, target date: unknown: 91.1 mhz; 600 w. Ant -397 ft TL: N40 58 28 W117 43 24. Hrs open: 219 Dodd Rd., Ringgold, GA, 30736. Phone: (706) 965-2355. Fax: (706) 965-3755. Licensee: Victor Broadcasting Inc. (acq 9-18-2008). ◆James E. Price III, pres.

KWNA(AM)— Jan 28, 1955: 1400 khz; 1 kw-U. TL: N40 57 23 W117 42 48. Hrs open: 24 Box 1400, 89446. Secondary address: 335 West 4th Street 89445. Phone: (775) 623-5203. Fax: (775) 625-1011.E-mail: BOBBOLTON1@AOL.com Licensee: Ely Radio LLC. (acq 11-6-2006; $500,000 with co-located FM). Natl. Network: ABC, . Gardner, Carton & Douglas. Format: News/talk. News staff: 2; News: 12 hrs wkly.

Target aud: General. Spec prog: Farm 2 hrs wkly. ◆Bob Bolton, gen mgr, gen sls mgr; Rodd Stowell, progmg dir; Rachael Marie, news dir; Sandy Crownover, traf mgr.

KWNA-FM— Apr 3, 1982: 92.7 mhz; 60 w. 2,120 ft TL: N41 00 40 W117 45 59. (CP: 140 w). Stereo. Hrs open: 24 Prog sep from AM Box 1400, 89446. Secondary address: 335 West 4th Street 89445. Phone: (775) 623-5203. Fax: (775) 625-1011.E-mail: BOBBOLTON1@AOL.com Natl. Network: ABC, . Format: C&W. Target aud: 25-54. ◆Bob Bolton, gen mgr, gen sls mgr; Rodd Stowell, progmg dir.

*KWNM(FM)—Not on air, target date: unknown: 89.7 mhz; 450 w. Ant 2,152 ft TL: N41 00 40 W117 45 57. Hrs open: 5077 Industrial Dr., Collegedale, TN, 37315. Phone: (615) 469-5122. Fax: (615) 216-7266. Web Site:www.lifetalk.net Licensee: Life Talk Radio Inc. ◆Don C. Schneider, pres.

New Hampshire

Bedford

WMLL(FM)— June 1996: 96.5 mhz; 730 w. Ant 935 ft TL: N42 59 02 W71 35 22. Hrs open: 500 Commercial St., Manchester, 03101. Phone: (603) 669-7979. Phone: (603) 669-5777. Fax: (603) 669-3299. Fax: (603) 669-4641. Web Site:www.965themill.com Licensee: Saga Communications of New England LLC. Group owner: Saga Communications Inc. (acq 9-29-97; $3.3 million). Population served: 300,000 Natl. Rep: Katz Radio,. Format: Classic rock. Target aud: 35-54; baby boomers. ◆Edward Christian, CEO; Raymond R. Garon, pres; Samuel Bush, CFO.

Belmont

WNHW(FM)— May 8, 1994: 93.3 mhz; 300 w. Ant 1,020 ft TL: N43 23 52 W71 33 03. Stereo. Hrs open: 11 Kimball Dr., Ste 114, Hooksett, 03106. Phone: (603) 225-1160. Fax: (603) 225-5938. Web Site:www.933thewolf.com Licensee: Nassau Broadcasting III L.L.C. Group owner: Nassau Broadcasting Partners L.P. (acq 10-1-2004; $8 million with WJYY(FM) Concord). Format: Country. ◆Brit Johnson, gen mgr; Dawn Parris, gen sls mgr; Matt Forrest, progmg dir; Steve Ordinetz, engrg mgr & chief of engrg.

Berlin

WKDR(AM)— 2009: 1490 khz; 1 kw-D, 930 w-N. TL: N44 28 58 W71 10 38. Hrs open: 297 Pleasant St., 03570. Phone: (603) 752-1230. Fax: (603) 752-3117. Licensee: Barry P. Lunderville. ◆Barry P. Lunderville, gen mgr.

WMOU(AM)— 1947: 1230 khz; 1 kw-U. TL: N44 27 32 W71 10 16. Hrs open: 24 Box 489, 297 Pleasant St., 03570. Phone: (603) 752-1230. Fax: (603) 752-3117.E-mail: wmou@ncia.net Licensee: Barry P. Lunderville. (acq 11-11-2003; $75,000). Population served: 35,000 Natl. Network: Westwood One, . Format: Adult standards. News staff: one; News: 6 hrs wkly. Target aud: 25-54; local residents of northern New Hampshire. Spec prog: Fr 3 hrs, talk 2 hrs, swap shop 3 hrs wkly. ◆Barry Lunderville, pres, progmg dir; Bob Barbin, opns dir; Randy Frank, gen sls mgr; Brian Lunderville, chief of engrg.

Campton

WLKC(FM)— 1997: 105.7 mhz; 125 w. Ant 2,001 ft TL: N43 57 32 W71 33 23. Stereo. Hrs open: 24 Rebroadcasts WXRU(FM) Wolfeboro 100%. 288 S. River Rd., Bedford, 03110. Phone: (603) 669-1250. Fax: (603) 528-1638.E-mail: nebco231@hotmail.com Licensee: Devon Broadcasting Co. Inc. (acq 3-5-99; $300,000). Format: AAA. Target aud: 25-54. ◆Steve Young, gen mgr; Dana Marshall, progmg dir; Lou Muise, chief of engrg; Stephanie Battaglia, traf mgr.

Claremont

WHDQ(FM)— 1948: 106.1 mhz; 9.51 kw. Ant 1,068 ft TL: N43 23 48 W72 18 01. Stereo. Hrs open: Prog sep from AM 106 N. Main St., Lebanon, 03784. Phone: (603) 298-0332. Fax: (603) 727-0134.E-mail: info@q106rock.com Web Site:www.q106rock.com Population served: 150,000 Format: Classic rock.

WTSV(AM)— 1948: 1230 khz; 1 kw-U. TL: N43 22 15 W72 19 42. Hrs open: 106 N. Main St., West Lebanon, 03784. Phone: (603) 298-0332.

Fax: (603) 727-0134.E-mail: espnthescore@aol.com Web Site:www.scoreradio.com Licensee: Nassau Broadcasting III L.L.C. Group owner: Nassau Broadcasting Partners L.P. (acq 8-2-2004; grpsl). Population served: 39,500 Natl. Network: ABC, ESPN Radio,. Rgnl rep: Roslin. Rini & Coran. Format: Sports. Target aud: 35 plus. ◆Jeffrey Shapiro, pres; Shirley Clark, gen mgr.

Concord

*WEVO(FM)— Aug 4, 1981: 89.1 mhz; 50 kw. 380 ft TL: N43 12 53 W71 34 28. Stereo. Hrs open: 24 207 N. Main St., 03301. Phone: (603) 228-8910. Fax: (603) 224-6052.E-mail: admin@nhpr.org Web Site:www.nhpr.org Licensee: New Hampshire Public Radio Inc. Natl. Network: NPR, PRI, . Garvey, Schubert & Barer. Wire Svc: AP Format: News/talk. News staff: 9; News: 42 hrs wkly. Target aud: 25-54; well educated adults. Spec prog: Folk 3 hrs wkly. ◆Elizabeth Gardella, pres; Mark Bevis, news dir; John Huntley, engrg dir.

WJYY(FM)— Sept 15, 1983: 105.5 mhz; 1.55 kw. 456 ft TL: N43 16 46 W71 30 15. Stereo. Hrs open: 24 11 Kimball Dr., Hooksett, 03106. Phone: (603) 225-1160. Fax: (603) 224-7280. Web Site:www.wjyy.com Licensee: Nassau Broadcasting III L.L.C. Group owner: Nassau Broadcasting Partners L.P. (acq 10-1-2004; $8 million with WNHW(FM) Belmont). Format: CHR. News staff: one; News: 6 hrs wkly. Target aud: 25-54. ◆Brit Johnson, gen mgr; Dawn Parris, gen sls mgr; Joe Dukette, progmg dir.

WKXL(AM)— June 15, 1946: 1450 khz; 1 kw-U. TL: N43 11 39 W71 33 17. Hrs open: 24 37 Redington Rd., 03301. Phone: (603) 225-5521 Office. Phone: (603) 224-1450 Studio. Fax: (603) 224-6404.E-mail: info@wkxl.com Web Site:www.wkxl1450.com Licensee: New Hampshire Family Radio LLC (acq 12-16-2004; $800,000). Population served: 80,000 Natl. Network: AP Radio, . Wire Svc: AP Format: News/talk. News staff: 2; News: 36 hrs wkly. Target aud: 35 plus; adults in Concord, Hillsboro, Manchester & contiguous towns. ◆Anthony Schilella, gen mgr, stn mgr, opns mgr & progmg dir.

WNNH(FM)—See Henniker

*WSPS(FM)— 1974: 90.5 mhz; 200 w. 110 ft TL: N43 11 37 W71 34 29. Hrs open: 24 St. Paul's School, 325 Pleasant St., 03301. Phone: (603) 228-4810. Phone: (603) 230-5810. Fax: (603) 229-4891.E-mail: wsps@sps.edu Web Site:www.wsps.sps.edu Licensee: St. Paul's School. Population served: 40,000 Drinker Biddle & Reath. Format: Div. Target aud: General. ◆David Harvey, gen mgr; Glenn Reider, stn mgr.

WTPL(FM)—(Hillsboro, Oct 1, 1989: 107.7 mhz; 580 w. Ant 738 ft TL: N43 09 00 W71 47 56. Stereo. Hrs open: 24 501 South St., Bow, 03304. Phone: (603) 545-0777. Fax: (603) 545-0781. Web Site:www.wtplfm.com Licensee: Great Eastern Radio LLC. (acq 6-3-2004; $1.5 million). Natl. Network: CBS Radio, ESPN Radio, . Format: News/talk, sports. News staff: 2; News: 50 hrs wkly. Target aud: 35 plus; adult audience in Merrimack & Hillsborough counties. ◆Mike Johnson, gen mgr; Bob Lipman, opns mgr; Jim Whedon, gen sls mgr.

*WVNH(FM)— Mar 7, 1999: 91.1 mhz; 650 w vert. Ant 331 ft TL: N43 23 54 W71 25 24. Hrs open: Box 40, 03302. Phone: (603) 227-0911.E-mail: info@wvnh.org Web Site:www.wvnh.org Licensee: New Hampshire Gospel Radio Inc. Format: Christian. ◆Peter Stohrer, gen mgr; Cheryl Eggert, stn mgr.

WWHK(FM)— Mar 7, 1972: 102.3 mhz; 3 kw. Ant 285 ft TL: N43 13 00 W71 34 34. Stereo. Hrs open: 24 11 Kimbell Dr., Suite 114, Hooksett, 03106. Phone: (603) 225-1160. Fax: (603) 225-8935.E-mail: jfronk@nassaubroadcasting.com Licensee: Capitol Broadcasting Corp. Inc. Group owner: Vox Radio Group L.P. (acq 8-12-99). Population served: 100,000 Format: Rock. Target aud: 25-54; adult audience in Merrimack county - south central NH. ◆Brid Johnson, gen mgr.

Conway

WBNC(AM)— Dec 21, 1955: 1050 khz; 1 kw-D, 63 w-N. TL: N43 58 48 W71 06 36. Hrs open: Dups FM 100% Box 2008, 03818. Secondary address: 2 Common Court, Unit A30, North Conway 03860. Phone: (603) 356-8870. Fax: (603) 356-8875.E-mail: office@wmwv.com Licensee: Mt. Washington Radio & Gramophone L.L.C. Format: Visitor Information. ◆Greg Frizzell, gen mgr.

WMWV(FM)— June 23, 1967: 93.5 mhz; 3 kw. 420 ft TL: N43 56 48 W71 08 24. Stereo. Hrs open: Mt. Washington Radio, Box 2008, 03818. Secondary address: FedEx/UPS, A30 Settlers Green OVP, Rt 16, North Conway 03860. Phone: (603) 356-8870. Fax: (603) 356-8875.E-mail: office@wmwv.com Web Site:www.wmwv.com Licensee: Mt. Washington Radio & Gramophone L.L.C. (group owner; acq

9-27-01; grpsl). Population served: 17,000 Natl. Rep: Roslin,. Format: AAA. ◆Ronald Frizzell, gen mgr; Charles Osgood, opns VP, chief of engrg.

*WPHH(FM)—Not on air, target date: unknown: 91.1 mhz; 1.1 kw horiz, 3 kw vert. Ant 358 ft TL: N43 56 48 W71 08 24. Hrs open: 17 Varney St., Lebanon, ME, 04027. Phone: (603) 767-5994. Licensee: New Life Media. ◆Ford Bishop, pres.

WVMJ(FM)— Oct 23, 1995: 104.5 mhz; 3 kw. 328 ft TL: N43 55 34 71 05 46. Stereo. Hrs open: 24 Box 2008, 03818. Secondary address: 2 Common Court, Unit A30, N. Conway 03860. Phone: (603) 356-8870. Fax: (603) 356-8875.E-mail: office@wmwv.com Web Site:www.conwaymagic.com Licensee: Mt. Washington Radio & Gramophone L.L.C. (group owner; acq 10-15-01; grpsl). Format: Adult contemp. ◆Greg Frizzell, gen mgr; Cooper Fox, progmg dir.

Derry

WDER(AM)— October 1983: 1320 khz; 10 kw-D, 1 kw-N, DA-2. TL: N42 51 59 W71 17 14. Hrs open: 24 Box 465, 8 Lawrence Rd., 03038-6465. Phone: (603) 437-9337. Phone: (603) 434-9302. Fax: (603) 434-1035.E-mail: wderam1320@aol.com Web Site:www.lifechangingradio.com Licensee: Blount Communications Inc. of NH. Group owner: Blount Communications Group (acq 9-5-00; $793,000). Natl. Network: Salem Radio Network, . Format: Talk, relg. Target aud: 25-54; male & female. ◆William Blount, pres; David Young, VP, gen mgr; Steve Sobozenski, opns mgr.

Dover

WOKQ(FM)— August 1970: 97.5 mhz; 50 kw. 492 ft TL: N43 13 26 W70 58 18. Stereo. Hrs open: 24 Box 576, 03821-0576. Secondary address: 292 Middle Rd. 03820-4901. Phone: (603) 749-9750. Fax: (603) 749-1459.E-mail: info@wokq.com Web Site:www.wokq.com Licensee: Citadel Broadcasting Co. Group owner: Citadel Broadcasting Corp. (acq 9-1-99; grpsl). Population served: 1,000,000 Natl. Network: CNN Radio, . Natl. Rep: Christal,. Paul, Hastings, Janofsky & Walker. Wire Svc: AP Format: Country. News staff: 2. Target aud: 25-54; general. ◆Farid Suleman, CEO; Judy Ellis, pres; Martin Lessard, gen mgr; Mark Ericson, opns mgr; Mark Jennings, progmg dir.

WTSN(AM)— August 1956: 1270 khz; 5 kw-U, DA-2. TL: N43 11 01 W70 51 14. Hrs open: 24 Box 400, 101 Back Rd., 03821-0400. Phone: (603) 742-1270. Phone: (603) 742-0987. Fax: (603) 742-0448. Web Site:www.987thebay.com Licensee: Garrison City Broadcasting Inc. (acq 3-18-83). Population served: 250,000 Natl. Rep: McGavren Guild,. Format: News/talk, sports. News staff: 3. Target aud: 35-64; very affluent. ◆Bob Demers, CEO; Rick Bean, gen mgr.

Durham

*WUNH(FM)— July 15, 1963: 91.3 mhz; 3 kw. 300 ft TL: N43 09 23 W70 56 26. Stereo. Hrs open: 24 Memorial Union Bldg., Univ. of New Hampshire, 03824. Phone: (603) 862-2541. Phone: (603) 862-2222. Fax: (603) 862-2543.E-mail: gm@wunh.unh.edu Web Site:www.wunh.unh.edu Licensee: University of New Hampshire. Population served: 500,000 Natl. Network: AP Radio, . Format: Progsv. News: 7 hrs wkly. Target aud: Diverse. Spec prog: Black 4 hrs, blues 3 hrs, jazz 5 hrs, Pol 2 hrs, folk 4 hrs, celtic 2 hrs wkly. ◆Josh Cilley, gen mgr; Alexandra Buchalski, opns dir; Abbie Crocker, prom dir; Augie Ciotti, progmg dir; Greg Falla, mus dir; John Bosselman, news dir; Peter Geremia, chief of engrg.

Exeter

WERZ(FM)— Sept 21, 1972: 107.1 mhz; 5.2 kw. 351 ft TL: N43 01 38 W70 52 51. Hrs open: Prog sep from AM 815 Lafayette Rd., Portsmouth, 03801. Phone: (603) 436-7300. Fax: (603) 430-9415.E-mail: info@werz.com Web Site:www.werz.com Population served: 499,000 Format: Top-40. ◆Michael O'Donnell, progmg dir; Beth La Rocque, traf mgr.

*WPEA(FM)— 1964: 90.5 mhz; 115 w. 170 ft TL: N42 58 44 W70 57 00. Stereo. Hrs open: Phillips Exeter Academy, 20 Main St., 03833-2460. Phone: (603) 777-4414.E-mail: WPEA@exeter.edu Licensee: Trustees of Phillips Exeter Academy. Population served: 25,000 Format: Var. Target aud: General; students.

WXEX(AM)— June 4, 1966: 1540 khz; 5 kw-D. TL: N42 59 23 W70 56 14. Hrs open: 815 Lafayette Rd., Portsmouth, 03801. Phone: (603) 436-7400. Fax: (603) 430-9415. Licensee: Aruba Capital Holdings LLC Group owner: Clear Channel Communications Inc. (acq 3-9-2009; $325,000). Population served: 80,000 Natl. Rep: McGavren Guild,.

Format: News/talk, sports. ◆Robert Greer, gen mgr; Dan Pierce, opns mgr, progmg dir; Judy Figliulo, gen sls mgr; Jennifer McElreavy, prom dir; Kelly Brown, news dir; Ken Neeman, chief of engrg; Beth LaRocque, traf mgr.

Farmington

*WNHI(FM)— July 9, 1999: 106.5 mhz; 2.9 kw. Ant 486 ft TL: N43 24 01 W71 09 27. Stereo. Hrs open: 24 Rebroadcasts KLVR(FM) Middletown, CA 100%. 2351 Sunset Blvd., Suite 170-218, Rocklin, CA, 95765. Phone: (916) 251-1600. Fax: (916) 251-1650. Web Site:www.klove.com Licensee: Educational Media Foundation. (acq 6-2-2008; $1 million). Population served: 320,000 Natl. Network: K-Love, . Davis Wright Tremaine LLP. Format: Contemp Christian. ◆Mike Novak, pres.

Fitzwilliam Depot

WZNH(AM)—Not on air, target date: unknown: 870 khz; 780 w-D, 400 w-N, DA-N. TL: N42 45 59 W72 06 59. Hrs open: 17 Knightsbridge Ct., Nanuet, NY, 10954. Phone: (845) 356-9613. Licensee: Steven Wendell. ◆Steven Wendell, gen mgr.

Franklin

WFTN(AM)— Oct 30, 1966: 1240 khz; 1 kw-U. TL: N43 27 16 W71 38 33. Hrs open: Box 941, 110 Babbitt Rd., 03235. Phone: (603) 934-2500. Fax: (603) 934-2933.E-mail: info@mix941fm.com Web Site:www.mix941fm.com Licensee: Northeast Communications Corp. (group owner; acq 9-30-74). Population served: 30,000 Format: Mus of your life. ◆Jeff Fisher, pres, gen mgr, stn mgr; Fred Caruso, opns mgr, progmg dir; Jeff Levitan, gen sls mgr; Rick Ganley, prom dir; Gary Ford, mus dir; Amy Bates, news dir; Cathy Keyser, traf mgr.

WFTN-FM— Apr 10, 1987: 94.1 mhz; 6 kw. 328 ft TL: N43 28 23 W71 36 20. Stereo. Hrs open: Box 941, 110 Babbitt Rd., 03235. Phone: (603) 934-2500. Fax: (603) 934-2933.E-mail: info@mix941fm.com Web Site:www.mix941fm.com Population served: 100,000 Format: Adult contemp.

Gorham

*WEVC(FM)— May 1995: 107.1 mhz; 6 kw. 151 ft TL: N44 27 32 W71 10 16. Stereo. Hrs open: 24 Rebroadcasts WEVO(FM) Concord 100%. 207 N. Main St., Concord, 03301. Phone: (603) 228-8910. Fax: (603) 224-6052.E-mail: admin@nhpr.org Web Site:www.nhpr.org Licensee: New Hampshire Public Radio Inc. Natl. Network: NPR, PRI, . Wire Svc: AP Format: News/talk. News staff: 9; News: 42 hrs wkly. Target aud: 25-54. Spec prog: Folk 3 hrs wkly. ◆Elizabeth Gardella, pres, gen mgr; Mark Bevis, news dir; John Huntley, engrg dir.

Groveton

WRNH(FM)—Not on air, target date: unknown: 101.5 mhz; 6 kw. Ant 318 ft TL: N44 37 50 W71 17 34. Hrs open: 339 North St., Medfield, MA, 02052. Phone: (508) 359-2700. Licensee: Liveair Communications Inc. ◆David M. Wang, pres.

Hampton

WSAK(FM)— August 1992: 102.1 mhz; 3 kw. 328 ft TL: N42 53 51 W70 53 02. Stereo. Hrs open: 24 Rebroadcasts WSHK(FM) Kittery, ME 100%. Box 576, Dover, 03821-0576. Secondary address: 292 Middle Rd., Dover 03820-4901. Phone: (603) 749-9750. Phone: (603) 749-2776. Fax: (603) 749-1459.E-mail: info@wokq.com Web Site:www.shark1053.com Licensee: Citadel Broadcasting Co. Group owner: Citadel Broadcasting Corp. (acq 7-7-99; grpsl). Natl. Network: CNN Radio, . Natl. Rep: Christal,. Wiley, Rein & Fielding. Wire Svc: AP Format: Classic rock. News staff: 2. Target aud: 25-49. ◆Farid Suleman, CEO; Judy Ellis, pres; Marty Lessard, gen mgr; Mark Ericson, opns mgr; Ken Hoffman, gen sls mgr; Jonathan Smith, progmg dir.

Hanover

WDCR(AM)— Mar 4, 1958: 1340 khz; 1 kw-U. TL: N43 41 59 W72 16 47. Stereo. Hrs open: 24 Box 957, 03755. Secondary address: 3rd Fl., Robinson Hall, Dartmouth College 03826. Phone: (603) 646-3313. Phone: (603) 646-3826. Fax: (603) 643-7655.E-mail: heath.cole@dartmouth.edu Web Site:www.webdcr.com Licensee: Trustees of Dartmouth College. Population served: 80,000 Format: Modern

rock. News staff: 2; News: 4 hrs wkly. Target aud: General. ◆Alex Belser, gen mgr; Heath Cole, opns mgr; Julie Kaye, gen sls mgr, traf mgr; Rob Demick, progmg dir.

*WEVH(FM)— October 1993: 91.3 mhz; 150 w. 1,180 ft TL: N43 42 30 W72 09 16. Hrs open: Rebroadcasts WEVO(FM) Concord 100%. 207 N. Main St., Concord, 03301. Phone: (603) 228-8910. Fax: (603) 224-6052. Web Site:www.nhpr.org Licensee: New Hampshire Public Radio Inc. Natl. Network: NPR, PRI, . Garvey, Schubert & Barer. Wire Svc: AP Format: News/talk. News staff: 9; News: 42 hrs wkly. Target aud: 25-54. Spec prog: Folk 3 hrs wkly. ◆Elizabeth Gardella, pres.

WFRD(FM)— Feb 19, 1976: 99.3 mhz; 6 kw. Ant 328 ft TL: N43 39 14 W72 17 44.2. Stereo. Hrs open: 24 Prog sep from AM Box 957, 03755. Secondary address: 3rd Fl., Robinson Hall, Dartmouth College 03826. Phone: (603) 646-3313. Phone: (603) 646-3826. Fax: (603) 643-7655. Web Site:www.wfrd.com Population served: 150,000 Format: Modern rock. News staff: 2. Target aud: 18-45. ◆Pauel Sotskov, progmg dir.

WGXL(FM)— Jan 12, 1987: 92.3 mhz; 6 kw. Ant 326 ft TL: N43 39 17 W72 17 41. Stereo. Hrs open: 31 Hanover, Lebanon, 03766. Phone: (603) 448-1400. Fax: (603) 448-1755. Licensee: Great Eastern Radio LLC. (acq 10-30-2007; grpsl). Format: Hot adult contemp. Target aud: 25-49.

WTSL(AM)— October 1950: 1400 khz; 1 kw-U. TL: N43 41 03 W72 17 46. Hrs open: 24 31 Hanover, Suite 4, Lebanon, 03766. Phone: (603) 448-1400. Fax: (603) 448-1755. Licensee: Great Eastern Radio LLC. Group owner: Clear Channel Communications Inc. (acq 10-30-2007; grpsl). Population served: 50,000 Natl. Network: CBS, . Rini Coran PC. Format: News/talk, sports. News staff: 2; News: 25 hrs wkly. Target aud: 35 plus. ◆Christopher Olsen, gen mgr; Michael Barrett, opns mgr, progmg dir, news dir; Gary Laperle, chief of engrg.

WXXK(FM)—See Lebanon

Haverhill

WYKR-FM— Feb 19, 1990: 101.3 mhz; 3 kw. 39 ft TL: N44 06 49 W71 58 54. Stereo. Hrs open: 6 AM-10 PM Box 675, Rt. 302, Wells River, VT, 05081. Secondary address: Box 1013, Woodsville 03785. Phone: (802) 757-2773. Fax: (802) 757-2774.E-mail: wykr@kingcon.com Web Site:www.wykr.com Licensee: Puffer Broadcasting Inc. Population served: 100,000 Natl. Network: Westwood One, NBC, Jones Radio Networks, . Natl. Rep: Roslin,. Fisher, Wayland, Cooper, Leader & Zaragoza. Format: Country. Target aud: 25 plus. ◆Stephen J. Puffer, pres, gen mgr, gen sls mgr, adv mgr, progmg dir; Teresa Puffer, opns mgr; Don Smith, chief of engrg.

Henniker

*WNEC-FM— Feb 9, 1971: 91.7 mhz; 120 w. -210 ft TL: N43 10 34 W71 49 22. Hrs open: 17 New England College, 28 Bridge St., 03242. Phone: (603) 428-2278. Phone: (603) 358-8863. Fax: (603) 428-7230.E-mail: A.Metzegen@nec.edu Licensee: New England College. Population served: 10,000 Format: Progsv, adult contemp, Black, jazz, new age, urban contemp. News: one hr wkly. Target aud: 18-25; college students. Spec prog: Blues 4 hrs, country 3 hrs, American Indian 18 hrs, folk 18 hrs, farm 4 hrs wkly. ◆Ambrose Metzegen, CEO; Chris Collord, progmg VP; Kristen Westhoven, mus dir; Dale Carlow, engrg VP.

WNNH(FM)— Nov 17, 1989: 99.1 mhz; 2.8 kw. Ant 479 ft TL: N43 12 49 W71 41 19. Stereo. Hrs open: 24 11 Kimball Dr., Unit 114, Hooksett, 03106. Phone: (603) 524-1324. Fax: (603) 528-5185. Web Site:www.franknh.com Licensee: Nassau Broadcasting III L.L.C. Group owner: Nassau Broadcasting Partners L.P. (acq 3-16-2004; grpsl). Natl. Rep: McGavren Guild,. Verner, Liipfert, Bernhard, McPherson & Hand. Format: Classic hits. News staff: 2; News: 20 hrs wkly. Target aud: 25-54; mass appeal. ◆Rob Fulmer, gen mgr; Andy Mack, opns mgr, progmg mgr; Ken Cail, news dir.

Hillsboro

WTPL(FM)—Licensed to Hillsboro. See Concord

Hinsdale

WYRY(FM)—Licensed to Hinsdale. See Keene

Jackson

WEVJ(FM)— 8/02: 99.5 mhz; 4.7 kw. Ant 171 ft TL: N44 10 30 W71 10 07. Hrs open: 24
Rebroadcasts WEVO(FM) Concord 100%.
New Hampshire Public Radio, 207 N. Main St., Concord, 03301-5003. Phone: (603) 228-8910. Fax: (603) 224-6052.E-mail: admin@nhpr.org Web Site:www.nhpr.org Licensee: New Hampshire Public Radio. Natl. Network: NPR, PRI, . Garvey,Schubert & Barer. Wire Svc: AP Format: News/talk. News staff: 9. Target aud: 25-54. ♦Betsy Gardela, pres; Elizabeth Gardella, gen mgr; Mark Bevis, news dir; John Huntley, engrg dir.

Jaffrey

WXNH(AM)—Not on air, target date: unknown: 540 khz; 250 w-D, 330 w-N, DA-2. TL: N42 50 55 W71 57 53. Hrs open: 17 Knightsbridge Ct., Nanuet, NY, 10954. Phone: (845) 356-9613. Licensee: Steven Wendell. ♦Steven Wendell, gen mgr.

Keene

***WEVN(FM)**— April 1994: 90.7 mhz; 1.5 kw. 938 ft Stereo. Hrs open: 24
Rebroadcasts WEVO(FM) Concord 100%.
207 N. Main St., Concord, 03301. Phone: (603) 228-8910. Fax: (603) 224-6052.E-mail: admin@nhpr.org Web Site:www.nhpr.org Licensee: New Hampshire Public Radio Inc. Natl. Network: NPR, PRI, . Garvey, Schubert & Barer. Wire Svc: AP Format: News/talk. News staff: 9; News: 42 hrs wkly. Target aud: 25-54. Spec prog: Folk 3 hrs wkly. ♦Elizabeth Gardella, pres; Mark Bevis, news dir; John Huntley, engrg dir.

WINQ(FM)—Winchester

WKBK(AM)— June 2, 1927: 1290 khz; 5 kw-U, DA-1. TL: N42 56 56 W72 18 22. Hrs open: Box 466, 03431. Secondary address: 69 Stanhope Ave. 03431. Phone: (603) 352-9230. Fax: (603) 357-3926.E-mail: info@wkbk.com Licensee: Saga Communications of New England LLC. Group owner: Saga Communications Inc. (acq 5-1-02; grpsl). Population served: 60,000 Natl. Network: CBS, . Natl. Rep: McGavren Guild,. Format: News, talk. Target aud: 25 plus. ♦Bruce Lyons, gen mgr; Stephen Hamel, opns dir; Vicky Lenahan, prom dir; Dan Mitchell, progmg dir; Paul Scheuring, news dir; Ira Wilner, chief of engrg; Jennifer Bond, traf mgr.

WKNE(FM)— May 1964: 103.7 mhz; 12.2 kw. 991 ft TL: N43 02 00 W72 22 04. Stereo. Hrs open: Box 466, 03431. Phone: (603) 352-9230. Fax: (603) 357-3926.E-mail: info@wkne.com Licensee: Saga Communications of New England LLC. Format: Adultcontemp, top-40. Target aud: 18-49. ♦Jennifer Bond, traf mgr.

***WKNH(FM)**— November 1975: 91.3 mhz; 274 w. 79 ft TL: N42 55 29 W72 16 42. (CP: 91.7 mhz, 192 w, ant 363 ft.). Stereo. Hrs open: 24 Keene State College, 229 Main St., 03435-2704. Phone: (603) 358-2420. Phone: (603) 358-2421. Fax: (603) 358-2417.E-mail: wknhinfo@aol.com Web Site:www.jumblue.com/wknh/ Licensee: Board of Trustees University System of New Hampshire. Population served: 30,000 Format: Progsv. News staff: 2; News: 3 hrs wkly. Target aud: General. Spec prog: Class 4 hrs, folk 6 hrs, jazz 3 hrs, blues 3 hrs, rap 4 hrs, new age 4 hrs, reggae 3 hrs, Christian 3 hrs, metal 4 hrs, experimental 3 hrs wkly. ♦James McCluskey, gen mgr.

WYRY(FM)—(Hinsdale, June 30, 1987: 104.9 mhz; 1.55 kw. 456 ft TL: N42 46 33 W72 27 19. (CP: 725 w, ant 669 ft.). Stereo. Hrs open: 24 30 Warwick Rd., Suite 10, Winchester, 03470. Phone: (603) 239-8200. Fax: (603) 239-6203. Web Site:www.wyry.com Licensee: Tri-Valley Broadcasting Corp. (acq 8-86). Natl. Network: Jones Radio Networks, . Reddy, Begley & McCormick. Format: Country. News staff: 3; News: 10 hrs wkly. Target aud: 25-49; upscale adults & business decision makers. ♦Brian McCormick, VP, gen mgr; Sean Patrik, sls VP & progmg dir; Dan Guy, chief of engrg.

WZBK(AM)— May 1959: 1220 khz; 1 kw-U. TL: N42 55 50 W72 17 56. Hrs open: 69 Stanhope Ave., 03431. Phone: (603) 352-9230. Fax: (603) 357-3926.E-mail: info@wkbkam.com Licensee: Saga Communications of New Hampshire LLC. Group owner: Saga Communications Inc. (acq 7-1-2002; $2.63 million with WOQL(FM) Winchester). Population served: 60,000 Booth, Freret, Imlay & Tepper P. Format: News/talk. Target aud: 25-54; general. ♦Bruce Lyons, stn mgr, prom VP; Susan Wells, gen sls mgr; Steve Hamill, progmg dir, chief of engrg; Paul Schering, news dir; Ira Wilner, chief of engrg; Jen Bond, traf mgr.

Laconia

WEMJ(AM)— Apr 9, 1961: 1490 khz; 1 kw-U. TL: N43 32 29 W71 27 45. Hrs open: Box 7326, Village W. Bldg 1, Gilford, 03247. Phone: (603) 524-1323. Fax: (603) 528-5185. Licensee: Nassau Broadcasting III L.L.C. Population served: 14,888 Natl. Network: CBS, . Natl. Rep: D & R Radio,. Format: Talk.

WEZS(AM)— Aug 22, 1922: 1350 khz; 5 kw-D, 112 w-N. TL: N43 30 27 W71 31 00. Hrs open: 277 Union Ave., 03246. Phone: (603) 524-6288. Fax: (603) 528-1638.E-mail: feedback@wezs.com Web Site:www.oldies1350.net Licensee: Gary W. Hammond. (acq 3-17-94; 6-6-94). Population served: 152,500 Natl. Network: USA, . Format: Oldies hits of the 60s & 70s. Target aud: 45 plus. ♦Gary W. Hammond, gen mgr.

WLNH-FM— Nov 22, 1965: 98.3 mhz; 3.8 kw. 413 ft TL: N43 35 46 W71 29 55. Hrs open: 24 hrs Box 7326, Village West Bldg. 1, Gilford, 03247. Phone: (603) 524-1323. Fax: (603) 528-5185.E-mail: info@wlnh.com Web Site:www.wlnh.com Licensee: Nassau Broadcasting III L.L.C. Group owner: Nassau Broadcasting Partners L.P. (acq 4-7-2004; grpsl). Population served: 40,000 Rosenman & Colin L.L.P. Format: Hot adult contemp. Target aud: 25-54. ♦Molly King, prom dir; Chris Ialuna, progmg dir.

Lancaster

WKBR(AM)—Not on air, target date: unknown: 1450 khz; 1 kw-D, 670 w-N. TL: N44 30 00 W71 33 50. Hrs open: Box 896, Littleton, 03561. Secondary address: 195 Main St. 03584. Phone: (603) 444-4102. Fax: (603) 788-3536.E-mail: kiss102@together.net Licensee: Radio New England Broadcasting LLC

WXXS(FM)— 1998: 102.3 mhz; 1.5 kw. Ant 964 ft TL: N44 23 39 W71 39 20. Stereo. Hrs open: 24 Box 896, Littleton, 03561. Secondary address: 195 Main St. 03584. Phone: (603) 444-4102. Phone: (603) 788-3636. Fax: (603) 788-3536.E-mail: kiss102@together.net Licensee: Radio New England Broadcasting LLC Natl. Network: CBS, . Format: Contemp hit/top-40. ♦Barry P. Lunderville, gen mgr; Brian Lunderville, opns mgr; Barry Lunderville, progmg dir; Danielle Corbiel, traf mgr.

Lebanon

WGXL(FM)—See Hanover

WHDQ(FM)—See Claremont

WUVR(AM)— 2004: 1490 khz; 640 w-U. TL: N43 39 12 W72 14 16. Hrs open: Box 2295, New London, 03257. Phone: (603) 448-0500. Fax: (603) 526-9372.E-mail: office@wntk.com Web Site:www.wntk.com Licensee: KOOR Communications Inc. Format: News/talk. ♦Robert Vinikoor, gen mgr, gen sls mgr, progmg dir; Dave Shurtleff, news dir; Russ McCallister, chief of engrg.

***WVFA(FM)**— Feb 6, 2004: 90.5 mhz; 7 w. Ant 695 ft TL: N43 37 17 W72 10 30. Hrs open: 24 Box 126, Hartford, VT, 05047-0126. Secondary address: 48 Wescott Rd., Enfield 03748. Phone: (802) 295-9683. Fax: (802) 295-9683.E-mail: vtpreacher@aol.com Licensee: Green Mountain Educational Fellowship Inc. Population served: 80,000 Wire Svc: AP Format: Inspirational, educ, relg. News: 11 hrs wkly. Target aud: 25-49; primary. ♦William A. Wittik, pres, CFO & gen mgr; Betsy Murray, opns mgr.

WXXK(FM)— Dec 18, 1990: 100.5 mhz; 22 kw. Ant 325 ft TL: N43 37 17 W72 10 30. Hrs open: 24 31 Hanover St., Suite 4, 03766. Phone: (603) 448-1400. Fax: (603) 448-1755. Web Site:www.kixx.com Licensee: Great Eastern Radio LLC. Group owner: Clear Channel Communications Inc. (acq 10-30-2007; grpsl). Population served: 150,000 Natl. Network: Westwood One, CNN Radio, . Format: Country. News staff: 3; News: 20 hrs wkly. Target aud: 25-54. ♦Cheryl Frisch, CFO, dev VP; Robert Frisch, gen mgr; Kenny Michaels, opns mgr, prom dir; Matt Cross, sls dir, traf mgr; Michael Barrett, progmg dir, news dir.

Lisbon

WLTN-FM—Licensed to Lisbon. See Littleton

Littleton

WLTN(AM)— Oct 10, 1963: 1400 khz; 1 kw-U. TL: N44 18 47 W71 46 08. Hrs open: 24 15 Main St., 03561. Phone: (603) 444-3911. Fax: (603) 444-7186.E-mail: mix967@roadrunner.com Licensee: Barry P. Lunderville L.L.C. (acq 6-30-2005; with WLTN-FM Lisbon). Population served: 150,000 Format: Oldies, Red Sox. News staff: one; News: 40 hrs wkly. Target aud: 21-65. ♦Barry Lunderville, gen mgr; Christina Brooks, gen sls mgr; Phil Rivera, progmg dir; Jim Clothey, news dir; Brian Lunderville, chief of engrg; Danielle Corbiel, traf mgr.

WLTN-FM—(Lisbon, Sept 1, 1991: 96.7 mhz; 6 kw. 295 ft TL: N44 13 11 W71 52 07. Stereo. Hrs open: 24 Prog sep from AM 15 Main St., 03561. Phone: (603) 444-3911. Fax: (603) 444-7186.E-mail: mix967@roadrunner.com Licensee: Barry P. Lunderville L.L.C. Population served: 200,000 Natl. Network: Westwood One, . Format: Bright adult contemp. News staff: one; News: 7 hrs wkly. Target aud: 25-54. ♦Danielle Corbiel, traf mgr.

WMTK(FM)— Feb 23, 1985: 106.3 mhz; 390 w. 1,256 ft TL: N44 21 14 W71 44 23. Stereo. Hrs open: 24 Box 106, 03561-0106. Phone: (603) 444-5106. Fax: (603) 444-1205.E-mail: thenotch@kington.net Licensee: Vermont Broadcast Associates Inc. (acq 8-2000; $250,000). Population served: 180,000 Bryan Cave. Format: Classic hits. News staff: one. Target aud: 30-50; slightly more males, active lifestyles. ♦Bruce James, gen mgr, progmg dir; Steve Nichols, gen sls mgr; Todd Wellington, news dir; Don Smith, chief of engrg.

Madbury

WWNH(AM)— May 20, 1989: 1340 khz; 1 kw-U. TL: N43 10 22 W70 55 00. Hrs open: 24 Box 69, Dover, 03821. Secondary address: 284 Rt. 155, Dover 03821. Phone: (603) 742-8575. Fax: (603) 743-6444.E-mail: info@loveradio.net Web Site:www.loveradio.net Licensee: Harvest Broadcasting. Natl. Network: USA, . Format: MOR. News: 3 hrs wkly. Target aud: General; 29 plus. Spec prog: Family 24 hrs wkly. ♦Patti Smith, CEO, gen mgr, stn mgr, gen sls mgr; Ernie Jenkins, chief of opns, progmg dir, news dir; Steve Donnell, engrg dir & chief of engrg.

Manchester

WFEA(AM)— Mar 8, 1932: 1370 khz; 5 kw-U, DA-2. TL: N42 54 26 W71 27 45. Hrs open: 500 Commercial St., 03101. Phone: (603) 669-5777. Fax: (603) 669-4641.E-mail: raydionh@wzid.com Licensee: Saga Communications of New England LLC. Group owner: Saga Communications Inc. (acq 6-2-92; grpsl, including co-located FM). Population served: 250,000 Rgnl rep: Katz. Smithwick & Belendiuk. Format: Adult standards. Target aud: 50 plus; "Modern Maturity" market. Spec prog: Fr 3 hrs, Sp 2 hrs wkly.

WGAM(AM)— Oct 1, 1946: 1250 khz; 5 kw-U, DA-2. TL: N43 00 40 W71 30 19. Hrs open: 5 AM-11 PM 1 Indian Head Plaza, 5th Fl., Nashua, 03060. Phone: (603) 880-9001. Fax: (603) 577-8682.E-mail: info@wgamradio.com Web Site:www.wgamradio.com Licensee: Absolute Broadcasting LLC. Group owner: Northeast Broadcasting Company Inc. (acq 11-21-2006; $1.6 million). Population served: 400,000 Natl. Network: Fox Sports, . Format: Sports. ♦Jerry DiGrezio, gen mgr.

WGIR(AM)— October 1941: 610 khz; 5 kw-D, 1 kw-N, DA-2. TL: N43 00 57 W71 28 48. Hrs open: 24 195 McGregor St., Suite 810, 03102. Phone: (603) 625-6915. Fax: (603) 669-0610.E-mail: info@wgiram.com Web Site:www.wgiram.com Licensee: Capstar TX L.P. Group owner: Clear Channel Communications Inc. (acq 8-30-00; grpsl). Population served: 200,000 Natl. Network: Fox News Radio, Westwood One, . Format: News/talk, sports. News staff: 2; News: 38 hrs wkly. Target aud: 35-54. ♦Joseph Graham, gen mgr.

WGIR-FM— June 5, 1963: 101.1 mhz; 11.5 kw. Ant 1,027 ft TL: N42 58 54 W71 35 21. Stereo. Hrs open: Prog sep from AM 195 McGregor St., Suite 810, 03105. Phone: (603) 625-6915. Fax: (603) 669-0610.E-mail: info@rock101fm.com Web Site:www.rock101fm.com Population served: 500,000 Format: AOR.

***WLMW(FM)**— September 1997: 90.7 mhz; 15 w. 869 ft TL: N42 58 59 W71 35 25. Stereo. Hrs open: Box 366, Auburn, 03032. Secondary address: 134 Hollis Rd., Amherst 03031. Phone: (603) 483-8950. Fax: (603) 483-8908.E-mail: jim@nhfamilyradio.org Web Site:www.nhfamilyradio.org Licensee: Knowledge For Life. Format: Christian family radio. ♦Jim Phelan, gen mgr.

WOKQ(FM)—See Dover

WZID(FM)— 1948: 95.7 mhz; 14.5 kw. 930 ft TL: N42 59 02 W71 35 22. Hrs open: 500 Commercial St., 03101. Phone: (603) 669-5777. Fax: (603) 669-4641.E-mail: raydionh@wzid.com Web Site:www.wzid.com Population served: 448,000 Format: Adult contemp. Target aud: 25-54. ♦Andy Orcutt, gen sls mgr; Dave Ashton, progmg dir.

Meredith

***WANH(FM)**— 2009: 91.5 mhz; 1.7 kw. Ant 26 ft TL: N43 41 25 W71 22 34. Hrs open: Box 40, Concord, 03302. Phone: (603) 227-0911.E-mail: info@wvnh.org Web Site:www.wvnh.org Licensee: New Hampshire Gospel Radio Inc. Format: Christian. ♦Peter Stohrer, gen mgr.

WWHQ(FM)— Nov 16, 1988: 101.5 mhz; 6 kw. Ant 328 ft TL: N43 35 46 W71 29 55. Stereo. Hrs open: Box 7326, Gilford, 03247. Phone: (603) 524-1323. Phone: (603) 225-1160. Fax: (603) 528-5185. Fax: (603) 882-0588. Web Site:www.thehawkrocks.com Licensee: Nassau Broadcasting III L.L.C. Group owner: Nassau Broadcasting Partners L.P. (acq 4-7-2004; grpsl). Format: Classic rock. ♦Louis Mercatanti, pres; Dominic Biello, opns dir; Rob Fulmer, gen mgr & gen sls mgr.

Moultonborough

WSCY(FM)— May 31, 1993: 106.9 mhz; 130 w. 2,096 ft TL: N43 46 09 W71 18 52. Stereo. Hrs open: Box 99, Franklin, 03235. Phone: (603) 253-8080. Fax: (603) 934-2933.E-mail: info@mix941fm.com Web Site:www.mix941fm.com Licensee: Northeast Communications Corp. (group owner; acq 5-4-93; $399,072; 5-24-93). Format: Hot country. ♦Jeff Fisher, pres, stn mgr; Amy Bates, sls VP, news dir; Jeff Levitan, opns mgr & gen sls mgr; Gene Terwilliger, chief of engrg.

Mt. Washington

WHOM(FM)— July 9, 1958: 94.9 mhz; 48 kw. 3,760 ft TL: N44 16 13 W71 18 13. (CP: Ant 46 ft.). Stereo. Hrs open: One City Center, Portland, ME, 04101. Phone: (207) 774-6364. Fax: (207) 774-8707.E-mail: whom@whom949.com Web Site:www.whom949.com Licensee: Citadel Broadcasting Co. Group owner: Citadel Broadcasting Corp. (acq 7-7-99; grpsl). Population served: 200,000 Natl. Rep: Christal,. Format: Light rock, adult contemp. Target aud: 35-64; professionals with active lifestyles. ♦Mike Sambrook, gen mgr; Tim Moore, progmg dir; Barbara Cole, adv.

Nashua

***WEVS(FM)**— 2005: 88.3 mhz; 3.5 kw horiz, 5 kw vert. Ant 69 ft TL: N42 45 00 W71 28 47. Stereo. Hrs open:
Rebroadcasts WEVO(FM) Concord 100%.
207 N. Main St., Concord, 03301-5003. Phone: (603) 228-8910. Fax: (603) 224-6052. Web Site:www.nhpr.org Licensee: New Hampshire Public Radio Inc. Natl. Network: NPR, PRI, . Format: News/talk. ♦Elizabeth Gardella, gen mgr; Mark Bevis, news dir; John Huntley, engrg dir.

WFNQ(FM)— Oct 19, 1987: 106.3 mhz; 950 w. Ant 541 ft TL: N42 44 07 W71 23 37. Stereo. Hrs open: 24 11 Kimball Dr., Suite 114, Hooksett, 03106. Phone: (603) 889-1063. Fax: (603) 882-0688. Web Site:www.1063frankfm.com Licensee: Nassau Broadcasting III L.L.C. Group owner: Nassau Broadcasting Partners L.P. (acq 3-16-2004; grpsl). Cole, Raywid & Braverman. Format: Hot adult contemp. News staff: one; News: 5 hrs wkly. Target aud: 18-49. ♦Louis F. Mercatanti, pres; Rob Fulmer, gen mgr; Andy Mack, opns dir; Phyllis Knight, gen sls mgr, traf mgr; Sarah Sullivan, progmg dir; Dirk Nadon, chief of engrg.

WGHM(AM)— 1991: 900 khz; 910 w-D, 60 w-N. TL: N42 45 34 W71 28 37. Hrs open: 6 AM-6 PM (Oct-Apr); 6 AM-10 PM (May-Sept) One Indian Head Plaza, 5th Fl., 03060. Phone: (603) 880-9001. Fax: (603) 577-8682.E-mail: info@wgamradio.com Web Site:www.wgamradio.com Licensee: Absolute Broadcasting LLC. (acq 11-2-2005; $925,000). Natl. Network: Fox Sports, . Format: Sports. Target aud: 35 plus. ♦Jerry DiGrezio, gen mgr; Marty Terrell, gen sls mgr; John Kosian, progmg dir, chief of engrg; Paul Hust, traf mgr.

WSMN(AM)— Mar 9, 1958: 1590 khz; 5 kw-U, DA-1. TL: N42 44 40 W71 29 52. Hrs open: 18 1 Indian Head Plaza, 03060. Phone: (603) 880-9001. Fax: (603) 577-8682.E-mail: info@wgamradio.com Web Site:www.wsmnradio.com Licensee: Absolute Broadcasting LLC. (acq 11-10-2005; $250,000). Population served: 90,000 Natl. Network: ESPN Radio, . Format: News/talk, sports. ♦Jerry DiGrezio, gen mgr.

New London

WNTK-FM— Nov 30, 1992: 99.7 mhz; 620 w. 712 ft TL: N43 26 52 W72 02 04. Hrs open: 24
Rebroadcasts WNTK(AM) Newport 50%.
Box 2295, 03257. Secondary address: 103 Hanover St., Lebanon 03766. Phone: (603) 448-0500. Fax: (603) 526-9372.E-mail: office@wntk.com Web Site:www.wntk.com Licensee: Koor Communications Inc. (group owner) Shaw Pittman. Format: Talk/news. News staff: 2. Target aud: 24-54. ♦Robert L. Vinikoor, CEO, gen mgr, progmg dir; Sheila E. Vinikoor, pres; Dave Shurtleff, news dir; Russ McCallister, chief of engrg.

***WSCS(FM)**— February 1996: 90.9 mhz; 63 w horiz, 250 w vert. 297 ft TL: N43 24 41 W71 58 33. Hrs open: Colby-Sawyer College, 541 Main St., 03257. Phone: (603) 526-3493. Fax: (603) 526-3452.E-mail: wscs@colby-sawyer.edu Web Site:www.colby-sawyer.edu/wscs Licensee: Colby-Sawyer College. Format: Educ. ♦Sean Joncas, stn mgr; James Kovach, disc jockey.

Newport

WCNL(AM)— Aug 11, 1960: 1010 khz; 10 kw-D, 37 w-N. TL: N43 21 52 W72 10 47. Hrs open: 24 Box 2295, New London, 03257. Phone: (603) 448-0500. Fax: (603) 448-6601.E-mail: bob@wntk.com Web Site:www.wntk.com Licensee: KOOR Communications. (group owner; (acq 8-88; $250,000; 8-29-88). Shaw Pittman. Format: Classic country/Americanna. Target aud: 25-54; informed adults. ♦Robert L. Vinikoor, pres, gen mgr; Robert Vinikoor, progmg dir, chief of engrg; Sheila Vinikoor, traf mgr & disc jockey.

North Conway

WPKQ(FM)— October 1952: 103.7 mhz; 21.5 kw horiz, 16.5 kw vert. Ant 3,874 ft TL: N44 16 14 W71 18 15. Stereo. Hrs open: 24
Rebroadcasts WOKQ(FM) Dover 80%.
P.O. Box 576, Dover, 03821-0576. Secondary address: 2617 White Mountain Hwy. 03860. Phone: (603) 749-9750. Fax: (603) 749-6589.E-mail: mail@wokq.com Web Site:www.wpkq.com Licensee: Citadel Broadcasting Co. Group owner: Citadel Broadcasting Corp. (acq 7-7-99; grpsl). Population served: 3,000,000 Natl. Network: CNN Radio, . Natl. Rep: Christal,. Wiley, Rein & Fielding. Wire Svc: AP Format: Country. News staff: 2. Target aud: 25-54; New England residents. ♦Farid Suleman, CEO; Judy Ellis, pres; Mark Ericson, gen mgr, opns mgr; Ken Hoffman, gen sls mgr; Mark Jennings, progmg dir.

Peterborough

WFEX(FM)— June 1971: 92.1 mhz; 180 w. Ant 1,332 ft TL: N42 51 42 W71 52 46. Stereo. Hrs open: 24
Rebroadcasts WFNX(FM) Lynn, MA 80%.
25 Exchange St., Lynn, MA, 01901. Secondary address: 32 Technology Way 2W8, Nashua 03060. Phone: (603) 882-9210. Fax: (603) 578-9210.E-mail: fnxradio@fnxradio.com Web Site:www.fnxradio.com Licensee: FNX Broadcasting of New Hampshire LLC. Group owner: Phoenix Media Communications Group (acq 11-29-99). Population served: 511,000 Rubin, Winston, Dierks, Harris, & Cooke. Wire Svc: AP Format: Alternative rock. News staff: one; News: 2 hrs wkly. Target aud: Adults 18-44; young, educated white collar professionals with extremely active lifestyles. Spec prog: Gay talk 2 hrs, jazz 6 hrs wkly. ♦Stephen Mindich, CEO; Gary Kurtz, gen mgr; Peter Cawley, gen sls mgr; Keith Dakin, progmg dir; Chris Hall, chief of engrg.

Plymouth

***WPCR-FM**— Sept 29, 1974: 91.7 mhz; 215 w. 95 ft TL: N43 45 25 W71 38 59. Hrs open: 24 WPCR HUB, Plymouth State College, 17 High St., 03264-1594. Phone: (603) 535-2242 (office). Phone: (603) 536-5000 (univ. switchboard). Fax: (603) 535-2783.E-mail: genmgr@wpcr.plymouth.edu Web Site:wpcr.plymouth.edu Licensee: Plymouth State College. Natl. Network: AP Radio, . Format: AOR, progsv. Target aud: 15-35; college students & those interested in progressive alternative music. Spec prog: Class 3 hrs, jazz 3 hrs, reggae 3 hrs, blues 3 hrs, comedy 3 hrs wkly.

WPNH(AM)— Nov 10, 1965: 1300 khz; 5 kw-D, DA-D. TL: N43 46 32 W71 42 20. Hrs open: 24 Box 99, Franklin, 03235. Secondary address: 110 Babbitt Rd., Franklin 03235. Phone: (603) 536-2500. Phone: (603) 536-2501. Fax: (603) 934-2933.E-mail: info@mix941fm.com Licensee: Northeast Communications Corp. (group owner; acq 2-9-99; with co-located FM). Population served: 29,100 Reddy, Begley & McCormick. Format: Big band. Target aud: 35 plus. Spec prog: Breakfast with the bands 6 hrs wkly. ♦Jeff Fisher, gen mgr; Fred Caruso, opns mgr, progmg dir; Jess Levitan, gen sls mgr; Amy Bates, news dir; Cathy Keizer, traf mgr.

WPNH-FM— Oct 1, 1975: 100.1 mhz; 2.35 kw. 364 ft TL: N43 45 41 W71 38 59. (CP: 4.9 kw, ant 358 ft.). Stereo. Hrs open: Dups AM 75% Box 99, Franklin, 03235. Secondary address: 110 Babbitt Rd., Franklin 03235. Phone: (603) 536-2500. Phone: (603) 536-2501. Fax: (603) 934-2933.E-mail: info@mix941fm.com Web Site:www.wpnhfm.com Licensee: Northeast Communications Corp. Population served: 64,000 Format: Alternative. ♦Rick Ganley, progmg dir, local news ed; Cathy Keizer, traf mgr; Bob Moulton, disc jockey.

***WPVH(FM)**—Not on air, target date: unknown: 90.7 mhz; 200 w vert. Ant 200 ft TL: N43 45 45.3 W71 39 00. Hrs open: 260 Cape Moonshine Rd., Wentworth, 03282. Phone: (603) 764-9800. Web Site:www.wentworthbaptistchurch.com/WVOH.html Licensee: Wentworth Baptist Church. ♦Jeremy Cochran, pres.

Portsmouth

WERZ(FM)—See Exeter

WHEB(FM)— Jan 14, 1964: 100.3 mhz; 50 kw. 459 ft TL: N43 03 11 W70 46 04. (CP: Ant 446 ft. TL: N43 03 05 W70 46 09). Stereo. Hrs open: 815 Lafayette Rd., 03801. Phone: (603) 436-7300. Fax: (603) 430-9415.E-mail: info@wheb.com Web Site:www.wheb.com Licensee: Capstar TX L.P. Group owner: Clear Channel Communications Inc. (acq 8-30-00; grpsl). Population served: 79,700 Format: Rock and roll. Target aud: 18-49. ♦Robert Greer, gen mgr; Christopher Garrett, opns mgr, progmg dir, mus dir; Christine Sieks, gen sls mgr; Kelly Brown, news dir; Kenneth Neelan, chief of engrg; Sandy Nagle, traf mgr; Greg Kretschmar, disc jockey.

WMYF(AM)— Dec 5, 1960: 1380 khz; 1 kw-U, DA-N. TL: N43 03 48 W70 47 09. Hrs open: 24 815 Lafayette Rd., 03801. Phone: (603) 436-7300. Fax: (603) 430-9415. Licensee: Capstar TX L.P. Format: Music of your life. Target aud: 25-54. ♦Judy Figliulo, gen sls mgr; Michael O'Donnell, progmg dir; Heather Salisbury, traf mgr.

WXEX(AM)—See Exeter

Rochester

WGIN(AM)— 1947: 930 khz; 5 kw-U, DA-N. TL: N43 17 13 W70 56 55. Hrs open: 24 Prog sep from FM 815 Lafayette Rd., Portsmouth, 03801. Phone: (603) 436-7300. Fax: (603) 430-9415. Licensee: Capstar TX L.P. Population served: 310,000 Format: News/talk, sports. Target aud: 25-64; decision-makers, heads of businesses, households. ♦Dan Pierce, progmg dir; Kelly Brown, news dir; Beth LaRocque, traf mgr.

WQSO(FM)— Oct 21, 1979: 96.7 mhz; 3 kw. Ant 328 ft TL: N43 17 14 W70 56 49. Stereo. Hrs open: 24 815 Lafayette Rd., Portsmouth, 03801. Phone: (603) 436-7300. Fax: (603) 430-9415. Licensee: Capstar TX L.P. Group owner: Clear Channel Communications Inc. (acq 8-30-2000; grpsl). Wiley, Rein & Fielding. Format: News/talk. News staff: 3; News: 12 hrs wkly. Target aud: 25-54. ♦Robert Greer, gen mgr.

Salem

WCCM(AM)— Jan 10, 1977: 1110 khz; 5 kw-D, DA-D. TL: N42 45 42 W71 16 13. Hrs open: 462 Merrimack St., Methuen, MA, 01844. Phone: (978) 686-9966. Phone: (978) 683-7171. Fax: (978) 687-1180.E-mail: traffic@1110wccmam.com Web Site:1110wccm.com/wccm/ Licensee: Costa-Eagle Radio Ventures L.P. (group owner; (acq 1996). Population served: 90,000 Natl. Rep: Roslin,. Bryan Cave. Format: News/talk. News staff: 2; News: 25 hrs wkly. Target aud: General. ♦Pat Costa, gen mgr; John Bassett, stn mgr; Bruce Arnold, progmg dir.

Somersworth

WBYY(FM)— Jan 25, 1995: 98.7 mhz; 6 kw. 315 ft TL: N43 14 12 W70 53 47. Hrs open: 24 Box 400, 101 Back Rd., Dover, 03820-0400. Phone: (603) 742-0987. Fax: (603) 742-0448.E-mail: info@987thebay.com Web Site:www.987thebay.com Licensee: Garrison City Broadcasting Inc. Format: Adult contemp. News staff: 2. Target aud: 25-54. ♦Bob Demers Sr., CEO; Michael L. Dafoe, gen mgr; Mike Pomp, news dir; Jeff Rosenberg, chief of engrg; Julie Michalik, traf mgr.

Stratford

WTTT(FM)—Not on air, target date: unknown: 98.7 nhz; 143 w. Ant 1,958 ft TL: N44 43 54 W71 32 10. Hrs open: 6139 Franklin Park Rd., McLean, VA, 22101. Phone: (703) 761-5013. Fax: (703) 761-5023. Licensee: Jackman Holding Company LLC. ♦A. Wray Fitch III, gen mgr.

Swanzey

WSNI(FM)— January 1983: 97.7 mhz; 1.75 kw. Ant 613 ft TL: N42 54 57 W72 19 48. Stereo. Hrs open: 24 69 Stanhope Ave., Keene, 03431. Phone: (603) 352-9230. Fax: (603) 357-3926. Web Site:www.sunnykeene.com Licensee: Saga Communications of New

England LLC. Group owner: Saga Communications Inc. (acq 4-1-2003; $400,000). Population served: 250,000 Natl. Network: ABC, . Format: Adult contemp. News staff: 2; News: 7 hrs wkly. Target aud: 25-54; 60% female, 40% male. ◆Robert Cox, VP, gen mgr; Steve Hamel, opns mgr; Vicki Lenanan, prom dir.

Walpole

WFYX(FM)— November 2000: 96.3 mhz; 320 w. Ant 407 ft TL: N43 08 14 W72 25 59. Hrs open:
Rebroadcasts WWOD(FM) Hartford, VT 100%.
106 N. Main St., West Lebanon, 03784. Phone: (603) 298-0332. Fax: (603) 298-7554. Fax: (603) 727-0134.E-mail: info@bestoldies104.com Web Site:www.bestoldies104.com Licensee: Nassau Broadcasting III L.L.C. Group owner: Nassau Broadcasting Partners L.P. (acq 8-13-2004; grpsl). Format: Oldies. ◆Camille Losapio, gen mgr.

Whitefield

WNYN-FM— 2007: 99.1 mhz; 460 w. Ant 1,135 ft TL: N44 21 10 W71 44 15. Hrs open: 169 River St., Montpelier, VT, 05602-3724. Phone: (802) 223-2396. Fax: (802) 223-1520. Licensee: White Park Broadcasting Inc. Format: Adult hits. ◆Steven A. Silberberg, pres; Ed Flanagan, gen mgr.

Winchester

WINQ(FM)— Oct 15, 1991: 98.7 mhz; 6 kw. Ant 328 ft TL: N42 49 56 W72 23 34. Stereo. Hrs open: 24 69 Stanhope Ave., Keene, 03431. Phone: (603) 352-9230. Fax: (603) 357-3926. Web Site:www.987wink.com Licensee: Saga Communications of New Hampshire LLC. Group owner: Saga Communications Inc. (acq 7-1-2002; $2.63 million with WZBK(AM) Keene). Population served: 100,000 Natl. Network: ABC, Jones Radio Networks, . Booth, Freret, Imlay & Tepper. Format: New country. News staff: 4; News: 8 hrs wkly. Target aud: 25-54. ◆Robert Cox, VP & gen mgr.

WZBK(AM)—See Keene

Wolfeboro

WASR(AM)— April 1970: 1420 khz; 5 kw-D, 137 w-N. TL: N43 35 31 W71 13 12. Hrs open: 5 AM-8 PM Box 900, 03894-0900. Secondary address: 73 Varney Rd. 03894-0900. Phone: (603) 569-1420. Fax: (603) 569-1900.E-mail: mail@wasr.net Web Site:www.wasr.net Licensee: Winnipesaukee Network Inc. (acq 3-31-2004; $350,000). Population served: 60,000 Format: Adult contemp, news. News staff: 4; News: 35 hrs wkly. Target aud: 25-54. ◆Grant P. Hatch, pres; Gary Hammond, engrg dir.

WLKZ(FM)— Feb 1, 1985: 104.9 mhz; 570 w. Ant 1,056 ft TL: N43 32 46 W71 22 42. Stereo. Hrs open: 24 Box 7326, Laconia, 03247-7326. Secondary address: 25 Country Club Rd., Bldg. One, Gilford 03249. Phone: (603) 524-1323. Fax: (603) 528-5185.E-mail: wlkz@metroczst.net Web Site:www.franknh.com Licensee: Nassau Broadcasting III L.L.C. Group owner: Nassau Broadcasting Partners L.P. (acq 3-16-2004; grpsl). Natl. Rep: McGavren Guild,. Haley, Bader & Potts. Format: Classic hits. News: 5 hrs wkly. Target aud: 25-54; baby boomers. ◆Louis F. Mercatanti, pres; Jim Cande, sr VP; Rob Fulmer, gen mgr; Pat Kelly, opns dir, progmg dir; Ron Piro, gen mgr & gen sls mgr; Andy Mack, prom dir; Dirk Nadon, chief of engrg.

New Jersey

Andover

WOF(AM)— Oct 8, 1946: 1000 khz; 1 kw-D, 250 w-N, DA-D (L-KQSL). TL: N35 48 31 W121 43 28. (CP: 5 kw-U). Stereo. Hrs open: 24 12 Coulter Pl., 07821. Fax: (908) 219-0182. Licensee: General Broadcasting Corp. (group owner; (acq 7-20-69; $255,000 with co-located FM;2-12-83). Rgnl. Network: Mountain State Network. Format: MOR, C&W. Spec prog: Sp 3 hrs wkly. ◆Edgar Adcock, gen mgr.

Asbury Park

WADB(AM)— 1926: 1310 khz; 2.5 kw-D, 1 kw-N, DA-2. TL: N40 13 47 W74 05 27. Hrs open: 2401 Rt. 66, Ocean, 07712. Phone: (732) 897-8282. Fax: (732) 897-8283.E-mail: info@1310espndeportes.com Web Site:www.1310espndeportes.com Licensee: Millennium Shore

License Holdco LLC. Group owner: Millennium Radio Group LLC (acq 6-11-2002; grpsl). Population served: 170,000 Natl. Network: Fox Sports, . Format: Sports. ◆Bill Saurer, gen mgr; Lou Russo, progmg dir; Jay Pierce, chief of engrg; John Surno, sls.

WHTG(AM)—See Eatontown

WJLK(FM)— Nov 20, 1947: 94.3 mhz; 1.3 kw. Ant 499 ft TL: N40 13 45 W74 05 24. Stereo. Hrs open: Prog sep from AM 2401 Rt. 66, Ocean, 07712. Phone: (732) 897-8282. Fax: (732) 897-8283. Web Site:www.getthepoint.com Population served: 757,000 Format: Hot adult contemp. ◆Lou Russo, opns mgr, progmg dir; Debbie Mazzella, mus dir; Tara Hessline, traf mgr.

*WYGG(FM)—Not on air, target date: unknown: Stn currently dark. 88.1 mhz; 100 w. 33 ft TL: N40 13 01 W74 00 35. Hrs open: 1488 New York Ave., Minority Business & Housing Development, Inc., Brooklyn, NY, 11210. Phone: (908) 775-0821. Web Site:www.radiobonnenouvelle.com Licensee: Minority Business & Housing Development, Inc. Format: Relg.

Atlantic City

WAJM(FM)— 1997: 88.9 mhz; 150 w vert. 102 ft TL: N39 21 54 W74 28 31. Hrs open: Atlantic City High School, 1400 N. Albany Ave., 08401. Secondary address: 1809 Pacific Ave. 08402. Phone: (609) 343-7300. Fax: (609) 343-7347.E-mail: plewis@acboe.org Web Site:www.acboe.org Licensee: Atlantic City Board of Education. Format: Div. ◆Pamela Lewis, gen mgr; Albert Horner, stn mgr.

WAYV(FM)— April 1961: 95.1 mhz; 50 kw. Ant 331 ft TL: N39 22 51 W74 27 04. Stereo. Hrs open: 24
Simulcast with WAIV(FM) Cape May 100%.
8025 Black Horse Pike, Suite 100-102, West Atlantic City, 08232. Phone: (609) 484-8444. Fax: (609) 646-6331.E-mail: gfequity@aol.com Web Site:www.wayv951fm@aol.com Licensee: Equity Communications L.P. (group owner; (acq 6-21-96; $3.1 million). Population served: 400,000 Natl. Rep: Katz Radio,. Latham & Watkins. Format: Hot adult contemp. Target aud: 18-49; adults. ◆Gary Fisher, sr VP, VP, gen mgr; Rob Garcia, progmg dir.

WENJ(AM)— 1940: 1450 khz; 1 kw-U. TL: N39 22 42 W74 26 53. Hrs open: 24 950 Tilton Rd., Suite 200, Northfield, 08225. Phone: (609) 645-9797. Fax: (609) 272-9228.E-mail: mike.ruble@mrgnj.com Licensee: Millennium Atlantic City License Holdco LLC. Group owner: Millennium Radio Group LLC (acq 5-11-2001; grpsl). Population served: 300,000 Natl. Network: ESPN Deportes, . Format: Sp sports. Target aud: 25 plus; the population of South Jersey. ◆Dan Sullivan, gen mgr; Mike Ruble, gen sls mgr; Jennifer Doughton, prom dir; Eric Johnson, progmg dir; Tom McNally, chief of engrg.

WFPG(FM)— September 1962: 96.9 mhz; 50 kw. 400 ft TL: N39 22 42 W74 26 53. Stereo. Hrs open: 24 Prog sep from AM 950 Tilton Rd., Suite 200, Northfield, 08225. Phone: (609) 645-9797. Fax: (609) 272-9228.E-mail: mike.ruble@mrgnj.com Web Site:www.literock969.com Population served: 500,000 Format: Light rock, soft adult contemp. News staff: one. Target aud: 25-54. ◆Gary Guida, progmg dir.

WJSE(FM)—(Petersburg, August 1991): 102.7 mhz; 3.3 kw. Ant 295 ft TL: N39 12 18 W74 39 33. Stereo. Hrs open: 24 1601 New Rd., Linwood, 08221. Phone: (609) 653-1400. Fax: (609) 601-0450. Web Site:www.theace1027.com Licensee: Atlantic Broadcasting of Linwood NJ Limited Liability Co. (acq 10-15-2008; grpsl). Population served: 325,000 Format: Active rock. ◆Brett DeNafo, CEO; Dick Irland, gen mgr.

WMGM(FM)— June 14, 1961: 103.7 mhz; 50 kw. 400 ft TL: N39 23 38 W74 30 34. Stereo. Hrs open: 24 1601 New Rd., Linwood, 08221. Phone: (609) 653-1400. Fax: (609) 601-0450.E-mail: wmgm1037@aol.com Web Site:www.theshark1037.com Licensee: Atlantic Broadcasting of Linwood NJ Limited Liability Co. Group owner: Access.1 Communications Corp. (acq 10-15-2008; grpsl). Population served: 545,000 Natl. Rep: McGavren Guild,. Format: Classic rock. Target aud: 25-54; men. ◆Brett DeNafo, CEO; Dick Irland, gen mgr; Nick Giorno, progmg dir; Dan Merlo, chief of engrg; Anne Pratt, traf mgr.

WMID(AM)— May 30, 1947: 1340 khz; 890 w-U. TL: N39 22 35 W74 27 08. Hrs open: 24 Equity Communications LP, 8025 Black Horse Pike, Suite 100, W. Atlantic City, 08232-2959. Phone: (609) 484-8444. Fax: (609) 646-6331.E-mail: gfequity@aol.com Web Site:www.classicoldieswmid.com Licensee: Equity Communications L.P. (group owner; (acq 3-29-2002; grpsl). Population served: 250,000 Natl. Rep: Katz Radio,. Latham & Watkins. Format: Classic oldies. Target aud: 35-64; adults. ◆Gary Fisher, VP, gen mgr, gen sls mgr; Rob Garcia, progmg dir.

*WNJN-FM— September 1996: 89.7 mhz; 25 w horiz, 6 kw vert. Ant 272 ft TL: N39 27 40 W74 41 06. Hrs open: Box 777, Trenton, 08625-0777. Phone: (609) 777-5036. Fax: (609) 777-5217.E-mail: radio@njn.org Web Site:www.njn.net Licensee: New Jersey Public Broadcasting Authority. Natl. Network: NPR, PRI, . Schwartz, Woods & Miller. Format: News/talk. Target aud: General. ◆Pharoah Cranston, stn mgr & opns mgr.

WOND(AM)—See Pleasantville

WPUR(FM)— June 1998: 107.3 mhz; 13.5 kw. Ant 449 ft TL: N39 21 40 W74 25 05. Hrs open: 950 Tilton Rd., Suite 200, Northfield, 08225. Phone: (609) 645-9797. Fax: (609) 272-9224. Web Site:www.catcountry1073.com Licensee: Millennium Atlantic City License Holdco LLC. Group owner: Millennium Radio Group LLC (acq 5-11-01; grpsl). Population served: 500,000 Natl. Rep: McGavren Guild,. Format: Country. Target aud: 25-54. ◆Andy Santoro, gen mgr; Joe Kelly, opns dir, progmg dir; Mike Ruble, sls dir, gen sls mgr; Hank Weisbecher, news dir; Tom McNally, chief of engrg.

WZBZ(FM)—See Pleasantville

Avalon

WIBG-FM— Mar 29, 1976: 94.3 mhz; 3 kw. Ant 300 ft TL: N39 07 48 W74 47 20. Stereo. Hrs open: 24 3208 Pacific Ave., Wildwood, 08260. Phone: (609) 522-1987. Fax: (609) 522-3666. Licensee: WIBG Limited Liability Co. (acq 7-3-2009; $1.475 million). Population served: 300,000 Format: Oldies. ◆Bob Maschio, gen mgr; Rick Rock, progmg mgr.

Barnegat

*WBNJ(FM)—Not on air, target date: unknown: 91.9 mhz; 4.5 kw vert. Ant 226 ft TL: N39 45 54 W74 19 12. Hrs open: Box 386, Waretown, 08758. Licensee: WWN Educational Radio Corp. ◆William E. Clanton Jr., pres.

Bass River Township

WBBO(FM)— Oct 1, 1972: 106.5 mhz; 1.45 kw. Ant 682 ft TL: N39 37 53 W74 21 12. Stereo. Hrs open: 24 2335 W. Bangs Ave., Neptune, 07753. Phone: (732) 774-4755. Fax: (732) 774-7315.E-mail: grockradio@grockradio.com Web Site:www.grockradio.com Licensee: Press Communications LLC. (acq 2-11-2005; $3.16 million). Population served: 500,000 Natl. Rep: McGavren Guild,. Format: Alternritive rock, modern adult contemp. News staff: one. Target aud: 18-49. ◆Frank Calderaro, gen mgr; John Kaszuba, gen sls mgr; Terrie Carr, progmg dir; Mike Heilman, chief of engrg; Annemarie Cassone, traf mgr.

Beach Haven West

*WVBH(FM)— 2003: 88.3 mhz; 1 w horiz, 100 w vert. Ant 426 ft TL: N39 42 56 W74 17 32. Hrs open:
Simulcast of WXHL (FM) Christiana 100%.
179 Stanton-Christiana Rd., Newark, DE, 19702. Phone: (302) 731-0690. Fax: (302) 738-3090. Web Site:www.thereachfm.com Licensee: Priority Radio Inc. (group owner; (acq 11-14-2003; $400,000). Format: Adult contemp chrisitan mus. ◆Steve Hare, gen mgr; Dan Edwards, opns mgr.

Belvidere

WWYY(FM)— Oct 15, 1992: 107.1 mhz; 1.2 kw. Ant 718 ft TL: N40 56 53 W75 09 38. Hrs open: 22 S. 6th St., Stroudsburg, PA, 18360. Phone: (570) 421-2100. Fax: (570) 421-2040.E-mail: info@lite935.com Web Site:www.107thebone.fm Licensee: Nassau Broadcasting Holdings Inc. Group owner: Nassau Broadcasting Partners L.P. (acq 2-25-03; grpsl). Natl. Network: ABC, . Format: Rock. ◆Maureen Barth, VP & gen mgr.

Berlin

*WNJS-FM— Aug 21, 1992: 88.1 mhz; 1 w horiz, 20 w vert. Ant 781 ft TL: N39 43 41 W74 50 39. (CP: 1 w horiz, 80 w vert, ant 941 ft). Hrs open: Box 777, Trenton, 08625-0777. Secondary address: 25 S. Stockton St., Trenton 08608. Phone: (609) 777-5000. Fax: (609) 777-5217. Web Site:www.njn.net Licensee: New Jersey Public Broadcasting Authority (acq 3-6-91;3-25-91). Natl. Network: NPR, PRI, . Schwartz, Woods & Miller. Format: News/talk. Target aud: General.

Blackwood

*WDBK(FM)— June 7, 1979: 91.5 mhz; 100 w. Ant 87 ft TL: N39 47 06 W75 02 19. Hrs open: Box 200, 08012. Phone: (856) 374-4881. Fax: (856) 374-4969.E-mail: info@wdbk.com Licensee: Camden County College. Population served: 75,000 Format: Alternative. ◆James Canonica, gen mgr; Greg Gaughan, stn mgr.

Blairstown

WHCY(FM)— Oct 21, 1973: 106.3 mhz; 340 w. 859 ft TL: N41 02 51 W74 58 22. Stereo. Hrs open: 24 45 Mitchell Ave., Franklin, 07416. Phone: (973) 827-2525. Fax: (973) 827-2135.E-mail: info@max1063.com Web Site:www.max1063.com Licensee: CC Licenses LLC. Group owner: Clear Channel Communications Inc. (acq 2-13-2001). Population served: 130,000 Natl. Rep: Katz Radio,. Format: Hot adult contemp. Target aud: 18-49; Women. Spec prog: Relg one hr wkly. ◆John Hogan, CEO; Dick Taylor, gen mgr, mktg mgr; Lois Burmester, sls dir; Frank Curci, prom dir; Rob Ryan, progmg dir.

Brick Township

*WBGD(FM)— June 1975: Stn currently dark. 91.9 mhz; 195 w horiz. Ant 56 ft TL: N40 06 17 W74 07 34. Stereo. Hrs open: Brick Memorial High School, 2001 Lanes Mill Rd., 08724. Phone: (732) 262-2500. Fax: (732) 836-9246. Licensee: Brick Township Board of Educ. Target aud: General. ◆Fran Bristol, gen mgr.

Bridgeton

*WNJB(FM)— 1998: 89.3 mhz; 1 w horiz, 2.5 kw vert. Ant 220 ft TL: N39 27 35 W75 09 28. Hrs open: 5 AM-midnight Box 777, Trenton, 08625-0777. Phone: (609) 777-5036. Fax: (609) 777-5217.E-mail: raido@njn.org Web Site:www.njn.net Licensee: New Jersey Public Broadcasting Authority. Natl. Network: NPR, PRI,. Schwartz, Woods & Miller. Format: News/talk. Target aud: General. ◆Pharoah Cranston, stn mgr, opns mgr, progmg dir; Steve Prido, adv mgr; Bill Schorbus, engrg dir.

WSNJ(AM)— August 1937: 1240 khz; 1 kw-U. TL: N39 27 40 W75 12 21. Hrs open: 5:30 AM-midnight 1771 S. Burlington Rd., 08302. Phone: (856) 451-2930. Fax: (856) 453-9440.E-mail: information@wsnjam.com Web Site:wsnjam.com Licensee: Quinn Broadcasting Inc. (acq 2-18-2004; $550,000). Population served: 20,435 Wiley, Rein & Fielding. Format: Var. News staff: one; News: 10 hrs wkly. Target aud: 25 plus. Spec prog: Big band, MOR, news/talk, farm 10 hrs wkly. ◆James F. Quinn, pres, exec VP; Toni Coogan, CFO; Greg Hennis, gen mgr; Fred Sharkey, gen sls mgr, progmg dir; John Casey, mus dir; Richard Arsenault, chief of engrg.

Bridgewater

WWTR(AM)— Dec 23, 1971: 1170 khz; 243 w-D, DA. TL: N40 33 30 W74 35 52. Hrs open: 6am - 8pm 2088 Highway 130 North, Monmouth Junction, 08852. Phone: (732) 821-6009. Fax: (732) 821-6003.E-mail: info@ebcmusic.com Web Site:www.ebcmusic.com Licensee: The Sentinel Publishing Co. Group owner: Greater Media Inc. (acq 7-12-2001; grpsl). Population served: 300,000 Format: South Asian ethnic. News staff: 5; News: new progmg one hr wkly. Indian. ◆Alka Agrawal, gen mgr; Kulraaj Anand, progmg VP, progmg dir; Neal Newman, chief of engrg.

Brigantine

*WWFP(FM)— 2006: 90.5 mhz; 77 w vert. Ant 307 ft TL: N39 22 46 W74 25 45. Hrs open: CSN International, Box 391, Twin Falls, ID, 83303. Phone: (208) 734-6633. Fax: (208) 736-1958. Web Site:www.csnradio.com Licensee: CSN International (group owner). ◆Mike Stocklin, gen mgr; Don Mills, progmg dir; Kelly Carlson, chief of engrg.

Burlington

WNUW(FM)— Jan 19, 1949: 97.5 mhz; 26 kw. Ant 682 ft TL: N40 04 57 W75 10 53. Stereo. Hrs open: One Bala Plaza, Mail Stop 429, Bala Cynwyd, PA, 19004-1428. Phone: (610) 771-9750. Web Site:www.nowismusic.com Licensee: Greater Philadelphia Radio Inc. (acq 11-15-2006; exchange for WCRB(FM) Lowell, MA). Population served: 500,000 Leventhal, Senter & Lerman. Format: Adult contemp. ◆Peter H. Smyth, chmn; John Fullam, gen mgr; Jim Brown, stn mgr; Chrissy Sirianni, prom dir; Don Gosselin, progmg dir; Margo Marano, mus dir.

Camden

WEMG(AM)— September 1925: 1310 khz; 1 kw-D, 250 w-N. TL: N39 57 28 W75 06 54. Stereo. Hrs open: 24 1341 N. Delaware Ave., Suite 509, Philadelphia, PA, 19125. Phone: (215) 426-1900. Fax: (215) 426-1550.E-mail: mtaub@davidsonmediagroup.com Web Site:http://mega1310am.com Licensee: Davidson Media Station WEMG Licensee LLC. Group owner: Mega Communications Inc. (acq 1-31-2006; $8.75 million). Population served: 5,500,000 Natl. Rep: Interep,. Format: Tropical Hispanic. News staff: 1; News: news in am/pm drive. ◆Marc Taub, gen mgr; Maria Del Pilar, progmg dir.

*WKDN-FM— July 23, 1968: 106.9 mhz; 38 kw. 600 ft TL: N39 54 33 W75 06 00. Stereo. Hrs open: 2906 Mt. Ephraim Ave., 08104. Phone: (215) 922-0282.E-mail: info@familyradio.com Web Site:www.familyradio.com Licensee: Family Stations Inc. (group owner; acq 7-23-68). Dow, Lohnes & Albertson. Format: Relg. Target aud: General; families. Spec prog: Class 2 hrs wkly. ◆Rich Archut, opns mgr.

WTMR(AM)— Nov 1, 1948: 800 khz; 5 kw-D, 500 w-N. TL: N39 54 33 W75 06 00. Hrs open: 2775 Mt. Ephraim Ave., 08104. Phone: (609) 962-8000. Fax: (609) 962-8004.E-mail: radioman@voicenet.com Licensee: KAAY License L.P. Group owner: Beasley Broadcast Group (acq 9-4-98; $8 million). Format: Relg talk. ◆Louise Bessler, gen mgr, gen sls mgr; Mike Smith, progmg dir.

Canton

WJKS(FM)— Jan 15, 1972: 101.7 mhz; 3 kw. 263 ft TL: N39 25 51 W75 20 13. Hrs open: First Federal Plaza Bldg., 704 King St., Suite 604, Wilmington, DE, 19801. Phone: (302) 622-8895. Fax: (302) 622-8678.E-mail: tonyq@wjks1017.com Web Site:www.wjks1017.com Licensee: QC Communication Inc. (acq 3-17-97; $1.8 million with WFAI(AM) Salem). Population served: 700,000 Format: Urban Contemporary. Target aud: 18-44. ◆Mel Brittingham, opns dir; Maria Sylvanus, gen sls mgr; Tony Quartarone, gen mgr & progmg dir; Jeff DePaulo, chief of engrg.

Cape May

WAIV(FM)— June 3, 1967: 102.3 mhz; 3.2 kw. Ant 292 ft TL: N39 00 33 W74 52 13. Stereo. Hrs open:
Simulcast with WAYV(FM) Atlantic City 100%.
8025 Black Horse Pike, Suite 100-102, West Atlantic City, 08232. Phone: (609) 484-8444. Fax: (609) 646-6331.E-mail: gfequity@aol.com Web Site:951wayv.com Licensee: Equity Communications L.P. (group owner; (acq 3-29-2002; grpsl). Population served: 200,000 Natl. Rep: Katz Radio,. Latham & Watkins. Format: Hot adult contemp. Target aud: 18-49; adults. ◆Gary Fisher, sr VP, VP, gen mgr; Rob Garcia, progmg dir.

*WWCJ(FM)— September 1999: 89.1 mhz; 15 kw. Ant 308 ft TL: N39 02 58 W74 51 14. Hrs open: 24
Rebroadcasts WWFM(FM) Trenton 100%.
Box B, Trenton, 08690. Phone: (609) 587-8989. Fax: (609) 570-3863.E-mail: wwfm@mccc.edu Web Site:www.wwfm.org Licensee: Mercer County Community College. Format: Classical. ◆Peter Fretwell, gen mgr.

Cape May Court House

*WJPG(FM)— 2004: 88.1 mhz; 550 w vert. Ant 213 ft TL: N39 07 32 W74 49 27. Hrs open: Joy Communications Inc., Box 603, Woodbine, 08270-0603. Phone: (609) 646-0057. Fax: (609) 861-3730.E-mail: letters@praise899.org Web Site:www.praise899.org Licensee: Maranatha Ministries. Population served: 450,000 Format: Praise & worship. News: 10 hrs wkly. Target aud: 25-54; women. Spec prog: Gospel one hr wkly. ◆Kenneth Manri, gen mgr.

*WNJZ(FM)— August 1999: 90.3 mhz; 6 kw. Ant 236 ft TL: N39 06 18 W74 48 06. Hrs open: Box 777, Trenton, 08625-0777. Phone: (609) 777-5036. Fax: (609) 777-5217.E-mail: radio@njn.org Web Site:www.njn.net Licensee: New Jersey Public Broadcasting Authority. Natl. Network: NPR, PRI,. Format: News/talk. ◆Pharoah Cranston, stn mgr.

WSNQ(FM)— Sept 5, 1985: 105.5 mhz; 3.3 kw. Ant 295 ft TL: N39 07 32 W74 49 26. Stereo. Hrs open: 24
Simulcast with WZBZ(FM) Atlantic City 100%.
8025 Black Horse Pike, Suite 100-102, West Atlantic City, 08232. Phone: (609) 484-8444. Fax: (609) 646-6331.E-mail: info@993thebuzz.com Web Site:993thebuzz.com Licensee: Equity Communications L.P. (group owner; (acq 5-31-2002; grpsl). Population served: 400,000 Natl. Rep: Katz Radio,. Latham & Watkins. Format: CHR. Target aud: 18-49; adults. ◆Gary Fisher, sr VP, VP, gen mgr; Rob Garcia, progmg dir; Denise Carrington, traf mgr.

Cherry Hill

*WKVP(FM)— Jan 7, 1985: 89.5 mhz; 50 w horiz, 2 kw vert. Ant 180 ft TL: N39 51 33 W74 57 00. Hrs open: 24
Rebroadcasts KLVR(FM) Santa Rosa, CA 100%.
2351 Sunset Blvd., Suite 170-218, Rocklin, CA, 95765. Phone: (916) 251-1600. Fax: (916) 251-1650. Web Site:www.klove.com Licensee: Educational Media Foundation. (acq 1-10-2007; $2.45 million). Population served: 800,000 Natl. Network: K-Love, . Format: Contemp Chirstian. ◆Richard Jenkins, pres.

Delaware Township

*WDVR(FM)— Feb 19, 1990: 89.7 mhz; 4.8 kw. Ant 302 ft TL: N40 30 37 W74 57 29. Stereo. Hrs open: 24 Box 191, Rt. 604, Sergeantsville, 08557-0191. Phone: (609) 397-1620. Fax: (609) 397-5991.E-mail: info@wdvr.com Web Site:www.wdvrfm.org Licensee: Penn-Jersey Educational Radio Corp. Natl. Network: ABC, . Schwartz, Woods & Miller. Format: Div. News: 2 hrs wkly. Target aud: 30 plus. Spec prog: Folk 6 hrs, relg 6 hrs, jazz 11 hrs, oldies 13 hrs, bluegrass 6 hrs, country classic, 12 hrs; Americana country 6 hrs wkly. ◆Frank W. Napurano, pres, gen mgr; Ginny Lee, prom dir; Frank Napurano, progmg dir; Carla Van Dyk, mus dir.

Dover

WDHA-FM— Feb 22, 1961: 105.5 mhz; 1 kw. Ant 574 ft TL: N40 51 19 W74 30 42. Stereo. Hrs open: 24 55 Horsehill Rd., Cedar Knolls, 07927. Phone: (973) 538-1250. Phone: (973) 455-1055. Fax: (973) 538-3060.E-mail: rock@wdhafm.com Web Site:www.wdhafm.com Licensee: The Sentinel Publishing Co. Group owner: Greater Media Inc. (acq 7-6-01; grpsl). Population served: 360,000 Natl. Rep: Katz Radio,. Pepper & Corazzini. Format: New & Classic Rock. Target aud: 18-49. ◆Nancy McKinley, stn mgr; Matt DeVoti, gen sls mgr; Pete Forester, natl sls mgr.

Dover Township

*WWNJ(FM)— December 1991: 91.1 mhz; 50 w horiz, 50 kw vert. Ant 151 ft TL: N39 58 07 W74 04 19. Stereo. Hrs open: 24
Rebroadcasts WWFM(FM) Trenton 100%.
Box B, Trenton, 08690. Phone: (609) 587-8989. Fax: (609) 570-3863.E-mail: wwfm@mccc.edu Web Site:www.wwfm.org Licensee: Mercer County Community College Board of Trustees. (acq 11-4-91). Natl. Network: PRI, . Format: Classical. Target aud: General. ◆Peter Fretwell, gen mgr & dev mgr.

East Orange

*WFMU(FM)— 1958: 91.1 mhz; 1.25 kw. Ant 495 ft TL: N40 47 19 W74 15 20. Stereo. Hrs open: 24 Box 2011, Jersey City, 07303-2011. Phone: (201) 521-1416. Fax: (201) 521-1286.E-mail: wfmu@wfmu.org Web Site:www.wfmu.org Licensee: Auricle Communications. Population served: 6,000,000 Format: Div, free-form. Target aud: General. Spec prog: International 15 hrs wkly. ◆Brian Turner, progmg dir, mus dir; John Fogarazzo, chief of engrg; Ken Freedman, gen mgr & spec ev coord.

Eatontown

WHTG(AM)— Nov 1, 1957: 1410 khz; 500 w-D, 126 w-N. TL: N40 16 10 W74 04 19. Hrs open: 2355 W. Bangs Ave., Neptune, 07753. Phone: (732) 774-4755. Fax: (732) 774-4974. Web Site:www.1410amradio.com Licensee: Press Communications L.L.C. (group owner; (acq 11-4-2000; $15 million with co-located FM). Population served: 1,000,000 Natl. Rep: Christal,. Format: Great gold. Target aud: 35 plus; general. Spec prog: Baseball 20 hrs, football 3 hrs, basketball 6 hrs wkly. ◆Robert McAllan, CEO & pres; Richard T. Morena, CFO; John Dziuba, gen mgr; Cindy Brennan, stn mgr; John Kaszuba, gen sls mgr; Mathew Schwenker, natl sls mgr, prom dir; Jack Aponte, progmg dir, mus dir; Mike Heilman, chief of engrg.

WHTG-FM— Oct 11, 1961: 106.3 mhz; 1.1 kw. Ant 528 ft TL: N40 16 41 W74 04 51. Stereo. Hrs open: 2355 W. Bangs Ave., Neptune, 07753. Phone: (732) 774-4755. Fax: (732) 774-4974.E-mail: g1063@g1063.com Web Site:www.grockradio.com Licensee: Press Communications L.L.C. Leventhal, Senter & Lerman. Format: Alternative rock, modern adult contemp. Target aud: 18-34. ◆John Kaszuba, opns dir, rgnl sls mgr; Michael Gavin, progmg mgr; Brian Phillips, mus dir.

Egg Harbor City

WSJO(FM)— Sept 23, 1971: 104.9 mhz; 10 kw. Ant 508 ft TL: N39 32 49 W74 38 19. Stereo. Hrs open: 109 Walters Ave., Trenton, 08638. Phone: (609) 771-8181. Fax: (609) 406-7956. E-mail: info@wsjo.com Web Site:www.sojo1049.com Licensee: Millennium Egg Harbor License Holdco LLC. Group owner: Nassau Broadcasting Partners L.P. (acq 11-23-2004; $14 million). Population served: 65,000 Natl. Network: AP Radio, . Format: Hot adult contemp. Target aud: 35 plus. Spec prog: Relg 4 hrs wkly. ◆Andy Santoro, pres & gen mgr.

Egg Harbor Township

*WXGN(FM)— 2000: 90.5 mhz; 500 w vert. Ant 82 ft TL: N39 16 46 W74 34 34. Hrs open: 24 1512 Atkinson Ave., Somers Point, 08244-1119. Phone: (609) 926-5182. Fax: (609) 926-5185. Web Site:wxgn.com Licensee: Joy Broadcasting Inc. Format: Contemp Christian. ◆Bob Green, gen mgr.

Elizabeth

WJDM(AM)— Mar 11, 1970: 1530 khz; 1 kw-D. TL: N40 38 56 W74 14 32. Hrs open: 412 Linden Ave., 07202. Phone: (908) 352-3400. Fax: (908) 352-4268. E-mail: info@1530restauradion.com Web Site:www.puertadepaz.com Licensee: Multicultural Radio Broadcasting Licensee LLC. Group owner: Multicultural Radio Broadcasting Inc. (acq 2-4-2004; grpsl). Population served: 2,000,000 Format: Sp. ◆Richard Dirocco, gen mgr; Didier Ugalde, stn mgr.

Ewing

WIMG(AM)—Licensed to Ewing. See Trenton

Flemington

*WCVH(FM)— April 1974: 90.5 mhz; 78 w. 449 ft TL: N40 33 25 W74 54 18. Stereo. Hrs open: 24/7 84 Rt. 31, 08822. Phone: (908) 782-9595. Fax: (908) 284-7109. E-mail: cpuorro@hcrhs.k12.nj.us Web Site:www.hcrhs.k12.nj.us Licensee: Hunterdon Central Board of Education. Population served: 300,000 Format: Country. Target aud: 18-54. ◆Chris Puorro, gen mgr, progmg dir; John Anastasio, opns dir, chief of engrg; Nick Biando, prom dir; Ryan Gill, mus dir.

WNJE(AM)— Jan 5, 1998: 1040 khz; 4.7 kw-D, 1 kw-N, DA-2. TL: N40 30 18 W74 58 37. (CP: 15 kw-D, 2.5 kw-N, 7.5 kw-CH, DA-3). Hrs open: 24
Rebroadcasts WEPN(AM) New York, NY 100%.
c/o WEPN(AM), 2 Penn Plaza, 17th Fl., New York, NY, 10121. Phone: (212) 613-3800. Fax: (212) 613-3861. Web Site:www.1050espnradio.com Licensee: Nassau Broadcasting II L.L.C. Group owner: Nassau Broadcasting Partners L.P. (acq 2-15-2002; grpsl). Population served: 5,511,450 Natl. Network: ESPN Radio, . Format: Sports. ◆Tim McCarthy, gen mgr.

Florence

WIFI(AM)— 1985: 1460 khz; 5 kw-D, 500 w-N, DA-2. TL: N40 04 53 W74 47 41. Hrs open: 24 2025 Burlington-Columbus Rd., Burlington, 08016. Phone: (609) 499-4800. Fax: (609) 499-4905. Licensee: Real Life Broadcasting. Population served: 2,000,000 Natl. Network: USA, . Format: Relg. ◆Ron Graban, gen mgr.

Franklin

WSUS(FM)— Feb 28, 1965: 102.3 mhz; 590 w. 745 ft TL: N41 08 37 W74 32 21. Stereo. Hrs open: 45 Mitchell Ave., 07416. Phone: (973) 827-2525. Fax: (973) 827-2135. E-mail: info@wsus1023.com Web Site:www.wsus1023.com Licensee: CC Licenses LLC. Group owner: Clear Channel Communications Inc. (acq 2-15-2001; grpsl). Natl. Rep: Katz Radio,. Wire Svc: AP Format: Adult contemporary. News: 10 hrs wkly. Target aud: 18-54; Adults & Families. ◆John Hogan, CEO; Ken O'Brien, opns mgr; Dick Taylor, mktg mgr; Maria Lake, opns mgr & progmg dir.

Freehold Township

*WRDR(FM)— Feb 20, 1997: 89.7 mhz; 10 w horiz, 2 kw vert. 170 ft TL: N40 11 19 W74 15 01. Stereo. Hrs open: 24 6550 Rt. 9 S., Howell, 07731. Phone: (732) 901-9953. Fax: (732) 901-0356. Web Site:www.bridgefm.org Licensee: Bridgelight LLC (acq 1-31-03; $875,000).

Population served: 6,700,000 Format: Christian. News staff: . Target aud: 25-62. Spec prog: Relg 6 hrs wkly. ◆Brian J. Rechton, gen mgr; John Gates, progmg dir.

Glassboro

*WGLS-FM— January 1964: 89.7 mhz; 750 w. 489 ft TL: N39 41 41 W75 17 55. Stereo. Hrs open: 24 Rowan Univ., 201 Mullica Hill Rd., 08028-1701. Phone: (856) 863-9457. Fax: (856) 256-4704. E-mail: wgls@rowan.edu Web Site:http://wgls.rowan.edu Licensee: Rowan University. Population served: 1,300,000 Natl. Network: ABC, . Booth, Freret, Imlay & Tepper, P.C. Format: Div, educ. News staff: one; News: one. Target aud: 18-45; general. Spec prog: Black 10 hrs wkly. ◆Frank J. Hogan, gen mgr; Mandy Rippert, pub affrs dir; Frank Sippel, chief of engrg.

Hackensack

WNYM(AM)— 1921: 970 khz; 50 kw-D, 5 kw-N, DA-2. TL: N40 54 40 W74 01 42. Hrs open: 777 Terrace Ave, 6th floor, Hasbrouck Heights, 07604-3100. Phone: (201) 298-9700. Fax: (201) 298-5797. E-mail: contact@nycradio.com Web Site:am970theapple.townhall.com Licensee: Salem Media of New York LLC. Group owner: Salem Communications Corp. (acq 8-3-94). Population served: 13,000,000 Format: News/talk. Target aud: 25-44. ◆Edward Atsinger, pres; Joe D. Davis, VP; Sean O'Neill, gen mgr; Tamela Kay Maxwell, gen sls mgr; Peter Thiele, progmg dir.

Hackettstown

*WNTI(FM)— Dec 5, 1957: 91.9 mhz; 5.6 kw. 510 ft TL: N40 51 07 W74 52 35. Stereo. Hrs open: 24 400 Jefferson St., 07550. Phone: (908) 852-4545. Phone: (908) 979-4355. Fax: (908) 852-8515. Web Site:www.wnti.org Licensee: Centenary College. Population served: 400,000 Natl. Network: PRI, . Format: Free form. News: 2 hrs wkly. Target aud: 15 plus. Spec prog: Big band 4 hrs, blues 11 hrs, heavy metal 6 hrs, reggae 3 hrs, oldies 3 hrs, jazz 9 hrs, relg 4 hrs wkly. ◆Paul Massen, gen mgr.

WRNJ(AM)— 1996: 1510 khz; 2.5 kw-ND, 230 w-N, DA-N. TL: N40 50 47 W74 48 16 (D), N40 48 55 W74 49 38 (N). Hrs open: Box 1000, 07840. Phone: (908) 850-1000. Fax: (908) 852-8000. E-mail: info@oldies1510.com Web Site:www.wrnj.com Licensee: WRNJ Radio Inc. Population served: 35,000 Natl. Network: ABC, . Shaw Pittman. Wire Svc: AP Format: News/talk, oldies. News staff: 3; News: 10 hrs wkly. Target aud: 25-50 plus; upwardly mobile. Spec prog: Talk 10 hrs wkly. ◆L.J. Tighe, pres; Norman Worth, gen mgr; Russ Long, opns dir; Dan Hollis, gen sls mgr, news dir; Chuck Reiger, progmg dir; Larry Tighe, chief of engrg; Pat Layton, traf mgr.

Hammonton

WGYM(AM)— May 11, 1961: 1580 khz; 1 kw-D, 7 w-N. TL: N39 37 33 W74 47 44. Hrs open: 24 hrs
Rebroadcasts WOND(AM) Atlantic City 100%.
1601 New Rd., Linwood, 08221. Phone: (609) 653-1400. Fax: (609) 601-0450. Web Site:www.wond1400am.com Licensee: Access.1 New Jersey License Co. LLC. Group owner: Access.1 Communications Corp. (acq 11-17-2003; grpsl). Population served: 545,000 Natl. Network: Westwood One, . Natl. Rep: McGavren Guild,. Rubin, Winston, Diercks, Harris & Cooke. Format: News/talk. Target aud: Adults 35+. ◆Sydney L. Small, chmn; Chesley Maddox-Dorsey, pres; Dick Irland, gen mgr; John De Lucia, gen sls mgr; Stuart Abrams, progmg dir, traf mgr; Dan Merlo, chief of engrg.

Hazlet

*WDDM(FM)— May 24, 1979: 89.3 mhz; 10 w. Ant 125 ft TL: N40 25 37 W74 11 40. Stereo. Hrs open: 49 Briscoe Terr., PA, 04714. Phone: (732) 452-0777. E-mail: info@dhoomfm.com Web Site:www.dhoomfm.com Licensee: WVRM Inc. (acq 5-2-2001; $175,000 for stock). Format: World Ethnic. ◆James Manfredonia, pres & gen mgr.

Hopatcong

*WDNJ(FM)— 2009: 88.1 mhz; 500 w vert. Ant 387 ft TL: N40 56 25 W74 36 48. Hrs open: 99 Clinton Rd., West Caldwell, 07006. Phone: (973) 852-0300. Licensee: Youngshine Media Inc. ◆Sun Young Joo, gen mgr.

Jersey City

WSNR(AM)— December 1948: 620 khz; 3 kw-D, 7.6 kw-N, DA-2. TL: N40 47 53 W74 06 24. (CP: 8.5 kw-D, 5 kw-N, DA-2. TL: N40 50 52 W74 20 22). Stereo. Hrs open: 475 Park Ave. S., New York, NY, 10016-6901. Phone: (847) 509-1661. Fax: (646) 424-2232. Fax: (847) 509-7750. Web Site:www.sportingnews.com Licensee: Rose City Radio Corp. (group owner; acq 3-23-01; grpsl). Population served: 9,000 Natl. Network: CBS, . Wire Svc: CBS Format: multicultural, sports. Target aud: General. ◆Clancy Woods, pres, gen mgr, progmg dir; Colleen Mamzella, chief of engrg & traf mgr.

WWRU(AM)— Dec 8, 1995: 1660 khz; 10 kw-U, DA-2. TL: N40 49 13 W74 04 09 (D), N40 49 13 W74 04 09 (N). (CP: TL: N40 49 13 W74 04 04 (D), N40 49 13 W74 04 09 (N). Hrs open: 449 Broadway, 5th Fl., New York, NY, 10013. Phone: (212) 966-8700. Fax: (212) 966-9580. Licensee: Multicultural Radio Broadcasting Licensee LLC. Group owner: Multicultural Radio Broadcasting Inc. (acq 2-4-2004; grpsl). Format: Korean. ◆Gene Heinemeyer, gen mgr.

Lakehurst

*WLNJ(FM)—Not on air, target date: unknown: 91.7 mhz; 4 kw. Ant 144 ft TL: N40 04 07 W74 28 09. Hrs open: Box 730, Manahawkin, 08050. Phone: (609) 978-1678. Fax: (609) 597-4146. Web Site:www.wyrs.org Licensee: WYRS Broadcasting. ◆Bob Wick, gen mgr.

Lakewood

WOBM(AM)— Nov 20, 1970: 1160 khz; 5 kw-D, 8.9 kw-N, DA-2. TL: N40 08 09 W74 13 48. Hrs open: 24 Box 927, Toms River, 08754. Phone: (732) 269-0927. Fax: (732) 269-9292. Web Site:www.wobmam.com Licensee: Millennium Shore License Holdco LLC. Group owner: Millennium Radio Group LLC (acq 5-14-02; grpsl). Population served: 452,000 Natl. Network: AP Radio, . Natl. Rep: Katz Radio,. Blair, Joyce & Silva. Format: Oldies, Big Band, talk. News staff: 5; News: 14 hrs wkly. Target aud: 45 plus; educated. Spec prog: Talk 12 hrs wkly. ◆Andy Santoro, gen mgr; John Furno, gen sls mgr; Steve Ardolina, progmg dir; Tom Mongelli, news dir; Jay Pierce, chief of engrg; Nancy Cordiano, traf mgr.

WOBM-FM—See Toms River

Lawrenceville

*WRRC(FM)— Sept 23, 1989: 107.7 mhz; 17 w. 36 ft TL: N40 16 44 W74 44 15. Stereo. Hrs open: 16 Rider Univ., Bart Luedeke Ctr., 2083 Lawrenceville Rd., 08648. Phone: (609) 896-5369. Fax: (609) 219-4729. Licensee: Rider University Board of Trustees. Format: Var. News staff: 3; News: 4 hrs wkly. Target aud: 16-21; high school & college students. Spec prog: Black 10 hrs, heavy metal 10 hrs wkly.

Lincroft

*WBJB-FM— Jan 13, 1975: 90.5 mhz; 11 kw. 135 ft TL: N40 19 19 W74 07 57. Stereo. Hrs open: 24 Brookdale Community College, 765 Newman Springs Rd., 07738. Phone: (732) 224-2490. Phone: (732) 224-2252. Fax: (732) 224-2494. E-mail: comments@wbjb.org Web Site:www.90.5thenight.org Licensee: Board of Trustees of Brookdale Community College. Population served: 1,000,000 Natl. Network: NPR, . Erwin, Campbell & Tannenwald. Format: AAA, news. News: 16 hrs wkly. Target aud: 18-54; general. Spec prog: Haitian 3 hrs, pub affrs 5 hrs, bluegrass 3 hrs, Sp 4 hrs, blues 4 hrs wkly. ◆Tom Brennan, stn mgr; Jeff Raspe, mus dir; Michelle McBride, pub affrs dir; George Marshall, chief of engrg.

Lindenwold

WTTM(AM)— May 1999: 1680 khz; 10 kw-D, 1 kw-N. TL: N39 53 15 W75 00 05. Hrs open: Multicultural Radio Broadcasting Inc., 449 Broadway, New York, NY, 10013. Phone: (212) 966-1059. Fax: (212) 966-9580. Licensee: Multicultural Radio Broadcasting Licensee LLC. Group owner: Multicultural Radio Broadcasting Inc. (acq 5-24-2002; grpsl). Format: Asian. ◆Troy Hall, gen mgr; C.W. Queen, stn mgr.

Long Branch

WWZY(FM)— June 1, 1960: 107.1 mhz; 4.7 kw. Ant 371 ft TL: N40 18 17 W73 59 08. Stereo. Hrs open: 2355 W. Bangs Ave., Neptune, 07753. Phone: (732) 774-4755. Fax: (732) 774-7315. E-mail: info@breezeradio.com Web Site:www.breezeradio.com Licensee: Press Communications LLC (group owner; acq 6-18-2003; $20 million). Population served: 1,000,000 Natl. Rep: Eastman Radio,. Wire Svc:

AP Format: Adult contemp. Target aud: Women; 25-54. ♦Frank Calderaro, gen mgr; John Kaszuba, gen sls mgr; Mike Fitzgerald, progmg dir; Mike Heilman, chief of engrg.

Madison

*WMNJ(FM)— Sept 15, 1980: 88.9 mhz; 8 w. Ant 75 ft TL: N40 45 30 W74 25 48. Stereo. Hrs open: 24 Drew Univ., 36 Madison Ave., 07940. Phone: (973) 408-4753. Phone: (973) 408-3000 (univ.). Fax: (973) 408-3939. Licensee: Drew University (acq 9-25-89). Format: Alternative, AOR. ♦Margaret E.L. Howard, VP; Alicia E. Lutes, progmg dir.

Mahwah

*WRPR(FM)— July 15, 1980: 90.3 mhz; 100 w. 30 ft TL: N41 04 51 W74 10 34. Stereo. Hrs open: 18 501 Ramapo Valley Rd., 07430. Phone: (201) 825-1234. Phone: (201) 825-7998. Fax: (201) 327-9036.E-mail: wrpr@ramapo.edu Web Site:phobos.ramapo.edu/wrpp Licensee: Ramapo College of New Jersey. Format: College contemp. News staff: 4; News: 10 hrs wkly. Target aud: 18-24; college students. Spec prog: Pub affrs 12 hrs wkly. ♦Evan Brown, gen mgr; Andrew Bernstein, progmg dir; Sarah Tucci, mus dir & news dir; Delores Smith, traf mgr.

Manahawkin

WCHR-FM— 2002: 105.7 mhz; 13 kw. Ant 459 ft TL: N39 42 56 W74 17 32. Hrs open: 2401 Rt. 66, Ocean, 07712. Phone: (732) 897-8282. Fax: (732) 897-8283.E-mail: info@105thehawk.com Web Site:www.1057thehawk.com Licensee: Millennium Shore License Holdco LLC. Group owner: Millennium Radio Group LLC (acq 3-15-2004; $12 million). Format: Classic rock. ♦Bill Saurer, gen mgr; Phil LoCascio, opns mgr; John Furno, gen sls mgr; Tom Monzeli, news dir; Jay Pierce, engrg dir.

WJRZ-FM— July 4, 1976: 100.1 mhz; 1.7 kw. Ant 436 ft TL: N39 47 54 W74 12 10. Stereo. Hrs open: 24 Box 1000, 1001 Beach Ave., 08050. Secondary address: 610 Main Street, Belmar 07719. Phone: (609) 597-1100. Phone: (732) 681-9591. Fax: (609) 597-4400. Fax: (732) 681-9431. Web Site:www.wjrz.com Licensee: Jersey Shore Broadcasting Corp. Group owner: Greater Media Inc. (acq 7-19-02). Population served: 1,100,000 Natl. Network: AP Radio, . Natl. Rep: Katz Radio,. Format: Classic Hits. News staff: one; News: 4 hrs wkly. Target aud: 35-54. ♦Dan Finn, exec VP, VP; Mike Normand, gen mgr; Jeff Rafter, opns mgr, progmg dir; Marge Guglielmo, gen sls mgr; Doug Sjonvall, prom dir; Bill Clanton Sr., chief of engrg; Sharon Zarnowski, traf mgr.

*WNJM(FM)— August 1999: 89.9 mhz; 1 w horiz, 200 w vert. Ant 259 ft TL: N39 41 57 W74 14 05. Hrs open: Box 777, Trenton, 08625-0777. Phone: (609) 777-5036. Fax: (609) 777-5217.E-mail: radio@njn.org Web Site:www.njn.net Licensee: New Jersey Public Broadcasting Authority. Natl. Network: NPR, PRI, . Format: News/talk. ♦Pharoah Cranston, stn mgr.

*WYRS(FM)— Mar 27, 1995: 90.7 mhz; 1 w horiz, 15 kw vert. Ant 262 ft TL: N39 38 24 W74 17 32. Stereo. Hrs open: 24 Box 730, 08050. Phone: (609) 978-1678. Fax: (609) 597-4146.E-mail: info@wyrs.org Web Site:www.wyrs.org Licensee: WYRS Broadcasting (acq 2-18-2005; $1). Natl. Network: AP Radio, . Format: Family & community. Target aud: General. ♦Bob Wick, CEO, gen mgr & chief of engrg.

Margate City

WTTH(FM)— Nov 19, 1991: 96.1 mhz; 2.8 kw. Ant 400 ft TL: N39 21 02 W74 26 55. Stereo. Hrs open: 24
Simulcast with WDTH(FM) Wildwood Crest 100%.
8025 Black Horse Pike, Suite 100-102, West Atlantic City, 08232. Phone: (609) 484-8444. Fax: (609) 646-6331.E-mail: gfequity@aol.com Web Site:www.961wtth.com Licensee: Equity Communications L.P. (group owner; (acq 5-30-2003; grpsl). Population served: 400,000 Natl. Rep: Katz Radio,. Laitham & Watkins. Format: Urban adult contemp. Target aud: 18-49; adults. Spec prog: Gospel 5 hrs, relg one hr wkly. ♦Gary Fisher, sr VP, VP, gen mgr; Rob Garcia, progmg dir.

Medford Lakes

*WVBV(FM)— 2005: 90.5 mhz; 21 kw vert. Ant 453 ft TL: N39 33 20 W74 44 48. Stereo. Hrs open: 24 Hope Christian Church of Marlton Inc., 55 E. Main St., Marlton, 08053. Phone: (856) 983-1662. Fax: (856) 983-1814.E-mail: info@ccmarlton.org Web Site:www.hopefm.net Licensee: Hope Christian Church of Marlton Inc. Fletcher, Heald & Hildreth. Format: Christian/talk, praise, worship & music. ♦William C. Luebkemann Jr., pres & gen mgr.

Millville

WENJ-FM— Feb 2, 1962: 97.3 mhz; 50 kw. Ant 466 ft TL: N39 19 15 W74 46 17. Stereo. Hrs open: 950 Tilton Rd., Suite 200, Northfield, 08225. Phone: (609) 771-8181. Fax: (609) 926-5907. Web Site:espnnj.com Licensee: Millennium Atlantic City II License Holdco LLC. Group owner: Millennium Radio Group LLC (acq 12-21-2001; grpsl). Population served: 139,000 Natl. Network: ESPN Radio, . Format: Sports. Target aud: 25-54. ♦Andy Santoro, gen mgr; Eric Johnson, progmg dir; Eric Scott, news dir; Frank Certo, chief of engrg.

WMVB(AM)— December 1953: 1440 khz; 1 kw-D, 65 w-N, DA-2. TL: N39 25 19 W75 01 14. Hrs open: 24
Simulcast with WSNJ(AM) Bridgeton.
415 N. High St., 08332. Phone: (856) 293-1440. Fax: (856) 327-0408.E-mail: greg@wmvb.net Web Site:www.wsmjam.com Licensee: Quinn Broadcasting Inc (acq 4-26-2000; $500,000). Population served: 342,917 Format: Var. News staff: 4. Target aud: 25-54; general public. Spec prog: Sp 2 hrs, gospel 8 hrs, children 3 hrs wkly. ♦Greg Hennis, gen mgr.

Morristown

*WJSV(FM)— Feb 22, 1971: 90.5 mhz; 124 w. 17 ft TL: N40 50 10 W74 29 16. Stereo. Hrs open: 8 AM-10 PM (M-F) WJSV c/o Morristown High School, 50 Early St., 07960. Phone: (973) 292-2168. Fax: (973) 539-5573.E-mail: norman.wallerstein@msdk12.net Licensee: Morris School District Board of Education. Population served: 750,000 Format: Free form AOR. News staff: one; News: 3 hrs wkly. Target aud: General. Spec prog: News/talk 3 hrs, sports 3 hrs wkly. ♦Norman Wallerstein, gen mgr; Dame Mallan, stn mgr; Lee Tyler, prom dir, adv mgr; Michael O'Brien, progmg dir.

WMTR(AM)— Dec 12, 1948: 1250 khz; 5 kw-D, 7 kw-N, DA-2. TL: N40 48 45 W74 27 36. Stereo. Hrs open: Box 1250, 07962-1250. Phone: (973) 538-1250. Fax: (973) 538-3060. Web Site:www.wmtram.com Licensee: The Sentinel Publishing Co. Group owner: Greater Media Inc. (acq 7-6-01; grpsl). Population served: 1,000,000 Pepper & Corazzini. Format: Oldies. Target aud: 35 plus. Spec prog: Community connection 5 hrs wkly. ♦Dan Finn, exec VP; Chris Edwards, opns mgr, mktg dir, progmg mgr; Matt DeVoti, gen sls mgr; Nancy McKinley, gen mgr & natl sls mgr.

Mount Holly

WWJZ(AM)— November 1992: 640 khz; 50 kw-D, 950 w-N, DA-2. TL: N40 05 28 W74 50 30. Hrs open: 501 Office Center Dr., Suite 190, Fort Washington, PA, 19034. Phone: (215) 591-0100. Fax: (215) 591-4527. Web Site:www.radiodisney.com Licensee: Radio Disney Group LLC. Group owner: ABC Inc. (acq 12-30-99). Format: Children, pre-teen. Target aud: 45 plus. ♦Robert Minton, gen mgr; Ray de la Garza, progmg dir.

Netcong

*WNJY(FM)— 2008: 89.3 mhz; 1 w horiz, 520 w vert. Ant 430 ft TL: N40 53 14 W74 41 55. Hrs open:
Rebroadcasts WNJT-FM Trenton 100%.
Box 777, Trenton, 08625-0777. Phone: (609) 777-5000. Fax: (609) 777-5217. Web Site:www.njn.net Licensee: New Jersey Public Broadcasting Authority. NJN Public Radio Format: News/talk.

New Brunswick

WCTC(AM)— Dec 12, 1946: 1450 khz; 1 kw-U. TL: N40 29 32 W74 25 11. Stereo. Hrs open: 24 Box 100, Broadcast Ctr., 08903. Secondary address: 78 Veronica Ave., Somerset 08873. Phone: (732) 249-2600. Fax: (732) 249-9010. Web Site:www.wctcam.com Licensee: The Sentinel Publishing Co. Group owner: Greater Media Inc. (acq 5-1-57). Population served: 2,000,000 Format: Oldies. News staff: 6; News: 15 hrs wkly. Target aud: 35-54. Spec prog: Rutgers Univ. & high school sports. ♦Dan Finn, VP; Frank Calderaro, gen mgr; Bruce Johnson, opns mgr, progmg dir, news dir, sports cmtr; Jack Cahill, gen sls mgr; Dave Kirby, prom dir; Keith Smeal, chief of engrg; Susan Young, traf mgr.

WMGQ(FM)— 1947: 98.3 mhz; 1 kw. 525 ft TL: N40 28 33 W74 29 34. Stereo. Hrs open: 24 Prog sep from AM Box 100, 08903. Secondary address: 78 Veronica Ave., Somerset 08873. Phone: (732) 249-2600. Fax: (732) 249-9010. Population served: 2,000,000 Format: Adult contemp. News: 3 hrs wkly. Target aud: 25-54. ♦Tim Tefft, progmg dir.

*WRSU-FM— April 1974: 88.7 mhz; 1.4 kw. 150 ft TL: N40 28 00 W74 26 15. Stereo. Hrs open: 24 126 College Ave., 08903. Phone: (732) 932-7800. Fax: (732) 932-1768.E-mail: wrsu@wrsu.rutgers.edu Web Site:www.wrsu.org Licensee: Board of Governors Rutgers University. Population served: 1,000,000 Wire Svc: AP Format: Var/div. News: 6 hrs wkly. Target aud: 15-30; college students, div group of young adults. ♦Danny Breslauer, gen mgr.

Newark

*WBGO(FM)— Feb 7, 1948: 88.3 mhz; 4.5 kw. Ant 430 ft TL: N40 44 11 W74 10 15. Stereo. Hrs open: 24 54 Park Pl., 07102. Phone: (973) 624-8880. Fax: (973) 824-8888.E-mail: jazz88@wbgo.org Web Site:www.wbgo.org Licensee: Newark Public Radio Inc. (acq 12-77). Population served: 375,000 Natl. Network: NPR, . Dow, Lohnes & Albertson. Wire Svc: AP Format: Jazz. News staff: 3; News: 5 hrs wkly. Target aud: General. ♦Tim Porter, chmn; Cephas Bowles, gen mgr; Amy Niles, gen sls mgr, rgnl sls mgr; Angelika Beener, mktg mgr; Thurston Briscoe, progmg dir; Doug Doyle, news dir; David Tallacksen, chief of engrg; Stevan Smith, traf mgr.

WCAA(FM)— August 1992: 105.9 mhz; 2.4 kw. Ant 722 ft TL: N40 45 04 W73 58 25. Hrs open: 485 Madison Ave., New York, NY, 10022. Phone: (212) 310-6000. Fax: (212) 888-3694. Web Site:www.univision.com Licensee: WADO-AM License Corp. ("WADO"). Group owner: Univision Radio (acq 9-22-2003; grpsl). Population served: 18,000,000 Format: Sp, reggaton. ♦Joe Pagan, gen mgr.

*WFME(FM)— 1959: 94.7 mhz; 38 kw. 570 ft TL: N40 47 18 W74 15 19. Stereo. Hrs open: 24 289 Mt. Pleasant Ave., West Orange, 07052. Phone: (973) 736-3600. Fax: (973) 736-4832.E-mail: wfme@wfme.com Web Site:www.familyradio.com Licensee: Family Stations Inc. (group owner; acq 3-10-66). Population served: 14,000,000 Natl. Network: Family Radio, . Format: Christian educ. Target aud: General. ♦Harold Camping, pres, gen mgr; Charles Menut, stn mgr, chief of engrg; Jason Frentses, pub affrs dir.

WHTZ(FM)— June 1, 1961: 100.3 mhz; 7.8 kw. 1,220 ft TL: N40 44 54 W73 59 10. Hrs open: 36th Fl., 101 Hudson St., Jersey City, 07302. Phone: (212) 239-2300. Fax: (212) 239-2308.E-mail: z100radio@aol.com Web Site:www.z100.com Licensee: AMFM Radio Licenses L.L.C. Group owner: Clear Channel Communications Inc. (acq 8-30-00; grpsl). Population served: 381,930 Natl. Rep: Christal,. Format: Top 40. ♦Rob Williams, exec VP, gen mgr; Tom Poleman, opns mgr; Bob McCuin, gen sls mgr; Josh Hadden, engrg dir, chief of engrg.

WNSW(AM)— 1947: 1430 khz; 5 kw-U, DA-N. TL: N40 42 32 W74 14 31. Stereo. Hrs open: 24 449 Broadway 2nd Fl., New York, NY, 10013. Phone: (212) 966-1059. Fax: (212) 966-9580.E-mail: geneh@mrbi.net Licensee: Multicultural Radio Broadcasting Licensee LLC. Group owner: Multicultural Radio Broadcasting Inc. (acq 1-30-98; grpsl). Population served: 13,000,000 Natl. Rep: Katz Radio,. Hopkins & Sutter. Format: Sp contemp Christian. ♦Gene Heinemeyer, gen mgr, progmg dir; Harold Chou, chief of engrg.

Newton

WNNJ(FM)— Oct 15, 1961: 103.7 mhz; 2.3 kw. 892 ft TL: N41 11 33 W74 45 13. Stereo. Hrs open: 24 Prog sep from AM 45 Mitchell Ave., Franklin, 07416. Phone: (973) 827-2525. Fax: (973) 827-2135.E-mail: info@wnnj.com Web Site:www.wnnj.com Licensee: CC Licenses LLC Population served: 250,000 Format: Rock. Target aud: 18-54; adults and families. ♦John Hogan, CEO; Dick Taylor, mktg mgr, mus dir; Krystal Reilly, pub affrs dir.

WTOC(AM)— Dec 15, 1953: 1360 khz; 2 kw-D, 320 w-N, DA-2. TL: N41 02 22 W74 44 19. Hrs open: 24 45 Mitchell Ave., Franklin, 07416. Phone: (973) 827-2525. Fax: (973) 827-2135. Web Site:www.oldies1360.com Licensee: CC Licenses LLC. Group owner: Clear Channel Communications Inc. (acq 1-31-2001; grpsl). Population served: 130,000 Natl. Network: Westwood One, . Natl. Rep: Katz Radio,. Wire Svc: AP Format: Oldies. News staff: 2; News: 5 hrs wkly. Target aud: 35 plus; mature adults with high incomes. Spec prog: Relg one hr, pub affrs one hr wkly. ♦John Hogan, CEO, pres, CFO; Randy Michaels, chmn; Andy Rosen, VP; Bob Dunphy, gen mgr; Vince Thomas, stn mgr, opns dir & opns mgr; Laura Brockman, sls dir; Elizabeth Toscano, prom dir; Rob Ryan, progmg dir; Alexandra Vallejo, news dir.

North Cape May

WKOE(FM)— 1993: 106.7 mhz; 3 kw. Ant 200 ft TL: N38 57 32 W74 55 23. Hrs open: 3208 Pacific Ave., Wildwood, 08260. Phone: (609) 522-1987 . Phone: (609) 522-3666.E-mail: info@1067coastcountry.com Web Site:www.1067coastcountry.com Licensee: Coastal Broadcasting Systems Inc. (acq 11-1-2004; $700,000). Natl. Network: USA, Moody, . Format: Country. Spec prog: Class 3 hrs wkly. ♦Bob Maschio, VP; Mark Hunter, progmg dir.

Oakland

WVNJ(AM)— Dec 13, 1993: 1160 khz; 20 kw-D, 2.5 kw-N, DA-2. TL: N41 03 26 W74 15 00. Stereo. Hrs open: 24 1086 Teaneck Rd., Suite 4F, Teaneck, 07666. Phone: (201) 837-0400. Fax: (201) 837-9664.E-mail: wvnj1160am@aol.com Web Site:www.wvnj.com Licensee: Universal Broadcasting of New York Inc. (group owner; acq 3-24-94; $12,050,000. with WTHE(AM) Mineola, NY;6-20-94) Population served: 8,250,000 Natl. Rep: Universal Broadcasting Inc,. Rgnl rep: Universal Broadcasting Inc Cohn & Marks. Format: News, talk, Information. News staff: one; News: 8 hrs wkly. Target aud: 35-64; upscale. Spec prog: Health related. ◆Miriam Warshaw, pres; Howard Warshaw, sr VP; Dr. Abe Warshaw, gen mgr; David Margalotti, opns dir, progmg dir, mus dir; Pete Bucky, prom dir, news dir & news dir.

Ocean Acres

WKMK(FM)— 1992: 98.5 mhz; 6 kw. Ant 328 ft TL: N39 45 06 W74 15 39. Hrs open: 24 2355 W. Bangs Ave., Neptune, 07753. Phone: (732) 774-4755. Fax: (732) 774-7315. Web Site:www.k985radio.com Licensee: Press Communications LLC. Group owner: Millennium Radio Group LLC (acq 8-9-2004; $17 million). Population served: 400,000 Format: Country. Target aud: 25-55; women. ◆ Mike Fitzgerald, stn mgr; Diana Pellegrino, mktg dir, prom dir.

Ocean City

WIBG(AM)— October 1992: 1020 khz; 1.9 kw-D, 680 w-CH. TL: N39 13 45 W74 40 54. Hrs open: Sunrise-sunset Traders Lane Professional Campus, 3328 Simpson Ave., 08226. Phone: (609) 398-1020. Fax: (609) 398-3736.E-mail: wibg@wibg.com Web Site:www.wibg.com Licensee: Enrico S. Brancadora. (acq 12-1-92; $140,000; 12-21-92). Format: Christian news/ talk. News staff: one; News: 7 hrs wkly. Target aud: 25-45; young urban-suburban professional. ◆Rick Brancadora, CEO & gen mgr; Josh Hennig, opns mgr; Harry Hurley, sls dir; David Angel, prom mgr, traf mgr.

*WRTQ(FM)— Sept 27, 1994: 91.3 mhz; 82 w horiz, 10.5 kw vert. Ant 384 ft TL: N39 19 15 W74 46 17. Hrs open: 24 Rebroadcasts WRTI(FM) Philadelphia 100%. 1509 Cecil B Moore Ave, Philadelphia, PA, 19121. Phone: (215) 204-8405. Fax: (215) 204-7027.E-mail: comments@wrti.org Web Site:www.wrti.org Licensee: Temple University of the Commonwealth System of Higher Education. Population served: 325,000 Natl. Network: NPR, AP Radio, . Rgnl. Network: Radio Pa. Radio Pa. Format: Jazz, class. News staff: one; News: 15 hrs wkly. Target aud: 30-65. ◆Dave Conant, gen mgr; Jack Moore, progmg dir; Jeff DePolo, chief of engrg; Lorna Dixon, traf mgr.

WTKU-FM— April 1983: 98.3 mhz; 6 kw. Ant 328 ft TL: N39 12 18 W74 39 33. Stereo. Hrs open: 24 1601 New Rd., Linwood, 08221. Phone: (609) 653-1400. Fax: (609) 601-0450. Web Site:www.kool983.com Licensee: Atlantic Broadcasting of Linwood NJ Limited Liability Co. Group owner: Access.1 Communications Corp. (acq 10-15-2008; grpsl). Population served: 545,000 Natl. Rep: McGavren Guild,. Format: Hits of the 60s & 70s. News: 5 hrs wkly. Target aud: 25-64. ◆Brett DeNafo, CEO; Dick Irland, gen mgr; Nick Giorno, progmg dir; Dan Merlo, chief of engrg; Anne Pratt, traf mgr.

Parsippany-Troy Hills

WXMC(AM)— Jan 13, 1973: 1310 khz; 1 kw-D, 88 w-N, DA-1. TL: N40 51 51 W74 21 06. Hrs open: 24 Box 160, TCB, West Orange, 07052. Phone: (973) 575-5561. Fax: (973) 575-5637.E-mail: hoyestudia@hotmail.com Licensee: James Chladek Chladek Broadcast Group (acq 1-15-93; $200,000;2-8-93). Population served: 500,000 KMZ Roseman. Format: Tropical, romantic Sp mus, relg. News staff: one; News: 4 hrs wkly. Target aud: 25 plus; young upper middle class business professionals. ◆James Chladek, CEO, gen mgr; Edwin Blas, stn mgr, chief of engrg; Otto Gust, chief of opns.

Paterson

WPAT(AM)— May 3, 1941: 930 khz; 5 kw-U, DA-2. TL: N40 50 59 W74 10 59. Stereo. Hrs open: 449 Broadway, New York, NY, 10013. Phone: (212) 966-1059. Fax: (212) 966-9580. Licensee: Multicultural Radio Broadcasting Licensee LLC. Group owner: Multicultural Radio Broadcasting Inc. (acq 7-22-98). Format: Multilingual, sports in Sp. ◆Gene Heinemeyer, gen mgr; Harold Chou, chief of engrg.

WPAT-FM— Mar 29, 1957: 93.1 mhz; 5.3 kw. 1,420 ft TL: N40 42 43 W74 00 49. (CP: 21.88 kw, and 338 ft.). Stereo. Hrs open: 26 W. 56th St., New York, NY, 10019. Phone: (212) 541-9200. Fax: (212) 246-9239. Licensee: WPAT Licensing Inc. Group owner: Spanish Broadcasting System Inc. (acq 1996; $83.5 million). Format: Sp adult contemp. ◆Raul Alarcon Jr., CEO, pres; Raul Alarcon Sr., chmn; Jose A. Garcia, CFO.

Pemberton

*WBZC(FM)— Jan 24, 1995: 88.9 mhz; 470 w horiz, 10 kw vert. Ant 220 ft TL: N39 50 34 W74 32 40. Stereo. Hrs open: 24 Burlington County College, 601 Pemberton Browns Mills Rd., 08068-1599. Phone: (609) 894-9311, EXT. 1189. Fax: (609) 894-9440.E-mail: bholcumb@bcc.edu Web Site:www.z889.org Licensee: Burlington County College. Population served: 500,000 Bechtel & Cole. Format: Rhythm crossover. News: 4 hrs wkly. Target aud: 18-35. Spec prog: Folk 4 hrs, jazz 4 hrs, bluegrass 4 hrs, reggae 4 hrs,. ◆Brett Holcomb, opns mgr, progmg dir; Neil Shore, mus dir.

Pennsauken

WRNB(FM)— 1946: 107.9 mhz; 780 w. Ant 905 ft TL: N39 57 09 W75 10 05. Stereo. Hrs open: 5:30 AM-midnight 1000 River Rd., Suite 400, Conshohocken, PA, 19428-2437. Phone: (610) 276-1100. Fax: (610) 279-1139. Licensee: Radio One Licenses LLC. Group owner: Radio One Inc. (acq 2-2-2004; $35 million). Population served: 100,000 Format: Urban contemp. ◆Chester Schofield, gen mgr.

Petersburg

WJSE(FM)—Licensed to Petersburg. See Atlantic City

Piscataway

*WVPH(FM)— May 1976: 90.3 mhz; 200 w. 7 ft TL: N40 32 45 W74 28 25. Hrs open: 100 Behmer Rd., 08854-4173. Phone: (732) 981-0153. Fax: (732) 981-1985.E-mail: wvph@pway.org Licensee: Board of Education Piscataway High School. Format: Educ, progsv, talk. ◆Patricia Cardinal, gen mgr.

Pleasantville

WMGM(FM)—See Atlantic City

WOND(AM)— July 1950: 1400 khz; 1 kw-U. TL: N39 23 26 W74 30 47. Hrs open: Rebroadcasts WGYM(AM) Hammonton 100%. 1601 New Rd., Linwood, 08221. Phone: (609) 653-1400. Fax: (609) 601-0450. Web Site:www.wond1400am.com Licensee: Atlantic Broadcasting of Linwood NJ Limited Liability Co. Group owner: Access.1 Communications Corp. (acq 10-15-2008; grpsl). Population served: 545,000 Natl. Network: Westwood One, . Natl. Rep: McGavren Guild,. Format: News/talk. Target aud: Adults 35 +. ◆Brett DeNafo, CEO; Dick Irland, gen mgr; John De Lucia, gen sls mgr; Dan Merlo, chief of engrg; Stuart Abrams, opns VP, natl sls mgr & traf mgr.

WTAA(AM)— Jan 1, 1955: 1490 khz; 400 w-U. TL: N39 23 24 W74 30 45. Hrs open: 24 hrs 1601 New Rd., Linwood, 08221. Phone: (609) 653-1400. Fax: (609) 601-0450. Web Site:www.kool983.com Licensee: Atlantic Broadcasting of Linwood NJ Limited Liability Co. Group owner: Access.1 Communications Corp. (acq 10-15-2008; grpsl). Population served: 27,000 Natl. Network: La Gran D, . Natl. Rep: McGavren Guild,. Rgnl Mexican. ◆Brett DeNafo, CEO; Dick Irland, gen mgr.

WZBZ(FM)— 1974: 99.3 mhz; 3 kw. Ant 328 ft TL: N39 22 35 W74 27 08. Stereo. Hrs open: 24 Simulcast with WGBZ(FM) Cape May Court House 100%. Equity Communications L.P., 8025 Black Horse Pike, Suite 100-102, West Atlantic City, 08232. Phone: (609) 484-8444. Fax: (609) 646-6331.E-mail: info@993thebuzz.com Web Site:993thebuzz.com Licensee: Equity Communications L.P. (group owner; acq 5-31-2002; grpsl). Population served: 400,000 Natl. Rep: Katz Radio,. Lathmam & Watkins. Format: CHR. Target aud: 18-49; adults. ◆Gary Fisher, sr VP, gen mgr; Rob Garcia, progmg dir.

Point Pleasant

WRAT(FM)— Oct 4, 1968: 95.9 mhz; 4 kw. Ant 293 ft TL: N40 10 17 W74 01 39. Stereo. Hrs open: 24 1731 Main St., Belmar, 07719-3051. Secondary address: 610 Main St., Belmar 07719. Phone: (732) 681-3800. Fax: (732) 681-5995. Web Site:www.wrat.com Licensee: The Sentinel Publishing Co. Group owner: Greater Media Inc. (acq 7-6-01; grpsl). Population served: 1,021,400 Natl. Rep: Katz Radio,. Format: Rock. Target aud: 21-44; men 25-54. ◆Dan Finn, VP, gen

mgr; Carl Craft, opns mgr, progmg dir; Marge Guglielmo, gen sls mgr; William Clanton Sr., chief of engrg.

Pomona

*WLFR(FM)— Oct 16, 1984: 91.7 mhz; 900 w. Ant 151 ft TL: N39 28 45 W74 32 23. Stereo. Hrs open: 6 AM-2 AM Stockton State College, Box 195, 08240. Phone: (609) 652-4781. Fax: (609) 652-4958. Web Site:www.wlfr.fm Licensee: Stockton State College Population served: 186,000 Format: Alternative, var. News: one hr wkly. Target aud: General. Spec prog: Folk 3 hrs, class 4 hrs, jazz 10 hrs wkly. ◆Christine Farina, gen mgr.

Pompton Lakes

WGHT(AM)— Oct 3, 1964: 1500 khz; 1 kw-D, DA-D. TL: N40 58 51 W74 17 06. Hrs open: Sunrise-sunset Box 316, 1878 Lincoln Ave., 07442. Phone: (973) 839-1500. Fax: (973) 839-2400.E-mail: livestudio@ghtradio.com Web Site:www.ghtradio.com Licensee: Mariana Broadcasting Inc. (acq 7-8-93; 8-23-93). Population served: 500,000 Natl. Network: AP Radio, . Format: Oldies, talk. News staff: 3; News: 10 hrs wkly. Target aud: 25-54; general. Spec prog: Relg 2 hrs, polka one hr, loc sports 3 hrs wkly. ◆John Silliman, pres, gen mgr, stn mgr; Tom Niven, opns VP; Mary Hamilton, gen sls mgr; Jimmy Howes, prom VP, progmg dir; Debra Valentine, news dir.

Port Republic

*WEHA(FM)— 2003: 88.7 mhz; 760 w vert. Ant 131 ft TL: N39 35 34 W74 26 15. Hrs open: 300 Philadelphia Ave., Little Egg Harbor, 08087. Phone: (609) 965-9100. Fax: (609) 965-9190.E-mail: wgxm@verison.net Licensee: WXXY Broadcasting Inc. Format: Gospel. ◆George Krementz, gen mgr.

Princeton

WHWH(AM)— Sept 7, 1963: 1350 khz; 5 kw-U, DA-2. TL: N40 22 00 W74 44 38. Hrs open: 24 Multicultural Radio Broadcasting Inc., 449 Broadway, New York, NY, 10013. Phone: (212) 431-4300. Fax: (212) 966-9580. Web Site:www.mrbi.net Licensee: Multicultural Radio Broadcasting Licensee LLC. Group owner: Multicultural Radio Broadcasting Inc. (acq 5-24-2002; grpsl). Population served: 358,000 Wiley Rein LLP. ◆Arthur S. Liu, pres.

WNUW(FM)—See Burlington

WPRB(FM)— October 1955: 103.3 mhz; 14 kw. 731 ft TL: N40 17 00 W74 41 20. Hrs open: 24 30 Bloomberg Hall, 08544. Phone: (609) 258-3655. Fax: (609) 258-1806.E-mail: manager@wprb.com Web Site:www.wprb.com Licensee: Princeton Broadcasting Service Inc. Format: Class, jazz, progsv. Target aud: 13-60. Spec prog: Asian Indian 6 hrs wkly. ◆Spencer Salazar, gen mgr.

Princeton Junction

*WWPH(FM)— November 1975: 107.9 mhz; 10 w. 36 ft TL: N40 18 20 W74 37 16. Hrs open: West Windsor-Plainsboro High School, 346 Clarksville Rd., 08550-1518. Phone: (609) 716-5050. Fax: (609) 716-5092.E-mail: wwph107.9fmlogin@ww-p.org Web Site:www.wwph1079.com Licensee: West Windsor Plainsboro Regional Board of Education. Format: Var. Target aud: 14-30; West Windsor & Plainsboro residents interested in their community. ◆Glenn Allison, gen mgr.

Salem

WFAI(AM)—Licensed to Salem. See Wilmington DE

WJKS(FM)—See Canton

South Belmar

WRAT(FM)—See Point Pleasant

South Orange

*WSOU(FM)— Apr 14, 1948: 89.5 mhz; 2.4 kw. 370 ft TL: N40 44 44 W74 14 50. Stereo. Hrs open: 24 Seton Hall University, 400 S. Orange Ave., 07079. Phone: (973) 313-6110. Fax: (973) 761-7593.E-mail: wsou@shu.edu Web Site:www.wsou.net Licensee: Seton Hall University.

Population served: 8,000,000 Booth, Freret, Imlay & Tepper. Wire Svc: AP Format: Active rock. News: 7 hrs wkly. Target aud: 18-34. Spec prog: Pol 2 hrs, Ethnic 10 hrs, pub affrs 5 hrs, relg 5 hrs wkly. ♦Mark Maben, gen mgr; Jen Wilcox, prom dir; Alexander Castiglione, progmg dir; Danielle Maffei, mus dir; Eric Bishop, news dir; Frank Scafidi, chief of engrg.

Stirling

WKMB(AM)— February 1972: 1070 khz; 250 w-D. TL: N40 40 35 W74 28 36. Hrs open: Sunrise-sunset 120 W. 7th, Suite 201, Plainfield, 07060. Phone: (908) 822-1515. Phone: (908) 647-4400. Fax: (908) 822-1927.E-mail: mprayer@harvestradio.com Web Site:www.harvestradio.net Licensee: World Harvest Communications Inc. (acq 1-15-03). Population served: 1,000,000 Format: Christian / Talk. ♦Gary Kirkwood Sr., CEO, pres; Melissa Prayer, gen mgr; Robert Hunt, opns mgr.

Sussex

***WNJP(FM)**— 1998: 88.5 mhz; 450 w. Ant 636 ft TL: N41 08 37 W74 32 18. Hrs open: Box 777, Trenton, 08625-0777. Phone: (609) 777-5036. Fax: (609) 777-5217. Web Site:www.njn.net Licensee: New Jersey Public Broadcasting Authority. Natl. Network: NPR, PRI, . Schwartz, Woods & Miller. Format: News/talk. Target aud: General. ♦Pharoah Cranston, opns mgr.

Teaneck

***WFDU(FM)**— Aug 30, 1971: 89.1 mhz; 550 w. 550 ft TL: N40 57 39 W73 55 23. Stereo. Hrs open: 1:15 AM-3:45 PM (M-F); 24 (S, Su) 1000 River Rd., 07666. Phone: (201) 692-2806. Fax: (201) 692-2807.E-mail: barrys@fdu.edu Web Site:www.wfdu.fm Licensee: Fairleigh Dickinson University. Population served: 18,000,000 Schwartz, Woods & Miller. Wire Svc: AP Format: Var/div. News: 2 hrs wkly. Target aud: General. Spec prog: Sp 3 hrs hrs wkly. ♦Carl J. Kraus, gen mgr; Barry Sheffield, opns mgr.

Toms River

***WNJO(FM)**— 2008: 90.3 mhz; 1 w horiz, 4 kw vert. Ant 121 ft TL: N39 54 52 W74 04 58. Hrs open:
Rebroadcasts WNJT-FM Trenton 100%.
Box 777, Trenton, 08625-0777. Phone: (609) 777-5000. Fax: (609) 777-5217. Web Site:www.njn.net Licensee: New Jersey Public Broadcasting Authority. Natl. Network: NPR, . NJN Public Radio Format: News/talk.

WOBM-FM— Mar 1, 1968: 92.7 mhz; 1.4 kw. 485 ft TL: N39 52 30 W74 09 52. Stereo. Hrs open: 24 Box 927, 08754. Phone: (732) 269-0927. Fax: (732) 269-9292.E-mail: wobm@wobm.com Web Site:www.wobm.com Licensee: Millennium Shore Holdco LLC. Group owner: Millennium Radio Group LLC (acq 5-14-02; grpsl). Population served: 452,000 William D. Silva. Format: Adult contemp. ♦Andy Santoro, gen mgr; John Furno, gen sls mgr; Teddy Maturo, prom dir, progmg dir; Steve Ardolina, progmg dir; Tom Mongelli, news dir.

Trenton

WCHR(AM)— Apr 11, 1941: 920 khz; 1.4 kw-D, 1 kw-N, DA-2. TL: N40 15 19 W74 51 44. Stereo. Hrs open: 24 119 Locktown Rd., Flemington, 08822. Phone: (610) 369-7777. Fax: (215) 321-5583.E-mail: csimpson@wchram.net Web Site:www.wchram.net Licensee: Nassau Broadcasting II L.L.C. (group owner; (acq 4-25-2002; with co-located FM). Cohn & Marks. Format: Relg. Target aud: General; relg adults. ♦John White, stn mgr; Curt Simpson, opns mgr; Chuck Zulker, sls dir.

WFJS(AM)— Jan 20, 1947: 1260 khz; 5 kw-D, 2.5 kw-N, DA-2. TL: N40 15 56 W74 45 27. Hrs open: Box 7509, 08628. Phone: (215) 269-4446. Phone: (866) 883-9357. Fax: (215) 269-6848. Web Site:www.wfjs.org Licensee: Domestic Church Media Foundation Group owner: Millennium Radio Group LLC (acq 9-12-2008; $2.3 million). Population served: 104,638 Natl. Network: EWTN Radio, . Law Office of Dennis J. Kelly. Format: Catholic. ♦James Manfredonia, pres.

WIMG(AM)—(Ewing, 1923: 1300 khz; 5 kw-D, 2.5 kw-N, DA-2. TL: N40 17 16 W74 52 23. Hrs open: 24 Box 9078, 08650. Secondary address: 1842 S. Broad St. 08610. Phone: (609) 695-1300. Fax: (609) 278-1588.E-mail: wimg1300@aol.com Web Site:www.wimg1300.com Licensee: Morris Broadcasting Co. of New Jersey Inc. (acq 12-3-93; 12-20-93). Population served: 580,000 Natl. Network: American Urban, NBC, Westwood One, . Natl. Rep: Williams Radio Sales,. Booth, Freret, Imlay & Tepper. Format: Urban adult contemp, gospel. News: 6 hrs wkly. Target aud: 25-54. ♦Johnny Morris, CEO; Louise E. Morris, chmn; Michael Morris, pres; Maggie Guzzardo, exec VP, gen mgr; Felicia Brannon, opns VP; Pamela Pruitt, dev VP.

WKXW(FM)— Aug 27, 1962: 101.5 mhz; 15.5 kw. Ant 902 ft TL: N40 16 58 W74 41 11. Stereo. Hrs open: Box 5698, 08638. Secondary address: 109 Walters Ave. 08638. Phone: (609) 771-8181. Fax: (609) 406-7956.E-mail: info@wkxw.com Web Site:www.nj1015.com Licensee: Millennium Central New Jersey License Holdco LLC. Population served: 400,000 Natl. Rep: Christal,. Format: Talk. News staff: 15; News: 75 hrs wkly. Target aud: General; New Jersey residents. ♦Eric Johnson, progmg dir; Laurie Roth, traf mgr.

***WNJT-FM**— May 20, 1991: 88.1 mhz; 110 w. Ant 689 ft TL: N40 16 58 W74 41 11. Hrs open: Box 777, 08625-0777. Phone: (609) 777-5036. Fax: (609) 777-5217.E-mail: pcrast@njn.org Web Site:www.njn.net Licensee: New Jersey Public Broadcasting Authority. Natl. Network: NPR, PRI, . Schwartz, Woods & Miller. Format: News/talk. Target aud: General. ♦Pharoah Cranston, stn mgr; Andre Butts, progmg dir.

WPST(FM)— Aug 7, 1965: 94.5 mhz; 50 kw. Ant 492 ft TL: N40 11 22 W74 50 47. Stereo. Hrs open: Prog sep from AM 619 Alexander Rd., 3rd Fl., Princeton, 08540-6003. Phone: (609) 419-0300. Fax: (609) 951-9778. Web Site:www.wpst.com Licensee: Nassau Broadcasting II L.L.C. (acq 4-25-2002; with co-located AM). Format: CHR. ♦Jim Spector, progmg dir, disc jockey; Angela Hartman, traf mgr; Randy Ellis, mus dir & disc jockey.

***WTSR(FM)**— September 1966: 91.3 mhz; 1.5 kw. 35 ft TL: N40 16 17 W74 46 55. Stereo. Hrs open: 24 The College of New Jersey, WTSR(FM), Box 7718, Ewing, 08628-7718. Phone: (609) 771-3200. Phone: (609) 771-2554. Fax: (609) 637-5113.E-mail: wtsr@wtsr.org Web Site:www.wtsr.org Licensee: The College of New Jersey Radio System. Population served: 106,638 Format: Progsv, alternative. News: 15 hrs wkly. Target aud: 13-40; people who listen to div mus formats. Spec prog: Gospel 6 hrs, pub affrs 8 hrs, folk 4 hrs, jazz 4 hrs, oldies 6 hrs wkly. ♦Patrick Lavery, stn mgr; Pat Hall, opns mgr; Jeff Rupert, progmg dir.

***WWFM(FM)**— Sept 6, 1982: 89.1 mhz; 1.15 kw. Ant 292 ft TL: N40 15 30 W74 38 59. Stereo. Hrs open: 24 P.O. Box B, 08690. Secondary address: 1200 Old Trenton Rd., West Windsor 08550. Phone: (609) 587-8989. Fax: (609) 570-3863.E-mail: wwfm@mccc.edu Web Site:www.wwfm.org Licensee: Mercer County Community College Board of Trustees. Population served: 400,000 Natl. Network: NPR, PRI, . Format: Classical. News: 3.5 hrs wkly. Target aud: General. ♦Heidi Jamieson, dev mgr; Alice Weiss, progmg dir.

Tuckerton

WBHX(FM)— 1999: 99.7 mhz; 5.3 kw. Ant 108 ft TL: N39 33 41 W74 14 27. Hrs open: 2355 West Bangs Ave., Neptune, 07753. Phone: (732) 774-4755. Fax: (732) 774-7315.E-mail: thebreezeradio @thebreezeradio.com Web Site:www.the breezeradio.com Licensee: Press Communications L.L.C. (group owner; acq 9-18-02; $1.15 million). Format: Adult Contemp. ♦Mike Fitzgerald, progmg dir.

Union Township

***WKNJ-FM**— January 1980: 90.3 mhz; 8.7 w. 88 ft TL: N40 40 35 W74 14 02. Stereo. Hrs open: Kean Univ., CAS 401, 1000 Morris Ave., Union, 07083. Phone: (908) 737-0440. Fax: (908) 737-0445.E-mail: wknjfm@yahoo.com Web Site:www. kean.edu/~cahss/acad_dept/comm /wknj/index/html Licensee: Kean University. Format: New mus. Spec prog: Black 2 hrs, jazz 8 hrs, new age 8 hrs wkly. ♦Scott McHugh, gen mgr; Cathleen Londino, stn mgr.

Upper Montclair

***WMSC(FM)**— Dec 9, 1974: 90.3 mhz; 10 w. 672 ft TL: N40 51 53 W74 12 03. Stereo. Hrs open: 7 AM-1 AM Student Ctr. Annex, Montclair State University, 07043. Phone: (973) 655-4257. Phone: (973) 655-4256. Fax: (973) 655-7433. Web Site:www.montclair.edu/org/wmsc Licensee: Montclair State University. Population served: 200,000 Format: Alternative. News: 5 hrs wkly. Target aud: Under 35. Spec prog: Black 4 hrs, gospel 2 hrs, jazz 2 hrs, Sp 2 hrs, sports 3 hrs wkly. ♦Walter Soto, gen mgr; Andrew Ward, opns dir; Dave Giumara, prom dir; Dan Maxwell, progmg dir; Lisa Hresko, mus dir.

Villas

WCZT(FM)— February 1992: 98.7 mhz; 3 kw. 292 ft TL: N39 00 33 W74 52 13. Hrs open: 24 3208 Pacific Ave., Wildwood, 08260. Phone: (609) 522-1987. Fax: (609) 522-3666.E-mail: coastalproduction@gmail.com Web Site:www.987thecoast.com Licensee: Coastal Broadcasting Systems Inc. (acq 5-21-2001; $1.4 million for stock). Format: Adult contemp. ♦Bob Maschio, gen mgr; Ed Rosenfeld, gen sls mgr; Scott Wahl, stn mgr & news dir; Ray Bradley, chief of engrg.

Vineland

WMIZ(AM)— Aug 19, 1959: 1270 khz; 500 w-D, 350 w-N, DA-2. TL: N39 29 53 W75 04 31. (CP: 360 w-D, 210 w-N). Hrs open: Prog sep from FM Box 689, 638 E. Landis Ave., 08362. Secondary address: 632 Maurice River Parkway 08360. Phone: (856) 692-8888. Fax: (856) 696-2568. Web Site:www.wmizradio.com Licensee: Clear Communications Inc. Population served: 52,600 Format: Spanish. Target aud: Hispanic. ♦Carl Hemple, Sr., CEO; W. Russell Withers, Jr., pres; Dana Withers, gen mgr; Scott Smolis, sls dir; Nicholas Lemay, news dir.

WVLT(FM)— October 1968: 92.1 mhz; 3 kw. 328 ft TL: N39 29 53 W75 04 31. Stereo. Hrs open: Box 689, 638 E. Landis Ave., 08360. Phone: (856) 692-8888. Fax: (856) 696-2568. Web Site:www.wvlt.com Licensee: Clear Communications Inc. (acq 8-1-86; $400,000; 5-12-86). Natl. Network: ABC, Jones Radio Networks, . Format: Oldies. Target aud: 25-54; baby boomers. ♦Carl Hemple, Sr., CEO; Cheryl Kinderman, gen mgr; Carson Raleton, stn mgr; Shaun Harvey, progmg dir; Heather Dooley, news dir; Chuck Niday, chief of engrg.

Washington Township

WNJC(AM)— July 29, 1946: 1360 khz; 5 kw-D, 800 w-N, DA-2. TL: N39 47 23 W75 06 11. Hrs open: 6 AM-midnight 123 Egg Harbor Rd., Ste 302, Sewell, 08080. Phone: (856) 227-1360. Fax: (856) 232-9093. Web Site:www.wnjc1360.com Licensee: Forsyth Broadcasting LLC (acq 1995; $161,000). Population served: 7,000,000 Bechtel & Cole. Format: Talk, progsv, gospel. News staff: 3; News: 20 hrs wkly. Target aud: 30 plus; 52% women, upper income. Spec prog: Relg 6 hrs wkly. ♦John Forsythe, pres; Al Jones, gen mgr, progmg dir.

Wayne

***WPSC-FM**— Nov 1, 1988: 88.7 mhz; 200 w. Ant 259 ft TL: N40 59 46 W74 16 51. Stereo. Hrs open: 9 am-3 am M-F; 6 am-3 am S-S Hobart Hall, 300 Pompton Rd., 07470. Phone: (973) 720-3319. Fax: (973) 720-2454.E-mail: wpsc887fm@wpunj.edu Licensee: William Paterson University of New Jersey. (acq 7-90; $1; 7-16-90). Population served: 1,700,000 Format: Alternative. Target aud: 18-35; independent thinking. Spec prog: Punk 3 hrs, hip hop 18 hrs, metal 18 hrs, classic rock 12 hrs, jazz 12 hrs wkly. ♦Ron Stotyn, gen mgr.

West Long Branch

***WMCX(FM)**— May 2, 1974: 88.9 mhz; 1 kw. 118 ft TL: N40 16 44 W74 00 26. Stereo. Hrs open: 24 Monmouth Univ., 400 Cedar Ave., 07764. Phone: (732) 571-3482. Fax: (732) 263-5145.E-mail: wmcxradio@monmouth.edu Web Site:www.wmcx.com Licensee: Monmouth University. Population served: 200,000 Natl. Network: AP Radio, . Format: Modern rock. News: 2.5 hrs wkly. Target aud: 18-25; college students, recent grads, young adults. Spec prog: Sports 11 hrs, jazz 3 hrs, changes w/semester. ♦Aaron Furgason, gen mgr.

Wildwood

WCMC(AM)— Nov 25, 1951: 1230 khz; 1 kw-U. TL: N39 00 09 W74 48 46. Hrs open: 24 8025 Black Horse Pike, Suite 100-102, West Atlantic City, 08232. Secondary address: 3010 New Jersey Ave. 08260. Phone: (609) 484-8444 x317. Fax: (609) 646-6331.E-mail: wcmc@aol.com Licensee: Equity Communications L.P. (group owner; (acq 11-4-97; $7.1 million with co-located FM). Population served: 200,000 Natl. Network: ABC, . Natl. Rep: Katz Radio,. Laitham & Watkins. Format: Adult standards. Target aud: Adults 35-64. ♦Gary Fisher, pres, VP, gen mgr, gen sls mgr; Jim MacMillan, progmg dir.

WZXL(FM)— Dec 17, 1959: 100.7 mhz; 38 kw. Ant 331 ft TL: N39 07 28 W74 45 56. Stereo. Hrs open: 24 8025 Black Horse Pike, Suite 100-102, West Atlantic City, 08232. Phone: (609) 484-8444 x 317. Fax: (609) 646-6331. Web Site:www.wzxl.com Population served: 400,000 Natl. Rep: Katz Radio,. Laitham & Watkins. Format: Classic rock. Target aud: Adults 18-49. ♦Steve Raymond, progmg dir.

Wildwood Crest

WEZW(FM)— Aug 15, 1993: 93.1 mhz; 4.2 kw. Ant 216 ft TL: N39 00 33 W74 52 13. Stereo. Hrs open: 24
Simulcast with WTTH(FM) Margate City 100%.
8025 Black Horse Pike, Suite 100-102, West Atlantic City, 08232. Phone: (609) 484-8444. Fax: (609) 646-6331. Web Site:www.961wtth.com

Licensee: Equity Communications L.P. (group owner; (acq 5-30-2003; grpsl). Population served: 200,000 Natl. Rep: Katz Radio,. Laitham & Watkins. Format: Urban adult contemp. Target aud: 18-49; adults. Spec prog: . ♦Gary Fisher, sr VP, VP, gen mgr; Rob Garcia, progmg dir; Denise Carrington, traf mgr.

Woodbine

***WJPH(FM)—** Feb 16, 1999: 89.9 mhz; 1 kw. Ant 105 ft TL: N39 16 51 W74 51 11. Stereo. Hrs open: 24 Box 603, 08270-0603. Phone: (609) 861-3700.E-mail: letters@praise899.org Web Site:www.praise899.org Licensee: Maranatha Ministries/Joy Communications Inc. Population served: 150,000 Booth, Freret, Imlay & Tepper. Format: Praise & worship. News: 10 hrs wkly. Target aud: 25-54; women. Spec prog: Gospel one hr wkly. ♦Kenneth Manri, pres.

Zarephath

WAWZ(FM)— Aug 22, 1954: 99.1 mhz; 28 kw. Ant 656 ft TL: N40 36 41 W74 34 12. Stereo. Hrs open: 24 Box 9058, 08890. Phone: (732) 469-0991. Fax: (732) 469-2115.E-mail: info@star991fm.com Web Site:www.star991fm.com Licensee: Pillar of Fire Inc. (group owner) Format: Adult contemp, Christian. Target aud: 25-54. ♦Rea Crawford, gen mgr; Scott Taylor, stn mgr; Allen Lewis Lewicki, opns dir; Stacey Stone, prom dir; Ed Abels, adv dir; Johnny Stone, progmg dir; Ron Habegger, engrg dir, chief of engrg.

New Mexico

Alamo

***KABR-FM—**Not on air, target date: unknown: 88.1 mhz; 400 w. Ant -195 ft TL: N34 25 01 W107 30 04. Hrs open: Box 907, Magdalena, 87825-0815. Phone: (505) 854-2632. Fax: (505) 854-2545. Licensee: Alamo Navajo School Board Inc. ♦Sarah Apache, gen mgr.

Alamo Community

***KABR(AM)—** August 1983: 1500 khz; 1 kw-D. TL: N34 25 01 W107 30 04. Hrs open: Box 907, Magdalena, 87825. Phone: (505) 854-2632. Phone: (505) 854-2641, Ext 1600-01. Fax: (505) 854-2545.E-mail: info@kabram.com Web Site:www.alamo.bia.edu Licensee: Alamo Navajo Community School. Format: Ethnic. Target aud: General; Native Americans, loc ranchers, tourists, teachers & health professionals. Spec prog: American Indian 10 hrs wkly. ♦Ann Kerr, pres; Sarah Apache, gen mgr & stn mgr.

Alamogordo

KINN(AM)— June 10, 1957: 1270 khz; 1 kw-D, 500 w-N. TL: N32 53 13 W105 57 04. Stereo. Hrs open: 24 Box 1848, 88311. Phone: (505) 434-1414. Fax: (505) 434-2213. Licensee: Burt Broadcasting Inc. (group owner; (acq 4-1-2001; with co-located FM). Baraff, Koerner & Olender. Format: News/talk. News: 22 hrs wkly. Target aud: 24-50; military & civil service personnel employed in high-tech jobs. ♦William F. Burt, pres & gen mgr; Lori Swinford, gen sls mgr; James White, progmg dir, news dir; Ken Bass, engrg dir; Donnie Burt, traf mgr.

KNMZ(FM)— 1997: 103.7 mhz; 47 kw. 1,338 ft TL: N33 10 45 W105 53 53. Hrs open: 24 Box 2710, 88311. Secondary address: 119 N. Canyon Rd. 88310. Phone: (575) 437-1505. Fax: (575) 437-5566.E-mail: Lhenke@snmradio.com Web Site:www.snmradio.com Licensee: WP Broadcasting LLC. Group owner: Runnels Broadcasting System L.L.C. (acq 5-19-2006; grpsl). Natl. Network: ABC, . Format: Classic hits. ♦Les Henke, gen mgr.

KQEL(FM)— 2006: 107.9 mhz; 3 kw. Ant -594 ft TL: N32 53 13 W105 57 04. Hrs open: 24 Box 1848, 88311. Phone: (505) 434-1414. Fax: (505) 434-2213. Licensee: Burt Broadcasting Inc. (group owner; (acq 10-29-2003; $93,000 for CP). Format: Late 50's - early 80's. ♦William F. Burt, gen mgr; Lori Swinford, gen sls mgr.

KRSY(AM)— June 28, 1950: 1230 khz; 1 kw-U. TL: N32 53 46 W105 56 42. Hrs open: 24 Box 2710, 119 N. Canyon Road, 88311. Phone: (575) 437-1505. Phone: (575) 437-1230. Fax: (575) 437-5566. Web Site:www.snmradio.com Licensee: WP Broadcasting LLC. Group owner: Runnels Broadcasting System L.L.C. (acq 5-19-2006; grpsl). Population served: 55300 Jones, Waldo, Holbrook & McDonough; Barry Wood. Format: Talk, sports. News staff: 2; News: 10 hrs wkly. Target aud: 25-54; active adults, community-oriented. Spec prog: Big band 6 hrs, farm one hr, gospel 8 hrs, relg 4 hrs wkly. ♦Les Henke, gen mgr.

KRSY-FM—(La Luz, Jan 17, 1987: 92.7 mhz; 6 kw. Ant -216 ft TL: N32 58 13 W105 59 21. Stereo. Hrs open: 24 Box 2710, 119 N. Canyon Road, 88311. Phone: (575) 437-1063. Phone: (575) 437-1063. Web Site:www.snmradio.com Licensee: WP Broadcasting LLC. Natl. Network: ABC, . Format: Today's Best Country. News staff: 2; News: 2 hrs wkly. Target aud: 18-34; active adults, young adults. Spec prog: NASCAR. ♦Les Henke, gen mgr & natl sls mgr.

***KUPR(FM)—** Oct 14, 2000: 91.7 mhz; 100 w. Ant 1,679 ft TL: N32 49 47 W105 53 10. Stereo. Hrs open: 24 3001 N. Florida Ave., 88310. Phone: (505) 437-0917. Fax: (505) 434-6060. Fax: (505) 437-9917.E-mail: kupr917@yahoo.com Licensee: Southern New Mexico Radio Foundation. Wood, Maines & Brown. Format: Country gospel loc. News: 4 hrs wkly. Target aud: 25-60; adults. ♦Bob Flotte, pres; Devere Johnson, opns dir.

***KYCM(FM)—** 2006: 89.9 mhz; 800 w. Ant 1,630 ft TL: N32 49 47 W105 53 13. Hrs open:
Rebroadcasts KYCC(FM) Stockton, CA 100%.
9019 West Ln., Stockton, CA, 95210-1401. Phone: (209) 477-3690. Fax: (209) 477-2762.E-mail: kycc@kycc.org Web Site:www.kycc.org Licensee: Your Christian Companion Network Inc. Format: Gospel, inspirational, adult contemp. ♦Shirley Garner, gen mgr.

KYEE(FM)— July 21, 1980: 94.3 mhz; 3 kw. -492 ft TL: N32 56 42 W105 56 47. Stereo. Hrs open: 24 Box 1848, 88311. Phone: (505) 434-1414. Fax: (505) 434-2213.E-mail: 94key@bbiradio.net Web Site:www.sos.state.nm.us/radio.htm Licensee: Burt Broadcasting Inc. (group owner; acq 11-88; $230,000;12-19-88). Population served: 60,000 Format: CHR. Target aud: 18-44; young adults. ♦Donnie L. Burt, VP; William F. Burt, pres & gen mgr; Lori Swinford, gen sls mgr.

KZZX(FM)— 1979: 105.3 mhz; 910 w. Ant 1,614 ft TL: N32 49 48 W105 53 12. Stereo. Hrs open: 24 Box 1848, 88311. Phone: (505) 434-1414. Fax: (505) 434-2213. Licensee: Burt Broadcasting Inc. Format: Country. News: 22 hrs wkly. Target aud: 20-55.

Albuquerque

KABQ(AM)— 1947: 1350 khz; 5 kw-D, 500 w-N, DA-N. TL: N35 06 02 W106 40 34. Hrs open: 8am - 5:30pm 5411 Jefferson N.E., 87109. Phone: (505) 338-7400. Fax: (505) 830-6543. Web Site:www.abqtalk.com Licensee: Clear Channel Broadcasting Licenses. Group owner: Clear Channel Communications Inc. (acq 3-01-00; grpsl). Population served: 243,751 Natl. Rep: Lotus Entravision Reps LLC,. Format: Progressive talk. Target aud: General. ♦Chuck Hammond, pres & gen mgr; Bill May, progmg dir, disc jockey; Chris Williams, chief of engrg.

KALY(AM)—(Los Ranchos de Albuquerque, 1982: 1240 khz; 1 kw-U. TL: N35 12 06 W106 35 56. Stereo. Hrs open: 24 2505 6th St. N.W., 87102. Phone: (505) 244-1100. Fax: (505) 244-0612. Web Site:www.radiodisney.com Licensee: Radio Disney Group LLC. Group owner: ABC Inc. (acq 2-21-03; $650,000). Format: Family Programing. Target aud: 25-49. ♦Lynn Southard, gen mgr.

***KANW(FM)—** October 1950: 89.1 mhz; 20 kw. 4,152 ft TL: N35 12 44 W106 26 57. Stereo. Hrs open: 24 2020 Coal Ave. S.E., 87106. Phone: (505) 242-7163. Phone: (505) 242-7848.E-mail: brasher@aps.edu Web Site:www.kanw.com Licensee: Board of Education of the City of Albuquerque. Population served: 850,000 Natl. Network: NPR, PRI, . Format: Sp. News staff: News progmg 20 hrs wkly ♦Michael Brasher, gen mgr.

KBQI(FM)— Apr 27, 1979: 107.9 mhz; 22.5 kw. 4,130 ft TL: N35 12 43 W106 26 57. Stereo. Hrs open: 24 5411 Jefferson St. N.E., Suite 100, 87109. Phone: (505) 830-6400. Fax: (505) 830-6543.E-mail: info@bigi1079.com Web Site:www.bigi1079.com Licensee: Citicasters Licenses L.P. Group owner: Clear Channel Communications Inc. (acq 9-28-99; grpsl). Format: Country. Target aud: 18-49. ♦Chuck Hammond, gen mgr; Bill May, chief of opns.

KBZU(FM)— November 1954: 96.3 mhz; 20 kw. Ant 4,110 ft TL: N35 12 44 W106 26 58. Stereo. Hrs open: 24 500 4th St. N.W., 5th Fl., 87102. Phone: (505) 767-6700. Fax: (505) 767-6767. Licensee: The Last Bastion Station Trust LLC, as Trustee Group owner: Citadel Broadcasting Corp. (acq 6-12-2007; grpsl). Population served: 523,000 Natl. Network: ESPN Deportes, . Natl. Rep: McGavren Guild,. Kaye, Scholer, Fierman, Hays & Handler. Format: Sp sports. ♦Eddie Haskell, opns dir, progmg dir; Jeff Berry, gen sls mgr & natl sls mgr; Art Ortega, pub affrs dir; Bill Harris, engrg dir.

KDAZ(AM)— 1969: 730 khz; 1 kw-D, 76 w-N, DA-2. TL: N35 00 31 W106 42 52. Hrs open: 24 Box 4338, 87196. Secondary address: 5010 4th St. N.W. 87107. Phone: (505) 345-7373. Fax: (505) 345-5669.E-mail: birga@kdaz.org Web Site:www.kdaz.org Licensee: Pan American Broadcasting Inc. (acq 11-17-2003). Population served: 662,380 Natl. Network: USA, . Gammon & Grange. Format: Variety. Target aud: 25-54. ♦Blackie Gonzalez, CEO, chmn, pres; Vickie Archiveque, CFO; Annette Garcia, VP, gen mgr; Jim Sandell, progmg dir.

KDEF(AM)— September 1953: 1150 khz; 5 kw-D, 500 w-N, DA-2. TL: N35 12 06 W106 35 54. Hrs open: 10424 Edith N.E., 87113. Phone: (505) 888-1150. Fax: (505) 899-1977.E-mail: info@kdefam.com Licensee: RAMH Corp. (acq 7-95; $125,000). Population served: 500,000 Natl. Network: CNN Radio, . Format: 80s & 90s music, youth sports, news. Target aud: General. ♦Henry Tafoya, gen mgr.

KDRF(FM)— Apr 20, 1988: 103.3 mhz; 22 kw. 4,069 ft TL: N35 12 50 W106 27 00. Stereo. Hrs open: 24 Citadel Southwest, 500 4th St. N.W., 5th Fl., 87102. Phone: (505) 767-6700. Fax: (505) 767-6767. Web Site:www.ed.fm Licensee: Citadel Broadcasting Co. Group owner: Citadel Broadcasting Corp. (acq 1996; $5 million). Natl. Rep: Christal,. Format: Best of the Hits. Target aud: 18-49. ♦Linda Rosenberg, gen sls mgr.

***KFLQ(FM)—** Feb 20, 1983: 91.5 mhz; 20 kw. Ant 4,041 ft TL: N35 12 51 W106 27 02. Stereo. Hrs open: 24 3801 Eubank N.E., 87111. Phone: (505) 296-9100. Fax: (505) 296-6262.E-mail: kflqonair@flc.org Web Site:915flr.org Licensee: Family Life Broadcasting System. Group owner: Family Life Communications Inc. (acq 1982). Population served: 500,000 Natl. Network: Moody, USA, . Format: Inspirational, praise & worship. Target aud: 35-54; female. ♦Randy Carlson, pres; Dan Rosecrans, stn mgr.

KIVA(AM)— Feb 22, 1971: 1550 khz; 5 kw-D, 20 w-N. TL: N35 06 02 W106 40 34. Hrs open: 24 1213 San Pedro N E, 87110. Phone: (505) 899-5029.E-mail: joyam@joyam Web Site:www.softfavorites1550.com Licensee: Vanguard Media L.L.C. (acq 1-21-2000; $112,000). Population served: 650,000 Format: Soft adult contemp. News: 5 hrs wkly. Target aud: 35-64; mature upscale adults. ♦Don Davis, CEO, pres; Craig Collins, gen mgr, opns mgr, mus dir; Josie Bunch, stn mgr; Crystal Felice, rgnl sls mgr, mktg mgr.

KKIM(AM)— Apr 15, 1972: 1000 khz; 10 kw-D. TL: N35 10 14 W106 37 51. Hrs open: Box 30925, 87190-0925. Secondary address: 4125 Carlisle Blvd. N.E. 87107-4806. Phone: (505) 878-0980. Fax: (505) 878-0098. Web Site:www.mykkim.com Licensee: AGM-Nevada L.L.C. Group owner: American General Media (acq 12-22-97; grpsl). Population served: 243,751 Format: Christian, talk. Target aud: 25-54. Spec prog: Black 2 hrs wkly. ♦Dewey Moede, stn mgr.

KKOB(AM)— Apr 5, 1922: 770 khz; 50 kw-U, DA-N. TL: N35 12 09 W106 36 41. Hrs open: 24 500 4th St. N.W., 87102. Phone: (505) 767-6700. Fax: (505) 767-6767.E-mail: kkobam@citcomm.com Web Site:www.770kkob.com Licensee: Citadel Broadcasting Co. Group owner: Citadel Broadcasting Corp. (acq 3-15-94; $7.8 million with co-located FM;4-11-94). Population served: 500,000 Natl. Rep: McGavren Guild,. Haley, Bader & Potts. Format: News/talk. ♦Milt McConnell, gen mgr; Matt Woodcock, rgnl sls mgr; Pat Frisch, opns mgr & progmg dir; Alex Cuellar, news dir; Art Ortega, pub affrs dir; Bill Harris, chief of engrg.

KKOB-FM— Aug 1, 1967: 93.3 mhz; 21.5 kw. 4,150 ft TL: N35 12 42 W106 26 59. Stereo. Hrs open: 24 Prog sep from AM 500 4th St. N.W., 87102. Phone: (505) 767-6700. Fax: (505) 767-6767. Licensee: Citadel Broadcasting Population served: 863,000 Format: Adult contemp. ♦Milt McConnell, gen mgr; Kris Abrans, opns dir, opns mgr; Tim Gannon, sls VP, rgnl sls mgr; Mark Anderson, mktg dir; Kris Abrams, progmg dir; Linda Land, traf mgr; Carlos Duran, disc jockey.

KKRG(FM)— October 1994: 101.3 mhz; 3.7 kw. Ant 420 ft TL: N35 04 06 W106 46 46. Hrs open: 24 8009 Marble Ave. N.E., 87110. Phone: (505) 262-1142. Fax: (505) 254-7106. Licensee: Univision Radio License Corp. Group owner: Univision Radio (acq 9-22-2003; grpsl). Format: Sp. Target aud: 35-54.

***KLYT(FM)—** Sept 11, 1976: 88.3 mhz; 4.1 kw. Ant 4,244 ft TL: N35 12 49 W106 27 01. Stereo. Hrs open: 24 4001 Osuna Rd. N.E., 87109. Phone: (505) 344-9146. Fax: (505) 344-9193. Web Site:www.m88.org Licensee: Calvary Chapel of Albuquerque, Inc. (acq 11-30-2000). Population served: 450,000 Format: Contemp Christian hits. ♦Chip Lusko, VP, gen mgr; Lynn Gilstrap, stn mgr; Darren Arnold, gen sls mgr.

KMGA(FM)—Listing follows KTBL(AM).

KNML(AM)— Mar 28, 1928: 610 khz; 5 kw-U, DA-N. TL: N35 01 56 W106 39 48. Hrs open: 24 500 4th St. N.W., 5th Flr., 87102. Phone: (505) 767-6700. Fax: (505) 767-6767.E-mail: knml@citcomm.com Web Site:www.610thesportsanimal.com Licensee: Citadel Broadcasting Co. Group owner: Citadel Broadcasting Corp. (acq 3-23-00; swap with KSVA(AM) Albuquerque). Population served: 100,000 Format: All sports. Target aud: 25-54. ♦Milt McConnell, gen mgr; Pat Frisch, opns dir; Ian Martin, progmg dir.

KPEK(FM)— December 1974: 100.3 mhz; 22.5 kw. 4,110 ft TL: N35 12 51 W106 27 02. Stereo. Hrs open: 8am - 5:30pm 5411 Jefferson N.E., Suite A100, 87109. Phone: (505) 830-6400. Fax: (505) 830-6543.E-mail: info@1003thepeak.com Web Site:www.1003thepeak.com Licensee: Citicasters Licenses L.P. Group owner: Clear Channel Communications Inc. (acq 9-28-99; grpsl). Population served: 369,900 Format: Modern adult contemp. Target aud: 25-54; adults, high income professional and technical. ♦Chuck Hammond, gen mgr; Bill May, chief of opns.

KQTM(FM)—See Rio Rancho

KRKE(AM)— May 14, 1956: 1600 khz; 10 kw-D, 128 w-N. TL: N35 10 14 W106 37 51. Hrs open: 24 307 Los Ranchos Rd. N.W., 87107. Phone: (505) 899-5029. Fax: (505) 899-6865.E-mail: realoldies1600@realoldies1600 Web Site:www.realoldies1600.com Licensee: Vanguard Media LLC (acq 12-20-2004; $650,000). Population served: 600,000 Natl. Network: CNN Radio, . Natl. Rep: Christal,. Format: Oldies. Target aud: 30-50. ♦Don Davis, CEO, pres, gen mgr; Craig Collins, opns mgr, progmg dir, mus dir; Crystal Felice, mktg mgr; Doris Budris, prom dir.

KRST(FM)— Sept 15, 1965: 92.3 mhz; 22.5 kw. 4,110 ft TL: N35 12 55 W106 27 02. Stereo. Hrs open: 24 5th Fl., 500 4th St. N.W., 87102. Phone: (505) 767-6700. Fax: (505) 767-6767. Web Site:www.923krst.com Licensee: Citadel Broadcasting Co. Group owner: Citadel Broadcasting Corp. (acq 9-30-96; grpsl). Population served: 600,000 Format: Hot new country. ♦Milt McConnell, gen mgr, gen sls mgr, natl sls mgr; Eddie Haskell, opns mgr, progmg dir; Richard Piombino, prom dir; Paul Bailey, mus dir; Art Ortega, pub affrs dir; Bill Harris, engrg dir, chief of engrg.

KRZY(AM)— June 1956: 1450 khz; 1 kw-U. TL: N35 07 56 W106 37 18. Stereo. Hrs open: 24 2725 F. Broadbent Parkway N E, 87107. Phone: (505) 342-4141. Fax: (505) 344-8714.E-mail: mwilder@entravision.com Web Site:www.entravision.com Licensee: Entravision Holdings LLC. Group owner: Entravision Communications Corp. (acq 3-14-2000; grpsl). Population served: 500,000 Format: Sp/rgnl Mexican. ♦Jeff Liberman, pres; Margarita Wilder, gen mgr & gen sls mgr; Juan Vavala, prom mgr.

KSVA(AM)— Mar 28, 1998: 920 khz; 1 kw-D, 130 w-N. TL: N35 07 56 W106 37 18. Hrs open: 24 Box 2378, Corrales, 87048. Phone: (800) 775-4673. Fax: (505) 890-0808.E-mail: tim@lifetalk.net Web Site:www.lifetalk.net Licensee: Lifetalk Radio Inc. (acq 4-7-2000; swap with KNML(AM) Albuquerque). Population served: 1000000 Natl. Network: USA, . Format: Inspirational Christian. News: 2 hrs wkly. Target aud: 35 plus; Christians. Spec prog: Sp 4 hrs wkly. ♦Phil Folett, CEO; Jep Choate, chmn; Ricardo Baratta, stn mgr; Robert Hardy, chief of opns; Clare Gallimore, dev dir; Jeremy Woodruff, progmg dir; Elvin Vence, chief of engrg.

KTBL(AM)—(Los Ranchos de Albuquerque, Dec 16, 1987: 1050 khz; 1 kw-D, 500 w-N, DA-1. TL: N34 58 46 W106 44 13. Hrs open: 500 4th St. N.W., 87102. Phone: (505) 767-6700. Fax: (505) 767-6767. Web Site:www.1050kbull.com Licensee: Citadel Broadcasting Co. Group owner: Citadel Broadcasting Corp. (acq 6-28-96; $5.725 million with KBZU(FM) Albuquerque). Population served: 100,000 Format: News/talk. Target aud: 25-54. ♦Milt McConnell, gen mgr; Blake Mendenhall, rgnl sls mgr; Glenn Herbert, mktg dir, prom dir; Pat Frisch, opns dir & progmg dir; Art Ortega, pub affrs dir; Bill Harris, chief of engrg; Lynda Ortega, traf mgr.

***KUNM(FM)**— Oct 17, 1966: 89.9 mhz; 13.6 kw. Ant 4,070 ft TL: N35 12 44 W106 26 57. Stereo. Hrs open: 24 MSC06 3520, Univ. of New Mexico, 87131-0001. Phone: (505) 277-4806. Fax: (505) 277-8004.E-mail: kunm@kunm.org Web Site:www.kunm.org Licensee: Regents of the University of New Mexico. Population served: 780,000 Natl. Network: NPR, PRI, . Dow, Lohnes & Albertson. Format: Div, news/talk. News staff: 3; News: 50 hrs wkly. Target aud: 25-54; those who enjoy NPR and diverse community-produced programs. Spec prog: Class 12 hrs, Sp 9 hrs, Indian 9 hrs wkly. ♦Richard Towne, gen mgr; Mary Bokuniewicz, dev dir.

KXKS(AM)— Dec 16, 1969: 1190 khz; 10 kw-D, 24 w-N. TL: N35 03 04 W106 38 34. Hrs open: 24 Wilkins Communications Network Inc., Box 444, Spartanburg, SC, 29304. Phone: (864) 585-1885. Fax: (864) 597-0687.E-mail: info@wilkinsradio.com Web Site:www.wilkinsradio.com Licensee: Wild West Radio Corp. (group owner; (acq 12-16-2004; $775,000). Population served: 886,000 Womble, Carlyle, Sandridge & Rice. Format: Christian Preaching/talk. Target aud: 35 plus. ♦Bob Wilkins, CEO; LuAnn Wilkins, exec VP; Doug Cekander, stn mgr.

KZRR(FM)— June 25, 1961: 94.1 mhz; 100 kw. 4,130 ft TL: N35 12 44 W106 26 58. Stereo. Hrs open: 24 5411 Jefferson St. N.E., Suite 100, 87109. Phone: (505) 830-6400. Fax: (505) 830-6543.E-mail: info@94rock.com Web Site:www.94rock.com Licensee: Clear Channel Broadcasting Licenses Inc. Group owner: Clear Channel Communications Inc. (acq 9-28-99; grpsl). Natl. Network: Westwood One, . Format: AOR. ♦Chuck Hammond, gen mgr.

Angel Fire

KKTC(FM)— Jan 15, 1990: 99.9 mhz; 1.75 kw. Ant 2,119 ft TL: N36 33 30 W105 11 38. Stereo. Hrs open: 24 5542 NDCBU, Taos, 87571-6122. Secondary address: 125A Camino de la Merced, Taos 87571-5119. Phone: (505) 758-4491. Fax: (505) 758-4452.E-mail: production@kxmt.com Web Site:radiotaos.com Licensee: DMC Broadcasting Inc. (acq 3-19-2003; $645,000 with KXMT(FM) Taos). Natl. Network: ABC, . Haley, Bader & Potts. Format: Todays country. News staff: one; News: 7 hrs wkly. Target aud: 25-54; adults middle-upper-income residents & tourists. Spec prog: Jazz 4 hrs, relg 8 hrs wkly. ♦Jeff Singer, opns mgr, progmg dir; Pattee Brown, gen sls mgr; Jennifer Trujillo, news dir.

Armijo, Albuquerque

KNKT(FM)— Dec 17, 1991: 107.1 mhz; 50 kw. 304 ft TL: N35 03 15 W106 51 31. (CP: 60 kw, 2,365 ft.). Stereo. Hrs open: 24 4001 Osuna Rd. N.E., Albuquerque, 87109. Phone: (505) 344-9146. Fax: (505) 344-9193. Web Site:www.calvaryabq.org Licensee: Calvary Chapel of Albuquerque Inc. (acq 9-29-94; $800,000 with KDEF(AM) Albuquerque; 11-21-94). Population served: 500,000 Format: Praise, worship, bible teaching. News: 4 hrs wkly. Target aud: 25-54. ♦Chip Lusko, gen mgr; Lynn Gilstrap, stn mgr; Darren Arnold, gen sls mgr.

Arroyo Seco

***KRRT(FM)**— Apr 3, 2008: 90.9 mhz; 6 kw. Ant -656 ft TL: N36 23 51 W105 32 34. Hrs open:
Rebroadcasts KUNM(FM) Albuquerque 100%.
Room 326 Onate Hall, University of New Mexico, Albuquerque, 87131. Phone: (505) 277-8009. Fax: (505) 277-8004.E-mail: kunm@kunm.org Web Site:www.kunm.org Licensee: Regents of the University of New Mexico. Format: Div, news/talk. ♦Richard Towne, gen mgr.

Artesia

KSVP(AM)— Nov 14, 1946: 990 khz; 1 kw-D, 250 w-N. TL: N32 49 29 W104 23 59. Hrs open: 24 317 W. Quay, 88210. Phone: (505) 746-2751. Fax: (505) 748-3748.E-mail: info@ksvpradio.com Web Site:www.ksvpradio.com Licensee: Pecos Valley Broadcasting Co. (acq 1993; $150,000 with co-located FM; 9-13-93). Population served: 150,000 Natl. Network: CBS, . Cohn & Marks. Format: Talk. News staff: one; News: 18 hrs wkly. Target aud: General. ♦Gene Dow, gen mgr, gen sls mgr & chief of engrg.

KTZA(FM)— May 9, 1969: 92.9 mhz; 100 kw. 1,089 ft TL: N32 47 39 W104 12 27. Stereo. Hrs open: 24 Prog sep from AM 121 S. Canal St., Suite C, Carlsbad, 88220. Phone: (505) 746-2751. Fax: (505) 748-3748.E-mail: info@kz93.com Web Site:www.kz93.com Population served: 150,000 Natl. Network: ABC, . Format: Country. News: 3 hrs wkly. Target aud: 25-54. ♦Gene Dow, VP.

Aztec

KCQL(AM)— Sept 4, 1959: 1340 khz; 1 kw-U. TL: N36 49 17 W107 59 58. Stereo. Hrs open: 24 200 E. Broadway, Farmington, 87401. Phone: (505) 325-1716. Fax: (505) 325-6797. Web Site:www.foxsports1340.com Licensee: Capstar TX L.P. Group owner: Clear Channel Communications Inc. (acq 8-30-2000; grpsl). Population served: 85,000 Natl. Network: Fox Sports, . Wire Svc: UPI Format: Sports. News: 14 hrs wkly. Target aud: 18-54. Spec prog: Sp 6 hrs wkly. ♦Bill Kruger, gen mgr; Steve Bortstein, progmg dir.

KWYK-FM— Jan 2, 1978: 94.9 mhz; 100 kw. Ant 433 ft TL: N32 47 39 W104 12 27. Stereo. Hrs open: 24 1515 W. Main, Farmington, 87401. Phone: (505) 325-1996. Fax: (505) 327-2019.E-mail: productionroom@basinbroadcasting.com Licensee: Basin Broadcasting Co. Format: Adult contemp. News: 15 hrs wkly. Target aud: 25-54; mainstream population. ♦Kerwin Gober, gen mgr; Dana Childs, progmg dir; Jim Burk, chief of engrg.

Bayard

KNFT(AM)— July 4, 1968: 950 khz; 5 kw-D. TL: N32 46 51 W108 11 58. Hrs open: Box 2577, Silver City, 88062. Secondary address: 5 Racetrack Rd., Silver City 88061. Phone: (505) 388-1958. Fax: (505) 388-5000.E-mail: events@silvercityradio.com Licensee: SkyWest Licenses New Mexico LLC. Group owner: Runnels Broadcasting System L.L.C. (acq 6-1-2006; grpsl). Population served: 100,000 Format: Talk, sports. ♦Matthew Runnell, gen mgr, gen sls mgr, progmg dir; Rita Niccum, chief of engrg; Anna Gallegos, traf mgr.

KNFT-FM— June 15, 1981: 102.9 mhz; 3 kw. 135 ft TL: N32 50 40 W108 14 18. (CP: 29.14 kw, ant 491 ft.). Hrs open: Prog sep from AM Secondary address: 5 Racetrack Rd., Silver City 88061. Phone: (505) 388-1958. Fax: (505) 388-5000.E-mail: events@silvercityradio.com Web Site:www.gilanet.com Format: C&W.

Belen

KARS(AM)— Oct 7, 1961: 860 khz; 1.3 kw-D, 186 w-N. TL: N34 41 43 W106 46 13. Stereo. Hrs open: 24 Box 860, 208 N. 2nd St., 87002. Phone: (505) 864-3024. Fax: (505) 864-2719.E-mail: info@karsam.com Licensee: AGM-Nevada L.L.C. Group owner: American General Media (acq 12-22-97; grpsl). Population served: 54,000 Natl. Rep: Lotus Entravision Reps LLC,. Format: Country. News staff: one; News: 30 hrs wkly. Target aud: 25 plus. Spec prog: Relg. ♦Scott Hutton, gen mgr; Ron Ortega, stn mgr, gen sls mgr; Ron Travis, mus dir, news dir; Bob Picknell, chief of engrg; Russ Ortego, disc jockey.

KDLW(FM)— 1982: 97.7 mhz; 100 kw. Ant 859 ft TL: N34 47 55 W106 48 59. Stereo. Hrs open: 24 Dups AM 18% 4125 Carlisle NE, Albuquerque, 87107. Phone: (505) 878-0980. Fax: (505) 878-0098. Web Site:www.americangeneralmedia.com Licensee: AGM-Nevada L.L.C. Population served: 600,000 Format: Sp. ♦Russ Ortego, disc jockey.

***KQGC(FM)**— 2004: 90.7 mhz; 1.6 kw. Ant 649 ft TL: N34 47 55 W106 48 59. Hrs open:
Rebroadcasts KLRD(FM) Yucaipa, CA 100%.
5700 W. Oaks Blvd., Rocklin, 95765. Phone: (916) 251-1600. Phone: (800) 525-5683. Fax: (916) 251-1650. Web Site:www.air1.com Licensee: Educational Media Foundation. Group owner: EMF Broadcasting. Natl. Network: Air 1, . Format: Christian. ♦Mike Novak, pres.

Bloomfield

KKFG(FM)— 1988: 104.5 mhz; 100 kw. Ant 1,086 ft TL: N36 38 33 W107 46 54. Stereo. Hrs open: 200 E. Broadway, Farmington, 87401. Phone: (505) 325-1716. Fax: (505) 325-6797. Web Site:www.kool1045.com Licensee: Capstar TX L.P. Group owner: Clear Channel Communications Inc. (acq 8-30-2000; grpsl). Format: Oldies. ♦Bill Kruger, gen mgr.

Bosque Farms

KABQ-FM— July 1, 1987: 104.7 mhz; 100 kw. Ant 843 ft TL: N34 46 12 W106 51 42. Stereo. Hrs open: 5411 Jefferson N.E., Suite A100, Albuquerque, 87109. Phone: (505) 830-6400. Fax: (505) 830-6543.E-mail: info@abtalk.com Web Site:www.classiccountry1047.com Licensee: Aloha Station Trust LLC, as Trustee group owner: Clear Channel Communication Inc. (acq 7-30-2008). Format: Classic country. News staff: one. Target aud: 25-54. ♦Bill May, pres, chief of opns; Chuck Hammond, gen mgr.

***KQRI(FM)**— Nov 16, 2001: 105.5 mhz; 97.58 kw. Ant 745 ft TL: N34 47 55 W106 48 59. Stereo. Hrs open: 24 2351 Sunset Blvd., Suite 170-218, Rocklin, CA, 95765. Phone: (916) 251-1600. Fax: (916) 251-1650.E-mail: klove@klove.com Web Site:www.klove.com Licensee: Educational Media Foundation. Group owner: EMF Broadcasting. Natl. Network: K-Love, . Shaw Pittman. Format: Contemp Christian mus. News staff: 3. Target aud: 25-44; Judeo-Christian, female. ♦Richard Jenkins, pres; Mike Novak, VP; Keith Whipple, dev dir; Eric Allen, natl sls mgr; David Pierce, progmg mgr, mus dir; Ed Lenane, news dir; Sam Wallington, engrg dir; Karen Johnson, news rptr.

Cannon AFB

***KKCJ(FM)**— 2006: 90.7 mhz; 25 kw. Ant 194 ft TL: N34 26 58 W103 37 03. Hrs open:
Rebroadcasts KSGR(FM) Portland, TX 100%.
c/o KSGR(FM), 3001 Rodd Field Rd., Corpus Christi, TX, 78414-3987. Phone: (361) 814-7775. Fax: (361) 814-7779.E-mail: jim.shepherd@csnradio.com Web Site:www.ksgr.org Licensee: CSN International (group owner). Natl. Network: CSN, . Format: Contemp Christian. ♦Jim Shepherd, stn mgr.

Carlsbad

KAMQ(AM)— June 10, 1938: 1240 khz; 1 kw-U. TL: N32 23 43 W104 14 48. Hrs open: Box 1538, 88220. Secondary address: 1609 Radio Blvd. 88220. Phone: (505) 887-5323. Fax: (505) 887-7000.E-mail: info@kdoveradio.com Licensee: KAMQ Inc. (acq 1-21-76). Population served: 40,000 Format: Adult contemp, Christian. ♦Don Hughes, gen mgr, gen sls mgr; Reginald James, progmg dir; Frank Nymeyer, chief of engrg.

KATK(AM)— May 17, 1950: 740 khz; 1 kw-D, 500 w-N. TL: N32 27 02 W104 12 47. Hrs open: 1609 Radio Blvd., 88220. Phone: (505) 887-7563. Fax: (505) 887-7000.E-mail: katk@pccnm.com Web Site:www.katkradio.com Licensee: Stubbs Broadcasting Co. Inc. (acq 3-31-00; $475,000 with co-located FM). Reddy, Begley & McCormick. Format: Adult standards. News: 70 hrs wkly. Target aud: 50 plus; bilingual Hispanics. Spec prog: Gospel 2 hrs wkly. ♦Don Hughes, gen mgr, gen sls mgr; Reginald James, progmg dir; Frank Nymeyer, chief of engrg.

KATK-FM— Sept 15, 1966: 92.1 mhz; 3 kw. 190 ft TL: N32 27 02 W104 12 47. Stereo. Hrs open: 1609 Radio Blvd., 88220. Phone: (505) 887-7563. Fax: (505) 887-7000. Web Site:www.katkradio.com Licensee: Stubbs Broadcasting Co. Inc. Format: Country. News: 70 hrs wkly. Target aud: 18-54.

KCCC(AM)— July 1, 1966: 930 khz; 1 kw-D, 60 w-N. TL: N32 24 20 W104 11 21. Hrs open: 24 930 N. Canal, 88220. Phone: (505) 887-5521. Fax: (505) 885-5481.E-mail: kccc@carlsbadnm.com Licensee: Compass Enterprises Inc. (acq 8-14-95). Population served: 55,000 Format: Oldies. ♦Nick Jenkins, pres, gen sls mgr, prom dir; Michelle McCutcheon, opns mgr, progmg dir; Phil Tozier, news dir; Frank Nymeyer, engrg mgr, chief of engrg.

KCDY(FM)— July 1989: 104.1 mhz; 100 kw. 676 ft TL: N32 34 22 W104 05 32. Hrs open: Prog sep from AM Box 1538, 88220. Secondary address: 1609 Radio Blvd. Phone: (505) 887-7563. Fax: (505) 887-7000. Licensee: KAMQ Inc. Format: Adult contemp. ♦Steve Sparks, progmg dir & progmg mgr.

KPZE-FM— 2000: 106.1 mhz; 39 kw. Ant 558 ft TL: N32 34 22 W104 05 32. Hrs open: 24 317 W. Quay Ave., Artesia, 88210. Phone: (505) 746-2751. Fax: (505) 748-3748.E-mail: info@kpze.com Web Site:www.kpze.com Licensee: Pecos Valley Broadcasting Co. Group owner: Runnels Broadcasting System L.L.C. (acq 2005; $475,000). Population served: 50,000 Cohn and Marks L.L.P. Format: Rgnl/Mexician. News staff: one; News: one hr wkly. ♦Gene Dow, gen mgr.

Chama

KZRM(FM)— Oct 8, 1999: 95.9 mhz; 1 kw. Ant 312 ft TL: N36 53 58 W106 36 07. Hrs open: 24 Box 307, 87520. Phone: (505) 756-1617. Fax: (505) 756-1317.E-mail: info@kzrm.com Web Site:www.kzrmradio.com Licensee: Lance Broadcasting LLC (acq 5-3-2004; $220,000). Format: Classic rock. ♦Scott Flury, gen mgr & gen sls mgr.

Churchrock

KYVA-FM— Aug 7, 1997: 103.7 mhz; 100 kw. 1,299 ft TL: N35 28 03 W108 14 25. Hrs open: 24 Box 420, Gallup, 87305. Phone: (505) 863-6851. Fax: (505) 863-2429.E-mail: mm1@cia-g.com Web Site:www.gallupradio.com Licensee: Millennium Media Inc. (acq 6-98). Natl. Network: ABC, . Format: Classic Hits. News staff: one; News: 12 hrs wkly. Target aud: 25+. 0. Spec prog: American Indian 10 hrs, Sp 4 hrs wkly. ♦George M. Malti, CEO, pub affrs dir; Sammy Chioda, pres; Tom Devlin, sls dir; John McBreen, news dir; Keith Desautels, chief of engrg; Al Zane, progmg.

Clayton

KLMX(AM)— Nov 10, 1949: 1450 khz; 1 kw-U. TL: N36 26 39 W103 11 24. Hrs open: Box 547, Union County Fairgrounds, 88415. Phone: (505) 374-2555. Fax: (505) 374-2557. Licensee: Johnson County Broadcasters Inc. (acq 11-10-78). Population served: 3,500 Format: Country. Spec prog: Sp 2 hrs wkly. ♦Avis Green Tucker, pres; Jim McCollum, VP; Janet Dillon, gen mgr, gen sls mgr; Paula V. Maestas-Ballew, progmg dir & news dir; Henry Walker, chief of engrg.

***KLXM(FM)**—Not on air, target date: unknown: 90.5 mhz; 1 kw horiz. Ant 256 ft TL: N36 26 39 W103 11 24. Hrs open: 116 Hillcrest Dr., Seminole, OK, 74868. Phone: (405) 380-3516.E-mail: info@bpba.us Web Site:bpba.us Licensee: Better Public Broadcasting Association. ♦Dennis Burton, gen mgr.

Cloudcroft

***KHII(FM)**— 2004: 88.9 mhz; 100 w. Ant 1,187 ft TL: N32 59 48 W105 42 38. Stereo. Hrs open: 24
Rebroadcasts KUPR(FM) Alamogordo 80%.
3001 N. Florida Ave., Alamogordo, 88310. Phone: (505) 437-0917. Fax: (505) 434-6060. Fax: (505) 437-9917.E-mail: khii889@yahoo.com Licensee: Southern New Mexico Radio Foundation. Format: All Gospel music formats. ♦Bob Flotte, pres; DeVere Johnson, progmg dir.

KNMB(FM)—Not on air, target date: unknown: 96.7 mhz; 25 kw. 2,880 ft Hrs open: Box 2010, Ruidoso Downs, 88346. Phone: (505) 258-9922. Fax: (505) 258-2363.E-mail: production@mtbradio.com Licensee: MTD Inc. (group owner) Format: Classic Country. ♦Tim Keithley, gen mgr.

Clovis

***KAQF(FM)**— March 1998: 91.1 mhz; 1 kw. 174 ft TL: N34 24 05 W103 12 12. Hrs open: Box 3206, American Family Radio, Tupelo, MS, 38803. Phone: (662) 844-8888. Fax: (662) 842-6791. Licensee: American Family Association. Group owner: American Family Radio Format: Inspirational Christian. ♦Marvin Sanders, gen mgr.

KCLV(AM)— February 1953: 1240 khz; 1 kw-U. TL: N34 22 40 W103 12 17. Hrs open: 24 Prog sep from FM Box 1907, 88101. Secondary address: 2112 Thornton St. 88101. Phone: (505) 763-4401. Fax: (505) 769-2564.E-mail: kclv@allsups.com Licensee: Zia Broadcasting Co. (Acq 7-1-71). Population served: 50,000 Natl. Network: ESPN Radio, . Format: Sports. ♦Lonnie D. Allsup, pres; Gary Jackson, chief of engrg; Lorraine Weingates, traf mgr.

KCLV-FM— Jan 8, 1970: 99.1 mhz; 74.2 kw. Ant 230 ft TL: N34 23 18 W103 11 07. Stereo. Hrs open: 24 Box 1907, 88102-1907. Secondary address: 2112 Thornton St. 88101. Phone: (505) 763-4401. Fax: (505) 769-2564.E-mail: kclv@allsups.com Licensee: Zia Broadcasting Co. (acq 11-12-81). Population served: 70,000 Natl. Network: ABC, . Format: Country. Target aud: 30 plus. ♦Rcik Keefer, gen sls mgr; Rick Keefer, gen mgr & progmg dir.

***KCOI(FM)**—Not on air, target date: unknown: 88.1 mhz; 1.1 kw. Ant 174 ft TL: N34 24 05 W103 12 12. Hrs open: Drawer 2440, Tupelo, MS, 38803. Phone: (662) 844-8888. Fax: (662) 842-6791. Licensee: Salt & Light Communications Inc. ♦Larry Durham, pres.

***KELU(FM)**— 2006: 90.3 mhz; 14 kw. Ant 397 ft TL: N34 26 21 W103 12 22. Hrs open:
Rebroadcasts KLVR(FM) Middletown, CA 100%.
2351 Sunset Blvd., Suite 170-218, Rocklin, CA, 95765. Phone: (916) 251-1600. Fax: (916) 251-1650. Web Site:www.klove.com Licensee: Educational Media Foundation. (acq 9-22-2005; $40,000 for CP). Natl. Network: K-Love, . Format: Contemp Christian. ♦Mike Novak, pres.

KICA(AM)— 1933: 980 khz; 50 kw-D, 188 w-N, DA-D. TL: N34 20 55 W102 57 18. Hrs open: 24 1000 Sycamore St., 88101. Phone: (505) 762-6200. Fax: (505) 762-8800.E-mail: info@kkyckica@plateautel.net Web Site:www.kkyckica@plateautel.net Licensee: Tallgrass Broadcasting LLC. (group owner; (acq 4-2-2007; grpsl). Population served: 100,000 Natl. Network: USA, . Shaw Pittman. Format: Talk. Target aud: 30 plus. Spec prog: Farm 5 hrs, high school sports 4 hrs wkly. ♦Dana Taylor, opns dir, progmg dir & news dir.

KKYC(FM)— 1993: 102.3 mhz; 25 kw horiz. Ant 177 ft TL: N34 24 31 W103 11 15. Hrs open: 24 1000 Sycamore St., 88101. Phone: (505) 762-6200. Fax: (505) 762-8800.E-mail: clovis@tallgrassnation.com Web Site:www.1023myfm.com Licensee: Tallgrass Broadcasting LLC. (acq 4-2-2007; grpsl). Population served: 60,000 Format: Top-40. News staff: one; News: 2 hrs wkly. Target aud: 25-54. ♦Anne Bradshaw, mktg dir; Mark "Mojo" Wilson, opns VP & progmg dir.

KRMQ-FM— 2003: 101.5 mhz; 100 kw. Ant 453 ft TL: N34 15 08 W103 14 21. Hrs open: 42437 U.S. 70, Portales, 88130. Phone: (505) 359-1759. Fax: (505) 359-0724. Web Site:q1015.com Licensee: Rooney Moon Broadcasting Inc. (group owner). (acq 1-13-2006; $595,000). Format: Oldies. ♦Steve Rooney, pres & gen mgr.

KSMX-FM— November 1982: 107.5 mhz; 100 kw. 550 ft TL: N34 11 34 W103 16 44. Stereo. Hrs open: 208 E. Grand Ave., 88101. Secondary address: 42437 U.S. 70, Portales 88130. Phone: (505) 763-4649. Fax: (505) 359-0724.E-mail: bettermix@bettermix.com Web Site:www.bettermix.com Licensee: Rooney Moon Broadcasting Inc. (group owner; (acq 7-15-2002; grpsl). Format: Hot adult contemp. ♦Duffy Moon, opns dir, mktg VP; Steve Rooney, pres, gen mgr & progmg dir; Kevin Robbins, news dir; Jeff Burmeister, chief of engrg; Lisa Schmidt, traf mgr.

KTQM-FM— Mar 1, 1963: 99.9 mhz; 100 kw. 360 ft TL: N34 21 48 W103 13 05. Stereo. Hrs open: 24 Box 869, 88102. Secondary address: 710 Curry Rd. K 88101. Phone: (505) 762-4411. Fax: (505) 769-0197.E-mail: ktqm@plateautel.net Web Site:www.ktqm.com Licensee: Curry County Broadcasting, Inc. 1980 Population served: 125,000 Natl. Network: ABC, . Format: Adult contemp. News: 3 hrs wkly. Target aud: 25-54; young affluent. ♦Hewel Jones, pres; Grant McGee, opns dir, progmg dir; Bob Coker, gen sls mgr; Marty Berry, traf mgr.

KWKA(AM)— 1971: 680 khz; 500 w-U, DA-1. TL: N34 21 48 W103 13 05. Hrs open: 24 Box 869, 88102. Secondary address: 710 Curry Rd. K 88101. Phone: (505) 762-4411. Fax: (505) 769-0197.E-mail: ktqm@plateautel.net Licensee: Curry County Broadcasting Inc. (acq 10-24-1980; $650,000; with co-located FM; 11-10-80). Population served: 125,000 Natl. Network: CNN Radio, . Rgnl rep: Rgnl Reps. Fletcher, Heald & Hildreth. Format: News/Talk. News: 3 hrs wkly. Target aud: 35 - 64. Spec prog: Sean Hannity Talk Show. ♦Hewel Jones, pres; Bob Coker, VP; Grant McGee, gen mgr, opns mgr; Marty Berry, natl sls mgr & traf mgr.

Corrales

KKNS(AM)— July 15, 1985: 1310 khz; 5000 kw-D, 500 w-N, DA-N. TL: N35 12 00 W106 35 59. Stereo. Hrs open: 24
95.9 FM Simulcast.
1606 Central Ave., Suite104, Albuquerque, 87106. Phone: (505) 255-5015. Fax: (505) 262-4792.E-mail: vcamino@elcaminocomm.com Web Site:www.elcaminocomm.com Licensee: El Camino Communications LLC Group owner: Simmons Media Group (acq 1-22-2007; $860,000). Format: Mexican rgnl. Target aud: H-18-49. ♦Victor Camino, pres & gen mgr.

KSYU(FM)— Apr 27, 1996: 95.1 mhz; 3 kw. Ant -531 ft TL: N35 14 42 W106 36 18. Hrs open: 24 5411 Jefferson St. N.E., Suite 100, Albuquerque, 87109. Phone: (505) 830-6400. Fax: (505) 830-6543. Web Site:www.951abq.com Licensee: Clear Channel Broadcasting Licenses Inc. Group owner: Clear Channel Communications Inc. (acq 9-28-99). Format: Rhythmic adult contemp. ♦Chuck Hammond, gen mgr.

Deming

KDEM(FM)— Apr 15, 1977: 94.3 mhz; 3 kw. 195 ft TL: N32 15 05 W107 45 28. Stereo. Hrs open: Prog sep from AM Box 1700, 1700 S. Gold, 88031. Phone: (575) 546-9011. Fax: (575) 546-9342.E-mail: radio@demingradio.com Web Site:www.demingradio.com Population served: 28,000 Natl. Network: Westwood One, . Wire Svc: AP Format: Adult contemp. News staff: one; News: 5 hrs wkly. Target aud: 18-54.

KOTS(AM)— Mar 10, 1954: 1230 khz; 1 kw-U. TL: N32 15 05 W107 45 28. Hrs open: 24 Box 470, 1700 S. Gold, 88031. Phone: (575) 546-9011. Fax: (575) 546-9342.E-mail: radio@demingradio.com Web Site:www.demingradio.com Licensee: Luna County Broadcasting Co. (acq 4-01-90). Population served: 28,000 Natl. Network: Westwood One, . Wire Svc: AP Format: Country. News staff: one; News: 13 hrs wkly. Target aud: General. Spec prog: Farm 5 hrs, Sp 8 hrs wkly. ♦Candie G. Sweetser, stn mgr.

***KZPI(FM)**— Mar 25, 1996: 91.7 mhz; 600 w. 62 ft TL: N32 15 31 W107 46 45. Hrs open: 24 Box 252, Paulino Bernal Evangelism, McAllen, TX, 78505. Phone: (956) 686-6382. Fax: (956) 686-2999. Licensee: Paulino Bernal Evangelism. (acq 2-13-98; $45,000). Format: Christian, relg, Sp. Target aud: General. ♦Paulino Bernal, pres.

Des Moines

***KENU(FM)**—Not on air, target date: unknown: 88.5 mhz; 3 kw. Ant 1,998 ft TL: N36 42 20 W103 52 36. Hrs open: Eastern New Mexico University, 52 Broadcast Center, Portales, 88130-9989. Phone: (575) 562-2112. Fax: (575) 562-2590.E-mail: kenwfm@enmu.edu Web Site:www.kenw.org Licensee: Eastern New Mexico University. ♦Duane W. Ryan, gen mgr.

KHOD(FM)— July 2007: Stn currently dark. 105.3 mhz; 82 kw. Ant 2,053 ft TL: N36 42 20 W103 52 36. Stereo. Hrs open: 520 Monticello Dr., Las Vegas, NV, 89107-3616. Phone: (702) 878-0773. Licensee: Hodson Broadcasting. ♦Richard Hodson, CEO, chief of engrg, sls & progmg.

Dexter

KALN(FM)— 2009: 96.1 mhz; 50 kw. Ant 453 ft TL: N33 23 57 W104 22 30. Hrs open: 500 N. Main St., Suite 904, Roswell, 88201. Phone: (575) 623-3914. Licensee: Hispanic Target Media Inc. ◆Francisco San Millan, pres.

Dulce

*KCIE(FM)— Dec 3, 1990: 90.5 mhz; 100 kw. 1,535 ft TL: N36 59 00 W106 58 12. Hrs open: 24 Box 603, A.I.E. Bldg., Narrow Gauge Rd., 87528. Phone: (575) 759-3681. Fax: (575) 759-9140.E-mail: kcie@zianet.com Licensee: Jicarilla Apache Tribe. Population served: 3,000 Format: Div. News staff: one; News: 2 hrs wkly. Target aud: General. ◆Lisa Vigil-Gomez, stn mgr; Romaine Wood, progmg dir; Darnell Muniz, mus dir; Jim Burt, chief of engrg.

Encino

KXNM(FM)—Not on air, target date: unknown: 88.7 mhz; 40 kw. Ant 341 ft TL: N34 41 41 W105 35 24. Hrs open: Torrance County Project Office, 809 S. First St., Suite A, Moriarty, 87035. Phone: (505) 832-0332. Fax: (505) 832-0601. Web Site:www.tcponm.com Licensee: Torrance County. Format: Educ. ◆Joy Ansley, gen mgr.

Espanola

KDCE(AM)— 1963: 950 khz; 4.2 kw-D, 90 w-N. TL: N36 00 08 W106 03 59. Hrs open: 403 W. Pueblo Dr., 87532. Phone: (505) 753-2201. Fax: (505) 753-8685.E-mail: kdce@zianet.com Web Site:www.kdce.net Licensee: Richard L. Garcia Broadcasting Inc. (acq 11-29-82; $625,000; 11-8-82). Population served: 200,000 Format: Sp. ◆Casey Gallegos, gen mgr; Richard Garcia, pres & gen sls mgr; Ray Casias, progmg dir; Ken Bass, chief of engrg; Ester Marquez, traf mgr.

*KRAR(FM)— Apr 1, 2008: 91.9 mhz; 5.9 kw. Ant 530 ft TL: N36 09 08 W106 02 21. Hrs open:
Rebroadcasts KUNM(FM) Albuquerque 100%.
Room 328 KUNM Onate Hall, University of New Mexico, Albuquerque, 87131. Phone: (505) 277-8009. Fax: (505) 277-8004.E-mail: kunm@kunm.org Web Site:www.kunm.org Licensee: Regents of the University of New Mexico (acq 9-25-2007; $15,000 for CP). Format: Div, news/talk. ◆Richard Towne, gen mgr.

KYBR(FM)— July 6, 1981: 92.9 mhz; 3 kw. Ant -249 ft TL: N36 00 08 W106 03 59. (CP: 50 kw, and 203 ft.). Hrs open: 403 W. Pueblo Dr., 87532. Phone: (505) 753-2201. Fax: (505) 753-8685.E-mail: kdce@zianet.com Web Site:www.kdce.net Licensee: Rio Chama Broadcasting Co. (acq 1995; $50,000). Format: Rgnl Mexican. ◆Efrem Galindo, progmg dir.

Eunice

KEJL(FM)— 1996: 100.9 mhz; 50 kw. Ant 295 ft TL: N32 28 10 W103 09 36. Stereo. Hrs open: 24 Box 5967, Hobbs, 88241. Secondary address: 1423 W. Bender, Hobbs 88241. Phone: (505) 393-6000. Fax: (505) 397-6088.E-mail: larryphilpot@basinbreadband.com Licensee: FiveStar Enterprises L.C. (acq 1999; $20,000). Population served: 47,000 Natl. Network: Jones Radio Networks, . Format: Classic rock. News staff: one. Target aud: 18-49. ◆Larry Philpot, gen mgr; Al Lobeck, gen sls mgr.

Farmington

KDAG(FM)— Sept 1, 1969: 96.9 mhz; 100 kw. Ant 1,010 ft TL: N36 39 49 W108 12 55. Stereo. Hrs open: 24 200 E. Broadway, 87401. Phone: (505) 325-1716. Fax: (505) 325-6797. Web Site:www.bigdog969.com Licensee: Capstar TX L.P. Group owner: Clear Channel Communications Inc. (acq 8-30-2000; grpsl). Population served: 250,000 Fisher, Wayland, Cooper, Leader & Zaragoza. Format: Classic rock. Target aud: 18-49. ◆Bill Kruger, gen mgr.

KENN(AM)— November 1951: 1390 khz; 5 kw-D, 1.3 kw-N, DA-N. TL: N36 42 27 W108 08 50. Hrs open: 212 W. Apache, 87401. Phone: (505) 325-3541. Fax: (505) 327-5796. Licensee: Winton Road Broadcasting Co. LLC (group owner; (acq 5-3-2001; grpsl). Population served: 38,000 Pepper & Corazzini. Format: News/talk, sports. Target aud: 25-54; upper middle class. ◆Dan Buctha, gen mgr; Randy Klock, gen sls mgr.

KISZ-FM—See Cortez, CO

KNDN(AM)— Aug 1, 1957: 960 khz; 5 kw-D, 163 w-N. TL: N36 43 48 W108 13 47. Hrs open: 6 AM-10 PM 1515 W. Main, 87401. Phone: (505) 325-1996. Fax: (505) 327-2019.E-mail: productionroom @basinbroadcasting.com Licensee: Basin Broadcasting Co. Format: Navajo Indian. Target aud: General; Navajo Indian reservation; all Navajo language. ◆Kerwin Gober, gen mgr & opns mgr; George Werito, progmg dir, news dir; Jim Burt, chief of engrg.

*KNMI(FM)— Mar 18, 1980: 88.9 mhz; 27 kw vert. Ant 663 ft TL: N36 40 16 W108 13 54. Stereo. Hrs open: 24 PO Box 1230, 87499. Secondary address: 2103 W. Main St. 87401. Phone: (505) 327-4357. Fax: (505) 325-9035.E-mail: email@verticalradio.org Web Site:www.verticalradio.org Licensee: Navajo Missions Inc. Population served: 120,000 Natl. Network: USA, . Format: Christian, talk, CHR hits. News: 9 hrs wkly. Target aud: 24-40; general. ◆Darren Nez, gen mgr.

KPCL(FM)— Dec 14, 1988: 95.7 mhz; 100 kw. 394 ft TL: N36 41 44 W108 13 11. Stereo. Hrs open: 24 Box 232, 87499. Secondary address: 1105 W. Apache 87401. Phone: (505) 327-7202. Fax: (505) 327-2163.E-mail: kpcl@kpcl.org Web Site:www.kpcl.org Licensee: Voice Ministries of Farmington Inc. Population served: 300,000 Natl. Network: Salem Radio Network, . Format: Christian contemp. News staff: one; News: 3 hrs wkly. Target aud: General; relg audience. Spec prog: Class one hr, Navajo 7 hrs wkly. ◆Fareed W. Ayoub, pres.

KRWN(FM)— 1974: 92.9 mhz; 30 kw. 430 ft TL: N36 41 45 W108 13 23. (CP: 62 kw, ant 394 ft.). Stereo. Hrs open: 24 Prog sep from AM 212 W. Apache, 87401. Phone: (505) 327-4449. Fax: (505) 327-5796. Web Site:www.krwn.com Licensee: Winton Road Broadcasting Co. LLC. Format: Classic rock. Target aud: 18-49. ◆Dan Buchta, gen mgr; Randy Klock, gen sls mgr.

KRZE(AM)— July 1, 1958: 1280 khz; 5 kw-D. TL: N36 49 03 W108 05 47. Hrs open: 24 Radio Fiesta, 204 E. Broadway, 87401. Phone: (505) 327-5287. Fax: (505) 326-1893. Licensee: J. Thomas Development of New Mexico Inc. (acq 12-18-91; with co-located FM). Population served: 100,000 Shaw Pittman. Format: Sp var. ◆Jeff Thomas, pres; Rogelio Esparva, gen mgr.

*KSJE(FM)— November 1990: 90.9 mhz; 15 kw. 390 ft TL: N36 41 52 W108 13 14. Stereo. Hrs open: 24 4601 College Blvd., 87402. Phone: (505) 566-3517. Fax: (505) 566-3385.E-mail: michlins@sanjuancollege.edu Web Site:www.ksje.org Licensee: San Juan College. Population served: 135,000 Natl. Network: PRI, . Format: Classical/jazz/news. News staff: one; News: 15 hrs wkly. Target aud: 25-65. Spec prog: Jazz 15 hrs, folk 15 hrs wkly. ◆Carol Spenser, pres; Scott Michlin, gen mgr; Constance Gotsch, progmg dir; Jim Burt, chief of engrg.

KTRA-FM— Feb 19, 1987: 102.1 mhz; 100 kw. Ant 1,033 ft TL: N36 48 52 W107 53 32. Stereo. Hrs open: 24 200 E. Broadway, 87401. Phone: (505) 325-1716. Fax: (505) 325-6797. Web Site:www.102ktra.com Licensee: Clear Channel Radio Licenses Inc. Group owner: Clear Channel Communications Inc. (acq 8-30-2000; grpsl). Population served: 250,000 Natl. Network: ABC, . Format: Classic country. Target aud: 25-54. ◆Dave Schaefer, progmg dir.

KUCU(AM)—Not on air, target date: unknown: 1060 khz; 10 kw-D, 250 w-N, DA-2. TL: N36 43 55 W108 06 38. Hrs open: 324 N. Vine #1, 87401. Phone: (505) 324-6434 . Licensee: Western Broadcasters Inc. ◆E. Boyd Whitney, pres & gen mgr.

*KUUT(FM)— 2008: 89.7 mhz; 1.35 kw vert. Ant 663 ft TL: N36 40 16 W108 13 54. Hrs open:
Rebroadcasts KUTE(FM) Ignacio, CO 100%.
Box 737, Ignacio, CO, 81137-0737. Phone: (970) 563-0255. Fax: (970) 563-0399.E-mail: info@ksut.org Web Site:www.ksut.org Licensee: KUTE Inc. Format: Triple A, americana. ◆Eddie Box Jr., pres; Beth Warren, gen mgr.

KWYK-FM—See Aztec

Flora Vista

*KUSW(FM)— 2008: 88.1 mhz; 4.1 kw vert. Ant 663 ft TL: N36 40 16 W108 13 54. Hrs open:
Rebroadcasts KUTE(FM) Ignacio, CO 100%.
Box 737, Ignacio, CO, 81137-0737. Phone: (970) 563-0255. Fax: (970) 563-0399.E-mail: info@ksut.org Web Site:www.ksut.org Licensee: KUTE Inc. (acq 6-7-2006). Format: Triple A, Americana. ◆Eddie Box Jr., pres; Beth Warren, gen mgr.

Fruitland

*KTGW(FM)— 91.7 mhz; 20 kw. 308 ft TL: N36 41 44 W108 13 11. Hrs open: 24 Attn: Fareed W. Ayoub, Box 232, Farmington, 87499. Secondary address: 1103 W. Apache St., Farmington 87401. Phone: (505) 327-7202. Fax: (505) 327-2163.E-mail: kpcl@kpcl.org Web Site:www.kpcl.org Licensee: Native American Christian Voice Inc. Southmayd & Miller. Format: Christian-talk. ◆Fareed Ayoub, pres; Annette Ayoub, exec VP.

Gallup

KFMQ(FM)— 1996: 106.1 mhz; 26 kw. 185 ft TL: N35 32 27 W108 44 32. Hrs open: 1632 S. 2nd St., 87301. Phone: (505) 863-9391. Fax: (505) 863-9393.E-mail: maryannarmijo@clearchannel.com Licensee: Clear Channel Broadcasting Licenses Inc. (Group owner: Clear Channel Communications Inc. (acq 4-17-97). Format: Rock. ◆Mary Ann Armijo, gen mgr, gen sls mgr; Ted Foster, opns mgr; Blas Saucedo, progmg dir.

KGAK(AM)— Feb 9, 1945: 1330 khz; 5 kw-D, 1 kw-N, DA-N. TL: N35 32 34 W108 44 11. Hrs open: 5am-10pm 401 E. Coal Ave., 87301. Phone: (505) 863-4444. Fax: (505) 722-7381.E-mail: kgak@cia-g.com Licensee: KRJG Inc. (acq 6-30-98; $102,600). Population served: 13,779 Natl. Network: CBS, . Format: Navajo, Indian. Target aud: 30-55. ◆Jim Gober, CEO, gen mgr; Jim Burt, gen sls mgr, chief of engrg; Leaudro Jodie, progmg dir.

*KGGA(FM)— 2008: 88.1 mhz; 1 kw. Ant 16 ft TL: N35 32 27 W108 44 36. Hrs open:
Rebroadcasts KLRD(FM) Yucaipa, CA 100%.
2351 Sunset Blvd., Suite 170-218, Rocklin, CA, 95765. Phone: (916) 251-1600. Fax: (916) 251-1650. Web Site:www.air1.com Licensee: Educational Media Foundation. (acq 7-23-2007; grpsl). Natl. Network: Air 1, . Format: Christian. ◆Mike Novak, pres.

*KGLP(FM)— Sept 1, 1992: 91.7 mhz; 160 w. Ant 1,145 ft TL: N35 36 13 W108 40 45. Stereo. Hrs open: 24
Rebroadcasts KSUT(FM) Ignacio, CO 50%.
Univ. of New Mexico, 200 College Rd., 87301. Phone: (505) 863-7626. Fax: (505) 863-7532. Fax: (505) 863-7633.E-mail: kglp@kglp.org Web Site:www.kglp.org Licensee: Gallup Public Radio. Population served: 50,000 Natl. Network: NPR, . Format: News, div. News: 40 hrs wkly. Target aud: General; adult professional, academic, business community. ◆David Pracy, opns mgr, progmg dir; Tom Funk, mus dir.

KGLX(FM)— Mar 1, 1989: 99.1 mhz; 51 kw. 1,249 ft TL: N35 36 18 W108 41 11. Stereo. Hrs open: 24 1632 S. 2nd St., 87301. Phone: (505) 863-9391. Fax: (505) 863-9393.E-mail: maryannarmijo @clearchannel.com Licensee: Clear Channel Broadcasting Licenses Inc. Group owner: Clear Channel Communications Inc. (acq 8-18-00; grpsl). Population served: 80,000 Bechtel & Cole. Format: Country. News staff: 2; News: 14 hrs wkly. Target aud: 25-54. Spec prog: American Indian 3 hrs wkly. ◆Mary Ann Armijo, gen mgr, adv dir; Sylvester Paquin, sls dir; Ted Foster, opns mgr & progmg dir; Pat Jarvison, sports cmtr.

KKOR(FM)— Oct 6, 1974: 94.5 mhz; 100 kw. 1,388 ft TL: N35 28 03 W108 14 25. Stereo. Hrs open: 24 Prog sep from AM Box 420, 87305. Secondary address: 300 West Aztec, Suite 200 87301. Phone: (505) 863-5567. Fax: (505) 863-2429.E-mail: mm1@cia-g.com Web Site:www.gallupradio.com Population served: 180,000 Natl. Network: ABC, . Format: Hot Adult contemp. News staff: one. Target aud: 25-44; young families with buying power. ◆George Malti, CEO; Sammy Chioda, pres; Tom Devlin, gen sls mgr; Keith Desantels, chief of engrg.

*KLLU(FM)— 2008: 88.9 mhz; 600 w. Ant 1,164 ft TL: N35 36 15 W108 41 10. Hrs open:
Rebroadcasts KLVR(FM) Middletown, CA 100%.
2351 Sunset Blvd., Suite 170-218, Rocklin, CA, 95765. Phone: (916) 251-1600. Fax: (916) 251-1650. Web Site:www.klove.com Licensee: Educational Media Foundation. Natl. Network: K-Love, . Format: Contemp Christian. ◆Mike Novak, pres.

*KNIZ(FM)—Not on air, target date: unknown: 89.9 mhz; 200 w. Ant 16 ft TL: N35 32 26.9 W108 44 35.6. Hrs open: Box 1434, Albuquerque, 87103-1434. Phone: (505) 768-4072. Licensee: Available Media Inc. ◆Robert Aly, pres.

KQLP(FM)—Not on air, target date: unknown: 101.5 mhz; 47.36 kw. Ant 1,325 ft TL: N35 36 21.9 W108 41 25.7. Hrs open: 2801 Via Fortuna Dr., Suite 675, Austin, TX, 78746. Phone: (512) 329-5843. Fax: (512) 329-5847. Web Site:www.matineemedia.com Licensee: Ace Radio Corp. ◆Stephen Hackerman, pres.

KXXI(FM)— Aug 15, 1975: 93.7 mhz; 62 kw. 161 ft TL: N35 36 22 W108 41 26. Stereo. Hrs open: 24 Box 420, 87301. Secondary address: 300 W. Aztec, Suite 200 87301. Phone: (505) 863-6851. Fax: (505) 863-2429.E-mail: mm1@cia-g.com Web Site:www.gallupradio.com Licensee: Millennium Media Inc. (acq 6-7-94). Population served: 200,000 Natl. Network: ABC, . Fletcher, Heald & Hildreth. Format: Classic rock. Target aud: 25-44. ♦George Malti, CEO; Sammy Chioda, pres, stn mgr; Tom Devlin, sls dir; John McBreen, news dir; Keith Desautels, chief of engrg.

KYVA(AM)— July 15, 1959: 1230 khz; 1 kw-U. TL: N35 32 02 W108 42 22. Stereo. Hrs open: 24 Box 420, 87305. Phone: (505) 863-6851. Fax: (505) 863-2429.E-mail: mm1@cia-g.com Web Site:www.gallupradio.com Licensee: Millennium Media Inc. (acq 3-77). Population served: 180,000 Natl. Network: ABC, . Format: Country. News staff: one; News: 12 hrs wkly. Target aud: 35-54; mature, with buying power. ♦George Malti, pres; Tom Devlin, sls dir; Brian Smith, prom dir, progmg dir; John McBreen, news dir; Keith DeSautels, chief of engrg.

Grants

KDSK(FM)— June 1, 1997: 92.7 mhz; 26 kw. Ant 171 ft TL: N35 07 09 W107 54 08. (CP: 45 kw, ant 1,351 ft. TL: N35 10 57.1 W107 36 12.7). Stereo. Hrs open: 24 733 Roosevelt, 87020. Phone: (505) 285-5598. Fax: (505) 285-5575. Licensee: KD Radio Inc. (acq 11-16-00; with KMIN(AM) Grants). Population served: 25,000 Format: Oldies. Target aud: 30-50; earning boom. ♦Derek Underhill, pres; Debbie Anderson, natl sls mgr; Tom Anderson, mktg VP.

***KIDS(FM)**—Not on air, target date: unknown: 88.1 mhz; 100 w. Ant 162 ft TL: N35 07 09 W107 54 02. Hrs open: 2020 Coal Ave. S.E., Albuquerque, 87106. Phone: (505) 242-7163.E-mail: brasher@aps.edu Web Site:www.kanw.com Licensee: Board of Education of the City of Albuquerque, NM. Population served: 30,000 ♦Michael Brasher, gen mgr.

***KLGQ(FM)**— 2006: 90.3 mhz; 1 kw. Ant 2,713 ft TL: N35 15 08 W107 35 45. Hrs open:
Rebroadcasts KLVR(FM) Santa Rosa, CA 100%.
2351 Sunset Blvd., Suite 170-218, Rocklin, CA, 95765. Phone: (916) 251-1600. Fax: (916) 251-1650. Web Site:www.klove.com Licensee: Educational Media Foundation. Natl. Network: K-Love, . Format: Contemp Christian. ♦Richard Jenkins, pres; Mike Novak, VP, progmg dir; Keith Whipple, dev dir; David Pierce, progmg mgr; Ed Lenane, news dir; Sam Wallington, engrg dir; Karen Johnson, news rptr.

KMIN(AM)— Sept 1, 1956: 980 khz; 1 kw-D, 250 kw-N. TL: N35 09 05 W107 52 31. Hrs open: 24 733 Roosevelt, 87020. Phone: (505) 285-5598. Fax: (505) 285-5575.E-mail: info@kmin980.com Web Site:www.kmin980.com Licensee: KD Radio Inc. (acq 1-2-01; $145,000 with KDSK(FM) Grants). Population served: 25,000 Format: Country. Target aud: 25-54; active, working adults. ♦Derek Underhill, pres, opns mgr; Debbie Anderson, natl sls mgr; Tom Anderson Jr., mktg VP.

Hatch

KVLC(FM)— Apr 1, 1994: 101.1 mhz; 100 kw. 1,033 ft TL: N32 41 35 W107 04 06. Stereo. Hrs open: 24 101 Perkins Dr., Las Cruces, 88005. Phone: (505) 527-1111. Fax: (505) 527-1100.E-mail: contact@101gold.com Web Site:www.101gold.com Licensee: Bravo Mic Communications LLC. (acq 1-7-2005; $1.3 million). Population served: 1,100,000 Format: Good time oldies. News staff: one; News: 3 hrs wkly. Target aud: 25-54. Spec prog: Bi-lingual Sp/English 6 hrs wkly. ♦Michael Smith, gen mgr; Allen Moore, opns mgr; K.C. Counts, progmg dir.

Hobbs

KHOB(AM)— Aug 7, 1954: 1390 khz; 5 kw-D, 500 w-N, DA-N. TL: N32 44 21 W103 10 48. Hrs open: 24 3301, N. Bensing Rd., 88240. Phone: (505) 392-9292. Fax: (505) 392-7579.E-mail: khobam@aol.com Licensee: American Asset Management Inc. (acq 2-28-90; $255,000; 3-19-90). Population served: 35,000 Format: Oldies. News staff: 2; News: 48 hrs wkly. Target aud: General; adult. ♦Harmon Hann, gen mgr; Pat Hann, progmg dir.

KIXN(FM)— Feb 1, 1996: 102.9 mhz; 100 kw. Ant 518 ft TL: N32 43 26 W103 34 34. Stereo. Hrs open: 24 619 N.Turner St., 88240. Phone: (505) 397-4969. Fax: (505) 393-4310.E-mail: paul@1radiosquare.com Web Site:www.1radiosquare.com Licensee: Noalmark Broadcasting Corp. (group owner; acq 1995; $53,000 for CP). Population served: 100,000 Format: Country. News staff: one; News: 5 hrs wkly. Target aud: Adults 18-49. ♦William C. Nolan, CEO & pres; Edwin Alderson, exec VP; Paul J. Starr, VP, gen mgr; Harry Harlan, sls dir, adv dir; Dawn Morgan, news dir; Ken Bass, engrg dir; Cathy Cox, traf mgr.

***KLHK(FM)**—Not on air, target date: unknown: 90.9 mhz; 11.8 kw vert. Ant 400 ft TL: N32 42 48 W103 05 28. Hrs open:
Rebroadcasts KLVR(FM) Middletown, CA 100%.
2351 Sunset Blvd., Suite 170-218, Rocklin, CA, 95765. Phone: (916) 251-1600. Fax: (916) 251-1650. Web Site:www.klove.com Licensee: Educational Media Foundation. (acq 7-23-2007; grpsl). Natl. Network: K-Love, . Format: Contemp Christian. ♦Mike Novak, pres.

KLMA(FM)— November 1993: 96.5 mhz; 100 kw. Ant 354 ft TL: N32 28 10 W103 09 36. Hrs open: 24 Box 457, 108 S. Willow, 88240. Phone: (575) 391-9650. Fax: (575) 397-9373. Web Site:www.klmaradio.com Licensee: Ojeda Broadcasting Inc. Group owner: Ojeda Broadcasting Inc. Mullin, Rhyne, Emmons & Topel. Format: Spanish. Target aud: Hispanic. ♦Hermilo Ojeda, CEO, gen mgr, gen sls mgr, mktg mgr; Pearl Ojeda, pres; Letiicia Ojeda, prom mgr.

***KOBH(FM)**—Not on air, target date: unknown: 91.7 mhz; 250 w. Ant 157 ft TL: N32 42 48 W103 05 28. Hrs open: Drawer 2440, Tupelo, MS, 38803. Phone: (662) 844-8888. Web Site:www.afr.net Licensee: American Family Association. (acq 8-27-2007). Natl. Network: American Family Radio, . ♦Donald E. Wildmon, chmn.

KPER(FM)— August 1965: 95.7 mhz; 25 kw. 328 ft TL: N32 43 27 W103 09 04. Stereo. Hrs open: 24 Box 5967, 88241-5967. Secondary address: 1423 W. Bender St. 88240. Phone: (505) 393-1551. Fax: (505) 397-6088. Web Site:www.hobbsradio.com Licensee: Noalmark Broadcasting Corp. (group owner; acq 1-99). Population served: 140,000 Format: Country. News staff: one. Target aud: 25-54. ♦Al Lobeck, gen mgr, gen sls mgr; Tyler Robinson, news dir; Ken Fine, chief of engrg.

KYKK(AM)— July 17, 1971: 1110 khz; 5 kw-D. TL: N32 48 59 W103 13 56. Hrs open: 6 AM-sunset Box 5967, 88241. Secondary address: 1423 W. Bender Blvd. 88240. Phone: (505) 393-1551. Fax: (505) 397-6088. Web Site:www.hobbsradio.com Licensee: Noalmark Broadcasting Corp. (group owner; acq 8-8-77). Population served: 140,000 Natl. Network: Premiere Radio Networks, Sporting News Radio Network, ABC, . Format: News/talk, sports. News staff: one; News: 10 hrs wkly. Target aud: 25-54; men & women. ♦William Nolan, pres; Al Lobeck, gen mgr, gen sls mgr; Tyler Robinson, news dir; Ken Fine, chief of engrg.

KZOR(FM)—Listing follows KYKK(AM).

Hurley

***KOOT(FM)**— 2009: 88.1 mhz; 2 kw vert. Ant 184 ft TL: N32 49 29 W108 14 54. Hrs open: 213 N. Bullard St., Silver City, 88061. Phone: (505) 534-0130.E-mail: cats-communityac@qwest.net Web Site:www.catsilver.org Licensee: Community Access Television of Silver. ♦James S. Bumpous, gen mgr.

KSIL(FM)— 2002: 105.5 mhz; 23 kw. Ant 1,063 ft TL: N32 50 40 W108 14 19. Stereo. Hrs open: 24 306 W. Broadway, Silver City, 88061. Phone: (505) 534-1055. Fax: (505) 534-1400.E-mail: info@ksilradio.com Web Site:www.ksilradio.com Licensee: James S. Bumpous dba Yellow Dog Radio. Population served: 25,000 Format: Div. News: 5 hrs wkly. Target aud: 25-54. ♦Steve Bumpous, gen mgr & progmg dir.

Jal

KPZA-FM— Nov 1, 1998: 103.7 mhz; 100 kw. Ant 371 ft TL: N32 25 53 W103 09 08. Hrs open: 24 KIXN(FM)KPZA-(FM)-KYKK(AM)-KZOR(FM), 619 N. Turner St., Hobbs, 88240. Phone: (505) 397-4969. Fax: (505) 393-4310.E-mail: paul@1radiosquare.com Web Site:www.1radiosquare.com Licensee: Noalmark Broadcasting Corp. (group owner; (acq 5-29-98; $10,000 for CP). Population served: 100,000 Format: Sp. News staff: one; News: 5 hrs wkly. Target aud: Hispanic. ♦William C. Nolan, CEO & pres; Edwin Alderson, sr VP; Paul J. Starr, gen mgr, opns VP; Tony Guerrero, stn mgr, news rptr; Harry Harlan, sls dir, adv dir; Cathy Cox, traf mgr.

Kirtland

KAZX(FM)— 1999: 102.9 mhz; 100 kw. Ant 1,007 ft TL: N36 48 52 W107 53 32. Hrs open: 200 E. Broadway, Farmington, 87401. Phone: (505) 325-1716. Fax: (505) 325-6797. Web Site:www.star1029.com Licensee: Capstar TX L.P. Group owner: Clear Channel Communications Inc. (acq 12-19-00; $1.26 million). Format: CHR. ♦Bill Kruger, gen mgr.

La Luz

KRSY-FM—Licensed to La Luz. See Alamogordo

Las Cruces

KGRT-FM— Sept 8, 1966: 103.9 mhz; 6 kw. 151 ft TL: N32 18 33 W106 49 24. Stereo. Hrs open: 24 Box 968, 88004. Secondary address: 1355 E. California St. 88001. Phone: (575) 525-9298. Fax: (575) 525-9419.E-mail: radiolc@kgrt.com Web Site:www.kgrt.com Licensee: Sunrise Broadcasting Inc. (acq 12-30-88; with co-located AM;12-19-88). Population served: 174,100 Natl. Network: CNN Radio, . Format: Country. News staff: 2. Target aud: 25-54; adults. ♦Allen Lumeyer, VP, gen mgr; Veronica Vaillancourt-Test, gen mgr; Ernesto Garcia, opns mgr, progmg dir; Tamara Blaeser, natl sls mgr, rgnl sls mgr; Sheila Kirsch, mus dir.

KHQT(FM)— Dec 12, 1974: 103.1 mhz; 1 kw. Ant 551 ft TL: N32 24 18 W106 45 41. Stereo. Hrs open: 24 Box 968, 88004. Secondary address: 1355 E. California 88001. Phone: (575) 525-9298. Fax: (575) 525-9419.E-mail: radiolc@kgrt.com Web Site:www.hot103.fm Licensee: Richardson Commercial Corp. (acq 10-2-2001; $1,650,000 with KKVS(FM) Truth or Consequences). Population served: 174,100 Fletcher, Heald & Hildreth. Format: CHR. News staff: 2. Target aud: 18-34; general. ♦Allen Lumeyer, VP, gen mgr; Ernesto Garcia, opns mgr, progmg dir; Tamara Blaeser, natl sls mgr, rgnl sls mgr; Veronica Vaillancourt-Test, rgnl sls mgr; Damien Willis, mus dir.

KKVS(FM)—See Truth or Consequences

***KMBN(FM)**— 2000: 89.7 mhz; 500 w. Ant 171 ft TL: N32 16 41 W106 54 39. Hrs open: Box 16691, 88004. Phone: (505) 521-8053.E-mail: kmbn@moody.edu Web Site:www.mbn.org/kmbn Licensee: Moody Bible Institute of Chicago. Group owner: The Moody Bible Institute of Chicago Format: Christian.

KMVR(FM)—See Mesilla Park

KOBE(AM)— April 1947: 1450 khz; 1 kw-U. TL: N32 18 07 W106 48 08. Hrs open: 24 Drawer 1838, 88004. Secondary address: 1832 W. Amador 88005. Phone: (505) 526-2496. Fax: (505) 523-3918.E-mail: kmvr-kobe@totacc.com Web Site:kobeam1450.com Licensee: Bravo Mic Communications II LLC. (acq 1-24-2007; $1.9 million with KMVR(FM) Mesilla Park). Population served: 167,000 Natl. Network: CBS, . Format: News/talk, sports. News staff: one; News: 25 hrs wkly. Target aud: 25 plus. ♦Larry Edwards, gen mgr; Amanda Riordan, opns VP, progmg dir, news dir, disc jockey; Keith Lamonica, chief of engrg, disc jockey.

***KRUC(FM)**— March 1998: 88.9 mhz; 500 w. 197 ft TL: N32 16 41 W106 54 39. Hrs open: 24 5128 Prince Edward Ave., El Paso, TX, 79924. Phone: (915) 544-9192. Web Site:www.wrn-rcm.org Licensee: World Radio Network Inc. (group owner) Format: Sp relg.

***KRUX(FM)**— Sept 20, 1989: 91.5 mhz; 1 kw. -194 ft TL: N32 17 03 W106 45 00. Hrs open: 7 AM-2 AM Box 30004, Corbett Ctr., 88003. Phone: (505) 646-4640. Fax: (505) 646-5219.E-mail: krux_music@hotmail.com Web Site:www.kruxradio.com Licensee: Board of Regents New Mexico State University. Format: Var. News staff: one; News: 2 hrs wkly. Target aud: General. ♦Melissa Aguilera, gen mgr; Mathias Ortiz, prom dir; Adrian Perez, progmg dir; Bianca Villani, news dir; Art Fountain, chief of engrg.

***KRWG(FM)**— Oct 3, 1964: 90.7 mhz; 100 kw. 350 ft TL: N32 15 24 W106 58 34. Stereo. Hrs open: 24 Box 3000, 88003. Secondary address: 2915 McFie Cir., Rm. 120 88003. Phone: (575) 646-2222. Fax: (575) 646-1974.E-mail: krwgfm@nmsu.edu Web Site:krwg.org Licensee: Regents of New Mexico State University. Population served: 250,000 Natl. Network: NPR, PRI, . Wiley, Rein & Fielding. Wire Svc: AP Format: Class, jazz, news, SP. News staff: 4; News: 39 hrs wkly. Target aud: 18-60. Spec prog: Sp 10 hrs, bluegrass/folk 8 hrs wkly. ♦Glen Cerny, gen mgr; Carrie Hamblen, chief of opns; L. Ford Ballard, dev dir; Fred Martino, news dir. Co-owned TV: *KRWG-TV affil

KSNM(AM)— Dec 15, 1955: 570 khz; 5 kw-D, 155 w-N. TL: N32 18 33 W106 49 24. Hrs open: 24 Box 968, 88004. Secondary address: 1355 E. California St. 88001. Phone: (575) 525-9298. Fax: (575) 525-9419. Web Site:www.ksnm570.am Licensee: Sunrise Broadcasting Inc. Population served: 174,100 Natl. Network: CNN Radio, . Format: News, talk and sports. News staff: 2; News: 15 hrs wkly. Target aud: 25 plus; adults. ♦Allen Lumeyer, VP, gen mgr; Ernesto Garcia, opns mgr, progmg dir; Tamara Blaeser, natl sls mgr & rgnl sls mgr.

KXPZ(FM)— May 1994: 99.5 mhz; 100 kw. Ant 1,023 ft TL: N32 41 35 W107 04 06. Stereo. Hrs open: 24 101 Perkins, 88005. Phone: (505) 527-1111. Fax: (505) 527-1100.E-mail: rocket@bravomic.com Web

Site:www.rocket995.com Licensee: Bravo Mic Communications LLC. (acq 4-18-2006; $1.4 million). Leventhal, Senter & Lerman. Format: Active rock. ◆Michael Smith, gen mgr; Edmundo Resendez, gen sls mgr; K.C. Counts, progmg dir; Glen Leffler, chief of engrg.

Las Vegas

KBAC(FM)— Nov 10, 1989: 98.1 mhz; 100 kw. Ant 1,036 ft TL: N35 22 20 W105 22 02. Stereo. Hrs open: 24 915 Orchid Point Way, Vero Beach, FL, 32963-9518. Phone: (772) 559-3790.E-mail: info@kbacfm.com Licensee: Hutton Broadcasting LLC. Group owner: Clear Channel Communications Inc. (acq 10-16-2007; $650,000). ◆Edward B. Hutton Jr., gen mgr.

KBQL(FM)— 2009: 92.7 mhz; 23 kw. Ant 341 ft TL: N35 34 23 W105 10 16. Hrs open: 304 S. Grand Ave., 87701. Phone: (505) 425-5669. Fax: (505) 425-3557. Licensee: Matias C. Martinez. Format: Real country. ◆Matt Martinez, gen mgr.

*KEDP(FM)— September 1968: Stn currently dark. 91.1 mhz; 72 w. Ant -215 ft TL: N35 35 46 W105 13 18. Hrs open: New Mexico Highlands Univ., Media Arts Dept., Studio 103, 87701. Phone: (505) 454-3238.E-mail: martinezda@nmhu.edu Web Site:www.nmhu.edu Licensee: Board of Regents, New Mexico Highlands University. Population served: 18,000 Format: Oldies rock mix. ◆Donna Martinez, gen mgr; David Chavez, mus dir; Doyle Hanschulz, engr.

KFUN(AM)— Dec 25, 1941: 1230 khz; 1 kw-U. TL: N35 35 48 W105 12 21. Hrs open: 24 Box 700, 87701. Phone: (505) 425-6766. Fax: (505) 425-6767.E-mail: jpbaca1946@yahoo.com Licensee: Meadows Media LLC. (acq 4-19-91; $400). Population served: 20,000 Format: Sp, C&W. Target aud: General. ◆Joseph Baca Jr., pres, gen mgr, gen sls mgr, news dir, sls; Loretta Baca, traf mgr.

KLVF(FM)— June 19, 1973: 100.7 mhz; 10 kw. Ant -75 ft TL: N33 35 48 W105 12 21. Stereo. Hrs open: 24 (CP: COL Pecos. 3.7 kw horiz, ant 686 ft. TL: N35 39 06 W105 33 15). Box 700, 87701. Phone: (505) 425-6766. Fax: (505) 425-6767.E-mail: jpbaca1946@yahoo.com Licensee: Meadows Media LLC. Format: Adult contemp. Target aud: 17-40.

KMDZ(FM)— 2000: 96.7 mhz; 4.4 kw. Ant 380 ft TL: N35 36 16 W105 15 35. Hrs open: 24 Sangre de Cristo Broadcasting Co., 304 S. Grand, 87701. Phone: (505) 425-5669. Fax: (505) 425-3557.E-mail: mattmartinez@knmx.com Licensee: Sangre de Cristo Broadcasting Co. Format: Classic rock. ◆Matt Martinez, gen mgr.

KNMX(AM)— Oct 1, 1980: 540 khz; 5 kw-D, DA. TL: N35 34 25 W105 10 17. Hrs open: Sunrise-sunset 304 S. Grand Ave., 87701. Phone: (505) 425-3555. Fax: (505) 425-3557.E-mail: mattmartinez@knmx.com Licensee: Sangre de Cristo Broadcasting Co. (acq 9-26-96; $235,000). Population served: 400,000 Format: Sp, news/talk. News staff: one; News: 15 hrs wkly. Target aud: 25-55; Hispanic, Anglo. ◆Matt Martinez, prom dir; Matt C. Martinez, pres, gen mgr & progmg dir; John Chichester, chief of engrg.

*KRRE(FM)— 2008: 91.9 mhz; 100 w. Ant -118 ft TL: N35 35 04 W105 12 07. Hrs open: Rebroadcasts KUNM(FM) Albuquerque 100%. Room 326 Onate Hall, University of New Mexico, Albuquerque, 87131. Phone: (505) 277-8009. Fax: (505) 277-8004.E-mail: kunm@kunm.org Web Site:www.kunm.org Licensee: Regents of the University of New Mexico. Natl. Network: NPR, . Format: Div, news/talk. ◆Richard Towne, gen mgr.

Lordsburg

KPSA-FM— July 4, 1986: 97.7 mhz; 250 w. Ant -134 ft TL: N32 20 57 W108 42 18. Stereo. Hrs open: 24 Box 2577, Silver City, 88062. Phone: (505) 538-3396. Fax: (505) 388-5000.E-mail: events@silvercityradio.com Licensee: SkyWest Licenses New Mexico LLC. Group owner: Runnels Broadcasting System L.L.C. (acq 6-1-2006; grpsl). Format: Classic rock. ◆Sabrina Pack, gen mgr, gen sls mgr; Ted Tucker, progmg dir.

Los Alamos

KABG(FM)— June 1956: 98.5 mhz; 100 kw. 1,781 ft TL: N35 53 08 W106 23 14. (CP: 100 kw, ant 1,906 ft.). Stereo. Hrs open: Box 30925, Albuquerque, 87190. Phone: (505) 878-0980. Fax: (505) 878-0098. Web Site:www.bigoldies.net Licensee: AGM-Nevada L.L.C. Population served: 840,000 Format: Oldies. Target aud: 25-54; affluent, upscale male professionals. ◆Scott Hutton, gen mgr; Scott Sherwood, progmg dir.

KLVO(FM)— Mar 19, 1987: 106.7 mhz; 15.5 kw. Ant 1,948 ft TL: N35 47 15 W106 31 35. Stereo. Hrs open: 24 4125 Carlisle N.E., Albuquerque, 87107. Phone: (505) 878-0980. Fax: (505) 878-0098. Web Site:www.radiolobo.net Licensee: A.G.M.-Nevada L.L.C. Group owner: American General Media (acq 8-9-2000; grpsl). Population served: 103,000 Format: Rgnl Mexican. News: 7 hrs wkly. Target aud: 25-54; mainstream audience with all socio-economic cells represented. ◆Scott Hutton, gen mgr.

KQBA(FM)— Mar 1, 1998: 107.5 mhz; 100 kw. Ant 298 ft TL: N36 01 34 W105 48 18. Hrs open: 2502C Camino Entrada, Santa Fe, 87507. Phone: (505) 471-1067. Fax: (505) 473-2667.E-mail: info@huntonbroadcasting.com Licensee: Hutton Broadcasting LLC. (acq 12-4-2000; $1 million). Format: Country. Target aud: 18-49; male. ◆Scott Hutton, gen mgr.

KRSN(AM)— Dec 9, 1949: 1490 khz; 1 kw-U. TL: N35 53 46 W106 17 21. Hrs open: 24 145 Central Park Square, 87544. Phone: (505) 663-1490. Fax: (505) 663-0011.E-mail: info@krsnam1490.com Web Site:www.krsnam1490.com Licensee: Gillian Sutton (acq 1996). Population served: 150,000 Natl. Network: CBS, Westwood One, . Format: Community news, loc sports & music. News staff: one; News: 20 hrs wkly. Target aud: 35 plus; well educated, affluent. Spec prog: Big Band 8 hrs, jazz 5 hrs wkly. ◆Gillian Sutton, CEO; David Sutton, chief of opns.

Los Lunas

KAGM(FM)— January 1995: 106.3 mhz; 100 kw. Ant 656 ft TL: N34 48 51 W106 50 29. Stereo. Hrs open: 24 4125 Carlisle Blvd. N.E., Albuquerque, 87107-4806. Phone: (505) 878-0980. Fax: (505) 878-0098. Licensee: AGM-Nevada L.L.C. Group owner: American General Media (acq 12-22-97; grpsl). Format: CHR. Target aud: 18-49. Spec prog: Club mix 18 hrs wkly. ◆Scott Hutton, gen mgr & mktg mgr; Matt Rader, prom dir.

KIOT(FM)— July 6, 1981: 102.5 mhz; 20 kw. Ant 4,159 ft TL: N35 12 55 W106 27 02. Stereo. Hrs open: 24 8009 Marble Ave. N.E., Albuquerque, 87110-7901. Phone: (505) 262-1142. Fax: (505) 254-7106. Licensee: The Univision Albuquerque Trust, Bob Woodward, Trustee Group owner: Univision Radio (acq 10-3-2007). Population served: 50,000 Jones, Waldo, Holbrook & McDonough. Format: Classic rock. News staff: one. Target aud: 25-49; hip adults who like diversity & have disposable income. Spec prog: Gospel 4 hrs wkly. ◆Chuck Morgan, gen mgr.

Los Ranchos de Albuquerque

KALY(AM)—Licensed to Los Ranchos de Albuquerque. See Albuquerque

KTBL(AM)—Licensed to Los Ranchos de Albuquerque. See Albuquerque

Lovington

KLEA(AM)— Dec 25, 1952: 630 khz; 500 w-D, 69 w-N. TL: N32 56 30 W103 19 12. Hrs open: 24 Box 877, Country Club Rd., 88260. Phone: (505) 396-2244. Fax: (505) 396-3355.E-mail: klea@valornet.com Web Site:www.107oldies.com Licensee: Lea County Broadcasting Co. Population served: 220,000 Format: Soft hits, Fox sports weekends. News staff: one; News: 12 hrs wlky. Target aud: 25-54. Spec prog: Relg 3 hrs wkly. ◆Keith Kelly, progmg dir; Susan Coe, gen mgr, gen sls mgr & news dir; Rita Niccum, chief of engrg; Annette Giese, traf mgr.

KLEA-FM— October 1965: 101.7 mhz; 25 kw. 280 ft TL: N32 56 30 W103 19 12. Stereo. Hrs open: 24 Dups AM 100% Box 877 , Country Club Rd., 88260. Phone: (505) 396-2244. Fax: (505) 396-3355.E-mail: klea@valornet.com Web Site:www.107oldies.com Population served: 150,000 Format: Oldies. News staff: one; News: 10 hrs wkly. ◆Susan Coe, exec VP.

*KYCV(FM)—Not on air, target date: unknown: 91.3 mhz; 6 kw. Ant 1,627 ft TL: N33 03 20 W103 49 12. Hrs open: 9019 N. West Ln., Stockton, CA, 95210. Phone: (209) 477-3690. Fax: (209) 477-2762.E-mail: kycv@kycc.org Web Site:www.kycc.org Licensee: Your Christian Companion Network Inc. ◆Shirley Garner, gen mgr.

Magdalena

KANM(FM)—Not on air, target date: unknown: 95.9 mhz; 100 kw. Ant 981 ft TL: N34 30 39 W107 13 16. Hrs open: 5842 Westslope Dr., Austin, TX, 78731. Phone: (512) 467-0643. Licensee: Matinee Radio LLC. ◆Robert Walker, pres.

Maljamar

*KMTH(FM)— Feb 14, 1985: 98.7 mhz; 100 kw. Ant 710 ft TL: N32 54 55 W103 46 31. Stereo. Hrs open: 24 Rebroadcasts KENW-FM Portales 100%. Eastern New Mexico Univ., 52 Broadcast Ctr., Portales, 88130. Phone: (505) 562-2112. Fax: (505) 562-2590. Web Site:kenw.org Licensee: Eastern New Mexico University. Population served: 350,000 Natl. Network: NPR, PRI, . Dow, Lohnes & Albertson. Wire Svc: AP Format: Class, btfl mus, news. News staff: one; News: 41 hrs wkly. Target aud: General. ◆Steven G. Gamble, pres; Ronnie Birdsong, VP; Duane W. Ryan, gen mgr; Shannon Hearn, opns dir; Carla Howard, dev dir; Virginia McReynolds, mktg dir; James Lee, news dir; Jeff Burmeister, engrg dir; Bob Scott, engrg mgr.

KWMW(FM)— Jan 17, 1990: 105.1 mhz; 100 kw. 917 ft TL: N32 52 40 W103 41 13. Hrs open: 1086 Mechem Drive, Ruidoso, 88345. Phone: (505) 396-0499. Fax: (505) 396-8349.E-mail: kruikwmw@trailnet.com Licensee: M.T.D. Inc. Group owner: MTD Inc. Format: Country. ◆Tim Keithley, gen mgr, gen sls mgr, progmg dir, news dir; Will Rooney, stn mgr.

Mentmore

*KPKJ(FM)—Not on air, target date: unknown: 88.5 mhz; 1.3 kw. Ant 491 ft TL: N35 33 36 W109 06 30. Hrs open: 4002 N. 3300 E., Twin Falls, ID, 83301. Phone: (208) 734-6633. Fax: (208) 736-1958. Web Site:www.csnradio.com Licensee: CSN International. ◆Mike Kestler, pres.

Mesilla Park

KMVR(FM)— June 1, 1974: 104.9 mhz; 3 kw. -32 ft TL: N32 18 07 W106 48 08. Stereo. Hrs open: 24 101 Perkins Dr., Las Cruces, 88005. Phone: (575) 527-1111. Fax: (575) 527-1100.E-mail: kmvr-kobe@totacc.com Web Site:www.kmvrfm.com Licensee: Bravo Mic Communications II LLC. (acq 1-24-2007; $1.9 million with KOBE(AM) Las Cruces). Population served: 167,000 Format: Hot adult contemp. Target aud: 18-54. ◆Larry Edwards, gen mgr.

Mesquite

*KELP-FM— February 2004: 89.3 mhz; 680 w. Ant 66 ft TL: N32 09 42 W106 42 03. Stereo. Hrs open: 24 6900 Commerce, El Paso, TX, 79915. Phone: (915) 779-0016. Fax: (915) 779-6641.E-mail: tina@kelpradio.com Licensee: Sky High Broadcasting Inc. (acq 3-28-02). Population served: 174,267 Natl. Network: Salem Radio Network, . Format: Christian. Target aud: 25-55 plus. ◆Jay Gilliland, opns dir.

Milan

KQNM(AM)— Sept 1, 1989: 1100 khz; 250 w-D, 20 w-N. TL: N35 05 51 W107 52 19. Hrs open: 24 809 Wellesly N.E., Albuqueque, 87106. Phone: (505) 899-5029. Fax: (505) 899-6865.E-mail: joy@joyam.com Licensee: Cibola Radio Co. (acq 7-12-99; $29,800). Population served: 22,000 Format: Soft adult contemp. Target aud: 25-54; upscale men. ◆Don Davis, pres.

*KXXQ(FM)— June 1991: 100.7 mhz; 100 kw. Ant 1,361 ft TL: N35 28 07 W108 14 24. Stereo. Hrs open: 24 Box 180, Tahoma, CA, 96142. Phone: (530) 584-5700. Fax: (530) 584-5705. Web Site:www.ihradio.org Licensee: IHR Educational Broadcasting. (acq 5-31-2005; $450,000). Format: Relg, catholic. ◆Douglas M. Sherman, pres.

Pecos

KLBU(FM)— Aug 1, 2001: 102.9 mhz; 3.7 kw horiz. Ant 686 ft TL: N35 39 06 W105 33 15. Hrs open: 551C Cordova Rd., Santa Fe, 87505. Phone: (505) 984-1029. Fax: (505) 984-0880.E-mail: info@klbu.com Web Site:www.blu1029.com Licensee: Hutton Broadcasting LLC. (acq 10-30-2007; $450,000). Wood, Maines & Brown, Chartered. Format: Modern adult contemp. ◆Edward B. Hutton, pres; Kerri Fama, gen mgr; Joann Orner, progmg dir.

KVSF-FM— 2004: 101.5 mhz; 25 kw. Ant 279 ft TL: N35 32 50 W105 45 54. Hrs open: Box 1863, Santa Fe, TX, 87504. Phone: (505) 438-7007. Fax: (505) 438-7007. Licensee: Hutton Broadcasting LLC. (acq 10-16-2007; $700,000). Format: Var. ♦James S. Bumpous, gen mgr.

Portales

***KENW-FM**— Oct 1, 1968: 89.5 mhz; 100 kw. Ant 590 ft TL: N34 15 08.11 W103 14 20.63. Stereo. Hrs open: 24 Eastern New Mexico Univ., 52 Broadcast Ctr., 88130. Phone: (505) 562-2112. Fax: (505) 562-2590.E-mail: kenwfm@enmu.edu Web Site:www.kenw.org Licensee: Eastern New Mexico University. Population served: 350,000 Natl. Network: NPR, PRI, . Rgnl. Network: N.M. Pub. Format: Btfl mus, class, news/talk. News staff: one; News: 41 hrs wkly. Target aud: General. ♦Steven G. Gamble, pres; Ronnie Birdsong, VP; Duane W. Ryan, gen mgr; Shannon Hearn, opns dir; Carla Howard, dev dir; James Lee, news dir; Jeff Burmeister, engrg dir; Bob Scott, engrg mgr. Co-owned TV: *KENW-TV affil

KSEL(AM)— February 1950: 1450 khz; 1 kw-U. TL: N34 11 51 W103 19 24. Hrs open: 24 42437 US 70, 88130. Phone: (505) 359-4649. Fax: (505) 359-0724. Licensee: Rooney Moon Broadcasting Inc. (group owner; (acq 7-15-2002; grpsl). Population served: 100,000 Natl. Network: CNN Radio, . Format: News/talk. News: 168 hrs wkly. Target aud: 35+. ♦Duffy Moon, opns mgr, prom dir; Steve Rooney, pres, gen mgr, sls dir & progmg dir; Jeff Burmeister, chief of engrg; Lisa Schmidt, traf mgr.

KSEL-FM— March 1980: 95.3 mhz; 6 kw. Ant 298 ft TL: N34 11 51 W103 19 24. Stereo. Hrs open: 42437 US 70, 88130. Phone: (505) 359-4649. Fax: (505) 359-0724. Licensee: Rooney Moon Broadcasting Inc. Population served: 150,000 Natl. Network: CNN Radio, . Garvey, Schubert & Barer. Format: Country. Target aud: 18-54. Spec prog: Farm 4 hrs wkly. ♦Lisa Schmidt, traf mgr.

Questa

KLNN(FM)— 2006: 103.7 mhz; 51 kw. Ant -211 ft TL: N36 39 23 W105 37 57. Hrs open: Box 1844, Taos, 87571. Phone: (505) 758-5826. Fax: (505) 758-8430.E-mail: ktaoo@newmex.com Web Site:www.luna1037.com Licensee: West Waves Inc. (acq 2-16-2006; $68,160 for CP). Format: Adult contemp. ♦David W. Rahn, pres; Dave Noll, gen mgr.

Ramah

***KTDB(FM)**— Apr 24, 1972: 89.7 mhz; 15 kw. 300 ft TL: N34 57 59 W108 25 31. (CP: Ant 288 ft.). Hrs open: 5 AM-11 PM Box 40, B.I.A. Rt. 125, Pine Hill, 87357. Phone: (505) 775-3215. Fax: (505) 775-3551.E-mail: info@ktkb.com Web Site:www.rnsbinc.com Licensee: Ramah Navajo School Board Inc. Population served: 80,000 Natl. Network: NPR, . Format: C&W, cultural info, educ. Target aud: General; Native American. Spec prog: Navajo. ♦Barbara Maria, gen mgr, prom mgr; Irene Beaver, progmg dir; Earl Ericcho, news dir; Bernard J. Bustos, chief of engrg.

Raton

KBKZ(FM)— Dec 20, 2001: 96.5 mhz; 5.4 kw. Ant 968 ft TL: N36 59 33 W104 28 24. Hrs open: 100 Fisher Dr., Trinidad, CO, 81082. Phone: (719) 846-3355. Fax: (719) 846-4711.E-mail: kcrt@comcast.net Licensee: Phillips Broadcasting Co. Inc. Group owner: Phillips Broadcasting Inc. Population served: 12,000 Format: Country. ♦Lory Phillips, gen mgr.

KRTN(AM)— 1948: 1490 khz; 1 kw-U. TL: N36 53 10 W104 26 35. Hrs open: 24 Box 638, 1128 State St., 87740. Phone: (505) 445-3652. Fax: (505) 445-2911.E-mail: krtn@bacavalley.com Licensee: Enchanted Air Inc. (acq 5-31-2005; $750,000 with co-located FM). Population served: 25,000 Format: Adult contemp. Target aud: General. ♦Bill Donati, stn mgr, prom mgr, progmg dir, mus dir; Adrean Slocum, progmg dir, traf mgr; Jim Veltri, chief of engrg.

KRTN-FM— April 1982: 93.9 mhz; 26 kw. Ant 1,446 ft TL: N36 40 59 W104 24 50. Stereo. Hrs open: 24 Box 638, 1128 State St., 87740. Phone: (505) 445-3652. Fax: (505) 445-2911. Format: Oldies. ♦Billy Donoti, disc jockey.

Red River

***KRDR(FM)**— 2002: 90.1 mhz; 3.2 kw vert. Ant 718 ft TL: N36 41 25 W105 33 43. Hrs open: Box 788, Questa, 87556. Phone: (505) 586-1919. Fax: (505) 586-2332.E-mail: krdr@newmex.com Web Site:www.krdr.com Licensee: Red River Radio Inc. Format: Classic rock, oldies. ♦Lynn Nolen, stn mgr, progmg dir; Mike Nolen, gen mgr & chief of engrg.

Reserve

KZXQ(FM)— 2005: Stn currently dark. 104.5 mhz; 500 w. Ant -751 ft TL: N33 42 35 W108 45 56. Hrs open: Box 333, 87830. Phone: (623) 907-0267. Licensee: New Star Broadcasting LLC (acq 12-18-2002; $80,000). Format: Talk. ♦Karey Barbee, pres; Vance Barbee, gen mgr.

Rio Rancho

KQTM(FM)— Nov 2, 1984: 101.7 mhz; 3 kw. Ant 98 ft TL: N35 11 35 W106 28 15. Hrs open: 8009 Marble Ave. N.E., Albuquerque, 87110. Phone: (505) 262-1142. Fax: (505) 254-7106. Licensee: Team Broadcasting Inc. Group owner: Univision Radio (acq 7-31-2008; $1.4 million). Population served: 90,000 Natl. Network: Fox Sports, . Natl. Rep: Christal,. Format: Sports. ♦Joe O'Neill, pres; Chuck Morgan, gen mgr.

Roswell

KBCQ(AM)— May 1947: 1230 khz; 800 w-U. TL: N33 23 24 W104 29 45. (CP: 620 w-D, 1 kw-N. TL: N33 23 37 W104 36 16). Hrs open: 24 Box 670, 88201. Secondary address: 5206 W. 2nd St. 88201. Fax: (505) 622-9041.E-mail: penny@roswellradio.org Web Site:www.roswellradio.org Licensee: Roswell Radio Inc. Group owner: Roswell Radio Inc./Quay Broadcasters Inc. (acq 2-28-2003). Population served: 67,000 Natl. Network: CNN Radio, . Format: Oldies. Target aud: 35-75. Spec prog: Talk 15 hrs wkly. ♦John M. Dunn, pres; Jeff Chace, stn mgr, progmg dir; Caiti Chace, gen sls mgr.

KBCQ-FM— Oct 15, 1977: 97.1 mhz; 100 kw. 300 ft TL: N33 24 05 W104 22 45. Stereo. Hrs open: 24 Box 670, 88202. Phone: (505) 622-6450. Fax: (505) 622-9041. Web Site:www.roswellradio.org Licensee: Roswell Radio Inc. Group owner: Roswell Radio Inc./Quay Broadcasters Inc. (acq 11-2000; grpsl). Population served: 200,000 Fletcher, Heald & Hildreth. Format: CHR. News staff: one. Target aud: 18-49. ♦John Dunn, CEO & exec VP; Jeff Chase, gen mgr; Gary Babcock, engrg VP.

KBIM(AM)— May 1953: 910 khz; 5 kw-D, 500 w-N, DA-N. TL: N33 26 26 W104 31 35. Hrs open: 24 Box 1953, 88202. Secondary address: 1301 N. Main 88201. Phone: (505) 623-9100. Fax: (505) 623-4775.E-mail: kbim@dfn.com Web Site:kbim-roswell.com Licensee: Noalmark Broadcasting Corp. (acq 11-30-2007; $1.5 million with co-located FM). Population served: 200,000 Natl. Network: ABC, . Format: News/talk. News: 16 hrs wkly. Target aud: 25-54; upscale male & active working female. ♦William C. Nolan Jr., pres; John King, gen mgr, natl sls mgr, rgnl sls mgr, progmg dir, progmg mgr; Michael Liles, opns dir, chief of engrg; Betty King, gen sls mgr.

KBIM-FM— June 1959: 94.9 mhz; 100 kw. 1,880 ft TL: N33 03 20 W103 49 12. Stereo. Hrs open: 24 Prog sep from AM Box 1953, 88202. Phone: (505) 623-9100. Fax: (505) 623-4775.E-mail: kbim@dfn.com Web Site:kbim-roswell.com Licensee: Noalmark Broadcasting Corp. Population served: 187,000 Dow, Lohnes & Albertson. Format: Adult contemp. News: 16 hrs wkly. Target aud: 25-54. ♦Betty King, sls dir, progmg dir; John King, gen sls mgr.

KCKN(AM)— Dec 20, 1965: 1020 khz; 50 kw-U, DA-2. TL: N33 27 53 W104 29 58. Hrs open: 24 Box 220, 88202. Phone: (505) 622-0658. Fax: (505) 622-0852.E-mail: kckn@swwmail.net Web Site:kckn1020.com Licensee: JCE Licenses L.L.C. Group owner: James Crystal Inc. (acq 2000; $2.5 million). Population served: 500,000 Natl. Network: AP Network News, Jones Radio Networks, . John Wells King. Format: Classic country/religious. News staff: 2; News: 5 hrs wkly. Target aud: 25-54; adult professionals. Spec prog: local news 6 X daily. ♦Jim Hilliard Jr., pres; Jerry Kiefer, gen mgr, prom dir, progmg dir; Don Niccum, opns mgr; Bob Souza, gen sls mgr; Bob Williams, rgnl sls mgr, mus dir; Don Nicuum, news dir; Kathi Silvas, traf mgr.

KCRX(AM)— Mar 15, 1927: 1430 khz; 5 kw-D, 1 kw-N, DA-N. TL: N33 26 11 W104 36 18. Hrs open: 24 Box 2052, 88202-2052. Secondary address: 200 W. 1st St. 88203-2052. Phone: (505) 622-1432. Fax: (505) 622-1432.E-mail: kcrx@digicominc.net Web Site:oldiesradioonline.com Licensee: Rosendo Casarez Jr. Population served: 300,000 Natl. Network: CBS, Westwood One, . Format: Good time rock and roll oldies. News staff: one. Target aud: 35 plus. ♦Rosendo Casarez Jr., pres & opns dir.

KEND(FM)— May 30, 1990: 106.5 mhz; 52 kw. 135 ft TL: N33 23 05 W104 43 22. Stereo. Hrs open: 24 317 Quay Ave., Artesia, 88210. Phone: (505) 625-2098. Fax: (505) 622-3877. Web Site:www.themix1065.com Licensee: Pecos Valley Broadcasting Co. (acq 4-1-2007; $500,000). Format: AOR. News: 6 hrs wkly. Target aud: 18-34; upscale adults. ♦Mike Winters, gen mgr; Sean McKellips, traf mgr.

***KGCN(FM)**— 2009: 91.7 mhz; 3.5 kw vert. Ant 394 ft TL: N33 21 47 W104 38 11. Hrs open:
Rebroadcasts KLVR(FM) Middletown, CA 100%.
2351 Sunset Blvd., Suite 170-218, Rocklin, CA, 95765. Phone: (916) 251-1600. Fax: (916) 251-1650. Web Site:www.klove.com Licensee: Educational Media Foundation. (acq 7-23-2007; grpsl). Natl. Network: K-Love, . Format: Contemp Christian. ♦Mike Novak, pres.

KMOU(FM)— August 1992: 104.7 mhz; 100 kw. Ant 328 ft TL: N33 24 49 W104 22 49. Stereo. Hrs open: 24 Box 670, 88202-0670. Secondary address: 5206 W. 2nd St. 88203. Phone: (505) 625-6450. Fax: (505) 622-9041. Web Site:www.,roswellradio.org Licensee: Roswell Radio Inc. Group owner: Roswell Radio Inc./Quay Broadcasters Inc. (acq 11-22-2000; $750,000). Population served: 200,000 Fletcher, Heald & Hildreth. Format: Country. News staff: 2; News: 12 hrs wkly. ♦John M. Dunn, CEO; Jeff Chace, stn mgr, progmg dir; Caiti Chace, gen sls mgr.

***KQAI(FM)**— 2007: 89.1 mhz; 2 kw vert. Ant 207 ft TL: N33 23 36 W104 37 27. Hrs open:
Rebroadcasts KLRD(FM) Yucaipa, CA 100%.
2351 Sunset Blvd., Suite 170-218, Rocklin, CA, 95765. Phone: (916) 251-1600. Fax: (916) 251-1650. Web Site:www.air1.com Licensee: Educational Media Foundation. (acq 9-22-2005; $40,000 for CP). Natl. Network: Air 1, . Format: Alternative rock, div. ♦Richard Jenkins, pres.

KRDD(AM)— 1963: 1320 khz; 1 kw-D. TL: N33 24 14 W104 28 12. Hrs open: Box 1615, 88202. Phone: (505) 623-8111.E-mail: krddam@yahoo.com Licensee: Media Mining Group LLC (acq 5-11-2004). Population served: 100,000 Format: Sp. ♦Carlos Espinoza, pres, gen mgr, prom mgr; Monica Cardeas, gen sls mgr; Ramiro Vasquez, progmg dir.

***KRLU(FM)**— 2004: 90.1 mhz; 2 kw vert. Ant 394 ft TL: N33 21 47 W104 38 11. Hrs open: 24
Rebroadcasts KLVR(FM) Middletown, CA 100%.
2351 Sunset Blvd., Suite 170-218, Rocklin, CA, 95765. Phone: (916) 251-1600. Fax: (916) 251-1650.E-mail: klove@klove.com Web Site:www.klove.com Licensee: Educational Media Foundation. Group owner: EMF Broadcasting. Natl. Network: K-Love, . Shaw Pittman. Format: Contemp Christian. News staff: 3. Target aud: 25-44; Judeo Christian, female. ♦Mike Novak, pres.

KSFX(FM)— Mar 15, 1991: 100.5 mhz; 100 kw. 122 ft TL: N33 28 54 W104 39 12. Hrs open: 24 Box 670, 88201. Secondary address: 5206 W. 2nd St. 88201. Phone: (505) 622-6450. Fax: (505) 622-9041. Web Site:roswellradio.org Licensee: Roswell Radio Inc. Group owner: Roswell Radio Inc./Quay Broadcasters Inc. (acq 11-2000; grpsl). Population served: 200,000. Fletcher, Heard & Hildreth. Format: Classic Hits. News staff: 2; News: 12 hrs wkly. Target aud: 25-49; mainstream upscale. ♦John Dunn, CEO; Gary Babock, exec VP; John M. Dunn, gen mgr; Jeff Chace, stn mgr, sls dir, progmg dir; Caiti Chace, gen sls mgr; Tony Clayton, prom dir; Gary Babcock, engrg VP, chief of engrg.

***KWFL(FM)**— Dec 21, 1989: 99.3 mhz; 16.5 kw. Ant 436 ft TL: N33 21 47 W104 38 11. Stereo. Hrs open: 24 3801 Eubank NE, Albuquerque, 87111. Phone: (800) 776-1050. Fax: (505) 296-6262.E-mail: kflqonair@flc.org Web Site:www.flc.org/flr/kwfl Licensee: Family Life Broadcasting System. Group owner: Family Life Communications Inc. (acq 5-24-2004; $1). Natl. Network: Moody, . Format: Relg. Target aud: Christian community. ♦Randy L. Carlson, pres; Dan Rosecrans, gen mgr.

Ruidoso

KBUY(AM)— November 1959: 1360 khz; 5 kw-D, 199 w-N. TL: N33 19 35 W105 40 02. Hrs open: 24 Box 39, 88355. Secondary address: 1096 Mechen Dr., Suite 230 88345. Phone: (505) 258-2222. Fax: (505) 258-2224.E-mail: kwesradio@kwes.net Web Site:www.kwes.net Licensee: Walton Stations New Mexico Inc. Group owner: Walton Stations (acq 10-22-82; $475,000 with co-located FM; 11-15-82). Natl. Network: Fox News Radio, . Format: Oldies. News staff: one; News: 14 hrs wkly. Target aud: 38 plus; 25-54 females. Spec prog: Sp 4 hrs wkly. ♦Steve Hall, progmg dir; Steve Swayze, chief of engrg; Gary Herron, traf mgr.

KIDX(FM)— 2000: 101.5 mhz; 920 w. Ant 2,850 ft TL: N33 24 14 W105 46 56. Hrs open: Box 2010, 88346. Phone: (505) 258-9922. Fax: (505) 258-2363.E-mail: production@mtbradio.com Licensee: MTD Inc. (group owner) Format: Classic rock. ♦Tim Keithley, gen mgr.

KWES(AM)— 2008: 1450 khz; 1 kw-D, 860 w-N. TL: N33 19 34 W105 40 14. Hrs open: 1096 Mechem Dr., Suite 230, 88345-7071. Phone: (575) 258-2222. Fax: (575) 258-2224.E-mail: shall@kwes.net Web Site:www.kwes.net Licensee: Walton Stations New Mexico Inc. Natl. Network: Fox Sports, . Format: Sports. ♦John Walton, pres; Steve Hall, gen mgr; Juanita Jones, gen sls mgr.

KWES-FM— 1982: 93.5 mhz; 25 kw. 58 ft TL: N33 23 12 W105 40 14. Stereo. Hrs open: 24 Prog sep from AM Box 39, 88355. Phone: (505) 258-2222. Fax: (505) 258-2224.E-mail: shall@kwes.net Web Site:www.kwes.net Licensee: Walton Stations New Mexico Inc. Natl. Network: Jones Radio Networks, . Format: C&W. News staff: one; News: 17 hrs wkly. Target aud: 18-54. ♦Steve Swayze, mus dir; Gary Herron, traf mgr.

***KYCT(FM)**— 2009: 91.3 mhz; 210 w. Ant 2,824 ft TL: N33 24 15.2 W105 46 54.7. Hrs open: 9019 N. West Ln., Stockton, CA, 95210. Phone: (209) 477-3690. Fax: (209) 477-2762.E-mail: kycc@kycc.org Web Site:www.kycc.org Licensee: Your Christian Companion Network Inc. ♦Shirley Garner, gen mgr.

Ruidoso Downs

KRUI(AM)— April 1984: 1490 khz; 1 kw-U. TL: N33 19 17 W105 35 24. Hrs open: 24 1086 Mechem Dr., Ruidoso, 88345. Phone: (505) 258-9922. Fax: (505) 258-2363.E-mail: production@mtbradio.com Licensee: MTD Inc. (group owner; acq 12-88; $20,000; 12-19-88). Natl. Network: Westwood One, . Format: News, talk, sports. News: 14 hrs wkly. ♦Tim Keithley, gen mgr.

Santa Clara

KNUW(FM)— 1996: 95.1 mhz; 7.7 kw. 1,548 ft TL: N32 51 47 W108 14 28. Hrs open: 24 106 S. Bullard St., Silver City, 88061. Phone: (505) 534-8700. Fax: (505) 534-8702.E-mail: knuw@zianet.com Licensee: Duran-Hill, Inc. Format: Sp. Target aud: General; Hispanic. ♦George H. Mesa, pres, gen mgr, progmg dir; Cecilia Soza, gen sls mgr; Ken Bass, engrg VP.

Santa Fe

KHFM(FM)— Aug 15, 1965: 95.5 mhz; 19 kw. 1,850 ft TL: N35 53 08 W106 23 14. Stereo. Hrs open: 24 4125 Carlisle N. E., Albuquerque, 87107. Phone: (505) 878-0980. Fax: (505) 889-0617.E-mail: lgold@americangeneralmedia.com Web Site:www.classicalkhfm.com Licensee: AGM-Nevada L.L.C. Format: Class. Target aud: 18-49. ♦Bob Bishop, progmg dir.

KJFA(FM)— Sept 28, 1985: 105.1 mhz; 100 kw. Ant 1,937 ft TL: N35 47 15 W106 31 35. Stereo. Hrs open: 8009 Marble Ave. N.E., Albuquerque, 87110-7901. Phone: (505) 262-1142. Fax: (505) 254-7106. Licensee: Univision Radio License Corp. Group owner: Univision Radio (acq 9-22-2003; grpsl). Format: Mexican rgnl. Target aud: 35-54. ♦Chuck Morgan, gen mgr.

KKIM-FM— 2000: 94.7 mhz; 100 kw. Ant 797 ft TL: N36 05 21 W106 01 41. Hrs open: 4125 Carlisle Blvd. N.E., Albuquerque, 87107. Phone: (505) 878-0980. Fax: (505) 878-0098. Web Site:www.mykkim.com Licensee: AGM Nevada LLC. (acq 1996; $96,250). Format: Christian news/talk. ♦Dewey Moede, stn mgr.

KKOB Exp Stn— 1986: 770 khz; 230 w-U. TL: N35 40 56 W105 58 21. Hrs open:
Rebroadcasts KKOB(AM) Albuquerque 100%.
500 4th St. N.W., Suite 500, Albuquerque, 87102. Phone: (505) 767-6700. Fax: (505) 767-6767. Web Site:www.770kkob.com Licensee: Citadel Broadcasting Co. Natl. Rep: McGavren Guild,. Format: MOR. ♦Milt McConnell, gen mgr, stn mgr; Dennis Logsdon, rgnl sls mgr; Glen Hebert, mktg dir, prom dir; Pat Frisch, opns mgr & progmg dir; Art Ortega, pub affrs dir; Mike Langner, chief of engrg.

KKSS(FM)— March 1969: 97.3 mhz; 94 kw. Ant 1,876 ft TL: N35 46 50 W106 31 55. (CP: 240 w, ant 85 ft. TL: N35 04 41 W106 35 06). Stereo. Hrs open: 24 8009 Marble Ave. N.E., Albuquerque, 87110. Phone: (505) 262-1142. Fax: (505) 254-7106. Licensee: Univision Radio License Corp. Group owner: Univision Radio (acq 9-22-2003; grpsl). Population served: 600,000 Natl. Rep: D & R Radio,. Format: CHR. Target aud: 18-34; Hispanic females. ♦Chuck Morgan, gen mgr.

***KQLV(FM)**— Mar 16, 1990: 90.7 mhz; 3 kw. Ant 199 ft TL: N35 40 41 W105 59 29. Stereo. Hrs open: 24 2351 Sunset Blvd., Suite 170-218, Rocklin, CA, 95765. Phone: (916) 251-1600. Fax: (916) 251-1650. Web Site:www.klove.com Licensee: Educational Media Foundation. (acq 2-5-2008; exchange for KSFR(FM) White Rock). Population served: 100,000 Natl. Network: K-Love, . Davis Wright Tremaine LLP. Format: Contemp Christian. ♦Ira Gordon, gen mgr; Lisa Clark, gen sls mgr.

KRZY-FM— Nov 2, 1983: 105.9 mhz; 100 kw. Ant 1,919 ft TL: N35 46 49 W106 31 34. Stereo. Hrs open: 24 2725 Broadbent Pkwy. N.E., Suite F, Albuquerque, 87107. Phone: (505) 342-4141. Fax: (505) 344-8714.E-mail: mwilder@entravision.com Licensee: Entravision Holdings LLC. Group owner: Entravision Communications Corp. (acq 3-14-2000; grpsl). Leventhal, Senter & Lerman. Format: Sp. Target aud: 18-34. ♦Margarita Wilder, gen mgr.

KSWV(AM)— June 1966: 810 khz; 5 kw-D. TL: N35 39 17 W106 00 05. Hrs open: Box 1088, 102 Taos St., 87504. Phone: (505) 989-7441. Fax: (505) 989-7607.E-mail: kswvanthonygonzales@yahoo.com Licensee: La Voz Broadcasting Co. (acq 12-20-90; $150,000). Format: Sp loc info & mus. Target aud: 25-54. ♦Celine V. Gonzales, pres; Anthony Gonzales, gen mgr, progmg dir; George Gonzales, gen sls mgr; John Chidester, progmg dir & chief of engrg.

KTEG(FM)— Nov 24, 1983: 104.1 mhz; 100 kw. Ant 1,876 ft TL: N35 46 50 W106 31 35. Stereo. Hrs open: 24 5411 Jefferson St. N.E., Suite 100, Albuquerque, 87109. Phone: (505) 830-6400. Fax: (505) 830-6599.E-mail: info@ktegfm.com Web Site:www.1041theedge.com Licensee: Citicasters Licenses Inc. Group owner: Clear Channel Communications Inc. (acq 1-27-2009). Thompson Hine LLP. Format: Alternative. ♦Chuck Hammond, VP & gen mgr; Bill May, chief of opns.

KTRC(AM)— 1935: 1260 khz; 5 kw-D, 1 kw-N. TL: N35 40 36 W105 58 21. Hrs open: 6 AM-midnight 2502 C Camino Entrada, 87505. Phone: (505) 438-3890. Fax: (505) 473-2667. Licensee: A.G.M.-Nevada L.L.C. Group owner: American General Media (acq 8-9-2000; grpsl). Population served: 155,000 Natl. Network: Air America, CNN Radio, . Jones, Waldo, Holbrook & McDonough. Format: Progressive talk. Target aud: 35-64; involved affluent adults. ♦Scott Matthews, gen mgr, progmg dir.

KVSF(AM)— Feb 20, 1947: 1400 khz; 1 kw-U. TL: N35 41 16 W105 56 04. Hrs open: 2502 Camino Entrada, Suite C, 87507. Phone: (505) 471-1067. Fax: (505) 473-2667.E-mail: scott@huttonbroadcasting.com Web Site:www.espnsantafe.com Licensee: Hutton Broadcasting LLC. Group owner: American General Media (acq 6-5-2006; $350,000). . Natl. Network: ESPN Radio, . Format: Sports. ♦Edward B. Hutton, pres; Scott Hutton, gen mgr; Marti Segura, prom dir; Ira Gordon, progmg dir.

Santa Rosa

KKJY(FM)— 2001: 95.9 mhz; 1.5 kw. Ant 118 ft TL: N34 56 47 W104 39 10. Hrs open:
Rebroadcasts KSSR(AM) Santa Rosa 100%.
HC 69 Box 78, 88435. Secondary address: 2818 Historic Rt. 66 88435. Phone: (505) 472-5777. Phone: (505) 472-3752. Fax: (505) 472-5777. Licensee: Cibola Radio Co. (acq 9-14-2006). Format: Adult contemp, country, Sp. ♦Gabriel Esquibel, gen mgr.

***KNLK(FM)**— 2004: 91.9 mhz; 100 w. Ant -26 ft TL: N34 57 20 W104 40 53. Hrs open: 2020 Coal Ave. S.E., Albuquerque, 87106. Phone: (505) 242-7163.E-mail: brasher@aps.edu Web Site:www.kanw.com Licensee: Board of Education of the City of Albuquerque, NM. Population served: 10,000 Format: Sp. ♦Michael Brasher, gen mgr.

KSSR(AM)— Nov 2, 1960: 1340 khz; 1 kw-U. TL: N34 56 40 W104 39 00. Hrs open: 24 HC 69 Box 78, 88435. Secondary address: 2818 Historic Rt. 66 88435. Phone: (505) 472-5777. Fax: (505) 472-5777.E-mail: kssrradio@yahoo.com Licensee: Joseph M. Esquibel (acq 1989; $50,000). Natl. Network: Westwood One, . Format: Adult contemp, country, Sp. News staff: one; News: 16 hrs wkly. Target aud: General; 85% Hispanic, plus largely transient motorists. ♦Gabriel Esquibel, gen mgr.

Shiprock

***KFDC(FM)**—Not on air, target date: unknown: 90.5 mhz; 11 kw. Ant 2,430 ft TL: N36 27 39.4 W109 05 45.7. Hrs open: Box 3841, 87420-3841. Phone: (505) 368-1028. Licensee: Dine Agriculture Inc. ♦Gilbert Yazzie, gen mgr.

Silver City

KSCQ(FM)— Nov 28, 1989: 92.9 mhz; 11.5 kw. Ant 1,023 ft TL: N32 50 40 W108 14 18. Stereo. Hrs open: 24 Box 2577, 88062. Secondary address: 1560 N. Corbin St. 88061. Phone: (505) 388-4116. Fax: (505) 388-1759.E-mail: events@silvercityradio.com Web Site:theq929.com Licensee: Skywest Media LLC (acq 10-31-2005; $330,000). Population served: 62,000 Format: Hot adult contemp. News: 3 hrs wkly. Target aud: 25-55; baby boomers, generation X. ♦Sabrina Pack, gen mgr, gen sls mgr; Ted Tucker, progmg dir.

Socorro

***KBOM(FM)**— Feb 15, 2008: 88.7 mhz; 100 w. Ant 1,876 ft TL: N34 04 17 W106 57 44. Hrs open:
Rebroadcasts KUNM(FM) Albuquerque 100%.
MSC06 3520, Onate Hall, 1 University of New Mexico, Alququerque, 87131-0001. Phone: (505) 277-4806. Fax: (505) 277-8004.E-mail: kunm@kunm.org Web Site:www.kunm.org Licensee: Regents of the University of New Mexico. Format: Div, news/talk. ♦Richard Towne, gen mgr.

KMXQ(FM)— Jan 22, 1995: 92.9 mhz; 6 kw. -177 ft TL: N34 02 43 W106 54 21. Hrs open: 24 Box 699, 87801. Secondary address: 834 Hwy. 60 W. 87801. Phone: (505) 835-1286. Fax: (505) 835-2015.E-mail: kmxq@sdc.org Licensee: Lakeshore Media L.L.C. (acq 10-29-2002; $450,000). Population served: 70,000 Format: Country. News staff: 4; News: 167 hrs wkly. Target aud: 12 plus. Spec prog: Farm 2 hrs, talk one hr wkly. ♦Virgil Vigil, gen mgr, gen sls mgr, mktg mgr & prom dir; John Gonzales, prom mgr, progmg VP, engrg dir.

***KVLK(FM)**— 2007: 89.5 mhz; 10 kw horiz. Ant 161 ft TL: N34 23 44 W107 00 42. Hrs open: 24
Rebroadcasts KLVR(FM) Santa Rosa, CA 100%.
2351 Sunset Blvd., Suite 170-218, Rocklin, CA, 95765. Phone: (916) 251-1600. Fax: (916) 251-1650. Web Site:www.klove.com Licensee: Educational Media Foundation. Group owner: EMF Broadcasting. Natl. Network: K-Love, . Format: Contemp Christian.

***KXFR(FM)**— 2008: 91.9 mhz; 25 kw. Ant 243 ft TL: N34 23 44 W107 00 42. Hrs open:
Rebroadcasts KUFR(FM) Salt Lake City, UT 100%.
c/o KUFR(FM), 136 East South Temple, Suite 1630, Salt Lake City, UT, 84111. Phone: (801) 359-3147. Fax: (801) 359-8112. Licensee: Family Stations Inc. Natl. Network: Family Radio, . Format: Christian.

KYRN(FM)— 2009: 102.1 mhz; 250 w. Ant -476 ft TL: N34 04 35 W106 54 29. Hrs open: Box 272, Green Bay, WI, 54305-0272. Phone: (920) 271-1000. Fax: (920) 271-1010.E-mail: info@sovcity.com Web Site:www.sovcity.com Licensee: Sovereign City Radio Services LLC. ♦Scott Krusinski, VP.

Taos

KKIT(FM)— 2005: 95.9 mhz; 4 kw. Ant -630 ft TL: N36 23 22 W105 35 09. Stereo. Hrs open: 24 5542 NDCBU, 87571-6122. Secondary address: 125A Camino de la Merced 87571-5119. Phone: (505) 758-4491. Phone: (877) 737-KKIT. Fax: (505) 758-4452.E-mail: production@kxmt.com Web Site:www.radiotaos.com Licensee: DMC Broadcasting Inc. Natl. Network: ABC, . Format: Adult hits. ♦Jeff Singer, opns mgr, progmg dir; Pattee Brown, gen sls mgr; Jennifer Trujillo, news dir.

KTAO(FM)— January 1978: 101.9 mhz; 1.05 kw. 2,824 ft TL: N36 14 48 W105 39 15. Stereo. Hrs open: 6 AM-2 AM Box 1844, 87571. Phone: (505) 758-5826. Fax: (505) 758-8430.E-mail: ktaoo@newmex.com Web Site:www.ktao.com Licensee: Taos Communications Corp. (acq 1-78). Population served: 110,000 Brown, Nietert & Kaufman. Format: AAA. News staff: 2; News: 7 hrs wkly. Target aud: 25-49; educated, responsive, upwardly mobile. Spec prog: Jazz 3 hrs, Roots & Wires, 5 hrs; maccasin wire, 3 hrs; world on tour, 2 hrs; celtic 4 hrs; Sonido del sol, 3 hrs. ♦Brad Hockmeyer, CEO, pres, progmg dir; Dave Noll, opns dir; Paddy Mac, mus dir.

KVOT(AM)— 2005: 1340 khz; 1 kw-U. TL: N36 23 22 W105 35 09. Hrs open: 24/7 5542 NDCBU, 87571-6122. Secondary address: 125A Camino de la Merced 87571-5119. Phone: (505) 758-4491. Fax: (505) 758-4452. Licensee: DMC Broadcasting Inc. (acq 12-20-2005). Natl. Network: ABC, . Format: Talk/ Air America. ♦Jeff Singer, opns mgr, progmg dir; Pattee Brown, gen sls mgr; Jennifer Trujillo, news dir.

KXMT(FM)— Dec 1, 2000: 99.1 mhz; 60 kw. Ant 2,135 ft TL: N36 51 32 W106 00 28. Hrs open: 5542 NDCBU, 87571-6122. Secondary address: 125A Camino de la Merced 87571-5119. Phone: (505) 758-4491. Fax: (505) 758-4452. Web Site:www.kxmt.com Licensee: DMC Broadcasting Inc. (acq 3-19-2003; $645,000 with KKTC(FM) Angel Fire). Format: Mexican rgnl. ♦Darren Cordova, pres; Jeff Singer, opns mgr, progmg dir; Pattee Brown, gen sls mgr; Jennifer Trujillo, news dir.

Tatum

KTUM(FM)— 2003: 107.1 mhz; 100 kw. Ant 918 ft TL: N32 52 50 W103 41 01. Hrs open: 1086 Mechem Drive, Ruidoso, 88345. Phone: (505) 396-0499. Fax: (505) 396-8349. Licensee: MTD Inc. (group owner) Format: Classic rock. ♦Tim Keithley, gen mgr, gen sls mgr, progmg dir, news dir; Will Rooney, stn mgr.

Thoreau

KXTC(FM)— Oct 21, 1991: 99.9 mhz; 100 kw. Ant 1,210 ft TL: N35 36 13 W108 40 45. Stereo. Hrs open: 24 1632 S. 2nd St., Gallup, 87301-5836. Phone: (505) 863-9391. Fax: (505) 863-9393.E-mail: maryannarmijo@clearchannel.com Web Site:www.999xtc.com Licensee: Clear Channel Broadcasting Licenses Inc. (acq 9-7-2000). Borsari & Paxson. Format: CHR. News staff: 2; News: 2 hrs wkly. Target aud: 18-44; Women. Spec prog: American Indian one hr, Sp 8 hrs wkly. ♦MaryAnn Armijo, gen mgr.

Truth or Consequences

KCHS(AM)— September 1944: 1400 khz; 1 kw-U. TL: N33 08 26 W107 13 55. Hrs open: 6am-11pm 7days a wk Box 351, 87901. Phone: (505) 894-2400. Fax: (505) 894-3998.E-mail: kchs@gpkmedia.com Web Site:www.gpkmedia.com Licensee: Myrna Baird-Kohs dba GPK Media LLC (acq 6-18-92). Population served: 10,000 Natl. Network: AP Radio, . Format: Country, news, oldies. News staff: 3. Target aud: General; area residents & visitors at lake. ♦Myrna Kohs, gen mgr, gen sls mgr, mus dir; Patrick Kohs, pres, prom VP, progmg dir & news dir.

KKVS(FM)— Nov 1, 1984: 98.7 mhz; 49 kw. Ant 2,644 ft TL: N32 58 15 W107 13 26. Stereo. Hrs open: 24 Box 968, Las Cruces, 88004. Secondary address: 1355 E. California St., Las Cruces 88001. Phone: (575) 525-9298. Fax: (575) 525-9419.E-mail: radiolc@kgrt.com Web Site:www.vista.fm Licensee: Richardson Commercial Corp. (acq 10-2-2001; $1,650,000 with KHQT(FM) Las Cruces). Population served: 174,100 Fletcher, Heald & Hildreth. Format: Rgnl Mexican. News staff: one. Target aud: 25-54; Hispanic. ♦Allen Lumeyer, VP, gen mgr; Veronica Vaillancourt-Test, rgnl sls mgr; Sara Holguin, progmg dir; Martin Cortez, mus dir.

Tse Bonito

KHAC(AM)— Mar 21, 1967: 880 khz; 10 kw-D, 430 w-N. TL: N35 38 41 W109 01 13. Hrs open: Box 9090, Western Indian Ministries, Window Rock, AZ, 86515. Phone: (505) 371-5587. Fax: (505) 371-5588.E-mail: wim@westernindian.org Web Site:www.westernindian.org Licensee: Western Indian Ministries. (group owner) Population served: 73,500 Format: Christian, CHR, Navajo. News staff: one. American Indian. ♦Larry Harper, gen mgr; Bruce Kinde, engrg mgr.

Tucumcari

***KENM(FM)**— 2009: 89.3 mhz; 165 w. Ant 869 ft TL: N35 08 04 W103 41 53. Hrs open: 52 Broadcast Center, Eastern New Mexico University, Portales, 88130-9989. Phone: (575) 562-2112. Fax: (575) 562-2590.E-mail: kenwfm@enmu.edu Web Site:www.kenw.org Licensee: Eastern New Mexico University. ♦Duane W. Ryan, gen mgr.

KQAY-FM— Jan 19, 1968: 92.7 mhz; 3 kw. 64 ft TL: N35 10 15 W103 42 25. Stereo. Hrs open: Prog sep from AM Box 668, 902 S. Date St., 88401. Phone: (505) 461-0522. Fax: (505) 461-0092.E-mail: ktmnkqay@yahoo.com Web Site:www.tucumari.was Format: Adult contemp.

KTNM(AM)— 1941: 1400 khz; 1 kw-U. TL: N35 10 15 W103 42 25. Hrs open: Box 668, 902 S. Date St., 88401. Phone: (505) 461-0522. Phone: (505) 461-1400. Fax: (505) 461-0092.E-mail: ktnmkqay@yahoo.com Web Site:www.tucumcari.ws Licensee: Quay Broadcasters Inc. Group owner: Roswell Radio Inc./Quay Broadcasters Inc. (acq 1-10-2003; with co-located FM). Population served: 15,000 Natl. Network: ABC, . Cohn & Marks. Format: C&W. Target aud: General. Spec prog: Sp 18 hrs wkly. ♦Diane Paris, gen mgr, gen sls mgr, prom mgr, news dir; Greg Carnefix, progmg dir.

***KVIJ(FM)**—Not on air, target date: unknown: 90.9 mhz; 500 w vert. Ant 850 ft TL: N34 57 50 W103 41 33. Hrs open: Box 667, 88401-0667. Secondary address: 823 S. 1st St. 88401. Phone: (505) 461-3106. Licensee: Trinity Baptist Church. ♦David P. McAfee, gen mgr.

***KVLP(FM)**— 2009: 91.7 mhz; 570 w. Ant 312 ft TL: N35 08 23 W103 44 35. Hrs open:
Rebroadcasts KLVR(FM) Middletown, CA 100%.
2351 Sunset Blvd., Suite 170-218, Rocklin, CA, 95765. Phone: (916) 251-1600. Fax: (916) 251-1650. Web Site:www.klove.com Licensee: Educational Media Foundation. (acq 3-23-2007; grpsl). Natl. Network: K-Love, . Format: Contemp Christian. ♦Mike Novak, pres.

Tularosa

***KNMA(FM)**— May 5, 2008: 88.1 mhz; 7 kw vert. Ant 1,900 ft TL: N32 49 49 W105 53 25. Hrs open:
Rebroadcasts KAWZ(FM) Twin Falls, ID 100%.
Box 391, Twin Falls, ID, 83303. Phone: (208) 734-6633. Fax: (208) 736-1958. Web Site:www.csnradio.com Licensee: Calvary Chapel of Twin Falls Inc. Natl. Network: CSN, . Format: Christian praise & worship, Bible teaching. ♦Mike Kestler, pres; Don Mills, stn mgr.

White Rock

KSFR(FM)— 1991: 101.1 mhz; 2.5 kw. Ant 1,863 ft TL: N35 53 09 W106 23 16. Stereo. Hrs open: 24 6401 S. Richards Ave., Santa Fe, 87508. Phone: (505) 428-1527. Fax: (505) 424-8938.E-mail: info@ksfr.org Web Site:www.ksfr.org Licensee: Santa Fe Community College (acq 2-5-2008; exchange for KQLV(FM) Santa Fe). Population served: 147,000 Garvey Schubert Barer. Format: News/talk, jazz. News staff: one; News: 14 hrs wkly. Target aud: General. Spec prog: American Indian 4 hrs, Sp 4 hrs wkly. ♦Dal Dearmin, gen mgr; Sean Conlon, opns mgr; William Dupuy, news dir.

Zuni

***KSHI(FM)**— Apr 6, 1978: 90.9 mhz; 100 w. Ant -249 ft TL: N35 05 18 W108 47 22. Stereo. Hrs open: 8am - 5pm Box 339, 87327. Phone: (505) 782-4144. Fax: (505) 782-5069.E-mail: zuniradio@gmail.com Licensee: Zuni Communications Authority. Population served: 10,000 Format: Educ. Target aud: 18-34; primarily Indian. Spec prog: Indian 20 hrs wkly. ♦Duane Chimoni, gen mgr.

New York

Acra

***WGXC(FM)**—Not on air, target date: June 2010: 90.7 mhz; 127 w horiz, 3.3 kw vert. Ant 312 ft TL: N42 19 43 W73 58 15. Hrs open: 5662 Rt. 23, 12405. Phone: (518) 622-2598.E-mail: tr@free103point9.org Web Site:www.free103point9.org Licensee: free103point9. ♦Melissa Dubbin, pres; Galen Joseph-Hunter, gen mgr; Tom Roe, progmg dir.

Albany

***WAMC(AM)**— 1934: 1400 khz; 1 kw-U. TL: N42 41 21 W73 47 37. Hrs open:
wamc(FM) 97%.
Box 66600, 12206. Secondary address: 318 Central Ave. 12206. Phone: (518) 465-5233. Fax: (518) 432-6974.E-mail: mail@wamc.org Web Site:www.wamc.org Licensee: WAMC. Group owner: WAMC/Northeast Public Radio (acq 4-24-03; $500,000). Population served: 114,873 Natl. Network: NPR, PRI, . Dow Lohnes & Albertson. Wire Svc: AP Format: News/talk. ♦David Galletly, VP.

***WAMC-FM**— Oct 1, 1958: 90.3 mhz; 10 kw. Ant 1,970 ft TL: N42 38 14 W73 10 07. Stereo. Hrs open: 24 Box 66600, 318 Central Ave., 12206. Phone: (518) 465-5233. Phone: (800) 323-9262. Fax: (518) 432-6974.E-mail: mail@wamc.org Web Site:www.wamc.org Licensee: WAMC. Group owner: WAMC/Northeast Public Radio (acq 7-1-82). Population served: 1,464,200 Natl. Network: NPR, PRI, . Dow, Lohnes & Albertson. Wire Svc: AP Format: News, talk. News staff: 11; News: 48 hrs wkly. Target aud: General. Spec prog: Jazz 18 hrs, folk 7 hrs. ♦Alan Chartock, CEO, chmn; David Galletly, VP.

***WCDB(FM)**— Mar 1, 1978: 90.9 mhz; 100 w. 222 ft TL: N42 41 16 W73 49 19. Stereo. Hrs open: 24 Campus Ctr. 316, 1400 Washington Ave., 12222. Phone: (518) 442-5234. Phone: (518) 442-5262. Fax: (518) 442-4366.E-mail: info@wcdb.com Web Site:www.wcdb.albany.edu Licensee: State University of New York. Population served: 1,000,000 Format: Div, AOR, urban contemp. News: 15 hrs wkly. Target aud: 15-55; students & surrounding community. Spec prog: Gospel 3 hrs, Sp 3 hrs, dance 3 hrs, jazz 10 hrs, metal 10 hrs wkly. ♦Michael Di Pietro, gen mgr & chief of engrg.

WDCD(AM)— May 1948: 1540 khz; 50 kw-U, DA-1. TL: N42 44 01 W73 51 49. Hrs open: 24 4243 Albany St., 12212. Phone: (518) 862-1540. Fax: (518) 862-1545.E-mail: info@crawfordbroadcasting.com Web Site:www.crawfordbroadcasting.com Licensee: Kimtron Inc. Group owner: Crawford Broadcasting Co. (acq 1995; $700,000). Population served: 790,000 Target aud: 30-54; educated, conservative, committed religious. ♦Donald Crawford, pres, gen mgr; Peter Kaye, prom dir & progmg dir.

WDDY(AM)— June 14, 1924: 1460 khz; 5 kw-U, DA-N. TL: N42 37 21 W73 48 09. Hrs open: 24 52 Corporate Cir., Suite K, 12203. Phone: (518) 464-1311. Fax: (518) 464-4185. Web Site:www.radiodisney.com Licensee: Radio Disney Group LLC. Group owner: ABC Inc. (acq 2-12-02; $2 million). Population served: 750,000 Natl. Network: ABC, . Natl. Rep: Katz Radio,. Format: Family & children programs. News staff: one. Target aud: 25-54; general. ♦Rob Thomson, gen mgr; Sarah Wiseman, prom mgr.

WGDJ(AM)—See Rensselaer

WGNA-FM— December 1973: 107.7 mhz; 12.5 kw. Ant 984 ft TL: N42 38 18 W73 59 51. Hrs open: 1241 Kings Rd., Schenectady, 12303. Phone: (518) 881-1515. Fax: (518) 881-1516.E-mail: wgna1077@aol.com Web Site:www.wgna.com Licensee: Regent Licensee of Mansfield Inc. Group owner: Regent Communications Inc. (acq 8-24-2001; grpsl). Latham & Watkins. Format: Country. ♦Robert Ausfeld, gen mgr; John Hirsch, stn mgr.

WGY(AM)—See Schenectady

WHAZ(AM)—See Troy

WHRL(FM)— Sept 1, 1966: 103.1 mhz; 6 kw. 328 ft TL: N42 39 46 W73 40 37. Stereo. Hrs open: 1203 Troy-Schenectady Rd., Latham, 12110. Phone: (518) 452-4800. Fax: (518) 452-4855.E-mail: feedback@channel1031.com Web Site:www.whrl.com Licensee: CC Licenses LLC. Group owner: Clear Channel Communications Inc. (acq 8-5-98; grpsl). Population served: 114,873 Natl. Rep: Clear Channel,. Format: Alternative. Target aud: 21-54; upscale arrivers. ♦Kristen Delaney, VP, gen mgr; John Cooper, stn mgr, progmg dir; Lisa Biello, opns dir.

WKLI-FM— 1972: 100.9 mhz; 6 kw. Ant 298 ft TL: N42 43 54 W73 52 56. Stereo. Hrs open: 24 6 Johnson Rd., Latham, 12110. Phone: (518) 786-6600. Fax: (518) 786-6610.E-mail: info@albanymagic.com Web Site:www.albanymagic.com Licensee: 6 Johnson Road Licenses Inc. Group owner: Pamal Broadcasting Ltd. (acq 10-9-2001). Population served: 103,200 Natl. Network: CBS Radio, . Format: Adult standards. Target aud: 25-54; upscale women. ♦Dan Austin, gen mgr; Kevin Callahan, opns mgr; Suzette Anthony, sls dir; Jillian Shuhart, prom dir; Jay Scott, progmg dir; Mike Carey, news dir.

WOFX(AM)—See Troy

WPYX(FM)— Sept 16, 1980: 106.5 mhz; 15.3 kw. 902 ft TL: N42 38 09 W74 00 05. Stereo. Hrs open: 24 1203 Troy-Schenectady Rd., Latham, 12110. Phone: (518) 452-4800. Fax: (518) 452-4855.E-mail: feedback@pyx106.com Web Site:www.pyx106.com Licensee: Capstar TX L.P. Group owner: Clear Channel Communications Inc. (acq 8-30-00; grpsl). Population served: 1,300,000 Format: Classic rock. Target aud: 25-54. ♦Kristen Delaney, VP, gen mgr; John Cooper, stn mgr; Nicholas Lombardi, gen sls mgr; Jill Manti, mktg dir; John Cooper, progmg dir.

WROW(AM)— Sept 30, 1947: 590 khz; 5 kw-D, 1 kw-N, DA-2. TL: N42 34 25 W73 47 12. Hrs open: 24 6 Johnson Rd., Lathan, 12110. Phone: (518) 786-6600. Fax: (518) 786-6610.E-mail: info@wrow.com Web Site:www.wrow.com Licensee: 6 Johnson Road Licenses Inc. Group owner: Pamal Broadcasting Ltd. (acq 10-19-2001; grpsl). Population served: 62,600 Natl. Network: CBS, . Natl. Rep: McGavren Guild,. Wire Svc: AP Format: News/talk. News staff: 3; News: 8 hrs wkly. Target aud: 35 plus; affluent, educated, white collar, upwardly mobile, homeowners. Spec prog: Gospel 3 hrs wkly. ♦Jim Morrell, pres; Dan Austin, gen mgr; Kevin Callahan, opns VP, opns mgr; Suzette Anthony, gen sls mgr; Paul Vandenburg, progmg VP; Mike Carey, news dir.

WTRY-FM—See Rotterdam

WYJB(FM)— October 1966: 95.5 mhz; 12 kw. 1,020 ft TL: N42 38 11 W74 00 00. Stereo. Hrs open: 6 Johnson Rd., Lathan, 12110. Phone: (518) 786-6600. Fax: (518) 786-6610.E-mail: info@b95.com Web Site:www.b95.com Population served: 1,179,500 Natl. Rep: McGavren Guild,. Format: Soft adult contemp. News staff: 3. Target aud: 25-54. ♦Kevin Callahan, opns dir & opns mgr; Chad O'Hara, mktg dir, news rptr; Darrin Kibbey, prom dir, progmg VP, mktg, prom; Chuck Taylor, progmg dir, mus dir.

Albion

***WJCA(FM)**— Dec 27, 2001: 102.1 mhz; 3.7 kw. Ant 423 ft TL: N43 11 19 W78 08 53. Hrs open: Box 262550, Baton Rouge, LA, 70826.

Secondary address: 8917 World Ministry Ave., Baton Rouge, LA 70810. Phone: (225) 768-3688. Phone: (225) 768-8300. Fax: (225) 768-3729.E-mail: kawikfish@yahoo.com Web Site:www.jsm.org Licensee: Family Worship Center Church Inc. (group owner; (acq 1-30-2006; $950,000). Format: Christian. ♦David Whitelaw, COO; Jimmy Swaggart, pres; John Santiago, progmg mgr.

Alfred

***WALF(FM)**— 1971: 89.7 mhz; 200 w. 73 ft TL: N42 15 17 W77 47 13. Stereo. Hrs open: One Saxon Dr., 14802. Phone: (607) 871-2287.E-mail: info@walf.org Web Site:www.walfradio.org Licensee: Alfred University. Population served: 25,000 Natl. Network: NPR, . Format: Div. ♦Ben Duffy, gen mgr & stn mgr.

***WETD(FM)**— Mar 19, 1973: 90.7 mhz; 360 w. 282 ft TL: N42 15 37 W77 47 51. Stereo. Hrs open: 24 WETD Studios, Alfred State College, 10 Upper Campus Dr., 14802. Phone: (607) 587-3694.E-mail: wetd@alfredstate.edu Web Site:web.alfredstate.edu/wetd Licensee: State University of New York. Format: Rock/AOR. Target aud: 18-22; college students.

WZKZ(FM)— Feb 28, 1999: 101.9 mhz; 1.3 kw. 699 ft TL: N42 12 20 W77 48 46. Hrs open: 24 3012 Eastside Ave., Wellsville, 14895. Phone: (585) 593-9553; (607) 733-5626. Fax: (585) 593-9554.E-mail: wzkz@wzkzradio.com Web Site:www.wzkzradio.com Licensee: Pembrook Pines Inc. Group owner: Pembrook Pines Media Group. Natl. Network: Jones Radio Networks, . Natl. Rep: Interep,. Wire Svc: AP Format: Hot country. News staff: 2; News: 10 hrs wkly. Target aud: 18-54. ♦Robert Pfuntner, CEO; Rod Biehler, gen mgr; Bob Weigand, opns mgr, news dir; Jim Davison, progmg.

Altamont

WZMR(FM)— June 26, 1968: 104.9 mhz; 530 w. Ant 932 ft TL: N42 38 11 W74 00 02. Hrs open: 24 6 Johnson Rd., Latham, 12110. Phone: (518) 786-6600. Fax: (518) 786-6610.E-mail: info@albanyedge.com Web Site:albanyedge.com Licensee: 6 Johnson Road Licenses Inc. Group owner: Pamal Broadcasting Ltd. (acq 10-19-2001; grpsl). Population served: 400,000 Format: Active rock. Target aud: 18-44; men. ♦Dan Austin, gen mgr; Kevin Callahan, opns mgr; Suzette Anthony, sls dir; Terry O'Donnell, mktg dir; Nick Rivers, progmg dir; Mike Carey, news dir.

Amherst

WUFO(AM)— 1948: 1080 khz; 1 kw-D. TL: N42 56 46 W78 49 43. Hrs open: Sunrise-sunset 89 LaSalle Ave., Buffalo, 14214. Phone: (716) 834-1080. Fax: (716) 837-1438.E-mail: wufo1080am@aol.com Web Site:www.wufoam.com Licensee: McL/McM New York LLC. (acq 3-1-72). Population served: 125,000 Natl. Network: American Urban, . Format: Gospel. News: 5 hrs wkly. Target aud: 25-54; Black adults, relg foundation, strong work ethics. Spec prog: Talk 8 hrs wkly. ♦Ron Davenport, pres; Alan Lincoln, gen mgr; Carol M. Salter, stn mgr, opns mgr, progmg dir.

Amsterdam

WCSS(AM)— Apr 8, 1948: 1490 khz; 1 kw-U. TL: N42 57 40 W74 10 35. Hrs open: 24 Box 1250 Riverfront Ctr., 12010. Phone: (518) 843-2500. Fax: (518) 684-6044.E-mail: wcss@cranesville.com Web Site:www.wcss1490.com Licensee: IZ Communications Corp. (acq 9-13-99; $188,000). Population served: 800,000 Natl. Network: Jones Radio Networks, USA, . Format: News/talk, AC, Mets Baseball. News staff: one; News: 20 hrs wkly. Target aud: 25 plus; adults interested in loc, community info & mus. Spec prog: Local progmg & talk 12 hrs wkly. ♦Joseph Isabel, gen mgr.

WEXT(FM)— Aug 1, 1975: 97.7 mhz; 1.6 kw. Ant 623 ft TL: N42 59 05 W74 10 49. Stereo. Hrs open: 4 Global View, Troy, 12180. Phone: (518) 880-3400. Fax: (518) 880-3409.E-mail: info@wmht.org Web Site:www.wmht.org Licensee: WMHT Educational Telecommunications (acq 9-19-2005; $1.5 million). Format: Classical. ♦Deborah Onslow, pres, gen mgr & stn mgr.

WVTL(AM)— Aug 16, 1961: 1570 khz; 1 kw-D, 207 w-N. TL: N42 54 38 W74 13 04. Hrs open: 24 5816 State Hwy. 30, 12010. Phone: (518) 843-9284. Fax: (518) 843-5225.E-mail: info@wvtl.com Web Site:www.1570wvtl.com Licensee: Roser Communications Network Inc. (acq 10-21-94; $400,000 with WBUG-FM Fort Plain; 12-5-94). Format: News, talk, sports. News staff: 2; News: 10 hrs wkly. Target aud: 25 plus. ♦Ken Roser Jr., gen mgr; Roxanne Roser, stn mgr; Grant Roser, gen sls mgr.

Arcade

***WCOF(FM)**— 2005: 89.5 mhz; 1 kw. Ant 593 ft TL: N42 27 41 W78 18 26. Hrs open:
Rebroadcasts WCIK(FM) Bath 100%.
Box 506, Bath, 14819. Phone: (607) 776-4151. Fax: (607) 776-6929.E-mail: mail@fln.org Web Site:www.fln.org Licensee: Family Life Ministries Inc. Group owner: Family Life Network. Natl. Network: Salem Radio Network, . Hardy, Carey, Chautin & Balkin, LLP. Wire Svc: Metro Weather Service Inc. Format: Contemp Christian. News staff: 3; News: 14 hrs wkly. Target aud: 30-54; general. ♦Dick Snavely, CFO; Rick Snavely, pres & gen mgr; John Owens, progmg dir; Jim Travis, chief of engrg.

Argyle

***WNGN(FM)**— August 1994: 91.9 mhz; 240 w. Ant 571 ft TL: N43 13 33 W73 26 34. Hrs open: 24 65 King Rd., Buskirk, 12028. Phone: (518) 686-0975. Fax: (518) 686-0975.E-mail: wngn@wngn.net Licensee: Northeast Gospel Broadcasting Inc. (acq 3-17-93; 4-5-93). Population served: 400,000 Natl. Network: Moody, . Format: Christian, inspirational. News: one hr wkly. Target aud: 35-54; general. ♦Brian Larson, pres.

Arlington

WRRB(FM)— December 1989: 96.9 mhz; 3 kw. 1,010 ft TL: N41 43 11 W73 59 45. (CP: 310 w). Stereo. Hrs open: 24
Rebroadcasts WDST(FM) Woodstock 100%.
Box 416, Poughkeepsie, 12602. Secondary address: 2 Pendell Rd., Poughkeepsie 12602. Phone: (845) 471- 1500. Fax: (845) 454-1204. Web Site:www.wrrv.com Licensee: Cumulus Licensing Corp. Group owner: Cumulus Media Inc. (acq 1-23-02; grpsl). Fisher, Wayland, Cooper, Leader & Zaragoza. Format: Progsv adult rock. News: 5 hrs wkly. Target aud: 25-54; upscale professionals. ♦Charles Benfer, gen mgr.

Attica

WLOF(FM)— Nov 9, 1977: 101.7 mhz; 3 kw. Ant 295 ft TL: N42 50 51 W78 21 01. Stereo. Hrs open: 6325 Sheridan Dr., Williamsville, 14221. Phone: (716) 839-6117. Fax: (716) 839-0400. Web Site:www.wlof.net Licensee: Holy Family Communications Inc. Group owner: Holy Family Communications acq 12-20-99; $655,000). Population served: 250000 Format: Relg. Target aud: 25-54; blue collar, housewives. ♦Jim Wright, gen mgr.

Au Sable

WYME(FM)—Not on air, target date: unknown: 97.9 mhz; 18 kw. Ant 830 ft TL: N44 46 30 W73 36 48. Hrs open: 1717 Dixie Hwy., Suite 650, Fort Wright, KY, 41011. Phone: (859) 331-9100. Licensee: Radioactive LLC. ♦Benjamin L. Homel, pres.

Auburn

WAUB(AM)— Dec 24, 1959: 1590 khz; 500 w-D, 1 kw-N, DA-2. TL: N42 54 34 W76 36 09. Hrs open: 5998 Experimental Blvd., Geneva, 13021. Phone: (315) 258-0937. Fax: (315) 258-9248.E-mail: tbaker@flradiogroup.com Web Site:www.fingerlakes1.com Licensee: Auburn Broadcasting Inc. Group owner: Finger Lakes Radio Group (acq 7-2-97; $70,000 plus additonal consideration). Population served: 34,599 Natl. Network: CBS, . James L. Oyster. Format: Talk radio. Target aud: General. ♦Bill Askew, gen sls mgr; Mike Smith, progmg dir; Ted Baker, news dir.

***WDWN(FM)**— Oct 31, 1972: 89.1 mhz; 3 kw. 102 ft TL: N42 56 40 W76 32 33. Stereo. Hrs open: 197 Franklin St., 13021. Phone: (315) 255-1743, EXT. 2282. Phone: (315) 253-0449. Fax: (315) 255-2690. Web Site:www.wdwn.fm Licensee: Cayuga County Community College. (acq 10-72). Population served: 250,000 Format: AOR. Target aud: 18-25; high school & college students, young adults. ♦Philip Gover, pres; Steven Keeler, gen mgr; Douglas Brill, chief of engrg.

WPHR-FM— May 20, 1949: 106.9 mhz; 14 kw. 941 ft TL: N42 48 05 W76 26 14. Stereo. Hrs open: 500 Plum St., Suite 100, Syracuse, 13204. Phone: (315) 472-9797. Fax: (315) 472-2333. Licensee: CC Licenses LLC. Group owner: Clear Channel Communications Inc. (acq 3-24-2000). Population served: 34,599 Format: Urban Contemp. Target aud: 25-54; educated, up-scale, high income, mobile, family oriented. ♦Joel Delmonico, gen mgr; Butch Charles, progmg dir; Kenny Dees, mus dir.

***WVWA(FM)**—Not on air, target date: unknown: 90.3 mhz; 4.3 kw. Ant 232 ft TL: N42 58 47 W76 32 40. Hrs open: 300 Pulteney St., Geneva, 14456-3397. Phone: (315) 781-3456. Fax: (315) 781-3916. Licensee: Colleges of the Seneca. ♦Aaron Read, gen mgr.

WWLF(AM)— Jan 26, 1927: 1340 khz; 1 kw-U. TL: N42 57 05 W76 35 05. Hrs open: 401 W. Kirkpatrick St., Syracuse, 13204. Phone: (315) 472-0222. Fax: (315) 478-7745.E-mail: info@radiodisney.com Web Site:www.radiodisney.com Licensee: WOLF Radio Inc. (group owner; acq 6-26-98; $103,000). Population served: 34599 Natl. Network: Radio Disney, . Format: Children. ♦Sam Furco, gen mgr; Becky Mullen, prom mgr.

Avon

WYSL(AM)— Jan 23, 1987: 1040 khz; 20 kw-D, 500 w-N, 13.2 kw-CH, DA-3. TL: N42 51 16 W77 42 39. Stereo. Hrs open: 24 Box 236, 14414-0236. Secondary address: 5620 S. Lima Rd. 14414. Phone: (585) 346-3000. Fax: (585) 346-0450.E-mail: info@wysl1040.com Web Site:www.wysl1040.com Licensee: Radio Livingston Ltd. Population served: 1,400,000 Natl. Network: ABC, Westwood One, . Format: News/sports. News staff: 3; News: 160 hrs wkly. Target aud: 35 plus; general. Spec prog: Relg 4 hrs wkly. ♦Robert Savage, CEO; Robert C. Savage, pres; James Stevenson, CFO; J.C. Delass, gen mgr, stn mgr; Bob D'Angelo, opns mgr.

Babylon

WBAB(FM)— Aug 27, 1958: 102.3 mhz; 6 kw. 269 ft TL: N40 47 58 W73 20 08. Stereo. Hrs open: 24 555 Sunrise Hwy., West Babylon, 11704-6009. Phone: (631) 587-1023. Fax: (631) 587-1282.E-mail: wbab@wbab.com Web Site:wbab.com Licensee: Cox Radio Inc. Group owner: Cox Broadcasting (acq 5-22-98; grpsl). Population served: 2,800,000 Natl. Rep: Christal,. Format: AOR. News staff: one; News: 2 hrs wkly. Target aud: 25-54; men. ♦Kim Guthrie, gen mgr.

WNYG(AM)— Jan 1, 1958: 1440 khz; 1 kw-D, 38 w-N. TL: N40 42 32 W73 21 53. Hrs open: 24 404 Rt. 109, West Babylon, 11704. Phone: (631) 321-9640. Fax: (631) 422-5992.E-mail: spiritny@optimum.net Web Site:www.wnygspiritofny.com Licensee: Multicultural Radio Broadcasting Licensee LLC. Group owner: Multicultural Radio Broadcasting Inc. (acq 6-14-00; $850,000). Population served: 2,500,000 Format: Contemp Christian. News staff: one; News: 3 hrs wkly. Target aud: 25-64. ♦Doug Edwards, pres, progmg dir; Phyllis Rose, gen mgr.

Baldwinsville

***WBXL(FM)**— Jan 29, 1975: 90.5 mhz; 175 w. 207 ft TL: N43 09 47 W76 18 47. Stereo. Hrs open: 7 AM-11 PM Baker High School, 29 E. Oneida St., 13027. Phone: (315) 638-6010. Phone: (315) 638-6000. Licensee: Baldwinsville Central School District. Population served: 250,000 Format: CHR. Family of school district students. ♦Peter Hunn, gen mgr.

WSEN(AM)— Feb 25, 1959: 1050 khz; 2.5 kw-D, DA. TL: N43 10 46 W76 20 19. Stereo. Hrs open: 24
Rebroadcasts WSEN-FM Baldwinsville.
Box 1050, 13027. Secondary address: 8456 Smoky Hollow Rd. 13027. Phone: (315) 635-3971. Fax: (315) 635-3490.E-mail: webmaster@wsenfm.com Web Site:www.wsenfm.com Licensee: Buckley Broadcasting of New York LLC. Group owner: Buckley Broadcasting Corp. (acq 8-20-80; $700,000 with co-located FM;8-11-80). Natl. Network: CBS, . Natl. Rep: McGavren Guild,. Format: Oldies. Target aud: 35 plus; well-educated professionals with disposable income. ♦Richard Buckley, pres; Judith Kelly, VP, gen mgr; Jody Frawley, gen sls mgr, rgnl sls mgr; Kristine Gladle, prom mgr; Jim Tate, progmg dir; Al Jenner, chief of engrg.

WSEN-FM— Nov 10, 1967: 92.1 mhz; 25 kw. 300 ft TL: N43 10 46 W76 20 19. Stereo. Hrs open: 24 Dups AM 100% Box 1050, 13027. Secondary address: 8456 Smoky Hollow Rd. 13027. Phone: (315) 635-3971. Fax: (315) 635-3490.E-mail: webmaster@wsenfm.com Web Site:www.wsenfm.com Natl. Rep: McGavren Guild,. Target aud: 35-64; well-educated professionals with disposable income.

Ballston Spa

WKKF(FM)— May 27, 1968: 102.3 mhz; 4.1 kw. 386 ft TL: N42 52 44 W73 51 47. Stereo. Hrs open: 24 1203 Troy-Schenectady Rd., Latham, 12110. Phone: (518) 452-4800. Fax: (518) 452-4885. Web Site:www.1023kissfm.com Licensee: CC Licenses LLC. Group owner: Clear Channel Communications Inc. (acq 3-6-97). Population served: 739900 Natl. Rep: Clear Channel,. Wilmer, Cutler & Pickering. Format: Contemp hit. Target aud: 18-34; upscale, hip women. ♦John Cooper, stn mgr; Rob Dawes, opns dir; Randy McMartin, progmg dir.

Batavia

WBTA(AM)— Feb 6, 1941: 1490 khz; 1 kw-D, 71 kw-N. TL: N42 58 35 W78 11 12. Hrs open: 24 113 Main St., 14020. Phone: (585) 344-1490. Fax: (585) 344-1441.E-mail: debbie@wbta1490.com Web Site:www.wbta1490.com Licensee: HPL Communications Inc. (acq 11-24-2003). Population served: 75,000 Natl. Rep: Rgnl Reps,. Format: News/talk, soft rock. News staff: news progmg 10 hrs wkly News: 2;. Older, upscale audience. Spec prog: Sports 9 hrs wkly. ♦Daniel C. Fischer, pres; Daniel Fischer, gen mgr, progmg dir; Lorne Way, gen sls mgr.

***WGCC-FM**— Nov 13, 1985: 90.7 mhz; 880 w. 164 ft TL: N43 01 03 W78 08 18. Stereo. Hrs open: 6 AM-1 AM One College Rd., 14020. Phone: (585) 343-0055, EXT. 6284. Phone: (585) 343-9422. Fax: (585) 345-6806.E-mail: cmplatt@genesee.edu Web Site:wgcc-fm.com Licensee: Genesee Community College Board of Trustees. Population served: 100,000 Format: Serious rock, rock/AOR, modern rock, classic rock. News staff: one; News: 5 hrs wkly. Target aud: 13-30; high school & college youth. ♦Chuck Platt, pres, engrg dir; Jeremy Canute, stn mgr; Andrew Scutt, mus dir.

Bath

WABH(AM)— Nov 2, 1962: 1380 khz; 500 w-D. TL: N42 20 11 W77 17 34. (CP: 5 kw-D, 350 w-N). Hrs open: 19 Box 72, E. Washington St. Ext., 14810. Phone: (607) 776-3326. Fax: (607) 776-6161.E-mail: wvinsales@stny.rr.com Web Site:www.wvinradio.com Licensee: Pembrook Pines Mass Media Inc. Group owner: Pembrook Pines Media Group (acq 4-13-90; with co-located FM;5-7-90). Population served: 150,000 Natl. Network: CBS, . Format: Oldies. Target aud: General. Spec prog: Farm one hr wkly. ♦Bill Fleishman, gen mgr.

***WCIK(FM)**— Aug 29, 1983: 103.1 mhz; 790 w. Ant 532 ft TL: N42 20 07 W77 27 27. Stereo. Hrs open: 24 Box 506, 7634 Campbell Creek Rd., 14810. Phone: (607) 776-4151. Fax: (607) 776-6929.E-mail: mail@fln.org Web Site:www.fln.org Licensee: Family Life Ministries Inc. Group owner: Family Life Network. Natl. Network: Salem Radio Network, . Hardy, Carey, Chautin & Balkin, LLP. Wire Svc: Metro Weather Service Inc. Format: Christian contemp. News staff: 3; News: 14 hrs wkly. Target aud: 30-54; general. ♦Dick Snavely, CFO, VP; Rick Snavely, pres & gen mgr; John Owens, progmg dir; Jim Travis, chief of engrg.

WVIN-FM— Oct 10, 1971: 98.3 mhz; 3 kw. 351 ft TL: N42 19 06 W77 21 27. (CP: 2.75 kw, ant 341 ft.). Stereo. Hrs open: 19 Box 72 , E. Washington St. Ext., 14810. Phone: (607) 776-3326. Fax: (607) 776-6161.E-mail: wvinsales@stny.rr.com Web Site:www.wvinradio.com Population served: 150,000 Format: Soft adult contemp. Spec prog: Jazz 2 hrs wkly.

Bay Shore

WBZO(FM)— February 1993: 103.1 mhz; 3 kw. 285 ft TL: N40 45 04 W73 12 52. Stereo. Hrs open: 24 234 Airport Plaza Blvd., Farmingdale, 11735. Phone: (631) 770-4200. Fax: (631) 770-0101. Web Site:www.b103.com Licensee: WCMB Broadcasting L.P. Group owner: Barnstable Broadcasting Inc. (acq 3-6-97; $12.45 million). Population served: 2,500,000 Natl. Rep: D & R Radio,. Verner, Liipfert, Bernhard, McPherson & Hand. Format: Oldies. News staff: one; News: 25 hrs wkly. Target aud: General. ♦Dave Widmer, gen mgr; Bill Wise, progmg dir; Frank Brinka, news dir, disc jockey; Michael Glaser, chief of engrg.

Beacon

WBNR(AM)— Dec 17, 1959: 1260 khz; 1 kw-D, 500 w-N, DA-2. TL: N41 29 32 W73 58 43. Stereo. Hrs open: 24
Simulcast with WLNA(AM) Peekskill 100%.
Box 310, 12508. Secondary address: 715 Rt. 52 12508. Phone: (845) 838-6000. Fax: (845) 838-2109. Web Site:www.hvradionet.com Licensee: 6 Johnson Road Licenses Inc. Group owner: Pamal Broadcasting Ltd. (acq 10-19-2001; grpsl). Population served: 200,000 Natl. Network: Fox Sports, . Format: Talk, sports. Target aud: 35 plus. ♦James Morrell, CEO; Jason Finkelberg, gen mgr; Bruce Owens, progmg dir.

WGNY-FM—See Newburgh

WSPK(FM)—See Poughkeepsie

Beekman

***WBKW(FM)**—Not on air, target date: unknown: 88.3 mhz; 3 w. Ant 679 ft TL: N41 34 22 W73 41 01. Hrs open: 375 Monroe Tpke., Monroe, CT, 06468. Phone: (203) 268-9667. Web Site:www.wmnr.org Licensee: Monroe Board of Education. ♦Kurt Anderson, gen mgr; Jane Stadler, opns mgr.

Big Flats

WENI-FM— April 1989: 97.7 mhz; 1.30 kw. Ant 482 ft TL: N42 09 43 W77 02 15. Hrs open: 24 21 E. Market St., Corning, 14830. Phone: (607) 937-8181. Fax: (607) 962-1138.E-mail: cnj@route81radio.com Licensee: WS2K Radio LLC. Group owner: Route 81 Radio LLC (acq 7-14-2008; grpsl). Population served: 50,000 Natl. Network: ABC, . Natl. Rep: Roslin,. Format: Oldies. Target aud: 25-54. ♦Jamie Evans, natl sls mgr; Paul Lyle, gen mgr & progmg dir; Dave Shoen, news dir.

Binghamton

WAAL(FM)— March 1954: 99.1 mhz; 8.7 kw. Ant 954 ft TL: N42 03 31 W75 57 06. Stereo. Hrs open: 24 P.O. Box 414, 13902. Secondary address: 59 Court St. 13901. Phone: (607) 772-8400. Fax: (607) 722-3438. Web Site:www.991thewhale.com Licensee: Citadel Broadcasting Co. Population served: 250,000 Format: Classic rock. News staff: one; News: 2 hrs wkly. Target aud: 18-49; CHR/rock listeners. ♦Don Morgan, progmg dir.

WENE(AM)—See Endicott

***WHRW(FM)**— Mar 1, 1966: 90.5 mhz; 1.45 kw. -47 ft TL: N42 05 24 W75 58 05. Stereo. Hrs open: 24 Box 2000, Univ. Union, Binghamton Univ., 13902-6000. Secondary address: 4400 Vestal Pkwy, P.O. Box 2000, Binghamton 13902-6000. Phone: (607) 777-2139. Fax: (607) 777-6501.E-mail: gm@whrwfm.org Web Site:www.whrwfm.org Licensee: State University of New York. Population served: 64,123 Wire Svc: UPI Format: Var/div. News: 5 hrs wkly. Target aud: General. Spec prog: It 3 hrs, Jazz 9 hrs, Pol 3 hrs, Relg 6 hrs, Sp 9 hrs wkly. ♦Mike Saltzman, gen mgr; Brian Napolitano, chief of engrg.

WHWK(FM)— September 1956: 98.1 mhz; 10 kw. 960 ft TL: N42 03 34 W75 57 06. Stereo. Hrs open: Prog sep from AM Box 414, 13902. Phone: (607) 772-8400. Fax: (607) 772-9806. Web Site:www.whwk.com Licensee: Citadel Broadcasting Co. Population served: 223,000 Format: Country. Target aud: 25-54. ♦Ed Walker, progmg dir.

***WIFF(FM)**— 1995: 90.1 mhz; 100 w. Ant 686 ft TL: N42 03 10 W75 42 07. Hrs open: 24 111 N. Main St., Elmira, 14901. Phone: (607) 732-2484. Fax: (607) 732-8704.E-mail: csnny@q969online.com Web Site:www.csnradio.com Licensee: CSN International (group owner; acq 5-30-2003; $67,000). Population served: 200,000 .Reddy, Begley & McCormick Format: Christian adult contemp. News staff: 2; News: 8 hrs wkly. Target aud: General. ♦Lorenzo Galletti, gen mgr; Gina Galletti, progmg mgr.

WINR(AM)— 1946: 680 khz; 5 kw-D, 500 w-N, DA-2. TL: N42 06 53 W75 51 16. Hrs open: 24 320 N. Jensen Rd., Vestal, 13850-2111. Phone: (607) 584-5800. Fax: (607) 584-5900. Licensee: AMFM Radio Licenses LLC. Group owner: Clear Channel Communications Inc. (acq 2-13-2001; $1 million). Population served: 64,123 Natl. Network: CBS, . Fisher, Wayland, Cooper, Leader & Zaragoza. Format: MOR, news/talk. News staff: one; News: 10 hrs wkly. Target aud: 35 plus. ♦Tom Barney, gen mgr; Doug Mosher, opns mgr.

WNBF(AM)— 1928: 1290 khz; 5 kw-U, DA-2. TL: N42 03 31 W75 57 14. Hrs open: Box 414, 13902. Phone: (607) 772-8400. Fax: (607) 772-9806. Web Site:www.wnbf.com Licensee: Citadel Broadcasting Co. Group owner: Citadel Broadcasting Corp. (acq 6-9-99; grpsl). Population served: 202,000 Format: News/talk. Target aud: 35-64. ♦Roger Neal, progmg dir; Bernie Fionte, news dir; Larry Hodge, chief of engrg.

***WSKG-FM**— Oct 22, 1975: 89.3 mhz; 10.2 kw. 942 ft TL: N42 03 22 W75 56 39. Stereo. Hrs open: 24 Box 3000, 13902. Phone: (607) 729-0100. Fax: (607) 729-7328. Fax: (607) 231-0996.E-mail: wskg_mail@wskg.pbs.org Web Site:www.wskg.com Licensee: WSKG Public Telecommunications Council. Population served: 273,000 Natl. Network: NPR, PRI, . Dow, Lohnes & Albertson. Format: Class, news. News staff: one; News: 33 hrs wkly. Target aud: General. Spec prog: Jazz, folk 5 hrs wkly. ♦Brian Sickora, pres; Nancy Christensen, opns dir; Linda Cohen, prom dir; Ken Campbell, progmg dir; William Snyder, mus dir; Mike Pufky, engrg dir, chief of engrg; Stacy Mosteller, traf mgr. Co-owned TV: *WSKG-TV affil.

***WSQX-FM**— Jan 17, 1995: 91.5 mhz; 3.5 kw. 380 ft TL: N42 07 54 W75 55 56. Stereo. Hrs open: 24 Box 3000, 13902. Phone: (607) 729-0100. Fax: (607) 729-7328.E-mail: wskg_mail@wskg.pbs.org Web Site:www.wskg.com Licensee: WSKG Public Telecommunications Council. Population served: 219,800 Natl. Network: NPR, PRI, . Dow, Lohnes & Albertson. Format: Jazz, news. Target aud: General. Spec prog: Talk 10 hrs wkly. ♦Brian Sickora, pres; Nancy Christensen, opns dir; Ken Campbell, progmg dir; Stacy Mosteller, traf mgr. Co-owned TV: *WSKG-TV affil

WYOS(AM)— June 1947: 1360 khz; 5 kw-D, 500 w-N, DA-2. TL: N42 04 03 W75 54 20. Hrs open: 24 59 Court St., 13901. Secondary address: Box 414 13902. Phone: (607) 772-8850. Fax: (607) 772-9806. Web Site:www.wnbf.com Licensee: Citadel Broadcasting Co. Group owner: Citadel Broadcasting Corp. (acq 6-9-99; grpsl). Population served: 64,123 Natl. Network: ESPN Radio, . Natl. Rep: McGavren Guild,. Format: Sports. ♦Roger Neal, gen sls mgr & progmg dir.

Black River

WBLH(FM)— Aug 11, 2008: 92.5 mhz; 6 kw. Ant 328 ft TL: N44 03 17.8 W75 57 15.3. Hrs open: 223 J.B. Wise Pl., Suite 10, Watertown, 13601. Phone: (315) 786-0925. Fax: (315) 786-0920. Licensee: Radioactive LLC. ♦Benjamin L. Homel, pres; Jennifer Loonan, gen mgr.

Blue Mountain Lake

***WXLH(FM)**— November 1992: 91.3 mhz; 78 w. 1,729 ft TL: N43 52 18 W74 24 02. Hrs open: 24
Rebroadcasts WSLU(FM) Canton 100%.
St. Lawrence Univ., North Country Public Radio, Canton, 13617. Phone: (315) 229-5356. Fax: (315) 229-5373.E-mail: info@ncpr.org Web Site:www.ncpr.org Licensee: St. Lawrence University. Donald E. Martin. Format: Eclectic public radio. News staff: 2; News: 35 hrs wkly. Target aud: General. Spec prog: Gospel, jazz, class, folk, pub affrs. ♦Ellen Rocco, gen mgr; Sandra Demarest, dev dir.

Boonville

WBRV(AM)— June 22, 1955: 900 khz; 1 kw-D, 52 w-N. TL: N43 30 47 W75 21 46. Hrs open: 24
Rebroadcasts WLLG(FM) Lowville 50%.
7606 N. State St., Lowville, 13367. Phone: (315) 942-4311. Phone: (315) 376-7500. Fax: (315) 376-8549.E-mail: sales@themoose.net Web Site:www.themoose.net Licensee: Flack Broadcasting Group L.L.C. Population served: 15,000 Natl. Network: USA, . Shaw Pittman. Format: Country. News: 18 hrs wkly. Target aud: General. ♦Sara Flack, sr VP; William Flack, pres, gen mgr & progmg dir; Brian Best, news dir; Dana Cowles, disc jockey.

WBRV-FM— Jan 31, 1989: 101.3 mhz; 5.5 kw. 348 ft TL: N43 26 53 W75 20 48. Stereo. Hrs open: 24
Rebroadcasts WLLG (FM) Lowville 50%.
7606 N. State St., Lowville, 13367. Phone: (315) 942-4311. Phone: (315) 376-7500. Fax: (315) 376-8549.E-mail: sales@themoose.net Web Site:www.themoose.net News: 10 hrs wkly. Target aud: General. Spec prog: Farm 3 hrs, relg 3 hrs wkly.

***WXLB(FM)**— 2009: 91.7 mhz; 100 w. Ant 351 ft TL: N43 26 53 W75 20 48. Hrs open:
Rebroadcasts WSLU(FM) Canton 100%.
North Country Public Radio, St. Lawrence University, Canton, 13617. Phone: (315) 229-5356. Fax: (315) 229-5373.E-mail: radio@ncpr.org Web Site:www.northcountrypublicradio.org Licensee: The St. Lawrence University. Natl. Network: NPR, PRI, . Format: Eclectic public radio. ♦Ellen Rocco, gen mgr.

Brentwood

***WXBA(FM)**— June 21, 1975: 88.1 mhz; 180 w. 90 ft TL: N40 46 19 W73 15 19. Stereo. Hrs open: 24 Ross High School, First & 5th Aves., 11717. Phone: (631) 434-2581. Phone: (631) 434-2582. Fax: (631) 273-6572.E-mail: wxba@88x.net Web Site:www.88x.net Licensee: Brentwood Public School District. Population served: 100,000 Format: Educ, CHR. News staff: 2; News: 3 hrs wkly. Target aud: 18-54; general. Spec prog: Black 5 hrs wkly. ♦Les Black, gen mgr; Jaimie Ottone, stn mgr; Charles Vollmer, progmg dir; Paul Bryant, news dir; Frank Lapple, chief of engrg; Pete Mandzych, sports cmtr.

Brewster

WPUT(AM)—Licensed to Brewster. See Patterson

Briarcliff Manor

WXPK(FM)— Apr 8, 1960: 107.1 mhz; 890 w. 590 ft TL: N41 04 49 W73 48 26. Stereo. Hrs open: 24 56 Lafayette Ave., White Plains,

10603. Phone: (845) 838-6000. Fax: (848) 838-2109.E-mail: info@1071thepeak.com Web Site:www.1071thepeak.com Licensee: 6 Johnson Road Licenses Inc. Group owner: Nassau Broadcasting Partners L.P. (acq 11-5-2004; $18.4 million). Population served: 2,000,000 Hogan & Hartson. Format: AAA. News staff: one. Target aud: 18-44; upscale, young, suburban. ♦Darren DiPrima, stn mgr.

Bridgehampton

WBAZ(FM)— 1996: 102.5 mhz; 4.8 kw. 367 ft TL: N40 53 58 W72 23 06. Stereo. Hrs open: 24 Box 7162, Amagansett, 11930. Secondary address: 249 Montauk Hwy., Amagansett 11930. Phone: (631) 267-7800. Fax: (631) 267-1018.E-mail: info@wbaz.com Web Site:www.wbaz.com Licensee: AAA Licensing LLC. Group owner: AAA Entertainment L.L.C. (acq 8-22-2000; $2.75 million with WBEA(FM) Southold). Population served: 1,500,000 Pepper & Corazzini. Format: Soft adult contemp. Target aud: 25-44; adults with active lifestyles. Spec prog: News, sports. ♦Don Maguire, pres; Hedy Krebs-DeMaio, gen mgr; Steve Harper, progmg dir, mus dir, chief of engrg & traf mgr.

Bridgeport

WTKW(FM)— Nov 9, 1992: 99.5 mhz; 5.7 kw. 338 ft TL: N43 09 07 W75 56 05. (CP: 2.85 kw). Stereo. Hrs open: 24 235 Walton St., Syracuse, 13202. Phone: (315) 472-9111. Fax: (315) 472-1888.E-mail: geninfo@tk99.net Web Site:www.tk99.net Licensee: Galaxy Syracuse Licensee LLC. (group owner; (acq 4-6-2000; grpsl). Leventhal, Senter & Lerman. Format: Classic rock. News staff: one; News: 3 hrs wkly. Target aud: 25-54 plus; stable, peak-earning adults. ♦Ed Levine, pres; Mike Lucarelli, CFO; Ed Levine, gen mgr; Lisa Morrow, sls VP; Mimi Grizwold, progmg VP.

Brighton

WZNE(FM)— November 1996: 94.1 mhz; 6 kw. 318 ft TL: N43 08 07 W77 35 07. (CP: 1.8 kw, ant 407 ft.). Stereo. Hrs open: 24 1700 HSBC Plaza, Rochester, 14604. Phone: (585) 399-5700. Fax: (585) 399-5750.E-mail: info@thezone941.com Web Site:www.thezone941.com Licensee: Stephens Media Group-Rochester LLC. Group owner: Infinity Broadcasting Corp. (acq 7-14-2008; grpsl). Natl. Network: CNN Radio, . Format: Alternative. Target aud: Men 18-34; affluent fans of alternative rock music. ♦Al Casazza, gen mgr; Adam Drexler, mktg dir.

Brockport

WASB(AM)— Feb 15, 1970: 1590 khz; 1 kw-U, DA-2. TL: N43 11 44 W77 57 05. Hrs open: 24 6675 4th Section Rd., 14420. Phone: (585) 637-7040. Licensee: David L. Wolfe (acq 12-21-2005; with WRSB(AM) Canandaigua). Population served: 16,000 Format: Christian. Target aud: All ages; rural audience, western Rochester & suburbs. ♦Daniel Wolfe, gen mgr, stn mgr; Gail Reed, progmg dir.

***WBSU(FM)**— Jan 14, 1981: 89.1 mhz; 7.33 kw. 160 ft TL: N43 12 45 W77 57 17. Stereo. Hrs open: 24 Seymour Union, 14420. Phone: (585) 395-2580. Fax: (585) 395-5334.E-mail: wkozires@brockport.edu Web Site:www.891thepoint.com Licensee: State University of New York. Population served: 500,000 Natl. Network: AP Radio, . Wire Svc: AP Format: CHR, AOR, alternative. News: 4 hrs wkly. Target aud: 17-34; college & young professional. Spec prog: Black one hr, pub affrs 8 hrs wkly. ♦Dr. John Halstead, pres; Warren Kozireski, gen mgr; Dean King, chief of engrg.

***WKDL-FM**— 1999: 104.9 mhz; 6 kw. Ant 328 ft TL: N43 09 51 W77 47 02. Hrs open: 2351 Sunset Blvd., Suite 170-218, Rocklin, CA, 95765. Phone: (916) 251-1600. Fax: (916) 251-1650. Web Site:www.klove.com Licensee: Brockport Licenses LLC. (acq 1-27-2006; $4 million). Natl. Network: K-Love, . Format: Contemp Chirstian. ♦Richard Jenkins, pres.

Bronxville

WFAS-FM—Licensed to Bronxville. See White Plains

Brooklyn

WKRB(FM)—Licensed to Brooklyn. See New York

WNYE(FM)—See New York

Brookville

***WCWP(FM)**— April 1965: 88.1 mhz; 100 w. 190 ft TL: N40 49 00 W73 35 49. Stereo. Hrs open: 24
Rebroadcasts WLIU(FM) Southampton 85%.
Long Island Univ., C.W. Post Campus., 11548. Phone: (516) 299-2683. Phone: (516) 299-2626. Fax: (516) 299-2767.E-mail: wcwp@cwpost.liu.edu Web Site:www.liu.edu/wcwp Licensee: Long Island University.8-13-90) Population served: 1,400,000 Natl. Network: NPR, . Format: News, jazz, NPR. News staff: one; News: 15 hrs wkly. Target aud: General. ♦Dan Cox, gen mgr; Nick Sekela, progmg dir.

Buffalo

WBBF(AM)— September 1947: 1120 khz; 1 kw-D. TL: N42 49 50 W78 47 54. Hrs open: 225 Delaware, Suite 1A, 14202. Phone: (716) 848-1120. Fax: (716) 848-9518.E-mail: totallygospel@adelphia.net Licensee: Citadel Broadcasting Co. Population served: 462,768 Format: Gospel. ♦Michael Brummer, gen mgr; John Young, opns.

WBEN(AM)— Sept 8, 1930: 930 khz; 5 kw-U, DA-N. TL: N42 58 42 W78 57 27. Hrs open: 24 500 Corporate Pkwy., Suite 200, Amherst, 14226. Phone: (716) 843-0600. Fax: (716) 832-2872. Web Site:www.wben.com Licensee: Entercom Buffalo License L.L.C. Group owner: Entercom Communications Corp. (acq 1999). Population served: 1,410,000 Natl. Network: CBS, . Natl. Rep: D & R Radio,. Format: News/talk, sports. News staff: 10; News: 20 hrs wkly. Target aud: 35-64; general. Spec prog: Buffalo Bills football. ♦L. Greene, gen mgr; Brian Meany, sls dir; Mike Krupa, natl sls mgr; Cheryl Klocke, prom mgr; Tim Wenger, progmg dir; John Zach, news dir; Kevin Keenan, pub affrs dir; Dennis Kavanaugh, engrg VP; Kevin Sylvester, sports cmtr.

***WBFO(FM)**— Jan 7, 1959: 88.7 mhz; 24 kw. 240 ft TL: N43 00 13 W78 45 54. (CP: 50 kw, ant 256 ft.). Stereo. Hrs open: 24 3435 Main St., 205 Allen Hall, 14214. Phone: (716) 829-2880. Phone: (716) 829-6000. Fax: (716) 829-2277.E-mail: mail@wbfo.org Web Site:www.wbfo.org Licensee: State University of New York. Population served: 462,768 Natl. Network: NPR, . Format: Jazz, news. News staff: 2; News: 50 hrs wkly. Target aud: General; educated professionals. Spec prog: Blues 8 hrs, bluegrass 3 hrs, class one hr, Pol 3 hrs wkly. ♦Carole Smith Petro, VP, gen mgr; Mark Wozniak, opns mgr; Joan Wilson, dev dir; Mark Scott, news dir.

WBLK(FM)—See Depew

***WBNY(FM)**— 1982: 91.3 mhz; 100 w. TL: N42 55 59 W78 52 59. Hrs open: 24 Campbell Student Union, 1300 Elmwood, 14222. Phone: (716) 878-5104. Phone: (716) 878-3080. Fax: (716) 878-6600.E-mail: wbny@hotmail.com Web Site:www.wbny.org Licensee: State University of New York. Population served: 10,000 Format: New mus, alternative rock. News: 6 hrs wkly. Target aud: 18-25; college student. Spec prog: Black 12 hrs, jazz 3 hrs, reggae 3 hrs, heavy metal 3 hrs, folk 3 hrs wkly. ♦Anthony Swinnich, progmg dir; Kevin Slattery, gen mgr & mus dir.

WBUF(FM)— 1947: 92.9 mhz; 93 kw. Ant 580 ft TL: N42 38 12 W78 42 58. Stereo. Hrs open: 14 Lafayette Sq., Suite 1300, 14203. Phone: (716) 852-9292. Fax: (716) 852-9290. Web Site:www.wbuf.com Licensee: Regent Broadcasting of Buffalo Inc. Group owner: Infinity Broadcasting Corp. (acq 12-15-2006; grpsl). Population served: 2000000 Natl. Network: CBS Radio, CNN Radio, . Natl. Rep: Christal,. Format: Talk. Target aud: 18-34; men. ♦Jeff Silver, sr VP, gen mgr; Dan Walding, gen sls mgr; Jean Tod, prom dir; Joe Russo, progmg dir; Bob Hill, news dir.

WDCX-FM— February 1963: 99.5 mhz; 115 kw. Ant 640 ft TL: N42 38 07 W78 46 05. (CP: 17 kw, ant 430 ft.). Stereo. Hrs open: 24 625 Delaware Ave., 14202. Phone: (716) 883-3010. Fax: (716) 883-3606.E-mail: wdcxinfo@crawfordbroadcasting.com Web Site:www.wdcxfm.com Licensee: Kimtron Inc. Group owner: Crawford Broadcasting Co. Population served: 6,000,000 Format: Christian & relg talk. Target aud: General. ♦Donald B. Crawford, pres; Nevin W. Larson, gen mgr.

WECK(AM)—See Cheektowaga

WEDG(FM)— 1947: 103.3 mhz; 49 kw. 340 ft TL: N42 55 33 W78 50 28. Stereo. Hrs open: 50 James E. Casey Dr., 14206. Phone: (716) 881-4555. Fax: (716) 884-2931. Web Site:www.wedg.com Licensee: Citadel Broadcasting Co. Group owner: Citadel Broadcasting Corp. (acq 2-23-00; grpsl). Natl. Rep: Eastman Radio,. Shaw Pittman. Format: Rock. Target aud: 18-44. ♦Chet Osadchey, gen mgr; Ross DiFranco, gen sls mgr; Jim Kurdrdziel, progmg dir; Tom Ragan, news dir.

***WFBF(FM)**— 1989: 89.9 mhz; 16 kw. Ant 295 ft TL: N42 41 19 W78 45 15. Hrs open: 4135 Northgate Blvd., Suite 1, Sacramento, CA, 95834. Fax: (410) 268-0931. Web Site:www.familyradio.com Licensee: Family Stations Inc. (group owner) Format: Relg. ♦Harold Camping, pres.

WGR(AM)— May 22, 1922: 550 khz; 5 kw-U, DA-2. TL: N42 46 04 W78 50 39. Stereo. Hrs open: 24 500 Corporate Pkwy., Suite 200, Amherst, 14226. Phone: (716) 843-0600. Fax: (716) 843-0250. Web Site:www.wgr550.com Licensee: Entercom Buffalo License LLC. Group owner: Entercom Communications Corp. (acq 12-13-99; grpsl). Population served: 3,800,000 Natl. Network: ESPN Radio, . Fisher, Wayland, Cooper, Leader & Zaragoza L.L.P. Format: Sports. Target aud: 25-54; men. ♦Greg Ried, VP; Tim Wenger, opns mgr; Jill Kowalski, gen sls mgr; Andy Roth, progmg dir, chief of engrg.

WGRF(FM)— Sept 14, 1959: 96.9 mhz; 24 kw. 712 ft TL: N42 57 14 W78 52 37. Stereo. Hrs open: 50 James E. Casey Dr., 14206. Phone: (716) 881-4555. Fax: (716) 882-ufax. Web Site:www.97rock.com Licensee: Citadel Broadcasting Co. Group owner: Citadel Broadcasting Corp. (acq 2-23-00; grpsl). Fisher, Wayland, Cooper, Leader & Zaragoza. Format: Classic rock. Target aud: 25-49; classic rock listeners. ♦Chet Osadchey, gen mgr, gen sls mgr; John Hager, opns mgr, progmg dir; Ryan McCrohan, prom dir; Chris Klein, news dir; Al Marranca, chief of engrg.

WHTT-FM— Oct 3, 1954: 104.1 mhz; 50 kw. Ant 500 ft TL: N42 49 50 W78 47 54. Stereo. Hrs open: 24 50 James E. Casey Dr., 14206. Phone: (716) 881-4555. Fax: (716) 884-2931. Web Site:www.whtt.com Licensee: Citadel Broadcasting Co. Group owner: Citadel Broadcasting Corp. (acq 2-23-2000; grpsl). Population served: 641,071 Natl. Network: ABC, . Natl. Rep: Eastman Radio,. Format: Classic hits. Target aud: 35-64; women and adults. ♦Chet Osadchey, gen sls mgr; Joe Siragusa, progmg dir.

WJYE(FM)— Nov 11, 1966: 96.1 mhz; 47.1 kw. 505 ft TL: N42 53 10 W78 52 25. Stereo. Hrs open: 24 14 Lafayette Sq., Suite 1200, 14203. Phone: (716) 856-3550. Fax: (716) 852-0537. Web Site:www.wjye.com Licensee: Regent Broadcasting of Buffalo Inc. Group owner: Infinity Broadcasting Corp. (acq 12-15-2006; grpsl). Population served: 220,800 Natl. Rep: Christal,. Format: Adult contemp. News staff: one; News: 23 hrs wkly. Target aud: 25-54. Spec prog: Pub affrs 2 hrs wkly. ♦Jeff Silver, sr VP, VP; Joe Chille, opns mgr, progmg dir; Andrea DeFazio, gen sls mgr; Katie Benson, prom dir; Bob Hill, news dir.

***WNED(AM)**— Oct 14, 1924: 970 khz; 5 kw-U, DA-1. TL: N42 44 41 W78 00 00. Hrs open: 24 Box 1263, 14240. Secondary address: 140 Lower Terr. 14202. Phone: (716) 845-7000. Fax: (716) 845-7043.E-mail: info@wned.org Web Site:www.wned.org Licensee: Western New York Public Broadcasting Assoc. (acq 8-14-76). Population served: 1,000,000 Natl. Network: PRI, NPR, . Format: News/talk. News staff: 8. Target aud: 35 plus. Spec prog: Pub affrs. ♦Donald K. Boswell, pres; Richard J. Daly, stn mgr; Cynthia Dwyer, dev VP; Jim Dimino, sls VP; Gwen Mysiak, prom dir; Al Wallack, progmg dir; Jon Herrington, engrg VP; Monica Wilson, local news ed; Sam Anson, local news ed & sports cmtr.

***WNED-FM**— June 6, 1960: 94.5 mhz; 105 kw. 710 ft TL: N42 38 13 W78 46 05. Stereo. Hrs open: Prog sep from AM Box 1263, 14240. Phone: (716) 845-7000. Fax: (716) 845-7043.E-mail: info@wned.org Web Site:www.wned.org Licensee: Western New York Public Broadcasting Assoc. Population served: 1,400,000 Natl. Network: PRI, . Schwartz, Woods & Miller. Format: Class. ♦Peter Goldsmith, progmg dir. Co-owned TV: *WNED-TV affil

WTSS(FM)— Nov 11, 1946: 102.5 mhz; 110 kw. 1,340 ft TL: N42 39 33 W78 37 33. Stereo. Hrs open: 24 Prog sep from AM 500 Corporate Pkwy., Suite 200, Amherst, 14226. Phone: (716) 843-0600. Fax: (716) 832-2872. Web Site:www.star1025.com Natl. Rep: D & R Radio,. Format: CHR, adult contemp. Target aud: 18-49. ♦Dave Gillen, progmg dir; Kevin Sylvester, sports cmtr.

WWKB(AM)— 1925: 1520 khz; 50 kw-U, DA-1. TL: N42 46 10 W78 50 34. Hrs open: 24 500 Corporate Pkwy., 14226. Phone: (716) 843-0600. Fax: (716) 832-3323. Web Site:www.kb1520.com Licensee: Entercom Buffalo License LLC. Group owner: Entercom Communications Corp. (acq 12-13-99; grpsl). Population served: 462,768 Natl. Rep: D & R Radio,. Format: Progressive talk. News staff: 4; News: 20 hrs wkly. Target aud: 25-54. ♦Gregory Ried, gen mgr, prom mgr; Tim Wenger, progmg dir.

WWWS(AM)— 1934: 1400 khz; 1 kw-U. TL: N42 55 33 W78 50 28. Hrs open: 500 Corporate Pkwy., 14226. Phone: (716) 843-0600. Fax: (716) 843-3323. Licensee: Entercom Buffalo License LLC. Group owner: Entercom Communications Corp. (acq 12-13-99; grpsl). Population served: 992,100 Natl. Rep: Katz Radio,. Format: Urban contemp. Target aud: 35-54. ♦Larry Robb, gen mgr; Sue O'Neil, progmg dir; Tom Karvelis, chief of engrg.

WYRK(FM)— Nov 14, 1962: 106.5 mhz; 50 kw. 390 ft TL: N42 53 10 W78 52 25. Stereo. Hrs open: 14 Lafayette Sq., Suite 1200, 14203. Phone: (716) 852-7444. Fax: (716) 852-5683.E-mail: info@wyrk.com Web Site:www.wyrk.com Licensee: Regent Broadcasting of Buffalo Inc. Group owner: Infinity Broadcasting Corp. (acq 12-15-2006; grpsl). Population served: 462,768 Natl. Rep: Katz Radio,. Wire Svc: UPI Format: Country. Target aud: 25-54; adults. ♦Jeff Silver, sr VP, VP; Mark Plimpton, gen sls mgr; Dean Sarago, prom dir; Wendy Lynn, progmg dir; Bob Hill, news dir.

Calcium

WOTT(FM)— 2009: 94.1 mhz; 21.5 kw. Ant 328 ft TL: N43 57 12.8 W75 50 34.3. Hrs open: 199 Wealtha Ave., Watertown, 13601. Phone: (315) 782-1240. Fax: (315) 782-0312. Licensee: Community Broadcasters LLC. (acq 1-8-2009; $200,000 for CP). Format: Rock. ♦James L. Leven, pres; David W. Mance, gen mgr; Lance Hale, progmg dir.

Calverton-Roanoke

WDRE(FM)— 1998: 105.3 mhz; 1 kw. Ant 492 ft TL: N40 51 18 W72 46 12. (CP: 660 w, ant 607 ft). Hrs open: 24 3075 Vets Memorial Hwy. #201, Ronkonkoma, 11779. Phone: (631) 648-2500. Fax: (516) 222-1391.E-mail: info@wlir.com Licensee: Jarad Broadcasting Co. of Calverton Inc. Group owner: The Morey Organization Inc. (acq 10-2-98). Natl. Rep: Christal,. Format: Rhythmic dance top-40. ♦Beverly Fortune, gen mgr.

Canajoharie

***WCAN(FM)**— October 1988: 93.3 mhz; 6 kw. 268 ft TL: N42 53 46 W74 35 45. Stereo. Hrs open: 24
Rebroadcasts WAMC-FM Albany 100%.
Box 66600, 318 Central Ave., Albany, 12206-6600. Phone: (518) 465-5233. Phone: (800) 323-9262. Fax: (518) 432-6974.E-mail: mail@wamc.org Web Site:www.wamc.org Licensee: WAMC. Group owner: WAMC/Northeast Public Radio Natl. Network: PRI, NPR, . Dow, Lohnes & Albertson. Wire Svc: AP Format: News, talk. News: 48 hrs wkly. Target aud: General. Spec prog: Jazz 17 hrs, folk 7 hrs wkly. ♦Alan Chartock, CEO; David Galletly, VP.

Canandaigua

WCGR(AM)— Apr 5, 1961: 1550 khz; 250 w-D. TL: N42 52 52 W77 15 02. Hrs open: 6 AM-6 PM 3568 Lenox Rd., Geneva, 14456. Phone: (315) 781-7000. Fax: (315) 781-7700. Licensee: The Fingerlakes Radio Group Inc. (acq 12-93; with co-located FM; 1-3-94). James L. Oyster. Format: News/talk, middle of the road. News staff: one; News: 10 hrs wkly. Target aud: General. ♦George Kimble, pres; Alan Bishop, gen mgr; Paula Triplett, gen sls mgr; Mike Smith, progmg dir; Ted Baker, news dir.

***WCIY(FM)**— Dec 14, 1992: 88.9 mhz; 680 w. Ant 1,063 ft TL: N42 44 44 W77 25 34. Stereo. Hrs open:
Rebroadcasts WCIK(FM) Bath 100%.
Box 506, Bath, 14810. Secondary address: 7634 Campbell Creek Rd., Bath Phone: (607) 776-4151. Fax: (607) 776-6929.E-mail: mail@fln.org Web Site:www.fln.org Licensee: Family Life Ministries Inc. Group owner: Family Life Network Natl. Network: Salem Radio Network, . Hardy, Carey, Chautin & Balkin, LLP. Wire Svc: Metro Weather Service Inc. Format: Contemp Christian. News staff: 3; News: 14 hrs wkly. Target aud: 30-54. ♦Dick Snavely, pres, CFO; Rick Snavely, pres, VP & gen mgr; John Owens, progmg dir; Jim Travis, chief of engrg.

WRSB(AM)— Apr 5, 1997: 1310 khz; 1 kw-U, DA-2. TL: N42 53 20 W77 19 09. Hrs open:
Rebroadcasts WASB(AM) Brockport 100%.
6675 Fourth Section Rd., Brockport, 14420. Phone: (585) 637-7040. Licensee: David Wolfe (acq 12-21-2005; with WASB(AM) Brockport). Natl. Network: ABC, . Format: Christian. Target aud: Everyone; all ages. ♦Dr. David Wolfe, gen mgr; Gail Reed, progmg dir.

WVOR(FM)— July 16, 1974: 102.3 mhz; 3.4 kw. 282 ft TL: N42 51 47 W77 19 22. Hrs open: 24 1700 HSBC Plaza, 100 Chestnut Street, Rochester, 14604. Phone: (585) 393-1240. Phone: (585) 454-4884. Fax: (585) 454-5081. Web Site:www.radiosunny.com Licensee: Citicasters Licenses L.P. Group owner: Clear Channel Communications Inc. (acq 5-4-99; grpsl). Population served: 40,000 Format: Adult contemp. News: 3 hrs wkly. Target aud: 25-54. ♦Karen Carey, VP & gen mgr; David LeFrois, opns mgr, progmg dir.

Canton

WNCQ-FM— July 1984: 102.9 mhz; 23.5 kw. Ant 338 ft TL: N44 32 10 W75 05 46. Stereo. Hrs open: 24 1 Bridge Plaza, Suite 204, Ogdensburg, 13369. Phone: (315) 393-1220. Fax: (315) 393-3974.E-mail: john@q1029.com Web Site:www.q1029.com Licensee: Stephens Media Group-Ogdensburg LLC. Group owner: Martz Communications Group Population served: 100,000 Taylor & Powell LLC. Format: Hot country. Target aud: 25-54; adults. ♦John Winter, gen mgr.

WRCD(FM)— Jan 1, 1997: 101.5 mhz; 2.4 kw. 364 ft TL: N44 32 01 W75 05 50. Stereo. Hrs open: 24 Box 210, Massena, 13662. Phone: (315) 769-3333. Fax: (315) 769-3299.E-mail: studio@1015thefox.com Web Site:www.1015thefox.com Licensee: Stephens Media Group-Massena LLC. Group owner: Martz Communications Group Taylor & Powell LLC. Format: Rock. News staff: 2; News: 7 hrs wkly. Target aud: 30-50; country fans. ♦Michael Boldt, gen mgr; Drew Scott, progmg dir; Bob Larue, news dir; Bob Sauder, chief of engrg.

***WSLU(FM)**— December 1964: 89.5 mhz; 40.3 kw. 299 ft TL: N44 32 01 W75 05 50. Hrs open: 24 St. Lawrence Univ., 13617. Phone: (315) 229-5356. Fax: (315) 229-5373.E-mail: info@ncpr.org Web Site:www.ncpr.org Licensee: St. Lawrence University. Population served: 1,000,000 Natl. Network: NPR, PRI, . Donald E. Martin. Format: Eclectic public radio. News staff: 2; News: 35 hrs wkly. Target aud: General. Spec prog: Gospel, jazz, class, folk, pub affrs, Black. ♦Ellen Rocco, gen mgr; Sandra Demarest, dev dir; Jacqueline Sauter, progmg dir; Martha Foley, news dir; Robert G. Sauter, chief of engrg.

***WXLE(FM)**—Not on air, target date: unknown: 88.7 mhz; 2.6 kw. Ant 233 ft TL: N44 32 01 W75 05 50. Hrs open: North Country Public Radio, St. Lawrence University, 13617. Phone: (315) 229-5356. Fax: (315) 229-5373. Web Site:www.northcountrypublicradio.org Licensee: The St. Lawrence University. ♦Ellen Rocco, stn mgr.

Cape Vincent

WLYK(FM)— Apr 21, 1997: 102.7 mhz; 6 kw. Ant 328 ft TL: N44 06 58 W76 20 21. Hrs open: 24 199 Wealtha Ave., Watertown, 13601. Phone: (315) 782-0103. Fax: (315) 782-0312. Fax: (315) 782-1240. Web Site:www.kix1027.com Licensee: Border International Broadcasting Inc. Group owner: Clancy-Mance Communications (acq 10-15-98; $50,000). Population served: 150,000 Natl. Rep: Roslin,. Format: Country. ♦David Mance, CEO, pres, gen mgr; Todd Dalessandro, opns VP; Dick Whelan, rgnl sls mgr.

***WMHI(FM)**— Oct 1, 1990: 94.7 mhz; 6 kw. 284 ft TL: N44 02 42 W76 15 37. Stereo. Hrs open: 24
Rebroadcasts WMHR(FM) Syracuse 98%.
4044 Makyes Rd., Syracuse, 13215. Phone: (315) 469-5051.E-mail: mhn@marshillnetwork.org Web Site:www.marshillnetwork.org Licensee: Mars Hill Broadcasting Co. Inc. dba Mars Hill Network. (group owner) Natl. Network: Moody, Salem Radio Network, . Wiley, Rein & Fielding. Wire Svc: AP Format: Relg, Christian. News: 6 hrs wkly. Target aud: General; Christian families. ♦Clayton Roberts, pres; Wayne Taylor, gen mgr; Chris Tetta, progmg dir; Valerie Smith, news dir; Rich McVicar, traf mgr.

***WSLZ(FM)**—Not on air, target date: unknown: 88.1 mhz; 1 kw. Ant 298 ft TL: N44 04 42 W76 15 26. Hrs open: North Country Public Radio, St. Lawrence University, Canton, 13617. Phone: (315) 229-5356. Fax: (315) 229-5373. Web Site:www.ncpr.org Licensee: The St. Lawrence University. ♦Ellen Rocco, gen mgr.

Carthage

WTOJ(FM)— Nov 1, 1984: 103.1 mhz; 6 kw. 500 ft TL: N43 57 16 W75 43 45. Stereo. Hrs open: 24 199 Wealtha Ave., Watertown, 13601. Phone: (315) 782-1240. Fax: (315) 782-0312.E-mail: blade@theborder.com Web Site:www.magic103.com Licensee: Community Broadcasters LLC. (group owner; (acq 2-8-2007; grpsl). Population served: 120,000 Natl. Rep: Roslin,. Format: Adult contemp. Target aud: 25-54. ♦James L. Leven, pres; David W. Mance, gen mgr; Joseph Brosk, stn mgr; Todd Dalesandro, opns dir.

Catskill

WCKL(AM)— Feb 6, 1970: 560 khz; 1 kw-D, DA. TL: N42 12 00 W73 50 07. Hrs open: 24 2271 Adam Clayton Powell Blvd., New York, 10030. Phone: (518) 828-5006. Fax: (518) 828-1080. Licensee: Black United Fund of New York Inc. (acq 6-10-2003; $100,000). Population served: 980,450 Format: Talk. ♦Kermit Eady, pres.

WCTW(FM)— September 1990: 98.5 mhz; 4.7 kw. Ant 374 ft TL: N42 12 03 W73 50 09. Stereo. Hrs open: 24 20 Tucker Drive, Poughkepsie, 12534. Phone: (845) 471-2300. Fax: (845) 471-2683. Web Site:www.985thecat.com Licensee: CC Licenses LLC. Group owner: Clear Channel Communications Inc. (acq 1-17-2002; grpsl). Natl. Network: Westwood One, . Natl. Rep: Katz Radio,. Format: Soft adult contemp. News staff: one; News: 2 hrs wkly. Target aud: 25-44; female. ♦Frank Curcio, gen mgr; Reggie Osterhoudt, opns dir; Jim Brady, gen sls mgr; Jeanette Relyea, natl sls mgr; Nick Smirnoff, prom dir; Michelle Taylor, progmg dir; Cameron Hendrix, news dir; Bill Draper, chief of engrg; Elizabeth Mele, sls.

Cazenovia

***WITC(FM)**— April 1978: 88.9 mhz; 129 w. 33 ft TL: N42 55 53 W75 51 15. Hrs open: Noon-midnight Cazenovia College, 22 Sullivan St., 13035. Phone: (315) 655-7154. Licensee: Cazenovia College. Population served: 15,000 Format: Alternative. News: 3 hrs wkly. Target aud: 15-35; college & young area residents. Spec prog: News/talk 3 hrs, div 10 hrs wkly. ♦Roger Benn, gen mgr.

Center Moriches

WLVG(FM)— Mar 3, 1997: 96.1 mhz; 2.65 kw. Ant 499 ft TL: N40 51 08 W72 45 55. Hrs open: 24 3241 Rt. 112, Bldg. #7, Medford, 11763. Phone: (631) 451-1039. Fax: (631) 451-0891.E-mail: info@wrcn.com Web Site:www.wrcn.com Licensee: IW Limited Liability Co. Group owner: Barnstable Broadcasting Inc. acq 1-13-2004; $3.75 million). Format: Adult contemp. ♦Dave Widmer, gen mgr; Sal Abetamarco, gen sls mgr; Megan Moir, prom dir; Charlie Lombardo, progmg dir; Jen Moran, news dir; Bob Anderson, chief of engrg, chief of engrg.

Champlain

WCHP(AM)— Aug 20, 1985: 760 khz; 35 kw-D, DA. TL: N44 56 44 W73 25 48. Hrs open: Sunrise-sunset Box 888, 137 Rapids Rd., 12919. Phone: (518) 298-2800. Fax: (518) 298-2604.E-mail: wchp@wchp.com Web Site:www.wchp.com Licensee: Champlain Radio Inc. (acq 1-31-91; 2-18-91). Population served: 4,000,000 Format: Relg, talk. Target aud: 25 plus. Spec prog: Fr, Sp. ♦Teri Billiter, gen mgr; Tonya Billiter, opns mgr; Brandi Lloyd, progmg dir.

Chateaugay

WYUL(FM)— Apr 15, 1997: 94.7 mhz; 1.9 kw. 2,081 ft TL: N44 41 43 W73 53 00. Stereo. Hrs open: 24 86 Porter Rd., Malone, 12953. Phone: (518) 483-1100. Fax: (518) 483-1382. Licensee: Cartier Communications Inc. Group owner: Martz Communications Group Population served: 3,500,000 Smithwick & Belendiuk. Format: CHR. ♦Timothy D. Martz, CEO, pres & CFO; Michael T. Boldt, gen mgr; Kim Scott, sls dir; Drew Scott, progmg dir; Neil Drew, news dir.

Cheektowaga

WECK(AM)— August 1956: 1230 khz; 1 kw-U. TL: N42 55 27 W78 46 41. Hrs open: 14 Lafayette Sq., Suite 1200, Buffalo, 14203. Phone: (716) 856-3550. Fax: (716) 852-0537. Web Site:www.weck1230.com Licensee: Culver Communications II Inc. Group owner: Infinity Broadcasting Corp. (acq 3-11-2008; $1.3 million). Population served: 100,000 Natl. Network: Westwood One, . Natl. Rep: Christal,. Format: Talk. Target aud: 35-64. Spec prog: Pol 2 hrs wkly. ♦Richard Greene, pres.

Chenango Bridge

WWYL(FM)— July 1, 1996: 104.1 mhz; 3.1 kw. 462 ft TL: N42 08 20 W75 52 24. Hrs open: Box 414, Binghamton, 13902. Phone: (607) 772-8400. Fax: (607) 772-9806. Web Site:www.wild104fm.com Licensee: Citadel Broadcasting Co. Group owner: Citadel Broadcasting Corp. (acq 6-9-99; grpsl). Format: CHR. ♦Mary Beth Walsh, gen mgr; Eric Donaldson, gen sls mgr; Andrew Smith, prom dir; Matt Johnson, progmg dir.

Cherry Valley

WJIV(FM)— 1949: 101.9 mhz; 11.5 kw. 1,027 ft TL: N42 47 36 W74 41 41. Stereo. Hrs open: 24 Box 507, 13320. Secondary address: 1668 Country Hwy. 50 13320. Phone: (607) 264-3062. Phone: (518) 437-1251. Fax: (607) 264-8277.E-mail: wjiv@hughes.net Licensee: Christian Broadcasting System Ltd. (group owner; acq 6-5-00; $1.3 million). Population served: 4,000,000 Bechtel & Cole. Wire Svc: UPI Format: Relg, talk. Target aud: 25-54. ♦John Yinger, pres; Rob Baltodano, gen mgr & progmg dir.

Clifton Park

WPTR(FM)— November 1985: 96.7 mhz; 4.7 kw. 328 ft TL: N42 52 44 W73 51 47. Stereo. Hrs open: 24 4243 Albany St., Albany, 12212. Phone: (518) 862-1540. Fax: (518) 862-1545.E-mail: info@crawfordbroadcasting.com Web Site:www.crawfordbroadcasting.com Licensee: Kimtron Inc. Group owner: Crawford Broadcasting Co. (acq 1996; $820,000). Population served: 850,000 Format: Big band, oldies. Target aud: 30-64; financially capable. ◆Donald Crawford, pres, gen mgr, stn mgr; Peter Kaye, progmg dir; David Groth, chief of engrg.

Clinton

*WHCL-FM— Feb 18, 1963: 88.7 mhz; 270 w. 97 ft TL: N43 03 04 W75 24 24. Stereo. Hrs open: 24 Hamilton College, 198 College Hill Rd., 13323. Phone: (315) 859-4200.E-mail: mngrwhcl@hamilton.edu Web Site:www.whcl.org Licensee: The Trustees of Hamilton College. Population served: 170,000 Format: Div, progsv, AOR. Target aud: General. Spec prog: Class 9 hrs, jazz 9 hrs, relg 2 hrs wkly. ◆Alex Price, gen mgr & mus dir.

Clyde

*WCOV-FM— Dec 5, 1995: 93.7 mhz; 3.8 kw. Ant 328 ft TL: N42 59 38 W76 51 59. Hrs open:
Rebroadcasts WCIK(FM) Bath 100%.
Box 506, Bath, 14810. Secondary address: 7634 Campbell Creek Rd., Bath 14810. Phone: (607) 776-4151. Fax: (607) 776-6929.E-mail: mail@fln.org Web Site:www.fln.org Licensee: Family Life Ministries Inc. Group owner: Family Life Network (acq 10-3-00). Natl. Network: Salem Radio Network, . Hardy, Carey, Chautin & Balkin, LLP. Wire Svc: Metro Weather Service Inc. Format: Contemp Christian. News staff: 3; News: 14 hrs wkly. Target aud: 30-54. ◆Dick Snavely, CFO; Rick Snavely, pres & gen mgr; John Owens, progmg dir; Jim Travis, chief of engrg.

Cobleskill

WQBJ(FM)— Sept 1, 1986: 103.5 mhz; 50 kw. Ant 492 ft TL: N42 58 21 W74 29 30. Stereo. Hrs open:
Rebroadcasts WQBK-FM Rensselaer 100%.
1241 Kings Rd., Schenectady, 12303. Phone: (518) 881-1515. Fax: (518) 881-1516. Web Site:www.wqbk.com Licensee: Regent Licensee of Mansfield Inc. Group owner: Regent Communications Inc. (acq 8-7-2000; grpsl). Haley, Bader & Potts. Format: Rock/AOR. Target aud: 18-49; general. ◆Robert Ausfeld, gen mgr; Bob O'Neal, chief of engrg.

WSDE(AM)— July 1, 1981: 1190 khz; 1 kw-D. TL: N42 41 26 W74 26 40. Hrs open: 6 AM-sunset Box 608, 12043. Phone: (518) 234-3400. Fax: (518) 234-4567. Web Site:www.wsde.com Licensee: Viva Communications Group LLC (acq 6-25-2004; $120,000). Population served: 1,000,000 Natl. Network: CNN Radio, . Format: Standards. Target aud: General.

Conklin

WKGB-FM— Feb 11, 1989: 92.5 mhz; 1.45 kw. Ant 676 ft TL: N42 06 48 W75 51 09. Stereo. Hrs open: 24 320 N. Jensen Rd., Vestal, 13850. Phone: (607) 584-5800. Fax: (607) 584-5900.E-mail: info@925kgb.com Web Site:www.925kgb.com Licensee: CC Licenses LLC. Group owner: Clear Channel Communications Inc. (acq 4-14-2000; grpsl). Natl. Rep: D & R Radio,. Carr, Morris & Graeff. Format: AOR, classic rock. News: one hr wkly. Target aud: 25-49; baby boomers who grew up with rock and roll of the 60s & 70s. Spec prog: Jazz 2 hrs, farm one hr wkly. ◆Tom Burney, gen mgr; Jim Free, opns mgr, progmg dir; Michele Page, sls dir; Tom Barney, mktg mgr.

Copenhagen

WBDR(FM)— 1994: 106.7 mhz; 1.7 kw. Ant 1,191 ft TL: N43 52 47 W75 43 11. Hrs open: 24 199 Wealthea Ave., Watertown, 13601. Phone: (315) 782-1240. Fax: (315) 782-0312.E-mail: blade@theborder.com Web Site:www.wbdr.com Licensee: Community Broadcasters LLC. Group owner: Clancy-Mance Communications (acq 2-8-2007; grpsl). Natl. Rep: Roslin,. Format: CHR. ◆James L. Leven, pres; David W. Mance, gen mgr; Todd Dalesandro, opns mgr; Dick Whelan, rgnl sls mgr.

Copiague

*WGSS(FM)—Not on air, target date: unknown: 89.3 mhz; 35 w. Ant 171 ft TL: N40 40 52 W73 23 04. Hrs open: 803 County Line Rd., North Amityville, 11701. Phone: (631) 224-1761. Licensee: Calvary Chapel of Hope. ◆Claude Stauffer, pres.

Corinth

WFFG-FM— June 26, 1967: 107.1 mhz; 2.85 kw. Ant 482 ft TL: N43 14 40 W73 46 18. Stereo. Hrs open: 24 89 Everts Ave., Queensbury, 12804. Phone: (518) 793-7733. Fax: (518) 793-0838. Web Site:www.froggy107.com Licensee: 6 Johnson Road Licenses Inc. Group owner: Pamal Broadcasting Ltd. (acq 4-1-2004; grpsl). Population served: 110,000 Format: Country. News staff: one; News: 2 hrs wkly. Target aud: 18-54. ◆Clay Ashworth, gen mgr; Walt Adams, opns mgr.

Corning

WCBA(AM)— November 1948: 1350 khz; 2 kw-D. TL: N42 07 01 W77 02 25. Hrs open: 24 21 E. Market St., 14830. Phone: (607) 937-8181. Fax: (607) 962-1138.E-mail: cnj@route81radio.com Licensee: WS2K Radio LLC. Group owner: Route 81 Radio LLC (acq 7-14-2008; grpsl). Population served: 250,000 Natl. Network: Westwood One, . Natl. Rep: Roslin,. Format: All sports. Target aud: 50 plus. ◆Jamie Evans, gen mgr & stn mgr.

WENI(AM)— November 1949: 1450 khz; 1 kw-D, 930 w-N. TL: N42 06 59 W77 02 24. Hrs open:
Rebroadcasts WENY(AM) Elmira 100%.
21 E. Market St., 14830. Phone: (607) 962-4646. Fax: (607) 962-1138.E-mail: cnj@route81radio.com Licensee: WS2K Radio LLC. Group owner: Route 81 Radio LLC (acq 7-14-2008; grpsl). Population served: 40,000 Natl. Network: USA, . Natl. Rep: McGavren Guild,. Format: News/talk. Target aud: 25-64. ◆Paul Lyle, gen mgr.

WGMM(FM)— February 1989: 98.7 mhz; 2 kw. Ant 393 ft TL: N42 09 38 W77 02 19. Stereo. Hrs open: 24
Rebroadcasts WENY-FM Elmira 100%.
21 E. Market St., 14830. Phone: (607) 937-8181. Fax: (607) 962-1138.E-mail: cnj@route81radio.com Licensee: WS2K Radio LLC. (acq 7-14-2008; grpsl). Natl. Network: ABC, . Natl. Rep: McGavren Guild,. Format: Adult contemp. ◆Paul Lyle, gen mgr.

WNKI(FM)— May 1947: 106.1 mhz; 40 kw. 532 ft TL: N42 09 43 W77 02 15. Stereo. Hrs open: 2205 College Ave., Elmira, 14903. Phone: (607) 732-4400. Fax: (607) 732-7774.E-mail: info@wink106.com Web Site:www.wink106.com Licensee: Chemung County Radio Inc. Group owner: Backyard Broadcasting LLC (acq 12-1-02; grpsl). Population served: 250,000 Natl. Rep: Christal,. Format: Adult contemp, CHR. News staff: one; News: one hr wkly. Target aud: 25-54; women. ◆Margaret Tollner, gen mgr; Scott Free, opns mgr; Brian Povancher, gen sls mgr.

*WSQE(FM)— 1995: 91.1 mhz; 3.6 kw. Ant 653 ft TL: N42 06 20 W76 52 17. Stereo. Hrs open: 24
Rebroadcasts WSKG-FM Binghamton 100%.
Box 3000, Binghamton, 13902. Phone: (607) 729-0100.E-mail: info@wskg.org Web Site:www.wskg.com Licensee: WSKG Public Telecommunications Council. Population served: 160,100 Natl. Network: NPR, PRI, AP Radio, . Dow, Lohnes & Albertson. Format: Class, news. News staff: one; News: 33 hrs wkly. Target aud: General. Spec prog: Jazz, folk 5 hrs wkly. ◆Brian Sickora, pres; Nancy Christensen, opns dir; Ken Campbell, progmg dir; Stacy Mosteller, traf mgr.

Cornwall

WWLE(AM)— Nov 22, 1969: 1170 khz; 1 kw-D, DA. TL: N41 26 24 W74 04 25. Hrs open: Box 2130, Newburgh, 12550. Phone: (845) 569-7010. Fax: (845) 562-1348. Licensee: 1170 Broadcast Radio Inc. (acq 1-1-00; $100,000). Natl. Network: USA, . Gammon & Grange. Format: News/talk. Spec prog: Farm one hr wkly. ◆Charles Stewart, gen mgr.

Cortland

WIII(FM)— Nov 15, 1947: 99.9 mhz; 24 kw. Ant 710 ft TL: N42 33 22 W76 09 17. Stereo. Hrs open: 24 1751 Hanshaw Rd., Ithaca, 14850. Phone: (607) 257-6400. Fax: (607) 257-6497.E-mail: i100@wiii.com Web Site:www.i100rocks.com Licensee: Saga Communications of New England LLC (acq 9-1-2007; $4 million with co-located AM). Population served: 200,000 Natl. Rep: Katz Radio,. Format: Classic rock. News staff: one; News: one hr wkly. Target aud: 25-54; men. ◆Susan Johnston, gen mgr; Chris Allinger, opns mgr.

Copiague (continued)

*WSUC-FM— Nov 17, 1976: 90.5 mhz; 241 w. -110 ft TL: N42 35 53 W76 11 13. Stereo. Hrs open: 24 State Univ. of New York, Brockway Hall, Graham Ave., 13045. Phone: (607) 753-2936. Fax: (607) 753-2807.E-mail: info@wsuc.com Licensee: State University of New York. Population served: 32,000 Natl. Network: AP Radio, . Format: Var/div, rock. Target aud: 12-50. ◆Peter Johams, gen mgr.

WYBY(AM)— Nov 15, 1947: 920 khz; 1 kw-D, 500 w-N, DA-N. TL: N42 33 22 W76 09 17. Hrs open: 24 11530 Carmel Commons Blvd., Charlotte, NC, 28226. Phone: (704) 523-5555.E-mail: bbn@bbnradio.org Web Site:www.bbnradio.org Licensee: Bible Broadcasting Network Inc. Group owner: Citadel Broadcasting Corp. (acq 9-1-2007; donation). Population served: 45,000 Format: Relg. ◆Lowell L. Davey, pres.

Dannemora

*WKVJ(FM)— 2005: 89.7 mhz; 4.4 kw. Ant 1,096 ft TL: N44 34 24 W73 40 31. Stereo. Hrs open: 24 American Educational Broadcasting Inc., 3185 S. Highland Dr., Suite 13, Las Vegas, NV, 89109. Secondary address: Box 888, Studio, Champlain 12919. Fax: (518) 298-2604.E-mail: wchp@wchp.com Licensee: American Educational Broadcasting Inc. Fletcher, Heald & Hildreth. Format: Christian. ◆Carl Auel, CEO; Carl J. Auel, pres; Fred Hodges, gen mgr.

WNMR(FM)— 2008: 107.1 mhz; 1 kw. Ant 276 ft TL: N44 43 15.8 W73 44 10.5. Hrs open: Box 212, Burlington, VT, 05402. Phone: (804) 759-4000. Licensee: Radioactive LLC. Format: Talk. ◆Benjamin L. Homel, pres.

Dansville

WDNY(AM)— Oct 20, 1978: 1400 khz; 1 kw-U. TL: N42 32 19 W77 40 57. Hrs open: 19 Dups FM 100% 195 Main St., 14437. Phone: (585) 335-2273. Fax: (585) 335-9677.E-mail: wdny@frontiernet.net Licensee: Miller Media Inc. (Acq 4-13-92; $290,000; 5-4-92). Population served: 20,000 Natl. Network: Jones Radio Networks, Westwood One, . Format: Music of your Life. News staff: one; News: 8 hrs wkly. ◆Mark Miller, progmg dir.

WDNY-FM— March 1990: 93.9 mhz; 570 w. 741 ft TL: N42 30 45 W77 38 07. Stereo. Hrs open: 24 195 Main St., 14437. Phone: (585) 335-2273. Fax: (585) 335-9677.E-mail: wdny@frontiernet.net Licensee: Miller Media Inc. Population served: 50,000 Natl. Network: Jones Radio Networks, Westwood One, . Format: Adult contemp. News staff: one; News: 8 hrs wkly. Target aud: 25-54. Spec prog: Relg one hr, big band 3 hrs, sports 4 hrs wkly. ◆Dorothy Hotchkiss, gen mgr.

Delhi

WDHI(FM)— Mar 16, 1992: 100.3 mhz; 770 w. Ant 643 ft TL: N42 22 40 W74 50 23. Stereo. Hrs open: 16 34 Chestnut St., Oneonta, 13820. Phone: (607) 432-1030. Fax: (607) 432-6909.E-mail: info@centralnewyorkradio.com Licensee: Double O Central New York Corp. (group owner; (acq 10-22-2004; grpsl). Natl. Network: USA, . Format: CHR. ◆George Wells, gen mgr.

WTBD-FM— 2008: 97.5 mhz; 6 kw. Ant 328 ft TL: N42 14 09 W74 57 12. Hrs open: 34 Chestnut St., Oneonta, 13820. Phone: (607) 432-1030. Fax: (607) 432-6909.E-mail: info@centralnewyorkradio.com Licensee: Double O Central New York Corp. ◆George Wells, gen mgr.

Depew

WBLK(FM)— December 1964: 93.7 mhz; 47 kw. Ant 505 ft TL: N42 53 10 W78 52 25. Stereo. Hrs open: Rand Bldg., 14 Lafayette Sq., Buffalo, 14203. Phone: (716) 852-9393. Fax: (716) 852-9390.E-mail: info@wblk.com Web Site:www.wblk.com Licensee: Regent Broadcasting of Buffalo Inc. Group owner: Infinity Broadcasting Corp. (acq 12-15-2006; grpsl). Population served: 462,768 Natl. Network: CBS Radio, . Natl. Rep: Katz Radio,. Format: Urban contemp. Target aud: General. ◆Jeff Silver, sr VP, VP; Rose Vecchiarelli, gen sls mgr; Chris Reynolds, progmg dir.

Deposit

WIYN(FM)— Jan 16, 1991: 94.7 mhz; 770 w. Ant 642 ft TL: N42 01 43 W75 28 25. Stereo. Hrs open: 16 34 Chestnut St., Oneonta, 13820. Phone: (607) 432-1030. Fax: (607) 432-6909.E-mail: info@centralnewyorkradio.com Licensee: Double O Central New York Corp. (group owner; (acq 10-22-2004; grpsl). Population served: 40,000 Format: Oldies. Target aud: 28-55. ◆George Wells, gen mgr.

DeRuyter

WVOA-FM— 1948: 105.1 mhz; 42 kw. Ant 541 ft TL: N42 46 58 W75 50 28. Stereo. Hrs open: 7095 Myers Rd., East Syracuse, 13057. Phone: (315) 656-2231.E-mail: programming@wvoaradio.com Web Site:www.wvoaradio.com Licensee: Foxfur Communications LLC Group owner: Clear Channel Communications Inc. (acq 5-1-2009; $1.25 million). Population served: 500,000 Format: Relg. ◆ Sam Furco, gen mgr.

Dewitt

WVOA(AM)—Not on air, target date: unknown: 720 khz; 2.5 kw-D, 390 w-N, DA-N. TL: N43 03 30 W76 10 01 (D), N42 56 02 W76 06 59 (N). Hrs open: 4853 Manor Hill Dr., Syracuse, 13215-1336. Phone: (315) 468-0908. Licensee: Cram Communications LLC. ◆ Sam Furco, gen mgr.

Dolgeville

*WVVC-FM—Not on air, target date: unknown: 88.5 mhz; 800 w vert. Ant -249 ft TL: N43 10 43 W74 42 08. Hrs open: 65 King Rd., Buskirk, 12028-2221. Phone: (518) 686-0975. Fax: (518) 686-0975. Licensee: Northeast Gospel Broadcasting Inc. ◆ Brian Larson, gen mgr.

Dundee

WFLR(AM)— Oct 1, 1956: 1570 khz; 5 kw-D, 442 w-N. TL: N42 32 40 W76 59 35. Hrs open: 24 30 Main St., 14837. Phone: (607) 243-7158. Phone: (607) 243-7070. Fax: (607) 243-7662.E-mail: wfir@linkny.com Web Site:www.linkny.com/wflr Licensee: Finger Lakes Radio Group Inc. Group owner: Finger Lakes Radio Group (acq 3-5-2004; $600,000 with co-located FM). Population served: 80,000 Natl. Network: Motor Racing Net., Format: Country, news/talk. News staff: one; News: 40 hrs wkly. Target aud: 25-55. Spec prog: Relg 5 hrs wkly. ◆ Dick Evans, gen mgr; Mark Feiock, prom dir.

Dunkirk

WDOE(AM)— Dec 24, 1949: 1410 khz; 1 kw-D, 500 w-N, DA-N. TL: N42 27 51 W79 21 21. Stereo. Hrs open: Box 209, Willow Rd., 14048. Phone: (716) 366-1410. Phone: (716) 366-8580. Fax: (716) 366-1416. Licensee: Chadwick Bay Broadcasting Corp. (acq 2-26-2001; with WBKX(FM) Fredonia). Population served: 75,000 Natl. Network: ABC, . Format: Oldies, news/talk. News staff: News progmg 12 hrs wkly Target aud: 45-65. Spec prog: Pol 6 hrs, Sp 2 hrs wkly. ◆ John Bulmer, pres; Chuck Telford, gen mgr.

East Aurora

WLKK(FM)—See Wethersfield Township

East Hampton

WEHN(FM)— Mar 1, 1993: 96.9 mhz; 4.3 kw. Ant 384 ft TL: N40 59 37 W72 10 19. Hrs open: 24
Simulcast with WEHM(FM) Southampton 100%.
Box 7162, Amagansett, 11930. Secondary address: 249 Montauk Hwy., Amagansett 11930. Phone: (631) 267-7800. Fax: (631) 267-1018. Web Site:www.wehm.com Licensee: AAA Licensing LLC. Group owner: AAA Entertainment L.L.C. (acq 5-31-2000; grpsl). Population served: 110,000 Natl. Network: CNN Radio, . Format: Progsv adult rock. Target aud: 24-54; upscale Hamptons residents and NYC second homeowners. ◆ Don Maguire, pres; Hedy Krebs-DeMaio, gen mgr; Steve Harper, opns mgr & progmg dir.

East Patchogue

WALK(AM)—Licensed to East Patchogue. See Patchogue

East Syracuse

WSIV(AM)—Licensed to East Syracuse. See Syracuse

Easthampton, Village

*WEER(FM)—Not on air, target date: unknown: 90.7 mhz; 3.8 kw vert. Ant 285 ft TL: N41 01 56.1 W71 58 32.1. (ST with KCBE(FM) Napeague). Hrs open: 192 Big Fresh Pond Rd., Southampton,

11968. Phone: (631) 283-0843.E-mail: info@hamptonscommunityradio.com Web Site:www.hamptonspublicradio.org Licensee: Hamptons Community Radio Corp. ◆ M.J. Stutterheim, chmn; Barbara Barri, gen mgr.

Ellenville

WELG(AM)— December 1964: 1370 khz; 5 kw-D. TL: N41 44 19 W74 23 48. Hrs open: 20 Tucker Dr., Poughkeepsie, 12603. Secondary address: 22 N. Main St. 12428. Phone: (845) 471-2300. Fax: (845) 471-2683. Web Site:www.1370welg.com Licensee: CC Licenses LLC. Group owner: Clear Channel Communications Inc. (acq 7-14-2000; grpsl). Population served: 50,000 Natl. Network: Jones Radio Networks, . Natl. Rep: Katz Radio,. Format: Nostalgia. Target aud: 30-64. ◆ Frank Curcio, gen mgr; Reggie Osterhoudt, opns mgr; Jim Brady, gen sls mgr; Jeanette Relyea, natl sls mgr; Nick Smirnoff, prom dir; Rick Knight, progmg dir; Cameron Hendrix, news dir.

WRWC(FM)— August 1970: 99.3 mhz; 115 w. Ant 1,630 ft TL: N41 41 06 W74 21 23. Stereo. Hrs open: 24
Simulcast with WRWD-FM Highland 100%.
20 Tucker Dr., Poughkeepsie, 12603. Phone: (845) 471-2300. Fax: (845) 471-2683. Web Site:www.wrwdfm.com Population served: 400,000 Natl. Network: Jones Radio Networks, . Natl. Rep: Katz Radio,. Format: Country. News staff: one. ◆ Frank Curcio, gen mgr; Reggie Osterhoudt, opns dir; Jim Brady, gen sls mgr; Jeanette Relyes, natl sls mgr; Nick Smirnoff, prom dir; Aaron McCord, progmg dir; Elizabeth Mele, sls.

Elmira

*WCIH(FM)— July 31, 1989: 90.3 mhz; 4 kw. Ant 526 ft TL: N41 53 39 W76 51 32. Stereo. Hrs open: 24
Rebroadcasts WCIK(FM) Bath 100%.
Box 506, Bath, 14810. Secondary address: 7634 Campbell Creek Rd., Bath 14810. Phone: (607) 776-4151. Fax: (607) 776-6929.E-mail: mail@fln.org Web Site:www.fln.org Licensee: Family Life Ministries Inc. Group owner: Family Life Network Natl. Network: Salem Radio Network, . Hardy, Carey, Chautin & Balkin, LLP. Wire Svc: Metro Weather Service Inc. Format: Contemp Christian. News staff: 3; News: 14 hrs wkly. Target aud: 30-54; general Christian public. ◆ Dick Snavely, CFO, VP; Rick Snavely, pres & gen mgr; John Owens, progmg dir; Jim Travis, chief of engrg.

*WECW(FM)— Jan 19, 1959: 107.7 mhz; 6 w. -312 ft TL: N42 05 52 W76 48 53. Stereo. Hrs open: Elmira College, One Park Pl., 14901. Phone: (607) 735-1885. Phone: (607) 735-1815.E-mail: wecw@elmira.edu Licensee: Elmira College. Population served: 55,000 Format: Classic rock, Top-40. Target aud: 18-30. ◆ Lauren Sanclementi, gen mgr; Paul Riley, progmg dir.

WEHH(AM)—See Elmira Heights-Horseheads

WELM(AM)— April 1947: 1410 khz; 5 kw-D, 1 kw-N, DA-N. TL: N42 07 11 W76 48 37. Stereo. Hrs open: 24 1705 L22 N. Main St.ake St., 14901. Phone: (607) 733-5626. Phone: (607) 732-1400. Fax: (607) 733-5627.E-mail: ppinesmedia1@stny.rr.com Licensee: Pembrook Pines Elmira Ltd. Group owner: Pembrook Pines Media Group (acq 10-1-77). Population served: 350,000 Natl. Network: CBS, . Bechtel & Cole. Format: Sports. News staff: one; News: 10 hrs wkly. Target aud: 25-54. Spec prog: Relg one hr wkly. ◆ Robert J. Pfuntner, CEO, pres & gen mgr; Gary Knight, opns dir; David Crum, gen sls mgr, adv mgr; Patrick Leiby, mktg dir; Bob Michaels, progmg dir, sports cmtr; Brian Stoll, mus dir; Mike Jacobs, news dir, local news ed; Nancy Nicastro, pub affrs dir.

WENY(AM)— 1939: 1230 khz; 1 kw-U. TL: N42 04 30 W76 46 55. Hrs open: 24
Rebroadcasts WCLI(AM) Corning 100%.
21 E. Market St., Corning, 14830. Phone: (607) 937-8181. Fax: (607) 962-1138.E-mail: cnj@route81radio.com Licensee: WS2K Radio LLC. Group owner: Route 81 Radio LLC (acq 7-14-2008; grpsl). Population served: 200,000 Natl. Rep: McGavren Guild,. Format: News/talk. Target aud: 30 plus. ◆ Paul Lyle, gen mgr.

WENY-FM— Aug 15, 1965: 92.7 mhz; 700 w. Ant 561 ft TL: N42 01 55 W76 47 02. Stereo. Hrs open: 24
Rebroadcasts WCBA-FM Corning 100%.
21 E. Market St., Corning, 14830. Phone: (607) 937-8181. Fax: (607) 962-1138.E-mail: cnj@route81radio.com Licensee: WS2K Radio LLC. (acq 7-14-2008; grpsl). Population served: 250,000 Natl. Network: ABC, . Format: Adult contemp.

WLVY(FM)— Aug 1, 1966: 94.3 mhz; 800 w. Ant 745 ft TL: N42 07 51 W76 47 26. Stereo. Hrs open: Prog sep from AM 1705 Lake St., 14901. Phone: (607) 733-5626. Phone: (607) 732-1400. Fax: (607) 733-5627.E-mail: airstaff@wlvy94rock.com Web Site:www.wlvy94rock.com Natl. Network: Westwood One, . Rgnl rep: Pembrook Pines Format:

CHR, hot adult contemp, Top 40s. News staff: one; News: 5 hrs wkly. Target aud: 18-36; young vibrant adults. ◆ Dave Crum, sls dir, adv dir; Sue Schneck, mktg dir; Bob Smith, prom dir; Mike Strobel, progmg dir, disc jockey; Jim Reed, engrg dir; Mark Saia, engrg mgr; Donna Vande Bogart, traf mgr; Allison Barden, disc jockey.

WNKI(FM)—See Corning

WPGI(FM)—See Horseheads

WWLZ(AM)—See Horseheads

Elmira Heights-Horseheads

WEHH(AM)— July 4, 1956: 1600 khz; 5 kw-D, 170 w-N, DA-2. TL: N42 07 11 W76 48 37. Hrs open: 24 1705 Lake St., Elmira, 14901. Phone: (607) 733-5626. Phone: (607) 732-1400. Fax: (607) 733-5627.E-mail: ppinesmedial@sty.rr.com Web Site:wehhradio.com Licensee: Pembrook Pines Elmira Ltd. Group owner: Pembrook Pines Media (acq 5-19-99). Population served: 100,000 Format: Adult classics. News: 2 hrs wkly. Target aud: 45 plus; upscale adults. ◆ Robert J. Pfuntner, CEO, gen mgr; Sue Schneck, opns VP.

Endicott

WENE(AM)— September 1947: 1430 khz; 5 kw-U, DA-N. TL: N42 04 56 W76 01 53. Stereo. Hrs open: 24 320 N. Jensen Rd., Vestal, 13850-2111. Phone: (607) 785-3351. Fax: (607) 584-5900.E-mail: info@1430theteam.com Web Site:www.1430theteam.com Licensee: CC Licenses LLC. Group owner: Clear Channel Communications Inc. (acq 4-14-2000; grpsl). Population served: 250,000 Natl. Network: Westwood One, . Natl. Rep: McGavren Guild,. Proskauer, Rose, Goetz & Mendelsohn, L. Format: Talk, sports. News staff: 2; News: 28 hrs wkly. Target aud: 35 plus. ◆ Tom Barney, gen mgr.

WMRV-FM— 1969: 105.7 mhz; 35 kw. 570 ft TL: N42 08 20 W75 59 58. Stereo. Hrs open: 24 Prog sep from AM 320 N. Jensen Rd., Vestal, 13850. Phone: (607) 785-3351. Fax: (607) 584-5900. Web Site:www.1430theteam.com Format: CHR. Target aud: 18-34.

Endwell

WBBI(FM)— 1998: 107.5 mhz; 1.1 kw. Ant 544 ft TL: N42 08 17 W75 59 59. Hrs open: 320 North Jensen Rd., Vestal, 13850. Phone: (607) 584-5800. Fax: (607) 584-5900. Web Site:www.1075thebear.com Licensee: CC Licenses LLC. Group owner: Clear Channel Communications Inc. (acq 4-14-2000; grpsl). Format: Classic rock. ◆ Joanna Alay, gen mgr.

Esperance

*WOPG(FM)—Not on air, target date: unknown: 89.9 mhz; 1.5 kw vert. Ant 971 ft TL: N42 46 28.6 W74 40 54.5. Hrs open: 14 Lincoln Town Rd., Clifton Park, 12065. Phone: (518) 877-6137. Licensee: Pax et Bonum Inc. Natl. Network: EWTN Radio, . ◆ Thomas Threlkeld, pres.

Essex

WCPV(FM)— Oct 1, 1994: 101.3 mhz; 1 kw. Ant 797 ft TL: N44 24 12 W73 26 02. Hrs open: 1500 Hegeman Ave., Colchester, VT, 05446. Phone: (802) 654-9300. Fax: (802) 655-0478.E-mail: info@champrocks.com Web Site:www.champrocks.com Licensee: Vox AM/FM LLC. Group owner: Clear Channel Communications Inc. (acq 7-25-2008; grpsl). Format: Classic rock. ◆ Karen Marshall, gen mgr; Steve Cormier, opns mgr; John Hill, sls dir.

Fairport

WFKL(FM)— 1993: 93.3 mhz; 4.4 kw. Ant 384 ft TL: N43 10 37 W77 28 39. Stereo. Hrs open: 24 Entercom Rochester LLC, 70 Commercial St., Rochester, 14614-1010. Phone: (585) 423-2900. Fax: (585) 325-5139. Web Site:www.wfkl-fm.fimc.net Licensee: Stephens Media Group-Rochester LLC. Group owner: Entercom Communications Corp. (acq 7-14-2008; grpsl). Natl. Rep: Katz Radio,. Taylor & Powell LLC. Format: Oldies. News staff: one. Target aud: 25-54; upscale. ◆ Michael Doyle, gen mgr; Mike Rockwell, natl sls mgr; Mike Johnson, rgnl sls mgr; Christine Neenan, prom dir; Steve Hausmann, news dir; Joe Fleming, chief of engrg.

Fenner

*WXXE(FM)— Dec 21, 1998: 90.5 mhz; 7 w. 413 ft TL: N42 58 12 W75 47 12. Hrs open: 826 Euclid Ave., Syracuse, 13210. Phone: (315) 863-6013.E-mail: info@wxxe.org Web Site:www.wxxe.org Licensee: Syracuse Community Radio Inc. Format: Var. ◆Dana Bonn, pres, mus dir; Danny Danhauser, gen mgr.

Fleming

*WTMI(FM)—Not on air, target date: unknown: 88.7 mhz; 174 w vert. Ant 354 ft TL: N42 47 52.6 W76 34 27.1. Hrs open: 17 Clymer St., Auburn, 13021. Phone: (315) 252-2937. Fax: (315) 252-4173. Licensee: Tyburn Academy. Natl. Network: EWTN Radio, . ◆Robert Faiola, pres.

Fort Plain

WBUG-FM— Mar 1, 1990: 101.1 mhz; 1.25 kw. Ant 718 ft TL: N42 52 44 W74 47 07. Stereo. Hrs open: 24 185 Genesee St., Suite 1601, Utica, 13501. Phone: (315) 734-9245. Fax: (315) 624-9245. Web Site:www.bugcountry.com Licensee: Roser Communications Network Inc. (acq 10-21-94; $400,000 with WVTL(AM) Amsterdam; 12-5-94). Natl. Network: ABC, . Format: C&W. News staff: 2; News: 10 hrs wkly. Target aud: 25 plus. ◆Ken Roser, gen mgr; Dave Silver, opns mgr, gen sls mgr.

Frankfort

WKLL(FM)—Licensed to Frankfort. See Utica

Fredonia

WBKX(FM)— April 1989: 96.5 mhz; 1.4 kw. Ant 686 ft TL: N42 22 02 W79 23 12. Stereo. Hrs open: 24 Box 209, 4561 Willow Rd., Dunkirk, 14048. Phone: (716) 366-8580. Phone: (716) 366-1410. Fax: (716) 366-1416. Web Site:www.96kix.com Licensee: Chadwick Bay Broadcasting Corp. (acq 2-26-2001; with WDOE(AM) Dunkirk). Population served: 75000 Natl. Network: ABC, . Format: Country. News staff: one; News: 12 hrs wkly. Target aud: 25-54. ◆Alan Bishop, pres; Chuck Telford, gen mgr; Mike McAdam, progmg dir; David Rowley, news dir.

*WCVF-FM— July 6, 1978: 88.9 mhz; 130 w. Ant -115 ft TL: N42 27 08 W79 20 14. Stereo. Hrs open: 24 115 McEwen Hall, State Univ. of New York, 14063. Phone: (716) 673-3420. Fax: (716) 673-3427.E-mail: fredoniaradio@gmail.com Web Site:www.fredoniaradio.com Licensee: State University of New York. Population served: 40,000 Natl. Network: NPR, . Wire Svc: UPI Format: Div, progsv. News: 28 hrs wkly. All ages of campus & community of Fredonia. Spec prog: Reggae 4 hrs, folk 4 hrs, world 4 hrs, spanish 4 hrs, new age 4 hrs, polka 3 hours weekly.

Freeport

WGBB(AM)— August 1924: 1240 khz; 1 kw-U. TL: N40 38 44 W73 34 38. Hrs open: 1850 Lausdown Ave., 404 Rte 109, W. Babylon, 11704. Phone: (516) 623-1240. Fax: (516) 623-1240.E-mail: support@am1240wgbb.com Web Site:www.am1240wgbb.com Licensee: WGBB-AM Inc. Group owner: Cox Broadbasting (acq 5-22-98; grpsl). Population served: 35,000 Format: Var. Target aud: 25-65. Spec prog: Relg 6 hrs, Sp 2 hrs wkly. ◆Josephine Chin, gen mgr; Jeff Lo, opns mgr.

Friendship

*WCID(FM)— 1989: 89.1 mhz; 7 kw. Ant 492 ft TL: N42 07 07 W78 10 43. Stereo. Hrs open: 24
Rebroadcasts WCIK(FM) Bath 100%.
Box 506, 7634 Campbell Creek Rd., Bath, 14810. Phone: (607) 776-4151. Fax: (607) 776-6929.E-mail: mail@fln.org Web Site:www.fln.org Licensee: Family Life Ministries Inc. Group owner: Family Life Network Natl. Network: Salem Radio Network, . Hardy, Carey, Chautin & Balkin, LLP. Wire Svc: Metro Weather Service Inc. Format: Christian, contemp. News staff: 3; News: 14 hrs wkly. Target aud: 30-54; general. ◆Dick Snavely, CFO; Rick Snavely, pres & gen mgr; John Owens, progmg dir; Jim Travis, chief of engrg.

Fulton

WAMF(AM)— Aug 19, 1949: 1300 khz; 1 kw-D. TL: N43 17 41 W76 26 35. Stereo. Hrs open: 24 401 W. Kirkpatrick St., Syracuse, 13204. Phone: (315) 472-0222. Fax: (315) 478-7745. Licensee: Cram Communications LLC. (acq 11-14-2007). Population served: 300,000

Natl. Network: ABC, . Format: Country. Target aud: 35 plus; hometown listeners, county coverage. Spec prog: It 2 hrs, Pol 5 hrs wkly. ◆Don Derosa, gen mgr.

WBBS(FM)— Aug 1, 1961: 104.7 mhz; 50 kw. 310 ft TL: N43 12 53 W76 23 44. (CP: Ant 479 ft.). Stereo. Hrs open: 500 Plum St., Suite 100, Bridgewater Pl., Syracuse, 13204. Phone: (315) 448-1047. Phone: (315) 472-9797. Fax: (315) 472-2323. Web Site:www.b1047.net Licensee: Citicasters Licenses L.P. Group owner: Clear Channel Communications Inc. (acq 5-4-99; grpsl). Population served: 550,000 Format: Country. ◆Joel Delmonico, gen mgr; Ron Nagy, gen sls mgr.

Garden City

*WHPC(FM)— Oct 12, 1972: 90.3 mhz; 500 w. Ant 213 ft TL: N40 43 47 W73 35 33. Stereo. Hrs open: 24 WHPC, One Education Dr., 11530-6793. Phone: (516) 572-7439. Fax: (516) 572-7831.E-mail: WHPC@NCC.EDU Web Site:www.sunynassau.edu Licensee: Nassau Community College Board of Trustees. Population served: 2,000,000 Format: Div, educ, adult contemp. News staff: 2; News: 5 hrs wkly. Target aud: 20-65; general. ◆Sean Fanelli, CEO; Jack Ostling, exec VP; Jim Green, opns mgr, progmg dir.

WQBU-FM— 1988: 92.7 mhz; 2 kw. Ant 521 ft TL: N40 45 26 W73 42 52. Stereo. Hrs open: 485 Madison Ave., New York, 10022. Phone: (212) 310-6000. Fax: (212) 310-6095.E-mail: info@univision.com Web Site:www.univision.com Licensee: Univision Radio License Corp. Group owner: Univision Radio (acq 1-12-2004; $60 million). Format: Rgnl Mexican. ◆Joe Pagan, VP & gen mgr.

Geneseo

*WGSU(FM)— Feb 18, 1963: 89.3 mhz; 1.8 kw. 11 ft TL: N42 47 51 W77 49 13. Stereo. Hrs open: 24 Blake B 104, 1 College Cir., 14454. Phone: (585) 245-5486. Fax: (585) 245-5240.E-mail: pruszyns@geneseo.edu Web Site:www.geneseo.edu/~wgsu/ Licensee: State University of New York. Population served: 10,000 Format: News, alternative. News: 7 hrs wkly. Target aud: 12-55; college, immediate community. ◆Chris Pruszynski, gen mgr.

Geneva

*WEOS(FM)— Mar 30, 1971: 89.7 mhz; 4 kw. 312 ft TL: N42 51 27 W76 59 21. Stereo. Hrs open: 24 300 Pulteney St., 14456. Secondary address: 113 Hamilton St. 14456. Phone: (315) 781-3456. Phone: (315) 781-3897. Fax: (315) 781-3916.E-mail: weos@hws.edu Web Site:www.weos.org Licensee: The Colleges of the Seneca. Population served: 300,000 Natl. Network: NPR, PRI, . Wire Svc: AP Format: Jazz, progsv, news/talk. News staff: one; News: 40 hrs wkly. Target aud: 18-plus. Spec prog: AAA 12 hrs, world 10 hrs, metal 6 hrs, gospel 3 hrs, reggae 3 hrs wkly. ◆Aaron Read, gen mgr; Greg Cotterill, stn mgr, dev dir; Genoa Boswell, progmg dir; Anessa Amer, mus dir; Sara Henegan, news dir.

WFLK(FM)— 1974: 101.7 mhz; 5.4 kw. Ant 125 ft TL: N42 51 34 W77 00 29. Stereo. Hrs open: 24 Box 1017, 14456. Phone: (315) 781-1101. Fax: (315) 781-6666.E-mail: k1017@rochester.rr.com Web Site:www.k1017.com Licensee: MB Communications Inc. (acq 1993). Population served: 300,000 Henry Crawford. Format: Super hit country. News staff: 2; News: 10 hrs wkly. Target aud: 25-49. ◆Russ Kimble, pres & stn mgr; John Thomas, opns mgr, pub affrs dir; Lori Rose, dev mgr; Deb Hunt, gen sls mgr; Matt Ripley, prom dir, progmg dir.

WGVA(AM)— 1947: 1240 khz; 1 kw-U. TL: N42 51 37 W77 00 59. Hrs open: 24 3568 Lenox Rd., 14456. Phone: (315) 781-1240. Fax: (315) 781-7700. Licensee: Geneva Broadcasting Inc. (acq 9-27-96). Population served: 325,000 James L. Oyster. Format: News/talk. News staff: one; News: 10 hrs wkly. Target aud: General. ◆George Kimble, pres; Alan Bishop, exec VP, VP, gen mgr; Paula Triplett, gen sls mgr; Mike Smith, progmg dir; Ted Baker, news dir.

WNYR-FM—See Waterloo

Glens Falls

WFFG-FM—See Corinth

*WGFR(FM)— January 1977: 92.7 mhz; 13 w. 49 ft TL: N43 18 44 W73 38 58. Hrs open: Adirondack Community College, 640 Bay Rd., Queensbury, 12804-1498. Phone: (518) 743-2311. Fax: (518) 745-1433. Web Site:www.wgfr.org Licensee: Board of Trustees

of Adirondack Community College. Population served: 50,000 Format: Progsv, AAA, Indie rock. Target aud: 18 plus; adults. ◆Kevin Ankeny, gen mgr; Steve Tefft, stn mgr.

*WLJH(FM)— 2001: 90.9 mhz; 360 w. Ant 663 ft TL: N43 19 55 W73 20 20. Hrs open:
Rebroadcasts WFGB(FM) Kingston 100%.
Box 777, Lake Katrine, 12449. Phone: (845) 336-6199. Fax: (845) 336-7205. Web Site:www.soundoflife.org Licensee: Sound of Life Inc. Format: Christian. ◆Tom Michael Zahradnik, gen mgr; Bob Conti, opns mgr; Joe Hunter, progmg dir.

WMML(AM)— May 28, 1959: 1230 khz; 1 kw-U. TL: N43 19 43 W73 38 58. Hrs open: 24 89 Everts Ave., Queensbury, 12804. Phone: (518) 793-7733. Fax: (518) 793-0838. Licensee: 6 Johnson Road Licenses Inc. Group owner: Pamal Broadcasting Ltd. (acq 4-1-2004; grpsl). Population served: 117,222 Natl. Network: ESPN Radio, . Format: Sports. News staff: one; News: 6 hrs wkly. Target aud: 18-54 plus. Spec prog: Relg 3 hrs wkly. ◆Clay Ashworth, gen mgr.

WNYQ(FM)—See Hudson Falls

WWSC(AM)— Dec 18, 1946: 1450 khz; 1 kw-U. TL: N43 18 46 W73 35 57. Hrs open: 24 128 Glen St., 12801. Phone: (518) 761-9890. Fax: (518) 761-9893. Web Site:www.radiowins.com Licensee: Regional Radio Group LLC. (acq 9-10-2008; grpsl). Population served: 104,000 Natl. Network: ABC, Wall Street, Westwood One, . Leventhal Senter & Lerman. Format: News/talk, sports. News staff: 1.5; News: 166 hrs wkly. Target aud: 12 plus; people who want full news radio & talk. ◆Clay Ashworth, gen mgr; Dan Miner, stn mgr; Mike Dubray, gen sls mgr; Pete Cloutier, prom dir; Jim Scott, news dir; Steve Babson, chief of engrg.

Gloversville

WENT(AM)— July 1, 1944: 1340 khz; 1 kw-U. TL: N43 01 30 W74 21 10. Hrs open: 5:30 AM-midnight Box 831, 138 Harrison St. Ext., 12078. Phone: (518) 725-7175. Fax: (518) 725-7177.E-mail: went@capital.net Web Site:www.am1340went.com Licensee: Whitney Radio Broadcasting Inc. Population served: 102,000 Natl. Network: CNN Radio, ESPN Radio, . Wire Svc: AP Format: Full service, adult contemp. News staff: 2; News: 14 hrs wkly. Target aud: 30 plus. Spec prog: Talk one hr wkly. ◆Jack Scott, pres, gen mgr; Jon W. Clark, VP; Shirley V. Clark, stn mgr.

WFNY(AM)— 3/2003: 1440 khz; 3.6 kw-D, 500 w-N, DA-N. TL: N43 01 57 W74 21 02. Hrs open: 101 S. Main St., 12078. Phone: (518) 725-1108. Fax: (518) 773-3349.E-mail: info@wfny.com Licensee: Michael A. Sleezer. Format: Hits past & present. ◆Michael A. Sleezer, gen mgr; Michael Sleezer, progmg dir.

*WNGG(FM)—Not on air, target date: unknown: 90.9 mhz; 1 kw. Ant 262 ft TL: N43 09 42 W74 31 00. Hrs open: 65 King Rd., Buskirk, 12028-0036. Phone: (518) 686-0975. Fax: (518) 686-0975.E-mail: wngn@wngn.org Web Site:www.wngn.org Licensee: Northeast Gospel Broadcasting Inc. ◆Brian Larson, pres & gen mgr.

Gouverneur

WGIX-FM— Dec 5, 1967: 95.3 mhz; 6 kw. Ant 328 ft TL: N44 20 22 W75 24 00. Stereo. Hrs open: 24 2315 Knox St., Ogdensburg, 13669. Phone: (315) 393-1100. Fax: (315) 393-6673. Web Site:www.coololdies.us Licensee: Community Broadcasters LLC. Group owner: Clancy-Mance Communications (acq 2-8-2007; grpsl). Population served: 120,000 Format: Oldies. News staff: 3; News: 7 hrs wkly. Target aud: 35-54. ◆James L. Leven, pres, gen mgr; Tobi Newcombe, sls dir & progmg dir; Ken Ruhland, chief of engrg.

*WSLG(FM)—Not on air, target date: unknown: 90.5 mhz; 1.4 kw. Ant 230 ft TL: N44 20 22 W75 24 00. Hrs open: North Country Public Radio, St. Lawrence University, Canton, 13617. Phone: (315) 229-5356. Fax: (315) 229-5373. Web Site:www.ncpr.org Licensee: The St. Lawrence University. ◆Ellen Rocco, stn mgr.

Grand Gorge

*WGKR(FM)— November 1997: 105.3 mhz; 60 w. 1,342 ft TL: N42 23 58 W74 35 27. Hrs open:
Rebroadcasts WFGB(FM) Kingston 100%.
Box 777, Lake Katrine, 12449. Secondary address: 199 Tuytenbridge Rd., Lake Katrine 12449. Phone: (845) 336-6199. Fax: (845) 336-7205.E-mail: email@soundoflife.org Web Site:www.soundoflife.org Licensee: Sound of Life Inc. Format: Contemp Christian. ◆Tom Michael Zahradnik, gen mgr; Bob Conti, opns mgr; Joe Hunter, progmg dir.

Greece

*WGMC(FM)— Nov 11, 1973: 90.1 mhz; 15 kw. Ant 138 ft TL: N43 14 40 W77 41 36. Stereo. Hrs open: 24 Box 300, North Greece, 14515-0300. Secondary address: 1139 Maiden Ln., Rochester 14615. Phone: (585) 966-2660. Fax: (585) 581-8185. Web Site:www.jazz901.org Licensee: Greece Central School District. Population served: 1,00,000 Dow, Lohnes & Albertson. Format: Jazz. Target aud: 25-50; upscale, educated, mus lovers. Spec prog: Pol 2 hrs, Sp 10 hrs, Lithuanian one hr, Turkish one hr, blues 3 hrs wkly. ◆Jack Mindy, opns mgr, disc jockey.

Hamilton

*WRCU-FM— Mar 22, 1970: 90.1 mhz; 1.9 kw. 155 ft TL: N42 48 38 W75 31 58. Stereo. Hrs open: Colgate University, 13346. Phone: (315) 228-7901. Fax: (315) 228-7028. Web Site:www.wrcu.colgate.edu Licensee: Colgate University. Population served: 3,636 Format: Progsv, div, jazz. Spec prog: Jazz 12 hrs, class 4 hrs, Black 10 hrs wkly. ◆Lydia Gulick, gen mgr; Tracy Hoole, progmg dir & progmg mgr; Paul Osmolskis, news dir.

Hampton Bays

WLIR-FM— Nov 20, 1980: 107.1 mhz; 4.1 kw. Ant 397 ft TL: N40 53 07 W72 41 33.6. Stereo. Hrs open:
Rebroadcasts WEPN(AM) New York 100%.
3075 Veterans Memorial Highway, Ronkonkoma, 11779. Phone: (631) 648-2500. Fax: (516) 222-1391.E-mail: info@wlir.com Licensee: Jarad Broadcasting Co. of Hampton Bays LLC Group owner: The Morey Organization Inc. (acq 2-27-2004; $2 million). Population served: 100,000 Natl. Network: ESPN Radio, . Natl. Rep: Roslin,. Format: Sports. ◆John Caracciolo, gen mgr; Harlan Friedman, progmg dir.

Hancock

WBZX(FM)— 2009: 107.1 mhz; 2.1 kw. Ant 111 ft TL: N41 57 43.4 W75 16 16.9. Hrs open: 149 Penn Ave., Scranton, PA, 18503. Phone: (570) 348-9103. Fax: (570) 346-6038. Licensee: The Scranton Times L.P. ◆William R. Lynett, pres.

Hempstead

WHLI(AM)— July 22, 1947: 1100 khz; 10 kw-D, DA. TL: N40 41 06 W73 36 38. Hrs open: Sunrise-sunset 234 Airport Plaza Blvd., #5, Farmingdale, 11735-3938. Phone: (631) 770-4200. Fax: (631) 770-0090.E-mail: info@whli.com Web Site:www.whli.com Licensee: Long Island Broadcasting Inc. Group owner: Barnstable Broadcasting Inc. (acq 12-15-84; $5 million with co-located FM; 9-24-84). Population served: 2,000,000 Natl. Rep: Katz Radio,. Format: Adult standards. News staff: one; News: 2 hrs wkly. Target aud: 35-64; adults. Spec prog: Black one hr wkly. ◆Dave Widmer, pres, gen mgr, progmg VP; Mike Banks, sls dir, gen sls mgr; Cheryl Kampanis, prom dir; Frank Brinka, news dir; Antoinette Rodriguez, traf mgr; Joe Satta, disc jockey.

WKJY(FM)— July 22, 1947: 98.3 mhz; 3 kw. Ant 328 ft TL: N40 41 08 W73 36 37. Hrs open: 24 234 Airport Plaza Blvd. #5, Farmingdale, 11735-3938. Phone: (631) 770-4200. Fax: (631) 770-0090.E-mail: info@whli.com Web Site:www.whli.com Licensee: Long Island Broadcasting Inc. Natl. Rep: Katz Radio,. Format: Adult contemp. News staff: one. Target aud: 25-54. Spec prog: Black one hr wkly. ◆Alissa Marty, mktg dir; Bill George, progmg dir; Antoinette Rodriguez, traf mgr; Bill Edwards, disc jockey; Mike Glaser, news rptr & engr.

*WRHU(FM)— June 9, 1959: 88.7 mhz; 470 w. 200 ft TL: N40 43 03 W73 36 12. Stereo. Hrs open: 24 Rm. 127, 111 Hofstra Univ., 11549-1110. Phone: (516) 463-5667. Fax: (516) 463-5668.E-mail: mail@wrhu.org Web Site:www.wrhu.org Licensee: Hofstra University. Population served: 2,500,000 Dow, Lohnes & Albertson. Wire Svc: AP Format: Div. News: 11 hrs wkly. Target aud: General. ◆Kathleen Reddington, stn mgr.

Henderson

WEFX(FM)— 1991: 100.7 mhz; 3 kw. 328 ft TL: N43 49 13 W76 05 29. (CP: 6 kw). Hrs open: 199 Wealtha Ave., Watertown, 13601. Phone: (315) 782-1240. Fax: (315) 782-0132. Web Site:www.realrock1007.com Licensee: Community Broadcasters LLC. (acq 2-8-2007; grpsl). Natl. Rep: Roslin,. Format: Active rock. ◆James L. Leven, pres; Glenn Curry, gen mgr; Todd Dalesandro, opns mgr; Vickie Fenn, sls dir; Johnny Keegan, progmg dir.

Henrietta

*WITR(FM)— Mar 7, 1975: 89.7 mhz; 910 w. 154 ft TL: N43 05 08 W77 40 05. Stereo. Hrs open: 24 32 Lomb Memorial Dr., Rochester, 14623. Phone: (585) 475-2000. Fax: (585) 475-4988. Web Site:www.witr.rit.edu Licensee: Rochester Institute of Technology. Population served: 750,000 Format: Modern music. Target aud: General. Spec prog: Reggae 5 hrs, jazz 8 hrs, contemp Christian rock 10 hrs, gospel 8 hrs hrs wkly. ◆Craig Ceremuga, gen mgr; Michelle Comeau, prom dir; Steve Montario, progmg dir.

Herkimer

WNRS(AM)— October 1956: 1420 khz; 1 kw-D. TL: N43 03 40 W75 01 44. Hrs open: 24 Box 927, Ilion, 13357. Phone: (315) 866-9200. Fax: (315) 866-6906.E-mail: wxur@hotmail.com Licensee: Arjuna Broadcasting Corp. (acq 10-23-96). Population served: 120,000 Natl. Network: ESPN Radio, . Natl. Rep: Roslin,. Cohn & Marks. Format: Sports. News staff: one. Target aud: 18 plus; men. ◆Mindy Barstein, pres, gen mgr; Tim Barstein, sls VP; Tom Davenport, opns VP & progmg dir; Anthony Falvo, chief of engrg.

*WVHC(FM)— October 1993: 91.5 mhz; 350 w vert. -115 ft Stereo. Hrs open: 24 Reservoir Rd., 13350. Phone: (315) 866-0300, EXT. 354. Fax: (315) 866-7253. Licensee: Herkimer County Community College. Format: Jazz. News: 5 hrs wkly. Target aud: General; residents of southern Herkimer county & college community. ◆Wade Lamb, gen mgr & stn mgr.

WXUR(FM)— Apr 28, 1979: 92.7 mhz; 6 kw. Ant 299 ft TL: N43 03 50 W75 01 44. Stereo. Hrs open: 24 Box 927, Ilion, 13357. Phone: (315) 866-9200. Fax: (315) 866-6906. Licensee: Arjuna Broadcasting Corp. Population served: 420,000 Natl. Network: Westwood One, . Format: Classic hits. News staff: one. ◆Tim Barstein, dev VP; Jenna Davenport, mktg mgr; Chris Miller, progmg VP, local news ed; Tony Falvo, engrg VP; Max Davenport, traf mgr; Robert Huyck, sports cmtr.

Highland

WJGK(AM)—Not on air, target date: unknown: 1200 khz; 4.7 kw-D, 1 kw-N, DA-2. TL: N41 44 07 W73 57 38. Hrs open: Box 2307, Newburgh, 12550-0451. Phone: (845) 561-2131. Fax: (845) 561-2138. Licensee: Sunrise Broadcasting Corp. ◆Joerg Klebe, pres.

WRWD-FM— Oct 3, 1989: 107.3 mhz; 330 w. Ant 968 ft TL: N41 41 58 W74 00 11. Stereo. Hrs open: 20 Tucker Dr., Poughkeepsie, 12603. Phone: (845) 454-2800. Fax: (845) 471-0793. Web Site:www.wrwdfm.com Licensee: AMFM Radio Licenses LLC. Group owner: Clear Channel Communications Inc. (acq 12-10-97; $7.5 million with WBWZ(FM) New Paltz). Population served: 660,000 Natl. Network: Jones Radio Networks, . Natl. Rep: Katz Radio,. Gammon & Grange. Format: C&W. Target aud: 18 plus. Spec prog: Farm one hr wkly. ◆Frank Curcio, gen mgr; Jim Brady, gen sls mgr; Jeanette Relyea, natl sls mgr; Nick Smirnoff, prom dir; Aaron McCord, progmg dir; Cameron Hendrix, news dir.

Homer

WXHC(FM)— 1991: 101.5 mhz; 1.3 kw. 489 ft TL: N42 41 12 W76 11 54. Stereo. Hrs open: 24 Box 386, 12 S. Main St., 13077. Phone: (607) 749-9942. Fax: (607) 749-2374.E-mail: johneves@wxhc.com Web Site:www.wxhc.com Licensee: John Eves. Population served: 75,000 Natl. Rep: Roslin,. Cole, Raywid & Braverman. Format: Oldies. News staff: one; News: 10 hrs wkly. Target aud: 25-54. ◆John Eves, pres; Bruce Eves, exec VP; Patricia Eves, VP; Sonny King, opns VP.

Honeoye Falls

WFXF(FM)— 1948: 95.1 mhz; 50 kw. Ant 479 ft TL: N43 02 01 W77 25 18. Stereo. Hrs open: 24 1700 HSBC Plaza, 100 Chestnut Street, Rochester, 14604. Phone: (585) 454-4884. Fax: (585) 454-5081. Web Site:www.fox951.com Licensee: Citicasters Licenses Inc. (NEW). Group owner: Clear Channel Communications Inc. (acq 1999; grpsl). Population served: 120,000 Format: Classic hits. Target aud: 25-54. ◆Karen Carey, VP & gen mgr; Dave LeFrois, opns mgr.

Hoosick Falls

WHAZ-FM— July 4, 1991: 97.5 mhz; 400 w. Ant 1,204 ft TL: N42 51 40 W73 13 59. (CP: 420 w, ant 1,184 ft. TL: N42 51 49 W73 13 59). Hrs open: 30 Park Ave., Cohoes, 12047-3330. Phone: (518) 237-1330. Fax: (518) 235-4468.E-mail: events@aliveradionetwork.com Web Site:www.whaz.com Licensee: Capital Media Corp. Group owner: Vox

Radio Group L.P. (acq 7-19-2005; $1.1 million). Format: Christian oldies. ◆Paul Lotters, gen mgr; Rex Gregory, progmg dir; Bill Rosenfeld, chief of engrg.

Hornell

WCKR(FM)— June 1981: 92.1 mhz; 2.55 kw. Ant 508 ft TL: N42 20 38 W77 37 36. Stereo. Hrs open: 24 5942 Ashbaugh Hill Rd., 14843. Phone: (607) 324-1480. Fax: (607) 324-5415.E-mail: kpd@wlea.net Web Site:www.wckr.com Licensee: PMJ Communications Inc. (acq 1991). Population served: 100,000 Natl. Network: USA, . Wire Svc: AP Format: Country. News staff: 2; News: 11 hrs wkly. Target aud: 21 plus. ◆Kevin P. Doran, pres, stn mgr; Glenn Lee, opns mgr, prom mgr, progmg dir; Tom Booth, gen sls mgr; Brian O'Neil, news dir; Ralph Van Derlinden, chief of engrg.

WHHO(AM)— 1949: 1320 khz; 5 kw-D. TL: N42 17 32 W77 40 27. Hrs open: Box 726, 1484 Beech St., 14843. Phone: (607) 654-0322. Fax: (877) 575-1320. Web Site:www.hornellradio.com Licensee: Bilbat Radio Inc. (acq 6-10-83; $450,000 with co-located FM; 5-30-83). Population served: 300,000 Format: Oldies. ◆Kevin White, CFO & gen mgr.

WKPQ(FM)— 1946: 105.3 mhz; 50 kw. Ant 530 ft TL: N42 17 32 W77 40 27. Stereo. Hrs open: 24 Box 726, 1484 Beech St., 14843. Phone: (607) 654-0322. Fax: (877) 575-1320. Web Site:www.hornellradio.com Licensee: Bilbat Radio Inc. Population served: 750,000 Format: Hot adult comtemp. Target aud: 18-54; females. ◆Kevin White, gen mgr.

WLEA(AM)— September 1951: 1480 khz; 2.5 kw-D. TL: N42 17 15 W77 38 47. Hrs open: 24 5942 Ashbaugh Hill Rd., 14843. Phone: (607) 324-1480. Fax: (607) 324-5415.E-mail: kpd@wlwa.net Web Site:www.wlea.net Licensee: PMJ Communications Inc. (acq 1991). Population served: 80,000 Wire Svc: AP Format: News/talk. News staff: 2; News: 16 hrs wkly. Target aud: 35 plus. ◆Tom Booth, gen mgr; Brian O'Neil, news dir.

*WSQA(FM)— 2000: 88.7 mhz; 4.5 kw. Ant 495 ft TL: N42 16 02 W77 37 55. Hrs open: Box 3000, Binghamton, 13902. Phone: (607) 729-0100. Fax: (607) 729-7328.E-mail: wskg_mail@wskg.pbs.org Web Site:www.wskg.com Licensee: WSKG Public Telecommunications Council. Format: Jazz, news. ◆Brian Sickora, pres; Nancy Christensen, opns dir; Ken Campbell, progmg dir; Stacy Mosteller, traf mgr.

Horseheads

WEHH(AM)—See Elmira Heights-Horseheads

WLNL(AM)— May 7, 1967: 1000 khz; 5 kw-D. TL: N42 09 14 W76 50 47. Hrs open: Sunrise-sunset 3134 Lake Rd., 14845. Phone: (607) 737-9208. Fax: (607) 737-9210.E-mail: inbox@wlnlradio.com Web Site:www.wlnlradio.com Licensee: Trinity Media Ltd. (acq 1-21-92; $256,000;11-11-91). Population served: 200,000 Natl. Network: USA, Salem Radio Network, . Format: Relg. Target aud: 25-54; Christian families, women/mothers who work at home. Spec prog: Country/bluegrass one hr wkly. ◆Heather Clark, pres, gen mgr, mus dir; Heather Clark, traf mgr; John Earley, sls.

WPGI(FM)— July 4, 1970: 100.9 mhz; 3 kw. 245 ft TL: N42 12 00 W76 51 30. Stereo. Hrs open: Prog sep from AM 2205 College Ave., Elmira, 14903. Phone: (607) 732-4400. Fax: (607) 732-7774. Licensee: Chemung County Radio Inc. Population served: 30,500 Format: Country. Target aud: General.

WWLZ(AM)— April 1966: 820 khz; 5 kw-D, 1 kw-N, DA-2. TL: N42 09 14 W76 50 47. Hrs open: 2205 College Ave., Elmira, 14903. Phone: (607) 732-4400. Fax: (607) 732-7774. Licensee: Chemung County Radio Inc. Group owner: Backyard Broadcasting LLC (acq 12-1-2002; grpsl). Population served: 30,500 Format: News/talk. Target aud: 25-54; baby boomers. ◆Kevin White, gen mgr; Jim Poteat, prom mgr, progmg dir.

Houghton

*WJSL(FM)— Jan 18, 1979: 90.3 mhz; 6 kw. 216 ft TL: N42 22 39 W78 10 45. Stereo. Hrs open: 24
Rebroadcasts WMHR(FM) Syracuse 70%.
Box 30021, Rochester, 14603. Phone: (585) 325-7500. Fax: (585) 258-0339.E-mail: newsroom@wxxi.org Web Site:www.wxxi.org Licensee: WXXI Public Broadcasting Council. Population served: 150,000 Format: Class. Target aud: 18-36; college. Spec prog: Class 5 hrs wkly. ◆Norm Silverstein, CEO, pres; Sue Rogers, VP.

Hudson

WHUC(AM)— 1947: 1230 khz; 1 kw-U. TL: N42 15 13 W73 45 45. Hrs open: 24 6620 Route 9 South, 12603. Secondary address: 5620 Rt. 96 12534. Phone: (518) 828-5006. Fax: (518) 828-1080. Licensee: CC Licenses LLC. Group owner: Clear Channel Communications Inc. (acq 1-17-2002; grpsl). Population served: 82,000 Natl. Network: Jones Radio Networks, . Natl. Rep: Katz Radio,. Format: Adult standards. News staff: one; News: 4 hrs wkly. Target aud: 35 plus; loc people in Columbia & Greene counties. ♦Frank Curcio, gen mgr; Reggie Osterhoudt, opns mgr; Jim Brady, gen sls mgr; Jeanette Relyea, natl sls mgr; Nick Smirnoff, prom dir; Bill Williams, progmg dir; Cameron Hendrix, news dir.

***WHVP(FM)**— May 1998: 91.1 mhz; 362 w vert. 991 ft TL: N42 17 52 W73 53 57. Stereo. Hrs open:
Rebroadcasts WFGB(FM) Kingston 100%.
Box 777, Lake Katrine, 12449. Phone: (845) 336-6199. Fax: (845) 336-7205.E-mail: email@soundoflife.org Web Site:www.soundoflife.org Licensee: Sound of Life Inc. Format: Christian. ♦Tom Michael Zahradink, gen mgr; Bob Conti, opns mgr; Joe Hunter, progmg dir.

WZCR(FM)— Jan 20, 1969: 93.5 mhz; 3 kw. Ant -15 ft TL: N42 15 13 W73 45 45. Stereo. Hrs open: 24 20 Tucker Dr., Poughkeepsie, 12603. Secondary address: 5620 Rt. 96 12534. Phone: (845) 471-2300. Fax: (845) 401-2683.E-mail: info@wczr.com Licensee: CC Licenses LLC. Natl. Network: Westwood One, . Natl. Rep: Katz Radio,. Format: Oldies. News: 3 hrs wkly. Target aud: General; adults 35-54.

Hudson Falls

WNYQ(FM)— Sept 19, 1983: 101.7 mhz; 4.6 kw. Ant 180 ft TL: N43 22 40 W73 39 56. Stereo. Hrs open: 24 89 Everts Ave., Queensbury, 12804. Phone: (518) 793-7733. Fax: (518) 793-0838. Licensee: 6 Johnson Road Licenses Inc. Group owner: Pamal Broadcasting Ltd. (acq 4-1-2004; grpsl). Format: Adult standards. News staff: one. Target aud: 35-64. ♦Clay Ashworth, gen mgr.

Huntington

WNYH(AM)— Sept 1, 1951: 740 khz; 25 kw-D, 43 w-N, DA-2. TL: N40 51 04 W73 26 16. (CP: 20 kw-D, 50 w-N, DA-2). Stereo. Hrs open: 24 100-25 Queens Blvd., Suite 1CC, Forest Hills, 11375. Secondary address: 131 Jericho Tpke., Suite 306, Jericho 11753. Phone: (718) 335-3333. Licensee: Win Radio Broadcasting Corp. (acq 9-1-2005). Population served: 1,500,000 Format: Adult. ♦Richard S. Yoon, pres & gen mgr.

Hyde Park

WCZX(FM)— Aug 18, 1970: 97.7 mhz; 300 w. 1,030 ft TL: N41 43 11 W73 59 45. Stereo. Hrs open: 24 Box 416, 2 Pendell Rd., Poughkeepsie, 12602. Phone: (845) 471-1500. Fax: (845) 454-1204. Web Site:www.mix97fm.com Licensee: Cumulus Licensing Corp. Group owner: Cumulus Media Inc. (acq 1-23-02; grpsl). Population served: 300,000 Natl. Rep: Katz Radio,. Format: Adult contemp. News staff: one; News: 10 hrs wkly. Target aud: 25-54. ♦John Dickie, CEO; Lew Dickie, pres; Charles Benfer, gen mgr.

WHVW(AM)— July 4, 1963: 950 khz; 500 w-D, 57 w-N. TL: N41 44 46 W73 54 46. Hrs open: 24 316 Main St., Poughkeepsie, 12601-3123. Phone: (845) 471-9500. Fax: (845) 452-8696.E-mail: whvw@whvw.net Web Site:www.whvw.org Licensee: Joseph-Paul Ferraro. (acq 3-9-92; $350,000; 3-30-92). Population served: 500,000 Format: Oldies. Target aud: 25-54. Spec prog: Ger one hr, It one hr, Irish one hr wkly. ♦J.P. Ferraro, pres & gen mgr.

Irondequoit

WKGS(FM)— March 1992: 106.7 mhz; 3.5 kw. 627 ft TL: N43 11 27 W77 37 11. Stereo. Hrs open: 24 1700 HSBC Plaza, 100 Chestnut Street, Rochester, 14604. Phone: (585) 454-4884. Fax: (585) 454-5081. Web Site:www.1067kissfm.com Licensee: Citicasters Licenses L.P. Group owner: Clear Channel Communications Inc. (acq 1999; grpsl). Population served: 830,000 Format: CHR. Target aud: 18-34. ♦Karen Carey, VP & gen mgr; Joe Bonacci, progmg dir.

Islip

WLIE(AM)— 1960: 540 khz; 2.5 kw-D, 220 w-N, DA-2. TL: N40 45 06 W73 12 50. Stereo. Hrs open: 24 2137 Deer Park Ave., Deer Park, 11729. Phone: (631) 243-5400. Fax: (631) 243-5444.E-mail: Info@wlie.com Web Site:www.wlie.com Licensee: Stuart Henry (acq 12-4-2003). . Population served: 2,500,000 Natl. Network: USA, Jones Radio Networks, . Thompson, Hine L.L.P. Format: Talk radio. News: 10 hrs wkly. Target aud: 45 plus. Spec prog: Relg 3 hrs wkly. ♦Stuart Henry, pres & gen mgr.

Ithaca

WHCU(AM)— Jan 23, 1923: 870 khz; 5 kw-D, 1 kw-N, DA-N. TL: N42 21 49 W76 36 20. Hrs open: 24 1751 Hanshaw Rd., 14850. Phone: (607) 257-6400. Fax: (607) 257-6497.E-mail: info@whcu870.com Licensee: Saga Communications of New England LLC. (acq 5-31-2005; grpsl). Population served: 680,000 Natl. Network: CBS, Westwood One, AP Radio, . Natl. Rep: Christal,. Richard Carr. Format: News/talk, sports. News staff: 3; News: 40 hrs wkly. Target aud: 25-64. ♦Edward K. Christian, pres; Susan Johnston, gen mgr; Chris Allinger, opns dir; Connie Fairfax-Ozmun, mktg dir; Geoff Dunn, progmg dir, news dir.

***WICB(FM)**— Jan 14, 1947: 91.7 mhz; 4.1 kw. Ant 135 ft TL: N42 25 07 W76 29 39. Stereo. Hrs open: 24 Ithaca College, 118 Park Hall, 14850. Phone: (607) 274-1040.E-mail: wicb@ithaca.edu Web Site:www.wicb.org Licensee: Ithaca College. Population served: 250,000 Natl. Network: ABC, . Format: Modern rock, urban contemp. News: 6 hrs wkly. Target aud: 18-34; young audience with taste for innovative mus. Spec prog: Jazz 13 hrs, folk 2 hrs, blues 2 hrs, reggae 2 hrs, world beat 2 hrs wkly. ♦Christopher Wheatley, gen mgr.

WIII(FM)—See Cortland

***WITH(FM)**—Not on air, target date: unknown: 90.1 mhz; 4.2 kw. Ant -315 ft TL: N42 25 47 W76 29 49. Hrs open: 300 Pulteney St., Geneva, 14456-3397. Phone: (315) 781-3456. Fax: (315) 781-3916.E-mail: weos@hws.edu Web Site:www.weos.org Licensee: The Colleges of the Seneca. ♦Aaron Read, gen mgr.

WNYY(AM)— April 1956: 1470 khz; 5 kw-D, 1 kw-N, DA-N. TL: N42 23 32 W76 28 29. Hrs open: 24 1751 Hanshaw Rd., 14850. Phone: (607) 257-6400. Fax: (607) 257-6497. Licensee: Saga Communications of New England LLC. (acq 5-31-2005; grpsl). Population served: 680,000 Natl. Network: Westwood One, . Natl. Rep: Christal,. Format: Progressive talk. News staff: 3. Target aud: 35-54. ♦Edward K. Christian, pres; Susan Johnston, gen mgr; Chris Allinger, opns dir; Connie Fairfax-Ozmun, mktg dir; Geoff Dunn, progmg dir, news dir.

WQNY(FM)— 1948: 103.7 mhz; 15.5 kw. Ant 879 ft TL: N42 23 13 W76 40 10. Stereo. Hrs open: 24 Prog sep from AM 1751 Hanshaw Rd., 14850. Phone: (607) 257-6400. Fax: (607) 257-6497. Licensee: Saga Communications of New England LLC Richard Carr. Format: Country. News staff: 3. Target aud: 25-54. ♦Chris Allinger, progmg dir.

***WSQG-FM**— 1988: 90.9 mhz; 5 kw. 294 ft TL: N42 34 55 W76 33 22. Stereo. Hrs open: 24
Rebroadcasts WSKG-FM Binghamton 100%.
Box 3000, Binghamton, 13902. Phone: (607) 729-0100. Fax: (607) 729-7328.E-mail: wskg_mail@wskg.pbs.org Web Site:www.wskg.com Licensee: WSKG Public Telecommunications Council. Population served: 83,200 Natl. Network: NPR, PRI, . Dow, Lohnes & Albertson. Format: Class, news. News staff: one; News: 33 hrs wkly. Target aud: General. Spec prog: Jazz 7 hrs, folk/bluegrass 5 hrs wkly. ♦Brian Sickora, pres; Nancy Christensen, opns dir; Ken Campbell, progmg dir; Stacy Mosteller, traf mgr.

WVBR-FM— June 7, 1958: 93.5 mhz; 3 kw. 250 ft TL: N42 25 42 W76 26 57. Stereo. Hrs open: 24 957-B Mitchell St., 14850. Phone: (607) 273-4000. Fax: (607) 273-4069.E-mail: concert@wvbr.com Web Site:www.wvbr.com Licensee: Cornell Radio Guild Inc. Population served: 100,000 Natl. Network: Westwood One, . Natl. Rep: Eastman Radio, Katz Radio,. Format: Full service, AOR. News: 10 hrs wkly. Target aud: 18-49; highly educated listeners. Spec prog: Oldies 5 hrs, heavy metal 6 hrs, folk 8 hrs,blues 5 hrs, Latin 5 hrs wkly. ♦Jordan Gremli, gen mgr, dev VP; Mike Estrich, opns VP & gen sls mgr; Michelle Bitman, prom dir; Dan Powers, progmg dir.

WYXL(FM)— Sept 1, 1947: 97.3 mhz; 26 kw. Ant 879 ft TL: N42 27 54 W76 22 23. Stereo. Hrs open: 1751 Hanshaw Rd., 14850. Phone: (607) 257-6400. Fax: (607) 257-6497. Licensee: Saga Communications of New England LLC. Format: Adult contemp. Target aud: 25-54. ♦Chris Allinger, progmg dir.

Jamestown

***WCOT(FM)**— Dec 14, 1992: 90.9 mhz; 12 kw. Ant 653 ft TL: N42 00 06 W79 03 19. Stereo. Hrs open:
Rebroadcasts WCIK(FM) Bath 100%.
Box 506, 7634 Campbell Creek Rd., Bath, 14810. Phone: (607) 776-4151. Fax: (607) 776-6929.E-mail: mail@fln.org Web Site:www.fln.org Licensee: Family Life Ministries Inc. Group owner: Family Life Network Natl. Network: Salem Radio Network, . Hardy, Carey, Chautin & Balkin, LLP. Wire Svc: Metro Weather Service Inc. Format: Contemp Christian. News staff: 3; News: 14 hrs wkly. Target aud: 30-54. ♦Dick Snavely, CFO; Rick Snavely, pres, VP & gen mgr; John Owens, progmg dir; Jim Travis, chief of engrg.

WHUG(FM)— Feb 1, 1965: 101.9 mhz; 3.3 kw. 298 ft TL: N42 07 55 W79 13 09. Stereo. Hrs open: Prog sep from AM Box 1199, 202 Front St., 1471. Phone: (716) 664-2313. Fax: (716) 488-1471.E-mail: A ahill@radiojamestown.com Web Site:www.whug.com Format: Country. News staff: 2; News: 2 hrs wkly.

WJTN(AM)— December 1924: 1240 khz; 500 w-D, 1 kw-N. TL: N42 06 18 W79 15 28. Hrs open: 24 Box 1139, 14702-1139. Secondary address: 2 Orchard Rd. W.E. 14701. Phone: (716) 487-1151. Fax: (716) 664-9326.E-mail: wjtn@wjtn.com Web Site:www.wjtn.com Licensee: Media One Group LLC (acq 8-30-2002; $5.05 million with co-located FM). Population served: 140,000 Natl. Network: Westwood One, . Natl. Rep: Rgnl Reps,. Wire Svc: AP Format: News, talk, sports. News staff: 3; News: 16 hrs wkly. Target aud: 35 plus; adults seeking full service progmg. Spec prog: It one hr, Sp one hr, Swedish one hr, farm one hr wkly. ♦Merrill Rosen, gen mgr; Nick Keefe, opns mgr, prom dir, progmg dir; Larry Sazacki, sls dir; Wayne Goff, chief of engrg; Kathy Roselle, traf mgr; Terry Frank, local news ed; Jason Sample, news rptr; Dennis Webster, farm dir; Matt Krieg, sports cmtr; Jim Roselle, disc jockey.

WKSN(AM)— Jan 26, 1948: 1340 khz; 500 w-D, 1 kw-N. TL: N42 05 46 W79 14 48. Hrs open: Box 1199, 202 Front St., 14701. Phone: (716) 664-2313. Fax: (716) 488-1471.E-mail: ahill@radiojamestown.com Web Site:www.wksn.com Licensee: Media One Group II LLC. Group owner: Vox Radio Group L.P. (acq 5-31-2005; grpsl). Population served: 39,795 Format: Oldies. News staff: 2; News: 3 hrs wkly. Spec prog: Relg 2 hrs, Swedish one hr wkly. ♦Daniel C. Fischer, VP, gen mgr; Guy Ditonto, gen sls mgr; Tom Marshall, progmg dir; Joel Keefer, news dir; Burton O. Waterman, chief of engrg; Roseanne De Frisco, traf mgr.

***WNJA(FM)**— 1991: 89.7 mhz; 6 kw. 754 ft TL: N42 02 48 W79 05 26. Hrs open: 24 Box 1263, Buffalo, 14240. Secondary address: 140 Lower Terr., Buffalo 14202-1263. Phone: (716) 845-7000. Fax: (716) 845-7043.E-mail: info@wnja.org Web Site:www.wned.org Licensee: Western New York Public Broadcasting Association. Schwartz, Woods & Miller. Format: Class. Target aud: 35 plus. ♦Donald K. Boswell, CEO, pres, gen mgr; Michael Sutton, CFO; Richard Daly, sr VP; Sylvia Bennett, dev VP; Peter Goldsmith, progmg dir.

***WUBJ(FM)**— July 11, 1994: 88.1 mhz; 265 w. Ant 558 ft TL: N42 05 06 W79 17 23. Hrs open: 24
Rebroadcasts WBFO(FM) Buffalo 100%.
c/o Radio Stn. WBFO(FM), 3435 Main St., 205 Allen Hall, Buffalo, 14214-3003. Phone: (716) 829-6000. Fax: (716) 829-2277.E-mail: mail@wbfo.org Web Site:www.wbfo.org Licensee: State University of New York. Population served: 117,000 Natl. Network: NPR, . Format: Jazz, news. News staff: 2; News: news progrmg 50 hrs wkly. Target aud: General; educated professional. Spec prog: Blues 8 hrs, bluegrass music 3 hrs, Pol 3 hrs wkly. ♦Carole Smith Petro, VP, gen mgr; Mark Wozniak, opns mgr; Joan Wilson, dev dir; Mark Scott, news dir.

WWSE(FM)— October 1947: 93.3 mhz; 26.5 kw. Ant 643 ft TL: N42 05 06 W79 17 23. Stereo. Hrs open: 24 Box 1139, 14702-1139. Secondary address: 2 Orchard Rd. W.E. 14701. Phone: (716) 664-9393. Fax: (716) 664-9326.E-mail: wwsefm@wwsefm.com Web Site:wwsefm.com Licensee: Media One Group LLC. Population served: 200,000 Format: Adult contemp. News staff: 3; News: 7 hrs wkly. Target aud: 12554; female. ♦Cheryl Akin, sls VP, news rptr; Nick Keefe, mus dir; Brian Papalia, asst music dir; Sammie Green, traf mgr; Matthew Hanley, news rptr; Andrew Hill, disc jockey.

Jeffersonville

WDNB(FM)— Nov 15, 1999: Stn currently dark. 102.1 mhz; 2.2 kw. Ant 535 ft TL: N41 44 30 W74 51 23. Stereo. Hrs open: 24 267 N. Main St., Suite 3, Liberty, 12754. Phone: (570) 253-1616. Fax: (570) 253-6297.E-mail: vbebedetti@boldgoldmedia.com Web Site:www.boldgoldmedia.com Licensee: Bold Gold Media Group L.P. (group owner; (acq 5-23-2005; grpsl). Schwartz, Woods & Miller. Format: Country. News staff: one; News: 5 hrs wkly. Target aud: 25 plus; male & female general high school education plus. ♦Vince Benedetto, CEO; Bob Vanderheyden, gen mgr; Brian Walker, gen sls mgr; Paul Ciliberto, prom dir; George Schmitt, progmg dir; Theresa Opeka, news dir.

***WJFF(FM)**— Feb 12, 1990: 90.5 mhz; 3.7 kw. 629 ft TL: N41 48 58 W74 47 15. Stereo. Hrs open: 24 Box 546, 4765 State Rt. 52, 12748. Phone: (845) 482-4141. Fax: (845) 482-WJFF.E-mail: wjff@wjffradio.org

Web Site:www.wjffradio.org Licensee: Radio Catskill. Natl. Network: NPR, PRI, . Haley, Bader & Potts. Format: News/talk/eclectic music. News: 75 hrs wkly. Target aud: 16-60; general. ◆Bill Duncan, pres; Christine Aherne, stn mgr.

WPDA(FM)— January 1993: 106.1 mhz; 1.6 kw. 627 ft TL: N41 48 57 W74 45 42. Stereo. Hrs open:
Rebroadcasts WPDH(FM) Poughkeepsie 100%.
Box 416, Poughkeepsie, 12602. Phone: (845) 471-1500. Fax: (845) 454-1204. Web Site:www.wpdh.com Licensee: Cumulus Licensing Corp. Group owner: Cumulus Media Inc. (acq 1-23-02; grpsl). Natl. Rep: Katz Radio,. Format: Main stream rock. ◆Charles Benfer, gen mgr.

Johnson City

WLTB(FM)— Sept 3, 1972: 101.7 mhz; 1.25 kw. Ant 699 ft TL: N42 03 45 W75 56 37. Stereo. Hrs open: Box 7, Vestal, 13851. Secondary address: 1808 Vestal Pkwy. E., Vestal 13851. Phone: (607) 748-9131. Fax: (607) 748-0061. Web Site:Web Site:www.magic1017fm.com Licensee: GM Broadcasting Inc. (acq 9-2-97; $176,000 with co-located AM). Population served: 400,000 Natl. Network: CNN Radio, . Natl. Rep: Christal,. Format: Adult contemp. Target aud: 25 - 54; emphasis on females. ◆Thomas Mollen, pres.

Johnstown

WENT(AM)—See Gloversville

WIZR(AM)— 1964: 930 khz; 1 kw-D. TL: N42 59 54 W74 21 31. Stereo. Hrs open: 24 135 Guy Park Ave., Amsterdam, 12010. Phone: (518) 762-4631. Fax: (518) 762-0105. Licensee: 6 Johnson Road Licenses Inc. Group owner: Pamal Broadcasting Ltd. (acq 10-19-2001; grpsl). Population served: 250,000 Shaw Pittman. Format: Adult Contemp. News staff: one; News: 6 hrs wkly. Target aud: 25-54. Spec prog: It one hr, Pol one hr, Sp one hr wkly. ◆Joey Caruso, gen mgr.

Kingston

*WAMK(FM)— March 1988: 90.9 mhz; 940 w. 1,486 ft TL: N42 04 35 W74 06 26. Stereo. Hrs open: 24
Rebroadcasts WAMC-FM Albany 100%.
Box 66600, 318 Central Ave., Albany, 12206-6600. Phone: (518) 465-5233. Phone: (800) 323-9262. Fax: (518) 432-6974.E-mail: mail@wamc.org Web Site:www.wamc.org Licensee: WAMC. Group owner: WAMC/Northeast Public Radio Natl. Network: PRI, NPR, . Dow, Lohnes & Albertson. Wire Svc: AP Format: News/talk. News: 77 hrs wkly. Target aud: General. Spec prog: Jazz 13 hrs, folk 7 hrs. ◆Alan Chartock, CEO, chmn, pres; David Galletly, VP, progmg dir; Selma Kaplan, VP & news dir.

WDST(FM)—See Woodstock

*WFGB(FM)— January 1985: 89.7 mhz; 3.1 kw. 1,486 ft TL: N42 04 35 W74 06 26. Stereo. Hrs open: 24 Box 777, Lake Katrine, 12449. Phone: (845) 336-6199. Fax: (845) 336-7205.E-mail: email@soundoflife.org Web Site:www.soundoflife.org Licensee: Sound of Life Inc. Population served: 350,000 Format: Christian. News: 3 hrs wkly. Target aud: General. ◆ Tom Michael Zahradnik, gen mgr; Bob Conti, opns mgr; Joe Hunter, progmg dir.

*WFRH(FM)— Sept 1993: 91.7 mhz; 950 w. 272 ft TL: N41 59 04 W74 02 56. Hrs open: 24 786 Murray Rd., 12401. Phone: (315) 331-7482. Fax: (410) 268-0931.E-mail: info@familyradio.com Web Site:www.familyradio.com Licensee: Family Stations Inc. (group owner) Population served: 175,000 Format: Relg. ◆Harold Camping, pres & gen mgr; Dan Elmendorf, stn mgr.

WGHQ(AM)— Mar 4, 1956: 920 khz; 5 kw-D, 262 w-N, DA-1. TL: N41 53 09 W73 58 15. Hrs open: 24 715 Rt. 52, Beacon, 12508. Phone: (845) 838-6000. Fax: (845) 838-2109. Web Site:www.hvradionet.com Licensee: 6 Johnson Road Licenses Inc. Group owner: Clear Channel Communications Inc. (acq 4-1-2007; grpsl). Population served: 160,000 Natl. Network: Fox Sports, . Format: Talk, sports. Target aud: 30 plus. ◆Jason Finkelberg, gen mgr.

WKNY(AM)— Aug 1, 1939: 1490 khz; 1 kw-U. TL: N41 56 11 W74 00 30. Hrs open: 24 718 Broadway, 12401. Secondary address: Box 1398 12402. Phone: (845) 331-1490. Fax: (845) 331-9569.E-mail: wknynews@pendellrd.com Web Site:1490wkny.com Licensee: Cumulus Licensing Corp. Group owner: Cumulus Media Inc. (acq 1-23-02; grpsl). Population served: 200,000 Natl. Network: CBS, . Natl. Rep: Katz Radio,. Wire Svc: AP Format: Adult contemp. News staff: 2; News: 26 hrs wkly. Target aud: 25-54; 60% female. Spec prog: Ger

one hr, Pol one hr, Irish one hr wkly. ◆Chuck Benfer, gen mgr; Dominic Fusco, gen sls mgr; Warren Lawrence, progmg dir; Linda Rosner, news dir.

WKXP(FM)— Dec 13, 1965: 94.3 mhz; 2.25 kw. Ant 544 ft TL: N41 53 44 W73 59 32. Stereo. Hrs open: 24 Box 416, Poughkeepsie, 12602-0416. Secondary address: 2 Pendell Rd., Poughkeepsie 12602. Phone: (845) 471-1500. Fax: (845) 454-1204.E-mail: newsroom@pendelled.com Web Site:www.943thewolf.com Licensee: Cumulus Licensing Corp. Group owner: Cumulus Media Inc. (acq 2-11-2004; $3.5 million). Population served: 200,000 Format: Country. Target aud: 18-49; women. ◆Charles Benfer, gen mgr; Beth Christy, prom dir.

Lake George

WCKM-FM— Apr 21, 1994: 98.5 mhz; 370 w. Ant 1,289 ft TL: N43 25 12 W73 45 37. Stereo. Hrs open: 24 128 Glen St., Glens Falls, 12801-4432. Phone: (518) 761-9890. Fax: (518) 761-9893.E-mail: staffmail@radiowins.com Web Site:www.radiowins.com Licensee: Regional Radio Group LLC. (acq 9-10-2008; grpsl). Population served: 300,000 Natl. Network: ABC, . Leventhal Senter & Lerman. Format: Hits of the 60s, 70s & 80s. News staff: 1.5; News: 7 hrs wkly. Target aud: 25-54; upscale baby boomers. Spec prog: Interviews. ◆Steve Babson, CEO; Robin Truax, exec VP, traf mgr; Clay Ashworth, gen mgr; Dan Miner, stn mgr, opns dir; Pete Cloutier, gen sls mgr, prom dir.

Lake Luzerne

WBAR-FM— June 30, 1992: 94.7 mhz; 300 w. 892 ft TL: N43 17 22 W73 44 35. Stereo. Hrs open: 24
Rebroadcasts WHAZ(AM) Troy 100%.
30 Park Ave., Cohoes, 12047-3330. Phone: (518) 237-1330. Fax: (518) 235-4468.E-mail: events@aliveradionetwork.com Web Site:www.whaz.com Licensee: Capital Media Corp. (group owner; acq 10-1-92; 11-9-92). Population served: 600,000 Format: Bible teaching & preaching. Target aud: 25-75. ◆Paul F. Lotters, pres, gen mgr; Steven L. Klob, opns dir, dev dir, sls dir, prom dir & adv dir; Rex Gregory, progmg dir, progmg mgr; Rex P. Gregory, news dir, pub affrs dir, disc jockey; Bill Rosenfeld, chief of engrg.

Lake Placid

WIRD(AM)— Nov 21, 1961: 920 khz; 5 kw-D, 250 w-N. TL: N44 15 36 W74 01 22. Hrs open: 24 Box 211, Saranac Lake, 12983. Phone: (518) 891-1544. Fax: (518) 891-1545.E-mail: brandy@mtnradio.com Licensee: Radio Lake Placid Inc. Group owner: Mountain Communications (acq 1-10-2005). Population served: 80,000 Natl. Network: ESPN Radio, . Tierney & Swift. Format: Sports. News staff: 2; News: 20 hrs wkly. Target aud: 25-54; working blue collar/college educated.

WLPW(FM)— October 1979: 105.5 mhz; 3 kw. Ant -236 ft TL: N44 15 36 W74 01 22. Stereo. Hrs open: 24 Box 211, Saranac Lake, 12983. Phone: (518) 891-1544. Fax: (518) 891-1545.E-mail: brandy@mtnradio.com Licensee: Radio Lake Placid Inc. Population served: 80,000 Format: Classic rock.

Lake Ronkonkoma

*WSHR(FM)— January 1966: 91.9 mhz; 2.8 kw. 141 ft TL: N40 50 00 W73 06 01. Stereo. Hrs open: 24 Sachem North High School, 212 Smith Rd., 11779. Phone: (631) 471-1472. Fax: (631) 471-1400. Fax: (631) 471-1491. Licensee: Board of Education Sachem Central School District at Holbrook. (acq 1967). Population served: 1,500,000 Format: Var. Target aud: General. ◆Mark Laura, gen mgr; Isaic Ramaswamy, stn mgr.

Lake Success

WKTU(FM)—Licensed to Lake Success. See New York

Lakewood

WKZA(FM)— Mar 2001: 106.9 mhz; 5.2 kw. 715 ft TL: N41 57 31 W79 16 11. Hrs open: 106 W. T/Ihird St., Suite 106, Jamestown, 14701. Phone: (716) 487-1106. Fax: (716) 488-2169.E-mail: morningshow@1069kissfm.com Web Site:www.1069kissfm.com Licensee: Cross Country Communications LLC. Format: Top-40 hits. ◆John Newman, gen mgr; Sherrie Brookmire, gen sls mgr; Steve Rockford, progmg dir.

*WYRR(FM)—Not on air, target date: unknown: 88.9 mhz; 420 w. Ant 335 ft TL: N42 10 33 W79 19 02. Hrs open: 4271 Muncy-Exchange Rd., Turbotville, PA, 17772. Phone: (570) 412-6295. Licensee: Muncy Hills Broadcasting Inc. ◆Van A. Michael, pres.

Lancaster

WXRL(AM)— 1964: 1300 khz; 5 kw-D, 2.5 kw-N, DA-2. TL: N42 52 58 W78 37 54. Hrs open: 24 Box 170, 5426 William St., 14086. Phone: (716) 681-1313. Fax: (716) 681-7172.E-mail: wxrl@aol.com Web Site:www.wxrl.com Licensee: Dome Broadcasting Inc. (acq 11-1-70). Population served: 1,000,000 Natl. Network: CNN Radio, . Smithwick & Belendiuk. Format: Country. Target aud: 35 plus; Mature men & women 35 and older. Spec prog: German one hr, Polish 19 hrs wkly. ◆Louis A. Schriver, pres, gen mgr; Joan C. Schriver, exec VP, progmg dir; Lori Arumygam, dev dir; Louis E. Schriver Jr., gen sls mgr; Linda Sukennik, prom dir, prom mgr, traf mgr; Lynn Carol Supparits, opns dir, opns mgr & mus dir.

Liberty

*WGWR(FM)— November 1997: 88.1 mhz; 60 w. 561 ft TL: N41 48 55 W74 45 48. Hrs open: 24
Rebroadcasts WFGB(FM) Kingston 100%.
Box 777, Lake Katrine, 12449. Phone: (845) 336-6199. Fax: (845) 336-7205.E-mail: wmial@soundoflife.org Web Site:www.soundoflife.org Licensee: Sound of Life Inc. Format: Christian. ◆Tom Michael Zahradnik, gen mgr; Bob Conti, opns mgr; Joe Hunter, progmg dir.

WVOS(AM)— 1947: 1240 khz; 1 kw-U. TL: N41 46 54 W74 43 49. Hrs open: 5 AM-11 PM 198 Bridgeville Rd., Monticello, 12701. Phone: (845) 794-9898. Fax: (845) 794-0125. Licensee: Watermark Communications LLC (acq 11-2-2005; $1.7 million with co-located FM). Population served: 35,000 Barry Skidelsky. Format: Hot country. ◆Helena Manzione, gen mgr.

WVOS-FM— December 1964: 95.9 mhz; 6 kw. Ant 328 ft TL: N41 45 09 W74 43 01. Hrs open: 24 Prog sep from AM 198 Bridgeville Rd., Monticello, 12701. Phone: (845) 794-9898. Fax: (845) 794-0125. Web Site:www.wvosfm.com Population served: 70,000 Format: Greatest hits of all time. Target aud: 25-54.

Lindenhurst

*WOBH(FM)—Not on air, target date: unknown: 89.7 mhz; 1.775 kw. Ant 92 ft TL: N40 38 04 W73 19 59. Hrs open: 803 County Line Rd., North Amityville, 11701. Phone: (631) 224-1761. Licensee: Calvary Chapel of Hope (acq 8-29-2008; $57,500 for CP). ◆Claude Stauffer, pres.

Little Falls

WIXT(AM)— June 10, 1952: 1230 khz; 1 kw-U. TL: N43 02 33 W74 51 31. Hrs open: 24 39 Kellogg Rd., Suite 500, New Hartford, 13413. Phone: (315) 797-0803. Fax: (315) 797-7813.E-mail: info@galaxycommunication.com Web Site:www.starsradionetwork.com Licensee: Galaxy Utica Licensee LLC. Group owner: Clear Channel Communications Inc. (acq 10-24-2007; grpsl). Population served: 200,000 Richard Hayes. Format: Sports. News staff: one; News: 16 hrs wkly. Target aud: 25-54. Spec prog: Farm one hr, relg one hr wkly. ◆Brian Delaney, gen mgr.

WKAJ(AM)—Not on air, target date: unknown: 1120 khz; 1.5 kw-D, 250 w-N, DA-N. TL: N43 01 19 W74 50 12. Hrs open: 41 Kathleen Crescent, Coram, 11727. Phone: (631) 928-6506. Licensee: Michael Celenza. ◆Michael Celenza, gen mgr.

WSKU(FM)— Jan 3, 1991: 105.5 mhz; 2.3 kw. 152 ft TL: N42 59 27 W74 55 06. Stereo. Hrs open: 24 185 Genesee St., Suite 1601, Utica, 13501. Phone: (315) 734-9245. Fax: (315) 624-9245. Web Site:www.cnykiss.com Licensee: Roser Communications Network Inc. Group owner: Clear Channel Communications Inc. (acq 10-24-2007; grpsl). Population served: 200,000 Natl. Rep: Roslin,. Richard Hayes. Format: CHR, rhythmic. News staff: one; News: one hr wkly. Target aud: 25-54. ◆Brian Delaney, gen mgr; Stephen Lawrence, opns mgr.

Lockport

WLVL(AM)— May 8, 1947: 1340 khz; 1 kw-U. TL: N43 10 30 W78 42 39. Hrs open: Box 477, 14095. Secondary address: 320 Michigan St. 14094. Phone: (716) 433-5944. Fax: (716) 433-6588.E-mail: wlvl@wlvl.com Web Site:www.wlvl.com Licensee: Culver Communications Inc. (acq 9-81; $600,000; 10-5-81). Population served: 45,000 Natl. Network:

Westwood One, . Format: News/talk, sports. Target aud: 25-64; adult Lockport area citizens. Spec prog: Farm one hr, lt 2 hrs, Pol one hr, relg 3 hrs wkly. ◆Richard C. Greene, pres & gen mgr; Richard Greene, progmg dir; Doug Young, news dir.

Loudonville

*WVCR-FM— Apr 26, 1963: 88.3 mhz; 2.8 kw. Ant 840 ft TL: N42 38 13 W74 00 05. Stereo. Hrs open: 24 515 Loudon Rd., 12211-1462. Phone: (518) 782-6750. Fax: (518) 782-6498.E-mail: info@wvcr.com Web Site:www.wvcr.com Licensee: Siena College. Population served: 1,000,000 Format: Variety/"We Play Anything". Target aud: 12-34; female. Spec prog: Pol 3 hrs, Sp 3 hrs, gospel 3 hrs, Irish 3 hrs. ◆Darrin S. Kibbey, gen mgr; Joseph Doty, opns mgr; Dean Charette, progmg mgr.

Lowville

WLLG(FM)— Apr 1, 1987: 99.3 mhz; 1 kw. 561 ft TL: N43 45 12 W75 33 50. Stereo. Hrs open: 24 7606 N. State St., 13367. Phone: (315) 376-7500. Fax: (315) 376-8549.E-mail: sales@themoose.net Web Site:www.themoose.net Licensee: The Flack Broadcasting Group L.L.C. Natl. Network: USA, . Shaw Pittman. Format: Country, news. News staff: one; News: 18 hrs wkly. Target aud: General. Spec prog: Farm 3 hrs, relg 2 hrs wkly. ◆William Flack, pres, gen mgr & progmg dir; Brian Best, news dir; Ken Ruhlend, chief of engrg.

Malone

WICY(AM)— Nov 4, 1946: 1490 khz; 1 kw-U. TL: N44 50 46 W74 16 07. Hrs open: 18 86 Porter Rd., 12953. Phone: (518) 483-1100. Fax: (518) 483-1382. Web Site:www.oldiesradioonline.com Licensee: Cartier Communications Inc. Group owner: Martz Communications Group (acq 6-30-97; $761,000 with co-located FM). Population served: 51,000 Natl. Rep: Rgnl Reps,. Arter & Hadden. Format: Oldies. News staff: 2; News: 15 hrs wkly. Target aud: 25-54. Spec prog: Farm one hr wkly. ◆Michael Boldt, gen mgr & gen sls mgr.

*WMHQ(FM)— Dec 3, 2003: 90.1 mhz; 3 kw. Ant 325 ft TL: N44 49 48 W74 22 35. Stereo. Hrs open: 24
Rebroadcasts WMHR(FM) Syracuse 99%.
4044 Makyes Rd., Syracuse, 13215. Phone: (315) 469-5051.E-mail: mhn@marshillnetwork.org Web Site:www.marshillnetwork.org Licensee: Mars Hill Broadcasting Co. Inc. Natl. Network: Moody, Salem Radio Network, . Wiley, Rein & Fielding. Wire Svc: AP Format: Christian. News: 6 hrs wkly. Target aud: General; Christian families. ◆Clayton Roberts, pres; Wayne Taylor, gen mgr; Chris Tetta, progmg dir; Jeremy Miller, news dir; Valerie Smith, traf mgr.

*WSLO(FM)— February 1989: 90.9 mhz; 200 w. 354 ft TL: N44 49 46 W74 22 31. Hrs open: 24
Rebroadcasts WSLU(FM) Canton 100%.
St. Lawrence Univ., Canton, 13617. Phone: (315) 229-5356. Fax: (315) 229-5373.E-mail: radio@ncpr.org Web Site:www.ncpr.org Licensee: St. Lawrence University. Donald E. Martin. Format: Eclectic public radio. News staff: 2; News: 35 hrs wkly. Target aud: General. ◆Ellen Rocco, gen mgr; Shelly Pike, opns mgr & chief of opns; Sandra Demarest, dev dir.

WVNV(FM)— May 1, 1993: 96.5 mhz; 2.4 kw. Ant 361 ft TL: N44 49 37 W74 22 46. Stereo. Hrs open: 20 86 Porter Rd., 12953. Phone: (518) 483-1100. Fax: (518) 483-1382. Web Site:www.country965.com Licensee: Cartier Communications Inc. Population served: 100,000 Format: Country. News staff: 2; News: 2 hrs wkly. Target aud: 18-54. ◆Drew Scott, progmg dir.

Malta

WBZZ(FM)— October 1996: 105.7 mhz; 7.1 kw. Ant 613 ft TL: N42 47 09 W73 37 43. Hrs open: 1241 Kings Rd., Schenectady, 12303. Phone: (518) 881-1515. Fax: (518) 881-1516.E-mail: comments@buzz1057.com Web Site:www.buzz1057.com Licensee: Regent Licensee of Mansfield Inc. Group owner: Vox Radio Group L.P. (acq 1-4-2007; $4.9 million). Population served: 275,000 Format: Hot adult contemp. Target aud: 18-54; general. ◆Robert Ausfeld, gen mgr.

Manlius

WAQX-FM— Aug 23, 1978: 95.7 mhz; 25 kw. 300 ft TL: N43 00 25 W76 05 38. Stereo. Hrs open: 24 1064 James St., Syracuse, 13203. Phone: (315) 472-0200. Fax: (315) 472-1146.E-mail: hunter.scott@citcomm.com Web Site:www.95x.com Licensee: Citadel Broadcasting Co. Group owner: Citadel Broadcasting Corp. (acq 4-26-01; grpsl). Natl. Network: ABC, . Natl. Rep: D & R Radio,. Shaw

Pittman. Format: AOR. News: 3 hrs wkly. Target aud: 19-49; male. Spec prog: Pub service one hr wkly. ◆Dan Austin, gen mgr; Tom Mitchell, opns dir & opns mgr; Angela Moonan, sls dir; Hunter Scott, progmg dir; Dave Edwards, chief of engrg.

Massena

WMSA(AM)— Oct 12, 1945: 1340 khz; 1 kw-U. TL: N44 54 14 W74 53 01. Hrs open: 5:30 AM-10:15 PM Box 210, 2155 State Rt. 420, 13662. Phone: (315) 769-3594. Fax: (315) 769-3299.E-mail: info@1340wmsa.com Web Site:www.1340wmsa.com Licensee: Stephens Media Group-Massena LLC. Group owner: Martz Communications Group Population served: 14,100 Format: Adult contemp. News staff: one; News: 16 hrs wkly. Target aud: 18 plus. ◆Michael Boldt, gen mgr; Bob Larue, news dir; Bob Sauder, chief of engrg.

WYBG(AM)— Aug 18, 1958: 1050 khz; 1 kw-D, 500 w-N. TL: N44 53 42 W74 56 05. Hrs open: 6 AM-7 PM Box 298, 24 Andrews St., 13662. Phone: (315) 764-0554. Fax: (315) 764-0118.E-mail: wybgradio@nnymail.com Web Site:www.wybg1050.com Licensee: Wade Communications Inc. (acq 8-15-88; $450,000; 8-15-88). Population served: 295,000 Natl. Network: USA, . Natl. Rep: Commercial Media Sales,. Format: News/talk. News staff: 2; News: 14 hrs wkly. Target aud: 25-65; baby boomers & seniors. Spec prog: American Indian, children, farm, folk. ◆Curran Wade, pres, gen mgr, progmg dir; Dorothy Wade, VP.

Mechanicville

WABY(AM)— Oct 19, 1981: 1160 khz; 5 kw-D, 570 w-N. TL: N42 55 12 W73 42 08. Hrs open: 24 100 Saratoga Village Blvd., Suite 21, Malta, 12020. Phone: (518) 899-3000. Fax: (518) 889-3057.E-mail: wadymoon@aol.com Web Site:www.wabymoon.com Licensee: The Anastos Media Group Inc. Group owner: Anastos Media Group Inc. (acq 12-7-00; $280,000). Natl. Network: ABC, . Format: Standards. News staff: one; News: 50 hrs wkly. Target aud: 40 plus; adults, male & female. ◆Scott Collins, pres & gen mgr; John Measey, stn mgr; John Meaney, opns mgr, progmg dir, progmg mgr, news dir; Fran Dingman, gen sls mgr; Amanda Albright, prom dir.

WTMM-FM— Jan 4, 1993: 104.5 mhz; 5 kw. Ant 351 ft TL: N42 52 44 W73 51 47. Stereo. Hrs open: 24 1241 Kings Rd., Schenectady, 12303. Phone: (518) 881-1515. Fax: (518) 881-1516. Web Site:www.wtmm.com Licensee: Regent Licensee of Mansfield Inc. Group owner: Regent Communications Inc. (acq 8-24-2001; grpsl). Natl. Network: ESPN Radio, . Format: Sports talk. Target aud: 25-54; serious sports fans. ◆Robert Ausfeld, gen mgr; Brian ' Sinkoff, progmg dir.

Medina

*WFWO(FM)—Not on air, target date: unknown: 89.7 mhz; 2.2 kw. Ant 216 ft TL: N43 13 23 W78 17 21. Hrs open: Box 287, Freeport, ME, 04032. Phone:(207) 865-3448. Fax:(207) 865-1763.E-mail: info@positive.fm Web Site:www.positive.fm Licensee: The Positive Radio Network. ◆Mie Stoddard, chmn; Paula K, gen mgr.

Mexico

WVOU(FM)— 1997: 103.9 mhz; 3 kw. Ant 292 ft TL: N43 28 36 W76 16 44. Hrs open: 7095 Myers Rd., East Syracuse, 13057. Phone: (315) 656-2231. Licensee: Renard Communications Corp. (acq 3-13-97; $3,000 for CP). Format: Relg. Spec prog: Ger 2 hrs, lt 2 hrs, Pol 4 hrs , Sp 15 hrs wkly. ◆Sam Furco, gen mgr.

Middletown

WALL(AM)— Aug 6, 1942: 1340 khz; 1 kw-U. TL: N41 27 25 W74 26 24. Hrs open: 24 Box 416, Poughkeepsie, 12602. Secondary address: 2 Pendel Rd., Poughkeepsie 12602. Phone: (845) 471-1500. Fax: (845)-454-1204. Web Site:www.cumulus.com Licensee: Cumulus Licensing Corp. Group owner: Cumulus Media Inc. (acq 1-23-02; grpsl). Population served: 305,000 Hogan & Hartson. Format: Radio Disney. News staff: 2; News: 30 hrs wkly. Target aud: 35-64; educated, upscale families. ◆Victor Goodman, gen sls mgr; Nick Robbins, progmg dir; Beth Christie, pub affrs dir; Bryan Jones, local news ed.

*WOSR(FM)— Feb 3, 1992: 91.7 mhz; 1.8 kw. Ant 630 ft TL: N41 36 04 W74 33 13. Stereo. Hrs open: 24
Rebroadcasts WAMC-FM Albany 100%.
Box 66600, Albany, 12206-6600. Secondary address: 318 Central Ave. 12206-6600. Phone: (518) 465-5233. Phone: (800) 323-9262. Fax: (518) 432-6974.E-mail: mail@wamc.org Web Site:www.wamc.org Licensee: WAMC. Group owner: WAMC/Northeast Public Radio Natl.

Network: NPR, PRI, . Dow, Lohnes & Albertson. Wire Svc: AP Format: News, talk. News: 77 hrs wkly. Target aud: General. Spec prog: Folk 7 hrs, jazz 13 hrs wkly. ◆Alan Chartock, CEO, chmn, pres; David Galletly, VP, progmg dir; Selma Kaplan, VP & news dir.

WRRV(FM)— Nov 11, 1966: 92.7 mhz; 3 kw. 300 ft TL: N41 27 21 W74 26 22. Stereo. Hrs open: 24 Prog sep from AM Box 416, Poughkeepsie, 12602. Phone: (845) 471-1500. Fax: (845) 454-1204. Web Site:www.cumulus.com Format: Alternative ROCK. News staff: one; News: 3 hrs wkly. Target aud: 18-44; younger, mobile, upscale families. Spec prog: New mus 2 hrs wkly. ◆Mike Harris, pres; Bill Palmeri, gen mgr; Greg O'Brien, progmg dir; Andrew Boris, mus dir.

WYNY(AM)—Not on air, target date: unknown: 1400 khz; 1 kw-U, DA-D. TL: N41 28 26 W74 27 01. Hrs open: 135 White Bridge Rd., 10940. Phone: (845) 355-4001. Fax: (845) 355-4002. Licensee: Digital Radio Broadcasting Inc. ◆Charles Williamson, gen mgr.

Mineola

WTHE(AM)— Jan 1, 1964: 1520 khz; 1 kw-D. TL: N40 44 45 W73 37 29. Hrs open: 260 E. Second St., 11501. Phone: (516) 742-1520. Fax: (516) 742-2878.E-mail: nygospelradio@aol.com Web Site:www.wthe1520am.com Licensee: Universal Broadcasting of New York Inc. (group owner; acq 7-10-69; $235,000). Population served: 12,000,000 Cohn and Marks, LLP. Format: Relg, Black gospel. News staff: one; News: 10 hrs wkly. Target aud: General. ◆Howard Warshaw, CEO, exec VP, gen mgr; Miriam Warshaw, pres; Abe Warshaw, sr VP, VP; Howard Warshaw Sr., VP; Darren Greggs, opns VP; Clara Mack, mus dir.

Minerva

*WGOR(FM)—Not on air, target date: unknown: 88.1 mhz; 325 w vert. Ant 52 ft TL: N43 51 53.4 W74 00 24.8. Hrs open: 89 Half Hollow Rd., Melville, 11747. Phone: (631) 387-1055. Licensee: Balfour Lake Foundation Inc. ◆David M. Cohen, pres.

WXMR(FM)—Not on air, target date: unknown: 100.7 mhz; 1 kw. Ant -115 ft TL: N43 47 14 W73 58 53. Hrs open: 1717 Dixie Hwy., Suite 650, Fort Wright, KY, 41011. Phone: (859) 331-9100. Licensee: Radioactive LLC. ◆Benjamin L. Homel, pres.

Minetto

WKRH(FM)— October 1996: 106.5 mhz; 5.1 kw. 328 ft TL: N43 25 45 W76 32 14. Hrs open: 235 Walton St., Syracuse, 13202-1351. Phone: (315) 472-9111. Fax: (315) 472-1888.E-mail: generalinfo@krock.com Web Site:www.krock.com Licensee: Galaxy Syracuse Licensee LLC. (acq 8-31-2000). Leventhal, Senter & Lerman. Format: Alt rock. News staff: one; News: 2 hrs wkly. Target aud: 18-49; men. ◆Ed Levine, pres; Michael Lucarelli, CFO; Lisa Morrow, sr VP; Mimi Grisworld, progmg VP; Scott Petibone, progmg dir.

Monroe

*WLJP(FM)— May 1991: 89.3 mhz; 200 w. 1,023 ft TL: N41 22 38 W74 07 55. (CP: Ant 1,038 ft.). Stereo. Hrs open:
Rebroadcasts WFGB(FM) Kingston 100%.
Box 777, Lake Katrine, 12449. Phone: (845) 336-6199. Fax: (845) 336-7205.E-mail: email@soundoflife.org Web Site:www.soundoflife.org Licensee: Sound of Life Inc. Population served: 350,000 Format: Contemp Christian. Target aud: General. ◆Tom Michael Zahradnik, gen mgr; Bob Conti, opns mgr; Joe Hunter, progmg dir.

Montauk

*WPKM(FM)— 2004: 88.7 mhz; 8 w horiz, 2.7 kw vert. Ant 226 ft TL: N41 01 53 W71 58 32. Hrs open:
Rebroadcasts WPKN(FM) Bridgeport, CT 100%.
244 University Ave., Bridgeport, CT, 06604. Phone: (203) 331-9756.E-mail: wpkn@wpkn.org Web Site:www.wpkn.org Licensee: WPKN Inc. Format: Div. ◆Harry Minot, gen mgr.

WXLM(FM)— Feb 19, 1993: 104.7 mhz; 6 kw. Ant 328 ft TL: N41 01 57 W71 58 31. Stereo. Hrs open: 24 7 Governor Winthrop Blvd., New London, 06320. Phone: (866) 441-9653. Fax: (860) 444-7970.E-mail: info@wxlm.fm Web Site:www.wxlm.fm Licensee: Citadel Broadcasting Co. Group owner: Citadel Broadcasting Corp. (acq 4-3-2003). Format: News/talk. News staff: 2; News: 5 hrs wkly. Target aud: 21-54; adults who grew up in the 60s & 70s. ◆Kevin O'Connor, opns dir; Julie Johnson, progmg dir.

Montgomery

***WNYX(FM)**— 2009: 88.1 mhz; 1.15 kw. Ant 115 ft TL: N41 28 37.4 W74 16 09.8. Hrs open: River Broadcasting Inc., 211 River Rd., Walden, 12586-2815. Phone: (845) 778-2400. Licensee: River Broadcasting Inc. ♦John H. Katonah, pres.

Monticello

WJUX(FM)— Nov 1, 1994: 99.7 mhz; 6 kw. 328 ft TL: N41 39 24 W74 43 40. Stereo. Hrs open: 24 6550 Rt. 9 S., Howell, NJ, 07731. Phone: (732) 901-9953. Fax: (732) 901-0356.E-mail: info@bridgefm.org Web Site:www.bridgefm.org Licensee: Bridgelight LLC (acq 11-13-03). Population served: 6,700,000 Koteen & Naftalin. Format: Relg. Target aud: 35-54. ♦Brian J. Rechten, gen mgr, stn mgr; Patti Gates, gen sls mgr.

WSUL(FM)— Apr 16, 1977: 98.3 mhz; 2.2 kw. 535 ft TL: N41 39 38 W74 41 14. Stereo. Hrs open: 24 Box 98.3, 198 Bridgeville Rd., 12701. Phone: (845) 794-9898. Phone: (845) 794-0242. Fax: (845) 794-0125.E-mail: office@wsul.com Web Site:www.wsul.com Licensee: Watermark Communications LLC (acq 3-17-2005; $2.5 million). Population served: 100,000 Wilkinson Barker Knauer. Format: Hot Adult Contemp. News staff: 2. Target aud: 25-54. ♦Helena Manzione, gen mgr; Joni Shaughnessy, opns mgr, progmg dir; Yannika Sonic, prom dir; Bill James, news dir.

WVOS-FM—See Liberty

Montour Falls

WNGZ(FM)— June 1973: 104.9 mhz; 1 kw. 480 ft TL: N42 15 05 W76 52 53. Stereo. Hrs open: 24 2205 College Ave., Elmira, 14903. Phone: (607) 732-4400. Fax: (607) 732-7774. Licensee: Chemung County Radio Inc. Group owner: Backyard Broadcasting LLC (acq 12-1-02; grpsl). Population served: 1,534 Format: Classic rock. News staff: one. Target aud: 20-49; baby boomers, young adults. ♦Margaret Tollner, gen mgr, gen sls mgr; Scott Free, opns mgr; Brian Povancher, gen sls mgr; Vinnie Pagano, progmg dir.

Morristown

WYSX(FM)— Noverber 1998: 96.7 mhz; 17 kw. Ant 354 ft TL: N44 34 43 W75 30 51. Stereo. Hrs open: 24 One Bridge Plaza, Suite 204, Ogdensburg, 13669. Phone: (315) 393-1220. Fax: (315) 393-3974.E-mail: john@yesfm.com Web Site:www.yesfm.com Licensee: Stephens Media Group-Ogdensburg LLC. Group owner: Martz Communications Group Population served: 112,000 Format: CHR. Target aud: 18-34. ♦John Winter, gen mgr.

Mount Hope

***WMFU(FM)**— September 1994: 90.1 mhz; 1.1 kw. Ant 600 ft TL: N41 25 36 W74 34 54. Stereo. Hrs open: 24 Box 2011, Jersey City, NJ, 07303-2011. Secondary address: 4th Floor, 43 Montgomery St., Jersey City, NJ 07302. Phone: (201) 521-1416. Fax: (201) 521-1286.E-mail: info@wxhd.com Web Site:www.wfmu.org Licensee: Auricle Communications. (acq 6-97). Haley, Bader & Potts. Format: Div, free form. Target aud: General. ♦Ken Freedman, pres & gen mgr; Brian Turner, progmg dir, mus dir; John Fogarazzo, chief of engrg.

Mount Kisco

WFAF(FM)— Jan 15, 1964: 106.3 mhz; 1.4 kw. Ant 440 ft TL: N41 11 56 W73 41 37. Stereo. Hrs open:
Rebroadcasts WPDH(FM) Poughkeepsie 100%.
365 Secor Rd., Hartsdale, 10530. Secondary address: 2 Pendell Rd., Poughkeepsie 12602. Phone: (914) 693-2400. Fax: (914) 693-4489. Web Site:www.wfafm.com Licensee: Cumulus Licensing Corp. Group owner: Cumulus Media Inc. (acq 1-23-2002; grpsl). Population served: 150000 Format: Adult contemp. ♦Rob Calarco, gen mgr.

WRVP(AM)— Oct 27, 1957: 1310 khz; 5 kw-D, 33 w-N, DA-2. TL: N41 11 37 W73 44 22. Hrs open: 6 AM-6 PM Box 2908, Patterson, NJ, 07509. Phone: (973) 881-8700. Fax: (973) 881-8324.E-mail: bobrod@radiovision.net Web Site:www.radiovision.net Licensee: Radio Vision Cristiana Management Corp. (acq 8-26-2002; $1.36 million). Population served: 100,000 Koteen & Naftalin. Format: Sp Christian. News staff: 3. Target aud: General. ♦Milton Donato, pres; Bob Rodriguez, gen mgr.

WWES(FM)—Not on air, target date: unknown: 88.9 mhz; 200 w vert. Ant 115 ft TL: N41 14 20 W73 42 48. Hrs open: 318 Central Ave., Albany, 12206. Phone: (518) 465-5233. Fax: (518) 432-6974. Web Site:www.wamc.org Licensee: WAMC. ♦Alan Chartock, CEO & pres.

Nanuet

WRCR(AM)—See Spring Valley

Napeague

***WEGB(FM)**—Not on air, target date: unknown: 90.7 mhz; 10 w horiz, 6.25 kw vert. Ant 315 ft TL: N41 01 56 W71 58 32. (ST with WEER(FM) Easthampton, Village). Hrs open: 2837 Noyac Rd., Sag Harbor, 11963. Phone: (631) 725-4155. Fax: (631) 725-4155. Web Site:cbchamptons.com Licensee: Community Bible Church. ♦Doug Kinney, pres.

New City

WRKL(AM)— July 4, 1964: 910 khz; 1 kw-D, 800 w-N, DA-2. TL: N41 10 52 W74 02 53. Hrs open: 24 1551 Rt. 202, Pomona, 10970. Phone: (845) 354-2000. Fax: (845) 354-4796.E-mail: wrkl@polskieradio.com Web Site:www.polskieradio.com Licensee: Polnet Communications Ltd. (group owner; acq 3-19-99). Population served: 300,000 Wiley, Rein and Fielding. Format: Polish language. News staff: one; News: 50 hrs wkly. Target aud: 18-54; Polish language audience. ♦Kent D. Gustafson, CEO, gen mgr; Walter Kotaba, pres; Grzegorz Sliwecki, opns mgr.

New Paltz

WBWZ(FM)— Nov 19, 1992: 93.3 mhz; 350 w. 1,328 ft TL: N41 41 58 W74 00 11. Hrs open: 24 20 Tucker Dr., Poughkeepsie, 12603. Phone: (845) 471-2300. Fax: (845) 471-2683.E-mail: DaveMcCord @ClearChannel.com Web Site:www.star933fm.com Licensee: AMFM Radio Licenses LLC. Group owner: Clear Channel Communications Inc. (acq 12-22-2000; with WRWD-FM Highland). Population served: 660,000 Natl. Network: Jones Radio Networks, . Natl. Rep: Katz Radio,. Format: Hot adult contemp hits. News staff: one; News: 7 hrs wkly. Target aud: 25-54; baby boomers. ♦Frank Curcio, gen mgr; Reggie Osterhoudt, opns dir; Jim Brady, gen sls mgr; Jeanette Relyea, natl sls mgr; Nick Smirnoff, prom dir; Aaron McCord, progmg dir; Cameron Hendrix, news dir.

New Rochelle

WVIP(FM)— 1953: 93.5 mhz; 3 kw. 325 ft TL: N40 57 45 W73 50 32. Stereo. Hrs open: 24 Prog sep from AM One Broadcast Forum, 10801. Phone: (914) 636-1460. Fax: (914) 636-2900.E-mail: don@wvox.com Population served: 7,000,000 Garvey, Schubert & Barer. Format: Adult standards. News staff: 2; News: 14 hrs wkly. Target aud: 18 plus; adults. Spec prog: It 6 hrs, Jewish one hr wkly. ♦William O'Shaughnessy, chmn; Don Stevens, stn mgr; Richard LittleJohn, sls VP, progmg dir.

WVOX(AM)— 1950: 1460 khz; 500 w-D. TL: N40 55 42 W73 46 30. Hrs open: 24 One Broadcast Forum, 10801. Phone: (914) 636-1460. Fax: (914) 636-2900. Web Site:www.wvox.com Licensee: Hudson-Westchester Radio Inc. (acq 5-1-68). Population served: 75,385 Natl. Network: Jones Radio Networks, AP Radio, . Garvey, Schubert & Barer. Format: News/talk. News staff: 4; News: 50 hrs wkly. Target aud: 24 plus; community minded. Spec prog: Black one hr, gospel one hr, relg 3, Irish one, Jewish 2 hrs, gay-lesbian one hr wkly. ♦Cindy Gallagher, CFO, exec VP; Nancy Curry, VP; Don Stevens, opns mgr; Matthew O'Shaughnessy, dev dir; Judy Fremont, sls VP, gen sls mgr; David O'Shaughnessy, progmg VP; Richard Littlejohn, mus dir; William O'Shaughnessy, CEO, pres, edit dir & political ed.

New York

WABC(AM)— Oct 7, 1921: 770 khz; 50 kw-U. TL: N40 52 50 W74 04 12. Hrs open: 17th Fl., 2 Penn Plaza, 10121. Phone: (212) 613-3800. Fax: (212) 613-3823.E-mail: info@wabc.com Web Site:www.wabcradio.com Licensee: Radio License Holding X LLC. (acq 6-12-2007; grpsl). Population served: 789,556 Natl. Rep: Interep,. Format: Talk. ♦Mitch Dolan, pres, gen mgr; Tim McCarthy, stn mgr & sls dir; Fred Bennett, gen sls mgr; Russ King, prom dir, pub affrs dir; Phil Boyce, progmg dir; Kevin Plumb, chief of engrg.

WADO(AM)— Mar 12, 1934: 1280 khz; 50 kw-D, 7.2 kw-N, DA-2. TL: N40 49 36 W74 04 32. Hrs open: 24 485 Madison Ave., 3rd Flr., 10022. Phone: (212) 310-6000. Fax: (212) 888-3694. Web Site:www.univision.com Licensee: Wado-Am License Corp. Group owner: Univision Radio (acq 9-22-2003; grpsl). Population served: 3,000,000 Natl. Rep: Katz Radio,. Format: Sp, news/talk, sports. News staff: 13; News: 50 hrs wkly. Target aud: 25-54; Hispanics in the NY metropolitan area. ♦Joe Pagan, gen mgr.

WAXQ(FM)— Dec 1, 1956: 104.3 mhz; 6 kw. 1,361 ft TL: N40 44 54 W73 59 10. Stereo. Hrs open: 1180 Ave. of the Americas, 10036. Phone: (212) 575-1043. Fax: (212) 302-7814. Web Site:www.q1043.com Licensee: AMFM Radio Licenses LLC. Group owner: Clear Channel Communications Inc. (acq 8-30-2000; grpsl). Population served: 1,000,000 Fleischman & Walsh. Format: Classic rock. News staff: one; News: 2 hrs wkly. ♦Rob Williams, gen mgr; Bob Buchmann, progmg dir; Eric Wellman, mus dir; Henry Behring, chief of engrg.

***WBAI(FM)**— January 1960: 99.5 mhz; 5.4 kw horiz, 3.9 kw vert. 1,220 ft TL: N40 44 54 W73 59 10. Stereo. Hrs open: 24 120 Wall St., 10th Fl., 10005. Phone: (212) 209-2800. Phone: (212) 209-2800. Fax: (212) 747-1698. Web Site:www.wbai.org Licensee: Pacifica Foundation. Group owner: Pacifica Foundation Inc. dba Pacifica Radio (acq 1-9-60). Population served: 18,000,000 Format: Div, educ, news/talk. News staff: 2; News: 5 hrs wkly. Target aud: General; NY metropolitan area. Spec prog: American Indian one hr, Black 10 hrs, class 5 hrs, folk 2 hrs, jazz 5 hrs, Sp 3 hrs wkly. ♦Indra Hardat, gen mgr; Bernard White, prom dir.

WBBR(AM)— Feb 13, 1991: 1130 khz; 50 kw-U, DA-N. TL: N40 48 39 W74 02 24. Hrs open: 731 Lexington Ave., 10022. Phone: (212) 318-2000. Fax: (917) 369-5000. Web Site:www.bloomberg.com Licensee: Bloomberg Communications Inc. (acq 11-4-92; $13.58 million; 11-23-92). Population served: 18,000,000 Format: Business news. ♦Ken Kohn, gen mgr.

WBLS(FM)— Sept 15, 1965: 107.5 mhz; 5.4 kw horiz, 3.8 kw vert. 1,220 ft TL: N40 44 54 W73 59 10. Hrs open: 24 Prog sep from AM 3 Park Ave., 10016. Phone: (212) 447-1000. Fax: (212) 447-5193.E-mail: info@wbls.com Web Site:www.wbls.com Licensee: Urban Radio I L.L.C. Natl. Network: ABC, . Format: Black, urban contemp. Target aud: 25-54; upscale, urban. ♦Pierre M. Sutton, CEO; Kernie Anderson, gen mgr; Vinny Brown, progmg dir; Bill Stallman, engrg dir; Lucella Duncan, traf mgr; Larry Hardesty, sports cmtr; Charles Mitchell, disc jockey.

WCBS(AM)— 1924: 880 khz; 50 kw-U. TL: N40 51 35 W73 47 09. Hrs open: 24 524 W. 57th St., 9th Fl., 10019. Phone: (212) 975-4321. Fax: (212) 975-4674.E-mail: desk@wcbs880.com Web Site:www.wcbs880.com Licensee: CBS Radio East Inc. Group owner: Infinity Broadcasting Corp. (acq 11-13-98; grpsl). Natl. Network: CBS, . Format: News. Target aud: 25-54. ♦Chad Brown, VP, gen mgr; Matt Timothy, gen sls mgr; Mary Butler, natl sls mgr; Manny Severin, mktg dir, prom dir, adv dir; Cry Quimby, progmg dir; Tim Scheld, news dir; Mark Olkowski, chief of engrg.

WCBS-FM— 1941: 101.1 mhz; 6.8 kw. Ant 1,353 ft TL: N40 44 54 W73 59 10. Hrs open: Prog sep from AM 1540 Broadway, 10036. Phone: (212) 258-6000. Fax: (212) 846-5188. Web Site:www.wcbsfm.com Population served: 1,000,000 Format: Oldies. ♦Chad Brown, VP, gen mgr; Ezio Torres, gen sls mgr; Joe McCoy, progmg dir.

WEPN(AM)— Aug 28, 1922: 1050 khz; 50 kw-U. TL: N40 48 26 W74 04 11. Stereo. Hrs open: 24 2 Penn Plaza, 17th Fl., 10121. Phone: (212) 613-3800. Fax: (212) 613-3861. Web Site:www.1050espnradio.com Licensee: New York AM Radio LLC. Group owner: ABC Inc. (acq 4-28-2003; $78 million). Population served: 15,340,000 Natl. Network: ESPN Radio, . Format: Sports, talk. News staff: 2. Target aud: Men 25-54. ♦Tim McCarthy, pres & gen mgr; Mike Thompson, progmg dir.

WFAN(AM)— 1930: 660 khz; 50 kw-U. TL: N40 51 35 W73 47 09. Stereo. Hrs open: 24 Kaufman-Astoria Studios, 34-12 36th St., Astoria, 11106. Phone: (718) 706-7690. Fax: (718) 361-1059.E-mail: info@fan.com Web Site:www.wfan.com Licensee: CBS Radio East Inc. Group owner: Infinity Broadcasting Corp. (acq 2-25-92; $70 million; 4-92). Population served: 18,000,000 Natl. Network: CBS, . Natl. Rep: CBS Radio,. Wire Svc: SportsTicker Wire Svc: Sports Wire Format: Sports, talk. News staff: 34. Target aud: 25-54; sports fans. ♦Chuck Ortick, gen mgr; Mark Chernoff, progmg dir; Tony Hammel, gen sls mgr & news dir.

***WFUV(FM)**— July 1947: 90.7 mhz; 46 kw. Ant 508 ft TL: N40 52 48 W73 52 40. Stereo. Hrs open: 24 441 E. Fordham Rd., Keating Hall B12, Bronx, 10458. Phone: (718) 817-4550. Fax: (718) 365-9815. Fax: (718) 817-5595.E-mail: thefolks@wfuv.org Web Site:www.wfuv.org Licensee: Fordham University, Executive Committee, Board of Trustees. Population served: 15,898,000 Natl. Network: NPR, PRI, . Renouf & Polivy. Wire Svc: AP Format: AAA, div. News staff: 2; News: 8 hrs wkly. Target aud: 25 plus; intelligent & sophisticated mus listeners. Spec prog: Irish 10 hrs wkly. ♦Joseph McShane, pres; John Hollwitz, VP; Ralph M. Jennings, gen mgr; George Evans, opns dir; John Platt, mktg dir; Janeen Shalteman, prom dir; Chuck Singleton, progmg dir; Rita Houston, mus dir; Julianne Welby, news dir; George Bodarky, pub affrs dir.

***WHCR-FM—** February 1985: 90.3 mhz; 10 w. 266 ft TL: N40 49 09 W73 56 59. Hrs open: 24 160 Convent Ave., Nac Building, Room 5217, 10031. Phone: (212) 650-7481. Fax: (212) 650-7480.E-mail: info@whcr.org Web Site:www.whcr.org Licensee: City College of New York. Format: Jazz, Sp, Black. News: 70 hrs wkly. Target aud: Community of Harlem. ♦Angela Harden, gen mgr.

WHTZ(FM)—See Newark, NJ

WINS(AM)— 1924: 1010 khz; 50 kw-U, DA-1. TL: N40 48 16 W74 06 25. (CP: TL: N40 48 39 W74 02 24). Hrs open: 24 345 Hudson St., 10th Fl., 10014. Phone: (212) 315-7000. Fax: (212) 315-7015.E-mail: info@1010wins.com Web Site:www.1010wins.com Licensee: CBS Radio East Inc. Group owner: Infinity Broadcasting Corp. Population served: 17,272,000 Natl. Network: ABC, CNN Radio, . Natl. Rep: CBS Radio,. Leventhal. Senter & Lerman. Wire Svc: AP Format: News. News staff: 50; News: 168 hrs wkly. Target aud: General. ♦Joel Hollander, CEO; Greg Janoff, gen mgr; Mike Felicetti, gen sls mgr; Mark Mason, progmg dir; Ben Mevorach, news dir; Mark Olkowski, engrg dir, engrg mgr. Co-owned TV: WCBS-TV affil.

***WKCR-FM—** October 1941: 89.9 mhz; 1 kw. 849 ft TL: N40 42 43 W74 00 49. (CP: 630 w, ant 1,419 ft.). Stereo. Hrs open: 24 2920 Broadway, Mailcode 2612, 10027. Phone: (212) 854-9920. Fax: (212) 854-9296.E-mail: bored@wkcr.org Web Site:www.wkcr.org Licensee: Trustees of Columbia University. Population served: 18,000,000 Format: Var/div, class, jazz. News: 3 hrs wkly. Target aud: General. Spec prog: Country 6 hrs, news/sports 6 hrs, international 8 hrs, Sp 10 hrs, Black 12 hrs wkly. ♦Jordan Paul, stn mgr; Shira Burton, prom dir.

WKDM(AM)— 1927: 1380 khz; 5 kw-U, DA-1. TL: N40 49 13 W74 04 09. (CP: 5 kw-D, 13 kw-N, DA-2). Hrs open: 2nd Fl., 449 Broadway, 10013. Phone: (212) 966-1059. Phone: (212) 431-1430. Fax: (212) 966-9580.E-mail: info@mrbi.net/wkdm.htm Web Site:www.mrbi.net/wkdm.htm Licensee: Multicultural Radio Broadcasting Licensee LLC. Group owner: Multicultural Radio Broadcasting Inc. (acq 6-30-2003; $37 million). Population served: 1,000,000 Format: Chinese Mandarin (M-F), Sp (weekends). ♦Arthur Liu, pres; Gene Heinemeyer, gen mgr.

***WKRB(FM)**—(Brooklyn, May 28, 1978: 90.3 mhz; 10 w. Ant 133 ft TL: N40 34 36 W73 56 04. Stereo. Hrs open: 24 Kingsborough Community College, 2001 Oriental Blvd., Brooklyn, 11235. Phone: (718) 368-5817. Fax: (718) 368-4776. Web Site:www.wkrb.org Licensee: Kingsborough Community College. Population served: 250,000 Format: Div, CHR. Target aud: General; young adults. ♦Regina S. Peruggi, pres; Rob Herklotz, gen mgr.

WKTU(FM)—(Lake Success, 1940: 103.5 mhz; 5.4 kw. 1,417 ft TL: N40 42 43 W74 00 49. Stereo. Hrs open: 24 32 Avenue of the Americas, Bldg. 1, 10013. Phone: (201) 420-3700. Fax: (201) 420-3737.E-mail: 1035ktu@clearchannel.com Web Site:www.ktu.com Licensee: AMFM Radio Licenses LLC. Group owner: Clear Channel Communications Inc. (acq 8-30-2000; grpsl). Population served: 13700000 Natl. Rep: D & R Radio,. Leventhal, Senter & Lerman. Format: Dance, radio. News staff: one. Target aud: 18-54. ♦Rob Williams, gen mgr.

WLIB(AM)— 1942: 1190 khz; 10 kw-D, 30 kw-N, DA. TL: N40 47 48 W74 06 06. Hrs open: 24 3 Park Ave., 10016. Phone: (212) 447-1000. Fax: (212) 447-5193.E-mail: info@wlib.com Web Site:www.wlib.com Licensee: Urban Radio I L.L.C. Group owner: Inner City Broadcasting (acq 7-72). Population served: 786,776 Natl. Rep: McGavren Guild,. Format: Black gospel. ♦Pierre M. Sutton, chmn; Deon Levingston, VP, gen mgr; Leon Van Gelder, gen sls mgr; Gwen Kingsberry, prom dir, prom mgr; Vinny Brown, opns mgr & progmg dir.

WLTW(FM)— Jan 26, 1961: 106.7 mhz; 5.4 kw horiz, 7.8 kw vert. 1,220 ft TL: N40 44 54 W73 59 10. Stereo. Hrs open: 32 Ave. of the Americas, 10013. Phone: (212) 377-7900. Fax: (212) 603-4602.E-mail: info@wltw.com Web Site:www.1067litefm.com Licensee: AMFM Radio Licenses LLC. Group owner: Clear Channel Communications Inc. (acq 8-30-2000; grpsl). Natl. Network: AP Radio, . Natl. Rep: Katz Radio,. Latham & Watkins. Format: Adult contemp. ♦Andrew Rosen, gen mgr; Steve Chessare, gen sls mgr; Bridget Sullivan, prom dir; Jim Ryan, progmg dir.

WMCA(AM)— 1925: 570 khz; 5 kw-U, DA-1. TL: N40 45 10 W74 06 15. (CP: 50 kw-D, 30 kw-N). Hrs open: 24 777 Terrace Ave., 6th floor, Hasbrouck Heights, NJ, 07604-3100. Phone: (201) 298-5700. Fax: (201) 298-5757.E-mail: office@nycradio.com Web Site:www.wmca.com Licensee: Salem Media of New York LLC. Group owner: Salem Communications (acq 9-15-89; $13 million; 8-14-89). Population served: 20,000,000 Format: Christian/talk. News: 5 hrs wkly. Target aud: General. Spec prog: Jewish 9 hrs wkly. ♦Edward G. Atsinger III, pres; Joe D. Davis, VP; M. Susan Lucchesi, gen mgr; Peter Thiele, opns mgr; Tamela Kay Maxwell, gen sls mgr.

***WNYC(AM)—** July 8, 1924: 820 khz; 10 kw-D, 1 kw-N, DA. TL: N40 45 10 W74 06 15. Hrs open: One Centre St., 10007. Phone: (212) 669-7800. Fax: (212) 669-8986. Web Site:www.wnyc.org Licensee: WNYC Radio Broadcasting Foundation (acq 10-3-96; $20 million with co-located FM). Population served: 15,000,000 Natl. Network: PRI, NPR, . Format: News/talk, info. Target aud: General. Spec prog: Big band 2 hrs, spoken word 3 hrs wkly. ♦Laura Walker, CEO, pres; Mitchell Heskel, CFO; Peter Wilderotter, dev VP; Ellen Reynolds, dev dir; Dean Cappello, progmg VP, progmg dir.

***WNYC-FM—** Sept 21, 1943: 93.9 mhz; 5.4 kw. 1,418 ft TL: N40 42 43 W74 00 49. Stereo. Hrs open: 24 Prog sep from AM One Centre St., 10007. Phone: (212) 669-7800. Fax: (212) 669-8986. Web Site:www.wnyc.com Licensee: WNYC Radio Broadcasting Foundation Format: News, class. News: 35 hrs wkly. Spec prog: Drama & literature 5 hrs, jazz 4 hrs wkly.

***WNYE(FM)—** November 1938: 91.5 mhz; 18 kw. Ant 430 ft TL: N40 41 21 W73 58 37. Hrs open: 24 112 Tillary St., 11201. Phone: (718) 250-5800. Fax: (718) 855-8863. Web Site:www.wnye.nycenet.edu Licensee: New York City Dept. of Info Technology & Telecommunications. Population served: 12,000,000 Natl. Network: NPR, PRI, . Rgnl. Network: NPR, PRI. Arnold & Porter. Format: Educ. Target aud: General. ♦Terence M. O'Driscoll, gen mgr; Chang Kim, chief of engrg. Co-owned TV: WNYE-TV affil

***WNYU-FM—** May 3, 1973: 89.1 mhz; 8.3 kw. 256 ft TL: N40 51 26 W73 54 48. Stereo. Hrs open: 4 PM-1 AM (M-F) 194 Mercer St., 5th Fl., 10012. Phone: (212) 998-1660. Fax: (212) 998-1652. Web Site:www.wnyu.org Licensee: New York University. Population served: 100,000 Natl. Network: ABC, . Format: AOR. News: 4 hrs wkly. Spec prog: Dance mus 13 hrs, Black 5 hrs, reggae 2 hrs, Sp 2 hrs, oldies 3 hrs wkly. ♦Robby Morris, gen mgr; Momo Araki, prom dir.

WOR(AM)— Feb 22, 1922: 710 khz; 50 kw-U, DA-1. TL: N40 47 30 W74 05 38. Hrs open: 24 111 Broadway, 10008. Secondary address: 166 West Putnam Ave., Greenwich, CT 06830. Phone: (212) 642-4500. Fax: (212) 642-4486. Web Site:www.wor710.com Licensee: Buckley Broadcasting/WOR LLC. Group owner: Buckley Broadcasting Corp. (acq 12-89; $25.1 million;12-11-89). Population served: 18,000,000 Natl. Rep: Eastman Radio,. Format: Info, news/talk. News staff: 5; News: 4 hrs wkly. Target aud: 35-64. Spec prog: Relg 4 hrs wkly. ♦Joseph Bilotta, COO, exec VP; Rick Buckley, pres; Eloise Maroney, opns dir.

WPLJ(FM)— Jan 18, 1960: 95.5 mhz; 6.7 kw. Ant 1,335 ft TL: N40 44 54 W73 59 10. Stereo. Hrs open: 24 17th Fl., 2 Penn Plaza, 10121. Phone: (212) 613-8900. Fax: (212) 613-8956. Fax: (212) 613-8950.E-mail: writeus@Plj.com Web Site:www.plj.com Licensee: Radio License Holding IX LLC. Population served: 8,000,000 Natl. Rep: Interep,. Format: Hot adult contemp. News: 5 hrs wkly. Target aud: 18-54; females. ♦Steven W. Borneman, stn mgr, gen sls mgr; Tom Cuddy, opns VP; Theresa Angela, prom dir; Scott Shannon, progmg dir; Tony Mascaro, mus dir; Patty Steele, news dir; Kevin Plumb, engrg dir.

WQEW(AM)— Dec 3, 1936: 1560 khz; 50 kw-U, DA-2. TL: N40 42 59 W73 55 04. Hrs open: c/o WABC(AM), 2 Penn Plaza, 17th Fl., 10121. Phone: (212) 615-3250. Fax: (212) 615-3268.E-mail: Jospeh.M.Weinholtz @radiodisney.com Web Site:www.radiodisney.com Licensee: Radio Disney New York LLC. (acq 5-24-2007; $40 million). Population served: 14,000,000 Wire Svc: Reuters Format: Children. Target aud: 25-64; educated & affluent. ♦Jospeh M. Weinholtz, gen mgr & stn mgr.

WQHT(FM)— 1940: 97.1 mhz; 6.7 kw. Ant 1,338 ft TL: N40 44 54 W73 59 10. Stereo. Hrs open: 24 395 Hudson St., 7th Floor, 10014. Phone: (212) 229-9797. Fax: (212) 929-8559. Web Site:www.hot97.com Licensee: Emmis License Corp. of New York. Group owner: Emmis Communications Corp. Population served: 2,000,000 Natl. Rep: Katz Radio,. Format: CHR. Target aud: General. ♦Alexandra Cameron, sr VP, gen mgr, gen mgr; Harry Clark, sls dir; Brian D'Aurelio, mktg dir; Ebro Darden, progmg dir.

WQXR-FM— Nov 8, 1939: 96.3 mhz; 6 kw. 1,361 ft TL: N40 44 54 W73 59 10. Stereo. Hrs open: 24 122 5th Ave., 3rd Fl., 10011. Phone: (212) 633-7600. Phone: (212) 633-7650. Fax: (212) 633-7666.E-mail: WQXR@WQXR.COM Licensee: The New York Times Electronic Media Co. Group owner: The New York Times Co. (acq 2-1-44). Wire Svc: Reuters Format: Class. ♦Tom Bartunek, pres & gen mgr; Hester Furman, mus dir.

WRKS(FM)— 1941: 98.7 mhz; 6 kw. 1, 361ft TL: N40 44 54 W73 59 10. Stereo. Hrs open: 24 395 Hudson St., 7th Floor, 10014. Phone: (212) 242-9870. Fax: (212) 929-8559.E-mail: 987kissfm@987kissfm.com Web Site:www.987kissfm.com Licensee: Emmis Radio License Corp. of New York. Group owner: Emmis Communications Corp. (acq 10-26-94; $68 million;12-5-94). Population served: 2,500,000 Natl. Rep: Katz Radio,. Format: Rhythm and blues, classic soul. News staff: one. Target aud: 25-54; African American. ♦Alexandra Cameron, sr VP, gen mgr, gen mgr; Harry Clark, sls dir; Brian D'Aurelio, mktg dir; Jill Strada, progmg dir.

WRXP(FM)— 1945: 101.9 mhz; 6.2 kw. Ant 1,355 ft TL: N40 44 54 W73 59 10. Stereo. Hrs open: 24 7th Fl., 395 Hudson St., 10014. Phone: (212) 352-1019. Fax: (212) 929-8559.E-mail: mail.1019@rxp.com Web Site:www.1019rxp.com Licensee: Emmis Radio License LLC. Group owner: Emmis Communications Corp. (acq 3-26-98; grpsl). Population served: 1,245,000 Natl. Rep: Katz Radio,. Format: New adult rock. News staff: one; News: 4 hrs wkly. ♦Alexandra Cameron, sr VP, gen mgr; Harry Clark, sls dir; Brian D'Aurelio, mktg dir; Leslie Fram, progmg dir.

***WSIA(FM)**—(Staten Island, Aug 31, 1981: 88.9 mhz; 10 w. 650 ft TL: N40 35 51 W74 06 53. Stereo. Hrs open: 24 2800 Victory Blvd., Staten Island, 10314. Phone: (718) 982-3050. Fax: (718) 982-3052.E-mail: mailbox@wsia.fm Web Site:www.wsia.fm Licensee: College of Staten Island. Format: Alternative rock. Target aud: General. ♦Philip Masciantonio, gen mgr; John Ladley, prom dir, chief of engrg.

WSKQ-FM— 1950: 97.9 mhz; 7.6 kw horiz, 5.4 kw vert. 1,220 ft TL: N40 44 54 W73 59 10. Stereo. Hrs open: 26 W. 56th St., 10019. Phone: (212) 541-9200. Fax: (212) 541-9408. Web Site:www.lamega.com Licensee: WSKQ Licensing Inc. Group owner: Spanish Broadcasting System Inc. (acq 2-1-89; $55 million). Population served: 15,000,000 Natl. Rep: McGavren Guild,. Format: Sp, tropical salsa. Target aud: 18-49; Hispanic. ♦Raul Alarcon Jr., CEO, pres; Raul Alarcon Sr., chmn; Jose Garcia, CFO.

WSNR(AM)—See Jersey City, NJ

WWFS(FM)— August 1958: 102.7 mhz; 6 kw. Ant 1,361 ft TL: N40 44 54 W73 59 10. Stereo. Hrs open: 24 345 Hudson St., 10th Fl., 10014. Phone: (212) 489-1027. Fax: (212) 489-1263. Web Site:www.fresh1027.com Licensee: CBS Radio East Inc. Group owner: Infinity Broadcasting Corp. (acq 12-89; grpsl; 12-11-89). Population served: 18,000,000 Natl. Network: Westwood One, . Format: Soft rock. Target aud: 24-44; women. ♦Maire Mason, VP, gen mgr; Mark Olkowski, chief of engrg.

WWPR-FM— Dec 14, 1953: 105.1 mhz; 6 kw. 1,362 ft TL: N40 44 54 W73 59 10. Stereo. Hrs open: 24 18th Fl., 1120 Ave. of Americas, 10036-6798. Phone: (212) 704-1051. Fax: (212) 398-3299.E-mail: info@power105fm.com Web Site:www.power1051fm.com Licensee: AMFM Radio Licenses LLC. Group owner: Clear Channel Communications Inc. (acq 8-30-00; grpsl). Wilkinson Barker Knauer. Format: Urban contemp. News staff: one. Target aud: 25-54. ♦Rob Williams, gen mgr.

WWRL(AM)— Aug 26, 1926: 1600 khz; 5 kw-U, DA-2. TL: N40 47 44 W74 03 18. Hrs open: 333 7th Ave. 14th, 10001. Phone: (212) 631-0800. Fax: (212) 239-7423. Web Site:www.wwrl1600.com Licensee: Access. 1 New York License Co. LLC. Group owner: Access.1 Communications Corp. (acq 9-28-89; $1.98 million;10-16-89). Natl. Network: Air America, ABC, Fox News Radio, Westwood One, . Rubin, Winston, Diercks, Harris & Cooke. Format: Progressive talk. ♦Adriane Gaines, pres, gen mgr; Rennie Bishop, progmg dir.

***WWRV(AM)—** May 1, 1972: 1330 khz; 5 kw-U, DA-1. TL: N40 32 45 W74 12 11. Hrs open: 24 Box 2908, Paterson, NJ, 07509. Secondary address: 419 Broadway, Paterson, NJ 07501. Phone: (973) 881-8700. Phone: (973) 881-1130. Fax: (973) 881-8324.E-mail: bobrod@radiovision.net Web Site:www.radiovision.net Licensee: Radio Vision Christiana Management Corp. (acq 6-30-89; $13 million; 5-15-89). Population served: 18,000,000 Format: Relg, Sp, Christian. News staff: one. Target aud: General. ♦Rev. Milton Donato, pres & gen mgr; Reverend Bob Rodriguez, stn mgr.

WXRK(FM)— 1951: 92.3 mhz; 6 kw. Ant 1,220 ft TL: N40 44 54 W73 59 10. Stereo. Hrs open: 24 40 W. 57th St., 14th Fl., 10019. Phone: (212) 314-9230. Fax: (212) 314-9282.E-mail: wxrk923@aol.com Web Site:www.923now.com Licensee: CBS Radio East Inc. Group owner: Infinity Broadcasting Corp. Natl. Network: ABC, . Natl. Rep: CBS Radio,. Format: Top-40. ♦Tom Chiusano, VP & gen mgr; Alan Leinwand, sls VP; Mike Peer, mus dir; Richard Herby, engrg mgr.

WZRC(AM)— 1925: 1480 khz; 5 kw-U, DA-2. TL: N40 50 42 W74 01 12. Hrs open: 449 Broadway, 2nd Fl., 10013. Phone: (212) 965-1480. Fax: (212) 965-8917.E-mail: info@mrbi.net/wzrc.htm Web Site:www.mrbi.net/wzrc.htm Licensee: Multicultural Radio Broadcasting Licensee LLC. Group owner: Multicultural Radio Broadcasting Inc. (acq 1-30-98; grpsl). Population served: 13,400,000 Format: Cantonese. Target aud: 12-34. ♦Sherman Ngan, gen mgr.

Newark

WACK(AM)— Oct 19, 1957: 1420 khz; 5 kw-D, 500 w-N, DA-2. TL: N43 01 08 W77 04 41. Hrs open: 24 Box 1420, 187 Vienna Rd.,

14513. Phone: (315) 331-1420. Fax: (315) 331-7101.E-mail: 1420wack@rochester.rr.com Web Site:www.1420wack.com Licensee: Waynco Radio Inc. Group owner: Pembrook Pines Media Group (acq 3-11-2005; $600,000). Population served: 250,000 Natl. Network: CNN Radio, Motor Racing Net, Westwood One, . Fletcher, Heald & Hildreth. Format: News/talk, sports. News staff: one; News: 30 hrs wkly. Target aud: 25-54; active, affluent, upscale audience. Spec prog: Farm 5 hrs wkly. ♦John Tickner, pres, gen mgr; John Derleth, rgnl sls mgr; Ken Synesael, progmg dir; Rus Jeffrey, news dir; Ralph Vanderlinden, engr.

Newburgh

WBNR(AM)—See Beacon

WGNY(AM)— Feb 25, 1933: 1220 khz; 5 kw-D, DA. TL: N41 29 57 W74 03 54. (CP: 5 kw-D, 180 w-N, DA-1. TL: N41 31 53 W74 06 48). Hrs open: 24 Box 2307, 12550. Secondary address: 661 Little Britain Rd., New Windsor 12553. Phone: (845) 561-2131. Phone: (845) 561-2132. Fax: (845) 561-2138. Web Site:www.wgny.net Licensee: Sunrise Broadcasting Corp. Group owner: Sunrise Broadcasting Corp. (acq 8-90; $10,000 with co-located FM;8-20-90). Natl. Rep: Katz Radio,. Rosenman & Colin L.L.P. Format: Oldies. Target aud: General. Spec prog: Relg 4 hrs, Sp one hr wkly. ♦Joerg Klebe, pres; Robert A. DeFelice, gen mgr; Robert Maines, opns VP, opns dir, chief of engrg; Hank Gross, news dir; Tom Morel, pub affrs dir.

WGNY-FM— Oct 29, 1966: 103.1 mhz; 6 kw. 275 ft TL: N41 28 22 W74 08 22. Stereo. Hrs open: Prog sep from AM Box 2307, 12550. Secondary address: 661 Little Britain Rd. 12553. Phone: (845) 561-2131. Phone: (845) 561-2132. Fax: (845) 561-2138. Web Site:www.wgnyfm.com Format: Adult contemp.

Newport Village

WBGK(FM)— 2001: 99.7 mhz; 1.4 kw. Ant 676 ft TL: N43 08 28 W75 01 49. Hrs open: 185 Genesee St., Suite 1601, Utica, 13501. Phone: (315) 734-9245. Fax: (315) 624-9245. Web Site:www.bugcountry.com Licensee: Roser Communications Network Inc. (acq 5-29-2001; $575,000). Natl. Network: ABC, . Format: Country. ♦Ken Roser, gen mgr; Roxanne Roser, stn mgr; Dave Silvers, opns mgr.

Niagara Falls

WHLD(AM)— May 20, 1940: 1270 khz; 5 kw-D, 1 kw-N, DA-2. TL: N42 44 41 W78 53 13. Hrs open: 19 2495 Main St., Ste 355, Buffalo, 14214. Phone: (716) 855-1270. Fax: (716) 855-4681.E-mail: Rmarks@whldam1270.com Web Site:www.whld1270.com Licensee: Citadel Broadcasting Co. Group owner: Citadel Broadcasting Corp. Population served: 1,500,000 Format: Gospel. ♦Brian Brown Cashdollar, CFO; Ray Marks, VP & gen mgr.

WJJL(AM)— Dec 21, 1947: 1440 khz; 1 kw-D, 55 w-N. TL: N43 04 43 W79 00 40. Hrs open: 24 920 Union Rd., West Seneca, 14224. Secondary address: portage&pine 14304. Phone: (716) 674-9555. Fax: (716) 674-0400.E-mail: radio1440@verizon.net Web Site:www.wjjl.com Licensee: M.J. Phillips Communications Inc. (acq 10-20-92; $600,000;11-23-92). Population served: 1,900,000 Leonard S. Joyce. Format: Old time rock & roll. News staff: one; News: 3 hrs wkly. Target aud: 25-54; baby boomers. Spec prog: Black 2 hrs, It 4 hrs, news/talk 5 hrs wkly, gospel one hr wky, Pol 2 hrs wkly. ♦Earl Morgan, chmn; John Phillips, pres; Dennis Westberg, CFO; Mark Phillips, CEO & opns VP; M.J. Phillips, opns dir.

WJYE(FM)—See Buffalo

WKSE(FM)— Jan 1, 1946: 98.5 mhz; 46 kw. 420 ft TL: N43 00 18 W78 59 35. Stereo. Hrs open: 24 500 Corporate Pkwy., Suite 200, Amherst, 14226. Phone: (716) 843-0600. Fax: (716) 843-0250. Fax: (716) 644-9fax.E-mail: Info@kiss985.com Web Site:www.kiss985.com Licensee: Entercom Buffalo License LLC. Group owner: Entercom Communications Corp. (acq 12-13-99; grpsl). Natl. Network: ABC, . Natl. Rep: D & R Radio,. Mullin, Rhyne, Emmons & Topel. Format: CHR. News staff: 3. Target aud: 12-49. ♦Larry Robb, gen mgr; Steve Fortunato, gen sls mgr; Sue O'Neil, progmg dir.

North Creek

***WXLG(FM)**— 1995: 89.9 mhz; 200 w. 1,994 ft TL: N43 40 22 W74 02 58. Hrs open: 24
Rebroadcasts WSLU(FM) Canton 100%.
St. Lawrence Univ., North Country Public Radio, Canton, 13617. Phone: (315) 229-5356. Fax: (315) 229-5373.E-mail: info@ncpr.org Web Site:www.ncpr.org Licensee: St. Lawrence University. Donald E. Martin. Format: Eclectic public radio. News staff: 2; News: 35 hrs wkly. Target aud: General. ♦Ellen Rocco, gen mgr; Shelly Pike, chief of opns; Sandra Demarest, dev dir; Jacqueline Sauter, progmg dir.

North Salem

***WJZZ(FM)**—Not on air, target date: unknown: 90.1 mhz; 100 w vert. Ant -102 ft TL: N41 19 44 W73 35 29. Hrs open: 19 Boas Ln., Wilton, CT, 06897-1301. Phone: (203) 762-9425. Licensee: Foothills Public Radio Inc. ♦Dennis Jackson, pres.

North Syracuse

WKRL-FM— March 1972: 100.9 mhz; 6 kw. 164 ft TL: N43 09 06 W76 07 58. Stereo. Hrs open: 235 Walton, Syracuse, 13202. Phone: (315) 472-9111. Fax: (315) 472-1888. Web Site:www.krock.com Population served: 600,000 Natl. Network: ABC, . Format: Modern rock. Target aud: 18-34; upscale, educated. ♦Kamala Dworski, gen mgr.

WTLA(AM)— Aug 1, 1959: 1200 khz; 1 kw-U, DA-N. TL: N43 09 06 W76 07 58. Hrs open: 24 235 Walton, Syracuse, 13202. Phone: (315) 472-9111. Fax: (315) 472-1888. Licensee: Galaxy Syracuse Licensee LLC. Group owner: Galaxy Communications LP (acq 4-6-2000; grpsl). Natl. Network: Jones Radio Networks, . James L. Oyster. Format: Adult standards. News staff: one; News: 2 hrs wkly. Target aud: 35-64; white collar executives. Spec prog: Ger 2 hrs, Pol 2 hrs, relg 2 hrs wkly. ♦Ed Levine, pres, gen mgr; Mimi Griswald, progmg dir; Tim Backer, chief of engrg.

Norwich

WBKT(FM)— June 1, 1997: 95.3 mhz; 470 w. Ant 841 ft TL: N42 26 08 W75 30 47. Hrs open: 24 34 Chestnut St., Oneonta, 13820. Phone: (607) 432-1030. Fax: (607) 432-6909.E-mail: info@centralnewyorkradio.com Licensee: Double O Central New York Corp. (group owner; (acq 10-22-2004; grpsl). Population served: 100,000 Natl. Network: ABC, . Format: Country. News staff: 2. Target aud: 25-54; general. ♦George Wells, gen mgr; Bud Williamson, chief of engrg.

WCHN(AM)— January 1953: 970 khz; 1 kw-D. TL: N42 30 24 W75 29 29. Hrs open: 24 34 Chestnut St., Oneonta, 13820. Phone: (607) 432-1030. Fax: (607) 432-6909. Licensee: Double O Central New York Corp. (group owner; (acq 10-22-2004; grpsl). Population served: 50,000 Natl. Network: ABC, . Format: Stardust memories. News: 20 hrs wkly. Target aud: 35-65; mature. ♦George Wells, gen mgr.

WKXZ(FM)— 1961: 93.9 mhz; 26 kw. 680 ft TL: N42 32 52 W75 27 07. Stereo. Hrs open: 5 AM-1 AM Prog sep from AM 34 Chestnut St., Oneonta, 13820. Phone: (607) 334-2218. Fax: (607) 334-9867. Population served: 500,000 Natl. Network: ABC, . Format: Hot adult contemp. News: 10 hrs wkly. Target aud: 25-54; growing families.

Norwood

WVLF(FM)— 2001: 96.1 mhz; 25 kw. Ant 328 ft TL: N44 54 11 W74 53 02. Hrs open: Box 210, Massena, 13662. Phone: (315) 769-3333. Fax: (315) 769-3299.E-mail: frank@valley961.com Web Site:www.valley961.com Licensee: Stephens Media Group-Massena LLC. Group owner: Martz Communications Group Format: Yesterday's favorites, today's hits. ♦Michael R. Guimond, gen mgr; Bob Larue, news dir; Bob Sauder, chief of engrg.

Noyack

***WSUF(FM)**— Sept 15, 1996: 89.9 mhz; 12 kw. 357 ft TL: N41 06 35 W72 22 05. Stereo. Hrs open: 24
Rebroadcasts WSHU(FM) Fairfield, CT 30%.
5151 Park Ave., Fairfield, CT, 06825. Phone: (203) 365-6604. Fax: (203) 371-7991.E-mail: lombardi@wshu.org Web Site:www.wshu.org Licensee: Sacred Heart University Inc. Natl. Network: NPR, PRI, . Mullin, Rhyne, Emmons & Topel. Wire Svc: AP Format: News/talk. News staff: 4; News: 45 hrs wkly. Target aud: General. Spec prog: Folk 5 hrs, new age 6 hrs wkly. ♦George Lombardi, gen mgr; Barbara Bashar, opns mgr; Gillian Anderson, dev dir.

Nyack

***WNYK(FM)**— May 5, 1982: Stn currently dark. 88.7 mhz; 10 w. 55 ft TL: N41 04 59 W73 55 45. Stereo. Hrs open: One South Blvd., Nyack College, 10960. Phone: (845) 358-1828. Phone: (845) 358-1710.E-mail: wnyk@nyack.edu Web Site:wwwnyack.edu/WNYK Licensee: Nyack College. Population served: 250,000 Target aud: 18-35; 60%/40% -F/M, well educated. Spec prog: Black 6 hrs, relg 2 hrs wkly.

Odessa

WFIZ(FM)— Aug 20, 1968: 95.5 mhz; 850 w. Ant 869 ft TL: N42 23 13 W76 40 11. Stereo. Hrs open: 24 179 Graham Rd., Ithaca, 14850. Phone: (607) 257-2059. Fax: (607) 257-2387. Web Site:www.z955.net Licensee: Finger Lakes Radio Group Inc. (acq 3-5-2004; $600,000 with co-located AM). Format: Top-40. ♦Frank Lischak, gen mgr; Tommy Franks, progmg dir.

***WINO(FM)**—Not on air, target date: unknown: 89.9 mhz; 250 w. Ant 341 ft TL: N42 18 07 W76 48 01. Hrs open: c/o Garvey Schubert Barer, 1000 Potomac St. N.W., 5th Fl., Washington, DC, 20007-3501. Phone: (202) 965-7880. Fax: (202) 965-1729. Licensee: Ithaca Community Radio Inc. ♦Diane Cohen, chmn; John Crigler, gen mgr.

Ogdensburg

WPAC(FM)— June 1998: 98.7 mhz; 3 kw. Ant 92 ft TL: N44 43 41 W75 26 36. Hrs open: 24 1 Bridge Plaza, Suite 204, 13369. Phone: (315) 393-1220. Fax: (315) 393-3974.E-mail: john@q1029.com Web Site:pac987.com Licensee: Stephens Media Group-Ogdensburg LLC. Group owner: Martz Communications Group Population served: 112,000 Format: Super hits of the 60s & 70s. News staff: one. ♦John Winter, gen mgr.

WQTK(FM)— July 1981: 92.7 mhz; 3 kw. Ant 310 ft TL: N44 42 21 W75 27 55. Stereo. Hrs open: 2315 Knox St., 13669. Phone: (315) 393-1100. Fax: (315) 393-6673. Licensee: Community Broadcasters LLC. (acq 2-8-2007; grpsl). Population served: 100,000 Natl. Network: CNN Radio, . Natl. Rep: Eastman Radio, Katz Radio,. Wire Svc: AP Format: Talk. News: 10 hrs wkly. Target aud: 25-49; community connected, active, mature, responsible & responsive. ♦Bryan Mallette, gen mgr.

WSLB(AM)— 1940: 1400 khz; 1 kw-U. TL: N44 42 21 W75 27 55. Hrs open: 24 2315 Knox St., 13669. Phone: (315) 393-1100. Fax: (315) 393-6673.E-mail: burgproduction@commbroadcasters.com Licensee: Community Broadcasters LLC. Group owner: Clancy-Mancy Communications (acq 2-8-2007; grpsl). Population served: 14,554 Natl. Network: ESPN Radio, . Natl. Rep: Eastman Radio, Katz Radio,. Shaw Pittman L.L.P. Wire Svc: AP Format: Sports. ♦James L. Leven, pres, gen mgr; Bryan Mallette, gen mgr, gen sls mgr; John Astolfi, opns mgr.

Olean

WHDL(AM)— February 1929: 1450 khz; 1 kw-U. TL: N42 04 39 W78 28 32. Hrs open: 24 3163 New State Rt. 417, 14760. Phone: (716) 372-0161. Fax: (716) 372-0164.E-mail: wpig.production@bybradio.com Web Site:www.whdlradio.com Licensee: Arrow Communication of N.Y. Inc. Group owner: Backyard Broadcasting LLC (acq 12-1-2002; grpsl). Population served: 32,000 Rgnl rep: Rgnl Reps. Wiley, Rein & Fielding. Format: Oldies. News staff: 2; News: 6 hrs wkly. Target aud: 25-54. ♦John J. Morton, gen mgr; Mark Thomson, progmg dir.

WMXO(FM)— Nov 1, 1978: 101.5 mhz; 1.55 kw. 405 ft TL: N42 06 24 W78 23 28. Stereo. Hrs open: Prog sep from AM 231 N. Union St. , 14760. Phone: (716) 375-1015. Fax: (716) 375-7705.E-mail: traffic@mix101.com Web Site:www.mix101.com Licensee: Pembroke Pines Inc. Natl. Network: CBS, Westwood One, . Format: Adult contemp. Target aud: 18-49.

WOEN(AM)— May 20, 1957: 1360 khz; 1 kw-D, 30 w-N. TL: N42 06 24 W78 23 28. Hrs open: 24 231 N. Union St., 14760. Phone: (716) 375-1015. Fax: (716) 375-7705.E-mail: traffic@mix101.com Web Site:www.mix101.com Licensee: Pembrook Pines Inc. Group owner: Vox Radio Group L.P. (acq 2-22-2005; $950,000 with co-located FM). Population served: 19169 Natl. Network: CBS, Westwood One, . Natl. Rep: Dome,. Format: MOR. News staff: one. Target aud: 45-65. ♦Robert J. Pfuntner, pres; John R. Sirianni, gen mgr; Michael McAdam, progmg dir; Ralph Vanderlinden, chief of engrg.

***WOLN(FM)**— March 1993: 91.3 mhz; 115 w. Ant 656 ft TL: N42 02 08 W78 26 47. Hrs open: 24
Rebroadcasts WBFO(FM) Buffalo 100%.
c/o WBFO(FM), 3435 Main St., 205 Allen Hall, Buffalo, 14214. Phone: (716) 829-2880. Fax: (716) 829-2277.E-mail: mail@wbfo.org Web Site:www.wbfo.org Licensee: State University of New York. Population served: 111,800 Natl. Network: NPR, . Format: News, jazz. News staff: 2; News: 50 hrs wkly. Target aud: General; educated professionals. Spec prog: Blues 8 hrs, bluegrass music 3 hrs, Pol 3 hrs wkly. ♦Carole Smith Petro, VP; Carole Smith Petro, gen mgr; Mark Wozniak, opns mgr; Joan Wilson, dev dir; Mark Scott, news dir.

WPIG(FM)— Feb 1, 1949: 95.7 mhz; 43 kw. Ant 740 ft TL: N42 02 08 W78 26 47. Stereo. Hrs open: 24 3163 New State Rt. 417, 14760.

Phone: (716) 372-0161. Fax: (716) 372-0164.E-mail: wpig.production@bybradio.com Web Site:www.wpig.com Licensee: Arrow Communications of N.Y. Inc. Population served: 350,000 Natl. Network: ABC, . Format: Contemp country.

Olivebridge

***WFSO(FM)—** Dec 27, 1996: 88.3 mhz; 100 w vert. Ant 69 ft TL: N41 54 30 W74 14 46. Hrs open: 314 Acorn Hill Rd., 12461. Phone: (845) 657-5723.E-mail: dce@redeemerbroadcasting.org Licensee: Redeemer Broadcasting Inc. Format: Relg. ♦Clarence Elmendorf, stn mgr.

Oneida

WMCR(AM)— Sept 26, 1956: 1600 khz; 1 kw-D, 20 w-N. TL: N43 05 04 W75 41 35. Hrs open: 16 237 Genesee St., 13421. Phone: (315) 363-6050. Fax: (315) 363-9149.E-mail: info@wmcr.com Licensee: Warren Broadcasting Co. Inc. (acq 1-3-2006). Format: Adult contemp, current CD's, oldies. Target aud: General. ♦Joel Meltzer, gen mgr, opns mgr & progmg dir.

WMCR-FM— September 1972: 106.3 mhz; 1.25 kw. Ant 718 ft TL: N43 02 48 W75 39 58. Hrs open: 237 Genesee St., 13421. Phone: (315) 363-6050. Fax: (315) 363-9149.E-mail: info@wmcr.com Licensee: Warren Broadcasting Co. Inc.

Oneonta

WDOS(AM)— Dec 1, 1947: 730 khz; 1 kw-D. TL: N42 27 29 W75 00 20. Hrs open: Box 649, 13820. Phone: (607) 432-1030. Fax: (607) 432-6909.E-mail: info@centralnewyorkradio.com Web Site:www.wdos.com Licensee: Double O Central New York Corp. (acq 11-4-2005; $3.8 million with co-located FM). Population served: 23,200 Haley, Bader & Potts. Format: Country. Target aud: General; adult. Spec prog: Big band 7 hrs, nostalgia 2 hrs, relg 7 hrs wkly. ♦Lou Cerra, gen mgr; Janet Laytham, progmg dir.

***WONY(FM)—** 1975: 90.9 mhz; 177 w. -72 ft TL: N42 28 02 W75 03 40. Stereo. Hrs open: 24 Alumni Hall, SUCO Campus, 13820. Phone: (607) 436-2712. Fax: (607) 436-2713. Licensee: State University of New York. Population served: 20,000 Format: Educ, div. Target aud: General.

***WRHO(FM)—** Jan 1, 1970: 89.7 mhz; 150 w. 150 ft TL: N42 27 24 W75 04 28. Stereo. Hrs open: 18 Hartwick College Dewar Hall, Radio Stn. WRHO, 13820. Phone: (607) 431-4555. Phone: (607) 431-4556. Fax: (607) 431-4064. Licensee: Hartwick College. Natl. Network: AP Radio, . Format: AOR, classic rock, progsv. News: 4 hrs wkly. Target aud: General; teenagers, college students & young adults. Spec prog: Folk 5 hrs, jazz 4 hrs, Sp 2 hrs, world beat 2 hrs, children's 2 hrs wkly. ♦Brian Knox, gen mgr.

***WSQC-FM—** 1992: 91.7 mhz; 570 w horiz, 2.3 kw vert. 528 ft TL: N42 25 27 W75 02 33. Hrs open: 24
Rebroadcasts WSKG-FM Binghamton 100%.
Box 3000, Binghamton, 13902. Phone: (607) 729-0100. Fax: (607) 729-7328.E-mail: wskg_mail@wskg.pbs.org Web Site:www.wskg.com Licensee: WSKG Public Telecommunications Council. Population served: 92,000 Natl. Network: NPR, PRI, . Dow, Lohnes & Albertson. Format: Class, news. News staff: one; News: 33 hrs wkly. Target aud: General. Spec prog: Jazz, folk 5 hrs wkly. ♦Brian Sickora, pres; Nancy Christensen, opns dir; Ken Campbell, mktg VP, progmg dir; Stacy Mosteller, traf mgr.

WSRK(FM)— Jan 26, 1970: 103.9 mhz; 850 w. 520 ft TL: N42 25 33 W75 02 47. (CP: 2.05 kw). Stereo. Hrs open: 5 AM-midnight Prog sep from AM Box 649, 13820. Phone: (607) 432-1030. Fax: (607) 432-6909.E-mail: info@centralnewyorkradio.com Web Site:www.wsrk.com Population served: 16,030 Format: Adult contemp. News: 5 hrs wkly. Target aud: 25-54; adult males & females. Spec prog: Class 2 hrs wkly.

WZOZ(FM)— Nov 28, 1972: 103.1 mhz; 2 kw. 360 ft TL: N42 25 28 W75 04 36. Hrs open: 24 34 Chestnut St., 13820-2466. Phone: (607) 432-1030. Fax: (607) 432-6909.E-mail: info@centralnewyorkradio.com Licensee: Double O Central New York Corp. (group owner; (acq 10-22-2004; grpsl). Population served: 100,000 Format: Hits of the 80s. News staff: 2; News: 8 hrs wkly. Target aud: 25-54. Spec prog: Jazz 2 hrs, blues 2 hrs, oldies 2 hrs wkly. ♦George Wells, gen mgr.

Ontario

WMJQ(AM)—Not on air, target date: unknown: 1330 khz; 1 kw-D, 2 kw-N, DA-2. TL: N43 10 49 W77 18 15. Hrs open: 135 White Bridge Rd., Middletown, 10940. Phone: (845) 355-4001. Fax: (845) 355-4002.E-mail: bud@dre.cc Licensee: Digital Radio Broadcasting Inc. Rini Coran. ♦Bud Williamson, pres.

Ossining

***WDFH(FM)—** July 15, 1995: 90.3 mhz; 53 w. Ant 476 ft TL: N41 09 07 W73 47 10. Stereo. Hrs open: 24 21 Brookside Ln., Dobbs Ferry, 10522. Phone: (914) 674-0900.E-mail: info@wdfh.org Web Site:www.wdfh.org Licensee: Hudson Valley Community Radio Inc. Population served: 625,000 Carter, Ledyard & Milburn. Format: Alternative, news. Target aud: 18+. Spec prog: Pub affrs 20 hrs wkly. ♦Marc Sophos, chmn & pres.

***WOSS(FM)—** Feb 22, 1972: 91.1 mhz; 10 w. 100 ft TL: N41 09 36 W73 51 38. (CP: 91.9 mhz, 16.42 w, ant 69 ft.). Stereo. Hrs open: 24 190 Croton Ave., 10562. Secondary address: 29 S. Highland Ave. 10562. Phone: (914) 762-5760 x370. Licensee: Board of Education Union Free School District 1. Population served: 21,659 Format: Top-40, educ, urban contemp. News staff: 3. Target aud: General. ♦Martin McDonald, stn mgr.

Oswego

WAMF(AM)—See Fulton

WBBS(FM)—See Fulton

***WNYO(FM)—** 1993: 88.9 mhz; 100 w. 10 ft TL: N43 27 07 W76 32 40. Hrs open: State Univ. of NY, 9B Hewitt Union, 13126. Phone: (315) 312-2101. Fax: (315) 312-3542.E-mail: wnyo@oswego.edu Web Site:www.oswego.edu/~wnyo Licensee: State University of New York. Format: Div, rock, urban contemp. Target aud: 13-34. Spec prog: Sp 6 hrs, news/talk 4 hrs wkly. ♦Tom Turner, gen mgr & progmg dir.

WOLF-FM— July 1990: 96.7 mhz; 3 kw. Any 328 ft TL: N43 29 12 W76 23 10. Stereo. Hrs open: 24 401 W. Kirkpatrick St., Syracuse, 13204. Phone: (315) 472-0222. Fax: (315) 478-7745.E-mail: programming@movin100.com Web Site:movin100.com Licensee: WOLF Radio Inc. (group owner; (acq 8-4-97; $65,000). Population served: 140,000 Rgnl rep: Rgnl Reps James L. Oyster. Format: Rhythmic adult contemp. ♦Sam Furco, gen mgr.

***WRVO(FM)—** Jan 6, 1969: 89.9 mhz; 50 kw. Ant 440 ft TL: N43 25 14 W76 32 39. Stereo. Hrs open: 24 7060 State Rt. 104, 13126. Phone: (315) 312-3690. Fax: (315) 312-3174.E-mail: feedback@wrvo.fm Web Site:www.wrvo.fm Licensee: State University of New York. Population served: 545,100 Natl. Network: NPR, . Wire Svc: AP Format: News/talk, old time radio. News staff: 4; News: 140 hrs wkly. Target aud: 25-55. ♦John E. Krauss, gen mgr; Fred Vigeant, opns dir, progmg dir; Matt Seubert, dev dir; Chris Vlanowski, news dir; Jeff Windsor, chief of engrg.

WSGO(AM)— 1960: 1440 khz; 1 kw-D, 42 w-N. TL: N43 24 56 W76 28 00. Hrs open: 24
Rebroadcasts WTLA(AM) North Syracuse 100%.
235 Walton Street, Syracuse, 13202. Phone: (315) 472-9111. Fax: (315) 472-1888. Licensee: Galaxy Syracuse Licensee LLC. Group owner: Galaxy Communications LP (acq 4-6-2000; grpsl). Population served: 150,000 Natl. Network: Jones Radio Networks, . Format: Adult standards. News: one hr wkly. Target aud: 40 plus; retired & mobile. Spec prog: Ger 2 hrs, Pol 2 hrs wkly. ♦Ed Levine, pres, gen mgr; Mimi Griswold, progmg dir; Tim Backer, chief of engrg.

WTKV(FM)— Mar 15, 1973: 105.5 mhz; 3 kw. 450 ft TL: N43 24 56 W76 27 54. Stereo. Hrs open: 24
Rebroadcasts WTKW(FM) Bridgeport 100%.
235 Walton Street, Syracuse, 13202. Phone: (325) 472-9111. Fax: (315) 472-1888. Web Site:www.classicrock.com Population served: 250,000 Format: Classic rock. News staff: one; News: 2 hrs wkly. Target aud: 25-54. Spec prog: Folk 3 hrs, blues one hr wkly. ♦Ed Levine, gen mgr; Mimi Griswold, progmg dir.

Owego

WEBO(AM)— July 27, 1957: 1330 khz; 5 kw-D, 50 w-N. TL: N42 06 19 W76 16 22. Hrs open: 5 AM-10 PM 212 Main St., 13827. Phone: (607) 687-9605. Fax: (607) 687-4184. Web Site:webo1330.com Licensee: Tioga Media Inc. (acq 6-30-00; $1). Population served: 150,000 Natl. Network: USA, . Natl. Rep: D & R Radio,. Baraff, Koerner & Olender. Format: News, talk. News staff: 2. Target aud: 35 plus. Spec prog: NASCAR racing 16 hrs, relg 6 hrs wkly. ♦Terry Coleman, gen mgr.

***WHVM(FM)—**Not on air, target date: unknown: 91.9 mhz; 990 w. Ant 525 ft TL: N41 57 37 W76 32 56. Hrs open: Box 236, Maine, 13802. Phone: (607) 754-0001. Web Site:www.mtstfrancis.com Licensee: Mount St. Francis Hermitage Inc. Natl. Network: EWTN Radio, .

Palmyra

WZXV(FM)— May 1993: 99.7 mhz; 2.8 kw. 485 ft TL: N43 02 00 W77 25 17. Hrs open: 24 Box 25099, Farmington, 14425. Secondary address: 1777 Rt. 332, Farmington 14425. Phone: (315) 597-9574; (585) 398-3569. Fax: (585) 398-3250.E-mail: wzxv@ccfingerlake.org Web Site:www.wzxv.org Licensee: Calvary Chapel of the Finger Lakes Inc. (acq 8-2-95; $70,000). Format: Christian worship, Bible teaching. ♦Jeff Gallatin, gen mgr & progmg dir.

Patchogue

WALK(AM)—(East Patchogue, May 20, 1952: 1370 khz; 500 w-D, 102 w-N. TL: N40 45 14 W72 59 14. Hrs open: 24 Box 230, 11772. Phone: (631) 475-5200. Fax: (631) 475-9016.E-mail: info@1370walk.com Web Site:www.1370walk.com Licensee: AMFM Radio Licenses LLC. Group owner: Clear Channel Communications Inc. (acq 8-30-00; grpsl). Population served: 300,000 Format: Bib band, oldies. News: 15 hrs wkly. Target aud: 50 plus. ♦Andy Rosen, VP, gen mgr; Jim Condron, gen sls mgr; Linda Healy, mktg dir; Bill Terry, prom dir; Rob Miller, progmg dir; John Lorentz, chief of engrg.

WALK-FM— December 1952: 97.5 mhz; 39 kw. 544 ft TL: N40 50 41 W73 02 01. Stereo. Hrs open: Box 230, 11772. Phone: (631) 475-5200. Fax: (631) 475-9016.E-mail: info@walkradio.com Web Site:walkradio.com Population served: 2,600,000 Format: Adult contemp. Target aud: 25-54. Spec prog: Hits of the 70s, love songs. ♦Cindi Clifford, disc jockey.

WBLI(FM)— Dec 1, 1958: 106.1 mhz; 49 kw horiz, 47 kw vert. 499 ft TL: N40 50 32 W73 02 25. Stereo. Hrs open: 24 555 Sunrise Hwy., W. Babylon, 11704. Phone: (631) 669-9254. Fax: (631) 376-0812. Fax: (631) 376-0569.E-mail: wbli@wbli.com Web Site:www.wbli.com Licensee: Cox Radio Inc. Group owner: Cox Broadcasting (acq 5-22-98; grpsl). Population served: 2,800,000 Natl. Network: AP Radio, . Natl. Rep: Christal,. Format: CHR. News staff: one; News: 5 hrs wkly. Target aud: 18-34; women. ♦Austin Vali, VP, gen mgr; Nancy Cambino, opns mgr; Suzanne Riccio, pub affrs dir.

WLIM(AM)— Dec 1, 1951: 1580 khz; 10 kw-D, 500 w-N, DA-N. TL: N40 47 45 W72 59 32. Stereo. Hrs open: 24 41 Pennsylvania Ave., Medford, 11763. Secondary address: 41 Pennsylvania Ave, Medford 11763. Phone: (631) 475-1580. Fax: (631) 475-1523.E-mail: radioformula @radio-formula.us Web Site:www.radio-formula.us Licensee: Polnet Communications Ltd. (group owner; acq 6-1-01; $850,000 including five-year noncompete agreement). Population served: 1,500,000 Wiley, Rein and Fielding. Format: Spanish variety. News staff: one; News: 20 hrs wkly. Target aud: 18-54; Spanish language audience. Spec prog: Spanish language 24 hrs/day, 7 days/week. ♦Kent Gustafson, CEO; Walter Kotaba, pres; Brad Behnke, stn mgr, opns mgr.

Patterson

WDBY(FM)— Jan 17, 1982: 105.5 mhz; 1.5 kw. 460 ft TL: N41 31 18 W73 38 06. Stereo. Hrs open: 24 1004 Federal Rd., Brookfield, CT, 06804. Phone: (203) 775-1212. Fax: (203) 775-6452.E-mail: info@105radio.com Web Site:www.y105radio.com Licensee: Cumulus Licensing Corp. Group owner: Cumulus Media Inc. (acq 1-23-2002; grpsl). Natl. Network: Westwood One, . Haley, Bader & Potts. Format: Adult contemp. News staff: 2; News: 4 hrs wkly. Target aud: 25-54. ♦Brett Beshore, gen mgr; Tim Sheehan, opns mgr; Tom Principi, gen sls mgr; Tony Wise, progmg dir; Lisa Harris, news dir; Peter Partenio, chief of engrg; Sheila Alexson, traf mgr.

WPUT(AM)—(Brewster, July 3, 1958: 1510 khz; 1 kw-D. TL: N41 24 34 W73 37 29. Hrs open: 1004 Federal Rd., Brookfield, 06804. Phone: (203) 775-1212. Fax: (203) 775-6452. Licensee: Cumulus Licensing Corp. Population served: 200,000 Natl. Network: ESPN Radio, . Format: Sports. ♦Matt Carey, progmg dir.

Pattersonville

***WPGL(FM)—** Aug 15, 1994: 90.7 mhz; 30 w. 653 ft TL: N42 51 00 W74 03 58. Stereo. Hrs open: 24
Rebroadcasts WFGB(FM) Kingston 95%.
Box 777, Lake Katrine, 12449. Secondary address: 199 Tuytenbridge Rd., Lake Katrine 12449. Phone: (845) 336-6199. Fax: (845) 336-7205.E-mail: email@soundoflife.org Web Site:www.soundoflife.org Licensee: Sound of Life Inc. Population served: 300,000 Format:

Christian. News: 3 hrs wkly. Target aud: General. ◆Tom Michael Zahradnik, gen mgr; Bob Conti, opns mgr; Joe Hunter, progmg dir.

Paul Smiths

*WPSA(FM)— Jan 10, 1973: 98.3 mhz; 10 w. -7 ft TL: N44 26 04 W74 15 04. Hrs open: Co-ordinator of Student Activities, Paul Smiths College, Rts. 86 & 30, 12970. Phone: (518) 327-6401. Fax: (518) 327-6369. Fax: (518) 327-6016. Licensee: Paul Smiths College of Arts & Sciences. Format: Educ, pub affrs, MOR.

Pawling

WDBY(FM)—See Patterson

Peekskill

WHUD(FM)— Oct 24, 1958: 100.7 mhz; 50 kw. 500 ft TL: N41 20 18 W73 53 41. Hrs open: Box 310, Beacon, 12508. Phone: (914) 838-6000. Fax: (914) 838-2109. Licensee: 6 Johnson Road Licenses Inc. Population served: 320,000 Natl. Network: ABC, . Format: Adult contemp. Target aud: Upscale adults. ◆Jason Finkleburg, gen mgr, opns mgr; Steven Petrone, progmg mgr.

WLNA(AM)— 1948: 1420 khz; 5 kw-D, 1 kw-N, DA-2. TL: N41 18 31 W73 55 00. Hrs open:
Simulcast with WBNR(AM) Beacon 100%.
Box 310, Beacon, 12508. Phone: (914) 838-6000. Fax: (914) 838-6094. Web Site:www.hvradionet.com Licensee: 6 Johnson Road Licenses Inc. Group owner: Pamal Broadcasting Ltd. (acq 10-19-2001; grpsl). Population served: 2,000,000 Natl. Network: Fox Sports, . Format: Talk, sports. Target aud: 35 plus. ◆Jason Finkelberg, gen mgr & progmg VP.

Penn Yan

WYLF(AM)— 1988: 850 khz; 1 kw-D, 47 w-N. TL: N42 39 41 W77 07 14. Hrs open: 24 100 Main St., 14527. Phone: (315) 536-0850. Fax: (315) 536-3299. Fax: (315) 781-6666.E-mail: wylf@airxcess.net Licensee: M.B. Communications. (acq 10-88). Population served: 550,000 Henry E. Crawford. Format: Adult standards. News staff: 2. Target aud: 35 plus. ◆Russ Kimble, pres, gen mgr & stn mgr; Don Radigan, opns mgr; Phil Mann, gen sls mgr.

Peru

*WXLU(FM)— 1991: 88.1 mhz; 1 kw. Ant 1,118 ft TL: N44 34 25 W73 40 29. Hrs open: 24
Rebroadcasts WSLU(FM) Canton 100%.
N. Country Public Radio, St. Lawrence Univ., Canton, 13617. Phone: (315) 229-5356.E-mail: radio@mcpr.org Web Site:www.ncpr.org Licensee: St. Lawrence University. Donald E. Martin. Format: Eclectic public radio. News staff: 2; News: 35 hrs wkly. Target aud: General. ◆Ellen Rocco, gen mgr.

Phoenix

WZUN(FM)— May 22, 1995: 102.1 mhz; 6 kw. 220 ft TL: N43 06 03 W76 16 56. Stereo. Hrs open: 24 235 Walton St., Syracuse, 13202. Phone: (315) 472-9111. Fax: (315) 472-1888. Web Site:www.thesunnyspot.com Licensee: Galaxy Syracuse Licensee LLC. (group owner; acq 12-15-2000; $3.75 million). Leventhal, Senter & Lerman. Format: Adult contemp. Target aud: 25-54; general. ◆Ed Levine, pres; Mike Lucarelli, CFO; Lisa Morrow, sls VP; Mimi Griswold, progmg VP; Ted Bradford, progmg dir.

Plainview

*WPOB-FM— September 1973: 88.5 mhz; 125 w. 150 ft TL: N40 46 53 W73 27 36. (CP: Ant 259 ft. TL: N40 47 48 W73 27 44). Hrs open: 50 Kennedy Dr., 11803-4098. Phone: (516) 937-6373. Phone: (516) 937-6344. Fax: (516) 937-6384. Licensee: Plainview-Old Bethpage Central School District. Format: Educ, AOR. Target aud: General. ◆Adam Weinstock, gen mgr; Joel Genero, opns dir.

Plattsburgh

WBTZ(FM)— Feb 3, 1960: 99.9 mhz; 100 kw. 984 ft TL: N44 46 13 W73 36 47. Stereo. Hrs open: 24 255 S. Champlain St., Burlington, VT, 05402. Phone: (802) 860-2465. Fax: (802) 860-1818.E-mail:

mailbag@99thebuzz.com Web Site:www.99thebuzz.com Licensee: Hall Communications Inc. (acq 7-31-2006; $2.5 million). Population served: 261,000 Format: Alternative rock. Target aud: 18-44. ◆Dan Dubonnet, gen mgr; Matt Grasso, progmg dir.

*WCEL(FM)— Jan 14, 1991: 91.9 mhz; 380 w. 852 ft TL: N44 46 27 W73 36 48. Stereo. Hrs open: 24
Rebroadcasts WAMC-FM Albany 100%.
Box 666000, Albany, 12206. Secondary address: 318 Central Ave., Albany 12206. Phone: (518) 465-5233. Phone: (800) 323-9262. Fax: (518) 432-6974.E-mail: mail@wamc.org Web Site:www.wamc.org Licensee: WAMC. Group owner: WAMC/Northeast Public Radio (acq 1996; $160,000). Natl. Network: PRI, NPR, . Dow, Lohnes & Albertson. Wire Svc: AP Format: News, talk. News: 77 hrs wkly. Target aud: General. Spec prog: Folk 7 hrs, jazz 13 hrs wkly. ◆Alan Chartock, CEO, chmn, pres; David Galletly, VP, progmg dir; Selma Kaplan, VP & reporter.

WEAV(AM)— Feb 3, 1935: 960 khz; 5 kw-U, DA-2. TL: N44 34 27 W73 26 54. Hrs open: 1500 Hegeman Ave., Colchester, VT, 05446. Phone: (802) 655-0093. Fax: (802) 655-0478.E-mail: info@wxzofm.com Web Site:www.wxzofm.com Licensee: Vox AM/FM LLC. Group owner: Clear Channel Communications Inc. (acq 7-25-2008; grpsl). Population served: 225,000 Format: Hot talk, sports. Target aud: General. ◆Karen Marshall, gen mgr; Steve Cormier, opns mgr.

WIRY(AM)— Jan 30, 1950: 1340 khz; 1 kw-D, 940 w-N. TL: N44 40 12 W73 26 41. Hrs open: 5 AM-midnight 301 Cornelia St., 12901. Phone: (518) 563-1340. Fax: (518) 563-1343.E-mail: wiry@wiry.com Web Site:www.wiry.com Licensee: Hometown Radio Inc. (acq 2-1-95; $175,000; 2-27-95). Population served: 25,000 Natl. Network: Westwood One, . Natl. Rep: Roslin,. Format: Adult contemp. News staff: 2; News: 11 hrs wkly. Target aud: 18 plus. ◆Dan Santa, exec VP; William D. Santa, pres & gen mgr.

WKOL(FM)— Aug 22, 1994: 105.1 mhz; 23.5 kw. 338 ft TL: N44 31 31 W73 31 07. Stereo. Hrs open: 24 Box 4489, Burlington, VT, 05406. Secondary address: 70 Joy Dr., South Burlington, VT 05403. Phone: (802) 658-1230. Fax: (802) 862-0786.E-mail: kool105@hallradio.com Web Site:www.wkol.com Licensee: Hall Communications Inc. (group owner; acq 6-13-95; $1.1 million). Natl. Rep: D & R Radio,. Fletcher, Heald & Hildreth. Wire Svc: AP Format: Classic Hits. Target aud: 25-54. ◆Bonnie Rowbotham, chmn; Arthur Rowbotham, pres; Bill Baldwin, exec VP; Dan Dubonnet, gen mgr; Rod Hill, opns dir & progmg mgr.

*WQKE(FM)— April 1979: 93.9 mhz; 10 w. 156 ft TL: N44 41 40 W73 28 00. Stereo. Hrs open: 7 AM-2:30 PM 101 Broad St., Kehoe 202, State University of NY, 12901. Phone: (518) 564-2727. Fax: (518) 564-3994. Licensee: State University of N.Y. Population served: 30,000 Format: College alternative. Target aud: 18-24. Spec prog: Heavy metal 10 hrs, classic rock 12 hrs, Black 9 hrs, relg 3 hrs wkly. ◆Phil Czterwastek, opns dir; Andy Martinez, mus dir.

WTWK(AM)— January 1998: 1070 khz; 5 kw-D. TL: N44 36 14 W73 27 18. Hrs open: 2 N. Main St., Suite 401, St. Albans, VT, 05478. Phone: (802) 524-2133. Fax: (802) 527-1450.E-mail: michaele@champlainradio.com Web Site:www.eve1070.com Licensee: Champlain Communications Corp. Group owner: Northeast Broadcasting Company Inc. (acq 1-11-2002; $150,000). Natl. Network: Air America, . Format: Talk. Target aud: 25-54; women. ◆Richard C. DeLancey Sr., gen mgr; J.J. Prieve, progmg dir.

Port Henry

WVTK(FM)— Sept 5, 1982: 92.1 mhz; 18 kw. Ant 10 ft TL: N44 01 38 W73 28 54. Stereo. Hrs open: 24 Box 1093, Burlington, VT, 05402. Phone: (802) 655-0093. Fax: (802) 655-0478.E-mail: info@trueoldieschannel.com Web Site:www.trueoldieschannel.com Licensee: Vox AM/FM LLC. Group owner: Clear Channel Communications Inc. (acq 7-25-2008; grpsl). Population served: 200,000 Rini Coran PC. Format: Oldies. News: one hr wkly. Target aud: 25-54. ◆Karen Marshall, gen mgr.

Port Jervis

WDLC(AM)— July 4, 1953: 1490 khz; 1 kw-U. TL: N41 21 49 W74 40 41. Hrs open: 24 15 Neversink Dr., 12771. Phone: (845) 856-5185. Fax: (845) 856-4757.E-mail: info@foxcountry.us Licensee: PJ Radio L.L.C. (acq 2-7-2005; $4 million with co-located FM). Population served: 50,000 Format: Oldies. ◆James Morley, gen mgr.

*WRPJ(FM)— October 1992: 88.9 mhz; 500 w. 590 ft TL: N41 25 36 W74 34 45. Stereo. Hrs open:
Rebroadcasts WFGB(FM) Kingston 100%.
Box 777, Lake Katrine, 12449. Secondary address: 199 Tuytenbridge Rd., Lake Katrine 12449. Phone: (845) 336-6199. Phone: (800)

724-8518. Fax: (845) 336-7205.E-mail: email@soundoflife.org Web Site:www.soundoflife.org Licensee: Sound of Life Inc. Population served: 300,000 Format: Christian. Target aud: General. ◆Tom Michael Zahradnik, gen mgr; Bob Conti, opns mgr; Joe Hunter, progmg dir.

WTSX(FM)— Oct 30, 1970: 96.7 mhz; 3 kw. Ant 300 ft TL: N41 22 24 W74 43 49. Stereo. Hrs open: 24 15 Neversink Dr., 12771. Phone: (845) 856-5185.E-mail: kevinhalpenny@foxcountry.us Format: Country. News staff: 2. ◆Judi Edwards, traf mgr; Bob Oefinger, disc jockey.

Portville

WBYB(FM)— Sept 18, 1985: 96.7 mhz; 460 w. Ant 508 ft TL: N42 03 04 W78 25 11. Stereo. Hrs open: 24 9 S. Main St., Coudersport, PA, 16915. Phone: (814) 274-8600. Phone: (814) 642-9396. Fax: (814) 274-0760. Web Site:www.twintiersbob.com Licensee: Colonial Radio Group Inc. (acq 6-22-2009; $275,000). Format: Country.

Potsdam

*WAIH(FM)— Sept 10, 1998: 90.3 mhz; 100 w. -16 ft TL: N44 39 43 W74 58 26. Hrs open: Student Union, 9050 Barrington Dr., 13676. Phone: (315) 267-4888. Fax: (315) 267-2798.E-mail: waih@potsdam.edu Web Site:www2.potsdam.edu/waih Licensee: State University of New York. Format: Music, talk. ◆Jon Foote, gen mgr.

WPDM(AM)— Apr 30, 1955: 1470 khz; 1 kw-D. TL: N44 38 38 W75 03 32. Hrs open: Box 348, 13676. Phone: (315) 265-5510. Fax: (315) 265-4040.E-mail: hits@99hits.com Licensee: St. Lawrence Radio Inc. Population served: 9,985 Cohn & Marks. Format: Adult contemp. News staff: one; News: 5 hrs wkly. Target aud: 25 plus; div audience. ◆Jane A. Kyle, pres; William Solomon, VP & gen mgr; Derry Loucks, gen sls mgr; Justin James, mus dir, disc jockey; Scott Dosztan, news dir; Dan Simmons, chief of engrg; Betty Bombarn, traf mgr; Andy Van Duyne, disc jockey.

WSNN(FM)— Oct 15, 1968: 99.3 mhz; 3 kw. Ant 155 ft TL: N44 38 38 W75 03 32. Hrs open: 6 AM-midnight Prog sep from AM Box 348, 13676. Phone: (315) 265-5510. Fax: (315) 265-4040.E-mail: hits@99hits.com Web Site:www.99hits.com Licensee: Zoe Communications Inc. Cohn & Marks. Format: Country. News staff: one; News: 5 hrs wkly. Target aud: 25-54. ◆Derry Loucks, stn mgr; Justin Gonyea, mus dir, traf mgr; Andy Van Duyne, disc jockey.

*WTSC-FM— Nov 3, 1963: 91.1 mhz; 700 w. 155 ft TL: N44 39 45 W75 00 07. Stereo. Hrs open: 24 hrs a day Clarkson University, Box 8743, 13699. Phone: (315) 268-7658.E-mail: radio@clarkson.edu Web Site:http://radio.clarkson.edu Licensee: Clarkson University. Population served: 9,985 Format: Alternative. ◆James Heroux, gen mgr; Chaz Adams, stn mgr.

Poughkeepsie

WEOK(AM)— October 1949: 1390 khz; 5 kw-D, DA. TL: N41 43 14 W73 54 29. Hrs open: 24 Box 416, 12602-0416. Secondary address: 2 Penvell Rd. 12602-0416. Phone: (845) 471-1500. Fax: (845) 454-1204. Web Site:www.cumulus.com Licensee: Cumulus Licensing Corp. Group owner: Cumulus Media Inc. (acq 1-23-2002). Population served: 245,000 Natl. Rep: Sp. News staff: 3. Target aud: 35 plus. Spec prog: Farm 2 hrs, Pol one hr, relg 2 hrs, talk 5 hrs, Sinatra 2 hrs wkly. ◆Charles Benfer, pres; Nick Robbins, opns dir, prom dir; Victor Goodman, gen sls mgr.

WKIP(AM)— June 1940: 1450 khz; 1 kw-U, DA-D. TL: N41 42 18 W73 53 16. Hrs open: 20 Tucker Dr., 12603-1644. Phone: (845) 471-2300. Fax: (845) 471-2683. Web Site:1450wkip.com Licensee: CC Licenses LLC. Group owner: Clear Channel Communications Inc. (acq 7-12-2000; grpsl). Population served: 222,900 Natl. Rep: Katz Radio. Format: News/talk. News staff: one; News: 2 hrs wkly. Target aud: 35-64. ◆Frank Curcio, gen mgr; Reggie Osterhoudt, opns dir, opns mgr; Jim Brady, gen sls mgr; Jeanette Relyea, natl sls mgr; Nick Smirnoff, prom dir; Rick Knight, progmg dir; Cameron Hendrix, news dir; Elizabeth Mele, sls.

WPDH(FM)— December 1962: 101.5 mhz; 4.5 kw. Ant 1,540 ft TL: N41 43 09 W73 59 47. Stereo. Hrs open: 24 Prog sep from AM Box 416, 12602. Phone: (845) 471-1500. Fax: (845) 454-1204. Web Site:www.wpdh.com Format: Classic rock. Spec prog: Blues deluxe, flashback 4 hrs wkly. ◆Nick Robbins, opns mgr; Greg O'Brien, progmg dir, mus dir.

WPKF(FM)— 1996: 96.1 mhz; 3 kw. Ant 171 ft TL: N41 44 46 W73 54 46. Hrs open: 24 20 Tucker Dr., 12603. Phone: (845) 471-2300. Fax: (845) 471-2683. Web Site:www.kissfmjams.com Licensee: CC

Licenses LLC. Group owner: Clear Channel Communications Inc. (acq 7-14-2000; grpsl). Natl. Network: Jones Radio Networks, . Natl. Rep: Clear Channel, Katz Radio,. Format: Rhythmic CHR. ♦Frank Curcio, gen mgr; Reggie Osterhoudt, opns dir; Jim Brady, gen sls mgr; Jeanette Relyea, natl sls mgr; Nick Smirnoff, prom dir; Aaron McCord, progmg dir; Cameron Hendrix, news dir; Elizabeth Mele, sls.

***WRHV(FM)**— Sept 5, 1990: 88.7 mhz; 230 w. 1,289 ft TL: N41 43 09 W73 59 47. Stereo. Hrs open:
Rebroadcasts Wmht-FM Schenectady 60%.
4 Global View, Troy, 12180. Phone: (518) 880-3400. Fax: (518) 880-3409.E-mail: info@wmht.org Web Site:www.wmht.org Licensee: WMHT Educational Telecommunications. Population served: 90,000 Natl. Network: PRI, . Schwartz, Woods & Miller. Format: Class. Target aud: 35-54; class mus lovers. Spec prog: Jazz 2 hrs, ethnic one hr wkly. ♦Deborah Onslow, pres; Dave Nicosia, chief of engrg.

WRNQ(FM)— June 30, 1989: 92.1 mhz; 2.15 kw. Ant 384 ft TL: N41 40 36 W73 49 14. Stereo. Hrs open: 24 Prog sep from AM 20 Tucker Dr., 12603. Phone: (845) 471-2300. Fax: (845) 471-2683. Web Site:www.921litefm.com Licensee: CC Licenses LLC. Population served: 500,000 Natl. Network: Jones Radio Networks, . Natl. Rep: Katz Radio,. Format: Soft adult contemp. News staff: one; News: 20 hrs wkly. Target aud: 35-54; primary market is women. ♦Reggie Oserhoudt, opns dir; Jim Brady, gen sls mgr; Jeanette Relyea, natl sls mgr; Frank Curcio, mktg mgr; Nick Smirnoff, prom dir; Michelle Taylor, progmg dir, mus dir; Elizabeth Mele, sls.

WSPK(FM)— Dec 7, 1947: 104.7 mhz; 7.4 kw. 1,260 ft TL: N41 29 19 W73 56 52. Stereo. Hrs open: 24 715 Rt. 52, 12508. Phone: (845) 838-8600. Phone: (845) 838-6000. Fax: (845) 838-2109. Web Site:www.k104online.com Licensee: 6 Johnson Road Licenses Inc. Group owner: Pamal Broadcasting Ltd. (acq 10-19-2001; grpsl). Population served: 500,000 Natl. Network: Westwood One, ABC, . Natl. Rep: Katz Radio,. Format: CHR. News staff: one. Target aud: 18-49. ♦James Morrell, CEO; Fred Bennett, VP, natl sls mgr; Jason Finkelberg, gen mgr; Arthur Heller, gen sls mgr; Paul Thurst, chief of engrg.

***WVKR-FM**— 1976: 91.3 mhz; 3.7 kw. 820 ft TL: N41 38 25 W74 01 16. Stereo. Hrs open: 24 Box 726, Vassar College, 12604. Phone: (845) 437-5475. Fax: (845) 437-7656. Web Site:www.wvkr.org Licensee: Vassar College. Population served: 1,500,000 Format: Div. News staff: 4; News: 5 hrs wkly. Target aud: General. ♦Nick De Leeuw, gen mgr.

Pulaski

***WGKV(FM)**— January 1987: 101.7 mhz; 5 kw. Ant 358 ft TL: N43 36 28 W75 58 23. Hrs open: 2351 Sunset Blvd., Suite 170-218, Rocklin, CA, 95765. Phone: (916) 251-1600. Fax: (916) 251-1650. Web Site:www.klove.com Licensee: Educational Media Foundation. (group owner; (acq 7-6-2007; grpsl). Natl. Network: K-Love, . Format: Contemp Christian. ♦Mike Novak, sr VP.

WSCP(AM)—See Sandy Creek-Pulaski

Queensbury

WCQL(FM)— September 1967: 95.9 mhz; 380 w. Ant 1,273 ft TL: N43 25 12 W73 45 37. Stereo. Hrs open: 24 128 Glen St., Glens Falls, 12801. Phone: (518) 761-9890. Fax: (518) 761-9893.E-mail: cashworth@regionalradiogroup.com Web Site:www.radiowins.com Licensee: Regional Radio Group LLC. (acq 9-10-2008; grpsl). Population served: 200,000 Natl. Network: Jones Radio Networks, . Format: Hits of the 80s, 90s & now. News staff: 1.5; News: 3 hrs wkly. Target aud: 18-49. ♦Clay Ashworth, gen mgr; Dan Miner, stn mgr; Mike Dubray, traf mgr.

Rapids

***WLNF(FM)**—Not on air, target date: unknown: 90.5 mhz; 250 w. Ant 74 ft TL: N43 05 12 W78 37 59. Hrs open: 293 Niagara St., Lockport, 14094. Phone: (716) 434-1733. Fax: (716) 434-2837.E-mail: lctv@lctv.net Web Site:www.lctv.net Licensee: Lockport Community Television. ♦Tom Riley, gen mgr.

Ravena

***WYKV(FM)**— 1991: 94.5 mhz; 3 kw. Ant 328 ft TL: N42 33 23 W73 52 05. Hrs open: 24 2351 Sunset Blvd., Suite 170-218, Rocklin, CA, 95765. Phone: (916) 251-1600. Fax: (916) 251-1650. Web Site:www.klove.com Licensee: Educational Media Foundation. Group owner: Galaxy Communications L.P. (acq 7-6-2007; grpsl). Natl. Network: K-Love, . Format: Contemp Christian. ♦Mke Novak, sr VP.

Remsen

WADR(AM)— Dec 12, 1966: 1480 khz; 5 kw-D. TL: N43 19 31 W75 10 29. Stereo. Hrs open: 24
Rebroadcasts WRNY(AM) Rome 100%.
239 Genesee St., Suite 500, Utica, 13501. Phone: (315) 797-0803. Fax: (315) 797-7813. Web Site:www.starsradionetwork.com Licensee: Roser Communications Network Inc. Group owner: Clear Channel Communications Inc. (acq 10-24-2007; grpsl). Population served: 175,000 Natl. Network: Westwood One, . Natl. Rep: Christal,. Latham & Watkins. Format: Sports. News: 3 hrs wkly. Target aud: 35 plus; 60% female, 40% male. ♦Brian Delaney, gen mgr; Gene Conte, progmg dir; Joe Petro, chief of engrg.

WOKR(FM)— Dec 1, 1982: 93.5 mhz; 1.15 kw. Ant 748 ft TL: N43 20 44 W75 15 00. Stereo. Hrs open: 24 2351 Sunset Blvd., Suite 170-218, Rocklin, CA, 95765. Phone: (916) 251-1600. Fax: (916) 251-1650. Web Site:www.klove.com Licensee: Educational Media Foundation. (acq 10-24-2007; $350,000). Population served: 275,000 Natl. Network: K-Love, . Format: Contemp Christian. ♦Mike Novak, sr VP.

***WRUN-FM**— Dec 16, 2008: 90.3 mhz; 1.2 kw. Ant 669 ft TL: N43 20 47.8 W75 13 58.8. Hrs open:
Rebroadcasts WAMC-FM Albany 100%.
318 Central Ave., Albany, 12206-2522. Phone: (518) 465-5233. Fax: (518) 432-6974. Web Site:www.wamc.org Licensee: WAMC. Format: News/talk. ♦Alan Chartock, CEO & pres.

Rensselaer

WGDJ(AM)— Dec 3, 1961: 1300 khz; 5 kw-U, DA-2. TL: N42 35 23 W73 44 37. Hrs open: 24 C/O TU Center, 51 South Pearl St., Albany, 12207. Phone: (518) 813-4975. Fax: (518) 813-9025.E-mail: patr@talk1300.com Web Site:www.talk1300.com Licensee: Capital Broadcasting Inc. Group owner: Regent Communications Inc. (acq 2-4-2008; $850,000). Population served: 800,000 Natl. Network: ABC, . Natl. Rep: Interep,. Format: Talk. Target aud: 35-64. ♦Paul Vandenburgh, pres & gen mgr; Patrick Ryan, sls VP; Mike Carey, news dir.

WQBK-FM— Dec 1, 1972: 103.9 mhz; 6 kw. Ant 302 ft TL: N42 35 06 W73 46 29. Stereo. Hrs open: 24 1241 Kings Rd., Schenectady, 12303. Phone: (518) 881-1515. Fax: (518) 881-1516. Web Site:www.wqbk.com Licensee: Regent Broadcasting of Albany Inc. (acq 2000; grpsl). Population served: 114,873 Format: Rock. ♦Bob Ausfeld, exec VP; John Hirsch, stn mgr; Jim Clifford, sls dir; Shawn Murphy, progmg dir.

Riverhead

WFTU(AM)— Aug 8, 1963: 1570 khz; 1 kw-D, 500 w-N, DA-2. TL: N40 54 48 W72 39 16. Hrs open: 305 N. Service Rd., Dix Hills, 11746. Phone: (631) 424-7000. Phone: (631) 656-3192. Web Site:www.wftu.net Licensee: Five Towns College (acq 5-24-01; $80,000). Population served: 100,000 Format: College radio. ♦Rob Stern, gen mgr.

WRCN-FM— Aug 14, 1962: 103.9 mhz; 1.5 kw. 466 ft TL: N40 51 07 W72 45 55. Stereo. Hrs open: 3241 Rt 112, Bldg. 7, Medford, 11763. Phone: (631) 451-1039. Fax: (631) 451-0891. Fax: (631) 451-0896.E-mail: info@wrcn.com Web Site:www.wrcn.com Licensee: IW L.L.C. Group owner: Barnstable Broadcasting Inc. (acq 10-1-97; grpsl). Population served: 750,000 Natl. Rep: Katz Radio,. Haley, Bader & Potts. Format: Classic hits, rock. Target aud: 18-49. ♦Mike Kaneb, pres; Dave Widmer, gen mgr, stn mgr; Sal Abetamarco, gen sls mgr; Megan Moir, prom dir; Charlie Lombardo, progmg dir; Jen Moran, news dir; Bob Anderson, chief of engrg.

WRIV(AM)— June 1955: 1390 khz; 1 kw-D, 64 w-N. TL: N40 55 22 W72 38 52. Hrs open: 6 AM-midnight Box 1390, 11901. Secondary address: 40 W. Main St. 11901. Phone: (631) 727-1390. Fax: (631) 369-WRIV (9748). Web Site:www.wrivonline.com Licensee: Crystal Coast Communications. (acq 10-87). Population served: 104,000 Format: Adult standards. News staff: one; News: 14 hrs wkly. Target aud: 35-64. Spec prog: Farm 8 hrs, Pol 4 hrs wkly. ♦Bruce Tria, gen mgr.

Rochester

WBEE-FM— February 1961: 92.5 mhz; 50 kw. 500 ft TL: N43 10 37 W77 28 39. Stereo. Hrs open: 24 70 Commercial St., 14614-1010. Phone: (585) 423-2900. Fax: (585) 325-5139. Fax: (585) 423-2947.E-mail: info@wbee.com Web Site:www.wbee.com Licensee: Entercom Rochester License LLC Group owner: Entercom Communications Corp. (acq 4-23-98; grpsl). Population served: 1,161,800 Natl. Network: Westwood One, . Format: Country. News staff: one; News: 4 hrs wkly. Target aud: 25-54. ♦Michael Doyle, gen mgr; Dave Symonds, opns mgr, chief of engrg; Sue Munn, gen sls mgr; Billy Kidd, progmg dir; Steve Hausmann, news dir; Joe Fleming, chief of engrg; Courtney Nourse, traf mgr.

***WBER(FM)**— 1974: 90.5 mhz; 2.5 kw. 417 ft TL: N43 02 00 W77 25 11. (CP: 50 kw). Stereo. Hrs open: 24 2596 Baird Rd., Penfield, 14526. Phone: (585) 419-8190. Fax: (585) 419-8191. Web Site:http: //wber.monroe.edu Licensee: Monroe B.O.C.E.S #1. Format: Alternative. Target aud: 25-34; male & female. ♦Joey Guisto, gen mgr.

WBZA(FM)— 1939: 98.9 mhz; 50 kw. 560 ft TL: N43 10 14 W77 40 23. Stereo. Hrs open: 24 Entercom Rocherster LLC, 70 Commercial St., 14614-1010. Phone: (585) 423-2900. Fax: (585) 325-5139. Fax: (585) 423-2947.E-mail: info@rochesterbuzz.com Web Site:www.rochesterbuzz.com Licensee: Entercom Rochester Inc. Group owner: Entercom Communications Corp. (acq 4-23-98; grpsl). Population served: 1,161,800 Natl. Network: Westwood One, . Natl. Rep: Katz Radio,. Akin, Gump, Strauss, Hauer & Feld. Format: Classic Hits. News staff: one. Target aud: 25-54; upscale. ♦Mike Johnson, VP; Michael Doyle, gen mgr.

WCMF-FM— June 9, 1960: 96.5 mhz; 50 kw. 457 ft TL: N43 08 07 W77 35 02. Stereo. Hrs open: 24 70 Commercial St., 14614. Phone: (585) 423-2900. Fax: (585) 325-5139. Web Site:www.wcmf.com Licensee: Entercom Rochester License LLC. Group owner: Infinity Broadcasting Corp. (acq 11-30-2007; grpsl). Population served: 296,233 Format: Classic rock. News staff: one; News: 10 hrs wkly. ♦John Thomas, opns mgr.

WDCX(AM)— February 1947: 990 khz; 5 kw-D, 2.5 kw-N, DA-2. TL: N43 13 54 W77 52 00. Hrs open: 24 2494 Browncroft Blvd., 14625. Phone: (585) 264-1027. Fax: (585) 264-1165.E-mail: info@legend1027.com Web Site:www.crawfordbroadcasting.com Licensee: Kimtron Inc. Group owner: Crawford Broadcasting Co. (acq 6-5-97; $650,000). Format: Christian.

WDKX(FM)— Apr 6, 1974: 103.9 mhz; 800 w. 540 ft TL: N43 09 17 W77 36 16. Stereo. Hrs open: 24 683 E. Main St., 14605. Phone: (585) 262-2050. Fax: (585) 262-2626. Web Site:www.wdkx.com Licensee: Monroe County Broadcasting Co. Ltd. (acq 9-19-02). Population served: 296,233 Format: Urban contemp. News staff: 2; News: 6 hrs wkly. Target aud: General. Spec prog: Jazz 4 hrs, gospel 7 hrs wkly. ♦Andrew A. Langston, CEO, gen mgr; Andrew Langston, pres; Marietta Avery, CFO; Camilla Maas, sr VP; Gloria M. Langston, stn mgr; Andre Langston, opns dir.

WDVI(FM)— 1962: 100.5 mhz; 50 kw. Ant 480 ft TL: N43 02 00 W77 25 17. Stereo. Hrs open: 24 1700 HSBC Plaza, 100 Chesnut Street, 14604. Phone: (585) 454-4884. Fax: (585) 454-5081. Web Site:www.mydrivefm.com Population served: 219,100 Format: Modern adult contemp. Target aud: 25-54. ♦Karen Carey, VP, gen mgr & gen sls mgr; Joe Bonacci, progmg dir, disc jockey.

WFXF(FM)—See Honeoye Falls

WHAM(AM)— July 11, 1922: 1180 khz; 50 kw-U. TL: N43 04 55 W77 43 30. Stereo. Hrs open: 24 1700 HSBC Plaza, 100 Chestnut Street, 14604. Phone: (585) 454-4884. Fax: (585) 454-5081. Fax: (585) 262-2334.E-mail: whamnews@wham1180.com Web Site:www.wham1180.com Licensee: Citicasters Licenses L.P. Group owner: Clear Channel Communications Inc. (acq 3-7-97; grpsl). Population served: 296,233 Natl. Network: CBS, . Format: News/talk. News staff: 6. Target aud: Adults: 25-54. ♦Karen Carey, VP, gen mgr; Jeff Howlett, stn mgr; Randy Gorbman, news dir.

WHIC(AM)— Sept 11, 1925: 1460 khz; 5 kw-U, DA-N. TL: N43 06 34 W77 34 20. (CP: 3.7 kw-D, 5 kw-N, DA-N. TL: N43 04 59 W77 38 52). Hrs open: 24 Box 25433, 14625. Secondary address: 2 Cambridge Pl., 1840 Winton Rd. S. 14618. Phone: (585) 271-0530. Fax: (585) 271-0530.E-mail: info@thestationofthewoss.com Web Site:www.thestationofthewoss.com Licensee: Holy Family Communications (group owner; acq 7-1-2003; $300,000). Population served: 1,500,000 Format: Catholic. ♦James N. Wright, pres; Jack Palvino, gen mgr.

WHTK(AM)— Nov 22, 1947: 1280 khz; 5 kw-U, DA-N. TL: N43 05 54 W77 35 00. Hrs open: 24 207 Midtown Plaza, 14604. Phone: (585) 454-4884. Phone: (585) 454-3942. Fax: (585) 262-2334.E-mail: info@whtk.com Web Site:www.whtk.com Licensee: Citicasters Licenses L.P. Group owner: Clear Channel Communications Inc. (acq 5-4-99; grpsl). Population served: 235,000 Natl. Rep: McGavren Guild,. Format: Talk. Target aud: 25-54; men. ♦Jeff Howlett, gen mgr, progmg dir; Scott Gordon, gen sls mgr.

***WIRQ(FM)**— January 1960: 104.7 mhz; 10 w. 485 ft TL: N43 12 59 W77 35 46. Stereo. Hrs open: 1 PM-8 PM (M-F); Sept-June 260 Cooper Rd., 14617. Phone: (585) 336-3065. Phone: (716) 336-3065.

Fax: (589) 336-2929. Licensee: Board of Education West, Irondequoit Central School District. Population served: 600,000 Format: Alternative. News: one hr wkly. Target aud: 13-45. Spec prog: Top-35 countdown 3 hrs, Progressive Pioneers 3 hrs, techno 3 hrs wkly. ♦Hannah Jacobs, gen mgr.

WJZR(FM)— Jan 22, 1993: 105.9 mhz; 3 kw. 180 ft TL: N43 09 35 W77 34 44. Stereo. Hrs open: 24 Fedder Industrial Park, 1237 E. Main St., 14609. Phone: (585) 288-5020. Licensee: North Coast Radio Inc. Population served: 650,000 Natl. Network: AP Radio, . Cohn & Marks. Format: Blues, jazz. News: 14 hrs wkly. Target aud: 25 plus. Spec prog: News review one hr wkly. ♦Lee Rust, pres & stn mgr; Barry Vee, gen sls mgr.

WPXY-FM— Sept 14, 1959: 97.9 mhz; 50 kw. 456 ft TL: N43 08 08 W77 35 02. Stereo. Hrs open: 70 Commercial St., 14614. Phone: (585) 423-2900. Fax: (585) 325-5139. Web Site:www.98pxy.com Licensee: Entercom Rochester License LLC. Group owner: Infinity Broadcasting Corp. (acq 11-30-2007; grpsl). Format: Pop contemp hits. ♦John Johnson, gen mgr, opns mgr; Mike Danger, progmg dir.

WRMM-FM— Nov 14, 1966: 101.3 mhz; 27 kw. 640 ft TL: N43 10 14 W77 40 23. Stereo. Hrs open: Phone: (585) 399-5700. Fax: (585) 399-5750.E-mail: info@warmradio.com Web Site:www.warmradio.com Licensee: Stephens Media Group-Rochester LLC. Group owner: Infinity Broadcasting Corp. (acq 7-14-2008; grpsl). Population served: 149,000 Format: Adult contemp. Target aud: 25-54; baby boomers. ♦Al Casazza, gen mgr.

WROC(AM)— 1947: 950 khz; 1 kw-U, DA-2. TL: N43 06 25 W77 35 51. Hrs open: 24 70 Commercial St., 14614-1010. Phone: (585) 423-2900. Fax: (585) 325-5139.E-mail: info@wroc.com Licensee: Entercom Rochester License LLC. Population served: 831,800 Natl. Network: ESPN Radio, . Format: Sports. ♦Joe Fleming, gen sls mgr, chief of engrg; Jim White, progmg mgr; Steve Hausmann, VP & news dir; Alana Katz, traf mgr.

***WRUR-FM**— Mar 6, 1966: 88.5 mhz; 3 kw. 348 ft TL: N43 09 23 W77 36 31. Stereo. Hrs open: 24 CPU Box 277356, Univ. of Rochester, 14627-7356. Phone: (585) 275-6400. Phone: (585) 275-7400. Fax: (585) 273-1357. Web Site:www.wrur.org Licensee: University of Rochester Broadcasting Corp. Population served: 1,500,000 Format: Div. News: 4 hrs wkly. Target aud: General. Spec prog: Jazz, gospel 3 hrs, relg one hr, world 10 hrs, folk 2 hrs, Sp 6 hrs, techno 5 hrs, death metal 8 hrs, industrial 3 hrs wkly. ♦Mike Lindsay, gen mgr; Paul Szymanski, opns mgr; Ally Miller, progmg dir.

***WXXI(AM)**— 1936: 1370 khz; 5 kw-U, DA-N. TL: N43 06 01 W77 34 23. Hrs open: 24 280 State St., 14614. Phone: (585) 325-7500. Fax: (585) 258-0339.E-mail: radio@wxxi.org Web Site:www.wxxi.org Licensee: WXXI Public Broadcasting Council. Population served: 941,600 Natl. Network: NPR, . Schwartz, Woods & Miller. Wire Svc: AP Format: News/talk. ♦Norm Silverstein, pres, gen mgr; Peter Iglinski, news dir; Bud Lowell, reporter.

***WXXI-FM**— December 1974: 91.5 mhz; 45 kw. 400 ft TL: N43 08 07 W77 35 03. Stereo. Hrs open: 24 Prog sep from AM 280 State St., 14614. Web Site:www.wxxi.org Licensee: WXXI Public Broadcasting Council Population served: 941,600 Natl. Network: PRI, . Format: Class. ♦Julia Figueras, mus dir, disc jockey; Morderai Lipshutz, disc jockey. Co-owned TV: *WXXI-TV affil.

WYSL(AM)—See Avon

Rome

WFRG-FM—See Utica

WODZ-FM— August 1968: 96.1 mhz; 7.4 kw. 600 ft TL: N43 02 14 W75 26 40. Stereo. Hrs open: 24 9418 State Rt.49, Marcy, 13403. Phone: (315) 768-9500. Fax: (315) 736-0720. Web Site:www.wodz.com Licensee: Regent License of Utica/Rome Inc. Group owner: Regent Communications Inc. (acq 11-5-99; grpsl). Population served: 267,900 Format: Oldies. ♦Mary Jo Beach, gen mgr; Tracy DeCarr, gen sls mgr; Bob Cain, progmg dir; Dave Andrews, news dir.

WRNY(AM)— Oct 12, 1959: 1350 khz; 500 w-D, 60 w-N. TL: N43 12 18 W75 29 08. Hrs open: 24 39 Kellogg Rd., Suite 500, New Hartford, 13413. Phone: (315) 797-0803. Fax: (315) 797-7813.E-mail: info@galaxycommunication.com Licensee: Galaxy Utica Licensee LLC. Group owner: Clear Channel Communications Inc. (acq 10-24-2007; grpsl). Population served: 44,000 Baraff, Koerner & Olender. Format: Sports. News staff: one. Target aud: 25 plus. Spec prog: Black 3 hrs wkly. ♦Brian Deleney, gen mgr; Chuck Hebbard, gen sls mgr; Gene Conte, progmg dir; Joe Petro, chief of engrg.

WRUN(AM)—See Utica

WUMX(FM)— May 1, 1983: 102.5 mhz; 27 kw. 649 ft TL: N43 02 14 W75 26 40. Stereo. Hrs open: 24 Prog sep from AM 39 Kellogg Rd., Suite 500, New Hartford, 13413. Phone: (315) 797-0803. Fax: (315) 797-7813.E-mail: info@galaxycommunication.com Web Site:www.1025kiss.com Population served: 280,000 Format: Country. News staff: one. Target aud: 18-49. Spec prog: Pub affrs one hr wkly. ♦Chris Spiwak, natl sls mgr, prom dir; Stew Schantz, progmg dir; Joe Petro, engrg mgr, chief of engrg; Ed O'Brien, sports cmtr.

WYFY(AM)— September 1946: 1450 khz; 1 kw-U. TL: N43 12 18 W75 28 48. Hrs open: 24 Box 7300, Charlotte, NC, 28241. Phone: (704) 523-5555. Fax: (704) 522-1967. Web Site:www.bbnradio.org Licensee: Bible Broadcasting Network Inc. Group owner: Bible Broadcasting Network (acq 5-7-99; $50,000). Population served: 275,000 Format: Relg. ♦Jason Padgett, stn mgr.

Rosendale

***WFNP(FM)**— Sept 5, 1990: 88.7 mhz; 230 w. 1,289 ft TL: N41 43 09 W73 59 47. Stereo. Hrs open: 7 PM-5 AM State Univ. of New York, SUB Rm. 413, New Paltz, 12561. Phone: (845) 257-3084. Phone: (845) 257-3094. Fax: (845) 257-3099. Web Site:www.wfnp.org Licensee: State University of New York, Albany. Population served: 330,000 Natl. Network: ABC, AP Radio, . Dow, Lohnes & Albertson. Format: Progsv, urban contemp. News: 3 hrs wkly. Target aud: General; demographic-specific programs. Spec prog: Black 14 hrs, jazz 4 hrs, Sp 3 hrs, news/talk 5 hrs, metal 7 hrs wkly. ♦William Clark, opns dir & opns mgr.

Rotterdam

WTRY-FM— Dec 15, 1986: 98.3 mhz; 6 kw. 318 ft TL: N42 44 43 W74 04 10. Stereo. Hrs open: 24 1203 Troy Schenectady Rd., Suite 201, Latham, 12110. Phone: (518) 452-4800. Fax: (518) 452-4855. Web Site:www.wtry.com Licensee: Capstar TX L.P. Group owner: Clear Channel Communications Inc. (acq 8-30-00; grpsl). Population served: 1,300,000 Natl. Rep: Clear Channel,. Format: Oldies. News staff: one; News: 20 hrs wkly. Target aud: 35-54. ♦Joseph Hennessy, gen mgr; John Cooper, stn mgr; Kristen Delaney, VP & mktg mgr.

Rouses Point

***WKYJ(FM)**— 2005: 88.7 mhz; 300 w vert. Ant 43 ft TL: N44 56 44 W73 25 41. Hrs open: 3185 S. Highland Dr., Suite 13, Las Vegas, NV, 89109. Phone: (702) 731-5588. Licensee: American Educational Broadcasting Inc. ♦Carl Auel, CEO; Carl J. Auel, pres; Fred Hodges, gen mgr.

Roxbury

***WIOX(FM)**—Not on air, target date: unknown: 91.3 mhz; 3.5 kw. Ant -600 ft TL: N42 17 03 W74 34 00. Hrs open: Box 189, 12474-0189. Phone: (607) 326-7641. Web Site:www.roxburyny.com Licensee: Town of Roxbury. ♦Thomas S. Hynes, gen mgr.

Sag Harbor

WLNG(FM)— Apr 13, 1969: 92.1 mhz; 5.3 kw. 350 ft TL: N40 58 19 W72 20 54. Hrs open: Box 2000, 11963. Secondary address: 23 Redwood Road 11963. Phone: (631) 725-2300. Fax: (631) 725-5897.E-mail: info@wlng.com Web Site:www.wlng.com Licensee: Mainstreet Broadcasting Co. Format: Oldies, Top-40. ♦Ann Buckhout, pres; Rusty Potz, exec VP; Gary Sapiane, VP.

Saint Bonaventure

***WSBU(FM)**— Apr 13, 1975: 88.3 mhz; 165 w. Ant -256 ft TL: N42 04 45 W78 29 07. Stereo. Hrs open: 24 Box O, Saint Bonaventure University, Rm. 210, Reilly Ctr., 14778. Phone: (716) 375-2307. Fax: (716) 375-2583.E-mail: webmaster@wsbu.net Licensee: St. Bonaventure University. Population served: 50,000 Format: AOR. News: 10 hrs wkly. Target aud: General; primarily students. ♦Dr. Robert Wickenheiser, pres; Joe O'Neil, stn mgr; Todd Lewandowski, spec ev coord.

Salamanca

WGGO(AM)— June 18, 1957: 1590 khz; 5 kw-D. TL: N42 10 24 W78 41 07. Hrs open: Box 100, Killbuck, 14748. Secondary address: 4104 Killbuck Rd. 14779. Phone: (716) 945-1590. Fax: (716) 945-1515.E-mail: wgrt983@direcway.com Licensee: Pembrook Pines Inc. (acq 6-9-2006; $1.25 million with co-located FM). Population served: 7,877 Natl. Network: ESPN Radio, . Format: Sports. Target aud: General. Spec prog: Country 5 hrs, Pol one hr wkly. ♦Robert J. Pfuntner, pres; Michael Washington, gen mgr, progmg dir; Sue Washington, gen sls mgr & mus dir; Scott Douglas, news dir; Russ Ehman, chief of engrg.

WQRS(FM)— Oct 15, 1988: 98.3 mhz; 1.6 kw. 430 ft TL: N42 06 32 W78 36 28. Stereo. Hrs open: Box 100, Killbuck, 14748. Secondary address: 4104 Killbuck Rd. 14779. Phone: (716) 945-1590. Fax: (716) 945-1515.E-mail: wqrt983@direcway.net Format: Classic rock.

Sandy Creek-Pulaski

WSCP(AM)— Aug 8, 1974: 1070 khz; 2.5 kw-D. TL: N43 36 19 W76 07 48. Hrs open: Box 640, 5090 U.S. Rt. 11, Pulaski, 13142. Phone: (315) 298-3185. Fax: (315) 298-6181. Web Site:www.wscp.net Licensee: Galaxy Syracuse Licensee LLC. (group owner; (acq 7-17-2001; $400,000 with WSCP-FM Pulaski). Natl. Network: Jones Radio Networks, . Format: Country. News staff: one; News: one hr wkly. Target aud: 35 plus. ♦Mimi Griswold, progmg dir.

Saranac Lake

WNBZ(AM)— Sept 11, 1927: 1240 khz; 1 kw-U. TL: N44 18 58 W74 07 08. Hrs open: 24 Box 211, 12983. Secondary address: Colony Ct. Ext. 12983. Phone: (518) 891-1544. Phone: (518) 891-3636. Fax: (518) 891-1545.E-mail: mail@wnbz.com Web Site:www.wnbz.com Licensee: Saranac Lake Radio L.L.C. Group owner: Mountain Communications (acq 6-1-98; $397,500 with co-located FM). Population served: 19,134 Irwin, Campbell, Crowe & Tannenwald. Format: Adult contemp. News staff: one; News: 36 hrs wkly. Target aud: 35 plus; loc community. ♦Ted Morgan, pres & gen mgr; John Gagnon, opns mgr, progmg dir; James Williams, gen sls mgr; Chris Knight, news dir; Crystal Tatro, pub affrs dir; Chris Brescia, chief of engrg; Steve Borst, disc jockey.

***WSLL(FM)**— July 1, 1989: 89.5 mhz; 200 w. 355 ft TL: N44 20 28 W74 07 43. Hrs open:
Rebroadcasts WSLU(FM) Canton 100%.
St. Lawrence Univ., Canton, 13617. Phone: (315) 229-5356. Fax: (315) 229-5373.E-mail: info@ncpr.org Web Site:www.ncpr.org Licensee: St. Lawrence University. Format: Eclectic public radio. Target aud: General. ♦Ellen Rocco, stn mgr; Sandra Demarest, dev dir.

WSLP(FM)— 2007: 93.3 mhz; 11 kw. Ant -207 ft TL: N44 15 36 W74 01 22. Hrs open: Box 368, Lake Placid, 12946. Phone: (518) 523-4900. Fax: (518) 523-4290.E-mail: info@wslpfm.com Web Site:www.wslpfm.com Licensee: North Country Radio Inc. Natl. Network: CNN Radio, . Format: Adult contemp. Target aud: 25-54. ♦Jon Lundin, gen mgr; Jim Williams, gen sls mgr.

WYZY(FM)— July 12, 1989: 106.3 mhz; 50 kw. Ant 394 ft TL: N44 20 28 W74 07 43. Stereo. Hrs open: 24 Prog sep from AM Box 211, 12983. Phone: (518) 891-1544. Fax: (518) 891-1545.E-mail: brandy@mtnradio.com Web Site:www.wnbz.com Licensee: Saranac Lake Radio LLC Population served: 30,000 Format: Adult contemp. News staff: 2; News: 10 hrs wkly. Target aud: 18-49; adults. ♦Crystal Tatro, opns mgr; Steve Borst, disc jockey.

Saratoga Springs

***WSPN(FM)**— Sept 9, 1974: 91.1 mhz; 253 w. 98 ft TL: N43 05 55 W73 47 10. Stereo. Hrs open: 24 Skidmore College, 12866. Phone: (518) 580-5783. Licensee: Skidmore College. Population served: 30,000 Natl. Network: AP Radio, . Format: College radio. News: 5 hrs wkly. Target aud: All ages. Spec prog: Folk 3 hrs, Pol 3 hrs, Sp 3 hrs, blues 9 hrs, world mus 3 hrs wkly. ♦Alissa DeVogel, gen mgr; Lily Gedney, mus dir.

***WSSK(FM)**— 2001: 89.7 mhz; 50 w. Ant 430 ft TL: N43 11 35 W73 45 25. Hrs open: Box 777, Lake Katrine, 12449. Phone: (845) 336-6199. Fax: (845) 336-7205.E-mail: info@soundoflife.org Web Site:www.soundoflife.org Licensee: Sound of Life Inc. Format: Contemp Christian. ♦Tom Michael Zahradnik, gen mgr; Bob Conti, opns mgr; Joe Hunter, progmg dir.

Saugerties

WBPM(FM)— 1999: 92.9 mhz; 6 kw. Ant 289 ft TL: N41 59 20 W74 01 08. Hrs open: 24 715 Rt. 52, Beacon, 12508. Phone: (845) 838-6000. Fax: (845) 838-6088. Web Site:www.wbpmfm.com Licensee: 6 Johnson Road Licenses Inc. Group owner: Clear Channel Communications Inc. (acq 4-1-2007; grpsl). Format: Classic hits. ♦Jason Finkelberg, gen mgr.

Schenectady

WGY(AM)— February 1922: 810 khz; 50 kw. TL: N42 47 37 W74 00 36. Hrs open: 24 1203 Troy-Schenectady Rd., Latham, 12110. Phone: (518) 452-4800. Fax: (518) 452-4855. Web Site:www.wgy.com Licensee: CC License LLC. Group owner: Clear Channel Communications Inc. (acq 8-5-98; grpsl). Population served: 800,000 Natl. Network: Fox News Radio, Premiere Radio Networks, . Natl. Rep: Clear Channel,. Wire Svc: AP Format: News/talk. News staff: 12; News: 23 hrs wkly. Target aud: 25-54; college graduate, married, homeowner. ◆Kristen Delaney, VP; Greg Foster, opns dir, opns mgr, progmg dir; Mark Scott, traf mgr; Don Weeks, disc jockey.

*WMHT-FM— June 8, 1972: 89.1 mhz; 11 kw. Ant 930 ft TL: N42 38 13 W74 00 06. Stereo. Hrs open: 4 Global View, Troy, 12180. Phone: (518) 880-3400. Fax: (518) 880-3409.E-mail: info@wmht.org Web Site:www.wmht.org Licensee: WMHT Educational Telecommunications. Format: Class. Spec prog: Jazz one hr wkly. ◆Deborah Onslow, gen mgr; Dave Nicosia, chief of engrg. Co-owned TV: *WMHT(TV) affil.

WOFX(AM)—See Troy

*WRUC(FM)— May 9, 1975: 89.7 mhz; 100 w. -88 ft TL: N42 49 04 W73 55 45. Stereo. Hrs open: Union College, 12308. Phone: (518) 388-6151. Phone: (518) 388-6154. Fax: (518) 388-6790. Licensee: Trustees of Union College. Population served: 950,000 Natl. Network: AP Radio, . Format: Alternative. Target aud: 18 plus; general. Spec prog: It one hr, Sp 3 hrs, jazz 15 hrs, sports 4 hrs wkly.

WRVE(FM)— April 1940: 99.5 mhz; 14.5 kw. 925 ft TL: N42 38 13 W73 59 48. Stereo. Hrs open: 24 Prog sep from AM 1203 Troy-Schenectady Rd., Latham, 12110. Phone: (518) 452-4800. Fax: (518) 452-4855. Web Site:www.wrve.com Natl. Network: Premiere Radio Networks, . Format: Adult contemp. News staff: one; News: 3 hrs wkly. Target aud: 25-54. ◆Randy McCarten, progmg dir.

WTRY-FM—See Rotterdam

WVKZ(AM)— Apr 15, 1942: 1240 khz; 1 kw-U. TL: N42 48 37 W73 59 04. Hrs open: 24 100 Saratoga Village Blvd., Ste. 21, Malta, 12020. Phone: (518) 899-3000. Fax: (518) 899-3057.E-mail: trueoldies@wvkz.com Web Site:www.wvkz.com Licensee: The Anastos Media Group Inc. Group owner: Anastos Media Group Inc. (acq 4-10-2000; $137,500). Population served: 247,000 Natl. Network: ABC, . Format: True oldies. News staff: one. Target aud: 25-54; men. ◆Phillip Anastos, pres; Fran Dingeman, gen mgr; John Meaney, stn mgr, news dir; John H. Meaney, opns mgr; Fran Dingman, gen sls mgr; Amanda Albright, prom dir.

Schoharie

WMYY(FM)— 1990: 97.3 mhz; 800 w. Ant 895 ft TL: N42 37 51 W74 16 01. Stereo. Hrs open: 24
Rebroadcasts WHAZ(AM) Troy 100%.
30 Park Ave., Cohoes, 12047-3330. Phone: (518) 237-1330. Fax: (518) 235-4468.E-mail: events@aliveradionetwork.com Web Site:www.whaz.com Licensee: Capital Media Corp. (group owner; acq 2-14-92; 2-17-92). Population served: 1,000,000 Format: Adult Christian. Target aud: 25-75; young to adult. Spec prog: Gospel, relg. ◆Paul F. Lotters, pres, gen mgr; Steven L. Klob, opns dir, dev dir, sls dir, prom dir & adv dir; Rex P. Gregory, progmg dir, news dir, pub affrs dir; Bill Rosenfeld, chief of engrg.

Schuyler Falls

*WOXR(FM)— 2004: 90.9 mhz; 2.7 kw. Ant 1,073 ft TL: N44 34 24 W73 40 31. Hrs open: Vermont Public Radio, 365 Troy Ave., Colchester, VT, 05446. Phone: (802) 655-9451. Fax: (802) 655-2799. Web Site:www.vpr.net Licensee: Vermont Public Radio (acq 8-29-2007; $1.1 million). Vermont Public Radio Format: Classical. ◆Mark Vogelzang, gen mgr.

Scotia

*WYAI(FM)— December 1981: 93.7 mhz; 1.25 kw. Ant 705 ft TL: N42 51 24 W74 04 03. Hrs open: 2351 Sunset Blvd., Suite 170-218, Rocklin, CA, 95765. Phone: (916) 251-1600. Fax: (916) 251-1650. Web Site:www.air1.com Licensee: Educational Media Foundation. (group owner; acq 7-6-2007; grpsl). Natl. Network: Air 1, . Format: Christian rock. ◆Mike Novak, sr VP.

Seneca Falls

WLLW(FM)— Nov 1, 1968: 99.3 mhz; 5 kw. Ant 358 ft TL: N42 59 38 W76 51 59. Stereo. Hrs open: 24 3568 Lenox Rd., Geneva, 14456. Phone: (315) 781-7000. Fax: (315) 781-7700. Format: Classic Rock. ◆Ken Paradise, progmg dir.

WSFW(AM)— Oct 1, 1968: 1110 khz; 1 kw-D. TL: N42 54 55 W76 46 28. Hrs open: Sunrise-sunset 3568 Lenox Rd., Geneva, 14456. Phone: (315) 781-7000. Fax: (315) 781-7700.E-mail: wnyr@flare.net Licensee: Auburn Broadcasting Inc. Group owner: Finger Lakes Radio Group (acq 3-2-2001; with co-located FM). Population served: 350,000 Natl. Rep: Rgnl Reps,. Borsari & Paxson. Format: Talk. News staff: one; News: 24 hrs wkly. Target aud: 25-54. Spec prog: Irish 2 hrs, It 2 hrs, jazz one hr, oldies 3 hrs, Pol 2 hrs wkly. ◆Allan Bishop, gen mgr.

Sidney

WCDO(AM)— 1983: 1490 khz; 1 kw-U. TL: N42 19 24 W75 22 57. Hrs open: 75 Main St., 13838. Phone: (607) 563-3588. Phone: (607) 563-3589. Fax: (607) 563-7805.E-mail: wcdo@wcdofm.com Licensee: CDO Broadcasting Inc. Group owner: Clancy-Mance Communications (acq 3-8-86; $180,000 with co-located FM; 1-13-86). Format: Adult contemp. Target aud: 25-54. ◆Craig Harris, gen mgr; Jim Tomeo, progmg dir.

WCDO-FM— May 1982: 100.9 mhz; 970 w. 577 ft TL: N42 17 33 W75 22 03. (CP: 1.88 kw). Hrs open: 75 Main St., 13838. Phone: (607) 563-3588. Phone: (607) 563-3589. Fax: (607) 563-7805.E-mail: wcdo@wcdofm.com Format: Adult contemp, oldies. Target aud: 25-54. ◆Craig Stevens, gen mgr, gen sls mgr; Greg Davie, sls dir.

Smithtown

*WFRS(FM)— Oct 17, 1988: 88.9 mhz; 1.5 kw horiz, 1.45 kw vert. 453 ft TL: N40 48 27 W73 10 48. Stereo. Hrs open: 24 289 MT.Pleasant Ave, West Orange, 07052. Phone: (631) 234-4151. Fax: (631) 234-4628. Web Site:www.familyradio.com Licensee: Family Stations Inc. (group owner; acq 9-27-83). Population served: 1,000,000 Natl. Network: Family Radio, . Format: Nondenominational Christian educ. News: 5 hrs wkly. Target aud: General. ◆Bruce Clark, gen mgr; Craig Hulsobus, progmg dir.

WMJC(FM)— May 21, 1957: 94.3 mhz; 2.6 kw. Ant 315 ft TL: N40 48 08 W73 17 12. Stereo. Hrs open: 24 234 Airport Plaza Blvd., Suite 5, Farmingdale, 11735. Phone: (631) 770-4200. Fax: (631) 770-0101.E-mail: jan@wmjcfm.com Web Site:www.island943.com Licensee: IW L.L.C. Group owner: Barnstable Broadcasting Inc. (acq 10-1-97; grpsl). Population served: 2,000,000 Natl. Network: AP Radio, . Rgnl. Network: Metronews Radio Net. Wire Svc: Standard Broadcast Wire Format: Hot adult contemp. News staff: one; News: 2 hrs wkly. Target aud: 25-54; men & women. ◆Dave Widmer, gen mgr.

Sodus

WUUF(FM)— 1991: 103.5 mhz; 6 kw. 243 ft TL: N43 16 05 W77 09 40. Hrs open: 24 Box 1420, Newark, 14513. Phone: (315) 331-9667. Fax: (315) 331-7101.E-mail: bigdogfm@rochester.rr.com Web Site:www.bigdog1035.com Licensee: Waynco Radio (acq 8-90; $10,000;8-13-90). Population served: 2,000,000 Natl. Network: Motor Racing Net, Westwood One, . Fletcher, Heald & Hildreth . Format: Country. News staff: one; News: one hr wkly. Target aud: 25-54. ◆John Tickner, pres, gen mgr; Jim Hill, opns dir; Rus Jeffrey, news dir.

South Bristol Township

WROO(FM)— Jan 22, 1996: 107.3 mhz; 650 w. Ant 994 ft TL: N42 44 47 W77 25 35. Hrs open: 24 1700 HSBC Plaza, 100 Chestnut St, Rochester, 14604. Phone: (585) 454-4884. Fax: (585) 454-5081. Web Site:www.mycountryfm.com Licensee: Citicasters Licenses L.P. Group owner: Clear Channel Communications Inc. (acq 1999; grpsl). Format: Country. Target aud: 25-54. ◆Karen Carey, VP & gen mgr; Dave LeFrois, opns mgr.

South Glens Falls

WENU(AM)— September 1988: 1410 khz; 1 kw-D, 126 w-N. TL: N43 16 07 W73 40 14. Hrs open: 24 89 Everts Ave., Queensbury, 12804. Phone: (518) 793-7733. Fax: (518) 793-0838. Licensee: 6 Johnson Road Licenses Inc. Group owner: Pamal Broadcasting Ltd. (acq 4-1-2004; grpsl). Population served: 233,000 Natl. Network: Westwood

One, . Format: Contemporary. News staff: one. Target aud: 35 plus. ◆James Morrell, pres; Mike Morgan, opns mgr.

Southampton

WEHM(FM)— July 21, 2003: 92.9 mhz; 6 kw. Ant 276 ft TL: N40 52 10 W72 34 37. Hrs open: Box 7162, Amagansett, 11930. Secondary address: 249 Montauk Hwy., Amagansett 11930. Phone: (631) 267-7800. Fax: (631) 267-1018.E-mail: info@wehm.com Web Site:www.wehm.com Licensee: AAA Licensing LLC. Group owner: AAA Entertainment L.L.C. (acq 4-30-2003). Format: Progsv adult rock. ◆Don Maguire, pres; Hedy Krebs-DeMaio, gen mgr; Steve Harper, opns mgr & progmg dir.

WHFM(FM)— October 1971: 95.3 mhz; 5 kw. 354 ft TL: N40 56 05 W72 23 15. Stereo. Hrs open: Box 674, Center Moriches, 11934. Phone: (631) 587-1023. Fax: (631) 283-9506. Web Site:www.wbab.com Licensee: Cox Radio Inc. Group owner: Cox Broadcasting (acq 5-22-98; grpsl). Population served: 150,000 Natl. Rep: Christal,. Format: Adult contemp, rock/AOR. Target aud: 25-49; upscale. ◆Kim Guthrie, VP; John Shea, gen mgr; Donovan Welsh, gen sls mgr; Vinny DiMarco, natl sls mgr; Chris Lloyd, progmg dir; Ted Ronneburger, chief of engrg; Lori DeFilliis, traf mgr.

*WLIU(FM)— Mar 3, 1979: 88.3 mhz; 5.9 kw horiz, 25 kw vert. 217 ft TL: N40 53 17 W72 26 43. (CP: 16 kw, ant 748 ft. TL: N40 51 18 W72 46 12). Stereo. Hrs open: 24
Rebroadcasts 88.1WCWP(FM) Brookville 60%.
239 Montauk Highway PO Bo 803, Southampton, 11969-0803. Phone: (631) 591-7000. Fax: (631) 591-7080.E-mail: wally@wliu.org Web Site:www.wliu.org Licensee: Long Island University. Population served: 115,000 Natl. Network: PRI, NPR, . Lawrence Bernstein. Wire Svc: AP Format: Jazz. News staff: 2; News: 34 hrs wkly. Target aud: 34-55; upscale, educ, public radio listeners. Spec prog: Pub affrs one hr wkly. ◆Dr. Wallace Smith, gen mgr; Jamie Berger, opns dir; Bonnie Grice, mus dir; Robert Anderson, chief of engrg.

*WRLI-FM— July 1999: 91.3 mhz; 10 kw. Ant 312 ft TL: N40 56 05 W72 23 15. Hrs open:
Rebroadcasts WPKT(FM) Meriden 100%.
1049 Asylum Ave., Hartford, CT, 06105. Phone: (860) 278-5310. Fax: (860) 244-9624.E-mail: info@wnpr.org Web Site:www.wnpr.org Licensee: Connecticut Public Television & Radio. Natl. Network: NPR, PRI, . Format: News/talk. ◆Jerry Franklin, CEO, pres; Kim Grehn, VP & gen mgr.

Southold

WBEA(FM)— July 3, 1985: 101.7 mhz; 6 kw. Ant 283 ft TL: N40 52 10 W72 34 37. Stereo. Hrs open: 24 Box 7162, Amagansett, 11930. Phone: (631) 267-7800. Fax: (631) 267-1018.E-mail: generaloffice @libroadcasting.com Web Site:www.1017blaze.com Licensee: AAA Licensing LLC. Group owner: AAA Entertainment L.L.C. (acq 8-22-2000; $2.75 million with WBAZ(FM) Bridgehampton). Population served: 1,500,000 Natl. Network: Westwood One, . Haley, Bader & Potts. Format: Hip hop. Target aud: 25-54; adults with active lifestyles. Spec prog: Health talk, financial news, CNN news. ◆Don Maguire, pres; Hedy Krebs-DeMaio, gen mgr; Steve Harper, opns mgr, gen sls mgr & progmg dir.

Southport

WOKN(FM)— Sept 15, 1993: 99.5 mhz; 1.25 kw. 485 ft TL: N42 07 49 W76 47 23. Hrs open: 24 1705 Lake St., Elmira, 14901. Phone: (607) 733-5626. Fax: (607) 733-4040. Fax: (607) 733-5627. Web Site:www.995wokn.com Licensee: Pembrook Pines Elmira Ltd. Group owner: Pembrook Pines Media Group. Population served: 350,000 Natl. Network: Jones Radio Networks, . Bechtel & Cole. Format: Country. News staff: one; News: 2 hrs wkly. Target aud: 18-49; female. ◆Robert J. Pfuntner, CEO & pres; Nancy E. Nicastro, gen mgr; Michael Williams, opns mgr.

Spencer

*WCII(FM)— Oct 1, 1989: 88.5 mhz; 17 kw. 590 ft TL: N42 00 50 W76 15 53. Stereo. Hrs open: 24
Rebroadcasts WCIK(FM) Bath 100%.
Box 506, 7634 Campbell Creek Rd., Bath, 14810. Phone: (607) 776-4151. Fax: (607) 776-6929.E-mail: mail@fln.org Web Site:www.fln.org Licensee: Family Life Ministries Inc. Group owner: Family Life Network Natl. Network: Salem Radio Network, . Hardy, Carey, Chautin & Balkin, LLP . Wire Svc: Metro Weather Service Inc. Format: Christian, inspirational, educ. News staff: 3; News: 14 hrs wkly. Target aud: 30-54; general public. Spec prog: News 14 hrs wkly. ◆Dick Snavely, CFO; Rick Snavely, pres, VP & gen mgr; John Owens, progmg dir; Jim Travis, chief of engrg.

Spring Valley

WRCR(AM)— Sept 15, 1977: 1300 khz; 500 w-D, 83 w-N, DA-2. TL: N41 05 48 W74 00 18. Hrs open: 24 Nanuet Mall, 75 W. Rt. 59, Ste. 2126, Nanuet, 10954. Phone: (845) 624-1313. Fax: (845) 624-1639.E-mail: mail@wrcr.com Web Site:www.wrcr.com Licensee: Alexander Broadcasting Inc. (acq 4-14-2000; $270,000). Population served: 400000 Natl. Network: USA, . Format: Adult contemp, news. News staff: 2; News: 18 hrs wkly. Target aud: 25-54; upscale. ♦Alexander Medakovic, pres & gen mgr; Alexander Madakovic, progmg dir.

Springville

WSPQ(AM)— Apr 20, 1986: 1330 khz; 1 kw-U, DA-2. TL: N42 29 53 W78 41 10. Hrs open: 24 51 Franklin St., 14141. Phone: (716) 592-9500. Fax: (716) 592-9522.E-mail: fredhaier@verizon.net Licensee: Hawk Communications Ltd. (acq 1996). Population served: 400,000 Natl. Network: CNN Radio, ESPN Radio, Motor Racing Net, . Format: Var/Diverse, adult contemp, country, sports. News staff: one; News: 10 hrs wkly. Target aud: 25-54. Spec prog: Farm 5 hrs, relg 2 hrs wkly. ♦Kevin Bower, gen mgr.

Staten Island

WSIA(FM)—Licensed to Staten Island. See New York

Stillwater

WQAR(FM)— Oct 3, 1988: 101.3 mhz; 2.9 kw. 470 ft TL: N43 00 42 W73 41 01. Stereo. Hrs open: 24 100 Saratoga Blvd., Ste. 21, Malta, 12020. Phone: (518) 899-3000. Phone: (518) 899-1013. Fax: (518) 899-3057.E-mail: star1013fm@aol.com Web Site:www.star1013.com Licensee: Anastos Media Group Inc. (group owner; acq 9-4-98; $900,000). Natl. Network: ABC, . Shaw Pittman. Format: Adult contemp. News staff: one; News: 6 hrs wkly. Target aud: 25-54; upscale. Spec prog: Saratoga Forum one hr. ♦Phillip Anastos, pres; Fran Dingeman, gen mgr; John Meaney, stn mgr, opns mgr, news dir; Fran Dingman, gen sls mgr; Amanda Albright, prom dir.

Stony Brook

***WUSB(FM)**— June 27, 1977: 90.1 mhz; 3.6 kw. 531 ft TL: N40 50 32 W73 02 23. Stereo. Hrs open: 24 Union Building, University at Stony Brook, 11794-3263. Phone: (631) 632-6501. Fax: (631) 632-7182.E-mail: info@wusb.org Web Site:www.wusb.org Licensee: State University of New York. Population served: 3,000,000 Dow, Lohnes & Albertson. Wire Svc: AP Format: News/talk, diversified, progsv. News: 20 hrs wkly. Target aud: 18-49; progsv & musically adventurous. Spec prog: Black 12 hrs, Pol one hr, Sp 3 hrs, Chinese one hr, Korean one hr, class 14 hrs, folk 15 hrs, jazz 20 hrs, blues 10 hrs wkly. ♦Norman L. Prusslin, gen mgr; Marko Srdanovic, opns dir.

Sylvan Beach

WWLF-FM— April 1999: 100.3 mhz; 6 kw. Ant 328 ft TL: N43 14 46 W75 46 25. Hrs open: 401 W. Kirkpatrick St., Syracuse, 13204. Phone: (315) 472-0222. Fax: (315) 478-7745.E-mail: programming@movin100.com Web Site:movin100.com Licensee: WOLF Radio Inc. (group owner; (acq 2-28-2002; $350,000). Format: Rhythmic adult contemp. ♦Sam Furco, gen mgr.

Syosset

***WKWZ(FM)**— July 24, 1973: 88.5 mhz; 125 w. 90 ft TL: N40 49 48 W73 28 57. (CP: Ant 259 ft.). Hrs open: 70 Southwoods Rd., 11791. Phone: (516) 364-5745. Phone: (516) 364-5746. Fax: (516) 364-5737.E-mail: BigDave5@aol.com Web Site:www.wkwz.org Licensee: Syosset Central School District. Population served: 400,000 Format: Div. Spec prog: C&W 6 hrs, class 6 hrs, jazz 12 hrs wkly. ♦David C. Favilla, gen mgr; Chris Hoffman, stn mgr; Roy Dippel, chief of engrg.

Syracuse

***WAER(FM)**— Apr 1, 1947: 88.3 mhz; 50 kw. Ant 276 ft TL: N43 02 01 W76 07 53. Stereo. Hrs open: 24 795 Olsrom Ave., 13244-2110. Phone: (315) 443-4021. Fax: (315) 443-2148.E-mail: waer@waer.org Web Site:www.waer.org Licensee: Syracuse University. Population served: 700,000 Natl. Network: NPR, . Arter & Hadden. Format: Jazz, sports, news. News staff: 3; News: 20 hrs wkly. Target aud: 25-49. Spec prog: Gospel 3 hrs, blues 3 hrs, world mus 4 hrs, new age 3 hrs wkly. ♦Joe Lee, gen mgr; Ron Ockert, progmg dir & progmg mgr; Eric Cohen, mus dir.

WAMF(AM)—See Fulton

WAQX-FM—See Manlius

WBBS(FM)—See Fulton

***WCNY-FM**— Dec 4, 1971: 91.3 mhz; 18.6 kw. 740 ft TL: N42 56 42 W76 01 28. Stereo. Hrs open: 5 AM-midnight Box 2400, 13220-2400. Secondary address: 506 Old Liverpool Rd., Liverpool 13088. Phone: (315) 453-2424. Fax: (315) 451-8824.E-mail: wcny-online@wcny.org Web Site:www.wcny.org Licensee: Public Broadcasting Council of Central New York. Population served: 80,000 Natl. Network: NPR, . Dow, Lohnes & Albertson. Format: Class. Target aud: General. Spec prog: Bluegrass 3 hrs, jazz 7 hrs wkly. ♦Colleen Edwards, CFO; Peter Hirsch, mktg dir; Don Dolloff, progmg dir; John Duffy, chief of engrg. Co-owned TV: *WCNY-TV affil

WFBL(AM)— Feb 4, 1922: 1390 khz; 5 kw-U, DA-N. TL: N43 05 30 W76 05 19. Hrs open: Box 1050, Baldwinsville, 13027. Phone: (315) 635-3971. Fax: (315) 635-3490. Web Site:www.wfbl.com Licensee: Buckley Broadcasting of New York LLC. Group owner: Buckley Broadcasting Corp. (acq 11-10-2003; $1.2 million). Format: Talk. ♦Judith C Kelly, VP, gen mgr & stn mgr; Bryan Richards, opns mgr.

WHEN(AM)— Apr 14, 1941: 620 khz; 5 kw-D, 1 kw-N, DA-N. TL: N43 05 35 W76 11 19. Stereo. Hrs open: 24 500 Plum St., Suite 100, 13204. Phone: (315) 472-9797. Fax: (315) 472-1904. Web Site:www.sportsradio620.com Licensee: CC Licenses LLC. Group owner: Clear Channel Communications Inc. (acq 1999). Population served: 179,800 Format: Sports. Spec prog: Syracuse Chiefs, Buffalo Bills, Syracuse Crunch. ♦Joel Delmonico, gen mgr.

***WJPZ-FM**— Jan 30, 1985: 89.1 mhz; 100 w. 120 ft TL: N43 02 01 W76 07 53. Stereo. Hrs open: 24 316 Waverly Ave., 13210. Phone: (315) 443-4689. Phone: (315) 443-2106. Fax: (315) 443-4379.E-mail: info@wjr.net Web Site:www.z89.com Licensee: WJPZ Radio Inc. Gardner, Carton & Douglas. Format: CHR. Target aud: 12-34; women & teenagers. Spec prog: Black 12 hrs, pub service 13 hrs wkly. ♦Geoff Herbert, gen mgr; Scott Purdy, opns VP; Louise Vazquez, dev VP; Joan Kump, prom dir; David McKinley, progmg dir.

WKRL-FM—See North Syracuse

WLTI(FM)— Apr 8, 1996: 105.9 mhz; 4 kw. 200 ft TL: N43 05 23 W76 09 10. Stereo. Hrs open: 24 1064 James St., 13203. Phone: (315) 472-0200. Fax: (315) 478-5625. Web Site:www.lite1059.com Licensee: Citadel Broadcasting Co. Group owner: Citadel Broadcasting Corp. (acq 2000; grpsl). Population served: 536,300 Natl. Network: CBS Radio, . Format: Soft adult contemp. Target aud: 25-54; general. ♦Dan Austin, gen mgr, progmg mgr; Tom Mitchell, opns dir; Angela Moonan, sls dir.

***WMHR(FM)**— Mar 9, 1969: 102.9 mhz; 20 kw. 784 ft TL: N42 58 00 W76 12 01. Stereo. Hrs open: 24 4044 Makyes Rd., 13215. Phone: (315) 469-5051.E-mail: mhn@marshillnetwork.org Web Site:www.marshillnetwork.org Licensee: Mars Hill Broadcasting Co. Inc. dba Mars Hill Network. (group owner) Population served: 1,546,800 Natl. Network: Moody, Salem Radio Network, . Wiley, Rein & Fielding. Wire Svc: AP Format: Christian. News: 6 hrs wkly. Target aud: General; Christian families. Spec prog: Children 11 hrs wkly. ♦Clayton Roberts, pres; Chris Tetta, CFO, mus dir; Jeremy Miller, VP, news dir; Wayne Taylor, gen mgr; Valerie Smith, traf mgr.

WNSS(AM)— 1946: 1260 khz; 5 kw-U, DA-2. TL: N43 09 10 W76 11 35. Hrs open: 24 Prog sep from FM 1064 James St., 13203. Phone: (315) 472-0200. Fax: (315) 478-5625. Web Site:www.espnradio1260.com Licensee: Citadel Broadcasting Co. Population served: 536,300 Natl. Network: ESPN Radio, . Format: Sports/Talk. Target aud: 25-54; men. ♦Dan Austin, gen mgr; Angela Moonan, sls dir; Tom Mitchell, progmg dir.

WNTQ(FM)— 1956: 93.1 mhz; 97 kw. 659 ft TL: N42 56 47 W76 01 32. Stereo. Hrs open: 24 1064 James St., 13203. Phone: (315) 472-0200. Fax: (315) 478-5625. Web Site:www.93q.com Licensee: Citadel Broadcasting Co. Group owner: Citadel Broadcasting Corp. (acq 4-26-01; grpsl). Population served: 536,300 Natl. Rep: McGavren Guild,. Format: CHR. Target aud: 25-54; women. ♦Dan Austin, gen mgr; Angela Moonan, sls dir; Janice Cole, progmg dir; Dave Edwards, chief of engrg; Elizabeth Marcy, traf mgr.

WOLF(AM)— Apr 27, 1940: 1490 khz; 620 w-D, 750 w-N, DA-D. TL: N43 03 30 W76 10 00. (CP: 1510 khz. TL: N42 57 42 W76 06 13). Stereo. Hrs open: 24 401 W. Kirkpatrick, 13204. Phone: (315) 472-0222. Fax: (315) 478-7745.E-mail: wolfam/fm@aol.com Web Site:www.radiodisney.com Licensee: WOLF Radio Inc. (group owner; (acq 10-5-82). Population served: 695,000 Natl. Network: Radio Disney, . James L. Oyster. Format: Children. ♦Sam Furco, gen mgr & opns dir.

***WRVD(FM)**— June 1, 1999: 90.3 mhz; 280 w. Ant 43 ft TL: N43 02 27 W76 08 22. Stereo. Hrs open: 24
Rebroadcasts WRVO(FM) Oswego 100%.
c/o WRVO(FM), Lanigan Hall, State Univ. College, Oswego, 13126. Phone: (315) 312-3690. Fax: (315) 312-3174.E-mail: feedback@wrvo.fm Web Site:wrvo.fm Licensee: State University of New York. Population served: 350,163 Natl. Network: NPR, . Format: News/talk, old time radio. News staff: 4; News: 140 hrs wkly. Target aud: 35-54. ♦John E. Krauss, gen mgr; Matt Seuert, dev dir; Fred Vigeant, progmg dir; Jeff Windsor, chief of engrg.

WSEN(AM)—See Baldwinsville

WSIV(AM)—(East Syracuse, Dec 6, 1955: 1540 khz; 1 kw-D. TL: N43 05 40 W76 02 00. (CP: 1.5 kw-D, 57 w-N). Hrs open: 24 7095 Myers Rd., East Syracuse, 13057. Phone: (315) 656-2231. Phone: (315) 956-2250. Fax: (315) 656-2259.E-mail: wvoaradio@msn.com Licensee: CRAM Communications L.L.C. (acq 1-6-97; $900,000 with WVOA(FM) DeRuyter). Population served: 350,000 Format: Christian, relg, Black gospel, music. Spec prog: Black 20 hrs, Gospel music. ♦Sam Furco, CEO; James Wall, gen mgr; Suzanne Anderson, stn mgr; Allen Elson, opns mgr; Keith Copes, gen sls mgr.

WSYR(AM)— 1922: 570 khz; 5 kw-U, DA-2. TL: N42 59 13 W76 09 09. Stereo. Hrs open: 24 Bridgewater Pl., 500 Plum St., 13204. Phone: (315) 472-9797. Fax: (315) 472-1904. Web Site:www.sybercuse.com Licensee: CC Licenses LLC. Group owner: Clear Channel Communications Inc. Population served: 600,000 Natl. Network: PRI, . Format: Full service, news/talk. News: 35 hrs wkly. Target aud: 25-54. ♦Joel Delmonico, gen mgr.

WTLA(AM)—See North Syracuse

WVOA-FM—See DeRuyter

WWHT(FM)— Sept 1, 1958: 107.9 mhz; 50 kw. Ant 490 ft TL: N42 57 21 W76 06 36. Stereo. Hrs open: 24 500 Plum St., Suite 100, 13204. Phone: (315) 472-9797. Fax: (315) 472-1904. Web Site:www.hot1079.com Licensee: CC Licenses LLC. Format: CHR.

WYYY(FM)— 1946: 94.5 mhz; 100 kw. 650 ft TL: N42 56 40 W76 07 08. Stereo. Hrs open: Prog sep from AM Bridgewater Pl., 500 Plum St., 13204. Phone: (315) 472-9797. Fax: (315) 472-1904. Web Site:www.sybercuse.com Format: Adult contemp.

Ticonderoga

***WANC(FM)**— Sept 6, 1982: 103.9 mhz; 1.55 kw. 380 ft TL: N43 49 55 W73 24 28. Stereo. Hrs open: 24
Rebroadcasts WAMC-FM Albany 100%.
Box 66600, 318 Central Ave., Albany, 12206-6600. Phone: (518) 465-5233. Phone: (800) 323-9262. Fax: (518) 432-6974.E-mail: mail@wamc.org Web Site:www.wamc.org Licensee: WAMC. Group owner: WAMC/Northeast Public Radio (acq 8-90; $400,000; 8-13-90). Natl. Network: NPR, PRI, . Dow, Lohnes & Albertson. Wire Svc: AP Format: News, Talk. Target aud: General. Spec prog: Folk 6 hrs, jazz 17 hrs wkly. ♦Alan Chartock, CEO, chmn, pres; David Galletly, VP.

WIPS(AM)— July 1955: 1250 khz; 1 kw-D. TL: N43 51 16 W73 23 24. Hrs open: 6 AM-sunset PO Box 600, Crown Point, 12928-0600. Phone: (518) 597-9477. Phone: (518) 597-3201. Fax: (518) 597-9479.E-mail: info@wipsradio.com Web Site:www.wipsradio.com Licensee: BisiBlue L.L.C. (acq 3-17-2004; $93,000). Population served: 5,000 Format: Oldies. News staff: one; News: 24 hrs wkly. Target aud: 25-54. Spec prog: Farm 6 hrs wkly. ♦Gregg Trask, pres, gen mgr; Patricia Knapp, chmn & CFO.

Troy

WFLY(FM)— August 1948: 92.3 mhz; 17 kw. 850 ft TL: N42 38 16 W73 59 55. Hrs open: 24 6 Johnson Rd., Latham, 12210. Phone: (518) 786-6600. Fax: (518) 786-6610. Licensee: 6 Johnson Road Licenses Inc. Group owner: Pamal Broadcasting Ltd. (acq 10-19-2001; grpsl). Population served: 220,000 Natl. Network: ABC, . Natl. Rep: McGavren Guild,. Format: CHR. News staff: one; News: 5 hrs wkly. Target aud: 18-49. ♦Dan Austin, gen mgr; Kevin Callahan, opns mgr; Suzette Anthony, sls VP; Justin Chabot, prom dir; Terry O'Donnell, progmg dir; Mike Carey, news dir.

WGNA-FM—See Albany

WHAZ(AM)— August 1922: 1330 khz; 1 kw-U. TL: N42 46 35 W73 41 10. Hrs open: 24 30 Park Ave., Cohoes, 12047-3330. Phone: (518) 237-1330. Fax: (518) 235-4468.E-mail: events@aliveradionetwork.com Web Site:www.whaz.com Licensee: Capital Media Corp. (group owner; (acq 9-24-87). Population served: 1,000,000 Format: Adult Christian. Target aud: 25-75; young to old. Spec prog: Gospel, rel. ♦Paul F. Lotters, pres, gen mgr; Steven L. Klob, opns dir & dev dir; Rex Gregory, progmg dir; Bill Rosenfeld, chief of engrg.

WOFX(AM)— Apr 15, 1940: 980 khz; 5 kw-U, DA-N. TL: N42 46 56 W73 50 07. Hrs open: River Hill Ctr., 1203 Troy Schenectady Rd., Suite 201, Latham, 12110. Phone: (518) 452-4800. Fax: (518) 452-4832.E-mail: info@wofx.com Web Site:www.wofx.com Licensee: Capstar TX L.P. Group owner: Clear Channel Communications Inc. (acq 8-30-00; grpsl). Population served: 1,300,000 Natl. Rep: Clear Channel,. Format: Sports talk. Target aud: 18-49. ♦Joseph Hennessy, gen mgr; John Cooper, stn mgr; Kristen Delaney, VP & mktg mgr.

WPYX(FM)—See Albany

***WRPI(FM)**— Nov 1, 1957: 91.5 mhz; 10 kw. 450 ft TL: N42 41 14 W73 42 22. Stereo. Hrs open: 6 AM-2 AM One WRPI Plaza, 12180. Phone: (518) 276-6248. Fax: (518) 276-2360. Web Site:www.wrpi.org Licensee: Rensselaer Polytechnic Institute. Population served: 1,500,725 Format: Div. News: 5 hrs wkly. Target aud: General; open minded, educated listeners. ♦John Corbett, pres; Colin Fredericks, gen mgr.

Trumansburg

WPIE(AM)— Jan 15, 1990: 1160 khz; 5 kw-D, 31 w-N, DA-2. TL: N42 32 42 W76 42 39. Hrs open: 24 1705 Lake St., Elmira, 14901. Phone: (607) 733-5626. Fax: (607) 733-5627.E-mail: ppinesmedia1@stny.rr.com Web Site:wpieradio.com Licensee: Pembrook Pines Ithaca Ltd. Group owner: Pembrook Pines Media Group (acq 3-3-93; $150,000;3-22-93). Population served: 250,000 Bechtel & Cole. Format: Sports. News staff: one; News: 18 hrs wkly. Target aud: 25-54; mature, upscale adults. ♦Bob Michaels, opns dir; Robert J. Pfuntner, pres, gen mgr & dev dir.

Tupper Lake

WRGR(FM)— Feb 29, 1980: 102.1 mhz; 140 w. Ant 1,446 ft TL: N44 09 35 W74 28 34. Stereo. Hrs open: 24
Rebroadcasts WLPW(FM) Lake Placid 100%.
Box 211, Saranac Lake, 12983-0211. Phone: (518) 891-1544. Fax: (518) 891-1545.E-mail: sales@wnbz.com Web Site:www.wnbz.com Licensee: Radio Lake Placid Inc. Group owner: Mountain Communications (acq 2003; grpsl). Population served: 20,000 Natl. Network: ABC, . Wire Svc: UPI Format: Classic rock, adult contemp. News staff: 2; News: 2 hrs wkly. Target aud: 25-54; men. Spec prog: Relg one hr, big band 2 hrs wkly. ♦Ted Morgan, pres & gen mgr.

***WXLS(FM)**—Not on air, target date: unknown: 88.3 mhz; 110 w. Ant 1,420 ft TL: N44 09 34 W74 28 34. Hrs open: North Country Public Radio, St. Lawrence University, Canton, 13617. Phone: (315) 229-5356. Fax: (315) 229-5373. Web Site:www.ncpr.org Licensee: The St. Lawrence University. ♦Ellen Rocco, gen mgr.

Utica

WFRG-FM— Oct 10, 1948: 104.3 mhz; 100 kw. Ant 500 ft TL: N43 03 27 W75 25 04. Stereo. Hrs open: 9418 River Rd., Marcy, 13403. Phone: (315) 768-9500. Fax: (315) 736-3311.E-mail: info@bigfrog104.com Web Site:www.bigfrog104.com Licensee: Regent Licensee of Utica/Rome Inc. (acq 11-5-99; grpsl). Population served: 264,900 Format: Country. Target aud: 25-54. ♦Mary Jo Beach, gen mgr; Tracy DeCarr, gen sls mgr; Bill McAdams, progmg dir; Dave Andrews, news dir.

WIBX(AM)— Dec 5, 1925: 950 khz; 5 kw-U, DA-1. TL: N43 06 16 W75 20 20. Hrs open: 24 9418 State Rt. 49, Marcy, 13403. Phone: (315) 768-9500. Fax: (315) 736-0720. Web Site:www.wibx950.com Licensee: Regent Licensee of Utica/Rome Inc. Group owner: Regent Communications Inc. (acq 2-11-2000; grpsl). Population served: 91,611 Natl. Network: CBS, . Format: News/talk, sports. News staff: 5. Target aud: 35-64; middle to upper income adults. Spec prog: Pol 3 hrs, farm 14 hrs wkly. ♦Tom Jacobson, gen mgr & opns dir.

WIXT(AM)—See Little Falls

WKLL(FM)—(Frankfort, Feb 12, 1990: 94.9 mhz; 50 kw. 276 ft TL: N43 03 26 W75 07 24. (CP: 34 kw, ant 567 ft.). Hrs open: 39 Kellogg Rd., New Hartford, 13413. Phone: (315) 797-1330. Fax: (315) 738-1073.E-mail: info@krock.com Web Site:www.krock.com Licensee: Galaxy Communications L.P. Group owner: Route 81 Radio LLC (acq 4-6-2000; grpsl). Natl. Network: ABC, . Natl. Rep: D & R Radio,. Format: Modern rock. ♦Beth Coughlin, gen mgr; Paul Sznal, opns mgr; Mimi Griswald, progmg VP.

***WKVU(FM)**— July 11, 1994: 100.7 mhz; 1.2 w. 551 ft TL: N43 09 12 W75 09 32. Hrs open: 24 1017 Higby Rd., New Hartford, 13413. Phone: (315) 793-1007. Fax: (315) 793-1044. Web Site:www.klove.com Licensee: Educational Media Foundation. Group owner: EMF Broadcasting (acq 6-7-01; $1.25 million). Natl. Network: K-Love, . Format: Christian music. Target aud: 25-45. ♦Bob Cain, chief of opns.

WLZW(FM)— Jan 1, 1972: 98.7 mhz; 25 kw. Ant 660 ft TL: N43 08 39 W75 10 45. Stereo. Hrs open: 24 9418 State Rt. 49, Marcy, 13403. Phone: (315) 768-9500. Fax: (315) 736-0720. Web Site:www.lite987.com Licensee: Regent Licensee of Utica/Rome Inc. Format: Lite adult contemp. News staff: 6. Target aud: 25-54; middle to upper income & educ levels. ♦Peter Naughton, progmg dir.

WOUR(FM)— June 1967: 96.9 mhz; 16 kw. Ant 790 ft TL: N43 08 46 W75 10 40. Stereo. Hrs open: 39 Kellogg Rd., New Hartford, 13413. Phone: (315) 797-0803. Web Site:www.wour.com Licensee: Galaxy Utica Licensee LLC. (acq 9-21-2007; grpsl). Population served: 91,611 Format: Rock/AOR. Target aud: 25-49; adults. ♦Brian Delaney, gen mgr; Jerry Kraus, prom mgr.

***WPNR-FM**— November 1977: 90.7 mhz; 450 w. 30 ft TL: N43 05 35 W75 16 21. Stereo. Hrs open: c/o Utica College, 1600 Burrstone Rd., 13502. Phone: (315) 792-3066. Phone: (315) 792-3069. Fax: (315) 792-3292. Licensee: Utica College. (acq 9-12-96). Format: Div, urban contemp, AOR. Spec prog: Class 10 hrs, jazz 14 hrs, reggae 5 hrs wkly. ♦Todd Hutton, pres.

WRCK(FM)— Apr 23, 1962: 107.3 mhz; 50 kw. Ant 499 ft TL: N43 08 40 W75 10 32. Stereo. Hrs open: 2351 Sunset Blvd., Suite 170-218, Rocklin, CA, 95765. Phone: (916) 251-1600. Fax: (916) 251-1650. Licensee: Educational Media Foundation. (acq 10-24-2007; $1,224,000). Population served: 8,500 Format: Contemp Christian. ♦Mike Novak, sr VP.

WRNY(AM)—See Rome

***WRUN(AM)**— Apr 24, 1948: 1150 khz; 5 kw-D, 1 kw-N, DA-2. TL: N43 10 31 W75 21 03. Hrs open:
Rebroadcasts WAMC-FM Albany 100%.
318 Central Ave., Albany, 12206. Phone: (518) 465-5233. Fax: (518) 432-6974.E-mail: mail@wamc.org Web Site:www.wamc.org Licensee: WAMC. Group owner: Regent Communications Inc. (acq 7-6-2005; $275,000). Population served: 91,611 Natl. Network: NPR, PRI, . Dow, Lohnes, & Albertson. Wire Svc: AP Format: News/talk. ♦Alan S. Chartock, CEO; David Galletly, VP.

***WRVN(FM)**— Jun 4, 1986: 91.9 mhz; 1.9 kw. Ant -62 ft TL: N43 08 31 W75 13 36. Stereo. Hrs open:
Rebroadcasts WRVO(FM) Oswego 100%.
7060 State Rt. 104, Oswego, 13126. Phone: (315) 312-3690. Fax: (315) 312-3174.E-mail: feedback@wrvo.fm Web Site:www.wrvo.fm Licensee: State University of New York. Population served: 216,000 Natl. Network: NPR, PRI, . Wire Svc: AP Format: News/talk, old time radio. News staff: 3; News: 140 hrs wkly. ♦John E. Krauss, gen mgr; Thomas Herbert, dev dir; Fred Vigeant, progmg dir; Chris Ulanowski, news dir; Jeff Windsor, chief of engrg.

WTLB(AM)— 1946: 1310 khz; 5 kw-D, 500 w-N, DA-2. TL: N43 03 24 W75 16 42. Hrs open: 24 39 Kellegg Rd., New Hartford, 13413. Phone: (315) 797-1330. Fax: (315) 738-1073.E-mail: info@krock.com Licensee: Galaxy Communications L.P. Group owner: Route 81 Radio LLC (acq 4-6-2000; grpsl). Population served: 25,000 Format: Btfl mus, MOR. News: one hr wkly. Target aud: 55 plus. ♦Ed Levine, pres; Jason Passante, gen mgr; Dave Doughty, chief of engrg.

WUMX(FM)—See Rome

***WUNY(FM)**— Oct 30, 1985: 89.5 mhz; 6.3 kw. 777 ft TL: N43 08 38 W75 10 40. Stereo. Hrs open: 5 AM-midnight Box 2400, 506 Old Liverpool Rd., Syracuse, 13220-2400. Phone: (315) 453-2424. Fax: (315) 451-8824.E-mail: wcny—online@wcny.org Web Site:www.wcny.org Licensee: Public Broadcasting Council of Central New York. Natl. Network: NPR, . Haley, Bader & Potts. Format: Class. Target aud: General. Spec prog: Bluegrass 3 hrs, jazz 7 hrs wkly. ♦Colleen Edwards, CFO; Peter Hirsch, mktg dir.

WUTQ(AM)— Jan 29, 1962: 1550 khz; 1 kw-D. TL: N43 06 48 W75 15 25. Stereo. Hrs open: 24
Rebroadcasts WRNY(AM) Rome 100%.
Mayro Bldg., 239 Genesee St., 13501. Phone: (315) 797-0803. Fax: (315) 797-7813. Licensee: Roser Communications Network Inc. Group owner: Clear Channel Communications Inc. (acq 10-24-2007; grpsl). Population served: 91,611 Natl. Network: Westwood One, . Natl. Rep: Christal,. Latham & Watkins. Format: Sports. Target aud: 35 plus; 60% female, 40% male. Spec prog: It 2 hrs, Pol 4 hrs wkly. ♦Brian Delaney, gen mgr; Gene Conte, progmg dir, traf mgr; Jack Moran, news dir; Joe Petro, chief of engrg.

Valhalla

***WARY(FM)**— Oct 3, 1973: 88.1 mhz; 171 w. 403 ft TL: N41 04 13 W73 47 25. Hrs open: 10 AM-10 PM (M-F) 75 Grasslands Rd., 10595. Phone: (914) 606-6752. Phone: (914) 606-6753. Fax: (914) 606-6260.E-mail: radprime1@aol.com Licensee: Westchester Community College. Population served: 500,000 Garvey, Schubert & Barer. Format: AOR. Target aud: 12-24. Spec prog: Pub svc 10 hrs wkly. ♦Radames Ocasio, gen mgr.

Vestal

WMXW(FM)— June 2, 1989: 103.3 mhz; 6 kw. 1,014 ft TL: N42 03 22 W75 56 39. (CP: 592 w). Stereo. Hrs open: 24 320 N. Jensen Rd., 13850-2111. Phone: (607) 584-5800. Fax: (607) 584-5900. Licensee: CC Licenses LLC. Group owner: Clear Channel Communications Inc. (acq 9-2000; grpsl). Natl. Rep: Katz Radio,. Format: Spectrum adult contemp. News staff: one. Target aud: 25-54. ♦Dave Lozzi, progmg dir & news dir.

Voorheesville

WAJZ(FM)— May 24, 1991: 96.3 mhz; 6 kw. 1,118 ft TL: N42 37 01 W74 00 46. Stereo. Hrs open: 24 6 Johnson Rd., Latham, 12110. Phone: (518) 786-6600. Phone: (518) 786-6620. Fax: (518) 786-6610.E-mail: info@jamz963.com Web Site:www.jamz963.com Licensee: 6 Johnson Road Licenses Inc. Group owner: Pamal Broadcasting Ltd. (acq 10-19-2001; grpsl). Population served: 73,200 Natl. Rep: McGavren Guild,. Format: Rhymthic CHR. News staff: 2; News: 3 hrs wkly. Target aud: 18-49. Spec prog: Relg one hr wkly. ♦Dan Austin, gen mgr; Suzette Anthony, sls VP; Peter Baumann, gen sls mgr; J.D. Reoman, mktg dir; Christa Gardner, prom dir; Rob Torres, progmg dir; Mike Carey, news dir.

Walton

WDLA(AM)— May 30, 1951: 1270 khz; 5 kw-D, 100 w-N. TL: N42 08 08 W75 04 52. Hrs open: Box 58, Rt. 206, 13856. Phone: (607) 865-4321. Fax: (607) 865-4189.E-mail: wdla@frontiernet.net Licensee: Double O Central New York Corp. (group owner; (acq 10-22-2004; grpsl). Population served: 44,000 Format: Timeless Favorites. Target aud: 28-55; general. Spec prog: When Radio Was. ♦George Wells, gen mgr; Donald L. Perkins, opns.

WDLA-FM— Nov 16, 1973: 92.1 mhz; 690 w. 656 ft TL: N42 08 10 W75 04 48. Hrs open: Box 58, Rt. 206, 13856. Phone: (607) 865-4321.E-mail: info@wdla.com

Warrensburg

WKBE(FM)— 1990: 100.3 mhz; 1.45 kw. 1,312 ft TL: N43 25 12 W73 45 39. Hrs open: 24 6 Johnson Rd., Latham, 12110. Phone: (518) 786-6600. Fax: (518) 786-6610. Licensee: 6 Johnson Road Licenses Inc. Group owner: Pamal Broadcasting Ltd. (acq 10-9-2001). Format: CHR. News staff: one; News: 10 hrs wkly. Target aud: 18-34; women. ♦Bill Hunt, gen mgr.

Warsaw

WCJW(AM)— May 16, 1973: 1140 khz; 2.5 kw-D, DA. TL: N42 43 35 W78 06 47. Hrs open: Sunrise-sunset Box 251, 3258 Merchant Rd., 14569. Phone: (585) 786-8131. Fax: (585) 786-2241.E-mail: wcjw@wcjw.com Web Site:www.wcjw.com Licensee: Lloyd Lane Inc. (acq 9-1-84). Population served: 750,000 Natl. Network: USA, . Rgnl rep: Regional Reps Format: Country. News staff: one; News: 20 hrs wkly. Target aud: 25-54; adults. Spec prog: Farm 11 hrs wkly. ♦Lloyd Lane, pres & gen mgr; Lee Richey, progmg dir; Jenny Snow, news dir.

***WCOU(FM)**— Dec 14, 1992: 88.3 mhz; 11 kw. Ant 535 ft TL: N42 49 36 W78 12 25. Stereo. Hrs open:
Rebroadcasts WCIK(FM) Bath 100%.
Box 506, Bath, 14810. Secondary address: 7634 Campbell Creek Rd., Bath 14810. Phone: (607) 776-4151. Fax: (607) 776-6929.E-mail: mail@fln.org Web Site:www.fln.org Licensee: Family Life Ministries Inc. Group owner: Family Life Network Natl. Network: Salem Radio Network, . Hardy, Carey, Chautin & Balkin, LLP. Wire Svc: Metro Weather Service Inc. Format: Contemp Christian. News staff: 3; News:

14 hrs wkly. Target aud: 30-54; general. ◆Dick Snavely, CFO; Rick Snavely, pres, VP & gen mgr; John Owens, progmg dir; Jim Travis, chief of engrg.

Warwick

WTBQ(AM)— July 24, 1969: 1110 khz; 500 w-D (non-directional). TL: N41 16 51 W74 21 46. Hrs open: Sunrise-sunset 62 N. Main St., Florida, 10921. Phone: (845) 651-1110. Fax: (845) 651-1025.E-mail: am1110@magiccarpet.com Web Site:www.wtbq.com Licensee: FST Broadcasting Corp. (acq 7-94; $150,000). Population served: 500,000 Natl. Network: ABC, Jones Radio Networks, . William D. Silva. Format: Oldies, talk. News staff: 2; News: 10 hrs wkly. Target aud: 24-55; affluent Orange County-New York City commuters. Spec prog: Folk one hr, Irish 2 hrs wkly. ◆Frank Truatt, pres, gen mgr, opns mgr; Rob McLean, gen sls mgr; Logan Moscovitz, progmg dir.

Waterloo

WNYR-FM— Apr 19, 1989: 98.5 mhz; 3.2 kw. 446 ft TL: N42 48 22 W76 50 47. Stereo. Hrs open: 24 3568 Lenox Rd., Geneva, 14456. Phone: (315) 781-7000. Fax: (315) 781-7700. Web Site:www.fingerlakes.com Licensee: Lake Country Broadcasting. Population served: 325,000 James L. Oyster. Format: Adult contemp. News staff: one; News: 5 hrs wkly. Target aud: 25-54. ◆George Kimble, pres; Alan Bishop, VP, gen mgr; Mike Smith, opns mgr, progmg dir; Paula Triplett, gen sls mgr; Ted Baker, news dir.

Watertown

WATN(AM)— Feb 3, 1941: 1240 khz; 1 kw-U. TL: N43 58 49 W75 56 12. Hrs open: 24 199 Wealtha Ave., 13601. Phone: (315) 782-1240. Fax: (315) 782-0312.E-mail: blade@theborder.com Licensee: Community Broadcasters LLC. (group owner; (acq 2-8-2007; grpsl). Population served: 120,000 Natl. Rep: Roslin,. Format: Talk. ◆James L. Leven, pres; David W. Mance, gen mgr; Todd Dalesandro, opns dir.

WCIZ-FM— Aug 25, 1986: 93.3 mhz; 6 kw. Ant 328 ft TL: N43 57 23 W75 50 45. Stereo. Hrs open: 24 134 Mullin St., 13601. Phone: (315) 788-0790. Fax: (315) 788-4379.E-mail: eliva.gaines@smgny.com Web Site:www.production@790wtny.com Licensee: Stephens Media Group-Watertown LLC. Format: Classic hits. News staff: 3; News: 2 hrs wkly. Target aud: 35-54.

WFRY-FM— Nov 22, 1968: 97.5 mhz; 100 kw. Ant 285 ft TL: N43 57 23 W75 50 45. Stereo. Hrs open: 134 Mullin St., 13601. Phone: (315) 788-0790. Fax: (315) 788-4379.E-mail: eliva.gaines@smgny.com Web Site:www.froggy97.com Licensee: Stephens Media Group-Watertown LLC. Format: Country. ◆Matt Raisman, progmg dir; Annie Croakly, disc jockey.

*WJNY(FM)— July 24, 1986: 90.9 mhz; 7.09 kw. 449 ft TL: N43 51 44 W75 43 40. Stereo. Hrs open: 5 AM-midnight
Rebroadcasts WCNY-FM Syracuse.
Box 2400, Syracuse, 13220-2400. Secondary address: 506 Old Liverpool Pl., Syracuse 13220. Phone: (315) 453-2424. Fax: (315) 451-8824.E-mail: wcny-online@wcny.org Web Site:www.wcny.org Licensee: Public Broadcasting Council of Central New York Inc. Natl. Network: NPR, . Haley, Bader & Potts. Format: Class. Spec prog: Bluegrass 3 hrs, jazz 5 hrs wkly. ◆Coleen Edwards, CEO, CFO; Peter Hirsch, mktg dir.

*WKWV(FM)— June 26, 2000: 90.1 mhz; 400 w. Ant 679 ft TL: N43 57 15 W75 43 45. Stereo. Hrs open: 24
Rebroadcasts KLVR(FM) Santa Rosa, CA 100%.
2351 Sunset Blvd., Suite 170-218, Rocklin, CA, 95765. Phone: (916) 251-1600. Fax: (916) 251-1650. Web Site:www.klove.com Licensee: Educational Media Foundation. (acq 1-13-2006; $300,000). Population served: 130,000 Natl. Network: K-Love, . Format: Contemp Christian. ◆Richard Jenkins, pres; Mike Novak, VP; Keith Whipple, dev dir; David Pierce, progmg mgr; Ed Lenane, news dir; Sam Wallington, engrg dir; Karen Johnson, news rptr.

WNER(AM)— Nov 2, 1959: 1410 khz; 3.5 kw-D, 58 w-N. TL: N43 56 47 W75 56 52. Hrs open: 134 Mullin St., 13601. Phone: (315) 788-0790. Fax:(315) 788-4379.E-mail: eliva.gaines@smgny.com Licensee: Stephens Media Group-Watertown LLC. Group owner: Regent Communications Inc. Population served: 30,787 Natl. Network: ESPN Radio, . Format: Sports. Target aud: 35-64. ◆Don Wagner, pres, CFO; Lance Thomas, progmg dir.

*WRVJ(FM)— July 1, 1989: 91.7 mhz; 1.6 kw. Ant 443 ft TL: N43 51 44 W75 43 40. Stereo. Hrs open: 24
Rebroadcasts WRVO(FM) Oswego 100%.
7060 State Rt. 104, Oswego, 13126. Phone: (315) 312-3690. Fax:

(315) 312-3174.E-mail: feedback@wrvo.fm Web Site:wrvd.fm Licensee: State University of New York. Population served: 71,650 Natl. Network: NPR, PRI, . Wire Svc: AP Format: News/talk, old time radio. News staff: 4; News: 140 hrs wkly. Target aud: 25-55. ◆John E. Krauss, gen mgr; Matt Seubert, dev dir; Fred Vigeant, progmg dir; Chris Ulanowski, news dir; Jeff Windsor, chief of engrg.

*WSLJ(FM)— 1992: 88.9 mhz; 200 w. 454 ft TL: N43 57 23 W75 50 28. Hrs open: 24
Rebroadcasts WSLU(FM) Canton 100%.
St. Lawrence Univ., Canton, 13617. Phone: (315) 229-5356. Fax: (315) 229-5373.E-mail: info@ncpr.org Web Site:www.ncpr.org Licensee: St. Lawrence University. Donald E. Martin. Format: Eclectic public radio. News staff: 2; News: 35 hrs wkly. Target aud: General. ◆Ellen Rocco, gen mgr; Shelly Pike, chief of opns; Sandra Demarest, dev dir; Jacqueline Sauter, progmg dir; Martha Foley, news dir; Robert Sauter, chief of engrg.

WTNY(AM)— Apr 29, 1941: 790 khz; 1 kw-U, DA-N. TL: N43 56 44 W75 56 54. Stereo. Hrs open: 24 134 Mullin St., 13601. Phone: (315) 788-0790. Fax: (315) 788-4379.E-mail: eliva.gaines@smgny.com Web Site:www.production@790wtny.com Licensee: Stephens Media Group-Watertown LLC. Group owner: Regent Communications Inc. Population served: 50,000 Natl. Network: CBS, . Taylor & Powell LLC. Format: News. News staff: 3; News: 20 hrs wkly. Target aud: 25 plus. Spec prog: Farm 3 hrs wkly. ◆Don Wagner, CFO, gen mgr; Lance Thomas, progmg dir.

Watervliet

WUAM(AM)— Mar 23, 1964: 900 khz; 400 w-D, 70 w-N. TL: N42 41 21 W73 47 37. Hrs open: 24 100 Saratoga Village Blvd., Sutie 21, Malta, 12020. Phone: (518) 899-3000. Fax: (518) 899-3057.E-mail: wabymoon@aol.com Web Site:www.capitalnews9.com Licensee: Anastos Media Group Inc. (group owner; (acq 9-99; $100,000). Population served: 170,000 Gammon & Grange. Format: News. Target aud: 25 plus. ◆Fran Dingman, gen mgr, gen sls mgr; Fran Dingham, prom dir; John H. Meaney, stn mgr, opns dir & news dir.

Watkins Glen

WNGZ(FM)—See Montour Falls

WRCE(AM)— June 22, 1968: 1490 khz; 400 w-U. TL: N42 21 11 W76 52 13. Hrs open: 2205 College Ave., Elmira, 14903. Secondary address: 1685 Four Mile Dr., Williamsport, PA 17701. Phone: (607) 732-4400. Fax: (607) 732-7774. Licensee: Chemung County Radio Inc. Group owner: Backyard Broadcasting LLC (acq 12-1-2002; grpsl). Population served: 16,700 Natl. Rep: D & R Radio,. Format: Country. Target aud: 20-49; baby boomers. ◆Margaret Tollner, gen mgr; Scott Free, opns mgr; Brian Povancher, gen sls mgr.

*WRFI(FM)—Not on air, target date: unknown: 91.9 mhz; 1.3 kw. Ant 108 ft TL: N42 24 16 W76 54 56. Hrs open: c/o Garvey Schubert Barer, 1000 Potomac St. N.W., 5th Fl., Washington, DC, 20007-3501. Phone: (202) 965-7880. Fax: (202) 965-1729. Licensee: Ithaca Community Radio Inc. ◆Diane Cohen, chmn; John Crigler, gen mgr.

Waverly

WATS(AM)—See Sayre, PA

WAVR(FM)— October 1974: 102.1 mhz; 4.1 kw. Ant 400 ft TL: N42 03 48 W76 31 28. Stereo. Hrs open:
Rebroadcasts WATS(AM) Sayre 100%.
204 Desmond St., Sayre, PA, 18840. Phone: (570) 888-7745. Fax: (570) 888-9005.E-mail: wats.wavr@cqservices.com Web Site:www.cyber-quest.com/watsvavr Licensee: Wats Broadcasting Inc. (acq 10-28-86). Format: Adult contemp. Target aud: 25-54; upscale bedroom community. ◆Charles C. Carver, pres, gen mgr; Meade T. Murtland, stn mgr.

Webster

*WFRW(FM)— October 1988: 88.1 mhz; 8.5 kw. 337 ft TL: N43 04 18 W77 05 35. Stereo. Hrs open: 24 117 C E Miller St., Newark, 14513. Phone: (315) 331-7482. Fax: (410) 268-0931.E-mail: info@familyradio.com Web Site:www.familyradio.com Licensee: Family Stations Inc. (group owner) Population served: 1,000,000 Format: Relg, educ. News: 4 hrs wkly. Target aud: General. Spec prog: Class 2 hrs wkly. ◆Harold Camping, pres & gen mgr.

WLGZ-FM— Feb 15, 1993: 102.7 mhz; 6 kw. Ant 328 ft TL: N43 10 14 W77 40 23. Hrs open: 24 2494 Browncroft Blvd., Rochester, 14625. Phone: (585) 264-1027. Fax: (585) 264-2165.E-mail: info@legend1027.com

Web Site:legends1027.com Licensee: Kimtron Inc. Group owner: Crawford Broadcasting Co. (acq 11-25-92; $950,000; 12-21-92). Format: Christian, talk. ◆Mark Shuttleworth, progmg dir; Brian Cunningham, chief of engrg.

*WMHN(FM)— Feb 29, 1988: 89.3 mhz; 1 kw. 75 ft TL: N43 13 45 W77 26 52. Stereo. Hrs open: 24
Rebroadcasts WMHR(FM) Syracuse 99%.
4044 Makyes Rd., Syracuse, 13215. Phone: (315) 469-5051.E-mail: mhn@marshillnetwork.org Web Site:www.marshillnetwork.org Licensee: Mars Hill Broadcasting Co. Inc. (group owner) Population served: 1,000,000 Natl. Network: Moody, Salem Radio Network, . Wiley, Rein & Fielding. Wire Svc: AP Format: Christian. News: 13 hrs wkly. Christian families. Spec prog: Children 11 hrs wkly. ◆Clayton Roberts, pres; Wayne Taylor, gen mgr & opns mgr; Chris Tetta, progmg dir; Jeremy Miller, news dir; Valerie Smith, traf mgr.

Wellsville

WJQZ(FM)— Feb 3, 1986: 103.5 mhz; 3 kw. 466 ft TL: N42 09 26 W77 55 26. Stereo. Hrs open: Prog sep from AM 82 Railroad Ave., 14895. Phone: (585) 593-6070. Fax: (585) 593-6212.E-mail: wjqzradio@yahoo.com Licensee: DBM Communications Inc. Format: Oldies. Target aud: 25-54. ◆Robert Mangels, progmg dir.

WLSV(AM)— Oct 31, 1955: 790 khz; 1 kw-D, 41 w-N. TL: N42 04 37 W77 55 47. Hrs open: 82 Railroad Ave., 14895. Phone: (585) 593-6070. Fax: (585) 593-6212.E-mail: wjqzradio@yahoo.com Licensee: DBM Communications Inc. (acq 8-21-98; $850,000 with co-located FM). Population served: 336,600 Baraff, Koerner & Olender. Format: Country. Target aud: General. ◆Richard Mangels, pres; Bob Mangels, news dir.

WQRW(FM)— Feb 14, 2007: 93.5 mhz; 1.1 kw. Ant 768 ft TL: N42 11 25 W77 49 17. Hrs open: 74 Main St., Hornell, 14843. Phone: (607) 281-1935. Fax: (607) 281-1936.E-mail: warw@93radioyahoo.com Licensee: Pembrook Pines Mass Media N.A. Corp. Format: Bright adult contemp. ◆Robert J. Pfuntner, pres.

Westhampton

WBON(FM)— Nov 18, 1993: 98.5 mhz; 950 w. Ant 525 ft TL: N40 51 18 W72 46 11. Stereo. Hrs open: 24 3075 Veterans Memorial Hwy., Suite 201, Ronkonkoma, 11779. Phone: (631) 648-2500. Fax: (631) 648-2510.E-mail: johnc@moreyorg.com Web Site:www.lafiestali.com Licensee: Jarad Broadcasting Co. of Westhampton Inc. Group owner: The Morey Organization Inc. Natl. Rep: Christal,. Format: Sp. ◆John Caracciolo, pres & chief of engrg.

Westhampton Beach

WRCN-FM—See Riverhead

Westport

WCLX(FM)— January 1995: 102.9 mhz; 6 kw. Ant 312 ft TL: N44 13 15 W73 24 41. Stereo. Hrs open: 24 Westport Broadcasting, 19 Boas Lane, Wilton, CT, 06897-1031. Secondary address: 3916 Otter Creek Road, Addison, VT 05491-9743. Phone: (203) 762-9425.E-mail: wwdj@optonline.net Web Site:www.wclxfm.com Licensee: Westport Broadcasting. Population served: 150,000 Cohn & Marks. Format: Progressive rock. Target aud: 25-54. ◆Dennis Jackson, CEO; Russ Kinsley, stn mgr; Diane Desmond, progmg dir.

Wethersfield Township

WLKK(FM)— 1948: 107.7 mhz; 19.5 kw. Ant 800 ft TL: N42 37 23 W78 17 16. Stereo. Hrs open: 24 500 Corporate Pkwy., Suite 200, Buffalo, 14226. Phone: (716) 843-0600. Fax: (716) 832-3323. Web Site:www.1077thelake.com Licensee: Entercom Buffalo License LLC. Group owner: Entercom Communications Corp. (acq 5-5-2004; $9 million). Population served: 1,200,000 Natl. Network: Westwood One, . Format: Progsv, classic rock. Target aud: 25-54; adults. ◆Larry Robb, gen mgr; Jeff Surdej, prom mgr; Hank Dole, progmg dir.

White Plains

WFAS(AM)— Aug 11, 1932: 1230 khz; 1 kw-U. TL: N41 01 32 W73 49 39. Hrs open: 365 Secor Rd., Hartsdale, 10530. Phone: (914) 693-2400. Fax: (914) 693-0000. Web Site:www.wfasam.com Licensee: Cumulus Licensing Corp. Group owner: Cumulus Media Inc. (acq 1-23-2002; grpsl). Population served: 785,500 Natl. Network: AP

Radio, . Natl. Rep: McGavren Guild,. Format: MOR. News staff: 2; News: 5 hrs wkly. Target aud: General. Spec prog: Sports progmg 8 hrs wkly. ◆Rod Colarco, gen mgr; Dave Ashton, opns mgr; Bob Barnum, progmg dir; Val Cichorek, traf mgr.

WFAS-FM—(Bronxville, Sept 1, 1947: 103.9 mhz; 600 w. Ant 667 ft TL: N41 01 32 W73 49 39. Stereo. Hrs open: Prog sep from AM 365 Secor Rd., Hartsdale, 10530. Phone: (914) 693-2400. Fax: (914) 693-0000.E-mail: music@wfasfm.com Web Site:www.wfasfm.com Format: Adult contemp. News: one hr wkly. Target aud: 25-54. ◆Robert Bongiardino, gen sls mgr; Misty Wien, prom dir; Dave Ashton, progmg dir; Pam Puso, news dir; Joan Franzino, pub affrs dir; Valencia Cichorek, traf mgr; Jim Killfield, news rptr.

WXPK(FM)—See Briarcliff Manor

Whitehall

WNYV(FM)— July 14, 1990: 94.1 mhz; 3 kw. 328 ft TL: N43 28 37 W73 26 56. Stereo. Hrs open: 5:30 AM-midnight Box 141, 12887. Secondary address: Box 568, East Poultney, VT 05741. Phone: (802) 287-9031. Licensee: Pine Tree Broadcasting. Natl. Rep: Commercial Media Sales,. Format: Adult contemp, country, oldies. News staff: one; News: 3 hrs wkly. Target aud: 25-55; active community oriented, working professional & families. Spec prog: Big band 3 hrs, pub affrs 5 hrs, relg 2 hrs, Pol one hr wkly. ◆Michael Leech, pres; Judith E. Leech, VP, gen mgr.

Whitesboro

WSKS(FM)— 1994: 97.9 mhz; 1.5 kw. 669 ft TL: N43 02 14 W75 26 40. Hrs open: Rebroadcasts WOWB(FM) Little Falls 100%. 185 Genesee St., Suite 1606, Utica, 13501. Phone: (315) 734-9245. Fax: (315) 624-9245. Web Site:www.cnykiss.com Licensee: Roser Communications Network Inc. Group owner: Clear Channel Communications Inc. (acq 10-24-2007; grpsl). Format: CHR, rhythmic. ◆Brian Delaney, gen mgr; Jack Moran, opns mgr; Ken Morrison, prom dir.

Willsboro

WXZO(FM)— 1997: 96.7 mhz; 1 kw. Ant 797 ft TL: N44 24 12 W73 26 02. Hrs open: 24 265 Hegeman Ave., Colchester, VT, 05446. Phone: (802) 654-9335. Fax: (802) 654-9381.E-mail: JamieDennis @ClearChannel.com Web Site:www.wxzofm.com Licensee: Vox AM/FM LLC. Group owner: Clear Channel Communications Inc. (acq 7-25-2008; grpsl). Format: Talk. ◆Tom Barney, gen mgr.

Windham

WRIP(FM)— Aug 5, 1999: 97.9 mhz; 580 w. Ant 1,056 ft TL: N42 17 06 W74 15 52. Stereo. Hrs open: 24 134 South St., P.O. Box 979, 12496-0979. Phone: (518) 734-4747. Fax: (413) 375-4711.E-mail: wrip@mhcable.com Web Site:www.wripfm.com Licensee: Rip Radio LLC. Population served: 125,000 Natl. Network: AP Network News, . Rgnl rep: Local Focus - NYC Cohn & Marks. Format: Adult contemp, full service. News: Approx 6 hrs wkly (net). Target aud: 25 plus; mass appeal. Spec prog: AAA 5 hours, Classic Hits 4 hrs, Jazz 2 hrs, Christian contemp 2 hrs wkly. ◆Dennis Jackson, CEO; Guy Patrick Garraghan, VP.

Windsor

WRRQ(FM)— 2006: 106.7 mhz; 680 w. Ant 643 ft TL: N42 03 10 W75 42 07. Hrs open: 24 101 Main St., Johnson City, 13790. Phone: (607) 772-1005. Fax: (607) 772-2945. Web Site:myq107.com Licensee: Equinox Broadcasting Corp. Natl. Rep: Katz Radio,. Format: Hot A/C, 80's rock. Target aud: 18-45. ◆George Hawras, pres.

Woodside

WWRL(AM)—See New York

Woodstock

WDST(FM)— Apr 29, 1980: 100.1 mhz; 2.9 kw. 308 ft TL: N41 59 04 W74 02 56. Stereo. Hrs open: 24 Box 367, 12498. Secondary address: 293 Tinker St. 12498. Phone: (845) 679-7266. Phone: (845) 679-7600. Fax: (845) 679-5395.E-mail: live@wdst.com Web Site:www.wdst.com Licensee: CHET-5 Broadcasting L.P. (acq 2-12-93; $1.65 million with WKNY(AM) Kingston; 3-8-93). Population served: 300,000 Natl. Network: CBS Radio, . Natl. Rep: Christal,. Shaw

Pittman. Format: Progsv adult rock. News staff: one; News: 5 hrs wkly. Target aud: 24-55; upscale professionals. ◆Gary H. Chetkof, chmn, pres; Greg Gattine, opns dir, progmg dir; Stan Beinstein, gen sls mgr; Ike Phillips, natl sls mgr; Jimmy Buff, progmg dir.

Wurtsboro

WZAD(FM)— Sept 1, 1990: 97.3 mhz; 620 w. Ant 718 ft TL: N41 36 04 W74 33 17. Stereo. Hrs open: 24 Box 416, 2 Pendell Rd., Poughkeepsie, 12602. Phone: (845) 471-1500. Fax: (845) 454-1204. Licensee: Cumulus Licensing Corp. Group owner: Cumulus Media Inc. (acq 1-23-2002; grpsl). Population served: 450,000 Akin, Gump, Strauss, Hauer & Feld. Format: Country. News staff: one; News: 5 hrs wkly. Target aud: 25-54; upscale, educated. ◆Lew Dickie, pres; Charles Benfer, gen mgr.

Yonkers

WVIP(FM)—See New Rochelle

Youngstown

WTOR(AM)— May 6, 1998: 770 khz; 9 kw-D. TL: N43 13 05 W78 56 53. Hrs open: 21700 Northwestern Hwy., Tower 14, Suite 1190, Southfield, MI, 48075. Phone: (716) 754-9514. Fax: (716) 754-9516.E-mail: sima@birach.com Web Site:www.birach.com Licensee: Birach Broadcasting Corp. (group owner; acq 1996; $409,000 less land cost for CP). Format: International mus. Ethnic, Serbian, Lithuanian, Sp, Pol, Macedonian. ◆Sima Birach, CEO, gen mgr & opns mgr.

North Carolina

Aberdeen

WEEB(AM)—See Southern Pines

WMGU(FM)—See Southern Pines

WQNX(AM)— January 1982: 1350 khz; 2.5 kw-D, 28 w-N, DA-2. TL: N35 07 20 W79 24 57. Hrs open: Box 1350, 28315. Phone: (910) 944-1350. Fax: (910) 944-8182.E-mail: qtalk@pinehurst.net Web Site:www.wqnxtalk.com Licensee: Golf Capital Broadcasting Inc. (acq 1987; $128,000; 4-20-87). Format: News/talk. ◆T.O. Calcutt, gen mgr.

Ahoskie

*WBKU(FM)— 2002: 91.7 mhz; 87 kw. Ant 430 ft TL: N36 05 45 W77 12 30. Hrs open: Drawer 3206, Tupelo, MS, 38803. Phone: (662) 844-8888. Fax: (662) 842-6791. Licensee: American Family Association. Group owner: American Family Radio Format: Christian. ◆Marvin Sanders, gen mgr.

WQDK(FM)— Sept 2, 1968: 99.3 mhz; 3 kw. 300 ft TL: N36 16 46 W77 01 59. Stereo. Hrs open: 24 332 Hwy. 42 W., 27910. Phone: (252) 332-7993. Fax: (252) 332-6887. Licensee: Max Radio of the Carolinas Licenses LLC. Group owner: MAX Media L.L.C. (acq 11-12-2002; grpsl). Population served: 23,616 Rgnl. Network: Agri-Net, Ray Sports Radio Net. Agrinet Format: Country. Spec prog: Farm 7 hrs wkly. ◆Don Upchurch, gen mgr & opns mgr.

WRCS(AM)— Apr 25, 1948: 970 khz; 1 kw-D. TL: N36 16 46 W77 01 59. Hrs open: 24 443 North Carolina Hwy 42 W, 27910. Phone: (252) 332-3101. Fax: (252) 332-3103.E-mail: wrcs@gate811.net Licensee: WRCS-AM 970 Inc. (acq 6-14-2002). Population served: 23,616 Format: Gospel. Target aud: 12-70. ◆J. C. Watford, gen mgr & opns mgr.

Albemarle

WPZS(FM)— February 1958: 100.9 mhz; 3 kw. Ant 200 ft TL: N35 22 40 W80 11 38. (CP: COL Indian Trail. 6 kw, ant 328 ft. TL: N35 07 29 W80 43 30). Stereo. Hrs open: 24 2303 W. Morehead St., Charlotte, 28208. Phone: (704) 358-0211. Fax: (704) 358-3752. Licensee: Radio One of North Carolina LLC. (group owner; (acq 11-12-2004; $11.5 million). Population served: 300,000 Format: Inspirational. ◆Debbie Kwei, gen mgr.

WSPC(AM)— July 1947: 1010 khz; 1 kw-D, 64 w-N. TL: N35 22 40 W80 11 38. Hrs open: 24 Box 549, 28002-0549. Secondary address: 1234 Magnolia St. 28001. Phone: (704) 983-1580. Fax: (704) 983-1436.E-mail: wspc@ctc.net Web Site:1010wspc.com Licensee: Stanly Communications Inc. (acq 2-5-2004; $600,000 with WZKY(AM) Albemarle). Population served: 150,000 Brooks, Pierce, McLendon, Humphrey & Leonard. Format: News/talk. News staff: one. Target aud: General. ◆Matt Smith, gen mgr & opns VP.

WZKY(AM)— July 9, 1956: 1580 khz; 1 kw-D, 12 w-N. TL: N35 21 38 W80 10 39. Stereo. Hrs open: 24 Box 549, 28002-0549. Phone: (704) 983-1580. Fax: (704) 983-1436.E-mail: wspc@ctc.net Web Site:www.1010wspc.com Licensee: Stanly Communications Inc. (acq 2-5-2004; $600,000 with WSPC(AM) Albemarle). Population served: 55,000 Rgnl. Network: N.C. News Net. N.C. News Net. Format: Oldies. Target aud: 30 plus. ◆Matt Smith, pres, sr VP, gen mgr, opns mgr; Sherri Smith, VP.

Asheboro

WKRR(FM)— November 1948: 92.3 mhz; 100 kw. 1,275 ft TL: N35 22 40 W80 11 38. Stereo. Hrs open: 24 192 E. Lewis St., Greensboro, 27408. Phone: (336) 274-8042. Fax: (336) 274-1629. Web Site:www.rock92.com Licensee: Dick Broadcasting Co. Inc. of Tennessee (acq 4-84). Format: Classic rock. Target aud: 18-49. ◆Bruce Wheeler, gen mgr; James Kerr, opns mgr.

WKXR(AM)— May 24, 1947: 1260 khz; 5 kw-D, 500 w-N, DA-2. TL: N35 43 26 W79 48 21. Hrs open: 24 1119 Eastview Dr., 27203. Phone: (336) 625-2187/ 625-1260.E-mail: wkxr@atomic.net Web Site:www.wkxr.com Licensee: Randolph Broadcasting Inc. (acq 8-4-86; $500,000; 7-7-86). Population served: 100,000 Natl. Network: AP Network News, Jones Radio Networks, . Rgnl. Network: N.C. News Net. N.C. News Net. Format: Country. News: 8 hrs wkly. Target aud: 18 plus. Spec prog: Farm one hr, gospel 10 hrs wkly. ◆Edward F. Swicegood II, pres, gen mgr; Ted Swicegood, opns mgr; Larry Reid, gen sls mgr, mktg dir, progmg dir, chief of engrg.

*WTJY(FM)— June 30, 1999: 89.5 mhz; 9.7 kw horiz, 7.8 kw vert. Ant 535 ft TL: N35 36 55 W79 53 28. Stereo. Hrs open: 24 Rebroadcasts WXRI(FM) Winston-Salem Newtwork. Box 25775, Winston-Salem, 27114. Phone: (336) 788-1155. Fax: (336) 788-7199.E-mail: office@joyfm.org Web Site:www.joyfm.org Licensee: Positive Alternative Radio Inc. Group owner: Baker Family Stations (Positive Radio Group) Natl. Network: Salem Radio Network, . Booth, Freret, Imlay & Tepper. Format: Southern gospel. ◆Daniel Britt, gen mgr & opns mgr.

WZOO(AM)— May 3, 1971: 710 khz; 1 kw-D, DA. TL: N35 45 50 W79 50 04. Hrs open: Box 460, 27204. Phone: (336) 672-0944. Licensee: Faith Enterprises Inc. (acq 11-15-86). Format: Southern gospel. ◆Huey Turner, gen mgr.

Asheville

*WCQS(FM)— 1975: 88.1 mhz; 1.6 kw. 1,168 ft TL: N35 35 23 W82 40 26. Stereo. Hrs open: 24 73 Broadway, 28801. Phone: (828) 253-6875. Fax: (828) 253-6700.E-mail: info@wcqs.org Web Site:www.wcqs.org Licensee: Western N.C. Public Radio Inc. (acq 1984). Population served: 500,000 Natl. Network: NPR, PRI, . Cohn & Marks. Format: Class, jazz, news. News staff: one; News: 35 hrs wkly. Target aud: 25 plus. Spec prog: Folk 9 hrs wkly. ◆Ed Subkis, gen mgr; Lee Wilcher, opns dir; Steve Busey, sls dir; Barbara Sayer, progmg dir; Richard J. Kowal, mus dir; David Hurand, news dir; Tom Spaight, chief of engrg.

WFGW(AM)—See Black Mountain

WISE(AM)— 1939: 1310 khz; 5 kw-D, 1 kw-N, DA-N. TL: N35 37 09 W82 34 21. Stereo. Hrs open: 24 1190 Patton Ave., 28806. Phone: (828) 253-1310. Fax: (828) 253-5619. Licensee: Saga Communications of North Carolina, LLC (acq 5-1-2002; $1.7 million). Population served: 500,800 Natl. Network: ESPN Radio, . Rgnl. Network: N.C. News Net. Format: Sports. News staff: one; News: 15 hrs wkly. Target aud: 35 plus; mature upscale audience. ◆Randy Cable, VP & gen mgr.

WKSF(FM)— August 1947: 99.9 mhz; 53 kw. 2,672 ft TL: N35 25 32 W82 45 25. Stereo. Hrs open: 24 Prog sep from AM 13 Summerlin Rd., 28806. Phone: (828) 257-2700. Fax: (828) 255-7850.E-mail: info@99kisscountry.com Web Site:www.99kisscountry.com Licensee: Capstar TX L.P. Format: Country. News: 3 hrs wkly. Target aud: 25-44.

*WLFA(FM)— 1975: 91.3 mhz; 440 w. 3,340 ft TL: N35 36 02 W82 45 07. Hrs open: 2420 Wade Hampton Blvd., Greenville, SC, 29615. Phone: (800) 849-8930. Phone: (828) 254-9532. Fax: (864) 292-8428.E-mail:

comments@hisradio.com Web Site:www.hisradio.com Licensee: Asheville Educational Association Inc. Format: Contemp Christian. ◆Alan Henderson, gen mgr.

WMIT(FM)—See Black Mountain

WMYI(FM)—See Greenville, SC

WSKY(AM)—Apr 11, 1947: 1230 khz; 1 kw-U. TL: N35 35 43 W82 33 57. Hrs open: 20 40 Westgate Pkwy., Suite F, 28806. Phone: (828) 251-2000. Fax: (828) 251-2135.E-mail: wsky@wilkinsradio.com Web Site:www.wilkinsradio.com Licensee: Wilkins Communications Network Inc. (group owner; (acq 1996). Population served: 450,000 Natl. Network: CBS, Salem Radio Network, . Womble, Carlyle, Sandridge & Rice. Format: Gospel, Christian teaching/talk. Target aud: 35 plus. ◆Bob Wilkins, pres; LuAnn Wilkins, exec VP; Mitchell Mathis, VP; Ruthie Spears, gen mgr; Greg Garrett, opns mgr; Tim Warner, engr.

WWNC(AM)—Feb 22, 1927: 570 khz; 5 kw-U, DA-N. TL: N35 35 49 W82 36 20. Hrs open: 24 13 Summerlin Rd., 28806. Phone: (828) 257-2700. Fax: (828) 255-7850.E-mail: info@wwnc.com Web Site:www.wwnc.com Licensee: Capstar TX L.P. Group owner: Clear Channel Communications Inc. (acq 8-30-2000; grpsl). Population served: 500,000 Natl. Network: Motor Racing Net, . Natl. Rep: McGavren Guild,. Format: News/talk. News staff: 3; News: 30 hrs wkly. Target aud: 25-54. Spec prog: Farm one hr, gospel 3 hrs, relg 3 hrs wkly.

Atlantic

WTKF(FM)—May 1992: 107.3 mhz; 7 kw. Ant 607 ft TL: N34 53 01 W76 30 21. Hrs open: Box 70, Newport, 28570-0070. Secondary address: 5447 Hwy. 70, Morehead City 28557. Phone: (252) 247-6343. Phone: (800) 818-2255. Fax: (252) 247-7343. Web Site:www.wtkf107.com Licensee: Atlantic Ridge Telecasters Inc. (acq 11-30-94; $430,000; 1-16-95). Natl. Network: Westwood One, Motor Racing Net, USA, . Rgnl. Network: N.C. News Net. N.C. News Net. Format: News/talk, sports. Target aud: 25 plus; educated, informed. ◆Lockwood Phillips, CEO; Ben Ball, gen mgr; Shane Willis, opns mgr.

Atlantic Beach

*WBJD(FM)—1999: 91.5 mhz; 50 kw. Ant 384 ft TL: N34 45 34 W76 51 16. Hrs open: 24 c/o WTEB(FM), 800 College Ct., New Bern, 28562. Phone: (252) 638-3434. Fax: (252) 638-3538. Web Site:www.publicradioeast.org Licensee: Craven Community College. Format: News & Ideas. ◆Kathleen Beal, gen mgr; Chris Wethington, stn mgr; Jill McGuire, dev dir; J. Howard Jones, chief of engrg; George Olsen, reporter.

Aurora

WSTK(FM)—Not on air, target date: unknown: Stn currently dark. 104.5 mhz; 4.2 kw. Ant 393 ft TL: N35 18 09 W76 34 00. (CP: COL Harkers Island. 16.5 kw, ant 403 ft. TL: N34 52 22 W76 24 56). Hrs open: 702 Hartness Rd., Statesville, 28677. Phone: (704) 878-9004. Licensee: Media East LLC. (acq 1-15-2003). ◆Ronald Benfield, pres & gen mgr.

*WZGO(FM)—Aug 1, 2006: 91.1 mhz; 40 kw. Ant 351 ft TL: N35 18 09 W76 34 00. Stereo. Hrs open: 24
Rebroadcasts WAGO(FM) Snow Hill.
Box 1895, Goldsboro, 27533. Phone: (252) 747-8887. Fax: (252) 747-7888.E-mail: wago@gomixradio.org Web Site:www.gomixradio.org Licensee: Pathway Christian Academy Inc. Natl. Network: Moody, Salem Radio Network, . Format: Christian. News staff: one; News: 14 hrs wkly. Target aud: General. ◆Dr. T.D. Worthington, pres, gen mgr; Ashley Lovett, prom dir; Keith Aycock, progmg dir; Tiffany Johnson, mus dir; Joe Patton, chief of engrg.

Banner Elk

WZJS(FM)—Aug 5, 1989: 100.7 mhz; 6 kw. Ant 758 ft TL: N36 10 34 W81 50 05. Hrs open: 24 738 Blowing Rock Rd., Boone, 28607. Phone: (828) 264-2411. Fax: (828) 264-2412.E-mail: info@1007macfm.com Web Site:www.1007macfm.com Licensee: High Country Adventures LLC. (group owner; (acq 3-3-2009; grpsl). Population served: 50,000 Natl. Network: Motor Racing Net, . Format: Eclectic for men 18-34. Target aud: 18-44. ◆Andy Glass, opns dir.

Bath

*WZPE(FM)—2005: 90.1 mhz; 675 w. Ant 128 ft TL: N35 28 32 W76 48 44. Stereo. Hrs open: 24 Box 828, Wake Forest, 27588. Phone: (919) 556-5178. Fax: (919) 556-9273. Web Site:www.wcpe.org Licensee: Educational Information Corp. Format: Classical. ◆Deborah S. Proctor, gen mgr; Rae Weaver, dev mgr; Dick Storck, progmg dir; Will Woltz, mus dir; John Graham, engr.

Bayboro

WNBB(FM)—2001: 97.9 mhz; 50 kw. Ant 433 ft TL: N35 00 02 W76 49 58. Stereo. Hrs open: 24 233 Middle St., Suite 107B, New Bern, 28562. Phone: (252) 638-8500. Fax: (252) 638-8597.E-mail: mail@bear979.com Web Site:www.bear979.com Licensee: Coastal Carolina Radio LLC (acq 11-25-2003; $800,000). Population served: 697,000 Natl. Network: Fox News Radio, . Natl. Rep: Rgnl Reps,. Format: Classic country. Target aud: 35-64; adults. ◆Dann Miller, gen mgr.

Beaufort

*WXBE(FM)—2005: 88.5 mhz; 1 kw. Ant 180 ft TL: N34 43 26 W76 43 18. Hrs open: Drawer 2440, Tupelo, MS, 38801. Phone: (662) 844-8888. Fax: (662) 842-6791. Web Site:www.afr.net Licensee: American Family Association. Group owner: American Family Radio. Format: Christian. ◆Marvin Sanders, gen mgr.

Beech Mountain

WECR-FM—1996: 102.3 mhz; 150 w. Ant 1,957 ft TL: N36 11 03 W81 52 48. Hrs open: 24 738 Blowing Rock Rd., Boone, 28607. Phone: (828) 264-2411. Fax: (828) 264-2412.E-mail: info@wecr1023.com Web Site:www.mix1023fm.com Licensee: High Country Adventures LLC. (group owner; (acq 3-3-2009; grpsl). Population served: 150,000 Natl. Network: CBS Radio, . Format: Lite adult contemp. News staff: 2; News: 2 hrs wkly. Target aud: 25-54.

Belhaven

WQZL(FM)—Oct 15, 1980: 101.1 mhz; 31 kw. Ant 607 ft TL: N35 18 18 W76 45 45. Stereo. Hrs open: 24
Rebroadcasts WQSL(FM) Jacksonville 100%.
1361 Colony Dr., New Bern, 28562. Phone: (252) 639-7900. Fax: (252) 639-7976.E-mail: info@wqzl.com Web Site:www.carolinatouch.com Licensee: NM Licensing LLC. Group owner: NextMedia Group L.L.C. (acq 11-26-2001; grpsl). Natl. Rep: Eastman Radio,. Format: Rhythm and blues. News: 3 hrs wkly. Target aud: 25-54. ◆Larry Weiss, gen mgr.

Belmont

WCGC(AM)—Dec 11, 1954: 1270 khz; 5 kw-D, 500 w-N, DA-2. TL: N35 15 05 W81 03 26. Stereo. Hrs open: 24 Box 1360, 6021 W. Wilkinson Blvd., 28012. Phone: (704) 825-2812. Fax:(704) 825-2127.E-mail: wcgc1270am@yahoo.com Licensee: WHVN Inc. Group owner: GHB Radio Group (acq 4-17-98; $250,000). Population served: 12,000 Natl. Network: Westwood One, . Format: Relg, talk. News staff: 2; News: 8 hrs wkly. Target aud: General. ◆Tom Gentry, pres & gen mgr.

Benson

WPYB(AM)—Sept 1, 1961: 1130 khz; 6.5 kw-D, 1 kw-CH. TL: N35 21 39 W78 34 09. Hrs open: Box 215, 27504. Secondary address: 2234 Hodges Chapel Road 27504. Phone: (919) 894-1130. Fax: (919) 894-1530.E-mail: wpyb@dockpoint.net Licensee: Benson-Dunn Broadcasting Inc. (acq 5-1-96; $250,000). Population served: 100,000 Format: Country, bluegrass, gospel. Target aud: General. ◆Jasper L. Tart, pres, gen mgr; Mable Sue Tart, exec VP.

Bethel

WNBR-FM—Dec 5, 1988: 98.9 mhz; 11.2 kw. Ant 489 ft TL: N35 47 29 W77 22 54. Stereo. Hrs open: 24 233 Middle Street, Suite 107B, New Bern, 28560. Phone: (252) 638-8500. Fax: (252) 638-8597.E-mail: mail@bear989.com Web Site:www.bear989.com Licensee: Coastal Carolina Radio LLC (group owner; (acq 5-17-2004; $1.07 million). Population served: 697 Natl. Network: Fox News Radio, . Natl. Rep: Rgnl Reps,. Format: Classic country. Target aud: 35-64; Adults. ◆Dann Miller, gen mgr.

Biltmore Forest

WOXL-FM—2002: 96.5 mhz; 1.85 kw. Ant 1,171 ft TL: N35 35 23 W82 40 26. Hrs open: 1190 Patton Ave., Asheville, 28806. Phone: (828) 259-9695. Fax: (828) 253-5619. Web Site:www.965woxl.com Licensee: Saga Communications of North Carolina LLC. (acq 1-31-2008; $8 million). Format: Light rock. ◆Bob Bolak, gen mgr; Holly Vandegrift, gen sls mgr; Will Candler, prom dir; Steve Marcus, progmg dir.

Black Mountain

WFGW(AM)—May 27, 1962: 1010 khz; 50 kw-D, 500 w-N, 19 kw-CH, DA-3. TL: N35 36 19 W82 21 00. Hrs open: 24 Box 159, 1330 U.S. Hwy. 70, 28711. Phone: (828) 669-8477. Fax: (828) 669-6983.E-mail: thankyou@brb.org Web Site:www.wfgw.org Licensee: Blue Ridge Broadcasting Corp. Population served: 366,000 Natl. Network: Salem Radio Network, . Pillsbury, Winthrop, Shaw Pittman. Format: Christian teaching, talk. News: 3 hrs wkly. Target aud: 35 plus. Spec prog: Black one hr wkly. ◆Billy Graham, chmn; Dr. David Bruce, pres; Jim Kirkland, gen mgr; Wayne Roper, dev mgr; Tom Greene, progmg dir; Keith Pittman, news dir; Paul Zettle, engr.

WMIT(FM)—June 1, 1942: 106.9 mhz; 36 kw. Ant 3,090 ft TL: N35 44 06 W82 17 10. Stereo. Hrs open: 24 Box 159, 1330 U.S. Hwy. 70, 28711. Phone: (828) 669-8477. Fax: (828) 669-6983. Web Site:www.wmit.org (Acq 1963). Population served: 1,500,000 Natl. Network: Fox News Radio, . Pillsbury, Winthrop, Shaw Pittman. Format: Contemp Christian music & teaching. Target aud: 35-54; women. ◆Matt Stockman, mus dir.

WZGM(AM)—Feb 26, 1966: 1350 khz; 1 kw-D, 74 w-N. TL: N35 37 19 W82 19 02. Hrs open: 24 Box 430, Lincolnton, 28093. Phone: (704) 735-8071. Fax: (828) 669-6224. Fax: (704) 732-9567. Web Site:www.z1350.com Licensee: HRN Broadcasting Inc. (acq 4-28-2005; $850,000). Population served: 22,000 Format: Southern gospel. Target aud: General. ◆D. Mark Boyd III, pres; Lanny Ford, gen mgr.

Bladenboro

*WRDK(FM)—Not on air, target date: 2010: 90.7 mhz; 780 w. Ant 308 ft TL: N34 33 19 W78 48 57. Stereo. Hrs open: Box 15, Chester, SC, 29706. Phone: (803) 581-9030. Fax: (803) 581-9932. Licensee: Richburg Educational Broadcasters Inc. ◆Jeff Sigmon, gen mgr.

Blowing Rock

WXIT(AM)—1983: 1200 khz; 10 kw-D, 7 kw-CH. TL: N36 09 17 W81 39 41. Hrs open: 738 Blowing Rock Rd., Boone, 28607. Phone: (828) 265-1023. Fax: (828) 264-8902.E-mail: wxit@newstalk1200.com Web Site:www.goblueridge.net Licensee: High Country Adventures LLC. (group owner; (acq 3-3-2009; grpsl). Natl. Network: CBS, . Format: News/talk. Target aud: 25-60; professionals. Spec prog: Relg 8 hrs, big band 4 hrs wkly. ◆Donna Hoffman, VP; Jonathan Hoffman, gen mgr; Andy Zlass, opns mgr, progmg dir.

Boiling Springs

*WGWG(FM)—Jan 22, 1974: 88.3 mhz; 50 kw. 302 ft TL: N35 13 52 W81 42 57. Stereo. Hrs open: 24 P.O. Box 876, 106 Emily Ln., 28017. Phone: (704) 406-3525. Fax: (704) 434-4338.E-mail: info@wgwg.org Web Site:www.wgwg.org Licensee: Gardner-Webb University. Population served: 315,000 Format: Triple A. News: one hr wkly. Target aud: General. Spec prog: Gospel 15 hrs wkly. ◆Frank Campbell, pres; Dan McClellan, stn mgr; Matt Webber, gen mgr & opns mgr.

Boone

*WASU-FM—May 18, 1972: 90.5 mhz; 220 w. 57 ft TL: N36 12 48 W81 41 10. Stereo. Hrs open: Appalachian State Univ., Wey Hall Suite 332, 28608. Phone: (828) 262-3170. Fax: (828) 262-6521. Licensee: Appalachian State University. Population served: 20,000 Format: Alternative. News: 2 hrs wkly. Target aud: 18-30; college students & area residents. Spec prog: Urban contemp 6 hrs, blues 2 hrs, Christian rock 3 hrs, country 8 hrs wkly. ◆Richard Davis, gen mgr.

WATA(AM)—September 1950: 1450 khz; 1 kw-U. TL: N36 12 59 W81 42 06. Hrs open: 5 AM-midnight (M-S); 6 AM-midnight (Su) 738 Blowing Rock Rd., 28607. Phone: (828) 264-2411. Fax: (828) 264-2412.E-mail: sindy@wecr1023.com Web Site:www.wataradio.com Licensee: High Country Adventures LLC. (group owner; (acq 3-3-2009; grpsl). Population served: 49,000 Natl. Network: ABC, . Format: Local newstalk. News staff: one; News: 4 hrs wkly. Target aud: 25-54. Spec

prog: Gospel 5 hrs, Paul Harvey 2.5 hrs.,Watauga High sports wkly. ◆Jonathan Hoffman, gen mgr; Andy Glass, opns mgr.

Brevard

WSQL(AM)— July 6, 1950: 1240 khz; 1 kw-U. TL: N35 13 23 W82 42 20. Hrs open: Box 1240, 28712. Secondary address: 1319 Wilson Rd., Pisgah Forest 28768. Phone: (828) 877-5252. Fax: (828) 877-5253.E-mail: info@wqsl.com Licensee: A & L Broadcasting Inc. (acq 3-14-97; $110,000). Population served: 26,000 Natl. Network: CBS, . Format: Talk, adult contemp, MOR. Target aud: General. Spec prog: Jazz 10 hrs, gospel 8 hrs, relg 4 hrs wkly. ◆Allen Reese, gen mgr, opns mgr, gen sls mgr; Leah Reese, progmg dir.

Bryson City

WBHN(AM)— Oct 1, 1967: 1590 khz; 500 w-D, 37 w-N. TL: N35 25 41 W83 26 18. Hrs open: Box 1309, 28713. Phone: (828) 488-2682. Fax: (828) 488-3594.E-mail: wbhn@verizon.net Web Site:www.1590wbhn.com Licensee: Starcast South Inc. Group owner: Starcast Systems Inc. (acq 10-84; $355,000;10-15-84). Population served: 10,000 Format: Classic hits. ◆Jack Mullen Jr., pres; Jason Nations, gen mgr, gen sls mgr & mus dir; J.B. Jacobs, chief of engrg.

Buie's Creek

*WCCE(FM)— Oct 7, 1974: 90.1 mhz; 15 kw vert. Ant 302 ft TL: N35 12 39 W78 50 01. Stereo. Hrs open: 24 Box 1030, Science Bldg., Campbell Univ., 27506. Phone: (910) 893-1745. Fax: (910) 893-1746.E-mail: wcce@mailcenter.campbell.edu Web Site:www.campbell.edu/wcce/ Licensee: Campbell University. Population served: 50,000 Format: Smooth jazz, soft rock, relg. News: 10 hrs wkly. Target aud: General. Spec prog: Bluegrass 3 hrs, big band 4 hrs wkly. ◆ Travis Autry, gen mgr; Carolyn Bowden, opns mgr.

Burgaw

WKXB(FM)— Dec 13, 1964: 99.9 mhz; 100 kw. Ant 774 ft TL: N34 14 37 W78 07 24. Stereo. Hrs open: 24 25 N. Kerr Ave., Wilmington, 28405. Phone: (910) 791-3088. Fax: (910) 791-0112.E-mail: stanleyb@nextmediagroup.com Web Site:www.jammin999sm.com Licensee: Sunrise Broadcasting LLC. (group owner) (acq 11-18-2008; grpsl). Population served: 182,000 Natl. Rep: McGavren Guild,. Format: Rhythmic gold. News staff: one; News: 3 hrs wkly. Target aud: 25-54. ◆Barry Brown, VP; Barbara Raybourne, gen mgr; Gayle Brown, gen sls mgr; Missy Andrus, prom dir; Stanley B., progmg dir; Doug Carlisle, news dir.

WVBS(AM)— June 21, 1963: 1470 khz; 1 kw-D, 93 w-N. TL: N34 32 05 W77 54 31. (CP: TL: N34 31 22 W77 54 17.) Hrs open: Sunrise-sunset Box 914, Bible Baptist Church, 2190 Hwy. 117 S., 28425. Phone: (910) 259-5718. Licensee: Grace Christian School. (acq 12-23-94; 2-27-95). Population served: 1,744 Format: Christian. ◆Carl Gibbs, gen mgr; Dick Jones, stn mgr.

Burlington

WPCM(AM)— September 1941: 920 khz; 5 kw-D, 55 w-N. TL: N36 05 50 W79 29 03. Hrs open: Box 1119, 27215. Secondary address: 1109 Tower Dr. 27215. Phone: (336) 584-0126. Fax: (336) 584-6333. Web Site:www.920wpcm.com Licensee: Carolina Radio Group Inc. Group owner: Curtis Media Group (acq 3-1-90). Population served: 100,000 Format: Oldies & beach music. Target aud: 25 plus; upscale. ◆Bill Whitley, gen mgr.

WZTK(FM)— December 1946: 101.1 mhz; 100 kw. Ant 1,191 ft TL: N35 56 31 W79 26 33. Stereo. Hrs open: 24 Prog sep from AM Box 1119, 27215. Secondary address: 1109 Tower Dr. 27215. Phone: (336) 584-0126. Fax: (336) 854-1039.E-mail: info@fmtalk1011.com Web Site:www.fmtalk1011.com Licensee: Carolina Radio Group Inc. Population served: 1,887,200 Format: Talk. Target aud: 25-54. Spec prog: Bluegrass 3 hrs wkly. ◆Bryon Tucker, progmg dir.

Burlington-Graham

WBAG(AM)— 1946: 1150 khz; 1 kw-D, 48 w-N. TL: N36 06 48 W79 27 00. Hrs open: 24 Box 2450, Burlington, 27216. Secondary address: 1745 Burch Bridge Rd. 27217. Phone: (336) 226-1150. Fax: (336) 226-1180. Web Site:www.wbag1150.com Licensee: Gray Broadcasting LLC (acq 10-27-98; $150,000). Population served: 108,000 Rgnl. Network: N.C. News Net. N.C. News Net. Format: Adult standards/talk. News staff: 2; News: 25 hrs wkly. Target aud: 25-54; general. Spec

prog: Relg 5 hrs wkly. ◆Joe Gray, gen mgr; Harry Myers, opns mgr, progmg dir; Gailes Stuckey, gen sls mgr; Tim Walker, chief of engrg; Bill Huff, sports cmtr.

WSML(AM)—See Graham

Burnsville

WKYK(AM)— May 28, 1967: 940 khz; 5 kw-D, 250 w-N, DA-N. TL: N35 55 32 W82 16 20. Stereo. Hrs open: 24 Box 744, Mark Group Bldg., 28714. Secondary address: 749 Sawmill Road 28714. Phone: (828) 682-3510. Phone: (828) 682-3798. Fax: (828) 682-6227. Fax: (828) 682-0998.E-mail: 940@wkyk.com Web Site:www.wkyk.com Licensee: Mark Media Inc. (acq 4-10-69). Population served: 463,000 Natl. Network: ABC, . Rgnl. Network: N.C. News Net. N.C. News Net. Format: Real country. News staff: one; News: 10 hrs wkly. Target aud: 18-55. Spec prog: Gospel 12 hrs wkly. ◆J. Ardell Sink, CEO, pres; Remelle Sink, exec VP; Michael Sink, VP, gen mgr, chief of engrg; Holly S. Hall, opns mgr, mktg dir; Mary Marsh, prom dir; Steve Murphy, news dir & pub affrs dir.

Buxton

*WBUX(FM)— 1999: 90.5 mhz; 5.9 kw. Ant 154 ft TL: N35 16 01 W75 32 38. Hrs open:
Rebroadcasts WCPE(FM) Wake Forest 99.9%.
120 Friday Center Dr., CB-0915, Chapel Hill, 27517-9495. Phone: (919) 966-5454. Fax: (919) 966-5955.E-mail: wunc@wunc.org Web Site:www.wunc.org Licensee: Board of Trustees/University of North Carolina at Chapel Hill. Population served: 3,434 Natl. Network: NPR, PRI, CBC Radio One, . Format: Classical. News staff: 7; News: 124 hrs wkly. Spec prog: Folk 20 hrs wkly. ◆Joan Rose, gen mgr.

WHDX(FM)— 2008: 99.9 mhz; 110 w. Ant 56 ft TL: N35 15 43 W75 31 23. Hrs open: 1400 12th St. N., Suite 5, Arlington, VA, 22209-3666. Phone: (703) 527-1434.E-mail: radiobuxton@yahoo.com Web Site:www.whdzx.com Licensee: David Wilson. ◆David Wilson, gen mgr.

WHDZ(FM)— 2008: 101.5 mhz; 110 w. Ant 66 ft TL: N35 15 43 W75 31 23. Hrs open: 1400 12th St. N., Suite 5, Arlington, VA, 22209-3666. Phone: (703) 527-1434.E-mail: radiobuxton@yahoo.com Web Site:www.whdzx.com Licensee: David Wilson. ◆David Wilson, gen mgr.

Calabash

WYNA(FM)— June 1964: 104.9 mhz; 15 kw. Ant 338 ft TL: N33 49 19 W78 46 18. Stereo. Hrs open: 3926 Wesley St., Suite 301, Myrtle Beach, SC, 29578. Phone: (843) 903-9962. Fax: (843) 903-1797. Web Site:www.1049bobfm.com Licensee: Qantum of Myrtle Beach License Co. LLC. (acq 4-23-2008; $4 million). Population served: 250,000 Format: Adult Hits. Target aud: 25-54; adults. ◆Frank D. Osborn, pres; Will Isaacs, gen mgr.

Camp Lejeune

WSME(AM)— Sept 8, 1980: Stn currently dark. 1120 khz; 6 kw-D, 4.2 kw-CH. TL: N34 43 03 W77 16 57. Hrs open: 337 E. Centre St., Jacksonville, 28540. Phone: (910) 355-9763. Fax: (910) 355-9763. Web Site:www.wsme1120.com Licensee: CTC Media Group Inc. (group owner). Format: Classic country. ◆Edwin Lee Afflerbach, VP.

Canton

WPTL(AM)— Aug 3, 1963: 920 khz; 500 w-D, 38 w-N. TL: N35 31 15 W82 48 24. Hrs open: 6 AM-6:30 PM Box 909, 133 Pisgah Dr., 28716. Phone: (828) 648-3576. Phone: (828) 648-3577. Fax: (828) 648-3577.E-mail: admin@wptlradio.net Web Site:www.wptlradio.net Licensee: Skycountry Broadcasting Inc. (acq 3-1-78). Population served: 50,000 Natl. Network: AP Radio, Jones Radio Networks, . Format: C&W, relg. News: 8 hrs wkly. Target aud: 25 plus; adult family. ◆Linda Reck, VP, stn mgr; William Reck, pres & gen mgr.

WYSE(AM)— July 12, 1954: 970 khz; 5 kw-D. TL: N35 31 58 W82 51 58. Hrs open: 1190 Patton Ave, Asheville, 28806. Phone: (828) 259-9695. Fax: (828) 253-5619. Web Site:www.1310bigwise.com Licensee: Saga Communications of North Carolina LLC. Group owner: Saga Communications Inc. (acq 3-11-2003). Population served: 50,000 Natl. Network: ESPN Radio, . Miller & Fields, P.C. Format: Sports. ◆Ed Christian, pres; Randy Cable, gen mgr.

Carolina Beach

WMYT(AM)— July 1, 1989: 1180 khz; 10 kw-D, DA. TL: N34 09 03 W78 04 48. Hrs open: Box 957, Wilmington, 28402-0957. Phone: (910) 763-2452. Fax: (910) 763-6578.E-mail: life@life905.com Web Site:www.life905.com Licensee: Carolina Christian Radio Inc. (group owner; acq 3-2-2001; $100,000 with WDVV(FM) Wilmington). Format: Relg Teaching & Talk. General Sp. ◆Jim Stephens, gen mgr; Roger Brace, engr.

WUIN(FM)— October 1996: 106.7 mhz; 5.6 kw. Ant 341 ft TL: N34 03 02 W77 57 20. Hrs open: 24
Simulcast with WPPG(FM) Fair Bluff.
122 Cinema Dr., Wilmington, 28403. Phone: (910) 772-6300.E-mail: info@carolinapenguin.com Web Site:www.carolinapenguin.com Licensee: Ocean Broadcasting II LLC (acq 7-3-2003; $1.5 million with WMFD(AM) Wilmington). Format: Triple A. ◆Paul Knight, gen mgr; Beau Gunn, progmg dir.

Cary

WKSL(FM)— 1946: 93.9 mhz; 100 kw. Ant 1,486 ft TL: N35 42 50 W78 49 04. Stereo. Hrs open: 3100 Smoketree Ct., Suite 700, Raleigh, 27604-1052. Phone: (919) 877-0939. Fax: (919) 786-2929. Licensee: Capstar TX L.P. Group owner: Clear Channel Communications Inc. (acq 8-30-2000; grpsl). Population served: 661,000 Format: Adult contemp. Target aud: 25-49; men. ◆Dick Harlow, gen mgr; Chris Shebel, progmg dir; Fred Pace, chief of engrg.

Chadbourn

WVOE(AM)— Apr 23, 1962: 1590 khz; 1 kw-D. TL: N34 21 05 W78 50 38. Hrs open: 1528 Old 74 Hwy. W., 28431. Phone: (910) 654-5621. Fax: (910) 654-4385.E-mail: wvoe@weblnk.net Licensee: Ebony Enterprises Inc. Population served: 500,000 Format: Rhythm and blues, jazz, gospel. Target aud: General; white & blue collar workers, housewives, students, sr citizens. ◆Willie J. Walls, pres; Willie J. Walls, gen mgr; Willie J. Walls, stn mgr.

Chapel Hill

WCHL(AM)— Jan 25, 1953: 1360 khz; 5 kw-D, 1 kw-N, DA-N. TL: N35 56 18 W79 01 36. Stereo. Hrs open: 24 88 VilCom Cir., Suite 100, 27514. Phone: (919) 933-4165. Fax: (919) 968-3748.E-mail: cdixon@wchl1360.com Web Site:www.wchl1360.com Licensee: Vilcom Interactive Media LLC (acq 8-5-2004; $775,000). Population served: 85,000 Natl. Network: ABC, CBS Radio, Jones Radio Networks, . N.C. News Net. Wire Svc: AP Format: News/talk. News staff: 3; News: 25 hrs wkly. Target aud: 25-54; educated adults with high median incomes. ◆Christy Jones Taylor, VP, gen mgr; Christy Dixon, stn mgr; Ron Stutts, progmg dir.

WDCG(FM)—See Durham

WKSL(FM)—See Cary

WLLQ(AM)— December 1973: 1530 khz; 10 kw-D, DA. TL: N35 58 07 W79 00 10. Hrs open: Sunrise-sunset Estuardo Valdemar Rodriguez and Leonor Rodriguez Stns, 1010 Vermont Ave. N.W. Suite 100, Washington, DC, 20005. Phone: (202) 638-1959. Fax: (202) 638-6127.E-mail: estuardovaldemar@hotmail.com Licensee: Estuardo Valdemar Rodriguez and Leonor Rodriguez. Group owner: WRTP Radio Network (acq 2-2-2005; grpsl). Population served: 95,438 Format: Mexican rgnl. Target aud: Spanish young adult. ◆Estuardo Valdemar Rodriguez, gen mgr.

*WUNC(FM)— Nov 3, 1952: 91.5 mhz; 100 kw. Ant 1,361 ft TL: N35 51 59 W79 10 00. Hrs open: 24 120 Friday Center Dr., CB-0915, 27517-9495. Phone: (919) 966-5454. Fax: (919) 966-5955.E-mail: wunc@wunc.org Web Site:www.wunc.org Licensee: University of North Carolina at Chapel Hill. Population served: 2,011,484 Natl. Network: NPR, PRI, CBC Radio One, . Brooks, Pierce, McLendon, Humphrey & Leonard, LLP. Format: News & info. News staff: 7; News: 124 hrs wkly. Target aud: 25-54; highly educated, pro-active in the community, concerned about local issues. Spec prog: Folk 20 hrs wkly. ◆Joan Siefert Rose, gen mgr; Kevin Wolf, opns mgr, traf mgr; Regina Yeager, dev dir; George Boosey, progmg dir, progmg mgr; Connie Walker, news dir; John Francioni, engrg dir, chief of engrg.

*WXYC(FM)— Mar 18, 1977: 89.3 mhz; 400 w. 280 ft TL: N35 54 15 W79 02 50. Stereo. Hrs open: 24 CB 5210, Carolina Union, 27599. Phone: (919) 962-8989.E-mail: info@wxyc.org Web Site:www.wxyc.org Licensee: Student Educational Broadcasting Inc. Population served: 25,000 Format: Div, free form. News: 3 hrs wkly. Target aud: General. ◆Lauren Brenner, stn mgr.

Charlotte

WBCN(AM)— Dec 1, 2003: 1660 khz; 10 kw-D, 1 kw-N. TL: N35 14 57 W80 51 41. Hrs open: 1520 South Blvd., Suite 300, 28203. Phone: (704) 342-2644. Fax: (704) 227-8985. Licensee: CBS Radio Holdings Inc. Group owner: Infinity Broadcasting Corp. Natl. Network: Sporting News Radio Network, . Natl. Rep: D & R Radio, Katz Radio,. Leventhal, Senter & Leman. Format: Sports. ♦Bill Schoening, gen mgr; D.J. Stout, opns mgr.

WBT(AM)— Apr 10, 1922: 1110 khz; 50 kw-U, DA-N. TL: N35 07 56 W80 53 23. Stereo. Hrs open: 24 One Julian Price Pl., 28208. Phone: (704) 374-3500. Fax: (704) 374-3889.E-mail: info@wbt.com Web Site:www.wbt.com Licensee: Greater Media of Charlotte Inc. (group owner; (acq 1-31-2008; grpsl). Population served: 889,000 Natl. Network: CBS, . Format: News/talk. News staff: 5; News: 20 hrs wkly. Target aud: 35-54; men. ♦Rick Jackson, sr VP, gen mgr; Lisa Gergely, gen mgr; Terry Mace, dev VP; Larry Rideaux, natl sls mgr; Matt Dubois, prom mgr; Bill White, progmg dir; Marshall Adams, news dir; Jerry Dowd, chief of engrg; Nancy Haynes, rsch dir; Nancy Albright, traf mgr; Jim Barroll, news rptr; Pete Kaliner, reporter.

WCGC(AM)—See Belmont

***WFAE(FM)**— June 29, 1981: 90.7 mhz; 100 kw. 760 ft TL: N35 15 06 W80 41 12. Stereo. Hrs open: 24 8801 J.M. Keynes Dr., Suite 91, 28262-8485. Phone: (704) 549-9323. Fax: (704) 547-8851.E-mail: wfae@wfae.org Web Site:www.wfae.org Licensee: University Radio Foundation Inc. (acq 4-12-93). Population served: 1,700,000 Natl. Network: NPR, PRI, . Garvey, Schubert & Barer. Format: News/talk. News staff: 4; News: 42 hrs wkly. Target aud: 35-49; professionals. ♦Roger Sarow, gen mgr; Tena Simmons, opns dir; Barbara Vermeire, dev dir; Renee Rallos, prom dir; Paul Stribling, progmg dir; Mark Rumsey, news dir; Renee Ballos, pub affrs dir; Jobie Sprinkle, engrg dir.

WFNZ(AM)— 1941: 610 khz; 5 kw-D, 1 kw-N, DA-2. TL: N35 17 53 W80 53 40. Hrs open: 1520 South Blvd # 300, 28203. Phone: (704) 319-9369. Fax: (704) 319-3934. Web Site:www.wfnz.com Licensee: CBS Radio Holdings Inc. Group owner: Infinity Broadcasting Corp. (acq 11-13-98; grpsl). Population served: 410,000 Format: Sports. Target aud: 18 plus; male, sports oriented. ♦Bill Schoening, gen mgr; D.J. Stout, opns mgr, progmg dir; Scott Vandivier, gen sls mgr; Chele Fassig, prom dir; Eric Lakey, chief of engrg.

WGFY(AM)— Jan 18, 1955: 1480 khz; 5 kw-U, DA-2. TL: N35 17 05 W80 52 34. Hrs open: 24 1100 S Troyn St., Suite 210, 28203. Phone: (704) 377-2223. Fax: (704) 373-2245.E-mail: info@radiodisney.com Web Site:www.radiodisney.com Licensee: Radio Disney Group LLC. Group owner: ABC Inc. (acq 8-22-00; grpsl). Fisher, Wayland, Cooper, Leader & Zaragoza. Format: Children, Tweens, Radio Disney. News staff: 6; News: 25 hrs wkly. Target aud: Under 12; kids, mothers, families. ♦Carolyn Renfro, prom mgr.

WGSP(AM)— Aug 23, 1958: 1310 khz; 5 kw-D. TL: N35 15 23 W80 51 52. Hrs open: 4801 E. Independence Blvd., Suite 803, 28212. Phone: (704) 442-7277. Fax: (704) 442-9518. Licensee: Norsan Consulting and Management Inc. (acq 12-13-2004; $2 million). Population served: 100,000 Format: Sp news/talk. ♦Norberto Sanchez, pres; Javier Placencia, progmg dir.

WHVN(AM)— 1958: 1240 khz; 1 kw-U, DA-1. TL: N35 12 00 W80 48 39. Hrs open: 5732 N. Tryon St., 28213. Phone: (704) 596-1240. Fax: (704) 596-6939.E-mail: whvn@bellsouth.net Licensee: WHVN Inc. Group owner: GHB Radio Group (acq 7-11-83). Population served: 241,178 Reddy, Begley & McCormick. Format: Relg. Target aud: 35 plus; Christian. ♦George Buck, pres; Tom Gentry, gen mgr, sls VP, mktg VP, prom VP & adv VP; Buddy Boone, progmg dir; Brant Hart, pub affrs dir; Gary Hattaway, chief of engrg.

WKQC(FM)— 1972: 104.7 mhz; 96 kw. Ant 1,210 ft TL: N35 15 06 W80 41 12. Stereo. Hrs open: 24 4015 Stuart Andrew Blvd., 28217. Phone: (704) 372-1104. Fax: (704) 523-1047. Web Site:www.star1047.com Licensee: Infinity Radio Holdings Inc. Group owner: Infinity Broadcasting Corp. (acq 11-13-98; grpsl). Population served: 1,200,000 Leventhal, Senter & Lerman. Format: Hits of the 70s & 80s. News staff: 2. Target aud: 25-54. ♦Keith Cornwell, gen mgr; John Reynolds, prom mgr.

WLNK(FM)— Aug 15, 1962: 107.9 mhz; 97 kw. Ant 1,692 ft TL: N35 21 51 W81 11 13. Stereo. Hrs open: 24 One Julian Price Pl., 28208. Phone: (704) 374-3500. Fax: (704) 338-3062. Web Site:www.1079thelink.com Licensee: Greater Media of Charlotte Inc. (acq 1-31-2008; grpsl). Format: Hot adult contemp. ♦Neal Sharpe, progmg dir; Derek James, mus dir; Nancy Haynes, rsch dir; Nancy Albright, traf mgr; Jim Barroll, news rptr; Pete Kaliner, reporter.

WNKS(FM)— July 21, 1962: 95.1 mhz; 100 kw. 1,542 ft TL: N35 21 44 W81 09 19. Stereo. Hrs open: 4015 Stuart Andrew Blvd., 28217. Phone: (704) 331-9510. Fax: (704) 344-8656. Web Site:www.kiss951.com Population served: 325,000 Format: CHR. ♦Keith Cornwell, gen mgr; John Renolds, opns mgr; Rob Whitehead, gen sls mgr; Natalie Kirby, mktg mgr; Chad Fitzsimmons, prom mgr.

WOGR(AM)— May 7, 1964: 1540 khz; 2.5 kw-D, DA. TL: N35 13 45 W80 58 32. (CP: TL: N35 16 26 W80 51 50). Hrs open: Sunrise-sunset Box 16408 Carrier Dr., 28297. Secondary address: 1501 N. Carrier Dr. 28216. Phone: (704) 393-1540. Phone: (704) 393-1588. Fax: (704) 393-1527.E-mail: whammond@wordnet.org Web Site:wordnet.org Licensee: Victory Christian Center Inc. (acq 7-27-88). Natl. Network: Salem Radio Network, . Gardner, Carton & Douglas. Format: Relg. Target aud: General. ♦Robyn Gool, pres; Wayne Hammond, gen mgr; James Sims, opns mgr; Terry Hammond, gen sls mgr, prom VP, prom dir, pub affrs dir, spec ev coord; Eleasah Hammond, mus dir; Tamma Wylie, traf mgr.

WPEG(FM)—See Concord

WSOC-FM— 1947: 103.7 mhz; 100 kw. 1,040 ft TL: N35 15 41 W80 43 38. (CP: Ant 1,059 ft.). Stereo. Hrs open: 1520 South Blvd, Suite 300 , 28203. Phone: (704) 522-1103. Fax: (704) 523-2104. Web Site:www.wsocfm.com Licensee: Infinity Radio Holdings Inc. Group owner: Infinity Broadcasting Corp. (acq 11-13-98; grpsl). Population served: 1,100,000 Leventhal, Senter & Lerman. Format: Country. Target aud: 25-54. ♦Bill Schoening, VP, gen mgr; D.J. Stout, opns mgr; Billy Grooms, gen sls mgr, rgnl sls mgr; Dustin Shearon, natl sls mgr; Chele Fassig, prom dir; Rick McCracken, mus dir; Frank Laseter, pub affrs dir; Eric Lakey, chief of engrg; Shirley Biers, traf mgr.

***WYFQ(AM)**— Oct 14, 1933: 930 khz; 5 kw-D, 1 kw-N, DA-N. TL: N35 16 00 W80 54 05. Hrs open: 24 Box 7300, 28241. Phone: (704) 523-5555. Fax: (704) 291-7807.E-mail: wyfq@bbnradio.org Web Site:www.bbnradio.org Licensee: Bible Broadcasting Network Inc. (group owner; acq 2-6-92; $475,000; 2-24-92). Population served: 325,000 Format: Traditional Christian. News: 3 hrs wkly. Target aud: General. ♦Rob Ferguson, gen mgr; John Woolery, progmg dir; Ron Muffley, engrg dir.

Cherry Point

WANG(AM)—See Havelock

WSSM(FM)—See Havelock

Cherryville

WCSL(AM)— June 28, 1967: 1590 khz; 10 kw-D, 30 w-N. TL: N35 22 27 W81 24 16. Hrs open: 24 Box 430, Lincolnton, 28093. Phone: (704) 735-8071. Fax: (704) 732-9567.E-mail: info@hrnb.com Web Site:www.hrnb.com Licensee: HRN Broadcasting Inc. (acq 4-14-2004; $500,000 with WLON(AM) Lincolnton). Population served: 5,258 Natl. Network: Westwood One, . Rgnl. Network: N.C. News Net. N.C. News Net. Format: Christian. Target aud: General. Spec prog: Loc sports 3 hrs wkly. ♦Mark Boyd, pres; Lanny Ford, gen mgr, adv dir, traf mgr; Calvin Hastings, sls dir, gen sls mgr; Milton Baker, progmg dir, sports cmtr, disc jockey; Wendy Stout, mus dir; Larry Seagle, news dir, pub affrs dir; Josh Pierce, chief of engrg; Richard Howell, sports cmtr; Tim Biggerstaff, disc jockey.

China Grove

WRNA(AM)— Nov 17, 1980: 1140 khz; 1 kw-D, 250 w-CH, DA-D. TL: N35 34 20 W80 35 21. Hrs open: 6 AM-2 hrs past sunset Box 8146, Kannapolis, 28083. Phone: (704) 857-1101. Fax: (704) 857-0680.E-mail: info@fordbroadcasting.com Web Site:www.fordbroadcasting.com Licensee: South Rowan Broadcasting Co. Group owner: Ford Broadcasting Inc. Population served: 500,000 Natl. Network: USA, . Format: Southern gospel. Target aud: General. ♦Carl Ford, pres, gen mgr, stn mgr, gen sls mgr, progmg mgr; Taylor Ford, exec VP; Angela Ford, sr VP.

Claremont

WCXN(AM)— Sept 5, 1985: 1170 khz; 10 kw-D. TL: N35 43 34 W81 08 52. Hrs open: 19 9th St. SW, Hickory, 28602. Phone: (828) 322-2683. Licensee: Birach Broadcasting Corp. Group owner: Davidson Media Group LLC (acq 8-1-2007; $800,000 with KXLQ(AM) Indianola, IA). Natl. Network: USA, . Format: Sp. Target aud: General. ♦Abel Orozco, gen mgr.

Clayton

WHPY(AM)— 1974: 1590 khz; 5 kw-D, DA. TL: N35 38 49 W78 30 21. Hrs open: Sunrise-sunset Box 535, Fellowship Baptist Church, 911 W. Main St., 27520. Phone: (919) 553-6774. Fax: (919) 359-0016.E-mail: WHPY@RADIO.COM Licensee: Fellowship Baptist Church Inc. dba Fellowship Christian Academy. (acq 8-4-97). Format: Christian. ♦Charles Ennis, pres; Keith Holland, gen mgr & stn mgr.

Clemmons

WMKS(FM)— May 3, 1947: 105.7 mhz; 34 kw. Ant 1,453 ft TL: N36 22 28 W80 22 31. Stereo. Hrs open: 24 2-B PAI Park, Greensboro, 27409. Phone: (336) 822-2000. Fax: (336) 887-0104. Web Site:www.1057kissfm.com Licensee: Clear Channel Broadcasting Licenses Inc. (group owner; (acq 9-12-2006;. $15.65 million). Format: Urban adult contemp. ♦Morgan Bohannon, gen mgr; Tim Satterfield, opns mgr; Pierre Proupe, sls dir; Brian Anthony, progmg dir.

Clinton

WCLN(AM)— Sept 27, 1975: 1170 khz; 5 kw-D. TL: N35 01 21 W78 20 58. Hrs open: Sunrise-sunset Box 28, 118 E. Main St., 28328. Phone: (910) 592-8949. Fax: (910) 592-3732.E-mail: grandpas@oldies1170.com Web Site:www.oldies1170.com Licensee: Christian Listening Network Inc. Population served: 100,000 Natl. Network: ABC, . N.C. News Net. Format: Oldies, beach. News staff: 4; News: 4.5 hrs. wkly. Spec prog: Community, gospel 8 hrs wkly. ♦George Wilson, pres; Pat Dixon, gen mgr; Nolan Wiggins, progmg dir; Don Smith, news dir; Debbie New, traf mgr.

WCLN-FM— June 11, 1967: 107.3 mhz; 13 kw. 453 ft TL: N35 02 14 W78 29 56. Stereo. Hrs open: 24 996 Helen St., Fayetteville, 28303. Phone: (910) 864-5028. Fax: (910) 864-6270.E-mail: wcln@christian107.com Web Site:www.christian107.com Licensee: Christian Listening Network Inc. (acq 7-94). Population served: 36,000 Format: Contemp Christian, inspirational. ♦George Wilson, pres; Dan DeBruler, gen mgr, sls dir; Cindy Long, prom dir; Steve Turley, progmg dir, progmg mgr; Van Clough, chief of engrg.

WRRZ(AM)— Apr 5, 1947: 880 khz; 1 kw-D. TL: N34 58 40 W78 18 15. Hrs open: Box 378, 28329. Phone: (910) 592-2165. Fax: (910) 592-8556.E-mail: wrrzradio@webtv.net Licensee: Sanchez Broadcasting Corp. (acq 10-14-2004). Population served: 50,000 Rgnl. Network: N.C. News Net. N.C. News Net. Brooks, Pierce, McLendon, Humphrey & Leonard. Format: Sp. Target aud: 25 plus. Spec prog: Black 5 hrs, relg 6 hrs, Sp 5 hrs wkly. ♦Victor Sanchez, pres; Martha Sanchez, gen mgr.

Columbia

WERX-FM— Mar 14, 1983: 102.5 mhz; 64 kw. 689 ft TL: N36 05 00 W76 36 00. Stereo. Hrs open: 24 Box 1418, Nags Head, 27959. Secondary address: 2422 S. Wrightsville Ave., Nags Head 27959. Phone: (252) 449-8331. Fax: (252) 449-8354. Web Site:www.1025theshark.com Licensee: East Carolina Radio of Elizabeth City Inc. Group owner: East Carolina Radio Group. Population served: 135,000 Format: Golden Oldies. Target aud: 18-49; moderate to high income, mobile professionals & families with children. Spec prog: Flashback, in concert, off the record, BBC classic tracks. ♦Rick Loesch, pres; R. Loesch, gen mgr; Tom Charity, opns mgr; John Maloney, gen sls mgr.

WRSF(FM)—Licensed to Columbia. See Elizabeth City

Concord

WEGO(AM)— Mar 5, 1943: 1410 khz; 1 kw-D, 182 w-N. TL: N35 24 29 W80 36 41. Hrs open: 5732 N. Tryon St., Charlotte, 28213. Phone: (704) 596-4900. Fax: (704) 596-6939.E-mail: wego@windstream.net Licensee: GHB of Waxhaw Inc. Group owner: GHB Radio Group (acq 10-28-2002; $450,000 with WSVM(AM) Valdese). Population served: 95,000 Rgnl. Network: N.C. News Net. N.C. News Net. Format: Timeless Classics. ♦Tom Gentry, gen mgr.

WPEG(FM)— June 15, 1962: 97.9 mhz; 95 kw. 1,608 ft TL: N35 21 44 W81 09 19. Stereo. Hrs open: 1520 South Blvd., Suite 300, Charlotte, 28203. Phone: (704) 342-2644. Fax: (704) 227-8979. Web Site:www.power98fm.com Licensee: Infinity Radio Holdings Inc. Group owner: Infinity Broadcasting Corp. (acq 11-13-98; grpsl). Population served: 900,000 Natl. Network: Westwood One, . Natl. Rep: Katz Radio,. Format: Urban contemp. News staff: one; News: 20 hrs wkly. Target aud: 12 plus; Black. Spec prog: Gospel 6 hrs, mix show 8 hrs wkly. ♦Bill Schoening, gen mgr; Terri Avery, opns mgr; Montressa Barber, gen sls mgr; Lindsay Slocum, progmg dir.

Creedmoor

WCMC-FM— Feb 1, 1993: 99.9 mhz; 22 kw. Ant 292 ft TL: N36 04 52 W78 28 27. Stereo. Hrs open: 24 711 Hillsboro St., Raleigh, 27605. Secondary address: Box 10100, Raleigh 27603. Phone: (919) 890-6299. Fax: (919) 890-6199.E-mail: info@999thefan.com Licensee: Capitol Broadcasting Co. Inc. Group owner: Joyner Radio Inc. (acq 4-22-2005; $7.25 million). Population served: 1,267,676 Natl. Rep: Katz Radio,. Holland & Knight. Wire Svc: AP Format: Sports. ♦Jim Goodmon, pres; Dan McGrath, CFO; Ardie Gregory, VP, gen mgr, prom VP; Joe Formicola, opns mgr; Karen Cates, gen sls mgr; Mark Tarak, natl sls mgr; Brandon Alexander, mktg mgr; Dave Shore, progmg dir.

Cullowhee

***WWCU(FM)**— Jan 15, 1977: 90.5 mhz; 760 w. -771 ft TL: N35 18 40 W83 10 34. Stereo. Hrs open: 24 Box 2728, Western Carolina Univ., 28723. Phone: (828) 227-7454. Phone: (828) 227-7173 (request line). Fax: (828) 227-7099.E-mail: info@wwcufm.com Web Site:www.wwcufm.com Licensee: Western Carolina University. Population served: 14,408 Natl. Network: ABC, . Wire Svc: Reuters Format: Classic sports. Target aud: 25-54; univ students & faculty, general public. ♦Kyle McCurry, gen mgr; Aaron D'Innocenzi, opns dir.

Dallas

WCRU(AM)— Jan 1, 1963: 960 khz; 1 kw-D, 500 w-N, DA-N. TL: N35 18 03 W81 10 13. Hrs open: 6 AM-midnight Box 477, 28034. Secondary address: 407 Robinson Clemmer Rd. 28034. Phone: (704) 922-3411. Phone: (704) 922-5960. Fax: (704) 922-6998.E-mail: monty@wzrh.com Web Site:www.wzrh.com Licensee: Truth Broadcasting Corp. (group owner; (acq 6-30-2004; $775,000). Population served: 1,500,000 Smithwick & Belendiuk. Format: Talk, teaching. News: 10 hrs wkly. Target aud: Male 25-59; college educ, income 50K. ♦Monty Monaghan, stn mgr; Stuart Epperson, pres & natl sls mgr.

***WSGE(FM)**— Oct 27, 1980: 91.7 mhz; 6 kw. Ant 853 ft TL: N35 24 26 W81 07 48. Stereo. Hrs open: 24 Ray Craig Classroom Bldg., 201 Hwy. 321 S., 28034-1499. Phone: (704) 922-4286. Phone: (704) 922-6552. Fax: (704) 922-2347.E-mail: hall.cathis@gaston.edu Web Site:www.wsge.org Licensee: Gaston College Board of Trustees. Population served: 1,500,000 Format: AAA, eclectic. News: 5 hrs wkly. Target aud: General. ♦Pat Skinner, pres; Cathis Hall, gen mgr, stn mgr; Cliff Anderson, mus dir.

Davidson

***WDAV(FM)**— Sept 1, 1973: 89.9 mhz; 100 kw. 807 ft TL: N35 26 55 W80 50 24. Stereo. Hrs open: 24 Box 8990, 28035-8990. Secondary address: 423 N. Main St. 28036. Phone: (704) 894-8900. Fax: (704) 894-2997.E-mail: wdav@wdav.org Web Site:www.wdav.org Licensee: Trustees of Davidson College. Population served: 2,000,000 Natl. Network: PRI, NPR, . Fletcher, Heald & Hildrreth. Format: Class. News: 2 hrs wkly. Target aud: General. ♦Benjamin K. Roe, gen mgr; Frank Dominguez, progmg dir; Ted Weiner, mus dir; Larry Schropp, chief of engrg; Jennifer Foster, disc jockey.

Dobson

WYZD(AM)— Oct 10, 1978: 1560 khz; 1 kw-D. TL: N36 23 36 W80 44 05. Hrs open: Box 797, 131 1/2 Atkin St., 27017. Phone: (336) 356-1560. Licensee: Gospel Broadcasting Inc. (acq 5-3-02). Rgnl. Network: N.C. News Net. N.C. News Net. Format: Gospel. ♦Ricky Cothren, gen mgr.

Dunn

WCKB(AM)— Dec 7, 1946: 780 khz; 7 kw-D, 1 w-N. TL: N35 17 00 W78 35 49. Hrs open: Sunrise-sunset PO Box 789, 28335. Secondary address: 17336 US Hwy 421 S. 28334. Phone: (910) 892-3133. Fax: (910) 892-3135.E-mail: wckb@wckb780.com Web Site:www.wckb780.com Licensee: N.C. Central Broadcasters Inc. (acq 9-15-89; $216,000; 10-2-89). Population served: 25,000 Rgnl. Network: N.C. News Net. N.C. News Net. Format: Southern gospel, religious. News: 6 hrs wkly. Target aud: 25 plus; Christian, family-oriented with regional interests. Spec prog: Buy-sell-trade 9 hrs wkly. ♦Charles Fowler, pres; Ronald Tart, gen mgr, gen sls mgr, natl sls mgr, rgnl sls mgr, prom mgr & adv dir; Lottie Squires, progmg dir, pub affrs dir, traf mgr, disc jockey; Neal Wood, asst music dir, disc jockey; Bill Lambert, chief of engrg; Al Myatt, news rptr, sports cmtr; Graden Blackman, disc jockey.

WRCQ(FM)— May 17, 1971: 103.5 mhz; 48 kw. 502 ft TL: N35 03 09 W78 38 54. Stereo. Hrs open: 24 1009 Drayton Rd., Fayetteville, 28303. Phone: (910) 864-5222. Fax: (910) 864-3065. Web Site:www.rock103rocks.com Licensee: Cumulus Licensing Corp. Group owner: Cumulus Media Inc. (acq 3-12-01; grpsl). Population served: 500,000 Natl. Network: ABC, . Borsari & Paxson. Format: Rock/AOR. News staff: one; News: one hr wkly. Target aud: 18-49. ♦Alan Buffaloe, gen mgr; Al Fields, progmg dir.

Durham

WDCG(FM)— Feb 28, 1948: 105.1 mhz; 73 kw. Ant 1,112 ft TL: N35 42 50 W78 49 04. Stereo. Hrs open: 3100 Smoketree Ct., Suite 700, Raleigh, 27604. Phone: (919) 871-1051. Fax: (919) 876-2929.E-mail: info@g105.com Web Site:www.g105.com Licensee: Capstar TX L.P. Group owner: Clear Channel Communications Inc. (acq 8-30-00; grpsl). Population served: 545,100 Natl. Network: ABC, . Format: Contemporary hit. Target aud: 18-49. ♦Ken Spitzer, gen mgr; Jon Robbins, opns dir; Tammy O'Dell, sls dir, disc jockey; Myron Bethea, gen sls mgr; Jessica Hayes, prom dir; Rick Schmidt, progmg dir; Dan McLeod, pub affrs dir; Fred Pace, chief of engrg; Tracy Leonard, traf mgr & farm dir.

WDNC(AM)— Apr 9, 1934: 620 khz; 5 kw-D, 1 kw-N, DA-2. TL: N36 02 10 W78 58 07. Hrs open: 24 4601 Six Forks Rd., Suite 520, Raleigh, 27609-5287. Phone: (919) 875-9100. Fax: (919) 510-6990.E-mail: info@wdnc.com Web Site:www.620thebull.com Licensee: WCHL-WDNC Inc. (Group owner: Curtis Media Group (acq 12-30-86). Natl. Network: Sporting News Radio Network, . Natl. Rep: McGavren Guild,. Wire Svc: AP Format: Sports. ♦Brian Maloney, gen mgr; Mike Stangl, prom dir; Adam Gold, progmg dir.

WDUR(AM)— 1947: 1490 khz; 1 kw-U. TL: N35 58 03 W78 53 18. Hrs open: 24 Box 48122, Doraville, GA, 30362. Phone: (770) 825-0095. Fax: (770) 246-0054. Web Site:www.prietobroadcasting.com Licensee: Prieto Broadcasting Inc. Group owner: Clear Channel Communications Inc. (acq 10-15-2007; $900,000). Population served: 95,438 Natl. Network: ESPN Radio, . Law office of David Tillotson. Format: Sports. ♦Filiberto Prieto, pres.

WFXC(FM)— May 15, 1971: 107.1 mhz; 2.6 kw. Ant 502 ft TL: N35 58 41 W78 48 59. Hrs open: 24 8001-101 Creedmoor Rd., Raleigh, 27613. Phone: (919) 848-9736. Fax: (919) 863-4859. Web Site:www.foxyhits.com Licensee: Radio One Licenses LLC. Group owner: Radio One Inc. (acq 11-8-2001; grpsl). Population served: 95,438 Wire Svc: UPI Format: Urban contemp. News staff: one; News: 5 hrs wkly. Target aud: 25-54; African American. Spec prog: Gospel 4 hrs wkly. ♦Gary Weiss, gen mgr; Cy Young, opns VP.

WKSL(FM)—Cary

***WNCU(FM)**— August 1995: 90.7 mhz; 50 kw. 433 ft TL: N36 03 33 W78 57 14. Stereo. Hrs open: 24 1801 Fayetteville St., Box 19875, 27707. Phone: (919) 560-9628. Fax: (919) 560-5283.E-mail: ethor@nccu.com Web Site:www.wncu.org Licensee: North Carolina Central University. Population served: 600,000 Natl. Network: NPR, PRI, . Format: Jazz, news/talk, info. News staff: one; News: 33 hrs wkly. Target aud: 25-54; middle class/middle age. ♦Edith Thorpe, gen mgr, mktg VP, prom VP, adv VP, progmg VP; Chris Whitfield, opns mgr; Uchenna Johnson, dev dir & sls dir; B.H. Hudson, mus dir; Kimberley Pierce, news dir, pub affrs dir; Jim Davis, engrg mgr.

WRJD(AM)— Oct 14, 1954: 1410 khz; 5 kw-D, 290 w-N, DA-2. TL: N36 01 44 W78 51 00. Hrs open: 24 707 Leon St., 27704-4125. Phone: (919) 220-3226. Fax: (919) 220-0006. Web Site:www.1410wrjd.com Licensee: Davidson Media Station WSRC Licensee LLC. Group owner: Willis Broadcasting Corp. (acq 3-20-2006; $1.2 million). Population served: 200,000 Format: Urban insp gospel/talk. News staff: 5. Target aud: 25-54. ♦Linda Greenwood, gen mgr.

WTIK(AM)— 1945: 1310 khz; 5 kw-D, 1 kw-N, DA-2. TL: N36 01 30 W78 54 08. Hrs open: 24 Box 2368, Davidson, 28036. Phone: (704) 987-3585.E-mail: info@wtik.com Licensee: Davidson Media Carolinas Stations LLC. Group owner: Davidson Media Group LLC (acq 5-10-2004; grpsl). Population served: 111,500 Format: Hispanic contemp. ♦Peter W. Davidson, pres.

***WXDU(FM)**— November 1983: 88.7 mhz; 1.18 kw. 103 ft TL: N36 02 08 W79 04 48. Stereo. Hrs open: 24 Box 90689, Duke Station, 27708. Phone: (919) 684-2957. Fax: (919) 684-3260.E-mail: wxdu@duke.edu Web Site:www.wxdu.org Licensee: Duke University. Format: Div. Target aud: General. Spec prog: Jazz 18 hrs, urban sound & hip hop 12 hrs wkly. ♦Jim Davis, chief of engrg.

East Fayetteville

***WWFJ(FM)**—Not on air, target date: unknown: 88.1 mhz; 1 kw. Ant 187 ft TL: N34 59 40 W78 48 24.1. Hrs open: 5587 U.S. Hwy. 1 North, Vass, 28394. Phone: (910) 693-7729. Licensee: Highland Baptist Church. ♦Bill Vaughn, pres.

Eden

WCLW(AM)— Aug 16, 1970: 1130 khz; 1 kw-D. TL: N36 31 21 W79 45 55. Hrs open: 116 S. Franklin St., Reidsville, 27320. Phone: (336) 634-1774. Fax: (336) 342-6497. Web Site:www.carolinabaptistcollege.com/radio.html Licensee: Dr. Jerry L. Carter dba Reidsville Baptist Church. (acq 6-26-98; $150,000). Format: Gospel. Target aud: 25-49. ♦Dean Lundy, gen mgr, opns mgr & progmg mgr.

WGBT(FM)— Mar 20, 1949: 94.5 mhz; 100 kw. Ant 981 ft TL: N36 20 48 W79 54 30. Stereo. Hrs open: 2-B Pai park, Greensboro, 27409. Phone: (336) 822-2000. Fax: (336) 887-0104. Licensee: Clear Channel Broadcasting Licenses Inc. Group owner: Clear Channel Communications Inc. (acq 1996; grpsl). Population served: 15,871 Natl. Rep: Clear Channel,. Format: Sp. ♦Morgan Bohannon, gen mgr; Pierre Proupe, sls dir; Carlos Pivano, progmg dir.

WLOE(AM)— Dec 20, 1946: 1490 khz; 1 kw-U. TL: N36 30 21 W79 46 18. Hrs open: 5 AM-10 PM
Rebroadcasts WMYN Mayodan NC 100%.
Box 279, Mayodan, 27027. Phone: (336) 427-9696; (336) 627-9563. Fax: (336) 548-4636.E-mail: info@wloewmyn.com Web Site:www.wloewmyn.com Licensee: Mayo Broadcasting Corp. (acq 6-90; $100,000; 6-4-90). Population served: 200,000 Natl. Network: Salem Radio Network, USA, . Format: Info, talk, relg. News staff: one; News: 30 hrs wkly. Target aud: 25 plus; general. ♦Richard D. Hall, pres; Mike Moore, gen mgr; Annette Moore, stn mgr.

Edenton

WBXB(FM)— June 18, 1976: 100.1 mhz; 50 kw. 302 ft TL: N36 07 11 W76 35 29. Stereo. Hrs open: 24 Box 765, 27932. Secondary address: 1900 Paradise Rd. 27932. Phone: (252) 482-8680. Fax: (252) 482-4260.E-mail: robbmal@aol.com Licensee: Willis Family Broadcasting Inc. (group owner; acq 3-4-92; grpsl; 3-23-92). Population served: 7,000 Natl. Network: American Urban, . Format: Gospel. News: 8 hrs wkly. Target aud: General. ♦Bishop L.E. Willis Sr., pres; Toina Willis, gen mgr.

WZBO(AM)— November 1955: 1260 khz; 1 kw-D, 34 kw-N. TL: N36 05 00 W76 36 00. Hrs open: Box 950, 27932. Phone: (252) 482-2104. Fax: (252) 482-5591.E-mail: swalker@ecri.net Web Site:www.ecri.net Licensee: East Carolina Radio of Elizabeth City Inc. Group owner: East Carolina Radio Group (acq 3-12-90; $400,000 with co-located FM; 4-2-90). Population served: 115,000 Rgnl. Network: N.C. News Net. Tharrington, Smith & Hargrove. Format: Hot hits rgnl Mexican. ♦Rick Loesch, pres, gen mgr, stn mgr; Tom Charity, opns mgr; Sam Walker, progmg dir.

Elizabeth City

WCNC(AM)— September 1939: 1240 khz; 1 kw-U. TL: N36 18 38 W76 13 56. Hrs open: 24 Box 1246, 27906-1246. Secondary address: 911 Parsonage St. Ext. 27909. Phone: (252) 335-4379. Fax: (252) 338-5275.E-mail: swalker@ecri.net Web Site:www.ecri.net Licensee: East Carolina Radio of Elizabeth City Inc. Group owner: East Carolina Radio Group (acq 10-29-98; $230,000). Population served: 120,000 Format: Hot hits rgnl Mexican. ♦Rick Loesch, pres; Cuervo Curtis, opns mgr, gen sls mgr; Tom Charity, gen sls mgr; Sam Walker, progmg dir, progmg mgr.

WGAI(AM)— Nov 2, 1947: 560 khz; 1 kw-D, 500 w-N, DA-2. TL: N36 20 16 W76 14 49. Stereo. Hrs open: 24 Box 1897, Kill Devil Hills, 27948. Phone: (252) 480-4655. Fax: (252) 441-8063.E-mail: info@wgai.com Licensee: Max Radio of the Carolinas Licenses LLC. Group owner: MAX Media L.L.C. (acq 11-12-2002; grpsl). Population served: 250,000 Natl. Network: CNN Radio, . Rgnl. Network: Agri-Net. Agrinet Format: News/talk, sports. News staff: 3; News: 30 hrs wkly. Target aud: General. Spec prog: Relg 4 hrs, farm 7 hrs, Black 4 hrs, relg 4 hrs wkly. ♦Mike Smith, gen mgr.

***WGPS(FM)**— February 2003: 88.3 mhz; 50 kw. Ant 446 ft TL: N36 18 40 W76 17 34. Hrs open: 905 Halstead Blvd., Suite 29, 27909. Phone: (252) 334-1883. Fax: (252) 333-1459.E-mail: wgpsradio@earthlink.net Web Site:www.wgpsradio.com Licensee: CSN International (group owner). Format: Christian teaching, praise & worship music. ♦Jeff Ozanne, gen mgr; Darla Ozanne, progmg dir; Maria Van DeWalker, mus dir.

WKJX(FM)— Aug 21, 1984: 96.7 mhz; 50 kw. Ant 407 ft TL: N36 12 10 W75 52 23. Stereo. Hrs open: 24 Box 1246, 27906. Secondary address: 911 Parsonage St. Ext. 27909. Phone: (252) 338-0196. Fax: (252) 338-5275.E-mail: swalker@ecri.net Web Site:www.ecri.net Licensee: East Carolina Radio of Elizabeth City Inc. Group owner: East Carolina Radio Group (acq 5-21-98; $475,000). Natl. Network: NBC Radio, Westwood One, . Rgnl. Network: N.C. News Net. N.C. News Net.

Format: Soft adult contemp. News staff: one; News: one hr wkly. Target aud: 18-55. ♦Rick Loesch, pres; Cuervo Curtis, opns mgr; Tom Charity, gen mgr & gen sls mgr; Sam Walker, progmg dir.

WRSF(FM)—(Columbia, June 13, 1983: 105.7 mhz; 100 kw. 613 ft TL: N35 53 18 W76 13 50. (CP: Ant 987 ft.). Stereo. Hrs open: 24 Box 1418, Nags Head, 27959. Secondary address: 2422 S. Wrightsville Ave., Nags Head 27959. Phone: (252) 449-8331. Fax: (252) 449-8354. Web Site:www.ecri.net Licensee: East Carolina Radio of Elizabeth City Inc. Group owner: East Carolina Radio Group (acq 1996). Population served: 550,000 Format: Hot Country. News staff: one; News: 5 hrs wkly. Target aud: 18-54; young & mid-range adults. ♦John Maloney, gen sls mgr, natl sls mgr; Jerry Barco, traf mgr; Ray Hall, disc jockey.

***WRVS-FM**— Mar 18, 1986: 89.9 mhz; 41 kw. 280 ft TL: N36 16 55 W76 12 44. Stereo. Hrs open: 24 1704 Weeksville Rd., Campus Box 800, Williams Hall, 27909. Phone: (252) 335-3515. Fax: (252) 335-3745. Licensee: Elizabeth City State University. Natl. Network: NPR, PRI, . Format: Urban contemp, var div, pub affrs. News staff: one; News: 5 hrs wkly. Target aud: 18-24; young adult, college. Spec prog: Jazz 6 hrs, Black 20 hrs, gospel 20. ♦Willie Gilchnist, CEO; Melbay Brown, gen mgr.

Elizabethtown

WBLA(AM)— Aug 3, 1956: 1440 khz; 5 kw-D, 197 w-N. TL: N34 37 32 W78 37 28. Hrs open: 24 Box 458, 512 Peanut Rd., 28337. Secondary address: Box 28 , Clinton 28329. Phone: (910) 862-3184. Phone: (910) 862-2000. Fax: (910) 872-0100.E-mail: wgqr1057@carolina.net Web Site:www.wgqr1057.com Licensee: Sound Business of Elizabethtown Inc. (acq 4-29-98; $525,000 with co-located FM). Population served: 92,000 Rgnl. Network: N.C. News Net. N.C. News Net. Format: Oldies, beach. News: 5 hrs wkly. Target aud: 25-54. Spec prog: Black gospel/relg 8 hrs wkly. ♦Lee Hauser, pres; Bruce Dickerson, VP; Patrick Dixon, gen mgr; Al Radlein, progmg dir, local news ed, disc jockey; Buddy Wommack, chief of engrg; Bill Monroe, disc jockey.

WGQR(FM)— December 1989: 105.7 mhz; 7.7 kw. Ant 583 ft TL: N34 44 05 W78 47 25. Stereo. Hrs open: 24 Dups AM 50% Box458, 512 Peanut Rd., Elizabethtowm, 28337. Secondary address: Box 28 28329. Web Site:www.wgqr1057.com Population served: 200,000 Format: Southern gospel. News: 6 hrs wkly. ♦Al Radlein, local news ed, disc jockey; Buddy Edwards, disc jockey.

Elkin

WIFM-FM— 1949: 100.9 mhz; 600 w. 709 ft TL: N36 11 33 W80 50 59. Hrs open: 24 Box 1038, 28621. Secondary address: 813 N. Bridge St. 28621. Phone: (336) 835-2511. Fax: (336) 835-5248.E-mail: wifm@wifmradio.com Web Site:www.wifmradio.com Licensee: Yadkin Valley Broadcasting Corp. (acq 1-12-2004; $1.15 million). Natl. Network: ABC, . Format: Classic hits/Today's hits, Adult contemp. News staff: one. Target aud: 25-45. ♦Gary York, pres; Paula Rice, gen mgr, gen sls mgr; Jerry Laws, progmg dir; Stony Owens, engrg mgr.

Elon

***WSOE(FM)**— November 1978: 89.3 mhz; 500 w. 104 ft TL: N36 06 25 W79 30 22. Stereo. Hrs open: Campus Box 6000, 27244. Phone: (336) 278-7210. Fax: (336) 278-7298.E-mail: wsoe@elon.edu Web Site:www.elon.edu/wsoe Licensee: Elon University. Format: Alternative Rock. ♦Nikki Wasikowski, gen mgr; Ryan Sweeney, progmg dir & progmg.

Enfield

WBOB-FM— July 14, 2007: 107.3 mhz; 4.1 kw. Ant 279 ft TL: N36 09 59 W77 46 46. Hrs open: 24 301 S. Church St., Suite 270, Rocky Mount, 27804. Phone: (252) 446-9262. Fax: (252) 446-9261.E-mail: bwilliams@newlitemedia.com Web Site:www.thepromise1073.com Licensee: Julie Epperson. Natl. Network: American Urban, . Format: Gospel. ♦Bronson Williams, progmg.

Erwin

***WUAW(FM)**— May 11, 1990: 88.3 mhz; 3 kw. 191 ft TL: N35 20 15 W78 39 49. Stereo. Hrs open: 24 Triton High School, 215 Maynard Lake Rd., 28339. Phone: (910) 897-8070. Fax: (910) 897-3148.E-mail: wuaw883fm@gaggle.net Web Site:www.wuaw.homestead.com Licensee: Central Carolina Community College. Format: Variety/Diverse. ♦Matt Garrett, pres; Ron McLamb, gen mgr & progmg dir; Dr. Jim Davis, chief of engrg.

Fair Bluff

WODR(FM)— 2003: 105.3 mhz; 11 kw. Ant 492 ft TL: N34 17 01 W78 48 09. Hrs open: 338 E. Mclver Rd., Florence, SC, 29506. Phone: (843) 665-1230. Licensee: The Padner Group LLC (acq 12-4-2003; $1.25 million). Format: Oldies. ♦William Polk, gen mgr.

WWKO(AM)— July 1988: Stn currently dark. 1480 khz; 1 kw-D, 48 w-N. TL: N34 19 23 W79 00 07. Hrs open: 24 Box 424, Cerrogordo, 28430. Secondary address: 12045 Andrew Jackson Hwy. 28439. Phone: (910) 649-1480. Fax: (910) 649-7266.E-mail: wsrc1480@emdarqmail.com Licensee: Rama Radio of North Carolina Inc. (acq 4-1-2006; $120,000). Population served: 250,000 Format: Oldies. ♦Anthony Lee, stn mgr.

Fairmont

WFMO(AM)— July 13, 1953: 860 khz; 1 kw-D, 12 w-N. TL: N34 31 03 W79 06 19. (CP: COL Conway, SC. 50 kw-D, 740 w-N, DA-2. TL: N33 49 40 W79 10 20). Hrs open: Box 668, Hwy 41 N., 28340. Phone: (910) 628-6781. Fax: (910) 628-6648. Licensee: Pro Media Inc. Group owner: Clark-Pittman Group (acq 12-31-86; $600,000 with co-located FM; 11-10-86). Population served: 150,000 Rgnl. Network: N.C. News Net. N.C. News Net. Format: Black, gospel, relg. Target aud: 25-54. Spec prog: Farm 5 hrs wkly. ♦James C. Clark, pres, gen mgr, stn mgr & gen sls mgr.

WSTS(FM)— August 1975: 100.9 mhz; 50 kw. Ant 489 ft TL: N34 16 17 W78 56 24. Stereo. Hrs open: Box 668, 28340. Phone: (910) 628-6781. Fax: (910) 628-6648.E-mail: wstf@carolina.net Licensee: Davidson Media Station WSTS Licensee LLC. (acq 10-31-2005). Population served: 500,000 Rgnl. Network: N.C. News Net. N.C. News Net. Format: Southern gospel. ♦James Clark, gen mgr; Shanna Todd, disc jockey.

Fairview

WPEK(AM)— July 4, 1997: 880 khz; 1.1 kw-D, DA. TL: N35 32 52 W82 28 16. Hrs open: 13 Summerlin Rd., Asheville, 28806. Phone: (828) 257-2700. Fax: (828) 255-7850.E-mail: info@880thepeak.com Web Site:www.880ThePEAK.com Licensee: Clear Channel Broadcasting Licenses Inc. Group owner: Clear Channel Communications Inc. (acq 3-21-01; grpsl). Population served: 225,000 Natl. Network: CBS, . Format: Talk. Target aud: 25-64; generally upscale adults. ♦Ken Salyer, gen mgr.

Farmville

WGHB(AM)— Dec 12, 1959: 1250 khz; 5 kw-D, 2.5 kw-N, DA-2. TL: N35 36 17 W77 34 29. Hrs open: 24 Box 3333, Greenville, 27836. Phone: (252) 317-1250. Fax: (252) 317-1255.E-mail: info@pirateradio1250.com Web Site:www.pirateradio1250.com Licensee: Pirate Media Group LLC (acq 11-25-03; $650,000). Population served: 500,000 Natl. Network: USA, . Format: Talk, sports. News: 8 hrs wkly. Target aud: 25-54. ♦Troy Dreyfus, gen mgr; Wesley Hines, disc jockey.

WTIB(FM)— Mar 24, 1974: 94.3 mhz; 3.9 kw. Ant 407 ft TL: N35 36 25 W77 28 05. Stereo. Hrs open: 24 211 Commerce St., Suite C, Greenville, 27835. Phone: (252) 355-1037. Fax: (252) 355-2234. Web Site:www.talkfm943.com Licensee: Inner Banks Media LLC. Group owner: Archway Broadcasting Group (acq 3-12-2007; grpsl). Population served: 100,000 Rgnl. Network: N.C. News Net. N.C. News Net. Cole, Raywid & Braverman. Format: Talk. News: 3 hrs wkly. Target aud: 25-54. ♦Henry Hinton, gen mgr & chief of engrg.

Fayetteville

WAZZ(AM)— 1947: 1490 khz; 1 kw-U. TL: N35 03 45 W78 54 30. Hrs open: 24 508 Person St., 28301. Phone: (910) 486-2055. Phone: (910) 484-1490. Fax: (910) 323-5635. Licensee: WFLB License L.P. Group owner: Beasley Broadcast Group (acq 1996; $228,635). Population served: 200,000 Rgnl. Network: Southern Farm. Natl. Rep: D & R Radio,. Format: Adults standards. News: 14 hrs wkly. Target aud: 35-64. Spec prog: Atlanta Braves baseball, Charlotte Bobcats basketball, auto racing. ♦George G. Beasley, CEO, gen mgr; Mac Edwards, VP, mktg mgr; Curt Nunnery, opns mgr, sls dir, gen sls mgr; Bryan Kusilka, natl sls mgr; Van Clough, chief of engrg.

WFAY(AM)— 1947: 1230 khz; 1 kw-U. TL: N35 04 15 W78 52 45. Hrs open: 24
Simulcast with WCIE(AM) Spring Lake 100%.
5418 Yadkin Rd., Suite D, 28303. Phone: (910) 222-1450. Fax: (704) 537-9735. Web Site:www.ncespn.com Licensee: Norsan Consulting and Management Inc. (acq 5-25-2006; $850,000). Natl. Network: ESPN Radio, . Rgnl. Network: N.C. News Net. Format: Sports. ♦Norberto Sanchez, CEO; Paul Lawing, gen mgr.

WFLB(FM)—See Laurinburg

WFNC(AM)— 1940: 640 khz; 10 kw-D, 1 kw-N. TL: N35 04 46 W78 55 58. Hrs open: 24 1009 Drayton Rd., 28303. Phone: (910) 864-5222. Fax: (910) 864-6208.E-mail: jimcooke@cumulus.com Web Site:www.wfnc640am.com Licensee: Cumulus Licensing Corp. Group owner: Cumulus Media Inc. (acq 3-12-2001; grpsl). Population served: 400,000 Natl. Network: CBS, . Wire Svc: AP Format: News/talk. News staff: 4; News: 20 hrs wkly. Target aud: 35 plus. ♦Alan Buffaloe, gen mgr; Jim Cooke, progmg dir; Gail Galbreath, engrg dir.

***WFSS(FM)**— Dec 7, 1977: 91.9 mhz; 100 kw. 440 ft TL: N35 04 22 W78 53 27. Stereo. Hrs open: 24 1200 Murchison Rd., 28301. Phone: (910) 672-1474. Fax: (910) 672-1964.E-mail: wfss@uncfsu.edu Web Site:wfss.org Licensee: Fayetteville State University Board of Trustees. Population served: 350,000 Natl. Network: NPR, PRI, . Wire Svc: AP Format: Jazz, news. News staff: one; News: 38 hrs wkly. Target aud: 18 plus; general. Spec prog: Gospel 2 hrs, African rhythms 2 hrs, class 5 hrs, folk 3 hrs wkly. ♦Jeffrey Womble, gen mgr; Yvonne Jackson, dev dir, mktg dir & prom dir; Janet G. Wright, progmg dir; Jimmy Miller, mus dir; Kathy Klaus, news dir; Ron Martin, chief of engrg; Arvetra Jones Jr., relg ed.

WIDU(AM)— Jan 20, 1958: 1600 khz; 5 kw-D, 147 w-N, DA-2. TL: N35 02 58 W78 51 33. Hrs open: 24 Box 2247, 28302. Secondary address: 1338 Bragg Blvd. 28301. Phone: (910) 483-6111. Phone: (910) 486-9438. Fax: (910) 483-6601.E-mail: widu1600@aol.com Web Site:www.rejoicewidu.com Licensee: Charles W. Cookman (acq 1-17-89). Population served: 300,000 Format: Black, gospel, news/talk. ♦Wes Cookman, pres; Sandra Lofton, gen mgr; Val Holiday, progmg dir.

WQSM(FM)— 1947: 98.1 mhz; 100 kw. 830 ft TL: N35 04 46 W78 55 58. Stereo. Hrs open: Prog sep from AM 1009 Drayton Rd., 28303. Phone: (910) 864-5222. Fax: (910) 864-6208.E-mail: jeffdavis@cumulus.com Web Site:www.cumulus.com Format: CHR. Target aud: General. ♦Chris Chaos, progmg dir; Paul Michels, rsch dir; Robin Duff, traf mgr; Rick Jensen, disc jockey.

***WYBH(FM)**— 2008: 91.1 mhz; 255 w. Ant 640 ft TL: N35 03 35 W78 59 24. Hrs open:
Rebroadcasts WYFQ(AM) Charlotte 100%.
Box 7300, Charlotte, 28241. Phone: (704) 523-5555. Web Site:www.bbnradio.org Licensee: Bible Broadcasting Network Inc. Natl. Network: Bible Bcstg Net, . Format: Christian. ♦Lowell Davey, pres.

WZFX(FM)—(Whiteville, Feb 21, 1962: 99.1 mhz; 100 kw. 1,000 ft TL: N34 44 05 W78 47 25. Stereo. Hrs open: Box 1809, 28302. Phone: (910) 486-4991. Fax: (910) 486-6720. Web Site:www.fox99.com Licensee: WDAS License L.P. Group owner: Beasley Broadcast Group (acq 5-8-97; $11.5 million). Natl. Rep: Katz Radio,. Format: Urban contemp. Target aud: 18-49. ♦George G. Beasley, CEO; Daniel Highsmith, VP; Mac Edwards, gen mgr; Tila Comstock, gen sls mgr; Mike Nicholson, progmg mgr; Van Clough, chief of engrg.

Fletcher

WQNQ(FM)— Feb 5, 1991: 104.3 mhz; 470 w. Ant 1,145 ft TL: N35 31 39 W82 29 49. Stereo. Hrs open: 24 13 Summerlin Rd., Asheville, 28806. Phone: (828) 257-2700. Fax: (828) 255-7850.E-mail: info@star1043.com Web Site:www.star1043.com Licensee: Clear Channel Broadcasting Licenses Inc. Group owner: Clear Channel Communications Inc. (acq 3-21-2001; grpsl). Population served: 150,000 Reddy, Begley & McCormick. Format: Hits of the 80s, 90s & now, hot adult contemp. News staff: 2; News: 10 hrs wkly. Target aud: 25-54. Spec prog: Relg 2 hrs, news/talk 5 hrs wkly. ♦Ken Salyer, gen mgr.

Forest City

WAGY(AM)— Oct 15, 1958: 1320 khz; 1 kw-D, 500 w-N, DA-N. TL: N35 21 19 W81 52 52. Hrs open: Box 280, 28043. Phone: (828) 245-9887. Fax: (828) 245-9880. Licensee: WAGY Inc. (acq 12-13-85; $310,000; 11-4-85). Natl. Network: ABC, . Format: Real country. ♦Malcolm Watson, gen mgr.

WTPT(FM)— Sept 10, 1947: 93.3 mhz; 93 kw. Ant 2,030 ft TL: N35 16 19 W82 14 00. Stereo. Hrs open: 25 Garlington Rd., Greenville, SC, 29615. Phone: (864) 271-9200. Fax: (864) 242-1567.E-mail: info@newrock933.com Web Site:www.newrock933.com Licensee: Entercom Greenville License LLC. Group owner: Barnstable Broadcasting Inc. (acq 10-7-2005; grpsl). Population served: 1,000,000 Format: Active

rock. ♦David J. Field, pres; Sharon Day, gen mgr; Mark Hendrix, progmg dir; Paige Pirtle, news dir.

WWOL(AM)— Sept 10, 1947: 780 khz; 10 kw-D. TL: N35 21 02 W81 54 04. Hrs open: Sunrise-sunset 1381 W. Main St., 28043. Phone: (828) 245-0078. Fax: (828) 245-8528.E-mail: wwol@rfci.net Licensee: Holly Springs Baptist Church. (acq 3-1-90; $150,000; 3-19-90). Population served: 608,804 Natl. Network: USA, . Format: Southern gospel, relg. News staff: 3. Target aud: General. Spec prog: Our community forum, NC family policy issues. ♦Wade H. Huntley, pres & stn mgr; Ray Davis, chief of opns, progmg dir, pub affrs dir; Terri Frashier, sls dir, gen sls mgr, mktg dir; Jean Bruce, traf mgr.

Franklin

***WFQS(FM)—** Mar 31, 1989: 91.3 mhz; 265 w. 2,304 ft TL: N35 10 24 W83 34 52. Stereo. Hrs open: 24
Rebroadcasts WCQS(FM) Asheville 100%.
73 Broadway, Asheville, 28801. Phone: (828) 253-6875. Fax: (828) 253-6700.E-mail: info@wcqs.org Web Site:www.wcqs.org Licensee: Western N.C. Public Radio Inc. Population served: 500,000 Natl. Network: NPR, PRI, . Cohn & Marks. Format: Class, jazz, news. News staff: one; News: 35 hrs wkly. Target aud: 25 plus. Spec prog: Folk 9 hrs wkly. ♦Edward Subkis, gen mgr; Lee Wilcher, opns dir; Steve Busey, sls dir; Barbara Sayer, progmg dir; Richard J. Kowal, mus dir; David Hurand, news dir; Tom Spaight, chief of engrg.

WFSC(AM)— May 5, 1957: 1050 khz; 1 kw-D. TL: N35 12 42 W83 22 07. Hrs open: 24 Box 470, 28744. Secondary address: 180 Radio Hill Rd. 28734. Phone: (828) 524-4418. Phone: (828) 524-5395. Fax: (828) 524-2788.E-mail: gibson@gacaradio.com Web Site:www.1050wfsc.com Licensee: Sutton Radiocasting Corp. Group owner: Georgia-Carolina Radiocasting Companies (acq 12-14-2001; grpsl). Population served: 75,000 Natl. Network: CBS, ABC, . Rgnl. Network: N.C. News Net. N.C. News Net. Dan J. Alpert. Format: Oldies. News staff: one; News: 12 hrs wkly. Target aud: 35 plus. ♦Douglas M. Sutton Jr., pres; Jeremy Duke, VP, gen mgr; Chad Dorsette, news dir; Tim Stephens, chief of engrg.

WNCC-FM— Sept 1, 1965: 96.7 mhz; 6 kw. 204 ft TL: N35 12 42 W83 22 07. Stereo. Hrs open: 24 Prog sep from AM Box 470, 28734. Secondary address: 180 Radio Hill Rd. 28744. Phone: (828) 524-4418. Phone: (828) 524-5395. Fax: (828) 524-2788.E-mail: gibson@gacaradio.com Web Site:www.967wncc.com Population served: 75,000 Natl. Network: ABC, . Format: Country. News staff: one; News: 6 hrs wkly. Target aud: 25 plus.

WPFJ(AM)— May 24, 1979: 1480 khz; 5 kw-D, 13 w-N. TL: N35 10 58 W83 21 27. Stereo. Hrs open: 24 185 Franklin Plaza, 28734. Phone: (828) 369-5033. Fax: (828) 369-3197.E-mail: thedove@wpfj.com Web Site:www.wpfj.com Licensee: Drake Enterprises Ltd. (acq 2-16-94; 3-28-94). Population served: 66,500 Natl. Network: Salem Radio Network, . Format: Relg. News: 12 hrs wkly. Target aud: 25-54. ♦Johnny Lee, gen sls mgr; Brenda Wooten, prom mgr; Rick Cruse, chief of engrg & disc jockey.

Fuquay-Varina

WNNL(FM)— Dec 1, 1980: 103.9 mhz; 7.9 kw. 577 ft TL: N35 35 47 W78 45 18. Stereo. Hrs open: 24 8001-101 Creedmoor Rd., Raleigh, 27613. Phone: (919) 848-9736. Fax: (919) 848-4724.E-mail: mmarinaro@radio-one.com Web Site:www.thelight1039.com Licensee: Radio One Licenses LLC. Group owner: Radio One Inc. (acq 11-8-01; grpsl). Population served: 870,000 Natl. Network: ABC, . Natl. Rep: Christal,. Format: Inspirational, gospel. News: 20 hrs wkly. Target aud: 25-54; educated, upper income, professionals. ♦Gary Weiss, gen mgr; Cy Young, opns dir; Kim Gattis, sls dir; Jodi Luke, natl sls mgr; Steven Walker, gen sls mgr & prom dir; Jerry Smith, progmg dir.

Garner

WRTG(AM)— Aug 11, 1969: 1000 khz; 1 kw-D. TL: N35 43 50 W78 36 12. Hrs open:
Rebroadcasts WRTP(AM) Chapel Hill 100%.
Estuardo Valdemar Rodriguez and Leonor Rodriguez Stns, 1010 Vermont Ave. N.W. Suite 100, Suite 100, Washington, DC, 20005. Phone: (202) 638-1959. Fax: (202) 638-6127.E-mail: estuardovaldemar@hotmail.com Licensee: Estuardo Valdemar Rodriguez and Leonor Rodriguez. Group owner: WRTP Radio Network (acq 2-2-2005; grpsl). Population served: 121,577 Natl. Network: USA, . Format: Mexican rgnl. ♦Estuardo Valdemar Rodriguez, gen mgr.

Gaston

WTRG(FM)— Nov 28, 1988: 97.9 mhz; 1.35 kw. Ant 488 ft TL: N36 27 38 W77 33 52. Stereo. Hrs open: 24 Box 910, Roanoke Rapids, 27870. Phone: (252) 538-9790. Fax: (252) 538-0378. Licensee: First Media Radio LLC. (group owner; (acq 7-22-2003; grpsl). Rgnl. Network: N.C. News Net., Va. News Net. Va. News Net. Format: Oldies. News: 2 hrs wkly. Target aud: 21-54. ♦Al Haskins, gen mgr; Les Atkins, opns dir.

Gastonia

WBAV-FM— September 1947: 101.9 mhz; 99 kw. Ant 987 ft TL: N35 13 56 W81 16 35. Stereo. Hrs open: 1520 South Blvd., Suite 300, Charlotte, 28203. Phone: (704) 342-2644. Fax: (704) 227-8985. Web Site:www.v1019.com Licensee: Infinity Radio Holdings Inc. Group owner: Infinity Broadcasting Corp. (acq 11-13-98; grpsl). Population served: 900,000 Natl. Rep: Christal,. Leventhal, Senter & Leman. Format: Adult contemp, rhythm and blues. News staff: one; News: 20 hrs wkly. Target aud: 25-54; black adults. Spec prog: Gospel 6 hrs, mixed shows 8 hrs wkly. ♦Bill Schoening, gen mgr; Terri Avery, opns mgr; Rob Grossman, gen sls mgr; Carol Crimminger, traf mgr.

WCRU(AM)—See Dallas

WGAS(AM)—See South Gastonia

WGNC(AM)— March 1939: 1450 khz; 1 kw-U. TL: N35 16 32 W81 12 04. Hrs open: 24 1511 W. Dixon Blvd., Shelby, 28152. Phone: (704) 868-8222. Fax: (704) 482-4680.E-mail: netoldies@aol.com Web Site:www.theboss.us Licensee: HRN Broadcasting Inc. (acq 10-6-2006; $1.5 million with WOHS(AM) Shelby). Population served: 47,142 Natl. Network: ABC, CBS Radio, Westwood One, . Rgnl. Network: N.C. News Net. N.C. News Net. Format: Oldies, sports, beach. News staff: one; News: 5 hrs wkly. Target aud: 18-49. ♦D. Mark Boyd III, pres; Terresa Hastings, VP; Calvin R. Hastings, gen mgr, gen sls mgr; Harold Watson, sls dir, adv dir; Lori Deitz, prom mgr; Mike Slade, progmg dir; Andy Foster, mus dir; Anna McGinnis, news dir, pub affrs dir; Larry Schropp, chief of engrg.

Goldsboro

WFMC(AM)— Nov 11, 1951: 730 khz; 1 kw-D, 98 w-N. TL: N35 22 25 W78 00 41. Hrs open: 24 2581 U.S. Hwy. 70 W., 27530. Phone: (919) 736-1150. Fax: (919) 736-3876.E-mail: bjohnston@curtismedia.com Web Site:www.730wfmc.com Licensee: New Age Communications Inc. Group owner: Curtis Media Group (acq 6-95; $300,000). Population served: 120,000 Rgnl. Network: Southern Farm, N.C. News Net. Format: Black gospel, relg. News staff: one; News: 10 hrs wkly. Target aud: 25+. ♦Donald W. Curtis, pres; Bill Johnston, gen mgr, gen sls mgr, disc jockey; Averill Williams, progmg dir; Ronyn Wade, news dir & disc jockey.

WGBR(AM)— 1939: 1150 khz; 5 kw-D, 800 w-N, DA-2. TL: N35 22 26 W78 00 42. Hrs open: 24 2581 U.S. Hwy. 70 W., 27530. Phone: (919) 736-1150. Fax: (919) 736-3876. Licensee: New Age Communications L.P. Group owner: Curtis Media Group (acq 2-15-89; $2.2 million with co-located FM; 3-6-89). Population served: 107,000 Natl. Network: CNN Radio, . Rgnl. Network: N.C. News Net. N.C. News Net. Wire Svc: AP Format: News/talk. News staff: one; News: 11 hrs wkly. Target aud: 25 plus. ♦Donald W. Curtis, pres; Bill Johnston, gen mgr, gen sls mgr; Kari DelaCruz, opns mgr, chief of engrg; Wayne Alley, progmg dir; Robyn Wade, news dir.

WKIX(FM)— Feb 2, 1972: 102.3 mhz; 2.1 kw. Ant 561 ft TL: N35 23 54 W78 00 38. Stereo. Hrs open: 24
Simulcast with WWMY(FM) Raleigh 100%.
3012 Highwoods Blvd., Suite 201, Raleigh, 27604. Phone: (919) 790-9392. Fax: (919) 790-8369.E-mail: bcampbell@curtismedia.com Web Site:www.y1029.com Licensee: New Age Communications Inc. Group owner: Curtis Media Group (acq 7-1-96; $550,000). Population served: 120,000 Format: Oldies 60s & 70s. News staff: 4. ♦Don Curtis, pres; Mike Hartel, gen mgr.

WRSV(FM)—See Rocky Mount

WSSG(AM)— Oct 22, 1955: 1300 khz; 1 kw-D, 49 w-N. TL: N35 24 08 W78 01 20. Hrs open: 116 W. Mulberry St., 27530. Phone: (919) 734-1300. Licensee: Robert Swinson (acq 12-18-97; $75,000). Format: Christian music. ♦Reginald Swinson, gen mgr.

WYMY(FM)— 1946: 96.9 mhz; 100 kw. 1,056 ft TL: N35 23 52 W78 08 07. Stereo. Hrs open: 24 Prog sep from AM 3012 Highwoods Blvd., Raleigh, 27604. Phone: (919) 790-9392. Fax: (919) 736-3876. Population served: 1,500,000 Rgnl. Network: N.C. News Net. N.C. News Net. Wire Svc: AP Format: Mexican, Sp. News: 2 hrs wkly. Target aud: 25-54. ♦Jon Bloom, gen mgr.

Graham

WBAG(AM)—See Burlington-Graham

WSML(AM)— Dec 2, 1967: 1200 khz; 10 kw-D, 1 kw-N, DA-N. TL: N36 08 01 W79 28 14. Hrs open: 24
Rebroadcasts WSJS-AM 600, Winston-Salem NC 90%.
875 W. 5th St., Winston Salem, 27101. Phone: (336) 227-4254. Fax: (336) 227-4254. Licensee: Crescent Media Group LLC. Group owner: Infinity Broadcasting Corp. (acq 2-14-2007; grpsl). Population served: 1,000,000 Miller & Fields,P.C. Format: News/talk. Spec prog: Black 18 hrs wkly. ♦Tom Hamilton, gen mgr & gen sls mgr; Larry Ingold, progmg dir; George Newman, chief of engrg.

Granite Falls

WYCV(AM)— Feb 22, 1963: 900 khz; 2.5 kw-D, 251 w-N. TL: N35 47 10 W81 25 00. Hrs open: 5 AM-11 PM (M-S); 6 AM-9 PM (Su) Box 486, 398 South Main St., 28630. Phone: (828) 396-3361. Phone: (828) 396-3362. Fax: (828) 396-9193. Web Site:www.gospel9.com Licensee: Freedom Broadcasting Corp. Group owner: Marvin L. Sizemore (acq 4-29-92). Population served: 684,000 Natl. Network: USA, AP Radio, . Smithwick & Belendiuk. Format: Relg, southern gospel. News staff: one; News: 2 hrs wkly. Target aud: 3-100. ♦Marvin Sizemore, pres; Buddy Sizemore, gen mgr, stn mgr; Clyde Smith, mus dir, sls; Ted Fuller, chief of engrg, engr; Teresa S. Sizemore, asst music dir & traf mgr.

Greensboro

WCOG(AM)— May 22, 1948: 1320 khz; 5 kw-U, DA-2. TL: N36 09 01 W79 54 48. Hrs open: 24 3404-H West Wendover Ave., 27407. Phone: (336) 294-0699. Fax: (336) 294-4988.E-mail: info@wcog.com Web Site:www.radiodisney.com Licensee: Radio Disney Group LLC. (acq 5-6-2005; $1.675 million). Population served: 144,076 Format: Family hits. Target aud: General. ♦Gerry Franzer., pres & stn mgr; Chris Nowak, prom mgr.

WEAL(AM)— Oct 5, 1962: 1510 khz; 1 kw-D, 250 w-CH. TL: N36 03 42 W79 47 35. Hrs open: Sunrise-sunset 7819 National Service Rd.Suite 401, 27409. Phone: (336) 605-5200. Fax: (336) 605-0138. Licensee: Entercom Greensboro License LLC Population served: 820,000 Natl. Rep: McGavren Guild,. Format: Gospel. Target aud: 25-54; North Carolina A&T State Univ. ♦Joseph Level, progmg dir.

WJMH(FM)—See Reidsville

WKEW(AM)— Feb 16, 1942: 1400 khz; 1 kw-U. TL: N36 04 00 W79 47 49. Hrs open: 24 hrs 7 days 4405 Providence Ln., #A, Winston Salem, 27106-3226. Phone: (336) 759-0363. Fax: (336) 759-0366.E-mail: info@1340thelight.com Web Site:www.1340thelight.com Licensee: Truth Broadcasting Corp. (group owner; acq 8-9-00; $800,000). Population served: 245,000 Format: Urban Gospel, Religious. Target aud: 35 plus; African-American. ♦Stuart Epperson, pres & gen mgr.

WMAG(FM)—See High Point

***WNAA(FM)—** 1979: 90.1 mhz; 10 kw. 467 ft TL: N36 04 58 W79 46 08. Stereo. Hrs open: 24 North Carolina A&T State Univ., Price Hall, Suite 200, 27411-1135. Phone: (336) 334-7936. Fax: (336) 334-7960. Web Site:www.aggienewsonline.com Licensee: North Carolina Agricultural & Technical State University. Population served: 900,000 Format: Gospel, Classic R&B, Jazz. News: 5 hrs wkly. Target aud: 35-45; general. Spec prog: Blues 4 hrs, Reggae 5 hrs, Gospel Hip Hop 3 hrs. ♦Tony Welborne, gen mgr & dev dir; Cherie Lofton, progmg dir; Ezinma Leak-Murphy, pub affrs dir; Larry Allen, chief of engrg.

WPAW(FM)—(Winston-Salem, April 1947: 93.1 mhz; 100 kw. Ant 1,050 ft TL: N36 16 33 W79 56 27. Stereo. Hrs open: 24 7819 National Service Rd., Suite 401, 27409. Phone: (336) 605-5200. Fax: (336) 605-5221.E-mail: info@wpaw.com Web Site:www.931wolfcountry.com Licensee: Entercom Greensboro License LLC. Group owner: Entercom Communications Corp. (acq 12-13-99; grpsl). Population served: 940,600 Natl. Network: CBS, . Natl. Rep: McGavren Guild,. Format: Country. ♦Brent Millar, gen mgr; Lisa Powell, sls dir, gen sls mgr; Greg Carpenter, gen sls mgr; Randy Bliss, progmg dir; Larry Allen, chief of engrg; Valerie Dickens, traf mgr.

WPET(AM)— 1954: 950 khz; 500 w-D. TL: N36 02 16 W79 47 42. Hrs open: 7819 National Service Rd., Ste. 401, 27409. Phone: (336) 605-5200. Fax: (336) 387-7206.E-mail: mcassady@intercom.com Web Site:www.wpetam950.com Licensee: Entercom Greensboro License

LLC. Group owner: Entercom Communications Corp. (acq 1-28-2002; $20.5 million with co-located FM). Population served: 13,200 Format: Southern gospel. Target aud: 25-54. ♦Brent Miller, gen mgr; Dave Compton, progmg dir.

WPOL(AM)—(Winston-Salem, Mar 25, 1937: 1340 khz; 1 kw-U. TL: N36 04 26 W80 15 19. Hrs open: 24 4405 Providence Ln., Winston-Salem, 27106. Phone: (336) 759-0363. Fax: (336) 759-0366.E-mail: info@1340thelight.com Web Site:www.1340thelight.com Licensee: Truth Broadcasting Corp. (acq 5-10-2000). Format: Relg, Urban gospel. News: one hr wkly. Relg. ♦Stuart Epperson Jr., pres & gen mgr.

***WQFS(FM)**— January 1970: 90.9 mhz; 1.9 kw. 200 ft TL: N36 05 39 W79 53 21. Stereo. Hrs open: 24 Box 17714, Founders Halls, 5800 W. Friendly Ave., 27410. Phone: (336) 316-2352. Phone: (336) 316-2444. Fax: (336) 316-2949.E-mail: wqts@guilford.edu Web Site:www.guilford.edu Licensee: Guilford College Board of Trustees. Population served: 280,000 Format: Free-form. News staff: one; News: 4 hrs wkly. Target aud: 15-50. ♦Elizabeth Bass, gen mgr.

WQMG-FM— July 8, 1962: 97.1 mhz; 100 kw. 1,289 ft TL: N36 05 09 W79 45 38. (CP: TL: N35 56 43 W79 51 44). Stereo. Hrs open: 24 7819 National Service Rd., Suite 401, 27409. Phone: (336) 605-5200. Fax: (336) 605-0138.E-mail: info@wqmg.com Web Site:www.wqmg.com Licensee: Entercom Greensboro License LLC Group owner: Entercom Communications Corp. (acq 12-13-99; grpsl). Population served: 1,000,000 Natl. Network: ABC, . Natl. Rep: McGavren Guild,. Format: Smooth rhythm and blues, classic soul. News staff: one. Target aud: 18-49; Black. ♦Brant Millar, gen mgr; Lisa Powell, sls dir; Joyce Staley, prom dir; Larry Allen, chief of engrg; Brian McCall, traf mgr.

WSMW(FM)— Jan 9, 1958: 98.7 mhz; 100 kw. 1,000 ft TL: N36 02 16 W79 47 42. Stereo. Hrs open: 24 Prog sep from AM 7819 National Service Rd., Ste. 401, 27409. Phone: (336) 605 5200. Fax: (336) 387-7206.E-mail: mcassady@intercom.com Web Site:www.987simon.com Licensee: Entercom Greensboro License LLC. Population served: 354,400 Format: Adult contemporary. Target aud: 18-49. ♦Sean Sellers, progmg dir.

***WUAG(FM)**— July 20, 1964: 103.1 mhz; 18.1 w. 230 ft TL: N36 03 51 W79 48 37. (CP: Ant 259 ft.). Stereo. Hrs open: 24 Taylor Bldg., Univ. of North Carolina at Greensboro, 27412. Phone: (336) 334-5450.E-mail: wuag@uncg.edu Web Site:www.wuag.net Licensee: University of North Carolina at Greensboro Board of Trustees. Population served: 170,000 Format: Progsv rock. News staff: one; News: 2 hrs wkly. Target aud: 12-40; high school & college students. Spec prog: Hip hop 6 hrs, world music 2 hrs, bluegrass 2 hrs, blues 4 hrs wkly. ♦Jack Bonney, gen mgr.

WWBG(AM)— 1998: 1470 khz; 3.5 kw-D, 5 kw-N, DA-2. TL: N36 12 46 W79 54 46. Hrs open: Box 12876, Winston-Salem, 27117. Phone: (336) 784-9004. Fax: (336) 784-8337.E-mail: quepasa@quepasamedia.com Web Site:www.quepasamedia.com Licensee: Davidson Media Station WWBG Licensee LLC. (acq 3-25-2005; swap with WTOB(AM) Winston-Salem for WDRU(AM) Wake Forest). Natl. Rep: Salem,. Format: Mexican rgnl. ♦Roger Martinez, gen mgr.

Greenville

WNCT(AM)— 1940: 1070 khz; 50 kw-D, 10 kw-N, DA-2. TL: N35 36 08 W77 25 35. Hrs open: 24 2929 Radio Station Rd., 27834. Phone: (252) 757-0011. Fax: (252) 757-0286. Web Site:www.1070wnct.com Licensee: WNCT License L.P. (acq 1996). Format: Beach, boogie and blues. Target aud: General. ♦Brad Hood, gen mgr & stn mgr.

WNCT-FM— Dec 22, 1963: 107.9 mhz; 100 kw. 1,800 ft TL: N35 21 55 W77 23 38. Stereo. Hrs open: 24 Phone: (252) 757-0011. Fax: (252) 757-0286. Web Site:www.oldies1079.com Licensee: WNCT License LP Population served: 451,000 Format: Oldies. ♦Jerry Wayne, progmg dir. Co-owned TV: WNCT-TV affil.

WRSV(FM)—See Rocky Mount

***WZMB(FM)**— Feb 2, 1982: 91.3 mhz; 282 w. 134 ft TL: N35 36 01 W77 21 53. Stereo. Hrs open: 8am - 5pm Mendenhall Student Ctr., East Carolina Univ., Rm 110, 27858. Phone: (252) 328-4751. Phone: (252) 328-4752. Fax: (252) 328-4773.E-mail: info@wzmd.ecu.edu Web Site:www.wzmb.ecu.edu Licensee: East Carolina University Media Board. (acq 2-82). Natl. Network: ABC, . Format: Alternative rock, Var, Div. News: 12 hrs wkly. Target aud: 18-24; univ students. ♦Charles Young, gen mgr.

Grifton

WXNR(FM)— Sept 11, 1989: 99.5 mhz; 16.5 kw. 830 ft TL: N35 12 07 W77 11 15. Stereo. Hrs open: 24 207 Glenbernie Dr., New Bern, 28560. Phone: (252) 633-1500. Fax: (252) 633-6546. Web Site:www.995thex.com Licensee: WXNR License L.P. Population served: 430,000 Rgnl. Network: N.C. News Net. Natl. Rep: D & R Radio,. Format: New rock. Target aud: 18-34. ♦Bruce Simel, gen mgr; Joe Peters, sls dir; Wilbur Vitols, gen sls mgr; Jeff Sanders, progmg dir; Richard Banks, chief of engrg.

Hamlet

WJSG(FM)— Aug 25, 1991: 104.3 mhz; 2.5 kw. 489 ft TL: N34 48 44 W79 43 38. Hrs open: 180 Airport Rd., Rockingham, 28379. Phone: (910) 895-3787. Fax: (910) 895-8811.E-mail: g104fm@104fm.com Web Site:www.g104fm.com Licensee: Jackson Broadcasting Co. Format: Christian country. ♦Sherrell Jackson, gen mgr & progmg dir; Jerry Stout, news dir.

WKDX(AM)— June 30, 1957: 1250 khz; 1 kw-D. TL: N34 53 06 W79 40 50. Hrs open: Box 827, 28345. Phone: (910) 582-1997. Fax: (910) 582-1920.E-mail: wkdx@carolina55.com Web Site:www.wkdx.net Licensee: The McLaurin Group (acq 5-19-00). Format: Gospel, ministry. ♦Howard McLaurin Jr., pres & gen mgr.

Harkers Island

WLGP(FM)— Aug 1, 1996: 100.3 mhz; 100 kw. Ant 485 ft TL: N34 48 17 W76 54 23. Stereo. Hrs open: 24 2278 Wortham Ln., Grovetown, GA, 30813. Phone: (706) 309-9610. Fax: (706) 309-9669.E-mail: ctbarinowski@gnnradio.org Web Site:www.gnnradio.org Licensee: Barinowski Investment Co. Group owner: Good News Network. Population served: 800,000 Format: Christian. ♦Clarence Barinowski, pres & gen mgr.

Harrisburg

WQNC(FM)— 1995: 92.7 mhz; 6 kw. Ant 328 ft TL: N35 16 20 W80 45 54. Hrs open: 2303 W. Morehead St., Charlotte, 28208. Phone: (704) 358-0211. Fax: (704) 358-3752. Web Site:www.q927fm.com Licensee: Radio One of North Carolina LLC. Group owner: Radio One Inc. (acq 6-7-2000). Natl. Rep: McGavren Guild,. Format: Talk, R&B. Target aud: Adults 25-54. ♦Debbie Kwei, gen mgr; Michael Taylor, gen sls mgr; Latoya Whitt, mktg dir, prom dir; Phil Woods, chief of engrg; Gaynell Nichols, traf mgr.

Hatteras

WCMS-FM— May 1999: 94.5 mhz; 91 kw. 981 ft TL: N35 29 10 W75 59 58. Stereo. Hrs open: 24 Box 1897, Kill Devil Hills, 27948. Phone: (252) 480-4655. Fax: (252) 441-8063.E-mail: info@wcms.com Web Site:www.wcms.com Licensee: Max Radio of the Carolinas Licenses LLC. Group owner: MAX Media L.L.C. (acq 11-12-2002; grpsl). Natl. Network: Jones Radio Networks, . Format: Hot country. News staff: 2. ♦Mike Smith, VP, gen mgr; Ray Turner, progmg dir.

WYND-FM— March 1995: 97.1 mhz; 48 kw. Ant 558 ft TL: N35 27 48 W76 02 07. Stereo. Hrs open: 24 637 Harbor Rd., Wanchese, 27981. Phone: (252) 475-1888. Fax: (252) 475-1881.E-mail: hunt@capsanmedia.com Licensee: CapSan Media LLC. Group owner: Convergent Broadcasting LLC (acq 6-30-2006; grpsl). Natl. Network: ESPN Radio, . Richard Hayes. Format: Sports. ♦William Whitlow, pres & gen mgr; Hunt Thomas, opns dir, progmg dir.

Havelock

WANG(AM)— June 16, 1962: 1330 khz; 1 kw-D. TL: N34 55 24 W76 56 37. Hrs open: Sunrise-sunset
Rebroadcasts WSSM-FM Morehead City 100%.
1361 Colony Dr., New Bern, 28562. Phone: (252) 639-7900. Fax: (252) 639-7979. Licensee: NM Licensing LLC. Group owner: NextMedia Group L.L.C. (acq 11-26-2001; grpsl). Population served: 5,283 Rgnl. Network: N.C. News Net. Natl. Rep: Eastman Radio,. Format: Adult hits. Target aud: 25-54. ♦Larry Weiss, gen mgr.

WSSM(FM)— Nov 12, 1971: 105.1 mhz; 18.5 kw. Ant 384 ft TL: N34 45 07 W76 52 57. Stereo. Hrs open: 1361 Colony Dr., New Bern, 28562. Phone: (252) 639-7900. Fax: (252) 639-7979. Licensee: NM Licensing LLC. Population served: 17,035 Natl. Rep: Eastman Radio,. Format: Adult standards.

Henderson

WCBQ(AM)—See Oxford

WHNC(AM)— June 20, 1945: 890 khz; 1 kw-D. TL: N36 21 04 W78 22 35. Hrs open: Sunrise-sunset
Rebroadcasts WCBQ(AM) Oxford 100%.
PO Box 1005, One Alvin Augustus Jones Way, 601 Henderson St., Oxford, 27565. Phone: (919) 693-3540. Phone: (919) 693-1340. Fax: (919) 693-9054. Licensee: The Paradise Network (TPN) of North Carolina Inc. (acq 6-6-2001; $650,000 with WCBQ(AM) Oxford). Population served: 37,000 Natl. Rep: Keystone (unwired net),. Rgnl rep: T-N. Format: Black gospel. News staff: one; News: 7 hrs wkly. Target aud: 18 plus. ♦Alvin Augustis Jones, chmn; Nathaniel Smith, stn mgr, relg ed; Jim Davis, engrg mgr; Ronald Smith, sls dir & chief of engrg; Jeff Rose, spec ev coord; Al Woodlief, news rptr, political ed; Aaron Woodlief, farm dir; Anita Woodlief, women's int ed.

WIZS(AM)— May 1, 1955: 1450 khz; 1 kw-U. TL: N36 19 31 W78 24 36. Hrs open: 24 Box 1299, 27536. Phone: (252) 492-3001. Fax: (252) 492-3002.E-mail: wizs@vance.net Web Site:www.wizs.com Licensee: Rose Farm and Rentals Inc. (acq 6-1-89; $265,000; 6-19-89). Population served: 215,000 Rgnl. Network: N.C. News Net. N.C. News Net. Format: Oldies, beach, country & Talk Radio. News staff: 2; News: 6 hrs wkly. Target aud: 25 plus; fans of Country, Oldies and Beach music. Spec prog: TownTalk, Tradio, Sports Mayhem. ♦George B. Rush, pres, gen mgr; Dan Simmons, opns mgr, progmg mgr, mus dir; Don Simmons, progmg dir, pub affrs dir; John D. Rose III, chief of engrg.

WYFL(FM)— 1948: 92.5 mhz; 100 kw. Ant 1,020 ft TL: N36 13 23 W78 12 07. Stereo. Hrs open: Box 733, Charlotte, 28241. Phone: 704) 523-5555.E-mail: wyfl@bbnradio.org Web Site:www.bbnradio.org Licensee: Bible Broadcasting Network Inc. (group owner; acq 10-3-81; $335,000; 9-14-81). Population served: 2,500,000 Format: Relg. Target aud: General. ♦Bryant Nelson, gen mgr & news dir.

Hendersonville

WHKP(AM)— Oct 24, 1946: 1450 khz; 1 kw-U. TL: N35 20 20 W82 27 20. Hrs open: 24/7 Box 2470, 1450 7th Ave. E., 28793. Phone: (828) 693-9061. Fax: (828) 696-9329.E-mail: 1450@whkp.com Web Site:www.whkp.com Licensee: Radio Hendersonville Inc. (acq 6-4-86). Population served: 100,000 Natl. Network: ABC, . Brooks, Pierce, McLendon, Humphrey & Leonard. Format: Variety. News staff: 10; News: 10 hrs wkly. Target aud: 25 plus; middle to upper income. Spec prog: Var 18 hrs wkly. ♦Art Cooley, pres, gen mgr, prom VP; Richard Rhodes, sls VP; Larry Freeman, progmg dir, news dir; Dave Lyons, chief of engrg; Marge Duncan, women's int ed; Abby Ramsey, disc jockey.

WMYI(FM)—Licensed to Hendersonville. See Greenville SC

WTZQ(AM)— Dec 25, 1964: 1600 khz; 1 kw-D, 12 w-N. TL: N35 18 53 W82 25 58. Hrs open: 24 Box 462, Flat Rock, 28731. Secondary address: 418 Duncun Rd. 28793. Phone: (828) 692-1600. Phone: (828) 697-1506. Fax: (828) 697-1416.E-mail: 1600@wtzq.com Web Site:www.wtzq.com Licensee: Houston Broadcasting Inc. (acq 5-3-2008). Population served: 125,000 Natl. Network: ABC, . Rgnl. Network: N.C. News Net. N.C. News Net. Format: Timeless classics. News staff: one; News: 8 hrs wkly. Target aud: 35 plus; mature upscale audiences. Spec prog: Gospel 4 hrs wkly. ♦J. Ardell Sink, pres; Mark Warwick, gen mgr, gen sls mgr, adv dir; Kathy Gallagher, prom dir, traf mgr; George Henry, news dir, disc jockey; Michael A. Sink, opns VP & chief of engrg.

Hertford

WFMZ(FM)— December 1997: 104.9 mhz; 50 kw. Ant 492 ft TL: N36 10 45 W76 21 12. Hrs open: 24 637 Harbor Rd., Wancheese, 27981. Phone: (252) 475-1888. Fax: (252) 475-1881.E-mail: 1049@capsanmedia.com Web Site:classichits1049.com Licensee: CapSan Media LLC. Group owner: Convergent Broadcasting LLC (acq 6-30-2006; grpsl). Population served: 250,000 Natl. Network: USA, . Format: Classic hits. Target aud: 25-54. ♦William Whitlow, pres; William Whitlow, gen mgr; Hunt Thomas, opns dir, progmg dir.

Hickory

WAIZ(AM)— Dec 5, 1948: 630 khz; 1 kw-D, 57 w-N. TL: N35 43 07 W81 18 36. Hrs open: 24 hrs Box 938, 28603. Secondary address: Box 430, Newton 28658. Phone: (828) 322-9472. Fax: (828) 464-9662.E-mail: totalradio@aol.com Licensee: Newton-Conover Communications Inc. (acq 10-5-94; $225,000). Population served:

701,000 Natl. Network: ABC, . Format: Oldiies. Target aud: 25 plus. ♦Dave Lingafelt, pres, gen mgr; Jim Turner, gen sls mgr; Karol Lowery, traf mgr.

***WFHE(FM)**— Aug 31, 1995: 90.3 mhz; 150 w. 804 ft TL: N35 39 27 W81 24 23. Hrs open: 24
Rebroadcasts WFAE(FM) Charlotte 100%.
c/o WFAE(FM), 8801 J.M. Keynes Dr., Suite 91, Charlotte, 28262-8485. Phone: (704) 549-9323. Fax: (704) 547-8851.E-mail: wfae@wfae.org Web Site:www.wfae.org Licensee: University Radio Foundation Inc. Population served: 200,000 Format: NPR/PRI Affiliate. ♦Roger Sarow, pres, gen mgr; Debra Peterson, CFO; Tena Simmons, opns dir; Barbara Vermeire, dev dir; Renee Rallos, prom dir, pub affrs dir; Paul Stribling, progmg dir; Mark Rumsey, news dir; Jobie Sprinkle, engrg dir.

WHKY(AM)— June 10, 1940: 1290 khz; 50 kw-D, 1 kw-N, DA-2. TL: N35 43 35 W81 18 02. Hrs open: 24 Box 1059, 526 Main Ave. S.E., 28603. Phone: (828) 322-1290. Fax: (828) 322-8256.E-mail: whky@whky.com Web Site:www.whky.com Licensee: Long Communications LLC (acq 12-31-01; with WHKY-TV Hickory). Population served: 1,200,000. Natl. Network: ABC, ESPN Radio, . Rgnl. Network: N.C. News Net. Natl. Rep: Rgnl Reps,. N.C. News Net. Rgnl rep: Rgnl Reps Hardy & Carey. Format: News/talk. News staff: 4; News: 50 hrs wkly. Target aud: 35-54. ♦Thomas E. Long, gen mgr; Jeff Long, stn mgr; Patty Guthrie, gen sls mgr; Heather Isenhour, traf mgr. Co-owned TV: WHKY-TV affil.

WLYT(FM)— Jan 20, 1959: 102.9 mhz; 31 kw. 1,545 ft TL: N35 24 26 W81 07 47. Stereo. Hrs open: 801 Wood Ridge Center Dr., Charlotte, 28217. Phone: (704) 714-9444. Fax: (704) 372-3208. Web Site:www.wlyt.com Licensee: Capstar TX L.P. Group owner: Clear Channel Communications Inc. (acq 8-30-00; grpsl). Population served: 150,000 Format: Adult contemp. Target aud: 25-54. ♦Morgan Johannon, gen mgr; Nick Allen, opns mgr; Kim Kyle, sls dir; Amanda Knepp, mktg dir; Anthony Testa, prom dir; Jeff Kent, progmg dir; Linda Silver, news dir; Alan Lane, chief of engrg.

***WPIR(FM)**— Dec 3, 1985: 88.1 mhz; 26.5 kw horiz, 21 kw vert. Ant 253 ft TL: N35 43 34 W81 08 52. Stereo. Hrs open: 24
Rebroadcasts WXRI(FM) East Bend 60%.
Box 909, Claremont, 28610. Secondary address: 3289 WCXN Radio Rd., Claremont 28610. Phone: (828) 459-2772. Fax: (828) 459-9805.E-mail: office@joyfm.org Licensee: Positive Alternative Radio Inc. Group owner: Baker Family Stations Format: Southern gospel, educ. ♦Brian Sanders, gen mgr.

***WRYN(FM)**—Not on air, target date: unknown: 89.1 mhz; 500 w. Ant 449 ft TL: N35 43 59 W81 19 51. Hrs open: Drawer 2440, Tupelo, MS, 38803-2440. Phone: (662) 844-5036. Web Site:www.afr.net Licensee: American Family Association. ♦Donald E. Wildmon, chmn.

WXRC(FM)— Dec 7, 1962: 95.7 mhz; 100 kw. 1,276 ft TL: N35 42 32 W81 31 32. Stereo. Hrs open: 24 1515 Mocking Bird Lane., Suite 910, Charlotte, 28208 - 28209. Phone: (704) 527-0957. Fax: (704) 527-2720.E-mail: totalradio@aol.com Web Site:957theride.com Licensee: Pacific Broadcasting Group Inc. (acq 10-5-94; $3.05 million; 10-17-94). Natl. Rep: McGavren Guild,. Format: Classic hits. Target aud: 18-49. ♦Dave Lingafelt, pres, gen mgr; Jim Turner, natl sls mgr; Peggy Barrett, prom dir; Karol Lowery, pub affrs dir, traf mgr; Larry Schropp, chief of engrg.

WYCV(AM)—See Granite Falls

High Point

WGOS(AM)— July 1947: 1070 khz; 1 kw-D. TL: N35 54 58 W80 01 00. Hrs open: Sunrise-sunset 6223 Old Mendenhall Rd., 27263-7624. Phone: (336) 434-5024. Fax: (336) 434-6018.E-mail: wgosradio@triad.rr.com Web Site:www.wgos.net Licensee: Iglesia Nueva Vida of High Point Inc. (acq 9-24-2008; $750,000). Natl. Network: USA, . Format: Loc talk, Sp. News: 2 hrs wkly. Target aud: General. Spec prog: Loc college sports 10 hrs wkly. ♦Javier Fernandez, pres; Lynn Ritchy, gen mgr, gen sls mgr; Max Parrish, stn mgr, chief of engrg; Simon Ritchy, progmg dir.

***WHPE-FM**— November 1947: 95.5 mhz; 100 kw. 440 ft TL: N35 55 10 W80 01 47. Stereo. Hrs open: 24 Box 7300, Charlotte, 28241. Phone: (336) 889-9473. Fax: (336) 889-9773.E-mail: whpe@bbnradio.org Web Site:www.bbnradio.org Licensee: Bible Broadcasting Network. (acq 10-74). Population served: 713,000 Natl. Network: USA, . Format: Relg. ♦Lowell Davey, pres; Dan Austin, gen mgr.

WJMH(FM)—See Reidsville

WMAG(FM)— 1946: 99.5 mhz; 100 kw. 1,500 ft TL: N35 52 13 W79 50 25. Stereo. Hrs open: 24 2 B PAI Park, Greensboro, 27409. Phone: (336) 822-2000. Fax: (336) 887-0104. Web Site:www.wmagradio.com Licensee: Capstar TX L.P. Group owner: Clear Channel Communications Inc. (acq 8-30-00; grpsl). Population served: 120,000 Format: Adult contemp. Target aud: 25-54. ♦Cheryl Salamone, VP; Morgan Bohannon, gen mgr; Scott Keith, opns mgr; Shannon Sopina, prom dir; Chris Morgan, news dir; Bill Flynn, disc jockey.

WMFR(AM)— Oct 15, 1935: 1230 khz; 1 kw-U. TL: N35 57 20 W80 00 22. Hrs open: 5:30 AM-1 AM 875 W. 5th St., Winston Salem, 27101-2505. Phone: (336) 777-3900. Fax: (336) 885-3299.E-mail: info@wmfr.com Web Site:www.wmfr.com Licensee: Crescent Media Group LLC. Group owner: Infinity Broadcasting Corp. (acq 2-14-2007; grpsl). Population served: 80,000 Format: News/talk. ♦Tom Hamilton, VP; Marty Holbrook, mktg dir, progmg dir; Bob Costner, news dir; George Newman, chief of engrg.

WVBZ(FM)— June 1953: 100.3 mhz; 100 kw. 1,049 ft TL: N35 58 09 W79 49 29. Stereo. Hrs open: 24 2-B PAI Park, Greensboro, 27409. Phone: (336) 822-2000. Fax: (336) 887-0104. Web Site:www.buzzardrocks.com Licensee: Capstar TX L.P. Group owner: Clear Channel Communications Inc. (acq 8-30-00; grpsl). Population served: 1,885,000 Format: Rock. Target aud: 25-54. ♦Morgan Bohannon, gen mgr; Brian Grube, sls dir; Tim Fattafield, progmg dir; Travis Moore, disc jockey.

WYSR(AM)— June 1953: 1590 khz; 1.4 kw-D, 14 w-N. TL: N35 59 04 W80 04 08. Hrs open: 808 English Rd., Suite 101, 27262. Phone: (336) 883-8852. Fax: (336) 882-1594.E-mail: wysr@northstate.net Licensee: Latino Broadcasting LLC (group owner; (acq 2-23-2006; $780,000). Population served: 100,000 Format: Talk, sports. Target aud: General. ♦Jose A. Isasi, pres; Carrie Armstrong, gen mgr; L.A. Batchelor, opns dir & opns mgr.

Highlands

WHLC(FM)— July 1993: 104.5 mhz; 460 w. Ant 1,158 ft TL: N35 03 40 W83 11 05. Stereo. Hrs open: 24 Box 1889, 28741. Secondary address: 2420 Hwy. 64 E. 28741. Phone: (828) 526-1045. Fax: (828) 526-4900.E-mail: info@whlc.com Web Site:www.whlc.com Licensee: Charisma Radio Corp. Population served: 680,000 Format: Easy lstng. Target aud: 35 plus. ♦Charles B. Cooper, pres, gen mgr; Will Amari, opns mgr.

Hope Mills

WCCG(FM)— July 1997: 104.5 mhz; 6 kw. 305 ft TL: N34 56 34 W78 51 41. Hrs open: 115 Gillespie St., Fayetteville, 28301. Phone: (910) 484-4932. Fax: (910) 485-5192.E-mail: ccg1045@aol.com Web Site:www.soul1045.com Licensee: James E. Carson. Format: Old School, Today's R&B. ♦James Carson, gen mgr.

Jacksonville

WAVQ(AM)— 2008: Stn currently dark. 1400 khz; 1 kw-U. TL: N34 44 56 W77 24 51. Hrs open: 702 Hartness Rd., Statesville, 28677. Phone: (704) 878-9004. Licensee: Conner Media Corp. ♦Ronald W. Benfield, pres.

WJCV(AM)— Oct 10, 1968: 1290 khz; 5 kw-D, 47 w-N. TL: N34 45 58 W77 23 28. Hrs open: 24 Box 1216, 28541. Phone: (910) 347-6141. Fax: (910) 347-1290. Web Site:www.wjcv.com Licensee: Down East Broadcasting Co. Inc. (acq 1996). Population served: 130,000 Natl. Network: USA, . Natl. Rep: Salem,. Format: Southern gospel, Christian. Target aud: 25-54; general. ♦Melvin Bland, stn mgr, opns mgr, progmg dir, disc jockey; Joe North, disc jockey.

***WJKA(FM)**— 2008: 90.1 mhz; 17 kw vert. Ant 280 ft TL: N34 38 52 W77 37 28. Hrs open:
Rebroadcasts WAFR(FM) Tupelo, MS 100%.
Box 2440, Tupelo, MS, 38803-2440. Phone: (662) 844-8888. Fax: (662) 842-6791. Web Site:www.afr.net Licensee: American Family Association. Natl. Network: American Family Radio, . Format: Contemp Christian. ♦Marvin Sanders, gen mgr.

WJNC(AM)— Oct 16, 1945: 1240 khz; 1 kw-U. TL: N34 44 56 W77 24 51. Hrs open: Box 70, Newport, 28570. Phone: (910) 455-7222. Fax: (252) 247-7343. Licensee: Heritage Broadcasting LLC. (acq 8-10-2001; $358,500). Population served: 25,000 Natl. Network: Westwood One, . Hogan & Hartson. Format: News/talk, sports. Target aud: 18-45 plus. ♦Ben Ball, gen mgr; Dave Gremoske, chief of engrg.

WLGD(FM)— Apr 28, 1965: 98.7 mhz; 100 kw. Ant 1,015 ft TL: N34 29 38 W77 29 18. Stereo. Hrs open: 24 25 N. Kerr Ave., Wilmington, 28405. Phone: (910) 791-3088. Fax: (910) 791-0112. Web Site:www.lagrand987.com Licensee: Sunrise Broadcasting LLC. Group owner: NextMedia Group L.L.C. (acq 11-18-2008; grpsl). Population served: 1,000,000 Format: Rgnl Mexican. ♦Jeff Sanchez, opns mgr.

WQSL(FM)— November 1993: 92.3 mhz; 22.5 kw. Ant 725 ft TL: N34 31 10 W77 26 52. Hrs open: 24 1361 Colony Dr., New Bern, 28562. Phone: (252) 639-7900. Fax: (252) 639-7979.E-mail: info@carolinatouch.com Web Site:www.carolinatouch.com Licensee: NM Licensing LLC. Group owner: NextMedia Group L.L.C. (acq 11-26-2001; grpsl). Natl. Rep: Eastman Radio,. Format: Urban Adult Contemporary. ♦Larry Weiss, gen mgr.

WSRP(AM)— June 21, 1954: Stn currently dark. 910 khz; 5 kw-U, DA-N. TL: N34 47 45 W77 29 24. Stereo. Hrs open: 24 3389 NC Highway 121, Farmville, 27828-9556. Phone: (910) 455-2202. Fax: (910) 355-2203. Licensee: Estuardo Valdemar Rodriguez & Leonor Rodriguez. (acq 6-30-2006; $475,000). ♦Henry Gonzalez, stn mgr.

WXQR(FM)— Mar 14, 1966: 105.5 mhz; 19 kw. Ant 794 ft TL: N34 31 10 W77 26 52. Stereo. Hrs open: 24 1361 Colony Dr., New Bern, 28562. Phone: (252) 639-7900. Fax: (252) 639-7979.E-mail: info@carolinaspurerock.com Web Site:www.carolinaspurerock.com Licensee: NM Licensing LLC. Group owner: NextMedia Group L.L.C. (acq 11-26-2001; grpsl). Population served: 142,500 Natl. Rep: Eastman Radio,. Format: Active rock. ♦Larry Weiss, gen mgr & stn mgr.

Jefferson

WMMY(FM)— October 1999: 106.1 mhz; 10.5 kw. Ant 508 ft TL: N36 19 53 W81 35 17. Hrs open: 738 Blowing Rock Rd., Boone, 28607. Phone: (828) 264-2411. Fax: (828) 264-2412.E-mail: sindy@wecr1023.com Web Site:www.highway106.com Licensee: High Country Adventures LLC. (group owner; (acq 3-3-2009; grpsl). Format: Country. Target aud: 18-49; adults. Spec prog: Southern Fried Friday Night; Mountainhome Music Live Bluegrass Saturday Nights.

Kannapolis

WRFX(FM)— October 1964: 99.7 mhz; 100 kw. 1,044 ft TL: N35 33 45 W80 42 40. (CP: 84 kw, ant 1,056 ft.). Stereo. Hrs open: 801 Wood Ridge Center Dr., Charlotte, 28217. Phone: (704) 714-9444. Fax: (704) 371-3238. Web Site:www.wrfx.com Licensee: Capstar TX L.P. Group owner: Clear Channel Communications Inc. (acq 8-30-2000; grpsl). Format: Classic rock, AOR. Target aud: 25-54; male. Spec prog: Talk 3 hrs wkly. ♦Morgan Bohannon, gen mgr; Nick Allen, opns mgr; Kim Kyle, sls dir; Amanda Knepp, mktg dir; Jeff Kent, progmg dir; Linda Silver, news dir; Ben Brinitzer, chief of engrg.

WRKB(AM)— Dec 11, 1960: 1460 khz; 500 w-D, 194 w-N. TL: N35 29 14 W80 36 18. Hrs open: 24
Rebroadcasts WRNA(AM) China Grove 90%.
Box 8146, 28083. Phone: (704) 857-1101. Fax: (704) 857-0680.E-mail: info@fordbroadcasting.com Web Site:www.fordbroadcasting.com Licensee: Ford Broadcasting Inc. (group owner; (acq 1994). Population served: 200,000 Natl. Network: USA, . Smithwick & Belendiuk. Format: Southern gospel. ♦Carl Ford, pres, gen mgr, opns mgr; Taylor Ford, exec VP; Angela Ford, sr VP.

Kernersville

WTRU(AM)— Aug 16, 1970: 830 khz; 50 kw-D, 10 kw-N, DA-2. TL: N36 11 58 W80 12 25. Hrs open: 24 4405 Providence Ln., Suite D, Winston-Salem, 27106. Phone: (336) 759-0363. Fax: (336) 759-0366.E-mail: info@wtru.com Web Site:www.wtru.com Licensee: Truth Broadcasting Corp. (group owner; (acq 7-20-2000; $3.5 million with WGTK(AM) Louisville, KY). Natl. Network: Salem Radio Network, . Format: News, Christian. News: 24 hrs wkly. Target aud: General. ♦Stuart Epperson, pres; Stuart Epperson Jr., gen mgr.

Kill Devil Hills

WCXL(FM)— January 1993: 104.1 mhz; 100 kw. 981 ft TL: N36 07 42 W75 49 39. Stereo. Hrs open: 24 Box 1897, 27948. Phone: (252) 480-4655. Fax: (252) 441-4827.E-mail: info@beach104.com Web Site:www.beach104.com Licensee: Max Radio of the Carolinas Licenses LLC. Group owner: MAX Media L.L.C. (acq 11-12-2002; grpsl). Format: Adult contemp. News staff: 2. Target aud: 18-54. Spec prog: Farm 2 hrs wkly. ♦Mike Smith, gen mgr; Bob Davis, gen sls mgr, rgnl sls mgr.

King

WKTE(AM)— Dec 4, 1963: 1090 khz; 1 kw-D. TL: N36 17 48 W80 22 18. Stereo. Hrs open: Phone: (336) 983-3111. Fax: (336) 368-1090.E-mail:

info@wktelogo.com Web Site:www.wktelogo.com Licensee: Booth-Newsom Broadcasting Inc. (acq 3-1-86; $105,000; 1-6-86). Population served: 80,000 Rgnl. Network: Southern Farm. Southern Farm Format: Gospel, bluegrass, country. Spec prog: Farm 2 hrs wkly. ◆P.W. Booth, pres; Rodney Booth, gen mgr; Mike Bertaux, progmg dir; Dan Sykes, chief of engrg; Ron Wishon, disc jockey; Elizabeth Club, sls.

Kings Mountain

WDYT(AM)— Mar 12, 1953: Stn currently dark. 1220 khz; 25 kw-D, 106 w-N, DA-D. TL: N35 17 12 W81 10 28. Stereo. Hrs open: 5 AM-midnight 131 Providence Rd., Charlotte, 28207. Phone: (704) 295-7901. Fax: (704) 295-7919. Web Site:www.1220wdyt.com Licensee: CRN Communications LLC (acq 3-31-2006; $950,000). Rgnl. Network: N.C. News Net. ◆Deanna Greco, gen mgr.

Kinston

WELS(AM)— September 1950: 1010 khz; 1 kw-D, 75 w-N. TL: N35 15 45 W77 37 35. (CP: TL: N35 17 02 W77 39 55). Hrs open: 8 AM-5 PM Box 3384, 28502. Secondary address: 313 N. Queen St. 28501. Phone: (252) 523-5151. Fax: (252) 523-9357.E-mail: welsradio@juno.com Licensee: Willis Broadcasting. (acq 1-13-95; 2-27-95). Population served: 180,000 Rgnl. Network: N.C. News Net., Tobacco. Natl. Rep: Clayton-Davis,. N.C. News Net. Format: Gospel. Target aud: 25-54; middle income. ◆Anthony Gonzales, gen mgr.

WELS-FM— Nov 21, 1990: 102.9 mhz; 3 kw. 295 ft TL: N35 17 03 W77 39 53. Hrs open: 24 Prog sep from AM Box 3384, 28502. Secondary address: 313 N. Queen St. 28501. Phone: (252) 523-5151. Fax: (252) 523-9357.E-mail: welsradio@juno.com Natl. Network: ABC, . Target aud: General; middle to upper income, married, working, college grads. Spec prog: East Carolina Univ. sports, Kinston Indians baseball. ◆Anthony Gonzales, disc jockey.

*WKNS(FM)— Mar 26, 1977: 90.3 mhz; 20 kw. 312 ft TL: N35 25 01 W77 48 57. Stereo. Hrs open:
Rebroadcasting WTEB(FM) New Bern 100%.
c/o WTEB(FM), 800 College Ct., New Bern, 28562. Phone: (252) 638-3434. Fax: (252) 638-3538. Web Site:www.publicradioeast.org Licensee: Craven Community College (acq 1-18-95; 6-19-95). Format: Information. Spec prog: Jazz 6 hrs wkly. ◆Kathleen Beal, gen mgr; Charles Wethington, stn mgr, opns mgr; Jill McGuire, dev dir; J. Howard Jones, chief of engrg; George Olsen, reporter.

WLNR(AM)— May 1954: Stn currently dark. 1230 khz; 1 kw-U. TL: N35 15 31 W77 36 33. Hrs open: 24 Radio La Grande, 1010 Vermont Ave. N.W., Suite 100, Washington, DC, 20005. Phone: (202) 638-1959. Fax: (202) 638-6127.E-mail: estuardovaldemar@hotmail.com Licensee: Estuardo Valdemar Rodriguez & Leonor Rodriguez. Group owner: Estuardo Valdemar Rodriguez and Leonor Rodriguez Stns (acq 1-2004; $315,000). Population served: 35,000 ◆Estuardo Rodriguez, gen mgr.

WRNS(AM)— Feb 28, 1937: 960 khz; 5 kw-D, 1 kw-N, DA-N. TL: N35 16 59 W77 39 01. Hrs open: 24 1361 Colony Dr., New Bern, 28562. Phone: (252) 639-7900. Fax: (252) 639-7979.E-mail: mail@wrns.com Web Site:www.wrns.com Licensee: NM Licensing LLC Population served: 40,000 Format: Country. Target aud: 25-64. ◆Wayne Carlyle, progmg dir.

WRNS-FM— Oct 12, 1968: 95.1 mhz; 100 kw. Ant 1,499 ft TL: N35 06 18 W77 20 15. Stereo. Hrs open: 24 1361 Colony Dr., New Bern, 28562. Phone: (252) 639-7900. Fax: (252) 639-7979.E-mail: mail@wrns.com Web Site:www.wrns.com Licensee: NM Licensing LLC Group owner: NextMedia Group L.L.C. (acq 11-26-01; grpsl). Population served: 420,000 Natl. Rep: Eastman Radio,. Wilmer, Cutler & Pickering. Format: Country. News staff: one. Target aud: 25-54. Spec prog: NASCAR racing 6 hrs wkly. ◆Larry Weiss, gen mgr.

La Grange

WZUP(FM)— January 1993: 104.7 mhz; 25 kw. Ant 249 ft TL: N35 15 31 W77 36 33. Hrs open: 3389 NC Highway 121, Farmville, 27828-9556. Phone: (252) 753-3202. Fax: (910) 355-2203. Licensee: Conner Media Corp. Format: Sp. ◆Rodney Rainey, gen mgr.

Laurinburg

WEWO(AM)— Sept 1, 1947: 1460 khz; 5 kw-U, DA-2. TL: N34 47 00 W79 30 40. Hrs open: 24 Box 788, 28353. Phone: (910) 280-5209. Fax: (910) 276-9787.E-mail: wewo1460@aol.com Licensee: Service Media Inc. (acq 5-27-98; $150,000). Population served: 8,859 Format: Gospel. Target aud: 25-54. ◆Westley Johnson, gen mgr.

WFLB(FM)— May 1, 1951: 96.5 mhz; 100 kw. Ant 1,043 ft TL: N34 46 50 W79 02 45. Stereo. Hrs open: 24 508 Person St., Fayetteville, 28301. Phone: (910) 486-4114. Fax: (910) 323-5635. Licensee: Beasley FM Acquisition Corp. Group owner: Beasley Broadcast Group (acq 7-31-96; $4.2 million with co-owned AM). Population served: 600,000 Natl. Rep: D & R Radio,. Format: contemporary hits. Target aud: 25-54; affluent men & women in their peak earning years. Spec prog: George Beasley, pres; Mac Edwards, VP; Angela Godwin, gen sls mgr; Bryan Kusilka, natl sls mgr; Dave Stone, progmg dir; Van Clough, chief of engrg; Clara Glover, traf mgr.

WLNC(AM)— Jan 2, 1962: 1300 khz; 500 w-D. TL: N34 47 00 W79 26 22. Hrs open: sunrise-sunset Box 1748, 28353. Secondary address: 1300 Lila Dr. 28352. Phone: (910) 276-1300.E-mail: wlncradio@carolina.net Web Site:www.wlncradio.com Licensee: Fox Broadcasting Inc. (acq 2-1-90; $325,000). Population served: 35,000 Format: Adult contemp. Target aud: General. Spec prog: Gospel 4 hrs wkly. ◆Fred Fox, gen mgr.

Leaksville

WGBT(FM)—See Eden

WLOE(AM)—See Eden

Leland

WAAV(AM)—Licensed to Leland. See Wilmington

WKXS-FM—Licensed to Leland. See Wilmington

Lenoir

WJRI(AM)— Mar 15, 1947: 1340 khz; 1 kw-U. TL: N35 53 47 W81 33 57. Hrs open: 24 827 Fairview Dr., 28645. Secondary address: Box 1678 28645. Phone: (828) 754-5361. Fax: (828) 757-3300.E-mail: info@foothillsradio.com Web Site:www.foothillsradio.com Licensee: Foothills Radio Group LLC (group owner; acq 11-28-01). Population served: 70,000 Rgnl. Network: N.C. News Net. N.C. News Net. Format: News/talk. News staff: one; News: 14 hrs wkly. Target aud: 20-45. ◆Al Bunch, pres, gen mgr, sls VP, mktg dir; Davy Crockett, opns VP, progmg dir, pub affrs dir; Steve Zushin, news dir; Stoney Owen, chief of engrg; Shannon Hefner, traf mgr; Rocky Brooks, disc jockey.

WKGX(AM)— Feb 13, 1969: 1080 khz; 5 kw-D. TL: N35 54 38 W81 33 35. Hrs open: 24 Box 1678 827 Fairview Dr., 28645. Phone: (828) 758-1033. Fax: (828) 757-3300.E-mail: wxgx@twave.net Licensee: Foothills Radio Group LLC (group owner; acq 11-28-01). Population served: 75,000 Format: Country, bluegrass. News staff: one; News: 6 hrs wkly. Target aud: 24-55; older, mature wise spenders. Spec prog: Trading post show 16 hrs wkly. ◆Patty Guthrie, gen mgr.

WKVS(FM)— Sept 27, 1993: 103.3 mhz; 910 w. Ant 843 ft TL: N35 58 30 W81 33 07. Hrs open: Box 1678, 827 Fairview Dr., 28645. Phone: (828) 758-1033. Fax: (828) 757-3300. Licensee: Foothills Radio Group LLC. (group owner; (acq 11-28-2001). Format: Hot new country. Target aud: 18-54. ◆Al Bunch, pres, gen mgr, sls dir, mktg dir; Davy Crockett, progmg dir, disc jockey; Steve Zushin, news dir, disc jockey; Rocky Brooks, pub affrs dir; Stonie Owen, engrg dir; Bill Nolin, disc jockey.

Lewisville

WSGH(AM)— 1986: 1040 khz; 10 kw-D, DA. TL: N36 08 06 W80 30 14. (CP: 10 kw-D, 182 w-N). Hrs open: 24 4015 Brownsboro Rd., Winston Salem, 27106. Phone: (336) 759-0524. Fax: (336) 759-9327. Web Site:www.radiolamovidita.com Licensee: Davidson Media Carolinas Stations LLC. Group owner: Davidson Media Group LLC (acq 5-10-2004; grpsl). Natl. Network: USA, . Format: Sp. Target aud: 17-28. ◆Marco Antonio Saucedo, pres; Lucy Saucedo, VP; Samuel Saucedo, gen mgr.

Lexington

WLXN(AM)— Sept 22, 1946: 1440 khz; 5 kw-D, 1 kw-N, DA-N. TL: N35 50 22 W80 14 02. Hrs open: 24 200 Radio Dr., 27292. Phone: (336) 248-2716. Fax: (336) 248-2800. Web Site:www.wlxn.com Licensee: Davidson County Broadcasting Co. Inc. Population served: 130,000 Rgnl. Network: N.C. News Net. N.C. News Net. Format: News/talk, sports. News staff: one; News: 30 hrs wkly. Target aud: 35 plus; those interested in news & sports. ◆Greeley N. Hilton Jr., pres; Tom Collins, opns VP, chief of opns; Bob Mahoney, news dir; Hal McGee, engrg dir; Hal V. McGee, disc jockey.

WTHZ(FM)— Aug 24, 1949: 94.1 mhz; 100 kw. 1,014 ft TL: N35 55 02 W80 17 37. Stereo. Hrs open: 24 Prog sep from AM 200 Radio Dr., 27292. Phone: (336) 248-2716. Fax: (336) 248-2800.E-mail: info@hitz94.com Web Site:www.hitz94.com Licensee: Davidson County Broadcasting Co. Inc. Population served: 1,000,000 Rgnl rep: T-N. Format: 80's hits, 90's hits & now. News staff: one; News: one hr wkly. Target aud: General; 25-49. ◆Greeley N. Hilton Jr., exec VP; Bob Campbell, progmg dir; Hal McGee, chief of engrg.

Lillington

*WLLN(AM)— Feb 12, 1979: 1370 khz; 5 kw-D, 49 w-N, DA-2. TL: N35 23 16 W78 48 22. Hrs open: Day time Box 969, 27546. Secondary address: 910 E. McNeil St. 27546. Phone: (910) 893-2811. Fax: (910) 893-2811. Licensee: Estuardo Valdemar Rodriguez (acq 9-21-99; $145,000). Population served: 300,000 Format: Spanish music. Target aud: General. ◆Estuardo Rodriguez, chmn, gen mgr; Leonor Rodriguez, pres; Helen Hernandez, stn mgr; Orlando Henao, mus dir.

Lincolnton

WLON(AM)— Aug 28, 1953: 1050 khz; 1 kw-D, 231 w-N. TL: N35 29 28 W81 16 03. Hrs open: 24
Rebroadcasts WCSL(AM) Cherryville 80%.
Box 430, 28093. Phone: (704) 735-8071. Fax: (704) 732-9567.E-mail: info@hrnb.com Web Site:www.hrnb.com Licensee: HRN Broadcasting Inc. (acq 4-14-2004; $500,000 with WCSL(AM) Cherryville). Population served: 35,000 Natl. Network: Westwood One, . Rgnl. Network: N.C. News Net. N.C. News Net. Format: Oldies, sports. Target aud: 25 plus. Spec prog: Gospel 5 hrs wkly. ◆Mark . Boyd, pres; Lanny Ford, gen mgr; Milton Baker, opns mgr.

Lockwoods Folly Town

*WGHW(FM)— 2006: 88.1 mhz; 10 kw vert. Ant 311 ft TL: N34 03 48 W78 05 32. Hrs open: 1460 Old Ocean Hwy., Bolivia, 28422. Phone: (910) 253-6593.E-mail: info@kjbbfm.com Web Site:www.kjbbfm.com Licensee: Church Planters of America (acq 5-18-2005). Fletcher, Heald & Hildreth. Format: Christian. ◆Danny Hawkins, pres & gen mgr.

Louisburg

WKXU(FM)— Dec 5, 1989: 102.5 mhz; 6 kw. 328 ft TL: N36 07 12 W78 22 48. Stereo. Hrs open: 24 Box 463, 27549. Phone: (919) 496-3105. Fax: (919) 496-5864. Licensee: New Century Media Group LLC Format: Country. News: 6 hrs wkly. Spec prog: News, birthday celebration, country exchange, sports. ◆Jackie Ayscue, traf mgr.

WYRN(AM)— Sept 12, 1958: 1480 khz; 500 w-D. TL: N36 06 46 W78 16 50. Hrs open: 24 Box 463, 27549. Phone: (919) 496-3105. Fax: (919) 496-5864. Licensee: New Century Media Group LLC. Group owner: Curtis Media Group (acq 6-1-2003; $2.8 million with co-located FM). Population served: 1,200,000 Rgnl. Network: N.C. News Net. N.C. News Net. Format: Talk. News staff: one; News: 20 hrs wkly. Target aud: Adults 25-54. Spec prog: Black. ◆Randy Jordan, gen mgr, opns mgr; William M. McClatchey Jr., pres, dev mgr & gen sls mgr; Jackie Ayscue, traf mgr.

Lumberton

WAGR(AM)— Nov 27, 1954: 1340 khz; 1 kw-U. TL: N34 35 58 W79 00 33. Hrs open: 24 PO Box 2247, Fayetteville, 28302. Secondary address: 1338 Bragg Blvd., Fayetteville 28301. Phone: (910)486-9438. Fax: (910) 739-1349.E-mail: wcookman@aol.com Licensee: WAGR Broadcasting Inc. (acq 6-30-98; $50,000). License and equipment only Population served: 20,000 Rgnl rep: Williams Format: Gospel. News: 4 hrs wkly. Target aud: 25-54. ◆Charles W. Cookman, pres; Sandra Lofton, gen mgr; Val Holiday, opns mgr & progmg dir.

WFVL(FM)— July 19, 1964: 102.3 mhz; 6 kw. Ant 267 ft TL: N34 35 58 W79 00 33. Stereo. Hrs open: 24 1009 Drayton Rd., Fayetteville, 28303. Phone: (910) 864-5222. Fax: (910) 864-3065. Web Site:www.oldiesradionc.com Licensee: Cumulus Licensing Corp. Group owner: Cumulus Media Inc. (acq 3-12-2001; grpsl). Population served: 103,000 Format: Oldies. Target aud: 18-54. ◆Alan Buffaloe, gen mgr & chief of engrg.

WKML(FM)— Dec 1, 1960: 95.7 mhz; 100 kw. 1,064 ft TL: N34 46 56 W79 04 42. Stereo. Hrs open: 24 Box 2563, Fayetteville, 28302. Secondary address: 508 Person St., Fayetteville 28301. Phone: (910) 483-9565. Fax: (910) 483-6008.E-mail: info@wkml.com Web Site:www.wkml.com Licensee: Beasley Broadcasting of Eastern North Carolina Inc. Group owner: Beasley Broadcast Group (acq 1981). Population served: 325,000 Natl. Rep: D & R Radio,. Brooks, Pierce, McLendon, Humphrey & Leonard. Format: C&W. News staff: one; News: 5 hrs wkly. Target aud: 25-54. ◆George G. Beasley, pres; J. Daniel Highsmith, gen mgr; Mac Edwards, opns VP, disc jockey; Angela Godwin, gen sls mgr; Bryan Kusilka, natl sls mgr; Paul Johnson, progmg dir; Van Clough, chief of engrg; Don Chase, disc jockey.

*WLPS-FM—Not on air, target date: unknown: 89.5 mhz; 2 kw vert. Ant 440 ft TL: N34 42 02 W79 06 32. Hrs open: 3463 Oakgrove Church Rd., 28360-3181. Phone: (910) 521-3101. Licensee: Billy Ray Locklear Evangelistic Association. ◆Billy Ray Locklear, chmn.

Manteo

WOBX-FM— 2001: 98.1 mhz; 50 kw. Ant 295 ft TL: N35 51 52 W75 39 01. Hrs open: 24 Box 1418, Nags Head, 27959. Secondary address: 2422 S. Wrightsville Ave., Nags Head 27959. Phone: (252) 449-8331. Fax: (252) 449-8354.E-mail: wobx@ecri.net Web Site:www.wobx.net Licensee: East Carolina Radio of Elizabeth City Inc. Format: Active rock. ◆R. Loesch, gen mgr; John Maloney, gen sls mgr.

*WUND-FM— 2004: 88.9 mhz; 50 kw horiz, 47 kw vert. Ant 1,371 ft TL: N35 54 00 W76 20 45. Hrs open: 24
Rebroadcasts WUNC(FM) Chapel Hill 99.9%.
120 Friday Center Dr., CB-0915, Chapel Hill, 27517-9495. Phone: (919) 966-5454. Fax: (919) 966-5955.E-mail: wunc@wunc.org Web Site:www.wunc.org Licensee: Board of Trustees of the University of North Carolina at Chapel Hill. Population served: 129,691 Natl. Network: NPR, PRI, . Format: News & info. News staff: 7; News 124 hrs wkly. Spec prog: Folk 20 hrs wkly. ◆Joan Siefert Rose, gen mgr.

*WURI(FM)— 1999: 90.9 mhz; 3.9 kw. Ant 187 ft TL: N35 54 28 W75 40 26. Hrs open: 24
Rebroadcasts WCPE(FM) Wake Forest 99.9%.
120 Friday Center Dr., CB-0915, Chapel Hill, 27517-9495. Phone: (919) 966-5454. Fax: (919) 966-5955.E-mail: wunc@wunc.org Web Site:www.wunc.org Licensee: Board of Trustees/University of North Carolina at Chapel Hill. Population served: 21,838 Natl. Network: CBC Radio One, NPR, PRI, . Format: Classical. Spec prog: Folk 20 hrs wkly. ◆Joan Rose, gen mgr; Kevin Wolf, opns mgr.

WVOD(FM)— Mar 28, 1986: 99.1 mhz; 50 kw. Ant 491 ft TL: N35 50 44 W75 38 50. Stereo. Hrs open: 24 637 Harbor Rd., Wanchese, 27981. Phone: (252) 475-1888. Fax: (252) 475-1881.E-mail: trimed@capsanmedia.com Web Site:www.991thesound.com Licensee: CapSan Media LLC. Group owner: Convergent Broadcasting LLC (acq 6-30-2006; grpsl). Population served: 28,000 Format: AAA. News staff: one. Target aud: 25-49. Spec prog: Class 6 hrs, blues 2 hrs, reggae 2 hrs wkly. ◆William Whitlow, gen mgr; Hunt Thomas, opns dir; Matt Cooper, progmg dir; Tad Abbey, mus dir; Andy Booth, chief of engrg; Sharon Pro, traf mgr.

Marion

WBRM(AM)— May 9, 1949: 1250 khz; 5 kw-D, 62 w-N. TL: N35 40 59 W82 02 08. Hrs open: 24 147 N. Garden St., 28752. Phone: (828) 652-9500.E-mail: wbrm@charterinternet.com 6 pm-6 am Westwood One Mainstream Country Licensee: WBRM Inc. (acq 12-1-88; $450,000). Population served: 75,000 Format: Country. News staff: one; News: 9 hrs wkly. Target aud: 25-55; young adult to mature. Spec prog: Gospel 5 hrs, relg 7 hrs wkly. ◆Annette Bryant, CEO, pres; Kevin Estes, opns mgr.

Mars Hill

*WYQS(FM)— 1974: 90.5 mhz; 250 w. Ant 1,276 ft TL: N35 53 12 W82 33 23. Stereo. Hrs open: 24 73 Broadway, Asheville, 28801. Phone: (828) 253-6875. Fax: (828) 253-6700.E-mail: info@wcqs.org Web Site:www.wcqs.org Licensee: Western North Carolina Public Radio Inc. (acq 12-10-2004; $177,000). Population served: 3,000 Natl. Network: NPR, . Format: News/talk. News staff: 3; News: 7 hrs wkly. Target aud: 14-30; college students & college community. ◆Ed Subkis, gen mgr; Lee Wilcher, opns dir; Steve Busey, sls dir; Barbara Sayer, progmg dir; David Hurand, news dir; Tom Spaight, chief of engrg.

Marshall

WHBK(AM)— Sept 20, 1956: 1460 khz; 500 w-D, 139 w-N. TL: N35 48 01 W82 40 34. Hrs open: 24 1055 Skyway Dr., 28753. Phone: (828) 649-3914. Fax: (828) 649-2869. Licensee: Southern Broadcasting Inc. (acq 10-22-91; $145,000). Population served: 30,000 Format: Southern gospel. Spec prog: Farm 3 hrs wkly. ◆Bruce Philips, pres; Ricky Seay, gen mgr; Ricky West, disc jockey.

Masonboro

WVNC(AM)—Not on air, target date: unknown: 820 khz; 50 kw-D, 3.3 kw-N, DA-2. TL: N34 16 19 W77 58 28. Hrs open: 16 Doe Run, Pittstown, NJ, 08867. Phone: (908) 730-7959. Licensee: Charles A. Hecht and Alfredo Alonso. ◆Charles A. Hecht, gen mgr.

Mayodan

WMYN(AM)— July 15, 1957: 1420 khz; 1 kw-D, 70 w-N, DA-2. TL: N36 24 58 W79 59 29. Hrs open: 5 AM-10 PM
Rebroadcasts WLOE(AM) Eden 100%.
Box 279, 27027. Phone: (336) 427-9696. Fax: (336) 548-4636.E-mail: info@wloewmyn.com Web Site:www.wloewmyn.com Licensee: Mayo Broadcasting Corp. (acq 1982; $110,000). Population served: 200,000 Natl. Network: Salem Radio Network, USA, . Format: Info, talk, relg. News staff: one; News: 30 hrs wkly. Target aud: 25 plus; general. ◆Richard D. Hall, pres; Mike Moore, gen mgr; Annette Moore, stn mgr.

Mebane

WGSB(AM)— Dec 7, 1973: Stn currently dark. 1060 khz; 1 kw-D, DA. TL: N36 03 28 W79 16 36. Hrs open: Sunrise-sunset
Rebroadcasts WRTP(AM) Chapel Hill 100%.
Estuardo Valdemar Rodriguez and Leonor Rodriguez Stns, 1010 Vermont Ave. N.W. - 100, Suite 100, Washington, DC, 20005. Phone: (202) 638-1959. Fax: (202) 638-6127.E-mail: estuardovaldemar@hotmail.com Licensee: Estuardo Valdemar Rodriguez and Leonor Rodriguez. Group owner: WRTP Radio Network (acq 2-2-2005; grpsl). Population served: 250,000 ◆Estuardo Valdemar Rodriguez, gen mgr.

Mint Hill

WNOW(AM)— Aug 1, 1987: 1030 khz; 10 kw-D, DA. TL: N35 08 30 W80 36 05. Hrs open: Sunrise-sunset 4321-E Stewart Andrew Blvd., Charlotte, 28217. Phone: (704) 665-9355. Fax: (208) 545-9888. Web Site:www.wnow.com Licensee: Davidson Media Carolinas Stations LLC. Group owner: Davidson Media Group LLC (acq 5-10-2004; grpsl). Population served: 400,000 Format: Tropical. ◆Peter W. Davidson, pres; Russ Douglass Jones, gen mgr, gen sls mgr, progmg dir; Aura Gavilan, prom mgr; Winston Hawkins, chief of engrg; Maria Zarate, traf mgr.

Mocksville

WDSL(AM)— October 1964: 1520 khz; 5 kw-D, 1 kw-CH. TL: N35 52 50 W80 32 26. Hrs open: Box 1520, 27028. Secondary address: 125 W. Deport St. 27028. Phone: (336) 751-9375.E-mail: wdslradio@mailcity.com Licensee: Davie Broadcasting Inc. (acq 10-26-90; $52,000; 11-19-90). Population served: 750,000 Format: Country, bluegrass, gospel. Target aud: 25-80; general.

Monroe

WDEX(AM)— December 1983: 1430 khz; 2.5 kw-U, DA-2. TL: N34 59 04 W80 36 14. Hrs open: 24 Box 3272, Kannapolis, 28111. Secondary address: Weddington Rd. 28110. Phone: (704) 289-9339. Fax: (704) 283-1255.E-mail: wdex1430am@yahoo.com Licensee: New Life Community Temple of Faith Inc. (acq 11-15-99). Smithwick & Belendink. Format: Traditional, contemp, gospel. Target aud: 25-55. ◆Ella Hood, CEO, gen mgr; Sharon Talford, pres & gen mgr.

WIXE(AM)— May 3, 1968: 1190 khz; 5 kw-D, 70 w-N. TL: N34 57 41 W80 32 40. Stereo. Hrs open: 24 Box 1007, 28111. Secondary address: 1700 Buena Vista Dr. 28112. Phone: (704) 289-2525. Fax: (704) 289-1416.E-mail: wixeradio@carolina.rr.com Web Site:www.wixe.com Licensee: Monroe Broadcasting Co. (acq 5-2-2000; $800,000). Population served: 1,300,000 N.C. News Net. Yelverton. Format: C&W, gospel, talk. News: 8 hrs wkly. Target aud: 18-55. Spec prog: Beach & oldies 5 hrs wkly. ◆Archie Morgan, pres & gen mgr.

Mooresville

WHIP(AM)— 1950: 1350 khz; 1 kw-D, 670 w-N. TL: N35 36 04 W80 48 51. Hrs open: 6 AM-6:30 PM Box 600, 2432 Statesville Hwy., 28115. Phone: (704) 664-9447. Fax: (704) 664-5551. Licensee: Mooresville Media Inc. Network: USA, . Format: Oldies. News: 13 hrs wkly. Target aud: 25-45. Spec prog: Black 6 hrs, relg 6 hrs wkly. ◆Glenn Hamrick, pres; Martha Hamrick, VP, traf mgr, women's int ed; Norman Tindal, sls VP, gen sls mgr, disc jockey; Harrill Hamrick, chief of engrg; Gary Trexler, sports cmtr, disc jockey; Vivian Brandon, disc jockey.

Morehead City

*WOTJ(FM)— Dec 12, 1988: 90.7 mhz; 24 kw. 466 ft TL: N34 46 41 W76 52 42. Stereo. Hrs open: 24 520 Roberts Rd., Newport, 28570. Phone: (252) 223-4600/223-6088. Fax: (252) 223-2201.E-mail: fbn@fbnradio.com Web Site:www.fbnradio.com Licensee: Grace Christian School. Natl. Network: USA, . Format: Relg. News: 8 hrs wkly. Target aud: General; family. ◆Michael D. Ebron, gen mgr.

WRHT(FM)— Dec 20, 1972: 96.3 mhz; 100 kw. 492 ft TL: N34 44 18 W76 48 40. Stereo. Hrs open: 24
Rebroadcasts WCBZ(FM) Williamston 100%.
1307 S. Glenburnie Rd., New Bern, 28562. Phone: (252) 672-5900. Fax: (252) 637-6872.E-mail: thehotfm@thehotfm.com Licensee: Inner Banks Media LLC. Group owner: Archway Broadcasting Group (acq 3-12-2007; grpsl). Population served: 450,000 Format: CHR. News staff: one; News: 7 hrs wkly. Target aud: 18-49; young active adults & military personnel. ◆Bill Bailey, gen mgr.

Morganton

WCIS(AM)— Mar 1, 1988: 760 khz; 3.5 kw-D. TL: N35 47 40 W81 43 12. Stereo. Hrs open: Day station Box 1806, 28680-1806. Secondary address: 1399 Bost Rd. 28655. Phone: (828) 584-3076. Fax: (828) 433-1498.E-mail: powerhouse76@aol.com Licensee: W.F.M. Inc. (acq 10-1-93; $65,000). Population served: 90,000 Natl. Network: USA, . Format: Southern gospel. ◆John L. Whisnant Sr., pres; Jeff Whisnant, VP; John L. Whisnant Jr., gen mgr; Jeff K. Whisnant, opns mgr.

WMNC(AM)— Sept 23, 1947: 1430 khz; 5 kw-D, 1 kw-N, DA-N. TL: N35 45 09 W81 43 03. Hrs open: 24 Box 969, 28680-0969. Secondary address: 1103 N. Green St. 28655. Phone: (828) 437-0521. Phone: (828) 437-0009. Fax: (828) 433-8855.E-mail: wmnc@bellsouth.net Web Site:www.bigdawg92fm.com Licensee: Cooper Broadcasting Co. (acq 9-23-47). Population served: 17,200 Natl. Network: CNN Radio, . Rgnl. Network: Southern Farm. Format: Classic country. ◆Joe Cooper, stn mgr; Cindy Byas, progmg dir; C.J. Stancil, news dir.

WMNC-FM— Aug 3, 1963: 92.1 mhz; 6 kw. 327 ft TL: N35 45 09 W81 43 19. Stereo. Hrs open: 24 Secondary address: 1102 N. Green Street 28655. Phone: (828) 437-0521. Fax: (828) 433-8855.E-mail: wmnc@bellsouth.net Web Site:www.bigdawg92fm.com Licensee: Cooper Broadcasting Co. Format: Hot new country.

WSVM(AM)—See Valdese

Mount Airy

WPAQ(AM)— February 1948: 740 khz; 10 kw-D, 1 kw-CH. TL: N36 04 W80 35 48. Hrs open: 6 AM-6:15 PM winter, loc sunset summer Box 907, 27030. Phone: (336) 786-6111. Fax: (336) 789-7792.E-mail: wpaq740am@earthlink.net Licensee: WPAQ Radio Inc. Population served: 25,000 Format: Bluegrass, old time, big band. News staff: one; News: 13 hrs wkly. Target aud: 25-64. Spec prog: Farm one hr, community affrs one hr, old time string mus 15 hrs wkly. ◆Kelly Epperson, gen mgr; Kelly D. Epperson, stn mgr; Kathy Edmonds, gen sls mgr; Susan Carroll, prom mgr; Bernie Phillips, news dir; John Mullins, chief of engrg.

WSYD(AM)— Oct 4, 1951: 1300 khz; 5 kw-D, 1 kw-N, DA-N. TL: N36 30 12 W80 35 35. Hrs open: 24 Box 1678, 27030. Phone: (336) 786-2147. Fax: (336) 789-9858. Licensee: Granite City Broadcasters Inc. (acq 1996). Population served: 60,000 Format: Gospel. News

staff: one; News: 8 hrs wkly. Target aud: General. ◆Kelly D. Epperson, pres & gen mgr; Deborah Cochran, progmg dir; Bernie Phillips, news dir; John Mullins, chief of engrg.

Mount Holly

WTCG(AM)— June 28, 1961: 870 khz; 5 kw-D. TL: N35 16 25 W80 51 40. Hrs open: 6 AM-sunset 1115 Honeysuckle Dr., Keene, TX, 76059. Phone: (817) 641-3495. Licensee: Family First Group owner: Georgia-Carolina Radiocasting Companies (acq 9-10-2008; $500,000). ◆Linda de Romanett, pres.

Mount Olive

WDJS(AM)— Dec 27, 1961: 1430 khz; 1 kw-D. TL: N35 12 16 W78 03 06. Hrs open: Box 479, 28365. Secondary address: 990 N. Center St., Ext. 28365. Phone: (919) 658-9751. Fax: (919) 658-4894. Licensee: The Mount Olive Broadcasting Co. Population served: 250,000 Format: Relg, Christian. Spec prog: Black 5 hrs, gospel 5 hrs, Sp 5 hrs wkly. ◆Ann W. Mayo, CEO, gen mgr; Nancy West, progmg dir.

Moyock

WCDG(FM)— Oct 17, 1974: 92.1 mhz; 18 kw. Ant 384 ft TL: N36 41 39 W76 02 57. Stereo. Hrs open: 1003 Norfolk Sq., Norfolk, VA, 23502-4948. Phone: (757) 466-0009. Fax: (757) 466-7043. Web Site:www.cool921.com Licensee: CC Licenses LLC. Group owner: Clear Channel Communications Inc. Population served: 1,700,000 Format: Hip Hop. Target aud: 18-34; males 18-49. ◆Lowery Mays, CEO; Reggie Jordan, gen mgr; Travis Dylan, opns mgr; Terry Ratliff, sls dir; Bill Davis, natl sls mgr; Toni B. Jones, prom dir; Michael Bov-e, chief of engrg.

Murfreesboro

WDLZ(FM)— Oct 11, 1970: 98.3 mhz; 3 kw. Ant 328 ft TL: N36 26 24 W77 08 10. Stereo. Hrs open: Prog sep from AM PO Box 38, 27855. Phone: (252) 398-4111. Fax: (252) 398-3581. Population served: 40,000 Format: Soft adult contemp.

WWDR(AM)— Mar 20, 1965: 1080 khz; 930 w-D. TL: N36 26 24 W77 08 10. Hrs open: Box 38, 27855. Secondary address: 1714 W. Main St. 27855. Phone: (252) 398-4111. Fax: (252) 398-3581. Licensee: First Media Radio LLC. (group owner; (acq 1-7-2003; grpsl). Population served: 40,000 Natl. Network: Moody, . Rgnl. Network: N.C. News Net. N.C. News Net. Format: Gospel. Spec prog: Farm 10 hrs wkly. ◆Earl Tellega, gen mgr; Neil Haskins, gen sls mgr; Frank White, prom mgr, chief of engrg; Bob Wood, progmg dir.

Murphy

WCNG(FM)— Oct 23, 1990: 102.7 mhz; 3 kw. 426 ft TL: N35 04 00 W83 59 58. (CP: Ant 236 ft.). Stereo. Hrs open: 5 AM-midnight Box 280, 28906. Phone: (704) 837-9264. Phone: (704) 837-5509.E-mail: info@wcng.com Population served: 175,000 Format: Soft rock. ◆Dennis Gene, gen mgr & disc jockey.

WCVP(AM)— Oct 12, 1958: 600 khz; 1 kw-D, 20 w-N. TL: N35 04 00 W83 59 58. Hrs open: 5 AM-10 PM Box 280, 28906. Phone: (828) 837-2151. Phone: (828) 837-2152.E-mail: info@wcvp.com Licensee: Cherokee Broadcasting Co. Population served: 220,000 Format: MOR, news, gospel. Target aud: All ages. Spec prog: Farm 3 hrs, class 20 hrs, C&W 12 hrs wkly. ◆Allan Blakemore, pres; Jane Blakemore, gen mgr, progmg dir, traf mgr; Dennis Blakemore, gen sls mgr, prom mgr, chief of engrg, rsch dir, sports cmtr; Skip Ballard, mus dir.

WKRK(AM)— Aug 8, 1958: 1320 khz; 5 kw-D, 62 w-N. TL: N35 06 42 W84 00 31. Hrs open: 24 427 Hill Street, 28906. Phone: (828) 837-1320. Fax: (828) 837-8610.E-mail: info@1320am.com Web Site:www.1320am.com Licensee: Radford Communications Inc. (acq 1995; $250,000). Population served: 120,000 Natl. Rep: Westwood One, . Natl. Rep: Keystone (unwired net),. Format: C&W, news/talk, relg. News: 7 hrs wkly. Target aud: 25-54. Spec prog: Pub affrs 3 hrs wkly. ◆Tim Radford, pres; Ab Radford, VP; Emma Ramsey, mktg mgr, adv mgr; Suzanne Crawford, prom mgr; Bill Yonce, disc jockey.

Nags Head

WZPR(FM)— Apr 4, 1990: 92.3 mhz; 18.5 kw. Ant 384 ft TL: N35 50 49 W75 38 19. Stereo. Hrs open: 24 637 Harbor Rd., Wanchese, 27981. Phone: (252) 475-1888. Fax: (252) 475-1881.E-mail: hunt@capsanmedia.com Web Site:www.classichits1049.com Licensee: CapSan Media LLC. Group owner: Convergent Broadcasting LLC (acq 6-30-2006; grpsl). Rgnl. Network: Capitol Radio Net., N.C. News Net. Format: Classic hits. Target aud: 25-54. ◆William Whitlow, pres & gen mgr; Hunt Thomas, opns mgr.

Nashville

WZAX(FM)— February 1997: 99.3 mhz; 6 kw. Ant 328 ft TL: N35 57 01 W77 57 26. Hrs open: 24 12717 East N.C 97, Rocky Mount, 27803. Phone: (252) 442-8092. Fax: (252) 977-6664. Web Site:www.jammin993.com Licensee: First Media Radio LLC (group owner; (acq 7-22-2003; grpsl). Natl. Rep: Interep,. Format: Rhythmic oldies. ◆Alex Kolobielski, pres; Mike Binkley, gen mgr & mktg mgr.

New Bern

*WAAE(FM)— 1997: 91.9 mhz; 1 kw. 164 ft TL: N35 09 17 W77 02 00. Hrs open:
Rebroadcasts WAFR(FM) Tupelo 100%.
Box 2440, Tupelo, MS, 38803. Phone: (662) 844-8888. Fax: (662) 840-3187.E-mail: info@afa.net Web Site:www.afr.net Licensee: American Family Association. Group owner: American Family Radio Format: Lite contemp, praise, talk. ◆Marvin Sanders, gen mgr; Joey Moody, chief of engrg.

WIKS(FM)— August 1977: 101.9 mhz; 100 kw. 1,020 ft TL: N35 12 07 W77 11 15. Stereo. Hrs open: 24 207 Glenburnie Dr., 28560. Phone: (252) 633-1500. Fax: (252) 633-6546. Web Site:www.1019online.com Licensee: Beasley FM Acquisition Corp. Population served: 924,300 Natl. Rep: D & R Radio,. Format: Urban adult contemp. Spec prog: Gospel 4 hrs, jazz 2 hrs wkly. ◆Bruce Beasley, pres; Bruce Simel, VP, gen mgr; J Dot, prom dir.

WNOS(AM)— Apr 23, 1942: 1450 khz; 1 kw-U. TL: N35 06 03 W77 04 33. Hrs open: 24 116 S. Business Plaza, 28562. Phone: (252) 638-8888. Fax: (252) 636-5848.E-mail: mike@rfenc.com Web Site:www.rfenc.com Licensee: CTC Media Group Inc. (group owner; acq 7-1-00; $65,000). Natl. Network: Fox Sports, Westwood One, . N.C. News Net. Format: Sports / Talk. Target aud: 12+, Male 12-45. ◆Lee Afflerbach, pres; Mike Afflerbach, gen mgr.

WSFL-FM— July 20, 1968: 106.5 mhz; 100 kw. 915 ft TL: N35 02 27 W77 21 11. Stereo. Hrs open: 24 207 Glenburnie Dr., 28560. Phone: (252) 633-1500. Fax: (252) 633-6546. Web Site:www.wsfl.com Licensee: W & B Media Inc. Group owner: Beasley Broadcast Group (acq 7-10-91; $500,000 with co-located AM; 7-29-91). Natl. Rep: D & R Radio,. Format: Classic rock, AOR. Target aud: 18-54. ◆Bruce Simel, gen mgr; Jeff Sanders, opns dir; Wendy Gatlin, prom dir; Richard Banks, engrg dir.

*WTEB(FM)— June 4, 1984: 89.3 mhz; 100 kw. 522 ft TL: N35 06 32 W77 06 10. Stereo. Hrs open: 24 800 College Ct., 28562. Phone: (252) 638-3434. Fax: (252) 638-3538. Web Site:www.publicradioeast.org Licensee: Board of Trustees, Craven Community College. Natl. Network: NPR, PRI, . Format: Class, news & info. News: 44 hrs wkly. Target aud: 35 plus; highly educated professionals. Spec prog: Jazz 4 hrs wkly. ◆Kathleen Beal, gen mgr; Charles Wethington, stn mgr, opns mgr; Jill McGuire, dev dir; J. Howard Jones, chief of engrg; George Olsen, reporter.

WWNB(AM)— July 5, 1953: 1490 khz; 1 kw-U. TL: N35 07 59 W77 03 56. Hrs open: 24 116 S. Business Plaza, 28562. Phone: (252) 633-1490. Fax: (252) 636-5848.E-mail: mike@rfenc.com Web Site:www.rfenc.com Licensee: CTC Media Group Inc. (group owner; acq 11-15-90; $75,000). Natl. Network: Westwood One, ESPN Radio, . Jimmy Young. Format: ESPN Sports Radio. Target aud: Men 12-54; general. ◆Mike Afflerbach, gen mgr; Chris Butler, gen sls mgr.

*WZNB(FM)— 2006: 88.5 mhz; 300 w. Ant 121 ft TL: N35 06 32 W77 06 10. Hrs open: Public Radio East, 800 College Ct., 28562. Phone: (252) 638-3434. Fax: (252) 638-3538. Web Site:www.publicradioeast.org Licensee: Craven Community College. Format: Information. ◆Charles Wethington, stn mgr; Jill McGuire, dev dir; J. Howard Jones, chief of engrg; George Olsen, reporter.

New Hope

WAUG(AM)— July 20, 1987: 750 khz; 500 w-D. TL: N35 47 28 W78 37 10. Stereo. Hrs open: 1315 Oakwood Ave., Raleigh, 27610. Phone:

(919) 516-4750.E-mail: waug@st-aug.edu Licensee: Saint Augustine's College. Natl. Network: American Urban, . Format: Relg, news/talk, gospel. Target aud: 18 plus; Black adults. ◆Dr. Diane Suber, pres; Alan Riggs, gen mgr, stn mgr; Frank Butler, opns mgr; John Hardee, chief of engrg.

Newland

WECR(AM)— Aug 14, 1978: 1130 khz; 1 kw-D. TL: N36 04 39 W81 54 59. Hrs open: 1281 Newland Hwy., 28657. Phone: (828) 733-0188. Fax: (828) 733-0189.E-mail: info@wecr.com Licensee: High Country Adventures LLC. (group owner; (acq 3-3-2009; grpsl). Population served: 55,000 Format: Country. Target aud: 25-54; middle class, blue collar. Spec prog: Gospel 10 hrs, relg 5 hrs, bluegrass 2 hrs wkly. ◆Jonathan Hoffman, gen mgr.

Newport

WMGV(FM)— Sept 4, 1983: 103.3 mhz; 100 kw. 980 ft TL: N34 45 06 W76 52 57. Hrs open: 24 207 Glenburnie Dr., New Bern, 28560. Phone: (252) 633-1500. Fax: (252) 633-0718.E-mail: info@wmgv.com Web Site:www.v1033.com Licensee: WMGV License L.P. Group owner: Beasley Broadcast Group Inc. (acq 2-3-2000; grpsl). Natl. Rep: D & R Radio,. Pepper & Corazzini. Format: Soft rock. Target aud: 18-54. ◆Bruce Simel, gen mgr; Colleen Jackson, progmg dir.

Newton

WNNC(AM)— June 18, 1948: 1230 khz; 1 kw-U. TL: N35 40 20 W81 14 12. Stereo. Hrs open: 24 Box 430, 28658. Phone: (828) 464-4041. Fax: (828) 464-9662.E-mail: info@aol.com Licensee: Newton-Conover Communications Inc. (acq 8-76). Population served: 202,000 Format: Adult contemp. News staff: one. Target aud: 25-49. Spec prog: Black 2 hrs, jazz 3 hrs wkly. ◆Dave Lingafelt, pres, gen mgr, chief of engrg; Jim Turner, gen sls mgr; Karol Lowery, traf mgr.

Newton Grove

*WYBJ(FM)— 2007: 90.7 mhz; 3 kw. Ant 354 ft TL: N35 13 54 W78 22 11. Hrs open: 520 Roberts Rd., Newport, 28570-8616. Phone: (252) 223-4600. Fax: (252) 223-2201. Web Site:www.fbnradio.com Licensee: Grace Missionary Baptist Church Inc. (acq 11-12-2008; $300,000). ◆Michael D. Ebron, gen mgr.

Norlina

*WJIJ(FM)— January 2001: 94.3 mhz; 6 kw. Ant 328 ft TL: N36 29 46 W78 11 14. Hrs open: 24
Rebroadcasts WAJC(FM) Zebulon 100%.
5 W. Hargett St., Raleigh, 27607. Phone: (919) 899-6778. Fax: (919) 899-6779. Licensee: CSN International (group owner; acq 12-18-98). Format: Christian teaching/praise & worship music. ◆Jim Walker, gen mgr.

*WZRN(FM)—Not on air, target date: unknown: 90.5 mhz; 2.3 kw. Ant 298 ft TL: N36 29 38 W78 11 23. Hrs open: 230-B Roanoke Ave., Roanoke Rapids, 27870. Phone: (252) 537-9999. Fax: (252) 537-3333. Web Site:www.wzru.org Licensee: Roanoke Valley Communications Inc. Format: Talk, class, news. ◆George Campbell, pres; Allen Garrett, gen mgr.

North Wilkesboro

WKBC(AM)— June 1947: 800 khz; 1 kw-D, 308 w-N. TL: N36 11 16 W81 08 30. Hrs open: 24 Box 938, 400 C St., 28659. Phone: (336) 667-2221. Fax: (336) 667-3677.E-mail: wkbctraffic@charter.net Licensee: Wilkes Broadcasting Co. Inc. (acq 1-24-03; with co-located FM). Population served: 60,000 Natl. Network: CBS Radio, . Wire Svc: AP Format: Country. News staff: one. ◆Robert Brown, pres & gen mgr; Ed Racey, news dir.

WKBC-FM— July 1962: 97.3 mhz; 100 kw horiz, 92 kw vert. Ant 1,322 ft TL: N36 04 34 W81 07 43. Stereo. Hrs open: 24 Box 938, 400 C St., 28659. Phone: (336) 667-2221. Fax: (336) 667-3677. Licensee: Wilkes Broadcasting Co. Inc. Population served: 1,200,000 Format: CHR. ◆Robert Brown, gen mgr; Bob Brown, progmg dir; Ed Racey, chief of engrg.

Oak Island

WSFM(FM)— July 2000: 98.3 mhz; 18.5 kw. 380 ft TL: N33 57 40 W78 01 37. Hrs open: 24 25 N. Kerr Ave., Suite C, Wilmington, 28405. Phone: (910) 791-3088. Fax: (910) 791-0112.E-mail: mud@surf983.com Web Site:www.surf983.com Licensee: Sunrise Broadcasting LLC. Group owner: NextMedia Group L.L.C. (acq 11-18-2008; grpsl). Format: Alternative. ◆Barbara Raybourne, gen mgr; Missy Andrus, prom dir; Mike Kennedy, mus dir; Walt Howard, engrg dir.

Ocean Isle Beach

WLQB(FM)— 1999: 93.5 mhz; 6 kw. Ant 328 ft TL: N33 55 37 W78 23 48. Hrs open:
Simulcast with WGTR(FM) Bucksport, SC 100%.
4841 Hwy. 17 Bypass S., Myrtle Beach, SC, 29577. Phone: (843) 293-0107. Fax: (843) 293-1717. Licensee: Qantum of Myrtle Beach License Co. LLC. Group owner: Qantum Communications Corp. (acq 7-2-2003; grpsl). Format: Country. ◆Michael Meeks, gen mgr; Serap Jackson, opns mgr & progmg mgr.

Ocracoke

***WOVV(FM)**—Not on air, target date: unknown: 90.1 mhz; 650 w. Ant 62 ft TL: N35 06 43 W75 58 38.2. Hrs open: 416 Irvin Garrish Hwy., 27960. Phone: (252) 921-0365. Licensee: Ocracoke Foundation. ◆Robin Payton Payne, pres.

Oriental

WNBU(FM)— Mar 18, 1993: 94.1 mhz; 11 kw. Ant 485 ft TL: N35 00 02 W76 49 58. Stereo. Hrs open: 24 1307 S. Glenburnie Rd., New Bern, 28562. Phone: (252) 672-5900. Fax: (252) 637-6872. Web Site:www.wnbufm.com Licensee: Inner Banks Media LLC. Group owner: Archway Broadcasting Group (acq 3-12-2007; grpsl). Population served: 250,000 Rgnl. Network: Capitol Radio Net. Pepper & Corazzini. Format: Talk. Target aud: 25 plus; adults with disposable incomes. ◆Henry Hinton, gen mgr.

Oxford

WCBQ(AM)— June 9, 1949: 1340 khz; 1 kw-U. TL: N36 18 27 W78 34 37. Stereo. Hrs open: 18
Rebroadcasts WHNC(AM) Henderson 100%.
PO Box 1005, One Alvin Augustus Jones Way, 601 Henderson St., 27565. Phone: (919) 693-3540. Phone: (919) 693-1340. Fax: (919) 693-9054.E-mail: alvin@dralvinjones.com Licensee: The Paradise Network (TPN) of North Carolina Inc. (acq 6-6-2001; $650,000 with WHNC(AM) Henderson). Population served: 25,000 Rgnl. Network: N.C. News Net. N.C. News Net. Rgnl rep: T-N. Format: Black gospel. News: 10 hrs wkly. Target aud: General. Spec prog: Farm, professional & college sports, news/talk. ◆Dr. Alvin Augustis Jones, gen mgr, chief of engrg; Jim Davis, engrg mgr; Jeff Rose, spec ev coord; Nathaniel Smith, min affrs dir & relg ed.

Pilot Mountain

***WGIW(FM)**— 2008: 89.7 mhz; 1.03 kw vert. Ant 198 ft TL: N36 26 27 W80 35 37. Hrs open: Box 159, Rural Hall, 27045. Phone: (605) 868-0525. Licensee: Church Planters of America. ◆Danny Hawkins, pres & gen mgr.

Pine Knoll Shores

WBNK(FM)— 2009: 92.7 mhz; 11.5 kw. Ant 748 ft TL: N34 53 00.4 W76 30 21.3. Hrs open: 5447 Hwy. 70, Morehead City, 28557. Phone: (561) 252-1194.E-mail: tvguyed@yahoo.com Licensee: Tower Investment Trust Inc. ◆William H. Brothers, pres.

Pinehurst

***WBFY(FM)**— September 2003: 90.3 mhz; 3.5 kw vert. Ant 328 ft TL: N35 09 13 W79 34 16. Hrs open: P.O. Drawer 2440, Tupelo, MS, 38803. Phone: (662) 844-8888. Fax: (662) 840-3187.E-mail: info@afa.net Web Site:www.afr.net Licensee: American Family Association. Group owner: American Family Radio Natl. Network: American Family Radio, . Format: Christian. News: 24 hours. ◆Marvin Sanders, gen mgr; Joey Moody, chief of engrg.

WEEB(AM)—See Southern Pines

WIOZ(AM)— Mar 25, 1980: 550 khz; 1 kw-D, 260 w-N, DA-2. TL: N35 09 04 W79 28 40. Hrs open: 24 200 Short Rd., Southern Pines, 28387. Phone: (910) 692-2107. Fax: (910) 692-6849. Licensee: Muirfield Broadcasting Inc. (group owner; acq 12-28-83). Population served: 62,000 Format: Adult standards. News staff: one; News: 5 hrs wkly. Target aud: General. ◆Walker Morris, pres; Tiffany Hewitt, gen mgr, gen sls mgr; Rich Rushforth, opns mgr.

WMGU(FM)—See Southern Pines

Pinetops

WPWZ(FM)— Dec 2, 1996: 95.5 mhz; 12.5 kw. 459 ft TL: N35 56 45 W77 39 37. Stereo. Hrs open: 24 12714 East NC 97, Rocky Mount, 27803. Phone: (252) 442-8092. Fax: (252) 977-6664. Licensee: First Media Radio LLC. (group owner; (acq 12-3-2003; grpsl). Natl. Rep: Interep,. Format: Urban. News staff: one. Target aud: 24-54. ◆Alex Kolobielski, pres; Mike Binkley, gen mgr & mktg mgr.

Pineville

WGIV(AM)— Mar 8, 1948: 1370 khz; 3 kw-D, 45 w-N. TL: N35 12 45 W80 52 06. (CP: COL Gastonia. 20 kw-D, 30 w-N. TL: N35 15 56 W81 09 01). Hrs open:
Rebroadcasts WRNA(AM) China Grove 90%.
Box 11584, Rock Hill, SC, 29731. Phone: (803) 329-2760. Fax: (803) 329-3317.E-mail: fneely@rejoiceradio.com Web Site:www.RejoiceRadio.com Licensee: Wisdom LLC. Group owner: Neely Enterprises (acq 2-2-2009; grpsl). Population served: 600,000 Natl. Network: USA, . Law office of David Tillotson. Format: Christian. Target aud: 30 plus. ◆Emma Neely, VP; Frank Neely, gen mgr, stn mgr; Frankie Hemphill, stn mgr.

Pisgah Forest

WGCR(AM)— Sept 16, 1985: 720 khz; 25 kw-D, 15 kw-CH. TL: N35 15 10 W82 40 28. Stereo. Hrs open: 3400New Hendersonville Hwy., 28768. Phone: (828) 884-9427. Fax: (828) 883-9427. Web Site:www.wgcr.net Licensee: Anchor Baptist Broadcasting Association. (acq 2-87). Natl. Network: USA, . Rgnl. Network: N.C. News Net. N.C. News Net. Format: Relg, news. Target aud: General. Spec prog: Gospel. ◆Randy C. Barton, pres, gen mgr, gen sls mgr; Shanna Barton, prom mgr & progmg dir; Shamma Barton, news dir; Lamar Owen, chief of engrg.

Plymouth

WJPI(AM)— Sept 11, 1959: 1470 khz; 5 kw-D. TL: N35 50 48 W76 45 22. Hrs open: Hwy. 64, 27962. Licensee: Free Temple Ministries Inc. (acq 12-14-98). ◆Terry Baylor, gen mgr.

WPNC-FM— December 1979: 95.9 mhz; 2.6 kw. 350 ft TL: N35 50 48 W76 45 22. Stereo. Hrs open: 24 930 Hwy. 32 S., 27962. Phone: (252) 793-9995. Fax: (252) 793-4673.E-mail: magic959production@yahoo.com Licensee: Durlyn Broadcasting Inc. (acq 1996). Population served: 100,000 Natl. Network: CBS Radio, . N.C. News Net. Format: Adult contemp. Target aud: 25-54. ◆Bill Benjamin, CEO, gen mgr; Marie Cox, VP; Alex Rains, opns mgr.

Raeford

WMFA(AM)— Apr 5, 1963: 1400 khz; 1 kw-U. TL: N35 58 43 W79 12 32. Hrs open: 6 AM-10 PM 1085 E. Central Ave., 28376. Phone: (910) 875-6225. Phone: (910) 875-6477. Fax: (910) 875-3220.E-mail: wmfa1400@yahoo.com Licensee: W & V Broadcasting Enterprises Inc. (acq 6-2-93; $12,000; 6-21-93). Population served: 300,000 Rgnl. Network: Capitol Radio Net. Format: Gospel. Target aud: General. Spec prog: Sp 6 hrs wkly. ◆William Hollingsworth, CEO & pres; Vera Hollingsworth, CFO; Jeremy Hollingsworth, gen mgr, opns mgr.

***WRAE(FM)**— 2006: 88.7 mhz; 2.25 kw vert. Ant 466 ft TL: N34 54 57 W79 07 28. Hrs open:
Rebroadcasts WAFR(FM) Tupelo, MS 100%.
Drawer 2440, Tupelo, MS, 38801-2440. Phone: (662) 844-8888. Fax: (662) 842-6791. Web Site:www.afr.net Licensee: American Family Association. Format: Christian. ◆Marvin Sanders, gen mgr.

Raleigh

WBBB(FM)— 1947: 96.1 mhz; 100 kw. 985 ft TL: N35 41 07 W78 43 14. Stereo. Hrs open: 24 3012 High Woods Blvd., Suite 200, 27604. Phone: (919) 876-6464. Fax: (919) 790-8893.E-mail: info@curtismedia.com Web Site:www.96rockonline.com Licensee: Carolina Media Group Inc. Group owner: Curtis Media Group (acq 1996; $16 million). Population

served: 1,700,000 Natl. Rep: McGavren Guild,. Format: Rock. Target aud: M 25-44. ◆Don Curtis, pres; Mike Hartel, gen mgr; Jay Naclis, progmg dir, progmg mgr; Allen Sherrill, chief of engrg; Ali Diatta, traf mgr; Shalon Lenfestey, prom dir & disc jockey.

WCLY(AM)— Aug 15, 1962: 1550 khz; 1 kw-D, 7 w-N. TL: N35 45 37 W78 39 27. Hrs open: 3012 Highwoods Blvd., Suite 200, 27604. Phone: (919) 954-1550. Fax: (919) 954-1556. Web Site:www.1550wcly.com Licensee: Triangle Broadcast Associates LLC. (acq 4-5-99). Format: Relg. Target aud: 25-65; primarily Black. ◆Rick Heilmann, gen mgr.

***WCPE(FM)**— July 17, 1978: 89.7 mhz; 96.7 kw. Ant 1,178 ft TL: N35 56 25 W78 28 45. Stereo. Hrs open: 24 Box 897, Wake Forest, 27588. Phone: (919) 556-5178. Fax: (919) 556-9273.E-mail: wcpe@wcpe.org Web Site:theclassicalstation.org Galaxy 14, Tr 8, Vert, 6.30/6.48 mhz Licensee: Educational Information Corp. Population served: 981,000 Brooks, Pierce, McLendon, Humphrey & Leonard. Format: Classical. Target aud: 35 plus; class music listeners. ◆Deborah S. Proctor, CEO, pres, gen mgr; Rae C. Weaver, dev dir; Dick Storck, progmg dir; William Woltz, mus dir; John Graham, engr.

WDCG(FM)—See Durham

WDOX(AM)— Dec 1, 1981: 570 khz; 500 w-D, 54 w-N. TL: N35 45 37 W78 39 27. Hrs open: 24 3012 Highwoods Blvd., 27604. Phone: (919) 855-9383. Fax: (919) 790-6654. Web Site:www.570wdox.com Licensee: Triangle Broadcast Associates LLC. Group owner: Curtis Media Group (acq 6-1-99). Population served: 600,000 Natl. Network: ABC, . Natl. Rep: McGavren Guild,. Format: News/talk. ◆Rick Heilmann, gen mgr; Peter Richon, progmg dir.

***WKNC-FM**— Oct 9, 1966: 88.1 mhz; 25 kw. 259 ft TL: N35 47 15 W78 40 14. Stereo. Hrs open: 24 343 Witherspoon Student Ctr., Campus Box 8607, 27695. Phone: (919) 515-2401. Fax: (919) 513-2693.E-mail: gm@wknc.org Web Site:www.wknc.org Licensee: North Carolina State University. Population served: 1,000,000 Format: Indie rock, hip hop, electronica, metal. News: 4 hrs wkly. Target aud: 18-59; adults & high school & college students of all demographics. ◆Kyle Robb, gen mgr; Phillip Smith, opns mgr; Nicole Griffin, prom dir; Adam Kincaid, progmg dir; Kelly Reid, mus dir; John Jeringan, chief of engrg; Will Patnaud, chief of engrg & engr.

WKSL(FM)—See Cary

WPJL(AM)— March 1939: 1240 khz; 1 kw-U. TL: N35 46 25 W78 27 09. Stereo. Hrs open: 5:30 AM-midnight Box 27946, 515 Bart St., 27611. Phone: (919) 834-6401. Licensee: WPJL Inc. (acq 7-86; $600,000; 4-21-86). Population served: 500,000 Natl. Network: USA, . Format: Full-time Christian. News: 10 hrs wkly. Target aud: 25-54; Evangelical Christian community of greater Raleigh area. Spec prog: Black gospel. ◆William C. Suttles, pres & gen mgr; LaRue Porter, opns mgr; Jon Hardee, chief of engrg.

WPTF(AM)— Sept 22, 1924: 680 khz; 50 kw-U, DA-N. TL: N35 47 38 W78 45 41. Stereo. Hrs open: 24 3012 Highwoods Blvd., Suite 201, 27604. Phone: (919) 790-9392. Fax: (919) 790-8369. Web Site:www.wptf.com Licensee: First State Communications. Population served: 236,600 Natl. Network: CBS, . Rgnl. Network: Southern Farm. Natl. Rep: McGavren Guild,. Southern Farm Format: News/talk. News: 20 hrs wkly. Target aud: 35-64. Spec prog: Farm 10 hrs wkly. ◆David Stuckey, gen mgr, gen sls mgr & progmg dir.

WQDR(FM)— August 1949: 94.7 mhz; 96 kw. 1,679 ft TL: N35 40 35 W78 32 09. Stereo. Hrs open: 24 3012 Highwoods Blvd., Suite 200, 27604. Phone: (919) 876-6464. Fax: (919) 790-8893.E-mail: info@curtismedia.com Web Site:www.wqdr.net Licensee: Carolina Media Group Inc. Population served: 1,000,000 Rgnl. Network: Southern Farm. Southern Farm Format: Modern country. News staff: one; News: 2 hrs wkly. Target aud: 25-54. Spec prog: NASCAR racing, bluegrass. ◆Trip Savery, gen mgr & gen sls mgr.

WQOK(FM)—(South Boston, VA) Oct 1, 1960: 97.5 mhz; 100 kw. 981 ft TL: N36 20 52 W78 40 00. Stereo. Hrs open: 24 8001-101 Creedmoor, Rd., 27613. Phone: (919) 848-9736. Fax: (919) 848-4724.E-mail: mmarinaro@radio-one.com Web Site:www.k975.com Licensee: Radio One Licenses LLC. Group owner: Radio One Inc. (acq 11-8-01; grpsl). Population served: 870,000 Natl. Network: ABC, . Natl. Rep: Christal,. Format: Urban contemp. News staff: one; News: 20 hrs wkly. Target aud: 25-54; upwardly mobile with discretionary income. Spec prog: Gospel 9 hrs wkly. ◆Gary Weiss, gen mgr; Cy Young, opns dir, progmg dir; Saundra Lemaster, sls dir & gen sls mgr; Jodi Luke, natl sls mgr.

WRAL(FM)— 1947: 101.5 mhz; 96 kw. 1,820 ft TL: N35 40 35 W78 32 09. Stereo. Hrs open: 24 Box 10100, 27605. Secondary address: 711 Hillsborough St. 27603. Phone: (919) 890-6101. Fax: (919) 890-6146.E-mail: mixonline@wralfm.com Web Site:www.wralfm.com Licensee: Capitol Broadcasting Co. Inc. (group owner; acq 1946).

Population served: 1,267,676 Rgnl. Network: N.C. News Net. Natl. Rep: Katz Radio,. N.C. News Net. Holland & Knight. Wire Svc: AP Format: Adult contemp. News: 7 hrs wkly news progmg. Target aud: 25-54. Spec prog: Public Afffairs Block - 6:30-8:00am Sundays. ♦Jim Goodmon, pres; Dan McGrath, CFO; Ardie Gregory, VP, gen mgr; Barry Fox, opns dir; Robert Wallace, gen sls mgr; Mark Turak, natl sls mgr; Kirk Kirkland, rgnl sls mgr; Paige Ellis Longest, prom dir; Keith Harrison, engrg dir. Co-owned TV: WRAL-TV affil.

WRBZ(AM)— 1947: 850 khz; 10 kw-D, 5 kw-N, DA-N. TL: N35 48 04 W78 48 51. Stereo. Hrs open: 24 4601 Six Forks Rd., Suite 520, Raliegh, 27609-5287. Phone: (919) 875-9100. Fax: (919) 510-6990.E-mail: brianm@850thebuzz.com Web Site:www.850thebuzz.com Licensee: McClatchey Broadcasting Co. LLC (acq 2-9-2005). Population served: 1,490,000 Natl. Network: Westwood One, Fox Sports, . Natl. Rep: McGavren Guild,. Wire Svc: AP Format: All sports. News: 5 hrs wkly. Target aud: 25-54. ♦Brian Maloney, gen mgr; Mike Stangl, prom mgr; Adam Gold, progmg dir; Ted Sawyer, traf mgr.

WRDU(FM)—(Wilson, Mar 1, 1961: 106.1 mhz; 100 kw. Ant 1,364 ft TL: N35 45 36 W78 11 04. Stereo. Hrs open: 24 3100 Smoketree Ct., Suite 700, 27604. Phone: (919) 876-1061. Fax: (919) 876-2929.E-mail: info@1061rdu.com Web Site:www.1061rdu.com Licensee: Clear Channel Communications Group owner: Clear Channel Communications Inc. (acq 8-30-2000; grpsl). Population served: 750,000 Fisher, Wayland, Cooper, Leader & Zaragoza. Format: Country. News staff: one; News: 3 hrs wkly. ♦Ken Spitzer, gen mgr.

WRTG(AM)—See Garner

WRVA-FM—(Rocky Mount, November 1947: 100.7 mhz; 100 kw. Ant 1,968 ft TL: N35 49 53 W78 08 50. Stereo. Hrs open: 3100 Smoketree Ct., Suite 700, 27604. Phone: (919) 878-1500. Fax: (919) 876-8578.E-mail: info@1007theriver.com Web Site:www.1007theriver.com Licensee: Capstar TX L.P. Group owner: Clear Channel Communications Inc. (acq 8-30-2000; grpsl). Population served: 750,000 Natl. Network: ABC, . Fisher, Wayland, Cooper, Leader & Zaragoza. Format: Classic rock. Target aud: 25-54; upscale adults. ♦Ken Spitzer, gen mgr; Jon Robbins, opns dir; Myron Bethea, sls dir, gen sls mgr; Jessica Hayes, prom dir; Fred Pace, engrg VP, chief of engrg; Tracy Leonard, traf mgr.

***WSHA(FM)—** Nov 18, 1968: 88.9 mhz; 50 kw. Ant 456 ft TL: N35 45 05 W78 36 01. Stereo. Hrs open: 24 118 E. South St., 27601. Phone: (919) 546-8432. Phone: (919) 546-8430. Fax: (919) 546-8315.E-mail: wsha@shawu.edu Web Site:www.wshafm.org Licensee: Shaw University. Population served: 511,619 Natl. Network: NPR, . Format: Jazz. News: 13.5 hrs wkly. Target aud: 25-55; high income, well educated. Spec prog: Sp 3 hrs, African 3 hrs, Caribbean 3 hrs, blues 8 hrs, gospel 6 hrs wkly. ♦Dr. Clarence G. Newsome, pres; Dr. Emeka Emekauwa, gen mgr; Rashad Mulhaimin, dev dir; Sharon Berry-Vivian, progmg dir; Azuka Molokwu, mus dir; Jim Davis, chief of engrg.

WWMY(FM)— 2000: Stn currently dark. 102.9 mhz; 1.7 kw. Ant 620 ft TL: N35 47 38 W78 45 41. Hrs open: 3012 Highwoods Blvd., Suite 201, 27604. Phone: (919) 790-6961. Fax: (919) 790-8369.E-mail: bcampbell@curtismedia.com Web Site:www.y1029.com Licensee: WWND LLC. Group owner: Curtis Media Group (acq 10-2-98; $495,000 for stock). Population served: 1,100,000 Natl. Rep: McGavren Guild,. Format: Oldies. ♦Mike Hartel, gen mgr; Shalon Lenfestry, prom dir; Bill Campbell, progmg dir; Allen Sherrill, chief of engrg; Ali Diatta, traf mgr.

Red Springs

WTEL(AM)— June 15, 1970: 1160 khz; 5 kw-D, 250 w-N. TL: N35 50 19 W79 10 36. Hrs open: 17 Box 711, 28377. Phone: (910) 843-5946. Fax: (910) 843-8694.E-mail: info@wtel.com Licensee: WDAS License L.P. Group owner: Beasley Broadcast Group Inc. (acq 6-12-97; $1.2 million with WUKS(FM) Saint Pauls). Population served: 200,000 Rgnl. Network: Southern Farm. Southern Farm Format: Southern gospel, Black gospel. News staff: 2. Target aud: 24-54. Spec prog: Farm 5 hrs wkly. ♦Danny Highsmith, gen mgr; Towanna Locklear, gen sls mgr, disc jockey; Deanna Hodges, prom mgr; Garrette Davis, progmg dir; Gilbert Baez, news dir; Van Clough, chief of engrg; George McPhaul, local news ed; Montana Locklear, disc jockey.

Reidsville

WJMH(FM)— Sept 6, 1948: 102.1 mhz; 100 kw. 1,203 ft TL: N36 16 33 W79 56 27. Stereo. Hrs open: 24 7819 National Service Rd., Suite 401, Greensboro, 27409. Phone: (336) 605-5200. Fax: (336) 605-5219.E-mail: info@102jamz.com Web Site:www.102jamz.com Licensee: Entercom Greensboro License LLC. Group owner: Entercom Communications Corp. (acq 12-13-99; grpsl). Population served: 940,600 Natl. Rep: McGavren Guild,. Format: Urban, Hip-Hop. Target aud: 16-35; 65% Black, 35% white. ♦Brent Millar, gen mgr; Erin Casey, gen sls mgr; Brian Douglas, progmg dir; Larry Allen, chief of engrg; Valerie Dickens, prom dir & traf mgr.

WREV(AM)— 1948: 1220 khz; 1 kw-D. TL: N36 23 19 W79 38 51. Hrs open:
Rebroadcasts WRTP(AM) Chapel Hill 100%.
1010 Vermont Ave. N.W., Suite 100, Washington, DC, 20005. Phone: (202) 638-1959. Fax: (202) 638-6127.E-mail: estuardovaldemar@hotmail.com Licensee: Estuardo Valdemar Rodriguez and Leonor Rodriguez. Group owner: Estuardo Valdemar Rodriguez and Leonor Rodriguez Stns (acq 8-5-2004; $125,000). Population served: 750,000 Format: Mexican reng. ♦Estuardo Valdemar Rodriguez, gen mgr.

Roanoke Rapids

WCBT(AM)— November 1940: 1230 khz; 1 kw-U. TL: N36 26 45 W77 39 51. Hrs open: 24 3 E. First St., Weldon, 27890. Phone: (252) 538-4184. Fax: (252) 538-0378.E-mail: haskinsal@yahoo.com Licensee: First Media Radio LLC. (group owner; (acq 7-22-2003; grpsl). Population served: 40,000 Natl. Network: ABC, ESPN Radio, . Rgnl. Network: N.C. News Net. N.C. News Net. Format: Sports. ♦Al Haskin, gen mgr; John Green, opns mgr; Allen Garrett, progmg dir; Frank White, chief of engrg.

***WPGT(FM)—** January 2001: 91.1 mhz; 2 kw. Ant 69 ft TL: N36 28 08 W77 39 02. Hrs open:
Rebroadcasts WGPS(FM) Elizabeth City 100%.
Winchester Stn., 905 Halstead Blvd., Elizabeth City, 27909. Phone: (252) 334-1883. Fax: (252) 333-1459.E-mail: wpgt@csnradio.com Licensee: CSN International (group owner; (acq 5-5-2000; $20,000 for CP). Format: Christian. News: one hr wkly. ♦Jeff Ozanne, gen mgr; Darla Ozanne, progmg dir; Maria VanDeWalker, mus dir.

WPTM(FM)— 1973: 102.3 mhz; 6 kw. 300 ft TL: N36 30 12 W77 44 47. (CP: 5.4 kw, ant 344 ft.). Stereo. Hrs open: 24 Box 910, 27870. Secondary address: 3 E. 4th St., Weldon 27890. Phone: (252) 536-3115. Fax: (252) 538-0378.E-mail: amyhmoran@yahoo.com Web Site:www.wptm1023.com Licensee: First Media Radio LLC. (group owner; (acq 7-22-2003; grpsl). Population served: 112,000 Rgnl. Network: Southern Farm. Southern Farm Wire Svc: UPI Format: Country. News staff: 3; News: 14 hrs wkly. Target aud: 25-54; females with spendable income, decision-makers. Spec prog: Farm15 hrs, relg 3 hrs wkly. ♦Al Haskins, gen mgr.

***WRTP(FM)—** July 4, 1994: 88.5 mhz; 24 kw. Ant 479 ft TL: N36 17 44 W78 06 21. Stereo. Hrs open: 24 7610 Falls of Neuse Rd., Suite 150, Raleigh, 27615. Phone: (919) 477-7222. Fax: (919) 477-4424.E-mail: wrtp@goodnews.org Web Site:www.hisradiowrtp.com Licensee: Radio Training Network Inc. (acq 4-29-2005; swap for WZRU(FM) Roanoke Rapids). Population served: 96,000 Natl. Network: Salem Radio Network, . Natl. Rep: Salem,. Format: Contemp Christian music. News: 14 hrs wkly. Target aud: 25-54; Christian. ♦Mark G. Parker, CEO, gen mgr, progmg dir; James Campbell, pres; Randy Jordan, sls dir.

WTRG(FM)—See Gaston

***WZRU(FM)—** Dec 8, 1972: 90.1 mhz; 760 w. Ant 174 ft TL: N36 26 13 W77 38 12. (CP: 11 kw, ant 505 ft. TL: N36 14 39 W77 34 40). Stereo. Hrs open: 24 232 Roanoke Ave., 27870-1916. Phone: (252) 308-0885. Fax: (252) 537-3333. Web Site:www.wzru.org Licensee: Roanoke Valley Communications Inc. (acq 5-6-2005; swap for WRTP(FM) Roanoke Rapids). Natl. Network: NPR, . Arter & Hadden. Format: Adult contemp. News staff: 2; News: 30 hrs wkly. Target aud: 35 plus; community oriented, above-average education. Spec prog: Gospel 6 hrs, jazz 6 hrs, folk 5 hrs, oldies 4 hrs, new age 10 hrs, big band 4 hrs wkly. ♦Allen Garrett, gen mgr.

Robbins

WLHC(FM)— June 2, 2003: 103.1 mhz; 6 kw. Ant 388 ft TL: N35 26 33 W79 26 37. Hrs open: 24 102 S. Steele St., Suite 301, Sanford, 27330. Secondary address: Box 1963, Pinehurst 28370. Phone: (919) 775-1031. Fax: (919) 775-1397.E-mail: whlc@life1031.com Web Site:www.life1031.com Licensee: Woolstone Corporation Natl. Network: ABC, . N.C. News Net. Format: Adult hits. News staff: one. Spec prog: Jazz 2 hrs, Christian 5 hrs, bluegrass 5 hrs wkly. ♦Alan Button, pres; Steve Koranda, stn mgr.

Robbinsville

WCVP-FM— 1987: 95.9 mhz; 60 w. 2,008 ft TL: N35 15 28 W83 47 44. Hrs open: 5:30 AM-10 PM (M-F); 6 AM-10 PM (S); 7 AM-10 PM (Su) Box 756, 129 N. By-Pass, 28771. Phone: (828) 479-8080. Phone: (828) 479-2296. Fax: (828) 479-2296.E-mail: info@wcvp.com Licensee: Cherokee Broadcasting Co. Format: C&W. Target aud: General. ♦Dennis G. Blakemore, pres, gen mgr, gen sls mgr, prom mgr, progmg dir, chief of engrg; Penny Wade, pub affrs dir.

Rockingham

WAYN(AM)— September 1946: 900 khz; 1 kw-U, DA-2. TL: N34 55 30 W79 44 35. Hrs open: 6 AM-10 PM Box 519, 28380. Secondary address: 1223 Rockingham Rd. 28380. Phone: (910) 895-4041. Fax: (910) 895-4993. Licensee: WAYN Inc. (acq 5-10-01). Population served: 23,600 Rgnl. Network: N.C. News Net. N.C. News Net. Cohn & Marks. Format: Adult contemp, info. News: 20 hrs wkly. Target aud: 25-49; event-conscious adults. ♦William F. Futterer, pres, gen mgr & gen sls mgr; Jim Smith, progmg dir, news dir, farm dir, women's int ed, disc jockey; Mary Futterer Morgan, mus dir; Gene Shaw, chief of engrg; Brent Goodwin, disc jockey.

WLWL(AM)— Oct 27, 1969: 770 khz; 5 kw-D. TL: N34 55 30 W79 47 11. Hrs open: Box 428, Ellerbe, 28338. Secondary address: 275 River Rd. 28379. Phone: (910) 997-2526. Fax: (910) 997-2527.E-mail: bigwaveradio@gmail.com Web Site:www.77bigwaves.com Licensee: Beach Music Broadcasting Co. Inc. Population served: 75,000 Rgnl. Network: N.C. News Net. N.C. News Net. Format: Beach, oldies. Target aud: 25-60. ♦Beth Ballard, gen mgr; Keith Davis, sls.

***WRSH(FM)—** May 1973: 91.1 mhz; 10 w. 60 ft TL: N34 57 03 W79 42 56. (CP: 339.7 w, ant 161 ft.). Hrs open: Box 1748, 28380. Secondary address: Richmond Sr. High School, 838 N. US Hwy. 1 28379. Phone: (910) 997-9812. Fax: (910) 997-9816. Licensee: Richmond County Board of Education. Format: Educ. ♦Kim Newton, gen mgr.

Rocky Mount

WDWG(FM)— Dec 18, 1989: 98.5 mhz; 16 kw. 417 ft TL: N35 54 43 W77 50 06. Hrs open: 12714 E. NC #97, 27803. Phone: (252) 442-8092. Fax: (252) 977-6664. Web Site:www.bigdawg985.com Natl. Rep: Interep,. Format: Country. Target aud: 18 plus. ♦Alex Kolobielski, pres; Mike Binkley, mktg mgr.

WEED(AM)— Sept 10, 1933: 1390 khz; 5 kw-D, 30 w-N. TL: N35 57 43 W77 49 35. Hrs open: 24 Box 2666, 27802. Secondary address: 115 N. Church St. 27802. Phone: (252) 443-5976. Fax: (252) 443-5977. Licensee: Northstar Broadcasting Corp. (acq 7-22-03; with co-located FM). Population served: 45,000 Natl. Network: Premiere Radio Networks, . Format: Relg. News staff: 10; News: 14 hrs wkly. Target aud: Males; 18+. ♦Charles Johnson II, VP, gen mgr, gen sls mgr; Sonya Johnson, opns mgr; Charles Johnson, II, progmg dir; Ethan Arrington, mus dir.

WFXK(FM)—See Tarboro

WRMT(AM)— Dec 15, 1958: 1490 khz; 1 kw-U. TL: N35 55 57 W77 49 49. Stereo. Hrs open: 24 12714 E. NC#97, 27803-0005. Phone: (252) 442-8092. Fax: (252) 977-6664. Licensee: First Media Radio LLC (group owner; (acq 1-7-2003; grpsl). Rgnl. Network: N.C. News Net. Natl. Rep: Interep,. N.C. News Net. Format: Sports. Target aud: 30 plus. ♦Alex Kolobielski, pres; Mike Binkley, gen mgr & mktg mgr.

***WRQM(FM)—** April 1, 1996: 90.9 mhz; 6 kw. Ant 626 ft TL: N35 48 40 W77 44 33. Hrs open: 24
Rebroadcasts WUNC(FM) Chapel Hill 99.9%.
120 Friday Ctr Dr., CB-0915, Chapel Hill, 27517-9495. Phone: (919) 966-5454. Fax: (919) 966-5955.E-mail: wunc@unc.edu Web Site:www.wunc.org Licensee: The Board of Trustees of the University of NC at Chapel Hill (acq 5-99). Population served: 250,665 Natl. Network: NPR, PRI, CBC Radio One, . Format: News & Info. News staff: 7; News: 124 hrs wkly. Target aud: 35 plus; educated, successful, community active. ♦Joan Rose, gen mgr; Kevin Wolf, opns mgr.

WRSV(FM)— 1949: 92.1 mhz; 2.35 kw. 531 ft TL: N35 48 40 W77 44 33. Stereo. Hrs open: 24 Prog sep from AM Box 2666, 27802. Secondary address: 115 N. Church St. 27802. Phone: (252) 937-7400. Fax: (252)443-5977.E-mail: soul92_2000@yahoo.com Web Site:www.soul92jams.com Population served: 557,400 Natl. Network: Premiere Radio Networks, . Format: Urban contemp. News staff: 25; News: 3 hrs wkly. Target aud: General; African American consumers of all age groups. ♦Charles Johnson, II, gen mgr, gen sls mgr, progmg dir; Sonya Johnson, opns mgr; Chuck Johnson, mus dir.

WRVA-FM—Licensed to Rocky Mount. See Raleigh

Rose Hill

WEGG(AM)— 1971: 710 khz; 250 w-D. TL: N34 51 48 W78 02 16. Hrs open: Sunrise-sunset Box 608, 28458. Secondary address: 3228 U.S. Hwy. 117 28458. Phone: (910) 289-2031. Fax: (910) 289-2032.E-mail: info@wegg.com Licensee: Conner Media Corp. Population served: 157,000 Rgnl. Network: Southern Farm. Natl. Rep: Keystone (unwired net),. Southern Farm Format: Gospel/relg, Black. Spec prog: Farm 9 hrs, bluegrass gospel 10 hrs wkly. ♦Don Brown, chief of engrg; Suzanne Wilson, gen mgr, opns mgr, progmg dir, news dir & farm dir; C.D. Melvin, relg ed.

Roxboro

WKRX(FM)— 1958: 96.7 mhz; 3 kw. 300 ft TL: N36 22 04 W78 59 58. Stereo. Hrs open: 5:30 AM-11 PM Dups AM Box 1176, 2070 Hurdle Mills Rd., 27573. Phone: (336) 599-0266. Fax: (336) 599-9411.E-mail: radio@aol.com Licensee: Roxboro Broadcasting Co. Natl. Network: ABC, . Rgnl. Network: N.C. News Net. N.C. News Net. Edmundson & Edmundson. News staff: one; News: 7 hrs wkly. Target aud: 18-49. ♦David Bradsher, mktg dir, prom VP, adv VP, progmg dir; Bill Lester, disc jockey.

WRXO(AM)— 1949: 1430 khz; 1 kw-D. TL: N36 22 04 W78 59 58. Hrs open: 6 AM-sunset
Simulcast with WKRX(FM) Roxboro.
Box 1176, 2070 Hurdle Mills Rd., 27573. Phone: (336) 599-0266. Fax: (336) 599-9411.E-mail: radiod@aol.com Licensee: Roxboro Broadcasting Co. (acq 5-8-92). Population served: 60000 Natl. Network: ABC, . Rgnl. Network: N.C. News Net., Tobacco. N.C. News Net. Edmundson & Edmundson. Format: Country. News staff: one; News: 7 hrs wkly. Target aud: 18-49. Spec prog: Black 4 hrs, farm 5 hrs, Southern gospel 5 hrs wkly. ♦David Bradsher, pres, gen mgr, gen sls mgr, adv mgr, progmg dir; Wayne Tuck, news dir; Conrad Kimbrough, chief of engrg; Bill Lester, disc jockey.

Rutherfordton

WCAB(AM)— Oct 19, 1966: 590 khz; 1 kw-D, 228 w-N. TL: N35 23 35 W81 55 23. Hrs open: 24 Box 511, 191 Whiteside Rd., 28139. Phone: (828) 287-3356. Fax: (828) 287-7182.E-mail: wcabam59@bellsouth.net Web Site:www.wcab59.com Licensee: Isothermal Broadcasting Corp. (acq 8-1-84; 7-16-84). Population served: 125,000 Rgnl. Network: N.C. News Net. N.C. News Net. Format: Country, news/talk, sports. News: 25 hrs wkly. Target aud: 25 plus; adult consumers. ♦James H. Bishop, pres, gen mgr; Van Austin, progmg dir; Lou Gilliam, traf mgr.

Saint Pauls

WUKS(FM)— Oct 16, 1994: Stn currently dark. 107.7 mhz; 6 kw. 328 ft TL: N34 46 59 W79 07 11. Hrs open: Box 710, 508 Person St., Fayetteville, 28302. Phone: (910) 486-4114. Fax: (910) 486-2124.E-mail: info@kiss1077.com Web Site:www.kiss1077.com Licensee: WDAS License L.P. Group owner: Beasley Broadcast Group (acq 6-12-97; $1.2 million with WTEL(AM) Red Springs). Population served: 600,000 Natl. Network: ABC, . Natl. Rep: D & R Radio,. Format: Urban adult contemp. Target aud: 25-54. ♦George Beasley, chmn; Bruce Beasley, pres; Caroline Beasley, CFO; Brian Beasley, exec VP; Mac Edwards, gen mgr, mktg mgr; Tila Comstock, gen sls mgr; Bryan Kusilka, natl sls mgr; Taylor Morgan, prom dir, mus dir; Jeff Anderson, progmg dir, progmg mgr; Val Jones, pub affrs dir; Dave Cooke, engrg dir; Van Clough, chief of engrg.

Salisbury

WEND(FM)— Mar 16, 1946: 106.5 mhz; 100 kw. 1,003 ft TL: N35 44 11 W80 38 52. (CP: 84 kw, ant 1,046 ft.). Stereo. Hrs open: 24 801 Woodbridge Center Dr., Charlotte, 28217-1908. Phone: (704) 376-1065. Fax: (704) 334-9525. Web Site:www.1065.com Licensee: Capstar TX L.P. Group owner: Clear Channel Communications Inc. (acq 3-12-01). Population served: 1,810,000 Natl. Rep: McGavren Guild,. Format: New rock, modern, alternative. Target aud: 18-34. ♦Jack Daniel, progmg dir, disc jockey; Liz Luke, pub affrs dir; Rob Caskey, chief of engrg; Chris Rozak, disc jockey.

***WOGR-FM**— November 1996: 93.3 mhz; 10 w. 180 ft TL: N35 40 03 W80 28 13. Hrs open:
Rebroadcasts WOGR(AM) Charlotte 100%.
Box 16408, Charlotte, 28297. Phone: (704) 630-1075. Fax: (704) 393-1527. Web Site:www.wordnet.org Licensee: Victory Christian Center Inc. Format: Christian contemp gospel. ♦Robyn Gool, pres; Wayne Hammond, gen mgr; Terry Hammond, sls dir, prom VP, pub affrs dir; Mayfield Harris, traf mgr, disc jockey; Lorenzo Peterson, disc jockey.

WSAT(AM)— June 1947: 1280 khz; 1 kw-U, DA-N. TL: N35 40 30 W80 30 30. Hrs open: 24 1525 Jake Alexander Blvd., 28145. Phone: (704) 633-0621. Fax: (704) 636-2955.E-mail: buddy@WSAT1280.com Web Site:www.1280wsat.com Licensee: Cap Communications Inc. (acq 6-28-02). Population served: 250,000 Natl. Network: Motor Racing Net, . Format: Adult standards. Target aud: 25-64; people that can afford high ticket items. ♦Charles Poole, pres; Bubby Poole, mus dir; Ted Fuller, chief of engrg; Buddy Poole, disc jockey.

WSTP(AM)— Jan 1, 1939: 1490 khz; 1 kw-U. TL: N35 41 12 W80 30 15. Stereo. Hrs open: 24 Box 4157, 28145-4157. Secondary address: 1105 Statesville Blvd. 28144. Phone: (704) 636-3811. Fax: (704) 637-1490.E-mail: newsradio1490@yahoo.com Web Site:www.1490wstp.com Licensee: Rowan Media INC. (acq 12-31-01). Population served: 180,000 Natl. Network: Fox News Radio, Talk Radio Network, Jones Radio Networks, . Rgnl. Network: N.C. News Net. N.C. News Net. Rgnl rep: Capital Radio Format: News/talk 24/7. News: 24 hrs daily. Target aud: 25-59. ♦Timothy H. Coates, pres; Mike Mangan, VP, gen mgr, gen sls mgr, natl sls mgr, rgnl sls mgr; Mark Brown, news dir, pub svc dir; Hal McGee, chief of engrg.

Sanford

***WDCC(FM)**— 1971: 90.5 mhz; 3 kw. 148 ft TL: N35 28 19 W79 08 36. Stereo. Hrs open: 24 1105 Kelly Dr., 27330. Phone: (919) 718-7257. Fax: (919) 718-7429.E-mail: wdcc@cccc.edu Web Site:www.wdccfm.com Licensee: Central Carolina Community College. Population served: 60,000 Format: CHR, Alternative Rock. ♦Bill Freeman, gen mgr, progmg VP & mus dir.

WFJA(FM)— 1950: 105.5 mhz; 2.3 kw. Ant 485 ft TL: N35 26 34 W79 18 41. Stereo. Hrs open: 24 Box 3457, 27331. Phone: (919) 775-3525. Fax: (919) 775-4503.E-mail: info@wfja.com Licensee: WWGP Broadcasting Corp. Population served: 150,000 Format: Hits of the 50s, 60s, 70 & 80s. News staff: one. Target aud: 25-54.

WWGP(AM)— 1946: 1050 khz; 1 kw-D, 161 w-N. TL: N35 26 28 W79 12 54. Hrs open: 6 AM-1 AM Box 3457, 27331. Phone: (919) 775-3525. Fax: (919) 775-4503.E-mail: production@wfjaradio.com Licensee: Richard K. Feindel. (acq 1-13-94; $190,000 with co-located FM; 2-7-94). Population served: 70,000 Format: Country. News staff: one; News: 7 hrs wklyone. Target aud: 18-54. Spec prog: Farm 7 hrs wkly. ♦Richard K. Feindel, pres & gen mgr; Audrey R. Mason, progmg dir; Margaret Murchison, news dir; Jim Vest, chief of engrg.

WXKL(AM)— Oct 2, 1952: 1290 khz; 1 kw-D, 44 w-N. TL: N35 27 01 W79 09 30. Hrs open: 6 AM-8 PM 1516 Woodland Ave., 27330. Phone: (919) 774-1290. Phone: (919) 774-1080. Fax: (919) 774-1118. Licensee: Thomas Broadcasting Inc. (acq 7-8-2003). Population served: 50,000 Natl. Network: NBC, . Format: Gospel. News: 6 hrs wkly. Target aud: 25 plus; general. ♦James Thomas, pres, gen mgr; Amos Marks, progmg dir, disc jockey; Danny Davis, disc jockey.

Scotland Neck

WYAL(AM)— Apr 3, 1960: 1280 khz; 5 kw-D. TL: N36 08 03 W77 25 53. Hrs open: 25539 Hwy. 125, 27874. Phone: (252) 826-3066. Licensee: Sky City Communications Inc. Population served: 2,869 Rgnl. Network: N.C. News Net., Tobacco. N.C. News Net. Format: Gospel. Spec prog: Farm 2 hrs wkly. ♦Richard Petway, pres & gen mgr.

Scotts Hill

***WZDG(FM)**— Mar 23, 2007: 88.5 mhz; 8.9 kw vert. Ant 544 ft TL: N34 30 07 W78 04 58. Stereo. Hrs open: Box 957, Wilmington, 28402-0957. Secondary address: 201 North Front Street, Suite 805, Wilmington 28401. Phone: (910) 202-0946. Fax: (910) 763-6578.E-mail: matt@edgeonover.com Web Site:www.edgeonover.com Licensee: Carolina Christian Radio Inc. Format: Christian alternative/rock. ♦Jim Stephens, gen mgr; Matt Wall, progmg dir.

Selma

WTSB(AM)— Aug 4, 1964: 1090 khz; 9 kw-D, 1.7 kw-CH. TL: N35 36 57 W78 24 33. Hrs open: Sunrise-sunset Box 90, Smithfield, 27577. Phone: (919) 934-6789.E-mail: info@wtsbradio.com Web Site:www.wtsbradio.com Licensee: Lamm Media Group LLC (acq 10-22-2007; $400,000). Population served: 90,000 Rgnl. Network: N.C. News Net. Format: Country. ♦Mickey S. Lamm, gen mgr.

Semora

WKVK(FM)— Mar 1, 1996: 106.7 mhz; 6 kw. Ant 328 ft TL: N36 29 24 W79 00 36. Hrs open: 2351 Sunset Blvd., Suite 170-218, Rocklin, CA, 95765. Phone: (843) 267-0036. Fax: (843) 399-9031. Web Site:www.klove.com Licensee: Educational Media Foundation. Natl. Network: K-Love, . Format: Christian Contemp. ♦Mike Novak, pres.

Shallotte

WBNE(FM)— Oct 31, 1977: 103.7 mhz; 25 kw. Ant 328 ft TL: N33 59 55 W78 22 25. (CP: COL Wrightsville Beach. 35 kw, ant 510 ft. TL: N34 03 02 W77 57 20). Hrs open: 24 122 Cinema Dr., Wilmington, 28403. Phone: (910) 772-6300. Fax: (910) 772-6310.E-mail: newsroom@seacomm.com Web Site:www.937thebone.com Licensee: Sea-Comm Inc. (group owner; (acq 12-30-2003; with WLTT(FM) Shallotte). Population served: 600,000 Natl. Network: Jones Radio Networks, . Format: Classic rock. News staff: one; News: 7 hrs wkly. Target aud: 25-54; upscale female. ♦Paul Knight, gen mgr, stn mgr; Max Deutsch, gen sls mgr; Jonathan Knight, prom mgr; Zach McHugh, progmg dir.

WLTT(FM)— Sept 20, 1986: 106.3 mhz; 6 kw. 328 ft TL: N34 02 50 W78 16 12. Stereo. Hrs open: 24 122 Cinema Dr., Wilmington, 28403. Phone: (910) 772-6300. Fax: (910) 772-6310.E-mail: info@thebigtalker1063fm.com Web Site:www.thebigtalker1063fm.com Licensee: Sea-Comm Inc. (group owner; (acq 12-30-2003; with WBNE(FM) Shallotte). Natl. Network: ABC, Jones Radio Networks, . Format: News/talk info. Target aud: 25 plus; mature professionals. Spec prog: Beach mus 6 hrs wkly. ♦Paul Knight, gen mgr; Max Deutsch, stn mgr.

WVCB(AM)— June 11, 1964: 1410 khz; 500 w-D. TL: N33 58 20 W78 23 02. Hrs open: Box 314, 28459. Secondary address: 4640 Main St. 28459. Phone: (910) 754-4512. Fax: (910) 754-3461.E-mail: wvcb@atmc.net Licensee: John G. Worrell. (acq 3-1-84; $30,000; 1-30-84). Population served: 897 Rgnl. Network: N.C. News Net. N.C. News Net. Format: Relg, gospel. Target aud: General. ♦Rhonda Worrell, stn mgr & opns mgr.

Sharpsburg

WNCM(FM)—Not on air, target date: unknown: 103.1 mhz; 6 kw. Ant 295 ft TL: N35 57 01 W77 57 26. Hrs open: 2619 Western Ave., Raleigh, 27606. Phone: (919) 821-8933. Fax: (919) 890-6095. Licensee: Capitol Broadcasting Co. Inc. (acq 10-1-2008; $825,000 for CP). ♦James F. Goodmon, pres.

Shelby

WADA(AM)— July 9, 1958: 1390 khz; 1 kw-D, 500 w-N, DA-N. TL: N35 19 28 W81 32 00. Stereo. Hrs open: 24 1366 Startown Rd, Lincolnton, 28092. Secondary address: Box 2266 28151-2266. Phone: (704) 482-1390. Fax: (704) 481-9007.E-mail: info@hrnb.com Web Site:www.us1390.com Licensee: HRN Broadcasting Inc. (acq 2006; $350,000). Population served: 250,000 Natl. Network: ABC, . Format: Country. Target aud: 25-54; middle and older. ♦D. Mark Boyd III, pres; Joe Martin, stn mgr & opns mgr; Andy Johnson, gen sls mgr.

WBT(AM)—See Charlotte

WIBT(FM)— 1948: 96.1 mhz; 100 kw. 1,738 ft TL: N35 21 44 W81 09 19. Stereo. Hrs open: 24 801 Woodbridge Center Dr., Charlotte, 28217-1908. Phone: (704) 338-9600. Fax: (704) 334-9525. Web Site:www.magic96.com Licensee: Clear Channel Broadcasting Licenses Inc. Group owner: Clear Channel Communications Inc. (acq 10-18-2000). Population served: 2,000,000 Natl. Rep: McGavren Guild,. Format: Hits of the 60s & 70s. News staff: one; News: 4 hrs wkly. Target aud: 25-54. ♦Morgan Bohannon, gen mgr; Graves Upchurch, gen sls mgr; Nick Allen, progmg dir; Linda Silver, news dir; Ben Brinitzer, chief of engrg; Brenda Grubb, traf mgr; Bobby Lane, disc jockey.

WOHS(AM)— Aug 21, 1946: 730 khz; 1 kw-D, 168 w-N. TL: N35 17 27 W81 34 05. Stereo. Hrs open: 24 1511 W. Dixon Blvd., 28152. Phone: (704) 482-4510. Phone: (704) 487-6313. Fax: (704) 482-4680.E-mail: thebossradio@bellsouth.net Web Site:www.theboss.us Licensee: HRN Broadcasting Inc. (acq 10-6-2006; $1.5 million with WGNC(AM) Gastonia). Population served: 500,000 Natl. Network: ABC, . Rgnl. Network: N.C. News Net. N.C. News Net. Rgnl rep: T-N. Format: Beach, Oldies, Sports. News staff: 2. Target aud: General. ♦D. Mark Boyd III, pres; Calvin R. Hastings, gen mgr.

Siler City

WNCA(AM)— Aug 19, 1952: 1570 khz; 5 kw-D, 290 w-N. TL: N35 43 40 W79 29 18. Hrs open: 6am - midnight Box 429, 17890 Hwy. 64 W., 27344. Phone: (919) 742-2135. Fax: (919) 663-2843. Licensee: Chatham Broadcasting Co. Inc. of Siler City. (acq 3-1-62). Population served: 50,000 Rgnl. Network: N.C. News Net. N.C. News Net. Smithwick & Belendiuk. Format: Loc prgmg, news/talk, christian, sports. News staff: 2; News: 15+ hrs wkly. Target aud: 25-55; rural, agri-oriented, blue-collar, growing spanish community. Spec prog: Gospel 5 hrs, relg 12 hrs, loc sports 6 hrs & Spanish 25 hrs wkly. ♦Barry Hayes, pres, gen mgr, news dir, engrg mgr; Dacia Hayes, dev VP; Renee Kennedy, stn mgr, opns dir, sls VP & sls dir; Debbie Applewhite, traf mgr; Jose Alvarado, spanish dir.

Smithfield

WMPM(AM)— 1950: 1270 khz; 5 kw-D. TL: N35 31 33 W78 20 01. Hrs open: Box 240, 27577. Phone: (919) 934-2434. Fax: (919) 989-6388.E-mail: blake_wpmp@yahoo.com Web Site:www.1270wmpm.com Licensee: Family Media Group LLC (acq 1-16-2009; $175,000). Population served: 90,000 Natl. Network: CBS, . Format: Country, bluegrass, gospel. Target aud: 30 plus; general. Spec prog: Farm 2 hrs, relg 8 hrs, news/talk 12 hrs wkly. ♦Ellis C. Barbour Jr., pres.

WTSB(AM)—See Selma

Snow Hill

***WAGO(FM)**— July 1, 1998: 88.7 mhz; 17 kw. Ant 310 ft TL: N35 30 07 W77 36 22. Stereo. Hrs open: 24 Box 1895, Goldsboro, 27533. Phone: (252) 747-8887. Fax: (252) 747-7888.E-mail: wago@gomixradio.org Web Site:www.gomixradio.org Licensee: Pathway Christian Academy Inc. Natl. Network: Moody, Salem Radio Network, . Steve Yelverton. Format: Christian. News staff: one; News: 14 hrs wkly. Target aud: General. ♦Dr. T.D. Worthington, pres, gen mgr; Ashley Worthington, prom dir; Keith Aycock, progmg dir; Tim Sutton, mus dir; Joe Patton, chief of engrg.

South Gastonia

***WGAS(AM)**— Aug 14, 1959: 1420 khz; 500 w-D. TL: N35 12 53 W81 10 31. Hrs open:
Rebroadcasts WOGR(AM) Charlotte.
1501 Carrier Dr., Charlotte, 28216. Phone: (704) 393-1540. Fax: (704) 393-1527. Web Site:www.wordnet.org Licensee: Victory Christian Center Inc. Population served: 150,000 Format: Gospel. Target aud: General. ♦Robyn Gool, pres; Terry Hammond, gen mgr.

Southern Pines

WEEB(AM)— Nov 15, 1947: 990 khz; 10 kw-D, 500 w-N. TL: N35 11 37 W79 24 42. Hrs open: 24 Box 1855, Midland Rd., 28388. Phone: (910) 692-7440. Fax: (910) 692-7372.E-mail: steve@weeb990.com Web Site:www.weeb990.com Licensee: Pinehurst Broadcasting Corp. (acq 8-31-91; $275,000; 6-10-91). Population served: 120,000 Natl. Network: ABC, Fox News Radio, Salem Radio Network, . Rgnl. Network: N.C. News Net. N.C. News Net. Maupin, Taylor, Ellis & Adams. Format: News/talk. News staff: 3; News: 26 hrs wkly. Target aud: 25 plus; business professionals, CEOs, retirees. Spec prog: High school & college sports, gospel 6 hrs wkly. ♦Rich McCarthy, opns mgr; Steve Adams, CFO, VP, gen mgr & progmg dir; Rose Sharp, relg ed.

WIOZ-FM— 1995: 102.5 mhz; 3.4 kw. 436 ft TL: N35 09 04 W79 28 40. Hrs open: 200 Short Rd., 28387. Phone: (910) 692-2107. Fax: (910) 692-6849. Web Site:www.star1025fm.com Licensee: Meridian Communications L.L.C. Group owner: Muirfield Broadcasting Inc. (acq 6-17-97; $316,500). Format: Adult contemp. ♦Walker Morris, pres; Tiffany Hewitt, gen mgr; Rich Rushforth, opns mgr.

WMGU(FM)— Aug 14, 1973: 106.9 mhz; 50 kw. Ant 492 ft TL: N35 09 04 W79 28 40. Stereo. Hrs open: 24 1009 Drayton Rd., Fayetteville, 28303. Phone: (910) 864-5222. Fax: (910) 864-3065. Web Site:www.oldiesradionc.com Licensee: Cumulus Licensing Corp. Group owner: Cumulus Media Inc. (acq 3-12-2001; $6.15 million). Population served: 600,000 Format: Urban contemp. News staff: 2; News: 18 hrs wkly. Target aud: 35 plus. ♦Alan Buffaloe, gen mgr; Jim Cook, progmg dir.

Southern Shores

WFMI(FM)— 2003: 100.9 mhz; 39 kw. Ant 485 ft TL: N36 12 10 W75 52 23. Hrs open: 4801 Columbus St., Suite 400, Virginia Beach, VA, 23462. Phone: (757) 490-9364. Fax: (757) 490-2524.E-mail: rejoice@rejoice100point9.com Web Site:www.rejoice1009.com Licensee: Communications Systems Inc. Format: Gospel, talk. ♦Mike Chandler, gen mgr; Karol Scott, stn mgr.

Southport

WAZO(FM)— Apr 15, 1978: 107.5 mhz; 32 kw. 594 ft TL: N34 03 02 W77 57 20. Stereo. Hrs open: 24 25 N. Kerr Ave., Wilmington, 28405. Phone: (910) 791-3088. Fax: (910) 791-0112.E-mail: mark@z1075.com Web Site:www.z1075.com Licensee: Sunrise Broadcasting LLC. (group owner) (acq 11-18-2008; grpsl). Population served: 182,000 Natl. Rep: McGavren Guild,. Format: CHR. News staff: one; News: one hr wkly. Target aud: 18-49; young, upwardly mobile professionals. ♦Barry Brown, VP; Bea Raybourne, gen mgr; Gayle Brown, gen sls mgr; Mark Jacobs, progmg dir; Doug Carlisle, news dir; Walt Howard, chief of engrg.

Sparta

WCOK(AM)— April 1967: 1060 khz; 800 w-D. TL: N36 28 55 W81 05 35. Hrs open: Box 578, 28675. Phone: (336) 372-8231. Fax: (336) 372-5863.E-mail: luke@ls.net Licensee: Mountain Empire Broadcasting Inc. (acq 10-1-99). Population served: 25,000 Format: C&W, relg. Target aud: General. ♦Andy Wright, pres, gen mgr, traf mgr, disc jockey; Jos Reynoso, gen mgr; Christy Galyan, disc jockey.

Spindale

WGMA(AM)— October 1982: 1520 khz; 500 w-D. TL: N35 21 00 W81 56 18. Hrs open: Sunrise-sunset Box 805, 301 W. Main St., 28160. Phone: (828) 287-5151. Phone: (828) 287-5150. Fax: 1-828-287-0081.E-mail: WGMA1520AM@BellSouth.Net Licensee: Moonglow Broadcasting Inc. (acq 5-16-03). Population served: 35,000 Smithwick & Belendiuk. Format: Southern gospel. News staff: one; News: 20 hrs wkly. Target aud: 30-50; adults. ♦Barbara Martin, pres, exec VP; Kaye Cantrell, gen mgr; Andy Foster, opns dir; Neil Murray, mus dir; Jerrell Bedford, chief of engrg, engr.

***WNCW(FM)**— Oct 13, 1989: 88.7 mhz; 17 kw. 3,054 ft TL: N35 44 05 W82 17 10. Stereo. Hrs open: 24 Box 804, 28160. Phone: (828) 287-8000. Fax: (828) 287-8012.E-mail: info@wncw.org Web Site:www.wncw.org Licensee: Isothermal Community College. Population served: 580,000 Natl. Network: PRI, NPR, . Schwartz, Woods & Miller. Format: AAA, news. News staff: one; News: 31 hrs wkly. Target aud: 35-49; anyone interested in diverse info & culture. Spec prog: Blues 4 hrs, jazz 5 hrs, folk 12 hrs, drama 3 hrs, gospel 2 hrs wkly. ♦David Gordon, gen mgr; Kate Barkschat, dev mgr, gen sls mgr, prom mgr; Elle Ellis, progmg dir; Martin Anderson, mus dir; Dennis Jones, chief of engrg, news rptr; Ele Ellis, traf mgr.

Spring Lake

WFBX(AM)— May 22, 1963: 1450 khz; 950 w-U. TL: N35 11 11 W78 57 35. Hrs open: 24
Simulcast with WFAY(AM) Fayetteville 100%.
5418 Yadkin Road, Fayetteville, 28303. Phone: (910) 222-1450. Fax: (910) 223-1451. Web Site:www.ncespn.com Licensee: WCIE-AM Inc. (acq 4-20-2001). Population served: 257,000 Natl. Network: ESPN Radio, . Rgnl. Network: Capitol Radio Net. Format: Sports.

***WZRI(FM)**— 2005: 89.3 mhz; 2 kw vert. Ant 179 ft TL: N35 10 14 W78 57 44. Stereo. Hrs open: 24 2351 Sunset Blvd., Suite 170-218, Rocklin, CA, 95765. Phone: (916) 251-1600. Fax: (916) 251-1650.E-mail: info@air1.com Web Site:www.air1.com Licensee: Educational Media Foundation. Group owner: EMF Broadcasting (acq 11-12-2002). Natl. Network: Air 1, . Shaw Pittman. Format: Contemp Christian. News staff: 3. Target aud: 18-35; Judeo-Christian, female. ♦Richard Jenkins, pres; Mike Novak, VP; Keith Whipple, dev dir; Liz Morton, mus dir; Ed Lenane, news dir; Sam Wallington, engrg dir; Karen Johnson, news rptr.

Spruce Pine

WTOE(AM)— Dec 24, 1955: 1470 khz; 5 kw-D, 100 w-N. TL: N35 54 24 W82 06 21. Hrs open: 24 Box 607, Mark Group Bldg., 749 Sawmill Rd., Burnsville, 28714. Secondary address: 749 Sawmill Road, Burnsville 28714. Phone: (828) 765-7441. Phone: (800) 949-3798. Fax: (828) 682-6227. Fax: (828) 682-0998.E-mail: 1470@wtoe.com Web Site:www.wtoe.com Licensee: Mountain Valley Media Inc. (acq 9-27-91). Population served: 104,000 Natl. Network: ABC, . Rgnl. Network: N.C. News Net. N.C. News Net. Format: Soft Oldies. News staff: one; News: 10 hrs wkly. Target aud: 25 plus. Spec prog: Relg 8 hrs wkly. ♦Remelle K. Sink, CEO, pres; J. Ardell Sink, exec VP; Michael Sink, VP, gen mgr, chief of engrg; Holly Hall, opns mgr, mktg dir; Mary Marsh, prom dir; Dennis Renfro, adv dir; Laura Phillips, news dir; Steve Murphy, pub affrs dir.

Statesville

WAME(AM)— Oct 7, 1957: 550 khz; 500 w-D. TL: N35 47 43 W80 51 17. Hrs open: 24 212 Signal Hill Dr., 28625. Phone: (704) 872-0550. Fax: (704) 872-0551.E-mail: wame@statesville.net Licensee: Statesville Family Radio Corp. Group owner: GHB Radio Group (acq 4-22-86; $210,000; 3-31-86). Population served: 150000 Natl. Network: USA, . Format: Adult standards. News: 2 hrs wkly. Target aud: 35-64. Spec prog: Gospel 5 hrs wkly.

WKKT(FM)— Mar 16, 1961: 96.9 mhz; 100 kw. 1,550 ft TL: N35 31 57 W80 47 47. Stereo. Hrs open: 24 801 Wood Ridge Center Dr., Charlotte, 28217. Phone: (704) 714-9444. Fax: (704) 332-8805.E-mail: info@wkktfm.com Web Site:www.wkktfm.com Licensee: Capstar TX L.P. Group owner: Clear Channel Communications Inc. (acq 8-30-00; grpsl). Population served: 1,200,000 Format: Country. Target aud: 25-54; middle to upper income adults. ♦Morgan Bohannon, gen mgr; Bruce Logan, opns mgr; Robin Colfax, natl sls mgr, rgnl sls mgr; Valerie Gladden, prom dir; John Roberts, progmg dir, news dir; Linda Silver, news dir, traf mgr; Ben Brinitzer, chief of engrg.

WSIC(AM)— May 3, 1947: 1400 khz; 1 kw-U. TL: N35 48 09 W80 53 30. Stereo. Hrs open: 24 1117 Radio Rd., 28677. Phone: (704) 872-6345. Fax: (704) 873-6921. Web Site:www.1400wsic.com Licensee: Iredell Broadcasting Inc. Group owner: Clear Channel Communications Inc. (acq 8-25-2006; $700,000). Population served: 19,996 Natl. Rep: Rgnl Reps,. Rgnl rep: T-N. Format: Sports, news. News staff: one; News: 21 hrs wkly. Target aud: 35 plus; upscale. ♦Mark Sanger, gen mgr; Billy Blevins, opns mgr, mus dir.

Swanquarter

***WHYC(FM)**— Mar 8, 1981: 88.5 mhz; 2.8 kw. Ant 262 ft TL: N35 26 27 W76 13 19. Stereo. Hrs open: 20472 Hwy. 264, 27885. Phone: (252) 926-7201. Licensee: Hyde County Board of Education. Format: Var. Target aud: General; eastern North Carolina population. ♦Vanessa Bryant, stn mgr.

Swansboro

***WKGV(FM)**— Sept 12, 1993: 104.1 mhz; 5.4 kw. Ant 345 ft TL: N34 43 26 W77 14 57. Stereo. Hrs open: 24
Rebroadcasts KLVR(FM) Middletown, CA 100%.
2351 Sunset Blvd., Suite 170-218, Rocklin, CA, 95765. Phone: (916) 251-1600. Fax: (916) 251-1650. Web Site:www.klove.com Licensee: Educational Media Foundation. (group owner; (acq 11-29-2007). Population served: 7,00.,000 Natl. Network: K-Love, . Davis Wright Tremaine LLP. Format: Contemp Christian. ♦Mike Novak, sr VP.

Sylva

WRGC(AM)— Nov 8, 1957: 680 khz; 1 kw-D, 250 w-N, DA-N. TL: N35 23 35 W83 11 38. 540 kHz; 5KW-D 210 w DA-N. Hrs open: 24 Box 1044, 1846 Skyland Dr., 28779. Phone: (828) 586-2221. Fax: (828) 586-6834.E-mail: jduke@gacaradio.com Web Site:www.wrgc.com Licensee: Georgia-Carolina Radiocasting Co. LLC. Group owner: Sutton Radiocasting Companies (acq 1-17-2002; $450,000). Population served: 86,663 Natl. Network: ABC, . N.C. News Net. Putbrese, Hunsaker & Trent, P.C. Format: Adult contemp/Local News/Community Involvement. News staff: one; News: 14 hrs wkly. Target aud: General. Spec prog: NASCAR/Local Sports. ♦Douglas M. Sutton Jr., pres; Jeremy Duke, VP; Jeremy, gen mgr; Eric Moore, opns mgr; Wiley Morris, news dir; Marty Lee, engrg dir, chief of engrg.

Tabor City

WTAB(AM)— July 1, 1954: 1370 khz; 5 kw-D, 109 w-N. TL: N34 09 00 W78 51 40. Hrs open: 6 AM-midnight Box 127, 28463. Secondary address: 210 Avon St. 28463. Phone: (910) 653-2131. Fax: (910) 653-5146.E-mail: wtab@wtabradio.com Web Site:www.wtabradio.com Licensee: WTAB Inc. (acq 7-1-95; $175,000). Population served: 40,000 Rgnl. Network: N.C. News Net. N.C. News Net. Format: Southern gospel, country. News: 7 hrs wkly. Target aud: General. Spec prog: Swap shop, 12hrs wkly. ♦Jack Miller, pres, gen mgr, sls VP; Bonnie Miller, exec VP; Bobby Pait, mus dir, disc jockey; Bob Gause, chief of engrg, engr; Lloyd Gore, disc jockey.

Tarboro

WCPS(AM)— January 1947: 760 khz; 1 kw-D. TL: N35 55 40 W77 34 15. Hrs open: Sunrise-sunset Box 1202, 27886. Secondary address: 1406 St Andrew St. 27886. Phone: (252) 824-7878. Fax: (252) 824-7818.E-mail: jwcpsam@embarqmail.com Web Site:ww.wcpsam760.com Licensee: Johnson Broadcast Ventures Ltd. (acq 5-6-00; $100,000). Population served: 13,000 Rgnl. Network: N.C. News Net. N.C. News Net. Format: Gospel/Blues. Target aud: General. ♦Jimmy Johnson, pres, gen mgr; Stephanie Randolph, stn mgr.

WFXK(FM)— September 1952: 104.3 mhz; 100 kw. 987 ft TL: N35 48 40 W77 44 33. Hrs open: 24
100% Simulcast with WFXC. WFXC, Durham, NC, 100%.
8001-101 Creedmoor Rd., Raleigh, 27613. Phone: (919) 848-9736. Fax: (919) 848-4724.E-mail: mmarinaro@radio-one.com Web Site:www.foxyhits.com Licensee: Radio One Licenses LLC. Group owner: Radio One Inc. (acq 11-8-01; grpsl). Population served: 870,000 Format: Adult contemp, urban. News staff: one; News: 3 hrs wkly. Target aud: 25-54. Spec prog: Gospel 3 hrs, jazz 4 hrs wkly. ♦Gary Weiss, gen mgr; Cy Young, opns dir, progmg dir; Kim Gattis, sls dir; Jodi Luke, natl sls mgr; Bruce Farmer, prom dir; Jodi Berri, mus dir; Jim Davis, chief of engrg.

Taylorsville

WACB(AM)— May 2, 1964: 860 khz; 1 kw-D. TL: N35 55 57 W81 10 19. Hrs open: 24 133 E. Main Ave., 28681. Phone: (828) 632-4621. Fax: (828) 632-9081. Licensee: Apple City Broadcasting Co. Inc. (acq 9-24-93; $70,239; 10-11-93). Population served: 500,000 N.C. News Net. Format: Modern country, oldies. News staff: 2; News: 4 hrs wkly. Target aud: General. Spec prog: Gospel 12 hrs wkly.Norris Keever, pres; Mary Alice Brown, VP; Joyce Brown, gen sls mgr; Lisa McLain, prom dir, women's int ed; Lonnie Carrigan, mus dir, disc jockey; Pete Ray, asst music dir, disc jockey; Roger Brown, CEO, exec VP, gen mgr, opns dir, news dir & pub affrs dir; Jeff Watts, chief of engrg; Dean Bruce, traf mgr; Rick Gilbert, sports cmtr; Mark Daniels, disc jockey

WTLK(AM)— June 17, 1962: 1570 khz; 1 kw-D, 248 w-N. TL: N35 55 45 W81 09 44. Hrs open: 133 E. Main Ave., 28681. Phone: (828) 632-4621. Fax: (828) 632-9081. Licensee: Apple City Broadcasting Co. Inc. (acq 6-95; $225,000). Population served: 28,000 Rgnl. Network: N.C. News Net. N.C. News Net. Format: Southern gospel, bluegrass gospel. ♦Norris Keever, pres; Mary Alice Brown, exec VP, mus dir; Roger Brown, CEO, gen mgr & opns dir; Joyce Brown, gen sls mgr; Lisa McLain, prom dir; Jeff Watts, chief of engrg.

Thomasville

WBLO(AM)— September 1947: 790 khz; 2.5 kw-D, 26 w-N. TL: N35 57 41 W80 02 13. Hrs open: 24 hrs Box 5663, High Point, 27262. Secondary address: 1607 Country Club Dr., High Point 27262. Phone: (336) 887-0983. Fax: (336) 887-3055. Web Site:www.790theball.com Licensee: GHB Radio Inc. Group owner: GHB Radio Group (acq 4-3-2001; $350,000). Natl. Network: Fox Sports, . Reddy, Begley & McCormick. Format: Sports/Talk. Target aud: Men 25-54. ♦George H. Buck Jr., pres; Susan Childress, gen mgr, gen sls mgr; Wes Jones, opns mgr; Drew Davis, progmg dir; Gary Hattaway, chief of engrg.

WIST-FM— April 1949: 98.3 mhz; 1.68 kw. Ant 429 ft TL: N35 57 41 W80 02 13. Stereo. Hrs open: 24 Box 5663, High Point, 27262. Secondary address: 1607 Country Club Dr., High Point 27262. Phone: (336) 887-0983. Fax: (336) 887-3055. Web Site:www.countrylegends983.com Licensee: WEAM Quality Radio Corp. Group owner: GHB Radio Group (acq 1997; $925,000). Population served: 800,000 Format: Classic Country. Target aud: 35 plus. ♦George H. Buck Jr., pres; Susan Childress, gen mgr, gen sls mgr; Wes Jones, opns mgr & prom dir; Ed Kasovic, engr.

Troy

WJRM(AM)— Dec 8, 1961: 1390 khz; 1 kw-D. TL: N35 21 43 W79 51 38. Hrs open: 5 AM-9 PM Box 706, 27371. Phone: (910) 576-1390. Fax: (910) 576-1393.E-mail: jeffrey@wjrm.com Web Site:wjrm.com Licensee: Family Worship Ministries Inc. (acq 6-10-02; $115,000). Population served: 33,000 Format: Christian gospel. News staff: one. ♦Harold Pope, pres, gen mgr; Jeffrey Pope, opns mgr & gen sls mgr.

Tryon

WJFJ(AM)— Oct 1, 1954: 1160 khz; 10 kw-D, 500 w-N, DA-N. TL: N35 14 07 W82 14 27. Hrs open: 24 Box 279, Courthouse St., Columbus, 28722. Phone: (828) 894-5858. Fax: (828) 894-2957.E-mail: wjfjradio@wjfjradio.com Web Site:www.wjfjradio.com Licensee: Columbus Broadcast Corp. Inc. (acq 1996; $265,000). Natl. Network: USA, . Format: Christian. News staff: one; News: 25 hrs wkly. Target aud: 25 plus; middle-to-upper income. ♦John Owens, gen mgr & opns mgr.

Valdese

WSVM(AM)— Oct 6, 1961: 1490 khz; 1 kw-U. TL: N35 44 03 W81 34 04. Hrs open: 24 Box 99, 1117 S. Praley St., 28690. Phone: (828) 874-0000. Fax: (828) 874-2123.E-mail: radio@1490wsvm.com Web Site:www.1490wsvm.com Licensee: GHB of Waxhaw Inc. Group owner: GHB Radio Group (acq 10-28-2002; $450,000 with WEGO(AM) Concord). Population served: 56,600 Natl. Network: ABC, . Rgnl. Network: N.C. News Net. N.C. News Net. Format: Oldies. News: 4 hrs wkly. Target aud: 25-64. Spec prog: Gospel 4 hrs, sports 15 hrs wkly. ♦Jerry Clegg, gen mgr.

Wadesboro

WADE(AM)— July 23, 1947: 1340 khz; 1 kw-U. TL: N34 57 01 W80 03 23. Hrs open: 24 Box 416, Waxhaw, 28173. Phone: (704) 843-5418. Fax: (704) 695-1495.E-mail: info@wade.com Licensee: Inspirational Deliverance Center Inc. (acq 6-8-93; $27,500; 6-28-93). Format: Adult contemp Christian. Spec prog: Farm one hr wkly. ♦Myra Davis, stn mgr.

***WYFQ-FM**— 1994: 93.5 mhz; 8.7 kw. Ant 554 ft TL: N35 02 57 W80 18 38. Stereo. Hrs open: 24 Box 7300, Charlotte, 28241. Phone: (704) 523-5555. Fax: (704) 522-1967. Web Site:www.bbnradio.org Licensee: Bible Broadcasting Network Inc. (group owner; acq 1996; $2,425,000). Smithwick & Belendiuk. Format: Relg. Target aud: 18-55. ♦Lowell L. Davey, CEO, pres; Rob Ferguson, gen mgr; Richard Johnson, opns mgr.

Wake Forest

WDRU(AM)— Sept 1, 1989: 1030 khz; 50 kw-D, DA. TL: N36 10 43 W78 45 30. Stereo. Hrs open: Daytime
Simulcast with WTRU(AM) Kernersville.
4405 Providence Lane, Ste D, Winston-Salem, 27106. Phone: (336) 759-0363. Fax: (336) 759-0366.E-mail: info@wtru.com Web Site:www.wtru.com Licensee: Truth Broadcasting Corp. Group owner: Davidson Media Group LLC (acq 5-2-2005; swap for WWBG(AM) Greensboro and WTOB(AM) Winston-Salem). Natl. Network: Salem Radio Network, . Format: Christian. Target aud: 25-54; middle-class families. ♦Bryan Brown, COO, gen sls mgr; Stuart W. Epperson Jr., pres; Stuart Epperson, Jr., gen mgr; Ed Park, progmg dir; Mandel Owens, chief of engrg.

Wallace

***WKBM-FM**—Not on air, target date: unknown: 89.5 mhz; 9 kw. Ant 249 ft TL: N34 37 46 W78 06 33. Hrs open: 511 Cedar Grove Rd., Clover, SC, 29710. Phone: (803) 684-2965. Licensee: Spirit Broadcasting Group Inc. ♦C. Curtis Sigmon, pres.

WZKB(FM)— July 20, 1972: 94.3 mhz; 3.3 kw. 300 ft TL: N34 45 29 W78 00 00. Stereo. Hrs open: Box 28, Clinton, 28329-0026. Phone: 910-864-5028. Fax: 910-864-6270.E-mail: dan@wgqe1057.com Web Site:www.wgqr.com Licensee: Christian Listening Network Inc. (acq 12-15-2003; $425,000). Population served: 120,000 Natl. Network: Salem Radio Network, . Natl. Rep: Salem,. Putbrese, Huntsaker & Trent. Format: Southern gospel. News: 11 hrs wkly. Target aud: 35-54; women. ♦George E. Wilson, pres; Dan DeBruler, gen mgr; Steve Turley, progmg dir.

Walnut Creek

WEQR(FM)— Sept 15, 1976: 97.7 mhz; 2.65 kw. Ant 501 ft TL: N35 17 28 W77 49 25. Stereo. Hrs open: 24 2581 US Hwy. 70 W., Goldsboro, 27530. Phone: (919) 736-1150. Fax: (919) 736-3876.E-mail: bjohnston@curtismedia.com Web Site:www.q977fm.com Licensee: New Age Communications Inc. Group owner: Curtis Media Group (acq 8-30-2004; $875,000). Population served: 200,000 Wire Svc: AP Format: Hot adult contemp. News staff: one; News: news prgmg 3 hrs/week. ♦Donald Curtis, pres, gen mgr; Bill Johnston, gen sls mgr; Jeff Farrow, progmg dir; Robyn Wade, news dir.

Wanchese

WOBR-FM— June 1, 1973: 95.3 mhz; 25 kw. Ant 295 ft TL: N35 51 52 W75 39 01. Stereo. Hrs open: 24 Prog sep from AM Box 1419, Nags Head, 27959. Phone: (252) 441-1024. Fax: (252) 441-2109.E-mail: jsweet@ecri.net Licensee: East Carolina Radio Inc. Population served: 22,000 Natl. Network: ABC, . Format: Classic rock. News staff: one. Target aud: 25-54; upscale, affluent baby boomers. ♦Eddie James, pres, progmg dir; Rich Laesch, gen mgr & opns mgr.

WOBX(AM)— May 29, 1970: 1530 khz; 1 kw-D, DA. TL: N35 51 52 W75 39 01. Hrs open: Sunrise-sunset Box 340, 27981. Secondary address: 3855 Mill Landing Rd., Hwy. 345 27981. Phone: (252) 473-5402. Fax: (252) 473-5838. Licensee: East Carolina Radio Inc. Group owner: East Carolina Radio Group (acq 8-82; $110,000;8-9-82). Population served: 25,000 Format: Relg, gospel. Target aud: Christian. ♦Elmo Daniels, pres, gen mgr; Jim Mills, chief of engrg.

Warrenton

WARR(AM)— 1970: 1520 khz; 5 kw-D, 1 kw-CH. TL: N36 24 18 W78 08 09. Hrs open: sun up-sun down 824 US 158 West, 27589. Phone: (252) 257-5557/257-9277. Web Site:www.warr-1520am.com Licensee: Quad Divisions Inc. dba Darensburg Broadcasting (acq 7-1-02). Rgnl. Network: N.C. News Net. N.C. News Net. Format: Soul gold gospel. News: 5 hrs wkly. Target aud: 25-56. ♦Logan Darensburg, pres & gen mgr; Ann Alston, stn mgr, prom dir.

Washington

WDLX(AM)— Mar 3, 1942: 930 khz; 5 kw-D, 1 kw-N, DA-N. TL: N35 31 34 W77 04 43. Hrs open: Box 3333, Greenville, 27836. Secondary address: 525 S. Evans St., Greenville 27858. Phone: (252) 317-1250. Fax: (252) 317-1255.E-mail: info@wdlx Web Site:www.pirateradio930.com Licensee: Pirate Media Group LLC Group owner: NextMedia Group L.L.C. (acq 6-27-2005; $400,000). Population served: 8,961 Rgnl. Network: N.C. News Net. N.C. News Net. Format: Talk. Target aud: 35 plus. ♦Troy Dreyfus, gen mgr.

WERO(FM)— Jan 20, 1961: 93.3 mhz; 100 kw. Ant 1,781 ft TL: N35 21 55 W77 23 38. Stereo. Hrs open: 24 1361 Colony Dr., New Bern, 28560. Phone: (252) 639-7900. Fax: (252) 946-0330. Web Site:www.bob933.com Licensee: NM Licensing LLC. (acq 11-26-2001; grpsl). Population served: 800,000 Natl. Rep: Eastman Radio,. Format: CHR. News staff: one; News: 12 hrs wkly. Target aud: 18-49. ♦Larry Weiss, gen mgr.

WLGT(FM)— December 1988: 98.3 mhz; 1.3 kw. Ant 490 ft TL: N35 29 14 W77 02 42. Stereo. Hrs open: 24 233 Middle St., Suite 207, New Bern, 28560. Phone: (252) 753-3202. Fax: (252) 753-5443.E-mail: audio@gloryradionet.com Web Site:www.gloryradionet.com Licensee: Media East LLC Group owner: Archway Broadcasting Group (acq 8-23-2007). Format: Gospel. Target aud: 25-54; upscale, affluent audience. ♦Wesley Hines, gen mgr.

Waxhaw

WOLS(FM)— Mar 1, 1995: 106.1 mhz; 32 kw. Ant 365 ft TL: N34 53 01 W80 47 37. Stereo. Hrs open: 24 4801 E. Independence Blvd., Suite 815, Charlotte, 28212. Phone: (704) 442-7277. Fax: (704) 405-3174. Licensee: GHB of Waxhaw Inc. Group owner: GHB Radio Group (acq 6-95; $325,000). Reddy, Begley & McCormick. Format: Rgnl Mexican. ♦George H. Buck Jr., pres; Edgar Saucedo, gen mgr.

Waynesville

WMXF(AM)— August 1947: 1400 khz; 1 kw-U. TL: N35 30 14 W82 58 25. Hrs open: 24 13 Summerlin Rd., Asheville, 28806. Phone: (828) 257-2700. Fax: (828) 281-3299. Licensee: Clear Channel Broadcasting Licenses Inc. Group owner: Clear Channel Communications Inc. (acq 3-21-2001; grpsl). Population served: 6488 Natl. Rep: Keystone (unwired net),. Format: Adult standards. News staff: one. Target aud: General. Spec prog: Relg 3 hrs wkly.

WQNS(FM)— October 1979: 104.9 mhz; 245 w. 1,581 ft TL: N35 34 07 W82 54 27. Stereo. Hrs open: 24 Prog sep from AM 1318-B Patton Ave., Asheville, 98806. Phone: (828) 257-2700. Fax: (828) 281-3299. Web Site:www.rock104rocks.com Licensee: Clear Channel Broadcasting Licenses Inc. Population served: 75,000 Format: Classic rock. Target aud: General.

Weaverville

WTMT(FM)— October 1989: 105.9 mhz; 9.7 kw. Ant 1,102 ft TL: N35 42 18 W82 50 01. Stereo. Hrs open: 24 1190 Patton Ave., Asheville, 28806. Phone: (828) 259-9695. Fax: (828) 253-3291.E-mail: amys@saganc.com Licensee: Saga Communications of North Carolina LLC. (acq 8-7-2006; $650,000). Format: Rock. ♦Edward K. Christian, pres; Randy Cable, VP & gen mgr; Chris Hoffman, gen sls mgr.

Weldon

WSMY(AM)— 1957: 1400 khz; 1 kw-U. TL: N36 24 43 W77 37 06. Hrs open: 24 Box 910, Roanoke Rapids, 27870. Phone: (252) 536-0209. Fax: (252) 538-0378.E-mail: info@wsmy1400.com Web Site:www.wsmy1400.com Licensee: First Media Radio LLC. (group owner; (acq 7-22-2003; grpsl). Population served: 112,000 Format: Urban, relg. Target aud: 18 plus; affluent adults. ♦Al Haskins, gen mgr; John Green, stn mgr; Allen Garrett, opns mgr.

Wendell-Zebulon

WETC(AM)— June 16, 1959: 540 khz; 5 kw-D, 500 w-N, DA-2. TL: N35 52 06 W78 25 56. (CP: 8 kw-D). Hrs open: 24 2865 Amwiler, Ste 650, Doraville, GA, 30360. Phone: (770) 825-0095. Fax: (770) 246-0054. Web Site:www.prietobroadcasting.com Licensee: Prieto Broadcasting Inc. (acq 6-1-2004; $1.8 million). Population served: 545,000 Format: Sp. ♦Everado Morales, stn mgr.

West Jefferson

WKSK(AM)— May 27, 1959: 580 khz; 5 kw-D, 34 w-N. TL: N36 24 39 W81 29 46. Hrs open: 24 Box 729, 28694. Phone: (336) 246-6001.E-mail: wksk@skybest.com Web Site:www.580wksk.com Licensee: Caddell Broadcasting, Inc. (acq 8-1-78). Population served: 80,000 Natl. Network: AP Radio, . Wire Svc: AP Format: C&W. News staff: one; News: 16 hrs wkly. Target aud: General. Spec prog: Farm 3 hrs, gospel 5 hrs, Sp one hr wkly. ♦Jan Caddell, pres & gen mgr; Graham Caddell, opns mgr.

Whiteville

WENC(AM)— July 14, 1946: 1220 khz; 5 kw-D, 152 w-N. TL: N34 18 30 W78 43 00. Hrs open: 6 AM-10 PM 108 Radio Station Rd., 28472. Phone: (910) 642-2133. Fax: (910) 642-5981. Licensee: DHA Communications. (acq 1-5-94; $135,000;1-17-94). Population served: 80,400 Rgnl. Network: N.C. News Net. N.C. News Net. Format: Urban contemp, gospel, blues. News staff: one; News: 10 hrs wkly. Target aud: 25-54; women. Spec prog: Farm 5 hrs, relg 4 hrs, talk 5 hrs wkly. ♦Jesse Lee Godwin, gen mgr.

WTXY(AM)— Jan 1, 1976: 1540 khz; 1 kw-D. TL: N34 19 23 W78 42 47. Hrs open: Sunrise-sunset Box 1038, 501 W. Virgil St., 28472. Phone: (910) 642-8214. Phone: (910) 642-8215. Fax: (910) 640-1540.E-mail: wtxy@earthlink.net Web Site:www.whitevillnc.com/wtxy Licensee: Stanley Broadcasting System Inc. (acq 2-2-87; $80,000; 12-22-86). Population served: 55,000 Natl. Network: Westwood One, Motor Racing Net, . Rgnl. Network: Tenn. Agri. Tenn. Agri-Net Format: News/talk. News staff: 2; News: 84 hrs wkly. Target aud: General. Spec prog: Farm 2 hrs, relg 10 hrs wkly. ♦John H. Stanley, exec VP; Thomas V. Stanley Jr., pres & gen mgr; Linda Shaver, opns mgr.

WZFX(FM)—Licensed to Whiteville. See Fayetteville

Wilkesboro

***WSIF(FM)**— Apr 6, 1977: Stn currently dark. 90.9 mhz; 1 kw. Ant -171 ft TL: N36 08 12 W81 11 02. Stereo. Hrs open: 24 Box 120, 28697. Secondary address: 1328 S. Collegiate Dr. 28697. Phone: (336) 838-6179. Phone: (336) 838-6222. Fax: (336) 838-6528.E-mail: al.delachica@wilkescc.edu Licensee: Wilkes Community College. Population served: 20,000 ♦Dr. Gordon G. Burns Jr., pres; Al de Lachica, gen mgr.

WWWC(AM)— Jan 26, 1970: 1240 khz; 1 kw-U. TL: N36 09 00 W81 09 42. Hrs open: Box 580, 28697. Secondary address: 413 Wilkesboro Blvd. 28697. Phone: (336) 838-1241/838-9992. Fax: (336) 838-9040.E-mail: onair@12403wc.com Web Site:www.12403wc.com Licensee: Foothills Media Inc. (acq 1994). Population served: 60000 Natl. Network: USA, . Rgnl. Network: N.C. News Net. N.C. News Net. Format: Southern gospel. Target aud: General. ♦John Wishon, pres, gen mgr, prom dir, progmg dir, chief of engrg; Petrice Edwards, gen sls mgr.

Williamston

WIAM(AM)— March 1951: 900 khz; 1 kw-D, 258 w-N. TL: N35 51 27 W77 02 34. Hrs open: 24 Box 590, 27892. Phone: (252) 792-4161. Fax: (252) 809-0039.E-mail: bryant@opendoorradio.com Web Site:www.opendoorradio.com Licensee: Lifeline Ministries Inc. (acq 6-18-90; 7-9-90). Population served: 30,000 Rgnl. Network: N.C. News Net. N.C. News Net. Format: Relg, gospel. Target aud: General. ♦Johnny Bryant, pres, gen mgr & progmg dir.

WRHD(FM)— Aug 1, 1962: 103.7 mhz; 100 kw. Ant 981 ft TL: N35 53 47 W76 58 58. Stereo. Hrs open: 24
Rebroadcasts WRHT(FM) Morehead City 100%.
408 W. Arlington Blvd., Suite 101-C, Greenville, 27834. Phone: (252) 355-1037. Fax: (252) 355-2234. Web Site:www.thehotfmonline.com Licensee: Inner Banks Media LLC. Group owner: Archway Broadcasting Group (acq 3-12-2007; grpsl). Population served: 300,000 Davis Wright Tremaine P.C. Format: Country. Target aud: 18-49; young adults. ♦Henry Hinton, gen mgr; Mike Biddle, opns mgr; Paul Kingman, gen sls mgr & mktg dir; Mike Middle, progmg dir; Eddie Harrell, chief of engrg; Donna Spivey, traf mgr.

Wilmington

WAAV(AM)—(Leland, Dec 20, 1957: 980 khz; 5 kw-U, DA-N. TL: N34 14 54 W78 00 09. Hrs open: 24 3233 Burnt Mill Rd., Ste 4, 28403-2654. Phone: (910) 763-9977. Fax: (910) 762-0456.E-mail: info@980waav.com Web Site:www.980waav.com Licensee: Cumulus Licensing Corp. Group owner: Cumulus Media L.L.C. (acq 7-2-97; $1.6 million with co-located FM). Population served: 60,000 Natl. Rep: McGavren Guild,. Wire Svc: AP Format: News/talk. Target aud: 35 plus. ♦Jim Principi, gen mgr; Perry Stone, opns mgr; Jennifer McLean, gen sls mgr; Jackie Jordon, mktg dir, prom dir; Mike Farow, progmg dir; Mark Ward, pub affrs dir; Tim Nelson, chief of engrg; Harvard Jennings, disc jockey.

***WDVV(FM)**— 1999: 89.7 mhz; 13.5 kw vert. Ant 348 ft TL: N34 10 52 W78 02 33. Stereo. Hrs open: Box 957, 28402. Secondary address: 201 North Front St., Suite 805 28401. Phone: (910) 763-2452. Fax: (910) 763-6578.E-mail: church@thedoveonline.org Web Site:www.thedoveonline.org Licensee: Carolina Christian Radio Inc. (group owner; (acq 2-16-2001; $100,000 with WMYT(AM) Carolina Beach). Natl. Network: USA, . Format: Christian praise & worship. ♦Jim Stephens, gen mgr; Roger Brace, chief of opns.

WGNI(FM)— Mar 1, 1970: 102.7 mhz; 100 kw. Ant 981 ft TL: N34 03 06 W78 04 57. Stereo. Hrs open: 24 3233 Burnt Mill Rd., Ste 4, 28403-2654. Phone: (910) 763-9977. Fax: (910) 762-0456.E-mail: info@cumulus.com Web Site:www.cumulus.com Licensee: Cumulus Licensing LLC. Group owner: Cumulus Media Inc. Population served: 200,000 Natl. Rep: McGavren Guild,. Wire Svc: AP Format: Hot adult contemp. News staff: 2. ♦Jim Principi, gen mgr; Perry Stone, opns dir; Jennifer McLean, gen sls mgr; David Carroll, prom dir, adv dir; Mike Farrow, progmg dir; Tim Nelson, chief of engrg.

***WHQR(FM)**— Apr 24, 1984: 91.3 mhz; 100 kw. Ant 1,141 ft TL: N34 07 53 W78 11 17. Stereo. Hrs open: 24 254 N. Front St., Wilminton, 28401. Phone: (910) 343-1640. Fax: (910) 251-8693.E-mail: whqr@whqr.org Web Site:www.whqr.org Licensee: Friends of Public Radio Inc. Population served: 320,000 Natl. Network: NPR, PRI, . Rgnl rep: Megan Gorham Schwartz, Woods & Miller. Wire Svc: AP Format: Class, news. News staff: 3; News: 63 hrs wkly. Target aud: 35 plus. ♦Bob Klorkmon, pres, progmg dir; John Milligan, gen mgr; George Scheibner, opns mgr, chief of engrg; Ann Berry, prom mgr; Catherine Welch, traf mgr.

WILT(FM)— February 1994: 104.5 mhz; 4.5 kw. Ant 377 ft TL: N34 16 15 W77 57 23. Hrs open: 25 N. Kerr Ave., 28405. Phone: (910) 791-3088. Fax: (910) 791-0112. Web Site:www.1045sunnyfm.com Licensee: Sunrise Broadcasting LLC. (acq 11-18-2008; grpsl). Format: Adult hits. Target aud: 25-54. ♦Dave Patella, gen mgr; Jennifer McLean-Bloech, sls dir; Brian White, progmg dir, progmg mgr.

WKXB(FM)—See Burgaw

WKXS-FM—(Leland, Dec 10, 1994: 94.5 mhz; 3.8 kw. Ant 416 ft TL: N34 12 35 W77 56 53. Hrs open: 24 Prog sep from AM 3233 Burnt Mill Rd., Ste 4, 28403. Phone: (910) 763-9977. Fax: (910) 762-0456.E-mail: info@980waav.com Format: Urban contemp. ♦Lou Bennett, progmg dir.

WLSG(AM)— Dec 24, 1946: 1340 khz; 1 kw-U. TL: N34 12 35 W77 56 53. Hrs open: 24 201 N. Front St., Suite 805, 28401. Secondary address: Box 957 28402. Phone: (910) 763-2452. Fax: (910) 763-6578.E-mail: jim@life905.com Web Site:www.godscountry1340.com Licensee: Carolina Christian Radio Inc. (group owner; (acq 6-30-2000; $75,000). Natl. Network: Salem Radio Network, . Format: Southern gospel, relg. Target aud: 30 plus. ♦Jim Stephens, gen mgr; Roger Brace, engr.

WMFD(AM)— Apr 15, 1935: 630 khz; 1 kw-U, DA-2. TL: N34 13 31 W77 59 17. Stereo. Hrs open: 24 25 N. Kerr Ave., 28405. Web Site:www.am630.net Licensee: Sunrise Broadcasting LLC. (acq 11-18-2008; grpsl). Population served: 65,000 Natl. Network: CBS, . Format: ESPN sports. News staff: one; News: 3 hrs wkly. Target aud: 30 plus; upscale audience.

WMNX(FM)— Feb 24, 1970: 97.3 mhz; 100 kw. Ant 883 ft TL: N34 03 06 W78 04 57. Stereo. Hrs open: 24 3233 Burnt Mill Dr., Ste 4, 28403-2654. Phone: (910) 763-9977. Fax: (910) 762-0456.E-mail: info@coast973.com Web Site:www.coast973.com Licensee: Cumulus Licensing Corp. Group owner: Cumulus Media Inc. (acq 3-12-2001; grpsl). Population served: 600,000 Natl. Rep: McGavren Guild,. Wire Svc: AP Format: Urban contemp. News staff: one. Target aud: 18-49; general. ♦Jim Principi, gen mgr; Perry Stone, opns dir.

WVBS(AM)—See Burgaw

WWIL(AM)— Aug 25, 1963: 1490 khz; 1 kw-U. TL: N34 13 52 W77 57 18. Hrs open: 24 Box 957, 28402-0957. Secondary address: 201 North Front St., Suite 805 28401. Phone: (910) 763-2452. Fax: (910) 763-6578.E-mail: life@life905.com Web Site:www.gospeljoy1490.com Licensee: Carolina Christian Radio Inc. (group owner; (acq 10-28-92; $35,000; 11-23-92). Population served: 150,000 Natl. Network: USA, . Format: Black gospel the light. Target aud: 25-49. ♦Jim Stephens, gen mgr; Pastor James Utley, stn mgr & mktg mgr.

***WWIL-FM**— December 1995: 90.5 mhz; 1 kw horiz, 20 kw vert. 328 ft TL: N34 10 52 W78 02 33. Hrs open: 24 Box 957, 28402. Secondary address: 201 North Front St., Suite 805 28401. Phone: (910) 763-2452. Fax: (910) 763-6578. Web Site:www.life905.com (Acq 6-95; 1-9-95). Population served: 300,000 Natl. Network: USA, . Format: Adult contemp, Christian. Target aud: 25-54. ♦Jim Stephens, gen mgr.

WWQQ-FM— Mar 31, 1969: 101.3 mhz; 50 kw. 525 ft TL: N34 13 31 W77 59 17. (CP: 40 kw, ant 544 ft.). Stereo. Hrs open: 24 3233 Burnt Mill Rd., Ste 4, 28403-2654. Phone: (910) 763-9977. Fax: (910) 762-0456.E-mail: info@cumulus.com Web Site:www.cumulus.com Licensee: Cumulus Licensing Corp. Group owner: Cumulus Media L.L.C. (acq 7-3-97; Population served: 110,000 Natl. Rep: McGavren Guild,. Wire Svc: AP Format: Today's Country. News staff: one. Target aud: 25-54. ♦Jim Principi, gen mgr; Perry Stone, opns mgr; Robin Batson, natl sls mgr; Dave Carroll, mktg dir, prom dir; Paul Johnson, progmg mgr; Tim Nelson, chief of engrg.

Wilson

WGTM(AM)— July 18, 1937: 590 khz; 5 kw-U, DA-2. TL: N35 43 04 W78 03 33. Hrs open: 8am - 5pm 4002 Hwy. 42 W., 27895. Phone: (252) 243-2188. Fax: (252) 237-8813.E-mail: wgtm590am@hotmail.com Licensee: Celestine L. Willis. Group owner: Willis Broadcasting Corp. (acq 12-15-89; $375,000; 3-3-86). Population served: 32,500 Format: Gospel. ♦Celestine L. Willis, gen mgr; Raymond Grant, progmg dir; Ray Taylor, disc jockey.

WLLY(AM)— 1961: 1350 khz; 1 kw-D, 79 w-N. TL: N35 43 24 W77 55 16. Hrs open: Daylight WLLY Radio Station, Box 637, 210 Beacon St. W., 27894-0637. Phone: (252) 237-5171. Fax: (252) 237-5172.E-mail: info@wlly.com Licensee: Estuardo Valdemar Rodriguez and Leonor Rodriguez, joint tenants. Group owner: Estuardo Valdemar Rodriguez and Leonor Rodriguez Stns (acq 10-11-2002; $255,000). Natl. Network: USA, . N.C. News Net. Format: Southern Gospel. Target aud: General.

WRDU(FM)—Licensed to Wilson. See Raleigh

WVOT(AM)— June 1948: Stn currently dark. 1420 khz; 1 kw-D, 500 w-N, DA-N. TL: N35 44 08 W77 53 02. Hrs open: 24 103 N. Jackson St., 27893. Phone: (252) 243-5157. Phone: (252) 243-1420. Fax: (252) 291-5000. Licensee: Kingdom Expansion Corp. (acq 1-18-2001; $100,000). Population served: 65,000 Format: Christian, sports. News: 25 hrs wkly. Target aud: 25-55. ♦M.K. Smith, pres; Joyce Farmer, gen mgr, stn mgr; Noel Johnson, sports cmtr.

Windsor

WBTE(AM)— 1969: 990 khz; 1 kw-D, 25 w-N. TL: N35 58 00 W76 56 54. Hrs open: Box 1008, 27983. Phone: (252) 794-5590. Fax: (252) 794-5151.E-mail: wbte@earthlink.net Licensee: Dr. Tine Hicks & Associate Group owner: Willis Broadcasting Corp. (acq 12-2-2005; $70,000). Format: Gospel. ♦Arbutis Walston, gen mgr.

WGTI(FM)— 1980: 97.7 mhz; 3 kw. Ant 300 ft TL: N36 04 06 W76 58 35. Hrs open: 24 Box 590, Williamston, 27892. Phone: (252) 792-4161. Fax: (252) 809-0039.E-mail: bryant@opendoorradio.com Web Site:www.opendoorradio.com Licensee: Lifeline Ministries Inc. (acq 12-13-2005; $300,000). Format: Gospel. ♦Johnny Bryant, pres & gen mgr.

Wingate

***WRCM(FM)**— June 14, 1993: 91.9 mhz; 17.7 kw. 515 ft TL: N35 03 33 W80 40 14. Stereo. Hrs open: 24 Box 17069, Charlotte, 28227. Secondary address: 1092 Radio Drive, Indian Trail 28079. Phone: (704) 821-9293. Phone: (704) 570-9200. Fax: (704) 821-9285.E-mail: newlife91.9@wrcm.org Web Site:www.wrcm.org Licensee: Columbia Bible College Broadcasting Co. Population served: 2,000,000 Natl. Network: Salem Radio Network, . Wire Svc: UPI Format: Adult contemp, Christian. Target aud: 25-44; female. ♦Joe Paulo, gen mgr; Elizabeth Poplin, prom dir, adv dir; Dwayne Harrison, progmg dir; Joyce Younts, pub affrs dir; Dave Morrison, chief of engrg; Steve McCranie, spec ev coord.

Winston-Salem

WBFJ(AM)— Oct 1, 1960: 1550 khz; 1 kw-D, DA. TL: N36 06 33 W80 14 47. Stereo. Hrs open: Sunrise-sunset 1249 Trade St., 27101. Phone: (336) 721-1560. Fax: (336) 777-1032.E-mail: live@wbfjfm.com Web Site:www.wbfj.org Licensee: Word of Life Broadcasting Inc. (acq 6-29-83). Population served: 375,000 Natl. Network: USA, . Format: Christian, talk, educational. Target aud: 29-54; general. ♦Philip T. Watson, pres, gen sls mgr; John Hill, progmg dir; Wally Decker, gen mgr & mus dir; Larry Schropp, chief of engrg.

***WBFJ-FM**— Sept 1, 1994: 89.3 mhz; 2.5 kw. 423 ft TL: N36 05 56 W80 15 00. Hrs open: 24 1249 Trade St., 27101. Phone: (336) 721-1560. Phone: (336) 777-1893. Fax: (336) 777-1032.E-mail: wbfj@wbfj.org Web Site:www.wbfj.fm Licensee: Triad Family Network Inc. Population served: 750,000 Natl. Network: USA, . Format: Contemp Christian mus. Target aud: 25-49. ♦Kurt Myers, prom mgr; Wally Decker, gen mgr, gen sls mgr & progmg dir; Verne Hill, news dir; Larry Shropp, chief of engrg.

***WFDD-FM**— Mar 13, 1961: 88.5 mhz; 60 kw. 345 ft TL: N35 58 12 W80 12 54. (CP: TL: N35 55 15 W80 17 37). Stereo. Hrs open: 24 Box 8850, 27109. Secondary address: 56 Wake Forest Rd. 27109. Phone: (336) 758-8850. Fax: (336) 758-5193.E-mail: wfdd@wfu.edu Web Site:www.wfdd.org Licensee: Trustees of Wake Forest University. Population served: 90,000 Natl. Network: PRI, NPR, . Rgnl rep: Public Radio Adv. Alliance Fletcher, Heald & Hildreth. Format: Class, news. News staff: 3; News: 29 hrs wkly. Target aud: General; educated/public radio. Spec prog: Jazz 16 hrs wkly. ♦Jay Banks, gen mgr & stn mgr; Denise Franklin, news dir.

WKTE(AM)—See King

WKZL(FM)— 1972: 107.5 mhz; 100 kw. 994 ft TL: N36 16 33 W79 56 27. Stereo. Hrs open: 192 E. Lewis St., Greensboro, 27406-1459. Phone: (336) 274-8042. Fax: (336) 274-1629. Web Site:www.1075kzl.com Licensee: Dick Broadcasting Co. Inc. of Tennessee (acq 11-23-92; $6.5 million with WGFX(FM) Gallatin, TN;12-14-92). Population served: 128,300 Kaye, Scholer, Fierman, Hays & Handler. Format: Contemp hit/Top-40. Target aud: 25-49; women. ♦Allen Dick, CEO, chmn, pres; Bruce Wheeler, VP, gen mgr; James Kerr, opns mgr, natl sls mgr; Jennifer Hart, gen sls mgr; Jason Goodman, progmg dir; Josie Paza, mus dir; Tom Caldwell, chief of engrg.

WMAG(FM)—See High Point

WPAW(FM)—Licensed to Winston-Salem. See Greensboro

WPIP(AM)— June 1, 1995: 880 khz; 900 w-D. TL: N36 06 33 W80 14 47. Hrs open: Sunrise-sunset 4135 Thomasville Rd., 27107. Phone: (336) 785-0527. Fax: (336) 785-0529.E-mail: wpip880am@triad.rr.com Web Site:www.wpipbereanradio.org Licensee: Berean Baptist Church. (acq 5-95; $80,000; 5-8-95). Natl. Network: USA, . Format: Conservative Christian. ♦Dr. Ron Baity, gen mgr; Jeff Baity, chief of opns.

WPOL(AM)—Licensed to Winston-Salem. See Greensboro

WSJS(AM)— Apr 17, 1930: 600 khz; 5 kw-D, 5 kw-N, DA-2. TL: N36 07 00 W80 21 26. Stereo. Hrs open: 875 W. 5th St., 27101. Phone: (336) 727-8826. Fax: (336) 777-3915. Web Site:www.wsjs.com Licensee: Crescent Media Group LLC. Group owner: Infinity Broadcasting Corp. (acq 2-14-2007; grpsl). Population served: 1,450,000 Natl. Network: Wall Street, . Natl. Rep: Clear Channel,. Format: News/talk. Target aud: 25-64. ♦Tom Hamilton, gen mgr & gen sls mgr; Marty Holbrook, prom dir; Beth Ann McBride, progmg dir; Bob Costner, news dir; George Newman, chief of engrg.

WSMX(AM)— October 1964: 1500 khz; 140 w-D. TL: N36 04 26 W80 15 19. Hrs open: Sunrise-sunset 1225 E. 5th St., Suite 104, 27101. Phone: (336) 391-1497. Fax: (336) 724-6368.E-mail: wsmxradio@aol.com Licensee: Gospel Media Inc. (acq 6-82). Population served: 140,000 Format: Gospel, community affrs. News: 12 hrs wkly. Target aud: 30-50 plus; blue collar, minorities, church members. ♦Joe Watson, pres & gen mgr.

***WSNC(FM)**— 1982: 90.5 mhz; 125 w. 92 ft TL: N36 05 36 W80 13 53. (CP: 10 kw, ant 194 ft. TL: N36 05 24 W80 13 20). Stereo. Hrs open: 24 601 Martin Luther King Dr., Hall-Patterson, F Fl., 27110. Phone: (336) 750-2321. Fax: (336) 750-2329.E-mail: WSNCFM@wssu.edu Web Site:www.wssu.edu Licensee: Winston-Salem State University. Natl. Network: NPR, PRI, . Format: Jazz, news, info. Target aud: 30-70; African-Americans. ♦Elvin Jenkins, gen mgr; Ben Donnelly, opns mgr; Monica Melton, progmg dir & mus dir; Baxter Griffin, chief of engrg.

WTIX(AM)— Oct 28, 1950: 980 khz; 1.3 kw-D, 49 w-N. TL: N36 06 40 W80 14 36. Hrs open: Box 5663, High Point, 27262. Secondary address: 1607 Country Club Dr., High Point 27262. Phone: (336) 887-0983. Fax: (336) 887-3055.E-mail: schildress@ghbradio.com Licensee: GHB Radio Inc. (acq 3-6-2006; $235,000). Population served: 150,000 Natl. Network: ESPN Radio, . Format: Sports/talk. Target aud: Men 25-54. ♦George H. Buck Jr., pres; Susan Childress, gen mgr, gen sls mgr; Wes Jones, opns mgr; Gary Hattaway, engr.

WTOB(AM)— Apr 22, 1947: 1380 khz; 5 kw-D, 2.5 kw-N, DA-2. TL: N36 08 53 W80 19 11. Stereo. Hrs open: 18 Box 12876, 27117. Phone: (336) 714-2774. Fax: (336) 714-8337.E-mail: quepasa@quepasamedia.com Web Site:www.quepasamedia.com Licensee: Davidson Media Station WTOB Licensee LLC. (acq 3-25-2005; swap with WWBG(AM) Greensboro for WDRU(AM) Wake Forest). Population served: 134,676 Rgnl. Network: N.C. News Net. N.C. News Net. Smithwick & Belendiuk. Format: Sp. Target aud: 35 plus; affluent audience. ♦Roger Martinez, gen mgr.

WTQR(FM)— Dec 1, 1947: 104.1 mhz; 100 kw. 1,420 ft TL: N36 22 28 W80 22 31. Stereo. Hrs open: 24 2-B PAI Park, Greensboro, 27409. Phone: (336) 822-2000. Fax: (336) 887-0104. Web Site:www.wtqr.com Licensee: Clear Channel Radio Licenses Inc. Group owner: Clear Channel Communications Inc. (acq 1996; grpsl). Population served: 1,450,000 Format: Country. Target aud: 25-54. Spec prog: NASCAR, bluegrass 2 hrs wkly. ♦Morgan Bohannon, gen mgr; Lisa Fields, gen sls mgr.

WVBZ(FM)—See High Point

***WXRI(FM)**— May 17, 1997: 91.3 mhz; 50 kw. Ant 216 ft TL: N36 08 06 W80 30 14. Stereo. Hrs open: 24 Box 25775, 27114. Phone: (336) 788-1155. Fax: (336) 788-7199.E-mail: office@joyfm.org Web Site:www.joyfm.org Licensee: Positive Alternative Radio Inc. Group owner: Baker Family Stations (Positive Radio Group) (acq 5-21-92). Population served: 115,000 Natl. Network: Salem Radio Network, . Booth, Freret, Imlay & Tepper. Format: Southern gospel. Target aud: Female; middle-aged. ♦Vernon H. Baker, pres; Brian Sanders, VP, gen mgr.

Winterville

WECU(AM)— Feb 7, 2006: 1570 khz; 3.8 kw-D, 200 w-N. TL: N35 32 15 W77 25 06. Hrs open: 24 1413 Evans St., Greenville, 27834. Phone: (252) 633-1490. Fax: (252) 931-9328.E-mail: wwnbwecu@yahoo.com Web Site:www.wecu1570.com Licensee: CTC Media Group. Group owner: CTC Media Group Inc. Format: Gospel. ♦Edwin Lee Afflerbach, pres; Michael Afflerbach, stn mgr.

Wrightsville Beach

WNTB(FM)— Nov 27, 2000: 93.7 mhz; 6 kw. Ant 328 ft TL: N34 18 04 W77 48 07. (CP: COL Topsail Beach). Hrs open: 24 122 Cinema Dr., Wilmington, 28403. Phone: (910) 772-6300. Fax: (910) 772-6310.E-mail: newsroom@seacomm.com Web Site:www.937thebone.com Licensee: Sea-Comm Inc. (group owner; (acq 6-30-2000; $1.2 million for CP). Format: Classic rock. ♦Paul Knight, gen mgr; Max Deutsch, gen sls mgr; Zach McHugh, progmg mgr; Jonathan Knight, news dir.

Yanceyville

WYNC(AM)— Nov 9, 1979: 1540 khz; 2.5 kw-D. TL: N36 24 52 W79 20 06. Hrs open: sun up-sun down Box 670, 27379. Secondary address: 545 Firetower Rd. 27379. Phone: (336) 694-7343. Fax: (336) 694-7514.E-mail: wync@earthlink.net Licensee: Semora Broadcasting Inc. (acq 12-9-91; $102,041; 1-6-92). Population served: 50,000 Natl. Network: Westwood One, . Format: Gospel. Target aud: General; rural Caswell county & Danville, VA. Spec prog: Gospel 16 hrs wkly. ♦George Thaxton, gen mgr, stn mgr; Leroy Connally, chief of engrg.

Zebulon

***WAJC(FM)**— May 1990: 90.5 mhz; 1.2 kw. Ant 210 ft TL: N35 49 19 W78 18 36. Hrs open: 24 5 W. Hargett St., Raleigh, 27601. Phone: (919) 899-6778. Fax: (919) 899-6779. Licensee: CSN International. (group owner; (acq 6-23-2000; $150,000). Format: Christian teaching. ♦Jim Walker, gen mgr.

North Dakota

Arthur

KVMI(FM)— April 1994: 103.9 mhz; 25 kw. Ant 328 ft TL: N47 07 20 W97 19 29. Hrs open: 4 Langer Ave., Casselton, 58012. Phone: (701) 866-0799. Fax: (218) 287-8274. Licensee: Vision Media Inc. (acq 2-25-2000). Natl. Network: Westwood One, . Format: Country. ♦Mike McCain, gen mgr.

Belcourt

***KEYA(FM)**— October 1975: 88.5 mhz; 19 kw. 263 ft TL: N48 50 37 W99 45 02. Stereo. Hrs open: 19 Box 190, Media Bldg., Hospital Rd., 58316. Phone: (701) 477-5686. Phone: (701) 477-5687. Fax: (701) 477-3252.E-mail: keya@utma.com Web Site:http://keya.utma.com/885 Licensee: KEYA Inc. Population served: 38,000 Natl. Network: NPR, . Steptoe & Johnson. Wire Svc: AP Format: C&W, oldies, rock/AOR. News: 7 hrs wkly. Target aud: General; members of the Turtle Mountain Band of Chippewa Indians. Spec prog: American Indian 6 hrs, relg 10 hrs, old-time fiddle mus 4 hrs, Chippewa 3 hrs wkly. ♦Kimberly Thomas, gen mgr; William Morin, adv dir; Jarle Kvale, progmg dir; Janice Keplin, chief of engrg.

***KSIH(FM)**—Not on air, target date: unknown: 90.1 mhz; 25 kw. Ant 302 ft TL: N48 50 37 W99 45 02. Hrs open: c/o Putbrese Hunsaker & Trent P.C., 200 S. Church St., Woodstock, VA, 22664. Phone: (540) 459-7646. Fax: (540) 459-7656. Web Site:www.radiomaria.us Licensee: Friends of Radio Maria Inc. ♦Florinda Iannace, pres; John C. Trent, gen mgr.

Beulah

KDKT(AM)— Oct 5, 1978: 1410 khz; 1 kw-D, 180 w-N. TL: N47 17 15 W101 45 46. Hrs open: 24 547 S. 7th Street, Bismarck, 58504. Secondary address: 547 S. 7th St., Suite 166, Box #166, Bismarck 58504. Phone: (701) 873-2215. Fax: (701) 873-2363.E-mail: info@dsnradio.com Web Site:www.foxsports1410.com Licensee: Digital Syndicate Network LLC (acq 2-27-2006; $150,000). Population served: 20,000 Natl. Network: Fox Sports, . Rgnl. Network: N.D. News Net., AgriAmerica. Format: Sports. News staff: 3.5; News: 14 hrs wkly. Target aud: 22-54; general. ♦Guy W. Giuliano, pres; Guy W. Giuliano, gen mgr; Dawson Austin, opns mgr.

KHRU(FM)—Not on air, target date: unknown: 97.9 mhz; 6 kw. Ant 315 ft TL: N47 18 23 W101 43 35. Hrs open: 5331 Mt. Alifan Dr., San Diego, CA, 92111. Phone: (858) 277-4991. Fax: (858) 277-1365. Web Site:www.horizonsd.org/radio.asp Licensee: Horizon Christian Fellowship. ♦Mike MacIntosh, pres.

Bismarck

KACL(FM)— Apr 22, 1997: 98.7 mhz; 100 kw. Ant 837 ft TL: N46 35 24 W100 47 46. Hrs open: 24 Box 1377, 1830 N. 11th St., 58501. Phone: (701) 250-6602. Fax: (701) 250-6632.E-mail: info@cumulus.com Web Site:www.cumulus.com Licensee: Cumulus Licensing Corp. Group owner: Cumulus Media Inc. (acq 5-11-98; grpsl). Format: Oldies. ♦Syd Stewart, gen mgr; Debbie Boechler, gen sls mgr; Bob Beck, progmg dir; Matt Murphy, news dir; Dennis Wilson, chief of engrg; Brian Kocher, traf mgr.

***KBFR(FM)**— October 2003: 91.7 mhz; 780 w. Ant 348 ft TL: N46 49 38 W100 46 28. Hrs open: 24 Family Stations Inc., 4135 Northgate Blvd., Suite 1, Sacramento, CA, 95834. Phone: (916) 641-8191. Fax: (916) 641-8238. Licensee: Family Stations Inc. (group owner). Format: Relg. ♦Harold Camping, pres.

***KBMK(FM)**— 2006: 88.3 mhz; 5.5 kw vert. Ant 380 ft TL: N46 49 38 W100 46 28. Hrs open:
Rebroadcasts KLVR(FM) Santa Rosa, CA 100%.
2351 Sunset Blvd., Suite 170-218, Rocklin, CA, 95765. Phone: (916) 251-1600. Fax: (916) 251-1650. Web Site:www.klove.com Licensee: Broadcasting for the Challenged Inc. Natl. Network: K-Love, . Format:

Contemp Christian. ♦Richard Jenkins, pres; Mike Novak, VP; Keith Whipple, dev dir; David Pierce, progmg mgr; Ed Lenane, news dir; Sam Wallington, engrg dir; Karen Johnson, news rptr.

KBMR(AM)— Aug 15, 1958: 1130 khz; 50 kw-D, DA. TL: N46 50 04 W100 31 19. (CP: 10 kw-D). Stereo. Hrs open: 24 3500 E. Rosser Ave., 58501. Phone: (701) 255-1234. Fax: (701) 222-1131.E-mail: kbmr@clearchannel.com Web Site:www.kbmr.com Licensee: CC Licenses LLC. Group owner: Clear Channel Communications Inc. (acq 2-13-2004;. grpsl). Population served: 71,000 Natl. Rep: McGavren Guild,. Borsari & Paxson. Format: C&W. Target aud: 25 plus. Spec prog: Farm 6 hrs wkly. ♦Bob Denver, gen mgr; Neil Cary, gen sls mgr; Charlie Williams, progmg dir; Jeff Alexander, news dir; Elliott Davidson, chief of engrg; Clarissa Lynn, disc jockey.

KBYZ(FM)— June 1, 1985: 96.5 mhz; 100 kw. Ant 963 ft TL: N46 35 24 W100 47 46. Hrs open: 1830 N. 11th St., 58501. Phone: (701) 663-6412.E-mail: info@bismanradio.com Web Site:bismanradio.com Population served: 250,000 Format: Classic rock. News staff: one. Target aud: 25-54. ♦Syd Stewart, mktg mgr; Dee Daniels, progmg dir.

***KCND(FM)**— Sept 1, 1981: 90.5 mhz; 50 kw. 1,216 ft TL: N46 35 23 W100 48 02. Stereo. Hrs open: 24 207 N 5th St., Fargo, 58102. Phone: (701) 224-1700. Fax: (701) 224-0555.E-mail: info@prairiepublic.org Web Site:www.prairiepublic.org Licensee: Prairie Public Broadcasting Inc. Population served: 65,000 Natl. Network: PRI, NPR, . Format: Class, jazz, news. News staff: 2; News: 40 hrs wkly. Target aud: General. Spec prog: American Indian 2 hrs, folk 6 hrs, blues 2 hrs wkly. ♦John Harris, CEO; John Harris, pres & gen mgr; Duane Lee, opns mgr; David Thompson, news dir. Co-owned TV: *KBME-TV affil.

KFYR(AM)— 1925: 550 khz; 5 kw-U, DA-N. TL: N46 51 12 W100 32 37. Stereo. Hrs open: Box 2156, 58502. Secondary address: 3500 E. Rosser Ave. 58501. Phone: (701) 255-1234. Fax: (701) 222-1131.E-mail: kfyr@clearchannel.com Web Site:www.kfyr.com Licensee: Citicasters Licenses L.P. Group owner: Clear Channel Communications Inc. (acq 5-4-99; grpsl). Population served: 192,200 Format: News/talk. ♦Bob Denver, gen mgr; Neil Cary, gen sls mgr.

KKCT(FM)— 1994: 97.5 mhz; 100 kw. Ant 837 ft TL: N46 35 24 W100 47 46. Hrs open: Box 1377, 1830 N. 11th St., 58501. Phone: (701) 250-6602. Fax: (701) 250-6632. Web Site:www.hot975fm.com Licensee: Cumulus Licensing Corp. Group owner: Cumulus Media Inc. (acq 5-11-98; grpsl). Format: CHR. ♦Syd Stewart, gen mgr; Dean Mastel, opns mgr; Bill Schmid, gen sls mgr; Chris Ryan, progmg dir; Larry Slabik, news dir; Jeff Foltz, chief of engrg; Connie Schroeder, traf mgr.

KLXX(AM)—(Bismarck-Mandan, 1925: 1270 khz; 1 kw-D, 250 w-N. TL: N46 48 37 W100 50 10. Hrs open: 24 Box 1377, 58502. Phone: (701) 663-6411. Phone: (701) 250-6602. Fax: (701) 663-8790. Fax: (701) 250-6632.E-mail: syd.stewart@cumulus.com Web Site:supertalk1270.com Licensee: Cumulus Licensing Corp. Group owner: Cumulus Media Inc. (acq 5-11-98; grpsl). Population served: 250,000 Natl. Network: CNN Radio, . Natl. Rep: Katz Radio,. Format: News/talk, sports. News staff: one; News: 90 hrs wkly. Target aud: 35 plus. Spec prog: Sports 6 hrs wkly. ♦Syd Stewart, gen mgr & gen sls mgr; Dean Mastel, progmg dir; Elliot Davidson, chief of engrg.

***KNRI(FM)**— 2006: 89.7 mhz; 250 w. Ant 157 ft TL: N46 51 00 W100 46 11. Hrs open: 24 2351 Sunset Blvd., Suite 170-218, Rocklin, CA, 95765. Phone: (916) 251-1600. Fax: (916) 251-1650.E-mail: info@air1.com Web Site:www.air1.com Licensee: Educational Media Foundation. Group owner: EMF Broadcasting. Natl. Network: Air 1, . Shaw Pittman. Format: Contemp Christian. News staff: 3. Target aud: 18-35; Judeo Christian female. ♦Richard Jenkins, pres; Mike Novak, VP; Keith Whipple, dev dir; David Pierce, progmg mgr; Ed Lenane, news dir; Sam Wallington, engrg dir; Karen Johnson, news rptr.

KQDY(FM)— Sept 13, 1968: 94.5 mhz; 100 kw. 1,117 ft TL: N46 51 31 W100 41 38. Stereo. Hrs open: 24 3500 E. Rosser, 58501. Phone: (701) 255-1234. Fax: (701) 222-1131.E-mail: info@kqdy.com Web Site:www.kqdy.com Licensee: CC Licenses LLC. Group owner: Clear Channel Communications Inc. (acq 2-13-2004; grpsl). Population served: 71,900 Format: Contemp country. News: 4 hrs wkly. Target aud: 18-49. ♦Bob Denver, gen mgr.

KSSS(FM)— Aug 1, 1994: 101.5 mhz; 100 kw. 987 ft TL: N46 56 31 W100 41 38. Hrs open: 24 3500 E. Rosser Ave., 58501. Secondary address: Box 2156 58502. Phone: (701) 255-1234. Fax: (701) 222-1131.E-mail: info@1015.fm Web Site:www.1015.fm Licensee: CC Licenses LLC. Group owner: Clear Channel Communications Inc. (acq 2-13-2004; grpsl). Format: Classic Rock. ♦Bob Denver, gen mgr; Terry Flack, gen sls mgr; Jeff Alexander, news dir; Cindy Lindsay, traf mgr.

KXMR(AM)— Mar 20, 1999: 710 khz; 50 kw-D, 4 kw-N, DA-3. TL: N46 50 04 W100 31 19 (D), N46 40 08 W100 46 33 (N). Hrs open: 24 3500 E. Rosser Ave., 58501. Secondary address: Box 2156 58502. Phone: (701) 255-1234. Fax: (701) 222-1131. Licensee: CC Licenses LLC. Group owner: Clear Channel Communications Inc. (acq 12-10-2003). Format: Sports. ♦Bob Denver, gen mgr.

KYYY(FM)— Aug 15, 1966: 92.9 mhz; 100 kw. Ant 1,180 ft TL: N46 36 19 W100 48 30. Stereo. Hrs open: Box 2156, 58502. Secondary address: 3500 E. Rosser Ave. 58501. Phone: (701) 255-1234. Fax: (701) 222-1131. Web Site:www.y93.com Licensee: Citicasters Licenses L.P. Format: Hot adult contemp. ♦Todd Mitchell, opns dir & progmg dir.

Bismarck-Mandan

KLXX(AM)—Licensed to Bismarck-Mandan. See Bismarck

Bottineau

KBTO(FM)— Nov 9, 1980: 101.9 mhz; 94 kw. 492 ft TL: N48 51 10 W100 20 01. Stereo. Hrs open: 24 1120 Highway 5 west, 58318. Phone: (701) 228-5151. Fax: (701) 228-2483.E-mail: sunnyradio@hotmail.com Licensee: Programmers Broadcasting Inc. (acq 1-2-2002; $595,000). Population served: 40,000 Natl. Network: ABC, . Rgnl. Network: Midwest Radio. American Ag Fletcher, Hildreth & Herald. Format: Country. News: 15 hrs wkly. ♦John Kircher, pres; Jean Kircher, VP, gen mgr; Jean Schemmp, stn mgr; J. Davis, gen sls mgr; Jeff Bliss, chief of engrg.

Bowman

KPOK(AM)— Aug 9, 1980: 1340 khz; 1 kw-U. TL: N46 10 48 W103 22 12. Hrs open: 24 Box 829, 11 1/2 N. Main, 58623. Phone: (701) 523-3883. Fax: (701) 523-3885.E-mail: kpok@ndsupernet.com Web Site:www.kpokradio.com Licensee: Tri-State Communications Inc. Population served: 50,000 Natl. Network: Westwood One, . Format: Country. News staff: one; News: 14 hrs wkly. Target aud: 25-54. Spec prog: Farm 2 hrs wkly. ♦Larry Kemnitz, pres; Richard Peterson, VP; Brian Fischer, gen mgr.

Burlington

KWGO(FM)— 2005: 102.9 mhz; 100 kw. Ant 512 ft TL: N48 03 04 W101 20 23. Hrs open: 24 1408 20th Ave. S.W. #1, Minot, 58701. Phone: (701) 852-7449. Fax: (701) 837-6925.E-mail: pbiminot@srt.com Licensee: Programmers Broadcasting Inc. Population served: 100,000 Fletcher, Heald & Hildreth. Format: Hot adult contemp. News: 5 hrs wkly. Target aud: 18-49. ♦John Kircher, pres; Jean Kircher, VP; Jean Schemmp, stn mgr; J. Davis, gen sls mgr; Jeff Bliss, chief of engrg.

Cannon Ball

KXRV(FM)— 2009: 107.5 mhz; 100 kw. Ant 777 ft TL: N46 34 19 W100 47 42. Hrs open: Box 5429, Twin Falls, ID, 83303-5429. Phone: (208) 733-3551. Licensee: World Radio Link Inc. ♦Earl Williamson, pres.

Carrington

KDAK(AM)— Oct 16, 1961: 1600 khz; 500 w-D, 90 w-N. TL: N47 25 43 W99 05 03. Hrs open: 24 Box 50, 58421. Secondary address: Box1170, Jamestown 58402. Phone: (701) 652-3151. Fax: (701) 652-2916.E-mail: kdakam@daktel.com Licensee: Two Rivers Broadcasting Inc. Group owner: Robert Ingstad Broadcast Properties (acq 7-1-94). Population served: 8,000 Natl. Network: ABC, . Rgnl. Network: N.D. News Net. N.D. News Net. Format: Country/news & info. Target aud: 30 plus. ♦Janice Ingstad, pres; Dave Reed, gen mgr, stn mgr.

KXGT(FM)— 1997: 98.3 mhz; 100 kw. Ant 866 ft TL: N47 05 38 W99 02 11. Stereo. Hrs open: P.O. Box 1170, Jamestown, 58402. Secondary address: 2625 8th Avenue SW, Jamestown 58401. Phone: (701) 252-1400. Fax: (701) 252-1402. Licensee: Two Rivers Broadcasting Inc. Format: Adult contemp. ♦Dave Reed, gen mgr.

Cavalier

KAOC(FM)— Sept 29, 1998: 105.1 mhz; 44 kw. 512 ft TL: N48 37 44 W98 00 35. Hrs open: 24 1420 3rd St., Langdon, 58249. Phone: (701) 256-1067. Fax: (701) 256-1051.E-mail: kndk1080@utma.com Licensee: Simmons Broadcasting Inc. (group owner; (acq 9-7-2004; $1). Format: Hot country. ♦Bob Simmons, gen mgr; Jen Taylor, opns mgr.

Devils Lake

KDLR(AM)— Jan 25, 1925: 1240 khz; 1 kw-U. TL: N48 06 42 W98 50 43. Hrs open: 318 W. Walnut St., 58301. Phone: (701) 662-7563. Fax: (701) 662-7564.E-mail: kdlrkdvl@stellarnet.com Web Site:lrradioworks.com Licensee: Double Z Broadcasting Inc. Group owner: Lake Region Radio Works (acq 1-1-2003; $820,000 with KDVL(FM) Devils Lake). Rgnl. Network: AgriAmerica, N.D. News Net. Format: Country, news. Target aud: 25 plus; general. Spec prog: Minnesota Twins baseball, Vikings football. ♦Curt Teigen, pres, gen mgr; Roger Mertens, sls dir; Eric Arndt, news dir.

***KDVI(FM)**— 2007: 89.9 mhz; 250 w. Ant 171 ft TL: N48 08 05 W98 46 20. Hrs open:
Rebroadcasts WAFR(FM) Tupelo, MS 100%.
Drawer 2440, Tupelo, MS, 38803. Phone: (662) 844-8888. Fax: (662) 842-6791. Web Site:www.afr.net Licensee: American Family Association. (acq 6-9-2006). Natl. Network: American Family Radio, . Format: Contemp Christian. ♦Donald E. Wildmon, chmn.

KDVL(FM)— Jan 1, 1967: 102.5 mhz; 100 kw. 471 ft TL: N47 59 16 W98 55 59. Stereo. Hrs open: 24 318 West Walnut St., Devil's Lake, 58301. Secondary address: 400 12 Ave. 58301. Phone: (701) 662-7563. Fax: (701) 662-7564.E-mail: kdlrkdvl@stellarnet.com Web Site:lrradioworks.com Licensee: Double Z Broadcasting Inc. Group owner: Lake Region Radio Works (acq 1-1-2003; $820,000 with KDLR(AM) Devils Lake). Population served: 90,000 Format: Oldies. News staff: one. Target aud: 18-54. ♦Curt Teigen, pres, gen mgr; Roger Mertens, sls dir; Bob Gunderson, progmg dir, disc jockey; Eric Arndt, news dir; Paul Clementich, traf mgr; Mark Beighley, sports cmtr; Kara Danelle, disc jockey.

***KPPD(FM)**— 2009: 91.7 mhz; 24 kw. Ant 703 ft TL: N48 03 47.8 W99 20 08.7. Hrs open:
Rebroadcasts KCND(FM) Bismarck 100%.
Box 3240, Fargo, 58108-3240. Phone: (701) 241-6900. Fax: (701) 224-0555. Web Site:www.prairiepublic.org Licensee: Prairie Public Broadcasting Inc. Format: Classical, jazz, news. ♦John Harris, gen mgr.

KQZZ(FM)— August 1996: 96.7 mhz; 45 kw. 512 ft TL: N47 58 46 W99 03 16. Hrs open: 24 318 W. Walnut St., 58301. Phone: (701) 662-7563. Fax: (701) 662-7564.E-mail: kdlrkdul@stellarnet.com Web Site:www.lrradioworks.com Licensee: Two Rivers Broadcasting Inc. Group owner: Lake Region Radio Works (acq 3-11-99; $250,000). Shaw Pittman. Format: Current & Classic Rock. ♦Curt Teigen, gen mgr & stn mgr.

KZZY(FM)— March 1984: 103.5 mhz; 100 kw. 433 ft TL: N47 59 28 W98 56 57. Stereo. Hrs open: 24 318 W. Walnut St., 58301. Phone: (701) 662-7563. Fax: (701) 662-7564.E-mail: kzzyfm@stellarnet.com Web Site:www.zzcountry.com Licensee: Double Z Broadcasting Inc. Group owner: Lake Region Radio Works (acq 4-11-90). Population served: 13,000 Format: C&W. News staff: one. ♦Curt Teigen, gen mgr, opns mgr, chief of engrg; Roger Mertens, gen sls mgr; Rob Hendricks, progmg dir; Kaye Schwab, traf mgr.

Dickinson

KCAD(FM)— Nov 20, 1996: 99.1 mhz; 100 kw. Ant 794 ft TL: N46 56 09 W102 43 55. Hrs open: 24 11291 39th St. SW, 58601-9206. Phone: (701) 227-1876. Fax: (701) 483-1959.E-mail: clearaudio@clearchannel.com Web Site:www.roughridercountry.net Licensee: CC Licenses LLC Group owner: Clear Channel Communications Inc. (acq 9-1-2000; grpsl). Natl. Network: AP Radio, Jones Radio Networks, . Format: Hot country. Target aud: 16-50; general. ♦Grant Giessinger, gen mgr & gen sls mgr; Bill Palenuk, progmg dir.

KDIX(AM)— 1947: 1230 khz; 1 kw-U. TL: N46 53 44 W102 47 06. Hrs open: 24 119 Second Ave. W., 58601. Phone: (701) 225-5133. Phone: (800) 934-1230. Fax: (701) 225-4136.E-mail: lee@kdix.net Licensee: Starrdak Inc. (acq 4-1-93). Population served: 47,000 Natl. Network: CBS, . Format: Adult contemp, oldies. News staff: 8; News: 6 hrs wkly. Target aud: 35-60. Spec prog: College sports. ♦Lee Leiss, chmn, gen mgr; Rod Kleinjan, opns dir.

***KDPR(FM)**— Oct 12, 1987: 89.9 mhz; 12.5 kw. 488 ft TL: N46 43 34 W102 54 56. Stereo. Hrs open: 24
Rebroadcast KCND(FM) Bismark 100%.
1814 N. 15th St., Bismarck, 58501. Phone: (701) 241-6900. Fax: (701) 239-7650.E-mail: program@prairiepublic.org Web Site:www.prairiepublic.org Licensee: Prairie Public Broadcasting Inc. Population served: 20,000 Natl. Network: PRI, NPR, . Format: Class, jazz, news. News staff: 2; News: 40 hrs wkly. Target aud: General. Spec prog: American Indian 2 hrs, folk 6 hrs wkly. ♦Bill Thomas, gen mgr; Duane Lee, opns mgr; Dave Thompson, news dir; Stephanie Chimeziri, spec ev coord.

KLTC(AM)— July 4, 1978: 1460 khz; 5 kw-U, DA-N. TL: N46 50 54 W102 49 49. Hrs open: 24 11291 39th St. S.W., 58601-9206. Phone: (701) 227-1876. Fax: (701) 483-1959.E-mail: clearaudio@clearchannel.com Licensee: CC Licenses LLC Population served: 80,000 Rgnl. Network: AgriAmerica. Natl. Rep: Hyett/Ramsland,. Format: Classic country. Target aud: General.

KZRX(FM)— Aug 15, 1983: 92.1 mhz; 10.5 kw. Ant 492 ft TL: N46 56 09 W102 43 55. Stereo. Hrs open: 5 AM-midnight 11291 39 St. SW, 58601. Phone: (701) 227-1876. Fax: (701) 483-1959.E-mail: clearaudio @clearchannel.com Web Site:www.z92fm.net Licensee: CC Licenses LLC. Group owner: Clear Channel Communications Inc. (acq 9-1-2000; grpsl). Population served: 35,000 Natl. Rep: Hyett/Ramsland,. Format: Rock. News staff: one. Target aud: 18-45. ♦George Smith, gen mgr; Don Reisenauer, gen sls mgr; Chad Barta, progmg dir; Brian Funk, chief of engrg; Kim Kramer, news dir & traf mgr.

Enderlin

KINV(FM)—Not on air, target date: unknown: 107.3 mhz; 100 kw. Ant 243 ft TL: N46 26 43 W97 39 07. Hrs open: 12310 Split Rail Pkwy., Austin, TX, 78750. Phone: (512) 789-3265. Licensee: Jose J. Garcia Jr. ♦Jose J. Garcia Jr., gen mgr.

Fargo

***KDSU(FM)**— Jan 17, 1966: 91.9 mhz; 100 kw. 991 ft TL: N47 00 48 W97 11 37. Stereo. Hrs open: 24 Box 3240, 58108. Phone: (701) 241-6900. Fax: (701) 231-8899.E-mail: info@kdsufm.com Web Site:www.prairiepublic.org Licensee: North Dakota State University. Population served: 500,000 Natl. Network: NPR, PRI, . Wire Svc: AP Format: Var/div. News staff: 3; News: 45 hrs wkly. Target aud: 24 plus; general. ♦John Harris, CEO; Bill Thomas, gen mgr; Nancy Wood, dev dir.

***KFBN(FM)**— Dec 8, 1997: 88.7 mhz; 30 kw horiz, 100 kw vert. 869 ft TL: N47 00 48 W97 11 37. Hrs open: Box 107, 58107. Phone: (701) 232-5500. Fax: (701) 241-4260.E-mail: info@kfbfm.com Web Site:www.kfbn.org Licensee: Fargo Baptist Church. Format: Mus, world news/rgnl weather, bible instruction. ♦T.C. Scheving, pres & gen mgr.

KFGO(AM)— Mar 14, 1948: 790 khz; 5 kw-U, DA-N. TL: N46 04 05 W96 48 05. Stereo. Hrs open: Box 10097, 58106. Phone: (701) 237-5346. Fax: (701) 237-0980.E-mail: studio@kfgo.com Web Site:www.kfgo.com Licensee: Radio Fargo-Moorhead Inc. Group owner: Clear Channel Communications Inc. (acq 1-19-2007; grpsl). Population served: 500,000 Natl. Network: CBS Radio, . Rgnl. Network: Minn. Pub. Natl. Rep: Eastman Radio,. MNN Wire Svc: AP Format: News/talk. News staff: 4. Target aud: 25 +. ♦Nancy Odney, COO; Joel Heitkamp, opns mgr; Jack Sunday, progmg dir.

***KFNW(AM)**—(West Fargo, Oct 28, 1955: 1200 khz; 10 kw-D, 1 kw-N, DA-N. TL: N46 48 06 W96 52 57. Hrs open: 24 5702 52nd Ave. S., 58104. Phone: (701) 282-5910. Fax: (701) 282-5781.E-mail: kfnw@kfnw.org Web Site:www.kfnw.org Licensee: Northwestern College. Group owner: Northwestern College & Radio. Format: Relg. News staff: one; News: 6 hrs wkly. Target aud: 25-54. ♦Gary D. Herr, stn mgr; Gary Ellingson, chief of engrg; Phil Kvamme, progmg dir & local news ed.

***KFNW-FM**— Mar 12, 1965: 97.9 mhz; 100 kw. Ant 1,000 ft TL: N46 48 07 W96 52 58. Stereo. Hrs open: 24 5702 52nd Ave. S., 58104. Phone: (701) 282-5910. Fax: (701) 282-5781.E-mail: knfw@knfw.org Licensee: Northwestern College. Format: Christian contemp. Target aud: 25-54.

KPFX(FM)— Jan 4, 1993: 107.9 mhz; 100 kw. Ant 713 ft TL: N46 32 41 W96 37 33. Stereo. Hrs open: 24 Box 9919, 58106. Secondary address: 2720 Seventh Ave. S. 58103. Phone: (701) 237-4500. Phone: (701) 237-4949. Fax: (701) 237-5400.E-mail: studio@1079thefox.com Web Site:www.1079thfox.com/ Licensee: Monterey Licenses LLC. Group owner: Triad Broadcasting Co. LLC (acq 8-18-99; grpsl). Population served: 194,800 Natl. Rep: Christal,. Shaw Pittman. Format: Classic rock. Target aud: 25-54; skews male. ♦Michael Brooks, gen mgr; Michael Kapel, opns mgr; David Howland, gen sls mgr; Moose Johnson, progmg dir.

KQWB-FM—(Moorhead, MN) November 1966: 98.7 mhz; 100 kw. 460 ft TL: N46 45 35 W96 36 26. Stereo. Hrs open: Box 9919, 58106-9919. Secondary address: 2720 7th Ave. S. 58103. Phone: (701) 237-4500. Phone: (701) 234-9898. Fax: (701) 235-9082.E-mail: studio@q98.com Web Site:www.q98.com Licensee: Monterey Licenses LLC. Group owner: Triad Broadcasting Co. LLC (acq 10-99; grpsl). Population served: 194,800 Natl. Rep: Christal,. Shaw Pittman. Format: Active rock. Target aud: 18-49; men. ♦Nancy Odney, VP & gen mgr; John Austin, opns dir; Anne Phibian, opns mgr.

KRWK(FM)— Feb 23, 1984: 101.9 mhz; 93 kw. Ant 1,000 ft TL: N47 00 37 W97 11 40. Stereo. Hrs open: Box 10097, 58108. Secondary address: 1020 25th St. S. 58103. Phone: (701) 237-5346. Fax: (701) 237-0980.E-mail: studio@rock102online.com Web Site:www.rock102online.com Licensee: Radio Fargo-Moorhead Inc. Natl. Rep: Eastman Radio,. Format: Classic rock. Target aud: Men 25-54. ♦Nancy Odney, COO; John Austin, opns mgr; Bret Amundson, progmg dir.

KVOX(AM)— 2007: 740 khz; 50 kw-D, 940 w-N, 7.5 kw-CH, DA-3. TL: N46 58 29 W96 30 12. Hrs open: 1020 25th St. S., 58108-2966. Secondary address: Box 10097 58106. Phone: (701) 237-5346. Fax: (701) 237-0980.E-mail: studio@740thefan.com Web Site:www.740thefan.com Licensee: Radio Fargo-Moorhead Inc. (acq 7-31-2007). Natl. Network: Fox Sports, . Natl. Rep: Eastman Radio,. Format: Sports. Target aud: 25-54; Men. ♦Nancy Odney, COO; Tank McNamara, progmg dir.

KVOX-FM—See Moorhead, MN

KVXR(AM)—See Moorhead, MN

WDAY(AM)— May 22, 1922: 970 khz; 5 kw-U, DA-N. TL: N46 52 43 W96 53 05. Stereo. Hrs open: 24 301 8th St. S., Box 2466, 58103. Phone: (701) 237-6500. Fax: (701) 241-5253.E-mail: wdaywday@qwestoffice.net Web Site:www.wday.com Licensee: Forum Communications Co. Inc. (group owner) Population served: 500,000 Natl. Rep: Christal,. Wire Svc: NWS (National Weather Service) Format: News/talk, farm, sports. News staff: 3; News: 35 hrs wkly. Target aud: 35-64. ♦William Marcil Sr., CEO & pres; Jack Sunday, progmg dir; Mike Tanner, news dir.

WDAY-FM— 1965: 93.7 mhz; 100 kw. 1,040 ft TL: N47 00 43 W97 11 58. Stereo. Hrs open: 24 1020 25th St. S., 58103. Secondary address: PO Box 10097 58106. Phone: (701) 237-5346. Fax: (701) 235-4042.E-mail: studio@y94.com Web Site:www.y94.com Licensee: Radio Fargo-Moorhead Inc. Group owner: Clear Channel Communications Inc. (acq 1-19-2007; grpsl). Natl. Rep: Eastman Radio,. Format: Top-40. Target aud: 18-49. ♦Nancy Odeny, COO; J T, progmg dir.

Flasher

KKBO(FM)— 2008: 105.9 mhz; 100 kw. Ant 912 ft TL: N46 35 23 W100 47 39. Hrs open: 3130 E. Broadway, Bismarck, 58501. Phone: (701) 751-8000. Web Site:www.1059bobfm.com Licensee: Connoisseur Media of Bismarck LLC. ♦Michael O. Driscoll, gen mgr.

Fort Totten

***KABU(FM)**— Mar 15, 1999: 90.7 mhz; 6 kw. Ant 328 ft TL: N47 59 28 W98 56 57. Hrs open: Box 7, 58335. Secondary address: KABU Radio Station, 7889 Hwy. 57, St. Michael 58370-9000. Phone: (701) 766-1995. Fax: (701) 766-4068.E-mail: kabu@stellarnet.com Licensee: Dakota Circle Tipi Inc. Population served: 9,001 Format: Educ, community, mus. Target aud: General; community on Spirit Lake Nation & surrounding areas to reach all age groups. Spec prog: American Indian 19 hrs, children 12 hrs, gospel 7 hrs, community & school 5 hrs wkly. ♦John Chaske, gen mgr & stn mgr.

Four Bears

***KMHA(FM)**— March 1984: 91.3 mhz; 100 kw. 380 ft TL: N47 44 23 W102 43 24. Stereo. Hrs open: 24 601 Lodge Rd., Newtown, 58763. Phone: (701) 627-3333/627-4306. Fax: (701) 627-3376.E-mail: kmha_fm@restel.net Licensee: Fort Berthold Communications Enterprise. Population served: 20,000 Format: Div. News staff: one. Target aud: Ranchers, farmers, Native Americans. Spec prog: American Indian-Mandan /Hidatsa/Arikara 4 hrs, country 8 hrs, farm one hr wkly. ♦Rose Crow Flies High, gen mgr; Clarence Sun, opns mgr.

Grafton

KAUJ(FM)— Sept 17, 1984: 100.9 mhz; 3 kw. 125 ft TL: N48 23 53 W97 26 56. Hrs open: 24 856 12th St. W., 58237. Phone: (701) 352-0431. Fax: (701) 352-0436.E-mail: kxpoaj@polarcomm.com Population served: 32,000 Format: Oldies radio. News staff: one; News: 2 hrs wkly. Target aud: 18-60. ♦Nick Amico, traf mgr.

KXPO(AM)— July 12, 1958: 1340 khz; 1 kw-U. TL: N48 23 53 W97 26 56. Hrs open: 6 AM-midnight 856 12th St. W., 58237. Phone: (701) 352-0431. Fax: (701) 352-0436.E-mail: kxpoaj@polarcomm.com Licensee: KGPC Co. (acq 12-12-72). Population served: 50,000 Natl. Network: ABC, . Rgnl. Network: American Net. N.D. News Net. Sam Miller. Wire Svc: AP Format: Country. News staff: 2; News: 15 hrs wkly. Target aud: 30-70. Spec prog: Farm 18 hrs, gospel 5 hrs, relg 4 hrs wkly. ♦Del Nygard, pres; Brian James, gen mgr, progmg dir; Todd Ingstad, adv mgr; Don Brintmall, chief of engrg; Nicki Amico, traf mgr.

Grand Forks

KCNN(AM)—See East Grand Forks, MN

***KFJM(FM)**— Mar 6, 1995: 90.7 mhz; 2.4 kw. 154 ft TL: N47 55 55 W97 04 26. Hrs open: 24 Box 8117, 58202-8117. Phone: (701) 777-2577. Licensee: University of North Dakota. Population served: 75,000 Natl. Network: NPR, PRI, . Format: AAA, jazz. News staff: 2; News: 15 hrs wkly. Target aud: 25-44; well-educated. Spec prog: Blues 3 hrs wkly. ♦Michael Olson, gen mgr, opns mgr & dev dir.

KJKJ(FM)— Aug 1, 1985: 107.5 mhz; 100 kw. 500 ft TL: N48 07 24 W97 04 20. Stereo. Hrs open: 24 Box 13598, 58206-3598. Secondary address: 505 University Ave. 58203. Phone: (701) 746-1417. Fax: (701) 746-1410.E-mail: patmclean@clearchannel.com Web Site:www.kjkj.com Licensee: Citicasters Licenses L.P. Group owner: Clear Channel Communications Inc. (acq 10-26-99; grpsl). Population served: 100,000 Format: AOR. News: 5 hrs wkly. Target aud: 18-49. ♦Jeff Hoberg, gen mgr; Pat McLean, stn mgr; Laura Hammack, gen sls mgr.

KKXL(AM)— 1941: 1440 khz; 1 kw-D, 500 w-N. TL: N47 57 52 W97 01 46. Stereo. Hrs open: 24 Box 13598, 58208-3598. Secondary address: 505 University Ave. 58203. Phone: (701) 746-1417. Phone: (701) 775-0575. Fax: (701) 746-1410.E-mail: patmclean@clearchannel.com Web Site:www.1440kkxl.com Licensee: Citicasters Licenses L.P. Group owner: Clear Channel Communications Inc. (acq 10-26-99; grpsl). Population served: 100,000 Natl. Network: Jones Radio Networks, . Format: Adult standards, news, mus of the 40s, 50s & 60s. News staff: one; News: 10 hrs wkly. Target aud: 25-54; farm community. ♦Pat McLean, gen mgr.

KKXL-FM— March 1975: 92.9 mhz; 63 kw. 385 ft TL: N47 57 52 W97 01 46. Stereo. Hrs open: Prog sep from AM Box 13598, 58208. Secondary address: 505 University Ave. 58203. Phone: (701) 746-1417. Phone: (701) 775-0575. Fax: (701) 746-1410.E-mail: patmclean@clearchannel.com Web Site:www.xl93.com Format: CHR. Target aud: 18-34.

KNOX(AM)— Sept 7, 1947: 1310 khz; 5 kw-U, DA-N. TL: N47 50 39 W97 01 30. Hrs open: 24 Box 13638, 58208-3638. Secondary address: Old Belmont Rd. S. 58208. Phone: (701) 775-4611. Fax: (701) 772-0540. Web Site:www.leightonbroadcasting.com Licensee: Leighton Enterprises Inc. (group owner; acq 10-23-96; $1.1 million with co-located FM). Population served: 39,008 Natl. Network: ABC, . Rgnl. Network: MNN. MNN Wire Svc: AP Format: Farm, news/talk. News staff: 3; News: 80 hrs wkly. Target aud: 35 plus. ♦Jack Hansen, gen mgr; Jarrod Thomas, opns mgr; Lynn Hodgson, gen mgr & gen sls mgr; Doug Barrett, news dir.

KNOX-FM— Feb 4, 1967: 94.7 mhz; 100 kw. Ant 325 ft TL: N48 00 20 W97 04 18. Stereo. Hrs open: 24 1185 9th St. N.E., Thompson, 58278-9343. Phone: (701) 775-4611. Fax: (701) 772-0540. Web Site:www.power947rocks.com Licensee: Leighton Enterprises Inc. Population served: 43,765 Natl. Network: ABC, . Format: Classic rock. Target aud: 18-45.

KQHT(FM)—(Crookston, MN) March 1986: 96.1 mhz; 100 kw. 413 ft TL: N47 50 43 W96 50 22. Stereo. Hrs open: 505 University Ave., 58203. Phone: (701) 746-1417. Fax: (701) 746-1410.E-mail: patmclean@clearchannel.com Web Site:www.961thefox.com Licensee: Citicasters Licenses L.P. Group owner: Clear Channel Communications Inc. (acq 10-26-99; grpsl). Rgnl rep: Hyett/Ramsland. Format: World class rock. Target aud: 18-49. ♦Pat McLean, gen mgr & gen sls mgr; Dave Schroeder, chief of engrg.

***KUND-FM**— May 30, 1976: 89.3 mhz; 38 kw. 215 ft TL: N47 55 55 W97 04 26. Stereo. Hrs open: Box 8117, 58202. Phone: (701) 777-2577. Licensee: University of North Dakota. Population served: 180,000 Format: Class. Spec prog: New age 5 hrs wkly. ♦Gary Olson, stn mgr.

***KWTL(AM)**— Oct 22, 1923: 1370 khz; 1 k-D, 250 w-N. TL: N47 55 55 W97 04 26. Hrs open: 24 Box 13703, 58208. Phone: (701) 795-0122. Web Site:www.youram1370.com Licensee: Real Presence Radio (acq 10-26-2004; $317,100). Population served: 200,000 Format: Catholic. ♦Steve W. Loegering, pres.

KYCK(FM)—See Crookston, MN

Harvey

KHND(AM)— July 21, 1981: 1470 khz; 1 kw-D, 160 w-N. TL: N47 45 23 W99 55 06. Hrs open: Box 6, 58341. Secondary address: 718 Lincoln Ave. 58341. Phone: (701) 324-4848. Fax: (701) 324-2043. E-mail: mrsj@khnd1470.com Web Site:khnd1470.com Licensee: Three Way Broadcasting Inc. (acq 1-16-03). Natl. Network: ABC, . Rgnl. Network: AgriAmerica. Format: Adult contemp. News: 15 hrs News Programing wkly. Target aud: 12 -85. Spec prog: weather, news, talk, classic rock programs, polka 3 hrs, talk show 8 hrs wkly. ◆ Rick Jensen, VP; Sheila Jensen, pres, gen mgr, stn mgr & gen sls mgr.

Harwood

KKLQ(FM)— 2001: 100.7 mhz; 25 kw. Ant 328 ft TL: N47 08 43 W96 58 18. Hrs open: 2351 Sunset Blvd., Suite 170-218, Rocklin, CA, 95765. Phone: (916) 251-1600. Fax: (916) 251-1650. Licensee: Educational Media Foundation. Group owner: EMF Broadcasting (acq 1-8-2004; $750,000). Natl. Network: K-Love, . Format: Christian. ◆ Richard Jenkins, pres; Mike Novak, VP; Keith Whipple, dev dir; David Pierce, progmg mgr; Ed Lenane, news dir; Sam Wallington, engrg dir; Karen Johnson, news rptr.

Hazelton

KUSB(FM)— 2006: 103.3 mhz; 100 kw. Ant 964 ft TL: N46 35 23.8 W100 47 46.2. Hrs open: 1830 N. 11th St., Bismarck, 58501. Phone: (701) 250-6602. Fax: (701) 250-6632. Licensee: Cumulus Licensing LLC. ◆ Syd Stewart, gen mgr.

Hettinger

KNDC(AM)— Mar 1, 1954: 1490 khz; 1 kw-U. TL: N46 01 11 W102 41 33. Hrs open: 12:00am - 11:59pm Box 151, 505 2nd Ave. S., 58639. Phone: (701) 567-2421. Phone (701) 567-2889. Fax: (701) 567-4636. E-mail: kndc1490@ndsupernet.com Web Site:www.kndc.com Licensee: Schweitzer Media Inc. (acq 5-19-99). Population served: 17,230 Natl. Network: ABC, . Rgnl. Network: AgriAmerica, N.D. News Net. S.D. News Net. Format: C&W. News: 24 hrs wkly. Target aud: 24-52; rural residents. Spec prog: Farm. ◆ Mike Schweitzer, pres; Nolan Dix, gen mgr, progmg dir, mus dir & sports cmtr.

KNDH(FM)—Not on air, target date: unknown: 93.5 mhz; 100 kw. Ant 958 ft TL: N46 09 12.97 W102 46 24.4. Hrs open: 1282 Smallwood Dr., Suite 372, Waldorf, MD, 20603. Phone: (202) 251-7589. Fax: (301) 645-1426. Licensee: Alma Corp. ◆ Dennis Wallace, gen mgr.

Hope

KMJO(FM)— 2002: 104.7 mhz; 100 kw. Ant 702 ft TL: N47 03 15 W97 24 44. Hrs open: 24 1020 25th St. S., Fargo, 58103. Secondary address: Box 10097, Fargo 58106. Phone: (701) 237-5346. Fax: (701) 237-0980. Web Site:www.mojo104.com Licensee: Radio Fargo-Moorhead Inc. Group owner: Clear Channel Communications Inc. (acq 1-19-2007; grpsl). Natl. Rep: Eastman Radio,. Format: Classic Hits. Target aud: 25-64; Adults. ◆ Nancy Odney, COO; Mike Waters, progmg dir.

Jamestown

*KJTW(FM)—Not on air, target date: unknown: 89.9 mhz; 400 w. Ant 154 ft TL: N46 53 30 W98 42 46. Hrs open: Drawer 2440, Tupelo, MS, 38803. Phone: (662) 844-8888. Web Site:www.afr.net Licensee: American Family Association. (acq 8-27-2007). Natl. Network: American Family Radio, . ◆ Donald E. Wildmon, chmn.

*KLUU(FM)— 2008: 88.9 mhz; 500 w vert. Ant 285 ft TL: N46 50 05 W98 41 31. Hrs open:
Rebroadcasts KLVR(FM) Middletown, CA 100%.
2351 Sunset Blvd., Suite 170-218, Rocklin, CA, 95765. Phone: (916) 251-1600. Fax: (916) 251-1650. Web Site:www.klove.com Licensee: Educational Media Foundation. Natl. Network: K-Love, . Format: Contemp Christian. ◆ Mike Novak, pres.

*KPRJ(FM)— 1993: 91.5 mhz; 18.5 kw. 354 ft TL: N46 46 36 W98 31 20. Hrs open: 24
Rebroadcasts KCND(FM) Bismarck 100%.
207 N 5th St., Fargo, 58102. Phone: (701) 241-6900. Fax: (701) 224-0555.E-mail: info@prairiepublic.org Web Site:www.prairiepublic.org Licensee: Prairie Public Broadcasting Inc. Natl. Network: NPR, PRI, . Format: Class, jazz, news. News staff: 3. Target aud: General. Spec prog: American Indian 2 hrs, folk 6 hrs wkly. ◆ John Harris, CEO & pres; Duane Lee, opns mgr; David Thompson, news dir.

KQDJ(AM)— Aug 12, 1954: 1400 khz; 1 kw-U. TL: N46 53 37 W98 41 20. Hrs open: 24 Box 1170, 58402. Secondary address: 2625 8th Ave. S.W. 58401. Phone: (701) 252-1400. Fax: (701) 252-1402.E-mail: bigdog@daktel.com Licensee: Two Rivers Broadcasting Inc. Group owner: Robert Ingstad Broadcast Properties (acq 1994; $600,000). Population served: 25,000 Natl. Network: Fox Sports, . Format: Sports. ◆ Dave Reed, gen mgr.

KSJB(AM)— 1937: 600 khz; 5 kw-U, DA-1. TL: N46 49 03 W98 42 34. Hrs open: 24 Box 5180, 58402-1840. Secondary address: 2400 8th Ave. S. W. 58402-1840. Phone: (701) 252-3570. Fax: (701) 252-1277.E-mail: info@ksjbam.com Licensee: Chesterman Communications Inc. (acq 8-20-90; $850,000 with co-located FM; 9-10-90). Population served: 16,500 Format: Classic country. News staff: one; News: 13 hrs wkly. Target aud: 25 plus. Spec prog: Farm 12 hrs wkly. ◆ Patrick Pfieffer, gen mgr; Patrick Pfeiffer, gen sls mgr, mktg mgr, prom mgr.

KSJZ(FM)— 1968: 93.3 mhz; 57 kw. 256 ft TL: N46 49 03 W98 42 34. Stereo. Hrs open: 6 AM-midnight Box 5180, 58402. Secondary address: 2400 8th Ave. S. W. 58402. Phone: (701) 252-3570. Fax: (701) 252-1277.E-mail: info@ksjbam.com Web Site:www.ksjbam.com Format: Adult hit radio. Target aud: 28-52; 60% male, 40% female.

KYNU(FM)— Aug 25, 1984: 95.5 mhz; 100 kw. Ant 398 ft TL: N46 51 52 W98 40 11. Stereo. Hrs open: 24 Box 1170, 58401. Secondary address: 2625 8th Ave. S.W. 58402. Phone: (701) 252-1400. Fax: (701) 252-1402. Licensee: Two Rivers Broadcasting Inc. Population served: 50,000 Natl. Network: ABC, . Format: Hot country. Target aud: 18-65. ◆ Dave Reed, gen mgr.

Kindred

*KFNL(FM)— June 6, 1986: 92.7 mhz; 25 kw. Ant 328 ft TL: N46 39 38 W96 43 01. Stereo. Hrs open: 24 3003 Snelling Ave. N., St. Paul, MN, 55113-1598. Phone: (651) 631-5000. Fax: (612) 631-5086. Licensee: Northwestern College. Group owner: Clear Channel Communications Inc. (acq 1-19-2007; donation). Population served: 150,000 Bryan Cave L.L.P. Format: Contemp Christian. ◆ Alan S. Cureton, pres.

Langdon

KNDK(AM)— June 27, 1967: 1080 khz; 1 kw-D. TL: N48 46 25 W98 21 50. Hrs open: 16 Box 9, Rt. 5, 58249. Phone: (701) 256-1080. Fax: (701) 256-1081.E-mail: kndk1080@utma.com Licensee: KNDK Inc. (group owner; (acq 12-1-87). Population served: 25,500 Natl. Network: CBS, . Haley, Bader & Potts. Format: News/talk, country. News staff: 3; News: 42 hrs wkly. Target aud: 25 plus. Spec prog: Farm 12 hrs, relg 4 hrs wkly. ◆ Bob Simmons, pres, gen mgr, gen sls mgr, progmg dir & chief of engrg.

KNDK-FM— Jan 15, 1992: 95.7 mhz; 6 kw. 328 ft TL: N48 45 18 W98 21 38. Hrs open: 24 Box 9, Rt. 5, 58249. Phone: (701) 256-1080. Fax: (701) 256-1081. (Acq 11-20-91; $90,000; 12-16-91). Format: Hot adult contemp.

Lincoln

*KGCD(FM)— 2006: 89.1 mhz; 950 w. Ant 693 ft TL: N46 35 24 W100 47 47. Hrs open: 24
Rebroadcasts KLVR(FM) Middletown, CA 100%.
2351 Sunset Blvd., Suite 170-218, Rocklin, CA, 95765. Phone: (916) 251-1600. Fax: (916) 251-1650.E-mail: @klove.com Web Site:www.klove.com Licensee: Educational Media Foundation. Group owner: EMF Broadcasting. Natl. Network: K-Love, . Shaw Pittman. Format: Contemp Christian. News staff: 3. Target aud: 25-44; Judeo Christian, female. ◆ Mike Novak, pres.

Lisbon

KQLX(AM)— November 1984: 890 khz; 1.8 kw-D. TL: N46 26 43 W97 39 07. Stereo. Hrs open: Box 1008, 1206 S. Main, 58054. Phone: (701) 683-5287. Fax: (701) 683-9029.E-mail: kqlx@kqlx.com Web Site:www.kqlx.com Licensee: Loomis Broadcasting Inc. Population served: 340,000 Rgnl. Network: AgriAmerica, Agri-Net, Agrinet Format: News/talk. News staff: one; News: 5 hrs wkly. Target aud: 18-65; farmers. Spec prog: Farm 18 hrs, Gospel 6 hrs wkly. ◆ Terry Loomis, pres; Rita Loomis, VP; Bruce Dougherty, gen mgr.

KQLX-FM— Oct 24, 1986: 106.1 mhz; 100 kw. Ant 714 ft TL: N46 44 39 W97 25 38. Stereo. Hrs open: Box 1008, 1206 S. Main, 58054. Phone: (701) 683-5287. Fax: (701) 683-9029.E-mail: kqlx@kqlx.com Web Site:www.kqlx.com Licensee: Sheyenne Valley Broadcasting Inc.

Population served: 12,000 Natl. Network: CNN Radio, . American Ag Format: Country. News staff: one; News: 5 hrs wkly. Target aud: 18-54; general.

Mandan

KLXX(AM)—See Bismarck

KNDR(FM)— June 19, 1977: 104.7 mhz; 100 kw. 852 ft TL: N46 35 11 W100 48 20. Stereo. Hrs open: 24 Box 516, 1400 NE 3rd Street, 58554. Phone: (701) 663-2345. Fax: (701) 663-2347.E-mail: kndr@midconetwork.com Web Site:www.kndr.fm Licensee: Central Dakota Enterprise Inc. Population served: 85,000 Wire Svc: AP Format: Christian, Adult Contemp. Target aud: 25-54; women and famlies (with children). ◆ LaRue Goetz, chmn; Brad Bales, gen mgr.

Mayville

KMAV-FM— Jan 10, 1977: 105.5 mhz; 25 kw. Ant 328 ft TL: N47 29 45 W97 21 03. Stereo. Hrs open: 24 Box 216, 58257. Phone: (701) 786-2335. Fax: (701) 786-2268. Web Site:kmav.com Licensee: KMSR Inc. (acq 9-8-2008; $480,000 with KMSR(AM) Mayville). Population served: 150,000 Natl. Network: ABC, . Format: Country. ◆ Marylou Keating, pres; Dan Keating, gen mgr.

KMSR(AM)— Oct 20, 1967: 1520 khz; 2.5 kw-D. TL: N47 29 45 W97 21 03. Hrs open: Sunrise-sunset Box 216, 58257. Phone: (701) 786-2335. Fax: (701) 786-2268.E-mail: sports@kmavradio.com Web Site:www.kmavradio.com Licensee: KMSR Inc. (acq 9-8-2008; $480,000 with KMAV-FM Mayville). Population served: 150,000 Natl. Network: ESPN Radio, . Rgnl. Network: N.D. News Net., AgriAmerica, Red River Farm Net. N.D. News Net. Format: Sports. Target aud: 25-55. ◆ Marylou Keating, pres; Rich Haraldson, exec VP; Dan Keating, gen mgr, adv mgr, progmg dir, sports cmtr; Jim Birkemeyer, sls dir; Eric Michaels, prom dir; Mary Keating, news dir.

Medina

KCVG(FM)—Not on air, target date: unknown: 92.3 mhz; 100 kw. Ant 699 ft TL: N47 05 38 W99 02 11. Hrs open: 5331 Mt. Alifan Dr., San Diego, CA, 92111. Phone: (858) 277-4991. Fax: (858) 277-1365. Web Site:www.horizonsd.org/radio.asp Licensee: Horizon Christian Fellowship. ◆ Mike MacIntosh, pres.

Minot

KCJB(AM)— September 1950: 910 khz; 5 kw-D, 1 kw-N, DA-2. TL: N40 11 57 W101 17 37. Hrs open: Box 10, 3425 S. Broadway, 58702. Phone: (701) 852-0361. Fax: (701) 852-1953. Licensee: CC Licenses LLC. Group owner: Clear Channel Communications Inc. (acq 1-12-2000; grpsl). Population served: 156,000 Natl. Network: CBS, . Fisher, Wayland, Cooper, Leader & Zaragoza L.L.P. Format: Full service, country. Target aud: 25 plus. Spec prog: Loc sports, various loc talk segments, farm 4 hrs wkly. ◆ Rick Stensby, gen mgr.

KHRT(AM)— Nov 17, 1957: 1320 khz; 2.5 kw-D, 310 w-N. TL: N48 11 48 W101 14 30. Hrs open: 24 Box 1210, 58702. Secondary address: 3600 County Rd. 195 S. 58702. Phone: (701) 852-3789. Fax: (701) 852-8498.E-mail: khrt@srt.com Licensee: Faith Broadcasting Inc. (acq 9-1-82; $188,248; 8-30-82). Population served: 107,300 Format: Relg, news/talk, Southern gospel. News staff: one; News: 10 hrs wkly. Target aud: 25-54; large families, loyal, upper-income professionals. Spec prog: Farm one hr wkly. ◆ Richard Leavitt, pres, gen mgr, gen sls mgr, progmg dir; Roy Leavitt, stn mgr; Johas Nelson, mus dir, disc jockey; John Kennedy, news dir; John McCann, chief of engrg, disc jockey; Marcia Leavitt, traf mgr.

KHRT-FM— 1992: 106.9 mhz; 26 kw. Ant 344 ft TL: N48 09 48 W101 17 55. Hrs open: Box 1210, 58702. Secondary address: 3600 County Rd. 195 S. 58702. Phone: (701) 852-3789. Fax: (701) 852-8498.E-mail: khrt@srt.com Licensee: Faith Broadcasting Inc. Format: Contemp Christian. ◆ Johas Nelson, progmg dir.

KIZZ(FM)— Sept 7, 1968: 93.7 mhz; 98 kw. 571 ft TL: N48 12 56 W101 19 05. Stereo. Hrs open: 24 Box 10, 58702. Secondary address: 101 S. Main St. 58701. Phone: (701) 852-2494. Fax: (701) 852-1390.E-mail: minotprod@clearchannel.com Licensee: CC Licenses LLC. Group owner: Clear Channel Communications Inc. (acq 9-1-2000; grpsl). Population served: 43,900 Format: Adult contemp. News staff: one; News: 3 hrs wkly. Target aud: 25-54. ◆ Rick Stensby, gen mgr, gen sls mgr; Allison Bostow, opns mgr, progmg dir; Don May, news dir; Brian Funk, chief of engrg; Rhonda Jensen, traf mgr; Bill Allen, disc jockey.

*KMPR(FM)— Nov 23, 1983: 88.9 mhz; 100 kw. 930 ft TL: N48 03 03 W101 23 24. (CP: 50 kw). Stereo. Hrs open: 24 Rebroadcasts KCND(FM) Bismarck 100%.
1814 N. 15th St., Bismarck, 58501. Phone: (701) 224-1700. Fax: (701) 224-0555.E-mail: info@prairiepublic.org Web Site:www.prairiepublic.org Licensee: Prairie Public Broadcasting Inc. Population served: 20,000 Natl. Network: PRI, NPR, . Format: Class, news, jazz. News staff: 2; News: 40 hrs wkly. Target aud: General. Spec prog: American Indian 2 hrs, folk 6 hrs wkly. ◆John Harris, CEO & pres; Duane Lee, opns mgr; David Thompson, news dir. Co-owned TV: *KSRE(TV) affil.

KMXA-FM— April 1984: 99.9 mhz; 100 kw. 500 ft TL: N48 10 57 W101 31 57. Stereo. Hrs open: 24 1000 20th Ave. S.W., 58701. Phone: (701) 852-2494. Fax: (701) 852-1390.E-mail: minotprod@clearchannel.com Web Site:www.mix999fm.com Licensee: CC Licenses LLC. Group owner: Clear Channel Communications Inc. (acq 1-12-2000; grpsl). Population served: 157,000 Format: Hot adult contemp. News: 4 hrs wkly. Target aud: 25-54; adult upper middle class with teens at home. ◆Rick Stensby, gen mgr & stn mgr; Allison Bostow, opns mgr.

KRRZ(AM)— Oct 28, 1929: 1390 khz; 5 kw-D, 1 kw-N. TL: N48 12 45 W101 14 30. Stereo. Hrs open: 1000 20th Ave. S.W., 58701. Phone: (701) 852-4646. Fax: (701) 852-1390.E-mail: mward.@kwhw.com Web Site:www.oldies1390.com Licensee: CC Licenses LLC. Group owner: Clear Channel Communications Inc. (acq 9-1-2000; grpsl). Population served: 32,290 Rgnl. Network: N.D. News Net. Natl. Rep: Roslin,. N.D. News Net. Format: Oldies. Target aud: 25-54. Spec prog: Sports. ◆Rick Stensby, gen mgr; Allison Bostow, opns mgr.

KYYX(FM)— Nov 15, 1966: 97.1 mhz; 100 kw. 984 ft TL: N48 03 02 W101 20 29. Stereo. Hrs open: 24 Prog sep from AM Box 10, 3425 S. Broadway, 58702. Phone: (701) 852-0361. Fax: (701) 852-1953. Licensee: CC Licenses LLC. News staff: one; News: 6 hrs wkly. Target aud: 18-49; young families. Co-owned TV: KXMC-TV affil.

KZPR(FM)— July 8, 1985: 105.3 mhz; 100 kw. 579 ft TL: N48 03 13 W101 26 03. Stereo. Hrs open: 24 Prog sep from AM 1000 20th Ave. S.W., 58701. Phone: (701) 852-4646. Fax: (701) 852-1390. Rgnl. Network: AgriAmerica. Format: Classic rock. News: 4 hrs wkly. Spec prog: Farm 4 hrs wkly. ◆Allison Bostow, adv dir, disc jockey; Rick Anthony, disc jockey.

New England

KCVD(FM)— 2008: 95.7 mhz; 700 w. Ant 610 ft TL: N46 27 48 W102 58 46. Hrs open: 5331 Mt. Alifan Dr., San Diego, CA, 92111. Phone: (858) 277-4991. Fax: (858) 277-1365. Licensee: Horizon Christian Fellowship. (acq 2-9-2006; grpsl). Format: Relg. ◆Mike MacIntosh, pres.

Oakes

KDDR(AM)— July 31, 1959: 1220 khz; 1 kw-D, 327 w-N. TL: N46 07 23 W98 05 21. Hrs open:
Rebroadcast KOVC(AM) Valley City.
Box 994, 136 Central Ave. N., Valley City, 58072. Phone: (701) 845-1490. Fax: (701) 845-1245.E-mail: kddr@drtel.net Licensee: Sioux Valley Broadcasting Co. Group owner: Robert Ingstad Broadcast Properties (acq 2-1-93; $85,000;2-22-93). Population served: 50,000 Rgnl. Network: N.D. News Net. N.D. News Net. Fletcher, Heald & Hildreth. Format: Country, news. Target aud: 28-59; farm/agriculture. ◆Tim Ost, gen mgr; Terry James, progmg dir.

Rugby

KZZJ(AM)— Aug 21, 1961: 1450 khz; 1 kw-U. TL: N48 21 14 W99 59 31. Hrs open: 24 230 Hwy. 2 S.E., 58368. Phone: (701) 776-5254. Fax: (701) 776-6154.E-mail: kzzj@kzzj.com Web Site:www.kzzj.com Licensee: Rugby Broadcasters Inc. (acq 7-6-89; $10,000;7-24-89). Population served: 38,000 Rgnl. Network: Midwest Radio Format: Modern country, farm. News staff: one. Target aud: 25-65. ◆Lila Brossart, gen mgr; Jay Schmalz, opns mgr, mus dir; Cheryl Holm, gen sls mgr, chief of engrg; Bruce Allen, news dir; Dee Dee Bishoff, traf mgr.

Sarles

KCVF(FM)—Not on air, target date: unknown: 105.9 mhz; 100 kw. Ant 459 ft TL: N48 37 58 W99 06 05. Hrs open: 5331 Mt. Alifan Dr., San Diego, CA, 92111. Phone: (858) 277-4991. Fax: (858) 277-1365. Licensee: Horizon Christian Fellowship. (acq 2-9-2006; grpsl). ◆Mike MacIntosh, pres.

South Heart

KDXN(FM)— Nov 1, 2008: 105.7 mhz; 100 kw. Ant 220 ft TL: N46 46 12 W103 12 37. Hrs open: Box 1322, Dickinson, 58602. Phone: (701) 483-8344. Fax: (701) 483-8345. Web Site:westernedgemedia.com Licensee: Western Edge Media LLC (acq 7-25-2008; $150,000 for CP). Format: Country. ◆Bill Palanuk, pres, gen mgr; Blake Messer, VP.

Tioga

KTGO(AM)— Feb 27, 1966: 1090 khz; 1 kw-D. TL: N48 23 30 W102 56 12. Hrs open: Box 457, 58852. Secondary address: 301 S.E. 2nd St. 58852. Phone: (701) 664-3322. Phone: (701) 664-3432. Fax: (701) 664-3322.E-mail: ktgo@wccray.com Licensee: Tioga Broadcasting Corp. Population served: 14,000 Natl. Network: CBS, . Format: Country. Target aud: 18-55. Spec prog: Gospel 11 hrs wkly. ◆David Guttormson, pres, gen mgr, gen sls mgr & progmg dir.

Valley City

KOVC(AM)— Oct 19, 1936: 1490 khz; 1 kw-U. TL: N46 54 48 W98 01 02. Hrs open: 19 136 Central Ave. N., 58072. Phone: (701) 845-1490. Fax: (701) 845-1245. Licensee: Sioux Valley Broadcasting Co. Group owner: Robert Ingstad Broadcast Properties. Population served: 68,500 Rgnl. Network: AgriAmerica. Format: Country, news, sports. News: 7 hrs wkly. Target aud: 25 plus. ◆Dave Reed, opns mgr; Ron Lee, prom dir, progmg dir, mus dir, disc jockey; Kerry Johnson, adv mgr; Ryan Cunningham, news dir; Don Brintnall, engrg mgr, chief of engrg; Terri Suhr, traf mgr; Rod Reel, edit dir, disc jockey; Dave Michaels, disc jockey.

KQDJ-FM— Aug 1, 1983: 101.1 mhz; 12 kw. Ant 1,000 ft TL: N46 54 24 W97 58 20. Hrs open: 19 136 Central Ave. N., 58072. Phone: (701) 845-1490. Fax: (701) 845-1245. Format: News/talk, sports info, adult standards. Target aud: 25-54. ◆Dave Reed, progmg mgr.

Velva

KTZU(FM)— 2005: 94.9 mhz; 98 kw. Ant 512 ft TL: N48 03 04 W101 20 23. Hrs open: 24 1408 20th Ave. S.W. #1, Minot, 58701. Phone: (701) 852-7449. Fax: (701) 837-6925.E-mail: pbiminot@srt.com Licensee: Programmers Broadcasting Inc. Population served: 100,000 Fletcher, Heald & Hildreth. Format: Classic rock. News: 5 hrs wkly. Target aud: 25-54. ◆John Kircher, pres; Jean Kircher, VP; Jean Schempp, stn mgr; J. Davis, gen sls mgr; Jeff Bliss, chief of engrg.

Wahpeton

KBMW(AM)—(Breckenridge, MN) Aug 28, 1948: 1450 khz; 1 kw-U. TL: N46 16 41 W96 35 19. Hrs open: 605 Dakota Ave., 58075. Phone: (701) 642-8747. Fax: (701) 642-9501.E-mail: studio@kbmwam.com Web Site:www.kbmwam.com Licensee: Monterey Licenses LLC. Group owner: Triad Broadcasting Co. LLC (acq 1-31-03; $1.2 million). Population served: 60,000 Format: Country. News staff: one; News: 18 hrs wkly. Target aud: 25-54; general. ◆Bill Dadlow, stn mgr.

KEGK(FM)— May 21, 1989: 106.9 mhz; 41 kw. Ant 538 ft TL: N46 32 46 W96 37 39. Stereo. Hrs open: 24 Box 1115, 58074. Secondary address: 605 Dakota Ave. 58075. Phone: (701) 642-8747. Phone: (701) 237-4500. Fax: (701) 642-9501.E-mail: studio@eagle1069.com Web Site:www.eagle1069.com Licensee: Guderian Broadcasting Inc. (acq 7-17-2002). Natl. Rep: Midwest Radio,. Rgnl rep: Quest Marketing. Format: Oldies. News staff: one; News: 5 hrs wkly. Target aud: 25-54. ◆Nancy Odney, gen mgr; John Austin, opns mgr, gen sls mgr; Michael Brooks, sls dir; Tim Murphy, adv mgr & progmg dir.

Walhalla

KYTZ(FM)— Sept 1, 1998: 106.7 mhz; 16 kw. Ant 836 ft TL: N48 38 38 W97 58 46. Hrs open: 24 1420 3rd St., Langdon, 58249. Phone: (701) 256-1067. Fax: (701) 256-1051.E-mail: kndk1080@vtma.com Licensee: Simmons Broadcasting Inc. (acq 9-7-2004). Format: Hot adult contemp. ◆Bob Simmons, gen mgr; Jen Taylor, opns mgr.

West Fargo

KFNW(AM)—Licensed to West Fargo. See Fargo

KQWB(AM)— Sept 1, 2000: 1660 khz; 10 kw-D, 1 kw-N. TL: N46 58 33 W96 35 02. Stereo. Hrs open: 2720 7th Ave. S., Fargo, 58103. Phone: (701) 237-4500. Fax: (701) 235-9082.E-mail: info@123fargo.com

Web Site:www.123fargo.com Licensee: Monterey Licenses LLC. Group owner: Triad Broadcasting Co. LLC (acq 8-18-99; grpsl). Natl. Network: Westwood One, . Natl. Rep: Christal,. Fisher, Wayland, Cooper, Leader & Zaragoza. Format: Talk/personality. Target aud: 35 plus. ◆David Benjamin, pres; Tom Douglas, CFO; Nancy Odney, gen mgr; Anne Phibian, opns mgr; John Austin, progmg dir.

Williston

KDSR(FM)— Feb 28, 1985: 101.1 mhz; 98 kw. Ant 800 ft TL: N48 03 30 W104 00 00. Stereo. Hrs open: 18 910 E. Broadway, 58801. Phone: (701) 572-4478. Fax: (701) 572-1419.E-mail: kdsr@dia.net Licensee: Williston Community Broadcasting Corp. dba KDSR(FM) (acq 6-28-2002). Population served: 90,000 Natl. Network: CNN Radio, . Booth, Freret, Imlay & Tepper. Format: Rock. News: 7 hrs wkly. ◆Stephen A. Marks, pres; Ben Buckles, opns mgr, chief of engrg; P. Sturlausson, progmg dir.

KEYZ(AM)— 1948: 660 khz; 5 kw-U, DA-2. TL: N48 14 20 W103 39 01. Stereo. Hrs open: 24 Box 2048, 58802-2048. Secondary address: 410 E. 6th 58801. Phone: (701) 572-5371. Fax: (701) 572-7511. Web Site:www.keyzradio.com Licensee: CCR-Williston IV LLC. Group owner: Cherry Creek Radio LLC (acq 12-19-2003; grpsl). Population served: 175,000 Natl. Network: ABC, . Rgnl. Network: AgriAmerica. American Ag Format: Classic Country, news/talk. News staff: one. Target aud: 25-54. Spec prog: Relg 5 hrs wkly. ◆Joel Swanson, gen mgr; Lyla Semenko, stn mgr; Scott Haugen, progmg dir.

*KJND-FM—Not on air, target date: unknown: 90.7 mhz; 10 kw. Ant 544 ft TL: N48 02 52 W103 59 01. Hrs open: Box 2426, Havre, MT, 59501-2426. Phone: (406) 265-5845. Fax: (406) 265-8860.E-mail: ynop@ynop.org Web Site:www.ynopradio.org Licensee: Hi-Line Radio Fellowship Inc. ◆Roger Lonnquist, gen mgr.

*KNDW(AM)—Not on air, target date: unknown: 91.7 mhz; 6 kw. Ant 118 ft TL: N48 10 45 W103 33 54. Hrs open: Drawer 2440, Tupelo, MS, 38803. Phone: (662) 844-8888. Licensee: Salt & Light Communications Inc. ◆Larry Durham, pres.

*KPPR(FM)— Nov 20, 1986: 89.5 mhz; 10.5 kw. 492 ft TL: N48 08 30 W103 53 34. Stereo. Hrs open: 24 Rebroadcasts KCND(FM) Bismarck 100%.
207 N 5th St., Fargo, 58102. Phone: (701) 224-1700. Phone: (800) 359-5566. Fax: (701) 224-0555.E-mail: info@prairiepublic.org Web Site:www.prairiepublic.org Licensee: Prairie Public Broadcasting. Population served: 40,000 Natl. Network: PRI, NPR, . Format: Jazz, class, news. News staff: 2; News: 40 hrs wkly. Target aud: General. Spec prog: American Indian 2 hrs, folk 6 hrs wkly. ◆John Harris, CEO & pres; Bill Thomas, stn mgr; Dave Thompson, news dir. Co-owned TV: KWSE(TV) affil

KYYZ(FM)— Dec 1, 1979: 96.1 mhz; 100 kw. Ant 873 ft TL: N48 02 52 W103 59 01. Stereo. Hrs open: 24 Box 2048, 58802-2048. Secondary address: 410 E. 6th 58801. Phone: (701) 572-5371. Fax: (701) 572-7511. Web Site:www.kyyzradio.com Licensee: CCR-Williston IV LLC. Population served: 68,000 Natl. Network: Fox News Radio, . Format: Hot country. News staff: one. Target aud: 25-54. ◆ Joel Swanson, gen mgr; Scott Haug, progmg dir; Penny Lalim, traf mgr.

Wimbledon

KRVX(FM)— 2005: 103.1 mhz; 99 kw. Ant 472 ft TL: N46 56 21 W98 18 30. Stereo. Hrs open: P.O. Box 1170, Jamestown, 58401. Secondary address: 2625 8th Ave. S.W., Jamestown 58402. Phone: (701) 252-1400. Fax: (701) 252-1402.E-mail: bigdog@daktel.com Licensee: James River Broadcasting Inc. Natl. Network: NBC Radio, . Format: Rock. Target aud: 18-54. ◆Dave Reed, gen mgr; Lynn Lambrecht, gen sls mgr.

Ohio

Ada

*WONB(FM)— Oct 18, 1991: 94.9 mhz; 3 kw. Ant 328 ft TL: N40 45 58 W83 50 14. Stereo. Hrs open: 24 Freed Ctr., 525 Main S. St., 45810. Phone: (419) 772-1194. Fax: (419) 772-2794.E-mail: wonb@onu.edu Web Site:www.wonbradio.net Licensee: Ohio Northern University. Natl. Network: CNN Radio, . Format: CHR. News: 8 hrs wkly. Target aud: 18-49; general. Spec prog: Relg one hr, gospel 3 hrs, smooth jazz 10 hrs wkly. ◆Dr. Kendall Baker, pres; Bob Ruble, CFO; G. Richard Gainey, gen mgr; Nichole Tebbe, progmg mgr.

Akron

WAKR(AM)— Oct 16, 1940: 1590 khz; 5 kw-U, DA-N. TL: N41 01 14 W81 30 20. Hrs open: 24 1795 W. Market St., 44313. Phone: (330) 869-9800. Fax: (330) 864-6799. Web Site:www.wakr.net Licensee: Rubber City Radio Group Inc. (group owner; acq 10-6-93; $9.3 million with co-located FM;10-25-93). Population served: 565,100 Natl. Network: ABC, . Natl. Rep: Christal,. Verner, Liipfert, Bernhard, McPherson & Hand. Wire Svc: AP Format: News, sports, oldies. News staff: 10; News: 40 hrs wkly. Target aud: 35 plus. ♦Thomas Mandel, CEO; Henry Zelman, CFO; Mark Biviano, sr VP; Chuck Collins, opns dir; Al Hruska, chief of opns, chief of engrg; Dominic Rizzo, gen sls mgr; Joyce Lagios, mktg dir, mktg mgr; Ed Esposito, progmg dir, news dir.

WAKS(FM)— 1950: 96.5 mhz; 31 kw. Ant 620 ft TL: N41 16 50 W81 37 22. Stereo. Hrs open: 6200 Oak Tree Blvd., Suite 400, Cleveland, 44131-6934. Phone: (216) 520-2600. Fax: (216) 981-8167. Web Site:www.waks.com Licensee: Aloha Station Trust LLC (acq 7-30-2008; grpsl). Format: CHR. ♦Mike Kenney, gen mgr; Kris Foley, gen sls mgr; Jeff Zukauckas, mktg dir, prom dir; Bo Matthews, progmg dir.

***WAPS(FM)**— Oct 4, 1955: 91.3 mhz; 800 w. Ant 151 ft TL: N41 03 18 W81 31 35. Stereo. Hrs open: 24 65 Steiner Ave., 44301. Phone: (330) 761-3099. Fax: (330) 761-3240.E-mail: tommybruno @913thesummit.com Web Site:www.913thesummit.com Licensee: Board of Education, Akron City School District. Population served: 300,000 Format: AAA, div. Target aud: 25-54; college educated adults. Spec prog: Ger 2 hrs, It 2 hrs, Hungarian one hr, Slovenian 2 hrs, Latin 2 hrs wkly. ♦Tommy Bruno, gen mgr; Andrew James, opns dir; Ryan Humbert, gen sls mgr.

WARF(AM)— 1926: 1350 khz; 5 kw-U, DA-1. TL: N41 10 05 W81 30 45. Hrs open: 7755 Freedom Ave., North Canton, 44720. Phone: (330) 492-4700. Fax: (330) 492-1350.E-mail: info@sportsradio1350.com Web Site:www.sportsradio1350.com Licensee: Capstar TX L.P. Group owner: Clear Channel Communications Inc. (acq 2000; grpsl). Population served: 275,425 Natl. Network: Fox Sports, . Format: Sports. ♦Dan Lankford, VP & gen mgr.

WCUE(AM)—See Cuyahoga Falls

WHLO(AM)— October 1944: 640 khz; 5 kw-D, 500 w-N, DA-2. TL: N41 04 47 W81 38 45. Stereo. Hrs open: 24 7755 Freedom Ave., N. Canton, 44720. Phone: (330) 836-4700. Fax: (330) 492-1350.E-mail: info@newstalk.com Web Site:www.newstalk.com Licensee: CC Licenses LLC. Group owner: Clear Channel Communications Inc. (acq 12-31-2001; $4.5 million). Population served: 275,425 Format: News/talk. ♦Don Lankford, gen mgr.

WJMP(AM)—See Kent

WNIR(FM)—See Kent

WONE-FM— October 1947: 97.5 mhz; 12 kw. 900 ft TL: N41 03 57 W81 34 59. Stereo. Hrs open: 1795 W. Market St., 44313. Phone: (330) 869-9800. Fax: (330) 864-6799. Fax: (330) 864-9750. Web Site:www.wone.net Format: Rock. Target aud: 18-49. ♦Brett Russell, prom mgr; T.K. O'Grady, progmg dir; Dana Durban, news rptr; Bob Campbell, disc jockey.

WQMX(FM)—(Medina, 1960: 94.9 mhz; 16.2 kw. Ant 880 ft TL: N40 04 58 W81 38 00. Stereo. Hrs open: 24 1795 W. Market St., 44313. Phone: (330) 869-9800. Fax: (330) 864-6799.E-mail: thom@wakr.net Web Site:wqmx.com Licensee: Rubber City Radio Group Inc. (group owner; (acq 1988). Population served: 565,100 Natl. Network: ABC, . Natl. Rep: Christal,. Verner, Liipfert, Bernhard, McPherson & Hand. Wire Svc: AP Format: Country. News staff: 10; News: 10 hrs wkly. Target aud: 25-54; adults. ♦Thomas Mandel, CEO; Al Hruska, COO; Mark Biviano, sr VP; Paul Christopherson, gen sls mgr; Joyce Lagios, mktg dir; Sue Wilson, progmg dir; Ken Steel, mus dir; Ed Esposito, news dir.

***WZIP(FM)**— Dec 10, 1962: 88.1 mhz; 7.5 kw. 827 ft TL: N41 04 58 W81 38 00. Stereo. Hrs open: 24 302 E. Buchtel Ave., Buchtel Mall, 44325-1004. Phone: (330) 972-7105. Fax: (330) 972-5521.E-mail: wzip@uakron.edu Web Site:www.wzip.fm Licensee: University of Akron. Population served: 1,000,000 Natl. Network: AP Network News, . Wire Svc: AP Format: CHR, AOR. Target aud: 18-34. Spec prog: Polka 4 hrs, pub affrs 11 hrs, sports talk 3 hrs wkly. ♦Thomas G. Beck, gen mgr; Blake Thompson, chief of engrg.

Alliance

WDJQ(FM)— April 1947: 92.5 mhz; 50 kw. 500 ft TL: N40 47 24 W81 06 26. Stereo. Hrs open: 24 Box 2356, 44601. Secondary address: 392 Smyth Ave. 44601. Phone: (330) 450-9250. Fax: (330) 821-0379.E-mail: radiosales@alliancelink.com Web Site:www.q92radio.com Licensee: D.A. Peterson Inc. Population served: 628,400 Format: Hot adult contemp. News staff: 2; News: 4 hrs wkly. Target aud: 25-54. ♦Don Peterson III, gen mgr; Mark O'Brian, sls dir; Mark O'Brien, gen sls mgr; John Stewart, progmg VP, progmg dir; Clint M, news dir; Steve Hundt, engrg dir & chief of engrg; Dee Zink, traf mgr.

WDPN(AM)— Sept 2, 1953: 1310 khz; 1 kw-D, 500 w-N, DA-2. TL: N40 55 34 W81 07 41. Hrs open: 24 Prog sep from FM Box 2356, 44601. Secondary address: 392 Smyth Ave. 44601. Phone: (330) 450-9250. Fax: (330) 821-0379.E-mail: info@wdpn.com Licensee: D.A. Peterson Inc. Population served: 50,000 Format: Unforgettable favorites. News staff: 2; News: 21 hrs wkly. Target aud: 35-64. Spec prog: Relg 4 hrs wkly. ♦Doug Lane, progmg dir; Rex Coombs, progmg dir & traf mgr.

***WRMU(FM)**— Oct 17, 1970: 91.1 mhz; 2.8 kw. 190 ft TL: N40 54 16 W81 06 45. Stereo. Hrs open: 24/7 Mount Union College, 1972 Clark Ave., 44601. Phone: (330) 823-2414. Phone: (330) 823-3777. Fax: (330) 829-4913.E-mail: wrmu@muc.edu Web Site:www.muc.edu/wrmu Licensee: Mount Union College. Population served: 26,547 Wire Svc: AP Format: Smooth jazz, Rock/AOR, oldies. News staff: one; News: 8 hrs wkly. Spec prog: Gospel 2 hrs, news/talk 5 hrs wkly. ♦Dr. Richard Giese, pres; Mark A. Bergmann, gen mgr; William Weisinger, chief of engrg.

Anna

***WHJM(FM)**— June 2006: 88.7 mhz; 3 kw vert. Ant 272 ft TL: N40 18 01 W84 12 25. Hrs open: 601 Washington St, Alexandria, LA, 71301. Phone: (888) 408-0201. Phone: (318) 561-6145. Fax: (318) 449-9954.E-mail: info.usa@radiomaria.org Web Site:www.radiomaria.us Licensee: Friends of Radio Maria Inc. Format: Catholic. ♦Father Duane Stenzel, opns mgr & progmg dir.

Archbold

***WBCY(FM)**— Dec 1, 1992: 89.5 mhz; 20 kw. Ant 315 ft TL: N41 28 59 W84 16 58. Hrs open: 24 c/o WBCL(FM), 1025 W. Rudisill Blvd., Fort Wayne, IN, 46807. Phone: (260) 745-0576. Fax: (260) 456-2913. Web Site:www.wbcl.org Licensee: Taylor University Broadcasting Inc. (acq 6-24-92). Population served: 889,000 Wire Svc: UPI Format: Contemp Christian. ♦Marsha Bunker, gen mgr; Craig Albrecht, opns mgr; Scott Tusleff, progmg dir & progmg mgr.

WMTR-FM— Mar 1968: 96.1 mhz; 3.8 kw. Ant 400 ft TL: N41 33 29 W84 11 08. Stereo. Hrs open: 24 303 1/2 N. Defiance St., 43502. Phone: (419) 445-9050. Fax: (419) 445-3531.E-mail: wmtr@rtecexpress.net Web Site:www.961wmtr.com Licensee: Nobco Inc. Population served: 125,000 Natl. Network: Westwood One, . Rgnl. Network: Agri Bcstg. Natl. Rep: Rgnl Reps,. Hogan & Hartson. Format: Adult top-40. News staff: one; News: 8 hrs wkly. Target aud: 25-54. ♦Max E. Smith Sr., pres; Max E. Smith Jr., gen mgr; Mark Knapp, mus dir; Larry Christy, news dir.

Ashland

WNCO(AM)— 1949: 1340 khz; 1 kw-U. TL: N40 50 25 W82 21 18. Hrs open: 24 1197 US Hwy. 42, 44805. Phone: (419) 289-2605. Phone: (419) 526-5825. Fax: (419) 289-0304. Web Site:www.wncoam.com Licensee: Capstar TX L.P. Group owner: Clear Channel Communications Inc. (acq 2-12-2001; grpsl). Population served: 53,900 Natl. Rep: Rgnl Reps,. Arent, Fox, Kintner, Plotkin & Kahn. Format: Talk. News staff: 2; News: 20 hrs wkly. Target aud: 35 plus. Spec prog: Farm 3 hrs wkly. ♦Diana Coon, gen mgr.

WNCO-FM— May 1947: 101.3 mhz; 50 kw. 500 ft TL: N40 50 25 W82 21 18. Stereo. Hrs open: 24 Prog sep from AM 1197 US Hwy. 42, 44805. Phone: (419) 289-2605. Fax: (419) 289-0304. Licensee: Capstar TX LP Population served: 230,000 Format: Country. News staff: 3; News: 14 hrs wkly. Target aud: 25 plus. ♦Dean Stampfli, opns dir, mktg dir; Martin Larsen, sls dir; Darla Stampfli, prom mgr, pub affrs dir; Lori Johnson, traf mgr; Gene Davis, local news ed; Steve Crabtree, sports cmtr.

***WRDL(FM)**— Aug 24, 1967: 88.9 mhz; 3 kw. 171 ft TL: N40 51 41 W82 19 11. Stereo. Hrs open: 6 AM-1 AM 401 College Ave., 44805. Phone: (419) 289-5678. Phone: (419) 289-5311. Fax: (419) 289-5329. Licensee: Ashland University. Population served: 250,000 Format: Rock, educ. News: 7 hrs wkly. Target aud: 18-35; general. Spec prog: Christian contemp 7 hrs, jazz 5 hrs, oldies 4 hrs wkly. ♦Dr. G. William Benz, pres; Tom Griffiths, gen mgr & chief of engrg.

Ashtabula

WFUN(AM)— November 1937: 970 khz; 5 kw-D, 1 kw-N, DA-2. TL: N41 48 52 W80 46 45. Hrs open: 24 3226 Jefferson Rd., 44004. Phone: (440) 993-2126. Fax: (440) 992-2658.E-mail: info@wfunam97.com Web Site:www.wfunam97.com Licensee: Sweet Home Ashtabula LLC. Group owner: Clear Channel Communications Inc. (acq 9-17-2007; grpsl). Natl. Network: ESPN Radio, . Format: Sports. Target aud: General. ♦Dana Schulte, VP; Dennis Brockman, pres & opns dir.

***WLGO(FM)**—Not on air, target date: unknown: 91.7 mhz; 4.5 kw. Ant 299 ft TL: N41 50 57.8 W80 42 20.7. Hrs open: 4459 Lake Road East, Geneva, 44041. Licensee: Lamb of God Communications. Natl. Network: EWTN Radio, . ♦Mary Malloy, pres.

WREO-FM— 1949: 97.1 mhz; 50 kw. 500 ft TL: N41 48 58 W80 46 52. Stereo. Hrs open: Prog sep from AM 3226 Jefferson Rd., 44004. Phone: (440) 993-2126. Fax: (440) 992-2658.E-mail: star97@star97.com Web Site:www.star97.com Population served: 1,200,000 Format: Adult contemp. Target aud: 25-54; professionals. ♦Dennis O'Brien, progmg dir.

WYBL(FM)— 2005: 98.3 mhz; 5.3 kw. Ant 344 ft TL: N41 50 23 W80 44 36. Hrs open: 3226 Jefferson Rd., 44004-9112. Phone: (440) 993-2126. Fax: (440) 992-2658. Web Site:www.983thebull.com Licensee: Sweet Home Ashtabula LLC. Group owner: Clear Channel Communications Inc. (acq 9-17-2007; grpsl). Format: News. ♦Dana Schulte, gen mgr.

WZOO-FM—See Edgewood

Athens

WATH(AM)— Oct 25, 1950: 970 khz; 1 kw-D, 160 w-N. TL: N39 20 40 W82 06 21. Hrs open: 24 Box 210, 45701. Secondary address: 300 Columbus Rd. 45701. Phone: (740) 593-6651. Phone: (740) 593-7982 (News). Fax: (740) 594-3488.E-mail: palmerd@wxtq.com Web Site:www.970wath.com Licensee: WATH Inc. (acq 9-5-73; with co-located FM). Population served: 155,000 Natl. Network: CBS Radio, . Natl. Rep: Rgnl Reps,. Rgnl rep: Rgnl Reps. Pepper & Corazzini. Wire Svc: AP Format: MOR, news/talk, sports. News staff: 3; News: 25 hrs wkly. Target aud: 40+. Spec prog: Big band 15 hrs wkly. ♦David W. Palmer, pres; Bob Stilson, VP; Thom Williams, gen mgr, stn mgr; Marianne Williams, natl sls mgr; Bob Beyette, news dir; Zahid Mumtaz, chief of engrg; Robin Barnes, pub svc dir.

WJKW(FM)— Sept 1, 1998: 95.9 mhz; 6 kw. 199 ft TL: N39 22 37 W81 57 46. Hrs open: 24 3809 Maple Ave., Castalia, 44824. Phone: (740) 592-9879. Fax: (740) 592-9952.E-mail: wjkw@cfbroadcast.net Licensee: Christian Faith Broadcast Inc. Group owner: Christian Faith Broadcasting Inc. Joseph E. Dunne III. Format: Adult contemp, Christian. Target aud: 25-44. ♦Rusty Yost, gen mgr; Kevin Ingle, stn mgr.

***WOUB(AM)**— Sept 14, 1957: 1340 khz; 500 w-D, 1 kw-N. TL: N39 19 45 W82 05 29. Stereo. Hrs open: 24 9 S. College St., 45701. Phone: (740) 593-4554. Fax: (740) 593-0240.E-mail: woub@woub.org Web Site:www.woub.org Licensee: Ohio University. Population served: 7,500 Natl. Network: NPR, PRI, . Format: News/talk, progsv. News staff: 3. Spec prog: Black 8 hrs wkly. ♦Carolyn Lewis, gen mgr; David Wiseman, opns VP, engrg VP; Steve Skidmore, opns dir; Scott Martin, opns mgr; Doug Partusch, mktg dir; Bryan Gibson, progmg dir, progmg mgr; Tim Sharp, news dir; Ted Ross, engrg dir.

***WOUB-FM**— Dec 13, 1949: 91.3 mhz; 50 kw. 500 ft TL: N39 18 50 W82 08 54. Stereo. Hrs open: 24 Prog sep from AM 9 S. College St. , 45701. Phone: (740) 593-4554. Fax: (740) 593-0240.E-mail: woub@woub.org Web Site:www.woub.org Licensee: Ohio University Population served: 70,000 Wire Svc: UPI Format: Adult contemp. News staff: 3. ♦Rusty Smith, progmg mgr; Jan Sole, asst music dir. Co-owned TV: *WOUB-TV affil.

WXTQ(FM)— Sept 16, 1964: 105.5 mhz; 6 kw. Ant 312 ft TL: N39 21 18 W82 05 32. Stereo. Hrs open: 24 Box 210, 45701. Secondary address: 300 Columbus Rd. 45701. Phone: (740) 593-6651. Phone: (740) 593-7982 (News). Fax: (740) 594-3488. Web Site:www.wxtq.com Licensee: WATH Inc. (acq 9-5-73). Population served: 100,000 Natl. Rep: Rgnl Reps,. Rgnl rep: Rgnl Reps Pepper & Corazzini. Wire Svc: AP Format: Hot adult Contemporary. News staff: 2; News: 5 hrs wkly. Target aud: 18-34. Spec prog: Ohio University Sports. ♦Dave Palmer, pres; Thom Williams, opns mgr; Kathy Malesick, gen sls mgr; Bob Beyette, news dir; Zahid Mumtaz, chief of engrg.

Bainbridge

***WKHR(FM)**— May 6, 1977: 91.5 mhz; 1.1 kw. 269 ft TL: N41 23 42 W81 18 25. (CP: 100 w). Stereo. Hrs open: Kenston High School,

17425 Snyder Rd., Chagrin Falls, 44023. Phone: (440) 543-9646. Fax: (440) 543-9012.E-mail: info@wkhr.com Web Site:www.wkhr.org Licensed: Kenston Local School District. Population served: 1,500,000 Format: Big band. Target aud: 55 plus; well established, mature. ◆Chris Kofron, gen mgr, opns dir & dev dir.

Barnesville

WBNV(FM)— July 1, 1991: 93.5 mhz; 6 kw. 489 ft TL: N39 54 10 W81 12 37. Stereo. Hrs open: 24 Box 338, 4988 Skyline Dr., Cambridge, 43725. Secondary address: Box 293, 175 E. Main St. 43713-0293. Phone: (740) 484-4430. Fax: (740) 425-9268. Fax: (740) 432-1991. Web Site:www.yourradioplace.com Licensed: W. Grant Hafley. Population served: 100,000 Natl. Network: USA, . Natl. Rep: Rgnl Reps,. Format: Adult contemp. News: 15 hrs wkly. Target aud: 25-54. ◆W. Grant Hafley, gen mgr; David L. Wilson, opns mgr.

Batavia

*WOBO(FM)— July 30, 1981: 88.7 mhz; 15.5 kw. 428 ft TL: N39 03 43 W84 05 50. Stereo. Hrs open: 24 Box 338, Owensville, 45160. Phone: (513) 724-3939/724-2969.E-mail: df1littman@cs.com Web Site:www.wobofm.com Licensed: Educational Community Radio Inc. Population served: 1,000,000 Format: Var/div. Target aud: 35 plus. Spec prog: Ger 5 hrs, Scottish one hr, Celtic 3 hrs, Pol 3 hrs wkly. ◆Mel Reifan, pres.

Beach City

*WOFN(FM)— Sept 27, 2000: 88.7 mhz; 3.3 kw horiz, 21 kw vert. Ant 358 ft TL: N40 35 41 W81 34 39. Stereo. Hrs open: 24 Box 1924, Tulsa, OK, 74101. Secondary address: 4916 Spruce Hill Dr., Suite 400, Canton 44617. Phone: (330) 244-9151. Phone: (918) 455-5693. Fax: (330) 244-0153.E-mail: mail@oasisnetwork.org Web Site:www.oasisnetwork.org Licensed: Creative Educational Media Corp. Inc. Format: Relg. Target aud: General. ◆David Ingles, pres; Bobbie Cook, gen mgr.

Beavercreek

WXEG(FM)— June 18, 1972: 103.9 mhz; 1.15 kw. 522 ft TL: N39 44 12 W84 09 25. Stereo. Hrs open: 24 101 Pine St., Dayton, 45402. Phone: (937) 224-1137. Fax: (937) 224-3667.E-mail: info@ccedayton.com Web Site:www.wxeg.com Licensed: Citicasters Licenses L.P. Group owner: Clear Channel Communications Inc. (acq 1999; grpsl). Population served: 830,200 Format: Alternative rock. News staff: one. Target aud: 18-34. ◆Robert Zurowesti, VP, gen mgr, mktg mgr; Steve Kramer, progmg dir.

Bellaire

WOMP(AM)— Dec 2, 1947: 1290 khz; 1 kw-D, 33 w-N. TL: N40 02 09 W80 46 16. Hrs open: 24 Box 448, Rt. 214, 56325 High Ridge Rd., 43906. Phone: (740) 676-5661. Fax: (740) 676-2742.E-mail: kool105@hotmail.com Licensed: Keymarket Licenses LLC. Group owner: Keymarket Communications LLC (acq 1-15-93; $575,000 with co-located FM;1-25-93). Population served: 156,400 Natl. Network: ESPN Radio, . Natl. Rep: Rgnl Reps,. Fleischman & Walsh L. Format: Sports. News staff: 2; News: 20 hrs wkly. Spec prog: Pol 2 hrs, Czech 2 hrs wkly. ◆Gerald Getz, pres; John Crawford, gen mgr.

WYJK-FM— 1947: 100.5 mhz; 48 kw. Ant 518 ft TL: N40 02 09 W80 46 16. Stereo. Hrs open: 24 Box 448, Rt. 214, 43906. Phone: (740) 676-5661. Fax: (740) 671-4487. Web Site:www.wompfm.com Licensed: Keymarket Licenses LLC. Wire Svc: AP Format: CHR. News staff: one. Target aud: 18-44; educated adults.

Bellefontaine

WBLL(AM)— 1951: 1390 khz; 500 w-D, 81 w-N. TL: N40 22 05 W83 44 02. Hrs open: 24 1501 Rd. 235, 43311-9506. Phone: (937) 592-1045. Fax: (937) 592-3299.E-mail: cwilkinson@wbll.com Web Site:www.wbll.com Licensed: V-Teck Communications Inc. (acq 12-2-87; grpsl; 10-19-87). Natl. Network: ABC, ESPN Radio, . Natl. Network: Agri Bcstg. Natl. Rep: Rgnl Reps,. ABN Radio Wire Svc: AP Format: News/talk, sports. News staff: 2; News: 126 hrs wkly. Target aud: General. Spec prog: Relg 6 hrs wkly. ◆Lou Vito, pres; Amie Huffman, gen mgr, adv dir, traf mgr; Chad Wilkinson, opns mgr, gen sls mgr, pub affrs dir; Sheryl Godwin, dev dir; Ken Keller, prom dir; Bill Tipple, news dir, news rptr, sports cmtr; Bill Bowin, chief of engrg; Jamie Ross, reporter.

WPKO-FM— July 15, 1969: 98.3 mhz; 1.75 kw. Ant 430 ft TL: N40 22 05 W83 44 02. Stereo. Hrs open: 24 1501 Rd. 235, 43311. Phone: (937) 592-1045. Fax: (973) 592-3299.E-mail: cwilkinson@wpko.com Web Site:www.wpko.com Format: Adult contemp. News staff: 2. Target aud: 12 plus. ◆Pam Allen, mktg dir & mktg mgr; Chad Wilkinson, mus dir, disc jockey; Louie Vito, asst music dir; Bill Bowin, engrg dir; Ken Keller, disc jockey.

Bellevue

WOHF(FM)— Apr 4, 1973: 92.1 mhz; 6 kw. Ant 328 ft TL: N41 14 19 W82 50 16. Stereo. Hrs open: 24 1281 North River Road, Fremont, 43420. Phone: (419) 332-8218. Fax: (419) 333-8226. Web Site:www.wohfradio.com Licensed: BAS Broadcasting Inc. (acq 10-1-2003; $550,000). Population served: 54,000 Natl. Network: ABC, . Rgnl. Network: Agri-Net. ABN Radio Rgnl rep: Rgnl Reps Format: Classic hits. News staff: one; News: 5 hrs wkly. ◆Tom Klein, CEO; Jim Lorenzen, pres.

Belpre

*WCVV(FM)— 1986: 89.5 mhz; 4.4 kw. Ant 384 ft TL: N39 19 27 W81 37 33. Stereo. Hrs open: 24 Box 405, 45714. Phone: (740) 423-5895. Fax: (740) 423-9951. Licensed: Belpre Educ. Broadcasting Foundation. Format: Christian, news. Target aud: General. ◆Clay Sloan, gen mgr, stn mgr; Ralph Matheny, chief of engrg.

*WLKP(FM)— May 1991: 91.9 mhz; 4.5 kw. Ant 325 ft TL: N39 20 46 W81 29 55. Hrs open: 2351 Sunset Blvd., Suite 170- 218, Rocklin, CA, 95765. Phone: (916) 251-1600. Fax: (916) 251-1650. Web Site:www.klove.com Licensed: Educational Media Foundation. (acq 3-31-2005; $700,000 with WLKV(FM) Ripley, WV). Natl. Network: K-Love, . Format: Christian. ◆Richard Jenkins, pres; Mike Novak, VP, news dir; Keith Whipple, dev dir; David Pierce, progmg mgr; Sam Wallington, engrg dir; Karen Johnson, news rptr.

WNUS(FM)— Sept 12, 1981: 107.1 mhz; 4.7 kw. 370 ft TL: N39 18 36 W81 35 49. Stereo. Hrs open: 24 Box 5559, Vienna, WV, 26105. Secondary address: 6006 Grand Central Ave., Vienna, WV 26105. Phone: (304) 295-9441. Phone: (740) 423-9687. Fax: (304) 295-4389.E-mail: roadcrew@wnus.com Web Site:www.wnus.com Licensed: CC Licenses LLC. Group owner: Clear Channel Communications Inc. (acq 4-17-2001; grpsl). Rgnl. Network: Ohio Radio Net., Metronews Radio Net. Natl. Rep: Clear Channel,. Format: Country. News staff: 2; News: 2 hrs wkly. Target aud: 18 plus. ◆Chuck Poet, gen mgr.

Berea

*WBWC(FM)— Mar 2, 1958: 88.3 mhz; 5 kw. Ant 256 ft TL: N41 25 05 W81 54 03. Stereo. Hrs open: 19 275 Eastland Rd., 44017. Phone: (440) 826-2145. Fax: (440) 826-3426.E-mail: jtaranto@bw.edu Web Site:www.wbwc.com Licensed: Baldwin-Wallace College. Population served: 1,400,000 Natl. Network: AP Radio, . Format: Modern rock. Target aud: 12-25; alternative mus listeners. ◆Allen Thompson, opns dir.

Bowling Green

*WBGU(FM)— November 1951: 88.1 mhz; 450 w. 178 ft TL: N41 22 33 W83 38 34. Hrs open: 24 120 W. Hall Bowling Green Univ., 43403. Phone: (419) 372-8657. Fax: (419) 372-0202. Web Site:www.wbgufm.com Licensed: Bowling Green State University. Population served: 110,000 Format: Div, jazz, Black. News: 7 hrs wkly. Target aud: General. Spec prog: Country 4 hrs, class 3 hrs, folk 4 hrs, Sp 4 hrs wkly. ◆Keely Miller, gen mgr; Jim Davis, chief of engrg. Co-owned TV: *WBGU-TV affil.

WJYM(AM)— December 1964: 730 khz; 1 kw-D, 359 w-N, DA-2. TL: N41 31 57 W83 33 55. Hrs open: 6 AM-midnight Box 262550, Baton Rouge, LA, 70826. Phone: (225) 768-3202. Fax: (225) 768-3729.E-mail: kawikfish@yahoo.com Web Site:www.jsm.org Licensed: Family Worship Center Church Inc. (group owner; acq 12-15-99). Population served: 5,000,000 Natl. Network: USA, . Format: Relg. News: 3 hrs wkly. Target aud: 25-49. ◆David Whitelaw, COO.

*WNOC(FM)—Not on air, target date: unknown: 89.7 mhz; 3.8 kw. Ant 312 ft TL: N41 24 33 W83 32 05. Hrs open: 350 Clark St., Toledo, 43605. Licensed: Ministry to Catholic Charismatic Renewal. ◆Roy Handy, gen mgr.

WRQN(FM)— June 1964: 93.5 mhz; 7 kw. Ant 397 ft TL: N41 27 28 W83 39 33. Hrs open: 3225 Arlington Ave., Toledo, 43614. Phone: (419) 725-5700. Fax: (419) 385-2902.E-mail: info@935wrqn.com Web Site:www.935wrqn.com Licensed: Cumulus Licensing Corp. Group

owner: Cumulus Media Inc. (acq 9-11-97; grpsl). Population served: 135,000 Format: Oldies. Target aud: 25-54. Spec prog: Pub service one hr wkly. ◆Skip Schmidt, gen mgr & stn mgr; Ron Finn, opns mgr, progmg dir.

Bridgeport

*WXHZ(FM)—Not on air, target date: unknown: 91.1 mhz; 125 w. Ant 157 ft TL: N40 06 31.7 W80 43 03.7. Hrs open: Box 5204, Wilmington, DE, 19808-5204. Phone: (302) 540-5690. Fax: (302) 738-3090. Web Site:www.thereachfm.com Licensed: Priority Radio Inc. ◆Steve Hare, gen mgr.

Brunswick

*WKJA(FM)—Not on air, target date: unknown: 91.9 mhz; 25 kw. Ant 318 ft TL: N40 54 56 W81 55 56. Hrs open: 3232 W. MacArthur Blvd., Santa Ana, CA, 92704. Phone: (714) 825-9663. Fax: (714) 825-9660. Licensed: CSN International. ◆Jeffrey W. Smith, pres.

Bryan

WBNO-FM— June 30, 1966: 100.9 mhz; 6 kw. Ant 299 ft TL: N41 28 44 W84 34 50. Hrs open: 24 12810 State Rd. 34, 43506-8809. Phone: (419) 636-3175. Fax: (419) 636-4570.E-mail: wbno@wbno-wqct.com Licensed: Impact Radio LLC (acq 8-1-2002; grpsl). Population served: 120,000 Natl. Network: ABC, . Rgnl rep: Rgnl Reps Irwin, Campbell & Tannenwald, P.C. Wire Svc: AP Format: Classic hits. News staff: one; News: 27 hrs wkly. Target aud: 25-54; loc oriented. ◆Dennis Rumsey, pres & gen mgr.

*WGBE(FM)— 1996: 90.9 mhz; 850 w. 387 ft TL: N41 28 30 W84 35 14. Hrs open: 24
Rebroadcasts WGTE-FM Toledo 100%.
1270 S. Detroit Ave., Toledo, 43614. Phone: (419) 380-4600. Fax: (419) 380-4710.E-mail: info@wgte.org Web Site:www.wgte.org Licensed: The Public Broadcasting Foundation of Northwest Ohio. Population served: 30,800 Natl. Network: NPR, PRI, . Schwartz, Woods & Miller. Format: Class, pub affrs, news. News: 23 hrs wkly. Target aud: General. Spec prog: Jazz 16 hrs wkly. ◆Marlon P. Kiser, CEO, pres, gen mgr; George Jones, chmn; Chris Pfeiffer, opns mgr; Ross Pffeiffer, dev dir.

WQCT(AM)— December 1962: 1520 khz; 500 w-D, 5 w-N, 250 w-CH. TL: N41 28 43 W84 34 49. Hrs open: 24 12810 State Rd. 34, 43506-8809. Phone: (419) 636-3175. Fax: 419) 636-4570. Licensed: Impact Radio LLC (group owner; . Population served: 120,000 Rgnl. Network: Agri Bcstg. Rgnl rep: Rgnl Reps Irwin, Campbell & Tannenwald, P.C. Format: Oldies. News staff: one; News: 3 hrs wkly. Target aud: 35-65; general.

Buchtel

WAIS(AM)— Dec 3, 1984: 770 khz; 1 kw-D. TL: N39 25 56 W82 12 02. Hrs open: Sunrise-sunset 15751 U.S. Rt. 33 S., Nelsonville, 45764. Phone: (740) 753-4094. Fax: (740) 753-4965.E-mail: wseo33@sbcglobal.net Licensed: Nelsonville TV Cable Inc. Natl. Network: ABC, . Frank Jazzo. Format: News/talk. News staff: 3; News: 21 hrs wkly. Target aud: 35 plus. Spec prog: Farm 5 hrs, gospel 3 hrs wkly. ◆Eugene Edwards, pres, gen mgr; Sharon Elliott, stn mgr.

Bucyrus

WBCO(AM)— Dec 22, 1962: 1540 khz; 500 w-D, DA. TL: N40 45 47 W82 56 05. Hrs open: Box 1140, 403 East Rensselaer St., 44820-1140. Phone: (419) 562-2222. Fax: (419) 562-0520.E-mail: comment@wqel.com Licensed: Franklin Communications Inc. Group owner: Saga Communications Inc. (acq 12-1-2003; $2.2 million with co-located FM). Population served: 30,000 Natl. Network: CBS, . Rgnl. Network: Agri Bcstg. Natl. Rep: Rgnl Reps,. Format: Adult standards. News staff: one; News: 25 hrs wkly. Target aud: 30-60. Spec prog: Farm 4 hrs, relg 4 hrs wkly. ◆Debbi Gifford, gen mgr, stn mgr, sls dir, prom dir; Dave Jones, gen sls mgr; Jim Radke, progmg dir, news dir, pub affrs rptr; Bill Bowin, chief of engrg; Sharon Shealy, traf mgr & farm dir.

WQEL(FM)— Sept 5, 1964: 92.7 mhz; 3 kw. 300 ft TL: N40 45 45 W82 55 50. Hrs open: 24 Prog sep from AM Box 1140, 403 East Rensselaer St., 44820. Phone: (419) 562-2222. Fax: (419) 562-0520. Natl. Network: CBS, . Natl. Rep: Rgnl Reps,. Format: Classic rock, sports. News staff: 2; News: 10 hrs wkly. Target aud: 25-54. ◆Jim Hahn, disc jockey.

Byesville

WILE-FM— Oct 29, 1994: 97.7 mhz; 1.8 kw. 413 ft TL: N40 02 24 W81 38 50. Hrs open: 24 Box 338, Cambridge, 43725. Secondary address: 4988 Skyline Dr., Cambridge 43725. Phone: (740) 432-5605. Fax: (740) 432-1991. Web Site:www.yourradioplace.com Licensee: AVC Communications Inc. (group owner; acq 7-13-00). Format: Adult standard. ◆Joel Losego, gen mgr; Dave Wilson, opns dir.

Cadiz

WCDK(FM)— Aug 28, 1985: 106.3 mhz; 6 kw. 360 ft TL: N40 15 14 W80 50 35. Stereo. Hrs open: 24 2307 Pennsylvania Ave., Weirton, WV, 26062. Phone: (304) 723-1444. Fax: (304) 723-1688.E-mail: wcdk@weir.net Web Site:www.106.3theriver.com Licensee: Priority Communications Ohio LLC. Group owner: Priority Communications (acq 12-98; $475,000 with WEIR(AM) Weirton, WV). Population served: 249,000 Natl. Network: Jones Radio Networks, . Natl. Rep: Dome,. Pepper & Corazzini. Format: Classic hits. News staff: one; News: 5 hrs wkly. Target aud: 25-54; general. Spec prog: OSU football, Cleveland Browns football, high school football. ◆Jay M. Philippone, pres, gen mgr; Jude Sheets, opns mgr; Judy Vavrek, stn mgr & sls dir.

Caldwell

WWKC(FM)— July 1, 1989: 104.9 mhz; 3 kw. 300 ft TL: N39 48 47 W81 56 38. Stereo. Hrs open: 24 Box 338, Cambridge, 43725. Secondary address: Box 19 43724. Phone: (740) 432-5605. Phone: (740) 732-7555. Fax: (740) 432-1991 . Web Site:www.yourradioplace.com Licensee: W. Grant Hafley. (acq 8-23-89; $15,000; 9-18-89). Rgnl. Network: Agri Bcstg. Natl. Rep: Rgnl Reps,. Format: Country. Target aud: 25-54. ◆W. Grant Hafley, gen mgr; David L. Wilson, opns mgr.

Caledonia

WYNT(FM)— Oct 1, 1986: 95.9 mhz; 4.6 kw. Ant 374 ft TL: N40 40 55 W83 00 27. Stereo. Hrs open: 19 1330 No. Main St., Marion, 43302. Phone: (740) 383-1131. Fax: (740) 387-3697. Web Site:www.majic959.com Licensee: CC Licenses LLC. Group owner: Clear Channel Communications Inc. (acq 4-2-2002; $825,000). Rgnl. Network: Agri Bcstg. Format: Adult contemp. Target aud: 27 plus; general. Spec prog: Farm 3 hrs wkly. ◆Diana Coon, gen mgr; Steve Scott, progmg dir; James Howell, news dir.

Cambridge

WCMJ(FM)— October 1964: 96.7 mhz; 2.3 kw. Ant 367 ft TL: N40 02 24 W81 38 50. Stereo. Hrs open: Box 338, 43725. Secondary address: 4988 Skyline Dr. 43725. Phone: (740) 432-5605. Fax: (740) 432-1991. Web Site:www.wcmj.com Licensee: AVC Communications Inc. (acq 5-5-83). Rgnl rep: Rgnl Reps Format: Adult contemp. News: 2. Target aud: 18-49. ◆Joel Losego, gen mgr.

WILE(AM)— Apr 9, 1948: 1270 khz; 1 kw-D. TL: N40 02 24 W81 38 50. Hrs open: 6505 County Road 109, Mt. Gilead, 43338. Phone: (419) 946-0016. Web Site:www.yourradioplace.com Licensee: St. Gabriel Radio Inc. (group owner; acq 8-29-2007; $750,000). Population served: 80,000 Natl. Network: ESPN Radio, . Format: Sports. Target aud: 25-54. ◆Christopher Gabrelcik, pres.

*WOUC-FM— May 11, 1987: 89.1 mhz; 5 kw. 500 ft TL: N40 05 32 W81 17 19. Stereo. Hrs open: 24
Rebroadcasts WOUB-FM Athens 100%.
9 S. College St., Athens, 45701. Phone: (740) 593-4554. Fax: (740) 593-0240.E-mail: woub@woub.org Web Site:www.woub.org Licensee: Ohio University. Natl. Network: PRI, NPR, . Format: News/talk. News staff: 3. ◆Carolyn Lewis, gen mgr; David Wiseman, opns VP; Steve Skidmore, opns dir; Scott Martin, opns mgr. Co-owned TV: *WOUC-TV affil

Campbell

WGFT(AM)—Licensed to Campbell. See Youngstown

WHOT-FM—See Youngstown

Canton

WCER(AM)— 1947: 900 khz; 500 w-D, 78 w-N. TL: N40 49 17 W81 25 34. Stereo. Hrs open: 4537 22nd St. N.W., 44708. Phone: (330) 478-6655. Fax: (330) 478-6651.E-mail: wcer@wcer.us Web Site:www.wcer.us Licensee: Melodynamic Broadcasting Corp. (acq 7-11-91; $85,000;7-29-91). Natl. Network: USA, . Format: Information, news/talk, sports. Spec prog: Farm 6 hrs, gospel 11 hrs, relg 5 hrs wkly. ◆Jack Ambrozic, gen mgr; Jeff Caldwell, progmg dir.

WDJQ(FM)—See Alliance

WDPN(AM)—See Alliance

WHBC(AM)— Mar 9, 1925: 1480 khz; 5 kw-U, DA-2. TL: N40 43 15 W81 26 28. Stereo. Hrs open: 550 Market Ave. S., 44702. Phone: (330) 456-7166. Fax: (330) 456-7199.E-mail: pcook@whbc.com Web Site:www.whbc.com Licensee: NM Licensing LLC. Group owner: NextMedia Group L.L.C. (acq 9-30-2000; with WHBC-FM Canton). Natl. Rep: Christal,. Cohn & Marks. Format: Full service, oldies. Target aud: 25 plus. Spec prog: Farm one hr wkly. ◆Richard Bossler, gen mgr.

WHBC-FM— Feb 2, 1948: 94.1 mhz; 50 kw. Ant 500 ft TL: N40 53 53 W81 19 07. Stereo. Hrs open: 550 Market Ave. S., 44702. Phone: (330) 456-7166. Fax: (330) 456-7199.E-mail: pcook@whbc.com Web Site:www.mix941.com Licensee: NM Licensing LLC. (acq 9-30-2000; with WHBC(AM) Canton). Format: Adult contemp. Target aud: 25-54. ◆ Terry Simmons, progmg dir.

WILB(AM)— Aug 11, 1946: 1060 khz; 5 kw-D, DA. TL: N40 50 04 W81 25 46. Hrs open: 4365 Fulton Dr. N.W., 44718. Phone: (330) 966-2903. Fax: (330) 966-3177. Web Site:www.livingbreadradio.com Licensee: Living Bread Radio Inc. (acq 7-1-2004; $300,000). Population served: 100,500 Format: Catholic talk. ◆Barbara Gaskell, pres; Kate Sell, stn mgr; Dan Clark, opns mgr.

WINW(AM)— Apr 14, 1966: 1520 khz; 1 kw-D, DA. TL: N40 50 41 W81 21 02. Hrs open: Sunrise-sunset 237 W. Tuscarawas, 44705. Phone: (330) 453-1520. Fax: (330) 454-3030.E-mail: christfirst@joy1520.com Web Site:www.joy1520.com Licensee: Pinebrook Corp. (acq 9-27-96; $75,000). Natl. Rep: Rgnl Reps,. Format: Gospel. Target aud: 35-54; professionals. ◆Patrick Barb, pres; Curtis Perry, gen mgr.

WKDD(FM)— Nov 19, 1961: 98.1 mhz; 50 kw. Ant 344 ft TL: N40 57 10 W81 19 20. Stereo. Hrs open: 24 7755 Freedom Ave. N.W., North Canton, 44720. Phone: (330) 492-4700. Fax: (330) 492-1350.E-mail: info@wkdd.com Web Site:www.wkdd.com Licensee: Citicasters Licenses L.P. Group owner: Clear Channel Communications Inc. (acq 12-22-2000; grpsl). Population served: 1,000,000 Format: Hot adult contemp. ◆Dan Lankford, gen mgr; Vince Ing, gen sls mgr; Keith Kennedy, progmg dir; Tom Duresky, news dir; John Hovenec, chief of engrg; Ellen Force, traf mgr.

WRQK(FM)— Mar 1, 1961: 106.9 mhz; 27.5 kw. Ant 340 ft TL: N40 49 17 W81 25 34. Stereo. Hrs open: 24 7755 Freedom Ave. N.W., North Canton, 44720. Phone: (330) 492-4700. Fax: (330) 492-1350.E-mail: wrqk@wrqk.com Web Site:www.wrqk.com Licensee: Capstar TX L.P. Group owner: Cumulus Media Inc. (acq 3-15-00; grpsl). Population served: 335,000 Format: Mainstream rock. News: one hr wkly. Target aud: 18-49; emphasis on men. ◆Don Lankford, gen mgr.

Carrollton

*WJDD(FM)—Not on air, target date: unknown: 90.9 mhz; 200 w. Ant 499 ft TL: N40 34 17 W81 10 51. Hrs open: Box 7317, Canton, 44705. Phone: (330) 875-7181. Web Site:www.dennyhazen.com Licensee: Denny and Marge Hazen Ministries Inc. ◆Denny Hazen, pres.

Castalia

WGGN(FM)— January 1975: 97.7 mhz; 1.25 kw. 660 ft TL: N41 23 48 W82 47 31. Hrs open: 24 3809 Maple Ave., 44824. Secondary address: P. O. Box 247 44824. Phone: (419) 684-5311. Fax: (419) 684-5378.E-mail: fm977@cfbroadcast.net Licensee: Christian Faith Broadcasting Inc. (group owner). Population served: 750,000 Natl. Network: USA, . Format: Adult contemp Christian. Target aud: 25-49; general. ◆Shelby Gillam, pres; Rusty Yost, gen mgr; Jeff Ferback, gen sls mgr; Dave Yost, prom dir, progmg dir.

Cedarville

*WCDR-FM— Dec 1, 1962: 90.3 mhz; 30 kw. 354 ft TL: N39 45 46 W83 53 05. Stereo. Hrs open: 24 Box 601, 45314-0601. Phone: (937) 766-7815. Fax: (937) 766-7927.E-mail: info@thepath.fm Web Site:www.thepath.fm Licensee: The Cedarville University. Population served: 400,000 Natl. Network: AP Radio, CNN Radio, Moody, . Format: Relg, full service. News staff: one; News: 16 hrs wkly. Target aud: 35-54. Spec prog: Black 2 hrs wkly. ◆William Brown, pres; Martin Clark, VP; Marv Sparks, gen mgr; Keith Hamer, opns mgr.

Celina

WCSM(AM)— Sept 11, 1963: 1350 khz; 500 w-D, 11 w-N, DA-1. TL: N40 32 17 W84 35 20. Hrs open: 24 Box 492, Meyers & Schunck Rds., 45822. Phone: (419) 586-5134. Fax: (419) 586-3814.E-mail: wcsm@bright.net Web Site:www.wcsmradio.com Licensee: Hayco Broadcasting Inc. (acq 1977). Population served: 80,000 Rgnl. Network: Ohio News Network, Agri-Net. Agrinet News staff: one; News: 20 hrs wkly. Target aud: 18-49. ◆John H. Coe, pres, gen mgr; Sue Heiser, gen sls mgr; Jim Hyatt, progmg dir, mus dir; Kevin Sandler, news dir, chief of engrg.

WCSM-FM— 1968: 96.7 mhz; 3 kw. Ant 328 ft TL: N40 33 08 W84 30 46. Hrs open: 24 Prog sep from AM Box 492, Meyers & Schunck Rds., 45822. Phone: (419) 586-5134. Fax: (419) 586-3814.E-mail: wcsm@bright.net Population served: 100,000 Natl. Network: ABC, Jones Radio Networks, . Rgnl. Network: Ohio Radio Net, Agri-Net. Agrinet Format: Sports.

WKKI(FM)— Dec 18, 1960: 94.3 mhz; 2.2 kw. 448 ft TL: N40 33 08 W84 30 46. Hrs open: 24 126 W. Fayette St., 45822. Phone: (419) 586-7715. Fax: (419) 586-1074.E-mail: k94@bright.net Web Site:www.wkki.net Licensee: The Sonshine Communications Corp. (acq 5-26-2004; $370,000 for stock). Population served: 250,000 Natl. Network: CNN Radio, Westwood One, . Natl. Rep: Roslin, Rgnl Reps,. Format: Adult contemp, sports. Target aud: 25-54. Spec prog: Contemp Christian 2 hrs wkly. ◆Paul Schmitmeyer, pres, pres & gen mgr; Hilany Dickey, stn mgr; Dan Dietz, chief of opns; Brian Mathews, progmg dir.

Centerville

*WCWT-FM— Sept 20, 1971: 101.5 mhz; 10 w. 110 ft TL: N39 37 39 W84 09 57. (CP: Ant 194 ft.). Hrs open: 500 E. Franklin, 45459. Phone: (937) 439-3558. Phone: (937) 439-3557. Fax: (937) 439-3574.E-mail: wcwt@centerville.k12.oh.us Licensee: Centerville City Board of Education. Population served: 30000 Format: Classic rock. Target aud: General. ◆Bob Romond, gen mgr & progmg dir.

Chillicothe

WBEX(AM)— September 1947: 1490 khz; 1 kw-U. TL: N39 19 56 W82 59 50. Hrs open: 24 Box 94, 45601. Secondary address: 45 W.Main St. 45601. Phone: (740) 773-3000. Fax: (740) 774-4494.E-mail: newsroom@wkkj.com Web Site:www.wbex.com Licensee: Citicasters Licenses L.P. Group owner: Clear Channel Communications Inc. (acq 1999; grpsl). Population served: 65,000 Natl. Network: CBS, Westwood One, . Natl. Rep: Katz Radio,. Format: News/talk, full service. News staff: 3; News: 10 hrs wkly. Target aud: 30-50. ◆Dan Latham, VP, gen mgr; Tracy Taylor, sls dir; Dan Ramey, progmg dir.

WCHI(AM)— Oct 1, 1951: 1350 khz; 1 kw-D, 28 w-N. TL: N39 19 13 W82 57 03. Hrs open: Box 94, 45 W. Main St., 45601. Phone: (740) 775-1350. Phone: (740) 773-3000. Fax: (740) 774-4494.E-mail: info@wchiam.com Web Site:www.wchiam.com Licensee: CC Licenses LLC. Group owner: Clear Channel Communications Inc. (acq 10-19-99; $4 million with co-located TM). Population served: 24,842 Natl. Network: ABC, . Natl. Rep: Katz Radio,. Format: Nostalgia. News staff: 2. Target aud: 25-65. ◆Dan Latham, gen mgr; Bob Neal, opns mgr; Tracy Taylor, sls dir.

WKKJ(FM)— Dec 22, 1978: 94.3 mhz; 25 kw. 266 ft TL: N39 19 52 W82 59 49. Stereo. Hrs open: 24 Prog sep from AM Box 94, 45 W. Main St., 45601. Phone: (740) 775-1350. Phone: (740) 773-3000. Fax: (740) 774-4494. Web Site:www.wkkj.com Natl. Network: ABC, . Format: Country. News staff: 3; News: 14 hrs wkly. ◆Dan Latham, VP; Mike Smith, news dir.

WLZT(FM)— July 1, 1961: 93.3 mhz; 50 kw. 335 ft TL: N39 19 52 W82 59 49. Stereo. Hrs open: 24 2323 W. Fifth Ave., Suite 200, Columbus, 43204. Phone: (614) 486-6101. Fax: (614) 487-2537.E-mail: info@933wlzt.com Web Site:www.933wlzt.com Licensee: CC Licenses LLC. Group owner: Clear Channel Communications Inc. (acq 4-11-2003). Population served: 100,000 Natl. Network: ABC, . Format: Adult contemp. News staff: 3. Target aud: 24-54. ◆Tom Thon, gen mgr; Dave Daugherty, gen sls mgr; Michael McCoy, progmg dir.

*WOHC(FM)— May 1, 1992: 90.1 mhz; 2 kw. 393 ft TL: N39 20 45 W83 11 15. Stereo. Hrs open: 24
Rebroadcasts WCDR(FM) Cedarville 100%.
Box 601, Cedarville, 45314. Phone: (937) 766-7815. Fax: (937) 766-7927.E-mail: info@thepath.fm Web Site:thepath.fm Licensee: The

Cedarville University. Natl. Network: AP Radio, CNN Radio, Moody, . Cohen & Berfield. Format: Relg, full service. News staff: one; News: 16 hrs wkly. Target aud: 35-54; information-oriented Christians and/or church members. Spec prog: Black 2 hrs wkly. ♦William Brown, pres; Marvin D. Sparks, gen mgr; Keith Hamer, opns mgr; Chad Bresson, news dir; John Tocknell, chief of engrg.

***WOUH-FM**— October 1992: 91.9 mhz; 750 w. 649 ft TL: N39 19 46 W82 48 08. Stereo. Hrs open: 24
Rebroadcasts WOUB-FM Athens 100%.
9 S. College St., Athens, 45701. Phone: (740) 593-4554. Fax: (740) 593-0240.E-mail: woub@woub.org Web Site:www.woub.org Licensee: Ohio University. Format: News/talk. News staff: 3. ♦Carolyn Lewis, gen mgr; David Wiseman, opns VP; Steve Skidmore, opns dir; Scott Martin, opns mgr; Tim Myers, progmg dir; Rusty Smith, progmg mgr; Tim Sharp, news dir; Kelly Martin, prom.

***WZCP(FM)**— Jan 15, 1988: 89.3 mhz; 2.5 kw. Ant 351 ft TL: N39 20 45 W83 11 15. Stereo. Hrs open: 24 881, East Johnstown Rd., Gahanna, 43230. Phone: 614-289-5700. Fax: 614-289-5793.E-mail: thepromise@promiseradionetwork.com Web Site:www.promiseradionetwork.com Licensee: Christian Voice of Central Ohio Inc. (acq 5-15-2007; grpsl). Rgnl. Network: Ohio Radio Net. Format: Christian talk, educ, Music. ♦Dan Baughman, gen mgr; Scott Saunders, progmg dir.

Cincinnati

WAKW(FM)— Nov 21, 1961: 93.3 mhz; 50 kw. 500 ft TL: N39 12 22 W84 33 23. Stereo. Hrs open: 24 6275 Collegevue Pl., 45224. Phone: (513) 542-9393. Fax: (513) 542-9333.E-mail: info@wakw.com Web Site:www.wakw.com Licensee: Pillar of Fire Inc. (group owner) Population served: 3,000,000 Natl. Network: Moody, . Format: Contemp Christian radio. News staff: one. Target aud: General; families. ♦Gerald Croucher, gen mgr & stn mgr.

WCIN(AM)— October 1953: 1480 khz; 4.5 kw-D, 300 w-N, DA-2. TL: N39 12 43 W84 29 20. Hrs open: 4445 Lake Forest Dr., 45242. Phone: (513) 281-7180. Fax: (513) 281-6125.E-mail: thepulseofthecity@hotmail.com Web Site:www.1480wdjo.com Licensee: Alchemy II Broadcasting LLC (acq 3-18-2009; $600,000). Population served: 452,524 Format: Oldies. Target aud: 50-64. ♦Brian Kauffmann, gen mgr.

WCKY(AM)— Sept 16, 1929: 1530 khz; 50 kw-U, DA-N, (LSS-Sacramento, CA). TL: N39 03 55 W84 36 27. Hrs open: 8044 Montgomery Rd., Suite 650, 45236. Phone: (513) 686-8300. Fax: (513) 333-4269. Web Site:www.wcky.com Licensee: Clear Channel Communications Group owner: Clear Channel Communications Inc. Population served: 300,000 Natl. Network: ESPN Radio, Fox Sports, Westwood One, . Format: Sports. Target aud: 35 plus; special focus on ages 35-64. ♦Darryl Parks, opns dir.

WCVG(AM)—See Covington, KY

WCVX(AM)— 1947: 1050 khz; 1 kw-D, 278 w-N. TL: N39 04 50 W84 31 18. Hrs open: 24 635 W. 7th St., Suite 400, 45203. Phone: (513) 579-1050. Phone: (513) 533-2500. Fax: (513) 421-0821. Fax: (513) 533-2527.E-mail: 1050am@wcux.com Web Site:www.wcux.com Licensee: Christian Broadcasting System Ltd. Group owner: Salem Communications Corp. (acq 2-10-2006; swap of WCVX(AM) and WQRT(AM) Florence, KY plus $6.75 million cash for WLQV(AM) Detroit, MI) Population served: 2,000,000 Natl. Network: Salem Radio Network, . Format: Relg, talk. News: 10 hrs wkly. Target aud: 24-54; family oriented young adults. Spec prog: Gospel 15 hrs, Sp 3 hrs wkly. ♦Jon R. Yinger, pres; Errol Dengler, VP; Gaither Stephens, gen mgr.

WDBZ(AM)— 1927: 1230 khz; 1 kw-U. TL: N39 06 27 W84 30 09. Hrs open: 24 705 Central Ave., Suite 200, 45202. Phone: (513) 679-6000. Fax: (513) 948-1985.E-mail: rporter@radio-one.com Web Site:www.1230thebuzz.com Licensee: Blue Chip Broadcasting Licenses Ltd. (acq 7-20-2007; $2.69 million). Population served: 452524 Natl. Rep: Christal,. Format: Gospel. News staff: one. Target aud: 25-54. ♦Lisa Thal, gen mgr; Lincoln Ware, opns mgr, progmg dir; Josh Guttman, gen sls mgr, natl sls mgr; Jeri Tolliver, prom dir.

WEBN(FM)— Aug 27, 1967: 102.7 mhz; 16.6 kw. 876 ft TL: N39 07 31 W84 29 57. Stereo. Hrs open: Prog sep from AM 8044 Montgomery Rd., Suite 650, 45236. Fax: (513) 749-3299. Web Site:www.webn.com Licensee: Jacor Broadcasting Corp. (Acq 2-86; $8 million;2-17-86). Population served: 1,340,000 Format: AOR.

WFTK(FM)—See Lebanon

WGRR(FM)—See Hamilton

***WGUC(FM)**— Sept 21, 1960: 90.9 mhz; 15 kw. Ant 960 ft TL: N39 07 27 W84 31 18. Stereo. Hrs open: 24 1223 Central Pkwy., 45214. Phone: (513) 241-8282. Fax: (513) 241-8456.E-mail: info@wguc.org Web Site:www.wguc.org Licensee: Cincinnati Public Radio, Inc. (acq 2-14-02). Population served: 1,300,000 Natl. Network: PRI, . Format: Class. Target aud: 35 plus; well-educated. ♦Richard Eiswerth, CEO; Barry Weinstein, CFO; Chris Phelps, gen mgr, mktg mgr; Robin Gehl, opns dir, progmg VP; Sherri Mancini, dev VP & dev dir; Gordon Bayliss, sls VP; Don Danko, engrg VP.

WIZF(FM)—See Erlanger, KY

***WJVS(FM)**— Apr 7, 1976: 88.3 mhz; 175 w. 105 ft TL: N39 17 21 W84 24 52. Stereo. Hrs open: 3254 E. Kemper Rd., 45241. Phone: (513) 771-8810. Fax: (513) 771-4928. Licensee: Great Oaks Institute of Technical and Career Development. (acq 1976). Format: Adult contemp. ♦Dave Angeline, gen mgr & progmg dir.

WKRC(AM)— 1922: 550 khz; 5 kw-D, 1 kw-N, DA-2. TL: N39 00 29 W84 26 39. Hrs open: 8040 Montgomery Rd., Suite 650, 45236. Phone: (513) 686-8300.E-mail: info@55krc.com Web Site:www.55krc.com Licensee: Jacor Broadcasting Corp. Group owner: Clear Channel Communications Inc. (acq 5-4-99; grpsl). Population served: 1,800,000 Natl. Network: Westwood One, CBS, . Hogan & Hartson. Format: News/talk info. Target aud: 35-64; adult, affluent, conservative. ♦Mike Kenney, VP; Karrie Sudbrack, gen mgr.

WKRQ(FM)— 1947: 101.9 mhz; 16 kw. 876 ft TL: N39 06 58 W84 30 05. Stereo. Hrs open: 2060 Reading Rd., Cincinatti, 45202. Phone: (513) 699-5102. Fax: (513) 699-5000. Web Site:www.wkrq.com Licensee: Bonneville Holding Co. Group owner: Infinity Broadcasting Corp. (acq 3-14-2008; grpsl). Population served: 400,000 Natl. Rep: Katz Radio,. Format: Hot adult contemp. ♦Jim Bryant, VP, gen mgr; Bryson Lair, sls dir, prom dir; Patti Marshall, progmg dir; Brian Douglas, mus dir.

WLW(AM)— Mar 22, 1922: 700 khz; 50 kw-U. TL: N39 21 11 W84 19 30. Hrs open: 8044 Montgomery Rd., Suite 650, 45236. Phone: (513) 686-8300. Fax: (513) 665-9700.E-mail: info@700wlw.com Web Site:www.700wlw.com Licensee: Jacor Broadcasting Corp. Group owner: Clear Channel Communications Inc. (acq 4-99; grpsl). Population served: 750,000 Format: News/talk.

WNNF(FM)— 1955: 94.1 mhz; 32 kw. Ant 600 ft TL: N39 06 18 W84 33 24. Stereo. Hrs open: 24 4805 Montgomery Rd., Suite 300, 45212. Phone: (513) 241-9898. Fax: (513) 241-6689.E-mail: info@radio941.net Web Site:www.radio941.com Licensee: Cumulus Licensing LLC. Group owner: Clear Channel Communications Inc. (acq 4-10-2009; grpsl). Population served: 452,524 Dickstein Shapiro LLP. Format: Adult contemp. News staff: one. Target aud: 25-54. ♦Bobby Dayer, gen mgr, progmg dir.

WOFX-FM— Aug 19, 1964: 92.5 mhz; 16 kw. Ant 866 ft TL: N39 06 59 W84 30 07. Hrs open: 4805 Montgomery Rd., Suite 300, 45212. Phone: (513) 241-9898. Fax: (513) 241-6689. Web Site:www.foxcincinnati.com Licensee: Cumulus Licensing LLC. (acq 4-10-2009; grpsl). Format: Classic rock. Target aud: 25-54. ♦Karrie Sudbrack, gen mgr.

WREW(FM)—See Fairfield

WRRM(FM)— Oct 1, 1959: 98.5 mhz; 17.5 kw. 807 ft TL: N39 07 19 W84 32 52. Stereo. Hrs open: 895 Centeral Ave., Suite 900, 45202. Phone: (513) 241-9898. Fax: (513) 749-3398. Fax: (513) 241-6689. Web Site:www.warm98.com Licensee: WRRM Lico Inc. Group owner: Susquehanna Radio Corp. (acq 1-72). Population served: 1,150,000 Format: Adult contemp. ♦TJ Holland, opns dir.

WSAI(AM)— June 7, 1923: 1360 khz; 5 kw-U, DA-N. TL: N39 14 51 W84 31 52. Hrs open: 24 8044 Montgomery Rd., Suite 650, 45236. Phone: (513) 686-8300. Fax: (513) 665-9700.E-mail: info@700wlw.com Web Site:www.1360espn.com Licensee: Clear Channel Communication Inc. Group owner: Clear Channel Communications Inc. (acq 4-29-99; grpsl). Natl. Network: ESPN Radio, . Wiley, Rein & Fielding. Format: Sports. ♦Mike Kenney, gen mgr; Darryl Parks, opns mgr, progmg VP; Mike Jamison, sls dir; Holly Nesser, mktg dir; Vince Marotta, prom dir; Ted Ryan, engrg dir.

WUBE-FM— July 20, 1949: 105.1 mhz; 14 kw. 920 ft TL: N39 07 31 W84 29 57. Stereo. Hrs open: 2060 Reading Rd., 45202. Phone: (513) 699-5105. Fax: (513-) 699-5000. Web Site:www.b105.com Licensee: Bonneville Holding Co. Group owner: Infinity Broadcasting Corp. (acq 3-14-2008; grpsl). Format: Country. ♦Jim Bryant, VP; Christine Mello, gen sls mgr; Duke Hamilton, mus dir, disc jockey.

***WVXU(FM)**— Oct 1, 1971: 91.7 mhz; 26.1 kw. Ant 683 ft TL: N39 07 31 W84 29 57. Stereo. Hrs open: 1223 Central Pkwy., 45214. Phone: (513) 352-9170. Fax: (513) 241-8456.E-mail: wvxu@cinradio.org Web Site:www.wvxu.org Licensee: Cincinnati Public Radio, Inc. (acq 8-22-2005; grpsl). Population served: 1,300,000 Natl. Network: PRI, NPR, . Rgnl. Network: Ohio Radio Net. Baker & Hostetler LLP. Format: News and info. News staff: 6; News: 107 hrs wkly. Target aud: 35 yrs plus; well educated. ♦Barry Weinstein, CFO; Richard Eiswerth, gen mgr; Sherri Mancini, dev VP; Chris Phelps, mktg VP; Robin Gehl, progmg VP; Maryanne Zeleznik, news dir, pub affrs dir; Don Danko, engrg VP.

Circleville

WNKK(FM)— Oct 1, 1965: 107.1 mhz; 3 kw. Ant 328 ft TL: N39 39 52 W82 51 04. Hrs open: 10th Floor, 280 Plaza N. High St., Columbus, 43215. Phone: (614) 233-9208. Fax: (614) 677-0083. Web Site:www.wink107.com Licensee: Wilks License Co.-Columbus LLC. Group owner: Infinity Broadcasting Corp. (acq 1-10-2007; grpsl). Population served: 250,000 Natl. Network: Westwood One, . Natl. Rep: Katz Radio,. Leventhal, Senter & Lerman. Format: Country. ♦Kathy Karnap, gen mgr, stn mgr; Ross Wagner, gen sls mgr; Scott Russell, rgnl sls mgr.

Cleveland

***WCPN(FM)**— Sept 8, 1984: 90.3 mhz; 50 kw. 500 ft TL: N41 22 18 W81 42 48. Stereo. Hrs open: 24 1375 Euclid Ave., 44115. Phone: (216) 916-6100. Fax: (216) 916-6101. Web Site:www.wcpn.org Licensee: Ideastream (acq 2-27-2001). Population served: 2,000,000 Natl. Network: PRI, NPR, . Schwartz, Woods & Miller. Format: News, talk, jazz. News staff: 16; News: 50 hrs wkly. Target aud: General. Spec prog: Ger one hr, Hungarian one hr, Lithuanian one hr, Pol one hr, Slovak one hr wkly. ♦Jerry Wareham, CEO; Keith Turner, opns dir, opns mgr; Maureen Paschke, dev VP & dev dir.

***WCRF(FM)**— Nov 23, 1958: 103.3 mhz; 25.5 kw. Ant 660 ft TL: N41 17 48 W81 39 27. Stereo. Hrs open: 24 9756 Barr Rd., 44141. Phone: (440) 526-1111. Fax: (440) 526-1319.E-mail: wcrf@moody.edu Web Site:wcrfradio.org Licensee: Moody Bible Institute of Chicago. (group owner) Population served: 4,000,000 Natl. Network: Moody, Salem Radio Network, . Southmayd. Wire Svc: AP Format: Inspirational. Target aud: 25-55. ♦Dr. Michael Easley, pres; Richard Lee, stn mgr; Phil Villareal, progmg dir; Doug Hainer, chief of engrg.

***WCSB(FM)**— May 10, 1976: 89.3 mhz; 1 kw. 190 ft TL: N41 30 12 W81 40 30. Stereo. Hrs open: 24 Cleveland State Univ., Rhodes Tower, 44115. Phone: (216) 687-3523.E-mail: promotions@wcsb.org Web Site:www.wcsb.org Licensee: Cleveland State University. Population served: 2,000,000 Format: Alternative, commerical. News: 7 hrs wkly. Target aud: General. ♦Eric Schulte, gen mgr; Brian Detrow, dev dir.

WDOK(FM)— Apr 30, 1950: 102.1 mhz; 12 kw. 1,004 ft TL: N41 23 02 W81 42 06. Stereo. Hrs open: One Radio Ln., 44114. Phone: (216) 696-0123. Fax: (216) 363-7189.E-mail: info@wdok.com Web Site:www.wdok.com Licensee: Infinity Radio Inc. Group owner: Infinity Broadcasting Corp. (acq 2000; grpsl). Population served: 3,330,500 Format: Soft rock. Target aud: 25-54; general. ♦Chris Maduri, gen mgr.

WENZ(FM)— July 14, 1959: 107.9 mhz; 70 kw. 750 ft TL: N41 28 03 W81 17 25. Stereo. Hrs open: 24 2510 Saint Clair Ave., 44114. Phone: (216) 579-1111. Fax: (216) 575-9141.E-mail: cforgy@radio-one.com Web Site:www.z1079fm.com Licensee: Radio One Licenses LLC. Group owner: Radio One Inc. (acq 11-8-01; grpsl). Population served: 175,000 Natl. Rep: Christal,. Format: Main stream urban. News staff: one. Target aud: 18-34. ♦Chris Forgy, VP, gen mgr; Kim Johnson, opns mgr; Paul Guy, gen sls mgr; Gary Zocolo, chief of engrg.

WERE(AM)—See Cleveland Heights

WFHM-FM— Apr 1, 1960: 95.5 mhz; 31 kw. 620 ft TL: N41 26 32 W81 29 28. Stereo. Hrs open: 24 4 Summit Park Dr., Suite 150, Independence, 44131. Phone: (216) 901-0921. Fax: (216) 901-1104.E-mail: office@whkradio.com Web Site:www.955thefish.com Licensee: Salem Media Group LLC. Group owner: Salem Communications Corp. (acq 12-22-2000; grpsl). Population served: 1,850,000 Natl. Rep: Salem,. Format: Christian/adult contemp. News: one hr wkly. Target aud: 25-54; female. ♦Edward Atsinger, pres; Errol Dengler, gen mgr, opns VP; Len Howser, progmg dir.

WGAR-FM— July 1948: 99.5 mhz; 50 kw. 500 ft TL: N41 22 18 W81 43 04. Stereo. Hrs open: 24 6200 Oak Tree Blvd., 4th Floor, Independence, 44131-2510. Phone: (216) 520-2600. Fax: (216) 524-2600. Web Site:www.wgar.com Licensee: Citicasters Licenses L.P. Group owner: Clear Channel Communications Inc. (acq 5-4-99; grpsl). Population served: 1,754,500 Natl. Network: AP Radio, . Natl. Rep: Christal,. Format: Contemp country. News staff: 2. Target aud: 25-54. ♦Mike Kenney, gen mgr; Bob Butts, gen sls mgr; Brian Jennings, progmg dir; Chuck Collier, mus dir.

WHK(AM)— July 28, 1921: 1420 khz; 5 kw-U, DA-N. TL: N41 21 30 W81 40 03. Hrs open: 4 Summit Park Dr., Suite 150, Independence, 44131. Phone: (216) 901-0921. Fax: (216) 901-5517.E-mail: office@whkradio.com Web Site:www.whkradio.com Licensee: Caron Broadcasting Inc. (acq 9-1-2004; $10 million). Population served: 1,728,000 Natl. Network: Salem Radio Network, . Hogan & Hartson. Wire Svc: AP Format: Conservative talk. Target aud: 25-54; male & female. ♦Len Howser, progmg dir.

WHKW(AM)— December 1930: 1220 khz; 50 kw-U, DA-1. TL: N41 18 26 W81 41 21. Stereo. Hrs open: 4 Summit Park Dr., Suite 150, 44131. Phone: (216) 901-0921. Fax: (216) 901-5517.E-mail: info@whkwradio.com Web Site:www.whkwradio.com Licensee: Caron Broadcasting Inc. Group owner: Salem Communications Corp. (acq 8-24-2000; grpsl). Format: Christian talk. ♦Errol Dengler, gen mgr.

WJMO(AM)— July 6, 1949: 1300 khz; 5 kw-U, DA-1. TL: N41 20 28 W81 44 29. Hrs open: 24 2510 St. Claire Ave. NE, 44114. Phone: (216) 579-1111. Fax: (216) 621-2176.E-mail: cforgy@radio-one.com Web Site:www.praise1300.com Licensee: Radio One Licenses LLC. Group owner: Radio One Inc. (acq 11-8-2001; grpsl). Population served: 750,903 Natl. Rep: Christal,. Format: Gospel. News staff: 2; News: 4 hrs wkly. Target aud: 25-54; Black adults. ♦Chris Forgy, VP; Haig Meguerditchian, gen mgr, gen sls mgr; Kim Johnson, opns mgr, gen sls mgr, prom mgr & mus dir.

WKNR(AM)— 1926: 850 khz; 50 kw-D, 4.7 kw-N, DA-2. TL: N41 19 00 W81 43 51. Stereo. Hrs open: 24 9446 Broadview Rd., 44147-2397. Phone: (440) 838-8585. Fax: (440) 838-1546. Web Site:www.espncleveland.com Licensee: Good Karma Broadcasting LLC. Group owner: Salem Communications Corp. (acq 2-7-2007; $7 million). Population served: 2,200,000 Natl. Network: ESPN Radio, . Format: Sports. Target aud: 25-54; male sports fans. ♦Craig Karmazin, CEO, pres; Sam Pines, stn mgr; Jason Gibbs, prom dir.

WKRK-FM—See Cleveland Heights

WMJI(FM)— Dec 6, 1948: 105.7 mhz; 27 kw. 900 ft TL: N41 23 09 W81 41 23. (CP: 15.5 kw, ant 1,020 ft.). Stereo. Hrs open: 24 6200 Oak Tree Blvd., 4th Fl., Independent, 44131. Phone: (216) 520-2600. Fax: (216) 524-3200. Web Site:www.wmji.com Licensee: Citicasters Licenses L.P. Group owner: Clear Channel Communications Inc. (acq 5-4-99; grpsl). Natl. Network: AP Radio, . Natl. Rep: Christal,. Wire Svc: UPI Format: Oldies. News staff: 4; News: 5 hrs wkly. Target aud: 25-54. ♦Mike Kenney, gen mgr; Kevin Metheny, opns dir, progmg dir; Roger Moorman, gen sls mgr.

WMMS(FM)— Nov 11, 1948: 100.7 mhz; 34 kw. 600 ft TL: N41 21 30 W81 40 03. Stereo. Hrs open: 6200 Oak Tree Blvd., South, 4th floor, Independence, 44131. Phone: (216) 520-2600. Fax: (216) 901-8166.E-mail: buzzard@wmms.com Web Site:www.wmms.com Licensee: Citicasters Licenses L.P. Group owner: Clear Channel Communications Inc. (acq 1999; grpsl). Population served: 1,500,000 Format: Rock. Target aud: 18-34. ♦Bo Matthews, opns mgr, mktg dir; Keith Hotchkiss, gen sls mgr, prom dir.

WMVX(FM)— May 4, 1960: 106.5 mhz; 11.3 kw. 1,036 ft TL: N41 22 45 W81 43 12. Stereo. Hrs open: 24 Prog sep from AM 6200 Oak Tree Blvd., 4th Fl., Independence, 44131. Phone: (216) 520-2600. Fax: (216) 520-3008. Web Site:www.wmvx.com Population served: 2,200,000 Format: Adult contemp. ♦Mike Kenney, stn mgr; Dawn Lesiak, traf mgr; Dave Snyder, sports cmtr.

WNCX(FM)— Oct 23, 1948: 98.5 mhz; 16 kw. 960 ft TL: N41 20 28 W81 44 29. Stereo. Hrs open: 24 1041 Huron Rd., 44115. Phone: (216) 861-0100. Fax: (216) 696-0385.E-mail: wncx@wncx.com Web Site:www.wncx.com Licensee: Infinity Radio License Inc. Group owner: Infinity Broadcasting Corp. Population served: 1,800,000 Natl. Network: ABC, Westwood One, . Leventhal, Senter & Lerman, PLLC. Format: Classic rock. Target aud: 25-54; adults. ♦Tom Herschel, VP & gen mgr; Linda Rodriguez, gen sls mgr; George Cohn, natl sls mgr; Marshall Goudy, mktg dir, prom dir, progmg dir.

WQAL(FM)— 1948: 104.1 mhz; 11 kw. 1,060 ft TL: N41 22 45 W81 43 12. Stereo. Hrs open: 24 One Radio Lane, 44114. Phone: (216) 696-0123. Fax: (216) 363-7199. Web Site:www.q104.com Licensee: Infinity Radio Inc. Group owner: Infinity Broadcasting Corp. (acq 12-14-00; grpsl). Population served: 750,903 Wiley, Rein & Fielding. Format: Hot adult contemp. News staff: one. Target aud: 25-49; women. ♦Chris Maduri, gen mgr.

***WRUW-FM**— Feb 26, 1967: 91.1 mhz; 15 kw. 292 ft TL: N41 31 14 W81 35 03. (CP: 14.5 kw, ant 276 ft.). Stereo. Hrs open: 24 11220 Bellflower Rd., 44106. Phone: (216) 368-2207. Phone: (216) 368-2208.E-mail: gm@wruw.org Web Site:www.wruw.org Licensee: Case Western Reserve University. Population served: 500,000 Format: Free-form/eclectic. Target aud: General; Cleveland & CWRU community. ♦Micah Waldstein, gen mgr; Peter McCall, stn mgr.

WTAM(AM)— 1923: 1100 khz; 50 kw-U. TL: N41 16 50 W81 37 22. Hrs open: 24 6200 Oak Tree Blvd., 4th Fl., 44131-2510. Phone: (216) 520-2600. Fax: (216) 901-8152 (progmg).E-mail: info@wtam.com Web Site:www.wtam.com Licensee: Clear Channel Broadcasting Inc. Group owner: Clear Channel Communications Inc. (acq 5-4-99; grpsl). Population served: 750,903 Hogan & Hartson. Format: News/talk, sports. News staff: 14; News: 25 hrs wkly. Target aud: 25-54. ♦Jim Meltzer, VP, gen mgr; Kevin Metheny, opns mgr; Gary Mincer, sls dir; Dave Ianni, gen sls mgr; Gaye Ramstrom, natl sls mgr; Jeff Zukauckas, prom dir; Ray Davis, progmg dir; R.C. Bauer, news dir; Cheryl Zivich, pub affrs dir; Dave Szucs, engrg dir, chief of engrg; Dawn Lesiak, traf mgr; Mike Snyder, sports cmtr.

WWGK(AM)— 1947: 1540 khz; 1 kw-D. TL: N41 30 10 W81 37 57. Hrs open: 9446 Broadview Rd, 44147-2397. Phone: (440) 838-8585. Fax: (440) 838-1546. Web Site:www.espncleveland.com Licensee: Good Karma Broadcasting L.L.C. (acq 10-27-2006; $2.5 million). Population served: 2,100,000 Natl. Network: ESPN Radio, Fox Sports, Premiere Radio Networks, . Format: Sports. Target aud: 25-54; males. ♦Craig Karmazin, CEO, pres; Sam Pines, stn mgr; Jason Gibbs, prom dir.

WWMK(AM)— Apr 3, 1950: 1260 khz; 10 kw-D, 5 kw-N. TL: N41 17 10 W81 38 34. Stereo. Hrs open: 24 175 Kenmar Industrial Pkwy., Broadview Heights, 44147. Phone: (440) 746-1010. Fax: (440) 746-1720. Web Site:www.radiodisney.com Licensee: Radio Disney Group LLC. Group owner: ABC Inc. (acq 8-26-98; $3.9 million). Natl. Network: USA, . Haley, Bader & Potts. Format: Family Hits. Target aud: 3-12, women 21-44; children & families. ♦Jeniffer Hansen, mktg dir; Michelle Kulball, stn mgr & prom dir.

WZAK(FM)— May 26, 1963: 93.1 mhz; 27.5 kw. 620 ft TL: N41 16 50 W81 37 22. Stereo. Hrs open: 24 2510 St. Clair Ave., 44114. Phone: (216) 579-1111. Fax: (216) 621-2176.E-mail: cforgy@radio-one.com Web Site:www.931wzak.com Licensee: Radio One Licenses LLC. Group owner: Radio One Inc. (acq 11-8-01; grpsl). Population served: 750,903 Natl. Rep: Christal,. Format: Urban adult contemp. News staff: one. Target aud: 25-54; Black adults. ♦Chris Forgy, gen mgr; Haig Megurditchian, gen sls mgr; Kim Johnson, opns mgr & mus dir.

Cleveland Heights

WERE(AM)— 1947: 1490 khz; 1 kw-U. TL: N41 30 48 W81 36 05. Hrs open: 24 2510 St. Clair Ave., Cleveland, 44114. Phone: (216) 579-1111. Fax: (216) 621-2176.E-mail: cforgy@radio-one.com Web Site:www.newstalk1490.com Licensee: Radio One Licenses LLC. Group owner: Radio One Inc. (acq 8-7-2000; grpsl). Population served: 1,737,300 Natl. Rep: Christal,. Format: News/talk. News staff: 4; News: 30 hrs wkly. ♦Cathy Hughes, CEO; Chris Forgy, VP, gen mgr; Haig Meguerditchian, gen sls mgr; Kimberly Hill, progmg dir.

WKRK-FM— Nov 23, 1960: 92.3 mhz; 40 kw. Ant 548 ft TL: N41 30 01 W81 33 59. Stereo. Hrs open: 24 1041 Huron Rd., Cleveland, 44115. Phone: (216) 861-0100. Fax: (216) 696-3710. Web Site:www.krockcleveland.com Licensee: CBS Radio Stations Inc. Group owner: Infinity Broadcasting Corp. (acq 12-14-2000; grpsl). Population served: 1,800,000 Natl. Network: ABC, . Leventhal, Senter & Lerman, PLLC. Format: Alternative rock. Target aud: 18-34; mass appeal, young adults. ♦Tom Herschel, VP & gen mgr; Jeff Miller, gen sls mgr; George Cohn, natl sls mgr, progmg dir; Marshall Goudy, mktg dir, prom dir.

Clyde

***WHVT(FM)**— December 1986: 90.5 mhz; 2.7 w. 154 ft TL: N41 17 45 W82 58 26. (CP: 2.6 kw, ant 154 ft.). Stereo. Hrs open: Box 273, 43410. Phone: (419) 547-8254. Fax: (419) 547-7195.E-mail: radio@whvtfm.com Web Site:www.whvtfm.com Licensee: Clyde Educ. Broadcasting Foundation. Format: Educ, relg. ♦James Lewis, pres & gen mgr.

WMJK(FM)— July 16, 1981: 100.9 mhz; 3 kw. 134 ft TL: N41 26 28 W82 41 14. Stereo. Hrs open: 24 1640 Cleveland Rd., Sandusky, 44870-4357. Phone: (419) 625-3380. Fax: (419) 625-1348.E-mail: paulmize@clearchannel.com Web Site:www.coast1009.com Licensee: BAS Broadcasting Inc. Group owner: Clear Channel Communications Inc. (acq 6-30-2008; grpsl). Population served: 500000 Natl. Network: ABC, . Natl. Rep: Katz Radio,. Rgnl rep: Rgnl Reps. Format: Country. News staff: 2; News: 4 hrs wkly. Target aud: 25-54. ♦Lisa J. Rich, gen mgr; Randy Hugg, opns mgr, progmg dir; Todd Lewis, gen sls mgr; Steve Shoffner, news dir; Gary Homza, chief of engrg.

WOHF(FM)—See Bellevue

Coal Grove

WBVB(FM)— Feb 1, 1990: 97.1 mhz; 3 kw. 472 ft TL: N38 25 27 W82 32 04. Hrs open: Box 2288, Huntington, WV, 25724. Secondary address: 134 4th Ave. 25701. Phone: (304) 525-7788. Fax: (304) 525-6281. Fax: (304) 525-7861 (Sales).E-mail: info@B97fm.com Web Site:www.B97fm.com Licensee: Capstar TX L.P. Group owner: Clear Channel Communications Inc. (acq 8-30-00; grpsl). Format: Oldies. Target aud: 18-34. Spec prog: Winston Cup racing. ♦Judy Jennings, gen mgr; Gloria Ward, sls dir; Mark Wood, progmg dir.

Columbus

WBNS(AM)— 1922: 1460 khz; 5 kw-D, 1 kw-N, DA-N. TL: N39 57 06 W82 54 23. Hrs open: 24 605 S. Front St., 43215. Phone: (614) 460-3850. Fax: (614) 460-3757. Web Site:www.1460thefan.com Licensee: RadiOhio Inc. Group owner: Dispatch Broadcast Group (acq 1933). Population served: 545,000 Natl. Network: ESPN Radio, . Rgnl. Network: Ohio News Net. Natl. Rep: Christal,. Wire Svc: AP Format: Sports. Target aud: Men 25-54. ♦Dave VanStone, gen mgr; Tom Bunyard, sls dir; Mike Kearney, gen sls mgr; Lorene Gillman, natl sls mgr; Todd Reigle, prom dir; Jimmy Powers, progmg dir; Steve Clawson, chief of engrg.

WBNS-FM— June 1959: 97.1 mhz; 20.5 kw. Ant 781 ft TL: N39 58 16 W83 01 40. Stereo. Hrs open: 605 S. Front St., Suite 300, 43215. Phone: (614) 460-3850. Fax: (614) 460-3757. Web Site:www.971thefan.com Licensee: RadiOhio Inc. Natl. Rep: Christal,. Wire Svc: AP Format: Sports. Target aud: Adults 25-54. ♦Dave Van Stone, pres, gen mgr, gen sls mgr; Mike Kearney, gen sls mgr; Todd Reigle, prom dir; Jimmy Powers, progmg dir.

***WCBE(FM)**— Sept 26, 1956: 90.5 mhz; 11 kw. 531 ft TL: N39 57 48 W83 00 17. Stereo. Hrs open: 24 540 Jack Gibbs Blvd., 43215. Phone: (614) 365-5555. Fax: (614) 365-5060.E-mail: wcbe@wcbe.org Web Site:www.wcbe.org Licensee: Board of Education, City School District of Columbus, Ohio. Natl. Network: NPR, PRI, . Ernest Sanchez. Wire Svc: AP Format: Var, news. News staff: 3; News: 37 hrs wkly. Target aud: 35-54. Spec prog: Jazz 4 hrs, blues 3 hrs, Celtic 4 hrs wkly. ♦Dan Mushalko, gen mgr, opns dir; Wendy Craver, dev dir; Maggie Brennan, mus dir; Jim Letizia, news dir, pub affrs dir.

WCKX(FM)— February 1996: 107.5 mhz; 1.9 kw. 413 ft TL: N39 57 46 W82 59 46. Hrs open: 24 350 E. 1st Ave., Suite 100, 43201. Phone: (614) 487-1444. Fax: (614) 487-5862.E-mail: info@wckx.com Web Site:www.power1075.com Licensee: Blue Chip Broadcasting Licenses Ltd. Group owner: Radio One Inc. (acq 4-30-01; grpsl). Natl. Network: ABC, . Natl. Rep: D & R Radio,. Format: Hip-Hop. News: one hr wkly. ♦Jeff Wilson, gen mgr.

WCOL-FM— 1947: 92.3 mhz; 22 kw. 754 ft TL: N39 58 16 W83 01 40. Stereo. Hrs open: 24 2323 W. Fifth Ave., Suite 200, 43204. Phone: (614) 486-6101. Fax: (614) 487-2554.E-mail: info@wcol.com Web Site:www.wcol.com Licensee: Citicasters Licenses L.P. Group owner: Clear Channel Communications Inc. (acq 5-4-99; grpsl). Format: Country. News staff: one. Target aud: 18-49. ♦Tom Thon, gen mgr.

***WHKC(FM)**— September 2007: 91.5 mhz; 15 kw. Ant 689 ft TL: N39 56 14 W83 01 16. Hrs open: 1630 Strathshire Hall Pl., Powell, 43065. Phone: (740) 548-5919. Fax: (740) 548-5911. Licensee: Christian Broadcasting Services Inc. Format: Christian teaching/music. ♦Holly Casagrande, gen mgr; Margaret Litton, progmg dir.

WJYD(FM)—See London

WLVQ(FM)— Apr 1, 1959: 96.3 mhz; 40 kw. 550 ft TL: N39 58 16 W83 01 40. Stereo. Hrs open: 24 10th Fl., 280 Plaza N. High St., 43215. Phone: (614) 227-9696. Fax: (614) 461-1059. Web Site:www.qfm96.com Licensee: Wilks License Co.-Columbus LLC. Group owner:Infinity Broadcasting Corp. (acq 1-10-2007; grpsl). Population served: 1,500,000 Natl. Network: Westwood One, . Natl. Rep: McGavren Guild,. Leventhal, Senter & Lerman. Format: Classic Rock. News staff: one; News: 2 hrs wkly. Target aud: 25-54. ♦Ross Wagner, sls dir; Scott Miller, VP & mktg dir; Marissa McClellan, prom dir; Chris Thomas, progmg dir.

WMNI(AM)— Apr 26, 1958: 920 khz; 1 kw-D, 500 w-N, DA-2. TL: N39 53 32 W83 02 51. Stereo. Hrs open: 24 Prog sep from FM 1458 Dublin Rd., 43215. Phone: (614) 481-7800. Fax: (614) 481-8070.E-mail: mail997@wrkz.com Web Site:www.wmni.com Licensee: North American Broadcasting Inc. Natl. Network: AP Network News, . Rgnl. Network: Agri Bcstg. Wire Svc: AP Format: Adult standards. News staff: 5; News: 20 hrs wkly. Target aud: 35 plus. Spec prog: Relg 4 hrs wkly.

WNCI(FM)— July 1961: 97.9 mhz; 175 kw. 560 ft TL: N39 58 10 W83 00 10. Stereo. Hrs open: 24 2323 W. 5th Ave., Suite 200, 43204. Phone: (614) 486-6101. Fax: (614) 487-3553. Web Site:www.wnci.com

Licensee: Citicasters Licenses L.P. Group owner: Clear Channel Communications Inc. (acq 1999; grpsl). Population served: 1,215,700 Holland & Knight. Format: Adult contemp. News staff: one; News: 4 hrs wkly. Target aud: 18-49. ♦Tom Thon, gen mgr; Dave Daugherty, gen sls mgr; Michael McCoy, progmg dir.

***WOSU(AM)**— Apr 24, 1922: 820 khz; 5 kw-D, 790 w-N (L-WBAP Ft. Worth, Tex.). TL: N40 01 44 W82 03 22. (CP: 1 kw-N). Hrs open: 24 2400 Olentangy River Rd., 43210. Phone: (614) 292-9678. Fax: (614) 292-0513. Web Site:www.wosu.org Licensee: Ohio State University. Population served: 1,200,000 Natl. Network: NPR, PRI, . Rgnl. Network: Ohio Radio Net. Dow, Lohnes & Albertson. Wire Svc: AP Format: Pub affrs, news/talk. News staff: 9; News: 114 hrs wkly. Target aud: 35 plus; general. Spec prog: Black one hr, bluegrass 12 hrs wkly. ♦Thomas Rieland, gen mgr; Tim Eby, stn mgr.

***WOSU-FM**— Dec 13, 1949: 89.7 mhz; 13.3 kw. 938 ft TL: N39 56 16 W83 01 16. Stereo. Hrs open: 24 Prog sep from AM 2400 Olentangy River Rd., 43210. Phone: (614) 292-9678. Fax: (614) 292-0513. Web Site:www.wosu.org Licensee: Ohio State University Population served: 1,000,000 Natl. Network: PRI, . Wire Svc: AP Format: Class music. Target aud: 25 plus. Co-owned TV: *WOSU-TV affil.

WRFD(AM)—(Columbus-Worthington, Sept 27, 1947: 880 khz; 23 kw-D. TL: N39 56 31 W83 01 20. Hrs open: Sunrise-sunset 8101 N. High St., Suite 360, 43235-1406. Phone: (614) 885-0880. Fax: (614) 885-6322.E-mail: mail@wrfd.com Web Site:www.wrfd.com Licensee: Christian Voice of Central Ohio Inc. Group owner: Salem Communications Corp. (acq 9-25-2008; $4 million). Population served: 6,888,826 Natl. Network: Salem Radio Network, . Natl. Rep: Christal, Salem,. Format: Relg, farm. News: one hr wkly. Target aud: 30-60; conservatives, Christians, farmers. ♦Dan Baughman, pres; David Ruleman, VP; Dan Craig, gen mgr; Ryan Moran, opns mgr, progmg dir; Tom Heyl, gen sls mgr; Greg Sauold, engrg dir.

WRKZ(FM)— Apr 26, 1962: 99.7 mhz; 20 kw. Ant 784 ft TL: N39 58 16 W83 01 40. Stereo. Hrs open: 24 1458 Dublin Rd., 43215. Phone: (614) 481-7800. Fax: (614) 481-8070.E-mail: mail@wbzx.com Web Site:www.wbzx.com Licensee: North American Broadcasting Co. Inc. (group owner) Population served: 1,200,000 Natl. Rep: D & R Radio,. Wire Svc: AP Format: Rock. News staff: 5. Target aud: 18-49. ♦Matthew Mnich, CEO, pres; Norma J. Mnich, chmn; Mark E. Jividen, VP, gen mgr; Jim Pontius, sls dir; Eric Feucht, gen sls mgr; Greg Moebius, prom dir; Hal Fish, progmg dir; Ronni Hunter, mus dir; Mark Nuce, news dir, pub affrs dir; Bill Bowin, engrg mgr.

WSNY(FM)— Aug 12, 1982: 94.7 mhz; 22 kw. 753 ft TL: N39 58 16 W83 01 40. Stereo. Hrs open: 4401 Carriage Hill Ln., 43220. Phone: (614) 451-2191. Fax: (614) 451-1831.E-mail: info@sunny95.com Web Site:www.sunny95.com Licensee: Franklin Communications Inc. Group owner: Saga Communications Inc. (acq 9-86). Population served: 1,382,200 Natl. Rep: Christal, Katz Radio,. Wire Svc: AP Format: Adult contemp. News staff: one; News: 3 hrs wkly. Target aud: 25-64; women, upscale families. ♦Alan Goodman, pres, VP, gen mgr; Katie Cyr, sls dir, news dir; Jill McCarron, gen sls mgr, natl sls mgr; Michelle Hurley, mktg dir.

WTVN(AM)— 1924: 610 khz; 5 kw-U, DA-N. TL: N39 52 26 W82 58 36. Hrs open: 24 2323 W. 5th Ave., Suite 200, 43204. Phone: (614) 486-6101. Fax: (614) 487-2559.E-mail: info@610wtvn.com Web Site:www.610wtvn.com Licensee: Citicasters Licenses L.P. Group owner: Clear Channel Communications Inc. (acq 1999; grpsl). Population served: 1,500,000 Koteen & Naftalin. Format: News/talk. Target aud: 25-54; leaning male. ♦Tom Thon, VP; Jeff Rehl, gen sls mgr; Bruce Collins, progmg dir; Bruce Kamp, news dir.

***WUFM(FM)**— Mar 22, 1996: 88.7 mhz; 5 kw. Ant 774 ft TL: N39 56 16 W83 01 16. Stereo. Hrs open: 24 Box 1887, Westerville, 43086-1887. Secondary address: 116 County Line Rd., Westerville 43082. Phone: (614) 839-7100. Fax: (614) 839-1329.E-mail: radiou@radiou.com Web Site:www.radiou.com GE-1 (ku) Licensee: Spirit Communications Inc. (acq 9-27-96; $95,000). Population served: 1,600,000 Gammon & Grange. Format: CHR, rock, progsv. Target aud: 12-24; Male. ♦John P. Shumate Sr., pres; Kathy Shumate, VP; Michael Buckingham, gen mgr; Cole Drake, prom dir; Nikki Cantu, progmg dir & mus dir.

WVKO(AM)— Nov 21, 1951: 1580 khz; 3.2 kw-D, 290 w-N, DA-2. TL: N40 03 42 W82 56 41. Hrs open: 24 4673 Winterset Dr., 43220-2010. Phone: (614) 538-1580.E-mail: info@stgabrielradio.com Web Site:www.stgabrielradio.com Licensee: Bernard Ohio LLC. (acq 1-22-2007; grpsl). Natl. Network: EWTN Radio, . Format: Catholic.

WVKO-FM—(Johnstown, June 16, 1975: 103.1 mhz; 1.6 kw. Ant 443 ft TL: N40 13 44 W82 39 35.8. Stereo. Hrs open: 74 S. 4th St., 43215. Phone: (614) 821-0002. Phone: (614) 469-1930. Fax: (614) 821-0002. Fax: (614) 224-6208.E-mail: wvko1580am@gmail.com Licensee: Bernard Ohio LLC. (acq 1-22-2007; grpsl). Natl. Rep: D & R Radio,. Format: Mexican Regional. Target aud: 18-54; upscale, professional; homeowners with disposable incomes. Spec prog: Jazz 10 hrs, relg 13 hrs, reggae 5 hrs wkly. ♦Hector Villarreal, gen mgr; Tom Morris, gen mgr & opns mgr.

WYTS(AM)— 1922: 1230 khz; 1 kw-U. TL: N39 56 31 W83 01 20. Stereo. Hrs open: 2323 W. Fifth Ave., Suite 200, 43204. Phone: (614) 487-2559. Web Site:talk1230wyts.com Licensee: Citicasters Licenses Inc. Natl. Network: Fox Sports, . Format: Sports. Target aud: 35 plus; general. ♦Jeff Rehl, gen sls mgr; Steve Konrad, progmg dir; Sis Campbell, traf mgr.

Columbus Grove

WLWD(FM)— 2003: 93.9 mhz; 14 kw. Ant 436 ft TL: N40 57 21 W84 07 59. Hrs open: 667 W. Market St., Lima, 45801. Phone: (419) 223-2060. Fax: (419) 229-3888.E-mail: russryder@clearchannel.com Web Site:www.wild939.com Licensee: CC Licenses LLC. Group owner: Clear Channel Communications Inc. (acq 8-10-2000). Format: CHR. News: one hr wkly. ♦Russ Ryder, opns mgr & progmg dir; Mark Gierhart, chief of engrg.

Columbus-Worthington

WRFD(AM)—Licensed to Columbus-Worthington. See Columbus

Conneaut

***WGOJ(FM)**— Apr 5, 1964: 105.5 mhz; 6 kw. 295 ft TL: N41 51 42 W80 31 01. Stereo. Hrs open: 24 Box 725, 44030. Secondary address: 235 Miill St. 44030. Phone: (440) 599-7252. Fax: (440) 593-4761.E-mail: wgoj@suite224.net Licensee: Developing Radio LLC (acq 1-28-2004; $750,000). Population served: 600,000 Natl. Network: Bible Bcstg Net, . Format: Christian. Target aud: General. ♦Dr. Roger P. Hogle, gen mgr; Robert Jackson, progmg dir.

WWOW(AM)— Oct 25, 1959: 1360 khz; 5 kw-D, 35 w-N. TL: N41 55 32 W80 32 32. Hrs open: 24 229 Broad St., 44030. Phone: (440) 593-2233. Fax: (440) 593-6885.E-mail: mlandon@1360wwow.com Web Site:www.1360wwow.com Licensee: Cause Plus Marketing LLC (acq 1-31-2007; $200,000). Population served: 14,552 Format: News/talk. ♦John Marra, pres; Marty Landon, opns mgr; Gary Gersin, progmg dir; Pat Williams, news dir.

Cortland

WKTX(AM)— Apr 1, 1985: 830 khz; 1 kw-D. TL: N41 24 56 W80 43 49. Hrs open: 11906 Madison Ave., Lakewood, 44107. Phone: (216) 221-0330. Fax: (216) 221-3638. Licensee: Miklos Kossanyi, Maria Kossanyi (acq 10-91). Natl. Network: USA, . Format: Variety, ethnic, polka. Target aud: 35 plus; homeowners. Spec prog: Slovenian 2 hrs, Greek 2 hrs, Pol one hr, German 5 hrs wkly. ♦Miklos Kossanyi, pres; Maria Kossanyi, VP; Jim Georgiades, opns dir, chief of opns; Jack Cory, progmg dir.

Coshocton

***WHVY(FM)**—Not on air, target date: unknown: 89.5 mhz; 5 kw. Ant 279 ft TL: N40 18 17 W81 44 04. Hrs open: Box 263, Clyde, 43410. Phone: (419) 547-8254. Fax: (419) 547-7195. Licensee: Clyde Educational Broadcasting Foundation. ♦Curtis J. Anstead, pres.

***WOSE(FM)**— 1996: 91.1 mhz; 6 kw. Ant 321 ft TL: N40 20 30 W81 57 56. Stereo. Hrs open:
Rebroadcasts WOSU-FM Columbus 100%.
2400 Olentangy River Rd., Columbus, 43210. Phone: (614) 292-9678. Fax: (614) 292-7625.E-mail: wosu@osu.edu Web Site:www.wosu.org Licensee: The Ohio State University. Natl. Network: PRI, NPR, . Dow, Lohnes & Albertson. Wire Svc: AP Format: Class. ♦Thomas Rieland, gen mgr; Tim Eby, stn mgr; Kevin Petrilla, opns mgr.

WTNS(AM)— Nov 9, 1947: 1560 khz; 1 kw-D. TL: N40 16 30 W81 49 37. Hrs open: 114 N. 6th St., 43812. Phone: (740) 622-1560. Fax: (740) 622-7940. Licensee: Coshocton Broadcasting Co. (group owner; acq 9-86; $560,653; 9-22-86). Population served: 13,747 Format: Country. ♦Bruce Wallace, pres, gen mgr; Tom Thompson, gen sls mgr; Mike Bechtol, mus dir; Ken Smailes, news dir; Jay Drummond, chief of engrg.

WTNS-FM— Apr 25, 1968: 99.3 mhz; 1.2 kw. 440 ft TL: N40 16 30 W81 49 37. Hrs open: 114 N. 6th St., 43812. Phone: (740) 622-1560. Fax: (740) 622-7940. Population served: 13,747 Format: Adult contemp. ♦Flo Murdock, women's int ed, disc jockey; Brad Haynes, disc jockey.

Covington

WPTW(AM)—See Piqua

Crestline

WYKL(FM)—Licensed to Crestline. See Mansfield

Crooksville

WYBZ(FM)— Oct 26, 1990: 107.3 mhz; 3 kw. 328 ft TL: N39 47 23 W82 05 39. (CP: Ant 302 ft.). Stereo. Hrs open: 24 Box 669, Zanesville, 43702-0669. Secondary address: 2895 A Maysville Pike, Zanesville 43701. Phone: (740) 453-6004. Fax: (740) 453-5865.E-mail: rick@wybz.com Web Site:www.wybz.com Licensee: Y Bridge Broadcasting Inc. (acq 12-26-90; $60,000; 1-14-91). Natl. Network: CNN Radio, . Smithwick & Belendiuk. Format: Oldies. News staff: one; News: 9 hrs wkly. Target aud: 25-55. ♦Monica Martinelli, sls VP, gen sls mgr; Rick Sabine, pres, gen mgr & progmg dir; Mark Hiner, chief of engrg.

Cuyahoga Falls

WAKS(FM)—See Akron

***WCUE(AM)**— 1950: 1150 khz; 5 kw-U, DA-2. TL: N41 12 05 W81 31 25. Hrs open: 24 13 Fairlane Dr., Joliet, IL, 60435. Secondary address: 4075 Bellaire Ln., Peninsula 44264. Phone: (815) 725-1331.E-mail: info@wcue.com Web Site:www.familyradio.com Licensee: Family Stations Inc. (group owner; acq 10-22-86). Population served: 275,425 Dow, Lohnes & Albertson. Format: Relg. News: 4 hrs wkly. Target aud: 25 plus; Christians. Spec prog: Class 2 hrs wkly. ♦Harold Camping, pres & gen mgr.

WQAL(FM)—See Cleveland

Dayton

WDAO(AM)— Mar 1, 1955: 1210 khz; 1 kw-D. TL: N39 43 36 W84 12 23. Hrs open: 1012 West 3rd St., 45402. Phone: (937) 222-9326. Fax: (937) 461-6100.E-mail: wdao1210@aol.com Web Site:www.wdaoradio.com Licensee: Johnson Communications Inc. (acq 1-88; $725,000; 1-18-88). Population served: 2,436,010 Natl. Rep: Christal,. Format: Rhythm and blues. ♦Jim Johnson, pres, VP, gen mgr; Sophia Carr, gen sls mgr; Jim Johnston, mus dir.

***WDPR(FM)**— Apr 9, 1977: 88.1 mhz; 600 w. Ant 781 ft TL: N39 43 16 W84 15 00. Stereo. Hrs open: 24 126 N. Main St., 45402. Phone: (937) 496-3850. Fax: (937) 496-3852.E-mail: gmw@dpr.org Web Site:www.dpr.org Licensee: Dayton Public Radio Inc. (acq 4-28-98). Population served: 500,000 Natl. Network: USA, . Format: Class. Target aud: 24-50. ♦Georganne M. Woessner, gen mgr; Larry Coressel, opns dir; Shaun Yu, progmg dir.

***WDPS(FM)**— 1976: 89.5 mhz; 6 kw. 198 ft TL: N39 45 28 W84 11 36. Stereo. Hrs open: 9:15 AM-4:30 PM 441 River Corridor Dr., 45402. Phone: (937) 542-7182. Fax: (937) 542-6714. Licensee: Dayton Public Schools. (acq 1976). Population served: 100,000 Format: Jazz, AAA. ♦Ken Kreitzer, gen mgr; P.R. Frank, opns dir, news dir; Christopher Hartley, mus dir; Jennifer Bryant, asst music dir; Tom Nornhold, chief of engrg.

WFCJ(FM)—See Miamisburg

WGTZ(FM)—See Eaton

WHIO(AM)— Feb 9, 1935: 1290 khz; 5 kw-U, DA-N. TL: N39 40 41 W84 07 53. Hrs open:
Simulcast with WHIO-FM Piqua 100%.
Box 1206, 45401. Secondary address: 1414 Wilmington Ave. 45420. Phone: (937) 259-2111. Fax: (937) 259-2168. Fax: (937) 259-2024.E-mail: info@1290whio.com Web Site:1290whio.com Licensee: Cox Radio Inc. Group owner: Cox Broadcasting Population served: 823,100 Natl. Rep: D & R Radio,. Dow, Lohnes & Albertson. Format: Full service, news/talk. News staff: 4; News: 30 hrs wkly. Target aud: 35-54. Spec prog: Relg 2 hrs wkly. ♦Donna Hall, VP, gen mgr; Lisa Allan, gen sls mgr; Marc Herbst, natl sls mgr; Kathy Eagle-Norris, rgnl sls mgr; Vicky Forrest, mktg dir; Tracey Slife, prom mgr; Larry Hansgen, progmg dir; Jim Barrett, news dir, pub affrs dir; Ron Gaier, chief of engrg. Co-owned TV: WHIO-TV affil.

WHKO(FM)— 1946: 99.1 mhz; 50 kw. Ant 1,066 ft TL: N39 44 02 W84 14 52. Stereo. Hrs open: Box 1206, 45401. Secondary address: 1414 Wilmington Ave. 45420. Phone: (937) 259-2111. Fax: (937) 259-2168.

Fax: (937) 259-2024.E-mail: info@1290whio.com Licensee: Cox Radio Inc. Population served: 838,400 Natl. Rep: Christal,. Format: Country. ♦Nick Roberts, opns mgr, progmg dir & mus dir. Co-owned TV: WHIO-TV affil.

WING(AM)— May 24, 1921: 1410 khz; 5 kw-U, DA-N. TL: N39 40 56 W84 09 33. Hrs open: 717 E. David Rd., 45429. Phone: (937) 294-5858. Fax: (937) 297-5233.E-mail: info@wingam.com Web Site:www.wingam.com Licensee: MLB-Dayton IV LLC. Group owner: Radio One Inc. (acq 9-12-2007; grpsl). Population served: 4,100 Natl. Network: CBS, Westwood One, . Natl. Rep: Katz Radio,. Format: ESPN, sports. Target aud: 25-54; well educated. ♦Andrea Scott, gen mgr.

WLQT(FM)—See Kettering

WMMX(FM)— September 1964: 107.7 mhz; 50 kw. 420 ft TL: N39 43 36 W84 12 23. Stereo. Hrs open: 24 101 Pine St., 45402. Phone: (937) 224-1137. Fax: (937) 224-3667.E-mail: info@ccedayton.com Web Site:www.wmmx.com Licensee: Citicasters Licenses L.P. Group owner: Clear Channel Communications Inc. (acq 1999; grpsl). Format: Hot Adult contemp. Target aud: 25-54. ♦Jeff Stevens, opns mgr, progmg dir; Robert Zurowesti, VP & mktg mgr.

WONE(AM)— Mar 20, 1949: 980 khz; 5 kw-U, DA-N. TL: N39 40 03 W84 10 01. Stereo. Hrs open: 24 101 Pine St., 45402. Phone: (937) 224-1137. Fax: (937) 224-3667.E-mail: info@ccedayton.com Web Site:www.wone.com Licensee: Citicasters Licenses L.P. Group owner: Clear Channel Communications Inc. (acq 5-4-99; grpsl). Population served: 115,300 Format: Sports. News staff: 3; News: 18 hrs wkly. Target aud: 35-64. ♦Robert Zurowesti, VP; Tony Tilford, opns mgr & progmg dir.

***WQRP(FM)**— 1976: 89.5 mhz; 6 kw. Ant 270 ft TL: N39 45 26 W84 12 24. Stereo. Hrs open: 2351 Sunset Blvd., Suite 170-218, Rocklin, CA, 95765. Phone: (916) 251-1600. Fax: (916) 251-1650. Web Site:www.klove.com Licensee: Educational Media Foundation. (acq 7-9-2008; $350,000). Natl. Network: K-Love, . Format: Contemp Christian. ♦Mike Novak, pres.

WTUE(FM)— 1959: 104.7 mhz; 50 kw. 499 ft TL: N39 43 19 W84 12 36. Stereo. Hrs open: 24 101 Pine St., 45402. Phone: (937) 224-1137. Fax: (937) 224-3667.E-mail: wtue@wtue.com Web Site:www.wtue.com Licensee: Citicasters Licenses L.P. Group owner: Clear Channel Communications Inc. Population served: 263,000 Format: AOR. News staff: one; News: 2 hrs wkly. Target aud: 18-49. ♦Robert Zurowesti, VP; Tony Tilford, opns mgr.

***WUDR(FM)**— 2003: 98.1 mhz; 13 w. Ant 90 ft TL: N39 47 14 W84 14 23. Hrs open: University of Dayton, 300 College Park, 45469-1679. Phone: (937) 229-2774. Web Site:flyer-radio.udayton.edu Licensee: University of Dayton. Format: Var. ♦Casey Drottar, gen mgr; Roy Flynn, opns mgr.

***WWSU(FM)**— Apr 4, 1977: 106.9 mhz; 10 w. 150 ft TL: N39 46 57 W84 03 43. Stereo. Hrs open: 24 Wright State University, 018 Student Union, 45435. Phone: (937) 775-5554. Phone: (937) 775-5555. Fax: (937) 775-5553.E-mail: wwsugeneralmanager@yahoo.com Web Site:www.listen.to/wwsu Licensee: Wright State University. Population served: 60,000 Format: Various/diverse. Target aud: 15-26; college & high school students. Spec prog: Black 12 hrs, relg 11 hrs, gospel 3 hrs, jazz 3 hrs, Sp 3 hrs wkly. ♦Johnathan Gallienne, gen mgr; Ashley Vance, progmg dir.

De Graff

***WDEQ-FM**— Sept 1, 1967: 103.3 mhz; 10 w. 23 ft TL: N40 18 48 W83 55 06. Hrs open: 2096 County Rd. 24 S., 43318. Phone: (937) 585-5981. Fax: (937) 585-4599. Web Site:www.riverside.k12.oh.us Licensee: Riverside Local Board of Education. Format: Educ. ♦Brian Yoder, gen mgr.

Defiance

WDFM(FM)— June 25, 1985: 98.1 mhz; 50 kw. 500 ft TL: N41 17 28 W84 32 17. Stereo. Hrs open: 24 118 Clinton St., 43512. Phone: (419) 782-9336. Fax: (419) 784-0306. Web Site:www.981mix.com Licensee: Citicasters Licenses L.P. Group owner: Clear Channel Communications Inc. (acq 5-4-99; grpsl). Natl. Network: CNN Radio, . Natl. Rep: Katz Radio,. Fletcher, Heald & Hildreth. Format: Adult contemp. News staff: one; News: 7 hrs wkly. Target aud: 25-54. Spec prog: Relg 3 hrs wkly. ♦Rick Small, pres, opns dir; Bob McLimans, gen mgr; Russ Ryder, progmg dir.

***WGDE(FM)**— Mar 14, 1999: 91.9 mhz; 6 kw. 305 ft TL: N41 17 41 W84 23 24. Hrs open: 24
Rebroadcasts WGTE-FM Toledo 100%.
1270 S. Detroit, Toledo, 43614. Phone: (419) 380-4600. Fax: (419) 380-4710.E-mail: info@wgte.com Web Site:www.wgte.org Licensee: Public Broadcast Foundation of NW Ohio. Schwartz, Woods & Miller. Format: Class, pub affrs, news. News: 23 hrs wkly. Target aud: General. Spec prog: Jazz 16 hrs, new age 4 hrs wkly. ♦George Jones, chmn; Marlon P. Kiser, CEO, pres & gen mgr.

WONW(AM)— 1949: 1280 khz; 1 kw-D, 500 w-N, DA-N. TL: N41 16 44 W84 23 50. Hrs open: 24 2110 Radio Dr., 43512. Secondary address: 709 N. Perry St., Napoleon 43545. Phone: (419) 782-8126. Fax: (419) 784-4154.E-mail: bobmclimans@clearchannel.com Web Site:www.wonw1280.com Licensee: CC Licenses LLC. Group owner: Clear Channel Communications Inc. (acq 11-5-99; grpsl). Natl. Network: CNN Radio, . Rgnl. Network: Agri Bcstg. Natl. Rep: Katz Radio,. Wire Svc: AP Format: News/talk, sports. News staff: one. Target aud: General. Spec prog: Rush Limbaugh. ♦Robert E. McLimans, VP, gen mgr; Rick Small, opns dir, opns mgr; John Schuette, gen sls mgr; Rusty Hoops, progmg dir.

WZOM(FM)— Aug 25, 1989: 105.7 mhz; 6 kw. 347 ft TL: N41 13 23 W84 22 36. Stereo. Hrs open: 24 2110 Radio Dr., 43512. Secondary address: 709 N. Perry St., Napoleon 43512. Phone: (419) 782-8126. Fax: (419) 784-4154.E-mail: 1057thebull@clearchannel.com Web Site:www.1057thebull.com Licensee: CC Licenses LLC. Group owner: Clear Channel Communications Inc. (acq 1-1-2000; grpsl). Natl. Rep: Katz Radio,. Rgnl rep: Rgnl Reps. Format: Country. News staff: one; News: 4 hrs wkly. Target aud: 25-54. Spec prog: Relg 6 hrs wkly. ♦Robert E. McLimans, sr VP, VP & gen mgr; Rick Small, opns dir; Bill Murphy, progmg dir.

Delaware

WDLR(AM)— Jan 18, 1961: 1550 khz; 500 w-D, 29 w-N, DA-2. TL: N40 17 56 W83 02 46. Hrs open: 24 1630 Strathshire Hall, Powell, 43065. Phone: (740) 368-9357. Fax: (740) 369-9463.E-mail: anuelrojas @laquebuenaohio.com Licensee: The Fifteen Fifty Corp. (acq 3-21-2006). Population served: 73,000 Format: Sp. ♦Luis Orozco, gen mgr & stn mgr.

***WJJE(FM)**— 2005: 89.1 mhz; 6 kw vert. Ant 328 ft TL: N40 24 01 W82 46 43. Hrs open: Drawer 2440, Tupelo, MS, 38803. Phone: (662) 844-8888. Fax: (662) 842-6791. Licensee: American Family Association. Group owner: American Family Radio (acq 12-15-2003; $10 for CP). Format: Relg. ♦Marvin Sanders, gen mgr.

***WSLN(FM)**— Apr 28, 1952: 98.7 mhz; 100 w. 105 ft TL: N40 17 46 W84 22 36. Stereo. Hrs open: Ohio Wesleyan Univ., 61 S. Sandusky St., 43015. Phone: (740) 368-2918. Fax: (740) 368-3649. Web Site:www.wslnowu.edu Licensee: The Trustees of Ohio Wesleyan University. Population served: 20,000 Format: Var, college. ♦Chris Andrus, stn mgr.

WVMX(FM)— June 21, 1991: 107.9 mhz; 6 kw. Ant 285 ft TL: N40 17 57 W83 02 45. Stereo. Hrs open: 24 4401 Carriage Hill Ln., Columbus, 43220. Phone: (614) 451-2191. Fax: (614) 451-1831.E-mail: info@b1079.com Web Site:www.themix1079.com Licensee: Franklin Communications Inc. Group owner: Saga Communications Inc. (acq 3-27-2003; $9 million). Population served: 350,000 Natl. Rep: Christal,. Wire Svc: AP Format: Hot adult contemp. News staff: one; News: 10 hrs wkly. Target aud: 25-44. ♦Alan Goodman, pres, gen mgr, gen mgr; Michelle Hurley, mktg dir; Bill Shannon, progmg dir.

Delhi Hills

***WORI(FM)**— July 1998: 90.1 mhz; 15 kw. Ant 335 ft TL: N39 13 34 W84 42 59. Hrs open: 24 2351 Sunset Blvd., Suite 170-218, Rocklin, CA, 95765. Phone: (916) 251-1600. Fax: (916) 251-1650.E-mail: info@air1.com Web Site:www.air1.com Licensee: Educational Media Foundation. Group owner: EMF Broadcasting (acq 10-2-2003; grpsl). Natl. Network: Air 1, . Shaw Pittman. Format: Contemp Christian. Target aud: 18-35; Judeo Christian, female. ♦Richard Jenkins, pres; Mike Novak, VP; Keith Whipple, dev dir; David Pierce, progmg mgr; Ed Lenane, news dir; Sam Wallington, engrg dir; Karen Johnson, news rptr.

Delphos

***WBIE(FM)**— 2001: 91.5 mhz; 5.5 kw. Ant 321 ft TL: N40 56 48 W84 15 24. Hrs open: Drawer 2440, Tupelo, MS, 38803-2440. Phone: (662) 844-8888. Fax: (662) 842-7798.E-mail: info@afa.net Web Site:www.afr.net Licensee: American Family Association. Group owner: American Family Radio Format: Classic gospel. ♦Marvin Sanders, gen mgr.

WDOH(FM)— Dec 16, 1972: 107.1 mhz; 3.3 kw. Ant 298 ft TL: N40 49 55 W84 21 11. Stereo. Hrs open: 1301 N. Cable Rd., Lima, 45805. Phone: (419) 331-1600. Fax: (419) 228-5085.E-mail: info@wdoh.com Web Site:www.wdoh.com Licensee: Maverick Media of Lima License LLC. (acq 11-15-2004; $1.15 million). Population served: 7,608 Natl. Network: CBS, . Fletcher, Heald & Hildreth. Format: Lite rock. News staff: one; News: 7 hrs wkly. Target aud: 25 plus. Spec prog: Farm 8 hrs wkly. ♦Gary S. Rozynek, pres; David P. Roach, gen mgr; Deb Klaus, opns dir; Matt Childers, gen sls mgr; Justin Kage, prom dir, mus dir.

Delta

WLQR-FM— September 1994: 106.5 mhz; 3 kw. Ant 328 ft TL: N41 35 13 W83 54 11. Hrs open: 3225 Arlington Ave., Toledo, 43614. Phone: (419) 725-5700. Fax: (419) 389-2902.E-mail: info@wrwk.com Web Site:www.1470theticket.com Licensee: Cumulus Licensing Corp. Group owner: Cumulus Media Inc. (acq 11-18-99; $4,925,000). Natl. Network: ESPN Radio, . Format: Sports. Target aud: 18-34; male. ♦Skip Sschmidt, gen mgr; Skip Schmidt, gen sls mgr; Dan McClintock, progmg dir.

Dover-New Philadelphia

WJER(AM)— Feb 10, 1950: 1450 khz; 1 kw-U. TL: N40 30 46 W81 27 24. Hrs open: 646 Boulevard, Dover, 44622. Phone: (330) 343-7755. Fax: (330) 364-4538.E-mail: wjer@wjer.com Web Site:www.wjer.com Licensee: WJER Radio LLC (acq 2-16-2007; $200,000). Natl. Rep: Rgnl Reps,. Format: Oldies. ♦Gary Petricola, pres; Bob Scanlon, gen mgr, progmg dir; Dan Pitzo, gen sls mgr; Jennifer Clark, news dir.

Dublin

WRXS(FM)— April 1953: 106.7 mhz; 7.3 kw. Ant 590 ft TL: N40 09 33 W82 55 23. Stereo. Hrs open: 2323 W. 5th Ave., Suite 200, Columbus, 43204. Phone: (614) 486-6101. Fax: (614) 487-3575.E-mail: tomthon@clearchannel.com Web Site:www.radio1067.com Licensee: Citicasters Licenses L.P. (acq 1999; grpsl). Format: Modern rock. ♦Tom Thon, gen mgr.

East Liverpool

WOGF(FM)— Apr 15, 1959: 104.3 mhz; 50 kw. 330 ft TL: N40 37 48 W80 36 10. (CP: Ant 492 ft.). Stereo. Hrs open: 24 131 Pleasant Dr., Suite 5U, Aliquippa, 15001. Phone: (724) 378-1271. Fax: (724) 378-4653. Web Site:www.froggyland.com Licensee: Keymarket Licenses LLC. Population served: 500000 Format: Country. Target aud: 25-54. ♦Ron Aughinbaugh, gen mgr; Kalen Boyd, progmg dir.

WOHI(AM)— Dec 1, 1949: 1490 khz; 1 kw-U. TL: N40 37 47 W80 36 09. (CP: 660 w-U). Hrs open: 131 Pleasant Dr., Suite 5U, Aliquippa, 15001. Phone: (724) 378-1271. Fax: (724) 378-4653. Licensee: Keymarket Licenses LLC. Group owner: Keymarket Communications LLC (acq 2000; grpsl). Population served: 50,000 Natl. Network: Jones Radio Networks, . Natl. Rep: Rgnl Reps,. Format: Oldies. Target aud: General. ♦Gerald Getz, pres; Ron Aughinbaugh, gen mgr; Kalen Boyd, progmg dir.

Eaton

WEDI(AM)— January 1979: 1130 khz; 250 w-D, DA. TL: N39 44 55 W84 35 02. Hrs open:
Rebroadcasts WBZI(AM) Xenia 80%.
23 E. Second St., Xenia, 45385. Phone: (937) 372-3531. Fax: (937) 372-3508.E-mail: myclassiccountry@myclassiccountry.com Web Site:www.myclassiccountry.com Licensee: Town and Country Broadcasting Inc. (acq 1-4-2005; $175,000). Population served: 825,000 Natl. Network: Fox News Radio, . Rgnl. Network: Agri Bcstg. Natl. Rep: Rgnl Reps,. Agrinet Reddy, Begley & McCormick, L.L.P. Wire Svc: AP Format: Classic country. News staff: 2; News: 3 hrs wkly. Target aud: 35-64; adults. Spec prog: Gospel 5 hrs., Farm 2 hrs. wkly. ♦Joe Mullins, pres, gen mgr; Roy Hatfield, progmg dir; Darrin Johnston, news dir; Megan Brugger, traf mgr.

WGTZ(FM)— Nov 28, 1960: 92.9 mhz; 31.6 kw. Ant 600 ft TL: N39 50 10 W84 24 16. Stereo. Hrs open: 24 717 E. David Rd., Dayton, 45429. Phone: (937) 294-5858. Fax: (937) 297-5233.E-mail: info@fly929.com Web Site:www.fly929.com Licensee: MLB-Dayton IV LLC. Group owner: Radio One Inc. (acq 9-12-2007; grpsl). Population served: 11,300 Natl. Rep: Katz Radio,. Format: Adult Hits. Target aud: 18-49; contemp middle America. ♦Andrea Scott, gen mgr.

Edgewood

WZOO-FM— Jan 23, 1989: 102.5 mhz; 5.8 kw. Ant 328 ft TL: N41 49 44 W80 49 28. Stereo. Hrs open: 24 3226 Jefferson Rd., Ashtabula, 44004-9112. Phone: (440) 993-2126. Web Site:www.102zoo.com Licensee: Sweet Home Ashtabula LLC. Group owner: Clear Channel Communications Inc. (acq 9-17-2007; grpsl). Population served: 100,000 Law Office of David Tillotson. Format: Oldies. News staff: 3. Target aud: General. ◆Dana Schulte, VP, gen mgr; Dennis O'Brien, opns dir.

Elyria

WEOL(AM)— October 1948: 930 khz; 1 kw-U, DA-2. TL: N41 16 10 W82 00 21. Hrs open: 24 Box 4006, 4th Fl., 538 Broad St., 44036. Phone: (440) 322-3761. Fax: (440) 284-3189. Licensee: Elyria-Lorain Broadcasting Co. (group owner) Population served: 275,000 Natl. Network: ABC, . Natl. Rep: McGavren Guild,. Rgnl rep: Rgnl Reps. Putbrese, Hunsaker & Trent. Wire Svc: AP Format: News/talk, sports. News staff: 4. Target aud: 35 plus. Spec prog: Sp 2 hrs wkly, H.S. Sports. ◆Lonnie Gronek, pres; Bruce VanDyke, gen mgr, progmg dir.

WNWV(FM)— October 1948: 107.3 mhz; 20 kw. Ant 781 ft TL: N41 16 10 W82 00 16. Stereo. Hrs open: Prog sep from AM Box 4006, 4th Fl., 44036. Phone: (4400 322-3761. Fax: (440) 284-3189.E-mail: info@wnwv.com Web Site:www.wnwv.com Natl. Rep: McGavren Guild,. Rgnl rep: Regional Reps Wire Svc: AP Format: Smooth jazz. News: 4 hrs wkly. Target aud: 25 plus; upscale. ◆Angie Handa, progmg dir.

Englewood

WDKF(FM)— Dec 15, 1993: 94.5 mhz; 6 kw. 328 ft TL: N39 57 17 W84 18 25. Hrs open: 24 101 Pine St., Dayton, 45402. Phone: (937) 224-1137. Fax: (937) 224-3667.E-mail: info@ccedayton.com Web Site:www.945kissfm.com Licensee: Aloha Station Trust LLC, as Trustee Group owner: Clear Channel Communications Inc. (acq 7-30-2008). Format: Top 40. Target aud: 18-34. ◆Robert Zurowesti, VP, mktg mgr; Tony Tilford, opns mgr & progmg dir.

Fairborn

WGNZ(AM)— Sept 1, 1968: 1110 khz; 2.5 kw-D, 1.7 kw-CH, DA. TL: N39 41 15 W83 57 55. Hrs open: Box 1100, Dayton, 45405-0879. Phone: (937) 454-9000. Fax: (937) 454-1980.E-mail: wgnz@wgnz.com Web Site:www.wgnz.com Licensee: L & D Broadcasters Inc. (acq 8-10-2009). Population served: 1,500,000 Natl. Network: Salem Radio Network, . Miller and Neely P.C. Format: Relg. Target aud: General; listeners who like family radio. ◆Tim Livingston, pres & gen mgr.

WXEG(FM)—See Beavercreek

Fairfield

WCNW(AM)— Feb 14, 1964: 1560 khz; 5 kw-D, DA. TL: N39 20 20 W84 31 30. Hrs open: 8686 Michael Ln., 45014. Phone: (513) 829-7700. Fax: (513) 829-1560.E-mail: info@wcnw.com Licensee: Vernon R. Baldwin Inc. (group owner; acq 6-11-84; $700,000; 3-19-84). Population served: 2,000,000 Format: Southern gospel. ◆Vernon R. Baldwin, pres, CFO & gen mgr; Mark Mitchell, stn mgr.

WREW(FM)— 1925: 94.9 mhz; 10.5 kw. Ant 1,056 ft TL: N39 12 01 W84 31 22. Stereo. Hrs open: 24 2060 Reading Rd., Cincinnati, 45202. Phone: (513) 699-5959. Fax: (513) 699-5000. Web Site:www.rewind949.com Licensee: Bonneville Holding Co. Group owner: Susquehanna Radio Corp. (acq 3-14-2008; grpsl). Wilkinson Barker Knauer L.L.P. Format: Classic hits. News: 8 hrs wkly. ◆Mike Fredrick, gen mgr; Christine Mello, gen sls mgr, prom mgr; Travis Moon, progmg dir.

Findlay

WBVI(FM)—See Fostoria

WFIN(AM)— Dec 15, 1941: 1330 khz; 1 kw-D, 79 w-N. TL: N41 00 36 W83 38 04. Hrs open: 24 Box 1507, 45839-1507. Secondary address: 551 Lake Cascades Pkwy. 45840. Phone: (419) 422-4545. Fax: (419) 422-6736.E-mail: wfin@wfin.com Web Site:www.wfin.com Licensee: Blanchard River Broadcasting Co. Group owner: Findlay Publishing Co. (acq 1949). Population served: 45,000 Natl. Network: ABC, . ABN Radio Rgnl rep: Rgnl Reps. Format: Local news/talk. News staff: 2. Target aud: 45 plus. Spec prog: Farm 7 hrs, sports 12 hrs wkly. ◆David Glass, pres, VP; Kurt Heminger, VP, opns dir; Sandy

Kozlevcar, gen mgr, gen sls mgr; Bill Rice, progmg dir; Tom Sheldon, news dir; Dennis Rund, chief of engrg; Vaun Wickerham, farm dir; Chris Miller, sports cmtr.

WKXA-FM— 1948: 100.5 mhz; 20 kw. Ant 440 ft TL: N40 55 00 W83 35 45. Stereo. Hrs open: 24 Box 1507, 45839-1507. Secondary address: 551 Lake Cascades Pkwy. 45840. Phone: (415) 422-4545. Fax: (419) 422-6736.E-mail: wkxa@wkxa.com Web Site:www.wkxa.com Licensee: Blanchard River Broadcasting Co. Rgnl rep: Regional Reps Format: Classic Hits. News staff: 2. Target aud: 25-54. ◆Dave Glass, pres; Kurt Heminger, VP; Sandy Kozlevcar, gen mgr, gen sls mgr; Meg Stevens, progmg dir, mus dir; Dennis Rund, chief of engrg; Vaun Wickerham, farm dir; Chris Miller, sports cmtr.

*WLFC(FM)— Nov 1, 1973: 88.3 mhz; 155 w. 66 ft TL: N41 03 11 W83 39 13. Stereo. Hrs open: 7 AM-midnight 1000 N. Main St., 45840. Phone: (419) 434-4747. Phone: (419) 434-9532. Fax: (419) 434-4822. Web Site:www.myspace.com/wlfc88_3 Licensee: University of Findlay. Population served: 45,000 Format: Indy Rock. News: 3 hrs wkly. Target aud: 18-40. Spec prog: Class 3 hrs, folk 3 hrs, relg 3 hrs, Sp 3 hrs wkly. ◆Chris Underation, gen mgr.

WPFX-FM—See North Baltimore

*WTKC(FM)— 07/2006: 89.7 mhz; 125 w. Ant 30 ft TL: N41 02 43 W83 39 02. Hrs open: Box 1212, 45840-1212. Phone: (419) 423-3285.E-mail: wtkc89.7@sbcglobal.net Web Site:www.wtkc897.com Licensee: Church of the Living God Ministries. Format: Christian music, talk. ◆Juan Salinas, gen mgr; Richard Lugo, progmg mgr.

Fort Shawnee

WZRX-FM— 1991: 107.5 mhz; 3 kw. 328 ft TL: N40 40 04 W84 01 41. Hrs open: 24 667 W. Market St., Lima, 45801. Phone: (419) 223-2060. Fax: (419) 229-3888.E-mail: comments@wzrx.com Web Site:www.x1075fm.com Licensee: Jacor Broadcasting Corp. Group owner: Clear Channel Communications Inc. (acq 5-4-99; grpsl). Population served: 150,000 Natl. Rep: Clear Channel,. Format: Oldies, rock/AOR. News: one hr wkly. Target aud: 18-49; male dominated. ◆Eric Michaels, opns mgr & progmg dir.

Fostoria

WBVI(FM)— 1946: 96.7 mhz; 3 kw. Ant 289 ft TL: N41 06 00 W83 28 32. Stereo. Hrs open: 24 P.O. Box 1157, 45830. Secondary address: Box 1624 45840. Phone: (419) 435-1430. Phone: (419) 422-9284. Fax: (419) 425-8019. Web Site:www.wbvi.com Licensee: TCB Holdings Inc. Population served: 660,000 Natl. Network: Westwood One, . Rgnl rep: OAB Format: Music (A/C). News staff: one. Target aud: 18-50. ◆Shannon Miller, gen sls mgr.

WFOB(AM)— Dec 9, 1952: 1430 khz; 1 kw-U, DA-2. TL: N41 06 06 W83 23 59. Hrs open: 24/7 Box 1157, 44830. Secondary address: Box 1624, Findlay 45840. Phone: (419) 435-1430. Phone: (419) 422-9284. Fax: (419) 435-6611.E-mail: production@wbvi.com Web Site:www.wfob.com Licensee: TCB Holdings Inc. c/o Roppe Corp. (acq 11-24-97; with co-located FM). Population served: 309,100 Natl. Network: CBS, . Natl. Rep: Rgnl Reps,. Baker & Hostetler. Format: Sports. Target aud: General. Spec prog: Sp 3 hrs wkly. ◆Brian Cooper, pres; Burley Stapley, opns mgr, chief of engrg; Shannon Miller, gen sls mgr & adv mgr.

Fredericktown

WXXR(FM)— Sept 14, 1987: 98.3 mhz; 1.8 kw. Ant 423 ft TL: N40 34 27 W82 30 27. Stereo. Hrs open: 24
Rebroadcasts WFXN-FM Galion 100%.
1197 US Hwy. Rt. 42, Ashland, 44805. Phone: (419) 289-2605. Fax: (419) 289-0304.E-mail: jeffschendel@clearchannel.com Licensee: Capstar TX L.P. Group owner: Clear Channel Communications Inc. (acq 2-12-2001; grpsl). Natl. Network: Fox News Radio, . Format: CHR. Target aud: 25-54; Male. Spec prog: Underground Garage, House of Hair. ◆Diana Coon, gen mgr; Joe Rinehart, stn mgr; Eric Hansen, opns mgr.

Fremont

WFRO-FM— Dec 15, 1946: 99.1 mhz; 11.5 kw. Ant 364 ft TL: N41 21 58 W83 05 20. Hrs open: 24 1281 N. River Rd., 43420. Phone: (419) 332-8218. Fax: (419) 333-8226. Web Site:www.wfroradio.com Licensee: BAS Broadcasting Inc. (acq 9-11-2002; $1.3 million). Population served: 400,000 Natl. Network: ABC, . Agrinet Rgnl rep: Rgnl Reps Erwin Krasnow. Format: Adult contemp. News staff: 2; News: 5 hrs wkly. Target aud: 25-54; adults. ◆Jim Lorenzen, pres; Tom Klein, CEO & gen mgr; Dave Campbell, opns mgr.

Gahanna

*WCVO(FM)— Oct 13, 1972: 104.9 mhz; 6 kw. 298 ft TL: N40 04 16 W82 48 35. Stereo. Hrs open: 24 Box 881, East Johnstown Rd., 43230. Secondary address: 4400 Reynoldsburg-New Albany Road, New Albany 43054. Phone: (614) 289-5700. Fax: (614) 289-5793.E-mail: theriver@1049theriver.com Web Site:www.1049theriver.com Licensee: Christian Voice of Central Ohio Inc. Population served: 1,500,000 Format: Christian, Adult Contempo. News: 1.5. Target aud: 25-54; Christian, politically aware, female, middle aged professionals. ◆Dan Baughman, pres, gen mgr, stn mgr, disc jockey; Todd Stack, progmg dir; Mike Russell, mus dir.

Galion

WFXN-FM— Nov 8, 1974: 102.3 mhz; 3.5 kw. Ant 430 ft TL: N40 45 26 W82 47 23. Hrs open: 24 1197 US Hwy. Rt 42, Ashland, 44805. Phone: (800) 529-1013. Fax: (419) 289-0304.E-mail: jeffschendel @clearchannel.com Web Site:www.foxclassicrock.com Licensee: Capstar TX L.P. Group owner: Clear Channel Communications Inc. (acq 2-12-2001; grpsl). Population served: 13,123 Natl. Network: Fox News Radio, . Format: Classic rock. Target aud: 25-54; Male. Spec prog: Underground Garage 2hrs, House of Hair 2hrs. ◆Diana Coon, gen mgr; Eric Hanson, opns mgr; Jeff Schendel, progmg dir.

Gallipolis

WJEH(AM)— June 19, 1950: 990 khz; 1 kw-D, 16 w-N, 250 w-CH. TL: N38 48 20 W82 13 23. Stereo. Hrs open: 24 Box 661, Gallipolis, 45631-0661. Secondary address: 117 Portsmouth Rd. 45631. Phone: (740) 446-3543. Fax: (740) 446-3001.E-mail: Sunny Broadcasting LLC (acq 10-6-2006; $625,000 with WNTO(FM) Racine). Population served: 90,000 Natl. Rep: Rgnl Reps,. Dean George Hill. Format: Music of your Life. News staff: one; News: 10 hrs wkly. Target aud: 35 plus. ◆Dave Diddle, gen mgr, stn mgr; Tina Merry, progmg dir; Bob Triplett, chief of engrg.

WXBW(FM)— Dec 15, 1961: 101.5 mhz; 50 kw. Ant 500 ft TL: N38 45 19 W82 13 36. Stereo. Hrs open: 24 Box 404, Huntington, WV, 25708. Secondary address: 919 Fifth Ave., Suite 210, Huntington, WV 25701. Phone: (304) 399-9603. Fax: (304) 399-9608. Web Site:www.bobfm1015.com Licensee: Connoisseur Media of WV-OH LLC. (acq 6-21-2006; $3.1 million). Population served: 500,000 Natl. Network: Westwood One, . Natl. Rep: McGavren Guild,. Format: Adult hits. Target aud: 24-49. ◆Newman Adkins, gen mgr.

Gambier

*WKCO(FM)— 1975: 91.9 mhz; 266 w. 190 ft TL: N40 22 25 W82 23 45. Stereo. Hrs open: 19 Box 312, Kenyon College, 43022. Phone: (740) 427-5412.E-mail: wkco@kenyon.edu Web Site:www.wkco.kenyon.edu Licensee: Kenyon College. Population served: 50,000 Format: Var. News: 8 hrs wkly. Target aud: 18-25; college population.

Geneva

WKKY(FM)— Nov 2, 1987: 104.7 mhz; 6 kw. 328 ft TL: N41 47 30 W81 05 31. Stereo. Hrs open: 24 95 W. Main St., 44041. Phone: (440) 466-9559. Fax: (440) 466-3138.E-mail: wkky@wkky.com Web Site:www.wkky.com Licensee: Music Express Broadcasting Corp. of Northeast Ohio. (acq 3-15-90; $441,965; 4-2-90). Population served: 128,000 Natl. Network: ABC, . Natl. Rep: Rgnl Reps,. Format: Country. News: 6 hrs wkly. Target aud: 25-54. Spec prog: Pub affrs 2 hrs wkly. ◆Warren Jones, pres; Gary Hayes, gen mgr; Cindy Steiner, traf mgr.

Gibsonburg

WIMX(FM)— Jan 24, 1989: 95.7 mhz; 3.5 kw. 433 ft TL: N41 28 19 W83 25 05. Stereo. Hrs open: 24 720 Water St, Toledo, 43604. Phone: (419) 868-7914. Fax: (419) 868-8765. Licensee: Urban Radio Licenses LLC. (acq 5-13-2005; $2 million). Natl. Rep: Interep,. Rgnl rep: Regional Reps Format: Urban Adult Contemporary. Target aud: 20-40. ◆Curtis Downey, gen mgr & mktg mgr.

Granville

*WDUB(FM)— Feb 7, 1962: 91.1 mhz; 100 w. 171 ft TL: N40 04 16 W82 31 24. Stereo. Hrs open: 24 Slayter Hall, Denison Univ., 43023. Phone: (740) 587-6382. Phone: (740) 587-0810. Fax: (740) 587-8364. Web Site:www.wdub.org Licensee: Denison University. Natl. Network: USA, . Wire Svc: UPI Format: Progsv, classic rock, free-form. News

staff: 3. Target aud: General; college students, faculty & loc residents. Spec prog: Black 9 hrs, reggae 2 hrs, Sp 2 hrs, Swedish 2 hrs wkly. ◆Jessie Kanelos, stn mgr.

Greenfield

WVNU(FM)— May 1, 1994: 97.5 mhz; 3.2 kw. 495 ft TL: N39 24 01 W83 26 48. Stereo. Hrs open: 24 Box 329, 321 Jefferson St., 45123. Phone: (937) 981-5050. Fax: (937) 981-2107.E-mail: wvnu@bright.net Web Site:wvnu.com Licensee: Southern Ohio Broadcasting Inc. (acq 1-12-94; $35,227; 2-7-94). Natl. Network: Jones Radio Networks, CNN Radio, . ABN Radio Pepper & Corazzini. Format: Lite adult contemp. Target aud: 24-54. ◆Patrick Hays, pres, gen mgr; Tom Archibald, VP; Nelson Eads, progmg dir.

Greenville

*WDPG(FM)— February 1994: 89.9 mhz; 50 kw. 403 ft TL: N40 08 49 W84 36 36. Hrs open: 24
Rebroadcasts WDPR(FM) West Carrollton 100%.
126 N. Main St., Dayton, 45402. Phone: (937) 496-3850. Fax: (937) 496-3852.E-mail: dpr@dpr.org Web Site:www.dpr.org Licensee: Dayton Public Radio Inc. Format: Class. ◆Georgie Woessner, gen mgr; Charles Wendelken-Wilson, mus dir.

WDSJ(FM)— Oct 26, 1990: 106.5 mhz; 50 kw. Ant 482 ft TL: N40 08 49 W84 36 36. Stereo. Hrs open: 24 101 Pine St., Dayton, 45402-2925. Phone: (937) 224-1137. Fax: (937) 224-3667.E-mail: info@ccedayton.com Web Site:www.1065thebull.com Licensee: Aloha Station Trust LLC, as Trustee Group owner: Clear Channel Communications Inc. (acq 7-30-2008). Population served: 544,000 Natl. Network: Jones Radio Networks, . Thompson Hine LLP. Format: Country. Target aud: 25-54. ◆Jeff Stevens, opns mgr, progmg dir; Robert Zurowesti, VP & mktg mgr.

*WMUO(FM)—Not on air, target date: unknown: 91.9 mhz; 6 kw. Ant 230 ft TL: N40 08 21 W84 37 04. Hrs open: 1223 Central Pkwy., Cincinnati, 45214. Phone: (513) 352-9170. Fax: (513) 241-8456.E-mail: WMUB@WMUB.org Web Site:www.wmub.org Licensee: The President & Trustees of Miami University. ◆Richard Eiswerth, gen mgr.

Grove City

WWCD(FM)— Aug 21, 1990: 101.1 mhz; 6 kw. 328 ft TL: N39 48 50 W83 03 19. Stereo. Hrs open: 24 503 S. Front St., Suite 101, Columbus, 43215. Phone: (614) 221-9923. Fax: (614) 227-0021.E-mail: webmaster@cd101.com Web Site:www.cd101.com Licensee: Fun With Radio LLC (acq 8-16-01). Drinker Biddle & Reath. Format: Alternative rock. Target aud: 21-40; well educated, upscale professionals with discretionary income. Spec prog: Jazz 3 hrs, acoustic 2 hrs, mix show 2 hrs wkly. ◆Roger Vaughan, pres & gen mgr; Randy Malloy, opns dir.

*WWGV(FM)— 2008: 88.1 mhz; 5.4 kw vert. Ant 272 ft TL: N39 43 16 W83 08 36. Hrs open:
Rebroadcasts WAFR(FM) Tupelo, MS 100%.
Drawer 2440, Tupelo, MS, 38803. Phone: (662) 844-5036. Fax: (662) 842-7798.E-mail: info@afa.net Web Site:www.afr.net Licensee: American Family Association. Natl. Network: American Family Radio, . Format: Contemp Christian. ◆Donald E. Wildmon, chmn.

Hamilton

WGRR(FM)— Apr 15, 1961: 103.5 mhz; 19.3 kw. Ant 790 ft TL: N39 16 24 W84 31 37. Stereo. Hrs open: 24 895 Central Ave., Suite 900, Cincinnati, 45202. Phone: (513) 241-9898. Fax: (513) 241-6689.E-mail: info@cumulus.com Web Site:www.wgrr.com Licensee: WVAE LICO Inc. Group owner: Infinity Broadcasting Corp. (acq 11-29-2007; exchange for WSWD(FM) Fairfield). Population served: 1,969,100 Format: Classic rock. ◆Joe Wickman, gen sls mgr; Keith Mitchell, prom dir.

*WHSS(FM)— May 12, 1975: 89.5 mhz; 190 w. 282 ft TL: N39 25 51 W84 37 40. Hrs open: Midnight-noon Hamilton High School, 1111 Eaton Rd., 45013. Phone: (513) 887-4818. Fax: (513) 887-4879.E-mail: whss@whss.org Web Site:www.895whss.org Licensee: Hamilton City Schools Board of Education. Population served: 432,000 Format: Rock, alternative. News: 3 hrs wkly. Target aud: 12 plus; general. ◆David P. Spurrier, gen mgr & progmg dir.

WMOH(AM)— Aug 15, 1944: 1450 khz; 1 kw-U. TL: N39 24 10 W84 31 54. Stereo. Hrs open: 24 2081 Fairgrove Ave., 45011. Phone: (513) 863-1111. Fax: (513) 863-6856.E-mail: christheiss@wmoh.com Web Site:www.wmoh.com Licensee: Vernon R. Baldwin Inc. (group owner;

acq 1-7-03; $950,000). Population served: 289,512 Natl. Network: ESPN Radio, . Natl. Rep: Rgnl Reps,. Format: Sports. News staff: 5; News: 25 hrs wkly. Target aud: 35-64; adults above medium income. ◆Chris Theiss, gen mgr, opns dir, opns mgr, gen sls mgr, sports cmtr; Bill Douglas, progmg dir; Steve Vaughn, news dir; Gail Moore, traf mgr; Jay Crawford, engr.

Harrison

WNLT(FM)— Sept 1, 1991: 104.3 mhz; 3 kw. 328 ft TL: N39 15 02 W84 50 10. Hrs open: 8686 Michael Ln., Fairfield, 45014. Phone: (513) 829-7700. Web Site:www.klove.com Licensee: Vernon R. Baldwin Inc. (group owner) Population served: 2,000,000 Natl. Network: K-Love, . Format: Contemp Christian. ◆Marci Baldwin, VP; Vernon R. Baldwin, pres & gen mgr.

Heath

WHTH(AM)— Oct 16, 1970: 790 khz; 1 kw-D, DA-1. TL: N40 03 05 W82 28 08. Hrs open: 24 Box 1057, 1000 N. 40th St., Newark, 43058-1057. Phone: (740) 522-8171. Fax: (740) 522-8174.E-mail: sales@wnko.com Web Site:www.wnko.com Licensee: Runnymede Corp. (acq 10-15-98; $100,000 for stock with WNKO(FM) Newark). Population served: 140,000 Natl. Network: CNN Radio, . Wire Svc: AP Format: Talk radio. Target aud: 35-54. ◆Charles Franks, pres; J. Thomas Swank, gen mgr; John Franks, opns VP.

WNKO(FM)—See Newark

Hicksville

WFGA(FM)— 2002: 106.7 mhz; 2.85 kw. Ant 482 ft TL: N41 19 16 W84 43 12. Hrs open: 450 N. Grand Staff Dr., Auburn, IN, 46706. Phone: (260) 920-3602. Fax: (260) 920-3604.E-mail: info@ilovefroggy.com Web Site:ilovefroggy.com Licensee: Fallen Timber Communications, LLC (acq 6-28-2000; $512,000). Format: Var. ◆Leann Didier, gen mgr.

Hilliard

WBWR(FM)— Feb 6, 1991: 105.7 mhz; 2.4 kw. 522 ft TL: N39 58 10 W83 00 10. Stereo. Hrs open: 24 2323 W. 5th Ave., Suite 200, Columbus, 43204. Phone: (614) 486-6101. Fax: (614) 487-3575.E-mail: tomthom@clearchannel.com Web Site:www.thebrew1057.com Licensee: Citicasters Licenses L.P. Group owner: Clear Channel Communications Inc. (acq 1999; grpsl). Natl. Network: ABC, . Format: Classic Rock. News staff: one. Target aud: 18-34. ◆Tom Thon, gen mgr; Rob O'Boyle, gen sls mgr, prom dir; John Crenshaw, progmg dir.

Hillsboro

WSRW(AM)— July 15, 1956: 1590 khz; 500 w-D. TL: N39 09 58 W83 36 25. Hrs open: Box 9, 45133. Secondary address: 5675 St., Rt. 247 45133. Phone: (937) 393-1590. Fax: (937) 393-1611.E-mail: wsrw@clearchannel.com Web Site:www.wsrwam.com Licensee: CC Licenses LLC. Group owner: Clear Channel Communcations Inc. (acq 10-26-99; $2.5 million with WSRW-FM Hillsboro). Population served: 75,000 Natl. Network: Jones Radio Networks, . Natl. Rep: Katz Radio,. Format: Classic Hit Country. News: 3 hrs wkly. Target aud: 35-54; general. ◆Dan Latham, sr VP, gen mgr; Kim Scaggs, opns mgr; John Barney, sls dir, gen sls mgr; Damon Scott, progmg dir; Paul Levo, chief of engrg.

WSRW-FM— 1962: 106.7 mhz; 50 kw. 300 ft TL: N39 09 58 W83 36 25. Stereo. Hrs open: 24 Box 9, 45133. Secondary address: 5675 St., Rt. 247 45133. Phone: (937) 393-1590. Fax: (937) 393-1611.E-mail: wsrw@clearchannel.com Web Site:www.wsrw.com Licensee: CC Licenses LLC. Group owner: Clear Channel Communications Inc. (acq 10-26-99; $2.5 million with WSRW(AM) Hillsboro). Population served: 3,000,000 Natl. Network: ABC, . Natl. Rep: Katz Radio,. Format: Country. News staff: one; News: 8 hrs wkly. Target aud: General. ◆Dan Latham, gen mgr; Kim Scaggs, opns mgr; Damon Scott, progmg mgr.

Holland

WPOS-FM— Sept 1, 1966: 102.3 mhz; 6 kw. 312 ft TL: N41 37 32 W83 42 41. Stereo. Hrs open: 24 Box 457, 43528. Secondary address: 7112 Angola Rd. 43528. Phone: (419) 865-5551. Fax: (419) 865-0112.E-mail: radio@wposfm.com Web Site:www.wposfm.com Licensee: Maumee Valley Broadcasting Association. (acq 8-1-65). Wiley, Rein & Fielding. Format: Christian. News: 10 hrs wkly. Spec prog: Gospel 20 hrs wkly. ◆Rick Waldron, gen mgr.

Hubbard

WRBP(FM)— Aug 16, 1993: 101.9 mhz; 3 kw. 328 ft TL: N41 05 29 W30 30 05. Hrs open: 20 Federal Plaza W., # T2, Youngstown, 44503. Phone: (330) 744-5115. Fax: (330) 744-4020.E-mail: skip@ytownradio.com Web Site:www.jamz1019.com Licensee: Bernard of Ohio LLC. (acq 1-22-2007; grpsl). Natl. Network: CNN Radio, . Format: hip-hop, R&B. Target aud: 25-54; general. Spec prog: Black, news/talk, jazz 12 hrs, relg 6 hrs, Sp 2 hrs wkly. ◆Skip Benarczyk, gen mgr, gen sls mgr, progmg dir; Tiffany Allen, prom dir.

Huron

WKFM(FM)— Apr 1, 1996: 96.1 mhz; 3.4 kw. 436 ft TL: N41 18 05 W82 29 16. Stereo. Hrs open: 24 10327 Milan Rd., US Rte. 250, Milan, 44846. Phone: (419) 609-5961. Fax: (419) 609-2679.E-mail: k96@wkfm.com Web Site:www.wkfm.com Licensee: Elyria-Lorain Broadcasting Co. (group owner; acq 7-1-96; $450,000). Natl. Network: Westwood One, . Putbrese, Hunsaker & Trent. Format: Country. News staff: one; News: one hr wkly. Target aud: General. ◆Gary Kneisley, pres; Lonnie Gronek, gen mgr; Tim Kelly, opns mgr; Bill Forthofer, gen sls mgr.

Ironton

WBKS(FM)— July 1, 1973: 107.1 mhz; 3.1 kw. Ant 449 ft TL: N38 31 23 W82 39 11. Hrs open: 18 Box 2288, Huntington, WV, 25724. Phone: (304) 525-7788. Fax: (304) 525-3299.E-mail: kiss107fm@clearchannel.com Web Site:www.1071kiss.com Licensee: Aloha Station Trust LLC Group owner: Clear Channel Communications Inc. (acq 7-30-2008; grpsl). Format: Hot CHR. News: 3 hrs wkly. Target aud: 35 plus; affluent, middle-aged. Spec prog: Relg 2 hrs wkly. ◆Judy Cornett, gen mgr; Matt Tweel, gen sls mgr; Jim Davis, progmg mgr; Gary Miller, mus dir; Bill Cornwell, news dir; Scott Hensley, chief of engrg.

WIRO(AM)— September 1951: 1230 khz; 1 kw-U. TL: N38 32 22 W82 40 17. Hrs open: 24 Box 2288, Huntington, WV, 25724. Phone: (304) 525-7788. Fax: (304) 525-6281.E-mail: paulswann@clearchannel.com Web Site:www.foxsports1230.com Licensee: Aloha Station Trust LLC Group owner: Clear Channel Communications Inc. (acq 7-30-2008; grpsl). Population served: 15,030 Natl. Network: Fox Sports, . Natl. Rep: Keystone (unwired net), Rgnl Reps,. Format: Sports. Target aud: 21-49. ◆Judy Jennings, gen mgr; Matt Tweel, gen sls mgr; Paul Swann, progmg dir & chief of engrg.

*WOUL-FM— Oct 12, 1987: 89.1 mhz; 50 kw. 400 ft TL: N38 31 23 W82 39 20. Stereo. Hrs open: 24
Rebroadcasts WOUB-FM Athens 100%.
9 S. College St., Athens, 45701. Phone: (740) 593-4554. Fax: (740) 593-0240.E-mail: woub@woub.org Web Site:www.woub.org Licensee: Ohio University. Population served: 70,000 Natl. Network: PRI, NPR, . Format: News/talk. News staff: 3. ◆David Wiseman, VP, opns VP; Carolyn Lewis, gen mgr; Steve Skidmore, opns dir; Scott Martin, opns mgr.

Jackson

WCJO(FM)— 1971: 97.7 mhz; 3 kw. 300 ft TL: N39 01 45 W82 35 51. Hrs open: 24 Box 667, 45640. Secondary address: 295 E. Main St. 45640. Phone: (740) 286-3023. Fax: (740) 286-6679.E-mail: jmossbarger@jcbiradio.com Licensee: Jackson County Broadcasting Inc. (group owner; acq 6-15-99; grpsl). Population served: 300,000 Natl. Network: Westwood One, . Fletcher, Heald & Hildreth. Format: Hot country. News staff: one; News: 8 hrs wkly. Target aud: General; current-country music lovers. ◆Jerry Mossbarger, gen mgr; Ron Speakman, gen sls mgr; John Pelletier, progmg dir, disc jockey.

Jefferson

*WCVJ(FM)— 1978: 90.9 mhz; 1.85 kw. Ant 643 ft TL: N41 37 50 W80 45 36. Stereo. Hrs open: 2351 Suset Blvd., Suite 170-218, Rocklin, CA, 95765. Phone: (916) 251-1600. Fax: (916) 251-1650. Licensee: Educational Media Foundation. (acq 10-14-2005; $650,000). Population served: 20,000 Format: Christian. ◆Richard Jenkins, pres; Mike Novak, VP; Keith Whipple, dev dir; David Pierce, progmg mgr; Ed Lenane, news dir; Sam Wallington, engrg dir; Karen Johnson, news rptr.

Johnstown

WVKO-FM—Licensed to Johnstown. See Columbus

Kent

WJMP(AM)— March 1964: 1520 khz; 1 kw-D, DA. TL: N41 09 35 W81 18 19. Hrs open: Box 2170, Akron, 44309-2170. Secondary address: 2449 S.R. 59 44240. Phone: (330) 673-2323. Fax: (330) 673-0301. Licensee: Media-Com Inc. (acq 1971). Population served: 300,000 Format: Talk. Target aud: 18 plus. ♦Richard M. Klaus, pres; William Klaus, stn mgr; Robert Klaus, sls VP; Jim Midock, news dir; Bob Sassman, chief of engrg; Mary Stein, traf mgr.

***WKSU-FM**— 1950: 89.7 mhz; 14.5 kw. Ant 909 ft TL: N41 04 58 W81 38 02. Stereo. Hrs open: 24 Box 5190, 44242-0001. Secondary address: 1613 E. Summit St. 44242-0001. Phone: (330) 672-3114. Fax: (330) 672-4107.E-mail: letters@wksu.org Web Site:www.wksu.org Licensee: Kent State University. Population served: 2,650,000 Natl. Network: PRI, NPR, AP Radio, . Dow, Lohnes & Albertson. Format: Class, news. News staff: 5; News: 35 hrs wkly. Target aud: 35-65; college grad, professional & upper income. Spec prog: Folk 12 hrs wkly. ♦Allen E. Bartholet, gen mgr; Mark Uryck, progmg dir; Ronald Bartlebaugh, engrg dir.

WNIR(FM)— Feb 19, 1962: 100.1 mhz; 4.2 kw. Ant 394 ft TL: N41 06 28 W81 21 19. Hrs open: Box 2170, Akron, 44309-2170. Secondary address: 2449 S.R. 59 44240. Phone: (330) 673-2323. Fax: (330) 673-0301. Licensee: Media-Com Inc. Population served: 2,000,000 Wombel, Carlyle, Sandridge & Rice. Wire Svc: AP Format: Talk. Target aud: General. ♦Mary Stein, traf mgr.

Kenton

WKTN(FM)— June 20, 1963: 95.3 mhz; 3 kw. 270 ft TL: N40 38 41 W83 33 59. Stereo. Hrs open: 5 AM-midnight 112 N. Detroit St., 43326. Phone: (419) 675-2355. Fax: (419) 673-1096.E-mail: wktn@dbscorp.net Web Site:www.wktn.com Licensee: Radio General Ltd. (acq 5-12-77). Population served: 40,000 Rgnl. Network: Agri Bcstg. Arent, Fox, Kintner, Plotkin & Kahn. Format: Adult contemp. News staff: one; News: 10 hrs wkly. Target aud: 25-54. Spec prog: Farm 2 hrs wkly. ♦Keith P. Gensheimer, pres & gen mgr.

Kettering

***WKET(FM)**— May 5, 1975: 98.3 mhz; 10 w. 150 ft TL: N39 41 46 W84 09 43. Hrs open: 3301 Shroyer Rd., 45429. Phone: (937) 296-7669. Fax: (937) 297-7435.E-mail: info@wket.com Licensee: Kettering City School District. Format: Educ, classic rock, AOR. Target aud: 13-18; high school students. ♦Karl Bremer, gen mgr & stn mgr.

WLQT(FM)— Feb 20, 1962: 99.9 mhz; 50 kw. 500 ft TL: N39 44 07 W84 10 10. Stereo. Hrs open: 24 101 Pine St., Dayton, 45402. Phone: (937) 224-1137. Fax: (937) 224-3667.E-mail: info@ccedayton.com Web Site:www.wlqt.com Licensee: Citicasters Licenses L.P. Group owner: Clear Channel Communications Inc. (acq 1999; grpsl). Format: Soft Adult contemp. Target aud: 35-64; persons 35-64. ♦Karrie Sudbrack, gen mgr; Jeff Stevens, opns mgr, progmg dir; Robert Zurowesti, VP & mktg mgr.

WQRP(FM)—See Dayton

Lancaster

***WFCO(FM)**— August 1988: 90.9 mhz; 1.2 kw vert. Ant 256 ft TL: N39 40 49 W82 35 51. Stereo. Hrs open: 24 201 S. Broad St., Studio 303, 43130. Phone: (740) 689-0909. Fax: (740) 654-8581.E-mail: wfco@wfcofm.com Web Site:wfcofm.com Licensee: Lancaster Educational Broadcasting Foundation. Population served: 200,000 Natl. Network: Salem Radio Network, . Format: Christian inspo, christian news/talk. News staff: one; News: one hr wkly. Target aud: 30 plus; Christian audience & those interested in community events. Spec prog: Live coverage of sports & community events. ♦Steve Rauch, gen mgr.

WHOK-FM— December 1958: 95.5 mhz; 50 kw. Ant 492 ft TL: N39 40 32 W82 40 34. Stereo. Hrs open: 24 10th Fl., 280 Plaza N. High St., Columbus, 43215. Phone: (614) 225-9465. Fax: (614) 677-0116. Web Site:www.955thehawk.com Licensee: Wilks License Co.-Columbus LLC. Group owner: Infinity Broadcasting Corp. (acq 1-10-2007; grpsl). Population served: 1,500,000 Natl. Network: Westwood One, . Natl. Rep: McGavren Guild,. Leventhal, Senter & Lerman. Format: Everything Country. News staff: one; News: 2 hrs wkly. Target aud: 25-54. ♦Ross Wagner, sls dir; Scott Miller, VP, gen mgr & mktg mgr; Marissa McClellan, prom dir; George Wolf, progmg dir.

WLOH(AM)— October 1948: 1320 khz; 1 kw-D, 28 w-N. TL: N39 44 21 W82 37 48. Hrs open: 24 2686 N. Columbus St., 43130. Phone: (740) 653-4373. Fax: (740) 653-0702.E-mail: community@wloh.net Web Site:www.wloh.net Licensee: Frontier Broadcasting LLC No. 3 (acq 2-13-01; $325,000). Population served: 108,000 Natl. Rep: D & R Radio,. Covington & Burling. Format: Talk radio. News staff: 2; News: 24 hrs wkly. Target aud: General; Fairfield, Franklin & surrounding county residents. Spec prog: Farm one hr wkly. ♦Bart Johnson, CEO; Mark Bohach, gen mgr, opns mgr; Michael O'Riley, gen sls mgr.

Lebanon

WFTK(FM)— May 26, 1958: 96.5 mhz; 19.5 kw. Ant 810 ft TL: N39 21 11 W84 19 30. Stereo. Hrs open: 24 c/o Radio Cincinnati, 895 Central Ave., Suite 900, Cincinnati, 45202. Phone: (513) 241-9898. Fax: (513) 241-6689. Web Site:www.supertalkfmgbs.com Licensee: WVAE Lico Inc. Group owner: Susquehanna Radio Corp. (acq 5-5-2006; grpsl). Population served: 67,865 Natl. Rep: Christal,. Format: Rock. ♦Gary Lewis, gen mgr, progmg dir; Jeff Davis, prom dir.

Lexington

***WFOT(FM)**— February 2007: 89.5 mhz; 360 w vert. Ant 304 ft TL: N40 43 36 W82 36 59. Hrs open: 1585 Bethel Rd, Suite 101-LL, Columbus, 43220-2010. Phone: (614) 442-1270. Fax: (714) 845-0411.E-mail: info@stgabrielradio.com Web Site:www.stgabrielradio.com Licensee: St. Gabriel Radio Inc. Natl. Network: EWTN Radio, . Format: Catholic talk. ♦Christopher Gabrelcik, pres; Michael Barone, stn mgr.

Lima

WCIT(AM)— Aug 22, 1963: 940 khz; 250 w-D, DA-2. TL: N40 43 21 W84 05 04. Stereo. Hrs open: 24 1301 N. Cable Rd., 45805. Phone: (419) 331-1600. Fax: (419) 222-5085. Licensee: Maverick Media of Lima License LLC. Group owner: Maverick Media LLC (acq 12-4-2003; grpsl). Population served: 220,000 Natl. Rep: Christal, Rgnl Reps,. Format: Oldies. News staff: 2; News: 20 hrs wkly. Target aud: 35-54; affluent, community involved. Spec prog: Jazz 2 hrs, relg 11 hrs wkly. ♦Gary S. Rozynek, pres; Matt Childers, gen mgr; Mark Mackey, stn mgr; Bill McAdams, opns mgr.

WEGE(FM)— Nov 25, 1970: 104.9 mhz; 3 kw. 260 ft TL: N40 43 21 W84 05 04. (CP: Ant 286 ft.). Stereo. Hrs open: 24 1301 N. Cable Rd., 45805. Phone: (419) 331-1600. Fax: (419) 222-3755. Licensee: Maverick Media of Lima License LLC. Group owner: Maverick Media LLC (acq 12-4-2003; grpsl). Population served: 150,000 Natl. Network: ABC, . Natl. Rep: Christal,. Format: Classic rock. Target aud: 25-54; affluent, community involved. ♦Dave Roach, gen mgr; Matt Childers, gen sls mgr; Bill Rice, progmg dir; Brandy Rader, traf mgr.

WFGF(FM)—See Wapakoneta

***WGLE(FM)**— Dec 2, 1981: 90.7 mhz; 50 kw. 420 ft TL: N40 39 15 W84 06 36. Stereo. Hrs open: 24
Rebroadcasts WGTE-FM Toledo 100%.
1270 S. Detroit Ave., Toledo, 43614. Phone: (419) 380-4600. Fax: (419) 380-4710.E-mail: info@wgte.com Web Site:www.wgte.org Licensee: The Public Broadcasting Foundation of Northwest Ohio. Population served: 458,318 Natl. Network: PRI, NPR, . Format: Class, News, Public Affairs. News: 23 hrs wkly. Target aud: General. Spec prog: Jazz 16 hrs, new age/eclectic 4 hrs wkly. ♦Marlon P. Kiser, CEO, pres, gen mgr; George Jones, chmn; Chris Pfeiffer, opns mgr; Ross Pfieffer, dev dir. Co-owned TV: *WGTE-TV affil.

WIMA(AM)— Dec 5, 1948: 1150 khz; 1 kw-U, DA-2. TL: N40 40 47 W84 06 34. Hrs open: 24 667 W. Market St., 45801. Phone: (419) 223-2060. Fax: (419) 229-3888.E-mail: comments@1150wima.com Web Site:www.1150wima.com Licensee: Jacor Broadcasting Corp. Group owner: Clear Channel Communications Inc. (acq 5-4-99; grpsl). Population served: 150,000 Natl. Network: Fox News Radio, Fox Sports, . Natl. Rep: Clear Channel,. Wire Svc: AP Format: News/talk, sports. News staff: one; News: 20 hrs wkly. Target aud: 35 plus. Spec prog: Farm 5 hrs wkly. ♦Art Versnick, VP, gen mgr; David Cook, stn mgr; Phil Austin, opns mgr; Jack Wheelbarger, natl sls mgr; Dave Woodward, progmg dir; Doug Jenkins, news dir; Mark Gierhart, chief of engrg.

WIMT(FM)— December 1948: 102.1 mhz; 13 kw. Ant 528 ft TL: N40 38 03 W84 12 29. Stereo. Hrs open: 24 667 W. Market St., 45801. Phone: (419) 223-2060. Fax: (419) 229-3888.E-mail: comments@t102.com Web Site:www.t102.com Licensee: Jacor Broadcasting Corp. (acq 5-4-99). Population served: 250,000 Wire Svc: AP Format: Country. News staff: one; News: one hrs wkly. Target aud: 25-54. ♦Brian Steel, rgnl sls mgr & progmg dir.

***WTGN(FM)**— Sept 27, 1966: 97.7 mhz; 6 kw. 300 ft TL: N40 45 26 W84 08 12. Stereo. Hrs open: 1600 Elida Rd., 45805. Phone: (419) 227-2525. Fax: (419) 222-5438.E-mail: wtgn@wcoil.com Web Site:www.wtgn.org Licensee: Associated Christian Broadcasters Inc. Population served: 53,734 Format: Christian. ♦Wesley Lytle, pres; Scott Young, gen mgr.

WWSR(FM)— 1985: 93.1 mhz; 3 kw. Ant 328 ft TL: N40 45 47 W84 10 59. Hrs open: 24 1301 N. Cable Rd., 45805. Secondary address: Box 1487 45802. Phone: (419) 331-1600. Fax: (419) 222-3755. Licensee: Maverick Media of Lima License LLC. Group owner: Maverick Media LLC (acq 12-4-2003; grpsl). Population served: 150,000 Format: Sports. Target aud: 25-54; young, affluent. Spec prog: Nascar Nextel Races. ♦Gary Rozynek, pres, prom dir; Matt Childers, gen mgr, mus dir; Bill McAdams, stn mgr; Stacy McAdams, prom dir; Brandy Rader, engrg dir, traf mgr.

***WYSM(FM)**— 2001: 89.3 mhz; 3 kw. Ant 220 ft TL: N40 39 15 W84 06 36. Hrs open: 5105 Glendale Ave., Suite C, Toledo, 43614. Phone: (419) 389-0893. Fax: (419) 381-0731.E-mail: yesfm@yeshome.com Web Site:www.yeshome.com Licensee: Side by Side Inc. Format: Christian rock. ♦J. Todd Hostetler, gen mgr; Jeff Howe, progmg dir.

Logan

WKNA(FM)— Dec 10, 1965: 98.3 mhz; 3 kw. Ant 240 ft TL: N39 31 47 W82 23 10. Stereo. Hrs open: 24 Box 429, One Radio Ln., 43138. Phone: (740) 385-2151. Fax: (740) 385-4022. Licensee: WLGN LLC. Population served: 250,000 Format: Country. News staff: one; News: 25 hrs wkly. ♦Scott Blazer, CEO, gen mgr; Vicki Lutz, traf mgr.

WLGN(AM)— December 1967: 1510 khz; 1 kw-D, 250 w-CH. TL: N39 31 47 W82 23 10. Stereo. Hrs open: Sunrise-sunset Box 429, 43138. Secondary address: One Radio Ln. 43138. Phone: (740) 385-2151. Fax: (740) 385-4022.E-mail: wlgn@magicohio.com Licensee: WLGN LLC. (acq 1-4-2005; $675,000 with co-located FM). Population served: 25,000 Natl. Network: ABC, . Natl. Rep: Rgnl Reps,. Format: Timeless favorites. Target aud: 18-54. ♦Scott Blazer, gen mgr; Vicki Lutz, gen sls mgr.

London

WJYD(FM)— 1965: 106.3 mhz; 6 kw. 328 ft TL: N39 53 05 W83 25 23. Stereo. Hrs open: 24 350 E. 1st Ave., Suite 100, Columbus, 43201. Phone: (614) 487-1444. Fax: (614) 487-5862.E-mail: info@wjod.com Web Site:www.joy106.com Licensee: Blue Chip Broadcasting Licenses Ltd. Group owner: Radio One Inc. (acq 4-30-01; grpsl). Population served: 1603000 Natl. Network: ABC, . Natl. Rep: D & R Radio,. Format: Gospel. News staff: 3. Target aud: 18-34. Spec prog: Gospel 10 hrs wkly. ♦Jeff Wilson, gen mgr.

Lorain

WCLV(FM)— April 1961: 104.9 mhz; 6 kw. Ant 328 ft TL: N41 28 32 W81 59 24. Stereo. Hrs open: 24 26501 Renaissance Pkwy., Cleveland, 44128. Phone: (216) 464-0900. Fax: (216) 464-2206.E-mail: wclv@wclv.com Web Site:www.wclv.com Licensee: Radio Seaway Inc. (acq 11-1-01). Population served: 1,500,000 Natl. Rep: D & R Radio, Interep,. Hogan & Hartson. Wire Svc: AP Format: Classical. News: 5 hrs wkly. Target aud: 35-64; high-income, college graduates & professionals. Spec prog: Jazz 5 hrs, financial news one hr wkly. ♦Robert D. Conrad, CEO & pres; Richard G. Marschner, CFO, exec VP; Jenny Northern, gen mgr, gen sls mgr; John Simna, opns mgr; Bill O'Connell, progmg mgr.

WDLW(AM)— December 1969: 1380 khz; 500 w-D, 67 w-N. TL: N41 25 48 W82 09 07. Hrs open: 24 Box 277, Oberlin, 44074. Secondary address: 45624 State Rt. 20, Oberlin 44047. Phone: (440) 774-1320. Fax: (440) 774-1336.E-mail: woblwdlw@yahoo.com Web Site:www.northcoastdailynews.com Licensee: WDLW Radio Inc. (acq 2-14-02; $250,000). Population served: 1,000,000 Wire Svc: AP Format: Oldies rock-n-roll. News staff: 3; News: 10 hrs wkly. Target aud: 35-64. ♦Doug Wilber, pres, gen mgr; Lorie Wilber, VP; Pamela Gard, progmg dir.

***WNZN(FM)**— 1992: 89.1 mhz; 2.2 kw. 374 ft TL: N41 18 34 W82 26 31. Hrs open: 24 9712 State Rd. 113, Berlin Heights, 44814. Phone: (419) 588-3700.E-mail: tony10491@adelphia.net Licensee: Spanish Cultural Network. Format: Sp. ♦Milton Velazquez, gen mgr & opns mgr.

Loudonville

WXXF(FM)—Licensed to Loudonville. See Wooster

Manchester

WAGX(FM)— 1992: 101.3 mhz; 3 kw. 299 ft TL: N38 40 58 W83 39 45. Hrs open: 24 9503 Mason Lewis Rd., Maysville, KY, 41056. Secondary address: Box 449 45144. Phone: (606) 564-8474. Fax: (606) 564-8383. Licensee: Jewell Schaeffer Broadcasting Inc. Population served: 100,000 Format: Oldies, adult contemp, classic rock. Target aud: 25-54; upscale adults. ◆James P. Wagner, CEO & pres.

Mansfield

WMAN(AM)— Dec 4, 1939: 1400 khz; 1 kw-U. TL: N40 46 13 W82 32 36. Hrs open: 24 1400 Radio Ln., 44906. Phone: (419) 529-2211. Fax: (419) 529-2516. Web Site:www.am1400.com Licensee: Capstar TX L.P. Group owner: Clear Channel Communications Inc. (acq 8-7-00; grpsl). Population served: 45,047 Natl. Network: CBS, Westwood One, . Format: News/talk. News staff: 3; News: 30 hrs wkly. Target aud: 35 plus; upscale, active mgmt/exec.

WNCO-FM—See Ashland

*WOSV(FM)— June 27, 1989: 91.7 mhz; 750 w. 450 ft TL: N40 42 33 W82 29 11. Stereo. Hrs open: 24
Rebroadcasts WOSU-FM Columbus 100%.
2400 Olentangy River Rd., Columbus, 43210. Phone: (614) 292-9678. Fax: (614) 292-7625.E-mail: wosu@osu.edu Web Site:www.wosu.org Licensee: The Ohio State University. Population served: 121,000 Natl. Network: PRI, NPR, . Dow, Lohnes & Albertson. Wire Svc: AP Format: Classical. News: 28 hrs wkly. Target aud: 35 plus. ◆Thomas Rieland, gen mgr; Tim Eby, stn mgr; Kevin Petrilla, opns mgr.

WRGM(AM)—See Ontario

*WVMC-FM— March 1979: 90.7 mhz; 170 w. Ant 100 ft TL: N40 43 19 W82 31 52. Stereo. Hrs open: 24 500 Logan Rd., 44907. Phone: (419) 756-5651 ext 225. Fax: (419) 756-7470. Web Site:www.wvmcfm.com Licensee: Mansfield Christian School. Population served: 35,000 Format: Christian. Target aud: 18-34; middle income adults, mostly female. ◆Josh Hooper, gen mgr.

WVNO-FM— Aug 11, 1962: 106.1 mhz; 40 kw. 545 ft TL: N40 45 50 W82 37 04. Stereo. Hrs open: 2900 Park Ave. W., 44906. Phone: (419) 529-5900. Fax: (419) 529-2319.E-mail: info@wvno.com Web Site:www.wvno.com Licensee: Johnny Appleseed Broadcasting Co. Population served: 350,000 Rgnl rep: Rgnl Reps Format: Adult contemp. News staff: 5; News: 10 hrs wkly. Target aud: 25-54; female. ◆Gunther S. Meisse, pres, gen mgr; Tony Mitchell, opns mgr.

WYHT(FM)— Oct 18, 1962: 105.3 mhz; 50 kw. Ant 371 ft TL: N40 46 09 W82 32 23. Stereo. Hrs open: 1400 Radio Ln., 44906. Phone: (419) 529-2211. Fax: (419) 529-2516. Web Site:www.wyht.com Licensee: Capstar TX L.P. Population served: 55,047 Format: Hot adult contemp.

*WYKL(FM)—(Crestline, Dec 10, 1990: 98.7 mhz; 1.8 kw. Ant 418 ft TL: N40 46 08 W82 46 03. Stereo. Hrs open: 24 2351 Sunset Blvd., Suite 170-218, Rocklin, CA, 95765. Phone: (916) 251-1600. Fax: (916) 251-1650.E-mail: klove@klove.com Web Site:www.klove.com Licensee: Educational Media Foundation. Group owner: EMF Broadcasting (acq 12-18-03; $900,000). Population served: 150,000 Natl. Network: K-Love, . Shaw Pittman. Format: Contemp Christian. Target aud: 25-44; Judeo Christian female. ◆Richard Jenkins, pres; Mike Novak, VP; Keith Whipple, dev dir; Eric Allen, natl sls mgr; David Pierce, progmg mgr; Ed Lenane, news dir; Sam Wallington, engrg dir; Karen Johnson, news rptr.

Mariemont

WKFS(FM)—See Milford

Marietta

*WCMO(FM)— Oct 1, 1960: 98.5 mhz; 40 w. 105 ft TL: N39 25 07 W81 26 32. Hrs open: Marietta College, 215 5th St., 45750. Phone: (740) 376-4802. Phone: (740) 376-4800. Fax: (740) 376-4807. Web Site:www.wmrtfm.com Licensee: Marietta College. Population served: 17,000 Format: AOR. ◆Marilee Morrow, gen mgr & progmg dir.

WLTP(AM)— May 8, 1996: 910 khz; 5 kw-D, 61 w-N, DA-2. TL: N39 26 07 W81 28 01. Stereo. Hrs open: 24 6006 Grand Central Ave., Vienna, WV, 26105. Phone: (304) 295-6070. Fax: (304) 295-4389.E-mail: info@wltp.com Web Site:www.wltp.com Licensee: CC Licenses LLC. Group owner: Clear Channel Communications Inc. (acq 9-4-2002). Population served: 16,861 Natl. Network: CBS, Westwood One, AP

Radio, . Format: New, talk. News staff: one; News: 8 hrs wkly. Target aud: 18-54; males. ◆Chuck Poet, gen mgr.

WMOA(AM)— Sept 8, 1946: 1490 khz; 1 kw-U. TL: N39 25 07 W81 28 34. Hrs open: 24 Box 708, 45750. Secondary address: 925 Lancaster St. 45750. Phone: (740) 373-1490. Fax: (740) 373-1717.E-mail: kwenzel@wmoa1490.com Web Site:www.wmoa1490.com Licensee: JAWCO Inc. (acq 7-11-97; $659,000 with WJAW(FM) McConnelsville). Population served: 15,000 Pepper & Corazzini. Format: Adult contemp, news, sports. News staff: 2; News: 5 hrs wkly. Target aud: 35 plus; mature, middle-class to affluent. Spec prog: Farm one hr, relg one hr, sports 15 hrs wkly. ◆John A. Wharff III, pres, gen mgr & gen sls mgr; Dan Castelli, mus dir.

*WMRT(FM)— Nov 13, 1975: 88.3 mhz; 9.2 kw. 205 ft TL: N39 25 07 W81 26 32. Stereo. Hrs open: Marietta College, 215 Fifth St., 45750. Phone: (740) 376-4802. Phone: (740) 376-4800. Fax: (740) 376-4807. Web Site:www.wmrtfm.com Licensee: Marietta College. Population served: 16,861 Format: Class, news/talk, jazz. ◆Marilee Morrow, gen mgr.

WRVB(FM)— Dec 1, 1964: 102.1 mhz; 25 kw. 400 ft TL: N39 25 07 W81 28 34. Stereo. Hrs open: 24 6006 Grand Central Ave., Box 5559, Vienna, WV, 26105. Phone: (304) 295-6070. Fax: (304) 295-4389.E-mail: info@102theriver.com Web Site:www.102theriver.com Licensee: CC Licenses LLC. Group owner: Clear Channel Communications Inc. (acq 4-17-2001; grpsl). Format: CHR. Target aud: 25-54; general. ◆Chuck Poet, gen mgr.

WXIL(FM)—See Parkersburg, WV

Marion

WMRN(AM)— Dec 23, 1940: 1490 khz; 1 kw-U. TL: N40 36 54 W83 07 54. Hrs open: 1330 N. Main St., 43302. Phone: (740) 383-1131. Fax: (740) 387-3697. Web Site:www.wmrn.com Licensee: Citicasters Licenses L.P. Group owner: Clear Channel Communications Inc. (acq 1999; grpsl). Population served: 38,646 Format: Oldies, news/talk. Spec prog: Farm 5 hrs wkly. ◆Diane Glassmeyer, gen mgr.

WMRN-FM— Feb 27, 1975: 94.3 mhz; 3 kw. Ant 300 ft TL: N40 36 27 W83 14 14. Stereo. Hrs open: 24 1330 N. Main St., 43302. Phone: (740) 383-1131. Fax: (740) 387-3697. Web Site:www.buckeyecountry943.com Licensee: Citicasters Licenses L.P. Group owner: Clear Channel Communications Inc. (acq 1999; grpsl). Population served: 150,000 Natl. Rep: Rgnl Reps,. Format: Country. Target aud: 25-54. ◆Diana Coon, gen mgr; Mike Mitchell, adv dir; Scott Shawver, opns mgr & mus dir.

*WOSB(FM)— Apr 14, 1998: 91.1 mhz; 2.5 kw horiz, 6.8 kw vert. 285 ft TL: N40 41 06 W83 15 24. Hrs open: 24
Rebroadcasts WOSU-FM Columbus.
2400 Olentangy River Rd., Columbus, 43210. Phone: (614) 292-9678. Fax: (614) 292-7625.E-mail: wosu@osu.edu Web Site:www.wosu.org Licensee: The Ohio State University. Natl. Network: NPR, . Wire Svc: AP Format: Classical. ◆Thomas Rieland, gen mgr.

*WXMF(FM)—Not on air, target date: unknown: 91.9 mhz; 15 w horiz, 500 w vert. Ant 315 ft TL: N40 36 46 W83 07 48. Hrs open: Box 158, Upper Sandusky, 43351. Licensee: Kayser Broadcast Ministries Inc. ◆Daniel L. Kayser, pres & gen mgr.

Marysville

WUCO(AM)— Dec 1, 1983: 1270 khz; 500 w-U, DA-2. TL: N40 14 46 W83 19 50. Hrs open: 24 1585 Bethel Rd, Suite 101-LL, Columbus, 43220-2010. Phone: (614) 442-1270. Fax: (714) 845-0411.E-mail: info@stgabrielradio.com Web Site:www.stgabrielradio.com Licensee: St. Gabriel Radio Inc (acq 4-10-2008). Population served: 40,000 Natl. Network: EWTN Radio, . Rgnl. Network: Agri-Net, Ohio News Net. Format: Catholic talk. ◆Chris Gabrelcik, pres; Michael Barone, stn mgr; Farris Wilhite, engr.

Massillon

WTIG(AM)— Aug 1, 1957: 990 khz; 250 w-D, 119-N, DA-2. TL: N40 49 56 W81 33 40. Hrs open: 24 Box 608, 44648. Secondary address: 3580 Karen Ave. N.W. 44647. Phone: (330) 837-9900. Fax: (330) 837-9844.E-mail: espn@espn990.com Web Site:www.espn990.com Licensee: WTIG Inc. (acq 1991; 8-12-85). Population served: 32,539 Rgnl. Network: Ohio News Net. Format: Sports. Target aud: 25-54; male. Spec prog: Loc church svcs 6 hrs wkly. ◆Donovan Resh, VP, opns dir, chief of opns, progmg dir; Ray Jeske, pres & gen mgr.

Maumee

*WYSZ(FM)— Nov 14, 1992: 89.3 mhz; 6.3 kw. 321 ft TL: N41 38 55 W83 42 22. Stereo. Hrs open: 24 5105 Glendale Ave., Suite C, Toledo, 43614. Phone: (419) 389-0893. Fax: (419) 381-0731. Licensee: Side By Side Inc. Population served: 500,000 Gammon & Grange. Format: Christian, CHR/Rock. Target aud: 15-25. ◆J. Todd Hostetler, gen mgr; Janet Yonke, dev dir, progmg dir; Jeff Howe, progmg dir.

McArthur

WYRO(FM)— 1994: 98.7 mhz; 6 kw. 328 ft TL: N39 08 59 W82 35 36. Hrs open: 24 Box 667, Jackson, 45640. Secondary address: 295 E. Main St., Jackson 45640. Phone: (740) 286-3023. Fax: (740) 286-6679.E-mail: jmossbarger@jcbiradio.com Licensee: Davis Broadcasting Media Inc. (acq 4-26-99). Natl. Network: Westwood One, . Format: Classic rock. News staff: one. Target aud: 18-65. ◆Jerry Mossbarger, gen mgr; Ron Speakman, gen sls mgr; John Pelletier, progmg mgr.

McConnelsville

WJAW-FM— October 1992: 100.9 mhz; 930 w. Ant 577 ft TL: N39 33 24 W81 51 06. Stereo. Hrs open: 24 Box 708, Marietta, 45750. Secondary address: 925 Lancaster St., Marietta 45750. Phone: (740) 373-1490. Fax: (740) 373-1717.E-mail: swiles@wmoa1490.com Web Site:www.wmao1490.com Licensee: JAWCO Inc. (acq 6-25-97; $659,300 with WMOA(AM) Marietta). Population served: 50,000 Natl. Network: ABC, . Rgnl. Network: Ohio Radio Net. Format: Sports. News staff: one. Target aud: 18-34; male. ◆John Wharff III, pres, sr VP & gen mgr.

Medina

WQMX(FM)—Licensed to Medina. See Akron

Miamisburg

WFCJ(FM)— Jan 7, 1961: 93.7 mhz; 50 kw. Ant 492 ft TL: N39 39 35 W84 18 53. Stereo. Hrs open: 24 Box 937, Dayton, 45449-0937. Secondary address: 7333 Manning Rd. 45342. Phone: (937) 866-2471. Fax: (937) 866-2062.E-mail: inspiration@wfcj.com Web Site:www.wfcj.com Licensee: Miami Valley Christian Broadcasting Association Inc. Population served: 2,600,000 Natl. Network: USA, Salem Radio Network, . Natl. Rep: Salem,. Miller & Neely. Wire Svc: AP Format: Relg, Christian. News: 10 hrs wkly. Target aud: 35-64; Evangelical Christians. Spec prog: Black 3 hrs, children 2 hrs wkly. ◆Bud Schindler, pres; Clair D. Miller, VP, gen mgr; Bill Nance, progmg dir; John Graham, chief of engrg.

Miamitown

*WMWX(FM)— Aug 5, 2006: 88.9 mhz; 4.6 kw. Ant 374 ft TL: N39 19 18 W84 57 33. Hrs open: 24 5114 Princeton-Glendale Rd., Hamilton, 45011. Phone: (513) 887-0590.E-mail: bspry@classxradio.com Web Site:classxradio.com Licensee: Spryex Communications Inc. Format: Classic rock. Target aud: 30-58. ◆William J. Spry Jr., pres.

Middleport

WYVK(FM)—Licensed to Middleport. See Middleport-Pomeroy

Middleport-Pomeroy

WMPO(AM)— Aug 28, 1959: 1390 khz; 5 kw-D, 120 w-N. TL: N39 00 35 W82 04 14. Hrs open: Box 71, 39520 Bradbury Rd., Middleport, 45760. Phone: (740) 992-6485. Fax: (740) 992-6486.E-mail: office@wyvk.com Web Site:www.wyvk.com Licensee: Positive Radio Group Inc. of Ohio. Group owner: Baker Family Stations (acq 1999; $492,000 with WYVK(FM) Middleport). Population served: 27,304 Natl. Network: ESPN Radio, . Natl. Rep: Rgnl Reps,. Format: Sports. Target aud: 35 plus. Spec prog: Relg 6 hrs, farm one hr, gospel 18 hrs wkly. ◆Rick Ash, pres; Brenda Merritt, gen mgr.

WYVK(FM)—(Middleport, Aug 27, 1973: 92.1 mhz; 4.7 kw. Ant 113 ft TL: N39 03 30 W82 02 31. Stereo. Hrs open: 19 Box 71, 39520 Bradbury Rd., Middleport, 45760. Phone: (740) 992-6485. Fax: (740) 992-6486.E-mail: brenda@wyvk.com Web Site:www.wyvk.com Licensee: Positive Radio Group Inc. of Ohio Population served: 37845 Format: Adult contemp. News: 3 hrs wkly. Target aud: 25-54. ◆Brenda Merritt, gen mgr & mus dir.

Middletown

WPFB(AM)— Sept 1, 1947: 910 khz; 1 kw-D, 100 w-N. TL: N39 30 57 W84 21 05. Hrs open: 24 4505 Central Ave., 45044. Phone: (513) 422-3625. Fax: (513) 424-9732.E-mail: info@wpfb.com Web Site:www.wpfb.com Licensee: Radio Stations WPAY/WPFB Inc. Group owner: WPAY/WPFB Inc. Population served: 2,000,000 Natl. Rep: Roslin,. Format: Classic country. News staff: 2; News: 26 hrs wkly. Spec prog: Radio Movie of the Week 2 hrs wkly. ◆Douglas L. Braden, pres & gen mgr.

WPFB-FM— July 1, 1959: 105.9 mhz; 34 kw. 590 ft TL: N39 30 57 W84 21 05. Stereo. Hrs open: 24 4505 Central Ave., 45044. Phone: (513) 422-3625. Fax: (513) 424-9732.E-mail: info@wpfb.com Web Site:www.therebel1059.com Licensee: Radio Stations WPAY/WPFB Inc. Population served: 48,767 Format: Country. Target aud: 25-54.

Milford

WKFS(FM)— Aug 1, 1969: 107.1 mhz; 3 kw. 299 ft TL: N39 06 16 W84 20 10. (CP: 6 kw). Stereo. Hrs open: 8044 Montgomery Rd., Suite 650, Cincinnati, 45236. Phone: (513) 686-8300.E-mail: info@kisscincinnati.com Web Site:www.kisscincinnati.com Licensee: Jacor Broadcasting Corp. Group owner: Clear Channel Communications Inc. (acq 5-4-99; grpsl). Verner, Liipfert, Bernhard, McPherson & Hand. Format: Top 40. ◆Mike Kenney, gen mgr; Chuck Fredrick, opns mgr, chief of opns; Mark Anderson, prom dir.

Millersburg

WKLM(FM)— 1988: 95.3 mhz; 3 kw. 328 ft TL: N40 29 07 W81 50 40. Stereo. Hrs open: 5:30 AM-midnight 7409 White Hill Ln., 44654. Phone: (330) 674-1953. Fax: (330) 674-9556.E-mail: wklmradio@earthlink.net Licensee: Coshocton Broadcasting Co. (group owner; acq 7-10-90; $490,000; 8-6-90). Natl. Network: ABC, . Format: Adult contemp. News staff: one; News: 12 hrs wkly. Target aud: General. Spec prog: Loc sports. ◆Bruce Wallace, pres, gen mgr; Tom Thompson, gen sls mgr; Matt Croy, progmg dir.

*WVML(FM)— June 2004: 90.5 mhz; 4.8 kw. Ant 367 ft TL: N40 36 08 W81 44 32. Stereo. Hrs open: 24
Rebroadcasts WCRF(FM) Cleveland 100%.
WCRF Radio, 9756 Barr Rd., Cleveland, 44141. Phone: (440) 526-1111. Fax: (440) 526-1319.E-mail: wcrf@moody.edu Web Site:wcrfradio.org Licensee: The Moody Bible Institute of Chicago (group owner). Southmayd. Wire Svc: AP Format: Inspirational. Target aud: 25-55; Adults. ◆Dr. Michael Easley, pres; Richard Lee, stn mgr; Phil Villareal, progmg dir; Doug Hainer, chief of engrg.

Montpelier

WLZZ(FM)— 1991: 104.5 mhz; 3 kw. Ant 328 ft TL: N41 30 54 W84 39 43. Hrs open: 24 209 W. Main St., 43543. Phone: (419) 485-5530. Phone: (800) 788-1045. Fax: (419) 485-5539.E-mail: wlzz@wlzzradio.com Licensee: Lake Cities Broadcasting Corp. Population served: 50,000 Format: Country. News staff: one; News: 12 hrs wkly. Target aud: 25-54. ◆Tom Andrews, CEO, chmn, pres; William Kerner, exec VP & gen mgr.

Morrow

*WLMH(FM)— 1970: 89.1 mhz; 100 w. 200 ft TL: N39 20 51 W84 08 13. Hrs open: 3001 E. US. 22nd & 3rd, 45152. Phone: (513) 899-3884. Fax: (513) 899-4912. Licensee: Little Miami Local Schools. Format: Educ, oldies, classic rock. ◆Wayne Lyke, opns mgr.

Mount Gilead

WVXG(FM)— March 1994: Stn currently dark. 95.1 mhz; 6 kw. Ant 328 ft TL: N40 35 15 W82 48 20. Stereo. Hrs open: Box 102, Powell, 43065. Phone: (740) 549-7002. Licensee: ICS Holdings Sub 1 Inc. (acq 12-17-2003; $384,588). Population served: 76,000 ◆Dan Baughman, gen mgr.

Mount Vernon

WMVO(AM)— Nov 26, 1953: 1300 khz; 500 w-D, DA. TL: N40 24 17 W82 26 23. Hrs open: 17421 Coshocton Rd., Box 348, 43050. Phone: (740) 397-1000. Fax: (740) 392-9300. Web Site:www.wmvo.com Licensee: BAS Broadcasting Inc. Group owner: Clear Channel Communications Inc. (acq 10-1-2005; $2 million with WQIO(FM) Mount Vernon). Population served: 20,000 Natl. Network: ABC, . Natl.

Rep: Rgnl Reps,. Wire Svc: AP Format: Var, news/talk. Spec prog: Relg 7 hrs wkly. ◆Diana Coon, gen mgr, mktg mgr; Michael Hayes, opns mgr & news dir.

*WNZR(FM)— May 1, 1986: 90.9 mhz; 100 w. 193 ft TL: N40 22 14 W82 28 05. Stereo. Hrs open: 24 800 Martinsburg Rd., 43050. Phone: (740) 392-9090. Fax: (740) 392-9155.E-mail: wnzr@mvnu.edu Web Site:www.wnzr.fm Licensee: Mt. Vernon Nazarene University. Population served: 53,309 Natl. Network: AP Radio, . Sciarrina & Associates. Wire Svc: AP Format: Christian adult contemp. News: 5 hrs wkly. Target aud: 25-54; Christian adults. ◆Marcy Rinehart, stn mgr.

WQIO(FM)— May 26, 1951: 93.7 mhz; 37 kw. Ant 565 ft TL: N40 24 18 W82 26 20. Stereo. Hrs open: 24 Prog sep from AM 17421 Coshocton Rd., Box 348, 43050. Phone: (740) 397-1000. Fax: (740) 392-9300.E-mail: info@wqiofm.com Web Site:www.wqiofm.com Licensee: BAS Broadcasting Inc. (acq 10-1-2005; $2 million with WMVO(AM) Mount Vernon). Population served: 13,373 Format: Adult contemp. News staff: one. Target aud: 35-54. Spec prog: Hit mus 4 hrs, gospel 2 hrs wkly.

Napoleon

WNDH(FM)— June 1972: 103.1 mhz; 3.3 kw. 300 ft TL: N41 18 00 W84 09 22. Stereo. Hrs open: 24 709 N. Perry St., 43545. Phone: (419) 592-8060. Fax: (419) 592-1085.E-mail: wndh@clearchannel.com Web Site:www.wndh1031.com Licensee: CC Licenses LLC. Group owner: Clear Channel Communications Inc. (acq 1-1-2000; grpsl). Natl. Network: CBS, . Rgnl. Network: Agri Bcstg, Ohio Radio Net. Rgnl rep: Rgnl Reps Wire Svc: AP Format: Adult contemp. News staff: one. Target aud: General. Spec prog: Ger Polka 2 hrs wkly. ◆Robert E. McLimans, sr VP, VP & gen mgr; Rick Small, opns dir; John Schuette, gen sls mgr.

Nelsonville

WSEO(FM)— September 1990: 107.7 mhz; 3 kw. 328 ft TL: N39 27 38 W82 13 09. Stereo. Hrs open: 24 15751 U.S. Rt. 33 S., 45764. Phone: (740) 753-4094. Phone: (740) 753-2154. Fax: (740) 753-4965.E-mail: wseo33@sbcglobal.net Licensee: Nelsonville TV Cable Inc. Format: True Country. News staff: 3; News: 15 hrs wkly. Target aud: 25-49. Spec prog: Farm. ◆Eugene R. Edwards, pres, gen mgr; Nick Brooks, mus dir.

New Boston

WIOI(AM)— Sept 2, 1959: 1010 khz; 1 kw-D, 22 w-N. TL: N38 43 48 W82 57 10. Hrs open: Box 1233, Portsmouth, 45662. Phone: (606) 932-4796. Fax: (606) 932-4796.E-mail: chip@wioiradio.com Web Site:www.wioiradio.com Licensee: Maillet Media Inc. (acq 1996). Population served: 27,633 Format: Adult standards. ◆Charles Maillet Jr., gen mgr.

New Concord

*WMCO(FM)— Jan 28, 1961: 90.7 mhz; 1.3 kw. 84 ft TL: N39 59 46 W81 43 18. Stereo. Hrs open: 6 AM-midnight Caldwell Hall, 163 Stormont St., 43762. Phone: (740) 826-8375.E-mail: wmco@muskingum.edu Web Site:www.muskingum.edu/~wmco Licensee: Muskingum College. Population served: 2,500 Format: Div, educ, progsv. News: 10 hrs wkly. Target aud: General. Spec prog: Class 4 hrs, jazz 10 hrs, relg 2 hrs wkly. ◆Jeffrey D. Harman, gen mgr; Lisa Marshall, stn mgr; Matthew Hott, progmg dir.

New Lexington

WWJM(FM)— May 1, 1978: 105.9 mhz; 1.7 kw. 627 ft TL: N39 46 37 W82 09 54. Stereo. Hrs open: 24 210 S. Jackson St., 43764. Secondary address: 247 Market St., Zanesville 43701. Phone: (740) 342-1988. Fax: (740) 342-1036.E-mail: wwjm@aol.com Web Site:www.wwjm.com Licensee: Perry County Broadcasting Co. Population served: 100,000 Natl. Network: Westwood One, . Format: Hot Adult contemp. News staff: one; News: 2 hrs wkly. Target aud: 18-54; young to middle-aged. ◆Charles Edwards, chmn, pres & gen mgr.

New Philadelphia

WJER(AM)—See Dover-New Philadelphia

*WKRJ(FM)— July 12, 1994: 91.5 mhz; 2 kw. 240 ft TL: N40 33 50 W81 31 05. Hrs open:
Rebroadcasts WKSU-FM Kent 100%.

c/o WKSU-FM, Box 5190, Kent, 44242-0001. Secondary address: 1613 E. Summit St, Kent 44242-0001. Phone: (330) 672-3114. Fax: (330) 672-4107.E-mail: letters@wksu.org Web Site:www.wksu.org Licensee: Kent State University. Population served: 76,525 Natl. Network: NPR, PRI, . Dow, Lohnes & Albertson. Format: Class, news. News staff: 5; News: 35 hrs wkly. Target aud: 35-65; college grad, professional & upper income. ◆Allen E. Bartholet, gen mgr; Robert Burford, mktg dir, prom dir; David Roden, mus dir; M.L. Schultze, news dir; Ronald Bartlebaugh, engrg dir.

WNPQ(FM)— Feb 2, 1969: 95.9 mhz; 3 kw. 400 ft TL: N40 35 51 W81 29 32. Stereo. Hrs open: 24 3969 Convenience Cir. N.W., Suite 205, Canton, 44718. Phone: (330) 492-9590. Fax: (330) 492-3702. Web Site:www.thelight959.com Licensee: Tuscarawas Broadcasting Co. Population served: 300,000 Natl. Network: CBS Radio, . Format: Christian contemp. Target aud: 18-49; family oriented. Spec prog: Black 4 hrs, southern gospel 4 hrs wkly. ◆James Natoli Jr., pres; Garry Meeks, gen mgr; Tom Bishop, gen sls mgr; Ed Franklin, prom dir.

WTUZ(FM)—(Uhrichsville, May 1, 1990: 99.9 mhz; 5.3 kw. 348 ft TL: N40 26 19 W81 26 01. Stereo. Hrs open: 24 2424 E. High Ave., 44663. Phone: (330) 339-2222. Fax: (330) 339-5930.E-mail: info@wtuz.com Web Site:www.wtuz.com Licensee: WTUZ Radio Inc. Population served: 120,000 Natl. Network: Fox News Radio, . Smithwick & Belendiuk. Wire Svc: AP Format: Country. News staff: 2; News: 7 hrs wkly. Target aud: General. Spec prog: Farm 2 hr, relg 4 hr wkly. ◆Edward A. Schumacher, pres, gen mgr; Melanie Osborn, gen sls mgr; Pat Smith, prom dir; Brad Shupe, progmg dir; Jennifer Lourenco, news dir; John Demuth, chief of engrg.

Newark

WCLT(AM)— Jan 4, 1949: 1430 khz; 500 w-D, 48 w-N. TL: N40 02 02 W82 24 08. Hrs open: 24 Box 5150, 43058-5150. Secondary address: 674 Jacksontown Rd. S.E., Heath 43056. Phone: (740) 345-4004. Fax: (740) 345-5775.E-mail: wclt@wclt.com Web Site:www.wclt.com Licensee: WCLT Radio Inc. (acq 1-1-58). Population served: 145,000 Natl. Network: AP Radio, Fox News Radio, . Wire Svc: AP Format: News/talk. News staff: 2; News: 12 hrs wkly. Target aud: General. ◆Robert H. Pricer, CEO; Douglas C. Pricer, pres, gen mgr.

WCLT-FM— Aug 7, 1947: 100.3 mhz; 50 kw. 390 ft TL: N40 02 02 W82 24 08. Stereo. Hrs open: 24 Prog sep from AM Box 5150, 43058. Secondary address: 674 Jacksontown Rd. S.E. 43056. Phone: (740) 345-4004. Fax: (740) 345-5775. Natl. Network: Fox News Radio, . Wire Svc: AP Format: Country. Target aud: 25-54.

WHTH(AM)—See Heath

WNKO(FM)— Dec 8, 1972: 101.7 mhz; 3 kw. Ant 298 ft TL: N39 38 W82 30 13. Stereo. Hrs open: 24 Box 1057, 1000 N. 40th St., 43058-1057. Phone: (740) 522-8171. Fax: (740) 522-8174.E-mail: sales@wnko.com Web Site:www.wnko.com Licensee: Runnymede Corp. (acq 10-15-98; $100,000 for stock with WHTH(AM) Heath). Population served: 140,000 Natl. Network: CNN Radio, . Wire Svc: AP Format: Classic hits. News staff: 2. Target aud: 25-54. ◆Charles Franks, pres; Tom Swank, gen mgr; John Franks, opns VP.

*WZNP(FM)— 2008: 89.3 mhz; 4.5 kw vert. Ant 325 ft TL: N39 58 45 W82 12 07. Hrs open: 881 E. Johnstown Rd., Gahanna, 43230. Phone: (614) 289-5700. Fax: (614) 289-5796. Web Site:newark.promiseradionetwork.com Licensee: Riverside Ministries. Format: Christian. ◆Dan Baughman, gen mgr.

Niles

WBBG(FM)— May 15, 1988: 106.1 mhz; 3 kw. 328 ft TL: N41 15 52 W80 45 35. Hrs open: 7461 South Ave., Boardman, 44512. Phone: (330) 965-0057. Fax: (330) 729-9991.E-mail: billkelly@clearchannel.com Web Site:www.wbbgfm.com Licensee: Citicasters Licenses L.P. Group owner: Clear Channel Communications Inc. (acq 5-4-99; grpsl). Cohn & Marks. Format: Oldies. Target aud: 18-49. ◆Bill Kelly, gen mgr; Dan Rivers, opns mgr; Jeff Kelly, progmg dir; John Nagy, news dir; John Clark, chief of engrg.

WRTK(AM)— Nov 1, 1963: 1540 khz; 500 w-D, DA. TL: N41 07 56 W80 45 40. Hrs open: Box 1798, Warren, 44482-1798. Secondary address: 124 N. Park Ave., Warren 44482. Phone: (330) 394-7700. Fax: (330) 394-7701. Web Site:www.freq1540.com Licensee: Beacon Broadcasting Inc. (acq 9-14-2005; $400,000). Population served: 100000 Format: Contemp Christian, gospel. Spec prog: It one hr, Pol one hr wkly. ◆Harold Glunt, pres, gen mgr; Richard Esbenshade, gen mgr, gen sls mgr & rgnl sls mgr.

North Baltimore

WPFX-FM— July 30, 1990: Stn currently dark. 107.7 mhz; 3 kw. Ant 328 ft TL: N41 07 04 W83 32 38. Stereo. Hrs open: 1281 N. River Rd., Fremont, 43420. Phone: (419) 332-8218. Licensee: BAS Broadcasting Inc. Group owner: Clear Channel Communications Inc. (acq 6-30-2008; grpsl). ◆James A. Lorenzen, pres.

North Canton

WHOF(FM)— Aug 29, 1968: 101.7 mhz; 6 kw. Ant 266 ft TL: N40 49 22 W81 25 41. Stereo. Hrs open: 24 7755 Freedom Ave. N.W., 44720. Phone: (330) 492-4700. Web Site:www.my1017.com Licensee: CC Licenses LLC. Group owner: Clear Channel Communications Inc. (acq 1-30-2004; $4.3 million with WJER(AM) Dover-New Philadelphia). Population served: 11,516 Format: Adult contemp. Spec prog: Farm 2 hrs wkly.

North Kingsville

WFXJ-FM— Apr 8, 2002: 107.5 mhz; 6 kw. Ant 328 ft TL: N41 54 10 W80 39 36. Hrs open: 3226 Jefferson Rd., Ashtabula, 44004-9112. Phone: (440) 998-1075. Fax: (440) 992-2658. Web Site:www.theforx1075.com Licensee: Sweet Home Ashtabula LLC. Group owner: Clear Channel Communications Inc. (acq 9-17-2007; grpsl). Format: Classic rock. Target aud: 18-54; males. ◆Dana Schulte, VP, gen mgr; Dennis O'Brien, opns dir; Michelle Baird, sls dir.

North Ridgeville

WJTB(AM)— Sept 16, 1984: 1040 khz; 5 kw-D. TL: N41 22 37 W82 00 27. Hrs open: 105 Lake Ave., Elyria, 44035. Phone: (440) 327-1844. Fax: (440) 322-8942.E-mail: wjtb1040am@aol.com Licensee: Taylor Broadcasting Co. Format: Urban contemp, gospel. ◆James Taylor, pres & gen mgr; Henry Dunn, opns mgr.

Norwalk

WLKR(AM)— Mar 18, 1968: 1510 khz; 500 w-D, DA. TL: N41 16 45 W82 39 23. Hrs open: Sunrise-sunset 10327 Milan Rd., U.S. Rt. 250, Milan, 44846. Phone: (419) 609-5961. Fax: (419) 609-2679.E-mail: wikr@acc.com Web Site:www.wlkrradio.com yes Licensee: Elyria-Lorain Broadcasting Co. (group owner; acq 4-9-02; with co-located FM). Population served: 150,000 Natl. Network: Westwood One, ESPN Radio, . Format: Oldies. News staff: one; News: 2 hrs wkly. Target aud: 40 plus. ◆Bill Hatheway, gen sls mgr; Shelly Luipold, rgnl sls mgr; Tim Kelly, stn mgr & progmg mgr; Scott Truxell, news dir, local news ed; Ken Wilde, chief of engrg; Mike Jeffries, traf mgr.

WLKR-FM— Sept 17, 1962: 95.3 mhz; 3 kw. 300 ft TL: N41 16 49 W82 39 27. Stereo. Hrs open: 24 Prog sep from AM 10327 Milan Rd., US Rt. 250, Milan, 44846. Phone: (419) 609-5961. Fax: (419) 609-2679.E-mail: info@wlkrradio.com Web Site:wlkrradio.com yes Licensee: Elyria-Lorain Broadcasting Co. Population served: 150,000 Format: Adult contemp. News staff: one; News: 3 hrs wkly. Target aud: General; residents of Huron & Erie counties. Spec prog: Farm 3 hrs wkly. ◆Tim Kelly, mus dir; Carol Walters, pub affrs dir; Mike Jeffries, traf mgr; Scott Truxel, local news ed.

*WNRK(FM)— 2004: 90.7 mhz; 4 kw. Ant 407 ft TL: N41 10 50 W82 23 21. Hrs open: 24
Rebroadcasts WKSU-FM Kent 100%.
c/o WKSU-FM, Box 5190, Kent, 44242-0001. Secondary address: 1613 E. Summit St., Kent 44242-0001. Phone: (330) 672-3114. Fax: (330) 672-4107.E-mail: letters@wksu.org Web Site:www.wksu.org Licensee: Kent State University. Natl. Network: AP Radio, NPR, PRI, . Dow, Lohnes & Albertson. Format: Classical, news. ◆Allen E. Bartholet, gen mgr; Mark Uryck, progmg dir; Ronald Bartlebaugh, engrg dir.

Oak Harbor

WJZE(FM)— August 1993: 97.3 mhz; 4.3 kw. Ant 387 ft TL: N41 28 19 W83 25 05. Stereo. Hrs open: 24 720 Water St., Toledo, 43604. Phone: (419) 868-7914. Fax: (419) 868-8765. Licensee: Urban Radio Licenses LLC. (acq 6-30-2005; $2.6 million). Population served: 500,000 Natl. Rep: Interep,. Rgnl rep: Regional Reps Smithwick & Belendiuk. Format: Rhythmic Contemporary Hits. News staff: one. Target aud: Adults 18-34. ◆Curtis Downey, gen mgr & mktg mgr.

Oberlin

*WOBC-FM— November 1951: 91.5 mhz; 440 w. 124 ft TL: N41 17 39 W82 13 26. (CP: 88.3 mhz, 3.5 kw). Stereo. Hrs open: 24 Wilder Hall, 135 W. Lorain St., 44074. Phone: (440) 775-8107. Phone: (440) 775-8139. Fax: (440) 775-6678. Web Site:www.wobc.org Licensee: Oberlin College Student Network Inc. Population served: 250,000 Format: Div, educ. News: 5 hrs wkly. Target aud: General. Spec prog: Folk 12 hrs, Fr one hr, jazz 15 hrs, electronic 20 hrs wkly. ◆Ian Page, stn mgr; Megan Snowe, opns mgr & dev dir.

WOBL(AM)— Dec 24, 1971: 1320 khz; 1 kw-U, DA-2. TL: N41 16 05 W82 12 40. Hrs open: 24 Box 277, 45624 Rt. 20 E., 44074. Phone: (440) 774-1320. Fax: (440) 774-1336.E-mail: woblwdlw@earthlink.net Licensee: WOBL Inc. Population served: 276,000 Rgnl. Network: Agri Bcstg. Reddy, Begley & McCormick, LLP. Wire Svc: AP Format: Gold country. News staff: 3; News: 14 hrs wkly. Target aud: 35-55. ◆Doug Wilber, gen mgr; Pamela Gard, progmg dir & progmg mgr.

Ontario

WRGM(AM)— July 17, 1987: 1440 khz; 1 kw-D, DA. TL: N40 46 05 W82 37 04. Stereo. Hrs open: 24 2900 Park Ave. W., Mansfield, 44906. Phone: (419) 529-5900. Fax: (419) 529-2319.E-mail: info@wrgm.com Web Site:www.wrgm.com Licensee: GSM Media Corp. Population served: 155,000 Natl. Network: ESPN Radio, . Natl. Rep: Rgnl Reps,. Format: Sports. News staff: 5; News: 10 hrs wkly. Target aud: 25 plus. Spec prog: High school football & basketball, NASCAR races. ◆Gunther Meisse, pres, gen mgr; Tony Mitchell, opns mgr.

Ottawa

WBUK(FM)— Feb 4, 1977: 106.3 mhz; 1.4 kw. Ant 489 ft TL: N40 57 21 W83 54 42. Stereo. Hrs open: 24 667 W. Market St., Lima, 45801. Phone: (419) 223-2060. Fax: (419) 229-3888.E-mail: info@wbuk.com Web Site:www.wbuk.com Licensee: The Blanchard River Broadcasting Co. Group owner: Clear Channel Communications Inc. (acq 12-3-2008; $500,000). Population served: 300,000 Rgnl. Network: Agri Bcstg. Format: Classic rock. News staff: one; News: 3 hrs wkly. Target aud: 18-49; affluent, upscale adults. Spec prog: Farm 5 hrs, sports 2 hrs, MOR 4 hrs wkly. ◆Kim Field, gen mgr.

Oxford

*WMUB(FM)— 1950: 88.5 mhz; 24.5 kw. Ant 499 ft TL: N39 33 26 W84 47 35. Stereo. Hrs open: 24 1223 Central Pkwy., Cincinnati, 45214. Phone: (513) 352-9170. Fax: (513) 241-8456.E-mail: WMUB@WMUB.org Web Site:www.wmub.org Licensee: President & Trustees of Miami University. Population served: 716,726 Natl. Network: NPR, PRI, . Ohio Educ. Telecommunications Baker & Hostetler. Wire Svc: AP Format: News/talk, jazz. Target aud: General. ◆Richard Eiswerth, gen mgr.

WOXY(FM)— Dec 24, 1959: 97.7 mhz; 3 kw. 255 ft TL: N39 28 44 W84 45 51. (CP: Ant 321 ft.). Stereo. Hrs open: 24 5120 College Corner Pike, 45056. Phone: (937) 378-6151. Fax: (513) 377-2200. Licensee: First Broadcasting Capital Partners LLC. Group owner: First Broadcasting Investment Partners LLC (acq 3-17-2004; $5.64 million). Population served: 1,000,000 Fletcher, Heald & Hildreth. Wire Svc: AP Format: Alternative. Target aud: 18-34. ◆Heather Frye, gen mgr.

Painesville

WABQ(AM)— Apr 25, 1956: 1460 khz; 1 kw-D, 500 w-N, DA-2. TL: N41 44 20 W81 14 09. Hrs open: 24 One Radio Pl., 44077. Phone: (440) 951-1460. Fax: (216) 231-9803. Fax: (440) 357-7701.E-mail: wbkc@wbkc.com Web Site:www.wbkc.com Licensee: Radio Advantage One LLC (acq 1-27-2005; $450,000). Population served: 30,000 Format: Gospel. ◆Dale Edwards, pres, gen mgr; Almira Byrd, exec VP; Danelle Caldwell, opns mgr.

*WHWN(FM)— 2009: 88.3 mhz; 700 w. Ant 144 ft TL: N41 42 17 W81 14 34. Hrs open: Attn: Nelson Cintron Jr., 3032 Vega Ave., Cleveland, 44113-5046. Licensee: La Cadena Mundial Hispana Inc.

Parma

WCCD(AM)— Jan 9, 1973: 1000 khz; 500 w-D, DA. TL: N41 19 11 W81 46 07. Hrs open: 3130 Mayfield Rd, Cleveland Heights, 44118. Phone: (216) 320-0000. Fax: (216) 321-9878.E-mail: Latreradio1000@yahoo.com Web Site:www.radio1000.org Licensee: New Spirit Revival Center Ministries, Inc. Group owner: Salem Communications Corp. 12/06 Population served: 12,807 Format:

Christian talk, Gospel. Target aud: 25-54. Spec prog: Black 3 hrs, Greek 2 hrs, Ukrainian one hr wkly. ◆Latre Mattis, gen mgr.

Paulding

WKSD(FM)— Aug 14, 1989: 99.7 mhz; 3 kw. 328 ft TL: N41 03 32 W84 35 30. Hrs open: 24 Box 487, Van Wert, 45891. Phone: (419) 238-1220. Fax: (419) 238-2578.E-mail: wert@bright.net Web Site:www.vwindependent.com Licensee: First Family Broadcasting Inc. (acq 1-3-95; $225,000; with WERT(AM) Van Wert; 3-6-95). Natl. Network: ESPN Radio, . Natl. Rep: Rgnl Reps,. Format: Oldies, Sports. ◆Chris Roberts, pres, gen mgr, progmg dir, news dir, chief of engrg; Mona Kennedy, gen sls mgr & traf mgr.

Pickerington

WJZA(FM)— Oct 7, 1989: 103.5 mhz; 4 kw. 435 ft TL: N39 51 52 W82 38 19. Stereo. Hrs open: 24 4401 Carriage Hill Ln., Columbus, 43220. Phone: (614) 451-2191. Fax: (614) 451-1831.E-mail: info@wjza.com Web Site:www.wjza.com Licensee: Franklin Communications Inc. Group owner: Saga Communications Inc. (acq 10-1-2003; $13 million). Population served: 1,500,000 Natl. Rep: Christal,. Wire Svc: AP Format: Smooth jazz. News: 2 hrs wkly. Target aud: 25-54. Spec prog: Various 15 hrs wkly. ◆Alan Goodman, pres, gen mgr; Katie Cyr, sls dir; Michelle Hurley, mktg dir; Bill Harman, progmg dir.

Piketon

WXZQ(FM)— December 1997: 100.1 mhz; 6 kw. 328 ft TL: N39 05 53 W82 57 20. Stereo. Hrs open: 24 Box 820, 45661. Phone: (740) 947-0059. Fax: (740) 947-4600.E-mail: wxiz@roadrunner.com Licensee: Piketon Communications. Population served: 30,000 Format: Current hit radio. Target aud: 18-49. ◆Gerald E. Davis, gen mgr; Brad Lambert, gen sls mgr.

Piqua

WHIO-FM— Nov 30, 1960: 95.7 mhz; 50 kw. Ant 476 ft TL: N40 13 02 W84 17 35. Stereo. Hrs open: 24
Simulcast with WHIO(AM) Dayton 100%.
1414 Wilmington Ave., Dayton, 45420. Phone: (937) 259-2111. Fax: (937) 259-2168.E-mail: info@1290whio.com Web Site:1290whio.com Licensee: Cox Radio Inc. Group owner: Cox Broadcasting (acq 1998; grpsl). Population served: 1,463,000 Format: News/talk. Target aud: 35-54. ◆Donna Hall, gen mgr; Nick Roberts, opns mgr; Todd Pitt, gen sls mgr.

WPTW(AM)— November 1947: 1570 khz; 250 w-U. TL: N40 08 14 W84 16 00. Hrs open: 24 1625 Covington Ave., 45356. Phone: (937) 773-3513. Fax: (937) 773-4345.E-mail: wptwnews@1570wptw.com Web Site:www.1570wptw.com Licensee: Miami Valley Radio LLC (acq 7-1-2008). Population served: 125,000 Natl. Network: CBS, . Rgnl. Network: Ohio Radio Net. ABN Radio Miller & Fields. Format: Oldies. News staff: one; News: 8 hrs wkly. Target aud: 35 plus. Spec prog: Farm 2 hrs, sports 30 hrs wkly.

Pleasant City

WBIK(FM)— 2002: 92.1 mhz; 6 kw. Ant 169 ft TL: N40 01 37 W81 33 09. Hrs open: 24 4988 Skyline Dr., Box 338, Cambridge, 43725. Phone: (740) 432-5605. Fax: (740) 432-1991. Web Site:wbik.com Licensee: David L. Wilson (acq 8-1-00). Rgnl rep: Rgnl Reps Format: Classic rock. ◆David L. Wilson, gen mgr.

Pomeroy

WMPO(AM)—See Middleport-Pomeroy

Port Clinton

WXKR(FM)— Oct 4, 1961: 94.5 mhz; 30 kw. 640 ft TL: N41 29 51 W83 16 12. Stereo. Hrs open: 24 3225 Arlington Ave., Toledo, 43614. Phone: (419) 725-5700. Fax: (419) 385-2902.E-mail: info@wxkr.com Web Site:www.wxkr.com Licensee: Cumulus Licensing Corp. Group owner: Cumulus Media L.L.C. (acq 12-19-97; $5 million cash). Population served: 658,000 Natl. Network: ABC, . Fletcher, Heald & Hildreth. Format: Classic Rock. News staff: one; News: one hr wkly. Target aud: 25-49. Spec prog: Sp one hr wkly. ◆Skip Schmidt, gen mgr & gen sls mgr; Ryan Young, prom dir; Dan McClintock, progmg dir; London Mitchell, news dir, edit dir; Kevin Hawley, engrg dir; Debbie Calevro, traf mgr.

Portsmouth

WNXT(AM)— Aug 30, 1951: 1260 khz; 5 kw-D, 1 kw-N, DA-2. TL: N38 48 38 W82 59 21. Hrs open: 24 Box 1228, Masonic Temple Bldg., 602 Chillicothe St., 45662. Phone: (740) 353-1161. Fax (740) 353-8080.E-mail: wnxtradio@yahoo.com Web Site:www.wnxtradio.com Licensee: Hometown Broadcasting of Portsmouth Inc. (acq 5-96; $477,500 with co-located FM). Population served: 83,000 Natl. Network: ABC, ESPN Radio, . Natl. Rep: Rgnl Reps,. Pepper & Corazzini. Format: ESPN sports radio/talk. News staff: one; News: 35 hrs wkly. Target aud: Adult males; 25-54. ◆ Phillip Bruce Leslie, pres; Steve Hayes, exec VP, opns mgr; Rick Mayne, gen mgr, gen sls mgr; Chris Smith, progmg dir; Sam McKibbin, news dir; Tyrone Henry, chief of engrg.

WNXT-FM— Sept 15, 1965: 99.3 mhz; 2.55 kw. 512 ft TL: N38 43 20 W83 00 05. Stereo. Hrs open: 24 Prog sep from AM Box 1228, Masonic Temple Bldg., 45662. Phone: (740) 353-1161. Fax: (740) 353-3191.E-mail: wnxtradio@yahoo.com Web Site:www.wnxtradio.com Population served: 83,000 Format: Adult contemp/gold. News staff: one; News: one hr wkly. Target aud: 25-54. ◆ Rick Mayne, stn mgr; Chris Smith, progmg mgr.

*WOHP(FM)— Feb 18, 1992: 88.3 mhz; 1 kw. 643 ft TL: N38 43 20 W83 00 05. Hrs open: 24
Rebroadcasts WCDR-FM Cedarville 100%.
Box 601, 251 N. Main St., Cedarville, 45314. Phone: (937) 766-7815. Fax: (937) 766-7927. Web Site:www.thepath.fm Licensee: The Cedarville University. Population served: 100,000 Cohen & Berfield. Format: Relg, full-service. News staff: one; News: 16 hrs wkly. Target aud: 35-54; church oriented audience. Spec prog: Black 2 hrs wkly. ◆ William Brown, pres; Marvin D. Sparks, gen mgr; Keith Hamer, opns mgr; Chad Bresson, news dir; John Tocknell, chief of engrg.

*WOSP(FM)— May 25, 1993: 91.5 mhz; 110 w. 1,207 ft TL: N38 45 42 W83 03 41. Stereo. Hrs open: 24
Rebroadcasts WOSU-FM Columbus 100%.
2400 Olentangy River Rd., Columbus, 43210. Phone: (614) 292-9678. Fax: (614) 292-7625.E-mail: wosu@osu.edu Web Site:www.wosu.org Licensee: The Ohio State University. Population served: 75,000 Natl. Network: PRI, NPR, AP Radio, . Dow, Lohnes & Albertson. Wire Svc: AP Format: Classical. Target aud: 35 plus. ◆ Thomas Rieland, gen mgr; Tim Eby, stn mgr; Kevin Petrilla, opns mgr. Co-owned TV: *WPBO-TV affil.

WPAY(AM)— Apr 15, 1935: 1400 khz; 800 w-U. TL: N38 43 22 W83 00 05. Hrs open: 1009 Gallia St., 45662-4140. Phone: (740) 353-5176. Fax: (740) 353-1715.E-mail: comments@f1400wpay.com Web Site:www.1400wpay.com Licensee: Radio Stations WPAY/WPFB Inc. Group owner: WPAY/WPFB Inc. (acq 2-1-57). Population served: 27,633 Natl. Network: CBS, . Format: Talk. Target aud: 18-65; young, affluent & upwardly mobile adults. Spec prog: Gospel 6 hrs wkly. ◆ Douglas Braden, pres; Frank Lewis, gen mgr; Lorenzo Bentley, news dir.

WPAY-FM— June 15, 1948: 104.1 mhz; 100 kw. Ant 1,486 ft TL: N38 41 00 W83 00 46. Stereo. Hrs open: Dups AM 10% 1009 Gallia St., 45662-4140. Phone: (740) 353-5176. Fax: (740) 353-1715. Web Site:www.104wpay.com Licensee: Radio Stations WPAY/WPFB Inc. Population served: 88,500 Natl. Network: CBS, . Format: Country.

WZZZ(FM)— January 2003: 107.5 mhz; 2.6 kw. Ant 495 ft TL: N38 43 22 W82 59 56. Stereo. Hrs open: 24 Box 1228, 45662. Secondary address: 602 Chillicothe St. 45662. Phone: (740) 353-1161. Fax: (740) 353-3191.E-mail: classicrock1075thebreeze@yahoo.com Web Site:www.wzzz.com Licensee: Hometown Broadcasting of Portsmouth 2 Inc. (acq 6-28-02). Rgnl rep: Rgnl Reps Smithwick & Bellendiuk, P.C. Format: Classic rock. News staff: one; News: .25 hrs wkly. Target aud: 35-54; working class & professional adults. ◆ Rick Mayne, gen mgr; Steve Hayes, opns mgr; Bill Murphy, progmg mgr; Sam McKibbin, news dir; Tyrone Henry, chief of engrg.

Proctorville

*WHKU(FM)— Jan 25, 1986: 91.9 mhz; 3.5 kw. Ant 220 ft TL: N38 27 14 W82 25 05. Stereo. Hrs open: 24 2351 Sunset Blvd., Suite 170-218, Rocklin, CA, 95765. Phone: (916) 251-1600. Fax: (916) 251-1650. Web Site:www.klove.com Licensee: Educational Media Foundation. (acq 2-29-2008; $900,000 with WCKU(FM) Clarksburg, WV). Natl. Network: K-Love, . Format: Christian. Target aud: General. ◆ Michael Novak, pres.

Racine

WNTO(FM)— July 15, 1996: 93.1 mhz; 4.1 kw. Ant 397 ft TL: N38 56 56 W82 03 02. Hrs open: Box 661, Gallipolis, 45631-0661. Secondary address: 117 Portsmouth Rd., Gallipolis 45631. Phone: (740) 446-3543. Fax: (740) 446-3001.E-mail: davediddle@sunny931.com Web

Site:www.sunny931.com Licensee: Sunny Boradcasting LLC Group owner: Legend Communications L.L.C. (acq 10-6-2006; $625,000 with WJEH(AM) Gallipolis). Format: Hot adult contemp. Target aud: 18-50; general. Spec prog: American Indian one hr, Black one hr, farm one hr, folk 2 hrs, gospel 7 hrs, relg 7 hrs wkly. ◆ Dave Diddle, stn mgr; Tina Merry, progmg dir.

Reading

*WMKV(FM)— 1995: 89.3 mhz; 410 watts. 236 ft TL: N39 13 23 W84 25 56. Stereo. Hrs open: 24 11100 Springfield Pike, Cincinnati, 45246. Phone: (513) 782-2427. Fax: (513) 782-2720.E-mail: gzahn@lifesphere.org Web Site:www.wmkvfm.org Licensee: Lifesphere. Format: Nostalgia. Target aud: 40 plus. ◆ George Zahn, stn mgr.

Richwood

WODB(FM)— Nov 30, 1995: 104.3 mhz; 3.4 kw. Ant 436 ft TL: N40 21 52 W83 15 34. Stereo. Hrs open: 24 4401 Carriage Hill Ln., Columbus, 43220. Phone: (614) 451-2191. Fax: (614) 451-1831.E-mail: info@wjza.com Web Site:www.bighits1043.com Licensee: Franklin Communications Inc. Group owner: Saga Communications Inc. (acq 10-1-2003; $13 million with WJZA(FM) Lancaster). Population served: 1,500,000 Natl. Rep: Christal,. Wire Svc: AP Format: Classic hits. News: 2 hrs wkly. Target aud: 25-54. Spec prog: Various 15 hrs wkly. ◆ Alan Goodman, gen mgr; Katie Cyr, sls dir; Michelle Hurley, mktg dir; Bill Harman, progmg dir.

Ripley

WAOL(FM)— 1993: 99.5 mhz; 3 kw. 328 ft TL: N38 45 14 W83 50 24. Hrs open: 8354 Fryer Rd., Georgetown, 45121. Phone: (937) 378-6151. Fax: (937) 377-2200.E-mail: info@waol.com Web Site:www.radiomaxfm.com Licensee: First Broadcasting Capital Partners LLC. Group owner: First Broadcasting Investment Partners LLC (acq 3-17-2004; $4.06 million with WAXZ(FM) Georgetown). Format: Adult Hits. ◆ Heather Frye, gen mgr; Brian Elliott, progmg dir.

Rossford

WNWT(AM)— Nov 28, 1966: 1520 khz; 500 w-D, 400 w-N, DA-2. TL: N41 30 32 W83 33 07. Hrs open: 2351 Sunset Blvd., Suite 170-218, Rocklin, CA, 95765. Phone: (916) 251-1600. Fax: (916) 251-1650. Web Site:www.klove.com Licensee: Educational Media Foundation. (acq 4-21-2009; $2,825,000 with WNKL(FM) Wauseon). Population served: 383,318 Natl. Network: K-Love, . Format: Contemp Christian. ◆ Mike Novak, pres.

Rushville

*WLRY(FM)— December 1998: 88.9 mhz; 1.1 kw vert. Ant 298 ft TL: N39 46 41 W82 25 26. Hrs open: 24 Box 220, Arcangel Broadcasting Foundation, 43150. Phone: (740) 536-0885. Fax: (740) 536-1885.E-mail: wlry@wlry.org Web Site:www.wlry.org Licensee: Arcangel Broadcasting Foundation. Population served: 120,000 Natl. Network: USA, . Format: Christian rock. News: 40 hrs wkly. Target aud: 15-55; youth & adult mentors. Spec prog: Issues talk 16 hrs wkly. ◆ Richard Finke, gen mgr.

Saint Mary's

WFGF(FM)—See Wapakoneta

WKKI(FM)—See Celina

WMLX(FM)— 1998: 103.3 mhz; 950 w. 823 ft TL: N40 38 03 W84 12 29. Hrs open: 24 667 W. Market St., Lima, 45801. Phone: (419) 223-2060. Fax: (419) 229-3888.E-mail: comments@wmlx.com Web Site:www.wmlx.com Licensee: Clear Channel Radio Licenses, Inc. Group owner: Clear Channel Communications Inc. (acq 5-4-99; grpsl). Population served: 150,000 Format: Hits of the 80s & 90s, adult contemp. News: 2 hrs wkly. Target aud: 18-49; women. ◆ Matt Nesler, sls dir; Jolene Molaski, natl sls mgr; Matt Bell, rgnl sls mgr; Renee Scott, opns mgr & progmg dir; Mark Gierhart, engrg dir.

Salem

WQXK(FM)— Nov 25, 1958: 105.1 mhz; 88 kw. Ant 430 ft TL: N40 53 06 W80 49 50. (CP: TL: N40 53 08 W80 49 55). Stereo. Hrs open: Prog sep from AM 4040 Simon Rd, Youngstown, 44512. Phone: (330) 783-1000. Fax: (330) 783-0060. Web Site:www.k105country.com

Population served: 1,400,000 Format: Country. Target aud: 25-54. ◆ Brian Schimmel, gen mgr & traf mgr.

WSOM(AM)— June 2, 1965: 600 khz; 1 kw-D, 45 w-N, DA-2. TL: N40 49 47 W80 55 54. Hrs open: 4040 Simon Rd, Youngstown, 44512. Phone: (330) 783-1000. Fax: (330) 783-2287. Web Site:www.600wsom.com Licensee: Cumulus Licensing Corp. Group owner: Cumulus Media Inc. (acq 3-15-00; grpsl). Population served: 600,000 Kaye, Scholer, Fierman, Hays & Handler. Format: Nostalgia. Target aud: 35 plus. Spec prog: Farm 2 hrs wkly. ◆ Lou Dickey, CEO; Brian Schimmel, gen mgr, progmg dir; Wes Boyd, chief of engrg.

Sandusky

WCPZ(FM)— Aug 15, 1959: 102.7 mhz; 50 kw. Ant 141 ft TL: N41 26 29 W82 41 12. Stereo. Hrs open: 1640 Cleveland Rd., 44870. Phone: (419) 625-1010. Fax: (419) 625-1348. Web Site:www.wcpz.com Licensee: BAS Broadcasting Inc. Group owner: Clear Channel Communications Inc. (acq 6-30-2008; grpsl). Population served: 1550000 Format: Hot adult contemp. News: 2 hrs wkly. Target aud: 18-54. ◆ Paul Mize, gen mgr; Randy Hugg, progmg dir; Tammy Harrison, traf mgr.

WGGN(FM)—See Castalia

*WHRQ(FM)—Not on air, target date: unknown: 88.1 mhz; 14.5 kw. Ant 256 ft TL: N41 25 54 W82 44 11. Hrs open: Box 546, Port Clinton, 43452-0546. Licensee: Port Clinton Knights of Columbus Home Association. Natl. Network: EWTN Radio, . ◆ Gerald Arnold, pres.

WLEC(AM)— Dec 7, 1947: 1450 khz; 1 kw-U. TL: N41 26 29 W82 41 10. Hrs open: 24 Prog sep from FM 1640 Cleveland Rd., 44870. Phone: (419) 625-1010. Fax: (419) 625-1348. Web Site:www.wlec.com Licensee: BAS Broadcasting Inc. (acq 6-30-2008; grpsl). Population served: 250,000 Rgnl rep: Rgnl Reps. Format: Sports. News: 2 hrs wkly.

*WVMS(FM)— December 1993: 89.5 mhz; 2.12 kw horiz, 5.36 kw vert. Ant 69 ft TL: N41 26 29 W82 48 20. Stereo. Hrs open: 24
Rebroadcasts WCRF(FM) Cleveland 100%.
c/o Radio Stn WCRF(FM), 9756 Barr Rd., Cleveland, 44141. Phone: (440) 526-1111. Fax: (440) 526-1319.E-mail: wcrf@moody.edu Web Site:wcrfradio.org Licensee: The Moody Bible Institute of Chicago. Southmayd. Wire Svc: AP Format: Inspirational, relg, Christian. Target aud: 25-55; Adults. ◆ Michael Easley, pres; Richard Lee, stn mgr; Gary Bittner, mus dir; Doug Hainer, chief of engrg.

Shadyside

WVKF(FM)— Sept 1, 1990: 95.7 mhz; 6.8 kw horiz, 6.67 kw vert. Ant 626 ft TL: N40 03 41 W80 45 09. Hrs open: 24 Clear Channel Communications, 1015 Main St., Wheeling, WV, 26003-2709. Phone: (304) 232-1170. Fax: (304) 234-0067.E-mail: info@wvkf.com Web Site:www.wvkffm.com Licensee: Capstar TX L.P. Group owner: Clear Channel Communications Inc. (acq 2-26-2004; $930,000). Natl. Rep: Christal,. Format: CHR. ◆ Scott Miller, gen mgr; Jon Dickerson, gen sls mgr; Keith Mac, progmg dir.

Shelby

*WAUI(FM)— November 1998: 88.3 mhz; 900 w. Ant 138 ft TL: N40 55 14 W82 38 51. Hrs open: Drawer 2440, Tupelo, MS, 38803-2440. Phone: (662) 844-8888. Fax: (662) 842-6791. Web Site:www.afr.net Licensee: American Family Association. Group owner: American Family Radio Format: Inspirational Christian. ◆ Marvin Sanders, gen mgr.

WSWR(FM)— Dec 1, 1981: 100.1 mhz; 3 kw. Ant 300 ft TL: N40 56 42 W82 39 42. Stereo. Hrs open: 1400 Radio Ln., Mansfield, 44906. Phone: (419) 529-2211. Fax: (419) 529-2516. Web Site:www.cruisin100.com Licensee: Capstar TX L.P. Group owner: Regent Communications Inc. (acq 8-24-2000; grpsl). Format: Oldies. ◆ Diana Coon, gen mgr.

Sidney

WMVR-FM— 1965: 105.5 mhz; 3 kw. Ant 155 ft TL: N40 18 04 W84 12 21. Stereo. Hrs open: 24 2929 W. Russell Rd., 45365. Phone: (937) 498-1055. Fax: (937) 498-2277.E-mail: hits@hits1055.com Licensee: Dean Miller Broadcasting Corp. (acq 6-10-2004). Population served: 16,332 Natl. Rep: Rgnl Reps,. Format: Adult contemp. Target aud: 18-54; women. ◆ Loretta Trent, gen mgr; Becca Woolley, prom dir.

Sinking Spring

*WOCU(FM)—Not on air, target date: unknown: 90.7 mhz; 3 kw. Ant 285 ft TL: N38 58 47 W83 23 32. Hrs open: 251 N. Main St., Cedarville, 45314. Phone: (937) 766-7815. Fax: (937) 766-7927. Web Site:www.thepath.fm Licensee: The Cedarville University. ◆Marv Sparks, gen mgr.

South Vienna

*WOAR(FM)— 2006: 88.3 mhz; 1 kw vert. Ant 278 ft TL: N39 55 54 W83 36 36. Hrs open: 5700 West Oaks Blvd., Rocklin, CA, 95765. Phone: (916) 251-1600. Fax: (916) 251-1650. Web Site:www.air1.com Licensee: Educational Media Foundation. (acq 3-23-2007; grpsl). Natl. Network: Air 1, . Format: Christian. ◆Richard Jenkins, pres.

South Webster

*WEKV(FM)— 1996: 94.9 mhz; 3 kw. Ant 328 ft TL: N38 45 39 W82 43 17. Hrs open: 24 2351 Sunset Blvd., Suite 170-218, Rocklin, CA, 95765. Phone: (916) 251-1600. Fax: (916) 251-1650. Web Site:www.klove.com Licensee: Educational Media Foundation. (acq 12-30-2005; $450,000). Population served: 140,000 Natl. Network: K-Love, . Format: Contemp Christian. ◆Richard Jenkins, pres.

*WTJM(FM)—Not on air, target date: unknown: 90.9 mhz; 5 kw vert. Ant 391 ft TL: N39 00 47.4 W82 41 30.1. Hrs open: 1585 Bethel Rd., Suite 101-LL, Columbus, 43220-2010. Phone: (614) 442-1270. Fax: (714) 845-0411.E-mail: info@stgabrielradio.com Web Site:www.stgabrielradio.com Licensee: St. Gabriel Radio Inc. ◆Chris Gabrelcik, pres; Mike Barone, stn mgr.

South Zanesville

*WCVZ(FM)— Jan 5, 1983: 92.7 mhz; 16 kw. Ant 407 ft TL: N39 42 52 W82 04 10. Stereo. Hrs open: 24 2477 E. Pike, 43701-4626. Secondary address: Box 3208, Zanesville 43701. Phone: (740) 455-3181. Fax: (740) 455-6195. Web Site:www.whiznews.com/fm/ Licensee: Southeastern Ohio Broadcasting Systems Inc. (acq 2-17-2009; $2,177,000). Population served: 250,000 Natl. Network: USA, . Format: Hot adult contemp. News: 10 hrs wkly. Target aud: General; young children 5-10 to senior citizens. ◆Henry C. Littick II, pres; Dan Baughman, gen mgr; Tate Luck, opns mgr; Michael James, progmg dir; Mike Russell, mus dir.

Spencerville

*WBCJ(FM)— Sept 1, 1997: 88.1 mhz; 2.6 kw. 492 ft TL: N40 42 41 W84 23 01. Hrs open: 1025 W. Rudisill Blvd., Fort Wayne, IN, 46807. Phone: (260) 745-0576. Fax: (260) 745-2001.E-mail: wbcl@wbcl.org Web Site:www.wbcl.org Licensee: Taylor University Broadcasting Inc. Format: Contemp Christian. ◆Craig Albrecht, opns mgr, chief of engrg; Jill Johnston, prom dir.

Springfield

WDHT(FM)— August 1958: 102.9 mhz; 50 kw. 492 ft TL: N39 57 11 W83 52 07. Stereo. Hrs open: 24 717 E. David Rd., Dayton, 45429. Phone: (937) 294-5858. Fax: (937) 297-5233.E-mail: info@hot1029.com Web Site:www.hot1029.com Licensee: MLB-Dayton IV LLC. Group owner: Radio One Inc. (acq 9-12-2007; grpsl). Population served: 81,926 Natl. Rep: Katz Radio,. Wire Svc: UPI Format: Hip-Hop. Target aud: General. ◆Andrea Scott, gen mgr.

*WEEC(FM)— Dec 15, 1961: 100.7 mhz; 50 kw. 469 ft TL: N39 57 42 W83 52 05. Stereo. Hrs open: 24 2265 Troy Rd., 45504. Phone: (937) 399-7837. Fax: (937) 399-7802.E-mail: info@weec.org Web Site:www.weec.org Licensee: World Evangelistic Enterprise Corp. Population served: 2,000,000 Natl. Network: USA, Moody, AP Radio, . Miller & Neely. Wire Svc: AP Format: Christian music, bible teaching, talk. News staff: one; News: 16 hrs wkly. Target aud: 40 plus; general. Spec prog: Black one hr, farm one hr wkly. ◆Duane Helman, pres; Newell Moore, VP; Tracy Figley, CEO & gen mgr; Chris Grindrod, progmg dir.

WIZE(AM)— Nov 1, 1940: 1340 khz; 1 kw-U. TL: N39 56 33 W83 47 15. Hrs open: 24
Simulcasts WONE(AM) Dayton 100%.
101 Pine St., Dayton, 45402. Phone: (937) 224-1137. Fax: (937) 224-3667.E-mail: info@ccedayton.com Web Site:www.wone.com Licensee: Citicasters Licenses L.P. Group owner: Clear Channel Communications Inc. (acq 5-4-99; grpsl). Format: Sports. News staff: one; News:

14 hrs wkly. Target aud: 25 plus; upper income, businesses, offices. ◆Robert Zurowesti, VP, gen mgr; Tony Tilford, progmg dir; Jeff Bennett, chief of engrg.

WULM(AM)— 1947: 1600 khz; 1 kw-D, 34 w-N. TL: N39 57 11 W83 52 07. Hrs open: 24 1529 Miracle Mile, 45503. Phone: (937) 390-1693. Fax: (937) 399-8767.E-mail: webmaster@1600wuim.net Licensee: Radio Maria Inc. (acq 5-30-2008; $225,000). Population served: 165,000 Putbrese, Hunsaker & Trent. Format: News and talk. ◆Robert Pitsch, gen mgr; Marco Simmons, stn mgr.

*WUSO(FM)— Feb 20, 1966: 89.1 mhz; 100 w. Ant 85 ft TL: N39 56 09 W83 48 41. Hrs open: 24 Box 720, Wittenberg Univ., 45501. Phone: (937) 327-7026. Fax: (937) 327-6340.E-mail: wusoprogrock@yahoo.com Web Site:wuso.org Licensee: Wittenberg University. Population served: 35,000 Format: Progsv, rock. Target aud: General; liberal arts students & residents of Springfield, OH. Spec prog: Jazz 6 hrs, class 3 hrs, blues 3 hrs, urban contemp 9 hrs wkly. ◆Brian Cataldi, gen mgr.

Steubenville

*WBJV(FM)— 2002: 88.9 mhz; 125 w. Ant 256 ft TL: N40 21 56 W80 43 36. Hrs open: Drawer 3206, Tupelo, MS, 38803. Phone: (662) 844-8888. Fax: (662) 842-6791. Licensee: American Family Association. Group owner: American Family Radio. Format: Christian. ◆Marvin Sanders, gen mgr.

WDIG(AM)— Sept 25, 1973: 950 khz; 1 kw-D, DA. TL: N40 26 49 W80 34 06. Hrs open: 24 4039 Sunset Blvd., 43952. Phone: (740) 264-1760. Fax: (740) 264-5035. Web Site:www.wdigradio.com Licensee: World Witness For Christ Ministries Inc. Population served: 30,771 Natl. Network: ABC, . Dan J. Alpert. Format: Urban, oldies. Target aud: 25-54; general. Spec prog: Gospel. ◆Roy Dawkins, CEO; Del King, gen mgr, engrg VP.

WKWK-FM—See Wheeling, WV

WSTV(AM)— Nov 4, 1940: 1340 khz; 1 kw-U. TL: N40 26 49 W80 34 06. Hrs open: 24 Box 1340, 43952. Secondary address: 320 Market St. 43952. Phone: (740) 283-4747. Fax: (740) 283-3655.E-mail: wstv@wstv.com Web Site: www.wstv.com Licensee: Keymarket Licences LLC. Group owner: Keymarket Communications LLC (acq 3-20-2000; grpsl). Population served: 141,000 Natl. Network: ESPN Radio, . Natl. Rep: Rgnl Reps,. Fleischman & Walsh L. Format: Sports. News staff: 2; News: 5 hrs wkly. Spec prog: Po 2 hrs, Czech 2 hrs wkly. ◆Gerald Getz, pres; Jim Seemiller, gen mgr; Joyce Nicholson, opns mgr, progmg mgr, pub affrs dir; Frank Bell, progmg VP; Marjie De Fede, news dir; Greg Harper, chief of engrg.

Streetsboro

*WSTB(FM)— September 1973: 88.9 mhz; 680 w. Ant 373 ft TL: N41 09 04 W81 20 13. Hrs open: 7 AM-midnight 1900 Annalane Dr., 44241. Phone: (330) 626-4906. Fax: (330) 626-4906.E-mail: mail@rock889.com Web Site:www.rock889.com Licensee: Streetsboro City Schools. Population served: 25,000 Format: Modern rock. News staff: one; News: 4 hrs wkly. Target aud: 16-34. ◆Robert L. Long, gen mgr; Billy Germani, opns mgr.

Struthers

*WKTL(FM)— Sept 6, 1965: 90.7 mhz; 15 kw. 23 ft TL: N41 03 06 W80 35 56. Hrs open: Struthers High School, 111 Euclid Ave., 44471. Phone: (330) 755-8578. Fax: (330) 755-4525. Licensee: Struthers Board of Education. Population served: 15,343 Format: Adult contemp, classic rock. ◆Tom Krestal, gen mgr.

Swanton

WJUC(FM)—Licensed to Swanton. See Toledo

Sylvania

WWWM-FM— Nov 29, 1968: 105.5 mhz; 2.15 kw. 390 ft TL: N41 38 48 W83 36 22. (CP: 2.7 kw). Stereo. Hrs open: 24 3225 Arlington Ave., Toledo, 43614. Secondary address: 2965 Pickle Rd., Oregon 43616. Phone: (419) 725-5700. Fax: (419) 385-2902.E-mail: info@star105toledo.com Web Site:www.star105toledo.com Licensee: Cumulus Licensing Corp. Group owner: Cumulus Media L.L.C. (acq 9-11-97; $10 million with WLQR(AM) Toledo). Population served: 377,600 Natl. Rep: D & R Radio,. Format: Hot Adult Contemp. Target aud: 25-54. ◆Skip

Schmidt, gen mgr, sls dir & gen sls mgr; London Mitchell, prom dir, news dir; Ron Finn, progmg dir; Kevin Hawley, chief of engrg; Debbie Calevro, traf mgr.

Thompson

*WKSV(FM)— June 1997: 89.1 mhz; 50 kw. Ant 472 ft TL: N41 41 34 W81 02 51. Stereo. Hrs open: 24
Rebroadcasts WKSU-FM Kent 100%.
c/o WKSU-FM, Box 5190, Kent, 44242-0001. Secondary address: 1613 E.Summit St, Kent 44242-0001. Phone: (330) 672-3114. Fax: (330) 672-4107.E-mail: letters@wksu.org Web Site:www.wksu.org Licensee: Kent State University. Population served: 191,723 Natl. Network: NPR, PRI, AP Radio, . Dow, Lohnes & Albertson. Format: Class, news. News staff: 5; News: 35 hrs wkly. Target aud: 35-65; college grad, professional & upper income. ◆Allen E. Bartholet, gen mgr; Mark Uryck, progmg dir, news dir; Ronald Bartlebaugh, engrg dir.

Tiffin

WCKY-FM— July 11, 1963: 103.7 mhz; 50 kw. Ant 492 ft TL: N41 08 20 W83 14 45. Stereo. Hrs open: 1624 Tiffin Ave., Findlay, 45840. Phone: (419) 425-1077. Fax: (419) 422-2954. Web Site:www.1037wcky.com Licensee: Citicasters Licenses L.P. Population served: 355,000 Format: Country. ◆Kim Field, gen mgr.

WTTF(AM)— Dec 19, 1959: 1600 khz; 500 w-D, 20 w-N, DA-1. TL: N41 07 32 W83 13 45. Hrs open: 6 AM-10 PM 1624 Tiffin Ave., Findlay, 45840. Phone: (419) 427-1077. Fax: (419) 422-2954. Web Site:www.wttf.com Licensee: BAS Broadcasting Inc. Group owner: Clear Channel Communications Inc. (acq 6-30-2008; grpsl). Population served: 65,000 Rgnl. Network: Agri Bcstg. Garvey Schubert Barer. Format: Adult contemp. News staff: 2; News: 18 hrs wkly. Target aud: General. ◆Jim Lorenzen, gen mgr & progmg dir.

Toledo

WCWA(AM)— Apr 10, 1938: 1230 khz; 1 kw-U. TL: N41 38 13 W83 33 52. Hrs open: 125 S. Superior, 43602. Phone: (419) 244-8321. Fax: (419) 244-7631.E-mail: wcwa@clearchannel.com Web Site:www.wcwa.com Licensee: Jacor Broadcasting Corp. Group owner: Clear Channel Communications Inc. (acq 1999; grpsl). Population served: 383,318 Natl. Rep: Clear Channel,. Hogan & Hartson. Format: News/talk. Target aud: 25-54; male. Spec prog: Ger one hr, Pol one hr, relg 3 hrs, sports 15 hrs wkly. ◆John Hogan, CEO; Andy Stuart, VP, gen mgr; Kellie Holeman, sls dir, mktg dir; Jack Jolly, gen sls mgr; Tom Riggs, prom mgr & progmg dir.

*WGTE-FM— May 2, 1976: 91.3 mhz; 13.5 kw. 949 ft TL: N41 39 27 W83 25 55. Stereo. Hrs open: 24 1270 S. Detroit Ave., 43614. Phone: (419) 380-4600. Fax: (419) 380-4710.E-mail: info@wgte.com Web Site:www.wgte.org Licensee: The Public Broadcasting Foundation of Northwest Ohio. Population served: 1,101,300 Natl. Network: NPR, PRI, . Schwartz, Woods & Miller. Format: Class, News, Public Affairs. News: 23 hrs wkly. Target aud: General. Spec prog: Jazz 16 hrs, new age 4 hrs wkly. ◆Marlon P. Kiser, CEO, pres, gen mgr; George Jones, chmn; Chris Pfeiffer, opns mgr; Ross Pfieffer, dev dir. Co-owned TV: *WGTE-TV affil.

WIOT(FM)— October 1949: 104.7 mhz; 50 kw. 540 ft TL: N41 40 23 W83 25 31. Stereo. Hrs open: 24 Prog sep from AM 125 S. Superior, 43602. Phone: (419) 244-8321. Fax: (419) 244-7631. Web Site:www.wiot.com (Acq 1997). Population served: 600,000 Format: Rock/AOR. Spec prog: Progsv rock 2 hrs, metal 2 hrs wkly. ◆Brian Kohler, gen sls mgr; Don Grosselin, progmg dir.

WJUC(FM)—(Swanton, Feb 27, 1997: 107.3 mhz; 3 kw. 328 ft TL: N41 38 30 W83 54 03. Hrs open: 24 Box 351450, 43635-1450. Secondary address: 5902 Southwyck Blvd. 43614. Phone: (419) 861-9582. Fax: (419) 861-2866.E-mail: wcharleswelch@aol.com Web Site:www.thejuice1073.com Licensee: Welch Communications Inc. Population served: 792,000 Rgnl rep: Interep J. Richard Carr. Wire Svc: AP Format: Urban, Hip-Hop, R & B. Target aud: 18-54; African Americans 70%, others 30%. Spec prog: Blues, gospel. ◆W. Charles Welch, CEO, chmn, pres & gen mgr.

WJYM(AM)—See Bowling Green

WKKO(FM)— Dec 7, 1956: 99.9 mhz; 50 kw. 499 ft TL: N41 40 05 W83 27 01. (CP: 6.8 kw, ant 180 ft. TL: N41 37 00 W83 37 19). Stereo. Hrs open: 24 Prog 90% of AM 3225 Arlington Ave., 43614. Phone: (419) 725-5700. Fax: (419) 385-2902.E-mail: info@k100country.com Web Site:www.k100country.com Population served: 386,000 Natl. Network: ABC, . ◆Gary Outlaw, mus dir.

WLQR(AM)— October 1954: 1470 khz; 1 kw-U, DA-2. TL: N41 37 55 W83 28 45. Hrs open: 3225 Arlington Ave., 43614. Phone: (419) 725-5700. Fax: (419) 385-2902.E-mail: info@1470theticket.com Web Site:www.1470theticket.com Licensee: Cumulus Licensing Corp. Group owner: Cumulus Media L.L.C. (acq 9-11-97; $10 million with WWWM-FM Sylvania). Population served: 383,318 Format: Sports. Target aud: 25-54. ♦Skip Schmidt, gen mgr.

***WOTL(FM)**— Mar 24, 1988: 90.3 mhz; 700 w. 377 ft TL: N41 38 48 W83 36 22. Stereo. Hrs open: 13 Fairlane Dr., Joliet, IL, 60435. Secondary address: 716 N. Westwood Ave. 43607. Phone: (815) 725-1331. Web Site:www.familyradio.com Licensee: Family Stations Inc. (group owner) Format: Relg. Target aud: General. ♦Harold Camping, pres; John Rorvik, gen mgr.

WRVF(FM)— Aug 11, 1946: 101.5 mhz; 19.1 kw. 810 ft TL: N41 41 00 W83 24 29. Stereo. Hrs open: Prog sep from AM 125 S. Superior St., 43602. Phone: (419) 244-8321. Fax: (419) 244-7631. Web Site:www.wrvf.com Population served: 1,000,000 Natl. Rep: Clear Channel,. Format: Adult contemp. Target aud: 25-54; mostly female. Spec prog: Jazz 6 hrs wkly. ♦Maureen DeTange, gen sls mgr; Don Gosselin, progmg dir.

WSPD(AM)— Apr 15, 1921: 1370 khz; 5 kw-U, DA-N. TL: N41 36 03 W83 32 11. Stereo. Hrs open: 125 S. Superior St., 43602. Phone: (419) 244-8321. Fax: (419) 244-7631. Web Site:www.wspd.com Licensee: Citicasters Licenses L.P. Group owner: Clear Channel Communications Inc. (acq 5-4-99; grpsl). Population served: 791,000 Rgnl. Network: Ohio Radio Network. Rgnl rep: Rgnl Reps. Hogan & Hartson. Format: News/talk. Target aud: 25-54; mostly males. Spec prog: Relg 5 hrs, farm 3 hrs wkly. ♦Andy Stuart, VP; Jack Jolly, gen sls mgr, rgnl sls mgr; Kellie Holeman, sls dir & natl sls mgr; A.T. Simen, prom dir, prom mgr; Al Brady Law, progmg dir.

WTOD(AM)— June 16, 1946: 1560 khz; 5 kw-D, DA. TL: N41 36 59 W83 37 22. Hrs open: 3225 Arlington Ave., 43614. Phone: (419) 725-5700. Fax: (419) 385-2902.E-mail: info@am1560wtod.com Web Site:www.am1560wtod.com Licensee: Cumulus Licensing Corp. Group owner: Cumulus Media Inc. (acq 9-11-97; grpsl). Population served: 383,318 Format: Contemp country. News staff: one; News: 3 hrs wkly. Target aud: 25-54; adults. Spec prog: Pol 4 hrs wkly. ♦Kathy Stinehour, gen mgr; Gary Shores, progmg dir; London Mitchell, news dir; Kevin Hawley, chief of engrg.

WVKS(FM)— Oct 14, 1957: 92.5 mhz; 50 kw. 480 ft TL: N41 31 55 W83 35 37. Stereo. Hrs open: 24 125 S. Superior, 43602. Phone: (419) 244-8321. Fax: (419) 244-7631. Web Site:www.925kissfm.com Licensee: Citicasters Licenses L.P. Group owner: Clear Channel Communications Inc. (acq 5-15-99; grpsl). Population served: 3,000,000 Natl. Rep: Clear Channel,. Hogan & Hartson. Wire Svc: AP Format: CHR. News staff: one; News: one hr wkly. Target aud: 18-49; educated, employed adults, mostly females. ♦Andrew Stuart, VP, gen mgr; Bill Michaels, opns dir, progmg dir; Kellie Holeman, sls dir; Amy Jo Simon, prom dir.

WWWM-FM—See Sylvania

***WXTS-FM**— February 1975: 88.3 mhz; 1 kw. 125 ft TL: N41 40 07 W83 33 15. Stereo. Hrs open: 24 2400 Collingwood Blvd., 43620. Phone: (419) 244-6875. Fax: (419) 249-8248. Licensee: Toledo Board of Education. Population served: 250,000 Format: Jazz. Target aud: 28-55. Spec prog: Blues 5 hrs wkly. ♦John Kuschell, gen mgr.

***WXUT(FM)**— Nov 4, 1990: 88.3 mhz; 100 w horiz. 190 ft TL: N41 39 26 W83 36 57. Stereo. Hrs open: 8 PM-2 AM (M-W); 8 PM-4 AM (Th, F); 9 AM-4 AM (S); 10 AM-2 AM (Su) Student Union, 2515 W. Bancroft St., 43606. Phone: (419) 530-4172. Phone: (419) 530-4455. Fax: (419) 530-2210.E-mail: wxut@wxut.com Web Site:www.wxut.com Licensee: University of Toledo. Population served: 262,000 Format: Alternative. News: 4 hrs wkly. Target aud: General. Spec prog: Black 8 hrs, heavy metal 4 hrs, rhythm and blues 2 hrs, poetry one hr, women 2 hrs wkly. ♦Terrance Teagarden, gen mgr; Colleen Drakage, stn mgr.

Troy

WHIO-FM—See Piqua

***WOKL(FM)**— 1991: 96.9 mhz; 3 kw. Ant 315 ft TL: N40 01 41 W84 11 28. Stereo. Hrs open: 24
Rebroadcasts KLVR(FM) Santa Rosa 100%.
2351 Sunset Blvd., Suite 170-218, Rocklin, CA, 95765. Phone: (916) 251-1600. Fax: (916) 251-1650.E-mail: klove@klove.com Web Site:www.klove.com Licensee: Educational Media Foundation. Group owner: EMF Broadcasting (acq 7-17-03; $1.2 million). Natl. Network: K-Love, . Shaw Pittman. Format: Contemp Christian. News staff: 3. Target aud: 25-44; Judeo Christian, female. ♦Richard Jenkins, pres; Mike Novak, VP; Keith Whipple, dev dir; David Pierce, progmg mgr; Ed Lenane, news dir; Sam Wallington, engrg dir; Karen Johnson, news rptr.

Uhrichsville

WBTC(AM)— Dec 13, 1963: 1540 khz; 250 w-D, 5 w-N. TL: N40 25 26 W81 21 47. Hrs open: 125 Johnson Dr., 44683. Phone: (740) 922-2700. Fax: (740) 922-2702.E-mail: wbtc@tusco.net Web Site:www.wbtcam.com Licensee: Tuscarawas Broadcasting Co. Population served: 8,000 Natl. Network: CBS, . Natl. Rep: Rgnl Reps,. Format: News/talk, sports. Target aud: 30-55. Spec prog: Relg 2 hrs wkly. ♦James Natoli Jr., pres, stn mgr & gen sls mgr; J.R. Richards, progmg dir.

WTUZ(FM)—Licensed to Uhrichsville. See New Philadelphia

Union City

WTGR(FM)— Dec 31, 1994: Stn currently dark. 97.5 mhz; 6 kw. Ant 328 ft TL: N40 11 32 W84 47 58. Hrs open: 24 514 Martin St., Greenville, 45331. Phone: (937) 548-5085. Fax: (937) 548-5089.E-mail: info@wtgr.com Web Site:www.wtgr.com Licensee: Positive Radio Group Inc. of Ohio. Group owner: Baker Family Stations. Population served: 70,000 Natl. Network: CNN Radio, . Ohio Educ. Telecommunications Format: Country. News staff: one; News: one hr wkly. Target aud: 25-54; 25-49 female. ♦Vernon H. Baker, CEO; Edward A. Baker, VP.

University Heights

***WJCU(FM)**— May 13, 1969: 88.7 mhz; 850 w. Ant 321 ft TL: N41 29 24 W81 31 54. (CP: 2.5 kw, ant 341 ft). Stereo. Hrs open: 24 John Carroll Univ., 20700 N. Park Blvd., Cleveland, 44118. Phone: (216) 397-4437. Phone: (216) 397-4438. Fax: (216) 397-4439.E-mail: wjcu@jcu.edu Web Site:www.wjcu.org Licensee: John Carroll University. Format: Div, modern, progsv. News: one hr wkly. Target aud: General. Spec prog: It 2 hrs, Chinese one hr, Pol 2 hrs, Lithuanian 2 hrs, Hungarian 3 hrs, Latino 4 hrs wkly. ♦Mark Krieger, gen mgr; Joe Madigan, stn mgr.

Upper Arlington

WXMG(FM)— May 25, 1989: 98.9 mhz; 3 kw. 328 ft TL: N39 58 16 W83 01 40. (CP: 2.6 kw, ant 505 ft.). Stereo. Hrs open: 24 350 E 1st Ave., Suite 100, Columbus, 43201. Phone: (614) 487-1444. Fax: (614) 487-5862.E-mail: info@wxmg.com Web Site:www.magic989.com Licensee: Blue Chip Broadcasting Licenses Ltd. Group owner: Radio One Inc. (acq 4-30-01; grpsl). Natl. Rep: Christal,. Shaw Pittman. Format: Soul/rhythm and blues. News staff: one. Target aud: 25-54; upscale, educated, active & responsive. ♦Jeff Wilson, gen mgr.

Upper Sandusky

***WXML(FM)**— Dec 26, 1992: 90.1 mhz; 15 kw vert. Ant 518 ft TL: N40 54 53 W83 07 32. Stereo. Hrs open: 24 Box 158, 1800 E. Wyandot Ave., 43351. Phone: (419) 294-2900. Fax: (419) 294-1786.E-mail: wxmlradio@udata.com Web Site:www.wxml.cc Licensee: Kayser Broadcast Ministries Inc. Population served: 695,051 Natl. Network: AP Network News, . Garvey, Schubert, Barer. Format: Relg. News: 8 hrs wkly. Target aud: General. ♦Daniel L. Kayser, CEO, pres, CFO, gen mgr; Richard Johnson, VP; Jon Bowlus, progmg dir.

Urbana

WKSW(FM)— Aug 1, 1965: 101.7 mhz; 3.2 kw. 407 ft TL: N40 02 57 W83 46 06. Stereo. Hrs open: 24 2963 Derr Rd., Springfield, 45503. Phone: (937) 399-5300. Phone: (937) 294-5858. Fax: (937) 399-3661.E-mail: email@kisscountry.com Web Site:www.kisscountry.com Licensee: MLB-Dayton IV LLC. Group owner: Radio One Inc. (acq 9-12-2007; grpsl). Population served: 250,000 Format: Country. Target aud: 25-54; above-average income, blue-collar. ♦Jim Beard, gen mgr; Kert Radel, stn mgr; Andy Lawrence, prom dir, prom mgr, disc jockey; Lee Riley, progmg dir, disc jockey; Chris Daniels, news dir, pub affrs dir, disc jockey; Gene Simmons, chief of engrg; Mickie Cooper, traf mgr.

Van Wert

WBYR(FM)— Oct 1, 1962: 98.9 mhz; 50 kw. 450 ft TL: N40 53 33 W84 31 40. Stereo. Hrs open: 1005 Production Rd., Fort Wayne, IN, 46808. Phone: (260) 471-5100. Fax: (260) 471-5224.E-mail: info@wbyrfm.com Web Site:www.989thebear.com Licensee: Pathfinder Communications Corp. Group owner: Federated Media (acq 1996; $5.85 million). Population served: 147,500 Format: Active rock. Target aud: 18-49; men. ♦Jim Allgeier, gen mgr.

WERT(AM)— Nov 27, 1958: 1220 khz; 250 w-U. TL: N40 52 19 W84 33 15. Hrs open: 24 Box 487, 45891. Phone: (419) 238-1220. Fax: (419) 238-2578.E-mail: wert@bright.net Web Site:www.vwindependent.com Licensee: First Family Broadcasting Inc. (acq 1-03-95; $225,000 with WKSD-FM Paulding; 11-7-94). Population served: 30,464 Natl. Network: ABC, . Rgnl. Network: Agri Bcstg. Natl. Rep: Rgnl Reps,. Format: Adult standards/Timeless favorites. News staff: 2; News: 30 hrs wkly. Target aud: 35 plus; spendable income. Spec prog: Gospel 3 hrs, Sp one hr wkly. ♦Chris Roberts, pres & gen mgr.

Wapakoneta

WFGF(FM)— July 1, 1964: 92.1 mhz; 3 kw. Ant 320 ft TL: N40 39 20 W84 06 54. Stereo. Hrs open: 24 Secondary address: 1301 N. Cable Rd., Lima 45805. Phone: (419) 331-1600. Fax: (419) 222-3755. Licensee: Maverick Media of Lima License LLC. Group owner: Maverick Media LLC (acq 12-4-2003; grpsl). Population served: 150,000 Natl. Rep: Christal,. Rgnl rep: Rgnl Reps. Format: Country. News staff: one; News: 6 hrs wkly. Target aud: 18-49; young, affluent women. ♦Gary S. Rozynek, pres; Matt Childers, VP, gen mgr; Dan Kennedy, progmg dir; Tiffany Binder, prom mgr & sls.

Warren

WANR(AM)— Apr 7, 1971: 1570 khz; 500 w-D, 116 w-N, DA-1. TL: N41 12 22 W80 50 29. Hrs open: 24 Box 1798, 44482-1798. Phone: (330) 394-7700. Fax: (330) 394-7701. Web Site:www.wanr1570.com Licensee: Beacon Broadcasting Inc. (group owner; (acq 9-14-2005; grpsl). Population served: 250,000 Natl. Network: Fox Sports, . Rgnl. Network: Ohio Radio Net. Format: Sports. Target aud: 25-49; adult men. ♦Harold Glunt, CFO; Rich Esbenshade, gen mgr.

WHKZ(AM)— Nov 11, 1941: 1440 khz; 5 kw-U, DA-2. TL: N41 09 52 W80 50 47. Hrs open:
Rebroadcasts WHKW(AM) Cleveland 100%.
4 Summit Park Dr., Suite 150, Independence, 44131. Phone: (216) 901-0921. Fax: (216) 901-5517.E-mail: office@whkradio.com Licensee: Pentecostal Temple Development Corp. Group owner: Salem Communications Corp. (acq 5-7-2008; $550,000). Population served: 75,000 Natl. Rep: Salem,. Format: Christian talk. ♦Errol Dengler, gen mgr.

Washington Court House

WCHO(AM)— February 1952: 1250 khz; 500 w-D. TL: N39 32 59 W83 27 10. Hrs open: 1535 N. North St., 43160. Phone: (740) 335-0941. Fax: (740) 335-6869.E-mail: info@wcho.com Web Site:www.wchoam.com Licensee: Citicasters Licenses L.P. Group owner: Clear Channel Communications Inc. (acq 5-4-99; grpsl). Population served: 250,000 Natl. Network: ABC, . Rgnl. Network: Agri Bcstg. Natl. Rep: Katz Radio,. Format: MOR. News: 18 hrs wkly. Spec prog: Farm 5 hrs wkly. ♦Dan Latham, sr VP, gen mgr; Kim Skaggs, opns VP; Tracy Taylor, sls dir; John Barney, gen sls mgr; Carl Staffan, mus dir, news dir; Todd Jellison, engrg mgr.

WCHO-FM— December 1968: 105.5 mhz; 3 kw. 300 ft TL: N39 32 59 W83 27 10. Hrs open: 1535 N. North St., 43160. Phone: (304) 342-8131. Fax: (304) 344-4745. Web Site:www.wcho.com Population served: 250,000 Natl. Network: ABC, . Format: Country.

***WEWH(FM)**—Not on air, target date: unknown: 91.1 mhz; 9 kw vert. Ant 348 ft TL: N39 24 27.8 W83 21 15.3. Hrs open: 1585 Bethel Rd., Suite 101-LL, Columbus, 43220-2010. Phone: (614) 442-1270. Fax: (714) 845-0411.E-mail: info@stgabrielradio.com Web Site:www.stgabrielradio.com Licensee: St. Gabriel Radio Inc. ♦Chris Gabrelcik, pres; Mike Barone, stn mgr.

Wauseon

WMTR-FM—See Archbold

***WNKL(FM)**— 2003: 96.9 mhz; 5 kw. Ant 358 ft TL: N41 36 03 W83 54 27. Hrs open: 2351 Sunset Blvd., Suite 170-218, Rocklin, CA, 95765. Phone: (916) 251-1600. Fax: (916) 251-1650. Web Site:www.klove.com Licensee: Educational Media Foundation. (acq 4-21-2009; $2,825,000 with WNWT(FM) Rossford). Natl. Network: K-Love, . Format: Contemp Christian. ♦Mike Novak, pres.

***WYSA(FM)**— 1996: Stn currently dark. 88.5 mhz; 10 kw. Ant 292 ft TL: N41 33 29 W84 11 08. Hrs open: 24 5105 Glendale Ave., Suite C, Toledo, 43614. Phone: (419) 389-0893. Fax: (419) 381-0731. Web

Site:www.yeshome.com Licensee: Side by Side Inc. Format: Christian, CHR, rock. Target aud: 15-25. ♦Jim Oedy, pres; J. Todd Hostetler, gen mgr; Jeff Howe, opns dir, progmg dir.

Waverly

***WWVY(FM)**—Not on air, target date: unknown: 88.5 mhz; 350 w vert. Ant 331 ft TL: N39 15 18 W82 57 17. Hrs open: Drawer 2440, Tupelo, MS, 38803. Phone: (662) 844-8888. Fax: (662) 842-6791. Licensee: American Family Association. (acq 3-4-2008; $10 for CP). ♦Donald E. Wildmon, chmn.

WXIC(AM)— 1954: 660 khz; 1 kw-D. TL: N39 07 50 W83 00 46. Hrs open: Sunrise-sunset Box 227, 6655 St. Rt. 220 W., 45690. Phone: (740) 947-2166. Fax: (740) 947-4600.E-mail: wxiz@roadrunner.com Web Site:am660wxic.com Licensee: Crystal Communications Corp. (acq 7-1-79). Population served: 4,858 Natl. Rep: Keystone (unwired net),. Format: Southern gospel mus. Gospel music lovers. ♦Gerald E. Davis, pres, gen mgr; Rick Schweinburg, opns mgr; Brad Lambert, sls dir, adv mgr; Rick Schweinsburg, prom mgr; Rick Schweinburgh, progmg mgr.

WXIZ(FM)— March 1971: 100.9 mhz; 920 w. 500 ft TL: N39 13 17 W82 59 33. Stereo. Hrs open: 24 Box 227 6655 State Rte. 220 W., 45690. Web Site:www.wxiz.com Licensee: Crystal Communications Corp. Population served: 4,858 Format: Country. News staff: one; News: 10 hrs wkly. Target aud: 25-50. ♦Gerald E. Davis, stn mgr; Brad Lambert, gen sls mgr, prom mgr; Tim Hughes, mus dir; Roy Belt, news dir.

Waynesville

***WYNS(FM)**— 2009: 89.3 mhz; 175 w. Ant 75 ft TL: N39 28 52 W84 04 20. Hrs open: 105 S. Main St., 45068. Phone: (724) 516-6252.E-mail: hybridfm@hotmail.com Web Site:www.hybridfm.net Licensee: 24-7 Broadcasting Inc. Format: Var. ♦Deborah Ives, VP.

Wellston

WKOV-FM— July 17, 1971: 96.7 mhz; 16.5 kw. 430 ft TL: N39 01 45 W82 35 51. Stereo. Hrs open: 24 Box 667 295 E. Main, Jackson, 45650. Phone: (740) 286-3023. Fax: (740) 286-6679. Licensee: Jackson County Broadcasting Inc. Population served: 585,000 Natl. Network: Westwood One, . Fletcher, Heald & Hildreth. Format: Hot adult contemp. News staff: one; News: 21 hrs wkly. Target aud: 20-55. ♦Jerry Mossbarger, gen mgr; Ron Speakman, gen sls mgr; John Pelletier, progmg dir.

WYPC(AM)— 1953: 1330 khz; 500 w-D, 50 w-N. TL: N39 06 22 W82 34 44. Hrs open: 24 Box 667, 295 E. Main, Jackson, 45640. Phone: (740) 286-3023. Fax: (740) 286-6679.E-mail: jmossbarger@jcbiradio.com Licensee: Jackson County Broadcasting Inc. (group owner; acq 9-14-70). Population served: 42,000 Natl. Network: Westwood One, . Format: Adult standards. News staff: one; News: 8 hrs wkly. Target aud: 50 plus. ♦Jerry Mossbarger, gen mgr; Ron Speakman, gen sls mgr; John Pelletier, progmg dir.

West Carrollton

WROU-FM— Nov 25, 1991: 92.1 mhz; 890 w. Ant 597 ft TL: N39 43 15 W84 15 39. Hrs open: 24 717 E. David Rd., Dayton, 45429. Phone: (937) 294-5858. Fax: (937) 297-5233.E-mail: info@921wrou.com Web Site:www.921wrou.com Licensee: MLB-Dayton IV LLC. Group owner: Radio One Inc. (acq 9-12-2007; grpsl). Natl. Network: ABC, . Natl. Rep: Katz Radio,. Format: Urban contemp. Target aud: 25-54. ♦Andrea Scott, gen mgr.

West Chester

***WLHS(FM)**— Sept 3, 1976: 89.9 mhz; 100 w. 338 ft TL: N39 19 10 W84 22 04. Hrs open: 9 AM-5 PM 6840 Lakota Ln., Liberty Township, 45044-9578. Phone: (513) 759-4163. Fax: (513) 759-4165. Licensee: Lakota School District. Population served: 500 Wire Svc: UPI Format: Educ, rock/AOR. Target aud: General; div, open minded crowd. ♦Mark Hattersley, stn mgr; R.C. Anderson, opns dir; Corey Wyatt, sls dir; Danny Hall, mus dir; Brandon Enright, asst music dir.

West Union

WRAC(FM)— Dec 15, 1981: 103.1 mhz; 3.3 kw. Ant 426 ft TL: N38 51 28 W83 36 42. (CP: COL Georgetown. 6 kw, ant 328 ft. TL: N38 52 14 W83 45 55). Stereo. Hrs open: 24 Box 103, 114 So. Manchester St., 45693. Phone: (937) 544-9722. Fax: (937) 544-5523.E-mail: c103country@yahoo.com Licensee: DreamCatcher Communications Inc. (group owner; acq 9-21-81; $4,820; 10-12-81). Natl. Rep: Rgnl Reps,. Format: Country, southern gospel. Target aud: General. Spec prog: Farm 10 hrs wkly. ♦Donald Bowles, pres, gen mgr; Venita Bowles, VP; Ted Foster, stn mgr, progmg dir; Brad Rolfe, mus dir, news dir.

***WZWP(FM)**— 1990: 89.5 mhz; 3.2 kw. Ant 330 ft TL: N38 51 36 W83 36 42. Stereo. Hrs open: 24
Simulcasts WZCP(FM) Chillicothe 100%.
881, Gahanna, 43230. Phone: 614-289-5700. Fax: (614) 289-5793.E-mail: thepromise@promiseradionetwork.com Web Site:www.promiseradionetwork.com Licensee: Christian Voice of Central Ohio Inc. (acq 5-15-2007; grpsl). Rgnl. Network: Ohio Radio Net. Format: Christain talk, educ, Music. ♦Dan Baughman, gen mgr; Scott Saunders, progmg dir.

Westerville

***WOBN(FM)**— Oct 8, 1958: 97.5 mhz; 29 w horiz. Ant 66 ft TL: N40 07 28 W82 56 06. Stereo. Hrs open: Otterbein College, 33 College view Rd., 43081. Phone: (614) 823-1725. Phone: (614) 823-1557. Fax: (614) 823-3367. Web Site:ocwobn.otterbein.edu Licensee: Otterbein College. Population served: 12,530 Format: Rock, alternative rock, progsv. News: one hr wkly. Target aud: General; Westerville & Otterbein College community. Spec prog: Black 2 hrs, jazz one hr, relg 4 hrs, heavy metal 2 hrs wkly. ♦Tom Hough, gen mgr.

WTDA(FM)— 1998: 103.9 mhz; 6 kw. Ant 328 ft TL: N40 09 33 W82 55 21. Stereo. Hrs open: 24 1458 Dublin Rd., Columbus, 43215. Phone: (614) 481-7800. Fax: (614) 481-8070.E-mail: mail997@wrkz.com Web Site:www.tedfm.com Licensee: North American Broadcasting Co. Inc. (group owner; (acq 1999; $5 million). Population served: 1,200,000 Natl. Network: Fox Sports, . Natl. Rep: D & R Radio,. Hogan & Hartson. Wire Svc: AP Format: Talk. ♦Matthew Mnich, CEO, pres; Norma J. Mnich, chmn; Mark E. Jividen, VP, gen mgr.

Weston

***WTPG(FM)**—Not on air, target date: unknown: 88.9 mhz; 3 kw. Ant 253 ft TL: N41 16 11 W83 39 43. Hrs open: 2521 W. Sunflower N3, Santa Ana, CA, 92704. Phone: (714) 545-7868. Fax: (208) 736-1958. Web Site:www.csnradio.com Licensee: CSN International. ♦Jeffrey W. Smith, pres.

Wilberforce

***WCSU-FM**— Dec 15, 1962: 88.9 mhz; 1 kw. 150 ft TL: N39 42 57 W83 52 27. Stereo. Hrs open: Box 1004, 45384-1004. Phone: (937) 376-6371. Fax: (937) 376-6436.E-mail: info@wcsu.com Web Site:www.wcsufm.org Licensee: Central State University. Population served: 150,000 Format: Urban jazz. Target aud: 12-49; African-Americans. ♦J.C. Logan, gen mgr; Tony Chappel, mus dir.

Willard

WLRD(FM)— January 2000: 96.9 mhz; 6 kw. Ant 328 ft TL: N40 57 36 W82 37 16. Hrs open: 3809 Maple Ave., Castalia, 44824. Phone: (419) 684-5311. Fax: (419) 684-5378.E-mail: fm977@cfbroadcast.net Licensee: Christian Faith Broadcast Inc. Group owner: Christian Faith Broadcasting Inc. Population served: 24 Format: Southern gospel. Target aud: 25-54. ♦Rusty Yost, gen mgr.

***WSHB(FM)**—Not on air, target date: unknown: 90.9 mhz; 700 w. Ant 167 ft TL: N40 56 42 W82 39 42. Hrs open: 500 Logan Rd., Mansfield, 44907. Phone: (419) 756-5651. Fax: (419) 756-7470. Licensee: Mansfield Christian School. ♦Josh Hooper, gen mgr.

Willoughby-Eastlake

WELW(AM)— Jan 25, 1965: 1330 khz; 500 w-D. TL: N41 38 56 W81 25 19. Hrs open: 24 Box 1330, Willoughby, 44096. Phone: (440) 946-1330. Fax: (440) 953-0320.E-mail: email@welw.com Web Site:www.welw.com Licensee: Spirit Broadcasting Corp. (acq 9-11-90; 10-1-90). Population served: 500,000 Natl. Network: Radio America, Talk Radio Network, Westwood One, USA, . Format: Talk, sports. Target aud: 35 plus; community adults. Spec prog: Ger one hr; Croation 3 hrs, It one hr; Pol one hr; Spanish contemporary 1 hr; Polka 15 hrs wkly. ♦Ray Somich, pres; Tony Petkovosek, exec VP; Van Lane, gen sls mgr; Kathy Gee, traf mgr.

Wilmington

WKFI(AM)— 1963: 1090 khz; 1 kw-D, DA. TL: N39 26 12 W83 51 21. Hrs open:
Rebroadcasts WBZI(AM) Xenia 80%.
23 E. 2nd St., Xenia, 45385. Phone: (937) 372-3531. Fax: (937) 372-3508.E-mail: myclassiccountry@myclassiccountry.com Web Site:www.myclassiccountry.com Licensee: Town and Country Broadcasting Inc. (group owner; (acq 12-16-2004; $300,000). Population served: 450,000 Natl. Network: Fox News Radio, . Natl. Rep: Rgnl Reps,. Agrinet Reddy, Belley & McCormick, L. Wire Svc: AP Format: Classic country. News staff: one; News: 3 hrs wkly. Target aud: General. Spec prog: Big band 5 hrs wkly. ♦Joe Mullins, gen mgr; Roy Hatfield, progmg dir; Megan Brugger, traf mgr; Darrin Johnston, news cmtr.

WKLN(FM)— 1974: 102.3 mhz; 3 kw. Ant 300 ft TL: N39 21 54 W83 46 08. Stereo. Hrs open: 8686 Michael Ln., Fairfield, 45014-3015. Phone: (513) 829-7700.E-mail: info@wkln.com Web Site:www.klove.com Licensee: Vernon R. Baldwin Inc. (acq 4-22-2003; $1.2 million with co-located AM). Population served: 600,000 Natl. Network: K-Love, . Format: Contemp Christian. ♦Vernon Baldwin, pres.

Wooster

***WCWS(FM)**— April 1968: 90.9 mhz; 1.05 kw. 230 ft TL: N40 48 34 W81 56 18. Stereo. Hrs open: 24 Box 3177, Wishart Hall, College of Wooster, 44691. Phone: (330) 263-2240. Fax: (330) 263-2690.E-mail: wcws@wooster.edu Web Site:www.woo91.wooster.edu Licensee: The College of Wooster. Population served: 70,000 Booth, Freret, Imlay & Tepper P.C. Format: Div, music mix. News: 10 hrs wkly. Target aud: General; college students & people of the surrounding area. Spec prog: Edu 8 hrs wkly.

***WKRW(FM)**— Mar 29, 1993: 89.3 mhz; 2.1 kw. 318 ft TL: N40 46 28 W81 55 05. Stereo. Hrs open: 24
Rebroadcasts WKSU-FM Kent 99%.
Box 5190, Kent, 44242-0001. Secondary address: 1613 E. Summit St, Kent 44242-0001. Phone: (330) 672-3114. Fax: (330) 672-4107.E-mail: letters@wksu.org Web Site:www.wksu.org Licensee: Kent State University. Population served: 91,826 Natl. Network: NPR, PRI, . Dow, Lohnes & Albertson. Format: Class, news. News staff: 5; News: 35 hrs wkly. Target aud: 35-65; college grad, professional & upper income. Spec prog: Folk 12 hrs wkly. ♦Allen Bartholet, gen mgr.

WKVX(AM)— 1947: 960 khz; 1 kw-D, 32 w-N. TL: N40 47 31 W81 54 17. Hrs open: 24 Box 39, 186 South Hillcrest Drive, 44691. Secondary address: 186 S. Hillcrest Dr. 44691. Phone: (330) 264-5122. Fax: (330) 264-3571.E-mail: wkvx@aol.com Web Site:www.wkvx.com Licensee: WWST Corp. L.L.C. Group owner: Dix Communications Population served: 85,000 Natl. Network: Westwood One, CNN Radio, . Rgnl rep: Rgnl Reps Baker & Hostetler. Wire Svc: AP Format: Oldies. ♦Craig . Walton, gen mgr; Ron Hamilton, progmg dir.

WQKT(FM)— 1947: 104.5 mhz; 52 kw. Ant 331 ft TL: N40 47 31 W81 54 17. Stereo. Hrs open: 24 Box 39, 186 South Hillcrest Drive, 44691. Secondary address: 186 S. Hillcrest Dr. 44691. Phone: (330) 264-5122. Fax: (330) 264-3571.E-mail: wqkt@aol.com Web Site:www.wqkt.com Licensee: WWST Corp. L.L.C. Population served: 85,000 Natl. Network: Westwood One, CNN Radio, . Rgnl rep: Rgnl Reps Baker & Hostetler. Wire Svc: AP Format: Country, sports. News staff: 3. Target aud: 35-54. ♦Craig A. Walton, gen mgr; Craig Walton, gen sls mgr; Ron Hamilton, progmg dir.

WXXF(FM)—(Loudonville, March 1990: 107.7 mhz; 6 kw. Ant 328 ft TL: N40 36 58 W82 05 34. Stereo. Hrs open: 24
Rebroadcasts WFXN-FM Galion 100%.
1197 US Hwy. Rt 42, Ashland, 44805. Phone: (419) 289-2605. Fax: (419) 289-0304.E-mail: jeffschendel@clearchannel.com Licensee: Capstar TX L.P. Group owner: Clear Channel Communications Inc. (acq 2-12-2001; grpsl). Population served: 250,000 Natl. Network: Fox News Radio, . Format: Classic rock. Target aud: 25-54; Male. Spec prog: Underground Garage, House of Hair. ♦Diana Coon, gen mgr; Joe Rinehart, stn mgr; Eric Hansen, opns mgr; Jeff Schendel, progmg dir.

Xenia

WBZI(AM)— Nov 11, 1963: 1500 khz; 500 w-D. TL: N39 42 48 W83 54 48. Hrs open: Sunrise-sunset 23 E. 2nd St., 45385. Phone: (937) 372-3531. Fax: (937) 372-3508.E-mail: myclassiccountry@myclassiccountry.com Web Site:www.wbzi.com; www.myclassiccountry.com Licensee: Town & Country Broadcasting Inc. (acq 10-4-95; $140,000). Population served: 825,000 Natl. Network: Fox News Radio, . Rgnl. Network: Ohio News Net. Natl. Rep: Rgnl Reps,. Agrinet Reddy, Begley, & McCormick L.L.P. Wire Svc: AP Format: Classic country. News staff: one; News: 3 hrs wkly. Target aud: 35-64; upper income, married, homeowners. Spec prog: Gospel

5 hrs, farm 2 hrs wkly. ♦Joe Mullins, gen mgr; Roy Hatfield, progmg dir; Darrin Johnston, news dir; Megan Brugger, traf mgr.

WGNZ(AM)—See Fairborn

WZLR(FM)— Mar 3, 1967: 95.3 mhz; 6 kw. 300 ft TL: N39 37 54 W83 53 49. Stereo. Hrs open: 24 1414 Wilmington Ave., Dayton, 45420. Phone: (937) 259-2111. Fax: (937) 259-2168.E-mail: info@953theeagle.com Web Site:953theeagle.com Licensee: Cox Radio Inc. Group owner: Cox Broadcasting (acq 1998; grpsl). Population served: 1,463,000 Natl. Rep: Christal,. Dow, Lohnes & Albertson. Format: Classic hits. Target aud: 25-54. ♦Donna Hall, VP, gen mgr; Kathy Eagle-Norris, gen sls mgr; Jason Michaels, progmg dir, mus dir.

Yellow Springs

***WYSO(FM)**— Feb 8, 1958: 91.3 mhz; 37 kw. 410 ft TL: N39 45 46 W83 53 05. Stereo. Hrs open: 24 795 Livermore St., 45387. Phone: (937) 767-6420. Fax: (937) 769-1382.E-mail: wyso@wyso.org Web Site:www.wyso.org Licensee: Antioch University. Population served: 1,400,000 Natl. Network: PRI, NPR, . Rgnl. Network: Ohio Educ Bcstg. Ohio Educ. Telecommunications Garvey, Schubert & Barer. Format: News, Americana, AAA. News staff: 2; News: 77 hrs wkly. Target aud: 25-54; college educated, professional, mid-upper income. Spec prog: Folk 2 hrs, jazz 12 hrs, blues 4 hrs, new age 4 hrs, Celtic/British Isles 3 hrs,bluegrass 6 hrs wkly. ♦Tom Faecke, CFO; Paul Maassen, gen mgr; Jacki Mayer, dev dir.

Youngstown

WAKZ(FM)—(Sharpsville, PA) Dec 28, 1976: 95.9 mhz; 3 kw. Ant 328 ft TL: N41 13 05 W80 33 43. Stereo. Hrs open: 7461 South Ave., Boardman, 44512. Phone: (330) 965-0057. Fax: (330) 729-9991. Web Site:www.959kiss.com Licensee: Citicasters Licenses L.P. Group owner: Clear Channel Communications Inc. (acq 1-15-2004; grpsl). Format: CHR. ♦Bill Kelly, gen mgr; Cornell Bogdon, gen sls mgr, rgnl sls mgr; John Thomas, prom dir & prom mgr.

WASN(AM)— May 9, 1976: 1500 khz; 500 w-D, 250 w-CH, DA. TL: N41 06 26 W80 34 57. Hrs open: Sunrise-sunset 20 Federal Plaza W., # T2, 44503. Phone: (330) 744-5115. Fax: (330) 744-4020.E-mail: skip@ytownradio.com Licensee: Bernard of Ohio LLC. (acq 1-22-2007; grpsl). Natl. Network: CNN Radio, . Format: Talk/news. News: 4 hrs wkly. Target aud: General; families. ♦Skip Bednarczyk, gen mgr, gen sls mgr & progmg dir.

WBBG(FM)—See Niles

WBBW(AM)— Feb 20, 1949: 1240 khz; 1 kw-U. TL: N41 04 50 W80 38 54. Hrs open: 4040 Simon Rd., 44512. Phone: (330) 783-1000. Fax: (330) 783-0060. Web Site:www.wbbw.com Licensee: Cumulus Licensing Corp. Group owner: Cumulus Media Inc. (acq 3-15-00; grpsl). Population served: 150,000 Natl. Network: Westwood One, . Format: Sports. Target aud: General. ♦Brian Schimmel, gen mgr.

WGFT(AM)—(Campbell, Oct 16, 1955: 1330 khz; 500 w-D, 1 kw-N, DA-2. TL: N40 58 30 W80 35 15. Hrs open: 20 Federal Plaza W., # T2, Youngtown, 44503. Phone: (330) 744-5115. Fax: (330) 744-4020.E-mail: skip@ytownradio.com Web Site:www.1330wgft.com Licensee: Bernard of Ohio LLC. (acq 1-22-2007; grpsl). Population served: 500,000 Natl. Network: CNN Radio, . Format: talk. Target aud: General; family. ♦Skip Bednarczyk, gen mgr; Tiffany Allen, prom dir.

WHKZ(AM)—See Warren

WHOT-FM— November 1959: 101.1 mhz; 24 kw. Ant 711 ft TL: N41 03 28 W80 38 24. (CP: 25 kw, ant 694 ft.). Stereo. Hrs open: 4040 Simon Rd., 44512. Phone: (330) 783-1000. Fax: (330) 783-0060. Web Site:www.hot101.com Putbrese, Hunsaker & Trent. Format: CHR. Target aud: 18-54. ♦Brian Schimmel, gen mgr & gen sls mgr.

WKBN(AM)— 1926: 570 khz; 5 kw-U, DA-N. TL: N40 59 07 W80 36 02. Hrs open: 24 Box 9248, 44513. Secondary address: 7461 South Ave., Boardman 44512. Phone: (330) 965-0057. Fax: (330) 965-8277. Licensee: Citicasters Licenses L.P. Group owner: Clear Channel Communications Inc. (acq 1-22-99; $11 million with co-located FM). Population served: 750,000 Natl. Network: ABC, CBS, . Format: News/talk, sports. Spec prog: Polka 2 hrs, Croation 2 hrs wkly. ♦Bill Kelly, VP, gen sls mgr; Dan Rivers, progmg dir.

WLOA(AM)—(Farrell, PA) Oct 3, 1954: 1470 khz; 1 kw-D, 500 w-N, DA-N. TL: N41 11 58 W80 31 22. Hrs open: Box 1798, Warren, 44482-1798. Phone: (330) 394-7700. Fax: (330) 394-7701. Licensee: Beacon Broadcasting Inc. (group owner; (acq 10-4-2005; $295,000). Population served: 11,022 Format: Classic country.

WMXY(FM)— Aug 26, 1947: 98.9 mhz; 4.5 kw. 1,370 ft TL: N41 03 24 W80 38 44. Stereo. Hrs open: Prog sep from AM Box 9248, Younstown, 44513. Phone: (330) 965-0057. Fax: (330) 965-8277. Licensee: Citicasters Licenses L.P. Format: Adult contemp.

WNCD(FM)— June 1959: 93.3 mhz; 50 kw. Ant 280 ft TL: N41 04 50 W80 38 54. Stereo. Hrs open: Prog sep from AM Box 9248, 445123. Phone: (330) 965-0057. Fax: (330) 965-8277.E-mail: info@wncd.com Web Site:www.wncd.com Licensee: Citicasters Licenses LP Format: Rock. Target aud: 25-54. ♦Thomas John, prom dir; Dan Rivers, progmg dir.

WNIO(AM)— Sept 7, 1939: 1390 khz; 9.5 kw-D, 4.8 kw-N, DA-N. TL: N41 07 17 W80 42 05 (day), N40 59 11 W80 35 54 (night). Stereo. Hrs open: 24 7461 South Ave., 44512. Phone: (330) 965-0057. Fax: (330) 965-8277.E-mail: info@wnio.com Web Site:www.wnio.com Licensee: Citicasters Licenses L.P. Group owner: Clear Channel Communications Inc. (acq 1-15-2004; grpsl). Population served: 535000 Format: Nostalgia. News staff: 2; News: 3 hrs wkly. Target aud: General. Spec prog: It 3 hrs wkly. ♦Bill Kelly, gen mgr, gen sls mgr; Dan Rivers, adv dir.

WRTK(AM)—See Niles

***WYSU(FM)**— September 1969: 88.5 mhz; 50 kw. 499 ft TL: N41 03 28 W80 38 42. Stereo. Hrs open: 24 Youngstown State University, One University Plaza, 44555. Phone: (330) 941-3363. Fax: (330) 941-1501.E-mail: info@wysu.org Web Site:www.wysu.org Licensee: Youngstown State University. Population served: 914,9000 Natl. Network: PRI, NPR, . Bakeer & Hostetler. Format: Class, news. News: 48 hrs wkly. Target aud: General. Spec prog: Folk 3 hrs wkly. ♦Gary Sexton, gen mgr; David Luscher, opns mgr, progmg dir; Ron Krauss, chief of engrg.

***WYTN(FM)**— May 1991: 91.7 mhz; 3 kw. 299 ft TL: N41 03 28 W80 38 42. Stereo. Hrs open: 24 13 Fairlane Dr., Joliet, IL, 60435. Secondary address: 3930 Sunset Blvd. 60435. Phone: (815) 725-1331. Web Site:www.familyradio.com Licensee: Family Stations Inc. (group owner) Dow, Lohnes & Albertson. Format: Relg. Target aud: 25 plus; Christians. Spec prog: Class 2 hrs wkly. ♦Harold Camping, pres; John Rorvik, gen mgr.

Zanesville

WHIZ(AM)— July 8, 1924: 1240 khz; 1 kw-U. TL: N39 55 42 W81 59 06. Hrs open: 24 629 Downard Rd., 43701. Phone: (740) 452-5431. Fax: (740) 452-6553. Web Site:www.whizamfmtv.com Licensee: Southeastern Ohio Broadcasting System Inc. (acq 6-47). Population served: 33,045 Natl. Rep: Roslin, Rgnl Reps,. Format: Adult standards, news/talk. News staff: 10; News: 30 hrs wkly. Target aud: 25-54; general. Spec prog: Farm progmg 2 hrs wkly. ♦N.J. Littick, chmn; Henry Littick, pres; Van Vannelli, VP; Jay Benson, stn mgr, sls dir, adv dir; Brian Wagner, opns dir, mktg dir, progmg dir, farm dir, disc jockey; George Hiotis, news dir, local news ed; Ken Cash, chief of engrg; Andy Jones, sports cmtr; Brenda Larrick, disc jockey.

WHIZ-FM— Dec 16, 1961: 102.5 mhz; 50 kw. Ant 495 ft TL: N39 55 42 W81 59 07. (CP: COL Baltimore. 11 kw, ant 499 ft. TL: N39 47 00 W82 45 21). Stereo. Hrs open: 24 629 Downard Rd., 43701. Phone: (740) 452-5431. Fax: (740) 452-6553. Web Site:www.whizamfmtv.com Licensee: Southeastern Ohio Broadcasting System Inc. Population served: 245,000 Format: Adult contemp. News: 12 hrs wkly. Target aud: 25 plus; general. Spec prog: Relg one hr, sports 3 hrs wkly. ♦George Hiotis, local news ed; Brian Wagner, farm dir, disc jockey; Andy Jones, sports cmtr; Jared Stewart, disc jockey. Co-owned TV: WHIZ-TV affil.

***WJIC(FM)**— 2000: 91.7 mhz; 6 kw. 276 ft TL: N40 04 16 W82 11 30. Hrs open: 24 c/o VCY/America, 3434 W. Kilbourn Ave., Milwaukee, WI, 53208. Phone: (414) 935-3000. Fax: (414) 935-3015.E-mail: wjic@vcyamerica.org Web Site:www.wcyamerica.org Licensee: VCY/America Inc. (group owner; Natl. Network: USA, . Format: Relg, Christian. ♦Vic Eliason, gen mgr; Jim Schneider, progmg dir; Andy Eliason, chief of engrg.

***WOUZ(FM)**— Nov 1, 1993: 90.1 mhz; 3 kw. 279 ft TL: N39 48 50 W81 57 21. Stereo. Hrs open: 24
Rebroadcasts WOUB-FM Athens 100%.
9 S. College St., Athens, 45701. Phone: (740) 593-4554. Fax: (740) 593-0240.E-mail: woub@woub.org Web Site:www.woub.org Licensee: Ohio University. Format: News/talk. News staff: 3. ♦Carolyn Lewis, gen mgr.

WYBZ(FM)—See Crooksville

Oklahoma

Ada

KADA(AM)— September 1934: 1230 khz; 1 kw-U. TL: N34 47 06 W96 40 44. Hrs open: Box 609, 74821. Secondary address: 1019 N. Broadway 74820. Phone: (580) 332-1212. Fax: (580) 332-0128.E-mail: kada@cable1.net Licensee: The Chickasaw Nation. Population served: 30,000 Rgnl. Network: Okla. Radio Net. Okla. News Net. Format: Sports. Target aud: 25-54. Spec prog: Gospel 5 hrs wkly. ♦Roger Harris, gen mgr, dev mgr, adv mgr & min affrs dir.

KADA-FM— 1979: 99.3 mhz; 5.5 kw. Ant 299 ft TL: N34 42 31 W96 44 24. Stereo. Hrs open: Box 609, 74821. Phone: (580) 332-1212. Fax: (580) 332-0128.E-mail: kada@cable1.net Licensee: The Chickasaw Nation (acq 7-88). Format: Country. ♦Roger Harris, mktg mgr & min affrs dir.

***KAJT(FM)**— 2006: 88.7 mhz; 31 kw. Ant 239 ft TL: N34 46 32 W96 35 15. Hrs open: 24 262550 Box, Baton Rouge, LA, 70826. Secondary address: 8919 World Ministry Ave. , Baton Rouge, LA 70810. Phone: (225) 768-3688. Fax: (225) 768-3729.E-mail: kawikfish@yahoo.com Web Site:www.jsm.org Licensee: Family Worship Center Church Inc. Group owner: American Family Radio. (acq 10-7-2005; $500,000 with CP for KSSO(FM) Norman). Population served: 65,000 Format: Southern gospel. ♦David Whitelaw, COO; Jimmy Swaggart, pres; John Santiago, progmg dir.

***KAKO(FM)**— 2006: 91.3 mhz; 100 kw vert. Ant 442 ft TL: N35 13 36 W96 55 42. Hrs open: Drawer 2440, Tupelo, MS, 38803. Phone: (662) 844-8888. Fax: (662) 842-6791. Web Site:www.afr.net Licensee: American Family Association. Natl. Network: American Family Radio, . Format: Christian classics. ♦Marvin Sanders, gen mgr.

***KCNP(FM)**— January 1999: 89.5 mhz; 5.8 kw. Ant 581 ft TL: N34 41 01 W96 45 44. Hrs open: 24 Box 1548, 74821. Phone: (580) 436-2603. Licensee: The Chickasaw Nation. (acq 9-24-2008; $470,000). ♦Brian Brashier, gen mgr.

Altus

KEYB(FM)— Dec 25, 1988: 107.9 mhz; 50 kw. Ant 492 ft TL: N34 46 15 W99 32 20. Stereo. Hrs open: 24 Box 1077, 73522. Secondary address: 808 N. Main St. 73521. Phone: (580) 482-1555. Fax: (580) 482-8353.E-mail: keyb@keyb.net Web Site:www.keyb.net Licensee: Altus FM Inc. (acq 2-5-91;12-31-90). Population served: 76,321. Natl. Network: Jones Radio Networks, AP Network News, . Shaw Pittman. Format: Country. News staff: one; News: 3 hrs wkly. Target aud: 25-54. Spec prog: Farm 2 hrs wkly. ♦Gayle Ledbetter, CEO, gen mgr; Sam Schroeder, progmg VP; Richard Bustos, engrg dir; Tracie Tobitt, traf mgr.

***KKVO(FM)**— 1985: 90.9 mhz; 400 w. Ant 121 ft TL: N34 42 44 W99 19 03. Stereo. Hrs open: 24 2351 Sunset Blvd., Suite 170-218, Rocklin, CA, 95765. Phone: (916) 251-1600. Fax: (916) 251-1650. Web Site:www.klove.com Licensee: Educational Media Foundation. (acq 6-6-2005; $150,000). Population served: 25,000 Natl. Network: K-Love, . Format: Relg, educ. ♦Richard Jenkins, pres; Mike Novak, VP, progmg dir; Lloyd Parker, gen mgr; Ed Lenane, opns dir, news dir; Keith Whipple, dev dir; Eric Allen, natl sls mgr; David Pierce, progmg mgr; Jon Rivers, mus dir; Sam Wallington, engrg dir; Arthur Vassar, traf mgr; Karen Johnson, news rptr.

***KOCU(FM)**— July 2002: 90.1 mhz; 5 kw. Ant 85 ft TL: N34 40 14 W99 20 13. Hrs open:
Rebroadcasts KCCU(FM) Lawton 100%.
2800 W. Gore, Lawton, 73505. Phone: (580) 581-2472. Fax: (580) 581-5571.E-mail: kccu@cameron.edu Web Site:www.kccu.org Licensee: Cameron University. Natl. Network: NPR, PRI, . Format: News, classical. ♦Ted Riley, gen mgr.

KRKZ(FM)— Apr 1, 1974: 93.5 mhz; 45 kw. Ant 528 ft TL: N34 37 35 W99 20 10. Stereo. Hrs open: Prog sep from AM Box 577, 73522. Secondary address: 212 W. Cypress 73522. Phone: (580) 482-1450. Fax: (580) 482-3420.E-mail: mward@kwhw.com Population served: 50,000 Format: Classic rock.

***KTHL(FM)**—Not on air, target date: unknown: 89.3 mhz; 15 kw. Ant 361 ft TL: N34 39 05 W99 26 00. Hrs open: Box 14, Ponca City, 74602-0014. Phone: (580) 767-1400. Fax: (580) 765-1700.E-mail: mail@thehousefm.com Web Site:www.thehousefm.com Licensee: The Love Station Inc. ♦Doyle Brewer, gen mgr; Tony Weir, progmg dir.

KWHW(AM)— Apr 2, 1947: 1450 khz; 1 kw-U. TL: N34 37 35 W99 20 10. Hrs open: Box 577, 73522. Secondary address: 212 W. Cypress 73522. Phone: (580) 482-1450. Fax: (580) 482-3420. E-mail: mward@kwhw.com Web Site:www.kwhw.com Licensee: Monarch Broadcasting Inc. (group owner; acq 12-31-2003; grpsl). Population served: 50,000 Rgnl. Network: Okla. Radio Net. Okla. News Net. Format: C&W, news/talk, agriculture info. Spec prog: Sp 16 hrs wkly. ◆Jimmy Young, gen mgr & gen sls mgr.

Alva

KALV(AM)— Oct 18, 1956: 1430 khz; 500 w-U, DA-2. TL: N36 49 06 W98 38 38. Stereo. Hrs open: 24 R.R. 1 Box 53, 73717. Phone: (405) 327-1430. Fax: (405) 327-1433.E-mail: kalvradio@yahoo.com Licensee: MM&K of Alva Inc. (acq 8-30-94; $165,000; 9-19-94). Population served: 7,440 Format: Oldies. News staff: one; News: 8 hrs wkly. Target aud: 45-70; loc residents. ◆Randy Mitchel, pres & gen mgr.

KPAK(FM)—Not on air, target date: unknown: 97.5 mhz; 50 kw. Ant 492 ft TL: N37 01 27 W98 41 22. Hrs open: 1310 Main St., Kiowa, KS, 67070. Phone: (620) 825-4027. Fax: (620) 825-4324. Web Site:www.kpak.net Licensee: George S. Flinn Jr. Format: Adult alternative. ◆George Flinn Jr., pres.

Antlers

KDOE(FM)— 2006: 102.3 mhz; 3.3 kw. Ant 276 ft TL: N34 13 35 W95 37 20. Hrs open: 404 E. Jackson St., Hugo, 74743. Phone: (580) 326-5541. Fax: (580) 326-5236. Licensee: Will Payne. Format: Diversified. ◆Will Payne, gen mgr.

Apache

KACO(FM)— Jan 1, 1989: 98.5 mhz; 18.5 kw. Ant 305 ft TL: N34 56 30 W98 22 33. Stereo. Hrs open: 24 115 W. Broadway, Anadarko, 73005. Phone: (405) 247-6682. Fax: (405) 247-1051.E-mail: krmptraffic @classicnet.net Web Site:www.perry_pub_broadcasting.com Licensee: Perry Publishing & Broadcasting (acq 1-5-98; $475,000). Population served: 75,000 Natl. Network: ABC, . Cordon & Kelly. Format: Real Country. Target aud: 25-54. ◆Kevin Perry, VP; Joy Chapman, gen mgr; Russell Perry, opns mgr, sls dir; Terry Monday, progmg mgr.

Ardmore

KKAJ-FM— June 24, 1974: 95.7 mhz; 100 kw. Ant 449 ft TL: N34 05 53 W97 10 54. Stereo. Hrs open: 24 1205 Northglen, 73401. Phone: (580) 226-0421. Fax: (580) 226-0464.E-mail: webmaster@kkaj.com Web Site:www.kkaj.com Licensee: LKCM Radio Group L.P. (acq 2-26-2007; grpsl). Population served: 512,000 Rgnl. Network: Agri-net. Format: Country. News staff: one; News: 25 hrs wkly. Target aud: 18-54. ◆Michael Baer, gen mgr; Dave Hilton, opns mgr.

*KLCU(FM)— June 19, 1998: 90.3 mhz; 25 kw. Ant 213 ft TL: N34 12 10 W97 09 12. Hrs open:
Rebroadcasts KCCU(FM) Lawton 98%.
c/o KCCU(FM), Admin. Bldg., 2800 W. Gore Blvd., Lawton, 73505. Phone: (580) 581-2425. Phone: (580) 581-2474. Fax: (580) 581-5571.E-mail: kccu@cameron.edu Web Site:www.kccu.org Licensee: Cameron University. Population served: 100,000 Natl. Network: NPR, PRI, . Format: Classical. ◆Ted Riley, gen mgr; Terry Anderson, dev dir & dev dir; Michael V. Leal, progmg dir.

*KQPD(FM)— 2003: 91.1 mhz; 250 w. Ant 167 ft TL: N34 11 01 W97 07 23. Hrs open: Drawer 2440, Tupelo, MS, 38803. Phone: (662) 844-8888. Fax: (662) 842-6791. Licensee: American Family Association. Group owner: American Family Radio. Format: Christian. ◆Marvin Sanders, gen mgr.

KVSO(AM)— September 1935: 1240 khz; 1 kw-U. TL: N34 10 54 W97 08 48. Stereo. Hrs open: 24 1205 Northglen, 73401. Phone: (580) 226-0421. Fax: (580) 226-0464.E-mail: webmaster@kvso.com Web Site:www.kvso.com Licensee: LKCM Radio Group L.P. Group owner: NextMedia Group L.L.C. Population served: 320,000 Rgnl. Network: Okla. Radio Net. Natl. Rep: Christal,. Format: Christian music. News staff: one; News: 4 hrs wkly. Target aud: 25 plus. ◆Michael Baer, gen mgr.

KYNZ(FM)—See Lone Grove

Atoka

KHKC-FM— June 15, 1984: 102.1 mhz; 3.3 kw. Ant 449 ft TL: N34 25 08 W96 11 24. Stereo. Hrs open: Box 810, 74525. Secondary address: Hwy. 75 N. 74525. Phone: (580) 889-3392. Phone: (580) 889-6300. Fax: (580) 889-9308.E-mail: khkc103@yahoo.com Web Site:www.khkc1021.com Licensee: Keystone Broadcasting Corp. (acq 10-23-2001; with co-located AM). Format: Country. ◆Ricky Chase, gen mgr & progmg dir.

KKNG-FM—See Newcastle

Bartlesville

KRIG-FM—(Nowata, 1965: 104.9 mhz; 8.3 kw. Ant 564 ft TL: N36 43 37 W95 46 18. Stereo. Hrs open: 24 Box 1100, 74005. Secondary address: 1200 S.E. Frank Phillips Blvd. 74003. Phone: (918) 336-1001. Phone: (918) 336-1400. Fax: (918) 336-6939.E-mail: radio@bartlesvilleradio.com Web Site:www.bartlesvilleradio.com Licensee: KCD Enterprises Inc. (group owner; acq 6-26-98; $775,000). Natl. Network: ABC, . Natl. Rep: Rgnl Reps,. Agrinet Rgnl rep: Rgnl Reps Lauren A. Colby. Wire Svc: AP Format: Country. News staff: 2; News: 20 hrs wkly. Target aud: 35-65; mature buyers. Spec prog: Gospel 4 hrs wkly. ◆Kevin Potter, pres, gen mgr; Charlie Taraboletti, opns mgr; Dorea Potter, prom mgr; Sharon Frahm, traf mgr.

KWON(AM)— April 1942: 1400 khz; 1 kw-U. TL: N36 45 53 W95 57 35. Stereo. Hrs open: 24 Box 1100, 74005. Secondary address: 1200 S.E. Frank Phillips Blvd. 74003. Phone: (918) 336-1001. Phone: (918) 336-1400. Fax: (918) 336-6939.E-mail: radio@bartlesvilleradio.com Web Site:www.bartlesvilleradio.com Licensee: KCD Enterprises Inc. (group owner; acq 2-1-97; $625,000 with co-located FM). Population served: 42,000 Natl. Network: CBS, . Rgnl. Network: Okla. Radio Net. Okla. News Net. Rgnl rep: Rgnl Reps Lauren A. Colby. Wire Svc: AP Format: News/talk. News staff: 2; News: 25 hrs wkly. Target aud: 25-54; general. Spec prog: Relg 5 hrs wkly. ◆Charlie Taraboletti, opns mgr, opns mgr, progmg dir, news dir, engrg dir, engrg mgr; Kevin Potter, pres, stn mgr, sls dir & gen sls mgr; Dorea Potter, prom dir.

*KWRI(FM)— 2004: 89.1 mhz; 100 kw vert. Ant 626 ft TL: N36 42 13 W95 30 57. Hrs open: 24 2351 Sunset Blvd., Suite 170-218, Rocklin, CA, 95765. Phone: (916) 251-1600. Fax: (916) 251-1650.E-mail: info@air1.com Web Site:www.air1.com Licensee: Educational Media Foundation. Group owner: EMF Broadcasting. Natl. Network: Air 1, . Shaw Pittman. Format: Contemp Christian. News staff: 3. Target aud: 18-35; Judeo-Christian, female. ◆Richard Jenkins, pres; Mike Novak, VP; Keith Whipple, dev dir; David Pierce, progmg mgr; Ed Lenane, news dir; Sam Wallington, engrg dir; Karen Johnson, news rptr.

KYFM(FM)— Nov 6, 1961: 100.1 mhz; 25 kw. Ant 695 ft TL: N36 37 42 W96 11 26. Stereo. Hrs open: 24 Box 1100 , 74005. Secondary address: 1200 S.E. Frank Phillips Blvd. 74003. Phone: (918) 336-1001. Fax: (918) 336_6939. Web Site:www.bartlesvilleradio.com Licensee: KCD Enterprises Inc. Population served: 72,000 Natl. Network: ABC, . Rgnl. Network: Okla. Radio Net. Agrinet Rgnl rep: Rgnl Reps Lauren A. Colby. Wire Svc: AP Format: Adult contemp. News: 15 hrs wkly. Target aud: 25-49. Spec prog: Gospel 4 hrs wkly. ◆Kevin Potter, gen mgr; Charlie Taraboletti, opns mgr; Dorea Potter, prom dir; sharon Frahm, traf mgr; Tami Brinkman, sls.

Beaver

*KLXO(FM)—Not on air, target date: unknown: 91.9 mhz; 1 kw horiz. Ant 49 ft TL: N36 51 28 W100 30 36. Hrs open: 116 Hillcrest Dr., Seminole, 74868. Phone: (405) 380-3516.E-mail: info@bpba.us Web Site:www.bpba.us Licensee: Better Public Broadcasting Association. ◆Dennis Burton, gen mgr.

Bennington

KZRC(FM)— Nov 1, 1979: 98.1 mhz; 3.5 kw. Ant 210 ft TL: N34 02 40 W96 01 10. Stereo. Hrs open: 5 AM-1 AM North Texas Radio Group L.P., 5946 Club Oaks Dr., Dallas, TX, 75248. Phone: (972) 931-6055. Fax: (972) 931-9141.E-mail: info@kfyzfm.com Licensee: North Texas Radio Group L.P. (acq 11-2-98; $1.15 million with co-located AM). ◆Richard E. Witkovski, gen mgr.

Bethany

KKWD(FM)—Licensed to Bethany. See Oklahoma City

Bixby

KJMM(FM)— November 1994: 105.3 mhz; 10 kw. 879 ft TL: N35 51 41 W95 46 03. Hrs open: 24 7030 S. Yale Ave., Suite 302, Tulsa, 74136. Phone: (918) 494-9886. Fax: (918) 494-9683. Web Site:www.per-ry_pub_broadcasting.com Licensee: KJMM Inc. Group owner: Perry Publishing & Broadcasting Co. (acq 1-95). Natl. Network: ABC,

American Urban, Westwood One, . Meyer, Faller, Weisman & Rosenberg. Format: Urban contemp. News staff: one; News: 10 hrs wkly. Target aud: 18-35; General. ◆Russell Perry, CEO; Martha Vaughn, gen mgr.

Blackwell

KLOR-FM—See Ponca City

KOKB(AM)— October 1952: 1580 khz; 1 kw-D, 49 w-N. TL: N36 48 35 W97 15 50. Hrs open: 6 AM-9 PM
Rebroadcasts KOKP(AM) Perry 80%.
Box 2509, Ponca City, 74602. Secondary address: 122 N. Third St., Ponca City 74602. Phone: (580) 765-2485. Fax: (580) 767-1103.E-mail: kokb@eteamradio.com Web Site:www.eteamradio.com Licensee: Team Radio LLC (group owner; acq 10-18-96; $90,000). Population served: 65,000 Format: Talk, sports. News: 30 hrs wkly. Target aud: 35-75; adult, upper-middle income. ◆Bill Coleman, pres, gen mgr & stn mgr.

Blanchard

KOJK(FM)— Aug 18, 1977: 97.3 mhz; 1 kw. Ant 800 ft TL: N35 10 38 W97 36 10. Stereo. Hrs open: 24 5101 S. Shields Blvd., Oklahoma City, 73129. Phone: (405) 616-5500. Fax: (405) 616-5505. Web Site:www.jackokc.com Licensee: Nick Radio LLC. (acq 1-31-2006; $1 million). Population served: 100,000 Natl. Rep: D & R Radio,. Format: Adult Hits. ◆Skip Stow, CEO & pres; Becca Sharp, stn mgr, gen sls mgr.

Boise City

*KJHL(FM)— 2009: 90.9 mhz; 10 kw. Ant 351 TL: N36 44 05 W102 29 53. Hrs open: Box 991, Meade, KS, 67864. Phone: (620) 873-2991. Fax: (620) 873-2755.E-mail: kjil@kjil.com Web Site:www.kjil.com Licensee: Great Plains Christian Radio Inc. ◆Robert D. Hughes, CEO.

Bristow

KREK(FM)— Nov 14, 1978: 104.9 mhz; 5 kw. 351 ft TL: N35 47 11 W96 27 35. Stereo. Hrs open: 24 Box 1280, 74010. Phone: (918) 367-5501. Fax: (918) 367-5502.E-mail: krekfm@yahoo.com Licensee: Big Chief Broadcasting Co. of Bristow Inc. Population served: 75,000 Format: Country. Target aud: 0-100. ◆Clifford W. Smith, pres & gen mgr.

Broken Arrow

*KNYD(FM)— Aug 19, 1986: 90.5 mhz; 100 kw. Ant 1,637 ft TL: N36 01 15 W95 40 32. Stereo. Hrs open: 24 Box 1924, Tulsa, 74101. Secondary address: 11717 S. 129th East Ave. 74011. Phone: (918) 455-5693. Fax: (918) 455-0411.E-mail: mail@oasisnetwork.org Web Site:www.oasisnetwork.org Licensee: Creative Educational Media Inc. (acq 1985). Format: Relg. Target aud: General. ◆David Ingles, pres & gen mgr.

KTBT(FM)— Dec 23, 1970: 92.1 mhz; 27 kw. 656 ft TL: N36 06 38 W96 01 57. Stereo. Hrs open: 24 2625 S. Memorial, Tulsa, 74129. Phone: (918) 388-5100. Fax: (918)388-5400. Web Site:www.921thebeat.com Licensee: Clear Channel Broadcasting Licenses Inc. Group owner: Clear Channel Communications Inc. Natl. Rep: Clear Channel,. Format: CHR. Target aud: 18-34; women. ◆Michael Oppenheimer, gen mgr; Don Cristi, opns mgr.

Broken Bow

*KBWW(FM)—Not on air, target date: unknown: 88.3 mhz; 30 kw vert. Ant 459 ft TL: N34 01 44 W95 06 11. Hrs open: Box 126, Golden, 74737. Phone: (580) 420-6687. Licensee: Golden Baptist Church. ◆Ron Carroll, gen mgr.

KKBI(FM)— January 1983: 106.1 mhz; 50 kw. 817 ft TL: N34 14 45 W94 46 58. Stereo. Hrs open: 24 Box 1016, 108 N. Broadway, 74728-1016. Phone: (580) 584-3388. Fax: (580) 584-3341.E-mail: kkbi@pine-net.com Web Site:www.kkbifm.com Licensee: J.D.C. Radio Inc. (acq 1-27-98; $800,000). Population served: 34,000 Natl. Network: Jones Radio Networks, . Putbrese, Hunsaker & Trent. Format: Country. News staff: one; News: 5 hrs wkly. Target aud: 24-55. Spec prog: Farm 5 hrs, gospel 4 hrs wkly. ◆David Smulyan, gen mgr; Jay Lindley, exec VP & progmg dir.

Byng

KYKC(FM)— Sept 17, 1992: 100.1 mhz; 50 kw. 492 ft TL: N34 43 43 W46 42 45. (CP: 12.87 kw, ant 459 ft.). Hrs open: 24 Box 609, Ada, 74821. Secondary address: 1019 N. Broadway, Ada 74820. Phone: (580) 436-1616. Fax: (580) 436-1617.E-mail: kykc@cableone.net Web Site:www.kykc.net Licensee: The Chickasaw Nation. (acq 1-14-2005; $900,000). Format: Country. Target aud: 12 plus; across the board. ◆Roger Harris, gen mgr; Pete Roper, gen sls mgr, adv mgr; Mike Manos, progmg mgr.

Cache

*KARU(FM)— 2005: 88.9 mhz; 440 w vert. Ant 259 ft TL: N34 38 10 W98 41 32. Stereo. Hrs open: 24 2351 Sunset Blvd., Suite 170-218, Rocklin, CA, 95765. Phone: (916) 251-1600. Fax: (916) 251-1650.E-mail: info@air1.com Web Site:www.air1.com Licensee: Educational Media Foundation. Group owner: EMF Broadcasting. Natl. Network: Air 1, . Shaw Pittman. Format: Contemp Christian. News staff: 3. Target aud: 18-35; Judeo-Christian, female. ◆Richard Jenkins, pres; Mike Novak, VP; Keith Whipple, dev dir; Eric Allen, natl sls mgr; David Pierce, progmg dir; Liz Morton, mus dir; Ed Leane, news dir; Sam Wallington, engrg dir; Karen Johnson, news rptr.

KJMZ(FM)—Licensed to Cache. See Lawton

Carnegie

*KJCC(FM)— 2005: 89.5 mhz; 350 w vert. Ant 194 ft TL: N35 06 59 W98 28 26. Hrs open: CSN International, 3232 W. MacArthur Blvd., Santa Ana, CA, 92704. Secondary address: 300 Towakkonie Rd., Fort Cobb 73038. Phone: (405) 643-2117. Fax: (405) 643-2851.E-mail: leannafarmer99@yahoo.com Web Site:www.csnintl.com Licensee: CSN International (group owner). Format: Christian praise & worship, Bible teaching. ◆Leanna Farmer, stn mgr.

Catoosa

KEOR(AM)— Jan 29, 1968: 1120 khz; 2 kw-D, DA. TL: N36 18 31 W95 58 25. Hrs open: Sunrise-sunset Box 690240, Tulsa, 74169-0240. Phone: (918) 294-1904.E-mail: info@dioceseoftula.org Licensee: Catholic Diocese of Tulsa Group owner: First Broadcasting Investment Partners LLC (acq 3-17-2009; $532,500). Target aud: General. ◆Edward J. Slattery, CEO.

KZLI(AM)— July 3, 1950: 1570 khz; 1 kw-D. TL: N36 15 55 W95 42 37. Hrs open: Daytime Box 702588, Tulsa, 74170. Phone: (918) 496-7700. Fax: (918) 746-7615. Licensee: Reunion Broadcasting L.L.C. (group owner; Population served: 825,031 Okla. News Net. Hardy, Carey & Chautin. Format: Adult standards. News staff: one; News: 10 hrs wkly. Target aud: 35 plus. ◆Stan Tacker, gen mgr; Terri Tacker, gen sls mgr.

Chelsea

KTFR(FM)— March 1, 2001: 100.7 mhz; 6 kw. 328 ft TL: N36 30 12 W95 26 29. Hrs open: 24 Rebroadcasts KXOJ-FM Sapulpa. 2448 E. 81st St., Suite 4500, Tulsa, 74137. Phone: (918) 492-2660. Fax: (918) 492-8840.E-mail: kxoj@kxoj.com Web Site:www.kxoj.com Licensee: Michael P. Stephens. Group owner: Adonai Radio Group (acq 2-17-95;5-15-95). Format: Contemp Christian. ◆Mike Stephens, pres; David Stephens, gen mgr; Bob Thornton, progmg dir.

Chickasha

*KFXU(FM)— 2008: 90.5 mhz; 10 kw. Ant 321 ft TL: N34 54 33 W97 57 29. Stereo. Hrs open: 1101 N. 81 Hwy., Marlow, 73055. Phone: (580) 658-9292.E-mail: kfxi@cableone.net Licensee: Sister Sherry Lynn Foundation Inc. Format: Standards. ◆Ken Austin, gen mgr; Sherry Lynn, gen sls mgr; Jennifer James, progmg dir; Steve Michaels, mus dir; James Wilson, engr.

KWCO-FM— Nov 4, 1966: 105.5 mhz; 3.3 kw. 443 ft TL: N35 00 38 W97 55 54. Stereo. Hrs open: 24 627 West Chickasha Ave., Oklahoma City, 73129. Phone: (405) 224-9105. Fax: (405) 224-2890. Web Site:www.ktuz.com Licensee: Kenny Communications Inc. (acq 1-1-2004; $114,400). Population served: 100,000 Okla. Jones Radio Networks, . Format: Classic rock. News: 10 hrs wkly. Target aud: 18-54; Spanish persons. ◆Matthew Mollman, gen mgr; Keith Michaels, progmg dir; George Plummer, news dir; Christopher Hoops, chief of engrg.

Claremore

*KRSC-FM— Aug 4, 1980: 91.3 mhz; 2.2 kw. 364 ft TL: N36 19 06 W95 38 18. Stereo. Hrs open: 7 AM-11 PM Rogers State University., 1701 W. Will Rogers Blvd., 74017-3252. Phone: (918) 343-7670. Phone: (918) 343-7669. Fax: (918) 343-7952.E-mail: sdoyle@rsu.edu Web Site:www.rsu.edu Licensee: Board of Regents of the University of Oklahoma. Population served: 300,000 Okla. News Net. Format: Alternative (college). Target aud: General; college & community, young & older adults. Spec prog: Folk 5 hrs, jazz 5 hrs, progsv 12 hrs, country 5 hrs wkly. ◆Cathy Coomer, gen mgr, stn mgr; Steve Doyle, opns mgr. Co-owned TV: *KRSC-TV affil.

KRVT(AM)— Jan 17, 1958: 1270 khz; 5 kw-D, 1 kw-N, DA-2. TL: N36 15 55 W95 42 37. Hrs open: 24 Box 702588, Tulsa, 74170. Phone: (918) 496-7700. Fax: (918) 746-7615.E-mail: krvt@krvt.com Web Site:www.krvt.com Licensee: Reunion Broadcasting L.L.C. (group owner; acq 2-25-2000). Population served: 744,600 Natl. Network: CBS Radio, . Hardy, Carey & Chautin. Format: Oldies. News: 4 hrs wkly. Target aud: 35 plus; upscale adults. Spec prog: St. Louis Cardinal Baseball. ◆D. Stanley Tacker, pres & gen mgr.

Cleveland

*KJOG(FM)—Not on air, target date: unknown: 91.1 mhz; 19 kw vert. Ant 308 ft TL: N36 18 47 W96 46 20. Hrs open: 102 Red Branch Ln., Simpsonville, SC, 29681. Phone: (864) 297-0216. Fax: (864) 297-0344.E-mail: info@networkofglory.org Web Site:networkofglory.com Licensee: Network of Glory Inc. ◆Lola Richey, pres.

Clinton

KCLI(AM)— Apr 15, 1949: 1320 khz; 1 kw-D, 108 w-N. TL: N35 29 00 W98 58 54. Hrs open: 5105 S. Shields Blvd., Oklahoma city, 73129. Phone: (580) 323-0617. Fax: (580) 323-0717.E-mail: sales@wrightradio.com Licensee: Wright Broadcasting Systems Inc. Group owner: Wright Broadcasting Systems (acq 9-13-2000; $25,000). Rgnl. Network: Okla. Radio Net. Okla. News Net. Fletcher, Heald & Hildreth. Format: Spanish. Target aud: General. ◆Harold Wright, gen mgr.

KWEY-FM— Apr 9, 1978: 95.5 mhz; 40 kw. Ant 492 ft TL: N35 27 04 W98 58 19. Stereo. Hrs open: 24 Box 587, Weatherford, 73096. Phone: (580) 772-5939. Fax: (580) 772-5930.E-mail: sales@wrightradio.com Web Site:www.kwey.com Licensee: Wright Broadcasting Systems Inc. Group owner: Wright Broadcasting Systems (acq 1996; $300,000). Natl. Network: ABC, . Putbrese, Hunsaker & Trent, P.C. Wire Svc: AP Format: Country. News: 8 hrs wkly. Target aud: 18-54; upwardly mobile adults. ◆Harold Wright, CEO, pres, gen mgr; Todd Brunner, opns mgr; Heston Wright, sls dir; Rob Grogan, progmg dir; Ray Bagby, engrg dir.

*KYCU(FM)— September 2002: 89.1 mhz; 40 kw. Ant 633 ft TL: N35 26 40 W98 59 22. Hrs open: Rebroadcasts KCCU(FM) Lawton 100%. 2800 W. Gore Blvd., Lawton, 73505. Phone: (580) 581-2425. Fax: (580) 581-5571. Licensee: Cameron University. Natl. Network: NPR, PRI, . Format: News, classical. ◆Ted Riley, gen mgr.

Coalgate

KXFC(FM)— Dec 7, 2001: 105.5 mhz; 20 kw. Ant 364 ft TL: N34 41 43 W96 23 17. Hrs open: 24 1188 North Hills Centre, Ada, 74820. Phone: (580) 332-1212. Fax: (580) 332-0128.E-mail: score@cableone.net Web Site:www.kxfcradio.com Licensee: The Chickasaw Nation. (acq 10-1-2008; $1.5 million with KTLS-FM Holdenville). Population served: 176,000 Natl. Network: AP Radio, Jones Radio Networks, . Davis Wright Tremaine LLP. Format: Rhythmic top-40. Target aud: 25+. ◆Howard Stone, sr VP; Rick Woodward, gen mgr; Craig Stone, progmg dir; Renae Woodward, traf mgr.

Collinsville

KIZS(FM)— June 25, 1996: 101.5 mhz; 6.2 kw. Ant 656 ft TL: N36 20 02 W95 47 08. Hrs open: 2625 S. Memorial, Tulsa, 74129. Phone: (918) 388-5100. Fax: (918) 388-5400. Web Site:www.tulsa.lapreciosa.com Licensee: Clear Channel Broadcasting Licenses Inc. Group owner: Clear Channel Communications Inc. (acq 10-6-97; $1.9 million). Format: Sp. Target aud: 25-54; general. ◆Michael Oppenheimer, gen mgr & stn mgr; Don Cristi, opns mgr.

Comanche

KDDQ(FM)— Apr 1, 1982: 105.3 mhz; 6 kw. Ant 298 ft TL: N34 26 12 W97 54 47. Stereo. Hrs open: 24 1701 W. Pine Ave., Duncan, 73533. Phone: (580) 255-1350. Fax: (580) 470-9993.E-mail: kken@cableone.net Licensee: Perry Broadcasting of Southwest Oklahoma Inc. Group owner: Perry Publishing & Broadcasting Co. (acq 1-9-2003; grpsl). Natl. Network: ABC, . Format: Classic rock. News staff: one; News: 4 hrs wkly. Target aud: 25-54; females with mid-level income. Spec prog: Gospel 2 hrs wkly. ◆Joy Chapman, gen mgr, sls dir & prom dir; Dale Weakley, chief of engrg.

Cordell

KCDL(FM)— Sept 1, 1988: 99.3 mhz; 10.5 kw. 505 ft TL: N35 26 49 W98 59 17. Hrs open: 24 700 Frisco Ave., Clinton, 73601. Phone: (580) 772-5939. Fax: (580) 323-0717.E-mail: sales@wrightradio.com Web Site:kcdl.com Licensee: Wright Broadcasting Systems Inc. Group owner: Wright Broadcasting Systems (acq 8-30-99; $350,000). Natl. Network: ABC, CNN Radio, . Rgnl. Network: Agri-Net. Agrinet Format: Classic rock. Target aud: General. ◆Harold Wright, CEO, pres, gen mgr; Todd Brunner, opns dir; Rob Grogan, progmg dir.

Coweta

*KDIM(FM)— February 2005: 88.1 mhz; 50 w horiz, 100 kw vert. Ant 551 ft TL: N35 42 24 W96 05 39. Stereo. Hrs open: 24 Box 1924, Tulsa, 74101. Secondary address: 11717 S. 129th E. Ave., Broken Arrow 74011. Phone: (918) 455-5693. Fax: (918) 455-0411.E-mail: mail@oasisnetwork.org Web Site:www.oasisnetwork.org Licensee: Creative Educational Media Corp. Inc. Format: Relg. Target aud: General. ◆David Ingles, pres & gen mgr.

Cushing

KUSH(AM)— 1953: 1600 khz; 1 kw-D, 70 w-N. TL: N35 39 11 W96 42 37. Hrs open: Box 791, 74023. Phone: (918) 225-0922. Fax: (918) 225-0925.E-mail: kush@yahoo.com Licensee: Cimarron Valley Broadcasters Inc. (acq 3-4-65). Format: News/talk, sports. ◆Sean Kelly, gen mgr.

Del City

KOCY(AM)— November 1946: 1560 khz; 1 kw-D, 250 w-N, DA-2. TL: N35 26 26 W97 29 24 (D), N35 26 27 W97 29 24 (N). Hrs open: 24 5101 S. Shields, Oklahoma City, 73129. Phone: (405) 616-5500. Fax: (405) 616-5551. Web Site:www.radio.disney.go.com Licensee: Oklahoma Land Co. L.L.C. Group owner: Tyler Media Broadcasting Corp. (acq 12-15-2003; $250,000). Population served: 45,000 Natl. Network: Radio Disney, . Format: Children. News staff: one; News: 8 hrs wkly. Target aud: 18 plus. Spec prog: Loc sports. ◆Skip Stow, gen mgr.

Dickson

KTRX(FM)— June 2001: 92.7 mhz; 5.5 kw. Ant 341 ft TL: N34 06 56 W97 00 06. Stereo. Hrs open: 24 1205 Northglen, Ardmore, 73401. Phone: (580) 226-0421. Fax: (580) 226-0464.E-mail: webmaster@texomarocks.com Web Site:www.texomarocks.com Licensee: LKCM Radio Group L.P. Group owner: NextMedia Group L.L.C. (acq 2-26-2007; grpsl). Population served: 310,000 Natl. Network: Jones Radio Networks, . Rgnl. Network: Agri-net. Natl. Rep: Christal,. Format: Classic rock. News staff: one; News: 25 hrs wkly. Target aud: 25-54; men. ◆Gerry Schlegel, VP; Michael Baer, gen mgr; Dave Hilton, opns mgr, progmg dir.

Duncan

KKEN(FM)— Dec 31, 1975: 102.3 mhz; 3 kw. Ant 207 ft TL: N34 40 43 W97 58 05. Stereo. Hrs open: Prog sep from AM 1701 Pine St., W., 73533. Phone: (580) 255-1350. Fax: (580) 470-9993.E-mail: kken@cableone.net Population served: 40,000 Format: Country. Target aud: 25-54. ◆Pam Peck, rgnl sls mgr.

KPNS(AM)— Oct 31, 1947: 1350 khz; 250 w-D, 100 w-N. TL: N34 40 43 W97 58 05. Stereo. Hrs open: 6 AM-midnight 1701 Pine St., W., 73533. Phone: (580) 255-1350. Fax: (580) 470-9993.E-mail: kken@cableone.net Licensee: Perry Broadcasting of Southwest Oklahoma Inc. Group owner: Perry Publishing & Broadcasting Co. (acq 11-22-02; grpsl). Population served: 40,000 Format: Sports talk. News staff: one; News: 20 hrs wkly. Target aud: General. ◆Jay Chapman, gen mgr; Peggy Richardson, opns mgr; Joy Chatman, gen sls mgr, adv mgr; Terry Monday, progmg VP & progmg dir.

Durant

*KAYC(FM)— 2000: 91.1 mhz; 403 w. Ant 210 ft TL: N34 01 17 W96 28 18. Hrs open: Box 3206, American Family Radio, Tupelo, MS, 38803. Phone: (662) 844-8888. Fax: (662) 842-6791. Web Site:www.afr.net Licensee: American Family Association. Group owner: American Family Radio. Format: Inspirational Christian. ◆Marvin Sanders, gen mgr.

KLBC(FM)— November 1958: 106.3 mhz; 21 kw. Ant 358 ft TL: N34 00 07 W96 25 19. Stereo. Hrs open: 24 1418 N. 1st Ave., Box 190, 74701. Phone: (580) 924-3100. Fax: (580) 920-1426.E-mail: scott@klbcfm.com Web Site:www.klbcfm.com yes Licensee: Texoma Broadcasting Inc. Natl. Network: ABC, . Format: Country. News staff: one; News: 20 hrs wkly. Target aud: General. ◆Todd Tidwell, gen mgr & gen sls mgr; Bob McKinzie, prom dir.

KSEO(AM)— May 1947: 750 khz; 250 w-D. TL: N34 00 07 W96 25 19. Hrs open: 6 AM-7 PM Box 190, 1418 N. 1st Ave, 74701. Phone: (580) 924-3100. Fax: (580) 920-1426.E-mail: margie@klbcfm.com Web Site:www.klbcfm.com yes Licensee: Texoma Broadcasting Inc. (acq 5-28-99; with co-located FM). Population served: 34,000 Format: Contemp Christian. News staff: one; News: 3 hrs wkly. Target aud: Adults; 18-54. ◆Bob McKenzie, opns dir, progmg dir; Todd Tidwell, pres, gen mgr & gen sls mgr; Jim Reagan, pub affrs dir.

*KSSU(FM)— Feb 1, 1972: 91.9 mhz; 1.5 kw. 341 ft TL: N34 00 45 W96 19 45. Stereo. Hrs open: 24 1405 N. 4th St., PMB 4129, 74701-0609. Phone: (580) 745-7483. Fax: (580) 745-7475. Licensee: Southeastern Oklahoma State University. Population served: 35,000 Format: CHR. Target aud: 18-25; college, high school students & area residents.

Edmond

*KCSC(FM)— April 1966: 90.1 mhz; 100 kw. Ant 840 ft TL: N35 34 24 W97 29 08. Stereo. Hrs open: 24 Univ. of Central Okla., 100 N. University Dr., 73034-5209. Phone: (405) 974-3333. Fax: (405) 974-3844.E-mail: kcscfm@ucok.edu Web Site:www.kcscfm.com Licensee: University of Central Oklahoma. Population served: 1,006,629 Natl. Network: PRI, . Format: Class. News: One. Target aud: 35 plus; educated, affluent. ◆Bradford Ferguson, gen mgr; Barbara Hendrickson, opns mgr; Susan Clark, dev dir.

*KOKF(FM)— September 1977: 90.9 mhz; 100 kw. Ant 480 ft TL: N35 33 59 W97 28 28. Stereo. Hrs open: 24 2351 Sunset Blvd., Suite 170-218, Rocklin, CA, 95765. Phone: (916) 251-1600. Fax: (916) 251-1650. Web Site:www.air1.com Licensee: Educational Media Foundation. (acq 5-25-2006; $4 million). Population served: 1,700,000 Natl. Network: Air 1, . Format: Christian. ◆Richard Jenkins, pres, gen sls mgr; Mike Novak, VP; Keith Whipple, dev dir; David Pierce, progmg mgr; Ed Lenane, news dir; Sam Wallington, engrg dir; Karen Johnson, news rptr.

WWLS-FM—Licensed to Edmond. See Oklahoma City

El Reno

KZUE(AM)— Sept 9, 1962: 1460 khz; 500 w-D. TL: N35 30 30 W97 54 00. Hrs open: Daytime only 2715 S. Radio Rd., 73036. Phone: (405) 262-1460. Fax: (405) 262-1886.E-mail: kzue@aol.com Web Site:www.latremendaok.com Licensee: La Tremenda Inc. (acq 12-8-93; $40,000; 1-3-94). Population served: 25,000 Natl. Rep: Keystone (unwired net),. Format: Sp. ◆Nancy Galvan, gen mgr.

Eldorado

KXOW(FM)—Not on air, target date: unknown: 96.9 mhz; 6 kw. Ant 328 ft TL: N34 27 00 W99 32 04. Hrs open: Box 880, Roma, TX, 78584. Phone: (956) 487-8015. Licensee: South Texas FM Investments LLC. (acq 9-16-2008; grpsl). ◆Eloy Vera, gen mgr.

Elk City

KADS(AM)— October 1932: 1240 khz; 1 kw-U. TL: N35 22 51 W99 24 25. Hrs open: 24 Box 945, 73648. Phone: (580) 225-9696. Fax: (580) 225-9699.E-mail: info@kads.com Web Site:kecofm.com Licensee: Paragon Communications Inc. (group owner; acq 6-15-01; $15,000). Population served: 20,000 Natl. Network: ESPN Radio, . Wire Svc: AP Format: Sports. News staff: one. ◆Blake Brewer, gen mgr.

KECO(FM)— July 20, 1982: 96.5 mhz; 100 kw. 500 ft TL: N35 24 22 W99 29 54. Stereo. Hrs open: 24 Box 945, 73648. Secondary

address: 220 S. Pioneer Rd. 73644. Phone: (580) 225-9696. Fax: (580) 225-9699.E-mail: info@keco.com Web Site:www.kecofm.com Licensee: Paragon Communications Inc. (group owner; acq 4-22-98; $100,000 for 72% with KXOO(FM) Elk City). Population served: 60,000 Bryan Cave. Format: Country. News staff: one; News: 2.5 hrs wkly. Target aud: General. ◆Blake Brewer, pres, gen mgr, gen sls mgr; Connie Legrand, opns mgr.

KTIJ(FM)— July 15, 2000: 106.9 mhz; 100 kw. Ant 981 ft TL: N34 58 39 W99 24 35. Hrs open: Phone: (580) 726-5656. Fax: (580) 726-2222.E-mail: thezone@itlnet.net Licensee: Fuchs Radio LLC. Format: CHR/pop. ◆Chad Fox, gen mgr; Shelly Fox, VP & opns mgr.

KXOO(FM)— April 1995: 94.3 mhz; 12 kw. 469 ft TL: N35 24 22 W99 29 54. Stereo. Hrs open: 24 Box 945, 73648. Phone: (580) 225-9696. Fax: (580) 225-9699.E-mail: info@kxoo.com Web Site:www.kxoofm.com Licensee: Paragon Communications Inc. (group owner; acq 4-22-98; $100,000 for 72% with KECO(FM) Elk City). Population served: 40,000 Format: Adult Contemp christian. News staff: one; News: 2 hrs wkly. ◆Blake Brewer, pres, gen mgr; Gabe Ednay, chief of engrg.

Enid

KCRC(AM)— 1926: 1390 khz; 1 kw-U, DA-1. TL: N36 25 11 W97 52 28. Hrs open: 24 Box 952, 73702. Phone: (580) 237-1390. Fax: (580) 242-1390.E-mail: ctbradio@yahoo.com Licensee: Chisholm Trail Holding Co. Inc. (acq 6-1-83; $1.38 million; 6-20-83). Population served: 50,195 Natl. Network: Jones Radio Networks, ESPN Radio, . Rgnl. Network: Okla. Radio Net. Okla. News Net. Format: News. News staff: one; News: 2 hrs wkly. Target aud: General. ◆Hiram Champlin, pres, gen mgr; Ricky Roggow, opns mgr, mus dir; Sandy Daniels, gen sls mgr; Suzi Lakin, prom mgr; Chad McKee, progmg dir; Rob Houston, news dir, pub affrs dir; G.B. Bonham, chief of engrg.

KFXY(AM)— January 2004: 1640 khz; 10 kw-D, 1 kw-N. TL: N36 25 14 W97 52 28. Hrs open: 24 Box 952, 73702. Secondary address: 316 E. Willow 73701. Phone: (580) 237-1390. Fax: (580) 242-1390.E-mail: hchamplin@knid.com Licensee: Chisholm Trail Broadcasting Co. Format: Sports. ◆Hiram Champlin, gen mgr; Ricky Roggow, opns mgr; Sandy Daniels, gen sls mgr; Suzi Lakin, prom mgr; Chad McKee, progmg dir.

KGWA(AM)— 1950: 960 khz; 1 kw-U, DA-1. TL: N36 26 13 W97 55 16. Hrs open: 24 Box 3128, 73702. Secondary address: 1710 W. Willow Rd., Suite 300 73703. Phone: (580) 234-4230. Fax: (580) 234-2971.E-mail: radio@kofm.com Web Site:www.kgwanews.com Licensee: Williams Broadcasting LLC. (acq 9-10-99; with co-located FM). Population served: 102,000 Natl. Network: Fox News Radio, . Okla. News Net. Putbrese, Hunsaker & Trent. Format: News Talk. News staff: 4; News: 15 hours weekly. Target aud: P25-54. Spec prog: Farm 3 hrs wkly. ◆Daniel J. Smith, pres, gen mgr; Cheryl Myatt, gen sls mgr; J. Curtis Huckleberry, gen mgr & news dir.

*KKRD(FM)— Oct 1, 1986: 91.1 mhz; 300 w. Ant 297 ft TL: N36 23 48 W97 52 38. Stereo. Hrs open: 24 2351 Sunset Blvd., Suite 170-218, Rocklin, CA, 95765. Phone: (916) 251-1600. Fax: (916) 251-1650.E-mail: info@air1.com Web Site:www.air1.com Licensee: Educational Media Foundation. (acq 10-15-2004; $102,500). Population served: 200,000 Natl. Network: Air 1, . Format: Relg. ◆Richard Jenkins, pres; Mike Novak, VP; Keith Whipple, dev dir; David Pierce, progmg mgr; Ed Lenane, news dir; Sam Wallington, engrg dir; Arthur Vassar, traf mgr; Karen Johnson, news rptr.

KOFM(FM)— March 1982: 103.1 mhz; 25 kw. Ant 298 ft TL: N36 26 14 W97 55 15. Stereo. Hrs open: 24 Box 3128, 73702. Secondary address: 1710 W. Willow Rd., Suite 300 73703. Phone: (580) 234-6371. Fax: (580) 234-2971.E-mail: radio@kofm.com Web Site:www.kofm.com Licensee: Williams Broadcasting LLC. Population served: 102,000 Natl. Network: Fox News Radio, . Format: Country. News staff: 3; News: 1 hour weekly. Target aud: P25-54. ◆Kyle Williams, pres; Daniel J. Smith, gen mgr.

KQOB(FM)— May 1, 1967: 96.9 mhz; 97.5 kw horiz, 100 kw vert. Ant 1,450 ft TL: N35 58 50 W97 41 42. Stereo. Hrs open: Box 952, 73702. Secondary address: 316 E. Willow 73701. Phone: (580) 237-1390. Fax: (580) 242-1390. Licensee: Champlin Broadcasting Inc. Population served: 250,000 Rgnl. Network: Okla. Radio Net. Okla. News Net. Format: Var hits. Target aud: 18-54.

Eufaula

KTNT(FM)— June 15, 1967: 102.5 mhz; 25 kw. 150 ft TL: N35 22 25 W95 34 00. Hrs open: 24 Box 956, 74432. Phone: (918) 689-3663. Fax: (918) 689-5451.E-mail: mrogers@k955.com Web Site:www.kfoxradio.com Licensee: K95.5 Inc. (group owner; acq

9-24-98; $400,000). Population served: 100,000 Natl. Network: Fox News Radio, . Rgnl. Network: Okla. Radio Net. Okla. News Net. Format: Today's country. Spec prog: Gospel 3 hrs wkly. ◆William H. Payne, pres; Mike Rogers, gen mgr, stn mgr, gen sls mgr, progmg dir, mus dir; Lisa Cotten, progmg dir, traf mgr.

Fairview

*KHEV(FM)— 2009: 90.3 mhz; 490 w. Ant 607 ft TL: N36 13 25 W98 36 07. Hrs open: Box 991, Meade, KS, 67864. Phone: (620) 873-2991. Fax: (620) 873-2755.E-mail: khym@khym.org Web Site:www.khym.org Licensee: Great Plains Christian Radio Inc. ◆Don Hughes, gen mgr.

Frederick

*KSYE(FM)— July 1992: 91.5 mhz; 100 kw. 390 ft TL: N34 21 52 W98 50 04. Stereo. Hrs open: 24 Phone: (866) 355-5793. Phone: (580) 335-5500. Fax: (580) 335-5900.E-mail: info@ksye.org Web Site:www.ksye.org Licensee: Criswell College. (group owner) Population served: 360,000 Natl. Network: ABC, . Format: Inspirational. Target aud: General. ◆Dr. Royce Laycock, chmn; Dr. Jerry Johnson, pres; Mike Tyrone, gen mgr; Keith Mayo, stn mgr, progmg dir.

KTAT(AM)— 1948: 1570 khz; 250 w-D. TL: N34 23 30 W99 01 51. Hrs open: Box 837, 73542. Secondary address: 207 W. Grand Ave. 73542. Phone: (580) 335-3874. Fax: (580) 335-7659. Licensee: Morey Broadcasting LLC (acq 12-18-90; $60,000 with co-located FM; 1-7-91). Population served: 6,800 Rgnl. Network: Okla. Radio Net. Format: Easy listening. ◆Brent Morey, gen mgr & gen sls mgr.

KYBE(FM)— Aug 15, 1982: 95.9 mhz; 6 kw. Ant 249 ft TL: N34 23 30 W99 01 51. Stereo. Hrs open: Box 1088, 73542. Phone: (580) 335-5923. Fax: (580) 335-7659. Web Site:www.coyotenews.com Licensee: Fort Worth Media Group G.P. LLC. (acq 9-9-2005; $325,000). Format: Country.

Glenpool

KTSO(FM)— May 24, 1976: 94.1 mhz; 100 kw. Ant 691 ft TL: N36 07 52 W96 04 13. Hrs open: 24 5810 E. Skelly Dr., Suite 801, Tulsa, 74135. Phone: (918) 665-3131. Fax: (918) 663-6622.E-mail: production @shamrocktuosa.com Web Site:www.941THESOUND.com Licensee: Shamrock Communications Inc. (group owner; acq 1996; $1.8 million). Natl. Rep: McGavren Guild,. Format: Classic hits. News staff: one; News: 35 hrs wkly. Target aud: 35-54. ◆Chuck Browning, gen mgr; William Lynett, CEO & opns mgr; Tom Holiday, sls dir; Paul Kaiegler, progmg dir.

Goltry

*KWGT(FM)—Not on air, target date: unknown: 90.5 mhz; 35 kw. Ant 397 ft TL: N36 40 47 W98 10 43. Hrs open: Box 697, Waukomis, 73773. Phone: (580) 758-3045. Licensee: Waukomis Baptist Church Inc. ◆Danny Marney, pres.

Goodwell

*KPSU(FM)— September 1977: 91.7 mhz; 380 w. 121 ft TL: N36 35 41 W101 38 10. Stereo. Hrs open: 10 AM to midnight Box 430, 73939. Phone: (580) 349-2611.E-mail: opsu@opsu.edu Web Site:www.opsu.edu Licensee: Oklahoma Panhandle State University. Population served: 3,000 Format: Div. Target aud: College age. ◆Dr. David Bryant, pres; Russell Guthrie, gen mgr.

Grandfield

*KWKL(FM)— Sept 19, 2003: 89.9 mhz; 11 kw vert. Ant 499 ft TL: N34 16 19 W98 25 30. Stereo. Hrs open: 24 2351 Sunset Blvd., Suite 170-218, Rocklin, CA, 95765. Phone: (916) 251-1600. Fax: (916) 251-1650.E-mail: klove@klove.com Web Site:www.klove.com Licensee: Educational Media Foundation. Group owner: EMF Broadcasting. Population served: 264,000 Natl. Network: K-Love, . Shaw Pittman. Format: Contemp Christian. News staff: 3. Target aud: 25-44; Judeo Christian, female. ◆Richard Jenkins, pres; Mike Novak, VP; Keith Whipple, dev dir; David Pierce, progmg mgr; Ed Lenane, news dir; Sam Wallington, engrg dir; Karen Johnson, news rptr.

Granite

*KHEB(FM)—Not on air, target date: unknown: 91.9 mhz; 3.2 kw. Ant 449 ft TL: N34 53 39 W99 36 39. Hrs open: Box 1343, Ada, 74821. Phone: (580) 332-0902.E-mail: email@thegospelstation.com Web Site:www.thegospelstation.com Licensee: South Central Oklahoma Christian Broadcasting Inc. ◆Randall Christy, pres; Rick Cody, gen mgr.

KZBS(FM)— 2008: 104.3 mhz; 1.7 kw. Ant 909 ft TL: N34 58 39 W99 24 35. Hrs open: Box 1343, Ada, 74820. Phone: (580) 332-0902. Fax: (580) 332-0922.E-mail: email@thegospelstation.com Web Site:www.thegospelstation.com Licensee: Bcvision. Format: Southern gospel. ◆ Randall Christy, pres; Rick Cody, gen mgr.

Grove

KGVE(FM)— Dec 12, 1980: 99.3 mhz; 15 kw. 312 ft TL: N36 36 49 W94 45 53. Stereo. Hrs open: 24 Box 451749, 74345. Phone: (918) 786-2211. Fax: (918) 786-2284.E-mail: info@kgvefm.com Licensee: Caleb Group. (acq 4-1-92; 3-16-92). Population served: 350,000 Natl. Network: ABC, . Rgnl. Network: Okla. Radio Net. Okla. News Net. Format: Country. News staff: one. Target aud: General. ◆Janell Hestand, VP, opns dir, progmg dir; Larry Hestand, pres, dev dir & prom dir.

*KWXC(FM)— 2008: 88.9 mhz; 6 kw vert. Ant 240 ft TL: N36 35 42 W94 38 05. Hrs open: 69601 E. 290 Rd., 74344. Phone: (918) 854-3523. Licensee: Grove Broadcasting Inc. Format: Talk radio. Target aud: 30-45. ◆Darral Martin, pres; Travis Martin, progmg mgr; Margaret Van Dyke, mktg.

Guthrie

KMFS(AM)— Nov 16, 1955: 1490 khz; 1 kw-U. TL: N35 52 56 W97 23 34. Hrs open: 24 Box 262550, Baton Rouge, LA, 70826. Secondary address: 8919 World Ministry Ave., Baton Rouge, LA 70810. Phone: (225) 768-3688/8300. Fax: (225) 768-3729.E-mail: kawikfish@yahoo.com Web Site:www.jsm.org Licensee: Family Worship Center Church Inc. (group owner) (acq 9-27-2002; $150,000). Population served: 18,000 Natl. Network: ABC, AP Radio, . Format: Relg teaching. ◆David Whitelaw, COO; Jimmy Swaggart, pres; John Santiago, gen mgr & progmg dir.

Guymon

KBIJ(FM)— 2008: 99.5 mhz; 100 kw. Ant 417 ft TL: N36 45 52 W101 12 32. Hrs open: Box 7441, Amarillo, TX, 79114. Phone: (806) 353-1488. Fax: (806) 353-1542.E-mail: info@krbgfm.com Web Site:www.gracechurchamarillo.com Licensee: Grace Community Church of Amarillo (acq 8-16-2006; $95,000 for CP). Format: Relg. ◆ William Gehm, pres & gen mgr.

KGYN(AM)— Dec 12, 1948: 1210 khz; 10 kw-U, DA-N. TL: N36 40 34 W101 22 58. Hrs open: 24 Box 130, 73942. Phone: (580) 338-1210. Phone: (800) 227-1210. Fax: (580) 338-8255.E-mail: kgyn@ptsi.net Web Site:www.kgynam1210.com Licensee: Telns Broadcasting Co. Inc. (acq 9-5-86; $400,000; 8-4-86). Population served: 450,000 Natl. Network: Jones Radio Networks, ABC, . Format: Country. News staff: one; News: 12 hrs wkly. Target aud: 25-65; broad based listenership. Spec prog: Relg 8 hrs, Sp 8 hrs wkly. ◆Ed Smith, pres; Richard Ryther, opns mgr.

*KJLG(FM)—Not on air, target date: unknown: 88.9 mhz; 25 kw. Ant 321 ft TL: N36 40 27 W101 28 09. Hrs open: Box 991, Meade, KS, 67864. Phone: (620) 873-2991 . Fax: (620) 873-2755.E-mail: kjil@kjil.com Web Site:www.kjil.com Licensee: Great Plains Christian Radio Inc. ◆Robert D. Hughes, CEO.

KKBS(FM)— Dec 25, 1983: 92.7 mhz; 11.5 kw. 485 ft TL: N36 42 43 W101 27 27. Stereo. Hrs open: 24 Phone: (580) 338-5493. Fax: (580) 338-0717.E-mail: kkbs@kkbs.com Web Site:www.kkbs.com Licensee: MLS Communications Inc. (acq 8-7-90; 8-27-90). Population served: 100,000 Natl. Network: Adult rock. News staff: 2; News: 17 hrs wkly. Target aud: 24-54+; working people, 2 income families, farmers. Spec prog: Financial markets 5 hrs wkly. ◆Marsha Strong, pres, gen mgr; Ramey Cozart, opns mgr.

Hammon

*KTHF(FM)—Not on air, target date: unknown: 89.9 mhz; 100 kw. Ant 577 ft TL: N35 47 46 W99 18 12. Hrs open: Box 14, Ponca City, 74602-0014. Phone: (580) 767-1400. Fax: (580) 765-1700.E-mail:

mail@thehousefm.com Web Site:www.thehousefm.com Licensee: The Love Station Inc. ◆Doyle Brewer, gen mgr; Tony Weir, progmg dir.

Healdton

*KAZC(FM)—Not on air, target date: unknown: 89.3 mhz; 3 kw. Ant 331 ft TL: N34 10 31 W97 24 20. Hrs open: Box 779, 73438. Phone: (580) 465-2352. Licensee: First Free Will Baptist Church of Healdton. ◆David Lomineck, gen mgr.

KICM(FM)— October 1978: 97.7 mhz; 25 kw. Ant 328 ft TL: N34 21 00 W97 27 35. Stereo. Hrs open: Box 1487, Ardmore, 73402. Phone: (580) 226-9797. Fax: (580) 226-5113.E-mail: mike@kicm.com Web Site:www.kicm.com Licensee: Keystone Broadcasting Corp. (acq 6-17-2005; $1.2 million). Population served: 80,000 Format: Country. Target aud: 21-49. Spec prog: Relg 6 hrs wkly. ◆Bill Countrymen, gen mgr.

Heavener

KPRV-FM— Oct 1, 1989: 92.5 mhz; 1.55 kw. 640 ft TL: N34 53 54 W94 34 30. Stereo. Hrs open: 24 Phone: (918) 647-3221. Fax: (918) 647-5092.E-mail: lbilly@clnk.com Web Site:www.kprvradio.com Licensee: LeRoy Billy. Natl. Network: ABC, . Rgnl. Network: Okla. Radio Net. Okla. News Net. Format: Country. News: 24 hrs wkly. Target aud: 24-54. ◆David Billy, progmg dir; LeRoy Billy, VP, gen mgr, gen sls mgr & mus dir; Allen Riley, chief of engrg.

Henryetta

*KVAZ(FM)— Dec 26, 1985: 91.5 mhz; 250 w. Ant 178 ft TL: N35 21 56 W96 00 34. Hrs open: 24 The Gospel Station Network, Box 1343, Ada, 74821. Phone: (580) 332-0902.E-mail: email@thegospelstation.com Web Site:www.thegospelstation.com Licensee: South Central Oklahoma Broadcasting Inc. (acq 7-1-2005; $25,000). Format: Southern gospel. ◆Randall Christy, pres; Rick Cody, gen mgr.

KXBL(FM)— Dec 20, 1966: 99.5 mhz; 100 kw. 984 ft TL: N35 50 02 W96 07 28. Stereo. Hrs open: 24 4590 E. 29th St., Tulsa, 74114. Phone: (918) 743-7814. Fax: (918) 743-7613.E-mail: info@bigcountry995.com Web Site:bigcountry995.com Licensee: Journal Broadcast Corp. Group owner: Journal Communications Inc. (acq 6-11-99; grpsl). Koteen & Naftalin. Format: Young country. Target aud: 18-34. ◆Carl Gardner, pres; Ron Kurtis, CFO; Randy Bush, VP; Randy Bush, gen mgr; Ric Hampton, opns mgr, mus dir, chief of engrg; Brian Gann, news dir; Ray Klotz, engrg dir.

Hobart

KQTZ(FM)— May 28, 1979: 105.9 mhz; 100 kw. Ant 1,020 ft TL: N34 52 15 W99 17 36. Stereo. Hrs open: 24 Box 577, Altus, 73522. Secondary address: 212 W. Cypress, Altus 73521. Phone: (580) 482-1450. Fax: (580) 482-3420.E-mail: mward@kwhw.com Web Site:www.kwhw.com Licensee: Monarch Broadcasting Inc. (group owner; (acq 12-31-2003; grpsl). Format: Adult contemp. Target aud: General; contemp adults during the day, rockers at night. ◆Matthew L. Ward, pres, gen mgr; Michael Barnes, opns dir.

KTJS(AM)— June 21, 1947: 1420 khz; 1 kw-D, 360 w-N. TL: N35 02 57 W99 05 48. Hrs open: 24 Box 311, 1515 N. Broadway, 73651. Phone: (580) 726-5656. Fax: (580) 726-2222.E-mail: thezone@itlnet.net Licensee: Fuchs Radio LLC. (acq 11-24-98; $182,000). Population served: 50,000 Format: Country, news/talk. News: 19 hrs wkly. Target aud: 30 plus; agri-related businessmen. Spec prog: Relg 12 hrs wkly. ◆Chad Fox, pres, gen mgr, progmg dir & mus dir.

Holdenville

KTLS-FM— Nov 30, 1991: 106.5 mhz; 25 kw. 328 ft TL: N34 54 50 W96 31 20. Hrs open: 24 1188 North Hills Centre, Ada, 74820. Phone: (580) 332-2211. Fax: (580) 436-1629.E-mail: ktls@ktlsradio.com Web Site:www.ktlsradio.com Licensee: The Chickasaw Nation. (acq 10-1-2008; $1.5 million with KXFC(FM) Coalgate). Population served: 170,000 Natl. Network: Jones Radio Networks, . Davis Wright Tremaine LLP. Format: Classic Rock. News staff: one. Target aud: 25-54. ◆Rick Woodward, gen mgr & opns dir; Craig Stone, progmg dir; Renae Woodward, traf mgr.

KWSH(AM)—See Wewoka

Hollis

KKRE(FM)— 2005: 92.5 mhz; 6 kw. Ant 328 ft TL: N34 36 34 W99 50 57. Hrs open: Box 1077, Altus, 73522. Secondary address: 808 N. Main St., Altus 73521. Phone: (580) 482-1555. Fax: (580) 482-8353.E-mail: keyb@keyb.net Web Site:www.keyb.net Licensee: Altus FM Inc. Format: New country. ◆Scott Wilmes, VP; Gayle Ledbetter, gen mgr.

Hugo

KIHN(AM)— October 1948: 1340 khz; 1 kw-U. TL: N34 00 15 W95 29 20. Hrs open: 16 Phone: (580) 326-6411. Fax: (580) 326-7921.E-mail: kihn@1starnet.com Licensee: Little Dixie Broadcasting Co. Population served: 25,000 Format: Var, news. News staff: one; News: 20 hrs wkly. Target aud: General. Spec prog: Gospel music 5 hrs, children one hr, farm one hr wkly. ◆Leeta M. Henson, pres & gen mgr.

KITX(FM)— June 1983: 95.5 mhz; 50 kw. Ant 492 ft TL: N33 54 56 W95 28 04. Stereo. Hrs open: 1600 W. Jackson St., 74743. Phone: (580) 326-2555. Fax: (580) 326-2623.E-mail: k955@neto.com Web Site:www.k955.com Licensee: K95.5 Inc. (acq 10-95; $400,000). Format: Country. Target aud: General. ◆Will Payne, gen mgr.

Idabel

KBEL-FM— Oct 1, 1973: 96.7 mhz; 25 kw. Ant 300 ft TL: N33 52 54 W94 49 10. Stereo. Hrs open: 24 Box 418, 74745. Secondary address: 813 Lincoln Rd. 74745. Phone: (580) 286-6642. Phone: (877) 329-8280. Fax: (580) 286-6643.E-mail: kbel967@yahoo.com Licensee: Box Broadcasting Corp. (acq 9-1-99; with co-located AM). Population served: 75,000 Natl. Network: Salem Radio Network, . Rgnl. Network: Quinstar. Agrinet Format: Country. News staff: one; News: 6 hrs wkly. Target aud: 18 plus; country audience. ◆Paul W. Box, CEO, pres & gen mgr.

KKBI(FM)—See Broken Bow

KQIB(FM)— Aug 1, 1999: 102.9 mhz; 6 kw. 318 ft TL: N33 59 57 W94 47 29. Stereo. Hrs open: 24 Phone: (580) 584-3388. Fax: (580) 584-3341.E-mail: kkbi@pine.net.com Web Site:www.kkbifm.com Licensee: JDC Radio Inc. (acq 9-2-98). Population served: 34,000 Natl. Network: ABC, . Putbrese, Hunsaker & Trent. Format: Hot adult contemp. News staff: one; News: 5 hrs wkly. Target aud: 25-44. ◆David Smulyan, gen mgr; Shellye Copeland, natl sls mgr & progmg dir.

*KXRT(FM)— 2003: 90.9 mhz; 500 w. Ant 210 ft TL: N33 53 33 W94 49 26. Hrs open: Drawer 2440, Tupelo, MS, 38801. Phone: (662) 844-8888. Fax: (662) 842-6791. Licensee: American Family Association. Group owner: American Family Radio (acq 1-31-2001). Format: Christian. ◆Marvin Sanders, gen mgr.

Ketchum

*KOSN(FM)— May 26, 1989: 107.5 mhz; 100 kw. Ant 981 ft TL: N36 46 13 W95 27 07. Stereo. Hrs open: 24
Simulcast with KOSU-FM Stillwater 100%.
Oklahoma State University, 302 PM Bldg., Stillwater, 74078. Phone: (405) 744-6352. Fax: (405) 744-9970.E-mail: info@kosu.org Web Site:www.kosu.org Licensee: PRC Tulsa I-LLC (acq 1-13-2005; $4 million). Population served: 1,000,000 Natl. Network: NPR, . Rgnl. Network: Okla. Radio Net. Format: Class, educ, news. News staff: 2; News: 18 hrs wkly. Target aud: General. Spec prog: American Indian one hr wkly. ◆Craig Beeby, gen mgr, progmg dir; Don Crider, dev dir; Rachel Hubbard, news dir; Dan Schroeder, chief of engrg.

Kingfisher

KINB(FM)— 2000: 105.3 mhz; 800 w. Ant 840 ft TL: N35 43 38 W97 52 30. Hrs open: 4045 N.W. 64th St., Suite 600, Oklahoma City, 73116. Phone: (405) 848-0100. Fax: (405) 843-5288.E-mail: info@laindomable.com Web Site:www.laindomable.com Licensee: The Last Bastion Station Trust LLC, as Trustee Group owner: Citadel Broadcasting Corp. (acq 6-12-2007; grpsl). Format: Sp. Target aud: 35-49 & 25-34; Yooung professionals. ◆Joe Jelddy, stn mgr; Luis Medina, opns mgr.

Lahoma

KXLS(FM)— Nov 1, 1995: 95.7 mhz; 9.6 kw. Ant 502 ft TL: N36 25 14 W98 01 12. Hrs open: Box 952, Enid, 73702. Secondary address: 316 E. Willow Rd., Enid 73701. Phone: (580) 237-1390. Fax: (580) 242-1390.E-mail: hchamplin@knid.com Licensee: Chisholm Trail Broadcasting Co. (acq 11-1-99; $525,000). Natl. Network: ABC, .

Format: Adult contemp. News staff: one; News: 2 hrs wkly. Target aud: 30-60; female. ♦Hiram Champlin, gen mgr; Sandy Daniels, gen sls mgr; Suzi Lakin, prom dir; Rob Houston, news dir; G.B. Bonham, chief of engrg.

Langston

***KALU(FM)**— Mar 3, 1975: 89.3 mhz; 150 w. Ant 200 ft TL: N35 56 36 W97 15 32. Hrs open: 24 c/o Gen. Mgr., Sanford Hall, Langston Univ., 73050. Phone: (405) 466-3428. Phone: (405) 466-3342. Fax: (405) 466-2921.E-mail: bishop@yahoo.com Web Site:www.lunet.edu Licensee: Langston University. Format: Jazz, relg, urban contemp. ♦Bishop Kendrick, gen mgr.

Lawton

KBZQ(FM)— May 1, 1992: 99.5 mhz; 16 kw. 338 ft TL: N34 35 31 W98 32 55. Stereo. Hrs open: 24 Box 6888, 73506-0888. Secondary address: 1006 N.W. 47th St., Suite B 73505. Phone: (580) 357-9950. Fax: (580) 357-9995.E-mail: kbzq@sbcglobal.net Web Site:www.hitsandfavorites.com Licensee: William R. Fritsch Jr. Population served: 113,000 Natl. Network: ABC, . Arter & Hadden. Format: Adult contemp. News staff: 3; News: one hr wkly. Target aud: 25-54; baby boomers, upscale white collar workers. Spec prog: Jazz 4 hrs, Hits of the 80s5 hrs, Sp 4 hrs wkly. ♦Chuck Pettigrew, opns dir, opns mgr, progmg dir; Rick Fritsch, gen mgr & sls dir; Lino Roldan, spanish dir.

***KCCU(FM)**— July 13, 1989: 89.3 mhz; 2 kw. Ant 463 ft TL: N34 37 26 W98 16 15. Stereo. Hrs open: 24 2800 W. Gore Blvd., 73505. Phone: (580) 581-2425. Fax: (580) 581-5571.E-mail: markn@cameron.edu Web Site:www.kccu.org Licensee: Cameron University. Population served: 100,000 Natl. Network: NPR, PRI, . Format: News, classical. News staff: 5; News: 40 hrs wkly. Target aud: General. Spec prog: Jazz. ♦Ted Riley, gen mgr.

KJMZ(FM)—(Cache, Oct 23, 1970: 97.9 mhz; 6 kw. Ant 292 ft TL: N34 35 31 W98 32 55. Stereo. Hrs open: 24 1525 S.E. Flowermound Rd., 73501. Phone: (580) 355-1050. Fax: (580) 355-1056.E-mail: spots@kjmz.com Web Site:www.kjmz.com Licensee: Perry Broadcasting of Lawton Inc. Population served: 800,000 Eugene T. Smith. Format: Rhythmic oldies. ♦Tony Foster, progmg dir.

***KJRF(FM)**— Jan 1, 2001: 91.1 mhz; 10 kw. Ant 413 ft TL: N34 41 22 W98 07 34. Hrs open: 24 The Christian Center Inc., 2405 S.W. Lee Blvd., 73505. Phone: (580) 357-4498. Fax: (580) 357-1818.E-mail: kjrf911@yahoo.com Web Site:www.thechristian-center.org Licensee: The Christian Center Inc. Format: Christian. ♦Reverend Paul Craig, pres; Alan Hampton, chief of opns; Randy Muirhead, stn mgr & progmg dir; Allan Hampton, engrg dir.

KKRX(AM)— May 27, 1956: 1050 khz; 250 w-D, DA. TL: N34 35 27 W98 21 10. Hrs open: 24 1525 S.E. Flowermound Rd., 73501. Phone: (580) 355-1050. Fax: (580) 355-1056.E-mail: spots@kjmz.com Web Site:www.kjmz.com Licensee: Perry Broadcasting of Lawton Inc. Group owner: Perry Publishing & Broadcasting Co. (acq 1-31-97; $486,000 with co-located FM). Natl. Rep: D & R Radio,. Format: Rhythmic Oldies. Spec prog: Ger one hr wkly. ♦Joy Chapman, gen mgr, opns mgr, gen sls mgr; Mark Edwards, news dir; Dale Weakley, chief of engrg.

KLAW(FM)— Jan 1, 1965: 101.3 mhz; 100 kw. Ant 584 ft TL: N34 32 59 W98 32 21. Stereo. Hrs open: 24 626 S.W. D. Ave., 73501. Phone: (580) 581-3600. Fax: (580) 357-2880.E-mail: klaw@gapbroadcasting.com Web Site:www.klaw.com Licensee: GAP Broadcasting Lawton License LLC. Group owner: Clear Channel Communications Inc. (acq 8-3-2007; grpsl). Population served: 117,000 Natl. Rep: Katz Radio,. Wiley, Rein & Fielding. Format: Country. News staff: one; News: 4 hrs wkly. Target aud: 25-54; adults. ♦Kim Dodds, gen mgr; David Crawford, opns mgr, progmg dir; JoAnne Taylor, gen sls mgr.

KMGZ(FM)— Nov 1, 1982: 95.3 mhz; 14 kw. 312 ft TL: N34 34 36 W98 28 30. Stereo. Hrs open: 24 1421 Great Plains Blvd., Suite C, 73505-2843. Phone: (580) 536-9530. Fax: (580) 536-3299.E-mail: gm@kmgz.com Web Site:www.kmgz.com Licensee: Broadco of Texas Inc. (acq 3-9-92; trade and joint venture agreement for KMGZ(FM); 4-6-92). Format: Adult contemp. News: one hr wkly. Target aud: 18-49. ♦Chuck Morgan, pres, gen mgr & gen sls mgr; Albert Young, progmg mgr.

***KVRS(FM)**— December 1989: 90.3 mhz; 1 kw vert. Ant 187 ft TL: N34 37 32 W98 31 43. Stereo. Hrs open: 24 1411 Parish Rd., Lake Charles, LA, 70611. Phone: (580) 536-8886. Fax: (580) 536-8891.E-mail: kvvs@kvvsfm.com Licensee: American Family Association. Group owner: American Family Radio (acq 4-29-2004; $10). Population served: 250,000 Natl. Network: American Family Radio, . Format: Christian, relg. News: 14 hrs wkly. Target aud: General. ♦Dan Meir, stn mgr & engrg VP.

KVRW(FM)— Mar 13, 1992: 107.3 mhz; 50 kw. Ant 492 ft TL: N34 36 27 W98 16 26. Stereo. Hrs open: 24 626 S.W. D Avenue, 73501. Phone: (580) 581-3600. Fax: (580) 357-2880.E-mail: my1073fm@gapbroadcasting.com Web Site:www.my1073.com Licensee: GAP Broadcasting Lawton License LLC. (acq 10-1-2007; grpsl). Population served: 89,900 Natl. Rep: Katz Radio,. Format: Adult contemp. News: 2 hrs wkly. Target aud: 25-54. ♦Kim Dodds, CEO, gen mgr; Joanne Taylor, gen sls mgr; Nancy Mace, progmg dir.

KXCA(AM)— May 1, 1941: 1380 khz; 1 kw-U, DA-2. TL: N34 35 24 W98 21 44. Hrs open: 24 1525 SE Flower Mound, 73501. Phone: (580) 355-1050. Fax: (580) 355-1056.E-mail: spots@kjmz.com Web Site:www.1380theticket.com Licensee: Perry Broadcasting of Southwest Oklahoma Inc. Group owner: Perry Publishing & Broadcasting Co. (acq 11-22-2002; grpsl). Population served: 1,090,000 Natl. Rep: Roslin,. Format: Sports, talk. Target aud: 35 plus. ♦Joy Chapman, gen mgr & gen sls mgr; James Stanley, progmg dir.

KZCD(FM)— June 8, 1987: 94.1 mhz; 18 kw. 524 ft TL: N34 34 24 W98 28 40. Stereo. Hrs open: 24 626 S.W. D Ave., 73501. Phone: (580) 581-3600. Fax: (580) 357-2880.E-mail: z94@gapbroadcasting.com Web Site:www.z94.com Licensee: GAP Broadcasting Lawton License LLC. Group owner: Clear Channel Communications Inc. (acq 8-3-2007; grpsl). Population served: 117,000 Natl. Rep: Katz Radio,. Wiley, Rein & Fielding. Format: Rock. News staff: one; News: 2 hrs wkly. Target aud: 18-49; males. ♦Kim Dodds, gen mgr; JoAnne Taylor, gen sls mgr; Don "Critter" Brown, progmg dir; Michelle Anders, engrg dir.

Lindsay

KBLP(FM)— Oct 1, 1988: 105.1 mhz; 850 w. 564 ft TL: N34 54 01 W97 33 56. Stereo. Hrs open: 24 204 S. Main, 73052. Phone: (405) 756-4438. Fax: (405) 756-2040.E-mail: jason@kblpradio.net Web Site:www.kblpradio.net Licensee: South Central Oklahoma Broadcasting & Advertising Corp. Rgnl. Network: Okla. Radio Net. Okla. News Net. Format: Country. News staff: 2; News: 10.5 hrs wkly. Target aud: 21-65; working consumers. ♦Charlie Jones, pres & gen mgr.

Locust Grove

KEMX(FM)— Feb 14, 1991: 94.5 mhz; 2.3 kw. 367 ft TL: N36 15 05 W95 13 21. Stereo. Hrs open: 24
Rebroadcasts KXOJ-FM Sapulpa 100%.
2448 E. 81st St., Suite 4500, Tulsa, 74137. Phone: (918) 492-2660. Fax: (918) 492-8840.E-mail: kxoj@kxoj.com Web Site:www.kxoj.com Licensee: KXOJ Inc. Group owner: Adonai Radio Group (acq 4-29-92; grpsl). Format: Contemp Christian music. Target aud: 18-35; young married or single Christians. ♦Mike Stephens, pres; David Stephens, gen mgr, sls dir, adv dir; Bob Thornton, progmg dir.

Lone Grove

KYNZ(FM)— May 25, 1988: 107.1 mhz; 24.5 kw. Ant 335 ft TL: N34 17 52 W97 09 12. Stereo. Hrs open: 24 1205 Northglen, Ardmore, 73401. Phone: (580) 226-0421. Fax: (580) 226-0464.E-mail: webmaster@kynz.com Web Site:www.kynz.com Licensee: LKCM Radio Group L.P. Group owner: NextMedia Group L.L.C. (acq 2-26-2007;. grpsl). Population served: 320,000 Rgnl. Network: Agri-Net. Natl. Rep: Christal,. Format: Goodtime Oldies. News staff: one; News: 25 hrs wkly. Target aud: 18-54. ♦Michael Baer, pres, gen mgr; Gerry Schlegel, VP, stn mgr; Dave Hilton, opns dir; Terry Bell, progmg dir.

Madill

KMAD(AM)— May 20, 1962: 1550 khz; 250 w-D. TL: N34 06 24 W96 46 30. Hrs open: Sunrise-sunset Box 1487, 6/10 Mile N. on Hwy 199, Ardmore, 73446. Phone: (580) 795-2345. Fax: (580) 795-5623.E-mail: kmad1550@yahoo.com Web Site:www.kmad1550.com Licensee: Robert S. Sullins (acq 3-20-98). Natl. Network: Jones Radio Networks, . Rgnl. Network: Agri-Net. Okla. News Net. Format: Classic hit country. News: 12 hrs wkly. Target aud: General. Spec prog: Farm 2 hrs wkly. ♦jason Smith, gen mgr.

Mangum

***KHIM(FM)**— 1998: 97.7 mhz; 540 w. Ant 1,079 ft TL: N34 58 39 W99 24 35. Hrs open: PO Box 311, Hobart, 73651. Secondary address: 1515 N. Broadway, Hobart 73651. Phone: (580) 726-5656. Fax: (580) 726-2222.E-mail: thezone@itlnet.net Licensee: Fuchs Radio L.L.C. (acq 4-4-2006; $250,000 with KJCM(FM) Snyder). Format: Mainstream rock. ♦Chad Fox, gen mgr & progmg dir.

Marlow

***KFXH(FM)**—Not on air, target date: unknown: 88.7 mhz; 500 w vert. Ant 184 ft TL: N34 41 43.73 W97 57 14.86. Hrs open: 1101 N. 81 Hwy., 73055. Phone: (580) 658-9292. Fax: (580) 658-2561. Licensee: The Sister Sherry Lynn Foundation. ♦Sherry Austin, pres.

KFXI(FM)— August 1987: 92.1 mhz; 100 kw. Ant 600 ft TL: N34 42 35 W98 03 00. Stereo. Hrs open: 24 1101 Hwy. 81 N., 73055. Phone: (580) 658-9292.E-mail: kfxi@cableone.net Web Site:www.kfxi.com Licensee: DFWU Inc. (group owner). Population served: 400,000 Southmayd & Miller. Format: Country. Target aud: 25-55. Spec prog: Gospel 8 hrs wkly. ♦K.D. Austin, gen mgr; Amy Helton, opns mgr; Sherry Lynn, gen sls mgr; Jennifer James, progmg dir.

McAlester

***KBCW-FM**— 1999: 91.9 mhz; 700 w. Ant 446 ft TL: N34 59 13 W95 42 10. Stereo. Hrs open: 24
Rebroadcasts KCSC(FM) Edmond 100%.
Univ. of Central Oklahoma, 100 N. University Dr., Edmond, 73034-5209. Phone: (405) 974-3333. Phone: (877) 359-3334. Fax: (405) 974-3844.E-mail: kcscfm@ucok.edu Web Site:www.kcscfm.com Licensee: The University of Central Oklahoma. Population served: 40,000 Natl. Network: PRI, . Format: Class. News: One. Target aud: 35 plus; educ, affluent. ♦Bradford Ferguson, gen mgr; Barbara Hendrickson, opns dir, news dir; Preston Walker, chief of engrg.

KNED(AM)— Mar 14, 1950: 1150 khz; 1 kw-D, 500 w-N, DA-N. TL: N34 56 12 W95 43 59. Stereo. Hrs open: 24 Box 1068, 74502-1068. Secondary address: 1801 E. Electric Ave. 74501. Phone: (918) 423-1460. Fax: (918) 423-7119.E-mail: kmcokned@mcalesterradio.com Web Site:mcalesterradio.com Licensee: Southeastern Oklahoma Radio LLC. (group owner; (acq 1-18-2005; $222,223). Population served: 175,000 Natl. Network: ABC, . Wiley, Rein & Fielding. Wire Svc: AP Format: C&W Classic. News: 10 hrs wkly. Target aud: 45 plus. ♦Lee Anderson, gen mgr, stn mgr; Sheila Turnbow, gen sls mgr; Megan Waters, progmg dir; John Yates, news dir.

KTMC(AM)— Mar 3, 1946: 1400 khz; 1 kw-U. TL: N34 57 00 W95 45 00. Hrs open: 24 Box 1068, 74502. Secondary address: 1801 E. Electric Ave. 74502. Phone: (918) 426-1050. Fax: (918) 423-7119.E-mail: kmconed@mclesterradio.com Web Site:mcalesterradio.com Licensee: Southeastern Oklahoma Radio LLC. (acq 1-18-2005; $444,445 with co-located FM). Population served: 60,000 Natl. Network: ABC, . Wiley, Rein & Fielding. Format: Timeless Classics. News: 2 hrs wkly. Target aud: 50 plus; older, middle-aged, mature & retired adults. Spec prog: Gospel 5 hrs wkly. ♦Lee Anderson, gen mgr, stn mgr; Sheila Turnbow, gen sls mgr; John Yates, news dir.

KTMC-FM— June 24, 1987: 105.1 mhz; 1.6 kw. 454 ft TL: N34 59 13 W95 42 10. Stereo. Hrs open: 24 Prog sep from AM Box 1068, 74502. Secondary address: 1801 E. Electric Ave. 74502. Phone: (918) 426-1050. Fax: (918) 423-7119. Web Site:www.mcalesterradio.com Population served: 100,000 Format: Classic rock. Target aud: 34-50. ♦Lee Anderson, gen mgr.

Miami

KGLC(FM)— December 1975: 100.9 mhz; 3.6 kw. Ant 273 ft TL: N36 53 27 W94 47 01. Stereo. Hrs open: Box 451750, Grove, 74345. Phone: (918) 542-1818. Phone: (918) 542-7175. Fax: (918) 542-1819.E-mail: info@kglc.com Licensee: Northeast Oklahoma Broadcast Network Inc. (acq 4-3-2006; $800,000 with KVIS(AM) Miami). Population served: 150,000 Natl. Network: USA, . Format: Contemp classics. Target aud: 25-44.

KVIS(AM)— February 1948: 910 khz; 1 kw-U, DA-1. TL: N36 53 27 W94 47 00. Hrs open: 24 Box 1555, 8400 S. Hwy. 137, 74355. Phone: (918) 542-1818. Phone: (918) 542-7175. Fax: (918) 542-1819.E-mail: info@kvis.com Licensee: Northeast Oklahoma Broadcast Network Inc. (acq 4-3-2006; $800,000 with KGLC(FM) Miami). Rgnl. Network: USA. Latham & Watkins. Format: Southern Gospel. News staff: one; News: 9 hrs wkly. Target aud: Christian/family. ♦Larry Hestand, pres; Robert Suman, gen mgr, gen sls mgr, progmg dir; Shanda Daugherty, prom dir & prom mgr; Kimberley Barnes, news dir; Rusty Wynn, chief of engrg.

Midwest City

KEBC(AM)—Licensed to Midwest City. See Oklahoma City

KTLV(AM)— April 1973: 1220 khz; 250 w-D, DA. TL: N35 23 50 W97 27 04. Hrs open: 6 am-7 pm 3336 S.E. 67th St., Oklahoma City, 73135. Phone: (405) 672-1220. Phone: (405) 672-3886. Fax: (405) 672-5858.E-mail: ktlv1220@aol.com Web Site:www.ktlv1220.com Licensee: First Choice Broadcasting Inc. (acq 6-19-92). Population served: 650,000 Format: Gospel, Christian. Target aud: 24 plus. ♦Howard D. Williams, pres; Dale Williams, gen mgr, progmg dir.

Moore

***KMSI(FM)**— Mar 26, 1991: 88.1 mhz; 50 kw vert. 597 ft TL: N35 12 07 W97 35 18. Stereo. Hrs open: 24 Box 1924, Tulsa, 74101. Secondary address: 120 S.W. 4th St. 73160. Phone: (405) 794-5674; (918) 455-5693. Fax: (405) 794-5112.E-mail: mail@oasisnetwork.org Web Site:www.oasisnetwork.org Licensee: Creative Educational Media Corp. Inc. Format: Relg. Target aud: General. ♦David Ingles, pres; Cherri Willis, gen mgr; David Warren, progmg dir; Hal Smith, chief of engrg.

WWLS(AM)— Sept 26, 1922: 640 khz; 1 kw-U, DA-N. TL: N35 17 21 W97 30 08. Hrs open: 4045 N.W. 64th St., Suite 600, Oklahoma, 73116. Phone: (405) 848-0100. Fax: (405) 848-5288.E-mail: info@wwls.com Web Site:www.thesportsanimal.com Licensee: Citadel Broadcasting Co. Group owner: Citadel Broadcasting Corp. (acq 10-28-99; grpsl). Population served: 1,000,000 Format: Sports/Talk. ♦Larry Bastida, gen mgr; Chris Baker, opns mgr; Dax Davis, progmg dir.

Muskogee

KBIX(AM)— May 1, 1936: 1490 khz; 450 w-U. TL: N35 46 56 W95 22 37. Hrs open: 24 215 N. State St., Ste 910, 74402. Phone: (918) 682-9700. Fax: (918) 682-6775.E-mail: info@kbixam.com Web Site:www.sportsanimaltulsa.com Licensee: KMMY Inc. Group owner: Adonai Radio Group (acq 12-11-2002; $1 million with KCXR(FM) Taft). Population served: 150,000 Format: Sports. ♦David Stephens, gen mgr.

KCXR(FM)—See Taft

KHTT(FM)— February 1972: 106.9 mhz; 100 kw. 1,005 ft TL: N35 51 41 W95 46 03. Stereo. Hrs open: 24 7030 S. Yale Ave., Suite 711, Tulsa, 74136. Phone: (918) 492-2020. Fax: (918) 496-2681.E-mail: info@khttfm.com Web Site:www.khits.com Licensee: Renda Broadcasting Corp. Group owner: Renda Broadcasting Corp.-Renda Radio Inc. (acq 4-15-93; $1.6 million; 5-3-93). Population served: 42,500 Format: Hot contemp hits. Target aud: 18-34; young adults. ♦Tony Renda, pres; Tod Tucker, opns mgr, progmg dir; Jon Phillips, gen sls mgr; Bill Sexauer, prom dir.

KYAL-FM— Jan 19, 1984: 97.1 mhz; 100 kw. Ant 1,274 ft TL: N35 17 05 W95 25 26. Stereo. Hrs open: 24 2448 E. 81 St, Suite 5500, Tulsa, 74137. Phone: (918) 492-2660. Fax: (918) 492-8840.E-mail: kxoj@kxoj.com Web Site:www.thesportsanimal.com Licensee: KMMY Inc. (acq 9-15-93; $500,000;10-11-93). Format: Sports. Target aud: 21-49; middle, upper-middle class. Spec prog: Farm 5 hrs wkly. ♦David Stephens, gen mgr.

Mustang

KZLS(FM)— Feb 1, 1981: 99.7 mhz; 39 kw. Ant 505 ft TL: N35 23 27 W97 45 24. Stereo. Hrs open: 24 Box 952, Enid, 73702. Secondary address: 316 E. Willow Rd., Enid 73701. Phone: (580) 237-1390. Fax: (580) 242-1390. Licensee: Chisholm Trail Holding Co. Inc. Population served: 132,000 Natl. Network: ABC, . Rgnl. Network: Mid-American Ag. Mid-America Ag Format: Country. News staff: one; News: 2 hrs wkly. Target aud: 25-49. ♦Hiram Champlin, pres; Sandy Daniels, gen mgr, gen sls mgr; Ricky Roggow, opns mgr, progmg dir; Suzi Lakin, prom dir; G.B. Bonham, chief of engrg.

Newcastle

KKNG-FM— Apr 15, 1971: 93.3 mhz; 100 kw. 797 ft TL: N35 11 28 W97 35 49. Stereo. Hrs open: 5101 S. Shields Blvd., Oklahoma City, 73129. Phone: (405) 616-5500. Fax: (405) 616-5505.E-mail: info@kkng.com Web Site:www.kkng.com Licensee: Tyler Broadcasting Corp. Group owner: Tyler Media Broadcasting Corp. (acq 10-95; $441,000). Population served: 19,300 Natl. Network: AP Radio, . Natl. Rep: D & R Radio,. Format: Country. Target aud: 25-54. Spec prog: Sunday Morning Gospel 7a-11a. ♦Skip Stow, CEO, pres & gen mgr; Kevin Young, opns dir, progmg dir; Harold Patterson, sls dir, news dir; Randy Mullinax, chief of engrg.

Norman

***KGOU(FM)**— Sept 25, 1970: 106.3 mhz; 6 kw. 300 ft TL: N35 17 22 W97 21 30. Stereo. Hrs open: 24 Copeland Hall, Rm. 300, University of Oklahoma, 73019. Phone: (405) 325-3388. Fax: (405) 325-7129.E-mail: manager@kgou.org Web Site:www.kgou.org Licensee: University of Oklahoma. Population served: 800,000 Natl. Network: NPR, . Dow, Lohnes & Albertson. Format: News/talk, jazz. News staff: one; News: 82 hrs wkly. Target aud: 25-54; general. Spec prog: Blues 8 hrs. ♦Karen Holp, gen mgr; Jolly Brown, dev dir; Jim Johnson, progmg dir; Brian Hardzinski, news dir; Patrick Roberts, chief of engrg.

KREF(AM)— November 1949: 1400 khz; 1 kw-U. TL: N35 13 04 W97 24 37. Hrs open: 24 2020 E. Alameda, 73071. Phone: (405) 321-1400. Fax: (405) 321-6820.E-mail: production@kref.com Web Site:www.kref.com Licensee: Fox Broadcasting, Co. (acq 1-9-98; $300,000). Population served: 700,000 Rgnl. Network: Okla. Radio Net. Okla. News Net. Garvey, Schubert & Barer. Format: Sports. News staff: one. Target aud: 25-54; middle, upper class adults. ♦John Fox, pres; Mike Holt, gen mgr, chief of opns; T.J. Perry, progmg dir.

***KSSO(FM)**— 2007: 89.3 mhz; 2.3 kw. Ant 163 ft TL: N35 13 22 W97 26 21. Hrs open: Box 262550, Baton Rouge, LA, 70826. Secondary address: 8919 World Ministry Ave. , Baton Rouge, LA 70810. Phone: (225) 768-3688. Phone: (225) 768-8300. Fax: (225) 768-3729.E-mail: kawikfish@yahoo.com Web Site:www.jsm.org Licensee: Family Worship Center Church Inc. (acq 10-7-2005; $500,000 for CP with KQUJ(FM) Ada). ♦David Whitelaw, COO; Jimmy Swaggart, pres; John Santiago, progmg dir.

North Enid

KNID(FM)— 2008: 107.1 mhz; 14 kw. Ant 449 ft TL: N36 32 13 W98 00 39. Hrs open: 24 316 E. Willow, Enid, 73701. Phone: (580) 237-1390. Fax: (580) 242-1390. Web Site:www.todaysbestcountryonline.com Licensee: Champlin Broadcasting Inc. Format: Today's best country. Target aud: 18-54; men and women. ♦Hiram H. Champlin, pres.

Nowata

KRIG-FM—Licensed to Nowata. See Bartlesville

Okarche

KTUZ-FM— September 1968: 106.7 mhz; 13 kw. Ant 958 ft TL: N35 36 49 W97 52 19. Stereo. Hrs open: 24 5101 S. Shields Blvd., Oklahoma City, 73129. Phone: (405) 616-9900. Fax: (405) 616-0328.E-mail: jake.f@tylermedia.com Web Site:www.ktuz.com Licensee: Tyler Broadcasting Corp. Group owner: Tyler Media Broadcasting Corp. (acq 1-27-98; $100,000 with co-located AM). Population served: 145,000 Natl. Rep: Univision Radio National Sales,. Format: Sp. News: 16 hrs wkly. Target aud: 18-65. ♦Ty Tyler, gen mgr.

Oklahoma City

KATT-FM— Oct 17, 1960: 100.5 mhz; 28.87 kw. Ant 1,542 ft TL: N35 33 37 W97 29 07. Stereo. Hrs open: 4045 N.W. 64th, Suite 600, 73116. Phone: (405) 848-0100. Fax: (405) 843-5288.E-mail: infor@katt.com Web Site:www.katt.com Licensee: Citadel Broadcasting Co. Group owner: Citadel Broadcasting Corp. (acq 10-28-99; grpsl). Population served: 632,300 Format: AOR. Target aud: 18-34; Men. ♦Larry Bastida, gen mgr; Tricia York, gen sls mgr; Chris Baker, progmg dir.

KEBC(AM)—(Midwest City, 1922: 1340 khz; 1 kw-U. TL: N35 29 58 W97 30 33. Stereo. Hrs open: 24 50 Penn Pl., Suite 1000, 73118. Phone: (405) 840-5271. Fax: (405) 840-5808.E-mail: derricknance@clearchannel.com Web Site:www.sportsradio1340.com Licensee: Clear Channel Broadcasting Licenses Inc. (acq 6-10-2002). Population served: 800,400 Natl. Network: Fox Sports, . Natl. Rep: McGavren Guild,. Kaye, Scholer, Fierman, Hays & Handler L.L.P. Format: Sports. ♦Bill Hurley, gen mgr; Derrick Nance, gen sls mgr; Ken Post, progmg dir.

KHBZ-FM— June 6, 1967: 94.7 mhz; 98 kw. 1,387 ft TL: N35 32 58 W97 29 50. Stereo. Hrs open: 24 Box 1000, 73101. Phone: (405) 840-5271. Fax: (405) 842-1315.E-mail: info@947thebuzz.com Web Site:www.947thebuzz.com Licensee: Clear Channel Broadcasting Licenses, Inc. Group owner: Clear Channel Communications Inc. (acq 1-94; $7.5 million). Population served: 850,000 Format: Alt rock. News staff: one. Target aud: 25-54. ♦Mr. Jrod, VP & progmg dir.

KJYO(FM)— Apr 9, 1961: 102.7 mhz; 98 kw. 900 ft TL: N35 32 52 W97 29 29. (CP: Ant 984 ft.). Stereo. Hrs open: 24 Prog sep from AM Box 1000, 73101. Phone: (405) 840-5271. Fax: (405) 858-5333. Web Site:www.kj103fm.com Licensee: Clear Channel Broadcasting Licenses, Inc. Format: CHR/Top 40. ♦Mike McCoy, progmg dir.

KKWD(FM)—(Bethany, Oct 29, 1965: 104.9 mhz; 3 kw. Ant 299 ft TL: N35 29 58 W97 37 08. Hrs open: 24 4045 Northwest 64th St., Suite 600, 73116. Phone: (405) 848-0100. Fax: (405) 843-5288.E-mail: info@wild1049hd.com Web Site:www.wild1049hd.com Licensee: The Last Bastion Station Trust LLC, as Trustee Group owner: Citadel Broadcasting Corp. (acq 6-12-2007; grpsl). Format: Urban hits. Target aud: 35-49 & 25-34; young, professional. ♦Larry Bastida, gen mgr; Chris Baker, stn mgr.

KMGL(FM)— Nov 25, 1965: 104.1 mhz; 100 kw. 1,425 ft TL: N35 32 58 W97 29 18. Stereo. Hrs open: 24 Box 14818, 73113. Secondary address: 400 E. Britton Rd. 73114. Phone: (405) 478-5104. Fax: (405) 478-0448.E-mail: sobrien@rendabroadcasting.com Web Site:www.magic104.com Licensee: Renda Broadcasting. (group owner; acq 4-88). Population served: 831,600 Format: Adult contemp. Target aud: 25-54; women. ♦Don Pollnow, gen mgr; Bob Delancey, gen sls mgr; Steve O'Brien, progmg dir; Dennis Orcutt, chief of engrg.

KOKC(AM)— Dec 24, 1922: 1520 khz; 50 kw-U, DA-N. TL: N35 20 00 W97 30 16. Stereo. Hrs open: 24 Box 14818, 73113. Secondary address: 400 E. Britton Rd. 73113. Phone: (405) 478-5104. Fax: (405) 478-0448.E-mail: jperkey@rendabroadcasting.com Web Site:www.1520kokc.com Licensee: Renda Broadcasting Corp. of Nevada. Group owner: Renda Broadcasting Corp. (acq 6-30-98; grpsl). Population served: 2,160,200 Natl. Network: ABC, . Natl. Rep: ABC Radio Sales,. Format: News/talk/sports. Target aud: 25-54. ♦Don Pallnow Jr., gen mgr; J. Perkey, progmg dir.

KOMA(FM)— 1964: 92.5 mhz; 98 kw. 984 ft TL: N35 32 52 W97 29 29. Stereo. Hrs open: 24 400 E. Britton Rd., 73114. Phone: (405) 478-5104. Fax: (405) 475-7021. Web Site:www.komaradio.com Licensee: Renda Broadcasting Corp. of Nevada. Group owner: Renda Broadcasting Corp. (acq 6-30-98; grpsl). Format: Classic Hits. Target aud: 25-54. ♦Don Pollnow, gen mgr; Kent Jones, progmg dir; Stephen Bennett, news dir; Lisa Sykes, prom.

KQCV(AM)— 1948: 800 khz; 2.5 kw-D, 500 w-N, DA. TL: N35 24 45 W97 40 26. Hrs open: 24 1919 N. Broadway Ave., 73103. Phone: (405) 521-0800. Fax: (405) 521-1391.E-mail: kqcv@bottradionetwork.com Web Site:www.bottradionetwork.com Licensee: Bott Broadcasting Co. Group owner: Bott Radio Network (acq 1-76). Population served: 1,600,000 Format: Christian info, news. Target aud: 25-54; family oriented. ♦Richard P. Bott, pres; Richard Bott II, VP; Paul Sublett, gen mgr; Jerry McCall, opns dir.

KRMP(AM)— 1140 khz; 1 kw-D. TL: N35 23 14 W97 29 56. Hrs open: 1528 N.E. 23rd St., 73111. Phone: (405) 427-5877. Fax: (405) 424-6708.E-mail: info@krmp.com Web Site:www.perry_pub-_broadcasting.com Licensee: Perry Broadcasting Co. Inc. Group owner: Perry Publishing & Broadcasting Co. (acq 3-3-93; $375,000;3-22-93). Population served: 632,300 Format: Urban contemp. ♦Russell Perry, CEO; Kevin Perry, gen sls mgr; Terry Monday, opns mgr & progmg dir.

KROU(FM)—See Spencer

KRXO(FM)— Aug 7, 1987: 107.7 mhz; 99 kw. 991 ft TL: N35 32 58 W97 29 18. Stereo. Hrs open: 24 Box 14818, 73113. Secondary address: 400 E. Britton Rd. 73113. Phone: (405) 478-5104. Fax: (405) 478-0448.E-mail: bwiley@krxo.com Web Site:www.krxo.com Licensee: Renda Broadcasting Corp of Nevada. Group owner: Renda Broadcasting Corp. Population served: 2,160,200 Format: Classic rock. ♦Don Pallnow, gen mgr; Buddy Wiley, progmg dir, traf mgr; Steve Bennett, news dir.

KTLR(AM)— 1946: 890 khz; 1 kw-D. TL: N35 33 59 W97 28 28. Hrs open: 24 5101 S. Shields Blvd., 73129. Phone: (405) 616-5500. Fax: (405) 616-5505. Web Site:www.ktlr.com Licensee: Tyler Broadcasting Corp. Group owner: Tyler Media Broadcasting Corp. (acq 1999; $40,000). Population served: 366481 Natl. Rep: D & R Radio,. Format: Community/talk. Target aud: 10-80. Spec prog: Sp 3 hrs wkly. ♦Skip Stow, CEO, pres & gen mgr; Mike Miller, stn mgr, gen sls mgr, progmg dir, chief of engrg, disc jockey.

KTOK(AM)— Jan 29, 1927: 1000 khz; 5 kw-U, DA-2. TL: N35 21 29 W97 27 48. Hrs open: 24 Box 1000, 73101. Secondary address: 1900 Northwest Expressway, Ste 1000 73118. Phone: (405) 840-5271. Fax: (405) 858-5333. Web Site:www.ktok.com Licensee: Clear Channel Broadcasting Licences, Inc. (group owner; acq 8-5-92). Population served: 865,000 Rgnl. Network: Okla. Radio Net. Natl. Rep: Clear Channel,. Okla. News Net. Format: News/talk. ♦Lee Matthews, CEO & progmg dir.

KTST(FM)— Mar 16, 1962: 101.9 mhz; 100 kw. 1,390 ft TL: N35 32 58 W97 29 50. Stereo. Hrs open: 24 Phone: (405) 840-5271. Fax:

(405) 858-5333.E-mail: tomtravis@clearchannel.com Web Site:www.thetwister.com Licensee: Clear Channel Broadcasting Licenses, Inc. (group owner; acq 1996; grpsl). Population served: 793,900 Format: Country. News staff: one. Target aud: 18-49. ♦Bill Hurley, gen mgr; Tom Travis, opns dir & progmg dir.

KVSP(FM)— September 1981: 103.5 mhz; 100 kw. Ant 1,968 ft TL: N35 15 04 W98 36 53. Stereo. Hrs open: 24 Phone: (405) 427-5877. Fax: (405) 424-8811.E-mail: rmperry@kvsp.com Web Site:www.perry_pub_broadcasting.com Licensee: Perry Broadcasting of Southwest Oklahoma Inc. Group owner: Perry Publishing & Broadcasting Co. (acq 11-22-2002; grpsl). Natl. Network: ABC, . Format: Hip Hop RB. Target aud: 18 plus. ♦Kevin Perry, gen mgr, local news ed; Russell M. Perry, chief of opns.

KXXY-FM— October 1964: 96.1 mhz; 100 kw. 1,167 ft TL: N35 32 58 W97 29 18. (CP: Ant 256 ft.). Stereo. Hrs open: 24 Box 1000, 73101. Phone: (405) 840-5271. Fax: (405) 842-1315. Web Site:www.kxy.com Licensee: Clear Channel Broadcasting Licenses Inc. Group owner: Clear Channel Communications Inc. (acq 1996; grpsl). Population served: 800,400 Format: Country. ♦Bill Reed, gen mgr & progmg dir.

KYIS(FM)— June 1969: 98.9 mhz; 100 kw. 1,108 ft TL: N35 33 36 W97 29 07. Stereo. Hrs open: 24 4045 N.W. 64th St., Suite 600, 73116. Phone: (405) 848-0100. Fax: (405) 843-5288.E-mail: info@klis.com Web Site:www.klis.com Licensee: Citadel Broadcasting Co. Group owner: Citadel Broadcasting Corp. (acq 10-28-99; grpsl). Population served: 1,000,000 Natl. Network: AP Radio, . Format: Hot adult contemp. News staff: one. Target aud: 25-54; female. ♦Larry Bastida, gen mgr; Tricia York, gen sls mgr; Don Sweeney, prom dir; Chris Baker, progmg dir.

***KYLV(FM)**— Nov 3, 1980: 88.9 mhz; 39 kw. Ant 673 ft TL: N35 34 24 W97 29 08. Stereo. Hrs open: 24
Rebroadcasts KLVR(FM) Middletown, CA 100%.
2351 Sunset Blvd., Suite 170-218, Rocklin, CA, 95765. Phone: (916) 251-1600. Fax: (916) 251-1650.E-mail: klove@klove.com Web Site:www.klove.com Licensee: Educational Media Foundation. Group owner: EMF Broadcasting (acq 11-9-98; $1.2 million). Population served: 790,000 Natl. Network: K-Love, . Shaw Pittman. Format: Contemp Christian. News staff: 3. Target aud: 25-44; Judeo-Christian female. Spec prog: Black 3 hrs, relg 2 hrs, gospel 4 hrs, pub affrs 4 hrs wkly. ♦Richard Jenkins, pres; Mike Novak, VP, progmg dir; Keith Whipple, dev dir; David Pierce, progmg mgr; Jon Rivers, mus dir; Ed Lenane, news dir; Sam Wallington, engrg dir; Karen Johnson, news rptr.

WKY(AM)— January 1920: 930 khz; 5 kw-U, DA-N. TL: N35 33 43 W97 30 27. Stereo. Hrs open: 24 4045 NW 64th, Ste 600, Okahoma City, 73116. Phone: (405) 848-0100. Fax: (405) 843-5288.E-mail: info@jox930.com Web Site:www.jox930.com Licensee: Citadel Broadcasting Co. Group owner: Citadel Broadcasting Corp. (acq 1-31-2003; $7.7 million). Population served: 759,100 Wiley, Rein & Fielding. Format: Sports. Target aud: 25-54; Men. ♦Larry Bastida, gen mgr & natl sls mgr; Dan Davis, progmg dir; Chris Baker, opns.

WWLS-FM—(Edmond, June 28, 1962: 97.9 mhz; 6 kw. Ant 315 ft TL: N35 34 11 W97 30 01. Stereo. Hrs open: 24 4045 N.W. 64, Suite 600, 73116. Phone: (405) 848-0100. Fax: (405) 843-5288.E-mail: info@thesportsanimal.com Web Site:www.thesportsanimal.com Licensee: Citadel Broadcasting Co. Group owner: Citadel Broadcasting Corp. (acq 10-28-99; grpsl). Birch, Horton, Bittner & Cherot. Format: Sports/Talk. Target aud: 25-54. ♦Larry Bastida, pres & gen mgr; Chris Baker, opns mgr; Jay Davis, gen sls mgr; Dax Davis, progmg dir; Dax Barry Jr., news dir.

Okmulgee

KOKL(AM)— October 1937: 1240 khz; 1 kw-U. TL: N35 36 31 W95 58 19. Hrs open: 24 100 E. 7th St., Suite 100, 74447. Phone: (918) 756-3646. Fax: (918) 756-1800.E-mail: okklradio@aol.com Web Site:www.kokl.net Licensee: Regency Radio Inc. (acq 2-22-94; 3-21-94). Population served: 60,000 Natl. Network: ABC, . Format: True Country/news/talk/sports. News staff: one; News: 16 hrs wkly. Target aud: 25 plus; mid to upper income. Spec prog: Tulsa Univ. sports 10 hrs. ♦James R. Brewer, pres; Paul Brown, gen mgr.

Owasso

KQLL-FM— Oct 1, 1981: 106.1 mhz; 100 kw. Ant 1,315 ft TL: N36 31 36 W95 39 12. Stereo. Hrs open: 24 2625 South Memorial, Tulsa, 74129. Phone: (918) 388-5100. Fax: (918) 388-5400. Web Site:www.kooltulsa.com Licensee: Clear Channel Broadcasting Licenses Inc. Group owner: Clear Channel Communications Inc. (acq 1997; grpsl). Format: Classic top-40. Target aud: Adults 35-54. ♦Michael Oppenheimer, gen mgr; Don Cristi, opns mgr.

Pauls Valley

KVLH(AM)— December 1947: Stn currently dark. 1470 khz; 890 w-D, 35 w-N, DA-2. TL: N34 42 15 W97 15 19. Hrs open: 1101 N. Hwy 81, Marlow, 73055. Phone: (580) 658-9292. Licensee: Armstrong of Oklahoma Inc. (group owner; (acq 8-1-2007; $125,000). Population served: 10,000 Rgnl. Network: . Garvey, Schubert & Barer. ♦James C. Hilliard, pres.

Pawhuska

KOSG(FM)— 1997: 103.9 mhz; 3 kw. 328 ft TL: N36 44 56 W96 17 51. Hrs open: 319 S.E. Dewey St., Bartlesville, 74003. Phone: (918) 333-8550. Fax: (918) 333-8553.E-mail: info@kosgfm.com Licensee: Tallgrass Broadcasting LLC (acq 10-25-2006; $294,000). Format: Adult hits. ♦Joe Walker, pres & gen mgr.

KPGM(AM)— Oct 19, 1963: 1500 khz; 500 w-D. TL: N36 45 42 W96 11 58. Hrs open: 6 AM-6 PM Box 1526, 74056. Secondary address: 129 W. Main 74056. Phone: (918) 287-1145. Fax: (918) 287-1473.E-mail: kpgm@bartlesvilleradio.com Web Site:www.bartlesvilleradio.com/kpgm Licensee: Potter Radio LLC. (acq 7-1-2005; $100,000). Population served: 40,893 Natl. Network: Salem Radio Network, . Lauren Colby. Format: News/Christian talk. News staff: one; News: 20 hrs wkly. ♦Kevin Potter, pres & gen mgr; Charlie Taraboletti, progmg dir.

Perry

KOKP(AM)— July 6, 1986: 1020 khz; 400 w-D, 250 w-N, DA-2. TL: N36 15 35 W97 13 01. Hrs open: 24 Box 2509, Ponca City, 74602. Phone: (580) 765-2485. Fax: (580) 767-1103.E-mail: bill@eteamradio.com Web Site:www.eteamradio.com Licensee: Team Radio L.L.C. (group owner; (acq 7-14-98; $308,000 with co-located FM). Population served: 225,000 Fletcher, Heald & Hildreth. Format: Sports. Target aud: 24 plus; agriculture-related country. ♦Bill Coleman, pres, gen mgr, stn mgr, gen sls mgr, edit dir; Chris Johnson, progmg dir.

KOSB(FM)— Nov 24, 1988: 105.1 mhz; 6 kw. Ant 328 ft TL: N36 14 15 W97 21 59. Stereo. Hrs open: 24 Prog sep from AM Box 2509, Ponca City, 74602. Phone: (580) 765-2485. Fax: (580) 767-1103.E-mail: bill@eteamradio.com Web Site:www.eteamradio.com Licensee: Team Radio, LLC Natl. Network: Westwood One, . Format: Sports. News staff: one. Target aud: 25-55. ♦Chris Johnson, disc jockey.

Piedmont

***KZTH(FM)**— April 2008: 88.5 mhz; 35 kw. Ant 597 ft TL: N35 31 17 W98 09 33. Hrs open:
Rebroadcasts KJTH(FM) Ponca City 100%.
Box 14, Ponca City, 74602-0014. Phone: (580) 767-1400. Fax: (580) 765-1700.E-mail: mail@thehousefm.com Web Site:www.thehousefm.com Licensee: The Love Station Inc. Format: Christian hits. ♦Doyle Brewer, gen mgr; Tony Weir, progmg dir.

Pocola

***KKRI(FM)**— June 11, 2002: 88.1 mhz; 26 kw vert. Ant 420 ft TL: N35 09 02 W94 13 48. Stereo. Hrs open: 24 2351 Sunset Blvd., Suite 170-218, Rocklin, CA, 95765. Phone: (916) 251-1600. Fax: (916) 251-1650.E-mail: info@air1.com Web Site:www.air1.com Licensee: Educational Media Foundation. Group owner: EMF Broadcasting. Population served: 256,600 Natl. Network: Air 1, . Shaw Pittman. Format: Contemp Christian. News staff: 3. Target aud: 18-35; Judeo-Christian, female. ♦Richard Jenkins, pres; Mike Novak, VP; Keith Whipple, dev dir; David Pierce, progmg dir; Sam Wallington, engrg dir; Arthur Vassar, traf mgr; Karen Johnson, news rptr.

Ponca City

KIXR(FM)— June 1984: 104.7 mhz; 25 kw. Ant 292 ft TL: N36 47 21 W97 02 53. Stereo. Hrs open: 24 Box 2631, 74602. Secondary address: 3924 Santa Fe Rd. 74602. Phone: (580) 765-5491. Fax: (580) 762-8329.E-mail: kixr@kixr.com Web Site:www.kixr.com Licensee: Mur-Thom Broadcasting Inc. (acq 8-10-94; $80,000; 9-12-94). Population served: 101,000 Natl. Network: Westwood One, . Format: Community radio. News staff: 5; News: 4 hrs wkly. Target aud: 24-55; core audience of females between the ages of 24-45. Spec prog: Native American 3 hrs wkly. ♦Carol Murphy, pres; Gordon Thompson, gen mgr & progmg dir; Dave Foster, chief of engrg.

***KJTH(FM)**— 2004: 89.7 mhz; 100 kw. Ant 1,007 ft TL: N36 35 42 W97 34 38. Hrs open: 24 Box 14, 74602. Secondary address: 6600 W. Hwy. 60 74601. Phone: (580) 767-1400. Fax: (580) 765-1700.E-mail: mail@thehousefm.com Web Site:www.thehousefm.com Licensee: The Love Station Inc. Format: Christian hits. Target aud: 25-45; young Christian adults. ♦Doyle Brewer, CEO, pres, gen mgr; Janelle Keith, prom dir; Tony Weir, progmg dir.

KLOR-FM— December 1965: 99.3 mhz; 3 kw. 300 ft TL: N36 46 59 W97 04 15. Stereo. Hrs open: 24 122 N. 3rd St., 74601. Phone: (580) 762-9930. Fax: (580) 767-1103.E-mail: billc@eteamradio.com Web Site:www.eteamradio.com Licensee: Team Radio L.L.C. (group owner; acq 3-18-99). Population served: 68,000 Rgnl. Network: Okla. Radio Net. Okla. News Net. Format: Classic rock, oldies. News staff: one; News: 75 hrs wkly. Target aud: 18-55. ♦Bill Coleman, pres, gen mgr; Darrel Dye, gen sls mgr; Sean Anderson, progmg dir.

***KLVV(FM)**— December 1992: 88.7 mhz; 11.5 kw. 479 ft TL: N36 41 25 W97 10 20. Stereo. Hrs open: 24 Box 14, 74602. Secondary address: 6600 W. Hwy. 60 74601. Phone: (580) 767-1400. Fax: (580) 765-1700.E-mail: mail@mypraisefm.com Web Site:www.klvv.com; www.mychristianfm.com Licensee: The Love Station Inc. Population served: 75,000 Format: Inspirational music, Christian teaching. Target aud: 25-45; young Christian adults. ♦Doyle Brewer, CEO, pres, gen mgr; Tony Weir, progmg dir.

KOKB(AM)—See Blackwell

KPNC(FM)— June 5, 1979: 100.7 mhz; 25 kw. Ant 253 ft TL: N36 46 59 W97 04 15. Stereo. Hrs open: 24 Box 2509, 74602. Secondary address: 122 N. 3rd St. 74601. Phone: (580) 765-2485. Phone: (580) 767-1101. Fax: (580) 767-1103.E-mail: billc@eteamradio.com Web Site:www.eteamradio.com Licensee: Team Radio L.L.C. (group owner; (acq 7-20-90). Population served: 50,000 Format: Country. News: 20 hrs wkly. Target aud: 25-54; working middle class. Spec prog: Farm 5 hrs wkly. ♦Bill Coleman, chmn, VP, gen mgr; Darrel Dye, sls dir, gen sls mgr; Ryan Diamond, progmg dir.

WBBZ(AM)— 1927: 1230 khz; 1 kw-U. TL: N36 41 46 W97 03 07. Stereo. Hrs open: 24 Phone: (580) 765-6607. Fax: (580) 765-6611.E-mail: wbbz@wbbz.com Web Site:www.wbbz.com Licensee: Ponca City Publishing Co. (acq 1949). Population served: 35,000 Natl. Network: AP Radio, . Format: Classic favorites. News staff: one; News: 12 hrs wkly. Target aud: 35 plus. Spec prog: Class 5 hrs, relg 5 hrs, big band 3 hrs wkly. ♦Tom Muchmore, CEO; Phil Turney, gen mgr, stn mgr, gen sls mgr.

Poteau

***KARG(FM)**— June 1998: 91.7 mhz; 3.25 kw. 1,866 ft TL: N35 04 17 W94 40 47. Hrs open: Box 3206, American Family Radio, Tupelo, MS, 38803. Phone: (662) 844-8888, EXT. 204. Fax: (662) 842-6791. Web Site:www.afr.net Licensee: American Family Association. Group owner: American Family Radio Format: Inspirational Christian. ♦Marvin Sanders, gen mgr.

KOMS(FM)— Oct 18, 1969: 107.3 mhz; 100 kw. 1,810 ft TL: N34 57 50 W94 22 34. Stereo. Hrs open: 24 4608 Radio Tower Rd., Van Buren, AR, 72956. Phone: (479) 474-3422. Fax: (479) 474-2649.E-mail: cindywilson@cumulus.com Web Site:www.bigcountry1073.com Licensee: Cumulus Licensing Corp. Group owner: Cumulus Media Inc. (acq 5-17-99; $950,000). Population served: 500,000 Natl. Network: CNN Radio, . Wire Svc: AP Format: Class country. News staff: News progmg 60 hrs wkly Target aud: 25-54. ♦J.P. Morgan, opns mgr, disc jockey; Smitty O'Loughlin, mktg mgr; Michael Hauser, progmg dir, disc jockey; Don Jones, engr.

KPRV(AM)— Nov 25, 1953: 1280 khz; 1 kw-D, 108 w-N. TL: N35 00 55 W94 39 06. Hrs open: 24 Box 368, 74953. Secondary address: 22153 Old Hwy. 59 74953. Phone: (918) 647-3221. Fax: (918) 647-5092.E-mail: billy@clnk.com Web Site:www.kprvradio.com Licensee: LeRoy Billy. Natl. Network: ABC, . Rgnl. Network: Okla. Radio Net. Okla. News Net. Robert Allen. Format: Adult standards. News: 24 hrs wkly. Target aud: 24-54. ♦Joann Billy, gen mgr; LeRoy Billy, gen sls mgr.

KZBB(FM)— 1967: 97.9 mhz; 100 kw. 2,000 ft TL: N35 04 19 W94 40 46. Hrs open: 24 311 Lexington Ave., Fort Smith, AR, 72901. Phone: (479) 782-8888. Fax: (479) 782-0366.E-mail: b98@kzbb.com Web Site:www.kzbb.com Licensee: Capstar TX L.P. Group owner: Clear Channel Communications Inc. (acq 8-30-00; grpsl). Population served: 500,000 Format: CHR. News: one hr wkly. Target aud: 18-49; upscale. Spec prog: Black 2 hrs, jazz 2 hrs, relg one hr wkly. ♦Paul Swint, gen mgr; Ralph Cherry, opns mgr; Phil Robken, sls dir; Gary Elmore, progmg dir; Allan Riley, chief of engrg.

Pryor

KMYZ-FM— July 3, 1969: 104.5 mhz; 78 kw. 1,250 ft TL: N36 18 04 W95 19 29. Stereo. Hrs open: 24 5810 E. Skelly Dr., Suite 801, Tulsa,

74135. Phone: (918) 665-3131. Fax: (918) 663-6622.E-mail: production @shamrocktuosa.com Web Site:www.edgetulsa.com Licensee: Shamrock Communications Inc. (group owner; acq 4-14-84). Format: Alternative rock. ◆William Lynett, CEO; Chuck Browning, gen mgr.

Rattan

*KDBQ(FM)—Not on air, target date: unknown: 89.7 mhz; 2.2 kw. Ant 479 ft TL: N34 11 06 W95 08 21. Hrs open: Box 217, Gainesville, TX, 76241. Phone: (940) 668-7971. Licensee: 1 A Chord Inc. ◆Mary Fay Jackson, gen mgr.

Roland

KREU(FM)— Dec 29, 1995: 92.3 mhz; 740 w. 932 ft TL: N35 31 22 W94 23 32. Hrs open: PO Box 3100, Fort Smith, AR, 72913. Phone: (479) 785-2527. Fax: (501) 782-9127. Licensee: Star 92 Co. (acq 6-13-2003; $10,000). Format: Spanish. ◆Gary Keifer, gen mgr; Fred Baker Jr., opns mgr, gen sls mgr; Carol Patterson, gen sls mgr; Dale Davenport, chief of engrg; Martin Miranda, progmg.

Sallisaw

KKBD(FM)— May 18, 1972: 95.9 mhz; 30 kw. 600 ft TL: N35 24 29 W94 41 13. Stereo. Hrs open: 24 311 Lexington ve., Fort Smith, AR, 72901. Phone: (479) 782-8888.E-mail: info@bigdog959.com Web Site:www.bigdog959.com Licensee: Clear Channel Radio Licenses, Inc. Group owner: Clear Channel Communiations Inc. (acq 8-30-00; grpsl). Population served: 250000 Format: Classic Rock. Target aud: 25-49; adults. ◆Paul Swint, gen mgr; Phil Robken, sls dir.

Sand Springs

KJMU(AM)— July 22, 1961: 1340 khz; 450 w-D, 900 w-N. TL: N36 07 58 W96 05 36. Hrs open: 24 21700 Northwestern Hwy., Suite 1190, Southfield, MI, 48075. Phone: (248) 557-3500. Fax: (248) 557-2950.E-mail: djpercy@perezmediagroup.com Licensee: Birach Broadcasting Corp. (group owner; (acq 1-31-2008; $1.5 million with KTUV(AM) Little Rock, AR). Population served: 750,000 Format: Urban contemp. ◆Sima Birach, pres & gen mgr.

KRMG-FM— June 1989: 102.3 mhz; 50 kw. Ant 492 ft TL: N36 12 39 W96 06 03. Hrs open: 24
Simulcast with KRMG(AM) Tulsa 100%.
7136 S. Yale, Suite 500, Tulsa, 74136. Phone: (918) 493-3434. Fax: (918) 493-5376.E-mail: info@krmg.com Web Site:www.krmg.com Licensee: Cox Radio Inc. Group owner: Cox Broadcasting (acq 3-16-99; $3.5 million). Format: News/talk. Target aud: 25-44. ◆Dan Lawrie, gen mgr; Drew Anderssen, progmg dir; Wayne Smith, opns mgr & chief of engrg.

Sapulpa

KXOJ-FM— Feb 22, 1977: 100.9 mhz; 5 kw. 360 ft TL: N36 03 38 W96 06 03. Stereo. Hrs open: 24 Phone: (918) 492-2660. Fax: (918) 492-8840.E-mail: kxoj@kxoj.com Web Site:www.kxoj.com Licensee: KXOJ, Inc. Population served: 400,000 Format: Contemp Christian mus. ◆Mike Stephens, CEO; David Stephens, gen mgr, stn mgr.

KYAL(AM)— June 15, 1962: 1550 khz; 2.5 kw-D, 47 w-N, DA-1. TL: N36 01 08 W96 05 55. Stereo. Hrs open: 24 Cityplex Towers, Ste 5500, 2448 E. 81st St., Tulsa, 74137-4272. Phone: (918) 492-2660. Fax: (918) 492-8840.E-mail: studio@sportsanimaltulsa.com Web Site:www.sportsanimaltulsa.com Licensee: KXOJ Inc. Group owner: Adonai Radio Group (acq 5-2-73). Population served: 350,000 Format: Sports. Target aud: 35 plus. ◆David Stephens, pres, gen mgr, opns mgr, sls dir & mktg dir.

Sayre

*KESG(FM)—Not on air, target date: unknown: 88.7 mhz; 7 kw. Ant 256 ft TL: N35 17 36 W99 41 52. Hrs open: Box 452, 73662. Phone: (580) 928-2345. Fax: (580) 928-3271. Licensee: Trinity Fellowship Ministries Inc. ◆Andy Taylor, pres.

Seminole

KIRC(FM)— 1986: 105.9 mhz; 4.4 kw. 384 ft TL: N35 18 28 W96 45 18. Stereo. Hrs open: 24 2 E. Main St., Shawnee, 74801-6906. Phone: (405) 878-1803. Phone: (405) 382-0105. Fax: (405) 878-0162.E-mail: kirc1059@aol.com Licensee: One Ten Broadcast Group Inc. (group

owner; (acq 4-16-2008). Population served: 250,000 Format: Country. News staff: 9; News: 2 hrs wkly. Target aud: 12-55; general. Spec prog: Area tribes one hr wkly. ◆Linda Jones, pres, VP; Dennis Burton, gen mgr; David Beerley, gen sls mgr, progmg dir; Jim Stanford, chief of engrg; Nichole Johnson, traf mgr.

KTLS-FM—See Holdenville

KWSH(AM)—See Wewoka

*KXTH(FM)— October 2003: 89.1 mhz; 2.3 kw vert. Ant 387 ft TL: N35 12 53 W96 44 26. Hrs open: 24 Box 14, Ponca City, 74602-0014. Secondary address: 6600 W. Hwy. 60, Ponca City 74601. Phone: (580) 767-1400. Fax: (580) 765-1700.E-mail: mail@thehousefm.com Web Site:www.thehousefm.com Licensee: The Love Station Inc. (acq 9-16-03). Format: Adult contemp, Christian. Target aud: 25-45; young Christian adults. ◆Doyle Brewer, CEO, pres, gen mgr; Janelle Keith, prom dir; Tony Weir, progmg dir.

Shawnee

KGFF(AM)— Dec 10, 1930: 1450 khz; 1 kw-U. TL: N35 21 39 W96 53 41. Hrs open: 24 Box 9, 74802. Secondary address: 1570 S. Gordon Cooper Drive 74801. Phone: (405) 273-4390. Fax: (405) 273-4530.E-mail: mike@kgff.com Web Site:www.kgff.com Licensee: Citizen Band Potawatomi Indian Tribe of Oklahoma Inc. (acq 11-10-98; $155,000). Population served: 45,000 Natl. Network: ABC, . Rgnl. Network: Okla. Radio Net., Texas State Net. Okla. News Net. Format: Adult standards. News staff: one; News: 20 hrs wkly. General. Spec prog: school, University of Oklahoma, Oklahoma Baptist University, St. Gregory's University, relg 4 hrs wkly. ◆Michael Askins, gen mgr & opns dir.

KQCV-FM— Apr 13, 1998: 95.1 mhz; 100 kw. 1,004 ft TL: N35 15 47 W96 22 43. Hrs open: 1919 N. Broadway, Oklahoma City, 73103. Phone: (405) 521-0800. Fax: (405) 521-1391. Web Site:www.bottradionetwork.com Licensee: Community Broadcasting Inc. Group owner: Bott Radio Network Format: Christian info & teaching. ◆Paul Sublett, gen mgr; Jerry McCall, opns mgr.

Snyder

*KJCM(FM)— 2000: 100.3 mhz; 18 kw. Ant 384 ft TL: N34 38 02 W99 05 03. Hrs open: PO Box 311, Hobart, 73651. Secondary address: 1515 N. Broadway, Hobart 73651. Phone: (580) 726-5656. Fax: (580) 726-2222.E-mail: thezone@itlnet.net Licensee: Fuchs Radio L.L.C. (acq 4-4-2006; $250,000 with KHIM(FM) Mangum). Format: Adult contemp. ◆Chad Fox, gen mgr; Lance Perritt, progmg dir.

Soper

KMMY(FM)— 2008: 96.5 mhz; 3.4 kw. Ant 443 ft TL: N33 59 25 W95 46 48. Hrs open: 24 404 E. Jackson St., Hugo, 74743. Phone: (580) 326-5541. Fax: (580) 326-5236. Licensee: Will Payne. Format: Rock. ◆Will Payne, gen mgr.

Spencer

*KROU(FM)— Jan 28, 1993: 105.7 mhz; 4 kw. Ant 328 ft TL: N35 35 22 W97 29 03. Stereo. Hrs open: 24 hrs
Rebroadcasts KGOU(FM) Norman 100%.
Copeland Hall, Room 300, Norman, 73019. Secondary address: The University of Oklahoma Phone: (405) 325-3388. Fax: (405) 325-7129.E-mail: manager@kgou.org Web Site:www.kgou.org Licensee: University of Oklahoma. Population served: 800,000 Natl. Network: NPR, . Dow, Lohnes & Albertson. Format: News/talk, jazz. News staff: one; News: 82 hrs wkly. Target aud: 25-54; general. Spec prog: Blues 8 hrs. ◆Karen Holp, gen mgr; Jim Johnson, progmg dir.

Sperry

KMUS(AM)— 2004: 1380 khz; 7 kw-D, 250 w-N, DA-2. TL: N36 15 59 W95 58 15. Hrs open: 24 8321 E. 61st St., Ste 202, Tulsa, 74145. Phone: (918) 250-8484. Fax: (918) 250-6464.E-mail: info@kmusam.com Web Site:www.radiodisney.com/tulsa Licensee: Radio Disney Group LLC. Group owner: ABC Inc. (acq 2-28-2003; $1.5 million). Population served: 270,000 Format: Family. ◆Barbara Jacaby, gen mgr; Mark Gould, gen sls mgr; Amanda Lucie, progmg dir, prom.

Stigler

*KTKL(FM)— 2003: 88.5 mhz; 1 w horiz, 22 kw vert. Ant 643 ft vert TL: N35 08 30 W95 21 20. Stereo. Hrs open: 24 2351 Sunset Blvd., Suite 170-218, Rocklin, CA, 95765. Phone: (916) 251-1600. Fax: (916) 251-1650.E-mail: klove@klove.com Web Site:www.klove.com Licensee: Educational Media Foundation. Group owner: EMF Broadcasting. Natl. Network: K-Love, . Shaw Pittman. Format: Christian contemp. News staff: 3. Target aud: 25-54; Judeo Christian, female. ◆Richard Jenkins, pres; Mike Novak, VP; Keith Whipple, dev dir; David Pierce, progmg mgr; Ed Lenane, news dir; Sam Wallington, engrg dir; Karen Johnson, news rptr.

Stillwater

KGFY(FM)— Feb 6, 1967: 105.5 mhz; 4.9 kw. Ant 361 ft TL: N36 10 31 W97 00 51. Stereo. Hrs open: 24 408 E. Thomas Rd., 74075. Phone: (405) 372-7800. Fax: (405) 372-6969.E-mail: stillwaterradio@coxinet.net Licensee: Stillwater Broadcasting LLC. Group owner: Mahaffey Enterprises Inc. (acq 9-28-2001). Population served: 75,000 Fletcher, Heald & Hildreth. Format: Country. News staff: 2; News: 5 hrs wkly. Target aud: 25-54; young, college community & upscale educated people. Spec prog: Contemp Christian 4 hrs wkly. ◆Steven Johns, gen mgr.

*KOSR(FM)—Not on air, target date: unknown: 88.3 mhz; 1.2 kw. Ant 110 ft TL: N36 07 46.5 W97 05 43.4. Hrs open: 303 Paul Miller Bldg., 74078-4055. Phone: (405) 744-6352. Fax: (405) 744-9970. Licensee: Oklahoma State University. ◆Rachel Hubbard, gen mgr.

*KOSU(FM)— Dec 29, 1955: 91.7 mhz; 100 kw. Ant 1,010 ft TL: N36 06 33 W97 11 43. Stereo. Hrs open: 24 Oklahoma State Univ., 303 P.M. Bldg., 74078. Phone: (405) 744-6352. Fax: (405) 744-9970.E-mail: info@kosu.org Web Site:www.kosu.org Licensee: Oklahoma State University. Population served: 1,500,000. Natl. Network: NPR, . Format: Class, educ, news. News staff: 2; News: 48 hrs wkly. Target aud: General. Spec prog: American Indian one hr wkly. ◆Craig Beeby, gen mgr, progmg dir; Don Crider, dev dir, dev mgr; Rachel Hubbard, news dir; Dan Schroeder, engr.

KSPI(AM)— June 1, 1947: 780 khz; 250 w-D. TL: N36 04 56 W97 03 13. Stereo. Hrs open: 6 AM-6 PM Box 1269, 74076. Secondary address: 408 E. Thomas Rd. 74076. Phone: (405) 372-7800. Fax: (405) 372-6969.E-mail: stillwaterradio@coxinet.net Web Site:www.stillwaterradio.net Licensee: Stillwater Broadcasting LLC. Group owner: Mahaffey Enterprises Inc. (acq 7-21-97; $650,000 with co-located FM). Population served: 150,000 Natl. Network: ESPN Radio, . Format: News/talk, sports. News staff: one; News: 12 hrs wkly. Target aud: 30 plus. Spec prog: News, sports, features. ◆John Mahaffey, pres; Steven Johns, gen mgr; Jay McRae, progmg mgr; Bill Van Ness, news dir.

KSPI-FM— Nov 1, 1947: 93.7 mhz; 16 kw. 886 ft TL: N36 06 31 W97 11 46. Stereo. Hrs open: 24 Prog sep from AM Box 1269, 74076. Secondary address: 408 E. Thomas Rd. 74076. Phone: (405) 372-7800. Fax: (405) 372-6969.E-mail: stillwaterradio@coxinet.net Web Site:www.stillwaterradio.net Licensee: Stillwater Broadcasting LLC Population served: 85,000 Format: Adult contemp. News staff: 2; News: 11 hrs wkly. Target aud: 18 plus. ◆Steven Johns, gen mgr & gen sls mgr; Jay McRae, progmg mgr; Bill Vanness, news dir.

KVRO(FM)— Apr 12, 1997: 101.1 mhz; 6 kw. Ant 328 ft TL: N36 13 10 W97 09 47. Stereo. Hrs open: 24 Box 1269, 74076-1269. Secondary address: 408 E. Thomas 74075. Phone: (405) 372-7800. Fax: (405) 372-6969.E-mail: stillwaterradio@coxinet.net Licensee: Stillwater Broadcasting LLC. Group owner: Mahaffey Enterprises Inc. (acq 9-28-2001). Population served: 150,000 Format: Oldies. News staff: 2; News: 24 hrs wkly. Target aud: 25-54. ◆Steven Johns, gen mgr; Jay McRae, opns mgr; Bill Van Ness, news dir.

Stuart

*KLRB(FM)— 2003: 89.3 mhz; 3 kw vert. Ant 272 ft TL: N34 54 57 W96 08 10. Hrs open: 24 Box 145, 74570. Phone: (918) 697-4019. Fax: (580) 892-3941.E-mail: whitehousefan@hotmail.com Licensee: Lighthouse of Prayer Inc. Format: Southern Gospel & Christian Country. ◆Walter Kuhlman, pres; Stephen Burke, gen mgr, stn mgr.

Sulphur

*KFXT(FM)— 2000: 90.7 mhz; 7 kw. Ant 298 ft TL: N34 32 57 W96 58 34. Hrs open: 24 Sister Sherry Lynn Foundation Inc., 1101 N. 81 Hwy., Marlow, 73055. Phone: (580) 658-9292. Licensee: Sister Sherry Lynn Foundation Inc. Southmayd & Miller. Format: Gospel. ◆Ken Austin, gen mgr; Sherry Lynn, gen sls mgr; Jennifer James, progmg dir; James Wilson, engr.

KIXO(FM)— Nov 11, 1979: 106.1 mhz; 2.65 kw. Ant 499 ft TL: N34 39 03 W96 59 24. Stereo. Hrs open: 24 1101 Hwy. 81 N., Marlow, 73055. Phone: (580) 658-9292. Licensee: DFWU Inc. (group owner; (acq 10-1-90). Population served: 80,000 Southmayd & Miller. Format: Country. Target aud: 25-52. ♦Ken Austin, gen mgr; Sherry Lynn, gen sls mgr; Jennifer James, progmg dir; Amy Helton, chief of engrg, traf mgr.

Taft

KCXR(FM)— Mar 20, 1990: 100.3 mhz; 6 kw. Ant 380 ft TL: N35 48 42 W95 34 12. Stereo. Hrs open: 24 2448 E. 81st, Suite 5500, Tulsa, 74137. Phone: (918) 492-2660. Fax: (918) 492-8840.E-mail: kxoj@kxoj.com Web Site:www.kxoj.com/muskogee Licensee: KXOJ Inc. (group owner; (acq 12-11-2002; $1 million with KBIX(AM) Mukogee). Population served: 828,000 Format: Christian Contemporary. Target aud: 25-54. ♦Michael P. Stephens, pres; David Stevens, gen mgr.

Tahlequah

KEOK(FM)— Aug 20, 1966: 102.1 mhz; 6 kw. Ant 285 ft TL: N35 53 42.67 W94 57 12.16. Stereo. Hrs open: Box 676, 74465. Phone: (918) 456-2511. Fax: (918) 456-3231.E-mail: info@lakescountry1021.com Web Site:www.lakescountry1021.com Licensee: Payne 5 Communications LLC Format: Country. Target aud: 25-60. ♦Shane Sellers, traf mgr; Cindy Lee Sellers, local news ed.

KTLQ(AM)— August 1957: 1350 khz; 1 kw-D, 61 w-N. TL: N35 53 43 W94 57 12. Stereo. Hrs open: 24 Box 676, 74465. Phone: (918) 456-2511. Fax: (918) 456-3231.E-mail: Ralph@ktlq1350.com Web Site:www.ktlq1350.com Licensee: Payne 5 Communications LLC (acq 11-24-2003; $1.15 million with co-located FM). Population served: 100,000 Natl. Network: Westwood One, . Format: Classic country, sports. News staff: one; News: 6 hrs wkly. Target aud: 25-54. ♦Ralph Lynch, gen mgr; Shane Sellers, opns mgr & progmg dir.

KEOK(FM)— Aug 20, 1966: 102.1 mhz; Aug 20, 1966. Aug 20, 1966 TL: Aug 20, 1966. Aug 20, 1966. Stereo. Box 676, 74465. Phone: (918) 456-2511. Fax: (918) 456-3231. E-mail: info@lakescountry1021.com Web Site:www.lakescountry1021.com Licensee: Payne 5 Communications LLC Format: Country. Target aud: 25-60. ♦Shane Sellers, traf mgr; Cindy Lee Sellers, local news ed.

Tishomingo

***KTGS(FM)**— Sept 29, 1998: 88.3 mhz; 5.5 kw. Ant 922 ft TL: N34 21 34 W96 33 34. Hrs open: Box 1343, Ada, 74821. Phone: (580) 332-0902.E-mail: email@thegospelstation.com Web Site:www.thegospelstation.com Licensee: South Central Oklahoma Christian Broadcasting Inc. Format: Southern gospel. ♦Randall Christy, pres; Rick Cody, gen mgr & opns mgr.

Tonkawa

***KAYE-FM**— June 1, 1976: 90.7 mhz; 1.2 kw. 67 ft TL: N36 40 42 W97 17 50. Stereo. Hrs open: 7 AM-midnight (M-F) Central Hall 306, 1220 E. Grand, 74653. Phone: (580) 628-6446. Phone: (580) 628-6200. Fax: (580) 628-6209.E-mail: kaye@north-ok.edu Web Site:www.north-ok.edu Licensee: Northern Oklahoma College. Population served: 60,000 Format: Top 40. News: 6 hrs wkly. Target aud: 13-25. ♦Dr. Joe Kinzer, pres.

Tulsa

KAKC(AM)— July 15, 1938: 1300 khz; 5 kw-D, 1 kw-N, DA-2. TL: N35 59 40 W95 51 27. Hrs open: 24 2625 S. Memorial, 74129. Phone: (918) 388-5100. Fax: (918) 388-5400. Web Site:1300thebuzz.com Licensee: Clear Channel Broadcasting Licenses Inc. (group owner; (acq 8-5-92). Natl. Network: ESPN Radio, Fox Sports, . Natl. Rep: Clear Channel,. Format: Sports. Target aud: 25-54; men. ♦M. Oppenheimer, gen mgr; Garry Weaver, prom dir.

KBEZ(FM)— March 1964: 92.9 mhz; 100 kw. 1,319 ft TL: N36 11 26 W96 05 50. Stereo. Hrs open: 24 7030 S. Yale Ave., Suite 711, 74136. Phone: (918) 496-9336. Fax: (918) 496-1937.E-mail: jobs@kbez.com Web Site:www.kbez.com Licensee: Renda Broadcasting Corp. (group owner; acq 6-8-90; grpsl;6-25-90). Population served: 648,300 Format: Adult contemp. Target aud: 25-54. ♦Jon Phillips, gen mgr; Dave Dallow, opns mgr, progmg dir; Samantha Matthews, prom dir & pub affrs dir; Richard Harley, chief of engrg.

KCFO(AM)— 1946: 970 khz; 2.5 kw-D, 1 kw-N, DA-2. TL: N36 11 46 W96 02 22. Hrs open: 24 5800 E. Skelly Dr., Ste 150, 74135-6416. Phone: (918) 622-0970. Fax: (918) 622-0985.E-mail: info@kcfo.com Web Site:www.kcfo.com Licensee: Friendship Broadcasting L.P. (acq 8-1-90; $953,000; 7-2-90). Population served: 750,000 Natl. Network: USA, . Format: Relg, talk, sports. News: 3 hrs wkly. Target aud: 25-54; Men & women. ♦Ray Clatworthy, pres; Kenneth Staley, gen mgr.

KFAQ(AM)— Jan 23, 1925: 1170 khz; 50 kw-U, DA-N. TL: N36 08 49 W95 48 27. Stereo. Hrs open: 24 4590 E. 29th, 74114. Phone: (918) 743-7814. Fax: (918) 743-7613.E-mail: bgann@journalbroadcastgroup.com Web Site:www.1170kfaq.com Licensee: Journal Broadcast Corp. Group owner: Journal Broadcast Group Inc. (acq 6-11-99; grpsl). Population served: 237,000 Natl. Network: Fox News Radio, . Natl. Rep: Clear Channel,. Dow, Lohnes & Albertson. Format: Talk. News staff: 3; News: 24 hrs wkly. Target aud: 35 plus. Spec prog: Farm 5 hrs, gospel 2 hrs wkly. ♦Carl Gardner, pres; Ron Kurtis, CFO; Randy Bush, gen mgr, gen sls mgr; Brian gann, opns mgr; April Sailsbury, prom dir; Brian Gann, progmg dir, mus dir, news dir; Ray Klotz, engrg dir.

KGTO(AM)— 1998: 1050 khz; 1 kw-D. TL: N36 09 40 W96 03 10. Hrs open: 7030 S. Yale Ave., Suite 302, 74136. Phone: (918) 494-9886. Fax: (918) 494-9683. Web Site:www.kgto.com Licensee: KJMM Inc. Group owner: Perry Publishing & Broadcasting Co. (acq 3-30-01; $455,000). Population served: 375,000 Natl. Network: Westwood One, . Format: Urban adult contemp. Target aud: 35-54. ♦Martha Vaughan, gen mgr.

KJMU(AM)—See Sand Springs

KJSR(FM)— Nov 1, 1966: 103.3 mhz; 100 kw. Ant 1,279 ft TL: N36 01 10 W95 39 24. Stereo. Hrs open: 24 7136 S. Yale, Suite 500, 74136. Phone: (918) 493-3434. Fax: (918) 493-5383.E-mail: info@kjsrfm.com Web Site:www.star103fm.com Licensee: Cox Radio Inc. Group owner: Cox Broadcasting (acq 3-28-97; grpsl). Population served: 650,000 Format: Classic rock/classic hits. News staff: one. Target aud: 25-44. Spec prog: Pub affrs 2 hrs wkly. ♦Dan Lawrie, gen mgr; Steve Hunter, opns mgr.

KMOD-FM— Oct 10, 1959: 97.5 mhz; 100 kw. 1,800 ft TL: N36 11 46 W96 05 53. Stereo. Hrs open: 2625 S. Memorial, 74129. Phone: (918) 388-5100. Fax: (918) 388-5400. Web Site:www.kmod.com Licensee: Clear Channel Broadcasting Licenses Inc. Format: AOR. Target aud: 25-49; men.

KRAV(FM)— Nov 21, 1962: 96.5 mhz; 100 kw. Ant 1,486 ft TL: N36 11 46 W96 05 53. Stereo. Hrs open: 7136 S. Yale, Suite 500, 74136. Phone: (918) 491-9696. Fax: (918) 493-5385. Web Site:www.mix96tulsa.com Licensee: Cox Radio Inc. Group owner: Cox Broadcasting (acq 11-21-96; $5.5 million with co-located AM). Population served: 640,000 Format: Hot adult contemp. Target aud: 25-54; 30% men, 70% women. ♦Robert Neil, pres; Marc Morgan, exec VP; Dan Lawrie, VP; Dan Lawrie, gen mgr.

KRMG(AM)— Dec 31, 1949: 740 khz; 50 kw-D, 25 kw-N, DA-2. TL: N36 04 50 W96 17 09. Stereo. Hrs open: 24 7136 S. Yale, 74136. Phone: (918) 493-7400. Fax: (918) 493-2376.E-mail: info@krmg.com Web Site:www.krmg.com Licensee: Cox Radio Inc. Group owner: Cox Broadcasting (acq 3-28-97; grpsl). Population served: 633,300 Format: News/talk. News staff: 7. Target aud: 25-54; those interested in news, info & issue oriented talk. ♦Dan Laurie, gen mgr; Bill Bromley, gen sls mgr; Drew Anderssen, progmg dir.

KRVT(AM)—See Claremore

KTBZ(AM)— Jan 22, 1934: 1430 khz; 5 kw-U, DA-N. TL: N36 14 10 W95 56 50. Hrs open: 2625 S. Memorial Dr., 74129-2600. Phone: (918) 388-5100. Fax: (918) 388-5400. Web Site:www.1430thebuzz.com Licensee: Clear Channel Broadcasting Licenses Inc. Group owner: Clear Channel Communications Inc. (acq 1997; grpsl). Population served: 600,000 Format: Sports. Target aud: 25-49; men. ♦Michael Oppenheimer, gen mgr.

KVOO-FM— Nov 16, 1973: 98.5 mhz; 100 kw. Ant 1,229 ft TL: N36 11 26 W96 05 50. Hrs open: 24 4590 E. 29th, 74114. Phone: (918) 743-7814. Fax: (918) 743-7613.E-mail: ljensen@journalbroadcastgroup.com Web Site:www.kvoo.com Licensee: Journal Broadcast Corp. Format: Today's country. Target aud: 25-54. ♦Carl Gardner, pres; Ron Kurtis, CFO; Randy Bush, gen mgr, gen sls mgr; Brian Gann, opns mgr, progmg dir, mus dir, news dir; April Sailsbury, prom dir; Ray Klotz, engrg dir.

KWEN(FM)— 1961: 95.5 mhz; 96 kw. 1,328 ft TL: N36 11 46 W95 05 53. Stereo. Hrs open: 24 Prog sep from AM 7136 S. Yale, 74136. Phone: (918) 493-7400. Fax: (918) 493-2376.E-mail: info@kwen.com Web Site:www.k955fm.com Licensee: Cox Radio, Inc Population served: 150,000 Wire Svc: NWS (National Weather Service) Format: Contemp country. News staff: one. Target aud: 25-54; country life group. ♦Jim Vidler, gen sls mgr; Karla Cantrell, progmg dir.

***KWGS(FM)**— Oct 19, 1947: 89.5 mhz; 50 kw. Ant 1,067 ft TL: N36 01 15 W95 40 32. Stereo. Hrs open: 24 800 S. Tucker Dr., 74104. Phone: (918) 631-2577. Fax: (918) 631-3695.E-mail: answers@publicradiotulsa.org Web Site:www.kwgs.org Licensee: The University of Tulsa. Population served: 753,163 Natl. Network: NPR, PRI, . Rgnl rep: Wayne Blackmon John D. Pellegrin. Format: News & info/public radio. News staff: one; News: 84 hrs wkly. Target aud: General. ♦Frank Christel, sr VP; Richard Fisher, gen mgr; P. Casey Morgan, dev dir; John Durkee, news dir; Brad Newman, chief of engrg.

***KWTU(FM)**— Oct 15, 2004: 88.7 mhz; 5 kw. Ant 1,066 ft TL: N36 01 15 W95 40 32. Hrs open: 24 The University of Tulsa, 800 S. Tucker Dr., 74104. Phone: (918) 631-2577. Fax: (918) 631-3695.E-mail: answers@publicradiotulsa.org Web Site:www.publicradiotulsa.org Licensee: The University of Tulsa. Rgnl rep: Wayne Blackmon Format: Classical. Target aud: 50+. ♦Rich Fisher, gen mgr.

KYAL(AM)—See Sapulpa

Vinita

KGND(AM)— Dec 7, 1954: 1470 khz; 500 w-D, 88 w-N. TL: N36 38 44 W95 07 35. Hrs open: 24 Box 961, 74301. Secondary address: 402 N. Wilson St. 74301. Phone: (918) 256-2255. Fax: (918) 256-2633.E-mail: don@kitofm.com Licensee: KXOJ Inc. Population served: 75,000 Format: Sports. Target aud: 30-50. ♦Don Turner, gen mgr.

KITO-FM— Apr 9, 1981: 96.1 mhz; 50 kw. 492 ft TL: N36 34 56 W95 01 35. Stereo. Hrs open: 24 Box 961, 74301. Secondary address: 402 N. Wilson St. 74301. Phone: (918) 256-2255. Fax: (918) 256-2633.E-mail: don@kitofm.com Licensee: KXOJ Inc. (acq 8-1-2007; $1.8 million with co-located AM). Population served: 750,000 Format: Classic Country. News: 28 hrs wkly. Target aud: General; traditional country music fans. ♦Don Turner, gen mgr, gen sls mgr; Larry Pierce, progmg dir.

Wagoner

KXTD(AM)— Mar 1, 1966: 1530 khz; 5 kw-D, DA. TL: N35 58 30 W95 29 30. Stereo. Hrs open: Daytime 5807 S. Garnett, Suite F, Tulsa, 74146. Phone: (918) 254-7556. Fax: (918) 252-0036.E-mail: kxtbr@tulsacoxmail.com Web Site:www.quebuenatulsa.com Licensee: Gaytan-Galvan Limited Liability Co. (acq 1-31-97). Format: Sp. ♦Maria DeLeon, gen mgr.

Warner

KTFX-FM— March 1995: 101.7 mhz; 25 kw. Ant 276 ft TL: N35 34 39 W95 12 36. Stereo. Hrs open: 24 401 W. Broadway, Muskogee, 74401. Phone: (918) 683-1017. Fax: (918) 686-6159.E-mail: ktfx@k955.com Web Site:www.okiecountry1017.com Licensee: K95.5 Inc. (group owner) Population served: 88,649 Womble, Carlyle, Sandridge & Rice. Format: Country. News staff: one; News: 2 hrs wkly. Target aud: 25-54; Adults. ♦William H. Payne, CEO & pres; Travis Reeves, gen mgr; Cliff Casteel, opns mgr, progmg dir; Mick Reed, news dir.

Watonga

KIMY(FM)— Dec 12, 1987: 93.9 mhz; 3 kw. Ant 328 ft TL: N35 54 17 W98 23 09. (CP: 4.2 kw, ant 394 ft. TL: N35 50 27 W98 19 09). Stereo. Hrs open: 24 Box 1343, Ada, 74821. Phone: (580) 332-0902.E-mail: email@thegospelstation.com Web Site:www.thegospelstation.com Licensee: South Central Oklahoma Broadcasting Inc. (acq 3-11-2004; $163,000). Population served: 10,000 Format: Southern gospel. Target aud: 25-54; general. ♦Randall Christy, pres; Rick Cody, gen mgr.

Weatherford

***KAYM(FM)**— 2000: 90.5 mhz; 2.7 kw. Ant 282 ft TL: N35 29 47 W98 44 10. Hrs open: Box 3206, American Family Radio, Tupelo, MS, 38803. Phone: (662) 844-8888, EXT. 204. Fax: (662) 842-6791.E-mail: comments@afr.net Web Site:www.afr.net Licensee: American Family Association. Group owner: American Family Radio Format: Inspirational Christian. ♦Marvin Sanders, gen mgr.

***KWEH(FM)**—Not on air, target date: unknown: 91.3 mhz; 1.4 kw. Ant 253 ft TL: N35 29 47 W98 44 10. Hrs open: Drawer 2440, Tupelo, MS, 38803. Phone: (662) 844-8888. Licensee: Abundant Life Broadcasting. ♦Tamra Durham, VP.

KWEY(AM)— June 1, 1970: 1590 khz; 1 kw-D, DA. TL: N35 33 33 W98 43 11. Hrs open: Box 587, Hwy. 54 N., 73096. Phone: (580) 772-5939. Fax: (580) 772-1590.E-mail: info@kwey.com Web Site:www.kwey.com Licensee: Wright Broadcasting Systems Inc. (acq

7-17-91; $407,435 with co-located FM; 8-5-91). Population served: 11,400 Natl. Network: ABC, . Rgnl. Network: Agri-Net. Okla. News Net. Putbrese, Hunsaker & Trent. Format: C&W. News staff: one; News: 14 hrs wkly. Target aud: 25 plus; full service station. ♦G. Harold Wright, CEO; Heston Wright, sls dir; Todd Brunner, opns mgr & progmg dir; Ray Bagby', engrg dir; Chuck Edwards, sports cmtr.

Wewoka

KSLE(FM)— October 1997: 104.7 mhz; 6 kw. 328 ft TL: N35 04 51 W96 35 03. Hrs open: 24 Dups AM 100% 2 E. Main, Shawnee, 74801. Phone: (405) 382-0186. Fax: (405) 382-0128.E-mail: onetenbroadcast@onetenbroadcast.org Licensee: One Ten Broadcast Group Inc. (acq 4-16-2008). Format: Oldies. ♦Linda Jones, prom dir.

KWSH(AM)— July 1951: 1260 khz; 1 kw-U, DA-N. TL: N35 10 10 W96 32 30. Hrs open: 2 E. Main, Shawnee, 74801. Phone: (405) 382-1260. Phone: (405)-257-5441. Fax: (405) 257-2011. Fax: (405) 382-0128.E-mail: onetenbroadcast@onetenbroadcast.com Licensee: One Ten Broadcast Group Inc. (group owner; (acq 4-16-2008). Population served: 126,400 Rgnl. Network: Okla. Radio Net. Okla. News Net. Format: Country. Target aud: 21-61. Spec prog: American Indian one hr wkly. ♦Dennis Burton, stn mgr; Garry Walker, opns mgr, progmg dir; Linda Jones, pres, gen mgr, sls dir, prom mgr & adv mgr; Jim Stanford, chief of engrg.

Wilburton

KMCO(FM)— November 1965: 101.3 mhz; 100 kw. 494 ft TL: N34 59 13 W95 42 10. Stereo. Hrs open: 24 Box 1068, McAlester, 74502. Secondary address: 1801 E. Electric Ave., McAlester 74502. Phone: (918) 426-1050. Fax: (918) 423-7119.E-mail: info@mcalesterradio.com Web Site:www.mcalesterradio.com (Acq 1-18-2005; $766,666). Population served: 250,000 Natl. Network: CNN Radio, . Wiley, Rein & Fielding. Format: Modern Country. News: 5 hrs wkly. Target aud: 18-45. ♦Lee Anderson, gen mgr; Sheila Turnbow, gen sls mgr.

KOCD(FM)— Nov 1, 2002: 103.7 mhz; 100 kw. Ant 607 ft TL: N34 59 13 W95 42 10. Stereo. Hrs open: 24 Box 1076, Oklahoma City, 73101. Phone: (800) 516-1037. Fax: (316) 665-6682.E-mail: Jason@Smoothjazzoklahoma.com Web Site:www.smoothjazzoklahoma.co Licensee: KESC Enterprises LLC (group owner) (acq 1-18-2005; $766,666). Natl. Network: AP Radio, . Wiley, Rein & Fielding. Format: Adult contemp. Target aud: 25-54. ♦Jason Schlitz, VP & gen mgr.

Woodward

***KJOV(FM)**— 1998: 90.7 mhz; 4 kw. 400 ft TL: N36 24 08 W99 25 47. Hrs open: Box 991, Meade, KS, 67854. Secondary address: 922 Webster 73802. Phone: (620) 873-2991. Fax: (620) 873-2755. Licensee: Christian Community Radio. Format: Contemp Christian. ♦Don Hughes, pres, gen mgr; Michael Luskey, opns dir; Delvin Kinser, news dir; Steve Larson, chief of engrg; Polly Hughes, traf mgr.

KMZE(FM)— Oct 15, 1989: 92.1 mhz; 2.15 kw. 1,099 ft TL: N36 16 06 W99 26 56. Stereo. Hrs open: 24 Box D, 2728 Williams Ave., 73801. Phone: (580) 256-3692. Fax: (580) 256-3825. Licensee: FM 92 Broadcasters Inc. (acq 8-17-89;9-5-89). Natl. Network: Jones Radio Networks, . Format: Adult contemp. News staff: one. Target aud: 25-54. ♦Mike Mitchel, CEO & chmn.

KSIW(AM)— September 1947: 1450 khz; 1 kw-U. TL: N36 25 42 W99 24 10. Hrs open: 24 Box 1600, 73802. Secondary address: 1922 22nd St. 73801. Phone: (580) 256-1450. Fax: (580) 254-9102. Web Site:www.woodwardradio.com Licensee: Classic Communications Inc. (acq 6-20-2005). Population served: 50,000 Format: Sports/Talk. Target aud: Male 18-49. ♦Sherre House, pres, gen mgr & gen sls mgr; Sam Piel, progmg dir.

KWDQ(FM)— Jan 9, 1990: 102.3 mhz; 100 kw. Ant 868 ft TL: N36 22 31 W99 28 31. Stereo. Hrs open: Box 1600, 73802. Phone: (580) 254-9103. Fax: (580) 254-9102. Web Site:www.woodwardradio.com Licensee: Classic Communications Inc. (acq 3-20-92). Format: Active rock. Target aud: 18-49. ♦Sherre House, CEO & gen mgr.

KWFX(FM)— Nov 1, 1974: 100.1 mhz; 100 kw. Ant 868 ft TL: N36 22 31 W99 28 31. Stereo. Hrs open: 24 Box 1600, 73802. Secondary address: 1922 22nd St. 73801. Phone: (580) 256-0935. Fax: (580) 254-9102. Web Site:www.woodwardradio.com Licensee: Classic Communications Inc. (acq 4-30-96). Format: Country. Target aud: 25-65; affluent, males & females. ♦Sherre House, pres; Bret Brewer, opns dir.

KWOX(FM)— Dec 16, 1983: 101.1 mhz; 100 kw. 1,204 ft TL: N36 16 06 W99 26 56. Stereo. Hrs open: 24 101 Centre, 2728 Williams Ave., 73801. Phone: (580) 256-4101. Fax: (580) 256-3825.E-mail: k101@k101online.com Licensee: Omni Communications Corp. Population served: 150,000 Natl. Network: Westwood One, ABC, . Womble, Carlyle, Sandridge & Rice. Format: Country. News staff: 2. Target aud: General. ♦J. Douglas Williams, CEO, chmn, pres, gen mgr; Justin Stephenson, CFO; C. J. Montgomery, weather dir. Co-owned TV: KOMI-TV affil.

KZCU(FM)— 2001: 95.9 mhz; 6 kw. Ant 328 ft TL: N36 24 40 W99 21 05. Hrs open: 2800 W. Gore Blvd., Lawton, 73505-6377. Phone: (580) 581-2425. Fax: (580) 581-5571.E-mail: kccu@cameron.edu Web Site:www.kccu.org Licensee: Cameron University (acq 12-2-2008; $50,000). ♦Ted Riley, gen mgr.

Oregon

Albany

KGAL(AM)—See Lebanon

KHPE(FM)— Jan 12, 1969: 107.9 mhz; 100 kw. 1,160 ft TL: N44 38 46 W123 16 11. Stereo. Hrs open: 24 Box 278, 34545 Hwy. 20, 97321. Phone: (541) 926-2233. Fax: (541) 926-3925.E-mail: info@hope1079.com Web Site:www.hope1079.com Licensee: Extra Mile Media Inc. Population served: 1,750,000 Gammon & Grange. Format: Contemp Christian. Target aud: 25-54; female. ♦Bill Zipp, pres, sls dir; Randy Davison, gen mgr, gen sls mgr; Jeff McMahon, opns mgr, progmg dir; John Kenneke, chief of engrg; Vicki Webber, traf mgr.

KRKT-FM— June 1978: 99.9 mhz; 100 kw. Ant 1,069 ft TL: N44 38 46 W123 16 11. Stereo. Hrs open: 2840 Marion St. S.E., 97322. Phone: (541) 926-8628. Fax: (541-928-1261. Web Site:www.krktcountry.com Format: Country. ♦Scott Schuler, progmg dir.

KSHO(AM)—See Lebanon

KTHH(AM)— 1959: 990 khz; 250 w-D. TL: N44 35 43 W123 07 54. Hrs open: 24 2840 Marion St. S.E., 97322. Phone: (541) 926-8628. Fax: (541) 928-1261. Licensee: Bicoastal Willamette Valley LLC. Group owner: Clear Channel Communications Inc. (acq 7-2-2007; grpsl). Population served: 245,000 Natl. Rep: Tacher,. Fisher, Wayland, Cooper, Leader & Zaragoza L.L.P. Format: Classic country. News staff: one; News: 10 hrs wkly. Target aud: 25-54. ♦Robert Dove, gen mgr, gen sls mgr; Scott Schuler, adv dir.

KWIL(AM)— Jan 14, 1941: 790 khz; 1 kw-U, DA-2. TL: N44 37 54 W123 00 57. Hrs open: 24 Prog sep from FM Box 278, 34545 Hwy. 20, 97321. Phone: (541) 926-2233. Fax: (541) 926-3925.E-mail: randy@hope1079.com Web Site:www.kwil.com Licensee: Extra Mile Media Inc. (Acq 7-1-57). Population served: 705,600 Format: Christian teaching.

Altamont

KRAT(FM)—Licensed to Altamont. See Klamath Falls

Ashland

KCMX-FM— July 20, 1978: 101.9 mhz; 31.5 kw. Ant 1,457 ft TL: N42 17 54 W122 44 59. (CP: 31.62 kw, ant 1,426 ft.). Stereo. Hrs open: 24 1438 Rossanley Dr., Medford, 97501. Phone: (541) 779-1550. Fax: (541) 776-2360.E-mail: info@lite102.com Web Site:www.lite102.com Licensee: Mapleton License of Medford LLC. Population served: 250,000 Natl. Network: ABC, . Format: Adult contemp. News staff: one. Target aud: 25-54. ♦Casey Baker, progmg dir, mus dir; Kelly Kline, disc jockey.

KGAY(AM)— 1946: 580 khz; 1 kw-U, DA-N. TL: N42 09 46 W122 38 51. Hrs open: 1438 Rossanley Dr., Medford, 97501. Phone: (541) 779-1550. Fax: (541) 776-2360. Licensee: Mapleton License of Medford LLC. (group owner; (acq 10-26-2001; grpsl). Population served: 150,000 Natl. Network: ABC, . Dow, Lohnes & Albertson. Format: Rgnl Mexican. ♦Ron Hren, VP & gen mgr; Jamy Gilinsky, sls dir; Devin Harpole, mktg dir, prom dir; Joe Mussio, mktg mgr; Maria Chaney, traf mgr; Robert Probert, engr.

KIFS(FM)— Nov 25, 1996: 107.5 mhz; 5.8 kw. Ant 1,374 ft TL: N42 17 54 W122 44 53. Hrs open: 3624 Avion Dr., Medford, 97504. Phone: (541) 858-5423. Fax: (541) 857-0326.E-mail: info@107kiss.com Web Site:www.107kiss.com Licensee: Bicoastal Rogue Valley LLC. Group owner: Clear Channel Communications Inc. (acq 7-2-2007; grpsl). Population served: 150,000 Natl. Rep: Tacher,. Format: Contemp hit. Target aud: 18-49. ♦Bill Nielsen, gen mgr.

***KORV(FM)**—Not on air, target date: unknown: 89.5 mhz; 190 w. Ant 1,975 ft TL: N42 11 53 W122 29 30. Hrs open: Box 67, Medford, 97501. Phone: (541) 482-3999.E-mail: mcaso@mcaso.org Web Site:www.mcaso.org Licensee: Multicultural Association of Southern Oregon. ♦Jim Bauermeister, pres.

KSJK(AM)—See Talent

***KSMF(FM)**— Nov 7, 1987: 89.1 mhz; 2.3 kw. 1,340 ft TL: N42 17 54 W122 44 59. Stereo. Hrs open: 5 AM-2 AM 1250 Siskiyou Blvd., 97520. Phone: (541) 552-6301. Fax: 9541) 552-8565. Web Site:www.ijpr.org Licensee: The State of Oregon, acting by and through the State Board of Higher Education. Population served: 700,000 Natl. Network: NPR, PRI, . Ernest Sanchez. Wire Svc: AP Format: Jazz, AAA, news. News staff: one; News: 45 hrs wkly. Target aud: General. Spec prog: Blues 6 hrs, folk 3 hrs, pub affrs 7 hrs wkly. ♦Ronald Kramer, CEO; Mitchell Christian, CFO; Bryon Lambert, opns dir; Jessica Robinson, engrg dir.

***KSOR(FM)**— April 1969: 90.1 mhz; 38 kw. 2,657 ft TL: N42 41 30 W123 13 44. Stereo. Hrs open: 5 AM-2 AM Southern Oregon University, 1250 Siskiyou Blvd., 97520. Phone: (541) 552-6301. Fax: (541) 552-8565.E-mail: info@ijpr.org Web Site:www.ijpr.org Licensee: The State of Oregon, acting by and through the State Board of Higher Education. Population served: 700,000 Natl. Network: PRI, NPR, . Ernest Sanchez. Wire Svc: AP Format: Class, news. News staff: one; News: 35 hrs wkly. Target aud: General. Spec prog: Pub affrs 7 hrs wkly. ♦Ronald Kramer, CEO.

***KSRG(FM)**— 1995: 88.3 mhz; 230 w. 410 ft TL: N42 17 52 W122 44 58. Hrs open: 5 AM- 2 AM Southern Oregon Univ., 1250 Siskiyou Blvd., 97520. Phone: (541) 552-6301. Fax: (541) 552-8565.E-mail: info@ijpr.org Web Site:www.ijpr.org Licensee: The State of Oregon, acting by and through the State Board of Higher Education, for the benefit of Southern Oregon State University. Natl. Network: NPR, PRI, . Ernest Sanchez. Wire Svc: AP Format: Div, classical. News staff: one; News: 35 hrs wkly. Target aud: General. ♦Ronald Kramer, CEO & gen mgr.

Astoria

KAST(AM)— 1922: 1370 khz; 1 kw-U, DA-N. TL: N46 10 31 W123 50 58. Hrs open: 5 AM-midnight 1006 W. Marine Dr., 97103. Phone: (503) 325-2911. Fax: (503) 325-5570. Licensee: New Northwest Broadcasters LLC. (group owner; (acq 10-26-99; grpsl). Population served: 35,000 Format: News/talk, sports. News: 50 hrs wkly. Target aud: 35 plus. ♦Paul Mitchell, gen mgr.

***KGIO(FM)**— 2006: 90.5 mhz; 48 w vert. Ant 469 ft TL: N46 10 56 W123 48 09. Hrs open:
Rebroadcasts KRUC(FM) Las Cruces, NM 100%.
Box 3765, McAllen, TX, 78502. Phone: (956) 787-9788. Fax: (956) 787-9783.E-mail: info@kvmv.com Licensee: Carlos Arana Ministries (group owner). (acq 4-9-2009; $45,000). Format: Sp language/evangelical. ♦Dr. William Haney, gen mgr.

KKEE(AM)— 1950: 1230 khz; 1 kw-U. TL: N46 11 15 W123 49 30. Hrs open: 24 1006 W. Marine Dr., 97103-5826. Phone: (503) 325-2911. Fax: (503) 325-5570.E-mail: kastam@newnw.com Web Site:kkee1230.com Licensee: New Northwest Broadcasters LLC (group owner; acq 8-24-99; grpsl). Population served: 75,000 Format: Talk. News staff: one; News: 7 hrs wkly. Target aud: 25-54; diverse. ♦Paul Mitchell, gen mgr.

***KLOY(FM)**— 2006: 88.7 mhz; 250 w. Ant 1,053 ft TL: N46 15 46 W123 53 09. Hrs open:
Rebroadcasts KLVR(FM) Santa Rosa, CA 100%.
2351 Sunset Blvd., Suite 170-218, Rocklin, CA, 95765. Phone: (916) 251-1600. Fax: (916) 251-1650. Web Site:www.klove.com Licensee: Educational Media Foundation. Group owner: EMF Broadcasting (acq 2-2-2004). Natl. Network: K-Love, . Format: Contemp Christian. ♦Richard Jenkins, pres; Mike Novak, VP, progmg dir; Lloyd Parker, gen mgr; Ed Lenane, opns dir, news dir; Keith Whipple, dev dir; Eric Allen, natl sls mgr; David Pierce, progmg dir; Jon Rivers, mus dir; Sam Wallington, engrg dir; Arthur Vassar, traf mgr; Karen Johnson, news rptr.

***KMUN(FM)**— Feb 2, 1982: 91.9 mhz; 3 kw. 1,060 ft TL: N46 15 46 W123 53 09. Stereo. Hrs open: 5 AM-1 AM Box 269, 97103. Secondary address: 1445 Exchange St. 97103. Phone: (503) 325-0010. Fax: (503) 325-3956.E-mail: kmun@kmun.org Web Site:www.kmun.org Licensee: Tillicum Foundation. Population served: 50,000 Natl. Network: NPR, . Haley, Bader & Potts. Format: Eclectic. News staff: one; News: 12 hrs wkly. Target aud: General. Spec prog: Folk 18 hrs, children's 6

hrs, Sp 3 hrs, American Indian 2 hrs, Black 2 hrs wkly. ♦Ray Merritt, pres; David Hammock, gen mgr; Stephanie Stern, dev dir.

***KWYA(FM)**— 2001: 89.7 mhz; 200 w. Ant 1,027 ft TL: N46 15 46 W123 53 09. Stereo. Hrs open: 24
KWYQ.
3609 Columbia Heights Rd., Longview, WA, 98632-9585. Phone: (360) 577-5433.E-mail: office@wayfm.com Web Site:kwyq.wayfm.com Licensee: WAY-FM Media Group Inc. (group owner; (acq 8-1-2003; $135,000 with KWYQ(FM) Longview, WA). Format: CCM. ♦Danny Houle, gen mgr & stn mgr.

Baker City

***KANC(FM)**—Not on air, target date: unknown: 89.9 mhz; 250 w. Ant 659 ft TL: N44 45 58 W117 52 54. Hrs open: Drawer 2440, Tupelo, MS, 38803. Phone: (662) 844-8888. Licensee: Abundant Life Broadcasting. ♦Tamara Durham, VP.

***KANL(FM)**— 2005: 90.7 mhz; 250 w. Ant 653 ft TL: N44 45 58 W117 52 54. Hrs open: Box 3206, Tupelo, MS, 38803. Phone: (662) 844-8888. Web Site:www.afr.net Licensee: American Family Association. Group owner: American Family Radio. Format: Christian. ♦Marvin Sanders, gen mgr.

KBKR(AM)— 1939: 1490 khz; 1 kw-U. TL: N44 47 18 W117 48 35. Hrs open: 24
Rebroadcasts KLBM(AM) La Grande 100%.
Box 907, 2510 E. Cove Ave., La Grande, 97850. Phone: (541) 963-4121. Phone: (541) 963-4122. Fax: (541) 963-3117.E-mail: supertalk@eoni.com Licensee: Pacific Empire Radio Corp. (group owner; acq 7-19-2004; grpsl). Population served: 40,000 Natl. Network: Westwood One, . Natl. Rep: McGavren Guild,. Format: News/talk. News staff: one; News: 25 hrs wkly. Target aud: 25-54. Spec prog: Farm 2 hrs wkly. ♦Mark Bolland, pres; Steve Ryner, gen mgr & stn mgr; Bobby Hollowwa, progmg dir.

KCMB(FM)— June 26, 1988: 104.7 mhz; 100 kw. 1,747 ft TL: N45 07 26 W117 46 48. Stereo. Hrs open: 1009-C Adams Ave., La Grande, 97850. Phone: (541) 963-3405. Fax: (541) 963-5090. Web Site:www.cappsbroadcastgroup.com/1047kcmb Licensee: Oregon Trail Radio Inc. Group owner: Capps Broadcast Group. Natl. Network: ABC, . Natl. Rep: Tacher,. Format: Country. Target aud: 25-54. ♦Randy McKone, gen mgr.

***KDJC(FM)**— 2005: 88.1 mhz; 500 w vert. Ant 1,810 ft TL: N45 07 26 W117 46 48. Hrs open: Calvary Chapel La Grande, 1433 Jefferson St., La Grande, 97850. Phone: (541) 963-5884.E-mail: wade.twilegar@csnradio.com Web Site:www.csnradio.com Licensee: CSN International. (group owner). Format: Relg. ♦Wade Twilegar, gen mgr.

KKBC-FM— Feb 1, 1981: 95.3 mhz; 6 kw. -200 ft TL: N44 47 18 W117 48 35. (CP: 25 kw). Stereo. Hrs open: 24 Prog sep from AM Box 907, 2510 E. Cove Ave., La Grande, 97850. Phone: (541) 523-4431. Fax: (541) 963-3117.E-mail: theboomer@eoni.com Licensee: Pacific Empire Radio Corp. Population served: 18,000 Natl. Rep: McGavren Guild,. Format: Oldies. News staff: one; News: 6 hrs wkly. Target aud: 25-54.

***KOBK(FM)**— 2007: 88.9 mhz; 600 w. Ant 1,834 ft TL: N44 35 57 W117 46 58. Stereo. Hrs open: 24
Rebroadcasts KOPB-FM Portland 100%.
Oregon Public Broadcasting, 7140 S.W. Macadam Ave., Portland, 97219-3099. Phone: (503) 244-9900. Fax: (503) 293-4877. Web Site:www.opb.org Licensee: Oregon Public Broadcasting. Natl. Network: NPR, . Ore. Pub. Bcstg Radio Net. Swarz, Woods & Miller. Format: News/talk. ♦Steve Bass, CEO; Jeff Douglas, opns VP.

Bandon

KBDN(FM)— October 1996: 96.5 mhz; 1.5 kw. Ant 1,296 ft TL: N42 57 27 W124 16 13. Hrs open: 320 Central Ave., Suite 519, Coos Bay, 97420. Phone: (541) 267-2121. Fax: (541) 267-5229. Web Site:www.kbdn.com Licensee: Bicoastal Media Licenses III LLC. Group owner: Bicoastal Media L.L.C. (acq 10-16-2003; grpsl). Natl. Rep: Tacher,. Format: Real country. Target aud: 25-54. ♦Ken Dennis, CEO, gen mgr; Mike O'Brien, opns mgr & chief of opns.

Banks

KXJM(FM)— June 1990: 107.5 mhz; 35 kw. Ant 1,443 ft TL: N45 30 58 W122 43 59. Hrs open: 24 4949 S.W. Macadam Ave., Portland, 97239-3912. Phone: (503) 323-6400. Fax: (503) 323-6664. Web Site:www.jamminfm.com Licensee: Citicasters Licenses Inc. Group owner: Infinity Broadcasting Corp. (acq 4-1-2009; grpsl). Population served: 1,500,000 Natl. Network: Westwood One, . Format: Hits and hip hop. Target aud: 25-49; adult. ♦Robert Dove, gen mgr.

Bay City

KIXT(FM)— 2005: 95.9 mhz; 450 w. Ant 1,181 ft TL: N45 27 59 W123 55 11. Hrs open: 1600 Gray Lynn Dr., Walla Walla, WA, 99362. Phone: (509) 527-1000. Fax: (509) 529-5534. Licensee: Alexandra Communications Inc. (acq 8-2-2005; $150,000 for CP). ♦Tom Hodgins, pres & gen mgr.

Beaverton

KKCW(FM)— February 1984: 103.3 mhz; 95 kw. Ant 1,542 ft TL: N45 31 21 W122 44 45. Stereo. Hrs open: 24 4949 S.W. MacAdam Ave., Portland, 97239. Phone: (503) 222-5103. Fax: (503) 222-0030.E-mail: info@kkcwfm.com Web Site:www.k103.com Licensee: Citicasters Licenses L.P. Group owner: Clear Channel Communications Inc. (acq 5-4-99; grpsl). Natl. Rep: D & R Radio,. Format: Adult contemp. News staff: 3. Target aud: 25-54. ♦Robert Dove, gen mgr; Tony Coles, opns mgr.

Bend

KBND(AM)— 1938: 1110 khz; 10 kw-D, 5 kw-N, DA-N. TL: N44 06 25 W121 14 39. Hrs open: 24 Box 5037, 97708. Secondary address: 711 N.E. Butler Market Rd. 97701. Phone: (541) 382-5263. Fax: (541) 388-0456.E-mail: news@kbnd.com Web Site:www.kbnd.com Licensee: Combined Communications. (group owner; acq 4-27-90). Population served: 100,000 Natl. Network: Fox News Radio, . Natl. Rep: McGavren Guild,. Dow, Lohnes & Albertson. Format: Sports, News, Talk. News staff: 2. Target aud: 35-64; upscale, professionals. ♦Mike Chaney, gen mgr & gen sls mgr; Dave Junis, progmg dir.

KBNW(AM)— Aug 25, 2008: 1340 khz; 1 kw-D, 500 w-N. TL: N44 04 47 W121 16 58. Hrs open: 24
Simulcast with KWLZ-FM Warm Springs 100%.
854 N.E. 4th St., 97701. Phone: (541) 383-3825. Fax: (541) 383-3403. Web Site:www.newsradiocentraloregon.com Licensee: Summit Broadcasting Group LLC (acq 8-19-2008; $40,000 for CP). Population served: 200,000 Natl. Network: ABC, Premiere Radio Networks, Westwood One, Jones Radio Networks, Talk Radio Network, . Natl. Rep: Christal,. Wire Svc: AP Format: News/talk. News staff: 3; News: 17.5 weekly (local). Target aud: Adults 25-54. ♦Keith Shipman, gen mgr; Brian Canady, sls dir; John Edwards, gen sls mgr; Annette Weston, progmg dir; Bill Baker, news dir, pub affrs dir.

KICE(AM)— Feb 4, 1960: 940 khz; 10 kw-D, 60 w-N, DA-2. TL: N44 04 50 W121 16 51. Hrs open: 24 705 SW Bonnett Way #1100, 97702. Phone: (541) 388-3300. Fax: (541) 388-3303.E-mail: mflanagan@bendradiogroup.com Web Site:www.espn940.com Licensee: GCC Bend LLC. (group owner); (acq 1999). Population served: 55000 Natl. Network: ESPN Radio, . Natl. Rep: Katz Radio,. Format: Sports talk. News staff: one; News: 2 hrs wkly. Target aud: 35 plus. ♦Jim Gross, gen mgr; Ed Lambert, opns dir, opns mgr; Mick Green, sls dir; Mike Flanagan, progmg dir & engrg dir.

***KLBR(FM)**—Not on air, target date: unknown: 88.1 mhz; 5 kw. Ant 850 ft TL: N44 02 49 W121 31 50. Hrs open:
Rebroadcasts KLCC(FM) Eugene 100%.
136 W. 8th Ave., Eugene, 97401-0640. Phone: (541) 463-6000. Fax: (541) 463-6046.E-mail: klcc@klcc.org Web Site:www.klcc.org Licensee: Lane Community College. ♦Steve Barton, gen mgr.

KLRR(FM)—(Redmond, June 17, 1985: 101.7 mhz; 27.5 kw. 985 ft TL: N44 04 41 W121 19 57. Stereo. Hrs open: Box 5037, 97708. Phone: (541) 382-5263. Fax: (541) 388-0456.E-mail: clear@clear1017.fm Web Site:www.clear1017.fm Licensee: Combined Communications. Population served: 125,000 Format: Rock adult contemp, AAA. Target aud: 25-54; upscale, professional women & men. Spec prog: Jazz 5 hrs wkly. ♦Chuck Chackel, CEO; Mike Cheney, gen mgr; Doug Donolo, progmg dir.

KMGX(FM)— July 4, 1973: 100.7 mhz; 50 kw horiz, 20 kw vert. Ant 518 ft TL: N44 04 40 W121 19 49. Stereo. Hrs open: 705 S.W. Bonnett Way, Suite 1100, 97702. Phone: (541) 388-3300. Fax: (541) 388-3303.E-mail: elambert@bendradiogroup.com Web Site:www.mixradiobend.com Licensee: GCC Bend LLC. (group owner). Population served: 125000 Rgnl rep: Allied Radio Partners. Format: Adult contemp. Target aud: 25 plus; middle to upper income consumers. ♦Jim Gross, gen mgr; Ed Lambert, opns mgr; Sean Leavitt, pres & sls dir.

KMTK(FM)— 2000: 99.7 mhz; 26 kw. Ant 682 ft TL: N44 04 39 W121 19 57. Hrs open: 24 711 N.E. Butler Market Rd., 97701. Phone: (541) 382-5263. Fax: (541) 388-0456.E-mail: country@mountain997.com Web Site:www.mountain997.com Licensee: Combined Communications Inc. Group owner: Combined Communications Population served: 150,000 Format: Country. ♦Chuck Chackel, CEO, pres; Mike Cheney, gen mgr; Steve Leon, progmg dir.

KNLR(FM)— Dec 31, 1984: 97.5 mhz; 97 kw. Ant 536 ft TL: N44 04 38 W121 19 49. Stereo. Hrs open: 24 Box 7408, 97708. Phone: (541) 389-8873. Fax: (541) 389-5291.E-mail: info@knlr.com Web Site:www.knlr.com Licensee: Cowan Broadcasting LLC. Natl. Network: USA, . Wire Svc: AP Format: Christian. ♦Terry A. Cowan, gen mgr.

***KOAB-FM**— 1994: 91.3 mhz; 25 kw. 604 ft TL: N44 04 41 W121 19 57. Hrs open: 7140 S.W. Macadam, Portland, 97219. Phone: (503) 293-1905. Fax: (503) 293-1919.E-mail: info@opb.org Web Site:www.opb.org Licensee: Oregon Public Broadcasting. (acq 9-20-93; grpsl; 10-11-93). Population served: 110,000 Natl. Network: NPR, . Format: News, info music. News staff: news progmg 146 hrs wkly News: 5;. ♦Jack Galmiche, COO, exec VP & gen mgr. Co-owned TV: *KOAB-TV affil.

KQAK(FM)— Sept 5, 1986: 105.7 mhz; 40 kw. Ant 592 ft TL: N44 04 40 W121 19 48. Stereo. Hrs open: 24 854 N.E. 4th St., 97701. Phone: (541) 383-3825. Fax: (541) 383-3403. Web Site:www.kqak.com Licensee: Horizon Broadcasting Group L.L.C. (group owner; acq 2000; $3.45 million). Population served: 200,000 Natl. Rep: Christal,. Format: Classic Hits. News staff: 1. Target aud: 25-54. Spec prog: Inside Central Oregon (Public Affairs). ♦Keith Shipman, pres, gen mgr & sls dir; John Edwards, gen sls mgr; Dan Dubay, progmg dir, news dir; Bill Baker, news dir, pub affrs dir.

KTWS(FM)— Dec 21, 1990: 98.3 mhz; 5.2 kw. Ant 731 ft TL: N44 04 39 W121 19 57. Stereo. Hrs open: 24 Box 5037, 97701. Secondary address: 711 N.E. Butler Market Rd. 97701. Phone: (541) 382-5263. Fax: (541) 388-0456.E-mail: thetwins@thetwins.com Web Site:www.thetwins.com Licensee: Combined Communications, Inc. (group owner; acq 9-1-96). Population served: 150,000 Natl. Rep: McGavren Guild,. Format: Classic rock. Target aud: 25-54. ♦Chuck Chackel, pres; Mike Cheney, gen mgr; Ron Alvarez, progmg dir.

***KVLB(FM)**— 2003: 90.5 mhz; 500 w. Ant 564 ft TL: N44 04 40 W121 19 48. Hrs open: 24 2351 Sunset Blvd., Suite 170-218, Rocklin, CA, 95765. Phone: (916) 251-1600. Fax: (916) 251-1650.E-mail: klove@klove.com Web Site:www.klove.com Licensee: Educational Media Foundation. Group owner: EMF Broadcasting (acq 3-11-03; grpsl). Natl. Network: K-Love, . Shaw Pittman. Format: Contemp Christian. News staff: 3. Target aud: 25-44; Judeo Christian, female. ♦Richard Jenkins, pres; Mike Novak, VP; Keith Whipple, dev dir; David Pierce, progmg mgr; Ed Lenane, news dir; Sam Wallington, engrg dir; Karen Vassar, news rptr.

KXIX(FM)— December 1974: 94.1 mhz; 86 kw. Ant 994 ft TL: N44 02 49 W121 31 50. Stereo. Hrs open: 705 SW Bonnett Way #1100, 97702. Phone: (541) 388-3300. Fax: (541) 388-3303.E-mail: mflanagan@bendradiogroup.com Web Site:www.power94.fm Licensee: GCC Bend LLC. (acq 2000) Population served: 240,000 Natl. Rep: Katz Radio,. Format: CHR. Target aud: 18-49. ♦Jim Gross, gen mgr; Ed Lambert, opns mgr; Mick Green, sls dir; Mike Flanagan, progmg dir; R. L. Garrigus, news dir; Pam Hudspeth, traf mgr.

Bonanza

KYSF(FM)— 1999: 102.9 mhz; 460 w. Ant 2,106 ft TL: N42 05 48 W121 37 57. Hrs open: Box 339, Klamath Falls, 97601. Secondary address: 4509 South 6th St., Klamath Falls 97603. Phone: (541) 882-8833. Fax: (541) 882-8836. Web Site:www.hot102-9.com Licensee: New Northwest Broadcasters LLC (group owner; acq 10-20-98; grpsl). Format: CHR. ♦Rob Siems, gen mgr.

Brightwood

***KZME(FM)**—Not on air, target date: unknown: 91.1 mhz; 380 w. Ant 1,663 ft TL: N45 19 58 W121 42 48. Hrs open: 829 N.E. 8th St., Gresham, 97030-5643. Phone: (503) 667-8848. Fax: (503) 667-7710. Licensee: MetroEast Community Media. ♦Rob Brading, CEO.

Brookings

***KMWR(FM)**— Oct 31, 2002: 90.7 mhz; 100 w. Ant 1,233 ft TL: N42 07 23 W124 17 56. Stereo. Hrs open: 24
Rebroadcasts KVIP-FM Redding, CA 100%.
1139 Hartnell Ave., Redding, CA, 96002. Phone: (530) 222-4455. Fax: (530) 222-4484.E-mail: info@kvip.org Web Site:www.kvip.org Licensee: Pacific Cascade Communications Corp. Population served: 15,000 Format: Inspirational, Christian. News staff: 2. ♦David L. Morrow, VP; Steve Hafen, gen mgr; Ted Hering, progmg dir; Paul Brown, chief of engrg.

KURY(AM)— May 2, 1958: 910 khz; 1 kw-D, 37 w-N. TL: N42 04 32 W124 18 52. Hrs open: 24 Box 1029, 605 Railroad, 97415. Phone: (541) 469-2111. Phone: (541) 469-2112. Fax: (541) 469-6397.E-mail: kury@kuryradio.com Licensee: Eureka Broadcasting Co. Inc. (acq 4-19-2005; $775,000 with co-located FM). Population served: 45,000 Natl. Network: Jones Radio Networks, . Format: Oldies, country classic. Target aud: General. ♦Hugo Papstein, pres; Brian Papstein, gen mgr; Debby Phillips, gen sls mgr; Kevin Bane, progmg dir; Tina Williams, traf mgr.

KURY-FM— May 1977: 95.3 mhz; 8.7 kw. 1,164 ft TL: N42 07 23 W124 17 56. Stereo. Hrs open: 24 Prog sep from AM Box 1029, 605 Railroad, 97415. Phone: (541) 469-2111. Fax: (541) 469-6397.E-mail: kury@charterinternet.com Format: Adult contemp. News staff: one; News: 11 hrs wkly. ♦Brian Papstein, stn mgr; Debby Phillips, gen sls mgr, adv mgr; Kevin Bane, progmg mgr, local news ed, sports cmtr; Tina Williams, traf mgr; Amy Terebesi, disc jockey.

Brownsville

KEHK(FM)— Apr 1, 1991: 102.3 mhz; 100 kw horiz, 43 kw vert. 918 ft TL: N44 00 08 W123 06 50. Stereo. Hrs open: 24 1200 Executive Pkwy., Suite 440, Eugene, 97401. Phone: (541) 284-8500. Fax: (541) 485-0969. Web Site:www.starfm1023.com Licensee: Cumulus Licensing Corp. Group owner: Cumulus Media Inc. (acq 8-24-00; grpsl). Natl. Network: Jones Radio Networks, . Natl. Rep: McGavren Guild,. Format: Hot adult contemp. News staff: one; News: 2 hrs wkly. Target aud: 25-54. ♦Bill Bradley, pres; Michael O'Shea, gen mgr.

Burns

***KOBN(FM)**—Not on air, target date: unknown: 90.1 mhz; 1.2 kw. Ant 882 ft TL: N43 34 23 W119 07 49. Hrs open: 7140 S.W. Macadam Ave., Portland, 97219-3099. Phone: (503) 244-9900. Fax: (503) 293-1919. Web Site:www.opb.org Licensee: Oregon Public Broadcasting. ♦Steven M. Bass, CEO & pres.

KQHC(FM)— Sept 1, 1997: 92.7 mhz; 750 w. 905 ft TL: N43 34 22 W119 07 50. Stereo. Hrs open: 24 Box 877, Fairgrounds Rd., 97720. Phone: (541) 573-2055. Fax: (541) 573-5223.E-mail: kzzr_amkqhc_fm@centurytel.net Population served: 10,000 Natl. Network: Jones Radio Networks, . Natl. Rep: Tacher,. Format: Classic hits. ♦Toni Carson, gen mgr & sls dir; Kristina Spurlock, progmg dir.

KZZR(AM)— Sept 28, 1957: 1230 khz; 1 kw-U. TL: N43 33 49 W119 03 22. Hrs open: 24 Box 877, 69470 S. Fairgrounds Rd., 97720. Phone: (541) 573-2055. Fax: (541) 573-5223. Licensee: B&H Radio Inc. (acq 10-1-2007; $209,700 with co-located FM). Population served: 7,500 Natl. Network: ABC, Jones Radio Networks, . Natl. Rep: Tacher,. Wire Svc: AP Format: Contemp country, news, talk. News: 30 hrs wkly. Target aud: 18-55. Spec prog: Farm 6 hrs wkly. ♦Kristina Spurlock, progmg dir; Toni Carson, gen mgr & traf mgr.

Cannon Beach

KCBZ(FM)— 1997: 94.9 mhz; 7 kw horiz, 1.2 kw vert. Ant 302 ft TL: N45 57 08 W123 56 14. Hrs open: 24 Calcomm Stations Oregon LLC, 615 Broadway, Seaside, 97138. Phone: (503) 738-8668. Fax: (503) 738-8778.E-mail: calbrady@pacbell.net Web Site:www.kcbzfm.com Licensee: Calcomm Stations Oregon LLC (acq 12-7-2004; $240,000). Format: Hot adult contemp. ♦Cal Brady, gen mgr; Renee Hartford, gen sls mgr; John Chapman, progmg dir.

Canyon City

KJDY-FM— Dec 13, 1996: 94.5 mhz; 51 kw. Ant 1,364 ft TL: N44 17 50 W119 02 09. Stereo. Hrs open: 24 Box 399, 413 N.W. Bridge St., John Day, 97845. Phone: (541) 575-1185. Fax: (541) 575-2313.E-mail: kjdy@centurytel.net Licensee: Blue Mountain Broadcasting Co. Inc. Population served: 8,000 Natl. Network: ABC, . Format: Country. Target aud: 25-54. ♦Phil Gray, gen mgr.

Cave Junction

KCNA(FM)— Apr 30, 1985: 102.7 mhz; 100 kw. 1,976 ft TL: N42 15 30 W123 39 38. (CP: 50.7 kw). Stereo. Hrs open: 24 511 Rossanley Dr., Medford, 97501. Phone: (541) 772-0322. Fax: (541) 772-4233.E-mail: jim@opusradio.com Web Site:1027TheDrive.com Licensee: Opus Broadcasting Systems Inc. (group owner; acq 12-94). Natl. Rep: Tacher,. Format: Classic hits. ♦Henry Flock, pres; Dean Flock, gen mgr.

Central Point

KFJL(AM)—Not on air, target date: unknown: 1400 khz; 1 kw-U. TL: N42 21 00 W122 54 27. Hrs open: 670 Mason Way, Medford, 97501. Phone: (541) 779-2233. Fax: (541) 773-9554. Licensee: Fjarli Broadcasting, a General Partnership. ♦Jo Ann Fjarli, gen mgr.

Chemult

***KSKX(FM)**—Not on air, target date: unknown: 89.5 mhz; 100 w. Ant 1,895 ft TL: N43 18 20 W121 42 58. Hrs open: Jefferson Public Radio, 1250 Siskiyou Blvd., Ashland, 97520. Phone: (541) 552-6301. Fax: (541) 552-8565. Web Site:www.ijpr.org Licensee: The State of Oregon Acting By and Through the Oregon State Board of Higher Education for Southern Oregon University. ♦Ron Kramer, gen mgr.

Condon

KWCQ(FM)— 2008: 93.5 mhz; 35 kw. Ant 909 ft TL: N45 14 09 W120 18 09. Hrs open: 620 E. Third St., The Dalles, 97058. Phone: (541) 298-4141. Fax: (541) 298-7775. Web Site:www.mix935.com Licensee: Haystack Broadcasting Inc. (acq 6-18-2008; $45,000 for CP). Format: Adult contemp. ♦Danny V. Manciu, pres.

Coos Bay

KDCQ(FM)— May 24, 1995: 92.9 mhz; 4.5 kw. Ant 523 ft TL: N43 21 15 W124 14 34. Stereo. Hrs open: 24 3505 S.E. Ocean Blvd., 97423. Phone: (541) 269-0935. Fax: (541) 267-9376.E-mail: oldies@kdcq.com Web Site:www.kdcq.com Licensee: Bay Cities Building Co. Inc. Population served: 60,000 Natl. Network: ABC, . Natl. Rep: Tacher,. Wire Svc: AP Format: Oldies. News: 5 hrs wkly. Target aud: 35-54; baby boomers. Spec prog: Wolfman Jack. ♦Bruce Latta, pres; Stephanie Kilmer, gen mgr; Mikel Chavez, opns mgr.

KHSN(AM)— Mar 15, 1928: 1230 khz; 1 kw-U. TL: N43 22 11 W124 12 54. Hrs open: 24 320 Central, Suite 519, 97420. Phone: (541) 267-2121. Fax: (541) 267-5229. Licensee: W7 Broadcasting LLC (acq 8-7-03). Population served: 65,000 Rgnl rep: Allied Radio Partners. Format: Radio. News: 14 hrs wkly. Target aud: 35- plus. ♦Lee Taft, gen mgr; Mike O'Brien, opns mgr.

***KJCH(FM)**— Apr 1, 2005: 90.9 mhz; 3.5 kw. Ant 1,462 ft TL: N42 57 32 W124 16 23. Stereo. Hrs open: 24 1190 Face Rock Dr., Bandon, 97411. Secondary address: CSN International, 4002 N 3300 E, Twin Falls, ID 83301. Phone: (541) 347-2709. Fax: (541) 347-1447.E-mail: joshuatanner@rocketmail.com Licensee: CSN International (group owner). Format: Relg. ♦Joshua Tanner, gen mgr.

KMHS(AM)— Dec 7, 1956: 1420 khz; 1 kw-D. TL: N43 21 45 W124 11 33. Hrs open: 10th & Ingersoll, 97420. Phone: (541) 267-1451. Phone: (541) 267-1420. Fax: (541) 269-0161.E-mail: stevew@coosbay.k12.or.us Web Site:www.marshfield.coos-bay.k12.or.us /kmhs/index.htm Licensee: Coos Bay School District No. 9 (acq 7-22-97; $8,505 donation). Format: Classic country. ♦Steve Walker, gen mgr.

***KMHS-FM**— 2008: 91.3 mhz; 10 kw. Ant -33 ft TL: N43 22 07 W124 12 11. Hrs open: 10th & Ingersoll, 97420. Phone: (541) 267-3104. Licensee: Coos Bay School District No. 9. Format: Top-40. ♦Steve Walker, gen mgr.

***KSBA(FM)**— Nov 4, 1988: 88.5 mhz; 2.2 kw. 532 ft TL: N43 23 26 W124 04 46. Stereo. Hrs open: 5 AM-2 AM 1250 Siskiyou Blvd., Ashland, 97520. Phone: (541) 552-6301. Fax: (541) 552-8565.E-mail: info@ijpr.org Web Site:www.ijpr.org Licensee: The State of Oregon, acting by and through the State Board of Higher Education. Natl. Network: NPR, PRI, . Ernest Sanchez. Wire Svc: AP Format: Jazz, news, AAA. News staff: one; News: 45 hrs wkly. Target aud: General. Spec prog: Blues 6 hrs, folk 3 hrs, pub affrs 7 hrs wkly. ♦Ronald Kramer, CEO & gen mgr.

KTEE(FM)—See North Bend

KYSJ(FM)— Nov 1, 1979: 105.9 mhz; 15 kw. Ant 902 ft TL: N43 27 49 W124 05 44. Stereo. Hrs open: 580 Kingwood Ave., 97420. Phone: (541) 269-2022. Fax: (541) 267-0114.E-mail: kysj@lighthouseradio.com Web Site:www.lighthouseradio.com Licensee: Lighthouse Radio Group. (acq 10-25-93; $64,400; 11-8-93). Population served: 844,401 Wire Svc: AP Format: Smooth Jazz/ NAC. ♦David DeAndrea, progmg dir; Rick Stevens, gen mgr & opns.

KYTT-FM— November 1978: 98.7 mhz; 31 kw. 551 ft TL: N43 23 26 W124 07 46. (CP: 12.8 kw, ant 962 ft.). Stereo. Hrs open: 24 580 Kingwood, 97420. Phone: (541) 269-2022. Fax: (541) 267-0114. Web Site:www.lighthouseradio.com Licensee: Lighthouse Radio Group. (acq 3-1-89). Natl. Network: Salem Radio Network, . Wire Svc: AP Format: Contemp Christian. News: 8 hrs wkly. ♦Rick Stevens, gen mgr; Dave DeAndrea, opns mgr; Steve Ramberg, gen sls mgr.

Coquille

KSHR-FM— Nov 1, 1981: 97.3 mhz; 61 kw. Ant 856 ft TL: N43 14 51 W124 06 46. Stereo. Hrs open: Box 180, Coos Bay, 97428. Secondary address: 1270 W. 13th 97423. Phone: (541) 396-2121. Fax: (541) 267-5229. Web Site:www.kshr.com Licensee: Bicoastal Media Licenses III LLC. Format: Hot country.

KWRO(AM)— Feb 1, 1949: 630 khz; 5 kw-D. TL: N43 10 17 W124 11 54. Hrs open: Box 180, Coos Bay, 97428. Secondary address: 1270 W. 13th 97423. Phone: (541) 396-2121. Fax: (541) 267-5229.E-mail: connie@crbradio.com Web Site:www.southcoastradio.com Licensee: Bicoastal Media Licenses III LLC. Group owner: Bicoastal Media L.L.C. (acq 10-16-2003; grpsl). Population served: 61,000 Natl. Rep: McGavren Guild,. Format: News/talk. ♦Connie Williamson, gen mgr.

Corvallis

***KBVR(FM)**— Oct 26, 1965: 88.7 mhz; 340 w. -80 TL: N44 33 50 W123 16 30. Stereo. Hrs open: 24 Oregon State Univ., M.U. East, Snell Hall, Rm. 210, 97331-1618. Phone: (541) 737-2008. Fax: (541) 737-4545.E-mail: info@kbvrfm.com Licensee: State Board of Higher Education. Population served: 45,000 Format: Jazz, urban contemp, alternative rock. Target aud: 15-45; general. Spec prog: Class 4 hrs, Sp 4 hrs, folk 4 hrs wkly. ♦Ian Rose, stn mgr.

KEJO(AM)— August 1955: 1240 khz; 1 kw-U. TL: N44 35 44 W123 14 54. Hrs open: 2840 Marion St. S.E., Albany, 97321-3978. Phone: (541) 926-8628. Fax: (541) 928-1261. Web Site:www.kejoam.com Licensee: Bicoastal Willamette Valley LLC. Group owner: Clear Channel Communications Inc. (acq 7-2-2007; grpsl). Population served: 76,600 Reddy, Begley & McCormick. Format: Talk. Target aud: 40 plus. ♦Gary Grossman, gen mgr; Glenn Nobel, opns mgr, opns mgr, prom mgr, mus dir; Robert Dove, gen sls mgr; Nicole Meltzer, sports cmtr.

KFLY(FM)— Oct 1, 1966: 101.5 mhz; 28 kw. 98 ft TL: N44 35 44 W123 14 54. Stereo. Hrs open: 500 Valley River Dr, suite 350, Box1120, Eugene, 97401. Phone: (541) 485-1120. Fax: (541) 484-5769.E-mail: info@kflyfm.com Web Site:www.kflyfm.com Licensee: Bicoastal Williamette Valley LLC. Format: Hot adult contemp. Target aud: 25-49; general.

KGAL(AM)—See Lebanon

KLOO(AM)— Aug 23, 1947: 1340 khz; 1 kw-U. TL: N44 33 25 W123 16 22. Hrs open: 24 2840 Marion St. S.E., Albany, 97322. Phone: (541) 926-8628. Fax: (541) 928-1261. Web Site:www.news1340.com Licensee: Bicoastal Willamette Valley LLC. Group owner: Clear Channel Communications Inc. (acq 7-2-2007; grpsl). Population served: 43,500 Format: News/talk, sports. News staff: one; News: 83 hrs wkly. Target aud: 35-54. ♦Robert Dove, gen mgr; Larry Rogers, gen sls mgr; Rick Rogers, news dir; Robin O'Kelley, chief of engrg.

KLOO-FM— January 1973: 106.1 mhz; 100 kw. 1,140 ft TL: N44 38 45 W123 16 13. Stereo. Hrs open: 24 Prog sep from AM 2840 Marion St. S.E., Albany, 97322. Phone: (541) 926-8628. Fax: (541) 928-1261. Web Site:www.kloo.com Population served: 650,000 Format: Classic rock. News: 15 hrs wkly. Target aud: 18-54.

***KOAC(AM)**— Dec 7, 1922: 550 khz; 5 kw-U, DA-2. TL: N44 38 12 W123 11 33. Hrs open: 5 AM-midnight 7140 S. W. Macadam Ave., 97219. Phone: (503) 293-1905. Phone: (541) 737-5332. Fax: (503) 293-1919.E-mail: info@opb.org Licensee: Oregon Public Broadcasting. (acq 9-20-93; grpsl; 10-11-93). Population served: 1,000,000 Natl. Network: PRI, NPR, . Format: News/talk. News staff: 5; News: 40 hrs wkly. Target aud: 25-54; college educated with an interest in news & mus. Spec prog: Jazz 12 hrs wkly. ♦Lynne Clendenin, opns mgr; Roger Dominigues, chief of engrg. Co-owned TV: *KOAC-TV affil

KSHO(AM)—See Lebanon

Cottage Grove

KDPM(FM)— Mar 21, 1994: 100.5 mhz; 6 kw. Ant 115 ft TL: N43 44 41 W123 05 29. Hrs open: 24 4222 Commerce St., Suite E, Box 10, Eugene, 97402. Phone: (541) 683-3392. Fax: (541) 338-7067. Licensee: Diamond Peak Investments LLC (acq 8-31-2005; $350,000).

Natl. Rep: Tacher,. Format: Rhythmic Contemp. News: 6 hrs wkly. Target aud: 25-49. ♦Steve Master, gen mgr.

KNND(AM)— August 1953: 1400 khz; 950 w-U. TL: N43 45 43 W123 04 42. Hrs open: 24 321 Main St., 97424. Phone: (541) 942-2468. Fax: (541) 942-5797.E-mail: paul@knnd.com Licensee: Schwartzberg Communications Inc. (acq 5-2-2005; $300,000). Population served: 30,000 Natl. Network: AP Radio, . Dow, Lohnes & Albertson. Format: Country, news/talk. News staff: one; News: 40 hrs wkly. Target aud: General. Spec prog: Relg 3 hrs wkly. ♦Paul Schwartzberg, pres & gen mgr.

Creswell

KUJZ(FM)— Sept 1, 1983: 95.3 mhz; 625 kw. 1,207 ft TL: N44 00 04 W123 06 45. Stereo. Hrs open: 1200 Executive Pkwy., Suite 440, Eugene, 97401. Phone: (541) 484-8500. Fax: (541) 485-0969. Web Site:www.1320thescore.com Licensee: Cumulus Licensing Corp. Group owner: Cumulus Media Inc. (acq 2-29-00;; grpsl). Population served: 200,000 Natl. Network: ESPN Radio, . Natl. Rep: Christal,. Format: Sports. Target aud: 18-34. ♦B.J. O'Brien, gen mgr.

Dallas

KWIP(AM)—Licensed to Dallas. See Salem

Eagle Point

KZZE(FM)— March 1995: 106.3 mhz; 900 w. 1,591 ft TL: N42 21 13 W122 47 05. Hrs open: 3624 Avion Dr., Medford, 97504. Phone: (541) 857-0340. Fax: (541) 857-0326.E-mail: info@kzze.com Web Site:www.kzze.com Licensee: Bicoastal Rogue Valley LLC. Group owner: Clear Channel Communications Inc. (acq 7-2-2007; grpsl). Population served: 175,000 Natl. Rep: Tacher,. Format: Rock/AOR. News staff: one; News: one hr wkly. Target aud: 18-49; rock listeners. ♦Bill Nielsen, pres & gen mgr.

Elgin

KRJT(FM)— 2005: 105.9 mhz; 160 w. Ant 1,916 ft TL: N45 26 26 W117 53 31. Hrs open: 24 Box 907, La Grande, 97850. Secondary address: 2510 E. Cove Ave., La Grande 97850. Phone: (541) 963-4121. Fax: (541) 963-3117. Licensee: Pacific Empire Radio Corp. Natl. Rep: Interep, McGavren Guild,. Format: Oldies. Target aud: 25-54. ♦Mark Bolland, pres; Linda Ashlock, gen mgr.

Enterprise

***KETP(FM)—**Not on air, target date: unknown: 88.7 mhz; 100 w. Ant 1,755 ft TL: N45 23 58 W117 23 16. Hrs open: 7140 S.W. Macadam Ave., Portland, 97219-3099. Phone: (503) 244-9900. Fax: (503) 293-1919. Web Site:www.opb.org Licensee: Oregon Public Broadcasting. ♦Steven M. Bass, CEO & pres.

KWVR(AM)— June 1, 1960: 1340 khz; 1 kw-U. TL: N45 26 14 W117 17 30. Hrs open: 24 220 W. Main St., 97828-1244. Phone: (541) 426-4577. Fax: (541) 426-4578.E-mail: kwvrcarollee@eoni.com Web Site:kwvr.com Licensee: Wallowa Valley Radio LLC (acq 3-1-2009; $650,000 with KWVR-FM Enterprise). Natl. Network: ABC, . Format: News/talk. News staff: news progmg 11 hrs wkly News: 2;. Target aud: General. Spec prog: Farm 4 hrs wkly. ♦Lee D. Perkins, pres, gen mgr, stn mgr; Carol-Lee Perkins, VP, opns mgr; Alyssa Werst, traf mgr; Patrick Channing, II, sls.

KWVR-FM— 1986: 92.1 mhz; 6 kw. Ant -689 ft TL: N45 19 19 W117 13 18. Stereo. Hrs open: 24 220 W. Main St., 97828. Phone: (541) 426-4577. Fax: (541) 426-4578.E-mail: kwvrcarollee@eoni.com Licensee: Wallowa Valley Radio LLC (acq 3-1-2009; $650,000 with KWVR(AM) Enterprise). Natl. Network: ABC, Jones Radio Networks, . Format: Country.

Eugene

KDUK-FM—(Florence, Nov 21, 1983: 104.7 mhz; 63 kw. 2,326 ft TL: N44 17 35 W123 32 15. Stereo. Hrs open: 24 1500 Valley River Dr., Suite 350, 97401. Secondary address: 1345 Olive St. 977401. Phone: (541) 485-1120. Fax: (541) 484-5769.E-mail: info@kduk.com Web Site:www.kduk.com Licensee: Bicoastal Willamette Valley LLC. Group owner: Clear Channel Communications Inc. (acq 7-2-2007; grpsl). Format: CHR/Top-40. ♦Larry Rogers, mktg mgr.

KKNU(FM)—(Springfield-Eugene, Dec 18, 1958: 93.3 mhz; 100 kw horiz, 43 kw vert. Ant 1,296 ft TL: N44 00 04 W123 06 45. Stereo. Hrs open: 24 925 Country Club Rd., Suite 200, 97401. Phone: (541) 484-9400. Fax: (541) 344-9424. Web Site:www.kknu.com Licensee: McKenzie River Broadcasting Co. Inc. Group owner: McKenzie River Broadcasting Group (acq 11-17-92; $1.01 million with KEED(AM) Eugene;12-14-92). Population served: 288,800 Natl. Rep: D & R Radio,. Holland & Knight. Format: New country. Target aud: 25-49; country life group. ♦John Tilson, pres & gen mgr; Dave Wiles, gen sls mgr; Jim Davis, progmg dir.

KKNX(AM)— 1992: 840 khz; 1 kw-D, 220 w-N. TL: N44 05 48 W123 04 18. Stereo. Hrs open: 24 945 Garfield St., 97402. Phone: (541) 342-1012. Fax: (541) 342-6201.E-mail: john@radio84.com Web Site:www.radio84.com Licensee: John S. Mielke, Susan J. Mielke. (acq 7-18-96; $150,000). Population served: 275,000 Natl. Network: AP Radio, . Rgnl rep: Tacher & Co. Wire Svc: AP Format: Oldies. News staff: one; News: 7 hrs wkly. Target aud: 25-64; general. Spec prog: Black 3 hrs wkly. ♦John S. Mielke, pres; John S. Mielke, gen mgr.

***KLCC(FM)—** Feb 17, 1967: 89.7 mhz; 81 kw horiz, 54 kw vert. Ant 1,161 ft TL: N44 00 05 W123 06 48. Stereo. Hrs open: 24 136 W. 8th Ave., 97401-0640. Phone: (541) 463-6000. Fax: (541) 463-6046.E-mail: klcc@klcc.org Web Site:www.klcc.org Licensee: Lane Community College. Population served: 750,000 Natl. Network: NPR, . Arter & Hadden. Format: News/talk, adult contemp. News staff: one; News: 60 hrs wkly. Target aud: 25-54. Spec prog: Sp 5 hrs, folk 12 hrs, Black 3 hrs, blues 4 hrs, world 3 hrs, electronic 6 hrs wkly. ♦Steve Barton, gen mgr; Paula Chan Carpenter, dev dir; Don Hein, progmg dir; Tripp Sommer, news dir.

KLZS(AM)— Sept 7, 1954: 1450 khz; 1 kw-U. TL: N44 04 54 W123 06 34. Hrs open: 24 985 Country Club Rd., Suite 200, 97401. Phone: (541) 343-4100. Fax: (541) 343-0448.E-mail: info@alzx660am.com Web Site:www.alax660am.com Licensee: Churchill Communications LLC Group owner: McKenzie River Broadcasting Group (acq 11-3-2004; $87,500). Natl. Network: CNN Radio, . Format: Progsv talk. News staff: 2; News: 30 hrs wky. Target aud: 25-54.

KMGE(FM)— Oct 10, 1965: 94.5 mhz; 49 kw horiz, 21 kw vert. Ant 1,299 ft TL: N44 00 04 W123 06 45. Stereo. Hrs open: 925 Country Club Rd., Suite 200, 97401. Phone: (541) 484-9400. Fax: (541) 344-9424. Web Site:www.kmge.com Licensee: McKenzie River Broadcasting Co. Inc. (acq 3-87; $950,000;9-29-86). Population served: 750,000 Format: Adult contemp. Target aud: 18-49. ♦John Tilson, pres; Jeff Baird, progmg dir.

KNRQ-FM— Dec 26, 1958: 97.9 mhz; 100 kw. 1,230 ft TL: N44 00 08 W123 06 50. Stereo. Hrs open: Prog sep from AM 1200 Executive Pkwy., Suite 440, 97405. Phone: (541) 284-8500. Fax: (541) 284-8500.E-mail: info@nrq.com Web Site:www.nrq.com Format: Alternative. ♦Chris Crowley, progmg dir.

KODZ(FM)— November 1968: 99.1 mhz; 100 kw. 1,945 ft TL: N44 06 56 W122 59 56. Stereo. Hrs open: Prog sep from AM 500 Valley River Dr., suite 350, 97401. Phone: (541) 485-1120. Fax: (541) 484-5769. Population served: 250,000 Format: Classic Hits / AC. Target aud: 25-54; working women. ♦Larry Rogers, mktg mgr.

KOPB(AM)— Sept 19, 1947: 1600 khz; 5 kw-D, 1 kw-N, DA-N. TL: N44 03 05 W123 03 48. Hrs open: 7140 S.W. Macadam Ave., Portland, 97219-3099. Phone: (503) 293-9900. Fax: (503) 293-1919. Web Site:www.opb.org Licensee: Oregon Public Broadcasting (acq 2-20-2008; $475,000). Natl. Network: NPR, . Ore. Pub. Bcstg Radio Net. Format: News/talk. ♦Steven M. Bass, pres.

KORE(AM)—See Springfield-Eugene

KPNW(AM)— July 22, 1968: 1120 khz; 50 kw-U, DA-1. TL: N43 57 24 W123 02 10. Hrs open: 24 1500 Valley River Dr., suite 350, 97401. Phone: (541) 485-1120. Fax: (541) 484-5769. Web Site:www.kpnw.com Licensee: Bicoastal Willamette Valley LLC. Group owner: Clear Channel Communications Inc. (acq 7-2-2007; grpsl). Population served: 250,000 Format: News/talk. News staff: 2. Target aud: 35 plus; upper income, conservative. Spec prog: Portland Trail Blazers. ♦Robert Dove, gen mgr & mktg mgr.

***KRVM(AM)—** Nov 9, 1949: 1280 khz; 5 kw-D, 1.5 kw-N, DA-N. TL: N44 06 03 W123 03 06. Hrs open: 24 P.M.B. 237, 1574 Cobug Rd., 97401. Phone: (541) 687-3370. Fax: (541) 687-3573.E-mail: info@krvm.org Web Site:www.krvm.org Licensee: Lane County School District 4J. (acq 1-10-97). Natl. Network: NPR, . Natl. Rep: McGavren Guild,. Format: Talk. ♦Randy Larson, gen mgr.

***KRVM-FM—** Dec 8, 1947: 91.9 mhz; 1.1 kw. Ant 745 ft TL: N44 00 08 W123 06 50. Stereo. Hrs open: 24 P.M.B. 237, 1574 Cobug Rd., 97401. Phone: (541) 697-3370. Fax: (541) 687-3573.E-mail: info@krvm.org Web Site:www.krvm.org Licensee: Lane County School District No. 4J. Population served: 200,000 Natl. Network: NPR, . Format: AAA, AOR, blues. Target aud: General. Spec prog: Black 2 hrs, country one hr, folk 3 hrs, Native American 2 hrs wkly.

KSCR(AM)— June 12, 1962: 1320 khz; 1 kw-D, 40 w-N. TL: N44 05 25 W123 06 43. Hrs open: 1200 Executive Pkwy., Suite 440, 97401. Phone: (541) 485-5846. Fax: (541) 485-0969. Licensee: Cumulus Licensing Corp. Group owner: Cumulus Media Inc. (acq 2-29-00; grpsl). Population served: 200,000 Natl. Network: ESPN Radio, . Rgnl. Network: Christal. Natl. Rep: Christal,. Format: Sports. Target aud: 18-44; general. ♦Steve Ries, gen mgr.

KUGN(AM)— July 4, 1946: 590 khz; 5 kw-D, 5 kw-N, DA-N. TL: N44 05 48 W123 04 18. Stereo. Hrs open: 24 1200 Executive Pkwy., Suite 440, 97405. Phone: (541) 284-8500. Fax: (541) 284-8500.E-mail: info@kugn.com Web Site:www.kugn.com Licensee: Cumulus Licensing Corp. Group owner: Cumulus Media Inc. (acq 6-15-00; grpsl). Population served: 220,000 Natl. Network: CBS, . Dow, Lohnes & Albertson. Wire Svc: NWS (National Weather Service) Format: News/talk. News staff: 6; News: 28 hrs wkly. Target aud: 30-65; general. ♦Bill Bradley, gen mgr; Troy Murphy, gen sls mgr; Wendy Wintrode, prom dir; Jerry Allen, progmg dir; Rick Little, news dir; Cory Schruth, chief of engrg.

***KWAX(FM)—** Apr 4, 1951: 91.1 mhz; 21.5 kw horiz, 12.5 kw vert. Ant 1,214 ft TL: N44 00 04 W123 06 45. Stereo. Hrs open: 24 75 Centennial Loop, 97401. Phone: (541) 345-0800.E-mail: info@kwax.com Web Site:www.kwax.com Licensee: State Board of Higher Education. Population served: 267,000 Akin, Gump, Strauss, Hauer & Feld. Format: Class. News: 7 hrs wkly. Target aud: 35 plus. ♦Paul Bjornstad, gen mgr.

***KWVA(FM)—** May 27, 1993: 88.1 mhz; 500 w. -56 ft TL: N44 00 07 W123 06 53. Hrs open: 24 Box 3157, ERB Memoral Union, Univ. of Oregon, 97403. Secondary address: Univ. of Oregon, EMU, Suite M-112 97403. Phone: (541) 346-4091. Fax: (541) 346-0648.E-mail: kwva@gladstone.uoregon.edu Web Site:gladstone.uoregon.edu/~kwva Licensee: Associated Students of University of Oregon. (acq 6-29-92; 7-20-92). Population served: 275,000 Format: Div, progsv, urban contemp. News: 12 hrs wkly. Target aud: 3-30; college, alternative, underrepresented, varying educ levels & music lover. Spec prog: Asian 4 hrs, Black 4 hrs, jazz 6 hrs, country 3 hrs, Japanese 2 hrs, Sp 6 hrs wkly. ♦Charlotte Nisser, gen mgr, opns dir, dev dir; Michael Zarkesh, prom dir; Anna Jensen, progmg dir.

KZEL-FM— Apr 22, 1962: 96.1 mhz; 100 kw. 1,093 ft TL: N44 00 04 W123 06 45. Stereo. Hrs open: 1200 Executive Way, ste 440, 97401. Phone: (541) 284-8500. Fax: (541) 485-4070.E-mail: kteige@cumuluseugene.com Web Site:www.96kzel.com/main Licensee: Cumulus Licensing Corp. Group owner: Cumulus Media Inc. (acq 2-29-00; grpsl). Population served: 221,000 Natl. Network: Westwood One, . Natl. Rep: Christal,. Format: Classic Rock. Target aud: 18-44. ♦Steve Ries, gen mgr; Russ Davidson, opns mgr.

Florence

KCFM(AM)— May 5, 1985: 1250 khz; 1 kw-D, 68 w-N. TL: N44 00 38 W124 05 37. Hrs open: 24 Box 20000, 97439. Secondary address: Radio Center Bldg., 4480 Hwy. 101 N. 97439. Phone: (541) 997-9136. Fax: (541) 997-9165.E-mail: radioway@kcst.com Web Site:www.kcst.com Licensee: Coast Broadcasting Co. Inc. (acq 12-18-97). Format: Music of your life. Target aud: 55+. ♦John Thompson, gen mgr.

KCST-FM— October 1992: 106.9 mhz; 2.3 kw. 508 ft TL: N43 57 19 124 04 26. Stereo. Hrs open: 24 Box 20,000, 97439. Secondary address: 4480 Hwy 101 N., Radio Centre Bldg. 97439. Phone: (541) 997-9136. Fax: (541) 997-9165.E-mail: radioway@kcst.com Web Site:www.kcst.com Licensee: Coast Broadcasting Co. Inc. Natl. Network: ABC, . Rgnl rep: Tacher Company Wire Svc: AP Format: Adult contemp, country, oldies. Target aud: 35+.

KDUK-FM—Licensed to Florence. See Eugene

***KLFO(FM)—** Aug 16, 1999: 88.1 mhz; 250 w. Ant 548 ft TL: N43 57 26 W124 04 26. Stereo. Hrs open: 24
Rebroadcasts KLCC(FM) Eugene 100%.
136 W. 8th Ave., 4000 E. 30th Ave., Eugene, 97401. Phone: (541) 463-6000. Fax: (541) 463-6046.E-mail: klcc@klcc.org Web Site:www.klcc.org Licensee: Lane Community College. Format: Var/div, jazz, news. ♦Steve Barton, gen mgr & stn mgr; Paula Chan Carpenter, dev dir; Don Hein, progmg dir; Chris Heck, chief of engrg.

***KWVZ(FM)—** 2001: 91.5 mhz; 150 w. Ant 548 ft TL: N43 57 26 W124 04 26. Hrs open:
Rebroadcasts KWAX(FM) Eugene 100%.

c/o KWAX(FM), 75 Centennial Loop, Eugene, 97401. Phone: (541) 345-0800.E-mail: info@kwax.com Licensee: Oregon State Board of Higher Education. Format: Classical.

Garibaldi

KDEP(FM)— 2001: 105.5 mhz; 320 w. Ant 1,181 ft TL: N45 27 59 W123 55 11. Hrs open: 1000 Main Ave. N., Ste 5, Tillamook, 97141-9272. Phone: (503) 842-3888. Fax: (503) 842-5640.E-mail: tommy@coast105.com Licensee: Alexandra Communications Inc. (acq 9-21-2005; $250,000). Format: 60's, 70's, 80's mix. ◆Tom Hodgins, gen mgr; Jim Bock, gen sls mgr; Tommy Steggell, progmg dir & mus dir.

Gladstone

KRYP(FM)— May 10, 1981: 93.1 mhz; 1.55 kw. Ant 1,269 ft TL: N45 29 20 W122 41 40. Stereo. Hrs open: 6400 S.E. Lake Rd., Suite 350, Portland, 97222. Phone: (503) 786-0600. Fax: (503) 786-1551. Web Site:www.931elrey.com Licensee: Salem Media of Oregon Inc. (acq 1-19-2005). Population served: 45,000 Format: Rgnl Mexican. ◆Dennis Hayes, gen mgr.

Gleneden Beach

*KOGL(FM)— 2008: 89.3 mhz; 210 w. Ant 73 ft TL: N44 53 08 W124 00 51. Hrs open:
Rebroadcasts KOPB-FM Portland 100%.
7140 S.W. Macadam Ave., Portland, 97219. Phone: (503) 293-1905. Fax: (503) 293-1919. Web Site:www.opb.org Licensee: Oregon Public Broadcasting. Ore. Pub. Bcstg Radio Net. ◆Steve Bass, gen mgr.

*KQOC(FM)— June 1, 2008: 88.1 mhz; 8.8 kw. Ant 928 ft TL: N44 45 23 W124 02 52. Hrs open:
Rebroadcasts KQAC(FM) Portland 100%.
KBPS Public Radio, 515 N.E. 15th Ave., Portland, 97232. Phone: (503) 943-5828. Fax: (503) 802-9456. Web Site:www.allclassical.org Licensee: KBPS Public Radio Foundation. Format: Classical. ◆James Draznin, pres.

KSHL(FM)— December 1992: 97.5 mhz; 17 kw. 843 ft TL: N44 45 22 W124 02 57. Stereo. Hrs open: 24 Box 1180, 131 N.E. 15th St., Newport, 97365. Phone: (541) 265-6477. Fax: (541) 265-6478.E-mail: info@kshl.com Licensee: Stephanie Linn. Rgnl rep: McGavren Guild Format: Modern country. News: 2 hrs wkly. Target aud: 25-55; general. ◆Dick Linn, gen mgr, opns mgr; Stephanie Linn, pres & gen sls mgr.

Gold Beach

KGBR(FM)— December 1984: 92.7 mhz; 265 w. 2700 TL: N42 23 50 W124 21 50. (CP: 42.06 kw, ant 2,700 ft. TL: N42 23 44 W124 21 47). Stereo. Hrs open: 24 Box 787, 97444. Phone: (541) 247-7211. Phone: (541) 247-7418. Fax: (541) 247-4155.E-mail: info@kgbr.com Web Site:www.kgbr.com Licensee: St. Marie Communications Inc. (acq 3-87; $60,000; 11-16-87). Population served: 20,000 Natl. Rep: Tacher,. Fisher, Wayland, Cooper, Leader & Zaragoza. Format: Adult contemp. News staff: 2; News: 4 hrs wkly. Target aud: 25-54. ◆Dale L. St. Marie, gen mgr.

Gold Hill

KRWQ(FM)— Aug 11, 1980: 100.3 mhz; 30 kw. Ant 991 ft TL: N42 27 07 W123 03 20. Stereo. Hrs open: 24 3624 Avion Dr., Medford, 97504. Phone: (541) 772-4170. Fax: (541) 858-5416. Web Site:www.krwq.com Licensee: Bicoastal Rogue Valley LLC. Group owner: Clear Channel Communications Inc. (acq 7-2-2007; grpsl). Population served: 250,000 Natl. Rep: Tacher,. Format: Contemp country. News staff: one. Target aud: 18-54. ◆Bill Nielsen, gen mgr.

Grants Pass

*KAGI(AM)— Dec 16, 1939: 930 khz; 5 kw-D, 123 w-N. TL: N42 25 24 W123 20 04. Hrs open: 24 hrs Jefferson Public Radio, 1250 Siskiyou Blvd., Ashland, 97520. Phone: (541) 552-6301. Fax: (541) 552-8565.E-mail: info@ijpr.org Web Site:www.ijpr.org Licensee: The State of Oregon, acting by and through the State Board of Higher Education, for the benefit of Southern Oregon University. (acq 7-11-91;7-29-91). Population served: 50,000 Natl. Network: PRI, NPR, . Ernest Sanchez. Format: News, info. Spec prog: Sp 6 hrs wkly. ◆Mitchell Christian, CFO; Bryon Lambert, opns dir; Paul Westhelle,

dev dir, mktg dir; Ronald Kramer, CEO, gen mgr & progmg dir; Eric Alan, mus dir; Darin Ransom, engrg dir.

KAJO(AM)— Aug 15, 1957: 1270 khz; 10 kw-D, 48 w-N. TL: N42 26 16 W123 21 27. Stereo. Hrs open: 24 888 Rogue River Hwy., 97527. Phone: (541) 476-6608. Fax: (541) 476-4018.E-mail: kajo@kajo.com Web Site:www.kajo.com Licensee: Grants Pass Broadcasting Corp. Population served: 80,000 Natl. Network: AP Radio, . Natl. Rep: Tacher Wire Svc: AP Format: Adult standards, news/talk. News staff: 2; News: 22 hrs wkly. Target aud: 35 plus. Spec prog: Gospel one hr, relg 8 hrs wkly. ◆Matt Wilson, CEO; Carl Wilson, CFO; Brian Diatte, gen sls mgr; Marty Sether, prom dir, progmg dir; Jill Hamm, mus dir, prom; Joe Torsistano, chief of engrg.

*KAPK(FM)— April 1998: 91.1 mhz; 250 w. 13 ft TL: N42 27 44 W123 18 33. Hrs open: Box 3206, American Family Radio, Tupelo, MS, 38803. Phone: (662) 844-8888. Fax: (662) 842-6791. Web Site:www.afr.net Licensee: American Family Association. Group owner: American Family Radio Format: Inspirational Christian. ◆Marvin Sanders, gen mgr.

KROG(FM)— Oct 2, 1981: 96.9 mhz; 25 kw. 2,058 ft TL: N42 22 56 W123 16 29. (CP: 74 kw). Stereo. Hrs open: 24 511 Rossanley Dr., Medford, 97501. Phone: (541) 772-0322. Fax: (541) 772-4233. Web Site:www.969therogue.com Licensee: Opus Broadcasting Systems Inc. (group owner; acq 3-6-91; $63,634 with KRTA(AM) Medford;7-29-91). Natl. Rep: Tacher,. Format: New rock. News staff: one. Target aud: 25-54; affluent middle America. ◆Dean Flock, gen mgr; Brian Fraser, opns dir, sls dir.

Gresham

*KMHD(FM)— January 1984: 89.1 mhz; 7.9 kw. Ant 1,433 ft TL: N45 30 58 W122 43 59. Stereo. Hrs open: 24 26000 S.E. Stark St., 97030. Phone: (503) 491-7333. Fax: (503) 491-6999.E-mail: station-manager@knhd.fm Web Site:www.kmhd.org Licensee: Mt. Hood Community College. Population served: 1,850,000 Natl. Network: NPR, . Garvey, Schubert & Barer. Format: Jazz/blues. News: 5 hrs wkly. Target aud: 35-65; music lovers. Spec prog: Blues 15 hrs, news 5 hrs wkly. ◆Doug Sweet, gen mgr; Dan Gurin, opns dir; Calvin Walker, dev dir; Greg Gomez, mus dir.

KSZN(AM)—Licensed to Gresham. See Portland

Harbeck-Fruitdale

KLDR(FM)— May 3, 1991: 98.3 mhz; 185 w. 2,096 ft TL: N42 22 56 W123 16 29. Stereo. Hrs open: 24 888 Rogue River Hwy., Grants Pass, 97527. Phone: (541) 474-7292. Fax: (541) 474-7300.E-mail: kldr@kldr.com Web Site:www.kldr.com Licensee: Grants Pass Broadcasting Corp. Population served: 80,000 Natl. Network: AP Network News, . Natl. Rep: Tacher,. Format: Adult contemp. News staff: 3; News: 10 hrs wkly. Target aud: 25-54; Middle Age demo- actually a wide range in listeners. ◆Carl Wilson, pres, CFO; Matt Wilson, CEO & gen mgr; Brian Diatte, gen sls mgr; Marty Sether, progmg dir.

Hermiston

KOHU(AM)— Feb 6, 1956: 1360 khz; 4.3 kw-D, 500 w-N, DA-N. TL: N45 51 57 W119 18 45. Hrs open: 24 Box 145, 80404 Cooney Ln., 97838. Phone: (541) 567-6500. Fax: (541) 567-6068.E-mail: kqfm@eotnet.net Licensee: Westend Radio L.L.C. (acq 4-16-97; with co-located FM). Population served: 30,000 Natl. Network: ABC, . Natl. Rep: Farmakis,. Rgnl rep: Target. Format: C&W. News staff: one; News: 10 hrs wkly. Target aud: General; two county loc audience. Spec prog: Sp 6 hrs wkly. ◆Angela Pursel, gen mgr, stn mgr, sls VP, gen sls mgr, farm dir, farm dir; Jeff Walker, opns dir, prom dir, progmg dir; Adam Russell, news dir; Richard Wilson, engrg dir; Pam Rebman, traf mgr.

KQFM(FM)— Sept 18, 1978: 100.5 mhz; 5.3 kw. Ant 298 ft TL: N45 51 57 W119 18 38. Stereo. Hrs open: 24 Prog sep from AM Box 145, 80404 Cooney Ln., 97838. Phone: (541) 567-6500. Fax: (541) 567-6068.E-mail: kqfm@eotnet.net Licensee: Westend Radio L.L.C. Population served: 175,000 Natl. Network: ABC, . Format: Pure gold, adult contemp. News staff: one; News: 5 hrs wkly. Target aud: 25-54. ◆Ron Hughes, gen mgr & prom VP; Jeff Walker, mus dir; Pam Rebman, traf mgr; Angela Pursel, farm dir.

Hillsboro

KUIK(AM)— 1954: 1360 khz; 5 kw-U, DA-N. TL: N45 29 13 W122 54 31. Hrs open: 24 Box 566, 97123. Secondary address: 3355 N.E. Cornell Rd. 97124. Phone: (503) 640-1360. Fax: (503) 640-6108.E-mail: dave@kuik.com Web Site:www.kuik.com Licensee: Westside Radio

Inc. (group owner; (acq 7-8-2009; $1 million). Population served: 455,000 Agrinet David Tillotson. Wire Svc: AP Format: News/talk, sports, Sp. News staff: one; News: 24 hrs wkly. Target aud: 25-54; Seekers of locally produced unique programming. Spec prog: Relg 2 hrs, Sp 21 hrs wkly. ◆Spencer Rubin, pres; Donna McCoun, sr VP; Don McCoun, gen mgr; Paul Warren, opns mgr.

Hood River

KCGB-FM— Dec 4, 1978: 105.5 mhz; 3 kw. Ant -460 ft TL: N45 42 07 W121 32 10. Hrs open: Box 360, 97031. Secondary address: 1190 22nd St. 97031. Phone: (541) 386-1511. Fax: (541) 386-7155. Licensee: Bicoastal Media Licenses IV LLC. (acq 12-1-2007; grpsl). Population served: 14,934 Natl. Network: ABC, . Format: Hot adult contemp. Target aud: 18-49. ◆Jeff Skye, progmg dir, farm dir; Gwen Troutner, traf mgr; Mark Bailey, local news ed.

*KHRV(FM)—Not on air, target date: unknown: 88.1 mhz; 26 w. Ant 741 ft TL: N45 39 45 W121 28 14. Hrs open: Oregon Public Broadcasting, 7140 S.W. Macadam Ave., Portland, 97219. Phone: (541) 293-1905. Fax: (503) 293-1919. Web Site:www.opb.org Licensee: Oregon Public Broadcasting. Ore. Pub. Bcstg Radio Net. ◆Steve Bass, gen mgr.

KIHR(AM)— Oct 17, 1950: 1340 khz; 1 kw-U. TL: N45 42 06 W121 32 05. Hrs open: 24 Box 360, 97031. Secondary address: 1190 22nd St. 97031. Phone: (541) 386-1511. Fax: (541) 386-7155.E-mail: info@kihrk105.com Web Site:www.kihrk105.com Licensee: Bicoastal Media Licenses IV LLC. (group owner; (acq 12-1-2007; grpsl). Population served: 18,334 Garvey Schubert Barer. Format: C&W. News staff: 3; News: 12 hrs wkly. Target aud: 25-54. ◆Kenneth R. Dennis, CEO; Gary Grossman, gen mgr, stn mgr; Rick Cavagnaro, sls VP & sls dir; Jeff Skye, mus dir, disc jockey; Mark Bailey, news dir, local news ed, edit dir, sports cmtr; Jim Keightley, engrg dir, chief of engrg; Gwen Troutner, traf mgr; Ismael Pinedo, spanish dir.

*KQHR(FM)— January 2002: 90.1 mhz; 44 w. Ant 1,105 ft TL: N45 43 20 W121 26 16. Hrs open: 24
Rebroadcasts KBPS-FM Portland 100%.
515 N.E. 15th Ave., Portland, 97323. Phone: (503) 943-5828. Fax: (503) 802-9456.E-mail: musicinfo@allclassical.org Web Site:www.allclassical.org Licensee: KBPS Public Radio Foundation. Population served: 30,000 Format: Classical. News: 5 hrs wkly. ◆Suzanne White, gen mgr.

John Day

KJDY(AM)— Dec 13, 1963: 1400 khz; 1 kw-U. TL: N44 25 17 W118 57 09. Hrs open: 24
Rebroadcasts KJDY-FM Canyon City 100%.
413 N.W. Bridge St., ., 97845. Phone: (541) 575-1400. Fax: (541) 575-2313.E-mail: kjdy@centurytel.net Licensee: Blue Mountain Broadcasting Co. (acq 11-87; $150,000; 11-9-87). Population served: 9,500 Natl. Network: ABC, . Rgnl rep: Tacher J. Dominic Monahan. Format: C&W. News staff: one. ◆Phil Gray, gen mgr; Patricia Webb, gen sls mgr; Kelly Workman, progmg dir; J. Kelly Carlson, engrg VP, chief of engrg.

*KOJD(FM)—Not on air, target date: unknown: 89.7 mhz; 900 w. Ant -128 ft TL: N44 26 03 W118 57 28. Hrs open: Oregon Public Broadcasting, 7140 S.W. Macadam Ave., Portland, 97219-3099. Phone: (503) 293-1905. Fax: (503) 293-1919. Web Site:www.opb.org Licensee: Oregon Public Broadcasting. Ore. Pub. Bcstg Radio Net. ◆Steven M. Bass, CEO & pres.

Jordan Valley

*KGCL(FM)— 2005: 90.9 mhz; 21.5 kw vert. Ant 2,161 ft TL: N43 00 26 W116 42 23. Stereo. Hrs open: 24 2351 Sunset Blvd., Suite 170-218, Rocklin, CA, 95765. Phone: (916) 251-1600. Fax: (916) 251-1650.E-mail: info@air1.com Web Site:www.air1.com Licensee: Educational Media Foundation. Group owner: EMF Broadcasting. Natl. Network: Air 1, . Shaw Pittman. Format: Contemp Christian. News staff: 3. Target aud: 18-35; Judeo-Christian, female. ◆Richard Jenkins, pres; Mike Novak, VP; Keith Whipple, dev dir; David Pierce, progmg mgr; Ed Lenane, news dir; Sam Wallington, engrg dir; Karen Johnson, news rptr.

Junction City

*KPIJ(FM)— 2008: 88.5 mhz; 550 w. Ant 2,313 ft TL: N44 16 44 W123 35 38. Hrs open:
Rebroadcasts KAWZ(FM) Twin Falls, ID 100%.
Box 391, Twin Falls, ID, 83303. Secondary address: 4002 N. 3300 E., Twin Falls, ID 83301. Fax: (208) 734-6633. Fax: (208) 736-1958. Web

Site:www.csnradio.com Licensee: CSN International. Natl. Network: CSN, . Format: Christian praise & worship, Bible teaching. ♦Mike Stocklin, gen mgr.

KXOR(AM)— 1998: 660 khz; 10 kw-D, 75 w-N. TL: N44 12 36 W123 10 56. Hrs open: 24 895 Country Club Rd., Suite A200, Eugene, 97401. Phone: (541) 343-4100. Fax: (541) 343-0448.E-mail: info@alax660am.com Web Site:www.lax660.com Licensee: Churchill Communications LLC. Group owner: Pamplin Broadcasting (acq 1-14-2005; $550,000). Population served: 270,000 Natl. Rep: Univision Radio National Sales,. Rgnl rep: Julie Schneidar & Paul Danitz Wire Svc: AP Format: Sp. News staff: 1; News: 6am-6pm on the hour. Target aud: 25-54; 18-49. ♦Paul Danitz, gen mgr, progmg dir, mus dir; Phil Polter, gen sls mgr.

Keizer

KYKN(AM)— 1951: 1430 khz; 5 kw-U. TL: N44 55 36 W122 57 19. Hrs open: 24 Box 1430, Salem, 97308. Secondary address: 4205 Cherry Ave. N.E. 97303. Phone: (503) 390-3014. Fax: (503) 390-3728.E-mail: mfrith@kykn.com Web Site:www.kykn.com Licensee: Willamette Broadcasting Co. Inc. (acq 10-27-01). Population served: 500,000 Natl. Network: Premiere Radio Networks, Talk Radio Network, Westwood One, Salem Radio Network, . Natl. Rep: McGavren Guild,. Rgnl rep: McGavern Guild Format: News/talk. News staff: 2; News: 20 hrs wkly. Target aud: 25-64; $50-90K income, homeowners, white collar. Spec prog: LOCAL TALK TRAFFIC/ WEATHER/ NEWS..RUSH LIMBAUGH, SEAN HANNITY, LAURA INGRAHAM, BILL POST, GLENN BECK. ♦Michael Frith, gen mgr & gen sls mgr.

Klamath Falls

KAGO(AM)— July 19, 1923: 1150 khz; 5 kw-D, 1 kw-N, DA-N. TL: N42 12 56 W121 47 51. Hrs open: Box 339, 97601. Phone: (541) 882-8833. Fax: (541) 882-8836. Licensee: New Northwest Broadcasters LLC (group owner; acq 3-16-99; $1.6 million with co-located FM). Population served: 100,000 Natl. Network: CBS, . Dan Alpert. Format: News/talk. Target aud: 35-65; upscale, professional. Spec prog: Farm 3 hrs, Sp 5 hrs wkly. ♦Rob Siems, gen mgr; Brian Mobley, opns mgr.

KAGO-FM— Oct 15, 1973: 99.5 mhz; 60 kw. 360 ft TL: N42 12 56 W121 47 56. (CP: 100 kw, ant 994 ft. TL: N42 13 08 W121 48 56). Stereo. Hrs open: Box 339, 97601. Phone: (541) 882-8833. Fax: (541) 882-8836. Licensee: New Northwest Broadcasters LLC Natl. Network: CBS, . Format: Classic rock. ♦Rob Siems, gen mgr & prom dir.

KFEG(FM)— 2002: 104.7 mhz; 51 kw. Ant 645 ft TL: N42 13 24 W121 49 02. Hrs open: 24 Box 938, 97601. Phone: (541) 850-5242. Fax: (541) 884-2845.E-mail: sales@theeagle1047.fm Web Site:www.theeagle1047.fm Licensee: Cove Road Publishing LLC (acq 3-1-01). Format: Classic rock. Target aud: 25-54. ♦Bill Ifft, pres & gen mgr.

KFLS(AM)— 1946: 1450 khz; 1 kw-U. TL: N42 12 19 W121 46 04. Stereo. Hrs open: 24 Box 1450, 1338 Oregon Ave., 97601. Phone: (541) 882-4656. Fax: (541) 884-2845.E-mail: bob@klamathradio.com Web Site:www.klamathradio.com Licensee: Wynne Enterprises LLC. (group owner; (acq 1-1-71). Population served: 50,000 Natl. Network: ABC, . Rgnl rep: Tacher. Format: News/talk, sports. Target aud: 35 plus. ♦Robert Wynne, CEO, chmn, pres, gen mgr & gen sls mgr.

***KKLJ(FM)**— Mar 14, 2003: 88.9 mhz; 110 w. Ant 2,184 ft TL: N42 04 05 W121 58 13. Stereo. Hrs open: 24
Rebroadcasts KLVR(FM) Middletown, CA 100%.
2351 Sunset Blvd., Suite 170-218, Rocklin, CA, 95765. Phone: (916) 251-1600. Fax: (916) 251-1650.E-mail: klove@klove.com Web Site:www.klove.com Licensee: Educational Media Foundation. Group owner: EMF Broadcasting. Natl. Network: K-Love, . Shaw Pittman. Format: Contemp Christian. News staff: 3. Target aud: 25-44; Judeo Christian, female. ♦Richard Jenkins, pres; Mike Novak, VP; Lloyd Parker, gen mgr; Keith Whipple, dev dir; Eric Allen, natl sls mgr; David Pierce, progmg mgr; Ed Lenane, news dir; Sam Wallington, engrg dir; Arthur Vassar, traf mgr.

KKRB(FM)— Apr 1, 1983: 106.9 mhz; 100 kw. Ant 1,200 ft TL: N42 13 26 W121 49 02. Stereo. Hrs open: Box 1450, 97601. Secondary address: 1338 Oregon Ave. 97601. Phone: (541) 882-4656. Fax: (541) 884-2845.E-mail: bob@klamathradio.com Licensee: Wynne Enterprises LLC. Format: Adult contemp, top 40.

KLAD(AM)— September 1955: 960 khz; 5 kw-U. TL: N42 09 42 W121 39 01. Hrs open: Box 339, 97601. Secondary address: 4509 S. 6th St., Suite 201 97601. Phone: (541) 882-8833. Fax: (541) 882-8836. Licensee: New Northwest Broadcasters LLC (group owner; (acq 10-20-98; grpsl). Population served: 50,000 Format: Sports. Target aud: 25-54; mature with spendable income. ♦Rob Siems, gen mgr & opns mgr; Aaron Bentson, progmg dir; James Boyd, chief of engrg.

KLAD-FM— July 19, 1974: 92.5 mhz; 63 kw. Ant 2,188 ft TL: N42 05 51 W121 37 58. Hrs open: Box 339, 97601. Secondary address: 4509 S. 6th St., Suite 201 97601. Phone: (541) 882-8833. Fax: (541) 882-8836. Natl. Network: ABC, . Rgnl rep: Allied Radio Partners. Dow, Lohnes & Albertson. Format: Country. ♦Rob Siems, gen mgr & disc jockey.

***KLMF(FM)**— 2002: 88.5 mhz; 95 w. Ant 2,162 ft TL: N42 05 50 W121 37 59. Hrs open: Jefferson Public Radio, 1250 Siskiyou Blvd., Ashland, 97520. Phone: (541) 552-6301. Phone: (541) 552-8565.E-mail: info@ijpr.org Web Site:www.ijpr.org Licensee: The State of Oregon, acting by and through the State Board of Higher Education, for the benefit of Southern Oregon University. Natl. Network: NPR, PRI, . Ernest Sanchez. Wire Svc: AP Format: Class, news. News staff: one; News: 35 hrs wkly. ♦Mitchell Christian, CFO; Ronald Kramer, CEO & gen mgr; Bryon Lambert, opns dir; Paul Westhelle, dev dir.

KRAT(FM)—(Altamont, 1991: 97.7 mhz; 22 kw. Ant 1,712 ft TL: N42 10 06 W122 09 06. Stereo. Hrs open: Box 235, 97601. Phone: (541) 884-8167. Fax: (541) 884-8226. Licensee: George J. Wade. Format: Oldies.

***KSKF(FM)**— Nov 10, 1989: 90.9 mhz; 2 kw. 2,253 ft TL: N42 05 50 W121 37 59. Stereo. Hrs open: 5 AM-2 AM 1250 Siskiyou Blvd., Ashland, 97520. Phone: (541) 552-6301. Fax: (541) 552-8565.E-mail: info@ijpr.org Web Site:ww.ijpr.org Licensee: The State of Oregon, acting by and through the State Board of Higher Education. Natl. Network: NPR, PRI, . Ernest Sanchez. Format: AAA, jazz, news. News staff: one; News: 45 hrs wkly. Target aud: General. Spec prog: Blues 6 hrs, folk 3 hrs, pub affrs 7 hrs wkly. ♦Mitchell Christian, CFO; Ronald Kramer, CEO & gen mgr; Bryon Lambert, opns dir; Paul Westhelle, dev dir; Jessica Robinson, news dir, disc jockey.

***KTEC(FM)**— Dec 19, 1950: 89.5 mhz; 250 w. 184 ft TL: N42 12 59 W121 47 57. (CP: Ant 597 ft. TL: N42 13 26 W121 49 02). Stereo. Hrs open: 9 AM-midnight Oregon Institute of Technology, Box 2009, 3201 Campus Dr., 97601. Phone: (541) 885-1840. Phone: (541) 885-1841. Fax: (541) 885-1857.E-mail: ktec@oit.edu Web Site:www.oit.edu/-ktec Licensee: Oregon State Board of Higher Education. Population served: 20,000 Format: Freeform (diversified). News staff: one; News: 5 hrs wkly. Target aud: 15 plus; eclectic, free thinking, progsv individuals. Spec prog: American Indian one hr, Black 3 hrs, folk 3 hrs, Sp 3 hrs, world mus 6 hrs, electronic 9 hrs wkly. ♦Carola Roufs, gen mgr; Jake Byron, progmg mgr; Len Simpson, mus dir.

La Grande

***KEOL(FM)**— October 1973: 91.7 mhz; 310 w. -750 ft TL: N45 19 16 W118 05 26. Stereo. Hrs open: 24 One Univ. Blvd., 1410 L Ave., 97850. Phone: (541) 962-3698.E-mail: info@keolfm.com Web Site:www.eou.edu/keol Licensee: Oregon State Board of Higher Education. Population served: 20,000 Format: CHR, div, progsv. Target aud: 14-25; college students & loc youth. Spec prog: Black 12 hrs, class 4 hrs, jazz 6 hrs, reggae 7 hrs wkly. ♦Dave McDermot, stn mgr.

KLBM(AM)— 1938: 1450 khz; 1 kw-U. TL: N45 19 45 W118 04 00. Hrs open: 24
Rebroadcasts KBKR(AM) Baker City 100%.
Box 907, 97850. Secondary address: 2510 E. Cove Ave. 97850. Phone: (541) 963-4121. Phone: (541) 963-4122. Fax: (541) 963-3117.E-mail: supertalk@eoni.com Licensee: Pacific Empire Radio Corp. (group owner; acq 7-19-2004; grpsl). Population served: 40,000 Natl. Network: Westwood One, ABC, . Rgnl rep: McGavren Guild Denise Moline, P.C. Format: News/talk. News staff: one; News: 25 hrs wkly. Target aud: 25-54. Spec prog: Farm 2 hrs wkly. ♦Mark Bolland, pres; Steve Ryner, gen mgr; Bobby Hollowwa, progmg dir.

***KTVR-FM**— 2004: 90.3 mhz; 400 w. Ant 2,519 ft TL: N45 18 33 W117 43 54. Hrs open: 7140 S.W. Macadam Ave., Portland, 97219. Phone: (503) 293-1905. Fax: (503) 293-1919.E-mail: info@opb.org Web Site:www.opb.org Licensee: Oregon Public Broadcasting. Format: News, info music. News staff: 5; News: 146 hrs wkly. ♦Jack Galmiche, COO & exec VP.

KUBQ(FM)— Aug 15, 1977: 98.7 mhz; 2.25 kw. 1,942 ft TL: N45 26 26 W117 53 31. Stereo. Hrs open: 24 Prog sep from AM Box 907, 97850. Secondary address: 2510 E. Cove Ave. 97850. Phone: (541) 963-4121. Phone: (541) 963-4122. Fax: (541) 963-3117.E-mail: q98@eoni.com Population served: 35,000 Natl. Rep: McGavren Guild,. Format: Classic rock. News staff: one; News: 6 hrs wkly. Target aud: 25-54.

KWRL(FM)— Sept 27, 1988: 99.9 mhz; 60 kw. 377 ft TL: N45 12 59 W118 00 00. Stereo. Hrs open: 24 1009 Adams Ave., Suite C, 97850. Phone: (541) 963-7911. Fax: (541) 963-5090.E-mail: 999@eoni.com Licensee: KSRV Inc. Group owner: Capps Broadcast Group (acq 12-14-98; $800,000). Natl. Network: ABC, Jones Radio Networks, . Natl. Rep: Tacher,. Rgnl rep: Tacher. Format: Adult contemp. Target aud: 18-49; general. ♦Dave Capps, pres; Randy McKone, gen mgr.

La Pine

***KKLP(FM)**— 2005: 90.1 mhz; 2.5 kw vert. Ant 131 ft TL: N43 34 50 W121 34 13. Stereo. Hrs open: 24
Rebroadcasts KLVR(FM) Santa Rosa, CA 100%.
2351 Sunset Blvd., Suite 170-218, Rocklin, CA, 95765. Phone: (916) 251-1600. Fax: (916) 2511650.E-mail: klove@klove.com Web Site:www.kove.com Licensee: Educational Media Foundation. Group owner: EMF Broadcasting. Natl. Network: K-Love, . Shaw Pittman. Format: Contemp Christian. News staff: 3. Target aud: 25-44; Judeo Christian, female. ♦Richard Jenkins, pres; Mike Novak, VP; Keith Whipple, dev dir; David Pierce, progmg mgr; Ed Lenane, news dir; Sam Wallington, engrg dir; Karen Johnson, news rptr.

Lake Oswego

KDZR(AM)—Licensed to Lake Oswego. See Portland

KLTH(FM)— Aug 1, 1977: 106.7 mhz; 100 kw. Ant 1,443 ft TL: N45 30 58 W122 43 59. Stereo. Hrs open: 24 4949 S.W. Macadam Ave., Portland, 97239-3912. Phone: (503) 323-6400. Fax: (503) 323-6664.E-mail: info@klthfm.com Web Site:www.khits1067.com Licensee: Citicasters Licenses Inc. Group owner: Infinity Broadcasting Corp. (acq 4-1-2009; grpsl). Population served: 1,674,000 Wiley Rein LLP. Format: Oldies. News staff: one. Target aud: 35-54; 55% women, 45% men. ♦Robert Dove, gen mgr.

Lakeview

KLCR(FM)— 2003: 95.3 mhz; 780 w. Ant 1,378 ft TL: N42 12 40 W120 19 35. Hrs open: 24 Box 723, 97630. Phone: (541) 947-3325.E-mail: warrenstation@gooseke.like.com Licensee: Woodrow Michael Warren. Group owner: Woodrow Michael Warren Stns. Format: Classic rock. ♦Mike Warren, gen mgr.

***KOAP(FM)**— 2000: 88.7 mhz; 170 w. Ant -590 ft TL: N42 10 42 W120 21 19. Stereo. Hrs open: Oregon Public Broadcasting, 7140 S.W. Macadam Ave., Portland, 97219. Phone: (503) 244-9900. Fax: (503) 293-4877. Web Site:www.opb.org Licensee: Oregon Public Broadcasting. Natl. Network: NPR, . Ore. Pub. Bcstg Radio Net. Swarz, Woods & Miller. Format: News, world beat. ♦Steve Bass, CEO; Jeff Douglas, opns VP.

KQIK(AM)— Dec 5, 1956: 1230 khz; 1 kw-U. TL: N42 12 30 W120 21 39. Stereo. Hrs open: 24 629 Center St., 97630. Phone: (541) 947-3351. Fax: (541) 947-2309.E-mail: kqik@tnet.biz Licensee: Crystal Clear Broadcasting Co. Inc. (acq 12-10-2003; $118,000 with co-located FM). Population served: 15,000 Natl. Network: ABC, . Wire Svc: AP Format: Country. News staff: one; News: 2 hrs wkly. Target aud: General. Spec prog: Relg 2 hrs wkly. ♦Tommie S. Dodd, gen mgr.

KQIK-FM— 1987: 93.5 mhz; 1 kw. Ant 951 ft TL: N42 12 18 W120 19 39. Stereo. Hrs open: 24 629 Center St., 97630. Phone: (541) 947-3351. Fax: (541) 947-2309.E-mail: kqik@tnet.biz Population served: 30,000 Natl. Network: ABC, . Wire Svc: AP Format: Adult contemp. Target aud: General. ♦Walt Lawton, progmg dir.

Lebanon

KGAL(AM)— Aug 5, 1995: 1580 khz; 1 kw-U, DA-1. TL: N44 34 30 W122 55 15. Hrs open: 24 36991 KGAL Dr., 97355. Phone: (541) 451-5425. Fax: (541) 451-5429.E-mail: kgal@kgal.com Web Site:www.kgal.com Licensee: EADS Broadcasting Corp. Population served: 350,000 Natl. Network: CBS, Westwood One, Salem Radio Network, Sporting News Radio Network, . Natl. Rep: McGavren Guild,. Crowell & Moring. Wire Svc: AP Format: News-Talk-Sports. News staff: 5; News: 22 hrs wkly. Target aud: 25-54; active listeners. Spec prog: Local interview show 5 hrs wkly. ♦Richard "Charlie" Eads, pres; Florence R. Eads, CFO; Jim Willhight, opns mgr; Ted Jenne, progmg dir; Weldon Greig, news dir.

***KGRI(FM)**— 2005: 88.1 mhz; 1 w horiz, 170 w vert. Ant 2,473 ft vert TL: N44 28 59 W122 34 55. Stereo. Hrs open: 24
Rebroadcasts KLRD(FM) Yucaipa, CA 100%.
2351 Sunset Blvd., Suite 170-218, Rocklin, CA, 95765. Phone: (916) 251-1600. Fax: (916) 251-1650.E-mail: info@air1.com Web Site:www.air1.com Licensee: Educational Media Foundation. Group

owner: EMF Broadcasting. Natl. Network: Air 1, . Shaw Pittman. Format: Contemp Christian. News staff: 3. Target aud: 18-35; Judeo-Christian, female. ◆Richard Jenkins, pres; Mike Novak, VP, progmg dir; Lloyd Parker, gen mgr; Ed Lenane, opns dir, news dir; Keith Whipple, dev dir; Eric Allen, natl sls mgr; David Pierce, progmg mgr; Jon Rivers, mus dir; Sam Wallington, engrg dir; Karen Johnson, news rptr.

KSHO(AM)— 1950: 920 khz; 1 kw-U, DA-1. TL: N44 34 30 W122 55 15. Hrs open: 24 36991 KGAL Dr., 97355. Phone: (541) 451-5425. Fax: (541) 451-5429.E-mail: kgal@kgal.com Web Site:www.ksho.net Licensee: Eads Broadcasting Corp. (acq 10-1-81; $425,000; 10-5-81). Population served: 350,000 Natl. Network: Jones Radio Networks, AP Radio, . Natl. Rep: McGavren Guild, . Crowell & Moring. Wire Svc: AP Format: Adult Standards/MOR. News staff: 5; News: 7 hrs wkly. Target aud: 35 plus; mature adults with money & leisure. ◆Richard "Charlie" Eads, pres; Florence R. Eads, CFO; Jim Willhight, opns mgr; Ted Jenne, progmg dir; Weldon Greig, news dir.

KXPC(FM)— Apr 8, 1974: Stn currently dark. 103.7 mhz; 100 kw. Ant 1,099 ft TL: N44 30 17 W122 57 20. Stereo. Hrs open: 1207 9th Ave. S.E., Albany, 97322. Phone: (541) 928-1926. Fax: (541) 791-1054.E-mail: kxpc@kxpc.com Web Site:www.kxpc.com Licensee: Portland Broadcasting L.L.C. (acq 4-11-2001; $4.1 million). Population served: 250,000 ◆Rich Coleman, gen mgr.

Lincoln City

KBCH(AM)— May 27, 1955: 1400 khz; 1 kw-U. TL: N44 59 27 W123 58 45. Hrs open: Box 1430, Newport, 97365. Phone: (541) 265-2266. Fax: (541) 265-6397.E-mail: info@kbcham.com Web Site:kbcham.com Licensee: Pacific West Broadcasting Inc. Population served: 12,000 Rgnl rep: Tacher Format: MOR, full service. News staff: 2; News: 4 hrs wkly. ◆David Miller, pres & gen mgr.

KCRF-FM— Nov 1, 1981: 96.7 mhz; 19.5 kw. Ant 872 ft TL: N44 45 22 W124 02 57. Stereo. Hrs open: 24 Box 1430, Newport, 97365. Phone: (541) 265-2266. Fax: (541) 265-6397.E-mail: info@kcrffm.com Web Site:kcrffm.com Licensee: Pacific West Broadcasting Inc. (group owner; acq 11-15-00; grpsl). Population served: 68,000 Rgnl rep: Tacher Format: Classic rock. News staff: 2; News: 2 hrs wkly. ◆David Miller, pres & gen mgr.

Malin

*KBUG(FM)— 2000: Stn currently dark. 100.9 mhz; 750 w. Ant 899 ft TL: N42 05 48 W121 37 57. Stereo. Hrs open: Box 111, Klamath Falls, 97601. Phone: (541) 884-8167. Licensee: Malin Christian Church Inc. (acq 7-1-99; $3,000). Format: Christian country.

McMinnville

KLYC(AM)— June 18, 1949: 1260 khz; 1 kw-U, DA-N. TL: N45 13 19 W123 10 21. Hrs open: 24 Box 1099, 97128. Secondary address: 1975 N.E. Colvin Ct. 97128. Phone: (503) 472-1260. Fax: (503) 472-3243.E-mail: klyc@viclink.com Licensee: Bohnsack Strategies Inc. (acq 10-2-90; $120,000; 10-22-90). Population served: 90,000 Natl. Network: CNN Radio, . Format: Oldies. News staff: one. Target aud: 25-54. ◆Larry Bohnsack, pres & gen mgr.

*KSLC(FM)— Jan 17, 1972: 90.3 mhz; 320 w. -46 ft TL: N45 12 06 W123 11 52. Stereo. Hrs open: 6 AM-noon Unit DD, 900 S.E. Baker St., 97128. Phone: (503) 883-2550. Web Site:www.kslcfm.com Licensee: Linfield College. Population served: 25,000 Format: Alternative rock. News: 3 hrs wkly. Target aud: 12-25; young people looking for new mus. Spec prog: Black 2 hrs, heavy metal 7 hrs wkly, relg 2 hrs wkly. ◆Nancy Cornwell, gen mgr.

Medford

KBOY-FM— February 1958: 95.7 mhz; 100 kw. 935 ft TL: N42 27 07 W23 03 20. (CP: 60 kw, ant 751 ft.). Stereo. Hrs open: 24 1438 Rossanley Dr., 97501. Phone: (541) 779-1550. Fax: (541) 776-2360.E-mail: cbaker@radiomedford.com Web Site:www.957kboy.com Licensee: Mapleton License of Medford LLC. (group owner; (acq 10-26-2001; grpsl). Population served: 140,000 Format: Classic rock. News: One. ◆Ron Hren, VP & gen mgr; Joe Mussio, mktg mgr; Casey Baker, progmg dir; Maria Chaney, traf mgr; Robert Probert, engr.

KCMX(AM)—(Phoenix, Apr 7, 1962: 880 khz; 1 kw-U. TL: N42 18 36 W122 48 41. Hrs open: 24 1438 Rossanley Dr., 97501. Phone: (541) 779-1550. Fax: (541) 776-2360.E-mail: info@kcmxam.com Web Site:www.kcmxam.com Licensee: Mapleton License of Medford LLC. (group owner; acq 10-26-2001; grpsl). Population served: 150,000

KCMX-FM—See Ashland

KCNA(FM)—See Cave Junction

*KDOV(FM)— Aug 1, 1995: 91.7 mhz; 26 kw. -364 ft TL: N42 20 13 W122 51 44. Hrs open: 24 1236 Disk Drive St. E., 97501. Phone: (541) 776-5368. Fax: (541) 776-0618.E-mail: kdov@kdov.net Web Site:www.kdov.net Licensee: UCB USA Inc. (acq 1-16-2004; $750,000). Natl. Network: Salem Radio Network, . Edmundson & Edmundson. Wire Svc: AP Format: Relg, news/talk. News staff: one; News: 5 hrs wkly. Target aud: 25-54; women. ◆Perry A. Atkinson, pres; Dallas Rhoden, VP; Perry Atkinson, gen mgr; Pat Daly, opns mgr.

*KEZX(AM)— May 31, 1954: 730 khz; 1 kw-D, 74 w-N. TL: N42 18 36 W122 48 41. Hrs open: 24 511 Rossanley Dr., 97501. Phone: (541) 772-0322. Fax: (541) 772-4233. Licensee: Opus Broadcasting Systems Inc. (group owner; (acq 12-17-2003; $70,000). Natl. Network: Fox Sports, . Natl. Rep: Tacher,. Format: Sports. News staff: 3. ◆Dean Flock, gen mgr; Brian Fraser, sls dir.

KGAY(AM)—See Ashland

KLDZ(FM)— Aug 19, 1991: 103.5 mhz; 100 kw. Ant 479 ft TL: N42 17 13 W123 00 15. Stereo. Hrs open: 24 3624 Avion Dr., 97504. Phone: (541) 774-1324. Fax: (541) 857-0326.E-mail: info@kool103.net Web Site:www.kool103.net Licensee: Bicoastal Rogue Valley LLC. Group owner: Clear Channel Communications Inc. (acq 7-2-2007; grpsl). Population served: 150,000 Natl. Rep: Tacher,. Format: Super hits. Target aud: 25 plus. ◆Bill Nielsen, gen mgr.

KMED(AM)— 1922: 1440 khz; 5 kw-D, 1 kw-N. TL: N42 18 36 W122 48 41. Hrs open: 24 3624 Avion Dr., 97504. Phone: (541) 773-1440. Fax: (541) 857-0326.E-mail: news@kmed.com Web Site:www.kmed.com Licensee: Bicoastal Rogue Valley LLC. Group owner: Clear Channel Communications Inc. (acq 7-2-2007; grpsl). Population served: 125,000 Natl. Network: Westwood One, CBS, . Format: News/talk. News staff: one; News: 14 hrs wkly. Target aud: 35 plus. ◆Bill Nielsen, gen mgr; Bill Meyer, stn mgr.

KRTA(AM)— October 1947: 610 khz; 5 kw-U, DA-2. TL: N42 23 15 W122 46 11. Stereo. Hrs open: 24 511 Rossanley Dr., 97501. Phone: (541) 772-0322. Fax: (541) 772-4233.E-mail: brian@opusradio.com Licensee: Opus Broadcasting Systems Inc. (group owner; acq 7-9-91; $63,634 with KROG(FM) Grants Pass;7-29-91). Population served: 209,031 Natl. Network: La Gran D, . Natl. Rep: Tacher,. Leibowitz & Spencer. Format: Rgnl Mexican. News: 9 hrs wkly. Target aud: 12 plus; Hispanic. ◆Dean Flock, gen mgr; Brian Fraser, sls dir; Oscar Bonilla, progmg dir.

KTMT-FM— Oct 15, 1970: 93.7 mhz; 31 kw. 7,580 ft TL: N42 04 55 W122 43 07. Stereo. Hrs open: 24 1438 Rossanley Dr., 97501. Phone: (541) 779-1550. Fax: (541) 776-2360.E-mail: info@937mike.com Web Site:www.937mike.com Licensee: Mapleton License of Medford LLC. Population served: 500,000 Dow, Lohnes & Albertson. Format: Adult hits. News staff: one; News: 3 hrs wkly. Target aud: 18-49. ◆Casey Baker, mktg dir, mus dir, disc jockey; Richard Tempelton, prom dir; Leslie Haze, disc jockey.

Merrill

KKKJ(FM)— 2008: 105.5 mhz; 18 kw. Ant 686 ft TL: N42 13 24 W121 49 02. Hrs open: Box 938, Klamath Falls, 97601. Phone: (541) 850-5242. Fax: (541) 884-2845.E-mail: webmaster@klamathradio.com Web Site:www.klamathradio.com/3KJ/3KJ_HomePage.htm Licensee: Klamath Basin Broadcasting. Format: Top-40. Target aud: 18-49. ◆William Ifft, gen mgr.

Milton-Freewater

*KLRF(FM)— Jan 1, 1999: 88.5 mhz; 5 kw. Ant 1,302 ft TL: N45 47 16 W118 10 31. Hrs open: 24 Box 3006, Collegedale, TN, 37315. Phone: (509) 524-0885. Fax: (509) 524-0884; (423) 884-2802.E-mail: office@lifetalk.net Web Site:www.lifetalk.net Licensee: Lifetalk Broadcasting Association. Format: Relg, Christian. ◆Grant McPherson, gen mgr.

KZTB(FM)— Sept 10, 1992: 97.9 mhz; 100 kw. Ant 899 ft TL: N45 47 41 W118 10 06. Stereo. Hrs open: 24 2730 West Lewis #8, Pasco, WA, 99301. Phone: (509) 543-3334. Fax: (509) 452-0541.E-mail: zorro@radiozorro.com Licensee: Bustos Media of Eastern Washington

License LLC. Group owner: Clear Channel Communications Inc. (acq 2-22-2006; $900,000 plus swap for KUJJ(FM) Weston). Format: Sp. ◆Bob Berry, gen mgr.

Milwaukie

KOOR(AM)— February 1988: 1010 khz; 4.5 kw-D. TL: N45 29 03 W122 24 40. Stereo. Hrs open: 5110 S.E. Stark St., Suite C, Portland, 97415. Phone: (503) 234-5550. Fax: (503) 234-5583.E-mail: rtatum@bustosmedia.com Web Site:www.bustosmedia.com Licensee: Bustos Media of Oregon License LLC. Group owner: Bustos Media Holdings (acq 11-19-2003; $1 million). Format: Adult standards. ◆Ricky Tatum, gen mgr; Chitra Gade, opns mgr; Tom Oberg, gen sls mgr; Henry Cualio, progmg dir; James Boyd, chief of engrg.

Molalla

KRSK(FM)—Licensed to Molalla. See Portland

Monmouth

KSND(FM)— Mar 23, 1995: 95.1 mhz; 1 kw. Ant 3,307 ft TL: N44 53 19 W123 36 26. Stereo. Hrs open: 24 285 Liberty St. N.E., #340, Salem, 97301. Phone: (503) 763-9951. Fax: (503) 763-2676.E-mail: ernie@ksnd.com Web Site:www.ksnd.com Licensee: Radio Beam LLC (acq 6-7-2002; $400,000). Wire Svc: AP Format: Adult contemp. News staff: one; News: 5 hrs wkly. Target aud: 25-54. ◆Ernie Hopseker, pres, gen mgr, gen mgr, gen sls mgr; Scott Forrest, progmg dir; Frank Rippey, pub affrs dir; Lyndi Miles, traf mgr.

Mount Angel

KTRP(AM)—Not on air, target date: unknown: 1130 khz; 25 kw-D, 490 w-N, DA-2. TL: N45 04 35 W122 48 27. Hrs open: Box 60991, Palo Alto, CA, 94306-0991. Phone: (650) 856-6823. Licensee: JNE Investments Inc. ◆Jeffrey N. Eustis, pres.

Myrtle Point

*KOOZ(FM)— Aug 1, 1996: 94.1 mhz; 1 kw. Ant 1,456 ft TL: N42 57 32 W124 16 23. Hrs open: 5 AM-2 AM Jefferson Public Radio, 1250 Siskiyou Blvd., Ashland, 97520. Phone: (541) 552-6301. Phone: (541) 552-8565.E-mail: info@ijpr.org Web Site:www.ijpr.org Licensee: JPR Foundation Inc. (acq 4-19-02; $83,700 with KTBR(AM) Roseburg). Population served: 90,000 Natl. Network: NPR, PRI, . Ernest Sanchez. Wire Svc: AP Format: Class, news. News staff: one; News: 35 hrs wkly. ◆Mitchell Christian, CFO; Ronald Kramer, CEO & gen mgr; Bryon Lambert, opns dir; Paul Westhelle, dev dir.

Newport

KCUP(AM)—See Toledo

*KLCO(FM)— Sept 11, 1990: 90.5 mhz; 3.2 kw. 256 ft TL: N44 45 22 W124 02 57. Stereo. Hrs open: 24
Rebroadcasts KLCC(FM) Eugene 100%.
136 W. 8th Ave., Eugene, 97401-0640. Phone: (541) 463-6000. Fax: (541) 463-6046.E-mail: klcc@klcc.org Web Site:www.klcc.org Licensee: Lane Community College. Population served: 50,000 Natl. Network: NPR, . Format: Jazz, div, news. News staff: one; News: 60 hrs wkly. Target aud: 25-54. Spec prog: Sp 5 hrs, Black 3 hrs, folk 12 hrs, blues 4 hrs, world 3 hrs, electronic 6 hrs wkly. ◆Jerry Moskus, pres; Steve Barton, gen mgr.

KNCU(FM)— June 2000: 92.7 mhz; 3.8 kw. 840 ft TL: N44 45 22 W124 02 57. Stereo. Hrs open: Box 1430, 97365. Phone: (541) 265-2266. Fax: (541) 265-6397.E-mail: info@u92fm.com Web Site:www.u92fm.com Licensee: Pacific West Broadcasting Inc. (group owner; acq 10-27-00; grpsl). Population served: 44,000 Rgnl rep: Tacher. Format: Country. News staff: one; News: 2 hrs wkly. Target aud: 24-54; adults. ◆David J. Miller, pres & gen mgr.

KNPT(AM)— June 28, 1948: 1310 khz; 5 kw-D, 1 kw-N, DA-N. TL: N44 37 40 W123 59 15. Hrs open: 24 Box 1430, 906 S.W. Alder St., 97365. Phone: (541) 265-2266. Fax: (541) 265-6397.E-mail: info@knptam.com Web Site:knptam.com Licensee: Yaquina Bay Communications Inc. (acq 1-96). Population served: 18,000 Rgnl rep: Tacher. Format: News/talk, sports. News staff: 2; News: 21 hrs wkly. Target aud: 34 plus. Spec prog: Relg 2 hrs wkly. ◆David J. Miller, pres, gen mgr; Vern Morris, gen sls mgr; Johnny Randolph, progmg dir.

KYTE(FM)— Oct 25, 1976: 102.7 mhz; Oct 25, 1976. Oct 25, 1976 TL: Oct 25, 1976. Oct 25, 1976. Stereo. 24 Box 1430, 906 S.W. Alder St., 97365. Phone: (541) 265-2266. Fax: (541) 265-6397.E-mail: info@kytefm.com Web Site:www.kytefm.com Licensee: Yaquina Bay Communications Inc. Population served: 120,000 Rgnl rep: Tacher. Format: Adult contemp. News staff: 2; News: 4 hrs wkly. Target aud: 24-49. ♦David Miller, pres, gen mgr; Johnny Randolph, disc jockey.

***KYOR(FM)**— 2006: 88.9 mhz; 35 w. Ant 899 ft TL: N44 45 23 W124 02 59. Hrs open:
Rebroadcasts KUFR(FM) Salt Lake City, UT 100%.
c/o Radio Station KUFR(FM), 136 E. S. Temple, Suite 1630, Salt Lake City, UT, 84111. Phone: (801) 359-3147. Fax: (801) 359-8112.E-mail: info@familyradio.com Web Site:www.familyradio.com Licensee: Family Stations Inc. Format: Christian relg. ♦Harold Camping, gen mgr.

KYTE(FM)— Oct 25, 1976: 102.7 mhz; 66 kw. Ant 881 ft TL: N44 45 22 W124 02 57. Stereo. Hrs open: 24 Box 1430, 906 S.W. Alder St., 97365. Phone: (541) 265-2266. Fax: (541) 265-6397.E-mail: info@kytefm.com Web Site:www.kytefm.com Licensee: Yaquina Bay Communications Inc. Population served: 120,000 Rgnl rep: Tacher. Format: Adult contemp. News staff: 2; News: 4 hrs wkly. Target aud: 24-49. ♦David Miller, pres, gen mgr; Johnny Randolph, disc jockey.

North Bend

KBBR(AM)— December 1950: 1340 khz; 1 kw-U. TL: N43 25 52 W124 12 23. Hrs open: 24 Box 180, Coos Bay, 97420. Secondary address: 320 Central Ave., Suite 519, Coos Bay 97420. Phone: (541) 267-2121. Fax: (541) 267-5229. Licensee: Bicoastal Media Licenses III LLC. Population served: 70,000 Natl. Network: CBS Radio, Jones Radio Networks, Westwood One, . Natl. Rep: Katz Radio, Tacher,. Format: News/talk. News: 40 hrs wkly. Target aud: 25-54. ♦Ken Dennis, CEO; Mike Wilson, pres.

KOOS(FM)— October 1990: 107.3 mhz; 51 kw. Ant 692 ft TL: N43 12 18 W124 18 07. Stereo. Hrs open: 24 Box 180, Coos Bay, 97420. Secondary address: 320 Central Ave., Suite 519, Coos Bay 97420. Phone: (541) 267-2121. Fax: (541) 267-5229. Licensee: Bicoastal Media Licenses III LLC. Group owner: Bicoastal Media L.L.C. (acq 10-16-2003; grpsl). Population served: 382,619 Natl. Network: Jones Radio Networks, . Rgnl rep: Tacher Format: CHR. News: 14 hrs wkly. Target aud: 18-44. ♦Ken Dennis, CEO; Mike O'Brien, opns mgr.

KTEE(FM)— Dec 10, 1979: 94.9 mhz; 89 kw. Ant 626 ft TL: N43 12 18 W124 18 07. Stereo. Hrs open: 320 Central Ave., Suite 519, Coos Bay, 97420. Phone: (541) 267-2121. Fax: (541) 267-5229. Web Site:www.southcoastradio.com Licensee: Bicoastal Media Licenses III LLC. Group owner: Bicoastal Media L.L.C. (acq 10-16-2003; grpsl). Population served: 120,000 Natl. Rep: Tacher,. Format: AAA/CHR/Classic Hits Mix. News: 8 hrs wkly. Target aud: 25-54. ♦Kenneth R. Dennis, CEO; Mike Wilson, rgnl sls mgr.

North Powder

***KEFS(FM)**— 2006: 89.5 mhz; 120 w. Ant 1,787 ft TL: N45 07 26 W117 46 48. Hrs open: 1433 Jefferson Ave., La Grande, 97850-2643. Phone: (541) 963-5884. Web Site:www.csnradio.com Licensee: CSN International. Format: Christian. ♦Mike Kestler, pres; Wade Twilegar, gen mgr.

Nyssa

***KARO(FM)**— 1997: 98.7 mhz; 82 kw. Ant 1,000 ft TL: N43 24 09 W116 54 09. Hrs open: 24
Rebroadcasts KLRD(FM) Yucaipa, CA 100%.
2351 Sunset Blvd., Suite 170-218, Rocklin, CA, 95765. Phone: (916) 251-1600. Fax: (916) 251-1650. Web Site:www.air1.com Licensee: Educational Media Foundation (acq 2-25-03; $1 million). Natl. Network: Air 1, . Format: Christian. ♦Mike Novak, pres.

Oakridge

***KAVE(FM)**— 2006: 88.5 mhz; 400 w. Ant -1,286 ft TL: N43 44 27 W122 26 50. Stereo. Hrs open: 24 Hot adult contemp Lane County School District 4J, 200 N. Monroe St., Eugene, 97402. Phone: (541) 687-3123. Fax: (541) 687-3573.E-mail: randy@krvm.org Web Site:www.krvm.org Licensee: Lane County School District 4J. Target aud: 18-35. ♦Ken Martin, progmg dir; Randy Larson, stn mgr & chief of engrg.

***KMKR(FM)**— Oct 22, 1990: 92.1 mhz; 580 w. Ant -817 ft TL: N43 44 34 W122 26 03. Hrs open: Oakridge High School, 47997 W. First St., 97463. Phone: (541) 782-2231. Fax: (541) 782-4692.E-mail: kave921@hotmail.com Web Site:www.geocites.com/kave921 Licensee: School District #76. Format: CHR. Target aud: General. ♦Debbie Gillespie, gen mgr & chief of opns; Abbie Pierce, prom dir; Aaron Stone, progmg dir.

Ontario

KSRV(AM)— Nov 23, 1946: 1380 khz; 5 kw-D, 1 kw-N, DA-N. TL: N44 02 45 W116 58 24. Hrs open: 24 Box 129, 1725 N. Oregon St., 97914. Phone: (541) 889-8651. Fax: (541) 889-8733.E-mail: dale@impactradiogroup.com Licensee: FM Idaho Co. LLC (acq 9-9-2004; $2.5 million with co-located FM). Natl. Network: ABC, . Dow, Lohnes & Albertson. Format: Country favorites. News staff: one; News: 15 hrs wkly. Target aud: 25-54 plus. Spec prog: Farm 15 hrs wkly. ♦Dale Jeffries, gen mgr, progmg dir, news dir; Mark Broz, gen sls mgr; Mitch Pruett, prom dir.

KSRV-FM— July 4, 1977: 96.1 mhz; 47 kw. Ant 2,673 ft TL: N43 45 18 W116 05 51. Stereo. Hrs open: 24 5660 Franklin Rd., Suite 200, Nampa, ID, 83686. Phone: (208) 465-9966. Fax: (208) 465-2922.E-mail: mikey@impactradiogroup.com Web Site:www.961bobfm.com Format: Adult hits. News: 40 hrs wkly. ♦Darrell Calton, gen mgr; Mikey Fuentes, opns mgr; Mark Broz, gen sls mgr.

Oregon City

KGDD(AM)— July 4, 1947: 1520 khz; 50 kw-D, 10 kw-N, DA-2. TL: N45 24 44 W122 34 37. Hrs open: 24 5110 SE Stark St., Portland, 97215. Phone: (503) 234-5550. Fax: (503) 234-5583. Web Site:www.lagrand1520.com Licensee: Bustos Media of Oregon License LLC. Group owner: Bustos Media Holdings (acq 11-17-2003; $2.8 million). Population served: 400,000 Natl. Rep: D & R Radio,. Format: Sp. News staff: one. ♦Amador Bustos, pres; Ricky Tatum, gen mgr; Tom Oberg, gen sls mgr; Henry Cualio, prom dir; James Boyd, chief of engrg; Chitra Gade, traf mgr.

KGON(FM)—See Portland

Pendleton

***KRBM(FM)**— Apr 18, 1970: 90.9 mhz; 25 kw. 587 ft TL: N45 35 21 W118 59 53. Stereo. Hrs open: 7140 S.W. Macadam Ave., Portland, 97219. Phone: (503) 293-1905. Phone: (1-888) 293-1982. Fax: (503) 293-1919.E-mail: info@opb.org Web Site:www.opb.org Licensee: Oregon Public Broadcasting. (acq 9-20-93; grpsl; 10-11-93). Population served: 25,000 Natl. Network: PRI, NPR, . Rgnl. Network: Ore. Pub. Bcstg Radio Net. Ore. Pub. Bcstg Radio Net. Format: News, info music. News staff: 5; News: 146 hrs wkly. Target aud: Teens to adults. ♦Jack Galmiche, COO, exec VP & VP.

KTIX(AM)— 1941: 1240 khz; 1 kw-U. TL: N45 39 49 W118 47 19. Stereo. Hrs open: 24 2003 NW 56th Dr., 97801. Phone: (541) 278-2500. Fax: (541) 276-1480. Licensee: KSRV Inc. Group owner: Capps Broadcast Group (acq 5-14-98; $1.2 million with co-located FM). Population served: 15,200 Natl. Network: ESPN Radio, . Natl. Rep: Tacher,. Format: Sports. News staff: one. Target aud: 25-54; upscale adults. ♦Randy McKone, pres & stn mgr; J.J. Ford, opns mgr; John Thomas, prom mgr, progmg dir.

KUMA(AM)— Aug 25, 1955: 1290 khz; 5 kw-U, DA-N. TL: N45 40 25 W118 44 48. Hrs open: 24 2003 N.W. 56th Dr., 97801. Phone: (541) 276-1511. Fax: (541) 276-1480. Licensee: Round-Up Radio Inc. Group owner: Capps Broadcast Group (acq 7-1-93; $340,000 with co-located FM;7-26-93). Population served: 50,000 Rgnl rep: Tacher. Format: Talk, news. News staff: one; News: 20 hrs wkly. Target aud: 25 plus; adults. Spec prog: Farm 10 hrs wkly. ♦Dave Capps, pres; Randy McKone, VP & gen mgr; J.J. Ford, opns dir, opns mgr; Butch Thurman, news dir.

KUMA-FM— Oct 1, 1978: 107.7 mhz; 72 kw. Ant 1,115 ft TL: N45 35 27 W118 34 47. Stereo. Hrs open: Prog sep from AM 2003 N.W. 56th Dr., 97801. Phone: (541) 276-1511. Fax: (541) 276-1480. Population served: 100,000 Natl. Network: ABC, . Format: Adult contemp. Target aud: 18 plus. ♦J.J. Ford, progmg mgr.

KWHT(FM)— May 1, 1984: 103.5 mhz; 100 kw. 720 ft TL: N45 47 51 W118 22 17. Stereo. Hrs open: 24 Prog sep from AM 2003 NW 56th Dr., 97801. Phone: (541) 278-2500. Fax: (541) 276-1480. Population served: 350,000 Natl. Network: ABC, . Format: Country. News: 2 hrs wkly. Target aud: 25-54; adults. ♦Randy McKone, CEO & gen mgr; Julie Thompson, gen sls mgr; J.J. Ford, engrg VP; Connie Shurtleff, engr.

Phoenix

KAKT(FM)— 1991: 105.1 mhz; 52 kw. 545 ft TL: N42 25 41 W123 00 04. Hrs open: 24 1438 Rossanley Dr., Medford, 97501. Phone: (541) 779-1550. Fax: (541) 776-2360.E-mail: info@kat105.com Web Site:www.kat105.com Licensee: Mapleton License of Medford LLC. (group owner; (acq 10-26-2001; grpsl). Population served: 150,000 Format: Country. News staff: one. Target aud: 25-49; female. ♦Ron Hren, VP & gen mgr; Casey Baker, opns mgr, prom dir; Joe Mussio, mktg mgr; Maria Chaney, traf mgr; Robert Probert, engr.

***KAPL(AM)**— Jan 2, 1977: 1300 khz; 20 kw-U, DA-N. TL: N42 17 44 W122 48 15. Hrs open: Box 1090, Jacksonville, 97530. Phone: (541) 899-5275. Fax: (541) 899-8068.E-mail: kapl@applegatefellowship.org Web Site:www.applegatefellowship.org Licensee: Applegate Media Inc. (acq 10-24-91). Population served: 200,000 Format: News/talk, Christian. Target aud: 25-54. ♦Chris Thompson, gen mgr & opns mgr.

KCMX(AM)—Licensed to Phoenix. See Medford

Pilot Rock

KVAN-FM— 2006: 92.1 mhz; 6.9 kw. Ant 633 ft TL: N45 35 21 W118 59 54. Hrs open: 45 Campbell Rd., Walla Walla, WA, 99362. Phone: (509) 527-1000. Fax: (509) 529-5534. Licensee: Bruton Broadcasting LLC (acq 1-29-2007). Format: Oldies. ♦Aaron Bruton, gen mgr.

Pine Grove

***KPFR(FM)**— June 22, 2005: 89.5 mhz; 7 kw vert. Ant 1,673 ft TL: N45 19 58 W121 42 48. Hrs open: 24 Family Stations Inc., 4135 Northgate Blvd., Suite 1, Sacramento, CA, 95834. Phone: (916) 641-8191. Fax: (916) 641-8238. Licensee: Family Stations Inc. (group owner; (acq 9-9-2002). Format: Christian. ♦Harold Camping, pres.

Portland

KBMS(AM)—See Vancouver, WA

KBNP(AM)— 1949: 1410 khz; 5 kw-D, 250 w-N. TL: N45 28 24 W122 39 36. Hrs open: 24 278 S.W. Arthur St., 97201. Phone: (503) 223-6769. Fax: (503) 223-4305.E-mail: kbnp@kbnp.com Web Site:www.kbnp.com Licensee: KBNP Radio Inc. (acq 8-8-90; $320,000; 8-27-90). Population served: 1,327,500 Womble Carlyle Sandridge & Rice PLLC. Format: Business news & info, financial. News staff: 2; News: 163 hrs wkly. Target aud: General; corporations & individuals concerned with how-to's of making & keeping money. Spec prog: People w/disabilities, computer shows, home improvement. ♦Keith P. Lyons, gen mgr.

***KBOO(FM)**— June 1968: 90.7 mhz; 25.5 kw. 1,266 ft TL: N45 29 20 W122 41 40. Stereo. Hrs open: 24 20 S.E. 8th Ave., 97214. Phone: (503) 231-8032. Fax: (503) 231-7145.E-mail: program@kboo.org Web Site:kboo.fm Licensee: KBOO Foundation. (acq 8-5-75). Population served: 1,614,744 Haley, Bader & Potts. Format: Div. News staff: 2; News: 5 hrs wkly. Target aud: General. Spec prog: Sp 10 hrs, Indian one hr, ethnic 4 hrs, African/reggae 10 hrs wkly. ♦Arthur Davis, gen mgr, prom mgr; Justin Miller, adv mgr; Chris Merrick, progmg dir; John Mackey, mus dir, chief of engrg.

***KBPS(AM)**— Mar 23, 1923: 1450 khz; 1 kw-U. TL: N45 31 38 W122 29 03. Hrs open: 18 515 N.E. 15th Ave., 97232. Phone: (503) 916-5830. Fax: (503) 916-2642.E-mail: music.info@allclassical.org Web Site:www.allclassical.org Licensee: School District No. 1 Multnomah County, OR. Population served: 1,500,000 Format: Children programs. News: one hr wkly. Spec prog: Sp one hr wkly. ♦Sally Lewis, dev dir & mktg dir.

***KBVM(FM)**— Dec 8, 1989: 88.3 mhz; 3.5 kw. Ant 1,433 ft TL: N45 30 58 W122 43 59. Stereo. Hrs open: 24 Box 5888, 97228-5888. Secondary address: 5000 N. Willamette, MSC 160 97203. Phone: (503) 285-5200. Fax: (503) 285-3322.E-mail: info@kbvm.com Web Site:www.kbvm.fm Licensee: Catholic Broadcasting NW Inc. Population served: 1,907,000 Format: Relg. Target aud: General; anyone desiring Christian mus, inspiration, Catholic prayer & evangelism. Spec prog: Sp 14 hrs wkly. ♦Dina Marie Hale, progmg dir.

KCMD(AM)— Oct 18, 1925: 970 khz; 5 kw-U, DA-N. TL: N45 30 56 W122 43 56. Stereo. Hrs open: 24 222 S.W. Columbia, 97201. Phone: (503) 223-0300. Fax: (503) 497-2314.E-mail: info@kufo.com Licensee: CBS Radio Stations Inc. Group owner: Infinity Broadcasting Corp. (acq 11-13-98; grpsl). Format: Country, class. Target aud: 35 plus. ♦Dave McDonald, gen mgr; Mark Whaler, gen sls mgr.

KDZR(AM)—(Lake Oswego, 1996: 1640 khz; 10 kw-D, 1 kw-N. TL: N45 27 14 W122 32 47. Hrs open: 3030 S.W. Moody, Suite 210, 97201. Phone: (503) 228-4322. Fax: (503) 228-4325.E-mail: info@kdzra.com Web Site:www.radiodisney.com Licensee: Radio Disney Group LLC. Group owner: ABC Inc. (acq 2-03; $3.8 million with KKSL(AM) Lake Oswego). Natl. Network: Radio Disney, . Format: Families. ♦Jean-Paul Colaco, pres, gen mgr; Pamela Herrold, stn mgr.

KEX(AM)— Dec 24, 1926: 1190 khz; 50 kw-U, DA-N. TL: N45 25 20 W122 33 57. Hrs open: 24 4949 S.W. Macadam Ave., 97201. Phone: (503) 225-1190. Fax: (503) 227-5873.E-mail: info@kexam.com Web Site:www.1190kex.com Licensee: Citicasters Licenses L.P. Group owner: Clear Channel Communications Inc. Population served: 1,600,000 Hogan & Hartson. Format: News, talk. News: 25 hrs wkly. Target aud: 25-54; general. Spec prog: Portland Trailblazers basketball. ♦Ron Saito, pres, gen mgr; Mike Dirkx, opns dir, progmg dir; dave Milner, sls dir, gen sls mgr; Mike Lulich, natl sls mgr; Scott Thompson, mktg VP, mktg dir; Teri Rodrigues, prom mgr; Brad Ford, news dir; Shane Ruark, chief of engrg.

KFXX(AM)— Jan 17, 1925: 1080 khz; 50 kw-D, 10 kw-N, DA-2. TL: N45 33 26 W122 29 08. Stereo. Hrs open: 0700 S.W. Bancroft St., 97239. Phone: (503) 223-1441. Fax: (503) 223-6909.E-mail: comments@koth.com Web Site:www.1080thefan.com Licensee: Entercom Portland License LLC. Group owner: Entercom Communications Corp. (acq 12-18-2003; $44 million with co-located FM). Population served: 1,598,900 Format: Sports. Target aud: 25-54. ♦Ron Carter, CFO & gen mgr.

KGON(FM)— December 1967: 92.3 mhz; 100 kw. 920 ft TL: N45 20 23 W122 41 47. Stereo. Hrs open: 24 0700 S.W. Bancroft, 97239. Phone: (503) 223-1441. Fax: (503) 223-6909.E-mail: jhutchison@entercom.com Web Site:www.kgon.com Licensee: Entercom Portland License LLC. Group owner: Entercom Communications Corp. (acq 8-1-95; grpsl). Population served: 400,000 Natl. Rep: D & R Radio,. Format: Classic rock. News staff: 3; News: one hr wkly. ♦David Field, pres; Jack Hutchinson, sr VP, VP; Erin Hubert, gen mgr; Dick Loughney, gen sls mgr, chief of engrg; Keevin Wagner, gen mgr & prom dir; Clark Ryan, progmg dir.

KINK(FM)— Dec 24, 1968: 101.9 mhz; 97 kw. Ant 1,446 ft TL: N45 30 58 W122 43 59. Stereo. Hrs open: 24 1501 S.W. Jefferson St., 97201. Phone: (503) 517-6000. Fax: (503) 517-6100.E-mail: lwarren@kink.fm Web Site:www.kink.fm Licensee: Infinity Radio Inc. Group owner: Infinity Broadcasting Corp. (acq 11-13-98; grpsl). Population served: 1,972,900 Natl. Network: AP Radio, . Format: AAA. News staff: 2; News: 3 hrs wkly. Target aud: 25-54; primary, secondary. ♦Stan Mak, gen mgr; Maureen Pulicella, gen sls mgr; Candace Gonzales, mktg dir; Dennis Constantine, progmg dir; Sheila Hamilton, news dir; Leana Warren, pub affrs dir.

KKCW(FM)—See Beaverton

KKPZ(AM)— Nov 12, 1923: 1330 khz; 5 kw-U, DA-1. TL: N45 27 13 W122 32 45. Hrs open: 5 am-12 am (M-F); 6 am-12 am (S, Su) 4700 S. W. Macadam Ave., Suite 102, 97239. Phone: (503) 242-1950. Fax: (503) 242-0155.E-mail: info@kkpz.com Web Site:www.kkpz.com Licensee: KPHP Radio Inc. Group owner: Crawford Broadcasting Co. (acq 1995; $2 million). Population served: 2,200,000 Format: Christian, talk. Target aud: 34-54. Spec prog: Hispanic Christian talk, Hispanic Christian music. ♦Donald Crawford Sr., pres; James Autry, stn mgr; John White, chief of engrg.

KKRZ(FM)— May 1946: 100.3 mhz; 95 kw. 1,433 ft TL: N45 31 22 W122 45 07. Stereo. Hrs open: 4949 S.W. Macadam Ave., 97201. Phone: (503) 226-0100. Fax: (503) 295-9281.E-mail: info@kkrzfm.com Web Site:www.2100portland.com Licensee: Citicasters Licenses L.P. Population served: 382,619 Format: Contemp hit. Target aud: 18-49. ♦Jen Dalton, prom mgr; Michael Hayes, progmg dir; Shane Raurk, news dir.

KLPM(AM)— July 4, 1954: 1150 khz; 5 kw-D, 47 w-N, DA-1. TL: N45 38 34 W122 36 49. Hrs open: 5110 S.E. Stark, 97215. Phone: (503) 234-5550. Fax: (503) 234-5583. Web Site:www.bustosmedia.com Licensee: Bustos Media of Oregon License LLC. Group owner: Bustos Media Holdings (acq 11-18-2003; $1.25 million). Population served: 2,000,000 Natl. Rep: Interep,. Format: Sp contemp. Target aud: 25-54; general. Spec prog: Black one hr, Scandinavian one hr, URDU Hindi one hr, It one hr wkly. ♦Ricky Tatum, gen mgr; Tom Oberg, gen sls mgr; Henry Cualio, prom dir; Chitra Gade, chief of engrg, traf mgr.

KLTH(FM)—See Lake Oswego

KNRK(FM)—(Camas, WA) Nov 1, 1992: 94.7 mhz; 6.3 kw. Ant 1,322 ft TL: N45 29 20 W122 41 40. Stereo. Hrs open: 24 0700 S.W. Bancroft, 97239. Phone: (503) 223-1441. Fax: (503) 223-6909.E-mail: info@947.fm Web Site:www.947.fm Licensee: Entercom Portland License L.L.C. Group owner: Entercom Communications Corp. Format: Alternative rock. News staff: one. Target aud: 25-54. ♦David Field, pres; Jack Hutchison, exec VP; Jaime Cooley, progmg dir.

***KOPB-FM**— 1962: 91.5 mhz; 70 kw horiz, 21 kw vert. Ant 1,558 ft TL: N45 31 22 W122 45 07. Stereo. Hrs open: 7140 S.W. Macadam Ave., 97219. Phone: (503) 293-1905. Fax: (503) 293-1919.E-mail: opbnews@opb.org Web Site:www.opb.org Licensee: Oregon Public Broadcasting. (acq 9-20-93; grpsl; 10-11-93). Population served: 1,000,000 Natl. Network: NPR, PRI, . Format: News, info music. News staff: 5; News: 146 hrs wkly. Target aud: 34-54. ♦Jack Galmiche, COO, exec VP, dev VP, news dir; Virginia Breen, VP. Co-owned TV: *KOPB-TV affil.

KPDQ(AM)— July 30, 1947: 800 khz; 1 kw-D, 500 w-N. TL: N45 28 45 W122 44 55. Hrs open: 24 Dups FM 18% 6400 S.E. Lake Rd., 97222. Phone: (503) 786-0600. Fax: (503) 786-1551. Web Site:www.kpdq.am Licensee: Salem Media of Oregon Inc. Format: Conservative talk, Christian. Target aud: 18-54; listeners of talk. ♦Dennis Hayes, gen mgr; Jordan Smith, prom dir; Justin Mansfield, progmg dir.

KPDQ-FM— 1961: 93.9 mhz; 50 kw. Ant 1,269 ft TL: N45 29 20 W122 41 40. Stereo. Hrs open: 24 6400 S.E. Lake Rd., 97222. Phone: (503) 786-0600. Fax: (503) 786-1551. Web Site:www.kpdq.com Licensee: Salem Media of Oregon Inc. Group owner: Salem Communications Corp. (acq 8-86; grpsl; 7-28-86). Population served: 1,500,000 Format: Christian talk. Target aud: 25-54; listeners of Christian talk progmg. ♦Dennis Hayes, gen mgr; Mark Durkin, gen sls mgr; Jordan Smith, mktg dir, prom dir; Justin Mansfield, progmg dir, progmg mgr; Georgene Rice, news dir; Don Perkins, chief of engrg.

KPOJ(AM)— Mar 25, 1922: 620 khz; 25 kw-D, 10 kw-N, DA-2. TL: N45 25 20 W122 33 57. Hrs open: 24 4949 S.W. Macadam, 97201. Phone: (503) 323-6400. Fax: (503) 323-6664.E-mail: deaveosporne @clearchannel.com Web Site:www.620kpoj.com Licensee: Citicasters Licenses L.P. Group owner: Clear Channel Communications Inc. (acq 1999; grpsl). Natl. Network: ABC, . Format: News/talk. Target aud: 25-54. ♦Robert Dove, gen mgr; Mike Dirkx, opns mgr.

***KQAC(FM)**— August 1983: 89.9 mhz; 8.7 kw. Ant 964 ft TL: N45 30 58 W122 43 59. Stereo. Hrs open: 24 515 N.E. 15th Ave., 97232. Phone: (503) 943-5828. Fax: (503) 802-9456. Web Site:www.allclassical.org Licensee: KBPS Public Radio Foundation (acq 12-15-2003; $5.5 million). Population served: 1,750,000 Natl. Network: PRI, . Garvey, Schubert & Barer. Format: Classical. News: 5 hrs wkly. ♦Sally Lewis, dev dir; Larry Holtz, chief of engrg.

***KRRC(FM)**— May 1958: 97.9 mhz; 8 w. Ant 13 ft TL: N45 28 51 W122 37 50. Hrs open: Reed College, 3203 S.E. Woodstock, 97202. Phone: (503) 771-1112. Fax: (503) 777-7769. Licensee: The Reed Institute. (acq 1959). Population served: 385,000 Format: Div. Target aud: 17-21; Reed College student body. Spec prog: Black 10 hrs, class 4 hrs, country 2 hrs, Fr 2 hrs, jazz 10 hrs, Sp 2 hrs wkly. ♦Nicholas Wright, gen mgr; Kristin Holmberg, opns dir, mus dir.

KRSK(FM)—(Molalla, July 3, 1970: 105.1 mhz; 21 kw. Ant 1,542 ft TL: N45 31 21 W122 44 45. Stereo. Hrs open: 0700 S.W. Bancroft St., 97239. Phone: (503) 223-1441. Fax: (503) 223-6909.E-mail: info@1051thebuzz.com Web Site:www.1051thebuzz.com Licensee: Entercom Portland License L.L.C. Group owner: Entercom Communications Corp. (acq 4-23-98; grpsl). Population served: 1,200,000 Format: Hot adult contemp. ♦David Field, pres; Erin Hubert, gen mgr; Brian Lee, gen sls mgr; Liz Kay, prom dir; Jeff McHugh, progmg dir; Sheryl Steward, mus dir.

KSZN(AM)—(Gresham, Sept 28, 1956: 1230 khz; 1 kw-U. TL: N45 29 35 W122 24 40. Stereo. Hrs open: 24 5110 S.E. Stark St., WA, 97215. Phone: (503) 234-5550. Fax: (503) 234-5583.E-mail: rtatum@bustosmedia.com Web Site:www.bustosmedia.com Licensee: Bustos Media of Oregon License LLC. Group owner: Bustos Media Holdings (acq 7-15-2003; $1.13 million). Population served: 300,000 Format: Sp. News: 3 hrs wkly. Target aud: 12-54; lower to upper middle income. Spec prog: News 3 hrs, relg one hr wkly. ♦Amador S. Bustos, pres; Rick Tatum, gen mgr; Tom Oberg, gen sls mgr; Henry Cuallo, prom dir; James Boyd, chief of engrg.

KUFO-FM— May 1, 1977: 101.1 mhz; 100 kw. 1,640 ft TL: N45 30 58 W122 43 59. Stereo. Hrs open: 24 Prog sep from AM 20040 S.W. 1st Ave., 97201. Phone: (503) 223-0300. Fax: (503) 497-2314.E-mail: info@kufo.com Web Site:www.kufo.com Licensee: Infinity Radio Inc. Population served: 250,000 Format: AOR.

KUPL-FM— 1948: 98.7 mhz; 37 kw. 1,443 ft TL: N45 30 58 W122 43 59. Stereo. Hrs open: 24 222 S.W. Columbia, Suite 350, 97201. Phone: (503) 223-0300. Fax: (503) 223-6995.E-mail: laura.klein @infinitybroadcasting.com Web Site:www.kupl.com Licensee: Radio Systems of Miami Inc. Group owner: Infinity Broadcasting Corp. (acq 11-13-98; grpsl). Population served: 1,674,000 Natl. Network: AP Radio, . Leventhal, Senter & Lerman. Format: Country. News staff: one. Target aud: 25-54. ♦Mel Karmazin, chmn; Dan Mason, pres; Mark Walen, gen mgr; Lee Rogers, opns mgr; Tom Hunter, prom mgr; Cary Rolfe, progmg dir.

KWJJ-FM— 1968: 99.5 mhz; 50 kw. Ant 1,266 ft TL: N45 29 20 W122 41 40. Stereo. Hrs open: 0700 S.W. Bancroft St., 97239. Phone: (503) 223-1441. Fax: (503) 223-6909.E-mail: info@thewolfonline.com Web Site:www.thewolfonline.com Licensee: Entercom Portland License LLC. Format: Country. Target aud: 25-54.

KXL(AM)— 1926: 750 khz; 50 kw-D, 20 kw-N, DA-2. TL: N45 24 05 W122 26 47. Hrs open: 0234 S.W. Bancroft, 97231. Phone: (503) 243-7595. Fax: (503) 417-7662. Web Site:www.kxl.com Licensee: Rose City Radio Corp. (group owner; (acq 11-30-98; $55 million with co-located FM). Population served: 1,473,700 Natl. Network: CBS, . Natl. Rep: McGavren Guild,. Format: News/talk. Target aud: 25-54. ♦Rose City Radio, CFO; Tim McNamara, gen mgr; James Derby, opns mgr; Bill Ashenden, gen sls mgr.

***KXPD(AM)**—(Tigard, June 28, 1993: 1040 khz; 2.2 kw-D, 200 w-N. TL: N45 28 26 W122 39 33. Stereo. Hrs open: 24 871 Country Club Rd., Eugene, 97401-6009. Phone: (541) 344-5500. Fax: (541) 485-2550.E-mail: info@kxpd.com Licensee: Churchill Communications LLC. Group owner: EMF Broadcasting (acq 7-31-2006; $1.8 million). Format: Sp. ♦Suzanne Arlie, gen mgr.

KXTG(FM)— June 18, 1965: 95.5 mhz; 100 kw. Ant 990 ft TL: N45 29 23 W122 41 47. Stereo. Hrs open: 24 0234 S.W. Bancroft, 97231. Phone: (503) 243-7595. Fax: (503) 417-7662. Web Site:www.955thegame.com Licensee: Rose City Radio Corp. Natl. Network: Fox Sports, . Format: Sports. ♦Tim McNamara, gen sls mgr; James Derby, progmg dir.

KYCH-FM— Apr 1, 1980: 97.1 mhz; 100 kw. Amt 1,266 ft TL: N45 29 20 W122 41 40. Stereo. Hrs open: 0700 S.W. Bancroft St., 97239. Phone: (503) 223-1441. Fax: (503) 223-6909.E-mail: cryan@entercom.com Web Site:www.charliefm.com Licensee: Entercom Portland License L.L.C. Group owner: Entercom (acq 4-23-98; grpsl). Population served: 230,000 Natl. Rep: Christal,. Format: Adult contemp hits. Target aud: 25-54. ♦David Field, pres; Jack Hutchinson, exec VP; Maureen Pulicella, gen sls mgr; Dan Persigehl, progmg dir; Shel Bailey, prom dir & news dir; Gary Hilliard, chief of engrg.

Prineville

KLTW-FM— Apr 8, 1981: 95.1 mhz; 100 kw. Ant 472 ft TL: N44 18 32 W120 55 47. Stereo. Hrs open: 24
Translators: 104.5 mhz Bend, OR and 104.5 mhz Madras, OR.
854 NE 4th Street, Bend, 97701. Phone: (541) 383-3825. Web Site:www.lite951.com Licensee: Horizon Broadcasting Group LLC. (acq 2000). Population served: 200,000 Natl. Rep: Christal,. Format: Adult Contemporary. News staff: 3. Target aud: 25-54. Spec prog: Inside Central Oregon (Public Affairs). ♦Keith Shipman, gen mgr; Brian Canady, sls dir; John Edwards, gen sls mgr; Jeffrey Brian Nelson, progmg dir; Bill Baker, news dir, pub affrs dir.

KNLX(FM)— 2008: 104.9 mhz; 860 w. Ant 2,214 ft TL: N44 26 13 W120 57 11. Hrs open: Box 7408, Bend, 97708-7408. Secondary address: 30 S.E. Bridgeford Blvd., Bend 97702. Phone: (541) 389-8873. Fax: (541) 389-5291. Web Site:www.knlr.com Licensee: Cowan Broadcasting LLC (acq 4-30-2008; $25,000 for CP). Format: Christian. ♦Terry A. Cowan, gen mgr.

KRCO(AM)— Feb 1, 1950: 690 khz; 1 kw-D, 77 w-N. TL: N44 20 30 W120 54 10. Hrs open: 24
Translator: 96.9 mhz Prineville, OR.
854 NE 4th Street, Bend, 97701. Phone: (541) 447-6770. Fax: (541) 383-3403. Web Site:www.krcoam.com Licensee: Horizon Broadcasting Group L.L.C (group owner; (acq 3-2-2000; grpsl). Population served: 200,000 Natl. Network: ABC, . Natl. Rep: Christal,. Format: Classic Country. News staff: 3. Target aud: 35-64. ♦Keith Shipman, pres & gen mgr; Brian Canady, sls dir; John Edwards, gen sls mgr, news dir; Jack Friday, progmg dir; Bill Baker, news dir, pub affrs dir.

Rainier

KPPK(FM)— November 2005: 98.3 mhz; 1.6 kw. Ant 640 ft TL: N46 10 59 W122 57 29. Hrs open: 1130 14th Ave., Longview, WA, 98632. Phone: (360) 425-1500. Fax: (360) 423-1554.E-mail: grodman@biocoastalmedia.com Licensee: Bicoastal Media Licenses IV LLC. Format: Adult contemp 70s, 80s, and 90s. ♦Kevin P. Mostyn, opns mgr.

Redmond

***KKJA(FM)**— July 18, 2008: 89.9 mhz; 750 w. Ant 2,217 ft TL: N44 26 17 W120 57 14. Hrs open:
Rebroadcasts KAWZ(FM) Twin Falls, ID 100%.
CSN International, 4002 N. 3300 E., Twin Falls, ID, 83301. Phone: (208) 734-6633. Fax: (208) 736-1958. Web Site:www.csnradio.com Licensee: CSN International. Natl. Network: CSN, . Format: Christian praise & worship, Bible teaching. ♦Mike Kestler, pres; Mike Stocklin, gen mgr.

KLRR(FM)—Licensed to Redmond. See Bend

KRDM(AM)— June 2004: 1240 khz; 750 w-U. TL: N44 16 41 W121 08 44. Hrs open: 24 Box 817, 97756. Secondary address: 416 S.W. Black Bute Blvd. 97756. Phone: (541) 548-7621. Fax: (541) 504-8145.E-mail: sales@radiolabronca.net Licensee: Red Mountain Broadcasting LLC (acq 5-3-2006; $500,000). Population served: 176,000 Format: Sp-Rgnl Mexico. ♦Juan Zendejas, pres & gen mgr.

KSJJ(FM)— Feb 4, 1981: 102.9 mhz; 100 kw. 885 ft TL: N44 10 25 W121 16 29. Stereo. Hrs open: 24 969 S.W. Colorado, Bend, 97702. Secondary address: 1500 N.E. Butler Market Rd., Bend 97702. Phone: (541) 388-3300. Fax: (541)389-7885.E-mail: info@ksjj.com Web Site:www.ksjj.com Licensee: GCC Bend LLC. (group owner; (acq 1999; grpsl). Arent, Fox, Kintner, Plotkin & Kahn. Format: Country. News staff: one; News: 8 hrs wkly. Target aud: 25-54. ♦Dana Horner, stn mgr & sls dir.

***KWRX(FM)**— 2002: 88.5 mhz; 250 w. Ant 2,198 ft TL: N44 26 14 W120 57 12. (CP: 720 w). Hrs open: Agate Hall, Univ. of Oregon, 97403. Phone: (541) 345-0800.E-mail: kwax@qwest.net Web Site:www.kwax.com Licensee: State Board of Higher Education for the University of Oregon. Format: Classical. ♦Paul C. Bjornstad, gen mgr.

Reedsport

KDUN(AM)— June 2, 1961: 1030 khz; 50 kw-D, 630 w-N. TL: N43 44 17 W124 04 30. Hrs open: 24 136 N. 7th St., 97467. Phone: (541) 271-1030. Fax: (541) 271-2598.E-mail: traffic.kdun@gmail.com Web Site:www.kdun.com Licensee: Bill Schweitzer dba WKS Broadcasting Inc. Group owner: Pamplin Broadcasting (acq 8-29-2006; $220,000). Population served: 50,000 Natl. Network: CBS Radio, . Rgnl rep: McGavren-Guild Format: News, Talk. Target aud: 25 plus. ♦Bill Schweitzer, gen mgr; Joe Zelinski, opns mgr.

KJMX(FM)— 1993: 99.5 mhz; 11 kw. Ant 400 ft TL: N43 40 40 W124 06 36. Hrs open: 24 Box180, Coos Bay, 97467. Phone: (541) 267-2121. Fax: (541) 267-5229. Web Site:www.kjmxfm.com Licensee: Bicoastal Media Licenses III LLC. Group owner: Bicoastal Media L.L.C. (acq 10-16-2003; grpsl). Format: Classic rock. News staff: one; News: 2 hrs wkly. ♦John Pundt, gen mgr; Mike O'Brien, opns mgr.

***KLFR(FM)**— 1999: 89.1 mhz; 1 kw. 400 ft TL: N43 43 21 W124 05 40. Hrs open: 24 136 W. 8th Ave., Eugene, 97401-0640. Phone: (541) 463-6000. Fax: (541) 463-6046.E-mail: klcc@klcc.org Web Site:www.klcc.org Licensee: Lane Community College (acq 1-5-01; $32,500 for CP). Format: News/talk, adult contemp. ♦Steve Barton, gen mgr; Paula Chan Carpenter, dev dir; Gayle Chisholm, prom mgr; Don Heim, progmg dir.

***KSYD(FM)**— March 1990: 92.1 mhz; 3 kw. 358 ft TL: N43 39 26 W124 11 10. Hrs open: 24
KRVM FM 92.1.
1574 Coburg Rd. # 237, Eugene, 97401. Phone: (541) 687-3370. Fax: (541) 687-3573.E-mail: info@krvm.org Web Site:www.krvm.org Licensee: School District 4J Lane County. Format: AAA. Target aud: 12-40. ♦Carl Sundberg, gen mgr, chief of engrg; Bobbie Cirel, dev dir, gen sls mgr; Ken Martin, progmg dir.

Riley

***KOHP(FM)**—Not on air, target date: unknown: 89.1 mhz; 2.5 kw. Ant 1,771 ft TL: N43 33 25 W120 04 23. Hrs open:
Rebroadcasts KOPB-FM Portland 100%.
Oregon Public Broadcasting, 7140 S.W. Macadam Ave., Portland, 97219-3099. Phone: (503) 293-1905. Fax: (503) 293-1919. Web Site:www.opb.org Licensee: Oregon Public Broadcasting. Ore. Pub. Bcstg Radio Net. ♦Steve Bass, CEO & pres.

Rockaway Beach

***KLON(FM)**— 2005: 90.3 mhz; 1.8 kw vert. Ant 342 ft TL: N45 36 18 W123 55 30. Hrs open: 24
Rebroadcasts KLVR(FM) Santa Rosa, CA 100%.
2351 Sunset Blvd., Suite 170-218, Rocklin, CA, 95765. Phone: (916) 251-1600. Fax: (916) 251-1650.E-mail: klove@klove.com Web Site:www.klove.com Licensee: Educational Media Foundation. Group owner: EMF Broadcasting. Natl. Network: K-Love, . Shaw Pittman. Format: Contemp Christian. News staff: 3. Target aud: 25-44; Judeo Christian, female. ♦Richard Jenkins, pres; Mike Novak, VP; Ed Lenane, opns dir, news dir; Keith Whipple, dev dir; David Pierce, progmg mgr; Sam Wallington, engrg dir; Karen Johnson, news rptr.

Rogue River

KRRM(FM)— October 1994: 94.7 mhz; 130 w. 2,043 ft TL: N42 26 44 W123 12 56. Hrs open: 24 225 Rogue River Hwy., Grants Pass, 97527. Phone: (541) 479-6497. Fax: (541) 479-5726.E-mail: krrm@krrm.com Web Site:www.krrm.com Licensee: Shirley M. Bell. Population served: 99,100 Format: Classic country. Target aud: 35 plus. ♦Herb Bell, gen mgr, opns dir, progmg mgr; Shirley Bell, opns dir & sls dir.

Roseburg

***KMPQ(FM)**— Nov 24, 2004: 88.1 mhz; 950 w. Ant 351 ft TL: N43 12 22 W123 21 50. Hrs open: 136 W. 8th Ave., Eugene, 97401-0640. Phone: (541) 463-6000. Fax: (541) 463-6046.E-mail: klcc@klcc.org Web Site:www.klcc.org Licensee: Lane Community College. Natl. Network: NPR, . Format: News/talk, adult contemp. ♦Steve Barton, gen mgr; Paula Carpenter, dev dir; Don Hein, progmg dir.

KQEN(AM)— Sept 19, 1950: 1240 khz; 1 kw-U. TL: N43 11 44 W123 21 33. Hrs open: 24 Box 5180, 97470. Phone: (541) 672-6641. Fax: (541) 673-7598. Web Site:www.am1240kqen.com Licensee: Brooke Communications Inc. (group owner; acq 5-1-86; $173,000). Population served: 90,000 Natl. Network: ESPN Radio, . Natl. Rep: Tacher,. Haley, Bader & Potts. Format: News/ talk, sports. News staff: 2; News: 4 hrs wkly. Target aud: 35 plus; general. Spec prog: Sports. ♦Patrick A. Markham, pres; Mike Carter, opns mgr; Brian Prawitz, news dir.

KRSB-FM— Oct 1, 1970: 103.1 mhz; 2.75 kw. 308 ft TL: N43 12 24 W123 21 47. (CP: 25.5 kw, ant 676 ft. TL: N43 13 59 W123 19 22). Stereo. Hrs open: 24 1445 W. Harvard Ave., 97470. Phone: (541) 672-6641. Fax: (541) 673-7598.E-mail: country@bciradio.com Web Site:www.bestcountry103.com Licensee: Brooke Communications Inc. (group owner; acq 4-30-89). Population served: 90,000 Natl. Network: ABC, . Natl. Rep: Tacher,. Garvey Schubert Barer. Format: Contemp country. News staff: 2; News: 15 hrs wkly. Target aud: 25-54. ♦Patrick A. Markham, pres & gen mgr; Mike Carter, chief of opns.

KSKR(AM)— August 1935: 1490 khz; 1 kw-U. TL: N43 11 35 W123 21 39. Hrs open: 24 1445 W. Harvard Ave., 97470. Phone: (541) 672-6641. Phone: (541) 673-5551. Fax: (541) 673-7598. Web Site:www.kskrthescore.com Licensee: Brooke Communications Inc. (acq 1-14-2005). Population served: 55,000 Natl. Network: ESPN Radio, . Natl. Rep: Tacher,. Garvey, Schubert & Barer. Format: Sports. News staff: 2. Target aud: 25 plus. ♦Patrick A. Markham, pres; Mike Carter, gen mgr, progmg dir, mus dir; Pam Houck, gen sls mgr.

***KSRS(FM)**— December 1990: 91.5 mhz; 2 kw. 305 ft TL: N43 12 24 W123 21 47. Stereo. Hrs open: 5 AM-2 AM 1250 Siskiyou Blvd., Ashland, 97520. Phone: (541) 552-6301. Fax: (541) 552-8565.E-mail: info@ijpr.org Web Site:www.ijpr.org Licensee: The State of Oregon, Acting By and Through the State Board of Higher Education, for the benefit of Southern Oregon University. Natl. Network: NPR, PRI, . Ernest Sanchez. Wire Svc: AP Format: Class, news. News staff: one; News: 35 hrs wkly. Target aud: General. ♦Ronald Kramer, CEO & gen mgr; Bryon Lambert, opns dir; Paul Westhelle, dev dir.

***KTBR(AM)**— November 1955: 950 khz; 1 kw-D, 20 w-N. TL: N43 10 08 W123 22 28. Hrs open: 24 hrs Jefferson Public Radio, 1250 Siskiyou Blvd., Ashland, 97520. Phone: (541) 552-6301.E-mail: info@ijpr.org Web Site:www.ijpr.org Licensee: JPR Foundation Inc. (acq 4-19-02; $83,700 with KOOZ(FM) Myrtle Point). Population served: 75,000 Natl. Network: NPR, PRI, . Ernest Sanchez. Format: News info. News staff: one. Target aud: General. ♦Mitchell Christian, CFO; Ronald Kramer, CEO & gen mgr; Bryon Lambert, opns dir; Paul Westhelle, dev dir.

Saint Helens

KOHI(AM)— Mar 2, 1960: 1600 khz; 1 kw-D, 12 w-N. TL: N45 51 15 W122 49 11. Hrs open: 24
Talkstar Radio Network.
36200 Pittsburg Rd., Ste C, 97051-1188. Phone: (503) 397-1600. Fax: (503) 397-1601.E-mail: kohiradio@gmail.com Web Site:www.am1600kohi.com Licensee: Volcano Broadcasting. (acq 5-21-82; $150,000; 6-14-82). Population served: 26,000 Natl. Rep: Keystone (unwired net),. Rgnl rep: Tacher Format: Talk, sports, news. News staff: one; News: 12 hrs wkly. Target aud: Adults 25-65. Spec prog: Sports Talk, Religion. ♦David Aldridge, pres; Marty Rowe, VP, gen mgr; Alex Rowe, progmg dir; Thad Houk, sports cmtr.

Salem

***KAJC(FM)**— 2006: 90.1 mhz; 560 w. Ant 128 ft TL: N44 45 33 W123 13 34. Hrs open: 24 1399 Monmouth St., Independence, 97351. Phone: (503) 838-2476. Fax: (503) 838-2476.E-mail: kajc@kajcfm.org Web Site:www.kajcfm.org Licensee: CSN International (group owner). Format: Relg.

KBZY(AM)— May 1957: 1490 khz; 1 kw-U. TL: N44 57 03 W123 02 43. Hrs open: 24 2659 Commercial St. SE, Ste 204, 97302-4496. Phone: (503) 362-1490. Fax: (503) 362-6545.E-mail: kbzy@com.net Web Site:www.kbzy.com Licensee: Capital Broadcasting Inc. (acq 6-15-82; $365,000; 7-5-82). Population served: 415,000 Rgnl rep: Tacher Format: Local svc oldies. Target aud: 25-54. ♦Roy Dittman, pres, gen mgr; Terry Sol, progmg dir.

KGAL(AM)—Lebanon

KPJC(AM)— Dec 12, 1961: 1220 khz; 1 kw-D, 171 w-N. TL: N44 58 57 W123 00 17. Hrs open: 24 Box 17008, 97305. Phone: (503) 316-1220. Fax: (503) 364-1022.E-mail: info@jctown.com Web Site:www.thejctown.com Licensee: KCCS LLC (acq 4-15-2004; $500,000). Population served: 250,000 Natl. Network: USA, . Natl. Rep: Broadcast Reps Canada,. Reddy, Begley & McCormick. Format: Christian Family Radio. News: 14 hrs wkly. Target aud: 25-54; family. ♦Christina Evans, gen mgr; Phil Swearingin, opns mgr.

KSHO(AM)—Lebanon

***KWBX(FM)**— Apr 1, 2002: 90.3 mhz; 135 w vert. Ant 46 ft TL: N44 52 57 W122 57 34. Stereo. Hrs open: 24 Corban College, 5000 Deer Park Dr. S.E., 97317. Phone: (503) 375-7591. Fax: (503) 585-4316.E-mail: kwbx@corban.edu Web Site:www.corban.edu/radio Licensee: Corban College. Population served: 200,000 Reddy, Begley & McCormick. Format: Christian hit music, positive alternative. News staff: one; News: one hr wkly. Target aud: 25-44; young adults. ♦Dr. Reno Hoff, pres; Steve Hunt, gen mgr; Josh Bartlett, stn mgr.

KWIP(AM)—(Dallas, Apr 15, 1955: 880 khz; 5 kw-D, 1 kw-N. TL: N44 55 45 W123 17 22. Stereo. Hrs open: 1405 E. Ellendale, Dallas, 97338. Phone: (503) 623-0245. Fax: (503) 623-6733.E-mail: info@kwip.com Web Site:www.kwip.com Licensee: Jupiter Communications Corp. (acq 6-10-91; $21,000; 7-1-91). Population served: 200,000 Format: Rgnl Mexican. Target aud: 18-54; families & blue collar workers. Spec prog: Talk 5 hrs wkly. ♦Diana Burns, gen mgr.

KWOD(AM)— 1934: 1390 khz; 5 kw-D, 690 kw-N. TL: N44 59 43 W123 04 15. Hrs open: 0700 S.W. Bancroft St., Portland, 97239. Phone: (503) 223-1441. Fax: (503) 223-6909. Web Site:www.espndeportesradio.com Licensee: Entercom Portland License LLC. Group owner: Entercom Communications Corp. (acq 10-22-98; $605,000). Population served: 300,000 Natl. Network: ESPN Deportes, . Rgnl rep: Allied Radio Partners. Format: Sp sports. ♦David Field, pres; Jack Hutchison, exec VP.

KYKN(AM)—See Keizer

Sandy

***KLVP(FM)**— 1997: 88.7 mhz; 245 w horiz, 3.7 kw vert. Ant 1,745 ft TL: N45 20 01 W121 42 45. Stereo. Hrs open: 24
Rebroadcasts KLVR(FM) Middletown, CA 100%.
2351 Sunset Blvd., Suite 170-218, Rocklin, CA, 95765. Phone: (916) 251-1600. Fax: (916) 251-1650.E-mail: klove@klove.com Web Site:www.klove.com Licensee: Educational Media Foundation. Group owner: EMF Broadcasting. Population served: 1,184,000 Natl. Network: K-Love, . Shaw Pittman. Format: Contemp Christian. News staff: 3. Target aud: 25-44; Judeo-Christian, female. ♦Mike Novak, pres.

Scappoose

KFIS(FM)— May 1986: 104.1 mhz; 6.9 kw. Ant 1,266 ft TL: N45 29 20 W122 41 40. Hrs open: 6400 S.E. Lake Rd., Suite 350, Portland, 97222. Phone: (503) 786-0600. Fax: (503) 786-1551. Web Site:www.1041thefish.com Licensee: Caron Broadcasting Inc. Group owner: Salem Communications Corp. (acq 9-20-2001; $35.8 million). Population served: 25,000 Gardner, Carton & Douglas. Format: Christian. Target aud: 25-54; women. ♦Dennis Hayes, gen mgr; Jordan Smith, mktg dir & prom dir; Dave Arthur, progmg dir.

Seaside

KCRX-FM— 1998: 102.3 mhz; 25 kw. Ant 328 ft TL: N45 57 08 W123 56 14. Hrs open: 1006 W. Marine St., Astoria, 97103. Phone: (503) 325-2911. Fax: (503) 325-5570.E-mail: kcrx@nnbradio.com Web Site:www.kcrx1023.com Licensee: New Northwest Broadcasters LLC (group owner; acq 8-24-99; grpsl). Format: Classic rock. ◆Paul Mitchell, gen mgr; Tom Freel, opns mgr; Bob Castle, progmg dir.

KCYS(FM)— Nov 26, 1996: 98.1 mhz; 6 kw. 174 ft TL: N45 57 8 W123 56 14. Stereo. Hrs open: 24 Box 1258, Astoria, 97103. Secondary address: 1324 N. Holladay Dr. 97138. Phone: (503) 717-9643. Fax (503) 717-9578.E-mail: info@kcysfm.com Licensee: Dave's Broadcasting Co. (acq 6-23-2005; for 66.66% of stock). Population served: 40,000 Rgnl rep: Tacher. Format: Country. Target aud: 35-44; working moms with kids, some college. ◆ Dave Heick, gen mgr.

KSWB(AM)— July 12, 1968: 840 khz; 1 kw-D, 500 w-N. TL: N45 58 55 W123 55 02. Hrs open: Box 354, 97138. Phone: (503) 738-8668. Fax: (503) 738-8778. Licensee: Cannon Beach Radio (acq 3-10-2000). Format: Oldies. ◆John Chapman, gen mgr.

Selma

*****KJKL(FM)**— 2003: 88.7 mhz; 9 kw vert. Ant 1,916 ft TL: N42 15 29 W123 39 32. Hrs open: 2351 Sunset Blvd., Suite 170-218, Rocklin, CA, 95765. Phone: (916) 251-1600. Fax: (916) 251-1650.E-mail: klove@klove.com Web Site:www.klove.com Licensee: Educational Media Foundation. Group owner: EMF Broadcasting. Natl. Network: K-Love, . Shaw Pittman. Format: Contemp Christian. News staff: 3. Target aud: 25-44; Judeo Christian, female. ◆Richard Jenkins, pres; Mike Novak, VP; Keith Whipple, dev dir; David Pierce, progmg mgr; Ed Lenane, news dir; Sam Wallington, engrg dir; Karen Johnson, news rptr.

Shaniko

*****KHJJ(FM)**—Not on air, target date: unknown: 90.9 mhz; 12.5 kw. Ant 239 ft TL: N44 55 57 W120 49 03. Hrs open: 2051 S.W. Ferry St., Albany, 97322. Phone: (541) 815-1480. Licensee: Educational Broadcast Service. ◆Dena Crane, pres.

Sisters

*****KVRA(FM)**— 2006: 89.3 mhz; 1.4 kw vert. Ant 633 ft TL: N44 04 40 W121 19 48. Hrs open:
Rebroadcasts KLRD(FM) Yucaipa, CA 100%.
2351 Sunset Blvd., Suite 170-218, Rocklin, CA, 95765. Phone: (916) 251-1600. Fax: (916) 251-1650. Web Site:www.air1.com Licensee: Educational Media Foundation. Natl. Network: Air 1, . Format: Alternative rock, div. ◆Richard Jenkins, pres; Mike Novak, VP; Keith Whipple, dev dir; David Pierce, progmg mgr; Ed Lenane, news dir; Sam Wallington, engrg dir; Karen Johnson, news rptr.

KWPK-FM— June 1, 2001: 104.1 mhz; 34 kw. Ant 590 ft TL: N44 04 40 W121 19 49. Hrs open: 24 854 N.E. 4th St., Bend, 97701. Phone: (541) 383-3825. Fax: (541) 383-3403. Web Site:www.thepeak1041.com Licensee: Horizon Broadcasting Group LLC. (acq 3-31-2005; $475,000). Population served: 200,000 Natl. Rep: Christal,. Format: Hot adult contemporary. News staff: 3. Target aud: 18-49. Spec prog: Inside Central Oregon (Public Affairs). ◆Keith Shipman gen mgr; Brian Canady, sls dir; John Edwards, gen sls mgr; Dave Clemens, progmg dir; Bill Baker, news dir, pub affrs dir.

Springfield

*****KQFE(FM)**— Mar 7, 1989: 88.9 mhz; 2 kw. 418 ft TL: N44 02 01 W123 00 25. Hrs open: 24 4135 Northgate Blvd., Sacramento, CA, 95834. Phone: (800) 835-4810. Fax: (541) 726-9156. Web Site:www.familyradio.com Licensee: Family Stations Inc. (group owner) Natl. Network: Family Radio, . Format: Relg. Target aud: 30 plus; older relg. ◆Harold Camping, gen mgr; Carmen Brambora, opns mgr.

KSCR(AM)—See Eugene

Springfield-Eugene

KKNU(FM)—Licensed to Springfield-Eugene. See Eugene

KORE(AM)— September 1927: 1050 khz; 5 kw-D, 149 w-N. TL: N44 04 07 W123 01 45. Hrs open: 24 2080 Laura St., 97477-2197. Phone:

(541) 747-5673.E-mail: kore@kore1050am.com Licensee: Support Christian Broadcasting Inc. (acq 8-87). Population served: 800,000 Natl. Network: USA, . Format: Christian. Target aud: 18 plus. ◆Larry Knight, gen mgr.

KPNW(AM)—See Eugene

KSCR(AM)—See Eugene

KUGN(AM)—See Eugene

Stanfield

KLKY(FM)— 2005: 96.1 mhz; 8.5 kw. Ant 1,178 ft TL: N45 29 12 W119 25 52. Hrs open: 45 Campbell Rd., Walla Walla, WA, 99362. Phone: (509) 527-1000. Fax: (509) 529-5534. Licensee: Alexandra Communications Inc. Format: Top-40. ◆Tom Hodgins, gen mgr.

Stayton

KCKX(AM)— June 1, 1987: 1460 khz; 1 kw-D, 15 w-N. TL: N44 48 10 W122 44 03. Hrs open: 24 1665 James St., Woodburn, 97071. Phone: (503) 981-9400. Phone: (503) 769-1460. Fax: (503) 981-3561.E-mail: sam@lapantera940.com Web Site:www.cowboycountryradio.net Licensee: Sanlee Broadcasting Corp. (acq 1-21-98; $130,000). Population served: 600,000 Natl. Network: ABC, . Rgnl rep: Allied Radio Partners. Format: Classic country/western. News: 3 hrs wkly. Target aud: 25 plus; stable, mature adults with above average income. Spec prog: Portland Trailblazers basketball, Forest Dragons arena football, high school sports, farm 15 hrs wkly. ◆ Donald Coss, pres & exec VP; Chris McCartney, gen mgr; Andy McGarrett, sls.

Sunriver

KRXF(FM)— 2006: 92.7 mhz; 18.5 kw. Ant 813 ft TL: N44 02 49 W121 31 50. Hrs open: 705 S.W. Bonnett Way, Suite 1100, Bend, 97702. Phone: (541)388-3300. Fax: (541) 388-3303.E-mail: info@927fm.com Web Site:mflanagan@bendradiogroup.com Licensee: Fields Pond Group. Natl. Rep: Katz Radio,. Format: Alternative. ◆Mike Flanagan, progmg dir.

Sutherlin

KSKR-FM— 1999: 101.1 mhz; 3.6 kw. Ant 859 ft TL: N43 22 19 W123 21 15. Hrs open: 24 1445 W. Harvard Ave., Roseburg, 97470. Phone: (541) 672-6641. Fax: (541) 673-7598.E-mail: sales@bciradio.com Web Site:www.kskrthescore.com Licensee: Brooke Communications Inc. (group owner; (acq 12-16-2002). Population served: 90,000 Natl. Network: ESPN Radio, . Rgnl rep: Tacher Garvey Shubert Barer. Format: Sports. ◆Pat Markham, pres & gen mgr; Mike Carter, opns dir, progmg dir; Pam Houck, gen sls mgr.

Sweet Home

KFIR(AM)— Aug 7, 1968: 720 khz; 1 kw-D, 184 w-D. TL: N44 24 52 W122 44 22. Hrs open: Box 720, 28041 Pleasant Valley Rd., 97386. Phone: (541) 367-5115. Fax: (541) 367-5233. Licensee: Radio Fiesta Network LLC (acq 4-13-2007; $500,000). Population served: 650,000 Rgnl rep: Allied Broadcast Partners. Format: Talk radio. Target aud: 25-54 plus. ◆Michael Astalis, gen mgr.

*****KLVU(FM)**— Sept 20, 1989: 107.1 mhz; 9 kw. 2,476 ft TL: N44 28 59 W122 34 55. Stereo. Hrs open: 24 2351 Sunset Blvd., Suite 170-218, Rocklin, CA, 95765. Phone: (916) 251-1600. Fax: (916) 251-1650.E-mail: klove@klove.com Web Site:www.klove.com Licensee: Educational Media Foundation. Group owner: EMF Broadcasting (acq 3-12-97; $4 million). Population served: 1,500,000 Natl. Network: K-Love, . Shaw Pittman. Format: Contemp Christian. News staff: 3. Target aud: 25-44; Judeo-Christian female. ◆Richard Jenkins, pres; Mike Novak, VP; Keith Whipple, dev dir; David Pierce, progmg mgr; Ed Lenane, news dir; Sam Wallington, engrg dir; Karen Johnson, news rptr.

Talent

*****KSJK(AM)**— October 1960: 1230 khz; 1 kw-U. TL: N42 13 27 W122 44 33. Hrs open: 24 hrs Southern Oregon State College, 1250 Siskiyou Blvd., Ashland, 97520. Phone: (541) 552-6301. Fax: (541) 552-8565.E-mail: info@ijpr.org Web Site:www.ijpr.org Licensee: The State of Oregon, acting by and through the State Board of Higher Education. for the benefit of Southern Oregon University. (acq 7-28-89). Population served: 200,000 Natl. Network: PRI, NPR, . Ernest Sanchez. Format: News, info. Target aud: General. Spec prog:

Talk 6 hrs wkly. ◆Mitchell Christian, CFO; Ronald Kramer, CEO & gen mgr; Bryon Lambert, opns dir; Paul Westhelle, dev dir.

The Dalles

KACI(AM)— June 1955: 1300 khz; 1 kw-D, 13 w-N. TL: N45 34 54 W121 07 53. Hrs open: 24 502 Washington St., 97058-8003. Phone: (541) 296-2211. Fax: (541) 296-2213.E-mail: info@kaci.com Licensee: Bicoastal Media Licenses IV LLC. (group owner; (acq 12-1-2007; grpsl). Population served: 40,000 Natl. Network: Jones Radio Networks, . Garvey Schubert Barer. Format: News/talk. News staff: one; News: 14 hrs wkly. Target aud: 25-54. Spec prog: Relg one hr, home improvement 3 hrs, financial talk 6 hrs, computer talk 3 hrs, farm one hr, gardening one hr, pub affrs one hr wkly. ◆Michael Wilson, CEO, pres; Gary M. Grossman, gen mgr, stn mgr, gen sls mgr; Greg LeBlanc, opns dir; Rick Cavagnaro, sls dir; Greg LaBlanc, news dir; Paulette LaRoque, traf mgr.

KACI-FM— Feb 1, 1985: 97.7 mhz; 5 kw. 890 ft TL: N45 38 56 W121 16 20. Stereo. Hrs open: 24 Dups AM 100% 502 Washington St., 97058-8003. Phone: (541) 296-2211. Fax: (541) 296-2213.E-mail: info@kaci.com Licensee: Bicoastal Media Licenses IV LLC. (acq 12-1-2007; grpsl). Population served: 65,000 Format: Oldies. ◆Brian Thompson, progmg mgr; Paulette LaRoque, chief of opns & traf mgr; Greg LeBlanc, local news ed.

KMCQ(FM)— Nov 28, 1968: 104.5 mhz; 100 kw. Ant 1,998 ft TL: N45 42 44 W121 06 50. (CP: COL Covington, WA. 25 kw, ant 318 ft. : N47 11 13 W121 54 11). Stereo. Hrs open: 24 Box 104, 719 E. 2nd St., 97058. Phone: (541) 298-5116. Phone: (541) 298-5117. Fax: (541) 298-5119.E-mail: q104@q104radio.com Web Site:www.q104radio.com Licensee: First Broadcasting Capital Partners LLC. (acq 3-22-2007; $5.1 million). Population served: 80,000 Natl. Network: CNN Radio, . Natl. Rep: McGavren Guild,. FCC Attorney Dominic Monahan, Luvaas Cobb, Eugene, Or. Format: Adult contemp. News staff: one; News: 3 hrs wkly. Target aud: Females 25-49; mothers & family friendly. Spec prog: Blues 4 hrs, teen show 3 hrs wkly. ◆Gary Lawrence, pres; John Huffman, VP, gen mgr; Linda Griswold, sls dir, gen sls mgr; Paula Fairclo, opns dir & progmg dir.

KMSW(FM)— Oct 1, 2002: 92.7 mhz; 3.4 kw. Ant 892 ft TL: N45 38 56 W121 16 20. Stereo. Hrs open: 502 Washington St., 97058-8003. Phone: (541) 296-2211. Fax: (541) 296-2213.E-mail: info@kaci.com Web Site:www.gorgeradio.com Licensee: Bicoastal Media Licenses IV LLC. (acq 12-1-2007; grpsl). Rgnl rep: Tacher Format: Classic rock. Target aud: 25-54. ◆Michael Wilson, pres; Gary Grossman, gen mgr; Rick Cavagnaro, sls dir.

KODL(AM)— Oct 12, 1940: 1440 khz; 5 kw-D, 1 kw-N, DA-N. TL: N45 35 31 W121 11 57. Hrs open: Box 1488, 97058. Secondary address: 404 E. 2nd St. 97058. Phone: (541) 296-2101. Fax: (541) 296-3766.E-mail: web-master@kodl.net Web Site:www.kodl.com Licensee: Larson-Wynn Inc. (acq 9-1-74). Population served: 55,000 Format: Adult standard. Spec prog: Farm 4 hrs, Sp 2 hrs wkly. ◆Al Wynn, pres, gen mgr; Marcia Wynn, opns dir.

*****KOTD(FM)**— 2008: 89.7 mhz; 12 w. Ant 1,932 ft TL: N45 42 43 W121 06 58. Hrs open:
Rebroadcasts KOPB-FM Portland 100%.
7140 S.W. Macadam Ave., Portland, 97219-3099. Phone: (503) 293-1905. Fax: (503) 293-1919. Web Site:www.opb.org/radio/ Licensee: Oregon Public Broadcasting. Natl. Network: NPR, . Ore. Pub. Bcstg Radio Net. Format: News/talk. ◆Steve Bass, gen mgr.

*****KQDL(FM)**— 2008: 88.1 mhz; 5 w horiz, 500 w vert. Ant -738 ft TL: N45 38 11 W121 10 35. Hrs open:
Rebroadcasts KBPS-FM Portland 100%.
515 N.E. 15th Ave., Portland, 97232. Phone: (503) 943-5828. Fax: (503) 802-9456. Web Site:www.allclassical.org Licensee: KBPS Public Radio Foundation. Format: Classical. ◆Jack Allen, CEO & pres.

Tigard

KXPD(AM)—Licensed to Tigard. See Portland

Tillamook

*****KAIK(FM)**— 2006: 88.5 mhz; 60 w vert. Ant 1,276 ft TL: N45 27 59 W123 55 11. Hrs open:
Rebroadcasts KLRD(FM) Yucaipa, CA 100%.
2351 Sunset Blvd., Sute 170-218, Rocklin, CA, 95765. Phone: (916) 251-1600. Fax: (916) 251-1650.E-mail: info@air1.com Web Site:www.air1.com Licensee: Educational Media Foundation. Group owner: EMF Broadcasting. Natl. Network: Air 1, . Shaw Pittman. Format: Contemp Christian. News staff: 3. Target aud: 18-35; Judeo Christian female. ◆Richard Jenkins, pres; Mike Novak, VP; Keith

Whipple, dev dir; David Pierce, progmg mgr; Ed Lenane, news dir; Sam Wallington, engrg dir; Karen Johnson, news rptr.

KMBD(AM)— August 1947: 1590 khz; 5 kw-D, 1 kw-N, DA-N. TL: N45 27 24 W123 52 36. Hrs open: Box 40, 97141. Secondary address: 170 W. 3rd St. 97141. Phone: (503) 842-4422. Fax: (503) 842-2755.E-mail: comments@ktil-kmbd.com Web Site:www.ktil-kmbd.com Licensee: Oregon Eagle Inc. (acq 12-29-86; $250,000; grpsl; 10-26-86). Population served: 4,500 Format: News/talk, sports. ♦ Van Moe, pres & gen mgr.

*KTCB(FM)— Aug 25, 2004: 89.5 mhz; 380 w. Ant 1,151 ft TL: N45 27 59 W123 55 11. Stereo. Hrs open: 24 Box 269, Astoria, 97103. Phone: (503) 325-0010. Fax: (503) 325-3956.E-mail: kmun@kmun.org Web Site:www.kmun.org Licensee: Tillicum Foundation (acq 1-23-2003; swap for KTMK(FM) Tillamook). Natl. Network: NPR, . Garvey, Schubert & Barer. Wire Svc: AP Format: Public/Eclectic. News: 35 hrs wkly. ♦David Hammock, gen mgr; Arlene Layton, dev dir; Elizabeth Grant, progmg dir; Joanne Rideout, news dir.

KTIL-FM— October 1998: 94.3 mhz; 1.8 kw. Ant 1,171 ft TL: N45 27 59 W123 55 11. Stereo. Hrs open: 24 Box 40, 170 3rd St., 97141. Phone: (503) 842-4422. Fax: (503) 842-2755.E-mail: comments@ktil-kmbol.com Web Site:www.ktil-kmbd.com Licensee: Oregon Eagle Inc. (acq 2-4-99). Format: MOR, Music of your life. Target aud: General. ♦ Van Moe, pres & gen mgr.

*KTMK(FM)— 2005: 91.1 mhz; 140 w. Ant 1,168 ft TL: N45 27 59 W123 55 11. Hrs open: Oregon Public Broadcasting, 7140 S.W. Macadam Ave., Portland, 97219-3099. Phone: (503) 244-1905. Fax: (503) 293-1919. Web Site:www.opb.org Licensee: Oregon Public Broadcasting (acq 1-16-2003; swap for KTCB(FM) Tillamook). ♦Steve Bass, gen mgr.

Toledo

KCUP(AM)— Sept 26, 1960: 1230 khz; 1 kw-U. TL: N44 37 47 W123 56 35. Hrs open: Box 456, 145 N. Coast Hwy., Newport, 97365. Phone: (541) 265-5000. Fax: (541) 265-9576. Licensee: Agpal Broadcasting Inc. (acq 3-14-90; grpsl; 4-2-90). Population served: 34,000 Natl. Rep: McGavren Guild,. Haley, Bader & Potts. Format: Oldies. Target aud: 25-54. ♦ Cheryl Harle, gen mgr; Ed Kowas, gen sls mgr.

KPPT-FM— December 1980: 100.7 mhz; 3 kw. 430 ft TL: N48 38 40 W124 00 52. Stereo. Hrs open: Box 456, Newport, 97365. Secondary address: 145 N. Coast Hwy., Newport, 97365. Phone: (541) 265-5000. Fax: (541) 265-9576. Licensee: Agpal Broadcasting Inc. Population served: 43,000 Format: Classic rock. ♦Cheryl Harle, VP.

Tri City

KKMX(FM)— June 1, 1993: 104.3 mhz; 5.6 kw. Ant 1,384 ft TL: N43 00 13 W123 21 26. Stereo. Hrs open: 24 1445 W. Harvard Ave., Roseburg, 97470. Phone: (541) 672-6641. Fax: (541) 673-7598.E-mail: kissfm@bciradio.com Web Site:www.1045kiss.com Licensee: Brooke Communications Inc. (group owner; acq 11-21-96). Population served: 90,000. Natl. Rep: Tacher,. Garvey, Schubert & Barer. Format: Adult contemp. News staff: 2; News: 2 hrs wkly. Target aud: 25-54; general. ♦ Pat Markham, CEO, pres & gen mgr; Mike Carter, opns dir.

Troutdale

KPAM(AM)— 1997: 860 khz; 50 kw-D, 5 w-N. TL: N45 33 24 W122 29 08. Hrs open: 24 6605 S.E. Lake Rd., Portland, 97222. Phone: (503) 223-4321. Fax: (503) 294-0074.E-mail: email@kpam.com Web Site:www.kpam.com Licensee: Pamplin Broadcasting-Oregon Inc. Group owner: Pamplin Broadcasting (acq 12-29-97; $652,500 for 87% of stock). Natl. Network: ABC, . Natl. Rep: Tacher,. Rgnl rep: The Tacher Co.,. Wire Svc: AP Format: News/talk. News staff: 11; News: 35.4 hrs wkly. Target aud: 35-54; adults. Spec prog: Wall St. Journal. ♦Paul Clithero, gen mgr; Mark Ail, opns dir; Margaret Evans, sls dir, gen sls mgr; Jeanne Winters, natl sls mgr; Misty Osko, prom mgr; Bill Gallagher, progmg dir, news dir; Dave Bischoff, chief of engrg; Paul Blaviding, traf mgr; Robert Eisinger, political ed; Phil Cassidy, sports cmtr.

Turner

*KMUZ(FM)—Not on air, target date: unknown: 88.5 mhz; 32 w. Ant 777 ft TL: N44 47 01 W122 59 45. Hrs open: Box 1027, Salem, 97308. Phone: (503) 931-6323.E-mail: salemfolklore@comcast.net Web Site:www.salemfolklore.org Licensee: Salem Folklore Community. ♦ Tim Crosby, pres; Karen Holman, gen mgr.

Veneta

KEUG(FM)— 1998: 105.5 mhz; 2.8 kw. Ant 994 ft TL: N44 00 11 W123 06 48. Hrs open: 24 925 Country Club Rd., Suite 200, Eugene, 97401. Phone: (541) 484-9400. Fax: (541) 344-9424. Web Site:bob1055.com Licensee: McKenzie River Broadcasting Co. Inc. Group owner: McKenzie River Broadcasting Group (acq 1-28-2004; $1.02 million). Natl. Rep: D & R Radio,. Holland & Knight. Format: Adult contemp, cllassic hits. Target aud: 25-54; adults. ♦John Tilson, pres & gen mgr; Dave Wiles, gen sls mgr; Jeff Baird, progmg dir.

Waldport

KORC(AM)— July 1, 1988: 820 khz; 1000 w-D, 15 w-N. TL: N44 26 05 W124 01 20. Hrs open: Box 495, 97394. Phone: (541) 563-5100. Fax: (541) 563-5116. Licensee: Larry D. and Margaret E. Profitt, a General Partnership (acq 10-7-2003; $185,000). Format: Rock. ♦Larry Profitt, gen mgr.

Warm Springs

KWLZ-FM— Jan 18, 1986: 96.5 mhz; 100 kw. Ant 1,092 ft TL: N44 50 24 W121 13 56. Stereo. Hrs open: 24 Simulcast with KBNW(AM) Bend 100%. 854 N.E. 4th St., Bend, 97701. Phone: (541) 383-3825. Fax: (541) 383-3403. Licensee: Horizon Broadcasting Group L.L.C. (group owner; (acq 3-2-2000; grpsl). Population served: 200,000 Natl. Network: ABC, Premiere Radio Networks, Westwood One, Jones Radio Networks, Talk Radio Network, . Natl. Rep: Christal,. Format: News/talk. News staff: 3; News: 17.5 weekly (local). Target aud: 25-64. Spec prog: Inside Central Oregon (public affairs). ♦ Keith Shipman, pres & gen mgr; Brian Canady, sls dir; John Edwards, gen sls mgr; Annette Weston, progmg dir; Bill Baker, news dir, pub affrs dir.

*KWSO(FM)— Sept 22, 1986: 91.9 mhz; 3.3 kw. 203 ft TL: N44 50 24 W121 13 56. Stereo. Hrs open: 18 Box 489, 97761. Secondary address: 97761 Kahneeta Hamlet Rd. 97761. Phone: (541) 553-1965. Fax: (541) 553-3348.E-mail: smatters@wstribes.org Web Site:www.ksmo.org Licensee: Confederated Tribes of Warm Springs. Format: Native American, adult contemp. Target aud: General. ♦Sue Matters, gen mgr.

Warrenton

*KCPB-FM— Apr 17, 2006: 90.9 mhz; 9 w. Ant 1,040 ft TL: N46 15 46 W123 53 09. Hrs open: Box 263, Astoria, 97103. Phone: (503) 325-0010. Fax: (503) 325-3956.E-mail: kmun@kmun.org Web Site:www.kmun.org Licensee: Tillicum Foundation (acq 3-19-2004). Natl. Network: NPR, . ♦Ray Merritt, pres.

Welches

*KZRI(FM)— May 10, 2001: 90.3 mhz; 280 w. Ant 1,568 ft TL: N45 19 57 W121 42 57. Stereo. Hrs open: 24 2351 Sunset Blvd., Suite 170-218, Rocklin, CA, 95765. Phone: (916) 251-1600. Fax: (916) 251-1650.E-mail: info@air1.com Web Site:www.air1.com Licensee: Educational Media Foundation. Group owner: EMF Broadcasting. Population served: 38,700 Natl. Network: Air 1, . Shaw Pittman. Format: Contemp Christian. News staff: 3. Target aud: 18-35; Judeo-Christian, female. ♦Richard Jenkins, pres; Mike Novak, VP; Keith Whipple, dev dir; David Pierce, progmg mgr; Ed Lenane, news dir; Sam Wallington, engrg dir; Arthur Vassar, traf mgr; Karen Johnson, news rptr.

West Klamath

KRAM(AM)— Dec 1, 1987: Stn currently dark. 1070 khz; 1 kw-D. TL: N42 10 38 W121 46 25. Hrs open: Sunrise-sunset Box 1270, Klamath Falls, 97601. Phone: (541) 884-8074. Fax: (541) 884-8226. Licensee: Scott D. MacArthur, Personal Rep., estate of Sandra A. Falk (acq 8-8-2007). ♦Scott D. MacArthur, gen mgr.

Weston

KUJJ(FM)— 1997: 101.9 mhz; 13.5 kw. Ant 958 ft TL: N45 47 41 W118 10 06. Stereo. Hrs open: 24 45 Campbell Rd., Walla Walla, WA, 99362. Phone: (509) 527-1000. Fax: (509) 529-5534. Licensee: Alexandra Communications Inc. (group owner; (acq 4-10-2006; swap for KMMG(FM) Milton-Freewater). Format: Smooth jazz. ♦Tom Hodgins, gen mgr.

Winchester

*KLOV(FM)— August 1997: 89.3 mhz; 3.8 kw. Ant 420 ft TL: N43 14 06 W123 19 20. Stereo. Hrs open: 24 2351 Sunset Blvd., Suite 170-218, Rocklin, CA, 95765. Phone: (916) 251-1600. Fax: (916) 251-1650.E-mail: klove@klove.com Web Site:www.klove.com Licensee: Educational Media Foundation. Group owner: EMF Broadcasting. Population served: 74,000 Natl. Network: K-Love, . Shaw Pittman. Format: Contemp Christian mus. News staff: 3. Target aud: 25-44; Judeo-Christian, female. ♦Richard Jenkins, pres; Mike Novak, VP; Keith Whipple, dev dir; David Pierce, progmg mgr; Ed Lenane, news dir; Sam Wallington, engrg dir; Arthur Vassar, traf mgr; Karen Johnson, news rptr.

Winston

KGRV(AM)— Feb 12, 1984: 700 khz; 25 kw-D, 500 w-N. TL: N43 03 26 W123 23 48. Hrs open: 24 Box 1598, 97496. Secondary address: 196 S.E. Main St. 97496. Phone: (541) 679-8185. Fax: (541) 679-6456.E-mail: info@kgru700.net Web Site:www.kgrv700.net Licensee: Pacific Cascade Communications Corp. (acq 4-15-85). Natl. Network: Moody, . Format: Christian, regl, inspirational music. News: 10 hrs wkly. Target aud: 25-54. Spec prog: Southern gospel 3 hrs wkly. ♦David Morrow, pres, exec VP; Phil Morrow, gen mgr.

Woodburn

KWBY(AM)— July 10, 1964: 940 khz; 10 k-D, 500 w-N. TL: N45 10 37 W122 50 58. Hrs open: 24 1665 James St., 97071. Phone: (503) 981-9400. Fax: (503) 981-3561.E-mail: sam@lapantera940.com Web Site:www.lapantera940.com Licensee: Donald D. Coss (acq 10-18-91; $300,000; 11-4-91). Population served: 1,250,000 Natl. Network: CNN Radio, . Natl. Rep: Lotus Entravision Reps LLC,. Format: Sp/rgnl Mexican. News staff: one; News: 35 hrs wkly. Target aud: 18-49; younger-larger-than-gen mkt average Hispanic families. Spec prog: Relg 5 hrs, gospel 3 hrs wkly. ♦Donald Coss, pres; Dorecia Luse, gen mgr, opns dir; Natasha Holstein, mktg VP & prom VP; Gilberto Galvan, progmg mgr.

Pennsylvania

Allentown

WAEB(AM)— 1949: 790 khz; 1 kw-U, DA-2. TL: N40 37 05 W75 26 58 (day), N40 39 37 W75 30 50 (night). (CP: 3.8 kw-D, 1.5 kw-N, DA-2. TL (night): N40 39 33 W75 30 48). Hrs open: 1541 Alta Dr., Suite 400, Whitehall, 18052. Phone: (610) 434-1742. Phone: (610) 434–3808 (News). Fax: (610) 434-6288.E-mail: info@waeb.com Web Site:www.waeb.com Licensee: Capstar TX L.P. Group owner: Clear Channel Communications Inc. (acq 8-30-00; grpsl). Population served: 109,527 Natl. Network: CBS, . Format: News/talk. Target aud: 35-64. ♦Chris Taylor, gen mgr; Pat Gremling, gen sls mgr; Leanne Costelli, rgnl sls mgr; Laura St. James, progmg dir.

WAEB-FM— June 30, 1961: 104.1 mhz; 50 kw. 500 ft TL: N40 43 13 W75 35 44. (CP: 19.4 kw, ant 164 ft.). Stereo. Hrs open: Prog sep from AM 1541 Alta Dr., Suite 400, Whitehall, 18052. Phone: (610) 434-1742. Phone: (610) 434-3808 (news). Fax: (610) 434-6288.E-mail: info@b104.com Web Site:www.b104.com Format: CHR. Target aud: 18-44. ♦Diane Lee, gen sls mgr & prom dir; Craig Stevens, progmg dir.

WBYN(AM)—(Lehighton, Apr 12, 1962: 1160 khz; 4 kw-D, 1 kw-N, DA-2. TL: N40 49 03 W75 41 31. Stereo. Hrs open: 24 Rebroadcasts WBYN-FM Boyertown 100%. 107 Paxinosa Rd. W., Easton, 18040-1344. Phone: (610) 258-6155. Fax: (610) 253-3384. Licensee: Nassau Broadcasting II LLC (acq 4-25-2003; $375,000). Population served: 300,000 Natl. Rep: Katz Radio,. Rgnl rep: Glenn Jones Format: Christian. ♦Rick Musselman, gen mgr.

*WDIY(FM)— Jan 8, 1995: 88.1 mhz; 100 w vert. 843 ft TL: N40 33 54 W75 26 26. Hrs open: 5 AM-1 AM 301 Broadway, Bethlehem, 18015. Phone: (610) 694-8100. Fax: (610) 954-9474.E-mail: info@wdiyfm.org Web Site:www.wdiy.org Licensee: Lehigh Valley Community Broadcasters Association Board of Directors Inc. Natl. Network: NPR, . Schwartz, Woods & Miller. Format: News, class, pub affrs. News: 30 hrs wkly. Target aud: General. Spec prog: Folk 12 hrs, jazz 10 hrs, Sp 3 hrs, Asian-Indian one hr, Arabic one hr, Jewish one hr wkly. ♦Bill Dautremont-Smith, pres, sls dir; Rick Weaver, VP; Burr Beard, stn mgr; Sharon Ettinger, dev dir.

WHOL(AM)— Sept 12, 1948: 1600 khz; 500 w-D, 100 w-N, DA-2. TL: N40 35 33 W75 28 42. Hrs open: 24 1125 Colorado St., 18103. Phone: (610) 434-4801.E-mail: info@WHOL1600.COM Licensee: Matthew P. Braccili (acq 11-25-2003; $940,000). Population served: 700,000 Natl. Network: USA, Radio Unica, . Natl. Rep: Salem,. Format: Contemp Spanish topical top 40. Target aud: 18-65. ♦Matthew Braccili, stn mgr.

***WJCS(FM)**— Feb 29, 1996: 89.3 mhz; 125 w vert. 804 ft TL: N40 33 54 W75 26 26. Hrs open: 24 Box 8900, 18105-8900. Secondary address: 300 E. Rock Rd., Suite 205 18103. Phone: (610) 791-7262. Fax: (610) 797-6922.E-mail: wjcs@wjcs.org Web Site:www.wjcs.org Licensee: Beacon Broadcasting Corp. Population served: 500,000 Natl. Network: Moody, . Format: Educ, relg, news/talk, Christian. Target aud: General. ♦Frank Ginther, stn mgr.

WLEV(FM)— July 1947: 100.7 mhz; 11 kw. 1,073 ft TL: N40 33 54 W75 26 26. Stereo. Hrs open: 2158 Avenue C, Suite 100, Bethlehem, 18017. Phone: (610) 266-7600. Fax: (610) 231-0400. Licensee: Citadel Broadcasting Co. Group owner: Citadel Broadcasting Corp. (acq 9-5-97; $23 million). Population served: 250,000 Natl. Rep: Christal, Katz Radio,. Format: Adult contemp. ♦John Fraunfelter, gen mgr; Elizabeth Pembleton, sls dir; Shelly Easton, opns mgr & progmg dir.

***WMUH(FM)**— Feb 6, 1966: 91.7 mhz; 500 w. -3 ft TL: N40 35 52 W75 30 38. Stereo. Hrs open: 24 Muhlenberg College, 2400 Chew St., 18104. Phone: (484) 664-3456. Fax: (484) 664-3539.E-mail: wmuh@muhlenberg.edu Web Site:www.muhlenberg.edu/wmuh Licensee: Muhlenberg College. Population served: 400,527 Natl. Network: NPR, . Format: Div. Target aud: General. Spec prog: Sp 4 hrs, Arabic 2 hrs, Ger 2 hrs, It 2 hrs, Pol 2 hrs wkly. ♦Joe A. Swanson, gen mgr; Mike Calcagno, stn mgr; Rich Gensiak, progmg dir.

WSAN(AM)— May 24, 1923: 1470 khz; 5 kw-U, DA-N. TL: N40 38 10 W75 29 06. Stereo. Hrs open: 1541 Alta Dr., Suite 400, Whitehall, 18052. Phone: (610) 434-1742. Fax: (610) 434-6288. Web Site:www.1470wyhm.com Licensee: Capstar TX L.P. Group owner: Clear Channel Communications Inc. (acq 8-30-2000; grpsl). Population served: 109,527 Natl. Rep: D & R Radio,. Format: Sports. ♦Alison Ruppe, gen sls mgr; Craig Stevens, progmg dir.

WTKZ(AM)— September 1948: 1320 khz; 5 kw-D, 1 kw-N, DA-2. TL: N40 37 40 W75 29 09. Hrs open:
WEEX-AM Simulcast.
107 Paxinosa Rd. W., Easton, 18040-1344. Phone: (610) 258-6155. Fax: (610) 253-3384.E-mail: tomf@espnlv.com Web Site:www.espnlv.com Licensee: Nassau Broadcasting II L.L.C. Group owner: Mega Communications Inc. (acq 2-14-2005; $500,000). Population served: 100,800 Natl. Network: ESPN Radio, . Natl. Rep: Katz Radio. Rgnl rep: Glenn Jones Format: Sports. Target aud: 18-49; Men. ♦Tom Fallon, gen mgr & progmg mgr.

WZZO(FM)—See Bethlehem

Altoona

WALY(FM)—(Bellwood, Mar 28, 1970: 103.9 mhz; 3 kw. 984 ft TL: N40 34 04 W79 26 26. Stereo. Hrs open: 18 One Forever Dr., Hollidaysburg, 16648-3029. Phone: (814) 944-2221. Fax: (814) 943-2754.E-mail: forever@radio.com Web Site:www.waly1039.com Licensee: Forever Broadcasting LLC. Group owner: Forever Broadcasting (acq 7-16-97; grpsl). Population served: 536,100 Natl. Network: AP Radio, . Natl. Rep: Katz Radio,. Rgnl rep: Dome. Format: Oldies. Target aud: 35-64; earlier boomers, socially & financially active. ♦Carol B. Logan, pres; Dave Davies, gen mgr; Bobbi Castelluci, gen sls mgr.

WFBG(AM)— Oct 30, 1924: 1290 khz; 5 kw-D, 1 kw-N, DA-N. TL: N40 27 20 W78 23 50. Stereo. Hrs open: 24 One Forever Dr., Hollidaysburg, 16648. Phone: (814) 941-9800. Phone: (814) 944-1290. Fax: (814) 943-2754. Fax: (814) 941-7198.E-mail: info@foreverradio.com Web Site:www.wfbg.com Licensee: Forever of PA L.L.C. Group owner: Forever Broadcasting (acq 12-24-90; $2.1 million with co-located FM;1-14-91). Population served: 69,900 Natl. Rep: Christal,. Format: Adult standards. News staff: 2; News: 2 hrs wkly. Target aud: 25-54. ♦Dave Davies, gen mgr.

WFGY(FM)— Oct 17, 1960: 98.1 mhz; 30 kw. Ant 941 ft TL: N40 34 01 W78 26 32. Stereo. Hrs open: 24 Prog sep from AM One Forever Dr., Hollidaysburg, 16648. Phone: (814) 941-9800. Phone: (814) 944-1290. Fax: (814) 943-2754. Fax: (814) 941-7198.E-mail: info@foreverradio.com Web Site:www.froggyradio.com Population served: 102,500 Natl. Network: CBS, . Format: Contemp country. News staff: one. Target aud: 25-64.

WRKY-FM—See Hollidaysburg

WRTA(AM)— June 12, 1946: 1240 khz; 1 kw-U. TL: N40 30 26 W78 25 15. Hrs open: 19 1417-19 12th Ave., 16603. Phone: (814) 943-6112. Fax: (814) 944-9782.E-mail: contactus@wrta.com Web Site:www.wrta.com Licensee: Handsome Brothers Inc. (acq 1-9-2004; $500,000). Population served: 155,000 Natl. Network: Westwood One, . Rgnl rep: Marv Roslin Pepper & Corazzini. Format: News/talk. News staff: 2; News: 15 hrs wkly. Target aud: 25 plus; middle/upper income, college educated, professional. Spec prog: Sports play-by-play/loc college & high schools. ♦David Barger, pres; David R. Wolf, gen mgr, gen sls mgr, edit dir, edit mgr, political ed; Dave Weaver, news dir, local news ed, news rptr; Bob Taylor, chief of engrg; Ken Maguda, stn mgr, opns mgr, rgnl sls mgr, progmg dir & traf mgr; Charlie Weston, sports cmtr.

WVAM(AM)— July 1948: 1430 khz; 5 kw-D, 1 kw-N, DA-N. TL: N40 29 42 W78 24 06. Hrs open: One Forever Dr., Hollidaysburg, 16648. Phone: (814) 941-9800. Fax: (814) 943-2754.E-mail: info@foreverradio.com Web Site:www.wvamam.com Licensee: Forever Broadcasting LLC. Group owner: Forever Broadcasting (acq 12-12-2003; $2.1 million with co-located FM). Population served: 62,900 Natl. Network: ESPN Radio, . Format: Sports. Target aud: 25 plus; white collar professionals. Spec prog: Pol one hr wkly. ♦Dave Davies, gen mgr; Rich DeLeo, progmg dir; Troy Barnhart, chief of engrg.

WWOT(FM)— July 1976: 100.1 mhz; 3 kw. Ant 954 ft TL: N40 34 11 W78 26 25. Stereo. Hrs open: Prog sep from AM One Forever Dr., Hollidaysburg, 16648. Phone: (814) 941-9800. Fax: (814) 943-2754.E-mail: info@foreverradio.com Web Site:www.hot100radio.com Population served: 70,000 Format: CHR. ♦Jonathan Reed, progmg dir; Mark Haze, news dir.

Ambridge

WMBA(AM)— May 1957: 1460 khz; 500 w-U, DA-2. TL: N40 35 08 W80 12 11. Hrs open: 24 Box 719, Beaver, 15010. Phone: (724) 846-4100. Fax: (724) 843-7771.E-mail: 1230@wbvp-wmba.com Web Site:www.wbvp-wmba.com Licensee: Iorio Broadcasting Inc. (acq 5-23-2000; $325,000). Population served: 400,000 Natl. Network: Talk Radio Network, . Wire Svc: AP Format: Talk, sports. News staff: one; News: 10 hrs wkly. Target aud: 35+. Spec prog: Polka review 2 hrs, oldies 3 hrs, Polish 2 hrs wkly. ♦Frank Iorio, pres; Mark Peterson, gen mgr; John Nuzzo, progmg dir; Pat Septak, local news ed & news rptr; Bob Barrickman, sports cmtr.

Annville-Cleona

WWSM(AM)— Aug 4, 1968: 1510 khz; 5 kw-D, DA. TL: N40 17 44 W76 27 46. Hrs open: 277 Gravel Hil Road, Palmyra, 17078. Phone: (717) 272-1510. Fax: (717) 832-0209.E-mail: listener@wwsm.us Web Site:www.wwsm.us Licensee: Patrick H. Sickafus. (acq 10-14-93; $1; 11-1-93). Population served: 28,572 Natl. Network: Westwood One, USA, . Format: Classic western. News staff: 2. Target aud: 34 plus. Spec prog: Polka 2 hrs, bluegrass 3 hrs, gospel music 3 hrs wkly. ♦Patrick H. Sickafus, pres; Gary Gruver, gen mgr.

Apollo

WAVL(AM)— Dec 13, 1947: 910 khz; 5 kw-D, 69 w-N, DA-2. TL: N40 35 01 W79 31 34. (CP: 1360 khz; 6.7 kw-D, 700 w-N, DA-2. TL: N40 27 42 W79 36 07). Hrs open: 120 Beale Rd., Sarver, 16055. Phone: (724) 295-2000. Fax: (724) 295-9009. Web Site:www.praise910.com Licensee: Evangel Heights Assembly of God (acq 5-16-01; $400,000). Population served: 3,000,000 Natl. Network: USA, . Format: Contemp Christian. News: 2 hrs wkly. ♦John P. Kuert, pres; Paul Barton, gen mgr; Jeff Bogaczyk, opns dir.

Avis

WQBR(FM)— Aug 11, 1989: 99.9 mhz; 570 w. Ant 1,053 ft TL: N41 13 45 W77 22 02. Stereo. Hrs open: 24 Box 999, McElhattan, 17748. Secondary address: 330 McElhattan Dr., McElhattan 17748. Phone: (570) 769-2327. Fax: (570) 769-7746.E-mail: bear@kcnet.org Web Site:www.bear999.com Licensee: Maximum Impact Communications Inc. (acq 9-9-93; $270,000; 10-4-93). Population served: 300,000 Natl. Network: Jones Radio Networks, . Natl. Rep: Dome,. Format: Country/Americana. News staff: one; News: 2 hrs wkly. Target aud: 25-54. ♦Karyn O'Brien Stratton, pres, gen mgr, opns mgr, progmg mgr; Dave Stratton, gen sls mgr, mktg dir, prom mgr, adv mgr, news dir; Michael Ferriola, engrg mgr; Patti Knepp, traf mgr.

Avoca

WILK-FM— Apr 2, 1976: 103.1 mhz; 6 kw. Ant 72 ft TL: N41 18 20 W75 45 38. Stereo. Hrs open: 24
Simulcast with WILK(AM) Wilkes-Barre 100%.
305 Hwy. 315, Pittstown, 18640. Phone: (570) 883-9850. Fax: (570) 883-9851.E-mail: jimr@102themountain.com Web Site:www.wilknetwork.com Licensee: Entercom Wilkes-Barre Scranton LLC. Group owner: Entercom Communications Corp. (acq 12-13-99; grpsl). Population served: 35,000 Format: News/talk. Target aud: 18-54; general. ♦Jim Rising, opns mgr; Andy Zapotek, gen sls mgr.

Beaver Falls

WAMO-FM—Licensed to Beaver Falls. See Pittsburgh

WBVP(AM)— May 25, 1948: 1230 khz; 5 kw-U. TL: N40 44 16 W80 17 47. Hrs open: 24 Box 719, 1316 7th Ave., 15010. Phone: (724) 846-4100. Phone: (412) 761-6600. Fax: (724) 843-7771.E-mail: 1230@wbvp-wmba.com Web Site:www.wbvp-wmba.com Licensee: Iorio Broadcasting Inc. (acq 1996). Population served: 170,000 Natl. Network: Talk Radio Network, . Rgnl. Network: Radio Pa. Wire Svc: AP Format: Full service, News, Talk, Sports. News staff: 2. Target aud: 35 plus. Spec prog: Polka music 2 hrs, relg 2 hrs, gospel 2 hsr wkly. ♦Frank Iorio, pres, gen mgr; Mark Peterson, stn mgr; John Nuzzo, opns mgr.

***WITX(FM)**— June 19, 1986: 90.9 mhz; 100 w. 167 ft TL: N40 47 05 W80 20 36. Hrs open: 501 37th St., 15010. Phone: (724) 846-8738. Phone: (877) 477-5219. Licensee: Beaver Falls Educational Broadcasting Foundation. Format: Relg. ♦Rev. Kenneth Manypenny, pres.

Beaver Springs

WLZS(FM)— Feb 21, 1993: 106.1 mhz; 175 w. Ant 1,312 ft TL: N40 42 04 W77 12 50. Stereo. Hrs open: 24 Box 209, Mexico, 17056. Secondary address: Box 146 17812. Phone: (717) 436-2135. Fax: (717) 436-8155. Licensee: Starview Media Inc. (acq 1996; $235,000). Population served: 220,000 Radio Pa. Format: Oldies. News staff: one; News: 2 hrs wkly. Target aud: 25-54. ♦Curt Dreibelbis, gen mgr; Shane Nelson, progmg.

Bedford

WAYC(FM)— Dec 22, 1966: 100.9 mhz; 190 w. ant 1,279 ft TL: N40 00 46 W78 33 12. Stereo. Hrs open: 24 P.O. Box 1, 15522. Secondary address: 134 E. Pitt St., 2nd Fl. 15522. Phone: (814) 623-1000. Fax: (814) 623-9692.E-mail: cesscomm@embarqmail.com Licensee: Cessna Communications Inc. (group owner; acq 3-22-93; $350,000 with WBFD(AM) Bedford;3-29-93). Population served: 50,000 Natl. Network: Fox News Radio, . Rgnl. Network: Radio Pa. Radio Pa. Rgnl rep: Commercial Media Sales. G S B Law. Format: Hot AC. News staff: one. Target aud: 18-49; general. Spec prog: Pittsburgh Steelers/ High School Sports. ♦Jay B. Cessna, pres; John H. Cessna, VP & gen mgr; Chris Collins, opns mgr.

WBFD(AM)— July 2, 1955: 1310 khz; 2.5 kw-D, 85 w-N. TL: N40 02 37 W78 30 11. Hrs open: 24 P.O. Box 1, 15522. Secondary address: 2nd Fl., 134 E. Pitt St. 15522. Phone: (814) 623-1000. Fax: (814) 623-9692.E-mail: cesscom@embarqmail.com Licensee: Cessna Communications Inc. (group owner; acq 3-22-93; $350,000 with WAYC(FM) Bedford; 3-29-93). Population served: 35,000 Natl. Network: Talk Radio Network, Premiere Radio Networks, Salem Radio Network, . Rgnl. Network: Radio Pa. Radio Pa. Rgnl rep: Commercial Media Sales. Format: News/talk. News staff: one. Target aud: 30 plus; general. Spec prog: Penn State Sports. ♦Jay B. Cessna, pres; John H. Cessna, VP & gen mgr; Chris Collins, opns mgr.

WBVE(FM)— Aug 15, 1988: 107.5 mhz; 370 w. Ant 1,309 ft TL: N40 00 46 W78 33 12. Stereo. Hrs open: 24 P.O. Box One, 15522. Secondary address: 2nd Fl., 134 E. Pitt St. 15522. Phone: (814) 623-1000. Fax: (814) 623-9692.E-mail: cesscomm@embarqmail.com Licensee: Cessna Communications Inc. Population served: 50,000 Natl. Network: Fox News Radio, . Rgnl rep: Commerical Media Sales Format: Classic Rock. News staff: one. Target aud: 25-54. Spec prog: Motor Racing Network. ♦Jay B. Cessna, pres; John Cessna, VP; Chris Collins, opns mgr.

WHJB(AM)— Aug 5, 1974: 1600 khz; 2.7 kw-D, 18 w-N. TL: N40 02 35 W78 30 13. Hrs open: 24 Box 1, 15522. Secondary address: 134 E. Pitt St., 2nd Fl. 15522. Phone: (814) 623-1000. Fax: (814) 623-9692.E-mail: johnwhjb@embarqmail.com Licensee: Cessna Communications Inc. (acq 2-29-2008; $15,000). Population served: 35,000 Natl. Network: Salem Radio Network, . Rgnl rep: CommercialMedia Sales G S B Law. Format: Adult Standards/Religious. News staff: 1. Target aud: 35 plus. ♦Jay B. Cessna, pres, gen mgr; John Cessna, VP; Chris Collins, opns mgr.

***WUFR(FM)**— 2008: 91.1 mhz; 2.5 kw vert. Ant 1,220 ft TL: N40 17 40 W78 34 25. Hrs open:
Rebroadcasts WFSI(FM) Annapolis, MD 100%.

918 Chesapeake Ave., Annapolis, MD, 21403. Phone: (410) 268-6200. Fax: (410) 268-0931. Web Site:www.familyradio.com Licensee: Family Stations Inc. Natl. Network: Family Radio, . Format: Relg, educ. ◆Harold Camping, pres; W.A. Sadlier, stn mgr.

Bellefonte

WBLF(AM)— Aug 1, 1958: 970 khz; 1 kw-D, 61 w-N. TL: N40 54 12 W77 46 06. Hrs open: 315 S. Atherton St., State College, 16801. Phone: (814) 272-1320. Fax: (814) 272-3291.E-mail: wblfproduction@yahoo.com Licensee: Magnum Broadcasting Inc. (group owner; (acq 8-31-2005; $150,000). . Population served: 110,000 Natl. Network: Fox News Radio, Fox Sports, . Natl. Rep: Interep,. Agrinet Format: News/talk. Target aud: Adults 25+. ◆Michael M. Stapleford, pres; Diana Stapleford, gen mgr; Michael Brennen, gen sls mgr.

WTLR(FM)—See State College

WZWW(FM)—Licensed to Bellefonte. See State College

Bellwood

WALY(FM)—Licensed to Bellwood. See Altoona

Benton

WGGI(FM)— Oct 4, 1985: 95.9 mhz; 6 kw. 328 ft TL: N41 10 16 W76 24 37. Hrs open: 305 Hwy. 315, Box 729, Dushore, 18640. Phone: (570) 883-9850. Fax: (570) 883-9851.E-mail: feedback@froggy101.com Web Site:www.froggy101.com Licensee: Entercom Scranton Wilkes-Barre License LLC. Group owner: Entercom Communications Corp. (acq 12-13-99; grpsl). Population served: 600,000 Format: Country. Target aud: 25-54. ◆John Burkavage, VP; Jim Rising, opns mgr.

Berwick

WFBS(AM)— Aug 1, 1957: 1280 khz; 1 kw-D, 175 w-N. TL: N41 04 36 W76 15 32. Hrs open: 114 N. Market St., 18603. Phone: (570) 752-8012. Fax: (570) 752-1131.E-mail: way750am@aol.com Licensee: Bold Gold Media Group L.P. (acq 1-11-2007; $10,000 plus assumption of debt). Population served: 50,000 Format: Oldies. ◆JoAnn Germers Hausen, VP; Kevin Fennessy, gen mgr.

WHLM-FM— Feb 14, 1992: 103.5 mhz; 4.1 kw. 387 ft TL: N41 05 11 W76 16 41. Hrs open: 124 E. Main St., Bloomsburg, 17815. Phone: (570) 784-1200. Fax: (570) 784-6060.E-mail: whlm@aol.com Web Site:www.wkab.net Licensee: Columbia FM Inc. (acq 2006; $800,000). Format: Classic hits. Target aud: 25-54; females at work, 18-39 men on weekends. ◆Joseph Reilly, gen mgr & stn mgr.

Bethlehem

WGPA(AM)— Feb 14, 1946: 1100 khz; 250 w-D. TL: N40 37 27 W75 21 19. Hrs open: Sunrise-sunset 528 N. New St., 18018. Phone: (610) 866-8074. Fax: (610) 866-9381.E-mail: joetimmer@jollyjoetimmer.com Web Site:www.regiononline.com/joetimmer Licensee: Joseph Timmer dba Timmer Broadcasting Co. (acq 6-19-92; $100,000; 7-13-92). Population served: 310,000 Natl. Network: USA, . Format: Var, news/talk. News staff: one; News: 2 hrs wkly. Target aud: General. Spec prog: Ger 2 hrs, polka 12 hrs, Sp 4 hrs wkly. ◆Joe Timmer, pres, gen mgr; Mark Staller, opns dir.

*WLVR(FM)— May 3, 1973: 91.3 mhz; 185 w. 60 ft TL: N40 36 22 W75 22 42. Stereo. Hrs open: 7 AM-4 AM Lehigh Univ., 29 Trembley Dr., 18015-3066. Phone: (610) 758-4187. Fax: (610) 758-4186.E-mail: info@wlvr.com Licensee: Lehigh University. Population served: 500,000 Format: Var. News: 10 hrs wkly. Target aud: General. Spec prog: Black 12 hrs, class 8 hrs, reggae 6 hrs, jazz 12 hrs wkly. ◆Aimee Van House, gen mgr; Killian O'Conner, progmg dir.

WZZO(FM)— Feb 14, 1946: 95.1 mhz; 30 kw. 631 ft TL: N40 37 13 W75 17 37. Stereo. Hrs open: 1541 Alta Dr., Suite 400, Whitehall, 18052. Phone: (610) 434-1742. Fax: (610) 434-6288.E-mail: webmaster@wzzo.com Web Site:www.wzzo.com Licensee: Capstar TX L.P. Group owner: Clear Channel Communications Inc. (acq 8-30-00; grpsl). Population served: 841,000 Natl. Rep: Katz Radio,. Format: AOR. ◆Rich Lewis, gen mgr, mktg mgr; Pat Gremling, gen sls mgr; Tori Thomas, progmg dir.

Blairsville

WLCY(FM)— Apr 15, 1985: 106.3 mhz; 2.4 kw. Ant 363 ft TL: N40 31 10 W79 13 26. Stereo. Hrs open: 24 840 Philadelphia St., Suite 100, Indiana, 15701. Phone: (724) 465-4700. Fax: (724) 349-6842. Licensee: The St. Pier Group LLC. Group owner: Renda Broadcasting Corp. (acq 8-1-2004; $900,000). Natl. Network: Jones Radio Networks, . Rgnl rep: Dome. Format: Country. News staff: 2; News: 2 hrs wkly. Target aud: 25-54. ◆Mark Bertig, gen mgr.

Bloomsburg

*WBUQ(FM)— Sept 16, 1986: 91.1 mhz; 600 w. 500 ft TL: N41 00 29 W76 26 51. Stereo. Hrs open: 16 Bloomsburg Univ., 400 E. Second St., 1250 McCormick Center for Human Services, 17815. Phone: (570) 389-4686. Fax: (570) 389-5071.E-mail: wbuq@bloomu.edu Web Site:www.wbuqfm.com Licensee: Bloomsburg University of Pennsylvania. Population served: 15,000 Format: Alternative, rock/AOR. News staff: one; News: 2 hrs wkly. Target aud: General; college & area high school students. Spec prog: Talk 10 hrs, urban 10 hrs, metal 15 hrs, indie 10 hrs wkly. ◆Ray Moskal, gen mgr; Chad Eddinger, progmg dir.

WFYY(FM)— September 1956: 106.5 mhz; 36.5 kw. 570 ft TL: N40 59 42 W76 29 51. Stereo. Hrs open: Box 90, Selinsgrove, 17870. Secondary address: 246 W. Main St. 17815. Phone: (570) 374-5711. Fax: (570) 784-1004.E-mail: sales@wfyyradio.com Web Site:www.wfyyradio.com Licensee: MMP License LLC. Group owner: MAX Media L.L.C. (acq 10-17-03; grpsl). Population served: 11,652 Natl. Network: Westwood One, . Rgnl rep: Dome. Format: Adult contemp. Target aud: 18-49. ◆John A. Trinder, pres; Scott Richards, VP, gen mgr; Dawn Marie, opns dir; Greg Adair, gen sls mgr; Ted Koppen, chief of engrg.

WHLM(AM)— Sept 26, 1947: 930 khz; 1 kw-D, 23 w-N. TL: N41 01 00 W76 27 44. Hrs open: 24 Box One, 105 W. Main St., 2nd FL, 17815-3329. Phone: (570) 784-1200. Fax: (570) 784-6060.E-mail: whlmam@aol.com Web Site:www.whlm.com Licensee: Columbia Broadcasting Co. (acq 9-5-01; $45,000). Population served: 63,500 Natl. Network: CBS Radio, . Radio Pa. Borsari & Paxson. Format: Var/div. News staff: one; News: 15 hrs wkly. Target aud: 25-54. Spec prog: Farm one hr, relg 2 hrs wkly. ◆Joseph Reilly, pres, gen mgr; Larry Hopper, gen sls mgr.

Boalsburg

WBUS(FM)— Apr 13, 1998: 93.7 mhz; 33 kw. Ant 1,361 ft TL: N40 45 08 W77 45 16. Stereo. Hrs open: 2551 Park Center Blvd., State College, 16801. Phone: (814) 237-9800. Fax: (814) 237-2477.E-mail: tony@thebus.net Web Site:www.thebus.net Licensee: Forever Broadcasting LLC. (group owner; (acq 5-1-2005; $2.65 million with WRSC(AM) State College). Population served: 116,000 Format: classic rock. Target aud: 25-54. ◆Chuck Hertzog, VP, gen mgr; Tony Riccardi, progmg dir; Bob Taylor, chief of engrg.

Boyertown

WBYN-FM— Oct 31, 1960: 107.5 mhz; 30 kw. Ant 610 ft TL: N40 24 15 W75 39 09. Stereo. Hrs open: 24 280 Mill St., 19512. Phone: (610) 369-7777. Fax: (610) 369-7780.E-mail: jwhite@nassaubroadcasting.com Web Site:frankfmonline.com Licensee: WDAC Radio Co. (acq 11-5-91; $3 million; 12-2-91). Population served: 7,100,000 Natl. Rep: Katz Radio,. Jones, Waldo, Holbrook & McDonough. Format: Classic Hits. Target aud: 25-54; families. ◆Richard Crawford, pres; John White, gen mgr.

Braddock

WLFP(AM)— June 1947: 1550 khz; 1 kw-D, 4 w-N. TL: N40 24 47 W79 51 14. (CP: COL Reserve Township. 2 kw-D, 12 w-N, DA-2. TL: N40 29 27 W79 58 05). Hrs open: 5 AM-midnight 4736 Penn Ave., Pittsburgh, 15224. Phone: (412) 942-0076. Web Site:www.theedge1550.com Licensee: WURP East Inc. Group owner: Inner City Broadcasting (acq 8-29-2007; $225,000). Natl. Network: American Urban, . Format: Talk. News staff: one; News: 6 hrs wkly. Target aud: 25-54. ◆Michael Metter, pres; Chris Squire, gen mgr; Shelia Corley, stn mgr; Coddy Anderson, dev dir.

WRRK(FM)— June 1959: 96.9 mhz; 44.7 kw. Ant 530 ft TL: N40 24 42 W79 55 53. Stereo. Hrs open: 650 Smithfield St., Suite 2200, Pittsburgh, 15222. Phone: (412) 316-3342. Fax: (412) 316-3388.E-mail: info@wrrk.com Web Site:www.wrrk.com Licensee: WPNT Associates. Population served: 2,500,000 Natl. Network: ABC, . Dow, Lohnes & Albertson. Format: Adult hits. ◆Greg Frischling, gen mgr; Chris

Kohan, gen sls mgr; Vicki Wolfe, prom dir; John Robertson, progmg dir; Amy Crago, news dir; Paul Carroll, chief of engrg; Ed Lang, traf mgr.

Bradford

WBRR(FM)— Dec 1, 1987: 100.1 mhz; 1.65 kw. 525 ft TL: N41 58 12 W78 42 03. Stereo. Hrs open: 24 Prog sep from AM Box 545, 1490 St. Francis Dr., 16701. Phone: (814) 368-4141. Fax: (814) 368-3180. Web Site:www.wbrrfm.com (Acq 10-87; $21,000; 10-12-87). Format: 70s/80s hits. Target aud: 25-54.

WESB(AM)— April 1947: 1490 khz; 1 kw-U. TL: N41 27 54 W78 42 01. Hrs open: 24 Box 545, 1490 St. Francis Dr., 16701. Phone: (814) 368-4141. Fax: (814) 368-3180.E-mail: 1490@wesb.com Web Site:www.wesb.com Licensee: Radio Station WESB Inc. Population served: 25,000 Natl. Network: CNN Radio, . Rgnl. Network: Radio Pa. Natl. Rep: Dome,. Radio Pa. Baraff, Koerner & Olender. Format: Adult contemp. News staff: one. Target aud: 25-54. ◆Donald J. Fredeen, pres, gen mgr; Frank Williams, opns dir, progmg dir; Peggy Austin, sls dir; Christine Brookins, prom dir; Anne Holliday, mus dir, news dir.

WBRR(FM)— Dec 1, 1987: 100.1 mhz; Dec 1, 1987. Dec 1, 1987 TL: Dec 1, 1987. Dec 1, 1987. Stereo. 24 Prog sep from AM Box 545, 1490 St. Francis Dr., 16701. Phone: (814) 368-4141. Fax: (814) 368-3180. Web Site:www.wbrrfm.com (Acq 10-87; $21,000; 10-12-87). Format: 70s/80s hits. Target aud: 25-54.

*WTWT(FM)—Not on air, target date: unknown: 90.5 mhz; 3.6 kw. Ant 459 ft TL: N42 05 55 W78 27 46. Hrs open: Box 579, Russell, 16345. Secondary address: Rt. 62 North, Russell 16345. Phone: (814) 757-8744. Fax: (814) 757-8745. Web Site:www.wtwtfm.org Licensee: Calvary Chapel of Russell. Format: Christian teaching and music. ◆Jeffrey York, gen mgr.

Bristol

*WLBS(FM)— April 1998: 91.7 mhz; 100 w vert. 68 ft TL: N40 09 33 W74 51 24. Hrs open: 24 Rebroadcasts WRDV(FM) Warminster 100%. Box 2012, Warminster, 18974. Phone: (215) 674-8002. Fax: (215) 674-4586.E-mail: info@wrdv.org Web Site:www.wrdv.org Licensee: Bux-Mont Educational Radio Association. Population served: 10,000 Wire Svc: AP Format: Variety. ◆Charles W. Loughary, chmn; Todd H. Allen, gen mgr.

Brookville

WKQL(FM)— Jan 17, 2000: 103.3 mhz; 10.5 kw. 508 ft TL: N41 04 04 W79 04 59. Hrs open: 24 904 N. Main St., Punxsutawney, 15767. Secondary address: Renda Radio Inc., Broadcast Plaza, Pittsburgh 15767. Phone: (814) 938-6000. Fax: (814) 938-4237.E-mail: rendaradio@comcast.net Licensee: Renda Radio Inc. Group owner: Renda Broadcasting Corp. Population served: 200,000 Natl. Network: ABC, . Latham & Watkins. Format: Oldies. News staff: one; News: 2 hrs wkly. Target aud: 35-54; adults. ◆Diana Albright, gen mgr.

WMKX(FM)— Aug 22, 1981: 105.5 mhz; 16 kw. Ant 418 ft TL: N41 07 21 W79 03 51. Stereo. Hrs open: 24 51 Pickering St., 15825. Phone: (814) 849-8100. Fax: (814) 849-4585.E-mail: megarock@alltel.net Licensee: Strattan Broadcasting Inc. Format: Classic rock. News staff: one; News: 5 hrs wkly. Target aud: 25-54; general. Spec prog: Jazz 3 hrs, rock classics 6 hrs, oldies 8 hrs wkly. ◆Jim Farley, pres, gen mgr; Nathan Sharp, gen sls mgr.

Brownsville

WASP(AM)— Aug 3, 1968: 1130 khz; 5 kw-D, DA. TL: N40 02 33 W79 54 20. Hrs open: daylight hours only 123 Blaine Rd., 15417. Phone: (724) 938-2000. Fax: (724) 938-7824.E-mail: rherring@keymarketradio.com Web Site:www.classichitsradioonline .com Licensee: Keymarket Licenses LLC. Group owner: Keymarket Communications LLC (acq 8-31-99; $2.875 million with WPKL(FM) Uniontown). Population served: 2,500,000 Natl. Network: ABC, . Format: Classic Hits. News: 4 hrs wkly. Target aud: 35-64. ◆Gerald Getz, pres; Andrew Powaski, gen mgr.

Burgettstown

WOGH(FM)— May 1, 1947: 103.5 mhz; 19.5 kw. Ant 810 ft TL: N40 20 33 W80 37 14. Stereo. Hrs open: 24 Prog sep from AM Box 1340, Steubenville, 43952. Secondary address: 320 Market St. 43952.

Phone: (740) 283-4747. Fax: (740) 283-3655. Web Site:www.froggyland.com Format: Country. Target aud: 25-54. ♦Stu Schroeder, prom mgr; Scott Feist, progmg dir, mus dir.

Burnham

WVNW(FM)— August 1994: 96.7 mhz; 450 w. 850 ft TL: N40 35 10 W77 41 40. Hrs open: 24 Box 911, One Juniata St., Lewistown, 17044. Phone: (717) 242-1493. Fax: (717) 242-3764.E-mail: traffic@star967.com Licensee: WVNW Inc. (acq 2-1-94; 4-25-94). Natl. Network: ABC, Fox News Radio, . Radio Pa. Format: Hot country. Target aud: 25-54. ♦Jed A. Donahue, VP; Jed A. Donahue, gen mgr; Tom Sheeder, progmg dir; Erik Lane, news dir; Dave Busman, sports cmtr.

Butler

WBUT(AM)— Mar 14, 1949: 1050 khz; 500 w-D, 65 w-N. TL: N40 53 51 W79 53 22. Hrs open: 24 112 Hollywood Dr., Suite 203, 16001. Phone: (724) 287-5778. Fax: (724) 283-3005.E-mail: frontdesk@bcnetwork.com Web Site:www.wbut.com Licensee: Butler County Radio Network Inc. (group owner; (acq 5-19-98; grpsl). Population served: 174,000 Natl. Network: CNN Radio, . Format: Country. News staff: 2. Target aud: General. ♦Victoria Hinterberger, gen mgr; Bill Davis, progmg dir, news dir.

WISR(AM)— Sept 26, 1941: 680 khz; 250 w-D, 50 w-N. TL: N40 52 39 W79 54 09. Hrs open: 24 112 Hollywood Dr., Suite 203, 16003-0151. Phone: (724) 283-1500. Fax: (724) 283-3005.E-mail: frontdesk@bcnetwork.com Web Site:www.insidebutlercounty.com Licensee: Butler County Radio Network Inc. (group owner; acq 5-19-98; grpsl). Population served: 130,000 Natl. Network: CBS, . Radio Pa. Format: News/talk, sports. News staff: 2; News: 28 hrs wkly. Target aud: 45 plus. Spec prog: Relg 6 hrs wlky. ♦Wes Briggs, CFO; Vicki Hinterberger, gen mgr; Dave Malarkey, progmg dir; Scott Briggs, engr.

WLER-FM— Mar 14, 1949: 97.7 mhz; 4.6 kw. 374 ft TL: N40 53 51 W79 53 22. Stereo. Hrs open: 24 Prog sep from AM 112 Hollywood Dr., 16001. Phone: (724) 287-5778. Fax: (724) 283-3005.E-mail: frontdesk@bcnetwork.com Web Site:www.wlerfm.com Population served: 275,000 Natl. Network: Westwood One, CNN Radio, . Format: All hits. News staff: 2. ♦Victoria Hinterberger, stn mgr; Jay Kline, progmg dir, disc jockey; Bill Davis, news dir.

California

***WCAL(FM)—** September 1973: 91.9 mhz; 3 kw. 160 ft TL: N40 02 57 W79 54 01. Stereo. Hrs open: 24 California Univ. of PA, 428 Hickory St., 15419. Phone: (724) 938-3000. Fax: (724) 938-5959.E-mail: wheeler@cup.edu Licensee: The Student Association Inc. (acq 6-3-78). Population served: 500,000 Natl. Network: Westwood One, . Format: Active rock. News: 5 hrs wkly. Target aud: 18-25; students at California Univ. Spec prog: Contemp Christian 6 hrs, urban contemp 12 hrs, rap 4 hrs, alternative 6 hrs, metal 5 hrs wkly. ♦J.R. Willer, gen mgr & opns mgr.

Cambridge Springs

WXMJ(FM)— July 14, 1997: 104.5 mhz; 2.65 kw. Ant 502 ft TL: N41 42 17 W80 09 53. Stereo. Hrs open: 24 484 Allegheny Blvd., Franklin, 16323. Phone: (814) 432-2188. Fax: (814) 437-9372.E-mail: radio@zoominternet.com Web Site:www.mykissfm.com Licensee: Forever Broadcasting LLC. Group owner: Forever Broadcasting (acq 7-21-2000; grpsl). Population served: 84,000 Format: Hot adult contemp. Target aud: 25-54. ♦Carol Logan, prs; Terry Deitz, gen mgr; Joe Elan, gen sls mgr; Todd Adkins, opns mgr & progmg dir.

Canonsburg

WWCS(AM)— Nov 28, 1957: 540 khz; 7.5 kw-D, 500 w-N, DA-2. TL: N40 17 22 W80 11 07. (CP: 5 kw-D, 500 w-N, DA-2). Hrs open: 24 38 Angerer Rd., 15317. Phone: (724) 745-5400. Fax: (724) 745-8790. Web Site:www.radiodisney.com Licensee: Birach Broadcasting Corp. (acq 5-28-92; $475,000;6-22-92). Population served: 5,000,000 Format: Children. Target aud: Educated adults, ethnic groups, open minded. ♦Sima Birach Sr., gen mgr.

Canton

WHGL-FM— Aug 30, 1978: 100.3 mhz; 3.9 kw. 846 ft TL: N41 44 32 W76 50 08. Stereo. Hrs open: 24 Box 100, Troy, 16947. Secondary address: 170 Redington Ave, Troy 16947. Phone: (570) 297-0100. Fax: (570) 297-3193.E-mail: whgl100@ptd.net Web Site:www.wiggle100.com Licensee: Cantroair Communications Inc. (acq 1-7-99; $560,000 for 85% of stock with WTZN(AM) Troy). Natl. Network: ABC, . Format: Country. News staff: one. Target aud: 25-54. ♦Mike Powers, pres, gen mgr; Bob Gisler, VP; David Rockwell, prom mgr; Shane Wilber, mus dir.

WTZN(AM)—See Troy

Carbondale

WCDL(AM)— January 1950: 1440 khz; 5 kw-D. TL: N41 33 28 W75 29 11. Hrs open: 1 N. Main St., Suite 1440, 18704. Phone: (570) 282-8700. Fax: (570) 282-1435. Web Site:www.wcdlam.com Licensee: WS2K Radio LLC. Group owner: Route 81 Radio LLC (acq 7-14-2008; grpsl). Population served: 500,000 Format: Sp.

***WFUZ(FM)—** 2005: 91.3 mhz; 70 w. Ant 735 ft TL: N41 28 41 W75 29 51. Hrs open:
Rebroadcasts WCIK(FM) Bath, NY 100%.
Box 506, Bath, NY, 14810. Phone: (607) 776-4151. Fax: (607) 776-6929.E-mail: mail@fln.org Web Site:www.fln.org Licensee: Family Life Ministries Inc. Natl. Network: Salem Radio Network, . Hardy, Carey, Chautin & Balkin, LLP. Wire Svc: Metro Weather Service Inc. Format: Contemp Christian. News staff: 3; News: 14 hrs wkly. Target aud: 30-54. ♦Dick Snavely, CFO; John Owens, progmg dir; Jim Travis, chief of engrg.

WLNP(FM)— 1965: 94.3 mhz; 1.1 kw. Ant 770 ft TL: N41 32 37 W75 27 44. Stereo. Hrs open: 24 957 Broadcast Ctr., Avoca, 18641. Phone: (570) 414-1943. Fax: (570) 414-1944. Web Site:www.lite943fm.com Licensee: WS2K Radio LLC. Group owner: Route 81 Radio LLC (acq 7-14-2008; grpsl). Population served: 2,000,000 Format: Soft adult contemp. ♦Ira Rosenblatt, stn mgr.

Carlisle

WCAT-FM— 1959: 102.3 mhz; 3 kw. Ant 328 ft TL: N40 17 23 W77 08 10. Stereo. Hrs open: 24 Box 450, Hershey, 17033. Secondary address: 1703 Walnut Bottom Rd. 17013. Phone: (610) 266-7600. Phone: (508) 752-1045. Fax: (717) 258-4638. Web Site:www.red1023.com Licensee: Citadel Broadcasting Co. Group owner: Citadel Broadcasting Corp. (acq 1999; $4.5 million with WHYL(AM) Carlisle). Population served: 80,000 Natl. Network: CNN Radio, . Format: Country. Target aud: 25-54. ♦Cindy Miller, gen mgr; John Fraunfelter, opns mgr; Jay Hunter, prom dir; Will Robinson, progmg dir.

***WDCV-FM—** January 1972: 88.3 mhz; 450 w. 150 ft TL: N40 12 09 W77 11 46. Stereo. Hrs open: 7 AM-2 AM Box 1773, Dickinson College, Student Activities Office, 17013-2896. Phone: (717) 245-1444. Fax: (717) 245-1899.E-mail: webmaster@dickinson.edu Web Site:www.the-freq.com Licensee: Board of Trustees Dickinson College. Format: Div. News staff: 5; News: 5 hrs wkly. Spec prog: Jazz 6 hrs, Ger one hr, Sp one hr, funk/rap 15 hrs, Russian one hr, politics one hr, blues 6 hrs wkly. ♦Nick Stamos, gen mgr.

WHYL(AM)— 1948: 960 khz; 5 kw-D, 22 w-N. TL: N40 11 34 W77 10 28. Hrs open: 24 1703 Walnut Bottom Rd., 17015. Phone: (717) 249-1717. Fax: (717) 258-4638. Web Site:www.whylradio.com Licensee: WS2K Radio LLC. Group owner: Route 81 Radio LLC (acq 7-14-2008; grpsl). Population served: 350,000 Natl. Rep: McGavren Guild,. Format: News/talk. News staff: one. Target aud: 45 plus; older, mature adults. Spec prog: Polka 2 hrs. ♦Bruce Collier, gen mgr, gen sls mgr; Kevin Kremer, opns mgr; Karen Peiffer, traf mgr.

WIOO(AM)— July 8, 1965: 1000 khz; 1 kw-D. TL: N40 09 30 W77 11 49. Hrs open: Sunrise-sunset 180 York Rd., 17013. Phone: (717) 243-1200. Fax: (717) 243-1277.E-mail: wioo@pa.net Web Site:www.carlisle-pa.com/wioo Licensee: Harold Swidler. Population served: 18,079 Rgnl. Network: Radio Pa. Radio Pa. Format: Classic country. News staff: 2; News: 15 hrs wkly. Target aud: 21 plus. Spec prog: Relg 5 hrs wkly. ♦Harold Swidler, pres; Florence Fisher, gen mgr, opns mgr.

***WPFG(FM)—**Not on air, target date: unknown: 91.3 mhz; 600 w. Ant 830 ft TL: N40 16 36 W77 16 38. Hrs open: Box 125, 17013. Phone: (717) 249-3520.E-mail: CVCRTheBridge@EmbarqMail.com Web Site:cumberlandvalleychristianradio.com Licensee: Cumberland Valley Christian Radio. ♦Frederick A. Leeds, pres.

Carnegie

WZUM(AM)— July 1962: 1590 khz; 1 kw-D, 24 w-N, DA-2. TL: N40 25 28 W80 05 05. Hrs open: 6 AM-sunset 4939 Buttermilk Hollow Rd., Suite 301, West Mifflin, 15122. Phone: (412) 466-3571. Licensee: Believe & Achieve Family and Educational Center Inc. (acq 8-6-2009; $800,000). Population served: 300,000 Format: Gospel. Target aud: General. ♦Katrina Chase, gen mgr.

Cashtown

***WFKJ(AM)—** Dec 7, 1988: 890 khz; 1 kw-D. TL: N39 52 59 W77 20 43. Hrs open: 7 AM-6 PM Box 115, 17310. Secondary address: 3425 Chambersburg Rd., Biglerville 17307. Phone: (717) 337-1635. Fax: (717) 334-8914.E-mail: jil@wordbroadcast.org Web Site:www.wordbroadcast.org Licensee: Jesus is Lord Ministries International. Natl. Network: Moody, . Format: Relg. Target aud: General. Spec prog: Country 4 hrs, children 12 hrs wkly. ♦Fred Bream, prom mgr, prom mgr, progmg dir, mus dir, pub affrs dir; Rev. Michael H. Yeager, pres, gen mgr, gen sls mgr & news dir; Larry Angle, chief of engrg.

Central City

WCCL(FM)— Oct 19, 1972: 101.7 mhz; 725 w. Ant 643 ft TL: N40 06 42 W78 51 33. Stereo. Hrs open: 24 970 Tripoli St., Johnstown, 15902. Phone: (814) 534-8975. Fax: (814) 534-8979.E-mail: info@cool101online.com Web Site:www.cool101online.com Licensee: 2510 Licenses LLC. (group owner; (acq 2-16-2005; grpsl). Format: Oldies. News staff: 4. Target aud: 25-54. Spec prog: Relg 4 hrs wkly. ♦Nick Ferrara, gen mgr.

Centre Hall

WMAJ-FM— May 24, 1989: 99.5 mhz; 850 w. Ant 1,368 ft TL: N40 45 09 W77 45 16. Stereo. Hrs open: 24 2551 Park Center Blvd., State College, 16801. Phone: (814) 237-9800. Fax: (814) 237-2477.E-mail: info@majic99.com Web Site:www.majic99.com Licensee: Megahertz Licenses LLC. Group owner: Forever Broadcasting (acq 4-29-2002; $875,000 with WHUN(AM) Huntingdon). Population served: 37,000 Rgnl rep: Commercial Media Sales. Format: variety favorites. ♦Dave Davies, gen mgr.

Chambersburg

WCHA(AM)— Aug 11, 1946: 800 khz; 1 kw-D, 196 w-N. TL: N39 55 41 W77 41 44. Stereo. Hrs open: 25 Penncraft Ave., 17201. Phone: (717) 263-0813. Fax: (717) 263-9649.E-mail: mix95@mix95.com Licensee: MLB-Hagerstown-Chambersburg IV LLC. (acq 7-20-2005; grpsl). Population served: 17,315 Natl. Network: ABC, . Latham Watkins. Format: News/talk. News staff: one. Target aud: 25-54. Spec prog: Relg 8 hrs, gospel 2 hrs wkly. ♦Rich Bateman, gen mgr; Craig Stevens, opns mgr, gen sls mgr; Rick Alexander, chief of opns, progmg mgr; Tammy Heckman, prom mgr.

WHGT(AM)— 1956: 1590 khz; 5 kw-D, 1 kw-N, DA-N. TL: N39 54 15 W77 39 45. (CP: 15 kw-D, 15 w-N, DA-2. TL: N39 49 55 W77 41 56). Hrs open: 24 Emmanuel Baptist Temple, 16221 National Pike, Hagerstown, MD, 21740-2150. Phone: (301) 582-0378. Fax: (301) 582-1620.E-mail: aikens@emmanuelbaptisttemple.org Web Site:www.emmanuelbaptisttemple.org Licensee: Emmanuel Baptist Temple (acq 2-15-2006; gift from M. Belmont Verstandig Inc.). Population served: 200,000 Reddy, Begley & McCormick, LLP. Format: Conservative Christian. News: 14 hrs wkly. Conservative Christian. Spec prog: Church worship svc one hr wkly. ♦Dr. Larry Aikens Jr., gen mgr.

WIKZ(FM)— Apr 15, 1948: 95.1 mhz; 50 kw horiz, 42 kw vert. 449 ft TL: N39 55 41 W77 41 44. Stereo. Hrs open: Prog sep from AM 25 Penncraft Ave., 17201. Phone: (717) 263-0813. Fax: (717) 263-9649.E-mail: info@wikz.com Web Site:www.mix95.com Population served: 206,000 Format: Adult contemp. News staff: one. Target aud: 25-44. ♦Lisa Harding, prom mgr, disc jockey; J.P. McCartney, asst music dir; Jeff Baker, engrg mgr; Barbara Turkenton, traf mgr; Lisa Kline, local news ed, news rptr; Artie Shultz, disc jockey.

***WZXQ(FM)—** 2005: 88.3 mhz; 110 w vert. Ant 1,155 ft TL: N39 57 40 W77 28 32. Hrs open:
Rebroadcasts WBYO(FM) Sellersville 100%.
Box 186, Sellersville, 18960. Phone: (215) 721-2141. Fax: (215) 721-9811.E-mail: wordfm@wordfm.org Web Site:www.wordfm.org Licensee: Four Rivers Community Broadcasting Corp. Format: Christian Adult Contemp., Religious. ♦David Baker, VP; Charles W. Loughery, gen mgr.

Charleroi

WFGI(AM)— 1947: 940 khz; 250 w-D, 5 w-N, U. TL: N40 07 24 W79 53 45. Hrs open: 24 123 Blaine Rd., Brownsville, 15417. Phone: (724) 938-2000. Fax: (724) 938-7824. Licensee: Keymarket Licenses LLC. Group owner: Keymarket Communications LLC (acq 12-15-99; $3.5

million with co-located FM). Population served: 200,000 Baraff, Koerner & Olender. Format: Country. News staff: one. Target aud: General; Mon Valley area. ◆Gerald Getz, pres; Andrew Powaski, gen mgr.

WOGI(FM)— July 10, 1967: 98.3 mhz; 6 kw. 300 ft TL: N40 07 24 W79 53 45. Stereo. Hrs open: 24 Dups AM 100% 100 Ryan Ct., Suite 98, Pittsburgh, 15205. Phone: (412) 279-5400. Fax: (412) 279-5500.E-mail: info@froggyland.com Web Site:www.froggyland.com Population served: 398,000 Target aud: 18-49. ◆G. Getz, gen sls mgr; Mark Lindow, progmg dir; Scott Tavares, mus dir; Hollywood Haley, disc jockey.

Chester

*WDNR(FM)**— Apr 22, 1977: 89.5 mhz; 10 w. 117 ft TL: N39 51 42 W75 21 20. Stereo. Hrs open: 9 Widener University, Box 1000, One University Pl., 19013. Phone: (610) 499-4439. Phone: (610) 499-4000. Fax: (610) 499-4531.E-mail: wdnr895@mail.widener.edu Web Site:www.wdnr.com Licensee: Widener University. Population served: 50,000 Format: Free-form. Target aud: 16-30; high school & college age population. Spec prog: Jazz 2 hrs, blues 2 hrs, oldies 2 hrs, children 2 hrs wkly. ◆Art Kalemkarian, gen mgr; Sean Sheenan, opns dir; Drena Gwin, progmg dir, mus dir; John Blazek, chief of engrg.

WPWA(AM)— October 1947: 1590 khz; 3.2 kw-D, 1 kw-N, DA-N. TL: N39 52 39 W75 27 22. Stereo. Hrs open: 24 12 Kent Rd., Aston, 19014. Phone: (610) 358-1400. Fax: (610) 358-1845.E-mail: poder1590@wpwa.net Web Site:www.wpwa.net Licensee: Mount Ocean Media L.L.C. (acq 8-20-2001; $675,000). Population served: 1,700,000 Booth, Freret, Imlay & Tepper P. Format: Gospel, Christian, relg. News: 20 hrs wkly. Target aud: 25-64; affluent, mature adults. ◆Steve Skalish, gen mgr.

WVCH(AM)— Apr 4, 1948: 740 khz; 1 kw-D. TL: N39 52 38 W75 24 24. (CP: 50 kw-D, 450 w-N, DA-1). Hrs open: 6 AM-6 PM Box 157, Blue Bell, 19477-0102. Secondary address: 308 Dutton Mill Rd., Brookhaven 19015. Phone: (610) 872-8861. Fax: (610) 279-9002.E-mail: wvch@juno.com Web Site:www.wvch.com Licensee: WVCH Communications Inc. (acq 10-74). Population served: 4,300,000 Natl. Network: Moody, USA, . Wiley, Rein & Fielding. Format: Relg, Christian. Target aud: General. ◆Thomas H. Moffit, pres; Tom Moffit Jr., sr VP; William Fenton, VP; Tom Harvey, gen mgr.

Clarendon

WKNB(FM)— Aug 31, 1995: 104.3 mhz; 4.7 kw. Ant 371 ft TL: N41 47 21 W79 08 29. Stereo. Hrs open: 24 Box 824, Warren, 16365. Secondary address: 310 Second Ave, Warren 16365. Phone: (814) 723-1310. Fax: (814) 723-3356.E-mail: info@kibcoradio.com Web Site:www.kibcoradio.com Licensee: Radio Partners LLC. (acq 9-30-2005; grpsl). Natl. Network: AP Radio, . Rgnl rep: Commercial Media Sales Borsari & Paxson. Wire Svc: AP Format: Country. News staff: one. Target aud: 18-45. ◆Frank Iorio, gen mgr; David Whipple, gen sls mgr; Dale Bliss, prom dir, sls; Mark Silvis, progmg dir, progmg mgr & news dir; Dana Simmons, traf mgr.

WNAE-FM— 2007: 102.7 mhz; 5.5 kw. Ant 341 ft TL: N41 41 36 W79 03 40. Hrs open: Box 824, Warren, 16365. Phone: (814) 723-1310. Fax: (814) 723-3356.E-mail: info@kibcoradio.com Web Site:www.kibcoradio.com Licensee: Iorio Broadcasting Inc. Format: Country. ◆Frank Iorio, pres.

Clarion

WCCR(FM)— June 28, 1985: 92.7 mhz; 3 kw. 400 ft TL: N41 14 41 W79 15 42. Stereo. Hrs open: 24 Prog sep from AM Box 688, 16214. Secondary address: 1168 Greenville Pike 16214. Phone: (814) 226-4500. Fax: (814) 226-5898.E-mail: clarionradio@comcast.net Web Site:www.clarioncountydailynews.com Rgnl rep: Dome & Associates Format: Adult contemp. News staff: one; News: 8 hrs wkly. Target aud: 25-54.

*WCUC-FM**— April 1977: 91.7 mhz; 3.2 kw. Ant 318 ft TL: N41 12 35 W79 22 39. Stereo. Hrs open: 24/7 Clarion Univ. of PA, 840 Wood St., G55 Becker Hall, 16214. Phone: (814) 393-2330. Phone: (814) 393-2514. Fax: (814) 393-2065.E-mail: bexley@clarion.edu Licensee: Clarion University of Pennsylvania. (acq 6-76). Population served: 43,500 Wire Svc: AP Format: Top 40. Spec prog: Urban 6 hrs, country 6 hrs, jazz 3 hrs, community 12 hrs wkly. ◆Bill Adams, gen mgr; Bruce Exley, chief of opns & engr.

WWCH(AM)— June 12, 1960: 1300 khz; 1 kw-D, 36 w-N. TL: N41 10 34 W79 20 22. Hrs open: 24 Box 688, 16214. Secondary address: 1168 Greenville Pike 16214. Phone: (814) 226-4500. Fax: (814) 226-5898.E-mail: clarionradio@comcast.net Web

Site:www.clarioncountydailynews.com Licensee: Clarion County Broadcasting Corp. Population served: 48,000 Natl. Network: CBS Radio, . Rgnl. Network: Radio Pa. Natl. Rep: Dome,. Radio Pa. Frederick Polner. Format: Classic country/news/talk. News staff: one; News: 8 hrs wkly. Target aud: 25-54. Spec prog: Pub affrs, relg 8 hrs wkly. ◆William S. Hearst, pres & gen mgr.

Clearfield

WCPA(AM)— 1947: 900 khz; 2.5 kw-D, 500 w-N, DA-2. TL: N41 02 32 W78 26 54. Hrs open: 801 E. Dubois Ave., Suite D, Du Bois, 15801. Phone: (814) 371-6100. Fax: (814) 371-6100. Licensee: First Media Radio LLC. (acq 1-23-2007; $750,000 with co-located FM). Population served: 80,176 Natl. Rep: Dome,. Format: Oldies. Target aud: 35 plus. ◆Francis Rosana, gen mgr.

WQYX(FM)— July 12, 1967: 93.1 mhz; 1.7 kw. Ant 941 ft TL: N41 04 05 W78 31 07. Stereo. Hrs open: 24 801 E. Du Bois Ave., Du Bois, 15801. Phone: (814) 371-6100. Fax: (814) 765-6333. Baraff, Koerner & Olender. Format: Hot adult contemp. Target aud: 18-44. ◆Francis Rosana, gen mgr.

Coatesville

WCOJ(AM)— Nov 29, 1949: 1420 khz; 5 kw-U, DA-N. TL: N40 01 21 W75 48 53. Hrs open: 24 Box 798, Doylestown, 18901. Phone: (215) 345-1570. Fax: (215) 345-1946.E-mail: 1570am@holyspiritradio.org Web Site:www.holyspiritradio.org Licensee: Holy Spirit Radio Foundation Inc. Group owner: Route 81 Radio LLC (acq 2-27-2009; $800,000). Population served: 485,000 Natl. Network: EWTN Radio, . Cohn and Marks LLP. Format: Catholic. ◆Dale W. Meier, gen mgr.

*WRTJ(FM)**—Not on air, target date: unknown: 89.3 mhz; 1 w horiz, 600 w vert. Ant 236 ft TL: N40 01 23 W75 48 56. Hrs open: 1509 Cecil B. Moore Ave., WRTI/3rd Fl., Philadelphia, 19121-3410. Phone: (215) 204-8405. Fax: (215) 204-4870. Web Site:www.wrti.org Licensee: Temple University of The Commonwealth System of Higher Education. ◆David S. Conant, gen mgr.

Columbia

WVZN(AM)— 1957: Stn currently dark. 1580 khz; 500 w-D, 5 w-N. TL: N40 00 53 W76 28 13. Hrs open: 24 10 S. Prince St., Suite 200, Lancaster, 17603. Phone: (717) 823-9300. Licensee: Esfuerzo de Union Cristiana (acq 2-1-2002; $165,000). Rgnl. Network: Metronews Radio Net, Radio PA. ◆Wilson Cortez, gen mgr.

Confluence

*WKEL(FM)**— 2008: 98.5 mhz; 1.1 kw. Ant 764 ft TL: N39 55 40 W79 25 06. Hrs open: 2351 Sunset Blvd., Suite 170-218, Rocklin, CA, 95765. Phone: (916) 251-1600. Fax: (916) 251-1650. Web Site:www.klove.com Licensee: Educational Media Foundation. Natl. Network: K-Love, . Format: Contemp Christian. ◆Mike Novak, pres.

Connellsville

*WSVP(FM)**—Not on air, target date: unknown: 88.7 mhz; 54 w horiz, 2.5 kw vert. Ant 771 ft TL: N39 55 40 W79 25 06. Hrs open: P.O. Box 195, Uniontown, 15401. Phone: (724) 439-4908. Fax: (724) 439-4908. Licensee: St. Vincent De Paul Society Uniontown Area Conference. Natl. Network: EWTN Radio, . ◆Roy Sarver, gen mgr.

WYJK(AM)— Apr 23, 1947: 1340 khz; 1 kw-U. TL: N40 01 27 W79 36 35. Hrs open: 24 123 Blaine Rd., Brownsville, 15417. Phone: (724) 938-2000. Fax: (724) 938-7824.E-mail: rherring@keymarketradio.com Web Site:www.classichitsradioonline.com Licensee: Keymarket Licenses LLC Group owner: Keymarket Communications LLC (acq 1-17-2001; $475,000 with WPKL(FM) Uniontown). Population served: 150,000 Natl. Network: ABC, . Format: Classic hits. News: 6a - - 10a. Target aud: 25-64. ◆Gerald Getz, pres; Andrew Ponaski, gen mgr, sports cmtr.

Cooperstown

WUUZ(FM)— 2002: 107.7 mhz; 4.5 kw. Ant 377 ft TL: N41 29 23 W79 44 07. Hrs open: 24 900 Water Street, Downtown Mall, Meadville, 16335. Phone: (814) 724-9800. Fax: (814) 333-9628.E-mail: radio@zoominternet.net Web Site:www.mywuzz.com Licensee: Forever Broadcasting LLC. Group owner: Forever Broadcasting (acq 7-5-01; $342,000 for CP). Format: Classic hits. ◆Terry Deitz, gen mgr.

Corry

WWCB(AM)— Apr 2, 1955: 1370 khz; 1 kw-D, 500 w-N, DA-N. TL: N41 56 10 W79 39 20. Hrs open: 6 AM-11 PM (M-F); 7 AM-11 PM (S); 7 AM-10 PM (Su) Box 4, 16407. Secondary address: 418 N. Center 16407. Phone: (814) 664-8694. Fax: (814) 664-8695. Licensee: Corry Communications Corp. (acq 1-22-89; $140,000; 1-15-90). Population served: 10,000 Natl. Network: Motor Racing Net, Westwood One, CBS, . Format: Adult contemp, classic rock, sports. Target aud: General. ◆William Hammond III, pres.

Coudersport

WFRM(AM)— May 1953: 600 khz; 1 kw-D, 46 w-N. TL: N41 45 11 W78 00 03. Hrs open: 9 S. Main St., 16915. Phone: (814) 274-8600. Phone: (814) 642-9396. Fax: (814) 274-0760.E-mail: gmiller@wfrm.net; radio@wfrm.net Web Site:www.wfrm.net Licensee: Farm & Home Broadcasting Co. Group owner: Allegheny Mountain Network Stations Population served: 2,831 Natl. Network: ABC, . Natl. Rep: Dome,. Borsari & Paxson. Format: Hit country, strong loc news/talk. Target aud: General. Spec prog: Farm 2 hrs wkly. ◆Gerri Miller, gen sls mgr, prom mgr & progmg mgr.

Covington

WDKC(FM)— 1994: 101.5 mhz; 1.9 kw. Ant 594 ft TL: N41 43 25 W77 02 46. Stereo. Hrs open: Box 101.5, Mansfield, 16933. Secondary address: 8767 Rt. 414, Liberty 16930. Phone: (570) 662-9000. Fax: (570) 324-1015.E-mail: kc101@sosbbs.com Licensee: Mid-Atlantic Broadcasting Inc. (acq 4-95; $105,000). Population served: 100,000 Format: Country. News staff: one; News: 3 hrs wkly. Target aud: 25-54; 70% female. ◆Kevin Thomas, CEO, pres; Thomas Gluszczak, chmn; Kevin Gluszczak, gen mgr.

Cresson

WBRX(FM)— November 1981: 94.7 mhz; 970 w. Ant 794 ft TL: N40 24 11 W78 31 35. Hrs open: 24 2513 6th Ave., Altoona, 16602. Phone: (814) 943-6112. Fax: (814) 944-9782. Web Site:www.wbrx.com Licensee: Sounds Good Inc. Population served: 225,000 Natl. Network: Westwood One, . Format: Adult contemp. News staff: one; News: 7 hrs wkly. Target aud: 18-54; males. ◆David Barger, gen mgr & stn mgr.

Curwensville

WOKW(FM)— Aug 1, 1989: 102.9 mhz; 350 w. Ant 945 ft TL: N41 04 29 W78 31 58. Stereo. Hrs open: 24 Box 589, Clearfield, 16830. Secondary address: 712 River Rd., Clearfield 16830. Phone: (814) 765-4955. Fax: (814) 765-7038.E-mail: news@wokw.com Web Site:www.wokw.com Licensee: Raymark Broadcasting Co. Inc. Population served: 250,000 Natl. Network: ABC, . Format: Adult contemp. News staff: one; News: 14 hrs wkly. Target aud: 21-54. Spec prog: Oldies 2 hrs wkly. ◆Mark E. Harley, pres; Yvonne Lehman, exec VP; Mark Harley, gen mgr.

Dallas

WCIG(FM)— Oct 10, 1990: 107.7 mhz; 1.25 kw. Ant 725 ft TL: N41 27 07 W76 00 33. Stereo. Hrs open: 24 Box 701, Tunkhannock, 18657. Phone: (570) 836-4200. Fax: (570) 836-7035. Web Site:www.fln.org Licensee: Family Life Ministries Inc. (acq 8-6-2009; $1 million). Format: Relg.

WSJR(FM)— May 29, 1989: 93.7 mhz; 750 w. 679 ft TL: N41 15 43 W75 58 04. (CP: 1.45 kw). Stereo. Hrs open: 24 Rebroadcasts WCTP(FM) Carbondale 100%. 600 Baltimore Dr., 2nd Fl., Wilkes-Barre, 18702. Phone: (570) 824-9000. Fax: (570) 820-0520. Web Site:www.jr937.us Licensee: Citadel Broadcasting Co. Group owner: Citadel Broadcasting Corp. (acq 2-4-98; grpsl). Population served: 2,000,000 Natl. Network: CBS, . Natl. Rep: Roslin,. Format: Country. News staff: one; News: 3 hrs wkly. Target aud: 25-54. Spec prog: Community affrs one hr wkly. ◆Bill Palmeri, mktg mgr; Erin Evans, prom dir; Mark Lindow, progmg dir.

Danville

*WPGM(AM)**— June 1963: 1570 khz; 2.5 kw-D. TL: N40 59 10 W76 37 37. Hrs open: 8 E. Market St., 17821. Phone: (570) 275-1570. Fax: (570) 275-4071.E-mail: info@wpgm.org Web Site:www.wpgm.info Licensee: Montrose Broadcasting Corp. (group owner; (acq 1-6-64). Format: Relg, btfl mus. Target aud: General; families. ◆George Vacca, gen sls mgr & progmg dir.

*WPGM-FM— Sept 6, 1968: 96.7 mhz; 340 w. 760 ft TL: N40 59 16 W76 32 51. Stereo. Hrs open: Dups AM 75% 8 E. Market St., 17821. Phone: (570) 275-1570. Fax: (570) 275-4071.E-mail: info@wpgm.org Web Site:www.wpgm.info Licensee: Montrose Broadcasting Corp. Population served: 300,000

Doylestown

WISP(AM)— 1948: 1570 khz; 5 kw-D, 900 w-N, DA-2. TL: N40 19 34 W75 09 40. Hrs open: 24 Box 798, 18901. Secondary address: 40 Rickerts Rd. , Doylestown 18901. Phone: (215) 345-1570. Fax: (215) 345-1946.E-mail: 1570am@holyspiritradio.org Web Site:www.holyspiritradio.org Licensee: Holy Spirit Radio Foundation Inc. (acq 1999; $1,023,750). Population served: 475,000 Cohn and Marks. Format: Relg. News: 14 hrs wkly. Target aud: General. ♦Dale W. Meier, CEO & gen mgr.

DuBois

WCED(AM)— February 1941: 1420 khz; 5 kw-D, 500 w-N, DA-N. TL: N41 08 31 W78 48 07. Hrs open: 24 12 W. Long Ave., Du Bois, 15801-2100. Phone: (814) 375-5260. Fax: (814) 375-5262. Web Site:www.1420wced.com Licensee: WCED Radio LLC. Group owner: Priority Communications acq 11-28-2003; $150,000). Population served: 40,000 Natl. Network: ABC, ESPN Radio, . Rgnl. Network: Radio Pa. Womble Carlyle. Format: News/Talk. News staff: one; News: 20 hrs wkly. ♦Jay Philippone, gen mgr; Lori Lewis, stn mgr; Lindsey Schoening, news dir; Polly Slie, traf mgr; Al Lockwood, engr.

WCOH-FM— Nov 12, 1975: 107.3 mhz; 50 kw. Ant 499 ft TL: N41 11 28 W78 41 27. Stereo. Hrs open: 24 28 W. Scribner Ave., 15801. Phone: (814) 371-1330. Fax: (814) 375-5650.E-mail: sales@wdba.com Web Site:www.fln.org Licensee: Family Life Ministries Inc. (acq 10-6-93; $360,000; 10-25-93). Population served: 270,000 Natl. Rep: Salem,. Wire Svc: AP Format: Inspirational, Christian. News: 6 hrs wkly. Target aud: 25-54; women. Spec prog: Children 2 hrs wkly, Southern Gospel 5 hrs wkly, Christian rock 5 hrs wkly. ♦Daniel Brownlee, pres; Dan Kennard, gen mgr, progmg mgr; Gerald Meloon, opns dir & opns mgr.

WOWQ(FM)— 1948: 102.1 mhz; 28 kw. Ant 663 ft TL: N41 02 43 W78 42 11. Stereo. Hrs open: 24 801 E. DuBois Ave., 15801. Phone: (814) 371-6100. Fax: (814) 371-7724.E-mail: q102@adelphia.net Web Site:www.q102radio.fm Licensee: First Media Radio LLC. (group owner; (acq 4-10-2002; $4.2 million with WCED(AM) DuBois). Population served: 250,000 Format: Country. News staff: one; News: 10 hrs wkly. Target aud: 18 plus. ♦Alex Kolobielski, CEO, chmn, pres; F. "Moose" Rosana, gen mgr.

Dunmore

WBHD(FM)—(Olyphant, 1991: 95.7 mhz; 300 w. 1,010 ft TL: N41 26 10 W75 43 45. Hrs open: 24
Simulcast with WBHT(FM) Mountaintop.
600 Baltmore Dr., 2nd Fl., Wilkes-Barre, 18702. Phone: (570) 824-9000. Fax: (570) 820-0520. Web Site:www.97bht.com Licensee: Citadel Broadcasting Co. Group owner: Citadel Broadcasting Corp. (acq 1999; $950,000). Format: CHR. Target aud: 18-49; men, sports fans. Spec prog: Talk. ♦Bill Palmeri, mktg mgr.

Dushore

*WEMR(FM)—Not on air, target date: unknown: 88.7 mhz; 720 w. Ant 12 ft TL: N41 31 59 W76 24 10. Hrs open: Box 20155, Scranton, 18502. Phone: (607) 427-0452. Licensee: Telikoja Educational Broadcasting Inc. ♦Kevin M. Fitzgerald, pres.

East Nottingham

*WZXE(FM)—Not on air, target date: unknown: 88.3 mhz; 1 w horiz, 540 w vert. Ant 453 ft TL: N39 44 00 W75 57 56. Hrs open: Box 186, Sellersville, 18960. Phone: (215) 721-2141. Fax: (215) 721-9811. Web Site:www.wordfm.org Licensee: Four Rivers Community Broadcasting Corp. ♦Charles W. Loughery, gen mgr.

East Stroudsburg

*WESS(FM)— Mar 10, 1971: 90.3 mhz; 1.37 kw. -165 ft TL: N40 59 55 W75 10 21. Stereo. Hrs open: McGarry Communications Ctr., East Stroudsburg Univ., 18301. Phone: (570) 422-3512. Fax: (570) 422-3777.E-mail: wess@esu.edu Web Site:www.esu.edu/wess Licensee: East Stroudsburg University Board of Trustees/Student Activities Association. (acq 3-79). Population served: 40,000 Format: Div, alternative, sports. Spec prog: Class 4 hrs, educ 7 hrs, jazz 6 hrs, news/talk 6 hrs,oldies 8 hrs wkly. ♦Jillian Kane, stn mgr, prom dir; Jennifer Haney, prom dir; Nicholas Frey, news dir.

Easton

WCTO(FM)— 1948: 96.1 mhz; 50 kw. 500 ft TL: N40 35 55 W75 25 12. Stereo. Hrs open: 24 2158 Avenue C, Suite 100, Bethlehem, 18017. Phone: (610) 266-7600. Fax: (610) 231-0400. Web Site:www.catcountry96.fm Licensee: Citadel Broadcasting Co. Group owner: Citadel Broadcasting Corp. Population served: 841,000 Natl. Rep: Christal, Katz Radio,. Format: Country. ♦John Fraunfelter, gen mgr; Shelly Easton, opns mgr; Elizabeth Penbleton, sls dir.

WEEX(AM)— May 1956: 1230 khz; 840 w-D, 1 kw-N, DA-D. TL: N40 42 30 W75 13 00. Hrs open: 107 Paxinosa Rd. W., 18040-1344. Phone: (610) 258-6155. Fax: (610) 258-6292.E-mail: tomf@espnlv.com Web Site:www.espnlv.com Licensee: Nassau Broadcasting II LLC. Group owner: Nassau Broadcasting Partners L.P. (acq 1-31-01; grpsl). Population served: 60,000 Natl. Network: ESPN Radio, . Natl. Rep: Katz Radio,. Rgnl rep: Glenn Jones Format: Sports. Target aud: 18-49; men. ♦Rick Musselman, gen mgr; Pat Lincoln, gen sls mgr; Tom Fallon, progmg dir.

WEST(AM)— Feb 17, 1936: 1400 khz; 1 kw-U. TL: N40 40 23 W75 12 30. Stereo. Hrs open: 24 436 Northampton St., 18042. Phone: (610) 258-9378. Fax: (610) 250-9675.E-mail: infor@am1400west.net Web Site:www.am1400west.net Licensee: Maranatha Broadcasting Co. Inc. Population served: 557,200 Natl. Rep: McGavren Guild,. Fleischman & Walsh L. Format: MOR, It. News staff: 2; News: 20 hrs wkly. Target aud: General. ♦David Hinson, gen mgr; John Richetta, gen sls mgr; Terry Rich, progmg dir; Bob Kratz, chief of engrg.

*WJRH(FM)— March 1953: 104.9 mhz; 8 w. 23 ft TL: N40 41 53 W75 12 30. (CP: 100 w). Stereo. Hrs open: 15 Box 9473, Hogg Hall, Lafayette College, 18042. Phone: (610) 330-5316. Fax: (610) 250-5318. Web Site:info@lafayette.com Licensee: Lafayette College. Population served: 200,000 Format: Var. News staff: 3; News: 6 hrs wkly. Target aud: General; college students & community. Spec prog: Jazz 9 hrs, reggae 6 hrs, metal 6 hrs, Sp 6 hrs, classic rock 4 hrs wkly. ♦Sergey Tosninski, gen mgr; Brian Hertz, progmg dir; Fred Lott, chief of engrg.

WODE-FM— June 1950: 99.9 mhz; 50 kw. Ant 449 ft TL: N40 42 30 W75 13 00. Stereo. Hrs open: 107 Paxinosa Rd. W., 18040. Phone: (610) 258-6155. Fax: (610) 253-3384. Licensee: Nassau Broadcasting II LLC. (acq 1-31-2001; grpsl). Population served: 30,256 Natl. Rep: Katz Radio,. Rgnl rep: Glenn Jones Format: Classic hits. ♦Bill Sheridan, progmg dir.

Ebensburg

WRDD(AM)— May 25, 1961: 1580 khz; 1 kw-D. TL: N40 29 33 W78 42 54. Stereo. Hrs open: Sunrise-sunset Box 1095, Northern Cambria, 15714. Secondary address: 104 S. Center St. 15931. Fax: (814) 471-0282.E-mail: whpa@verizon.net Licensee: Vernal Enterprises Inc. (group owner; acq 3-19-97; $20,000 with WNCC(AM) Northern Cambria). Population served: 250,000 Natl. Network: USA, . Format: news/talk. News: 4 hrs wkly. Target aud: General; church goers. ♦Denny Pompa, pres; Larry Schrecongost, gen mgr.

WRKW(FM)— July 15, 1962: 99.1 mhz; 50 kw. Ant 499 ft TL: N40 24 41 W78 46 29. Stereo. Hrs open: 109 Plaza Dr., Suite 2, Johnstown, 15905. Phone: (814) 255-4186. Fax: (814) 255-6145.E-mail: info@hot92fm.net Web Site:www.rocky99.com Licensee: Forever Broadcasting LLC. (group owner; (acq 5-1-2005; $2.73 million with WJHT(FM) Johnstown). Population served: 42,476 Format: Rock. ♦Verla Price, gen mgr; Tina Perry, gen sls mgr; Mike Stevens, progmg dir; Rick Shepard, news dir; Jim Boxler, chief of engrg.

WWGE(AM)—See Loretto

Edinboro

*WFSE(FM)— Apr 3, 1979: 88.9 mhz; 3 kw. 312 ft TL: N41 52 41 W80 10 40. Stereo. Hrs open: 24 Edinboro Univ. of Pa., Faculty Annex 110, 16444. Phone: (814) 732-2641. Phone: (814) 732-2889 (request line).E-mail: dumbluck77@hotmail.com Licensee: Edinboro University. Population served: 230,000 Format: Alternative, modern rock. News: 18 hrs wkly. Target aud: 18-25; college students with community interest. Spec prog: Football & basketball, Black 15 hrs, relg 4 hrs, loc news 3 hrs, swing 2 hrs wkly. ♦Dr. Frank Pogue, CEO; Terrence Warburton, chmn; Chris Volack, gen mgr; Richard Smith, dev dir.

WXTA(FM)— Oct 15, 1988: 97.9 mhz; 10 kw. 505 ft TL: N41 57 59 W80 06 40. Stereo. Hrs open: 24 471 Robison Rd., Erie, 16509. Phone: (814) 864-4835. Fax: (814) 868-1876. Web Site:www.country98wxta.com Licensee: Citadel Broadcasting Co. Group owner: Citadel Broadcasting Corp. (acq 5-12-2004; grpsl). Natl. Rep: Katz Radio,. Format: Country. Target aud: Adults; 25-64. ♦Farid Suleman, CEO; Jim Riley, gen mgr; Stephanie Lancaster, gen sls mgr; Fred Horton, progmg dir; Dave Benson, news dir.

Elizabethtown

WMHX(FM)—(Hershey, Apr 30, 1964: 106.7 mhz; 14 kw. Ant 928 ft TL: N40 10 16 W76 35 50. Stereo. Hrs open: 24 515 S. 32nd St., Camp Hill, 17011. Phone: (717) 635-7000. Fax: (717) 635-7551. Web Site:www.mix1067fm.com Licensee: Citadel Broadcasting Co. Group owner: Citadel Broadcasting Corp. (acq 5-29-97; grpsl). Population served: 1,500,000 Fleischman & Walsh. Format: Adult hits. ♦Bob Adams, gen mgr.

WPDC(AM)— May 1958: 1600 khz; 1 kw-D, 18 w-N. TL: N40 09 45 W76 34 36. Hrs open: 24 1051 Dairy Lane, 17022. Phone: (717) 367-1600.E-mail: teamespn@earthlink.net Licensee: JVJ Communications Inc. (acq 10-1-84; $125,000; 10-15-84). Population served: 20,000 Natl. Network: ESPN Radio, . Rgnl. Network: Radio Pa. Format: Sports. News: 10 hrs wkly. Target aud: 25-54; men. ♦Vincent Grande, pres & gen mgr; Bill Wilson, opns VP; Sam Conrad, opns dir.

*WWEC(FM)— Aug 25, 1990: 88.3 mhz; 100 w. 373 ft TL: N40 08 83 W76 35 38. Stereo. Hrs open: 18 Elizabethtown College, One Alpha Dr., 17022-2298. Phone: (717) 361-1413. Phone: (717) 361-1589. Fax: (717) 361-1180.E-mail: wwec@etown.edu Web Site:www.etown.edu Licensee: Elizabethtown College. Population served: 25,000 Format: Progressive, Alternative. News: 6 hrs wkly. Target aud: General; college students, high school, churches, community. ♦Dr. Randyll K. Yoder, gen mgr; John Treese, stn mgr; Sara Robinson, dev dir; Adam Steiner, mktg dir; Kate Norton, prom dir.

Elizabethville

WYGL-FM— Dec 7, 1989: 100.5 mhz; 1.2 kw. 515 ft TL: N40 37 24 W76 49 54. Stereo. Hrs open: 24 Box 90, Selinsgrove, 17870. Phone: (570) 374-8819. Fax: (570) 374-7444.E-mail: bigcountryrequest@hotmail.com Web Site:www.bigcountrynow.com Licensee: MMP License LLC. Group owner: MAX Media L.L.C. (acq 10-17-03; grpsl). Natl. Network: USA, . Kaye, Scholer, Fierman, Hays & Handler. Format: Contemp country. News staff: one; News: 8 hrs wkly. Target aud: 25-54. ♦John A. Trinder, pres; Scott Richards, VP, gen mgr; Greg Adair, gen sls mgr; Ted Koppen, chief of engrg.

Ellwood City

WKPL(FM)— July 4, 1968: 92.1 mhz; 2.5 kw. Ant 512 ft TL: N40 46 09 W80 16 56. Stereo. Hrs open: 100 Ryan Ct., Pittsburg, 15205. Phone: (724) 378-1271. Fax: (412) 279-5500. Licensee: Keymarket Licenses LLC. Group owner: Keymarket Communications LLC (acq 6-30-2004; grpsl). Population served: 18,458 Format: Oldies.

Emporium

WLEM(AM)— Mar 2, 1958: 1250 khz; 2.5 kw-D, 30 w-N. TL: N41 30 22 W78 13 26. Hrs open: 16 145 E. 4th, 15834. Phone: (814) 486-3712. Fax: (814) 486-1772. Licensee: Salter Communications Inc. (acq 11-9-2006; $700,000 with co-located FM). Population served: 25,000 Natl. Network: Westwood One, . Natl. Rep: Commercial Media Sales,. Pepper & Corazzini. Format: Country. News staff: one; News: 3 hrs wkly. Target aud: 25-65. ♦John M. Salter, pres; J. Philippone, gen mgr; Gary Mitchell, opns mgr, progmg dir.

WQKY(FM)— May 20, 1985: 98.9 mhz; 2 kw. 548 ft TL: N41 29 32 W78 15 19. Stereo. Hrs open: Prog sep from AM 145 E. 4th, 15834. Phone: (814) 486-3712. Fax: (814) 486-1772. Format: Adult contemp.

Ephrata

WIOV-FM— Nov 9, 1962: 105.1 mhz; 25 kw. 702 ft TL: N40 10 30 W76 09 31. Stereo. Hrs open: 44 Bethany Rd., 17522-2416. Phone: (717) 738-1191. Fax: (717) 738-1661.E-mail: dick.raymond@citcomm.com Web Site:www.wiov.com Licensee: Citadel Broadcasting Co. Group owner: Citadel Broadcasting Corp. (acq 5-12-2004; grpsl). Population served: 1,000,000 Natl. Rep: McGavren Guild,. Format: Country. ♦Mitch Carroll, gen sls mgr; Dick Raymond, progmg dir; Carrie Rey, traf mgr.

*WRTL(FM)— 2000: 90.7 mhz; 1 w horiz, 850 w vert. Ant 869 ft TL: N40 19 22 W76 11 52. Hrs open: 24

Rebroadcasts WRTI(FM) Philadelphia 100%.
1509 Cecil B. Moore ave., Philadelphia, 19121-3410. Phone: (215) 204-8405. Fax: (215) 204-7027. Web Site:www.wrtl.org Licensee: Temple University of The Commonwealth System of Higher Education. Format: Classical jazz. ◆ Dave Conant, gen mgr.

Erie

*WEFR(FM)— March 1992: 88.1 mhz; 630 w. 430 ft TL: N41 57 59 W80 06 40. Stereo. Hrs open: 24 Family Stations Inc., 4135 Northgate Blvd., Sacramento, CA, 95834-1226. Phone: (916) 641-8191. Fax: (916) 641-8238. Licensee: Family Stations Inc. (group owner) Format: Relg. Target aud: General. ◆ Harold Camping, pres; John Rorvik, opns mgr.

*WERG(FM)— Dec 1, 1972: 90.5 mhz; 2.75 kw. Ant 374 ft TL: N42 02 34 W80 03 57. Stereo. Hrs open: 24 90.5 WERG, 109 University Sq., 16541. Phone: (814) 871-5841. Fax: (814) 871-7652.E-mail: laprice002@gannon.edu Web Site:www.wergfm.com Licensee: Gannon University. Population served: 237,800 Format: Alternative rock/var, urban. News: 3 hrs wkly. Target aud: 18 plus. Spec prog: Sp 3 hrs, Polka 4 hrs wkly. ◆ Chet LaPrice, gen mgr & opns mgr.

WFNN(AM)— 1947: 1330 khz; 5 kw-U, DA-2. TL: N42 03 18 W80 02 24. Hrs open: One Boston Store Place, 16501. Phone: (814) 461-1000. Fax: (814) 874-0011. Fax: (814) 455-6000. Licensee: Connoisseur Media of Erie LLC. Group owner: NextMedia Group L.L.C. (acq 3-31-2006; grpsl). Population served: 129,231 Natl. Network: Fox Sports, . Natl. Rep: Katz Radio,. Format: Sports. ◆ David Bevins, gen mgr.

WJET(AM)— 1951: 1400 khz; 1 kw. TL: N42 07 28 W80 03 54. Hrs open: 24 1 Boston Store Pl., 16501. Phone: (814) 461-1000. Phone: (814) 874-0011. Fax: (814) 874-0011.E-mail: jet1400@jet1400.com Web Site:www.jetradio1400.com Licensee: Connoisseur Media of Erie LLC. Group owner: NextMedia Group L.L.C. (acq 3-31-2006; grpsl). Population served: 236,700 Rgnl. Network: Radio Pa. Radio Pa. Format: News/talk. News staff: one. Target aud: 35 plus; middle to upper middle income, business owners, upscale. ◆ Rick Rambaldo, gen mgr & stn mgr.

*WMCE(FM)— Feb 2, 1989: 88.5 mhz; 750 w. Ant 499 ft TL: N42 05 25 W79 56 37. Stereo. Hrs open: 24 501 E. 38th St., 16546. Phone: (814) 824-2260. Phone: (814) 824-2261. Fax: (814) 824-2590.E-mail: wshannon@mercyhurst.edu Web Site:www.mercyhurst.edu Licensee: Mercyhurst College. Population served: 280,000 Natl. Network: AP Radio, . Format: Class. News: 6 hrs wkly. Target aud: General; Adults 45+. Spec prog: Pol 3 hrs, Ger 4 hrs, Sp 3 hrs, jazz 4 hrs wkly. ◆ William T. Shannon, gen mgr.

WPSE(AM)— Apr 21, 1935: 1450 khz; 1 kw-U. TL: N42 08 11 W80 02 25. Hrs open: 24 Penn State-Behrend, Station Rd., 16563-1450. Phone: (814) 898-6495. Phone: (814) 898-6491. Licensee: Board of Trustees, Pennsylvania State University. (acq 12-23-89). Natl. Network: CBS, Westwood One, . Format: Business news, sports. Target aud: General. ◆ Ron Slomski, gen mgr.

WQHZ(FM)— Oct 15, 1951: 102.3 mhz; 1.7 kw. Ant 613 ft TL: N42 02 25 W80 04 08. Stereo. Hrs open: 24 471 Robison Rd. W., 16509. Phone: (814) 868-5355. Fax: (814) 868-1876. Web Site:www.z1023online.com Licensee: Citadel Broadcasting Co. Group owner: Citadel Broadcasting Corp. (acq 5-12-2004; grpsl). Natl. Rep: Katz Radio,. Format: Classic rock. News staff: one. Target aud: 25-54; Adults. ◆ Farid Suleman, CEO; Jim Riley, gen mgr, natl sls mgr; Stephanie Lancaster, gen sls mgr; Adam Reese, progmg dir; Dave Benson, news dir.

*WQLN-FM— Jan 7, 1973: 91.3 mhz; 35 kw. 500 ft TL: N42 02 35 W80 03 59. Stereo. Hrs open: 24 8425 Peach St., 16509. Phone: (814) 864-3001. Fax: (814) 864-4077.E-mail: dmiller@wqln.org Web Site:www.wqln.org Licensee: Public Broadcasting of Northwest Pennsylvania Inc. Population served: 129,231 Natl. Network: NPR, PRI, . Dow, Lohnes & Albertson. Format: Classical; news; jazz. News staff: one; News: 24 hrs wkly. Target aud: General. Spec prog: Sp one hr, pub affrs 5 hrs, new age 2 hrs, call-in show 3 hrs wkly. ◆ Dwight Miller, pres; Cindy Spizarny, VP; Sue Allen, progmg dir; Kim Young, news dir. Co-owned TV: *WQLN(TV) affil.

WRIE(AM)— 1941: 1260 khz; 5 kw-U, DA-2. TL: N42 03 18 W80 02 24. Hrs open: 24 471 Robison Rd. W., 16509. Phone: (814) 868-5355. Fax: (814) 868-1876. Licensee: Citadel Broadcasting Co. Group owner: Citadel Broadcasting Corp. (acq 5-12-2004; grpsl). Natl. Network: ESPN Radio, . Natl. Rep: Katz Radio,. Format: Sports talk. ◆ Farid Suleman, CEO; Judy Ellis, COO; Gary Spurgeon, gen mgr, gen sls mgr; Marcia Diehl, opns mgr; Donna Palowitz, sls dir; Tina Achhammer, prom mgr; Ron Arlen, progmg dir; Heather Rose, mus dir; traf mgr; Dave Benson, news dir; Rick Pogson, chief of engrg.

WRKT(FM)—See North East

WRTS(FM)— May 1, 1969: 103.7 mhz; 50 kw. 499 ft TL: N42 05 25 W79 56 37. Stereo. Hrs open: 24 1 Boston Store Pl., 16501. Phone: (814) 461-1000. Fax: (814) 455-6000.E-mail: star104@star104.com Web Site:www.star104.com Licensee: Connoisseur Media of Erie LLC. Group owner: NextMedia Group L.L.C. (acq 3-30-2006; grpsl). Population served: 226,600 Fletcher, Heald & Hildreth. Format: Top 40. News staff: one; News: one hr wkly. Target aud: 25-54. Spec prog: PSA one hr wkly. ◆ Richard Rambaldo, gen mgr.

WXBB(FM)— Sept 1, 1993: 94.7 mhz; 1.7 kw. Ant 613 ft TL: N42 02 31 W80 03 57. Hrs open: 24 1 Boston Store Place, 16501. Phone: (814) 461-1000. Fax: (814) 874-0011. Web Site:www.947bobfm.com Licensee: Connoisseur Media of Erie LLC. Group owner: NextMedia Group L.L.C. (acq 3-30-2006; grpsl). Format: Adult hits. ◆ Rick Rambaldo, gen mgr.

WXKC(FM)— 1949: 99.9 mhz; 50 kw. 492 ft TL: N42 05 24 W79 57 12. Stereo. Hrs open: 24 Prog sep from AM 471 Robison Rd. W., 16509. Phone: (814) 868-5355. Fax: (814) 868-1876. Web Site:www.classy100.com Format: Adult contemp. News staff: one. Target aud: Adults; 35-64. ◆ Heather Rose, traf mgr.

WYNE(AM)—See North East

Everett

WSKE(FM)— Mar 15, 1988: 104.3 mhz; 820 w. Ant 886 ft TL: N40 00 11 W78 23 58. Stereo. Hrs open: 24 Prog sep from AM Box 133, 15537-0133. Secondary address: 151 E 1st Ave 15537-1351. Phone: (814) 652-2600. Fax: (814) 652-9347.E-mail: wske@penn.com Licensee: New Millennium Communications Group Inc. acq 09/27/01 Natl. Network: ABC, Jones Radio Networks, . Radio Pa. Rgnl rep: Dome & Associates Format: Modern Country. News staff: one; News: 7 hrs wkly. Target aud: 25-54. Spec prog: Bluegrass, Classic Country, Southern Gospel. ◆ Shane Imler, pres; John Imler, gen mgr.

WZSK(AM)— Mar 15, 1963: 1040 khz; 10 kw-D. TL: N40 00 26 W78 21 44. Hrs open: Box 133, 15537-0133. Phone: (814) 652-2600. Fax: (814) 652-9347.E-mail: wzsk@penn.com Licensee: New Millennium Communications Group Inc. (acq 9-27-01; with co-located FM). Natl. Network: Radio America, ABC, Jones Radio Networks, . Rgnl. Network: Radio Pa. Radio Pa. Rgnl rep: Dome & Associates Fletcher, Heald & Hildreth. Format: News/talk. News staff: one; News: 10 hrs wkly. Target aud: 25-54. ◆ John C. Imler, gen mgr, progmg dir; Shane S. Imler, pres & adv dir; Shane Imler, chief of engrg.

Fairless Hills

WKXW(FM)—See Trenton, NJ

Fairview

WTWF(FM)— October 2001: 93.9 mhz; 3 kw. Ant 469 ft TL: N41 57 59 W80 06 40. Hrs open: One Boston Store Pl., Erie, 16501. Phone: (814) 461-1000. Fax: (814) 874-0011.E-mail: us939@us939.com Web Site:www.us939.com Licensee: Connoisseur Media of Erie LLC. Group owner: NextMedia Group L.L.C. (acq 3-30-2006; grpsl). Format: Country. ◆ Richard Rambaldo, gen mgr.

Farmington Township

WCOP(FM)—Not on air, target date: unknown: 106.1 mhz; 4.12 kw. Ant 387 ft TL: N41 29 48 W79 25 52. Hrs open: Box 5429, Twin Falls, ID, 83303-5429. Phone: (208) 733-3551. Licensee: World Radio Link Inc. ◆ Earl Williamson, pres.

Farrell

WAKZ(FM)—See Youngstown, OH

WLOA(AM)—Licensed to Farrell. See Youngstown OH

Folsom

*WRSD(FM)— Jan 5, 1983: 94.9 mhz; 1.4 kw. 20 ft TL: N39 53 12 W75 20 01. Hrs open: Ridley School District Admin. Bldg., 901 Morton Ave., Ste. 100, 19033. Phone: (610) 534-1900. Fax: (610) 237-9641. Licensee: Ridley School District. Format: Div, adult contemp. ◆ Ann Brutch, gen mgr.

Forest City

WQFN(FM)— 2000: 100.1 mhz; 750 w. Ant 935 ft TL: N41 35 35 W75 25 56. Hrs open:
Simulcast with WQFM(FM) Nanticoke.
149 Penn Ave., Scranton, 18503. Phone: (570) 346-6555. Fax: (570) 346-6038.E-mail: tbass@shamrocknepa.com Web Site:www.921qfm.com Licensee: The Scranton Times L.P. Group owner: Shamrock Communications Inc. (acq 3-23-2000). Format: Adult contemp. Target aud: 35-64; adults. ◆ William R. Lynett, CEO; Jim Loftus, gen mgr.

Franklin

*WAWN(FM)— 1998: 89.5 mhz; 1 kw. 315 ft TL: N41 23 39 W49 46 20. Hrs open: Box 3206, Tupelo, MS, 38803. Phone: (662) 844-8888. Fax: (662) 842-6791.E-mail: comments@afr.net Web Site:www.afr.net Licensee: American Family Association. Group owner: American Family Radio Format: Christian, inspirational. ◆ Marvin Sanders, gen mgr.

WFRA(AM)— Apr 13, 1958: 1450 khz; 1 kw-U. TL: N41 23 27 W79 48 43. Hrs open: 6 AM-midnight Box 908, 484 Allegheny Blvd., 16323. Phone: (814) 432-2189. Fax: (814) 437-9372.E-mail: radio@zoominternet.com Licensee: Forever Broadcasting LLC. Group owner: Forever Broadcasting (acq 7-20-2000; grpsl). Population served: 64,000 Reddy, Begley & McCormick. Format: MOR, news, sports. News staff: one; News: 12 hrs wkly. Target aud: 45 plus. ◆ Carol Logan, pres; Terry Deitz, gen mgr; Tim Snyder, progmg dir & news dir; Lynn Deppen, engrg VP, chief of engrg; Tim Shaw, sports cmtr.

WHMJ(FM)— Mar 5, 1971: 99.3 mhz; 7.3 kw. Ant 600 ft TL: N41 26 16 W79 55 29. Stereo. Hrs open: 6 AM-midnight Prog sep from AM Box 908, 484 Allegheny Blvd., 16323. Phone: (814) 432-2189. Fax: (814) 437-9372.E-mail: radio@zoominternet.com Population served: 180,000 Format: Hot adult contemp. News: 4 hrs wkly. Target aud: 18-44. ◆ Tim Snyder, prom dir; Tim Shaw, sports cmtr.

Galeton

*WCOG-FM— 1996: 100.7 mhz; 7.7 kw. Ant 492 ft TL: N41 39 36 W77 38 02. Hrs open:
Rebroadcasts WCIK(FM) Bath, NY 100%.
Box 506, Bath, NY, 14810. Secondary address: 7634 Campbell Creek Rd., Bath, NY 14810. Phone: (607) 776-4151. Fax: (607) 776-6929.E-mail: mail@fln.org Web Site:www.fln.org Licensee: Family Life Ministries Inc. Group owner: Family Life Network (acq 10-1-96; $20,130). Natl. Network: Salem Radio Network, . Hardy, Carey, Chautin & Balkin, LLP. Wire Svc: Metro Weather Service Inc. Format: Contemp Christian. News staff: 3; News: 14 hrs wkly. Target aud: 30-54; general. ◆ Rick Snavely, pres, pres, CFO, VP, gen mgr & stn mgr; John Owens, progmg dir; Jim Travis, chief of engrg.

Gallitzin

WHPA(FM)— 1999: 93.5 mhz; 1.25 kw. Ant 727 ft TL: N40 29 36 W78 32 31. Stereo. Hrs open: 24 Box 1095, Northern Cambria, 15714-3095. Phone: (814) 472-4060. Fax: (814) 472-9370.E-mail: whpa@verizon.net Licensee: Vernal Enterprises Inc. (group owner). Format: Oldies. News: 2 hrs wkly. ◆ Larry Schrengost, gen mgr.

Gettysburg

WGET(AM)— Aug 27, 1950: 1320 khz; 1 kw-D, 500 w-N, DA-2. TL: N39 50 30 W77 13 25. Hrs open: 24 Box 3179, 1560 Fairfield Rd., 17325. Phone: (717) 334-3101. Fax: (717) 334-5822. Web Site:www.wget.com Licensee: Times and News Publishing Co. Population served: 150,000 Natl. Network: CBS, . Rgnl. Network: Radio Pa. Radio Pa. Hogan & Hartson. Wire Svc: AP Format: Adult contemp, news, sports. News staff: 3; News: 40 hrs wkly. Target aud: 35-64; mainstream mature adults. ◆ Philip Jones, CEO; Cindy Ford, pres; Dave Jackson, opns mgr; John C. Martin, gen sls mgr; Kim Alexander, news dir; Daryl Hancock, engrg mgr, chief of engrg; Shannon Weishaar, traf mgr; Larry Rhoten, spec ev coord.

WGTY(FM)— July 5, 1962: 107.7 mhz; 16 kw. 829 ft TL: N39 51 23 W76 56 57. Stereo. Hrs open: 24 Prog sep from AM Box 3179, 1560 Fairfield Rd., 17325. Phone: (717) 334-3101. Fax: (717) 334-5822. Web Site:www.wgty.com Licensee: Times and News Publishing Co. Population served: 400,000 Wire Svc: AP Format: Country. News: 2 hrs wkly. Target aud: 25-54. ◆ Cindy Ford, gen mgr, opns mgr; Lisa Snedden, prom mgr; Scott Donato, progmg dir; Dan Douglas, mus dir; Daryl Hancock, chief of engrg; Lou Ann Milhimes, traf mgr.

***WZBT(FM)**— Oct 23, 1976: 91.1 mhz; 180 w. 380 ft TL: N39 50 15 W77 14 09. Hrs open: 8 AM-2 AM Gettysburg College, Box 435, 17325. Secondary address: 300 N. Washington St. 17325. Phone: (717) 337-6000. Fax: (717) 337-6666.E-mail: wzbtexec@gettysburg.edu Web Site:www.gettesburg.edu/~wzbt/ Licensee: Gettysburg College. Population served: 100,000 Format: Progsv. Target aud: General. Spec prog: Class 3 hrs, folk 6 hrs, jazz 4 hrs, Sp 4 hrs, gospel one hr wkly. ♦Ryan Gottschall, stn mgr; Laura Benincasa, progmg dir.

Glen Mills

***WZZE(FM)**— May 20, 1975: 97.3 mhz; 18 w. 180 ft TL: N39 55 15 W75 29 58. (CP: Ant 184 ft.). Hrs open: Box 5001, Concordville, 19331. Secondary address: Glen Mills Schools, Glen Mills Rd. 19342. Phone: (610) 459-8100, ext: 307. Phone: (610) 459-4829.E-mail: msmith@glenmillerschools.org Licensee: Glen Mills Schools. (acq 2-28-84). Natl. Network: ABC, . Format: CHR. ♦C.D. Ferrainola, pres; Mark Smith, opns mgr.

Grantham

***WVMM(FM)**— Sept 29, 1989: 90.7 mhz; 100 w. 300 ft TL: N40 09 34 W76 59 00. Stereo. Hrs open: 24/7 beginning 8/27 Messiah College, One College Ave., Box 3058, 17027. Phone: (717) 691-6081. Fax: (717) 796-5241.E-mail: earke@messiah.edu Web Site:www.messiah.edu/wvmm Licensee: Messiah College. Natl. Network: PRI, . Format: Christian rock, AAA, Indy. News: 25 hrs/week. Target aud: 13-25. Spec prog: Praise and worship—7hrs, Gospel—5hrs, Big Band—Bluegrass & World music—1 hr each. ♦Edward T. Arke, gen mgr; Sheryl Ezbiansky, prom dir & chief of engrg.

Greencastle

WQCM(FM)— May 6, 1967: 94.3 mhz; 3.5 kw. 430 ft TL: N39 47 29 W77 40 30. Stereo. Hrs open: 24 25 Penncraft Ave., Chambersburg, 17201. Phone: (717) 263-0813. Fax: (717) 263-9649.E-mail: info@wqcm.com Web Site:www.wqcmfm.com Licensee: MLB-Hagerstown-Chambersburg IV LLC. (group owner; (acq 7-20-2005; grpsl). Population served: 212,913 Latham & Watkins. Format: Classic rock. News staff: one. Target aud: 25-44. ♦Rich Bateman, gen mgr; Tammy Heckman, prom dir; Mike Holder, progmg dir.

Greensburg

WGSM(FM)— Feb 2, 2006: 107.1 mhz; 2.3 kw. Ant 535 ft TL: N40 15 54 W79 20 24. Stereo. Hrs open: 24 2000 Tower Way, Suite 2040, 15601. Phone: (724) 216-1200. Fax: (724) 216-1201. Licensee: The St. Pier Group LLC. (group owner). (acq 3-5-2007; $2.2 million). Fletcher, Heald & Hildreth. Format: Var hits. News staff: one; News: one hr wkly.

Greenville

WEXC(FM)— July 1965: 107.1 mhz; 3 kw. Ant 328 ft TL: N41 22 50 W80 24 48. Stereo. Hrs open: 24 44 McCracken Rd., 16125. Secondary address: 124 N. Park Avenue, Warren, OH 44481. Phone: (724) 588-8000. Fax: (724) 588-2470.E-mail: myspace@thefreq107.com Web Site:www.thefreq107.com Licensee: Beacon Broadcasting Inc. (group owner; (acq 9-14-2005; grpsl). Population served: 9,960 Format: Positive rock, Christian. News staff: one. Target aud: 14-34. ♦Harold Glunt, gen mgr; Dana Schroyer, disc jockey.

WGRP(AM)— Sept 19, 1959: 940 khz; 1 kw-D, 2 w-N, DA-2. TL: N41 23 10 W80 24 35. Hrs open: 24 Box 1798, Warren, OH, 44482-1798. Phone: (330) 394-7700. Fax: (330) 394-7701. Web Site:www.classiccountry940.com Licensee: Beacon Broadcasting Inc. (acq 9-14-2005; grpsl). Population served: 9,960 Hogan & Hartson. Format: Classic country. ♦Harold Glunt, pres; Rich Esbenshade, gen mgr.

Grove City

***WSAJ-FM**— September 1968: 91.1 mhz; 3 kw. 125 ft TL: N41 09 20 W80 04 47. Stereo. Hrs open: 24 Grove City College, 100 Campus Dr., 16127. Phone: (724) 458-2077. Fax: (724) 458-2329.E-mail: wsaj@gcc.edu Licensee: Grove City College. Population served: 100,000 Format: Class. News staff: one. Target aud: General; listeners who are generally unfamiliar with class mus & arts. ♦Darren Morton, gen mgr & stn mgr.

WWGY(FM)— Sept 10, 1962: 95.1 mhz; 19 kw. Ant 805 ft TL: N41 15 08 W80 21 28. Stereo. Hrs open: 24 219 Savannah Gardner Rd., New Castle, 16101. Phone: (724) 346-5070. Fax: (724) 346-5075.E-mail: webmaster@foreverradio.com Web Site:fforeverradio.com Licensee: Forever Broadcasting LLC. Group owner: Forever Broadcasting (acq 2-23-2004; $2.28 million). Format: Country. News staff: one; News: 2 hrs wkly. Target aud: 18-34. ♦Scott D. Cohagan, gen mgr; John Thomas, progmg dir.

Halifax

***WLVU(FM)**— 2008: 88.5 mhz; 1.4 kw. Ant 354 ft TL: N40 27 26 W76 54 13. Hrs open:
Rebroadcasts KLVR(FM) Middletown, CA 100%.
2351 Sunset Blvd., Suite 170-218, Rocklin, CA, 95765. Phone: (916) 251-1600. Fax: (916) 251-1650. Web Site:www.klove.com Licensee: Educational Media Foundation. (acq 7-23-2007; grpsl). Natl. Network: K-Love, . Format: Contemp Christian. ♦Mike Novak, pres.

Hanover

WHVR(AM)— Jan 9, 1949: 1280 khz; 5 kw-D, 500 w-N, DA-2. TL: N39 49 11 W77 00 25. Hrs open: Box 234, 17331. Secondary address: 275 Radio Rd. Phone: (717) 637-3831. Fax: (717) 637-9006. Licensee: Radio Hanover Inc. Population served: 35,000 Format: Classic country. ♦Joan McAnall, gen mgr; Rick McCauslin, gen sls mgr; Deanna Forney, news dir; Daryll Harcock, chief of engrg.

WYCR(FM)—(York-Hanover, Dec 22, 1962: 98.5 mhz; 10.5 kw. Ant 928 ft TL: N39 51 30 W76 56 52. Stereo. Hrs open: Box 234, 17331. Secondary address: 275 Radio Rd. 17331. Phone: (717) 637-3831. Fax: (717) 637-9006.E-mail: info@thepeak.com Web Site:www.thepeak985.com Licensee: Radio Hanover Inc. Population served: 93,200 Format: Classic hits. ♦Beth Mowren, traf mgr; Davy Crockett, disc jockey.

Harrisburg

WHGB(AM)— May 28, 1945: 1400 khz; 1 kw-U. TL: N40 14 58 W76 52 03. Hrs open: 24 2300 Vartan Way, 17110-9720. Phone: (717) 238-1041. Fax: (717) 234-4842. Web Site:www.espnradio1400.com Licensee: Cumulus Licensing Corp. Group owner: Cumulus Media Inc. (acq 11-28-2000; grpsl). Population served: 510,000 Natl. Network: ESPN Radio, . Format: Sports. Target aud: 25-54; men. ♦Ron Vioanviannell, mktg mgr.

WHKF(FM)— July 1965: 99.3 mhz; 6 kw. 328 ft TL: N40 15 44 W76 54 37. Stereo. Hrs open: Prog sep from AM 600 Corporate Cir., 17110. Phone: (717) 540-8800. Fax: (717) 540-8814.E-mail: info@wwklfm.com Web Site:www.wwklfm.com Population served: 550,000 Target aud: 35-54. ♦Doug Baker, gen sls mgr; Kraig Nace, prom mgr; Peter MacArthur, news dir; Tom Presite, chief of engrg.

WHP(AM)— 1924: 580 khz; 5 kw-U, DA-N. TL: N40 18 11 W76 57 07. Stereo. Hrs open: 24 600 Corporate Circle, 17110. Phone: (717) 540-8800. Fax: (717) 541-0094. Fax: (717) 540-9268. Web Site:www.whp580.com Licensee: Clear Channel Radio License Inc. Group owner: Clear Channel Communications Inc. (acq 8-5-98; grpsl). Population served: 392,400 Natl. Network: Westwood One, . Format: News/talk. News staff: 4. Target aud: 35-64. ♦Ron Roy, gen sls mgr & natl sls mgr.

***WITF-FM**— Apr 1, 1971: 89.5 mhz; 5.9 kw. Ant 1,361 ft TL: N40 20 45 W76 52 06. Stereo. Hrs open: 24 Box 2954, 17105. Secondary address: 1982 Locust Ln. 17109. Phone: (717) 236-6000. Fax: (717) 232-7612.E-mail: info@witf.org Web Site:www.witf.org Licensee: WITF Inc. Population served: 12,500 Natl. Network: NPR, PRI, . Dow, Lohnes & Albertson. Format: Class, news/talk. News staff: 3; News: 43 hrs wkly. ♦Kathleen Pavelko, pres; Mitzi Trostle, gen mgr & stn mgr. Co-owned TV: *WITF-TV affil.

WKBO(AM)— 1922: 1230 khz; 48 kw-U. TL: N40 16 52 W76 52 06. Hrs open: 24 600 Corporate Cir., 17110-9787. Phone: (717) 540-8800. Fax: (717) 540-8814.E-mail: fortress1230am@oneheartministries.com Web Site:www.oneheartministries.com Licensee: Clear Channel Broadcasting Licenses Inc. Group owner: Clear Channel Communications Inc. (acq 8-5-98; grpsl). Population served: 68,061 Natl. Rep: Salem,. Format: Contemp Christian. News staff: 6; News: 168 hrs wkly. Target aud: 35-54; well educated, upscale professionals. Spec prog: Pop standards, Music of Your Life. ♦Pete Hamel, gen mgr, stn mgr & gen sls mgr.

WNNK-FM— 1962: 104.1 mhz; 22.5 kw. 725 ft TL: N40 18 59 W76 57 04. Stereo. Hrs open: 24 2300 Vartan Way, 17110. Phone: (717)238-1041. Fax: (717) 234-4842.E-mail: info@cumulus.com Web Site:www.cumulus.com Format: CHR. News staff: 2; News: 15 hrs wkly.

WRBT(FM)— Sept 30, 1962: 94.9 mhz; 25 kw. 699 ft TL: N40 18 57 W76 57 02. Stereo. Hrs open: 24 600 Corporate Cir., 17110. Phone: (717) 671-9949. Fax: (717) 540-8814.E-mail: info@bobradio.com Web Site:www.bobradio.com Licensee: Clear Channel Radio License Inc. Group owner: Clear Channel Communications Inc. (acq 8-5-98; grpsl). Population served: 1,000,000 Natl. Rep: Christal,. Latham & Watkins. Format: Hot country. News staff: one. Target aud: 25-54. ♦Ronald Roy, gen mgr. Co-owned TV: WHP-TV.

WRVV(FM)— 1946: 97.3 mhz; 17 kw. Ant 840 ft TL: N40 20 44 W76 52 09. Stereo. Hrs open: 24 600 Corporate Circle, 17110. Phone: (717) 540-8800. Fax: (717) 541-0094. Fax: (717) 540-9268. Web Site:www.wrvv.com Licensee: Clear Channel Radio License Inc. Format: Rock, adult contemp. Target aud: 25-54.

WSJW(FM)—See Starview

WTKT(AM)— February 1948: 1460 khz; 5 kw-D, 4.2 kw-N, DA-N. TL: N40 18 32 W76 56 13. Hrs open: 24 600 Corporate Cir., 17110. Phone: (717) 540-8800. Fax: (717) 540-8814.E-mail: info@theticket.com Web Site:www.1460theticket.com Licensee: Clear Channel Radio License Inc. Group owner: Clear Channel Communications Inc. (acq 8-5-98; grpsl). Population served: 550,000 Natl. Rep: Clear Channel,. Fisher, Wayland, Cooper, Leader & Zaragoza L.L.P. Format: Oldies, sports. News staff: 4; News: 30 hrs wkly. Target aud: General. Spec prog: Gospel 2 hrs, pub service 2 hrs wkly. ♦Ken Austin, progmg dir.

***WZXM(FM)**— 1995: 88.1 mhz; 540 w. Ant 105 ft TL: N40 15 44 W76 53 11. Hrs open: 24 Box 186, Sellersville, 18960. Phone: (215) 721-2141. Fax: (215) 721-9811.E-mail: wordfm@wordfm.org Web Site:www.wordfm.org Licensee: Four Rivers Community Broadcasting Corp. (acq 10-30-2007; exchange for WXPH(FM) Middletown). Population served: 400,000 Format: Contemp Christian. ♦Charles Loughery, pres; Charlie Loughery, gen mgr; Dave Baker, VP & stn mgr.

Havertown

***WHHS(FM)**— Dec 6, 1949: 107.9 mhz; 14 w. Ant 161 ft TL: N39 58 59 W75 18 10. Stereo. Hrs open: 2 PM-10 PM (M-F) 200 Mill Rd., 19083. Phone: (610) 446-7111. Fax: (610) 853-5952.E-mail: whhsnewsdirector@yahoo.com Web Site:www.whhs.org Licensee: School District of Haverford Township. Population served: 50,000 Format: Div. Target aud: General. ♦Kevin Moran, gen mgr & opns mgr.

Hawley

***WBYH(FM)**— December 2000: 89.1 mhz; 200 w. 525 ft TL: N41 24 43 W75 09 51. Hrs open: 24
Rebroadcasts WYBO (FM) Sellersville 100%.
Box 186, Sellersville, 18960. Phone: (215) 721-2141. Fax: (215) 721-9811.E-mail: wordfm@wordfm.org Web Site:www.wordfm.com Licensee: Four Rivers Communications Broadcasting Co. Population served: 50,000 Schwartz, Woods & Miller. Format: Christian Adult Contemp., Religious. ♦David Baker, VP.

WYCY(FM)— Sept 13, 1993: 105.3 mhz; 2.9 kw. 479 ft TL: N41 35 01 W75 10 30. Stereo. Hrs open: 24 575 Grove St., Honesdale, 18431. Phone: (570) 253-1616. Fax: (570) 253-6297.E-mail: vbenedetto@boldgoldmedia.com Web Site:www.boldgoldmedia.com Licensee: Bold Gold Media Group L.P. (group owner; (acq 5-23-2005; grpsl). Natl. Network: ABC, . Format: Oldies. News staff: one; News: 5 hrs wkly. Target aud: 25-55. ♦Vincent Benedetto, CEO; Bob Vanderheyden, gen mgr; Brian Wilken, gen sls mgr; Paul Ciliberto, prom dir; George Schmitt, progmg mgr; Theresa Opeka, news dir; Jessica Baglieri, traf mgr.

Hazleton

WAZL(AM)— Dec 19, 1932: 1490 khz; 1 kw-U. TL: N40 56 24 W75 58 04. Hrs open: 24 8 W. Broad St., 18201. Phone: (570) 455-1490. Fax: (570) 501-1112.E-mail: wazl.prod@yahoo.com Licensee: WS2K Radio LLC. Group owner: Route 81 Radio LLC (acq 7-14-2008; grpsl). Population served: 120,000 Natl. Network: Fox News Radio, . Wire Svc: Metro Weather Service Inc. Format: Classic Hits. News staff: 5; News: 1.5 hrs wkly. Target aud: 18-64. ♦Mike Moran, gen mgr; Tony Pacelli, progmg dir.

WBSX(FM)— 1949: 97.9 mhz; 6.3 kw. 1334 ft TL: N41 10 56 W75 52 22. Stereo. Hrs open: 24 600 Baltimore Dr., 2nd Fl., Wilkes-Barre, 18702. Phone: (570) 824-9000. Fax: (570) 820-0520. Web Site:www.979x.com Licensee: Citadel Broadcasting Co. Group owner: Citadel Broadcasting Corp. (acq 5-29-97; grpsl). Natl. Network: ABC, Moody, . Pepper & Corazzini. Format: Active rock. Target aud: 18-34. ♦John Crawford, gen sls mgr; Bill Palmeri, mktg mgr; Jim McKay, progmg dir; Phil Galasso, chief of engrg.

Hershey

WMHX(FM)—Licensed to Hershey. See Elizabethtown

Hollidaysburg

*WHHN(FM)— 2008: 88.1 mhz; 850 w horiz, 670 w vert. Ant 1,352 ft TL: N40 29 19 W78 21 20. Hrs open: Radio Maria Inc., 601 Washington St., Alexandria, LA, 71301. Phone: (318) 561-6145. Fax: (318) 449-9954. Web Site:www.radiomaria.us Licensee: Friends of Radio Maria. Format: Christian, relg, talk.

WKMC(AM)—See Roaring Spring

WRKY-FM— Dec 1, 1978: 104.9 mhz; 280 w. Ant 1,417 ft TL: N40 29 15 W78 21 09. Stereo. Hrs open: One Forever Dr., Hollidaysburg, 16648. Phone: (814) 941-9800. Fax: (814) 943-2754.E-mail: xman@rocky1049.com Web Site:www.rocky1049.com Licensee: Forever of PA L.L.C. Group owner: Forever Broadcasting (acq 2-18-97; $2 million with WKMC(AM) Roaring Spring). Population served: 140,000 Natl. Rep: Roslin,. Format: Rock, adult contemp. Target aud: 25-54; adults with significant income. ◆Carol B. Logan, pres; David Davies, gen mgr.

Homer City

WCCS(AM)— Oct 25, 1983: 1160 khz; 10 kw-D, 1 kw-N, DA-1. TL: N40 34 18 W79 10 12. Stereo. Hrs open: 204 Philadelphia St., Suite 100, Indiana, 15701. Phone: (724) 479-1160. Phone: (724) 465-4700.E-mail: mbertig@rendabroadcasting.com Web Site:www.1160wccs.com Licensee: The St. Pier Group LLC. Group owner: Renda Broadcasting Corp. (acq 10-4-2002; $650,000). Population served: 95,000 Natl. Network: ABC, . Rgnl rep: Dome & Associates Wire Svc: AP Format: Adult contemp. News staff: 2; News: 14 hrs wkly. Target aud: 25-49. Spec prog: Pol 3 hrs, oldies 9 hrs wkly. ◆Tony Renda Sr., CEO & pres; Mark A. Bertig, gen mgr; Alan Serena, opns VP; Jack Benedict, opns dir; Ron Nocco, news dir.

Honesdale

WDNH-FM— Oct 12, 1981: 95.3 mhz; 3 kw. Ant 256 ft TL: N41 34 23 W75 11 30. Stereo. Hrs open: 24 Prog sep from AM 575 Grove St., 18431. Phone: (570) 253-9595. Fax: (570) 253-6297.E-mail: info@boldgoldmedia.com Web Site:www.wdnh.com Licensee: Bold Gold Media Group L.P. Population served: 150,000 Natl. Network: USA, . Format: Hot adult contemp. News staff: one; News: 6 hrs wkly. Target aud: 25-54. ◆George Schmitt, progmg dir.

WPSN(AM)— September 1972: 1590 khz; 2.5 kw-D. TL: N41 33 13 W75 15 18. Hrs open: 575 Grove St., 18431. Phone: (570) 253-1616. Fax: (570) 253-6297. Web Site:www.infocow.net Licensee: Bold Gold Media Group L.P. (group owner; (acq 5-23-2005; grpsl). Population served: 90000 Natl. Rep: Dome,. Schwartz, Woods & Miller. Format: Sports. Target aud: General. ◆George Schmitt, progmg dir; John Emerson, news dir.

*WZZH(FM)— 2008: 90.9 mhz; 200 w. Ant 912 ft TL: N41 35 35 W75 25 56. Hrs open:
Rebroadcasts WBYO(FM) Sellersville 100%.
Box 186, Sellersville, 18960-0186. Phone: (215) 721-2141. Fax: (215) 721-9811.E-mail: wordfm@wordfm.org Web Site:www.wordfm.org Licensee: Four Rivers Community Broadcasting Corp. Format: Contemp Christian. ◆Charles W. Loughery, pres.

Hughesville

WRKK(AM)— Aug 4, 1985: 1200 khz; 10 kw-D, 250 w-N, DA-2. TL: N41 12 43 W78 44 56. Hrs open: 24
Rebroadcasts WRAK(AM) Williamsport 100%.
Box 3638, Williamsport, 17701. Secondary address: 1559 W. 4th St., Williamsport 17701. Phone: (570) 327-1400. Fax: (570) 327-8156.E-mail: wrak@wrak.com Web Site:www.wrak.com Licensee: Clear Channel Broadcasting License Inc. Group owner: Clear Channel Communications Inc. (acq 8-5-98; grpsl). Natl. Network: ABC, Westwood One, . Format: News/talk, rock. News staff: one. Target aud: 35 plus. ◆Bryan Kell, gen mgr; Duke Rice, opns dir & progmg dir.

Huntingdon

WHUN(AM)— Mar 2, 1947: 1150 khz; 5 kw-D, 36 w-N. TL: N40 27 18 W77 58 50. Hrs open: 24
Simulcast with WRSC(AM) State College.
RR 3 Box 225A, Huntington, 16652-8804. Phone: (814) 542-8648.

Fax: (814) 643-9625. Web Site:www.newsradio1390.com Licensee: Megahertz Licenses LLC. Group owner: Forever Broadcasting (acq 4-29-2002; $875,000 with WLTS(FM) Mount Union). Population served: 56,000 Rgnl rep: Commercial Media Sales Inc. Format: News/talk. News staff: one; News: 15 hrs wkly. Target aud: 25 plus; general. Spec prog: Relg 2 hrs wkly. ◆Kristin Cantrell, gen mgr.

*WKVR-FM— March 1978: 92.3 mhz; 10 w. -376 ft TL: N40 30 00 W78 00 52. Stereo. Hrs open: 22 Juniata College, 16652. Phone: (814) 643-5031. Phone: (814) 641-3341. Fax: (814) 643-4477. Licensee: Juniata College Board of Trustees. Population served: 4,000 Format: Classic rock, progsv, AOR. News: 8 hrs wkly. Target aud: 18-25; college students. Spec prog: CHR 15 hrs, jazz 3 hrs, Black 10 hrs, contemp Christian 3 hrs, reggae 3 hrs wkly. ◆Chad Herzog, gen mgr; J. Andrew Scott, prom dir.

WLAK(FM)— Sept 12, 1967: 103.5 mhz; 160 w. 1,427 ft TL: N40 29 51 W78 08 00. Stereo. Hrs open: 24
Rebroadcasts WMRF-FM Lewistown 95.7%.
Box 667, Lewistown, 17044. Secondary address: 12 East Market St., 2nd Floor , Lewistown 17044. Phone: (717) 248-6757. Fax: (717) 248-6759.E-mail: pete@merfradio.com Web Site:www.merfradio.com Licensee: First Media Radio LLC. (group owner; (acq 3-28-2001; grpsl). Population served: 50,000 Format: Adult contemp. Target aud: 18-44. ◆Peter Herman, gen mgr; Jeff Stevens, opns dir, progmg dir, disc jockey; Mary Lee Shaffer, news dir.

Hustontown

*WZXF(FM)—Not on air, target date: unknown: 91.7 mhz; 11 w. Ant 1,263 ft TL: N40 00 38 W78 08 43. Hrs open: Box 186, Sellersville, 18960. Phone: (215) 721-2141. Fax: (215) 721-9811. Web Site:www.wordfm.org Licensee: Four Rivers Community Broadcasting Corp. (acq 8-30-2007). ◆Charles W. Loughery, pres & gen mgr.

Indiana

WCCS(AM)—See Homer City

WDAD(AM)— Nov 4, 1945: 1450 khz; 1 kw-U. TL: N40 37 01 W79 07 55. Hrs open: 24 840 Philadelphia St., Suite 100, 15701. Phone: (724) 465-4700. Fax: (724) 349-6842.E-mail: info@wdadradio.com Web Site:www.wdadradio.com Licensee: The St. Pier Group. Group owner: Renda Broadcasting Corp. (acq 2-13-2004; $3.25 million). Population served: 16,100 Natl. Network: CBS, . Natl. Rep: Dome,. Pepper & Corazzini. Format: Good time oldies. News staff: one. Target aud: 35 plus. Spec prog: Relg 2 hrs wkly. ◆Mark Bertig, gen mgr.

*WIUP-FM— October 1969: 90.1 mhz; 1.6 kw. 88 ft TL: N40 36 57 W79 09 40. Stereo. Hrs open: 7 AM-2 AM Indiana Univ. of Pa., 121 Davis Hall, 15705. Phone: (724) 357-9487. Licensee: Indiana University of Pennsylvania. Population served: 92,000 Format: Div. News: 11 hrs wkly. Target aud: General. Spec prog: Black 14 hrs, class 15 hrs, folk 4 hrs, gospel one hr, jazz 15 hrs, new age 4 hrs, radio drama one hr wkly. ◆James Rogers, gen mgr. Co-owned TV: *WIUP-TV affil.

WQMU(FM)— Aug 14, 1968: 92.5 mhz; 3 kw. 108 ft TL: N40 38 17 W79 08 47. Stereo. Hrs open: 24 Prog sep from AM 840 Philadelphia St., Suite 100, 15701. Phone: (724) 465-4700. Fax: (724) 349-6842.E-mail: info@wqmuradio.com Web Site:www.wqmuradio.com Population served: 16,100 Rgnl rep: Dome Format: Adult hits. Target aud: 21-41.

Irwin

WKHB(AM)—Licensed to Irwin. See Pittsburgh

Jackson Township

*WRTY(FM)— Aug 23, 1991: 91.1 mhz; 3.5 kw. 862 ft TL: N41 02 40 W75 22 45. Stereo. Hrs open: 24
Rebroadcasts WRTI(FM) Philadelphia 100%.
1509 Cecil B. Moore Ave., 3rd Fl., Philadelphia, 19121. Phone: (215) 204-8405. Fax: (215) 204-7027.E-mail: comments@wrti.org Web Site:www.wrti.org Licensee: Temple University of The Commonwealth System of Higher Education. Population served: 1,000,000 Natl. Network: NPR,. Rgnl. Network: Radio Pa. Radio Format: Jazz, class. News staff: one; News: 15 hrs wkly. Target aud: 30-65. ◆Dave Conant, gen mgr.

Jeannette

WKFB(AM)— Jan 28, 1974: 770 khz; 750 w-D, 750 w-CH. TL: N40 17 20 W79 42 04. Hrs open: Sunrise-sunset Box 990, Greensburg,

15601-0990. Secondary address: 1918 Lincoln Hwy., North Versailles 15137. Phone: (412) 823-7000. Licensee: Broadcast Communications Inc. (group owner; (acq 4-98). Population served: 376,000 Format: Var. ◆Ashley R. Stevens, VP; Robert M. Stevens, pres & gen mgr.

Jenkintown

WPPZ-FM— Nov 1, 1960: 103.9 mhz; 270 w. Ant 1,109 ft TL: N40 02 29.6 W75 14 11.4. Hrs open: 24 1000 River Rd., Suite 400, Conshohocken, 19428. Fax: (215) 884-9400. Web Site:www.praise1039.com Licensee: Radio One Licenses LLC. Group owner: Radio One Inc. (acq 11-8-2001; grpsl). Dickstein Shapiro Morin & Oshinsky. Format: Relg. Target aud: 18-34. ◆Chester Schofield, gen mgr; Daisy Davis, progmg dir.

Jersey Shore

WJSA(AM)— July 10, 1979: 1600 khz; 1 kw-D, 20 w-N. TL: N41 13 32 W77 16 01. Hrs open: 24 262 Allegheny St., Suite 4, 17740-1442. Phone: (570) 398-7200. Fax: (570) 398-7201.E-mail: mail@wjsaradio.com Web Site:www.wjsaradio.com Licensee: Covenant Broadcasting Co. Population served: 160,000 Natl. Network: Salem Radio Network, Moody, . Natl. Rep: Salem,. Gammon & Grange. Format: Relg. News staff: one; News: 14 hrs wkly. Target aud: General. Spec prog: Sacred Classics one hr, southern gospel 4 hrs, Christian bluegrass one hr wkly. ◆John K. Hogg Jr., gen mgr; Ann L. Hogg, mus dir; Liz Brady, news dir.

WJSA-FM— Nov 1, 1984: 96.3 mhz; 4.4 kw. Ant 777 ft TL: N41 13 28 W77 22 48. Stereo. Hrs open: 24 262 Allegheny St., Suite 4, 17740-1442. Phone: (570) 398-7200. Fax: (570) 398-7201.E-mail: mail@wjsaradio.com Web Site:www.wjsaradio.com Licensee: Covenant Broadcasting Co. Population served: 300,000 Natl. Network: Moody, Salem Radio Network, . Natl. Rep: Salem,. Format: Relig. News staff: one; News: 14 hrs wkly. Spec prog: Sacred classics one hr, southern gospel 3 hrs, Christian bluegrass one hr wkly. ◆John K. Hogg Jr., gen mgr; Liz Brady, news dir; Ann L. Hogg, traf mgr.

Johnsonburg

WJNG(FM)— July 1998: 100.5 mhz; 1.3 kw. 666 ft TL: N41 23 11 W78 41 32. Hrs open: 24
Rebroadcasts WMKX(FM) Brookville 100%.
517 Market St., 15845. Phone: (814) 965-2921. Fax: (814) 965-2921. Licensee: Strattan Broadcasting Inc. Format: Classic rock. ◆James W. Farley, gen mgr; Kevin Heinrick, opns mgr, progmg dir; Nathan Sharpe, gen sls mgr; Cindy Perucci, traf mgr.

WKBI-FM—See Saint Marys

Johnstown

WCRO(AM)— September 1947: 1230 khz; 1 kw-U. TL: N40 19 55 W78 54 46. Hrs open: 24 222 Central Ave., 15904. Secondary address: 1089 Broad St 15906. Phone: (814) 533-5533. Fax: (814) 533-5698. Licensee: Greater Johnstown School District. (acq 1-11-99; $75,000). Population served: 100,000 Wire Svc: AP Format: Adult standards. News: 35 hrs wkly. Target aud: 45 - 64; Fastest growing and most financially secure demographically. Spec prog: University of Pittsburgh Football, basketball, NASCAR racing. ◆Ed Scherlock, stn mgr; Ed Sherlock, pres & opns mgr.

WFGI-FM— Aug 1949: 95.5 mhz; 57 kw. Ant 1,060 ft TL: N40 22 18 W78 58 57. Stereo. Hrs open: 109 Plaza Dr., Suite 2, 15905. Phone: (814) 255-4186. Fax: (814) 255-6145. Web Site:www.myfroggy95.com Licensee: Forever Broadcasting LLC Format: Country. Target aud: 25-54. ◆Terry Deitz, gen mgr; Tina Perry, gen sls mgr; Lara Mosby, progmg dir; Rick Shepard, news dir.

*WFRJ(FM)— June 6, 1986: 88.9 mhz; 5.5 kw vert. Ant 1,214 ft TL: N40 22 17 W78 58 56. Hrs open: 24 13 Fair Lane Dr., Suite 5, Jolette, IL, 60435. Phone: (916) 641-8191. Fax: (916) 641-8238.E-mail: info@familyradio.com Web Site:www.familyradio.com Licensee: Family Stations Inc. (group owner) Population served: 600,000 Format: Conservative Christian. News: 6 hrs wkly. Target aud: General; every age group. ◆Harold Camping, pres; Gary Johnson, opns mgr.

WJHT(FM)— Sept 1, 1974: 92.1 mhz; 580 w. Ant 1,043 ft TL: N40 22 15 W78 59 02. Stereo. Hrs open: 24 109 Plaza Dr., Suite 2, 15905. Phone: (814) 255-4186. Fax: (814) 255-6145.E-mail: info@hot92fm.net Web Site:www.hot92fm.net Licensee: Forever Broadcasting LLC. (group owner; (acq 5-1-2005; $2.73 million with WRKW(FM) Ebensburg). Population served: 209,000 Format: Contemporary hit. ◆Terry Deitz, gen mgr; Tina Perry, gen sls mgr; Mitch Edwards, progmg dir; Rick Shepard, news dir.

WKGE(AM)— April 1925: 850 khz; 10 kw-U, DA-1. TL: N40 10 54 W78 53 20. Hrs open:
Simulcasts WWGE(AM) Loretto 100%.
109 Plaza Dr., 15905. Phone: (814) 255-4186. Fax: (814) 255-6145. Licensee: Birach Broadcasting Corp. Group owner: Forever Broadcasting (acq 4-10-2008; $230,000). Population served: 200,000 Natl. Rep: McGavren Guild, Dome,. Format: News/talk, sports. ♦Sima Birach, pres; Verla Price, gen mgr & gen sls mgr; Mike Stevens, progmg dir; Rick Shepard, news dir; Jim Boxler, chief of engrg.

WKYE(FM)— Aug 14, 1973: 96.5 mhz; 50 kw. Ant 489 ft TL: N40 19 45 W78 53 54. Stereo. Hrs open: 24 109 Plaza Dr., 15905. Phone: (814) 255-4186. Fax: (814) 255-6145.E-mail: info@hot92fm.net Web Site:www.96key.com Licensee: Forever Broadcasting LLC. (acq 1-30-2004; $9.13 million with co-located AM). Population served: 890,300 Format: Adult contemp. ♦Verla Price, gen mgr; Jack Michaels, progmg dir; Brian Wolfe, mus dir; Jim Boxler, chief of engrg.

WNTJ(AM)— August 1946: 1490 khz; 1 kw-U. TL: N40 19 25 W78 53 49. Hrs open: 24 109 Plaza Dr., Suite 2, 15905. Phone: (814) 255-4186. Fax: (814) 255-6145.E-mail: info@hot92fm.net Web Site:www.ntjnetwork.com Licensee: 2510 Licenses LLC. Group owner: Forever Broadcasting (acq 5-1-2005; grpsl). Population served: 125,400 Format: News/talk. Target aud: 18-54. ♦Terry Deitz, gen mgr; Mike Stevens, progmg dir.

***WQEJ(FM)**— Oct 1, 1998: 89.7 mhz; 3.3 kw. Ant 1,036 ft TL: N40 22 17 W78 58 58. Hrs open: 24
Rebroadcasts WQED-FM Pittsburgh 100%.
c/o WQED-FM, 4802 5th Ave., Pittsburgh, 15213. Phone: (412) 622-1436. Fax: (412) 622-7073.E-mail: radio@wqed.org Web Site:www.wqed.org Licensee: WQED Multimedia. Natl. Network: AP Radio, NPR, PRI, . Schwartz, Woods & Miller. Format: Classical. Target aud: 35-64; educated, influential, professional, community leaders, mid to high income. ♦George L. Miles Jr., CEO, pres; Deborah Acklin, exec VP, gen mgr; Paul Byers, chief of engrg.

WRKW(FM)—See Ebensburg

Kane

WLMI(FM)— Sept 17, 1984: 103.9 mhz; 3 kw. Ant 300 ft TL: N41 39 34 W78 48 42. Stereo. Hrs open: 24 29 Fraley St., 16735. Phone: (814) 837-9564. Fax: (814) 975-1098.E-mail: wlmi@colonial.cc Web Site:www.wlmi.net Licensee: Colonial Radio Group Inc. (acq 8-2-2006; $390,000). Population served: 75,000 Natl. Network: ABC, . Rgnl rep: Dome, Commercial Media Sales Garvey, Schubert & Barer. Format: Country. News staff: one; News: 12 hrs wkly. Target aud: 25-49; families. Spec prog: Polka one hr, bluegrass one hr wkly. ♦Jeffrey Andrulonis, pres & gen mgr.

***WPSX(FM)**— 1995: 90.1 mhz; 17 kw. 761 ft TL: N41 37 04 W78 48 14. Stereo. Hrs open:
Rebroadcasts WPSU(FM) 100%.
WPSU-FM, 120 Outreach Bldg/, University Park, 16802. Phone: (814) 865-1877. Fax: (814) 865-4043.E-mail: wpsu@psu.edu Web Site:wpsu.org Licensee: The Pennsylvania State University. Natl. Network: NPR, PRI, . Paul, Hastings, Janufsky & Walker. Wire Svc: AP Format: Public radio. News staff: one; News: 35 hrs wkly. Upscale educated adults. Spec prog: Folk 10 hrs, jazz 3 hrs, blues 2 hrs wkly. ♦Ted Krichels, gen mgr; Greg Petersen, stn mgr; Steve Shipman, opns dir; Ashear Barr, gen sls mgr; Kris Allen, progmg mgr; Carl Fisher, chief of engrg; Leslie Dyer, traf mgr.

Kearsarge

WCXJ(AM)—Not on air, target date: unknown: 1590 khz; 500 w-D, 900 w-N, DA-2. TL: N42 01 47 W80 07 06. Hrs open: 4039 Sunset Blvd., Steubenville, OH, 43952. Phone: (412) 936-1500. Licensee: Eaton-Dietterich Partnership. ♦Randy Dietterich, gen mgr.

King of Prussia

WFYL(AM)— December 1976: 1180 khz; 420 w-D. TL: N40 08 06 W75 23 27. Hrs open: 2400 W. Main St., Jeffersonville, 19403-3071. Phone: (610) 539-5015. Licensee: Langer Broadcasting Group L.L.C. (group owner). Population served: 80,000 Format: Talk. ♦Helen Lenza, gen mgr.

Kittanning

WTYM(AM)— 1948: 1380 khz; 1 kw-D, 28 w-N. TL: N40 47 19 W79 32 05. Hrs open: Box 14A, R.D. 7, 16201. Phone: (724) 543-1380. Fax: (724) 543-1140.E-mail: wtym@alltel.net Web Site:www.wtym.8m.com Licensee: Vernal Enterprises Inc. (group owner; acq 7-22-92; $85,000;6-15-92). Population served: 150,000 Haley, Bader & Potts. Format: Oldies, sports. Target aud: 20-55. Spec prog: Relg 4 hrs wkly. ♦Larry L. Schrecongost, pres, gen mgr, opns mgr; Nancy W. Schrecongost, VP; John DeFeo, gen sls mgr, chief of engrg.

Kulpmont

***WBYK(FM)**—Not on air, target date: unknown: 91.9 mhz; 600 w. Ant 535 ft TL: N40 49 01 W76 27 00. Hrs open: Box 186, Sellersville, 18960. Phone: (215) 721-2141. Fax: (215) 721-9811. Web Site:www.wordfm.org Licensee: Four Rivers Community Broadcasting Corp. ♦Charles W. Loughery, pres & gen mgr.

Laceyville

***WCOZ(FM)**—Not on air, target date: unknown: 90.5 mhz; 200 w. Ant 56 ft TL: N41 40 32 W76 11 40. Hrs open: Box 20155, Scranton, 18502. Phone: (607) 427-0452. Licensee: Telikoja Educational Broadcasting Inc. ♦Kevin M. Fitzgerald, pres.

Lancaster

WDAC(FM)— Dec 13, 1959: 94.5 mhz; 19 kw. 810 ft TL: N39 53 46 W76 14 22. Stereo. Hrs open: Box 3022, 17604. Secondary address: for UPS, Fed-Ex only:, 683 Lancaster Pike, New Providence 17560. Phone: (717) 284-4123. Fax: (717) 284-2300.E-mail: postmaster@wdac.com Web Site:www.wdac.com Licensee: WDAC Radio Co. Population served: 417,000 Natl. Network: Moody, Salem Radio Network, . Wiley, Rein & Fielding. Format: Christian, talk. News staff: one; News: 8 hrs wkly. Target aud: 25-49; Evangelical Christians, families. Spec prog: Farm 4 hrs wkly. ♦Doug Myer, COO, gen mgr; Richard Crawford, pres; Mike Stike, opns mgr; Joe Hartman, sls dir; John E. Eby, progmg dir.

***WFNM(FM)**— May 1973: 89.1 mhz; 100 w. 150 ft TL: N40 02 43 W76 19 14. Stereo. Hrs open: 20 Box 3220, Franklin and Marshall College, 17604-3003. Phone: (717) 291-4098. Fax: (717) 358-4437. Web Site:wfnm.fandm.edu Licensee: Franklin and Marshall College. Population served: 300,000 Format: Var/div. News: 4 hrs wkly. Target aud: 13-35. Spec prog: Black 6 hrs, sports talk 2 hrs, class 2 hrs, jazz 8 hrs wkly.

***WJTL(FM)**— Aug 27, 1984: 90.3 mhz; 4.7 kw. 198 ft TL: N40 04 13 W76 17 19. (CP: 11.8 kw, ant 495 ft.). Stereo. Hrs open: Box 1614, 17608. Phone: (717) 392-3690. Fax: (717) 390-2892.E-mail: contact@wjtl.com Web Site:www.wjtl.com Licensee: Creative Ministries Inc. (acq 11-30-90; $500,000; 12-31-90). Natl. Network: USA, . Fisher, Wayland, Cooper, Leader & Zaragoza. Format: Contemp Christian. ♦Fred McNaughton, stn mgr.

WLAN(AM)— Aug 9, 1946: 1390 khz; 5 kw-D, 1 kw-N, DA-2. TL: N40 03 12 W76 20 26. Hrs open: 24 1685 Crown Ave., Suite 100, 17601. Phone: (717) 295-9700. Fax: (717) 295-7329.E-mail: webmaster@1390wlan.com Web Site:www.1390wlan.com Licensee: Clear Channel Radio Licenses Inc. Group owner: Clear Channel Communications Inc. (acq 1996; $7 million with co-located FM). Population served: 420,000 Natl. Network: ABC, . Natl. Rep: Clear Channel,. Wire Svc: AP Format: Adult standards. News staff: 3; News: 9 hrs wkly. Target aud: 35-64. ♦Dick Taylor, gen mgr & gen sls mgr.

WLAN-FM— January 1948: 96.9 mhz; 50 kw. 500 ft TL: N40 02 52 W76 27 25. Stereo. Hrs open: 24 1685 Crown Ave., Suite 100 , 17601. Phone: (717) 295-9700. Fax: (717) 295-7329.E-mail: webmaster@fm97.com Web Site:www.fm97.com Population served: 420,000 Wire Svc: AP Format: Adult contemp, Top-40. News staff: 3; News: 9 hrs wkly. Target aud: 18-49.

***WLCH(FM)**— Sept 14, 1987: 91.3 mhz; 160 w. 135 ft TL: N40 04 13 W76 17 19. Hrs open: 30 N. Ann St., 1st Fl., 17602. Phone: (717) 295-7996. Fax: (717) 295-7759.E-mail: radiocentr@aol.com Licensee: Spanish American Civic Association for Equality Inc. Format: Sp, educ, div. Target aud: General; Hispanics. ♦Mayra Guevar, CEO & pres; Carlos Groupera, exec VP, mktg mgr; Enid Vazquez, gen mgr.

WLPA(AM)— 1922: 1490 khz; 600 w-U. TL: N40 03 38 W76 18 59. Stereo. Hrs open: 24 Box 4368, 17604. Secondary address: 1996 Auction Rd., Manheim 17545. Phone: (717) 653-0800. Phone: (800) 222-1013. Fax: (717) 653-0122. Web Site:www.wlpa.com Licensee: Hall Communications Inc. (group owner; (acq 2-13-77). Population served: 63,000 Natl. Network: Fox Sports, . Rgnl. Network: Radio Pa. Radio Pa. Fletcher, Heald & Hildreth. Format: Sports. News: 8 hrs wkly. Target aud: 25-54; men. ♦Bonnie H.M. Rowbotham, chmn; Arthur J. Rowbotham, pres; William S. Baldwin, exec VP, sr VP & gen mgr; Sue Sensenig, progmg dir.

WROZ(FM)— 1944: 101.3 mhz; 50 kw. 1,289 ft TL: N40 02 04 W76 37 08. Stereo. Hrs open: 24 Prog sep from AM Box 4368, 17604. Phone: (717) 653-0800. Fax: (717) 653-0122.E-mail: wroz@hallradio.com Web Site:www.roseradio.com Licensee: Hall Communications Inc. Population served: 3,000,000 Format: Soft adult contemp. News staff: one. Target aud: 25-54; women. ♦Bonnie Hall Rowbotham, chmn, disc jockey; Art Rowbotham, pres; Bill Baldwin, exec VP, gen mgr; Michael C. Anthony, progmg dir, mus dir; Justin Broka, news dir; Dennis Mitchell, disc jockey.

Lansdale

WNPV(AM)— Oct 17, 1960: 1440 khz; 2.5 kw-D, 500 w-N, DA-2. TL: N40 14 18 W75 19 00. Hrs open: 24 Box 1440, 1210 Snyder Rd., 19446. Phone: (215) 855-8211. Fax: (215) 368-0180. Web Site:www.wnpv1440.com Licensee: WNPV Inc. (acq 10-1-80). Population served: 1,200,000 Natl. Network: Fox News Radio, . Rgnl. Network: Radio Pa. Radio Pa. Pillsbury, Winthrop, Shaw & Pittman. Format: News/talk, sports. News staff: 2; News: 20 hrs wkly. Target aud: 30 plus. Spec prog: Big band 3 hrs, relg 5 hrs, sports 6 hrs wkly. ♦Phillip Hunt, pres; Darryl Berger, VP, progmg dir; Phillip N. Hunt, gen mgr; Linda Moskal, gen sls mgr; Randy Brock, news dir; David McCrork, engr.

Lansford

WLSH(AM)— Dec 24, 1952: 1410 khz; 5 kw-D, 59 w-N, DA-D. TL: N40 50 40 W75 50 37. Hrs open: 24 2147 Market St., Nesquehoning, 18240. Secondary address: Box D 18232. Phone: (570) 645-3123. Fax: (570) 645-2159.E-mail: wmgh@ptdprolog.net Web Site:www.wmgh.com Licensee: J-Systems Franchising Corp. (group owner; acq 1-89; $300,000;1-16-89). Population served: 5,168 Natl. Network: Westwood One, USA, . Radio Pa. Format: Oldies. Target aud: 35-64; Mature adults. Spec prog: Big Band 4 hrs, Oldies 18 hrs wkly. ♦Harold G. Fulmer, III, CEO, chmn & pres; Christopher G. Fulmer, VP; Bill Lakatas, gen mgr.

Laporte

***WCIJ(FM)**—Not on air, target date: unknown: 90.9 mhz; 250 w. Ant 148 ft TL: N41 26 06 W76 28 28. Hrs open: Box 506, Bath, NY, 14810. Phone: (607) 776-4151. Fax: (607) 776-6929.E-mail: mail@fln.org Web Site:www.fln.org Licensee: Family Life Ministries Inc. ♦Rick Snavely, gen mgr.

***WEVP(FM)**—Not on air, target date: unknown: 91.7 mhz; 190 w. Ant 161 ft TL: N41 26 06 W76 28 28. Hrs open: Box 20155, Scranton, 18502. Phone: (607) 427-0452. Licensee: Telikoja Educational Broadcasting Inc. ♦Kevin M. Fitzgerald, pres.

WNKZ(FM)— August 1998: 103.9 mhz; 6 kw. Ant 276 ft TL: N41 26 06 W76 28 28. Stereo. Hrs open: 24 Box 230, 201 Bernice Rd., Suite 2, Dushore, 18614. Phone: (570) 928-7200. Fax: (570) 928-2100.E-mail: contact_us@cozy.com Web Site:www.cozyradio.com Licensee: Geos Communications. (acq 8-1-2008). Population served: 20,000 Format: Adult contemp. News: 4 hrs wkly. Target aud: 25-54; adults. ♦Ben Smith, gen mgr, progmg VP; Cindi McCarty, adv mgr; Kevin Fitzgerald, engrg VP.

Latrobe

WCNS(AM)— Aug 11, 1956: 1480 khz; 500 w-D, 1 kw-N, DA-N. TL: N40 16 12 W79 23 13. Hrs open: 24 400 Unity St., Suite 200, 15650. Phone: (724) 537-3338. Fax: (724) 539-9798.E-mail: info@wcnsradio.com Web Site:www.1480wcns.com Licensee: Longo Media Group. (acq 1-89). Population served: 147,444 Natl. Network: Westwood One, . Format: full service. News staff: 3; News: 15 hrs wkly. Target aud: 25 +; general. Spec prog: Relg 2 hrs wkly. ♦John Longo, pres; Greg Zahornacky, stn mgr; Dow Carnahan, opns mgr, progmg dir.

WQTW(AM)— 1952: 1570 khz; 1 kw-D, 220 w-N. TL: N40 18 07 W79 21 26. Hrs open:
Rebroadcasts WLSW(FM) Scottdale.
Box 208, George St., 15650. Phone: (724) 532-1778. Fax: (724) 532-1779. Licensee: L. Stanley Wall. (acq 4-84; $66,000; 4-23-84). Population served: 11,749 Format: Hot adult contemp. ♦L. Stanley Wall, pres & gen mgr.

Lebanon

WADV(AM)— July 4, 1976: 940 khz; 1 kw-D, 5 w-N. TL: N40 22 22 W76 21 53. Stereo. Hrs open: 19 720 E Kercher Ave., 17046. Phone: (717) 273-2611. Fax: (717) 273-7293. Licensee: WADV Radio Inc. (acq 12-4-01). Population served: 800,000 Natl. Network: Moody, .

Format: Southern & bluegrass gospel, country. News staff: one; News: 18 hrs wkly. Target aud: 25 plus; loyal, exclusive. ♦Jennifer Taylor Kochel, pres; Earl Kochel, gen mgr; Julie Kochel, opns VP.

WLBR(AM)— Nov 13, 1946: 1270 khz; 5 kw-D, 1 kw-N, DA-2. TL: N40 21 35 W76 27 30. Hrs open: 5 AM-1 AM 440 Rebecca St., 17042. Phone: (717) 272-7651. Fax: (717) 274-0161. Licensee: Lebanon Broadcasting Co. (acq 4-16-2007; with co-located FM). Population served: 112,000 Rgnl. Network: Radio Pa. Natl. Rep: Roslin,. Radio Pa. Rgnl rep: Dome Shaw Pittman. Format: News/talk. News staff: 2. Target aud: 25-64. ♦Robert D. Etter, VP, gen mgr, progmg dir; Mickey Santora, gen sls mgr; Greg Lyons, mus dir, disc jockey; Gordon Weise, news dir; Glenn Waybright, chief of engrg; Gayle Reich, traf mgr; Laura Lebeau, news rptr; Dave Eisenhauer, disc jockey.

WQIC(FM)— January 1948: 100.1 mhz; 3 kw. 267 ft TL: N40 21 37 W76 27 31. Stereo. Hrs open: 5 AM-1 AM Prog sep from AM 440 Rebecca St., 17042. Phone: (717) 272-7651. Fax: (717) 274-0161. Format: Adult contemp. Target aud: 25-54. ♦Mike Ebersole, mus dir, disc jockey; Gayle Reich, traf mgr; Scott Bradley, sports cmtr; John Tuscano, disc jockey.

WWSM(AM)—See Annville-Cleona

Lehighton

WBYN(AM)—Licensed to Lehighton. See Allentown

Levittown-Fairless Hills

WBCB(AM)— Dec 8, 1957: 1490 khz; 1 kw-U. TL: N40 10 08 W74 50 08. Hrs open: 24 200 Magnolia Dr., Levittown, 19054. Phone: (215) 949-1490. Fax: (215) 949-3671. Web Site:www.wbcb1490.com Licensee: Progressive Broadcasting Co. (acq 11-13-92; $550,000; 11-30-92). Population served: 750,000 Natl. Network: USA, . Format: Community radio. Target aud: 18 plus; varied programming appeals to different age groups. Spec prog: Sports. ♦Pasquale T. Deon Sr., pres; Merrill Reese, VP, gen mgr; Erica Darragh, opns mgr; Lee Alexander, sls dir, gen sls mgr; Paul Baroli, progmg dir.

Lewisburg

WCXR(FM)— Oct 18, 1990: 103.7 mhz; 3 kw. 418 ft TL: N40 56 40 W76 52 45. (CP: 103.7 mhz, 1.35 kw, ant 715 ft.). Stereo. Hrs open: 24
Rebroadcasts WZXR(FM) South Williamsport 100%.
1685 Four Mile Dr., Williamsport, 17740. Phone: (570) 323-8200. Fax: (570) 327-9138.E-mail: dan.farr@bybradio.com Licensee: South Williamsport SabreCom Inc. Group owner: Backyard Broadcasting LLC (acq 12-1-02; grpsl). Population served: 311,000 Natl. Network: ABC, . Natl. Rep: Christal,. Format: Classic rock. News staff: 3. Target aud: 25-54. ♦Barry Drake, pres; Robin Smith, CFO; Dan Farr, gen mgr.

***WGRC(FM)**— Apr 22, 1988: 91.3 mhz; 3 kw. Ant 321 ft TL: N40 56 40 W76 52 45. Stereo. Hrs open: 24 101 Armory Blvd., 17837-9504. Phone: (570) 523-1190. Fax: (570) 523-1114.E-mail: email@wgrc.com Web Site:www.wgrc.com Licensee: Salt and Light Media Ministries Inc. Population served: 592,000 Natl. Network: Salem Radio Network, . Miller & Neely. Wire Svc: AP Format: Christian, adult contemp. News staff: 3; News: 16 hrs wkly. Target aud: 25-54; young to middle-aged adult. ♦Larry Weidman, gen mgr; Jim Diehl, progmg dir, news rptr; John Callahan, news dir, news rptr; Lamar Smith, chief of engrg; Linda Dantonio, traf mgr; Chris Miller, engr.

***WVBU-FM**— October 1965: 90.5 mhz; 500 w. -120 ft TL: N40 57 18 W76 52 46. (CP: 225 w, ant 66 ft.). Stereo. Hrs open: 8 AM-2 AM Box C-3956, Bucknell Univ., 701 Moore Ave., 17837. Phone: (570) 577-2000. Phone: (570) 577-3824. Fax: (570) 577-1174.E-mail: wvbu@bucknell.edu Web Site:www.orgs.bucknell.edu/wvbu Licensee: Bucknell University. Population served: 60,000 Format: Modern Rock. News: 7 hrs wkly. Target aud: 18-23; college students. Spec prog: Jazz 3 hrs, dance/club 6 hrs, prison request 2 hrs, modern/new age one hr wkly.

Lewistown

WCHX(FM)— July 1, 1987: 105.5 mhz; 3 kw. 817 ft TL: N40 39 43 W77 34 28. (CP: 465 w, ant 816 ft.). Stereo. Hrs open: 24 Box 911, 17044. Secondary address: 114 N. Logan Blvd., Burnham 17009. Phone: (717) 242-1493. Fax: (717) 242-3764. Web Site:www.chx105.com Licensee: Mifflin County Communications Inc. Population served: 125,000 Natl. Network: Fox News Radio, . Radio Pa. Wilkinson Barker Knauer. Format: Classic rock. News staff: one; News: 10 hrs wkly. Target aud: 25-54; mature, affluent, middle & upper class adults. ♦Anna Hain, pres; Jed A. Donahue, VP; Scott Shaw, gen mgr.

WIEZ(AM)— June 1, 1941: 670 khz; 5.4 kw-D. TL: N40 36 30 W77 34 45. Hrs open: Sunrise-sunset Box 667, 17044. Secondary address: 12 E. Market St. 2nd Floor 17044. Phone: (717) 248-6757. Fax: (717) 248-6759.E-mail: pete@merfradio.com Licensee: First Media Radio LLC. (group owner; (acq 3-28-2001; grpsl). Population served: 75,000 Natl. Rep: Dome,. Format: News, info. News staff: 2; News: 12 hrs wkly. Target aud: 45 plus; adults who control the area's disposable income. ♦Pete Herman, gen mgr; Jeff Stevens, opns mgr; Mary Lee Schaeffer, news dir.

***WJRC(FM)**— July 1996: 90.9 mhz; 100 w. 1,128 ft TL: N40 34 58 W77 29 48. Stereo. Hrs open: 24
Rebroadcasts WGRC(FM) Lewisburg 100%.
101 Armory Blvd., Lewisburg, 17837-0279. Phone: (570) 523-1190. Fax: (570) 523-1114.E-mail: email@wgrc.com Web Site:www.wgrc.com Licensee: Salt and Light Media Ministries Inc. Population served: 76,000 Natl. Network: Salem Radio Network, . Miller & Neely. Wire Svc: AP Format: Contemp Christian. News staff: 3; News: 9 hrs wkly. Target aud: 25-54. ♦Larry Weidman, gen mgr; John Callahan, news dir, news rptr; Lamar Smith, chief of engrg; Linda Dantonio, traf mgr; Jim Diehl, news rptr; Chris Miller, engr.

WKVA(AM)— Dec 4, 1949: 920 khz; 1 kw-D, 500 w-N, DA-N. TL: N40 34 45 W77 34 18. Hrs open: 5 AM-midnight Box 911, 17044. Secondary address: 114 N. Logan Blvd., Burnham 17009. Phone: (717) 242-1055. Phone: (717) 242-1495. Fax: (717) 242-3764.E-mail: wkva@oldies920.com Web Site:www.oldies920.com Licensee: Mifflin County Communications Inc. (acq 2-18-98; $277,692). Population served: 75,000 Natl. Network: ABC, CBS Radio, . Rgnl. Network: Radio Pa. Radio Pa. Putbrese, Hunsaker & Trent, P.C. Format: Oldies, full service. News staff: 2; News: 31 hrs wkly. Target aud: 25-54; blue collar mix of agricultural & industrial adults. ♦Anna A. Hain, pres; Jed A. Donahue, VP; Erik Lane, news dir.

WMRF-FM— Oct 1, 1964: 95.7 mhz; 3.9 kw. 407 ft TL: N40 36 30 W77 34 45. Stereo. Hrs open: 24 12 E. Market St., 2nd Floor, 17044. Phone: (717) 248-6757. Fax: (717) 248-6759.E-mail: pete@merfradio.com Web Site:www.merfradio.com Licensee: First Media Radio LLC. (group owner; (acq 5-14-2001; grpsl). Population served: 60,000 Format: Hot adult contemp. News staff: 2; News: 8 hrs wkly. Target aud: 18-44. ♦Peter Herman, gen mgr; Jeff Stevens, opns dir, progmg dir, progmg mgr; Mary Lee Sheaffer, news dir.

Lincoln University

***WWLU(FM)**— Aug 1, 1975: 88.7 mhz; 10 w. 100 ft Hrs open: Box 179, 1570 Baltimore Pike, 19352. Phone: (610) 932-8300. Fax: (610) 932-1095. Licensee: Lincoln University. Population served: 23,000 Format: Urban contemp, hip hop. ♦Whitney G. Walton, gen mgr.

Linesville

WMVL(FM)— May 4, 1970: 101.7 mhz; 1.4 kw. Ant 554 ft TL: N41 42 38 W80 16 29. Stereo. Hrs open: 24 Box 846, Meadville, 16335. Secondary address: 16271Conneaut Lake Rd., Ste 102, Meadville 16335. Phone: (814) 337-8440. Fax: (814) 333-2562.E-mail: wmvl@zoominternet.net Web Site:cool1017online.com Licensee: Vilkie Communications Inc. (acq 4-1-2003; $330,000). Population served: 980,000 Natl. Network: ABC, . Rgnl rep: Regional Reps, CLE, OH Hogan & Hartson. Format: Oldies. News: 8 hrs wkly. Target aud: 29 plus. ♦Eugene Vilkie, VP; Joseph M. Vilkie, pres & gen mgr; Dave Hanahan, gen sls mgr; Chuck Stopp, progmg dir; Jenna Wagner, sls.

Lock Haven

WBPZ(AM)— Feb 20, 1947: 1230 khz; 1 kw-U. TL: N41 08 03 W77 28 09. Hrs open: 24 Box 420, 17745. Secondary address: 21 E. Main St. 17745. Phone: (570) 748-4038. Fax: (570) 748-0092.E-mail: wbpz@kcnet.org Licensee: Lipez Broadcasting Corp. (acq 3-27-86). Population served: 50,000 Natl. Rep: Keystone (unwired net), Dome,. Format: Oldies. News staff: one; News: 10 hrs wkly. Target aud: General. Spec prog: Loc sports. ♦John Lipez, pres, gen mgr; John Lupez, gen sls mgr; Randy Dorey, progmg dir; Bill Daney, mus dir; Mark Sohmer, news dir; Dennis Sherman, chief of engrg; Michelle Grove, traf mgr.

WSNU(FM)— September 1965: 92.1 mhz; 3 kw. 255 ft TL: N41 08 49 W77 29 16. (CP: Ant 328 ft.). Stereo. Hrs open: 24 Prog sep from AM Box 420, 17745. Secondary address: 21 E. Main St. 17745. Phone: (570) 748-4038. Fax: (570) 748-0092.E-mail: wbpz@kcnet.org Population served: 70,000 Format: Adult contemp. News staff: one; News: 6 hrs wkly. Target aud: 21-48. ♦Michelle Grove, traf mgr.

Loretto

WWGE(AM)— Dec 7, 1963: 1400 khz; 1 kw-U. TL: N40 30 12 W78 38 10. Hrs open: 24 Box 88, Ebensburg, 15931. Secondary address: 104 S. Center St. , Suite 401 , Ebensburg 15931. Phone: (814) 255-9943. Fax: (814) 255-3343. Web Site:www.edge1400.com Licensee: Pennsylvania Radiowerks LLC (acq 10-15-98; $100,000). Population served: 100,000 Natl. Network: Jones Radio Networks, . Format: News/talk, sports. ♦Rev. Michael H. Yeager, pres; Jennifer Strelnik, gen mgr.

Mansfield

WNBQ(FM)— June 1999: 92.3 mhz; 800 w. 643 ft TL: N41 53 53 W77 05 38. Hrs open: 24
Rebroadcasts WNBT-FM Wellsboro 100%.
Box 98, Wellsboro, 16901. Secondary address: 12385 Rt. 6 Box 198-B, Wellsboro 16901. Phone: (570) 724-1490. Fax: (570) 724-6971.E-mail: wnbt@ptd.net Web Site:www.wnbt.net Licensee: Farm & Home Broadcasting Co. Group owner: Allegheny Mountain Network Stations Natl. Network: Westwood One, . Rgnl rep: Dome & Assoc. . Borsari & Paxson Format: Bright adult contemporary. ♦Cary Simpson, pres; Al Harer, gen mgr.

***WNTE(FM)**— Sept 15, 1968: 89.5 mhz; 115 w. -320 TL: N41 48 22 W77 04 27. Hrs open: Box 84, South Hall, Mansfield Univ., 16933. Phone: (570) 662-4653. Fax: (570) 662-4654. Web Site:mustuweb.mnsfld.edu Licensee: Mansfield University (acq 9-15-78). Population served: 8,500 Format: AOR, Top-40. Target aud: 17-25; college students/community. Spec prog: Black 5 hrs, jazz 2 hrs wkly.

Markleysburg

***WLOG(FM)**— 2002: Stn currently dark. 89.1 mhz; 100 w vert. Ant 328 ft TL: N39 43 32 W79 28 53. Hrs open: Box 5459, Twin Falls, ID, 83301. Phone: (208) 733-3551. Fax: (208) 734-0674. Web Site:www.edgewaterbroadcasting.com Licensee: Edgewater Broadcasting Inc. (acq 5-27-2005; $10,000). ♦Clark Parrish, pres.

Martinsburg

WJSM-FM— Apr 19, 1965: 92.7 mhz; 640 w. Ant 964 ft TL: N40 17 37 W78 15 38. Hrs open: Box 87 Rt. 2, 16662. Phone: (814) 793-2188. Fax: (814) 793-9727. Licensee: Martinsburg Broadcasting Inc. Population served: 350,000 Natl. Network: USA, . Format: Relg, news/talk, gospel. ♦Bill Reed, local news ed; Deborah J. Walters, news rptr; William Reed, reporter; Hap Ritchey, mus critic, disc jockey; Cheryl A. Walters, women's int ed; Deborah Walters, disc jockey.

WKMC(AM)—See Roaring Spring

WWBJ(AM)— Feb 27, 1968: 1110 khz; 1 kw-D. TL: N40 18 14 W78 15 59. Hrs open: Box 87, Rt. 2, 16662. Phone: (814) 793-2188. Fax: (814) 793-9727. Licensee: Martinsburg Broadcasting Inc. (acq 10-1-89). Population served: 275,000 Harold McCombs. Format: Relg, news, talk. Target aud: General. Spec prog: Farm one hr wkly. ♦Deborah J. Walters, opns mgr; Bill Reed, news dir; Deborah Walters, news rptr, disc jockey; Cheryl A. Walters, women's int ed; Larry S. Walters, pres, gen mgr, progmg dir & disc jockey.

Masontown

***WRIJ(FM)**— November 1990: 106.9 mhz; 3 kw. 328 ft TL: N39 47 15 W79 59 20. Stereo. Hrs open: 19
Rebroadcasts WAIJ(FM) Grantsville, MD 100%.
Box 540, Grantsville, MD, 21536. Phone: (301) 895-3292. Fax: (301) 895-3293.E-mail: hesalive@hesalive.net Web Site:www.hesalive.net Licensee: He's Alive Inc. (group owner) Population served: 500,000 Natl. Network: USA, . Format: Gospel, Christian, relg, adult contemp. Target aud: 18-35. ♦Sharon Johnson, pres.

***WYFU(FM)**— 2003: 88.5 mhz; 16 kw vert. Ant 328 ft TL: N39 47 15 W79 59 20. Hrs open: Box 7300, Charlotte, NC, 28241. Phone: (704) 523-5555. Fax: (704) 522-1967.E-mail: bbn@bbnradio.org Web Site:www.bbnradio.org Licensee: Bible Broadcasting Network Inc. Group owner: Bible Broadcasting Network (acq 2-12-99; $250,000). Format: Christian. ♦Richard Johnson, gen mgr.

McConnellsburg

WEEO-FM— 1997: 103.7 mhz; 135 w. 1,555 ft TL: N39 55 25 W77 57 20. Hrs open: 37 South Main St., Suite 103, Chambersburg, 17201. Phone: (717) 709-0800. Phone: (717) 709-0801. Fax: (717) 709-0802.

Web Site:revolution1037.net Licensee: Allegheny Mountain Network. Group owner: Allegheny Mountain Network Stations (acq 10-95; $18,000). Rgnl rep: Dome Borsari & Paxson. Format: Modern Rock. ◆John F. Simpson, CEO & pres.

*WWCF(FM)— 2005: 88.7 mhz; 9 w. Ant 1,194 ft TL: N39 54 58 W77 57 25. Hrs open: 611 Longview Rd., 17233-9740. Phone: (717) 485-5526. Licensee: Morris Broadcasting & Communications Inc. Format: Children. ◆Glenn Morris, pres & gen mgr.

McKean

WQHZ(FM)—See Erie

McKeesport

WEDO(AM)— 1947: 810 khz; 1 kw-D. TL: N40 21 52 W79 48 49. Hrs open: Sunrise-sunset 1985 Lincoln Way, White Oak, 15131. Phone: (412) 664-4431. Fax: (412) 664-1236.E-mail: wedoradio@comcast.net Web Site:www.am81wedo.com Licensee: 810 Inc. (acq 5-72). Population served: 2,300,000 Format: Talk, health, var. Target aud: 35-65, 25-54, 65+. Spec prog: Slovenian one hr, Slovak one hr, Greek one hr, Croation one hr, It one hr wkly. ◆Judith Baron, pres; John James, VP, gen mgr; Bill Korch, progmg dir.

WMNY(AM)— April 1947: 1360 khz; 5 kw-D, 1 kw-N, DA-N. TL: N40 24 30 W79 55 40. (CP: COL Mount Lebanon. 910 khz; 7 kw-D, DA. TL: N40 16 05 W79 59 01). Hrs open: 24 3rd Fl., 900 Parish St., Pittsburgh, 15220. Phone: (412) 875-9500. Fax: (412) 875-9474. Web Site:www.wmnyradio.com Licensee: Renda Broadcasting Corp. of Nevada. (acq 9-10-97). Natl. Network: ABC, . Natl. Rep: McGavren Guild,. Wire Svc: AP Wire Svc: Metro Weather Service Inc. Format: Talk. News: 15 hrs wkly. Target aud: 25-54. Spec prog: Oldies 9 hrs, polka 2 hrs wkly. ◆Tony Renda Sr., CEO; Tony Renda Jr., gen mgr.

Meadville

*WARC(FM)— Feb 3, 1963: 90.3 mhz; 150 w. 86 ft TL: N41 38 55 W80 08 45. (CP: 340 w, ant 75 ft.). Stereo. Hrs open: Box C, Allegheny College, 520 N. Main St., 16335. Phone: (814) 332-3376.E-mail: info@warc.org Web Site:www.warcallegheny.org Licensee: Allegheny College. Population served: 40,000 Format: Alternative. Spec prog: Black 8 hrs, class 10 hrs, jazz 4 hrs wkly. ◆Jennifer Knapp, gen mgr.

WGYY(FM)— 1947: 100.3 mhz; 20 kw. 587 ft TL: N41 37 53 W80 10 37. Stereo. Hrs open: Prog sep from AM Box 397, Downtown Mall, 16335. Phone: (814) 724-1111. Fax: (814) 333-9628. Web Site:www.radio @zoominternet.net Licensee: Forever Broadcasting LLC Population served: 1,000,000 Format: Country.

WMGW(AM)— 1947: 1490 khz; 1 kw-U. TL: N41 37 53 W80 10 37. Hrs open: Box 397, Downtown Mall, 16335. Phone: (814) 724-1111. Fax: (814) 333-9628. Web Site:www.radio@zoominternet.net Licensee: Forever Broadcasting LLC. Group owner: Forever Broadcasting (acq 7-20-00; grpsl). Population served: 100,000 Format: News/talk, sports, info. Target aud: 25-54. ◆Terry Dietz, gen mgr & gen sls mgr; Dave Galentine, progmg dir.

*WVME(FM)— 2002: 91.9 mhz; 4.4 kw. Ant 308 ft TL: N41 37 50 W80 10 38. Stereo. Hrs open: 24 Rebroadcasts WCRF(FM) Cleveland, OH 100%. WCRF Radio, 9756 Barr Rd., Cleveland, OH, 44141. Phone: (440) 526-1111. Fax: (440) 526-1319.E-mail: wcrf@moody.edu Web Site:www.wcrfradio.org Licensee: The Moody Bible Institute of Chicago. (group owner) Southmayd. Wire Svc: AP Format: Inspirational. Target aud: 25-55; Adults. ◆Michael Easley, pres; Richard Lee, stn mgr; Phil Villareal, progmg dir; Gary Bittner, local news ed.

Mechanicsburg

WTPA(FM)— Nov 1, 1978: 93.5 mhz; 1.25 kw. 718 ft TL: N40 10 38 W76 52 38. Stereo. Hrs open: Cumulus Media, 2300 Vartan Way, Harrisburg, 17110-9720. Phone: (717) 238-1041. Fax: (717) 234-4842.E-mail: info@935wtpa.com Web Site:www.935WTPA.com Licensee: Cumulus Licensing Corp. Group owner: Cumulus Media Inc. (acq 2000; grpsl). Population served: 86,500 Wilkinson Barker Knauer. Format: Active rock. Target aud: 18-49. ◆Ron Giovaniello, stn mgr; John O'Dea, opns VP; Karen Richards, sls VP; John Butler, gen sls mgr; Diane Sohanuch, prom dir; Chris James, progmg dir; Dave Supplee, chief of engrg.

Media

WPHI-FM— November 1982: 100.3 mhz; 35 kw. Ant 600 ft TL: N39 58 29 W75 25 22. (CP: 17 kw, ant 863 ft. TL: N40 02 36 W75 14 33). Stereo. Hrs open: 24 1000 River Rd., Suite 400, Conshohocken, 19428-2437. Phone: (610) 276-1100. Fax: (610) 276-1139.E-mail: 1003@thebeatphilly.com Web Site:www.1003thebeaatphilly.com Licensee: Radio One Licenses LLC. Group owner: Radio One Inc. (acq 11-8-2001; grpsl). Population served: 4,000,000 Format: Rhythm and blues. News staff: one. Target aud: 18-44: savvy suburban educated professional. ◆Chester Schofield, gen mgr; Helen Little, opns mgr & chief of engrg.

Mercer

WLLF(FM)— January 1985: 96.7 mhz; 1.4 kw. ant 485 ft TL: N41 18 43 W80 16 39. Stereo. Hrs open: 24 2030 Pine Hollow Blvd., Hermitage, 16148. Phone: (724) 346-4113. Fax: (724) 981-4545. Web Site:www.967theriver.com Licensee: Cumulus Licensing Corp. Group owner: Cumulus Media Inc. (acq 3-15-00; grpsl). Natl. Network: Jones Radio Networks, . Format: Soft adult contemp. ◆Brian Schimmel, gen mgr; Joe Bilo, natl sls mgr, news dir; Bob Popa, progmg dir; Wes Boyd, chief of engrg.

WWIZ(FM)— October 1972: 103.9 mhz; 3 kw. 300 ft TL: N41 12 10 W80 21 30. Stereo. Hrs open: 4040 Simon Rd., Youngstown, OH, 44512. Phone: (330) 783-1000. Fax: (330) 783-0060. Web Site:www.realrock104.com Licensee: Cumulus Licensing Corp. Group owner: Cumulus Media Inc. (acq 3-15-00; grpsl). Population served: 200,000 Format: Active rock. Target aud: 25-54. ◆Brian Schimmell, gen mgr.

Mercersburg

WPPT(FM)— Mar 23, 1976: 92.1 mhz; 3.3 kw. 295 ft TL: N39 48 34 W77 48 22. (CP: 2.7 kw, ant 465 ft.). Stereo. Hrs open: 24 Box 788, 10960 John Wayne Dr., Greencastle, 17225. Phone: (717) 597-9200. Fax: (717) 597-9210.E-mail: webmaster@wayz.com Web Site:www.mylegends921.com Licensee: M. Belmont VerStandig Inc. Group owner: VerStandig Broadcasting (acq 10-1-93; $1.6 million with WCBG(AM) Chambersburg;9-6-93). Population served: 225,000 Leventhal, Senter & Lerman. Format: Classic Country. Target aud: 25-54; double income households. ◆Blake Truman, gen mgr.

Mexico

WJUN(AM)— Sept 8, 1955: 1220 khz; 1 kw-D, 46 w-N. TL: N40 32 06 W77 20 26. Hrs open: 24 Box 209, Old Rt. 22 E., 17056. Phone: (717) 436-2135. Fax: (717) 436-8155.E-mail: wjun@nmax.net Licensee: Starview Media Inc. (acq 11-16-89; grpsl; 12-19-88). Population served: 61,500 Natl. Network: ESPN Radio, . Rgnl. Network: Radio Pa. Radio Pa. Format: Sports. News staff: 2. Target aud: 25-54. Spec prog: Relg 2 hrs wkly. ◆Douglas George, pres; Curt Dreibelbis, gen mgr, gen sls mgr; Dan Roland, news dir; John Hess, chief of engrg; Laurie Hower, traf mgr & outdoor ed.

WJUN-FM— July 4, 1989: 92.5 mhz; 440 w. Ant 1,181 ft TL: N40 34 58 W77 29 48. Stereo. Hrs open: 24 Box 209, 17056. Secondary address: Old Rt. 22 E. 17056. Phone: (717) 436-2135. Fax: (717) 436-8155. Licensee: Starview Media Inc. Natl. Network: Motor Racing Net, . Rgnl. Network: Radio Pa. Radio Pa. Format: Country. News staff: one; News: 5 hrs wkly. ◆Mel Thomas, progmg dir.

Meyersdale

WQZS(FM)— 1992: 93.3 mhz; 630 w. 964 ft TL: N39 47 49 W79 10 05. Hrs open: 128 Hunsrick Rd., 15552. Phone: (814) 634-9111. Fax: (814) 634-0882.E-mail: helenwahl27@hotmail.com Licensee: Roger Wahl. Format: Oldies. News staff: one. Target aud: 25-60; females 60%, males 40%. Spec prog: Gospel 5 hrs wkly. ◆Helen E. Wahl, gen mgr, progmg dir; Jessy Chabol, gen sls mgr.

Middletown

*WMSS(FM)— Sept 7, 1978: 91.1 mhz; .56 w. 73 ft TL: N40 11 52 W76 43 30. Stereo. Hrs open: 7 AM-9 PM 215 Oberlin Rd, 17057. Phone: (717) 948-9136.E-mail: sales@wmssfm.com Web Site:www.wmssfm.com Licensee: Middletown Area School District. Population served: 250,000 Va. News Net. Format: Adult contemp, progsv, educ. News: one hr wkly. Target aud: General. Spec prog: Sports 5 hrs, relg 8 hrs wkly. ◆John Wilsbach, gen mgr; Maureen Denis, opns dir; Steve Leedy, opns mgr.

*WXPH(FM)— 2006: 88.7 mhz; 75 w horiz, 7 kw vert. Ant 708 ft TL: N40 02 07 W76 37 19. Hrs open: Rebroadcasts WXPN(FM) Philadelphia 100%. 3025 Walnut St., Philadelphia, 19104. Phone: (215) 898-6677. Fax: (215) 898-0707.E-mail: wxpndesk@xpn.org Web Site:www.xpn.org Licensee: The Trustees of the University of Pennsylvania (acq 10-30-2007; exchange for WZXM(FM) Harrisburg). Format: Adult alternative. ◆Roger LaMay, gen mgr; Quyen Shanahan, dev VP.

Mifflinburg

WWBE(FM)— 1975: 98.3 mhz; 1.4 kw. 482 ft TL: N40 53 27 W76 59 54. Stereo. Hrs open: 24 Rebroadcasts WUNS(FM) Lewisburg 100%. Box 90, Rt. 204 & State School Rd., Selinsgrove, 17870-0090. Phone: (570) 374-8819. Fax: (570) 374-7444.E-mail: bigcountryrequest@hotmail.com Web Site:www.bigcountrynow.com Licensee: MMP License LLC. Group owner: MAX Media L.L.C. (acq 10-17-03; grpsl). Population served: 225,000 Natl. Network: Westwood One, Jones Radio Networks, . Natl. Rep: Dome,. Format: Country. News staff: one; News: 2 hrs wkly. Target aud: 25-54. Spec prog: Gospel 2 hrs wkly. ◆Scott Richards, gen mgr; Greg Adair, stn mgr, gen sls mgr; Dawn Marie, progmg dir; Ted Koppen, chief of engrg.

Mifflintown

*WQJU(FM)— Oct 15, 1985: 107.1 mhz; 370 w. Ant 1,302 ft TL: N40 34 20 W77 30 51. Hrs open: 24 Rebroadcasts WTLR(FM) State College 100%. 2020 Cato Ave., State College, 16801. Phone: (814) 237-9857.E-mail: mail@cpci.org Licensee: Central Pennsylvania Christian Institute. (acq 1-22-93; $132,500; 2-15-93). Population served: 164,464 Natl. Network: Moody, USA, . Wire Svc: AP Format: Christian. News staff: one; News: 8 hrs wkly. Target aud: 30-55; adults, family oriented. ◆Mark Van Ouse, gen mgr & stn mgr.

Milford

WQCD(AM)—Not on air, target date: unknown: 1450 khz; 1 kw-U. TL: N41 20 10 W74 47 45. Hrs open: 135 White Bridge Rd., Middletown, NY, 10940. Phone: (845) 355-4001. Fax: (845) 355-4002. Licensee: Digital Radio Broadcasting Inc. ◆Charles Williamson, gen mgr.

Mill Hall

WVRT(FM)— Aug 20, 1979: 97.7 mhz; 6 kw. Ant 295 ft TL: N41 13 14 W77 16 39. Stereo. Hrs open: 24 Box 3238, Williamsport, 17701. Secondary address: 1559 W 4th Street, Williamsport 17701. Phone: (570) 327-1400. Fax: (570) 327-8156.E-mail: kcote@clearchannel.com Web Site:www.variety977.com Licensee: Clear Channel Radio Licenses, Inc. Group owner: Clear Channel Communications Inc. (acq 3-12-01; $1.5 million). Population served: 136,000 Natl. Rep: Christal,. Format: Hot adult contemp. Target aud: 18-49. ◆Karen Cote, gen sls mgr, adv mgr; Tom Scott, progmg dir; Mike Myer, engrg dir.

Millersburg

WQLV(FM)— Feb 24, 1992: 98.9 mhz; 780 w. 895 ft TL: N40 30 18 W77 07 03. Stereo. Hrs open: 24 234 Union St., 17061. Phone: (717) 692-2193. Fax: (717) 692-2080.E-mail: bob@wqlvfm.com Web Site:www.wqlvfm.com Licensee: UPOD Radio, LLC Population served: 210,000 Natl. Network: ABC, . Format: adult contemporary. News: Every hour. Target aud: 25 plus. Spec prog: seasonal High school sports. ◆Ric Cooper, pres; JD Cooper, gen mgr, mktg VP; Mark West, progmg dir.

Millersville

*WIXQ(FM)— 1978: 91.7 mhz; 129 w. 69 ft TL: N39 59 53 W76 21 20. Hrs open: 7 AM-3 AM Box 1002, Millersville Univ., 17551. Phone: (717) 872-3518. Phone: (717) 871-2317. Fax: (717) 872-3383.E-mail: comments@wixg.com Web Site:www.wixg.com Licensee: Millersville University. Format: Progsv, Black, div. News: one hr wkly. Target aud: 18-24; college students. Spec prog: Jazz 2 hrs wkly. ◆Greg Park, stn mgr; Paul Galvin, prom dir; Steve Entrekin, progmg dir.

Millvale

WAMO(AM)—Licensed to Millvale. See Pittsburgh

Milroy

*WRYV(FM)—Not on air, target date: unknown: 88.7 mhz; 1 w horiz, 2.5 kw vert. Ant 800 ft TL: N40 35 10 W77 41 40. Hrs open: 925 Houserville Rd., State College, 16801. Phone: (814) 867-3836. Fax: (814) 867-1922.E-mail: info@revfm.net Web Site:www.revfm.net Licensee: Invisible Allies Ministries. ◆Michael Schomer, gen mgr.

Milton

WMLP(AM)— Oct 27, 1955: 1380 khz; 1 kw-D, 18 w-N. TL: N40 59 52 W76 52 17. Stereo. Hrs open: 24 Box 1070, Sunbury, 17801. Secondary address: 1227 County Line Rd., Selinsgrove 17870. Phone: (570) 286-5838. Fax: (570) 743-7837.E-mail: valley@wvly.com Web Site:www.1380wmlp.com Licensee: Sunbury Broadcasting Corp. (acq 2006; $3 million with co-located FM). Population served: 167,100 Natl. Network: CNN Radio, . Natl. Rep: Dome, Roslin,. Format: Talk. News staff: 4; News: 12 hrs wkly. Target aud: 25-54. ◆Roger Haddon Jr., pres, gen mgr; Kevin Herr, opns mgr, progmg VP; Tricia Cease, gen sls mgr; Matt Farrand, news dir; Harry Bingaman, chief of engrg.

WVLY-FM— Oct 1, 1967: 100.9 mhz; 1.3 kw. Ant 715 ft TL: N40 57 12 W76 45 05. Stereo. Hrs open: 24 Prog sep from AM Box 1070, Sunbury, 17870. Secondary address: 1227 County Line Rd., Selinsgrove 17870. Phone: (570) 286-5838. Fax: (570) 743-7837.E-mail: equest@wvly.com Web Site:www.wvly.com Licensee: Sunbury Broadcasting Corp. Population served: 167,100 Natl. Rep: Dome, Roslin,. Format: Adult contemp. News staff: 4; News: 5 hrs wkly. Target aud: 25-54; adults. Spec prog: Smooth jazz 6 hrs wkly. ◆Roger S. Haddon Jr., CEO, pres; Kevine Herr, opns mgr; Tricia Cease, gen sls mgr; Matt Farrand, news dir; Harry Bingaman, chief of engrg.

Monroeville

WPGR(AM)— Sept 27, 1964: 1510 khz; 5 kw-D, 1 w-N, 2.5 kw-CH, DA-2. TL: N40 28 13 W79 51 04. Hrs open: 24 960 Penn Ave., Suite 200, Pittsburgh, 15222. Secondary address: Sheridan Broadcasting Co., 960 Penn Ave., Pittsburgh 15222. Phone: (412) 456-4064. Fax: (412) 391-3559.E-mail: mdouglass@sbcol.com Web Site:www.wamo.com Licensee: McL/McM Pennsylvania LLC. (group owner; (acq 9-28-2001; $625,000). Population served: 300000 Natl. Rep: McGavren Guild,. Fletcher, Heald & Hildreth, P.L.C. Format: Urban gospel. Target aud: 25-54; middle class & higher income households. Spec prog: Relg 6 hrs wkly. ◆Ronald Davenport Jr., chmn & pres; Michael Douglass, gen mgr.

Montrose

*WPEL(AM)— May 30, 1953: 1250 khz; 1 kw-D. TL: N41 51 16 W75 51 50. (CP: 800 khz; 1 kw-D, 135 w-N). Hrs open: 6 AM-sunset 251 High St., P.O. Box 248, 18801. Phone: (570) 278-2811. Fax: (570) 278-1442.E-mail: mail@wpel.org Web Site:wpel.org Licensee: Montrose Broadcasting Corp. (group owner) Population served: 40,000 Natl. Network: AP Network News, . Rgnl. Network: Radio Pa. Radio Pa. Gammon & Grange. Wire Svc: AP Format: Southern gospel music. News: 7 hrs wkly. Target aud: General; families. Spec prog: Class one hr, farm one hr wkly. ◆Larry Souder, pres, gen mgr; Lloyd Sheldon, opns mgr; LaVerne Sollick, prom mgr; Robert Brigham, chief of engrg.

*WPEL-FM— June 5, 1961: 96.5 mhz; 57 kw. 459 ft TL: N41 51 16 W75 51 50. Stereo. Hrs open: 24 Dups AM 50% 251 High St., P.O. Box 248, 18801. Phone: (570) 278-2811. Fax: (570) 278-1442.E-mail: mail@wpel.org Web Site:wpel.org Licensee: Montrose Broadcasting Corp. Population served: 523,042 Natl. Network: Moody, AP Network News, Salem Radio Network, . Rgnl. Network: Radio Pa. Radio Pa. Wire Svc: AP Format: btfl mus, relg. News: 12 hrs wkly. Target aud: General. ◆Larry Souder, gen mgr; Lloyd Sheldon, opns mgr; Robert Brigham, chief of engrg.

Mount Carmel

WVRZ(FM)— March 1993: 99.7 mhz; 790 w. Ant 646 ft TL: N40 49 09 W76 27 45. Hrs open: 24 1559 W. 4th St., Williamsport, 17701. Phone: (570) 327-1400. Fax: (570) 327-8156. Web Site:www.variety997.com Licensee: Clear Channel Broadcasting Licenses Inc. (acq 5-26-2005; $460,000). Population served: 250,000 Format: CHR. Target aud: 25-65. ◆Jim Dabney, gen mgr.

Mount Cobb

*WFTE(FM)—Not on air, target date: unknown: 90.3 mhz; 3 kw. Ant 95 ft TL: N41 23 09 W75 24 07. Hrs open: 1520 Lakeland Dr., Jermyn, 18433. Phone: (570) 504-5803. Licensee: Center for Creative Cooperation Inc. ◆Don Noll, pres.

Mount Pleasant

WKVE(FM)— Apr 21, 1978: 103.1 mhz; 4.4 kw. Ant 800 ft TL: N39 54 49.6 W79 37 57.4. Stereo. Hrs open: 24 369 Tower Rd., Waynesburg, 15370. Phone: (724) 627-5555. Fax: (724) 627-4021.E-mail: radiowanb@gmail.com Licensee: Broadcast Communications Inc. (group owner; (acq 4-1-2002; with co-located AM). Rgnl. Network: Radio Pa. Natl. Rep: Dome,. Format: Country. Target aud: 20 plus. ◆Judy E. Rastoka, gen mgr; Doug Wilson, progmg dir; Rick Williams, chief of engrg; Marcia Mackey, traf mgr.

Mount Pocono

WPLY(AM)— Apr 8, 1981: 960 khz; 1 kw-D, 24 w-N, DA-2. TL: N41 04 41 W75 22 49. Simulcast with WVPO(AM) Stroudsburg 100%. 22 S. 6th St., Stroudsburg, 18360. Phone: (570) 421-2100. Fax: (570) 421-2040.E-mail: info@lite935.com Licensee: Nassau Broadcasting II LLC. Group owner: Nassau Broadcasting Partners L.P. (acq 6-28-2000). Format: News, talk. ◆Rick Musselman, VP & gen mgr.

Mount Union

WBSS(FM)— Mar 30, 1992: 106.3 mhz; 120 w. Ant 1,440 ft TL: N40 24 53 W77 54 13. Stereo. Hrs open: 24 Simulcast with WBUS(FM) Boalsburg 100%. R.R. 3 Box 225-A, Huntingdon, 16652. Phone: (814) 643-9620. Phone: (814) 643-1063. Fax: (814) 643-9625. Web Site:www.thebus.net Licensee: Megahertz Licenses LLC. Group owner: Forever Broadcasting (acq 3-13-2002; $620,000). Population served: 82,345 Natl. Rep: Dome,. Mullin, Rhyne, Emmons & Topel. Format: Classic rock. News staff: one. ◆Kristen Cantrell, gen mgr.

Mountain Top

WBHT(FM)— September 1992: 97.1 mhz; 500 w. 1,102 ft TL: N41 10 57 W75 52 19. Hrs open: 24 600 Baltimore Dr., 2nd Fl., Wilkes-Barre, 18702. Phone: (570) 824-9000. Fax: (570) 820-0520. Web Site:www.97bht.com Licensee: Citadel Broadcasting Co. Group owner: Citadel Broadcasting Corp. (acq 10-23-98; grpsl). Cohn & Marks. Format: CHR. Target aud: 18-34. ◆Bill Palmeri, mktg mgr; A.J., progmg dir.

Muncy

WBZD-FM—Licensed to Muncy. See Williamsport

Murrysville

*WRWJ(FM)— July 1994: 88.1 mhz; 250 w. 243 ft TL: N40 28 51 W79 43 26. Hrs open: 19 Rebroadcasts WAIJ(FM) Grantsville, MD 100%. Box 540, Grantsville, MD, 21536-0540. Phone: (301) 895-3292. Fax: (301) 895-3293.E-mail: hesalive@hesalive.net Web Site:www.hesalive.net Licensee: He's Alive Inc. Natl. Network: USA, . Format: Gospel, Christian, relg, adult contemp. Target aud: 18-35. ◆Sharon Johnson, pres.

Nanticoke

WNAK(AM)— February 1947: 730 khz; 1 kw-D, 38 w-N. TL: N41 13 10 W75 59 28. Stereo. Hrs open: 957 Broadcast Ctr., Avoca, 18641. Phone: (570) 414-1943. Fax: (570) 414-1944. Licensee: WS2K Radio LLC. Group owner: Route 81 Radio LLC (acq 7-14-2008; grpsl). Population served: 16,632 Format: Sp hits. Target aud: 35 plus. ◆Ira Rosenblatt, stn mgr.

WQFM(FM)— Oct 31, 1973: 92.1 mhz; 280 w. Ant 1,056 ft TL: N41 10 59 W75 52 31. Stereo. Hrs open: 24 Simulcast with WQFN(FM) Forest City. 149 Penn Ave., Scranton, 18503. Phone: (570) 346-6555. Fax: (570) 346-6038.E-mail: tbass@shamrocknepa.com Web Site:www.921qfm.com Licensee: The Scranton Times L.P. Group owner: Shamrock Communications Inc. (acq 8-10-94). Natl. Rep: Roslin,. Format: Adult contemp. News staff: one; News: 5 hrs wkly. Target aud: 25-54. Spec prog: Pol 3 hrs wkly. ◆William R. Lynett, CEO; Jim Loftus, gen mgr.

*WSFX(FM)— Oct 25, 1987: 89.1 mhz; 100 w. 50 ft TL: N41 11 42 W75 59 28. Stereo. Hrs open: Luzerne County Community College, Prospect St. & Middle Rds., 18634. Phone: (570) 740-0632. Fax: (570) 740-0605. Licensee: Luzerne County Community College. Format: Div. Target aud: 16-25; college age alternative mus audience. ◆Ron Reino, gen mgr.

Nanty Glo

*WPKV(FM)— 2006: 90.7 mhz; 2.1 kw vert. Ant 482 ft TL: N40 30 20 W78 48 12. Hrs open: 5700 West Oaks Blvd., Rocklin, CA, 95765. Phone: (916) 251-1600. Fax: (916) 251-1650. Licensee: Educational Media Foundation. (acq 3-23-2007; grpsl). Format: Christian. ◆Richard Jenkins, pres.

New Berlin

*WBGM(FM)— September 1996: 88.1 mhz; 550 w. 417 ft TL: N40 53 27 W76 59 54. Hrs open: Rebroadcasts WPGM-FM Danville 100%. 8 E. Market St., Danville, 17821. Phone: (570) 275-1570. Fax: (570) 275-4071.E-mail: info@wbgm.org Licensee: Montrose Broadcasting Corp. (group owner) Format: Relg, Christian. ◆George Vacca, gen mgr; Deanna Force, mus dir.

New Castle

WJST(AM)— Oct 23, 1938: 1280 khz; 4.9 kw-D, 1 kw-N, DA-N. TL: N40 57 14 W80 19 05. Hrs open: 219 Savannah Gardner Rd., 16101-5546. Phone: (724) 346-5070. Fax: (724) 654-3101. Licensee: Forever Broadcasting LLC. Group owner: Forever Broadcasting (acq 6-30-2004; grpsl). Population served: 38,559 Natl. Network: ABC, . Natl. Rep: Dome, Rgnl Reps,. Format: Oldies. Target aud: 30 plus. Spec prog: Black one hr, class one hr wkly. ◆Scott D. Cohagan, gen mgr.

WKST(AM)— Aug 25, 1968: 1200 khz; 5 kw-D, 1 kw-N, DA-N. TL: N40 56 22 W80 23 38. Hrs open: 5:30 AM-1 AM 219 Savanah Gardner Rd., 16101. Phone: (724) 346-5070. Fax: (724) 654-3101. Web Site:www.wkst.com Licensee: Forever Broadcasting LLC. Group owner: Forever Broadcasting (acq 6-30-2004; grpsl). Population served: 38559 Rgnl rep: Commercial Media Sales. Format: News/talk, sports. News staff: 2; News: 7 hrs wkly. Target aud: 34 plus. Spec prog: Ger one hr, Pol one hr, Greek one hr wkly. ◆Scott D. Cohagan, gen mgr; Ken Hlebovy, progmg dir; Wade Sutton, news dir.

*WVMN(FM)— Nov 22, 1995: 90.1 mhz; 2 kw. Ant 236 ft TL: N41 00 47 W80 17 36. Stereo. Hrs open: 24 Rebroadcasts WCRF(FM) Cleveland, OH 100%. c/o Radio Stn WCRF(FM), 9756 Barr Rd., Cleveland, OH, 44141. Phone: (440) 526-1111. Fax: (440) 526-1319.E-mail: wcrf@moody.edu Web Site:www.wcrfradio.org Licensee: Moody Bible Institute of Chicago. (group owner) Southmayd. Wire Svc: AP Format: Inspirational. Target aud: 25-55. ◆Michael Easley, pres; Richard Lee, stn mgr; Gary Bittner, mus dir; Doug Hainer, chief of engrg.

New Kensington

WGBN(AM)— October 1940: 1150 khz; 1 kw-D, 70 w-N, DA-1. TL: N40 34 24 W79 46 58. Hrs open: 24 560 7th St., 15068. Phone: (724) 337-3588. Fax: (724) 337-1318. Licensee: Pentecostal Temple Development Corp. (acq 11-3-92; 11-23-92). Population served: 1,209,000 Natl. Network: USA, . Natl. Rep: Dome,. Fletcher, Heald & Hildreth. Format: Gospel. News staff: one; News: 19 hrs wkly. Target aud: 30 plus; older, upscale. Spec prog: Pol 3 hrs, It 2 hrs, Irish 2 hrs, relg 2 hrs wkly. ◆Lauren Mann, gen mgr; Calvin Penny, progmg dir; Del King, chief of engrg.

WPGB(FM)—See Pittsburgh

WZPT(FM)— Aug 17, 1967: 100.7 mhz; 17 kw. Ant 850 ft TL: N40 29 43 W80 00 18. Stereo. Hrs open: 24 651 Holiday Dr., Foster Plaza Five, Pittsburgh, 15220. Phone: (412) 920-9400. Fax: (412) 920-9444.E-mail: wbzw@cbfradio.com Web Site:www.1007.com Licensee: Infinity Radio Holdings Inc. Group owner: Infinity Broadcasting Corp. (acq 6-8-98; grpsl). Format: Hot adult contemp. Target aud: 18-49. ◆Joel Hollander, pres; Scott Herman, exec VP; Keith Clark, sr VP, opns VP, progmg VP, progmg dir; Don Oylear, VP, gen mgr; Keith Belden, sls dir, natl sls mgr; Ronda Zegarelli, gen sls mgr; Susie Barker, prom mgr; Jonny Hortwell, mus dir; Kerri Griffith, news dir, pub affrs dir; Chris Hudak, chief of engrg.

New Wilmington

*WWNW(FM)— Jan 31, 1968: 88.9 mhz; 4 kw vert. Ant 128 ft TL: N41 06 41 W80 20 21. Stereo. Hrs open: 24 Box 89, Westminster College, 16172. Phone: (724) 946-7242. Fax: (724) 946-7070.E-mail: barnerdl@westminster.edu Web Site:titanradio.net Licensee: Westminster College Board of Trustees. Population served: 60,000 Natl. Network: ABC, . Wire Svc: AP Format: Hot adult contemp. News: 3 hrs wkly.

Target aud: 18-35; college students & staff. Spec prog: Relg 3 hrs wkly. ♦R. Thomas Williamson, pres; David L. Barner, gen mgr; Charles Chirozzi, chief of engrg.

Norristown

WNAP(AM)— Aug 6, 1946: 1110 khz; 4.8 kw-D, DA. TL: N40 08 05 W75 18 48. Hrs open: 2311 Old Arch Rd., 19401. Phone: (610) 272-7600. Fax: (610) 272-5793.E-mail: gospel@wnap1110am.com Licensee: George H. Buck. Group owner: GHB Radio Group (acq 12-15-87; $725,000; 4-2-84). Population served: 3,500,000 Rgnl. Network: Metronews Radio Net. Format: Black gospel. Target aud: General. ♦Fred Blain, gen mgr, progmg dir; Orey Ferrell, gen sls mgr; Dave McCrork, chief of engrg.

North East

WRKT(FM)— Mar 29, 1970: 100.9 mhz; 4.2 kw. 252 ft TL: N42 11 51 W79 45 10. Stereo. Hrs open: 24 Boston Store Pl., Erie, 16501. Phone: (814) 461-1000. Fax: (814) 461-1500.E-mail: rocket101@rocket101.com Licensee: Connoisseur Media of Erie LLC. Group owner: NextMedia Group L.L.C. (acq 3-30-2006; grpsl). Population served: 226,600 Fletcher, Heald & Hildreth. Format: Classic rock. News staff: one; News: one hr wkly. Target aud: 25-54. Spec prog: Loc bands one hr wkly. ♦Richard Rambaldo, gen mgr; Michael Malpiedi, gen sls mgr.

WYNE(AM)— Nov 24, 1966: 1530 khz; 1 kw-D, 250 w-CH. TL: N42 12 05 W79 51 43. Stereo. Hrs open: Sunrise-set 16 West Division St., 16428. Phone: (814) 725-6243. Web Site:northeast.mercyhurst.edu Licensee: Mercyhurst College (acq 2-18-2005; $110,000). Population served: 12,000 Format: Oldies. Target aud: 35-64; men & women. ♦William T. Shannon, gen mgr.

Northern Cambria

WNCC(AM)— Oct 15, 1950: Stn currently dark. 950 khz; 500 w-D. TL: N40 40 47 W78 44 26. Hrs open: 24 Box 1095, 15714. Phone: (814) 472-4060. Fax: (814) 948-0950.E-mail: whpa@verizon.net Licensee: Vernal Enterprises Inc. (group owner; (acq 3-19-97; $20,000 with WRDD(AM) Ebensburg). Population served: 40000 Format: Adult contemp, oldies. News staff: one; News: 6 hrs wkly. Target aud: 35 plus; females & males in the 35 plus age range. ♦Larry Schrengost, gen mgr.

WPCL(FM)— Sept 30, 1991: 97.3 mhz; 6 kw. 610 ft TL: N40 38 26 W78 47 45. Stereo. Hrs open: 19
Rebroadcasts WAIJ (FM) Grantsville, MD 100%.
Box 540, 34 Spring Rd., Grantsville, MD, 21536. Phone: (301) 895-3292. Fax: (301) 895-3293.E-mail: hesalive@hesalive.net Web Site:www.hesalive.com Licensee: He's Alive Inc. (group owner; acq 3-18-97; $105,000). Natl. Network: USA, . Natl. Rep: Commercial Media Sales,. Format: Gospel, christian, adult contemp, relg. Target aud: 18-35. ♦Sharon Johnson, pres.

Northumberland

WEGH(FM)— Aug 22, 1994: 107.3 mhz; 900 w. Ant 843 ft TL: N40 47 10 W76 41 49. Stereo. Hrs open: 24 Box 1070, Sunbury, 17801. Secondary address: 1227 County Line Rd., Selinsgrove 17870. Phone: (570) 286-5838. Phone: (570) 743-1841. Fax: (570) 743-7837.E-mail: eagle107@eagle107.com Web Site:www.eagle107.com Licensee: Sunbury Broadcasting Corp. Population served: 167,100 Natl. Rep: Roslin,. Rgnl rep: Dome. Format: Classic Hits. News staff: 4; News: one hr wkly. Target aud: 25-54. ♦Roger S Haddon Jr., CEO; Roger S. Haddon Jr., pres; Kevin Herr, opns mgr; Tricia Cease, gen sls mgr & mktg mgr; Amy Knight, prom dir; Rob Senter, progmg dir, mus dir.

Oil City

WGYI(FM)— May 1, 1957: 98.5 mhz; 20 kw. 299 ft TL: N41 25 04 W79 72 53. Stereo. Hrs open: Prog sep from AM BOX 908, 484 Allegheny Blvd, Franklin, 16323. Phone: (814) 676-5744. Fax: (814) 437-9372.E-mail: radio@zoominternet.com Licensee: Forever Broadcasting LLC. Population served: 180,000 Format: America's Best Country.

WKQW(AM)— Dec 1, 1986: 1120 khz; 1 kw-D. TL: N41 23 45 W79 39 53. Hrs open: 222 Seneca St., 16301. Phone: (814) 676-8254. Fax: (814) 677-4272.E-mail: traffic@wkqw.com Web Site:www.kqw.com Licensee: Clarion County Broadcasting Corp. (acq 4-8-2005; $540,000 with co-located FM). Population served: 65,000 Natl. Network: CBS Radio, . Natl. Rep: Dome,. Format: Oldies. News staff: one; News: 4 hrs wkly. Target aud: 25-54. ♦Tim Shaw, progmg dir; Mark Heim, news dir; Steve Truitt, traf mgr; Bill Hearst, disc jockey.

WKQW-FM— September 1992: 96.3 mhz; 6 kw. Ant 328 ft TL: N41 23 45 W79 39 53. Stereo. Hrs open: 24 222 Seneca St., 16301. Phone: (814) 676-8254. Fax: (814) 677-4272.E-mail: traffic@kqw.com Web Site:www.venangocountydailynews.com Licensee: Clarion County Broadcasting Corp. Population served: 120,000 Natl. Network: CBS Radio, . Rgnl rep: Dome & Assoc. Polner Law Office. Format: Adult contemp, loc info. News staff: one; News: 4 hrs wkly. ♦William Hearst, pres; Tim Shaw, progmg mgr; Mark Heim, news dir; Steve Truitt, traf mgr; Sammy Gordon, sls.

WOYL(AM)— Feb 14, 1946: 1340 khz; 1 kw-U, DA-D. TL: N41 25 04 W79 42 53. Hrs open: 6 AM-midnight Box 908, 484 Allegheny Blvd, Franklin, 16323. Phone: (814) 676-5744. Fax: (814) 437-9372.E-mail: radio@zoominternet.com Licensee: Forever Broadcasting LLC. Group owner: Forever Broadcasting (acq 7-20-00; grpsl). Population served: 15,033 Natl. Rep: Dome, Keystone (unwired net),. Format: MOR, news/talk. News staff: one. ♦Terry Deitz, gen mgr; Joe Elan, sls dir, gen sls mgr; Todd Adkins, progmg dir; Paul Joseph, news dir.

Oliver

WOGG(FM)— June 11, 1993: 94.9 mhz; 1.65 kw. Ant 1,233 ft TL: N39 52 11 W79 38 22. Stereo. Hrs open: 24 123 Blaine Rd., Brownsville, 15417. Phone: (724) 938-2000. Fax: (724) 938-7824.E-mail: jtrunzo@zoominternet.net Web Site:foggyland.com Licensee: Keymarket Licenses LLC. Group owner: Keymarket Communications LLC (acq 8-31-99; $2.875 million with WASP(AM) Brownsville). Population served: 2,500,000 Format: Country. News staff: one. Target aud: 25-54. ♦Gerald Getz, pres; Andrew Powaski, gen mgr, gen sls mgr; Jeffrey Trunzo, chief of engrg.

Olyphant

WBHD(FM)—Licensed to Olyphant. See Dunmore

WQOR(AM)— July 20, 1987: 750 khz; 1.6 kw-D. TL: N41 28 34 W75 29 41. Hrs open: Sunrise-sunset 6325 Sheridan Dr., Williamsville, NY, 14221. Phone: (716) 839-6117. Fax: (716) 839-0400. Web Site:www.holyfamily.ws Licensee: Holy Family Communications (group owner; acq 3-24-2003; $170,000). Population served: 750,000 Format: Catholic radio. ♦James Wright, pres.

Palmyra

WWKL(FM)— Sept 22, 1959: 92.1 mhz; 3.3 kw. Ant 300 ft TL: N40 19 35 W76 36 33. Stereo. Hrs open:
Rebroadcasts WTPA(FM) Mechanicsburg 100%.
Cumulus Media-WNNK FM-WTCY AM, 2300 Vartan Way, Harrisburg, 17110-9720. Phone: (717) 238-1041. Fax: (717) 234-4842.E-mail: info@hot92.com Web Site:www.hot92.com Licensee: Cumulus Licensing Corp. Group owner: Cumulus Media Inc. (acq 11-28-2000; grpsl). Population served: 500,000 Rgnl. Network: Radio Pa. Radio Pa. Wilkinson Barker Knauer. Format: CHR/ rhythmic. Target aud: 25-54. Spec prog: Relg 6 hrs, Sp 14 hrs, Hershey Bears hockey, Hershey Wildcats soccer wkly. ♦Ron Giovanniello, gen mgr; Karen Richards, sls dir; Todd Matthews, gen sls mgr; John O'Dea, progmg dir; Amy Warner, mus dir; Dave Supplee, chief of engrg.

Patton

WBXQ(FM)— 1991: 94.3 mhz; 2.1 kw. Ant 548 ft TL: N40 39 17 W78 40 34. Hrs open: 2513 6th Ave., Altoona, 16602. Phone: (814) 944-9320. Fax: (814) 944-9782. Web Site:www.wbxq.com Licensee: Sherlock Broadcasting Inc. (acq 3-95; $450,000; 6-26-95). Format: Country. Target aud: 35-65. ♦David Barger, gen mgr.

Pen Argyl

***WWPJ(FM)**— 2001: 89.5 mhz; 1 w horiz, 40 w vert. Ant 1,125 ft TL: N40 53 03 W75 15 43. Hrs open: 24
Rebroadcasts WWFM(FM) Trenton, NJ 100%.
Mercer County Community College, 1200 Old Trenton Rd., Trenton, NJ, 08690. Phone: (609) 587-8989.E-mail: wwfm@mccc.edu Licensee: Mercer County Community College. Format: Classical. ♦Jeffery Sekerka, gen mgr.

Philadelphia

KYW(AM)— 1921: 1060 khz; 50 kw-U, DA-1. TL: N40 06 12 W75 14 56. Stereo. Hrs open: 24 400 Market St, 10th floor, 19106. Phone: (215) 238-1060. Fax: (215) 238-4657.E-mail: newstips@kyw1060info.com Web Site:www.kyw1060.com Licensee: CBS Radio East Inc. Group owner: Infinity Broadcasting Corp. Population served: 4,500,000 Natl. Network: ABC, CBS, CNN Radio, . Natl. Rep: CBS Radio,. Leventhal Senter & Lerman. Wire Svc: AP Format: News. News staff: 34; News: 168 hrs wkly. Target aud: 25-54; adults. ♦David Yadgaroff, VP, gen mgr; Michael Berkowitz, natl sls mgr; Rich Iovanisci, rgnl sls mgr; Kyle Ruffin, mktg dir; Dee Patel, news dir; Frank Sippel, chief of engrg. Co-owned TV: KYW-TV affil.

WBEB(FM)— May 13, 1963: 101.1 mhz; 14 kw. Ant 941 ft TL: N40 02 21 W75 14 13. Stereo. Hrs open: 24 225 E City Ave, Suite 200, Bala Cynwyd, 19004. Phone: (610) 667-8400. Fax: (610) 667-6795. Web Site:www.b101radio.com Licensee: WEAZ-FM Radio Inc. (acq 3-9-2006; $85,158,226). Population served: 500,000 Natl. Rep: McGavren Guild,. Borsari & Paxson. Format: Adult contemp. Target aud: 25-54. ♦Blaise Howard, VP; William Boone, stn mgr; Bonnie Hoffman, prom mgr; Chuck Knight, progmg dir; Emily Scheivert, pub affrs dir; Chris Sarris, engrg dir, chief of engrg; Maribeth Hoban, traf mgr.

WBEN-FM— Mar 1, 1949: 95.7 mhz; 50 kw. Ant 500 ft TL: N40 03 33 W75 14 20. Stereo. Hrs open: 24 One Bala Plaza, Suite 424, Bala Cynwyd, 19004. Phone: (610) 771-0933. Fax: (610) 771-9690.E-mail: gdefrancesco@greaterphila.com Web Site:www.957benfm.com Licensee: Greater Philadelphia Radio Group. Group owner: Greater Media Inc. (acq 5-29-97; $41.8 million). Population served: 4,000,000 Shaw Pittman. Format: Adult hits. News: 3 hrs wkly. Target aud: 25-54; professional, upscale executives. ♦John Fullam, gen mgr; Bill Schultz, opns mgr; Bill Burns, gen sls mgr; Jules Riley, progmg dir.

WDAS-FM— 1959: 105.3 mhz; 3.3 kw. 870 ft TL: N40 02 30 W75 14 24. (CP: 16.3 kw). Stereo. Hrs open: Prog sep from AM 111 Presidential Blv, Suite 100, Bala Cynwyd, 19004. Phone: (610) 617-8500. Fax: (610) 617-8501.E-mail: info@wdasfm.com Web Site:www.wdas.fm.com Format: Black adult contemp. Target aud: 25-54.

WFIL(AM)— 1922: 560 khz; 5 kw-U, DA-2. TL: N40 05 42 W75 16 38. Hrs open: 24 117 Ridge Pike, Lafayette Hill, 19444. Phone: (610) 941-9560. Fax: (610) 828-8879.E-mail: wfil@wfil.com Web Site:www.wfil.com Licensee: Pennsylvania Media Associates Inc. Group owner: Salem Communications Corp. (acq 11-1-93; $4 million). Population served: 11,792,380 Natl. Network: Salem Radio Network, . Natl. Rep: Salem,. Borsari & Paxson. Format: Relg, Christian, talk. News: 2 hrs wkly. Target aud: 35-64; parents & grandparents. ♦Russ Whitnah, VP & gen mgr; Kevin Manna, opns dir; Carol Healey, gen sls mgr; Rolanda Myers, mktg dir, chief of engrg; Mark Daniels, mktg mgr, progmg mgr; Rene Tetro, chief of engrg.

WHAT(AM)— 1925: 1340 khz; 1 kw-U. TL: N40 00 06 W75 12 35. Hrs open: 10 Shurs Ln., Suite 204, 19127. Phone: (267) 285-5161. Fax: (267) 285-5185. Web Site:www.martiniloungeradio.com Licensee: Marconi Broadcasting Co. LLC Group owner: Inner City Broadcasting (acq 1-12-2007; $5 million). Population served: 194,806 Format: Standards. ♦Tom Kelly, pres & gen mgr; David Direnzo, gen sls mgr.

***WHYY-FM**— 1954: 90.9 mhz; 13.5 kw. 920 ft TL: N40 02 30 W75 14 24. Stereo. Hrs open: 24 150 N. 6th St., Independence Mall West, 19106. Phone: (215) 351-1200. Phone: (215) 351-9204. Fax: (215) 351-3352.E-mail: talkback@whyy.org Web Site:www.whyy.org Licensee: WHYY Inc. Population served: 3,987,600 Natl. Network: NPR, PRI, . Schwartz, Woods & Miller. Format: News, info. News staff: 7; News: 35 hrs wkly. Target aud: 35-49. Spec prog: Opera 4 hrs, folk 4 hrs, jazz 4 hrs wkly. ♦William J. Marrazzo, pres; Paul Gluck, gen mgr.

WIOQ(FM)— 1941: 102.1 mhz; 27 kw. 669 ft TL: N40 02 40 W75 14 30. Stereo. Hrs open: 24 One Bala Plaza, Suite 243, Bala Cynwyd, 19004. Phone: (610) 667-8100. Fax: (610) 668-4657. Web Site:www.q102philly.com Licensee: AMFM Radio Licenses LLC. Group owner: Clear Channel Communications Inc. (acq 8-30-00; grpsl). Population served: 4,065,300 Format: CHR. Target aud: 18-34; females & teens. Spec prog: Pub affrs. ♦Rich Lewis, VP, gen mgr; Cassandra Banko, gen sls mgr; Lisa Acchione, mktg dir; Jeff Jordan, prom dir; Brian Bridgman, progmg dir; Marian Newsome, mus dir; Wendy McClure, pub affrs dir; Michael Guidotti, chief of engrg; Chris Marino, disc jockey.

WIP(AM)— Mar 16, 1922: 610 khz; 5 kw-U, DA-1. TL: N39 51 56 W75 06 43. Hrs open: 2 Bala Plaza, Bala Cynwyd, 19004. Phone: (610) 949-7800. Fax: (610) 949-7880.E-mail: info@610wip.com Web Site:www.610wip.com Licensee: CBS Radio Inc. of Philadelphia. Group owner: Infinity Broadcasting Corp. (acq 8-12-93; 8-30-93). Population served: 6,000,000 Natl. Network: Westwood One, . Natl. Rep: CBS Radio,. Format: All sports. ♦Cecil R. Forster Jr., VP, gen mgr; Tom Bigby, progmg mgr.

WISX(FM)— Nov 11, 1959: 106.1 mhz; 22 kw. Ant 740 ft TL: N40 04 58 W75 10 54. Stereo. Hrs open: 111 Presidential Blvd., Suite 100, Bala Cynwyd, 19004. Phone: (610) 508-1200. Phone: (610) 784-3333. Fax: (610) 784-0501.E-mail: info@phillys1061.com Web Site:www.phillys1061.com Licensee: AMFM Radio Licenses LLC. Group owner: Clear Channel Communications Inc. (acq 8-30-2000;

grpsl). Population served: 750,000 Natl. Rep: Christal,. Latham & Watkins. Format: Adult contemp. Target aud: 25-54.

***WKDU(FM)—** 1970: 91.7 mhz; 110 w. 155 ft TL: N39 57 36 W75 11 27. Stereo. Hrs open: 24 3210 Chestnut St., 19104. Phone: (215) 895-5920. Phone: (215) 895-5917. Fax: (215) 895-1050. Web Site:www.wkdu.org Licensee: Drexel University. Population served: 2,500,000 Format: Progsv, alternative rock, free format. Target aud: General. Spec prog: International 12 hrs, rhythm & blues 3 hrs, gospel 4 hrs, Israeli 3 hrs, new age 2 hrs, metal 4 hrs, Black 8 hrs wkly. ♦Evan Caposerri, gen mgr; Casey Ross, progmg dir; Ryan McIntyre, pub affrs dir; Jim Cavanaugh, chief of engrg.

WMGK(FM)— 1942: 102.9 mhz; 8.9 kw. Ant 1,148 ft TL: N40 02 21 W75 14 13. Stereo. Hrs open: 24 Prog sep from AM One Bala Plaza, Suite 339, Bala Cynwyd, 19004. Phone: (610) 667-8500. Fax: (610) 771-9692.E-mail: ckirchner@wmgk.com Web Site:www.wmgk.com Licensee: Greater Philadelphia Radio Inc. Population served: 1,800,000 Format: Classic rock. ♦Chris Kirchner, gen sls mgr; Ed Marshall, prom dir.

WMMR(FM)— Apr 20, 1942: 93.3 mhz; 18 kw. 827 ft TL: N39 57 09 W75 10 05. Stereo. Hrs open: 24 One Bala Plaza, Suite 424, Bala Cynwyd, 19004. Phone: (610) 771-0933. Fax: (610) 771-9710. Web Site:www.wmmr.com Licensee: Greater Philadelphia Radio Inc. Group owner: Greater Media Inc. (acq 7-23-97; grpsl). Natl. Network: Westwood One, . Natl. Rep: McGavren Guild,. Format: Main stream rock. News staff: one; News: 5 hrs wkly. Target aud: 25-54; suburban rockers. ♦Richard D. Feinblatt, sr VP; John Fullam, gen mgr; Paul Blake, gen sls mgr; Scott Segelbeum, mktg dir; Bill Weston, progmg dir; Ken Zipeto, mus dir; Larry Paulauski, chief of engrg; Queen Chandler, traf mgr.

WNTP(AM)— 1923: 990 khz; 50 kw-D, 10 kw-N, DA-2. TL: N40 05 43 W75 16 37. Hrs open: 24 117 Ridge Pike, Lafayette Hill, 19444. Phone: (610) 940-0990. Fax: (610) 828-8879.E-mail: wntp@wntp.com Web Site:www.wntp.com Licensee: Pennsylvania Media Associates Inc. Group owner: Salem Communications Corp. (acq 1994; $3.5 million grpsl). Population served: 7,927,724 Natl. Network: Salem Radio Network, . Borsari & Paxson. Format: News/talk. News: 4 times per hr. Target aud: 35-64; Adults. Spec prog: Sports, Sp. ♦Russ Whitnah, VP & gen mgr; Kevin Manna, opns mgr; Carol Healey, gen sls mgr; Rolanda Myers, mktg dir; Mark Daniels, mktg mgr, progmg mgr; Rene Tetro, chief of engrg.

WNWR(AM)— July 11, 1947: 1540 khz; 50 kw-D, DA. TL: N40 02 46 W75 14 15. (CP: COL Bala Cynwyd). Hrs open: 200 Monument Rd., Suite 6, Bala Cynwyd, 19004. Phone: (610) 664-6780. Fax: (610) 664-8529. Web Site:www.wnwr.com Licensee: Global Radio L.L.C. (acq 6-95; $1.4 million). Population served: 250,000 Natl. Rep: Roslin,. Taylor, Thiemann & Aitken. Format: Var/div, ethnic multicultural. Target aud: 25-54. ♦Jim Weitzman, pres; Sam Speiser, gen mgr, stn mgr; Shawn Laughlin, opns mgr.

WOGL(FM)— May 16, 1944: 98.1 mhz; 9.6 kw. Ant 1,109 ft TL: N40 02 29.6 W75 14 11.4. Stereo. Hrs open: 24 Prog sep from AM Two Plaza, Suite 800, Bala Cynwyd, 19004. Phone: (610) 668-5900. Fax: (610) 668-5977.E-mail: questions@wogl.com Web Site:www.wogl.com Licensee: CBS Radio East Inc. Population served: 4,000,000 Leventhal, Senter & Lerman. Format: Hits of the 60s & 70s. News staff: one; News: 1.25 hrs wkly. Target aud: 25-54. ♦James F. Loftus, gen mgr; Kerry Mulvey, gen sls mgr; Diane Santilippo, natl sls mgr; Cindy Webster, mktg dir; Anne Gress, progmg dir; Tommy McCarthy, mus dir; Dave Skalish, chief of engrg; LeeAnn Smith, traf mgr.

***WPEB(FM)—** May 15, 1981: 88.1 mhz; 1 w. Ant 49 ft TL: N39 57 33 W75 12 13. Hrs open: 4134 Lancaster Ave., 3rd Fl., 19104. Phone: (215) 387-6155.E-mail: info@radiovolta.org Web Site:www.radiovolta.org Licensee: West Philadelphia Educational Broadcasting Foundation. Population served: 1,500,000 Format: Div. Target aud: General.

WPEN(AM)— April 1929: 950 khz; 5 kw-U, DA-N. TL: N39 58 28 W75 16 30. Stereo. Hrs open: 24 One Bala Plaza, Mail Stop 429, Bala Cynwyd, 19004-1428. Phone: (610) 667-8500. Fax: (610) 771-9692.E-mail: bdeblois@950espn.com Web Site:sr950.com Licensee: Greater Philadelphia Radio Inc. Group owner: Greater Media Inc. (acq 1-6-75). Population served: 4,000,000 Natl. Network: ESPN Radio, . Format: Sports. ♦John Fullam, gen mgr; Bob DeBlois, stn mgr; Paul Blake, sls dir; Ralph Nieves, gen sls mgr; Mike McMonagle, prom dir; Matt Nahigian, progmg dir, progmg mgr.

WPHE(AM)—See Phoenixville

WPHT(AM)— 1922: 1210 khz; 50 kw-U. TL: N39 58 46 W74 59 13. Hrs open: Two Plaza, Suite 800, Bala Cynwyd, 19004. Phone: (610) 668-5800. Fax: (610) 667-5886.E-mail: talkradio1210@cbs.com Web Site:www.thebigtalker1210.com Licensee: CBS Radio East Inc. Group owner: Infinity Broadcasting Corp. (acq 8-58). Population served: 4,000,000 Natl. Network: CBS, Westwood One, . Natl. Rep: CBS Radio,. Leventhal, Senter & Lerman PLLC. Format: Talk. News: 2. Target aud: 25-64; adults. ♦David Yadgaroff, gen mgr; Mike Baldini, stn mgr; Grace Blazer, progmg dir; Dave Skalish, chief of engrg; Jennifer Miller, traf mgr.

WRDW-FM— 1957: 96.5 mhz; 17 kw. Ant 866 ft TL: N40 02 21 W75 14 13. Stereo. Hrs open: 24 555 City Line Ave., Ste. 330, Bala Cynwyd, 19004. Phone: (610) 667-9000. Fax: (610) 667-2972. Web Site:www.wired965.com Licensee: WDAS License L.P. Group owner: Beasley Broadcast Group (acq 3-11-97). Population served: 7,218,400 Natl. Network: Wall Street, . Natl. Rep: D & R Radio,. Fisher, Wayland, Cooper, Leader & Zaragoza. Format: CHR. Target aud: 18 plus; general. ♦Bruce Beasley, CEO, chmn, pres, progmg dir; Lynn Bruder, gen mgr; Rob Keegan, gen sls mgr; Don Melnyk, chief of engrg.

WRFF(FM)— February 1965: 104.5 mhz; 12.5 kw. Ant 1,008 ft TL: N40 02 30 W75 14 24. Stereo. Hrs open: 24 111 President Blvd., Suite 100, Bala Cynwyd, 19004. Phone: (610) 784-3333. Fax: (610) 784-2011. Web Site:www.radio1045.com Licensee: AMFM Radio Licenses LLC. Group owner: Clear Channel Communications Inc. (acq 8-30-2000; grpsl). Population served: 4,114,800 Format: Rock. News staff: one. ♦L. Lowry Mays, CEO; Manuel Rodriguez, VP; Ron Decastro, sls dir; Becki West, gen sls mgr; Shelvia Williams, prom dir; Brian Check, progmg dir; Margo Marano, mus dir; Jennifer Ryan, news dir, pub affrs dir; Sandra Johnson, traf mgr.

***WRTI(FM)—** July 9, 1953: 90.1 mhz; 12.5 kw. 1,010 ft TL: N40 02 21 W75 14 13. Stereo. Hrs open: 24 1509 Cecil B. Moore Blvd., 3rd Fl., 19121. Phone: (215) 204-8405. Fax: (215) 204-7027.E-mail: comments@wrti.org Web Site:www.wrti.org Licensee: Temple University of The Commonwealth System of Higher Education. Population served: 7,500,000 Natl. Network: NPR, PRI, . Rgnl. Network: Radio Pa. Radio Pa. Wire Svc: AP Format: Class, jazz. News staff: one; News: 15 hrs wkly. Target aud: 30-65. ♦David S. Conant, CEO, gen mgr; Vic Scarpato, CFO; William P. Johnston, stn mgr; Tobias Poole, opns dir; Patricia Prevost, dev dir; Rick Torpey, natl sls mgr; Porsche Blakey, mktg mgr; Jack Moore, progmg dir; Windsor Johnston, news dir; Jeff DePolo, chief of engrg; Lorna Nixon, traf mgr; Lesley Valdes, mus critic.

WTMR(AM)—See Camden, NJ

WUBA(AM)— 1923: 1480 khz; 5 kw-D, 1 kw-N, DA-2. TL: N39 59 53 W75 12 43. Hrs open: 24 111 Presidential Blv, Suite 100, Bala Cynwyd, 19004. Phone: (610) 617-8500. Fax: (610) 617-8501. Web Site:www.rumba1045.com Licensee: AMFM Radio Licenses LLC. Group owner: Clear Channel Communications Inc. (acq 8-30-2000; grpsl). Population served: 560,000 Format: Sp. ♦Joseph Tamburro, gen mgr, gen sls mgr & progmg dir.

WURD(AM)— July 23, 1958: 900 khz; 1 kw-D, 105 w-N, DA-2. TL: N39 55 02 W75 13 18. Hrs open: 1341 N. Delaware Ave., Suite 300, 19125. Phone: (215) 425-7875. Fax: (215) 634-6003.E-mail: kanderson@levescomm.com Licensee: Levas Communications LLC Group owner: Levas Communications LLC (acq 4-30-2003;. $4.25 million). Population served: 4,334,000 Natl. Network: CNN Radio, . Natl. Rep: McGavren Guild,. Womble, Carlyle, Sandridge & Rice. Format: Urban talk. Spec prog: Gospel 9 hrs, It 3 hrs wkly. ♦Art Camiolo, pres; Cody Anderson, gen mgr; Steve Ballard, opns dir; Bill Anderson, progmg dir; Kia Long, traf mgr.

WUSL(FM)— 1961: 98.9 mhz; 18 kw. 830 ft TL: N40 02 31 W75 14 11. Stereo. Hrs open: 24 111 Presidential Blvd., Suite 100, Bala Cynwyd, 19004. Phone: (610) 784-3333. Fax: (610) 784-0507. Web Site:www.power99.com Licensee: Clear Channel Radio Licenses, Inc. Group owner: Clear Channel Communications Inc. (acq 8-30-00; grpsl). Population served: 4,729,000 Latham & Watkins. Format: Urban contemp. News staff: 2; News: 4 hrs wkly. Target aud: 18-49. Spec prog: Gospel 4 hrs wkly. ♦Richard Lewis, VP, gen sls mgr & progmg dir.

WWDB(AM)— 1925: 860 khz; 10 kw-D, DA. TL: N40 09 15 W75 22 10. (CP: 500 w-N, DA-2). Hrs open: Daytime 555 City Line Ave., Suite 330, Bala Cynwyd, 19004. Phone: (610) 822-1321. Phone: (610) 822-1320. Fax: (610) 667-5978. Web Site:www.wwdbam.com Licensee: Beasley Broadcasting of Eastern Pennsylvania Inc. Group owner: Beasley Broadcast Group (acq 9-9-86; $2.4 million;8-11-86). Population served: 400,000 Format: Talk. Target aud: 18-49. ♦Bruce Gilbert, gen mgr; Tim Halloran, opns mgr.

***WXPN(FM)—** April 1957: 88.5 mhz; 5 kw. Ant 918 ft TL: N40 02 36 W75 14 33. Stereo. Hrs open: 24 3025 Walnut St., 19104. Phone: (215) 898-6677. Fax: (215) 898-0707.E-mail: wxpndesk@xpn.org Web Site:www.xpn.org Licensee: Trustees of the University of Pennsylvania. Population served: 4,315,028 Natl. Network: PRI, NPR, . Levanthol Senter & Lerman. Format: Adult alternative. News: 3 hrs wkly. Target aud: 25-54; educated. Spec prog: Children 5 hrs, folk 5 hrs wkly. ♦Roger LaMay, gen mgr; Quyen Shanahan, dev VP, mktg dir; Jay Ricci, sls VP; Tom Mara, gen sls mgr; Debby Seitz, prom mgr, spec ev coord; Bruce Warren, progmg dir, mus critic; Dan Reed, mus dir; Bob Bumbera, news dir, local news ed, sports cmtr; Jay Goldman, engrg dir; nda Myers, traf mgr; Deb D'Alessandro, women's int ed; Ali Costellini, disc jockey.

WXTU(FM)— September 1958: 92.5 mhz; 15 kw. Ant 915 ft TL: N40 02 19 W75 14 14. Stereo. Hrs open: 24 555 City Line Ave., Suite 330, Bala Cynwyd, 19004. Phone: (610) 667-9000. Fax: (610) 667-1355.E-mail: comments@925xtu.com Web Site:www.925xtu.com Licensee: Beasley Broadcasting of Eastern Pennsylvania Inc. Group owner: Beasley Broadcast Group (acq 7-83; $6 million;7-11-83). Natl. Rep: D & R Radio,. Format: Contemp country. Spec prog: Sundays 6am-6:30am-Philadelphia Focus. ♦Bruce Beasley, pres, VP; Natalie Conner, VP, gen mgr; Mark Vizza, mktg dir; Bob McKay, progmg dir; Don Melnyk, chief of engrg; Andie Summers, disc jockey.

WYSP(FM)— August 1971: 94.1 mhz; 9.6 kw. Ant 1,109 ft TL: N40 02 29.6 W75 14 11.5. Stereo. Hrs open: 400 MarketnSt, 9th Fl, 19106. Phone: (215) 625-9460. Fax: (215) 625-6560.E-mail: info@94wysp.com Web Site:www.94wysp.com Licensee: CBS Radio East Inc. (acq 11-1-81; grpsl; 9-28-81). Natl. Network: Westwood One, . Natl. Rep: CBS Radio,. Format: Rock. ♦Peter Kleiner, gen mgr; Gil Edwards, progmg dir.

Philipsburg

WJOW(FM)— March 1989: 105.9 mhz; 710 w. Ant 951 ft TL: N40 47 34 W78 10 29. Stereo. Hrs open: 24 1884 Port Matilda Hwy., Radio Park, 16866. Phone: (814) 272-1320. Fax: (814) 342-9742.E-mail: buzz@buzzfm.com Web Site:www.buzzfm.com Licensee: Magnum Broadcasting Inc. Population served: 350,000 Format: Modern rock/alternative. News: 2.5 hrs wkly. Target aud: 18-49; men & women. ♦Austin Davis, progmg dir, disc jockey; Sherry Flick, local news ed; Tor Michaels, news rptr; Jill Gleeson, disc jockey.

WPHB(AM)— June 1, 1956: 1260 khz; 5 kw-D, 34 w-N. TL: N40 53 39 W78 11 51. Hrs open: 24 1884 Port Matilda Hwy., Radio Park, 16866. Phone: (814) 342-2300. Fax: (814) 342-WPHB/9742.E-mail: wphb1260@gmail.com Web Site:www.wphbradio.com Licensee: Magnum Broadcasting Inc. (acq 11-24-2004; $2,022,527 with co-located FM). Population served: 50,000 Natl. Network: CNN Radio, . Rgnl. Network: Radio Pa. Radio Pa. Rgnl rep: Dome & Assoc Haley, Bader, Potts. Format: Classic country & news/talk, sports. Target aud: Men & women; generally 25+. Spec prog: Bluegrass 4 hrs, polka 6 hrs, Gospel 6 hrs, big band 5 hrs wkly. ♦Michael M. Stapleford, pres; Laura Shore Mack, gen mgr; Cliff Mack, chief of opns; Marian Kovach, gen sls mgr; Jason Torrance, prom dir; C.J. Daniels, progmg dir; Sherry Flick, pub affrs dir; Joe Portelli, chief of engrg; Mary Beth Thompson, traf mgr; Tor Michaels, news rptr; Bud O'Brien, sports cmtr; Sheldon Sharpless, disc jockey.

Phoenixville

WPHE(AM)— Aug 23, 1978: 690 khz; 1 kw-D, DA. TL: N40 08 08 W75 33 37. Hrs open: Box 46327, Philadelphia, 19160. Secondary address: 321 W. Sedgley Ave., Philadelphia 19140. Phone: (215) 291-7532. Fax: (215) 739-1337.E-mail: rs@radiosalvation.com Web Site:www.radiosalvation.com Licensee: Salvation Broadcasting Co. (acq 12-1-88). Population served: 400,000 Format: Sp, relg, div. Spec prog: Por 3 hrs wkly. ♦Sarrial Salva, pres; Mr. Sarrial Salva, gen mgr; Isabel Salva, sls dir; Juan Izquierdo, progmg dir; Juan Pydeck, chief of engrg.

Pittsburgh

KDKA(AM)— Nov 2, 1920: 1020 khz; 50 kw-U. TL: N40 33 33 W79 57 11. Hrs open: 24 One Gateway Center, 15222. Phone: (412) 575-2320.E-mail: madams@kdka.com Web Site:www.KDKAradio.com Licensee: Infinity Broadcasting East Inc. Group owner: Infinity Broadcasting Corp. Population served: 640,000 Natl. Network: AP Network News, Premiere Radio Networks, Westwood One, CBS Radio, . Natl. Rep: CBS Radio,. Wire Svc: AP Wire Svc: Accu-Weather Format: News/talk. News staff: 35; News: 75 hrs wkly. Target aud: P25-54. ♦Michael J. Young, VP, gen mgr; Marshall Adams, gen sls mgr, progmg dir; Amy Mauk, prom dir; Dan Wonders, news dir, edit mgr; Vic Pasquarelli, engrg dir & chief of engrg; Jeff Hathhorn, local news ed.

KQV(AM)— Nov 19, 1919: 1410 khz; 5 kw-U, DA-2. TL: N40 31 17 W80 00 34. Hrs open: 24 Centre City Tower, 650 Smithfield St., Suite 620, 15222. Phone: (412) 562-5900. Phone: (412) 562-5960. Fax: (412) 562-5936. Fax: (412) 563-5603.E-mail: kqvnews@kqv.com Web Site:www.kqv.com Licensee: Calvary Inc. (acq 12-1-82; $1.75 million; 1-3-83). Population served: 1,250,000 Natl. Network: Wall Street, AP Radio, . Radio Pa. Wire Svc: AP Format: Newsradio. News staff: 15; News: 168 hrs wkly. Target aud: 35 plus; affluent, info-oriented adults.NFL football (regular season, playoffs & Superbowl), Notre Dame football, Duquesne University men's basketball, MSA Sports

Network (high school sports), When Radio Was, Imagination Theater, Twilight Zone, Mystery Theater ♦Robert W. Dickey Sr., pres, gen mgr; Susan Selby, chief of opns; Judith Ross, gen sls mgr; Frank Gottlieb, news dir; Steve Conti, chief of engrg.

WAMO(AM)—(Millvale, Aug 1, 1948: 860 khz; 1 kw-D, 830 w-N, DA-2. TL: N40 29 27 W79 58 55. Hrs open: 24 960 Penn Ave., Suite 200, 15222. Phone: (412) 456-4064. Fax: (412) 391-3559.E-mail: wamo@wamo.com Web Site:www.wamo.com Licensee: McL/McM Pennsylvania LLC. (acq 3-1-73). Population served: 40,200 Natl. Network: American Urban, . Natl. Rep: McGavren Guild,. Fletcher, Heald & Hildreth, P.L.C. Format: Smooth rhythm and blues, classic soul. ♦Ronald Davenport Sr., chmn; Ronald Davenport Jr., pres; Michael L. Davenport, gen mgr; Kathy Gersha, opns VP; Mickey Baker, natl sls mgr; Jon Plesser, rgnl sls mgr, mus dir; Laura Varner-Norman, mktg mgr; Tammy Sadler, prom dir; George Cook, progmg dir; Kode Wred, mus dir; Tene Croom, news dir & pub affrs dir; Bob Sharkey, chief of engrg.

WAMO-FM—(Beaver Falls, 1960: 106.7 mhz; 37 kw. Ant 554 ft TL: N40 37 11 W80 05 36. Stereo. Hrs open: 24 960 Penn Ave., Suite 200, 15222. Phone: (412) 456-4064. Fax: (412) 391-3559.E-mail: mdouglass@sbcol.com Web Site:www.wamo.com Licensee: McL/McM Pennsylvania LLC. (group owner). Population served: 235,800 Natl. Network: American Urban, . Natl. Rep: McGavren Guild,. Fletcher, Heald & Hildreth. Format: Urban & hip hop. News: 2 hrs wkly. ♦Ronald Davenport Jr., pres; Michael Douglass, gen mgr; Kathy Gersna, opns VP; Mickey Baker, natl sls mgr; Jon Plesser, rgnl sls mgr; Tammy Sadler, prom dir; Ron Atkins, progmg dir; Tene Croom, news dir; Bob Sharkey, chief of engrg.

WBGG(AM)— 1932: 970 khz; 5 kw-U, DA-2. TL: N40 30 30 W80 00 30. Hrs open: 24 200 Fleet St., 15220. Phone: (412) 937-1441. Fax: (412) 937-0323. Web Site:www.fox970.com Licensee: AMFM Radio Licenses L.L.C. Group owner: Clear Channel Communications Inc. (acq 8-30-2000; grpsl). Population served: 550,000 Natl. Network: Fox Sports, . Format: Sports. ♦John Rohm, gen mgr; Fred Traynor, gen sls mgr.

WBZW-FM— July 19, 1948: 93.7 mhz; 41 kw. Ant 550 ft TL: N40 26 28 W80 01 32. Stereo. Hrs open: 651 Holiday Dr., Suite 310, Foster Plaza Bldg 5, 15220. Phone: (412) 920-9400. Fax: (412) 920-9444.E-mail: wbzw@cbfradio.com Web Site:www.b94.com Licensee: CBS Radio Holdings Inc. Group owner: Infinity Broadcasting Corp. (acq 11-13-98; grpsl). Population served: 625,000 Format: Hit music. ♦Joel Hollander, pres; Jacques Tortoroli, CFO; Scott Herman, exec VP; Michael Young, VP, gen mgr; Keith Clark, opns VP; Norm Slemenda, gen sls mgr; Brandon Davis, prom dir; Shelley Duffy, news dir & pub affrs dir; Chris Hudak, chief of engrg.

WDSY-FM— September 1962: 107.9 mhz; 17.5 kw. Ant 827 ft TL: N40 28 20 W79 59 41. Stereo. Hrs open: Foster Five, 651 Holiday Dr., 15220. Phone: (412) 920-9400. Fax: (412) 920-9449.E-mail: info@wdsy.com Web Site:www.y108.com Licensee: Infinity Radio Holdings Inc. Group owner: Infinity Broadcasting Corp. (acq 12-14-00; grpsl). Population served: 2,019,400 Natl. Network: Westwood One, . Natl. Rep: Katz Radio,. Leventhal, Senter & Lerman, P.L.L.C. Format: Country. Target aud: 25-54; general. ♦Joel Hollander, pres; Jacques Tortoroli, CFO; Scott Herman, exec VP; Don Oyleaar, VP; Don Oylear, gen mgr; Keith Clark, opns VP, opns dir; Christine Fallon-McKenna, gen sls mgr, news dir; Keith Belden, natl sls mgr; Norm Slemanda, rgnl sls mgr, traf mgr; Michael Young, mktg mgr, chief of engrg; Jane O'Malia, prom dir; Stoney Richards, mus dir.

***WDUQ(FM)**— Dec 15, 1949: 90.5 mhz; 25 kw. 480 ft TL: N40 25 52 W80 00 26. Stereo. Hrs open: 24 600 Forbes Ave., 15282-0001. Phone: (412) 396-6030. Fax: (412) 396-5061.E-mail: info@wduq.org Web Site:www.wduq.org Licensee: Duquesne University. Natl. Network: NPR, PRI, . Natl. Rep: Interep,. Cohn & Marks. Format: Jazz, news, pub affrs,. News staff: 5; News: 47 hrs wkly. Educated, moderately affluent. ♦Scott Hanley, gen mgr; Helen Wigger, opns dir; Fred Serrino, dev dir; Mary Lloyd, sls dir; Cynthia Ference-Kelly, mktg dir, prom dir; Shaunna Morrison, mus dir; Kevin Gavin, news dir; Chuck Leavens, engrg dir.

WDVE(FM)— May 10, 1962: 102.5 mhz; 55 kw. 820 ft TL: N40 29 38 W80 01 09. Stereo. Hrs open: 200 Fleet St., 4th Fl., 15220. Phone: (412) 937-1441. Fax: (412) 937-0323.E-mail: info@dve.com Web Site:www.dve.com Licensee: Capstar TX L.P. Group owner: Clear Channel Communications Inc. (acq 8-00; grpsl). Population served: 2,000,000 Natl. Rep: Christal,. Format: News, all talk. News staff: one. Target aud: 25-54. ♦Missy Gawaldo, gen sls mgr.

WEAE(AM)— May 1922: 1250 khz; 5 kw-U, DA-N. TL: N40 23 50 W79 57 43. Hrs open: 24 400 Ardmore Blvd., 15221. Phone: (412) 731-1250. Fax: (412) 244-4596. Web Site:www.1250ESPN.com Licensee: Sports Radio Group LLC. Group owner: ABC Inc. (acq 4-26-99; $5 million). Population served: 800,000 Natl. Network: ESPN Radio, . Natl. Rep: ABC Radio Sales,. Format: Sports, talk. Target aud: Men 25-54. Spec prog: Penn State University football & basketball. ♦Mike Thompson, pres, gen mgr; Nanci Rich, gen sls mgr; David Waugaman, natl sls mgr; Greg Plumb, prom dir; Jim Graci, progmg dir; Thad Mazur, engrg mgr; Michelle Freeman, traf mgr.

WEDO(AM)—See McKeesport

WJAS(AM)— Oct 19, 1921: 1320 khz; 5 kw-U, DA-N. TL: N40 25 11 W79 54 38. (CP: 7 kw-D, 3.3 kw-N, DA-2. TL: N40 28 46 W79 54 12). Hrs open: 900 Parish St., 15220. Phone: (412) 875-4800. Phone: (412) 875-9500. Fax: (412) 875-9570. Web Site:www.1320wjas.com Licensee: Renda Broadcasting Corp. (group owner; (acq 7-16-85; $700,000; 12-17-84). Population served: 1,821,000 Format: Big band, nostalgia, MOR. Target aud: 35 plus; older, upscale. Spec prog: Big band jump, Frank Sinatra 2 hrs wkly. ♦Anthony F. Renda, pres; Lawrence Weiss, gen mgr; David Pavlic, gen sls mgr; Chris Shovlin, prom dir; Mike McGann, progmg dir; Phil Lenz, chief of engrg.

WKHB(AM)—(Irwin, Oct 28, 1934: 620 khz; 5.5 kw-D, 50 w-N. TL: N40 17 20 W79 42 04. Stereo. Hrs open: 24 1918 Lincoln Hwy., North Versailles, 15137. Phone: (412) 823-7000. Licensee: Broadcast Communications Inc. (group owner; (acq 10-9-96; $300,000). Population served: 2,481,152 Rgnl. Network: Radio Pa. Format: Var. Target aud: Adults. ♦Ashley R. Stevens, VP; Robert M. Stevens, pres & gen mgr; Barry Banker, stn mgr; Clark Ingram, opns mgr.

WKST-FM— Aug 8, 1960: 96.1 mhz; 44 kw. 522 ft TL: N40 23 49 W79 57 43. Stereo. Hrs open: 200 Fleet St., 4th Fl., 15220. Phone: (412) 937-1441. Fax: (412) 937-0323.E-mail: info@kissfm961.com Web Site:www.kissfm961.com Licensee: Capstar TX L.P. Group owner: Clear Channel Communications Inc. (acq 8-30-00; grpsl). Format: CHR. ♦Missy Gawaldo, gen sls mgr.

WLFP(AM)—See Braddock

WLTJ(FM)— Apr 4, 1942: 92.9 mhz; 47 kw. Ant 890 ft TL: N40 29 38 W80 01 09. Hrs open: 24 650 Smith Field St., Suite 2200, 15222. Phone: (412) 316-3342. Fax: (412) 316-3388.E-mail: info@wltj.com Web Site:q929fm.com Licensee: WPNT Inc. (acq 4-84; $3 million; 3-19-84). Population served: 2,002,000 Rgnl. Network: Metronews Radio Net. Natl. Rep: McGavren Guild,. Format: Lite rock. Target aud: 25-54; affluent, professional, working public. ♦Saul Frischling, pres; Greg Frischling, gen mgr; Chris Kohan, gen sls mgr; Vicki Wolfe, prom dir; Chuck Stevens, progmg dir; Amy Crago, news dir; Paul Carroll, chief of engrg.

WORD-FM— 1948: 101.5 mhz; 48 kw. 505 ft TL: N40 29 02 W79 59 34. Stereo. Hrs open: 24 Seven Parkway Ctr., Suite 625, 15220. Phone: (412) 937-1500. Fax: (412) 937-1576.E-mail: word@wordfm.com Web Site:www.wordfm.com Licensee: Pennsylvania Media Associates Inc. Group owner: Salem Communications Corp. Population served: 520,117 Format: Christian. Target aud: 25-49. ♦Chuck Gratner, CEO, gen mgr; Randy Dietterich, chmn, chief of engrg; Kenny Woods, opns mgr, progmg dir; Smitty Boros, gen sls mgr; Shaun Pierce, news dir; Lisa Cook, traf mgr.

WPGB(FM)— Feb 4, 1963: 104.7 mhz; 13 kw. Ant 827 ft TL: N40 28 20 W79 59 41. Stereo. Hrs open: 24 200 Fleet, 4th Fl., 15220. Phone: (412) 937-1441. Fax: (412) 937-0323.E-mail: info@wpgb.com Web Site:www.wpgb.com Licensee: Capstar TX L.P. Group owner: Clear Channel Communications Inc. (acq 8-30-00; grpsl). Population served: 2,500,000 Natl. Network: Fox News Radio, . Wire Svc: AP Format: News, all talk, sports. News staff: 0; News: 5 hrs wkly. Target aud: 25-54; white collar workers. ♦John Rohm, VP; Fred Traynor, gen sls mgr, chief of engrg; Jay Bohannon, progmg dir.

WPIT(AM)— 1947: 730 khz; 5 kw-D. TL: N40 29 02 W79 59 34. Hrs open: Seven Parkway Ctr., Suite 625, 15220. Phone: (412) 937-1500. Fax: (412) 937-1576.E-mail: wpit@wpitam.com Web Site:www.wpitam.com Licensee: Pennsylvania Media Associates Inc. (Acq 12-2-92; $6.5 million;12-21-92). Format: Christian.

***WPTS-FM**— Aug 26, 1984: 92.1 mhz; 16 w. 462 ft TL: N40 26 39 W79 57 12. Stereo. Hrs open: 24 Univ. of Pittsburgh, 411 William Pitt Union, 15260. Phone: (412) 648-7990. Fax: (412) 648-7988.E-mail: wpts@freelist.org Web Site:www.wpts.pitt.edu Licensee: University of Pittsburgh. (acq 8-26-84). Population served: 30,000 Format: Eclectic, contemp, progsv. News staff: 3; News: 10 hrs wkly. Target aud: General. ♦Gregory Weston, gen mgr.

***WQED-FM**— Jan 25, 1973: 89.3 mhz; 43 kw. Ant 500 ft TL: N40 26 46 W79 57 51. Stereo. Hrs open: 24 4802 5th Ave., 15213. Phone: (412) 622-1300. Fax: (412) 622-1488.E-mail: radio@wqed.org Web Site:www.wqed.org Licensee: WQED Multimedia. Population served: 2,500,000 Natl. Network: NPR, PRI, . Schwartz, Woods & Miller. Format: Class. News: 5 hrs wkly. Target aud: 35-64; educated, influential, professional, community leaders, mid to high income. ♦George L. Miles Jr., pres; B.J. Leber, sr VP, stn mgr, prom VP; Michelle Pagano Heck, gen mgr; Ted Sohier, opns mgr, disc jockey; Lilli Mosco, dev VP, dev mgr; Rick Vaccarielli, sls dir; Karen Colbert, mktg dir; Gigi Saladna, prom mgr, progmg mgr; George Hazimanois, adv dir; Paul Byers, chief of engrg; Bob Walsh, disc jockey. Co-owned TV: *WQED(TV) affil.

***WRCT(FM)**— April 1974: 88.3 mhz; 1.75 kw. 53 ft TL: N40 26 39 W79 56 37. Stereo. Hrs open: 24 One WRCT Plaza, 5000 Forbes Ave., 15213. Phone: (412) 621-0728. Phone: (412) 621-9728. Fax: (412) 268-6549.E-mail: info@wrct.org Web Site:www.wrct.org Licensee: Carnegie Mellon Student Government Corp. Population served: l,500,000 Putbrese, Hunsaker & Trent. Format: Div, educ. News: 10 hrs wkly. Target aud: General. Spec prog: Black 12 hrs, class 3 hrs, country 3 hrs, folk 3 hrs, experimental 12 hrs, jazz 18 hrs wkly. ♦Matt Siko, gen mgr; Pauline Law, progmg dir.

WRRK(FM)—See Braddock

WSHH(FM)— Mar 8, 1948: 99.7 mhz; 10.5 kw. Ant 928 ft TL: N40 27 47 W80 00 17. Stereo. Hrs open: 900 Parish St., 15220. Phone: (412) 875-4800. Phone: (412) 875-9500. Fax: (412) 875-9474. Web Site:www.wshh.com Licensee: Renda Broadcasting Corp. (acq 11-83; $2.7 million; 11-14-83). Format: Soft adult contemp. News staff: one. Target aud: 25-54; white collar, upscale office workers, professionals, managers. Spec prog: Pub affrs one hr wkly. ♦Susan Kelly, gen sls mgr; Ron Antill, progmg dir; Allan Freed, pub affrs dir.

WWCS(AM)—See Canonsburg

WWNL(AM)— 1947: 1080 khz; 50 kw-D, DA. TL: N40 36 17 W79 57 37. Hrs open: Sunrise-sunset 5316 William Flynn Hwy., Unit 3N, Gibsonia, 15044. Phone: (724) 443-4844. Fax: (724) 443-4847.E-mail: wwnl@wilkinsradio.com Web Site:www.wilkinsradio.com Licensee: Steel City Radio Inc. Group owner: Wilkins Communications Network Inc. (acq 6-14-2001). Population served: 3,200,000 Womble, Carlyle, Sandridge & Rice. Format: Christian teaching, talk. Target aud: 35 plus. ♦Bob Wilkins, CEO; Mitchell Mathis, COO & pres; LuAnn Wilkins, exec VP; Fred Brucker, gen mgr, stn mgr; Greg Garrett, opns mgr; Art White, engr.

WWSW-FM— 1940: 94.5 mhz; 50 kw. Ant 810 ft TL: N40 27 48 W80 00 18. Stereo. Hrs open: 200 Fleet St., 15220. Phone: (412) 937-1441. Fax: (412) 937-0323. Web Site:www.3wsradio.com Licensee: AMFM Radio Licenses L.L.C. Format: Classic hits. ♦John Rohm, gen mgr.

WXDX-FM— 1960: 105.9 mhz; 72 kw. 440 ft TL: N40 29 27 W79 58 55. Stereo. Hrs open: 200 Fleet St., 15220. Phone: (412) 937-1441. Fax: (412) 937-0323.E-mail: info@wxdx.com Web Site:www.wxdx.com Licensee: Capstar TX L.P. Group owner: Clear Channel Communications Inc. (acq 8-30-00; grpsl). Population served: 2,000,000 Natl. Rep: Christal,. Format: Alternative. Target aud: 18-34. ♦Missy Gawaldo, gen sls mgr.

***WYEP-FM**— Apr 30, 1974: 91.3 mhz; 18.2 kw. 265 ft TL: N40 24 42 W79 55 33. Stereo. Hrs open: 24 67 Bedford Sq., 15203. Phone: (412) 381-9131. Phone: (412) 381-9900. Fax: (412) 381-9126.E-mail: info@wyep.org Web Site:www.wyep.org Licensee: Pittsburgh Community Broadcasting Corp. Population served: 2,500,000 Natl. Network: PRI, NPR, . Format: AAA. Target aud: 25-49; socially, politically & culturally aware & active; well-educated. Spec prog: Folk 9 hrs, blues 7 hrs, bluegrass 4 hrs, soul 3 hrs, celtic 2 hrs wkly. ♦Blaine Lucas, chmn; Sean Sebastian, pres; Lee Ferraro, gen mgr; Tony Pirollo, sls dir; Rosemary Welsch, progmg dir; Joe Resch, disc jockey.

WZUM(AM)—See Carnegie

Pittston

WDMT(FM)— November 1983: 102.3 mhz; 5.8 kw. Ant 72 ft TL: N41 18 20 W75 45 38. Stereo. Hrs open: 305 Hwy. 315, 18640. Phone: (570) 883-9850. Fax: (570) 883-9851.E-mail: info@102themountain.com Web Site:www.102themountain.com Licensee: Entercom Wilkes-Barre Scranton LLC. Group owner: Entercom Communications Corp. (acq 12-13-99; grpsl). Natl. Network: Jones Radio Networks, . Natl. Rep: D & R Radio,. Format: AAA. Target aud: 35-64; female. Spec prog: Philadelphia Eagles, Penn State football. ♦John Burkavage, gen mgr; Jim Rising, stn mgr; Andy Zapotek, gen sls mgr; Michael Ignatz, prom dir; Jerry Padden, progmg dir; Elizabeth Masich, mus dir; Lamar Smith, chief of engrg.

WITK(AM)— June 21, 1953: 1550 khz; 10 kw-D, 500 w-N, DA-2. TL: N41 20 45 W75 47 08. Hrs open: Box 851, 18640. Phone: (570) 207-6515. Fax: (877) 711-8500. Web Site:www.holyfamily.ws Licensee: Steel City Radio Inc. Group owner: Citadel Communications Corp. (acq 10-10-2007; $400,000). Population served: 22000 Format: Catholic radio. ♦James N. Wright, gen mgr.

Plains

WYCK(AM)— 1923: 1340 khz; 810 w-U. TL: N41 15 01 W75 49 32. Hrs open: 24
Rebroadcasts WICK(AM) Scranton 98%.
1049 N. Sekol Rd., Scranton, 18504. Phone: (570) 344-1221. Phone: (570) 655-6660. Fax: (570) 344-0996. Web Site:www.thegame-radio.com Licensee: Bold Gold Media WBS L.P. (acq 3-13-2006; grpsl). Population served: 350,000 Natl. Network: Fox Sports, . Smithwick & Belendiuk. Wire Svc: Metro Weather Service Inc. Format: Sports. News staff: one; News: 8 hrs progmg wkly. Target aud: Adults 35-64; adults who love original hits of top 40 era. Spec prog: Relg 3 hrs wkly, Polish 3 hrs wkly. ◆Bob Vanderheyden, gen mgr; Brian Spinelli, gen sls mgr.

Pleasant Gap

WWSH(FM)— 1997: 98.7 mhz; 2.2 kw. Ant 551 ft TL: N40 55 58 W77 45 40. Hrs open: 160 W. Clearview Ave., State College, 16803. Phone: (814) 238-5085. Fax: (814) 238-7932. Licensee: 2510 Licenses LLC. Group owner: Forever Broadcasting (acq 7-2-2008; $1.2 million). Format: Adult contemp. ◆Nick Ferrara, gen mgr.

Pocono Pines

WPZX(FM)— 2000: 105.9 mhz; 6 kw. Ant 328 ft TL: N41 05 06 W75 38 09. Hrs open:
Simulcast with WEZX(FM) Scranton.
149 Penn Ave., Scranton, 18503. Phone: (570) 346-6555. Fax: (570) 346-6038. Web Site:www.rock107.com Licensee: The Scranton Times L.P. Group owner: Shamrock Communications Inc. (acq 9-8-00). Format: Classic rock. ◆ William R. Lynett, CEO; Jim Loftus, COO, gen mgr; Tim Durkin, sls dir; Jenny Arndt, natl sls mgr; Mark Hoover, prom dir; Eric Logan, mus dir; Ruth Miller, news dir; Kevin Fitzgerald, chief of engrg; Krista Saar, traf mgr.

Port Allegany

WHKS(FM)— 1990: 94.9 mhz; 1.15 w. Ant 758 ft TL: N41 48 36 W78 23 10. Stereo. Hrs open: 24 42 N. Main St., 16743. Secondary address: 59 Lent Hollow Rd., Coudersport 16915. Phone: (814) 642-7004. Phone: (814) 274-5368. Fax: (814) 642-9491.E-mail: whks@verizon.net Web Site:whksradio.com Licensee: L-Com Inc. Population served: 30,000 Natl. Network: Jones Radio Networks, AP Radio, . Rgnl. Network: Radio Pa. Natl. Rep: Dome;. Radio Pa. Rgnl rep: Commercial Media Sales. Format: Adult contemp. News: 2 hrs wkly. Target aud: 25-54; general. Spec prog: Relg 2 hrs wkly. ◆David F. Lent, pres, gen mgr, opns dir, opns mgr, progmg mgr, news dir, traf mgr; Joe Taylor, gen sls mgr & mktg mgr.

Port Matilda

WKVB(FM)— Oct 17, 1994: 107.9 mhz; 450 w. Ant 1,174 ft TL: N40 55 11 W77 58 28. Hrs open: 24 160 W. Clearview Ave., State College, 16803. Phone: (814) 238-5085. Fax: (814) 238-8993. Web Site:www.klove.com Licensee: 2510 Licenses LLC. (group owner; (acq 2-16-2005; grpsl). Natl. Network: K-Love, . Format: Contemp Christian. ◆Nick Ferrara, gen mgr.

Portage

WLKJ(FM)— Nov 15, 1990: 105.7 mhz; 3 kw. Ant 321 ft TL: N40 22 59 W78 39 31. Stereo. Hrs open: 24 970 Tripoli St., Johnstown, 15902. Phone: (814) 534-8975. Fax: (814) 534-8979.E-mail: info@klove.com Web Site:www.klove.com Licensee: 2510 Licenses LLC. Group owner: Forever Broadcasting. (acq 5-1-2005; grpsl). Natl. Network: K-Love, . Format: Contemp Christian. Target aud: 18-54; middle to upper income. ◆Nick Ferrara, opns mgr.

Pottstown

WPAZ(AM)— Oct 1, 1951: 1370 khz; 1 kw-D. TL: N40 16 35 W75 37 44. Hrs open: 6 AM-7 PM 224 Maugers Mill Rd., 19464. Phone: (610) 326-4000. Phone: (610) 326-6832. Fax: (610) 326-7984. Web Site:www.1370wpaz.com Licensee: Faye Scott. Group owner: Great Scott Broadcasting Population served: 125,000 Format: News/talk. News staff: 2; News: 8 hrs wkly. Target aud: 25 plus; most affluent people. Spec prog: Pol one hr, relg 12 hrs wkly. ◆Faye Scott, pres; Mike LiCata, gen mgr, sls VP; Jay Warren, progmg dir; Paul Fanelli, news dir; Terry Dalton, chief of engrg.

WRFY-FM—See Reading

Pottsville

WAVT-FM— Nov 20, 1948: 101.9 mhz; 50 kw. 540 ft TL: N40 49 50 W76 12 32. Stereo. Hrs open: 24 Prog sep from AM Box 540, 212 S. Centre St. , 17901. Phone: (570) 622-1360. Fax: (570) 622-2822. Web Site:www.t102radio.com Licensee: Pottsville Broadcasting Co. Inc. Population served: 775,000 Format: CHR. ◆James A. Bowman, stn mgr, gen sls mgr, adv mgr; Chad Gerber, progmg dir, disc jockey; Deb Dougherty, women's int ed; Courtney Roberts, disc jockey.

WPAM(AM)— 1946: Stn currently dark. 1450 khz; 1 kw-U. TL: N40 41 27 W76 11 39. Hrs open: 24 145 Lawtons Hill, 17901. Secondary address: PO Box 732 17901-0732. Phone: (570) 622-1450. Fax: (570) 622-4690.E-mail: bob@phoenix1450.com Web Site:www.phoenix1450.com Licensee: Curran Communications Inc. (acq 1-76). Population served: 155,000 Natl. Network: Jones Radio Networks, . Rgnl. Network: Radio Pa. Blair, Joyce & Silva. Format: Classic rock. Target aud: 25-54; active, upwardly mobile adults. Spec prog: Gospel, Talk 6 hrs wkly. ◆Robert Murray, gen mgr.

WPPA(AM)— May 9, 1946: 1360 khz; 5 kw-D, 500 w-N, DA-2. TL: N40 41 56 W76 11 43. Hrs open: 24 Box 540, 212 S. Centre St., 17901. Phone: (570) 622-1360. Fax: (570) 622-2822.E-mail: info@wpparadio.com Web Site:www.wpparadio.com Licensee: Pottsville Broadcasting Co. Inc. Population served: 155,000 Natl. Network: CBS, . Format: Adult contemp. News staff: 2; News: 14 hrs wkly. Target aud: 25-54. ◆Argie D. Tidmore, pres, gen mgr, chief of engrg; Les Blankenhorn, opns mgr, disc jockey; William Tidmore, gen sls mgr & adv mgr; Al Kovy, progmg dir, progmg mgr; Jay Levan, news dir; Deb Daugherty, pub affrs dir, women's int ed, disc jockey; Dave Michaels, disc jockey.

Punxsutawney

WECZ(AM)— Mar 18, 1953: 1540 khz; 5 kw-D, 1 kw-CH. TL: N40 57 36 W79 00 08. Hrs open: 12 904 N. Main St., 15767. Phone: (814) 938-6000. Fax: (814) 938-4237. Licensee: Renda Radio Inc. (group owner; acq 6-1-81; $512,000; 5-11-81). Population served: 48,000 Natl. Network: Westwood One, . Latham & Watkins. Format: News, talk. News staff: 2; News: 10 hrs wkly. Target aud: 45 plus. Spec prog: Pol 3 hrs wkly. ◆Anthony F. Renda, pres; Doug Metherey, gen mgr, stn mgr; Jennifer Black, gen sls mgr; Marty Palmer, engrg dir; Jim Costanzo, disc jockey.

WPXZ-FM— Dec 12, 1973: 104.1 mhz; 3 kw. 300 ft TL: N40 57 36 W79 00 08. Stereo. Hrs open: 24 Prog sep from AM 904 N. Main St., 15767. Phone: (814) 938-6000. Fax: (814) 938-4237.E-mail: rendaradio@comcast.net Population served: 60,000 Natl. Network: ABC, . Format: Adult contemp. Target aud: 35-64. ◆Larry McGuire, mus dir.

Radnor Township

*WYBF(FM)— August 1991: 89.1 mhz; 700 w. 223 ft TL: N40 03 22 W75 22 30. Hrs open: 7 AM-2 AM (M, W, F); noon-2 AM (Su) Rebroadcasts WXVU(FM) Villanova.
Widener Ctr., 610 King of Prussia Rd., Radnor, 19087-3698. Phone: (610) 902-8457. Fax: (610) 902-8285. Licensee: Cabrini College. Format: Div, contemp hit, news/talk. ◆Dr. Jerry Zurek, chmn; Krista Mazzeo, gen mgr.

Reading

WBYN-FM—See Boyertown

WEEU(AM)— 1931: 830 khz; 20 kw-D, 6 kw-N, DA-2. TL: N40 30 54 W76 07 24. Hrs open: 24 34 N. 4th St., 19601-3996. Phone: (610) 376-7335. Fax: (610) 376-7756.E-mail: weeu@weeu.com Web Site:www.weeu.com Licensee: WEEU Broadcasting Co. (acq 12-46). Population served: 340,000 Natl. Rep: McGavren Guild;. Cohn & Marks. Format: Full service, news/talk, sports. News staff: 2; News: 6 hrs wkly. Target aud: 30 plus; mature. Spec prog: Folk 3 hrs, Ger 2 hrs wkly. ◆Dave Kline, gen mgr & stn mgr.

WIOV(AM)— Sept 1, 1946: 1240 khz; 1 kw-U. TL: N40 19 28 W75 56 31. Hrs open: 44 Bethany Rd., Ephrata, 17522-2416. Phone: (717) 738-1191. Fax: (717) 738-1661.E-mail: widv@ptd.net Web Site:www.espn1240.com Licensee: Citadel Broadcasting Co. Group owner: Citadel Broadcasting Corp. (acq 5-12-2004; grpsl). Population served: 315,000 Natl. Network: ESPN Radio, . Format: Sports. Target aud: 35-54; Male. ◆Mitch Carroll, VP, gen mgr, gen sls mgr, natl sls mgr; Jim Rudley, opns mgr; Brenda Perkins, natl sls mgr; Crissy Wall, rgnl sls mgr, adv mgr; CJ Taylor, prom dir; Susie Summer, prom mgr; Bob Moody, progmg VP; Dick Raymond, progmg mgr; Steve Haage, progmg mgr; Shanon Robinson, traf mgr.

WRAW(AM)— September 1922: 1340 khz; 1 kw-U. TL: N40 19 27 W75 55 10. Stereo. Hrs open: 24 1265 Perkiomen Ave., 19602. Phone: (610) 376-7173. Phone: (610) 376-6671. Fax: (610) 376-1270. Web Site:www.1340praiseradio.com Licensee: Clear Channel Radio Licenses Inc. Group owner: Clear Channel Communications Inc. (acq 1996; grpsl). Population served: 49,600 Arent, Fox, Kintner, Plotkin & Kahn. Format: Contemp Christian. ◆John Rizzuto, gen mgr; Brian Check, opns mgr; Nick Harris, prom dir; Al Burke, progmg dir; Steve McKenzie, chief of engrg.

WRFY-FM— Sept 23, 1962: 102.5 mhz; 19 kw. 807 ft TL: N40 19 19 W75 53 41. Stereo. Hrs open: 1265 Perkiomen Ave., 19602. Phone: (610) 376-7173. Fax: (610) 376-6671. Fax: (610) 376-1270. Web Site:www.y102.com Population served: 250,000 Format: CHR. Target aud: 18-49. ◆Al Burke, progmg mgr.

*WXAC(FM)— 1967: 91.3 mhz; 200 w. 33 ft TL: N40 22 08 W75 54 37. Stereo. Hrs open: 1621 N. 13th St., 19612-5234. Phone: (610) 921-7545. Fax: (610) 921-7685.E-mail: wxac@albright.edu Licensee: Albright College. Population served: 300,000 Format: Progsv, Jazz, AOR, Sp. Target aud: General; Albright college community & Reading area. ◆Mindy Cohen, stn mgr.

Red Lion

WGLD(AM)— Oct 22, 1950: 1440 khz; 1 kw-D, 56 w-N. TL: N39 54 17 W76 34 49. Hrs open: 5989 Susquehanna Plaza Dr, York, 17406. Phone: (717) 764-1155. Fax: (717) 252-4708. Web Site:www.espn1440.com Licensee: Susquehanna License Co. LLC. (acq 5-11-2005; $280,000). Population served: 5,645 Natl. Network: ESPN Radio, . Format: Sports. ◆John Dickey, pres; Todd Toerper, gen mgr & mktg mgr.

WSOX(FM)— October 1960: 96.1 mhz; 13.5 kw. Ant 951 ft TL: N39 54 16 W76 34 48. Stereo. Hrs open: 5989 Susquehanna Plaza Dr, York, 17408. Phone: (717) 764-1155. Fax: (717) 252-4708.E-mail: info@oldies961.com Web Site:www.oldies961.com Licensee: Susquehanna License Co. LLC. Group owner: Susquehanna Radio Corp. (acq 8-1-2003; $23 million). Population served: 5,645 Format: Oldies. ◆Todd Toerper, mktg mgr; Bobby D., progmg dir; Bob Poff, chief of engrg.

Renovo

WZYY(FM)— Sept 19, 1996: 106.9 mhz; 800 w. Ant 876 ft TL: N41 14 15 W77 45 02. Hrs open: 240 11th Street, 17764. Phone: (570) 923-9106. Fax: (570) 923-9106.E-mail: morninghive@yahoo.com Web Site:www.1069thesurge.com Licensee: Magnum Broadcasting Inc. (acq 7-21-2004; $200,000). Format: Classic Rock. ◆Michael M. Stapleford, pres; Diana Stapleford, gen mgr; Glenn Brooks, stn mgr; Michael Brennen, gen sls mgr.

Reynoldsville

WDSN(FM)— Feb 14, 1990: 106.5 mhz; 6 kw. 328 ft TL: N41 08 41 W78 52 41. Stereo. Hrs open: 24 12 W. Long Ave., Du Bois, 15801-2100. Phone: (814) 375-5260. Fax: (814) 375-5262. Web Site:www.sunny1065.fm Licensee: Priority Communications. (acq 11-6-90; $275,000; 11-26-90). Population served: 115,000 Natl. Network: Jones Radio Networks, Fox News Radio, . Rgnl rep: Commerical Media Sales Womble, Carlyle, Sandridge & Rice, LLP. Wire Svc: AP Format: Adult contemp. News staff: one; News: 18 hrs wkly. Target aud: 25-54. ◆Jay M. Philippone, pres, gen mgr; Lori Lewis, stn mgr, opns mgr; Beth Walters, opns dir; Lindsay Schoening, news dir; Al Lockwood, pub affrs dir; Polly Slie, traf mgr.

Ridgebury

WREQ(FM)— 1991: 96.9 mhz; 3.6 kw. Ant 430 ft TL: N41 55 43 W76 46 58. Hrs open: 24 111 N. Main St., Elmira, NY, 14901. Phone: (607) 732-2484. Fax: (607) 732-8704.E-mail: wreq@csnradio.com Web Site:q969online.com Licensee: CSN International. (group owner; (acq 6-14-2001; $300,000). Reddy, Begley & McCormick. Format: Edu, contemp Christian mus, modern praise & worship. News: 4 hrs wkly. Target aud: 25-44; women with families (small children), heads of households. ◆Mike Kessler, pres; Lorenzo Galletti, gen mgr; Gina Galletti, progmg dir.

Ridgway

WKBI(AM)—See Saint Marys

WKBI-FM—See Saint Marys

Riverside

WLGL(FM)— Oct 25, 1990: 92.3 mhz; 440 w. 833 ft TL: N40 57 30 W76 42 53. Stereo. Hrs open: 24
Rebroadcasts WYGL(AM) Selinsgrove.
Box 90, Rt. 204, State School Rd, Selinsgrove, 17870. Phone: (570) 374-8819. Fax: (570) 374-7444. E-mail: bigcountryrequest@hotmail.com Licensee: MMP License LLC. Group owner: MAX Media L.L.C. (acq 10-17-03; grpsl). Population served: 150,000 Natl. Network: Jones Radio Networks, CNN Radio, . Rgnl rep: Dome & Associates. Kaye, Scholer, Fierman, Hays & Handler. Format: Contemp hot country. News staff: one; News: 5 hrs wkly. Target aud: 25-54. ◆Scott Richards, gen mgr; Dawn Marie, opns dir, news dir; Greg Adair, gen sls mgr, mktg dir; Shelly Marx, prom dir, mus dir; Ted Koppen, chief of engrg.

Roaring Spring

WKMC(AM)— May 1, 1955: 1370 khz; 5 kw-D, 38 w-N, DA-2. TL: N40 19 26 W78 23 40. Stereo. Hrs open: 2513 6th Ave., 16602. Phone: (814) 224-7501. Fax: (814) 224-7504. E-mail: wkmc@cove.net Web Site: www.wkmcam.com Licensee: Handsome Brothers Inc. Group owner: Allegheny Mountain Network Stations. (acq 5-1-2005; $80,000). Population served: 140,000 Format: Adult standard. Target aud: 45 plus; mature, loyal listeners. ◆David Barger, pres; Mike Martin, gen mgr, mktg dir, prom dir, progmg dir, news dir; Robert Lynn, chief of engrg.

WRKY-FM—See Hollidaysburg

Russell

WQFX-FM— Nov 11, 1984: 103.1 mhz; 2.5 kw. 351 ft TL: N41 57 48 W79 09 42. Stereo. Hrs open: Box 1199, Jamestown, NY, 14702-1199. Phone: (716) 664-2313. Fax: (716) 488-1471. E-mail: A ahill@radiojamestown.com Licensee: Media One Group II LLC. (acq 5-31-2005; grpsl). Population served: 140000 Natl. Rep: Dome, Fisher, Wayland, Cooper, Leader & Zaragoza. Format: Classic rock. Target aud: 25-54. ◆Merrill Rosen, gen mgr; Jason Sample, progmg dir; Joel Keefer, news dir.

Saegertown

WUZZ(FM)— Jan 19, 1979: 94.3 mhz; 3 kw. 298 ft TL: N41 42 23 W80 10 09. Stereo. Hrs open: 900 Water St., Downtown Mall, Meadville, 16335. Phone: (814) 724-1111. Fax: (814) 333-9628. Web Site: www.mywuzz.com Licensee: Forever Broadcasting LLC. Group owner: Forever Broadcasting (acq 7-20-2000; grpsl). Format: Classic rock. ◆James R. Shields, gen mgr.

Saint Marys

WDDH(FM)— Apr 22, 1986: 97.5 mhz; 23 kw. 705 ft TL: N41 37 04 W78 48 14. (CP: 19.5 kw, ant 800 ft.). Stereo. Hrs open: 24 14902 Bootjack Rd., PO Box 0, Ridgway, 15853. Phone: (814) 772-9700. Fax: (814) 772-9750. E-mail: doug@houndcountry.com Web Site: www.houndcountry.com Licensee: Laurel Media Inc. (acq 5-2008). Population served: 620,000 Natl. Network: Jones Radio Networks, . Natl. Rep: Rgnl Reps,. Rgnl rep: Dome & Associates Commercial Media Sales Format: Country. Target aud: 25-54. ◆Dennis D. Heindl, pres; Doug Metheney, gen mgr.

WKBI(AM)— July 23, 1950: 1400 khz; 1 kw-U. TL: N41 24 56 W78 33 56. Hrs open: 24 Box 466, 137 Melody Rd., 15857. Phone: (814) 834-2821. Phone: (814) 834-2822. Fax: (814) 834-4319. E-mail: b94@wkbi.net Web Site: www.wkbi.net Licensee: Elk-Cameron Broadcasting Co. Group owner: Allegheny Mountain Network Stations Population served: 53,200 Natl. Network: Westwood One, . Rgnl. Network: Allegheny Mtn. Net. Natl. Rep: Dome,. Allegheny Mtn. Net. Borsari & Paxson. Format: Adult contemp, oldies, sports. News staff: one; News: 10 hrs wkly. Target aud: 35-55. ◆Cary H. Simpson, pres; Ted Simpson, gen mgr; Erik Lane, opns dir, pub affrs dir, disc jockey; Nancy Bowser, prom mgr; Phil Leslie, news dir; Robert Lynn, chief of engrg; Chris O'Donnell, disc jockey.

WKBI-FM— August 1966: 93.9 mhz; 2.35 kw. 800 ft TL: N41 23 11 W78 41 32. Stereo. Hrs open: 24 Box 466, 137 Melody Rd., 15857. Phone: (814) 834-2821. Fax: (814) 834-4319. Web Site: www.wkbi.net Licensee: Elk-Cameron Broadcasting Co. Population served: 6,022 Natl. Network: Westwood One, Jones Radio Networks, . Target aud: General; young adults. Spec prog: Relg 2 hrs wkly. ◆Chris O'Donnell, disc jockey.

*WRWV(FM)—Not on air, target date: unknown: 91.1 mhz; 110 w. Ant 610 ft TL: N41 23 11 W78 41 32. Hrs open: 925 Houserville Rd., State College, 16801. Phone: (814) 867-3836. Fax: (814) 867-1922. E-mail: info@revfm.net Web Site: www.revfm.net Licensee: Invisible Allies Ministries. ◆Michael Schomer, gen mgr.

Salladasburg

WBYL(FM)— 1989: 95.5 mhz; 3.9 kw. 239 ft TL: N41 14 00 W77 12 09. Stereo. Hrs open: Box 3638, Williamsport, 17701. Secondary address: 1559 W 4th Street, Williamsport 17701. Phone: (570) 327-1400. Fax: (570) 327-8156. E-mail: bill@billcountry.com Web Site: www.billcountry.com Licensee: Clear Channel Radio License Inc. Group owner: Clear Channel Communications Inc. (acq 8-5-98; grpsl). Population served: 250,000 Format: Country. News staff: one; News: 4 hrs wkly. Target aud: 35 plus. ◆James Dabney, gen mgr; Ken Sawyer, opns dir; Joe Daniels, gen sls mgr; Gary Chrisman, prom dir; Tom Scott, progmg dir; Kathy Thomas, news dir; Mike Myer, engrg dir.

Sayre

WATS(AM)— June 1950: 960 khz; 5 kw-D. TL: N41 59 48 W76 30 03. Hrs open:
Rebroadcasts WAVR-FM Waverly, NY 100%.
204 Desmond St., 18840. Phone: (570) 888-7745. Fax: (570) 888-9005. E-mail: wats.wavr@cqservices.com Licensee: WATS Broadcasting Inc. (acq 10-17-86). Population served: 100,000 Format: Adult contemp. Target aud: 25-54. Spec prog: Farm one hr wkly. ◆Charles C. Carver Jr., VP & gen mgr.

WAVR(FM)—See Waverly, NY

Schnecksville

*WXLV(FM)— Sept 23, 1983: 90.3 mhz; 420 w. 230 ft TL: N40 39 52 W75 36 40. (CP: 420 w, ant 230 ft.). Stereo. Hrs open: 24 4525 Education Park Dr., 18078. Phone: (610) 799-4141. Fax: (610) 799-1571. E-mail: bbeard@lccc.edu Web Site: www.wxlv.com Licensee: Lehigh Carbon Community College. Population served: 800,000 Format: Americana. Target aud: General. Spec prog: Country, Bluegrass, Rock. ◆Burr Beard, gen mgr & progmg dir.

Scottdale

WLSW(FM)— Dec 21, 1971: 103.9 mhz; 325 w. 780 ft TL: N40 00 51 W79 31 01. Stereo. Hrs open: 24 Box 763, Connellsville, 15425. Phone: (724) 628-2800. Fax: (724) 628-7380. E-mail: info@wlsw.com Web Site: www.wlsw.com Licensee: Wall Broadcasting. Population served: 70,000 Natl. Network: Westwood One, . Format: Hot adult contemp, oldies. Target aud: 25-54; general. ◆L. Stanley Wall, pres; Chris Molton, gen mgr, gen sls mgr, chief of engrg; Debbie Larson, progmg dir, disc jockey; Connie LaPorte, traf mgr; Charlie Apple, disc jockey.

Scranton

WARM(AM)— 1940: 590 khz; 5 kw-U, DA-2. TL: N41 28 44 W75 52 51. Hrs open: 24 600 Baltimore Dr., Wilkes Barre, 18702. Phone: (570) 824-9000. Fax: (570) 820-0520. E-mail: phil.galasso@citcomm.com Licensee: Citadel Broadcasting Co. Group owner: Citadel Broadcasting Corp. (acq 7-1-97; grpsl). Population served: 1,064,000 Natl. Network: ABC, . Format: Oldies. News staff: 1; News: 1 hrs wkly. Target aud: 35 plus. Spec prog: Sinatra, 2 hrs wkly. ◆John Crawford, sls dir; Bill Palmeri, mktg mgr; Erin Evans, prom mgr; Brian Hughes, news dir; Phil Galasso, progmg dir & chief of engrg; Lori Law, traf mgr.

WBAX(AM)—See Wilkes-Barre

WBZU(AM)— Jan 12, 1925: 910 khz; 1 kw-D, 500 w-N. TL: N41 22 56 W75 41 51. Hrs open: 24
Rebroadcasts WILK(AM) Wilkes Barre 100%.
305 Hwy. 315, Pittston, 18640. Phone: (570) 883-9850. Fax: (570) 883-0832. E-mail: info@wilknewsradio.com Web Site: www.wilknewsradio.com Licensee: Entercom Scranton Wilkes-Barre License LLC. Group owner: Entercom Communications Corp. (acq 12-16-99; grpsl). Population served: 103,564 Natl. Rep: D & R Radio,. Wire Svc: ABC Wire Svc: AP Wire Svc: Metro Weather Service Inc. Format: News/talk. News staff: 6; News: 25 hrs wkly. Target aud: 25-54; affluent, educated. Spec prog: Relg one hr wkly. ◆John Burkavage, gen mgr; Jim Rising, opns dir; Andy Zapotell, gen sls mgr; Bob DeMono, natl sls mgr; Liz Masich, prom mgr; Nancy Kman, progmg dir; Joe Thomas, news dir, sports cmtr; Lamar Smith, chief of engrg; Shannon Ball, traf mgr; Tom Ragan, news rptr; Shadol Steel, mus critic.

WEJL(AM)— Nov 29, 1922: 630 khz; 500 w-D, 32 w-N. TL: N41 24 35 W75 40 41. Hrs open:
Rebroadcasts WBAX(AM) Wilkes Barre 100%.
149 Penn Ave., 18503. Phone: (570) 346-6555. Fax: (570) 346-6038. Web Site: www.wejl-wbax.com Licensee: The Scranton Times LP. Group owner: Shamrock Communications Inc. (acq 1922). Population served: 103,564 Format: Sports. ◆William R. Lynett, CEO; Jim Loftus, COO, gen mgr; Tim Durkin, sls dir; Jenny Arndt, natl sls mgr; Mark Hoover, mktg dir; Michael Neff, progmg dir; Ruth Miller, news dir; Kevin Fitzgerald, chief of engrg; Krista Saar, traf mgr.

WEZX(FM)— Nov 1, 1967: 106.9 mhz; 1.45 kw. Ant 617 ft TL: N41 20 52 W75 39 03. Stereo. Hrs open: 149 Penn Ave., 18503. Phone: (570) 346-6555. Fax: (570) 346-6038. E-mail: info@wejl-wbax.com (Acq 1967). Population served: 103,564 Format: Classic rock. ◆Mark Hoover, prom mgr; Kevin Fritzgerald, engrg dir; Krista Saar, traf mgr.

WGGY(FM)— Dec 25, 1948: 101.3 mhz; 7 kw. 1,110 ft TL: N41 25 38 W75 44 53. Stereo. Hrs open: 305 Hwy. 315 , Pittston, 18640. Phone: (570) 883-1111. Fax: (570) 883-1360. Web Site: www.froggy101.com Natl. Network: CBS, . Natl. Rep: Interep,. Format: Country. ◆John Burkavage, VP, gen mgr; Jim Rising, opns mgr; Andy Zapotek, gen sls mgr; Bob De Mono, natl sls mgr; Elizabeth Masieh, mktg dir; Cheryl Willis, prom mgr, reporter; Mike Krinik, progmg dir; Jaymie Gordon, mus dir, news rptr; Laman Smith, chief of engrg; Shannon Ball, traf mgr; Shadol Steele, mus critic; Joe Thomas, sports cmtr.

WICK(AM)— Apr 17, 1954: 1400 khz; 1 kw-U. TL: N41 25 05 W75 39 43. Stereo. Hrs open: 24 1049 N. Sekol Rd., 18504. Phone: (570) 344-1221. Fax: (570) 344-0996. Web Site: www.thegame-radio.com Licensee: Bold Gold Media WBS L.P. (acq 3-13-2006; grpsl). Population served: 550,000 Natl. Network: Fox Sports, . Smithwick & Belendiuk. Format: Sports. News staff: 2; News: 8 hrs wkly. Target aud: 35-64; adults who love original hits of Top 40 Era. Spec prog: Relg 3 hrs, Pol 3 hrs wkly. ◆Bob Vanderheyden, gen mgr; Brian Spinelli, gen sls mgr.

WILK(AM)—See Wilkes-Barre

WITK(AM)—See Pittston

WKRZ(FM)—See Wilkes-Barre

WMGS(FM)—See Wilkes-Barre

*WUSR(FM)— Feb 27, 1993: 99.5 mhz; 300 w. 1,014 ft TL: N41 26 09 W75 43 33. Stereo. Hrs open: 11 AM-2 AM Univ. of Scranton, St. Thomas Hall, 800 Linden St., 18510. Phone: (570) 941-7648. Fax: (570) 941-4628. E-mail: wusr@scranton.edu Web Site: www.scranton.edu/wusr Licensee: University of Scranton. Population served: 368,664 Wire Svc: Metro Weather Service Inc. Format: Alternative, jazz, rock/AOR, blues. Target aud: General. Spec prog: Class 5 hrs, relg 4 hrs, loud rock 8 hrs, urban contemp 6 hrs, Latin 10 hrs wkly. ◆Ken Sandrowicz, gen mgr; Margo Christiansen, stn mgr.

*WVIA-FM— Apr 23, 1973: 89.9 mhz; 5 kw. 1,250 ft TL: N41 10 55 W75 52 17. Stereo. Hrs open: 24 100 Wvia Way, Pittston, 18640-6197. Phone: (570) 655-2808. Phone: (570) 826-6144. Fax: (570) 655-1180. E-mail: webadmin@wvia.org Web Site: www.wvia.org Licensee: N.E. Pa. Educational TV Association. Population served: 1,500,000 Natl. Network: NPR, PRI, . Rgnl. Network: Pa. Pub. Pennsylvania Public Television Network Format: Class, jazz, news. News: 31 hrs wkly. ◆A. William Kelly, CEO, pres; Chris Norton, VP; George Graham, mus dir; Joseph Glynn, engrg VP. Co-owned TV: *WVIA-TV affil.

*WVMW-FM— September 1974: 91.7 mhz; 2 kw. Ant -285 ft TL: N41 25 57 W75 38 06. Stereo. Hrs open: 14 Marywood University, 2300 Adams Ave., 18509. Phone: (570) 348-6202. Fax: (570) 961-4769. E-mail: mengoni@marywood.edu Web Site: www.vmfm917.com Licensee: Marywood College. Population served: 40,000 Format: Alternative. News staff: 2; News: 7 hrs wkly. Target aud: 15-25; young adults. Spec prog: Black 2 hrs, class 7 hrs, jazz 10 hrs wkly. ◆Earnest Mengoni, stn mgr; George Graham, chief of engrg.

WWRR(FM)— Nov 26, 1964: 104.9 mhz; 270 w. Ant 1,092 ft TL: N41 26 06 W75 43 35. Stereo. Hrs open: 24 Phone: (570) 344-1221. Fax: (570) 344-0996. Web Site: www.105theriver.net Licensee: Bold Gold Media WBS L.P. Population served: 650,000 Format: Classic hits. News staff: one; News: 8 hrs wkly. Target aud: 25-54; men & women. ◆Bob Vanderheyden, gen mgr; Brian Spinelli, gen sls mgr.

WYCK(AM)—See Plains

Selinsgrove

*WQSU(FM)— September 1967: 88.9 mhz; 12 kw. 620 ft TL: N40 57 06 W75 45 03. Stereo. Hrs open: 24 Susquehanna Univ., 514 University Ave., 17870. Phone: (570) 372-4030. Fax: (570) 372-2757. E-mail: augustin@susqu.edu Web Site: www.wqsu.com Licensee: Susquehanna

University. Population served: 225,000 Natl. Network: AP Radio, . Wire Svc: AP Format: Modern rock. News: 7 hrs wkly. Target aud: 18-34. Spec prog: Classic country 6 hrs, sports 4 hrs, bluegrass 7 hrs wkly. ♦Larry D. Augustine, gen mgr; Harry Bingaman, chief of engrg; Patricia Wendt, traf mgr.

WYGL(AM)— Jan 16, 1967: 1240 khz; 1 kw-U. TL: N40 48 59 W76 52 13. Hrs open: 24 Box 90, Rt. 204 & State School Rd., 17870. Phone: (570) 374-1155. Phone: (570) 374-8819. Fax: (570) 374-7444.E-mail: bigcountryrequest@hotmail.com Web Site:www.bigcountrynow.com Licensee: MMP License LLC. Group owner: MAX Media L.L.C. (acq 10-17-03; grpsl). Population served: 150,000 Natl. Network: USA, . Kaye, Scholer, Fierman, Hays & Handler L.L.P. Format: Contemp hot country. News staff: one; News: 8 hrs wkly. Target aud: 18 plus. ♦John A. Trinder, pres; Scott Richards, VP, gen mgr; Dawn Marie, opns dir; Greg Adair, gen sls mgr; Shelly Marks, prom dir, asst music dir; Lisa Richards, mus dir; Nat O'Brien, news dir; Ted Koppen, chief of engrg.

Sellersville

***WBYO(FM)—** March 1991: 88.9 mhz; 900 w. Ant 436 ft TL: N40 23 02 W75 21 02. Stereo. Hrs open: 24 Box 186, 18960. Phone: (215) 721-2141. Fax: (215) 721-9811.E-mail: wordfm@wordfm.org Web Site:www.wordfm.org Licensee: Four Rivers Community Broadcasting Corp. Population served: 300,000 Schwartz, Woods & Miller. Format: Adult contemp, Christian, religious. News staff: one; News: 10 hrs wkly. Target aud: General. Spec prog: Country gospel 2 hrs, gospel bluegrass 2 hrs wkly. ♦Charles W. Loughery, pres, gen mgr, engrg mgr, chief of engrg; Nancy K. Loughery, CFO; David Baker, VP, stn mgr; Kristine McClain, progmg mgr.

Shamokin

WBLJ-FM— 1968: 95.3 mhz; 1.25 w. 505 ft TL: N40 45 36 W76 32 19. Stereo. Hrs open:
Rebroadcasts WBYL(FM) Salladasburg 100%.
Box 3638, Williamsport, 17701-3638. Phone: (570) 327-1400. Fax: (570) 327-8156.E-mail: bill@billcountry.com Web Site:www.billcountry.com Licensee: Clear Channel Broadcasting Licenses Inc. Group owner: Clear Channel Communications Inc. (acq 10-4-01; $800,000 with co-located AM). Format: Country. ♦Jim Dabney, gen mgr; Joe Daniels, gen sls mgr; Gary Chrisman, prom dir; Tom Scott, progmg dir; Kathy Thomas, news dir.

Sharon

WPIC(AM)— Oct 25, 1938: 790 khz; 1.3 kw-D, 58 w-N. TL: N41 13 10 W80 28 25. Hrs open: 24 2030 Pine Hollow Blvd., Hermitage, 16148. Phone: (724) 346-4113. Fax: (724) 981-4545. Web Site:www.wpic790.com Licensee: Cumulus Licensing Corp. Group owner: Cumulus Media Inc. (acq 3-15-00; grpsl). Population served: 22,653 Natl. Network: ABC, Jones Radio Networks, Talk Radio Network, Westwood One, . Format: News/talk. News staff: one. Target aud: 35 plus. Spec prog: Pol 3 hrs, It 2 hrs, relg 2 hrs, infomercials 12 hrs wkly. ♦Brian Schimmel, gen mgr; Bob Popa, progmg dir; Wes Boyd, chief of engrg.

WYFM(FM)— Oct 25, 1947: 102.9 mhz; 44 kw. Ant 455 ft TL: N41 13 10 W80 28 25. Stereo. Hrs open: Prog sep from AM 4040 Simon Rd., Youngstown, 44512. Phone: (330) 783-1000. Fax: (330) 783-0060. Web Site:www.y-103.com Licensee: Cumulus Licensing Corp. Population served: 445,000 Natl. Network: Westwood One, . Format: Classic hits, classic rock. Target aud: 25-54. ♦Brian Schimmel, gen mgr; Scott Kennedy, progmg dir; Dave Messersmith, disc jockey.

Sharpsville

WAKZ(FM)—Licensed to Sharpsville. See Youngstown OH

Shenandoah

***WCIM(FM)—** 2008: 91.5 mhz; 600 w. Ant 7182 ft TL: N40 50 58 W76 06 55. Hrs open:
Rebroadcasts WCIK(FM) Bath, NY 100%.
Box 506, Bath, NY, 14810-0506. Phone: (607) 776-4151. Fax: (607) 776-6929. Web Site:www.fln.org Licensee: Family Life Ministries Inc. (acq 7-24-2007; $800,000 for CP). Format: Contemp Christian. ♦Rick Snavely, gen mgr.

Shippensburg

WEEO(AM)— Dec 5, 1961: 1480 khz; 460 w-D, 9 w-N. TL: N40 04 30 W77 32 09. Hrs open: 6 AM-10 PM 37 S. Main St., Chambersburg, 17201. Phone: (717) 709-0801. Fax: (717) 709-0802. Licensee: Shippensburg Broadcasting Inc. (acq 10-30-2005; $65,000). Population served: 35536 Rgnl. Network: Radio Pa. Radio Pa. Format: Adult contemp. Target aud: 30 plus. ♦Eric Swidler, pres; Matthew J. Becker, prom dir & prom mgr.

***WSYC-FM—** February 1975: 88.7 mhz; 100 w. 155 ft TL: N40 03 32 W77 31 20. (CP: TL: N40 04 30 W77 31 15). Stereo. Hrs open: 24 Shippensburg Univ., 1871 Old Main Dr., Seddia Union Bldg. 3rd Fl., Shippenburg, 17257. Phone: (717) 532-6006. Fax: (717) 477-4024. Web Site:www.wsyc.org Licensee: Shippensburg University. Population served: 10,000 Natl. Network: Westwood One, . Format: Var/div. News staff: 7; News: 3 hrs wkly. Target aud: 16-25; college & area high school students. Spec prog: Black 9 hrs, class 2 hrs, jazz 3 hrs, blues 2 hrs, wkly. ♦Sage Ober, gen mgr; Jim Shaffer, progmg dir; Jeff Hollinshead, chief of engrg.

Shiremanstown

WWII(AM)— June 1987: 720 khz; 2 kw-D. TL: N40 11 28 W76 57 09. Stereo. Hrs open: 6 AM-sunset 8 W. Main St., 17011. Phone: (717) 731-9944. Fax: (717) 731-4002.E-mail: rkwillard@juno.com Web Site:www.720therock.com Licensee: Hensley Broadcasting. Format: Christian. News: 2 hrs wkly. Target aud: 25 plus; Christian. Spec prog: Gospel 2 hrs, polka 7 hrs, Indian one hr, blues 4 hrs wkly. ♦Joe Green, gen mgr, sls dir; Tom Sullivan, progmg dir.

Slippery Rock

***WSRU(FM)—** Sept 20, 1991: 88.1 mhz; 100 w. 79 ft TL: N41 03 43 W80 02 35. Stereo. Hrs open: 14 Box C-211, Univ. Union, 16057. Phone: (724) 738-2655. Phone: (724) 738-2931. Fax: (724) 738-2754.E-mail: rockradio@hotmail.com Web Site:organizations.sru.edu/WRSK/index.asp Licensee: Slippery Rock University. Population served: 10,000 Natl. Network: ABC, . Format: Classic rock, progsv, var/div. News staff: one; News: 14 hrs wkly. Target aud: 18-24; on & off campus students. Spec prog: Relg one hr, campus info one hr, sports one hr wkly. ♦Matt Miller, gen mgr, sports cmtr; Jami LoAlbo, prom dir; Paul Joseph, progmg dir; Sara Faletti, mus dir; Werner Ullrich, chief of engrg; Jason Fialkovich, traf mgr.

Smethport

WXMT(FM)— January 1990: 106.3 mhz; 1.03 kw. Ant 788 ft TL: N41 48 36 W78 23 10. Stereo. Hrs open: 24 29 Fraley St., Kane, 16735. Phone: (814) 837-9564. Fax: (814) 975-1098.E-mail: wxmt@colonial.cc Web Site:www.colonial.cc/rockwithoutthehardedge/ Licensee: Colonial Radio Group Inc. Group owner: Allegheny Mountain Network Stations (acq 11-3-2008; $290,000). Rgnl. Network: Allegheny Mtn. Net. Format: 70s and early 80s rock. Target aud: Men. ♦Jeffrey Andrulonis, pres & gen mgr.

Somerset

WBHV(AM)— June 15, 1981: 1330 khz; 5 kw-D, 35 w-N, DA-1. TL: N39 59 33 W79 05 41. Hrs open: 24 970 Tripoli St., Johnstown, 15902. Phone: (814) 534-8975. Fax: (814) 534-8979.E-mail: info@klove.com Licensee: 2510 Licenses LLC. (group owner; (acq 2-16-2005; grpsl). Natl. Network: ESPN Radio, . Rgnl. Network: Radio Pa. Format: Sports. Target aud: 35-64. ♦Nick Ferrara, opns mgr.

WLKH(FM)— June 15, 1966: 97.7 mhz; 3.5 kw. Ant 430 ft TL: N40 01 31 W79 05 42. Hrs open: 24 970 Tripoli St., Johnstown, 15902. Phone: (814) 534-8975. Fax: (814) 534-8979.E-mail: info@klove.com Web Site:www.klove.com Licensee: 2510 Licenses LLC. (acq 5-1-2005; grpsl). Population served: 280,000 Natl. Network: K-Love, . Format: Contemp Christian. ♦Nick Ferrara, opns mgr.

WNTW(AM)— Jan 15, 1951: 990 khz; 10 kw-D, 75 w-N, DA-1. TL: N40 01 31 W79 05 42. Hrs open: 24
Rebroadcasts WLYE(AM) Johnstown 100%.
109 Plaza Dr. Suite 2, Johnstown, 15501-1212. Phone: (814) 255-4186. Fax: (814) 255-6145.E-mail: info@hot92fm.net Licensee: Forever Broadcasting LLC. Group owner: Forever Broadcasting (acq 9-9-97; grpsl). Population served: 325,000 Format: Country. News staff: one; News: 8 hrs wkly. Target aud: 35-55. ♦Carol Logan, pres; Verla Price, gen mgr & gen sls mgr; Mike Stevens, progmg dir; Rick Sheppard, news dir, pub affrs dir; Jim Boxler, chief of engrg; Tegan Hayes, traf mgr.

South Waverly

WPHD(FM)— 2003: 96.1 mhz; 920 w. Ant 612 ft TL: N41 58 04 W76 40 02. Stereo. Hrs open: 24 734 Chemung St., Horseheads, NY, 14845. Secondary address: 495 Court St., 2nd Fl., Binghamton 13904. Phone: (607) 795-0795. Phone: (607) 772-1005. Fax: (607) 795-1095. Fax: (607) 772-2945.E-mail: themetrocks@aol.com Web Site:cool96oldies.com Licensee: Fitzgerald and Hawras Partnership (acq 3-22-01). Natl. Rep: Katz Radio,. Format: Oldies. Target aud: 35-64; adults. ♦Kevin Fitzgerald, VP, chief of engrg; George Harris, gen mgr; Stephen Shimer, opns mgr.

South Williamsport

WZXR(FM)— June 1, 1968: 99.3 mhz; 410 w. Ant 1,237 ft TL: N41 12 42 W76 57 16. Stereo. Hrs open: 1685 Four Mile Dr., Williamsport, 17740. Phone: (570) 323-8200. Fax: (570) 327-9138. Web Site:www.wzxr.com Licensee: South Williamsport SabreCom Inc. Group owner: Backyard Broadcasting LLC (acq 12-1-02; grpsl). Population served: 400,000 Natl. Network: ABC, . Natl. Rep: Christal,. Format: AOR, classic rock. News staff: 3; News: 7 hrs wkly. Target aud: 25-54. ♦Barry Drake, pres; Robin Smith, CFO; Dan Farr, gen mgr; Bob Pawlikowski, sls dir; Ted Minier, progmg dir; John Finn, news dir; Tom Atkins, chief of engrg.

Starview

WSJW(FM)— Nov 22, 1971: 92.7 mhz; 700 w. Ant 954 ft TL: N40 04 32 W76 48 03. Stereo. Hrs open: 24 Box 4368, Lancaster, 17604. Secondary address: 1996 Auction Rd., Manheim 17545. Phone: (717) 653-0800. Phone: (800) 222-1013. Fax: (717) 653-0122.E-mail: bbaldwin@hallradio.com Web Site:smoothjazz927.com Licensee: Hall Communications Inc. (group owner: acq 1-16-96; $2.3 million). Population served: 1,315,500 Natl. Rep: D & R Radio,. Fletcher, Heald & Hildreth. Format: Smooth jazz. News staff: one. Target aud: 25-54; adult. ♦Bonnie H. Rowbotham, chmn; Arthur J. Rowbotham, pres; Bill Baldwin, exec VP, gen mgr; Paul Scott, prom dir & progmg dir.

State College

WBHV-FM— Oct 23, 1991: 94.5 mhz; 940 w. Ant 581 ft TL: N40 54 04 W77 50 20. Stereo. Hrs open: 160 W. Clearview Ave., 16803. Phone: (814) 238-5085. Fax: (814) 238-8993. Web Site:www.b945live.com Licensee: 2510 Licenses LLC. Group owner: Forever Broadcasting (acq 2-1-2006; $1.2 million). Population served: 100,000 Natl. Rep: Christal,. Format: Christian. ♦Nick Ferrara, gen mgr.

WBLF(AM)—See Bellefonte

WFGE(FM)—See Tyrone

***WKPS(FM)—** 1995: 90.7 mhz; 100 w. 85 ft TL: N40 47 58 W77 52 11. Hrs open: 24 125 Hub-Robeson Ctr., University Park, 16802. Phone: (814) 865-7983. Phone: (814) 865-9577. Fax: (814) 865-2751.E-mail: lion-officers@psu.edu Web Site:www.thelion.fm Licensee: Board of Trustees of Pennsylvania State University. Population served: 100,000 Format: Var. News: 4 hrs wkly. Target aud: University students. Spec prog: Jazz 11 hrs, Sp 8 hrs wkly. ♦Tom Shakely, VP, stn mgr, progmg dir; Brandon Peach, gen mgr; Tristan Vaughan, opns dir.

WOWY(FM)—(University Park, April 1965: 97.1 mhz; 3 kw. Ant 403 ft TL: N40 48 27 W77 56 29. Stereo. Hrs open: 160 W. Clearview Ave., 16803. Phone: (814) 238-5085. Fax: (814) 238-7932. Web Site:www.wowyonline.com Licensee: 2510 Licenses LLC. (acq 2-16-2005; grpsl). Population served: 38,000 Format: Oldies. ♦Nick Ferrara, gen mgr.

***WPSU(FM)—** Dec 6, 1953: 91.5 mhz; 1.7 kw. Ant 1,197 ft TL: N40 48 32 W77 50 28. Stereo. Hrs open: 24 174 Outreach Bldg, University Park, 16802. Phone: (814) 865-1877. Fax: (814) 865-4043.E-mail: wpsu@psu.edu Web Site:www.wpsu.org Licensee: Pennsylvania State University. Population served: 100,000 Natl. Network: PRI, NPR, . Paul, Hastings, Janofsky & Walker. Wire Svc: AP Format: News, class, public radio. News staff: one; News: 35 hrs wkly. Target aud: General; upscale, educated adults. Spec prog: Folk 10, jazz 3 hrs, blues 2 hrs wkly. ♦Ted Krichels, gen mgr; Greg Petersen, stn mgr; Steve Shipman, opns dir; Ashear Barr, sls dir; Bill Hiergeist, rgnl sls mgr; Kristine Allen, progmg dir; Carl Fisher, chief of engrg; Leslie Dyer, traf mgr.

WQWK(AM)— 1945: 1450 khz; 1 kw-U. TL: N40 48 32 W77 50 28. Hrs open: 24 2551 Park Center Blvd., 16801. Phone: (814) 237-9800. Fax: (814) 237-2477. Web Site:www.qwkrock.com Licensee: Forever Broadcasting LLC. Group owner: Forever Broadcasting (acq 3-10-98; $2.9 million with co-located FM). Population served: 110,000 Natl. Network: ESPN Radio, . Natl. Rep: Christal,. Format: Sports. Target aud: 30 plus; college educated, upscale. ♦Carol Logan, pres; Andrew Sumereau, gen mgr; Glen Turner, opns mgr; Bob Taylor, progmg dir, chief of engrg; Pat Boland, news dir & sports cmtr.

WRSC(AM)— May 29, 1961: 1390 khz; 2 kw-D, 1 kw-N, DA-N. TL: N40 48 50 W77 53 30. Hrs open: 2551 Park Center Blvd., 16801. Phone: (814) 237-9800. Fax: (814) 237-2477.E-mail: programming @newsradio1390.com Web Site:www.newsradio1390.com Licensee: Forever Broadcasting LLC. (group owner; (acq 5-1-2005; $2.65 million with WBUS(FM) Boalsburg). Population served: 112,000 Rgnl. Network: Radio Pa. Format: News/talk. ◆Chuck Hertzog, gen mgr; Pat Boland, progmg dir; Bob Taylor, news dir, chief of engrg.

WRSC-FM— 1965: 103.1 mhz; 3 kw. Ant -55 ft TL: N40 48 32 W77 50 28. Stereo. Hrs open: 24 2551 Park Center Blvd., 16801. Phone: (814) 237-9800. Fax: (814) 237-2477.E-mail: mail@hot1031.com Web Site:www.hot1031.com Licensee: Forever Broadcasting LLC Format: CHR. News staff: one. Target aud: 18-34; college-aged youth, young adults. ◆Joe Trimarchi, sls dir; Mike Martin, prom dir; Glen Turner, progmg dir.

*WRXV(FM)— June 18, 2004: 89.1 mhz; 1 w horiz, 4.4 kw vert. Ant 1,099 ft TL: N40 43 56 W78 19 33. Hrs open: 24 925 Houserville Rd., 16801. Phone: (814) 867-3836. Fax: (814) 867-1922.E-mail: info@revfm.net Web Site:www.revfm.net Licensee: Invisible Allies Ministries. Format: Contemp Christian. ◆Michael Schomer, gen mgr; Erik Lane, stn mgr; Jim Schomer, chief of engrg.

*WTLR(FM)— Jan 1, 1978: 89.9 mhz; 25 kw. 584 ft TL: N40 53 32 W77 51 49. Stereo. Hrs open: 24 2020 Cato Ave., 16801. Phone: (814) 237-9857. Licensee: Central Pennsylvania Christian Institute Inc. Population served: 500,000 Wire Svc: AP Format: Christian. News staff: one; News: 9 hrs wkly. Target aud: 30-55; Adults, family oriented. ◆Mark Van Ouse, gen mgr.

*WXFR(FM)— 2008: 88.3 mhz; 10 w horiz, 1.8 kw vert. Ant 686 ft TL: N40 53 35 W77 51 48. Hrs open: 24
Rebroadcasts WFSI(FM) Annapolis, MD 100%.
918 Chesapeake Ave., Annapolis, MD, 21403. Phone: (410) 268-6200. Fax: (410) 268-0931.E-mail: info@familyradio.org Web Site:www.familyradio.com Licensee: Family Stations Inc. Natl. Network: Family Radio, . Format: Relg, educ. ◆Harold Camping, pres; W.A. Sadlier, stn mgr.

WZWW(FM)—(Bellefonte, Sept 15, 1986: 95.3 mhz; 790 w. Ant 636 ft TL: N40 53 35 W77 51 48. Stereo. Hrs open: 24 863 Benner Pike, Suite 200, 16801. Phone: (814) 231-0953. Fax: (814) 231-0950.E-mail: nancy@3wz.com Web Site:www.3wz.com Licensee: First Media Radio LLC. (group owner; (acq 11-2-2000). Population served: 124,000 Natl. Network: CNN Radio, . Rgnl rep: Commercial Media Sales. Format: Adult contemp. News staff: 2; News: 7 hrs wkly. Target aud: 25-54; upscale families. Spec prog: Sports 3 hrs wkly. ◆Alex Kolobielski, pres; Mike McGough, gen mgr; Dave Kurten, gen sls mgr, progmg dir; Steve Jones, mus dir & sports cmtr.

Stroudsburg

*WBYX(FM)— Oct. 1, 1999: 88.7 mhz; 1 w horiz, 4 kw vert. Ant 794 ft TL: N41 02 40 W75 22 45. Stereo. Hrs open: 24
Rebroadcasts WBYO(FM) Sellersville 100%.
Box 186, Sellersville, 18960. Phone: (215) 721-2141. Fax: (215) 721-9811.E-mail: wordfm@wordfm.org Web Site:www.wordfm.org Licensee: Four Rivers Community Broadcasting Corp. Natl. Network: ABC, . Schwartz, Woods & Miller. Format: Adult contemp, Christian, religious. Target aud: 25-45. Spec prog: Bluegrass Gospel;. ◆Nancy Loughery, CFO; David W. Baker, VP; Charles W. Loughery, gen mgr; Kristine McClain, progmg dir.

WSBG(FM)— Oct 1, 1964: 93.5 mhz; 550 w. Ant 764 ft TL: N40 56 56 W57 09 29. Stereo. Hrs open: Prog sep from AM 22 S. 6th St., 18360. Phone: (570) 421-2100. Fax: (570) 421-2040.E-mail: info@lite935.com Web Site:www.lite935.com Format: Lite rock. Target aud: 20 plus. Spec prog: Modern rock 3 hrs wkly.

WVPO(AM)— 1947: 840 khz; 250 w-D. TL: N40 58 26 W75 11 43. Hrs open: 22 S. 6th St., 18360. Phone: (570) 421-2100. Fax: (570) 421-2040.E-mail: info@lite935.com Licensee: Nassau Broadcasting II L.L.C. Group owner: Nassau Broadcasting Partners L.P. (acq 2-15-02; grpsl). Population served: 120,000 Natl. Format: Adult standards. Target aud: 35 plus. ◆Peter Tonks, CFO; Rick Musselman, gen mgr; Michele Stevens, progmg VP; Rod Bauman, progmg dir; Bob Matthews, news dir; Tony Gervasi, engrg VP; George Guilda, engrg mgr.

Summerdale

*WJAZ(FM)— Jan 10, 1991: 91.7 mhz; 140 w. 683 ft TL: N40 18 16 W76 55 53. Stereo. Hrs open: 24
Rebroadcasts WRTI(FM) Philadelphia 100%.
1509 Cecil B. Moore Ave., 2nd Fl., ., Philadelphia, 19122. Phone: (215) 204-8405. Fax: (215) 204-7027.E-mail: comments@wrti.org Web Site:www.wrti.org Licensee: Temple University of the Commonwealth System of Higher Education (acq 12-88; $5,000;12-5-88). Population served: 1,450,000 Rgnl. Network: Radio Pa. Format: Classical, jazz. News staff: one; News: 15 hrs wkly. Target aud: 30-65. ◆Dave Conant, CEO, gen mgr; Vic Scarpato, CFO; Tobias Poole, opns dir; Rick Torpey, gen sls mgr, mktg mgr; Porsche Blakey, prom dir; Jack Moore, progmg dir; Windsor Johnson, news dir; Jeff DePolo, chief of engrg; Lorna Nixon, traf mgr.

Sunbury

WKOK(AM)— 1933: 1070 khz; 10 kw-D, 1 kw-N, DA-N. TL: N40 52 46 W76 49 18. Hrs open: 24 Box 1070, 17801. Secondary address: 1227 County Line Rd., Selinsgrove 17870. Phone: (570) 286-5838. Phone: (570) 743-1841. Fax: (570) 743-1605.E-mail: wkok@wkok.com Web Site:www.wkok.com Licensee: Sunbury Broadcasting Corp. (acq 5-33). Population served: 237,000 Natl. Network: CBS, CNN Radio, Fox News Radio, Wall Street, . Natl. Rep: Roslin,. Rgnl rep: Dome. Wilkinson Barker Knauer. Wire Svc: AP Format: News/talk, sports. News staff: 4; News: 168 hrs wkly. Target aud: 35-64. ◆Roger Haddon Jr., CEO, pres, gen mgr; Kevin Herr, opns mgr, news dir; Tricia Cease, gen sls mgr & mktg mgr; Mark Lawrence, progmg dir.

WQKX(FM)— Sept 15, 1948: 94.1 mhz; 16 kw. 879 ft TL: N40 47 07 W76 41 51. Stereo. Hrs open: 24 Prog sep from AM Box 1070, 17801. Secondary address: 1227 County Line Rd., Selinsgrove 17870. Phone: (570) 286-5838. Phone: (570) 743-1841. Fax: (570) 743-7837.E-mail: equest@wqkx.com Web Site:www.wqkx.com Population served: 167,100 Natl. Rep: Roslin,. Rgnl rep: Dome Format: Hot AC. News staff: 4; News: 7 hrs wkly. Target aud: 25-54. ◆Roger S. Haddon, Jr., CEO, pres; Tricia Cease, sls dir; Drew Kelly, progmg dir; Rob Senter, mus dir; Matt Farrand, news dir.

Susquehanna

WCDW(FM)— March 1995: 100.5 mhz; 1.35 kw. Ant 692 ft TL: N42 03 10 W75 42 07. Stereo. Hrs open: 24 101 Main St., Johnson City, NY, 13790. Phone: (607) 772-1005. Fax: (607) 772-2945.E-mail: cool100oldies@aol.com Web Site:www.cool100oldies.com Licensee: Equinox Broadcasting Corp. Natl. Rep: Katz Radio,. Format: Oldies. Target aud: 35-64. Spec prog: Polish 5 hrs wkly. ◆George Hawras, pres.

Swarthmore

*WSRN-FM— Dec 31, 1939: 91.5 mhz; 110 w. 140 ft TL: N39 54 18 W75 21 16. Stereo. Hrs open: Swarthmore College, 500 College Ave., 19081. Phone: (610) 328-8336. Phone: (610) 328-8335. Web Site:www.wsrnfm.org Licensee: Swarthmore College. Population served: 500,000 Format: Div. ◆Roger Shaw, gen mgr.

Sweet Valley

*WRGN(FM)— Oct 15, 1984: 88.1 mhz; 500 w. 239 ft TL: N41 17 54 W76 07 28. (CP: Ant 302 ft.). Hrs open: 24 2457 State Rt. 118, Hunlock Creek, 18621. Phone: (570) 477-3688. Fax: (570) 477-2310.E-mail: wrgn@epix.net Web Site:www.wrgn.com Licensee: Gospel Media Institute Inc. Format: Relg. ◆Burl F. Updyke, pres, gen mgr, gen sls mgr, chief of engrg; Shirley J. Updyke, prom dir & progmg dir.

Sykesville

WZDB(FM)—Not on air, target date: unknown: 95.9 mhz; 1.52 kw. Ant 643 ft TL: N41 02 43 W78 42 11. Hrs open: 306 Port St., Easton, MD, 21601. Phone: (410) 822-3301. Fax: (410) 822-0576. Licensee: First Media Radio LLC. ◆Alex Kolobielski, pres.

Tafton

*WLKA(FM)— 2002: 88.3 mhz; 580 w. Ant 968 ft TL: N41 35 36 W75 25 56. Hrs open: 2351 Sunset Blvd., Suite 170-218, Rocklin, CA, 95765. Phone: (916) 251-1600. Fax: (916) 251-1650. Web Site:www.klove.com Licensee: Educational Media Foundation. (acq 11-17-2006; $675,000). Natl. Network: K-Love, . Format: Contemp Christian. ◆Richard Jenkins, pres.

Tamaqua

WMGH-FM— June 14, 1965: 105.5 mhz; 1.4 kw. 485 ft TL: N40 47 14 W76 01 59. Stereo. Hrs open: 24 2147 Market St., Nesquehoning, 18240. Secondary address: P.O. Box D, Lansford 18232. Phone: (570) 668-2992. Phone: (570) 645-2105. Fax: (570) 645-2159.E-mail: wmgh@ptdprolog.net Web Site:www.wmgh.com Licensee: J-Systems Franchising Corp. (group owner; acq 2-28-87; $300,000;12-15-86). Population served: 120,000 Natl. Network: Westwood One, ABC, USA, . Radio Pa. Format: Adult contemp. Target aud: 25-54; primary women, secondary adults. Spec prog: Oldies 7 hrs, polka 3 hrs wkly. ◆Harold G. Fulmer III, pres; Christopher G. Fulmer, VP, gen sls mgr; Bill Lakatas, gen mgr, progmg dir; Mark Marek, news dir, edit dir; Joe Manjack, chief of engrg, disc jockey; Cheryl Lee, disc jockey.

Tarentum

WZPT(FM)—See New Kensington

Telford

*WBMR(FM)— June 1967: 91.7 mhz; 115 w. Ant 249 ft TL: N40 18 15 W75 17 39. Hrs open: 300 E. Rock Rd., Allentown, 18103. Phone: (610) 797-4530. Fax: (610) 791-3000.E-mail: info@wbmr.com Licensee: United Ministries. (acq 8-30-2002). Format: Relg.

Tioga

WMTT(FM)— May 23, 1991: 94.7 mhz; 820 w. 895 ft TL: N41 54 36 W77 00 40. (CP: 12 kw). Stereo. Hrs open: 24 734 Chemung St., Horseheads, NY, 14845. Secondary address: 495 Court St., 2nd Fl, Binghamton, NY 13904. Phone: (607) 795-0795. Phone: (607) 772-1005. Fax: (607) 795-1095. Fax: (607) 772-2945.E-mail: themetrocks@aol.com Web Site:www.themetrocks.com Licensee: Europa Communications (acq 5-22-92). Population served: 116,966 Natl. Rep: Katz Radio,. Format: Classic rock, AOR. News: 2 hrs wkly. Target aud: 25-49. ◆Kevin Fitzgerald, CEO, VP, chief of engrg; George Harris, gen mgr, opns dir; Robert Smith, stn mgr; Justin McGregor, prom dir; Stephen Shimer, opns mgr & progmg dir.

Titusville

WTIV(AM)— Nov 27, 1955: 1230 khz; 1 kw-U. TL: N41 37 00 W79 41 34. Hrs open: 6 AM-midnight 900 Water St., Downtown Mall, Meadville, 16335. Phone: (814) 432-2188. Fax: (814) 827-1679. Licensee: Forever Broadcasting LLC. Group owner: Forever Broadcasting (acq 7-20-00; grpsl). Population served: 25,000 Rgnl. Network: Radio Pa. Radio Pa. Reddy, Begley & McCormick. Format: News/talk info. News: 13 hrs wkly. Target aud: 22-54; mixed. ◆Thomas J. Sauber, gen mgr.

Tobyhanna

WKRF(FM)— Jan 15, 1993: 107.9 mhz; 5.7 kw. 564 ft TL: N41 07 04 W75 22 43. Stereo. Hrs open: 24
Rebroadcasts WKRZ(FM) Wilkes-Barre 100%.
305 Hwy. 315, Pittston, 18640. Phone: (570) 839-5858. Fax: (570) 883-9851.E-mail: info@wkrf.com Web Site:www.wkrf.com Licensee: Entercom Wilkes-Barre Scranton LLC. Group owner: Entercom Communications Corp. (acq 5-11-00). Population served: 80,000 Natl. Network: Jones Radio Networks, . Format: Top-40. News staff: one; News: one hr wkly. Target aud: 25-54. ◆John Burkavage, gen mgr; Jim Rising, stn mgr, opns mgr; Andy Zapotek, gen sls mgr; Bob Demono, natl sls mgr; Michael Ignatz, prom dir; Jerry Padden, progmg dir; Elizabeth Masich, mus dir; Lamar Smith, chief of engrg; Tracy Iannaprone, traf mgr; Joe Thomas, local news ed; Tom Regan, news rptr.

Towanda

WTTC(AM)— 1959: 1550 khz; 500 w-D. TL: N41 45 55 W76 29 10. Hrs open: 204 Desmond St., Sayre, 18840. Phone: (570) 888-7745. Fax: (570) 888-9005. Licensee: WATS Broadcasting Inc. (acq 5-1-96; $175,000 for stock with co-located FM). Population served: 30,000 Natl. Network: Motor Racing Net, . Format: Oldies. Target aud: General. ◆Charles C Carver Jr., pres; Charles C. Carver Jr., gen mgr; Meade T. Murtland, stn mgr.

WTTC-FM— November 1959: 95.3 mhz; 3 kw. 125 ft TL: N41 45 55 W76 29 10. Hrs open: 6 AM-11 PM Dups AM 100% 204 Desmond St., Sayre, 18840. Phone: (570) 888-7745. Fax: (570) 888-9005. ◆Joel Clawson, adv dir.

Trout Run

*WCIT-FM— 2001: 90.1 mhz; 350 w. Ant 295 ft TL: N41 27 26 W77 06 55. Hrs open:
Rebroadcasts WCIK(FM) Bath, NY 100%.

Box 506, Bath, NY, 14810. Secondary address: 7634 Campbell Creek Rd., Bath, NY 14810. Phone: (607) 776-4151. Fax: (607) 776-6929.E-mail: mail@fln.org Web Site:www.fln.org Licensee: Family Life Ministries Inc. Group owner: Family Life Network Natl. Network: Salem Radio Network, . Hardy, Carey, Chautin & Balkin, LLP. Wire Svc: Metro Weather Service Inc. Format: Contemp Christian. News staff: 3; News: 14 hrs wkly. Target aud: 30-54. ◆Rick Snavely, pres, gen mgr; Dick Snavely, CFO; Roger Settje, prom mgr; John Owens, progmg dir; Jim Travis, chief of engrg.

Troy

WHGL-FM—See Canton

WTZN(AM)— Mar 3, 1982: 1310 khz; 1 kw-D, 72 w-N. TL: N41 46 51 W76 49 09. Hrs open: Box 100, 16947. Secondary address: 170 Redington Ave. 16947. Phone: (570) 297-0100. Fax: (570) 297-3193.E-mail: whgl100@ptd.net Web Site:www.wtzn.com Licensee: Cantroair Communications Inc. (acq 1-7-99; $560,000 for 85% of stock with WHGL-FM Canton). Format: All sports. Target aud: 25-54. ◆Bob Gisler, VP, gen sls mgr; Mike Powers, pres, gen mgr & progmg dir; Kevin Smith, chief of engrg.

Tunkhannock

WGMF(AM)— June 13, 1986: 1460 khz; 5 kw-D, 1.25 kw-N, DA-2. TL: N41 33 46 W75 58 11. Hrs open: 18 Box 230, Dushore, 18614. Phone: (570) 928-7200. Fax: (570) 928-2100. Licensee: GEOS Communications. (acq 1-30-2004; $515,000 with co-located FM). Format: News/talk. ◆Ben Smith, gen mgr.

Tyrone

WFGE(FM)— Aug 15, 1961: 101.1 mhz; 8.5 kw. Ant 1,171 ft TL: N40 55 10 W77 58 28. Stereo. Hrs open: 24 2551 Park Center Blvd., State College, 16801. Phone: (814) 237-9800. Fax: (814) 237-2477. Licensee: Forever Broadcasting LLC. (acq 7-2-2008; $2.5 million). Population served: 650,000 Rgnl. Network: Allegheny Mtn. Net. Kaye Scholer LLP. Format: Country. ◆Chuck Hertzog, gen mgr; Monty Buehler, gen sls mgr.

WTRN(AM)— Jan 12, 1955: 1340 khz; 1 kw-U. TL: N40 39 48 W78 15 24. Hrs open: 24 Box 247, 16686. Secondary address: Washington Ave. & 1st St. 16686. Phone: (814) 684-3200. Fax: (814) 684-1220.E-mail: amnnet@aol.com Web Site:www.wtrn.net Licensee: Allegheny Mountain Network. (group owner) Population served: 7,072 Natl. Network: Jones Radio Networks, . Rgnl. Network: Allegheny Mtn. Net. Natl. Rep: Dome,. Allegheny Mtn. Net. Borsari & Paxson. Format: Adult contemp. News: 16 hrs wkly. Target aud: General; total community targeted. Spec prog: Relg 4 hrs wkly. ◆Cary H. Simpson, pres; Peg Baney, gen sls mgr; Rich Saupp, progmg dir; Jean Dixon, news dir; Robert Lynn, chief of engrg.

Union City

WCTL(FM)— Apr 23, 1967: 106.3 mhz; 3.4 kw. 430 ft TL: N42 00 04 W79 52 33. Stereo. Hrs open: 10912 Peach St., Waterford, 16441-9151. Phone: (814) 796-6000. Fax: (814) 796-3200.E-mail: wctl@wctl.org Web Site:www.wctl.org Licensee: Inspiration Time Inc. (acq 3-72). Population served: 300,000 Natl. Network: USA, . Natl. Rep: Salem,. Hogan & Hartson. Format: Adult contemp, Christian. News staff: one; News: 2.5 hrs wkly. Target aud: 25-54; Christian families. Spec prog: Children one hr wkly. ◆Ed Mattson, pres; Adam Frase, progmg dir, mus dir.

Uniontown

WMBS(AM)— July 15, 1937: 590 khz; 1 kw-U, DA-N. TL: N39 51 35 W79 44 44. Hrs open: 24 44 S. Mt. Vernon Ave., 15401. Phone: (724) 438-3900. Fax: (724) 438-2406.E-mail: sales590@wmbs590.com Web Site:www.wmbs590.com Licensee: Fayette Broadcasting Corp. Population served: 60,000 Natl. Network: CBS Radio, Westwood One, . Natl. Rep: Commercial Media Sales,. Rgnl rep: West Media Group Pillsbury, Winthrop, Shaw, Pittman, LLP. Wire Svc: AP Wire Svc: Metro Weather Service Inc. Format: Var/div. News staff: one; News: 24 hrs wkly. Target aud: 25 plus; General. Spec prog: Talk shows, polka 3 hrs wkly, Pittsburgh Pirates, Pittsburgh Steelers, Pittsburgh Penguins, Pitt Panthers, Westwood One Sports, CBS News. ◆Bob Pritts, pres; Brian Mroziak, gen mgr, sports cmtr; Doreen Minafee, opns VP, traf mgr; Sandy Tracy, sls VP; Michael Pasqua, gen sls mgr; Jim Morgan, news dir; Timothy Schwer, pub affrs dir; Larry Campbell, chief of engrg; Tim Schwer, women's cmtr, disc jockey.

WPKL(FM)— Dec 20, 1968: 99.3 mhz; 3 kw. Ant 300 ft TL: N39 53 09 W79 46 29. Stereo. Hrs open: 24 123 Blaine Rd., Brownsville, 15417. Phone: (724) 938-2000. Fax: (724) 938-7842.E-mail: rherring@keymarketradio.com Web Site:oldiesradiooonline.com Licensee: Keymarket Licenses LLC Group owner: Keymarket Communications LLC (acq 1-17-2001; $475,000 with WYJK(AM) Connellsville). Population served: 150,000 Natl. Rep: Dome,. Format: Oldies. Target aud: 25 plus. ◆Gerald Getz, pres; Andrew Powaski, gen mgr, sls dir, gen sls mgr, progmg dir.

University Park

WOWY(FM)—Licensed to University Park. See State College

Upton

WPPT(FM)—See Mercersburg

Villanova

*WXVU(FM)— August 1991: 89.1 mhz; 710 w. 223 ft TL: N40 03 22 W75 22 30. (CP: 100 w vert, ant 279 ft. TL: N40 01 58 W75 20 15). Hrs open: Villanova University, 210 Dougherty Hall, 800 Lancaster Ave., 19085-1699. Phone: (610) 519-7200. Phone: 610-519-7201. Fax: (610) 519-7956.E-mail: info@wxvufm.com Web Site:www.wxvufm.com Licensee: Villanova University. Population served: 150,000 Format: free form, var, eclectic. Target aud: 15-25; youngsters. Spec prog: Black 10 hrs, relg 2 hrs wkly. ◆Kevin Moran, gen mgr; Andrew Moriarty, progmg dir; Suzanne Lee, mus dir; Kaitlin Santana, pub affrs dir.

Warminster

*WRDV(FM)— Sept 6, 1976: 89.3 mhz; 1 kw horiz, 100 w vert. 118 ft TL: N40 12 19 W75 06 27. Stereo. Hrs open: 24 Box 2012, 18974. Secondary address: 126 S. York Rd., Hatboro 19040. Phone: (215) 674-8002. Fax: (215) 674-4586. Web Site:wrdv.org Licensee: Bux-Mont Educational Radio Associates. (acq 3-80). Population served: 50,000 Format: Variety. News: 2 hrs wkly. Target aud: General. Spec prog: C&W 4 hrs, blues 3 hrs, folk 4 hrs, new age 3 hrs, jazz 3 hrs wkly. ◆Charles W. Loughery, pres; Todd H. Allen, gen mgr & progmg dir.

Warren

WNAE(AM)— Dec 31, 1946: 1310 khz; 5 kw-D, 94 w-N. TL: N41 48 50 W79 10 04. Hrs open: 24 Box 824, 16365. Secondary address: 310 2nd Ave. 16365. Phone: (814) 723-1310. Fax: (814) 723-3356.E-mail: info@kibcoradio.com Web Site:www.kibcoradio.com Licensee: Radio Partners LLC. (acq 9-30-2005; grpsl). Population served: 12,998 Natl. Network: AP Network News, . Rgnl. Network: Radio Pa. Wire Svc: AP Format: Talk. News staff: one; News: 11 hrs wkly. Target aud: General. ◆David Whipple, gen mgr, stn mgr, gen sls mgr; Karen White, opns mgr; Dale Bliss, prom dir, sls; Mark Silvis, progmg dir & news dir; Dana Simmons, traf mgr.

WRRN(FM)— March 1948: 92.3 mhz; 50 kw. 410 ft TL: N41 48 50 W79 10 04. Stereo. Hrs open: 24 Dups AM 14% Box 824, 16365. Phone: (814) 723-1310. Fax: (814) 723-3356.E-mail: info@kibcoradio.com Web Site:www.kibcoradio.com Licensee: Radio Partners LLC Format: Oldies. ◆Dave Whipple, stn mgr.

Warwick

*WZZD(FM)— December 2000: 88.1 mhz; 180 w vert. 587 ft TL: N40 07 45 W75 52 43. Stereo. Hrs open: 24 Rebroadcasts WBYO(FM) Sellersville 90%. Box 186, Sellersville, 18960. Phone: (215) 721-2141. Fax: (215) 721-9811.E-mail: wordfm@wordfm.org Web Site:www.wordfm.org Licensee: Four Rivers Community Broadcasting Corp. Population served: 75,000 Format: Christian Adult Contemp., Religious. Spec prog: Bluegrass/gospel 3 hrs wkly. ◆David Baker, VP; Charles W. Loughery, gen mgr.

Washington

WJPA(AM)— Feb 1, 1941: 1450 khz; 1 kw-U. TL: N40 11 23 W80 14 02. Hrs open: 24 98 S. Main St., 15301. Phone: (724) 222-2110. Fax: (724) 228-2299.E-mail: email@wjpa.com Web Site:www.wjpa.com Licensee: Washington Broadcasting Co. Population served: 220,000 Rgnl. Network: Radio Pa. Radio Pa. Format: Oldies. News staff: 2; News: 6 hrs wkly. ◆Michael S. Siegel, pres, gen mgr; Bob Gregg,

opns dir, chief of opns, gen sls mgr; Dale Allen, prom mgr; Pete Povich, progmg dir; Margie Konstantinou, mus dir; Jim Jefferson, news dir.

WJPA-FM— Sept 26, 1964: 95.3 mhz; 2.15 kw. Ant 390 ft TL: N40 11 23 W80 14 02. (CP: 4.2 kw). Hrs open: 24 98 S. Main St., 15301. Phone: (724) 222-2110. Fax: (724) 228-2299. Web Site:www.wjpa.com Licensee: Washington Broadcasting Co. Format: Oldies.

WKZV(AM)— August 1968: 1110 khz; 1 kw-D, DA. TL: N40 13 16 W80 14 34. Hrs open: Daylight 80 E. Chestnut St., 15301. Phone: (724) 228-6678. Fax: (724) 228-6678. Licensee: My-Key Broadcasting Inc. (acq 11-9-92; $100,000; 11-30-92). Population served: 210,000 Natl. Rep: Dome,. Format: Country. Target aud: 35 plus. Spec prog: Pol 3 hrs, polka 2 hrs, Croatian one hr, gospel one hr, racing one hr, relg one hr wkly. ◆Helen C. Supinski, pres; Michael Panjuscek, VP, gen mgr, progmg dir & traf mgr.

*WNJR(FM)— Nov 26, 1972: 91.7 mhz; 950 w. Ant 112 ft TL: N40 10 13 W80 14 43. Stereo. Hrs open: 24 60 S. Lincoln St., 15301. Phone: (724) 503-1001 x3345 (gen mgr). Phone: (724) 223-6039 (studio).E-mail: wnjr@washjeff.edu Web Site:www.wasjeff.edu/wnjr Licensee: Washington and Jefferson College. Population served: 1,200,000 Wire Svc: AP Format: Var/Div/Free Form. News: 4 hrs wkly. Target aud: All ages; college students, staff, community, alumni.

Waynesboro

WBHB-FM— Feb 3, 1959: 101.5 mhz; 50 kw horiz, 48 kw vert. Ant 230 ft TL: N39 49 44 W77 33 10. Stereo. Hrs open: Box 788, Greencastle, 17225. Secondary address: 10960 John Wayne Dr. 17225. Phone: (717) 597-9200. Fax: (717) 597-9210.E-mail: info@myrock1015.com Web Site:www.myrock1015.com Licensee: HJV L.P. Population served: 250,000 Format: Rock. ◆Blake Truman, stn mgr; Ed Chapa, progmg dir.

WCBG(AM)— Aug 19, 1953: 1380 khz; 1 kw-D. TL: N39 44 20 W77 36 10. Hrs open: Box 788, Greencastle, 17225. Secondary address: 10960 John Wayne Dr., Greencastle 17225. Phone: (717) 597-9200. Fax: (717) 597-9210. Licensee: HJV L.P. Group owner: VerStandig Broadcasting (acq 1-6-97; $1,068,699 with co-located FM). Population served: 10,011 Format: ESPN Radio. Target aud: 25-54. ◆Blake Truman, gen mgr & stn mgr.

Waynesburg

WANB(AM)— Sept 27, 1956: 1580 khz; 720 w-D. TL: N39 52 12 W80 08 01. (CP: 1210 khz; 5 kw-D, 710 w-CH). Hrs open: Sunrise-sunset Dups FM 100% 369 Tower Rd., 15370. Phone: (724) 627-5555. Fax: (724) 627-4021.E-mail: wanbradio@gmail.com Licensee: Broadcast Communications Inc. Population served: 5,152 ◆Marcia Mackay, traf mgr.

*WCYJ-FM— July 6, 1979: 88.7 mhz; 18 w. -33 ft TL: N39 53 59 W80 11 07. Stereo. Hrs open: 24 Waynesburg University, 51 W. College St., 15370. Phone: (724) 852-3310. Phone: (724) 852-3297. Fax: (724) 627-4757.E-mail: wcyj@waynesburg.edu Web Site:www.waynesburg.edu Licensee: Waynesburg College. (acq 7-3-79). Population served: 10,000 Format: Hot AC. News staff: one. Target aud: 18-25; college & high school students. Spec prog: Oldies 3 hrs, country 3 hrs, Christian 3 hrs, R&B 3 hrs, classic rock 3 hrs wkly. ◆Ariel Dugan, gen mgr; Mark Perry, stn mgr; Travis Gongaware, opns dir.

Wellsboro

WNBT(AM)— May 13, 1955: 1490 khz; 1 kw-U. TL: N41 44 41 W77 17 35. Hrs open: 24 Box 98, 16901. Secondary address: 198-B RR 7 16901. Phone: (570) 724-1490. Phone: (570) 662-7100. Fax: (570) 724-6971.E-mail: wnbt@ptd.net Web Site:www.wnbt.net Licensee: Farm & Home Broadcasting Co. Group owner: Allegheny Mountain Network Stations Population served: 4,003 Natl. Network: Westwood One, . Rgnl. Network: Radio Pa. Natl. Rep: Dome,. Radio Pa. Borsari & Paxson. Format: Adult standards. News staff: one; News: 10 hrs wkly. Target aud: 45+. ◆Cary Simpson, pres.

WNBT-FM— July 2, 1969: 104.5 mhz; 50 kw. 380 ft TL: N41 44 17 W77 21 50. Stereo. Hrs open: 24 Box 98, 16901. Phone: (570) 724-1490. Fax: (570) 724-6971.E-mail: wnbt@ptd.net Web Site:www.wnbt.net Licensee: Farm & Home Broadcasting Co. Natl. Network: Westwood One, . Format: CHR, popular music, adult contemp. News staff: one; News: 2 hrs wkly. Target aud: 18-55.

West Chester

WCHE(AM)— Oct 4, 1963: 1520 khz; 1000 w-D. TL: N39 58 06 W75 37 59. Hrs open: Sunrise-sunset 105 W. Gay St., 19380. Phone: (610) 692-3131. Fax: (610) 692-3133.E-mail: wche@wche1520.com Web Site:www.wche1520.com Licensee: Chester County Radio Inc. (acq 7-11-97; $230,000). Population served: 500,000 Natl. Network: USA, Westwood One, . Pepper & Corazzini. Format: Talk, Alternative Rock. News staff: one; News: 20 hrs wkly. Target aud: 24-64; upscale. Spec prog: Relg 8 hrs, country 2 hrs wkly. ♦David S. Shur, pres, sls dir, progmg dir, news dir; Jay Shur, gen mgr, opns mgr, chief of opns, prom dir & pub affrs dir.

WCOJ(AM)—See Coatesville

***WCUR(FM)**— 1999: 91.7 mhz; 100 w. Ant 108 ft TL: N39 57 02 W75 35 58. Hrs open: West Chester University, Sykes Union Bldg., 19383. Phone: (610) 436-2414. Fax: (610) 436-2477.E-mail: wcur@yahoo.com Web Site:www.wcur.fm Licensee: Student Services Inc. Format: Diversified.

West Hazleton

WKZN(AM)— 1982: 1300 khz; 5 kw-D, 500 w-N, DA-2. TL: N40 56 26 W76 00 07. Hrs open: 24
Rebroadcasts WILK(AM) Wilks-Barre 100%.
Box 729, 305 Hwy. 315, Pittstown, 18640. Phone: (570) 883-9850. Fax: (570) 883-0832.E-mail: info@wilknewsradio.com Web Site:www.wilknewsradio.com Licensee: Entercom Scranton Wilkes-Barre License LLC. Group owner: Entercom Communications Corp. (acq 12-13-99; grpsl). Population served: 25,000 Rgnl. Network: Radio Pa. Natl. Rep: D & R Radio,. Wire Svc: ABC Wire Svc: AP Format: News/talk. News staff: 6; News: 25 hrs wkly. Target aud: General; affluent, educated. Spec prog: Relg one hr wkly. ♦John Burkavage, gen mgr; Jim Rising, opns dir; Andy Zapotek, gen sls mgr; Bob DeMond, natl sls mgr; Casey Consagra, prom mgr; Nancy Kman, progmg dir; Joe Thomas, news dir, sports cmtr; Lamar Smith, chief of engrg; Shannon Ball, traf mgr; Tom Ragan, news rptr; Shadoe Steele, mus critic.

Whitneyville

WLIH(FM)— Mar 15, 1987: 107.1 mhz; 3.3 kw. Ant 298 ft TL: N41 46 13 W77 12 08. Stereo. Hrs open: 6 AM-Midnight Box 97, Wellsboro, 16901. Secondary address: 2352 Charleston Rd, Wellsboro 16901. Phone: (570) 724-4272. Fax: (570) 724-2302.E-mail: wlih107@quik.com Web Site:www.wlih.com Licensee: Good Christian Radio Broadcasting Inc. Natl. Network: USA, . Format: Relg, Christian, news. News: 28 hrs wkly. Target aud: General; serving the Christian community of the county. ♦Robert Makin, pres; Carol Makin, gen mgr.

Wilkes-Barre

WARM(AM)—See Scranton

WBAX(AM)— May 1, 1922: 1240 khz; 1 kw-U. TL: N41 15 13 W75 54 25. Hrs open: 24
Simulcasts with WEJL (AM) Scranton.
149 Penn Ave., Scranton, 18503. Phone: (570) 346-6555. Fax: (570) 346-6038.E-mail: INFO@WEJL-WBAX.COM Web Site:www.wejl-wbax.com Licensee: The Scranton Times L.P. Population served: 58,856 Format: Sports. News staff: one; News: 5 hrs wkly. Target aud: 18 + men. Spec prog: sports. ♦William R. Lynett, CEO; Jim Loftus, COO, gen mgr; Tim Durkin, sls dir; Jerry Arndt, natl sls mgr; Mark Hoover, mktg dir, prom mgr; Michael Neff, progmg dir; Ruth Miller, news dir; Kevin Fitzgerald, engrg dir; Krista Saar, traf mgr.

WBZU(AM)—See Scranton

***WCLH(FM)**— Feb 6, 1972: 90.7 mhz; 175 w. 1,020 ft TL: N41 10 58 W75 52 21. Stereo. Hrs open: 24 84 W. South St., Wilkes University, Wilkes Barre, 18766. Phone: (570) 408-5907. Fax: (570) 408-5908.E-mail: wclh@wilkes.edu Web Site:www.wclh.org Licensee: Wilkes University. Population served: 700,000 Natl. Network: AP Network News, . Format: Metal, hip hop, alternative. News: 7 hrs wkly. Target aud: 12-44. Spec prog: Ger 3 hrs, Sp 3 hrs wkly. ♦Renee Loftus, gen mgr; Ariel Cohen, progmg dir.

WEJL(AM)—See Scranton

WGGY(FM)—See Scranton

WICK(AM)—See Scranton

WILK(AM)— Feb 13, 1947: 980 khz; 5 kw-D, 1 kw-N, DA-N. TL: N41 13 42 W75 56 53. Stereo. Hrs open: 24 305 Hwy. 315, Pittston, 18640. Phone: (570) 883-9800. Fax: (570) 883-9851.E-mail: feedback@thewilknetwork.com Web Site:www.wilknetwork.com Licensee: Entercom Scranton Wilkes-Barre License LLC. Group owner: Entercom Communications Corp. (acq 12-13-99; grpsl). Population served: 72,500 Format: News/talk. Target aud: 15-54. Spec prog: Relg one hr wkly. ♦Joseph Fields, pres; John Burkavage, gen mgr.

WITK(AM)—See Pittston

WKRZ(FM)— 1947: 98.5 mhz; 8.7 kw. 1,171 ft TL: N41 11 56 W75 49 06. Stereo. Hrs open:
Rebroadcasts WKRZ(FM) Tobyhanna 100%.
305 Hwy. 315, Box 729, Pittston, 18640. Phone: (570) 883-9850. Fax: (570) 883-9851.E-mail: info@wkrz.com Web Site:www.wkrz.com Licensee: Entercom Scranton Wilkes-Barre License LLC. Group owner: Entercom Communications Corp. (acq 12-13-99; grpsl). Population served: 200,000 Format: CHR. Target aud: 19-54; women. ♦John Burkavage, gen mgr; Jim Rising, opns mgr; Ryan Flynn, gen sls mgr, sls; Tias Schuster, progmg dir; Elizabeth Masich, mus dir; Lamar Smith, chief of engrg.

WMGS(FM)— 1946: 92.9 mhz; 5.3 kw. Ant 1,384 ft TL: N41 10 58 W75 52 26. Stereo. Hrs open: 24 600 Baltimore Dr., 2nd Floor, 18702. Phone: (570) 824-9000. Fax: (570) 820-0520. Web Site:www.magic93fm.com Licensee: Citadel Broadcasting Co. Group owner: Citadel Broadcasting Corp. (acq 7-1-97; grpsl). Format: Soft rock. News staff: one; News: 2 hrs wkly. Target aud: 25-54; adult women. Spec prog: Farm one hr, relg 3 hrs wkly. ♦Bill Palmeri, mktg mgr; Erin Evans, prom dir; Stan Phillips, progmg dir.

WNAK(AM)—See Nanticoke

***WRKC(FM)**— Sept 18, 1968: 88.5 mhz; 440 w. -470 ft TL: N41 14 57 W75 52 26. Stereo. Hrs open: 7 AM-2 AM 133 N. Franklin St., 18711. Phone: (570) 208-5931. Fax: (570) 825-9049.E-mail: wrkc@kings.edu Web Site:www.kings.edu/~wrke/ Licensee: King's College. Population served: 300,000 Format: Rock, AOR, reading for the blind. Target aud: General; people who need wide-ranging svcs. ♦Sue Henry, gen mgr; Pat Barton, stn mgr; Katie Moore, progmg dir; Michael Wasenda, mus dir.

WWRR(FM)—See Scranton

Wilkinsburg

WPYT(AM)— Aug 25, 1960: 660 khz; 260 w-D. TL: N40 24 47 W79 51 14. Hrs open: Daylight 4736 Penn Ave., Pittsburgh, 15224. Phone: (412) 661-6001. Fax: (412) 661-7195. Licensee: Langer Broadcasting Group L.L.C. (group owner; acq 5-22-98). Rgnl. Network: Radio Pa. Reddy, Begley & McCormick. Format: Talk. ♦Ed Dehart, gen sls mgr; Stephen Zelenko, gen mgr, gen mgr & progmg dir.

Williamsport

WBZD-FM—(Muncy, Aug 11, 1983: 93.3 mhz; 1.7 kw. Ant 1,220 ft TL: N41 12 42 W76 57 16. Stereo. Hrs open: 24 1685 Four Mile Dr., 17701. Phone: (570) 323-8200. Fax: (570) 327-9138.E-mail: dan.farr@bybradio.com Web Site:www.wbzd.com Licensee: South Williamsport SaberCom Inc. Group owner: Backyard Broadcasting LLC (acq 12-1-02; grpsl). Population served: 300,000 Natl. Rep: Christal,. Format: Oldies. News staff: one; News: 3 hrs wkly. Target aud: 18-54; adult oriented, mass appeal. ♦Barry Drake, pres; Robin Smith, CFO; Dan Farr, gen mgr; Bob Pawlikowski, gen sls mgr; Ted Minier, progmg dir; Brian Hill, chief of engrg, engr.

***WCRG(FM)**— Feb 20, 2002: 90.7 mhz; 3 kw. Ant -216 ft TL: N41 13 50 W77 08 59. Stereo. Hrs open: 24
Rebroadcasts WGRC(FM) Lewisburg 100%.
101 Armory Blvd., Lewisburg, 17837. Phone: (570) 523-1190. Fax: (570) 523-1114.E-mail: email@wgrc.com Web Site:www.wgrc.com Licensee: Salt & Light Media Ministries Inc. Population served: 150,000 Miller & Neely. Wire Svc: AP Format: Contemp Christian. News staff: 3; News: 12 hrs wkly. Target aud: 25-54. ♦Larry Weidman, gen mgr; Lamar Smith, chief of engrg; Linda Dantonio, traf mgr; Jim Diehl, news rptr; Chris Miller, engr.

WILQ(FM)— July 31, 1949: 105.1 mhz; 9.2 kw. Ant 1,135 ft TL: N41 11 43 W76 58 18. Stereo. Hrs open: 24 1685 Four Mile Dr., 17701. Phone: (570) 323-8200. Fax: (570) 327-9138.E-mail: dan.farr@bybradio.com Web Site:www.wilq.com Licensee: South Williamsport SabreCom Inc. Group owner: Backyard Broadcasting LLC (acq 12-1-02; grpsl). Population served: 350,000 Natl. Rep: Christal,. Format: Country. News staff: 4; News: 7 hrs wkly. Target aud: 25 plus; adults in a 10 county area. ♦Barry Drake, pres; Robin Smith, CFO; Dan Farr, gen mgr; Doug Dodge, gen sls mgr; Ted Minier, progmg dir; John Finn, news dir.

WKSB(FM)— Apr 1, 1948: 102.7 mhz; 53 kw. 1,270 ft TL: N41 11 21 W76 58 53. Stereo. Hrs open: 24 Prog sep from AM Box 3638, 1559 W. 4th St., 17701. Phone: (570) 327-1400. Fax: (570) 327-8156.E-mail: wksb@wksb.com Web Site:www.wksb.com Population served: 71,000 Format: Adult contemp. News staff: one. Target aud: 25-54. ♦Russell Davidson, opns dir; Tom Scott, progmg dir; Tom Turner, asst music dir; Mark Lawrence, pub affrs dir; Dan Milliken, engrg dir; Liz Stroup, traf mgr.

WLMY(FM)— Aug 16, 1989: 107.9 mhz; 360 w. Ant 1,289 ft TL: N41 12 39 W76 57 17. Stereo. Hrs open: 24 1685 Four Mile Dr., 17701. Phone: (570) 323-8200. Fax: (570) 327-9138. Licensee: South Williamsport SabreCom Inc. Group owner: Backyard Broadcasting LLC (acq 12-1-2002; grpsl). Population served: 311,200 Natl. Network: ABC, . Natl. Rep: Christal,. Format: Adult contemp. News staff: one; News: one hr wkly. Target aud: 25-54. ♦Barry Drake, pres; Robin Smith, CFO; Dan Farr, gen mgr.

WLYC(AM)— June 1951: 1050 khz; 1 kw-D, 36 w-N. TL: N41 15 44 W77 01 59. Hrs open: 24 101 Phillips Park Dr., So. Williamsport, 17702-7063. Phone: (570) 327-1300. Fax: (570) 327-1331.E-mail: wlyc1050@yahoo.com Web Site:www.sports1050.com Licensee: Sentry Communications License LLC (acq 7-19-2005; $75,000). Population served: 350,000 Natl. Network: ESPN Radio, Westwood One, . Radio Pa. Rgnl rep: . Miller and Neely, PC. Format: Sports. News: Sports news only. Target aud: 25-54; male. ♦James R. McKowne, gen mgr; Jeffrey Andruionis, opns mgr; Christy Andruionis, sls.

***WPTC(FM)**— Sept 3, 1980: 88.1 mhz; 494 w. -101 ft TL: N41 14 11 W77 01 26. Stereo. Hrs open: 24 One College Ave., 17701. Phone: (570) 326-3761, EXT. 7548. Fax: (570) 320-2423.E-mail: wptc@pct.edu Web Site:www.pct.edu/wptc Licensee: Pennsylvania College of Technology. (acq 3-14-90). Population served: 99,000 Wire Svc: AP Format: Jazz, modern rock. News: one hr wkly. Target aud: 18-24; college students. Spec prog: Lost Radio (1 hr). ♦Davie Gilmour, pres; Brad Nason, gen mgr.

WRAK(AM)— Apr 10, 1930: 1400 khz; 1 kw-U. TL: N41 14 22 W77 02 27. Hrs open: 24
Rebroadcasts WRKK(AM) Hughesville 100%.
Box 3638, 1559 W. 4th St., 17701. Phone: (570) 327-1400. Fax: (570) 327-8156.E-mail: wrak@wrak.com Web Site:www.wrak.com Licensee: Clear Channel Radio License Inc. Group owner: Clear Channel Communications Inc. (acq 8-5-98; grpsl). Population served: 37,918 Natl. Network: Westwood One, . Format: News/talk, sports. News staff: one; News: 3 hrs wkly. Target aud: 35 plus. ♦James Dabney, gen mgr, gen sls mgr; Tom Scott, mktg dir; Ken Sawyer, progmg dir.

***WRLC(FM)**— Apr 5, 1976: 91.7 mhz; 740 w. -298 ft TL: N41 14 42 W76 59 50. Stereo. Hrs open: 24 Mass Communication Bldg., Lycoming College, 700 College Place, 17701. Phone: (570) 321-4060. Fax: (570) 321-4372.E-mail: wrlc@lycoming.edu Web Site:www.lycoming.edu/orgs/wrlc Licensee: Lycoming College. (acq 1-76). Population served: 35,000 Format: Alternative, Hip Hop, Oldies. News: 15 hrs wkly. Target aud: General; Lycoming College & its surrounding communities. Spec prog: Class one hr, gospel 6 hrs, pub affrs 2 hrs, Christian rock 3 hrs, jazz 8 hrs, blues 3 hrs wkly. ♦Alan Jackson, gen mgr, stn mgr; Skip Smith, chief of engrg.

WVRT(FM)—See Mill Hall

***WVYA(FM)**— 2003: 89.7 mhz; 3.3 kw. Ant -16 ft TL: N41 14 54 W77 01 52. Stereo. Hrs open: 24
Rebroadcasts WVIA-FM Scranton.
100 Wvia Way, Pittston, 18640-6197. Phone: (570) 655-2808. Fax: (570) 655-1180.E-mail: webadmin@wvia.org Web Site:www.wvia.org Licensee: Northeastern Pennsylvania Educational TV Association. Natl. Network: NPR, . Dow, Lohnes & Albertson. Wire Svc: AP Format: Class, jazz, news. News staff: one; News: 30 hrs wkly. Target aud: Upscale, mature audience. ♦A. William Kelly, CEO, gen mgr; A William Kelly, pres; Chris Norton, VP; Larry Vojtko, progmg mgr.

WWPA(AM)— May 22, 1949: 1340 khz; 1 kw-U. TL: N41 13 45 W77 00 45. Hrs open: 24 1685 Four Mile Dr., 17701. Phone: (570) 323-8200. Fax: (570) 327-9138. Licensee: South Williamsport SabreCom Inc. Group owner: Backyard Broadcasting LLC (acq 12-1-02; grpsl). Population served: 136,000 Natl. Network: CSN, . Natl. Rep: Christal,. Format: News/talk. News staff: one; News: 168 hrs wkly. Target aud: 35 plus. Spec prog: Sports. ♦Barry Drake, pres; Robin Smith, CFO; Dan Farr, gen mgr.

WZXR(FM)—See South Williamsport

Wyomissing

*WYTL(FM)— 2005: 91.7 mhz; 10 w horiz, 320 w vert. Ant 840 ft TL: W40 19 22 W76 11 52. Hrs open: Rebroadcasts WBYO (FM) Sellersville 100%.
Box 186, Sellersville, 18960. Phone: (215) 721-2141. Fax: (215) 721-9811.E-mail: wordfm@wordfm.org Web Site:www.wordfm.org Licensee: Four Rivers Community Broadcasting Corp. Format: Adult contemp Religious. ◆David Baker, VP.

York

WARM-FM— Sept 1, 1962: 103.3 mhz; 6.4 kw. 1,305 ft TL: N40 01 38 W76 36 08. Stereo. Hrs open: 24 Prog sep from AM Box 910, 17402. Secondary address: 5989 Susquehanna Plaza Dr. 17406. Phone: (717) 764-1155. Fax: (717) 252-4708.E-mail: info@warm103.com Web Site:www.warm103.com Format: Adult contemp. ◆ Tom Ranker, VP & stn mgr; Tina Heim, gen sls mgr; Bob Hurbert, prom mgr; Kelly West, progmg dir, disc jockey; Joel Murphy, traf mgr; Gina Koch, spec ev coord; Dennis Wagner, disc jockey.

WOYK(AM)— March 1932: 1350 khz; 5 kw-D, 1 kw-N, DA-N. TL: N39 56 00 W76 49 06. Hrs open: 24 Box 20249, 17402. Secondary address: 1051 Dairy Ln., Elizabethtown 17022. Phone: (717) 840-0355. Fax: (717) 840-0355.E-mail: woyk1350@att.net Web Site:sportsradioespn1350.com Licensee: WOYK Inc. (acq 12-87). Natl. Network: Sporting News Radio Network, . Radio Pa. Format: Sports. Target aud: 25-64; men. ◆Douglas George, pres; Vincent Grande, gen mgr; SAM CONRAD, opns dir.

WQXA-FM— 1948: 105.7 mhz; 25 kw. Ant 705 ft TL: N39 59 56 W76 41 43. Stereo. Hrs open: 515 S. 32nd St., Camp Hill, 17011. Phone: (717) 635-7700. Fax: (717) 635-7551. Licensee: Citadel Broadcasting Co. (acq 5-29-97; grpsl). Population served: 1,800,000 Format: Active rock. Target aud: 18-49. ◆Bob Adams, gen mgr & progmg mgr.

WSBA(AM)— Sept 1, 1942: 910 khz; 5 kw-D, 1 kw-N, DA-2. TL: N39 59 53 W76 44 42. Hrs open: 24 Box 910, 17402-0910. Secondary address: 5989 Susquehanna Plaza Dr. 17406. Phone: (717) 764-1155. Fax: (717) 252-4708.E-mail: info@wsba910.com Web Site:www.wsba910.com Licensee: WSBA Lico Inc. Group owner: Susquehanna Radio Corp. Population served: 1,000,000 Format: News/talk. News staff: 5. Spec prog: Black 3 hrs, farm 4 hrs wkly. ◆ Tom Rawker, gen mgr; Bob Popa, prom mgr, chief of engrg; Jim Horn, progmg dir.

WSJW(FM)—See Starview

*WVYC(FM)— Nov 18, 1976: 99.7 mhz; 370 w. 97 ft TL: N39 56 49 W76 43 47. (CP: 99.7 mhz). Stereo. Hrs open: 18 York College of Pennsylvania, 439 Country Club Rd., 17405-7199. Phone: (717) 815-1932. Phone: (717) 815-1311.E-mail: tgibson@ycp.edu Web Site:www.wvyc.org Licensee: York College of Pennsylvania. Format: Educ, Div/Var, free form. News staff: one; News: 3 hrs wkly. Target aud: 14-24; new mus lovers. Spec prog: Class 8 hrs, jazz 8 hrs, Sp one hr wkly. ◆Michelle Gorecki, gen mgr.

WYYC(AM)— 1948: 1250 khz; 1 kw-D. TL: N39 59 56 W76 41 43. Stereo. Hrs open: 24 919 Buckingham Blvd., Elizabethtown, 17022. Phone: (717) 757-9402.E-mail: wyyc@wilkinsradio.com Web Site:www.wilkinsradio.com Licensee: Steel City Radio Inc. Group owner: Citadel Broadcasting Corp. (acq 10-11-2005; $250,000). Population served: 1,154,000 Womble, Carlyle, Sandridge & Rice. Format: Chrisitian teaching/talk. Target aud: 35 plus. ◆Bob Wilkins, CEO, stn mgr; LuAnn Wilkins, exec VP; Bob Moore, gen mgr, stn mgr.

York-Hanover

WYCR(FM)—Licensed to York-Hanover. See Hanover

Youngsville

*WTMV(FM)— Jan 19, 1999: 88.5 mhz; 100 w. -335 ft TL: N41 51 01 W79 18 41. Stereo. Hrs open: 24 409 E. Main St., 16371. Phone: (814) 563-4903. Fax: (814) 563-4903.E-mail: wtmv@verizon.net Web Site:www.wtmv.com Licensee: Living Word of Faith Christian Outreach. Population served: 5,000 Natl. Network: American Family Radio, Moody, . Format: Christian. News staff: 5; News: 7-11. Target aud: 21 plus; Christians of all ages. Spec prog: Children 10 hrs, class 2.5 hrs wkly. ◆Rev. Patricia A. Baker, VP, mus dir; Rev. William E. Baker, pres & gen mgr; Kathy Joy, pub affrs dir; Khlare Bracken, mus critic.

Rhode Island

Block Island

WCRI(FM)— June 13, 1994: 95.9 mhz; 6 kw. 174 ft TL: N41 10 21 W71 33 52. Stereo. Hrs open: 24 400 S. County Trail, Exeter, 02822. Phone: (401) 294-9274. Fax: (401) 596-6782.E-mail: mail@classical959.com Web Site:www.classical959.com Licensee: Judson Group Inc. (acq 11-22-2006; $1.6 million with WCNX(AM) Hope Valley). Population served: 50,000 Format: Class. Target aud: General. Spec prog: New age 4 hrs, folk 4 hrs, big band 4 hrs, relg 2 hrs wkly. ◆Christopher S. Jones, pres; Mark Halliday, gen mgr; Michael Abranson, stn mgr.

WJZS(FM)— Oct 3, 1988: 99.3 mhz; 6 kw. Ant 256 ft TL: N41 10 28 W71 34 20. Stereo. Hrs open: 24 Box 367, Newport, 02480. Phone: (401) 846-1540. Fax: (401) 846-1598.E-mail: rmelfi@wadk.com Web Site:www.wjzs.com Licensee: Astro Tele-Communications Corp. (acq 8-24-99). Population served: 1,000,000 Shaw Pittman. Format: Adult contemp/variety. Target aud: 30-50; total community. ◆Robert Melfi, gen mgr; Maurice B. Polayes, chief of engrg; Lisa Lancaster, traf mgr.

Bristol

*WQRI(FM)— April 1989: 88.3 mhz; 100 w. 75 ft TL: N41 38 49 W91 15 34. Hrs open: One Old Ferry Rd., Campus Program, 02809. Phone: (401) 254-3283. Phone: (401) 254-3282. Fax: (401) 254-3355. Licensee: Roger Williams University. Format: AOR. ◆Becky Riopel, gen mgr.

Charlestown

WKFD(AM)—Not on air, target date: unknown: 1370 khz; 2.5 kw-D, 5 kw-N, DA-2. TL: N41 22 38 W71 39 50. Hrs open: 24 20 Freeman Pl., Needham, MA, 02192. Phone: (781) 444-4754. Fax: (781) 444-8630. Licensee: Astro Tele-Communications Corp. ◆Maurice B. Polayes, pres.

Coventry

*WCVY(FM)— Oct 19, 1978: 91.5 mhz; 200 w. 36 ft TL: N41 41 10 W71 35 37. Stereo. Hrs open: 40 Reservoir Rd., 02816-6404. Phone: (401) 822-9499. Fax: (401) 822-9492. Licensee: Coventry Public Schools. Format: Top-40. Target aud: 12-30. Spec prog: Sports 2 hrs wkly. ◆Jason Murry, stn mgr.

East Greenwich

WARV(AM)—See Warwick

*WRJI(FM)—Not on air, target date: unknown: 91.5 mhz; 100 w. Ant 157 ft TL: N41 39 35 W71 30 00. Hrs open: 39 Julian St., Providence, 02909. Licensee: Educational Radio for the Public of the New Millennium.

Greenville

WALE(AM)—Licensed to Greenville. See Providence

Hope Valley

WCNX(AM)— Oct 7, 1985: 1180 khz; 1.8 kw-D. TL: N41 31 36 W71 44 35. Stereo. Hrs open: 400 S. County Trail, Exeter, 02822. Phone: (401) 596-6795. Fax: (401) 596-6782.E-mail: mail@classical959.com Web Site:www.newsradio1180.com Licensee: Judson Group Inc. (acq 11-22-2006; $1.6 million with WCRI(FM) Block Island). Population served: 750,000 Natl. Network: USA, . Smithwick & Belendiuk. Format: Loc news. ◆Christopher S. Jones, pres; Mark Halliday, gen mgr; Mike Abramson, stn mgr & chief of engrg.

Kingston

*WRIU(FM)— Feb 16, 1964: 90.3 mhz; 3.44 kw. 415 ft TL: N41 29 52 W71 31 42. Stereo. Hrs open: 24 326 Memorial Union, 02881. Phone: (401) 874-4949. Fax: (401) 874-4349. Licensee: University of Rhode Island. Population served: 1,000,000 Format: Div, rock. Target aud: Diverse. Spec prog: Folk 15 hrs, gospel 5 hrs, heavy metal 6 hrs, blues 3 hrs, reggae 7 hrs, Sp 3 hrs wkly. ◆James Proctor, gen mgr.

Middletown

WKKB(FM)— Oct 6, 1978: 100.3 mhz; 1.55 kw. Ant 656 ft TL: N41 35 48 W71 11 24. Stereo. Hrs open: 24 1185 N. Main St., Providence, 02904. Phone: (401) 331-1003. Fax: (401) 521-5077.E-mail: marcklowan@supermaxfm.com Web Site:latina 1003.com Licensee: Davidson Media Rhode Island Stations LLC. Group owner: Citadel Broadcasting Corp. (acq 1-31-2005; $7.5 million with WAKX(FM) Narragansett Pier). Population served: 40,000 Format: Sp tropical. News staff: one; News: 7 hrs wkly. Target aud: 12+; Latino Americans 1st & 2nd generation. ◆Craig Rapoza, gen mgr; Cesar Salas, gen sls mgr; Enrique Ortaga, progmg VP; Juan Gonzalez, progmg dir.

Narragansett Pier

WRNI-FM— July 15, 1990: 102.7 mhz; 1.95 kw. Ant 226 ft TL: N41 25 27 W71 28 38. Stereo. Hrs open: 19 One Union Station, Providence, 02903. Phone: (401) 351-2800. Fax: (401) 351-0246. Web Site:www.wrni.org Licensee: Rhode Island Public Radio Group owner: Citadel Communications Corp. (acq 5-16-2007; $2.56 million). Population served: 1,000,000 Natl. Network: NPR, . Format: News/talk. ◆Eugene B. Mihaly, pres; Joe O'Connor, gen mgr.

Newport

WADK(AM)— Nov 6, 1948: 1540 khz; 1 kw-D, 20 w-N. TL: N41 30 13 W71 18 43. Hrs open: 6am-6pm Box 367, 02840. Phone: (401) 846-1540. Fax: (401) 846-1598.E-mail: rmelfi@wadk.com Web Site:www.wadk.com Licensee: Astro Tele-Communications Corp. (acq 8-24-99). Population served: 78,000 Natl. Network: ABC, Talk Radio Network, . Shaw Pittman. Format: News/talk/sports. News staff: 2; News: 17.5 hrs wkly. Target aud: 35 +. Spec prog: Jazz 7 hrs wkly; gardening 1 hr; Real Estate 1 hr; Law 1 hr; Pet Care 2 hrs; Irish Music 2hrs. ◆Robert Melfi, gen mgr; Lisa Lancaster, progmg dir, traf mgr; Maurice Polayes, chief of engrg.

Pawtucket

WDDZ(AM)— Feb 12, 1950: 550 khz; 1 kw-D, 500 w-N, DA-N. TL: N41 54 20 W71 23 56. Stereo. Hrs open: 24 hrs 203 Concord St., Suite 453, 02860. Phone: (401) 722-0839. Fax: (401) 722-1459. Licensee: Radio Disney Group LLC. Group owner: ABC Inc. (acq 5-29-2001; $2.05 million). Population served: 30,000 Natl. Network: Radio Disney, . Format: Children. Target aud: Children & Teens 3-14, Parents 25-54, esp. moms. ◆Michael Kellogg, gen mgr; Jaccalen Grillo, prom mgr.

Portsmouth

*WJHD(FM)— Apr 3, 1972: 90.7 mhz; 360 w. 80 ft TL: N41 36 06 W71 16 20. Hrs open: Portsmouth Abbey School, Cory's Ln., 02871. Phone: (401) 683-2000. Fax: (401) 683-5888. Licensee: The Order of St. Benedict. Population served: 12,000 Format: Div. ◆Edmund Adams, gen mgr.

Providence

WALE(AM)—(Greenville, 1948: Stn currently dark. 990 khz; 50 kw-D, 5 kw-N, DA-2. TL: N41 57 18 W71 35 39. Hrs open: 6 AM-midnight 1185 N. Main St., Greenville, 02904. Phone: (401) 521-0990. Fax: (401) 521-5077. Licensee: Cumbre Communications Corp., debtor in possession (acq 8-10-2004). Population served: 2,500,000 Format: Sp. Target aud: . ◆Manolo Pazos, gen mgr.

WBRU(FM)— Feb 21, 1966: 95.5 mhz; 20 kw. 440 ft TL: N41 49 40 W71 22 09. (CP: 50 kw, and 492 ft. TL: N41 48 28 W71 28 12). Stereo. Hrs open: 24 88 Benevolent St., 02906. Phone: (401) 272-9550. Fax: (401) 272-9278.E-mail: promotions@wbru.com Web Site:www.wbru.com Licensee: Brown Broadcasting Service Inc. Population served: 180,000 Format: Alternative Urban contemp. News: 3 hrs wkly. Target aud: 18-34; highly educated professionals. Spec prog: Black 20 hrs, jazz 18 hrs wkly. ◆Jon Zucker, gen mgr, prom dir; Marianna Faircloth, stn mgr; Mark Stackowski, gen sls mgr; Olivia Hoffman, prom dir; Chris Novello, progmg dir; Kaitlyn Laabs, news dir.

WCTK(FM)—(New Bedford, MA) Dec 9, 1946: 98.1 mhz; 47.3 kw. 508 ft TL: N41 37 21 W70 55 07. Stereo. Hrs open: 24 Prgmg separate from AM 75 Oxford St., 02905. Phone: (401) 467-4366. Fax: (401) 941-2795.E-mail: twall@hallradio.com Web Site:www.wctk.com Licensee: Hall Communications Inc. Population served: 1,594,300 Natl. Rep: Eastman Radio,. Fletcher, Heald & Hildreth. Format: Country. Target aud: 25-54. ◆Arthur Rowbotham, pres.

*WDOM(FM)— Mar 15, 1966: 91.3 mhz; 125 w. 130 ft TL: N41 50 39 W71 26 14. Stereo. Hrs open: 18 Providence College, 02918. Phone: (401) 865-2460. Fax: (401) 865-2822.E-mail: wdom@studentweb.providence.edu Web Site:www.listen.to/wdom Licensee: Providence College. Population served: 179,213 Format: College alternative. News: one hr wkly. Target aud: General; college students & professionals. Spec prog: Urban contemp 16 hrs, metal 6 hrs, country 2 hrs, classic rock 3 hrs, sports 2 hrs wkly. ◆Scott Seseske, gen mgr, dev dir, pub affrs dir, sports cmtr; Brian Wall, opns dir, mktg dir, progmg dir; Carlin Corrigan, prom dir; Dan Devine, mus dir, mus critic; Jaclyn Schede, asst music dir; Sott Seseske, spec ev coord.

*WELH(FM)— September 1994: 88.1 mhz; 150 w. 98 ft TL: N41 51 30 W71 19 04. Hrs open: 24 216 Hope St., 02906. Phone: (401) 421-8100. Fax: (401) 751-7674. Web Site:www.wheelerschool.org Licensee: The Wheeler School. Fletcher, Heald & Hildreth. Format: Div, jazz, Sp. Target aud: General. ◆Dave Schiano, gen mgr.

WHJJ(AM)— Sept 6, 1922: 920 khz; 5 kw-U, DA-N. TL: N41 46 53 W71 19 55. Hrs open: 24 75 Oxford St., 02905. Phone: (401) 781-9979. Fax: (401) 781-9329. Web Site:www.920whjj.com Licensee: Capstar TX L.P. Group owner: Clear Channel Communications Inc. (acq 8-30-2000; grpsl). Population served: 184,000 Natl. Network: CBS, . Natl. Rep: Clear Channel,. Wilkinson, Barker, Knauer & Quinn. Format: News/talk. Target aud: 35-64. ◆Jim Corwin, gen mgr; Kevin Hickey, sls dir; Bill George, progmg dir.

WHJY(FM)— Mar 14, 1966: 94.1 mhz; 50 kw. Ant 546 ft TL: N41 49 40 W71 22 09. Stereo. Hrs open: 75 Oxford St., 02905. Phone: (401) 781-9979. Fax: (401) 781-9329. Web Site:www.whjy.com Licensee: Capstar TX L.P. Population served: 250,000 Format: AOR. Target aud: 18-34; adults. ◆Scott Laudani, progmg dir.

WLKW(AM)—(West Warwick, Aug 12, 1986: 1450 khz; 1 kw-U. TL: N41 41 38 W71 31 26. Hrs open: 24 75 Oxford St., 02905. Phone: (401) 467-4366. Fax: (401) 941-2795.E-mail: twall@hallradio.com Licensee: Hall Communications Inc. (group owner; acq 6-4-01; $410,000). Population served: 30,000 Natl. Network: ESPN Radio, . Natl. Rep: Eastman Radio,. Fletcher, Heald and Hildreth. Format: All Sports. News staff: one. Target aud: 35-64. Spec prog: Pol 2 hrs wkly. ◆Bonnie Rowbotham, CEO; Arthur Rowbotham, pres; Tom Wall, gen mgr.

WNBH(AM)—(New Bedford, MA) May 21, 1921: 1340 khz; 1 kw-U. TL: N41 37 21 W70 55 07. Hrs open: 24 Simulcast with WLKW(AM) West Warwick, RI. 888 Purchase St., New Bedford, MA, 02740. Phone: (508) 979-8003. Phone: (401) 467-4366. Fax: (508) 979-8009.E-mail: twall@hallradio.com Web Site:wnbhradio.com Licensee: Hall Communications Inc. (group owner; acq 10-1-66). Population served: 101,777 Natl. Network: ABC, . Natl. Rep: D & R Radio,. Fletcher, Heald & Hildreth. Format: Btfl mus. News: 3 hrs wkly. Target aud: 35-64. Spec prog: Pol 2 hrs wkly. ◆Bonnie H. Rowbotham, chmn; Arthur J. Rowbotham, pres; Tom Wall, VP & gen mgr.

WPMZ(AM)— Apr 15, 1947: 1110 khz; 5 kw-D. TL: N41 49 40 W71 22 09. Hrs open: 1270 Mineral Spring Ave., North Providence, 02904. Phone: (401) 726-8413. Fax: (401) 726-8649.E-mail: wpmz@aol.com Web Site:www.poder1110.com Licensee: Videomundo Broadcasting Co. L.L.C. (acq 1-27-98; $900,000). Population served: 1,200,000 Format: Sp. Target aud: General. ◆Dilson Mendez, pres; Tony Mendez, gen mgr; Johanna Petrarca, sls dir; Zoilo Garcia, progmg dir.

WPRO(AM)— Oct 16, 1931: 630 khz; 5 kw-U, DA-N. TL: N41 46 28 W71 19 23. Hrs open: Simulcast with WEAN-FM Wakefield-Peacedale 100%. 1502 Wampanoag Tr., East Providence, 02915. Phone: (401) 433-4200. Fax: (401) 433-5967. Web Site:www.630wpro.com Licensee: Citadel Broadcasting Co. Group owner: Citadel Broadcasting Corp. (acq 5-29-97; grpsl). Population served: 179,213 Natl. Rep: McGavren Guild,. Format: News/talk, sports. ◆Barbara Haynes, gen mgr; Joe Lembo, sls dir.

WPRO-FM— April 1949: 92.3 mhz; 39 kw. 550 ft TL: N41 48 18 W71 28 24. (CP: 45.4 kw, ant 489 ft.). Stereo. Hrs open: Prog sep from AM 1502 Wampanoag Tr., East Providence, 02915. Phone: (401) 433-4200. Fax: (401) 433-5967. Web Site:www.92wpro.com Licensee: Citadel Broadcasting Co. Population served: 346,100 Format: CHR. ◆Steve Maully, rgnl sls mgr; Tony Brisco, progmg dir.

WPRV(AM)— June 2, 1922: 790 khz; 5 kw-U, DA-N. TL: N41 50 03 W71 21 56. Stereo. Hrs open: 1502 Wampanoag Tr., East Providence, 02915. Phone: (401) 433-4200. Fax: (401) 433-2932. Web Site:www.790thescore.com Licensee: Citadel Broadcasting Co. Group owner: Citadel Broadcasting Corp. (acq 5-29-97; grpsl). Population served: 1,792,130 Natl. Rep: McGavren Guild,. Format: Talk, business talk. Target aud: 25-64; upper class, affluent, college educated. ◆Barbara Haynes, VP & gen mgr.

WRNI(AM)— April 1948: 1290 khz; 5 kw-U, DA-2. TL: N41 51 21 W71 26 41. Hrs open: 24 One Union Station, 02903. Phone: (401) 351-2800. Fax:(401) 351-0246.E-mail: info@wrni.org Web Site:www.wrni.org Licensee: WRNI Foundation (acq 7-1-98). Natl. Network: NPR, PRI, . Natl. Rep: Rgnl Reps,. Format: News/talk. News staff: 8; News: 80 hrs wkly. Target aud: 25-54; intelligent adults interested in news & politics. ◆Joe O'Connor, gen mgr; Steve Callahan, chief of engrg.

WSNE-FM—See Taunton, MA

WSTL(AM)— June 16, 1946: 1220 khz; 1 kw-D, 166 w-N. TL: N41 49 15 W71 23 07. Hrs open: 24 95 Sagamore Rd., Seekonk, MA, 02771-3428. Phone: (508) 336-4233. Fax: (508) 343-2159.E-mail: patricia.varner@shineradio.us Web Site:shineradio.us Licensee: New England Christian Media Inc. (acq 10-1-2006; $1.9 million). Population served: 79,000 Format: Christian broadcasting. ◆Patricia Varner, gen mgr; Mike Laliberte, progmg dir.

WWBB(FM)— June 7, 1968: 101.5 mhz; 13.5 kw horiz, 12 kw vert. 951 ft TL: N41 52 13 W71 17 47. Stereo. Hrs open: 24 75 Oxford St., 3rd Fl., 02905. Phone: (401) 781-9979. Fax: (401) 781-9329. Web Site:www.b101.com Licensee: Clear Channel Radio Licenses Inc. Group owner: Clear Channel Communications Inc. Population served: 1,278,800 Natl. Network: AP Radio, Premiere Radio Networks, . Natl. Rep: Clear Channel,. Format: Classic hits. Target aud: 35-54; indispensable & powerful adults. ◆Jim Corwin, gen mgr; Mark Cottey, sls dir, pub affrs dir; Michelle Maker, mktg dir; Steve Lariviere, chief of engrg.

WWLI(FM)— July 11, 1948: 105.1 mhz; 50 kw. Ant 500 ft TL: N41 48 22 W71 28 12. Stereo. Hrs open: 1502 Wampanoag Tr., East Providence, 02915. Phone: (401) 433-4200. Fax: (401) 433-5967. Web Site:www.lite105.com Licensee: Citadel Broadcasting Co. Population served: 220,000 Format: Light rock. Target aud: 25-54; mid to upper income professionals, general appeal format. ◆Barbara Haynes, gen mgr.

Smithfield

*WJMF(FM)— Aug 1, 1974: 88.7 mhz; 225 w. 130 ft TL: N41 55 13 W71 32 26. Stereo. Hrs open: 7 AM-2 AM Box 6, Bryant College, 1150 Douglas Pike, 02917. Phone: (401) 232-6044. Phone: (401) 232-6160. Fax: (401) 232-6748. Web Site:www.wjmf887.com Licensee: Bryant College of Business Administration. Population served: 10,000 Format: Urban, alternative. News staff: one; News: 12 hrs wkly. Target aud: 16-30; from teenagers to young executives. Spec prog: Folk 4 hrs, gospel 2 hrs, relg 2 hrs wkly. ◆Bryan Adams, gen mgr.

Wakefield-Peacedale

WEAN-FM— June 1995: 99.7 mhz; 2.3 kw. Ant 535 ft TL: N41 25 31 W71 34 59. Hrs open: 24 Simulcast with WPRO(AM) Providence 100%. 1502 Wampanoag Trail, East Providence, 02915. Phone: (401) 433-4200. Fax: (401) 437-3297. Web Site:www.630wpro.com Licensee: Citadel Broadcasting Co. Group owner: Citadel Broadcasting Corp. (acq 8-6-97; $8.5 million with WKKB(FM) Middletown). Population served: 1,100,000 Wiley, Rein & Fielding. Format: News/talk. ◆Barbara Haynes, gen mgr; Duffy Egan, chief of engrg.

Warwick

WARV(AM)— Aug 12, 1959: 1590 khz; 5 kw-U, DA-2. TL: N41 43 40 W71 27 46. Hrs open: 24 19 Luther Ave., 02886. Phone: (401) 737-0700. Fax: (401) 737-1604.E-mail: warv@aol.com Web Site:www.warv.net Licensee: Blount Communications Inc. Group owner: Blount Communications Group (acq 7-7-78). Population served: 1,500,000 Natl. Network: Salem Radio Network, . Format: Relg. Target aud: 25-54; Adults. Spec prog: Black 2 hrs wkly. ◆Deborah C. Blount, exec VP; David O. Young, VP; William A. Blount, pres & gen mgr; Kevin Linegan, opns mgr.

West Warwick

WLKW(AM)—Licensed to West Warwick. See Providence

Westerly

WEEI-FM— Oct 17, 1967: 103.7 mhz; 37 kw. 570 ft TL: N41 34 22 W71 37 55. Stereo. Hrs open: 24 150 Chestnut St., Providence, 02903. Phone: (401) 751-9334. Fax:(401) 351-8109.E-mail: info@weei.com Web Site:www.fnxradio.com Licensee: Entercom Providence License LLC. Group owner: Entercom Communications Corp. (acq 6-15-2004; $14.5 million). Population served: 250,000 Natl. Network: Westwood

One, . Format: Sports, talk. News staff: one. Target aud: 25-49. ◆David J. Field, CEO; Joseph M. Field, chmn, VP; Joseph Harrington, stn mgr; Rod Morrison, prom dir & prom mgr.

*WKIV(FM)— Dec 8, 1997: 88.1 mhz; 1 w horiz, 1.2 kw vert. Ant 105 ft TL: N41 26 13 W71 52 55. Stereo. Hrs open: Rebroadcasts KLVR(FM) Middletown, CA 100%. 2351 Sunset Blvd., Suite 170-218, Rocklin, CA, 95765. Phone: (916) 251-1600. Fax: (916) 251-1650. Web Site:www.klove.com Licensee: Educational Media Foundation (acq 3-21-2008; $100,000). Natl. Network: K-Love, . Format: Contemp Christian. ◆Mike Novak, gen mgr.

WXNI(AM)— July 1949: 1230 khz; 1 kw-U. TL: N41 21 57 W71 50 11. Hrs open: Rebroadcasts WRNI(AM) Providence 100%. One Union Station, Providence, 02903. Phone: (401) 351-2800. Fax: (401) 351-0246.E-mail: info@wrni.org Web Site:www.wrni.org Licensee: WRNI Foundation (acq 3-26-99). Natl. Network: NPR, PRI, . Format: News, talk. News: 80 hrs wkly. Target aud: 25-54; intelligent adults interested in news & politics. ◆Joe O'Connor, gen mgr; Steve Callahan, chief of engrg.

Wickford

WKKB(FM)—See Middletown

Woonsocket

WNRI(AM)— Nov 28, 1954: 1380 khz; 2.5 kw-D, 16 w-N. TL: N42 00 58 W71 29 30. Stereo. Hrs open: 786 Diamond Hill Rd., 02895. Phone: (401) 769-6925. Fax: (401) 762-0442.E-mail: rogerwnri@prodigy.net Web Site:www.wnri.com Licensee: Bouchard Broadcasting Inc. (group owner; (acq 10-20-2004; $900,000). Population served: 100,000 Natl. Network: USA, . Format: News/talk. Target aud: 35 plus. Spec prog: Fr 4 hrs, Pol 2 hrs, Por 2 hrs wkly. ◆Roger Bouchard, gen mgr.

WOON(AM)— Nov 11, 1946: 1240 khz; 1 kw-U. TL: N41 59 35 W71 30 33. (CP: TL: N41 59 34 W71 30 20). Hrs open: 985 Park Ave., 02895-6332. Phone: (401) 762-1240. Fax: (401) 769-8232.E-mail: email@onworldwide.com Web Site:www.onworldwide.com Licensee: O-N Radio Inc. (acq 10-19-99). Format: Full service. Target aud: 35 plus. Spec prog: Fr one hr, Pol 3 hrs, Black one hr, gospel one hr wkly. ◆Dave Richards, gen mgr.

WWKX(FM)— July 1, 1949: 106.3 mhz; 1.15 kw. Ant 518 ft TL: N41 59 43 W71 26 54. Stereo. Hrs open: 1502 Wampanoaq Tr., East Providence, 02915. Phone: (401) 433-4200. Fax: (401) 433-5967.E-mail: hot1063@hot1063.com Web Site:www.hot1063.com Licensee: Citadel Broadcasting Co. Group owner: Citadel Communications Corp. (acq 1-24-2005; $16.5 million with WAKX(FM) Narragansett Pier). Population served: 900,000 Natl. Network: Westwood One, . Rgnl rep: Christal. Format: Rhythm/dance, CHR. Target aud: 18-49. ◆Barbara Haynes, gen mgr; Duffy Egan, chief of engrg.

South Carolina

Abbeville

WABV(AM)— March 1956: 1590 khz; 1 kw-D, 27 w-N. TL: N34 09 03 W82 23 34. Hrs open: 75 Hwy. 28 South , 29620. Phone: (864) 366-9228.E-mail: info@wabv1590.com Web Site:www.wabv1590.com Licensee: Hellinger Broadcasting Inc. (acq 4-14-97). Population served: 100,000 Format: Country. ◆Mark Hellinger, pres; Paul B. Walker Jr., opns mgr & progmg dir.

WZLA-FM— Jan 1, 1990: 92.9 mhz; 6 kw. Ant 243 ft TL: N34 11 13 W82 19 28. Stereo. Hrs open: 24 Box 548, 29620. Secondary address: 112 N. Main St. 29620. Phone: (864) 366-5785. Fax: (864) 366-9391.E-mail: z93@wctel.net Web Site:z93oldies.com Licensee: Shelley Reid. Natl. Network: Motor Racing Net, Salem Radio Network, . Fletcher, Heald & Hildreth. Format: Oldies. Target aud: 25-65. Spec prog: Gospel 8 hrs wkly. ◆Shelley Reid, pres, gen mgr, opns dir, progmg dir, chief of engrg; Oscar H. Reid Jr., stn mgr, gen sls mgr; Oscar Reid, traf mgr; Wayne Stevenson, sports cmtr.

Aiken

WGUS-FM—See New Ellenton

WKSP(FM)— Sept 17, 1966: 96.3 mhz; 17.5 kw. Ant 846 ft TL: N33 41 06 W81 55 36. Hrs open: 2743 Perimeter Pkwy. Bldg. 100, Suite 300, Augusta, GA, 30909. Phone: (706) 396-6000. Fax: (706) 396-6010. Web Site:www.kiss963.com Licensee: Capstar TX L.P. Group owner: Clear Channel Communications Inc. (acq 12-19-00; grpsl). Format: Rhythm and blues, oldies. ◆Mark Bass, gen mgr.

WKXC-FM— August 1966: 99.5 mhz; 22.5 kw. 728 ft TL: N33 38 44 W21 55 40. Stereo. Hrs open: 4051 Jimmie Dyess Pky, Augusta, GA, 30909. Phone: (706) 396-7000. Fax: (706) 396-7092. Web Site:www.kicks99.com Licensee: WGAC License LLC. Group owner: Beasley Broadcast Group Inc. (acq 4-2-2001; $12 million with WHHD(FM) Clearwater). Population served: 45,000 Format: Country. ◆Kent Dunn, gen mgr; Mark Haddon, gen sls mgr; T. Gentry, progmg dir.

*WLJK(FM)— 1990: 89.1 mhz; 10 kw. 1,374 ft TL: N33 24 18 W81 50 15. Stereo. Hrs open: 24
Rebroadcasts WRJA-FM Sumter 100%.
1101 George Rogers Blvd., Columbia, 29201. Phone: (803) 737-3420. Fax: (803) 737-3552.E-mail: gasque@scetv.org Web Site:www.scern.org Licensee: South Carolina Educational TV Commission. Natl. Network: NPR, PRI, . Dow, Lohnes & Albertson. Format: NPR news. News: News progrmg 120 hrs wkly. ◆Moss Bresnahan, pres; Tom Holloway, dev dir; John Gasque, progmg dir.

Allendale

WDOG(AM)— Jan 1, 1966: 1460 khz; 1 kw-D. TL: N33 01 22 W81 19 58. (CP: COL Barnwell. 320 w-D, 45 w-N. TL: N33 13 25 W81 21 35). Hrs open: 2447 Agusta Hwy., 29810. Phone: (803) 584-3500. Fax: (240) 358-7473. Licensee: Good Radio Broadcasting Inc. Population served: 50,000 Rgnl. Network: S.C. Net. S.C. News Net. Format: C&W, Black. ◆H. Carl Gooding, pres, gen mgr, gen sls mgr, chief of engrg; Rick Gooding, prom mgr, progmg dir, disc jockey; Lisa Gooding, news dir, traf mgr, women's int ed; Jim Lowe, local news ed, disc jockey; Carl Gooding, farm dir; Ron Lopez, disc jockey.

WDOG-FM— Aug 29, 1983: 93.5 mhz; 3 kw. 300 ft TL: N33 01 22 W81 19 58. Stereo. Hrs open: Dups WDOG AM 100% 2447 Agusta Hwy., 29810. Phone: (803) 584-3500. Fax: (240) 358-7473. ◆Lisa Gooding, traf mgr, women's int ed; Jim Lowe, local news ed, disc jockey; Carl Gooding, farm dir; Rick Gooding, disc jockey.

Anderson

WAIM(AM)— April 1935: 1230 khz; 1 kw-U. TL: N34 31 52 W82 36 50. Hrs open: 2203 Old Williamston Rd., 29621. Phone: (864) 226-1511. Phone: (864) 225-1230. Fax: (864) 226-1513.E-mail: waimrd@carol.net Licensee: Palmetto Broadcasting Corp10-19-92) Population served: 50,000 Format: News/talk. Target aud: 25-64. ◆Rick Driver, gen mgr, gen sls mgr, progmg dir, disc jockey; Craig More, disc jockey.

WANS(AM)— June 1, 1949: 1280 khz; 5 kw-D, 1 kw-N, DA-N. TL: N34 32 17 W82 41 28. Hrs open: 24 141 Powell Rd., 29625. Phone: (864) 224-9267. Licensee: FM 103 Inc. (acq 10-28-96). Population served: 30,000 Format: Sports. ◆Ray Morris, gen mgr.

WJMZ-FM— Aug 1, 1963: 107.3 mhz; 100 kw. 1,008 ft TL: N34 42 06 W82 36 20. Stereo. Hrs open: 24 220 N. Main St., Suite 402, Greenville, 29601. Phone: (864) 235-1073. Fax: (864) 370-3403. Web Site:www.1073jamz.com Licensee: Cox Radio Inc. Group owner: Cox Communications Inc. (acq 2-1-2001; grpsl). Population served: 1,408,400 Format: Urban contemp. ◆Steve Sinicropi, VP & gen mgr; Bob Grossmall, gen sls mgr; Cathy Tabor, natl sls mgr; Laurie Madden, mktg dir, prom mgr; Doug Davis, mus dir, disc jockey; K.J. Bland, asst music dir; Ed Bailey, news dir; Lemont Bryant, chief of engrg; Kenny Mac Miles, disc jockey.

WROQ(FM)— 1947: 101.1 mhz; 100 kw. 994 ft TL: N34 38 51 W82 16 13. Stereo. Hrs open: 25 Garlington Rd., Greenville, 29615. Phone: (864) 271-9200. Fax: (864) 242-1567.E-mail: info@wroq.com Web Site:www.wroq.com Licensee: Entercom Greenville License LLC. Group owner: Barnstable Broadcasting Inc. (acq 10-7-2005; grpsl). Population served: 675,000 Format: Classic rock. Target aud: 25-54; baby boomers. ◆David J. Field, pres; Sharon Day, gen mgr; Mark Hendrix, progmg dir.

WTBI(AM)—See Pickens

Andrews

WGTN-FM—Licensed to Andrews. See Georgetown

Atlantic Beach

WMIR(AM)— Oct 1, 1997: 1200 khz; 690 w-D. TL: N33 50 10 W78 51 08. Hrs open: Sunrise-sunset 4337 Big Barn Dr., Little River, 29566. Phone: (843) 399-2653. Fax: (843) 399-2659.E-mail: wradio@sc.rr.com Licensee: Atlantic Beach Radio Inc. (acq 1-31-97). Population served: 175,000 Format: Relg. Target aud: 25-65; Urban Black gospel. ◆Dr. Gardner Altman, pres; Reggie Dyson, CEO & gen mgr.

WSEA(FM)— 1998: 100.3 mhz; 12 kw. Ant 476 ft TL: N33 47 03 W78 52 44. Hrs open: 11640 Hwy. 17 Bypass S., Murrells Inlet, 29576-9332. Phone: (843) 651-7869. Fax: (843) 651-3197.E-mail: info@hot100fm.com Web Site:www.hot100fm.com Licensee: Cumulus Licensing Corp. Group owner: Cumulus Media Inc. (acq 7-16-98; $1.3 million). Format: CHR. ◆Bill Hazen, gen mgr.

Bamberg-Denmark

WVCD(AM)— June 23, 1957: 790 khz; 1 kw-D, 100 w-N. TL: N33 18 50 W81 04 43. Hrs open: Box 678, Denmark, 29042. Phone: (803) 703-7002. Fax: (803) 703-7022. Licensee: Voorhees College (acq 1-29-03; $112,500). Population served: 10,000 Rgnl. Network: S.C. Net. S.C. News Net. Format: Relg. Spec prog: Farm one hr wkly. ◆Annette Gantt, gen mgr.

Batesburg

WBLR(AM)— May 10, 1956: 1430 khz; 5 kw-D, 142 w-N. TL: N33 54 58 W81 31 42. Hrs open: 24 2278 Wortham Lane, Grovetown, GA, 30813. Phone: (706) 309-9610.E-mail: ctbarinowski@comcast.net Web Site:www.gnnradio.org Licensee: Barinowski Investment Company Group owner: Good News Network. (acq 8-18-98). Population served: 45,000 Rgnl. Network: S.C. Net. Format: Sp. Target aud: General. ◆Clarence Barinowski, pres & gen mgr.

WZMJ(FM)— Aug 5, 1965: 93.1 mhz; 2.1 kw. Ant 561 ft TL: N33 54 02 W81 24 25. Stereo. Hrs open:
Simulcast with WOIC(AM) Columbia 100%.
1900 Pineview Rd., Columbia, 29209. Phone: (803) 695-8600. Fax: (803) 695-8605.E-mail: mhanisch@innercity.sc.com Licensee: Urban Radio II L.L.C. Group owner: Inner City Broadcasting (acq 5-30-2003; $11.1 million with WHXT(FM) Orangeburg). Population served: 472,800 Natl. Network: ESPN Radio, Jones Radio Networks, . Format: Sports. ◆Steve Patterson, gen mgr; Scott Norton, gen sls mgr; Dave Stewart, progmg dir, chief of engrg.

Beaufort

*WAGP(FM)— Oct 10, 1987: 88.7 mhz; 6 kw. 302 ft TL: N32 24 05 W80 44 21. Stereo. Hrs open: 24 Box 119, 29901. Secondary address: 4 Grober Hill Rd., Suite C 29901. Phone: (843) 525-1859. Fax: (843) 522-3691.E-mail: waagp@islc.net Web Site:www.wagp.net Licensee: The Christian Broadcasting Corp. of Beaufort. Natl. Network: Moody, . Format: Relg. News: 20 hrs wkly. Target aud: General; evangelical Christians. ◆Carl J. Broggi, pres; Richard Forschner, gen mgr.

WGZO(FM)—See Parris Island

*WJWJ-FM— Aug 1, 1980: 89.9 mhz; 47 kw. Ant 1,096 ft TL: N32 42 42 W80 40 54. Stereo. Hrs open: 24
Rebroadcasts WRJA(AM) Sumter 100%.
1101 George Rogers Blvd., Columbia, 29201. Phone: (803) 737-3420. Fax: (803) 737-3552.E-mail: gasque@scetv.org Web Site:www.etvradio.org Licensee: South Carolina Educational TV Commission. Natl. Network: NPR, PRI, . Format: NPR news. News: 120 hrs wkly. Target aud: General. ◆Moss Brenahan, pres & gen mgr; John Gasque, progmg dir.

WVGB(AM)— 1959: 1490 khz; 1 kw-U. TL: N32 26 08 W80 41 54. Hrs open: 806 Monson St., 29901. Phone: (843) 524-4700. Fax: (843) 524-9742. Fax: (843) 524-1329.E-mail: vgbradio@earthlink.net Licensee: Vivian Broadcasting Inc. (acq 1-21-83). Population served: 95,000 Natl. Network: American Urban, . Format: Relg, gospel. Target aud: 18-65; African American. Spec prog: Community progmg, sports. ◆William A. Galloway, pres; Vivian M. Galloway, gen mgr, opns VP, sls VP; Darryl Jamison, stn mgr; Derrick Moon, progmg mgr.

WYKZ(FM)— Aug 8, 1962: 98.7 mhz; 100 kw. 1,001 ft TL: N32 19 50 W80 56 19. Stereo. Hrs open: 24 245 Alfred St., Savannah, GA, 31408. Phone: (912) 964-9414.E-mail: info@987theriver.com Web Site:www.987theriver.com Licensee: Capstar TX L.P. Group owner: Clear Channel Communications Inc. (acq 8-30-00; grpsl). Population served: 350,000 Wiley, Rein & Fielding. Format: Light adult contemp. News staff: one; News: 3 hrs wkly. Target aud: 25-54; female. Spec prog: Oldies 5 hrs wkly. ◆Steve Richards, opns mgr; Sheryl Collison, sls dir; Mark Robertson, progmg dir; Marty Foglia, chief of engrg.

Belton

*WEPC(FM)— May 1994: 88.5 mhz; 50 kw. 298 ft TL: N34 23 43 W82 29 49. Hrs open: 24
Rebroadcasts WRAF-FM Toccoa Falls, GA 100%.
Secondary address: 292 Old Clarkesville Hwy., Toccoa Falls, GA 30577. Phone: (706) 282-6030. Phone: (800) 251-8326. Fax: (706) 282-6090.E-mail: radio@tfc.edu Web Site:www.myfavoritestation.net Licensee: Toccoa Falls College. Format: Christian, MOR, educ. ◆David Cornelius, gen mgr.

WROP(AM)— October 1956: 1390 khz; 1 kw-D, 17 w-N. TL: N34 35 19 W82 32 17. Hrs open: 129 Edgerton Ln., Lexington, 29072. Licensee: Big Fish Broadcasting LLC (acq 10-15-2007; $100,000). Population served: 145,000 Target aud: General. ◆Jeffrey S. Roper, gen mgr.

Belvedere

*WAFJ(FM)— August 1994: 88.3 mhz; 4.5 kw. Ant 1,387 ft TL: N33 24 29 W81 50 36. Stereo. Hrs open: 24 102 LeCompte Ave., N. Augusta, 29841. Phone: (803) 819-3125. Fax: (803) 819-3129.E-mail: info@wafj.com Web Site:www.wafj.com Licensee: Radio Training Network Inc. (acq 1994; $291,000). Population served: 522,000 Natl. Network: Fox News Radio, . Format: Contemp Christian. News staff: one. Target aud: 25-54; women. ◆Steve Swanson, gen mgr, progmg dir & mus dir; Cleve Walker, news dir.

Bennettsville

WBSC(AM)— June 1947: 1550 khz; 10 kw-D, 5 kw-N, DA-N. TL: N34 40 52 W79 42 04. Hrs open: Box 1275, 29512-1275. Phone: (843) 479-7121. Fax: (843) 479- 4474.E-mail: wbsc@aol.com Web Site:www.wbsc1550.com Licensee: D. Mitch Broadcasting Inc. (acq 4-95). Population served: 87,000 Natl. Network: ABC, . Natl. Rep: Dora-Clayton,. Format: Oldies, gospel. Spec prog: Black 15 hrs wkly. ◆Dwight Johnson, CEO, pres, VP, gen mgr; Richard Gehm, chief of opns.

Bishopville

WAGS(AM)— Feb 24, 1954: 1380 khz; 1 kw-D. TL: N34 12 35 W80 13 34. Hrs open: 6:30 AM-6 PM 142 Wags Dr., 29010. Phone: (803) 484-5415.E-mail: wagsradio@sc.rr.com Licensee: Beaver Communications (acq 11-01-99; $27,500). Population served: 22,000 Natl. Network: USA, . Format: Country, bluegrass. News: 6 hrs wkly. Target aud: 25-55 plus. Spec prog: Live remotes-parades, civic events, festivals 2 hrs, relg 7 hrs wkly. ◆James D. Jenkins, gen mgr & chief of opns.

Blackville

WIIZ(FM)— April 1996: 97.9 mhz; 50 kw. 433 ft TL: N33 06 52 W81 23 13. Hrs open: 8968 Marlboro Ave., Barnwell, 29812. Phone: (803) 259-9797. Fax: (803) 541-9700. Web Site:WWW.WIIZFM.COM Licensee: NicWild Communications Inc. (acq 10-9-96; $340,000). Format: Urban contemp. ◆Bobby Nichols, gen mgr & progmg dir.

Bluffton

WGZR(FM)— June 22, 1988: 106.9 mhz; 100 kw. ant 800 ft TL: N32 13 36 W80 50 53. Stereo. Hrs open: 24 401 Mall Blvd., Suite 101 D, Savannah, GA, 31406. Phone: (912) 351-9830. Fax: (912) 352-4821.E-mail: mhalverson@adventureradio.fm Web Site:luckydogcountry1069.com Licensee: Monterey Licenses LLC. Group owner: Triad Broadcasting Co. LLC (acq 8-8-2000; grpsl). Population served: 500,000 Natl. Rep: Christal,. Format: Country. News staff: one. ◆Robert Leonard, gen mgr.

Blythwood

WBAJ(AM)— 1999: 890 khz; 50 kw-D, 8.5 kw-CH. TL: N34 06 31 W81 04 28. Hrs open: 241-A Riverchase Way, Lexington, 29072. Phone: (803) 794-9673.E-mail: radio@wbaj.net Web Site:www.wbaj.net Licensee: Family First (acq 8-29-98; $60,000). Format: Christian. ◆Linda de Romanett, pres & gen mgr.

Bowman

WSPX(FM)— October 1997: 94.5 mhz; 3.5 kw. Ant 434 ft TL: N33 19 13 W80 43 52. Hrs open: 24 Box 1445, Orangeburg, 29116. Secondary address: 1236 Five Chop Rd., Orangeburg 29115. Phone: (803) 539-9450. Fax: (803) 539-9458.E-mail: email@wfmv.com Web Site:wspx@sc.rr.com Licensee: Glory Communications Inc. (group owner; acq 4-19-01; $400,000). Population served: 175,000 Format: Gospel. ♦Alex Snipes Jr., gen mgr.

Branchville

WGFG(FM)— Dec 13,1993: 105.1 mhz; 2.9 kw. Ant 478 ft TL: N33 26 35 W80 48 16. Hrs open: 24 200 Regional Pkwy., Bldg. C, Suite 200, Orangeburg, 29118. Phone: (803) 536-1710. Fax: (803) 531-1089.E-mail: mail@miller.fm Web Site:www.miller.fm Licensee: Miller Communications Inc. (group owner; (acq 4-30-2003; $1.25 million with WQKI-FM Orangeburg). Population served: 175,000 Natl. Network: ABC, . Format: Oldies. Target aud: 25-64; baby boomers. ♦Harold Miller Jr., pres; Theresa Miller, gen mgr; Russ T. Fender, opns mgr.

Briarcliff Acres

WRXZ(FM)— Apr 5, 1975: 107.1 mhz; 50 kw. Ant 492 ft TL: N33 56 14 W78 57 53. Stereo. Hrs open: 18 4841 Hwy. 17 Bypass S., Myrtle Beach, 29577. Phone: (843) 293-0107. Fax: (843) 293-1717.E-mail: info@thesound1071.com Web Site:www.thesound1071.com Licensee: Qantum of Myrtle Beach License Co. LLC. Group owner: Qantum Communications Corp. (acq 7-2-2003; grpsl). Format: Rock. ♦Jimmy Feuger, gen mgr.

Bucksport

WGTR(FM)— June 1, 1993: 107.9 mhz; 20 kw. Ant 784 ft TL: N33 35 45 W79 03 11. Hrs open: 4841 Hwy.17 by-pass South, Myrtle Beach, 29577. Phone: (843) 293-0107. Fax: (843) 293-1717.E-mail: info@gator1079.com Web Site:www.gator1079.com Licensee: Qantum of Myrtle Beach License Co. LLC. Group owner: Qantum Communications Corp. (acq 7-2-2003; grpsl). Population served: 271,400 Format: Country. Spec prog: Motor racing 8 hrs wkly. ♦Jimmy Feuger, gen mgr.

Camden

WCAM(AM)— July 23, 1948: 1590 khz; 1 kw-D, 27 w-N. TL: N34 13 36 W80 40 45. Stereo. Hrs open: 6 AM-11 PM Box 753, 29020. Secondary address: 5 The Commons Ward Rd., Lugoff 29078. Phone: (803) 438-9002. Fax: (803) 408-2288.E-mail: wpubradio@camden.net Web Site:www.kol1027.com Licensee: Kershaw Radio Corp. (acq 8-87; $75,000; 5-5-86). Population served: 42,000 Rgnl. Network: S.C. Net. S.C. News Net. Format: Nostalgia, adult standards. Target aud: 45 plus. ♦Chris Johnson, gen mgr; Bill Rogers, progmg dir.

WEAF(AM)— Dec 10, 1970: 1130 khz; 5 kw-D, 7 w-N. TL: N34 15 32 W80 34 47. (CP: COL Springdale. 1 kw-D, 9 w-N, 1 kw-CH. TL: N33 57 34 W81 02 28). Hrs open: Box 1165, 29021. Phone: (803) 432-8717. Fax: (803) 939-9469.E-mail: wsmvproduction@wsmv.com Licensee: Glory Communications Inc. Group owner: GHB Radio Group (acq 7-13-2006; $222,500). Format: Gospel quartet. ♦Alex Snipe, gen mgr.

WPUB-FM— December 1974: 102.7 mhz; 3.3 kw. 299 ft TL: N34 13 31 W80 40 44. Stereo. Hrs open: Box 753, 29020. Secondary address: 5 The Commons Ward Rd. 29020. Phone: (803) 438-9002. Fax: (803) 408-2288.E-mail: wpubradio@camden.net Web Site:www.kol1027.com Population served: 44,000 Format: Oldies. Target aud: 25-55.

Cameron

WTQS(AM)— 2008: 1490 khz; 1 kw-U. TL: N33 33 09 W80 44 38. Hrs open: Box 2355, West Columbia, 29171. Phone: (803) 939-9530. Fax: (803) 939-9469.E-mail: wsmvproduction@wsmv.com Licensee: Glory Communications Inc. (acq 2-10-2006; $50,000 for CP). ♦Alex Snipe, pres.

Cayce

WGCV(AM)— Aug 22, 1958: 620 khz; 2.5 kw-D, 126 w-N. TL: N33 57 34 W81 02 28. Hrs open: 24 2440 Millwood Ave., Colombia, 29205. Phone: (803) 748-9620. Fax: (803) 799-1620.E-mail: wgcvproduction@wgcv.net Web Site:www.wgcv.net Licensee: Glory Communications Inc. (group owner; acq 10-8-99). Natl. Network: American Urban, . Format: Gospel. News staff: one. Target aud: 34-65; Black adults. ♦Alex Snipe, pres, gen mgr; Rev. Isaac Heyward, stn mgr, prom dir; Tezra Haire, gen sls mgr; Tony Green, progmg dir.

WLTY(FM)—Licensed to Cayce. See Columbia

***WYFV(FM)**— Oct 10, 1990: 88.5 mhz; 50 kw. Ant 171 ft TL: N33 54 32 W81 05 57. Stereo. Hrs open: 24 Bible Broadcasting Network, Charlotte, NC, 28214-7300. Phone: (800) 888-7077. Web Site:bbnradio.org Licensee: Bible Broadcasting Network Inc. (group owner; acq 6-26-90; 7-23-90). Format: Relg, bible preaching & teaching. News: 10 hrs wkly. Target aud: General. ♦Lowell Davey, pres.

Charleston

WALC(FM)— Apr 4, 1990: 100.5 mhz; 17.5 kw. Ant 394 ft TL: N32 49 20 W79 58 45. Stereo. Hrs open: 24 2420 Wade Hampton Blvd., Greenville, 29615. Phone: (864) 292-6040. Fax: (864) 292-8428. Web Site:www.hisradio.com Licensee: Radio Training Network Inc. Group owner: Clear Channel Communications Inc. (acq 1-26-2009; $2.3 million). Natl. Rep: Katz Radio,. Format: Contemp Christian. ♦Allen Henderson, gen mgr.

WEZL(FM)— Oct 3, 1970: 103.5 mhz; 100 kw. Ant 659 ft TL: N32 49 04 W79 50 08. (CP: Ant 987 ft.). Stereo. Hrs open: 24 950 Houston Northcutt Blvd., Mount Pleasant, 29464. Phone: (843) 884-2534. Fax: (843) 884-1218.E-mail: info@wezlfm.com Web Site:www.wezlfm.com Licensee: Citicasters Licenses L.P. Group owner: Clear Channel Communications Inc. (acq 5-4-99; grpsl). Population served: 420,800 Format: C&W. News staff: one; News: 3 to 4 hrs wkly. ♦Paul Smith, gen mgr; Scott Johnson, progmg mgr; Teri Hegel, mus dir, sls; Brian Worboys, traf mgr, outdoor ed; Willie Bennett, news dir & engr.

***WFCH(FM)**— December 1986: 88.5 mhz; 29.6 kw. 305 ft TL: N32 49 04 W79 50 08. Hrs open: Box 1505, Mount Pleasant, 29465. Phone: (843) 881-9450. Phone: (510) 568-6200. Fax: (510) 568-6190.E-mail: famradio@familyradio.com Web Site:www.familyradio.com Licensee: Family Stations Inc. (group owner) Natl. Network: Family Radio, . Format: Relg. ♦Harold Camping, gen mgr; Joe Papp, chief of engrg.

WIOP(FM)—(Isle of Palms, May 1967: 95.9 mhz; 50 kw. Ant 340 ft TL: N32 49 28 W80 00 10. Stereo. Hrs open: 2294 Clements Ferry Rd., 29492. Phone: (843) 972-1100. Fax: (843) 972-1200. Licensee: Apex Broadcasting Inc. (group owner; (acq 8-4-2008; $1.5 million). Population served: 20,000 Format: Rock & roll classics. ♦G. Dean Pearce, pres.

WIWF(FM)— Apr 1, 1948: 96.9 mhz; 100 kw. Ant 1,750 ft TL: N32 55 28 W79 41 58. Stereo. Hrs open: 4230 Faber Place Drive, Suite 100, North Charleston, 29405. Phone: (843) 277-1200. Fax: (843) 277-1212.E-mail: info@sunny969.com Web Site:www.sunny969.com Licensee: Citadel Broadcasting Co. Group owner: Citadel Broadcasting Corp. Natl. Rep: McGavren Guild,. Format: Country. ♦Paul O'Malley, gen mgr; Bocky Gilleath, gen sls mgr; Brian Driver, progmg dir; J.T. Tucker, chief of engrg.

WLTQ(AM)— 1947: Stn currently dark. 730 khz; 1 kw-D, 100 w-N. TL: N32 46 22 W80 00 58. Hrs open: 24 426 S. River Rd., Tryon, NC, 28782-7879. Phone: (828) 859-6982.E-mail: info@thedrive100.com Licensee: Indigo Radio LLC Group owner: Clear Channel Communications Inc. (acq 7-15-2008; $608,230). Population served: 66,945 ♦Mark W. Jorgenson, gen mgr.

WQNT(AM)— 1948: 1450 khz; 1 kw-U. TL: N32 48 15 W79 57 43. Hrs open: 60 Markfield Dr., Suite 4, 29407. Phone: (843) 763-6631. Fax: (843) 766-1239.E-mail: ted@kirkmanbroadcasting.com Licensee: Kirkman Broadcasting Inc. (group owner; (acq 1995). Population served: 460,000 Natl. Network: Fox Sports, . Brian Madden & Assoc. Format: Sports. Target aud: 25-54; Men. Spec prog: Relg one hr wkly. ♦Gil Kirkman, pres; Ted Byrne, opns mgr, progmg dir; Rick Howze, gen sls mgr; Wally Momeier, chief of engrg.

WQSC(AM)— 1946: 1340 khz; 1 kw-U. TL: N32 49 07 W79 57 43. Hrs open: 24 60 Markfield Dr., Suite 4, 29407. Phone: (843) 763-6631. Fax: (843) 766-1239.E-mail: ted@kirkmanbroadcasting.com Web Site:www.1340theboardwalk.net Licensee: Kirkman Broadcasting Inc. (group owner; acq 11-1-94). Population served: 66,945 Rgnl. Network: S.C. Net. Format: Beach Music. Target aud: 25-54; Adults. ♦Don Seehafer, pres; Rick Howze, gen mgr, gen sls mgr; Ted Byrne, opns mgr; John Dixon, news dir; Wally Momeier, chief of engrg.

***WSCI(FM)**— 1973: 89.3 mhz; 97 kw. 540 ft TL: N32 47 44 W79 50 27. Stereo. Hrs open: 24
Rebroadcasts WLTR(FM) Columbia 95%.
1101 George Rogers Blvd., Columbia, 29201. Phone: (803) 737-3420. Fax: (803) 737-3552.E-mail: gasque@scetv.org Web Site:www.etvradio.org Licensee: South Carolina Educational TV Commission. Population served: 66,945 Natl. Network: NPR, PRI, . Format: NPR news, class. News: 70 hrs wkly. ♦Moss Bresnahan, pres; Tom Holloway, sls dir; John Gasque, progmg dir; Hap Griffin, engrg VP; Connie Murray, traf mgr.

WSPO(AM)— May 14, 1930: 1390 khz; 5 kw-U, DA-N. TL: N32 49 26 W80 00 06. Stereo. Hrs open: 24 2294 Clements Ferry Rd., 29492. Phone: (843) 972-1100. Fax: (843) 972-1200. Web Site:wsposports.com Licensee: Apex Broadcasting Inc. Group owner: Citadel Broadcasting Corp. (acq 8-24-2007; $70,000). Population served: 66,945 Natl. Rep: McGavren Guild,. Putbrese Hunsaker & Trent P.C. Format: Sports. ♦Chris Johnson, gen mgr.

WSSX-FM— 1945: 95.1 mhz; 100 kw. 361 ft TL: N32 49 20 W79 58 45. (CP: Ant 1,000 ft.). Stereo. Hrs open: 24 4230 Faber Place Dr., Ste. 100, No. Charleston, 99405. Phone: (843) 277-1200. Fax: (843) 277-1212.E-mail: info@95fx.com Web Site:www.95fx.com Licensee: Citadel Broadcasting Co. Group owner: Citadel Broadcasting Corp. (acq 6-9-99; grpsl). Population served: 100,000 Natl. Network: Westwood One, . Format: Adult contemp, Top-40. News staff: one. Target aud: 18-34. ♦Paul O'Mailey, gen mgr.

WTMA(AM)— 1939: 1250 khz; 5 kw-D, 1 kw-N, DA-N. TL: N32 49 20 W79 58 45. Hrs open: 24 4230 Faber Place Dr., Suite 100, N. Charleston, 29405. Phone: (843) 277-1200. Fax: (843) 227-1212.E-mail: mike.edwards@citcomm.com Web Site:www.wtma.com Licensee: Citadel Broadcasting Co. Group owner: Citadel Broadcasting Corp. (acq 6-9-99; grpsl). Population served: 15,000 Natl. Network: Westwood One, ABC, . Wire Svc: AP Format: News/talk. News staff: 2; News: 5 hrs wkly. Target aud: 25-54. ♦Paul O'Malley, gen mgr; Mike Edwards, opns dir.

WXLY(FM)—See North Charleston

WYBB(FM)—See Folly Beach

WZJY(AM)—See Mt. Pleasant

Cheraw

WCRE(AM)— July 1953: 1420 khz; 1 kw-D, 97 w-N / 250 24 hrs. TL: N34 40 48 W79 53 58. (Simulcast on FM translator W230AS Cheraw on 93.9 mhz). Stereo. Hrs open: 24 Box 160, 29520. Secondary address: 541 Hwy. #1 S. 29520. Phone: (843) 537-7887. Fax: (843) 537-7307.E-mail: janepigg@gmail.com Web Site:www.wcreradio.com Licensee: Pee Dee Broadcasting LLC (acq 2-27-2004; $50,000). Format: Adult contemp, oldies. News staff: one; News: 12 hrs wkly. Target aud: 25 plus; Adults. Spec prog: Black 5 hrs wkly.

WJMX-FM— July 17, 1979: 103.3 mhz; 44 kw. 525 ft TL: N34 30 19 W79 54 15. (CP: 50 kw, ant 492 ft.). Stereo. Hrs open: 181 E. Evans St., Suite 311, Florence, 29501. Phone: (843) 667-9569. Fax: (843) 673-7390. Web Site:www.wjmx.com Licensee: Qantum of Florence License Co. LLC. Group owner: Qantum Communications Corp. (acq 7-2-2003; grpsl). Population served: 278,000 Rgnl. Network: S.C. Net. Natl. Rep: McGavren Guild,. S.C. News Net. Format: CHR. Target aud: 18-34. ♦Jonathan Brewster, gen mgr & stn mgr; Gary Downes, opns dir; Craig Dallariva, gen sls mgr, engrg dir.

Chester

WBT-FM— Aug 30, 1969: 99.3 mhz; 7.6 kw. Ant 603 ft TL: N34 47 29 W81 16 01. Stereo. Hrs open: 24
Rebroadcasts WBT(AM) Charlotte 100%.
One Julian Price Pl., Charlotte, NC, 28208. Phone: (704) 374-3500. Fax: (704) 338-3062. Web Site:www.wbt.com Licensee: Greater Media of Charlotte Inc. (group owner; (acq 1-31-2008; grpsl). Population served: 1,105,000 Format: News/talk. News staff: 7; News: 6 hrs wkly. Target aud: 25-54; information, sports seekers. Spec prog: Gospel 6 hrs wkly. ♦Rick Jackson, VP, gen mgr; Tom Jackson, opns dir; Terry Mace, dev VP.

WGCD(AM)— July 19, 1948: 1490 khz; l kw-U. TL: N34 41 54 W81 12 06. Hrs open: Box 11584, Rock Hill, 29731. Phone: (803) 329-2760. Fax: (803) 329-3317. Web Site:www.rejoynetwork.com Licensee: Wisdom LLC. Group owner: Neely Enterprises (acq 2-2-2009; grpsl). Format: Gospel. ♦Frank K. Neeley, gen mgr; Frankie Hemphill, stn mgr.

Chesterfield

***WRFE(FM)**— 2007: 89.3 mhz; 1.5 kw. Ant 197 ft TL: N34 43 15 W80 05 18. (CP: 33 kw, ant 279 ft. TL: N34 45 59 W80 15 55). Stereo. Hrs open: Box 25775, Winston-Salem, NC, 27114. Phone: (336) 788-1155.

Fax: (336) 788-7199. Web Site:www.joyfm.org Licensee: Positive Alternative Radio Inc. (acq 1-16-2008; $500,000). Population served: 203,000 Format: Southern gospel. ♦Edward A. Baker, pres; Brian Sanders, gen mgr.

WVSZ(FM)— 1993: 107.3 mhz; 4.5 kw. 328 ft TL: N34 43 12 W80 05 45. Hrs open: Box 307, Rock Hill, 29731. Phone: (843) 286-1071. Phone: (843) 623-3299. Fax: (803) 324-2860.E-mail: almiller@wrhi.com Web Site:www.wrhi.com Licensee: Our Three Sons Broadcasting L.L.P. (group owner; acq 2-28-97; $142,500). Natl. Network: ABC, . S.C. News Net. Format: Country. ♦Allan M. Miller, gen mgr; Steven Stone, opns mgr; Mike Crowder, news dir.

Clearwater

WHHD(FM)— April 1987: 98.3 mhz; 11.5 kw. Ant 485 ft TL: N33 30 44 W82 04 48. Stereo. Hrs open: 24 4051 Jimmie Dyess Pky., Augusta, GA, 30909. Phone: (706) 396-7000. Fax: (706) 396-7100.E-mail: mail@whhd.com Web Site:www.hd983.com Licensee: WGAC License LLC. Group owner: Beasley Broadcast Group Inc. (acq 4-2-2001; $12 million with WKXC-FM Aiken). Format: Top 40/Mainstream. Target aud: 18-49; females. Spec prog: Kidd Kraddick in the Morning. ♦Kent Murphy, gen sls mgr; Kent Dunn, mktg VP; Bryan Axelson, prom dir; Chuck Whitaker, progmg dir; Charlie McCoy, chief of engrg.

Clemson

WAHT(AM)— July 27, 1969: 1560 khz; 1 kw-D, 500 w-CH. TL: N34 42 04 W82 49 30. Hrs open: 6 AM-8 PM Box 1560, 202 Lawrence Rd., 29631. Phone: (864) 654-1560. Fax: (864) 654-3300.E-mail: waht@wahtam.com Web Site:www.wahtam.com Licensee: Golden Corners Broadcasting Inc. (acq 9-28-89; $100,000; 10-16-89). Population served: 150,000 S.C. News Net. Wire Svc: CBS Format: Oldies. News staff: one; News: 35 hrs wkly. Target aud: 35-58; older yuppies. ♦George W. Clement, pres, gen mgr; Faye Clement, VP; Jeff Bright, stn mgr, gen sls mgr, progmg dir & chief of engrg.

WCCP-FM— Apr 8, 1993: 104.9 mhz; 4.6 kw. Ant 371 ft TL: N34 38 13 W82 42 30. Stereo. Hrs open: 24 Box 1560, 202 Lawrence Rd., 29631. Phone: (864) 654-4004. Fax: (864) 654-3300.E-mail: info@wccpfm.com Web Site:www.wccpfm.com Population served: 900,000 Natl. Network: CBS, Sporting News Radio Network, . Format: Sports. Target aud: 25-50. ♦George Clement, CEO; Aly Darby, stn mgr, progmg dir; Barry Clement, opns VP, opns mgr, prom dir; Pam Ponder, gen sls mgr.

***WSBF-FM**— Mar 16, 1961: 88.1 mhz; 3 kw. 200 ft TL: N34 40 42 W82 49 15. Stereo. Hrs open: Clemson University, 210 Hendrix Student Ctr., 29634. Phone: (864) 656-4010. Fax: (864) 656-4011.E-mail: program@wsbf.net Web Site:www.wsbf.net Licensee: Clemson University Board of Trustees. Population served: 50,000 Natl. Network: Westwood One, . Format: Progsv. Target aud: 16-25.

Clinton

WPCC(AM)— Sept 11, 1957: 1410 khz; 1 kw-D, 100 w-N. TL: N34 26 42 W81 53 24. Hrs open: 24 Box 1455, 29325. Secondary address: 1766 Hwy 72 West, West Clinton 29325. Phone: (864) 833-1410. Fax: (864) 833-2467.E-mail: wpcc@charter.net Web Site:www.sportsradio1410wpcc.com Licensee: Laurens County Communications Inc. (acq 12-83; $90,000; 12-5-83). Population served: 250,000 Natl. Network: ESPN Radio, . Format: Sports. News staff: one; News: one hr wkly. Target aud: General. Spec prog: Moring Show- The Doghouse, Local and Regional Sports. ♦A. Cruickshanks, pres; Rhonda Cruickshanks, gen mgr, opns mgr & mktg dir; Chris Burgin, progmg dir.

Cokesbury

***WKRI(FM)**—Not on air, target date: unknown: 91.9 mhz; 1.25 kw horiz, 25 kw vert. Ant 315 ft TL: N34 17 01 W82 10 49. Hrs open: 511 Cedar Grove Rd., Clover, 29710. Phone: (803) 684-2965. Licensee: Spirit Broadcasting Group Inc. ♦C. Curtis Sigmon, pres.

Columbia

WARQ(FM)— Feb 6, 1971: 93.5 mhz; 2.8 kw. 443 ft TL: N34 02 00 W80 58 56. Stereo. Hrs open: 24 Box 9127, 29290. Secondary address: 1900 Pineview Rd. 29290. Phone: (803) 695-8600. Fax: (803) 695-8605.E-mail: info@warq.com Web Site:www.warq.com Licensee: Urban Radio II L.L.C. Group owner: Inner City Broadcasting (acq 8-7-2000; grpsl). Population served: 461,000 Natl. Network: Westwood One, . Wire Svc: Accu-Weather Format: Rock. News staff: one; News: 5 hrs wkly. Target aud: 18-49. ♦Steve Patterson, gen mgr; Scott Norton, gen sls mgr; Jamie Muldrow, prom dir; Dave Stewart, progmg dir.

WCEO(AM)— Jan 1, 1994: 840 khz; 50 kw-D, DA. TL: N34 12 42 W80 50 05. Stereo. Hrs open: Sunrise-sunset 108 Columbia N.E. Dr., Suite F, 29223. Phone: (803) 419-7366. Fax: (803) 419-7363. Web Site:latremendaradio.com Licensee: Norsan Broadcasting WCEO LLC. (group owner; (acq 10-1-2006; $1.6 million). Tom McCoy. Format: Sp. ♦Lino Cruz, stn mgr.

WCOS(AM)— 1939: 1400 khz; 1 kw-U. TL: N34 00 18 W81 00 43. Hrs open: 24 316 Greystone Blvd., 29210-8007. Phone: (803) 343-1100. Fax: (803) 798-5255. Licensee: Capstar TX L.P. Group owner: Clear Channel Communications Inc. (acq 9-1-00; grpsl). Population served: 450,000 Natl. Rep: Clear Channel,. Format: Sports. Target aud: Men 25-54. ♦Bobby Martin, gen mgr; Gary Barboza, opns mgr, progmg dir; Gary Frakes, prom dir; Gary Robinson, engrg dir; Mary Pais, traf mgr; Christopher Thompson, news rptr.

WCOS-FM— March 1951: 97.5 mhz; 100 kw. 981 ft TL: N34 08 23 W81 03 22. Stereo. Hrs open: 24 Prog sep from AM 316 Greystone Blvd., 29210. Phone: (803) 343-1100. Fax: (803) 798-5255. Web Site:www.wcosfm.com Format: Country. News staff: one. Target aud: 25-54. ♦Margret Wallace, sls dir, gen sls mgr; Susan Brown, prom mgr; Ron Brooks, progmg dir, news dir; Glen Garrett, mus dir; Gary Robinson, chief of engrg.

WISW(AM)— June 30, 1954: 1320 khz; 5 kw-D, 2.5 kw-N, DA-N. TL: N34 00 16 W81 04 15. Hrs open: 24 1801 Charleston Hwy., Cayce, 29033. Phone: (803) 796-7600. Fax: (803) 796-5502. Licensee: Citadel Broadcasting Co. Group owner: Citadel Broadcasting Corp. Natl. Rep: Christal,. Reddy, Begley & McCormick. Format: Talk Radio. News staff: 5; News: 168 hrs wkly. Target aud: 35-64. Spec prog: Sports. ♦William L. McElveen, pres & gen mgr; Tim Miller, opns mgr; Bill MacAvine, gen sls mgr; Al Conner, progmg dir; Ray Allen, news dir; Ed Noyes, engrg dir.

***WLTR(FM)**— July 1, 1976: 91.3 mhz; 96 kw. 761 ft TL: N34 07 07 W80 56 12. Stereo. Hrs open: 24 1101 George Rogers Blvd., 29201. Phone: (803) 737-3420. Fax: (803) 737-3552.E-mail: gasque@scetv.org Web Site:www.etvradio.org Licensee: South Carolina Educ. TV Commission. Population served: 450,000 Natl. Network: NPR, PRI, . Dow, Lohnes & Albertson. Format: Classical, NPR news. ♦Moss Bresnahan, pres, VP; Tom Holloway, dev dir; John Gasque, progmg dir.

WLTY(FM)—(Cayce, July 11, 1974: 96.7 mhz; 3.3 kw. 443 ft TL: N34 00 04 W81 02 05. Stereo. Hrs open: 316 Greystone Blvd., 29250. Phone: (803) 343-1100. Fax: (803) 779-9727.E-mail: info@wlty.com Web Site:www.lite967.com Licensee: Capstar TX L.P. Group owner: Clear Channel Communications Inc. (acq 8-30-00; grpsl). Natl. Rep: Clear Channel,. Format: Light Adult Contemp. News: 6 hrs wkly. Target aud: 25-44; professionals & young adults. ♦Bob Huntley, gen mgr.

WLXC(FM)— Apr 15, 1989: 103.1 mhz; 6 kw. Ant 308 ft TL: N34 03 05 W81 00 07. Stereo. Hrs open: 1801 Charleston Hwy., Cayce, 29033. Phone: (803) 796-7600. Fax: (803) 796-5502. Licensee: Citadel Broadcasting Co. Format: Urban contemp. News staff: one; News: one hr wkly. Target aud: 25-54; upward, mobile, higher income. ♦William L. McElveen, gen mgr; Ray Allen, prom dir; Al Conner, news dir.

WMFX(FM)—(Saint Andrews, Jan 23, 1985: 102.3 mhz; 6 kw. 322 ft TL: N34 05 55 W81 04 48. Stereo. Hrs open: 24 Box 9127, 29290-0127. Secondary address: 1900 Pineview Rd. 29209. Phone: (803) 695-8600. Fax: (803) 695-8605.E-mail: mhanisch@innercity.sc.com Web Site:www.fox102.com Licensee: Urban Radio II L.L.C. Group owner: Inner City Broadcasting (acq 8-7-2000; grpsl). Population served: 461,000 Format: Classic rock, AOR. News staff: one; News: one hr wkly. Target aud: 18-49. ♦Maggie Hanisch, gen mgr; Scott Norton, gen sls mgr; Jamie Bowman, prom dir; Dave Stewart, progmg dir.

***WMHK(FM)**— Aug 30, 1976: 89.7 mhz; 100 kw. 1,398 ft TL: N34 05 49 W80 45 51. Stereo. Hrs open: Box 3122, 29230. Phone: (803) 754-5400. Fax: (803) 714-0849.E-mail: wmhk@wmhk.com Web Site:www.wmhk.com Licensee: Columbia Bible College Broadcasting Co. Population served: 713,200 Format: Contemp christian music. Target aud: 25-44; women. ♦Joe Paulo, gen mgr; John Owens, opns mgr; Steve Sunshine, progmg dir.

WNOK(FM)— July 15, 1959: 104.7 mhz; 100 kw. 1,014 ft TL: N34 09 06 W80 54 36. (CP: 96 kw, ant 1,033 ft. TL: N34 09 03 W80 54 36). Stereo. Hrs open: 24 316 Greystone Blvd, 29210. Phone: (803) 343-1080. Fax: (803) 256-1968. Web Site:www.wnok.com Licensee: Capstar TX L.P. Group owner: Clear Channel Communications Inc. (acq 8-30-00; grpsl). Population served: 390,000 Format: CHR. Target aud: 18-34; landed gentry. ♦Bob Hentley, gen mgr.

WOIC(AM)— Jan 1, 1947: 1230 khz; 1 kw-U, DA-N. TL: N33 59 34 W81 02 45. Hrs open: Box 9127, 29290. Phone: (803) 776-1013. Fax: (803) 695-8605. Web Site:www.espn1230am.com Licensee: Urban Radio II L.L.C. Group owner: Inner City Broadcasting (acq 8-7-2000; grpsl). Population served: 461,000 Natl. Network: USA, . Natl. Rep: D & R Radio,. Format: Talk. News: 3 hrs wkly. Target aud: 25-54; Male. ♦Steve Patterson, gen mgr.

WQXL(AM)— June 15, 1945: 1470 khz; 5 kw-D, 138 w-N. TL: N34 01 44 W81 02 23. Hrs open: 6 AM-8:30 PM POB 2355, West Columbia, 29171. Phone: (803) 779-7911. Fax: (803) 252-2158.E-mail: wqxl1470@aol.com Licensee: Glory Communications Inc. (acq 5-11-2007; $200,000). Population served: 153,542 Natl. Network: USA, . Format: Praise & worship. Target aud: 25-49. ♦Alex Snipe, pres; Donna Moore, stn mgr; Olin Jenkins, opns mgr.

WTCB(FM)—See Orangeburg

***WUSC-FM**— Jan 17, 1977: 90.5 mhz; 2.5 kw. 233 ft TL: N34 00 02 W81 01 19. (CP: Ant 253 ft.). Stereo. Hrs open: 24 Drawer B, Univ. of South Carolina, 1400 Greene St., 29208. Phone: (803) 777-5468. Fax: (803) 777-6482. Web Site:wusc.sc.edu Licensee: University of South Carolina. Population served: 400,000 Format: Var. News staff: one; News: 3 hrs wkly. Target aud: General; alternative generation. ♦Will Belenger, stn mgr.

WVOC(AM)— July 10, 1930: 560 khz; 5 kw-U, DA-N. TL: N34 02 00 W81 08 32. Stereo. Hrs open: 24 316 Greystone Blvd., 29210-8007. Phone: (803) 343-1100. Fax: (803) 256-1968. Web Site:www.wvoc.com Licensee: Capstar TX L.P. Group owner: Clear Channel Communications Inc. (acq 8-30-00; grpsl). Population served: 415,800 Natl. Network: CNN Radio, . Rgnl. Network: S.C. Net. S.C. News Net. Wire Svc: Dow Jones Financial News Services Format: News/talk, sports. News staff: 2; News: 40 hrs wkly. Target aud: 35-64. ♦Tim McFalls, gen mgr.

WXBT(FM)—(West Columbia, Aug 5, 1975: 100.1 mhz; 5.9 kw. 331 ft TL: N34 04 08 W81 04 16. Stereo. Hrs open: 24 316 Greystone Blvd., 29210. Phone: (803) 343-1100. Fax: (803) 252-9267. Licensee: Capstar TX L.P. Group owner: Clear Channel Communications Inc. (acq 8-30-00; grpsl). Population served: 462,000 Natl. Network: CBS, . Format: Rhythm and blues, urban contemp. News staff: one; News: 17 hrs wkly. Target aud: 35 plus; mature adults. ♦Bryan Anthony, progmg dir, chief of engrg; Tim McFalls, gen mgr & news dir.

Conway

***WHMC-FM**— Sept 15, 1985: 90.1 mhz; 30 kw. 706 ft TL: N33 57 05 W79 06 31. Hrs open: 24
Rebroadcasts WRJA-FM Sumter 100%.
1101 George Rogers Blvd., Columbia, 29201. Phone: (803) 737-3420. Fax: (803) 737-3552.E-mail: gasque@scetv.org Web Site:www.etvradio.org Licensee: South Carolina Educational Television Commission. Natl. Network: NPR, PRI, . Format: NPR news. News: New progrmg 120 hrs wkly. ♦Moss Bresnahan, pres; John Gasque, VP, progmg dir.

WIQB(AM)— Feb 23, 1977: 1050 khz; 5 kw-D, 473 w-N, DA-2. TL: N33 50 56 W79 05 03. Stereo. Hrs open: 24 11640 Hwy. 17 Bypass, Murrells Inlet, 29576. Phone: (843) 651-7869. Fax: (843) 397-3197. Licensee: Cumulus Licensing Corp. Group owner: Cumulus Media Inc. (acq 12-29-97; grpsl). Population served: 256,000 Rgnl. Network: S.C. Net. S.C. News Net. Gardner, Carton & Douglas. Format: Sports. News staff: one. Target aud: 50 plus; affluent retirees. ♦Ron Raybourne, gen mgr; Dave Solomon, progmg dir; Robert Kesler, news dir; Buddy Womack, chief of engrg.

WJXY-FM— October 1990: 93.9 mhz; 3.7 kw. Ant 420 ft TL: N33 50 07 W78 52 06. Stereo. Hrs open: 24 11640 Hwy. 17 Bypass, Murrells Inlet, 29576. Phone: (843) 651-7869. Fax: (843) 397-3197. Licensee: Cumulus Licensing Corp. Natl. Network: ABC, . Format: Sports. News: 2 hrs wkly. Target aud: 18-34. ♦Lou Dickey, pres & opns dir; Dave Solomon, adv dir, pub affrs dir; Lisa Van Horn, pub affrs dir.

WPJS(AM)— August 1945: 1330 khz; 5 kw-D, 500 w-N, DA-N. TL: N33 50 57 W79 04 11. Hrs open: Box 961, 29528. Phone: (843) 248-9040. Fax: (843) 248-6365. Licensee: WPJS Broadcasters Inc. Format: Black gospel. Target aud: 12 plus. ♦P.J. Parrish, gen mgr.

Cross Hill

WYOR(FM)— September 1999: 94.1 mhz; 3.6 kw. Ant 417 ft TL: N34 12 16 W81 54 37. Hrs open: 637 E. Durst Ave., Greenwood, 29649. Phone: (864) 223-8553. Fax: (864) 943-0314. Web Site:www.941thebull.com Licensee: Peregon Broadcasting LLC (acq 11-6-2006; $800,000 with WCRS(AM) Greenwood). Format: Country. ♦Carl Pundt, gen mgr.

Darlington

WDAR-FM— December 1965: 105.5 mhz; 4.1 kw. 400 ft TL: N34 18 58 W79 53 17. (CP: 17 kw). Stereo. Hrs open: 24hrs Box 103000, Florence, 29501. Secondary address: 181 E. Evans St., Suite 311, Florence 29506. Phone: (843) 667-4600. Fax: (843) 673-7390. Web Site:www.sunny1055online.com Licensee: Qantum of Florence License Co. LLC Group owner: Qantum Communications Corp. (acq 7-2-2003; grpsl). Format: Easy lstng, adult contemp. ◆Craig Dalla Riva, gen mgr; Sherry Miller, gen sls mgr; Gail Nichols, progmg dir; Thoma Lesieur, news dir; David Jones, chief of engrg; Veronica Wingate, traf mgr.

WWRK(AM)— 1955: 1400 khz; 1 kw-U. TL: N34 18 58 W79 53 17. Hrs open: Box 103000, Florence, 29501. Secondary address: 181 E. Evans St., Suite 311, Florence 29506. Phone: (843) 667-4600. Fax: (843) 673-7390. Licensee: Qantum of Florence License Co. LLC Population served: 200,000 Format: Black gospel. Target aud: 25 plus. ◆ Terri Burgess, traf mgr.

Dillon

*WDLL(FM)— 2007: 90.5 mhz; 25 kw vert. Ant 276 ft TL: N34 19 53 W79 33 37. Hrs open:
Rebroadcasts WAFR(FM) Tupelo, MS 100%.
Box 2440, Tupelo, MS, 38803-2440. Phone: (662) 844-8888. Fax: (662) 842-6791. Web Site:www.afr.net Licensee: American Family Association. Format: Christian. ◆Donald E. Wildmon, chmn.

WDSC(AM)— May 22, 1946: 800 khz; 1 kw-D, 382 w-N. TL: N34 22 11 W79 24 08. Hrs open: 24 Box 103000, Florence, 29501. Secondary address: 181 E. Evans St., Florence 29506. Phone: (843) 667-4600. Fax: (843) 673-7390. Licensee: Qantum of Florence License Co. LLC. Group owner: Qantum Communications Corp. (acq 7-2-2003; grpsl). Population served: 100,780 Format: Gospel. Target aud: General. ◆Craig Dalla Riva, gen mgr; Sherry Miller, gen sls mgr.

WEGX(FM)— Feb 16, 1954: 92.9 mhz; 100 kw. Ant 1,801 ft TL: N34 21 53 W79 19 49. Stereo. Hrs open: 24 Box 103000, Florence, 29501. Secondary address: 181 E. Evans St., Suite 311, Florence 29506. Phone: (843) 667-4600. Fax: (843) 673-7390. Web Site:www.eagle929online.com Licensee: Qantum of Florence License Co. LLC. (acq 7-2-2003; grpsl). Population served: 481,400 Format: Country. Spec prog: Jazz one hr wkly. ◆Randy Wilcox, progmg dir.

Dorchester Terrace-Brentwood

WTMZ(AM)—Licensed to Dorchester Terrace-Brentwood. See North Charleston

Easley

WELP(AM)— Mar 4, 1951: 1360 khz; 5 kw-D, 36 w-N. TL: N34 50 20 W82 38 24. Hrs open: 24 100 Cross Hill Rd., 29640. Phone: (864) 855-9300. Fax: (864) 855-8444.E-mail: welp@wilkinsradio.com Web Site:www.wilkinsradio.com Licensee: Upstate Radio Inc. Group owner: Wilkins Communications Network Inc. (acq 1999; $150,000). Population served: 775,000 Womble, Carlyle, Sandridge & Rice. Format: Christian teaching/talk. News staff: 2; News: 22 hrs wkly. Target aud: 35 plus. ◆Bob Wilkins, pres, gen sls mgr; LuAnn Wilkins, exec VP; Mitchell Mathis, VP; Greg Garrett, gen mgr, stn mgr, opns mgr, mus dir; Ted McCall, chief of engrg & engr.

WOLI-FM— 1964: 103.9 mhz; 6 kw. Ant 328 ft TL: N34 50 21 W82 31 37. Stereo. Hrs open: 225 S. Pleasantburg Dr., Suite 3B, Greenville, 29607. Phone: (864) 751-0113. Licensee: Davidson Media Station WOLI Licensee LLC. Group owner: Entercom Communications Corp. (acq 10-6-2005; grpsl). Population served: 72,900 Format: Sp contemp. ◆Tom Durney, gen mgr & prom dir.

Eastover

WNKT(FM)— Jan 5, 1971: 107.5 mhz; 40 kw. Ant 548 ft TL: N33 45 46 W80 49 23. Stereo. Hrs open: 24 1801 Charleston Hwy., Suite J, Cayce, 29033. Phone: (803) 796-7600. Fax: (803) 796-5502. Licensee: Citadel Broadcasting Co. Group owner: Citadel Broadcasting Corp. (acq 6-9-99; grpsl). Population served: 500,000 Natl. Rep: McGavren Guild,. Format: Sports. ◆William L. McElveen, gen mgr.

Elloree

WORG(FM)—Licensed to Elloree. See Elloree-Santee

Elloree-Santee

WORG(FM)—(Elloree, May 1988: 100.3 mhz; 25 kw. 328 ft TL: N33 21 42 W80 41 05. Stereo. Hrs open: 24 1675 Chestnut St., Orangeburg, 29115. Phone: (803) 516-8400. Fax: (803) 516-0704.E-mail: worg@worg.com Web Site:www.worg.com Licensee: Garris Communications Inc. (acq 7-95). Population served: 400,000 Format: Adult contemp. News: 6am, 7am, 8am. Target aud: 25-54. Spec prog: John Tesh Nightly. ◆Marion R. Garris, pres & gen mgr.

Enoree

*WNRE(FM)—Not on air, target date: unknown: 88.1 mhz; 175 w. Ant 253 ft TL: N34 38 06 W81 58 47. Hrs open: 511 Cedar Grove Rd., Clover, 29710. Phone: (803) 684-2965. Licensee: Spirit Broadcasting Group Inc. ◆C. Curtis Sigmon, pres.

Florence

WDSC(AM)—See Dillon

WEGX(FM)—See Dillon

WJMX(AM)— July 13, 1947: 970 khz; 5 kw-D, 3 kw-N, DA-N. TL: N34 13 47 W79 48 07. Stereo. Hrs open: 24 Box 103000, 29501. Secondary address: Florence Bus. & Tech. Ctr., 181 E. Evans St., Ste. 311 29506. Phone: (843) 667-4600. Phone: (843) 665-0970. Fax: (843) 673-7390. Web Site:newstalk970online.com Licensee: Qantum of Florence License Co. LLC. Group owner: Qantum Communications Corp. (acq 7-2-2003; grpsl). Population served: 300,000 Natl. Network: CBS, AP Radio, . Rgnl. Network: S.C. Net. Natl. Rep: McGavren Guild,. S.C. News Net. Format: Talk, news. News staff: one; News: 49 hrs wkly. Target aud: 25-54. Spec prog: Big band 3 hrs wkly. ◆Jonathan Brewster, gen mgr; Craig Dalla Riva, stn mgr.

WJMX-FM—See Cheraw

*WLPG(FM)— May 15, 1993: 91.7 mhz; 10 kw horiz, 9.2 kw vert. 492 ft TL: N34 07 45 W79 50 06. Hrs open: 24 2278 Wortham Ln., Grovetown, GA, 30802. Phone: (706) 309-9610.E-mail: ctbarinowski@comcast.net Web Site:www.gnnradio.org Licensee: Augusta Radio Fellowship Institute Inc. Format: Christian. News: 12 hrs wkly. ◆Clarence Barinowski, gen mgr.

WOLH(AM)— Nov 18, 1937: 1230 khz; 1 kw-U. TL: N34 13 48 W79 44 49. Hrs open: 24 338 E. McIver Rd., 29506. Phone: (843) 665-1230. Fax: (843) 665-8786.E-mail: jjones1990@sc.rr.com Licensee: Miller Communications Inc. Group owner: GHB Radio Group (acq 4-29-2008; $275,000 with WHYM(AM) Lake City). Population served: 110,000 Natl. Network: ABC, . Rgnl rep: Jim D. Jones Format: Sports/talk. News staff: one; News: 4 hrs wkly. Spec prog: Farm one hr, gospel 4 hrs, jazz 4 hrs, talk 16 hrs wkly. ◆Harold Miller Jr., pres; Jeffrey Andrew Lonas, gen mgr.

WYNN(AM)— Nov 5, 1958: 540 khz; 250 w-U. TL: N34 13 05 W79 48 22. Hrs open: 24 2014 N. Irby St., 29501. Phone: (843) 661-5000. Fax: (843) 661-0888. Licensee: Cumulus Licensing Corp. Group owner: Cumulus Media Inc. (acq 12-17-98; with co-located FM). Population served: 150,000 Natl. Network: American Urban, . Scott Johnson. Format: Black gospel, blues, Black classics. News staff: one; News: 12 hrs wkly. Target aud: 35 plus; Black. Spec prog: Jazz. ◆Jerry Stevens, gen mgr, gen sls mgr; Matt Scurry, opns mgr; Ollie Williams, progmg dir; Daniel Tindal, asst music dir.

WYNN-FM— Oct 1, 1964: 106.3 mhz; 1.1 kw. 507 ft TL: N34 14 03 W79 46 52. (CP: 1.7 kw). Stereo. Hrs open: 24 Prog sep from AM 2014 N. Irby St., 29501. Licensee: Cumulus Licensing Corp. Format: Urban contemp. News staff: one; News: one hr wkly. Target aud: 12-34. ◆Gerald McSwain, progmg dir.

Folly Beach

WYBB(FM)— July 4, 1988: 98.1 mhz; 50 kw. 500 ft TL: N32 39 57 W80 03 11. Stereo. Hrs open: 24 59 Windermere Blvd., Charleston, 29407. Phone: (843) 769-4799. Fax: (843) 769-4797. Web Site:www.98xonline.com Licensee: L.M. Communications of South Carolina Inc. Group owner: L.M. Communications Inc. (acq 5-17-88). Population served: 500,000 Natl. Network: ABC, . Leventhal, Senter & Lerman. Format: New rock. News: 28 hrs wkly. Target aud: 25-49; men. ◆Lynn Martin, pres; Charlie Cohn, gen mgr; Mike Allen, opns dir.

Forest Acres

WWNQ(FM)— 2005: 94.3 mhz; 2.55 kw. Ant 446 ft TL: N34 00 04 W81 02 05. Hrs open: 1010 Gervais St., Suite 100, Columbia, 29201-3130. Phone: (803) 753-6803. Fax: (803) 753-6806.E-mail: comments@flashback943.com Web Site:www.flashback943.com Licensee: Double O South Carolina Corp. (acq 9-10-2004; $4.73 million for CP). Format: Classic hits. Target aud: 25-50. ◆Chuck McKay, gen mgr; Tyler Ryan, progmg dir.

Forestbrook

WKZQ-FM— Mar 11, 1985: 96.1 mhz; 8.5 kw. Ant 871 ft TL: N33 27 W79 02 55. Stereo. Hrs open: 24 1016 Ocala St., Myrtle Beach, 29577. Phone: (843) 448-1041. Fax: (843) 626-5988. Web Site:www.wkzq.net Licensee: NM Licensing LLC. (group owner; (acq 10-28-2008; swap for WAVF(FM) Hanahan). Format: New rock. Target aud: 18-34. ◆Steven Dinetz, CEO; Jeff Dinetz, COO; Carl Hirsch, chmn; Skip Weller, pres; Barry Brown, gen mgr; Art Greene, sls dir; Liza Van Horne, prom mgr; Mark McKinney, progmg dir; Paul Matthews, chief of engrg; Trimeshia Jeffery, traf mgr.

Fort Mill

*WFBK(FM)—Not on air, target date: unknown: 91.5 mhz; 100 w. Ant 118 ft TL: N35 00 26 W80 58 50. Hrs open: Box 15, Chester, 29706. Phone: (803) 581-9030. Fax: (803) 581-9932. Licensee: Richburg Educational Broadcasters Inc. ◆Jeff Sigmon, gen mgr.

Fountain Inn

WFIS(AM)— October 1956: 1600 khz; 1 kw-D, 29 w-N. TL: N34 42 28 W82 13 40. Hrs open: 24 Box 156, 29644. Secondary address: 1318 N. Main St. 29644. Phone: (864) 963-5991. Fax: (864) 963-5992.E-mail: wfis16@aol.com Licensee: Golden Strip Broadcasting Inc. (acq 1-7-2008). Population served: 45,000 Natl. Network: Westwood One, Jones Radio Networks, ABC, . Rgnl. Network: S.C. Net. Natl. Rep: Rgnl Reps,. S.C. News Net. Format: Talk, sports. News staff: one; News: 3 hrs wkly. Target aud: 25-49; working adults. Spec prog: Gospel 4, Black 4 hrs, Christian 3 hrs wkly. ◆Joseph E. LaStringer, gen mgr.

Gaffney

WFGN(AM)— 1948: 1180 khz; 2.5 kw-D. TL: N35 02 59 W81 38 42. Hrs open: 6 AM-8 PM 470 Leadmine Rd., 29342. Phone: (864) 489-9430. Fax: (864) 489-9440. Licensee: Hope Broadcasting Inc. (acq 8-7-90; $160,000; 8-27-90). Population served: 100,000 Format: Relg. ◆Eddie Leroy Bridges Jr., pres; Ed Ridges, gen mgr; Charles Montgomery, opns mgr, disc jockey; Rev. Eula Miller, gen sls mgr; Caroline Allen, disc jockey.

WNOW-FM— 1959: 105.3 mhz; 100 kw. Ant 1,190 ft TL: N35 25 05 W81 46 32. Stereo. Hrs open: 24 Box 1210, 29342. Secondary address: 340 Providence Rd. 29341. Phone: (864) 489-9066. Fax: (864) 489-9069.E-mail: feedback@wagifm.com Web Site:www.wagifm.com Licensee: Gaffney Broadcasting Inc. (acq 10-18-2007; $22 million with co-located AM). Population served: 1,000,000 Natl. Network: CNN Radio, . Wire Svc: AP Format: Contemp country, gospel. News staff: one. Target aud: 18-54. Spec prog: Clemson Univ. sports, loc sports, talk 10 hrs wkly. ◆Ronald Owenby, gen mgr; Dennis Fowler, stn mgr, news dir; Ernie Payne, Jr., gen sls mgr; Jonathan Fitch, mus dir; Claudella Moss, traf mgr.

*WYFG(FM)— Oct 12, 1982: 91.1 mhz; 100 kw. 574 ft TL: N35 06 37 W81 46 42. Stereo. Hrs open: 24 Bible Broadcasting Network, Charlotte, NC, 28241-7300. Phone: (800) 888-7077. Licensee: Bible Broadcasting Network Inc. (group owner) Population served: 1,000,000 Natl. Network: USA, . Format: Relg/Conservative Christian. News staff: one. Target aud: General. ◆Lowell Davey, pres; Stan Schenkel, gen mgr.

WZZQ(AM)— Sept 28, 1962: 1500 khz; 1 kw-D, 500 w-N. TL: N35 05 18 W81 38 40. Hrs open: Box 1210, 29342. Secondary address: 340 Providence Rd. 29341. Phone: (864) 489-9066. Fax: (864) 489-9069.E-mail: feedback@wagifm.com Web Site:http://www.wagifm.com/ Licensee: Gaffney Broadcasting Inc. Population served: 13,253 Rgnl. Network: S.C. Net. S.C. News Net. Wire Svc: AP Format: Country. News staff: one; News: 2 hrs wkly. Target aud: 18-54.

Garden City

WWXM(FM)— Sept 25, 1971: 97.7 mhz; 100 kw. Ant 718 ft TL: N33 35 45 W79 03 11. Stereo. Hrs open: 24 4841 Hwy. 17 By-pass S., Myrtle Beach, 29577. Phone: (843) 293-0107. Fax: (843) 293-1717.E-mail: info@977online.com Web Site:www.977online.com Licensee: Qantum of Myrtle Beach License Co. LLC. Group owner: Qantum Communications Corp. (acq 7-2-2003; grpsl). Population served: 200,000 Fletcher, Heald & Hildreth. Format: CHR. News staff: one; News: 2 hrs wkly. Target aud: 18-49. ♦Jimmy Feuger, gen mgr.

Georgetown

WGTN(AM)— July 1, 1949: 1400 khz; 1 kw-U. TL: N33 24 15 W79 19 36. Stereo. Hrs open: 24 Box 1400, 29442. Phone: (843) 546-1400. Fax: (843) 527-2337. Web Site:www.wgtnradio.com Licensee: R.J. Stalvey (acq 1-24-2001). Population served: 10,449 Natl. Network: Fox News Radio, . Format: News/talk. News staff: one; News: 12 hrs wkly. Target aud: 25-54; upscale adult; bus, professional and technical. ♦Rod Stalvey, gen mgr.

WGTN-FM—(Andrews, Aug 19, 1985: 100.7 mhz; 3.1 kw. Ant 446 ft TL: N33 24 03 W79 27 30. Stereo. Hrs open: 24 3926 Wesley St., Suite 301, Myrtle Beach, 29578. Phone: (843) 903-9962. Fax: (843) 903-1797. Licensee: Coastline Communications of Carolina Inc. (acq 10-12-2000; $800,000). Format: Adult Hits. Target aud: 25-54; Adults. ♦Will Isaacs, gen mgr; Jerome Bresson, news dir.

WLFF(FM)— May 1, 1973: 106.5 mhz; 50 kw. 530 ft TL: N33 26 20 W79 08 11. Stereo. Hrs open: 24 11640 Hwy. 17 By-pass S., Murrells Inlet, 29576. Phone: (843) 651-7869. Fax: (843) 651-3197. Web Site:www.sunny1065.net Licensee: Cumulus Licensing Corp. Group owner: Cumulus Media Inc. (acq 1-27-98). Format: Oldies. ♦Bill Hazen, gen mgr.

WLMC(AM)— March 1962: 1470 khz; 1 kw-D. TL: N33 22 15 W79 16 39. Stereo. Hrs open: Box 2865, 29442. Phone: (843) 546-8863. Fax: (843) 546-6281.E-mail: wlmcradio@aol.com Licensee: Cumberland A & A Corp. (acq 2-10-2003; $200,000). Natl. Network: ABC, . Format: Gospel, Christian, inspirational. Target aud: 25 plus; African-Americans. Spec prog: Talk 4 hrs wkly. ♦Reggie Dyson, CEO.

WXJY(FM)— Sept 1, 1990: 93.7 mhz; 6 kw. 328 ft TL: N33 16 09 W79 17 49. Stereo. Hrs open: 24 11640 Highway 17 Bypass, Murrells Inlet, GA, 29576. Phone: (404) 949-0700. Fax: (404) 949-0740. Web Site:www.teammyrtlebeach.com Licensee: Cumulus Licensing Corp. Group owner: Cumulus Media Inc. (acq 12-29-97; grpsl). Population served: 50,000 Format: Sports. News: 4 hrs wkly. Target aud: 25-49; career-oriented, college-educated adults. ♦Lyne Ryan, gen mgr; Roderick Smith, opns mgr; Kellly Broderick, progmg dir.

Goose Creek

WSCC-FM— May 19, 1983: 94.3 mhz; 25 kw. Ant 328 ft TL: N32 49 04 W79 50 08. Stereo. Hrs open: 950 Houston Northcutt Blvd., Mt. Pleasant, 29464. Phone: (843) 856-6100. Fax: (843) 884-1218.E-mail: bjkay@clearchannel.com Web Site:www.wscfm.com Licensee: Clear Channel Broadcasting Licenses Inc. Group owner: Clear Channel Communications Inc. (acq 7-29-2003). Natl. Network: Fox News Radio, . Natl. Rep: McGavren Guild,. Format: Talk. News staff: 3. Target aud: 25-54. ♦Paul Smith, gen mgr; Willie Bennett, chief of engrg.

Gray Court

WSSL-FM—Licensed to Gray Court. See Greenville

Greenville

WCSZ(AM)—(Sans Souci, May 26, 1966: Stn currently dark. 1070 khz; 50 kw-D, 1.5 kw-N, DA-3. TL: N34 55 05 W82 27 21. Stereo. Hrs open: 24 200 N. Hwy. 25 Bypass, 29617. Phone: (864) 294-1071. Fax: (864) 246-8695. Licensee: WHYZ Radio L.P. (acq 1996; $200,000 for foreclosure). Population served: 700000 Natl. Network: Westwood One, American Urban, . Format: Inspirational gospel. Target aud: 25-54; $50,000 plus houshold income, college educated, 60% male, 40% female. ♦Glenn Cherry, CEO; Jerry Young, gen mgr & stn mgr.

***WEPR(FM)**— Sept 3, 1972: 90.1 mhz; 85 kw. 1,184 ft TL: N34 56 26 W82 24 38. Stereo. Hrs open: 24
Rebroadcasts WLTR(FM) Columbia 100%.
1101 George Rogers Blvd., Columbia, 29201. Phone: (803) 737-3420. Fax: (803) 737-3552.E-mail: gasque@scetv.org Web Site:www.etvradio.org Licensee: South Carolina Educ. TV Commission. Natl. Network: NPR, PRI, . Dow, Lohnes & Albertson. Format: NPR news, classical. News: New progrmg 70 hrs wkly. ♦Moss Bresnahan, pres; Paul Zweimiller, stn mgr; John Gasque, progmg dir; Hap Griffin, engrg VP; Connie Murray, traf mgr.

WESC-FM— March 1948: 92.5 mhz; 100 kw. 2,000 ft TL: N35 08 16 W82 36 31. Stereo. Hrs open: 24 Box 100, 29602. Secondary address: 7 N. Laurens St., Suite 700 29601. Phone: (864) 242-4660. Fax: (864) 242-8813. Web Site:www.wescfm.com Licensee: Clear Channel Broadcasting Licenses Inc. Group owner: Clear Channel Communications Inc. (acq 1998; grpsl). Population served: 281,700 Format: Country. ♦Bill McMartin, gen mgr; Bob Hooper, sls dir; Sandra Dill, mktg VP; Vicky Sexton, prom VP; Scott Johnson, progmg dir; John Landrum, mus dir; Roger Davis, news dir; Jim Graham, chief of engrg; Goldia Williams, traf mgr; Charlie Munson, disc jockey.

WFBC-FM— March 1947: 93.7 mhz; 100 kw. 1,850 ft TL: N35 06 40 W82 36 17. Stereo. Hrs open: 24 Prog sep from AM 25 Garlington Rd., 29615. Phone: (864) 271-9200. Fax: (864) 242-1567.E-mail: info@b937online.com Web Site:www.b937online.com Licensee: Entercom Greenville License LLC Population served: 650,000 Format: Adult contemp. News staff: 4; News: one hr wkly. Target aud: 35-64. Spec prog: Alternative 2 hrs wkly. ♦Niki Knight, CFO & progmg dir; Heidi Aiken, news dir.

WGVL(AM)— 1950: 1440 khz; 5 kw-U, DA-N. TL: N34 52 06 W82 28 04. Hrs open: 24 6119 White Horse Rd., Suite 16, 29611. Phone: (864) 220-1115. Fax: (864) 220-1120.E-mail: info@lainvasora1440.com Web Site:www.lainvasora1440.com Licensee: Capstar TX L.P. Group owner: Clear Channel Communications Inc. (acq 8-30-00; grpsl). Wiley Rein LLP. Format: Hispanic. News staff: 2; News: 4 hrs wkly. Target aud: 25-54.

WLFJ(AM)— March 1947: 660 khz; 50 kw-D, 10 kw-CH. TL: N34 53 10 W82 28 03. Hrs open: 2420 Wade Hampton Blvd., 29615. Phone: (864) 292-6040. Fax: (864) 292-8428.E-mail: comments@hisradio.com Web Site:www.christiantalk660.com Licensee: Clear Channel Broadcasting Licenses Inc. Group owner: Clear Channel Communications Inc. (acq 1998; grpsl). Population served: 61,208 Natl. Network: Fox News Radio, . Format: Christian Talk. Target aud: 25-54. ♦Allen Henderson, gen mgr; Gary Miller, stn mgr; Isaac Fineman, sls dir.

***WLFJ-FM**— May 1983: 89.3 mhz; 41 kw. 1,100 ft TL: N34 56 26 W82 24 44. Stereo. Hrs open: 24 2420 Wade Hampton Blvd., 29615. Phone: (864) 292-6040. Phone: (864) 292-5683. Fax: (864) 292-8428.E-mail: comments@hisradio.com Web Site:www.hisradio.com Licensee: Radio Training Network Inc. (acq 8-31-89). Population served: 850000 Format: Contemp Christian. ♦Allen Henderson, gen mgr; Rob Dempsey, progmg dir; Ted McCall, chief of engrg.

WMUU-FM— Aug 15, 1960: 94.5 mhz; 100 kw. Ant 1,200 ft TL: N34 56 29 W82 24 41. Stereo. Hrs open: 24 920 Wade Hampton Blvd., 29609. Phone: (864) 242-6240. Fax: (864) 370-3829.E-mail: generalmanager@wmuu.com Web Site:www.wmuu.com Licensee: WMUU Inc. Format: Btfl mus. Target aud: 35 plus. Spec prog: Class 14 hrs, relg 20 hrs wkly. ♦Paul Wright, gen mgr; Jeff Gainous, prom dir, outdoor ed; Brigette Barrett, progmg dir; Joe Norris, engrg dir.

WMYI(FM)—(Hendersonville, NC) Apr 15, 1958: 102.5 mhz; 20 kw. 1,778 ft TL: N35 13 22 W82 32 57. Stereo. Hrs open: 24 7 N. Laurens St., Suite 700, 29601-2744. Phone: (864) 235-1025. Fax: (864) 242-2536. Web Site:www.wmyi.com Licensee: Clear Channel Radio Licenses, Inc. Group owner: Clear Channel Communications Inc. (acq 8-30-00; grpsl). Population served: 150,000 Format: Adult contemp. News staff: one. ♦Bill McMartin, gen mgr.

WPCI(AM)— Feb 8, 1954: 1490 khz; 1 kw-U. TL: N34 51 38 W82 24 31. Hrs open: 840 N. Hwy. 25 Bypass, 29617. Phone: (864) 834-3193, EXT. 35. Phone: (864) 836-3551. Licensee: Hunter Broadcast Group. (acq 12-88; $15,000; 2-20-89). Format: Rhythm oldies. ♦Randy Mathena, pres & gen mgr.

WPJF(AM)— Sept 15, 1949: 1260 khz; 5 kw-D, 29 w-N. TL: N34 53 16 W82 23 27. Hrs open: 20 Grand Ave., Suite C, 29607. Phone: (864) 241-5355. Fax: (864) 241-5353. Licensee: WMUU Inc. (acq 3-27-75). Population served: 61,208 Fletcher, Heald & Hildreth. Format: Sp relg. Target aud: 35 plus. ♦Ed Dos Santos, gen mgr; Joe Norris, chief of engrg.

WSSL-FM—(Gray Court, November 1960: 100.5 mhz; 100 kw. Ant 1,250 ft TL: N34 34 18 W82 06 44. Hrs open: 24 Box 100, 29602. Phone: (864) 242-1005. Fax: (864) 271-3830. Web Site:www.wsslfm.com Licensee: Capstar TX L.P. Population served: 172,200 Rgnl. Network: S.C. Net. S.C. News Net. Format: Country. ♦Bill McMartin, VP, gen mgr; Steve Geofferies, opns mgr; Libby Spencer, sls dir; Vicky Sexton, prom dir; Kix Layton, mus dir; Jim Graham, chief of engrg.

***WTBI-FM**— June 1991: 91.7 mhz; 3 kw. 328 ft TL: N34 49 43 W82 26 59. Stereo. Hrs open: 24 3931 White Horse Rd., 29611. Phone: (864) 295-2145. Fax: (864) 295-6313.E-mail: jwatts@tabernacleministries.org Web Site:www.wtbi.org Licensee: Tabernacle Baptist Bible College. Format: Relg music, educ, gospel. Target aud: General. ♦Charles Garrett, Sr., gen mgr.

WYRD(AM)— May 1933: 1330 khz; 5 kw-U, DA-N. TL: N34 51 18 W82 25 24. Hrs open: 24
Rebroadcasts WORD(AM) Spartanburg.
25 Garlington Rd., 29615. Phone: (864) 271-9200. Fax: (864) 242-1567.E-mail: info@newsradioword.com Web Site:www.newsradioword.com Licensee: Entercom Greenville License LLC. Group owner: Entercom Communications Corp. (acq 12-13-99; grpsl). Population served: 85,000 Natl. Network: ABC, Salem Radio Network, . Format: News/talk info. Target aud: 30-64. ♦Tom Durney, gen mgr.

Greenwood

WCRS(AM)— Sept 1, 1941: 1450 khz; 1 kw-U. TL: N34 12 34 W82 09 05. Hrs open: 24 2881 Peachtree Rd. N.E., Apt. 2405, Atlanta, GA, 30305. Phone: (864) 223-1450. Fax: (864) 943-0314. Web Site:1450wcrsam.com Licensee: Peregon Broadcasting LLC (acq 11-6-2006; $800,000 with WYOR(FM) Cross Hill). Population served: 100,000 Natl. Network: CBS, . Rgnl. Network: S.C. Net. S.C. News Net. Format: Adult standards, news/talk. News staff: 2; News: 20 hrs wkly. Target aud: 25 plus; middle & upper income adults. ♦Mike Hatfield, opns mgr.

WCZZ(AM)— June 20, 1973: 1090 khz; 5 kw-D, 2.25 kw-CH. TL: N34 09 46 W82 11 41. Stereo. Hrs open: Sunrise-sunset 210 Montague Ave., 29649. Phone: (864) 223-4300. Fax: (864) 223-4096.E-mail: sunny@sunny103-5.com Licensee: Broomfield Broadcasting LLC (acq 7-28-2005; $1.03 million with co-located FM). Population served: 211,400 Natl. Network: Westwood One, . Wiley, Rein & Fielding. Format: Rejoice Black gospel. News: 12 hrs wkly. Target aud: 25-65. ♦John Broomfield, pres; Dave Fezler, exec VP, progmg dir; Rick Prusator, sls VP; Kathleen Prusator, mktg VP, prom VP; Tonya Branyon, traf mgr; Stephanie White, prom.

WZSN(FM)— March 1989: 103.5 mhz; 25 kw. 328 ft TL: N34 09 46 W82 11 41. Stereo. Hrs open: 24 210 Montague Ave., 29649. Phone: (864) 223-4300. Fax: (864) 223-4096. Web Site:www.sunny103-5.com Natl. Network: Westwood One, . Format: Adult contemp. News: 3 hrs wkly. Target aud: 25-54. ♦Stephanie White, prom.

Greer

WCKI(AM)— Mar 3, 1955: 1300 khz; 1 kw-D. TL: N34 55 39 W82 15 42. Hrs open: 6 AM-6 PM Box 170022, Spartanburg, 29652-0905. Phone: (864) 877-8458. Phone: (864) 877-8459. Fax: (864) 877-8500.E-mail: mbrennan@mediatrixsc.org Licensee: Mediatrix SC Inc. (acq 10-13-2004; $280,000). Population served: 10,642 Format: Christian, talk radio. News: one hr wkly. Target aud: 25-54; working people who spend money. ♦Mike Brannen, pres; Gary Powery, stn mgr.

WOLT(FM)— January 1993: 103.3 mhz; 2.7 kw. Ant 495 ft TL: N34 59 13 W82 09 56. Hrs open: 225 S. Pleasantburg Dr., Suite 3 B, Greenville, 29607. Phone: (864) 751-0113. Fax: (864) 569-0945. Web Site:www.wolt-fm.com Licensee: Davidson Media Station WOLT Licensee LLC. Group owner: Entercom Communications Corp. (acq 10-6-2005; grpsl). Format: Oldies. ♦Robert Freese, gen mgr; Bill Prather, opns mgr, progmg dir; Ann Freese, natl sls mgr.

WPJM(AM)— June 15, 1949: 800 khz; 1 kw-D, 438 w-N. TL: N34 56 59 W82 14 43. Hrs open: 305 N. Tryon St., 29651. Phone: (864) 877-1821. Fax: (864) 877-0342. Licensee: Full Gospel WPJM 800 AM Radio Inc. (acq 11-28-97; $200,000). Population served: 1,000,000 Rgnl. Network: S.C. Net. S.C. News Net. Format: Gospel. Target aud: General. ♦Bobby Cohen, pres, gen mgr; J.B. Adams, progmg dir.

Hampton

WBHC-FM— September 1970: 92.1 mhz; 6 kw. Ant 328 ft TL: N32 50 38 W81 07 31. Stereo. Hrs open: Box 607, 29924. Phone: (803) 943-2831. Fax: (803) 943-5450. Web Site:www.varietyhits921.com Licensee: Bocock Communications LLC (acq 6-1-2004; $375,000 with co-located AM). Natl. Network: CNN Radio, . Rgnl. Network: S.C. Net. S.C. News Net. Rgnl rep: Interep Format: Adult contemp. News staff: one. Target aud: Adults. Spec prog: Relg 11 hrs wkly. ♦John Bocock, pres, gen sls mgr, adv dir; Kevin Coan, opns mgr.

WHGS(AM)— September 1957: 1270 khz; 10 kw-D, 219 w-N. TL: N32 50 38 W81 07 32. Hrs open: 24 Box 607, 29924. Phone: (803) 943-2831. Fax: (803) 943-5450. Licensee: Bocock Communications LLC (acq 6-1-2004). Population served: 260,560 Natl. Network: CNN Radio, . Natl. Rep: Salem,. S.C. News Net. Rgnl rep: Interep Format: News Talk. News staff: one. ◆John Bocock, pres & gen mgr.

Hanahan

WAVF(FM)— July 3, 1969: 101.7 mhz; 100 kw. Ant 782 ft TL: N32 49 04 W79 50 08. Stereo. Hrs open: 24 2294 Clements Ferry Rd., Charleston, 29492. Phone: (843) 972-1100. Fax: (843) 972-1200. Web Site:wavf-fm.fimc.net Licensee: Apex Broadcasting Inc. Group owner: NextMedia Group L.L.C. (acq 10-28-2008; swap for WKZQ-FM Forestbrook). Natl. Rep: Christal,. Format: Variety hits. ◆Dean Pearce, CEO, pres; Chris Johnson, gen mgr; John Anthony, opns VP.

Hardeeville

WLVH(FM)— Aug 30, 1992: 101.1 mhz; 50 kw. 476 ft TL: N32 05 48 W81 19 17. Stereo. Hrs open: 24 245 Alfred St., Savannah, GA, 31408. Phone: (912) 964-7794. Fax: (912) 964-9414.E-mail: garyyoung@clearchannel.com Web Site:www.love1011.com Licensee: Capstar TX L.P. Group owner: Clear Channel Communications Inc. (acq 8-30-00; grpsl). Natl. Network: ABC, . Format: Adult urban contemp. News: one hr wkly. Target aud: 25-54; affluent Black adults. ◆Craig Scott, gen mgr; Steve Richards, opns mgr; Sheryl Collison, sls dir; Gary Young, progmg dir; Marty Foglia, chief of engrg.

Hartsville

WBZF(FM)— Nov 19, 1992: 98.5 mhz; 6 kw. Ant 328 ft TL: N34 21 16 W80 04 06. Hrs open: 2014 N. Irby St., Florence, 29501. Phone: (843) 661-5000. Fax: (843) 661-0888. Web Site:www.glory985-com Licensee: Cumulus Licensing Corp. Format: Black, inspirational. ◆Ollie Williams, progmg dir.

WHSC(AM)— Oct 1, 1946: 1450 khz; 1 kw-U. TL: N34 21 15 W80 04 20. Hrs open: 24 2014 N. Irby St., Florence, 29501. Phone: (843) 661-5000. Fax: (843) 661-0888. Web Site:www.cumulus.com Licensee: Cumulus Licensing Corp. Group owner: Cumulus Media Inc. (acq 4-20-98; 700,000 with co-located FM). Population served: 95,000 Rgnl. Network: Tobacco, S.C. Net. S.C. News Net. Reddy, Begley & McCormick. Format: CHR. News: 12 hrs wkly. Target aud: 19-49; those with buying power. Spec prog: Farm 3 hrs, gospel 3 hrs, relg 6 hrs, big band 3 hrs, oldies 6 hrs wkly. ◆Jerry Stevens, gen mgr; Matt Scurry, opns mgr; Gale Gilbraith, chief of engrg.

WJDJ(AM)— Dec 4, 1972: 1490 khz; 1 kw-U. TL: N34 21 47 W80 04 28. Hrs open: 6:30 AM-6PM
WAGS—WAGS/WJDJ are simulcast. Program originates at WAGS. 142 Wags Dr., Bishopville, 29010. Phone: (803) 484-5415.E-mail: wagsradio@sc.rr.com Licensee: Beaver Communications (acq 4-26-02). Population served: 24,000 Natl. Network: USA, . Format: Country, bluegrass, gospel, Live Radio, Real People in Real Time. News: 6 hrs wkly. Target aud: 28 & up; Adults 28 & up. Spec prog: live remotes 2 hrs wkly, religious 7 hrs wkly. ◆James D. Jenkins, pres & gen mgr.

Hemingway

*WLGI(FM)— July 1, 1984: 90.9 mhz; 50 kw. Ant 505 ft TL: N33 43 09 W79 19 50. Stereo. Hrs open: 15 1272 Williams Hill Rd., 29554. Phone: (843) 558-9544. Phone: (843) 558-9100. Fax: (843) 558-5778.E-mail: wlgi@ufbnb.org Licensee: Regional Baha'i Council of the Southern States. Population served: 800,000 Reddy, Begley & McCormick. Wire Svc: Weather Wire Format: Gospel, Black, urban contemp. Target aud: General. Spec prog: Jazz.

Hilton Head Island

WFXH(AM)— Feb 14, 1983: 1130 khz; 1 kw-D, 500 w-N, DA-N. TL: N32 12 01 W80 43 27. Stereo. Hrs open: 24 One Saint Augustine Pl., 29928. Phone: (843) 785-9569. Fax: (843) 842-3369.E-mail: info@adventureradio.com Web Site:www.adventureradio.com Licensee: Monterey Licenses LLC. Group owner: Triad Broadcasting Co. LLC (acq 7-18-00; grpsl). Population served: 50,000 Format: ESPN sports & news. News staff: one; News: 5 hrs wkly. Target aud: 35 plus. ◆Robert Leonard, gen mgr.

WFXH-FM— July 14, 1973: 106.1 mhz; 10.5 kw. 794 ft TL: N32 19 50 W80 56 19. (CP: 25 kw, ant 594 ft.). Stereo. Hrs open: Prog sep from AM 401 Mall Blvd., Suite 101 D, Savannah, GA, 31406. Phone: (912) 351-9830. Fax: (912) 352-4821.E-mail: mhalverson@adventureradio.fm Web Site:www.adventureradio.com Population served: 100,000 Natl.

Rep: Christal,. Format: Rock. News staff: 2. Target aud: 18-49; more male than female. ◆Robert Leonard, gen mgr.

WWJN(FM)—(Ridgeland, July 15, 1986: 104.9 mhz; 16 kw. Ant 410 ft TL: N32 26 10 W80 55 23. Stereo. Hrs open: 24 210 Montaque Ave., Greenwood, 29649. Phone: (864) 223-4300. Licensee: JB Broadcasting LLC Group owner: Triad Broadcasting Co. LLC (acq 11-2-2006; $800,000). Population served: 500,000 Format: Oldies. News staff: 2. Target aud: 18-49; general. ◆Robert Leonard, gen mgr.

Holly Hill

WJBS(AM)— Dec 1, 1972: 1440 khz; 1 kw-D, 98 w-N. TL: N33 20 23 W80 26 18. Hrs open: Box 1087, 29059. Phone: (803) 496-5352. Fax: (803) 496-2526.E-mail: wjbsam@yahoo.com Licensee: Eugene Schoebinger. (acq 7-1-85). Population served: 8,000 Format: Gospel. Spec prog: Black 17 hrs, fishing/hunting 2 hrs, farm 2 hrs wkly. ◆Harry Govan, gen mgr, gen sls mgr; Robert Small, prom dir.

Hollywood

WXST(FM)— July 15, 1988: 99.7 mhz; 70 kw. Ant 781 ft TL: N32 49 04 W79 50 08. Stereo. Hrs open: 24 2294 Clements Ferry Rd., Charleston, 29492-7729. Phone: (843) 972-1100. Fax: (843) 972-1200.E-mail: info@star997.com Web Site:www.star997.com Licensee: Apex Broadcasting Inc. (group owner; acq 11-20-01). Population served: 350,000 Natl. Network: Jones Radio Networks, . Garvey Schubert Barer. Format: Adult urban contemp. Target aud: 25-54; urban professional. ◆Dean Pearce, CEO, pres, gen mgr; John Anthony, opns mgr; Carl Wine, gen sls mgr, prom dir; Walt Rosen, sls.

Homeland Park

WRIX(AM)— Sept 1, 1986: 1020 khz; 10 kw-D. TL: N34 28 14 W82 38 03. Hrs open: 102 E. Shockley Ferry Rd., Anderson, 29624. Phone: (864) 224-6733. Fax: (864) 224-0260. Licensee: AM 1020 Inc. (acq 10-28-99). Rgnl. Network: S.C. Net. S.C. News Net. Format: Relg. Spec prog: Black 7 hrs wkly. ◆Karen Small, pres & gen mgr.

Honea Path

WRIX-FM— June 10, 1977: 103.1 mhz; 6 kw. 392 ft TL: N34 23 43 W82 29 49. Stereo. Hrs open: 24 102 E. Shockley Ferry Rd., Anderson, 29624. Phone: (864) 224-9749. Fax: (864) 224-0260. Licensee: FM 103 Inc. (acq 10-28-99). Natl. Network: ABC, . Rgnl. Network: S.C. Net. S.C. News Net. Format: News/talk. Spec prog: Talk 20 hrs wkly. ◆Karen Small, gen mgr.

Irmo

WWNU(FM)— May 23, 1987: 92.1 mhz; 15 kw. Ant 427 ft TL: N34 04 55 W81 07 36. Stereo. Hrs open: 24 1010 Gervais St., Suite 100, Columbia, 29201-3130. Phone: (803) 753-6800. Fax: (803) 753-6806. Web Site:www.new92.com Licensee: Double O South Carolina Corp. (acq 11-1-2004; $4.7 million). Rgnl. Network: S.C. Net. Format: Country. News: 7 hrs wkly. ◆Chuck McKay, gen mgr; Tyler Ryan, opns mgr & progmg dir.

Isle of Palms

WIOP(FM)—Licensed to Isle of Palms. See Charleston

Johnsonville

WALD(AM)— August 1947: 1080 khz; 9 kw-D, 2.7 kw-CH. TL: N33 54 36 W79 40 09. Hrs open: sunup-sundown Box 2480, Walterboro, 29488. Phone: (843) 538-4780. Fax: (843) 538-5392.E-mail: rswaldradio@lowcountry.com Licensee: Glory Communications, Inc. (acq 5-28-2002; with WBGC(AM) Chipley, FL). Population served: 20,000 Format: Gospel. ◆Jesse Bowers, gen mgr; Annette Gantt, opns mgr; Ronda Simpson, progmg dir.

WPDT(FM)— May 1995: 105.1 mhz; 2.95 kw. Ant 472 ft TL: N33 54 36 W79 40 09. Hrs open: 109 N. McAllister St., Lake City, 29560. Phone: (843) 374-5255. Fax: (843) 374-5256.E-mail: wpdt@ftc-i.net Web Site:www.wfmv.com Licensee: Glory Communications Inc. (group owner; acq 5-20-02). Format: Urban inspiration. ◆Alex Snipes Jr., gen mgr; Tersa Haire, sls dir; Tony Gee, progmg VP.

Johnston

WKSX-FM— Aug 26, 1985: 92.7 mhz; 1.8 kw. Ant 577 ft TL: N33 45 19 W81 50 44. Stereo. Hrs open: Drawer 1, 29832. Secondary address: 102 Slide Hill Rd. 29832. Phone: (803) 275-4444. Fax: (803) 275-3185.E-mail: fdavisksx@bellsouth.net Licensee: Edgefield Saluda Radio Co. Inc. (acq 4-85; $3,586; 4-8-85). Natl. Network: CNN Radio, . Natl. Rep: Keystone (unwired net),. S.C. News Net. Format: Oldies/Beach. ◆Mike Casey, pres; Frank Davis, opns mgr; Fayne Anderson, chief of engrg; Tony Baughman, traf mgr.

Kershaw

WKSC(AM)— Dec 21, 1961: 1300 khz; 500 w-D. TL: N34 33 30 W80 33 34. Hrs open: 24 Box 516, 203 E. Hilton St., 29067. Phone: (803) 475-8585. Fax: (805) 966-3530.E-mail: wksc@wkscradio.com Web Site:www.wkscradio.com Licensee: Kershaw Broadcasting Corp. (acq 7-23-03). Population served: 1,818 Natl. Network: ABC, . Format: Oldies. Target aud: 35-64. ◆John Griffin, pres; Johnny Knight, gen mgr.

Kiawah Island

WCOO(FM)— Dec 7, 1969: 105.5 mhz; 50 kw. Ant 436 ft TL: N32 39 57 W80 03 11. Stereo. Hrs open: 24 c/o WYBB(FM), 59 Windermere Blvd., Charleston, 29407. Phone: (843) 769-4799. Fax: (843) 769-4797. Web Site:www.thebridgeat1055.com Licensee: L.M. Communications II of South Carolina Inc. Group owner: L.M. Communications Inc. (acq 3-30-95; 6-26-95). Natl. Network: ABC, . Leventhal Senter & Lerman. Format: Rhythmic oldies. Target aud: 25-54; general. ◆Lynn Martin, pres; Charlie Cohn, gen mgr; Mike Allen, opns mgr.

Kingstree

WDKD(AM)— July 1949: 1310 khz; 5 kw-D, 67 w-N. TL: N33 42 11 W79 49 08. Hrs open: 24 51 Commerce St., Sumter, 29150. Phone: (803) 775-2321. Fax: (803) 773-4856.E-mail: production@miller.fm Web Site:www.miller.fm Licensee: Miller Communications Inc. (group owner; (acq 12-18-2001; $1,415,456 assumption of debt with co-located FM). Population served: 39,960 Natl. Network: ABC, . Rgnl. Network: S.C. Net. S.C. News Net. Format: Soft adult contemp. Target aud: 25-54. ◆Harold T. Miller Jr., CEO; Harold T. Miller, Jr., pres; Theresa Miller, VP & gen mgr; Dave Baker, opns VP, progmg VP; John Mcleod, pub affrs dir; Sarah Skinner, traf mgr.

WRZE(FM)— 1998: 94.1 mhz; 6 kw. 328 ft TL: N33 43 32 W79 58 19. (CP: 6 kw). Hrs open: 24 Box 103000, BTC-311, 181 E. Evans St., Florence, 29506. Phone: (843) 667-4600. Phone: (843) 665-0970. Fax: (843) 673-7390. Licensee: Qantum of Florence License Co. LLC. Group owner: Qantum Communications Corp. (acq 7-2-2003; grpsl). Format: Gospel. Target aud: 25-54; urban & caucasian. ◆Jonathan Brewster, gen mgr; Craig Dalla Riva, stn mgr.

WWKT-FM— May 28, 1966: 99.3 mhz; 11 kw. Ant 492 ft TL: N33 54 07 W79 59 52. Stereo. Hrs open: 24 Prog sep from AM 51 Commerce St., Sumter, 29150. Phone: (803) 775-2321. Fax: (803) 773-4856.E-mail: production@miller.fm Web Site:www.miller.fm Population served: 300,000 Smithwick & Belendiuk. Format: Rhythmic CHR. News staff: one; News: 14 hrs wkly. ◆Johnny Green, progmg dir, disc jockey; Vakenya Brunson, traf mgr; Gary "Thrills" Mills, disc jockey.

Ladson

WJNI(FM)— June 15, 1998: 106.3 mhz; 6 kw. 328 ft TL: N32 55 42 W80 06 13. Stereo. Hrs open: 24 60 Markfield Drive, Charleston, 29407. Phone: 8437636631. Fax: 8437635636. Web Site:wjnifm.com Licensee: Thomas B. Daniels. Group owner: Jabar Communications. Population served: 800,000 Natl. Rep: Interep,. Format: Urban contemp, inspirational. Target aud: 25 plus. ◆Michael Baynard, gen mgr.

*WKCL(FM)— Jan 11, 1982: 91.5 mhz; 100 kw. 305 ft TL: N33 00 24 W80 05 17. Stereo. Hrs open: 24 526 College Park Rd., 29456. Phone: (843) 553-5420. Fax: (843) 553-0636.E-mail: wkcl@msn.com Web Site:www.wkclradio.com Licensee: Chapel of the Holy Spirit and Holy Spirit Bible College. Population served: 500,000 Format: Contemp MOR, southern gospel. Target aud: General; baby boomers. ◆Carl L. Wiggins Sr., pres & gen mgr.

Lake City

WHYM(AM)— Oct 9, 1953: 1260 khz; 5 kw-D, 55 w-N. TL: N33 51 42 W79 44 15. Hrs open: 6 AM-6 PM

Simulcasts WOLS(AM) Florence 75%.
Box 1177, ., 29560. Secondary address: 925 E. Main St. 29560. Phone: (843) 665-1230. Licensee: Miller Communications Inc. (group owner; (acq 4-29-2008; $275,000 with WOLH(AM) Florence). Population served: 175,000 Natl. Network: ABC, . Rgnl. Network: S.C. Net. S.C. News Net. Rgnl rep: Jim D.Jones Format: Country. News staff: one; News: 5 hrs wkly. Target aud: 35 plus. Spec prog: Loc news. ◆Jeff Andrew Lonis, gen mgr.

WWFN-FM— May 11, 1977: 100.1 mhz; 3.3 kw. 433 ft TL: N33 51 42 W79 44 15. Stereo. Hrs open: 2014 N. Irby St., Florence, 29501. Phone: (843) 661-5000. Fax: (843) 661-0888. Licensee: Cumulus Licensing Corp. Group owner: Cumulus Media Inc. (acq 3-12-2001; $850,000). Format: Sports. Target aud: 25-54. ◆Jerry Stevens, gen mgr.

Lamar

WSIM(FM)— October 1992: 93.7 mhz; 2.8 kw. Ant 485 ft TL: N34 12 12 W79 51 52. Hrs open: 24 51 Commerce St., Sumter, 29151. Phone: (803) 775-2321. Fax: (803) 773-4856.E-mail: production@miller.fm Licensee: Miller Communications Inc. (group owner; (acq 11-14-2000; grpsl). Population served: 18,000 Natl. Network: ABC, . Smithwick & Belendiuk. Format: Soft rock. News staff: one. Target aud: 35-64; adults. ◆Harold T. Miller Jr., CEO, pres; Theresa Miller, VP & gen mgr; Dave Baker, opns VP, opns mgr.

Lancaster

WAGL(AM)— Aug 7, 1962: 1560 khz; 50 kw-D, DA. TL: N34 49 53 W80 52 08. Stereo. Hrs open: Box 28, 29721. Secondary address: 101 S. Woodland Dr. 29720. Phone: (803) 283-8431. Fax: (803) 286-4702.E-mail: waglradio@conporium.net Web Site:www.waglradio.com Licensee: Palmetto Broadcasting System Inc. Population served: 1,000,000 + Format: Gospel, oldies. News staff: 6. ◆B.L. Phillips Jr., pres & gen mgr.

WRHM(FM)— July 27, 1964: 107.1 mhz; 3.3kw. 436 ft TL: N34 48 05 W80 47 51. Stereo. Hrs open: Box 307, Rock Hill, 29731. Secondary address: 142 N. Confederate Ave., Rock Hill 29730. Phone: (803) 286-1071. Fax: (803) 324-2860.E-mail: almiller@wrhi.com Web Site:fm107.com Licensee: Our Three Sons Broadcasting L.L.P. (acq 10-1-87). Population served: 800,000 Natl. Network: ABC, . Rgnl. Network: S.C. Net. S.C. News Net. Format: Country, news, sports. Target aud: 25-54. ◆Allan M. Miller, gen mgr; Steven Stone, opns mgr; Mike Crowder, news dir.

Latta

WCMG(FM)— Sept 18, 1970: 94.3 mhz; 10.5 kw. 502 ft TL: N34 11 14 W79 31 23. Stereo. Hrs open: 24 2014 N. Irby St., Florence, 29501. Phone: (843) 661-5000. Fax: (843) 661-0888. Web Site:www.cumulus.com Licensee: Cumulus Licensing Corp. Group owner: Cumulus Media Inc. (acq 6-99; $525,000). Population served: 96,581 Natl. Network: USA, . Smithwick & Belendiuk. Format: Ault urban contemp. News staff: one; News: 8 hrs wkly. Target aud: 21-54; African-American. ◆Gerry Stevens, gen mgr, gen sls mgr; Matt Scurry, opns mgr; Pam Mathis, progmg dir; Gail Gilbreath, chief of engrg; Martha Clark, traf mgr.

Laurens

WLBG(AM)— Mar 1, 1947: 860 khz; 1 kw-D, 12 w-N. TL: N34 30 13 W82 01 06. Hrs open: 24 Box 1289, 315 Hillcrest, 29360. Phone: (864) 984-3544. Fax: (864) 984-3545.E-mail: mail@wlbg.com Web Site:www.wlbg.com Licensee: Southeastern Broadcast Associates Inc. (acq 8-5-83). Population served: 200,000 Natl. Network: Fox News Radio, Fox Sports, . Pepper & Corazzini. Format: Var. News: 4 hrs wkly. Target aud: 30 plus; Black. ◆Emil J. Finley, pres; Michael C. Johnson, dev VP.

Leesville

WBLR(AM)—See Batesburg

Lexington

WOMG(FM)— Aug 31, 1994: 98.5 mhz; 6 kw. Ant 328 ft TL: N33 52 42 W81 12 59. Hrs open: 24 Box 5106, Columbia, 29250. Secondary address: 1801 Charleston Hwy., Suite J, Cayce 29033. Phone: (803) 796-9975. Fax: (803) 796-5502.E-mail: doug.william@citcomm.com Licensee: Citadel Broadcasting Co. Group owner: Citadel Broadcasting

Corp. (acq 5-30-2000; grpsl). Population served: 525,000 Fletcher, Heald & Hildreth. Format: Oldies. Target aud: 25-54. ◆William McElveen, gen mgr.

WQVA(AM)— 1983: 1170 khz; 10 kw-D. TL: N33 58 17 W81 16 43. Hrs open: Sunrise-sunset Box 537, Irmo, 29063. Phone: (803) 407-5223. Fax: (803) 407-6160.E-mail: info@myritmo.com Web Site:myritmo.com Licensee: Peregon Communications Inc. Group owner: Levas Communications LLC (acq 4-28-2005; $575,000). Format: Sp. ◆Sergio Perez, gen mgr & stn mgr; Beth Well, gen sls mgr.

Loris

WLSC(AM)— August 1958: 1240 khz; 1 kw-U. TL: N34 02 41 W78 53 39. Hrs open: 6 AM-midnight Box 578, 29569. Phone: (843) 756-1183.E-mail: infor@wlsc.com Licensee: JARC Broadcasting Inc. (acq 8-15-88). Population served: 1,741 Rgnl. Network: S.C. Net. Natl. Rep: Keystone (unwired net),. S.C. News Net. Format: Full service. Target aud: 21-54. ◆Jerry Jenrette, gen mgr.

WVCO(FM)— Nov 19, 1993: 94.9 mhz; 11 kw. Ant 489 ft TL: N33 59 39 W78 46 16. Hrs open: 24 Box 3689, North Myrtle Beach, 29582. Phone: (843) 445-9491. Fax: (843) 445-9490. Web Site:www.949thesurf.com Licensee: Carolina Beach Music Broadcasting Corp. (acq 6-18-03; $2.2 million). Population served: 300,000 Format: Beach & boogie. News: 2 hrs wkly. Target aud: 25-45. ◆Earl P. Taylor, CEO, VP; Selene Graham, sr VP.

Manning

WYMB(AM)— July 15, 1957: 920 khz; 2.3 kw-D, 1 kw-N. TL: N33 41 22 W80 16 16. (CP: 920 khz; 2.3 kw-D, 1 kw-N, DA-N. TL: N33 41 22 W80 16 16). Hrs open: 2014 N. Irby St., Florence, 29501. Phone: (843) 661-5000. Fax: (843) 661-0888. Licensee: Cumulus Media Inc. Group owner: Cumulus Media Inc. (acq 3-24-99; with co-located FM). Population served: 4,025 Natl. Network: AP Radio, . Natl. Rep: Katz Radio,. Format: Top 40. Target aud: General. ◆Jerry Stevens, gen mgr.

Marion

WHLZ(FM)— August 1991: 100.5 mhz; 21.5 kw. 354 ft TL: N34 19 36 W79 32 35. Hrs open: 2014 N. Irby St., Florence, 29501. Phone: (843) 661-5000. Fax: (843) 661-0888.E-mail: ernie.frieson@cumulus.com Web Site:www.cumulus.com Licensee: Cumulus Media Inc. Group owner: Cumulus Media Inc. (acq 3-24-99; $3.8 million with WMXT(FM) Pamplico). Format: Country. ◆Jerry Stevens, gen mgr; Matt Scurry, opns mgr & progmg dir; Gail Gilbreath, chief of engrg, engr.

Mauldin

WBZT-FM— Apr 28, 1965: 96.7 mhz; 700 w. Ant 964 ft TL: N34 55 16 W82 24 05. Stereo. Hrs open: 24 Box 100, Greenville, 29602. Secondary address: 7 N. Laurens St., Suite 700, Greenville 29601. Phone: (864) 242-1005. Fax: (864) 242-8813.E-mail: info@wbtz.com Web Site:www.shine967.com Licensee: Clear Channel Broadcasting Licenses Inc. Group owner: Clear Channel Communications Inc. (acq 12-22-00). Population served: 300,000 Wire Svc: AP Format: Christian. ◆Marc Chase, exec VP; Bruce Logan, VP; Bill McMartin, gen mgr; Craig Debolt, stn mgr; Scott Johnson, opns mgr.

McClellanville

WWIK(FM)— Dec 1, 1994: 98.9 mhz; 50 kw. Ant 492 ft TL: N33 11 20 W79 33 25. Stereo. Hrs open: 24 5081 Rivers Ave., North Charleston, 29406. Phone: (843) 554-1063. Fax: (843) 554-1088.E-mail: traffic@jabarcommunications.com Web Site:www.jabarcommunications.com Licensee: 98.9 Inc. Group owner: Jabar Communications (acq 1-5-2001). Population served: 800,000 Format: Sp top-40. Target aud: 18-25; adults. ◆Michael Baynard, gen mgr.

Moncks Corner

WIHB(FM)— Apr 16, 1973: 92.5 mhz; 100 kw. Ant 777 ft TL: N32 49 04 W79 50 08. (CP: 56 kw, ant 1,776 ft. TL: N32 55 28 W79 41 58). Stereo. Hrs open: 24 2294 Clements Ferry Rd., Charleston, 29492-7729. Phone: (843) 972-1100. Fax: (843) 972-1200.E-mail: info@coast925.com Web Site:www.coast925.com Licensee: Apex Broadcasting Inc. (group owner; (acq 10-17-2001; $3 million). Population served: 1,000,000

Format: Adult contemp. ◆Dean Pearce, CEO, pres, gen mgr, stn mgr; John Anthony, opns VP; Carl Wine, prom dir; Bruce Roberts, chief of engrg; Walt Rosen, sls.

WJKB(AM)— December 1963: 950 khz; 10 kw-D, 6 kw-N, DA-2. TL: N33 12 20 W80 03 54. Hrs open: 24 60 Markfield Dr., Suite 4, Charleston, 29407. Phone: (843) 763-6631. Fax: (843) 766-1239. Web Site:am950.net Licensee: Kirkman Broadcasting Inc. (group owner; (acq 11-29-2000; $150,000). Population served: 400,000 Natl. Network: Jones Radio Networks, Motor Racing Net, . Rgnl. Network: S.C. Net Brian Madden. Format: Classic country. Target aud: 25-54; male. Spec prog: Nascar. ◆Gil Kirkman, pres; John Dixon, gen mgr, news dir; Ted Byrne, opns mgr; Rick Howze, gen sls mgr; Wally Momeier, chief of engrg.

Mt. Pleasant

WRFQ(FM)— June 1, 1985: 104.5 mhz; 100 kw. 659 ft TL: N32 49 04 W79 50 09. Stereo. Hrs open: 24 950 Houston Northcutt Blvd., 29464. Phone: (843) 884-2534. Fax: (843) 884-6096.E-mail: kevin@qious.com Web Site:q1045.com Licensee: Citicasters Licenses L.P. Group owner: Clear Channel Communications Inc. (acq 5-4-99; grpsl). Population served: 500,000 Format: Classic rock. Target aud: 25-54; adults, men. ◆Paul Smith, VP, mktg mgr; Scott Johnson, opns mgr; Tom Bustard, sls dir; Kevin Harbison, progmg dir.

WZJY(AM)— May 21, 1982: 1480 khz; 1 kw-D, 44 w-N. TL: N32 48 59 W79 50 18. Hrs open: 24 5081 Rivers Ave., North Charleston, 29406. Phone: (843) 554-1063. Fax: (843) 554-1088. Licensee: Thomas B. Daniels Group owner: Levas Communications LLC (acq 6-24-2007; $375,000). Population served: 300,000 Natl. Rep: Interep,. Format: Urban talk. News staff: 5; News: 24 hrs wkly. ◆Michael Baynard, gen mgr.

Mullins

WJAY(AM)— June 1, 1949: 1280 khz; 5 kw-D, 270 w-N. TL: N34 11 30 W79 18 55. Hrs open: 18 Box 1020, Marion, 29571. Phone: (843) 423-1140. Fax: (843) 423-2829. Web Site:www.wjay.com Licensee: The Greater Highway Church of Christ. Population served: 50,000 Natl. Network: ABC, . Rgnl. Network: S.C. Net, Tobacco. S.C. News Net. Format: Gospel. News: 8 hrs wkly. Target aud: General. Spec prog: Farm 10 hrs wkly. ◆Curtis Campbell, pres, gen mgr & progmg dir.

Murrell's Inlet

***WMBJ(FM)**— 1997: 88.3 mhz; 1.8 kw vert. Ant 331 ft TL: N33 26 35 W79 08 21. Hrs open: 24
His Radio Network.
2420 Wade Hampton Blvd., Greenville, 29615. Phone: (864) 292-6040. Fax: (864) 292-8428.E-mail: comments@hisradio.com Web Site:www.hisradio.com Licensee: Radio Training Network Inc. (acq 7-20-99; $5,000 cash). Format: Contemporary Christian. ◆Allen Henderson, gen mgr.

WYEZ(FM)— Apr 7, 1991: 94.5 mhz; 25 kw. Ant 328 ft TL: N33 33 13 W79 13 14. Stereo. Hrs open: 24 Box 2830, Myrtle Beach, 29578. Secondary address: 3926 Wesley St., Suite 301, Myrtle Beach 29579. Phone: (843) 903-9962. Fax: (843) 903-1797.E-mail: general@movin945.net Web Site:www.movin945.net Licensee: Fidelity Broadcasting Corp. (acq 11-30-2000; $1 million). Format: Rhythmic Oldies. News staff: one; News: 40 hrs wkly. Target aud: Adults 25-54. ◆Will Isaacs, gen mgr; Bob Gauss, engrg dir.

Myrtle Beach

WMYB(FM)— Jan 11, 1965: 92.1 mhz; 94 kw. Ant 863 ft TL: N33 35 27 W79 02 55. Stereo. Hrs open: 24 1016 Ocala St., 29577. Phone: (843) 448-1041. Fax: (843) 626-5988. Web Site:www.star921.net Licensee: NM Licensing LLC. Group owner: NextMedia Group L.L.C. (acq 11-26-01; grpsl). Population served: 175000 Cohn & Marks. Format: Adult contemporary. Target aud: Women: 25-54. ◆Steven Dinetz, CEO; Jeff Dinetz, COO; Carl Hirsch, chmn; Skip Weller, pres; Barry Brown, gen mgr; Art Greene, sls dir; Liza Van Horne, prom dir; Bill Catcher, progmg dir; Paul Matthews, chief of engrg; Ginny Batchelder, traf mgr.

WRNN(AM)— Apr 24, 1965: 1450 khz; 5 kw-D, DA. TL: N33 42 20 W78 58 23. Hrs open: 1016 Ocala St., 29577. Phone: (843) 448-1041. Fax: (843) 626-5988. Licensee: NM Licensing LLC. Group owner: NextMedia Group LLC (acq 11-26-2001; grpsl). Population served: 150,000 Format: Sports. Target aud: 25-60. ◆Steven Dinetz, CEO; Carl Hirsch, chmn; Skip Weller, pres; Barry Brown, gen mgr; Dave Priest, progmg dir.

WYAV(FM)— July 1964: 104.1 mhz; 100 kw. Ant 981 ft TL: N33 35 27 W79 02 55. Stereo. Hrs open: 1016 Ocala St., 29577. Phone: (843) 448-1041. Fax: (843) 626-5988. Web Site:www.wave104.net Licensee: NM Licensing LLC. Group owner: NextMedia Group L.L.C. (acq 11-26-01; grpsl). Population served: 300,000 Format: Classic rock. Target aud: 18-49. ♦Steven Dinetz, CEO; Jeff Dinetz, COO; Carl Hirsch, chmn; Skip Weller, pres; Barry Brown, gen mgr; Art Greene, sls dir; Liza Van Horne, prom dir; Mark McKinney, progmg dir; Paul Matthews, chief of engrg; Trimeshia Jeffery, traf mgr.

New Ellenton

WGUS-FM— December 1989: 102.7 mhz; 4.3 kw. Ant 387 ft TL: N33 30 49 W81 38 03. Hrs open: 24 4051 Jimmie Dyess Pkwy., Augusta, 30909. Phone: (706) 396-7000. Fax: (706) 396-7092. Web Site:www.oldies107.com Licensee: WGAC License LLC. Group owner: Beasley Broadcast Group (acq 12-22-94; $700,000; 2-13-95). Format: Oldies. News: 7 hrs wkly. Target aud: 35-64; affluent audience loyal fan base. ♦Kent Dunn, gen mgr; T. Gentry, opns dir; Zach Taylor, progmg dir.

Newberry

WKDK(AM)— October 1946: 1240 khz; 1 kw-U. TL: N34 17 30 W81 37 15. Hrs open: 24 hrs Box 753, 3000 Hazel St., 29108. Phone: (803) 276-2957. Fax: (803) 276-3337.E-mail: jcoggins@wkdk.com Web Site:www.wkdk.com Licensee: Newberry Broadcasting Co. (acq 1951). Population served: 31,111 Natl. Network: ABC, . Rgnl. Network: S.C. Net. S.C. News Net. Format: Adult contemp, oldies. Target aud: General. ♦James P. Coggins, VP & gen mgr; Heather Hawkins, opns mgr.

WKMG(AM)— May 22, 1968: 1520 khz; 1 kw-D. TL: N34 15 12 W81 35 44. Hrs open: Sunrise-sunset 1840 Glenn St. Extention, 29108. Phone: (803) 405-0111. Fax: (803) 276-5677. Licensee: Cornell Blakely (acq 3-20-01; $10,000). Population served: 31,000 Format: Hispanic. Spec prog: Relg 2 hrs, gospel 3 hrs, Sp 10 hrs wkly. ♦Cornell Blakely, gen mgr.

North Augusta

WKZK(AM)— May 9, 1962: 1600 khz; 4 kw-D, 27 w-N. TL: N33 29 37 W81 59 52. Hrs open: 6 AM-sunset Box 1454, Augusta, GA, 30903. Secondary address: 2 Milledge Rd., Augusta, GA 30904. Phone: (706) 738-0044. Fax: (706) 481-8442.E-mail: wkzk1600@bellsouth.net Web Site:wkzk.net Licensee: Gospel Radio Inc. (acq 9-22-83; $190,000; 10-10-83). Natl. Network: American Urban, . Natl. Rep: Dora-Clayton,. Format: Black gospel, relg. Target aud: Black adults. ♦Garfield Turner, gen mgr & progmg dir.

WTHB(AM)—See Augusta, GA

WYNF(AM)—Licensed to North Augusta. See Augusta GA

North Charleston

WTMZ(AM)—(Dorchester Terrace-Brentwood, Nov 17, 1960: 910 khz; 500 w-U, DA-N. TL: N34 09 03 W82 23 34. Hrs open: 24 60 Markfield Dr., #4, Charleston, 29407. Phone: (843) 763-6631. Fax: (843) 766-1239.E-mail: ted@kirkmanbroadcasting.com Web Site:www.910theteam.net Licensee: Kirkman Broadcasting Inc. Group owner: Citadel Broadcasting Corp. (acq 1-5-2005; $500,000). Natl. Network: ESPN Radio, . Format: Sports. ♦Gil Kirkman, gen mgr; Ted Byrne, opns mgr; Rick Howze, gen sls mgr.

WXLY(FM)— July 17, 1962: 102.5 mhz; 100 kw. Ant 659 ft TL: N32 49 04 W79 50 09. Stereo. Hrs open: 24 950 Houston Northcutt Blvd., 2nd Fl., Mt. Pleasant, 29464. Phone: (843) 856-6100. Fax: (843) 884-1218.E-mail: lisacooper@clearchannel.com Web Site:www.wxly.com Licensee: Citicasters Licenses L.P. Group owner: Clear Channel Communications Inc. (acq 5-4-99; grpsl). Population served: 405,000 Format: Oldies/classic hits. News staff: 2. Target aud: 25-54. ♦Paul Smith, VP, gen mgr, mktg mgr; Scott Johnson, opns mgr; Tom Bustard, sls dir; Michelle Kelly, gen sls mgr; Chris Rivers, progmg dir; Willie Bennett, chief of engrg.

***WYFH(FM)**— July 7, 1984: 90.7 mhz; 50 kw. 492 ft TL: N32 58 23 W80 13 54. Stereo. Hrs open: 11530 Carmel Commons Blvd., Charlotte, NC, 28226. Phone: (704) 523-5555. Fax: (704) 522-1967.E-mail: bbn@bbnradio.org Web Site:www.bbnradio.org Licensee: Bible Broadcasting Network Inc. (group owner) Natl. Network: Bible Bcstg Net, . Format: Relg, Christian. ♦Dave Phillps, pres.

North Myrtle Beach

WEZV(FM)— Aug 15, 1972: 105.9 mhz; 17 kw. Ant 360 ft TL: N33 49 19 W78 46 18. Stereo. Hrs open: 24 Box 2830, Myrtle Beach, 29578. Secondary address: 3926 Wesley St., Suite 301, Myrtle Beach 29579. Phone: (843) 903-9962. Fax: (843) 903-1797. Web Site:www.wezv.com Licensee: Fidelity Broadcasting Corp. (acq 4-1-2000; $2.6 million with WNMB(AM) North Myrtle Beach). Population served: 125000 Format: Easy lstng. Target aud: 35 plus. ♦Matt Sedota, gen mgr & gen sls mgr.

***WKVC(FM)**— Sept 9, 1997: 88.9 mhz; 100 kw vert. 587 ft TL: N34 05 46 W78 28 28. Hrs open: 24 4337 Big Barn Dr., Little River, 29566. Phone: (843) 399-9649. Fax: (843) 399-9031.E-mail: kreeder@klove.com Web Site:www.klove.com Licensee: Educational Media Foundation. Group owner: EMF Broadcasting (acq 5-11-00; $1.2 million). Natl. Network: K-Love, . Format: Relg. Target aud: 25-65; contemp Christian. ♦Richard Jenkins, CEO & pres; Kurt Reeder, gen mgr.

WNMB(AM)— Apr 1, 1983: 900 khz; 500 w-U, DA-2. TL: N33 49 26 W78 45 59. Hrs open: 429 Pine Ave., 29582. Phone: (843) 249-6662. Fax: (843) 249-7823. Licensee: Norman Communications NMB Inc. (acq 6-4-2004; $250,000). Format: Relg. ♦Bill Norman, gen mgr.

Orangeburg

WHXT(FM)— September 1973: 103.9 mhz; 9.2 kw. Ant 531 ft TL: N33 40 13 W80 52 25. Stereo. Hrs open: 1900 Pineview Rd., Columbia, 29209. Phone: (803) 695-8680. Phone: (803) 376-1039. Fax: (803) 695-8605.E-mail: mhanisch@innercity.sc.com Web Site:www.hot1039fm.com Licensee: Urban Radio II L.L.C. Group owner: Inner City Broadcasting (acq 5-30-2003; $11.1 million with WZMJ(FM) Batesburg). Population served: 130,100 Format: Urban contemp. ♦Steve Patterson, gen mgr.

WPJK(AM)— Nov 3, 1958: 1580 khz; 1 kw-D. TL: N33 28 43 W80 52 46. Hrs open: Sunrise-sunset 175 Cannon Bridge Rd., 29115. Phone: (803) 534-4848. Fax: (803) 534-0888. Licensee: Radio Orangeburg Partnership. (acq 6-86). Natl. Network: USA, . Format: Relg, urban contemp, gospel. ♦Bose Gowdy, pres, gen mgr; Rev. Pinckney Palmer Jr., opns mgr.

WQKI-FM— Oct 10, 1987: 102.9 mhz; 2.7 kw. Ant 492 ft TL: N33 27 55 W80 56 44. Stereo. Hrs open: 24 200 Regional Pkwy., Bldg. C, Suite 200, 29118. Phone: (803) 536-1710. Fax: (803) 531-1089.E-mail: mail@miller.fm Web Site:miller.fm Licensee: Miller Communications Inc. (group owner; acq 4-30-03; $1.25 million with WGFG(FM) Branchville). Population served: 175,000 Natl. Network: ABC, . Format: Classic rock. News staff: one; News: 10 hrs wkly. Target aud: 25-54. Spec prog: Relg 6 hrs wkly. ♦Harold Miller Jr., pres; Russ T. Fender, opns mgr, progmg dir; Sonny Pagan, sls VP; Theresa Miller, gen mgr & gen sls mgr; Dave Baker, progmg VP; Dave Dalesky, engrg VP, chief of engrg.

***WSSB-FM**— Mar 15, 1985: 90.3 mhz; 90 kw. 225 ft TL: N33 29 55 W80 50 30. Stereo. Hrs open: 24 Box 7619, Nance B-114, 29117. Phone: (803) 536-8196. Fax: (803) 533-3652.E-mail: info@wssb.com Web Site:www.scsu.edu Licensee: South Carolina State University. Natl. Network: American Urban, NPR, . Format: Urban contemp, gospel, jazz. News staff: one; News: 7 hrs wkly. Target aud: 8-65. Spec prog: Jazz 10 hrs, reggae 4 hrs, blues 2 hrs, rap 4 hrs wkly. ♦Marion White, progmg dir, mus dir; Milton E. McKissick, gen mgr & news dir; Ken Durst, chief of engrg.

WTCB(FM)— July 6, 1967: 106.7 mhz; 100 kw. 787 ft TL: N33 46 52 W80 55 14. Stereo. Hrs open: Box 5106, Columbia, 29250. Secondary address: 1801 Charleston Hwy., Suite J, Cayce 29033. Phone: (803) 796-7600. Fax: (803) 796-9291.E-mail: info@wtcb.com Web Site:www.b106fm.com Licensee: Citadel Broadcasting Co. Group owner: Citadel Broadcasting Corp. (acq 5-30-00; grpsl). Population served: 771,000 Natl. Rep: Christal,. Format: Adult contemp. Target aud: 25-54; affluent, upscale young adults. ♦William L. McElveen, pres & gen mgr; Brent Johns, opns mgr.

Pageland

WGSP-FM— Feb 22, 1975: 102.3 mhz; 2.55 kw. Ant 512 ft TL: N34 53 57 W80 25 46. Stereo. Hrs open: Box 2148, Tucker, GA, 30085. Phone: (843) 672-7839. Phone: (704) 442-7222. Fax: (843) 672-1023. Web Site:www.latremendaradio.com Licensee: Norsan Media Group of South Carolina LLC. (acq 7-13-2006; $975,000). Population served: 100,000 Natl. Network: Salem Radio Network, . Format: Sp (Mexican rgnl). ♦Norberto Sanchez, pres.

Pamplico

WMXT(FM)— Nov 1, 1990: 102.1 mhz; 50 kw. 500 ft TL: N34 04 56 W79 37 19. Stereo. Hrs open: 24 2014 N. Irby St., Florence, 29501-1504. Phone: (843) 661-5000. Fax: (843) 661-0888.E-mail: buzz.bowman@cumulus.com Web Site:www.cumulus.com Licensee: Cumulus Licensing Corp. Group owner: Cumulus Media Inc. (acq 3-24-99; $3.8 million with WHLZ(FM) Marion). Population served: 178,000 Fletcher, Heald & Hildreth. Format: Classic rock. News staff: 2; News: 3 hrs wkly. Target aud: 25-54. Spec prog: Beach music 5 hrs wkly. ♦Jerry Stevens, gen mgr; Matt Scurry, opns mgr; Buzz Bowman, prom dir, progmg dir; Gail Gilbreath, chief of engrg.

Parris Island

WGZO(FM)— July 1985: 103.1 mhz; 17.5 kw. 328 ft TL: N32 26 10 W80 55 23. Stereo. Hrs open: 24 401 Mall Blvd., Suite 101 D, Savannah, GA, 31406. Phone: (912) 351-9830. Fax: (912) 352-4821.E-mail: mhalverson@adventureradio.fm Web Site:www.1031thedrive.com Licensee: Zip Communications Inc. (acq 7-10-01; $100,000). Population served: 500,000 Natl. Rep: Christal,. Format: The Drive. News staff: 2. Target aud: 12-34; young, hip, trendy adults. ♦Robert Leonard, gen mgr.

Pawley's Island

WDAI(FM)— Oct 2, 1993: 98.5 mhz; 6.1 kw. Ant 666 ft TL: N33 35 27 W79 02 55. Stereo. Hrs open: 24 11640 Highway 17 Bypass, Murrells Inlet, 29576. Phone: (843) 651-7869. Fax: (843) 651-3197.E-mail: info@985kissfm.net Web Site:www.985kissfm.net Licensee: Cumulus Licensing Corp. Group owner: Cumulus Media Inc. (acq 1-27-98). Natl. Network: Westwood One, . Format: Urban contemporary. News staff: one; News: 6 hrs wkly. Target aud: 25-54. ♦Bill Hazen, gen mgr.

Pendleton

WVGC(FM)—Not on air, target date: unknown: 95.9 mhz; 4.5 kw. Ant 383 ft TL: N34 42 33.3 W82 55 28.7. Hrs open: 3671 W. Wheeler Rd., Lakeland, FL, 33801. Phone: (863) 248-4650. Licensee: Georgia-Carolina Wireless LLC. ♦Megan Sutton Lightfoot, gen mgr.

Pickens

WTBI(AM)— Aug 3, 1967: 1540 khz; 10 kw-D. TL: N34 51 37 W82 43 25. Hrs open: Sunrise-sunset
Rebroadcasts WTBI-FM Greenville.
3931 White Horse, Greenville, 29611. Phone: (864) 295-2145. Fax: (864) 295-6313.E-mail: jwatts@tabernacleministries.org Web Site:www.wtbi.org Licensee: Tabernacle Christian Schools (acq 11-83; $150,000; 1-30-84). Population served: 94,000 Natl. Network: USA, . Format: Christian, educational. Target aud: All ages. ♦Dr. Melvin Aiken, pres; Charles Garrett Sr., stn mgr, opns mgr, gen sls mgr; John Watts, progmg dir, disc jockey; Fay Frazier, traf mgr; Jeremy Chisam, disc jockey.

Port Royal

WLOW(FM)— February 1988: 107.9 mhz; 24 kw. Ant 725 ft TL: N32 13 36 W80 50 53. Hrs open: 24 One St. Augustine Pl., Hilton Head Island, 29928. Phone: (843) 785-9569. Fax: (843) 842-3369.E-mail: wlow1079@adventureradio.fm Web Site:www.wlow.com Licensee: Monterey Licenses LLC. Group owner: Triad Broadcasting Co. LLC (acq 7-18-2000; grpsl). Population served: 500,000 Natl. Rep: Christal,. Format: The coast. Target aud: 45 plus; active, affluent, older. ♦Robert Leonard, gen mgr.

Ravenel

WMGL(FM)— February 1986: 101.7 mhz; 3 kw. 482 ft TL: N32 46 44 W80 10 37. (CP: 6.5 kw, ant 689 ft. TL: N32 38 59 W80 19 00). Stereo. Hrs open: 24 4230 Faber Place Dr., Suite 100, North Charleston, 29405. Phone: (843) 277-1200. Fax: (843) 277-1212.E-mail: info@magic1017.com Web Site:www.magic1017.com Licensee: The Last Bastion Station Trust LLC, as Trustee Group owner: Citadel Broadcasting Corp. (acq 6-12-2007; grpsl). Cole, Raywid & Braverman. Format: New adult contemp. News staff: 2; News: 6 hrs wkly. Target aud: 25-54; upscale adults. ♦Paul O'Malley, gen mgr.

Richburg

***WRBK(FM)**— 1998: 90.3 mhz; 7.5 kw horiz, 7.3 kw vert. Ant 538 ft TL: N34 41 46 W81 01 23. Stereo. Hrs open: 24 Box 15, Chester, 29706. Phone: (803) 581-9030. Fax: (803) 581-9932.E-mail:

WRBK@Truvista.net Licensee: Richburg Educational Broadcasters Inc. Format: Beach mus, oldies. Target aud: 30-60; middle aged adults who like beach flavored oldies. ♦Jeff Sigmon, pres & gen mgr.

Ridgeland

WNFO(AM)— 1964: 1430 khz; 1 kw-D, 880 w-N. TL: N32 28 07 W81 00 15. (CP: COL: Sun City-Hilton Head, 213 w-D. TL: N32 21 24 W80 55 23). Hrs open: Sunrise-sunset Box 6567, Hilton Head Island, 29938. Phone: (843) 785-5769. Fax: (843) 785-8139. Licensee: Walter M. Czura (acq 7-9-91; $22,500;7-29-91). Population served: 135,000 Format: Hispanic. Target aud: General; incoming visitors to South Carolina & Spanish speaking people. Spec prog: Spanish. ♦Walter M. Czura, pres & gen mgr.

WWJN(FM)—Licensed to Ridgeland. See Hilton Head Island

Ridgeville

WPAL-FM— September 1968: 100.9 mhz; 5.7 kw. Ant 682 ft TL: N33 05 07.9 W80 22 17.4. Stereo. Hrs open: 24 Phone: (843) 529-9293. Fax: (843) 746-9299. Web Site:wayx.wayfm.com Licensee: Charles W. Cherry, Receiver for Gresham Communications Inc. (acq 4-4-2007). Population served: 20,000 Rgnl. Network: S.C. Net. Garvey Schubert Barer. Format: Contemp Christian. ♦Bret Bremberg, gen mgr.

Rock Hill

WAGL(AM)—See Lancaster

WAVO(AM)— May 18, 1948: 1150 khz; 1 kw-D, 57 w-N. TL: N34 57 02 W81 00 16. Hrs open: 24 Box 1024, 29731. Secondary address: 400 Pineview Rd. 29731. Phone: (704) 327-1150. Phone: (704) 596-4900. Fax: (704) 596-6939.E-mail: bboonewhvn@bellsouth.net Licensee: WHVN Inc. Group owner: GHB Radio Group (acq 2-4-92; $115,000; 2-24-92). Reddy, Begley & McCormick. Format: Adult standards. News staff: one; News: 15 hrs wkly. Target aud: 25-54; career-oriented. Spec prog: College football & baseball. ♦Tom Gentry, gen mgr, stn mgr & gen sls mgr; Buddy Boone, progmg dir; Brant Hart, mus dir, pub affrs dir; Gary Hattaway, chief of engrg.

WBT-FM—See Chester

WBZK(AM)—See York

*WNSC-FM— Jan 3, 1978: 88.9 mhz; 100 kw. Ant 600 ft TL: N34 50 24 W81 01 07. Stereo. Hrs open: 24 1101 George Rogers Blvd., Columbia, 29201. Phone: (803) 737-3420. Fax: (803) 737-3552.E-mail: gasque@scetv.org Web Site:www.etvradio.org Licensee: South Carolina Educational Television Commission. Natl. Network: NPR, PRI, . Format: NPR news. ♦Moss Bresnahan, pres; Tom Holloway, dev dir; John Gasque, progmg dir.

WRHI(AM)— Dec 14, 1944: 1340 khz; 1 kw-U. TL: N34 54 51 W81 00 42. Hrs open: 24 hours Box 307, 29731. Secondary address: 142 N. Confederate Ave. 29730. Phone: (803) 324-1340. Fax: (803) 324-2860.E-mail: newsroom@wrhi.com Web Site:www.wrhi.com Licensee: Our Three Sons Broadcasting L.L.P. (group owner; acq 10-1-84). Population served: 225,000 Natl. Network: ABC, . Rgnl. Network: S.C. Net. S.C. News Net. Format: News/talk, sports. News staff: 2; News: 14 hrs wkly. Target aud: 30 plus. ♦Allan M. Miller, gen mgr; Steven Stone, opns mgr; Mike Crowder, news dir.

Saint Andrews

WMFX(FM)—Licensed to Saint Andrews. See Columbia

Saint George

WQIZ(AM)— Aug 23, 1962: 810 khz; 5 kw-D. TL: N33 08 51 W80 33 47. Hrs open: 173 Radio Rd., 29477. Phone: (904) 859-0980. Licensee: Mediatrix SC Inc. (acq 7-29-2008). Population served: 80,000 Format: Catholic. ♦Paul Danese, gen mgr; Bert Artlip, stn mgr.

Saint Matthews

WIGL(FM)— 1990: 93.9 mhz; 1.75 kw. Ant 607 ft TL: N33 45 46 W80 49 23. Hrs open: 24 200 Regional Pkwy., Bldg. C, Suite 200, Orangeburg, 29118. Phone: (803) 534-2777. Fax: (803) 531-1089.E-mail:

mail@miller.fm.com Licensee: Miller Communications Inc. (acq 6-30-2003; $900,000 with co-located AM). Population served: 100,000 ♦Theresa Miller, gen mgr.

WPOG(AM)— Aug 15, 1975: 710 khz; 1 kw-D, DA. TL: N33 37 04 W80 46 50. Hrs open: 6 AM-6 PM 4305 Columbia Rd., Orangeburg, 29118-1268. Phone: (803) 536-4300. Licensee: Grace Baptist Church of Orangeburg (group owner; acq 10-6-2005; $235,000). Population served: 100,000 Format: Gospel. ♦Gene G. Soult, gen mgr.

Saint Stephen

WTUA(FM)— May 1990: 106.1 mhz; 3 kw. 328 ft TL: N33 29 36 W79 53 21. Hrs open: Box 1240, 29479. Secondary address: 4013 Burns Dr. 29479. Phone: (843) 567-2091. Fax: (843) 567-3088.E-mail: wtuaradio@direcway.com Licensee: Praise Communications Inc. (acq 1-27-2005). Format: Gospel. News staff: one; News: 5 hrs wkly. Target aud: 20-65; African American. ♦Lynette L. Nelson, gen mgr.

Saluda

WJES(AM)— June 12, 1961: 1190 khz; 350 w-D. TL: N33 57 27 W81 47 34. (CP: 1200 khz; 10 kw-D, 4 w-N, 6.1 kw-CH). Hrs open: 125 N. Main St., 29138. Phone: (864) 445-9537.E-mail: info@1190wjes.com Web Site:www.1190wjes.com Licensee: Carolina Broadcast Partners LLC (acq 6-26-2006; $100,000). Population served: 3,150 Rgnl. Network: S.C. Net. Format: Country, beach and oldies. ♦Jeffery S. Roper, pres.

Sans Souci

WCSZ(AM)—Licensed to Sans Souci. See Greenville

Scranton

WZTF(FM)— 1991: 102.9 mhz; 2.9 kw. Ant 466 ft TL: N34 00 39 W79 45 24. Hrs open: Box 103000, Florence, 29501. Phone: (843) 667-4600. Phone: (843) 667-0970. Fax: (843) 673-7390. Licensee: Qantum of Florence License Co. LLC. Group owner: Qantum Communications Corp. (acq 7-2-2003; grpsl). Format: Urban contemp. ♦Jonathan Brewster, gen mgr.

Seneca

WHZT(FM)— June 6, 1953: 98.1 mhz; 100 kw. 1,004 ft TL: N34 41 14 W82 59 12. Stereo. Hrs open: 24 220 N. Main St., Suite 402, Greenville, 26901. Phone: (864) 232-9810. Fax: (864) 370-3403. Web Site:www.hot981.com Licensee: Cox Radio Inc. Group owner: Cox Communications Inc. (acq 2-1-2001; grpsl). Population served: 800,000 Natl. Network: Westwood One, CBS, . Dickstein Shapiro Morin & Oshinsky. Format: CHR. News staff: 2; News: 18 hrs wkly. Target aud: 25-54; affluent adults. ♦Steve Sinicropi, VP & gen mgr; Rob Grossman, gen sls mgr; Cathy Tabor, natl sls mgr; Laurie Madden, mktg VP, prom dir, news dir; Murph Dawg, mus dir, traf mgr; Lemont Bryant, chief of engrg.

WSNW(AM)— June 1, 1949: 1150 khz; 1 kw-D, 58 w-N. TL: N34 41 11 W82 59 27. Hrs open: 24
W277BX FM Translator.
Box 1251, 29679. Secondary address: 103 Ram Cat Alley 29678. Phone: (864) 882-9769. Fax: (864) 886-0082.E-mail: allgood@gacaradio.com Web Site:www.wsnwradio.com Licensee: Tugart Properties LLC. Group owner: Georgia-Carolina Radiocasting Companies (acq 9-28-2001). Population served: 72,510 Natl. Network: CBS Radio, . S.C. News Net. Dan J. Alpert. Wire Svc: AP Format: MOR Oldies, Talk, local news. News staff: one; News: 12 hrs wkly. Target aud: Adults 35 plus. Spec prog: Local Sports. ♦Art Sutton, pres; Tug Carter, VP; Adam Wright, stn mgr; Ian Lundin, opns mgr; Chad Dorsette, news dir; Marty Lee, chief of engrg.

Simpsonville

WFIS(AM)—See Fountain Inn

WYRD-FM— July 10, 1989: 106.3 mhz; 25 kw. Ant 328 ft TL: N34 50 33 W82 09 59. Stereo. Hrs open: 24 25 Garlington Rd., Greenville, 29615-4613. Phone: (864) 271-9200. Web Site:www.wyrd.com Licensee: Entercom Greenville License LLC. Group owner: Barnstable Broadcasting Inc. (acq 10-7-2005; grpsl). Latham & Watkins. Format: News/talk. Target aud: 25-54; adults. ♦David J. Field, pres; Sharon Day, gen mgr.

Socastee

WRNN-FM— 1997: 99.5 mhz; 14.5 kw. 430 ft TL: N33 49 30 W78 51 47. Hrs open: 1016 Ocala St., Myrtle Beach, 29577. Phone: (843) 448-1041. Fax: (843) 626-5988. Web Site:www.wrnn.net Licensee: NM Licensing LLC. Group owner: NextMedia Group L.L.C. (acq 11-26-2001; grpsl). Format: Talk. ♦Steven Dinetz, CEO; Jeff Dinetz, COO; Carl Hirsch, chmn; Skip Weller, pres; Barry Brown, gen mgr; Art Greene, sls dir; Liza Van Horne, prom dir; Dave Priest, progmg dir; Paul Matthews, chief of engrg; Ginny Batchelder, traf mgr; Kim Johnson, spec ev coord.

Society Hill

*WEBK(FM)—Not on air, target date: 2010: 91.1 mhz; 1.4 kw. Ant 223 ft TL: N34 32 51 W79 53 02. Stereo. Hrs open: Box 15, Chester, 29706. Phone: (803) 581-9030. Fax: (803) 581-9932. Licensee: Richburg Educational Broadcasters Inc. ♦Jeff Sigmon, gen mgr.

South Congaree

WFMV(FM)— 1993: 95.3 mhz; 6 kw. 328 ft TL: N33 53 58 W81 13 29. Hrs open: 24 Box 2355, West Columbia, 29171. Secondary address: 2440 Millwood Ave., Columbia 29205. Phone: (803) 939-9530. Fax: (803) 939-9469.E-mail: email@wfmv.com Web Site:www.wfmv.com Licensee: Glory Communications. Group owner: Glory Communications Inc. Population served: 471,800 Format: Urban inspirational. Target aud: Primary : adult 25-54; secondary: Women 25-54. ♦Alex Snipe Jr., gen mgr; Tezra Haire, gen sls mgr.

Spartanburg

WASC(AM)— Jan 15, 1968: 1530 khz; 1 kw-D, 250 w-CH. TL: N34 56 58 W81 57 33. Hrs open: Box 5686, 29304. Secondary address: 840 Wofford St. 29304. Phone: (864) 585-1530. Fax: (864) 573-7790. Licensee: New South Broadcasting Corp. (acq 2-9-76). Population served: 49,000 Format: Black, Urban Gold. ♦Sam E. Floyd, pres; K. Joseph Sessoms, VP, chief of engrg; K. Joseph Sessmos, gen mgr; Ed Waddell, min affrs dir, farm dir.

WOLI(AM)— Sept 1, 1940: 910 khz; 3.6 kw-D, 960 w-N. TL: N35 01 10 W82 00 36. Hrs open: 24
Rebroadcasts WYRD(AM) Greenville 100%.
6665 Pottery Rd., 29303. Phone: (864) 641-6370. Web Site:www.woli-am.com Licensee: Davidson Media Station WSPA Licensee LLC. Group owner: Entercom Communications Corp. (acq 10-6-2005; grpsl). Natl. Network: CBS, ABC, . Format: News/talk, sports. News staff: 4; News: 50 hrs wkly. Target aud: 35-64. Spec prog: Atlanta Falcons football, Univ. of South Carolina football and basketball, relg 5 hrs, sports 12 hrs wkly. ♦Jimmy Vineyard, gen mgr; Jim Kirkland, opns mgr; Tom Durney, gen sls mgr; Kelly Cowen, prom dir; Peter Phiele, progmg dir; Lisa Rollins, news dir, news rptr; Jerry Massey, chief of engrg; Katherine Lambert, traf mgr; Amy Hierder, news rptr; John Boone, sports cmtr.

WORD(AM)— Feb 17, 1930: 950 khz; 5 kw-U, DA-N. TL: N34 58 53 W81 59 14. Hrs open: 24 25 Garlington Rd., Greenville, 29615. Phone: (864) 271-9200. Fax: (800) 967-9329. Fax: (864) 242-1567. Web Site:www.newsradioword.com Licensee: Entercom Greenville License L.L.C. Group owner: Entercom Communications Corp. (acq 12-13-99; grpsl). Population served: 600,000 Natl. Network: CBS, Motor Racing Net, . Rgnl. Network: S.C. Net. S.C. News Net. Format: News/talk. News staff: 4; News: 45 hrs wkly. Target aud: 35-64. ♦David J. Field, CEO; Steve Fisher, CFO; Tom Durney, gen mgr; Jim Kirkland, opns mgr.

WSPA-FM— Aug 29, 1946: 98.9 mhz; 100 kw. 1,910 ft TL: N35 10 12 W82 17 27. Stereo. Hrs open: 24 Prog sep from AM 25 Garlington Rd., Greenville, 29615. Phone: (864) 271-9200. Fax: (864) 370-1473. Web Site:www.magic989online.com Licensee: Entercom Greenville License LLC. (acq 12-13-99; grpsl). Population served: 1,200,000 Format: Light adult contemp. News: one hr wkly. Spec prog: Relg 3 hrs, jazz 6 hrs, 70s oldies 10 hrs wkly. ♦Jerry Stevens, gen sls mgr; David Patella, natl sls mgr; Michael McKeel, progmg dir; Stephen Hester, traf mgr; Lisa Rollins, news rptr; Jeff Cross, disc jockey.

WSPG(AM)— Sept 1, 1952: 1400 khz; 1 kw-U. TL: N34 58 26 W81 55 37. Hrs open: Box 193, 29304. Secondary address: 340 Garner Rd. 29303. Phone: (864) 573-1400. Fax: (864) 573-8699.E-mail: info@espn1400am.com Licensee: Fulmer Broadcasting Inc. (acq 12-30-2003; $300,000). S.C. News Net. Wire Svc: AP Format: News/talk, sports. Target aud: Adult male 25-54. ♦Matthew Y. Fulmer, pres; J. Dwayne Corn, gen mgr; Jan Scruggs, progmg dir, progmg.

Summerton

WLJI(FM)— 1997: 98.3 mhz; 6 kw. 328 ft TL: N33 42 58 W80 20 44. Hrs open: 24
Simulcast of WFMV(FM) South Congaree 100%.
Box 1348, Sumter, 29151. Phone: (803) 774-5512. Fax: (803) 774-5534.E-mail: wlji@ftc-i.net Licensee: Glory Communications Inc. (group owner; acq 4-1-97). Format: Urban inspirational. Target aud: Adults 25-54. ◆Alex Snipe Jr., gen mgr; Tony Jamison, opns mgr; Tezra Haire, gen sls mgr.

Summerville

WAZS(AM)— June 7, 1963: 980 khz; 1 kw-D, 131 w-N. TL: N33 01 57 W80 12 00. Hrs open: 24
simulcast w/ WZJY-AM.
5081 Rivers Ave., North Charleston, 29406. Phone: (843) 554-1063. Fax: (843) 554-1088.E-mail: traffic@jaborcommunications.com Web Site:jaborcommunications.com Licensee: Thomas B. Daniels. Group owner: Jabar Communications (acq 9-1-2000). Population served: 200,000 Natl. Rep: Interep,. Format: Spanish. Target aud: 18-35. ◆Michael Baynard, gen mgr.

WWWZ(FM)— May 10, 1974: 93.3 mhz; 50 kw. Ant 492 ft TL: N33 06 54 W79 54 25. Hrs open: 4230 Faber Place Drive, Suite 100, North Charleston, 29405. Phone: (843) 277-1200. Fax: (843) 277-1212.E-mail: info@z93jams.com Web Site:www.z93jams.com Licensee: Citadel Broadcasting Co. Group owner: Citadel Broadcasting Corp. (acq 6-9-99; grpsl). Population served: 3,704 Format: Urban contemp. ◆Paul O'Malley, gen mgr; Star Israel, gen sls mgr; Terry Base, progmg dir; Judy Herold, news dir; Justin Tucker, chief of engrg; Stephanie Gaines, women's int ed.

Sumter

WDXY(AM)— May 23, 1960: 1240 khz; 1 kw-U. TL: N33 54 16 W80 19 25. Hrs open: 24 Box 1269, 29151. Secondary address: 51 Commerce St. 29150. Phone: (803) 775-2321. Fax: (803) 773-4856.E-mail: production@miller.fm Web Site:www.newsstalk1240.am Licensee: Miller Communications Inc. (group owner; acq 1-2-2001; grpsl). Population served: 244,000 Natl. Rep: Rgnl Reps,. Smith & Belendiuk. Format: Talk. News staff: one; News: 6 hrs wkly. Target aud: 35 plus. ◆Harold T. Miller, CEO, pres; Theresa Miller, VP & gen mgr; Dave Baker, opns VP.

*WRJA-FM— Aug 25, 1975: 88.1 mhz; 98 kw. 1,000 ft TL: N33 52 32 W80 16 14. Stereo. Hrs open: 24 1101 George Rogers Blvd., Columbia, 29201. Phone: (803) 737-3420. Fax: (803) 737-3552.E-mail: gasque@scetv.org Web Site:www.etvradio.org Licensee: South Carolina Educational TV Commission. Population served: 24,555 Natl. Network: NPR, PRI,. Format: NPR news. News progmg 120 hrs wkly. ◆Moss Bresnahan, pres; Tom Holloway, sls dir; John Gasque, progmg dir; Connie Murray, traf mgr.

WSSC(AM)— Apr 27, 1953: 1340 khz; 1 kw-U. TL: N33 55 45 W80 19 29. Hrs open: 6 AM-midnight 201 Oswego Rd., 29150. Phone: (803) 469-0288. Fax: (803) 469-0297. Web Site:www.sumterbaptisttemple.com Licensee: Sumpter Baptist Temple Inc. (acq 2-28-94; $157,500; 5-2-94). Population served: 26,536 Rgnl. Network: S.C. Net. S.C. News Net. Format: Christian radio. Target aud: 25-54. ◆Eddie Richardson, pres & gen mgr.

WWBD(FM)— June 21, 1995: 94.7 mhz; 3 kw. Ant 479 ft TL: N33 51 55 W80 17 09. Hrs open: 24 Box 1269, 29151. Secondary address: 51 Commerce St. 29150. Phone: (803) 773-1859. Fax: (803) 773-4856.E-mail: Tmiller55@aol.com Web Site:www.miller.fm Licensee: Miller Communications Inc. (group owner; acq 9-27-2001). Population served: 297,000 Natl. Network: American Urban, . Smithwick & Belendiuk. Format: Classic hits. News staff: one. Adults 25 to 49 & secondary females 25-54. ◆Harold T. Miller, Jr., CEO, pres; Dave Baker, opns VP, sls dir; Theresa Miller, chmn, VP, gen mgr & gen sls mgr.

WWDM(FM)— 1961: 101.3 mhz; 100 kw. 1,322 ft TL: N33 52 52 W80 16 14. Stereo. Hrs open: 24 1900 Pineview Rd., Columbia, 29209. Phone: (803) 695-8600. Fax: (803) 695-8605.E-mail: mhanisch@innercity.sc.com Web Site:www.thebigdm.com Licensee: Urban Radio II L.L.C. Group owner: Inner City Broadcasting (acq 8-7-2000; grpsl). Population served: 461,000 Natl. Network: ABC, Westwood One, . Natl. Rep: D & R Radio,. Format: Urban contemp. News staff: one; News: 6 hrs wkly. Target aud: 18-49. ◆Maggie Hanisch, gen mgr; Mike Love, opns dir, progmg dir; Mark Fitzmayer, gen sls mgr; Susan Morningstar, VP & prom dir.

WWHM(AM)— Mar 16, 1940: 1290 khz; 1 kw-U, DA-N. TL: N33 55 16 W80 16 59. Hrs open: 16 Box 1269, 29151-1269. Phone: (803) 775-2321. Fax: (803) 773-4856.E-mail: production@miller.fm Web

Site:www.miller.fm Licensee: Miller Communications Inc. (acq 11-12-2007; $60,000). Population served: 25,000 ◆David Baker, VP.

Surfside Beach

WSYN(FM)— Apr 4, 1977: 103.1 mhz; 12.5 kw. 325 ft TL: N33 34 32 W79 02 29. (CP: 11.5 kw, ant 485 ft. TL: N33 43 22 W79 03 43). Stereo. Hrs open: 24
Rebroadcasts WVCO(FM) Loris 100%.
11640 Hwy. 17 Bypass, Murrells Inlet, 29576. Phone: (843) 651-7869. Fax: (843) 651-3197.E-mail: info@sunny1065.net Web Site:www.cumulus.com Licensee: Cumulus Licensing Corp. Group owner: Cumulus Media Inc. (acq 4-30-2001; swap of WSYN(FM) for WQSL(FM) & WXQR(FM) Jacksonville, NC). Population served: 250,000 Natl. Network: Westwood One, . Fisher, Wayland, Cooper, Leader & Zaragoza. Format: Country. News staff: one; News: 4 hrs wkly. Target aud: 25-54; adults & families of loc towns & tourists. ◆John Sheftic, gen mgr.

Union

WBCU(AM)— Aug 27, 1949: 1460 khz; 1 kw-U, DA-N. TL: N34 43 10 W81 39 44. Hrs open: 24 210 E. Main, 29379. Phone: (864) 427-2411. Phone: (864) 427-2412. Fax: (864) 429-2975.E-mail: chris@wbcuradio.com Web Site:www.wbcuradio.com Licensee: Union-Carolina Broadcasting Co. Inc. (acq 3-3-2006; $240,000 for all of the stock). Population served: 50,000 Natl. Network: ABC, . Rgnl. Network: S.C. Net. S.C. News Net. Dan J. Alpert. Format: Country standards, loc news, weather. News staff: 2; News: 24 hrs wkly. Target aud: 30 plus; working class adult buyers. Spec prog: Sports 10 hrs, news//talk 10 hrs wkly. ◆James C. Woodson, CEO, pres, gen mgr; Daniel Prince, opns mgr; Linda Comer, gen sls mgr; Kevin Shehan, news dir; Tim Stephens, chief of engrg.

Walhalla

WGOG(FM)— Sept 1, 1991: 96.3 mhz; 6 kw. Ant 302 ft TL: N34 51 33 W83 03 31. Stereo. Hrs open: 24 Box 10, 29691. Secondary address: 2058 Westminster Hwy. 29691. Phone: (864) 638-3616. Fax: (864) 638-6810.E-mail: wgog@wgog.com Web Site:www.wgog.com Licensee: Appalachian Broadcasting Co. Inc. (acq 10-16-2001; with co-located AM). Population served: 442,686 Natl. Network: ABC, . Rgnl. Network: S.C. Net. Dan J. Alpert. Format: Country. News staff: one; News: 15 hrs wkly. Target aud: 25-54. ◆Douglas M. Sutton Jr., pres; M. Terry Carter, VP; Gary Butts, gen mgr; Wayne Morton, opns mgr; Tim Stephens, progmg dir, chief of engrg; Dick Mangrum, news dir, local news ed.

WJTP(AM)— Apr 15, 1959: 1000 khz; 1 kw-D. TL: N34 44 29 W83 04 18. (CP: COL Lithia Springs, GA. 890 khz; 5 kw-D. TL: N33 48 39 W84 37 02). Hrs open: Sunrise-sunset Box 10, 29691. Phone: (864) 638-3616. Fax: (864) 638-6810.E-mail: gary@wgog.com Licensee: New Life Broadcasting Inc. Group owner: Georgia-Carolina Radiocasting Companies (acq 10-10-2008; $1 million). Population served: 168,603 Natl. Network: ABC, . Fletcher, Heald & Hildreth. Format: Oldies, talk. News staff: one; News: 6 hrs wkly. Target aud: 25-54; emphasis on women. ◆Juan Carlos Matos, pres; Gary Butts, VP, gen mgr; Dick Mangrum, news dir; Tim Stephens, chief of engrg.

Walterboro

WALI(FM)— Dec 13, 1991: 93.7 mhz; 6 kw. 345 ft TL: N32 49 54 W80 43 30. Hrs open: 24 724 S. Jefferies Blvd., 29488. Phone: (843) 549-1543. Fax: (843) 549-2711.E-mail: info@wali.com Licensee: Hess Communications L.L.C. (acq 1996; $285,000). Population served: 37,000 Rgnl. Network: S.C. Net. S.C. News Net. Rgnl rep: Rgnl Reps. Format: Country, sports. News: 3 hrs wkly. Target aud: General. Spec prog: Gospel 5 hrs wkly. ◆Karl Hess, pres, gen mgr, opns VP, mus dir, chief of engrg; Thomas Heirs, sls dir, adv dir; Belinda Pierpaoli, progmg dir, asst music dir, pub affrs dir; Samantha Hess, mus dir; Susan Linder, spec ev coord; Dennis Hall, disc jockey.

Wedgefield

WIBZ(FM)— Mar 1, 1985: 95.5 mhz; 4.4 kw. Ant 387 ft TL: N33 56 56 W80 23 34. Stereo. Hrs open: 24 Box 1269, Sumter, 29151. Secondary address: 51 Commerce St., Sumter 29150. Phone: (803) 773-1859. Fax: (803) 773-4856.E-mail: production@miller.fm Licensee: Miller Communicatins Inc. (group owner; acq 11-14-00; grpsl). Population served: 264,000 Natl. Network: ABC, . Smithwick & Belendiuk. Format: Solid gold. News staff: one. Target aud: 18-49. ◆Harold T. Miller, CEO, pres; Dave Baker, opns VP; Theresa Miller, VP & gen sls mgr.

West Columbia

WGCV(AM)—See Cayce

WLTY(FM)—See Columbia

WXBT(FM)—Licensed to West Columbia. See Columbia

Whitmire

*WNBK(FM)— 2009: 90.9 mhz; 1.8 kw. Ant 335 ft TL: N34 29 52 W81 32 55. Hrs open: Box 15, Chester, 29706. Phone: (803) 581-9030. Fax: (803) 581-9932. Licensee: Richburg Educational Broadcasters Inc. Format: Beach music, oldies. ◆Jeff Sigmon, gen mgr.

Williston

WAAW(FM)— Aug 12, 1994: 94.7 mhz; 2.11 kw. 561 ft TL: N33 28 33 W81 32 57. Stereo. Hrs open: 24 2166 Park Ave S.E., Aiken, 29801. Phone: (803) 641-6499. Fax: (803) 641-8844.E-mail: frank@rejoiceradio.com Licensee: Wisdom LLC. Group owner: Neely Enterprises (acq 2-2-2009; grpsl). Population served: 68,376 Format: Gospel music. ◆Rev. Leaster Smalls, stn mgr.

Woodruff

WDRF(AM)— July 7, 1967: 1510 khz; 1 kw-D, 250 w-CH. TL: N34 45 22 W82 03 18. Hrs open: Box 547, 29388. Phone: (864) 476-7184. Fax: (864) 476-0474. Licensee: B&B Media Inc. (acq 8-10-99). Format: Relg. ◆T.C. Lewis, gen mgr.

York

WBZK(AM)— Apr 19, 1956: 980 khz; 3.15 kw-D, 291 w-N, DA-2. TL: N34 59 50 W81 15 09. Hrs open: 24 4201-J Stuart Andrew Blvd., Charlotte, NC, 28217. Phone: (704) 665-8240. Fax: (208) 545-9888.E-mail: ann@wnow.com Web Site:www.wbzk.com Licensee: 980 AM Inc. Group owner: Davidson Media Group LLC (acq 9-16-2008; exchange for WPYR(AM) Baton Rouge, LA). Population served: 893,630 Natl. Network: ABC, . Format: Spanish, Christian. News: 6 hrs wkly. Target aud: 22-54. Spec prog: Chinese 10 hrs, Greek 10 hrs wkly. ◆Michael B. Glinter, pres; Russ Jones, gen mgr; Robert Freeze, opns dir; Humberto Martinez, progmg dir; Winston Hawkins, chief of engrg.

South Dakota

Aberdeen

KBFO(FM)— Feb 20, 1999: 106.7 mhz; 100 kw. 338 ft TL: N45 27 57 W98 20 08. Hrs open: 24 Box 1930, 57401. Secondary address: 13541 386th Ave. 57401. Phone: (605) 225-1560. Fax: (605) 229-4849. Licensee: Armada Media - Aberdeen Inc. Group owner: Clear Channel Communications Inc. (acq 10-31-2006; grpsl). Population served: 70,000 Rgnl rep: Jones Satellite Audio. Format: Hot adult contemp. Target aud: 18-35. ◆DaLime LeGrand, gen mgr; Rob Feller, gen sls mgr; Doug Pitts, progmg mgr.

*KEEA(FM)—Not on air, target date: unknown: 90.1 mhz; 6 kw. Ant 98 ft TL: N45 28 22 W98 30 16. Hrs open: Drawer 2440, Tupelo, MS, 38803. Phone: (662) 844-8888. Fax: (662) 842-6791. Web Site:www.afr.net Licensee: American Family Association. (acq 4-7-2008). Natl. Network: American Family Radio, . ◆Donald E. Wildmon, chmn.

KGIM(AM)— September 1933: 1420 khz; 1 kw-D, 232 w-N. TL: N45 29 07 W98 29 46. Hrs open: 13541 386th Ave., 57401. Phone: (605) 229-3632. Fax: (605) 229-4849. Licensee: Armada Media - Aberdeen Inc. Group owner: Robert Ingstad Broadcast Properties (acq 10-31-2006; grpsl). Population served: 77,107 Fisher, Wayland, Cooper, Leader & Zaragoza L.L.P. Format: Country, news, sports. News staff: 10 hrs wkly Target aud: 25 plus; general. Spec prog: Weather, farm 12 hrs wkly. ◆Jim Coursolle, pres; Brian Lundquist, gen mgr.

*KKAA(AM)— Sept 12, 1974: 1560 khz; 10 kw-D, 5 kw-N, DA-2. TL: N45 25 05 W98 28 36. Hrs open: 24 Family Stations Inc., 4135 Northgate Blvd., Suite 1, Sacramento, CA, 95834. Phone: (916) 641-8191. Fax: (916) 641-8238. Licensee: Family Stations Inc. Group owner: Clear Channel Communications Inc. (acq 11-30-2004; $75,000 with KQKD(AM) Redfield). Population served: 100,000 Format: Relg. ◆Harold Camping, pres.

KLRJ(FM)— September 1979: 94.9 mhz; 100 kw. Ant 446 ft TL: N45 27 57 W98 20 08. Stereo. Hrs open: 5 AM-1 AM Rebroadcasts KLVR(FM) Santa Rosa, CA. 2351 Sunset Blvd., Suite 170-218, Rocklin, CA, 95765. Phone: (916) 251-1600. Fax: (916) 251-1650. Web Site:www.klove.com Licensee: Educational Media Foundation. (acq 11-30-2004; $200,000). Population served: 250,000 Natl. Network: K-Love, . Format: Christian music. ◆Richard Jenkins, pres; Mike Novak, VP; Keith Whipple, dev dir; David Pierce, progmg mgr; Sam Wallington, engrg dir; Karen Johnson, news rptr.

KSDN(AM)— Apr 16, 1947: 930 khz; 5 kw-D, 1 kw-N, DA-2. TL: N45 25 29 W98 31 03. Hrs open: Box 1930, 57402. Secondary address: 13541 386th Ave. 57401. Phone: (605) 225-1560. Fax: (605) 229-4849.E-mail: info@aberdeenradioranch.com Web Site:www.aberdeenradioranch.com Licensee: Armada Media - Aberdeen Inc. Group owner: Clear Channel Communications Inc. (acq 10-31-2006; grpsl). Population served: 100,000 Natl. Network: ABC, . Format: Talk. News staff: one; News: 15 hrs wkly. Target aud: 25-54. Spec prog: Farm 15 hrs wkly. ◆Ron Feller, gen sls mgr; Doug Pitts, progmg dir.

KSDN-FM— Nov 18, 1979: 94.1 mhz; 100 kw. 440 ft TL: N45 25 27 W98 31 00. Stereo. Hrs open: Box 1930, 57401. Phone: (605) 225-1560. Fax: (605) 229-4849. Population served: 50,000 Format: Classic rock.

Arlington

*KSRJ(FM)—Not on air, target date: unknown: 89.9 mhz; 14 kw. Ant 466 ft TL: N44 20 23 W97 09 17. Hrs open: 4604 Airpark Blvd., Duluth, MN, 55811-5751. Phone: (218) 722-3017. Fax: (218) 279-5010. Web Site:www.refugeradio.com Licensee: Refuge Media Group. ◆Mike Marrone, pres; Paulette Kutzler, gen mgr.

Belle Fourche

KBFS(AM)— July 22, 1959: 1450 khz; 1 kw-U. TL: N44 40 02 W103 51 22. Hrs open: 24 Rebroadcasts KYDT(FM) Sundance, WY 99%. Box 787, 57717. Phone: (605) 892-2571. Fax: (605) 892-2573.E-mail: kbfs@mato.com Web Site:www.kbfs.com Licensee: Ultimate Caps Inc. (acq 3-17-94; $95,000; 6-20-83). Population served: 25,000 Natl. Network: Jones Radio Networks, ESPN Radio, Motor Racing Net, CBS Radio, Westwood One, . Rgnl rep: Colorado Avalanche, Colorado Rockies Wire Svc: AP Format: Country, sports, news, talk. News: 20 hrs wkly. Target aud: 25-54; farmers, ranchers, sports fans. Spec prog: Farm 20 hrs, relg 2 hrs wkly. ◆Cynthia A. Grimmelmann, pres; Karl Grimmelmann, exec VP, gen mgr & opns mgr.

KFMH(FM)—Not on air, target date: unknown: 102.1 mhz; 7 kw. Ant -12 ft TL: N44 39 48 W103 51 26. Hrs open: Bad Lands Broadcasting Co. Inc., 288 S. River Rd., Bedford, NH, 03110. Phone: (603) 668-6400. Fax: (603) 668-6470. Licensee: Bad Lands Broadcasting Co. Inc. Group owner: Kona Coast Radio LLC (acq 9-6-2005; $915,000). ◆Steven A. Silberberg, pres.

KZZI(FM)— Sept 22, 1995: 95.9 mhz; 100 kw. Ant 1,788 ft TL: N44 19 35 W103 50 06. Stereo. Hrs open: 24 2827 E. Colorado Blvd., Spearfish, 57783. Phone: (605) 642-85747. Fax: (605) 642-7849. Web Site:www.kzcountry.com Licensee: Western South Dakota Broadcasting L.L.C. (acq 1999; $79,006). Population served: 150,000 Natl. Rep: Katz Radio,. Format: Country. Target aud: 18-54. ◆Steve Duffy, gen mgr; Les Tuttle, gen sls mgr.

Box Elder

KXMZ(FM)— 2008: 102.7 mhz; 50 kw. Ant 449 ft TL: N44 05 33 W103 14 53. Hrs open: 136 Main St., Suite 202, Westport, CT, 06880-3304. Phone: (203) 227-1978. Fax: (203) 227-2373.E-mail: hits1027@hits1027.com Web Site:www.hits1027.com Licensee: Connoisseur Media LLC.

Brandon

KDEZ(FM)— 2007: 100.1 mhz; 2.15 kw. Ant 558 ft TL: N43 31 07 W96 32 05. Hrs open: 5100 S. Tennis Ln., Sioux Falls, 57108. Phone: (605) 361-0300. Fax: (605) 361-5410. Web Site:www.easy1001.com Licensee: Cumulus Licensing LLC. Format: Adult contemp. ◆Lew Dickey, pres; Don Jacobs, gen mgr; Barry Roberts, progmg dir.

Brookings

KBRK(AM)— July 28, 1955: 1430 khz; 1 kw-D, 100 w-N. TL: N44 18 13 W96 46 10. (CP: TL: N44 18 12 W96 46 01). Hrs open: 227 22nd

Ave. S., 57006. Phone: (605) 692-1430. Fax: (605) 692-6434.E-mail: brookingsradio@brookings.net Web Site:www.brookingsradio.com Licensee: Three Eagles Communications Co. Group owner: Three Eagles Communications Population served: 125,000 Format: Traditional radio today. Spec prog: Farm 9 hrs wkly. ◆Cami Powers, gen mgr.

KBRK-FM— Aug 10, 1968: 93.7 mhz; 36 kw. 571 ft TL: N44 20 22 W96 09 16. Hrs open: 24 227 22nd Ave. S., 57006. Phone: (605) 692-1430. Fax: (605) 692-4441. Web Site:www.b937.com Licensee: Three Eagles of Huron Inc. Population served: 35,000 Natl. Network: Westwood One, . Format: Adult contemp. Target aud: 20-45. ◆Cami Powers, gen mgr.

*KESD(FM)— July 1967: 88.3 mhz; 50 kw. 623 ft TL: N44 20 10 W97 13 41. Stereo. Hrs open: Box 2218B Pugsely Ctr., 57007. Phone: (605) 688-4191. Fax: (605) 677-5010.E-mail: sdpr@sdpb.org Web Site:www.sdpb.org Licensee: South Dakota Board of Directors for Educational Telecommunications. Population served: 278,000 Natl. Network: NPR, PRI, . Format: News, class. Target aud: 35-65; upscale, higher educated & arts-oriented. ◆Julie Andersen, pres; Joe Tlustos, stn mgr; Terry Spencer, dev dir. Co-owned TV: *KESD-TV affil.

KJJQ(AM)—(Volga, May 6, 1981: 910 khz; 500 w-U. TL: N44 15 01 W96 57 22. Hrs open: 24 227 22nd Ave. S., 57006. Phone: (605) 692-1430. Fax: (605) 692-6434.E-mail: brookingsradio@brookings.net Web Site:www.brookingsradio.com Licensee: Three Eagles of Joliet Inc. Group owner: Three Eagles Communications (acq 7-1-2004; grpsl).. Population served: 43,000 Natl. Network: ESPN Radio, . Rgnl. Network: AgriAmerica, S.D. News Net. Pepper & Corazzini. Format: Sports, talk, info. Target aud: 25-54; 60% male, 40% female. ◆Cami Powers, gen mgr.

KKQQ(FM)—(Volga, Apr 15, 1984: 102.3 mhz; 25 kw. Ant 243 ft TL: N44 15 01 W96 57 22. Stereo. Hrs open: 227 22nd Ave. S., 57006. Phone: (605) 692-9125. Fax: (605) 692-6434.E-mail: brookingsradio@brookings.net Web Site:www.kcountry.com Licensee: Three Eagles of Joliet Inc. (acq 7-1-2004; grpsl). Format: Hot country. Target aud: 18-54. ◆Cami Powers, gen mgr.

*KSDJ(FM)— 1993: 90.7 mhz; 1 kw. 148 ft TL: N44 19 01 W96 47 02. Stereo. Hrs open: 24 Box 2815, Rm. 069-D, 57007-2815. Phone: (605) 688-5559.E-mail: newrock907ksdj@hotmail.com Web Site:www.907ksdj.com Licensee: South Dakota State University. (group owner) Population served: 25,000 Format: Alternative. News staff: one; News: 5 hrs wkly. Target aud: 17-22; college students. Spec prog: Black 8 hrs, jazz 2 hrs wkly. ◆Peggy Gordon-Miller, pres; Jay Buchholz, gen mgr.

Canton

KYBB(FM)— 1996: 102.7 mhz; 50 kw. 485 ft TL: N43 28 48 W96 41 05. Hrs open: 5100 S. Tennis Ln., Sioux Falls, 57108. Phone: (605) 339-9999. Fax: (605) 339-2735. Web Site:www.81027.com Licensee: Cumulus Licensing LLC. Group owner: Cumulus Media Inc. (acq 3-29-2004; grpsl). Natl. Rep: Christal,. Format: Classic rock. Target aud: 25-49; men. ◆Don Jacobs, gen mgr; Scott Maguire, opns dir; Dan Rahman, progmg dir.

Clear Lake

KDBX(FM)— 1999: 107.1 mhz; 15 kw. 430 ft TL: N44 52 36 W96 52 28. Hrs open: 227 22nd Ave. S., Brookings, 57006. Phone: (605) 692-9125. Fax: (605) 692-6434.E-mail: brookingsradio@brookings.net Web Site:www.brookingsradio.com Licensee: Three Eagles of Joliet Inc. Group owner: Waitt Radio Inc. (acq 5-17-2005; $250,000). Format: Classic rock. ◆Cami Powers, gen mgr.

Custer

KAWK(FM)— November 1996: 105.1 mhz; 6.5 kw. Ant 1,312 ft TL: N43 44 41 W103 28 52. Hrs open: Box 611, Hot Springs, 57747. Phone: (605) 745-3637. Fax: (605) 745-3517.E-mail: info@kawk.com Licensee: Mt. Rushmore Broadcasting Inc. Format: Oldies.

KFCR(AM)— May 1, 1988: 1490 khz; 830 w-U. TL: N43 43 03 W103 35 00. Hrs open: Box 611, Hot Springs, 57747. Secondary address: 145 Mount Rushmore Rd. 57730. Phone: (605) 745-3637. Fax: (605) 745-3517. Licensee: Mount Rushmore Broadcasting Inc. (group owner; (acq 5-6-92; 5-25-92). Format: Adult contemp. ◆Gary Baker, gen mgr.

Deadwood

KDSJ(AM)— July 2, 1947: 980 khz; 5 kw-D, 1 kw-N, DA-N. TL: N44 22 57 W103 39 44. Hrs open: Box 567, 57732. Phone: (605) 578-1826. Fax: (605) 578-1827. Web Site:www.kdsj980.com Licensee: Goldrush Broadcasting. (acq 7-1-82). Population served: 100,000 Rgnl. Network: S.D. News Net. S.D. News Net. Format: Top-40, oldies, news, sports. Target aud: 25-50. ◆Al Decker, pres & gen mgr.

KSQY(FM)— Sept 4, 1982: 95.1 mhz; 100 kw. 1,707 ft TL: N44 19 49 W103 50 10. Stereo. Hrs open: 24 Box 1680, Rapid City, 57709. Secondary address: 306 E. St. Joe, Rapid City 57709. Phone: (605) 343-0888. Fax: (605) 342-3075. Web Site:www.95ksky.com Licensee: Haugo Broadcasting Inc. (group owner) Population served: 160,000 Natl. Rep: Midwest Radio,. Rgnl rep: Midwest Radio. Format: Triple A. News: 2 hrs wkly. Target aud: 18-49; young, active adults within a 5 state region. ◆Houston Haugo, CEO & pres; Chris Haugo, exec VP, gen mgr.

Dell Rapids

KSQB-FM— Oct 2, 1998: 95.7 mhz; 25 kw. 328 ft TL: N43 45 48 W96 48 27. Stereo. Hrs open: 24 500 South Phillips Ave., Sioux Falls, 57104. Phone: (605) 331-5350. Fax: (605) 336-0415. Licensee: Backyard Broadcasting South Dakota Licensee LLC. (acq 8-1-2006; grpsl). Population served: 175,000 Natl. Rep: Rgnl Reps,. Wire Svc: AP Format: Classic hits. Target aud: 20-40; young, active adults with spending ability. ◆Mark Nelson, opns mgr.

Faith

KPSD(FM)— June 1, 1989: 97.1 mhz; 100 kw. 1,525 ft TL: N45 03 14 W102 15 47. Hrs open: Rebroadcasts KUSD(FM) Vermillion. Box 5000, Vermillion, 57069. Secondary address: 555 N. Dakota St. 57069. Phone: (605) 677-5861. Fax: (605) 677-5010.E-mail: sdpr@sdpb.org Web Site:www.sdpb.org Licensee: South Dakota Board of Directors for Educational Telecommunications. Natl. Network: NPR, . Format: Classical, jazz, news. ◆Julie Andersen, pres; Terry Spencer, dev dir; Carol Robertson, prom dir; Owen DeJong, progmg dir.

Flandreau

KXQL(FM)— October 2000: 107.9 mhz; 21 kw. Ant 761 ft TL: N43 57 56 W96 49 11. Stereo. Hrs open: 24 500 South Phillips Ave., Sioux Falls, 57104. Phone: (605) 331-5350. Fax: (605) 336-0415. Licensee: Backyard Broadcasting South Dakota Licensee LLC. (acq 8-1-2006; grpsl). Population served: 175,000 Natl. Network: Jones Radio Networks, . Natl. Rep: Rgnl Reps,. Format: Good Time Great Oldies. Target aud: Adults; 35-65. ◆Mark Nelson, opns mgr & progmg dir.

Fort Pierre

KJBI(FM)— Dec 1, 2007: 100.1 mhz; 51 kw. Ant 530 ft TL: N44 18 30 W100 20 49. Hrs open: 24 Box 1197, Pierre, 57501. Secondary address: 214 W. Pleasant Dr., Pierre 57501. Phone: (605) 224-8686. Fax: (605) 224-8984. Licensee: James River Broadcasting Inc. (acq 7-31-2007; $450,000 for CP). Format: Classic hits. ◆Mark A. Swendsen, gen mgr.

Frankfort

*KTUT(FM)—Not on air, target date: unknown: 89.5 mhz; 100 kw. Ant 479 ft TL: N44 48 20 W97 45 55. Hrs open: Box 217, Gainesville, TX, 76241. Phone: (940) 668-7971. Licensee: 1 A Chord Inc. ◆Dorothy Fay Jones, gen mgr.

Freeman

*KVCF(FM)— 2002: 90.5 mhz; 9 kw. Ant 807 ft TL: N43 29 22 W97 26 33. Stereo. Hrs open: 3434 W. Kilbourn Ave., Milwaukee, WI, 53208-3313. Phone: (414) 935-3000. Fax: (414) 935-3015. Web Site:www.vcyamerica.org Licensee: VCY America Inc. Format: Relg, Christian. ◆Vic Eliason, gen mgr; Jim Schneider, progmg dir; Andy Eliason, chief of engrg.

Gregory

*KVCX(FM)— May 8, 1982: 101.5 mhz; 100 kw. 640 ft TL: N43 07 41 W99 26 10. Stereo. Hrs open: 3434 W. Kilbourn Ave., Milwaukee, WI, 53208. Phone: (414) 935-3000. Fax: (414) 935-3015.E-mail:

kvcx@vcyamerica.org Web Site:www.vcyamerica.org Licensee: VCY/America Inc. (group owner; acq 4-87). Natl. Network: USA, Moody, . Format: Relg, Christian. ◆Dr. Randall Melchert, pres; Vic Eliason, VP & gen mgr; Jim Schneider, progmg dir, pub affrs dir; Tom Schlueter, mus dir; Gordon Morris, news dir; Andrew Eliason, chief of engrg.

Hermosa

*KWRC(FM)— 2008: 90.9 mhz; 400 w. Ant 1,269 ft TL: N43 44 40 W103 28 52. Hrs open:
Rebroadcasts KAWZ(FM) Twin Falls, ID 100%.
4002 N. 3300 E., Twin Falls, ID, 83301. Phone: (208) 734-6633. Fax: (208) 736-1958. Web Site:www.csnradio.com Licensee: Calvary Chapel of Twin Falls Inc. Format: Christian praise & worship, Bible teaching. ◆Mike Kestler, VP.

Hot Springs

KZMX(AM)— July 4, 1958: 580 khz; 2.3 kw-D, 310 w-N. TL: N43 27 24 W103 28 34. Hrs open: Box 611, 57747. Secondary address: North Wind Cave Rd. 57747. Phone: (605) 745-3637. Fax: (605) 745-3517.E-mail: themorningshow@email.com Web Site:info@kzmx.com Licensee: Mount Rushmore Broadcasting Inc. (group owner; (acq 5-20-93; $45,000 with co-located FM;6-14-93). Population served: 5,000 Format: Real country. Spec prog: Farm 6 hrs wkly. ◆Gary Baker, gen mgr, gen sls mgr & progmg dir.

KZMX-FM— Feb 10, 1981: 96.7 mhz; 1.4 kw. Ant 440 ft TL: N43 26 34 W103 27 27. Stereo. Hrs open: Box 611, 57747. Secondary address: North Wind Cave Rd. 57747. Phone: (605) 745-3637. Fax: (605) 745-3517.E-mail: info@kzmx.com Format: Real country.

Hoven

*KCFE(FM)—Not on air, target date: unknown: 88.3 mhz; 500 w. Ant 36 ft TL: N45 16 33.05 W99 48 12. Hrs open: Box 102, 57450. Phone: (605) 948-2495. Web Site:www.gloryboundbaptistchurch.com Licensee: Glory Bound Baptist Church. ◆James Ruckman, pres.

Huron

KIJV(AM)— July 1, 1947: 1340 khz; 1 kw-U. TL: N44 20 46 W98 12 34. Hrs open: 24 1726 Dakota Ave. S., 57350. Phone: (605) 352-8621. Fax: (605) 352-8622. Licensee: Dakota Communications Ltd. (group owner; acq 3-11-2004; $400,000 with co-located FM). Population served: 14,299 Format: Oldies, talk, sports. News staff: one. Target aud: 35 plus. ◆Duane D. Butt, pres; John Speeney, gen mgr, gen sls mgr; Matt Price, progmg dir; Curt Coleman, news dir; Sheri Barth, sports cmtr; Nick Rottum, disc jockey.

KOKK(AM)— Jan 13, 1976: 1210 khz; 5 kw-D, 1 kw-N, DA-2. TL: N44 21 44 W98 09 09. Hrs open: 1726 Dakota Ave. S., 57350. Phone: (605) 352-8621. Fax: (605) 352-0911.E-mail: traffic@kokk.com Web Site:www.kokk.com Licensee: Dakota Communications Ltd. (group owner). Population served: 14,000 Format: Country. ◆Linda Marcus, gen mgr; Dick Schultz, chief of engrg.

*KVCH(FM)—Not on air, target date: unknown: 88.7 mhz; 100 kw vert. Ant 279 ft TL: N44 20 33 W98 14 38. Hrs open: 3434 W. Kilbourn Ave., Milwaukee, WI, 53208-3313. Phone: (414) 935-3000. Fax: (414) 935-3015. Web Site:www.vcyamerica.org Licensee: VCY America Inc. ◆Vic Eliason, VP.

KZKK(FM)— 1993: 105.1 mhz; 6 kw. 154 ft TL: N44 21 44 W98 09 09. Hrs open: 5:30 AM-midnight Box 931, 57350. Secondary address: 1835 Dakota Ave. 57350. Phone: (605) 352-1933. Fax: (605) 352-0911. Web Site:www.kokk.com Population served: 35,000 Format: Adult contemp. News staff: one.

Ipswich

KABD(FM)— December 2007: 107.7 mhz; 51 kw. Ant 354 ft TL: N45 27 13 W98 48 10. Hrs open: 426 N. Hwy. 281, Suite 4, Aberdeen, 57401. Phone: (605) 725-5551. Fax: (605) 725-5553. Web Site:www.1077kabd.com Licensee: Dakota Broadcasting LLC (acq 10-31-2007; with KMOM(FM) Roscoe). Population served: 90,000 Format: Adult hits. News staff: 9; News: 6a-5p.

*KAJF(FM)—Not on air, target date: unknown: 88.5 mhz; 20 kw vert. Ant 34 ft TL: N45 26 56.2 W99 15 08.8. Hrs open: 1460 Old Ocean Hwy., Bolivia, NC, 28422. Phone: (910) 368-1581. Licensee: Shining Light Ministries. ◆Joshua Hawkins, pres.

Lake Andes

*KDKO(FM)—Not on air, target date: unknown: 89.5 mhz; 6 kw. Ant 433 ft TL: N43 04 59 W98 28 23. Hrs open: Box 572, 57356. Phone: (605) 487-7072. Fax: (605) 487-7964. Licensee: Native American Community Board Inc. ◆Charon Asetoyer, gen mgr.

Lemmon

KBJM(AM)— Apr 1, 1966: 1400 khz; 1 kw-U. TL: N45 55 05 W102 11 55. Hrs open: 24 Box 540, 57638. Secondary address: 500 First Ave. E. 57638. Phone: (605) 374-5747. Fax: (605) 374-5332. Web Site:www.kbjm.com Licensee: Media Associates Inc. (acq 1-17-91; $108,240; 2-4-91). Population served: 15,000 Natl. Rep: Keystone (unwired net),. Format: C&W, oldies, farm. News: 30 hrs wkly. Target aud: General. ◆Mike Schweitzer, pres, gen mgr & gen sls mgr; James Schwab, progmg dir.

Lennox

KSOO-FM— 2008: 99.1 mhz; 25 kw. Ant 328 ft TL: N43 22 36 W96 48 19. Hrs open: 5100 S. Tennis Ln., Sioux Falls, 57108. Phone: (605) 361-0300. Fax: (605) 361-5410. Licensee: Cumulus Licensing LLC. Natl. Network: ESPN Radio, . Format: Sports. ◆Don Jacobs, gen mgr.

Little Eagle

*KLND(FM)— June 25, 1997: 89.5 mhz; 100 kw. Ant 679 ft TL: N45 44 54 W100 48 30. Stereo. Hrs open: 6 AM-midnight 11420 SD Hwy. 63, McLaughlin, 57642. Phone: (605) 823-4661. Fax: (605) 823-4660.E-mail: info@klndfm.com Web Site:www.klnd.org Licensee: Seventh Generation Media Services Inc. Natl. Network: PRI, . Morrison & Foerster LLP. Format: Var. News staff: one; News: 5 hrs wkly. Target aud: General; tribal people on the Standing Rock & Cheyenne River Nations. Spec prog: Gospel 3 hrs, children 4 hrs, Spo one hr, elders 2 hrs, news/talk 5 hrs wkly. ◆Jana Shields Gipp, chmn; Beau Fontenalla, gen mgr, stn mgr.

Lowry

KMLO(FM)— 1996: 100.7 mhz; 100 kw. 587 ft TL: N45 16 26 W99 58 21. Hrs open:
Rebroadcasts KPLO-FM Reliance 100%.
c/o KMLO-FM, 214 W. Pleasant Dr., Pierre, 57501. Phone: (605) 224-8686. Fax: (605) 224-8984.E-mail: drgprod1@amfmradio.biz Licensee: James River Broadcasting Inc. Group owner: Robert Ingstad Broadcast Properties. Format: Country. ◆Robert Inqstad, pres; Mark A. Swendsen, gen mgr.

*KQSD-FM— 1994: 91.9 mhz; 100 kw. 725 ft TL: N45 16 34 W99 59 03. Hrs open: Box 5000, Vermillion, 57069. Secondary address: 555 N. Dakota St. 57069. Phone: (605) 677-5861. Fax: (605) 677-5010. Web Site:www.sdpb.org Licensee: South Dakota Board of Directors for Educational Telecommunications. Format: Classical, news, pub affrs, jazz. ◆Owen DeJong, progmg dir.

Madison

KJAM(AM)— Dec 3, 1959: 1390 khz; 500 w-D, 62 w-N. TL: N44 00 37 W97 10 18. Hrs open: 18 101 S. Egan Ave., 57042. Phone: (605) 256-4515. Fax: (605) 256-6477.E-mail: info@kjamradio.com Web Site:www.kjamradio.com Licensee: Three Eagles of Brookings Inc. Group owner: Three Eagles Communications (acq 12-8-99; $1.2 million with co-located FM). Population served: 164,000 Format: Soft rock, news/talk. News staff: 13; News: 15 hrs wkly. Target aud: 21 plus. Spec prog: National agriculture talk program 11 hrs wkly. ◆Gary Buchanan, pres; Lorin Larsen, gen mgr, dev dir; Jim Hockett, gen sls mgr; Peg Nordling, progmg dir; Sue Bergheim, news dir; Bob Cook, chief of engrg; Dave Borman, farm dir; Joyce Wiesman, women's int ed.

KJAM-FM— Dec 17, 1967: 103.1 mhz; 33 kw. Ant 305 ft TL: N43 59 08 W97 07 41. Stereo. Hrs open: 24 101 S. Egan Ave., 57042. Phone: (605) 256-4515. Fax: (605) 256-6477.E-mail: manager@kjamradio.com Web Site:www.kjamradio.com Licensee: Three Eagles of Brookings Inc. Population served: 200,000 Format: Country, news. News staff: 2; News: 20 hrs wkly. Target aud: 21 plus. ◆Nicole Nordbye, news rptr; Dan Sudenga, farm dir; James Wyngaard, sports cmtr.

Martin

*KZSD-FM— July 3, 1991: 102.5 mhz; 100 kw. 754 ft TL: N43 26 06 W101 33 14. Hrs open: Box 5000, Vermillion, 57069. Secondary address: 555 N. Dakota St. 57069. Phone: (605) 677-5861. Fax: (605) 677-5010.E-mail: sdpr@sdpb.org Web Site:www.sdpb.org Licensee: South Dakota Board of Directors for Educational Telecommunications. Format: Classical, jazz, folk, news. News staff: 10. ◆Owen DeJong, progmg dir.

Milbank

KCGN-FM—(Ortonville, MN) Sept 23, 1983: 101.5 mhz; 98 kw. Ant 1,000 ft TL: N45 22 29 W97 02 20. Stereo. Hrs open: 24 Box 247, Osakis, MN, 56360. Phone: (320) 859-3000. Fax: (320) 859-3010.E-mail: info@praisefm.org Web Site:www.praisefm.org Licensee: Praise Broadcasting Inc. (acq 10-24-2003). Population served: 500,000 Format: Praise & worship, adult contemp Christian. Target aud: 25-44; middle-aged women. ◆David McIver, gen mgr; Jack Zitzmann, progmg dir, news dir; Sherrie McIver, mus dir; Steve Kneprath, chief of engrg; Michelle Anderson, traf mgr.

KKSD(FM)— Feb 4, 1991: 104.3 mhz; 100 kw. 981 ft TL: N45 10 31 W96 59 15. Stereo. Hrs open: 24 921 9th Ave., Watertown, 57201-4960. Phone: (605) 882-1480. Fax: (605) 886-2121.E-mail: A mneudecker@kwat.threeeagles.com Web Site:www.ksdr.com Licensee: Three Eagles of Joliet Inc. Group owner: Three Eagles Communications (acq 7-1-2004; grpsl). Format: Oldies. Target aud: 25-54. Spec prog: Sports 5 hrs wkly. ◆Nancy Linneman, gen mgr.

KMSD(AM)— Mar 20, 1975: 1510 khz; 5 kw-D, 14 w-N, 1 kw-CH. TL: N45 11 42 W96 38 18. Hrs open: PO Box 1005, 57252. Phone: (605) 432-5516. Fax: (605) 432-4231.E-mail: kmsd@tnics.com Licensee: Armada Media-Watertown Inc. Group owner: Robert Ingstad Broadcast Properties (acq 8-3-2007; grpsl). Population served: 126,000 Rgnl. Network: S.D. News Net., AgriAmerica, S.D. News Net. Wire Svc: UPI Format: News/talk, oldies. Target aud: General. Spec prog: Farm 6 hrs wkly. ◆Jeff Kurtz, gen mgr.

KXLG(FM)— Nov 1, 1972: 99.1 mhz; 37 kw. Ant 564 ft TL: N45 03 55 W96 49 23. Stereo. Hrs open: 1726 Dakota Ave. S., Huron, 57350. Phone: (605) 352-8621. Fax: (605) 352-8622. Web Site:www.performance-radio.com Licensee: Dakota Communications Ltd. Format: Hot country. Target aud: 25-54. ◆Linda Marcus, gen mgr.

Mitchell

KMIT(FM)— Mar 10, 1975: 105.9 mhz; 100 kw. 549 ft TL: N43 41 25 W98 00 27. Stereo. Hrs open: 24 Box 520, 57301. Secondary address: 501 S. Ohlman Place, 57301. Phone: (605) 996-9667. Fax: (605) 996-0013.E-mail: kmit@kmit.com Web Site:www.kmit.com Licensee: Saga Communications of South Dakota LLC. Group owner: Saga Communications Inc. (acq 5-1-2001; $4.05 million with KUQL(FM) Wessington Springs). Population served: 185,000 Format: Modern country. News staff: 2. Target aud: 18-54. Spec prog: Farm 18 hrs wkly. ◆Nikki Frederickson, gen sls mgr; Lisa Youngstrom, prom mgr; Joel VanDover, progmg dir; John Cyr, chief of engrg; Eric Roozen, disc jockey.

KORN(AM)— 1947: 1490 khz; 1 kw-U. TL: N43 42 14 W97 59 57. Hrs open: 24 Box 921, 57301. Secondary address: 319 N. Main 57301. Phone: (605) 996-1490. Fax: (605) 996-6680.E-mail: kornstudio@kornq107.com Licensee: Sorenson Broadcasting Corp. (group owner; (acq 7-1-97; $1.2 million with co-located FM). Population served: 15,000 Natl. Network: Westwood One, ABC, . Wire Svc: AP Format: Talk, news/talk, sports. News staff: one; News: 15 hrs wkly. Target aud: 35 plus; mature adults. Spec prog: Farm 10 hrs wkly. ◆Mary Quass, pres; John Koons, gen mgr, gen sls mgr, news rptr; Clayton Mick, progmg dir; J.P. Skelly, news dir.

KQRN(FM)— Aug 17, 1980: 107.3 mhz; 100 kw. 450 ft TL: N43 41 46 W98 03 35. Stereo. Hrs open: 24 Prog sep from AM Box 921, 57301. Secondary address: 319 N. Main 57301. Phone: (208) 983-1230. Fax: (605) 996-1490. Web Site:q107radio.com Population served: 50,000 Wire Svc: AP Format: Adult Contemp, CHR. News staff: one; News: 4 hrs wkly. Target aud: 10-49; adult female. ◆Steve Morgan, progmg dir.

Mobridge

KOLY(AM)— Aug 10, 1956: 1300 khz; 5 kw-D, 111 w-N. TL: N45 32 07 W100 20 45. Hrs open: 24 Box 400, 118 E. 3rd St., 57601. Phone: (605) 845-3654. Fax: (605) 845-5094.E-mail: koly@westriv.com Licensee: James River Broadcasting Co. Group owner: Robert Ingstad Broadcast Properties (acq 7-8-97; $890,742 with co-located FM). Population served: 50,000 Format: Pop standards. News staff: one; News: 21 hrs wkly. Target aud: General. Spec prog: Farm, American Indian. ◆Mark Swendsen, gen mgr; Dawn Konold, gen sls mgr; John Schreier,

progmg dir; Nate Duehlmeier, news dir; Rolland Cory, chief of engrg; Pat Morrison, sports cmtr; Andy Shumacher, disc jockey.

KOLY-FM— Oct 1, 1973: 99.5 mhz; 56 kw. 560 ft TL: N45 31 50 W100 20 30. (CP: 100 kw, ant 361 ft. TL: N45 32 07 W100 20 45). Stereo. Hrs open: Dups AM 5% Box 400, 118 E. 3rd St., 57601. Phone: (605) 845-3654. Fax: (605) 845-5094.E-mail: koly@westriv.com Format: Adult contemp. ♦Dawn Konold, stn mgr, disc jockey; Cindy Dafnis, opns mgr, traf mgr; John Schreier, news rptr; Nate Duehlmeier, news dir & women's int ed.

Newell

KXZT(FM)—Not on air, target date: unknown: 103.7 mhz; 4.8 kw horiz. Ant 1,492 ft TL: N44 19 40 W103 50 06. Hrs open: 194 McGee Rd., Versailles, KY, 40383. Phone: (859) 879-0818. Licensee: JER Licenses LLC. ♦Jon E. Robinson, gen mgr.

Pierpont

***KDSD-FM**— Apr 1, 1984: 90.9 mhz; 70 kw. 1,057 ft TL: N45 29 55 W97 40 35. Stereo. Hrs open:
Rebroadcasts KUSD(FM) Vermillion.
Box 5000, Vermillion, 57069. Secondary address: 555 N. Dakota St., Vermillion 57069. Phone: (605) 677-5861. Fax: (605) 677-5010.E-mail: sdpr@sdpb.org Web Site:www.sdpb.org Licensee: South Dakota Board of Directors for Educational Telecommunications. Population served: 152,300 Natl. Network: PRI, NPR, . Rgnl. Network: S.D. Pub. S.D. Pub Format: News, class, jazz. News staff: 8. ♦Terry Spencer, dev dir; Owen DeJong, progmg dir.

Pierre

KCCR(AM)— Feb 4, 1959: 1240 khz; 1 kw-U. TL: N44 21 02 W100 19 08. Hrs open: 5:30 AM-midnight 106 West Capital Ave., 57501. Phone: (605) 224-1240. Fax: (605) 224-0095.E-mail: info@todaykccr.com Web Site:todaykccr.com Licensee: Sorenson Broadcasting Corp. (acq 3-1-72). Population served: 15,000 Natl. Network: CBS, . Format: Oldies, News/talk. News staff: 2; News: 24 hrs wkly. Target aud: 35 plus; well-educated, upper income, politically aware business people, retirees, housewives. ♦Dean Sorenson, pres; Steve White, gen mgr; Tanya Martin, gen sls mgr; Dan Myer, progmg dir.

KGFX(AM)— 1927: 1060 khz; 10 kw-D, 1 kw-N, DA-2. TL: N44 17 12 W100 20 18. Hrs open: 24 Box 1197, 57501. Secondary address: 214 W. Pleasant Dr. 57501. Phone: (605) 224-8686. Fax: (605) 224-8984. Web Site:www.dakotaradiogroup.com Licensee: James River Broadcasting. Group owner: Robert Ingstad Broadcast Properties (acq 11-15-68). Population served: 40,000 Natl. Network: ABC, . Rgnl. Network: S.D. News Net. S.D. News Net. Shaw Pittman. Wire Svc: AP Format: Country, farm. News staff: one; News: 20 hrs wkly. Target aud: 25-54. ♦Janice Ingstad, pres; Mark A. Swendsen, gen mgr, gen sls mgr; Paul Rollie, progmg dir; Jeri Thomas, news dir, political ed; Dorene Foster, farm dir.

KGFX-FM— Jan 4, 1982: 92.7 mhz; 3 kw. Ant 245 ft TL: N44 22 15 W100 24 17. Stereo. Hrs open: 24 Box 1197, 57501. Secondary address: 214 W. Pleasant Dr. 57501. Phone: (605) 224-8686. Fax: (605) 224-8984. Licensee: Robert E. Ingstad Properties. Format: Adult contemp. Target aud: 25-49. ♦Patrick Callahan, news rptr.

KLXS-FM— Apr 15, 1981: 95.3 mhz; 49 kw. Ant 299 ft TL: N44 22 15 W100 24 17. Stereo. Hrs open: 106 West Capital Ave., 57501. Phone: (605) 224-7381.E-mail: info@todaykccr.com Licensee: Sorenson Broadcasting Corp. Natl. Network: Westwood One, . Format: Adult contemp. Target aud: 18-34; 55% female, 45% male.

***KVFL(FM)**— 2006: 89.1 mhz; 400 w vert. Ant 371 ft TL: N44 25 33 W100 21 28. Stereo. Hrs open: 24 3434 W. Kilbourn Ave., Milwaukee, WI, 53208-3313. Phone: (414) 935-3000. Fax: (414) 935-3015.E-mail: kvfl@vcyamerica.org Web Site:www.vcyamerica.org Licensee: VCY America Inc. Format: Relg, Christian. ♦Vic Eliason, VP & gen mgr; Jim Schneider, progmg dir.

Pine Ridge

KVAR(FM)— July 2008: Stn currently dark. 93.7 mhz; 12 kw. Ant 479 ft TL: N42 49 47 W102 39 80. Stereo. Hrs open: Box 563, Tanner, AL, 35671. Secondary address: 709 Coleman Ave., Athens, AL 35611. Phone: (256) 497-4502. Fax: (443) 342-2478.E-mail: varietyrock@hotmail.com Licensee: Alleycat Communications. Format: Var rock. Target aud: 18-54. ♦Richard W. Dabney, gen mgr.

***KVKR(FM)**—Not on air, target date: unknown: 88.3 mhz; 10 kw. Ant 436 ft TL: N42 49 47 W102 39 08. Hrs open: Box 563, Tanner, AL, 35671. Phone: (256) 497-4502. Licensee: Southern Cultural Foundation. ♦Richard W. Dabney, gen mgr.

Porcupine

***KILI(FM)**— 1984: 90.1 mhz; 100 kw. Ant 508 ft TL: N43 10 48 W102 19 25. Hrs open: Box 150, 57772. Secondary address: 901 Lamont Ln. 57772. Phone: (605) 867-5002. Fax: (605) 867-5634.E-mail: info@kilifm.com Web Site:www.kiliradio.org Licensee: Lakota Communications Inc. Format: Native American, var. ♦Melanie Janis, gen mgr.

Rapid City

***KASD(FM)**— 2006: 90.3 mhz; 1 kw. Ant 407 ft TL: N44 04 13 W103 15 01. Hrs open:
Rebroadcasts WAFR(FM) Tupelo, MS 100%.
Drawer 2440, Tupelo, MS, 38803. Phone: (662) 844-8888. Fax: (662) 842-6791. Web Site:www.afr.net Licensee: American Family Association. Natl. Network: American Family Radio, . Format: Christian. ♦Marvin Sanders, gen mgr.

KBHB(AM)—See Sturgis

***KBHE-FM**— 1984: 89.3 mhz; 9.8 kw. 410 ft TL: N44 03 09 W103 14 38. Stereo. Hrs open: Box 5000, Vermillion, 57069. Phone: (605) 677-5861. Fax: (605) 677-5010. Web Site:www.sdpb.org Licensee: South Dakota Board of Educational Telecommunications. Population served: 122,500 Natl. Network: PRI, NPR, . Rgnl. Network: S.D. Pub. S.D. Pub Format: Classical Jazz, News. ♦Joe Tlustos, gen mgr.

KFXS(FM)— Apr 11, 1977: 100.3 mhz; 100 kw. 450 ft TL: N44 04 14 W103 15 01. Stereo. Hrs open: 24 Box 2480, 57709. Secondary address: 660 Flormann St., Suite 100 57709. Phone: (605) 343-6161. Fax: (605) 343-9012.E-mail: request@foxradio.com Web Site:www.foxradio.com Licensee: New Rushmore Radio Inc. Group owner: Triad Broadcasting Co. LLC (acq 10-23-2006; grpsl). Natl. Rep: Christal,. Shaw Pittman. Format: Classic rock. News staff: one; News: 3 hrs wkly. Target aud: 25-54. ♦Lia Green, gen mgr; Charlie O'Douglas, opns mgr; Jake Michaels, progmg dir; Kay Duda, traf mgr; Gary Peterson, engr.

KIMM(AM)— Mar 16, 1962: 1150 khz; 5 kw-D, 500 w-N, DA-N. TL: N44 04 35 W103 08 49. Hrs open: Box 2480, 57709. Phone: (605) 343-6161. Fax: (605) 343-9012.E-mail: prod@newrushmore.com Licensee: Aasen Publishing Inc. (acq 2-17-2009; $100,000). Population served: 157,900 Natl. Rep: Christal,. Format: Classic country. Target aud: 35-64. Spec prog: Colorado Rockies baseball, farm one hr wkly. ♦Carson Aasen, pres; Ron Hansen, gen mgr; Gary Peterson, chief of opns, chief of engrg; Michael Goodroad, sls dir; Gail Hanson, gen sls mgr; Wayne Janke, progmg dir, news dir & pub affrs dir; Dan Rahman, disc jockey.

KIQK(FM)— Jan 7, 1992: 104.1 mhz; 100 kw. 515 ft TL: N44 01 50 W103 15 34. Stereo. Hrs open: 24 Box 1680, 57709. Phone: (605) 343-0888. Fax: (605) 342-3075. Format: Country. News staff: one; News: 3 hrs wkly. Target aud: 25-54. ♦Christian Haugo, gen mgr & prom dir.

KKLS(AM)— June 7, 1959: 920 khz; 5 kw-D, 100-N, DA-2. TL: N44 03 43 W103 10 29. Stereo. Hrs open: 24 Box 2480, 57709-2480. Phone: (605) 343-6161. Fax: (605) 343-9012.E-mail: prod@newrushmore.com Web Site:www.kkls.net Licensee: New Rushmore Radio Inc. Group owner: Triad Broadcasting Co. LLC (acq 10-23-2006; grpsl). Population served: 164,100 Natl. Network: Westwood One, . Natl. Rep: Christal,. Wilmer Hale. Wire Svc: AP Format: Oldies. Target aud: 35-64. ♦Lia Green, gen mgr; Charlie O'Douglas, opns mgr; Michael Goodroad, sls dir & gen sls mgr.

KKMK(FM)— 1971: 93.9 mhz; 100 kw. 650 ft TL: N44 02 48 W103 14 46. Stereo. Hrs open: 24 Prog sep from AM Box 2480, 57709. Phone: (609) 343-6161. Fax: (605) 343-9012.E-mail: kkmk@rapidnet.comm Web Site:www.kkmk.com Natl. Rep: Christal,. Wilmer Hale. Wire Svc: AP Format: Adult contemp. Target aud: 25-54.

***KLMP(FM)**— Feb 17, 2005: 88.3 mhz; 63 kw. Ant 1,712 ft TL: N44 19 42 W103 50 03. Hrs open: 1853 Fountain Plaza Dr., 57702. Phone: (605) 342-6822. Fax: (605) 342-0854.E-mail: info@klmp.com Web Site:www.klmp.com Licensee: Bethesda Christian Broadcasting Inc. Natl. Network: Fox News Radio, . Format: Inspirational programs & music. Target aud: 35 plus; general. ♦Tom Schoenstedt, gen mgr; Joe Standish, chief of engrg.

KOTA(AM)— November 1936: 1380 khz; 5 kw-U, DA-N. TL: N44 02 00 W103 11 15. Stereo. Hrs open: 24 Box 1760, 518 St. Joseph St., 57709-1760. Phone: (605) 342-2000. Fax: (605) 721-5732.E-mail: les@dberadio.com Web Site:www.kotaradio.com Licensee: Duhamel Broadcasting Enterprises. (group owner; acq 5-54). Population served: 216,000 Natl. Network: CBS, . Natl. Rep: Katz Radio,. Shaw Pittman. Wire Svc: AP Format: News/talk. News staff: 2; News: 10 hrs wkly. Target aud: 35 plus. ♦William F. Duhamel, pres; Les Tuttle, stn mgr. Co-owned TV: KOTA-TV affil

KOUT(FM)— 1993: 98.7 mhz; 100 kw. 515 ft TL: N44 01 50 W103 15 34. Hrs open: 24 Box 2480, 57709-2480. Secondary address: 660 Flormann St., Suite 100 57701. Phone: (605) 343-6161. Fax: (605) 343-9012.E-mail: prod@newrushmore.com Web Site:www.katcountry.com Licensee: New Rushmore Radio Inc. Group owner: Triad Broadcasting Co. LLC (acq 10-23-2006; grpsl). Population served: 87,000 Natl. Rep: Christal,. Shaw Pittman. Format: Country. Target aud: Adults 25-54. ♦Lia Green, gen mgr; Charlie O'Douglas, opns mgr; Mark Houston, progmg dir; Kay Duda, traf mgr; Gary Peterson, engr.

***KQFR(FM)**— Aug. 5, 2005: 89.9 mhz; 2.3 kw. Ant 1,843 ft TL: N44 19 42 W103 50 03. Hrs open: 24 Family Stations Inc., 4135 Northgate Blvd., Suite 1, Sacramento, CA, 95834. Phone: (916) 641-8191. Fax: (916) 641-8238.E-mail: kebr@jps.net Licensee: Family Stations Inc. (group owner). Format: Relg. ♦Harold Camping, pres; John Rorvik, opns mgr & rgnl sls mgr; Joe Papp, chief of engrg.

KQRQ(FM)— October 2002: 92.3 mhz; 86 kw. Ant 581 ft TL: N44 04 07 W103 15 02. Hrs open: 24 Box 1760, 57709. Phone: (605) 342-2000. Fax: (605) 721-5732.E-mail: leskota@rushmore.com Web Site:www.q923.com Licensee: New Generation Broadcasting LLC. Natl. Rep: Katz Radio,. Wire Svc: AP Format: Classic hits. Target aud: Adults 25-44. ♦Les Tuttle, gen mgr.

KRCS(FM)—See Sturgis

KTOQ(AM)— Sept 26, 1953: 1340 khz; 1 kw-U. TL: N44 04 06 W103 10 11. Hrs open: 24 Box 1680, 306 1/2 E. St. Joseph St., 57709. Phone: (605) 343-0888. Fax: (605) 342-3075. Licensee: Haugo Braodcasting Inc. (group owner; acq 11-20-98; $1.97 million with co-located FM). Population served: 150,000 Natl. Rep: McGavren Guild,. Booth, Freret, Imlay & Tepper. Format: Talk. News staff: 2; News: 3 hrs wkly. Target aud: 35 plus; upscale. Spec prog: Farm 2 hrs wkly. ♦Houston Haugo, CEO, pres; Christian Haugo, VP, gen mgr; Georgia McGaa, gen sls mgr; Brad Anderson, news dir, disc jockey; Rose Jeffert, pub affrs dir; Tracy Krsnak, chief of engrg; Phil Amundson, traf mgr.

KTPT(FM)— Oct 1, 1968: 97.9 mhz; 100 kw horiz. Ant 390 ft TL: N44 02 46 W103 14 41. Stereo. Hrs open: 24 1853 Fountain Plaza Dr., 57702. Phone: (605) 342-6822. Fax: (605) 342-0854.E-mail: info@ktpt.com Web Site:www.979thepoint.com Licensee: Bethesda Christian Broadcasting Inc. Group owner: Bethesda Christian Broadcasting (acq 6-25-96; $350,000). Population served: 65,000 Format: Contemp Christian. ♦Mitch Hildebrandt, pres; Tom Schoenstadt, gen mgr; John Derrek, gen sls mgr; Jennifer Crawford, progmg dir.

KZLK(FM)— 2001: 106.3 mhz; 92 kw. Ant 695 ft TL: N44 04 07 W103 15 02. Stereo. Hrs open: 24 Box 1760, 57709. Phone: (605) 342-2000. Fax: (605) 721-5732.E-mail: leskota@rushmore.com Web Site:www.1063maxfm.com Licensee: Steven E. Duffy. Population served: 90,000 Natl. Rep: Katz Radio,. Shaw Pittman. Wire Svc: AP Format: Jack. Target aud: Adult 25-54. ♦Les Tuttle, gen mgr.

Redfield

KGIM-FM— Apr 7, 1991: 103.7 mhz; 100 kw. Ant 564 ft TL: N45 12 52 W98 40 54. Stereo. Hrs open: 5:30 AM-midnight 13541 386th Ave., Aberdeen, 57401. Phone: (605) 229-3632. Fax: (605) 229-4849. Licensee: Armada Media - Aberdeen Inc. (acq 10-31-2006; grpsl). Format: Country. News staff: one. Target aud: 25-49. ♦Jim Coursolle, pres.

KNBZ(FM)— 1999: 97.7 mhz; 62 kw. Ant 190 ft TL: N44 54 30 W98 19 40. Hrs open: Box 1930, Aberdeen, 57402. Secondary address: 13541 386th Ave., Aberdeen 57401. Phone: (605) 229-3632. Fax: (605) 229-4849.E-mail: info@hubcityradio.com Web Site:www.hubcityradio.com Licensee: Armada Media - Aberdeen Inc. Group owner: Robert Ingstad Broadcast Properties. (acq 10-31-2006; grpsl). Format: Adult contemp. ♦Brian Lundquist, gen mgr; Doc Sebastian, progmg dir.

***KQKD(AM)**— December 1962: 1380 khz; 500 w-D, 140 w-N, DA-2. TL: N44 53 53 W98 30 23. Hrs open: 24 4135 Northgate Blvd., Suite 1, Sacramento, CA, 95834. Phone: (916) 641-8191. Licensee: Family Stations Inc. Group owner: Robert Ingstad Broadcast Properties (acq

11-30-2004; $75,000 with KKAA(AM) Aberdeen). Population served: 12,000 Format: Relg. ♦Harold Camping, pres.

Reliance

KPLO-FM— January 1986: 94.5 mhz; 95 kw. 1,000 ft TL: N43 57 55 W99 36 11. Stereo. Hrs open: 24 214 W. Pleasant Dr., Pierre, 57325. Phone: (605) 734-4000. Phone: (605) 224-8686. Fax: (605) 224-8984.E-mail: drgprod1@amfmradio.biz Licensee: James River Broadcasting Co. Group owner: Robert Ingstad Broadcast Properties (acq 8-21-98; $98,000). Format: Country. Target aud: 25-54. Spec prog: Farm 5 hrs wkly. ♦Mark Swendsen, gen mgr.

***KTSD-FM—** 1984: 91.1 mhz; 100 kw. 1,480 ft TL: N43 57 55 W99 35 56. Stereo. Hrs open:
Rebroadcasts KUSD-FM, Vermillion,SD 89.7%.
Box 5000, Vermillion, 57069. Secondary address: 555 N. Dakota St. , Vermillion 57069. Phone: (605) 677-5861. Fax: (605) 677-5010.E-mail: sdpr@sdpb.org Web Site:www.sdpb.org Licensee: S.D. Board of Educational Telecommunications. Population served: 150,000 Natl. Network: PRI, NPR, . Format: Classical, jazz , news. Spec prog: Sioux one hr wkly. ♦Joe Tlustos, gen mgr; Owen DeJong, progmg dir.

Roscoe

KMOM(FM)— Dec 11, 2007: 105.5 mhz; 100 kw. Ant 456 ft TL: N45 27 13 W98 48 10. Hrs open: 24 426 N. Hwy 281, Suite 4, Aberdeen, 57401. Phone: (605) 725-5551. Fax: (605) 725-5553. Web Site:www.dakotabroadcasting.com Licensee: Dakota Broadcasting LLC (acq 10-31-2007; with KABD(FM) Ipswich). Population served: 100,000 Format: Country. News staff: 9. Target aud: 18-34, 25-54.

Rosebud

***KOYA(FM)—**Not on air, target date: unknown: 88.1 mhz; 51 kw vert. Ant 640 ft TL: N43 13 01 W100 47 28. Hrs open: Box 430, 57570. Phone: (605) 747-2381. Licensee: Rosebud Sioux Tribe. ♦Ronald L. Neiss, gen mgr.

Saint Francis

KINI(FM)—See Crookston, NE

Salem

KIKN-FM— Nov 4, 1993: 100.5 mhz; 100 kw. 981 ft TL: N43 29 18 W97 26 34. Stereo. Hrs open: 24 5100 S. Tennis Ln., Sioux Falls, 57108. Phone: (605) 361-0300. Fax: (605) 361-5410. Web Site:www.kikn.com Licensee: Cumulus Licensing LLC. Group owner: Cumulus Media Inc. (acq 4-1-2004; grpsl). Population served: 350,000 Natl. Rep: Christal,. Format: New country. News staff: one. Target aud: 18-49. ♦Lew Dickey, pres; Don Jacobs, gen mgr; J.D. Collins, progmg dir.

Sioux Falls

***KAUR(FM)—** Oct 9, 1972: Stn currently dark. 89.1 mhz; 680 w. Ant 184 ft TL: N43 31 37 W96 44 18. Stereo. Hrs open: 10 AM-3 AM Box 751, KAUR-FM, Augustana College, 57197. Secondary address: 2001 S. Summit Ave. 57197. Phone: (605) 274-0770. Fax: (605) 336-5465.E-mail: kaurfm@gmail.com Web Site:kaur.augie.edu Licensee: Augustana College Association. Population served: 150,000 Target aud: General. ♦Chuck Carlson, gen mgr.

***KCFS(FM)—** July 1985: 94.5 mhz; 2 kw. Ant 197 ft TL: N43 31 56 W96 44 20. Hrs open: Sioux Falls College, 1101 W. 22nd St., 57105. Phone: (605) 331-6691. Fax: (605) 331-6615.E-mail: kcfs@thecoo.edu Web Site:www.usiouxfalls.edu/campus/radio/index.html Licensee: University of Sioux Falls. Population served: 110,000 Format: Div. Spec prog: Urban 6 hrs wkly. ♦Jesse Logterman, gen mgr; Chris Stafford, stn mgr; Jason Peiser, progmg dir.

***KCSD(FM)—** July 1, 1985: 90.9 mhz; 2.35 kw. 190 ft TL: N43 31 57 W96 44 20. Stereo. Hrs open: 24 1101 W. 22nd St., 57105. Phone: (605) 331-6690. Fax: (605) 331-6692.E-mail: sdpr@sdpb.org Web Site:www.sdpb.org Licensee: University of Sioux Falls. Natl. Network: NPR, . Rgnl. Network: S.D. Pub. S.D. Pub Format: Class. News staff: one; News: 44 hrs wkly. Target aud: 25 plus; educated males & females. Spec prog: Folk 5 hrs, jazz 10 hrs wkly. ♦Janice Davis, stn mgr.

KDLO-FM—See Watertown

KELO(AM)— 1937: 1320 khz; 5 kw-U, DA-N. TL: N43 29 17 W96 38 14. Stereo. Hrs open: 24 Prog sep from FM 500 S. Phillips, 57104. Phone: (605) 331-5350. Fax: (605) 336-0415. Web Site:kelo.com Licensee: Backyard Broadcasting South Dakota Licensee LLC Group owner: Midcontinent Media Inc. Population served: 222,000 Natl. Network: Fox News Radio, . Natl. Rep: Katz Radio,. Format: News/talk, weather. News staff: 6. Target aud: 25-54. ♦Craig R. Hodgson, VP.

KELO-FM— July 11, 1965: 92.5 mhz; 100 kw. Ant 1,820 ft TL: N43 31 07 W96 32 05. Stereo. Hrs open: 24 500 S. Phillips, 57104. Phone: (605) 331-5350. Fax: (605) 336-0415. Web Site:kelofm.com Licensee: Backyard Broadcasting South Dakota Licensee LLC (acq 4-2005; grpsl). Population served: 368,000 Natl. Rep: Katz Radio,. Leventhal, Senter & Lerman. Format: Adult contemp. ♦Barry Drake, pres; Craig Hodgson, gen mgr.

KKLS-FM— March 1975: 104.7 mhz; 100 kw. 860 ft TL: N43 43 46 W97 05 10. Stereo. Hrs open: Prog sep from AM 5100 S. Tennis Ln, 57108. Phone: (605) 361-0300. Fax: (605) 361-5410. Format: Contemp hit. Target aud: 18-49. ♦Lew Dickey, pres; Don Jacobs, stn mgr; Andy Erickson, progmg dir, progmg mgr.

KMXC(FM)— Oct 1, 1973: 97.3 mhz; 60 kw. 221 ft TL: N43 35 48 W96 38 20. Stereo. Hrs open: 5100 S. Tennis Ln., Suite 200, 57108. Phone: (605) 339-1140. Fax: (605) 339-2735. Web Site:www.mix97-3.com Format: Adult contemp. Target aud: 25-44; females. ♦Lew Dickey, pres; Don Jacobs, stn mgr; Scott Maguire, progmg dir.

***KNWC(AM)—** March 1961: 1270 khz; 5 kw-D, 2.3 kw-N, DA-2. TL: N43 17 07 W96 45 53. Hrs open: 24 6300 S. Tallgrass Ave., 57108-8107. Phone: (605) 339-1270. Fax: (605) 339-1271.E-mail: knwc@knwc.org Web Site:www.knwc.org Licensee: Northwestern College. Group owner: Northwestern College & Radio (acq 1961). Population served: 150,000 Bryan Cave. Format: Relg, news. News staff: one; News: 24 hrs wkly. Target aud: 35-54. ♦David Martin, opns dir; Jeff Rupp, gen mgr, progmg dir, local news ed & news rptr.

***KNWC-FM—** Mar 28, 1969: 96.5 mhz; 100 kw. 1,600 ft TL: N43 31 07 W96 32 05. Stereo. Hrs open: 24 Dup AM 50% 6300 S. Tallgrass Ave., 57108. Phone: (605) 339-1270. Fax: (605) 339-1271. Web Site:www.knwc.org Population served: 200,000 Bryan Cave. Format: Christian. News staff: one; News: 24 hrs wkly. Target aud: 20-54. ♦Tim Unsinn, prom dir & progmg dir.

KRRO(FM)— May 6, 1969: 103.7 mhz; 38 kw. Ant 394 ft TL: N43 27 28 W96 40 14. Stereo. Hrs open: 24 500 S. Phillips, 57104. Phone: (605) 331-5350. Fax: (605) 336-0415. Web Site:www.krro.com Licensee: Backyard Broadcasting South Dakota Licensee LLC (acq 4-2005; grpsl). Population served: 220,000 Natl. Rep: Katz Radio,. Shaw Pittman. Wire Svc: AP Format: AOR. Target aud: 25-49; young adults, family-rearing age with disposable income. ♦Barry Drake, pres; Craig Hodgson, gen mgr.

***KRSD(FM)—** May 11, 1985: 88.1 mhz; 2 kw. Ant 183 ft TL: N43 31 37 W96 44 18. Stereo. Hrs open: 24 Box 7011, Collegeville, MN, 56321. Phone: (605) 335-6666. Fax: (320) 363-4948.E-mail: mail@mpr.org Web Site:www.mpr.org Licensee: Minnesota Public Radio. Natl. Network: NPR, PRI, . Format: Class, news. News staff: one. Target aud: General. ♦William H. Kling, pres; Kristi Booth, stn mgr; Mike Edgerly, news dir; Vince Fuhs, chief of engrg.

***KSFS(FM)—** 2006: 90.1 mhz; 1 kw. Ant 57 ft TL: N43 32 41 W96 45 45. Hrs open: 2351 Sunset Blvd., Suite 170-218, Rocklin, CA, 95765. Phone: (916) 251-1600. Fax: (916) 251-1650. Web Site:www.klove.com Licensee: Educational Media Foundation. (acq 1-30-2009; $650,000). Natl. Network: K-Love, . Format: Contemp Christian. ♦Mike Novak, pres.

KSOO(AM)— 1926: 1140 khz; 10 kw-D, 5 kw-N, DA-N. TL: N43 28 47 W96 41 04. Hrs open: 5100 S. Tennis Ln., Suite 200, 57108. Phone: (605) 339-1140. Fax: (605) 339-2735. Web Site:www.ksoo.com Licensee: Cumulus Licensing LLC. Group owner: Cumulus Media Inc. (acq 3-29-2004; grpsl). Population served: 150,000 Natl. Rep: Christal,. Format: News/talk, sports. Target aud: 35-54. ♦Lew Dickey, pres, gen mgr; Don Jacobs, stn mgr; Dave Roberts, progmg dir; Gene Hetland, news dir; Mike Langford, chief of engrg.

KSQB(AM)— June 13, 1970: 1520 khz; 500 w-D. TL: N43 33 28 W96 47 46. Hrs open: 500 South Phillips Ave., 57104. Phone: (605) 331-5350. Fax: (605) 336-0415. Licensee: Backyard Broadcasting South Dakota Licensee LLC. (acq 8-1-2006; grpsl). Population served: 150,000 Natl. Network: Jones Radio Networks, . Natl. Rep: Rgnl Reps,. Law Offices of Richard J. Hayes. Wire Svc: AP Format: Good Times Great Oldies. Target aud: 35-65. ♦Mark Nelson, progmg dir.

KSQB-FM—See Dell Rapids

KTWB(FM)— May 5, 1990: 101.9 mhz; 34 kw. 580 ft TL: N43 45 11 W96 53 22. Stereo. Hrs open: 24 500 S. Phillips Ave., 57104. Phone: (605) 331-5350. Fax: (605) 336-0415.E-mail: ktwb@bybradio.com Web Site:www.ktwb.com Licensee: Backyard Broadcasting South Dakota Licensee LLC. Group owner: Midcontinent Media Inc. (acq 4-2005; grpsl). Population served: 198,530 Natl. Rep: Katz Radio,. Richard Hayes. Wire Svc: AP Format: Country. News staff: one; News: 10 hrs wkly. Target aud: 25-54; adult. ♦Barry Drake, pres; Craig Hodgson, gen mgr.

KWSN(AM)— May 6, 1948: 1230 khz; 1 kw-U. TL: N43 33 31 W96 46 10. Hrs open: 24 500 S. Phillips, 57104. Phone: (605) 331-5350. Fax: (605) 336-0415. Web Site:www.kwsn.com Licensee: Backyard Broadcasting South Dakota Group owner: Midcontinent Media Inc. . Population served: 220,000 Natl. Network: Fox Sports, . Natl. Rep: Katz Radio,. Wire Svc: AP Format: All sports. News staff: 2; News: 27 hrs wkly. Target aud: 25-54; adults with disposable income, business leaders.

KXQL(FM)—See Flandreau

KXRB(AM)— February 1969: 1000 khz; 10 kw-D, DA. TL: N43 29 13 W96 35 48. Hrs open: 24 5100 S. Tennis Ln, 57108. Phone: (605) 361-0300. Fax: (605) 361-5410. Licensee: Cumulus Licensing LLC. Group owner: Cumulus Media Inc. (acq 3-29-2004; grpsl). Population served: 300,000 Natl. Network: CNN Radio, . Rgnl. Network: CNN. Natl. Rep: Christal,. Wire Svc: UPI Format: Country, farm. News staff: one; News: 5 hrs wkly. Target aud: 25-54. ♦Lew Dickey, pres; Don Jacobs, gen mgr; Mike Langford, progmg dir, chief of engrg; Randy McDaniel, progmg dir & mus dir; Jerry Dohmen, news dir.

Sisseton

KBWS-FM— Dec 28, 1983: 102.9 mhz; 100 kw. 496 ft TL: N45 36 52 W97 24 51. Stereo. Hrs open: 509 Veterans Ave., 57262. Phone: (605) 698-3471. Fax: (605) 698-3330.E-mail: kbws@tnics.com Web Site:www.phcountry.com Licensee: Armada Media-Watertown Inc. Group owner: Robert Ingstad Broadcast Properties. (acq 8-3-2007; grpsl). Format: Country. Target aud: General. ♦Jim Coursolle, pres; Jeff Kurtz, gen mgr; Randy Peterson, rgnl sls mgr; John Seiber, progmg dir, news dir; Terry Heitman, pub affrs dir; Don Brittnal, chief of engrg; Jamie Rothe, traf mgr.

Spearfish

***KBHU-FM—** Oct 18, 1974: 89.1 mhz; 100 w. 55 ft TL: N44 29 48 W103 52 13. Stereo. Hrs open: 24 Unit 9003, 1200 University St., 57799. Phone: (605) 642-6011. Phone: (605) 642-6265. Fax: (605) 642-6762.E-mail: kbhufm@hotmail.com Web Site:www.kbhufm.com Licensee: Black Hills State University. Population served: 12,000 Natl. Network: Westwood One, . Wire Svc: AP Format: Alternative. News: 3 hrs wkly. Target aud: 12-35. ♦Dave Diamond, CEO; Kay Schallenkamp, pres; Cody Oliver, gen mgr; Stephen Webb, stn mgr; Cody Holliwell, dev dir; Erica Morris, sls dir; David Martin, progmg dir.

KDDX(FM)— July 19, 1985: 101.1 mhz; 100 kw. 1,604 ft TL: N44 19 40 W103 50 14. (CP: Ant 1,817 ft. TL: N44 19 36 W103 50 12). Stereo. Hrs open: 24 2827 E. Colorado Blvd., 57783. Phone: (605) 642-5747. Fax: (605) 642-7849. Web Site:www.xrock.fm Licensee: Duhamel Broadcasting Enterprises. (group owner; acq 3-16-92; $525,000; 3-30-92). Population served: 150,000 Format: Active rock. News staff: one; News: 3 hrs wkly. Target aud: 18-49. ♦Les Tuttle, gen mgr; Ted Peiffer, gen sls mgr; Jim Kallas, progmg dir.

***KJKT(FM)—**Not on air, target date: unknown: 90.7 mhz; 700 w. Ant 1,643 ft TL: N44 19 42 W103 50 03. Hrs open: 5700 West Oaks Blvd., Rocklin, CA, 95765. Phone: (916) 251-1600. Fax: (916) 251-1650. Licensee: Educational Media Foundation. (acq 3-23-2007; grpsl). ♦Mike Novak, pres.

KSLT(FM)— Feb 17, 1984: 107.3 mhz; 100 kw. 1,702 ft TL: N44 19 36 W103 50 12. Stereo. Hrs open: 24 1853 Fountain Plaza Dr., Rapid City, 57702-9315. Phone: (605) 342-6822. Fax: (605) 342-0854.E-mail: info@kslt.com Web Site:www.kslt.com Licensee: Bethesda Christian Broadcasting Inc. Natl. Network: Fox News Radio, . Format: Contemp Christian. Target aud: 25-49; affluent, educated, 60% female, 40% male. ♦Mitch Hildebrandt, pres; Tom Schoenstadt, gen mgr; John Derrek, rgnl sls mgr; Dave Masters, progmg dir, mus dir; Joe Standish, chief of engrg.

Sturgis

KBHB(AM)— Sept 27, 1962: 810 khz; 21 kw-D. TL: N44 25 23 W103 25 38. Hrs open: Sunrise-sunset Box 99, Hwy. 79 N., 57785. Phone: (605) 347-4455. Fax: (605) 347-5120.E-mail: info@kbham.com Licensee: New Rushmore Radio Inc. Group owner: Triad Broadcasting Co. LLC (acq 10-23-2006; grpsl). Population served: 100,000 Natl. Network:

ABC, . Rgnl. Network: Agri-Net, AgriAmerica. Agrinet Format: Farm. News staff: one; News: 17 hrs wkly. Target aud: 35 plus. Spec prog: American Indian one hr, gospel 3 hrs wkly. ♦Dean Kinney, gen mgr, gen sls mgr; Toni Kinney, opns mgr; Gary Matthews, progmg dir; Gary Maki, news dir; Gary Peterson, chief of engrg.

KRCS(FM)— Dec 5, 1972: 93.1 mhz; 100 kw. 1,059 ft TL: N44 19 58 W103 32 20. Stereo. Hrs open: Prog sep from AM Box 2480, Rapid City, 57709. Phone: (605) 343-6161. Fax: (605) 343-9012.E-mail: prod@newrushmore.com Web Site:www.hot931.com Licensee: New Rushmore Radio Inc. Format: Continuous hit radio. ♦Lia Green, gen mgr; Charlie O'Douglas, opns mgr; Leah Green, sls dir, gen sls mgr; Chad Bower, progmg dir; D. Ray Knight, news dir; Gary Peterson, chief of engrg.

Tulare

***KAMF(FM)**—Not on air, target date: unknown: 91.7 mhz; 10 kw. Ant 192 ft TL: N44 34 03.8 W98 34 07.2. Hrs open: Box 159, Rural Hall, NC, 27045. Phone: (605) 868-0525. Licensee: Church Planters of America. ♦Danny Hawkins, pres & gen mgr.

Vermillion

***KAOR(FM)**— September 1986: 91.1 mhz; 120 w. 107 ft TL: N42 47 01 W96 55 26. Stereo. Hrs open: 18 Contemporary Media & Journalism, 414 E. Clark, 57069-2390. Phone: (605) 677-5477. Fax: (605) 677-4250.E-mail: kaor@usd.edu Web Site:www.usd.edu/kaor Licensee: The University of South Dakota. Population served: 35,000 Cohn & Marks. Format: AOR, CHR, progsv. News: 2 hrs wkly. Target aud: 16-30; college age students & faculty. Spec prog: American Indian 2 hrs wkly. ♦Ramon Chavez, chmn; Kent Osborne, gen mgr; Don Harris, chief of engrg.

***KUSD(FM)**— Oct 1, 1967: 89.7 mhz; 50 kw horiz, 21.5 kw vert. 518 ft TL: N43 03 00 W96 47 12. (CP: 32 kw, ant 663 ft.). Stereo. Hrs open: Box 5000, 57069. Secondary address: 555 N. Dakota St. 57069. Phone: (605) 677-5861. Fax: (605) 677-5010.E-mail: sdpr@sdpb.org Web Site:www.sdpb.org Licensee: South Dakota Board of Directors/Educational Telecommunications. Population served: 150,000 Natl. Network: NPR, PRI, . Rgnl. Network: S.D. Pub. S.D. Pub Format: Classical, news & pub affrs, jazz. Spec prog: Sioux one hr wkly. ♦Julie Anderson, pres; Owen DeJong, gen mgr, progmg dir; Terry Spencer, dev dir. Co-owned TV: *KUSD-TV affil.

KVHT(FM)— Nov 16, 1967: 106.3 mhz; 50 kw. 390 ft TL: N42 59 45 W96 49 25. Stereo. Hrs open: 24 Box 718, Yankton, 57078. Secondary address: 210 W. 3rd St., Yankton 57078. Phone: (605) 665-2600. Fax: (605) 665-8875.E-mail: classichits1063@kvht.com Web Site:www.kvht.com Licensee: Culhane Communications Inc. (acq 5-6-93; $340,000 with co-located AM; 5-24-93). Population served: 350,000 Natl. Network: ABC, . Shaw Pittman. Wire Svc: AP Format: Classic hits 60's, 70's, 80's. News staff: one; News: 42 hrs wkly. Target aud: 25-64. ♦Kevin Culhane, gen mgr, gen sls mgr, chief of engrg; Randy Eichelburg, opns mgr & progmg dir; Joe Van Goor, news dir; Dina Anderson, traf mgr.

KVTK(AM)— Nov 16, 1967: 1570 khz; 500 w-D. TL: N42 47 32 W97 00 03. Stereo. Hrs open: 24 Box 718, Yankton, 57078. Secondary address: 210 W. 3rd St., Yankton 57078. Phone: (605) 665-2600. Fax: (605) 665-8875. Web Site:www.kvtk.com Licensee: Culhane Communications Inc. Population served: 100000 Natl. Network: ESPN Radio, Westwood One, . Format: Sports. News staff: one; News: 20 hrs wkly. Target aud: 25-54; general. ♦Kevin Culhane, CEO; Kevin Culhane, gen mgr; Randy Hammer, opns mgr.

Volga

KJJQ(AM)—Licensed to Volga. See Brookings

KKQQ(FM)—Licensed to Volga. See Brookings

Wall

KXZS(FM)—Not on air, target date: unknown: 107.5 mhz; 100 kw horiz. Ant 479 ft TL: N44 05 50 W102 35 48. Hrs open: 194 McGee Rd., Versailles, KY, 40383. Phone: (859) 879-0818. Licensee: JER Licenses LLC. ♦Jon E. Robinson, gen mgr.

Wasta

***KVSD(FM)**—Not on air, target date: unknown: 88.9 mhz; 100 kw vert. Ant 466 ft TL: N44 02 34 W102 22 46. Hrs open: 3434 W. Kilbourn Ave., Milwaukee, WI, 53208-3313. Phone: (414) 935-3000.E-mail: vcy@vcyamerica.org Licensee: VCY America Inc. ♦Vic Eliason, VP.

Watertown

KDLO-FM— Mar 1, 1968: 96.9 mhz; 100 kw. 1,571 ft TL: N44 57 57 W97 35 22. Stereo. Hrs open: 24 921 9th Ave. S., 57201. Phone: (605) 886-8444. Fax: (605) 886-9306.E-mail: A mneudecker @kwat.threeeagles.com Licensee: Three Eagles of Joliet Inc. Group owner: Three Eagles Communications (acq 7-1-2004; grpsl). Population served: 60,000 Natl. Network: USA, . Format: C&W. News staff: one. Target aud: 25-54. ♦Dean Johnson, gen mgr; Bruce Erlandson, opns mgr.

KIXX(FM)— Sept 29, 1968: 96.1 mhz; 97 kw. Ant 977 ft TL: N45 10 31 W96 59 15. Stereo. Hrs open: 6 AM-1 AM Box 950, 57201. Secondary address: 921 9th Ave S. E. 57201. Phone: (605) 886-9696. Fax: (605) 886-9306.E-mail: A mneudecker@kwat.threeeagles.com Licensee: Three Eagles of Joliet Inc. (acq 7-1-2004; grpsl). Format: Adult contemp. Target aud: 25-54. ♦Curt Crawford, progmg dir.

***KJBB(FM)**— August 2000: 89.1 mhz; 200 w vert. Ant 20 ft TL: N44 53 57 W97 06 18. Hrs open: 24 6704 Highway H. South, Germantown, NC, 27019. Phone: (605) 884-0156.E-mail: dannyhawkins@dailypost.com Web Site:www.kjbbfm.com Licensee: Church Planters of America (acq 7-20-2003). Population served: 20,500 Format: Educational. ♦Ms. Sheila Hawkins, VP; Danny Hawkins, gen mgr.

***KRFW(FM)**—Not on air, target date: unknown: 91.9 mhz; 750 w. Ant 236 ft TL: N44 51 56 W97 06 20. Hrs open: 4604 Airpark Blvd., Duluth, MN, 55811-5751. Phone: (218) 722-3017. Fax: (218) 722-1650.E-mail: airstaff@refugeradio.com Web Site:www.refugeradio.com Licensee: Refuge Media Group. ♦Brett M. Gibson, gen mgr.

KSDR(AM)— Apr 16, 1961: 1480 khz; 1 kw-D, 53 w-N. TL: N44 55 58 W97 06 19. Hrs open: 6 AM-midnight 3 E. Kemp, Suite 300, 57201. Phone: (605) 886-5747. Fax: (605) 886-2121.E-mail: A mnuedecker @kwat.threeeagles.com Licensee: Three Eagles of Brookings Inc. Group owner: Three Eagles Communications (acq 6-19-00; $3.25 million with co-located FM). Population served: 50,000 Tierney & Swift. Format: Talk. News staff: 3; News: 15 hrs wkly. Target aud: 25-54. ♦Gary Buchanan, pres; Dean Johnsson, gen mgr, mus dir.

KSDR-FM— Mar 10, 1992: 92.9 mhz; 97 kw. 977 ft TL: N45 10 31 W96 59 15. Stereo. Hrs open: 24 3 E. Kemp, Suite 300, 57201. Phone: (605) 886-5747. Fax: (605) 886-2121.E-mail: A mneudecker @kwat.threeeagles.com Population served: 100,000 Rgnl. Network: Tribune. Tribune Radio Networks Format: C&W. News staff: one; News: 12 hrs wkly. Target aud: General; rgnl country stn with wide var of ages. Spec prog: Farm 8 hrs, sports 8 hrs wkly.

KWAT(AM)— Mar 8, 1940: 950 khz; 1 kw-U, DA-N. TL: N44 52 12 W97 06 49. Hrs open: 5 AM-midnight Box 950, 57201. Secondary address: 921 9th Ave S. E. 57201. Phone: (605) 886-8444. Fax: (605) 886-9306.E-mail: A mneudecker@kwat.threeeagles.com Licensee: Three Eagles of Joliet Inc. Group owner: Three Eagles Communications (acq 7-1-2004; grpsl). Population served: 15,571 Natl. Network: CBS, . Format: MOR, news, farm. Target aud: 35 plus. ♦Gary Buchanan, pres; Dean Johnson, VP, gen mgr, gen sls mgr; Bruce Erlandson, opns mgr; Mike Blakenship, mus dir; David Law, news dir; Jim Thoreson, farm dir; Todd Enderson, disc jockey.

Wessington Springs

KJRV(FM)— 2005: 93.3 mhz; 65 kw. Ant 623 ft TL: N44 11 39 W98 19 05. Hrs open: 1726 Dakota Ave. S., Huron, 57350. Phone: (605) 352-1933. Phone: (605) 352-8623. Fax: (605) 352-1934.E-mail: mlyon@kokk.com Web Site:www.bigjimrocks.com Licensee: Alpena Broadcasting Co. Format: Classic rock. ♦Linda Marcus, gen mgr; Mike Lyon, gen sls mgr.

KUQL(FM)— 1999: 98.3 mhz; 100 kw. Ant 899 ft TL: N43 45 28 W98 24 39. Hrs open: Box 520, Mitchell, 57301. Secondary address: 501 S. Ohlman, Mitchell 57301. Phone: (605) 996-9667. Phone: (605) 996-1100. Fax: (605) 996-0013. Web Site:www.kool98.com Licensee: Saga Communications of South Dakota LLC. Group owner: Saga Communications Inc. (acq 5-1-2001; $4.05 million with KMIT(FM) Mitchell). Format: Oldies. ♦Tim Smith, gen mgr; Nikki Frederickson, gen sls mgr; Kory Hartman, progmg dir; John Cyr, chief of engrg.

Winner

KWYR(AM)— Sept 27, 1957: 1260 khz; 5 kw-D, 146 w-N. TL: N43 22 57 W99 54 38. Stereo. Hrs open: 24 346 Main St., 57580. Secondary address: Box 491 57580. Phone: (605) 842-3333. Fax: (605) 842-3875.E-mail: 937radio@gwtc.net Web Site:www.kwyr.com Licensee: Midwest Radio Corp. (acq 12-2-2005; $378,000 for stock with co-located FM). Population served: 30,000 Wire Svc: AP Format: Country. News staff: one; News: 14 hrs wkly. Target aud: 25-60. ♦John Driscoll, VP; Scott Schramm, pres & gen mgr.

KWYR-FM— Nov 25, 1971: 93.7 mhz; 100 kw. Ant 560 ft TL: N43 17 46 W99 52 02. Stereo. Hrs open: 24 346 Main St., 57580. Secondary address: Box 491 57580. Phone: (605) 842-3693. Fax: (605) 842-3875. Web Site:www.kwyr.com Licensee: Midwest Radio Corp. Population served: 30,000 Natl. Network: Jones Radio Networks, . Wire Svc: AP Format: Adult contemp, CHR. Target aud: 18-45. ♦John Driscoll, gen sls mgr & engrg dir.

Yankton

KKYA(FM)— May 25, 1982: 93.1 mhz; 100 kw. 469 ft TL: N42 43 49 W97 24 13. Stereo. Hrs open: 24 Prog sep from AM Box 628, 57078. Secondary address: 202 W. 2nd St. 57078. Phone: (605) 665-7892. Fax: (605) 665-0818.E-mail: davelee@kk93.com Web Site:www.kk93.com Population served: 50,000 Waitt Farm Net. Format: Country. News staff: 2; News: 1.5 hrs wkly. ♦Curt Dykstra, gen mgr; Dave Lesher, opns mgr; Cynthia Miller, gen sls mgr; David Leonard, news dir; Tammy Hauger, traf mgr.

***KPCJ(FM)**—Not on air, target date: unknown: 91.9 mhz; 4.5 kw. Ant 403 ft TL: N42 36 33 W97 22 02. Hrs open: 1460 Old Ocean Hwy., Bolivia, NC, 28422. Phone: (910) 368-1581. Licensee: Shining Light Ministries. ♦Joshua Hawkins, pres.

KYNT(AM)— Mar 15, 1955: 1450 khz; 1 kw-U. TL: N42 53 30 W97 25 10. Hrs open: 24 Box 628, 57078. Secondary address: 202 W. 2ndn St. 57078. Phone: (605) 665-7892. Fax: (605) 665-0818.E-mail: kynt1450@kynt1450.com Web Site:www.kynt1450.com Licensee: Sorenson Broadcasting Corp. (group owner; (acq 7-1-73). Population served: 14,500 Natl. Network: ABC, . Waitt Farm Net. Format: Adult contemp. News staff: 2; News: 25 hrs wkly. Target aud: General. Spec prog: Farm 5 hrs, polka one hr, Pol one hr wkly. ♦Curt Dykstra, gen mgr; Dave Lesher, opns mgr; Cynthia Miller, gen sls mgr; Dave Leonard, news dir; Tammy Hauger, traf mgr; Troy Cowman, pub svc dir.

WNAX(AM)— November 1922: 570 khz; 5 kw-U, DA-N. TL: N42 54 47 W97 18 58. Hrs open: 24 1609 E. Hwy. 50, 57078. Phone: (605) 665-7442. Fax: (605) 665-8788.E-mail: wnax@wnax.com Web Site:www.wnax.com Licensee: Saga Communications Inc. (acq 1996). Population served: 3,500,000 Natl. Network: CBS, . Rgnl. Network: MNN. Natl. Rep: Katz Radio,. MNN Smithwick & Belendiuk. Wire Svc: NOAA Weather Wire Svc: Knight-Ridder/Tribune Information Services Format: News/talk, farm. News staff: 4; News: 23 hrs wkly. Target aud: 35 plus; farmers & agri-businesses. Spec prog: Relg 16 hrs, sports 10 hrs, weather 15 hrs, farm news 35 hrs wkly. wkly. ♦Edward Christian, pres; Bill Holst, gen mgr; Steve Crawford, opns mgr; Jim Reimler, progmg mgr, mus dir; Jerry Oster, news dir.

WNAX-FM— Aug 9, 1973: 104.1 mhz; 97 kw. 981 ft TL: N42 38 24 W97 03 21. Stereo. Hrs open: 24 Prog sep from AM 1609 E. Hwy. 50, 57078. Phone: (605) 665-7442. Fax: (605) 665-8788. Web Site:www.wnax.com Licensee: Saga Communications Inc. Population served: 400000 Wire Svc: NOAA Weather Format: Country. News staff: one; News: 3 hrs wkly. Target aud: 25-54.

Tennessee

Alamo

WCTA(AM)— October 1983: 810 khz; 250 w-D, DA. TL: N35 47 59 W89 07 20. Hrs open: Box 246, 14 S. Johnson St., 38001. Phone: (731) 696-2781.E-mail: billy@wcta810.com Licensee: Billy H. Williams (acq 5-1-96; $119,933). Population served: 25,000 Format: News, talk. Target aud: 30 plus. Spec prog: Relg 9 hrs wkly. ♦Billy H. Williams, pres, gen mgr; Billy Williams, progmg mgr; Dave Hacker, chief of engrg.

WWGM(FM)— Aug 10, 1989: 93.1 mhz; 25 kw. 443 ft TL: N35 43 31 W89 03 25. Stereo. Hrs open: 24 25 Stonebrook Pl., Suite G, 322, Jackson, 38305. Phone: (731) 616-4015. Fax: (731) 855-1600.E-mail: lennis931@aol.com Web Site:www.gracebroadcasting.com Licensee: Grace Broadcasting Services Inc. (acq 8-18-97; $800,000). Population served: 150,000 Miller & Miller. Format: Southern gospel, relg. News staff: one; News: 3 hrs wkly. Target aud: 24-54; upscale women. ♦Lacy Ennis, pres & stn mgr.

Alcoa

WBCR(AM)— Aug 25, 1957: 1470 khz; 1 kw-D. TL: N35 47 47 W83 56 17. Hrs open: Box 130, 37701. Secondary address: 118 Defoe Cir. 37701. Phone: (865) 984-1470. Fax: (865) 983-0890.E-mail: truthradioam1470@yahoo.com Licensee: Blount County Broadcasting Co. (acq 2-20-96). Format: News/talk. News staff: one; News: 10 hrs wkly. Target aud: 35+. ♦Harry Grothjahn, gen mgr.

***WYLV(FM)**— Feb 14, 1993: 89.1 mhz; 4.5 kw. 994 ft TL: N36 00 13 W83 56 35. Stereo. Hrs open: 24 1621 E. Magnolia Ave., Knoxville, 37917. Phone: (865) 521-8910. Fax: (865) 521-8923.E-mail: info@love89.org Web Site:www.love89.org Licensee: Foothills Broadcasting Inc. Population served: 600,000 Format: Contemp Christian. ♦David Wells, gen mgr, opns mgr; Marisa Lykins, prom dir; Jonathan Unthank, progmg dir.

Algood

WATX(AM)— Oct 5, 1981: 1590 khz; 1 kw-D, 500 w-N. TL: N36 11 02 W85 25 03. Hrs open: 6 AM-9 PM 259 S. Willow Ave., Cookeville, 38501. Phone: (931) 528-6064. Fax: (931)520-1590.E-mail: jimstapleton @jwcbroadcasting.com Licensee: JWC Broadcasting (group owner; acq 8-3-01). Population served: 150,000 Natl. Network: Salem Radio Network, . Natl. Rep: Rgnl Reps,. Format: Christian. News staff: 2; News: 34 hrs wkly. Target aud: General. Spec prog: Gospel. ♦Jim Stapleton, gen mgr.

Ashland City

WQSV(AM)— July 14, 1982: 790 khz; 2 kw-D, 35 w-N. TL: N36 17 08 W87 05 00. Hrs open: Box 619, 37015-0619. Secondary address: 208 1/2 N. Main St. 37015-1316. Phone: (615) 792-6789. Fax: (615) 792-7795.E-mail: wqsvradio@bellsouth.net Web Site:www.wqsvam790.com Licensee: Sycamore Valley Broadcasting Inc. (acq 12-20-91; $55,000; 1-13-92). Natl. Network: ABC, . Rgnl. Network: Tenn. Radio Net. Tenn. Radio Net. Format: Var. News staff: 4. Target aud: General. ♦Richard Albright, CEO, gen mgr & stn mgr.

Athens

WJSQ(FM)— Dec 1, 1979: 101.7 mhz; 7.5 kw. 528 ft TL: N35 31 19 W84 27 29. Stereo. Hrs open: 24 Prog dups AM 100% 2110 Oxnard Rd., 37303. Phone: (423) 745-1000. Fax: (423) 745-2000.E-mail: 1017wlar@bellsouth.net Web Site:www.1017wlar.com Format: Country.

WLAR(AM)— May 15, 1946: 1450 khz; 1 kw-U. TL: N35 26 44 W84 36 43. Hrs open: 24 2110 Oxnard Rd., 37303. Phone: (423) 745-1000. Fax: (423) 745-2000.E-mail: 1017wlar@bellsouth.net Web Site:www.1017wlar.com Licensee: James C. Sliger. (acq 4-18-83; $200,000; 5-9-83). Population served: 18,600 Format: Contemp country. Spec prog: Farm 2 hrs wkly. ♦James Sigler, gen mgr & gen sls mgr.

WJSQ(FM)— Dec 1, 1979: 101.7 mhz; Dec 1, 1979. Dec 1, 1979 TL: Dec 1, 1979. Dec 1, 1979. Stereo. 24 Prog dups AM 100% 2110 Oxnard Rd., 37303. Phone: (423) 745-1000. Fax: (423) 745-2000.E-mail: 1017wlar@bellsouth.net Web Site:www.1017wlar.com Format: Country.

WYXI(AM)— Oct 5, 1966: 1390 khz; 2.5 kw-D, 62 w-N. TL: N35 26 48 W84 34 19. Hrs open: 6 AM-7 PM Box 1390, 112 E. Madison Ave., 37371-1390. Phone: (423) 746-1390. Fax: (423) 744-1390.E-mail: wyxi@bellsouth.net Web Site:wyxi.com Licensee: Cornerstone Broadcasting Inc. (acq 9-11-86; $75,000; 7-21-86). Population served: 48,000 Natl. Network: ABC, . Rgnl rep: Rgnl Reps Fletcher, Heald & Hildreth, PLC. Format: Talk. News staff: one; News: 10 hrs wkly. Target aud: 25-64; mature middle class. Spec prog: Black one hr, relg 8 hrs wkly. ♦Bob Ketchersid, VP, opns dir, progmg dir; Mark Lefler, pres & stn mgr.

Atwood

WTKB-FM— 1992: 93.7 mhz; 6 kw. Ant 328 ft TL: N35 57 25 W88 41 44. (CP: 15 kw, ant 325 ft). Hrs open: 24 25 Stonebrook Place, Suite G, 322, Jackson, 38305. Phone: (731) 616-4015. Fax: (731) 855-1600.E-mail: lennis931@aol.com Licensee: Grace Broadcasting Services Inc. Group owner: Thunderbolt Broadcasting Co./Gibson County Broadcasting (acq 1-7-2005; grpsl). Population served: 350,000 Format: Christian music. ♦Lacy Ennis, gen mgr.

Bartlett

WMFS-FM— May 1994: 92.9 mhz; 6 kw. Ant 328 ft TL: N35 10 20 W89 56 40. Hrs open: 24 1835 Moriah Woods Blvd., Bldg. 1, Memphis, 38117. Phone: (901) 726-0555. Phone: (901) 767-0104. Fax: (901) 725-5101. Web Site:www.680wsmb.com Licensee: Entercom Memphis License LLC. Group owner: Infinity Broadcasting Corp. (acq 11-30-2007; grpsl). Population served: 1,000,000 + Natl. Network: ESPN Radio, . Natl. Rep: Interep,. Leventhal, Senter & Lerman. Wire Svc: Metro Weather Service Inc. Format: Sports. ♦Terry Wood, pres, VP & gen mgr; Kory Myers, gen sls mgr; Scott Speropoulas, natl sls mgr; Rob Cressman, progmg dir.

WMPS(AM)—Licensed to Bartlett. See Memphis

Baxter

WBXE(FM)— October 1995: 93.7 mhz; 25 kw. 328 ft TL: N36 18 53 W85 32 00. Hrs open: 24 259 S. Willow Ave., Cookeville, 38501. Phone: (931) 528-6064. Fax: (931) 520-1590.E-mail: jstapleton @jwcbroadcasting.com Web Site:www.brock937.com Licensee: JWC Broadcasting (group owner; acq 8-29-01). Natl. Network: Westwood One, . Natl. Rep: Rgnl Reps,. Format: Rock. News staff: one. Target aud: 18-45; Men 25 plus. ♦Jim Stapleton, gen mgr.

Bells

WNWS(AM)—See Brownsville

Benton

WBIN(AM)— May 18, 1977: 1540 khz; 1 kw-D, 2 w-N, 500 w-CH. TL: N35 11 15 W84 38 13. (CP: 1 kw-D, 4 w-N, 500 w-CH. TL: N35 10 50 W84 38 34). Hrs open: Sunrise-sunset 108 Lifestyle Way, 37307. Phone: (423) 338-2864.E-mail: craig@craigharding.com Licensee: John A. Sines and L. Jane Sines, JTWROS (acq 12-29-99; $79,000). Population served: 100,000 ABN Radio Format: Relg. Target aud: All ages; Includes baby boomers and seniors. ♦Chris Harding, gen mgr, progmg dir & disc jockey.

WSAA(FM)— November 1996: 93.1 mhz; 5 kw. Ant 358 ft TL: N35 05 40 W84 53 45. Stereo. Hrs open: 24 Box 9170, Chattanooga, 37412. Phone: (423) 485-8987. Fax: (423) 485-8946. Licensee: LB Radio of Chattanooga, LLC Format: Sp hits. Target aud: 25-54. Spec prog: Pub affrs 2 hrs, talk, Univ. of Tennessee sports, loc sports wkly.

***WTSE(FM)**— 2005: 91.1 mhz; 8.5 kw vert. Ant 466 ft TL: N35 19 25 W84 17 54. Hrs open: Box 5459, Twin Falls, ID, 83303. Phone: (208) 733-3551. Fax: (208) 734-0674. Web Site:www.edgewaterbroadcasting.com Licensee: Radio Assist Ministry Inc. (acq 9-13-2004; $1 for CP). Sciarrino & Associates. ♦Clark Parrish, pres.

Berry Hill

WVOL(AM)— December 1951: 1470 khz; 5 kw-D, 1 kw-N, DA-2. TL: N36 12 01 W86 46 47. Hrs open: 24 1320 Brickchurch Pike, Nashville, 37207. Phone: (615) 226-9510. Fax: (615) 226-0709.E-mail: wvol1470@aol.com Web Site:www.wvol1470.com Licensee: Heidelberg Broadcasting LLC. (acq 4-24-00). Population served: 1,636,000 Format: Classic oldies, rhythm and blues. Target aud: 25-54; relg. Spec prog: Gospel 6 hrs wkly. ♦John Heidelberg, chmn, pres, gen mgr, gen sls mgr, min affrs dir; Roderick M. Heidelberg, opns mgr, progmg dir; Watt Harriston, chief of engrg; Betty Fykes, traf mgr.

Blountville

WXSM(AM)— Sept 20, 1967: 640 khz; 10 kw-D, 810 w-N, DA-N. TL: N36 31 19 W81 25 25. Stereo. Hrs open: 24 Box 8668, Gray, 37615. Phone: (423) 477-1000. Fax: (423) 477-4747.E-mail: SportsMonster@640wxsm.com Web Site:www.640wxsm.com Licensee: Citadel Broadcasting Co. Group owner: Citadel Broadcasting Corp. (acq 5-30-2000; grpsl). Population served: 500,000 Natl. Network: ESPN Radio, . Natl. Rep: Dora-Clayton,. Format: Sports. ♦Bill Meade, pres, progmg dir; Don Raines, gen mgr; Debbie Caso, sls dir; Paul Overbay, gen sls mgr; Al LeFevre, chief of engrg.

Bolivar

WBOL(AM)— Oct 19, 1962: 1560 khz; 250 w-D. TL: N35 15 30 W88 58 50. Hrs open: Box 191, 123 W. Market, 38008. Phone: (731) 658-3633. Phone: (731) 658-3690. Fax: (731) 658-3408.E-mail: wojg@aeneas.net Licensee: Shaw's Broadcasting Co. Format: Blues, light jazz, oldies. ♦Johnny W. Shaw, gen mgr; Dewayne Dickerson, gen sls mgr; Opal Shaw, progmg dir.

WMOD(FM)— Jan 27, 1975: 96.7 mhz; 3 kw. 300 ft TL: N35 15 00 W88 53 28. Stereo. Hrs open: 24 PO Box 438, 38008. Phone: (731) 658-4320. Fax: (731) 658-7328. Fax: (731) 658-4320.E-mail: wmo@newwavecomm.net Licensee: WMOD Inc. (acq 6-17-97; $320,000). Natl. Network: ABC, . Rgnl. Network: Tenn. Radio Net. Tenn. Radio Net. Rgnl rep: Midsouth. Format: Country. News: 7 hrs wkly. Target aud: 25-55; males & females. ♦D. Richard Teubner, pres, gen mgr; Gail R. Teubner, opns mgr & traf mgr.

WOJG(FM)— June 1992: 94.7 mhz; 6 kw. 328 ft TL: N35 16 39 W88 55 41. Hrs open: Box 191, 123 W. Market, 38008. Phone: (731) 658-3633. Fax: (731) 658-3408.E-mail: wojg@aeneas.net Licensee: Johnny W. Shaw & Opal J. Shaw. Format: Gospel. ♦Dwayne Dickerson, opns dir & sls dir; Dave Hacker, chief of engrg.

Brentwood

WNSR(AM)— Sept 4, 1985: 560 khz; 4.5 kw-D, 75 w-N, DA-2. TL: N35 54 32 W86 46 13. Hrs open: 1815 Division St., Suite 110, Nashville, 37203. Phone: (615) 844-1039. Fax: (615) 777-2284.E-mail: info@wnsr.com Web Site:www.wnsr.com Licensee: Southern Wabash Communications Middle Tennessee Inc. Group owner: Southern Wabash Communications Corp. (acq 11-25-97; $245,000). Format: Sports. Target aud: 18-54; men. ♦Ted Johnson, gen mgr.

Bristol

***WHCB(FM)**— Aug 10, 1984: 91.5 mhz; 1.5 kw. Ant 2,326 ft TL: N36 26 03 W82 08 03. Stereo. Hrs open: 24 Box 2061, 37621-2061. Secondary address: 340 Edgemont Ave., Suite 100 37620. Phone: (423) 878-6279. Fax: (423) 878-6520.E-mail: whcb@aecc.org Web Site:www.whcbradio.org yes Licensee: Appalachian Educational Communication Corp. Population served: 2,000,000 Natl. Network: Moody, Salem Radio Network, . Format: Talk, educ, Christian. News staff: one; News: 14 hrs wkly. Target aud: General. Spec prog: Class one hr, Appalachian culture 2 hrs, farm one hr, folk one hr, Sp one hr, Jewish one hr, black 3 hrs, children 10 hrs, gospel 15 hrs wkly. ♦Kenneth C. Hill, pres & gen mgr.

WIGN(AM)— Aug 18, 1962: 1550 khz; 5 kw-D, 6 w-N. TL: N36 33 58 W82 09 30. Hrs open: Sunrise-sunset Box 68, 37621. Phone: (276) 591-5800. Fax: (276) 591-5278.E-mail: wignradio@bvunet.net Web Site:www.wignradio.com Licensee: Sunshine Broadcasters Inc. (acq 8-4-2005; $245,000 for stock). Population served: 520,000 Format: Southern gospel. News: 3 hrs wkly. Target aud: 25-54 yrs. ♦Rick Mitchell, gen mgr.

WKPT(AM)—See Kingsport

WOPI(AM)— June 15, 1929: 1490 khz; 1 kw-U. TL: N36 35 45 W82 09 42. Hrs open: 24 222 Commerce St., Kingsport, 37660. Secondary address: 288 Delaney St. 37620. Phone: (423) 764-5131. Fax: (423) 246-6261. Fax: (423) 247-9836.E-mail: davidw@wtfm.com Web Site:www.wopi.com Licensee: Holston Valley Broadcasting Corp. Group owner: Glenwood Communications Corp. (acq 5-16-96; $140,000; 5-7-90). Population served: 200,000 Natl. Rep: McGavren Guild,. Cordon & Kelly. Format: Oldies. News staff: 2. Target aud: 35 plus. ♦George DeVault, pres; Bettte Lawson, CFO; David Widener, exec VP, gen mgr; Aaron Teffeteller, progmg dir, pub affrs dir.

WQUT(FM)—See Johnson City

WXBQ-FM— 1945: 96.9 mhz; 67 kw. 2,200 ft TL: N36 25 59 W82 08 11. Stereo. Hrs open: Box 1389, VA, 24203. Secondary address: 901 E. Valley Dr., VA 24201. Phone: (276) 669-8112. Fax: (276) 669-0541.E-mail: info@wxbq.com Web Site:www.wxbq.com Licensee: Bristol Broadcasting Inc. Group owner: Nininger Stations Population served: 188,600 Natl. Rep: McGavren Guild,. Format: Country. Target aud: 25-54. ♦W.L. Nininger, pres; Pete Nininger, gen mgr; Winnie Quaintance, gen sls mgr; Roger Bowldin, prom dir, prom mgr; Bruce Clark, progmg dir; George Dixon, news dir; Chuck Lawson, chief of engrg.

Brownsville

WNWS(AM)— Oct 14, 1963: 1520 khz; 250 w-D. TL: N35 36 30 W89 14 40. Hrs open: Sunrise-sunset Box 198, 42 S. Washington Ave. 2nd Floor, 38012. Phone: (731) 772-3700. Phone: (731) 423-8316. Fax: (731) 423-8304. Licensee: The Wireless Group Inc. (group owner; acq 4-80; $320,000 with co-located FM;3-31-80). Population served: 20,000 Natl. Network: ABC, . Format: Sp Talk. ♦Carlton Veirs, pres, gen mgr; Tanya Garcia, progmg dir.

***WRRI(FM)**—Not on air, target date: unknown: 88.3 mhz; 500 w. Ant 125 ft TL: N35 35 33 W89 14 50. Hrs open: 2351 Sunset Blvd., Suite 170-218, Rocklin, CA, 95765. Phone: (916) 251-1600. Fax: (916) 251-1650. Licensee: Educational Media Foundation. (acq 11-1-2006; grpsl). ♦Richard Jenkins, pres.

WTBG(FM)— Nov 9, 1965: 95.3 mhz; 5 kw. 150 ft TL: N35 36 30 W89 14 40. (CP: 6 kw, ant 328 ft.). Stereo. Hrs open: 24
Rebroadcasts WNWS-FM Jackson 30%.
Box 198, 42 S. Washington Ave., TX, 38012. Phone: (901) 772-3700. Web Site:www.brownsvilleradio.com Licensee: The Wireless Group Inc. Wyatt, Tarrant & Combs. Format: Country, news/talk. News staff: one. Target aud: 25-54. ♦Carlton Veirs, CEO & gen mgr.

Bulls Gap

WBGQ(FM)— 2001: 100.7 mhz; 6000 w. Ant 1,260 ft TL: N36 22 48 W83 10 47. Stereo. Hrs open: 24 Cherokee Broadcasting System, Box 519, Morristown, 37815. Phone: (423) 235-4640.E-mail: www.wbgqfm@planetc.com Web Site:wjdtfm@planetc.com Licensee: Cherokee Broadcasting (acq 5-14-2008). Population served: 500,000 Natl. Network: CNN Radio, . Format: Rhythm mix. Target aud: 18-54; female 65% & male 35%. ♦Clark Quillen, CEO, gen mgr; David Quillen, opns VP.

Byrdstown

WLSQ(FM)—Not on air, target date: unknown: 98.9 mhz; 1.1 kw. Ant 760 ft TL: N36 29 26 W85 01 47. Hrs open: 224 Charleston Ln., Unit 102, Crossville, 38555. Phone: (931) 248-4360. Licensee: Brandon Tollett (acq 8-29-2007; $100,000 for CP). ♦Brandon Tollett, gen mgr.

Calhoun

WCLE-FM— August 1993: 104.1 mhz; 2.3 kw. Ant 522 ft TL: N35 15 59 W84 50 23. Stereo. Hrs open: 24 Box 2695, Cleveland, 33730. Secondary address: 1860 Executive Park, Suite E, Cleveland 37312. Phone: (423) 472-6700. Fax: (423) 476-4686.E-mail: info@mymix1041.com Licensee: Hartline LLC (group owner; (acq 12-7-2007; $2.1 million with WCLE(AM) Cleveland). Format: Adult contemp. News staff: one. Target aud: 25-54. ♦Steve Hartline, gen mgr.

Camden

WFWL(AM)— Sept 18, 1956: 1220 khz; 250 w-D, 140 w-N. TL: N36 03 10 W88 05 15. Hrs open: 24 Box 539, 117 Vicksburg Ave., 38320. Phone: (731) 584-7570. Phone: (731) 584-4444. Fax: (731) 584-7553.E-mail: wfwlwrjb@bellsouth.net Web Site:www.morningcoffeebreak.com Licensee: Community Broadcasting Services Inc. (acq 4-30-98; $767,000 exercise of option with co-located FM). Population served: 45,000 Rgnl. Network: Tenn. Radio Net. Natl. Rep: Keystone (unwired net),. Tenn. Radio Net. Rgnl rep: Midsouth. Miller & Fields, P.C. Format: C&W. Target aud: 25-49; adult. Spec prog: Gospel 8 hrs wkly. ♦Stan Medlin, pres; Ron Lane, gen mgr, gen sls mgr, prom mgr; Jim Hart, progmg dir, news dir, disc jockey; Larry Nunnery, engrg mgr; Bobby Melton, disc jockey.

WRJB(FM)— June 20, 1976: 98.3 mhz; 3 kw. Ant 300 ft TL: N36 03 25 W88 06 10. Stereo. Hrs open: 24 Box 539, 117 Vicksburg Ave., 38320. Phone: (731) 584-7570. Phone: (731) 584-4444. Fax: (731) 584-7553.E-mail: wfwlwrjb@bellsouth.net Licensee: Community Broadcasting Services Inc. Population served: 372,000 Format: Adult contemp. News: 4 hrs wkly. Target aud: 20-50. ♦Stan Medlin, pres, CFO; Charles Ennis, exec VP; Larry Nannery, engrg VP; Vickie Dodson, traf mgr; Jim Hart, disc jockey.

Carthage

WRKM(AM)— June 20, 1959: 1350 khz; 1 kw-D, 91 w-N. TL: N36 14 42 W85 56 44. Hrs open: 12 Box 179, 37030. Secondary address: 104 Z Country Ln. 37030. Phone: (615) 735-1350. Fax: (615) 735-0381.E-mail: am1350@smithcounty.com Web Site:www.wucz-wrkm.com Licensee: Wood Broadcasting Inc. (acq 8-20-2007; $500,000 for stock). Population served: 250,000 Natl. Network: Sporting News Radio Network, . Rgnl. Network: Tenn. Radio Net. Format: Sports. News staff: one; News: 2 hrs wkly. Target aud: 35 plus. ♦Dennis M. Banka, pres; John Wood, gen mgr, gen sls mgr; Dennis Banka, prom dir, progmg dir; Carl Campbell, chief of engrg; Tracy Banka, traf mgr.

WUCZ(FM)— July 18, 1975: 104.1 mhz; 6 kw. 300 ft TL: N36 18 43 W85 57 08. Stereo. Hrs open: 24 Prog sep from AM Box 179, 37030. Secondary address: 104 Z Country Ln. 37030. Phone: (615) 735-1350. Fax: (615) 735-0381.E-mail: z104@smithcounty.com Web Site:www.wucz-wrkm.com Population served: 500,000 Natl. Network: Westwood One, . Rgnl. Network: Tenn. Radio Net. Format: Country. News staff: one; News: 2 hrs wkly. Target aud: 18-35. ♦John Wood, stn mgr, opns mgr; Tracy Banka, traf mgr.

Celina

WVFB(FM)— August 1994: 101.5 mhz; 6 kw. 328 ft TL: N36 33 15 W85 36 39. Stereo. Hrs open: 24 341 Radio Station Rd., Tompkinsville, KY, 42167. Phone: (270) 487-6119. Fax: (270) 487-8462.E-mail: wtky@alltel.net Licensee: Paul Burrow, Executor. Population served: 329,321 Natl. Network: USA, . Natl. Rep: Rgnl Reps,. Format: Sports talk. News staff: 2; News: 2 hrs wkly. Target aud: Male 18-55. ♦Jeff Wix, gen mgr, gen sls mgr.

Centerville

WNKX(AM)— Nov 16, 1955: 1570 khz; 5 kw-D, 77 w-N. TL: N35 45 29 W87 27 35. Hrs open: 24 25 Stonebrook Pl., Suite G #322, Jackson, 38305. Phone: (731) 664-9497. Fax: (731) 661-9064.E-mail: info@gracebroadcasting.com Web Site:www.gracebroadcasting.com Licensee: Grace Broadcasting Services Inc. (acq 11-1-2008; $75,000). Population served: 20,000 Rgnl. Network: Tenn. Radio Net. Sciarrino & Shubert PLLC. ♦Charles Ennis, pres.

WNKX-FM— May 1974: 96.7 mhz; 6 kw. 300 ft TL: N35 49 39 W87 34 02. Stereo. Hrs open: 24 Dups AM 50% Box 280, 37033. Phone: (931) 729-5191. Fax: (931) 729-5467.E-mail: kix96fm@bellsouth.net Web Site:www.countrykix96.com Licensee: Hickman County Broadcasting Co. Inc. Population served: 100,000 Natl. Rep: Dora-Clayton,. Tenn. Radio Net. Rgnl rep: Midsouth McCampbell & Young. Format: Country. News staff: 3; News: 30 hrs wkly. Target aud: 6-80. ♦Mickey Bunn, opns mgr, asst music dir, news rptr, farm dir; Steve Turner, stn mgr & progmg mgr; Brent Atkinson, disc jockey.

Chattanooga

WDEF(AM)— Dec 31, 1940: 1370 khz; 5 kw-U, DA-N. TL: N35 02 25 W85 20 22. Hrs open: 24 2615 Broad Street, 37408. Secondary address: 2615 S. Broad St. 37408. Phone: (423) 321-6200. Fax: (423) 321-6270.E-mail: dhoward@wdefradio.com Licensee: Bahakel Communications. Population served: 366,100 Natl. Network: Fox Sports, . Format: News/talk, Sports. Target aud: 25-64; males. ♦Jeff Fontana, gen sls mgr.

WDEF-FM— Sept 15, 1964: 92.3 mhz; 100 kw. 1,180 ft TL: N35 08 06 W85 19 25. Stereo. Hrs open: 24 2615 Broad Street, 37408. Secondary address: 2615 Broad St. 37408. Phone: (423) 321-6200. Fax: (423) 321-6270.E-mail: info@sunny923.com Licensee: Bahakel Communications (group owner; acq 1996; grpsl). Population served: 750,000 Natl. Network: CBS, . Format: Adult Contemporary. News staff: one; News: 5 hrs wkly. Target aud: 25-54; upscale adults. ♦Bernie Barker, gen mgr; Danny Howard, progmg dir.

WDOD(AM)— Apr 13, 1925: 1310 khz; 5 kw-U, DA-N. TL: N35 04 54 W85 20 14. Hrs open: 24 2615 Broad Street, 37408. Secondary address: 2615 Broad St. 37408. Phone: (423) 321-6200. Fax: (423) 321-6270. Web Site:chattanoogaradioadvertising.com Licensee: WDOD of Chattanooga Inc. Group owner: Bahakel Communications (acq 6-62). Population served: 250,000 Format: Oldies. Target aud: 35 plus; empty nesters. ♦Bernie Barker, gen mgr; Jeff Fontana, gen sls mgr.

WDOD-FM— February 1960: 96.5 mhz; 100 kw. 1,080 ft TL: N35 09 39 W85 19 11. Stereo. Hrs open: Prog sep from AM 2615 Broad Street, 37408. Phone: (423) 321-6200. Fax: (423) 321-6270.E-mail: dhoward@wdefradio.com Web Site:www.965themountain.com Population served: 375,000 Format: Top 40. Target aud: 18-54; upscale, contemp adults. ♦Jeff Fontana, gen sls mgr.

***WDYN-FM**— June 1, 1968: 89.7 mhz; 100 kw. 205 ft TL: N35 10 17 W85 18 58. Stereo. Hrs open: 24 1815 Union Ave., 37404. Phone: (423) 493-4382. Phone: (423) 493-4383. Fax: (423) 493-4526.E-mail: wdyn@wdyn.com Web Site:www.wdyn.com Licensee: Tennessee Temple University. Population served: 1,300,000 Natl. Network: USA, . Format: Relg. News staff: one; News: 2 hrs wkly. Target aud: General; conservative Christians. ♦Tommy L. Sneed, gen mgr & opns dir.

WFLI(AM)—See Lookout Mountain

WGOW(AM)— 1936: 1150 khz; 5 kw-D, 1 kw-N, DA-N. TL: N35 04 05 W85 20 04. Hrs open: Box 11202, 37401. Secondary address: 821 Pineville Rd. 37405. Phone: (423) 756-6141. Fax: (423) 266-3629. Web Site:www.wgow.com Licensee: Citadel Broadcasting Co. Group owner: Citadel Broadcasting Corp. (acq 5-30-00; grpsl). Population served: 174,000 Natl. Rep: Christal,. Reddy, Begley & McCormick. Format: News/talk. ♦Dan Brown, pres, VP & gen mgr; Bill Lockhart, progmg dir.

WGOW-FM—(Soddy-Daisy, July 14, 1977: 102.3 mhz; 6 kw. 287 ft TL: N35 11 45 W85 13 45. Stereo. Hrs open: Box 11202, 37401. Secondary address: 821 Pineville Rd. 37405. Phone: (423) 756-6141. Fax: (423) 266-3629. Web Site:www.wgow.com Licensee: Citadel Broadcasting Co. Group owner: Citadel Broadcasting Corp. (acq 5-30-00; grpsl). Format: News/talk. Target aud: 18-54; baby boomers. ♦Dan Brown, gen mgr; Kennard Yamada, sls dir, sls dir, gen sls mgr; Bill Lockhart, progmg dir; Kevin West, news dir; Dave Fisher, chief of engrg.

WJBP(FM)—See Red Bank

WJOC(AM)— July 4, 1948: 1490 khz; 1 kw-U. TL: N35 03 07 W85 16 24. Hrs open: 805 Chickamauga Ave., Rossville, GA, 30741. Phone: (706) 861-0800. Phone: (888) 963-9562. Fax: (706) 861-2299. Web Site:www.joy1490.com Licensee: Sara Margarett Fryar. (acq 8-11-97; $230,000). Population served: 500,000 Natl. Network: USA, . Format: Southern gospel, Christian mus. ♦Trey Searcy, gen mgr.

WJTT(FM)—See Red Bank

WLMR(AM)— 1961: 1450 khz; 1 kw-U. TL: N35 02 54 W85 16 26. Hrs open: 24 3809 Ringgold Rd., 37412. Phone: (423) 624-4200. Fax: (423) 624-4722.E-mail: wlmr@wilkinsradio.com Web Site:www.wilkinsradio.com Licensee: Grace Media Inc. Population served: 475,000 Natl. Network: USA, . Womble, Carlyle, Sandridge & Rice. Format: Christian teaching/talk. Target aud: 35 plus. ♦Bob Wilkins, pres; LuAnn J. Wilkins, exec VP, VP; John M. Burks, stn mgr; Greg Garrett, opns mgr, prom VP; Mitchell Mathis, VP & progmg dir; Charlie Edwards, chief of engrg, engr.

***WMBW(FM)**— Aug 1, 1969: 88.9 mhz; 100 kw. 1,505 ft TL: N34 57 43 W85 22 40. Stereo. Hrs open: 24
WMKW 89.3FM; WFCM 91.7FM; WFCM-AM710.
Box 73026, 37407. Secondary address: 1920 E. 24th St. PL. 37404. Phone: (423) 629-8900. Fax: (423) 629-0021.E-mail: wmbw@moody.edu Web Site:www.wmbw.org Licensee: Moody Bible Institute of Chicago. (group owner; acq 5-18-73). Population served: 500,000 Natl. Network: Moody, . Southmayd & Miller. Format: Educ, relg. News: 12 hrs wkly. Target aud: 25-54. Spec prog: Black one hr wkly. ♦Edward Cannon, pres; Leighton LeBoeuf, gen mgr, mktg dir; Andy Napier, prom dir, progmg dir, mus dir, spec ev coord; Paul Martin, mus dir; Kate Klos, news dir, disc jockey; David Morais, chief of engrg; Jim Young, news rptr.

WMPZ(FM)—(Ringgold, GA) Jan 1, 1995: 93.7 mhz; 4.9 kw. 302 ft TL: N34 53 51 W85 10 25. Hrs open: 24 1305 Carter St., 37402. Phone: (423) 265-9494. Fax: (423) 266-2335.E-mail: info@power94.com Web Site:groove93.com Licensee: J.L. Brewer Broadcasting L.L.C. (acq 11-96). Natl. Network: ABC, . Natl. Rep: D & R Radio,. Format: Urban adult contemp. Target aud: 25-54; adults. ♦Jim Brewer II, pres, VP, gen mgr; Keith Landecker, opns mgr.

WNOO(AM)— June 1951: 1260 khz; 5 kw-D. TL: N35 03 08 W85 16 22. Hrs open: 24 Box 5597, 37406-0597. Phone: (423) 698-8617. Fax: (423) 698-8796. Web Site:www.wnooradio.com Licensee: Clear Media LLC Group owner: Willis Broadcasting Corp. (acq 11-17-2006). Population served: 465,161 Natl. Network: American Urban, . Format: Gospel, talk. News staff: 8. Target aud: 25-54; mature Black adults & children. ♦Lee Clear, pres & gen mgr.

WRXR-FM—See Rossville, GA

WSKZ(FM)— November 1960: 106.5 mhz; 100 kw. 1,080 ft TL: N35 09 42 W85 19 06. Stereo. Hrs open: Prog sep from AM Box 11202, 37401. Secondary address: 821 Pineville Rd. 37405. Phone: (423) 756-6141. Fax: (423) 266-3629. Web Site:www.wskz.com Format: Adult rock. ♦Kelly McCoy, progmg dir.

WSMC-FM—See Collegedale

***WUTC(FM)**— March 1980: 88.1 mhz; 30 kw. 889 ft TL: N35 12 28 W85 16 46. (CP: 30 kw). Stereo. Hrs open: 24 615 McCallie Ave., 37403. Phone: (423) 425-4756. Fax: (423) 425-2379. Web Site:www.wutc.org Licensee: Board of Trustees of University of Tennessee. Population served: 460,000 Natl. Network: NPR, PRI, AP Radio, . Format: Information, AAA. Target aud: General. ♦John McCormack, gen mgr; Ken Dryden, dev dir, sls dir; Mark Colbert, progmg dir.

Church Hill

WEYE(FM)—(Surgoinsville, November 1990: 104.3 mhz; 4.1 kw. Ant 397 ft TL: N36 32 05 W82 47 52. Stereo. Hrs open: 24 Box 128, 37642. Secondary address: 439 Richmond St. 37642. Phone: (800) 450-1043. Fax: (423) 357-3635.E-mail: dsandz@yahoo.com Web Site:www.eagle1043fm.com Licensee: ASRadio LLC (acq 6-21-2005; $1.2 million). Population served: 50,000 Natl. Network: USA, . Natl.

Rep: Rgnl Reps,. Bryan Cave. Format: Country. ♦David W. DeFranzo, stn mgr & progmg dir; Daryl Smith, chief of engrg.

WMCH(AM)— May 8, 1954: 1260 khz; 1 kw-D. TL: N36 31 15 W82 44 54. Hrs open: Box 128, 37642. Phone: (423) 357-5601. Fax: (423) 357-3635.E-mail: wmchradio@yahoo.com Web Site:www.wmch.us Licensee: Tri-City Radio L.L.C. (acq 10-11-2001). Population served: 150,000 Natl. Network: USA, . Format: Southern gospel, relg teaching. Target aud: 25-54; adult audience. ♦Randall Seaver, gen mgr.

Clarksville

***WAPX-FM**— Oct 1, 1984: 91.9 mhz; 6 kw. Ant 194 ft TL: N36 32 13 W87 21 26. Stereo. Hrs open: 24 Box 4627, Austin Peay State Univ., 37044. Phone: (931) 221-7378. Fax: (931) 221-7265. Web Site:www.apsu.edu/comm_thea/student_activities/wapxfm.htm Licensee: Austin Peay State University. Population served: 100,000 Format: Consistently Diverse. News: 8 hrs wkly. Target aud: 18-34; college students & young professionals. Spec prog: Black 6 hrs, jazz 6 hrs wkly. ♦Dr. David Michael von Palko, gen mgr.

***WAYQ(FM)**— Oct 22, 2003: 88.3 mhz; 14 kw. Ant 745 ft TL: N36 17 36 W87 18 21. Hrs open: 24 1095 W. McEwen Dr., Franklin, 37067. Phone: (615) 261-9293. Fax: (615) 261-3967. Web Site:www.wayfm.com Licensee: WAY-FM Media Group Inc. (group owner). Format: Christian hit radio. ♦Teresa White, dev dir; Jeff Brown, progmg dir.

WJZM(AM)— Oct 19, 1941: 1400 khz; 1 kw-U. TL: N36 30 57 W87 20 57. Hrs open: 24 Box 648, 37040. Secondary address: 925 Martin St. 37040. Phone: (931) 645-6414. Fax: (931) 551-8432.E-mail: 14jzm@wjzm.com Web Site:www.wjzm.com Licensee: Cumberland Radio Partners Inc. Population served: 115,000 Format: News/talk, sports. News: 8 hrs wkly. Target aud: 25-60; blue collar, working women, businessmen. Spec prog: Relg. ♦Hank Bonecutter, gen mgr, gen sls mgr, news dir; John Bastin, opns mgr; Ivan Davis, chief of engrg; Angie Brown, disc jockey.

WKFN(AM)— Nov 12, 1954: 540 khz; 1 kw-D, 54.5 w-N. TL: N36 32 28 W87 19 33. Hrs open: 24 1640 Old Russelville Pike, 37043. Phone: (931) 648-7720. Fax: (931) 648-7769. Licensee: Saga Communications of Tuckessee L.L.C. Group owner: Saga Communications Inc. (acq 2-1-2001; grpsl). Population served: 158,200 Format: Sports/talk. News staff: 2; News: 36 hrs wkly. Target aud: 25-54. ♦Katie Gambill, gen mgr; Scott Chase, opns dir & progmg dir.

WQZQ(AM)— Jan 24, 1980: 1550 khz; 2.5 kw-D, 250 w-N, DA-N. TL: N36 32 12 W87 22 24. Hrs open: 24 Box 290099, Nashville, 37217. Phone: (931) 645-1550. Fax: (615) 361-9873.E-mail: akamer@cromwell.radio.com Licensee: Winston Communications Inc. Group owner: The Cromwell Group Inc. (acq 10-17-91). Pepper & Corazzini. Format: Black gospel, talk. Target aud: 24-56; talk radio audience. ♦Bayard Walters, pres; Tincy Crouse, gen mgr; David Wilson, opns mgr.

Cleveland

WBAC(AM)— June 18, 1945: 1340 khz; 1 kw-U. TL: N35 09 54 W84 51 13. Hrs open: 24 2640 Commerce Drive N.E., 37311. Phone: (423) 242-7656. Fax: (423) 472-5290. Web Site:www.wbacradio.com Licensee: East Tennessee Radio Group III L.P. Group owner: Brewer Broadcasting Corp. (acq 5-30-2008; grpsl). Population served: 88,850 Natl. Network: ABC, . Rgnl. Network: Tenn. Radio Net. Natl. Rep: D & R Radio,. Tenn. Radio Net. Format: News/talk. News staff: one; News: 16 hrs wkly. Target aud: 35-64. ♦Charles Sells, gen mgr; John Holland, gen sls mgr; Corky Whitlock, progmg dir; Mike Powers, opns mgr & news dir.

WCLE(AM)— May 2, 1957: 1570 khz; 5 kw-D, 84 w-N. TL: N35 10 55 W84 50 55. Hrs open: Box 2695, 37320. Phone: (423) 472-6700. Fax: (423) 476-4686.E-mail: info@mymix1041.com Web Site:www.1570wcle.com Licensee: Hartline LLC (group owner; (acq 12-7-2007; $2.1 million with WCLE-FM Calhoun). Population served: 100,000 Fletcher, Heald & Hildreth. Format: News/talk. Target aud: 25-54. ♦Steve Hartline Jr., pres.

WSMC-FM—See Collegedale

WUSY(FM)— Aug 1, 1961: 100.7 mhz; 100 kw. 1,191 ft TL: N35 12 26 W85 17 10. Stereo. Hrs open: 24 7413 Old Lee Hwy., Chattanooga, 37421. Phone: (423) 892-3333. Fax: (423) 899-7224. Fax: (423) 642-9329.E-mail: jcruze@clearchannel.com Web Site:www.us101country.com Licensee: Capstar TX L.P. Group owner: Clear Channel Communications Inc. (acq 8-7-2000; grpsl). Format: Contemp country. ♦Sammy George, gen mgr; Rhonda Rollins, gen sls mgr; Jay Cruze, progmg dir; Ed Buice, news dir; Andre Johnson, chief of engrg; Vick Grabitt, traf mgr.

Clifton

WLVS-FM— 2002: 106.5 mhz; 3.8 kw. Ant 416 ft TL: N35 28 41 W88 06 36. Hrs open:
Rebroadcasts WXFL(FM) Florence 100%.
624 Sam Philips St., Florence, AL, 35630. Phone: (256) 764-8121. Fax: (256) 764-8169. Web Site:www.kix96country.com Licensee: Gold Coast Broadcasting Co. (acq 8-3-00; $75,000 for 51% of CP). Format: Country. ♦Nick Martin, gen mgr; Rocky Reich, sls dir; Fletch Brown, progmg mgr; Greg Pace, chief of engrg.

Clinton

***WDVX(FM)**— November 1997: 89.9 mhz; 200 w. 1,960 ft TL: N36 11 53 W84 13 51. Hrs open: Box 27568, Knoxville, 37927. Phone: (865) 494-2020. Fax: (865) 494-3299.E-mail: mail@wdvx.com Web Site:www.wdvx.com Licensee: Cumberland Communities Communications Corp. Format: Americana music. ♦Tony Lawson, gen mgr.

***WYFC(FM)**— July 4, 1966: 95.3 mhz; 540 w. 669 ft TL: N36 04 21 W84 01 18. Stereo. Hrs open: 24 11530 Carmel Commons Blvd., Charlotte, NC, 28226-3976. Phone: (704) 523-5555. Fax: (704) 522-1967.E-mail: bbn@bbnradio.org Web Site:www.bbnradio.com Licensee: Bible Broadcasting Network Inc. (group owner; acq 8-18-89; $450,000; 9-5-89). Format: Traditional Christian. ♦Lowell Davey, pres; Hank Crull, gen mgr; Grant Bishop, stn mgr.

WYSH(AM)— November 1960: 1380 khz; 1 kw-D, 500 w-N, DA-N. TL: N36 06 48 W84 08 30. Stereo. Hrs open: 24 Box 329, 37717. Secondary address: 111 Hillcrest Dr. 37716. Phone: (865) 457-1380. Fax: (865) 457-4440.E-mail: ron@merle.com Web Site:www.wyshradio.com Licensee: Clinton Broadcasters Inc. (acq 6-10-91; 11-19-90). Population served: 518,000 Natl. Network: AP Radio, . Rgnl. Network: Tenn. Radio Net. Natl. Rep: Keystone (unwired net),. Tenn. Radio Net. Format: Classic country. News staff: one; News: 15 hrs wkly. Target aud: 25-54; families, blue collar to upper income. Spec prog: Relg 15 hrs wkly. ♦Ronald C. Meredith Jr., pres, gen mgr & opns mgr.

Coalmont

WSGM(FM)— June 21, 1994: 104.7 mhz; 1 kw. 548 ft TL: N35 20 22 W85 46 10. Stereo. Hrs open: 6 AM-10 PM Box 1269, Fire Tower Rd., Tracy City, 37387. Phone: (931) 592-7777. Fax: (931) 592-7778.E-mail: wsgmfm@hotmail.com Licensee: Cumberland Communication Corp. Population served: 25,100 Donald E. Martin. Format: Div, relg, gospel. News: 30 hrs wkly. Target aud: General; interested in community affrs. ♦Dr. Byron Harbolt, pres, exec VP, stn mgr; Sam Harbolt, sr VP; Geniveve Harbolt, VP; Tom Wiseman, chief of engrg; Gina Brady, disc jockey.

Collegedale

***WSMC-FM**— November 1961: 90.5 mhz; 100 kw. 554 ft TL: N35 01 20 W85 04 32. (CP: 1,029 ft. TL: N35 15 20 W85 13 34). Stereo. Hrs open: Box 870, 37315. Phone: (423) 236-2905. Fax: (423) 236-1905. Web Site:www.wsmc.org Licensee: Southern Adventist University. Population served: 3,000 Natl. Network: PRI, NPR, . Format: Class, news. Target aud: 25-54. ♦Gordon Bietz, pres; David Brooks, gen mgr; Myrna Ott, opns dir & opns mgr.

Collierville

WCRV(AM)— Oct 1, 1966: 640 khz; 50 kw-D, 500 w-N, DA-N. TL: N34 59 35 W89 53 58. Hrs open: 24 6401 Poplar Ave., Suite 640, Memphis, 38119. Phone: (901) 763-4640. Fax: (901) 763-4920. Licensee: Bott Broadcasting. (group owner) Natl. Network: USA, . Natl. Rep: Salem,. Format: Christian info. Target aud: 25-54; family oriented. ♦Richard P. Bott, pres; Richard Bott II, VP; Shirley Gossett, opns mgr; Todd Payne, gen mgr & gen sls mgr; Byron Tyler, progmg dir.

Collinwood

WMSR-FM— July 1991: 94.9 mhz; 7.7 kw. Ant 594 ft TL: N35 01 46 W87 47 07. Hrs open: 24 509 N. Main St., Tuscumbia, 35674. Phone: (256) 383-2525. Fax: (256) 383-4450.E-mail: thechief@star94.net Web Site:www.star94.net Licensee: Urban Radio Licenses LLC (acq 12-3-2007; $1.2 million). Population served: 250,000 Natl. Network: Fox News Radio, . Natl. Rep: Katz Radio,. Fletcher, Heald & Hildreth PLC. Format: CHR. News: 8 hrs wkly. Target aud: 18-49; primary women, secondary adults. ♦Kevin Wagner, gen mgr; Derrick Robbinson, gen sls mgr; Kevin Whoreton, prom dir; Jon Marte, progmg dir.

Colonial Heights

WPWT(AM)— Dec 31, 1984: 870 khz; 10 kw-D. TL: N36 27 40 W82 27 12. Hrs open: Sunrise-sunset Box 2061, Bristol, 37621. Secondary address: 340 Edgemont Ave., Suite 100, Bristol 3720. Phone: (423) 878-6279. Fax: (423) 878-6520.E-mail: wpwt@aecc.org Web Site:www.powertalk870.com Licensee: Information Communications Corp. (acq 6-29-2001). Population served: 2,000,000 Natl. Network: Fox News Radio, Salem Radio Network, Talk Radio Network, Premiere Radio Networks, . Format: talk radio. News staff: one; News: 5 hrs wkly. Target aud: Adults 25-54. Spec prog: Health Education one hr wkly. ♦Kenneth C. Hill, gen mgr; Rusty Cury, sls VP; Jerome Jackson III, prom dir; Mathew Hill, progmg dir; Art Countiss, news dir.

WRZK(FM)— Apr 4, 1997: 95.9 mhz; 7.4 kw. Ant 1,253 ft TL: N36 31 36 W82 35 13. Stereo. Hrs open: 24 222 Commerce St., Kingsport, 37660. Phone: (423) 246-9578. Fax: (423) 247-9836.E-mail: scott@hvbcgroup.com Web Site:www.wrzk.com Licensee: Holston Valley Broadcasting Corp. (acq 8-14-2008; $3.65 million). Population served: 396,400 Natl. Network: ABC, . Natl. Rep: McGavren Guild,. Law office of Dennis J. Kelly. Format: Active rock. News staff: 2. Target aud: 18-44; general. ♦David Widener, exec VP, gen mgr; Tim Loy, gen sls mgr; Scott Onks, progmg dir; Duane Nelson, news dir.

Columbia

***WAYM(FM)**— 1992: 88.7 mhz; 16.5 kw. 508 ft TL: N35 49 27 W86 49 28. Stereo. Hrs open: 24 1095 W. McEwen Dr., Franklin, 37067. Phone: (615) 261-9293. Fax: (615) 261-3967.E-mail: wayfm@wayfm.com Web Site:www.wayfm.com Licensee: WAY-FM Media Group Inc. (group owner; acq 3-13-91;4-1-91). Population served: 1,209,000 Format: Christian hit radio. Target aud: 12-34; females. ♦Teresa White, dev dir; Jeff Brown, progmg.

WKOM(FM)— Jan 1, 1967: 101.7 mhz; 4.1 kw. Ant 400 ft TL: N35 37 04 W87 02 34. Stereo. Hrs open: 24 Box 1377, 38402. Secondary address: 315 W. 7th St. 38401. Phone: (931) 388-3636. Fax: (931) 381-1017. Licensee: Middle Tennessee Broadcasting Co. (acq 9-1-72). Population served: 200,000 Natl. Network: Motor Racing Net, ABC, . Format: Pure gold. News staff: one; News: 8 hrs wkly. Target aud: 30-50. ♦Robert McKay III, CEO.

WKRM(AM)— Nov 25, 1946: 1340 khz; 1 kw-U. TL: N35 36 38 W87 03 22. Hrs open: 24 Box 1377, 38402. Secondary address: 315 W. 7th St. 38401. Phone: (931) 388-3636. Fax: (931) 381-1017. Licensee: Robert M. McKay III. (acq 12-26-89). Population served: 75,000 Natl. Network: ABC, Motor Racing Net, Premiere Radio Networks, . Format: Adult contemp. News staff: one; News: 8 hrs wkly. Target aud: 25-54. Spec prog: Relg 4 hrs wkly. ♦Robert M. McKay III, pres & gen mgr.

WMCP(AM)— Nov 12, 1956: 1280 khz; 5 kw-D, 500 w-N, DA-N. TL: N35 37 08 W86 58 52. Hrs open: 24 Box 711, 38402. Secondary address: 1st Farmer & Merchants Bank Bldg., 816 S. Garden, Suite 306 38401. Phone: (931) 388-3241. Fax: (931) 381-2510.E-mail: wmcp@edge.net Licensee: Maury County Boosters Corp. (acq 12-79). Population served: 261,998 Rgnl. Network: Tenn. Radio Net. Tenn. Radio Net. Format: Country. News staff: one; News: 13 hrs wkly. Target aud: 18 plus. Spec prog: Farm 4 hrs weekly. ♦Edna Williford, pres; Mack Shaw, VP & gen mgr.

WMRB(AM)— Aug 14, 1982: 910 khz; 500 w-D, 88 w-N. TL: N35 36 24 W87 01 30. Hrs open: 1014 S. Garden St., 38401. Phone: (931) 381-7100. Fax: (931) 381-0088. Web Site:www.wmrb910am.som Licensee: Ogilvie Family Ministries Inc. (acq 7-3-97; $50,000). Natl. Rep: Dora-Clayton,. Format: Gospel, Black, relg. Target aud: General; Christian families. ♦Trent Ogilvie, gen mgr & opns mgr.

Cookeville

WGIC(FM)— Mar 26, 1964: 98.5 mhz; 50 kw. Ant 492 ft TL: N36 08 34 W85 28 02. Stereo. Hrs open: 20 698 S. Willow Ave., 38501. Phone: (931) 526-7144. Fax: (931) 528-8400.E-mail: email@magic985.com Web Site:www.magic985.com Licensee: Cookeville Communications LLC. (acq 5-30-2008; grpsl). Natl. Network: ABC, . Natl. Rep: Clear Channel,. Format: Hot adult Contemp. News staff: one; News: 8 hrs wkly. ♦Marty McFly, progmg dir; Helen Daniels, traf mgr.

WGSQ(FM)— Mar 8, 1963: 94.7 mhz; 100 kw. 1,319 ft TL: N36 10 26 W85 20 37. Stereo. Hrs open: 24 698 S. Willow, 38501. Phone: (931) 526-7144. Fax: (931) 528-8400. Licensee: Cookeville Communications LLC. (acq 5-30-2008; grpsl). Population served: 1,500,000 Format: Country. News staff: 2; News: 28 hrs wkly.

***WHRS(FM)**— Oct 1, 1996: 91.7 mhz; 500 w. 384 ft TL: N36 08 34 W85 28 02. Hrs open:
Rebroadcasts WPLN(FM) 90.3, Nashville; 100%.

630 Mainstream Dr., Nashville, 37228-1204. Phone: (615) 760-2903. Fax: (615) 760-2904.E-mail: info@wpln.org Web Site:www.wpln.org Licensee: Nashville Public Radio. Format: Class, news. Spec prog: Bluegrass one hr, song writers one hr wkly. ♦William Ivey, chmn; Robert Gordon, gen mgr.

WHUB(AM)— July 20, 1940: 1400 khz; 1 kw-U. TL: N36 10 25 W85 30 40. Hrs open: 24 698 S. Willow Ave., 38501. Phone: (931) 526-7144. Fax: (931) 528-8400. Licensee: Cookeville Communications LLC. Group owner: Clear Channel Communications Inc. (acq 5-30-2008; grpsl). Population served: 50,000 Natl. Network: CBS, . Rgnl. Network: Tenn. Radio Net. Tenn. Radio Net. Format: Classic country, Southern gospel. News staff: one; News: 18 hrs wkly. Target aud: General. Spec prog: Sports 10 hrs, gospel 11 hrs wkly. ♦Dave Thomas, gen mgr; Marty McFly, opns dir; Jim Stapleton, sls dir, natl sls mgr; Lehra Heidel, mktg dir; Lehar Heidel, prom dir; Jim Herrin, news dir; Mike Dinger, mus dir & chief of engrg; Jennifer Henson, traf mgr.

WPTN(AM)— July 10, 1962: 780 khz; 1 kw-D. TL: N36 09 30 W85 31 15. Hrs open: 698 S. Willow, 38501. Phone: (931) 526-7144. Fax: (931) 528-8400. Licensee: Cookeville Communications LLC. Group owner: Clear Channel Communications Inc. (acq 5-30-2008; grpsl). Population served: 80,000 Natl. Rep: Clear Channel,. Dow, Lohnes & Albertson. Format: News/talk. Target aud: General. ♦David Roederer, gen mgr; Bruce Welker, sls VP; Lehra Mayfield, prom VP; Marty Selby, progmg VP; Jim Herrin, news dir; Dave Johnson, pub affrs dir.

***WTTU(FM)**— May 22, 1972: 88.5 mhz; 2.25 kw. 168 ft TL: N36 10 26 W85 30 12. (CP: 2 kw horiz, ant 164 ft.). Stereo. Hrs open: 24/7 Box 5113, University Ctr., Dixie Ave., 38505. Phone: (931) 372-3688. Fax: (931) 372-6225.E-mail: davewttu@gmail.com Web Site:www.tntech.edu/wttu Licensee: Tennessee Technological University. Population served: 60,000 Format: Alternative. News staff: one; News: 5 hrs wkly. Target aud: 14-25. Spec prog: Jazz, Metal, American, Folk, Rap represented with specialty shows.

***WWOG(FM)**— 1994: 90.9 mhz; 40 kw. Ant 697 ft TL: N36 11 05 W85 22 30. Hrs open: 24
Rebroadcasts WSGP(FM) Glasgow, KY and WTHL(FM) Somerset, KY 100%.
Box 1423, Somerset, KY, 42502. Secondary address: 93 Rainbow Terr., Somerset 42503. Phone: (606) 679-6300. Fax: (606) 679-1342.E-mail: dcradio@alltel.net Web Site:www.kingofkingsradio.net Licensee: Somerset Educational Broadcasting Foundation. Format: Conservative, traditional relg, educ. ♦David Carr, gen mgr; Carolyn Jones, progmg dir; Marvin Whittaker, chief of engrg.

Copperhill

WLSB(AM)— Dec 2, 1958: 1400 khz; 1 kw-U. TL: N34 58 04 W84 19 39. Hrs open: 6 AM-10 PM
Simulcast with WYHG(AM) Young Harris, GA.
Box 430, 37317. Phone: (423) 496-3311. Fax: (423) 496-2635.E-mail: info@wlsb.com Web Site:www.wolfcreekbroadcasting.com Licensee: Copper Basin Broadcasting Co., Inc. (acq 9-26-2002). Format: Country, bluegrass. ♦Rebecca St. John, stn mgr.

Covington

WKBL(AM)— Aug 16, 1954: 1250 khz; 800 w-D, 106 w-N. TL: N35 35 10 W89 38 35. Hrs open: 24 101 WKBL Dr., 38019. Phone: (901) 476-7129. Fax: (901) 476-7120.E-mail: billy.thomas@us51country.com Web Site:www.us51country.com Licensee: Covington Broadcasting Inc., LMA in 2007 by 51 Radio, Inc. (acq 2-22-99; $600,000 with co-located FM). Population served: 100,000 Natl. Network: Jones Radio Networks, . Rgnl. Network: Tenn. Radio Net. Tenn. Radio Net. Rgnl rep: N/A Format: Classic country. News staff: one; News: 14 hrs wkly. Target aud: 35 - 64. Spec prog: Black 4 hrs wkly. ♦Gloria Thomas, gen mgr; Gary Murdock, progmg dir.

WKBQ(FM)— Aug 31, 1965: 93.5 mhz; 6 kw. Ant 328 ft TL: N35 35 12 W89 38 21. Stereo. Hrs open: 24 101 WKBL Dr., 38019. Phone: (901) 476-7129. Fax: (901) 476-7120.E-mail: david.lane@us51country.com Web Site:www.us51country.com Licensee: Covington Broadcasting Inc. 4/1/99 Population served: 170,000 Natl. Network: AP Radio, Jones Radio Networks, . Tenn. Radio Net. Rgnl rep: N/A Format: Today's Country. News staff: one; News: 6.5 hrs wkly. Target aud: 18 - 54; Adults. Spec prog: University of Tennessee Football, University of Memphis Basketball, Local High School Football. ♦Gary Murdock, progmg dir.

Cowan

WZYX(AM)— Mar 10, 1957: 1440 khz; 5 kw-D, 100 w-N. TL: N35 09 39 W86 01 51. Stereo. Hrs open: 24 540 W. Cumberland St., 37318-0398. Phone: (931) 967-7471. Phone: (931) 967-7472. Fax: (931) 962-1440.E-mail: wzyxradio@bellsouth.net Web Site:www.wzyxradio.com Licensee: Tims Ford Broadcasting Co. Inc. (acq 4-26-2004). Population served: 50,000 Natl. Network: CNN Radio, . Wire Svc: NOAA Weather Format: Country, oldies, talk. News staff: one; News: 15 hrs wkly. Target aud: 35-55; middle-of-the-road working people. Spec prog: Talk, gospel 10 hrs, farm 2 hrs, relg 12 hrs wkly. ♦Jeff Pennington, VP; Mary Lou Garner, CEO, pres & stn mgr.

Crossville

WAEW(AM)— 1952: 1330 khz; 1 kw-D. TL: N35 56 59 W85 02 08. (CP: TL: N35 57 01 W85 02 09). Hrs open: 24 961 Miller Ave., 38555. Phone: (931) 707-1102. Fax: (931) 707-1220. Web Site:www.1330waew.com Licensee: Peg Broadcasting Crossville LLC (group owner; acq 10-1-2003; grpsl). Population served: 35,000 Natl. Network: ABC, . Format: Talk. News staff: 2; News: 13 hrs wkly. Target aud: 35-64; adult. ♦Jeff Shaw, gen mgr, mktg mgr; Gordon Stack, opns mgr; Steve Sweeney, sls dir; Christy Lewis, news dir; Kendra Williams, traf mgr; Houston McDavitt, engr.

WCSV(AM)— June 15, 1968: 1490 khz; 1 kw-U. TL: N35 56 46 W85 02 13. (CP: TL: N35 57 01 W85 02 09). Hrs open: 24 961 Mlller Ave., 38555. Phone: (931) 707-1102. Fax: (931) 707-1220. Web Site:www.1490wcsv.com Licensee: Peg Broadcasting Crossville LLC (group owner; acq 10-1-2003; grpsl). Population served: 35,000 Natl. Network: ABC, . Format: Sports. News staff: 2; News: 13 hrs wkly. Target aud: 25-54; men. ♦Jeff Shaw, gen mgr, mktg mgr; Gordon Stack, opns mgr; Steve Sweeney, sls dir; Christy Lewis, news dir; Kendra Williams, traf mgr; Houston McDavitt, engr.

***WMKW(FM)**— November 1996: 89.3 mhz; 500 w. 1,395 ft TL: N35 46 38 W84 58 34. Hrs open: 24
Rebroadcasts WMBW(FM) Chattanooga 100%.
1920 E. 24th Street Pl., Chattanooga, 37404. Secondary address: Box 73026, Chattanooga 37407. Phone: 423-629-8900. Fax: (423) 629-0021. Web Site:www.moody.edu Licensee: The Moody Bible Institute of Chicago. Population served: 50,000 Southmayd & Miller. Format: Educ, relg, news/talk. Target aud: General. ♦Edward Cannon, pres; Leighton LeBoeuf, gen mgr, mktg dir; Andy Napier, prom dir, progmg dir; Paul Martin, mus dir; David Morais, chief of engrg; Jim Young, local news ed.

WOWF(FM)— June 15, 1990: 102.5 mhz; 25 kw. 308 ft TL: N36 01 22 W85 00 07. Stereo. Hrs open: 24 961 Miller Ave., 38555. Phone: (931) 707-1102. Fax: (931) 707-1220. Web Site:www.1025wowcountry.com Licensee: Peg Broadcasting Crossville LLC (group owner; acq 1-3-01; $2.5 million). Population served: 138,426 Natl. Network: Jones Radio Networks, Fox News Radio, . Rgnl rep: Rgnl Reps. Wire Svc: AP Format: Country. News staff: 2; News: 10 hrs wkly. Target aud: 25 -54; adults. ♦Houston McDavitt, gen mgr, engr; Gordon Stack, opns mgr, progmg mgr; Steve Sweeney, sls dir & gen sls mgr; Christy Lewis, news dir; Kendra Williams, traf mgr.

WPBX(FM)— May 12, 1967: 99.3 mhz; 6 kw. 259 ft TL: N35 57 01 W85 02 09. Stereo. Hrs open: 24 961 Miller Ave., 38555. Phone: (931) 484-5115. Fax: (931) 707-1220.E-mail: info@993.net Web Site:mix993.net Licensee: Peg Broadcasting Crossville LLC (group owner; acq 10-1-2003: grpsl). Population served: 40,000 Natl. Network: ABC, . Natl. Rep: Clear Channel,. Format: Adult contemp. News staff: 2; News: 10 hrs wkly. Target aud: 25-54; women. ♦Jeffrey H. Shaw, gen mgr; Steve J. Sweeney, gen sls mgr; Jeffrey Shaw, mktg mgr; Gordon Stack, progmg dir, chief of engrg; Christy Lewis, news dir; Kendra Williams, traf mgr.

Dayton

WDNT(AM)— Dec 6, 1957: 1280 khz; 1 kw-D, 345 w-N. TL: N35 28 12 W85 02 15. Hrs open:
Rebroadcasts WBAC(AM) Cleveland 100%.
2640 Commerce Dr., N.E., Cleveland, 37311. Phone: (423) 242-7656. Fax: (423) 472-5290. Web Site:www.wbacradio.com Licensee: East Tennessee Radio Group III L.P. Group owner: Brewer Broadcasting Corp. (acq 5-30-2008; grpsl). Population served: 28,604 Natl. Network: ABC, . Natl. Rep: D & R Radio,. Tenn. Radio Net. Format: MOR. News staff: one; News: 26 hrs wkly. Target aud: 45 plus. ♦Charles Sells, gen mgr; Mike Powers, opns mgr; John Holland, gen sls mgr; Corky Whitlock, progmg dir.

Decatur

WAYA(FM)— October 1989: 93.9 mhz; 16.5 kw. Ant 402 ft TL: N35 21 55 W84 45 22. Hrs open: 24 2540 Commerce Dr. N.E., Cleveland, 37311. Phone: (423) 472-4053. Fax: (423) 472-5290. Licensee: East Tennessee Radio Group III L.P. (acq 5-30-2008; grpsl). Population served: 87,000 Natl. Rep: D & R Radio,. Format: Country. News staff: one; News: one hr wkly. Target aud: 25-54.

Dibrell

***WRCC(FM)**—Not on air, target date: unknown: 88.3 mhz; 85 w. Ant 344 ft TL: N35 50 20 W85 47 02. Hrs open: 5210 S.E. Washington Blvd., Bartlesville, OK, 74006. Phone: (918) 333-8700. Licensee: Pearl Communications Group. ♦Danny Hester, pres.

Dickson

WDKN(AM)— Jan 1, 1955: Stn currently dark. 1260 khz; 5 kw-D. TL: N36 06 31 W87 22 14. Hrs open: 6 AM-6:30 PM 106 E. College St., 37055. Phone: (615) 446-4000. Phone: (615) 446-0752. Fax: (615) 446-9681.E-mail: wdkn@bellsouth.net Licensee: Edmission & Eubank Communications Inc. (acq 6-15-87; $220,000;5-18-87). Population served: 100,000 McCampbell & Young, P. Target aud: General. ♦Tommy Edmisson, pres; Oscar Eubank, VP; Leroy Kennell, gen mgr.

***WNRZ(FM)**— Apr 7, 1997: 91.5 mhz; 8 kw. Ant 262 ft TL: N36 00 36 W87 30 47. Stereo. Hrs open: 24
Rebroadcasts WNAZ-FM Nashville 100%.
333 Murfreesboro Rd., Nashville, 37210. Phone: (615) 248-1689. Fax: (615) 248-7786.E-mail: info@wnrz.com Licensee: Trevecca Nazarene University Inc. Population served: 80,000 Format: Christian, progsv contemp. Target aud: 14-28; Christians. ♦Dr. Dan Boone, pres; Mark Myers, CFO; David Deese, gen mgr; Paul Eby, stn mgr; Dave Queen, opns mgr.

Donelson

WCRT(AM)—Licensed to Donelson. See Nashville

Dresden

WCDZ(FM)— Apr 10, 1992: 95.1 mhz; 21.5 kw. Ant 276 ft TL: N36 15 50 W88 40 03. Stereo. Hrs open: 24 Box 318, Martin, 38237. Phone: (731) 587-9526. Fax: (731) 587-5079.E-mail: oldies951@crunet.com Licensee: Thunderbolt Broadcasting Co. Group owner: Thunderbolt Broadcasting Co./Gibson County Broadcasting (acq 1-28-94; $320,000;2-21-94). Population served: 158,033 Womble, Carlyle, Sandridge & Rice. Format: Oldies. News staff: one; News: one hr wkly. Spec prog: Atlanta Braves and Tennessee Vols. ♦Paul Tinkle, pres.

Dunlap

WSDQ(AM)— Nov 1, 1980: 1190 khz; 5 kw-D. TL: N35 21 41 W85 22 33. Hrs open: 16 Main St. N., 37327-6129. Phone: (423) 949-4114. Fax: (423) 949-5143.E-mail: wsdq@bledsoe.net Licensee: Rodgson Inc. (acq 7-18-02; $165,000). Rgnl. Network: Tenn. Radio Net. Tenn. Radio Net. Format: Country, bluegrass. Spec prog: Gospel 7 hrs wkly. ♦Charles Rodgers, pres; Earl Nunley, gen mgr.

Dyer

WTJJ(FM)— Feb 1, 1995: 94.3 mhz; 6 kw. Ant 328 ft TL: N36 06 12 W89 07 45. Hrs open: 24 122 Radio Rd., Jackson, 38301. Phone: (731) 427-3316. Fax: (731) 427-9338. Licensee: Forever South Licenses LLC. (acq 7-31-2006; grpsl). Population served: 150,000 Format: Country. ♦Verla Price, gen mgr.

Dyersburg

WASL(FM)— July 1, 1968: 100.1 mhz; 26 kw. Ant 676 ft TL: N36 06 00 W89 29 12. Stereo. Hrs open: 24 Prog sep from AM Box 100, 38025. Secondary address: 2555 Huish Rd. 38024. Phone: (731) 285-1450. Phone: (731) 285-1339. Fax: (731) 287-0100.E-mail: roger@burksb.com Web Site:wasl.net Population served: 300,000 Natl. Network: ABC, . Natl. Rep: Rgnl Reps,. Wire Svc: AP Format: Rock. News staff: one. Target aud: 18-54. Spec prog: John Boy and Billy, Tenn Titans. ♦Roger Vestal, VP & gen mgr; Natalie Burks, sls dir; Dan DeFilippo, progmg dir; Brian Thomas, traf mgr; Dave Hacker, engr.

WTRO(AM)— July 13, 1946: 1450 khz; 1 kw-U. TL: N36 03 02 W89 22 07. Hrs open: 24
FM Translator 101.7.
Box 100, 38025. Secondary address: 2555 Huish Rd. 38024. Phone: (731) 285-1450. Phone: (731) 285-1339. Fax: (731) 287-0100. Licensee: Dr. Pepper/Pepsi Cola Bottling Co. of Dyersburg Inc. (acq 1991). Population served: 100,000 Natl. Network: ABC, . Rgnl. Network: Yancey Action. Bryan Cave. Wire Svc: AP Format: Oldies. News staff: one; News: news prgmg 5 hrs/week. Target aud: 35 plus. Spec prog: St. Louis Cardinals, Tenn Vols. ♦Roger Vestal, exec VP, gen mgr; Natalie Burks, gen sls mgr; Tom Hunt, progmg dir.

*WZKV(FM)— Oct 30, 1992: 90.7 mhz; 100 kw. Ant 373 ft TL: N36 06 00 W89 29 12. Stereo. Hrs open: 24 5700 West Oaks Blvd., Rocklin, CA, 95765. Phone: (916) 251-1600. Fax: (916) 251-1650. Licensee: Educational Media Foundation. (acq 3-29-2007; $825,000). Population served: 310,000 Davis Wright Tremaine LLP. Format: Christian. ◆Richard Jenkins, pres.

East Ridge

WOGT(FM)— Nov 9, 1990: 107.9 mhz; 25 kw. Ant 328 ft TL: N35 07 33 W85 17 25. Hrs open: 24 Box 11202, Chattanooga, 37401. Phone: (423) 756-6141. Fax: (423) 756-0292. Web Site:www.1079dukefm.com Licensee: Citadel Broadcasting Co. Group owner: Citadel Broadcasting Corp. (acq 5-30-00; grpsl). Format: Country. ◆Dan Brown, gen mgr.

Elizabethton

WBEJ(AM)— July 1946: 1240 khz; 1 kw-U. TL: N36 20 07 W82 13 03. Hrs open: 24 510 Broad St., 37643-2718. Phone: (423) 542-2184. Fax: (423) 542-3912.E-mail: wbej@planetc.com Web Site:www.wbej.com Licensee: CB Radio Inc. (acq 9-24-82; $335,000; 10-18-82). Population served: 500,000 Natl. Network: Westwood One, . Format: Country. News staff: one; News: 8 hrs wkly. Target aud: 25-49. ◆Don Crisp, pres; Cleo Reed, VP, gen mgr; David A. Miller, opns dir, dev dir, gen sls mgr.

WTZR(FM)— May 17, 1968: 99.3 mhz; 3.6 kw. Ant 810 ft TL: N36 24 07 W82 12 12. Stereo. Hrs open: Box 1389, Bristol, VA, 24203. Secondary address: 901 E. Valley Dr., Bristol, VA 24201. Phone: (276) 669-8112. Fax: (276) 669-0541.E-mail: info@mix993.com Web Site:www.mix993.com Licensee: Bristol Broadcasting Co. Group owner: Bristol Broadcasting Co. Inc. (acq 2-13-97; $3 million). Population served: 390,000 Natl. Rep: Christal,. Format: Alternative rock. Target aud: 18-49. ◆W.L. Nininger, pres, gen mgr; Bruce Clark, stn mgr, prom dir, progmg dir; Winnie Quaintance, gen sls mgr; Chuck Lawson, chief of engrg; Anna Honaker, traf mgr.

*WUMC(FM)— 1999: 90.5 mhz; 500 w. -285 ft TL: N36 17 58 W82 17 28. Hrs open: Box 9, Milligan College, 37682. Phone: (423) 461-8464. Phone: (423) 461-8700. Licensee: Milligan College. Format: CHR, Contemp Christian music. ◆Carrie Swanay, gen mgr.

Englewood

WENR(AM)— Apr 21, 1967: 1090 khz; 1 kw-D. TL: N35 25 35 W84 30 57. Hrs open: Box 676, Etowah, 37331-0676. Phone: (423) 263-5555. Fax: (423) 263-2555.E-mail: wenrradio@yahoo.com Licensee: Paul Wilson dba 1090 Radio, a Tennessee sole proprietorship (acq 10-2-98; $75,000). Rgnl. Network: Tenn. Radio Net. Format: Gospel. ◆Carolyne Wilson, gen mgr.

Erwin

WEMB(AM)— May 17, 1956: 1420 khz; 5 kw-D. TL: N36 06 58 W82 26 49. Hrs open: Box 280, 101 Riverview Rd., 37650. Phone: (423) 743-6123. Phone: (423) 743-6124. Fax: (423) 743-6122. Licensee: WEMB Inc. (acq 4-1-61). Population served: 50,000 Rgnl. Network: Tenn. Radio Net. Tenn. Radio Net. Format: Country, gospel, sports. Spec prog: Bluegrass 2 hrs, gospel 10 hrs wkly. ◆Jim Crawford, pres, gen mgr; Charles W. Ray, opns mgr, progmg dir, chief of engrg; Kathy Thornberry, news dir; Fred Lance, edit dir.

WXIS(FM)—Listing follows WEMB(AM).

Etowah

WCPH(AM)— 1955: 1220 khz; 1 kw-D, 109 w-N. TL: N35 19 15 W84 30 34. Hrs open: Box 676, 37331. Phone: (423) 263-5555. Fax: (423) 263-2555.E-mail: wcphradio@yahoo.com Licensee: Starr Mountain Broadcasting Co. (acq 3-18-97; $39,000). Population served: 3,736 Format: News/talk, sports, easy listening mus. ◆Carolyne Wilson, gen mgr.

WLLJ(FM)— 1977: 103.1 mhz; 50 kw. 492 ft TL: N35 27 24 W84 40 43. Stereo. Hrs open: 24
Rebroadcasts WBDX(FM) Trenton, GA 100%.
Box 9396, Chattanooga, 37412. Secondary address: Box 212 , McDonald 37353. Phone: (423) 892-1200. Fax: (423) 892-1633.E-mail: debbie@j103.com Web Site:www.j103.com Licensee: Friendship Broadcasting LLC. (acq 2-13-98). Population served: 1,000,000 Natl. Network: Salem Radio Network, . Format: Adult contemp, Christian. News staff: one; News: 2 hrs wkly. Target aud: 18-49; female. ◆Bob

Lubell, CEO, pres; Dave Skinner, CFO; Debbie Lubell, gen mgr, mktg dir; Elizabeth Gearu, chief of engrg & traf mgr; Dawn Manor, local news ed.

Fairview

WPFD(AM)— May 28, 1982: 850 khz; 500 w-D. TL: N36 00 29 W87 08 38. Hrs open: 6 AM-sunset 1074 Hwy. 96 N., 37062. Phone: (615) 799-8585. Fax: (615) 799-2999. Licensee: Fairview Broadcasting. Format: Country. Target aud: 18-54. ◆Sam Warden, pres; Chuck Hussey, gen mgr, mus dir, news dir; John Almon, chief of engrg.

Farragut

WMTY(AM)— Nov 10, 1988: 670 khz; 500 w-D. TL: N35 53 12 W84 14 48. Stereo. Hrs open: 517 Watts Rd., Knoxville, 37922. Phone: (865) 671-7419. Fax: (865) 675-4859. Licensee: Horne Radio L.L.C. Group owner: Horne Radio Group (acq 1999; $275,000). Natl. Network: USA, . Format: Talk. Target aud: 25-54; upscale adults. ◆Doug Horne, pres.

Fayetteville

WEKR(AM)— Oct 1, 1948: 1240 khz; 1 kw-U. TL: N35 09 28 W86 35 25. Hrs open: 4:30 AM-10 PM Box 656, 37334. Secondary address: 7 Boonshill Rd. 37334. Phone: (931) 433-3545. Fax: (931) 438-0620. Licensee: Joseph D. Young, Wanda Young & Mary Elizabeth Miller. (acq 2-22-94; $194,000; 3-21-94). Population served: 30,000 Natl. Network: CNN Radio, . Rgnl. Network: Tenn. Radio Net. Tenn. Radio Net. Format: Country, southern gospel, sports. News staff: one; News: 5 hrs wkly. Target aud: 25 plus; general. Spec prog: Farm one hr wkly. ◆Joseph D. Young, CEO; Jim Young, stn mgr, chief of opns, gen sls mgr, adv mgr, pub affrs dir, spec ev coord; Joseph Young, progmg dir.

WYTM-FM— Mar 27, 1970: 105.5 mhz; 3 kw. 295 ft TL: N35 07 37 W86 34 47. (CP: 2.25 kw, and 495 ft.). Stereo. Hrs open: 5 AM-10 PM Box 717, 37334. Phone: (931) 433-1531. Fax: (931) 433-4110. Licensee: Time Broadcasters Inc. Population served: 185,000 Natl. Network: ABC, . Format: Country. ◆Joseph D. Young, pres & gen mgr; Debbie Kawiecki, opns mgr.

Franklin

WAKM(AM)— Mar 18, 1953: 950 khz; 5 kw-D, 80 w-N. TL: N35 57 25 W86 50 03. (CP: 2.5 kw-D). Hrs open: 24 222 Mallory Station Rd., 37065. Phone: (615) 794-1594. Fax: (615) 794-1595.E-mail: wakm950@comcast.net Licensee: Franklin Radio Associates Inc. (acq 10-1-82; $310,600; 10-18-82). Population served: 128,000 Natl. Network: CNN Radio, . Rgnl. Network: Tenn. Radio Net. Tenn. Radio Net. Format: Country, news/talk. News staff: 2; News: 14 hrs wkly. Target aud: 24 plus; community interested adults. Spec prog: Relg 6 hrs, NASCAR racing 6 hrs wkly. ◆Jim Hayes, pres, chief of engrg; Linda Jackson Carden, sls dir; Tom Lawrence, VP, gen mgr & gen sls mgr; Darrell Williams, progmg dir; Charles Dibrell, news dir.

WHEW(AM)— Feb 1, 1969: 1380 khz; 2.8 kw-D, 500 w-N, DA-N. TL: N35 54 22 W86 54 21. Hrs open: 18 1811 Carters Creek Pike, 37064. Phone: (615) 595-0595. Fax: (615) 591-4007.E-mail: laley1330@laley1380.net Web Site:www.laley1380.net Licensee: SG Communications Inc. (acq 7-29-99; $208,398). Population served: 300,000 Natl. Network: CNN Radio, . Format: Spanish, sports, news/talk. News staff: one. Target aud: General; Hispanics. ◆Victor Guzman, CEO; Salvador Guzman, pres, gen mgr; Claudio Vazquez, sls dir; Enrique Garcia, progmg dir.

WRLT(FM)— Nov 16, 1961: 100.1 mhz; 3 kw. 1,134 ft TL: N36 02 06 W86 50 54. Stereo. Hrs open: 24 1310 Clinton St., Suite 200, Nashville, 37203. Phone: (615) 242-5600. Fax: (615) 523-2153.E-mail: comments@WRLT.com Web Site:www.WRLT.com Licensee: Tuned In Broadcasting Inc. (acq 1996). Natl. Network: Westwood One, . Natl. Rep: Roslin,. Davis, Wright, Tremaine. Format: AAA. Target aud: Adults 18+. Spec prog: Retro Rock 4 hrs, Local Music 3 hrs, Music Business Talk 2 hrs, Indie Rock 1 hr, Blues 1 hr weekly. ◆Lester Turner Jr., CEO, chmn, pres; Fred Buc, gen mgr, gen sls mgr; David Hall, prom dir, progmg dir; Tom Hansen, chief of engrg.

Gallatin

WGFX(FM)— Dec 1, 1960: 104.5 mhz; 49 kw. 1,312 ft TL: N36 16 05 W86 47 16. Hrs open: 24 506 2nd Ave. S., Nashville, 37210. Phone: (615) 244-9533. Fax: (615) 259-1271.E-mail: ken.bailey@citcom.com Web Site:www.104thezone.com Licensee: Citadel Broadcasting Co. Group owner: Citadel Broadcasting Corp. (acq 4-26-01; grpsl).

Population served: 1,000,000 Natl. Rep: Katz Radio,. Kaye, Scholer, Fierman, Hays & Handler. Format: Sports/talk. Target aud: 18-49. ◆Ken Bailey, gen mgr.

WHIN(AM)— Aug 2, 1948: 1010 khz; 5 kw-D. TL: N36 26 00 W86 28 00. Stereo. Hrs open: 24 Box 1685, 37066. Phone: (615) 451-0450. Phone: (615) 451-0451. Fax: (615) 452-9446.E-mail: whinam@comcast.net Licensee: WHIN Inc. (acq 10-84). Population served: 100,000 Format: Country. News staff: one; News: 14 hrs wkly. Target aud: 25-54; upper middle to lower middle income. Spec prog: Black 2 hrs, farm 5 hrs wkly. ◆Jack Williams, pres & gen mgr.

WMRO(AM)— Feb 19, 1994: 1560 khz; 1 kw-D, 3 w-N. TL: N36 24 03 W86 27 03. Hrs open: Daytime Box 1445, 37066. Phone: (615) 451-2131. Fax: (615) 206-4207.E-mail: wmroam@bellsouth.net Web Site:www.magic1560.com Licensee: Classic Broadcasting Inc. (acq 10-28-93; $40,000). Population served: 103,000 Natl. Network: ABC, . Rgnl rep: . Miller & Neeley. Format: Hot adult contemp. News staff: 2; News: 4 hrs wkly. Target aud: 25-54; middle to upper class adults. Spec prog: Relg 11 hrs. wkly. ◆Scott Bailey, pres & gen mgr.

*WVCP(FM)— Jan 4, 1979: 88.5 mhz; 1 kw. 390 ft TL: N36 28 02 W86 28 35. Stereo. Hrs open: 24 1480 Nashville Pike, Suite 101, Ramer Bldg., 37066. Phone: (615) 230-3618. Fax: (615) 230-4803.E-mail: holly.nimmo@volstate.edu Web Site:www.volstate.edu Licensee: Volunteer State Community College. Wire Svc: AP Format: Black, CHR, adult contemp, oldies. News: 5 hrs wkly. Target aud: General. Spec prog: Black 8 hrs, metal 15 hrs, gospel 6 hrs, bluegrass 2 hrs wkly. ◆Dr. Warren R. Nichols, pres; Howard Espravnik, gen mgr; Holly Nimmo, opns dir.

WYXE(AM)— Nov 1, 1966: Stn currently dark. 1130 khz; 2.3 kw-D. TL: N36 24 38 W86 27 16. Hrs open: 1079 E. Trinity Ln., Nashville, 37216. Phone: (615) 227-1130. Web Site:www.radiovida1130.com Licensee: Iglesia De Dios Hispana Pentecostal De Nashville Tennessee (acq 1-31-2006; $600,000). Format: Sp relg. ◆Richard D. Deck Jr., gen mgr.

Gatlinburg

WSEV-FM— January 1983: 105.5 mhz; 650 w. 964 ft TL: N35 42 13 W83 33 57. Stereo. Hrs open: 24 196 W. Dumplin Valley Rd., Kodak, 37764. Phone: (865) 932-6002. Fax: (865) 932-0167.E-mail: bill@easttennesseeradio.com Licensee: East Tennessee Radio Group L.P. (acq 3-22-2000; $1.45 million with WSEV(AM) Sevierville). Population served: 65000 Natl. Network: Fox News Radio, . Rgnl. Network: Tenn. Radio Net. Tenn. Radio Net. Format: Adult Contemporary. News staff: one. Target aud: 25-54; loc adults, tourists. ◆Bill Burkett, stn mgr; Steve Hartford, opns mgr & news dir.

Germantown

WHBQ-FM— June 1994: 107.5 mhz; 3.9 kw. Ant 407 ft TL: N35 10 30 W89 44 26. Stereo. Hrs open: 24 6080 Mt. Mariah Rd., Memphis, 38115. Phone: (901) 375-9324. Fax: (901) 375-0041.E-mail: info@q1075.com Web Site:www.q1075.com Licensee: Flinn Broadcasting Corp. (acq 1997; $4). Format: Top-40. ◆Donald Biggs, gen mgr.

WKQK(FM)—Licensed to Germantown. See Memphis

WOWW(AM)—Licensed to Germantown. See Memphis

Goodlettsville

WRQQ(FM)— Dec 3, 1999: 97.1 mhz; 43 kw. Ant 518 ft TL: N36 17 50 W86 45 11. Hrs open: 24 10 Music Cir. E., Nashville, 37203. Phone: (615) 321-1067. Fax: (615) 321-5771.E-mail: danielle.haese@cumulus.com Web Site:www.classichits971.com Licensee: Cumulus Licensing Corp. Group owner: Cumulus Media Inc. (acq 3-28-2002; grpsl). Format: Classic hits. ◆John Columbus, gen mgr; Steve Grant, gen sls mgr; Derick Corbett, progmg dir; Troy Pennington, chief of engrg.

Graysville

WAYB-FM— 1994: 95.7 mhz; 6 kw. Ant 328 ft TL: N35 24 39 W85 07 54. Hrs open: Box 262550, Baton Rouge, LA, 70826. Secondary address: 8919 World Ministry Ave, Baton Rouge, LA 70810. Phone: (225) 768-3688. Phone: (225) 768-8300. Fax: (225) 768-3729.E-mail: kawikfish@yahoo.com Web Site:www.jsm.org Licensee: Family Worship Center Church Inc. (group owner; acq 5-20-02). Format: Christian. ◆David Whitelaw, COO; Jimmy Swaggart, pres; John Santiago, progmg dir.

Greeneville

WAEZ(FM)— 1956: 94.9 mhz; 100 kw. 1,090 ft TL: N36 04 34 W82 41 28. Stereo. Hrs open: 24 901 E. Valley Dr., Bristol, VA, 24201. Phone: (276) 669-8112. Fax: (276) 669-0541.E-mail: info@electric949.com Web Site:www.electric949.com Licensee: Bristol Broadcasting Co. Inc. (group owner; acq 6-22-00). Population served: 175000 Natl. Rep: Rgnl Reps,. Format: CHR. News staff: 2. Target aud: 25-49. Spec prog: Univ. of Tennessee football & basketball. ♦Pete Nininger, pres; Bill Hickey, opns mgr.

WGRV(AM)— 1946: 1340 khz; 1 kw-U. TL: N36 10 10 W82 50 52. Hrs open: 24 Prog sep from FM. Box 278, 37744. Secondary address: 1004 Arnold Rd. 37743. Phone: (423) 638-4147.E-mail: wgrv@greeneville.com Licensee: Radio Greeneville Inc. Population served: 55,000 Rgnl. Network: Tenn. Radio Net. Tenn. Radio Net. Format: Modern country. News staff: 3. ♦Betty Fletcher, traf mgr; Maxine Humphreys, local news ed, women's int ed; Nancy Ensor, news rptr; Al Wrinn, farm dir; Charlie Hicks, disc jockey.

WIKQ(FM)—(Tusculum, February 1996: 103.1 mhz; 6 kw. -223 ft TL: N36 07 40 W82 37 57. Hrs open: 24 Box 278, 37744. Secondary address: 1004 Arnold Rd. 37743. Phone: (423) 639-1831. Fax: (423) 638-1979.E-mail: wsmg@greeneville.com Licensee: Radio Greeneville Inc. (group owner; (acq 6-22-2000; $1.8 million with WSMG(AM) Greeneville). Population served: 70,000 Format: Country. News staff: one. Target aud: 25-55; middle to upper middle income. ♦Ron P. Metcalf, gen mgr; Ron P. Metcalfe, pres & opns VP; Brian Stayton, progmg dir; Nathan Humbard, mus dir; Bobby Rader, news dir; Ray C. Elliott, chief of engrg.

WSMG(AM)— Dec 1, 1961: 1450 khz; 1 kw-U. TL: N36 10 30 W82 50 18. Hrs open: 24 Box 278, 37744. Secondary address: 10004 Arnold Rd. 37743. Phone: (423) 638-3188. Fax: (423) 638-1979.E-mail: wsmg@greeneville.com Licensee: Radio Greeneville Inc. (group owner; acq 6-22-00; $1.8 million with WIKQ(FM) Tusculum). Population served: 57,000 Format: Oldies. Target aud: General. ♦Ronnie Metcalfe, pres, gen mgr & opns mgr.

Halls Crossroads

WMYL(FM)— Aug 15, 1991: 96.7 mhz; 1.9 kw. Ant 489 ft TL: N36 04 21 W84 01 18. Stereo. Hrs open: Box 329, Clinton, 37717. Secondary address: 111 Hillcrest Dr., Clinton 37716. Phone: (865) 457-1380. Fax: (865) 457-4440.E-mail: ron@merle.com Licensee: M & M Broadcasting (acq 4-18-2006; $1 million). Population served: 150,000 Natl. Network: ABC, CNN Radio, . Rgnl. Network: Ky. Net., Tenn. Radio Net., Va. News Net. Natl. Rep: Rgnl Reps,. Format: Country. Target aud: 25-54; community-oriented adults. Spec prog: Farm 2 hrs, gospel 2 hrs, relg 2 hrs wkly. ♦Ronald C. Meredith Jr., gen mgr.

Harriman

WIJV(FM)— Jan 21, 1981: 92.7 mhz; 690 w. Ant 964 ft TL: N35 59 04.8 W84 44 06.7. (CP: 6 kw, ant 328 ft. TL: N35 52 04 W84 25 56). Stereo. Hrs open: Box 810, Crossville, 38557. Phone: (931) 484-1057. Licensee: Progressive Media Inc. (group owner; (acq 7-2-2007; $2.4 million). Format: Classic rock. ♦Kirk Tollett, gen mgr, gen sls mgr, progmg dir, chief of engrg; Scott Humphrey, news dir; Jennifer Tollett, traf mgr.

Harrogate

WCXZ(AM)— Nov 10, 1980: 740 khz; 900 w-D, 7 w-N. TL: N36 33 40 W83 39 21. Hrs open: 24 Box 2025, 37752. Phone: (423) 869-6335. Fax: (423) 869-6435. Web Site:www.74wcxz.com Licensee: Lincoln Memorial University (acq 3-28-2008). Population served: 125,000 Format: Country.

***WLMU(FM)**— Aug 5, 1987: 91.3 mhz; 190 w. 284 ft TL: N36 35 10 W83 39 54. Stereo. Hrs open: 24 Box 2025, Sigmon Communications Ctr., Hwy. 25 E., 37752. Phone: (423) 869-6331.E-mail: info@wlmu.com Web Site:www.913thegap.com Licensee: Lincoln Memorial University. Population served: 30,000 Format: Country/Bluegrass. Target aud: 25-54. ♦Dr. Nancy Moody, pres; Travis Moody, gen mgr; Dustin McCoy, opns mgr.

Hartsville

WTNK(AM)— Sept 1, 1966: 1090 khz; 1 kw-D, 2 w-N. TL: N36 23 17 W86 09 55. Hrs open: 24 165 Marlene St., 37074. Phone: (615) 374-2111. Fax: (615) 374-3544. Licensee: G & L Aircasters Inc. (acq 2-14-2003; $160,000). Population served: 500,000 Natl. Rep: Keystone (unwired net),. Format: Country. News: 5 hrs wkly. Target aud: 35 plus. Spec prog: Gospel 4 hrs wkly. ♦Gary Frank, CEO, pres, gen mgr, stn mgr, chief of opns; Jerry Richmond, news dir; Lisa Frank, COO, CFO, exec VP, pub affrs dir & traf mgr.

Henderson

***WFHU(FM)**— May 22, 1967: 91.5 mhz; 10.5 kw. 300 ft TL: N35 27 50 W88 41 10. Stereo. Hrs open: 24 158 E. Main St., 38340. Phone: (731) 989-6691. Phone: (731) 989-6749.E-mail: wfhu@wfhu.edu Web Site:www.fhu.edu/radio Licensee: Freed-Hardeman University. Population served: 100,000 Format: Jazz, classic rock, classical. News staff: one; News: 5 hrs wkly. Target aud: General; young adults to senior citizens. Spec prog: Class 10 hrs, gospel 9 hrs, jazz 45 hrs wkly. ♦Milton Sewell, pres; Ron Means, gen mgr.

WFKX(FM)— Feb 1, 1984: 95.7 mhz; 4.4 kw. Ant 383 ft TL: N35 29 52 W88 42 29. Stereo. Hrs open: 24 111 W. Main St., Jackson, 38301. Phone: (731) 427-9616. Fax: (731) 424-2473.E-mail: cthomas@wwyn.fm Web Site:wfkx.fm Licensee: Thomas Radio LLC (group owner; (acq 11-9-2001; grpsl). Population served: 230,000 Natl. Network: ABC, . Borsari & Paxson. Format: Urban contemp, Black. News: 5 hrs wkly. Target aud: 18-54; the general Black population & contemp women. Spec prog: Gospel 3 hrs wkly. ♦Billy Thomas, pres; Chip Thomas, gen mgr; Jim Smith, chief of engrg.

WHHM-FM— Nov 19, 1990: 107.7 mhz; 50 kw horiz, 49.07 kw vert. Ant 459 ft TL: N35 27 23 W88 37 36. Stereo. Hrs open: 24 111 W. Main St., Jackson, 38301. Phone: (731) 427-9616. Fax: (731) 424-2473.E-mail: info@star1077.fm Web Site:www.star1077.fm Licensee: Thomas Radio LLC (group owner; (acq 11-9-2001; grpsl). Population served: 370,000 Rgnl. Network: Tenn. Agri. Tenn. Agri-Net McFadden, Evans & Sill. Wire Svc: AP Format: Var, adult contemp. News staff: one; News: 5 hrs wkly. Target aud: 25-54; adults. Spec prog: Gospel 10 hrs wkly. ♦Chip Thomas, gen mgr; Phil Hickerson, gen sls mgr; Shane Connor, opns mgr & progmg mgr; Jim Smith, chief of engrg.

Hendersonville

WQQK(FM)— Oct 16, 1970: 92.1 mhz; 3 kw. 462 ft TL: N36 17 50 W86 45 11. Stereo. Hrs open: 24 10 Music Cir. E., Nashville, 37203. Phone: (615) 321-1067. Fax: (615) 321-5771.E-mail: danielle.haese@cumulus.com Web Site:www.cumulus.com Licensee: Cumulus Licensing LLC. Group owner: Cumulus Media Inc. (acq 3-28-2002; grpsl). Natl. Network: ABC, . Pepper & Corazzini. Format: Adult urban contemp. Target aud: 18-49; relg. Spec prog: Gospel 6 hrs wkly. ♦John Columbus, gen mgr; Timothy J. Meagher, gen sls mgr; Kenny Smoov, progmg dir; Troy Pennington, chief of engrg.

Henry

WMUF-FM— Apr 12, 1999: 104.7 mhz; 2.9 kw. Ant 476 ft TL: N36 08 19 W88 15 52. Stereo. Hrs open: 24
Rebroadcasts WMUF(AM) Paris 100%.
110 India Rd., Paris, 38242. Phone: (731) 644-9455. Fax: (731) 644-9970.E-mail: wmuf@bellsouth.net Web Site:www.wmufradio.com Licensee: Benton-Weatherford Broadcasting Inc. of Tennessee (group owner). Population served: 50,000 Natl. Network: ABC, . Format: Country. Target aud: 25-54. ♦Gary Benton, pres, gen mgr; Janice Benton, opns VP.

Hohenwald

***WAUO(FM)**— 1998: 90.7 mhz; 950 w. Ant 233 ft TL: N35 33 56 W87 33 27. Hrs open: Box 3206, American Family Radio, Tupelo, MS, 38803. Phone: (662) 844-8888. Phone: (662) 844-8893 (call-in). Fax: (662) 842-6791.E-mail: comments@afr.net Web Site:www.afr.net Licensee: American Family Association. Group owner: American Family Radio Format: Christian classics. ♦Marvin Sanders, gen mgr.

WMLR(AM)— July 4, 1970: 1230 khz; 1 kw-U. TL: N35 31 22 W87 32 40. Hrs open: 24 184 Switzerland Rd., 38462. Phone: (931) 796-5966. Fax: (931) 796-7353.E-mail: harold@wmlr1230am.com Licensee: Cochran Communication Corp. of Lewis County. (acq 6-4-99; $67,500). Population served: 15,000 Natl. Network: ABC, . Format: C&W. Spec prog: Gospel. ♦Harold Cochran, pres, gen mgr; Celeste Cochran, news dir; Benjamin Cochran, weather dir; Josiah Cochran, mus critic & disc jockey.

Humboldt

WIRJ(AM)— Jan 20, 1949: 740 khz; 250 w-D, 50 w-N. TL: N35 48 52 W88 54 51. Hrs open: Box 740, 38343-0740. Secondary address: 2606 East End Dr. 38343. Phone: (731) 784-5000. Fax: (731) 784-2533.E-mail: BRANDY@CLICK1.NET Licensee: John F. Warmath. (acq 1996; $45,000). Format: Oldies, talk. ♦John F. Warmath, gen mgr.

WLLI(AM)— July 5, 1972: 1190 khz; 420 w-D. TL: N35 50 41 W88 54 08. Hrs open: 122 Radio Rd., Jackson, 38301. Phone: (731) 427-3316. Fax: (731) 427-9338. Web Site:www.realcountryonline.com Licensee: Forever South Licenses LLC. (acq 7-31-2006; grpsl). Population served: 200,000 Format: Country. ♦Verla Price, gen mgr.

WTJW(FM)— Jan 19, 1989: 105.3 mhz; 3 kw. Ant 328 ft TL: N35 50 41 W88 54 08. Stereo. Hrs open: 24 122 Radio Rd., Jackson, 38301. Phone: (731) 427-3316. Fax: (731) 427-9338. Licensee: Forever South Licenses LLC Format: CHR. Target aud: 18-49. ♦Dave Hacker, engrg dir.

WZDQ(FM)— Sept 1, 1964: 102.3 mhz; 6 kw. Ant 305 ft TL: N35 45 45 W88 51 42. Stereo. Hrs open: 24 111 W. Main St., Jackcon, 38301. Phone: (731) 427-9616. Fax: (731) 424-2473.E-mail: info@wzdq.fm Web Site:www.wzdq.fm Licensee: Thomas Radio LLC. (group owner; (acq 11-9-2001; grpsl). Population served: 500,000 Natl. Network: CNN Radio, . Format: Rock. Target aud: 25-49; middle to upper class. ♦Chip Thomas, gen mgr; Marsha Hulsey, gen sls mgr; Shane Connor, opns mgr & prom dir.

Huntingdon

WVHR(FM)— November 1979: 100.9 mhz; 6 kw. 300 ft TL: N35 57 05 W88 27 47. Stereo. Hrs open: 24 215 Baker Rd., Huntington, 38344. Phone: (731) 986-0242. Fax: (731) 986-8557.E-mail: wvhr@aeneas.net Licensee: Jim W. Freeland. (acq 9-16-2005; $650,000). Rgnl. Network: Tenn. Radio Net. Tenn. Radio Net. Format: Classic hit country. ♦Jerry Vandiver, gen mgr, sls dir; Michael Ray, opns dir, progmg dir & news dir; Dave Hacker, chief of engrg.

WWDX(AM)— Oct 21, 1975: 1530 khz; 1 kw-D. TL: N36 00 04 W88 26 02. Hrs open: 7 AM-5 PM 9662 H'way 77, 38344. Phone: (731) 986-9746. Fax: (731) 986-9704. Licensee: Jim W. Freeland. (acq 3-13-2007; $110,000). Population served: 32,000 Format: Country. News staff: 2. Target aud: General. ♦Mark C. Johnson, gen mgr; Sarah Dunning, gen sls mgr; Jay Jackson, news dir.

Jackson

***WAMP(FM)**— 1995: 88.1 mhz; 750 w. 134 ft TL: N35 39 38 W88 51 30. Hrs open: American Family Radio, Box 3206, Tupelo, MS, 38803. Phone: (662) 844-8888. Phone: (662) 844-8893. Fax: (662) 842-6791.E-mail: comments@afr.net Web Site:www.afr.net Licensee: American Family Association. Group owner: American Family Radio Format: Christian. ♦Marvin Sanders, gen mgr.

WDXI(AM)— Oct 31, 1948: 1310 khz; 5 kw-D, 1 kw-N, DA-N. TL: N35 39 50 W88 49 20. Hrs open: 24 Box 3845, 38303-3845. Secondary address: 1 Radio Park Dr. 38305-4124. Phone: (731) 427-9611. Phone: (731) 424-1310. Fax: (731) 424-1321. Licensee: Gerald W. Hunt (acq 1-15-93; $480,000 with co-located FM;2-8-93). Population served: 55,000 Natl. Rep: D & R Radio,. Format: Business news. News staff: one; News: 10 hrs wkly. Target aud: 25 plus. Spec prog: Farm 12 hrs, gospel 16 hrs, sports 16 hrs wkly. ♦Gerald W. Hunt, gen mgr, gen sls mgr & progmg mgr.

WJAK(AM)— Nov 14, 1954: 1460 khz; 1 kw-D, 128 w-N. TL: N35 38 37 W88 46 24. Hrs open: 24 111 W. Main St., 38301. Phone: (731) 427-9616. Fax: (731) 427-9302. Licensee: Thomas Radio L.L.C. (group owner; (acq 7-21-2004; $318,000). Population served: 100,000 Natl. Network: Moody, USA, . Natl. Rep: Rgnl Reps,. Format: Urban Gospel. News: 14 hrs wkly. Target aud: 18-54; primarily Black Christian middle-class families with low to moderate income. ♦Chip Thomas, gen mgr.

***WKNP(FM)**— Dec 17, 1990: 90.1 mhz; 17 kw. 528 ft TL: N35 38 46 W88 49 57. Stereo. Hrs open: 24
Rebroadcasts WKNO-FM Memphis 100%.
7151 Cherry Farms Rd., Memphis, 38016. Phone: (901) 458-2521. Fax: (901) 325-6505. Web Site:www.wknofm.org Licensee: Mid-South Public Communications Foundation. Population served: 120,000 Natl. Network: NPR, PRI, . Schwartz, Woods & Miller. Format: News and Classical. News staff: 2; News: 51 hrs wkly. Target aud: 35 plus. ♦Michael LaBonia, pres; Dan Campbell, gen mgr, stn mgr; Darel Snodgrass, opns mgr; Charles McLarty, dev dir. Co-owned TV: *WKNO-TV affil

WMXX-FM— May 9, 1979: 103.1 mhz; 42 kw. Ant 538 ft TL: N35 32 39 W88 47 18. Stereo. Hrs open: Prog sep from AM Box 3845, 38303.

Secondary address: 1 Radio Park Dr. 38303. Phone: (731) 427-9611. Phone: (731) 424-1310. Fax: (731) 424-1321. Format: Oldies. Target aud: 25-54.

WNWS-FM— August 1993: 101.5 mhz; 3 kw. 300 ft TL: N35 38 59 W88 46 11. Stereo. Hrs open: 24 207 W. Lafayette St., 38301. Phone: (731) 423-8316. Fax: (731) 423-8304.E-mail: newstalk@wnws.com Web Site:www.wnws.com Licensee: Radiocorp of Jackson Inc. Group owner: The Wireless Group Inc. (acq 12-6-00; $925,000). Population served: 50,000 Natl. Network: CBS, . Format: News/talk. News staff: 2; News: 25 hrs wkly. Target aud: 25 plus; upscale adults. ♦Greg Wood, opns mgr; Larry Wood, gen mgr & progmg dir.

WOGY(FM)— 1947: 104.1 mhz; 100 kw. 679 ft TL: N35 38 46 W88 49 57. Stereo. Hrs open: Prog sep from AM 122 Radio Rd., 38301. Phone: (731) 427-3316. Fax: (731) 427-4576.E-mail: info@eagle104.net Web Site:eagle104.net Population served: 426,852 Format: Country. Target aud: 18-54. ♦Deb Smith, prom dir; Rusty Mac, news dir & news rptr.

WTJS(AM)— 1931: 1390 khz; 5 kw-D, 1 kw-N, DA-N. TL: N35 38 50 W88 50 00. Hrs open: 24 122 Radio Rd., 38301. Phone: (731) 427-3316. Fax: (731) 427-4576. Licensee: Forever South Licenses LLC. Group owner: Clear Channel Communications Inc. (acq 5-12-2006; grpsl). Population served: 290,120 Rgnl. Network: Tenn. Radio Net. Tenn. Radio Net. Format: News/talk. News staff: 3; News: 30 hrs wkly. Target aud: 35 plus; general. ♦Roger Vestal, gen mgr; Dave Hacker, opns mgr, chief of engrg; Gina Langley, gen sls mgr; Connie Cain, traf mgr; Todd Starnes, news dir & local news ed.

WYNU(FM)—See Milan

Jamestown

WCLC(AM)— Oct 28, 1957: 1260 khz; 1 kw-D. TL: N36 26 10 W84 55 42. Hrs open: Box 1509, 38556. Phone: (931) 879-8188. Fax: (931) 879-1733.E-mail: wclc@twlakes.net Licensee: Bible Believers Network Inc. Population served: 40,000 Format: Bible believers network, relg. Spec prog: Farm 2 hrs, bluegrass 3 hrs wkly. ♦Connie Cody, gen mgr; Ryan Smith, opns mgr; Jim Cody, gen sls mgr; Cheryl Wright, progmg dir, progmg mgr; Steve Boutelle, news dir; Sheliah Hughes, traf mgr.

WCLC-FM— 1985: 105.1 mhz; 1.1 kw. 605 ft TL: N36 26 31 W84 55 28. (CP: 2.85 kw, ant 476 ft.). Stereo. Hrs open: Dups AM 100% Box 1509, 38556. Phone: (931) 879-8188. Fax: (931) 879-1733. Population served: 100,000 Format: Relg.

WDEB(AM)— Jan 12, 1968: 1500 khz; 1 kw-D, 500 w-CH. TL: N36 25 31 W84 56 32. Hrs open: Sunrise-sunset Box 69, 38556. Secondary address: 403 Livingston Ave. 38556. Phone: (931) 879-8164. Phone: (931) 879-9332. Fax: (931) 879-7437.E-mail: wdebaudio@twlakes.net Web Site:wderadio.com Licensee: BAZ Broadcasting Inc. (acq 4-1-72). Population served: 201,225 Rgnl. Network: Tenn. Radio Net. Tenn. Radio Net. Format: Country, relg. News staff: 7; News: 10 hrs wkly. Target aud: 18-54; household members who spend money in the marketplace. Spec prog: Farm 3 hrs wkly. ♦N.A. Baz, pres, gen mgr, prom dir, adv dir, news dir; Jean Baz, VP; Gary Crocket, progmg dir; Kevin R. Baz, mus dir; Gunther Muhsemann, chief of engrg; Gary Clark, reporter, disc jockey.

WDEB-FM— Oct 10, 1972: 103.9 mhz; 1.6 kw. 450 ft TL: N36 25 55 W84 56 33. Stereo. Hrs open: 5 AM-10:15 PM Dups AM 80% Box 69, 38556. Secondary address: 403 Livingston Ave. 38556. Phone: (931) 879-8164. Phone: (931) 879-9332. Fax: (931) 879-7437. Web Site:wderaudio@twlakes.net Wire Svc: NOAA Weather Format: Modern country, gospel. ♦Jean Baz, sls dir; N. A. Baz, rgnl sls mgr, mktg mgr, prom mgr; Cindy Mitchell, women's int ed; John Mullinix, disc jockey.

Jasper

WWAM(AM)— Mar 2, 1987: 820 khz; 5 kw-D. TL: N35 04 23 W85 37 39. Stereo. Hrs open: Box 279, 37347. Secondary address: 4896 Main St. 37347. Phone: (423) 942-1700. Phone: (931) 592-5588. Fax: (423) 942-1700. Licensee: Shelton Broadcasting System. Natl. Network: USA, . Format: Gospel. Target aud: 25-49. Spec prog: Bluegrass one hr, acappella one hr wkly. ♦Rick Shelton, gen mgr.

Jefferson City

WJFC(AM)— Nov 1, 1961: 1480 khz; 500 w-D. TL: N36 06 15 W83 29 10. Hrs open: 6 AM-6 PM Box 430, 37760. Phone: (865) 475-3825. Fax: (865) 475-3800.E-mail: wjfcteam80@charterinternet.com Licensee: Lakeway Broadcasting LLC (acq 10-12-2006; $100,000). Population served: 25,124 Timothy K. Brady. Format: Country. News staff: one; News: 10 hrs wkly. Target aud: 25 plus; Jefferson, Grainger & Hamblen counties. Spec prog: Farm one hr, relg 4 hrs wkly. ♦M. Edward Stiner Jr., pres; Kenneth C. Hill, gen mgr.

WNRX(FM)— Feb 1, 1976: 99.3 mhz; 3 kw. 654 ft TL: N36 04 28 W83 34 56. Hrs open: 24 415 Middle Creek Rd., Sevierville, 37862. Phone: (865) 453-2844. Fax: (865) 428-2601. Licensee: Citadel Broadcasting Co. Group owner: Citadel Broadcasting Corp. (acq 7-20-2004; $1.65 million). Population served: 600,000 Format: CHR. News staff: one; News: 17 hrs wkly. Spec prog: Gospel 4 hrs, relg 2 hrs wkly.

Jellico

WEKX(FM)— 1993: 102.7 mhz; 630 w. 1,008 ft TL: N36 37 55 W84 08 31. Hrs open: 24 522 Main St., Williamsburg, KY, 40769. Phone: (606) 549-1027. Fax: (606) 549-5565.E-mail: wekx@bellsouth.net Licensee: Whitley Broadcasting Co. Inc. (group owner; (acq 5-31-2002; grpsl). Population served: 500,000 Rgnl rep: Rgnl Reps. Format: Classic Rock. News: 5 hrs wkly. ♦David Estes, gen mgr; Frank Folsom, gen sls mgr, chief of engrg; Rick Campbell, stn mgr & progmg mgr.

WJJT(AM)— Feb 1, 1972: 1540 khz; 1 kw-D, 1 w-N, 500 w-CH. TL: N36 34 59 W84 08 10. Hrs open: Sunup to Sundown PO Box 88, 37762. Phone: (423) 494-1582.E-mail: wjjtradio@gmail.com Web Site:www.wjjtradio.com (streaming) Licensee: Southeast Broadcasting Corp. (acq Aug-4-2007; $250,000). Population served: 60,000 Natl. Network: Salem Radio Network, . Rgnl. Network: Tenn. Radio Net. Format: Gospel. News staff: 3; News: 4 hrs wkly. ♦Glenda Kilgore, exec VP; James Kilgore, pres, gen mgr & stn mgr.

Johnson City

WETB(AM)— Oct 1, 1947: 790 khz; 5 kw-D, 72 w-N. TL: N36 19 43 W82 24 39. Hrs open: 6 AM-11 PM Box 4127, 37602. Secondary address: 231 Brandonwood Dr. 37604. Phone: (423) 928-7131. Fax: (423) 928-8392.E-mail: webb@mounet.com Licensee: Mountain Signals Inc. (acq 12-5-90; 12-31-90). Population served: 50,000 Natl. Network: USA, . Format: Gospel. News staff: one; News: 3 hrs wkly. Target aud: General. ♦Paul Gobble Jr., gen mgr & pres; Bob Morrison, stn mgr, opns mgr, progmg dir; Loretta Gouge, gen sls mgr.

***WETS(FM)**— Feb 26, 1974: 89.5 mhz; 66 kw. 2,273 ft TL: N36 26 02 W82 08 08. Stereo. Hrs open: 24 c/o East Tennessee State University, Box 70630, Ellis Hall, 37614-1709. Phone: (423) 439-6440. Phone: (423) 439-6441. Fax: (423) 439-6449.E-mail: winklerw@etsu.edu Web Site:www.wets.org Licensee: East Tennessee State University. Population served: 500,000 Natl. Network: NPR, PRI, . Format: Class, folk, news/talk. News: 22 hrs wkly. Target aud: General. Spec prog: Blues 12 hrs, Sp one hr wkly. ♦Paul E. Stanton, pres; Wayne Winkler, gen mgr; Larry Mayer, progmg dir; Jim Blalock, mus dir; Mitch Sandidge, chief of engrg; Mike Strickland, min affrs dir; Susan Lachmann, women's int ed.

WJCW(AM)— Dec 13, 1938: 910 khz; 5 kw-D, 1 kw-N, DA-N. TL: N36 24 37 W82 27 13. Hrs open: 24 Box 8668, Gray, 37615. Phone: (423) 477-1000. Fax: (423) 477-4747.E-mail: TalkRadio@wjcw.com Web Site:www.wjcw.com Licensee: Citadel Broadcasting Co. Group owner: Citadel Broadcasting Corp. (acq 5-30-2000; grpsl). Population served: 57,000 Natl. Network: CBS, ABC, . Reddy, Begley & McCormick. Format: Talk. Target aud: 25 plus. Spec prog: Relg 4 hrs wkly. ♦Don Raines, VP, gen mgr; Bob Gordon, opns dir; Debbie Caso, sls dir; Paul Overbay, gen sls mgr; Bob Lawrence, mktg dir, prom dir; Brian Bishop, progmg dir; Richard Lovette, news dir; Al F. LeFevere, chief of engrg.

WKTP(AM)—See Jonesborough

WQUT(FM)— Mar 1, 1948: 101.5 mhz; 100 kw. Ant 1,500 ft TL: N36 16 07 W82 20 21. Stereo. Hrs open: 24 Box 8668, Gray, 37615. Phone: (423) 477-1015. Fax: (423) 477-4747.E-mail: classiccrock@wqut.com Web Site:www.wqvt.com Licensee: Citadel Broadcasting Co. Population served: 375,000 Format: Classic rock. News staff: 2; News: 3 hrs wkly. Target aud: 18-49. ♦Randy Ross, gen sls mgr; Jeri George, prom dir, disc jockey; John Patrick, progmg dir, disc jockey; Susan Rines, traf mgr; "John Boy & Billy", disc jockey.

WTFM(FM)—See Kingsport

Jonesborough

WKTP(AM)— October 1958: 1590 khz; 5 kw-U, DA-2. TL: N36 19 54 W82 28 27. Hrs open: 24
Rebroadcasts WKPT(AM) Kingsport 90%.
222 Commerce St., Kingsport, 37660. Phone: (423) 246-9578. Fax: (423) 247-9836.E-mail: davidw@wtfm.com Web Site:www.wkptam.com Licensee: Holston Valley Broadcasting Corp. Group owner: Glenwood Communications Corp. (acq 1-25-90; $90,000; 3-5-90). Population served: 200,000 Natl. Network: ABC, . Natl. Rep: McGavren Guild,. Cordon & Kelly. Wire Svc: AP Format: Oldies. News staff: 2; News: 24 hrs wkly. Target aud: 35 plus. ♦George Devault, pres; N. David Widener, exec VP, gen mgr & stn mgr; Aaron Teffeteller, progmg dir.

WTZR(FM)—See Elizabethton

Karns

WCYQ(FM)— Jan 8, 1989: 93.1 mhz; 1.2 kw. Ant 515 ft TL: N35 58 59 W84 04 37. (CP: 2.4 kw, ant 512 ft. TL: N35 57 46 W84 01 23). Hrs open: 1533 Amherst Rd., Knoxville, 37909. Phone: (865) 693-1020. Fax: (865) 693-8493.E-mail: info@wmyu.com Web Site:www.q93country.com Licensee: Journal Broadcast Corp. Group owner: Journal Communications Inc. (acq 5-19-97). Format: Country. ♦Andy Laird, VP, progmg dir, engr; Chris Protzman, gen mgr; Bruce Patrick, progmg dir.

Kingsport

***WCQR-FM**— December 1996: 88.3 mhz; 1.2 kw. Ant 2,132 ft TL: N36 25 53 W82 08 16. Stereo. Hrs open: 2312 Oak St., Gray, 37615-8039. Phone: (423) 477-5676. Fax: (423) 477-7060.E-mail: office@wcqr.org Web Site:www.wcqr.org Licensee: Positive Alternative Radio Inc. Group owner: Baker Family Stations/Positive Alternative Radio Inc. Natl. Network: Salem Radio Network, . Booth, Freret, Imlay & Tepper. Format: Contemp Christian music. Target aud: 25-54. ♦Mike Perry, gen mgr.

***WCSK(FM)**— Nov 5, 1984: 90.3 mhz; 195 w. 23 ft TL: N36 31 37 W82 35 12. Stereo. Hrs open: 1701 East Center St., 37664. Phone: (423) 378-2111. Fax: (423) 378-8473.E-mail: jhall@k12k.com Web Site:http://kcs.kk12k.com/index Licensee: Kingsport Board of Education. Population served: 70,000 Format: Educational/Eclectic Music Mix. ♦Jeff Hall, stn mgr.

WGOC(AM)— October 1951: 1320 khz; 5 kw-D, 500 w-N, DA-N. TL: N36 33 59 W82 33 22. Hrs open: 24 Box 8668, Gray, 37615. Secondary address: 162 Freehill Rd. 37615. Phone: (423) 477-1000. Fax: (423) 477-4747.E-mail: sportsmonster@640wxsm.com Web Site:www.640wxsm.com Licensee: Citadel Broadcasting Co. Group owner: Citadel Broadcasting Corp. (acq 5-30-2000; grpsl). Population served: 52,000 Natl. Network: ESPN Radio, CBS Radio, . Natl. Rep: Katz Radio,. Wiley, Rein & Fielding. Wire Svc: AP Format: sports. ♦Don Raines, gen mgr; Bob Gordon, opns dir; Debbie Caso, sls dir; Paul Overbay, gen sls mgr; Bob Lawrence, mktg dir, prom dir; Al LeFevere, chief of engrg.

WHGG(AM)— June 1967: 1090 khz; 10 kw-D. TL: N36 27 40 W82 27 12. Hrs open: 12 Box 2061, Bristol, 37621. Secondary address: 340 Edgemont Ave., Suite 100, Bristol 37620. Phone: (423) 878-6279. Fax: (423) 878-6520. Web Site:www.mighty1090.com Licensee: Information Communication Corp. (acq 1-1-2006; $250,000 with WABN(AM) Abingdon, VA). Population served: 2,000,000 Format: Oldies. News staff: one; News: 10 hrs wkly. Target aud: 24-55. ♦Kenneth C. Hill, pres, gen mgr; Matthew J. Hill, stn mgr; Rusty Curs, sls dir.

WJCW(AM)—See Johnson City

WKOS(FM)— Feb 21, 1970: 104.9 mhz; 2.75 kw. Ant 492 ft TL: N36 33 14 W82 27 00. Stereo. Hrs open: Box 8668, Gray, 37615. Secondary address: 162 Freehill Rd. 37615. Phone: (423) 477-1000. Fax: (423) 477-4747.E-mail: BestMusicMix@wkos.com Web Site:www.wkos.com Licensee: Citadel Broadcasting Co. Population served: 100,000 Natl. Network: Westwood One, . Format: Adult contemp. Target aud: 25-54. ♦Debbie Caso, gen mgr; Larry Harris, gen sls mgr; Bob Lawrence, mktg dir, prom dir; J.B. Stone, progmg dir.

WKPT(AM)— July 14, 1940: 1400 khz; 1 kw-U. TL: N36 32 37 W82 31 21. Stereo. Hrs open: 24 222 Commerce St., 37660. Phone: (423) 246-9578. Fax: (423) 247-9836.E-mail: davidw@wtfm.com Web Site:www.wkptam.com Licensee: Holston Valley Broadcasting Corp. Group owner: Glenwood Communications Corp. (acq 6-1-66). Population served: 650,000 Natl. Network: ABC, . Natl. Rep: McGavren Guild,. Cordon & Kelly. Wire Svc: AP Format: Oldies. News staff: 2. Target aud: 35 plus. ♦George Devault, pres; N. David Widener, exec VP, gen mgr; Charles Aesque, gen sls mgr; Aaron Teffeteller, progmg dir, progmg mgr; Duane Nelson, news dir, local news ed; Emily Pridemore, traf mgr; Roger Epperson, news rptr.

WQUT(FM)—Johnson City

WTFM(FM)— February 1948: 98.5 mhz; 74 kw. Ant 2,241 ft TL: N36 25 54 W82 08 15. Stereo. Hrs open: 24 222 Commerce St., 37660. Phone: (423) 246-9578. Fax: (423) 247-9836.E-mail: davidw@wtfm.com Web Site:www.wtfm.com Population served: 1,000,000 Natl. Network:

ABC, . Natl. Rep: McGavren Guild,. Cordon & Kelly. Wire Svc: AP Format: Adult contemp. News staff: 2. Target aud: 25-54. ♦N. David Widener, gen mgr; Tim Loy, gen sls mgr; Mark Baker, progmg mgr; Duane Nelson, news dir; Lyle Musser, chief of engrg; Emily Pridemore, traf mgr; Steve Mann, sports cmtr, disc jockey; Elva Marie, disc jockey. Co-owned TV: WKPT-TV affil

Kingston

WBBX(AM)— July 1978: 1410 khz; 500 w-D. TL: N35 52 49 W84 30 56. Hrs open: 8 AM-6 PM Box 389, 37763. Secondary address: 705 Greenwood St. 37763. Phone: (615) 376-6954. Licensee: Pilgrim Pathway Inc. (acq 6-30-92; $35,000; 7-27-92). Format: Gospel. Target aud: General. ♦Grant Carter, pres & gen mgr.

***WKTS(FM)**— 9/11/2006: 90.1 mhz; 55 w vert. Ant 633 ft TL: N35 45 57 W84 34 33. Hrs open: 24 331 Skyline View Ln., 37763. Phone: (865) 717-3335.E-mail: thebridgefm@yahoo.com Web Site:www.bridgeradiofm.org Licensee: Foothills Broadcasting, Inc. Format: Christian Contemp. News staff: one; News: 3 hrs wkly. Spec prog: 2 church services, 2hrs. ♦David Wells, gen mgr; Darrin Wilcox, stn mgr.

Kingston Springs

WFFI(FM)— Jan 15, 1993: 93.7 mhz; 1.15 kw. Ant 754 ft TL: N36 08 10 W86 59 04. Hrs open: 24
Simulcasts with WFFH(FM) Smyrna.
402 BNA Dr., Suite 400, Nashville, 37217. Phone: (615) 367-2210. Fax: (615) 367-0758.E-mail: 94fm@thefish.com Web Site:www.94fmthefish.net Licensee: Caron Broadcasting Inc. Group owner: Salem Communications Corp. (acq 12-18-2002; $5.6 million with WFFH(FM) Smyrna). Natl. Network: Salem Radio Network, . Natl. Rep: Salem,. Format: Contemp Christian. Target aud: 25-54; adults. ♦Michael S. Miller, gen mgr; Kevin R. Anderson, gen sls mgr; Dick Marsh, prom dir; Kim Bindel, news dir, news dir; Carl Campbell, chief of engrg; Ed Evenson, traf mgr; Vance Dillard, progmg dir & disc jockey.

Knoxville

WETR(AM)— July 5, 1995: 760 khz; 2.5 kw-D. TL: N36 02 34 W84 02 51. (CP: 2.4 kw). Hrs open: Day-time 1621 E. Magnolia Ave., 37917. Phone: (865) 525-1060. Fax: (865) 521-8923.E-mail: info@talkradio760.com Web Site:www.talkradio760.com Licensee: Thomas H. Moffit Jr. (acq 1995). Population served: 850,000 Natl. Network: Salem Radio Network, Talk Radio Network, . Format: News/talk. Target aud: 25-54; blue collar men & women. ♦David Wells, gen mgr; David Wells, progmg dir.

WIFA(AM)— Jan 21, 1941: 1240 khz; 1 kw-U. TL: N35 57 17 W83 57 04. Hrs open: 24 Box 50840, 37950. Secondary address: 818 N. Cedar Bluff Rd. 37923. Phone: (865) 531-2005. Fax: (865) 531-2006. Web Site:www.1240radio.com Licensee: Progressive Media Inc. (acq 8-6-2004; $550,000). Format: Adult contemp Christian music & talk. ♦Barry Culberson, pres; Brian Brooks, gen mgr.

WIMZ-FM— October 1949: 103.5 mhz; 100 kw. 1,723 ft TL: N36 08 06 W83 43 29. Stereo. Hrs open: 1100 Sharps Ridge Rd., 37917. Phone: (865) 525-6000. Fax: (865) 525-2000.E-mail: rcchambers@sccradio.com Web Site:www.wimz.com Licensee: South Central Communications Corp. (group owner; (acq 2-23-93; $3.5 million with co-located AM;3-15-93). Population served: 174,587 Format: Classic rock. ♦Randy Ross, sls dir; Neda Gayle, natl sls mgr; Terry Gillingham, VP & mktg mgr; Randy Chambers, progmg dir; Billy Kidd, mus dir; Nikki Roberts, pub affrs dir; Jeff Cutshaw, traf mgr.

WITA(AM)— Sept 1, 1960: 1490 khz; 1 kw-U. TL: N35 58 11 W83 57 56. Hrs open: 24 hrs 7212 Kingston Pike, 37919. Phone: (865) 588-2974. Phone: (865) 588-2975.E-mail: wita1490@aol.com Web Site:www.wwcr.com Licensee: RR Broadcast Group Inc. (group owner; (acq 2-18-2005; $425,000). Population served: 500,000 Format: Christian talk. Target aud: General. Spec prog: Black 8 hrs wkly. ♦Rex D. Palmer, pres; Gail Scott, gen mgr; Greg McMahon, opns mgr.

WIVK-FM— Dec 16, 1965: 107.7 mhz; 91 kw. 2,053 ft TL: N35 48 41 W83 40 10. Stereo. Hrs open: 24 Box 11167, 37939. Fax: (423) 588-3725. Web Site:www.wivk.com Licensee: Citadel Broadcasting Co. Population served: 200,000 Format: C&W. ♦John Crooks, progmg dir.

WJXB-FM— Apr 10, 1967: 97.5 mhz; 96 kw. 1,296 ft TL: N36 00 36 W83 55 57. Stereo. Hrs open: 24 1100 Sharps Ridge Mem Park Dr., 37917. Phone: (865) 525-6000. Fax: (865) 656-3292.E-mail: jjarnigan@sccradio.com Web Site:www.b975.com Licensee: South Central Communications Corp. (group owner). Population served: 174,589 Wire Svc: UPI Format: Adult contemp. Target aud: 25-54. ♦Terry Gillingham, VP & gen mgr; Randy Ross, sls dir; Jeff Jarnigan, progmg dir; Susan Hollingsworth, traf mgr.

***WKCS(FM)**— December 1952: 91.1 mhz; 250 w. 73 ft TL: N35 59 36 W83 55 24. Hrs open: 8 AM-3:30 PM Fulton High School, 2509 Broadway N.E., 37917. Phone: (865) 594-1259.E-mail: wkcsradio@hotmail.com Licensee: Fulton High School. Population served: 250,000 Format: Oldies. News: 3 hrs wkly. Target aud: 18 plus; University of Tennessee. ♦Russell Mayes, gen mgr.

WKGN(AM)— Sept 28, 1947: 1340 khz; 1 kw-U. TL: N35 57 20 W83 58 14. Stereo. Hrs open: Box 10005, 37919. Phone: (865) 546-7900. Fax: (865) 546-7965.E-mail: info@wkgn.com Licensee: Norsan Consulting and Management Inc. (acq 3-8-2006; $500,000). Natl. Network: Westwood One, . Natl. Rep: Roslin,. Format: Urban contemp, gospel. Target aud: 18-34; young, mobile adults. Spec prog: Relg 5 hrs, medicine/health one hr wkly. ♦Norberto Sanchez, pres; Robert L. Stewart, gen mgr; Thomas Henderson, progmg dir; Ed Martin, chief of engrg.

WKHT(FM)— November 1991: 104.5 mhz; 6 kw. 394 ft TL: N36 00 36 W83 55 57. (CP: 2.3 kw, ant 528 ft.). Hrs open: 1533 Amhearst Rd., 37909. Phone: (865) 693-1020. Phone: (865) 824-1021. Fax: (865) 824-1880.E-mail: dmckee@journalbroadcastinggroup.com Web Site:www.1045thebone.com Licensee: Journal Broadcast Corp. (group owner; (acq 3-4-98; $5.745 million with WQBB(AM) Powell). Natl. Rep: Roslin,. Format: Classic rock. Target aud: 35 plus; female. Spec prog: Pub affrs 2 hrs wkly. ♦Chris Protzman, gen mgr; Rich Bailey, opns mgr; Eddy Roy, sls dir, news dir, traf mgr; Dodie Manalac, gen sls mgr; Russ Allen, progmg dir; Mark Lucas, chief of engrg.

WKTI(AM)—(Powell, Aug 15, 1984: 1040 khz; 10 kw-D. TL: N36 02 34 W84 02 51. Stereo. Hrs open: 1533 Amhearst Rd., 37909. Secondary address: Box 50158 37950. Phone: (865) 824-1021. Fax: (865) 824-1880.E-mail: bpatrick@journalbroadcastgroup.com Web Site:www.studio1040.com Licensee: Journal Broadcast Corp. Natl. Network: AP Radio, Jones Radio Networks, . Format: Standards. ♦Dan McKee, sls dir; Bruce Patrick, progmg dir.

WKVL(AM)— Jan 16, 1989: 850 khz; 50 kw-D, DA. TL: N36 04 12 W83 58 19. Stereo. Hrs open: 517 Watt Rd., 37922. Phone: (865) 675-4105. Fax: (865) 675-4859. Licensee: Horne Radio L.L.C. Group owner: Horne Radio Group (acq 10-15-99; grpsl). Format: Talk. Target aud: 25 plus; educated, informed adults. ♦Brian Tatum, CEO & gen mgr.

WKXV(AM)— February 1953: 900 khz; 1 kw-D, 258 w-N. TL: N35 58 52 W83 59 15. Hrs open: 24 5106 Middlebrook Pike, 37921. Phone: (865) 558-0900. Fax: (865) 588-5848.E-mail: wkxv@bellsouth.net Licensee: Ratel Broadcasting Co. Inc. Population served: 174,587 Format: Relg, Southern gospel. Target aud: 18+. ♦Ted H. Lowe Sr., pres; Ted H. Lowe Jr., gen mgr, gen sls mgr; Rick Whisman, news dir; Frank Folsom, chief of engrg; Ted Lowe Jr., mus critic; Eva Ruffin, women's int ed.

WNFZ(FM)—See Oak Ridge

WNML(AM)— Mar 23, 1953: 990 khz; 10 kw-U, DA-N. TL: N36 02 33 W83 53 59. Stereo. Hrs open: 24 WIVK711, Box 11167, 37939. Secondary address: 4711 Old Kingston Pike 37919. Phone: (865) 588-6511. Fax: (865) 558-4218. Web Site:www.newstalk99.com Licensee: Citadel Broadcasting Co. Group owner: Citadel Broadcasting Corp. (acq 4-26-2001; grpsl). Population served: 520,184 Format: News/talk, sports. News staff: 8; News: 28 hrs wkly. Target aud: 25-54. ♦Farid Suleman, CEO; Donna Heffner, CFO; Ed Brantley, gen mgr, gen sls mgr; Mike Hammond, opns mgr; Charles Sells, sls dir; Lisa Rotton, natl sls mgr; Jack Lee Gillette, rgnl sls mgr; Steve Queisser, mktg dir; John Crooks, progmg dir; Tom Graham, news dir; Tim Berry, chief of engrg.

WNOX(FM)—(Oak Ridge, Apr 20, 1974: 100.3 mhz; 100 kw. Ant 2,001 ft TL: N36 11 53 W84 13 51. Stereo. Hrs open: Box 11167, 37939. Secondary address: 4711 Old Kingston Pike 37919. Phone: (865) 588-6511. Fax: (865) 588-3725. Web Site:www.wnoxnewstalk.com Licensee: Oak Ridge FM Inc. Population served: 1,201,600 Natl. Rep: Katz Radio,. Wire Svc: AP Format: News/talk. ♦Ed Brantley, VP, gen mgr; Mike Hammond, opns mgr, progmg dir; Jack Lee, gen sls mgr; Laura Hall, mktg dir; Catherine Howell, news dir; Tim Berry, chief of engrg.

WNPZ(AM)— May 21, 1961: Stn currently dark. 1580 khz; 5 kw-D, 1 kw-CH. TL: N35 54 42 W83 53 33. Hrs open: Metropolitan Management Corp. of Tennessee, 1515 Magnolia Ave., 37917. Licensee: Metropolitan Management Corp. of Tennessee (acq 5-10-02; $280,000). ♦Randal A. Mangham, pres.

WNRX(FM)—See Jefferson City

WRJZ(AM)— Feb 12, 1927: 620 khz; 5 kw-U, DA-N. TL: N35 59 24 W83 50 15. Hrs open: 24 Christian Media Ctr., 1621 E. Magnolia Ave., 37917. Phone: (865) 525-0620. Fax: (865) 521-8910.E-mail: joy62@wrjz.com Web Site:www.wrjz.com Licensee: Tennessee Media Associates. (acq 10-84). Population served: 650,000 Natl. Network: Salem Radio Network, . Natl. Rep: Salem,. Format: Christian, talk. News: 5 hrs wkly. Target aud: 25-54; white collar men & woman. ♦Thomas Moffit Jr., pres; David Wells, gen mgr, progmg dir.

***WUOT(FM)**— October 1949: 91.9 mhz; 100 kw. 1,580 ft TL: N36 00 19 W83 56 23. Stereo. Hrs open: 24 Univ. of Tennessee, 209 Communications Bldg., 37996-0322. Phone: (865) 974-5375. Fax: (865) 974-3941.E-mail: wuot@utk.edu Web Site:www.wuot.org Licensee: University of Tennessee. Population served: 600,000 Natl. Network: PRI, NPR, . Cohn & Marks. Wire Svc: AP Format: News, classical, jazz. News staff: 3; News: 37 hrs wkly. Target aud: 35-54. ♦Regina Dean, gen mgr; Greg Hill, opns dir; Dan Berry, progmg dir; Matt Shafer Powell, news dir; Mike Murvell, chief of engrg.

***WUTK-FM**— Jan 4, 1982: 90.3 mhz; 800 w. 23 ft TL: N35 57 09 W83 55 34. Stereo. Hrs open: 24 Univ. of Tenn., P-103 Andy Holt Tower, 37996. Phone: (865) 974-2228. Phone: (865) 974-2229. Fax: (865) 974-2814.E-mail: wutk@utk.edu Web Site:www.wutkradio.com Licensee: University of Tennessee. (acq 8-31-88). Population served: 350,000 Format: New rock. Target aud: 18-45; male/female. ♦Benny Smith, gen mgr, prom dir & progmg dir.

WVLZ(AM)— June 1, 1988: 1180 khz; 10 kw-D, 2.6 kw-CH. TL: N35 58 48 W83 49 09. Hrs open: 802 S. Central Ave., 37902. Phone: (865) 546-4653. Fax: (865) 637-7133. Web Site:www.wvlz.com Licensee: Kirkland Wireless Broadcasters Inc. (acq 3-25-02; $400,000 with WKCE(AM) Maryville). Population served: 400,000 Format: Sports. Target aud: 30 plus; young, married with small children. ♦John Hodge, gen mgr & stn mgr.

WWST(FM)—See Sevierville

WYFC(FM)—See Clinton

La Follette

WLAF(AM)— May 17, 1953: 1450 khz; 1 kw-U. TL: N36 22 52 W84 07 32. Hrs open: 24 Drawer 1409, 37766. Secondary address: 210 N 5th St 37766. Phone: (423) 562-1450. Phone: (423) 562-3557. Fax: (423) 562-5764.E-mail: wlaf@campbellcounty.com Licensee: Stair Co. Inc. (acq 12-15-88; $125,000; 1-16-89). Population served: 40,000 Natl. Network: USA, . Rgnl. Network: Tenn. Radio Net. Tenn. Radio Net. Format: Gospel. News staff: one; News: 7 hrs wkly. Target aud: 12+ or 25+. Spec prog: Bluegrass 7 hrs wkly. ♦Jim Stair, pres; Bill Waddell, VP, opns VP, dev VP.

WQLA(AM)— Sept 1, 1983: 960 khz; 1 kw-D. TL: N36 22 02 W84 08 50. Hrs open: Box 1539, 37766. Phone: (423) 566-1000. Fax: (865) 457-5900.E-mail: wqla@bellsouth.net Licensee: La Follette Broadcasters Inc. (acq 8-24-99; with co-located FM). Natl. Rep: Roslin,. Format: Southern gospel. Target aud: General. ♦Cliff Jennings, pres & gen mgr.

WTNQ(FM)— Sept 1, 1982: 104.9 mhz; 1.1 kw. Ant 499 ft TL: N36 21 08 W84 05 20. (CP: 900 w). Stereo. Hrs open: 24 Box 1530, 37766. Phone: (423) 566-1000. Fax: (423) 457-5900. Population served: 35,000 Format: C&W, sports. Target aud: 18 plus. ♦Barbara Nuls, gen sls mgr.

La Vergne

WBUZ(FM)— May 1, 1962: 102.9 mhz; 100 kw. Ant 954 ft TL: N35 48 01 W86 37 17. Stereo. Hrs open: 24 1824 Murfreesboro Rd., Nashville, 37217. Phone: (615) 399-1029. Fax: (615) 399-1023.E-mail: programming@1029thebuzz.com Web Site:www.1029thebuzz.com Licensee: WYCQ Inc. Group owner: The Cromwell Group Inc. (acq 11-28-89). Population served: 876,500 Rgnl. Network: Tenn. Agri. Format: New rock. Target aud: 18-34; residents in middle TN. Spec prog: Farm one hr wkly. ♦Bayard Walters, pres; Bob Reich, stn mgr; Shauna Conner, prom dir; Russ Schenck, progmg dir; Jim Patrick, news dir; David Wilson, chief of engrg; Andra Kramer, traf mgr.

Lafayette

WEEN(AM)— Nov 3, 1958: 1460 khz; 1 kw-D, 138 w-N. TL: N36 32 06 W86 00 27. Hrs open: Daytime 231 Chaffin Rd., 37083. Phone: (615) 666-2169. Fax: (615) 666-8056.E-mail: wlct@nctc.com Licensee:

Lafayette Broadcasting Co. Inc. (acq 11-1-01). Population served: 40,000 Natl. Network: Salem Radio Network, . Rgnl. Network: Tenn. Radio Net. Tenn. Radio Net. Format: Solid Gospel. Target aud: General; 25-54 year olds. Spec prog: Farm 5 hrs wkly. ♦Ivan Davis, CEO, pres; Randall Swaffer, gen mgr, stn mgr & opns dir.

WLCT(FM)— July 1, 1995: 102.1 mhz; 6 kw. Ant 325 ft TL: N36 32 06 W86 00 27. Stereo. Hrs open: 5 AM-11 PM 231 Chaffin Rd., 37083. Phone: (615) 666-2169. Fax: (615) 666-8056.E-mail: wlct@nctc.com Licensee: Lafayette Broadcasting Co. Inc. Population served: 50,000 Format: Country. Target aud: 20-60. ♦Melinda White, gen mgr, traf mgr; Randy Swaffer, gen mgr & opns mgr; Jamie Dallas, mktg mgr, sls, mktg; Jamie DAllas, prom.

Lakeland

WMQM(AM)—Licensed to Lakeland. See Memphis

Lakesite

WALV-FM— July 1, 1976: 105.1 mhz; 850 w. Ant 879 ft TL: N35 15 20 W85 13 34. Stereo. Hrs open: 24 1305 Carter St., Chattanooga, 37402. Phone: (423) 265-9494. Fax: (423) 266-2335. Licensee: J.L. Brewer Broadcasting of Cleveland LLC. Population served: 420,000 Natl. Rep: Eastman Radio,. Wiley Rein LLP. Format: Sports. Target aud: 18 plus; adults. ♦Jim Brewer, CEO; Jim Brewer II, pres, gen mgr; Dave Strycker, stn mgr; Mike Lee, progmg dir.

Lawrenceburg

***WAWI(FM)**— 1999: 89.7 mhz; 6 kw. Ant 148 ft TL: N35 16 04 W87 19 25. Hrs open: Box 3206, American Family Radio, Tupelo, MS, 38803. Phone: (662) 844-8888. Fax: (662) 842-6791.E-mail: comments@afr.net Web Site:www.afr.net Licensee: American Family Association. Group owner: American Family Radio Format: Relg. ♦Marvin Sanders, gen mgr.

WDXE(AM)— July 21, 1951: 1370 khz; 1 kw-D, 44 w-N. TL: N35 15 25 W87 18 24. Hrs open: 29 Public Square, 38464. Phone: (931) 762-4411. Fax: (931) 762-4789.E-mail: wdxe@wdxe.com Licensee: Lakewood Communications LLC (acq 9-11-02; $450,000 with co-located FM). Population served: 12,000 Rgnl. Network: Tenn. Radio Net. Tenn. Radio Net. Format: Classic country. ♦Jack Cheatwood, gen mgr, stn mgr, news dir; Ron Fisher, gen sls mgr, progmg dir, disc jockey; Phillip Kemper, chief of engrg; Paula Walker, women's int ed; Ronnie Allen, disc jockey.

WDXE-FM— Aug 28, 1964: 106.7 mhz; 6 kw. Ant 292 ft TL: N35 15 25 W87 18 24. Hrs open: Prog sep from AM 29 Public Square, 38464. Phone: (931) 762-4411. Fax: (931) 762-4789.E-mail: wdxe@wdxe.com Format: Adult contemp. ♦Jack Cheatwood, gen mgr & progmg dir.

WLLX(FM)— May 1991: 97.5 mhz; 2.3 kw. 535 ft TL: N35 12 18 W87 19 39. Stereo. Hrs open: 24 Box 156, 38464. Secondary address: 1212 N. Locust Ave. 38464.E-mail: wllxradio@lorettotel.net Licensee: Roger W. Wright dba Prospect Communications Format: Country. News staff: one. Target aud: 25-54. ♦Janet Wright, mktg mgr, adv mgr; Dan Hollander, mus dir, disc jockey; Roger Wright, pub affrs dir; Carolyn Thompson, disc jockey.

WWLX(AM)— June 21, 1987: 590 khz; 600 w-D, 133 w-N. TL: N35 12 18 W87 19 39. Stereo. Hrs open: 24 Box 156, 38464. Secondary address: 1212 N. Locust Ave. 38464. Phone: (931) 762-6200. Fax: (931) 762-6200.E-mail: ben@wlxonline.com Licensee: Roger W. Wright dba Prospect Communications. Format: C&W. News staff: one; News: 10 hrs wkly. Target aud: General. Spec prog: Oldies R&R 8 hrs, old country 8 hrs wkly. ♦Janet Wright, gen sls mgr, prom mgr; Dan Hollander, progmg dir, disc jockey; Michele Tankersley, news dir; Roger Wright, pres, gen mgr & chief of engrg; Carolyn Thompson, disc jockey.

***WZXX(FM)**— 2005: 88.5 mhz; 300 w. Ant 276 ft TL: N35 15 18 W87 19 30. Hrs open: Box 5459, Twin Falls, ID, 83303-5459. Phone: (208) 733-3551. Fax: (208) 733-3548. Web Site:www.edgewaterbroadcasting.com Licensee: Radio Assist Ministry Inc. (group owner). (acq 5-5-2005; $85,000). ♦Clark Parrish, pres.

Lebanon

WANT(FM)— Oct 1, 1993: 98.9 mhz; 5 kw. 320 ft TL: N36 12 24 W86 16 02. Stereo. Hrs open: 24 510 Trousdale Ferry Pike, 37087. Phone: (615) 444-0900. Fax: (615) 443-4235. Web Site:www.wantfm.com Licensee: Bay-Pointe Broadcasting Co. Inc. Population served: 850,000 Tierney & Swift. Format: Country. News staff: one. Target aud: General. ♦Billy Goodman, opns mgr, news dir; Susan H. James, pres, gen mgr & progmg dir; M.J. Lucas, mus dir; Albert S. Jarratt Sr., chief of engrg.

WCOR(AM)— Dec 7, 2005: 1490 khz; 1 kw-U. TL: N36 12 26 W86 16 03. Stereo. Hrs open: 24 510 Trousdale Ferry Pike, 37087. Phone: (615) 444-0900. Fax: (615) 443-4235.E-mail: Susie@WANTFM.com Licensee: Finbar Broadcasting Company Inc. Population served: 150,000 Natl. Network: ABC, . Irwin, Campbell & Tannenwald. Format: News/talk, sports. ♦William O. Barry, pres & gen mgr; Harry P. Stephenson, gen sls mgr; Billy Goodman, news dir; Gary M. Brown, chief of engrg.

***WFMQ(FM)**— Dec 15, 1966: 91.5 mhz; 500 w. Ant 82 ft TL: N36 12 13 W86 18 01. (CP: 1 kw, ant 262 ft. TL: 36 12 24 W86 16 02). Stereo. Hrs open: 24 One Cumberland Sq., 37087-3554. Phone: (615) 444-2562. Fax: (615) 444-2569.E-mail: wfmq@cumberland.edu Web Site:cumberland.edu/campus_life/wfmq Licensee: Cumberland University. Population served: 185,000 Irwin, Campbell & Tannenwald. Format: Jazz. Spec prog: Class 6 hrs wkly. ♦Dr. Harvill Eaton, pres; Jeremiah McElwain, stn mgr; Albert Jarratt Sr., chief of engrg.

WKDA(AM)— Oct 5, 1949: 900 khz; 5 kw-D, 136 w-N. TL: N36 12 26 W86 16 03. Hrs open: 24 510 Trousdale Ferry Pike, 37087. Phone: (615) 444-0900. Fax: (615) 443-4235. Web Site:www.wantfm.com Licensee: WCOR Inc. (acq 4-93; 3-15-93). Population served: 500,000 Irwin, Campbell, & Tannewald. Format: Country, big band. News staff: one. Target aud: General. ♦Susan H. James, pres & gen mgr; Billy Goodman, news dir; Gary Brown, chief of engrg.

***WRSN(FM)**—Not on air, target date: unknown: 88.1 mhz; 1.65 kw. Ant 328 ft TL: N36 24 10 W86 11 32. Hrs open: 501 N. Water Ave., Gallatin, 37066. Phone: (615) 230-7048. Web Site:www.saintjohnvianney.org/school.html Licensee: St. John Vianney Roman Catholic School. Natl. Network: EWTN Radio, . ♦John Sappenfield, gen mgr.

WRVW(FM)— Aug 31, 1962: 107.5 mhz; 46 kw. Ant 1,342 ft TL: N36 15 50 W86 47 39. Stereo. Hrs open: 24 55 Music Sq. W., Nashville, 37203. Phone: (615) 664-2400. Fax: (615) 664-2434.E-mail: programming @1075theriver.com Web Site:www.1075theriver.com Licensee: Capstar TX L.P. Group owner: Clear Channel Communications Inc. (acq 8-30-00; grpsl). Population served: 1,000,000 Format: CHR. News staff: one; News: 4 hrs wkly. Target aud: 18-49. ♦Gene McKay, gen mgr; Keith Kaufman, opns mgr; Darren Smith, sls dir; Tom Schurr, mktg mgr; Temple Hancock, prom mgr; Rich Davis, progmg dir.

Lenoir City

WBLC(AM)— June 15, 1965: 1360 khz; 1 kw-D, 24 w-N. TL: N35 47 32 W84 17 45. Hrs open: 24 Box 247, 37771. Secondary address: 4787 Browder Hollow Rd. 37771. Phone: (865) 986-5332. Fax: (865) 986-5332.E-mail: wblc3abn@bellsouth.net Licensee: Three Angels Broadcasting Network Inc. (acq 8-13-02; $55,000). Population served: 600,000 Format: Christian, relg. Target aud: 35 plus. ♦Jim Morris, gen mgr & stn mgr.

WKZX-FM— Sept 19, 1967: 93.5 mhz; 6 kw. 165 ft TL: N35 46 12 W84 16 47. Hrs open: Box 340, 406 E. Broadway, 37771. Phone: (865) 986-9850. Fax: (865) 986-1716.E-mail: wkzx@aol.com Licensee: B.P. Broadcasters L.L.C. Format: Rgnl Mexician. News staff: one; News: 20 hrs wkly. Target aud: General; Adults. ♦Dale Anthony, gen mgr & chief of engrg.

WLIL(AM)— May 30, 1950: 730 khz; 1 kw-D, 280 w-N. TL: N35 46 12 W84 16 47. Hrs open: 24 Box 520, 37771. Phone: (865) 986-7536. Fax: (865) 986-1716.E-mail: wlilcountry@aol.com Licensee: B.P. Broadcasters L.L.C. (acq 8-01-2000; $1 million with co-located FM). Population served: 31,189 Natl. Network: CNN Radio, . Natl. Rep: Keystone (unwired net),. Rgnl rep: Rgnl Reps. Format: Classic country. News staff: one; News: 20 hrs wkly. Target aud: General; adults. Spec prog: Black one hr, farm one hr, gospel 18 hrs, American Indian one hr wkly. ♦Dale Anthony, gen mgr.

Lewisburg

WAXO(AM)— Sept 1, 1980: 1220 khz; 1 kw-D. TL: N35 25 42 W86 46 22. Hrs open: 217 W. Commerce St., 37091. Phone: (931) 359-6641. Fax: (931) 270-9290.E-mail: waxo@waxo.com Web Site:www.waxo.com Licensee: Marshall County Radio Corp. (acq 9-1-82; $250,000; 8-23-82). Population served: 25,000 Natl. Network: USA, . Format: Country. Spec prog: Gospel 12 hrs wkly. ♦Bob Smartt, pres & gen mgr.

WJJM(AM)— May 15, 1947: 1490 khz; 1 kw-U. TL: N35 27 03 W86 46 57. Hrs open: Box 2025, 37091. Secondary address: 344 E. Church St. 37091. Phone: (931) 359-4511. Fax: (931) 270-9556.E-mail: wjjm@wjjm.com Web Site:www.wjjm.com Licensee: WJJM Inc. (acq 3-26-2004; $230,000 with co-located FM). Population served: 7,207 Rgnl. Network: Tenn. Radio Net. Natl. Rep: Keystone (unwired net),. Tenn. Radio Net. Fletcher, Heald & Hidreth. Format: Country. News staff: one; News: one hr wkly. Target aud: 25-65; manufacturing, business, family programming. ♦Michelle W. Haislip, pres; Lisa Savage, gen mgr; Michelle W. Haislip, stn mgr, sls dir; Jeff Haislip, progmg mgr; Doug Hazelwood, mus dir; Tommy Allen, news dir; Don Roden, chief of engrg.

WJJM-FM— Feb 20, 1969: 94.3 mhz; 5.5 kw. Ant 115 ft TL: N35 27 03 W86 46 57. Stereo. Hrs open: 17 Box 2025, 37091. Secondary address: 344 E. Church St. 37091. Phone: (931) 359-4511. Fax: (931) 270-9556. Web Site:www.wjjm.com Licensee: WJJM Inc. Population served: 20,000 Format: Country. ♦Doug Cheek, adv dir; Chris Bates, disc jockey.

Lexington

WDXL(AM)— July 1954: 1490 khz; 1 kw-U. TL: N35 38 05 W88 23 34. Hrs open: 24 Box 279, 38351. Secondary address: 584 Smith Ave. 38351. Phone: (731) 968-3500. Phone: (731) 968-9990. Fax: (731) 968-0380.E-mail: wzlt@netease.net Licensee: Lexington Broadcast Service Inc. (acq 1955). Population served: 21,000 Natl. Network: Jones Radio Networks, . Format: Southern gospel. News staff: one; News: 10 hrs wkly. Target aud: 30 plus. Spec prog: Black 4 hrs, gospel 10 hrs wkly. ♦Dan Hughes, gen mgr, gen sls mgr, sports cmtr; Terry Rhodes, progmg dir.

***WIGH(FM)**— Sept 30, 1995: 88.7 mhz; 15 kw. Ant 548 ft TL: N35 42 12 W88 36 10. (CP: 14 kw, ant 538 ft. TL: N35 43 19 W88 36 07). Stereo. Hrs open: 24 Box 3206, Tupelo, MS, 38803. Secondary address: 107 Park Gate Dr., Tupelo, MS 38801. Phone: (662) 844-8888. Fax: (662) 842-6791. Licensee: American Family Association. Group owner: American Family Radio (acq 5-22-03; $20,000). Population served: 250,000 Natl. Network: American Family Radio, . Format: Christian. Target aud: Visually & physically impaired. ♦Marvin Sanders, gen mgr.

WZLT(FM)— September 1964: 99.3 mhz; 5 kw. 150 ft TL: N35 38 05 W88 23 34. Stereo. Hrs open: 24 Prog sep from AM Box 279, 38351. Secondary address: 584 Smith Ave. 38351. Phone: (731) 968-9990. Fax: (731) 968-0380.E-mail: wzlt@netease.net Licensee: Lexington Broadcast Service Inc. Population served: 30,000 Format: Adult contemp. Target aud: General. ♦Todd Buttrey, progmg dir.

Livingston

WLIV(AM)— Nov 26, 1956: 920 khz; 1 kw-D. TL: N36 22 28 W85 18 20. Hrs open: 24 Box 359, 1130 W. Main St., 38570. Phone: (931) 823-1226. Fax: (931) 823-6005. Licensee: Sunny Broadcasting G.P. (acq 1996; $100,000 with co-located FM). Population served: 21,504 Natl. Network: CNN Radio, . Rgnl. Network: Tenn. Radio Net. Natl. Rep: Keystone (unwired net),. Tenn. Radio Net. Format: News, Sports. News staff: 2; News: 7 hrs wkly. Target aud: General. Spec prog: Farm 2 hrs, relg 15 hrs, gospel 18 hrs wkly. ♦Millard V. Oakley, pres; Joel Upton, gen mgr; Carolyn Peterman, stn mgr; Craig Cantrell, opns dir; Austin Stinnett, chief of engrg; Shirley Burnette, traf mgr.

WLQK(FM)— December 1966: 95.9 mhz; 20 kw. 784 ft TL: N36 11 36 W85 20 41. Stereo. Hrs open: 259 S. Willow Ave., Cookeville, 38501. Phone: (931) 526-6064. Fax: (931) 520-1590.E-mail: jimstapleton @jwcbroadcasting.com Web Site:www.literock959.com Licensee: JWC Broadcasting (group owner; acq 12-18-98). Natl. Rep: Rgnl Reps,. Format: Soft rock. Target aud: General. ♦Jim Stapleton, gen mgr & stn mgr.

Lobelville

WFGZ(FM)— October 1974: 94.5 mhz; 22 kw. Ant 715 ft TL: N35 45 56 W87 49 50. Stereo. Hrs open: 24 25 Stonebrook Place, Suite G 322, Jackson, 38305. Phone: (888) 855-9394. Fax: (731) 855-1600.E-mail: info@gracebroadcasting.com Web Site:www.gracebroadcasting.com Licensee: Grace Broadcasting Services Inc. (acq 11-28-2003; $487,000). Population served: 250,000 Format: Contemp Christian. News staff: one; News: 14 hrs wkly. Target aud: 18-54; mid to upper income adults with purchasing power. ♦Charles M. Ennis, pres; Lacy Ennis, gen mgr & opns mgr.

Lookout Mountain

WFLI(AM)— Feb 20, 1961: 1070 khz; 50 kw-D, 2.5 kw-N, DA-2. TL: N35 02 42 W85 21 44. Hrs open: 24 621 O' Grady Dr., Chattanooga, 37419. Phone: (423) 821-3555. Fax: (423) 821-3557.E-mail: flipaul@aol.com

Licensee: WFLI Inc. Population served: 400,000 Natl. Network: USA, . Format: Relg, southern gospel. Target aud: 18-54. ◆Ying Hua Benns, pres & gen mgr; Paul White, stn mgr, opns mgr.

Loretto

WJHX(AM)—See Lexington, AL

WKSR-FM— Jan 12, 1970: 98.3 mhz; 18 kw. Ant 377 ft TL: N35 09 00 W87 17 45. Stereo. Hrs open: Box 738, Pulaski, 38478. Secondary address: 104 S. Second St., Pulaski 38478. Phone: (931) 363-2505. Fax: (931) 424-3157. Licensee: Pulaski Broadcasting Inc. (acq 1-1-84; $350,000; 12-19-83). Population served: 75,000 Natl. Network: ABC, . Format: Country. News staff: 2. ◆Ronnie Rose, gen mgr; Ed Carter, progmg dir.

Loudon

WFIV-FM— May 20, 1991: 105.3 mhz; 6 kw. 328 ft TL: N35 48 40 W84 16 02. Stereo. Hrs open: 24 517 Watt Rd., Knoxville, 37922. Phone: (865) 675-4105. Fax: (865) 675-4859.E-mail: horneradio@nxs.net Web Site:www.wkvl.com Licensee: Horne Radio L.L.C. Group owner: Horne Radio Group (acq 8-29-2001; grpsl). Population served: 350,000 Natl. Network: CBS, . Format: AAA. News: 3 hrs wkly. Target aud: 25-50; baby boomers. ◆Douglas A. Horne, pres; Jim Christensen, gen mgr; Shawn Nunally, gen sls mgr; Todd Ethridge, progmg dir; Brian Tatum, chief of engrg; Martha Lee, traf mgr.

WLOD(AM)— Jan 1, 1983: 1140 khz; 1 kw-D. TL: N35 43 35 W84 20 49. Hrs open: Sunrise-sunset 517 Watt Rd., Knoxville, 37922. Phone: (865) 675-4105. Fax: (865) 675-4859. Licensee: Horne Radio LLC. Group owner: Horne Radio Group (acq 8-29-01; grpsl). Natl. Network: ABC, . Format: News/Talk. News staff: one. Target aud: 35 plus. ◆Bill Tatum, gen mgr.

WNML-FM— Jan 5, 1989: 99.1 mhz; 6 kw. 328 ft TL: N35 47 10 W84 17 24. Stereo. Hrs open: 24 Simulcast with WNML (AM) & WNRX (FM) Knoxville. Box 11167, Knoxville, 37939-1167. Secondary address: 4711 Old Kingston Pike, Knoxville 37919. Phone: (865) 588-6511. Fax: (865) 558-4217. Web Site:www.sportsanimal99.com Licensee: Citadel Broadcasting Co. Group owner: Citadel Broadcasting Corp. (acq 8-2-00; grpsl). Natl. Network: ABC, Westwood One, . Natl. Rep: Katz Radio,. Rgnl rep: Rgnl Reps. Wire Svc: AP Format: Sports talk. Target aud: 25-54. ◆Ed Brantley, gen mgr; Mike Hammond, opns mgr; Jack Lee, gen sls mgr; Mickey Dearstone, mktg dir; Tim Berry, chief of engrg.

Lynchburg

*WGBQ(FM)—Not on air, target date: unknown: 91.9 mhz; 470 w. Ant 226 ft TL: N35 20 10 W86 20 31. Hrs open: 102 Red Branch Ln., Simpsonville, SC, 29681. Phone: (864) 297-0216. Fax: (864) 297-0344.E-mail: info@networkofglory.org Web Site:networkofglory.com Licensee: Network of Glory Inc. ◆Lola Richey, pres.

Madison

WPLN(AM)—Licensed to Madison. See Nashville

WRLT(FM)—See Franklin

Madisonville

WRKQ(AM)— July 12, 1967: 1250 khz; 500 w-D, 86 w-N. TL: N35 30 29 W84 22 45. Hrs open: 6 AM-6 PM Box 489, 37354. Phone: (423) 442-1446. Fax: (423) 440-9636. Web Site:www.wrkq.net Licensee: Beverly Broadcasting Co. LLC (acq 5-4-2004; $40,000). Population served: 2,858 Natl. Network: CBS Radio, . Format: News/talk. News staff: one. Target aud: General. ◆Mike Beverly, pres & gen mgr.

WYGO(FM)— Nov 15, 1992: 99.5 mhz; 2.51 kw. 515 ft TL: N35 30 20 W84 27 21. Stereo. Hrs open: 24 Box 933, Athens, 37371. Secondary address: 2110 Oxnard Rd., Athens 37303. Phone: (423) 337-0995. Phone: (423) 746-0995. Fax: (423) 745-2000. Licensee: Major Broadcasting Corp. Format: Music of 80s & 90s, hot adult contemp. Target aud: 18-54. ◆Randy Sliger, gen mgr.

Manchester

WFTZ(FM)— Nov 16, 1992: 101.5 mhz; 3 kw. 345 ft TL: N35 23 51 W86 08 39. Stereo. Hrs open: 24 Box 1015, 37349. Secondary address: 1025 Hillsboro Blvd. 37355. Phone: (931) 723-1015. (931) 728-3458. Fax: (931) 723-1099.E-mail: kahuna@fantasyradio.com Web Site:www.fantasyradio.com Licensee: Phase Two Communications Inc. (acq 10-21-91). Population served: 250,000 Natl. Network: ABC, . Timothy K. Brady. Wire Svc: AP Format: Adult contemp. News staff: one; News: 4 hrs wkly. Target aud: 25-45; white collar, educated. ◆Roger H. Dotson, CEO, pres, gen mgr, opns mgr, chief of engrg; Marsha T. Dotson, gen sls mgr; Amber Dotson, prom VP, traf mgr; Taylor VanWormer, progmg dir; Wayne D. Hudgens, news dir & pub affrs dir.

WMSR(AM)— Apr 7, 1957: 1320 khz; 5 kw-D, 79 w-N. TL: N35 28 03 W86 05 42. Hrs open: 24 1030 Oakdale St., 37355. Phone: (931) 728-3526. Phone: (931) 728-1320. Fax: (931) 728-3527.E-mail: wmsr@thunder1320.com Web Site:www.thunder1320.com Licensee: Coffee County Broadcasting Inc. (acq 8-22-2005; $700,000). Wire Svc: AP Format: Oldies, sports, talk. News staff: one; News: 21 hrs wkly. Target aud: General. Spec prog: High school sports, farm. ◆Scott Vaughn, gen mgr.

WWTN(FM)— June 20, 1962: 99.7 mhz; 100 kw. 2,033 ft TL: N35 28 03 W86 05 42. Stereo. Hrs open: 10 Music Cir. E., Nashville, 37203. Phone: (615) 321-1067. Fax: (615) 321-5771. Fax: (615) 871-6099. Web Site:www.997wtn.com Licensee: Cumulus Licensing Corp. Group owner: Cumulus Media Inc. (acq 7-21-2003; $65 million with WSM-FM Nashville). Population served: 1,233,170 Natl. Network: ABC, CBS Radio, . Wire Svc: UPI Format: News/talk, sports. Target aud: 25-54; general. ◆John Columbus, gen mgr; Mark McLaughlin, gen sls mgr.

Martin

WCMT(AM)— June 8, 1957: 1410 khz; 700 w-D, 58 w-N. TL: N36 21 45 W88 50 56. Hrs open: 24 Box 318, 1410 N. Lindell St., 38237. Phone: (731) 587-9526. Fax: (731) 587-5079.E-mail: wcmt@crunet.com Web Site:www.wcmt.com Licensee: Thunderbolt Broadcasting Co. Group owner: Thunderbolt Broadcasting Co./Gibson County Broadcasting (acq 3-1-80;2-18-80). Population served: 420,335 Natl. Network: Westwood One, AP Radio, . Womble, Carlyle, Sandridge & Rice. Format: News/talk, oldies. News: 10 hrs wkly. Target aud: 25-54; baby boomers. ◆Paul F. Tinkle, pres.

WCMT-FM—(South Fulton, Sept 26, 1967: 101.3 mhz; 22 kw. Ant 308 ft TL: N36 29 00 W88 57 10. Stereo. Hrs open: 24 Prog sep from AM Box 318, Marten, 38232. Phone: (731) 587-9526. Fax: (731) 587-5079.E-mail: wcmt@crunet.com Web Site:www.wcmt.com Population served: 507,170 Womble, Carlyle, Sandridge & Rice. Format: AC. News: 25 hrs wkly. ◆Paul Tinkle, pres.

*WUTM(FM)— Sept 1, 1971: 90.3 mhz; 185 w. 250 ft TL: N36 20 28 W88 51 39. Stereo. Hrs open: 6 AM-midnight 220 Gooch Hall, Univ. of Tenn. at Martin, 38238. Phone: (731) 881-7095. Fax: (731) 881-7550.E-mail: wutm@utm.edu Web Site:www.utm.edu /organizations/wutm Licensee: University of Tennessee. Population served: 10,000 Tenn. Radio Net. Format: CHR. Target aud: General; Univ.

Maryville

WBCR(AM)—See Alcoa

WGAP(AM)— Aug 13, 1947: 1400 khz; 1 kw-U. TL: N35 45 41 W83 58 57. Hrs open: 24 517 Watt Rd., Knoxville, 37934. Phone: (865) 983-4310. Phone: (865) 983-4105. Fax: (865) 983-4314. Fax: (865) 675-4859. Licensee: Horne Radio LLC. Group owner: Horne Radio Group (acq 8-29-01; grpsl). Population served: 412,000 Natl. Network: Motor Racing Net, . Natl. Rep: Rgnl Reps,. Pepper & Corazzini. Format: Country. News staff: one; News: 18 hrs wkly. Target aud: 25 plus; general. ◆Brian Tatum, gen mgr.

WKCE(AM)— 1989: 1120 khz; 500 w-D. TL: N35 45 08 W83 35 04. Stereo. Hrs open: 802 S. Central, Knoxville, 37902. Phone: (865) 546-4653. Fax: (865) 637-7133. Licensee: Kirkland Wireless Broadcasters Inc. (acq 3-25-2002; $400,000 with WVLZ(AM) Knoxville). Natl. Network: ESPN Deportes, . Format: Sp sports. ◆Rob Robinson, opns mgr.

WQJK(FM)— Feb 2, 1990: 95.7 mhz; 6 kw. Ant 321 ft TL: N35 49 53 W84 01 25. Stereo. Hrs open: 24 1100 Sharps Ridge Mem Park Dr., Knoxville, 37917. Phone: (865) 525-6000. Fax: (865) 656-4386.E-mail: rchambers@sccradio.com Web Site:www.jackfmknoxville.com Licensee: South Central Communications Corp. (group owner) Population served: 785,000 Format: JACK-FM/adult hits. Target aud: 35-59;

adults. ◆J.P. Engelbrecht, CEO; Craig Jacobus, pres, gen mgr; Terry Gillingham, opns mgr; Randy Chambers, prom mgr, progmg dir; Judy Dyke, traf mgr.

Maynardville

*WDLF(FM)— 2001: 88.3 mhz; 2.85 kw horiz. Ant 1,489 ft TL: N36 00 13 W83 56 34. Hrs open: 1621 E. Magnolia Ave., Knoxville, 37917. Phone: (865) 521-8910. Fax: (865) 521-8923.E-mail: info@ez88.org Web Site:life883.org Licensee: Foothills Broadcasting Inc. Population served: 650,000 Format: Christian. ◆David Wells, gen mgr; Mike Blakemore, progmg dir; Marisa Lykins, prom.

McKenzie

*WAJJ(FM)— 2002: 89.3 mhz; 1 kw. Ant 328 ft TL: N36 06 55 W88 30 38. Hrs open: 24 1415 Island Ford Rd., Madisonville, KY, 42431. Phone: (270) 825-3004.E-mail: comments@wsof.org Web Site:www.wajjradio.org Licensee: Temple Broadcasting Co. (acq 7-25-2005; $90,000). Format: Christian educ. ◆Gary Hall, gen mgr.

WHDM(AM)— Jan 29, 1954: 1440 khz; 500 w-D, 91 w-N. TL: N36 07 20 W88 31 31. Hrs open: 110 India Rd., Paris, 38242. Phone: (731) 644-9455. Fax: (731) 644-9970.E-mail: wmvf@bellsouth.net Web Site:www.whdmradio.com Licensee: WHDM Broadcasting Inc. (acq 1-4-2002; $69,000). Population served: 5,651 Natl. Network: ABC, . Format: Oldies. News staff: one; News: 4 hrs wkly. ◆Gary D. Benton, pres; Janice Benton, gen mgr & opns VP.

WWYN(FM)— Feb 11, 1963: 106.9 mhz; 100 kw. Ant 892 ft TL: N35 54 06 W88 46 55. (CP: ant 886 ft. TL: N35 54 05 W88 46 51). Stereo. Hrs open: 24 111 W. Main St., Jackson, 38301. Phone: (731) 427-9616. Fax: (731) 424-2773.E-mail: cthomas@wwyn.fm Web Site:www.wwyn.fm Licensee: Rainbow Media Inc. Group owner: Thomas Radio LLC (acq 11-9-2001). Population served: 386,000 Format: Modern country. News staff: one; News: 4 hrs wkly. Target aud: 25-54; adults. ◆Chip Thomas, gen mgr; Shane Conner, progmg dir; Ellen Bennet, news dir; Jim Smith, chief of engrg.

McKinnon

WTPR-FM— 1992: 101.7 mhz; 1.8 kw. Ant 607 ft TL: N36 24 39 W87 58 06. Stereo. Hrs open: 24 Rebroadcasts WTPR(AM) Paris 100%. 206 N. Brewer St., Paris, 38242. Phone: (731) 642-7100. Fax: (731) 642-9367.yes Licensee: WENK of Union City Inc. (group owner; (acq 1996; $200,000). Population served: 55,000 Rgnl rep: Rgnl Reps. Shainis & Peltzman. Format: 60s & 70s oldies. News staff: one; News: 12 hrs wkly. Target aud: 35-54. ◆Terry Hailey, gen mgr, progmg dir & engr.

McMinnville

WAKI(AM)— 1947: 1230 khz; 1 kw-U. TL: N35 41 42 W85 46 33. Hrs open: 5 AM-midnight 230 W. Coville St, 37110. Phone: (931) 473-9253. Fax: (931) 473-4149.E-mail: jeffbarnes@clearchannel.com Licensee: Peg Broadcasting Crossville LLC. Group owner: Clear Channel Communications Inc. (acq 6-30-2008; grpsl). Population served: 85,000 Putbrese, Hunsaker & Trent. Format: News/talk info. News staff: one; News: 24 hrs wkly. Target aud: 25-54; general. Spec prog: Farm 2 hrs wkly. ◆David Roederer, gen mgr.

WBMC(AM)— May 1, 1955: 960 khz; 500 w-D. TL: N35 40 00 W85 46 00. Hrs open: 5 AM-8 PM 230 W. Coville St, 37110. Phone: (931) 473-2104. Fax: (931) 473-4149. Licensee: Peg Broadcasting Crossville LLC. Group owner: Clear Channel Communications Inc. (acq 6-30-2008; grpsl). Population served: 90,000 Natl. Network: ABC, . Format: Country, Top-40, gospel. News staff: one; News: 10 hrs wkly. Target aud: General. Spec prog: Farm 5 hrs wkly. ◆Bryan Kell, gen mgr, stn mgr, gen sls mgr; Jeff Barnes, progmg dir; Jay Walker, news dir; Homer Wilson Jr., chief of engrg; Kathy Klasek, traf mgr.

*WCPI(FM)— February 1997: 91.3 mhz; 1.6 kw. 182 ft TL: N35 40 41 W85 45 06. Stereo. Hrs open: 24 110 S. Court Sq., 37110. Phone: (931) 506-9274. Fax: (931) 507-1005.E-mail: wcpi@blomand.net Licensee: Warren County Education Foundation. Population served: 90,763 Wire Svc: AP Format: Educ. Target aud: 6 plus. ◆Dr. Norman Rone, pres; Gloria Grissom, stn mgr; Mary Cantrell, mktg dir; Richard Myers, chief of engrg.

Memphis

KQPN(AM)—See West Memphis, AR

KWAM(AM)— 1946: 990 khz; 10 kw-D, 450 w-N, DA-2. TL: N35 08 04 W90 05 38. Hrs open: 2650 Thousand Oaks Blvd., Suite 4100, 38118. Phone: (901) 259-1300. Fax: (901) 259-6449. Licensee: Concord Media Group Inc. (acq 11-2-2000; $1 million). Population served: 800,000 Format: Talk/news. Target aud: 25 plus; general. ♦Tim Davies, gen mgr; Jeffrey Jones, gen sls mgr; Leonard Blakely, progmg dir.

WBBP(AM)— Apr 11, 1964: 1480 khz; 5 kw-D, 100 w-N. TL: N35 03 18 W90 05 15. Hrs open: 24 369 GE Patterson Ave., 38126. Phone: (901) 278-7878. Fax: (901) 332-1707. Web Site:www.bbless.org Licensee: Bountiful Blessings Inc. (acq 10-25-90; $462,000; 11-19-90). Population served: 942,000 Format: Gospel. Target aud: 25-54; Listeners who enjoy a variety of gospel. ♦Bishop G.E. Patterson, pres, gen mgr; Sterlene Chavers, traf mgr.

WCRV(AM)—See Collierville

WDIA(AM)— June 7, 1947: 1070 khz; 50 kw-D, 5 kw-N, DA-2. TL: N35 16 05 W90 01 03. Hrs open: 24 2650 Thousand Oaks Blvd., Suite 4100, 38118. Phone: (901) 259-1300. Fax: (901) 259-6451.E-mail: info@am1070wdia.com Web Site:www.am1070wdia.com Licensee: CC Licenses LLC. Group owner: Clear Channel Communications Inc. (acq 1996; grpsl). Population served: 670,000 Natl. Network: ABC, . Natl. Rep: Clear Channel,. Format: Black urban contemp. Target aud: 25-54; Black adults. Spec prog: Gospel. ♦Tim Davies, gen mgr; Ralph Salierno, sls dir; Franklin Gilbert Jr., prom dir; Bobby O'Jay, progmg dir; Alonzo Pendleton, chief of engrg.

WEGR(FM)— March 1967: 102.7 mhz; 100 kw. 970 ft TL: N35 10 52 W89 49 56. Stereo. Hrs open: 24 Prog sep from AM 2650 Thousand Oaks Blvd., Suite 4100, 38118. Phone: (901) 259-1300. Fax: (901) 259-6451.E-mail: rock103@aol.com Web Site:www.rock103.com Population served: 1,700,000 Natl. Rep: Clear Channel,. Format: Classic rock. News staff: one; News: 15 hrs wkly. Target aud: 25-54; 25-34 core audience-70% male, 30% female. Spec prog: Rockline, flashback, blues show. ♦Tim Spencer, opns mgr; Felicia Moore, prom mgr. Co-owned TV: WPTY-TV, WLMT(TV) affils

***WEVL(FM)**— May 1, 1976: 89.9 mhz; 9.3 kw. 374 ft TL: N35 08 05 W89 45 38. Stereo. Hrs open: 20 Box 40952, 38174-0952. Secondary address: 518 S. Main St. 38103. Phone: (901) 528-0560. Phone: (901) 528-0561.E-mail: wevl@wevl.org Web Site:www.wevl.org Licensee: Southern Communication Volunteers Inc. Population served: 1,000,000 Format: Var, educ, blues. News: 2 hrs wkly. Target aud: General. Spec prog: Jazz 15 hrs, C&W 15 hrs, Fr one hr, Irish 4 hrs, Indian subcontinent one hr wkly. ♦Dan Phillips, pres; Judy Dorsey, stn mgr, opns dir & dev dir.

WGKX(FM)— Jan 10, 1968: 105.9 mhz; 100 kw. Ant 993 ft TL: N35 09 16 W89 49 20. Stereo. Hrs open: 24 5629 Murray Rd., 38119. Phone: (901) 682-1106. Fax: (901) 767-9531. Web Site:www.kix106.com Licensee: Citadel Broadcasting Co. Group owner: Citadel Broadcasting Corp. (acq 3-23-2004; grpsl). Population served: 1,800,000 Natl. Rep: Katz Radio,. Format: Country. Target aud: 25-54. ♦Sheri Sawyer, gen mgr, sls dir; Dan Barron, sls dir, chief of engrg; Gennora Reed, gen sls mgr, prom dir; Tim Jones, progmg dir; Paula Davis, prom.

WGSF(AM)— February 1984: 1030 khz; 50 kw-D, 1 kw-N, 10 kw-CH. TL: N35 10 59 W89 56 17. Hrs open: 24 Stn currently dark 3654 Park Ave., 38111. Phone: (901) 454-9948. Fax: (901) 454-1027. Licensee: Arlington Broadcasting Co. Inc. Natl. Network: Westwood One, CBS, . Format: Spanish. ♦Daniel Ybarra, gen mgr.

WHBQ(AM)— Mar 18, 1925: 560 khz; 5 kw-D, 1 kw-N, DA-2. TL: N35 15 12 W90 02 51. Hrs open: 24 6080 Mt. Moriah, 38115. Phone: (901) 375-9324. Fax: (901) 375-4117. Web Site:www.sports56whbq.com Licensee: Flinn Broadcasting Corp. (acq 10-1-88). Population served: 1,735,400 Natl. Network: CBS, . Rgnl. Network: Conference Call. Format: Sports. News: 2 hrs wkly. Target aud: 18-54. ♦George S. Flinn, pres; Chris Coates, gen mgr; Eli Savoie, progmg dir, chief of engrg.

WHRK(FM)— Jan 1, 1961: 97.1 mhz; 100 kw. Ant 530 ft TL: N35 13 23 W90 02 33. Stereo. Hrs open: 24 Prog sep from AM 2650 Thousand Oaks Blvd., Suite 4100, 38118. Phone: (901) 259-1300. Fax: (901) 259-6451.E-mail: info@k97fm.com Web Site:www.k97fm.com Population served: 751,000 Format: Urban contemp. Target aud: 18-49. ♦Devin Steel, progmg dir.

***WKNO-FM**— Mar 1, 1972: 91.1 mhz; 100 kw. 580 ft TL: N35 09 17 W89 49 20. Stereo. Hrs open: 24 7151 Cherry Farms Rd., 38016. Phone: (901) 458-2521. Fax: (901) 325-6505. Web Site:www.wknofm.org Licensee: Mid-South Public Communications Foundation. Population served: 623,530 Natl. Network: NPR, PRI, . Schwartz, Woods & Miller. Format: News and Classical. News staff: 2; News: 51 hrs wkly. Target aud: 35 plus. ♦Michael LaBonia, pres; Dan Campbell, gen mgr; Darel Snodgrass, opns mgr; Charles McCarty, dev dir. Co-owned TV: *WKNO-TV affil

WKQK(FM)—(Germantown, Apr 15, 1977: 94.1 mhz; 50 kw. Ant 472 ft TL: N34 59 22 W89 51 45. Stereo. Hrs open: 24 1835 Moriah Woods Blvd., Bldg. 1, 38117. Phone: (901) 767-0104. Fax: (901) 682-2804. Web Site:www.941kqk.com Licensee: Entercom Memphis License LLC. Group owner: Entercom Communications Corp. (acq 12-13-99; grpsl). Population served: 1,200,000 Format: Classic hits. News staff: one; News: 2 hrs wkly. Target aud: 18-49; adults with discretionary income. ♦Dan Barron, gen mgr.

WLOK(AM)— Mar 1, 1956: 1340 khz; 1 kw-U. TL: N35 07 01 W90 00 59. Hrs open: 24 363 S. 2nd St., 38103. Phone: (901) 527-9565. Fax: (901) 528-0335. Web Site:www.wlok.com Licensee: Gilliam Communications Inc. (acq 1-12-77). Population served: 1,000,000 Natl. Rep: McGavren Guild,. Format: Gospel, talk. News staff: one. Target aud: 25-54. ♦H. Gilliam Jr., gen mgr; Jerry Bafford, gen sls mgr, natl sls mgr; Kim Harper, progmg dir; Delsa Fleming, mus dir; Jay Mumphrey, news dir; Falesha Stafford, pub affrs dir.

WMC(AM)— Jan 21, 1923: 790 khz; 5 kw-U, DA-N. TL: N35 10 09 W89 53 12. Stereo. Hrs open: 24 1835 Moriah Woods Blvd., Bldg. 1, 38117. Phone: (901) 726-0555. Fax: (901) 726-5847.E-mail: info@wmc79.com Web Site:www.wmc79.com Licensee: Entercom Memphis License Inc. Group owner: Infinity Broadcasting Corp. (acq 11-30-2007; grpsl). Population served: 1,008,400 Natl. Rep: CBS Radio,. Wire Svc: Metro Weather Service Inc. Format: Country. News staff: one. ♦Terry Wood, sr VP, VP, gen mgr, gen mgr & opns mgr.

WMC-FM— May 22, 1947: 99.7 mhz; 300 kw. 970 ft TL: N35 10 09 W89 53 12. Stereo. Hrs open: 24 1835 Moriah Woods Blvd., Bldg. 1, 38117. Fax: (901) 726-0555. Web Site:www.fm100memphis.com Licensee: Entercom Memphis License Inc Population served: 1,008,400 Format: Adult contemp. Target aud: 25-54; adults.

WMFS(AM)— March 1925: 680 khz; 10 kw-D, 5 kw-N, DA-N. TL: N35 13 23 W90 02 33. Stereo. Hrs open: 1835 Moriah Woods Blvd., Bldg. 1, 38117. Phone: (901) 767-0104. Fax: (901) 767-0582. Licensee: Entercom Memphis License LLC. Group owner: Entercom Communications Corp. (acq 12-13-99; grpsl). Population served: 733,300 Natl. Network: Fox Sports, . Format: Sports. ♦Dan Barron, VP, gen mgr; Kory Myers, gen sls mgr; Rondi Atkinson, mktg dir; Dennis Fuller, progmg dir, progmg mgr; Mike Schwartz, chief of engrg.

WMPS(AM)—(Bartlett, Aug 19, 1986: 1210 khz; 10 kw-D, 250 w-N, DA-2. TL: N35 18 27 W89 38 21. Hrs open: 24 6080 Mt. Moriah Rd. Ext., 38115. Phone: (901) 375-9324. Fax: (901) 375-0041.E-mail: mail@flinn.com Licensee: Arlington Broadcasting Co. Inc. Rgnl. Network: Tenn. Radio Net. Tenn. Radio Net. Format: Music of Your Life. Target aud: 25 plus. Spec prog: Relg progmg 7 hrs wkly. ♦Fred Flinn, pres; Shea Flinn, gen mgr.

WMQM(AM)—(Lakeland, Apr 27, 1955: 1600 khz; 50 kw-D, 35 w-N. TL: N35 10 34 W89 56 10. Hrs open: 24 3704 Whittier, 38108. Secondary address: Sale Office, 1300 WWCR Ave., Nashville 37218. Phone: (901) 327-2500. Fax: (901) 327-2777.E-mail: info@wwcr.com Web Site:www.wwcr.com Licensee: WMQM Inc. Group owner: F.W. Robbert Broadcasting Co. Inc. Population served: 2,000,000 Format: Relg. Target aud: General. ♦Fred P. Werstenberger, pres; George McClintock, gen mgr; David Brown, stn mgr; Adam Lock, opns mgr.

WOWW(AM)—(Germantown, October 1955: 1430 khz; 2.5 kw-U, DA-N. TL: N35 04 20 W89 51 40 (day); N35 12 50 W89 47 46 (night). (CP: 2.8 kw-U, DA-2. TL: N34 59 22 W89 51 45 (one-site)). Hrs open: 6080 Mt. Mariah Rd. Ext., 38115. Phone: (901) 375-9324. Fax: (901) 375-0041.E-mail: info@radiodisney.com Web Site:www.radiodisney.com Licensee: Flinn Broadcasting Corp. (acq 9-22-93; $695,000; 10-11-93). Format: Radio disney. Target aud: 25-54. ♦George S. Flinn, pres; Lonnie Treadaway, gen mgr.

***WPLX(AM)**—(Turrell, AR) April 1987: 1180 khz; 5 kw-D, 26 w-N, 3.5 kw-CH. DA-3. TL: N35 08 31 W90 08 06. Hrs open: Sunrise-sunset 2351 Sunset Blvd., Suite 170-218, Rocklin, CA, 95765. Phone: (916) 251-1600. Fax: (916) 251-1650.E-mail: klove@klove.com Web Site:www.klove.com Licensee: Educational Media Foundation. Group owner: EMF Broadcasting (acq 10-20-2000; grpsl). Population served: 1,500,000 Natl. Network: K-Love, . Davis Wright Tremaine LLP. Format: Contemp Christian mus. News staff: 3. Target aud: 25-44; female (Judeo-Christian). ♦Richard Jenkins, pres; Mike Novak, VP; Keith Whipple, dev dir; David Pierce, progmg mgr; Ed Lenane, news dir; Sam Wallington, engrg dir; Karen Johnson, news rptr.

***WQOX(FM)**— Apr 8, 1974: 88.5 mhz; 30 kw. 430 ft TL: N35 09 17 W89 49 20. Stereo. Hrs open: 24 Telecommunications Center, 2485 Union Ave., 38112. Phone: (901) 320-3460. Fax: (901) 454-7673. Web Site:www.wqoxmes/admin/avery/mes.com Licensee: Board of Education Memphis City Schools. Population served: 1,000,000 Format: Urban adult contemp, educ, pub affrs. News staff: one. Target aud: 12-54; Students, teachers, parents & admin staff. ♦Derek Wagner, gen mgr, opns mgr; Derek A. Wagner, opns mgr; Paul Gubala, progmg mgr, mus dir; Chris Malone, asst music dir, pub affrs dir; Sherman Austin, progmg dir & pub affrs dir; Derick McMillan, chief of engrg.

WREC(AM)— September 1922: 600 khz; 5 kw-U, DA-2. TL: N35 11 51 W90 00 31. Hrs open: 24 2650 Thousand Oaks Blvd., Suite 4100, 38118. Phone: (901) 259-1300. Fax: (901) 259-6451.E-mail: info@recradio.com Web Site:www.wrecradio.com Licensee: CC Licenses LLC. Group owner: Clear Channel Communications Inc. (acq 1996; grpsl). Population served: 1700000 Natl. Network: Westwood One, ABC, . Rgnl. Network: Prog Farm, Tenn. Radio Net. Natl. Rep: Clear Channel,. Tenn. Radio Net. Wire Svc: NWS (National Weather Service) Format: News/talk, sports & info. News staff: 2; News: 5 hrs wkly. Target aud: 35 plus; upscale, professional, males 70%. Spec prog: Farm 3 hrs, relg 4 hrs wkly. ♦Timothy P. Davies, gen mgr; Alonzo Pendleton, opns mgr, chief of engrg; Ralph Salierno, sls dir; Frank Gilbert, prom dir, prom mgr; Steve Versnick, progmg dir.

WRVR(FM)— Sept 15, 1968: 104.5 mhz; 100 kw. 751 ft TL: N35 09 17 W89 49 20. Stereo. Hrs open: Prog sep from AM 1835 Moriah Woods Blvd., Bldg. 1, 38117. Phone: (901) 767-0104. Fax: (901) 767-0582.E-mail: river104@wrvr.com Web Site:www.wrvr.com Population served: 897,700 Format: Adult contemp. News staff: one; News: 2 hrs wkly. ♦Dan Barron, VP, gen mgr; Rondi Atkinson, sls dir; Rachel Dewitt, gen sls mgr, disc jockey; Jerry Dean, progmg dir; Mike Schwartz, chief of engrg, disc jockey.

***WUMR(FM)**— August 1979: 91.7 mhz; 25 kw. 394 ft TL: N35 09 17 W89 51 28. Stereo. Hrs open: 6 AM-midnight Univ. of Memphis, 3745 Central Ave., 38152. Phone: (901) 678-3176. Phone: (901) 678-4843. Fax: (901) 678-4331.E-mail: rmcdowll@memphis.edu Licensee: The University of Memphis. (acq 1979). Population served: 1,000,000 Schwartz, Woods & Miller. Format: Jazz, sports. News staff: one; News: 2 hrs wkly. Target aud: 18-49; upscale, college-educated. ♦Robert McDowell, gen mgr.

WXMX(FM)—(Millington, Apr 12, 1960: 98.1 mhz; 100 kw. 1,240 ft TL: N35 28 03 W90 11 27. (CP: Ant 768 ft.). Stereo. Hrs open: 5629 Murray Rd., 38119. Phone: (901) 682-1106. Fax: (901) 767-9531. Web Site:www.981themax.com Licensee: Citadel Broadcasting Co. Group owner: Citadel Broadcasting Corp. (acq 3-23-2004; grpsl). Format: Classic hits, oldies. Target aud: 25-54; adults, upwardly mobile with above average income. ♦Sherri Sawyer, gen mgr; Dan Baron, sls dir; Gennora Reed, gen sls mgr; Michael Webb, progmg dir; Paula Davis, prom.

***WYPL(FM)**— Apr 17, 1991: 89.3 mhz; 100 kw. Ant 1,253 ft TL: N35 28 03 W90 11 27. Stereo. Hrs open: 24 Memphis Public Library, 3030 Poplar Ave., 38111. Phone: (901) 415-2752. Fax: (901) 323-7902.E-mail: info@memphislibrary.org Web Site:www.memphislibrary.org Licensee: Memphis Public Library & Information Center. Reddy, Begley & McCormick. Format: News. News: 110 hrs wkly. Target aud: General. Spec prog: Sp one hr wkly. ♦Tommy Warren, gen mgr.

Middleton

WYDL(FM)— 2001: 100.7 mhz; 25 kw. Ant 328 ft TL: N35 00 13 W88 39 39. Hrs open: 102 N. Cass St., Suite D, Corinth, MS, 38834. Phone: (662) 284-4611. Fax: (662) 284-9609.E-mail: mike@wydl.com Web Site:www.wydl.com Licensee: Flinn Broadcasting Corp. Format: CHR, top-40, adult contemp. ♦Mike Brandt, gen mgr; Wendy Sherrod, gen sls mgr.

Milan

WYNU(FM)— Dec 12, 1964: 92.3 mhz; 100 kw. 991 ft TL: N35 54 06 W88 46 55. Stereo. Hrs open: 24 122 Radio Rd., Jackson, 38301. Phone: (731) 427-3316. Fax: (731) 427-4576.E-mail: steveburke@clearchannel.com Web Site:www.rock923.net Licensee: Forever South Licenses LLC. Group owner: Clear Channel Communications Inc. (acq 5-12-2006; grpsl). Population served: 1,000,000 Mullin, Rhyne, Emmons & Topel. Format: Classic rock. News staff: one; News: 5 hrs wkly. Target aud: 18-54; middle/upper income adults with disposable income & buying power. ♦Roger Vestal, gen mgr; Dave Hacker, opns mgr; Gina Langley, gen sls mgr; Steve Burke, progmg dir.

Millersville

WNFN(FM)— 1998: 106.7 mhz; 2.95 kw. Ant 965 ft TL: N36 15 50 W86 47 39. Hrs open: 10 Music Circle E., Nashville, 37203. Phone: (615) 321-1067. Fax: (615) 321-5771.E-mail: danielle.haese@cumulus.com Web Site:www.i106hits.com Licensee: Cumulus Licensing Corp. Group

owner: Cumulus Media Inc. (acq 2-12-2002; grpsl). Format: Top-40. ♦John Columbus, gen mgr; Derick Corbett, progmg dir; Dan Goodman, chief of engrg; Dave Elliott, sls.

Millington

WLRM(AM)— June 22, 1962: 1380 khz; 2.5 kw-D, 1 kw-N, DA-2. TL: N35 18 56 W89 55 23. Hrs open: 3665 Kirby Pkwy, Memphis, 38115. Phone: (901) 473-3434. Licensee: CPT & T Radio Station Inc. (acq 12-28-2004; $400,000). Format: Inspirational love. ♦Michelle Price, gen mgr.

WXMX(FM)—Licensed to Millington. See Memphis

Minor Hill

WEUZ(FM)— Sept 2, 1983: 92.1 mhz; 1.2 kw. 460 ft TL: N35 07 18 W87 11 17. Stereo. Hrs open:
Simulcast with WEUP-FM Moulton, AL; 100%.
2609 Jordan Ln. N.W., Huntsville, AL, 35816. Phone: (256) 837-9387. Fax: (256) 837-9404.E-mail: news@103weup.com Web Site:www.103weup.com Licensee: Broadcast One Inc. (acq 12-2-93; $310,000; 1-3-94). Format: Urban contemp, hip hop, rhythm and blues. ♦Hundley Batts, pres, gen sls mgr; Steve Murry, stn mgr; John Hain, chief of engrg; Yvonne Craighead, traf mgr.

Monterey

WKXD(FM)— Mar 3, 1986: 106.9 mhz; 23 kw. 735 ft TL: N36 07 13 W85 14 44. Stereo. Hrs open: 24 259 S. Willow Ave., Cookeville, 38501. Phone: (931) 528-6064. Fax: (931) 520-1590.E-mail: jstapleton @jwcbroadcasting.com Web Site:www.1069kicksfm.com Licensee: JWC Broadcasting (group owner; acq 8-3-01). Population served: 700,000 Natl. Network: ABC, . Natl. Rep: Rgnl Reps,. Format: Rock. News staff: one; News: one hr wkly. Target aud: 18-49; young, adult & affluent audiences. ♦Jim Stapleton, gen mgr.

WLIV-FM— Jan 8, 1997: 104.7 mhz; 1.25 kw. 712 ft TL: N36 15 42 W85 16 35. Stereo. Hrs open: 24 1130 West Main St., Livingston, 38570. Phone: (931) 823-1226. Fax: (931) 823-6005. Licensee: Sunny Broadcasting G.P. (acq 9-7-99). Population served: 40,000 Natl. Network: Fox News Radio, . Wire Svc: AP Format: Country, major sports. News staff: one; News: 4 hrs wkly. Target aud: General. ♦Millard V. Oakley, pres; Joel Upton, gen mgr; Carolyn Peterman, stn mgr; Craig Cantrell, opns dir; Austin Stinnett, chief of engrg; Shirley Burnette, traf mgr; Mark Young, pub svc dir.

Morrison

WOWC(FM)— Aug 2, 1964: 105.3 mhz; 6 kw. Ant 243 ft TL: N35 37 27 W85 53 37. Stereo. Hrs open: 24 520 N. Spring St., Sparta, 38583. Phone: (931) 836-1055. Phone: (931) 836-2824. Fax: (931) 836-2320. Web Site:rockdog1055.com Licensee: Peg Broadcasting Crossville LLC. (acq 6-30-2008; grpsl). Population served: 400,000 Format: Classic rock. News staff: one. Target aud: 18-34. ♦Don Howard, opns mgr & local news ed.

Morristown

WCRK(AM)— October 1947: 1150 khz; 5 kw-D, 500 w-N, DA-N. TL: N36 14 11 W83 18 33. Hrs open: 24 Box 220, 37815-0220. Phone: (423) 586-9101. Fax: (423) 587-2866.E-mail: wcrk@lcs.net Web Site:www.wcrk.com Licensee: Radio Acquisition Corp. (acq 7-13-98; $250,000). Population served: 59,000 Natl. Network: ABC, . Natl. Rep: Rgnl Reps,. Format: Top 40 hits. News staff: one; News: 45 hrs wkly. Target aud: 25-54; slighty more female, average income $50,000 yearly. ♦S. Herschel Lake, pres; Geraldine Lake, VP; Edwin Arnold, gen mgr, sls dir; Matt Keaton, progmg dir; Mike Rypel, news dir; Dan Trombley, engrg mgr, engr.

WJDT(FM)—See Rogersville

WMTN(AM)— Oct 19, 1957: 1300 khz; 5 kw-D, 100 w-N. TL: N36 12 15 W83 19 57. Hrs open: Box 220, 37815. Phone: (423) 586-9101. Web Site:www.wmtnradio.com Licensee: Radio Acquisition Corp. Group owner: Horne Radio Group (acq 10-12-2006). Population served: 500,000 Natl. Network: USA, . Rgnl. Network: Tenn. Radio Net. Tenn. Radio Net. Format: Classic country. ♦ED Dodson, gen mgr.

WMXK(FM)— May 31, 1964: 94.1 mhz; 920 w. Ant 771 ft TL: N36 13 40 W83 19 58. Stereo. Hrs open: 5700 W. Oaks Blvd., Rocklin, CA, 95765. Phone: (916) 251-1600. Fax: (916) 251-1650. Web Site:www.klove.com Licensee: Educational Media Foundation. (acq 6-17-2008; $640,000). Population served: 60,000 Natl. Network: K-Love, . Format: Contemp Christian. ♦Mike Novak, pres.

Mount Pleasant

WXRQ(AM)— Dec 15, 1981: 1460 khz; 1 kw-D, 170 w-N. TL: N35 31 21 W87 11 34. Hrs open: 6 AM-8 PM Box 31, 209 Bond St., 38474. Phone: (931) 379-3119. Fax: (931) 379-3129.E-mail: wxrq@yahoo.com Licensee: New Life Broadcasting Inc. (acq 1-17-89; $75,000; 1-30-89). Population served: 66,000 Natl. Network: USA, . Format: Southern gospel. News staff: one; News: 7 hrs wkly. Target aud: General. Spec prog: Black 4 hrs wkly. ♦Donald Paul, pres, gen mgr; Monty Gilliam, gen sls mgr, mus dir; Tim Wright, progmg dir & news dir.

Mountain City

WMCT(AM)— Dec 8, 1967: 1390 khz; 1 kw-D. TL: N36 29 23 W81 47 12. Hrs open: 6 AM-6 PM 1211 N. Church St., 37683. Phone: (423) 727-6701. Fax: (423) 727-9454.E-mail: jim@wmct-1390.com Web Site:www.wmctradio.com Licensee: Johnson County Broadcasting Co. Population served: 20,000 Natl. Network: ABC, . Rgnl. Network: Tenn. Radio Net. Natl. Rep: Rgnl Reps,. Tenn. Radio Net. Rgnl rep: Linley Grande Format: Classic & hit country gospel. News staff: one. Target aud: 25-50. ♦Janice Russell, pres & gen mgr.

Munford

WKIM(FM)— 1948: 98.9 mhz; 40 kw. Ant 1,135 ft TL: N35 28 03 W90 11 27. Stereo. Hrs open: 5629 Murray Rd., Memphis, 38119. Phone: (901) 680-9898. Fax: (901) 767-9531. Web Site:www.989kimfm.com Licensee: Citadel Broadcasting Co. Group owner: Citadel Broadcasting Corp. (acq 3-23-2004; grpsl). Population served: 10,100 Natl. Rep: Katz Radio,. Format: Adult hits. ♦Sherri Sawyer, gen mgr; Dan Barron, sls dir; Amy Goodman, gen sls mgr; Marvin Nugent, progmg dir; Marvin Emilien, prom.

Murfreesboro

WCJK(FM)— Aug 10, 1963: 96.3 mhz; 52 kw. 1,286 ft TL: N36 15 50 W86 47 38. Stereo. Hrs open: 24 Box 40506, Nashville, 37204. Secondary address: 504 Rosedale Ave., Nashville 37211. Phone: (615) 259-4567. Fax: (615) 259-4594. Web Site:www.963jackfm.com Licensee: South Central Communications Corp. (group owner; (acq 2-4-94; $6 million; 3-28-94). Natl. Rep: Katz Radio,. Bryan Cave. Wire Svc: NWS (National Weather Service) Format: Adult Hits. News staff: one. Target aud: A 25-54. ♦Marty Linck, CEO, progmg dir; Dennis Gwiazdon, gen mgr; Craig Jones, sls dir, prom dir; Meredith Mazanek, pres & mktg dir; Clinton Hooper, chief of engrg.

***WFCM-FM**— September 1997: 91.7 mhz; 1 kw. 902 ft TL: N35 43 52 W86 41 25. Hrs open: 24
Rebroadcasts WMBW(FM) Chattanooga 100%.
1920 E. 24th Street Pl., Chattanooga, 37404. Phone: (423) 629-8900. Fax: (423) 629-0021.E-mail: wfcm@moody.edu Web Site:www.wfcm.org Licensee: The Moody Bible Institute of Chicago. Natl. Network: Moody, . Southmayd & Miller. Format: Educ, relg. Target aud: 25-54. ♦Edward Cannon, pres; Leighton LeBoeuf, gen mgr; Andy Napier, progmg dir; Paul Martin, mus dir; David Morais, chief of engrg.

WGNS(AM)— Dec. 31, 1946: 1450 khz; 1 kw-U. TL: N35 50 26 W86 23 27. Hrs open: 24 306 S. Church St., 37130-3732. Phone: (615) 893-5373. Fax: (615) 867-6397.E-mail: news@1450wgns.com Web Site:www.wgnsradio.com Licensee: The Rutherford Group Inc. (acq 1984;10-15-84). Population served: 250,000 Natl. Network: ABC, . Tenn. Radio Net. Format: News/talk, sports. News: 80 hrs wkly. Target aud: 25 plus; active adults, "movers & shakers" in economic & educ groupings. Spec prog: Black 7 hrs, farm 3 hrs, relg 6 hrs wkly. ♦Bart Walker, pres, gen mgr; Lee Ann Walker, VP; Scott Walker, sr VP & stn mgr; Melissa McCullough, opns mgr; Jeff Jordan, prom mgr, progmg dir; Gary Brown, chief of engrg. Co-owned TV: WETV-LP

WMGC(AM)— Nov 1, 1953: 810 khz; 5 kw-D, 6 w-N. TL: N35 50 14 W86 25 00. Hrs open:
Rebroadcasts WNSR(AM) Brentwood 55%.
435 37th Ave. N., Nashville, 37209. Phone: (615) 844-1039. Licensee: Radio 810 Nashville Ltd. Group owner: Southern Wabash Communications Corp. (acq 7-10-01). Population served: 550,000 Natl. Network: ABC, . Format: Sp. Target aud: 18-54; adults. Spec prog: Relg 4 hrs wkly. ♦Ted Johnson, gen mgr.

***WMOT(FM)**— Apr 9, 1969: 89.5 mhz; 100 kw. Ant 676 ft TL: N36 05 07 W86 26 22. Stereo. Hrs open: 24 Box 3, Middle Tennessee State Univ., 37132. Phone: (615) 898-2800. Phone: (615) 255-9071. Fax: (615) 898-2774.E-mail: wmot@mtsu.edu Web Site:www.wmot.org Licensee: Middle Tennessee State University. Population served: 800,000 Natl. Network: NPR, AP Radio, . Format: Jazz. News staff: 2; News: 10 hrs wkly. Target aud: 24 plus; general. ♦John L. High, gen mgr; John Egly, opns mgr; Keith Palmer, dev dir.

***WMTS-FM**— 1996: 88.3 mhz; 680 w. Ant 138 ft TL: N35 50 56 W86 21 11. Hrs open: 24 Box 58, Middle Tenn. State Univ., 37132. Phone: (615) 898-5051. Phone: (615) 898-2636. Fax: (615) 898-5682. Web Site:www.wmtsradio.com Licensee: Middle Tennessee State University. Population served: 50,000 Format: Black, Sp, div. Target aud: 18-26; College age, diverse. Spec prog: Polka 2 hrs, electronic 10 hrs, jazz 4 hrs, funk 2 hrs wkly.

Nashville

WAMB(AM)— Dec 21, 2001: 1200 khz; 50 kw-D, 3.8 kw-CH. TL: N36 12 32 W86 52 21. Stereo. Hrs open: 24 1617 Lebanon Rd., Suite 100, 37210. Phone: (615) 889-1960. Fax: (615) 902-9108.E-mail: wamb@bellsouth.net Web Site:www.wamb.net Licensee: Great Southern Broadcasting Co. Inc. (acq 7-1-2006; $2 million). Population served: 750,000 Natl. Network: CNN Radio, . Irwin, Campbell & Tannenwald. Format: Adult standards/MOR. ♦Will C. Baird Jr., VP; William O. Barry, pres & gen mgr; Harry P. Stephenson, gen sls mgr; Ronald W. Johnson, progmg dir; Gary M. Brown, chief of engrg; Beth Lane, traf mgr.

WCJK(FM)—See Murfreesboro

WCRT(AM)—(Donelson, Apr 12, 1971: 1160 khz; 50 kw-D, 1 kw-N, DA-N. TL: N36 09 49 W86 42 56. Stereo. Hrs open: 24 Two Lakeview Place, 15 Century Blvd., Suite 101, 37214-3692. Phone: (615) 871-1160. Fax: (615) 871-9355.E-mail: ruselton@bottradionetwork.com Licensee: Bott Communications Inc. (acq 1-11-2006; $5 million). Population served: 1,500,000 Fletcher, Heald & Hildreth. Format: Christian. ♦Richard P. Bott, pres; Richard P. Bott II, VP; Randy Uselton, gen mgr.

WENO(AM)— May 23, 1988: 760 khz; 1 kw-D. TL: N36 08 28 W86 45 23. Hrs open: Sunrise-sunset 333 Murfreesboro Rd., 37210. Phone: (615) 248-1689. Fax: (615) 248-7786.E-mail: info@weno.com Web Site:www.weno.com Licensee: WENO Inc. (acq 5-7-90; $300,000; 5-21-90). Population served: 750,000 Natl. Network: AP Radio, . Format: Christian, relg. News: 6 hrs wkly. Target aud: 25-54. ♦Dan Boone, pres; Mark Myers, CFO; David Deese, gen mgr; Dave Queen, stn mgr; Dan Klimkowski, chief of engrg; Jennifer Houchin, traf mgr.

***WFSK-FM**— Apr 14, 1973: 88.1 mhz; 700 w horiz. Ant 6 ft TL: N36 10 00 W86 48 17. Stereo. Hrs open: 24 Fisk Univ., 1000 17th Ave. N., 37208-3051. Phone: (615) 329-8754. Fax: (615) 329-9305.E-mail: xlawson@fisk.edu Web Site:www.fisk.edu/wfsk Licensee: Fisk University. Population served: 750,000 Natl. Network: PRI, . Format: Smooth jazz-smooth grooves, talk radio. ♦Sharon Kay, gen mgr; Xuam Lawson, progmg dir; Clinton Hooper, chief of engrg.

WGFX(FM)—See Gallatin

WJXA(FM)— Apr 3, 1976: 92.9 mhz; 100 kw. 1,086 ft TL: N36 07 14 W86 58 07. Stereo. Hrs open: 24 Box 40506, 37204-0506. Secondary address: 504 Rosedale Ave. 37211. Phone: (615) 259-4567. Fax: (615) 259-4594. Web Site:www.mix929.com Licensee: South Central Communications Corp. (group owner) Natl. Rep: Katz Radio,. Bryan Cave. Format: Adult contemp. Target aud: A 25-54. ♦Dennis Gwiazdon, gen mgr; Craig Jones, sls dir; Meredith Mazanek, mktg dir; Barbara Bridges, progmg dir; Anna Marie Ritter, news dir; Clinton Hooper, chief of engrg; Gillian Baxter, traf mgr.

WKDF(FM)— Jan 1, 1967: 103.3 mhz; 100 kw. 1,233 ft TL: N36 02 08 W86 50 56. Stereo. Hrs open: 506 2nd Ave. S., 37210. Phone: (615) 244-9533. Fax: (615) 259-1271.E-mail: ken.bailey@citcom.com Web Site:www.1-3WKDF.com Licensee: Citadel Broadcasting Co. Group owner: Citadel Broadcasting Corp. acq 4-26-01; grpsl). Format: Country. Target aud: 18-34; general. ♦Dave Kelly, gen mgr, progmg dir; Cindy Francis, prom mgr; Bud Ford, progmg dir; Eddy Foxx, mus dir; Cameron Adkins, chief of engrg; Jennifer Boucher, traf mgr.

WLAC(AM)— Nov 24, 1926: 1510 khz; 50 kw-U, DA-N. TL: N36 16 15 W86 45 24. Hrs open: 24 55 Music Sq. W., 37203. Phone: (615) 664-2400. Fax: (615) 664-2457.E-mail: info@1510wlac.com Web Site:www.1510wlac.com Licensee: Capstar TX L.P. Group owner: Clear Channel Communications Inc. (acq 8-30-00; grpsl). Population served: 486,000 Natl. Network: Wall Street, ABC, . Haley, Bader & Potts. Format: News/talk, relg. News staff: 3; News: 18 hrs wly. Target aud: 35-64; professionals, business owners & managers. Spec prog: Black 20 hrs wkly. ♦Dave Alpert, pres; Keith Kaufman, opns dir, mktg dir; Darren Smith, sls dir; Temple Hancock, prom dir; Bruce Collins, progmg mgr; Mike Gideon, chief of engrg.

WMDB(AM)— Aug 15, 1983: 880 khz; 2.5 kw-D. TL: N36 12 43 W86 49 09. Hrs open: 209 10th Ave. S., Cummins # 342, 37203. Phone: (615) 242-1411. Fax: (615) 242-8223. Web Site:www.rejoice880.com Licensee: Davidson Media Station WMDB Licensee LLC. (acq 9-1-2005; $1.6 million). Format: Gospel. Target aud: 18 plus; general. ◆Armando Quintero, pres & gen mgr.

WNAH(AM)— Dec 24, 1949: 1360 khz; 1 kw-U. TL: N36 11 30 W86 46 26. Hrs open: 24 44 Music Sq. E., 37203. Phone: (615) 254-7611. Fax: (615) 467-8600.E-mail: mail@wnah.com Web Site:www.wnah.com Licensee: Hermitage Broadcasting Corp. Format: Southern gospel. News: 5 hrs wkly. Target aud: 21-50. ◆Van T. Irwin Jr., pres & gen mgr; Tony Cappuccilli, gen sls mgr; Bill Grist, prom mgr; Hoyt M. Carter Jr., progmg dir, chief of engrg; Bobby Lynn II, mus dir.

*WNAZ-FM— May 23, 1967: 89.1 mhz; 1.4 kw. Ant 200 ft TL: N36 08 28 W86 45 23. Stereo. Hrs open: 24 Prog sep from AM 333 Murfreesboro Rd., 37210. Phone: (615) 248-1689. Fax: (615) 248-7786.E-mail: info@wnaz.com Web Site:www.wnaz.com Licensee: Trevecca Nazarene University Inc. Population served: 447,877 Format: Progsv Christian. News: 3 hrs wkly. Target aud: 18-30; college & young professionals.

WNQM(AM)— July 1, 1948: 1300 khz; 50 kw-D, 5 kw-N, DA-N. TL: N36 12 30 W86 53 38. Hrs open: 24 1300 WWCR Ave., 37218. Phone: (615) 255-1300. Fax: (615) 255-1311.E-mail: wnqm@wwcr.com Web Site:www.wnqm1300.com Licensee: WNQM Inc. Group owner: F.W. Robbert Broadcasting Co. Inc. (acq 1-83; $700,000; 12-19-83). Population served: 2,000,000 Natl. Network: USA, . Format: Relg, Sp. News: 2 hrs wkly. Target aud: General. Spec prog: Sp. ◆Fred P. Westenberger, pres; Eric Westenberger, gen mgr; Brady Murray, opns mgr.

WNRQ(FM)— 1953: 105.9 mhz; 100 kw. 1,226 ft TL: N30 02 08 W86 50 56. Stereo. Hrs open: 24 Prog sep from AM 55 Music Sq. W., 37203. Phone: (615) 664-2400. Fax (615) 664-2457.E-mail: info@1059.com Web Site:www.1059.com Population served: 1,700,000 Format: Adult contemp. News staff: one; News: 3 hrs wkly. Target aud: 25-54; upwardly mobile adults. Spec prog: Christian 6 hrs wkly. ◆David Alpert, gen mgr, mktg mgr; Keith Kaufman, opns mgr; Temple Hancock, prom mgr.

WNVL(AM)— 1948: 1240 khz; 1 kw-U. TL: N36 09 24 W86 46 15. Hrs open: 24 Cummins Stn, 209 Tenth Ave. S., Suite 342, 37203. Phone: (615) 242-1411. Fax: (615) 242-3823.E-mail: gerente@activa1240.com Licensee: Davidson Media Station WNSG Licensee LLC. (acq 8-1-2005; $2.7 million). Population served: 447,877 Format: Rgnl Mexican. Target aud: 25-54. ◆Armando Quintero, gen mgr; Orlalndo Rosa, opns mgr; Alberto Pena, mus dir; Jay Shoemaker, chief of engrg.

WPLN(AM)—(Madison, Sept 14, 1958: 1430 khz; 5 kw-D, 1 kw-N, DA-N. TL: N36 16 19 W86 42 53. 15 kw-D, 1 kw-N, DA-N. Stereo. Hrs open: 24 630 Mainstream Dr., 37228. Phone: (615) 760-2903. Fax: (615) 760-2904.E-mail: info@wpln.org Web Site:www.wpln.org Licensee: Nashville Public Radio (acq 2-15-02; $3 million). Population served: 850,000 Tierney & Swift. Format: News/talk. Target aud: General. ◆Rob Gordon, pres & gen mgr.

*WPLN-FM— Dec 17, 1962: 90.3 mhz; 80 kw. Ant 1,132 ft TL: N36 02 08 W86 50 56. Stereo. Hrs open: 630 Mainstream Dr., 37228-1204. Phone: (615) 760-2903. Fax: (615) 760-2904.E-mail: info@wpln.org Web Site:www.wpln.org Licensee: Nashville Public Radio. Population served: 1,000,000 Natl. Network: NPR, PRI, . Format: Class, cultural, news, bluegrass. Target aud: General. ◆Robert Gordon, gen mgr; Laura Landress, gen sls mgr; Henry Fennell, progmg dir; Will Griffin, mus dir; Anita Bugg, news dir; Tom Knox, chief of engrg, news rptr; Wendy Poston, traf mgr; Nina Cardona, spec ev coord.

WPRT-FM—See Pegram

WQQK(FM)—See Hendersonville

*WRVU(FM)— Dec 3, 1971: 91.1 mhz; 14.5 kw. 457 ft TL: N36 08 27 W86 51 56. Stereo. Hrs open: 24 Box 9100-B, Vanderbilt Univ., 128 Sarratt Student Ctr., 37235. Phone: (615) 322-3691. Phone: (615) 322-7625. Fax: (615) 343-2582. Web Site:www.wrvu.org Licensee: Vanderbilt Student Communications. Population served: 447,877 Natl. Network: ABC, . Format: Progsv rock, jazz, div. Target aud: General; div, adventurous individuals. ◆Jennifer Sexton, gen mgr; David Cash, progmg dir.

WSIX-FM— 1948: 97.9 mhz; 100 kw. 1,140 ft TL: N36 02 49 W86 49 49. Stereo. Hrs open: 24 55 Music Sq. W., 37203. Phone: (615) 664-2400. Fax: (615) 664-2457. Licensee: Capstar TX L.P. Group owner: Clear Channel Communications Inc. (acq 8-30-00; grpsl). Population served: 1,000,000 Format: Country. News staff: 2; News: one hr wkly. Target aud: 25-54. ◆David Alpert, gen mgr; Keith

Kaufman, opns mgr, mktg dir, prom dir; Temple Hancock, prom dir; Mike Moore, progmg dir, pub affrs dir; Al Voecks, news dir; Mike Gideon, chief of engrg.

WSM(AM)— Oct 5, 1925: 650 khz; 50 kw-U. TL: N35 59 50 W86 47 32. Stereo. Hrs open: 24 2804 Opryland Dr., 37214. Phone: (615) 889-6595. Fax: (615) 458-2445. Web Site:www.wsmonline.com Licensee: Grand Ole Opry LLC (acq 11-14-2000; grpsl). Population served: 447,877 Natl. Network: ABC, . Natl. Rep: Christal,. Format: Country. News staff: 12; News: 11 hrs wkly. Target aud: 35 plus; high school graduates, married homeowners, income $25,000 plus. Spec prog: Farm 6 hrs, Grand Ole Opry 12 hrs wkly. ◆Chris Kulick, gen mgr; Bill Hutcherson, gen sls mgr, pub affrs dir.

WSM-FM— Nov 1, 1962: 95.5 mhz; 100 kw. Ant 1,279 ft TL: N36 08 27 W86 51 56. Stereo. Hrs open: 10 Music Circle E., 37203. Phone: (615) 321-1067. Fax: (615) 321-5808. Web Site:www.955thewolf.com Licensee: Cumulus Licensing LLC. Group owner: Cumulus Media Inc. (acq 7-21-2003; $65 million with WWTN(FM) Manchester). Population served: 294,200 Format: Country. Target aud: 25-54. ◆Michael Dickey, gen mgr.

WVOL(AM)—See Berry Hill

WYFN(AM)— Jan 7, 1927: 980 khz; 5 kw-U, DA-N. TL: N36 12 25 W86 40 25. Hrs open: 11530 Carmel Commons Blvd., Charlotte, NC, 28226. Phone: (704) 523-5555. Fax: (704) 522-1967.E-mail: bbn@bbnradio.org Web Site:www.bbnradio.org Licensee: Bible Broadcasting Network. (group owner; acq 1-31-91; $600,000; 2-18-91). Natl. Rep: McGavren Guild,. Format: Relg. ◆Aaron Tuttle, gen mgr & stn mgr.

New Johnsonville

*WAYW(FM)— 2001: 89.9 mhz; 3.1 kw. Ant 466 ft TL: N35 56 17 W87 53 39. Hrs open: 24 1095 W. McEwen Dr., Franklin, 37067. Phone: (615) 261-9293. Fax: (615) 261-3967.E-mail: waym@wayfm.com Web Site:www.wayfm.com Licensee: WAY-FM Media Group Inc. (group owner; acq 2-1-01). Population served: 111,815 Format: Christian. ◆Teresa White, dev dir; Jeff Brown, progmg dir.

Newport

WGGQ(AM)— September 1978: 1060 khz; 1 kw-D. TL: N35 59 10 W83 10 46. Hrs open: 377 Graham St., 37821. Phone: (423) 623-8743. Phone: (423) 623-8744. Fax: (423) 623-0545. Licensee: Bristol Broadcasting Co. Inc. (acq 6-16-2006; $800,000 with co-located FM). Natl. Network: ABC, . Roberts & Eckard. Format: Country. Target aud: 25-49. ◆W.L. Nininger, pres; Mona Sizemore, gen mgr; Brian Fredette, prom mgr, progmg dir.

*WGSN(FM)— 2008: 90.7 mhz; 1 kw vert. Ant 2,296 ft TL: N35 54 20 W83 17 48. Hrs open: Box 1509, Jamestown, 38556. Phone: (931) 879-8188. Fax: (931) 879-1733. Web Site:www.newlife105.com Licensee: Bible Believers Network Inc. ◆Fred Allred, pres; Connie Cody, gen mgr.

WLIK(AM)— Apr 9, 1954: 1270 khz; 5 kw-D, 500 w-N, DA-N. TL: N35 57 49 W83 12 31. Hrs open: 24 640 W. Hwy. 25/70, 37821. Phone: (423) 623-3095. Fax: (423) 623-3096.E-mail: wlik@planetc.com Web Site:wlik.net Licensee: WLIK Inc. Population served: 300,000 Natl. Network: CNN Radio, . Rgnl. Network: Tenn. Radio Net. Tenn. Radio Net. Rgnl rep: Regional Reps Format: Oldies. News staff: one; News: 7 hrs wkly. Target aud: General. Spec prog: Relg 18 hrs wkly. ◆Dwight D. Wilkerson, pres, gen mgr, stn mgr; Angie Wilkerson, VP; Johnnie Swann, chief of opns.

WNPC-FM— February 1993: 92.9 mhz; 3.1 kw. 459 ft TL: N35 57 27 W83 05 03. Stereo. Hrs open: 24 Dups AM 90% Rebroadcasts WNPC(AM) Newport 100%. 377 Graham St., 37821. Phone: (423) 623-8743. Fax: (423) 623-8744. Fax: (423) 623-0545. ◆Jim Phillips, progmg VP.

Norris

WRJK(FM)— April 2001: 106.7 mhz; 1.1 kw. Ant 751 ft TL: N36 07 12 W83 55 30. Stereo. Hrs open: 24 Rebroadcasts WTXM(FM) Maryville 100%. Box 27100, Knoxville, 37927-7100. Phone: (865) 525-6000. Fax: (865) 525-2000.E-mail: jjarnigan@sccradio.com Web Site:WWW.JACKFMKNOXVILLE.COM Licensee: South Central Communications Corp. (group owner; acq 6-14-2001; $2.5 million). Population served: 607,600 Wire Svc: AP Format: JACK-FM. ◆Craig Jacobus, pres; Judy Berkley, natl sls mgr; Terry Gillingham, VP & mktg mgr; Jeff Jarnigan, progmg dir.

Oak Ridge

WATO(AM)— Feb 1, 1948: 1290 khz; 5 kw-D, 500 w-N, DA-2. TL: N36 03 02 W84 12 38. Hrs open: 24 517 Watt Rd., Knoxville, 37922. Phone: (865) 482-1290. Phone: (865) 675-4105. Fax: (865) 675-4859. Licensee: Horne Radio LLC. Group owner: Horne Radio Group (acq 8-29-01; grpsl). Population served: 518,000 Natl. Network: Westwood One, . Format: Oldies. News staff: one. Target aud: 25-54. ◆Alex Carroll, sls dir, chief of engrg; Brian Tatum, stn mgr & progmg dir.

WNFZ(FM)— February 1967: 94.3 mhz; 2.5 kw. 515 ft TL: N35 56 28 W84 09 28. Stereo. Hrs open: Box 27100, Knoxville, 37927-7100. Secondary address: 1100 Sharps Ridge Rd., Knoxville 37917. Phone: (865) 525-6000. Fax: (865) 525-2000.E-mail: SCOX@SCCRADIO.COM Web Site:WWW.943THEX.COM Licensee: John A. Pirkle. Population served: 450,000 Format: Alternative Rock. Target aud: General. ◆John W. Pirkle, CEO, chmn; Johnathan W. Pirkle, pres; Terry Gillingham, VP & gen mgr; Jeff Cutshaw, natl sls mgr; Shane Cox, progmg dir.

WNOX(FM)—Licensed to Oak Ridge. See Knoxville

Olive Hill

*WDNX(FM)— Jan 10, 1975: 89.1 mhz; 100 kw. 249 ft TL: N35 12 30 W88 03 46. Stereo. Hrs open: 24 HHA Administration Bldg., 3575 Lonesome Pine Rd., Savannah, 38372. Secondary address: WDNX Bldg., 3730 Lonesome Pine Rd., Savannah 38372. Phone: (731) 925-9236. Fax: (731) 925-4238.E-mail: sheriwdnx@yahoo.com Web Site:www.lifetalk.net Licensee: Rural Life Foundation. Population served: 250,000 Format: Inspirational music, Christian teaching & inspiration. News staff: one; News: 5 hrs wkly. Target aud: General; families. Spec prog: Class 5 hrs, farm one hr wkly. ◆Charles Harris, chmn; Steven Dickman, pres, CFO, exec VP, stn mgr & dev mgr; Sheri Durbin, gen sls mgr, mktg mgr, pub affrs dir; Steve Dickman, chief of engrg.

Oliver Springs

WJRV(FM)— 2009: 106.1 mhz; 190 w. Ant 1,746 ft TL: N36 06 29 W84 20 08. Hrs open: 408 N. Cedar Bluff Rd., Suite 252, Knoxville, 37923. Phone: (865) 246-3848. Fax: (865) 246-7979. Web Site:river106.com Licensee: Momentum Broadcasting LLC. Format: Hot adult contemp. ◆Norman R. Alpert, pres; Jeff Alpert, gen mgr.

WOKI(FM)— Sept 15, 1989: 98.7 mhz; 8 kw. Ant 571 ft TL: N36 06 48 W84 03 44. Hrs open: 24 Box 11167, Knoxville, 37939. Secondary address: 4711 Old Kingston Pike, Knoxville 37919. Phone: (865) 588-6511. Fax: (865) 656-7487. Web Site:www.987earlfm.com Licensee: Citadel Broadcasting Co. Group owner: Citadel Broadcasting Corp. (acq 4-26-2001; grpsl). Population served: 336,335 Natl. Rep: Katz Radio,. Rgnl rep: Rgnl Reps. Wire Svc: AP Format: Oldies. Target aud: 18 plus. ◆Mike Hammond, pres, opns mgr; Ed Brantley, VP, gen mgr; Tammy Browning, gen sls mgr; Shanna Lingerfelt, mktg dir; Joe Stutler, progmg dir.

Oneida

WBNT-FM— June 10, 1965: 105.5 mhz; 3 kw. Ant 285 ft TL: N36 30 03 W84 29 24. Stereo. Hrs open: 18 Box 4370, 37841. Phone: (423) 569-8598. Fax: (423) 569-5572.E-mail: wbnt@highland.net Web Site:www.hive105.com Licensee: Oneida Broadcasters Inc. Population served: 20,000 Natl. Network: ABC, . Rgnl. Network: Tenn. Radio Net. Tenn. Radio Net. Format: Adult contemp, country. Target aud: 16-56; male/female working class-retirees. ◆Hillard Mattie, gen mgr & stn mgr.

WOCV(AM)— Aug 1, 1959: 1310 khz; 1 kw-D. TL: N36 30 03 W84 29 24. Hrs open: 6 AM-sunset Rebroadcasts WBNT-FM Oneida 100%. Box 4370, 37841. Phone: (423) 569-8598. Fax: (423) 569-5572.E-mail: wbnt@highland.net Web Site:www.hive105.com Licensee: Oneida Broadcasters Inc. (acq 12-14-2006; $525,000 for 70% of stock with co-located FM). Population served: 19,500 Natl. Network: ABC, . Tenn. Radio Net. Format: Adult contemp, country. News staff: 4; News: 15 hrs wkly. Target aud: 22-55; male & female. ◆Hillard Mattie, gen mgr; Darrel E. Smith, chief of engrg.

Ooltewah

WPLZ(FM)— Feb 27, 1980: 95.3 mhz; 11 kw. Ant 499 ft TL: N34 57 23 W85 17 32. Stereo. Hrs open: 24 1305 Carter St., Chattanooga, 37402. Phone: (423) 265-9494. Fax: (423) 266-2335.E-mail: Jim2@BrewerRadio.com Web Site:www.chattanoogapulse.com Licensee: J.L. Brewer Broadcasting of Cleveland LLC. Population served:

22,500 Natl. Rep: Katz Radio,. Format: News/talk. ◆Mike Powers, progmg dir; Ed Ramsey, mus dir, pub affrs dir.

Paris

WAKQ(FM)— September 1967: 105.5 mhz; 3.7 kw. 419 ft TL: N36 16 45 W88 20 31. Stereo. Hrs open: Prog sep from AM Rebroadcasts WWKF(FM) Union City 100%.
206 N. Brewer St., 38242. Phone: (731) 642-7100. Fax: (731) 642-9367.E-mail: info@kf99kg105.com Web Site:kf99kg105.com Format: CHR. News staff: one; News: one hr wkly. Target aud: 12-34. ◆Terry Hailey, mus dir.

WLZK(FM)— Nov 1, 1991: 94.1 mhz; 10.5 kw. 328 ft TL: N36 18 50 W88 17 33. Stereo. Hrs open: 24 110 India Rd., 38242. Phone: (731) 644-9455. Fax: (731) 644-9970.E-mail: wlzk@bellsouth.net Web Site:www.wmvfradio.com Licensee: Benton-Weatherford Broadcasting Inc. of Texas (Acq 3-15-91; 4-8-91). Population served: 75,000 Natl. Network: Jones Radio Networks, . Format: Adult contemp. News staff: one; News: 7 hrs wkly.

WMUF(AM)— May 9, 1980: 1000 khz; 5 kw-D, DA. TL: N36 18 50 W88 17 33. Hrs open: 110 India Rd., 38242. Phone: (731) 644-9455. Fax: (731) 644-9970.E-mail: wmuf@bellsouth.net Web Site:www.wmufradio.com Licensee: Benton-Weatherford Broadcasting Inc.of Tennessee (group owner; acq 4-1-85). Population served: 50,000 Natl. Network: ABC, . Format: Country. News staff: one; News: 3 hrs wkly. Target aud: 25-54; people with disposable income. Spec prog: Farm 2 hrs wkly. ◆Gary D. Benton, pres; Gary Benton, gen mgr.

WPRH(FM)— 2009: 90.9 mhz; 5.4 kw vert. Ant 315 ft TL: N36 15 29 W88 11 11. Hrs open:
Rebroadcasts WAFR(FM) Tupelo, MS 100%.
Drawer 2440, Tupelo, MS, 38803. Phone: (662) 844-8888. Fax: (662) 842-6791. Web Site:www.afr.net Licensee: American Family Association. (acq 1-16-2007). Natl. Network: American Family Radio, . Format: Christian. ◆Donald E. Wildmon, chmn.

WTPR(AM)— May 7, 1947: 710 khz; 750 w-D. TL: N36 16 47 W88 20 32. Stereo. Hrs open: Sunrise-sunset
Rebroadcasts WTPR-FM Paris 100%.
206 N. Brewer St., 38242. Phone: (731) 642-7100. Fax: (731) 642-9367.E-mail: thailey@wenkwtpr.com Web Site:wenkwtpr.com Licensee: WENK of Uniion City Inc. (group owner; acq 10-28-89; 8-14-89). Population served: 125,000 Natl. Network: ABC, . Rgnl. Network: Reg reps. Rgnl rep: Rgnl Reps Shaninis & Peltzman. Format: Oldies. News staff: one; News: 12 hrs wkly. Target aud: 35-54. ◆Terry Hailey, pres, gen mgr & progmg dir; Brad Hosford, chief of engrg.

Parker's Crossroads

WBFG(FM)— 1999: 96.5 mhz; 6 kw. Ant 328 ft TL: N35 45 33 W88 23 15. Hrs open: Box 279, Lexington, 38351. Secondary address: 584 Smith Ave., Lexington 38351. Phone: (731) 968-9990. Fax: (731) 968-0380.E-mail: wbfg965@yahoo.com Web Site:www.wbfg965.com Licensee: Crossroads Broadcasting LLC. (acq 4-14-99). Natl. Network: ESPN Radio, . Format: Sports. ◆Dan Hughes, gen mgr; Lori Becker, opns mgr.

Parsons

WKJQ(AM)— Oct 3, 1970: 1550 khz; 1 kw-D. TL: N35 39 26 W88 09 07. Hrs open: Box 576, 38363. Secondary address: 109 Iron Hill Rd. 38363. Phone: (731) 847-3011. Fax: (731) 847-4600.E-mail: ralphclenney@yahoo.com Licensee: Clenney Broadcasting Corp. (acq 4-1-89). Population served: 30,000 Robert S. Stone. Format: Relg. Target aud: General. ◆Ralph D. Clenney, pres & gen mgr.

WKJQ-FM— June 4, 1990: 97.3 mhz; 6 kw. 256 ft TL: N35 39 39 W88 07 05. Stereo. Hrs open: 24 Prog sep from AM Box 576, 38363. Phone: (731) 847-3011. Fax: (731) 847-4600.E-mail: ralphclenney@yahoo.com Licensee: Clenney Broadcasting Corp. Population served: 27,569 Format: Country. Target aud: 25-54.

Pegram

WPRT-FM— Apr 27, 1964: 102.5 mhz; 100 kw. Ant 974 ft TL: N36 17 36 W87 18 20. Stereo. Hrs open: 24 Box 150846, Nashville, 37215. Phone: (615) 399-1029. Fax: (615) 361-9873.E-mail: programming @1025theparty.com Web Site:www.v1025.com Licensee: Montgomery Broadcasting. Group owner: The Cromwell Group Inc. (acq 1990). Population served: 1,000,000 Natl. Rep: McGavren Guild,. Womble Carlyle. Format: Hot adult contemp. Target aud: 18-34; S. KY

residents. ◆Bayard H. Walters, pres; Tincy Crouse, gen mgr; Troy Hanson, opns mgr; David Wilson, chief of engrg.

Pigeon Forge

WPFT(FM)— 2007: 106.3 mhz; 500 w. Ant 1,117 ft TL: N35 42 13 W83 33 57. Hrs open: 112 Jordan Dr., Chattanooga, 37421. Phone: (423) 485-8987. Licensee: East Tennessee Radio Group L.P. ◆Paul G. Fink, gen mgr.

Pikeville

WUAT(AM)— Dec 19, 1972: 1110 khz; 250 w-D. TL: N35 36 18 W85 11 14. Hrs open: Box 128, 37367. Secondary address: 101 N. Main 37367. Phone: (423) 447-2906. Fax: (423) 447-7309.E-mail: info@uatradio.com Web Site:www.wuatradio.com Licensee: Joyce V. Bownds. (acq 6-28-99; $1,500). Population served: 1,454 Lukas, McGowan, Nace & Gutierrez. Format: Country, gospel, bluegrass. Spec prog: Farm 5 hrs, relg 15 hrs wkly. ◆Joyce Bownds, pres, gen mgr, gen sls mgr & progmg dir.

Portland

WQKR(AM)— July 15, 1980: 1270 khz; 1 kw-D, 59 w-N, DA-2. TL: N36 36 11 W86 32 01. Hrs open: 24 100 Main St., Suite 201, 37148-1218. Phone: (615) 325-3250. Fax: (615) 325-0803.E-mail: wqkr@comcast.net Licensee: Venture Broadcasting LLC (acq 8-8-2005; $50,000). Population served: 100,000 Natl. Network: ABC, . Tenn. Radio Net. Format: Oldies. News staff: one. Target aud: 25-54. ◆Lee Dorman, gen mgr.

Powell

WKTI(AM)—Licensed to Powell. See Knoxville

Pulaski

WKSR(AM)— May 6, 1947: 1420 khz; 1 kw-U, DA-N. TL: N35 12 04 W87 03 20. Hrs open: Box 738, 38478. Secondary address: 104 S. Second St. 38478. Phone: (931) 363-2505. Fax: (931) 424-3157. Web Site:www.wksr.com Licensee: Pulaski Broadcasting Inc. (acq 4-4-80; $481,300; 4-21-80). Population served: 13,500 Natl. Network: ABC, . Format: Oldies. News: one. Target aud: 25-54. ◆Ronnie Rose, gen mgr; Ed Carter, progmg dir.

Red Bank

*WJBP(FM)— Sept 12, 1980: 91.5 mhz; 11 kw. 951 ft TL: N35 09 42 W85 19 06. Stereo. Hrs open: 24 7355 N. Oracle Rd., Tucson, AZ, 85704. Phone: (520) 742-6976. Web Site:www.myflr.org/default.asp Licensee: Family Life Broadcasting Inc. (acq 12-10-2008; $1.5 million). Population served: 250,000 Format: Contemp Christian. ◆Dr. James L. Catanzaro, pres; Bob Riley, gen mgr, chief of engrg; Linda Miller, mktg VP; Patty Brown, prom VP; Sandy Smith, adv dir; Don Hixson, progmg dir; Jake Land, pub affrs dir.

WJTT(FM)— November 1972: 94.3 mhz; 4.7 kw. 429 ft TL: N35 07 32 W85 17 23. Stereo. Hrs open: 24 1305 Carter St., Chattanooga, 37402. Phone: (423) 265-9494. Fax: (423) 266-2335.E-mail: info@power94.com Web Site:www.power94.com Licensee: Brewer Broadcasting of Chattanooga Inc. (acq 12-26-93; $1.68 million). Population served: 366,800 Natl. Rep: D & R Radio. Format: Urban contemp. Target aud: 18-49. Spec prog: Relg 4 hrs wkly. ◆Jim L. Brewer Sr., pres; Jim L. Brewer II, VP, gen mgr; Jerry Ware, gen sls mgr; Brad Guagriri, natl sls mgr; Jay Holloway, prom mgr; Keith Landecker, progmg dir; Donna Harrison, news dir; Parks Hall, chief of engrg.

Ripley

*WAUV(FM)— 2000: 89.7 mhz; 5.3 kw. Ant 394 ft TL: N35 46 31 W89 28 18. Hrs open: Box 3206, American Family Radio, Tupelo, MS, 38803. Phone: (662) 844-8888. Fax: (662) 842-6791.E-mail: comments@afr.net Web Site:www.afr.net Licensee: American Family Association. Group owner: American Family Radio. Format: Relg. ◆Marvin Sanders, gen mgr.

WTRB(AM)— Dec 11, 1954: 1570 khz; 1 kw-D, 50 w-N. TL: N35 43 46 W89 32 33. (CP: 28 kw-D, 534 w-N). Hrs open: 17 Box 410, 372 S. Jefferson St., 38063. Phone: (731) 635-1570. Fax: (731) 635-9722. Licensee: West Tennessee Regional Broadcasting Inc. (group owner).

(acq 11-16-2004; $265,000). Population served: 25,000 Rgnl. Network: Tenn. Radio Net. Natl. Rep: Keystone (unwired net),. Tenn. Radio Net. Format: C&W. Spec prog: Gospel 6 hrs wkly. ◆Phillip Ennis, pres; Don Paris, gen mgr, gen sls mgr, disc jockey; April Goodrich, disc jockey.

Rockwood

WIHG(FM)— July 9, 1991: 105.7 mhz; 1.65 kw. Ant 1,233 ft TL: N35 52 05 W84 53 18. Hrs open: Box 810, Crossville, 38557. Phone: (931) 484-1057. Fax: (931) 707-0580. Licensee: Southern Media Group Inc. (acq 6-10-2003). Population served: 384,900 Natl. Network: CNN Radio, . Rgnl rep: Rgnl Reps Wire Svc: AP Format: Classic rock. News: 4 hrs wkly. Target aud: 25-54.

WYHM(AM)— May 12, 1957: 580 khz; 1 kw-D, 49 w-N. TL: N35 49 40 W84 39 19. Hrs open: Box 810, Crossville, 38557. Phone: (931) 484-1057. Fax: (931) 707-0580. Licensee: The Holler Inc. (group owner; (acq 8-25-2008; $225,000). Population served: 607,315 Natl. Network: ABC, . Natl. Rep: Rgnl Reps,. Format: Country. News staff: 3; News: news progmg 3 hrs wkly. Target aud: 35 plus; adults. ◆Kirk Tollett, gen mgr.

Rogersville

WJDT(FM)— Dec 1, 1990: 106.5 mhz; 6000 w. Ant 1,378 ft TL: N36 22 51 W83 10 47. Stereo. Hrs open: 24 Box 519, Morristown, 37815-0519. Secondary address: N. Davy Crockett Pkwy., Morristown 37814. Phone: (423) 235-4640. Phone: (865) 993-3639.E-mail: wjdtfm@planetc.com Web Site:www.wjdtfm.com Licensee: C & S Broadcasting. Population served: 500,000 Natl. Network: CNN Radio, . Larry Perry. Format: Country. News: 6 hrs wkly. Target aud: 18-59; female 65%, male 35%. ◆Clark Quillen, pres; David C. Quillen, opns mgr.

WRGS(AM)— Aug 20, 1954: 1370 khz; 1 kw-D, 40 w-N. TL: N36 24 58 W82 59 04. Hrs open: 24 211 Burem Rd., 37857. Phone: (423) 272-3900. Fax: (423) 272-0328.E-mail: stationmanager@wrgsradio.com Web Site:www.wrgsradio.com Licensee: WRGS Inc. Population served: 50,000 Natl. Network: USA, . Rgnl. Network: Tenn. Radio Net. Natl. Rep: Rgnl Reps,. Format: Country, gospel. Target aud: General. ◆Debbie Beal, gen mgr; Jay Phillips, progmg dir, progmg mgr; Mike Reeves, news dir; Chuck Windham, chief of engrg.

Saint Joseph

WMXV(FM)— 1991: 101.5 mhz; 2.85 kw. Ant 484 ft TL: N34 55 47 W87 31 44. Hrs open: Box 374, 37 Old Jackson Hwy., 38481. Phone: (931) 845-4172. Phone: (256) 757-9455. Fax: (931) 845-4172. Licensee: Urban Radio Licenses LLC. (acq 5-13-2005; grpsl). Format: Classic country, Southern gospel. ◆Rick Brown, gen mgr; Randy Paul, opns dir; Lance Knoll, gen sls mgr; Tony Fowler, prom dir; Jane Hoslan, adv dir, adv mgr; Lonnie Box, progmg dir; Sandi Summers, news dir; Craig Westbrook, chief of engrg.

Savannah

*WAZD(FM)— 2001: 88.1 mhz; 380 w. Ant 128 ft TL: N35 12 58 W88 14 30. Hrs open: Box 3206, American Family Radio, Tupelo, MS, 38803. Phone: (662) 844-8888. Fax: (662) 842-6791.E-mail: comments@afr.net Web Site:www.afr.net Licensee: American Family Association. Group owner: American Family Radio Format: Relg. ◆Marvin Sanders, gen mgr.

WKWX(FM)— June 23, 1980: 93.5 mhz; 25 kw. Ant 298 ft TL: N35 17 08 W88 10 03. Stereo. Hrs open: Box 40, 38372. Secondary address: 695 Wayne Rd. 38372. Phone: (731) 925-9600. Fax: (731) 925-8828.E-mail: wkwx@bellsouth.net Licensee: Melco Inc. (acq 12-19-02). Natl. Network: AP Radio, . Tenn. Radio Net. Format: New Hit Country. ◆Steve Carnal, pres; Jane Haggard, gen mgr; Jim Jerrolds, gen sls mgr; Dennis Brown, progmg dir, chief of engrg; Tom Treadway, chief of engrg.

WORM(AM)— June 29, 1956: 1010 khz; 250 w-D, 27 w-N. TL: N35 14 24 W88 14 29. Hrs open: 165 Bowen Dr., 38372. Phone: (731) 925-4981. Phone: (731) 925-7102. Fax: (731) 925-4981.E-mail: thewormq105@yahoo.com Licensee: Gerald W. Hunt. Population served: 5,576 Rgnl. Network: Tenn. Radio Net. Radio Net. Format: Pure Gold. ◆Gerald W. Hunt, pres, gen mgr, gen sls mgr, chief of engrg; Dave Morgan, progmg dir; Randy Tucker, mus dir.

WORM-FM— Aug 25, 1966: 101.7 mhz; 3 kw. 175 ft TL: N35 14 24 W88 14 29. Stereo. Hrs open: 165 Bowen Dr., 38372. Phone: (731) 925-4981. Phone: (731) 925-7102. Fax: (731) 925-4981.E-mail:

thewormq105@yahoo.com Licensee: Gerald W. Hunt Population served: 5,576 Format: Hot country.

Selmer

WDTM(AM)— Oct 31, 1967: 1150 khz; 1 kw-D. TL: N35 11 27 W88 35 21. Hrs open: 25 Stonebrook Pl., Suite G322, Jackson, 38305. Phone: (731) 663-3931. Fax: (731) 663-9804. Licensee: Grace Broadcasting Services Inc. (acq 7-25-2005; $200,000 with co-located FM). Population served: 113,495 Format: Contemp Christian. ◆Lacy Ennis, pres & gen mgr.

WSIB(FM)— January 1990: 93.9 mhz; 6 kw. Ant 328 ft TL: N35 11 27 W88 35 21. Stereo. Hrs open: 24 25 Stonebrook Pl., Suite G322, Jackson, 38305. Phone: (731) 663-3931. Fax: (731) 663-9804. Web Site:www.gracebroadcasting.com Format: Inspirational gospel. Target aud: 20-45.

***WXKV(FM)**— 2008: 90.5 mhz; 20 kw. Ant 413 ft TL: N35 10 44 W88 33 45. Hrs open:
Rebroadcasts KLVR(FM) Middletown, CA 100%.
2351 Sunset Blvd., Suite 170-218, Rocklin, CA, 95765. Phone: (916) 251-1600. Fax: (916) 251-1650. Web Site:www.klove.com Licensee: Educational Media Foundation. (acq 11-1-2006; grpsl). Natl. Network: K-Love, . Format: Contemp Christian. ◆Richard Jenkins, pres.

WXOQ(FM)— June 15, 1986: 105.5 mhz; 6 kw. Ant 298 ft TL: N35 13 11 W88 40 23. Stereo. Hrs open: 24 165 Bowen Dr., Savannah, 38372. Phone: (731) 645-9880. Fax: (731) 925-4981.E-mail: thewormQ105@yahoo.com Licensee: Gerald W. Hunt. (acq 6-28-94; $185,000; 7-11-94). Natl. Network: Westwood One, . Format: Country. News staff: 2. Target aud: General. ◆Gerald W. Hunt, pres, gen mgr, chief of engrg; Dave Morgan, progmg dir; Randy Tucker, mus dir.

Sevierville

WSEV(AM)— Apr 23, 1955: 930 khz; 5 kw-D, 148 w-N. TL: N35 52 42 W83 33 18. Stereo. Hrs open: 24 415 Middle Creek Rd., 37862. Phone: (865) 453-2844. Fax: (865) 429-2601. Licensee: Grand Crowne Resorts of Pigeon Forge LLC (acq 4-28-2008; $212,500). Population served: 65,000 Natl. Network: CBS, . Rgnl. Network: Tenn. Radio Net. Natl. Rep: Rgnl Reps,. Tenn. Radio Net. Format: Adult contemp. News staff: one; News: 6 hrs wkly. Target aud: 25 plus. ◆Paul Sink, gen mgr, stn mgr; Bill Burkett, opns mgr; Steve Hartford, progmg dir & news dir.

WWST(FM)— Feb 3, 1961: 102.1 mhz; 15 kw. 1,979 ft TL: N35 48 41 W83 40 08. Stereo. Hrs open: 24 Journal Broadcast Group, 1533 Amhearst Rd., Knoxville, 37909-1204. Phone: (865) 693-1020. Phone: (865)   824-1021. Fax: (865)   824-1880.E-mail: dmckee@journalbroadcastgroup.com Web Site:www.star1021fm.com Licensee: Journal Broadcast Corp. Group owner: Journal Communications Inc. (acq 5-19-97). Population served: 350,000 Natl. Network: ABC, . Hogan & Hartson. Format: CHR. News: 4 hrs wkly. Target aud: 25-54. ◆Chris Protzman, gen mgr, natl sls mgr; Rich Bailey, opns dir, progmg dir, pub affrs dir; Dan McKee, rgnl sls mgr; Justin Buznedo, prom dir; Scott Bohannon, mus dir; Ashey Adams, disc jockey.

Sewanee

***WUTS(FM)**— May 1972: 91.3 mhz; 200 w. 658 ft TL: N35 12 20 W85 55 07. (CP: 88.5 mhz). Hrs open: Univ. of the South, 735 University Ave., 37383. Phone: (931) 598-1206. Phone: (931) 598-1112. Fax: (931) 598-1145.E-mail: wuts@sewanee.edu Licensee: University of the South. Population served: 2,341 Format: Div, progsv. Target aud: General; college students. Spec prog: Black 2 hrs, class 4 hrs, country 2 hrs, jazz 4 hrs, Fr 2 hrs wkly. ◆John Lee, gen mgr; Austin Lacy, mus dir; Greg Banworth, chief of engrg.

Seymour

WJBZ-FM— Mar 31, 1991: 96.3 mhz; 3 kw. 328 ft TL: N35 54 32 W83 40 59. Hrs open: 24 Box 2526, Knoxville, 37901. Phone: (865) 577-4885. Fax: (865) 579-4667.E-mail: info@praise963.com Web Site:www.praise963.com Licensee: Seymour Communications. Format: Southern gospel. ◆Charlotte Mull, CEO; Doug Hutchison, pres, gen mgr; Mike Clark, opns mgr; Jamie Lewis, gen sls mgr, prom mgr; Tim Guinn, mus dir; Tim Berry, chief of engrg; Staci Beal, traf mgr.

Shelbyville

***WBIA(FM)**— 1999: 88.3 mhz; 250 w. Ant 46 ft TL: N35 28 54 W86 27 28. Hrs open: Drawer 2440, Tupelo, MS, 38803. Phone: (662)

844-8888. Fax: (662) 842-6791. Web Site:www.afr.net Licensee: American Family Association. Group owner: American Family Radio Format: Christian. ◆Marvin Sanders, gen mgr; John Riley, progmg dir; Joey Moody, chief of engrg.

WLIJ(AM)— Dec 2, 1959: 1580 khz; 5 kw-D, 12 w-N. TL: N35 27 21 W86 27 09. Hrs open: 24 Box 7, 236 Woodland Dr., 37160. Phone: (931) 684-1514. Phone: (931) 684-1515. Fax: (931) 684-3956. Licensee: Hopkins-Hall Broadcasting Inc. (acq 7-19-90; $110,000; 8-6-90). Population served: 12,262 Garvey, Schubert & Barer. Format: Country, bluegrass, gospel. News staff: one; News: 14 hrs wkly. Target aud: General. Spec prog: Black one hr, farm 3 hrs, relg 11 hrs wkly. ◆Nadine Hopkins, pres; Keith Cook, gen sls mgr, disc jockey; Rusty Reed, gen mgr, progmg dir & news dir; Paul Hopkins, chief of engrg; Hal Ball, disc jockey.

WZNG(AM)— December 1946: 1400 khz; 1 kw-U. TL: N35 28 26 W86 26 45. Hrs open: 24 Box 7, 37162. Secondary address: 236 Woodland Dr. 37160. Phone: (931) 680-1214. Fax: (931) 684-3956. Licensee: Hopkins-Hall Broadcasting Inc. (acq 12-19-96; $250,000). Population served: 36,000 Garvey, Schubert & Barer. Format: Radio America, talk star. Target aud: General; residents of the loc area. Spec prog: Relg 5 hrs wkly. ◆Nadine Hopkins, pres; Paul Hopkins, sr VP; Rusty Reed, gen mgr & stn mgr.

Signal Mountain

WLND(FM)— Aug 29, 1994: 98.1 mhz; 1 kw. Ant 794 ft TL: N35 05 16 W85 21 47. Hrs open: 24 7413 Old Lee Hwy., Chattanooga, 37421. Phone: (423) 892-3333. Fax: (423) 642-0097.E-mail: miller@981thelegend.com Web Site:www.thelegendonline.com Licensee: Capstar TX L.P. Group owner: Clear Channel Communications Inc. (acq 8-15-2000; grpsl). Kaye, Scholer, Fierman, Hays & Handler. Format: Classic country. News staff: one; News: 4 hrs wkly. Target aud: 35-54. ◆Sammy George, gen mgr; Jay Cruze, opns mgr, progmg dir; Rhonda Rollins, gen sls mgr.

Smithville

WJLE(AM)— Apr 11, 1964: 1480 khz; 1 kw-D, 34 w-N. TL: N35 55 31 W85 49 14. Hrs open: 16 2606 McMinnville Hwy., 37166-5071. Phone: (615) 597-4265. Fax: (615) 597-6025.E-mail: wjle@dtccom.net Web Site:www.wjle.com Licensee: Center Hill Broadcasting Corp. Population served: 300,000 Format: Country. News staff: one; News: 14 hrs wkly. Target aud: General. Spec prog: Gospel 15 hrs wkly. ◆W.E. Vanatta, pres & gen mgr; Dwayne Page, sls dir, progmg dir, news dir; Homer Wilson Jr., chief of engrg.

WJLE-FM— 1970: 101.7 mhz; 3 kw. Ant 195 ft TL: N35 55 31 W85 49 14. Hrs open: 16 2606 McMinnville Hwy., 37166-5071. Phone: (615) 597-4265. Fax: (615) 597-6025. Web Site:www.wjle.com Licensee: Center Hill Broadcasting Corp. Format: Country.

Smyrna

***WFCM(AM)**— 1993: 710 khz; 250 w-D. TL: N35 58 31 W86 33 16. Hrs open: Sunrise-sunset
Rebroadcasts WMBW(FM) Chattanooga 100%.
1920 E. 24th Street Pl., Chattanooga, 37404. Secondary address: 615 Potomac Pl. 37167. Phone: (423) 629-8900. Fax: (423) 629-0021.E-mail: wfcm@moody.edu Web Site:www.wfcm.org Licensee: The Moody Bible Institute of Chicago. (group owner; acq 5-16-97; $162,500). Natl. Network: Moody, . Format: Educ, relg, news/talk. ◆Edward Cannon, pres; Wayne Pederson, VP; Leighton LeBoeuf, gen mgr, stn mgr; Andy Napier, progmg dir; Paul Martin, mus dir; David Morais, chief of engrg.

WFFH(FM)— Oct 7, 1993: 94.1 mhz; 3.2 kw. Ant 305 ft TL: N36 01 14 W86 38 18. Stereo. Hrs open: 24
Simulcasts with WFFI(FM) Kingston Springs.
402 BNA Dr., Suite 400, Nashville, 37217. Phone: (615) 367-2210. Fax: (615) 367-0758. Web Site:www.94fmthefish.net Licensee: Caron Broadcasting Inc. Group owner: Salem Communications Corp. (acq 12-18-02; $5.6 million with WFFI(FM) Kingston Springs). Natl. Network: Salem Radio Network, . Natl. Rep: Salem,. Format: Contemp Christian. Target aud: 25-54; adults. ◆Michael S. Miller, gen mgr; Dick Marsh, prom dir; Vance Dillard, progmg dir; Kim Bindel, news dir; Carl Campbell, chief of engrg; Ed Evenson, traf mgr.

Soddy-Daisy

WGOW-FM—Licensed to Soddy-Daisy. See Chattanooga

WSDT(AM)— Feb 27, 1970: 1240 khz; 1 kw-U. TL: N35 16 16 W85 10 28. Hrs open: 24 11563 Argonne Rd, Festus, MO, 63028-2951. Secondary address: 4513 Hixson Pike, Suite 105, Hixson 35373.

Phone: (636) 586-8697. Fax: (636) 586-8697.E-mail: svicomm@hughes.net Web Site:www.svicommunications.com Licensee: Serendipity Ventures II LLC (group owner; (acq 2006). Population served: 35,000 Natl. Network: USA, . Format: Oldies. News: TOH-Daytime. ◆Steve Vogt, gen mgr.

Somerville

WSTN(AM)— Nov 29, 1982: Stn currently dark. 1410 khz; 500 w-U, DA-2. TL: N35 14 31 W89 19 03. Hrs open: 8919 World Ministry Ave., Baton Rouge, LA, 70826. Phone: (225) 768-8300. Web Site:www-jsm.org Licensee: Family Worship Center Church Inc. (group owner; (acq 12-4-2002). ◆David Whitelaw, COO; Jimmy Swaggart, pres; John Santiago, gen mgr & progmg dir.

South Fulton

WCMT-FM—Licensed to South Fulton. See Martin

South Pittsburg

WEPG(AM)— July 9, 1954: 910 khz; 5 kw-D, 95 w-N. TL: N35 00 57 W85 42 00. Hrs open: Box 8, 37380. Secondary address: 105 N. Ash Ave. 37380. Phone: (423) 837-0747. Fax: (423) 837-2974.E-mail: wepgtv6@aol.com Licensee: Stone/Collins Communications Inc. (acq 2-1-02). Population served: 80,000 Format: Country. Target aud: 18-50; females. Spec prog: Gospel 10 hrs wkly. ◆Roger Spears, gen mgr; Glenda Frame, prom dir; Rogers Spears, gen sls mgr & progmg dir.

WUUQ(FM)— Nov 5, 1990: 97.3 mhz; 16 kw. Ant 856 ft TL: N34 58 21 W85 37 58. Stereo. Hrs open: 24 Box 4743, Chattanooga, 37405. Secondary address: 307 N Market St, Chattanooga 37414. Phone: (423) 643-2212. Fax: (423) 642-0096. Fax: (423) 643-2215. Web Site:www.wuuqradio.com Licensee: 3 Daughters Media Inc. Group owner: Clear Channel Communications Inc. (acq 6-22-2007; grpsl). Format: Classic Hits. News staff: 2; News: 20 hrs wkly. Target aud: 18-54. ◆Joe Mule, gen mgr; Dale Mitchell, progmg dir.

Sparta

WSMT(AM)— Apr 26, 1953: 1050 khz; 1 kw-D, 181 w-N. TL: N35 57 00 W85 28 50. Hrs open: 24 520 N. Spring St., 38583-1305. Phone: (931) 836-1055. Phone: (931) 836-2824. Fax: (931) 836-2320. Licensee: Peg Broadcasting Crossville LLC. Group owner: Clear Channel Communications Inc. (acq 7-1-2008; grpsl). Population served: 200,000 Format: Southern gospel. News staff: one; News: 10 hrs wkly. Target aud: General. Spec prog: Relg 10 hrs wkly. ◆Bryan Kell, CEO, gen mgr; Duke Rice, opns mgr; Anthony Griffen, engr.

WTZX(AM)— Nov 26, 1971: 860 khz; 1 kw-D, 9.9 w-N. TL: N35 55 20 W85 26 50. Hrs open: 24 520 N. Spring St., 38583-1305. Phone: (931) 836-1055. Fax: (931) 836-2320. Licensee: Peg Broadcasting Crossville LLC. Group owner: Clear Channel Communications Inc. (acq 7-1-2008). Population served: 200,000 Format: Oldies. News staff: one. Target aud: General. ◆Bryan Kell, gen mgr; Duke Rice, stn mgr & opns mgr; Anthony Griffen, engr.

Spencer

WTRZ(FM)— Aug 1, 1993: 107.3 mhz; 2 kw. Ant 508 ft TL: N35 39 55 W85 31 19. Hrs open: 230 W. Colville St., Mc Minnville, 37110. Phone: (931) 473-9253. Fax: (931) 473-4149.E-mail: bryankell@clearchannel.com Web Site:www.kiss107radio.com Licensee: Peg Broadcasting Crossville LLC. Group owner: Clear Channel Communications Inc. (acq 6-30-2008; grpsl). Format: CHR. ◆Bryan Kell, gen mgr, sls; Jeff Edwards, progmg dir; Homer Wilson, chief of engrg.

***WZYZ(FM)**— 2003: 90.1 mhz; 30 w. Ant 590 ft TL: N35 44 03 W85 27 33. Hrs open: 24 Trinity Ln., 38585. Phone: (931) 946-7777.E-mail: questions@wzyz.org Licensee: Church Faith Trinity Assemblies (acq 8-1-02). Format: Relg. ◆Daniel Lawson, gen mgr.

Spring City

***WLNQ(FM)**—Not on air, target date: unknown: 88.5 mhz; 850 w vert. Ant -278 ft TL: N35 39 58.7 W84 52 44.1. Hrs open: Box 604, Loudon, 37774. Phone: (865) 458-9563. Fax: (865) 458-0959. Licensee: Corporation for Radio Education Inc. ◆Richard S. Lynn, pres.

WXQK(AM)— July 12, 1979: 970 khz; 500 w-D. TL: N35 39 59 W84 52 44. Hrs open: 6 AM-6 PM

Rebroadcasts WBAC(AM) Cleveland 100%.
2640 Commerce Dr. N.E., Cleveland, 37311. Phone: (423) 242-7656. Fax: (423) 472-5290. Web Site:www.wbacradio.com Licensee: East Tennessee Radio Group III L.P. Group owner: Brewer Broadcasting Corp. (acq 5-30-2008; grpsl). Population served: 28,608 Natl. Network: ABC, . Natl. Rep: D & R Radio, Tenn. Radio Net. Format: News/talk. News staff: one; News: 16 hrs wkly. Target aud: 35-64. ◆Charles Sells, gen mgr; Mike Powers, opns mgr; John Holland, gen sls mgr; Corky Whitlock, progmg dir.

Springfield

WDBL(AM)— July 24, 1950: 1590 khz; 1 kw-D, 30 w-N. TL: N36 29 43 W86 54 26. (CP: 710 w-D. TL: N36 29 42 W86 54 22). Hrs open: 19 1640 Old Russellville Pike, Clarksburg, 37043. Phone: (931) 648-7720. Fax: (931) 648-7769. Licensee: Lightning Broadcasting LLC (acq 7-28-2004; $150,000). Population served: 42,000 Rgnl. Network: Tenn. Radio Net. Tenn. Radio Net. Format: Contemp Christian. News staff: one; News: 16 hrs wkly. Target aud: 18 plus. Spec prog: Farm 10 hrs, gospel 10 hrs wkly. ◆Susan Quesenberry, gen mgr; Lee Logan, opns mgr, progmg dir; J.C. Morrow, mus dir, chief of engrg.

WSGI(AM)— Dec 15, 1982: 1100 khz; 1 kw-D. TL: N36 31 00 W86 53 30. Hrs open: 6 AM-sunset Box 909, 37172. Phone: (615) 384-9744. Fax: (615) 384-9746.E-mail: wsgi1100@yahoo.com Licensee: Lightning Broadcasting LLC (acq 3-2001; $155,000). Tenn. Radio Net. Format: Variety. Target aud: General. Spec prog: Relg, farm 5 hrs, gospel 16 hrs wkly. ◆Jo Petersen, VP; Neil Petersen, pres & gen mgr; Billy Gray, gen sls mgr, news dir.

Static

WSBI(AM)— Apr 7, 1986: 1210 khz; 1 kw-D. TL: N36 37 22 W85 05 15. Hrs open: Sunrise-sunset Box 160508, Nashville, 37216. Phone: (615) 227-1130. Fax: (606) 387-8126.E-mail: wsbiam.com Web Site:www.radiovida1130.com Licensee: Donnie S. Cox (acq 11-3-99; $60,000). Natl. Network: USA, . Format: Sp Christian. Target aud: 25 plus. ◆Donnie Cox, gen mgr; Robert Huddleston, chief of engrg.

Sunbright

*WJCG(FM)—Not on air, target date: unknown: 91.5 mhz; 100 w horiz, 16.5 kw vert. Ant 462 ft TL: N36 01 00 W84 56 00. Hrs open: 2864 Alcoa Hwy., Knoxville, 37920. Phone: (865) 609-1385. Fax: (865) 579-4932. Web Site:www.calvaryknoxville.org Licensee: Calvary Chapel of Knoxville. ◆Mark Kirk, pres; Greg Hilt, gen mgr.

Surgoinsville

WEYE(FM)—Licensed to Surgoinsville. See Church Hill

Sweetwater

WDEH(AM)— 1955: 800 khz; 1 kw-D, 379 w-N. TL: N35 36 49 W84 27 33. Hrs open: 24 Box 330, 37874. Phone: (423) 337-5025. Fax: (423) 337-5026.E-mail: wlodwdeh@yahoo.com Licensee: Horne Radio L.L.C. Group owner: Horne Radio Group (acq 1999; $425,000 with co-located FM). Population served: 500,000 Format: Gospel.

WLOD-FM— September 1967: 98.3 mhz; 6 kw. Ant 135 ft TL: N35 36 49 W84 27 33. Stereo. Hrs open: 24 Box 330, 37874. Phone: (423) 337-5025. Fax: (423) 337-5026. Population served: 250,000 Format: Oldies.

Tazewell

WNTT(AM)— July 1, 1960: 1250 khz; 500 w-D. TL: N36 27 09 W83 34 23. Hrs open: 6 AM-Sunset Box 95, 115 Bluetop Rd., 37879-0095. Phone: (423) 626-4203. Fax: (423) 626-3040.E-mail: aileen@wntt1250am.co Web Site:www.wntt1250am.com Licensee: WNTT Inc. (acq 9-1-94; $90,000). Population served: 25,860 Natl. Network: ABC, . Format: Country, oldies, news. News: 12 hrs wkly. Target aud: 18-65; general. ◆Aileen S. Craft, CEO, gen sls mgr, progmg dir, progmg mgr, news dir, local news ed; Frank Folsom, chief of engrg; Jennifer Duff, opns mgr, chief of opns & disc jockey.

Tiptonville

WTNV(FM)— July 1, 2007: 97.3 mhz; 6 kw. Ant 328 ft TL: N36 20 59 W89 22 12. Hrs open: P.O. Box 100, 2555 Huish Rd., Dyersburg,

38025-0100. Phone: (731) 285-1339. Fax: (731) 287-0100. Web Site:eagle973.net Licensee: Dr. Pepper Pepsi-Cola Bottling Co. of Dyersburg. Natl. Network: Fox News Radio, . Tenn. Radio Net. Rgnl rep: Rgnl Reps Format: Country. Target aud: 18-54. ◆W.E. Burks, pres; Natalie Burks, sls dir; Dan Defilippo, progmg dir; Dave Hacker, engr.

Trenton

WTNE(AM)— Dec 9, 1966: 1500 khz; 250 w-D, 6 w-N. TL: N35 58 52 W88 55 32. Hrs open: 24 25 Stonebrook Place, Suite G, 322, Jackson, 38305. Phone: (731) 616-4015. Fax: (731) 855-1600. Licensee: Grace Broadcasting Services Inc. Population served: 100,000 Rgnl rep: Midsouth. Format: Adult contemp. Target aud: General; Gibson county, news oriented people. Spec prog: Sports. ◆Lacy Ennis, pres.

WTNE-FM— August 1980: 97.7 mhz; 50 kw. Ant 328 ft TL: N36 05 10 W88 54 39. Stereo. Hrs open: 24 25 Stonebrook Place, Suite G, 322, Jackson, 38305. Phone: (731) 616-4015. Fax: (731) 855-1600.E-mail: lennis931@aol.com Licensee: Grace Broadcasting Services Inc. Group owner: Thunderbolt Broadcasting Co./Gibson County Broadcasting (acq 1-7-2005; grpsl). Population served: 500,000 Format: News Talk, sports. News staff: one. Target aud: 25-60. Spec prog: High school sports 10 hrs, college football 10 hrs wkly. ◆Lacy Ennis, pres.

Tullahoma

*WAUT-FM— 1998: 88.5 mhz; 1.9 kw. 177 ft TL: N35 20 30 W86 11 05. Hrs open: Box 3206, American Family Radio, Tupelo, MS, 38803. Phone: (662) 844-8888. Phone: (662) 844-8893. Fax: (662) 842-6791.E-mail: comments@afr.net Web Site:www.afr.net Licensee: American Family Association. Group owner: American Family Radio Format: Relg. ◆Marvin Sanders, gen mgr.

WJIG(AM)— Aug 1, 1947: 740 khz; 250 w-D, 67 w-N. TL: N35 20 36 W86 12 00. Hrs open: 24 WJIG AM 740, 2214 N. Jackson St., 37388. Phone: (931) 455-7426. Fax: (931) 455-7438.E-mail: wjig@charterinternet.com Licensee: NRS Enterprises Inc. (acq 2-21-97; $163,000). Population served: 18,000 Natl. Network: Salem Radio Network, . Rgnl. Network: Tenn. Radio Net. Tenn. Radio Net. Format: Christian. Target aud: 35 plus. ◆Roy Woods, pres; Joyce Woods, gen mgr; Heath Laws, disc jockey.

*WTML(FM)— 2001: 91.5 mhz; 1.55 kw. Ant 269 ft TL: N35 23 53 W86 08 40. Hrs open:
Rebroadcasts WPLN-FM Nashville 100%.
Nashville Public Radio, 630 Mainstream Dr., Nashville, 37228-1204. Phone: (615) 760-2903. Fax: (615) 760-2904.E-mail: info@wpln.org Web Site:www.wpln.org Licensee: Nashville Public Radio. Format: Classical, news, bluegrass. ◆Robert Gordon, gen mgr; Scott Smith, opns mgr; Laura Landress, gen sls mgr; Henry Fennell, progmg dir; Will Griffin, mus dir; Anita Bugg, news dir; Tom Knox, chief of engrg; Wendy Poston, traf mgr.

Tusculum

WIKQ(FM)—Licensed to Tusculum. See Greeneville

*WZTH(FM)—Not on air, target date: unknown: 91.1 mhz; 500 w horiz, 10 kw vert. Ant 321 ft TL: N36 05 53 W82 56 37. Hrs open: 6 Surrey Ct., Marlton, NJ, 08053. Phone: (856) 983-1055. Licensee: Solid Foundation Broadcasting Corp. ◆James M. Smith, pres.

Union City

WENK(AM)— Oct 26, 1946: 1240 khz; 1 kw-U. TL: N36 25 28 W89 02 17. Stereo. Hrs open: 24
Rebroadcasts WTPR-FM McKinnon 100%.
1729 Nailling Dr., 38261. Phone: (731) 885-1240. Fax: (731) 885-3405.E-mail: thailey@wenkwtpr.com Licensee: WENK of Union City Inc. Group owner: WENK Broadcast Group Inc. (acq 1-74). Population served: 96,579 Natl. Rep: Rgnl Reps., Shainis & Peltzman. Format: Oldies. News staff: one; News: 15 hrs wkly. Target aud: 35-54. ◆Richard Hall, sls dir; Brad Hosford, chief of engrg; Terry Hailey, pres, gen mgr, progmg dir & edit mgr.

WQAK(FM)— March 1994: 105.7 mhz; 24 kw. Ant 328 ft TL: N36 31 07 W89 05 41. Stereo. Hrs open: Box 5000, 38281. Secondary address: 233 Westgate 38281. Phone: (731) 885-0051. Fax: (731) 885-0250.E-mail: ptinkle@crunet.com Web Site:www.wqakradio.com Licensee: Thunderbolt Broadcasting Co. (acq 12-29-2005; $900,000 with WYVY(FM) Union City). Population served: 263,874 Womble, Carlyle, Sandridge & Rice. Format: Classic Hits. News staff: one. ◆Paul F. Tinkle, pres.

*WTAI(FM)— 2005: 88.9 mhz; 860 w vert. Ant 623 ft TL: N36 24 48 W89 08 59. Hrs open: 5700 West Oaks Blvd., Rocklin, CA, 95765. Phone: (916) 251-1600. Fax: (916) 251-1650. Licensee: Educational Media Foundation. (acq 6-21-2005; $25,000 for CP). Format: Christian. ◆Richard Jenkins, pres.

WYVY(FM)— Sept 20, 1974: 104.9 mhz; 6 kw. Ant 328 ft TL: N36 28 25 W88 56 41. Stereo. Hrs open: 24 Box 5000, 38281. Secondary address: 223 Westgate Dr. 38261. Phone: (731) 885-0051. Fax: (731) 885-0250.E-mail: ptinkle@crunet.com Web Site:www.kytnradio.com Licensee: Thunderbolt Broadcasting Co. (acq 12-29-2005; $900,000 with WQAK(FM) Union City). Population served: 301,843 Rgnl. Network: Tenn. Radio Net. Womble, Carlyle, Sandridge & Rice. Format: Country. News staff: one; News: 25 hrs wkly. Target aud: 18 plus. ◆Paul F. Tinkle, pres.

Walden

WURV(FM)— Jan 23, 1964: 103.7 mhz; 25 kw. Ant 292 ft TL: N35 07 33 W85 17 25. Stereo. Hrs open: 24 7413 Old Lee Hwy., Chattanooga, 37421. Phone: (423) 892-3333. Fax: (423) 899-7224. Web Site:www.1037theriver.com Licensee: Citicasters Licenses L.P. Population served: 225,000 Format: Adult contemp. Target aud: 18-40. ◆Bryan Kell, sls dir; Greg Rambin, progmg dir.

Wartburg

WECO(AM)— Aug 31, 1970: 940 khz; 5 kw-D. TL: N36 05 48 W84 35 31. Hrs open: Box 100, 37887. Secondary address: 305 N. Church St. 37887. Phone: (423) 346-3900. Fax: (423) 346-7686.E-mail: wecoradio@highland.net Licensee: Morgan County Broadcasting Co. Inc. Rgnl. Network: Tenn. Radio Net. Tenn. Radio Net. Format: Gospel. ◆Sandy Lavender, gen mgr; Gary Stone, progmg dir; Carl Stump, chief of engrg.

WECO-FM— August 1988: 101.3 mhz; 500 w. 770 ft TL: N36 05 25 W78 38 05. Hrs open: Box 100 , 37887. Secondary address: 305 N. Church St. 37887. Phone: (423) 346-3900. Fax: (423) 346-7686.E-mail: wecoradio@highland.net (Acq 1-30-89). Format: Country. Target aud: 25-49.

*WLNB(FM)—Not on air, target date: unknown: 90.3 mhz; 550 w vert. Ant -47 ft TL: N36 05 48 W84 35 31. Hrs open: Box 604, Loudon, 37774. Phone: (865) 458-9563. Web Site:www.wlntfm.com Licensee: Corporation for Radio Education Inc. ◆Richard S. Lynn, pres.

Waverly

WQMV(AM)— Sept 25, 1963: 1060 khz; 1 kw-D, 4 w-N. TL: N36 05 15 W87 51 18. Hrs open: 24 Box 610, 37185. Phone: (931) 296-9768. Fax: (931) 296-9892.E-mail: wqmv@comcast.net Web Site:www.wqmv1060.com Licensee: C & L Broadcasting Corp. (acq 10-16-2003; $60,000). Population served: 6,000 Natl. Network: ABC, . Tenn. Radio Net. Format: Music from the 50s, 60s, 70s, 80s. Target aud: Adults 35-65. ◆Richard Albright, pres.

WVRY(FM)— Sept 26, 1972: 105.1 mhz; 50 kw. Ant 492 ft TL: N36 05 16 W87 51 19. Stereo. Hrs open: 24 2263 N. Highland Ave., 25 Stonebrook Pl., Suite #322, Jackson, 38305. Phone: (731) 855-9394. Fax: (731) 855-1600.E-mail: info@salemmusicnetwork.com Web Site:www.gracebroadcasting.com Licensee: Reach Satellite Network Inc. Group owner: Salem Communications Corp. (acq 3-31-2000; $3.1 million for stock with WBOZ(FM) Woodbury). Population served: 1,500,000 Natl. Network: Salem Radio Network, . Rgnl. Network: Tenn. Radio Net. Natl. Rep: Salem,. Tenn. Radio Net. Fletcher, Heald & Hildreth. Format: Southern gospel. Target aud: 25-54. ◆Jim Cumbee, CEO; Rodney Minyard, gen mgr.

Waynesboro

WWON(AM)— Jan 31, 1970: 930 khz; 500 w-D. TL: N35 18 30 W87 44 44. Hrs open: 24 Box 999, 38485. Secondary address: 100 Public Sq. S. 38485. Phone: (931) 722-3631. Fax: (931) 722-3632.E-mail: wwon@netease.net Web Site:www.bigoldies930.com Licensee: Small Potatoes Broadcasting Co. LLC (acq 6-12-2008; $118,000). Population served: 20000 Law Offices of Timothy K. Brady. Format: Oldies. News: 13 hrs wkly. Target aud: 18-54; listeners interested in rgnl & natl issues. ◆Chris Lash, gen mgr.

White Bluff

WQSE(AM)— July 18, 1982: 1030 khz; 1 kw-D, DA-N. TL: N36 08 03 W87 12 58. Hrs open: 201 Hall Ln., 37187. Phone: (615) 797-9785.

Fax: (615) 797-9788.E-mail: dvanedjwqse@aol.com Licensee: Canaan Communications Inc. (acq 3-19-03; $85,000). Format: Southern gospel. ♦Duane Jeffrey, pres, gen mgr; Kerry Lampley, sls dir; Mary Jeffrey, mus dir, disc jockey; Shery Swaw, sports cmtr.

Winchester

WCDT(AM)— Mar 8, 1948: 1340 khz; 1 kw-U. TL: N35 10 51 W86 05 34. Hrs open: 24 1201 S. College St., 37398. Phone: (931) 967-2201. Phone: (931) 967-2202. Fax: (931) 967-2201.E-mail: wcdt@bellsouth.net Web Site:www.wcdt1340.com Licensee: Franklin County Radio & Broadcasting Co. Inc. (acq 8-1-56). Population served: 65,000 Natl. Network: ABC, . Rgnl. Network: Tenn. Radio Net. Tenn. Radio Net. Format: U.S. Country. News staff: one; News: 15 hrs wkly. Target aud: General. Spec prog: Farm 15 hrs, Relg 6 hrs wkly. ♦John T. Yarbrough, pres; Darryl Basham, gen mgr; Jan Tavalin, news dir, spec ev coord; Al Tipps, disc jockey; Sharon Price, mktg dir & sls.

Woodbury

WBOZ(FM)— Oct 5, 1994: 104.9 mhz; 6 kw. Ant 328 ft TL: N35 49 33 W86 09 28. Stereo. Hrs open: 24 312 S. Church St., Murfreesboro, 37130. Secondary address: 402 BNA Dr., Suite 400, Nashville 37217. Phone: (615) 890-3233. Fax: (615) 890-2990.E-mail: info@salemmusicnetwork.com Web Site:www.solidgospel105.com Licensee: Reach Satellite Network Inc. Group owner: Salem Communications Corp. (acq 4-1-00; $3.1 million for stock with WVRY(FM) Waverly). Population served: 130,000 Natl. Network: Salem Radio Network, . Natl. Rep: Salem,. Format: Christian country, southern gospel. News: 14 hrs wkly. Target aud: 35+; adults. Spec prog: Sports 5 hrs wkly. ♦Greg R. Anderson, pres; Michael S. Miller, gen mgr; Kevin R. Anderson, stn mgr; Dick Marsh, prom dir; Vance Dillard, progmg dir; Carl Campbell, chief of engrg.

WBRY(AM)— Oct 24, 1963: 1540 khz; 500 w-D. TL: N35 49 53 W86 06 42. (Simulcast on FM translator W244CJ Woodbury on 96.7 mhz). Hrs open: 24 Box 7, 37190. Secondary address: 153 Mile Valley Rd. 37190. Phone: (615) 563-2313. Fax: (615) 563-6229.E-mail: askus@wbry.com Web Site:www.wbry.com Licensee: Volunteer Broadcasting LLC (acq 3-2-2005; $130,000). Population served: 25,000 Natl. Network: ABC, . Format: Traditional country. News staff: one; News: 7 hrs wkly. Target aud: 25 plus; adults. ♦Doug Combs, pres & gen mgr.

Texas

Abilene

***KACU(FM)**— June 2, 1986: 89.7 mhz; 33 kw. 215 ft TL: N32 28 34 W99 42 22. Stereo. Hrs open: 24 ACU Box 27820, 79699. Phone: (325) 674-2441. Fax: (325) 674-2417.E-mail: bestj@acu.edu Web Site:www.kacu.org Licensee: Abilene Christian University. Natl. Network: NPR, . Format: Adult contemp, class, news. News: 42 hrs wkly. Target aud: 35 plus; middle-to-upper income professionals. Spec prog: Jazz 3 hrs wkly. ♦John Best, gen mgr, opns dir; Kim Seidman, dev dir.

***KAGT(FM)**— Nov 5, 2002: 90.5 mhz; 100 kw. Ant 341 ft TL: N32 30 37 W99 44 28. Stereo. Hrs open: 24 2351 Sunset Blvd., Suite 170-218, Rocklin, CA, 95765. Phone: (916) 251-1600. Fax: (916) 251-1650. Licensee: Educational Media Foundation. (acq 12-31-2006; $450,000). Population served: 200,000 Format: Christian. ♦Richard Jenkins, pres.

***KAQD(FM)**— 1998: 91.3 mhz; 1 kw. Ant 177 ft TL: N32 28 36 W99 44 56. Hrs open: Box 3206, American Family Radio, Tupelo, MS, 38803. Phone: (662) 844-8888. Fax: (662) 842-6791.E-mail: comments@afr.net Web Site:www.afr.net Licensee: American Family Association. Group owner: American Family Radio Format: Inspirational Christian. ♦Marvin Sanders, gen mgr.

KBCY(FM)—See Tye

KEAN-FM— July 1, 1969: 105.1 mhz; 100 kw. Ant 810 ft TL: N32 16 35 W99 35 39. Stereo. Hrs open: 24 3911 S. First St., 79605. Phone: (325) 676-7711. Fax: (325) 676-3851.E-mail: kean@keanradio.com Web Site:www.keanradio.com Population served: 250,000 Natl. Network: ABC, . Format: Country. ♦Karen Brakefield Hines, gen mgr; Rudy Fernandez, progmg dir.

KEYJ-FM— Apr 30, 1961: 107.9 mhz; 100 kw. 670 ft TL: N32 17 06 W99 38 38. Stereo. Hrs open: 3911 S. First St., 79605. Phone: (325) 677-7225. Phone: (325) 676-7711. Fax: (325) 676-3851.E-mail: info@keyj.com Web Site:www.keyj.com Licensee: GAP Broadcasting Abilene License LLC. Group owner: Clear Channel Communications Inc. (acq 8-3-2007; grpsl). Format: Alternative rock. Target aud: 18-49; men. ♦Dale Harris, gen mgr; James Cameron, opns mgr; Frank Payne, progmg dir.

KFGL(FM)— September 1974: 100.7 mhz; 100 kw. 1,260 ft TL: N32 24 48 W100 06 25. Stereo. Hrs open: 3911 S. First St., 79605. Phone: (325) 676-7111. Fax: (325) 676-3851. Web Site:www.keyj.com Licensee: GAP Broadcasting Abilene License LLC. Group owner: Clear Channel Communications Inc. (acq 8-3-2007; grpsl). Population served: 200,000 Format: Classic rock. Target aud: 18-34; women. Spec prog: Oldies 2 hrs wkly. ♦Ted Warren, gen mgr; James Cameron, opns mgr; Renee Gonzalez, gen sls mgr.

***KGNZ(FM)**— Mar 7, 1981: 88.1 mhz; 75 kw. 710 ft TL: N32 17 46 W99 43 01. Stereo. Hrs open: 24 542 Butternut St., 79602. Secondary address: 1001 Cedar Crest St. 79601. Phone: (325) 673-3045. Fax: (325) 672-7938.E-mail: studio@kgnz.com Web Site:www.kgnz.com Licensee: Christian Broadcasting Co. Natl. Network: USA, . Format: Adult contemp, Christian. Spec prog: Black 2 hrs, gospel 2 hrs wkly. ♦Larry Jack Hill, pres, gen mgr; Doug Harris, opns mgr; Randy Martinez, dev dir.

KGXL(FM)—See Winters

KKHR(FM)— June 1988: 106.3 mhz; 50 kw. Ant 184 ft TL: N32 28 34 W99 42 22. Stereo. Hrs open: 24 402 Cypress St., Suite 510, 79601. Phone: (325) 672-5442. Fax: (325) 672-6128.E-mail: parker@radioabilene.com Web Site:radioabilene.com Licensee: Canfin Enterprises Inc. (acq 3-25-2005; $684,000). Natl. Rep: Lotus Entravision Reps LLC,. Format: Latino mix. News: 3 hrs wkly. Target aud: 18-49. ♦Parker Cannon, gen mgr; Ben Gonzalez, progmg dir; James Thompson, chief of engrg.

KORQ(FM)—See Baird

KSLI(AM)— June 15, 1957: 1280 khz; 500 w-D, 226 w-N. TL: N32 26 30 W99 43 08. Hrs open: 24 Box 3098, 79604. Secondary address: 3911 S. First St. 79605. Phone: (325) 676-7711. Fax: (325) 676-3851. Web Site:www.keyj.com Licensee: GAP Broadcasting Abilene License LLC. Group owner: Clear Channel Communications Inc. (acq 8-3-2007; grpsl). Population served: 235,000 Natl. Network: Jones Radio Networks, . Format: Music of your life. News: 4 hrs wkly. Target aud: 18-49; Hispanic. ♦Dale Harris, gen mgr.

KULL(FM)— Apr 1, 1998: 92.5 mhz; 27.5 kw. Ant 663 ft TL: N32 16 35 W99 35 38. Hrs open: 3911 S. 1st St., 79605. Phone: (325) 677-7225. Fax: (325) 677-3851.E-mail: info@kull.com Licensee: GAP Broadcasting Abilene License LLC. Group owner: Clear Channel Communications Inc. (acq 8-3-2007; grpsl). Population served: 250,000 Natl. Network: ABC, . Format: Oldies. ♦Ted Wrenn, VP; James Cameron, opns mgr.

KWKC(AM)— June 19, 1948: 1340 khz; 1 kw-U. TL: N32 25 14 W99 43 54. Hrs open: 24 Box 3498, 79604-3498. Phone: (325) 672-5442. Fax: (325) 672-6128.E-mail: parker@radioabilene.com Web Site:www.radioabilene.com Licensee: Canfin Enterprises Inc. Population served: 150,000 Natl. Network: CBS Radio, . Rgnl. Network: Texas State Net. Texas State Networks Format: News/talk. News staff: 2. Target aud: 25 plus. ♦Parker Cannan, pres, gen mgr & opns VP.

KYYW(AM)— Oct 1, 1936: 1470 khz; 5 kw-D, 1 kw-N, DA-N. TL: N32 29 26 W99 45 02. Hrs open: 3911 S. First St., 79605. Phone: (325) 676-7711. Fax: (325) 676-3851. Web Site:www.keanradio.com Licensee: GAP Broadcasting Abilene License LLC. Group owner: Clear Channel Communications Inc. (acq 8-3-2007; grpsl). Population served: 250,000 Natl. Network: CBS, . Kenkel & Associates. Format: Classic country. ♦Randy Jones, gen mgr & progmg dir; Gary Smith, engrg dir, chief of engrg.

KZQQ(AM)— Aug 29, 1962: 1560 khz; 500 w-D, 45 w-N. TL: N32 27 21 W99 47 59. Hrs open: 24 Box 3498, 79604-3498. Phone: (325) 672-5442. Fax: (325) 672-6128. Web Site:www.radioabilene.com Licensee: Canfin Enterprises Inc. Population served: 120000 Natl. Network: ESPN Radio, . Texas State Networks Format: ESPN sports, talk. News staff: one. Target aud: 18 plus. ♦Parker Cannan, gen mgr.

Alamo

KJAV(FM)— Aug 17, 1980: 104.9 mhz; 6 kw. Ant 328 ft TL: N26 12 49 W98 05 21. Hrs open: 1201 N. Jackson Rd., Suite 900, McAllen, 78501. Phone: (956) 992-8895. Fax: (956) 992-8897.E-mail: info@bmpradio.com Web Site:www.bmpradio.com Licensee: BMP RGV License Company L.P. (acq 1-26-2005; $7 million). Format: Adult hits. ♦Thomas Castro, pres; Jose Luis Munoz, gen mgr; Jeff Koch, opns mgr, progmg dir.

Alamo Heights

KDRY(AM)—Licensed to Alamo Heights. See San Antonio

KLUP(AM)—See Terrell Hills

Albany

KNOS(FM)—Not on air, target date: unknown: 98.9 mhz; 6 kw. Ant 328 ft TL: N32 37 25 W99 26 26. Hrs open: 2801 Via Fortuna, Suite 675, Austin, 78746. Licensee: Matinee Radio LLC.

Alice

***KIFR(FM)**—Not on air, target date: unknown: 88.3 mhz; 23.5 kw vert. Ant 292 ft TL: N27 53 55 W98 05 55. Hrs open: 4135 Northgate Blvd., Suite 1, Sacramento, CA, 95834-1226. Phone: (916) 641-8191. Fax: (916) 641-8238. Licensee: Family Stations Inc. ♦Harold Camping, pres; Peggy Renschler, gen mgr.

KNDA(FM)— Jan 1, 1974: 102.9 mhz; 50 kw. 492 ft TL: N27 42 26 W97 46 54. Stereo. Hrs open: 2001 Saratoga, Suite 100, Corpus Christi, 78417. Phone: (361) 814-1030. Phone: (361) 814-1029. Fax: (361) 814-1036.E-mail: lilrichardabomb@aol.com Licensee: Encarnacion A. Guerra (acq 5-95). Population served: 27,500 Format: Hip-hop, R&B. ♦Jesse Rodriguez, gen mgr.

KOPY(AM)— 1947: 1070 khz; 1 kw-U, DA-N. TL: N27 46 39 W98 04 53. Hrs open: 24 Box 731, 78333. Secondary address: 2722 N. Business Hwy. 281 78332. Phone: (361) 664-1884. Fax: (361) 664-1886. Licensee: Claro Communications Ltd. (acq 8-31-2007; $300,000 with KOPY-FM Alice). Population served: 60,000 Format: Country. News staff: 12; News: 2 hrs wkly. Target aud: 18-59. ♦Bobby Pena, gen mgr, stn mgr; Jackie Hinojosa, gen sls mgr, prom mgr, progmg dir & news dir.

KOPY-FM— Jan 20, 1976: 92.1 mhz; 3 kw. Ant 300 ft TL: N27 46 39 W98 04 53. Stereo. Hrs open: 24 Box731, 78333. Secondary address: 2722 N. Business Hwy. 281 78332. Phone: (361) 664-1884. Fax: (361) 664-1886. Licensee: Claro Communications Ltd. (acq 8-31-2007; $300,000 with KOPY(AM) Alice). Format: Tejano. News: 8 hrs wkly. Target aud: General. ♦Bobby Pena, progmg dir.

KUKA(FM)—See San Diego

Allen

KESN(FM)— Dec 1, 1981: 103.3 mhz; 100 kw. Ant 1,968 ft TL: N33 32 08 W96 49 54. Stereo. Hrs open: 400 E. Las Colinas Blvd., Suite 1033, Irving, 75039. Phone: (214) 258-2800. Fax: (214) 258-2809. Web Site:www.espn1033.com Licensee: WBAP-KSCS Operating Ltd. Group owner: ABC Inc. (acq 8-9-2000; $18 million). Natl. Network: ESPN Radio, . Format: Sports. Target aud: 25-54; males and females. ♦Peter Dits, CEO, gen mgr; Tom Lee, gen mgr & progmg dir.

Alpine

KALP(FM)— September 1986: 92.7 mhz; 2.37 kw. 328 ft TL: N30 19 09 W103 37 04. Hrs open: 6 AM-10 PM Box 9650, 79831. Secondary address: 500 Hendryx Ave. 79830. Phone: (432) 837-2144. Fax: (915) 837-3984.E-mail: alpineradio@brooksdata.net Licensee: Rio Grande Broadcasting Co. Format: C&W. ♦Gene Ray Hendryx, gen mgr, progmg dir, chief of engrg & pres.

KVLF(AM)— Feb 27, 1947: 1240 khz; 1 kw-U. TL: N30 22 30 W103 39 36. Hrs open: 6 AM-10 PM Drawer 779, 79831. Secondary address: 500 Hendryx Ave. 79831. Phone: (432) 837-2144. Fax: (432) 837-3984.E-mail: alpineradio@brooksdata.net Licensee: Big Bend Broadcasters. Population served: 13,700 Natl. Network: ABC, . Format: Div. News: 21 hrs wkly. Spec prog: Sp 10 hrs wkly. ♦Gene Ray Hendryx Jr., pres; Ray Hendryx, gen mgr; Jerry Sotello, gen sls mgr.

Alvin

***KACC(FM)**— Nov 1, 1993: 89.7 mhz; 5.6 kw. 338 ft TL: N29 24 01 W95 12 13. Stereo. Hrs open: 24 3110 Mustang Rd., 77511. Phone: (281) 756-3766. Fax: (281) 756-3885. Web Site:www.kaccradio.com Licensee: Alvin Community College. Garvey, Schubert & Barer. Wire Svc: AP Format: AOR. News staff: one; News: 3 hrs wkly. Target aud: General. ♦A. Rodney Allbright, pres; Mark Moss, chief of opns & progmg dir.

KTEK(AM)— November 1981: 1110 khz; 2.5 kw, DA. TL: N29 22 51 W95 14 15. Hrs open: Sunrise-sunset 3050 Post Oak Blvd., Suite 1680, Houston, 77056-6573. Phone: (713) 979-2700. Web Site:www.bizradio.com Licensee: BusinessRadio Houston Licensee LLC Group owner: Salem Communications Corp. (acq 3-28-2008; $7.75 million). Natl. Network: USA, . Format: Talk. Target aud: 25-54; upscale families, 60% women, 40% male. ♦Daniel Frishberg, pres.

Amarillo

***KACV-FM—** Mar 15, 1976: 89.9 mhz; 100 kw. 1,041 ft TL: N35 20 33 W101 49 21. Stereo. Hrs open: 6 AM-midnight Box 447, 79178. Secondary address: 2408 S. Jackson 79109. Phone: (806) 371-5222. Fax: (806) 345-5576.E-mail: kacvfm90@actx.edu Web Site:www.kacvfm.org Licensee: Amarillo Junior College District. Population served: 420,000 Natl. Network: ABC, . Format: Alternative/block. Spec prog: Jazz 12 hrs, Texas 6 hrs wkly. ♦Linda Pitner, gen mgr; Brian Frank, progmg dir. Co-owned TV: *KACV-TV affil.

KARX(FM)—(Claude, Apr 12, 1992: 95.7 mhz; 100 kw. 391 ft TL: N35 06 16 W101 39 28. Stereo. Hrs open: 24 301 S. Polk, Suite 100, 79101. Phone: (806) 342-5200. Fax: (806) 342-5202.E-mail: chris.matchett@cumulus.com Web Site:www.cumulus.com Licensee: Cumulus Licensing Corp. Group owner: Cumulus Media Inc. (acq 2-2-98; $675,000). Population served: 85,000 Format: Classic rock. News staff: one; News: 10 hrs wkly. Target aud: 25-54; male. ♦Jim Worthington, gen mgr; Stan Ross, sls dir; Shea White, prom dir; Eric Slayter, progmg dir; Dale Miller, mus dir; Matt Darby, news dir; J.P. Wolf, chief of engrg; Shannon Urton, sls.

KATP(FM)— Mar 11, 1976: 101.9 mhz; 100 kw. 935 ft TL: N35 20 33 W101 49 21. Stereo. Hrs open: 24 6214 W. 34th St., 79109. Phone: (806) 355-9777. Fax: (806) 359-0136.E-mail: gap@broadcasting.com Web Site:www.catcountry1019.com Licensee: GAP Broadcasting Amarillo License LLC. Group owner: Clear Channel Communications Inc. (acq 10-1-2007; grpsl). Population served: 250,000 Format: Classic country. News: 2 hrs wkly. Target aud: 18-49. ♦Kevin Meyer, gen mgr; Les Montgomery, dev mgr; Debbie Davis, gen sls mgr.

***KAVW(FM)—** July 1998: 90.7 mhz; 1 kw. 213 ft TL: N35 11 50 W101 49 59. Hrs open: Box 3206, Tupelo, MS, 38803. Phone: (662) 844-8888. Fax: (662) 842-6791.E-mail: comments@afr.net Web Site:www.afr.net Licensee: American Family Association. Group owner: American Family Radio Format: Inspirational Christian. ♦Marvin Sanders, gen mgr.

KBZD(FM)— March 1994: 99.7 mhz; 21.5 kw. 351 ft TL: N35 06 50 W101 49 16. Hrs open: 3639 Wolflin Ave., 79103. Phone: (806) 355-1044. Fax: (806) 457-0642.E-mail: ctonzalze@tegasb.com Licensee: Tejas Broadcasting Ltd. LLP Group owner: Amigo Broadcasting L.P. (acq 11-15-2004; grpsl). Format: Tejano/Regional Mexican. ♦Mac Douglas, gen mgr; Brad Gonzalez, gen sls mgr; Israel Salazar, progmg dir; Charlie Singleton, chief of engrg; Emelia Chacon, traf mgr.

KDJW(AM)— Sept 15, 1955: 1360 khz; 500 w-D, 137 w-N. TL: N35 14 49 W101 49 13. Hrs open: 701 S. Pierce St., Suite 101, 79101. Phone: (806) 350-1360. Fax: (806) 350-1360.E-mail: ffeedlot@aol.com Web Site:www.kdjw.com Licensee: Avondale Operating Inc. (acq 12-8-03). Format: Classic country. Target aud: 45 plus; adults with money. ♦Ron Slover, pres.

KGNC(AM)— May 19, 1922: 710 khz; 10 kw-U, DA-2. TL: N35 25 12 W101 33 20. Hrs open: 24 Box 710, 79189-0710. Secondary address: 3505 Olsen Blvd., Suite 117 79109. Phone: (806) 355-9801. Fax: (806) 354-8779. Web Site:www.kgncam.com Licensee: Morris Communications Corp. Group owner: Morris Communications Inc. (acq 12-22-97; grpsl). Population served: 400,000 Natl. Network: ABC, . Rgnl. Network: Texas State Net. Natl. Rep: Katz Radio,. Texas State Networks Wiley, Rein & Fielding. Wire Svc: Reuters Format: News/talk. Target aud: General; upscale adults & agricultural business listeners. ♦Dan Gorman, gen mgr; Chris Albracht, progmg dir.

KGNC-FM— Dec 24, 1958: 97.9 mhz; 100 kw. Ant 1,285 ft TL: N35 18 52 W101 50 47. Stereo. Hrs open: 24 Box 710, 79189-0710. Phone: (806) 355-9801. Fax: (806) 354-8779. Licensee: Morris Communications Corp. Population served: 300,000 Wire Svc: Reuters Format: Country. ♦Dan Gorman, stn mgr.

KIXZ(AM)— June 1947: 940 khz; 5 kw-D, 1 kw-N, DA-2. TL: N35 09 17 W101 45 28. Hrs open: 24 6214 W. 34th., 79109. Phone: (806) 355-9777. Fax: (806) 355-5832.E-mail: kixz@clearchannel.com Web Site:www.newsradio940.com Licensee: GAP Broadcasting Amarillo License LLC. Group owner: Clear Channel Communications Inc. (acq 10-1-2007; grpsl). Population served: 250,000 Akin, Gump, Strauss, Hauer & Feld. Format: News/talk. News staff: one; News: 8 hrs wkly. Target aud: General. Spec prog: Talk 2 hrs, gospel 6 hrs wkly. ♦Kevin Meyer, gen mgr; Dusty Cagle, sls dir, gen sls mgr; Lori Crofford, prom dir; David Emmons, progmg dir; Charles Fuller, news dir, chief of engrg; Jennifer Stephenson, traf mgr.

***KJJP(FM)—** Dec 6, 1991: 105.7 mhz; 6 kw. 236 ft TL: N35 12 28 W101 51 18. Hrs open: 24 210 N. 7th St., Garden City, KS, 67846. Phone: (620) 275-7444. Phone: (800) 678-7444. Fax: (620) 275-7496. Web Site:www.hppr.org Licensee: Kanza Society Inc. (acq 8-17-2004; $1.25 million). Format: Christian. Target aud: General. ♦Richard Hicks, gen mgr.

***KJRT(FM)—** Apr 1, 1994: 88.3 mhz; 20 kw. 265 ft TL: N35 11 57 W101 48 43. Hrs open:
Rebroadcasts KPDR(FM) Wheeler 100%.
Box 8088, 5754 Canyon Dr., 79114. Phone: (806) 359-8855. Fax: (806) 354-2039.E-mail: kjrt@kingdomkeys.org Web Site:www.kingdomkeys.org Licensee: Top o'Texas Educational Broadcasting Foundation. Format: Relg, educ. ♦Ricky Pfeil, gen mgr.

KMXJ-FM— March 1946: 94.1 mhz; 100 kw. Ant 1,082 ft TL: N35 20 33 W101 49 21. Stereo. Hrs open: 24 6214 W. 34th, 79109. Phone: (806) 355-9777. Fax: (806) 355-5832.E-mail: kmxj@clearchannel.com Web Site:www.mix941kmxj.com Licensee: GAP Broadcasting Amarillo License LLC. Group owner: Clear Channel Communications Inc. (acq 10-1-2007; grpsl). Population served: 200000 Natl. Network: ABC, . Format: Adult contemp. News staff: one; News: 2 hrs wkly. Target aud: General. ♦Kevin Meyer, gen mgr; Les Montgomery, dev mgr; Debbie Davies, gen sls mgr; Lori Crofford, prom dir; Johnny McQueen, progmg dir, progmg mgr; Charlie Fuller, chief of engrg; Jennifer Stephenson, traf mgr.

KPRF(FM)— October 1979: 98.7 mhz; 100 kw. Ant 480 ft TL: N35 11 02 W101 58 11. Stereo. Hrs open: 24 Prog sep from AM 6214 W. 34th St., 79109. Phone: (806) 355-9777. Fax: (806) 355-5832.E-mail: info@987jackfm.com Web Site:www.987jackfm.com Licensee: GAP Broadcasting Amarillo License LLC. (acq 10-1-2007; grpsl). Population served: 200000 Natl. Network: ABC, . Format: Adult hits. News staff: one; News: 2 hrs wkly. Target aud: General. ♦Kevin Meyer, gen mgr; Marshal Blevins, progmg dir; Jennifer Stephenson, traf mgr.

KPUR(AM)— Aug 1, 1949: 1440 khz; 5 kw-D, 1 kw-N, DA-N. TL: N35 07 20 W101 48 09. Stereo. Hrs open: 24 301 S. Polk, Suite 100, 79101. Phone: (806) 342-5200. Fax: (806) 342-5202.E-mail: rickmatchett@cumulus.com Web Site:www.cumulus.com Licensee: Cumulus Licensing Corp. Group owner: Cumulus Media Inc. (acq 3-12-98; $820,000 with KPUR-FM Canyon). Population served: 175,000 Format: Talk, sports. Target aud: 25-54. ♦Jim Worthington, gen mgr; Craig Vaughn, prom dir; Matt Darby, progmg dir; J.P. Wolf, chief of engrg.

KQFX(FM)—(Borger, March 1975: 104.3 mhz; 100 kw. 590 ft TL: N35 25 54 W101 36 47. Stereo. Hrs open: 3639B Wolfin Ave., 79103. Phone: (806) 355-1044. Fax: (806) 457-0642. Licensee: Tejas Broadcasting Ltd. LLP. Group owner: Amigo Broadcasting L.P. (acq 11-15-2004; grpsl). Population served: 200,000 Format: Regional. ♦Matt Douglas, gen mgr; Willie Palacios, sls dir & gen sls mgr; Israel Salavar, progmg dir; Charlie Singleton, chief of engrg.

KQIZ-FM— November 1976: 93.1 mhz; 100 kw. 700 ft TL: N35 17 33 W101 50 48. Stereo. Hrs open: 24 301 S. Polk, Suite 100, 79101. Phone: (806) 342-5200. Fax: (806) 342-5202.E-mail: rick.matchett@cumulus.com Web Site:www.cumulus.com Licensee: Cumulus Licensing Corp. Group owner: Cumulus Media L.L.C (acq 3-5-98; $3.057 million). Population served: 162,000 Format: CHR. Target aud: 18-44; young families. Spec prog: Relg 2 hrs wkly. ♦Jim Worthington, gen mgr; Shea White, prom dir; Deana McGuire, progmg dir; J.P. Wolf, chief of engrg.

KRGN(FM)— Oct 6, 1986: 103.1 mhz; 25 kw. 300 ft TL: N35 16 04 W101 53 06. Hrs open: 24 Box 10050, 79116. Secondary address: 910 S. Lamar 79106. Phone: (806) 376-5746. Fax: (806) 376-4212.E-mail: krgn@flc.org Web Site:www.krgn.org Licensee: Family Life Broadcasting Inc. Group owner: Family Life Broadcasting System (acq 6-24-98; grpsl). Natl. Network: USA, . Format: MOR Christian inspirational, news/talk, educ. News: 4 hrs wkly. Target aud: 28 plus; mature Christian, mainstream evangelical. ♦Steve Wright, stn mgr; Steve Johnson, news dir.

KTNZ(AM)— 1946: 1010 khz; 5 kw-D, 500 w-N, DA-2. TL: N35 11 03 W101 41 28. Hrs open: 3639 Wolfin Ave., 79103. Phone: (806) 355-1044. Fax: (806) 457-0642.E-mail: ctonzale@tegasb.com Licensee: Tejas Broadcasting Ltd. LLP Population served: 200,000 Format: Christian. ♦Israel Salazar, progmg VP & news dir.

KXGL(FM)— November 1997: 100.9 mhz; 100 kw. Ant 1,305 ft TL: N35 18 53 W101 50 47. Stereo. Hrs open: 24 1616 S. Kentucky, Suite C-215, 79102. Phone: (806) 351-2345. Fax: (806) 331-3170.E-mail: jameykarr@1009theeagle.com Licensee: JMJ Broadcasting Co. Inc. (acq 1-15-2004). Population served: 184,900 Natl. Rep: Katz Radio,. Larry Bernstein. Wire Svc: AP Format: Classic hits. News staff: one; News: 5 hrs wkly. Target aud: 25-54. ♦Herbert W. McCord, pres; Bob Russell, gen mgr; Jamey Karr, opns mgr, progmg dir; Brice Edwards, gen sls mgr; Kelly James, news dir.

***KXLV(FM)—** August 1989: 89.1 mhz; 3 kw. 328 ft TL: N35 15 39 W101 52 53. Stereo. Hrs open: 24 2351 Sunset Blvd., Suite 170-218, Rocklin, CA, 95765. Phone: (916) 251-1600. Fax: (916) 251-1650.E-mail: klove@klove.com Web Site:www.klove.com Licensee: Educational Media Foundation. Group owner: EMF Broadcasting (acq 11-4-99; $450,000). Population served: 200000 Natl. Network: K-Love, . Shaw Pittman. Format: Contemp Christian music. News staff: 3. Target aud: 25-44; Judeo Christian, female. ♦Richard Jenkins, pres; Mike Novak, VP; Keith Whipple, dev dir; Russ Lloyd, rgnl sls mgr; David Pierce, progmg dir; Jon Rivers, mus dir; Ed Lenane, news dir; Sam Wallington, engrg dir; Karen Johnson, news rptr.

***KXRI(FM)—** November 1993: 91.9 mhz; 2.25 kw. Ant 292 ft TL: N35 14 31 W101 48 43. Hrs open: 24 2351 Sunset Blvd., Suite 170-218, Rocklin, CA, 95765. Phone: (916) 251-1600. Fax: (916) 251-1650.E-mail: info@air1.com Web Site:www.air1.com Licensee: Educational Media Foundation. Group owner: EMF Broadcasting (acq 5-1-2000; $750,000 with KKLU(FM) Lubbock). Natl. Network: Air 1, . Shaw Pittman. Format: Contemp Christian. News staff: 3. Target aud: 18-35; Judeo Christian female. ♦Richard Jenkins, pres; Mike Novak, VP; Keith Whipple, dev dir; Eric Allen, natl sls mgr; David Pierce, progmg mgr; Ed Lenane, news dir; Sam Wallington, engrg dir.

KXSS-FM— March 1985: 96.9 mhz; 100 kw. Ant 613 ft TL: N35 17 33 W101 50 48. Stereo. Hrs open: 24 6214 W. 34th St., 79109. Phone: (806) 355-9777. Fax: (806) 355-5832.E-mail: kmml@kmml.com Web Site:www.969kmml.com Licensee: GAP Broadcasting Amarillo License LLC. Group owner: Clear Channel Communications Inc. (acq 10-1-2007; grpsl). Population served: 200,000 Natl. Network: ABC, . Format: CHR. News staff: one; News: 2 hrs wkly. Target aud: General. ♦Kevin Meyer, gen mgr; Les Montgomery, dev mgr, progmg dir; Debbie Davis, gen sls mgr; Lori Crofford, prom dir; Charlie Fuller, chief of engrg; Jennifer Stephenson, traf mgr.

KZIP(AM)— Sept 15, 1955: 1310 khz; 1 kw-D. TL: N35 11 02 W101 58 11. Hrs open: 6 AM-10 PM 3639 B. Wolflin, 79102. Phone: (806) 355-1044. Fax: (806) 352-6525.E-mail: cgonzzales@tejasbroadcasting.com Licensee: Del Norte Communications Inc. (acq 5-22-2001). Population served: 200,000 Format: Talk radio. News staff: one; News: one hr wkly. Target aud: General. ♦Mac Douglas, gen mgr.

KZRK(AM)—(Canyon, May 8, 1962: 1550 khz; 1 kw-D, 219 w-N. TL: N34 58 54 W101 57 18. Hrs open: 6 AM-6 PM 301 S. Polk, Suite 100, 79101. Phone: (806) 342-5200. Fax: (806) 342-5202.E-mail: rickmatchett@cumulus.com Licensee: Cumulus Licensing Corp. Format: Sports talk.

KZRK-FM—(Canyon, Sept 30, 1985: 107.9 mhz; 100 kw. 476 ft TL: N35 13 36 W102 00 24. Stereo. Hrs open: 24 301 S. Polk, Suite 100, 79101. Phone: (806) 342-5200. Fax: (806) 342-5202.E-mail: chris.knight@cumulus.com Web Site:www.kzrk.com Licensee: Cumulus Licensing Corp. Group owner: Cumulus Media Inc. (acq 3-3-98; $1 million with co-located AM). Population served: 300,000 Natl. Network: Westwood One, . Natl. Rep: Roslin,. Format: AOR. News staff: one; News: 3 hrs wkly. Target aud: 18-34; general. ♦Rick Matchett, gen mgr; Eric Slayter, opns mgr, prom mgr, progmg dir; Stan Ross, sls dir; D'Lisa Pohnert, mktg dir; Chris Collins, mus dir; J. Curry, asst music dir; J.P. Wolf, chief of engrg; Matt Darby, local news ed.

Andrews

KACT(AM)— Jan 12, 1955: 1360 khz; 1 kw-D. TL: N32 20 50 W102 33 23. Hrs open: 2125 N. Highway 385, 79714. Secondary address: Box 524 Phone: (432) 523-2845. Fax: (432) 523-5671.E-mail: kact1055@windstream.net Web Site:www.kactradio.com Licensee: Zia Broadcasting Co. (acq 5-26-76). Population served: 12,500 Natl. Network: CBS Radio, Radio America, Talk Radio Network, Westwood One, . Format: news, talk, sports. News staff: hourly News: 1;. ♦Lonnie Allsup, pres; Gerald Reid, gen mgr, news dir; Rick Keefer, gen sls mgr.

KACT-FM— 1980: 105.5 mhz; 3 kw. Ant 210 ft TL: N32 20 50 W102 33 23. Stereo. Hrs open: 2125 N. Highway 385, 79714. Secondary address: Box 524 Phone: (432) 523-2845. Fax: (432) 523-5671.E-mail: kact1055@windstream.net Web Site:www.kactradio.com Licensee: Zia Broadcasting Co. Format: Country. ♦Gerald Reid, gen mgr.

Anson

KTLT(FM)— June 1988: 98.1 mhz; 50 kw. Ant 305 ft TL: N32 39 49 W99 51 18. Stereo. Hrs open: 24 2525 S. Danville Dr., Abilene, 79605.

Phone: (325) 793-9700. Fax: (325) 692-1576. Web Site:www.kbcy.com Licensee: Cumulus Licensing Corp. Group owner: Cumulus Media Inc. (acq 1999). Kaye, Scholer, Fierman, Hays & Handler. Format: Alternative rock. ♦Jim Christoferson, gen mgr; John Scott, opns mgr & progmg dir; Chris Andrews, chief of engrg.

Aransas Pass

***KKWV(FM)—** 2008: 88.1 mhz; 28 kw vert. Ant 367 ft TL: N27 52 02 W97 13 07. Hrs open:
Rebroadcasts KLRD(FM) Yucaipa, CA 100%.
2351 Sunset Blvd., Suite 170-218, Rocklin, CA, 95765. Phone: (916) 251-1600. Fax: (916) 251-1650. Web Site:www.air1.com Licensee: Educational Media Foundation. (acq 7-23-2007; grpsl). Natl. Network: Air 1, . Format: Christian. ♦Mike Novak, pres.

Arlington

KLTY(FM)—Licensed to Arlington. See Dallas

Athens

***KATG(FM)—** 2006: 88.1 mhz; 80 kw vert. Ant 544 ft TL: N32 02 41 W95 40 37. Hrs open: Box 2440, Tupelo, MS, 38803-2440. Phone: (662) 844-8888. Fax: (662) 842-6791. Web Site:www.afr.net Licensee: American Family Association. Format: Christian classics. ♦Marvin Sanders, gen mgr.

KCKL(FM)—See Malakoff

KLVQ(AM)— May 17, 1948: 1410 khz; 1 kw-U. TL: N32 10 20 W95 50 36. Hrs open: 24 Box 489, Hwy. 31 E., Malakoff, 75148. Phone: (903) 489-1238. Fax: (903) 489-2671. Web Site:www.kcklklvq.com Licensee: Lake Country Radio L.P. Group owner: Routt Radio Companies Inc. (acq 11-5-2005;. $550,000 with KCKL(FM) Malakoff). Population served: 40,000 Natl. Network: Salem Radio Network, . Wire Svc: NOAA Weather Wire Svc: UPI Format: Southern gospel. News staff: one; News: 7 hrs wkly. Target aud: 35 plus. Spec prog: Black one hr, relg 8 hrs wkly. ♦John Weeks, gen mgr; Pat Isaacson, opns mgr, sls dir, pub affrs dir; Rich Flowers, progmg dir, news dir; Wayne Blackwelder, chief of engrg.

Atlanta

KNRB(FM)— Dec 22, 1978: 100.1 mhz; 50 kw. Ant 492 ft TL: N33 15 18 W94 05 16. Stereo. Hrs open: 24 Box 262550, Baton Rouge, LA, 70826. Secondary address: 8919 World Ministry Ave., Baton Rouge, LA 70810. Phone: (225) 768-3688. Phone: (225) 768-8300. Fax: (225) 768-3729.E-mail: kawikfish@yahoo.com Web Site:www.jsm.org Licensee: Family Worship Center Church Inc. (acq 3-7-2002; grpsl). Population served: 200000 Rgnl rep: Riley. Format: Southern gospel. News: 15 hrs wkly. Target aud: General. ♦David Whitelaw, COO; Jimmy Swaggart, pres; John Santiago, progmg dir.

KPYN(AM)— Oct 18, 1950: 900 khz; 1 kw-D, 33 w-N. TL: N33 04 58 W94 10 58. Hrs open: 24 Box 900, 75531. Secondary address: State Hwy. 43 S. 75551. Phone: (903) 796-2817. Fax: (903) 769-1000. Web Site:www.amen900.com Licensee: Freed AM Corp. (group owner; (acq 8-3-2005; $100,000). Format: Contemp Christian. Target aud: . ♦Robert A. Delgiorno Jr., pres & gen mgr; Jeff Akin, progmg dir.

Austin

KAMX(FM)—See Luling

KASE-FM— Mar 30, 1969: 100.7 mhz; 100 kw. 1,100 ft TL: N30 19 10 W97 48 06. Stereo. Hrs open: 24 Clear Channel Radio KVET-KASE, 3601 South Congress, Bldg. F, 78704. Phone: (512) 684-7300. Fax: (512) 684-7441. Web Site:www.kase101.com Licensee: Capstar TX L.P. Group owner: Clear Channel Communications Inc. (acq 8-30-00; grpsl). Population served: 507,300 Format: Country. Target aud: 18-44. ♦Pam McKay, gen mgr, mktg mgr; Mac Daniels, opns mgr; Mel Jones, sls dir, mktg dir; Mitch Bordeno, gen sls mgr; Gil Garcia, chief of engrg, disc jockey; Suzanne Munoz, traf mgr.

***KAZI-FM—** Aug 29, 1982: 88.7 mhz; 1.6 kw. 351 ft TL: N30 16 37 W97 49 34. Hrs open: 24 8906 Wall St., Suite 203, 78754. Phone: (512) 836-9544. Phone: (512) 836-9545. Fax: (512) 836-9563.E-mail: steve@katzfm.org Web Site:www.kazifm.org Licensee: Austin Community Radio. Population served: 100,000 Haley, Bader & Potts. Format: Gospel, reggie, rap, rhythm and blues, blues, jazz. News staff: one; News: 12 hrs wkly. Target aud: General; all ages, all ethnic groups. Spec prog: Reggae 6 hrs, blues 6 hrs, gospel 18 hrs, talk 10 hrs wkly. ♦David Bursell, chmn; Steven Savage, gen mgr; Sharon Jones, mktg VP, prom mgr; Marion Nickerson, progmg dir; Avis Thomas, mus dir; James Davis, engrg VP, chief of engrg.

KBPA(FM)—(San Marcos, 1971: 103.5 mhz; 95.5 kw. 1,256 ft TL: N30 02 42 W97 52 50. Stereo. Hrs open: 24 8309 N. Hwy 35, Suite 967, 78753. Phone: (512) 832-4000. Fax: (512) 832-4071.E-mail: info@oldies103austin.com Web Site:www.oldies103austin.com Licensee: Emmis Austin Radio Broadcasting Co. L.P. Group owner: Emmis Communications Corp. (acq 4-25-2003; grpsl). Population served: 1,000,000 Natl. Rep: Clear Channel,. Wiley, Rein & Fielding. Format: Oldies. News staff: one; News: 4 hrs wkly. Target aud: 25-64. ♦Bruce Walden, gen mgr; Jeff Carrol, opns mgr; Brad Copland, gen sls mgr, natl sls mgr; Mike Paterson, prom dir; Bo Chase, progmg dir, progmg mgr; Lisa Melton, news dir, traf mgr; Jim Henkle, chief of engrg.

KFIT(AM)—(Lockhart, Feb 1, 1967: 1060 khz; 2 kw-D, DA. TL: N30 19 13 W97 38 59. Hrs open: 6 AM-8 PM Box 160158, 78716. Secondary address: 110 Wild Basin Rd., Suite 375 78746. Phone: (512) 328-8400. Fax: (512) 328-8437.E-mail: kfitam@yahoo.com Licensee: KFIT Inc. (acq 6-25-91; $400,000; 7-15-91). Population served: 500,000 Natl. Network: Westwood One, . Dow, Lohnes & Albertson. Format: Gospel. News staff: 2. Target aud: 18-65. ♦Darrell Marshi, CEO; Terri Lewis, gen mgr & opns mgr.

KFON(AM)— 1922: 1490 khz; 1 kw-U. TL: N30 15 13 W97 42 25. Stereo. Hrs open: 24 912 S. Capital of Texas Hwy., 78746. Phone: (512) 416-1100. Fax: (512) 416-8205. Licensee: BMP Austin License Company L.P. (acq 2-10-2005; grpsl). Population served: 500,000 Format: Rgnl Mexician. Target aud: 18 plus; men. ♦Pedro Gasc, gen mgr.

KGSR(FM)—(Bastrop, 1966: 107.1 mhz; 46 kw. 518 ft. TL: N30 07 18 W97 34 45. Stereo. Hrs open: 24 8309 N. IH 35, 78753. Phone: (512) 832-4000. Fax: (512) 832-4042. Web Site:www.kgsr.com Licensee: LBJS Broadcasting Co. L.P. Group owner: Emmis Communications Corp. (acq 4-25-03; grpsl). Natl. Rep: Christal,. Format: AAA. News staff: one. Target aud: 25-44; upscale, active, educated adults. Spec prog: Jazz 6 hrs wkly. ♦Beverley Wimer, VP, traf mgr; Bruce Walden, gen mgr; Tatjana Deegan, gen sls mgr; Jyl Hershman-Ross, prom dir; Lynn Barstow, progmg dir; Susan Castle, mus dir; Todd Jeffries, news dir; Jim Henkel, chief of engrg.

KIXL(AM)—(Del Valle, Aug 8, 1959: 970 khz; 1 kw-U, DA-2. TL: N30 19 13 W97 37 25. Hrs open: 24 11615 Angus Rd., Suite 102, 78759. Phone: (512) 390-5495. Fax: (512) 241-0510.E-mail: KIXL@relevantradio.com Web Site:www.relevantradio.com Licensee: Starboard Media Foundation Inc. (acq 1-20-2006; $3.58 million). Population served: 1,165,000 Format: Catholic talk. ♦Ted Wrenn, gen mgr; Ruben Villarreal, stn mgr, opns mgr.

KJCE(AM)—(Rollingwood, Aug 12, 1958: 1370 khz; 5 kw-D, 500 w-N. TL: N30 18 16 W97 38 53. Hrs open: 4301 Westbrook Dr., Escalade B, 3rd Fl., 78746. Phone: (512) 327-9595. Fax: (512) 329-6255. Web Site:www.talkradio137am.com Licensee: Entercom Austin License LLC Group owner: Infinity Broadcasting Corp. . Natl. Network: Westwood One, ABC, Salem Radio Network, . Texas State Networks Format: Talk. News staff: one; News: 10 hrs wkly. Target aud: Males 18-54.

KKMJ-FM— Jan 5, 1968: 95.5 mhz; 100 kw horiz, 87 kw vert. Ant 1,000 ft TL: N30 19 23 W97 47 58. Stereo. Hrs open: 24 4301 Westbank Dr., Escalade B, 3rd Fl., 78746. Phone: (512) 327-9595. Fax: (512) 329-6255.E-mail: jdhiatt@cbs.com Web Site:www.majic.com Licensee: Entercom Austin License LLC (acq 11-30-2007; grpsl). Population served: 1,000,000 Natl. Rep: Katz Radio,. Leventhal, Senter & Lerman. Format: Adult contemp. Target aud: 25-54. ♦Clint Culp, sr VP, sls dir; John Hiatt, sr VP & gen mgr.

KLBJ(AM)— 1939: 590 khz; 5 kw-D, 1 kw-N, DA-N. TL: N30 14 14 W97 37 44. Hrs open: 24 8309 N. I-35, 78753. Phone: (512) 832-4000. Fax: (512) 832-4081.E-mail: info@590klbj.com Web Site:www.590klbj.com Licensee: LBJS Broadcasting Co. L.P. Group owner: Emmis Communications Corp. (acq 4-25-03; grpsl). Population served: 625,000 Natl. Network: ABC, Wall Street, . Natl. Rep: McGavren Guild,. Wire Svc: NWS (National Weather Service) Format: News/talk. News staff: 6; News: 14 hrs wkly. ♦Brooke Gallagher, VP; Bruce Walden, gen mgr; Julie Springer, prom dir; Mark Caesar, progmg dir; Hal Kemp, news dir; Jim Henkel, engrg dir.

KLBJ-FM— 1960: 93.7 mhz; 100 kw. Ant 1,050 ft TL: N30 18 36 W97 47 33. Stereo. Hrs open: 8309 N. I-35, 78753. Phone: (512) 832-4000. Fax: (512) 832-4081.E-mail: info@590klbj.com Web Site:www.klbjfm.com Licensee: Emmis Austin Radio Broadcasting Co. L.P. (acq 7-1-2003; grpsl). Population served: 625,000 Format: Rock. ♦Bob Sinclair, exec VP; Scott Gillmore, opns dir; Jeff Carroll, progmg dir; Loris Lowe, news dir.

***KMFA(FM)—** January 1967: 89.5 mhz; 40 kw. Ant 1,306 ft TL: N30 19 23 W97 47 58. Stereo. Hrs open: 24 3001 N. Lamar, Suite 100, 78705. Phone: (512) 476-5632. Fax: (512) 474-7463.E-mail: info@kmfa.org Web Site:www.kmfa.org Licensee: Capitol Broadcasting Association Inc. Population served: 821,600 Garvey, Schubert, Barer. Format: Class. Target aud: General. Spec prog: Educ 2 hrs wkly. ♦Frank Bash, chmn; Joan Kobayashi, gen mgr; Rich Upton, opns mgr.

KPEZ(FM)— Aug 13, 1976: 102.3 mhz; 26 kw. Ant 686 ft TL: N30 13 24 W97 49 39. Stereo. Hrs open: 24 3601 South Congress, #F, 78704-7213. Phone: (512) 684-7300. Fax: (512) 684-7441.E-mail: info@z1023.com Web Site:www.z1023.com Licensee: CCB Texas Licenses L.P. Group owner: Clear Channel Communications Inc. (acq 7-24-92). Population served: 900,000 Natl. Rep: Clear Channel,. Cohn & Marks. Format: Positive music. News staff: one; News: 3 hrs wkly. Target aud: 25-54; young adults with families, above average income, education. ♦Ginger Nelson, VP, sls dir; Mac Daniels, opns dir, progmg dir; Mel Jones, sls dir; Pam McKay, mktg mgr; Gil Garcia, chief of engrg; Tracy Walker, mktg dir & disc jockey.

KTXZ(AM)—See West Lake Hills

***KUT(FM)—** Nov 10, 1958: 90.5 mhz; 100 kw. Ant 680 ft TL: N30 18 51 W97 51 58. Stereo. Hrs open: 1 University Station A0704, Univ.of Texas, 78712-1090. Phone: (512) 471-1631. Fax: (512) 471-3700.E-mail: kut@kut.org Web Site:www.kut.org Licensee: University of Texas at Austin. Population served: 1,000,000 Natl. Network: NPR, PRI, . Cohn & Marks. Format: Music & news. News staff: 5; News: 25 hrs wkly. Target aud: 25-54; educated; influential decision makers & arts community. Spec prog: Folk 4 hrs, blues 6 hrs wkly. ♦Stewart Vanderwilt, gen mgr; Sylvia Carson, dev dir; Chris Collins, gen sls mgr, engrg mgr; Jody Evans, progmg dir; Emily Donahue, news dir.

KVET(AM)— 1946: 1300 khz; 5 kw-D, 1 kw-N, DA-2. TL: N30 22 31 W97 42 59. Stereo. Hrs open: 24 Clear Channel Radio KVET-KASE, 3601 South Congress, Bldg. F, 78704. Phone: (512) 684-7300. Fax: (512) 684-7441. Web Site:www.sportsradio1300.com Licensee: Capstar TX L.P. Format: Talk, sports. News staff: 6; News: 25 hrs wkly. Target aud: 25-64. ♦Mac Daniels, opns dir, progmg dir; Mel Jones, sls dir, sports cmtr; Tracy Walker, mktg dir; Pam McKay, mktg mgr; Gil Garcia, chief of engrg.

KVET-FM— 1950: 98.1 mhz; 100 kw. 686 ft TL: N30 13 24 W97 49 39. Stereo. Hrs open: 24 3601 South Congress, Bldg. F, 78704. Phone: (512) 684-7300. Fax: (512) 684-7441. Web Site:www.kvet.com Licensee: Capstar TX L.P. Group owner: Clear Channel Communications Inc. (acq 8-30-00; grpsl). Natl. Network: Westwood One, . Format: Country. News staff: 4. Target aud: 35-64. ♦John Hogan, pres; Charlie Ranilly, sr VP; Pam McKay, gen mgr, mktg mgr; Mac Daniels, opns dir; Mel Jones, sls dir; Tracy Walker, mktg dir; Gil Garcia, chief of engrg.

***KVRX(FM)—** November 1994: 91.7 mhz; 3 kw. 85 ft TL: N30 16 00 W97 40 27. Hrs open: PO Box D, c/o UT Austin, 78713. Phone: (512) 471-5106. Fax: (512) 232-5793.E-mail: kvrx@kvrx.com Web Site:www.kvrx.org Licensee: University of Texas at Austin. Population served: 900,000 Format: Alternative,indie. Target aud: 18-34; general. Spec prog: Share frequency with KOOP-FM. ♦Andrew Thompson, stn mgr; Michael McAfee, progmg mgr; Chelsey Blackmon, mus dir.

***KYLR(FM)—**(Hutto, February 1980: 92.1 mhz; 1.65 kw. Ant 449 ft TL: N30 32 04 W97 34 52. Stereo. Hrs open: 2351 Sunset Blvd., Suite 170-218, Rocklin, CA, 95765. Phone: (916) 251-1600. Fax: (916) 251-1650. Web Site:www.klove.com Licensee: Educational Media Foundation. (acq 3-31-2006; $6 million with KMLR(FM) Gonzales). Population served: 180,000 Format: Contemp Christian. ♦Richard Jenkins, pres; Mike Novak, VP; Keith Whipple, dev dir; David Pierce, progmg dir; Ed Lenane, news dir; Sam Wallington, engrg dir; Karen Johnson, news rptr.

Azle

KTCY(FM)— June 29, 1967: 101.7 mhz; 92 kw. Ant 2,034 ft TL: N33 26 13 W97 29 05. Stereo. Hrs open: 24 4201 Pool Rd., Colleyville, 76034. Phone: (817) 868-2900. Fax: (817) 868-2116. Web Site:www.xoradio1017.com Licensee: Liberman Broadcasting of Dallas License LLC. Group owner: Entravision Communications Corp. (acq 11-2-2006; grpsl). Population served: 6,153,500 Natl. Rep: Lotus Entravision Reps LLC,. Format: Sp contemp. Target aud: 18-34; Hispanics. ♦Rosa Cuellar, gen mgr.

Baird

KORQ(FM)— Sept 9, 1999: 95.1 mhz; 100 kw. Ant 872 ft TL: N32 17 06 W99 38 39. Hrs open: 24 1740 N. First, Abilene, 79603. Phone: (325) 437-9596. Fax: (325) 673-1819.E-mail: doudmediagroup@aol.com Web Site:www.95a.fm Licensee: Doud Media Group LLC Acq 9-2-02 Population served: 500,000 Natl. Network: Fox News Radio, . Dennis

J. Kelly. Format: CHR. News staff: one; News: news prgmg 10 hrs wkly. Target aud: 18-49; women & teens. ♦Richard Doud, gen mgr; Kid Cruz, opns mgr; Justin Riggan, sls dir; James Thompson, engrg dir.

Balch Springs

KSKY(AM)—Licensed to Balch Springs. See Dallas

Ballinger

KKCN(FM)— August 1977: 103.1 mhz; 100 kw. Ant 456 ft TL: N31 39 37 W100 05 23. Hrs open: 24 1301 S. Abe St., San Angelo, 76903. Phone: (325) 655-7161. Fax: (325) 658-7377. Web Site:www.103kkcn.com Licensee: Double O Texas Corp. Group owner: Encore Broadcasting LLC (acq 3-15-2006; grpsl). Population served: 150,000 Format: Country. ♦John Kerr, gen mgr; Randy Phair, gen sls mgr; Boomer Kingston, progmg dir; Garry Vaughn, engr.

KRUN(AM)— August 1947: 1400 khz; 1 kw-U. TL: N31 43 31 W99 57 42. Hrs open: 24 hrs Box 230, 1920 Hutchings Ave., 76821. Phone: (325) 365-5500. Fax: (325) 365-3407.E-mail: krun1400@hotmail.com Web Site:www.krunam.com Licensee: Graham Brothers Communications L.L.C. (acq 12-11-98; $395,000 with co-located FM). Population served: 4,203 Natl. Network: ABC, . Rgnl. Network: Texas State Net. Voice of Southwest Agriculture Radio Format: Country, sports. News staff: one; News: 2 hrs wkly. Target aud: 25-54. Spec prog: Christian 4 hrs wkly. ♦Andy Allen, gen mgr; Glynne Collenbark, opns mgr; Kody Mac, progmg dir; Toby Virden, gen mgr & traf mgr.

Bandera

KEEP(FM)— July 11, 1981: 103.1 mhz; 1.65 kw. 430 ft TL: N29 51 21 W99 05 26. Stereo. Hrs open: 24
Rebroadcasts KFAN-FM Johnson City 100%.
Box 311, 210 Woodcrest, Fredericksburg, 78624. Phone: (830) 997-2197. Fax: (830) 997-2198.E-mail: txradio@ktc.com Web Site:www.texasrebelradio.com Licensee: J. & J. Fritz Media Ltd. (group owner; acq 7-99; $108,000). Fletcher, Heald & Hildreth. Format: Americana AAA. News staff: one. Target aud: 25-49. ♦Jayson Fritz, pres, gen mgr, gen sls mgr; Jan Fritz, VP, mktg VP, adv mgr; Gloria Ottmers, opns mgr; Ariana Carruth Fritz, prom mgr; Mac McClennahan, progmg dir; Rick Star, mus dir; Duncan Black, chief of engrg; Robbi Frantzen, local news ed.

Bastrop

KGSR(FM)—Licensed to Bastrop. See Austin

***KHIB(FM)**— 1998: 88.5 mhz; 4 kw. Ant 308 ft TL: N30 12 57 W97 08 31. Hrs open: Houston Christian Broadcasters Inc., 2424 South Blvd., Houston, 77098-5196. Phone: (713) 520-5200. Web Site:www.khcb.org Licensee: Houston Christian Broadcasters Inc. (acq 1-19-2005; $112,000). Natl. Network: Moody, . Format: Christian. ♦Bruce Munsterman, gen mgr.

Bay City

***KEDR(FM)**— 2007: 88.1 mhz; 3.57 kw. Ant 1,433 ft TL: N28 48 03 W96 07 32. Hrs open:
Rebroadcasts WBFR(FM) Birmingham, AL 100%.
c/o WBFR(FM), 244 Goodwin Crest Dr., Suite 118, Birmingham, AL, 35209. Phone: (205) 942-3530. Fax: (510) 568-6190. Licensee: Family Stations Inc. Format: Relg, evangelical. ♦Stanley Jackson, gen mgr.

KMKS(FM)— July 27, 1984: 102.5 mhz; 50 kw. 492 ft TL: N28 47 47 W96 09 17. (CP: 100 kw). Stereo. Hrs open: 24 Box 789, 77404-0789. Secondary address: 2309 5th St. 77414. Phone: (979) 244-4242. Fax: (979) 245-0107.E-mail: kmks@kmks.com Web Site:www.kmks.com Licensee: Sandlin Broadcasting Co. Inc. Format: Hot C&W. News staff: 4; News: one hr wkly. Target aud: 24-54.Margaret K. Sandlin, pres; Larry Sandlin, gen mgr, opns mgr, chief of engrg; Judith Gardiner, gen sls mgr, mktg mgr; Helen Linley, prom mgr, news dir, disc jockey; C.W. Simon, progmg dir, disc jockey; Teresa Kaufmann, pub affrs dir; Kay Sandlin, local news ed, news rptr, farm dir, political ed, women's int ed, disc jockey; Glen Richards, disc jockey

KXGJ(FM)— Sept 25, 1995: 101.7 mhz; 100 kw. 449 ft TL: N28 43 53 W96 05 26. Hrs open:
Simulcast KQQK Jefferson.
3000 Bering Dr., Houston, 77057. Phone: (713) 315-3400. Fax: (713) 314-3506. Licensee: Liberman Broadcasting of Houston License LLC. Group owner: Liberman Broadcasting Inc. (acq 10-11-2002; $3.15 million with KNTE-FM El Campo). Population served: 670,000 Natl. Network: ABC, . Format: Sp. ♦Leonard Liberman, CEO, pres, progmg mgr; Winter Horton, VP & gen mgr; Ezequiel Gonzalez, progmg dir; Meliza Posada, traf mgr; Mike Todd, engr.

***KZBJ(FM)**— 2005: 89.5 mhz; 35 kw. Ant 479 ft TL: N29 08 58 W95 59 14. Hrs open:
Rebroadcasts KSBJ(FM) Humble 100%.
Box 187, Humble, 77347. Phone: (281) 446-5725. Fax: (281) 540-2198. Web Site:www.ksbj.org Licensee: KSBJ Educational Foundation (acq 5-31-2003). Format: Contemp Christian. ♦Tim McDermott, gen mgr.

Baytown

KWWJ(AM)— October 1947: 1360 khz; 5 kw-D, 1 kw-N, DA-2. TL: N29 46 28 W95 00 55. Stereo. Hrs open: 24 Box 419, 77522. Secondary address: 4638 Decker Dr. 77522. Phone: (281) 837-8777. Fax: (281) 424-7588.E-mail: kwwj1360@yahoo.com Web Site:www.kwwj.org Licensee: Salt of the Earth Broadcasting Inc. (acq 8-88). Population served: 69,000 Natl. Network: American Urban, . Format: Gospel. News staff: one. Target aud: General. ♦Darrell E. Martin, pres, gen mgr, gen sls mgr, prom mgr & pub affrs dir.

Beaumont

KFNC(FM)— 1948: 97.5 mhz; 100 kw. Ant 1,955 ft TL: N29 41 52 W94 24 09. Stereo. Hrs open: 24 2700 Post Oak Blvd., Suite 2300, Houston, 77056. Phone: (713) 300-3500. Fax: (713) 300-3585. Licensee: CMP KC Licensing LLC. Group owner: Cumulus Media Inc. (acq 5-3-2006; grpsl). Natl. Network: ESPN Radio, . Format: Sports. ♦Pat Fant, mktg mgr.

***KGHY(FM)**— Jan 10, 2009: 88.5 mhz; 13.5 kw vert. Ant 344 ft TL: N30 16 23 W93 57 23. Hrs open: 24 Box 34321, Houston, 77234-4321. Phone: (713) 941-3676. Web Site:www.thegospelhiway.org Licensee: CCS Radio Inc. Format: Southern gospel. ♦Otis Dyson, pres.

KIKR(AM)— 1938: 1450 khz; 1 kw-U. TL: N30 03 52 W94 07 12. Hrs open: 755 S. 11th, Suite 102, 77701. Phone: (409) 833-9421. Fax: (409) 833-9296.E-mail: info@cumulus.com Web Site:www.cumulus.com Licensee: Cumulus Licensing Corp. Group owner: Cumulus Media Inc. (acq 3-9-98; grpsl). Population served: 115,919 Natl. Rep: McGavren Guild,. Scott Johnson. Format: Sports. Target aud: 25-54. ♦Zanatta Kelley, gen mgr; Jim West, opns dir, mus dir; Mark Guzman, prom mgr; Greg Davis, chief of engrg; Liz Soileau, traf mgr.

***KLBT(FM)**— Aug 17, 2006: 88.1 mhz; 7 kw vert. Ant 476 ft TL: N29 54 52 W94 17 06. Hrs open: Box 5928, 77726. Phone: (409) 833-0045.E-mail: info@thekingsmusician.org Web Site:www.thekingsmusician.org Licensee: The King's Musician Educational Foundation Inc (acq 1-31-2006; $450,000 for CP). Format: Contemp Christian. ♦Leslie E. Jones, pres.

KLVI(AM)— 1924: 560 khz; 5 kw-U, DA-N. TL: N30 02 42 W93 52 07. Stereo. Hrs open: 24 2885 Interstate 10 East, 77702. Secondary address: 2885 I-10 E. 77726. Phone: (409) 896-5555. Fax: (409) 896-5599. Web Site:www.klvi.com Licensee: Clear Channel Group owner: Clear Channel Communications Inc. (acq 8-30-00; grpsl). Population served: 288,600 Fisher, Wayland, Cooper, Leader & Zaragoza L.L.P. Format: News/talk. News staff: 4; News: 5 hrs wkly. Target aud: 25-54; informed professionals.John Hogan, CEO; Randall Mays, CFO; Charlie Rahilly, sr VP; Mark Kopelman, VP; Vesta Brandt, gen mgr; Trey Poston, opns dir; Jim Love, opns mgr, pub affrs dir; Elizabeth Blackstock, sls dir; Rob Windham, gen sls mgr, natl sls mgr; Shon Hodgkinson, prom dir; Al Caldwell, progmg dir, disc jockey; Neil Harrison, news dir; T. J. Bordelon, chief of engrg; Gaile Darbone, traf mgr; Bob West, disc jockey

KQBU-FM—See Houston

KQQK(FM)— July 10, 1967: 107.9 mhz; 100 kw. 1,000 ft TL: N30 02 09 W94 08 31. Stereo. Hrs open: 24
Simulcasts KXGJ(FM) Matagorda.
3000 Bering Dr., Houston, 77057. Phone: (731) 315-3400. Fax: (713) 314-3506. Web Site:www.xoradio.com Licensee: Liberman Broadcasting of Houston License LLC. Group owner: Liberman Broadcasting Inc. (acq 10-11-2002; $24 million). Population served: 520,000 Format: Sp, rock. Target aud: 18-49; bilingual Hispanics. ♦Lenard Liberman, CEO, pres; Winter Horton, VP & gen mgr; Brad Branson, gen sls mgr; Ezequiel Gonzalez, progmg dir; Meliza Posada, traf mgr; Mike Todd, engr.

KQXY-FM— September 1966: 94.1 mhz; 100 kw. 1,099 ft TL: N30 06 56 W94 00 00. Stereo. Hrs open: 24 755 S. 11th St., Suite 102, 77701. Phone: (409) 833-9421. Fax: (409) 833-9296.E-mail: psanders@qt.rr.com Web Site:www.kqxy.com Licensee: Cumulus Licensing Corp. Group owner: Cumulus Media Inc. (acq 3-9-98; grpsl). Population served: 328,800 Format: Contemp hit. News staff: one; News: 5 hrs wkly. Target aud: 18-49; skewed female. ♦Rick Prusator, gen mgr; Mike Simpson, gen sls mgr; Greg Davis, chief of engrg.

KRCM(AM)— July 1947: 1380 khz; 1 kw-D, 127 w-N. TL: N30 02 09 W94 08 31. (CP: COL Shenandoah. 250 w-D, 69 w-N. TL: N30 11 42 W95 23 25). Hrs open: 6 AM-6 PM
Rebroadcasts KOLE(AM) Port Arthur 50%.
27 Sawyer St., 77702. Phone: (409) 835-1340. Phone: (409) 835-1340. Fax: (409) 832-5686.E-mail: manager@newsradiofox.com Web Site:www.newsradiofox.com Licensee: Voice Broadcasting Inc. (acq 1-29-03). Population served: 115,917 Natl. Network: Fox News Radio, Talk Radio Network, USA, . Texas State Networks Gammon & Grange. Format: News/talk. News staff: 2; News: 40 hrs wkly. ♦Ralph McBride, pres, gen mgr; Brent Bobbitt, gen sls mgr; Jeanette Harvey, progmg dir, traf mgr; Dominick Brascia, progmg mgr; Jeff Roberts, pub affrs dir; Russ Ingram, engr.

KTCX(FM)— 1996: 102.5 mhz; 50 kw. 492 ft TL: N29 59 22 W94 14 44. Hrs open: 755 South 11th St., Suite 102, Box 870, 77704. Phone: (409) 833-9421. Fax: (409) 833-9296. E-mail: info@ktcx.com Web Site:www.ktcx.com Licensee: Cumulus Licensing Corp. Group owner: Cumulus Media Inc. (acq 3-26-98; $3.6 million). Format: Adult urban. ♦Zanetta Kelley, gen mgr; Ed Turner, stn mgr; Jim West, opns mgr; Walter Brickhouse, sls VP; Wes Matejka, sls dir; Marco Camacho, rgnl sls mgr; Mark Guzman, prom dir; Douglas Harris, progmg dir; Adrian Scott, asst music dir; Greg Davis, chief of engrg.

***KTXB(FM)**— Jan 23, 1990: 89.7 mhz; 9 kw. 567 ft TL: N30 09 27 W93 48 06. Hrs open: 24 4135 Northgate Blvd., Suite #1, 77701. Phone: (409) 745-1737.E-mail: info@ktxb.com Web Site:www.familyradio.com Licensee: Family Stations Inc. (group owner) Format: Christian. ♦Harold Camping, pres; Martha Tallent, stn mgr & opns mgr.

***KVLU(FM)**— 1974: 91.3 mhz; 40 kw. 450 ft TL: N30 06 40 W94 03 10. Stereo. Hrs open: 24 Box 10064, 77710. Phone: (409) 880-8164.E-mail: kvlu@hal.lamar.edu Web Site:www.kvlu.org Licensee: Lamar University. Population served: 350,000 Natl. Network: NPR, . Format: Class, jazz, news. Target aud: 35 plus. Spec prog: Sp 5 hrs wkly. ♦Byron Balentine, gen mgr; Melanie Dishman, dev dir.

KYKR(FM)— Feb 1, 1966: 95.1 mhz; 100 kw. 500 ft TL: N30 08 57 W94 07 59. Stereo. Hrs open: 24 2885 Interstate 10 E., 77702. Secondary address: 2885 Interstate 10 E. 77726. Phone: (409) 896-5555. Fax: (409) 896-5599. Web Site:www.kykr.com Licensee: Capstar TX L.P. Group owner: Clear Channel Communications Inc. (acq 8-30-2000; grpsl). Population served: 288,600 Natl. Rep: Clear Channel,. Shaw Pittman. Wire Svc: AP Format: Country. News staff: 3; News: 2 hrs wkly. Target aud: 18-54.John Hogan, CEO; Lowry Mays, chmn; Mark Mays, pres; Randall Mays, CFO; Mark Kopelman, sr VP, VP, opns mgr; Vesta Brandt, gen mgr; Joey Armstrong, opns dir; Elizabeth Blackstock, sls dir; Rick Miles, natl sls mgr; Cutter McIntyre, prom dir; Mickey Ashworth, progmg dir, disc jockey; Harold Mann, news dir; Jim Love, pub affrs dir; Dave Smith, chief of engrg; Gaile Darbone, traf mgr; Vicki Cleveland, spec ev coord; Big Dave Bubba, disc jockey

KZZB(AM)— May 1, 1947: 990 khz; 1 kw-U, DA-1. TL: N30 08 57 W94 07 59. Hrs open: 24 2531 Calder Ave., 77702. Phone: (409) 833-0990. Fax: (409) 833-0995.E-mail: info@kzzb.com Web Site:www.kzzbradio.com Licensee: Martin Broadcasting Inc. (acq 7-28-92; 8-17-92). Natl. Rep: Christal,. Haley, Bader & Potts. Format: Gospel. News staff: one. Target aud: 18-49. ♦Darrell Martin, pres, gen mgr; Willie Mae McIver, progmg dir.

Beeville

KIBL(AM)— Oct 20, 1949: 1490 khz; 1 kw-U. TL: N28 23 08 W97 43 42. Hrs open: 5 AM-10 PM Box 252, McAllen, 78505. Phone: (956) 781-5528. Fax: (956) 686-2999. Licensee: Paulino Bernal (acq 3-7-97; $50,600). Population served: 560,730 Format: Christian, Sp Christian. ♦Eloy Bernal, gen mgr, progmg dir, disc jockey; John Ross, chief of engrg & disc jockey.

KRXB(FM)— Dec 2, 1988: 107.1 mhz; 1.25 kw. Ant 305 ft TL: N28 25 40 W97 45 36. Stereo. Hrs open: 24 110 E. Bowie Ste. B, 78102. Phone: (361) 358-4941. Fax: (361) 358-0601.E-mail: krxbfm@sbcglobal.net Licensee: Shaffer Communications Group Inc. (acq 10-95; $380,000). Natl. Network: Jones Radio Networks, . Format: Classic rock. News staff: 4. Target aud: 25 plus. ♦Joe Shaffer, pres; Marlene Rivera, natl sls mgr; Joy Burkhardt, traf mgr.

KTKO(FM)— Dec 12, 1976: 105.7 mhz; 25 kw. 328 ft TL: N28 28 16 W97 48 39. Stereo. Hrs open: 5 AM-10 PM 2300 S. Washington,

78102. Phone: (361) 358-1490. Fax: (361) 358-7814.E-mail: bebekicker106 @lonestarinternet.net Licensee: Texas Gulfwest Broadcasting Inc. (acq 6-01-02; $325,000). Population served: 485,355 Gardner, Carton & Douglas. Wire Svc: NOAA Weather Format: Country. News staff: one; News 13 hrs wkly. Target aud: 18-64. ◆Bebe Adamez, gen mgr, opns mgr & opns mgr.

*KVFM(FM)— 2000: 91.3 mhz; 1 kw vert. Ant 302 ft TL: N28 26 42 W97 45 50. Hrs open: Box 252, McAllen, 78505. Phone: (956) 781-5528. Fax: (956) 686-2999. Licensee: Paulino Bernal Evangelism.

Bellaire

KGOW(AM)— June 7, 1961: 1560 khz; 500 w-D. TL: N29 37 15 W95 25 04. Hrs open: 6 AM-sunset 5353 W. Alabama St., Suite 415, Houston, 77056-5922. Phone: (713) 479-5300. Fax: (713) 479-5333.E-mail: info@kgowam.com Web Site:1560thegame.com Licensee: Gow Communications L.L.C. (acq 4-10-2007; $9 million). Population served: 22,000 Format: Sports. ◆David F. Gow, pres, farm dir; Richard Topper, gen mgr.

Bells

KMKT(FM)— September 1997: 93.1 mhz; 6.8 kw. 626 ft TL: N33 41 31 W96 26 36. Hrs open: 101 E. Main, Suite 255, Denison, 75020. Phone: (903) 465-6200. Fax: (903) 463-9816.E-mail: jason@931kmkt.com Web Site:www.931kmkt.com Licensee: NM Licensing LLC. Group owner: NextMedia Group L.L.C. (acq 11-26-01; grpsl). Format: Country. ◆Steven Dinetz, CEO; Jeff Dinetz, pres; Sean Stover, CFO; David Smith, gen mgr; Jason Taylor, opns mgr, progmg dir; Anne Oliver, prom dir; Tiffany Reynolds, news dir; Vince Richardson, chief of engrg; David MacMullen, sls.

Bellville

KNUZ(AM)— Aug 8, 1974: 1090 khz; 250 w-D. TL: N29 56 50 W96 15 54. Hrs open:
Rebroadcasts KLTR(FM) Caldwell 100%.
530 W. Main St., Brenham, 77833. Phone: (979) 836-9411. Fax: (979) 836-9435.E-mail: lorihenderson01@hotmail.com Licensee: Roy E. Henderson Group owner: Bayport Broadcast Group (acq 4-17-90; $150,000). Format: Adult contemp. ◆Roy Henderson, pres.

Belton

KOOC(FM)— Apr 25, 1970: 106.3 mhz; 11.5 kw. Ant 489 ft TL: N31 03 46 W97 31 54. Stereo. Hrs open: 24 608 Moody Ln., Temple, 76504. Phone: (254) 773-5252. Fax: (254) 773-0115.E-mail: info@b1063.com Web Site:www.b1063.net Licensee: Cumulus Licensing LLC. Group owner: Cumulus Media Inc. (acq 2-2-2000; grpsl). Population served: 162,000 Format: Rhythmic. Target aud: 25-54. ◆Bourdon Wooten, gen mgr; Brian Mack, stn mgr, progmg dir; Mikie Cummings, gen sls mgr; Chris Cummings, news dir.

KTON(AM)— Dec 1, 1961: 940 khz; 1 kw-D, DA. TL: N31 02 37 W97 25 46. Hrs open: 24 Box 1387, 76513. Phone: (818) 939-9377. Licensee: JLF Communications LLP. (group owner; (acq 2-8-2007; $900,000). Population served: 187,000 Natl. Network: USA, . Format: Country gold. Target aud: 25-54. ◆James Harrison, gen mgr, stn mgr, opns VP; Jim Cooper, engrg mgr.

Benbrook

KDXX(FM)— January 1990: 107.1 mhz; 74 kw. Ant 1,050 ft TL: N32 35 10 W97 49 52. Stereo. Hrs open: 24 7700 Carpenter Fwy., Dallas, 75247. Phone: (214) 525-0400. Fax:(214) 631-1196. Web Site:univision.com Licensee: KCYT-FM License Corp. Group owner: Univision Radio (acq 9-22-2003; grpsl). Population served: 3,000,000 Gammon & Grange. Format: Sp adult contemp. ◆Frank Carter, gen mgr; Andy Lockridge, opns dir; Cipriano Robles, sls dir; Betsy Galleguillos, natl sls mgr; Oscar Espinosa, prom dir; Herminio "Chayan" Ortuno, progmg dir; Patrick Parks, chief of engrg; Myrna Vera, rsch dir; Mirentxu Smith, traf mgr.

Benjamin

KBTY(FM)—Not on air, target date: unknown: 95.3 mhz; 13 kw. Ant 459 ft TL: N33 46 28 W99 48 21. Hrs open: 6117 Lemon Thyme Dr., Alexandria, VA, 22310. Phone: (571) 228-1258. Fax: (703) 299-6626. Licensee: Miriam Media Inc. ◆Darryl K. Delawder, pres & gen mgr.

Big Lake

KPDB(FM)— 2001: 98.3 mhz; 50 kw. Ant 430 ft TL: N31 11 45 W101 25 40. Hrs open: Box 252, McAllen, 78505. Phone: (956) 686-6382.E-mail: radiodesafio@radiodesafio.org Web Site:www.radiodesafio.org Licensee: Centro Cristiano de Fe Inc. (acq 5-13-02; $300,000). Format: Christian, Sp, relg.

KWTR(FM)— 2004: 104.1 mhz; 500 w. Ant 62 ft TL: N31 11 54 W101 27 45. Hrs open: Box 1041 Phone: (325) 884-3451. Licensee: Woodrow Michael Warren. Group owner: Woodrow Michael Warren Stns. Format: Country. ◆Woodrow Michael Warren, gen mgr.

Big Sandy

*KTAA(FM)— Nov 6, 1995: 90.7 mhz; 5.8 kw. Ant 515 ft TL: N32 37 50 W94 53 44. Hrs open: 24 10550 Barkley St., Overland Park, KS, 66212. Phone: (913) 642-7770. Fax: (913) 642-1319.E-mail: comments@bottradionetwork.com Web Site:www.bottradionetwork.com Licensee: Community Broadcasting Inc. (acq 9-6-2006; $450,000). Natl. Network: USA, . Format: Christian talk. Target aud: 25-54; adults. ◆Richard P. Bott II, exec VP; Pat Rulon, natl sls mgr; Rachel Moser, mktg mgr; Jason Potocnik, traf mgr.

Big Spring

*KBCX(FM)— 2001: 91.5 mhz; 250 w. Ant 331 ft TL: N32 11 06 W101 27 56. Hrs open: Box 3206, Tupelo, MS, 38803. Phone: (662) 844-8888. Fax: (662) 842-6791.E-mail: comments@afr.net Web Site:www.afr.net Licensee: American Family Association. Group owner: American Family Radio Format: Inspirational Christian. ◆Marvin Sanders, gen mgr.

KBQX(AM)—Not on air, target date: unknown: 730 khz; 230 w-D, 300 w-N, DA-2. TL: N32 13 04 W101 29 25. Hrs open: 227 N. Walnut St., Kermit, 79745. Phone: (432) 352-9110. Licensee: Trade Media Corp. ◆Mark Nolte, VP.

KBST(AM)— Dec 23, 1936: 1490 khz; 1 kw-U. TL: N32 15 44 W101 27 37. Stereo. Hrs open: Box 1632, 79721. Secondary address: 608 Johnson St. 79720. Phone: (432) 267-1490. Fax: (432) 267-1579.E-mail: onair@kbst.com Licensee: Rhattigan Broadcasting (Texas) LP (group owner/; (acq 8-19-2004; grpsl). Population served: 28,735 Natl. Network: Fox Sports, . Natl. Rep: Riley,. Texas State Networks Format: News, talk, sports. Target aud: 25 plus. ◆Michael Rhattigan, CEO, disc jockey; Malinda Ellison Flenniken, gen mgr; Tim Knox, opns mgr & progmg dir; Mike Henry, news dir.

KBST-FM— 1961: 95.7 mhz; 33 kw. Ant 459 ft TL: N32 13 13 W101 26 25. Stereo. Hrs open: Box 1632, 79721. Secondary address: 608 Johnson St. 79720. Phone: (432) 267-6391. Fax: (432) 267-1579.E-mail: onair@kbst.com Web Site:www.kbst.com Licensee: Rhattigan Broadcasting (Texas) LP. (group owner; (acq 8-19-2004; grpsl). Population served: 33,000 Natl. Network: ABC, . Texas State Networks Format: News/talk, country. ◆Michael Rhattigan, CEO; Malinda Flenniken, gen mgr; Tim Knox, opns mgr; Mike Henry, news dir.

KBTS(FM)— Aug 14, 1995: 94.3 mhz; 8.3 kw. Ant 561 ft TL: N32 13 13 W101 26 25. Hrs open: Box 1632, 79721. Secondary address: 608 Johnson St. 79720. Phone: (432) 267-6391. Fax: (432) 267-1579.E-mail: onair@kbst.com Licensee: Rhattigan Broadcasting (Texas) LP (group owner; (acq 6-3-2004; grpsl). Format: Hot adult contemp. ◆Michael Rhattigan, CEO, gen mgr; Malinda Flenniken, gen mgr; Tim Knox, opns dir & progmg dir.

KBYG(AM)— 1948: 1400 khz; 1 kw-U. TL: N32 13 22 W101 28 35. Hrs open: 24 2801 Wasson Dr., 79720-7301. Phone: (432) 263-6351. Fax: (432) 263-8223.E-mail: david.pappajohn@kbyg.net Licensee: Ballard Drew. (acq 4-9-90). Population served: 150,000 Rgnl. Network: S.W. Agri-Radio. Southwest Agri-Radio Format: Oldies, Sp, talk. News staff: one. Target aud: 25-54; Anglo-Hispanic. ◆David M. Pappajohn, gen mgr; Vents Allyn, progmg dir.

*KPBD(FM)— 2005: 89.3 mhz; 3 kw. Ant 328 ft TL: N32 09 51 W101 25 27. Hrs open: Box 252, McAllen, 78505. Phone: (956) 686-6382. Fax: (956) 686-2999. Licensee: Paulino Bernal Evangelism. ◆Paulino Bernal Jr., pres.

Bishop

KMZZ(FM)— June 15, 1980: 106.9 mhz; 25 kw. Ant 298 ft TL: N27 39 10 W97 54 59. (CP: Ant 246 ft. TL: N27 40 16 W97 44 17). Stereo. Hrs open: 24 701 Benys Rd., Corpus Christi, 78408. Phone: (361) 289-0999. Fax: (361) 289-0810.E-mail: davilabroadcasting@bizstx.rr.com

Licensee: Claro Communications Ltd. (acq 11-4-2004; $550,000). Population served: 300,000 Baraff, Koerner & Olender. Format: Relg. News staff: one. Target aud: 18-49; people with buying power. ◆Lionel Davila, gen mgr; Mike Aradillias, sls VP; Jeremy Lopez, progmg dir; George Sanders, chief of engrg.

Bloomington

*KHVT(FM)— 2006: 91.5 mhz; 46 kw. Ant 482 ft TL: N29 00 04 W97 00 05. Hrs open:
Rebroadcasts KHCB-FM Houston 95%.
KHCB Radio Network, 2424 South Blvd., Houston, 77098-5110. Phone: (713) 520-5200.E-mail: email@khcb.org Web Site:www.khcb.org Licensee: Houston Christian Broadcasters Inc. (group owner). Format: Christian. Spec prog: Sp Christian 6 hrs wkly. ◆Bruce Munsterman, gen mgr.

KLUB(FM)— December 1992: 106.9 mhz; 25 w. 269 ft TL: N28 42 16 W96 50 08. Stereo. Hrs open: 24 107 N. Star Dr., Victoria, 77904. Secondary address: Box 3325, Victoria 77904. Phone: (361) 573-0777. Fax: (361) 578-0059.E-mail: kixs@gapbroadcasting.com Web Site:www.1069therock.com Licensee: GAP Broadcasting Victoria License LLC. Group owner: Clear Channel Communications Inc. (acq 10-1-2007; grpsl). Format: Classic rock. News staff: one; News: 4 hrs wkly. Target aud: 25-59; listeners in a growth & acquisition mode. Spec prog: Blues. ◆Jeff Lyon, gen mgr; Natalie Franz, gen sls mgr; Adam West, progmg mgr; James Love, news dir; Charles Smithey, engrg mgr, engr; Becky Snell, traf mgr.

Boerne

KBRN(AM)— May 10, 1982: 1500 khz; 250 w-D. TL: N29 48 44 W98 43 41. Hrs open: 11737 Nelon Dr., Corpus Christi, 78410. Phone: (361) 774-4354. Fax: (361) 241-7945. Licensee: Claro Communications Ltd. (acq 6-25-2004; $200,000). Population served: 250,000 Format: Sp. ◆Gerry Benavides, gen mgr.

Bonham

KFYN(AM)— May 1948: 1420 khz; 250 w-D, 148 w-N. TL: N33 34 40 W96 09 55. Stereo. Hrs open: 5 AM-1 AM 811 E. Sam Rayburn Dr., 75418-4928. Secondary address: Box 248 75418-4928. Phone: (903) 583-3151. Fax: (903) 583-2728.E-mail: kfyn@kfyn1420.com Web Site:www.kfyn1420.com Licensee: Vision Media Group Inc. (acq 12-4-02). Population served: 238,000 Natl. Network: ABC, . Rgnl. Network: Texas State Net. Texas State Networks Format: Country. Spec prog: Farm 6 hrs, relg 6 hrs, oldies rock 6 hrs wkly. ◆C.L. Carter II, pres, gen mgr; Jeff Davis, opns mgr & progmg dir.

Borger

*KASV(FM)— 1998: 88.7 mhz; 10 kw horiz, 3 kw vert. 203 ft TL: N35 40 42 W101 23 18. Hrs open: 24
Rebroadcasts KJRT(FM) Amarillo 100%.
Box 8088, Amarillo, 79114. Phone: (806) 359-8855. Fax: (806) 354-2039. Web Site:www.kingdomkeys.org Licensee: Top O' Texas Ed. Broadcasting. Format: Relg, educ. ◆Ricky Pfeil, gen mgr.

KQFX(FM)—Licensed to Borger. See Amarillo

KQTY(AM)— Jan 10, 1947: 1490 khz; 1 kw-U. TL: N35 41 05 W101 23 20. Stereo. Hrs open: 24 Box 165, 113 Union, 79007. Phone: (806) 273-7533. Phone: (806) 273-5889. Fax: (806) 273-3727.E-mail: kqtyradio@yahoo.com Web Site:kqtyradio.com Licensee: Zia Broadcasting. (acq 12-1-79). Population served: 26,800 Format: News/talk, live sports. Target aud: 25-54; blue collar workers with traditional values & beliefs. ◆Lonnie Ausups, CEO; Rick Keefer, gen mgr; George Grover, stn mgr.

KQTY-FM— 1999: 106.7 mhz; 6 kw. Ant 259 ft TL: N35 41 05 W101 23 12. Stereo. Hrs open: 24 Box 165, 79008-0165. Secondary address: 113 Union 79007. Phone: (806) 273-5889. Fax: (806) 273-3727.E-mail: kqtyradio@yahoo.com Web Site:www.kqtyradio.com Licensee: Zia Broadcasting Co. Population served: 26,800 Natl. Network: ABC, . Format: Country. News: 15 hrs wkly. Target aud: 25-54; Blue collar workers w/traditional values & beliefs. Spec prog: Religious, 1hr; southern gospel, 3hrs; christian country, 5hrs; Texas country, 10hrs. ◆Lonnie Allsups, CEO; George Grover, stn mgr.

Bovina

KKNM(FM)— 2008: 96.5 mhz; 50 kw. Ant 459 ft TL: N34 41 17 W102 56 53. Hrs open: 1227 W. Magnolia Ave., Suite 300, Fort Worth,

76104-4400. Phone: (817) 920-7599. Fax: (817) 920-9606. Licensee: Tejas Broadcasting Ltd. LLP. ♦Charles J. Brooks, pres.

***KOVA(FM)**—Not on air, target date: unknown: 90.9 mhz; 5 kw. Ant 141 ft TL: N34 39 08 W102 50 42. Hrs open: 282 Country Estate Dr., Springer, OK, 73458. Phone: (580) 653-2777. Licensee: Ron Elmore Ministries Inc. ♦Ron Elmore, pres.

Bowie

KNTX(AM)— May 29, 1959: 1410 khz; 500 w-D, DA. TL: N33 35 10 W97 48 23. Stereo. Hrs open: 24 hrs Box 1080, State Hwy 59 & FM 1758, 76230. Phone: (940) 872-2288. Fax: (940) 872-1228.E-mail: chenderson@kntxradio.com Web Site:kntxradio.com Licensee: Henderson Broadcasting Co. L.P. (acq 3-13-03). Population served: 30,000 Natl. Network: ABC, CBS Radio, . Rgnl. Network: Texas State Net. Texas State Networks Reddy, Begley & McCormick. Format: Oldies. News staff: one; News: 15 hrs wkly. Target aud: 25-54. Spec prog: . Gospel 4 hrs wkly ♦Charley M. Henderson, pres, gen mgr, engrg dir, chief of engrg; Pamela A. Henderson, VP, sls dir; Jackie Hopson, prom VP; Wendy Hill, opns dir & progmg dir; Charley Henderson, mus dir; Doris McGuffey, news dir.

Brady

KNEL(AM)— December 1935: 1490 khz; 1 kw-U. TL: N31 07 48 W99 19 21. Hrs open: Box 630, 76825. Secondary address: 117 S. Blackburn St. 76825. Phone: (325) 597-2119. Fax: (325) 597-1925.E-mail: knel@airmail.net Web Site:www.knelradio.com Licensee: Farris Broadcasting Inc. (acq 10-12-95; $475,000 with co-located FM). Population served: 15,750 Natl. Network: ABC, . Rgnl. Network: Texas State Net. Texas State Networks Format: Oldies. Target aud: General. ♦Lynn Farris, pres, gen mgr; Stan Cooper, chief of engrg.

KNEL-FM— Aug 21, 1979: 95.3 mhz; 3 kw. 299 ft TL: N31 07 27 W99 21 34. Stereo. Hrs open: Box 630, 76825. Secondary address: 117 S. Blackburn St. 76825. Phone: (325) 597-2119. Fax: (325) 597-1925. Web Site:www.knelradio.com Population served: 15,500 Rgnl. Network: Texas State Net. Texas State Networks Format: Country. Target aud: General. ♦Lynn Farris, gen mgr.

Breckenridge

KBWM(FM)—Not on air, target date: unknown: 100.1 mhz; 6 kw. Ant 250 ft TL: N32 47 32 W98 56 24. Hrs open: 3654 W. Jarvis Ave., Skokie, IL, 60076. Phone: (847) 674-0864. Fax: (847) 674-9188. Web Site:www.kmcommunications.com Licensee: KM Communications Inc. ♦Kevin Joel Bae, VP & gen mgr.

***KDRG(FM)**—Not on air, target date: unknown: 89.9 mhz; 17.9 kw. Ant 325 ft TL: N32 35 48 W98 44 26. Hrs open: Box 497933, Garland, 75049. Phone: (469) 245-3604. Licensee: Gospel American Network. ♦William R. Wright, gen mgr.

KLXK(FM)— Aug 1, 1982: 93.5 mhz; 50 kw. 446 ft TL: N32 45 31 W98 56 00. Stereo. Hrs open: Box 1507, Graham, 76450. Secondary address: 101 E. Walker St., Suite 201 76424. Phone: (254) 559-6543. Fax: (254) 559-6545. Natl. Network: ABC, . Rgnl. Network: Vsa Radio. Format: Country. News staff: one; News: 1.5 hrs wkly. Target aud: 25-54; general. Spec prog: Agricultural programming 5 hrs wkly. ♦Joe Graham, gen mgr, sports cmtr; Greg Tiller, progmg dir; Jim Jones, news dir; Roy Robinson, VP & traf mgr.

KROO(AM)— September 1947: 1430 khz; 1 kw-D, 17 w-N. TL: N32 45 11 W98 55 57. Hrs open: 24 Box 1507, Graham, 76450. Secondary address: 101 E. Walker St., Suite 201 76424. Phone: (254) 559-6543. Fax: (254) 559-6545.E-mail: klxk@brazosnet.com Licensee: Graham Newspapers Inc. (group owner; (acq 4-12-2001; with co-located FM). Population served: 70,000 Natl. Network: ABC, . Format: Adult Contempory. News staff: one; News: 2.5 hrs wkly. Target aud: Adults 25-54; adults. ♦Roy Robinson, VP; Joe Graham, gen mgr; Greg Tiller, progmg dir; Jim Jones, news dir, chief of engrg.

Brenham

KLTR(FM)— August 1988: 94.1 mhz; 6 kw. 328 ft TL: N30 08 31 W96 25 00. Stereo. Hrs open: 24 Light rock 530 W. Main, 77833-9247. Phone: (979) 836-9411. Fax: (979) 836-9435.E-mail: lorihenderson01@hotmail.com Licensee: Roy E. Henderson. (group owner; (acq 5-31-2001; $1.5 million). Fletcher, Heald & Hildreth. Format: Adult contemp. News staff: one; News: 18 hrs wkly. Target aud: 18-49. Spec prog: Gospel 10 hrs wkly. ♦Roy Henderson, pres, gen mgr; Ryan Henderson, gen sls mgr; Amber Kyle, progmg dir; Lori Henderson, traf mgr.

KTTX(FM)— Sept 15, 1964: 106.1 mhz; 50 kw. 492 ft TL: N30 21 49 W96 34 33. Stereo. Hrs open: Progmg separate from AM Box 1280, 77834. Phone: (979) 836-3655. Fax: (979) 830-8141.E-mail: mail@ktex.com Web Site:www.ktex.com Population served: 300,000 Format: Contemp country. News staff: one; News: 1.5 hrs wkly. Target aud: 18-49. ♦Tom D. Whitehead, VP, gen sls mgr & natl sls mgr; Carolyn Warmke, rgnl sls mgr; Ken Murray, progmg dir, traf mgr; Shelly Granke, pub affrs dir, disc jockey; Michele Daniels, traf mgr, disc jockey.

***KUBJ(FM)**— 2008: 89.7 mhz; 17.5 kw. Ant 407 ft TL: N30 03 17 W96 30 26. Hrs open: Box 187, Humble, 77347. Phone: (281) 446-5725. Fax: (281 540-2198. Web Site:www.ksbj.org Licensee: KSBJ Educational Foundation. (acq 12-12-2007; $100,000 for CP). Format: Contemp Christian. ♦Tim McDermott, gen mgr.

KWHI(AM)— Apr 15, 1947: 1280 khz; 1 kw-D, 89 w-N. TL: N30 10 05 W96 25 20. Hrs open: Box 1280, 77834. Secondary address: 223 E. Main St. 77833. Phone: (979) 836-3655. Fax: (979) 830-8141.E-mail: mail@kwhi.com Web Site:www.kwhi.com Licensee: Tom S. Whitehead Inc. (acq 5-1-47). Population served: 100,000 Natl. Network: ABC, . Natl. Rep: Rgnl Reps,. Format: Country, news/talk. News staff: 2; News: 14 hrs wkly. Target aud: 25-54. Spec prog: Polka 2 hrs, relg 3 hrs, farm 3 hrs wkly. ♦Tom Whitehead Jr., pres; Ken Murray, opns mgr; Tom D. Whitehead, gen sls mgr; Kelly Outlaw, prom dir; Craig Mantey, progmg dir; Frank Wagner, news dir; Mark Whitehead, chief of engrg; Elizabeth Pomykal, traf mgr; Tom S. Whitehead, edit dir; Ed Pothul, sports cmtr.

Bridgeport

KBOC(FM)— Aug 2, 1982: 98.3 mhz; 6 kw. Ant 226 ft TL: N33 13 28 W97 47 51. Stereo. Hrs open: 24 4201 Pool Rd., Colleyville, 76034-5017. Phone: (817) 868-2900. Fax: (817) 868-2929. Web Site:www.elnorteenlinea.com Licensee: Liberman Broadcasting of Dallas License LLC. (acq 11-2-2006; grpsl). Population served: 250,000 Format: Rgnl Mexican. ♦Alex Sanchez, gen mgr.

Brookshire

KCHN(AM)— 2001: 1050 khz; 410 w-D, DA. TL: N29 52 45 W96 02 08. Hrs open: 1782 W. Sam Houston Pkwy. N., Houston, 77043. Phone: (713) 490-2538. Fax: (713) 984-1721. Web Site:www.mrbi.net Licensee: KCHN Licensee LLC. Population served: 700,000 Format: Multi-ethnic. ♦Terry Lowry, gen mgr.

Brownfield

KKUB(AM)— August 1949: 1300 khz; 1 kw-D. TL: N33 10 49 W102 14 51. Hrs open: Box 411, 79316-0411. Secondary address: 1722 Tahoka Rd. 79316. Phone: (806) 637-4531. Fax: (806) 637-4610. Licensee: Dios Llega Al Hombre Ministries (acq 5-10-2001). Population served: 10,387 Rgnl. Network: Texas State Net. Format: Sp music, classic country. Target aud: 24 and up. ♦Adolph Hernandez, gen mgr.

***KMLU(FM)**— 2008: 90.7 mhz; 130 w. Ant 276 ft TL: N33 10 30 W102 17 20. Hrs open:
Rebroadcasts KLVR(FM) Middletown, CA 100%.
2351 Sunset Blvd., Suite 170-218, Rocklin, CA, 95765. Phone: (916) 251-1600. Fax: (916) 251-1650. Web Site:www.klove.com Licensee: Educational Media Foundation. (acq 11-1-2006; grpsl). Natl. Network: K-Love, . Format: Contemp Christian. ♦Richard Jenkins, pres.

***KPBB(FM)**— 1999: 88.5 mhz; 4.5 kw. Ant 377 ft TL: N33 09 18 W102 16 51. Hrs open: Box 252, McAllen, 78505. Secondary address: 4501 N. McCall Rd., McAllen 78504. Phone: (956) 686-6382. Fax: (956) 686-2999. Licensee: Paulino Bernal Evangelism. Format: Sp, Christian. ♦Paulino Bernal, gen mgr.

KTTU-FM— Nov 12, 1984: 104.3 mhz; 50 kw. Ant 466 ft TL: N33 25 08 W102 08 58. Stereo. Hrs open: 24 9800 University Ave., Lubbock, 79423. Phone: (806) 745-3434. Fax: (806) 748-2470.E-mail: idee@ramar.com Licensee: Ramar Communications II Ltd. (group owner; (acq 3-26-99; $1.025 million). Format: Sports. Target aud: 25-54. ♦Diana Dee, gen sls mgr; Lew Dee, gen mgr & progmg dir.

Brownsville

***KBNR(FM)**— Apr 10, 1984: 88.3 mhz; 5.5 kw. 289 ft TL: N25 55 10 W97 31 44. Stereo. Hrs open: 24 Box 5480, 78523-5480. Secondary address: 901 Mexico Blvd. 78520. Phone: (956) 542-6933. Fax: (956) 542-0523.E-mail: kbnr@lwrn.org Web Site:www.radiokbnr.org Licensee: World Radio Network Inc. Population served: 1,100,000 Format: Relg, educ, Sp. News: 3 hrs wkly. Target aud: 20-45; Hispanic, middle & upper income. ♦Ted Haney, pres; Abelardo Limon, VP; Moises Flores, stn mgr.

KKPS(FM)— Jan 17, 1978: 99.5 mhz; 100 kw. 1,034 ft TL: N26 04 53 W97 49 44. Stereo. Hrs open: 24 801 N. Jackson Rd., McAllen, 78501. Phone: (956) 661-6000. Fax: (956) 661-6082.E-mail: mquinn@entravision.com Licensee: Entravision Holdings L.L.C. Group owner: Entravision Communications Corp. (acq 7-20-00; grpsl). Population served: 700,000 Rosenman & Colin. Format: Sp mus, Tejano. News staff: one. Target aud: 18-49; Hispanic females, young adults. ♦Scott Savage, gen mgr.

KRIO(AM)—See McAllen

KVNS(AM)— 1999: 1700 khz; 8.8 kw-D, 880 w-N. TL: N25 56 57 W97 33 15. Stereo. Hrs open: 24 901 E. Pike Blvd., Weslaco, 78596. Phone: (956) 973-9202. Phone: (866) 973-1041. Fax: (956) 973-9355. Licensee: Clear Channel Broadcasting Licenses Inc. Group owner: Clear Channel Communications Inc. (acq 12-9-2003; grpsl). Shaw Pittman. Format: News/talk. ♦Tim Thomas, gen mgr; Billy Santiago, opns mgr; Cyndi Torres, sls dir, gen sls mgr; Ken Meek, chief of engrg.

Brownwood

***KBUB(FM)**— Mar 12, 1987: 90.3 mhz; 550 w. 308 ft TL: N31 43 10 W99 00 57. Hrs open: Box 1549, 76804. Phone: (325) 641-2223. Phone: (325) 646-3420. Fax: (325) 643-9772. Licensee: Living Word Church of Brownwood Inc. (acq 12-18-96). Format: Christian praise music, teaching. ♦Angelia Schum, gen mgr.

KBWD(AM)— Aug 17, 1941: 1380 khz; 1 kw-D, 500 w-N. TL: N31 42 36 W98 57 36. Hrs open: Box 280, 76804. Secondary address: 300 Carnegie St. 76801. Phone: (325) 646-3505. Fax: (325) 646-2220.E-mail: upfront@koxe.com Web Site:www.koxe.com Licensee: Brown County Broadcasting Co. Population served: 25,672 Format: Adult contemp. ♦Don Dillard, VP; Barbara McAnally, gen mgr.

***KHBW(FM)**— September 1998: 91.7 mhz; 290 w. Ant 571 ft TL: N31 43 32 W99 00 48. Stereo. Hrs open: 24 Houston Christian Broadcasters Inc., 2424 South Blvd., Houston, 77098. Phone: (713) 520-5200. Web Site:www.khcb.org Licensee: Houston Christian Broadcasters Inc. (acq 2-27-2009; $40,000). Population served: 25,000 Southmayd & Miller. Format: Christian. ♦Bruce Munsterman, gen mgr.

KOXE(FM)— May 17, 1975: 101.3 mhz; 100 kw. Ant 577 ft TL: N31 43 45 W99 01 12. Stereo. Hrs open: Box 280, 76804. Phone: (325) 646-3505. Fax: (325) 646-2220. Web Site:www.koxe.com Licensee: Brown County Broadcasting Co. Format: Country. ♦Barbara McAnally, gen mgr.

***KPBE(FM)**— 2000: 89.3 mhz; 6 kw. Ant 328 ft TL: N31 46 37 W98 50 30. Hrs open: Box 252, McAllen, 78505. Secondary address: 4501 N. McCall Rd., McAllen 78504. Phone: (956) 686-6382. Fax: (956) 686-2999. Licensee: Paulino Bernal Evangelism. Format: Sp, Christian. ♦Paulino Bernal, pres & gen mgr.

KPSM(FM)— Apr 11, 1981: 99.3 mhz; 100 kw. Ant 446 ft TL: N31 43 10 W99 00 57. Stereo. Hrs open: Box 1549, 76804. Secondary address: 901 C.C. Woodson Rd. 76801. Phone: (325) 646-5993. Fax: (325) 643-9772.E-mail: rock@web-access.net Web Site:www.kpsm.net Licensee: Living Word Church of Brownwood Inc. (acq 1996). Population served: 186,132 Natl. Network: Salem Radio Network, . Format: Contemp Christian music. Spec prog: Children 3 hrs, Christian hip hop 5 hrs, Southern Gospel 2 hrs wkly. ♦Jack Ruth, CEO; Angelia Schum, gen mgr; Brigitte Rittenour, stn mgr, opns dir, sls dir, mktg dir; Kevin Koontz, prom VP; Erich Schnitz, progmg dir; Tom Zintgraff, chief of engrg.

KXYL(AM)— 1953: 1240 khz; 1 kw-U. TL: N31 42 21 W98 59 45. Hrs open: 24 Prog sep from FM 600 Fisk Dr, 76801. Phone: (325) 646-3535. Fax: (325) 646-5347.E-mail: ksta1000@web-access.net Web Site:wattsradio.net Licensee: Tackett-Boazman Broadcasting LP Population served: 35,000 Rgnl. Network: Texas State Net. Natl. Rep: Roslin,. Texas State Networks Format: Btfl mus, Sp. News staff: 2; News: 8 hrs wkly. Target aud: 18+; Spanish. Spec prog: Christian Sp 36 hrs wkly. ♦Chema Martinez, progmg dir; Helen Lehman, traf mgr.

KXYL-FM— September 1965: 96.9 mhz; 74 kw. Ant 321 ft TL: N31 42 16 W99 00 05. Stereo. Hrs open: 24 600 Fisk Dr, 76801. Phone: (325) 646-3535. Fax: (325) 646-5347.E-mail: ksta1000@web-access.net Web Site:wattsradio.net Licensee: Tackett-Boazman Broadcasting LP (group owner; (acq 4-11-2006; grpsl). Population served: 50,000 Natl. Network: ABC, . Cohn & Marks. Format: News/talk. News staff: 3. Target aud: 18+. ♦Cathy Hail, gen mgr, progmg dir; Helen Lehman,

opns mgr, prom dir, traf mgr; Ted Wrenn, sls dir; Kyle Dennis, news dir; sports cmtr; Stan Cooper, chief of engrg; Will Prickett, disc jockey.

Bryan

KAGC(AM)— Dec 27, 1977: 1510 khz; 500 w-D. TL: N30 41 21 W96 21 35. Hrs open: Box 3248, 77805. Secondary address: 2700 Rudder Fwy. S., Suite 5000, College Station 77845. Phone: (979) 695-9595. Fax: (979) 695-1933.E-mail: kagcradio@cox-internet.com Web Site:kagcradio.com Licensee: Divcon Associates Inc. (acq 3-87). Population served: 133,719 Natl. Network: Salem Radio Network, . Verner, Liipfert, Bernhard, McPherson & Hand. Format: Contemp Christian. News: 6 hrs wkly. Target aud: 25-54; upscale, higher income & conservative. Spec prog: Black 2 hrs, Czech music 2 hrs wkly. ◆Bill Hicks, pres; Ben Downs, gen mgr; Keith Kane, opns mgr, prom mgr, progmg dir; Sam Jones, gen sls mgr; Michele McNew, adv dir; Chris Dusterhoff, chief of engrg.

KKYS(FM)— July 28, 1984: 104.7 mhz; 50 kw. 350 ft TL: N30 42 59 W96 22 20. Stereo. Hrs open: 24 1716 Briarcrest Dr., Ste. 150, 77802. Phone: (979) 846-5597. Fax: (979) 268-9090.E-mail: leslieguidry @clearchannel.com Web Site:www.mix1047.com Licensee: CCB Texas Licenses L.P. Group owner: Clear Channel Communications Inc. (acq 10-10-00; grpsl). Population served: 100,000 Format: Hot adult contemp. News: 15 hrs wkly. Target aud: 18-49; heavy office lstng.

KNDE(FM)—See College Station

KNFX-FM— Oct 7, 1991: 99.5 mhz; 6 kw. Ant 328 ft TL: N30 39 02 W96 20 58. Hrs open: 24 1716 Briarcrest Dr., Suite 150, 77802. Phone: (979) 846-5597. Fax: (979) 268-9090.E-mail: leslieguydry @clearchannel.com Web Site:www.995thefox.com Licensee: CCB Texas Licenses L.P. Group owner: Clear Channel Communications Inc. (acq 7-20-01; $2.5 million). Population served: 150,000 Leventhal, Senter & Lerman. Format: Class rock. Target aud: General.

KORA-FM— Apr 1, 1966: 98.3 mhz; 900 w. Ant 528 ft TL: N30 39 00.985 W96 20 57.34. Stereo. Hrs open: Box 3069, 77805. Secondary address: 1240 Villa Maria Rd. 77802. Phone: (979) 776-1240. Fax: (979) 776-0123. Licensee: Brazos Valley Communications Ltd. Population served: 150,000 Natl. Rep: Katz Radio,. Format: Country. Target aud: P18-49, P25-54. Spec prog: ABC News. ◆Nathan Peacock, gen sls mgr; Roger Garrett, progmg dir; Lance Parr, chief of engrg.

KTAM(AM)— Sept 10, 1947: 1240 khz; 1 kw-U. TL: N30 39 02 W96 20 59. Hrs open: Box 3069, 77805. Secondary address: 1240 Villa Maria Rd. 77802. Phone: (979) 776-1240. Fax: (979) 776-0123. Licensee: Brazos Valley Communications Ltd. (group owner; acq 8-31-2006; grpsl). Population served: 150,000 Natl. Rep: Univision Radio National Sales,. Format: Regional Mexican. Target aud: 18-34, 18-49. Spec prog: GLR News, ESPN Deportes. ◆Chris Kiske, gen mgr; Nathan Peacock, gen sls mgr; Carolyn Benavides, progmg dir; Lance Parr, chief of engrg.

KZNE(AM)—See College Station

Buda

KROX-FM— Sept 1, 1984: 101.5 mhz; 12.5 kw. Ant 843 ft TL: N30 19 23 W97 47 58. Stereo. Hrs open: 24 8309 N. IH 35, Austin, 78753. Phone: (512) 832-4000. Fax: (512) 832-4071.E-mail: info@oldies103austin.com Web Site:www.krox.com Licensee: LBJS Broadcasting Co. L.P. Group owner: Emmis Communications Corp. (acq 4-25-03; grpsl). Population served: 1,000,000 Natl. Rep: McGavren Guild,. Format: Alternative, new rock. Target aud: 18-34; young adults. ◆Bruce Walden, gen mgr; James White, sls dir; Melody Lee, progmg dir; Todd Jeffries, news dir; Jim Henkle, chief of engrg; Lisa Melton, traf mgr.

Burkburnett

KYYI(FM)— June 1, 1989: 104.7 mhz; 100 kw. 1,017 ft TL: N34 05 35 W98 52 44. Stereo. Hrs open: 24 4302 Callfield Rd., Wichita Falls, 76308. Phone: (940) 691-2311. Fax: (940) 696-2255.E-mail: bear104@bear104.com Web Site:www.bear104.com Licensee: Cumulus Licensing Corp. Group owner: Cumulus Media Inc. (acq 10-3-97; grpsl). Cohn & Marks. Format: Classic Rock. ◆Lindy Parr, gen mgr; Brent Warner, opns mgr; Johnny Tidwell, gen sls mgr; Keith Vaughn; progmg dir; Jeff Chancey, chief of engrg; Dana Jameson, traf mgr.

Burleson

KCLE(AM)— July 22, 1922: 1460 khz; 5 kw-D, 700 w-N, DA-2. TL: N32 34 43 W97 16 50. Hrs open: 24 Box 1629, Cleburne, 76033.

Phone: (817) 645-6643. Fax: (817) 645-6644.E-mail: info@countrygoldradio.com Web Site:www.countrygoldradio.com Licensee: M&M Broadcasters Ltd. (group owner; acq 4-26-99; $450,000). Population served: 105,000 Format: Classic country. ◆Gary Moss, gen mgr.

Burnet

KBEY(FM)— April 1993: 92.5 mhz; 1.8 kw. Ant 604 ft TL: N30 44 29 W98 19 05. Hrs open: 5526 N. Hwy. 281, Marble Falls, 78654-3804. Phone: (830) 693-5551. Fax: (830) 693-5107.E-mail: realcountry@kbay.com Web Site:www.radiohillcountry.com Licensee: Munbilla Broadcasting Properties Ltd. (group owner). Format: Real country. ◆Cindi Ashford, gen mgr; Bill Woleben, opns dir.

KRHC(AM)— Aug 19, 1963: 1340 khz; 1 kw-U. TL: N30 46 04 W98 13 49. Hrs open: 24 5526 Hwy 281 N, Marble Falls, 78654. Phone: (830) 693-5551. Fax: (830) 693-5107.E-mail: comments@khlb.com Web Site:www.khlb.com Licensee: Munbilla Broadcasting Properties Ltd. (group owner; acq 12-4-2003; $1 million with co-located FM). Population served: 4,300 Rgnl. Network: Texas State Net. Texas State Networks Format: News, info, nostalgia. News staff: 2; News: 3 hrs wkly. Target aud: 35 plus. ◆Cindi Ashford, gen mgr; Ben Shields, progmg dir; Bill Woleben, chief of engrg, disc jockey.

Bushland

*KTXP(FM)— 2004: 91.5 mhz; 1 kw. Ant 262 ft TL: N35 08 51 W102 05 56. Hrs open: 24
Rebroadcasts KANZ(FM) Garden City 100%.
High Plains Public Radio, 210 N. 7th St., Garden City, KS, 67846. Phone: (620) 275-7444. Fax: (620) 275-7496. Web Site:www.hppr.org Licensee: Kanza Society Inc. Natl. Network: NPR, AP Radio, PRI, . Format: News, div. ◆Richard Hicks, gen mgr; Diana Gonzales, dev dir; Debra Stout, prom dir; Bob Kirby, progmg dir; Mary Palmer, mus dir; Chuck Springer, chief of engrg.

Byrne

*KLRW(FM)— 2004: 88.5 mhz; 500 w vert. Ant 522 ft TL: N31 25 16 W100 32 36. Hrs open: 2351 Sunset Blvd., Suite 170-218, Rocklin, CA, 95765. Phone: (916) 251-1600. Fax: (916) 251-1650. Web Site:www.klove.com Licensee: Educational Media Foundation. Group owner: EMF Broadcasting (acq 5-8-2003; $75,000 for CP). Natl. Network: K-Love, . Format: Christian. ◆Richard Jenkins, pres; Mike Novak, VP; Keith Whipple, dev dir; Eric Allen, natl sls mgr; David Pierce, progmg mgr; Ed Lenane, news dir; Sam Wallington, engrg dir; Karen Johnson, news rptr.

Caldwell

*KALD(FM)—Not on air, target date: October 2008: 91.9 mhz; 6 kw. Ant 328 ft TL: N30 33 24 W96 48 29. Hrs open: 2424 South Blvd., Houston, 77098. Phone: (713) 520-5200.E-mail: email@khcb.org Web Site:www.khcb.org Licensee: Houston Christian Broadcasters Inc. (acq 4-9-2007; $10,000 for CP). ◆Bruce Munsterman, gen mgr.

KAPN(FM)— 2002: 107.3 mhz; 6 kw. Ant 328 ft TL: N30 33 31 W96 34 50. Hrs open: 24 1240 E. Villa Maria Dr., Bryan, 77802. Phone: (979) 776-1240. Fax: (979) 776-0123. Licensee: Brazos Valley Communications Ltd. Group owner: Bayport Broadcast Group (acq 11-18-2008; $875,000). ◆Chris Kiske, gen mgr.

Callisburg

*KPFC(FM)— April 1998: 91.9 mhz; 300 w. 62 ft TL: N33 40 11 W97 00 50. Hrs open: 24 Box 918, Camp Sweeney, Gainesville, 76241. Phone: (940) 665-2011. Fax: (940) 665-9467.E-mail: kpfc@gmail.com Web Site:www.kpfc.org Licensee: Camp Sweeney. Format: Contemporary hits. ◆Dr. Ernie Fernandez, gen mgr; Skip Rigsby, progmg mgr.

Cameron

KJXJ(FM)— Apr 8, 1985: 103.9 mhz; 25 kw. Ant 695 ft TL: N30 44 14 W96 50 14. Stereo. Hrs open: 24 Box 3069, Bryan, 77805. Secondary address: 1240 E. Villa Maria, Bryan 77802. Phone: (979) 776-1240. Fax: (979) 776-6074. Licensee: Brazos Valley Communications Ltd. Group owner: Equicom Inc. (acq 8-31-2006; grpsl). Natl. Network: ABC, . Natl. Rep: Katz Radio,. Fletcher, Heald & Hildreth. Format: Jack-FM-adult hits. Target aud: 18-49; 25-54. ◆Chris Kiske, VP, gen mgr, opns dir; John Sellars, progmg dir; Lance Parr, chief of engrg.

KMIL(FM)— 2002: 105.1 mhz; 15 kw. Ant 328 ft TL: N30 51 30 W97 01 47. Hrs open: Box 832, 76520. Phone: (254) 697-6633. Fax: (254) 697-6330.E-mail: kmil@kmil.com Web Site:www.kmil.com Licensee: Cameron Broadcasting Co. Natl. Network: CBS Radio, . Format: Country. ◆Clay Gish, gen mgr.

KTAE(AM)— September 1955: 1330 khz; 500 w-D, 97 w-N. TL: N30 50 48 W96 57 55. Hrs open: Drawer 832, 76520. Secondary address: 901 E. First 76520. Phone: (254) 697-6633. Fax: (254) 697-6330.E-mail: kmil@tlab.net Web Site:www.kmil.com Licensee: Milam Broadcasting Co. (acq 12-31-97). Population served: 25,000 Natl. Rep: Keystone (unwired net),. Format: C&W, Sp. Target aud: General. Spec prog: Gospel 6 hrs, Czech 8 hrs wkly. ◆Joe Smitherman, gen mgr, sls dir, news dir; Sarah Haussecker, traf mgr; Nonito Martinez, spanish dir; A.T. Sheffield, disc jockey.

Camp Wood

KAYG(FM)— 2001: 99.1 mhz; 965 w. Ant 226 ft TL: N29 42 53 W100 00 56. Hrs open: Box 252, McAllen, 78505. Secondary address: 4501 N. McCall Rd., McAllen 78504. Phone: (956) 686-6382. Fax: (956) 686-2999. Licensee: La Radio Cristiana Network Inc. Format: Sp, Christian. ◆Paulino Bernal, pres & gen mgr.

*KHPS(FM)—Not on air, target date: unknown: 89.7 mhz; 500 w. Ant 361 ft TL: N29 42 53 W100 00 56. Hrs open: 2424 South Blvd., Houston, 77098-5110. Phone: (713) 520-5200.E-mail: email@khcb.org Web Site:www.khcb.org Licensee: Houston Christian Broadcasters Inc. ◆Bruce Munsterman, pres.

Campbell

KRVA-FM— Aug 1, 1969: 107.1 mhz; 3.6 kw. Ant 423 ft TL: N33 07 31 W95 44 35. Stereo. Hrs open: 115 W. 3rd St., Fort Worth, 76102. Phone: (817) 332-0959. Licensee: LKCM Radio Group L.P. (group owner; acq 5-21-2004; $1 million with KRVF(FM) Kerens). Population served: 5,000,000 Format: Oldies. News staff: 2. ◆Gerry Schlegel, pres; Joel Gough, sls dir; Molly Prince, prom dir; Chuck Taylor, mus dir; Michael Margrave, chief of engrg; Jane Wasson, traf mgr.

Canadian

*KHHC(FM)—Not on air, target date: unknown: 91.1 mhz; 100 w. Ant -13 ft TL: N35 54 50 W100 22 57. Hrs open: 1006 S. Main St., Wheeler, 79096. Phone: (806) 826-5202. Licensee: Solid Rock Foundation. ◆Gary D. Ware, pres.

Canton

KRDH(AM)— Sept 12, 1963: 1510 khz; 500 w-D. TL: N32 41 02 W95 29 44. Hrs open: Sunrise-suset Box 868, Forney, 75126. Phone: (903) 567-5566. Fax: (903) 567-5567.E-mail: info@krdh.com Licensee: RDH Land & Cattle Co. Inc. (acq 10-20-2006; $185,000). Population served: 50,000 Format: Contemp Christian. News: 6 hrs wkly. Target aud: General. ◆Eric Jontra, gen mgr & stn mgr; Dee Cox, opns mgr, sls dir, progmg dir.

Canyon

KPUR-FM— Jan 12, 1981: 107.1 mhz; 6 kw. 315 ft TL: N35 05 09 W101 54 48. Stereo. Hrs open: 24 301 S. Polk, Suite 100, Amarillo, 79101. Phone: (806) 342-5200. Fax: (806) 342-5202.E-mail: rickmatchett@cumulus.com Web Site:www.kpur.com Licensee: Cumulus Licensing Corp. Group owner: Cumulus Media L.L.C (acq 5-98; $820,000 with KPUR(AM) Amarillo). Population served: 200,000 Format: Oldies. News staff: one; News: 5 hrs wkly. Target aud: 35-55; boomers. ◆Jim Worthington, gen mgr; Eric Stevens, opns mgr, progmg dir; Shannon Urton, sls dir, gen sls mgr; Shea White, prom dir; J.P. Wolf, chief of engrg.

*KWTS(FM)— 1971: 91.1 mhz; 6 kw. 141 ft TL: N34 58 59 W101 55 10. Stereo. Hrs open: 24 Box 1514, Wt. Stn, 79016. Phone: (806) 651-2797. Phone: (806) 651-2911. Fax: (806) 651-2818.E-mail: kwts@wtamu.edu Web Site:www.wtamu.edu/kwts Licensee: West Texas A & M University. Population served: 10,922 Format: Rock. News staff: 2; News: 3 hrs wkly. Target aud: 16-25. Spec prog: Class 4 hrs, jazz 3 hrs, Black 3 hrs, techo 5 hrs, acoustic 3 hrs, Britsh rock 3 hrs, Sp 3 hrs wkly. ◆Dr. Leigh Browning, pres; Evan Kolius, gen mgr; Elizabeth Wiseman, sls dir; Andi Law, prom dir; Anthony Smith, progmg dir; Randy Ray, chief of engrg.

KZRK(AM)—Licensed to Canyon. See Amarillo

KZRK-FM—Licensed to Canyon. See Amarillo

Carrizo Springs

KAJP(FM)— 2008: 93.5 mhz; 6 kw. Ant 328 ft TL: N28 27 09 W99 54 15. Hrs open: c/o Lerman Senter PLLC, 2000 K St. N.W., Suite 600, Washington, DC, 20006-1809. Phone: (202) 429-8970. Fax: (202) 293-7783. Licensee: Hispanic Target Media Inc. ◆Francisco San Millan, pres; Meredith Senter, gen mgr.

KBEN(AM)— Aug 9, 1955: 1450 khz; 1 kw-U. TL: N28 31 15 W99 51 30. Hrs open: 203 S. 4th St., 78834. Phone: (830) 876-3205. Licensee: Sylvia Mijares (acq 9-30-97; $41,250). Population served: 15,000 Rgnl. Network: Texas State Net. Borsari & Paxson. Format: Relg, Sp. Target aud: English & Sp listeners. ◆Gordon Baehre, gen mgr.

KCZO(FM)— 1991: 92.1 mhz; 3 kw. 296 ft TL: N28 33 24 W99 53 49. Hrs open: Box 252, McAllen, 78505. Secondary address: 4501 N. Mc Call Rd., McAllen 78504. Phone: (956) 686-6382. Fax: (956) 686-2999. Licensee: Paulino Bernal Evangelism. Format: Sp, Christian. ◆Eloy Bernal, gen mgr.

Carrollton

KJON(AM)— Dec 17, 1970: 850 khz; 5 kw-D, DA. TL: N33 16 42 W96 49 16. Hrs open: 521 E. Bolt St., Fort Worth, 76110. Phone: (817) 923-3424. Fax: (817) 923-3451.E-mail: info@kjonam.com Licensee: Chatham Hill Foundation Inc. (acq 12-13-2006; grpsl). Format: Sp Catholic. ◆Bob Prouse, gen mgr.

Carthage

KGAS(AM)— October 1955: 1590 khz; 2.5 kw-D, 130 w-N. TL: N32 09 12 W94 18 52. Hrs open: 215 S. Market St., 75633-2623. Phone: (903) 693-6668. Fax: (903) 693-7188. Web Site:www.kgasradio.com Licensee: Jerry T. Hanszen (acq 9-1-88). Population served: 20,000 Rgnl. Network: Texas State Net. Texas State Networks Wire Svc: NOAA Weather Format: All sports. Target aud: General. ◆Jerry Hanszen, gen mgr.

KGAS-FM— Aug 1, 1992: 104.3 mhz; 6 kw. Ant 328 ft TL: N32 08 11 W94 23 07. Stereo. Hrs open: 215 S. Market St., 75633-2623. Phone: (903) 693-6668. Fax: (903) 693-7188. Web Site:www.kgasradio.com Licensee: Jerry T. Hanszen. Population served: 80,000 Natl. Network: ABC, Westwood One, . Format: Country. ◆Jerry Hanszen, gen mgr.

KTUX(FM)—Licensed to Carthage. See Shreveport LA

Cedar Park

KDHT(FM)— Aug 1, 1961: 93.3 mhz; 100 kw. Ant 1,948 ft TL: N30 43 34 W97 59 23. Stereo. Hrs open: 8309 N. I-35, Austin, 78753. Phone: (512) 832-4000. Fax: (512) 832-4081.E-mail: info@590klbj.com Web Site:www.kxmg.com Licensee: Emmis Austin Radio Broadcasting Co. L.P. Group owner: Emmis Communications Corp. (acq 4-25-03; grpsl). Population served: 2,000,000 Format: CHR, dance. Target aud: 18-34; women & men who like current music. Spec prog: Pub service 2 hrs, Sp one hr, Latino one hr wkly. ◆Bruce Walden, gen mgr; Jeff Carrol, opns mgr; Brad Copland, gen sls mgr; Bob Lewis, progmg dir; Bradley Grein, mus dir; Todd Jeffries, news dir; Jim Henkel, chief of engrg; Lisa Melton, traf mgr.

Center

KDET(AM)— Feb 22, 1949: 930 khz; 1 kw-D, 36 w-N. TL: N31 50 03 W94 12 53. Hrs open: Box 400, 307 San Augustine St., 75935. Phone: (936) 598-3304. Fax: (936) 598-9537. Licensee: Center Broadcasting Co. Inc. (group owner; (acq 3-26-98; grpsl). Population served: 29,000 Rgnl. Network: Texas State Net. Natl. Rep: Riley,. Texas State Networks Format: Southern gospel, country, Sp. ◆Lori Collins, stn mgr; Rob Rockett, opns mgr; Rachel Sanz, news dir.

KQBB(FM)— July 5, 1978: 100.5 mhz; 2.05 kw. Ant 567 ft TL: N31 43 34 W94 15 27. Stereo. Hrs open: Box 930, 75935. Secondary address: 307 San Augustine St. 75935. Phone: (936) 598-3304. Fax: (936) 598-9537. Licensee: Center Broadcasting Co. Inc. Format: Country. Shelby County. ◆Lori Alvis, gen mgr, gen sls mgr; Rob Rockett, opns mgr; Rachel Sanz, news dir.

Centerville

KKEV(FM)—Not on air, target date: unknown: 103.5 mhz; 6 kw. Ant 283 ft TL: N31 16 46 W95 59 00. Hrs open: 3654 W. Jarvis Ave., Skokie, IL, 60076. Phone: (847) 674-0864. Fax: (847) 674-9188. Web Site:www.kmcommunications.com Licensee: KM Communications Inc. ◆Kevin Joel Bae, VP & gen mgr.

KUZN(FM)— 2001: 105.9 mhz; 25 kw. Ant 328 ft TL: N31 16 56 W95 53 42. Stereo. Hrs open: 24 912 Curtis Ave., Pasedena, 77504. Phone: (713) 589-1336. Fax: (713) 589-1335.E-mail: info@radioaleluya.org Web Site:www.radioaleluya.org Licensee: Aleluya Christian Broadcasting Inc. (acq 2-26-2008). Pillsbury Winthrop Shaw Pittman LLP. Format: Sp relg. ◆Ruben Villarreul, gen mgr.

Charlotte

KSAQ(FM)—Not on air, target date: unknown: 102.3 mhz; 6 kw. Ant 328 ft TL: N28 45 29 W98 38 01. Hrs open: 11700 S.W. Tangerine Ct., Palm City, FL, 34990-5801. Phone: (772) 215-1634. Licensee: Gary S. Hess (acq 11-7-2008; grpsl). ◆Gary S. Hess, gen mgr.

Childress

KCHT(FM)—Not on air, target date: unknown: 104.1 mhz; 50 kw. Ant 253 ft TL: N34 13 41 W100 18 17. Hrs open: 6117 Lemon Thyme Dr., Alexandria, VA, 22310. Phone: (571) 228-1258. Fax: (703) 299-6626. Licensee: Miriam Media Inc. ◆Darryl Delawder, pres & gen mgr.

KCTX(AM)— May 8, 1947: 1510 khz; 250 w-D. TL: N34 25 41 W100 13 47. Hrs open: 6:30 AM-6 PM Box 540, 79201-0540. Secondary address: 1111 16th St. N.W. 79201. Phone: (940) 937-6316. Fax: (940) 937-6551.E-mail: kctxradio@gmail.com Licensee: James G. Boles (acq 1-9-2006 $232,000 with KCTX-FM Childress plus land in Turkey, TX). Population served: 6,870 Rgnl. Network: Voice of the S.W. Format: Oldies. ◆James Boles, gen mgr; Chao Ware, gen sls mgr; J. Scott, progmg dir; Mona Boles, traf mgr.

KCTX-FM— July 1, 1984: 96.1 mhz; 50 kw. 520 ft TL: N34 26 20 W100 13 10. Stereo. Hrs open: Box 540, 79201. Secondary address: 1111 16th St. N.W. 79201. Phone: (940) 937-6316. Fax: (940) 937-6551.E-mail: kctxradio@gmail.com Licensee: James G. Boles (acq 1-9-2006; $232,000 with KCTX(AM) Childress plus land in Turkey, TX). Natl. Rep: Riley,. Format: Country. Target aud: General. Spec prog: Relg 5 hrs wkly. ◆James Boles, gen mgr; Chad Ware, gen sls mgr, news dir; J. Scott, progmg dir.

*KFCH(FM)—Not on air, target date: unknown: 89.5 mhz; 150 w. Ant 186 ft TL: N34 25 21.8 W100 12 12.8. Hrs open: 401 Avenue B S.E., 79201-5533. Phone: (940) 937-8015. Licensee: Centro de Milagros Congregation Inc. Format: Sp. ◆Daniel Garcia, pres.

Clarendon

KEFH(FM)— September 2000: 99.3 mhz; 44 kw. Ant 522 ft TL: N35 04 36 W100 53 33. Hrs open: 24 Box 370, 79226-0370. Phone: (806) 874-2296. Fax: (806) 874-4411.E-mail: kefh@ka1993.net Licensee: RoHo Broadcasting Co. Format: Oldies. ◆Ken Meinhart, gen mgr, progmg dir; Patrick Robertson, rgnl sls mgr; John Wolfe, chief of engrg; Carol Hinton, traf mgr.

Clarksville

KCAR(AM)— Apr 27, 1956: 1350 khz; 500 w-D, 50 w-N. TL: N33 36 41 W95 01 01. Hrs open: 24 228 W. Main St., 75426. Phone: (903) 427-3861. Fax: (903) 427-5524.E-mail: kool985@@neato.net Licensee: American Media Investments Inc. Group owner: Petracom Media LLC (acq 2-17-2009; grpsl). Population served: 14,497 Natl. Network: Jones Radio Networks, . Rgnl. Network: VSA Radio, Texas State Net. Texas State Networks Wiley Rein LLP. Format: Classic country. News: 10 hrs wkly. Target aud: General; rural, agricultural, middle-aged. Spec prog: Gospel 6 hrs, sports 10 hrs, farm 2 hrs wkly. ◆Mike Monday, progmg dir; Dale Gorsuch, chief of engrg; Tex Phillips, gen mgr, sls dir & disc jockey.

KGAP(FM)— Dec 11, 1990: 98.5 mhz; 50 kw. Ant 328 ft TL: N33 35 47 W95 01 03. Stereo. Hrs open: 24 228 W. Main St., 75426. Phone: (903) 427-3861. Fax: (903) 427-5524.E-mail: kool985@neato.net Licensee: American Media Investments Inc. (acq 2-17-2009; grpsl). Natl. Network: ABC, . Format: Oldies. News: one hr wkly. Target aud: 25-64. ◆Tex Phillips, CEO & sls dir.

Claude

KARX(FM)—Licensed to Claude. See Amarillo

Cleburne

KHFX(AM)— April 1947: 1140 khz; 5 kw-D, 710 w-N, DA-2. TL: N32 16 57 W97 24 47. Hrs open: 24 Box 1629, 76033. Secondary address: 305 Milsap Hwy., Mineral Wells 76067. Phone: (817) 645-1150. Fax: (817) 645-3944.E-mail: info@kcleam.com Licensee: Siga Broadcasting Corp. Group owner: First Broadcasting Investment Partners LLC (acq 9-24-2008; $1.4 million). Population served: 100,000 Rgnl. Network: Texas State Net. Format: Country. ◆Gabriel Arango, pres.

Cleveland

KTHT(FM)— Jan 17, 1993: 97.1 mhz; 100 kw. Ant 1,847 ft TL: N30 32 06 W95 01 04. Stereo. Hrs open: 1990 Post Oak Blvd., Suite 2300, Houston, 77056. Phone: (713) 622-5533. Fax: (713) 993-9300. Web Site:www.countrylegends971.com Licensee: Cox Radio Inc. Group owner: Cox Broadcasting (acq 8-15-2000; grpsl). Format: Country classics. ◆Caroline Devine, gen mgr; Judy Lakin, gen sls mgr; John Chaing, progmg dir; Ed Wilson, engr.

Clifton

KWOW(FM)— 1989: 104.1 mhz; 16 kw. Ant 459 ft TL: N31 44 05 W97 19 17. Stereo. Hrs open: 24 6401 Cobbs Dr., Waco, 76710-2536. Phone: (254) 772-6104. Fax: (254) 772-0642. Web Site:www.laley104.com Licensee: BMP Waco License Company L.P. Group owner: Amigo Broadcasting L.P. (acq 11-9-2004; grpsl). Natl. Rep: Lotus Entravision Reps LLC,. Blooston, Mordkofsky, Jackson & Dickens. Format: Sp, Mexican rgnl. Target aud: 18-54; adults. ◆Bob Proud, sr VP; Cynthia Lopez, gen mgr, opns mgr; Jaime Martinez, progmg dir; Darrel Heckendorf, chief of engrg.

Coahoma

KWDC(FM)— 2006: 105.5 mhz; 5.1 kw. Ant 358 ft TL: N32 21 52 W101 19 35. Hrs open: Rebroadcasts KSRD(FM) Saint Joseph, MO 100%. c/o KSRD(FM), 1212 Faraon St., Saint Joseph, MO, 64501. Phone: (816) 233-5773. Fax: (816) 233-5777. Web Site:www.ksrdradio.com Licensee: Horizon Christian Fellowship. (acq 2-9-2006; grpsl). Format: Christian. ◆Mike MacIntosh, pres; Brian KC Jones, gen mgr.

Cockrell Hill

KRVA(AM)—Licensed to Cockrell Hill. See Dallas

Coleman

KQBZ(FM)— 1974: 102.3 mhz; 12 kw. Ant 689 ft TL: N31 44 54 W99 19 57. Stereo. Hrs open: Dups AM 100% Box 100, Brownwood, 76804. Phone: (325) 646-3535. Fax: (541) 889-8733. Population served: 9,900 ◆Kyle Dennis, gen mgr & progmg dir.

KSTA(AM)— Nov 1, 1947: 1000 khz; 250 w-D. TL: N31 51 16 W99 25 36. Hrs open: 600 Fisk Dr, Brownwood, 76801. Phone: (325) 646-3535. Fax: (325) 646-5347.E-mail: ksta1000@web-access.net Licensee: Tackett-Boazman Broadcasting LP. (group owner; (acq 4-11-2006; grpsl). Population served: 20,000 Natl. Network: Jones Radio Networks, . Rgnl. Network: Texas State Net., VSA Radio. Texas State Networks Format: Classic country. Target aud: General. Spec prog: Farm 14 hrs, Sp 5 hrs, gospel 7 hrs wkly. ◆Mikey Wayne, gen mgr, progmg dir; Stan Cooper, chief of engrg.

College Station

*KAMU-FM— Mar 30, 1977: 90.9 mhz; 32 kw. 340 ft TL: N30 37 48 W96 20 33. (CP: 2.4 kw horiz, 32 kw vert). Stereo. Hrs open: 6 AM-midnight Moore Communications Ctr., 4244 TAMU, 77843-4244. Phone: (979) 845-5613. Fax: (979) 845-1643.E-mail: kamu@tamu.edu Web Site:kamutamu.edu Licensee: Texas A&M University. Population served: 120,000 Natl. Network: NPR, PRI, . Format: Bluegrass, news, class, jazz. News: 35 hrs wkly. Target aud: General. Spec prog: Folk 3 hrs, new age 5 hrs, international 5 hrs wkly. ◆Rodney L. Zent, gen mgr; Penny Zent, stn mgr; Elaine Hoyak, dev dir; Richard Howard, progmg dir; Ken Nelson, engrg dir; Ed Hadden, chief of engrg; Yildiz McNew, traf mgr.

***KEOS(FM)**— Mar 25, 1995: 89.1 mhz; 100 w vert. 254 ft TL: N30 38 54 W96 23 23. (CP: 1 kw). Stereo. Hrs open: 24 Box 78, 77841. Secondary address: 207 E. Carson St., Bryan 77801-1404. Phone: (979) 779-5367. Fax: (979) 779-7259.E-mail: keos@keos.org Web Site:www.keos.org Licensee: Brazos Educational Radio. Population served: 130,000 Natl. Network: PRI, . Format: News/talk, educ. News staff: News progmg 25 hrs wkly Target aud: General. Spec prog: Folk 10 hrs, gospel 3 hrs, jazz 3 hrs, Jewish & Israeli 2 hrs wkly. ♦Mark McCann, pres; Linda Gunderson, CFO; Jeff White, gen mgr, progmg dir; Tom Schwerdt, opns dir; Chad Brinkley, dev dir; John Roths, mus dir; George Weber, pub affrs dir; Lance Parr, chief of engrg; Mark Purcell, traf mgr; Leann Weatherby, spec ev coord; Reta Taylor, relg ed; Harvey John Miller, disc jockey.

KKYS(FM)—See Bryan

***KLGS(FM)**— 2007: 89.9 mhz; 8.4 kw vert. Ant 358 ft TL: N30 28 35 W96 25 57. Hrs open:
Rebroadcasts WAFR(FM) Tupelo, MS 100%.
Drawer 2440, Tupelo, MS, 38803. Phone: (662) 844-8888. Fax: (662) 842-6791. Web Site:www.afr.net Licensee: American Family Association. (acq 1-3-2006; $10 for CP). Format: Christian. ♦Marvin Sanders, gen mgr.

KNDE(FM)— Aug 8, 1964: 95.1 mhz; 36 kw. Ant 571 ft TL: N30 41 18 W96 25 35. Stereo. Hrs open: Prog sep from AM 2700 Earl Rudder Fwy. S., Suite 5000, 77845. Phone: (979) 846-1150. Fax: (979) 846-1933.E-mail: radio@wtaw.com Format: Top 40 hits. ♦Bobby Mason, progmg dir.

KTAM(AM)—See Bryan

KZNE(AM)— Oct 2, 1922: 1150 khz; 1 kw-D, 500 w-N, DA-N. TL: N30 38 05 W96 21 20. Stereo. Hrs open: 24 2700 Earl Rudder Fwy. S., Suite 5000, 77845. Phone: (979) 846-1150. Fax: (979) 846-1933.E-mail: radio@wtaw.com Web Site:www.kzne.com Licensee: Bryan Broadcasting Corp. (group owner; acq 8-7-97; with co-located FM). Population served: 120000 Format: Sports. News staff: 3; News: 58 hrs wkly. Target aud: 25-54. Spec prog: Farm 10 hrs wkly. ♦William R. Hicks, pres; Benjamin D. Downs, gen mgr; Sam Jones, sls dir, gen sls mgr; Louie Belina, progmg dir; Chace Murphy, news dir.

WTAW(AM)— May 2000: 1620 khz; 10 kw-D, 1 kw-N. TL: N30 37 54 W96 21 28. Hrs open: Box 3248, Bryan, 77805. Secondary address: 2700 Rudder Fwy., Suite 5000 77845. Phone: (979) 846-1150. Fax: (979) 846-1933.E-mail: radio@wtaw.com Web Site:www.wtaw.com Licensee: Bryan Broadcasting Corp. (group owner). Format: News/talk. ♦Benjamin D. Downs, gen mgr; Sam Jones, gen sls mgr; Scott Delucia, progmg dir; Chris Dusterhoff, chief of engrg; Alisa Dusterhoff, traf mgr.

Colorado City

KAUM(FM)— Mar 29, 1983: 107.1 mhz; 3 kw. Ant 157 ft TL: N32 23 15 W100 53 33. Stereo. Hrs open: Box 990, 79512. Phone: (325) 728-5224. Fax: (325) 728-5224. Web Site:www.realcountryonline.com Population served: 5,227 Format: Country. ♦Jim Baum, gen mgr & farm dir.

KVMC(AM)— June 16, 1950: 1320 khz; 1 kw-D. TL: N32 23 15 W100 53 33. Hrs open: Box 990, 79512. Phone: (325) 728-5224. Fax: (325) 728-5224. Web Site:www.realcountryonline.com Licensee: James G. Baum (acq 2-13-81; $395,000;3-9-81). Population served: 5,227 Rgnl. Network: Texas State Net. Texas State Networks Format: Country. ♦Jim Baum, pres & gen mgr; Gary Graham, chief of engrg.

Columbus

KULM-FM— Sept 3, 1973: 98.3 mhz; 6 kw. Ant 253 ft TL: N29 42 03 W96 34 24. Stereo. Hrs open: 24 Box 111, 78934. Secondary address: 325 Radio Ln. 78934. Phone: (979) 732-5766. Fax: (979) 732-6377.E-mail: kulmradio@aol.com Licensee: Roy E. Henderson. Group owner: Fort Bend Broadcasting Co. (acq 5-16-2000; grpsl). Population served: 30,000 Natl. Network: ABC, . Rgnl. Network: Texas State Net. Texas State Networks Format: C&W. News: 12 hrs wkly. Target aud: General. Spec prog: Polka 12 hrs wkly. ♦Roy Henderson, pres; Steve Smith, CFO; Carl Geisler, stn mgr, sls dir, progmg dir; Ray Nelson, chief of engrg; Judy Barrett, traf mgr.

Comanche

KCOM(AM)— Apr 1, 1962: 1550 khz; 250 w-D. TL: N31 53 54 W98 35 14. Hrs open: 24 218 N Austin St., 76442-2429. Phone: (325) 356-2558. Fax: (325) 356-3120.E-mail: kcom@comanchetx.com Web Site:www.kcomam.com Licensee: CCR-Stephenville III LLC. (acq 8-2-2005; $164,000). Population served: 21,000 Rgnl. Network: Texas State Net. Texas State Networks Format: Country Gospel. Target aud: 35-64; Men & Women. Spec prog: Gospel 5 hrs wkly. ♦Joseph Schwartz, pres; Marcus Nettleton, gen mgr, opns mgr; John Barnes, gen sls mgr; Peggy Vineyard, progmg dir, pub affrs dir, traf mgr, disc jockey; Stan Cooper, chief of engrg; Bill Cole, disc jockey.

KYOX(FM)— March 1999: 94.3 mhz; 32 kw. 620 ft TL: N31 54 51 W98 41 48. Stereo. Hrs open: 218 N. Austin St., 76442. Phone: (325) 356-3090. Fax: (325) 356-3120.E-mail: kyox@comanchetx.com Web Site:www.kyoxfm.com Licensee: CCR-Stephenville III LLC. Group owner: Cherry Creek Radio LLC (acq 6-10-2004; grpsl). Population served: 94,000 Format: Traditional country. Target aud: 35-64; men & women. ♦Richard Niblett, gen mgr; Jerri Lynn Robinson, gen sls mgr, mus dir; Pam Niblett, progmg dir, news dir; Justin McClure, chief of engrg.

Comfort

KGSX(FM)— Feb 26, 1994: 95.1 mhz; 100 kw. Ant 659 ft TL: N29 38 03 W98 47 57.8. Stereo. Hrs open: 24 1717 N. E. Loop 410, Suite 400, San Antonio, 78217. Phone: (210) 829-1075. Licensee: Univision Radio License Corp. Group owner: Univision Radio (acq 9-22-2003; grpsl). Population served: 1,367,500 Thompson, Hine & Flory. Format: Sp. News staff: one; News: 4 hrs wkly. Target aud: 25-54; average, middle income with small town & rural lifestyle. ♦Mac Tichenor, pres; Dan Wilson, gen mgr; Rick Thomas, opns dir & opns mgr.

Commerce

***KETR(FM)**— Apr 7, 1975: 88.9 mhz; 100 kw. 400 ft TL: N33 14 17 W95 55 27. Stereo. Hrs open: 24 Box 4504, Performing Arts Ctr., 2600 S. Neal, 75429. Phone: (903) 886-5848. Fax: (903) 886-5850.E-mail: ketr@ketr.org Web Site:ketr.org Licensee: Board of Regents Texas A&M University-Commerce. Natl. Network: NPR, . Format: Jazz, adult contemp, news. News staff: one; News: 7 hrs wkly. Target aud: 21-66; general. Spec prog: Bluegrass 3 hrs wkly. ♦Beverly Nanos, gen sls mgr; Vicki Holloway, gen mgr, stn mgr & progmg dir; Mark Chapman, mus dir; Kevin Jeffries, news dir; Robert Goodwin, chief of engrg; Deborah Smith, traf mgr; Brad Kellar, news rptr.

***KYJC(FM)**— 2005: 91.3 mhz; 350 w horiz. Ant 174 ft TL: N33 15 37 W95 52 59. Hrs open: CSN International Inc., 4022 N. 3300 E., Twin Falls, ID, 83301. Phone: (208) 734-6633. Fax: (208) 736-1958. Web Site:www.csnradio.com Licensee: CSN International Inc. Group owner: CSN International (acq 3-6-2003). ♦Mike Stocklin, gen mgr; Don Mills, progmg dir; Kelly Carlson, chief of engrg.

Comstock

KOAH(AM)—Not on air, target date: unknown: 1450 khz; 1 kw-U. TL: N29 40 50 W101 13 00. Hrs open: 8320 W. 66th Ave., Arvada, CO, 80004. Phone: (303) 431-0103. Licensee: Better Life Ministries. ♦Claud Pettit, pres.

Conroe

***KAFR(FM)**— October 1998: 88.3 mhz; 100 kw vert. Ant 443 ft TL: N30 27 52 W95 30 20. Hrs open: American Family Radio, Box3206, Tupelo, MS, 38803. Phone: (662) 844-8888. Fax: (662) 842-6791.E-mail: comments@afr.net Web Site:www.afr.net Licensee: American Family Association. Group owner: American Family Radio. Format: Inspirational Christian. ♦Marvin Sanders, gen mgr.

KHPT(FM)— Feb 14, 1965: 106.9 mhz; 91.6 kw. Ant 1,899 ft TL: N30 13 53 W95 07 26. Stereo. Hrs open: 1990 Post Oak Blvd., Suite 2300, Houston, 77056. Phone: (713) 963-1200. Fax: (713) 622-5457. Web Site:www.1069thepoint.com Licensee: Cox Radio Inc. Group owner: Cox Broadcasting (acq 8-24-2000; grpsl). Format: Hits of the 80s music. ♦Mark Krieschen, VP, gen mgr; Beth Lavine, gen sls mgr; Mike Murray, natl sls mgr; Shana Sonnier, mktg dir; Dain Craig, progmg dir.

KJOJ(AM)— Apr 16, 1951: 880 khz; 10 kw-D, 1 kw-N, DA-2. TL: N30 17 38 W95 25 55. Stereo. Hrs open: Little Saigon Radio, 7080 Southwest Fwy., Houston, 77074. Phone: (713) 271-7888. Fax: (713) 271-9333. Web Site:www.littlesaigonradio.com Licensee: Liberman Broadcasting of Houston License LLC. Group owner: Liberman Broadcasting Inc. (acq 3-20-2001; grpsl). Format: Ethnic Vietnamese. ♦Winter Horton, gen mgr.

KYOK(AM)— Apr 13, 1981: 1140 khz; 5 kw-D, DA. TL: N30 20 40 W95 27 32. Hrs open: 300 E. Bryant Rd., 77301. Phone: (936) 441-1140. Fax: (936) 788-1140.E-mail: info@kyokradio.com Web Site:www.kyokradio.com Licensee: Martin Broadcasting Inc. (acq 2-10-92; $175,000; 3-2-92). Population served: 35000 Format: Gospel. Target aud: 24-55. ♦Darrell Martin, pres, stn mgr; Nicholas Martin, stn mgr; Roland Booker, sls dir, prom dir & progmg dir; Dave Biondi, chief of engrg.

Converse

KTMR(AM)— July 28, 1980: 1130 khz; 25 kw-D, DA. TL: N29 19 10 W97 58 35. Hrs open: 1302 N. Shepherd Dr., Houston, 77008. Phone: (713) 868-5559. Fax: (713) 868-9631.E-mail: docarango@houston.rr.com Web Site:www.bizradio.com Licensee: SIGA Broadcasting Corp. (group owner; (acq 5-4-99; $333,750). Format: Business talk. ♦Gabriel Arango, gen mgr.

Copperas Cove

KNCT-FM—See Killeen

KSSM(FM)— Nov 21, 1977: 103.1 mhz; 8.6 kw. 276 ft TL: N31 05 05 W97 57 07. Stereo. Hrs open: 24 608 Moody Ln., Temple, 76504. Phone: (254) 773-5252. Fax: (254) 773-0115.E-mail: bourdon.wooter@cumulus.com Web Site:www.1031kissfm.com Licensee: Cumulus Licensing Corp. Group owner: Cumulus Media Inc. (acq 2-2-00). Population served: 250000 Natl. Rep: Interep,. Cohn & Marks. Format: Urban adult contemp. News: 3 hrs wkly. Target aud: 25-54. Spec prog: Gospel. ♦Bourdon Wooten, gen mgr; Mikie Cummings, gen sls mgr; Jamie Garrett, prom dir, news dir; Mark Raymond, progmg dir; Doug Bernhardt, chief of engrg, engr.

Corpus Christi

***KBNJ(FM)**— January 1985: 91.7 mhz; 5 kw. 500 ft TL: N27 46 43 W97 37 57. Stereo. Hrs open: 24 Box 270068, 78427. Phone: (361) 855-0975/76. Fax: (361) 855-0977.E-mail: kbnj@lwrn.org Web Site:www.kbnj.org Licensee: World Radio Network Inc. (group owner; acq 6-5-84; $36,000; 5-21-84). Natl. Network: Moody, USA, . Format: Relg, educ, English. News: 7 hrs wkly. Target aud: General. ♦Joe Fahl, gen mgr, stn mgr & progmg mgr; Jimmy Stinson, mus dir, chief of engrg.

KBSO(FM)— 1992: 94.7 mhz; 3 kw. 285 ft TL: N27 49 50 W97 32 34. Hrs open: 701 Benys Rd., 78408. Phone: (361) 289-0999.E-mail: davilabroadcasti@bizstx.rr.com Licensee: Reina Broadcasting Inc. Format: Texas radio. ♦Manuel Davila Jr., gen mgr.

KCCT(AM)— June 1954: 1150 khz; 1 kw-D, 500 w-N, DA-2. TL: N27 48 01 W97 28 44. Stereo. Hrs open: 24 701 Benys Rd., 78408. Phone: (361) 289-0999. Fax: (361) 289-0810.E-mail: davilabroadcasti@bizstx.rr.com Licensee: Radio KCCT Inc. (acq 8-15-74). Population served: 240,000 Format: Talk. ♦Manuel Davila Jr., pres, VP, gen sls mgr & progmg dir; George Sanders, chief of engrg.

KCTA(AM)— Oct 24, 1959: 1030 khz; 50,000 kw-D. TL: N27 56 01 W97 15 34. Hrs open: Sunrise-sunset 1602 S. Brownlee Blvd., 78404. Phone: (361) 882-7711. Fax: (361) 882-3038.E-mail: kcta@usawide.net Web Site:www.kctaradio.com Licensee: Broadcasting Corp. of the Southwest. (acq 1959). Population served: 210,000 Natl. Network: USA, . Format: Relg. Target aud: 35 plus. Spec prog: Sp 6 hrs wkly. ♦Bill York, pres, gen mgr; David Freymiller, opns mgr.

KDAE(AM)—(Sinton, 1954: 1590 khz; 1 kw-D, 500 w-N, DA-2. TL: N28 01 16 W97 28 14. Stereo. Hrs open: 24 Box 260715, 78426. Secondary address: 929 N. Padre Island Dr. 78406. Phone: (361) 299-1982. Fax: (361) 299-1049. Web Site:www.radiolibertad.net Licensee: The Worship Center of Kingsville. (acq 1-11-99). Population served: 353,000 Natl. Network: ABC, . Natl. Rep: McGavren Guild,. Fisher, Wayland, Cooper, Leader & Zaragoza L.L.P. Format: MOR, Spanish, Christian. News staff: one; News: 2 hrs wkly. Target aud: 35-64. Spec prog: Farm 6 hrs wkly. ♦Rufino Sendejo, gen mgr; A.J. Solis, progmg dir; George Sanders, chief of engrg.

***KEDT-FM**— Mar 2, 1982: 90.3 mhz; 100 kw. 802 ft TL: N27 39 12 W97 33 55. Stereo. Hrs open: 24 4455 S. Padre Island Dr., Suite 38, 78411-4481. Phone: (361) 855-2213. Fax: (361) 855-3877.E-mail: info@kedt.pbs.org Web Site:www.kedt.org Licensee: South Texas Public Broadcasting System Inc. Natl. Network: NPR, . Schwartz, Woods & Miller. Format: Class, news, jazz. Latin. News staff: one; News: 37 hrs wkly. Target aud: General. Spec prog: Sp 4 hrs wkly. ♦Don Dunlap, pres, gen mgr; Myra Lombardo, VP; Bob Scott, chief of engrg.

KEYS(AM)— March 1941: 1440 khz; 1 kw-U, DA-N. TL: N27 47 02 W97 27 29. Hrs open: 24 Box 9757, 78469. Secondary address: 2117 Leopard St. 78408. Phone: (361) 883-3516. Fax: (361) 882-9767.E-mail: johngifford1440@yahoo.com Web Site:www.1440keys.com Licensee:

Malkan AM Associates L.P. (acq 1965). Population served: 285,000 Natl. Network: ABC, . Natl. Rep: Katz Radio,. Texas State Networks Thompson Hine. Wire Svc: Accu-Weather Format: News/talk, sports. News: . Target aud: 25 +. ♦Glen Powers, pres, gen mgr, progmg dir; Janice Raleigh, sls dir; Nick Russo, prom dir.

KFTX(FM)—See Kingsville

KKBA(FM)—See Kingsville

***KKLM(FM)**— Mar 11, 1991: 88.7 mhz; 8 kw. Ant 866 ft TL: N27 44 29 W97 36 09. Stereo. Hrs open: 24
Rebroadcasts KLVR(FM) Middletown, CA 100%.
5700 W. Oaks Blvd., Rocklin, CA, 95765. Phone: (860) 434-8400. Fax: (916) 251-1650.E-mail: info@klove.com Web Site:www.klove.com Licensee: Educational Media Foundation. Group owner: EMF Broadcasting (acq 6-5-2002; $500,000). Population served: 350,000 Natl. Network: K-Love, . Format: Comtemp Christian. News: 10 hrs wkly. Target aud: 35 plus. ♦Richard Jenkins, pres; Keith Whipple, gen mgr.

KKTX(AM)— 2002: 1360 khz; 1 kw-U. TL: N27 48 01 W97 27 41. Hrs open: 24 Prog sep from FM Radio Plaza, 501 Tupper Ln., Corpus Cristi, 78417. Phone: (361) 289-0111. Fax: (361) 289-5024.E-mail: scottjohnson@clearchannel.com Web Site:www.1360online.com Licensee: Capstar TX L.P. Population served: 300,000 Natl. Network: ABC, . Format: News/talk. Target aud: 2-18; children. ♦Matt Martrin, gen mgr; Zee Zepola, sls dir; Scott Johnson, progmg dir; Russell Vaughan, chief of engrg.

KLTG(FM)— Sept 1, 1967: 96.5 mhz; 97 kw. 955 ft TL: N27 44 28 W97 36 08. Stereo. Hrs open: Box 898, 78403. Phone: (361) 883-1600. Fax: (361) 888-5685. Web Site:www.thebeach965online.com Licensee: Tejas Broadcasting Ltd. LLP. Group owner: Amigo Broadcasting L.P. (acq 11-15-2004; grpsl). Population served: 500,000 Format: Hot AC. Target aud: 25-54. ♦Gloria Apolinario, gen mgr & progmg dir.

KMIQ(FM)—(Robstown, July 23, 1989: 104.9 mhz; 3 kw. Ant 298 ft TL: N27 40 39 W97 38 20. (CP: 104.9 mhz; 50 kw, ant 492 ft. TL: N27 56 08 W97 56 19). Stereo. Hrs open: Box 270547, 78427. Phone: (361) 289-8877. Fax: (361) 289-7722. Licensee: Cotton Broadcasting. Format: Tejano. Target aud: 18 plus. Spec prog: Relg 6 hrs wkly. ♦Carlo Lopez, gen mgr; Santos Leal, progmg dir.

KMJR(FM)—See Portland

KMXR(FM)— January 1970: 93.9 mhz; 100 kw. 840 ft TL: N27 46 50 W97 38 03. Stereo. Hrs open: 24 501 Tupper Ln., 78417. Phone: (361) 289-0111. Fax: (361) 289-5035.E-mail: oldies939@aol.com Web Site:www.939online.com Licensee: Capstar TX L.P. Group owner: Clear Channel Communications Inc. (acq 8-30-00; grpsl). Population served: 422,300 Natl. Network: AP Radio, . Format: Oldies. News staff: one; News: 5 hrs wkly. Target aud: 25-54. ♦Matt Martin, gen mgr.

KNCN(FM)—(Sinton, July 1, 1972: 101.3 mhz; 100 kw. 401 ft TL: N27 55 24 W97 25 26. Stereo. Hrs open: 24 Radio Plaza, 501 Tupper Ln., 78417. Phone: (361) 289-0111. Fax: (361) 289-5035.E-mail: c101@clearchannel.com Web Site:www.c101.com Licensee: Capstar TX L.P. Group owner: Clear Channel Communications Inc. (acq 8-30-00; grpsl). Population served: 275,000 Format: Active rock. News: one hr wkly. Target aud: 18-49; active. Spec prog: Coastal Bend Forum one hr, In Concert 2 hrs, In the Studio one hr, Flashback 2 hrs wkly. ♦Matt Martin, gen mgr.

KOUL(FM)—(Sinton, May 20, 1968: 103.7 mhz; 100 kw. 941 ft TL: N28 02 05 W97 26 10. Stereo. Hrs open: Box 898, 78403. Secondary address: 1300 Antelope 78401. Phone: (361) 883-1600. Fax: (361) 883-9303. Web Site:www.koul1037.com Licensee: Tejas Broadcasting Ltd. LLP. Group owner: Amigo Broadcasting L.P. (acq 11-15-2004; grpsl). Format: C&W. Target aud: 25-49; general. ♦Chuck Brooks, pres; Kent Cooper, gen mgr, stn mgr; Clayton Allen, opns mgr, progmg dir; Shannon Mortenson, gen sls mgr; KC Sheperd, prom dir; Paul Danitz, adv mgr; Lisa Del Rey, pub affrs dir; Russell Vaughan, chief of engrg; Debra Reid, traf mgr.

KRYS-FM— Dec 5, 1982: 99.1 mhz; 100 kw. 1,049 ft TL: N27 45 07 W97 38 18. (CP: 97 kw). Stereo. Hrs open: 24 Radio Plaza, 501 Tupper Ln., 78417. Phone: (361) 289-0111. Fax: (361) 289-5024.E-mail: info@krysfm.com Web Site:www.krysfm.com Licensee: Capstar TX L.P. Group owner: Clear Channel Communications Inc. (acq 8-30-00; grpsl). Population served: 360,000 Natl. Network: ABC, . Format: Country. News staff: one. Target aud: 25-54. ♦Matt Martin, gen mgr; Zee Zepola, sls dir & gen sls mgr; Frank Edwards, prom dir, progmg dir; Lou Ramirez, mus dir; Russell Vaughn, chief of engrg; Pamela Anaya, traf mgr.

KSIX(AM)— September 1947: 1230 khz; 1 kw-U. TL: N27 48 09 W97 27 14. Stereo. Hrs open: 24 710 Buffalo St., Suite 608, 78416. Phone: (361) 882-5749. Fax: (361) 884-1240.E-mail: info@espn1230ksix.com Web Site:www.espn1230ksix.com Licensee: Withers Family Texas Holding LP (acq 10-28-02). Population served: 232,000 Natl. Network: ESPN Radio, . Format: Sports. ♦Jim Withers, gen mgr; Scott Howe, gen sls mgr; Bill Doerner, progmg dir; Valerie Smith, traf mgr.

KUNO(AM)— May 1950: 1400 khz; 1 kw-U. TL: N27 45 36 W97 26 14. Stereo. Hrs open: 24 Radio Plaza, 501 Tupper Ln., 78417-9736. Phone: (361) 289-0111. Fax: (361) 289-5035. Licensee: Capstar TX L.P. Group owner: Clear Channel Communications Inc. (acq 8-30-00; grpsl). Population served: 360,000 Format: Sp. News: 17 hrs wkly. Target aud: 25-64. ♦Matt Martin, gen mgr.

KZFM(FM)— Dec 7, 1964: 95.5 mhz; 100 kw. Ant 991 ft TL: N27 39 33 W97 34 12. Stereo. Hrs open: 24 Box 9757, 78469. Secondary address: 2117 Leopard St. 78408. Phone: (361) 883-3516. Fax: (361) 882-9767.E-mail: thechief@star94.net Web Site:www.hotz95.com Licensee: Malkan FM Associates L.P. Group owner: Malkan Broadcast Assoc. (acq 1976). Population served: 500,000 Natl. Rep: Katz Radio,. Thompson Hine. Format: CHR. Target aud: 18-34; female. ♦Glen Powers, pres, stn mgr; Janice Raleigh, gen sls mgr, prom dir; Gino Flores, prom dir; Ed Ocanas, progmg dir; Arlene Cordell, mus dir; John Gifford, chief of engrg.

Corrigan

KYTM(FM)—Not on air, target date: unknown: 99.3 mhz; 6 kw. Ant 282 ft TL: N31 06 48 W94 48 29. Hrs open: 1819 Cherokee Rose Cir., Mt. Pleasant, SC, 29466. Licensee: Tammy L. Pearce. ♦Tammy Pearce, gen mgr.

Corsicana

KAND(AM)— May 17, 1937: 1340 khz; 1 kw-U. TL: N32 06 53 W96 27 47. Hrs open: 24 1504 N. Beaton St., 75110. Secondary address: Box 2998 75151. Phone: (903) 874-7421. Phone: (903) 874-1340. Fax: (903) 874-0789. Web Site:www.kandradio.com Licensee: Yates Communications LLC (acq 5-17-2008; $105,000). Population served: 22,900 Rgnl. Network: Texas State Net. Texas State Networks Format: Talk. News staff: one; News: 25 hrs wkly. Target aud: General. ♦Mike Taylor, gen mgr; Mary Sikes, gen sls mgr, traf mgr, disc jockey; Bob Belcher, progmg dir; Dick Aldama, news dir; Jim Wiggins, chief of engrg, disc jockey.

Crane

KMMZ(FM)— 1995: 101.3 mhz; 100 kw. Ant 485 ft TL: N31 41 02 W102 19 13. Stereo. Hrs open: 24 Box 60375, Midland, 79711. Secondary address: 12200 W. I-20 E. 79711. Phone: (432) 563-2266. Fax: (432) 563-2288.E-mail: traffic@lacaliente101.com Licensee: Don L. Cook. Population served: 428,000 Thompson, Hine & Flory. Format: Sp Top 40. Target aud: 25-54. ♦Don L. Cook, gen mgr.

KXOI(AM)— December 1959: 810 khz; 1 kw-D, 500 w-N, DA-1. TL: N31 28 39 W102 20 24. Hrs open: 6 AM-midnight Box 2344, Odessa, 79760. Phone: (432) 333-5061. Fax: (432) 333-6067. Licensee: Hispanic Outreach Ministries Inc. Format: Sp. Target aud: General. ♦Rev. Pedro Emiliano, pres; Eli Emiliano, gen mgr, progmg dir; Don Cook, chief of engrg.

Creedmoor

KZNX(AM)— Dec 8, 1962: 1530 khz; 10 kw-D, 12 w-N, 1 kw-CH, DA-3. TL: N30 04 38 W97 38 08. Stereo. Hrs open: Sunrise-sunset 1050 E. 11th St., Suite 300, Austin, 78702. Phone: (512) 346-8255. Fax: (512) 346-8262.E-mail: controlroom@espnaustin.com Web Site:www.espnaustin.com Licensee: Simmons-Austin, LS LLC. Group owner: Simmons Media Group (acq 6-2-2004; $2 million). Population served: 1,000,000 Natl. Network: ESPN Radio, Westwood One, . Format: Talk, sports. News: 63 hrs wkly. Target aud: 25-54; 51% male, 49% female. ♦J. Cole McClellan, chief of engrg; Flavia Chen, traf mgr.

Crockett

KBHT(FM)— Nov 15, 1982: 93.5 mhz; 50 kw. 479 ft TL: N31 20 03 W95 47 13. Stereo. Hrs open: 24 Box 430, 206 S. Main St., Grapeland, 75844. Phone: (936) 544-9350. Fax: (936) 544-9695.E-mail: lesia@kbht.com Web Site:www.kbht.com Licensee: Weston Entertainment L.P. (acq 10-4-2005; $1.43 million). Rgnl. Network: Texas AP. Format: Classic country. News staff: 7. Target aud: 25-54. Spec prog: Gospel 6 hrs wkly. ♦Dennis W Goodman, gen mgr; Jeri Sulewski, sls dir.

***KCKT(FM)**— February 2003: 88.5 mhz; 250 w. Ant 161 ft TL: N31 19 37 W95 28 26. Hrs open: Box 3206, Tupelo, MS, 38803. Phone: (662) 844-8888. Fax: (662) 842-6791.E-mail: comments@afr.net Web Site:www.afr.net Licensee: American Family Association. Group owner: American Family Radio (acq 1-17-01). Format: Christian. ♦Marvin Sanders, gen mgr.

KIVY(AM)— Nov 11, 1949: 1290 khz; 2.5 kw-D, 175 w-N. TL: N31 18 20 W95 27 06. Hrs open: 24 102 S. Fifth St., 75835. Phone: (936) 544-2171. Phone: (936) 544-KIVY. Fax: (936) 544-4891.E-mail: leon@kivy.com Web Site:www.kivy.com Licensee: Leon Hunt (acq 9-19-2002; $1.1 million with co-located FM). Population served: 150,000 Natl. Network: ABC, . Rgnl. Network: Texas State Net. Texas State Networks Format: Classic oldies. Target aud: General. ♦Leon Hunt, pres, gen mgr, gen sls mgr & progmg dir; Chester Leediker, chief of engrg.

KIVY-FM— June 1, 1970: 92.7 mhz; 50 kw. Ant 497 ft TL: N31 18 18 W95 27 06. Stereo. Hrs open: 24 102 S. Fifth St., 75835. Phone: (936) 544-2171. Phone: (936) 544-5489. Fax: (936) 544-4891.E-mail: leon@kivy.com Web Site:www.kivy.com Licensee: Leon Hunt. Population served: 250,000 Natl. Network: ABC, . Rgnl. Network: Texas State Net. Texas State Networks Format: Country.

Crystal Beach

KSTB(FM)— 1996: 101.5 mhz; 14 kw. 449 ft TL: N29 33 52 W94 23 59. Stereo. Hrs open: 24 755 S. 11th St., Ste.102, Beaumont, 77701. Phone: (409) 833-9421. Fax: (409) 833-9296. Licensee: Cumulus Licensing Corp. Group owner: Cumulus Media Inc. (acq 5-20-02; $2.5 million). Population served: 600,000 Natl. Rep: Roslin,. Fisher, Wayland, Cooper, Leader & Zaragoza. Format: Country. News staff: 2; News: 12 hrs wkly. Target aud: 18-49. ♦Rick Prusater, gen mgr & stn mgr; Jim West, opns VP, progmg dir; Greg Davis, chief of engrg; Liz Ferguson, traf mgr.

Crystal City

KHER(FM)— Sept 5, 1985: 94.3 mhz; 3 kw. 135 ft TL: N28 39 57 W99 48 58. Hrs open: Box 743, 65 Big Wells Hwy., 78839. Phone: (830) 374-2203.E-mail: kherfm@yahoo.com Licensee: Sylvia Mijares. (acq 9-4-97). Rgnl. Network: Texas State Net. Texas State Networks Borsari & Paxson. Format: Sp, news/talk. Target aud: 18-54; 90% Hispanic, 10% non-minority. Spec prog: Relg 2 hrs wkly. ♦Sylvia Mijares, pres & gen mgr; Rudy Gomez, sls VP; Marie Thelma Martinez, news dir, pub affrs dir; Charlie Schmele, chief of engrg; Becky P. Reyes, traf mgr.

Cuero

***KTLZ(FM)**— 2003: Stn currently dark. 89.9 mhz; 5 kw. Ant 243 ft TL: N29 02 23 W97 19 24. Hrs open: 24 Box 5459, Twin Falls, ID, 83303-5459. Phone: (208) 733-3551. Fax: (208) 734-0674. Web Site:www.edgewaterbroadcasting.com Licensee: Radio Assist Ministry Inc. (acq 9-21-2004; $50,000). ♦Clark Parrish, pres.

Cypress

KYND(AM)— December 1991: 1520 khz; 3 kw-D, DA. TL: N30 00 37 W95 41 40. Hrs open:
Rebroadcasts KJOJ(AM) Conroe 100%.
Little Saigon Radio, 7080 Southwest Fwy., Houston, 77074. Phone: (713) 271-7888. Fax: (713) 271-9333.E-mail: radio@littlesaigonradio.com Web Site:www.littlesaigonradio.com Licensee: Matthew Provenzano. Format: Ethnic, Vietnamese. Target aud: General. ♦Matt Provenzano, CEO.

Daingerfield

KNGR(AM)— August 1966: 1560 khz; 1.5 kw-D, 60 w-N. TL: N33 01 35 W94 42 22. Stereo. Hrs open: 24 Box 474, 75638. Phone: (903) 645-4325. Fax: (903) 645-4357. Web Site:www.kingcountry.org Licensee: Network Communications Co. (acq 2-21-91; $50,000;3-11-91). Population served: 40,000 Format: Country. News: 3 hrs wkly. ♦Bob Wilson, chmn; Glory Wilson, gen mgr & progmg dir.

Dalhart

KIXK(AM)— 1948: 1240 khz; 1 kw-U. TL: N36 05 45 W102 30 38. Stereo. Hrs open: 24 Box 1359, Hwy. 385 N., 79022. Phone: (806) 249-4747.E-mail: kxit@kxit.net Web Site:www.kxit.com Licensee: Dalhart Radio Inc. (acq 12-3-2001; $325,000 with co-located FM). Population served: 8,500 Rgnl. Network: Texas State Net. Texas State Networks

Format: Country. Spec prog: Farm 7 hrs wkly. ♦George Chambers, pres, gen mgr; Jusin Bliss, progmg dir.

***KTDA(FM)**— 2009: 91.7 mhz; 870 w. Ant 128 ft TL: N36 03 20 W102 30 34. Hrs open:
Rebroadcasts WAFR(FM) Tupelo, MS 100%.
Drawer 2440, Tupelo, MS, 38803. Phone: (662) 844-8888. Fax: (662) 842-6791. Web Site:www.afr.net Licensee: American Family Association. (acq 6-9-2006). Natl. Network: American Family Radio, . Format: Christian. ♦Donald E. Wildmon, chmn.

KXIT(FM)— 1962: 96.3 mhz; 100 kw. Ant 472 ft TL: N35 53 46 W102 23 03. Stereo. Hrs open: 24 Box 1359, Hwy. 385 N., 79022. Phone: (806) 249-4747. Licensee: Radio Dalhart (acq 12-3-2001; $325,000 with co-located AM). Population served: 12,500 Format: Classic rock, oldies. ♦George Chambers, gen mgr.

Dallas

KAAM(AM)—(Garland, 1973: 770 khz; 10 kw-D, 1 kw-N, DA-2. TL: N33 01 58 W96 34 31. Stereo. Hrs open: 24 3201 Royalty Row, Irving, 75062. Phone: (972) 445-1700. Fax: (972) 438-6574.E-mail: cbcstand@aol.com Web Site:www.kaamradio.com Licensee: Dontron Inc. Group owner: Crawford Broadcasting Co. (acq 1979). Population served: 6000000 Format: Adult standards. Target aud: 35 plus; Christian. ♦Don Crawford, pres; Don Crawford Jr., gen mgr.

KBFB(FM)— 1965: 97.9 mhz; 99 kw. 1,611 ft TL: N32 35 15 W96 57 59. Stereo. Hrs open: 13331 Preston Rd., Suite 1180, 75240. Phone: (972) 331-5400. Fax: (972) 331-5560.E-mail: info@979tlpeat.com Web Site:www.979tlpbeat.com Licensee: Radio One Licenses LLC. Group owner: Radio One Inc. (acq 2000; grpsl). Population served: 3,000,000 Natl. Rep: CBS Radio,. Format: Urban contemp. Target aud: 25-50. ♦Alfred Liggine, pres; George Laughlin, gen mgr; John Candelaria, opns mgr, progmg dir; Shawn Nunn, sls dir; Joe Libios, mktg dir, prom dir; Tony Fields, progmg dir; Don Stevenson, chief of engrg; Rowena Montgomery, traf mgr.

***KCBI(FM)**— May 19, 1976: 90.9 mhz; 100 kw. 1,509 ft TL: N32 35 22 W96 58 10. Stereo. Hrs open: 24 Box 619000, 75261-9000. Phone: (817) 792-3800. Fax: (817) 277-9929.E-mail: kcbi@kcbi.org Web Site:www.kcbi.org Licensee: Criswell College. (group owner) Population served: 4,500,000 Natl. Network: AP Radio, . Format: Inspirational, Christian. News staff: 4; News: 4 hrs wkly. Target aud: 35-54; Christian families. ♦Ronald L. Harris, CEO; Royce Laycock, chmn; Heidi Graham, pres, sls dir; Todd Chatman, stn mgr; Doug Price, opns VP; James Nance, dev VP; Troy Kriechbaum, prom dir & prom mgr; Marc Anderson, progmg VP, mus dir; L.B. Lyon, news dir; Doug Watson, engrg dir.

KDGE(FM)—See Fort Worth-Dallas

KDMX(FM)— 1965: 102.9 mhz; 100 kw. 1,164 ft TL: N32 34 54 W96 58 32. Hrs open: 24 14001 N. Dallas Pkwy., Suite 300, 75240. Phone: (214) 866-8000. Fax: (214) 866-8201.E-mail: info@kdmxfm.com Web Site:www.mix1029.com Licensee: Citicasters Licenses L.P. Group owner: Clear Channel Communications Inc. (acq 5-4-99; grpsl). Format: Hot adult contemp. News: 3 hrs wkly. Target aud: 25-49; upper income females. ♦J.D. Freeman, gen mgr; Pat McMahon, opns dir; Jeff Mitchell, gen sls mgr; Steve Lee, mktg dir; Rick O'Bryan, progmg dir; Louis Sutton, engrg dir.

KEGL(FM)—See Fort Worth

***KERA(FM)**— July 11, 1974: 90.1 mhz; 95 kw. 1,260 ft TL: N32 34 43 W96 57 12. Stereo. Hrs open: 3000 Harry Hines Blvd., 75201. Phone: (214) 871-1390. Fax: (214) 740-9369.E-mail: kerafm@kera.org Web Site:www.kera.org Licensee: North Texas Public Broadcasting. Population served: 3,600,000 Natl. Network: NPR, PRI, . Arnold & Porter. Wire Svc: AP Format: News/talk, progsv. News staff: 5; News: 80 hrs wkly. Target aud: 35-54; general. ♦Kevin Martin, COO, pres, pres, CFO, exec VP; Barger Tygart, chmn; Jeff Luchsinger, stn mgr; Patricia Lyons, dev VP & engrg dir.

KFJZ(AM)—See Fort Worth

KFLC(AM)—See Fort Worth

KFXR(AM)— 1947: 1190 khz; 50 kw-D, 5 kw-N, DA-2. TL: N32 47 10 W96 57 00. Hrs open: 24 14001 Dallas Pkwy., Suite 300, 75240. Phone: (214) 866-8000. Fax: (214) 866-8059. Licensee: Capstar TX L.P. Group owner: Clear Channel Communications Inc. (acq 3-27-2001; $16 million). Population served: 4,000,000 Natl. Network: CNN Radio, . Format: All news. Target aud: 25-54; general.

KGGR(AM)— June 8, 1947: 1040 khz; 3.3 kw-D, 2.8 kw-CH. TL: N32 46 43 W96 43 51. Hrs open: 5787 S. Hampton Rd., Suite 285, 75232. Phone: (972) 572-5447. Phone: (972) 988-1040. Fax: (214) 330-6133.E-mail: info@kggram.com Web Site:www.kggram.com Licensee: MBC of Texas-KGGR Inc. Group owner: Mortenson Broadcasting Co. (acq 5-1-96; $1.15 million). Population served: 58,000 Natl. Network: American Urban, . Format: Relg, talk, Black. Target aud: 18 plus. ♦Ann Arnold, gen mgr; Christie Wafer, gen sls mgr.

KHKS(FM)—See Denton

KHVN(AM)—See Fort Worth

KJKK(FM)— Dec 25, 1965: 100.3 mhz; 97 kw. Ant 1,883 ft TL: N32 35 05 W96 57 46. Hrs open: 7901 Carpenter Fwy., 75247. Phone: (214) 630-3011. Fax: (214) 905-5052.E-mail: info@wild100.com Web Site:www.wild100.com Licensee: CBS Radio Partner I Inc. Group owner: Infinity Broadcasting Corp. (acq 11-13-98; grpsl). Population served: 450,000 Natl. Network: ABC, . Natl. Rep: CBS Radio,. Format: CHR. Target aud: 18-49. ♦Mel Karmazin, CEO; Dave Siebert, gen mgr; David Henry, sls dir; Joel Gough, gen sls mgr; Amy Gomoll, prom dir; Alex Valentine, progmg dir; Bethany Parks, mus dir; Lori Dodd, pub affrs dir; Bob Henke, chief of engrg; Connie Pena, traf mgr.

KKDA(AM)—See Grand Prairie

KKDA-FM— June 8, 1947: 104.5 mhz; 100 kw. 1,585 ft TL: N32 35 22 W96 58 10. Stereo. Hrs open: 24 Box 530860, Grand Prairie, 75053. Secondary address: 621 N.W. 6th St., Grand Prairie 75050. Phone: (972) 263-9911. Fax: (972) 558-0010.E-mail: staff@k104fm.com Web Site:www.k104fm.com Licensee: Service Broadcasting Group LLC. (acq 5-76). Population served: 500,000 Natl. Rep: Christal,. Format: Urban contemp. ♦Hymen Childs, pres; Chuck Smith, gen mgr; Skip Cheatham, progmg dir; Gary Wachter, chief of engrg.

KLIF(AM)— June 26, 1922: 570 khz; 5 kw-U, DA-2. TL: N32 56 40 W96 59 25. Hrs open: 24 3500 Maple Ave., Suite 1600, 75219. Phone: (214) 526-2400. Phone: (214) 263-4141. Fax: (214) 520-4343.E-mail: info@klif.com Web Site:www.klif.com Licensee: KLIF Lico Inc. Group owner: Susquehanna Radio Corp. (acq 12-15-89). Population served: 4,418,400 Natl. Network: Fox News Radio, . Format: News/talk. News staff: 1; News: 15 hrs wkly. Target aud: 25-54; men. ♦John Dickey, COO, exec VP, VP; Lew Dickey, CEO, chmn & pres; Dan Bennett, VP, mktg mgr.

KLNO(FM)—See Fort Worth

KLTY(FM)—(Arlington, April 1949: 94.9 mhz; 99 kw. Ant 1,666 ft TL: N32 35 19 W96 58 05. Stereo. Hrs open: 24 6400 Belt Line Rd., Suite 120, Irving, 75063. Phone: (972) 870-9949. Fax: (214) 561-2156.E-mail: info@klty.com Web Site:www.klty.com Licensee: Inspiration Media of Texas LLC. Group owner: Salem Communications Corp. 2000 Population served: 4,761,200 Natl. Rep: Katz Radio,. Format: Adult Contemporary. News staff: 1; News: 2 hrs wkly. Target aud: 25-54; female dominant, family oriented, upscale, conservative. ♦John L. Peroyea, VP & gen mgr.

KLUV(FM)— 1961: 98.7 mhz; 98 kw. 1,584 ft TL: N32 35 22 W96 58 10. Stereo. Hrs open: 24 4131 N. Central Expwy., Suite 700, 75204. Phone: (214) 526-9870. Fax: (214) 443-1570. Fax: (214) 522-5588.E-mail: info@kluv.com Web Site:www.kluv.com Licensee: CBS Radio Partner I Inc. Group owner: CBS Radio (acq 9-17-94; $51 million). Population served: 4,727,800 Format: Oldies. News staff: 2. Target aud: 35-54. ♦Mel Karmazin, pres; David Henry, gen mgr; John Phillips, gen sls mgr; Liz Balon, prom mgr; Jay Cresswell, mus dir; Kathy Jones, news dir, pub affrs dir; Bill Taylor, chief of engrg; Julie Davis, traf mgr.

KMNY(AM)—See Hurst

KMVK(FM)—See Fort Worth

KNIT(AM)— 1952: 1480 khz; 5 kw-D, 1.9 kw-N, DA-2. TL: N32 39 42 W96 39 20. Hrs open: 24 400 E. Las Colinas Blvd., Suite 1033, Irving, 75039. Phone: (214) 258-2800. Fax: (214) 258-2809. Licensee: JCE Licenses LLC. Group owner: Univision Radio (acq 2-3-2006; swap in exchange for WORL(AM) Altamonte Springs, FL). Natl. Network: ESPN Deportes, . Format: Sp sports. ♦Peter Dits, gen mgr.

***KNON(FM)**— Aug 3, 1983: 89.3 mhz; 55 kw. Ant 850 ft TL: N32 35 24 W96 58 21. Stereo. Hrs open: 24 Box 710909, 75371. Secondary address: 5353 Maples Ave. 75235. Phone: (214) 828-9500. Fax: (214) 823-3051. Web Site:www.knon.org Licensee: Agape Broadcasting Foundation Inc. (acq 8-83). Population served: 1,000,000 Format: Var. Target aud: General. ♦Dave Chaos, stn mgr; Christian Lee, mus dir; Pamela Parker, sls dir & news dir.

KPLX(FM)—See Fort Worth

KRLD(AM)— October 1926: 1080 khz; 50 kw-U, DA-N. TL: N32 53 25 W96 38 44. Hrs open: 24 4131 N. Central Expwy., Suite 500, 75204. Phone: (214) 525-7000. Fax: (214) 525-7370. Web Site:www.krld.com Licensee: CBS Radio Partner I Inc. Group owner: Infinity Broadcasting Population served: 3,352,500 Rgnl. Network: Texas State Net. Natl. Rep: CBS Radio,. Texas State Networks Format: News/talk, news, sports. News staff: 35; News: 119 hrs wkly. Target aud: 25-54. Spec prog: Texas Rangers baseball. ♦Brian Purdy, VP, gen mgr; Gavin Spittle, gen mgr, progmg dir; Tom Bigby, opns dir; Bob Waterman, gen sls mgr; Eric Disen, chief of engrg.

KRLD-FM— Apr 5, 1968: 105.3 mhz; 97 kw. Ant 1,883 ft TL: N32 35 05 W96 57 46. Stereo. Hrs open: 24 7901 Carpenter Fwy, 75247. Phone: (214) 630-3011. Fax: (214) 905-5052.E-mail: info@live1053.com Web Site:www.1053thefan.com Licensee: CBS Radio Partner I Inc. Group owner: Infinity Broadcasting Corp. (acq 11-13-98; grpsl). Population served: 4,761,200 Natl. Network: Fox Sports, . Natl. Rep: CBS Radio,. Leventhal, Senter & Lerman. Format: Sports. Target aud: 18-49; general. ♦Mel Karmazin, CEO; Brian Purdy, gen mgr; Steve Sullivan, gen sls mgr; Lynn Sornsen, natl sls mgr; Jeff Burkett, prom dir; Gavin Spittle, progmg dir; Bob Henke, chief of engrg; Susan Wade, traf mgr.

KRVA(AM)—(Cockrell Hill, Sept 29, 1947: 1600 khz; 5 kw-D, 1 kw-N, DA-2. TL: N32 44 25 W96 42 38. Hrs open: 24 4965 Preston Park Blvd., Suite 120, Plano, 75093. Licensee: Mortenson Broadcasting Co. of Texas Inc. (group owner; (acq 8-30-2004; $3.5 million). Population served: 5,000,000 Format: Ethnic, Indian, Pakistani. ♦Rehan Siddiqi, gen mgr; Naheed Raheel, progmg dir.

KRVA-FM—See Campbell

KSKY(AM)—(Balch Springs, Sept 30, 1941: 660 khz; 10 kw-D, 660 w-N, DA-N. TL: N29 22 51 W95 14 15. Hrs open: 24 6400 N. Beltline, Suite 110, Irving, 75063. Phone: (214) 561-9660. Fax: (214) 561-9662.E-mail: myopinion@ksky.com Web Site:www.ksky.com Licensee: Bison Media Inc. Group owner: Salem Communications Corp. (acq 4-24-2000; $7.5 million plus seller gets KMOM(FM) Fountain, CO). Population served: 1,000,000 Latham & Watkins. Format: News, talk. Target aud: 35-59; middle income white female. Spec prog: High school, college sports. ♦John L. Peroyea, CFO & gen mgr; David Darling, opns VP, opns mgr, progmg dir; Bob Johnson, gen sls mgr; David Sparkman, prom dir; Andy Pickard, chief of engrg.

KSOC(FM)—(Gainesville, 1958: 94.5 mhz; 100 kw. 1,896 ft TL: N33 33 36 W96 57 35. Stereo. Hrs open: 24 13331 Preston Rd., Suite 1180, 75234. Phone: (972) 331-5400. Fax: (972) 726-0940. Licensee: Radio One Licenses LLC. Group owner: Radio One Inc. (acq 11-8-01; grpsl). Population served: 4,800,000 Latham & Watkins. Format: Urban / adult contemp. News staff: one; News: one hr wkly. Target aud: 18-44; affluent generation X'ers. ♦George Laughlin, gen mgr; John Candelaria, progmg dir.

KTCK(AM)— 1920: 1310 khz; 5 kw-D, 5 kw-N, DA-2. TL: N32 56 41 W96 56 25. Stereo. Hrs open: 24 3500 Maple Ave., Suite 1310, 75219. Phone: (214) 526-7400. Fax: (214) 525-2525. Web Site:www.theticket.com Licensee: KRBE Lico Inc. Group owner: Susquehanna Radio Corp. (acq 1996; $14 million). Population served: 4,500,000 Format: Sports, talk. Target aud: 25-54; men & sport enthusiasts. ♦Dan Bennett, VP, gen mgr, mktg mgr; Jim Quirk, sls dir, mktg mgr; Ken Roberts, gen sls mgr; Jami Williams, natl sls mgr; Jamey Garner, prom dir; Jeff Catlin, progmg dir; Rob Chickering, engrg dir; Kimberly Jolly, traf mgr.

KVCE(AM)—See Highland Park

KVIL(FM)—See Highland Park

***KVTT(FM)**— Jan 26, 1950: 91.7 mhz; 100 kw. 1,099 ft TL: N32 35 24 W96 58 21. Stereo. Hrs open: 24 11061 Shady Tr., 75229. Phone: (214) 351-6655. Fax: (469) 522-0992.E-mail: kvtt@kvtt.org Web Site:www.kvtt.org Licensee: Covenant Educational Media Inc. (acq 9-21-2004; $16.5 million). Population served: 4,500,000 Format: Teaching, educ, music. News: one hr wkly. Spec prog: Radio Verdad (Hispanic Christian) 6 hrs wkly. ♦Douglas Price, gen mgr & stn mgr; Bryan Reeder, progmg dir, mus dir.

KZPS(FM)— Apr 1, 1948: 92.5 mhz; 100 kw. 1,590 ft TL: N32 35 22 W96 58 10. Stereo. Hrs open: 24 14001 N. Dallas Pkwy., Suite 300, 75240. Phone: (214) 866-8000. Web Site:www.kzps.com Licensee: AMFM Texas Licenses L.P. Group owner: Clear Channel Communications Inc. (acq 8-30-2000; grpsl). Population served: 325,000 Format: Classic rock. News staff: one. Target aud: 25-44; upscale young adults. ♦J.D. Freeman, gen mgr; Pat McMahon, opns dir; Kelly Kibler, sls dir, progmg VP; Tracy Martin, gen sls mgr & rgnl sls mgr; Steve Lee, mktg dir; Don Davis, prom dir, progmg dir; Anna DeHaro, news dir; Louis Sutton, chief of engrg; Sylvia Sanchez, traf mgr.

WBAP(AM)—See Fort Worth

WRR(FM)— 1948: 101.1 mhz; 100 kw. 1,510 ft TL: N32 35 22 W96 58 10. Stereo. Hrs open: 24 Box 159001, 75315-9001. Secondary address: 1516 First Ave. 75210. Phone: (214) 670-8888. Fax: (214) 670-8394. Web Site:www.wrr101.com Licensee: City of Dallas. Population served: 300,000 Natl. Network: AP Network News, . Natl. Rep: McGavren Guild,. Kaye, Scholer, Fierman, Hays & Handler. Format: Classical. News staff: 22. Target aud: 25-54; all ages. Spec prog: Children 2 hrs wkly. ◆Gregory T. Davis, VP & gen mgr.

Decatur

*KDKR(FM)— 1998: 91.3 mhz; 40 kw horiz, 100 kw vert. Ant 1,784 ft TL: N33 23 12 W97 33 57. Hrs open: 24 5617 Diamond Oaks Dr. S., Fort Worth, 76117. Phone: (817) 831-9130.E-mail: kdkr@csnradio.com Web Site:www.kdkr.org Licensee: CSN International (group owner; acq 7-12-2000). Format: Positive easy gospel, relg. ◆Chris Rohloff, gen mgr; Kelly Rasulo, opns dir; Stephanie Rohloff, progmg dir.

KRNB(FM)— Aug 15, 1968: 105.7 mhz; 100 kw. 492 ft TL: N32 11 11 W98 17 26. (CP: Ant 1,673 ft.). Stereo. Hrs open: 24 621 N.W. 6th St., Grand Prairie, 75050. Phone: (972) 263-9911. Fax: (972) 558-0010. Web Site:www.krnb.com Licensee: Service Broadcasting Group LLC. (acq 2-28-95; 5-22-95). Population served: 75,000 Natl. Network: ABC, . Format: Urban adult contemp. ◆Hymen Childs, pres; Chuck Smith, gen mgr; Shay Moore, progmg dir; Gary Wachter, chief of engrg.

Del Mar Hills

KVOZ(AM)— Apr 15, 1952: 890 khz; 10 kw-D, 1 kw-N, DA-N. TL: N27 32 57 W99 22 21. Hrs open: Box 252, McAllen, 78505. Phone: (956) 781-5528. Phone: (956) 686-6382. Fax: (956) 686-2999. Web Site:www.laradiochristiana.com Licensee: Consolidated Radio Inc. (acq 3-27-97). Population served: 3,600,000 Format: Sp gospel. Target aud: 18 plus. ◆Paulino Bernal, gen mgr; Eloy Bernal, stn mgr; Pete Guzman, opns mgr.

Del Rio

*KDLI(FM)— 2007: 89.9 mhz; 1 kw. Ant 171 ft TL: N29 25 24 W100 54 21. Hrs open:
Rebroadcasts WAFR(FM) Tupelo, MS 100%.
Box 2440, Tupelo, MS, 38803-2440. Phone: (662) 844-8888. Fax: (662) 842-6791. Web Site:www.afr.net Licensee: American Family Association. Format: Contemp Christian. ◆Marvin Sanders, gen mgr.

KDLK-FM— Aug 15, 1966: 94.1 mhz; 18 kw. Ant 276 ft TL: N29 25 45 W100 54 17. Stereo. Hrs open: 24 Prog sep from AM Box 1489, 78841. Phone: (830) 775-9583. Fax: (830) 774-4009. Web Site:www.kdlk.com Natl. Network: Westwood One, . Format: Country. Target aud: 18 plus. ◆Larry Mariner, pres, gen mgr; Rudy Briones, opns mgr; Jay Gonzalez, progmg dir; Christina Rangel, traf mgr.

KTDR(FM)— Mar 31, 1986: 96.3 mhz; 100 kw. 490 ft TL: N29 32 25 W101 07 21. Stereo. Hrs open: 24 307 E. 8th St., 78840. Phone: (830) 775-6291. Phone: (830) 775-6291. Fax: (830) 775-6545.E-mail: production@themix96.com Web Site:www.themix96.com Licensee: Grande Broadcasting of Del Rio Inc. Population served: 43,000 Borsari & Paxson. Format: Adult contemp. News: 1 hr wkly. Target aud: 25-54; male. Spec prog: Relg 3 hrs wkly. ◆Frank Mendoza, pres, gen mgr; Chris Russell, gen sls mgr, disc jockey; Charlene Duncan, chief of engrg, traf mgr; Margaritta Martinez, rsch dir.

KTJK(AM)— 1947: 1230 khz; 860 w-U. TL: N29 25 45 W100 54 17. Hrs open: 24 Box 1489, 78840. Phone: (830) 775-9583. Fax: (830) 774-4009. Web Site:www.ktjk.com Licensee: Forum Broadcasting Inc. (acq 12-10-02; with co-located FM). Population served: 50,000 Format: Tejano music format. Target aud: 25-54. ◆Larry Mariner, pres, gen mgr; Rudy Briones, opns mgr; Jay Gonzalez, progmg mgr; Christina Rangel, traf mgr.

KWMC(AM)— Aug 20, 1967: 1490 khz; 1 kw-U. TL: N29 22 17 W100 51 55. Hrs open: 24 903 E. Cortinas St., 78840. Phone: (830) 775-3544. Fax: (830) 775-3546.E-mail: kwmc1490@wcsonline.net Licensee: Minerva Garza Valdez. Population served: 37,000 Rgnl. Network: Texas State Net. Texas State Networks Wire Svc: NOAA Weather Format: Rock oldies. News staff: 2. Spec prog: Relg 5 hrs wkly. ◆Alfredo Garza, pres, gen mgr, chief of engrg; Minerva Garza-Valdez, VP; Guillermo Garza, stn mgr, prom dir, progmg dir, traf mgr; Javier Martinez, gen sls mgr.

Del Valle

KIXL(AM)—Licensed to Del Valle. See Austin

Denison

KJIM(AM)—See Sherman

*KYFB(FM)— Jan 19, 2007: 91.5 mhz; 4.5 kw. Ant 220 ft TL: N33 42 10 W96 34 05. Hrs open: Box 7300, Charlotte, NC, 28241. Phone: (704) 523-5555. Fax: (704) 522-1967. Web Site:www.bbnradio.org Licensee: Bible Broadcasting Network Inc. Format: Relg. ◆Lowell L. Davey, pres.

Denton

KFZO(FM)— September 1988: 99.1 mhz; 100 kw. Ant 1,168 ft TL: N33 23 22 W97 33 53. Stereo. Hrs open: 24 7700 Carpenter Fwy., Dallas, 75247. Phone: (214) 525-0400. Phone: (214) 630-8531. Fax: (214) 689-3818. Fax: (214) 631-1196 (sales).E-mail: info@kfzofm.com Web Site:www.kick991.com Licensee: KHCK-FM License Corp. Group owner: Univision Radio (acq 9-22-2003; grpsl). Format: Sp, Tejano. News staff: one; News: one hr wkly. Target aud: 25-54; affluent/educated adults. ◆Frank Carter, gen mgr; Andy Lockridge, opns dir; Howard Toole, sls dir; Cipriano Robles, gen sls mgr; Betsy Galleguillos, natl sls mgr; Oscar Espinosa, prom dir; Frank "Pancho" Gonzales, progmg dir; Myrna Vera, mus dir, rsch dir; Patrick Parks, chief of engrg; Mirentxu Smith, traf mgr; Claudia Torrescano, pub svc dir.

KHKS(FM)— 1947: 106.1 mhz; 100 kw. 1,584 ft TL: N32 35 22 W96 58 10. Stereo. Hrs open: 24 14001 N. Dallas Parkway, Suite 300, Dallas, 75240. Phone: (214) 866-8000. Fax: (214) 866-8588.E-mail: info@khksfm.com Web Site:www.1061kissfm.com Licensee: AMFM Texas Licenses L.P. Group owner: Clear Channel Communications Inc. (acq 8-30-00; grpsl). Population served: 700,000 Reed, Smith, Shaw & McClay. Format: CHR. News staff: one. Target aud: 18-49. ◆J.D. Freeman, gen mgr; Jeff Mitchell, gen sls mgr; Kelly Parker, natl sls mgr; Shawn McCalister, rgnl sls mgr; Steve Lee, mktg dir; Sarah Hannon, prom dir; Patrick Davis, progmg dir; Louis Sutton, engrg dir, chief of engrg; Sylvia Sanchez, traf mgr.

Devine

KRPT(FM)— Nov 17, 1982: 92.5 mhz; 50 kw. Ant 492 ft TL: N28 55 32 W99 02 53. Stereo. Hrs open: 24 6222 N.W. IH 10, San Antonio, 78201. Phone: (210) 736-9700. Fax: (210) 735-8811. Licensee: CCB Texas Licenses L.P. Group owner: Clear Channel Communications Inc. (acq 10-2-98; $1.5 million). Population served: 70,000 Format: Country. ◆Matt Martin, gen mgr.

Diboll

KAFX-FM—Licensed to Diboll. See Lufkin

KSML(AM)—Licensed to Diboll. See Lufkin

Dilley

KKDL(FM)—Not on air, target date: unknown: 93.7 mhz; 2.5 kw. Ant 266 ft TL: N28 38 53 W99 10 50. Hrs open: 2702 Pine St., Laredo, 78046-1614. Phone: (956) 726-4738. Licensee: La Nueva Cadena Radio Luz Inc. (acq 4-3-2008; $40,000 for CP). ◆Israel Tellez, pres & gen mgr.

KLMO-FM— 2001: 98.9 mhz; 92 kw. Ant 722 ft TL: N28 56 34 W99 16 47. Hrs open: Dilley Broadcasters, 115 West Ave. D, Robstown, 78320. Phone: (210) 532-9858. Fax: (361) 289-7722. Licensee: Dilley Broadcasters. Format: Sp var.

KVWG-FM— March 1984: 95.3 mhz; 100 w. Ant 121 ft TL: N28 40 23 W99 10 08. Stereo. Hrs open: Box K, 78061. Licensee: Pearsall Radio Works Ltd. Population served: 37,000

Dimmitt

KDHN(AM)— Dec 22, 1963: 1470 khz; 500 w-D, 149 w-N. TL: N34 35 11 W102 18 35. Hrs open: 704 W. Cleveland St., 79027. Phone: (806) 647-4161. Fax: (806) 647-4715.E-mail: kdhn@1984yoohoo.com Licensee: Collins Communications Co. (acq 12-12-84). Population served: 45,000 Format: C&W, relg, Sp. News: 8 hrs wkly. Target aud: General. Spec prog: Sp 17 hrs wkly. ◆Wayne Collins, pres & gen mgr.

KNNK(FM)—Licensed to Dimmitt. See Hereford

Doss

*KGLF(FM)—Not on air, target date: unknown: Stn currently dark. 88.1 mhz; 6 kw. Ant 328 ft TL: N30 22 22 W99 05 02. Hrs open: 5700 W. Oaks Blvd., Rocklin, 95765. Phone: (707) 528-9236. Licensee: Legacy Austin Broadcasting Foundation Inc. (acq 10-15-2003; $100,000 for CP). ◆Keith Whipple, gen mgr.

Dripping Springs

*KLLR(FM)— 2007: 91.9 mhz; 1.1 kw. Ant 472 ft TL: N30 11 53 W98 00 45. Hrs open:
Rebroadcasts KLVR(FM) Santa Rosa, CA 100%.
5700 West Oaks Blvd., Rocklin, CA, 95765. Phone: (916) 251-1600. Fax: (916) 251-1650. Web Site:www.klove.com Licensee: Educational Media Foundation. Natl. Network: K-Love, . Format: Contemp Christian. ◆Richard Jenkins, pres; Mike Novak, VP, progmg dir; Lloyd Parker, gen mgr; Ed Lenane, opns dir, news dir; Keith Whipple, dev dir; Eric Allen, natl sls mgr; David Pierce, progmg mgr; Jon Rivers, mus dir; Sam Wallington, engrg dir; Arthur Vassar, traf mgr; Karen Johnson, news rptr.

KXBT(FM)— 1984: 104.9 mhz; 2.35 kw. Ant 531 ft TL: N30 11 54 W98 00 46. Stereo. Hrs open: 24 912 S. Capital of Texas Hwy., Suite 400, Austin, 78746-3896. Phone: (512) 416-3000. Fax: (512) 416-8205. Licensee: BMP Austin License Company L.P. Group owner: Amigo Broadcasting L.P. (acq 11-9-2004; grpsl). Kenkel & Associates. Format: Sp contemp. Target aud: 25-54; upscale, retired, affluent. ◆Jerry Del Core, gen mgr.

Dublin

KSTV-FM— Aug 15, 1968: 93.1 mhz; 7.9 kw. 580 ft TL: N32 11 12 W98 17 44. Hrs open: 24 Box 289, 3209 W. Washington (Dublin Hwy.), Stephenville, 76401. Phone: (254) 968-2141. Fax: (254) 968-6221.E-mail: kstv@htcomp.net Web Site:www.377net.com Licensee: CCR-Stephenville III LLC. Group owner: Cherry Creek Radio LLC (acq 6-24-2004; grpsl). Format: Country. ◆Robert Elliot, gen mgr; Robert Haschke, gen sls mgr; Tony Hart, progmg dir; Nyki Wyatt, news dir; Justin McClure, chief of engrg; Troy Stark, traf mgr.

Dumas

KDDD(AM)— May 1, 1948: 800 khz; 250 w-D. TL: N35 51 42 W101 55 50. Hrs open: 6 AM-sunset Box 555, 79029. Secondary address: 408 N. Dumas Ave. 79029. Phone: (806) 935-4141. Fax: (806) 935-3836.E-mail: kddd@amaonline.com Licensee: PBI LLC Population served: 19,771 Format: Country. Target aud: General. ◆Candy Bray, traf mgr.

KDDD-FM— June 29, 1960: 95.3 mhz; 3 kw. 260 ft TL: N35 51 51 W101 55 45. Stereo. Hrs open: 24 Box 555, 79029. Secondary address: 408 N. Dumas Ave. 79029. Phone: (806) 935-4141. Fax: (806) 935-3836. Licensee: PBI LLC (acq 6-29-2007; $20,000 for 50% ownership interest with co-located AM). Population served: 20000 Natl. Network: ABC, . Format: Oldies. News staff: one; News: 13 hrs wkly. Target aud: 25-65; farmers, community, factory. Spec prog: Farm 5 hrs, gospel 5 hrs wkly. ◆Kandi Bray, gen mgr, gen sls mgr, traf mgr; Steve Bayless, opns mgr & progmg mgr; Ali Allison, news dir; Stephen White, chief of engrg.

Eagle Pass

*KEPI(FM)— May 13, 1995: 88.7 mhz; 1 kw. 180 ft TL: N28 39 26 W100 25 00. Hrs open: 24 Box 895, 2477 El Indio Hwy., 78853. Phone: (830) 757-0887. Fax: (830) 757-8950. Licensee: World Radio Network Inc. Population served: 150,000 Format: Contemp Christian. ◆James Gamblin, gen mgr.

KEPS(AM)— August 1957: 1270 khz; 1 kw-D. TL: N28 43 45 W100 29 30. Hrs open: Box 1123, 78852. Secondary address: 127 Kilowatt Dr. 78852. Phone: (830) 773-9247. Fax: (830) 773-9500.E-mail: kinlkepsrg@bizzstx.rr.com Licensee: Rhattigan Broadcasting (Texas) LP (group owner; (acq 8-19-2004; grpsl). Format: Tejano. Target aud: 18-49; middle income, Texas-born Hispanics. ◆Rosa T. De La Garza, gen mgr; Rosa T. De La Garza, gen sls mgr; Jose Perez, progmg dir; Mario Martinez, news dir; Gary Graham, chief of engrg.

*KEPX(FM)— Sept 9, 1994: 89.5 mhz; 52 kw. 256 ft TL: N28 39 26 W100 25 00. Stereo. Hrs open: 24 Box 895, 2477 El Indio Hwy., 78853. Phone: (830) 757-0895. Fax: (830) 757-8950. Web Site:www.kepx.net

Licensee: World Radio Network Inc. Population served: 500,000 Bryan Cave. Format: Sp, Christian. News: 3 hrs wkly. Target aud: Hispanic; Mexican. ♦Arturo Lazano, VP & gen mgr.

KINL(FM)— Nov 2, 1971: 92.7 mhz; 20 kw. 184 ft TL: N28 43 57 W100 29 34. Stereo. Hrs open: Box 1123, 78852. Secondary address: 127 Kilowatt Dr. 78852. Phone: (830) 773-9247. Fax: (830) 773-9500.E-mail: kinlkepsrg@bizzstx.rr.com Licensee: Rhattigan Broadcasting (Texas) LP. Format: Oldies hits of the 60s, 70s & 80s. ♦Cesar Galindo, progmg dir.

Eastland

KATX(FM)— Sept 1, 1986: 97.7 mhz; 3 kw. Ant 203 ft TL: N32 23 47 W98 46 26. Stereo. Hrs open: 24 611 W. Commerce, 76448. Phone: (254) 629-2621. Fax: (254) 629-8520.E-mail: radio@txol.net Licensee: Partnership Broadcasting Inc. (acq 2-1-2000; with co-located AM). Format: Country, talk. News staff: one; News: 8 hrs wkly. Target aud: 25-54; adults. ♦David Bacon, pres; Chuck Statler, exec VP.

KEAS(AM)— August 1953: 1590 khz; 500 w-D. TL: N32 23 47 W98 46 26. Hrs open: 6 am-sunset Dups FM 100% 611 W. Commerce, 76448. Phone: (254) 629-2621. Fax: (254) 629-8520.E-mail: radio@cebrodge.net Licensee: Partnership Broadcasting Inc. Population served: 3,178 Natl. Network: Westwood One, . Rgnl. Network: Texas State Net. Texas State Networks News staff: one; News: 8 hrs wkly. Target aud: 25-54. Spec prog: Gospel 5 hrs wkly. ♦Chuck Startler, pres; Thad McKinney, gen mgr.

***KQXE(FM)**— 2008: 91.1 mhz; 14 kw. Ant 335 ft TL: N32 20 48 W98 42 50. Hrs open: 905 Palo Pinto St., Weatherford, 96086-4135. Phone: (817) 341-2337. Fax: (817) 596-9842. Web Site:www.qxfm.com Licensee: CSSI Non-Profit Educational Broadcasting Corp. ♦John Peterson, gen mgr.

Edinburg

KBFM(FM)— February 1972: 104.1 mhz; 100 kw. 990 ft TL: N26 05 59 W97 50 16. Stereo. Hrs open: 24 901 E. Pike St., Weslaco, 78596. Phone: (956) 973-9202. Fax: (956) 973-9355.E-mail: kbfmm@aol.com Web Site:www.b104.net Licensee: Capstar TX L.P. Group owner: Clear Channel Communications Inc. (acq 8-15-00; grpsl). Population served: 750,000 Natl. Rep: Christal,. Format: CHR. News staff: one. Target aud: 18-34; females. Spec prog: Community affrs. ♦Danny Fletcher, VP, gen mgr; Billy Santiago, opns mgr; Cyndi Torres, rgnl sls mgr; Bobby Macias, mus dir; Gloria Garcia, traf mgr, disc jockey; Ken Meek, chief of engrg & disc jockey.

***KOIR(FM)**— Feb 5, 1983: 88.5 mhz; 3 kw. 285 ft TL: N26 07 49 W98 10 51. Stereo. Hrs open: 24 4300 S. Business Hwy. 281, 78539-9699. Phone: (956) 380-8100. Phone: (956) 380-3435. Fax: (956) 380-8156.E-mail: correo@radioesparanza.com Licensee: Rio Grande Bible Institute Inc. Population served: 10,000 Bryan Cave. Wire Svc: UPI Format: Relg, educ, Sp. Target aud: General. ♦Gerardo Lorenzo, gen mgr, progmg dir; Jerry Jeske, chief of engrg.

KURV(AM)— October 1947: 710 khz; 1 kw-U, DA-2. TL: N26 19 43 W98 09 35. Hrs open: 24 1201 N. Jackson Rd., Suite 900, McAllen, 78501. Phone: (956) 992-8895. Fax: (956) 992-8897.E-mail: talk@kurv.com Web Site:www.kurv.com Licensee: BMP RGV License Co. L.P. Group owner: Border Media Partners LLC (acq 2-6-2004; $7.5 million with KSOX(AM) Raymondville). Population served: 800,000 Natl. Network: CBS, . Rgnl. Network: Texas State Net. Texas State Networks Gammon & Grange. Format: News/talk, sports. News staff: 2; News: 30 hrs wkly. Target aud: 35-64. ♦Jose Luis Munoz, gen mgr.

KVLY(FM)— 1974: 107.9 mhz; 100 kw. 765 ft TL: N26 15 01 W97 55 21. Stereo. Hrs open: 801 Jackson Rd., McAllen, 78501. Phone: (956) 661-6000. Fax: (956) 661-6082.E-mail: mquinn@entravision.com Licensee: Entravision Holdings L.L.C. Group owner: Entravision Communications Corp. (acq 7-20-00; grpsl). Population served: 750,000 Format: Adult contemp Spanish. Target aud: 25-54. ♦Willie Rosales, gen mgr, gen mgr, stn mgr, opns mgr & gen sls mgr; Alex Duran, progmg dir; Lilly Lopez, mus dir; Shirley Kennedy, news dir; Sonny Cavazos, chief of engrg; Dora Borjas, traf mgr.

Edna

KIOX-FM— Sept. 20, 1998: 96.1 mhz; 13 kw. Ant 456 ft TL: N29 06 05 W96 27 19. Hrs open: 11675 Jollyville Rd., Suite 100, Austin, 78759. Phone: (512) 236-1884. Licensee: Buckalew Media Inc. Group owner: Fort Bend Broadcasting Co. (acq 6-5-2008; $70,000). Format: Country. ♦Ryan Henderson, gen mgr.

El Campo

KNTE-FM— September 1968: 96.9 mhz; 100 kw. 981 ft TL: N29 05 44 W96 27 25. (CP: TL: N28 53 35 W96 21 40). Hrs open: 24 3000 Bering Dr., Houston, 77057. Phone: (713) 315-3400. Fax: (713) 315-3565.E-mail: Houstoninfo@lbimedia.com Web Site:www.xoradio.com Licensee: Liberman Broadcasting of Houston License LLC. Group owner: Liberman Broadcasting Inc. (acq 10-11-2002; $3.15 million with KXGJ(FM) Bay City). Pepper & Corazzini. Format: Tejano. Target aud: 18-49; college, plant workers, business & agriculture. ♦Cheryl Kirk, gen mgr.

KULP(AM)— 1948: 1390 khz; 500 w-D, 180 w-N. TL: N29 12 34 W96 15 50. Hrs open: 6 AM-10 PM Box 390, 77437. Secondary address: 515 E. Jackson St. 77437. Phone: (979) 543-3303. Fax: (979) 543-1546.E-mail: contact@kulpradio.com Web Site:www.kulpradio.com Licensee: Wharton County Radio Inc. (acq 5-2-00; $240,000). Population served: 13,500 Texas State Networks Format: Classic country, news/talk, sports. News staff: 2; News: 5 hrs wkly. Target aud: 25 plus. Spec prog: Sp 14 hrs, Czech 5 hrs wkly. ♦Bob Buckalew, pres, VP; Jerry Aulds, gen mgr; Clint Robinson, opns mgr, mus dir; Bob Nason, news dir, pub affrs dir; Mike Wenglar, engrg dir; Kate Manrriquez, traf mgr.

El Paso

KAMA(AM)— July 13, 1972: Stn currently dark. 750 khz; 10 kw-D, 1 kw-N, DA-1. TL: N31 46 21 W106 16 56. Hrs open: 24 2211 E. Missouri, 79903. Secondary address: South 300 Phone: (915) 544-9797. Fax: (915) 544-1247.E-mail: info@netmio.com Web Site:www.univision.com Licensee: Tichenor Media System Inc. Group owner: Univision Radio (acq 9-22-2003; grpsl). Population served: 462,000 Format: Sp, oldies. News staff: one; News: 8 hrs wkly. Target aud: 25-54; women. ♦MacHenry Tichenor Jr., pres; Cecilia Uebel, gen mgr; Carlos Fourzan, gen sls mgr; Pedro Skaggs, progmg dir; Fernando Rubio, news dir; Michael McCabe, chief of engrg; Patricia Villasenor, traf mgr.

KBNA-FM— Aug 15, 1969: 97.5 mhz; 100 kw horiz, 48 kw vert. Ant 1,088 ft TL: N31 47 34 W106 28 47. Stereo. Hrs open: Dups AM 100% 2211 E. Missouri, Suite 300, 79903. Phone: (915) 544-9797. Fax: (915) 544-1247.E-mail: info@netmio.com Web Site:www.univision.com Population served: 550,000 ♦Cecilia Uebel, gen mgr; Carlos Fourzan, gen sls mgr; Michael McCabe, chief of engrg; Patricia Villasenor, traf mgr.

KELP(AM)— Apr 10, 1959: 1590 khz; 5 kw-D, 800 w-N. TL: N31 46 12 W106 25 37. (CP: TL: N31 44 38 W106 23 45). Stereo. Hrs open: 24 6900 Commerce, 79915. Phone: (915) 779-0016. Fax: (915) 779-6641.E-mail: tina@kelpradio.com Web Site:www.kelpradio.com Licensee: McClatchey Broadcasting. (acq 2-14-84; $590,000; 1-30-84). Population served: 1,500,000 Natl. Network: Salem Radio Network, . Format: Christian talk, information. Target aud: 25-54; Christian community of El Paso, Las Cruces, Northern Mexico. Spec prog: Spanish 12 hrs wklly. ♦Arnold McClatchey, pres; Tina Casano, gen mgr; Jay Gilliland, opns dir, gen sls mgr.

KHEY(AM)— Aug 22, 1929: 1380 khz; 5 kw-D, 500 w-N. TL: N31 45 42 W106 24 36. Hrs open: 24 4045 N. Mesa St., 79902. Phone: (915) 351-5400. Fax: (915) 351-3102.E-mail: info@khey1380.com Web Site:www.khey1380.com Licensee: CCB Texas Licenses L.P. Group owner: Clear Channel Communications Inc. (acq 5-29-98; $10.5 million with co-located FM). Population served: 680,000 Rgnl. Network: Texas AP. Natl. Rep: Clear Channel,. Format: Sports. Target aud: General. ♦Bill Struck, gen mgr; Karen Daniels-Pearson, gen sls mgr; Chris Lucy, mktg dir; Frank Rodriquez, prom dir; Paul Whittler, progmg dir & pub affrs dir; Enrique Lopez, chief of engrg; Julie Bustillos, traf mgr.

KHEY-FM— Aug 1, 1974: 96.3 mhz; 100 kw. 1,390 ft TL: N31 47 47 W106 28 55. Stereo. Hrs open: 24 4045 N. Mesa St, 79902. Phone: (915) 351-5400. Fax: (915) 351-3102.E-mail: info@khey.com Web Site:www.khey.com Natl. Network: ABC, . Format: Country. Target aud: 25-54. ♦Michelle Haston, sls dir; Steve Gramzay, progmg dir; Bobby Gutierrez, news dir, pub affrs dir, local news ed; Enrique Lopez, engrg dir; Amy Page, traf mgr.

KHRO(AM)— June 1958: 1150 khz; 5 kw-D, 380 w-N. TL: N31 45 15 W106 25 11. Stereo. Hrs open: 24 5426 N. Mesa St., 79912-5421. Phone: (915) 581-1126. Fax: (915) 585-4611.E-mail: info@ksve.com Licensee: Entravision Communications Co. L.L.C. Natl. Rep: Lotus Entravision Reps LLC,. Format: Talk. Target aud: 18-54.

KINT-FM— July 4, 1975: 93.9 mhz; 96.2 kw. 1,420 ft TL: N31 47 36 W106 28 50. Hrs open: 5426 N. Mesa St., 79912-5421. Phone: (915) 581-1126. Fax: (915) 585-4611.E-mail: info@kint.com Licensee: Entravision Communications Co. L.L.C. Group owner: Entravision Communications Co. L.L.C. (acq 6-4-97; grpsl). Natl. Rep: Lotus Entravision Reps LLC,. Format: Sp, adult contemp. News: 4 hrs wkly. Target aud: 25-54. ♦David Candelaria, gen mgr; Joe Garcia, opns mgr; Phil Gabbard, gen sls mgr, natl sls mgr; Leo Lugo, prom mgr; Abel Rodriguez, pub affrs dir; Ron Haney, chief of engrg.

***KKLY(FM)**— May 1, 1985: 89.5 mhz; 175 w. Ant 1,007 ft TL: N31 47 33 W106 28 48. Hrs open: 24 2351 Sunset Blvd., Suite 170-218, Rocklin, CA, 95765. Phone: (916) 251-1600. Fax: (916) 251-1650.E-mail: klove@klove.com Licensee: Educational Media Foundation. Group owner: EMF Broadcasting (acq 11-18-2002; $1 million). Natl. Network: K-Love, . Shaw Pittman. Format: Contemp Christian music. News staff: 3. Target aud: 25-44. ♦Richard Jenkins, pres; Mike Novak, VP; Keith Whipple, dev dir; David Pierce, progmg dir; Ed Lenane, news dir; Sam Wallington, engrg dir; Karen Johnson, news rptr.

KLAQ(FM)— Oct 1, 1978: 95.5 mhz; 88 kw. 1,390 ft TL: N31 47 47 W106 28 55. Stereo. Hrs open: Prog sep from AM 4150 Pinnacle, 79902. Phone: (915) 544-9550. Fax: (915) 532-6342.E-mail: info@klaq.com Web Site:www.klaq.com Format: Rock/AOR. Target aud: 18-49; adults who grew up on FM rock and roll. ♦Brad Dubow, gen mgr; Mike Ramey, progmg dir; Ron Haney, chief of engrg.

KOFX(FM)— June 6, 1978: 92.3 mhz; 100 kw. 1,860 ft TL: N31 48 55 W106 29 20. Stereo. Hrs open: 24 5426 N. Mesa, 79912. Phone: (915) 581-1126. Fax: (915) 532-4970.E-mail: info@923thefox.com Web Site:www.923thefox.com Licensee: Entravision Holdings L.L.C. Group owner: Entravision Communications Co. L.L.C. (acq 10-19-99). Population served: 750,000 Format: Oldies. News staff: 2. Target aud: 25-54; upscale. ♦David Candelaria, gen mgr; Joe Garcia, opns mgr; Phil Gabbard, gen sls mgr; Al Jones, progmg dir; Jim Lotspeich, chief of engrg; Susan Graham, traf mgr.

KPAS(FM)—See Fabens

KPRR(FM)— Dec 5, 1969: 102.1 mhz; 100 kw horiz, 66 kw vert. 1,289 ft TL: N31 47 34 W106 28 47. Stereo. Hrs open: 24 4045 N. Mesa St, 79902. Phone: (915) 351-5400. Fax: (915) 351-3102.E-mail: info@kprr.com Web Site:www.kprr.com Licensee: CCB Texas Licenses L.P. Group owner: Clear Channel Communications Inc. (acq 5-16-96; grpsl). Population served: 550,000 Natl. Rep: Clear Channel,. Format: CHR. Target aud: 18-34. ♦L. Lowry Mays, CEO, chmn, pres; Randall T. Mays, CFO; Bill Struck, VP, gen mgr; Michelle Haston, gen sls mgr; Christopher Lucy, mktg dir; Frank Rodriquez, prom dir; Bobby Ramos, progmg dir; Patti Diaz, news dir, local news ed; Andrea Thomas, pub affrs dir; Enriquez Lopez, chief of engrg; Amy Page, traf mgr.

KQBU(AM)— June 1947: 920 khz; 1 kw-D, 360 w-N, DA-N. TL: N31 45 41 W106 26 14. Hrs open: 2211 E. Missouri, Suite 300, 79903. Phone: (915) 544-9797. Fax: (915) 544-1247. Licensee: Tichenor License Corp. Group owner: Univision Radio (acq 9-22-2003; grpsl). Population served: 1,000,000 Format: Talk. ♦MacHenry Tichenor Jr., pres; Cecilia Uebel, gen mgr; Carlos Fourzan, gen sls mgr; Leonel Arias, prom mgr; Michael McCabe, chief of engrg; Patricia Villasenor, traf mgr.

KROD(AM)— June 1, 1940: 600 khz; 5 kw-U, DA-N. TL: N31 54 56 W106 23 33. Hrs open: 24 4150 Pinnacle, 79902. Phone: (915) 544-9550. Fax: (915) 532-6342.E-mail: info@krod.com Web Site:www.krod.com Licensee: Regent Broadcasting of El Paso Inc. Group owner: Regent Communications Inc. (acq 12-1-99; grpsl). Population served: 425,000 Rgnl. Network: Texas State Net. Natl. Rep: D & R Radio,. Texas State Networks Format: News/talk, sports. News staff: one; News: 3 hrs wkly. Target aud: 25-54; adult listeners who grew up on the roots of rock and roll. ♦Brad Dubow, gen mgr; Steve Kaplowitz, progmg dir; Ron Haney, chief of engrg.

KSII(FM)— Dec 30, 1975: 93.1 mhz; 100 kw. 1,422 ft TL: N31 47 34 W106 28 47. Stereo. Hrs open: 24 4150 Pinnacle, Suite 120, 79902. Phone: (915) 544-9300. Fax: (915) 544-9536.E-mail: info@ksii.com Web Site:www.ksiiinfo.com Licensee: Regent Broadcasting of El Paso Inc. Group owner: Regent Communications Inc. (acq 12-1-99; grpsl). Population served: 462,000 Wilmer, Cutler & Pickering. Format: Hot adult contemp. News staff: one; News: 2 hrs wkly. Target aud: 25-54; 60% male, 40% female. ♦Brad Dubow, gen mgr; Kelly Calvillo, gen sls mgr; Chris Elliot, progmg dir; Diana Rivas, pub affrs dir, traf mgr; Robert King, chief of engrg.

KSVE(AM)— Feb 11, 2004: 1650 khz; 8.5 kw-D, 850 w-N. TL: N31 45 13 W106 24 58. Hrs open: 5426 N. Mesa St., 79912-5421. Phone: (915) 581-1126. Fax: (915) 532-4970. Licensee: Entravision Holdings LLC. Group owner: Entravision Communications Corp. Format: Sp. ♦David Candelaria, gen mgr; Joe Garcia, opns mgr; Phil Gabbard, sls dir; Leo Lugo, prom dir; Jim Lotspeich, chief of engrg; Susan Fleming, traf mgr.

***KTEP(FM)**— Sept 14, 1950: 88.5 mhz; 94 kw. 731 ft TL: N31 47 17 W106 28 46. Stereo. Hrs open: 24 500 W. University Ave., 79968-0556. Phone: (915) 747-5152. Phone: (915) 880-5837. Fax: (915) 747-5641.E-mail: ktep@utep.edu Web Site:www.ktep.org Licensee: University of Texas

at El Paso. Population served: 600,000 Natl. Network: PRI, NPR, . Format: Class, jazz, news. News staff: one; News: 39 wkly. Target aud: 35 plus; college educated, upper-income. Spec prog: Gospel 4 hrs, folk 3 hrs wkly. ♦Dennis Woo, opns dir, mus dir; Joe Torres, dev dir, prom dir; Patrick J. Piotrowaski, gen mgr & progmg VP; Louie Saenz, news dir; Norbert Miles, chief of engrg; Norma Martinez, traf mgr.

KTSM(AM)— 1947: 690 khz; 10 kw-U, DA-2. TL: N31 58 11 W106 21 15. Stereo. Hrs open: 24 4045 N. Mesa St, 79902. Phone: (915) 351-5400. Fax: (915) 351-3102.E-mail: info@ktsmradio.com Web Site:www.ktsmradio.com Licensee: CCB Texas Licenses L.P. Group owner: Clear Channel Communications Inc. (acq 5-16-96; grpsl). Population served: 550,000 Natl. Rep: Clear Channel,. Format: News/talk. Target aud: 25-54; men. Spec prog: Relg 3 hrs, radio health journal one hr, El Paso public forum one hr wkly. ♦L. Lowry Mays, CEO, chmn, pres; Randall T. May, CFO; Bill Struck, VP, gen mgr; Karen Daniels-Pearson, gen sls mgr; Christopher Lucy, mktg dir; Frank Rodriquez, prom dir; Tom Connelly, progmg mgr; Melissa Kerr, news dir; Michael Calderon, pub affrs dir; Enrique Lopez, chief of engrg; Krystal Watkins, traf mgr.

KTSM-FM— June 11, 1962: 99.9 mhz; 87 kw. Ant 1,820 ft TL: N31 48 19 W106 28 57. Stereo. Hrs open: 4045 N. Mesa St., 79902. Phone: (915) 351-5400. Fax: (915) 351-3102.E-mail: info@ktsmradio.com Licensee: CCB Texas Licenses L.P. Natl. Network: CBS, . Format: Adult contemp. ♦Bill Clifton Tole, progmg dir; Sam Cassiano, mus dir; Melissa Kerr, pub affrs dir; Enrique Lopez, engrg dir; Krystal Watkins, traf mgr.

***KVER(FM)**— Jan 1, 1993: 91.1 mhz; 510 w. 1,118 ft TL: N31 47 34 W106 28 47. Stereo. Hrs open: 24 Box 12008, 79913-0008. Phone: (915) 544-9190.E-mail: kver@hcjb.org Web Site:www.kver.org Licensee: World Network Radio Inc. (group owner) Format: Sp, relg, educ. Hispanic. ♦Marcos Barraza, stn mgr; Gracel Calleros, progmg dir.

KVIV(AM)— Dec 3, 1949: 1340 khz; 1 kw-U. TL: N31 46 24 W106 24 52. Hrs open: 4900 Montana Ave., 79903. Phone: (915) 565-2999. Fax: (915) 562-3156.E-mail: radiovictoria@mail.com Licensee: El Paso y Juarez Companerismo-Cristiano (acq 10-20-2006). Population served: 450,000 Dow, Lohnes & Albertson. Format: Sp, relg. Target aud: Mexican-American. ♦Alfonso Cabrera, pres, gen mgr; Jesus Cruz, progmg dir.

KXPL(AM)— Sept 16, 1985: 1060 khz; 10 kw-D. TL: N31 48 41 W106 31 53. Hrs open: 2211 E. Missouri Ave., E-237, 79903-3837. Phone: (915) 587-8822. Fax: (915) 587-8602.E-mail: newsroomlavoz@yahoo.com Licensee: New Radio System Inc. (acq 7-21-2004). Format: Sp info/news. ♦Maria Elena Lazo, gen mgr; Jose Camacho, progmg dir, traf mgr; Paul Gregg, chief of engrg.

KYSE(FM)— Nov 29, 1958: 94.7 mhz; 97 kw horiz, 65 kw vert. Ant 1,191 ft TL: N31 47 34 W106 28 47. Stereo. Hrs open: 24 5426 N. Mesa, 79902. Phone: (915) 581-1126. Fax: (915) 532-4970.E-mail: info@superestrella947.com Web Site:www.superestrella947.com Licensee: Entravision Holdings L.L.C. Group owner: Entravision Communications Co. L.L.C. (acq 10-19-99). Natl. Rep: Lotus Entravision Reps LLC,. Format: Sp, Top-40. Target aud: 18-34. ♦David Candelaria, gen mgr; Joe Garcia, opns dir; Phil Gabbard, gen sls mgr; Susan Graham, traf mgr.

Eldorado

KLDE(FM)— 2007: 104.9 mhz; 6 kw. Ant 302 ft TL: N30 51 55 W100 35 36. Hrs open: Box 717, 76936. Phone: (325) 853-1049. Licensee: Tenn-Vol Corp. (acq 3-25-2008; $13,209 for CP). Format: Oldies. ♦Danny Ray Boyer, gen mgr.

Electra

***KOLI(FM)**— January 1998: 94.9 mhz; 50 kw. 492 ft TL: N34 05 01 W98 59 29. Hrs open: 4302 Callfield Rd., Wichita Falls, 76308. Phone: (940) 691-2311. Fax: (940) 696-2255.E-mail: info@cumulus.com Web Site:www.culumus.com Licensee: Cumulus Licensing Corp. Group owner: Cumulus Media Inc. (acq 8-10-99; $238,400). Format: Classic Country. ♦Lindy Parr, gen mgr; Brent Warner, opns mgr, progmg dir; Andrea Lewis, gen sls mgr; Jim Russell, news dir; Jeff Chan, chief of engrg; Dana Jameson, traf mgr.

Elgin

KXXS(FM)— Aug 14, 1992: 92.5 mhz; 1.6 kw. Ant 449 ft TL: N30 19 00 W97 20 22. Hrs open: 24 912 South Capital of Texas Hwy, Suite 400, Austin, 78746. Phone: (512) 453-1491. Fax: (512) 453-6809.E-mail: jdelcore@bmpradio.com Licensee: BMP Austin License Company L.P. (acq 2-10-2005; grpsl). Natl. Network: CNN Radio, . Bechtel & Cole. Format: Sp, Tejano. ♦Pedro Gasc, gen mgr.

Fabens

KPAS(FM)— Mar 24, 1979: 103.1 mhz; 3 kw. 300 ft TL: N31 35 42 W106 11 58. Stereo. Hrs open: 18 Box 371010, El Paso, 79937. Phone: (915) 851-3382. Fax: (915) 851-4360. Web Site:www.kpasfmradio.com Licensee: Algie A. Felder. (acq 6-27-86; 5-12-86). Population served: 2,000,000 Natl. Network: USA, . Format: Relg. News: 6 hrs wkly. ♦Algie A. Felder, pres & gen mgr.

Fairfield

KNES(FM)— Dec 1, 1983: 99.1 mhz; 11.5 kw. Ant 482 ft TL: N31 40 55 W96 01 22. Stereo. Hrs open: 24 PO Box 347, 627 W. Commerce, 75840. Phone: (903) 389-5637. Fax: (903) 389-7172.E-mail: texas99@texas99.com Web Site:www.texas99.com Licensee: J & J Communications Inc. (acq 11-19-90; $209,000; 12-10-90). Natl. Network: Jones Radio Networks, . Rgnl. Network: Texas State Net. Natl. Rep: Riley,. Texas State Networks Format: Country. News staff: one; News: 6 hrs wkly. Target aud: General. Spec prog: Farm 3 hrs, talk 15 hrs, Black 3 hrs, gospel 3 hrs wkly. ♦Buzz Russell, progmg dir; Joe Reid, gen mgr, rgnl sls mgr & traf mgr.

Falfurrias

KDFM(FM)—Not on air, target date: unknown: 103.3 mhz; 3 kw. 328 ft TL: N27 15 28 W98 07 07. Hrs open: Box 252, McAllen, 78505. Phone: (956) 686-6382. Phone: (956) 686-2992. Fax: (956) 686-2999. Licensee: La Radio Cristiana Network Inc. Format: Sp.

KLDS(AM)— Jan 1, 1953: 1260 khz; 500 w-D, 330 w-N. TL: N27 14 11 W98 10 22. Hrs open: 6 AM-midnight Box 401, 78355. Secondary address: 215 W. Adam St. 78355. Phone: (361) 325-1212. Fax: (361) 325-5003. Licensee: The Evangelistic Worship Center (acq 10-27-97; $75,000). Population served: 250,000 Baraff, Koerner & Olender. Format: Sp/ Christian. Target aud: General. ♦Timothy Trevino, gen mgr & progmg dir; Steve Cantu, chief of engrg.

KPSO-FM— Nov 1, 1983: 106.3 mhz; 6 kw. Ant 184 ft TL: N27 14 11 W98 10 22. Stereo. Hrs open: 6 AM-10 PM 304 E. Rice St., 78355-3624. Phone: (361) 325-2112. Fax: (361) 325-2112.E-mail: kpso@awesomenet.net Licensee: Brooks Broadcasting Corp. Population served: 100,000 Texas State Networks Koerner & Olender. Format: Tejano (Sp), country. News: 15 hrs wkly. Target aud: All groups. ♦Raymond O. Creely, gen mgr, chief of engrg; Steve Cantu, exec VP, gen sls mgr & spanish dir.

***KTPM(FM)**—Not on air, target date: unknown: 88.1 mhz; 100 w vert. Ant 220 ft TL: N27 17 20 W98 07 23. Hrs open: Box 18400, Corpus Christi, 78480. Phone: (361) 937-4201. Licensee: Texas Pelican Media. ♦Nancy J. Doerner, gen mgr.

Fannett

***KZFT(FM)**— Oct 31, 2003: 90.5 mhz; 35 kw vert. Ant 361 ft TL: N29 53 33 W94 08 06. Hrs open: Drawer 3206, Tupelo, MS, 38803. Phone: (662) 844-8888. Fax: (662) 842-6791. Licensee: American Family Association. Group owner: American Family Radio. Format: Christian. ♦Marvin Sanders, gen mgr.

Farmersville

KFCD(AM)— November 1947: 990 khz; 7 kw-D, 920 w-N, DA-2. TL: N33 07 01 W96 16 47. Stereo. Hrs open: 24 Box 12345, Dallas, 75225. Phone: (972) 354-1990. Fax: (972) 354-0820. Licensee: Bernard Dallas LLC (acq 1-31-2007; $9 million with KHSE(AM) Wylie). Population served: 385,200 Natl. Network: CNN Radio, . Rgnl. Network: Texas State Net. Format: Talk. Target aud: 35 plus; men. ♦Jerry Overton, gen mgr; Dave Marcum, opns mgr, progmg mgr, pub affrs dir; Ed Wodka, rgnl sls mgr, adv mgr; Dave Schum, chief of engrg; Leslie Cooke, traf mgr.

KXEZ(FM)— Sept 1, 1998: 92.1 mhz; 1.95 kw. Ant 584 ft TL: N33 16 31 W96 22 02. Stereo. Hrs open: Box 940670, Plano, 75094. Phone: (903) 482-6750. Phone: (972) 396-1640. Fax: (972) 396-1643.E-mail: info@kxez.com Web Site:www.kxez.com Licensee: Metro Broadcasters-Texas Inc. (acq 12-3-98). Natl. Network: Jones Radio Networks, . Format: Classic country. ♦Ken Jones, CEO, pres, gen mgr, chief of engrg; Glenda Jones, CFO; Jack Bishop, opns dir, pub affrs dir; Joshua Jones, sls dir, gen sls mgr, mktg VP, mktg dir, prom dir; Hal Mayfield, news dir; Ron Eudaly, engrg dir.

Farwell

KICA-FM— Sept 15, 1984: 98.3 mhz; 50 kw. Ant 223 ft TL: N34 23 22 W103 10 27. (CP: 100 kw, ant 384 ft. TL: N34 29 36 W103 23 46). Stereo. Hrs open: 24 1000 Sycamore St., Clovis, NM, 88101. Phone: (505) 762-6200. Fax: (505) 762-8800. Licensee: Tallgrass Broadcasting LLC. (group owner; (acq 4-2-2007; grpsl). Population served: 80,000 Format: World class rock. News staff: one; News: 3 hrs wkly. Target aud: 18-49. ♦Dana Taylor, progmg dir, sports cmtr; Shannon Phillips, mus dir & traf mgr.

KIJN(AM)— Apr 17, 1958: 1060 khz; 10 kw-D, DA. TL: N34 23 14 W103 01 51. Hrs open: Box 458, 79325. Phone: (806) 481-3318. Fax: (806) 481-3835.E-mail: kijn@email.com Licensee: Metropolitan Radio Group Inc. (group owner; (acq 9-97; with co-located FM). Population served: 150,000 Format: Christian music, relg, Sp Christian. Target aud: General. ♦Mike Rodriquez, gen mgr; David Pollard, progmg dir.

KIJN-FM— Aug 1, 1985: 92.3 mhz; 100 kw. Ant 354 ft TL: N34 32 26 W102 47 56. Stereo. Hrs open: 24 Box 458, 79325. Phone: (806) 481-3318. Fax: (806) 481-3835. Licensee: Joseph Walker (acq 5-26-2009; $90,000). Population served: 150,000 Format: Christian music, relg.

KMUL(AM)— July 6, 1956: 830 khz; 1.1 kw-D, 10 w-N. TL: N34 29 42 W103 23 39. Hrs open: 600 W 8th St., Muleshoe, 79347-3330. Phone: (806) 272-4273. Phone: (806) 272-4087. Fax: (806) 272-5067.E-mail: info@kmulam.com Licensee: Tallgrass Broadcasting LLC. (group owner; (acq 4-2-2007; grpsl). Population served: 4,525 Format: Sp. Spec prog: Farm 3 hrs wkly. ♦Noe Anzaldua, gen mgr, progmg dir; Martha Alvarado, progmg dir; Rick Keefer, chief of engrg.

Ferris

KDFT(AM)— July 13, 1988: 540 khz; 1 kw-D, 249 w-N, DA-2. TL: N32 30 47 W96 34 28 (D), N32 30 52 W96 34 26 (N). Hrs open: 24 5801 Marvin D. Love Fwy., Suite 409, Dallas, 75237. Phone: (972) 572-1540. Fax: (972) 572-1263.E-mail: kdft-kmny@mrbi.net Web Site:kdft540.com Licensee: Way Broadcasting Licensee LLC (acq 4-19-2000; grpsl). Rgnl rep: In Language Radio, San Francisco Format: Sp Christian. Target aud: 25-59; Sp. ♦Sean Kim, COO; Arthur Liu, pres; Ted Sauceman, gen mgr; Yary Uhing, opns mgr.

Floresville

***KJMA(FM)**— 1993: 89.7 mhz; 9 kw. Ant 138 ft TL: N29 13 55 W98 03 05. Hrs open: 1905 10th St., 78114. Phone: (830) 393-6116. Fax: (830) 393-3817. Web Site:www.grnonline.com Licensee: La Promesa Foundation. (acq 6-25-2007; $130,000). Population served: 45,000 Natl. Network: EWTN Radio, . Format: Catholic radio. ♦Leonard J. Oswald, pres; Cissy Gonzalez, gen mgr.

KTFM(FM)— June 15, 1977: 94.1 mhz; 40 kw. Ant 548 ft TL: N29 11 03 W98 30 49. Stereo. Hrs open: 24 4500 Eisenhauer Rd., San Antonio, 78218. Phone: (210) 654-5100. Fax: (210) 340-1775. Licensee: BMP San Antonio License Co. L.P. Group owner: Border Media Partners LLC (acq 4-28-2004; $24.4 million with KSAH(AM) Universal City). Population served: 1,400,000 Format: Rhythmic CHR. Target aud: 18-49. ♦Lance Hawkins, gen mgr; Bob Brown, sls dir.

Flower Mound

KPMZ(FM)— Oct 23, 2006: 96.7 mhz; 92 kw. Ant 2,034 ft TL: N33 26 13 W97 29 05. Stereo. Hrs open: 24 2221 E. Lamar Blvd., Suite 300, Arlington, 76006. Phone: (817) 695-3500. Fax: (817) 695-0860. Web Site:www.platinum967.com Licensee: Radio License Holding IV LLC. Group owner: ABC Inc. (acq 6-12-2007; . grpsl). Population served: 132,000 Natl. Network: ABC, . Natl. Rep: McGavren Guild,. Format: Adult hits. Target aud: 18-34; adults. ♦Victor Sansone, gen mgr; Neal Peden, chief of engrg.

Floydada

KFLP(AM)— 1951: 900 khz; 250 w-D. TL: N33 58 20 W101 21 00. Hrs open: Box 658, 79235. Phone: (806) 983-5704. Fax: (806) 983-5705.E-mail: kflp@kflp.net Web Site:www.kflp.net Licensee: Anthony L. Ricketts. (acq 8-4-99; with co-located FM). Population served: 20,000 Natl. Network: USA, . Natl. Rep: Interep,. American Ag Format: Farm. News staff: one; News: 12 hrs wkly. Farmers. ♦Tony St. James, gen mgr & progmg dir.

KFLP-FM— Apr 1, 1985: 106.1 mhz; 25 kw. Ant 233 ft TL: N33 58 07 W101 21 15. Stereo. Hrs open: 24 Box 658, 79235. Phone: (806) 983-5704. Fax: (806) 983-5705. Web Site:www.kflp.net Licensee:

Anthony L. Ricketts. Population served: 20,000 Rgnl. Network: VSA Radio. Natl. Rep: Interep,. Format: Country. Target aud: 18-49; adults.

Fort Stockton

KFST(AM)— May 8, 1954: 860 khz; 250 w-U. TL: N30 52 37 W102 53 30. Hrs open: 24 954 S US Hwy. 385, 79735. Phone: (432) 336-2228. Phone: (432) 336-5834. Fax: (432) 336-5834.E-mail: kfst@sbcglobal.net Licensee: Fort Stockton Radio Co Inc. (acq 1-1-86). Population served: 226,422 Rgnl. Network: Texas State Net. Texas State Networks Wire Svc: NOAA Weather Format: Adult contemp, relg. News staff: 2; News: 6 hrs wkly. Target aud: General. ◆Ken Ripley, gen mgr, dev dir, progmg dir, chief of engrg & local news ed.

KFST-FM— November 1974: 94.3 mhz; 3 kw. Ant 236 ft TL: N30 52 37 W102 53 30. Stereo. Hrs open: 954 S. US Hwy. 385, 79735. Phone: (432) 336-2228. Phone: (432) 336-5834. Fax: (432) 336-5834.E-mail: kfst@sbcglobal.net Licensee: Fort Stockton Radio Co. Inc. Wire Svc: NOAA Weather Format: Country, Sp.

*KRAF(FM)—Not on air, target date: unknown: 88.3 mhz; 300 w. Ant 26 ft TL: N30 52 00 W102 51 54. Hrs open: 902 W. Michigan, Midland, 79701. Phone: (432) 686-9522. Licensee: Christian Television Radio Ministry. ◆David Chavez, gen mgr.

Fort Worth

KBFB(FM)—See Dallas

KDMX(FM)—See Dallas

KDXX(FM)—See Benbrook

KEGL(FM)— April 1959: 97.1 mhz; 99 kw. Ant 1,666 ft TL: N32 35 19 W96 58 05. Stereo. Hrs open: 24 14001 N. Dallas Pkwy., Suite 300, Dallas, 75240. Phone: (214) 866-8000. Web Site:www.kegl.com Licensee: Citicasters Licenses L.P. Group owner: Clear Channel Communications Inc. (acq 5-4-99; grpsl). Population served: 517,600 Format: Rock. ◆J.D. Freeman, gen mgr; Pat McMahon, opns mgr.

KFJZ(AM)— Feb 15, 1947: 870 khz; 500 w-D. TL: N32 45 42 W97 18 49. Hrs open: 521 E. Bolt St., 76110. Phone: (817) 923-3424. Licensee: SIGA Broadcasting Corp. (acq 1-10-2008; $1.8 million). Population served: 3,600,000 Format: Sp. ◆Gabriel Arango, pres & gen mgr.

KFLC(AM)— 1922: 1270 khz; 50 kw-D, 5 kw-N, DA-2. TL: N32 43 36 W97 11 30. Stereo. Hrs open: 24 7700 Carpenter Fwy., Dallas, 75247. Phone: (214) 525-0400. Fax: (214) 631-1196. Web Site:www.univision.com Licensee: KESS-AM License Corp. Group owner: Univision Radio (acq 9-22-2003; grpsl). Population served: 4,000,000 Format: Sp, news/talk, sports. News staff: 2; News: 11 hrs wkly. Target aud: 25-54. ◆Frank Carter, gen mgr; Andy Lockridge, opns dir; Cipriano Robles, sls dir; Ivonne Flaherty, gen sls mgr; Karen Hocking, natl sls mgr; Oscar Espinosa, prom dir; Herminio (Chayan) Ortuno, progmg dir; Myrna Vera, news dir, rsch dir; Patrick Parks, engrg mgr & chief of engrg; Mirentxu Smith, rsch dir, traf mgr; Claudia Torrescano, pub svc dir.

KFXR(AM)—See Dallas

KHVN(AM)— Dec 6, 1946: 970 khz; 1 kw-D, 270 w-N. TL: N32 47 56 W97 17 43. Hrs open: 24 5787 S. Hampton Rd., Dallas, 75232. Phone: (214) 331-5486. Fax: (214) 331-1908.E-mail: traffic@khvanam.com Web Site:www.khvnam.com Licensee: Mortenson Broadcasting Co. of Texas Inc. (group owner; (acq 5-31-2002; $4.5 million with KNAX(AM) Fort Worth). Population served: 600,000 Natl. Rep: Interep,. Format: Gospel. News staff: one; News: 10 hrs wkly. Target aud: 25-54. ◆Jack Mortenson, CEO & VP; Dion Mortenson, gen mgr.

KJKK(FM)—See Dallas

KKDA-FM—See Dallas

KKGM(AM)— 2002: 1630 khz; 10 kw-D, 1 kw-N. TL: N32 48 35 W97 07 24. Hrs open: 24 hrs 5787 S. Hampton Rd., Suite 108, Dallas, 75232. Phone: (214) 337-5700. Fax: (214) 337-5707.E-mail: traffic@kkgmam.com Web Site:www.kkgmam.com Licensee: Mortenson Broadcasting Co. of Texas Inc. (group owner; (acq 5-31-2002; with KHVN(AM) Fort Worth). Population served: 6,000,000 Format: Southern gospel, ministry, sports. Target aud: 30-64. ◆Lon Sosh, gen mgr; Jack Davis, progmg dir; Mike Price, chief of engrg.

KLIF(AM)—See Dallas

KLNO(FM)— Dec 24, 1964: 94.1 mhz; 100 kw. Ant 1,585 ft TL: N32 35 22 W96 58 10. Stereo. Hrs open: 24 7700 Carpenter Hwy., Dallas, 75247. Phone: (214) 525-0400. Fax: (214) 525-0473. Fax: (214) 631-1196 (sales).E-mail: info@klnofm.com Licensee: HBC License Corp. Group owner: Univision Radio (acq 9-22-2003; grpsl). Population served: 250000 Natl. Network: ABC, . Format: Mexican regional. ◆Frank Carter, gen mgr; Andy Lockridge, opns dir; Cipriane Robles, sls dir; Ivonne Flaherty, gen sls mgr; Karen Hecking, natl sls mgr; Oscar Espinosa, prom dir; Herminio (Chayan) Ortuno, progmg dir; Patrick Parks, chief of engrg; Myrna Vera, rsch dir; Mirentxu Smith, traf mgr; Claudia Torrescano, pub svc dir.

KLTY(FM)—See Dallas

KLUV(FM)—See Dallas

KMVK(FM)— Feb 8, 1965: 107.5 mhz; 16.5 kw. Ant 1,883 ft TL: N32 35 02 W96 57 48. Stereo. Hrs open: 24 7901 Carpenter Fwy., Dallas, 75247. Phone: (214) 526-9870. Fax: (214) 905-5052. Web Site:www.mega1075.com Licensee: CBS Radio Partner I Inc. Group owner: CBS Radio (acq 6-26-96; grpsl). Format: Sp hot adult contemp. Target aud: 25-54. ◆Julie Davis, CEO, traf mgr; Mel Karmazin, pres; David Henry, gen mgr; Rick Frisch, gen sls mgr; Dave Dillon, natl sls mgr; Liz Balon, prom dir; Kurt Johnson, progmg dir; Mark Sanford, mus dir; Bill Taylor, news dir, chief of engrg; Vance Henley, engrg mgr.

KPLX(FM)— Dec 15, 1962: 99.5 mhz; 100 kw. 1,680 ft TL: N32 34 54 W96 58 32. Stereo. Hrs open: 24 3500 Maple Ave., Suite 1600, Dallas, 75219. Phone: (214) 526-2400. Fax: (214) 520-4343.E-mail: info@kplzfm.com Web Site:www.995thewolf.com Licensee: KPLX Lico Inc. Group owner: Susquehanna Radio Corp. (acq 1974). Population served: 4,418,400 Natl. Network: AP Network News, . Format: Country. News staff: one; News: 4 hrs wkly. Target aud: 25-54; loyal listeners throughout the day. ◆Dan Bennett, pres, mktg mgr; Jim Quirk, sls dir; Rob Chickering, chief of engrg.

KRLD(AM)—See Dallas

KRLD-FM—See Dallas

KRVA(AM)—See Dallas

KSCS(FM)— Mar 8, 1949: 96.3 mhz; 99 kw. Ant 1,610 ft TL: N32 35 15 W96 57 59. Stereo. Hrs open: 24 Prog sep from AM 2221 E. Lamar, Suite 300, Arlington, 76006. Phone: (817) 695-1820. Fax: (817) 695-0014. Web Site:www.kscs.com Population served: 3,000,000 Natl. Rep: ABC Radio Sales,. Format: Country. ◆Greg Heitzman, natl sls mgr; Robert Shiflet, mktg dir.

KSKY(AM)—See Dallas

*KTCU-FM— Oct 6, 1964: 88.7 mhz; 3 kw. 320 ft TL: N32 42 40 W97 22 00. Stereo. Hrs open: 6 AM-1 AM Box 298020, Moudy Bldg., Texas Christian Univ., 76129. Phone: (817) 257-7631. Phone: (817) 257-7634. Fax: (817) 257-7637.E-mail: ktcu@tcu.edu Web Site:www.ktcu.net Licensee: Board of Trustees Texas Christian University. Population served: 1,000,000 Format: Americana, Rock, AAA. Spec prog: some specialty shows. ◆Russell Scott, gen mgr.

KZPS(FM)—See Dallas

WBAP(AM)— May 2, 1922: 820 khz; 50 kw-U. TL: N32 36 38 W97 10 00. Stereo. Hrs open: 24 2221 E. Lamar, Suite 300, Arlington, 76006. Phone: (817) 695-1820. Fax: (817) 695-0014. Web Site:www.wbap.com Licensee: Radio License Holding IV LLC. Group owner: ABC Inc. (acq 6-12-2007; grpsl). Population served: 3,500,000 Natl. Rep: ABC Radio Sales,. Format: News/talk. News staff: 7; News: 37 hrs wkly. Target aud: 25-54. Spec prog: Dallas Stars, farm 6 hrs wkly. ◆Pete Dits, gen mgr, gen sls mgr; Stephanie Calahan, gen sls mgr; Bob Shomper, progmg dir; Neal Reden, chief of engrg.

Fort Worth-Dallas

KDGE(FM)— Apr 10, 1962: 102.1 mhz; 100 kw. Ant 1,591 ft TL: N32 34 54 W96 58 32. Stereo. Hrs open: 24 14001 N. Dallas Pkwy., Suite 300, Dallas, 75240. Phone: (214) 866-8000. Fax: (214) 866-8091. Web Site:www.kdge.com Licensee: Capstar TX L.P. Group owner: Clear Channel Communications Inc. (acq 8-30-2000; grpsl). Population served: 3,000,000 Natl. Rep: CBS Radio,. Format: Alternative rock. News staff: one; News: 5 hrs wkly. Target aud: 20-44. ◆J.D. Freeman, gen mgr; Tracy Martin Taylor, stn mgr; John Roberts, opns mgr.

Franklin

KBXT(FM)— Nov 7, 1994: 101.9 mhz; 25 kw. Ant 328 ft TL: N30 56 04 W96 26 15. Hrs open: 24 Box 3069, Bryan, 77802. Phone: (979) 776-1240. Fax: (979) 776-0123. Licensee: Brazos Valley Communications Ltd. (group owner; (acq 8-31-2006; grpsl). Format: Rhythmic contemp hit radio. ◆Edward Sanchez, gen mgr.

Frankston

KOYE(FM)— June 15, 1970: 96.7 mhz; 50 kw. Ant 492 ft TL: N32 02 22 W95 24 39. Stereo. Hrs open: 24 East Texas Radio Group, 210 S. Broadway, Tyler, 75702. Phone: (903) 581-9966. Fax: (903) 534-5300.E-mail: request@koye.com Web Site:www.lainvasora.fm Licensee: Access.1 Texas License Company LLC. Group owner: Waller Broadcasting (acq 1-7-2005; grpsl). Population served: 300,000 Natl. Rep: McGavren Guild,. Format: Rgnl Mexican. Target aud: 18-49. ◆Rick Guest, gen mgr; Genni Causey, gen sls mgr; Robert Taylor, natl sls mgr; Jessie Duron, progmg dir.

Fredericksburg

*KBLC(FM)— August 2008: 91.5 mhz; 3.1 kw. Ant 394 ft TL: N30 11 49 W98 38 19. Hrs open: 2424 South Blvd., Houston, 77098-5196. Phone: (713) 520-5200. Licensee: Houston Christian Broadcasters Inc. ◆Bruce Munsterman, pres.

KNAF(AM)— November 1947: 910 khz; 1 kw-D, 174 w-N. TL: N30 17 12 W98 52 58. Hrs open: Box 311, 78624. Secondary address: 210 Woodcrest 78624. Phone: (830) 997-2197. Fax: (830) 997-2198.E-mail: texasrebelradio@fbgn Licensee: J. & J. Fritz Media Ltd. (group owner; (acq 1-23-91;2-11-91). Population served: 200,000 Rgnl. Network: Texas State Net. Format: Country, full service, talk. Spec prog: Farm 5 hrs, Polka 4.5 hrs wkly. ◆Jayson Fritz, pres, gen mgr; Jan Fritz, sr VP; Arziana Carruth, prom dir; Rick Star, progmg dir; Holley Day, mus dir.

KNAF-FM— 2005: 105.7 mhz; 9.1 kw. Ant 538 ft TL: N30 21 49 W98 54 47. Stereo. Hrs open: Box 311, 78624. Secondary address: 210 Woodcrest 78624. Phone: (830) 997-2197. Fax: (830) 997-2198.E-mail: txradio@ktc.com (group owner). Format: Country. Target aud: 18-54. ◆Jayson Fritz, engrg VP.

Freeport

KJOJ-FM— 1987: 103.3 mhz; 100 kw. Ant 994 ft TL: N28 48 57 W95 36 03. Hrs open: 3000 Bering Dr., Houston, 77057. Phone: (713) 315-3400. Fax: (713) 315-3565.E-mail: Houstoninfo@lbimedia.com Web Site:www.laraza.fm Licensee: Liberman Broadcasting of Houston License LLC. Group owner: Liberman Broadcasting Inc. (acq 3-20-2001; grpsl). Population served: 4,000,000 Format: Rgnl Mexican. ◆Lenard Liberman, CEO, pres; Winter Horton, VP; Gerardo Reyes, gen sls mgr; Cheque Gonzalez, progmg dir; Meliza Posada, traf mgr.

Freer

KBRA(FM)— Jan 18, 1985: 95.9 mhz; 190 w horiz. Ant 466 ft TL: N27 51 17 W98 35 49. Hrs open: 850 Brandon Ave., Jackson, MS, 39209. Phone: (601) 906-0836. Licensee: Cobra Broadcasting Co. L.L.C. Population served: 5,000

*KPBN(FM)— 2004: 90.7 mhz; 700 w. Ant 312 ft TL: N27 48 55 W98 41 45. Hrs open: Box 252, McAllen, 78505. Phone: (956) 686-6382. Fax: (956) 686-2999. Licensee: Paulino Bernal Evangelism. Format: Sp, Christian. ◆Paulino Bernal Jr., pres.

Friona

KGRW(FM)— Nov 1, 1994: 94.7 mhz; 50 kw. Ant 492 ft TL: N34 41 17 W102 56 53. Hrs open: Rebroadcasts KQFX(FM) Borger 100%. 3639 Wolfin Ave., Amarillo, 79102. Phone: (806) 355-1044. Fax: (806) 457-0642.E-mail: CTOMZA;ZE@TEGASB.COM Licensee: Tejas Broadcasting Ltd. LLP. Group owner: Amigo Broadcasting L.P. (acq 11-15-2004; grpsl). Format: Sp, Tejano. Target aud: 25-54; working class Texas born Hispanic audience. ◆Matt Douglas, gen mgr; Brad Gonzalez, gen sls mgr; Israel Salazar, progmg dir; Charles Singleton, chief of engrg; Emilia Chacon, traf mgr.

Frisco

KATH(AM)— October 1936: 910 khz; 1 kw-D, 500 w-N, DA-2. TL: N33 12 55 W96 53 56. Hrs open: 8828 N. Stemmons Fwy., Suite 106, Dallas, 75247. Phone: (214) 634-7780. Fax: (214) 634-7523. Licensee: Chatham Hill Foundation Inc. Group owner: Amigo Broadcasting L.P. (acq 12-13-2006; grpsl). Format: Sp, sports. Target aud: Ages 18-44; Hispanic sports & music fans. ◆Gus Perez, gen mgr; Fernando Gonzalez, sls dir; Arturo Canizalez, progmg dir; Adriana Balero, traf mgr.

Gainesville

KGAF(AM)— 1947: 1580 khz; 250 w-U, DA-N. TL: N33 37 42 W97 06 25. Hrs open: P. O. Box 368, 107-A S. Commerce St., 76241. Phone: (940) 665-5546. Fax: (940) 665-1580.E-mail: info@kgaf1580.com Web Site:www.kgaf1580.com Licensee: First IV Media Inc. (acq 11-15-74). Population served: 16,210 Texas State Networks Format: Adult contemp, oldies, news/talk. News staff: one. Target aud: 25-54; m/f. Spec prog: Farm 3 hrs, sports 3 hrs wkly. ◆Steve Eberhart, gen mgr; Curt Spain, gen sls mgr; Dee Blanton, progmg dir; Stephen Monahan, news dir; Frank Bonner, chief of engrg; Chad Henderson, disc jockey.

KSOC(FM)—Licensed to Gainesville. See Dallas

Galveston

KGBC(AM)— May 1947: 1540 khz; 1 kw-D, 250 w-N, DA-N. TL: N29 18 51 W94 48 16. Hrs open: 24 1302 N. Shepherd Dr., Houston, 77008-3752. Phone: (713) 868-5559. Fax: (713) 868-9631.E-mail: KGBC1540@gmail.com Web Site:www.kgbc1540.com Licensee: SIGA Broadcasting Corp. (group owner; acq 5-9-2002; $900,000). Population served: 150,000 Format: Favorite songs from the 60s, 70s and 80s. Target aud: 30 plus; general. ◆Julian Arango, stn mgr; Bobby Coles, adv mgr.

KHCB(AM)—Licensed to Galveston. See Houston

KOVE-FM— July 2001: 106.5 mhz; 100 kw. Ant 1,322 ft TL: N29 24 40 W94 57 04. Stereo. Hrs open: 24 5100 Southwest Fwy., Houston, 77056. Phone: (713) 965-2300. Fax: (713) 965-2401.E-mail: info@univision.com Web Site:www.univision.com Licensee: HBC License Corp. Group owner: Univision Radio (acq 9-22-2003; grpsl). Population served: 4,000,000 Format: Sp super hits. News staff: one; News: 3 hrs wkly. Target aud: 18-49; assimilated Hispanics. ◆Mark Masepohl, sr VP, VP; Dave Burdette, stn mgr; Arnulfo Ramirez, opns dir; Marie Barden, gen sls mgr; Kim Mercier, natl sls mgr; Frances Jones, prom dir; Angel Basulto, progmg dir; Renzo Heredia, pub affrs dir; Marty Scruggs, engrg dir; Carole Van Matre, rsch dir; Claudetta Wallace, traf mgr.

Ganado

KHTZ(FM)— Nov 26, 1997: 104.7 mhz; 50 kw. Ant 459 ft TL: N28 55 37 W96 46 54. Stereo. Hrs open: 24 102 Jason Plaza, Suite 1, Victoria, 77901. Phone: (979) 836-9411. Fax: (361) 579-4105.E-mail: ego@lonestarfm.com Web Site:www.lonestarfm.com Licensee: Roy E. Henderson. (group owner; (acq 5-10-2001; $1.5 million). Texas State Networks Format: Country. Target aud: 25-64; skews males. ◆Ryan Henderson, gen mgr.

Gardendale

KFZX(FM)— Jan 9, 1984: 102.1 mhz; 100 kw. Ant 984 ft TL: N31 57 55 W102 46 10. Stereo. Hrs open: 24 1330 E. 8th St., Suite 207, Odessa, 79761. Phone: (432) 563-9102. Fax: (432) 580-9102. Web Site:www.1021jackfm.com Licensee: GAP Broadcasting Midland-Odessa License LLC. Group owner: Clear Channel Communications (acq 10-1-2007; grpsl). Population served: 200,000 Natl. Rep: Eastman Radio,. Format: Adult hits. Target aud: 25-54. ◆Mike Gatons gen mgr; Robert Hallmark, progmg dir; Rodney Norris, chief of engrg.

Garland

KAAM(AM)—Licensed to Garland. See Dallas

Gatesville

*KYAR(FM)— Apr 6, 1976: 98.3 mhz; 200 w. Ant 239 ft TL: N31 27 07 W97 42 14. Stereo. Hrs open: 24 2351 Sunset Blvd., Suite 170-218, Rocklin, CA, 95765. Phone: (916) 251-1600. Fax: (916) 251-1650.

Licensee: Educational Media Foundation. Group owner: EMF Broadcasting (acq 3-21-2003; $100,000). Population served: 130,000 Natl. Network: Air 1, . Rgnl. Network: Texas State Net. Shaw Pittman. Format: Christian. News staff: 3. Target aud: 25-44; Judeo Christian, female. ◆Richard Jenkins, pres; Mike Novak, VP; Keith Whipple, dev dir; David Pierce, progmg mgr; Ed Lenane, news dir; Sam Wallington, engrg dir; Karen Johnson, news rptr.

George West

KGWT(FM)— 2008: 93.5 mhz; 22.5 kw. Ant 344 ft TL: N28 17 37 W98 13 16. Hrs open: 206 1/2 Houston St., 78022-3457. Phone: (361) 449-1315. Licensee: Hispanic Target Media Inc. ◆Francisco San Millan, pres.

Georgetown

KHFI-FM— Mar 1, 1972: 96.7 mhz; 100 kw. 951 ft TL: N30 19 20 W97 48 03. Stereo. Hrs open: 24 3601 S. Congress Ave., #F, Austin, 78704-7213. Phone: (512) 684-7300. Fax: (512) 684-7441.E-mail: info@967kissfm.com Web Site:www.967kissfm.com Licensee: CCB Texas Licenses L.P. Group owner: Clear Channel Communications Inc. (acq 3-9-93; $3.5 million;3-29-93). Population served: 900,000 Natl. Rep: Clear Channel,. Format: Hit rock. News staff: one; News: one hr wkly. Target aud: 18-49; adult women. ◆Pam McKay, gen mgr, mktg mgr; Mac Daniels, opns dir; Mel Jones, sls dir; Melody Caldwell, gen sls mgr; Tracy Walker, mktg dir; Gil Garcia, chief of engrg.

KHZS(FM)— Oct 31, 1991: 107.7 mhz; 25 kw. Ant 508 ft TL: N30 42 17 W97 38 32. Hrs open: 24 57 W. South Temple, Suite 107, Salt Lake City, UT, 84101. Phone: (512) 419-1077. Fax: (512) 340-7169.E-mail: info@kinvfm.com Web Site:www.netmio.com Licensee: Univision Radio License Corp. Group owner: Univision Radio (acq 9-22-2003; grpsl). Jones, Waldo, Holbrook & McDonough. Format: Sp, adult hits. Target aud: 18-34; male.

Giddings

*KANJ(FM)— Oct 28, 1999: 91.1 mhz; 450 w. Ant 335 ft TL: N30 09 56 W96 52 15. Hrs open: 24 Rebroadcasts KHCB-FM Houston 95%. 2424 South Blvd., Houston, 77098. Phone: (713) 520-5200.E-mail: email@khcb.org Web Site:www.khcb.org Licensee: Houston Christian Broadcasters Inc. (group owner) Natl. Network: Moody, . Format: Christian. ◆Bruce Munsterman, gen mgr.

Gilmer

KFRO-FM— July 24, 1980: 95.3 mhz; 5.9 kw. Ant 666 ft TL: N32 37 50 W94 53 44. Stereo. Hrs open: 24 402 S. Ragsdale St., Jacksonville, 75766. Phone: (903) 586-2527. Fax: (903) 589-0677. Licensee: Walller Media LLC. Group owner: Waller Broadcasting (acq 6-15-98; $1.425 million with KFRO(AM) Longview). Population served: 300,000 Natl. Rep: Roslin,. Kaye, Scholer, Fierman, Hays & Handler. Format: Hot adult contemp. Target aud: 25-49. ◆Dudley Waller, gen mgr.

Gladewater

KEES(AM)— 1947: 1430 khz; 5 kw-D, 1 kw-N, DA-N. TL: N32 31 46 W94 52 50. Hrs open: Box 6, Tyler, 75710-0006. Secondary address: 1001 E Southeast Loop 323, Suite 455, Tyler 75701-9600. Phone: (903) 593-2519. Fax: (903) 597-8378.E-mail: info@ktbb.com Web Site:www.ktbb.com Licensee: Gleiser Communications LLC (group owner; acq 11-21-03; grpsl). Population served: 25,000 Natl. Network: Westwood One, . Natl. Rep: Riley,. Format: Talk. ◆Paul Gleiser, gen mgr & gen sls mgr; Mike LaRoux, chief of engrg; Angie Mapes, traf mgr.

Glen Rose

KTFW-FM— 1989: 92.1 mhz; 25 kw. Ant 1,417 ft TL: N32 16 31 W98 01 22. Stereo. Hrs open: 115 W. 3rd. St., Fort Worth, 76102. Phone: (817) 332-0959. Fax: (817) 348-8373. Web Site:www.countrylegends921.com Licensee: LKCM Radio Group L.P. (group owner; (acq 1-13-2006; $10,142,816). Population served: 1,300,000 Rgnl. Network: Texas State Net. Texas State Networks Fletcher, Heald & Hildreth. Format: Classic country. Target aud: 40 plus. ◆Gerry Schlegel, pres, gen mgr; George Marti, VP; Mike Crow, progmg dir & progmg mgr.

Goldsmith

KTXO(FM)—Not on air, target date: unknown: 94.7 mhz; 6 kw. Ant 328 ft TL: N31 52 02 W102 39 18. Hrs open: 5842 Westslope Dr., Austin, 78731. Phone: (512) 467-0643. Licensee: Matinee Radio LLC. ◆Robert Walker, pres.

Goliad

KHMC(FM)— 1995: 95.9 mhz; 25 kw. Ant 321 ft TL: N28 40 57 W97 18 50. Hrs open: 24 Box 407, Victoria, 77902. Phone: (361) 575-9533. Fax: (361) 575-9502.E-mail: majictejano@yahoo.com Licensee: Cinco de Mayo Broadcasting. Population served: 180,000 Format: Tejano/Sp. ◆Homer Lopez, gen mgr; Ralph Salezar, gen sls mgr.

Gonzales

KCTI(AM)— Dec 17, 1947: 1450 khz; 1 kw-U. TL: N29 30 35 W97 24 51. Hrs open: 615 Saint Paul St., 78629. Phone: (830) 672-3631. Fax: (830) 672-9603.E-mail: kcti@kcti1450.com Web Site:www.kcti1450.com Licensee: Gonzales Communications, a Texas L.P. (acq 3-1-95; with co-located FM;5-22-95). Population served: 110000 Rgnl. Network: Texas State Net. Texas State Networks Format: Country. Target aud: General. ◆Marina Mann, pres; Steven Oakes, gen mgr; Syble Kline, gen sls mgr; Dian Bowman, progmg mgr, traf mgr; L.D. Decker, news dir; Bill Woleben, chief of engrg.

*KMLR(FM)— March 1986: 106.3 mhz; 15 kw. Ant 423 ft TL: N29 41 17 W97 40 39. Hrs open: 2351 Sunset Blvd., Suite 170-218, Rocklin, CA, 95765. Phone: (916) 251-1600. Fax: (916) 251-1650. Web Site:www.klove.com Licensee: Educational Media Foundation. (acq 3-31-2006; $6 million with KYLR(FM) Hutto). Natl. Network: K-Love, . Format: Contemp Christian. ◆Richard Jenkins, pres; Mike Novak, VP, progmg dir; Lloyd Parker, gen mgr; Ed Lenane, opns dir, news dir; Keith Whipple, dev dir; Eric Allen, natl sls mgr; David Pierce, progmg mgr; Jon Rivers, mus dir; Sam Wallington, engrg dir; Arthur Vassar, traf mgr; Karen Johnson, news rptr.

*KZAR(FM)— 2008: 88.1 mhz; 1.3 kw. Ant 384 ft TL: N29 29 09 W97 29 17. Hrs open: Rebroadcasts KLRD(FM) Yucaipa, CA 100%. 2351 Sunset Blvd., Suite 170-218, Rocklin, CA, 95765. Phone: (916) 251-1600. Fax: (916) 251-1650. Web Site:www.air1.com Licensee: Educational Media Foundation. (acq 2-28-2006; $36,000 for CP). Natl. Network: Air 1, . Format: Christian. ◆Richard Jenkins, pres; Mike Novak, VP; Keith Whipple, dev dir; David Pierce, progmg mgr; Ed Lenane, news dir; Sam Wallington, engrg dir; Karen Johnson, news rptr.

Graford

*KWCB(FM)—Not on air, target date: unknown: 90.3 mhz; 64 kw vert. Ant 220 ft TL: N33 08 43 W98 28 37. Hrs open: 111 E. Columbia, Weatherford, 76086. Phone: (817) 596-7807. Fax: (817) 596-0529. Licensee: Weatherford Christian School. ◆Ricky Harman, gen mgr.

Graham

KSWA(AM)— 1948: 1330 khz; 500 w-D. TL: N33 07 37 W98 35 35. Hrs open: 24 Box 1507, 76450. Phone: (940) 549-1330. Fax: (940) 549-8628.E-mail: gm@kwkq-kswa.com Licensee: Graham Newspapers Inc. (group owner; (acq 1996). Texas State Networks Garvey, Schubert & Barer. Format: Legends of Country. News staff: one; News: 10 hrs wkly. Target aud: Adults 35 plus. Spec prog: Bluegrass 2 hrs, gospel 2 hrs, Texas mus 2 hrs wkly. ◆Roy Robinson, VP; Joe Graham, gen mgr; Cindy Lewis, gen sls mgr; Greg Tiller, progmg dir; James M. Jones, news dir, chief of engrg; Christy Garcia, traf mgr.

KWKQ(FM)— August 1975: 94.7 mhz; 10.5 kw. Ant 485 ft TL: N33 02 30 W98 46 44. Stereo. Hrs open: 24 Prog sep from AM Box 1507, 76450. Phone: (940) 549-1330. Fax: (940) 549-8628. Texas State Networks Format: Classic Rock. News staff: one; News: 5 hrs wkly. Target aud: Adults 25-54. Spec prog: Alternative 6 hrs wkly. ◆Joe Graham, gen mgr, disc jockey; Jim Jones, news dir; Roy Robinson, VP & disc jockey.

Granbury

KPIR(AM)— Mar 13, 1980: 1420 khz; 500 w-U, DA-2. TL: N32 27 43 W97 47 19. Hrs open: 24 1620 Weatherford Hwy., 76048. Phone: (817) 736-0360. Fax: (817) 736-0344. Web Site:www.kpir.com Licensee: Pirate Broadcasters Inc. (acq 8-13-02). Population served: 250,000 Format: Real country. News staff: one; News: 21 hrs wkly. Target aud:

25-55; general. Spec prog: Farm one hr wkly. ◆Bob Haschke, gen mgr, sls dir; Shayne Hollinger, progmg mgr; Justin McClure, chief of engrg; Sue Haschke, traf mgr.

Grand Prairie

KKDA(AM)— Aug 1, 1957: 730 khz; 500 w-U. TL: N32 45 52 W96 59 36. Hrs open: Box 530860, 75053. Phone: (972) 263-9911. Fax: (972) 558-0010. Web Site:www.k104fm.com Licensee: Service Broadcasting Group LLC. (acq 12-22-76). Population served: 500,000 Format: Rhythm and blues oldies. ◆Hymen Childs, pres; Chuck Smith, gen mgr; Willis Johnson, progmg dir; Gary Wachter, chief of engrg.

Greenville

KESN(FM)—See Allen

KGVL(AM)— Mar 26, 1946: 1400 khz; 1 kw-U. TL: N33 10 02 W96 05 55. Stereo. Hrs open: Box 1015, 75403. Secondary address: 1517 Wolfe City Dr. 75401. Phone: (903) 455-1400. Phone: (903) 450-1400. Fax: (903) 455-5485.E-mail: info@kgvl.com Licensee: KGVL Radio LLC (acq 6-18-2009; $600,000 with KIKT(FM) Greenville). Population served: 70,000 Rgnl. Network: Texas State Net. Networks Dow, Lohnes & Albertson. Format: 70, 80, 90 country. Target aud: 25 plus. Spec prog: Black one hr, farm 5 hrs, relg 6 hrs wkly. ◆Frank Janda, gen mgr; Jim Patrick, progmg dir; Jason Russell, chief of engrg.

KIKT(FM)— Sept 15, 1978: 93.5 mhz; 1.8 kw. Ant 328 ft TL: N33 11 00 W96 03 19. (CP: COL Cooper. 12.4 kw, ant 407 ft. TL: N33 13 16 W95 41 20). Stereo. Hrs open: 24 Box 1015, 75403. Secondary address: 1517 Wolfe City Dr. 75401. Phone: (903) 450-0935. Phone: (903) 455-1460. Fax: (903) 455-5485.E-mail: info@kikt.com Web Site:www.kiktradio.com Licensee: KGVL Radio LLC (acq 6-18-2009; $600,000 with KGVL(AM) Greenville). Natl. Network: ABC, . Format: Country. News: 15 hrs wkly. Target aud: General. ◆Frank Janda, gen mgr.

*KTXG(FM)— 2006: 90.5 mhz; 38 kw. Ant 722 ft TL: N33 19 00 W96 24 27. Hrs open:
Rebroadcasts WAFR(FM) Tupelo, MS 100%.
Drawer 2440, Tupelo, MS, 38801. Phone: (662) 844-8888. Fax: (662) 842-6791. Web Site:www.afr.net Licensee: American Family Association. Format: Chirstian. ◆Marvin Sanders, gen mgr.

Gregory

KPUS(FM)— 1999: 104.5 mhz; 14 kw. Ant 446 ft TL: N27 52 00 W97 13 09. Stereo. Hrs open: 24 826 S. Padre Island Dr., Corpus Christi, 78416. Phone: (361) 814-3800. Fax: (361) 855-3770.E-mail: info@classicrook1045.com Web Site:classicrock1045.com Licensee: Convergent Broadcasting Corpus Christi LP. Group owner: Convergent Broadcasting LLC (acq 1-12-2004; grpsl). Population served: 313,600 Format: Classic rock. Target aud: Adults; 25-54. ◆Mark White, gen mgr; Dallas Garcia, gen sls mgr; Scott Holt, opns mgr & progmg dir; Molly Cox, mus dir; Amanda Moreno, traf mgr.

Groves

KCOL-FM— Sept 17, 1983: 92.5 mhz; 50 kw. 440 ft TL: N30 01 45 W93 52 59. Stereo. Hrs open: 24 Box 5488, Beaumont, 77726. Phone: (409) 896-5555. Fax: (409) 896-5566.E-mail: info@cool1925.com Web Site:www.cool925.com Licensee: Clear Channel Broadcasting Licenses Inc. Group owner: Clear Channel Communications Inc. (acq 1-29-2004; $4.5 million). Population served: 320,000 Format: Oldies. Target aud: 35 plus. ◆John Hogan, CEO; Randall Mays, CFO; Charlie Rahilly, sr VP; Mark Kopelman, VP; Vesta Brandt, gen mgr; Trey Poston, opns dir.

Groveton

KKUL-FM—Not on air, target date: unknown: 98.1 mhz; 6 kw. Ant 328 ft TL: N31 05 18 W94 58 56. Hrs open: 5842 Westslope Dr., Austin, 78731. Phone: (512) 467-0643. Licensee: Matinee Radio LLC. ◆Robert Walker, pres.

Hallettsville

KHLT(AM)— Sept 5, 1979: 1520 khz; 250 w-D. TL: N29 26 38 W96 57 22. Hrs open: Sunrise-sunset 111 N. Main St., 77964. Phone: (361) 798-4333. Fax: (361) 798-3798.E-mail: texasthunderradio@yahoo.com Licensee: Matthew Provenzano Group owner: Fort Bend Broadcasting

Co. (acq 6-20-2008; $25,000). Rgnl. Network: Texas State Net. Texas State Networks Wire Svc: NWS (National Weather Service) Format: Country. News staff: one; News: 13 hrs wkly. Target aud: General. Spec prog: Farm 5 hrs, Czech 5 hrs, Ger 5 hrs wkly. ◆Laura Kremling, gen mgr, stn mgr; Travis Kremling, progmg dir & chief of engrg.

KTXM(FM)— Oct 29, 1997: 99.9 mhz; 6 kw. Ant 131 ft TL: N29 26 38 W96 57 22. Hrs open:
Rebroadcasts KYKM(FM) Yoakum 100%.
111 N. Main St., 77964. Phone: (361) 798-4333. Fax: (361) 798-3798.E-mail: texasthunderradio@yahoo.com Licensee: Kremling Enterprises Inc. (acq 5-12-2008; $250,000 with KYKM(FM) Yoakum). Format: Country. ◆Laura Kremling, stn mgr; Travis Kremling, progmg dir & chief of engrg.

Haltom City

KDBN(FM)— 1995: 93.3 mhz; 50 kw. Ant 276 ft TL: N32 54 44 W97 11 18. Hrs open: 3500 Maple Ave., 13th Fl., Dallas, 75219. Phone: (214) 526-7400. Fax: (214) 525-2525. Web Site:fm933qualityrock.com Licensee: Susquehanna Radio Corp. Group owner: Susquehanna Radio Corp. (acq 1-28-97). Format: Rock. News: 2 hrs wkly. ◆Lew Dickey, CEO, chmn & pres; John Dickey, exec VP; Dan Bennett, VP, gen mgr; Carmen Lee, gen sls mgr; John Winchestor, prom dir; Jerome Fischer, progmg dir; Hue Beavers, chief of engrg.

Hamilton

KCLW(AM)— May 22, 1948: 900 khz; 250 w-D. TL: N31 43 08 W98 08 39. Hrs open: 24 Box 631, 76531. Secondary address: 115 A N. Rice 76531. Phone: (254) 386-8804 phone/fax.E-mail: info@kclw.com Web Site:www.kclw.com Licensee: Lasting Value Broadcasting Group Inc. (acq 8-22-00; $380,000). Population served: 5,000 Natl. Network: CBS, Jones Radio Networks, . Format: Classic country. News staff: one; News: 6 hrs wkly. Target aud: 18-65. Spec prog: Relg 6 hrs, Sp 12 hrs wkly. ◆Meredith Beal, pres; Sammie Casey, gen mgr; Ronald Beal, opns VP.

Hamlin

KCDD(FM)— Jan 30, 1987: 103.7 mhz; 100 kw. 985 ft TL: N32 43 31 W100 04 19. Stereo. Hrs open: 2525 S. Danville Dr., Abilene, 79605. Phone: (325) 793-9700. Fax: (915) 692-1576. Web Site:info@cumulus.com Licensee: Cumulus Licensing Corp. Group owner: Cumulus Media Inc. (acq 2-13-98; grpsl). Format: CHR. ◆Trace Michaels, gen mgr; Brad Elliott, progmg dir; Chris Andrews, chief of engrg.

Harker Heights

KRMY(AM)—See Killeen

KUSJ(FM)—Licensed to Harker Heights. See Temple

Harlingen

KBTQ(FM)— July 1975: 96.1 mhz; 100 kw. Ant 449 ft TL: N26 10 34 W97 46 59. Stereo. Hrs open: 200 S. 10th, Suite 600, McAllen, 78501. Phone: (956) 631-5499. Fax: (956) 631-0090.E-mail: info@netmio.com Web Site:www.netmio.com Licensee: Tichenor License Corp. (TLC). Population served: 101,500 Format: Tejano. ◆Alex Quintero, progmg dir.

KFRQ(FM)— January 1960: 94.5 mhz; 100 kw. 1,158 ft TL: N26 08 55 W97 49 17. Stereo. Hrs open: 24 801 N. Jackson Rd., McAllen, 78501. Phone: (956) 661-6000. Fax: (956) 661-6082.E-mail: mquinn@entravision.com Web Site:www.kfrq.com Licensee: Entravision Holdings LLC. (group owner; acq 1996; $6.1 million with KKPS(FM) Brownsville). Population served: 750,000 Format: Adult rock. News staff: one. Target aud: 25-54. ◆Alex Duran, VP, gen mgr & progmg dir.

KGBT(AM)— 1941: 1530 khz; 50 kw-D, 10 kw-N, 50 kw-CH, DA-2. TL: N26 22 33 W97 53 43. Stereo. Hrs open: 24 200 S. 10th, Suite 600, McAllen, 78501. Phone: (956) 631-5499. Fax: (956) 631-0090.E-mail: info@netmio.com Web Site:www.netmio.com Licensee: Tichenor License Corp. ("TLC"). Group owner: Univision Radio (acq 9-22-2003; grpsl). Population served: 525,900 Format: Sp. News staff: 2. Target aud: 18 plus. ◆Joe Morales, gen mgr; Hugo Delacruz, progmg dir; Jorge Garza, chief of engrg.

*KMBH-FM— Apr 30, 1991: 88.9 mhz; 3 kw. Ant 298 ft TL: N26 10 46 W97 30 06. Stereo. Hrs open: 24 Box 2147, 78551. Secondary address: 1701 Tennessee 78551. Phone: (956) 421-4111. Fax: (956) 421-4150.E-mail: kmbhkhid@aol.com Web Site:www.kmbh.org Licensee:

RGV Educational Broadcasting Inc. Population served: 950,000 Natl. Network: NPR, . Format: News, class, jazz. News: 34 hrs wkly. Target aud: General. Spec prog: Sp 3 hrs wkly. ◆Fr. Pedro Briseno, CEO, pres & gen mgr; Chris Maley, progmg dir. Co-owned TV: *KMBH(TV) affil

Hart

*KKFC(FM)—Not on air, target date: unknown: 89.3 mhz; 15 kw. Ant 351 ft TL: N34 30 04 W102 06 19. Hrs open: Box 217, Gainesville, 76241. Phone: (940) 668-7971. Licensee: 1 A Chord Inc. ◆Mary Fay Jackson, gen mgr.

Harts Bluff

*KPKP(FM)—Not on air, target date: unknown: 89.1 mhz; 3 kw vert. Ant 134 ft TL: N33 23 22.5 W94 50 28.7. Hrs open: 1039 CR 2920, Pittsburg, 75686. Phone: (903) 466-6791. Licensee: Millennium Broadcasting Corp. ◆James Furlow Jr., pres.

Haskell

KVRP-FM— Apr 8, 1981: 97.1 mhz; 100 kw. 531 ft TL: N33 09 40 W99 48 57. Stereo. Hrs open: 24 Box 1118, 1406 N. First, 79521. Phone: (940) 864-8505. Fax: (940) 864-8001.E-mail: gary@kvrp.com Web Site:www.kvrp.com Licensee: 1 Chronicles 14 L.P. (acq 8-4-2004; $700,000 with KVRP(AM) Stamford). Population served: 45,000 Rgnl. Network: Texas State Net. Texas State Networks Format: Country. News: 5 hrs wkly. Target aud: 25 plus. Spec prog: Farm 5 hrs, relg 6 hrs wkly. ◆Greg Weston, pres, VP; Gary Barrett, gen mgr, gen sls mgr, prom mgr; Dave Harrison, progmg dir; Tony St. James, farm dir.

Hearne

*KEDC(AM)—Not on air, target date: unknown: 88.5 mhz; 5.7 kw vert. Ant 272 ft TL: N30 56 22.7 W96 35 05.6. Hrs open: 3601 E. 29th St., Suite 8, Bryan, 77802. Phone: (979) 846-2825. Fax: (979) 846-0389.E-mail: info@coalitionforlife.com Licensee: Brazos Valley Coalition for Life. Natl. Network: EWTN Radio, . ◆Shawn Carney, gen mgr.

KVJM(FM)— May 15, 1985: 103.1 mhz; 5 kw horiz, 4.9 kw vert. Ant 361 ft TL: N30 45 35 W96 28 00. Hrs open: Box 3989, Bryan, 77805. Phone: (979) 779-3337. Fax: (979) 779-3444.E-mail: kvjmv103@aol.com Licensee: Equal Access Media Inc. Format: Sp. Target aud: 18-54. ◆Pluria Marshall Jr., gen mgr, sls VP; Edward Sanchez, stn mgr, mus dir, asst music dir, news dir, pub affrs dir; Plyria Marshall Jr., natl sls mgr; Lester Pace, progmg dir; Ed Loftis, chief of engrg.

Hebronville

*KAZF(FM)— November 2000: 91.9 mhz; 3 kw. 266 ft TL: N27 21 44 W98 40 09. Hrs open: Box 252, McAllen, 78505. Phone: (956) 686-6382. Fax: (956) 686-2999.E-mail: paulinobernal@laradiocristina.com Web Site:www.laradiocristina.com Licensee: Paulino Bernal Evangelism. Format: Christian contemp. ◆Gilbert Martinez, stn mgr.

KEKO(FM)— 2003: 101.7 mhz; 3 kw. Ant 328 ft TL: N27 18 46 W98 39 51. Hrs open: Box 1614, Laredo, 78044. Phone: (956) 726-4738. Fax: (928) 569-0456.E-mail: info@israelsr.com Web Site:www.lacadenaradioluz.com/keko.htm Licensee: La Nueva Cadena Radio Luz Inc. Format: Sp Christian. ◆Israel Tellez, pres & gen mgr; Hiram Tellez, progmg mgr.

Helotes

KONO-FM— Feb 18, 1971: 101.1 mhz; 98 kw. 1,368 ft TL: N29 50 26 W98 49 32. Stereo. Hrs open: 24 8122 Datapoint Dr., Suite 500, San Antonio, 78229. Phone: (210) 615-5400. Fax: (210) 615-5300. Web Site:www.kono101.com Licensee: Cox Radio Inc. Group owner: Cox Broadcasting (acq 2-12-98; $23 million with KONO(AM) San Antonio). Population served: 1,300,000 Natl. Rep: Katz Radio,. Wire Svc: AP Format: Oldies. News staff: one; News: one hr wkly. Target aud: 25-54; total audience appeal. ◆Bob Neil, CEO; Marty Choate, VP, gen mgr; Connie Tyra Kremer, gen sls mgr; Jeff Scott, natl sls mgr; Vera Flores, prom dir; Roger Allen, progmg dir; Chrissie Murnin, news dir; Paul Reynolds, chief of engrg; Connye Rodriguez, traf mgr; Dave Griffith, disc jockey.

Hemphill

KPBL(AM)— Feb 16, 1978: Stn currently dark. 1240 khz; 1 kw-U. TL: N31 22 03 W93 50 10. Hrs open: R.R. 5 Box 2095, 75948. Phone: (409) 787-4796. Fax: (409) 787-2696. Licensee: Phillip Burr Broadcasting Co. Population served: 35,000 Format: Country. ♦Phillip Burr, pres & gen mgr.

KTHP(FM)— November 2000: 103.9 mhz;; 6 kw. Ant 243 ft TL: N31 20 28 W93 50 44. (CP: 4.5 kw, ant 377 ft. TL: N31 25 24 W93 50 30). Hrs open: 24 605 San Antonio Ave., Many, LA, 71449. Phone: (318) 256-5177. Fax: (318) 256-0950.E-mail: kthp@sabinenet.com Web Site:www.bdcradio.com Licensee: Baldridge-Dumas Communications Inc. (group owner). Format: Classic country. ♦Rhonda Benson, gen mgr; Cindy Ezernack, stn mgr.

Hempstead

KTWL(FM)— 1999: 105.3 mhz; 9.2 kw. Ant 544 ft TL: N30 18 19 W96 01 40. Hrs open:
Simulcasts KLTR(FM) Caldwell 100%.
530 W. Main St., Brenham, 77833. Phone: (979) 836-9411. Fax: (979) 836-9435.E-mail: lorihenderson01@hotmail.com Licensee: Farmers Communications. Group owner: Bayport Broadcast Group Robert J. Buenzle. Format: Adult comtemp. ♦Roy E. Henderson, CEO, pres; Steve Britewell, engrg VP.

Henderson

KWRD(AM)— March 1956: 1470 khz; 5 kw-D. TL: N32 10 55 W94 47 49. Hrs open: 1101 Kilgore Dr., 75652. Phone: (903) 655-1800. Fax: (903) 655-1808.E-mail: info@kwrdonline.com Web Site:www.kwrdonline.com Licensee: Jerry Hanszen dba Hanszen Broadcasting Co. (acq 5-7-2001; with KOFY(AM) Gilmer). Population served: 50,000 Natl. Network: ESPN Radio, . Rgnl. Network: Texas State Net. Format: Sports. Target aud: General. ♦Jerry Hanszen, gen mgr.

Hereford

KJNZ(FM)— Dec 12, 2000: 103.5 mhz; 50 kw. Ant 279 ft TL: N34 45 00 W102 22 54. Hrs open: 1013 W. Park Ave., 79045. Phone: (806) 364-0277. Fax: (806) 363-6567.E-mail: joelwithlaley@yahoo.com Licensee: Hereford Broadcasting LLC Group owner: The Formby Stations (acq 4-25-2007; $400,000). Booth, Freret, Imlay & Tepper P.C. Format: Rgnl Mexican. ♦Joel Gallegos, gen mgr.

KNNK(FM)—(Dimmitt, June 13, 1998: 100.5 mhz; 43 kw. Ant 489 ft TL: N34 44 49 W102 29 37. Stereo. Hrs open: 24 Box 1635, 207 S. 25-Mile Ave., 79045-9998. Phone: (806) 363-1005. Fax: (806) 364-0226.E-mail: knnk@wtrt.net Web Site:www.knnk.net Licensee: James D. Peeler. Population served: 253,002 Natl. Network: Moody, . Format: Southern gospel, beautiful music. Target aud: General; mature adults. Spec prog: Soft instrumentals 20 hrs wkly. ♦James "Buddy" D. Peeler, gen mgr.

KPAN(AM)— August 1948: 860 khz; 250 w-D, 231 w-N. TL: N34 47 33 W102 25 45. Hrs open: 24 Box 1757, 218 E. 5th St., 79045. Phone: (806) 364-1860. Fax: (806) 364-5814.E-mail: kpan@kpanradio.com Web Site:www.kpanradio.com Licensee: KPAN Broadcasters. Group owner: Formby Stations Population served: 350,000 Natl. Network: CBS, . Rgnl. Network: Texas State Net. Texas State Networks Shaw Pittman. Wire Svc: AP Format: Contemp country. News staff: one; News: 20 hrs wkly. Target aud: General. Spec prog: Tejano 15 hrs, farm 12 hrs wkly. ♦Chip Formby, gen mgr.

KPAN-FM— Sept 1, 1965: 106.3 mhz; 30 kw. 259 ft TL: N34 47 33 W102 25 45. Stereo. Hrs open: 24
Rebroadcasts KPAN(AM) Hereford.
Box 1757, 218 E. 5th St., 79045. Phone: (806) 364-1860. Fax: (806) 364-5814. Web Site:www.kpanradio.com Natl. Network: CBS Radio, . Rgnl. Network: Texas State Net. Texas State Networks Shaw Pittman. Wire Svc: AP Target aud: General. ♦Chip Formby, gen mgr.

***KRBG(FM)**— 2008: 88.7 mhz; 9.5 kw. Ant 374 ft TL: N34 53 50 W102 14 08. Hrs open: Box 7441, Amarillo, 79114-7441. Phone: (806) 353-1488. Fax: (806) 353-1542. Licensee: Grace Christian Church of Amarillo Inc. (acq 4-30-2009; $210,000). ♦William Gehm, pres.

***KRLH(FM)**— 2009: 90.9 mhz; 130 w. Ant 269 ft TL: N34 51 02 W102 23 38. Hrs open:
Rebroadcasts KLVR(FM) Middletown, CA 100%.
2351 Sunset Blvd., Suite 170-218, Rocklin, CA, 95765. Phone: (916) 251-1600. Fax: (916) 251-1650. Web Site:www.klove.com Licensee: Educational Media Foundation. (acq 3-23-2007; grpsl). Natl. Network: K-Love, . Format: Contemp Christian. ♦Mike Novak, pres.

Hewitt

KDRW(FM)—Not on air, target date: unknown: 106.7 mhz; 21.5 kw. Ant 354 ft TL: N31 24 45 W97 12 40. Hrs open: 1551 Queens Rd., Los Angeles, CA, 90069. Phone: (323) 656-0796. Licensee: William W. McCutchen III. ♦William W. McCutchen III, gen mgr.

Highland Park

KVCE(AM)— Mar 1, 1960: 1160 khz; 35 kw-D, 1 kw-N, DA-2. TL: N33 10 37 W97 40 36 (D), N33 02 21 W96 56 34 (N). Hrs open: 24 222 W. Las Colinas Blvd., Irving, 75039. Phone: (888) 839-2717. Web Site:www.kvceradio.com Licensee: Dallas Broadcasting LLC Group owner: First Broadcasting Investment Partners LLC (acq 8-23-2006; $9.25 million). Population served: 50,000 Format: Talk. ♦Dan Patrick, gen mgr.

KVIL(FM)—(Highland Park-Dallas, Aug 14, 1961: 103.7 mhz; 100 kw. Ant 1,571 ft TL: N32 34 54 W96 58 32. Stereo. Hrs open: 24 4131 N. Central Expwy., Suite 1200, Dallas, 75204. Phone: (214) 526-9870.E-mail: feedback@kvil.com Web Site:www.kvil.com Licensee: CBS Radio Partner I Inc. Group owner: CBS Radio (acq 7-2-87). Population served: 500,000 Natl. Network: CBS, . Format: Light rock. ♦David Henry, gen mgr.

Highland Park-Dallas

KVIL(FM)—Licensed to Highland Park-Dallas. See Highland Park

Highland Village

KWRD-FM— Nov 15, 1988: 100.7 mhz; 100 kw. Ant 1,840 ft TL: N33 33 37 W96 57 34. Stereo. Hrs open: 18 6400 N. Belt Line Rd., Suite 110, Irving, 75063-6037. Phone: (214) 561-9673. Fax: (214) 561-9662.E-mail: theword@thewordfm.com Web Site:www.thewordfm.com Licensee: Inspiration Media of Texas LLC. Group owner: Salem Communications Corp. (acq 1-17-2001; grpsl). Population served: 38,000 Format: Christian talk. ♦John L. Peoryea, gen mgr; David Darling, opns mgr; Ezio Torres, sls dir; David Sparkman, prom dir; Andy Pickard, chief of engrg.

Hillsboro

KBRQ(FM)— Oct 20, 1959: 102.5 mhz; 100 kw. Ant 449 ft TL: N31 49 23 W97 09 35. Stereo. Hrs open: 24 314 W. State Hwy. 6, Waco, 76712. Phone: (254) 776-3900. Fax: (254) 761-6371.E-mail: brenthenslee@clearchannel.com Web Site:www.1025thebear.com Licensee: Aloha Station Trust LLC, as Trustee Group owner: Clear Channel Communications Inc. (acq 7-30-2008). Thompson Hine LLP. Format: Classic rock. Target aud: 25-49; men. ♦Evan Armstrong, gen mgr; Zack Owen, opns dir; Vernon Riggs, sls dir, gen sls mgr; Brent Henslee, progmg dir.

KHBR(AM)— May 21, 1948: 1560 khz; 250 w-D. TL: N32 01 00 W97 06 32. Hrs open: 12 Box 569, 76645. Secondary address: 335 Country Club Rd. 76645. Phone: (254) 582-3431. Fax: (254) 582-3800.E-mail: info@khbrhillsboro.com Web Site:www.khbrhillsboro.com Licensee: KHBR Radio Inc. (acq 1955). Population served: 42,750 Rgnl. Network: Texas State Net. Texas State Networks Wire Svc: NOAA Weather Format: Classic country. News: 18 hrs wkly. Target aud: General. Spec prog: Czech 1.5 hrs, gospel 6 hrs wkly. ♦Roger Galle, pres; Rick Bailey, gen mgr; Roger Creech, progmg dir.

Holliday

***KGVB(FM)**—Not on air, target date: unknown: 90.9 mhz; 20 kw. Ant 364 ft TL: N33 42 31 W98 57 10. Hrs open: Box 1343, Ada, OK, 74821. Phone: (580) 332-0902. Licensee: South Central Oklahoma Christian Broadcasting Inc. ♦Randall Christy, pres & gen mgr.

Hondo

KCWM(AM)— Feb 13, 1970: 1460 khz; 500 w-D, 226 w-N. TL: N29 21 42 W99 07 42. Hrs open: 6 AM-10 PM Box 447, 78861. Secondary address: 1605 Ave. K 78861. Phone: (830) 741-5296. Fax: (830) 426-3368. Licensee: Hondo Communications Inc. (acq 10-11-96). Population served: 35,000 Rgnl. Network: Texas State Net. Natl. Rep: Keystone (unwired net),. Texas State Networks Format: C&W. News staff: one; News: 20 hrs wkly. Target aud: General. ♦Mike Carr, pres, gen mgr, progmg dir; Tim Copeland, gen sls mgr, mktg dir, prom mgr; Paul McKay, chief of engrg; Tom Fusselmen, traf mgr.

KMFR(FM)— 1993: 105.9 mhz; 6 kw. Ant 328 ft TL: N29 18 48 W99 16 03. Stereo. Hrs open: 8023 Vantage Dr., Suite 840, San Antonio, 78230. Phone: (888) 522-7437. Fax: (210) 341-1777. Licensee: Hondo RadioWorks Ltd. (acq 12-12-2000; $74,925). Format: Classic rock. ♦John W. Barger, CEO.

Hooks

KPWW(FM)— Dec 22, 1985: 95.9 mhz; 11.5 kw. 449 ft TL: N33 27 25 W94 10 59. (CP: 11.3 kw, ant 485 ft.). Stereo. Hrs open: 24 2324 Arkansas Blvd., Texarkana, 71854. Phone: (870) 772-3771. Fax: (870) 772-0364.E-mail: info@power959.com Web Site:www.power959.com Licensee: GAP Broadcasting Texarkana License LLC. Group owner: Clear Channel Communications Inc. (acq 8-3-2007; grpsl). Population served: 200,000 Natl. Rep: McGavren Guild,. Format: Modern Top 40. News staff: one. Target aud: 18-49; contemp adults, upscale middle America. ♦Ron Bird, gen mgr; Phil Robken, natl sls mgr; John Williams, news dir; Wes Spicher, progmg dir & chief of engrg; Cindy Esterling, traf mgr.

Hornsby

***KOOP(FM)**— November 1994: 91.7 mhz; 3.13 kw. 85 ft TL: N30 16 00 W97 40 27. (CP: Ant 197 ft.). Stereo. Hrs open: 9 AM-7 PM (M-F); 9 AM-10 PM (S, Su) Box 2116, Austin, 78768. Secondary address: 304 E. 5th St., Austin 78768. Phone: (512) 472-1369. Phone: (512) 472-5667. Fax: (512) 472-6149.E-mail: info@koop.org Web Site:www.koop.org Licensee: Texas Educational Broadcasting Inc. Population served: 750,000 Format: Var of music & info. News: 14 hrs wkly. Spec prog: American Indian one hr, Black 2 hrs, folk 7 hrs, Ger 5 hrs, Pol 5 hrs, Sp 10 hrs wkly. ♦Amy Wright, stn mgr; Lonny Stern, prom dir; Joanna Garfinkel, mus dir.

Houston

KAMA-FM—(Missouri City, Aug 8, 1968: 104.9 mhz; 2.7 kw. Ant 981 ft TL: N29 45 30 W95 22 03. Stereo. Hrs open: 5100 Southwest Fwy., 77056. Phone: (713) 965-2400. Fax: (713) 965-2401.E-mail: info@univision.com Licensee: Tichenor License Corp. Group owner: Univision Radio (acq 9-22-2003; grpsl). Population served: 4,000,000 Format: Sp. ♦Mark Masepohl, sr VP, gen mgr; Dave Burdette, gen sls mgr; Kim Guerrero, natl sls mgr; Nestor Enriquez, prom dir; Arnulfo Ramirez, progmg dir; Renzo Heredia, pub affrs dir.

KBME(AM)— Oct 16, 1944: 790 khz; 5 kw-U, DA-2. TL: N29 54 54 W95 27 42. Stereo. Hrs open: 24 200 West Loop S., Suite 300, 77027. Phone: (713) 212-8000. Fax: (713) 212-8790.E-mail: info@kbmeam.com Web Site:www.790kbme.com Licensee: AMFM Texas Licenses L.P. Group owner: Clear Channel Communications Inc. (acq 8-30-2000; grpsl). Population served: 425,000 Natl. Network: ESPN Radio, . Natl. Rep: Christal,. Format: Sports. ♦Mark Copelman, gen mgr; Pam McKay, gen sls mgr; Ken Charles, natl sls mgr, progmg VP; Dan Endom, rgnl sls mgr; Melissa Brezner, mktg dir, prom dir; Tim Collins, progmg dir; Bryan Erickson, news dir; Peggy Tuck, pub affrs dir; David Armstrong, chief of engrg.

KBXX(FM)— January 1958: 97.9 mhz; 100 kw. 1,920 ft TL: N29 34 34 W95 30 36. Stereo. Hrs open: 24 Greenway Plaza, Suite 1508, 77046. Phone: (713) 623-2108. Fax: (713) 623-0344.E-mail: scorpio@kbxx.com Web Site:www.kbtt.com Licensee: Radio One Licenses LLC. Group owner: Radio One Inc. (acq 2000). Population served: 3,000,000 Natl. Rep: Clear Channel,. Dickstein Shapiro Morin & Oshinsky L.L.P. Format: Hip hop. Target aud: 18-29; females. ♦Ernest Jackson, pres, disc jockey; Carl Hamilton, VP; Mark McMillen, gen mgr; Tom Callococci, opns mgr.

KCOH(AM)— 1952: 1430 khz; 5 kw-D. TL: N29 45 22 W95 16 37. Stereo. Hrs open: 24 5011 Almeda Rd., 77004. Phone: (713) 522-1001. Fax: (713) 521-0769.E-mail: dsamuel@kcohradio.com Web Site:www.kcohradio.com Licensee: KCOH Inc. (acq 9-27-76). Population served: 2,250,000 Natl. Network: Westwood One, . Natl. Rep: Roslin,. Cavelll, Mertz & Davis. Format: Black, urban contemp, talk. News staff: 2; News: 15 hrs wkly. Target aud: 25-54; upbeat, knowledgeable, civic & politically minded adults. Spec prog: Sports.Mike Petrizzo, exec VP, gen mgr, gen sls mgr, adv dir; Travis O. Gardner, VP, opns VP, prom mgr, mus dir, min affrs dir, mus critic; Michael Harris, progmg dir, news dir, local news ed, edit dir, edit mgr, political ed, relg ed, disc jockey; Don Samuel, asst music dir, disc jockey; A.D. Rigmaiden, engrg dir, chief of engrg; Myasha Smith-Trent, traf mgr; Ralph Cooper, sports cmtr; Lisa Berry-Dockery, women's cmtr; Steven R. Talton, disc jockey

KEYH(AM)— November 1974: 850 khz; 10 kw-D, 185 w-N, DA-1. TL: N29 39 19 W95 40 19. Hrs open: 3000 Bering Dr., 77057. Phone: (713) 315-3400. Fax: (713) 315-3506. Licensee: Liberman Broadcasting of Houston License LLC. Group owner: Liberman Broadcasting Inc. (acq 4-22-2003; $5.70 million). Population served: 500,000 Format:

Sp. Target aud: 24-65; Hispanic, recent immigrants & primarily Sp speakers. ♦Lenard Liberman, CEO, pres; Winter Horton, gen mgr; Gerardo Reyes, gen sls mgr; Ezequiel Gonzalez, progmg dir; Meliza Posada, news dir, traf mgr; Mike Todd, chief of engrg, engr.

KGLK(FM)—See Lake Jackson

***KHCB(AM)**—(Galveston, 1922: 1400 khz; 1 kw-U. TL: N29 17 24 W94 50 12. (CP: COL League City. 1 kw-U, DA-2. TL: N29 25 35 W95 08 00). Hrs open: 24 2424 South Blvd., 77098-5196. Phone: (713) 520-5200. Fax: (713) 520-8104. Web Site:www.khcb.org Licensee: Houston Christian Broadcasters Inc. (group owner; (acq 12-4-90; $150,000). Population served: 250,000 Format: Sp, relg. News staff: one. Target aud: General. Spec prog: Chinese 13 hrs, Vietnamese 4 hrs wkly. ♦Bruce Munsterman, pres, stn mgr, progmg dir; Dolly Martin, progmg mgr, disc jockey; Miguel Jacinto, mus dir, news dir, disc jockey; Dan Wales, chief of engrg; Rebecca Aguilar, disc jockey.

***KHCB-FM**— Mar 10, 1962: 105.7 mhz; 100 kw. Ant 1,614 ft TL: N29 34 06 W95 29 57. Stereo. Hrs open: 24 2424 South Blvd., 77098-5196. Phone: (713) 520-5200.E-mail: email@khcb.org Web Site:www.khcb.org Licensee: Houston Christian Broadcasters Inc. Population served: 5,000,000 Natl. Network: Moody, . Format: Christian. Spec prog: Sp 10 hrs, Chinese one hr wkly. ♦Bruce Munsterman, gen mgr; Bonnie C. BeMent, mus dir, news dir; Dan Wales, engrg dir.

KHJK(FM)—(La Porte, 1992: 103.7 mhz; 94.86 kw. Ant 1,935 ft TL: N29 56 09 W94 30 38. Hrs open: 9801 Westheimer Rd., Suite 700, 77042. Phone: (713) 266-1000. Licensee: CMP KC Licensing LLC. Group owner: Cumulus Media Inc. (acq 5-3-2006; grpsl). Format: Adult alternative. ♦Patrick Fant, gen mgr.

KHMX(FM)— 1961: 96.5 mhz; 100 kw. Ant 1,952 ft TL: N29 34 34 W95 30 36. Stereo. Hrs open: 24 Greenway Plaza, Suite 1900, 77046. Phone: (713) 881-5100. Fax: (713) 881-5150.E-mail: info@khmx.com Web Site:www.khmx.com Licensee: CBS Radio Holdings Inc. Group owner: Clear Channel Communications Inc. (acq 4-1-2009; grpsl). Population served: 4,500,000 Format: Hot adult contemp. Target aud: 25-40. ♦Brian Purdy, gen mgr.

KHPT(FM)—See Conroe

KIKK(AM)—See Pasadena

KILT(AM)— 1948: 610 khz; 5 kw-U, DA-2. TL: N29 55 04 W95 25 33. Hrs open: 8:30-5:00 24 Greenway Plaza, Suite 1900, 77046. Phone: (713) 881-5100. Phone: (713) 881-5957. Fax: (713) 881-5150. Web Site:www.sportsradio610.com Licensee: CBS Radio Partner I Inc. Group owner: Infinity Broadcasting Corp. (acq 12-89). Population served: 1,594,086 Natl. Rep: CBS Radio,. Format: Sports, talk. ♦Laura Morris, VP; Moose Rosenfeld, gen mgr; Bill Van Rysdam, progmg dir; Dan Woodard, chief of engrg.

KILT-FM— 1961: 100.3 mhz; 100 kw. Ant 1,920 ft TL: N29 34 34 W95 30 36. Stereo. Hrs open: 24 24 Greenway Plaza, Suite 1900, 77046. Phone: (713) 881-5100. Phone: (713) 881-5957. Fax: (713) 881-5150. Web Site:www.kilt.com Licensee: CBS Radio Partner I Inc. Format: Country. ♦Nick Peterson, gen sls mgr; Jeff Garrison, progmg dir; Jim Carola, news dir.

KKBQ-FM—See Pasadena

KKHH(FM)— Oct 4, 1959: 95.7 mhz; 100 kw. Ant 1,971 ft TL: N29 34 34 W95 30 36. Stereo. Hrs open: 24 24 Greenway Plaza, Suite 1900, 77046. Phone: (713) 881-5100. Fax: (713) 881-5250. Web Site:www.hothitshouston.com Licensee: CBS Radio Partner I Inc. Group owner: Infinity Broadcasting Corp. (acq 11-13-98; grpsl). Population served: 3,348,800 Natl. Network: CBS, . Natl. Rep: CBS Radio,. Leventhal, Senter & Lerman. Format: CHR. Target aud: 25-54. ♦Laura Morris, VP; Diane Holt, sls dir; Maxine Todd, progmg dir; Dan Woodard, chief of engrg.

KKRW(FM)— Jan 1, 1964: 93.7 mhz; 100 kw. 1,779 ft TL: N29 34 27 W95 29 37. Stereo. Hrs open: 200 West Loop S., Suite 300, 77027. Phone: (713) 212-8000. Fax: (713) 830-8099. Web Site:www.kkrw.com Licensee: Capstar TX L.P. Group owner: Clear Channel Communications Inc. (acq 8-30-00; grpsl). Population served: 2,905,350 Format: Classic rock. Target aud: 25-54. ♦Vince Richards, progmg dir.

KLAT(AM)— July 31, 1961: 1010 khz; 5 kw-U, DA-2. TL: N29 53 47 W95 17 25. (CP: 3.6 kw-N). Stereo. Hrs open: 5100 Southwest Fwy., 77056. Phone: (713) 407-1415. Fax: (713) 965-2401.E-mail: info@univision.com Web Site:www.univision.com Licensee: Tichenor License Corp. Group owner: Univision Radio (acq 9-22-2003; grpsl). Population served: 1,026,000 Format: Sp, news/talk. Target aud: 25-54; Hispanic. ♦Mark Masepohl, sr VP, gen mgr, sls dir; Dave Burdette, VP, stn mgr; Arnulfo Ramirez, opns mgr; Kim McBride, natl sls mgr, pub affrs dir; Manuel Cardona, rgnl sls mgr; Frances Jones, prom dir; Pilar Torres, prom mgr; Rolando Becerra, progmg dir; Renzo Heredia, news dir, disc jockey; Marty Scruggs, chief of engrg.

KLOL(FM)— 1947: 101.1 mhz; 100 kw. Ant 1,920 ft TL: N29 34 34 W95 30 36. Stereo. Hrs open: 24 Greenway Plaza, Suite 1900, 77046. Phone: (713) 881-5100. Fax: (713) 881-5150.E-mail: info@klol.com Web Site:www.mega101fm.com Licensee: CBS Radio Holdings Inc. (acq 4-1-2009; grpsl). Population served: 425,000 Natl. Rep: CBS Radio,. Format: Sp. Target aud: 18-54. ♦Charlie Wilkinson, gen mgr.

KLTN(FM)— Oct 4, 1960: 102.9 mhz; 100 kw. Ant 1,049 ft TL: N29 45 26 W95 20 18. Stereo. Hrs open: 24 5100 Southwest Fwy., 77056. Phone: (713) 965-2300. Fax: (713) 965-2401.E-mail: info@univision.com Web Site:www.univision.com Licensee: Univision Radio Houston License Corp. Group owner: Univision Radio (acq 9-22-2003; grpsl). Population served: 4,000,000 Format: Rgnl Mexican hits. News staff: one. Target aud: 18-49; Hispanics. ♦Mark Masepohl, sr VP, gen mgr; Dave Burdette, stn mgr, gen sls mgr; Arnulfo Ramirez, opns mgr; Kim Mercier, natl sls mgr; Frances Jones, prom dir; Raul Brindis, progmg dir; Renzo Heredia, news dir & pub affrs dir; Marty Scruggs, chief of engrg.

KLVL(AM)—See Pasadena

KMIC(AM)— 1955: 1590 khz; 5 kw-U, DA-N. TL: N29 50 38 W95 26 51. Hrs open: 24 3050 Post Oak Blvd., Suite 220, 77056. Phone: (713) 552-1590. Fax: (713) 552-1588.E-mail: info@kmic.com Web Site:www.disney.com Licensee: Radio Disney Group LLC. Group owner: ABC Inc. (acq. 1999). Population served: 3,000,000 Natl. Network: Radio Disney, . Format: Family progmg. Target aud: 6-14; 25-49; kids, parents. ♦Chris Martin, gen mgr, gen sls mgr, adv dir; A. D. Rigmaiden, chief of engrg; Johanna Anderson, traf mgr; Laura Pena, prom mgr & spec ev coord.

KMJQ(FM)— Feb 1, 1964: 102.1 mhz; 100 kw. 1,719 ft TL: N29 34 27 W95 29 37. Stereo. Hrs open: 24 24 Greenway Plaza, Suite 1508, 77046-2467. Secondary address: Box 22900 77227-2900. Phone: (713) 623-2108. Fax: (713) 623-0106.E-mail: info@kmjqfm.com Web Site:www.kmjq.com Licensee: Radio One Licenses LLC. Group owner: Radio One Inc. (acq 11-8-01; grpsl). Population served: 583,400 Natl. Network: ABC, . Natl. Rep: Clear Channel,. Wiley, Rein & Fielding. Format: Adult urban contemp. News staff: 2. Target aud: 25-54; African-Americans. Spec prog: Talk 3 hrs wkly. ♦Tom Callococci, pres, opns mgr; Carl Hamilton, VP, disc jockey; Mark McMillen, gen mgr; Jerome Hutchinson, gen sls mgr; Brenda Ford-Jones, natl sls mgr; Cindy Webster, rgnl sls mgr; Bobrie Jefferson, prom mgr; Sam Choice, progmg dir, progmg mgr; Carmen Watkins, news dir; David Ainslie, engrg mgr, chief of engrg; Vickie Duke, traf mgr.

KNTH(AM)— Jan 17, 1968: 1070 khz; 10 kw-D, 5 kw-N, DA-2. TL: N29 59 33 W95 29 33. Hrs open: 6161 Savoy, Suite 1200, 77036. Phone: (713) 260-3600. Fax: (713) 260-3628.E-mail: comment@knth.net Licensee: South Texas Broadcasting Inc. Group owner: Salem Communications Corp. (acq 1-6-95; $2.5 million;3-6-95). Natl. Rep: Salem,. Format: News/talk. ♦Chuck Jewell, gen mgr; Paul Baker, opns mgr, mktg mgr, progmg dir; Dan Doster, gen sls mgr; Ken Garza, pub affrs dir; Sidney Jones, chief of engrg; Kent McDonald, traf mgr.

KODA(FM)— Nov 9, 1958: 99.1 mhz; 95 kw. 1,920 ft TL: N29 34 34 W95 30 36. Stereo. Hrs open: 24 2000 West Loop S., Suite 300, 77027. Phone: (713) 212-8000. Fax: (713) 830-8099. Web Site:www.sunny99.com Licensee: AMFM Texas License L.P. Group owner: Clear Channel Communications Inc. (acq 8-30-00; grpsl). Population served: 3,184,200 Latham & Watkins. Format: Adult contemp. News staff: one; News: 22 hrs wkly. Target aud: 25-54. Spec prog: Jazz 4 hrs wkly. ♦Mark Kopelman, gen mgr; Sandy Capell, gen sls mgr; Vince Richards, progmg dir; Donna McCoy, mus dir.

***KPFT(FM)**— March 1970: 90.1 mhz; 100 kw. 433 ft TL: N29 55 26 W95 32 17. (CP: 28 kw, ant 672 ft.). Stereo. Hrs open: 24 419 Lovett Blvd., 77006. Phone: (713) 526-4000. Fax: (713) 526-5750. Web Site:www.kpft.org Licensee: Pacifica Foundation Inc. Group owner: Pacifica Foundation Inc. dba Pacifica Radio Population served: 4,000,000 Natl. Network: PRI, . Haley, Bader & Potts. Format: Div, news. Target aud: General. Spec prog: Black 15 hrs. ♦Dwande Bradley, gen mgr; Donna Platt, dev dir; Otis Maclay, progmg dir; Phil Edwards, mus dir; Ernesto Aguilar, news dir; Steve Brightwell, engrg dir.

KPRC(AM)— May 9, 1925: 950 khz; 5 kw-U, DA-N. TL: N29 48 14 W95 16 42. Hrs open: 24 2000 W. Loop S., Suite 300, 77027. Phone: (713) 212-8000. Fax: (713) 212-8970.E-mail: info@950kprc.com Web Site:www.950kprc.com Licensee: CCB Texas Licenses L.P. Group owner: Clear Channel Communications Inc. (acq 3-14-95; 6-5-95). Population served: 3,580,000 Natl. Network: CBS, Fox News Radio, Westwood One, . Rgnl. Network: Texas State Net. Natl. Rep: Clear Channel,. Texas State Networks Dow, Lohnes & Albertson. Format: News/talk info. News staff: 15; News: 32 hrs wkly. Target aud: 25-54. Spec prog: Gardening 7 hrs, home handyman 6 hrs, automotive 3 hrs wkly. ♦Mark Kopelman, gen mgr; Michael Berry, opns mgr; Paul Lambert, gen sls mgr; Ken Charles, progmg dir; Brian Erickson, news dir; David Armstrong, chief of engrg; Matt Thomas, sports cmtr.

KQBU-FM—(Port Arthur, July 4, 1969: 93.3 mhz; 100 kw. Ant 1,952 ft TL: N30 03 05 W94 31 37. Stereo. Hrs open: 24 5100 Southwest Fwy., 77056. Phone: (713) 965-2400. Fax: (713) 965-2401. Licensee: Tichenor License Corp. Format: Rgnl Mexican. Target aud: 18-34; urban/Latin audience. ♦Mark Masepohl, sr VP.

KQUE(AM)— Feb 18, 1948: 1230 khz; 1 kw-U. TL: N29 45 26 W95 20 18. Hrs open: 24
Simacasts KKRW (FM) Houston.
3000 Bering Dr., Suite 1170, 77057. Phone: (713) 315-3400. Fax: (713) 315-3506. Licensee: Liberman Broadcasting of Houston License LLC. Group owner: Liberman Broadcasting Inc. (acq 3-20-2001; grpsl). Population served: 3,941,000 Fisher, Wayland, Cooper, Leader & Zaragoza L.L.P. Format: Mexican rgnl. News: 14 hrs wkly. Target aud: 35 plus; mature, upscale, high-income. ♦Lenard Liberman, CEO, VP; Winter Horton, VP & gen mgr; Cheque Gonzalez, stn mgr, progmg dir; Gerardo Reyes, gen sls mgr, chief of engrg; Ezequiel Gonzalez, progmg dir; Meliza Posada, traf mgr.

KRBE(FM)— Nov 8, 1959: 104.1 mhz; 100 kw. 1,920 ft TL: N29 34 34 W95 30 36. Stereo. Hrs open: 9801 Westheimer, Suite 700, 77042. Phone: (713) 266-1000. Fax: (713) 954-2344. Web Site:www.104krbe.com Licensee: KRBE Lico Inc. Group owner: Susquehanna Radio Corp. (acq 11-86; $25 million with co-located AM;10-6-86). Population served: 451,000 Format: CHR. Target aud: 18-34; general.Peter Brubaker, chmn; David Kennedy, pres; Nancy Vaeth, sr VP; Mark Shecterle, gen mgr; Amy Dewbre, gen sls mgr; Beth Lavine, natl sls mgr; Mike Paterson, mktg dir; Lesley Brotamante, prom mgr, adv mgr; Tracy Austin, progmg dir & progmg mgr; Leslie Whittle, mus dir; Maria Todd, news dir; Benny Boone, pub affrs dir; Andy Hudack, engrg mgr; Chuck Underwood, chief of engrg

KROI(FM)—See Seabrook

KRTX(AM)—(Rosenberg-Richmond, Nov 15, 1948: 980 khz; 1 kw-D, 212 w-N. TL: N29 33 10 W95 47 00. (CP: 5 kw-U, DA-2). Stereo. Hrs open: 24 912 Curtis St., Pasadena, 77502. Phone: (713) 589-1336. Fax: (713) 589-1335. Licensee: Aleluya Christian Broadcasting Inc. Group owner: Univision Radio (acq 12-17-2008; $3 million). Population served: 4,000,000 Law Office of Dan J. Alpert. Format: Sp relg. ♦Ruben Villarreal, gen mgr.

KTBZ-FM— Nov 1, 1964: 94.5 mhz; 100 kw. 2,000 ft TL: N29 34 34 W95 30 36. Stereo. Hrs open: 2000 W. Loop S., Suite 300, 77027. Phone: (713) 212-8000. Fax: (713) 212-8970.E-mail: info@thebuzz.com Web Site:www.thebuzz.com Licensee: AMFM Texas Licenses L.P. Group owner: Clear Channel Communications Inc. (acq 8-30-00; grpsl). Population served: 350,000 Natl. Rep: D & R Radio,. Format: Oldies. Target aud: 25-54; baby boomers. Spec prog: Talk 2 hrs, relg one hr, pub affrs one hr wkly. ♦Ellen Cavanaugh, gen mgr; Jim Trapp, progmg dir.

KTEK(AM)—See Alvin

KTRH(AM)— Mar 29, 1930: 740 khz; 50 kw-U, DA-2. TL: N29 57 57 W94 56 32. Hrs open: 2000 West Loop South, Suite 300, 77027. Phone: (713) 526-5874. Fax: (713) 360-3666.E-mail: info@ktrh.com Web Site:www.ktrh.com Licensee: AMFM Texas Licenses L.P. Group owner: Clear Channel Communications Inc. (acq 8-30-2000; grpsl). Population served: 2,900,000 Natl. Network: ABC, . Natl. Rep: Christal,. Dow, Lohnes & Albertson. Format: News, sports. Target aud: 25-54. ♦Mark Kopelman, gen mgr; Betty Scott, progmg dir.

***KTRU(FM)**— May 20, 1971: 91.7 mhz; 50 kw. 492 ft TL: N30 03 54 W95 16 10. Stereo. Hrs open: 24 Rice University, 6100 S. Main, 77005. Phone: (713) 348-4098.E-mail: ktru@ktru.org Web Site:www.ktru.org Licensee: Rice University. Population served: 2,000,000 Format: Div. Target aud: General.Eclectic 104 hrs, world 2 hrs, americana 1 hr, experimental 3 hrs, post-punk 1 hr, local 2 hrs, hip hop 3 hrs, reggae 2 hrs, blues 2 hrs, sixties 2 hrs, funk 1 hr, bluegrass 2 hrs, punk 3 hrs, electronic 2 hrs, electronic dance 3 hrs, east indian 2 hrs, children's 1 hr, african 2 hrs, modern classical 3 hrs, spoken word 1 hr, jazz 10 hrs, ska 1 hr, heavy metal 3 hrs wkly. ♦Will Robedee, gen mgr; Rachel Orosco, stn mgr.

***KTSU(FM)**— October 1973: 90.9 mhz; 18.5 kw. 285 ft TL: N29 43 25 W95 21 52. Stereo. Hrs open: 24 3100 Cleburne st., 77004. Phone: (713) 313-7591. Fax: (713) 313-7479. Licensee: Board of Regents Texas Southern University. Population served: 216,600 Format: Educ, div, jazz. News staff: one; News: 10 hrs wkly. Target aud: 25-54. Spec prog: Reggae 8 hrs wkly. ♦Dr. John Rudley, pres; George Thomas, gen mgr; Charles Hudson, opns mgr, progmg dir; Larry Johson, dev mgr; Maurice Hopethompson, news dir; Dave Biondi, chief of engrg.

***KUHF(FM)**— Nov 6, 1950: 88.7 mhz; 100 kw. 1,800 ft TL: N29 34 28 W95 29 37. Stereo. Hrs open: 24 4343 Elgin, 3rd Fl., 77204-0887. Phone: (713) 743-0887. Fax: (713) 743-0868.E-mail: kuhf@kuhf.org Web Site:www.kuhf.org Licensee: University of Houston. Population served: 3,100,000 Natl. Network: NPR, PRI, . Dow, Lohnes & Albertson. Format: Class, news. News staff: 7; News: 25 hrs wkly. Target aud: 25 plus. ♦John Proffitt, gen mgr; Debra Fraser, stn mgr, prom dir; Regina Scruggs, opns mgr; Victor C. Kendall, dev dir; Kathy Rogers, adv mgr; Capella Tucker, progmg dir, news dir; Jack Williams, news dir, news rptr; Alex Schneider, engrg dir, chief of engrg; Ed Mayberry, news rptr; St. John Flynn, cultural affrs dir.

KXYZ(AM)— Aug 8, 1930: 1320 khz; 5 kw-U, DA-N. TL: N29 42 37 W95 10 29. Hrs open: 1782 W. Sam Houston Pkwy. N., 77043. Phone: (713) 490-2538. Fax: (713) 984-1721. Licensee: Multicultural Radio Broadcasting Licensee LLC. Group owner: Multicultural Radio Broadcasting Inc. (acq 12-1-2003; grpsl). Population served: 1,594,000 Format: Contemp Sp, talk. ♦Terry Lowry, gen mgr.

Howe

KHYI(FM)— April 1949: 95.3 mhz; 16 kw. Ant 413 ft TL: N33 23 43 W96 35 50. Stereo. Hrs open: 24 Box 940670, Plano, 75094. Secondary address: 12225 Greenville Ave. Ste.356, Suite 120, Dallas, TN 75074. Phone: (972) 633.0953. Fax: (972) 633-0957.E-mail: ken.jones@kxez.com Web Site:www.khyi.com Licensee: Metro Broadcasters-Texas Inc. Population served: 4,761,200 Natl. Network: Jones Radio Networks, . Fletcher, Heald & Hildreth. Format: Americana/Texas country. News staff: one; News: 3 hrs wkly. Target aud: 25-54; affluent, white collar, middle to upper income listeners. ♦Ken Jones, CEO, pres, gen mgr, news dir, chief of engrg; Glenda Jones, CFO; Lou Rogers, opns dir, opns mgr, pub affrs dir; Joshua Jones, sls dir, gen sls mgr, mktg VP, mktg dir, prom dir; Chance Cody, progmg dir; Mike Doyal, engrg dir.

Hudson

KZXL(FM)— 2002: 96.3 mhz; 1.35 kw. Ant 695 ft TL: N31 21 55 W94 45 59. Hrs open: Box 150455, Lufkin, 75915. Phone: (877) 963-9696. Web Site:www.963zxl.com Licensee: The Turning Leaf LLC (acq 1-22-2008; $400,000). Format: Rock. ♦Vance Barbee, gen mgr.

Humble

KGOL(AM)— July 18, 1984: 1180 khz; 50 kw-D, 1 kw-N, DA-3. TL: N30 08 21 W95 17 24. Stereo. Hrs open: 5 AM-midnight 5821 Southwest Fwy., Suite 600, Houston, 77057. Phone: (713) 349-9880. Fax: (713) 349-0647. Fax: (713) 600-3338.E-mail: caguilar@entravision.com Licensee: Entravision Holdings LLC. Group owner: Entravision Communications Corp. (acq 7-28-00; grpsl). Luther & Watkins. Format: Foreign/Ethnic. News staff: one. Target aud: General; Ethnic & Asian. Spec prog: Hindi 15 hrs wkly. ♦Walter Ulloa, CEO; Jeff Liberman, pres; Carmen Aguilar, gen mgr; David Padgett, opns mgr, progmg mgr; Rick Hunt, engrg VP.

***KSBJ(FM)**— July 6, 1982: 89.3 mhz; 100 kw. Ant 840 ft TL: N30 12 26 W95 05 28. Stereo. Hrs open: 24 Box 187, 77347. Secondary address: 1722 Treble Dr. 77338. Phone: (281) 446-5725. Fax: (281) 540-2198.E-mail: info@ksbj.org Web Site:www.ksbj.org Licensee: KSBJ Educational Foundation. Population served: 4,000,000 Format: Contemp Christian. News staff: 31; News: 4 hrs wkly. Target aud: 25-49; Christian adults. ♦Tim McDermott, gen mgr; Jason Ray, prom dir; John Hull, progmg dir; Jim Beeler, mus dir, disc jockey; Amanda Carroll, news dir; George Schank, chief of engrg; J.R. Hernandez, spec ev coord; Duane Allen, disc jockey.

Hunt

KRZS(FM)— 2009: 99.9 mhz; 14.5 kw. Ant 200 ft TL: N30 05 08 W99 16 23. Hrs open: 604-D Junction Hwy., Kerrville, 78028. Phone: (830) 890-5229. Fax: (830) 890-5232.E-mail: rick@roseradio999.com Web Site:www.roseradio999.com Licensee: Munbilla Kerrville Ltd. ♦B. Shane Fox, gen mgr.

Huntington

KSML-FM— March 1, 1994: 101.9 mhz; 15 kw. Ant 827 ft TL: N31 20 05 W94 40 10. Stereo. Hrs open: 24 Yates Broadcasting, 121 Cotton Sq., Lufkin, 75902. Phone: (936) 634-4584. Fax: (936) 632-5722.E-mail: keith@yatesbroadcasting.com Web Site:www.ksml.net Licensee: Yates Broadcasting Corp. Format: Sp. ♦Steven Yates, gen mgr; Keith Sims, opns mgr, progmg dir.

Huntsville

***KHCH(AM)**— Oct 4, 1982: 1410 khz; 250 w-D, 87 w-N. TL: N30 42 54 W95 31 42. Hrs open: 24 2424 South Blvd., Houston, 77098. Phone: (713) 520-5200.E-mail: email@khcb.org Web Site:www.khcb.org Licensee: KHCB Inc. Group owner: Houston Christian Broadcasters Inc. (acq 10-97; $145,000). Format: Sp Christian. ♦Bruce Munsterman, gen mgr; Dolly Martin, progmg dir; Miguel Jacinto, news dir.

KHVL(AM)— Nov 3, 1938: 1490 khz; 1 kw-U. TL: N30 41 48 W95 33 08. Hrs open: 24 P.O. Box 330, 77342. Secondary address: 622 Interstate 45 S. 77340. Phone: (936) 295-2651. Fax: (936) 295-8201.E-mail: steveeverett@ksam1017@.com Web Site:www.khvl.com Licensee: HEH Communications LLC (acq 12-21-2000; $1.9 million with co-located FM). Population served: 65,000 Natl. Network: ABC, . Format: Classic Hits 60s & 70s. News staff: one; News: 5 local news casts per day. Target aud: 30 plus. Spec prog: Black 5 hrs wkly. ♦Steve Everett, gen mgr; Brooke Addams, opns mgr; Larry Crippen, news dir; Stacy Selman, traf mgr.

KSAM-FM— Aug 1, 1965: 101.7 mhz; 6 kw. Ant 420 ft TL: N30 41 48 W95 33 08. Stereo. Hrs open: 24 P.O. Box 330, 77342. Secondary address: 622 Interstate 45 S. 77340. Phone: (936) 295-2651. Fax: (936) 295-8201.E-mail: ksammail@yahoo.com Web Site:www.ksam1017.com Licensee: HEH Communications LLC (acq 12-21-2000; $1.9 million with co-located AM). Population served: 65,000 Format: Country. News staff: one; News: 6 local news casts per day. Target aud: 25-54; women. ♦Steve Everett, gen mgr; Brooke Addams, opns mgr; Larry Crippen, news dir; Stacey Selman, traf mgr.

***KSHU(FM)**— October 1973: 90.5 mhz; 3 kw. 255 ft TL: N30 42 50 W95 32 58. Stereo. Hrs open: 24 Box 2207, 1804 Avenue J, 77341. Phone: (936) 294-3939. Phone: (936) 294-1342. Fax: (936) 294-1888.E-mail: rtf_kshu@shsu.edu Web Site:www.shsu.edu/~rtf_kshu Licensee: Sam Houston State University. Population served: 40,000 Format: Class, CHR, jazz. News: 25 hrs wkly. Target aud: General; rural. Spec prog: Sp 4 hrs wkly. ♦James Jones, gen mgr; Amanda Sebesta, opns dir; Jimmy Wehr, progmg dir; Steve Sandlin, chief of engrg.

Hurst

KMNY(AM)— April 1947: 1360 khz; 50 kw-D, 890 w-N, DA-2. TL: N32 46 28 W96 57 53. Hrs open: 24 5801 Marvin D. Love Fwy., Suite 409, Dallas, 75237. Phone: (972) 572-1540. Fax: (972) 572-1260. Web Site:www.rationalradio.org Licensee: Multicultural Radio Broadcasting Licensee LLC. Group owner: Multicultural Radio Broadcasting Inc. (acq 2-4-2004; grpsl). Natl. Network: Air America, USA, . Format: Talk. ♦Ted Sauceman, gen mgr.

Hutto

KYLR(FM)—Licensed to Hutto. See Austin

Idalou

KRBL(FM)— Sept 18, 1995: 105.7 mhz; 6 kw. 328 ft TL: N33 40 06 W101 37 52. Hrs open: 916 Main St., Suite 617, Lubbock, 79401. Phone: (806) 749-1057. Fax: (806) 749-1177. Licensee: Triumph Communications Inc. Format: Classic country. Target aud: 24-64. ♦Paul Beane, gen mgr, opns mgr, news dir; Steve Ritchie, gen sls mgr, adv dir; Anthony Garza, progmg dir, chief of engrg; Wanda Byers, traf mgr.

Ingleside

KRSR(FM)— 1996: 107.3 mhz; 14 kw. Ant 446 ft TL: N27 52 00 W97 13 08. Stereo. Hrs open: 24 826 S. Padre Island Dr., Corpus Christi, 78416. Phone: (361) 814-3800. Fax: (361) 855-3770.E-mail: info@1073jakefm.com Web Site:www.star1073radio.com Licensee: Convergent Broadcasting Corpus Christi LP. Group owner: Convergent Broadcasting LLC (acq 1-12-2004; grpsl). Population served: 313,600 Format: Light rock. Target aud: 25-54; adults. ♦Mark White, gen mgr; Dallas Garcia, adv mgr; Scott Holt, progmg dir; William Hooper, engr.

Ingram

KSYY(FM)— 2007: 96.5 mhz; 8.4 kw. Ant 430 ft TL: N30 07 04 W99 11 40. Hrs open: 1717 Dixie Hwy., Fort Wayne, 41011. Licensee: Radioactive LLC. ♦Benjamin L. Homel, pres.

***KTXI(FM)**— November 1998: 90.1 mhz; 50 kw. 453 ft TL: N30 06 14 W99 04 36. Stereo. Hrs open: 24
Rebroadcasts KPAC(FM) San Antonio 75% , KSTX(FM) San Antonio 25%.
Texas Public Radio, 8401 Datapoint Dr., Suite 800, San Antonio, 78229. Phone: (210) 614-8977. Fax: (210) 614-8983.E-mail: info@ktxi.fm Web Site:www.ktxi.fm Licensee: Texas Public Radio. Population served: 50000 Natl. Network: NPR, PRI, . Garvey, Schubert & Barer. Format: Class, news. Target aud: 25 plus. ♦Dan Skinner, pres, gen mgr; Nathan Cone, opns mgr, progmg dir; Laverne Dittx, dev mgr; Janet Grojean, progmg dir, sls; Randy Anderson, mus dir; Dave Davies, news dir; Wayne Coble, engrg dir.

Iowa Park

KXXN(FM)— 2009: 96.3 mhz; 6 kw. Ant 256 ft TL: N33 58 20 W98 45 35. Hrs open: 819 S.W. Federal Hwy., Suite 106, Stuart, FL, 34994. Phone: (772) 215-1634.E-mail: info@toweritrust.com Web Site:www.toweritrust.com Licensee: Tower Investment Trust Inc. ♦William H. Brothers, pres.

Jacksboro

KJKB(FM)— Oct 6, 1996: 95.5 mhz; 6 kw. Ant 328 ft TL: N33 19 43 W98 16 46. Hrs open: 24 101 N Main St, Ste 206, 76458. Phone: (940) 567-6600. Fax: (940) 567-6602.E-mail: kjkb@boss9055.com Licensee: Hunt Broadcasting Inc. Group owner: On-Air Family LLC (acq 1995; $6,000). Population served: 12,000 Format: Classic Rock. ♦Janice Hunt, CEO, gen mgr; Jim Hunt, exec VP; Debbie Watts, stn mgr; Jerrod Knight, progmg dir.

Jacksonville

***KBJS(FM)**— May 16, 1987: 90.3 mhz; 3 kw. 266 ft TL: N31 58 16 W95 15 51. (CP: 19 kw, ant 1,286 ft. TL: N32 03 40 W95 18 50). Stereo. Hrs open: Box 193, 75766. Phone: (903) 586-5257. Fax: (903) 586-4986.E-mail: info@kbjs.org Web Site:www.kbjs.org Licensee: East Texas Media Association Inc. Natl. Network: Moody, . Format: Relg, Christian. Spec prog: Black one hr, Sp one hr wkly. ♦Bob Shivery, pres, gen mgr; Randy Featherston, stn mgr; Eddie Baiseri, progmg dir, progmg mgr.

KEBE(AM)— Jan 12, 1947: 1400 khz; 1 kw-U. TL: N31 58 11 W95 15 52. Hrs open: 24 Box 1648, 75766. Secondary address: Radio Ctr., 402 S. Ragsdale 75766. Phone: (903) 586-2527. Fax: (903) 586-1394.E-mail: info@wallerbroadcasting.com Web Site:www.kooi.com Licensee: Waller Broadcasting Inc. Group owner: Waller Broadcasting (acq 11-58; $75,000). Population served: 12,724 Natl. Rep: McGavren Guild,. Format: Classic country. News staff: 2; News: 6 hrs wkly. Target aud: 25-54. Spec prog: Farm 9 hrs wkly. ♦Dudley Waller, CEO, pres, gen mgr; Tina Harper, CFO; Alan Mather, opns dir, opns mgr.

KLJT(FM)— 1993: 102.3 mhz; 50 kw. Ant 492 ft TL: N31 52 18 W95 10 00. Stereo. Hrs open: 24 Box 1648, 75766. Secondary address: 402 S. Ragsdale 75766. Phone: (903) 586-2527. Fax: (903) 589-0677.E-mail: dudley2@wallerbroadcasting.com Web Site:www.wallerbroadcast.com Licensee: Waller Media LLC. Group owner: Waller Broadcasting (acq 12-9-02). Natl. Network: ABC, . Natl. Rep: McGavren Guild,. David Tillotson. Wire Svc: AP Format: Adult favorites. News staff: one; News: 6 hrs wkly. ♦Dudley Waller, CEO & gen mgr.

KOOI-FM— Sept 9, 1967: 106.5 mhz; 100 kw. Ant 1,468 ft TL: N32 03 40 W95 18 50. Stereo. Hrs open: 24 Box 7820, Tyler, 75711. Secondary address: 210 S. Broadway, Tyler 75702. Phone: (903) 581-9966. Fax: (903) 534-5300.E-mail: kooi@etradiogroup.com Web Site:www.kooi.com Licensee: Access.1 Texas License Company LLC. (acq 1-7-2005; grpsl). Population served: 848,000 Natl. Network: ABC, . Rgnl. Network: Texas State Net. Natl. Rep: McGavren Guild,. Texas State Networks Format: Adult contemp. Target aud: 25-54. ♦Rick Guest, gen mgr, opns mgr, mktg mgr, mus dir; Genni Causey, gen sls mgr; Paul Orr, progmg dir; Shelley Miller, traf mgr.

Jasper

KCOX(AM)— Aug 6, 1948: 1350 khz; 5 kw-D, 37 w-N. TL: N30 55 11 W93 58 13. Hrs open: 24 Box 2008, 75951. Secondary address: 1408 E. Gibson 75951. Phone: (409) 384-4500. Fax: (409) 384-4525.E-mail: crosstexas@sbcglobal.net Web Site:www.crosstexasmedia.com Licensee: Cross Texas Media Inc. (acq 8-29-2007; $890,000 with co-located FM). Population served: 300,000 Natl. Network: Salem Radio Network, . Rgnl. Network: Texas State Net. Format: Contemp Christian. Target aud: 18-35. ♦Rick Tallent, gen mgr; Dale Cucancic, gen sls mgr; T.J. Bordelon, opns dir & engrg dir; Barbara Bordelon, traf mgr.

KJAS(FM)— 1996: 107.3 mhz; 8 kw. Ant 328 ft TL: N30 58 31 W93 59 24. Stereo. Hrs open: 24 765 Hemphill St., 75951. Phone: (409) 384-2626. Fax: (409) 383-1979.E-mail: presff@kjas.com Web Site:www.kjas.com Licensee: DBA Rayburn Broadcasting Co. Population

served: 72,000 Booth, Freret, Imlay & Tepper. Format: Adult contemp. News staff: one; News: 4 hrs wkly. Target aud: 24-54; females/buying group. Spec prog: Oldies 4 hrs wkly. ◆Mike Lout, gen mgr; Melaney Dickerson, opns mgr; Debra Foster, sls VP, gen sls mgr; Crystal Mouton, pub affrs dir.

KTXJ-FM— November 1964: 102.7 mhz; 26 kw. Ant 440 ft TL: N31 03 36 W93 57 42. (CP: 50 kw, ant 492 ft). Stereo. Hrs open: 24 Prog sep from AM Box 2008, 75951. Secondary address: 1408 E. Gibosn 75951. Phone: (409) 384-4500. Fax: (409) 384-4525.E-mail: crosstexas@sbcglobal.net Web Site:www.crosstexasmedia.com Licensee: Cross Texas Media Inc. Population served: 400,000 Natl. Network: Salem Radio Network, . Format: Southern gospel music. Very broad receptive demographic.

Jefferson

*KHCJ(FM)— 2003: 91.9 mhz; 3.1 kw. Ant 462 ft TL: N32 49 23 W94 28 32. Hrs open: 24
Rebroadcasts KHCB-FM Houston 95%.
Houston Christian Broadcasters Inc., 2424 South Blvd., Houston, 77098. Phone: (713) 520-5200.E-mail: email@khcb.org Web Site:www.khcb.org Licensee: Houston Christian Broadcasters Inc. (group owner). Natl. Network: Moody, . Format: Christian. ◆Bruce E. Munsterman, gen mgr.

KJTX(FM)— October 1990: 104.5 mhz; 2.3 kw. 531 ft TL: N32 49 23 W94 28 32. (CP 4.4 kw, ant 384 ft.). Stereo. Hrs open: 24 Box 150508, Longview, 75615. Phone: (903) 759-1243. Fax: (903) 759-9725.E-mail: kjtxlr@juno.com Web Site:www.kjtx1045fm.com Licensee: Wisdom Ministries Inc. (acq 4-16-93; $140,000; 5-3-93). Population served: 500,000 Format: Gospel, Christian. News: 2 hrs wkly. Target aud: 16 plus. ◆Leroy Richardson, pres, pres, gen mgr, progmg dir, chief of engrg; Jocelyn Jordan, mus dir; Sharon Herbert, traf mgr.

Johnson City

KFAN-FM— 1991: 107.9 mhz; 37.2 kw. 492 ft TL: N30 11 49 W98 38 19. Stereo. Hrs open: 24 Box 311, 210 Woodcrest, Fredericksburg, 78624. Phone: (830) 997-2197. Fax (830) 997-2198.E-mail: txradio@ktc.com Web Site:www.texasrebelradio.com Licensee: J. & J. Fritz Media Ltd. (group owner). Population served: 200,000 Fletcher, Heald + Hildreth. Format: Americana AAA. News staff: one. Target aud: 25-49. Spec prog: Jazz 5 hrs wkly. ◆Jayson Fritz, pres, gen mgr, gen sls mgr; Jan Fritz, sr VP, mktg VP, adv VP; Ariana Carruth, prom VP; Rick Star, progmg dir; Robbie Fish, news dir; Kyle Province, pub affrs dir; Duncan Black, chief of engrg.

Jourdanton

KLEY-FM— 2001: 95.7 mhz; 11 kw. Ant 1,036 ft TL: N28 54 57.4 W98 39 39. Hrs open: 4500 Eisenhauer Rd, San Antonio, 78218. Phone: (210) 654-5100. Fax: (210) 340-1775. Licensee: BMP San Antonio License Co. L.P. (group owner; (acq 12-23-2004; $7.5 million). Format: Mexican rgnl. ◆Lance Hawkins, gen mgr; Bob Brown, sls dir.

Junction

KMBL(AM)— 1953: 1450 khz; 1 kw-U. TL: N30 29 34 W99 45 41. Hrs open: 24 2125 Sidney Baker, Kerrville, 78028. Secondary address: 214 Pecan St. 76899. Phone: (830) 896-1230. Fax (830) 792-4142.E-mail: generalmanager@krvl.com Licensee: Foster Charitable Foundation Inc. Group owner: Hill Country Broadcasting Corp. (acq 5-31-2007). Population served: 2,654 Natl. Network: Westwood One, . Rgnl. Network: Texas State Net. Texas State Networks Format: Country. News staff: one; News: 6 hrs wkly. Target aud: General. Spec prog: Farm 6 hrs wkly. ◆David L. Greenwald, pres; Monte Spearman, gen mgr, dev dir, mktg dir; Harley Belew, opns dir; Glen Taylor, prom dir; Monte Speaman, adv dir; A.J. Hernandez, progmg dir; Charles Rodaiquez, news dir; Carolyn Anderson, pub affrs dir; Steve Alex, stn mgr, sls dir & engrg VP; Debbie Adams, traf mgr; Laurel Bradford, local news ed.

KOOK(FM)— 1997: 93.5 mhz; 50 kw. 492 ft TL: N30 29 31 W100 02 03. Hrs open: 24 2125 Sidney Baker St, Kerrville, 78028. Phone: (830) 896-1230. Fax: (830) 792-4142. Licensee: Foster Charitable Foundation Inc. Group owner: Hill Country Broadcasting Corp. (acq 5-31-2007). Natl. Network: ABC, . Rgnl. Network: Texas State Net. Texas State Networks Format: Country. Spec prog: Gospel 2 hrs wkly. ◆Monte Spearman, gen mgr; Donna Keese, opns mgr.

Karnes City

KTXX(FM)— March 2005: 103.1 mhz; 34 kw. Ant 587 ft TL: N29 00 52 W97 40 02. Hrs open: 4500 Eisenhauer Rd, San Antonio, 78218. Phone: (210) 654-5100. Fax: (210) 340-1775. Licensee: Palm Broadcasting Co. Format: Sp Christian. ◆Lance Hawkins, gen mgr; Bob Brown, sls dir.

Keene

*KJCR(FM)— June 13, 1974: 88.3 mhz; 23 kw. 180 ft TL: N32 24 19 W97 19 55. Stereo. Hrs open: 24 304 N. College Dr., 76059. Phone: (817) 202-6788. Fax: (817) 202-6790. Web Site:www.kjcr.org Licensee: Southwestern Adventist University. Population served: 1,500,000 Donald E. Martin. Format: Relg. News: 8 hrs wkly. Target aud: 18 plus; general. ◆Don Sahly, pres; Randy Yates, gen mgr; Christina Osborn, opns mgr, progmg dir, news dir; Karen Knaubert, sls dir, prom dir; Marianne Dale, mus dir; Ron Macomber, chief of engrg.

Kempner

KHLE(FM)— Dec 15, 1978: 106.9 mhz; 2.3 kw. Ant 538 ft TL: N31 06 01 W97 55 39. Stereo. Hrs open: 581 Pan American Dr., Suite 8, Harker Heights, 76548. Phone: (254) 833-5855. Fax: (254) 833-8844. Web Site:www.piratefmonline.com Licensee: Munbilla Fort Hood Ltd. Natl. Network: ABC, . Format: Adult hits. News staff: 2; News: 3 hrs wkly. Target aud: 25-54.

Kenedy

KTNR(FM)—Licensed to Kenedy. See Kenedy-Karnes City

Kenedy-Karnes City

KAML(AM)— November 1954: 990 khz; 250 w-D, 70 w-N. TL: N28 51 02 W97 52 48. Hrs open: 24 R. 1 Box 990, Kenedy, 78119-9719. Secondary address: Box 990, Karnes City 78118. Phone: (830) 583-2990. Fax: (830) 583-0700.E-mail: info@kamlam.com Licensee: SIGA Broadcasting Corp. (group owner; acq 1-17-2002). Population served: 197,000 Natl. Rep: Dome,. Wire Svc: U.S. Weather Service Format: Country, news, sports. News staff: 2; News: 8 hrs wkly. Target aud: 24-54; male-female. ◆Gabriel Arango, pres; Clyde Eckols, gen mgr; Clyde S. Eckols, mktg dir, sls; Steve Eckols, progmg dir.

*KTNR(FM)—(Kenedy, Sept 1, 1982: 92.1 mhz; 6 kw. Ant 262 ft TL: N28 45 35 W97 51 45. Stereo. Hrs open: 8500 N. Stemmons Fwy., Dallas, 75247. Phone: (214) 879-0081. Fax: (214) 879-0083. Licensee: Hispanic Christian Community Network Inc. (acq 9-19-2007; $175,000). ◆Antonio Cesar Guel, pres & gen mgr.

Kerens

KRVF(FM)— May 23, 1979: 106.9 mhz; 21.5 kw. Ant 365 ft TL: N32 06 12 W96 22 33. Stereo. Hrs open: 1373 S.E. Country Rd. 0070, Coriscana, 75109. Phone: (903) 872-4757. Fax: (903) 885-9107. Licensee: LKCM Radio Group L.P. (group owner; (acq 5-21-2004; $1 million with KRVA-FM Campbell). Population served: 5,000,000 Format: Oldies. ◆Bert Goldman, exec VP; Chris McMurray, gen mgr.

Kermit

KERB(AM)— June 1950: 600 khz; 1 kw-D, DA. TL: N31 50 05 W103 08 10. Hrs open: Box 252, McAllen, 78505. Phone: (956) 781-5528. Fax: (956) 686-2999. Licensee: La Radio Cristiana Network Inc. (acq 5-20-97; $80,000 with co-located FM). Population served: 15,000 Rgnl. Network: Texas State Net. Natl. Rep: Keystone (unwired net),. Texas State Networks Format: Christian, Sp Christian. ◆Eloy Bernal, gen mgr; Gilbert Martinez, progmg dir.

KERB-FM— 1983: 106.3 mhz; 3 kw. 276 ft TL: N31 50 05 W103 08 10. Hrs open: Dups AM 100% Box 252, McAllen, 78505. Phone: (956) 781-5528. Fax: (956) 686-2999. Web Site:www.laradiocristiana.com Licensee: La Radio Cristiana Network Inc. Population served: 15,000

Kerrville

KERV(AM)— Nov 5, 1948: 1230 khz; 990 w-U. TL: N30 04 14 W99 11 07. Stereo. Hrs open: 24 21125 Sidney Baker N., Kerville, 78028. Phone: (830) 896-1230. Fax: (830) 792-4142.E-mail: info@kerv.com Web Site:www.kerv.com Licensee: Foster Charitable Foundation Inc. Group owner: Hill Country Broadcasting Corp. (acq 5-31-2007).

Population served: 50,000 Natl. Network: ABC, . Format: Talk, smooth jazz. News staff: one; News: 3 hrs wkly. Target aud: 45 plus; educated professionals.

KGSX(FM)—See Comfort

*KHKV(FM)— 1998: 91.1 mhz; 300 w. 207 ft TL: N30 02 37 W99 07 17. Hrs open: 24
Rebroadcasts KHCB(AM) Houston-Galveston 80%.
2424 South Blvd., Houston, 77098. Phone: (713) 520-5200.E-mail: email@khcb.org Web Site:www.khcb.org Licensee: Houston Christian Broadcasters Inc. (group owner). Format: Christian, Sp. ◆Bruce Munsterman, gen mgr; Dolly Martin, progmg dir; Miguel Jacinto, news dir.

*KKER(FM)— Dec 8, 2000: 88.7 mhz; 52 kw. Ant 571 ft TL: N30 03 30 W99 03 50. Hrs open: 24 Houston Christian Broadcasters Inc., 2424 South Blvd., Houston, 77098. Phone: (713) 520-5200.E-mail: email@khcb.org Web Site:www.khcb.org Licensee: Houston Christian Broadcasters Inc. (group owner; acq 11-24-00; $3,500 for CP with CP of KHCP(FM) Paris). Natl. Network: Moody, . Format: Christian. Spec prog: Sp 6 hrs, Chinese one hr wkly. ◆Bruce Munsterman, gen mgr.

KKVR(FM)— Sept 1, 2007: 106.1 mhz; 6 kw. Ant 328 ft TL: N30 02 27 W99 10 19. Hrs open: 24 3505 Fredricksburg Rd., 78028. Phone: (830) 896-4990. Fax: (830) 896-4991. Licensee: E-String Wireless Ltd. Format: Classic hits. ◆Bret Huggins, gen mgr.

KRNH(FM)— June 1994: 92.3 mhz; 20 kw. Ant 666 ft TL: N30 03 42 W99 03 43. Hrs open: 24 3505 Fredricksburg Rd., 78028. Phone: (830) 896-4990. Fax: (830) 896-4991.E-mail: mary@theranchfm92.com Web Site:www.theranchfm92.com Licensee: Radio Ranch Ltd. (acq 9-6-00; $245,000). Baraff, Koerner & Olender. Format: Real Country. Target aud: 18-64. ◆Ben McGiffert, gen mgr.

KRVL(FM)— Sept 12, 1975: 94.3 mhz; 33 kw. Ant 400 ft TL: N30 15 08 W99 08 01. Stereo. Hrs open: 24 2125 Sidney Baker N., 78028. Phone: (830) 896-1230. Fax: (830) 792-4142.E-mail: info@revfmradio.com Web Site:www.revfmradio.com Licensee: Foster Charitable Foundation Inc. (acq 5-31-2007). Population served: 300,000 Natl. Network: ABC, . Format: Americana. Target aud: 25-49. Spec prog: Gospel one hr, local church service one hr wkly. ◆Jana Smith, gen mgr; Marti Ashcraft, opns mgr; Glenn Taylor, progmg dir; Diane Philips, traf mgr; Gordon Ames, sls.

Kilgore

KDOK(AM)— Dec 26, 1936: 1240 khz; 1 kw-U. TL: N32 25 02 W94 51 15. Hrs open: 3810 Brookside Dr., Tyler, 75701. Phone: (903) 581-0606. Fax: (903) 581-2011.E-mail: craigreininger@gapbroadcasting.com Web Site:www.kktx.com Licensee: GAP Broadcasting Tyler License LLC. Group owner: Clear Channel Communications Inc. Population served: 150,000 Natl. Rep: Katz Radio, Target Broadcast Sales,. Target aud: 25-54.

KKTX-FM— Dec 23, 1976: 96.1 mhz; 50 kw. Ant 492 ft TL: N32 22 14 W94 56 20. Stereo. Hrs open: 3810 Brookside Dr., Tyler, 75701. Phone: (903) 581-0606. Fax: (903) 581-2011.E-mail: craigreininger @gapbroadcasting.com Web Site:www.kktx.com Licensee: GAP Broadcasting Tyler License LLC (acq 8-3-2007; grpsl). Population served: 550,000 Format: Classic rock. Target aud: 25-54. ◆Craig Reininger, sls dir; Chris Jones, rgnl sls mgr; Lisa Nix, progmg dir.

*KZLO(FM)— Feb 4, 1991: 88.7 mhz; 63 kw horiz, 79 kw vert. Ant 551 ft TL: N32 20 14 W95 02 41. Stereo. Hrs open: 19 5700 West Oaks Blvd., Rocklin, CA, 95765. Phone: (916) 251-1600. Fax (916) 251-1650. Web Site:www.klove.com Licensee: Educational Media Foundation. (acq 2-15-2007; $2 million). Natl. Network: K-Love, . Davis Wright Tremaine LLP. Format: Contemp Christian. ◆Richard Jenkins, pres.

Killeen

KIIZ-FM— Dec 10, 1990: 92.3 mhz; 6 kw. Ant 239 ft TL: N31 06 29 W97 39 50. Stereo. Hrs open: 24 100 West Central Expressway, Harker Heights, 76348. Phone: (254) 699-5000. Fax: (254) 399-8134.E-mail: babysitter@clearchannel.com Web Site:www.kiiz.com Licensee: Capstar TX L.P. Group owner: Clear Channel Communications Inc. (acq 8-30-2000; grpsl). Format: Urban contemp. News: 2 hrs wkly. Target aud: 18-49. ◆Tim Thomas, gen mgr & stn mgr; Chuck Redden, sls dir, gen sls mgr; Terry Steele, prom mgr; Julia Conner, news dir, traf mgr; Brett Gilbert, chief of engrg.

*KNCT-FM— Nov 23, 1970: 91.3 mhz; 50 kw. 1,170 ft TL: N30 59 12 W97 37 47. Stereo. Hrs open: 24 Box 1800, Central Texas College,

6200 W. Central Texas Expwy., 76542. Phone: (254) 526-1176. Fax: (254) 526-1850.E-mail: knctfm@knctfm.com Web Site:www.knct.org Licensee: Central Texas College. Population served: 240,000 Natl. Network: AP Network News, . Rgnl. Network: Texas AP. Format: Btfl mus, class. Target aud: 45 plus. Spec prog: Jazz 15 hrs wkly, big band 6 hrs wkly. ♦Max Rudolph, gen mgr; Dan Hull, progmg dir; Steve Sulzer, chief of engrg. Co-owned TV: *KNCT(TV) affil

KRMY(AM)— July 4, 1955: 1050 khz; 250 w-D. TL: N31 06 53 W97 42 00. Hrs open: 4638 Decker Dr., Baytown, 77520. Secondary address: 314 N. 2nd St. 76514. Phone: (254) 628-7071. Fax: (254) 634-5263. Licensee: Martin Broadcasting Inc. (group owner; acq 11-89; grpsl;11-27-89). Population served: 50,000 Format: Gospel. Target aud: 18-44. ♦Darrell Martin, gen mgr; Horatio Martinez, progmg dir.

KUSJ(FM)—See Temple

Kingsville

KFTX(FM)— May 2, 1970: 97.5 mhz; 100 kw. 1,000 ft TL: N27 30 54 W97 51 58. Stereo. Hrs open: 24 1520 S. Port Ave., Corpus Christi, 78405. Phone: (361) 883-5987. Fax: (361) 883-3648. Web Site:www.kftx.com Licensee: Quality Broadcasting Corp. (acq 11-29-2006). Wood, Maines & Brown. Format: Country. News staff: one; News: 2 hrs wkly. Target aud: 25-49; educated, affluent young adults. ♦Bruce Nelson Stratton, gen mgr, stn mgr; Cyndi Rowden, sls dir, gen sls mgr; Chuck Abel, progmg dir; Austin Daniels, mus dir; Mark Earle, chief of engrg; Wendy Hatley, traf mgr.

KINE(AM)— November 1948: 1330 khz; 1 kw-D, 250 w-N. TL: N27 36 36 W97 47 42. Hrs open: 24 115 W. Avenue D, Rob Towns, 78380. Phone: (361) 855-1330. Fax: (361) 289-7722. Licensee: Cotton Broadcasting. (acq 9-28-90; $50,000; 10-22-90). Population served: 500,000 Format: Rgnl Sp, relg. Target aud: 25-54. ♦Humberto L. Lopez, CEO; Humberto Lopez, pres; Carlos Lopez, gen mgr; Minerva R. Lopez, dev VP; Ernest Lopez, sls VP; Manuel Lopez, prom VP; Homer Lopez, mus dir; Tommy Greg, chief of engrg.

KKBA(FM)— November 1981: 92.7 mhz; 12.5 kw. 869 ft TL: N27 32 07 W97 53 06. Stereo. Hrs open: 24 Box 9757, Corpus Christi, 78469. Secondary address: 2117 Leopard St. , CorpusChristi 78408. Phone: (361) 883-3516. Fax: (361) 882-9767.E-mail: thechief@star94.net Web Site:www.927kkba.com Licensee: Malkan Broadcasting L.P. Group owner: Malkan Broadcast Assoc. (acq 9-13-95;10-2-95). Population served: 315,000 Natl. Rep: Katz Radio,. Thompson Hines, LLP. Format: Adult contemp. News staff: one; News: 20 hrs wkly. Target aud: 25-54. ♦Glen Powers, pres, gen mgr; Janice Raleigh, sls dir; Norma Morales, prom dir; John Gifford, engrg dir, chief of engrg; Bart Allison, progmg.

***KTAI(FM)**— Feb 23, 1970: 91.1 mhz; 100 w. 98 ft TL: N27 31 24 W97 52 42. Stereo. Hrs open: Noon-12:30 AM (M-F); 4 PM-10 PM (Su) 700 University Blvd., MSC 178, Texas A & M Univ.-Kingsville, 78363. Phone: (361) 593-3489.E-mail: ktaifm@hotmail.com Web Site:www.tamuk.edu/ktai Licensee: Texas A&M University-Kingsville. Population served: 28,711 Format: Rock. Target aud: 16-25; high school & college ages. Spec prog: Black 8 hrs, gospel 6 hrs, mus from India 3 hrs, mus from Mexico 3 hrs wkly. ♦Cark Saltarelli, pres, gen mgr; Kirk Notarianni, opns mgr; Christin Rycroft, progmg dir.

Knox City

KTSX(FM)—Not on air, target date: unknown: 107.3 mhz; 6 kw. Ant 328 ft TL: N33 25 40 W99 40 00. Hrs open: Box 880, Roma, 78584. Phone: (956) 487-8015. Licensee: South Texas FM Investments LLC. (acq 9-16-2008; grpsl). ♦Eloy Vera, gen mgr.

Krum

KNOR(FM)— Nov 11, 1984: 93.7 mhz; 15.5 kw. Ant 1,969 ft TL: N33 29 05 W97 24 44. Stereo. Hrs open: 24 4201 Pool Rd., Colleyville, 76034. Phone: (817) 868-2900. Fax: 817-868-2116.E-mail: Dallasinfo@lbimedia.com Web Site:www.laraza937.com Licensee: Liberman Broadcasting of Dallas License LLC. Group owner: Liberman Broadcasting Inc. (acq 5-13-2004; $15.5 million). Population served: 100,000 Rgnl. Network: Okla. Radio Net. Natl. Rep: Roslin,. Fletcher, Heald & Hildreth. Format: Sp. Target aud: HISPANIC. ♦Rosa Cuellar-Khraish, gen mgr.

La Grange

KBUK(FM)— Dec 21, 1970: 104.9 mhz; 3 kw. 203 ft TL: N29 52 57 W96 51 58. (CP: Ant 328 ft.). Stereo. Hrs open: Dups AM 100% FM Rd. 155, 78945. Phone: (979) 968-3173. Fax: (979) 968-6196.E-mail: info@kvlgkbuk.com Web Site:www.kvlgkbuk.com Population served: 35,000 ♦Roy Cerney, stn mgr.

KVLG(AM)— June 27, 1959: 1570 khz; 250 w-D, DA-1. TL: N29 52 58 W96 51 57. Hrs open: Box 609, 78945. Secondary address: FM 155 S. 78945. Phone: (979) 968-3173. Phone: (979) 743-4050. Fax: (979) 968-6196.E-mail: info@kvlgkbuk.com Web Site:www.kvlgkbuk.com Licensee: Fayette Broadcasting Corp. Population served: 30,000 Rgnl. Network: Texas State Net., VSA Radio. Texas State Networks Format: Country. Target aud: General. Spec prog: Ger one hr, Black one hr, farm 4 hrs, Pol/Czech 12 hrs, relg 5 hrs wkly. ♦Roy Cerney, gen mgr & progmg dir.

La Porte

KHJK(FM)—Licensed to La Porte. See Houston

Lake Jackson

KGLK(FM)— April 1963: 107.5 mhz; 100 kw. Ant 2,000 ft TL: N29 17 16 W95 13 53. Stereo. Hrs open: 24 1990 Post Oak Blvd., Suite 2300, Houston, 77056. Phone: (713) 963-1200. Fax: (713) 622-5457. Web Site:www.1075theeagle.com Licensee: Cox Radio Inc. Group owner: Cox Television (acq 8-30-2000; grpsl). Population served: 196,100 Format: Oldies. News staff: 2; News: 5 hrs wkly. Target aud: 25-54; college grads from the 60s, 70s & 80s. ♦Mark Krieschen, VP, gen mgr; Rob Hienaman, gen sls mgr; Mike Murray, natl sls mgr; Bill Tatar, mktg dir; Ed Scarborough, progmg dir; Paul Christy, mus dir.

***KYBJ(FM)**— 1995: 91.1 mhz; 5 kw. 459 ft TL: N29 02 37 W95 20 11. Hrs open:
Rebroadcasts KSBJ(FM) Humble 100%.
1722 Treble, c/o KSBJ(FM), Humble, 77338. Phone: (281) 446-5725. Fax: (281) 540-2198.E-mail: mwanner@ksbj.org Web Site:www.ksbj.org Licensee: Educational Media Foundation of Brazosport. Format: Contemporary Christian. Target aud: 25-49. ♦Tim McDermott, gen mgr; Jon Hull, progmg dir, news dir.

Lamesa

***KBKN(FM)**—Not on air, target date: unknown: 91.3 mhz; 250 w. Ant 157 ft TL: N32 45 34 W101 57 09. Hrs open: 1406 E. Garden Ln., Midland, 79702. Phone: (432) 638-1150. Fax: (432) 682-5230.E-mail: robertd@grnonline.com Web Site:www.lapromesa.org Licensee: La Promesa Foundation. (acq 5-4-2004; $108,000 including six translator stns). Format: Christian. ♦Leonard Oswald, pres & gen mgr.

KPET(AM)— May 21, 1947: 690 khz; 250 w-U. TL: N32 42 27 W101 56 11. Hrs open: 24 Box 1188, One Radio Rd., 79331. Phone: (806) 872-6511. Phone: (806) 872-6537. Fax: (806) 872-6514.E-mail: kpet@pics.net Licensee: DCB License Sub LLC (acq 10-5-2007; $290,000). Population served: 16,000 Natl. Network: ABC, . Rgnl. Network: Texas State Net. Texas State Networks Format: C&W. News staff: one; News: 2 hrs wkly. Target aud: 18-65. ♦Don Sitton, gen mgr, opns dir, progmg dir; Elaine Githens, gen sls mgr, adv mgr; Grover Clifft, news dir; Anthony Garza, chief of engrg; DeeAnn Martin, traf mgr.

KTXC(FM)— May 1, 1988: 104.7 mhz; 100 kw. 800 ft TL: N32 23 47 W101 57 24. Stereo. Hrs open: 24 11320 WCR 127, Midland, 79711. Phone: (432) 570-6670. Fax: (432) 567-9992. Licensee: Graham Brothers Comm. L.L.C. (acq 1999; $270,000). Population served: 500,000 Format: Rgnl Mexican. Target aud: 25-54; college-educated, upper-income families. ♦Richard Esparza, gen mgr & stn mgr.

Lampasas

KCYL(AM)— 1948: 1450 khz; 1 kw-U. TL: N31 04 31 W98 11 02. Hrs open: 5 AM-11 PM 505 N. Key Ave., 76550. Phone: (512) 556-6193. Phone: (512) 556-3671. Fax: (512) 556-2197.E-mail: info@lampasasraio.com Licensee: Ronald K. Witcher. (acq 2-12-85). Population served: 12,000 Rgnl. Network: Texas State Net. Texas State Networks Format: C&W. News staff: 3; News: 15 hrs wkly. Target aud: 30 plus; agriculture, farm & ranch. Spec prog: Farm 5 hrs, loc news & community service 14 hrs, sports 8 hrs, relg 10 hrs wkly. ♦Joe Lombardi, prom mgr, progmg dir, disc jockey; Ronnie Witcher, pres, gen mgr, opns mgr, gen sls mgr & chief of engrg; Lela Cooper, traf mgr.

Langtry

KHTW(AM)—Not on air, target date: unknown: 1400 khz; 1 kw-U. TL: N29 47 30 W101 30 30. Hrs open: 8320 W. 66th Ave., Arvada, CO, 80004. Phone: (303) 431-0103. Licensee: Better Life Ministries. ♦Claud Pettit, pres.

Laredo

***KBNL(FM)**— July 27, 1985: 89.9 mhz; 100 kw. Ant 604 ft TL: N27 39 27 W99 35 10. Stereo. Hrs open: 24 Box 440029, 78044. Secondary address: 1620 E. Plum St. 78043. Phone: (956) 724-9090/724-9211. Fax: (956) 724-9919.E-mail: kbnl@lwrn.org Web Site:www.kbnl.org Licensee: World Radio Network Inc. (group owner; (acq 10-24-85). Population served: 250,000 Format: Religous, Spanish. News: 2 hrs wkly. Target aud: Male-Females 18-54. ♦Arturo Lozano, gen mgr.

***KHOY(FM)**— November 1985: 88.1 mhz; 1.8 kw. 348 ft TL: N27 31 14 W99 31 19. Hrs open: 1901 Corpus Christi, 78043. Phone: (956) 722-4167. Fax: (956) 722-4464.E-mail: info@khoyfm.com Web Site:www.khoy.org Licensee: Laredo Catholic Communications Inc. Format: Adult contemp, Sp. Target aud: General. ♦Bennett McBride, gen mgr, news dir; Jose Angel Jimenez, progmg dir.

KJBZ(FM)— Dec 29, 1982: 92.7 mhz; 3 kw. 289 ft TL: N27 31 04 W99 31 20. Stereo. Hrs open: 24 6402 N. Bartlett Ste. 1, 78041. Phone: (956) 726-9393. Fax: (956) 724-9915. Licensee: Encarnacion A. Guerra. (acq 12-14-89; $750,000; 1-8-90). Format: Regional Mexican. Target aud: General; all ages. ♦Belinda Guerra, CEO, VP, mus dir; Jorge A. Arredondo, gen mgr, mktg dir; Laura Lafaire, gen sls mgr; Luis "Bird" Rodriguez, progmg dir; Arturo Trevino, chief of engrg.

KLAR(AM)— 1956: 1300 khz; 1 kw-D, 80 w-N. TL: N27 31 45 W99 31 15. Stereo. Hrs open: 24 Box 2517, 78044. Secondary address: 3320 Anna Ave. 78040-1070. Phone: (956) 723-1300. Fax: (956) 723-9539.E-mail: info@klaramfeytoder.com Licensee: Faith and Power Communications Inc. (acq 1996). Population served: 230,000 Format: Sp Christian. News staff: 2; News: 18 hrs wkly. Target aud: 18-54; Hispanic & Anglo middle to upper-middle class. ♦Hector Patino, pres, gen mgr & gen sls mgr.

KLNT(AM)— Apr 20, 1990: 1490 khz; 1 kw-U. TL: N27 29 41 W99 28 16. Hrs open: 24 107 Calle Del Norte, Suite 212, 78041. Phone: (956) 725-1000. Fax: (956) 794-9155.E-mail: info@klntam.com Licensee: BMP 100.5 FM L.P. Group owner: Amigo Broadcasting L.P. (acq 11-9-2004; grpsl). Fisher, Wayland, Cooper, Leader & Zaragoza L.L.P. Format: Rgnl Mexican. ♦Thomas H. Castro, pres; Raul Rodriguez, gen mgr; Ruben Villareal, opns dir; Joe Flores, sls.

KNEX(FM)— 1992: 106.1 mhz; 3 kw. 213 ft TL: N27 33 12 W99 24 17. Hrs open: 107 Calle Del Norte, Suite 212, 78041. Phone: (956) 725-1000. Fax: (956) 794-9155. Web Site:www.hot1061.net Licensee: BMP 100.5 FM L.P. Group owner: Amigo Broadcasting L.P. (acq 11-9-2004; grpsl). Format: CHR, Sp. ♦Miguel Villarreal, gen mgr.

KQUR(FM)— Feb 2, 1972: 94.9 mhz; 100 kw. Ant 1,000 ft TL: N27 31 14 W99 31 19. Stereo. Hrs open: 107 Calle Del Norte, Suite 212, 78041. Phone: (956) 725-1000. Fax: (956) 718-1000. Licensee: Border Broadcasters Inc. Population served: 1000000 Natl. Rep: Roslin,. Fisher, Wayland, Cooper, Leader & Zaragoza. Format: Hot adult contemp. Target aud: 25-54; general. ♦Miguel Villarreal, gen mgr.

KRRG(FM)— October 1982: 98.1 mhz; 100 kw. Ant 737 ft TL: N27 31 14 W99 31 19. Stereo. Hrs open: 6402 N. Bartlett Ste. 1, 78041. Phone: (956) 724-9800. Fax: (956) 724-9915.E-mail: superdave@krrg.com Web Site:www.bigbuck98.com Licensee: Guerra Enterprises (acq 11-20-92; $1.2 million; 12-21-92). Natl. Rep: D & R Radio,. Format: Country. ♦Belinda Guerra, CEO, pres; Jorge A. Arredondo, gen mgr, stn mgr, opns dir & gen sls mgr; David Gonzalez, progmg dir; Arturo Trevino, chief of engrg; Jeannette Alvarado, traf mgr.

Leakey

KBDK(FM)—Not on air, target date: unknown: 93.1 mhz; 50 kw. Ant 397 ft TL: N29 46 41 W99 45 06. Hrs open: 3654 W. Jarvis Ave., Skokie, IL, 60076. Phone: (847) 674-0864. Licensee: KM Communications Inc. ♦Kevin Joel Bae, VP.

KBLT(FM)— June 10, 1997: 104.3 mhz; 1 kw. 594 ft TL: N29 41 34 W99 48 56. Hrs open: Box 56, 78873. Secondary address: 935 East Main, Uvalde 78801. Phone: (830) 278-3693. Fax: (830) 278-2329.E-mail: kbradioranch@hotmail.com Licensee: Radio Cactus Ltd. (acq 10-23-00; $60,916 for 51% of stock with KBNU(FM) Uvalde). Population served:

10,000 Format: Contemp Christian. Target aud: General. ♦John Furr, pres, chief of engrg; Regenia Tumbarello, gen mgr.

KRKP(FM)—Not on air, target date: unknown: 107.7 mhz; 1 kw. Ant 269 ft TL: N29 47 24 W99 42 51. Hrs open: 194 McGee Rd., Versailles, KY, 40383. Phone: (859) 879-0818. Licensee: JER Licenses LLC. ♦Jon E. Robinson, gen mgr.

Leander

KHHL(FM)— May 16, 1976: 98.9 mhz; 29 kw. Ant 515 ft TL: N30 23 26 W97 50 13. Stereo. Hrs open: 24 912 Capital of Texas Hwy, Suite 400, Austin, 78746. Phone: (512) 416-1100. Fax: (512) 416-8205. Licensee: BMP Austin License Company L.P. Group owner: Amigo Broadcasting L.P. (acq 11-9-2004; grpsl). Population served: 926,300 Natl. Network: ABC, Westwood One, . Natl. Rep: D & R Radio,. Wilkinson Barker Knauer. Format: Rgnl Mexican. Target aud: 25-54; adults. ♦Paul Danitz, gen mgr; Ian Hernandez, opns mgr; Daniel Martinez, progmg dir.

Levelland

KJDL-FM— Nov 8, 1983: 105.3 mhz; 23.5 kw. Ant 712 ft TL: N33 25 24 W102 07 41. Stereo. Hrs open: 1603 13th St., Suite 210, Lubbock, 79401. Phone: (806) 744-6864. Fax: (806) 744-8018.E-mail: info@kjdlfm.com Web Site:1053jack.com Licensee: Walker FM Holdings LLC (acq 10-12-2007; $900,000). Format: Country. ♦Dave Walker, gen mgr.

KLVT(AM)— August 1949: 1230 khz; 1 kw-U. TL: N33 35 49 W102 23 09. Hrs open: Box 967, 79336. Secondary address: 611 N. West Ave. 79336. Phone: (806) 894-3134. Fax: (806) 894-3135.E-mail: office@hprnetwork.com Licensee: Profit Programming of Northern Texas (acq 1-7-2007; $200,000). Rgnl. Network: Texas State Net. Texas State Networks Format: Classic country. ♦Jody Rose, gen mgr, opns mgr & progmg dir; Anthony Garza, chief of engrg.

Lewisville

KESS-FM— Apr 10, 1999: 107.9 mhz; 100 kw. Ant 981 ft TL: N33 19 42 W97 03 56. Hrs open: 24 7700 John Carpenter Fwy., Dallas, 75247. Phone: (214) 525-0400. Fax: (214) 631-1154.E-mail: info@kessfm.com Web Site:www.univisionradio.com Licensee: KECS-FM License Corp. Group owner: Univision Radio (acq 9-22-2003; grpsl). Format: Mexican rgnl. ♦Frank Carter, gen mgr; Andy Lockridge, opns dir; Cipriano Robles, sls dir; Karen Hocking, natl sls mgr; Oscar Espinosa, prom dir; Herminio (Chayan) Ortuno, progmg dir.

Liberty

KSHN-FM— November 1977: 99.9 mhz; 26 kw. 679 ft TL: N30 03 05 W94 31 37. Stereo. Hrs open: 24 2099 Sam Houston St., 77575-4817. Phone: (936) 336-5793. Fax: (936) 336-5250.E-mail: info@kshn.com Web Site:www.kshn.com Licensee: Trinity River Valley Broadcasting Co. (acq 11-77). Population served: 700,000 Rgnl. Network: Texas State Net. Texas State Networks Format: Adult contemp, oldies, country. News staff: one; News: 36 hrs wkly. Target aud: 34 plus; Adults. Spec prog: Black 3 hrs, bluegrass 2 hrs, relg 5 hrs wkly. ♦Bill Buchanan, CEO, pres, gen mgr, gen sls mgr, adv mgr, sports cmtr; Eric Latz, progmg dir, news rptr, disc jockey; Tiffany York, dev dir & news dir; Barbara Moss, pub affrs dir, traf mgr; James Stephenson, chief of engrg; Kevin Ladd, reporter; Bill Buchannan, edit dir; Larry Wilburn, outdoor ed; Larry Wazeck, sports cmtr; Allen Wayne, disc jockey.

Littlefield

KZZN(AM)— 1947: 1490 khz; 1 kw-U. TL: N33 56 17 W102 20 38. Hrs open: Box 967, Levelland, 79336. Phone: (806) 385-4474. Phone: (806) 385-1490. Fax: (806) 894-3135.E-mail: hprn@gmail.com Web Site:www.hprnetwork.com Licensee: Juan Alejandro Ibarra (acq 2-1-2009; $250,000). Population served: 20,000 Natl. Network: USA, . Rgnl. Network: Texas State Net., Texas Agribus. Texas State Networks Format: Country, gospel. Target aud: General; try to reach all ages. Spec prog: Farm 7 hrs, relg 5 hrs wkly. ♦Paul Beane, gen mgr; Mike Rader, opns mgr, progmg dir; Emil Macha, sls dir; Anthony Garza, chief of engrg.

Livingston

KETX(AM)— June 28, 1957: 1440 khz; 5 kw-D. TL: N30 44 23 W94 55 30. Hrs open: 6 AM-midnight 701 W. Church St., 77351. Phone: (936) 327-8916. Fax: (936) 327-8477. Licensee: Peggy Sue Marsh, administrator Population served: 32,000 Rgnl. Network: Texas State Net. Format: Country. ♦Curtis G. Walzel, pres.

KETX-FM— Sept 1, 1970: 92.3 mhz; 32 kw. Ant 607 ft TL: N30 44 18 W94 55 26. Stereo. Hrs open: 701 W. Church St., 77351. Secondary address: 115 Radio Road 77351. Phone: (936) 327-8916. Fax: (936) 327-8477.E-mail: classichits@livingston.net Web Site:www.923theeagle.com Licensee: Peggy Sue Marsh, administrator (acq 2-27-2007; with co-located AM). Population served: 7,000 Eugene T. Smith. Format: Classic Hits. Target aud: General. ♦Curtis G. Walzel, gen mgr; Ken Luck, gen sls mgr.

Llano

KAJZ(FM)— 2000: Stn currently dark. 96.3 mhz; 2.9 kw. Ant 459 ft TL: N30 41 12 W98 34 16. Hrs open: 1777 N.E. Loop 410, Suite 400, San Antonio, 78217. Phone: (210) 821-6548. Fax: (210) 804-7825. Licensee: Rawhide Radio LLC. Group owner: Univision Radio (acq 9-22-2003; grpsl). Format: Adult standards. ♦Dan Wilson, gen mgr.

KITY(FM)— 2004: 102.9 mhz; 2 kw. Ant 495 ft TL: N30 40 37 W98 33 59. Hrs open: 1809 Lightsey Rd., Austin, 78704. Phone: (512) 444-9268.E-mail: kity@tstar.net Licensee: Bryan A. King (acq 3-9-2004; grpsl). Natl. Network: CNN Radio, Westwood One, . Format: Oldies. ♦Bryan King, gen mgr.

Lockhart

KFIT(AM)—Licensed to Lockhart. See Austin

Lometa

KACQ(FM)— 1996: 101.9 mhz; 6 kw. 328 ft TL: N31 14 33 W98 19 19. Hrs open: 505 N. Key Ave., Lampasas, 76550. Phone: (512) 556-6193. Fax: (512) 556-2197. Web Site:lampasasradio.com Licensee: Debra L. Witcher. Format: Country. ♦Norma Spinner, sls dir; Joe Lombardi, progmg dir; Lela Cooper, news dir, traf mgr; Ronnie Witcher, gen mgr & chief of engrg.

Longview

KFRO(AM)— Feb 6, 1935: 1370 khz; 1 kw-U, DA-N. TL: N32 30 07 W94 42 12. Stereo. Hrs open: 24 4408 N US Highway 259, 75605-7703. Phone: (903) 663-9800. Fax: (903) 663-9458.E-mail: gnimmons@etradiogroup.com Web Site:www.kykx.com Licensee: Access.1 Texas License Company LLC. Group owner: Waller Broadcasting (acq 1-7-2005; grpsl). Population served: 150,000 Natl. Network: ABC, Westwood One, . Rgnl. Network: Texas State Net. Kaye, Scholer, Fierman, Hays & Handler L.L.P. Format: News/talk, sports. News staff: one; News: 30 hrs wkly. Target aud: 25-54; general. Spec prog: Black 3 hrs wkly. ♦Sydney L. Small, CEO; Chesley Maddox-Dorsey, pres; Debbie Tilley, CFO; Richard Guest, gen mgr; Robert Taylor, sls dir; Dru Laborde, progmg dir; Sans Hawkins, engrg dir; Shelley Miller, traf mgr.

KYKX(FM)— July 1, 1974: 105.7 mhz; 100 kw. 1,156 ft TL: N32 36 04 W94 52 15. Stereo. Hrs open: 24 Box 5818, 481 E. Loop 281, 75608-5818. Phone: (903) 663-9800. Phone: (903) 663-3700. Fax: (903) 663-9458.E-mail: gnimmons@etradiogroup.com Web Site:www.kykx.com Licensee: Access.1 Texas License Company LLC. Group owner: Waller Broadcasting (acq 1-7-2005; grpsl). Population served: 250,000 Natl. Rep: McGavren Guild,. Format: Modern country. News staff: one; News: 6 hrs wkly. Target aud: General. ♦Richard Guest, gen mgr; Ginger Nimmons, gen sls mgr; Dru LaBorde, progmg dir; Tom Metzger, gen mgr & news dir; Sans Hawkins, chief of engrg; Shirley Bread, traf mgr.

Lorenzo

KKCL(FM)— 1989: 98.1 mhz; 50 kw. 431 ft TL: N33 36 32 W101 43 45. Stereo. Hrs open: 24 4413 82nd St., Suite 300, Lubbock, 79424. Phone: (806) 798-7078.E-mail: INFO@KKCLF.COM Web Site:98kool.com Licensee: GAP Broadcasting Lubbock License LLC. Group owner: Clear Channel Communications Inc. (acq 8-3-2007; grpsl). Population served: 350,000 Natl. Network: ABC, . Format: Oldies. News staff: 8; News: 14 hrs wkly. Target aud: 25-54; upscale 55% male, 45% female. Spec prog: Talk 17 hrs wkly. ♦Scott Parsons, gen mgr.

Los Ybanez

KBXJ(FM)— December 1990: 98.5 mhz; 50 kw. Ant 459 ft TL: N32 43 22 W102 01 50. Stereo. Hrs open: 24 10133 McRee, Dallas, 75238. Phone: (214) 341-3887. Licensee: KYMI License Sub LLC (acq 11-21-2007). Population served: 20,000 ♦David Stewart, gen mgr.

Lovelady

KHMR(FM)— 2009: 104.3 mhz; 10.6 kw. Ant 500 ft TL: N31 11 30 W95 29 32. Hrs open: Rt. 2 Box 187, 75851. Phone: (936) 636-2859. Web Site:www.kmcommunications.com Licensee: KM Communications Inc. ♦Kevin Joel Bae, VP & gen mgr.

Lubbock

***KAMY(FM)**— Oct 1, 1990: 90.1 mhz; 200 w. 492 ft TL: N33 30 08 W101 52 20. Stereo. Hrs open: 24 5124-C 69th St., 79424. Phone: (806) 794-1766. Fax: (806) 798-3251.E-mail: kamy@flc.org Web Site:kamyfm.org Licensee: Family Life Broadcasting Inc. Group owner: Family Life Broadcasting System (acq 6-24-98; grpsl). Population served: 207,000 Format: Christian. Target aud: 28 plus; 35-54 female; Christian community of Lubbock. ♦Dave Borowsky, prom dir; Don Webster, gen mgr, gen sls mgr & prom mgr.

KBZO(AM)— April 1953: 1460 khz; 1 kw-D, 250 w-N. TL: N33 32 53 W101 49 24. Hrs open: 24 1220 Broadway, Ste. 600, 79401. Phone: (806) 763-6051. Fax: (806) 744-8363.E-mail: jsauceda@cntravision.com Web Site:www.kbzo-am.entravision.com Licensee: Entravision Holdings LLC. Group owner: Entravision Communications Corp. (acq 10-7-99). Population served: 250,000 Natl. Rep: Lotus Entravision Reps LLC,. Format: Mexican rgnl. Target aud: Hispanic. ♦Jose Sauceda, gen mgr.

KDAV(AM)— May 14, 1947: 1590 khz; 1 kw-U, DA-2. TL: N33 31 16 W101 46 28. Hrs open: 1714 Buddy Holly Ave., 79401. Phone: (806) 744-5859. Phone: (806) 770-5328.E-mail: radio@door.net Web Site:www.kdav.com Licensee: Renaissance Broadcasting Inc. (acq 7-29-98; $150,000). Population served: 250,000 Wire Svc: ESSA Weather Service Format: Oldies, rock and roll. News staff: one; News: 5 hrs. wkly. Target aud: 50 plus. ♦Bill Clement, pres; Bob Holtan, gen mgr.

KEJS(FM)— 1993: 106.5 mhz; 34 kw. 587 ft TL: N33 30 08 W101 52 20. Hrs open: 1607 13th St., 79401. Phone: (806) 747-5951. Fax: (806) 747-3524.E-mail: ebarton@kejsfm.com Web Site:www.jalapenomix.com Licensee: Barton Broadcasting Co. Format: Tejano. ♦Ernest Barton, gen mgr; Debra Alcorte, mktg dir, traf mgr; Gilbert Esparza, progmg dir.

KFMX-FM— Aug 1, 1966: 94.5 mhz; 100 kw. 817 ft TL: N33 31 05 W101 51 25. Stereo. Hrs open: 4413 82nd St. Suite 300, 79424-3366. Phone: (806) 798-7078. Fax: (806) 798-7052. Licensee: Gap Broadcasting Lubbock License LLC. Population served: 376,900 Format: AOR. ♦Wes Nessman, progmg dir.

KFYO(AM)— Sept 6, 1927: 790 khz; 5 kw-D, 1 kw-N, DA-3. TL: N33 27 50 W101 55 30. Stereo. Hrs open: 24 4413 82nd St., Suite 300, 79424. Phone: (806) 798-7078. Fax: (806) 798-7052. Licensee: GAP Broadcasting Lubbock License LLC. Group owner: Clear Channel Communications Inc. (acq 8-3-2007; grpsl). Population served: 186,000 Natl. Network: CBS, . Rgnl. Network: Texas State Net. Texas State Networks Format: News/talk. News staff: 2; News: 12 hrs wkly. Target aud: General. ♦Scott Parsons, gen mgr; Robert Snyder, progmg dir, traf mgr; Roger Taylor, chief of engrg.

KJAK(FM)—(Slaton, Feb 12, 1978: 92.7 mhz; 100 kw. 584 ft TL: N33 32 32 W101 50 14. Stereo. Hrs open: 24 Box 6490, 79493. Phone: (806) 745-6677. Fax: (806) 745-8140.E-mail: kjak@kjak.com Web Site:www.kjak.com Licensee: G.O. Williams Oil Co. Inc. dba Williams Broadcasting Group (acq 6-19-81; 7-13-81). Population served: 750,000 Format: Christian. Target aud: General; Christians & those looking for answers to everyday problems. Spec prog: Sports 5 hrs wkly. ♦Woody Van Dyke, gen mgr, gen sls mgr, prom mgr & mus dir; Bob Howell, news dir; Roger Taylor, chief of engrg.

KJDL(AM)— Nov 15, 1966: 1420 khz; 500 w-U, DA-N. TL: N33 36 49 W101 52 30. Hrs open: 18 1603 13th St., Suite 210, 79401. Phone: (806) 741-1420. Phone: (806) 744-6864. Fax: (806) 744-8018.E-mail: dwalker@newsradio1420.com Web Site:www.newsradio1420.com Licensee: Walker Broadcasting & Communications Ltd. (acq 9-14-2005; $350,000). Population served: 179,000 Rgnl. Network: Texas State Net. Texas State Networks Format: News/talk. ♦David Walker, pres, gen mgr; Bill Enloe, chief of engrg; Helen Castro, prom mgr, progmg dir & traf mgr.

KJTV(AM)— Nov 1, 1946: 950 khz; 5 kw-D, 500 w-N, DA-2. TL: N33 34 53 W101 49 38. Hrs open: 24 Box 3757, 79452. Secondary address: 9800 University Ave. 79423. Phone: (806) 745-3434. Fax: (806) 748-2470. Licensee: Ramar Communications II Ltd. Texas State

Networks Format: News/talk info. News staff: one; News: 147 hrs wkly. Target aud: 25-54. ♦Brad Moran, gen mgr.

KKAM(AM)— Jan 1, 1955: 1340 khz; 1 kw-U. TL: N33 33 24 W101 51 46. Hrs open: 4413 82nd St., Suite 300, 79424-3366. Phone: (806) 798-7078. Fax: (806) 798-7052.E-mail: info@kfmx.com Web Site:www.kfmx.com Licensee: GAP Broadcasting Lubbock License LLC. Group owner: Clear Channel Communications Inc. (acq 8-3-2007; grpsl). Natl. Network: ABC, CBS, . Format: Sports. ♦Scott Parsons, gen mgr; Wes Nessman, opns dir; Matt Martin, sls dir; Mark Finkner, progmg dir.

***KKLU(FM)**— Oct 24, 1993: 90.9 mhz; 13.5 kw. Ant 236 ft TL: N33 32 30 W101 49 16. Stereo. Hrs open: 24 5700 W. Oaks Blvd., Rocklin, 95765. Phone: (916) 251-1600. Fax: (916) 251-1650. Web Site:www.klove.com Licensee: Educational Media Foundation. Group owner: EMF Broadcasting (acq 5-1-2000; $750,000 with KXRI(FM) Amarillo). Natl. Network: K-Love, . Format: Contemp Christian mus. Target aud: All ages. ♦Richard Jenkins, pres & gen mgr; Mike Novak, progmg VP.

KLLL-FM— Mar 1, 1958: 96.3 mhz; 100 kw. 817 ft TL: N33 31 05 W101 51 25. Stereo. Hrs open: 24 33 Briercroft Office Park., 79412. Phone: (806) 762-3000. Fax: (806) 770-5363. Web Site:www.klll.com Licensee: Wilks License Co. -Lubbock LLC. Group owner: NextMedia Group L.L.C. (acq 8-19-2005; grpsl). Population served: 400,000 Natl. Network: ABC, . Format: Country. Target aud: 25-54. ♦Jay Richardson, gen mgr, gen sls mgr; Jeff Scott, opns mgr, progmg dir; Randy Smith, prom dir & prom mgr; Neely Yates, mus dir; Kelli D'Angelo, news dir; Randy Hayes, chief of engrg; Celeste Collins, traf mgr, women's int ed.

***KOHM(FM)**— January 1973: 89.1 mhz; 70 kw. Ant 567 ft TL: N33 34 55 W101 53 25. Stereo. Hrs open: 24 1901 University Ave., Suite 603-B, Texas Tech Univ., 79410. Secondary address: Box 45891 79409. Phone: (806) 742-3100. Fax: (806) 742-3716.E-mail: kohm@ttu.edu Web Site:www.kohm.org Licensee: Texas Tech University. (acq 11-87). Population served: 250,000 Natl. Network: NPR, PRI, . Format: Classical. ♦Derrick Ginter, gen mgr; Sherril Skibell, dev dir; Clinton Barrick, progmg dir. Co-owned TV: *KTXT-TV affil.

KONE(FM)— 1975: 101.1 mhz; 100 kw. 882 ft TL: N33 30 08 W101 52 20. Stereo. Hrs open: 24 33 Briercroft Office Park, 79412. Phone: (806) 762-3000. Fax: (806) 762-8419. Web Site:www.cr101.com Licensee: Wilks License Co.-Lubbock LLC. Group owner: NextMedia Group L.L.C. (acq 8-19-2005; grpsl). Population served: 400,000 Natl. Network: ABC, . Format: Soft adult contemp, classic rock. Target aud: 25-54. ♦Scott Harris, gen mgr; Jeff Scott, opns mgr, progmg VP, progmg dir; Jay Richards, gen sls mgr; Rick Gilbert, prom dir; Kelly Greene, mus dir; Stacey James, news dir; Randy Hayes, chief of engrg; Julia Aguilar, traf mgr.

KQBR(FM)— July 15, 1964: 99.5 mhz; 100 kw. 817 ft TL: N33 31 05 W101 51 25. Stereo. Hrs open: Box 53120, 4413 82nd St., Suite 300, 79424. Phone: (806) 798-7078. Fax: (806) 798-7052.E-mail: info@kqbr.com Web Site:www.kqbr.com Licensee: GAP Broadcasting Lubbock License LLC. Group owner: Clear Channel Communications Inc. (acq 8-3-2007; grpsl). Population served: 125000 Format: Country. ♦Scott Parsons, gen mgr; Wes Nessmann, opns dir; Leslie Tucker, gen sls mgr; Jackie Neal, progmg dir; Landon King, news dir; Roger Taylor, chief of engrg; Kris Torres, traf mgr.

KRFE(AM)— Sept 19, 1953: 580 khz; 500 w-D, 290 w-N, DA-2. TL: N33 32 00 W101 49 14. Hrs open: 24 6602 Martin Luther King Blvd., 79404. Phone: (806) 745-1197. Fax: (806) 745-1088. Web Site:www.krfeam580.com Licensee: KRFE Radio Inc. (acq 2-94). Population served: 300,000 Natl. Network: ABC, . Format: Easy lstng, news/talk. News staff: one; News: 5 hrs wkly. Target aud: 40 plus. Spec prog: News/talk 15 hrs wkly. ♦Wade Wilkes, gen mgr & prom VP.

***KTXT-FM**— Apr 1, 1961: 88.1 mhz; 35 kw. Ant 423 ft TL: N33 34 55 W101 53 25. Stereo. Hrs open: 24 Box 45891, 79409. Phone: (806) 742-3100. Fax: (806) 742-3716.E-mail: kohm@ttu.edu Web Site:www.kohm.org Licensee: Texas Tech University. Population served: 250,000 Format: Jazz. ♦Derrick Ginter, gen mgr.

KXTQ-FM— November 1963: 93.7 mhz; 100 kw. 740 ft TL: N33 30 57 W101 50 54. Stereo. Hrs open: 24 Box 3757, 79452. Secondary address: 9800 University Ave. 79423. Phone: (806) 745-3434. Fax: (806) 748-2470.E-mail: cheinz@ramarcom.com Web Site:www.magic937fm.com Licensee: Ramar Communications II Ltd. (group owner; (acq 9-93; $362,500). Population served: 375,000 Natl. Rep: Univision Radio National Sales,. Leventhal, Senter & Lerman. Format: Tejano, Sp. Target aud: 18-49. ♦Brad Moran, pres; Chuck Heinz, gen mgr; Connie Hayes, sls dir, gen sls mgr; Eddie Moreno, progmg dir, progmg mgr; Susie Gonzales, traf mgr.

KZII-FM— Mar 10, 1982: 102.5 mhz; 100 kw. Ant 850 ft TL: N33 31 05 W101 51 25. Stereo. Hrs open: 24 4413 82nd St., Suite 300, 79424. Phone: (806) 798-7078. Web Site:www.z102.com Licensee: GAP Broadcasting Lubbock License LLC. Format: CHR. Target aud: 18-49. ♦George Parsons, gen mgr & progmg dir.

Lufkin

KAFX-FM—(Diboll, June 29, 1960: 95.5 mhz; 100 kw. Ant 567 ft TL: N31 24 28 W94 45 53. Stereo. Hrs open: 24 Box 2209, 75902-2209. Secondary address: 1216 S. 1st St. 75901-4716. Phone: (936) 639-4455. Fax: (936) 639-5540.E-mail: johnnylathrop@gapbroadcasting.com Web Site:kfox95.com Licensee: GAP Broadcasting Lufkin License LLC. Group owner: Clear Channel Communications Inc. (acq 10-1-2007; grpsl). Population served: 250,000 Format: Hot adult contemp. News staff: one; News: 2 hrs wkly. Target aud: 25-44; female. ♦Johnny Lathrop, gen mgr; Tami Koonce, sls dir & natl sls mgr.

KAGZ(FM)— 2008: 93.9 mhz; 1.7 kw. Ant 610 ft TL: N31 21 55 W94 45 59. Hrs open: 24018 Middle Fork, San Antonio, 78258. Phone: (830) 980-7111. Licensee: E-String Wireless Ltd. ♦Bret D. Huggins, gen mgr.

***KAVX(FM)**— Dec 25, 1998: 91.9 mhz; 20 kw. 787 ft TL: N31 22 08 W94 38 43. Stereo. Hrs open: 24 Box 151340, 75915-1340. Phone: (936) 639-5673. Fax: (936) 639-5677.E-mail: alross@kavx.org Web Site:www.kavx.org Licensee: Lufkin Educational Broadcasting Foundation. Population served: 146,000 Natl. Network: USA, . Gammon & Grange. Format: Teaching & talk. Target aud: Persons 30 plus. Spec prog: Praise and Worship - Weekends. ♦Dwyan Calvert, gen mgr; Drew Wilson, prom dir; Al Ross, prom mgr; Michelle Ross, opns mgr, progmg dir & mus dir.

***KLDN(FM)**— May 2, 1991: 88.9 mhz; 50 kw. Ant 649 ft TL: N31 24 28 W94 45 53. Stereo. Hrs open: 24
Rebroadcasts KDAQ(FM) Shreveport, LA 100%.
Box 5250, Shreveport, LA, 71135. Phone: (318) 797-5150. Phone: (800) 552-8502. Fax: (318) 797-5265.E-mail: listenermail@redriverradio.org Web Site:www.redriverradio.org Licensee: Board of Supervisors of Louisiana State University. Natl. Network: NPR, PRI, . Format: Classical, news, jazz. Target aud: 25+. ♦Kermit Poling, gen mgr; Rick Shelton, opns mgr.

KRBA(AM)— May 3, 1938: 1340 khz; 1 kw-U. TL: N31 21 51 W94 43 09. Hrs open: 24 Box 1345, 75901. Secondary address: 121 Cotton Sq. 75901. Phone: (936) 634-6661. Fax: (936) 632-5722.E-mail: kybi@lcc.net Web Site:www.krba.net Licensee: Stephen W. Yates. Population served: 30,000 Format: Var/div. News staff: one; News: 7 hrs wkly. Target aud: General. ♦Stephen Yates, gen mgr; Kevin Sims, progmg dir, disc jockey; Jeremy Chance, traf mgr, disc jockey.

KSML(AM)—(Diboll, June 2, 1957: 1260 khz; 4.5 kw-D, 72 w-N. TL: N31 21 53 W94 43 08. Hrs open: 24 121 Cotton Sq., 75901. Phone: (936) 632-8444. Fax: (936) 632-8451.E-mail: info@ksml.com Licensee: Stephen W. & Karla Yates. (acq 5-95; 5-22-95). Format: Sp. News staff: one; News: 14 hrs wkly. ♦Stephen W. Yates, pres, gen mgr; Oscar Chavez, progmg dir; Steve Comer, chief of engrg.

***KSWP(FM)**— Aug 31, 1985: 90.9 mhz; 380 w. 174 ft TL: N31 23 17 W94 46 43. (CP: 90.9 mhz, 30 kw, ant 787 ft.). Stereo. Hrs open: 24 151 Holmes Rd., 75904. Phone: (936) 639-5673. Fax: (936) 639-5677.E-mail: alross@kavx.org Web Site:www.kswp.org Licensee: Lufkin Educational Broadcasting Foundation. Natl. Network: USA, . Format: Contemporary Christian music. Target aud: Woman 25-54, Persons 25-54. Spec prog: Pub affrs talk show 2 hrs wkly. ♦Dwyan Calvert, pres, gen mgr; Drew Wilson, prom dir; Michelle Ross, progmg dir & mus dir.

KYBI(FM)— May 1, 1978: 100.1 mhz; 25 kw. Ant 699 ft TL: N31 24 28 W94 45 53. Stereo. Hrs open: 24 Box 1345, 75901. Secondary address: 121 Cotton Sq. 75902. Phone: (936) 634-4584. Fax: (936) 632-5722.E-mail: info@kybi.com Web Site:www.kybi.com Population served: 150,000 Format: Adult contemp. Target aud: 25-54. ♦Stephen Yates, gen mgr.

KYKS(FM)— July 9, 1976: 105.1 mhz; 100 kw. 1,066 ft TL: N31 22 08 W94 38 45. Stereo. Hrs open: 24 Box 2209, 75901. Secondary address: 1216 S. First St. 75901. Phone: (936) 639-4455. Fax: (936) 632-5957. Fax: (936) 639-5540.E-mail: info@kyks.com Web Site:www.kicks105.com Licensee: GAP Broadcasting Lufkin License LLC. Group owner: Clear Channel Communications Inc. (acq 10-1-2007; grpsl). Population served: 250,000 Fletcher, Heald & Hildreth. Format: Country. News staff: one. Target aud: 25-54. ♦Larry Gunter, gen mgr; Johnny Lathrop, sls dir; Danny Merrell, prom dir, progmg dir, pub affrs dir; Sean Ericson, mus dir; Brandy Abney, traf mgr.

Luling

KAMX(FM)— Mar 22, 1987: 94.7 mhz; 99 kw. 1,305 ft TL: N30 19 23 W97 47 58. Stereo. Hrs open: 24 4301 Westbank Dr., Escalade B—3rd Fl., Bldg. B. Suite 350, Austin, 78746. Phone: (512) 327-9595. Fax: (512) 329-6255.E-mail: jdhiatt@cbs.com Web Site:mix947.com Licensee: Entercom Austin License LLC. Group owner: Infinity Broadcasting Corp. (acq 11-30-2007; grpsl). Population served: 700,000 Natl. Rep: Katz Radio,. Levanthal, Senter & Lerman. Format: Modern adult contemp. Target aud: 18-49; upscale adults. Spec prog: Pub affrs 2 hrs wkly. ♦Clint Culp, sr VP, sls dir; John Hiatt, sr VP, mktg dir & mktg mgr.

Lytle

***KZLV(FM)**— Jan 20, 1990: 91.3 mhz; 2.95 kw. 302 ft TL: N29 14 39 W98 44 27. Stereo. Hrs open: 24 1566 N.E. Loop 410, San Antonio, 78209. Phone: (210) 824-9100. Fax: (210) 824-8870.E-mail: info@kzlv.com Web Site:www.klove.com Licensee: Educational Media Foundation. Group owner: EMF Broadcasting (acq 4-28-99). Natl. Network: K-Love, . Format: Adult contemp, Christian. Target aud: 25-49; professional adult & parents. ♦Dick Jenkins, pres; Lloyd Parker, gen mgr; Ed Lenane, opns dir.

Mabank

KTXV(AM)— 2007: 890 khz; 20 kw-D, 250 w-N, DA-2. TL: N32 17 13 W95 58 39. Hrs open: 10613 Bellaire Blvd., Suite 900, Houston, 77072. Phone: (713) 917-0050. Fax: (713) 917-0213. Web Site:www.radiosaigonhouston.com Licensee: Bustos Media Holdings L.L.C. (acq 9-5-2007; $1 million). Format: Ethnic. ♦Thuy Vu, gen mgr.

Madisonville

KAGG(FM)— Dec 5, 1989: 96.1 mhz; 50 kw. 500 ft TL: N30 48 02 W96 07 00. Stereo. Hrs open: 24 1716 Briarcrest Dr., Suite 150, Bryan, 77802. Phone: (979) 268-9696. Fax: (979) 268-9090.E-mail: info@aggie96.com Web Site:www.aggie96.com Licensee: CCB Texas Licenses L.P. Group owner: Clear Channel Communications Inc. (acq 10-10-00; grpsl). Fletcher, Heald & Hildreth. Format: Country.

***KHML(FM)**— 2006: 91.5 mhz; 95 kw. Ant 341 ft TL: N31 06 39.6 W95 57 08.6. Stereo. Hrs open: 24
Rebroadcasts KHCB-FM Houston 95%.
2424 South Blvd., Houston, 77098-5110. Phone: (713) 520-5200.E-mail: email@khcb.org Web Site:www.khcb.org Licensee: Houston Christian Broadcasters Inc. Natl. Network: Moody, . Format: Christian. Spec prog: Sp Christian 6 hrs wkly. ♦Bruce Munsterman, gen mgr.

KKLB(FM)—Not on air, target date: unknown: 101.3 mhz; 3.1 kw. Ant 462 ft TL: N31 00 00 W95 59 58. Hrs open: 3500 Maple Ave., Suite 1320, Dallas, 75219-1622. Phone: (214) 363-6030. Licensee: Katherine Pyeatt. ♦Katherine Pyett, gen mgr.

KMVL(AM)— October 1989: 1220 khz; 500 w-D, 12 w-N. TL: N30 57 56 W95 53 52. Hrs open: 24 102 W. Main, 77864. Phone: (936) 348-9200. Fax: (936) 348-9201.E-mail: kmvl@kmvl.net Web Site:www.kmvl.net Licensee: Hunt Broadcasting. (acq 7-17-91; 8-5-91). Rgnl. Network: Texas State Net. Texas State Networks Format: Adult standards. News staff: one; News: 15 hrs wkly. Target aud: General. ♦Leon Hunt, gen mgr.

KMVL-FM— April 1997: 100.5 mhz; 13 kw. 449 ft TL: N31 00 42 W96 02 27. Hrs open: 24 102 W. Main St., 77864. Phone: (936) 348-9200. Fax: (936) 348-9201. Web Site:www.kmvl.net Natl. Network: ABC, . Format: Country. Target aud: 25-49. ♦Leon Hunt, gen mgr.

Malakoff

KCKL(FM)— Aug 8, 1983: 95.9 mhz; 6 kw. Ant 295 ft TL: N32 08 48 W95 58 25. Stereo. Hrs open: 24 Box 489, Hwy. 31 E., 75148. Phone: (903) 489-1238. Fax: (903) 489-2671.E-mail: kcklklvq@tvec.net Web Site:www.kcklklvq.com Licensee: Lake Country Radio L.P. Group owner: Routt Radio Companies Inc. (acq 11-5-2005; $550,000 with KLVQ(AM) Athens). Population served: 100,000 Natl. Network: ABC, . Format: Real country. News staff: one; News: 10 hrs wkly. Target aud: 25-54; country/city folk, weekenders & visitors to Cedar Creek Lake. Spec prog: Relg 7 hrs wkly. ♦Adabeth Routt, gen mgr; Pat Isaacson, opns mgr, gen sls mgr; Mike Lallande, progmg dir; Rich Flowers, news dir; Wayne Blackwelder, chief of engrg.

Manor

KELG(AM)— Apr 22, 1981: 1440 khz; 800 w-D, 500 w-N, DA-2. TL: N30 19 36 W97 32 35. Hrs open: 24 912 S. Capital of Texas Hwy., Suite 400, White Lake Hills, 78741. Phone: (512) 416-1100. Fax: (512) 314-7742. Licensee: Encino Broadcasting LLC. (acq 2-15-2008; grpsl). Bechtel & Cole. Format: Rgnl Mexican. ◆Jerry Del Core, gen mgr; Chayan Ortuno, progmg dir; Ben Rippy, chief of engrg; Pam Walker, traf mgr.

KTXW(AM)—Not on air, target date: unknown: 1120 khz; 250 w-D, 153 w-N, DA-2. TL: N30 20 51 W97 31 23. Hrs open: Box 60991, Palo Alto, CA, 94306. Phone: (650) 856-6823. Licensee: JNE Investments Inc. ◆Jeffrey N. Eustis, pres.

Marathon

KHRX(AM)—Not on air, target date: unknown: 1470 khz; 10 kw-D, 250 w-N, DA-N. TL: N30 13 09 W103 14 02. Hrs open: 8320 W. 66th Ave., Arvada, CO, 80004. Phone: (303) 431-0103. Licensee: Better Life Ministries. ◆Claud M. Pettit, pres.

Marble Falls

*KBMD(FM)— 2002: 88.5 mhz; 6 kw. Ant 89 ft TL: N30 33 12 W98 15 30. Hrs open: 24
EWTN.
1903 S. Lemesa Rd., Midland, 78701. Phone: (432) 638-1150. Fax: (432) 682-5230.E-mail: robertd@gmonline.com Web Site:www.gmonline.com Licensee: La Promesa Foundation. (acq 2-24-2005; $130,000). Format: Catholic relg. News staff: 2. ◆Leonard Oswald, pres; Dick Bigelow, gen mgr.

Marfa

KRTS(FM)— 2007: 93.5 mhz; 5.32 kw. Ant 1,427 ft TL: N30 33 50.2 W104 09 44.8. Hrs open: Box 238, 79843. Secondary address: 111 S. Highland Ave. 79843. Phone: (432) 729-4578.E-mail: info@marfapublicradio.org Web Site:www.marfapublicradio.org Licensee: Matinee Radio LLC. ◆Tom Michael, gen mgr.

Marion

KBIB(AM)—Licensed to Marion. See San Antonio

Markham

KKHA(FM)— August 2000: 92.5 mhz; 6 kw. Ant 328 ft TL: N28 52 26 W96 08 22. Stereo. Hrs open: 24 1717 7th street, Bay City, 77414. Phone: (979) 323-7771. Fax: (775) 719-2182.E-mail: lee@happyradioonline.com Web Site:www.kkhafm.com Licensee: Edwards Broadcasting Co. (acq 9-28-2007; $400,000). Format: Classic Hits. News staff: 1. Target aud: 25-54; White equally mixed gender. ◆Dick Witkovski, pres; Lee Parkinson, gen mgr; Ernie Cunnar, opns mgr.

Marlin

KBBW(AM)—See Waco

KLRK(FM)— Apr 2, 1977: 92.9 mhz; 3 kw. 500 ft TL: N31 19 31 W96 54 36. (CP: 50 kw, ant 492 ft. TL: 31 24 45 W97 12 40). Stereo. Hrs open: 24 220 S. 2nd St., Apt. 282, Waco, 76701. Phone: (254) 772-0930. Fax: (254) 753-0499.E-mail: info@star929fm.com Web Site:star929fm.com Licensee: Simmons Austin, LS LLC. Group owner: Simmons Media Group (acq 6-4-2004; grpsl). Population served: 109000 Natl. Rep: Roslin,. Leventhal, Senter & Lerman. Format: Bright adult contemp. News staff: one. Target aud: 25-49. ◆Daryl O'Neal, gen mgr; Rob Reed, opns mgr; Bill LeGrande, sls dir; Dustin Drew, progmg dir; Cole McClellan, chief of engrg; Flavia Chen, traf mgr.

Marshall

*KBWC(FM)— March 1977: 91.1 mhz; 100 w. 110 ft TL: N32 32 12 W94 22 29. Stereo. Hrs open: 24 711 Wiley Ave., 75670. Phone: (903) 927-3266. Phone: (903) 927-3307. Fax: (903) 935-0153.E-mail: info@kbwcfm.com Licensee: Wiley College. Population served: 40,000 Natl. Network: American Urban, . Format: Urban/mix. Target aud: 18-34. ◆Shanon Levingston, gen mgr.

KCUL(AM)— Oct 7, 1957: 1410 khz; 500 w-D, 90 w-N, DA-2. TL: N32 29 30 W94 21 52. Hrs open: 5:30 AM-11 PM Box 7820, Tyler, 75711. Secondary address: 621 Chase Dr., Tyler 75701. Phone: (903) 581-9966. Fax: (903) 534-5300. Licensee: Access. 1 Texas License Co. LLC. Group owner: Access.1 Communications Corp. (acq 5-9-2000; grpsl). Population served: 86,000 Natl. Network: Fox News Radio, . Rgnl. Network: Texas State Net. Texas State Networks Format: News, classic country. News staff: one; News: 15 hrs wkly. Target aud: General. Spec prog: Farm 3 hrs wkly. ◆Rick Quest, gen mgr.

KCUL-FM— Jan 1, 1992: 92.3 mhz; 5.8 kw. Ant 328 ft TL: N32 32 26 W94 24 03. Stereo. Hrs open: 24 Box 7820, Tyler, 75711. Secondary address: 621 Chase Dr., Tyler 75701. Phone: (903) 581-9966. Fax: (903) 534-5300. Licensee: Access: 1 Texas License Co. LLC. Population served: 175,000 Rgnl. Network: Texas State Net. Texas State Networks Format: Mexican rgnl. Target aud: 25 plus.

KMHT(AM)— 1947: 1450 khz; 1 kw-U. TL: N32 33 50 W94 21 04. Hrs open: 2323 Jefferson Ave., 75670. Phone: (903) 923-8000. Fax: (903) 935-2481. Licensee: Hanszen Broadcast Group Inc. (acq 9-17-2002; $400,000 with co-located FM). Population served: 27,345 Format: All sports. ◆Chris Paddie, gen mgr.

KMHT-FM— Sept 4, 1977: 103.9 mhz; 3 kw. Ant 300 ft TL: N32 33 50 W94 21 04. Hrs open: 2323 Jefferson Ave., 75670. Phone: (903) 923-8000. Fax: (903) 935-2481. Population served: 50,000 Format: Country. ◆Chris Paddie, gen mgr.

Mart

*KSUR(FM)— 2007: 88.9 mhz; 100 kw vert. Ant 623 ft TL: N31 23 02 W97 16 38. Hrs open:
Rebroadcasts WAFR(FM) Tupelo, MS 100%.
6304 Gardendale Dr., Waco, 76710. Phone: (254) 772-1900. Web Site:www.kbderadio.net Licensee: American Family Association. Format: Christian. ◆Marvin Sanders, gen mgr.

Mason

KHLB(FM)— 2005: 102.5 mhz; 26 kw. Ant 630 ft TL: N30 42 03 W99 13 59. Hrs open: 5526 N. Hwy. 281, Marble Falls, 78654. Phone: (830) 693-5551. Fax: (830) 593-5107. Licensee: Munbilla Broadcasting Properties Ltd. (group owner). Format: Country. ◆Cindi Ashford, gen mgr; Ben Shields, progmg dir; Bill Woleban, chief of engrg.

KOTY(FM)— 2004: 95.7 mhz; 50 kw. Ant 436 ft TL: N30 33 53 W99 27 13. Hrs open: 1809 Lightsey Rd., Austin, 78704. Phone: (512) 444-9268.E-mail: kity@tstar.net Licensee: Bryan A. King (acq 2-13-2004; grpsl). ◆Bryan King, gen mgr.

KYRT(FM)—Not on air, target date: unknown: 99.7 mhz; 6 kw. Ant 279 ft TL: N30 44 48 W99 14 58. Hrs open: 381 Casa Linda Plaza, Suite 347, Dallas, 75218. Phone: (972) 241-2110. Fax: (830) 693-5107. Licensee: Munbilla Broadcasting Properties Ltd. ◆B. Shane Fox, gen mgr.

McAllen

KGBT-FM— 1964: 98.5 mhz; 100 kw. 997 ft TL: N26 07 14 W97 49 18. (CP: Ant 997 ft.). Stereo. Hrs open: 200 S. 10th, Suite 600, 78501. Phone: (956) 631-5499. Fax: (956) 631-0090.E-mail: info@netmio.com Web Site:www.netmio.com/radio/kgbt-fm Licensee: Tichenor License Corp. Group owner: Univision Radio (acq 9-22-2003; grpsl). Population served: 500,000 Format: Mexican rgnl. ◆Mac Tichenor Jr., pres; Joe Morales, gen mgr; Angela Navarrete, gen sls mgr; Hugo de la Cruze, progmg dir; Jorge Garza, chief of engrg; Odie Francisco Chavez, news dir & traf mgr.

*KHID(FM)— July 16, 1992: 88.1 mhz; 2.1 kw. 253 ft TL: N26 21 44 W98 19 26. Stereo. Hrs open: 24
Rebroadcasts KMBH-FM Harlingen.
Box 2147, Harlingen, 78551. Secondary address: 1701 E. Tennessee Ave., Harlingen 78550. Phone: (956) 421-4111. Fax: (956) 421-4150.E-mail: kmbhkhid@aol.com Web Site:www.kmbh.org Licensee: RGV Educational Broadcasting Inc. Population served: 950,000 Format: News, class, jazz. News: 34 hrs wkly. Target aud: General. ◆Pedro Briseno, gen mgr.

KIRT(AM)—See Mission

KJAV(FM)—See Alamo

KRIO(AM)— 1947: 910 khz; 5 kw-U, DA-2. TL: N26 18 02 W98 12 38. Hrs open: 24 4300 S. Business 281, Edinburg, 78539. Phone: (956)

380-3435. Fax: (956) 380-8156.E-mail: correo@radioesperanza.com Web Site:www.radioesperanza.com Licensee: Rio Grande Bible Institute Inc. (acq 5-30-86). Population served: 750,000 Bryan Cave. Wire Svc: UPI Format: Relg, educ, Sp. News: 5 hrs wkly. Target aud: General. ◆Larry Windle, pres; Gerardo Lorenzo, gen mgr, progmg dir; Jerry Joske, chief of engrg.

KVLY(FM)—See Edinburg

KVMV(FM)— March 1972: 96.9 mhz; 100 kw. 1,160 ft TL: N26 04 53 W97 49 44. Stereo. Hrs open: 24 Box 3333, 78502. Secondary address: 715 E. Thomas Dr., Pharr 78502. Phone: (956) 787-9700. Fax: (956) 787-9783.E-mail: info@kvmv.com Web Site:www.kvmv.org Licensee: World Radio Network Inc. (group owner; acq 8-27-84). Population served: 600,000 Natl. Network: Moody, . Format: Contemp Christian. News: 4 hrs wkly. Target aud: 30-65; general. ◆James Gamblin, gen mgr & progmg dir; Bob Malone, mus dir.

McCamey

KPBM(FM)—Not on air, target date: unknown: 95.3 mhz; 3 kw. 758 ft TL: N31 12 42 W102 16 29. Hrs open: Box 252, McAllen, 78502. Licensee: Paulino Bernal. ◆Paulino Bernal, gen mgr.

McCook

*KCAS(FM)— Jan 1, 2001: 91.5 mhz; 2.5 kw. Ant 358 ft TL: N26 28 51 W98 23 45. Stereo. Hrs open: 24 Faith Baptist Church Inc., 4301 N. Shary Rd., Mission, 78574. Secondary address: P. O. Box 8106, Mission 78572. Phone: (956) 424-9098. Fax: (956) 581-7786.E-mail: mail@kcasradio.org Web Site:www.kcasradio.org Licensee: Faith Baptist Church Inc. Population served: 650,000 Natl. Network: USA, . Format: Relg. News: 12 hrs wkly. Target aud: 30-85; male & female. ◆Joel Mangin, gen mgr, opns mgr & progmg dir; Jerry Jeske, chief of engrg.

McKinney

*KNTU(FM)— November 1969: 88.1 mhz; 100 kw. 443 ft TL: N33 17 24 W97 08 10. Stereo. Hrs open: 24 Box 310881, Denton, 76203. Secondary address: 1179 Union Cir., Suite 262, Denton 76201. Phone: (940) 565-3688. Phone: (940) 565-3459. Fax: (940) 565-2518.E-mail: kntu@unt.edu Web Site:www.kntu.com Licensee: University of North Texas. Population served: 5,000,000 Natl. Network: AP Radio, . Rgnl. Network: Texas State Net. Wire Svc: AP Format: Jazz. News: 8 hrs wkly. Target aud: 18 +. Spec prog: Class 6 hrs, Sp 6 hrs, new mus 3 hrs, pub affrs 2 hrs wkly. ◆Russ Campbell, gen mgr; Mark Lambert, progmg mgr, news dir; Larry Gregg, chief of engrg.

McQueeney

KLTO-FM— July 1989: 97.7 mhz; 100 kw. Ant 981 ft TL: N29 20 45 W97 38 44. Stereo. Hrs open: 24 1777 N.E. Loop 410, San Antonio, 78217. Phone: (210) 829-1075. Fax: (210) 824-9971. Licensee: Rawhide Radio LLC. Group owner: Univision Radio (acq 9-22-2003; grpsl). Population served: 1,206,495 Format: Active Rock. Target aud: 12-17, 18-34. ◆Rory Charitan, sls dir; Bret Huggins, progmg dir, chief of engrg.

Memphis

KLSR-FM— 1982: 105.3 mhz; 100 kw. 485 ft TL: N34 41 13 W100 30 23. Stereo. Hrs open: 24 Box 400, 114 N. 7th, 79245. Phone: (806) 259-3511. Fax: (806) 259-2397.E-mail: klsr105fm@arn.net Licensee: Davis Broadcast Company Inc. (acq 7-15-86; $78,348 with co-located AM; 7-28-86). Population served: 50,000 Format: C&W, div, contemp. Spec prog: Sp 6 hrs, good time oldies 60s & 70s 10 hrs, relg 5 hrs wkly. ◆Donna Davis, pres; Brandi Davis-Tatum, VP, gen sls mgr; Joe Davis, gen mgr.

Mercedes

KHKZ(FM)— Sept 10, 1982: 106.3 mhz; 1.65 kw. 649 ft TL: N26 13 50 W98 20 18. Stereo. Hrs open: 24 901 E. Pike Blvd., Weslaco, 78596. Phone: (866) 973-1041. Fax: (956) 544-0311. Licensee: Clear Channel Broadcasting Licenses Inc. Group owner: Clear Channel Communications Inc. (acq 12-9-2003; grpsl). Natl. Network: USA, . Fisher, Wayland, Cooper, Leader & Zaragoza. Format: Hot adult contemp. News staff: 3. Target aud: General. Spec prog: Black 3 hrs, southern gospel 2 hrs, Christian rock 3 hrs wkly. ◆Danny Fletcher, gen mgr; Billy Santiago, opns mgr; Cyndia Torres, gen sls mgr; J. Contu, progmg dir; Ken Meek, chief of engrg; Gloria Garcia, traf mgr.

KTEX(FM)— January 1975: 100.3 mhz; 100 kw. Ant 1,223 ft TL: N26 06 01 W97 50 21. Stereo. Hrs open: 24 901 E. Pike Blvd., Weslaco, 78596. Phone: (956) 973-9202. Fax: (956) 973-9335.E-mail: ktexx@aol.com Web Site:www.ktex.net Licensee: Capstar TX L.P. Group owner: Clear Channel Communications Inc. (acq 8-15-2000; grpsl). Population served: 750,000 Format: Country. News staff: one. Target aud: 25-54; male & female. ♦Billy Santiago, VP, opns mgr; Danny Fletcher, gen mgr.

Meridian

KOME-FM—Not on air, target date: unknown: Stn currently dark. 95.3 mhz; 25 kw. Ant 328 ft TL: N32 02 06 W97 50 02. Hrs open: 301 Commerce St., Suite 1600, Fort Worth, 76102. Phone: (817) 332-0959. Licensee: LKCM Radio Group LP. ♦Gerry Schlegel, pres.

Merkel

KHXS(FM)— Nov 4, 1983: 102.7 mhz; 100 kw. 1,486 ft TL: N32 22 00 W99 58 42. Stereo. Hrs open: 24 2525 S. Danville, Abilene, 79608. Phone: (325) 793-9700. Fax: (325) 692-1576. Web Site:www.102thebear.com Licensee: Cumulus Licensing Corp. Group owner: Cumulus Media Inc. (acq 6-15-98; $1.6 million). Format: Classic rock. ♦Jim Christoferson, gen mgr; John Scott, opns mgr, progmg dir; Chris Andrews, chief of engrg; Lori Barrett, traf mgr.

KMXO(AM)— June 1, 1963: 1500 khz; 250 w-D. TL: N32 28 17 W100 00 19. Hrs open: 604 N. 2nd St., 79536. Phone: (325) 928-3060. Fax: (325) 928-4683. Licensee: Ray R. Silva. Format: Chirstian. ♦Zacarias Serrato, gen mgr.

Mertzon

***KMEO(FM)**— 2006: 91.9 mhz; 6.5 kw vert. Ant 522 ft TL: N31 25 16 W100 32 36. Hrs open: Box 2440, Tupelo, MS, 38803. Phone: (662) 844-8888. Fax: (662) 842-6791. Web Site:www.afr.net Licensee: American Family Association. (acq 8-9-2005). Format: Christian classics. ♦Marvin Sanders, gen mgr.

Mesquite

***KEOM(FM)**— Sept 4, 1984: 88.5 mhz; 61 kw. 514 ft TL: N32 45 46 W96 38 04. Stereo. Hrs open: 24 2600 Motley Dr., Suite 300, 75150. Phone: (972) 888-7560.E-mail: pbrooks@mesquiteisd.org Web Site:www.keom.fm Licensee: Mesquite Independent School District. Rgnl. Network: Texas State Net. Texas State Networks Format: Div. Target aud: General; citizens of Mesquite & surrounding area. ♦Peggy Brooks, stn mgr.

Mexia

KRQX(AM)— May 21, 1956: 1590 khz; 500 w-D, 128 w-N. TL: N31 41 10 W96 27 18. Hrs open: 24 Box 1590, 76667. Secondary address: 1006-B Milam St. 76667. Phone: (254) 562-5328. Fax: (254) 562-6729.E-mail: radio@kycxfm.com Licensee: Simmons Austin, LS LLC. (acq 8-19-2005; $390,000 with co-located FM). Population served: 30,000 Natl. Network: ABC, . Rgnl. Network: Texas State Net. Texas State Networks Format: Country. Target aud: General; 20-59. Spec prog: Farm 12 hrs, Gospel 3 hrs wkly. ♦Susan Cholopisa, gen mgr; Bill Ferris, opns dir, gen sls mgr; Jan Phillips, news dir; Brandi Garza, traf mgr; Dave Campbell, sports cmtr.

KRQX-FM— Aug 29, 1983: 104.9 mhz; 2.85 kw. Ant 482 ft TL: N31 38 39 W96 36 51. Stereo. Hrs open: Dups AM 100% Box 1590, 76667. Phone: (254) 562-5328. Fax: (254) 562-6729. Population served: 30,000 Natl. Network: CBS, . Roy F. Perkins. ♦Bill Ferris, chief of opns; Susan Cholopisa, stn mgr & progmg dir; Brandi Garza, traf mgr; Dave Campbell, sports cmtr.

Midland

KCHX(FM)— Aug 15, 1988: 106.7 mhz; 100 kw. 613 ft TL: N31 54 53 W101 57 49. Stereo. Hrs open: 24 1330 E. 8th St., Suite 207, Odessa, 79761. Phone: (432) 563-9102. Fax: (432) 580-9102.E-mail: info@mymix1067.com Web Site:www.mymix1067.com Licensee: GAP Broadcasting Midland-Odessa License LLC. Group owner: Clear Channel Communications Inc. (acq 10-1-2007; grpsl). Population served: 350,000 Format: Adult contemp. News: 2 hrs wkly. Target aud: 25-54; general. ♦Gloria Apolinario, gen mgr; Laura Florez, gen sls mgr; Rob Norris, chief of engrg & engr.

KCRS(AM)— Dec 20, 1935: 550 khz; 5 kw-D, 1 kw-N, DA-2. TL: N32 04 10 W102 01 46. Hrs open: 24 1330 E. 8th St., Suite 207, Odessa, 79761. Phone: (432) 563-9102. Fax: (432) 580-9102. Web Site:www.newstalkkcrs.com Licensee: GAP Broadcasting Midland-Odessa License LLC. Group owner: Clear Channel Communications Inc. (acq 8-3-2007; grpsl). Population served: 200,000 Rgnl. Network: Texas State Net. Texas State Networks Dow, Lohnes & Albertson. Format: News/talk. News staff: 2; News: 30 hrs wkly. Target aud: 25-54. ♦Gloria Apolinario, gen mgr; Robert Hallmark, opns mgr, prom dir, progmg dir, pub affrs dir, spec ev coord; Jesse Grimes, news dir, local news ed, news rptr; Rod Norris, engrg mgr; Shelly Todd, traf mgr.

KCRS-FM— May 25, 1976: 103.3 mhz; 100 kw. 920 ft TL: N32 05 11 W102 17 11. Hrs open: 24 Prog sep from AM 1330 E. 8th St., Suite 207, Odessa, 79761. Phone: (432) 563-9102. Fax: (432) 580-9102.E-mail: info@1033kissfm.net Web Site:www.1033kissfm.net Licensee: GAP Broadcasting Midland-Odessa License LLC. Population served: 200,000 Format: Adult contemp. ♦Ric Elliott, progmg dir; Jesse Grimes, pub affrs dir, local news ed, news rptr, edit dir; Shelly Todd, traf mgr; Robert Hallmark, spec ev coord.

KLPF(AM)— Aug 6, 1950: 1150 khz; 1 kw-D. TL: N31 58 55 W102 03 30. Hrs open: 24
EWTN.
1903 S. Lamesa Rd., 79701. Phone: (432) 638-1150. Fax: (432) 682-5230.E-mail: robertd@grnonline.com Web Site:www.grnonline.com Licensee: La Promesa Foundation. (acq 2-11-2002; $85,000). Population served: 250,000 Format: Catholic progmg. News staff: 3. ♦Robert Dominguez, gen mgr; Toya Hall, progmg dir.

KMCM(FM)—See Odessa

KMND(AM)— Nov 27, 1963: 1510 khz; 2.4 kw-D. TL: N31 57 49 W102 04 53. Hrs open: Bldg. #2, 11300 Hwy. 191, 79707. Phone: (432) 563-5636. Fax: (432) 563-3823.E-mail: jmesher@aol.com Web Site:www.kmnd.com Licensee: Cumulus Licensing Corp. Group owner: Cumulus Media Inc. (acq 12-17-98; grpsl). Natl. Network: ESPN Radio, . Format: Sports. Spec prog: Jazz one hr wkly. ♦George Demarco, gen mgr; Mike Baer, sls dir, gen sls mgr; Robi Burns, progmg dir; Garry Vaughn, chief of engrg.

KNFM(FM)— Nov 2, 1959: 92.3 mhz; 100 kw. Ant 985 ft TL: N32 05 51 W102 17 21. Stereo. Hrs open: Bldg. # 2, 11300 Hwy. 191, 79707. Phone: (432) 563-5636. Fax: (432) 563-3823. Web Site:www.lonestar92.com Population served: 300,000 Format: Country. ♦George DeMarco, gen mgr; John Moesch, opns mgr, progmg dir; Spencer Bennett, progmg dir; Aleese Fielder, sls; Tonya Calloway, prom; Robbie Green, engr.

***KPBJ(FM)**— 2005: 90.1 mhz; 1.85 kw. Ant 417 ft TL: N31 57 39 W101 54 25. Hrs open:
Rebroadcasts KCZO(FM) Carrizo Springs 100%.
Box 252, McAllen, 78505. Phone: (956) 686-6382. Fax: (956) 686-2999. Licensee: Paulino Bernal Evangelism. Format: Sp. ♦Paulino Bernal Jr., pres.

KQRX(FM)—Licensed to Midland. See Odessa

***KVDG(FM)**— Sept 1, 2006: 90.9 mhz; 1.5 kw. Ant 430 ft TL: N31 54 32 W102 04 01. Stereo. Hrs open: 1406 E. Garden Ln., 79701. Phone: (432) 682-1485. Fax: (432) 682-5230.E-mail: robertd@grnonline.com Licensee: La Promesa Foundation. (acq 11-6-2007; $175,000). Natl. Network: EWTN Radio, . ♦Leonard J. Oswald, pres.

KWEL(AM)— April 1957: 1070 khz; 2.5 kw-D. TL: N31 57 44 W102 04 07. Hrs open: 6 AM-9 PM 1611 W. College Ave., 79701. Secondary address: 310 W. Wall, Ste 104 79701. Phone: (432) 620-9393. Fax: (432) 620-9591.E-mail: craiganderson@kwel.com Web Site:www.kwel.com Licensee: Faustino Quiroz. (acq 5-1-93; $140,000; 4-5-93). Population served: 220,000 Natl. Network: ABC, . Format: Talk, news. News: 60 hrs wkly. Target aud: 35 plus; adults. ♦Craig Anderson, CEO, gen mgr, progmg dir; Doris Anderson, traf mgr, traf mgr, opns; Garry Vaughn, engr.

KZBT(FM)— 1974: 93.3 mhz; 100 kw. Ant 500 ft TL: N31 57 30 W102 03 59. Stereo. Hrs open: 24 11300 Hwy 191, Bldg. 2, 79707. Phone: (432) 563-9300. Fax: (915) 563-3823. Web Site:www.b93.net Licensee: Cumulus Licensing Corp. Group owner: Cumulus Media Inc. (acq 12-17-98; grpsl). Population served: 220,000 Format: Contemp hit/top-40. News staff: one; News: 2 hrs wkly. Target aud: 18-44. ♦George DeMarco, gen mgr; John Moesch, opns mgr; Aleese Fielder, gen sls mgr; Rebecca Cruz, prom dir; Leo Caro, progmg dir; Robbie Green, chief of engrg.

Mineola

KMOO-FM— Sept 1, 1977: 99.9 mhz; 6 kw. Ant 295 ft TL: N32 45 04 W95 33 18. Stereo. Hrs open: 24 Box 628, 75773. Secondary address: Hwy. 69 N. 75773. Phone: (903) 569-3823. Fax: (903) 569-6641.E-mail: jason@kmoo.com Web Site:www.kmoo.com Licensee: Hightower Radio Inc. (acq 5-26-98; $600,000 for stock). Rgnl. Network: Texas State Net. Texas State Networks Wiley Rein LLP. Format: Country. News staff: one; News: 3 hrs wkly. Target aud: 25-64. ♦Jason Hightower, pres, gen mgr, gen sls mgr, prom dir, progmg dir; Amy Castleberry, opns dir; Marlene Keahey, pub affrs dir.

Mineral Wells

KFWR(FM)— Mar 1, 1970: 95.9 mhz; 80 kw. Ant 1,079 ft TL: N32 39 50 W98 09 47. Stereo. Hrs open: 24 115 W. 3rd St., Fort Worth, 76102. Phone: (817) 332-0959. Fax: (817) 348-8373.E-mail: info@959theranch.com Web Site:959theranch.com Licensee: LKCM Radio Group L.P. (group owner; acq 9-30-02; $6 million). Population served: 1,000,000 Format: Tex country. Target aud: 25-54; local, Texas country. ♦Gerry Schlegel, pres; Joel Gough, sls dir; Molly Prince, prom dir; Chuck Taylor, mus dir; Michael Margrave, chief of engrg; Jane Wasson, traf mgr.

KJSA(AM)— Dec 1, 1946: 1110 khz; 20 kw-D, DA. TL: N33 19 49 W97 44 08. Hrs open: 6 AM-sunset 305 Millsap Hwy., 76067. Phone: (940) 325-1140. Fax: (940) 325-1164.E-mail: info@kjsaam.com Licensee: M&M Broadcasters Ltd. (group owner; (acq 2-22-2006; grpsl). Population served: 75,000 Format: Sp. ♦Gary Moss, gen mgr.

Mirando City

KBDR(FM)— Apr 1, 1993: 100.5 mhz; 42 kw. Ant 551 ft TL: N27 21 17 W99 13 52. Stereo. Hrs open: 24 107 Calle Del Norte, Suite 102, Laredo, 78041. Phone: (956) 725-1000. Fax: (956) 718-1000.E-mail: mrillstrsl@kbdrfm.com Licensee: BMP 100.5 FM LP. Group owner: Border Media Partners LLC (acq 5-30-2003; $8 million with KBUC(FM) Raymondville). Population served: 1000000 Format: Regional Sp. Target aud: 18-45; upper-income bracket. ♦Tom Castro, CEO; Hugo Del Pozzo, CFO; Steve Stephenson, VP, gen mgr; Nestor Cobos, stn mgr; Issac Carrillo, opns mgr, sls dir; Robert Garcia, prom dir; Joe Flores, adv dir; Rogelio Botello Rios, progmg dir; Joe Espinoza, chief of engrg.

Mission

KGBT-FM—See McAllen

KIRT(AM)— Feb 23, 1958: 1580 khz; 1 kw-D, 302 w-N. TL: N26 17 36 W89 19 50. Hrs open: Box 3509, 78573. Phone: (956) 519-9999. Fax: (956) 581-0546.E-mail: kirtradio@aol.com Web Site:www.radioimagen.net Licensee: Bravo Broadcasting Co. Inc. (acq 10-25-01). Population served: 20,000 Rgnl. Network: Texas State Net. Texas State Networks Format: Sp. ♦Walter Gomez, gen mgr; Rosie Pedraza, gen sls mgr, traf mgr; Armando Pedraza, progmg dir; John Pankratz, chief of engrg.

KQXX-FM— 1989: 105.5 mhz; 3 kw. 300 ft TL: N26 13 50 W98 20 18. Stereo. Hrs open: 24
Rebroadcasts KTJN(FM) Brownsville 100%.
901 E. Pike Blvd., Weslaco, 78596. Phone: (956) 973-9202. Fax: (956) 544-0311.E-mail: billysantiago@clearchannel.com Web Site:www.oldies1055.net Licensee: Clear Channel Broadcasting Licenses Inc. Group owner: Clear Channel Communications Inc. (acq 12-9-2003; grpsl). Population served: 300,000 Format: Oldies. News staff: 3. ♦Danny Fletcher, gen mgr; Billy Santiago, opns mgr; Cyndia Torres, gen sls mgr; Ken Meek, chief of engrg; Gloria Garcia, traf mgr.

Missouri City

KAMA-FM—Licensed to Missouri City. See Houston

KBRZ(AM)— October 1952: 1460 khz; 5 w-D, 125 w-N. TL: N29 33 52 W95 42 06. Hrs open: 912 Curtis Ave., Pasadena, 77502. Phone: (713) 589-1336. Fax: (713) 589-1335. Licensee: Aleluya Christian Broadcasting Inc. (acq 3-1-2001; $700,000). Population served: 85,000 Format: Sp Christian. ♦Ruben Villarreal, gen mgr.

Monahans

KBAT(FM)—Licensed to Monahans. See Odessa

KCKM(AM)— Mar 12, 1947: 1330 khz; 5 kw-D, 1 kw-N, DA-N. TL: N31 38 45 W103 00 04. Hrs open: 24 Box 3069, Odessa, 79760-3069. Phone: (432) 943-2588. Fax: (432) 943-7314.E-mail: info@kckmam.com Licensee: Sandhills Communication Inc. (acq 2001; $175,000). Population served: 8,333 Natl. Network: CBS, . Rgnl. Network: Texas State Net.

Natl. Rep: Riley,. Texas State Networks Roberts & Eckard. Format: Oldies. News staff: one. Target aud: 25-54; general. Spec prog: Gospel 3 hrs wkly. ◆Rick Anderson, gen mgr; David McCaffity, progmg dir; Allen Martin, news dir; Dexter Nichols, sports cmtr.

Morton

*KPGA(FM)— Jan 16, 2009: 91.9 mhz; 100 kw. Ant 522 ft TL: N33 33 01 W102 13 07. Hrs open:
Rebroadcasts KLRD(FM) Yucaipa, CA 100%.
2351 Sunset Blvd., Suite 170-218, Rocklin, CA, 95765. Phone: (916) 251-1600. Fax: (916) 251-1650. Web Site:www.air1.com Licensee: Educational Media Foundation. Natl. Network: Air 1, . Format: Christian. ◆Mike Novak, pres.

Mount Pleasant

KIMP(AM)— Oct 8, 1948: 960 khz; 1 kw-D, 75 w-N. TL: N33 09 54 W95 00 27. Hrs open: Box 990, 75456. Secondary address: 1798 U.S. Hw. 67 West 75455. Phone: (903) 572-8726. Fax: (903) 572-7232. Web Site:easttexasradio.com Licensee: East Texas Broadcasting Inc. (group owner; (acq 11-21-91; $850,000 with co-located FM; 12-16-91). Population served: 50,000 Rgnl. Network: Texas State Net. Format: Rgnl Mexican. News staff: 10; News: 10 hrs wkly. Target aud: General. ◆John Mitchell, chmn; Bud Kitchens, pres, VP, gen mgr; Darrin Tripp, opns dir, progmg dir; Bryan Frimesth, gen sls mgr; Clint Cooper, news dir, pub affrs dir, farm dir; Bill Hughes, chief of engrg; Justice Thornburg, traf mgr; Jesse Carillo, spanish dir; Tammy Ray, disc jockey.

*KPIP(FM)—Not on air, target date: unknown: 88.3 mhz; 3 kw vert. Ant 149 ft TL: N33 10 10.4 W95 05 59.3. Hrs open: 1039 CR 2920, Pittsburg, 75686. Phone: (903) 466-6791. Licensee: Millennium Broadcasting Corp. ◆James Furlow Jr., pres.

Mountain Home

KMHO(FM)—Not on air, target date: unknown: 102.1 mhz; 6 kw. Ant 272 ft TL: N30 10 34 W99 23 02. Hrs open: Box 717, Pickerington, OH, 43147-0717. Phone: (239) 877-4605. Licensee: In Phase Broadcasting Inc. ◆Peter L. Cea, pres.

Muenster

*KTMU(FM)—Not on air, target date: unknown: 88.7 mhz; 4.5 kw vert. Ant 535 ft TL: N33 43 43 W97 31 36. Hrs open: Box 217, Gainesville, 76241. Phone: (940) 668-7971. Licensee: 1 A Chord Inc. ◆Mary Fay Jackson, pres.

KZZA(FM)— Dec 23, 1991: 106.7 mhz; 75 kw. Ant 2,034 ft TL: N33 26 13 W97 29 05. Stereo. Hrs open: 24 4201 Pool Rd. , Coleyville, 76034. Fax: (817) 868-2900. Fax: (817) 868-2929. Web Site:casa1067.com Licensee: Liberman Broadcasting of Dallas License LLC. Group owner: Entravision Communications Corp. (acq 11-2-2006; grpsl). Population served: 6,153,500 Natl. Rep: Eastman Radio,. Thompson Hine. Format: Rgnl Mexican. Target aud: 18-34. ◆Alex Sanchez, gen mgr.

Muleshoe

KMUL-FM— Feb 6, 1966: 103.1 mhz; 6 kw. Ant 75 ft TL: N34 13 39 W102 44 10. Stereo. Hrs open: 1000 Sycamore St., Clovis, NM, 88101. Phone: (505) 762-6200. Fax: (505) 762-8800. Licensee: Tallgrass Broadcasting LLC. (acq 4-2-2007; grpsl). Population served: 4,525 Format: Country.

Nacogdoches

KJCS(FM)— May 1967: 103.3 mhz; 100 kw. 476 ft TL: N31 34 51 W94 40 16. Stereo. Hrs open: 910 North St., 75961. Phone: (936) 559-8800. Fax: (936) 559-8801.E-mail: info@kjcsfm.com Licensee: Radio Licensing Inc. Population served: 105,000 Natl. Network: ABC, . Format: Country. Spec prog: Gospel 3 hrs wkly. ◆Bill Vance Jr., gen mgr; Carolyn Gage, stn mgr, natl sls mgr; Della Huse, gen sls mgr; Lou Bennett, progmg dir & pub affrs dir; Gwen Jordan, traf mgr.

*KSAU(FM)— July 5, 1975: 90.1 mhz; 3.5 kw. Ant 450 ft TL: N31 37 45 W94 40 44. Stereo. Hrs open: 10 AM-2 AM Box 13048, 75962. Secondary address: 1936 North St., Boynton Building 75961. Phone: (936) 468-4000. Fax: (936) 468-1331.E-mail: ksau@sfasu.edu Web Site:www.sfasu.edu/ksau Licensee: Stephen F. Austin State University. Population served: 120,000 Natl. Network: ABC, . Wire Svc: AP

Format: Jazz, indie rock, alt rock. News: 3 hrs wkly. Target aud: 18-54. ◆Sherry Williford, gen mgr; John Chapman, engr.

KSFA(AM)— June 2, 1947: 860 khz; 1 kw-D, 175 w-N. TL: N31 31 36 W94 39 29. Stereo. Hrs open: 1216 South First, Lufkin, 75901. Phone: (936) 639-4455. Fax: (936) 639-4440.E-mail: info@ksfa.com Web Site:www.ksfa860.com Licensee: GAP Broadcasting Lufkin License LLC. Group owner: Clear Channel Communications Inc. (acq 10-1-2007; grpsl). Population served: 140,250 Format: News/talk. Target aud: 25 plus; upscale, upper income level men. Spec prog: Houston Astros baseball, farm 7 hrs wkly. ◆Larry Gunter, gen mgr; Danny Merrell, progmg dir.

KTBQ(FM)— July 15, 1967: 107.7 mhz; 50 kw. Ant 492 ft TL: N31 42 30 W94 41 18. Stereo. Hrs open: 24 1216 South First, Lufkin, 75901. Phone: (936) 639-4455. Fax: (936) 639-4440.E-mail: info@ktbq.com Web Site:www.q1077.com Licensee: GAP Broadcasting Lufkin License LLC. (acq 10-1-2007; grpsl). Population served: 100,000 Format: Classic rock. News staff: one. Target aud: 18-49; upscale women.

KYKS(FM)—See Lufkin

Natalia

*KYRQ(FM)—Not on air, target date: unknown: 90.3 mhz; 2.3 kw. Ant 148 ft TL: N29 09 13 W98 55 16. Hrs open: Box 6767, Athens, GA, 30604. Phone: (706) 425-0739. Licensee: Community Public Radio Inc. (acq 8-8-2008; CP exchange for CP of WBRQ(FM) La Grange, GA.) ◆Penny Jackson, pres.

Navasota

KWBC(AM)— Sept 21, 1960: Stn currently dark. 1550 khz; 250 w-D, 26 w-N. TL: N30 22 48 W96 06 01. (CP: COL College Station. 1.4 kw-D, 24 w-N, DA-D. TL: N30 37 54 W96 21 28). Hrs open: 303 E. Washington, Suite A, 77868. Phone: (936) 825-9007. Fax: (936) 825-1019.E-mail: news@navasotanews.com Web Site:navasotanews.com Licensee: Bryan Broadcasting Corp. (acq 7-31-2007; $275,000). Population served: 92,000 Format: Local news/talk. ◆Ben Downs, gen mgr; Dave Hill, stn mgr; Tom Turner, news dir; Chris Dusterhoff, chief of engrg; Michelle McNew, sls.

KWUP(FM)— Mar 1, 1989: Stn currently dark. 92.5 mhz; 6 kw. Ant 263 ft TL: N30 24 58 W96 04 43. Stereo. Hrs open: 24 Box 187, Humble, 77347. Phone: (281) 446-5725. Fax: (281) 540-2198.E-mail: info@thehippo.com Licensee: KSBJ Educational Foundation (group owner; (acq 6-5-2008; $1.03 million). Population served: 200,000 ◆Tim McDermott, gen mgr.

Nederland

KBED(AM)— Jan 11, 1969: 1510 khz; 5 kw-D, DA-D. TL: N30 03 35 W93 58 49. Hrs open: Sunrise-sunset 755 S. 11th St., Suite 102, Beaumont, 77704. Phone: (409) 833-9421. Fax: (409) 833-9296.E-mail: info@cumulus.com Web Site:www.cumulus.com Licensee: Cumulus Licensing Corp. Group owner: Cumulus Media Inc. (acq 3-9-98; grpsl). Population served: 15,000 Natl. Network: ESPN Radio, . Format: Sports. News staff: one; News: 5 hrs wkly. Target aud: 18-49; males. Spec prog: Relg 4 hrs wkly. ◆Zanetta Kelley, gen mgr; Wes Matejka, sls dir; Mark Guzman, prom dir, spec ev coord; Jim West, progmg dir; Richard Core, news dir; Greg Davis, chief of engrg; Liz Ferguson, traf mgr.

New Boston

KEWL-FM— July 1995: 95.1 mhz; 25 kw. Ant 325 ft TL: N33 26 15 W94 25 11. Hrs open: 24 1323 College Dr., Texarkana, 75503. Phone: (903) 793-1109. Fax: (903) 794-4717. Web Site:www.kool951.com Licensee: American Media Investments Inc. Group owner: Petracom Media LLC (acq 2-17-2009; grpsl). Format: Oldies. Target aud: 35-64. ◆Charlotte Hartwell, gen mgr.

KLBW(AM)— Nov 16, 1969: 1530 khz; 2.5 kw-D. TL: N33 28 56 W94 25 25. Hrs open: 6 AM-6 PM 1198 Daniels Chaper Rd., 75570. Phone: (903) 628-2561.E-mail: info@knboam.com Licensee: Chapel of Light (acq 9-5-2008; $70,000). Population served: 100,000 Format: MOR, Christian. Target aud: General. ◆Carmen Johnson, gen mgr.

KTTY(FM)— 2009: 105.1 mhz; 4.3 kw. Ant 387 ft TL: N33 28 00 W94 27 48. Hrs open: 1305 S. Glenburnie Rd., New Bern, NC, 28562. Phone: (252) 636-3333. Fax: (252) 633-3997. Web Site:texarkana.bigfishfm.com Licensee: Tower Investment Trust Inc. Format: Contemp Christian. ◆Bill Brothers, gen mgr; Blake Larson, opns mgr.

KZRB(FM)— Nov 16, 1997: 103.5 mhz; 50 kw. 492 ft TL: N33 24 54 W94 38 10. Stereo. Hrs open: 24 710 W. Ave. A, Hooks, 75561. Phone: (903) 547-3223. Fax: (903) 547-3095. Web Site:kzrb.com Licensee: B & H Broadcasting System Inc. (acq 4-16-93; $1.5 million;5-3-93). Population served: 450,000 Natl. Network: American Urban, . Rgnl. Network: Texas State Net. Natl. Rep: Christal,. Format: Adult contemp, oldies, urban contemp. News staff: one; News: 9 hrs wkly. Target aud: 25-54; all age buyers. ◆Ray C. Bursey Jr., CEO, pres, gen mgr, sls VP; Sandy Hunter, opns mgr & prom VP; Brigette Talbert, progmg VP, mus dir; Gray Graham, engrg VP.

New Braunfels

KGNB(AM)— Apr 1, 1950: 1420 khz; 1 kw-D, 196 w-N. TL: N29 39 45 W98 10 29. Hrs open: 24 1540 Loop 337 N., 78130. Phone: (830) 625-7311. Fax: (830) 625-7336.E-mail: localnews@kgnb.com Web Site:www.kgnb.com Licensee: New Braunfels Communications Inc. Population served: 175,000 Natl. Network: CNN Radio, Westwood One, . Southmayd & Miller, P.C. Format: Loc news, country music. News staff: 3; News: 26 hrs wkly. Target aud: 25-54; men. ◆Bill Rainer, CEO; Mattson Rainer, VP & gen mgr.

KNBT(FM)— Nov 22, 1968: 92.1 mhz; 6 kw. 300 ft TL: N29 43 50 W98 07 15. Stereo. Hrs open: 24 Prog sep from AM 1540 Loop 337 N., 78130. Phone: (830) 625-7311. Fax: (830) 625-7336.E-mail: mattson@knbtfm.com Web Site:www.knbtfm.com Licensee: New Braunfels Communications Inc. Format: Americana. Target aud: 25-54. Spec prog: Relg 3 hrs wkly. ◆Mattson Rainer, gen mgr.

New Deal

KLZK(FM)— September 1961: 97.3 mhz; 30.5 kw. Ant 613 ft TL: N33 30 08 W101 52 20. Stereo. Hrs open: 24 Box 3757, Lubbock, 79452. Secondary address: 9800 University, Lubbock 79423. Phone: (806) 745-3434. Fax: (806) 748-2470. Web Site:www.stars1043.com Licensee: Ramar Communications II Ltd. (group owner; acq 7-12-2002; $750,000). Population served: 350,000 Natl. Rep: Univision Radio National Sales,. ◆Chuck Heinz, gen mgr; Connie Hayes, gen sls mgr; Eddie Moreno, progmg dir; Gilbert Saldana, mus dir; Lee Thomas, chief of engrg; Susie Gonsales, traf mgr.

New Ulm

KNRG(FM)— 1999: 92.3 mhz; 6 kw. Ant 328 ft TL: N29 53 50 W96 32 35. Stereo. Hrs open: Box 111, Columbus, 78934. Phone: (979) 732-5766. Fax: (979) 732-6377. Licensee: New Ulm Broadcasting Co. Group owner: Bayport Broadcast Group Population served: 30,000 Format: Classic hits. ◆Carl Geisler, gen mgr.

Nolanville

KLFX(FM)— 1994: 107.3 mhz; 1.35 kw. Ant 548 ft TL: N31 05 38 W97 34 51. Hrs open: 100 W. Central Texas Expwy., Suite 306, Harker Heights, 76548. Phone: (254) 699-5000. Fax: (254) 680-4212.E-mail: klfx@klfx.com Web Site:1073rocks.com Licensee: Clear Channel Broadcasting Licenses Inc. Group owner: Clear Channel Communications Inc. (acq 1-15-2004; $2.6 million). Format: Rock. ◆Evan Armstrong, gen mgr.

Odem

KLHB(FM)— Feb 18, 1985: 98.3 mhz; 50 kw. Ant 433 ft TL: N27 47 26 W97 27 02. Stereo. Hrs open: 24 1300 Antelope, Corpus Christi, 78401. Phone: (361) 883-1600. Fax: (361) 883-9303.E-mail: johnnyo@johnnyoradio.com Licensee: Tejas Broadcasting Ltd. LLP. Group owner: Amigo Broadcasting L.P. (acq 11-15-2004; grpsl). Population served: 400,000 Format: Sp. Target aud: 18-49; progsv, affluent, middle class Hispanics. ◆Kent Cooper, gen mgr.

Odessa

KBAT(FM)—(Monahans, Nov 1, 1983: 99.9 mhz; 100 kw. Ant 574 ft TL: N31 45 40 W102 31 28. Stereo. Hrs open: 24 11300 Hwy. 191, Bldg. 2, Midland, 79707. Phone: (432) 563-5499. Fax: (432) 563-5530.E-mail: info@kbatfm.com Licensee: Cumulus Licensing Corp. Group owner: Cumulus Media Inc. (acq 12-17-98; grpsl). Jones, Waldo, Holbrook & McDonough. Format: Contemp Christian. Target aud: 25-54; general. ◆George DeMarco, gen mgr; John Moesch, opns mgr; Aleese Fielder, gen sls mgr; Brian Hill, prom dir, mus dir; Kevin Chase, progmg dir; Robbie Green, chief of engrg.

*KBMM(FM)— 2004: 89.5 mhz; 25 kw. Ant 535 ft TL: N31 40 35 W102 21 32. Hrs open: Drawer 3206, Tupelo, MS, 38803. Phone: (662)

844-8888.E-mail: info@kbmmfm.com Web Site:afr.net Licensee: American Family Association. Group owner: American Family Radio Format: Christian. ♦Marvin Sanders, gen mgr.

***KFLB(AM)**— Jan 29, 1947: 920 khz; 1 kw-D, 500 w-N, DA-1. TL: N31 49 14 W102 25 42. Hrs open: 24 7355 N. Oracle Rd., Suite 200, Tucson, 85704. Phone: (520) 742-6976. Fax: (520) 469-7312.E-mail: kflb@flc.org Web Site:www.flr.org Licensee: Family Life Broadcasting System. (group owner; (acq 6-24-98; grpsl). Population served: 260,000 Format: Christian, relg. Target aud: 34-59; females. ♦Dawn Bumstead, gen mgr.

KFZX(FM)—See Gardendale

KHKX(FM)— July 1, 1977: 99.1 mhz; 100 kw. Ant 407 ft TL: N32 03 10 W102 17 38. Stereo. Hrs open: 24 Box 9400, Midland, 79708. Phone: (432) 520-9912. Fax: (432) 520-0112. Licensee: Double O Texas Corp. (group owner; (acq 2006; grpsl). Population served: 850,000 Natl. Network: USA, . Format: Country. News: one hr wkly. Target aud: 25-54; general. ♦Terry Bond, CEO & gen mgr.

***KLVW(FM)**— Sept 1, 1989: 90.5 mhz; 28 kw. Ant 453 ft TL: N31 53 50 W102 33 57. Hrs open: 24 2351 Sunset Blvd., Suite 170-218, Rocklin, CA, 95765. Phone: (916) 251-1600. Fax: (916) 251-1650. Licensee: Educational Media Foundation. (acq 6-15-2009; exchange for KFLB-FM Stanton). Population served: 260,000 Format: Christian. ♦Mike Novak, pres.

KMCM(FM)— January 1961: 96.9 mhz; 100 kw. 500 ft TL: N32 05 13 W102 17 12. Stereo. Hrs open: 3303 N. Midkiff Rd., Suite 115, Midland, 79705. Phone: (432) 520-9912. Fax: (432) 520-0112. Web Site:www.97gold.com Licensee: Double O Texas Corp. (group owner; (acq 2006; grpsl). Population served: 220,000 Natl. Rep: Katz Radio,. Wiley, Rein & Fielding. Format: Classic hits. News: 2 hrs wkly. Target aud: 25-54; men. ♦Terry Bond, CEO.

KMRK-FM— Aug 23, 1991: 96.1 mhz; 27.5 kw. Ant 948 ft TL: N32 05 11 W102 17 10. Stereo. Hrs open: 24 1330 E. 8th St., Suite 207, 79761. Phone: (432) 563-9102. Fax: (432) 580-9102. Fax: (915) 580-4800. Web Site:www.mycountry961.com Licensee: GAP Broadcasting Midland-Odessa License LLC. Group owner: Clear Channel Communications Inc. (acq 10-1-2007; grpsl). Population served: 200,000 Natl. Network: American Urban, . Wire Svc: AP Format: Country. News staff: one; News: 2 hrs wkly. Target aud: 18-34. ♦Gloria Apolinario, gen mgr; Steve Driscoll, opns mgr.

KNFM(FM)—See Midland

***KOCV(FM)**— Jan 6, 1964: 91.3 mhz; 5 kw. 300 ft TL: N31 51 30 W102 23 00. (CP: Ant 289 ft.). Stereo. Hrs open: 6 AM-midnight Odessa College, 201 W. University Blvd., 79764. Phone: (432) 580-9130. Fax: (915) 337-0529.E-mail: cevan@odessa.edu Web Site:www.odessa.edu Licensee: Odessa College. Population served: 78,380 Natl. Network: NPR, . Format: News, eclectic, class. News staff: one; News: 33 hrs wkly. Target aud: 35 plus; educated, affluent adults. Spec prog: Jazz 4 hrs, opera 4 hrs, folk 4 hrs, blues 4 hrs, bluegrass 2 hrs, Celtic 4 hrs wkly. ♦Carl Evans, gen mgr & opns mgr.

KODM(FM)— 1965: 97.9 mhz; 100 kw. 361 ft TL: N31 47 40 W102 10 44. Stereo. Hrs open: 24 11300 Hwy. 191, Bldg. 2, Midland, 79707. Phone: (432) 563-5499. Fax: (432) 563-5330.E-mail: spencer.bennett@cumulus.com Web Site:www.kodm.com Licensee: Cumulus Licensing Corp. Group owner: Cumulus Media Inc. (acq 12-17-98; grpsl). Population served: 220,000 Natl. Network: ABC, . Format: Lite rock, adult contemp. Target aud: 25-54; women. ♦George DeMarco, gen mgr; John Moesch, opns mgr; Aleese Fielder, gen sls mgr; Tonya Calloway, progmg dir; Robbie Green, chief of engrg.

KOZA(AM)— Jan 20, 1947: Stn currently dark. 1230 khz; 1 kw-U. TL: N31 49 52 W102 22 09. Hrs open: 24 1319 S. Crane Ave., 79763. Phone: (432) 332-1230. Fax: (432) 335-0064. Licensee: Stellar Media Inc. (acq 4-20-89). Population served: 225,000 Target aud: 18-54. ♦Benjamin Velasquez, gen mgr.

KQLM(FM)— Mar 11, 1996: 107.9 mhz; 100 kw. 846 ft TL: N32 05 51 W102 17 21. Hrs open: 24 1319 S. Crane, 79763. Phone: (432) 333-1227. Fax: 432) 335-0064. Web Site:www.9108fm.com Licensee: Stellar Media Inc. (acq 12-30-02). Population served: 250,000 Haley, Bader & Potts. Format: Regional Mexican. News: 10 hrs wkly. Target aud: General; Hispanics/Latinos. ♦Benjamin Velasquez, CEO & gen mgr.

KQRX(FM)—(Midland, Oct 20, 1995: 95.1 mhz; 10.35 kw. Ant 505 ft TL: N32 03 10 W102 17 38. Hrs open: 24 3303 N. Midkiff, Suite 115, Midland, 79705. Phone: (432) 520-9510. Fax: (432) 520-9505.E-mail: ooradio01@aol.com Web Site:www.boblivesintaxes.com Licensee: Double O Texas Corp. (group owner; (acq 2006; grpsl). Population served: 250,000 Natl. Rep: Katz Radio,. Fletcher, Heald & Hildreth. Format: Adult hits. ♦Tommy Vascocu, gen mgr; Michael Todd, progmg dir.

KRIL(AM)— June 1946: 1410 khz; 1 kw-U, DA-N. TL: N31 49 00 W102 21 00. Hrs open:
Rebroadcasts KMND(AM) Midland 100%.
11300 Hwy 191, Bldg. 2, Midland, 79707. Phone: (432) 563-5636. Fax: (432) 563-3823.E-mail: jmesher@aol.com Web Site:www.kmnd.com Licensee: Cumulus Licensing Corp. Group owner: Cumulus Media Inc. (acq 8-10-99; $110,000). Population served: 200,000 Natl. Network: ESPN Radio, . Format: Sports. Target aud: 25 plus; higher educ level, higher income level. ♦George Demarco, gen mgr; Robie Burns, progmg dir; Gary Vaugn, chief of engrg.

KXOI(AM)—See Crane

Olney

KAHA(FM)—Not on air, target date: unknown: 104.3 mhz; 50 kw. Ant 472 ft TL: N33 15 20 W98 49 53. Hrs open: Box 880, Roma, 78584. Phone: (956) 487-8015. Licensee: South Texas FM Investments LLC. (acq 9-16-2008; grpsl). ♦Eloy Vera, gen mgr.

Orange

KIOC(FM)— Feb 28, 1977: 106.1 mhz; 100 kw. 1,225 ft TL: N30 09 31 W93 59 11. Stereo. Hrs open: 24 2885 Interstate 10 E., Beaumont, 77702. Phone: (409) 896-5555. Fax: (409) 896-5599.E-mail: bigdog106@bigdog106.com Web Site:www.bigdog106.com Licensee: Capstar TX L.P. Group owner: Clear Channel Communications Inc. (acq 8-30-00; grpsl). Population served: 375,000 Format: Classic rock. Target aud: 18-49; adults who have discretionary income. ♦John Hogan, CEO; Lowry Mays, chmn; Mark Mays, pres; Randall Mays, CFO; Charlie Rahilly, sr VP; Mark Kopelman, VP; Vesta Brandt, gen mgr; Gaile Darbone, opns dir, traf mgr; Elizabeth Blackstock, sls dir; Mike Davis, progmg dir, disc jockey; Jim Love, pub affrs dir; Shon Hodgkinson, chief of engrg, spec ev coord.

KKMY(FM)— 1972: 104.5 mhz; 100 kw. 440 ft TL: N30 08 07 W93 50 39. (CP: 98 kw, ant 984 ft. TL: N30 08 04 W93 56 59). Stereo. Hrs open: 2885 Interstate 10 E., Beaumont, 77702. Phone: (409) 896-5555. Fax: (409) 896-5500.E-mail: info@kkmyfm.com Web Site:www.mix1045.com Licensee: Capstar TX L.P. Group owner: Clear Channel Communications Inc. (acq 8-30-00; grpsl). Population served: 500,000 Fisher, Wayland, Cooper, Leader & Zaragoza. Format: Adult contemp. Target aud: 25-54; at-work lstng audience.John Hogan, CEO; Lowry Mays, chmn; Mark Mays, pres; Randall Mays, CFO; Charlie Rahilly, sr VP; Mark Kopelman, VP; Trey Poston, opns dir, progmg dir; Gaile Darbone, opns mgr, traf mgr; Elizabeth Blackstock, sls dir; Vesta Brandt, gen mgr & natl sls mgr; Kaleb Dainwood, prom dir, progmg dir, spec ev coord; Harold Mann, news dir; Jim Love, pub affrs dir; Scott Rice, chief of engrg; Nunee Oakes, disc jockey, disc jockey

KOGT(AM)— January 1948: 1600 khz; 1 kw-U, DA-N. TL: N30 08 25 W93 45 11. Hrs open: Box 1667, 77631-1667. Secondary address: 5304 Meeks Dr. 77632. Phone: (409) 883-4381. Fax: (409) 883-7996.E-mail: news@kogt.com Web Site:www.kogt.com Licensee: G-CAP Communications Inc. (acq 8-7-92; 8-24-92). Population served: 90,000 Rgnl. Network: Texas State Net. Texas State Networks Format: C&W, news, sports. Target aud: 25 plus. ♦Gary Stelly, pres, gen mgr, progmg dir; Richard Corder, gen sls mgr, disc jockey; Glenn Earle, news dir; Russ Ingram, engrg dir; Iva Key Odom, traf mgr; Clay Williams, disc jockey.

Ore City

KAZE(FM)— May 1991: 106.9 mhz; 8.2 kw. 502 ft TL: N32 41 54 W94 37 04. Hrs open: 212 Grande Blvd., Suite B-100, Tyler, 75703. Phone: (903) 581-5259. Fax: (903) 939-3473.E-mail: chelle@theblaze.cc Web Site:www.theblaze.cc Licensee: Reynolds Radio Inc. (group owner; acq 1-9-97). Format: Rhythmic Contemporary Hit Radio. ♦Rusty Reynolds, pres; Rick Reynolds, gen mgr; Robin George, gen sls mgr; Charlie O'Douglas, progmg dir; Marcus Love, mus dir; James McWain, engrg dir; Chelle Wright-Peterson, traf mgr.

Overland

***KKVI(FM)**— 2008: 89.9 mhz; 120 w vert. Ant 98 ft TL: N33 04 00 W95 46 10. Hrs open: Box 497933, Garland, 75049. Phone: (469) 245-3604. Licensee: Gospel American Network. ♦William R. Wright, gen mgr.

Overton

KPXI(FM)— Oct 8, 1961: 100.7 mhz; 8.1 kw. Ant 571 ft TL: N32 09 07 W95 03 27. Stereo. Hrs open: 24 1101 Kilgore Dr., Henderson, 75652. Phone: (903) 655-1800. Fax: (903) 655-1808.E-mail: info@kwrdonline.com Web Site:www.kwrdonline.com Licensee: Inspiration Media of Texas LLC. Group owner: Sunburst Media L.P. (acq 11-6-2000; with KWRD-FM Highland Village). Population served: 1,500,000 Format: Country. ♦Jerry Hanszen, gen mgr.

Ozona

KYXX(FM)— Nov 25, 1976: 94.3 mhz; 3 kw. Ant 394 ft TL: N30 42 42.6 W101 07 28.7. Stereo. Hrs open: 680 Hwy. 277 S., Sonora, 76950. Phone: (325) 387-3553. Fax: (325) 387-3554.E-mail: khoskyxx@verizon.net Licensee: Foster Charitable Foundation Inc. Group owner: Hill Country Broadcasting Corp. (acq 5-31-2007). Population served: 63884 Natl. Network: ABC, . Texas State Networks Format: Classic Country. Target aud: 12-50 plus. ♦Marti Ashcraft, opns mgr; Eddy Smith, engr.

Palacios

KROY(FM)— November 1996: 99.7 mhz; 50 kw. 331 ft TL: N28 43 53 W96 05 26. Hrs open: 102 Jason Plaza, Suite 2, Victoria, 77901. Phone: (361) 572-0105. Fax: (361) 798-3798. Licensee: Roy E. Henderson. (group owner; (acq 1-22-99). Format: Texas country. ♦Egon Barthels, gen mgr; Ryan Henderson, opns mgr; Lori Beusin, gen sls mgr; Robi Austynn, progmg dir; Ray Nelson, chief of engrg; Kim Brazil, traf mgr.

Palestine

***KLTB(FM)**—Not on air, target date: unknown: 91.1 mhz; 2 kw. Ant 246 ft TL: N31 50 39 W95 42 35. Hrs open: Box 465, Brownsboro, 75756. Phone: (903) 852-3701. Fax: (903) 852-3957. Licensee: Brownsboro Independent School District. ♦Joel Irwin, pres.

KNET(AM)— Jan 2, 1936: 1450 khz; 1 kw-U. TL: N31 46 26 W95 37 00. Hrs open: 24 Box 3649, 75802. Secondary address: 800 W. Palestine Ave. 75801. Phone: (903) 729-6077. Fax: (903) 729-4742.E-mail: traffic@kyyk.com Web Site:www.kyyk.com Licensee: Tomlinson-Leis Communications L.P. (acq 9-30-2005; $1.2 million with co-located FM). Population served: 45,300 Woble, Carlyle, Sandridge & Rice. Format: Classic country. News staff: one; News: 6 hrs wkly. Target aud: 35 plus. Spec prog: Relg 7 hrs, farm 6 hrs wkly. ♦Edward B. Tomlinson II, pres; Jason Hightower, gen mgr; Tamie Armstrong, opns dir & sls dir; Dave Peterson, progmg dir.

***KYFP(FM)**— May 15, 2000: 89.1 mhz; 100 kw. Ant 485 ft TL: N32 00 12 W95 43 06. Stereo. Hrs open: 24 Box 7300, Charlotte, NC, 28241. Phone: (704) 523-5555. Fax: (704) 522-1967. Web Site:www.bbnradio.org Licensee: Bible Broadcasting Network Inc. Group owner: Bible Broadcasting Network Smithwick & Belendiuk PC. Format: Relg. ♦Lowell Davey, pres; Richard Johnson, opns mgr; Hank Iarrior, progmg dir; Ron Muffley, chief of engrg.

KYYK(FM)— Aug 20, 1976: 98.3 mhz; 5 kw. Ant 728 ft TL: N31 55 33 W95 38 48. Stereo. Hrs open: 24 Box 3649, 75802. Secondary address: 800 W. Palestine Ave. 75801. Phone: (903) 729-6077. Fax: (903) 729-4742. Web Site:www.youreasttexas.com Population served: 115,000 Format: Country. News staff: one; News: 2 hrs wkly. Target aud: 18-54. ♦Edward Tomlinson II, pres; Lee Parkinson, gen mgr; Buddy Jackson, progmg dir.

Pampa

***KAVO(FM)**— July 1998: 90.9 mhz; 17 kw. Ant 364 ft TL: N35 33 08 W101 02 42. Hrs open:
Rebroadcasts WAFR(FM) Tupelo, MS 100%.
Box 3206, Tupelo, MS, 38803. Phone: (662) 844-8888. Fax: (662) 842-6791.E-mail: comments@afr.net Web Site:www.afr.net Licensee: American Family Association. Group owner: American Family Radio Natl. Network: American Family Radio, . Format: Inspirational Christian. ♦Marvin Sanders, gen mgr.

KGRO(AM)— 1947: 1230 khz; 1 kw-U. TL: N35 34 39 W100 57 08. Hrs open: Box 1779, 79066-1779. Phone: (806) 669-6809. Fax: (806) 669-0662.E-mail: production@kgrokomxradio.com Web Site:www.kgrokomxradio.com Licensee: Pampa Broadcasters Inc. (acq 8-1-67). Population served: 30,000 Natl. Network: Jones Radio Networks, ABC, . Format: Adult contemp. Target aud: 18-45. ♦James Hughes, pres; Darrell Sehorn, gen mgr, gen sls mgr, progmg dir;

Donny Hooper, news dir, sports cmtr; Greg Campbell, chief of engrg; Linda Sehorn, traf mgr; Jimmy Story, disc jockey.

KOMX(FM)— May 18, 1981: 100.3 mhz; 32 kw. Ant 300 ft TL: N35 34 39 W100 57 08. Stereo. Hrs open: Box 1779, 79066-1779. Phone: (806) 669-6809. Fax: (806) 669-0662. Licensee: Pampa Broadcasters Inc. Population served: 125,000 Natl. Network: ABC, Jones Radio Networks, . Rgnl. Network: Texas State Net. Texas State Networks Format: Country. Target aud: 20 plus. ♦Linda Sehorn, traf mgr; Donny Hooper, sports cmtr; Jimmy Story, disc jockey.

Paris

KBUS(FM)— June 3, 1985: 101.9 mhz; 50 kw. 500 ft TL: N33 37 15 W95 32 50. Stereo. Hrs open: 24 5409 90th St., Lubbock, 79424-4305. Phone: (903) 785-1068. Fax: (903) 785-7176.E-mail: jyoung@easttexasradio.com Web Site:www.easttexasradio.com Licensee: East Texas Broadcasting Inc. (group owner; acq 5-11-01; grpsl). Population served: 50,000 Pepper & Corazzini. Format: Classic rock, news. News staff: one; News: 20 hrs wkly. Target aud: 25-54. Spec prog: Farm 6 hrs wkly. ♦Bud Kitchens, pres; Jimmy Young, gen mgr; Trey Elliott, opns mgr; Jay James, progmg dir, pub affrs dir; Dave Johnson, news dir; Deanna Thorpe, traf mgr.

***KHCP(FM)**— Jan 10, 2001: 89.3 mhz; 21 kw. Ant 354 ft TL: N33 49 36 W95 27 49. Hrs open: 24 Houston Christian Broadcasters Inc, 2424 South Blvd, Houston, 77098. Phone: (713) 520-5200.E-mail: email@khcb.org Web Site:www.khcb.org Licensee: Houston Christian Broadcasters Inc. (group owner; acq 11-24-00; $3,500 for CP with CP of KKER(FM) Kerrville). Natl. Network: Moody, . Format: Christian. ♦Bruce Munsterman, gen mgr.

KOYN(FM)— Oct 6, 1988: 93.9 mhz; 50 kw. 492 ft TL: N33 49 36 W95 27 49. Stereo. Hrs open: 24 Box 1038, 75461. Secondary address: 2810 Pine Mill Rd. 75461. Phone: (903) 785-1068. Fax: (903) 785-7176.E-mail: jyoung@easttexasradio.com Web Site:www.easttexasradio.com Licensee: East Texas Broadcasting Inc. (group owner; acq 5-11-01; grpsl). Population served: 150,000 Natl. Network: USA, . Pepper & Corazzini. Format: Country. News staff: 2; News: 3 hrs wkly. Target aud: 12 plus. ♦Bud Kitchens, exec VP; Jimmy Young, gen mgr, stn mgr; Trey Elliott, opns mgr; Jay James, progmg dir; Dave Johnson, news dir; Deanna Thorpe, traf mgr.

KPLT(AM)— Nov 19, 1936: 1490 khz; 1 kw-U. TL: N33 38 07 W95 33 14. Hrs open: 24 Box 9, 75461. Secondary address: 2305 S.E. 3rd St. 75461. Phone: (903) 785-1068. Fax: (903) 785-7176. Web Site:www.kpltfm.com Licensee: East Texas Broadcasting Inc. (group owner; acq 5-11-01; grpsl). Population served: 55,000 Natl. Network: ABC, . Rgnl. Network: Texas State Net. Texas State Networks Pepper & Corazzini. Format: Classic country. Target aud: General. Spec prog: Gospel 15 hrs wkly. ♦John Mitchell, pres; Bob Gipson, exec VP, gen mgr, sls dir, gen sls mgr; Kim Good, prom dir, prom mgr; Trey Elliott, opns dir, opns mgr, progmg VP & progmg dir; Dave Johnson, news dir; Christy Storey, pub affrs dir; Bill Hughes, engrg dir, chief of engrg.

KPLT-FM— Aug 14, 1966: 107.7 mhz; 50 kw. Ant 492 ft TL: N33 44 55 W95 24 53. Hrs open: Box 9 , 75461. Secondary address: 2305 S.E. 3rd St. 75461. Phone: (903) 785-1068. Fax: (903) 785-7176. Web Site:www.kpltfm.com Population served: 150,000 Natl. Network: ABC, . Format: Hot adult contemp. Target aud: 18-35; heavy female/listen at work.

KZHN(AM)— September 1950: 1250 khz; 500 w-D, 95 w-N. TL: N33 43 21 W95 32 50. Stereo. Hrs open: 24 4140 North Main St, 75460. Secondary address: 402 Munson Ave, Rockwall 75087. Phone: (903) 784-1234. Fax: (903) 784-2344.E-mail: kzhn@koyote.com/kzhn@hughes.net Web Site:www.txn1250.com Licensee: Eiffel Tower Broadcasting (acq 10-19-2005). Natl. Network: USA, . Agrinet Rgnl rep: Eiffel Tower Broadcasting Womble-Carlyle, Sandridge & Rice. Wire Svc: AP Format: Country gold classics. News staff: 4; News: 24 hrs wkly. Target aud: 24-54+. Spec prog: Variety/diversified. ♦Larry Ryan, CEO; B.J. Clayton, gen mgr; MaryAnn Ryan, gen sls mgr; Crystal Jewel, progmg dir; Jesse Gilbert, chief of engrg.

Pasadena

***KFTG(FM)**— February 1981: 88.1 mhz; 440 w. Ant 110 ft TL: N29 40 02 W95 09 17. Hrs open: 24 912 Curtis Ave., 77502. Phone: (713) 589-1336. Fax: (713) 589-1335. Licensee: Aleluya Christian Broadcasting Inc. (acq 3-21-2003; $482,500). Population served: 250,000 Format: Southern gospel. ♦Roberto R. Villarreal, gen mgr.

KIKK(AM)— October 1957: 650 khz; 250 w-D. TL: N29 41 18 W95 10 29. Hrs open: Sunrise-sunset Suite 1900, 24 Greenway Plaza, Houston, 77046. Phone: (713) 881-5100. Fax: (713) 881-5250. Web Site:www.businessradio650.com Licensee: CBS Radio Partner I Inc. Group owner: Infinity Broadcasting Corp. (acq 10-20-93; 11-8-93). Population served: 123,280 Natl. Network: CBS, . Natl. Rep: CBS Radio,. Format: Business radio. Target aud: 25-44. ♦Laura Morris, VP, gen mgr; Josh Mednick, sls dir; Dan Blanchard, gen sls mgr, natl sls mgr; Richard Topper, natl sls mgr; Pam Kehoe, mktg dir, prom mgr; Brent Clanton, progmg dir; Dan Woodard, chief of engrg; Judy Hart, traf mgr.

KKBQ-FM— August 1962: 92.9 mhz; 100 kw. 1,919 ft TL: N29 34 34 W95 30 36. Stereo. Hrs open: 24 1990 Post Oak Blvd. #2300, Houston, 77056. Phone: (713) 961-0093. Fax: (713) 993-9300. Web Site:www.KKBQ.com Licensee: Cox Radio Inc. Group owner: Cox Broadcasting (acq 8-7-2000; grpsl). Population served: 3,458,300 Reed, Smith, Shaw & McClay. Format: Country. Target aud: 25-54. ♦Caroline Devine, gen mgr; Doug Abernethy, sls dir; Judy Lakin, gen sls mgr; Mike Murray, natl sls mgr; Bill Tatar, mktg dir; Remo Mazzini, prom dir; Christi Brooks, mus dir; Mike Mollett, pub affrs dir; Jed Wilkinson, chief of engrg; Emily Gerald, traf mgr; "Cactus Jack" Talley, disc jockey.

KKHH(FM)—See Houston

KLVL(AM)— May 5, 1950: 1480 khz; 1 kw-D, 500 w-N, DA-N. TL: N29 41 02 W95 11 09. Hrs open: 1302 N. Shepherd Dr., Houston, 77008. Phone: (713) 665-8994. Phone: (713) 868-6166. Fax: (713) 868-9631.E-mail: diddierugalde@hotmail.com Web Site:www.klvl1480.com Licensee: SIGA Broadcasting Corp. (group owner; acq 5-16-97; $1.25 million). Population served: 500,000 Format: Sp Christian, var, sports talk. Spec prog: Black 4 hrs wkly. ♦Dr. Gabriel Arango, pres; Hector Guevara, gen mgr.

Pearsall

KRIO-FM— Aug 4, 2002: 104.1 mhz; 100 kw. Ant 981 ft TL: N28 44 53 W98 50 14. Hrs open: 24 4500 Eisenhauer Rd, San Antonio, 78218. Phone: (210) 654-5100. Fax: (210) 340-1775. Licensee: BMP San Antonio License Co. L.P. (acq 7-23-2004; $10.25 million). Fletcher, Heald & Hildreth. Format: Sp contemp. ♦Lance Hawkins, gen mgr; Bob Brown, sls dir.

KSAG(FM)—Not on air, target date: unknown: 103.3 mhz; 6 kw. Ant 328 ft TL: N29 01 04 W99 09 25. Hrs open: 11700 S.W. Tangerine Ct., Palm City, FL, 34990-5801. Phone: (956) 489-1013. Licensee: Gary S. Hess (acq 11-7-2008; grpsl). ♦Gary S. Hess, gen mgr.

KVWG(AM)— Nov 3, 1962: Stn currently dark. 1280 khz; 500 w-D. TL: N28 53 13 W99 06 40. Hrs open: Box K, 78061. Secondary address: 205 S. Walnut St. 78061. Phone: (830) 334-8900. Fax: (830) 334-3448.E-mail: info@kvwg.com Licensee: Pearsall Radio Works Ltd. (acq 10-20-98; $200,000 with co-located FM). Population served: 47,000 Rgnl. Network: Texas State Net. ♦John W. Barger, pres.

Pecan Grove

KREH(AM)— 1952: 900 khz; 5 kw-D, 10 w-N, DA-2. TL: N29 38 38 W96 05 46. Hrs open: Sunrise-sunset 10613 Bellaire Blvd., Suite 900, Houston, 77072. Phone: (713) 917-0050. Fax: (713) 917-0213. Licensee: Bustos Media Holdings LLC. Group owner: Bustos Media Holdings (acq 6-11-2002). Format: Ethnic. ♦Thuy Vu, gen mgr.

Pecos

KGEE(FM)— 1999: 97.3 mhz; 300 w. Ant 70 ft TL: N31 25 07 W103 30 58. Hrs open:
Simulcast with KZBT(FM) Midland 100%.
11300 Hwy. 191, Bldg. 2, Midland, 79707. Phone: (432) 563-5636. Fax: (432) 563-3823. Web Site:www.b93.net Licensee: Cumulus Licensing LLC. (acq 6-11-2002; $1 million). Format: Hip hop, rhythm and blues. ♦George DeMarco, gen mgr.

KIUN(AM)— Oct 23, 1935: 1400 khz; 1 kw-U. TL: N31 26 09 W103 30 14. Hrs open: 24 Box 469, 79772. Phone: (432) 445-2497. Fax: (432) 445-4092.E-mail: kiun@valornet.com Web Site:www.98xfm.com Licensee: Pecos Radio Co. (acq 3-16-2006; with co-located FM). Population served: 13,000 Rgnl. Network: Texas State Net. Texas State Networks Sanchez Law Firm. Format: Country. Target aud: General. ♦Bill Cole, gen mgr, progmg dir & chief of engrg.

***KPKO(FM)**—Not on air, target date: unknown: 91.3 mhz; 20 kw. Ant 62 ft TL: N31 25 06 W103 30 55. Hrs open: Drawer 2440, Tupelo, MS, 38803-2440. Phone: (662) 844-8888. Fax: (662) 842-6791. Web Site:www.afr.net Licensee: American Family Association. Natl. Network: American Family Radio, . ♦Donald E. Wildmon, chmn.

KPTX(FM)— Aug 3, 1981: 98.3 mhz; 9.5 kw. Ant 423 ft TL: N31 29 56 W103 19 50. Stereo. Hrs open: 6 AM-10 PM Box 469, 79772. Phone: (432) 445-2497. Fax: (432) 445-4092.E-mail: info@98xfm.com Web Site:www.98xfm.com Licensee: Parday Inc. Natl. Network: ABC, . Sanchez Law Firm. Format: Adult contemp. Target aud: 25 plus; adult. ♦Bill Cole, gen mgr.

Perryton

KEYE(AM)— Nov 19, 1948: 1400 khz; 1 kw-U. TL: N36 23 20 W100 49 37. Hrs open: Box 630, 79070. Phone: (806) 435-5458. Fax: (806) 435-5393.E-mail: keye@ptsin.net Web Site:www.keye.net Licensee: Perryton Radio Inc. (acq 8-69). Population served: 40,000 Rgnl. Network: Texas State Net. Texas State Networks Format: Country. Spec prog: Farm 2 hrs, relg 3 hrs wkly. ♦Chris Samples, gen mgr, gen sls mgr, progmg dir; Lynlee Mullins, traf mgr.

KEYE-FM— January 1978: 96.1 mhz; 8.5 kw. Ant 400 ft TL: N36 21 54 W100 46 48. Stereo. Hrs open: Box 630, 79070. Phone: (806) 435-5458. Fax: (806) 435-5393.E-mail: keye@ptsin.net Web Site:www.keye.net Licensee: Perryton Radio Inc. Population served: 50,000 Format: Oldies.

Pflugerville

KOKE(AM)— 2001: 1600 khz; 5 kw-D, 700 w-N, DA-2. TL: N30 20 44 W97 32 46. Hrs open: 9434 Parkfield Dr., Austin, 78757. Phone: (512) 453-1491. Fax: (512) 834-1491. Licensee: Encino Broadcasting LLC. Group owner: Amigo Broadcasting L.P. (acq 2-15-2008; . grpsl). Format: Mexican rgnl. ♦Jose Garcia, gen mgr.

Pharr

KVJY(AM)— February 1985: 840 khz; 5 kw-D, 1 kw-N, DA-2. TL: N26 19 00 W98 06 16. Stereo. Hrs open: 1201 No. Jackson, Suite 900, McAllen, 78501. Phone: (212) 966-1059. Phone: (956) 992-8895. Fax: (956) 992-8897.E-mail: info@radiounica.com Web Site:www.radiounica.com Licensee: BMP RGV License Co. L.P. Group owner: Multicultural Radio Broadcasting Inc. (acq 3-31-2005; grpsl). Format: Country. ♦Thomas Castro, pres; Jose Luis Munoz, gen mgr; Jeff Koch, opns dir, progmg dir.

Pilot Point

KZMP-FM— Oct 17, 1983: 104.9 mhz; 15.7 kw. Ant 1,755 ft TL: N33 33 37 W96 57 34. Stereo. Hrs open: 4201 Pool Rd., Coleyville, 76034. Phone: (817) 868-2900. Fax: (817) 868-2929. Licensee: Liberman Broadcasting of Dallas License LLC. Group owner: Entravision Communications Corp. (acq 11-2-2006; grpsl). Population served: 6,153,500 Format: Ethnic. ♦Rosa Cuellar, gen mgr.

Pittsburg

KDVE(FM)— Dec 15, 1986: 103.1 mhz; 10 kw. Ant 672 ft TL: N32 52 50 W94 58 13. Stereo. Hrs open: 24 Box 1648, Jacksonville, 75766. Secondary address: 402 S. Ragsdale, Jacksonville 75766. Phone: (903) 586-2527. Fax: (903) 589-0677.E-mail: dudleyw@wallerboradcasting.com Licensee: Waller Media LLC. (group owner; (acq 8-24-2005; $975,000 with KXAL-FM Tatum). Population served: 280,000 Format: Sp adult contemp. News staff: one; News: 6 hrs wkly. ♦Dudley Waller, gen mgr.

***KGWP(FM)**— 2003: 91.1 mhz; 800 w vert. Ant 128 ft TL: N33 01 41 W95 02 57. Stereo. Hrs open: 24 1511 Jefferson Ave., Mount Pleasant, 75455. Phone: (951) 675-8661. Fax: (903) 575-1984. Licensee: Andres Serranos Ministries Inc. (acq 4-5-2006; $83,332). Format: Christian Sp contemp. News staff: one; News: 10 hrs wkly. Target aud: 30-55 plus. ♦Rafael Garcia, pres.

***KPIT(FM)**— 2008: 91.7 mhz; 450 w vert. Ant 131 ft TL: N33 02 45.5 W95 03 23.2. Hrs open: 1039 CR 2920, 75686. Phone: (903) 466-6791. Licensee: Millennium Broadcasting Corp. ♦James Furlow, pres.

KSCN(FM)— Mar 1, 1999: 96.9 mhz; 14 kw. 390 ft TL: N33 00 31 W95 04 14. Stereo. Hrs open: 24 Box 990, Mount Pleasant, 75456. Secondary address: 1798 US Hwy. 67 W., Mount Pleasant 75455. Phone: (903) 572-8726. Fax: (903) 572-7232.E-mail: bud@easttexasradio.com Web Site:www.easttexasradio.com Licensee: East Texas Broadcasting Inc. (group owner). Population served: 68,000 Format: Country. News staff: 2; News: 3 hrs wkly. Target aud: 25-54; general. ♦John Mitchell, chmn; Bud Kitchens, pres, gen mgr;

Bryan Friesth, gen sls mgr; Darrin Tripp, progmg dir; Clint Cooper, news dir, pub affrs dir; Bill Hughes, chief of engrg; Justice Thornburg, traf mgr.

Plains

*KPHS(FM)— Nov 14, 1977: 90.3 mhz; 220 w. 135 ft TL: N33 11 16 W102 49 20. Hrs open: 8:30 AM-3:15 PM Box 479, 79355. Phone: (806) 456-7401. Fax: (806) 456-4325. Licensee: Plains Independent School District. Format: Educ. ◆Rennetta O'Quinn, gen mgr.

Plainview

*KBAH(FM)— Mar 18, 2004: 90.5 mhz; 75 kw. Ant 426 ft TL: N34 03 58 W101 42 16. Hrs open: Box 3206, Tupelo, MS, 38803. Phone: (662) 844-8888 ext. 204.E-mail: info@kbahfm.com Web Site:afr.net Licensee: American Family Association. Group owner: American Family Radio Population served: 285,000 Format: Christian classics. ◆Marvin Sanders, gen mgr.

KKYN-FM— 1987: 106.9 mhz; 50 kw. Ant 469 ft TL: N34 15 47 W101 40 30. Stereo. Hrs open: 24 Prog sep from AM 3218 N. Quincy, 79072. Secondary address: Box 147 79073. Phone: (806) 296-2771. Fax: (806) 293-5732. Web Site:www.kkyn.net Licensee: Rhattigan Broadcasting (Texas) LP Format: Country. News staff: one; News: 5 hrs wkly. Target aud: 35 plus. ◆Michael Rhattigan, gen mgr; Jerry Larsen, stn mgr; Brandy Haines, progmg dir; Tom Hall, opns mgr, mktg dir, prom dir & pub affrs dir; Dana Huggin, traf mgr.

*KPMB(FM)—Not on air, target date: unknown: 88.5 mhz; 3 kw. Ant 282 ft TL: N34 13 14 W101 42 52. Hrs open: Box 252, McAllen, 78505. Phone: (956) 686-6382. Fax: (956) 686-2999. Licensee: Paulino Bernal Evangelism. Format: Sp relg.

KREW(AM)— Aug 14, 1944: 1400 khz; 1 kw-U. TL: N34 12 20 W101 42 59. Hrs open: 24 3218 N. Quincy, 79072. Secondary address: Box 1420 79072. Phone: (806) 293-2661. Fax: (806) 293-5732. Web Site:kkyn.net Licensee: Rhattigan Broadcasting (Texas) LP (group owner; (acq 8-19-2004; grpsl). Population served: 60,000 Rgnl. Network: Texas State Net. Texas State Networks Wire Svc: AP Format: Sp, oldies. News: 7 hrs wkly. Target aud: Adults 35+; baby boomers. ◆Michael Rhattigan, gen mgr; Brandy Haines, progmg dir; Tom Hall, stn mgr, opns mgr & news dir; Dana Huggins, traf mgr.

KRIA(FM)— 1999: 106.9 mhz; 50 kw. 469 ft TL: N34 15 47 W101 40 30. Hrs open: 3218 N. Quincy, 79072. Secondary address: Box 1420 79073. Phone: (806) 293-2661. Fax: (806) 293-5732. Web Site:kkyn.net Licensee: Rhattigan Broadcasting (Texas) LP Natl. Network: CSN, . Fisher, Wayland, Cooper, Leader & Zaragoza. Format: Classic rock. News: 10 hrs wkly. Target aud: Hispanic; 18-49. ◆Michael Rhattigan, CEO, gen mgr; Tom Hall, opns mgr.

KVOP(AM)— Oct 1, 1974: 1090 khz; 5 kw-D, 500 w-N, DA-2. TL: N34 05 32 W101 38 26. Hrs open: 24 3218 N. Quincy, 79072. Secondary address: Box 147 79073. Phone: (806) 296-2771. Fax: (806) 293-5732. Licensee: Rhattigan Broadcasting (Texas) LP (group owner; (acq 8-19-2004; grpsl). Natl. Rep: Katz Radio,. Format: Talk/Sports. News: 10 hrs wkly. Target aud: Adults; 25-54. Spec prog: Farm 12 hrs wkly. ◆Michael Rhattigan, gen mgr; Brandy Haines, progmg dir; Tom Hall, opns mgr & news dir.

*KWLD(FM)— 1952: 91.5 mhz; 370 w. 105 ft TL: N34 11 14 W101 43 32. Stereo. Hrs open: 24 1900 W. 7th St., #230, ., PLainview, 79072. Phone: (806) 291-1091. Fax: (806) 291-1963.E-mail: kwld@wbu.edu Web Site:www.wbu.edu Licensee: Wayland Baptist University. Population served: 40,000 Natl. Network: USA, . Format: CHR, Christian music, jazz. News: 14 hrs wkly. Target aud: 15-30; high school through college, young adult, afternoon & evening. ◆Paul Armes, pres; Jim Smith, CFO; Bill Hardage, exec VP; Betty Donaldson, VP; Steve Long, gen mgr; Paul Sutton, stn mgr, progmg dir; David Carr, chief of engrg.

Plano

KMKI(AM)— July 15, 1999: 620 khz; 5 kw-D, 4.5 kw-N, DA-2. TL: N33 14 34 W96 32 29. Stereo. Hrs open: 24 2221 E. Lamar Blvd., Suite 300, Arlington, 76006. Phone: (817) 695-1333. Fax: (817) 695-3556. Web Site:www.radiodisney.com Licensee: Radio Disney Dallas LLC. Group owner: ABC Inc. (acq 9-4-98; $12.1 million). Population served: 2,000,000 Natl. Network: Radio Disney, . Natl. Rep: Interep,. Format: Top-40. Target aud: 6-12; 25-49; women adults. ◆Jamie Ramsey, stn mgr; Molly Bunker, prom dir.

Pleasant Valley

KZAM(FM)— 2008: 98.7 mhz; 6 kw. Ant 318 ft TL: N34 02 54 W98 39 38. Hrs open: Box 880, Roma, 78584. Phone: (956) 487-8015. Licensee: South Texas FM Investments LLC. (acq 9-16-2008; grpsl). ◆Eloy Vera, gen mgr.

Pleasanton

*KWMF(AM)— Feb 8, 1951: 1380 khz; 4 kw-D, 160 w-N, DA-D. TL: N29 00 00 W98 31 50. Hrs open: 24 hrs 1903 S. Lamesa Rd., Midland, 79701-1706. Secondary address: 3308 Broadway, San Antonio 78209. Phone: (210) 821-5050. Fax: (432) 684-5588.E-mail: robertd@grnonline.com Web Site:www.grnonline.com Licensee: La Promesa Foundation. Group owner: Border Media Partners LLC (acq 12-13-2006; grpsl). Population served: 30,000 Natl. Network: EWTN Radio, . Rgnl. Network: Texas State Net. Format: Catholic, Sp. ◆Robert Dominguez, gen mgr.

Point Comfort

KJAZ(FM)— Dec 10, 1998: 94.1 mhz; 25 kw. 194 ft TL: N28 46 08 W96 42 39. Stereo. Hrs open: 24 102 Jason Plaza, Suite 2, Victoria, 77901. Phone: (361) 572-0105. Fax: (361) 798-3798. Licensee: Roy E. Henderson. Group owner: Fort Bend Broadcasting Co. (acq 4-13-2001; $400,000). Format: Classic rock. Target aud: Baby boomers; active, affluent adults. ◆Ryan Henderson, gen mgr & progmg dir.

Port Arthur

*KDEI(AM)— August 1934: 1250 khz; 5 kw-D, 1 kw-N, DA-N. TL: N29 57 04 W93 52 46. Hrs open: 24 601 Washington St., Alexandria, LA, 71301. Phone: (318) 561-6145. Fax: (318) 449-9954.E-mail: info.usa@radiomaria.org Web Site:www.radiomaria.us Licensee: Radio Maria Inc. (group owner; acq 9-20-99). Population served: 57,371 Natl. Network: American Urban, . Format: Christian, Relg, talk. News: 10.5 hrs wkly. Target aud: General; isolated and under-represented groups in society, sick, elderly etc. ◆Dale DePerrodil, gen sls mgr; Duane Stenzel, gen mgr & progmg dir; Danny Brou, chief of engrg, disc jockey.

KOLE(AM)— 1947: 1340 khz; 1 kw-U. TL: N29 54 15 W93 56 10. Hrs open: 24 27 Sawyer St., Beaumont, 77702. Phone: (409) 835-2222. Phone: (866) 835-1340. Fax: (409) 832-5686.E-mail: sima@birach.com Web Site:www.birach.com/kole.htm Licensee: Birach Broadcasting Corp. (acq 3-20-2008; $450,000). Population served: 57,371 Natl. Network: USA, Fox News Radio, Talk Radio Network, . Texas State Networks Law Office of Lauren A. Colby. Format: News/talk. News staff: 2; News: 40 hrs wkly. Target aud: 25 plus. ◆Sima Birach, pres; Ralph McBride, gen mgr; Brent Bobbitt, gen sls mgr; Dominick Brascia, progmg dir, progmg mgr; John St.John, news dir; Jeff Roberts, pub affrs dir; Russ Ingram, chief of engrg, engr; Jeanette Harvey, traf mgr.

KQBU-FM—Licensed to Port Arthur. See Houston

KTJM(FM)— Apr 15, 1963: 98.5 mhz; 100 kw. Ant 1,952 ft TL: N30 03 05 W94 31 37. Stereo. Hrs open: 3000 Bering Dr., Houston, 77057. Phone: (713) 315-3400. Fax: (713) 315-3405. Web Site:www.laraza.fm Licensee: Liberman Broadcasting of Houston License LLC. Group owner: Liberman Broadcasting Inc. (acq 3-20-2001; grpsl). Format: Rgnl Mexican. ◆Heraldo Reyes, gen mgr & stn mgr.

Port Isabel

KNVO-FM— 1992: 101.1 mhz; 3 kw. Ant 360 ft TL: N25 57 52 W97 14 38. Stereo. Hrs open: 24 801 Jackson Rd., McAllen, 78501. Phone: (956) 661-6000. Fax: (956) 661-6081.E-mail: msomonth@entravision.com Licensee: Entravision Holdings L.L.C. Group owner: Entravision Communications Co. L.L.C. (acq 7-20-2000; grpsl). Population served: 350,000 Natl. Network: Westwood One, . Fletcher, Heald & Hildreth. Format: Sp contemp. News staff: one; News: one hr wkly. Target aud: 25-55. ◆Willie Rosales, gen mgr & gen sls mgr; Mando Sanroman, progmg dir; Sonny Cabazos, chief of engrg; Dora Borjas, traf mgr.

Port Lavaca

KITE(FM)—Licensed to Port Lavaca. See Victoria

Port Neches

KBPO(AM)— June 13, 1959: 1150 khz; 500 w-D, 63 w-N, DA-2. TL: N30 04 45 W93 57 05. Hrs open: Box 1290, Weslaco, 78599. Phone: (956) 968-7777. Fax: (956) 968-5143.E-mail: egarza@radiovida.com Web Site:www.radiovida.com Licensee: Vision Latina Broadcasting Inc. (acq 9-8-93; $75,000; 9-27-93). Population served: 27,000 Format: Sp, relg. ◆Enrique Garza, gen mgr.

Port O'Connor

*KHPO(FM)— 2007: 91.9 mhz; 4 kw. Ant 308 ft TL: N28 25 44 W96 26 54. Hrs open:
Rebroadcasts KHCB-FM Houston 95%.
2424 South Blvd., Houston, 77098-5110. Phone: (713) 520-5200. Web Site:www.khcb.org Licensee: Houston Christian Broadcasters Inc. Natl. Network: Moody, . Format: Christian. News: 6 hrs wkly. ◆Bruce Munsterman, pres.

Portland

KMJR(FM)— Dec 15, 1979: 105.5 mhz; 1.9 kw. 354 ft TL: N27 47 48 W97 23 51. Stereo. Hrs open: 24 1300 Antelope, Corpus Christi, 78401. Phone: (361) 883-1600. Fax: (361) 888-5685. Licensee: Tejas Broadcasting Ltd. LLP. Group owner: Amigo Broadcasting L.P. (acq 11-15-2004; grpsl). Format: Rgnl Mexican. Target aud: 18-49; general. ◆Eddie Alonzo, gen mgr; Julie Garza, progmg dir; Lon Gonzalez, news dir; Henry Turner, chief of engrg; Debbie Reid, traf mgr.

KOUL(FM)—See Corpus Christi

*KSGR(FM)— October 2000: 91.1 mhz; 3 kw. Ant 298 ft TL: N28 00 06 W97 15 01. Hrs open: 3001 Rodd Field Rd., Corpus Christi, 78414. Phone: (361) 814-7775. Fax: (361) 814-7779.E-mail: info@ksgr.org Web Site:www.ksgr.org Licensee: Coastlands Radio Inc. (group owner; (acq 7-25-2008; $120,000). Format: Contemp Christian. ◆Jim Sheperd, gen mgr.

Post

KGCE(FM)— May 1, 1991: 107.3 mhz; 22 kw. Ant 748 ft TL: N33 13 23 W101 26 26. Hrs open: 24 2351 Sunset Blvd., Suite 170-218, Rocklin, CA, 95765. Phone: (916) 251-1600. Fax: (916) 251-1650. Web Site:www.godscountryradionetwork.com Licensee: Educational Media Foundation. Group owner: EMF Broadcasting (acq 5-21-2004; $550,000). Population served: 200,000 Format: Country, gospel. ◆Richard Jenkins, pres; Mike Novak, VP, progmg dir; Lloyd Parker, gen mgr; Ed Lenane, opns dir, news dir; Keith Whipple, dev dir; Eric Allen, natl sls mgr; David Pierce, progmg mgr; Jon Rivers, mus dir; Sam Wallington, engrg dir; Arthur Vassar, traf mgr; Karen Johnson, news rptr.

Prairie View

*KPVU(FM)— Nov 26, 1981: 91.3 mhz; 98.3 kw. 410 ft TL: N30 05 21 W95 59 46. Stereo. Hrs open: 24 P.O. Box 519, Mail Stop 1415, 77446. Phone: (936) 261-3769. Fax: (936) 261-3769.E-mail: kpvu_fm@pvamu.edu Web Site:www.pvamu.edu/kpvu Licensee: Prairie View A&M University. Population served: 250,000 Natl. Network: NPR, . Format: Smooth jazz, adult contemp, gospel. News staff: News progmg 14 hrs wkly Target aud: 18 plus. Spec prog: Black 6 hrs wkly. ◆Cheryl Granger Brooks, gen mgr; Jeffrey Kelley, progmg dir; Dave Cassels, chief of engrg; Leonard Moon, news dir & sports cmtr.

Premont

KMFM(FM)— 1989: 104.9 mhz; 3 kw. 299 ft TL: N27 22 19 W98 11 21. (CP: 100.7 mhz, 25 kw, ant 285 ft. TL: N27 28 30 W98 03 23). Hrs open: Box 252, McAllen, 78502. Phone: (956) 686-6382. Fax: (956) 686-2999. Licensee: Radio Cristiana Network. Format: Sp, relg. ◆Eloy Bernal, gen mgr; Paulino Bernal Jr., stn mgr & progmg mgr; John Ross, chief of engrg.

Presidio

KHUA(AM)—Not on air, target date: unknown: 1230 khz; 800 w-D, 710 w-N. TL: N29 36 00 W104 25 14. Hrs open: 8320 W. 66th Ave., Arvada, CO, 80004. Phone: (303) 431-0103. Licensee: Better Life Ministries. ◆Claud Pettit, pres.

Quanah

KOLJ(AM)— May 11, 1951: 1150 khz; 500 w-D, DA. TL: N34 18 58 W99 44 49. Hrs open: 6 AM-sunset Box 396, 79252-0396. Phone: (940) 663-5711. Fax: (940) 663-2125.E-mail: john@radio1150.net Web Site:www.radio1150.net Licensee: John L. White (group owner; (acq 9-15-2008; $5,000). Population served: 85,000 Format: Classic country. Target aud: General. ◆John White, stn mgr.

KWFB(FM)— Sept 1, 1982: 100.9 mhz; 50 kw. Ant 492 ft N34 15 21 W99 30 05. Stereo. Hrs open: 24 719 Scott Ave., Suite 1009, Wichita Falls, 76301. Phone: (940) 322-1009. Fax: (940) 767-3299.E-mail: kixc@broadcast.net Web Site:www.bobradio.fm Licensee: KIXC-FM L.L.C. Format: Var. News: 10 hrs wkly. Target aud: General. Spec prog: Farm 3 hrs, relg 2 hrs wkly. ◆Glen Ingram, pres, gen sls mgr; Michael Reeves, gen mgr; John White, opns dir, progmg dir.

Ralls

KCLR(AM)— May 31, 1963: 1530 khz; 5 kw-D, 1 kw-CH. TL: N33 40 00 W101 22 44. Hrs open: Box 252, McAllen, 78505. Phone: (956) 686-6382. Fax: (956) 686-2999.E-mail: paulinobernal@hotmail.com Web Site:www.laradiocristiana.com Licensee: Paulino Bernal (acq 10-19-2001). Population served: 1,962 Format: Sp, Christian. ◆Paulino Bernal, gen mgr; Eloy Bernal, stn mgr; Pete Guzman, opns mgr.

Ranger

KCUB-FM— July 1, 1990: 98.5 mhz; 5.8 kw. Ant 335 ft TL: N32 20 48 W98 42 50. Stereo. Hrs open: 24 471 N. Harbin Dr., Suite 102, Stephenville, 76401. Phone: (254) 968-7459. Fax: (254) 968-6258.E-mail: john@mandatoryfm.com Web Site:www.mandatoryfm.com Licensee: Mandatory Broadcasting Inc. (acq 5-17-2007; $600,000). Natl. Network: Jones Radio Networks, . Rgnl. Network: Texas State Net. Texas Networks Format: Texas country. News staff: 0. Target aud: 20-65; all-important age group of today's buying public. ◆John Hollinger, gen mgr; Jon Gibson, gen sls mgr & progmg dir; Jim Rhodes, chief of engrg.

Raymondville

KBIC(FM)— October 1996: 105.7 mhz; 1.8 kw. Ant 426 ft TL: N26 26 37 W97 42 08. Hrs open: 24 Box 1290, Weslaco, 78599. Phone: (956) 968-7777. Fax: (956) 968-5143.E-mail: info@radiovida.com Web Site:www.radiovida.com Licensee: Christian Ministries of the Valley Inc. (acq 2-4-93; 3-1-93). Format: Sp, relg. ◆Enrique Garza, gen mgr.

KBUC(FM)— 1979: 102.1 mhz; 17.9 kw. Ant 758 ft TL: N26 38 09 W97 50 10. Stereo. Hrs open: 6 AM-midnight Dups AM 100% 1201 N. Jackson Rd., Suite 900, McAllen, 78501. Phone: (956) 992-8895. Fax: (956) 992-8897. Licensee: BMP RGV License Company L.P. Group owner: Border Media Partners LLC (acq 5-30-2003; $8 million with KBDR(FM) Mirando City). Format: Regional Mexican. ◆Jose Luis Munoz, gen mgr; Rogelio Botelleo Rios, opns mgr; Maria Alvarez, gen sls mgr; Joe Espinoza, chief of engrg; Angela Pina, traf mgr.

KSOX(AM)— June 1, 1957: 1240 khz; 1 kw-U. TL: N26 27 28 W97 46 55. Hrs open: 6 AM-midnight 2921 North Closner, Edinburg, 78541. Phone: (956) 992-8895. Fax: (956) 992-8897. Licensee: BMP RGV License Co. L.P. Group owner: Border Media Partners LLC (acq 2-6-2004; $7.5 million with KURV(AM) Edinburg). Population served: 7,987 Format: Sports. Target aud: 25-55. ◆Angela Pina, traf mgr.

Refugio

KTKY(FM)— Oct 5, 1979: Stn currently dark. 106.1 mhz; 25 kw. Ant 328 ft TL: N28 08 15 W97 12 45. (CP: COL Taft. 50 kw, ant 446 ft. TL: N27 52 00 W97 13 08). Stereo. Hrs open: 710 Buffalo St., Suite 608, Corpus Christi, 78401. Phone: (314) 345-1030. Phone: (361) 882-5749. Fax: (361) 884-1240.E-mail: jim@koplar.com Licensee: Pacific Broadcasting of Missouri L.L.C. (acq 4-24-98; $725,000). Population served: 400,000 ◆James G. Withers, gen mgr.

Reno

KLOW(FM)— 2009: 98.9 mhz; 5.9 kw. Ant 331 ft TL: N33 38 54 W95 36 12. Hrs open: 1305 S. Glenburnie Rd., New Bern, NC, 28562. Phone: (252) 636-3333. Fax: (252) 633-3997. Web Site:paris.bigfishfm.com Licensee: Tower Investment Trust Inc. Format: Contemp Christian. ◆Bill Brothers, gen mgr; Blake Larson, opns mgr.

Richardson

KKLF(AM)— 1999: 1700 khz; 10 kw-D, 1 kw-N. TL: N33 25 23 W96 39 45. Hrs open: Rebroadcasts KTCK(AM) Dallas 100%. 3500 Maple Ave., Suite 1310, Dallas, 75219. Phone: (214) 526-7400. Fax: (214) 525-2525. Web Site:www.theticket.com Licensee: KRBE Lico Inc. Group owner: Susquehanna Radio Corp. (acq 4-30-98). Format: Sports.

Richmond

KAMA-FM—See Houston

KRTX(AM)—See Houston

Rio Grande City

KQBO(FM)— April 1985: 107.5 mhz; 1.41 kw. 420 ft TL: N26 25 47 W98 49 25. Stereo. Hrs open: 5 AM-midnight 102 KCTM-FM 103 Rd., 78582-9805. Phone: (956) 487-8224. Fax: (815) 361-6185.E-mail: info@kqbofm.com Licensee: Gustavo Valadez Jr. (acq 6-13-03). Format: Latin pop. News: 5 hrs wkly. Target aud: 18-45. ◆Gustavo "Gus" Valadez Jr., pres.

KRGX(FM)—Not on air, target date: unknown: 95.1 mhz; 6 kw. Ant 328 ft TL: N26 26 04.9 W98 55 45.3. Hrs open: 2768 Pharmacy Rd., 78582. Phone: (956) 487-5621. Licensee: James Falcon. ◆James Falcon, gen mgr.

Robinson

KHCK-FM— Nov 1, 1972: 107.9 mhz; 6 kw. Ant 328 ft TL: N31 30 33 W97 10 03. Stereo. Hrs open: 24 10801 N. Mopac Expwy. 2-250, Austin, 78759-5457. Phone: (512) 340-7100. Phone: (214) 525-0400. Web Site:www.univision.com Licensee: KICI-FM License Corp. Group owner: Univision Radio (acq 9-22-2003; grpsl). Population served: 35,000 Format: Mexican, rgnl. Target aud: 18-54. ◆Tim McCoy, gen mgr; Randall Garcia, gen sls mgr; Alejandro Covarrubias, progmg dir; Samantha Martinez, traf mgr.

Robstown

*KLUX(FM)— Mar 17, 1985: 89.5 mhz; 60 kw. Ant 954 ft TL: N27 46 50 W97 38 03. Stereo. Hrs open: 24 1200 Lantana, Corpus Christi, 78407. Phone: (361) 289-2487. Fax: (361) 289-1420.E-mail: klux@goccn.org Web Site:www.klux.org Licensee: Diocesan Telecommunications Corp. Population served: 500,000 Natl. Network: USA, . Ross & Hardies. Format: Easy lstng. News staff: one; News: 13 hrs wkly. Target aud: 35 plus; total persons. Spec prog: Sp 3 hrs wkly. ◆Rev. Msgr. Michael Howell, chmn; Marty Wind, exec VP, gen mgr; Russ Martin, opns mgr & progmg dir.

KMIQ(FM)—Licensed to Robstown. See Corpus Christi

KROB(AM)— Feb 22, 1963: 1510 khz; 500 w-D. TL: N27 46 39 W97 37 55. Hrs open: 400 SPID, Suite 107, Corpus Christi, 78405. Phone: (361) 299-6000. Fax: (361) 299-6002.E-mail: krobam1510@sbcglobal.net Licensee: B Communications Joint Venture. (acq 1-4-2002). Format: Spanish Oldies. Target aud: 25-54. ◆Jerry Benavides, pres; Jerry Benevides, gen mgr; Ben Benavides, sls dir; Bob Pena, progmg dir; Gary Graham, chief of engrg; Peter Hemphill, traf mgr.

KSAB(FM)— Oct 13, 1966: 99.9 mhz; 96 kw. 955 ft TL: N27 44 28 W97 36 08. Stereo. Hrs open: 501 Tupper Ln., Radio Plaza, Corpus Christi, 78417. Phone: (361) 289-0111. Fax: (361) 289-5035.E-mail: ksabfm@aol.com Web Site:www.ksabfm.com Licensee: Capstar TX L.P. Group owner: Clear Channel Communications Inc. (acq 8-30-00; grpsl). Format: Tejano, Sp. ◆Matt Martin, gen mgr; Dan Pena, prom dir, progmg dir.

Rockdale

KRXT(FM)— Feb 27, 1989: 98.5 mhz; 6 kw. 328 ft TL: N30 38 32 W97 02 13. Stereo. Hrs open: 24 hrs 1095 W. Highway 79, 76567. Phone: (512) 446-6985. Fax: (512) 446-6987.E-mail: krxtl@farm-market.net Web Site:www.krxt.com Licensee: KRXT Inc. Rgnl. Network: Texas State Net. Texas State Networks Format: Country. News staff: one; News: 20 hrs wkly. Target aud: General. ◆Charles W. McGregor, pres, gen mgr & stn mgr.

Rockport

KKPN(FM)— October 1986: 102.3 mhz; 50 kw. 371 ft TL: N28 00 03 W97 04 34. Stereo. Hrs open: 24 826 S. Padre Island Dr., Corpus Christi, 78416. Phone: (361) 814-3800. Fax: (361) 855-3770. Web Site:info@planet1023.com Licensee: Convergent Broadcasting Corpus Christi LP. Group owner: Convergent Broadcasting LLC (acq 1-12-2004; grpsl). Population served: 313,600 Format: CHR/Top40. Target aud: Adult; 18-49. ◆Mark White, gen mgr; Dallas Garcia, gen sls mgr, adv mgr; Scott Holt, progmg dir; William Hooper, chief of engrg.

KTKY(FM)—See Refugio

Rocksprings

KDRX(FM)—Not on air, target date: unknown: 106.9 mhz; 50 kw. Ant 492 ft TL: N29 58 30 W100 25 15. Hrs open: 819 S.W. Federal Hwy., Suite 106, Stuart, FL, 34994. Phone: (772) 286-5586. Licensee: William H. Brothers. ◆William H. Brothers, gen mgr.

KHES(FM)—Not on air, target date: unknown: 92.5 mhz; 25 kw. Ant 328 ft TL: N29 58 34 W100 25 00. Hrs open: 11700 S.W. Tangerine Ct., Palm City, FL, 34990. Phone: (772) 215-1634.E-mail: info@toweritrust.com Licensee: Gary S. Hess. ◆Gary S. Hess, gen mgr.

Rollingwood

KJCE(AM)—Licensed to Rollingwood. See Austin

Roma

KBMI(FM)— Apr 30, 1983: 97.7 mhz; 3 kw. 298 ft TL: N26 24 22 W99 00 37. Hrs open: 18 1201 N. Jackson Rd., Suite 900, McAllen, 78501. Phone: (956) 992-8895. Fax: (956) 992-8897. Licensee: Horizon Broadcasting Inc. (acq 10-26-98; $119,742). Population served: 50,000 Natl. Network: CNN Radio, . Format: Country. Target aud: General; Sp speaking audience. ◆Arturo Gonzalez, gen mgr, progmg dir & chief of engrg.

Rosenberg-Richmond

KRTX(AM)—Licensed to Rosenberg-Richmond. See Houston

Round Rock

KFMK(FM)— October 1998: 105.9 mhz; 4.5 kw. 1,302 ft TL: N30 19 23 W97 47 58. Hrs open: 3601 South Congress, Bldg. F, Austin, 78704. Phone: (512) 684-7300. Fax: (512) 684-7441. Web Site:www.jammin1059.com Licensee: Aloha Station Trust LLC Group owner: Clear Channel Communications Inc. (acq 7-30-2008; grpsl). Format: Rhythmic adult contemp. ◆Mack Daniels, chief of opns; Mel Jones, sls dir; Melody Caldwell, gen sls mgr; Tracy Walker, mktg dir; Pam McKay, mktg mgr; Gil Garcia, chief of engrg.

*KNLE-FM— Aug 17, 1981: 88.1 mhz; 3 kw. 233 ft TL: N30 26 58 W98 48 48. Stereo. Hrs open: 24 Box 907, 78759. Secondary address: 12703 Research Dr., Suite 222, Austin 78759. Phone: (512) 257-8881. Fax: (512) 257-8880.E-mail: webmaster@candle88.com Web Site:www.candle88.com Licensee: Ixoye Productions Inc. (acq 6-23-03). Population served: 1,000,000 Format: Adult contemp, CHR. News: 6 hrs wkly. Target aud: 18-49; primarily female. Spec prog: Children 4 hrs wkly. ◆Sherland Priest, gen mgr, progmg dir, news dir & chief of engrg.

KZNX(AM)—See Creedmoor

Rudolph

*KTER(FM)—Not on air, target date: unknown: 90.7 mhz; 2.4 kw. 282 ft TL: N26 41 13 W97 45 52. Hrs open: 24 Faith Pleases God Church Corp., 4501 West Expwy. 83, Harlingen, 78552. Phone: (956) 412-5600. Fax: (956) 428-7556. Licensee: Faith Pleases God Church Corp. Format: Educ, Christian, Sp. Target aud: General. Spec prog: Children 4 hrs wkly. ◆Aracelis Ortiz, CEO; Clark Ortiz, pres; Ricardo Mejia, gen mgr; Tonya Porter, opns VP.

Rusk

KTLU(AM)— 1955: 1580 khz; 840 w-D, 165 w-N. TL: N31 49 12 W95 10 19. Hrs open: 24 Box 475, 75785. Secondary address: 618 N. Main St. 75785. Phone: (903) 586-7771. Phone: (903) 683-2257. Fax: (903) 683-5104.E-mail: kwrw@mediactr.com Licensee: E.H. Whitehead. Population served: 20,000 Natl. Network: ABC, . Rgnl. Network: Texas State Net. Texas State Networks Format: Oldies. News staff: one; News: 3 hrs wkly. Target aud: 35-65. Spec prog: Sp 10 hrs wkly. ♦Marie Whitehead, pres; Robert Gonzalez, gen mgr.

KWRW(FM)— July 1, 1981: 97.7 mhz; 14.5 kw. 407 ft TL: N31 49 12 W95 10 19. Stereo. Hrs open: 24 Dup AM 99% Box 475, 75785. Secondary address: 618 N. Main St. 75785. Phone: (903) 586-7771. Fax: (903) 683-5104. Population served: 400,000 Target aud: 25-54. Spec prog: Sp 10 hrs wkly.

San Angelo

KCLL(FM)— Aug 17, 1995: 100.1 mhz; 50 kw. Ant 385 ft TL: N31 31 49 W100 29 05. Hrs open: 24 2824 Sherwood Way, 76901. Phone: (325) 949-2112. Fax: (325) 944-0851.E-mail: kyzzfm@cs.com Web Site:www.kcll-fm.com Licensee: Foster Communications Co. Inc. (group owner; (acq 5-19-2004; $450,000). Format: Tejano. Target aud: 18-49; Hispanics, demographics. ♦Fred M. Key, pres; Audrey Carver Luna, gen mgr, natl sls mgr, prom mgr, pub affrs dir; Wilburn Luna, CFO & opns mgr; Doug Smith, gen sls mgr; Freddy Maskill, prom mgr; Juan Vela, progmg dir, progmg mgr; Jeff Rottman, news dir; Richard Whitworth, chief of engrg; Freddy Maskill, traf mgr.

KCRN(AM)— 1947: 1340 khz; 1 kw-U. TL: N31 28 43 W100 27 50. Hrs open: 24 Box 32, 76902-0032. Secondary address: 17 S. Chadbourne, Suite 500 76903. Phone: (325) 655-6917. Fax: (325) 655-7806. Web Site:www.kcrn.org Licensee: Criswell College (group owner; Population served: 100,000 News: 2 hrs wkly. Target aud: 35-54; adults with children in the home. ♦Mark Mohr, gen mgr; Keith Mayo, chief of engrg.

KCRN-FM— Feb 1, 1965: 93.9 mhz; 100 kw. Ant 649 ft TL: N31 42 11 W100 19 20. Stereo. Hrs open: 24 Box 32, 76902-0032. Secondary address: 17 S. Chadbourne, Suite 500 76903. Phone: (325) 655-6917. Fax: (325) 655-7806.E-mail: kcrn@kcrn.org Web Site:www.kcrn.org Licensee: Criswell College (acq 6-18-91; $350,000 with co-located AM;7-8-91). Population served: 200,000 Format: Inspirational Christian, relg. News: 2 hrs wkly. Target aud: 25 plus. ♦Mark Mohr, gen mgr; Keith Mayo, chief of engrg.

KDCD(FM)— June 1, 1980: 92.9 mhz; 100 kw. Ant 729 ft TL: N31 26 08 W100 34 08. Stereo. Hrs open: 3434 Sherwood Way, 76901. Phone: (325) 947-0899. Fax: (325) 947-0996.E-mail: terry.radio@lonestarmix.com Web Site:www.texaslonestarcountry.com Licensee: Four R Broadcasting Inc. (acq 1-11-2007; $1.5 million with KMDX(FM) San Angelo). Population served: 180,000 Format: Young country. Target aud: 18-49. Spec prog: Relg 2 hrs wkly. ♦Frank A. De Francesco, pres; Terry Hucks, gen mgr.

KELI(FM)— November 1986: 98.7 mhz; 100 kw. Ant 1,290 ft TL: N31 22 01 W100 02 48. Stereo. Hrs open: 24 1301 S. Abe St., 76903. Phone: (325) 655-7161. Fax: (325) 658-7377. Web Site:www.bob987.com Licensee: Double O Texas Corp. Group owner: Encore Broadcasting LLC (acq 3-15-2006; grpsl). Format: Adult hits. News staff: one; News: 6 hrs wkly. Target aud: 25-54. Spec prog: Relg 6 hrs wkly. ♦John Kerr, exec VP, gen mgr, adv dir; Randy Phair, gen sls mgr; Garry Vaughn, prom mgr, engr; Boomer Kingston, progmg dir.

KGKL(AM)— Dec 4, 1928: 960 khz; 5 kw-D, 1 kw-N, DA-N. TL: N31 29 39 W100 24 55. Hrs open: Box 1878, 76902. Secondary address: 1301 S. Abe 76903. Phone: (325) 655-7161. Fax: (325) 658-7377. Web Site:960kgkl.com Licensee: Double O Texas Corp. Group owner: Encore Broadcasting LLC (acq 3-15-2006; grpsl). Population served: 100,000 Natl. Rep: Katz Radio,. Format: News, talk, sports. News: 10 hrs wkly. Target aud: 35 plus. Spec prog: Farm 6 hrs wkly. ♦John Kerr, gen mgr; Boomer Kingsten, opns mgr.

KGKL-FM— Dec 24, 1965: 97.5 mhz; 100 kw. Ant 500 ft TL: N31 29 46 W100 24 50. Stereo. Hrs open: 24 Box 1878, 76902. Secondary address: 1301 S. Abe 76903. Phone: (325) 655-7161. Fax: (325) 658-7377. Web Site:www.975kgkl.com Licensee: Double O Texas Corp. Population served: 100,000 Natl. Network: ABC, . Kenkel & Associates. Format: Country. News: 3 hrs wkly. Target aud: 25-54. ♦John Kerr, gen mgr; Boomer Kingston, opns mgr; Randy Phair, gen sls mgr.

KIXY-FM— October 1966: 94.7 mhz; 100 kw. Ant 446 ft TL: N31 29 14 W100 26 57. Stereo. Hrs open: 24 Prog sep from AM 2824 Sherwood Way, 76901. Phone: (325) 949-3333.E-mail: kixy@kixyfm.com Web Site:www.kixyfm.com Natl. Network: CNN Radio, . Natl. Rep: McGavren Guild,. Format: Top-40, adult contemp. News staff: one. Target aud: 18-49. ♦David Carr, progmg dir; Shannon J. Roach, CFO & traf mgr.

KKSA(AM)— Nov 28, 1954: 1260 khz; 540 w-D, 71 w-N. TL: N31 29 14 W100 26 57. Stereo. Hrs open: 24 Box 2191, 76902. Secondary address: KIXY Complex, 2824 Sherwood Way 76902. Phone: (325) 949-2112. Fax: (325) 944-0851.E-mail: kixy@kixyfm.com Web Site:www.kksa-am.com Licensee: Foster Communications Company Inc. Group owner: Foster Communications Co. (acq 4-9-84). Population served: 125,000 Natl. Network: Westwood One, CBS, . Rgnl. Network: Texas State Net. Natl. Rep: McGavren Guild,. Texas State Networks Leventhal, Senter & Lerman. Wire Svc: UPI Format: News/talk, sports. News staff: one; News: 20 hrs wkly. Target aud: 25-54. ♦Fred M. Key, CEO, pres; Jay Michaels, opns mgr; Doug Smith, gen sls mgr.

***KLTP(FM)—** 2008: 90.9 mhz; 2.915 kw. Ant 626 ft TL: N31 25 16 W100 32 36. Hrs open: 542 Butternut, Abilene, 79602. Phone: (325) 673-3045. Fax: (325) 672-7938.E-mail: studio@kgnz.com Web Site:www.kgnz.com Licensee: Christian Broadcasting Co. Inc. (acq 8-14-2008). Format: Contemp Christian. ♦Gary Hill, gen mgr.

KMDX(FM)— Dec 5, 1998: 106.1 mhz; 50 kw. Ant 456 ft TL: N31 26 08 W100 34 08. Hrs open: 3434 Sherwood Way, 76901. Phone: (325) 947-0899. Fax: (325) 947-0996.E-mail: terry.radio@lonestarmix.com Web Site:www.themixonline.com Licensee: Four R Broadcasting Inc. (acq 1-11-2007; $1.5 million with KDCD(FM) San Angelo). Natl. Network: Jones Radio Networks, . Natl. Rep: Interep,. Format: Hot adult contemp. News staff: one. Target aud: 25-54. ♦Frank De Francesco, CEO, pres; Aaron Harris, opns mgr, progmg VP, mus dir; Terry Hucks, chmn, gen mgr & adv VP; Biss Casey, news dir; Len Martinez, engrg VP; Debbie Smith, traf mgr.

***KNAR(FM)—** 2006: 89.3 mhz; 1 kw. Ant 800 ft TL: N31 41 59 W100 26 30. Hrs open:
Rebroadcasts KLRD(FM) Yucaipa, CA 100%.
2351 Sunset Blvd., Suite 170-218, Rocklin, CA, 95765. Phone: (916) 251-1600. Fax: (916) 251-1650. Web Site:www.air1.com Licensee: Educational Media Foundation. (acq 9-22-2005; $40,000 for CP). Natl. Network: Air 1, . Format: Christian. ♦Richard Jenkins, pres; Mike Novak, VP; Keith Whipple, dev dir; David Pierce, progmg mgr; Ed Lenane, news dir; Sam Wallington, engrg dir; Karen Johnson, news rptr.

KSJT-FM— Oct 7, 1985: 107.5 mhz; 100 kw. 656 ft TL: N31 26 19 W100 34 18. Stereo. Hrs open: 24 209 W. Beauregard Ave., 76903. Phone: (325) 655-1717. Fax: (325) 6557-0601. Licensee: La Unica Broadcasting Co. Format: Sp. Target aud: 18-55. ♦Louis Perez, pres; Armando Martinez, stn mgr; Cody Austin, gen sls mgr; Jesus Zapata, progmg dir; Arturo Madrid, news dir; Dania Salas, traf mgr.

***KUTX(FM)—** Apr 1, 1996: 90.1 mhz; 5 kw. 909 ft TL: N31 35 21 W100 31 00. Hrs open:
Rebroadcasts KUT(FM) Austin 100%.
1 University Station A 0704, Univ. of Texas, Austin, 78712-1090. Phone: (512) 471-1631.E-mail: kut@kut.org Licensee: University of Texas at Austin. Population served: 100,000 Natl. Network: NPR, PRI, . Cohn & Marks. Format: Music & news. Target aud: 25-54; educated opinions, leaders and arts community. Spec prog: Folk 4 hrs, blues 6 hrs wkly. ♦Stewart Vanderwilt, gen mgr.

KWFR(FM)— November 1995: 101.9 mhz; 100 kw. 807 ft TL: N31 29 29 W100 26 03. Hrs open: 24 Box 2191, 76902. Secondary address: KIXY Complex, 2824 Sherwood Way 76901. Phone: (325) 949-2112. Fax: (325) 944-0851.E-mail: kixy@kixyfm.com Web Site:www.kwfrfm.com Licensee: Foster Communications Co. Inc. (group owner; acq 12-1-94; $219,000 with KFXJ(FM) Abilene;2-13-95). Natl. Rep: McGavren Guild,. Leventhal, Senter & Lerman. Format: Classic rock. News staff: one. ♦Fred M. Key, pres; Jay Michaels, opns mgr; Doug Smith, gen sls mgr; Chase O'Reily, progmg dir; Jeff Rottman, news dir; Adolph Ganza, chief of engrg.

San Antonio

KAHL(AM)— 1948: 1310 khz; 5 kw-D, 280 w-N, DA-2. TL: N29 24 53 W98 20 36. Hrs open: 24 8023 Vantage Drive, Suite 840, 78230. Phone: (210) 341-1310. Fax: (210) 694-5456. Licensee: Pearsall RadioWorks Ltd. Group owner: Univision Radio (acq 3-26-2008). Population served: 1,367,500 Natl. Rep: McGavren Guild,. Cohn & Marks. Format: Adult standards. ♦John Barger, pres & gen mgr.

KAJA(FM)— 1951: 97.3 mhz; 100 kw. 984 ft TL: N29 25 20 W98 29 22. Stereo. Hrs open: 24 6222 N.W. IH 10, 78201. Phone: (210) 736-9700. Fax: (210) 735 8811. Web Site:www.kj97.com Licensee: CCB Texas Licenses L.P. Population served: 175,000 Natl. Rep: Clear Channel,. Format: Country. News: 2 hrs wkly. Target aud: 18-54. ♦Matt Martin, gen mgr; George King, prom mgr, progmg dir.

***KBIB(AM)—**(Marion, Sept 21, 1989: 1000 khz; 250 w-D, DA. TL: N29 34 09 W98 09 47. Hrs open: 290 N. Santa Clara Rd., Marion, 78124. Phone: (830) 914-2083.E-mail: kbibam@juno.com Web Site:www.kbib.org Licensee: Hispanic Community College. Population served: 2,000,000 Wiley, Rein & Fielding. Format: Relg, Sp. Target aud: General. ♦Pastor Ken Hutchinson, gen mgr.

KCHL(AM)— June 1960: 1480 khz; 2.5 kw-D, 90 w-N, DA-2. TL: N29 24 45 W98 24 52. Hrs open: 15 1211 W. Hein Rd., 78220. Phone: (210) 337-1480. Fax: (210) 333-0081.E-mail: kchlradio@yahoo.com Web Site:www.kchl.org Licensee: Martin Broadcasting Inc. (group owner; acq 6-4-92; 6-22-92). Population served: 1,000,000 Natl. Rep: McGavren Guild,. Latham & Watkins. Format: Gospel. News staff: one. Target aud: 25-54. ♦Darrel Martin, gen mgr; Shouting Gail Barrett, gen sls mgr, progmg dir, progmg dir & mus dir; Brett Huggins, chief of engrg.

KCOR(AM)— Feb 1, 1946: 1350 khz; 5 kw-U, DA-N. TL: N29 31 27 W98 37 05. Hrs open: 1777 N.E. Loop 410, Suite 400, 78217. Phone: (210) 821-6548. Fax: (210) 804-7825. Licensee: Tichenor License Corp. Group owner: Univision Radio (acq 9-22-2003; grpsl). Population served: 1,367,500 Cohn & Marks. Format: Sp, news/talk. Target aud: 25-54; adults. ♦Dan Wilson, gen mgr.

KCYY(FM)— June 25, 1966: 100.3 mhz; 100 kw. 984 ft TL: N29 31 25 W98 43 25. Stereo. Hrs open: 24 Prog sep from AM 8122 Datapoint, # 500 , 78229. Phone: (210) 615-5400. Fax: (210) 615-5300. Web Site:www.y100fm.com Population served: 1,300,000 News staff: one. Target aud: 25-54. ♦Alyce Ian, pub affrs dir; Connye Rodriguez, traf mgr.

KDRY(AM)—(Alamo Heights, Nov 8, 1963: 1100 khz; 11 kw-D, 1 kw-N, DA-N. TL: N29 33 26 W98 22 35. Hrs open: 24 16414 San Pedro Ave., Suite 575, 78232-2246. Phone: (210) 545-1100. Fax: (210) 545-1139. Web Site:www.kdry.com Licensee: KDRY Radio Inc. Population served: 888,199 Format: Relg teaching. Target aud: General. ♦Diane Rainey, gen mgr.

KEDA(AM)— Mar 17, 1966: 1540 khz; 5 kw-D, 1 kw-N, DA-N. TL: N29 21 30 W98 21 05. Stereo. Hrs open: 510 S. Flores St., 78204. Phone: (210) 226-5254. Fax: (210) 227-7937.E-mail: kedakid@aol.com Web Site:www.kedaradio.com Licensee: D & E Broadcasting Co. (acq 3-7-66). Population served: 250,000 Rgnl. Network: Texas State Net. Texas State Networks Format: Tex Mex, Cajun. Target aud: 25-54. Spec prog: Salsa 4 hrs wkly. ♦Madeline Davila, pres, disc jockey; Alberto P. Davila, VP, gen mgr, natl sls mgr, mktg VP; Ricardo P. Davila, progmg dir; Bret Huggins, chief of engrg; Danny Casanova, disc jockey.

KFIT EXP STN— 1989: 1060 khz; 1 kw-D, DA. TL: N29 17 32 W98 31 57. Hrs open: 6 AM-8 PM
Rebroadcasts KFIT(AM) Lockhart.
Box 160158, Austin, 78716. Secondary address: 110 Wild Basin Rd., Suite 375, Austin 78716. Phone: (512) 328-8400. Fax: (512) 328-8437. Licensee: KFIT Inc. Population served: 500,000 Format: Gospel. ♦Rev. Darrell Martin, gen mgr; Terri Lewis, progmg dir.

KISS-FM— December 1946: 99.5 mhz; 97.7 kw. Ant 1,486 ft TL: N29 16 29 W98 15 52. Stereo. Hrs open: 8122 Datapoint Dr., Suite 600, 78229. Phone: (210) 646-0105. Fax: (210) 646-9711.E-mail: virgil.thompson@cox.com Web Site:www.kissrocks.com Licensee: Cox Radio Inc. Group owner: Cox Broadcasting (acq 8-4-97; grpsl). Population served: 1,400,000 Natl. Rep: Christal,. Format: AOR. Target aud: 18-44; men. ♦Virgil Thompson, gen mgr; Janis Maxymof, gen sls mgr; Jennifer Schultz, prom dir; Kevin Vargas, progmg dir; C.J. Cruz, mus dir, asst music dir; Steve Hahn, news dir, pub affrs dir; Richard Schuh, chief of engrg.

KJXK(FM)— 1969: 102.7 mhz; 100 kw horiz, 70 kw vert. 670 ft TL: N29 25 09 W98 29 06. Stereo. Hrs open: Prog sep from AM 4050 Eisenhauer Rd., 78218. Phone: (210) 528-5500. Fax: (210) 599-5588. Web Site:www.1027krock.com Format: CHR, top-40. Target aud: 12 plus. ♦John Cook, progmg dir.

KKYX(AM)— 1926: 680 khz; 50 kw-D, 10 kw-N, DA-N. TL: N29 30 03 W98 49 54. Stereo. Hrs open: 24 8122 Datapoint, # 500, 78229. Phone: (210) 615-5400. Fax: (210) 615-5300. Web Site:www.kkyx.com Licensee: Cox Radio Inc. Group owner: Cox Broadcasting (acq 3-28-97; grpsl). Population served: 1,300,000 Format: Country. News staff: one; News: 3 hrs wkly. Target aud: 35-64. Spec prog: Pub affrs 2 hrs wkly. ♦Bob Neil, CEO; Ben Reed, VP, gen mgr; Marty Choate, gen sls mgr; Jim Bratt, natl sls mgr; Julie Busse, mktg dir; Jim Kinney, prom dir; George King, progmg dir, progmg mgr; Chrissie Murnin, news dir, pub affrs dir; Paul Reynolds, chief of engrg; Connye Rodriguez, traf mgr.

KONO(AM)— January 1927: 860 khz; 5 kw-D, 1 kw-N, DA-N. TL: N29 26 14 W98 25 19. Stereo. Hrs open: 24 8122 Datapoint Dr., Suite 500,

78229. Phone: (210) 615-5400. Fax: (210) 615-5339. Web Site:www.kono101.com Licensee: Cox Radio Inc. Group owner: Cox Broadcasting (acq 2-12-98; $23 million with KONO-FM Helotes). Population served: 1,300,000 Format: Oldies. News staff: one; News: one hr wkly. Target aud: 25-64; total audience appeal. ♦Marty Choate, VP, gen mgr; Connie Tyra-Kremer, gen sls mgr; Roger Allen, progmg dir; Paul Reynolds, chief of engrg.

KONO-FM—See Helotes

***KPAC(FM)**— Nov 7, 1982: 88.3 mhz; 100 kw. 656 ft TL: N29 31 25 W98 43 25. Stereo. Hrs open: 24 Prog sep from FM 8401 Datapoint Dr., Suite 800, 78229. Phone: (210) 614-8977. Fax: (210) 614-8983.E-mail: info@tpr.org Web Site:www.tpr.org Licensee: Texas Public Radio. Population served: 1,500,000 Natl. Network: PRI, . Garvey, Schubert & Barer. Format: Class. News: 3 hrs wkly. Target aud: 25 plus; educated, upscale financially, mature, influential opinion leaders. ♦Dan Skinner, pres, gen mgr; Laverne Ditts, dev dir; Nathan Cone, progmg dir; Randy Anderson, mus dir; Wayne Coble, engrg dir; Janet Grojean, sls.

KPWT(FM)—See Terrell Hills

KQXT(FM)— Nov 19, 1967: 101.9 mhz; 100 kw. Ant 663 ft TL: N29 25 06 W98 29 01. Stereo. Hrs open: 24 6222 N.W. IH-10, 78201. Phone: (210) 736-9700. Fax: (210) 736-9776. Fax: (210) 735-8811. Licensee: CCB Texas Licenses L.P. Group owner: Clear Channel Communications Inc. (acq 1-27-93; $8 million;3-8-93). Population served: 985,000 Rgnl rep: Clear Channel. Format: Soft adult contemp. News staff: one; News: 2 hrs wkly. Target aud: 25-54; core target is women 30-44. Spec prog: Contemp jazz 4 hrs, relg 2 hrs, pub affrs one hr wkly. ♦L. Lowry Mays, CEO; Mark Mays, COO, pres; Randall Mays, CFO; Linda Hardy, gen mgr, gen sls mgr; Mike McDonald, sls dir; Marian Holdsworth, natl sls mgr; Tim Kiesling, mktg dir; Bill Rohde, prom dir; Ed Scarborough, progmg dir; Stan Kelly, news dir; Dan Walthers, chief of engrg; Diane Travis, disc jockey.

KRDY(AM)— Nov 13, 1961: 1160 khz; 10 kw-D, 1 kw-N, DA-2. TL: N29 32 11 W98 41 08. Stereo. Hrs open: 24 84 N.E. Loop 410, Suite 143, 78216. Phone: (210) 530-5360. Fax: (210) 530-5304. Licensee: Radio Disney Group LLC. Group owner: ABC Inc. (acq 5-30-2003; $3.2 million). Natl. Network: Radio Disney, . Format: Children. ♦Fred Stockwell, gen mgr.

KROM(FM)— June 1947: 92.9 mhz; 100 kw. 1,016 ft TL: N29 11 03 W98 30 49. Stereo. Hrs open: 1777 N.E. Loop 410, Suite 400, 78217. Phone: (210) 821-6548. Fax: (210) 804-7825.E-mail: info@netmio.com Web Site:www.netmio.com Licensee: Tichenor License Corp. Population served: 1,367,500 Cohn & Marks. Format: Regional Mexican, Sp. Target aud: 19-49; male. ♦Jd Gonzalez, opns dir; Rosemary Scott, rsch dir; Norma Perez, traf mgr.

***KRTU(FM)**— Jan 22, 1976: 91.7 mhz; 8.9 kw. 120 ft TL: N29 27 51 W98 28 56. Stereo. Hrs open: 24 Trinity University, One Trinity Place, 78212-7200. Phone: (210) 999-8917. Fax: (210) 999-8355.E-mail: krtu@trinity.edu Web Site:www.krtu.org Licensee: Trinity University. Population served: 1,200,000 Cohn & Marks. Format: Jazz. News: 5 hrs wkly. Target aud: 35-64; people from all walks of life who love jazz music. Spec prog: Christian rock 2 hrs; Blues 2 hrs wkly. ♦Dr. William G. Christ, gen mgr; Dr. Rob Huesea, stn mgr; Ryan Weber, opns mgr; Chris Helfrich, dev dir; Aaron Prado, progmg dir; Brett Huggins, chief of engrg.

KSAH(AM)—See Universal City

KSLR(AM)— Dec 26, 1926: 630 khz; 5 kw-U, DA-2. TL: N29 23 24 W98 21 00. Hrs open: 24 9601 McAllister Fwy., Suite 1200, 78216-4686. Phone: (210) 344-8481. Fax: (210) 340-1213.E-mail: kslr@kslr.com Web Site:www.kslr.com Licensee: Salem Media of Texas Inc. Group owner: Salem Communications Corp. (acq 8-6-94). Population served: 1,421,729 Natl. Network: Salem Radio Network, . Format: Christian, educ teaching, talk. News staff: one. Target aud: 18-54; women & families. Spec prog: Sp 18 hrs wkly. ♦David Ziebell, gen mgr; Baron Wiley, opns mgr; James Herring, gen mgr & gen sls mgr.

***KSTX(FM)**— October 1988: 89.1 mhz; 100 kw. 656 ft TL: N29 31 33 W98 43 21. Stereo. Hrs open: 24 8401 Datapoint Dr., Suite 800, 78229. Phone: (210) 614-8977. Fax: (210) 614-8983.E-mail: info@tpr.org Web Site:www.tpr.org Licensee: Texas Public Radio. Population served: 1,500,000 Natl. Network: NPR, PRI, . Garvey, Schubert & Barer. Wire Svc: AP Format: News & info. News staff: 5; News: 67 hrs wkly. Target aud: 25 plus; educated, upscale financially, influential opinion leaders. Spec prog: Jazz 6 hrs, var talk 6 hrs, folk 5 hrs, blues 6 hrs wkly. ♦Dan Skinner, pres, gen mgr; Nathan Cone, opns mgr, progmg dir; Laverne Pitts, dev dir, progmg dir; Dave Davies, news dir; Wayne Coble, news dir & engrg dir; Janet Grojean, sls.

***KSYM-FM**— Sept 15, 1966: 90.1 mhz; 5.7 kw. 128 ft TL: N29 26 50 W98 29 55. Stereo. Hrs open: 24 1300 San Pedro Ave., 78212-4299. Phone: (210) 733-2787. Fax: (210) 733-2801.E-mail: ksym@accd.edu Web Site:www.ksym.org Licensee: San Antonio College. Population served: 1,000,000 Format: AAA, Texas mus., new alternative. Target aud: 12-54; depending on block format. ♦John Onderdonk, gen mgr; Marlene Romo, sls dir; Michael Botsford, progmg dir; Shalom Topps, mus dir; Victor Pfau, chief of engrg.

KTKR(AM)— May 10, 1984: 760 khz; 50 kw-D, 1 kw-N, DA-2. TL: N29 26 58 W98 18 33. Stereo. Hrs open: 24 6222 N.W. IH-10, 78201. Phone: (210) 736-9700. Fax: (210) 735-8811. Web Site:www.ticketsports.com Licensee: CCB Texas Licenses L.P. Group owner: Clear Channel Communications Inc. (acq 6-16-93; $800,000;7-5-93). Natl. Network: Westwood One, . Natl. Rep: Clear Channel,. Format: Sports. Target aud: 25-49; male. ♦Matt Martin, gen mgr; Peter Bolger, progmg dir.

KTSA(AM)— May 9, 1922: 550 khz; 5 kw-U, DA-N. TL: N29 29 41 W98 24 52 (D), N29 29 46 W98 24 54 (N). Hrs open: 24 4050 Eisenhauer Rd., 78218. Phone: (210) 528-5500. Fax: (210) 599-5588. Web Site:www.ktsa.com Licensee: BMP San Antonio License Co. L.P. Group owner: Infinity Broadcasting Corp. (acq 5-31-2007; $45 million with co-located FM). Population served: 654,153 Cohn & Marks. Format: News/talk. News staff: 11; News: 35 hrs wkly. Target aud: 25-54. ♦Lance Hawkins, gen mgr.

KXTN-FM— Dec 31, 1967: 107.5 mhz; 100 kw. Ant 1,514 ft TL: N29 16 29 W98 15 52. Stereo. Hrs open: Prog sep from AM 1777 N.E. Loop 410, Suite 400, 78217. Phone: (210) 829-1075. Fax: (210) 822-2372. Web Site:www.kxtn.com Licensee: Tichenor License Corp. Population served: 1,367,500 Format: Tejano, Sp. Target aud: 25-49; contemp Sp, affluent, upscale. ♦Kriby Kaden, VP; Kirby Kaden, rgnl sls mgr; Colleen Carnahan, progmg dir, rsch dir; Norma Perez, traf mgr.

KXXM(FM)— May 5, 1964: 96.1 mhz; 100 kw. 479 ft TL: N29 38 00 W98 37 50. (CP: 99 kw, ant 328 ft.). Stereo. Hrs open: 24 6222 N.W. I-10, 78201. Phone: (210) 736-9700. Fax: (210) 736-8811.E-mail: tonytarvatto@clearchannel.com Web Site:www.mix961.com Licensee: CCB Texas Licenses L.P. Group owner: Clear Channel Communications Inc. (acq 6-19-98; $15 million). Population served: 654,153 Format: CHR. News staff: one; News: 3 hrs wkly. Target aud: 18-34; females. ♦Tom Glade, VP & gen mgr; Mike Hall, gen sls mgr; Tim Kiesling, mktg dir; Cesar Campa, prom dir.

***KYFS(FM)**— Nov 7, 1982: 90.9 mhz; 100 kw. 476 ft TL: N29 40 20 W98 14 43. Stereo. Hrs open: 24 11540 Carmel Commons Blvd., Suite 808, Charlotte, 28226. Fax: (704) 522-1967.E-mail: bbn@bbnradio.org Web Site:www.bbnradio.org Licensee: Bible Broadcasting Network Inc. (group owner; acq 11-20-91; $75,000; 12-9-91). Population served: 1,200,000 Smithwick & Belendiuk. Format: Christian. Target aud: 2 plus. ♦John D. Woolery, gen mgr & opns mgr.

KZDC(AM)— Jan 1, 1953: 1250 khz; 1 kw-U, DA-N. TL: N29 24 29 W98 26 39. Stereo. Hrs open: 24 4500 Eisenhauer Rd., 78218. Phone: (210) 654-5100. Fax: (210) 340-1775. Licensee: BMP San Antonio License Co. L.P. Group owner: Multicultural Radio Broadcasting Inc. (acq 3-312005; grpsl). Natl. Network: ESPN Radio, . Format: Sports. ♦Lance Hawkins, gen mgr; Bob Brown, sls dir.

KZEP-FM— Oct 1, 1966: 104.5 mhz; 100 kw. Ant 663 ft TL: N29 25 06 W98 29 01. Stereo. Hrs open: 24 427 E. 9th St., 78215. Phone: (210) 226-6444. Fax: (210) 225-5736.E-mail: kzepp@kzep.com Web Site:www.kzep.com Licensee: Citicasters Licenses L.P. Group owner: Lotus Communications Corp. (acq 7-29-2008; exchange for KVMX(FM) Bakersfield, CA and KWID(FM) Las Vegas, NV). Population served: 140,000 Natl. Rep: D & R Radio,. Format: Classic rock. News staff: one; News: 3 hrs wkly. Target aud: 25-54; males. ♦Jay A. Levine, pres, VP, gen mgr; Trish Levine, prom dir; Craig Chambers, progmg dir; Tom Scheppke, mus dir; Dave Delgado, news dir; Eddie Miles, chief of engrg; Becky Talamandes, traf mgr.

WOAI(AM)— Sept 29, 1922: 1200 khz; 50 kw-U. TL: N29 30 05 W98 07 09. Hrs open: 24 6222 N.W. IH-10, 78201. Phone: (210) 736-9700. Fax: (210) 735-8811. Web Site:www.woai.com Licensee: CCB Texas Licenses L.P. Group owner: Clear Channel Communications Inc. (acq 1975). Population served: 1,203,100 Natl. Network: Fox News Radio, . Natl. Rep: Clear Channel,. Texas State Networks Wire Svc: AP Format: News/talk info. News staff: 13; News: 20 hrs wkly. Target aud: 35-64; general. ♦Matt Martin, gen mgr; Peter Bolger, progmg dir; Dan Walthers, chief of engrg.

San Augustine

KQSI(FM)— Dec 29, 1993: 92.5 mhz; 1.4 kw. Ant 220 ft TL: N31 31 44 W94 05 59. Hrs open: 24
Rebroadcasts KDET(AM) Center 100%.
Box 930, Center, 75935. Phone: (936) 275-3242. Fax: (936) 598-9537. Licensee: Center Broadcasting Co. Inc. (group owner; acq 3-26-98; grpsl). Population served: 25,000 Natl. Network: ABC, . Texas State Networks Format: C & W, Sp. News staff: one. Target aud: 35-65. ♦Lori Alvis, gen mgr, gen sls mgr; Rob Rockett, progmg dir; Rachel Shanz, news dir; Harlan Riley, chief of engrg.

San Diego

KUKA(FM)— July 14, 1993: 105.9 mhz; 25 kw. 450 ft TL: N27 45 04 W98 07 28. Stereo. Hrs open: 24 Box 589, Alice, 78333. Phone: (361) 668-6666. Fax: (361) 668-6661.E-mail: info@kuka.com Licensee: Claro Communications Ltd. (acq 11-30-2007; $250,000). Population served: 447,510 Booth, Freret, Imlay & Tepper P.C. Format: Sp. News staff: one; News: one hr wkly. Target aud: 18-34; middle to upper class. ♦Teo Pena, gen mgr, disc jockey; Estela Nava, opns mgr, chief of engrg, traf mgr; Zulema Z. Marroquin, dev VP; Javier Villanueva, rgnl sls mgr; Tio Pena, mktg dir; Armando Marroquin Jr., mktg mgr, prom mgr, adv mgr; Pedro Vasquez, progmg dir, disc jockey; Peter Vasquez, news dir; Henry Turner, chief of engrg, traf mgr; Ted Pena, reporter, mus critic.

San Juan

KUBR(AM)— 1991: 1210 khz; 10 kw-D, 1 kw-N, DA-2. TL: N26 14 41 W98 05 25. Hrs open: 24 Box 252, McAllen, 78505. Phone: (956) 686-6382. Fax: (956) 686-2999.E-mail: paylinobernal@hotmail.com Web Site:www.laradiocristiana.com Licensee: Radio Christiana Network. Format: Sp, Christian. ♦Paulino Bernal, gen mgr; Eloy Bernal, stn mgr; Pete Guzman, opns mgr.

San Marcos

KBPA(FM)—Licensed to San Marcos. See Austin

***KTSW(FM)**— Apr 15, 1992: 89.9 mhz; 10.5 kw. Ant 213 ft TL: N29 39 20 W98 07 59. Stereo. Hrs open: 24 Old Main 106, 601 University Dr., 78666-4616. Phone: (512) 245-3485. Fax: (512) 245-3732.E-mail: ktsw@txstate.edu Web Site:www.ktsw.net Licensee: Texas State University-San Marcos. Dow, Lohnes & Albertson, PLLC. Format: College alternative, news/talk, sports. News: 9 hrs wkly. Target aud: 18-24; college students & young adults. ♦Dan Schumacher, gen mgr, sls; Jayce Beasley, stn mgr; Brian Shelton, prom dir; Evan Hilliard, progmg dir; Kristen Hennessey, mus dir; Tom Bruce, engrg dir; Lotta Bucks, traf mgr.

KUOL(AM)— 1948: 1470 khz; 250 w-U, DA-N. TL: N29 53 53 W97 54 44. Hrs open: 5:30 AM-midnight Box 252, McAllen, 78505. Phone: (956) 686-6382. Fax: (956) 686-2999.E-mail: paulinobernal@hotmail.com Web Site:www.laradiocristiana.com Licensee: Radio Christiana Network. (acq 3-26-97). Population served: 56,000 Format: Sp, Christian. ♦Paulino Bernal, gen mgr; Eloy Bernal, stn mgr; Pete Guzman, opns mgr.

San Saba

KBAL-FM— 1996: 106.1 mhz; 3 kw. Ant 20 ft TL: N31 11 26 W98 42 55. Hrs open: 24 705 S. Live Oak, 76877. Phone: (325) 372-5225. Fax: (325) 372-3817. Web Site:www.kbalradio.com Licensee: Roy E. Henderson (acq 5-16-2000; grpsl). Format: Country. Target aud: General. ♦Shay Hardy, gen mgr.

KNVR(AM)— 1954: 1410 khz; 800 w-D, 203 w-N. TL: N31 11 26 W98 42 55. Hrs open: 24 Box 126, 76877. Phone: (325) 372-5225. Fax: (325) 372-3817. Web Site:www.kbalradio.com Licensee: Roy E. Henderson (acq 5-16-2000; grpsl). Population served: 5,000 Texas State Networks Fletcher, Heald & Hildreth. Format: Adult contemp. ♦Steve Smith, CFO; Shay Hardy, gen mgr, progmg dir.

Sanger

KTDK(FM)— December 1989: 104.1 mhz; 6.2 kw. Ant 630 ft TL: N33 28 47 W97 03 22. Stereo. Hrs open: 24 3500 Maple Ave., Suite 1310, Dallas, 75219. Phone: (214) 526-7400. Fax: (214) 525-2525. Web Site:www.theticket.com Licensee: KRBE Lico Inc. Group owner: Susquehanna Radio Corp. (acq 4-30-98; $3.683 million). Format: Sports. Target aud: 24-55; men & sports enthusiasts. ♦Dan Bennett, VP, gen mgr; Jim Quirk, sls dir; Kim Roberts, gen sls mgr; Jeff Catlin, progmg dir; Rob Chickering, chief of engrg; Kimberly Jolly, traf mgr.

***KVRK(FM)**— July 8, 1999: 89.7 mhz; 14 kw. 1,699 ft TL: N33 33 36 W96 57 35. Hrs open: Research Educational Foundation Inc., 11061 Shady Tr., Dallas, 75229. Phone: (214) 353-8970. Fax: (214) 351-6809.E-mail: chris@897powerfm.com Web Site:www.897powerfm.com

Licensee: Research Educational Foundation Inc. Format: Christian, rock. ◆Stanley Thomas, gen mgr; Ron Evans, stn mgr; Devin Wickham, opns dir; Krystal Coleman, prom dir; Chris Goodwin, progmg dir; Kent Loney, chief of engrg.

Santa Anna

KBWT(FM)—Not on air, target date: unknown: 105.5 mhz; 19 kw. Ant 266 ft TL: N31 40 20.09 W99 10 57.07. Hrs open: 2801 Via Fortuna Dr., Suite 675, Austin, 78746. Phone: (713) 528-2517. Licensee: Ace Radio Corp. ◆Stephen Hackerman, pres.

Savoy

KQDR(FM)— 2009: 107.3 mhz; 2.3 kw. Ant 534 ft TL: N33 37 30 W96 20 03. Hrs open: 900 E. Pecan Grove Rd., Sherman, 75092. Phone: (903) 893-5625. Web Site:www.1073docfm.com Licensee: Prophecy Radio Group LLC. Format: Adult hits. ◆Brad LaRock, gen mgr & gen sls mgr.

Schertz

KBBT(FM)— Feb 1, 1976: 98.5 mhz; 97 kw. Ant 991 ft TL: N29 31 25 W98 43 25. Stereo. Hrs open: 24 1777 N.E. Loop 410, Suite 400, San Antonio, 78217. Phone: (210) 829-1075. Fax: (210) 804-7825.E-mail: info@netmio.com Web Site:www.netmio.com Licensee: Univision Radio License Corp. Group owner: Univision Radio (acq 9-22-2003; grpsl). Population served: 1,367,500 Format: Hip Hop. ◆Mac Tichenor, CEO & pres; Jeff Hinson, CFO; Dan Wilson, gen mgr; J. D. Gonzalez, opns mgr.

Seabrook

KROI(FM)— Apr 23, 1984: 92.1 mhz; 50 kw. Ant 981 ft TL: N29 16 33 W95 22 45. Stereo. Hrs open: 24 24 Greenway Plaza, Suite 900, Houston, 77046. Phone: (713) 623-2108. Fax: (713) 623-8166. Licensee: Radio One Licenses LLC. Group owner: Radio One Inc. (acq 7-20-2004; $72.5 million). Format: Gospel. Target aud: General. ◆Alfred C. Liggins III, pres; Scott R. Royster, exec VP; Doug Abernethy, gen mgr.

Seadrift

KMAT(FM)— May 1999: 105.1 mhz; 38.5 kw. Ant 456 ft TL: N28 26 17.1 W96 26 54.6. Stereo. Hrs open: 24 2424 South Blvd., Houston, 77098. Phone: (713) 520-7900. Fax: (713) 520-8104. Licensee: Cordell Communications Inc. Population served: 89,470 Leventhal, Senter & Lerman. Format: Sp Christian. News: 2 hrs wkly. Target aud: 30-50. ◆Bill Cordell, pres, gen mgr; Dolly Martin, progmg dir.

Sealy

*****KCPC(FM)**—Not on air, target date: unknown: 90.7 mhz; 1.7 kw. Ant 446 ft TL: N29 50 05 W96 16 10. Hrs open: 2424 South Blvd., Houston, 77098-5110. Phone: (713) 520-5200.E-mail: email@khcb.org Web Site:www.khcb.org Licensee: Houston Christian Broadcasters Inc. ◆Bruce Munsterman, pres.

Seguin

KSMG(FM)— Sept 9, 1970: 105.3 mhz; 100 kw. 1,240 ft TL: N29 16 29 W98 15 52. Stereo. Hrs open: 24 8122 Datapoint Dr., Suite 600, San Antonio, 78229. Phone: (210) 646-0105. Fax: (210) 646-9711.E-mail: virgil.thompson@cox.com Web Site:www.magic1053.com Licensee: Cox Radio Inc. Group owner: Cox Broadcasting (acq 8-4-97; grpsl). Population served: 1,400,000 Natl. Rep: Christal,. Leventhal, Senter & Lerman. Format: Hot adult contemp. News staff: one; News: 5 hrs wkly. Target aud: 25-49; females. ◆Virgil Thompson, gen mgr; Rory Charitan, gen sls mgr; Robert John, progmg dir; Katrina Curtiss, mus dir; Karen Clauss, news dir, pub affrs dir; Richard Schuh, chief of engrg; Cathy Sheehan, traf mgr.

KWED(AM)— Sept 9, 1948: 1580 khz; 1 kw-D, 253 w-N. TL: N29 34 48 W97 59 05. Hrs open: 24 609 E. Court St., 78155. Phone: (830) 379-2234. Fax: (830) 379-2238.E-mail: contact@kwed1580.com Web Site:www.seguintoday.com Licensee: Guadalupe Media, Ltd. (acq 7 - 1 - 07 $940,000). Population served: 300,000 Natl. Network: Westwood One, CNN Radio, Premiere Radio Networks, . Natl. Rep: Rgnl Reps,. Southmayd & Miller. Wire Svc: AP Format: Country, news/talk. News staff: 5; News: 30 hrs wkly. Target aud: 35-64. Spec prog: Farm 6 hrs wkly. ◆Hal Widsten, gen mgr; Richard Schuh, chief of engrg; Christine Penalver, sports cmtr.

Seminole

KIKZ(AM)— Apr 15, 1954: 1250 khz; 1 kw-D, 250 w-N. TL: N32 41 58 W102 38 12. Hrs open: 24 105 N.W. 11th St., 79360. Phone: (432) 758-5878. Fax: (432) 758-5474. Licensee: Gaines County Broadcasting LLC (acq 6-9-93; $193,276 with co-located FM; 7-5-93). Population served: 25,000 Rgnl. Network: Texas State Net. Texas State Networks Format: Country. Target aud: General. ◆Mike Elder, gen mgr.

KSEM-FM— Mar 15, 1985: 106.3 mhz; 3 kw. Ant 174 ft TL: N32 41 58 W102 38 12. Stereo. Hrs open: 24 105 N.W. 11th St., 79360. Phone: (432) 758-5878. Fax: (432) 758-5474. Licensee: Gaines County Broadcasting LLC. Format: Country. ◆Mike Elder, gen mgr.

Seymour

KSEY(AM)— Oct 26, 1950: 1230 khz; 1 kw-U. TL: N33 35 49 W99 16 42. Hrs open: #1 Radio Ln., 73680. Phone: (940) 889-2637. Fax: (940) 889-2665.E-mail: frnksey@aol.com Licensee: Mark Aulabaugh. (acq 11-95). Population served: 100,000 Wire Svc: NWS (National Weather Service) ◆Mark Aulabaugh, gen mgr; Orlando Jariez, progmg dir.

KSEY-FM— June 26, 1981: 94.3 mhz; 3 kw. 112 ft TL: N33 35 49 W99 16 42. (CP: 93.9 mhz, 50 kw, ant 492 ft. TL: N33 42 00 W99 08 12). Stereo. Hrs open: Dups AM 100% Box 471, 76380. Phone: (940) 889-2637. Fax: (940) 889-2637.E-mail: info@ksey.com Web Site:www.radioksey.com Format: Full service. ◆Mark Aulabaugh, gen mgr; Joe Gaither, progmg dir.

KZNO(FM)—Not on air, target date: unknown: 92.3 mhz; 50 kw. Ant 492 ft TL: N33 34 49 W99 18 00. Hrs open: Box 880, Roma, 78584. Phone: (956) 487-8015. Licensee: South Texas FM Investments LLC. (acq 9-16-2008; grpsl). ◆Eloy Vera, gen mgr.

Sherman

KJIM(AM)— Dec 19, 1947: 1500 khz; 1 kw-D, DA. TL: N33 41 30 W96 33 29. Hrs open: 4367 Woodlawn Rd., Denison, 75021-8037. Phone: (903) 893-1197. Licensee: Bob Mark Allen Productions Inc. Natl. Network: Westwood One, CBS, . Format: Original hits of the 50s, 60s, 70s & 80s, news, sports. Target aud: 40-65. ◆Bob Mark Allen, pres.

Silsbee

KAYD-FM— June 21, 1980: 101.7 mhz; 10.5 kw. Ant 502 ft TL: N30 06 54 W93 59 56. Stereo. Hrs open: 755 S. 11th St., Suite 102, Beaumont, 77704. Phone: (409) 833-9421. Fax: (409) 833-9296.E-mail: info@kayd.com Web Site:www.kayd.com Licensee: Cumulus Licensing LLC. (acq 11-8-2004; $2.1 million). Format: Country. News: 20 hrs wkly. Target aud: 25-54; persons. ◆Zanetta Kelley, gen mgr; Jim West, opns mgr, progmg dir; Wes Matejka, sls dir; Mark Guzman, prom mgr; Liz Ferguson, traf mgr; J.P. White, sports cmtr.

KSET(AM)— Oct 13, 1959: 1300 khz; 500 w-D. TL: N30 21 02 W94 13 39. Hrs open: 24 Box 455, 77656. Phone: (409) 385-2883. Fax: (409) 386-1001.E-mail: kset@kset1300.com Web Site:www.kset1300.com Licensee: Proctor-Williams Inc. (acq 2-14-01; with co-located FM). Population served: 7271 Rgnl. Network: Texas State Net. Texas State Networks Format: All sports. Target aud: General. ◆Dave Collier Sr., CEO & gen mgr.

Sinton

KDAE(AM)—Licensed to Sinton. See Corpus Christi

KNCN(FM)—Licensed to Sinton. See Corpus Christi

KOUL(FM)—Licensed to Sinton. See Corpus Christi

Slaton

KJAK(FM)—Licensed to Slaton. See Lubbock

Snyder

*****KGWB(FM)**— Aug 4, 2008: 91.1 mhz; 200 w. Ant 315 ft TL: N32 45 34 W100 54 46. Hrs open: Western Texas College, 6200 College Ave., 79549. Phone: (325) 574-7980. Fax: (325) 573-9321. Web Site:wtc.edu/kgwb/ Licensee: Scurry County Junior College District. Format: Var. ◆Michael Dreith, pres; Bob Lewis, gen mgr.

KLYD(FM)— 2003: 98.9 mhz; 5.6 kw. Ant 341 ft TL: N32 45 23 W100 54 09. Hrs open: 24 Box 1008, 79550. Phone: (325) 573-9322. Fax: (325) 573-7445.E-mail: dink@ksnyradio.com Licensee: Delbert Foree. Format: Modern rock. ◆Dink Foree, gen mgr.

KSNY(AM)— Dec 22, 1949: 1450 khz; 1 kw-U. TL: N32 43 33 W100 56 30. Hrs open: 24 Box 1008, 79550. Secondary address: 2301 Ave. R 79549. Phone: (325) 573-9322. Fax: (325) 573-7445.E-mail: lydia@ksnyradio.com Licensee: Snyder Broadcasting Co. (acq 8-20-2007; with co-located FM). Population served: 11,171 Natl. Network: ABC, . Format: Country. Target aud: General. ◆Lydia Foree, pres; Dink Foree, gen mgr.

KSNY-FM— Sept 2, 1980: 101.5 mhz; 35 kw. 500 ft TL: N32 53 29 W101 06 29. Stereo. Hrs open: 24 Prog dups AM 5% Box 1008, 79550. Secondary address: 2301 Ave. R 79550. Phone: (325) 573-9322. Fax: (325) 573-7445.E-mail: ksnyfm@snydertex.com Format: Country. News staff: one; News: 5 hrs wkly. Target aud: 25-54.

Somerset

KYTY(AM)— Mar 1, 1988: 810 khz; 250 w-U, DA-2. TL: N29 18 48 W98 30 29. Hrs open: 24 Box 701582, San Antonio, 78270. Phone: (210) 545-0810. Fax: (210) 545-6713.E-mail: staram810@yahoo.com Web Site:www.star810.com Licensee: Maranatha Broadcasting Inc. (Group owner: Clear Channel (acq 3-11-98; $750,000). Population served: 1,200,000 Format: Contemp Christian music. Target aud: 35-45; female. ◆Myron Wade, gen mgr; Mary Kaye, opns mgr; Reuben O. Garcia, progmg dir.

Somerville

*****KNCH(FM)**—Not on air, target date: unknown: 88.1 mhz; 196 w vert. Ant 343 ft TL: N30 23 21.1 W96 35 03.7. Hrs open: University of Texas at Austin, 1 University Station (A0704), Austin, 78712. Phone: (512) 471-1631. Fax: (512) 471-3700. Web Site:www.kut.org Licensee: The University of Texas at Austin. ◆Stewart Vanderwilt, gen mgr.

Sonora

KHOS-FM— May 1979: 92.1 mhz; 3 kw. Ant 298 ft TL: N30 33 33 W100 37 54. Stereo. Hrs open: 24 680 Hwy. 277 S., 76950. Phone: (325) 387-3553. Fax: (325) 387-3554.E-mail: khoskyxx@verizon.net Licensee: Foster Charitable Foundation Inc. Group owner: Hill Country Broadcasting Corp. (acq 5-31-2007). Population served: 10,000 Natl. Network: ABC, . Voice of Southwest Agriculture Radio Format: Classic Country. Target aud: 12-50 plus. ◆Marti Ashcraft, opns mgr; Eddy Smith, engr.

South Padre Island

KESO(FM)— Aug 27, 1996: 92.7 mhz; 3 kw. Ant 298 ft TL: N26 04 04 W97 13 16. Stereo. Hrs open: 24 1201 N. Jackson Rd., Suite 900, McAllen, 78501. Phone: (956) 992-8895. Fax: (956) 992-8897. Licensee: BMP RGV License Company L.P. (acq 1-28-2005; $6.6 million with KZSP(FM) South Padre Island). Population served: 500,000 Format: Mexican rgnl. ◆Terry Kimball, gen mgr & stn mgr; Jim Wilson, progmg dir.

KZSP(FM)— July 27, 1990: 95.3 mhz; 2.5 kw. Ant 353 ft TL: N26 04 04 W97 13 16. Stereo. Hrs open: 24
Simulcast with KURV(AM) Edinburg 100%.
1201 N. Jackson Rd., Suite 900, McAllen, 78501. Phone: (956) 992-8895. Fax: (956) 992-8897. Licensee: BMP RGV License Company L.P. (acq 1-28-2005; $6.6 million with KESO(FM) South Padre Island). Population served: 500,000 Format: News/talk. ◆Jose Luis Munoz, gen mgr.

Spearman

*****KTOT(FM)**— 2003: 89.5 mhz; 100 kw. Ant 1,066 ft TL: N36 03 44 W101 01 56. Hrs open: 24 High Plains Public Radio, 210 N. 7th St., Garden City, KS, 67846. Phone: (620) 275-7444. Fax: (620) 275-7496. Web Site:www.hppr.org Licensee: Kanza Society Inc. Natl. Network: AP Radio, NPR, PRI, . Format: Class music, news. Target aud: 25-80; educated. ◆Richard Hicks, gen mgr; Diana Gonzales, dev dir; Bob Kirby, progmg mgr; Chuck Springer, chief of engrg.

KXDJ(FM)— Dec 16, 1963: 98.3 mhz; 17.5 kw. Ant 836 ft TL: N36 03 44 W101 01 56. Stereo. Hrs open: 24 Box 307, 79081. Phone: (806) 658-2650. Fax: (806) 648-2652. Licensee: Chris Samples Broadcasting (acq 3-12-2009; $360,000). Population served: 77,200 Natl. Network:

CBS Radio, AP Radio, . Rgnl. Network: Texas State Net. Format: Country. News: 25 hrs wkly. ♦Chris Samples, pres, VP; Chris Samples, gen mgr.

Springtown

***KSQX(FM)**— August 1985: 89.1 mhz; 3 kw. Ant 184 ft TL: N32 58 53 W97 42 18. Hrs open: 24 905 Palo Pinto St., Weatherford, 76086. Phone: (817) 341-2337. Fax: (817) 613-0230.E-mail: chb890@swbell.net Web Site:www.kyqx.com Licensee: CSSI Non-Profit Educational Broadcasting Corp. Population served: 2,355.316 Hill & Welch. Format: Oldies, big band, talk shows, news, sports. News staff: 3; News: 5 hrs wkly. ♦Charles Beard, CEO; Mindy Beard, pres & gen mgr.

Stamford

KLGD(FM)— Feb 22, 1999: 106.9 mhz; 40 kw. 548 ft TL: N32 56 16 W99 57 20. Hrs open: 209 S. Danville, Suite B-105, Abilene, 79605. Phone: (915) 691-5400. Fax: (915) 691-5653.E-mail: bruce@texas96.com Web Site:countrylegends.com Licensee: Texas Gulfwest Communications Corp. (acq 6-26-01). Population served: 150,000 Format: Country. Target aud: 35 plus; adults. ♦Bill Hooten, CEO, gen mgr; Pete Garcia, progmg mgr & mus dir.

KVRP(AM)— July 1947: 1400 khz; 1 kw-U. TL: N32 55 52 W99 47 00. Hrs open: 24 Box 1118, 1406 N. First St., Haskell, 79521. Phone: (940) 864-8505. Fax: (940) 864-8001.E-mail: gary@kvrp.com Web Site:www.kvrp.com Licensee: 1 Chronicles 14 L.P. (acq 8-4-2004; $700,000 with KVRP-FM Haskell). Population served: 50,000 Rgnl. Network: Texas State Net. Format: Praise & Worship/ Christian. Target aud: 35+. ♦Gregg Weston, pres, gen mgr; Gary Barrett, gen mgr, stn mgr, gen sls mgr; Dave Harrison, progmg dir; Megan Cox, chief of engrg & traf mgr.

Stanton

***KFLB-FM**— 2005: 88.1 mhz; 100 kw. Ant 457 ft TL: N32 05 44 W101 48 47. Stereo. Hrs open: 24 Box 35300, Tucson, AZ, 85740. Phone: (520) 742-6976. Fax: (520) 742-6979. Web Site:www.myflr.org Licensee: Family Life Broadcasting Inc. Group owner: EMF Broadcasting. (acq 6-15-2009; exchange for KLVW(FM) Odessa). Bryan Cave LLC. Format: Relg. News staff: 3. ♦Tim L. Walker, VP.

KKJW(FM)— 1998: 105.9 mhz; 37 kw. Ant 400 ft TL: N31 51 19 W101 47 32. Hrs open: 4411 Brookdale Dr., Midland, 79703. Licensee: Unique Broadcasting L.L.C. (acq 7-23-97). Format: Classic country. ♦Dick Baze, gen mgr.

Stephenville

***KEQX(FM)**—Not on air, target date: unknown: 89.7 mhz; 6 kw vert. Ant 492 ft TL: N32 07 24 W97 58 48. Stereo. Hrs open: 24 905 Palo Pinto St., Weatherford, 76086. Phone: (817) 341-8950. Fax: (817) 596-9842.E-mail: qxfmnews@yahoo.com Web Site:kyqx.com Licensee: CSSI Non-Profit Educational Broadcasting Corp. Population served: 203,881 Hill & Welch. Format: Hard country. ♦Jean Hudgens, gen mgr.

***KQXS(FM)**— 2004: 89.1 mhz; 1.2 kw vert. Ant 424 ft TL: N32 16 09 W98 18 51. Hrs open: 905 Palo Pinto St., Weatherford, 76086. Phone: (817) 341-8950. Fax: (817) 596-9842.E-mail: qxfmnews@yahoo.com Web Site:kyqx.com Licensee: CSSI Non-Profit Educational Broadcasting Corp. (acq 11-25-2002). Population served: 205,570 Hill & Welch. Format: Oldies, big band, news. News staff: 3. ♦Jean Hudgens, gen mgr.

KSTV(AM)— 1947: 1510 khz; 500 w-D. TL: N32 12 08 W98 14 54. Hrs open: Box 289, 3209 W. Washington (Dublin Hwy), 76401. Phone: (254) 968-2141. Fax: (254) 968-6221.E-mail: kstv@htcomp.net Web Site:www.kstvfm.com Licensee: CCR-Stephenville III LLC. Group owner: Cherry Creek Radio LLC (acq 6-24-2004; grpsl). Population served: 75,000 Format: Mexican hits. Target aud: 54 plus; general. Spec prog: Farm 5 hrs, relg 6 hrs wkly. ♦Robert Elliott, gen mgr; Bob Haschke, gen sls mgr; Jose Perez, prom mgr, progmg dir; Lorena Rodriquez, news dir; Justin McClure, chief of engrg; Troy Stark, traf mgr.

***KTRL(FM)**— 2008: 90.5 mhz; 3.8 kw. Ant 1,322 ft TL: N32 16 31 W98 01 22. Hrs open: Box T-0415, 76402. Phone: (254) 968-9880. Licensee: Tarleton State University (acq 7-21-2009). ♦Rickey Richardson, gen mgr.

Sterling City

KNRX(FM)— Dec 1, 1998: 96.5 mhz; 40 kw. Ant 544 ft TL: N31 35 56 W100 50 42. Hrs open: 24 1301 S. Abe St., San Angelo, 76903. Phone: (325) 655-7161. Fax: (325) 658-7377. Web Site:965therock.com Licensee: Double O Texas Corp. Group owner: Encore Broadcasting LLC (acq 3-15-2006; grpsl). Format: Classic rock. Target aud: 25-64. ♦John Kerr, gen mgr; Randy Phair, adv dir; Boomer Kingston, progmg dir; Garry Vaughn, engrg dir.

Stratford

***KLXN(FM)**—Not on air, target date: unknown: 91.1 mhz; 100 w horiz. Ant 118 ft TL: N36 19 31 W102 03 11. Hrs open: 116 Hillcrest Dr., Seminole, OK, 74868. Phone: (405) 380-3516.E-mail: info@bpba.us Web Site:www.bpba.us Licensee: Better Public Broadcasting Association. ♦Dennis Burton, gen mgr.

Sulphur Bluff

KYZQ(FM)—Not on air, target date: unknown: 99.7 mhz; 6 kw. Ant 318 ft TL: N33 27 29 W95 19 35. Hrs open: 410 N. Jefferson Ave., Suite 298, Mt. Pleasant, 75455. Phone: (903) 717-8305. Licensee: La Ke Manda Broadcasting. ♦Leo Ashcraft, gen mgr.

Sulphur Springs

KSCH(FM)— Aug 30, 1982: 95.9 mhz; 6 kw. 285 ft TL: N33 09 07 W95 36 12. Stereo. Hrs open: 24
Rebroadcasts KSCN(FM) Pittsburg 90%.
930 S. Gilmer, 75482. Phone: (903) 885-1546. Fax: (903) 572-7232.E-mail: hitmusic@klake.net Web Site:www.easttexasradio.com Licensee: East Texas Broadcasting Inc. (group owner; acq 9-30-99). Population served: 100,000 Fletcher, Heald & Hildreth. Format: Country. News staff: 3; News: 13 hrs wkly. Target aud: 18-60. ♦J.R. "Bud" Kitchens Jr., pres; Daniel Osuna, gen mgr, gen sls mgr.

KSST(AM)— March 1947: 1230 khz; 1 kw-U. TL: N33 07 00 W95 35 05. Hrs open: 24 Box 284, 75483. Secondary address: 717 Shannon Rd. E. 75482. Phone: (903) 885-3111. Fax: (903) 885-4160.E-mail: ksst@neto.com Web Site:www.ksstradio.com Licensee: Hopkins County Broadcasting Co. (acq 1948). Population served: 30,000 Natl. Network: ABC, . Rgnl. Network: Texas State Net. Texas State Networks Format: Full service, adult standards. News staff: 2; News: 30 hrs wkly. Target aud: 25-54. ♦Dwayne Grimes, opns dir, gen sls mgr, progmg dir, outdoor ed; Enola Gay, prom dir, mus dir, reporter, women's cmtr, disc jockey; Patsy Bradford, adv dir; Don Julian, news dir, pub affrs dir, local news ed, sports cmtr; Dolly Kelly, min affrs dir; William Bradford, CEO, pres, gen mgr, chief of engrg & edit mgr.

Sweetwater

KXOX(AM)— November 1939: 1240 khz; 1 kw-U. TL: N32 29 16 W100 23 31. Stereo. Hrs open: 24 Box 570, 79556. Secondary address: 1801 Hoyt Ln. 79556. Phone: (325) 236-6655. Fax: (325) 235-4391.E-mail: kxox@sweetwaternet.com Licensee: Stein Broadcasting Inc. (acq 1956). Population served: 14,000 Rgnl. Network: Texas State Net. Texas State Networks Wire Svc: AP Format: Country. News: 2 plus hrs wkly. Target aud: 25-54. Spec prog: Farm 5 hrs, Sp 8 hrs, gospel 4 hrs wkly. ♦Jack Stein, pres; Jeff Stein, gen mgr, prom mgr, news dir, local news ed, disc jockey; Rosie Tovar, gen sls mgr; Richard Ferguson, progmg dir, women's int ed; Gary Graham, chief of engrg.

KXOX-FM— Apr 7, 1976: 96.7 mhz; 2.9 kw. Ant 154 ft TL: N32 29 16 W100 23 31. Stereo. Hrs open: 18 Box 570, 79556. Secondary address: 1801 Hoyt Ln. 79556. Phone: (325) 236-6655. Fax: (325) 235-4391. Licensee: Stein Broadcasting Co. Inc. (acq 1976). Wire Svc: AP News staff: one. ♦Richard Ferguson, progmg dir, women's int ed; Jeff Stein, local news ed; Lillie Guttierez, spanish dir; Gary Graham, disc jockey, engr.

Tahoka

KAMZ(FM)— 2001: 103.5 mhz; 20 kw. Ant 328 ft TL: N33 19 26 W101 48 15. Hrs open: 24 1220 Broadway, Suite 1035, Lubbock, 79401. Phone: (806) 741-0701. Fax: (806) 741-0705. Licensee: Albert Benavides. Format: Mexican regional. ♦Rick Benavides, gen mgr; Bob Benavides, mus dir; Bill Enloe, chief of engrg; Connie Ledesima, traf mgr.

KMMX(FM)— Aug 13, 1987: 100.3 mhz; 100 kw. 800 ft TL: N33 26 30 W101 52 42. Stereo. Hrs open: 24 33 Briercroft Park., Lubbock, 79412. Phone: (806) 762-3000. Fax: (806) 762-8419. Web Site:www.kmmx.com Licensee: Wilks License Co.-Lubbock LLC. Group owner: NextMedia Group L.L.C. (acq 8-19-2005; grpsl). Population served: 400,000 Natl. Network: ABC, . Format: Adult contemp. News staff: one; News: 5 hrs wkly. Target aud: 25-54; females. ♦Scott Harris, gen mgr; Jeff Scott, opns mgr; Jay Richards, gen sls mgr; Damon Scott, progmg dir; Stacey James, news dir; Randy Hayes, chief of engrg; Julie Aguilar, traf mgr.

Tatum

KXAL-FM— Aug 1, 1965: 100.3 mhz; 2.45 kw. Ant 518 ft TL: N32 22 37 W94 34 18. Stereo. Hrs open: 24 Box 1648, Jacksonville, 75766. Secondary address: 402 Ragsdale, Jacksonville 75766. Phone: (903) 586-2527. Fax: (903) 589-0677.E-mail: dudleyw@wallerbroadcasting.com Licensee: Waller Media LLC. Group owner: On-Air Family LLC (acq 8-24-2005; $975,000 with KDVE(FM) Pittsburg). Population served: 250,000 Format: Sp. Target aud: 25-54. ♦Dudley Waller, gen mgr; Chris Ousley, gen sls mgr; Victor Covarrubias, progmg dir.

Taylor

KLQB(FM)— Apr 4, 1975: 104.3 mhz; 48 kw. Ant 492 ft TL: N30 26 04 W97 21 53. Stereo. Hrs open: 24 4301 Westbank Dr., Escalade B-3rd Fl., Austin, 78746-4400. Phone: (512) 327-9595. Fax: (512) 329-6255. Licensee: Entercom Austin License Inc. Group owner: Infinity Broadcasting Corp. (acq 11-30-2007; grpsl). Population served: 908,000 Natl. Rep: Katz Radio,. Leventhal, Senter & Lerman. Format: Rgnl Mexican. ♦Clint Culp, sr VP; John Hiatt, gen mgr, mktg mgr; Rodney Brown, gen sls mgr; Carla Spears, mktg dir; Dusty Hayes, progmg VP; Darell Heckendorf, engrg dir.

KWNX(AM)— Apr 1, 1948: 1260 khz; 1 kw-D. TL: N30 36 19 W97 24 51. Hrs open: 24 1050 E. 11th St., Suite 300, Austin, 78702. Phone: (512) 346-8255. Fax: (512) 346-8262.E-mail: controlroom@espnaustin.com Web Site:www.espnaustin.com Licensee: Simmons-Austin, LS LLC. Group owner: Simmons Media Group (acq 5-17-2004; $950,000). Population served: 1,000,000 Natl. Network: ESPN Deportes, . Format: Sp sports. ♦Neil Parker, prom dir; Steve Wilder, gen mgr & progmg dir; J. Cole McClellan, chief of engrg; Flavia Chen, traf mgr.

Temple

***KBDE(FM)**— 2001: 89.9 mhz; 11.5 kw vert. Ant 489 ft TL: N31 16 05 W97 21 34. Hrs open: 6304 Gardendale Dr., Waco, 76710. Phone: (254) 772-1900.E-mail: kbse89@afo.net Web Site:www.kbderadio.net Licensee: American Family Association. Group owner: American Family Radio Format: Christian. ♦Marvin Sanders, gen mgr.

KLTD(FM)— 1995: 101.7 mhz; 16.5 kw. 410 ft TL: N31 16 24 W97 23 31. Hrs open: 108 E. Ave. E., Copperas Cove, 76522. Phone: (254) 773-5252. Fax: (254) 547-2394.E-mail: info@kltdfm.com Web Site:www.cumulus.com Licensee: Cumulus Licensing Corp. Group owner: Cumulus Media Inc. (acq 4-20-01; $1.5 million including $50,000 noncompete agreement). Format: Classic Rock. ♦Bourdon Wooten, gen mgr; Mikie Cummings, gen sls mgr; Jamie Garrett, prom dir; Tom Rivers, progmg dir; Chris Cummings, news dir; Doug Bernhardt, chief of engrg; Thalesa Hector-Dixon, traf mgr.

KTEM(AM)— Nov 25, 1936: 1400 khz; 950 w-U. TL: N31 04 01 W97 23 57. Hrs open: 24 608 Moody Ln., 76504. Phone: (254) 773-5252. Fax: (254) 773-0115.E-mail: jamie.garrett@cumulus.com Web Site:www.myktem.com Licensee: Cumulus Licensing Corp. Group owner: Cumulus Media Inc. (acq 3-12-01; $425,000). Population served: 300,000 Natl. Network: CBS, . Rgnl. Network: Texas State Net. Format: News/talk, sports. News staff: one; News: 30 hrs wkly. Target aud: 35-64; affluent, educated, politically active. Spec prog: Czech 3 hrs wkly. ♦Bourdon Wooten, gen mgr, natl sls mgr; Mikie Cummings, gen sls mgr; Brian Brown, prom mgr; Jamie Garrett, progmg dir; Doug Bernhardt, chief of engrg.

KUSJ(FM)—(Harker Heights, June 1987: 105.5 mhz; 930 w. 587 ft TL: N31 05 23 W97 35 55. (CP: 33 kw, ant 600 ft. TL: N30 59 09 W97 37 51). Stereo. Hrs open: 608 Moody Ln., 76504. Phone: (254) 773-5252. Fax: (254) 773-0015.E-mail: info@kusj.com Web Site:us105.com Licensee: Cumulus Licensing Corp. Group owner: Cumulus Media Inc. (acq 2-2-00; grpsl). Format: Country. Target aud: 25-54. ♦Bourdon Wooten, gen mgr; Mikie Cummings, gen sls mgr; Jamie Garrett, prom dir; Doug Bernhardt, chief of engrg, engr.

***KVLT(FM)**— May 1, 2003: 88.5 mhz; 5 kw vert. Ant 617 ft TL: N30 59 08 W97 37 56. Stereo. Hrs open: 24 American Educational Broadcasting Inc., 3185 S. Highland Dr. #13, Las Vegas, NV, 89109. Secondary address: 3411 Market Loop, Studio, Suite 108 76502. Phone: (254) 791-5251. Fax: (254) 791-0200.E-mail: james@kvltfm.com Licensee: American Educational Broadcasting Inc. Natl. Network:

K-Love, . Fletcher, Heald & Hildreth. Format: Contemp Christian music. ◆Carl J. Auel, pres; James E. Auel, gen mgr.

Terrell

KPYK(AM)— October 1947: 1570 khz; 270 w-D, 6 w-N. TL: N32 45 17 W96 14 22. Hrs open: 24 Box 157, 75160. Secondary address: Town West Plaza, 1412-C W. Moore Ave. 75160. Phone: (972) 524-5795. Fax: (972) 524-5795.E-mail: kpyk@broadcast.net Web Site:www.kpyk.com Licensee: Mohnkern Electronics Inc. (acq 4-1-92; $25,000 plus assumption of debt; 3-16-92). Population served: 115,000 Natl. Network: USA, . Format: big band, adult standards, old radio programs. News staff: one; News: 15 hrs wkly. Target aud: 40 plus; mature adults. ◆Chuck Mohnkern, pres, gen mgr, chief of opns, gen sls mgr, progmg dir, news dir, chief of engrg, local news ed; Liz Mohnkern, asst music dir, disc jockey; Chris Babler, sports cmtr; Susan Pinson, prom dir, pub affrs dir, traf mgr & women's int ed.

Terrell Hills

KLUP(AM)— Oct 17, 1947: 930 khz; 5 kw-D, 1 kw-N, DA-N. TL: N29 31 06 W98 24 25. Hrs open: 24 9601 McAllister Fwy., Suite 1200, San Antonio, 78216. Phone: (210) 344-8481. Fax: (210) 340-1213.E-mail: myopinion@klup.com Web Site:www.klup.com Licensee: South Texas Broadcasting Inc. Group owner: Salem Communications Corp. (acq 7-27-00; grpsl). Natl. Network: Salem Radio Network, . Format: News/talk. Target aud: 35-64; upper & middle income, empty nesters. ◆Baron Wiley, gen mgr, opns mgr, progmg dir, progmg dir; James Herring, gen sls mgr.

KPWT(FM)— July 18, 1979: 106.7 mhz; 100 kw. Ant 1,017 ft TL: N29 11 03 W98 30 49. Stereo. Hrs open: 24 8122 Datapoint Dr., # 500, San Antonio, 78229. Phone: (210) 615-5400. Fax: (210) 615-5300. Web Site:www.fmtalk1067.com Licensee: Cox Radio Inc. Group owner: Cox Communications Inc. (acq 3-28-97; grpsl). Population served: 1,300,000 Wire Svc: AP Format: Talk. News staff: one. Target aud: 18-34. ◆Bob Neil, CEO; Marty Choate, VP, gen mgr; Mark Bowka, gen sls mgr; Jeff Scott, natl sls mgr; Adam Micheals, prom dir; Doug Bennett, progmg dir; Paul Reynolds, chief of engrg.

Texarkana

KCMC(AM)— Feb 26, 1932: 740 khz; 1 kw-U, DA-1. TL: N33 26 17 W94 08 33. Hrs open: 24 615 Olive St., 75501. Phone: (903) 793-4671. Fax: (903) 792-4261. Licensee: ArkLaTex LLC. (group owner; (acq 1-3-2007; grpsl). Population served: 200,000 Natl. Network: ESPN Radio, . Natl. Rep: Interep,. Format: Sports. Target aud: 18 plus; sports fans. ◆Harold Sudbury, CEO; Scott Gray, CFO, VP & progmg dir.

KEWL-FM—See New Boston

KHTA(FM)—See Wake Village

KKTK(AM)— 1946: 1400 khz; 1 kw-U. TL: N33 26 28 W94 03 16. Hrs open: 24 1323 College Dr., 75503. Phone: (903) 793-1100. Fax: (903) 794-4717. Licensee: American Media Investments Inc. Group owner: Petracom Media LLC (acq 2-17-2009; grpsl). Natl. Network: Fox News Radio, . Format: Talk. Target aud: 35 plus. ◆Charlotte Hartwell, gen mgr.

KKYR-FM— July 15, 1965: 102.5 mhz; 100 kw. 445 ft TL: N33 22 24 W94 01 00. Stereo. Hrs open: 2324 Arkansas Blvd., AR, 71854. Phone: (870) 772-3771. Fax: (870) 772-0364.E-mail: wesspicher @gapbroadcasting.com Web Site:www.kkyr.com Licensee: GAP Broadcasting Texarkana License LLC. Group owner: Clear Channel Communications Inc. (acq 8-3-2007; grpsl). Population served: 150,000 Format: Country. Target aud: General. ◆Ron Bird, gen mgr; Mitzi Dowd, gen sls mgr; Mario Garcia, progmg dir; John Williams, news dir; Wes Spicher, chief of engrg.

KOSY(AM)—See Texarkana, AR

KRMD(AM)—See Shreveport, LA

KRMD-FM—See Shreveport, LA

KTAL-FM— 1945: 98.1 mhz; 100 kw horiz, 61 kw vert. 1,360 ft TL: N32 54 11 W94 00 22. Hrs open: 24 208 N. Thomas Dr., Shreveport, LA, 71137. Phone: (318) 222-3122. Fax: (318) 459-1493.E-mail: info@98rocks.fm Web Site:www.98rocks.fm Licensee: Access. 1 Louisiana Holding Co. LLC. Group owner: Access.1 Communications Corp. (acq 12-20-02; grpsl). Format: Classic rock. News staff: one.

Target aud: 25-54. ◆Cary Camp, gen mgr; Don Zimmerman, gen sls mgr; Greg Hanson, progmg dir; Eddie Thurmand, chief of engrg.

KTFS(AM)— Oct 23, 1961: 940 khz; 2.5 kw-D, 11 w-N. TL: N33 24 28 W94 02 45. Hrs open: 24 615 Olive St., 75501. Phone: (903) 793-4671. Fax: (903) 792-4261. Licensee: ArkLaTex LLC. (group owner; (acq 1-3-2007; grpsl). Population served: 200,000 Natl. Network: Premiere Radio Networks, Radio America, Fox News Radio, Talk Radio Network, . Natl. Rep: Interep,. Format: News/talk. News staff: one; News: 25 hrs wkly. Target aud: 35 plus. ◆Harold Sudbury, CEO; Scott Gray, CFO & VP.

*KTXK(FM)— Feb 1, 1984: 91.5 mhz; 5.2 kw. 335 ft TL: N33 23 33 W94 14 44. Stereo. Hrs open: 24 2500 N. Robinson, 75599. Phone: (903) 838-4541. Fax: (903) 832-5030.E-mail: ktxktc@yahoo.com Licensee: Texarkana College. Population served: 270,000 Natl. Network: PRI, NPR, . Format: Btfl mus, class. News staff: one; News: 35 hrs wkly. Target aud: 35 plus. Spec prog: Jazz 15 hrs wkly. ◆Steve Mitchell, pres, gen mgr & chief of opns.

Texas City

KYST(AM)— November 1947: 920 khz; 5 kw-D, 1 kw-N, DA-2. TL: N29 25 03 W94 56 12. Hrs open: 7322 S.W. Fwy., Suite 500, Houston, 77074. Phone: (713) 779-9292. Fax: (713) 779-1651.E-mail: info@kyst.com Web Site:www.radiodeporte.com Licensee: Hispanic Broadcasting Inc. (acq 10-1-93; $548,000; 10-18-93). Population served: 76,400 Format: Sp. ◆Cruz Velasquez, gen mgr.

Thorndale

KLGO(FM)— Sept 30, 2005: 99.3 mhz; 6 kw. Ant 328 ft TL: N30 29 23 W97 17 56. Stereo. Hrs open: 24 6633 E. Hwy 290, Austin, 78723. Phone: (512) 637-9300. Fax: (512) 352-5425.E-mail: info@klgo.net Web Site:www.theword993.com Licensee: Jackson Lake Broadcasting Co. Natl. Network: Moody, Salem Radio Network, . Hardy, Carey & Chautin. Format: Christian, talk. News: 10 hrs wkly. Spec prog: Black 6 hrs wkly. ◆Dean Clark, opns dir; Gene Bender, gen mgr & gen sls mgr.

Three Rivers

KEMA(FM)— 2003: 94.5 mhz; 48 kw. Ant 492 ft TL: N28 43 10 W98 02 34. Hrs open: 1010 W. William Cannon Dr., Suite 402, Austin, 78745. Phone: (512) 383-1112. Licensee: Roy E. Henderson (acq 3-24-2000; $25,000 for CP). ◆Roy E. Henderson, gen mgr.

Tom Bean

KLAK(FM)— Jan 6, 1984: 97.5 mhz; 32 kw. Ant 617 ft TL: N33 28 30 W96 26 45. Stereo. Hrs open: 24 1700 Redbud Blvd., McKinney, 75069. Phone: (972) 542-9755. Phone: (866) 416-2995. Fax: (972) 838-1330.E-mail: webrequest@975klak.com Web Site:www.975klak.com Licensee: NM Licensing LLC. Group owner: NextMedia Group L.L.C. (acq 11-26-2001; grpsl). Population served: 1,100,000 Natl. Network: ABC, . Format: Adult contemp. News staff: one; News: 7 hrs wkly. Target aud: 25-54; women. ◆Steven Dinetz, CEO; Jeff Dinetz, pres; Sean Stover, CFO; Randy Friend, gen mgr; Jennifer Isbell, prom dir.

Tomball

KSEV(AM)— Dec 1, 1986: 700 khz; 25 kw-D, 1 kw-N, DA-2. TL: N30 11 34 W95 35 40. Hrs open: 11451 Katy Fwy., Suite 215, Houston, 77079. Phone: (281) 588-4800. Fax: (832) 358-9556.E-mail: thevoice@ksevradio.com Web Site:www.ksevradio.com Licensee: Liberman Broadcasting of Houston License LLC. Group owner: Liberman Broadcasting Inc. (acq 3-20-2001; grpsl). Population served: 4,500,000 Format: News/talk. ◆Dan Patrick, gen mgr; Bonny English, stn mgr, sls dir; Chuck McLeod, chief of engrg.

Tulia

KBTE(FM)— Apr 1, 1991: 104.9 mhz; 96.6 kw. Ant 977 ft TL: N33 57 35 W101 35 22. Hrs open: 24 33 Briercroft Office Park, Lubbock, 79412. Phone: (806) 762-3000. Fax: (806) 770-5363. Licensee: Wilks License Co.-Lubbock LLC. (acq 8-29-2005; $1,265,000). Natl. Network: ABC, . Format: Rhythm CHR. Target aud: 18-34. ◆Jay Richardson, gen mgr; Jeff Scott, opns mgr; Dee Brown, progmg dir; Randy Hayes, chief of engrg; Julia Aguilar, traf mgr.

KTUE(AM)— November 1954: 1260 khz; 1 kw-D, 53 w-N. TL: N34 31 34 W101 46 56. Hrs open: 24 Box 252, McAllen, 78505-0252. Phone:

(956) 686-6382. Fax: (956) 686-2999. Licensee: Paulino Bernal (acq 9-24-2004). Population served: 600,000 Rgnl. Network: Texas State Net. Format: Sp relg. Target aud: General. ◆Paulino Bernal, gen mgr.

Tye

KBCY(FM)— October 1983: 99.7 mhz; 100 kw. 744 ft TL: N32 24 39 W100 06 26. Stereo. Hrs open: 24 Box 3157, 2525 S. Danvile, Abilene, 79605. Phone: (325) 793-9700. Fax: (325) 692-1576.E-mail: info@kbcy.com Web Site:www.kbcy.com Licensee: Cumulus Licensing Corp. Group owner: Cumulus Media Inc. (acq 2-13-98; grpsl). Population served: 125,000 Format: Country. News: 21 hrs wkly. Target aud: 25-49; upscale adults. Spec prog: Relg 5 hrs wkly. ◆Jim Christoferson, gen mgr; John Scott, opns mgr; Kelly Jay, progmg dir; Chris Andrews, chief of engrg; Lori Barrett, traf mgr.

KWFA(AM)—Not on air, target date: unknown: 1030 khz; 5 kw-D, 370 w-N, DA-2. TL: N32 27 37 W99 50 03. Hrs open: 6720 Lakeview Dr., Carmichael, CA, 95608. Licensee: Marlene V. Borman. ◆Marlene V. Borman, gen mgr.

Tyler

KGLD(AM)— May 11, 1956: 1330 khz; 1 kw-D, 77 w-N. TL: N32 22 35 W95 15 55. Stereo. Hrs open: 24 2737 S Broadway, Suite 101, 75701. Phone: (903) 526-1330.E-mail: kgldradio@yahoo.com Web Site:www.kgld.org Licensee: Salt of the Earth Broadcasting Inc. (acq 6-30-2004; $160,000). Population served: 127,000 Natl. Network: ABC, . Gardner, Carton & Douglas. Format: Gospel. Spec prog: S. ◆Darrell Martin, gen mgr & progmg dir.

*KGLY(FM)— June 1988: 91.3 mhz; 12 kw. 462 ft TL: N32 21 06 W95 16 00. Stereo. Hrs open: 24 Box 8525, 75711. Secondary address: 2721 E. Erwin St. 75708. Phone: (903) 593-5863. Fax: (903) 593-2663.E-mail: kkgly@kgly.com Web Site:www.encouraagementfm.com Licensee: Educational Radio Foundation of East Texas Inc. Natl. Network: Moody, USA, . Format: Relg. News: 3 hrs wkly. Target aud: 35 plus. ◆Dan Bolin, gen mgr; John Paul Little, stn mgr; Leah Coombs, mus dir; Sans Hawkins, chief of engrg.

KISX(FM)—See Whitehouse

KKUS(FM)— 1990: 104.1 mhz; 50 kw. 492 ft TL: N32 29 40 W95 28 55. Stereo. Hrs open: 24 Box 7820, 75711. Secondary address: 210 S Broadway 75702. Phone: (903) 581-9966. Fax: (903) 534-5300.E-mail: kkus@etradiogroup.com Web Site:www.theranch.fm Licensee: Access.1 Texas License Company LLC. Group owner: Waller Broadcasting. (acq 1-7-2005; grpsl). Population served: 300,000 Natl. Network: Fox News Radio, . Natl. Rep: McGavren Guild,. Format: Classic Country. Target aud: 35+. ◆Tom Perryman, gen mgr; Genni Causey, gen sls mgr; Robert Taylor, natl sls mgr; Chuck McKinley, progmg dir.

KNUE(FM)— Dec 31, 1964: 101.5 mhz; 100 kw. 1,074 ft TL: N32 15 35 W94 57 02. Stereo. Hrs open: 24 3810 Brookside, 75701. Phone: (903) 581-0606. Fax: (903) 581-2011.E-mail: craigreininger @gapbroadcasting.com Web Site:www.knue.com Licensee: GAP Broadcasting Tyler License LLC. Group owner: Clear Channel Communications Inc. (acq 8-3-2007; grpsl). Population served: 750,000 Format: Country. Target aud: General. ◆Steve Joos, gen mgr; Craig Reininger, sls dir; Chris Jones, prom dir, adv dir; Michael Gibson, progmg dir, mus dir; Dave Goldman, news dir; Laura Conway, traf mgr.

KTBB(AM)— Aug 28, 1947: 600 khz; 5 kw-D, 2.5 kw-N, DA-2. TL: N32 16 18 W95 12 23. Stereo. Hrs open: 24 Box 6, 75710-0006. Phone: (903) 593-2519. Fax: (903) 593-4918. Web Site:www.ktbb.com Licensee: Gleiser Communications LLC (group owner; acq 11-21-2003; grpsl). Population served: 533,000 Rgnl. Network: Texas State Net. Texas State Networks Gardner, Carton & Douglas. Format: Full service, news/talk, sports & info. News staff: 7; News: 70 hrs wkly. Target aud: 35 plus. Spec prog: Gospel 5 hrs wkly. ◆Paul L. Gleiser, CEO, pres, gen mgr & sls dir; Garth Maier, progmg dir, news dir; Barry Davis, news dir; Mike LaRoux, chief of engrg; Angie Mapes, traf mgr.

KTBB-FM— November 1975: 92.1 mhz; 9.6 kw. Ant 443 ft TL: N32 22 28 W95 16 24. Stereo. Hrs open: 24 Box 92, 75710-0092. Phone: (903) 593-2519. Phone: (903) 592-5200. Fax: (903) 597-4141. Web Site:www.ktbb.com Licensee: Gleiser Communications LLC acq 11-21-2003; grpsl). Format: Talk. News staff: one; News: 2 hrs wkly. Target aud: 35 plus. Spec prog: Tyler Junior Collete football, Saturday Night Big Band Dance Party. ◆Paul Berry, progmg dir, news dir; Mark Lavoux, chief of engrg; Deborah Harrington, traf mgr, political ed; Barry Davis, news rptr; Bill Davis, disc jockey.

KTYL-FM— February 1966: 93.1 mhz; 82 kw. Ant 938 ft TL: N32 15 35 W94 57 02. Stereo. Hrs open: 24 3810 Brookside Dr., 75701-9420. Phone: (903) 581-0606. Fax: (903) 581-2011.E-mail: craigreininger

@gapbroadcasting.com Web Site:www.mix931.com Licensee: GAP Broadcasting Tyler License LLC. Group owner: Clear Channel Communications Inc. (acq 8-3-2007; grpsl). Population served: 825,000 Format: Hot adult contemp. Target aud: 18-54. ♦Steve Joos, gen mgr; Craig Reininger, sls dir; Chris Jones, gen sls mgr; Jeff Evans, progmg dir.

***KVNE(FM)—** Oct 15, 1983: 89.5 mhz; 100 kw. 899 ft TL: N32 32 21 W95 13 16. (CP: 96 kw). Stereo. Hrs open: 24 Box 8525, 75711. Phone: (903) 593-5863. Web Site:www.kvne.com Licensee: Educational Radio Foundation of East Texas Inc. Format: Relg. News: 6 hrs wkly. Target aud: 20-45; families. Spec prog: Gospel 4 hrs, children 4 hrs, Sp 2 hrs wkly. ♦Mike Harper, stn mgr.

KYZS(AM)— 1930: 1490 khz; 1 kw-U. TL: N32 22 30 W95 16 05. Stereo. Hrs open: 24 Box 6, 75710. Phone: (903) 593-2519. Fax: (903) 597-4141. Web Site:www.ktbb.com Licensee: Gleiser Communications LLC (group owner; acq 11-21-2003; grpsl). Format: ESPN radio-sports. ♦Paul Gleiser, gen mgr & opns mgr; Garth Maier, progmg dir; Mike LaRoux, chief of engrg; Angie Mapes, traf mgr.

KZEY(AM)— 1958: 690 khz; 1 kw-D, 92 w-N, DA-2. TL: N32 22 52 W95 20 52. Hrs open: 24 Box 4248, 75712. Phone: (903) 593-1744. Licensee: Community Broadcast Group Inc. Population served: 150,000 Format: Urban contemp. Target aud: General. ♦Esther Milton, gen mgr.

Universal City

KSAH(AM)— Nov 1, 1986: 720 khz; 10 kw-D, 1 kw-N, DA-2. TL: N29 31 51 W98 10 39. Stereo. Hrs open: 24 4500 Eisenhauer Rd., San Antonio, 78218. Phone: (210) 654-5100. Fax: (210) 340-1775. Licensee: BMP San Antonio License Co. L.P. Group owner: Border Media Partners LLC (acq 4-28-2004; $24.4 million with KTFM(FM) Floresville). Format: Accordian-based music of northern Mexico. News staff: one; News: 2 hrs wkly. Target aud: 18-49. ♦Lance Hawkins, gen mgr; Bob Brown, sls dir.

University Park

KTNO(AM)— 1938: 1440 khz; 15 kw-D, 350 w-N, DA-2. TL: N32 45 02 W96 43 22. Hrs open: 24 5787 S. Hampton Rd., Suite 340, Dallas, 75232. Phone: (214) 330-5866. Fax: (214) 330-9885.E-mail: radiovida@ktno.com Web Site:www.ktnoam.com Licensee: Mortenson Broadcasting Co. of Texas Inc. (group owner; (acq 8-8-97; $650,000). Population served: 39,874 Natl. Network: ABC, . Format: Sp, talk info, Christian. News staff: 2; News: 40 hrs wkly. Target aud: 25 plus. ♦Jose Alfredo Castillo, gen mgr, gen sls mgr, progmg dir; Mike Benhauser, chief of engrg; Erica Garcia, traf mgr.

KZMP(AM)— 1999: 1540 khz; 32 kw-D, 750 kw-N, DA-2. TL: N32 48 45 W97 00 30. Hrs open: 24 400 E. Las Colinas Blvd., Suite 1033, Irving, 75039. Phone: (214) 258-2800. Fax: (214) 258-2809. Licensee: Liberman Broadcasting of Dallas License LLC. Group owner: Entravision Communications Corp. (acq 11-2-2006; grpsl). Population served: 6,153,500 Natl. Network: ESPN Deportes, . Natl. Rep: Lotus Entravision Reps LLC,. Wiley, Rein & Fielding. Format: Sp sports. ♦Peter Dits, gen mgr.

Uvalde

KBNU(FM)— 1996: 93.9 mhz; 25 kw horiz, 14.3 kw vert. Ant 292 ft TL: N29 16 34 W99 41 44. Stereo. Hrs open: 24
Rebroadcast KBLT(FM) Leakey 100%.
1010 Garner Field Rd., 78801. Phone: (830) 278-3693. Fax: (830) 278-2329.E-mail: kbradioranch@hotmail.com Web Site:wwwkbnu.fm Licensee: Radio Cactus Ltd. (acq 10-23-00; $60,916 for 51% of stock with KBLT(FM) Leakey). John Mc Veigh. Format: Classic country. News staff: 0. Target aud: General; 18-49. ♦John Furr, CEO, progmg dir, chief of engrg; Paula Furr, CFO; Regenia Tumbarello, gen mgr, gen sls mgr & prom dir.

KUVA(FM)— Aug 20, 1984: 102.3 mhz; 3 kw. 280 ft TL: N29 11 46 W99 46 48. Stereo. Hrs open: 24 Box 758, 1400 Batesville Rd., 78801. Phone: (830) 278-2555. Fax: (830) 278-9461.E-mail: production @uvalderadio.com Web Site:www.uvalderadio.com Licensee: Rhattigan Broadcasting (Texas) LP (group owner; acq 6-3-2004; grpsl). Population served: 100,000 Natl. Network: ABC, . Texas State Networks Baraff, Koerner & Olender. Format: Sp, Tejano. News staff: one; News: 6 hrs wkly. Target aud: 16-60; Hispanic. ♦Glenn Tryon, gen mgr.

KVOU(AM)— Apr 4, 1947: 1400 khz; 1 kw-U. TL: N29 11 16 W99 46 36. Hrs open: 24 Box 758, 78802-0758. Secondary address: 1400 Batesville Rd. 78801. Phone: (830) 278-2555. Fax: (830) 278-9461.E-mail: production@uvalderadio.com Web Site:www.uvalderadio.com Licensee: Rhattigan Broadcasting (Texas) LP (group owner; (acq 8-19-2004; grpsl). Population served: 85,800 Rgnl. Network: VSA Radio. Texas State Networks Baraff, Koerner & Olender. Format: Christian Adult Contemp. News staff: one; News: 15 hrs wkly. Target aud: 25-54; general. Spec prog: Farm 12 hrs wkly. ♦Glenn Tryon, gen mgr.

KVOU-FM— Sept 9, 1976: 104.9 mhz; 25 kw. 263 ft TL: N29 11 16 W99 46 36. Stereo. Hrs open: 24 Box 758, 78802-0758. Secondary address: 1400 Batesville Rd. 78801. Phone: (830) 278-2555. Fax: (830) 278-9461.E-mail: production@uvalderadio.com Web Site:www.uvalderadio.com Licensee: Rhattigan Broadcasting (Texas) LP (group owner; (acq 8-19-2004; grpsl). Texas State Networks Baraff, Koerner & Olender. Format: Country. News staff: 1; News: 15+ hrs wkly. Target aud: 18-49. Spec prog: High school play-by-play sports. ♦Glenn Tryon, gen mgr.

Van Horn

***KVHR(FM)—**Not on air, target date: unknown: 91.5 mhz; 100 w. Ant -95 ft TL: N31 02 02 W104 51 19. Hrs open: Drawer 2440, Tupelo, MS, 38803. Phone: (662) 844-5036. Fax: (662) 842-7798.E-mail: info@afa.net Web Site:www.afr.net Licensee: American Family Association. ♦Donald E. Wildmon, chmn.

Vernon

KVWC(AM)— July 1939: 1490 khz; 1 kw-U. TL: N34 09 12 W99 16 09. Hrs open: 6 AM-10 PM Box 1419, 76385. Secondary address: 302 E. Wilbarger 76384. Phone: (940) 552-6221. Fax: (940) 553-4222.E-mail: kvwc@kvwc.com Web Site:www.kvwc.com Licensee: KVWC Inc. (acq 6-1-61). Population served: 25,000 Natl. Rep: Riley,. Format: Oldies, farm, country. News staff: one; News: 10 hrs wkly. Target aud: General; Wilbarger & surrounding counties. Spec prog: Gospel 16 hrs wkly. ♦Mike Klappenbach, pres, gen mgr, progmg dir & chief of engrg.

KVWC-FM— Apr 10, 1972: 103.1 mhz; 6 kw. Ant 141 ft TL: N34 09 12 W99 16 09. Stereo. Hrs open: 6 AM-10 PM Dups AM 100% Box 1419, 76385. Secondary address: 302 E. Wilbarger 76384. Phone: (940) 552-6221. Fax: (940) 553-4222. Web Site:www.kvwc.com Population served: 100,000 ♦Mike Klappenbach, gen mgr.

Victoria

***KAYK(FM)—** October 2003: 88.5 mhz; 50 kw vert. Ant 282 ft TL: N28 46 43 W97 02 51. Hrs open: Box 3206, Tupelo, MS, 38803. Phone: (662) 844-8888.E-mail: info@kaykfm.com Web Site:www.afr.net Licensee: American Family Association. Group owner: American Family Radio Population served: 122,000 Format: Christian. ♦Marvin Sanders, gen mgr.

KBAR-FM— Feb 2, 1989: 100.9 mhz; 6 kw. Ant 272 ft TL: N28 47 20 W97 03 00. Hrs open: Box 3487, 77903. Secondary address: 3613 N. Main St. 77901. Phone: (361) 576-6111. Fax: (361) 572-0014. Licensee: Victoria RadioWorks Ltd. (group owner; (acq 1999; $27,500). Population served: 1,000,000 Format: Modern Rock. ♦Cindy Cox, gen mgr.

KITE(FM)—(Port Lavaca, Aug 1, 1976: 93.3 mhz; 100 kw. Ant 318 ft TL: N28 42 22 W96 48 03. Stereo. Hrs open: Box 3487, 77903. Secondary address: 3613 N. Main St. 77903. Phone: (361) 576-6111. Fax: (361) 572-0014. Licensee: Victoria RadioWorks Ltd. (group owner; (acq 10-29-98; $500,000). Population served: 500,000 Natl. Rep: McGavren Guild,. Format: Oldies. Spec prog: Farm one hr wkly. ♦Cindy Cox, gen mgr.

KIXS(FM)— Dec 4, 1980: 107.9 mhz; 100 kw. Ant 505 ft TL: N28 42 24 W96 50 06. Stereo. Hrs open: Box 3325, 77903. Secondary address: 107 North Star Dr. 77904. Phone: (361) 573-0777. Fax: (361) 578-0059.E-mail: kixs@gapbroadcasting.com Web Site:www.kixs.com Licensee: GAP Broadcasting Victoria License LLC. Group owner: Clear Channel Communications Inc. (acq 10-1-2007; grpsl). Population served: 187,000 Format: C&W. Target aud: 25-49; listeners in a growth & acquisition mode. ♦Jeff Lyon, gen mgr; Natalie Franz, gen sls mgr, natl sls mgr; James Love, prom dir, news dir, pub affrs dir; Eric Sharp, progmg dir; Joe Bob Burris, mus dir, disc jockey; Charles Smithey, chief of engrg; Joe Friday, disc jockey.

KNAL(AM)— Apr 16, 1948: 1410 khz; 500 w-U, DA-N. TL: N28 46 48 W97 00 08. Hrs open: 24 Box 3487, 77903. Secondary address: 3613 N. Main St. 77901. Phone: (361) 576-6111. Fax: (361) 572-0014. Licensee: Victoria RadioWorks Ltd. (group owner; (acq 2-1-2002; $100,000). Population served: 100,000 Fletcher, Heald & Hildreth. Format: Adult standards. ♦Cindy Cox, gen mgr.

KQVT(FM)— Dec 1, 1990: 92.3 mhz; 6 kw. Ant 298 ft TL: N28 46 04 W96 59 12. Stereo. Hrs open: 24 107 North Star Dr., 77904. Phone: (361) 573-0777. Fax: (361) 578-0059.E-mail: kixs@gapbroadcasting.com Web Site:www.kqvt.com Licensee: GAP Broadcasting Victoria License LLC. Group owner: Clear Channel Communications Inc. (acq 10-1-2007; grpsl). Population served: 100,000 Format: Adult contemp. ♦Jeff Lyon, gen mgr; Natalie Franz, gen sls mgr & natl sls mgr; James Love, prom dir, prom dir, news dir, pub affrs dir; J.P. Stone, progmg mgr; Charles Smithey, chief of engrg.

KTXN-FM— Dec 1, 1994: 98.7 mhz; 100 kw. Ant 253 ft TL: N28 48 46 W97 03 45. Stereo. Hrs open: 24 107 N. Star Dr., 77904-2082. Phone: (361) 573-0777. Fax: (361) 578-0059. Web Site:www.987jack.com Licensee: Broadcast Equities Texas Inc. Population served: 58,035 Drinker Biddle & Reath LLP. Format: Adult hits. Target aud: 18-54; general. ♦Jeff Lyon, gen mgr.

KVIC(FM)— Apr 8, 1976: 95.1 mhz; 13 kw. Ant 459 ft TL: N28 46 55 W96 56 29. Stereo. Hrs open: 24 Box 3487, 77903. Secondary address: 3613 N. Main St. 77901. Phone: (361) 576-6111. Fax: (361) 572-0014). Format: Adult contemp, CHR. Target aud: 18-49.

KVNN(AM)— January 1940: 1340 khz; 1 kw-U. TL: N28 49 49 W97 00 33. Hrs open: 24 Box 3487, 77903. Secondary address: 3613 N. Main St. 77901. Phone: (361) 576-6111. Fax: (361) 572-0014. Licensee: Victoria RadioWorks Ltd. (group owner; (acq 10-26-98; $2.1 million with co-located FM). Population served: 300,000 Rgnl. Network: Texas State Net. Natl. Rep: McGavren Guild,. Texas State Networks Format: Traditional country. Target aud: 25-54; adults. ♦Cindy Cox, gen mgr.

***KVRT(FM)—** 1995: 90.7 mhz; 30 kw. 328 ft TL: N28 46 55 W96 56 30. Hrs open:
Rebroadcasts KEDT-FM Corpus Christi 100%.
4455 S. Padre Island Dr., Suite 38, Corpus Christi, 78411-1690. Phone: (361) 855-2213. Fax: (361) 855-3877. Licensee: South Texas Public Broadcasting System Inc. Natl. Network: NPR, . Format: Class, news, jazz. ♦Don Dunlap, pres, gen mgr; Myra Lombardo, exec VP & VP; Bob Scott, chief of engrg.

***KXBJ(FM)—** Sept 1, 1994: 89.3 mhz; 18.5 kw. 336 ft TL: N28 49 20 W96 58 20. Stereo. Hrs open:
Rebroadcasts KSBJ(FM) Humble 100%.
Box 187, Humble, 77347. Secondary address: 2207 Wildwood St. 77901. Phone: (361) 574-8936. Fax: (361) 575-0175.E-mail: kxbj@ksbj.org Web Site:www.kxbj.org Licensee: KSBJ Educational Foundation. Population served: 72,596 Natl. Network: USA, . Hardy & Carey. Format: Contemp Christian mus, relg. Target aud: 25-54. ♦Dr. Billy Powell, pres; Tim McDermott, gen mgr; Bard Letsinger, stn mgr; Jon Hull, progmg dir.

Waco

KBBW(AM)— April 1953: 1010 khz; 10 kw-D, 2.5 kw-N, DA-2. TL: N31 34 09 W97 00 00. Hrs open: 1019 Washington Ave., 76701. Phone: (254) 757-1010. Fax: (254) 752-5339.E-mail: info@1010kbw.com Web Site:www.1010kbw.com Licensee: Steve Williams dba American Broadcasting of Texas. (acq 6-16-86; 5-12-86). Population served: 4,500,000 Format: Christian. Target aud: 25-54. ♦Elizabeth Layne, stn mgr, opns dir; Ryan Williams, opns dir, prom dir; Steve Williams, pres, gen mgr, gen sls mgr & progmg dir; Dave Fricker, chief of engrg.

KBCT-FM— Aug 1, 1996: 94.5 mhz; 3.2 kw. Ant 453 ft TL: N31 30 31 W97 10 03. Hrs open: 24 4701 W. Waco Dr., 76710. Phone: (254) 388-5945.E-mail: info@kbct.com Web Site:www.lonestar94.com Licensee: Kennelwood Broadcasting Co. Inc. Population served: 225,405 Format: News/talk. ♦Jerry Lenamon, pres & gen mgr.

KBGO(FM)— Sept 6, 1959: 95.7 mhz; 24 kw. 505 ft TL: N31 30 51 W97 11 43. Stereo. Hrs open: 24 314 W. State Hwy. 6, 76712. Phone: (254) 776-3900. Fax: (254) 761-6371.E-mail: brenthenslee @clearchannel.com Web Site:www.oldies95online.com Licensee: Capstar TX L.P. Group owner: Clear Channel Communications Inc. (acq 8-30-00; grpsl). Population served: 450,000 Format: Oldies. Target aud: 35-64. ♦Evan Armstrong, gen mgr; Zack Owen, opns dir & opns mgr; Vernon Riggs, sls dir; Brett Henslee, progmg dir, chief of engrg.

KBRQ(FM)—See Hillsboro

KRZI(AM)— 2001: 1660 khz; 10 kw-D, 1 kw-N. TL: N31 24 46 W97 12 18. Hrs open: 220 S. 2nd St., Apt. 2B2, 76701-2250. Phone: (254) 772-0930. Fax: (254) 753-0499.E-mail: production@hot.rr.com Web Site:www.1660espn.com Licensee: Simmons Austin, LS LLC. Group owner: Simmons Media Group (acq 6-4-2004; grpsl). Natl. Network: ESPN Radio, . Format: Sports. ♦Daryl O'Neal, gen mgr; Bill Le Grand, sls dir; Tom Barfield, opns mgr & progmg dir.

*KVLW(FM)— 2005: 88.1 mhz; 16.5 kw vert. Ant 1,096 ft TL: N31 18 53 W97 19 36. Hrs open: American Educational Broadcasting Inc., 3185 S. Highland Dr., Suite 13, Las Vegas, NV, 89109. Secondary address: 3411 Market Loop, Studio, Suite 108, Temple 76502. Phone: (254) 791-5251. Fax: (254) 791-0200. Licensee: American Educational Broadcasting Inc. Natl. Network: K-Love, . Fletcher, Heald & Hildreth. Format: Contemp Christian music. ◆Carl Auel, pres; James E. Auel, gen mgr.

*KWBU-FM— Mar 15, 1966: 107.1 mhz; 3 kw. 190 ft TL: N31 31 51 W97 09 10. Hrs open: 7-1 am One Bear Pl. #972961, 76798-7296. Phone: (254) 710-4470. Phone: (254) 710-6909. Fax: (254) 710-1563.E-mail: kwbu@baylor.edu Web Site:www.baylor.edu/kwbu Licensee: Baylor University. Population served: 146600 Natl. Network: NPR, PRI, . Format: Class, div. News staff: one; News: 10 hrs wkly. Target aud: under 45; college age. Spec prog: Jazz 10 hrs wkly. ◆Polly Anderson, pres; Brodie Bashaw, gen mgr, stn mgr; Derek Smith, news dir, pub affrs dir, sports cmtr; Tony Poole, engrg dir & chief of engrg.

KWTX(AM)— May 1, 1946: 1230 khz; 5 kw-D, 250 w-N, DA-2. TL: N31 31 42 W97 07 14. Hrs open: 24 314 W. State Hwy. 6, 76712. Phone: (254) 776-3900. Fax: (254) 761-6371.E-mail: info@newstalk1230.com Web Site:newstalk1230.com Licensee: Capstar TX L.P. Group owner: Clear Channel Communications Inc. (acq 8-30-2000; grpsl). Natl. Network: ABC, . Natl. Rep: Clear Channel,. Format: News/talk. Target aud: 35-64; adults. ◆Michael Oppenheimer, gen mgr; Zack Owen, opns mgr; Evan Armstrong, gen sls mgr; Gloria Norris, natl sls mgr; Max Watson, progmg dir; Steve Keating, chief of engrg.

KWTX-FM— Dec 1, 1970: 97.5 mhz; 97 kw. 1,568 ft TL: N31 19 19 W97 18 58. Stereo. Hrs open: 24 Prog sep from AM 314 W. State Hwy. 6, 76712. Phone: (254) 776-3900. Fax: (254) 761-6371.E-mail: info@975online.com Web Site:www.975online.com Population served: 143,000 Format: CHR. Target aud: 25-49; women. ◆Jay Charles, progmg dir.

WACO-FM— June 1960: 99.9 mhz; 90 kw. 1,660 ft TL: N31 20 15 W97 18 37. Stereo. Hrs open: 314 W. State Hwy. 6, 76712. Phone: (254) 776-3900. Fax: (254) 761-6371.E-mail: info@waco100.com Web Site:www.waco100.com Licensee: Capstar TX L.P. Group owner: Clear Channel Communications Inc. (acq 8-30-00; grpsl). Population served: 500,000 Format: Country. ◆Evan Armstrong, gen mgr, gen sls mgr; Zack Owen, opns dir & progmg dir; Brett Gilbert, chief of engrg; Darla Walson, traf mgr.

Wake Village

*KHTA(FM)— Sept 22, 2000: 92.5 mhz; 25 kw. Ant 328 ft TL: N33 24 53 W93 58 12. Hrs open: 24 Houston Christian Broadcasters Inc., 2424 South Blvd., Houston, 77098. Phone: (713) 520-5200.E-mail: email@khcb.org Web Site:www.khcb.org Licensee: Houston Christian Broadcasters Inc. (group owner) Natl. Network: Moody, . Format: Bible teaching, inspirational music. Target aud: General; all ages, families. ◆Bonnie BeMent, pres; Bruce Munsterman, gen mgr & stn mgr.

Waskom

KQHN(FM)— 1968: 97.3 mhz; 42 kw. Ant 533 ft TL: N32 29 36 W93 45 55. Stereo. Hrs open: 24 Box 5459, Bossier City, LA, 71171. Secondary address: 270 Plaza Loop, Bossier City 71111. Phone: (318) 549-8500. Fax: (318) 549-8505.E-mail: cumulus.shreveport@cumulus.com Web Site:mixfm973.com Licensee: Cumulus Licensing LLC. Group owner: Cumulus Media Inc. (acq 11-1-2002; $1.75 million). Rgnl. Network: Ark. Radio Net. Format: Hot adult contemp. ◆Susan Lucchesi, gen mgr; Phil Robkin, sls dir; Casey Ryan Buddia, gen sls mgr; Paul Furnham, rgnl sls mgr; Gary Robinson, prom dir, progmg dir; John Sherman, news dir; Jasen Bragg, engrg dir.

Waxahachie

KBEC(AM)— June 1955: 1390 khz; 480 w-D, 260 w-N, DA-2. TL: N32 26 45 W96 48 15. Hrs open: 24 711 Ferris Ave., 75165. Phone: (972) 923-1390. Fax: (972) 935-0871.E-mail: info@kbec.com Web Site:www.kbec.com Licensee: Faye and Richard Tuck Inc. Population served: 400,000 Rgnl. Network: Texas State Net. Texas State Networks Format: Classic country. News staff: one; News: 15 hrs wkly. Target aud: 25-54. Spec prog: Farm 5 hrs. ◆Ken Roberts, gen mgr; Barry Wolverton, gen sls mgr; Richard Adams, news dir; Cristi Beaver, spec ev coord; Coco Coco, disc jockey.

Weatherford

*KMQX(FM)— 1995: 92.9 mhz; 6 kw. Ant -177 ft TL: N34 02 43 W106 54 21. Hrs open: 24 905 Palo Pinto St., 76086-4135. Phone: (817)

341-2337. Fax: (817) 613-0230.E-mail: chb890@swbell.net Web Site:www.kyqx.com Licensee: CSSI Non-Profit Educational Broadcast Inc. Population served: 1,361,541 Hill & Welch. Format: Oldies 40s-60s, loc sports, news. News staff: 3. ◆Charles H. Beard, CEO; Mindy Beard, VP.

*KYQX(FM)— Jan 5, 1986: 89.5 mhz; 4.5 kw. Ant 518 ft TL: N32 51 05 W98 06 31. Hrs open: 24 905 Palo Pinto St., 76086-4135. Phone: (817) 341-2337. Fax: (817) 613-0230.E-mail: chb890@swbell.net Web Site:www.qxfm.com Licensee: CSSI Non Profit Educational Broadcasting Corp. Population served: 1,943,645 Tim Welch. Format: Lite rock. News staff: 3; News: 7 hrs wkly. ◆Charles Beard, CEO, pres; John Peterson, gen mgr.

KZEE(AM)— Aug 12, 1956: 1220 khz; 500 w-D, 8 w-N. TL: N32 47 09 W97 47 55. Hrs open: Box 54803, Hurst, 76054. Phone: (817) 594-1220. Phone: (817) 849-1971. Web Site:www.radio1220am.com Licensee: Tarrant Radio Broadcasting Inc. (acq 9-5-01; $800,000). Population served: 25,000 Format: Christian Gospel. ◆Parvez Malik, pres; Cima Hernandez, gen mgr.

Wellington

KXME(FM)—Not on air, target date: unknown: 98.5 mhz; 25 kw. Ant 328 ft TL: N34 48 37 W100 19 46. Hrs open: Box 880, Roma, 78584. Phone: (956) 487-8015. Licensee: South Texas FM Investments LLC. (acq 9-11-2008; grpsl). ◆Eloy Vera, gen mgr.

Wells

KVLL-FM— 1993: 94.7 mhz; 50 kw. Ant 384 ft TL: N31 06 47 W94 48 32. Hrs open: 24 Box 2209, Lufkin, 75902-2209. Secondary address: 1216 S. 1st St., Lufkin 75901-4716. Phone: (936) 639-4455. Fax: (936) 639-5540.E-mail: johnnylathrop@gapbroadcasting.com Licensee: GAP Broadcasting Lufkin License LLC. (acq 10-2-2007; $750,000). Format: Oldies. ◆Johnny Lathrop, gen mgr.

Weslaco

KHKZ(FM)—See Mercedes

KRGE(AM)— 1926: 1290 khz; 5 kw-U, DA-N. TL: N26 12 36 W97 54 33. Hrs open: 24 Box 1290, 2720 W Hwy Business 83, 78596. Phone: (956) 968-7777. Fax: (956) 968-5143.E-mail: egarza@radiovida.com Web Site:www.radiovida.com Licensee: Christian Ministries of the Valley. (acq 1-31-91; 2-18-91). Population served: 20,007 Format: Christian, Sp. News: 3 hrs wkly. Target aud: 18-34. ◆Enrique Garza, gen mgr.

West Lake Hills

KTXZ(AM)— June 9, 1982: 1560 khz; 2.5 kw-U, DA-2. TL: N30 21 38 W97 39 11. Hrs open: 24 2211 S. IH 35, Suite 401, Austin, 78741. Phone: (512) 416-1100. Fax: (512) 453-6809. Web Site:www.ktxz.com Licensee: Encino Broadcasting LLC. (acq 2-15-2008; grpsl). Natl. Network: CNN Radio, Westwood One, . Format: Tejano. News: 14 hrs wkly. Target aud: 18-54; bilingual, Hispanic, male & female. Spec prog: Christian mus 6 hrs wkly. ◆Paul Danitz, gen mgr.

West Odessa

*KFRI(FM)— 2001: 88.7 mhz; 100 kw. Ant 426 ft TL: N31 50 53 W102 27 04. Hrs open: 24 2351 Sunset Blvd., Suite 170-218, Rocklin, CA, 95765. Phone: (916) 251-1600. Fax: (916) 251-1650.E-mail: klove@klove.com Web Site:www.klove.com Licensee: Educational Media Foundation. Group owner: EMF Broadcasting. Natl. Network: K-Love,. Shaw Pittman. Format: Contemp Christian. News staff: 3. Target aud: 25-44; Judeo Christian, female. ◆Richard Jenkins, pres; Mike Novak, VP; Keith Whipple, dev dir; David Pierce, progmg mgr; Ed Lenane, news dir; Sam Wallington, engrg dir; Karen Johnson, news rptr.

Wharton

KANI(AM)— June 17, 1962: 1500 khz; 500 w-U, DA-N. TL: N29 19 22 W96 03 32. Hrs open: Box 350, 77488. Secondary address: 215 E. Milam St. 77488. Phone: (979) 532-3800. Fax: (979) 532-8510.E-mail: kaniam1500@yahoo.com Licensee: Martin Broadcasting Inc. Population served: 43,000 Rgnl. Network: Texas State Net. Texas State Networks Format: Relg Christian. Spec prog: Sp 3 hrs, Pol 6 hrs wkly. ◆Sandra Stewart, gen mgr, gen sls mgr, progmg dir & news dir.

Wheeler

*KBDW(FM)—Not on air, target date: unknown: 91.3 mhz; 100 w horiz. Ant 321 ft TL: N35 25 57 W100 16 31. Hrs open: 1006 S. Main St., 79096. Phone: (806) 826-5202. Licensee: Solid Rock Foundation. ◆Gary D. Ware, pres.

*KLXL(FM)—Not on air, target date: unknown: 88.3 mhz; 100 w horiz. Ant 341 ft TL: N35 25 57 W100 16 31. Hrs open: 116 Hillcrest Dr., Seminole, OK, 74868. Phone: (405) 380-3516.E-mail: info@bpba.us Web Site:www.bpba.us Licensee: Better Public Broadcasting Association. ◆Dennis Burton, gen mgr.

*KPDR(FM)— Aug 31, 1986: 90.5 mhz; 10 kw. 482 ft TL: N35 25 57 W100 16 31. Stereo. Hrs open: 24 Box 8088, 5754 Canyon Dr., Amarillo, 79114. Phone: (806) 359-8855. Fax: (806) 354-2039.E-mail: kjrt@kingdomkeys.org Web Site:www.kingdomkeys.org Licensee: Top O' Texas Educational Broadcasting Foundation. Natl. Network: USA, . Dow, Lohnes & Albertson. Format: Relg, educ. Target aud: General. Spec prog: Sp 5 hrs wkly. ◆Ricky Pfeil, pres & gen mgr.

White Oak

KZTK(FM)— May 17, 2002: 99.3 mhz; 34 kw. Ant 541 ft TL: N32 35 17 W94 58 53. Hrs open: 24 212 Grande Blvd., , B 100, Tyler, 75703. Phone: (903) 581-5259. Fax: (903) 939-3473.E-mail: chelle@theblaze.cc Web Site:www.993jackfm.com Licensee: Reynolds Radio Inc. (group owner) Format: Adult hits. ◆Robin George, gen sls mgr; Charlie O'Douglas, progmg dir; Chelle Wright-Peterson, traf mgr.

Whitehouse

KISX(FM)— Aug 15, 1982: 107.3 mhz; 50 kw. Ant 500 ft TL: N32 17 19 W95 11 56. Stereo. Hrs open: 24 3810 Brookside Dr., Tyler, 75701. Phone: (903) 581-0606. Fax: (903) 581-2011.E-mail: craigreininger @gapbroadcasting.com Web Site:www.kiss107i.com Licensee: GAP Broadcasting Tyler License LLC. Group owner: Clear Channel Communications Inc. (acq 8-3-2007; grpsl). Population served: 750,000 Format: CHR. Target aud: 18-44. ◆Steve Joos, gen mgr; Craig Reininger, sls dir; Larry Thompson, progmg dir.

Whitesboro

KMAD-FM— June 1, 1985: 102.5 mhz; 18 kw. Ant 672 ft TL: N33 41 31 W96 26 36. Stereo. Hrs open: 24 101 E. Main St., Suite 255, Denison, 75021. Phone: (903) 463-6800. Fax: (903) 463-9816.E-mail: info@kmad.com Web Site:www.theclassicrockexperience.com Licensee: NM Licensing LLC. Group owner: NextMedia Group L.L.C. (acq 11-26-2001; grpsl). Format: Classic rock. ◆David Smith, gen mgr; Jennifer Isbell, prom dir; Jason Taylor, progmg dir.

Wichita Falls

KBZS(FM)— Nov 15, 1984: 106.3 mhz; 2.4 kw. 423 ft TL: N33 53 18 W98 34 08. (CP: 15.5 kw, ant 899 ft. TL: N33 53 23 W98 33 31). Stereo. Hrs open: 24 2525 Kell Blvd., Suite 200, 76308. Phone: (940) 763-1111. Fax: (940) 322-3166. Web Site:www.1063thebuzz.com Licensee: GAP Broadcasting Wichita Falls License LLC. Group owner: Clear Channel Communications Inc. (acq 8-3-2007; grpsl). Natl. Network: Westwood One, . Natl. Rep: McGavren Guild,. Format: AOR, adult contemp. Target aud: 18-49. ◆George Laughlin, pres; Kim Dodds, gen mgr; Chris Walters, opns mgr, news dir; Melissa Detrick, sls dir; Kara Tucker, prom dir; Liz Ryan, progmg dir; Scott Maingi, chief of engrg.

KLUR(FM)— Apr 14, 1963: 99.9 mhz; 100 kw. Ant 808 ft TL: N33 54 04 W98 32 21. Stereo. Hrs open: 4302 Callfield Rd., 76308. Phone: (940) 691-2311. Fax: (940) 696-2255.E-mail: info@klur.com Web Site:www.klur.com Licensee: Cumulus Licensing Corp. Group owner: Cumulus Media Inc. (acq 10-3-97; grpsl). Population served: 97,564 Format: New country. ◆Jim Marks, gen mgr, natl sls mgr; Lindy Parr, sls dir; Andrea Lewis, rgnl sls mgr; Zach Morton, progmg dir; Jeff Chancey, chief of engrg.

*KMCU(FM)—Not on air, target date: unknown: 88.7 mhz; 5 w horiz, 3 kw vert. Ant 253 ft TL: N33 56 30 W98 34 06. Stereo. Hrs open: 24 KCCU,KLW,KOCU,KYCU Lawton,Clinton,Ardmore,Altus, Oaklahoma, 90%. c/o KCCU(FM), Cameron University, 2800 W. Gore Blvd., Lawton, OK, 73505. Phone: (580) 581-2425. Fax: (580) 581-5571.E-mail: kccu@cameron.edu Web Site:www.cameron.edu/kccu/ Licensee: Cameron University. Natl. Network: NPR, PRI, . Format: News-classical & jazz music. News staff: 2; News: 36 hrs wkly. Target aud: 35 plus. ◆Ted Riley, gen mgr.

*KMOC(FM)— July 9, 1987: 89.5 mhz; 3 kw. 672 ft TL: N33 54 04 W98 32 21. Stereo. Hrs open: 24 hours Box 41, 76307. Secondary address: 1040 W. Wenonah St. 76309. Phone: (940) 767-3303. Fax: (940) 723-5807.E-mail: kmocfm@wf.net Web Site:www.kmocfm.com Licensee: Christian Service Foundation Inc. Population served: 250,000 Format: Christian. Target aud: 25-54. ◆Daniel Boyd, progmg dir; Delvin Kinser, news dir.

KNIN-FM— May 12, 1975: 92.9 mhz; 100 kw. 930 ft TL: N33 54 04 W98 32 21. Stereo. Hrs open: 24 2525 Kell Blvd., Suite 200, 76308. Phone: (940) 763-1111. Fax: (940) 322-3166.E-mail: info@929nin.com Web Site:www.929nin.com Licensee: GAP Broadcasting Wichita Falls License LLC. Group owner: Clear Channel Communications Inc. (acq 8-3-2007; grpsl). Population served: 356,600 Natl. Rep: McGavren Guild,. Format: CHR. Target aud: 18-49. ◆Kim Dodds, gen mgr; Chris Walters, opns mgr; Melissa Detrick, sls dir; Kara Tucker, prom dir; Liz Ryan, progmg dir; Vicki Vox, asst music dir; Scott Maingi, chief of engrg; Pamela Tracy, traf mgr.

KQXC-FM— Jan 7, 1994: 103.9 mhz; 4.5 kw. Ant 315 ft TL: N33 56 30 W98 34 07. Stereo. Hrs open: 24 4302 Callfield Rd., 76308. Phone: (940) 691-2311. Fax: (940) 696-2255.E-mail: info@cumulus.com Web Site:www.cumulus.com Licensee: Cumulus Licensing Corp. Group owner: Cumulus Media Inc. (acq 10-3-97; grpsl). Population served: 105,000 Natl. Network: ABC, . Format: Rhythmic CHR. Target aud: 18-45; males. ◆Jim Marks, gen mgr, opns mgr, natl sls mgr; Belda Holt, rgnl sls mgr; Susan Adkins, mktg dir, prom dir; Zach Morton, progmg dir; Jeff Chancey, chief of engrg.

KWFS(AM)— 1948: 1290 khz; 5 kw-D, 250 w-N. TL: N33 57 38 W98 33 42. Hrs open: 24 2525 Kell Blvd., Suite 200, 76308. Phone: (940) 763-1111. Fax: (940) 322-3166.E-mail: info@newstalk1290.com Web Site:www.newstalk1290.com Licensee: GAP Broadcasting Wichita Falls License LLC. Group owner: Clear Channel Communications Inc. (acq 8-3-2007; grpsl). Population served: 100,000 Rgnl. Network: Texas State Net. Natl. Rep: Clear Channel,. Texas State Networks Format: News/talk. News staff: one; News: 12 hrs wkly. Target aud: 25 plus. Spec prog: Sp 4 hrs wkly. ◆Chris Walters, pres, opns mgr, progmg mgr; Kim Dodds, gen mgr; Melissa Detrick, gen sls mgr; Kara Tucker, prom dir; Scott Maingi, chief of engrg; Joe Tom White, local news ed, farm dir.

KWFS-FM— 1961: 102.3 mhz; 100 kw. Ant 449 ft TL: N33 53 51 W98 32 32. Stereo. Hrs open: 24 2525 Kell Blvd., 76308. Phone: (940) 763-1111. Fax: (940) 322-3166.E-mail: info@lonestar1023.com Web Site:www.lonestar1023.com Population served: 323,000 Format: Country. News: one hr wkly. Target aud: 18-49. ◆Joe Tom White, local news ed & farm dir.

*KZKL(FM)— Sept 1, 1993: 90.5 mhz; 7 kw. Ant 430 ft TL: N33 53 50 W98 32 33. Hrs open: 24 2351 Sunset Blvd., Suite 170-218, Rocklin, CA, 95765. Phone: (916) 251-1600. Fax: (916) 251-1650. Web Site:www.klove.com Licensee: Educational Media Foundation. (acq 10-20-2005; $600,000). Population served: 200,000 Natl. Network: K-Love, . Format: Contemp Christian. ◆Richard Jenkins, pres; Mike Novak, VP; Keith Whipple, dev dir; David Pierce, progmg mgr; Ed Lenane, news dir; Sam Wallington, engrg dir; Karen Johnson, news rptr.

Willis

KVST(FM)— 1998: 99.7 mhz; 2.55 kw. Ant 504 ft TL: N30 26 55 W95 31 48. Hrs open: 1212 S. Frazier, Conroe, 77301. Phone: (936) 788-1035. Fax: (936) 788-2525.E-mail: info@kvst.com Web Site:www.kvst.com Licensee: New Wavo Communication Group Inc. (acq 7-16-98; $158,218). Format: Country. ◆Ben Amato, pres, gen mgr; William Boggs, gen sls mgr; Larry Galla, progmg mgr; Mike Shilo, news dir; Dade Moore, engrg dir; John Erle, traf mgr.

Winfield

KALK(FM)— Sept 27, 1987: 97.7 mhz; 22.5 kw. 328 ft TL: N33 11 01 W95 12 32. Stereo. Hrs open: 24 Box 990, Mount Pleasant, 75456. Secondary address: 1798 US Hwy. 67 W., Mount Pleasant 75455. Phone: (903) 577-9770. Phone: (903) 572-8726. Fax: (903) 572-7232.E-mail: hitmusic@klake.net Web Site:www.easttexasradio.com Licensee: East Texas Broadcasting Inc. (group owner; acq 1999; $600,000). Population served: 68,000 Format: Hot adult contemp. News staff: one; News: one hr wkly. Target aud: 18-54; younger, upwardly mobile, white collar. Spec prog: Gospel one hr wkly. ◆Bud Kitchens, pres, VP, gen mgr; Craig Morgan, opns dir.

Wink

KNIW(AM)—Not on air, target date: unknown: 1480 khz; 1 kw-D, 250 w-N, DA-N. TL: N31 45 20 W103 08 40. Hrs open: 227 N. Walnut St., Kermit, 79745. Phone: (432) 352-9110. Licensee: Trade Media Corp. ◆Mark Nolte, VP.

Winnie

KKHT-FM— Dec 1, 1987: 100.7 mhz; 100 kw. Ant 1,952 ft TL: N30 03 05 W94 31 37. Stereo. Hrs open: 24 6161 Savoy, Suite 1200, Houston, 77036. Phone: (713) 260-3600. Fax: (713) 260-3628.E-mail: comments@kkht.com Web Site:www.kkht.com Licensee: Salem Media of Illinois LLC. Group owner: Univision Radio (acq 1-7-2005; with WIND(AM) Chicago, IL and KNIT(AM) Dallas in exchange for WPPN(FM) Des Plaines, IL). Natl. Rep: Salem,. Format: Christian talk. ◆Chuck Jewell, gen mgr; Paul Baker, opns mgr, mktg mgr, progmg dir; Dan Doster, gen sls mgr; Marsha Lambeth, mus dir; Ken Garza, pub affrs dir; Sidney Jones, chief of engrg; Kent McDonald, traf mgr.

KPTY(FM)— November 1989: Stn currently dark. 105.3 mhz; 50 kw. Ant 492 ft TL: N29 48 51 W94 13 30. Stereo. Hrs open: 5100 Southwest Fwy., Houston, 77056. Phone: (713) 965-2300. Fax: (713) 965-2401. Licensee: Tichenor License Corp. Group owner: Univision Radio (acq 9-22-2003; grpsl). Population served: 250,000 ◆Mark Masepohl, VP & gen mgr.

Winnsboro

KWNS(FM)— Sept 1, 1983: 104.7 mhz; 2.75 kw. Ant 492 ft TL: N32 56 32 W95 18 53. Stereo. Hrs open: 24 Box 54, 215 Market St., 75494. Phone: (903) 342-3501.E-mail: kwns-fm@cox-internet.com Licensee: Lottie L. Foster, executor of estate of Richard E. Foster. Format: Southern gospel. News staff: one. Target aud: 35-70. ◆Lottie Foster, pres & gen mgr.

Winona

KBLZ(FM)—Not on air, target date: unknown: 102.7 mhz; 9.3 kw. 531 ft TL: N32 23 09 W95 06 43. Hrs open: 212 Grande Blvd., Suite B100, Tyler, 75703. Phone: (903) 581-5259. Phone: (903) 759-1061. Fax: (903) 939-3473. Web Site:www.theblaze.cc Licensee: S.O. 2,000 LLC. Group owner: Reynolds Radio Inc. (acq 8-26-99). Format: Urban Contemporary. ◆Rick Reynolds, gen mgr.

Winters

KGXL(FM)— Nov 1, 1981: 96.1 mhz; 50 kw. Ant 492 ft TL: N32 12 52 W99 53 22. Stereo. Hrs open: 24 1740 N. 1st St., Abilene, 79603. Phone: (325) 437-9596. Fax: (325) 673-1819. Licensee: Doud Media Group LLC Population served: 425,000 Natl. Network: Fox News Radio, . Format: Country. News staff: 1; News: news prgmg 10 hrs/week. Target aud: 25-54; 18-49. ◆Richard Doud, gen mgr; Kid Cruz, opns mgr; Justin Riggan, sls dir; James Thompson, engrg dir.

Wolfforth

KAIQ(FM)— 2000: 95.5 mhz; 100 kw. Ant 676 ft TL: N33 31 03 W101 51 24. Hrs open: 24 1220 Broadway, Suite 500, Lubbock, 79401. Phone: (806) 763-6051. Fax: (806) 744-8363. Licensee: Entravision Holdings LLC. (acq 2-10-2005; $1.5 million). Natl. Rep: Lotus Entravision Reps LLC,. Format: Spanish CHR. Target aud: Hispanic. ◆Jose Sauceda, gen mgr.

Woodville

KWUD(AM)— Jan 4, 1968: 1490 khz; 1 kw-U. TL: N30 44 52 W94 25 56. Hrs open: 24 Box 129, 75979. Secondary address: 105 E Wheat 75979. Phone: (409) 283-2777. Fax: (409) 283-2283.E-mail: kwud_main@sbcglobal.net Web Site:www.kwud1490.com Licensee: Carroll Texas Broadcasting Ltd. Group owner: Jimmy Ray Carroll Stns (acq 12-1-2001). Population served: 22,000 Natl. Network: ABC, Jones Radio Networks, . Rgnl. Network: Texas State Net. Texas State Networks Format: Old country, real country. News staff: one; News: 12 hrs wkly. Target aud: 18-55. Spec prog: Farm 2 hrs, gospel 6 hrs, relg 3 hrs wkly. ◆Jim Carroll, gen mgr, gen sls mgr; Richard McCullough, gen sls mgr & progmg dir; Chester Leediker, chief of engrg; Carol Carroll, traf mgr.

Wylie

KHSE(AM)— 2004: 700 khz; 250 w-U, DA-2. TL: N33 01 58 W96 17 56. Hrs open: 24 12900 Preston Rd., Suite 100, Dallas, 7523025. Phone: (972) 354-1990. Licensee: Bernard Dallas LLC (acq 1-31-2007; $9 million with KFCD(AM) Farmersville). Population served: 4,700,695 Format: Ethnic, Indian, Pakistani. ◆Otter Miller, gen mgr.

Yoakum

KYKM(FM)— January 1982: 92.5 mhz; 3 kw. 300 ft TL: N29 21 03 W97 11 32. Stereo. Hrs open: 24 111 N. Main St., Halletsville, 77964. Phone: (361) 798-4333. Fax: (361) 798-3798.E-mail: texasthunderradio@yahoo.com Licensee: Kremling Enterprises Inc. Group owner: Fort Bend Broadcasting Co. (acq 5-12-2008; $250,000 with KTXM(FM) Hallettsville). Population served: 75,000 Format: Country. News staff: one. Target aud: General. Spec prog: Polka 9 hrs wkly. ◆Laura Kremling, gen mgr; Travis Kremling, progmg dir & chief of engrg.

Yorktown

KGGB(FM)— 2009: 96.3 mhz; 6 kw. Ant 328 ft TL: N29 02 43 W97 24 23. Hrs open: 11737 Nelon Dr., Corpus Christi, 78410. Phone: (361) 241-7944. Fax: (361) 241-7945. Licensee: Gerald Benavides. ◆Gerald Benavides, gen mgr.

Zapata

KBAW(FM)— 2001: 93.5 mhz; 25 kw. Ant 328 ft TL: N26 54 43 W99 17 09. Hrs open: 2702 Pine St., Laredo, 78043. Phone: (956) 726-4738.E-mail: radiooluz@border.net Web Site:www.lacadenaradioluz.com/kbaw-93.htm Licensee: La Nueva Cadena Radio Luz Inc. Format: Sp, Christian. ◆Isreal Tellez, stn mgr.

KJJS(AM)—Not on air, target date: unknown: 103.9 mhz; 6 kw. Ant 328 ft TL: N26 55 03 W99 15 00. Hrs open: Lerman Senter PLLC, 2000 K St. N.W., Suite 600, Washington, DC, 20006-1809. Phone: (202) 429-8970. Fax: (202) 293-7783. Licensee: Hispanic Target Media Inc. ◆Francisco San Millan, pres; Meredith Senter, gen mgr.

Utah

Beaver

*KEZB(FM)—Not on air, target date: unknown: 90.7 mhz; 1.7 kw. Ant -210 ft TL: N38 09 14.1 W112 36 31.2. Hrs open: W142N7919 Thorndell Dr., Menomonee Falls, WI, 53051. Phone: (414) 617-0498. Licensee: Christian Vision Inc. ◆Lois McLario, pres.

Blanding

KBDX(FM)—Not on air, target date: unknown: 92.7 mhz; 594 w horiz, 255 w vert. Ant 3,405 ft TL: N37 50 24 W109 27 41. Hrs open: 8am-5pm 74-5605 Luhia St. B7, Kailua-Kona, HI, 96740. Phone: (808) 329-8090. Fax: (808) 443-0888.E-mail: info@lava105.com Web Site:www.lava105.com Licensee: Skynet, Hawaii LLC (acq 12-10-03; $300,000). Format: Oldies. ◆Joe Williams, gen mgr; Chip Begay, opns mgr.

Bountiful

KJMY(FM)— Mar 15, 1988: 99.5 mhz; 39 kw. Ant 2,952 ft TL: N40 36 29 W112 09 33. Hrs open: 24 2801 S. Decker Lake Dr., Salt Lake City, 84119. Phone: (801) 908-1300. Fax: (801) 908-1449.E-mail: info@kjmy.com Web Site:www.my995fm.com Licensee: Citicasters Licenses L.P. Group owner: Clear Channel Communications Inc. (acq 1999; grpsl). Population served: 1,000,400 Natl. Rep: Clear Channel, Katz Radio,. Hogan & Hartson. Format: Modern alternative, retro classics. Target aud: 18-49; adults. ◆Stu Stanek, gen mgr; Bill Betts, opns mgr; Bill Matthews, sls dir, prom dir; Emily Hunt, gen sls mgr; Mark Christiansen, progmg dir.

Brian Head

KREC(FM)— Nov 14, 1988: 98.1 mhz; 56 kw. 2,526 ft TL: N37 32 32 W113 04 05. Stereo. Hrs open: 24 750 W. Ridgeview Dr., Suite 204, Saint George, 84770. Phone: (435) 673-3579. Fax: (435) 673-8900.E-mail: star98fm@bonnevillesg.com Licensee: Bonneville International Corp. (acq 8-10-2006; grpsl). Population served: 112,000 Format: Soft adult contemp. Target aud: 25-54. ◆Chris McCarthy, sls dir, gen sls mgr; Rick Parrish, gen mgr & mktg mgr; Dave Cory, chief of engrg.

Brigham City

KEGH(FM)— Oct 20, 1972: 106.9 mhz; 81 kw. Ant 2,165 ft TL: N41 47 03 W112 13 55. Stereo. Hrs open: 2801 S. Decker Lake Dr., Salt Lake City, 84119. Phone: (801) 908-4100. Fax: (801) 908-4122. Licensee: Simmons-SLC, LS LLC. Group owner: Simmons Media Group (acq 4-19-2004; $3.95 million). Format: Hip hop, rhythm and blues.

KXOL(AM)— July 1, 1998: 1660 khz; 10 kw-D, 1 kw-N. TL: N41 18 54 W112 04 43. Hrs open: 24 80 S Redwood Rd, Suite 211, North Salt Lake City, 84054. Phone: (801) 936-0706. Fax: (801) 936-0670.E-mail: info@kxol.com Web Site:www.incacommunications.com Licensee: Simmons-SLC, LS, LLC. Group owner: Simmons Media Group (acq 4-1-2003; $925,000 with KSOS(AM) Brigham City). Format: Regional Mexican. ◆Jennifer Rodriguez, gen mgr, opns mgr; Daniel Advincule, gen sls mgr; Valentin Alvarez, progmg dir.

Castle Dale

KEMR(FM)—Not on air, target date: unknown: 102.1 mhz; 4.2 kw. Ant 1,555 ft TL: N39 10 19 W110 37 07. Hrs open: 980 N. Michigan Ave., Suite 1880, Chicago, IL, 60611. Phone: (312) 204-9900. Licensee: College Creek Media LLC. ◆Neal J. Robinson, pres.

Cedar City

*KCHG(FM)—Not on air, target date: unknown: 88.9 mhz; 6.7 kw. Ant 2,604 ft TL: N37 32 29 W113 04 04. Hrs open: 1142 N. Airport Rd. , 84720. Phone: (435) 867-8188. Licensee: Calvary Chapel Cedar City Inc. ◆Joe Carroll, pres.

KCIN(FM)— May 10, 1974: 94.9 mhz; 55 kw. Ant -121 ft TL: N37 45 51 W113 06 15. Stereo. Hrs open: 750 W. Ridgeview Dr., Suite 204, Saint George, 84770. Phone: (435) 673-3579. Fax: (435) 673-8900. Licensee: CCR-St. George IV LLC. (acq 5-3-2006; grpsl). Format: CHR. ◆Chris McCarthy, sls dir; Rick Parrish, mktg mgr.

KOBY(AM)— 1971: Stn currently dark. 940 khz; 10 kw-D. TL: N37 45 51 W113 06 15. Hrs open: Box 1450, Saint George, 84771. Phone: (435) 628-1000. Fax: (435) 628-6636. Licensee: Radio 940 LLC. (group owner; (acq 2-9-2009; $150,000). Population served: 9,595 ◆E. Morgan Skinner Jr., gen mgr.

KSUB(AM)— July 4, 1937: 590 khz; 5 kw-D, 1 kw-N, DA-N. TL: N37 41 55 W113 10 44. Hrs open: 24 251 W. Hilton Dr., Saint George, 84770. Phone: (435) 586-5900. Fax: (435) 673-8228. Web Site:www.590ksub.com Licensee: CCR-St. George IV LLC. (group owner; (acq 5-3-2006; grpsl). Population served: 20,000 Natl. Network: CBS, . Rgnl rep: Target Radio. Format: News/talk, info. News staff: one; News: 15 hrs wkly. Target aud: 35-65; adults. Spec prog: Relg, loc talk, farm 6 hrs wkly. ◆Brent Miner, gen mgr; Steve Miner, progmg dir; Dan Hobson, chief of engrg.

*KSUU(FM)— October 1966: 91.1 mhz; 10 kw. -462 ft TL: N37 38 55 W113 05 32. Stereo. Hrs open: 6 AM-midnight (winter); 10 AM-10 PM (summer) 351 W. Ctr., 84720. Phone: (435) 865-8224. Fax: (435) 865-8352.E-mail: rollins@fuu.edu Web Site:www.suu.edu/ksuu Licensee: Southern Utah University. Population served: 18,000 Format: CHR. News: 2 hrs wkly. Target aud: 12-34; children, university students. Spec prog: News, class 3 hrs, rhythm and blues 4 hrs, rock 4 hrs wkly. ◆Cal Rollins, stn mgr; Alex May, progmg dir; Alisia Brooks, mus dir; Camie Stables, news dir; Lance Jackson, chief of engrg.

KXBN(FM)— Oct 15, 1976: 92.5 mhz; 41.6 kw. Ant 1,690 ft TL: N37 38 41 W113 22 28. Stereo. Hrs open: 24 251 W. Hilton Dr., 84770. Phone: (435) 586-5900. Fax: (435) 673-8228. Population served: 50,000 Natl. Network: Jones Radio Networks, . Format: Oldies. News: 5 hrs wkly.

Centerville

KNRS-FM— Dec 24, 1979: 105.7 mhz; 25 kw. Ant 3,739 ft TL: N40 39 34 W112 12 05. Stereo. Hrs open: 24 2801 S. Decker Lake Dr., Salt Lake City, 84119. Phone: (801) 908-1300. Fax: (801) 908-1569.E-mail: info@ktmy.com Web Site:www.knrs.com Licensee: Citicasters Licenses L.P. Group owner: Clear Channel Communications Inc. (acq 5-3-2004; $22 million with KOSY-FM Spanish Fork). Population served: 175,885 Natl. Network: Fox News Radio, . Natl. Rep: Clear Channel, Katz Radio,. Format: Talk. Target aud: 25-54; adults. ◆Stu Stanek, gen mgr; Bill Betts, opns mgr; Bill Matthews, sls dir, chief of engrg; Kimberly Dickerson, gen sls mgr; Frank Bell, progmg dir.

KTUB(AM)— Dec 1, 1957: 1600 khz; 5 kw-D, 1 kw-N, DA-N. TL: N40 54 08 W111 55 40. Stereo. Hrs open: 24 2722 S. Redwood Rd., Suite 1, Salt Lake City, 84119. Phone: (801) 908-8777. Fax: (801) 908-8782.E-mail: info@bustosmedia.com Web Site:www.bustosmedia.com Licensee: Bustos Media of Utah License LLC. Group owner: Bustos Media Holdings (acq 9-1-2004; $1.5 million). Natl. Network: Ke-Buena, . Format: Rgnl Mexican. ◆Edward Distel, gen mgr.

Coalville

KJQN(FM)— 2004: 103.1 mhz; 89 kw horiz. Ant 2,122 ft TL: N40 52 16 W110 59 43. Hrs open: Simmons Media Group, 515 South 700 East, Salt Lake City, 84102. Phone: (801) 524-2600. Fax: (801) 524-6002.E-mail: reception@simonmedia.com Web Site:www.simmonsmedia.com Licensee: Simmons-SLC, LS LLC. Group owner: Simmons Media Group (acq 5-20-2004; $4.4 million for CP). Format: Alternative. ◆G. Craig Hanson, gen mgr.

KZZQ(FM)— Sept 6, 2005: 97.5 mhz; 89 kw horiz. Ant 2,122 ft TL: N40 52 16 W110 59 43. Hrs open: 2835 East 3300 South, Salt Lake City, 84109. Phone: (801) 412-6040. Fax: (801) 412-6041. Web Site:www.theblazeonline.com Licensee: 3 Point Media - Franklin L.L.C., debtor-in-possession (acq 7-17-2007). Wiley Rein LLP. Format: Rock. ◆Randy Rodgers, gen mgr.

Delta

*KEYD(FM)—Not on air, target date: unknown: 91.9 mhz; 5 kw. Ant 166 ft TL: N39 20 52 W112 34 01. Hrs open: 307 South 1600 West, Provo, 84601-3932. Phone: (801) 374-5210. Fax: (801) 374-2910. Web Site:www.keyy.com Licensee: Biblical Ministries Worldwide. ◆Steven Rygh, gen mgr.

KMGR(FM)— Sept 5, 1989: 95.9 mhz; 100 kw horiz. Ant 961 ft TL: N39 43 58 W111 56 34. Stereo. Hrs open: 24 3 Point Media - Delta LLC, 980 N. Michigan Ave., Suite 1880, Chicago, IL, 60611. Phone: (312) 204-9900. Licensee: 3 Point Media - Delta LLC. (acq 8-1-2003; $1.25 million). ◆Bruce Buzil, gen mgr.

KNAK(AM)— Feb 25, 1974: 540 khz; 1 kw-U. TL: N39 20 12 W112 33 21. Hrs open: 24 Box 636, 84624-0626. Secondary address: 1259 N. 100 W., American Fork 84003. Phone: (435) 864-5111. Fax: (801) 406-0067.E-mail: info@knakam.com Web Site:www.radioforthefamily.com Licensee: Accent Radio Inc. (acq 3-16-2000; $185,000). Population served: 50,000 Format: Relg. News: 15 hrs wkly. Target aud: 20-50. Spec prog: Farm 5 hrs wkly. ◆Jedidiah Harrison, pres; Curt Crosby, gen sls mgr, news dir, farm dir; Sam Bushman, gen mgr, stn mgr & progmg dir; Julie Bushman, traf mgr.

Elsinore

KCYQ(FM)— 1978: 97.7 mhz; 43 kw. Ant 2,883 ft TL: N38 32 30 W112 03 31. Stereo. Hrs open: Box 40, Manti, 84642. Phone: (435) 896-4456. Fax: (435) 896-9333. Web Site:www.kcyq.com Licensee: Mid-Utah Radio Inc. (acq 3-1-2006; swap for KLGL(FM) Richfield). Format: Country hits. ◆Marianne Barton, pres; Douglas Barton, gen mgr; Dave Gunderson, sls VP; J.D. Fox, progmg VP, mus dir; Kirk Williams, engrg VP.

Ephraim

*KAGJ(FM)—Not on air, target date: unknown: 89.5 mhz; 100 w. -321 ft TL: N39 21 37 W111 34 54. Hrs open: Snow College, 150 E. College Ave., 84627. Phone: (435) 283-7425/7000.E-mail: kagj_fm@hotmail.com Web Site:www.snow.edu/~kage Licensee: Snow College. Format: Classic rock with a kick. ◆Gary Chidester, gen mgr.

Huntington

KHUN(FM)—Not on air, target date: unknown: 107.1 mhz; 1 kw. Ant 1,748 ft TL: N39 12 35 W111 08 29. Hrs open: 980 N. Michigan Ave., Suite 1880, Chicago, IL, 60611. Phone: (312) 204-9900. Licensee: College Creek Media LLC. ◆Neal J. Robinson, pres.

Hurricane

KBZB(FM)— 2002: Stn currently dark. 98.9 mhz; 15.5 kw. Ant 1,952 ft TL: N36 50 49 W113 29 28. Hrs open: 515 S. 700 E., Suite 1C, Salt Lake City, 84102. Phone: (801) 524-2600. Licensee: CBL Investments LLC (acq 3-9-2009). ◆Bret J. Leifson, gen mgr.

Kanab

KPLD(FM)— 1986: 101.1 mhz; 99 kw. Ant 786 ft TL: N36 43 18 W112 12 57. Stereo. Hrs open: 24 204 Playa Della Rosita, Washington, 84780. Phone: (435) 628-3643. Fax: (435) 673-1210.E-mail: kony@infowest.com Licensee: Marathon Media Group L.L.C. (acq 1999; $1.75 million with KUNF(AM) Washington). Format: Hot adult contemp. ◆Carl Lamar, VP & gen mgr.

Levan

KQMB(FM)— 2001: 96.7 mhz; 67 kw horiz. Ant 1,919 ft TL: N39 20 12 W111 27 06. Hrs open: 1454 W. Business Park Dr., Orem, 84058. Phone: (801) 224-1400. Fax: (801) 224-1524. Licensee: Zeta Holdings LLC. Format: Hot adult contemp. ◆Robert H. Morey, gen mgr.

Logan

KBLQ-FM— August 1977: 92.9 mhz; 50 kw. 154 ft TL: N41 52 18 W111 48 31. Stereo. Hrs open: Prog sep from AM Box 3369, 94321. Phone: (435) 752-1390. Fax: (435) 752-1392. Web Site:www.q92.fm Format: Adult contemp. Target aud: 25-54; general. Spec prog: Gospel 8 hrs, jazz 4 hrs wkly. ◆Laurie Gill, traf mgr; Bill Walter, disc jockey.

KGNT(FM)—See Smithfield

KLGN(AM)— March 1968: 1390 khz; 5 kw-D, 500 w-N, DA-N. TL: N41 44 04 W111 51 13. Hrs open: Box 3369, 84323. Secondary address: 810 W. 200 N. 84321. Phone: (435) 752-1390. Fax: (435) 752-1392. Web Site:www.1390.com Licensee: Sun Valley Radio Inc. (group owner; acq 12-27-91; $572,279 with co-located FM). Population served: 140,000 Natl. Network: Westwood One, CBS, . Format: Adult standards, memories MOR. Target aud: 45 plus. Spec prog: Talk. ◆Kent Frandsen, pres; Jay Eubanks, gen mgr, gen sls mgr, mktg mgr, prom mgr; Michael Carver, opns mgr & progmg dir; Dan Baker, chief of engrg.

*KUSR(FM)— March 1999: 89.5 mhz; 800 w. -617 ft TL: N41 44 44 W111 48 16. Hrs open: 24 hours Utah Public Radio, 8505 Old Main Hill, 84322-8505. Phone: (435) 797-3138. Fax: (435)797-3150.E-mail: upr@upr.usu.edu Web Site:www.upr.org Licensee: Utah State University of Agricultural and Applied Science. Natl. Network: NPR, . Format: Classical, News/Talk. ◆Richard Meng, gen mgr.

*KUSU-FM— April 1953: 91.5 mhz; 90 kw. 1,140 ft TL: N41 53 11 W112 04 17. Stereo. Hrs open: 24 Utah Public Radio, 8505 Old Main Hill, 84322-8505. Phone: (435) 797-3138. Phone: (800) 826-1495. Fax: (435) 797-3150.E-mail: upr@upr.usu.edu Web Site:www.upr.org Licensee: Utah State University. Population served: 250,000 Natl. Network: NPR, PRI, . Dow, Lohnes & Albertson. Format: Class, news/talk. News staff: 2. Target aud: General. ◆Cathy Ives, gen mgr; Lee Austin, progmg dir; Nora Zambreno, pub affrs dir; Clifford J. Smith, chief of engrg; Craig Hislop, reporter.

KVFX(FM)— Nov 11, 1974: 94.5 mhz; 70 kw. 1,148 ft TL: N41 53 50 W111 57 39. Stereo. Hrs open: Prog sep from AM Box 267, 84323. Secondary address: 810 W. 200 N. 84321. Phone: (435) 752-5141. Fax: (435) 753-5555. Population served: 85,000 Format: CHR. News: 2 hrs wkly. Target aud: 18-35. ◆Blair Carter, progmg dir, progmg mgr; Kenton Frat Boy, disc jockey.

KVNU(AM)— Nov 20, 1938: 610 khz; 5 kw-D, 1 kw-N, DA-N. TL: N41 40 30 W111 56 06. Hrs open: 24 Box 267, 84323-0267. Secondary address: 810 W. 200 N. 84321. Phone: (435) 752-5141. Fax: (435) 753-5555.E-mail: kvnu@cvradio.com Web Site:610kvnu.com Licensee: Sun Valley Radio Inc. (group owner; acq 1996; $900,000 with co-located FM). Population served: 100,000 Natl. Network: ABC, . Format: News/talk. News: 15 hrs wkly. Target aud: General. Spec prog: Farm 2 hrs, relg 2 hrs wkly. ◆Al Lewis, gen mgr, progmg dir, outdoor ed, sports cmtr; James Murdock, gen sls mgr; Bill Walter, chief of engrg; Jennie Christensen, news dir & local news ed; Eric Frandsen, news rptr; Heather Bailey, reporter.

*KZCL(FM)— 2008: 90.5 mhz; 1 kw. Ant 367 ft TL: N41 36 41 W111 57 05. Hrs open: 1971 West North Temple, Salt Lake City, 84116. Phone: (801) 363-1818. Fax: (801) 533-9136. Licensee: Listeners Community Radio of Utah Inc. ◆Donna Land Maldonado, gen mgr.

Manti

KAUU(FM)— December 1978: 105.1 mhz; 48 kw horiz. Ant 2,244 ft TL: N39 45 37 W111 34 38. Stereo. Hrs open: 24 hours 2835 East 3300 South, Salt Lake City, 84109. Phone: (801) 412-6040. Fax: (801) 412-6041. Web Site:www.theblazeonline.com Licensee: Millcreek Broadcasting L.L.C. (group owner; (acq 4-17-2001). Format: Rock. ♦Randy Rodgers, gen mgr.

KMTI(AM)— June 7, 1976: 650 khz; 10 kw-D, 1 kw-N, DA-2. TL: N39 17 39 W111 38 13. Hrs open: 24 Box 40, 1600 W. 500 N., 84642. Phone: (435) 835-7301. Fax: (435) 835-2250. Web Site:www.kmtiradio.com Licensee: Sanpete County Broadcasting Co. Population served: 100,000 Natl. Network: ABC, . Rosenman & Colin. Wire Svc: AP Format: Country, news, full service. News staff: one; News: 20 hrs wkly. Target aud: 25-60. Spec prog: Farm 5 hrs wkly. ♦Douglas Barton, pres, gen mgr; Willy Akers, gen sls mgr; Larry Masco, progmg dir; Bruce Mehew, news dir; Beau Lund, chief of engrg.

Midvale

KSL-FM— 1995: 102.7 mhz; 25 kw. Ant 3,739 ft TL: N40 39 34 W112 12 05. Stereo. Hrs open: 24
Rebroadcasts KSL(AM) Salt Lake City 100%.
55 North 300 West, Salt Lake City, 84180. Phone: (801) 575-5555. Fax: (801) 526-1070. Web Site:www.ksl.com Licensee: Bonneville Holding Co. Group owner: Bonneville International Corp. (acq 12-5-2003; grpsl). Format: News/talk, sports. ♦Chris Redgrave, gen mgr.

Milford

KCDC(FM)—Not on air, target date: unknown: 98.5 mhz; 10.3 kw. Ant 3,982 ft TL: N38 31 12 W113 17 08. Hrs open: Box 11060, Jackson, WY, 83002. Licensee: Cochise Broadcasting LLC. ♦Ted Tucker, gen mgr.

Moab

KCYN(FM)— Sept 20, 1998: 97.1 mhz; 29 kw. Ant 1,292 ft TL: N38 31 37 W109 18 21. Stereo. Hrs open: 24 Box 1119, 84532. Secondary address: 1030 S. Bowling Alley Ln. #3 84532. Phone: (435) 259-1035. Fax: (435) 259-1037.E-mail: kcyn@kcynfm.com Web Site:www.kcynfm.com Licensee: Moab Communications LLC. (acq 8-15-97). Population served: 25,000 Natl. Network: Jones Radio Networks, Fox News Radio, . Natl. Rep: Rgnl Reps,. Wire Svc: Metro Weather Service Inc. Format: Country. News staff: one; News: 12 hrs wkly. Target aud: 18-54. ♦Phillip Mueller, gen mgr & gen sls mgr; Kenneth Meyer, chief of engrg; Holly Wilson, traf mgr.

***KZMU(FM)**— April 1992: 90.1 mhz; 400 w. Ant 1,279 ft TL: N38 31 37 W109 18 21. Stereo. Hrs open: 24 Box 1076, 84532. Secondary address: 1734 Rocky Rd. 84532. Phone: (435) 259-5968. Phone: (435) 259-8824. Fax: (435) 259-8763.E-mail: info@kzmu.org Web Site:www.kzmu.org Licensee: Moab Public Radio. Population served: 10,000 Format: Var/div, public radio. News staff: one; News: 8 hrs wkly. Target aud: General. Spec prog: Asian one hr, American Indian 5 hrs, Black 3 hrs, Sp one hr, folk 6 hrs, blues 19 hrs wkly. ♦Jeff Flanders, gen mgr; Christy Williams, progmg dir; Glen Peart, mus dir, asst music dir; Bob Owen, engrg dir.

Monroe

KMXD(FM)— Aug 1, 2007: 100.5 mhz; 33 kw. Ant 3,257 ft TL: N38 23 08 W112 19 57. Stereo. Hrs open: 24 Box 40, Manti, 84642. Phone: (435) 835-7301. Fax: (435) 835-2250. Licensee: Sanpete County Broadcasting Co. Population served: 125,000 Natl. Network: ABC, . Format: Soft adult contemp. Target aud: 30-65. ♦Douglas L. Barton, pres & gen mgr.

Monticello

KRZX(FM)—Not on air, target date: unknown: 106.1 mhz; 100 kw. Ant 1,378 ft TL: N38 31 36 W109 18 26. Hrs open: Box 36148, Tucson, AZ, 85740. Phone: (520) 797-4434.E-mail: in@krzxfm.com Licensee: Skywest Media L.L.C. ♦Ted Tucker, gen mgr.

Murray

KJQS(AM)— Nov 8, 1948: 1230 khz; 1 kw-U. TL: N40 39 57 W111 54 26. Stereo. Hrs open: 24 434 Bearcat Dr., Salt Lake City, 84115. Phone: (801) 485-6700. Fax: (801) 487-5369. Licensee: Citadel Broadcasting Co. Group owner: Citadel Broadcasting Corp. (acq 2-29-00; $104,202). Natl. Network: ESPN Radio, . Format: Sports. ♦Eric Hauenstein, gen mgr; Terry Mathis, sls dir & gen sls mgr; Scott Gerard, progmg dir; Richard Bauer, chief of engrg; Liz Mills, traf mgr.

Naples

KCUA(FM)— 1993: 92.5 mhz; 840 w. Ant 1,660 ft TL: N40 32 16 W109 41 57. Hrs open: R.R. 2 Box 2384, Roosevelt, 84066. Phone: (801) 412-6080. Fax: (435) 645-0963. Licensee: 3 Point Media - Coalville LLC. (acq 5-28-2004; $1.7 million). Format: Classic Rock. ♦Joe Evans, stn mgr.

Nephi

***KBJF(FM)**—Not on air, target date: unknown: 90.5 mhz; 75 kw. Ant 2,214 ft TL: N39 45 37 W111 34 38. Hrs open: 65 S. Main St., 84648. Phone: (435) 623-5440. Fax: (435) 623-5617. Licensee: First Baptist Church of Nephi, Utah. ♦Keith South, gen mgr.

KUDE(FM)— May 9, 1990: 103.9 mhz; 74 kw horiz. Ant 2,244 ft TL: N39 45 37 W111 34 38. Stereo. Hrs open: 24
Rebroadcasts KUDD(FM) Roy 100%.
2835 East 3300 South, Salt Lake City, 84109. Phone: (801) 412-6040. Fax: (801) 412-6041. Licensee: Millcreek Broadcasting L.L.C. (group owner; (acq 4-17-2001). Population served: 244,000 Format: Adult contemp. Target aud: 18-45. ♦Randy Rodgers, gen mgr; Brian Michel, opns mgr; Lutisha Merrill, gen sls mgr; Scott St. John, mktg mgr; Kevin Terry, engrg VP.

North Ogden

***KNKL(FM)**— Jan 29, 2004: 88.7 mhz; 7.3 kw vert. Ant 984 ft TL: N41 35 30 W112 14 57. Hrs open: 24 2351 Sunset Blvd., Suite 170-218, Rocklin, CA, 95765. Phone: (916) 251-1600. Fax: (916) 251-1650.E-mail: klove@klove.com Web Site:www.klove.com Licensee: Educational Media Foundation. Group owner: EMF Broadcasting. Population served: 449,000 Natl. Network: K-Love, . Shaw Pittman. Format: Contemp Christian. News staff: 3. Target aud: 25-44; female-Judeo Christian. ♦Richard Jenkins, pres; Mike Novak, VP, progmg dir; Lloyd Parker, gen mgr; Ed Lenane, opns dir, news dir; Keith Whipple, dev dir; Eric Allen, natl sls mgr; Dan Beck, rgnl sls mgr; Chris Joyce, prom dir; David Pierce, progmg mgr; Sam Wallington, engrg dir; Arthur Vassar, traf mgr; Karen Johnson, news rptr.

North Salt Lake City

KALL(AM)— Sept 22, 1981: 700 khz; 50 kw-D, 10 kw-N, DA-2. TL: N40 53 29 W111 56 29. Stereo. Hrs open: 24 515 South 700 East, Salt Lake City, 84102. Phone: (801) 524-2600. Fax: (801) 521-9234.E-mail: reception@simmonsmedia.com Web Site:www.kall700sports.com Licensee: Utah Radio Acquisition LLC Group owner: Clear Channel Communications Inc. (acq 3-17-2006; $4.1 million). Population served: 2,000,000 Natl. Rep: Clear Channel,. Format: Sports/talk. News staff: one; News: 20 hrs wkly. Target aud: 18-49; men. ♦Jeff Nemelka, gen sls mgr.

Oakley

KEGA(FM)— 2003: 101.5 mhz; 89 kw horiz, 38 kw vert. Ant 2,122 ft TL: N40 52 16 W110 59 43. Hrs open: Simmons Media Group, 515 South 700 E. #1C, Salt Lake City, 84102. Phone: (801) 524-2600. Fax: (801) 521-8100. Web Site:www.1015theeagle.com Licensee: Simmons-SLC, LS LLC. Group owner: Simmons Media Group (acq 4-4-2001; grpsl). Population served: 10,000 Format: Country. ♦Craig Hanson, pres; Stephen Johnson, gen mgr.

Ogden

KBER(FM)— July 13, 1976: 101.1 mhz; 25 kw. 3,740 ft TL: N40 39 35 W112 12 05. Stereo. Hrs open: 24 434 Bearcat Dr., Salt Lake City, 84115. Phone: (801) 485-6700. Fax: (801) 487-5369.E-mail: info@kber.com Web Site:www.kber.com Licensee: Citadel Broadcasting Co. Group owner: Citadel Broadcasting Corp. (acq 1996; $7.7 million). Natl. Rep: Katz Radio,. Format: AOR. News staff: one. Target aud: 18-49; men. ♦Eric Hauenstein, gen mgr; Zandi Wilcox, gen sls mgr; Diane Curtis, natl sls mgr; Joel Smith, prom dir, mus dir; Kelly Hamer, progmg dir; Richie Bauer, engrg dir.

KBZN(FM)— 1978: 97.9 mhz; 26 kw. Ant 3,770 ft TL: N40 39 35 W112 12 05. Hrs open: 257 East 200 South, Suite 400, Salt Lake City, 84111. Phone: (801) 364-9836. Fax: (801) 364-8068.E-mail: breeze@kbzn.com Web Site:www.kbzn.com Licensee: Capitol Broadcasting Inc. (acq 4-5-91; 4-29-91). Format: Smooth adult contemp. ♦John Webb, gen mgr; Dan Jessop, opns dir; Jan Bagley, gen sls mgr.

KENZ(FM)— Aug 1, 1964: 101.9 mhz; 25 kw. Ant 3,739 ft TL: N40 39 34 W112 12 05. Stereo. Hrs open: 24 2835 E. 3300 S., Salt Lake City, 84107. Phone: (801) 412-6040. Fax: (801) 412-6041. Web Site:www.1019popfm.com Licensee: Citadel Broadcasting Co. Group owner: Citadel Broadcasting Corp. (acq 7-30-2004; $16 million). Population served: 1,000,400 Natl. Network: ABC, . Format: Modern country. News staff: one; News: 6 hrs wkly. Target aud: 25-54. ♦Randy Rodgers, gen mgr.

KLO(AM)— 1924: 1430 khz; 5 kw-U, DA-N. TL: N41 10 44 W112 04 09. (CP: TL: N41 02 48 W112 01 38). Hrs open: 257 East 200 South, Suite 400, Salt Lake City, 84111. Phone: (801) 627-1430. Fax: (801) 627-0317.E-mail: info@kloam.com Web Site:www.kloradio.com Licensee: KLO Broadcasting Co. Population served: 1,159,700 Format: Talk, News, Sports. ♦John Webb, pres, gen mgr; Dan Jessop, opns mgr, progmg dir; Jan Bagley, gen sls mgr; Patrick Gleason, chief of engrg; Sheri Jensen, traf mgr.

KOGN(AM)— April 1948: 1490 khz; 1 kw-U. TL: N41 14 23 W111 58 58. Hrs open: 24 1506 Gibson Ave., 84404. Phone: (801) 395-5600. Fax: (801) 395-1490. Licensee: AM Radio 1490 Inc. (acq 4-10-2006; $520,000). Population served: 69,478 Natl. Network: CNN Radio, Westwood One, . Dan J. Alpert. Format: Adult standard, CNN radio news. ♦E. Morgan Skinner Jr., CEO & pres; Dick Carter, stn mgr.

KSVN(AM)— Jan 1, 1946: 730 khz; 1 kw-D, 66 w-N. TL: N41 11 17 W112 04 52. Hrs open: 24 4215 W. 4000 S., West Haven, 84401. Phone: (801) 292-1799. Fax: (801) 731-4445.E-mail: info@aztecautah.com Web Site:www.aztecautah.com Licensee: Azteca Broadcasting Corp. (group owner; acq 2-1-86). Population served: 1,200,000 Format: Rgnl Mexican. ♦Alex Collantes, pres, gen mgr, progmg dir; Maria Coria, gen sls mgr & traf mgr.

***KWCR-FM**— May 21, 1966: 88.1 mhz; 3 kw. -470 ft TL: N41 11 30 W111 56 37. (CP: Ant 315 ft.). Stereo. Hrs open: 24 2188 University Cir., 84408-2188. Phone: (801) 626-8800. Fax: (801) 626-6935.E-mail: kwcrradio@mail.weber.edu Web Site:www.weber.edu/kwcr Licensee: Weber State University Board of Trustees. Population served: 200,000 Wire Svc: UPI Format: Contemp hits, rock. News: 4 hrs wkly. Target aud: 18-26; college students, male & female. Spec prog: Relg 3 hrs, gospel 3 hrs, Sp 16 hrs wkly. ♦Mark Howard, gen mgr & sls dir.

***KYFO-FM**— June 1983: 95.5 mhz; 100 kw. Ant 718 ft TL: N41 14 59 W112 14 11. Stereo. Hrs open: 24 11530 Carmel Commons Blvd., Charlotte, NC, 28226. Phone: 704) 523-5555. Fax: (704) 522-1967.E-mail: bbn@bbnradio.org Web Site:www.bbnradio.org Licensee: Bible Broadcasting Network. (acq 1994). Population served: 1,000,000 Format: Christian. ♦Lowell Davey, pres; Hank Crull, gen mgr.

Orem

KKAT-FM— Nov 15, 1978: 107.5 mhz; 45 kw. Ant 2,850 ft TL: N40 16 48 W111 56 05. Stereo. Hrs open: 24 434 Bearcat Dr., Salt Lake City, 84115-2520. Phone: (801) 485-6700. Fax: (801) 487-5369.E-mail: info@1075.com Web Site:www.1075.com Licensee: Citadel Broadcasting Co. Group owner: Citadel Broadcasting Corp. (acq 12-18-96). Format: Country. Target aud: 25-54. ♦Eric Hauenstein, gen mgr; Diane Curtis, adv mgr; Bruce Jones, progmg dir; Kurt Johnson, prom.

***KOHS(FM)**— October 1994: 91.7 mhz; 1.75 kw. -831 ft TL: N40 17 48 W111 41 04. (CP: Ant -869 ft. TL: N40 17 32 W111 40 56). Stereo. Hrs open: 175 S. 400 E., 84058. Phone: (801) 224-9236. Fax: (801) 538-5690. Licensee: Orem Hl. Sch. Population served: 350,000 Format: Alternative.

KSRR(AM)—See Provo

Paragonah

***KRRA(FM)**—Not on air, target date: unknown: 91.3 mhz; 1.5 kw. Ant -741 ft TL: N37 54 56 W112 46 07. Hrs open: 282 Country Estate Dr., Springer, OK, 73458. Phone: (580) 653-2777. Licensee: Ron Elmore Ministries Inc. ♦Ron Elmore, pres.

Park City

***KPCW-FM**— July 2, 1980: 91.9 mhz; 105 w. Ant -23 ft TL: N40 40 59 W111 31 22. Stereo. Hrs open: Box 1372, 84060. Secondary address: KPCW City Hall Bldg., 445 Marsac 84060. Phone: (435) 649-9004. Fax: (435) 645-9063.E-mail: letters@kpcw.org Web Site:www.kpcw.org Licensee: Community Wireless of Park City. Population served: 13,000 Format: AAA, news. Spec prog: Class 17 hrs, C&W 18 hrs, jazz 12 hrs wkly. ♦Blair Feulner, gen mgr; Karen Thomas, progmg dir; Leslie Thatcher, news dir; Dennis Silver, chief of engrg.

Parowan

KENT(AM)— Oct 6, 2006: 1400 khz; 1 kw-U. TL: N37 48 22 W112 56 40. Hrs open: Box 115, Cedar City, 84721. Secondary address: 141 East College Ave., Cedar City 84720. Phone: (435) 477-2000. Fax: (435) 477-1400.E-mail: legacy1@infowest.com Licensee: AM Radio 1400 Inc. Group owner: Diamond Broadcasting Corp. (acq 11-16-2004). Population served: 38,311 Natl. Network: CNN Radio, Westwood One, . Dan J. Alpert. Format: Adult standards. News staff: 3. Target aud: 25-65. ♦E. Morgan Skinner, pres.

Payson

KTCE(FM)— November 1993: 92.1 mhz; 125 w. Ant 2,155 ft TL: N40 05 21 W111 49 15. Hrs open: 2835 E. 3300 S., Salt Lake City, 84603. Phone: (801) 412-6040. Fax: (801) 412-6041. Licensee: Moenkopi Communications Inc. (acq 9-28-2005). Format: Hot adult contemp.

Pleasant Grove

***KPGR(FM)**— May 1976: 88.1 mhz; 115 w. -1,128 ft TL: N40 21 48 W111 43 30. Stereo. Hrs open: 6:30 AM-10 PM 700 E. 200 S., 84062. Phone: (801) 785-5747. Phone: (801) 785-8700. Fax: (801) 785-8744. Web Site:www.kpgr.tripod.com Licensee: Alpine School District. Population served: 25,000 Format: Var. Target aud: 12-18; students. Spec prog: All Pleasant Grove High football, basketball, baseball games 4 hrs wkly.

Price

KARB(FM)— July 1977: 98.3 mhz; 7 kw. Ant -105 ft TL: N39 36 33 W110 48 50. Stereo. Hrs open: Box 875, 84501. Secondary address: 1899 North Carbonville Rd. 84501. Phone: (435) 637-1167. Fax: (435) 637-1177.E-mail: koal@emerytelcom.net Web Site:www.koal.net Licensee: Eastern Utah Broadcasting Co. Format: Country. ♦Tom Anderson, gen mgr.

***KCEU(FM)**—Not on air, target date: unknown: 89.9 mhz; 6 kw. Ant -584 ft TL: N39 32 35 W110 25 07. Hrs open: College of Eastern Utah, 451 E. 400 N., 84501. Phone: (435) 613-5668. Fax: (435) 613-5042. Licensee: College of Eastern Utah. ♦Ryan Thomas, pres; Troy Hunt, gen mgr.

***KEYP(FM)**—Not on air, target date: unknown: 91.9 mhz; 3 kw. Ant 1,748 ft TL: N39 12 35 W111 08 29. Hrs open: 307 South 1600 West, Provo, 84601-3932. Phone: (801) 374-5210. Fax: (801) 374-2910.E-mail: mail@keyy.com Web Site:www.keyy.com Licensee: Biblical Ministries Worldwide. ♦Christopher A. Bauer, pres.

KOAL(AM)— October 1936: 750 khz; 10 kw-U, 6.8 kw-N, DA-N. TL: N39 34 02 W110 47 53. Hrs open: Box 875, 84501. Phone: (435) 637-1167. Fax: (435) 637-1177.E-mail: koal@castlenet.com Web Site:www.koal.net Licensee: Eastern Utah Broadcasting Co. Population served: 34,900 Rgnl. Network: Intermountain Farm/Ranch Network. Format: News/talk, sports. Spec prog: Farm 5 hrs wkly. ♦Keith Mason, progmg dir; Thomas Anderson, pres, gen mgr & chief of engrg.

KSLL(AM)— Sept 6, 1980: 1080 khz; 10 kw-D. TL: N39 33 43 W110 46 36. Stereo. Hrs open: Box 1080, 84501. Secondary address: 163 E. 100 N. 84501. Phone: (435) 637-1080. Fax: (435) 637-8191.E-mail: kwsa@preciscom.net Web Site:www.kusaonline.com Licensee: Against the Wind Broadcasting Inc. (acq 6-21-02; $250,000 with co-located FM). Population served: 100,000 Format: Country. Target aud: General. ♦Randy J. Timothy, pres; David B. Smith, gen mgr, progmg dir; Dennis Silver, chief of engrg.

KWSA(FM)— December 1985: 100.9 mhz; 3 kw. 111 ft TL: N39 32 42 W110 48 56. Stereo. Hrs open: 24 Box 1980 , 84501. Secondary address: 163 E. 100 N. 84501. Phone: (435) 637-1080. Fax: (435) 637-8191.E-mail: kwsa@preciscom.net Web Site:www.kusaonline.com Population served: 50,000 Format: Adult contemp.

Provo

***KBYU-FM**— November 1960: 89.1 mhz; 32 kw. 2,913 ft TL: N40 36 28 W112 09 33. Stereo. Hrs open: 24 C302 Harris Fine Arts Ctr., 84602. Phone: (801) 422-3552. Fax: (801) 422-0922.E-mail: kbyu@byu.edu Web Site:www.kbyu.org Licensee: Brigham Young University. Population served: 1,099,000 Natl. Network: PRI, AP Radio, NPR, . Format: Class, news/talk. News staff: 2; News: 5 hrs wkly. Target aud: 35 plus. ♦Derek Marquis, CEO; Walter B. Rudolph, gen mgr; Daniel Hubbard, mktg dir, prom dir; Eric Glissmeyer, progmg dir, mus dir; Wes Sims, news dir; Lynn Edwards, engrg dir; Christine Nokleby, prom. Co-owned TV: *KBYU-TV affil.

***KEYY(AM)**— December 1949: 1450 khz; 1 kw-U. TL: N40 13 49 W111 41 12. Hrs open: 24 307 S. 1600 W., 84601-3932. Phone: (801) 374-5210. Fax: (801) 374-2910.E-mail: mail@keyy.com Web Site:www.keyy.com Licensee: Biblical Ministries Worldwide. (acq 5-10-88). Population served: 450,000 Natl. Network: Moody, Salem Radio Network, . Garvey, Schubert & Barer. Format: Christian. News staff: 0; News: 13 hrs wkly. Target aud: General. Spec prog: Sp 5 hrs wkly. ♦Chris Allinger, progmg dir.

KHTB(FM)— November 1979: 94.9 mhz; 47 kw. Ant 2,798 ft TL: N40 16 58 W111 56 11. Stereo. Hrs open: 24 434 Bearcat Dr., Salt Lake City, 84115. Phone: (801) 485-6700. Fax: (801) 487-5369. Web Site:949zrock.com Licensee: Citadel Broadcasting Co. (acq 8-13-2008). Format: Rock. ♦Judith A. Ellis, COO.

KOVO(AM)— Sept 12, 1939: 960 khz; 5 kw-D, 1 kw-N, DA-N. TL: N40 12 44 W111 40 13. (CP: COL Bluffdale. 50 kw-D, 940 w-N, DA-2. TL: N40 35 06 W112 04 20). Hrs open: 24
Rebroadcasts KZNS (AM) Salt Lake City 100%.
80 South Redwood Rd., # 211, North Salt Lake, 84054. Phone: (801) 936-0706. Fax: (801) 936-0670. Web Site:www.incacommunications.com Licensee: Simmons-SLC, LS LLC. Group owner: Simmons Media Group (acq 4-19-2004; $1 million). Population served: 500,000 Natl. Rep: D & R Radio,. Format: Sports Talk. Target aud: 35 plus; upper income affluent males & females 35-65. ♦Craig Hanson, pres; Stephen Johnson, gen mgr; Kevin Graham, progmg dir.

KSRR(AM)— Nov 24, 1947: 1400 khz; 1 kw-U. TL: N40 15 29 W111 42 24. Hrs open: 24 Box 828, Orem, 84058. Secondary address: 1454 W. Business Park Dr., Orem 84058. Phone: (801) 224-1400. Fax: (801) 224-1524. Licensee: Zeta Holdings LLC (acq 8-27-97). Population served: 550,000 Womble, Carlyle, Sandridge & Rice. Format: Adult contemp. News: one hr wkly. Target aud: 18-54. ♦Robert H. Morey, gen mgr.

KXRK(FM)— Feb 14, 1968: 96.3 mhz; 38 kw. Ant 2,952 ft TL: N40 36 28 W112 09 26. Stereo. Hrs open: 24 515 South 700 East, Suite 1C, Salt Lake City, 84102. Phone: (801) 524-2600. Fax: (801) 521-9234.E-mail: xmail@x96.com Web Site:www.x96.com Licensee: Simmons-SLC, LS LLC. Group owner: Simmons Media Group (acq 4-4-2001; grpsl). Population served: 1,200,000 Fletcher, Heald & Hildreth. Format: Alternative. Target aud: 18-34; young, affluent executives. ♦Craig Hanson, pres; Bruce Thomas, CFO; Stephen C. Johnson, gen mgr; Alan Hague, opns dir; Mike Lund, gen sls mgr; Kris Burton, natl sls mgr; Natalie Divino, mktg dir, prom dir; Scott Matthews, chief of engrg; Rachel Wilson, traf mgr; Bill Allred, disc jockey.

Randolph

KDUT(FM)— 2001: 102.3 mhz; 89 kw horiz. Ant 2,122 ft TL: N40 52 16 W110 59 43. Hrs open: 24 2722 S. Redwood Rd., Suite 1, Salt Lake City, 84119. Phone: (801) 908-8777. Fax: (801) 908-8782.E-mail: info@bustosmedia.com Web Site:www.bustosmedia.com Licensee: Bustos Media of Utah License LLC. Group owner: Bustos Media Holdings (acq 7-1-2004; $9 million). Format: Sp CHR. ♦Edward Distel, gen mgr.

Richfield

***KEYR(FM)**—Not on air, target date: unknown: 91.7 mhz; 6 kw. Ant 338 ft TL: N38 44 12 W112 00 49. Hrs open: 307 South 1600 West, Provo, 84601-3932. Phone: (801) 374-5210. Fax: (801) 374-2910.E-mail: mail@keyy.com Web Site:www.keyy.com Licensee: Biblical Ministries Worldwide. ♦Christopher A. Bauer, pres.

KLGL(FM)— 2000: 93.7 mhz; 66 kw. Ant 2,355 ft TL: N39 19 17 W111 46 11. Stereo. Hrs open: 24 Box 40, Manti, 84642. Phone: (435) 835-7301. Fax: (435) 835-2250. Web Site:www.klgl.com Licensee: Sanpete County Broadcasting Co. (acq 3-1-2006; swap for KCYQ(FM) Elsinore). Population served: 125,000 Format: Super hits. News staff: one; News: 11 hrs wkly. Target aud: General. ♦J.D. Fox, mus dir.

KSVC(AM)— September 1947: 980 khz; 10 kw-D, 1 kw-N. TL: N38 47 17 W112 00 41. Hrs open: 24 390 E. Annabella Rd., 84701. Phone: (435) 896-4456. Fax: (435) 896-9333. Web Site:midutahradio.com Licensee: Mid-Utah Radio Inc. (acq 9-15-94; $275,000 with co-located FM; 10-24-94). Population served: 62,000 Borsari & Paxson. Format: News/talk, sports. News: 18 hrs wkly. Target aud: 18-54. Spec prog: Farm one hr wkly. ♦Kevin Kitchen, gen mgr, sls dir; Bruce Mehew, news dir; Kirk Williams, chief of engrg.

***KUSL(FM)**—Not on air, target date: unknown: 89.3 mhz; 2 kw vert. Ant 3,157 ft TL: N38 23 08 W112 19 57. Hrs open: Utah Public Radio, 8505 Old Main Hill, Logan, 84322-8505. Phone: (435) 797-3138. Fax: (435) 797-3150. Web Site:www.upr.org Licensee: Utah State University of Agriculture and Applied Science. ♦Cathy Ives, gen mgr.

KYHR(AM)—Not on air, target date: unknown: 1490 khz; 1 kw-U. TL: N38 47 06 W112 04 52. Hrs open: 8320 W. 66th Ave., Arvada, CO, 80004. Phone: (303) 431-0103. Licensee: Better Life Ministries. ♦Claud Pettit, pres.

Roosevelt

KIFX(FM)— Dec 14, 1987: 98.5 mhz; 2.65 kw. 1,853 ft TL: N40 31 15 W109 42 17. (CP: 3.19 kw, ant 1,689 ft. TL: N40 32 16 W109 41 57). Stereo. Hrs open: 24 The Fox 98.5, Rt. 2, Box 2384, 84066. Secondary address: 2242 E. 1000 S. 84066. Phone: (435) 722-5011. Phone: (435) 789-5101. Fax: (435) 722-5012. Web Site:www.hitsandfavorites.com Licensee: Evans Broadcasting Inc. (acq 5-31-91; $283,750; 6-24-91). Rgnl rep: Art Moore. Format: Adult contemp. News staff: one; News: 5 hrs wkly. Target aud: 21-45. ♦Joseph L. Evans, pres, gen mgr; Teddie Evans, VP; Vickie Reary, opns dir; Teena Christopherson, gen sls mgr; Earl Hawkins, progmg dir; Jean Liddell, news dir; Steve Sprouce, chief of engrg.

KNEU(AM)— Jan 6, 1978: 1250 khz; 5 kw-D, 129 w-N. TL: N40 17 13 W109 57 32. Hrs open: 5 AM-11 PM Rt. 2, Box 2384, 84066. Secondary address: 2242 E 1000 S 84066. Phone: (435) 722-5011. Fax: (435) 722-5012.E-mail: radio@ubtanet.com Web Site:www.realcountryonline.com Licensee: Country Gold Broadcasting. (acq 2-84; $419,419; 2-20-84). Population served: 32,000 Format: Real Country. News staff: one; News: 10 hrs wkly. Target aud: 25-54. ♦Joseph L. Evans, pres, gen mgr; Teddie Evans, VP, gen sls mgr; Teena Christopherson, gen sls mgr; Earl Hawkins, progmg dir; Jean Liddell, news dir; Jonathan Hawkins, chief of engrg.

KXRQ(FM)— Dec 18, 1998: 94.3 mhz; 17.5 kw. Ant 1,863 ft TL: N40 31 15 W109 42 25. Stereo. Hrs open: 1420 E. 2850 S., Suite 200, Vernal, 84078. Phone: (435) 722-0940. Phone: (435) 781-1100. Fax: (435) 781-1500.E-mail: cruise@channelx94.com Web Site:www.channelx94.com Licensee: Uinta Broadcasting L.C. (acq 2-15-01; $450,000). Population served: 60,000 Wire Svc: Metro Weather Service Inc. Format: CHR. hot adult contemp. Target aud: 25-54. Spec prog: Relg 8 hrs wkly. ♦Charles D. Hahl, gen mgr; Charles Hall, opns dir, gen sls mgr, prom dir, engrg dir, chief of engrg; Amy Jensen, progmg dir; Natasha Huber, traf mgr; Bradon Johnson, local news ed.

Roy

***KANN(AM)**— September 1961: 1120 khz; 10 kw-D, 1 kw-N, DA-2. TL: N41 03 31 W112 04 10. Hrs open: 24 Box 3880, Ogden, 84409. Secondary address: 2500 W. 3700 S., Syracuse 84075. Phone: (801) 776-0249.E-mail: bobalzugarat@aol.com Web Site:www.sosradio.net Licensee: Faith Communications Corp. Population served: 1,100,000 Format: Christian, Adult Contemp. News: 6 hrs wkly. Target aud: 25-44; young families. ♦Bob Alzugarat, gen mgr; Brad Staley, pres & opns mgr.

KUDD(FM)— September 1986: 107.9 mhz; 67 kw. Ant 2,383 ft TL: N41 15 27 W112 26 24. Hrs open: 24
Rebroadcasts KUDD(FM) Nephi.
2835 E. 3300 S., Suite 800, Salt Lake City, 84107. Phone: (801) 412-6040. Fax: (801) 412-6041. Licensee: Millcreek Broadcasting L.L.C. (group owner; (acq 4-17-2001; grpsl). Natl. Rep: Interep,. Robert Olender. Format: Modern adult contemp. Target aud: General. ♦Randy Rodgers, gen mgr; Lutisha Merrill, gen sls mgr; Scott St. John, prom VP; Brian Michel, progmg dir; Kevin Terry, chief of engrg.

Saint George

***KAER(FM)**— 2006: 89.5 mhz; 7 kw. Ant 1,820 ft TL: N36 50 49 W113 29 28. Hrs open: 24
Rebroadcasts KLRD(FM) Yucaipa, CA 100%.
2351 Sunset Blvd., SUIte 170-218, Rocklin, CA, 95765. Phone: (916) 251-1600. Fax: (916) 251-1650.E-mail: info@air1.com Web Site:www.air1.com Licensee: Educational Media Foundation. Group owner: EMF Broadcasting. Natl. Network: Air 1, . Shaw Pittman. Format: Contemp Christian. News staff: 3. Target aud: 19-35; Judeo Christian female. ♦Richard Jenkins, pres; Lloyd Parker, gen mgr; Ed Lenane, opns dir, news dir; Keith Whipple, dev dir; Eric Allen, natl sls mgr; Mike Novak, progmg dir; David Pierce, progmg mgr; Sam Wallington, engrg dir.

KDXU(AM)— July 3, 1957: 890 khz; 10 kw-U, DA-N. TL: N37 04 04 W113 31 04. Hrs open: 750 W. Ridgeview Dr., Suite 204, 84770.

Phone: (435) 673-3579. Fax: (435) 673-8900. Licensee: CCR-St. George IV LLC. Group owner: Bonneville International Corp. (acq 8-10-2006; grpsl). Population served: 70,000 Format: News/talk. Target aud: 25-54. Spec prog: Relg 4 hrs wkly. ♦Joseph D. Schwartz, CEO; Chris McCarthy, sls dir, gen sls mgr; Rick Parrish, gen mgr & mktg mgr; Peter Gardner, progmg dir; Dave Cory, chief of engrg; Debbie Calobeer, traf mgr.

KONY(FM)— Nov 12, 1994: 99.9 mhz; 89 kw. Ant 2,053 ft TL: N36 50 49 W113 29 28. Stereo. Hrs open: 24 Box 910850, 84791. Secondary address: 204 W Playa Della Rosita, Washington 84780. Phone: (435) 628-3643. Fax: (435) 673-1210.E-mail: kony@infowest.com Web Site:www.999konycountry.com Licensee: Canyon Media Corp. Group owner: Legacy Communications Corp. Population served: 150,000 Natl. Network: Fox News Radio, . Natl. Rep: Katz Radio,. Rgnl rep: Kathy Bingham Format: Country. Target aud: 25-64; male & female. ♦M. Kent Frandsen, pres; Carl Lamar, gen mgr.

***KSGU(FM)**— 2005: 90.3 mhz; 2 kw. Ant 1,820 ft TL: N36 50 49 W113 29 28. Stereo. Hrs open:
Rebroadcasts KNPR(FM) Las Vegas, NV 100%.
1289 S. Torrey Pines Dr., Las Vegas, NV, 89146. Phone: (702) 258-9895. Fax: (702) 258-5646.E-mail: reception@knpr.org Web Site:www.ksgu.org Licensee: Nevada Public Radio (acq 3-10-2005; $250,000 for CP). Population served: 120,000 Format: All news and info. ♦Florence Rogers, gen mgr.

KSNN(FM)— June 15, 1973: 93.5 mhz; 3 kw. -125 ft TL: N37 06 54 W113 34 23. Stereo. Hrs open: Dups AM 5% 750 W. Ridgeview Dr., Suite 204, 84770. Phone: (435) 673-3579. Fax: (435) 673-8900. Licensee: CCR-St. George IV LLC. Format: Adult contemp. Target aud: 12-49. ♦Chris McCarthy, sls dir; Rick Parrish, mktg mgr.

KUNF(AM)—(Washington, June 6, 1982: 1210 khz; 10 kw-D, 250 w-N. TL: N37 08 38 W113 30 03. Hrs open: 24 750 W. Ridge View Dr., Suite 204, St. George, 84770. Phone: (435) 673-3579. Fax: (435) 673-8900. Web Site:www.sportsradio1210.com Licensee: CCR-St. George IV LLC. Group owner: Bonneville International Corp. (acq 8-10-2006; grpsl). Natl. Network: ESPN Radio, . Format: Sports, Talk. Target aud: 18-64. ♦Chris McCarthy, sls dir, gen sls mgr; Rick Parrish, mktg mgr; Mike McGary, progmg dir; Dave Cory, chief of engrg; Michelle Matthews, traf mgr.

***KXDS(FM)**— 2009: 91.3 mhz; 360 w. Ant 1,862 ft TL: N36 50 49 W113 29 28. Hrs open: 225 South 700 East, 84770. Phone: (435) 879-4264. Web Site:new.dixie.edu/classical91/ Licensee: Dixie College. ♦Paul Bulkley, gen mgr & progmg dir.

KZHK(FM)— January 1997: 95.9 mhz; 96.6 kw. 1,965 ft TL: N36 50 50 W113 29 28. Hrs open: 204 Playa Della Rosita, Washington, 84780. Phone: (435) 628-3643. Fax: (435) 673-1210.E-mail: kony@infowest.com Licensee: Marvin Kent Frandsen. Group owner: Sun Valley Radio Inc. Format: Classic rock. ♦M.K. Frandsen, pres; Carl Lamar, gen mgr, news dir; John Van Wagoner, gen sls mgr; Aaronee Allen, mktg dir, prom dir, pub affrs dir; Marty Lane, stn mgr & progmg dir; Kelton Lloyd, chief of engrg.

KZNU(AM)— Oct 9, 1957: 1450 khz; 1 kw-U. TL: N37 05 02 W113 33 26. Stereo. Hrs open: 24 Box 910850, 84791. Secondary address: 204 Playa Della Rosita, Washington 84780. Phone: (435) 628-3643. Fax: (435) 673-1210.E-mail: info@1450newsradio.com Web Site:www.1450newsradio.com Licensee: Canyon Media Corp. Group owner: Legacy Communications Corp. (acq 7-31-2004). Natl. Network: Fox News Radio, . Natl. Rep: Katz Radio,. Rgnl rep: Kathy Bingham Format: News/talk. ♦Carl Lamar, gen mgr.

Salt Lake City

KALL(AM)—See North Salt Lake City

KBEE(FM)— 1947: 98.7 mhz; 40 kw. 2,932 ft TL: N40 36 30 W112 09 34. Stereo. Hrs open: 434 Bearcat Dr., 84115. Phone: (801) 485-6700. Fax: (801) 487-5369.E-mail: info@b987.com Web Site:www.b987.com Licensee: Citadel Broadcasting Co. Group owner: Citadel Broadcasting Corp. (acq 7-18-97; $2,873,027 with co-located AM). Format: Adult contemp. Target aud: General. ♦Eric Hauenstein, gen mgr; Ed Hill, opns mgr; Jim Bratt, gen sls mgr; Jaelyn Carillo, prom dir; Rusty Keys, progmg dir; Richie Bauer, chief of engrg; Susan Wasescha, traf mgr.

KBJA(AM)—(Sandy, June 2001: 1640 khz; 10 kw-D, 1 kw-N. TL: N40 42 47 W111 55 53. Hrs open: 24 10348 S. Redwood Rd., South Jordan, 84095. Phone: (801) 254-7699. Fax: (801) 254-7688.E-mail: superradio1640@gmail.com Licensee: United Broadcasting Co. Inc. Format: Sp var. News staff: 5; News: 41.5 hrs wkly. Target aud: Hispanic adults; adult Hispanic market. ♦Jose L. Rivera, gen mgr, sls dir; Karla Hernandez, dev dir; Patricia Rivera, mktg dir; Christian Rivera, prom dir, spec ev coord; Jose Rivera, adv dir, pub affrs dir, political ed; Daniel Rivera, progmg dir, traf mgr; Carmen Vargas, news dir, local news ed; Dennis Silver, chief of engrg.

***KCPW-FM**— 1992: 88.3 mhz; 750 w. Ant -587 ft TL: N40 45 33 W111 49 48. Hrs open: 24 Box 510730, 84151-0730. Phone: (801) 359-5279. Fax: (801) 746-2708.E-mail: news@kcpw.org Web Site:www.kcpw.org Licensee: Community Wireless of Park City Inc. Natl. Network: NPR, PRI, . Format: News/talk. Target aud: 25 plus. ♦Vicki Mann, gen mgr; Bryan Schott, stn mgr, mus dir.

KDYL(AM)—(South Salt Lake, Sept 2, 1967: 1060 khz; 10 kw-D, 149 w-N. TL: N40 32 18 W112 04 38. Hrs open: 24 3606 South 500 West, 84115. Secondary address: 3606 South 500 W. 84115. Phone: (801) 262-5624. Fax: (801) 266-1510.E-mail: kdylam@aros.net Web Site:www.kdylam.com Licensee: Holiday Broadcasting Co. Group owner: Carlson Communications International Population served: 1,500,000 Wire Svc: CNN Format: Oldies. News: 13 hrs wkly. Target aud: 35-64; general. ♦Brent J. Carlson, VP; Ralph J. Carlson, gen mgr; R. Steve Carlson, opns VP.

KENZ(FM)—See Ogden

KFNZ(AM)— 1923: 1320 khz; 50 kw-D, 200 w-N. TL: N40 38 36 W111 55 24. Stereo. Hrs open: 434 Bearcat Dr., 84115. Phone: (801) 485-6700. Fax: (801) 487-5369. Licensee: Citadel Broadcasting Co. Population served: 175,885 Format: Sports. ♦Zandi Wilcox, gen sls mgr; Joel Smith, prom dir; Jeff Austin, progmg dir; Julie Allen, traf mgr; Dave Coons, sports cmtr.

KJQS(AM)—See Murray

KKAT(AM)— Nov 15, 1955: 860 khz; 10 kw-D, 195.8 w-N, 3 kw-CH. TL: N40 42 47 W111 55 53. Stereo. Hrs open: 434 Bearcat Dr., 84115. Phone: (801) 485-6700. Fax: (801) 487-5369. Licensee: Citadel Broadcasting Co. Group owner: Citadel Broadcasting Corp. Natl. Rep: Christal,. Format: Country. Target aud: 25-54. ♦Larry Wilson, CEO, chmn; Bob Proffitt, sr VP; Eric Hauenstein, gen mgr; Susie Harris Carlson, gen sls mgr; Rusty Keys, prom mgr, progmg dir; Richie Bauer, chief of engrg.

KMRI(AM)—(West Valley City, Nov 16, 1956: 1550 khz; 10 kw-D, 500 w-N. TL: N40 43 29 W112 00 43. Hrs open: 24 314 S. Redwood Rd., 84104. Phone: (801) 886-1550. Fax: (801) 973-7145. Web Site:www.exitos1550.com Licensee: Alpha & Omega Communications LLC (acq 8-15-2007; $500,000). Population served: 1,300,000 Wood, Maines & Borwn. Format: Christian, rgnl Mexican music. News staff: 2; News: 40 hrs wkly. Target aud: 16-50. ♦Pat Openshaw, pres; Andy Acosta, gen mgr, sls dir, progmg dir, chief of engrg.

KNRS(AM)— Aug 1, 1938: 570 khz; 5 kw-U, DA-2. TL: N40 49 09 W111 55 56. Hrs open: 24 2801 S. Decker Lake Dr., 84119. Phone: (801) 908-1300. Fax: (801) 908-1310. Web Site:www.knrs.com Licensee: Citicasters Licenses L.P. Group owner: Clear Channel Communications Inc. (acq 1999; grpsl). Population served: 1,400,400 Natl. Rep: Clear Channel,. Format: News/talk. News staff: one; News: 2 hrs wkly. Target aud: 25-54; adults. ♦Stu Stanek, gen mgr; Jeff Cochran, opns mgr; Bill Mathews, sls dir; Jim Vandiver, gen sls mgr; Greg Foster, progmg dir. Co-owned TV: KTVX(TV)

KNRS-FM—See Centerville

KODJ(FM)— Dec 1, 1968: 94.1 mhz; 21.5 kw. Ant 3,998 ft TL: N40 39 35 W112 12 05. Stereo. Hrs open: 24 2801 S. Decker Lake Dr., 84119. Phone: (801) 908-1300. Fax: (801) 908-1429.E-mail: robboshard @clearchannel.com Web Site:www.kodj.com Licensee: Citicasters Licenses L.P. Group owner: Clear Channel Communications Inc. (acq 5-4-99; grpsl). Population served: 1,361,800 Natl. Rep: Clear Channel, Katz Radio,. Format: Hits of the 60s & 70s. News: 2 hrs wkly. Target aud: 25-54; adults. ♦Stu Stanek, gen mgr; Bill Betts, opns mgr; Kimberly Dickerson, gen sls mgr; Rob Boshard, progmg dir. Co-owned TV: KUTV(TV) affil

***KRCL(FM)**— Dec 3, 1979: 90.9 mhz; 16.5 kw. 3,770 ft TL: N40 39 35 W112 12 05. Stereo. Hrs open: 24
Rebroadcasts KZMU(FM) Moab 50%.
1971 W. North Temple, 84116-3046. Phone: (801) 363-1818. Fax: (801) 533-9136.E-mail: mailman@krcl.org Web Site:www.krcl.org Licensee: Listeners Community Radio of Utah Inc. Population served: 45,000 Format: Div, educ, folk. News staff: one; News: 3 hrs wkly. Target aud: General. Spec prog: Black 20 hrs, Sp 9 hrs, American Indian 4 hrs, Asian 4 hrs, Polynesian one hr, wkly. ♦Donna Land Maldonado, pres, gen mgr; Kami St. John, dev VP, dev dir, mktg dir; Troy Mumm, opns dir & progmg dir; Doug Young, mus dir; Gena Edualson, pub affrs dir; Felix Gonzalez, engrg mgr; Lewis Downey, chief of engrg.

KRSP-FM— Aug 21, 1968: 103.5 mhz; 25 kw. Ant 3,739 ft TL: N40 39 34 W112 12 05. Stereo. Hrs open: 55 North 300 West, 84180. Phone: (801) 575-5555. Fax: (801) 526-1070. Web Site:www.arrow1035.com Licensee: Bonneville Holding Co. Group owner: Bonneville International Corp. (acq 12-5-2003; grpsl). Population served: 241,100 Format: Classic rock. Target aud: 18-34. ♦Chris Redgrave, gen mgr.

KSFI(FM)— Dec 26, 1946: 100.3 mhz; 25 kw. Ant 3,740 ft TL: N40 39 34 W112 12 05. Stereo. Hrs open: 55 North 300 West, 84180. Phone: (801) 575-5555. Fax: (801) 526-1070. Web Site:www.fm100.com Licensee: Bonneville Holding Co. Group owner: Bonneville International Corp. (acq 12-5-2003; grpsl). Format: Adult contemp. Target aud: 25-54; general. ♦Chris Redgrave, gen mgr; Paulette Cary, sls dir; Dain Craig, progmg dir; Christa Lee Durrant, mus dir; Peggy Ijams, news dir; Trina Bodily, traf mgr.

KSL(AM)— May 6, 1922: 1160 khz; 50 kw-U. TL: N40 46 46 W112 05 56. Stereo. Hrs open: 24 55 N. 300 W., 84180. Phone: (801) 575-5555. Fax: (801) 526-1070. Web Site:www.ksl.com Licensee: Bonneville International Corp. (group owner) Population served: 1,180,000 Natl. Network: CBS, . Wire Svc: Reuters Wire Svc: UPI Format: News/talk, sports. News staff: 12. Target aud: 25-54. ♦Bruce Reese, CEO; Robert Johnson, CFO; Chris Redgrave, gen mgr; Lora Woodbury, natl sls mgr; Paulette Cary, rgnl sls mgr; Kevin Larue, progmg dir; Monica Leger, pub affrs dir; John Dehnel, chief of engrg; Janet Johnson, traf mgr; Greg Wrubell, sports cmtr. Co-owned TV: KSL-TV affil.

KSOP(AM)—(South Salt Lake, Feb 1, 1955: 1370 khz; 5 kw-D, 500 w-N, DA-N. TL: N40 43 12 W111 55 42. Hrs open: 24 Box 25548, 84125. Secondary address: 1285 W. 2320 S. 84125. Phone: (801) 972-1043. Fax: (801) 974-0868. Web Site:www.goldcountryam1370.com Licensee: KSOP Inc. Population served: 175,885 Natl. Rep: D & R Radio,. Format: Classic country. News staff: one. Target aud: 25-54+. ♦Greg Hilton, pres, gen mgr, gen sls mgr; Don Hilton, progmg dir; Debbie Turpin, mus dir; Dick Jacobson, news dir; Bill Traue, chief of engrg; John Greenwell, farm dir, disc jockey; Bill Buckly, disc jockey.

KSOP-FM— Dec 10, 1964: 104.3 mhz; 25 kw. Ant 3,650 ft TL: N40 39 35 W112 12 05. Stereo. Hrs open: 24 Box 25548, 84125. Secondary address: 1285 W. 2320 S. 84125. Phone: (801) 972-1043. Fax: (801) 974-0868. Web Site:www.ksopcountry.com Licensee: KSOP Inc. Natl. Rep: McGavren Guild,. Format: Hot country. News staff: 1. Target aud: 18 plus. ♦Greg Hilton, gen mgr, gen sls mgr; Bill Buckley, disc jockey.

KTKK(AM)—(Sandy, May 13, 1960: 630 khz; 1 kw-D, 500 w-N, DA-2. TL: N40 41 30 W111 55 30. Hrs open: 24 10348 S. Redwood Rd., South Jordan, 84095. Phone: (801) 253-4883. Fax: (801) 253-9085.E-mail: webmaster@k-talk.com Web Site:www.k-talk.com Licensee: United Broadcasting Co. (acq 12-1-63). Population served: 175,885 Format: Talk. Target aud: 35 plus. ♦Richard Perry, pres, gen mgr; Janet Kelly, sls dir, prom dir; Tom Draschil, progmg dir & news dir; Dennis Silver, engrg dir.

KTUB(AM)—See Centerville

KUBL-FM— July 31, 1965: 93.3 mhz; 25 kw. Ant 3,739 ft TL: N40 39 34 W112 12 05. Stereo. Hrs open: 434 Bearcat Dr., 84115. Phone: (801) 485-6700. Fax: (801) 464-8580. Web Site:www.kbull93.com Licensee: Citadel Broadcasting Co. Format: Country 90s. ♦Ed Hill, opns mgr, progmg dir; Terry Mathis, sls dir & gen sls mgr; Randi P' Poll, prom VP, prom dir; Richie Bauer, chief of engrg; Julie Johnson, traf mgr.

***KUER(FM)**— June 4, 1960: 90.1 mhz; 38 kw. 2,900 ft TL: N40 36 30 W112 09 34. Stereo. Hrs open: University of Utah, 101 Wasatch Dr., #235, 84112. Phone: (801) 581-6625.E-mail: radiowest@kuer.org Web Site:www.kuer.org Licensee: University of Utah. Population served: 60,000 Natl. Network: NPR, PRI, . Format: NPR news, info & jazz music progmg. ♦John Greene, gen mgr; Susan Kropf, dev dir & news dir.

***KUFR(FM)**— Dec 14, 1989: 91.7 mhz; 220 w. Ant -318 ft TL: N40 46 09 W111 53 12. Hrs open: 24 136 East South Temple, Suite 1630, 84111. Phone: (801) 359-3147. Fax: (801) 359-8112.E-mail: info@familyradio.com Web Site:www.familyradio.com Licensee: Family Stations Inc. (group owner) Format: Christian relg. ♦Harold Camping, pres, gen mgr; Roger Crawford, stn mgr, chief of engrg; James Abrahamson, opns mgr; Thad McKinney, rgnl sls mgr.

KWDZ(AM)— 1945: 910 khz; 5 kw-D, 1 kw-N, DA-2. TL: N40 30 48 W112 00 23. Stereo. Hrs open: 24 2801 S. Decker Lake Dr., Suite 100, 84119. Phone: (801) 908-5152. Fax: (801) 908-7844.E-mail: ginger.m.buchanan@disney.com Web Site:www.radiodisney.com/saltlakecity Licensee: Radio Disney Group LLC. Group owner: ABC Inc. (acq 4-30-03; $3.7 million). Population served: 1,361,800 Natl. Network: Radio Disney, . Format: Children. ♦Ginger Buchanan, gen mgr; Cori Rampton, prom mgr; Barry McClellen, chief of engrg; Reba George, traf mgr.

KZHT(FM)— Feb 1, 1961: 97.1 mhz; 25 kw. Ant 3,739 ft TL: N40 39 34 W112 12 05. Stereo. Hrs open: 24 2801 S. Decker Lake Dr., 84119. Phone: (801) 908-1300. Fax: (801) 908-1389.E-mail: info@kzhfm.com Web Site:www.971zht.com Licensee: CC Licenses LLC. Group owner: Clear Channel Communications Inc. (acq 7-10-2000). Population served: 534,700 Natl. Rep: Katz Radio,. Format: CHR. Target aud: 18-49. ◆Bill Betts, gen mgr, opns mgr; Bill Mathews, sls dir; Emily Hunt, gen sls mgr; Stacy Sappenfield, prom dir; Jeff McCartney, progmg dir.

KZNS(AM)— February 1945: 1280 khz; 5 kw-D, 500 w-N, DA-N. TL: N40 44 47 W111 54 42. Hrs open: 515 S. 700 East, Suite 1C, 84102. Phone: (801) 524-2600. Fax: (801) 521-9234.E-mail: reception@simmonsmedia.com Web Site:www.1280thezone.com Licensee: Simmons-SLC, LS LLC. Group owner: Simmons Media Group (acq 4-4-2001; grpsl). Natl. Network: Westwood One, CNN Radio, . Rgnl. Network: CNN. Natl. Rep: CBS Radio,. Format: Sports talk. Target aud: 35 plus; retired, affluent, responsible & loyal. ◆David Simmons, chmn; G. Craig Hanson, pres; Stephen C. Johnson, gen mgr; Kevin Graham, progmg dir, news dir; Scott Matthews, chief of engrg.

Sandy

KBJA(AM)—Licensed to Sandy. See Salt Lake City

KTKK(AM)—Licensed to Sandy. See Salt Lake City

Smithfield

KGNT(FM)— February 1983: 103.9 mhz; 3 kw. Ant -131 ft TL: N41 48 44 W111 47 31. Hrs open: 810 W. 200 N., Logan, 84321. Phone: (435) 752-1390. Fax: (435) 752-1392. Web Site:www.thegiant.com Licensee: Frandsen Media Co. LLC. Group owner: Sun Valley Radio Inc. (acq 2-4-02; $775,000). Population served: 150,000 Natl. Network: CBS, Westwood One, . Dan J. Alpert. Format: Oldies. Target aud: 18-49; 55% female, 45% male middle class. ◆Jay Eubanks, stn mgr; Lori Gill, gen sls mgr; David Denton, progmg dir, news dir; Paul Anderson, chief of engrg.

South Jordan

KUUU(FM)— Sept 1, 1979: 92.5 mhz; 500 w. Ant 3,929 ft TL: N40 39 35.2 W112 12 04.7. Stereo. Hrs open: 24 2835 E. 3300 S., Salt Lake City, 84109. Phone: (801) 412-6040. Fax: (801) 412-6041. Licensee: Millcreek Broadcasting L.L.C. (group owner; acq 4-17-2001; grpsl). Population served: 28,000 Natl. Rep: Interep,. Format: Hip hop, rhythm. News staff: one; News: 15 hrs wkly. Target aud: General. ◆Randy Rodgers, gen mgr; Brian Michel, opns mgr; Lutisha Merrill, gen sls mgr; Scott St. John, prom mgr; Kevin Cruise, mus dir; Kevin Terry, engrg VP.

South Salt Lake

KDYL(AM)—Licensed to South Salt Lake. See Salt Lake City

KSOP(AM)—Licensed to South Salt Lake. See Salt Lake City

Spanish Fork

KHQN(AM)— July 24, 1960: 1480 khz; 1 kw-D. TL: N40 04 30 W111 39 42. Hrs open: Box 328, Delta, 84624. Phone: (801) 798-8610. Fax: (435) 864-3842. Web Site:www.khqnradio.com Licensee: Robyn Howell (acq 8-9-2006). Population served: 9,560 Format: News/talk, Sports. ◆Sam Bushman, gen mgr.

KOSY-FM— Nov 1, 1967: 106.5 mhz; 25 kw. Ant 3,739 ft TL: N40 39 34 W112 12 05. Hrs open: 24 2801 S. Decker Lake Dr., Salt Lake City, 84119. Phone: (801) 908-1300. Fax: (801) 908-1459. Web Site:www.kosy.com Licensee: Citicasters Licenses L.P. Group owner: Clear Channel Communications Inc. (acq 5-3-2004; $22 million with KXRV(FM) Centerville). Natl. Rep: Clear Channel, Katz Radio,. Format: Soft adult contemp. Target aud: 25-44; women. ◆Stu Stanek, gen mgr; Bill Betts, opns mgr; Bill Matthews, sls dir; Jim Vandiver, gen sls mgr; Steve Clem, progmg dir.

Spanish Valley

KCPX(AM)— 2009: 1490 khz; 1 kw-U. TL: N38 28 04 W109 26 18. Hrs open: 24 Box 1119, Moab, 84532. Secondary address: 1030 S. Bowling Alley Ln #3, Moab 84532. Phone: (435) 259-1035. Fax: (435) 259-1037. Licensee: Moab Communications LLC. Population served:

12,000 Natl. Network: Fox News Radio, Premiere Radio Networks, . Format: Talk. ◆Ralph J. Carlson, pres; Phillip Mueller, gen mgr.

Taylorsville

KUTR(AM)— May 9, 2005: 820 khz; 50 kw-D, 2.5 kw-N, 50 kw-CH, DA-2. TL: N40 19 48 W112 04 09. Hrs open: 55 North 300 West, Salt Lake City, 84180. Phone: (801) 575-5555. Fax: (801) 526-1070. Web Site:www.utaham820.com Licensee: Julie Epperson Group owner: Bonneville International Corp. (acq 6-30-2008; $600,000). Format: Contemp Christian. ◆Chris Redgrave, VP, stn mgr; Paulette Cary, gen sls mgr; Rod Arquette, opns VP & progmg VP; John Dehnel, chief of engrg.

Tooele

KIHU(AM)— July 3, 1956: 1010 khz; 50 kw-D, 13 w-N. TL: N40 32 36 W112 18 33. Hrs open: 24 Box 1372, Park City, 84060. Phone: (435) 649-9004. Fax: (435) 645-9063.E-mail: letters@kpcw.org Web Site:www.ihradio.org/stations/state/UT Licensee: IHR Educational Broadcasting. (acq 8-19-2009; $900,000). Population served: 12,539 Rgnl. Network: Metronews Radio Net. Format: Catholic. ◆Ed Sweeney, pres; Jonathan Klein, gen mgr.

Tremonton

KNFL(AM)— Jan 27, 2006: 1470 khz; 1 kw-D, 880 w-N, DA-N. TL: N41 34 42 W112 06 03. Hrs open: 24 1506 Gibson Ave., Odgen, 84404. Phone: (435) 628-1000.E-mail: kognradio@comcast.net Licensee: AM Radio 1470 Inc. Group owner: Diamond Broadcasting Corp. (acq 12-6-2004; grpsl). Natl. Network: CNN Radio, Westwood One, . Dan J. Alpert. Format: Adult standards/CNN radio news. Target aud: 35 plus. ◆E. Morgan Skinner Jr., CEO; Richard Carter, stn mgr.

Vernal

*KEYV(FM)—Not on air, target date: unknown: 91.7 mhz; 910 w. Ant 1,637 ft TL: N40 32 16 W109 41 57. Hrs open: 307 South 1600 West, Provo, 84601-3932. Phone: (801) 374-5210. Fax: (801) 374-2910.E-mail: mail@keyy.com Web Site:www.keyy.com Licensee: Biblical Ministries Worldwide. ◆Christopher A. Bauer, pres.

KLCY(FM)— May 1, 1975: 105.5 mhz; 3.3 kw. Ant 1,699 ft TL: N40 32 16 W109 41 57. Hrs open: 24 Box 307, 2425 N. Vernal Ave., 84078. Phone: (435) 789-0920. Fax: (435) 789-6977.E-mail: kvel@ubtanet.com Licensee: Ashley Communications Inc. Natl. Network: ABC, Jones Radio Networks, . Format: Eagle country. News: 2 hrs wkly. Target aud: 18-54; active.

KVEL(AM)— Jan 19, 1947: 920 khz; 4.5 kw-D, 1 kw-N, DA-N. TL: N40 29 30 W109 31 45. Hrs open: 24 Box 307, 2425 N. Vernal Ave., 84078. Phone: (435) 789-0920. Phone: (435) 789-1059. Fax: (435) 789-6977.E-mail: kvel@ubtanet.com Licensee: Ashley Communications Inc. (acq 8-11-98; $10,000 for stock with co-located INF). Population served: 30,000 Reddy, Begley & McCormick. Format: Sports, news/talk. News staff: one; News: 20 hrs wkly. Target aud: 35-64; affluent, upscale. Spec prog: Farm 2 hrs, relg, Sp, pub affrs one hr wkly. ◆Steve Evans, gen mgr, gen sls mgr; Clay Johnson, progmg dir; Steve Sprouse, chief of engrg.

Washington

KUNF(AM)—Licensed to Washington. See Saint George

Wellington

KRPX(FM)— 2006: 95.3 mhz; 6 kw. Ant -138 ft TL: N39 36 33 W110 48 50. Hrs open: Box 875, Price, 84501. Phone: (435) 637-1167. Fax: (435) 637-1177.E-mail: koal@emerytelcom.net Licensee: College Creek Media LLC. Format: Light rock hits. ◆Neal J. Robinson, pres; Tom Anderson, gen mgr.

West Jordan

KLLB(AM)— 1982: 1510 khz; 10 kw-D. TL: N40 33 06 W111 58 17. Hrs open: 868 E. 5900 South, Murray, 84107. Phone: (801) 487-0247. Fax: (801) 262-6200.E-mail: kllbam@yahoo.com Licensee: United Security Financial Inc. (acq 6-18-91; $180,001; 7-8-91). Format: Gospel. ◆Lois Johnson, gen mgr; Joel Cosby, gen sls mgr; D.J. Stone, progmg dir, traf mgr; Darrell Cosby, chief of engrg.

West Valley City

KMRI(AM)—Licensed to West Valley City. See Salt Lake City

Woodruff

KYMV(FM)— June 2002: 100.7 mhz; 88 kw horiz. Ant 2,122 ft TL: N40 52 16 W110 59 43. Hrs open: 515 S. 700 E., Suite 1C, Salt Lake City, 84102. Phone: (801) 524-2600. Fax: (801) 521-9234.E-mail: reception@simmonsmedia.com Web Site:movin1007.com Licensee: Simmons-SLC, LS LLC. Group owner: Simmons Media Group (acq 4-4-2001; grpsl). Format: Rhythmic adult contemp. ◆Stephen Johnson, gen mgr; Jacquie Louie, gen sls mgr; Naziol Nazarina, prom dir; Alan Hague, progmg VP.

Vermont

Addison

WUSX(FM)— 1999: 93.7 mhz; 21 kw. Ant 354 ft TL: N44 13 15 W73 24 37. Hrs open: 372 Dorset St., South Burlington, 05403. Phone: (802) 863-1010. Fax: (802) 861-7256. Web Site:www.crusin937.com Licensee: Addison Broadcasting Co. Inc. Group owner: Northeast Broadcasting Company Inc. (acq 12-19-2000; $434,000). Natl. Network: Jones Radio Networks, . Format: Oldies. ◆Rich Delancy, gen mgr; Rich Delancey, gen sls mgr; J.J. Prieve, progmg dir; Chris Fells, news dir; Mike Raymond, chief of engrg.

Barre

*WCMD-FM— Aug 1, 1998: 89.9 mhz; 940 w. 590 ft TL: N44 07 32 W72 28 36. Stereo. Hrs open: 24 Rebroadcasts WCMK(FM) Bolton 99%. 140 Main St., Essex Junction, 05452. Secondary address: Box 8310, Essex 05451-8310. Phone: (802) 878-8885. Fax: (802) 879-6835.E-mail: cmi.radio@verizon.net Web Site:thelightradio.net Licensee: Christian Ministries Inc. Natl. Network: Moody, . Joseph E. Dunne III. Format: Inspirational, Christian. News: 15 hrs wkly. Target aud: General; Christian, middle income. ◆Mark Kinsley, pres; Richard McClary, gen mgr; Karlo Salminen, opns dir, progmg dir; Darlene Lamos, gen sls mgr; Peter Morton, chief of engrg.

WORK(FM)— Aug 5, 1974: 107.1 mhz; 1.5 kw. Ant 410 ft TL: N44 09 30 W72 28 46. Hrs open: Prog sep from AM 41 Jacques St., 05641. Phone: (802) 476-4168. Fax: (802) 479-5893. Web Site:www.1071workfm.com Population served: 180,000 Format: Classic hits. ◆T.J. Michaels, progmg dir.

WSKI(AM)—See Montpelier

WSNO(AM)— Oct 13, 1959: 1450 khz; 1 kw-U. TL: N44 11 40 W72 30 52. Hrs open: 24 41 Jacques St., 05641. Phone: (802) 476-4168. Fax: (802) 479-5893. Web Site:www.wsno1450.net Licensee: Nassau Broadcasting III L.L.C. Group owner: Nassau Broadcasting Partners L.P. (acq 8-2-2004; grpsl). Population served: 40,000 Natl. Network: CBS, . Format: News/talk, sports. ◆Ken Barlow, gen mgr; Jim Severance, progmg dir.

Barton

WJPK(FM)— 2008: 100.3 mhz; 100 w. Ant 525 ft TL: N44 45 57 W72 09 10. Hrs open: Box 97, Lyndonville, 05851. Phone: (802) 626-9800. Fax: (802) 626-8500.E-mail: wjpk@gmail.com Licensee: Vermont Broadcast Associates Inc. Format: Country. ◆Bruce James, gen mgr.

Bellows Falls

WZLF(FM)— November 1981: 107.1 mhz; 1 kw. 530 ft TL: N43 12 33 W72 19 58. Stereo. Hrs open: 24 Rebroadcasts WSSH(FM) Marlboro 100%. Box 1230, Claremont, NH, 03743. Phone: (603) 542-7735. Fax: (603) 542-8721. Web Site:www.bobcountrysm.com Licensee: Nassau Broadcasting III L.L.C. Group owner: Nassau Broadcasting Partners L.P. (acq 8-2-2004; grpsl). Natl. Rep: Roslin,. Format: Country. News staff: one; News: 5 hrs wkly. Target aud: 25-54; general. Spec prog: Farm one hr wkly. ◆Courtney Galluzzo, gen mgr, gen sls mgr, rgnl sls mgr; Doug Daniels, opns mgr; Heath Cole, progmg dir & news dir.

Bennington

WBTN(AM)— Sept 23, 1953: 1370 khz; 1 kw-D. TL: N42 54 19 W73 12 32. Hrs open: WBTN Svc., 982 Mansion Dr., 05201. Secondary address: 407 Harwood Hill 05201. Phone: (802) 442-6321. Fax: (802) 442-3112.E-mail: wbtn@svcedu Licensee: Southern Vermont College (acq 8-20-2003). Population served: 47,950 Natl. Network: Westwood One, . Wire Svc: AP Format: News/talk, music; student progmg. Target aud: 24-54. ♦Ben Runnels, pres, chief of opns; Rich Ryder, gen mgr; Megan Williams, traf mgr.

WBTN-FM— Nov 4, 1978: 94.3 mhz; 3 kw. 110 ft TL: N42 56 52 W73 10 36. Stereo. Hrs open: 5:30 AM-midnight 365 Troy Ave., Colchester, 05446. Phone: (802) 655-9451. Fax: (802) 655-2799.E-mail: contact@vpr.net Web Site:www.vpr.net Licensee: Vermont Public Radio. (acq 11-24-99) $901,000 with co-located AM). Format: Classical. News staff: one; News: 4 hrs wkly. Target aud: 18-45. ♦Mark Vogelzang, pres, gen mgr, stn mgr & disc jockey.

Berlin

WWFY(FM)— Apr 2, 1975: 100.9 mhz; 5.2 kw. Ant 718 ft TL: N44 07 38 W72 28 48. Stereo. Hrs open: 24 41 Jacques St., Barre, 05641. Phone: (802) 476-4168. Fax: (802) 479-5893. Web Site:www.froggy1009.com Licensee: Nassau Broadcasting III L.L.C. Group owner: Nassau Broadcasting Partners L.P. (acq 8-2-2004; grpsl). Population served: 100,000 Gardner, Carton & Douglas. Format: Country. Target aud: 18-49; young professionals. ♦John Gales, gen mgr; Jim Severance, sls VP, progmg dir.

Bolton

*WGLY-FM— 1996: 91.5 mhz; 2 kw. Ant 935 ft TL: N44 21 53 W72 55 52. Stereo. Hrs open: 24
Rebroadcasts WCMD(FM) Barre 100%.
140 Main St., Essex Junction, 05452. Secondary address: Box 8310, Essex 05451-8310. Phone: (802) 878-8885. Fax: (802) 879-6835.E-mail: cmi.radio@verizon.net Web Site:thelightradio.net Licensee: Christian Ministries Inc. Natl. Network: Moody, . Joseph E. Dunne III. Format: Inspirational. ♦Mark Kinsley, pres; Richard McClary, gen mgr; Karlo Salminen, opns dir, dev mgr, progmg dir; Darlene Lamos, gen sls mgr; Peter Morton, chief of engrg.

Brandon

WEXP(FM)— May 2000: 101.5 mhz; 350 w. Ant 1,305 ft TL: N43 39 31 W73 06 26. Stereo. Hrs open: 24 1 Scale Ave., Suite 84, Rutland, 05761-4459. Phone: (802) 773-9264. Fax: (802) 747-0553. Web Site:www.101thefox.com Licensee: Nassau Broadcasting III L.L.C. Group owner: Vox Radio Group L.P. (acq 1-21-2005; $2.5 million with WTHK(FM) Wilmington). Natl. Network: Westwood One, . Format: Classic rock, Rock/AOR. Target aud: 25-54; male. ♦John Gales, gen mgr; Glenn Novak, gen sls mgr; Kemy Chambers, prom dir; Kelly Kowalski, progmg dir.

Brattleboro

WINQ(FM)—See Winchester, NH

WKVT(AM)— Nov 29, 1959: 1490 khz; 1 kw-U. TL: N42 50 51 W72 34 56. Hrs open: 24 458 Williams St., 05301. Phone: (802) 254-2343. Fax: (802) 254-6683. Web Site:www.1490wkvt.com Licensee: Saga Communications of New England LLC. Group owner: Saga Communications Inc. (acq 5-1-2002; grpsl). Population served: 12,239 Natl. Network: CBS, . Wire Svc: AP Format: News/talk. News staff: one; News: 30 hrs wkly. Target aud: 35-64; news & info oriented adults. ♦Dan Guin, gen mgr; Peter Case, opns mgr & news dir.

WKVT-FM— 1980: 92.7 mhz; 6 kw. 610 ft TL: N42 53 45 W72 39 49. Stereo. Hrs open: 24 458 Williams St., 05301. Phone: (802) 254-2343. Fax: (802) 254-6683. Population served: 100,000 Natl. Network: AP Radio, . Wire Svc: AP Format: Classic Hits. News staff: one; News: 8 hrs wkly. Target aud: 18-44. ♦Dan Guin, gen mgr.

WTSA(AM)— Apr 19, 1950: 1450 khz; 1 kw-U. TL: N42 52 13 W72 33 35. Hrs open: 24 Box 819, 05302. Secondary address: 464 Putney Rd. 05301. Phone: (802) 254-4577. Fax: (802) 257-4644.E-mail: info@wtsa.net Web Site:www.wtsa.net Licensee: Tri-State Broadcasters Inc. (acq 7-1-86; grpsl; 5-26-86). Population served: 12,239 Natl. Rep: D & R Radio, . Cohn & Marks. Format: Sports. News staff: one. Target aud: General. ♦John Kilduff, pres, opns dir; Tim Johnson, news dir & chief of engrg.

WTSA-FM— Dec 15, 1975: 96.7 mhz; 5.2 kw. 167 ft TL: N42 53 21 W72 36 47. Stereo. Hrs open: Prog sep from AM Box 819, 05301. Secondary address: 464 Putney Rd. 05301. Phone: (802) 254-4577. Fax: (802) 257-4644.E-mail: info@wtsa.net Web Site:www.wtsa.net Licensee: Tri-State Broadcasters Inc. Population served: 50,000 Format: Adult contemp. Target aud: 12 plus. Spec prog: Oldies 16 hrs wkly.

WYRY(FM)—See Keene, NH

Brighton

WVTI(FM)—Not on air, target date: unknown: 106.9 mhz; 1.42 kw. Ant 679 ft TL: N44 47 02 W71 53 14. Hrs open: Vermont Public Radio, 365 Troy Ave., Colchester, 05446. Phone: (802) 655-9451. Fax: (802) 655-2799. Web Site:www.vpr.net Licensee: Vermont Public Radio. ♦Mark Vogelzang, pres & gen mgr.

Bristol

WTNN(FM)— 2007: 97.5 mhz; 8.7 kw. Ant 518 ft TL: N44 24 23.1 W73 08 12.8. Hrs open: 4049 Williston Rd., South Burlington, 05403. Phone: (802) 864-9750. Fax: (802) 864-9777.E-mail: info@eaglecountry975.com Web Site:www.eaglecountry975.com Licensee: Impact Radio Inc. Format: Country. ♦Arthur V. Belendiuk, pres; John Fuller, gen mgr.

*WXLQ(FM)— 2009: 90.5 mhz; 160 w. Ant 594 ft TL: N44 13 24 W73 07 27. Hrs open:
Rebroadcasts WSLU(FM) Canton, NY 100%.
North Country Public Radio, St. Lawrence University, Canton, NY, 13617. Phone: (315) 229-5356. Fax: (315) 229-5373. Web Site:www.ncpr.org Licensee: The St. Lawrence University. Natl. Network: NPR, . Format: Eclectic public radio. ♦Ellen Rocco, gen mgr.

Burlington

WCAT(AM)— Apr 19, 1954: 1390 khz; 5 kw-U, DA-N. TL: N44 29 47 W73 12 49. Stereo. Hrs open: 24 372 Dorset St., South Burlington, 05403. Phone: (802) 655-6753. Fax: (802) 860-4721. Web Site:www.wcat1390.com Licensee: Radio Broadcasting Services Inc. Group owner: Radio Vermont Group Inc. (acq 8-3-2006; $400,000). Population served: 300,000 Natl. Network: ESPN Radio, . Natl. Rep: McGavren Guild,. Wire Svc: AP Format: Sports. ♦Steven A. Silberberg, pres; Richard C. DeLancey Sr., gen mgr; J.J. Prieve, progmg dir; Chris Fells, sports cmtr.

WEZF(FM)— July 19, 1968: 92.9 mhz; 46 kw. 2,703 ft TL: N44 31 40 W72 48 58. Stereo. Hrs open: 24 265 Hegeman Ave., Colchester, 05446. Secondary address: Box 1093 05402-1093. Phone: (802) 655-0093. Fax: (802) 655-0478. Web Site:www.star929.com Licensee: Vox AM/FM LLC. Group owner: Clear Channel Communications Inc. (acq 7-25-2008; grpsl). Population served: 100,000 Natl. Rep: Clear Channel,. Rini Coran PC. Format: Adult contemp. News staff: one; News: 7 hrs wkly. Target aud: 25-54. ♦Karen Marshall, gen mgr; Gale Parmalee, opns mgr.

WIZN(FM)—(Vergennes, Nov 15, 1983: 106.7 mhz; 50 kw. 373 ft TL: N44 18 40 W73 14 34. Stereo. Hrs open: 24 Box 4489, 05406. Phone: (802) 860-2440. Fax: (802) 860-1818.E-mail: wizn@wizn.com Web Site:www.wizn.com Licensee: Hall Communications Inc. Group owner: Deer River Broadcasting Group (acq 10-31-2005; $17 million). Natl. Rep: Katz Radio,. Format: Rock/AOR, live. Target aud: 18-49. Spec prog: Oldies 3 hrs, reggae one hr, progsv one hr, blues 3 hrs wkly. ♦Jennifer McCann, gen mgr; Tracy Ovitt, gen sls mgr; Matt Grasso, progmg dir, mus dir.

WJOY(AM)— Sept 14, 1946: 1230 khz; 1 kw-U. TL: N44 27 03 W73 11 51. Hrs open: 24 Box 4489, 05406-4489. Secondary address: 70 Joy Dr., South Burlington 05403. Phone: (802) 658-1230. Fax: (802) 862-0786.E-mail: wjoy@hallradio.com Web Site:www.wjoy.com Licensee: Hall Communications Inc. (group owner; (acq 12-1-83; 12-5-83). Natl. Network: Westwood One, . Natl. Rep: D & R Radio,. Fletcher, Heald & Hildreth. Format: News, easy lstng. News staff: one; News: 4 hrs wkly. Target aud: General; affluent, empty nesters, well educated. ♦Bonnie Rowbotham, chmn; Arthur J. Rowbotham, pres; Richard P. Reed, exec VP; Bill Baldwin, sr VP; Dan Dubonnet, gen mgr; Steve Pelkey, opns dir, progmg dir, disc jockey; Lee Bodette, gen sls mgr; Wendy Naylor, prom dir; Ginny McGehee, news dir, disc jockey; Dennis Snyder, chief of engrg.

WOKO(FM)— June 26, 1962: 98.9 mhz; 100 kw. Ant 307 ft TL: N44 27 03 W73 11 51. Stereo. Hrs open: 24 Box 4489, 05406-4489. Secondary address: 70 Joy Dr., South Burlington 05403. Phone: (802) 658-1230. Fax: (802) 862-0786. Web Site:www.woko.com Licensee: Hall Communications Inc. Format: Country. ♦Dan Dubonnet, VP; Bill Sargent, mus dir, disc jockey; Laura Lacasse, traf mgr; Ginny McGehee, local news ed; C.K. Coin, disc jockey.

*WRUV(FM)— Oct 3, 1965: 90.1 mhz; 460 w. 145 ft TL: N44 28 37 W73 11 59. (CP: Ant 131 ft.). Stereo. Hrs open: 24 Univ. of Vermont, Billings Student Ctr., 05405. Phone: (802) 656-4399. Phone: (802) 656-0796. Fax: (802) 656-2281.E-mail: wruv@zoo.uvm.edu Web Site:www.wruv.org Licensee: University of Vermont & State Agricultural College. Population served: 250,000 Format: Div, educ, jazz. Spec prog: Non-commercial free format, progmg varies. ♦Jake Davignon, stn mgr.

WTWK(AM)—See Plattsburgh, NY

WVMT(AM)— May 20, 1922: 620 khz; 5 kw-U, DA-N. TL: N44 29 47 W73 12 49. Hrs open: 24 Box 620, 118 Malletts Bay Ave, Colchester, 05446. Phone: (802) 655-1620. Fax: (802) 655-1329.E-mail: paulg@95triplex.com Web Site:www.newstalk620wvmt.com Licensee: Sison Broadcasting Inc. (acq 3-3-97; $2,939,014 with WXXX(FM) South Burlington). Population served: 250,000 Natl. Network: ABC, . Natl. Rep: McGavren Guild,. Format: News/talk & Sports. News staff: 2; News: 14 hrs wkly. Target aud: 35-65. ♦Paul S. Goldman, pres; Mark Esbjerg, opns mgr.

*WVPS(FM)— Oct 15, 1980: 107.9 mhz; 48.8 kw. Ant 2,716 ft TL: N44 31 32 W72 48 58. Stereo. Hrs open: 24 365 Troy Ave., Colchester, 05446. Phone: (802) 655-9451. Fax: (802) 655-2799. Fax: (802) 655-9117.E-mail: contract@vpr.net Web Site:www.vpr.net Licensee: Vermont Public Radio. Natl. Network: NPR, PRI, . Haley, Bader & Potts. Format: Class, jazz, news. News staff: 9; News: 43 hrs wkly. Target aud: General. Spec prog: Switchboard call-in progmg 3 hrs, opera 5 hrs, folk 4 hrs, children .5 hrs wkly. ♦Mark Vogelzang, CEO, pres, gen mgr; Brian Donahue, CFO; Victoria St. John, opns dir; Robin Turnau, dev dir; Cheryl Willoughby, progmg dir; Walter Parker, mus dir; John VanHoesen, news dir; Richard Parker, chief of engrg; Betty Smith, spec ev coord.

Castleton

*WIUV(FM)— Oct 1, 1976: 91.3 mhz; 227 w. -235 ft TL: N43 36 29 W73 10 54. Hrs open: Castleton State College, 86 Seminary St., 05735. Phone: (802) 468-5611. Phone: (802) 468-1264. Fax: (802) 468-5237. Web Site:www.castleton.edu Licensee: Board of Trustees. Population served: 55,000 Format: Progsv, variety. Target aud: General; smart people. Spec prog: Jazz 10 hrs, reggae 6 hrs, rap-urban 5 hrs, folk 4 hrs, Sp one hr wkly. ♦Robert Gershon, gen mgr.

Colchester

*WWPV-FM— Aug 10, 1973: 88.7 mhz; 100 w. 82 ft TL: N44 29 38 W73 09 51. Hrs open: 8 AM-2 PM St. Michaels College, Box 274, Winooski Park, 05439. Phone: (802) 654-2334. Fax: (802) 654-2336.E-mail: wwpv@smcvt.edu Web Site:personalweb.smcvt.edu/wwpv Licensee: Board of Trustees, St. Michaels College. Format: Free-form. Target aud: 14-65; varies by time of day & progmg. ♦Mike McCarthy, stn mgr; Jon Van Luling, progmg dir.

Danville

WDOT(FM)— 1996: 95.7 mhz; 3.8 kw. Ant 246 ft TL: N44 24 58 W72 03 32. Hrs open:
Rebroadcasts WNCS(FM) Montpelier 90%.
Box 374, St. Johnsbury, 05819. Phone: (802) 748-4055. Phone: (877) 367-6468. Fax: (802) 748-6939.E-mail: klm@pointfm.com Web Site:www.pointfm.com Licensee: Montpelier Broadcasting Inc. Group owner: Northeast Broadcasting Company Inc. (acq 1996; $152,500 for CP). Format: AAA. ♦Kim Buckminster, gen mgr, gen sls mgr; Jamie Canfield, progmg dir; John Hosford, chief of engrg.

Derby Center

WMOO(FM)— Apr 1, 1991: 92.1 mhz; 2.25 kw. 619 ft TL: N44 58 23 W72 04 30. Stereo. Hrs open: 24 Box 92, Derby/Newport Ave., 05829. Phone: (802) 766-9236. Fax: (802) 766-8067.E-mail: dprudhomme @nassaubroadcasting.com Web Site:www.northstarhits.com Licensee: Nassau Broadcasting III L.L.C. (acq 12-22-2004; $2.35 million with WIKE(AM) Newport). Population served: 65,000 Shaw Pittman. Wire Svc: AP Format: Hot adult contemp. News staff: one; News: 16 hrs wkly. Target aud: General. Spec prog: Community events 8 hrs wkly. ♦Dawn Prudhomme, opns mgr; Doug Weldon, progmg dir.

Essex Junction

WVVT(AM)—Not on air, target date: unknown: 670 khz; 50 kw-D, 300 w-N, 20 kw-CH, DA-3. TL: N44 29 40 W73 08 37. Hrs open: 16 Doe Run, Pittstown, NJ, 08867. Phone: (908) 730-7959. Licensee: Charles A. Hecht and Alfredo Alonso. ◆Charles A. Hecht, gen mgr.

Hartford

WWOD(FM)— Mar 15, 1992: 104.3 mhz; 5.6 kw. Ant 495 ft TL: N43 39 15 W72 21 32. Stereo. Hrs open: 24 106 N. Main St., West Lebanon, NH, 03784. Phone: (603) 298-0332. Phone: (603) 542-7735. Fax: (603) 727-0134.E-mail: info@bestoldies104.com Web Site:www.bestoldies104.com Licensee: Family Broadcasting Inc. Group owner: Nassau Broadcasting Partners L.P. (acq 8-2-2004; grpsl). Natl. Network: USA, . May & Dunne. Format: Oldies. News staff: one. Target aud: 25 plus. Spec prog: Children 3 hrs, country gospel 2 hrs wkly. ◆Shirley Clark, gen mgr & natl sls mgr; Doug Welldon, progmg dir.

Johnson

*WJSC-FM— July 16, 1972: 90.7 mhz; 200 w. Ant -489 ft TL: N44 38 29 W72 40 20. Stereo. Hrs open: Box 75, c/o Johnson State College., 05656. Phone: (802) 635-1355. Phone: (802) 635-1434. Fax: (802) 635-1202.E-mail: wjsc907@hotmail.com Web Site:www.wjsc.findhere.org Licensee: Board of Trustees, Vermont State College. Population served: 15,000 Format: Alternative, div. Spec prog: Class 3 hrs, C&W 3 hrs wkly. ◆Andrew Frappier, gen mgr.

Killington

WJEN(FM)— Aug 4, 1993: 105.3 mhz; 50 kw. Ant 2,240 ft TL: N43 38 22 W72 50 12. Stereo. Hrs open: 24 Box 30, Rutland, 05702. Phone: (802) 775-7500. Fax: (802) 775-7555.E-mail: catcountry @catamountradio.com Web Site:www.catcountryvermont.com Licensee: 6 Johnson Road Licenses Inc. Group owner: Pamal Broadcasting Ltd. (acq 10-19-2001; grpsl). Population served: 180,000 Verner, Liipfert, Bernhard, McPherson & Hand. Format: Country. Target aud: 18-49; adult, income $35,000 plus, homeowners. ◆Debbie Grembowicz, gen mgr; Terry Jaye, opns mgr; Brian Collamore, sls dir, gen sls mgr; Ken Gilbert, prom dir; Judy Anderson, progmg VP, progmg dir.

Lunenburg

WOTX(FM)— May 5, 2008: 93.7 mhz; 460 w. Ant 915 ft TL: N44 23 39 W71 39 20. Hrs open: Box 896, Littleton, NH, 03561. Phone: (603) 788-3636. Fax: (603) 788-3536.E-mail: kiss102@together.net Licensee: Alexxon Corp. Format: Classic rock. ◆Barry P. Lunderville, pres & gen mgr.

Lyndon

WGMT(FM)— May 19, 1990: 97.7 mhz; 600 w. 1,883 ft TL: N44 34 15 W71 53 40. Stereo. Hrs open: 24 Box 97, 10 Church St., Lyndonville, 05851. Phone: (802) 626-9800. Phone: (802) 626-0977. Fax: (802) 626-8500.E-mail: wgmt@kingcon.com Web Site:www.kingcon.com Licensee: Vermont Broadcast Associates Inc. Population served: 75,000 Natl. Network: CNN Radio, . Natl. Rep: Roslin,. Bryan Cave. Format: Adult contemp. News staff: 2; News: 5 hrs wkly. Target aud: 22-54; families, more female, disposable income, mobile. ◆Bruce James, pres, gen mgr; Steve Nichols, gen sls mgr; Mike Barrett, progmg dir; Don Smith, chief of engrg.

Lyndonville

*WWLR(FM)— Feb 4, 1977: 91.5 mhz; 3 kw. -75 ft TL: N44 32 04 W72 01 36. Stereo. Hrs open: 24 hrs Box F, Lyndon State College, 05851. Phone: (802) 626-6214. Fax: (802) 626-4806.E-mail: impulse915@hotmail.com Web Site:www.lsc.vsc.edu Licensee: Board of Trustees, Vermont State Colleges. Population served: 100,000 Format: Rock/AOR. Target aud: Everyone. Spec prog: Class 2 hrs, jazz 3 hrs wkly. ◆P.J. Cioffi, gen mgr; Jim Champine, opns dir.

Manchester

WEQX(FM)— November 1984: 102.7 mhz; 1.25 kw. 2,490 ft TL: N43 09 58 W73 06 59. Stereo. Hrs open: 24 Box 1027, 05254. Secondary address: 161 Elm St., Manchester Center 05255. Phone: (802) 362-4800. Phone: (802) 362-4875. Fax: (802) 362-5555. Fax: (802) 362-4885.E-mail: eqx@weqx.com Web Site:www.weqx.com Licensee: Northshire Communications Inc. Natl. Network: AP Radio, . Format:

Alternative. News: 5 hrs wkly. Target aud: 25-44. Spec prog: Jazz 4 hrs, AAA 4 hrs, locl 2 hrs, new music 3 hrs wkly. ◆A. Brooks Brown, pres, gen mgr; Melinda Brown, VP, opns mgr; Tim Bronson, progmg dir.

*WVNK(FM)—Not on air, target date: unknown: 91.1 mhz; 195 w. Ant 317 ft TL: N43 14 12.1 W73 01 43.7. Hrs open: 365 Troy Ave., Colchester, 05446. Phone: (802) 655-9451. Fax: (802) 655-2799. Web Site:www.vpr.net Licensee: Vermont Public Radio. Vermont Public Radio ◆Robin Turnau, gen mgr.

Marlboro

WRSY(FM)— July 1996: 101.5 mhz; 120 w. Ant 745 ft TL: N42 50 46 W72 41 16. Hrs open:
Rebroadcasts WRSI(FM) Turners Falls, MA 100%.
15 Hampton Ave., Northampton, MA, 01060-3809. Phone: (413) 586-7400. Fax: (413) 585-0927. Web Site:www.wrsi.com Licensee: Saga Communications of New England LLC. Group owner: Saga Communications Inc. (acq 2-13-2004; grpsl). Format: AAA. Target aud: 35 plus; women. ◆Dave Muscante, opns dir, gen sls mgr; Scott Howard, prom dir; Sean O'Mealy, gen mgr, progmg dir & news dir; Howard Frost, chief of engrg.

Middlebury

WFAD(AM)— Dec 24, 1965: 1490 khz; 1 kw-U. TL: N43 59 57 W73 09 35. Hrs open: 24 372 Dorset St., South Burlington, 05403. Phone: (802) 388-9000. Fax: (802) 388-3000.E-mail: firstnamelastinitial @champlainradio.com Web Site:www.wtwk1070.com Licensee: Addison Broadcasting Co. Inc. Group owner: Northeast Broadcasting Company Inc. (acq 6-22-2001). Population served: 45,000 Natl. Network: ESPN Radio, . Mullin, Rhyne, Emmons & Topel. Format: Sports. ◆Bob Rowe, VP; Richard C. DeLancey Sr., gen mgr; J.J. Prieve, progmg dir; Mike Raymond, chief of engrg.

*WOXM(FM)—Not on air, target date: unknown: 90.1 mhz; 1.2 kw. Ant 317 ft TL: N44 01 34 W73 09 44. Hrs open: Vermont Public Radio, 365 Troy Ave., Colchester, 05446. Phone: (802) 655-9451. Fax: (802) 655-2799. Web Site:www.vpr.net Licensee: Vermont Public Radio. ◆Robin Turnau, gen mgr.

*WRMC-FM— May 1949: 91.1 mhz; 2.9 kw. Ant -30 ft TL: N44 00 25 W73 10 40. Stereo. Hrs open: 24 Middlebury College, 05753. Phone: (802) 443-2471. Phone: (802) 443-6324. Fax: (802) 443-5108.E-mail: wrmc@wrmc.middlebury.edu Web Site:www.wrmc.middlebury.edu Licensee: President and Fellows of Middlebury College. Population served: 100,000 Natl. Network: AP Radio, . Format: Div, progsv. News: 8 hrs wkly. Target aud: General. Spec prog: Urban contemp 12 hrs, class 15 hrs, folk 15 hrs, relg one hr, blues 10 hrs, jazz 10 hrs, Sp one hr wkly. ◆Ryan Abernnathey, gen mgr.

Montpelier

WNCS(FM)— June 13, 1977: 104.7 mhz; 1.9 kw. 2,093 ft TL: N44 18 14 W72 37 18. Stereo. Hrs open: 24 169 River St., 05602-3724. Phone: (802) 223-2396. Fax: (802) 223-1520.E-mail: info@studiopointfm.com Web Site:www.pointfm.com Licensee: Montpelier Broadcasting Co. Inc. Group owner: Northeast Broadcasting Company Inc. (acq 2-12-87). Population served: 350,000 Format: AAA. Target aud: 25-40; above-average income & educated, baby boomers. Spec prog: Folk 4 hrs, jazz 5 hrs wkly. ◆Steven Silberberg, pres; Terry Lieberman, gen mgr; Caroline Scribner, gen sls mgr; Jamie Canfield, progmg dir; John Hosford, chief of engrg.

WORK(FM)—See Barre

WSKI(AM)— Dec 7, 1947: 1240 khz; 1 kw-U. TL: N44 14 40 W72 32 47. Stereo. Hrs open: 169 River St., 05602. Phone: (802) 223-5275. Fax: (802) 223-1520.E-mail: terry@pointfm.com Web Site:www.pointfm.com Licensee: Galloway Communications Inc. Group owner: Northeast Broadcasting Company Inc. (acq 5-2-00; grpsl). Population served: 85,000 Format: Oldies. Target aud: 35-64; 60% female, 40% male. ◆Terry Lieberman, gen mgr; Caroline Scribner, gen sls mgr; Jamie Canfield, progmg dir, progmg dir; John Hosford, chief of engrg.

WSNO(AM)—See Barre

Morrisville

WLVB(FM)— August 1993: 93.9 mhz; 5.4 kw. 121 ft TL: N44 34 24 W72 38 11. Hrs open: Box 94, 05661. Phone: (802) 888-4294. Fax: (802) 888-8523.E-mail: wlvb@radiovermont.com Web Site:www.wlvbradio.com Licensee: Radio Vermont Inc. Group owner:

Radio Vermont Group Inc. Format: Country. ◆Ken Squier, pres; Eric Michaels, gen mgr; Craig Ladd, opns mgr.

Newport

WIKE(AM)— Oct 12, 1952: 1490 khz; 1 kw-U. TL: N44 56 28 W72 13 35. Stereo. Hrs open: 24 P.O. Box 666, 05855. Secondary address: Derby Newport Rd., Derby 05829. Phone: (802) 766-9236. Fax: (802) 766-8067. Web Site:www.moo92.com Licensee: Nassau Broadcasting III L.L.C. (acq 12-22-2004; $2.35 million with WMOO(FM) Derby Center). Population served: 55,000 Covington & Burling. Format: Country. News staff: one; News: 4 hrs wkly. Target aud: 18 plus. Spec prog: Loc info/entertainment 5 hrs wkly. ◆William J. Macek, gen mgr; Dawn Prudhomme, opns mgr.

Northfield

*WNUB-FM— Dec 8, 1967: 88.3 mhz; 285 w. -387 ft TL: N44 08 32 W72 39 31. Stereo. Hrs open: 24 158 Harmon Dr., Comm. Ctr., Norwich Univ., 05663. Phone: (802) 485-2483. Fax: (802) 485-2565.E-mail: wnub@norwich.edu Web Site:www.norwich.edu Licensee: The Trustees of Norwich University. Population served: 7,500 Format: Rock/AOR, Triple A, Modern. Target aud: 15-40. ◆Doug Smith, gen mgr.

Norwich

*WNCH(FM)— 2004: 88.1 mhz; 100 w horiz, 1.6 kw vert. Ant 2,257 ft TL: N43 26 15 W72 27 08. Hrs open: 24 Vermont Public Radio, 365 Troy Ave., Colchester, 05446. Phone: (802) 655-9451. Fax: (802) 655-2799. Web Site:www.vpr.net Licensee: Vermont Public Radio. Natl. Network: NPR, . Vermont Public Radio Format: Cultural music svc. ◆Mark Vogelzang, pres & gen mgr.

Plainfield

*WGDR(FM)— May 11, 1973: 91.1 mhz; 800 w. -350 ft TL: N44 17 04 W72 26 28. Stereo. Hrs open: Box 336, Goddard College, 05667. Phone: (802) 454-7762. Phone: (802) 454-9962. Fax: (802) 454-1451.E-mail: wgdr@goddard.edu Web Site:www.wgdr.org Licensee: Goddard College Corp. Population served: 50,000 Format: Div. Target aud: Multiple. ◆Christine Farren, gen mgr, spec ev coord; Bert Klunder, opns mgr; Jen Isaacs, mus dir.

Poultney

WVNR(AM)— Aug 1, 1981: 1340 khz; 1 kw-U. TL: N43 30 16 W73 12 11. Hrs open: 5:30 AM-midnight Box 568, East Poultney, 05741. Secondary address: 1214 Rt. 30 S. 05764. Phone: (802) 287-9030.E-mail: wvnrwnyv@yahoo.com Licensee: Pine Tree Broadcasting Co. (acq 4-86). Format: Adult contemp, country, oldies. News staff: one; News: 3 hrs wkly. Target aud: 25-54; active, community oriented, working and professional, and families. Spec prog: Big band 3 hrs, loc sports 6 hrs, swap shop one hr, Polish one hr, gospel one hr wkly. ◆Michael J. Leech, pres; Judith E. Leech, exec VP, gen mgr.

Putney

*WCMK(FM)— 2003: 91.9 mhz; 150 w. Ant 758 ft TL: N42 58 28 W72 36 12. Hrs open: Box 8310, Essex, 05451-8310. Phone: (802) 878-8885. Fax: (802) 879-6835.E-mail: cmi.radio@verizon.net Web Site:thelightradio.net Licensee: Christian Ministries Inc. Format: Christian. ◆Ric McClary, gen mgr.

Randolph

WCVR-FM— Oct 25, 1982: 102.1 mhz; 11 kw. Ant 436 ft TL: N43 57 20 W72 36 10. Stereo. Hrs open: 24 62 Radio Dr., 05060. Phone: (802) 728-4411. Fax: (802) 728-4013. Web Site:www.champrocks.com Licensee: Vox AM/FM LLC. (acq 7-25-2008; grpsl). Population served: 315,000 Format: Classic rock. News: 6 hrs wkly. Target aud: 25-54; 50% men & 50 % women. ◆Tom Barney, gen mgr.

WTSJ(AM)— Nov 26, 1968: 1320 khz; 1 kw-D, 66 w-N. TL: N43 56 21 W72 38 13. Hrs open: 62 Radio Dr., 05060. Secondary address: 265 Hegeman Ave., Colchester 05446. Phone: (802) 728-4411. Fax: (802) 654-9381.E-mail: randolphradio@clearchannel.com Licensee: Vox AM/FM LLC. Group owner: Clear Channel Communications Inc. (acq 7-25-2008; grpsl). Population served: 25,000 Rini Coran PC. Format: News/talk. Target aud: 18-49. ◆Tom Barney, gen mgr.

Randolph Center

***WVTC(FM)**— Aug 29, 1983: 90.7 mhz; 300 w horiz. 203 ft TL: N43 56 07 W72 36 10. Stereo. Hrs open: 24 Vermont Technical College, Box 500, 05061. Phone: (802) 728-1550. Fax: (802) 728-1550. Web Site:www.wvtc.net Licensee: Vermont State Colleges Vermont Technical College. Population served: 2,115 Format: Punk, rap, rock, alternative. Target aud: General. ♦Marcus Jacobus-Petter, stn mgr.

Royalton

WRJT(FM)— 1996: 103.1 mhz; 1.35 kw. 682 ft TL: N43 46 28 W72 23 55. Hrs open:
Rebroadcasts WNCS(FM) Montpelier 90%.
c/o WNCS(FM), 169 River St., Montpelier, 05602. Phone: (802) 223-2396. Fax: (802) 223-1520. Web Site:www.pointfm.com Licensee: Lisbon Communications Inc. Group owner: Northeast Broadcasting Company Inc. (acq 11-30-01). Format: AAA. ♦Ed Flanagan, gen mgr; Tanya Stepasiuk, prom dir; Mark Miller, progmg dir; Jon Hosford, chief of engrg.

Rupert

WMNV(FM)— Apr 10, 1990: 104.1 mhz; 4.3 kw horiz. Ant 200 ft TL: N43 16 01 W73 15 21. Stereo. Hrs open: 24
Rebroadcasts WHAZ(AM) Troy, NY 100%.
30 Park Ave., Cohoes, NY, 12047-3330. Phone: (518) 237-1330. Fax: (518) 235-4468.E-mail: events@aliveradionetwork.com Web Site:www.whaz.com Licensee: Capital Media Corp. (group owner; acq 4-15-97). Population served: 500,000 Format: Adult Christian. Target aud: 25-75. Spec prog: Gospel, relg. ♦Paul F. Lotters, pres, gen mgr; Steven L. Klob, opns dir & dev dir; Rex P. Gregory, progmg dir, mus dir; Bill Rosenfeld, chief of engrg.

Rutland

WDVT(FM)— October 1988: 94.5 mhz; 6 kw. Ant 389 ft TL: N43 36 49 W73 01 33. Stereo. Hrs open: 24 Box 30, 05702. Phone: (802) 775-7500. Fax: (802) 775-7555.E-mail: catcountry@catamountradio.com Web Site:www.945thedrive.com Licensee: 6 Johnson Road Licenses Inc. Group owner: Pamal Broadcasting Ltd. (acq 10-19-2001; grpsl). Format: Classic hits. ♦Debbie Grembowicz, gen mgr; Terry Jaye, opns mgr; Brian Collamore, gen sls mgr; Carrie Allen, natl sls mgr; Dave Tibbs, prom dir; Ed Kelly, progmg dir.

***WFTF(FM)**— Jan 10, 1987: 90.5 mhz; 720 w. -560 ft TL: N43 37 09 W72 59 04. Hrs open: 24 2 Meadow Ln., 05701. Phone: (802) 775-0358. Phone: (802) 773-2863.E-mail: cbcoffice@cbcvt.org Web Site:www.cbcvt.org Licensee: Calvary Bible Church. Population served: 25,000 Natl. Network: Moody, . Format: Christian. ♦Ronald Systo, pres & gen mgr.

WJJR(FM)— Mar 25, 1971: 98.1 mhz; 1.15 kw. 2,591 ft TL: N43 36 17 W72 49 14. Stereo. Hrs open: 24 Box 30, 05702. Secondary address: 67 Merchants Row, Ruthland 05702. Phone: (802) 775-7500. Fax: (802) 775-7555.E-mail: wjjr@catamountradio.com Web Site:www.wjjr.net Licensee: 6 Johnson Road Licenses Inc. Group owner: Pamal Broadcasting Ltd. (acq 10-19-2001; grpsl). Population served: 847,178 Hogan & Hartson. Format: Adult contemp. News staff: one; News: one hr wkly. Target aud: 25-54; in-office managerial, professional. Spec prog: News, pub affrs one hr wkly. ♦Harry Weinhagen, gen mgr; Debbie Grembowiez, gen sls mgr; Ed Kelly, prom dir, news dir; Terry Jayl, progmg dir.

***WRVT(FM)**— Jan 10, 1989: 88.7 mhz; 2.77 kw. 1,328 ft TL: N43 39 32 W73 06 25. Hrs open:
Rebroadcasts WVPS(FM) Burlington 100%.
365 Troy Ave., Colchester, 05446. Phone: (802) 655-9451. Fax: (802) 655-2799. Fax: (802) 655-1801.E-mail: contact@vpr.net Web Site:www.vpr.net Licensee: Vermont Public Radio. Natl. Network: NPR, PRI, . Vermont Public Radio Format: Class, jazz, news. Target aud: General. Spec prog: Switchboard call-in 3 hrs, folk 4 hrs wkly. ♦Mark Vogelzang, pres, gen mgr; Victoria St. John, opns dir; Robin Turnau, dev VP, dev dir; Cheryl Willoughby, progmg dir; Walter Parker, mus dir; John VanHoesen, news dir; Rich Parker, chief of engrg.

WSYB(AM)— Dec 10, 1930: 1380 khz; 5 kw-D, 1 kw-N, DA-D. TL: N43 35 35 W72 59 25. Hrs open: Box 940, 05702-0940. Secondary address: 250 Dorr Dr. 05701. Phone: (802) 775-5597. Fax: (802) 775-6637. Licensee: 6 Johnson Road Licenses Inc. Group owner: Clear Channel Communications Inc. (acq 4-1-2007; grpsl). Population served: 70,000 Natl. Rep: McGavren Guild,. Format: News/talk. Target aud: 35-64. ♦Dave Ryeron, progmg dir; Glen Dudley, chief of engrg.

WZRT(FM)— 1974: 97.1 mhz; 1.15 kw. 2,591 ft TL: N43 36 17 W72 49 14. Stereo. Hrs open: 24 Dups AM 30% Box 940, 05702. Secondary address: 250 Dorr Dr. 05701. Phone: (802) 775-5597. Fax: (802) 775-6637. Population served: 58,000 Format: Adult contemp. News staff: 2; News: 5 hrs wkly. Target aud: 18-49.

Saint Albans

WLFE-FM— April 1970: 102.3 mhz; 20 w. Ant 364 ft TL: N44 45 53 W73 35 16. Stereo. Hrs open: 24 Box 712, 2 Main St., 05478. Phone: (802) 524-2133. Fax: (802) 527-1450.E-mail: michaele@champlainradio.com Web Site:www.purerock102.com Licensee: Radio Broadcasting Services Inc. Population served: 270000 Format: Active rock. News staff: one; News: 5 hrs wkly. Target aud: 18-49; men. ♦Bob Rowe, gen mgr; Carolyn Seifert, gen sls mgr; J.J. Prieve, progmg dir.

WRSA(AM)— 1930: 1420 khz; 1 kw-D, 110 w-N. TL: N44 50 12 W73 04 57. Hrs open: 24 Box 712, 2 Main St., 05478. Phone: (802) 524-2133. Fax: (802) 527-1450.E-mail: michaele@champlainradio.net Licensee: Champlain Communications Corp. Group owner: Northeast Broadcasting Company Inc. (acq 9-18-98; $500,000 with co-located FM). Population served: 60,000 Format: Talk radio. News staff: one; News: 20 hrs wkly. Target aud: General. ♦Mike Kmack, gen mgr, opns mgr & progmg dir.

Saint Johnsbury

***WCKJ(FM)**— Aug 1, 1998: 90.5 mhz; 1 kw. 738 ft TL: N44 24 40 W71 58 13. Stereo. Hrs open:
Rebroadcasts WGLY(FM) Bolton 100%.
Box 8310, Essex, 05451-8310. Secondary address: 140 Main St., Essec Junction 05452. Phone: (802) 878-8885. Fax: (802) 879-6835.E-mail: cmi.radio@verizon.net Web Site:thelightradio.net Licensee: Christian Ministries Inc. Natl. Network: Moody, . Joseph E. Dunne III. Format: Inspirational. ♦Ric McClary, gen mgr.

WKXH(FM)— Aug 1, 1985: 105.5 mhz; 400 w. Ant 712 ft TL: N44 24 38 W71 58 13. Stereo. Hrs open: 24 Box 249, 1303 Concord Ave., 05819. Phone: (802) 748-2345. Fax: (802) 748-2361.E-mail: kix105@kix1055.com Web Site:www.kix1055.com Licensee: Vermont Broadcast Associates Inc. Population served: 160,000 Natl. Network: ABC, Westwood One, . Format: Hot country. News staff: 2. Target aud: 24-55; families.

WSTJ(AM)— July 10, 1949: 1340 khz; 1 kw-U. TL: N44 25 06 W71 59 45. Hrs open: 24 Box 249, 1303 Concord Ave., 05819. Phone: (802) 748-1340. Fax: (802) 748-2361.E-mail: kix105@kix1055.com Licensee: Vermont Broadcast Associates Inc. (acq 4-3-98; $630,000 with co-located FM). Population served: 37,500 Natl. Network: ABC, Jones Radio Networks, . Bryan Cave. Format: Adult standards. News staff: one; News: 20 hrs wkly. Target aud: 35-75; adults and work places. ♦Bruce James, pres, gen mgr; Candis Leopold, opns mgr; Dave Labounty, progmg dir; Don Smith, chief of engrg.

***WVPA(FM)**— 1999: 88.5 mhz; 290 w vert. Ant 1,863 ft TL: N44 34 15 W71 53 38. Hrs open: Vermont Public Radio, 365 Troy Ave., Colchester, 05446. Phone: (802) 655-9451. Fax: (802) 655-2799.E-mail: mvogelzang@vpr.net Web Site:www.vpr.net Licensee: Vermont Public Radio. Natl. Network: NPR, . Vermont Public Radio Format: Class, jazz, news. ♦Mark Vogelzang, gen mgr; Victoria St. John, opns dir; Robin Turnau, dev VP; Cheryl Willoughby, progmg dir; Walter Parker, mus dir; John VanHoesen, news dir; Richard Parker, chief of engrg.

South Burlington

WXXX(FM)— Nov 16, 1984: 95.5 mhz; 25 kw. 236 ft TL: N44 30 35 W73 11 05. Stereo. Hrs open: 24 Box 620, 118 Malletts Bay Ave., Colchester, 05446. Phone: (802) 655-9550. Fax: (802) 655-1329.E-mail: paulg@95triplex.com Web Site:www.95triplex.com Licensee: Sison Broadcasting Inc. (acq 3-3-97; $2,939,014 with WVMT(AM) Burlington). Population served: 250,000 Natl. Rep: McGavren Guild,. Format: CHR. News staff: one; News: one hr wkly. Target aud: 18-49. ♦Paul Goldman, gen mgr; Mark Esbjerg, opns mgr; Ben Hamilton, progmg dir; Chantal Paulino, news dir.

Springfield

WCFR(AM)— May 26, 1954: 1480 khz; 5 kw-D. TL: N43 16 54 W72 29 21. Hrs open: 24 19 Main St., 05156. Phone: (802) 885-1480. Web Site:www.wcfram.com Licensee: KOOR Communications Inc. (group owner; (acq 12-19-2001; $75,000). Population served: 65,000 Format: Classic hits. News staff: one; News: 7 hrs wkly. Target aud: 45 plus; 35-54. ♦Bob Vinikoor, pres; Ray Lemire, gen mgr, opns dir & progmg dir.

WEEY(FM)— Jan 1, 1972: 93.5 mhz; 1.45 kw. Ant 472 ft TL: N43 18 55 W72 27 37. (CP: COL Swanzey, NH. 2 kw, ant 574 ft. TL: N42 54 57 W72 19 52). Stereo. Hrs open: 31 Hanover St., Suite 4, Lebanon, NH, 03766. Phone: (603) 448-1400. Fax: (603) 448-1755. Licensee: Great Eastern Radio LLC. Group owner: Clear Channel Communications Inc. (acq 10-30-2007; grpsl). Population served: 120,000 Format: Sports. Target aud: 25-54. ♦Tim Plante, gen mgr; Michael Barrett, opns dir, progmg dir; Chris Olsen, gen sls mgr.

Stowe

WCVT(FM)— Feb 28, 1977: 101.7 mhz; 130 w. 2,066 ft TL: N44 25 14 W72 49 42. Stereo. Hrs open: 24 Box 3536, Mountain Rd., 05672. Secondary address: 9 Stowe St., Waterbury 05676. Phone: (802) 244-1764. Fax: (802) 244-1771.E-mail: wcvt@classicvermont.com Web Site:www.wcvtradio.com Licensee: Radio Vermont Classics L.L.C. Group owner: Radio Vermont Group Inc. (acq 6-19-97; $450,000). Population served: 185,000 Natl. Rep: McGavren Guild,. Format: Classical. Target aud: 25-54; educated, upscale adults & families with active lifestyles. Spec prog: Children one hr wkly. ♦Eric Michaels, gen mgr; Thomas B. Beardsley, stn mgr; Frankie Allen, opns dir.

Sunderland

***WVTQ(FM)**— May 1, 1991: 95.1 mhz; 96 w. Ant 2,398 ft TL: N43 09 58 W73 07 02. Stereo. Hrs open: 24
Rebroadcasts WNCH(FM) Norwich 100%.
Vermont Public Radio, 365 Troy Ave., Colchester, 05446. Phone: (802) 655-9451. Fax: (802) 655-2799. Web Site:www.vpr.net Licensee: Vermont Public Radio Group owner: Pamal Broadcasting Ltd. (acq 11-15-2006; $625,000). Natl. Network: NPR, . Vermont Public Radio Format: Classical. Target aud: 18-49. ♦Mark Vogelzang, pres & gen mgr.

Swanton

***WNGF(FM)**—Not on air, target date: unknown: 89.9 mhz; 10 kw. Ant 118 ft TL: N44 53 10 W73 09 57. Hrs open: 65 King Rd., Buskirk, NY, 12028-0036. Phone: (518) 686-0975. Fax: (518) 686-0975.E-mail: wngn@wngn.org Web Site:www.wngn.org Licensee: Northeast Gospel Broadcasting Inc. ♦Brian A. Larson, pres & gen mgr.

Vergennes

WIZN(FM)—Licensed to Vergennes. See Burlington

Warren

WDEV-FM— Aug 11, 1989: 96.1 mhz; 3 kw. 4,000 ft TL: N44 07 37 W72 55 43. Stereo. Hrs open: 24
Rebroadcasts WDEV(AM) Waterbury 100%.
Box 550, Waterbury, 05676. Secondary address: 9 Stowe St., Waterbury 05676. Phone: (802) 244-7321. Fax: (802) 244-1771.E-mail: wdev@radiovermont.com Web Site:www.wdevradio.com Licensee: Radio Vermont Inc. Group owner: Radio Vermont Group Inc. (acq 10-15-92; $643,000 with WKDR(AM) Burlington; 11-23-92). Population served: 300,000 Natl. Network: ABC, . Wiley, Rein & Fielding. Format: News/talk, sports, music. News staff: one; News: 2 hrs wkly. Target aud: 25-54; affluent, upscale baby boomer generation. ♦Ken D. Squier, pres; Eric Michaels, gen mgr; Fred Hill, gen sls mgr; Jack Donovan, progmg dir; Rick Haskell, news dir; Tom Laffin, chief of engrg.

Waterbury

WDEV(AM)— July 16, 1931: 550 khz; 5 kw-D, 1 kw-N, DA-2. TL: N44 21 17 W72 45 07. Hrs open: Box 550, 9 Stowe St., 05676. Phone: (802) 244-7321. Fax: (802) 244-1771.E-mail: wdev@radiovermont.com Web Site:www.wdevradio.com Licensee: Radio Vermont Inc. Group owner: Radio Vermont Group Inc. (acq 1969). Population served: 250,000 Format: News, sports, div. Spec prog: Class one hr wkly. ♦Eric Michaels, gen mgr; Fred Hill, gen sls mgr; Jack Donovan, progmg dir; Rich Haskell, news dir; Tom Laffin, chief of engrg.

WWMP(FM)— Feb 14, 1985: 103.3 mhz; 3 kw. Ant 912 ft TL: N44 21 52 W72 55 53. Stereo. Hrs open: 24 372 Dorset St., South Burlington, 05403. Phone: (802) 863-1010. Fax: (802) 860-4721. Licensee: Radio Broadcasting Services Inc. Group owner: Northeast Broadcasting Company Inc. (acq 5-4-2000). Natl. Network: USA, . Joseph E. Dunne III. Format: Variety hits. News staff: one; News: 16 hrs wkly. Target aud: 25-54. Spec prog: Children 3 hrs wkly. ♦Rich Delancey, gen mgr & stn mgr; J.J. Prieve, progmg dir; Mike Raymond, chief of engrg.

Wells River

WTWN(AM)— Oct 3, 1976: 1100 khz; 5 kw-D. TL: N44 08 55 W72 04 02. Hrs open: Sunrise-sunset Box 675, 1047 Rt. 302, 05081. Phone: (802) 757-3311. Fax: (802) 757-2774.E-mail: wtwngch@kingcon.com Web Site:www.wtwnradio.com Licensee: Puffer Broadcasting Inc. (acq 10-3-73). Population served: 50,000 Natl. Network: Moody, . Natl. Rep: Roslin,. Shaw Pittman. Format: Relg. News: 9 hrs wkly. Target aud: 25 plus. Spec prog: Children, gospel. ◆Stephen J. Puffer, pres, gen mgr; Glenn Hatch, stn mgr, mktg dir; Teresa Puffer, opns mgr.

Westminster

WKKN(FM)— 1971: 101.9 mhz; 1.05 kw. Ant 774 ft TL: N43 02 00 W72 22 03.7. Stereo. Hrs open: 24 31 Hanover St., Suite 4, Lebanon, NH, 03766-1312. Phone: (603) 448-1400. Fax: (603) 448-1755. Licensee: Great Eastern Radio LLC. Group owner: Clear Channel Communications Inc. (acq 10-30-2007; grpsl). Natl. Network: Westwood One, . Format: Rock. News staff: one. Target aud: 25-54. ◆Tim Plante, gen mgr.

White River Junction

WNHV(AM)— Feb 28, 1963: 910 khz; 1 kw-D, 84 w-N. TL: N43 37 19 W72 21 04. Hrs open: 24 106 N. Main St., West Lebanon, NH, 03784. Phone: (603) 298-0332. Fax: (603)727-0134.E-mail: espnthescore@aol.com Licensee: Nassau Broadcasting III L.L.C. Group owner: Nassau Broadcasting Partners L.P. (acq 8-2-2004; grpsl). Population served: 8,000 Natl. Rep: Roslin,. Format: All sports. Target aud: 18-55. ◆Shirley Clark, gen mgr.

WTSL(AM)—See Hanover, NH

WXLF(FM)— Feb 1, 1969: 95.3 mhz; 3 kw. 225 ft TL: N43 39 14 W72 17 43. Stereo. Hrs open: 106 N. Main St., West Lebanon, NH, 03784. Phone: (603) 298-0332. Fax: (603) 727-0134. Web Site:www.953thewolf.com Licensee: Nassau Broadcasting III LLC Population served: 70,000 Natl. Network: Jones Radio Networks, Westwood One, . Format: Hot country. News: one hr wkly. Target aud: 35-54. ◆Mike Trombly, gen mgr.

WXXK(FM)—See Lebanon NH

Wilmington

WTHK(FM)— June 1, 1989: 100.7 mhz; 135 w. Ant 1,460 ft TL: N42 57 33 W72 55 22. Stereo. Hrs open: 24
Simulcast with WEXP(FM) Brandon 100%.
1 Scale Ave., Skuite 84, Rutland, 05761-4459. Secondary address: Box 850, West Dover 05356. Phone: (802) 464-1350. Fax: (802) 464-1112. Web Site:www.101thefox.com Licensee: Nassau Broadcasting III L.L.C. (group owner; acq 1-21-2005; $2.5 million with WEXP(FM) Brandon). Population served: 100,000 Natl. Rep: McGavren Guild,. Dan Alpert. Format: Classic rock. Target aud: 25-54; residents, tourists, upscale Mt. ◆John Gales, gen mgr, stn mgr; Kelly Kowalski, progmg dir.

Windsor

*****WVPR(FM)**— Aug 13, 1977: 89.5 mhz; 1.78 kw. 2,160 ft TL: N43 26 17 W72 27 08. Stereo. Hrs open:
Rebroadcasts WVPS(FM) Burlington 100%.
365 Troy Ave., Colchester, 05446. Phone: (802) 655-9451. Fax: (802) 655-2799. Fax: (802) 655-9117. Web Site:www.vpr.net Licensee: Vermont Public Radio. Population served: 90,000 Natl. Network: NPR, PRI, . Haley, Bader & Potts. Format: Jazz, class, news. Target aud: General. Spec prog: Switchboard call-in 3 hrs, folk 6 hrs wkly. ◆Mark Vogelzang, CEO, pres, gen mgr; Brian Donahue, CFO; Michael Crane, opns dir; Victoria St. John, opns mgr; Robin Turnau, dev dir; Cheryl Willoughby, progmg dir; Walter Parker, mus dir; Richard Parker, chief of engrg.

Woodstock

*****WGLV(FM)**— 2003: 91.7 mhz; 100 w. Ant 2,276 ft TL: N43 38 22 W72 50 12. Hrs open:
Rebroadcasts WGLY-FM Bolton 100%.
Box 8310, Essex, 05451-8310. Secondary address: 140 Main St., Essex Junction 05452. Phone: (802) 878-8885. Fax: (802) 879-6835.E-mail: cmi.radio@verizon.net Web Site:thelightradio.net Licensee: Christian Ministries Inc. Natl. Network: Salem Radio Network, Moody, . Format: Inspirational. ◆Ric McClary, gen mgr.

WMXR(FM)— Apr 18, 1989: 93.9 mhz; 670 w. Ant 682 ft TL: N43 36 17 W72 28 03. Stereo. Hrs open: 24 31 Hanover St., Suite 4, Lebanon, NH, 03766. Phone: (603) 448-1400. Fax: (603) 448-1755. Licensee: Great Eastern Radio LLC. Group owner: Clear Channel Communications Inc. (acq 10-30-2007; grpsl). Population served: 65,000 Format: News/talk, sports. ◆Tim Plante, gen mgr; Chris Olsen, gen sls mgr; Steven Smith, progmg dir.

Virginia

Abingdon

WABN(AM)— Dec 10, 1956: 1230 khz; 1 kw-U. TL: N36 43 07 W81 56 55. Hrs open: 6 AM-midnight Box 7, 24212. Phone: (276) 623-0030. Fax: (423) 878-6520.E-mail: wabn@aecc.org Web Site:www.wabn1230.com Licensee: Information Communication Corp. (acq 1-1-2006; $250,000 with WHGG(AM) Kingsport, TN). Population served: 220,000 Format: Oldies. ◆Kenneth C. Hill, pres; Kenneth Hill, gen mgr; Rusty Cury, stn mgr, gen sls mgr & progmg dir; Glen Zeigler, chief of engrg.

WFHG-FM— Dec 10, 1966: 92.7 mhz; 1.8 kw. 371 ft TL: N36 43 07 W81 56 55. Stereo. Hrs open: 24 Box 1389, Bristol, 24203. Secondary address: Bristol Broadcasting Co Inc, 901 E Valley Dr, Bristol 24201. Phone: (276) 669-8112. Fax: (276) 669-0541.E-mail: bhagy@wxbg.com Web Site:www.supertalkwfhg.com Licensee: Bristol Broadcasting Co. Inc. (group owner; acq 11-30-99; with co-located AM). Population served: 225,000 Format: News talk. News: 2 hrs wkly. Target aud: 12 plus; progsv, contemp & urban. ◆Bill Hagy, gen mgr & mus dir.

Accomac

WVES(FM)— Aug 13, 1990: 99.3 mhz; 22 kw. 344 ft TL: N37 47 05 W75 36 16. Stereo. Hrs open: 24 27214 Muttonhunk Rd., Parksley, 23421. Phone: (757) 665-6500. Fax: (757) 665-7178.E-mail: hotcountry@tassnet.net Web Site:www.wves.bravehost.com Licensee: Chincoteague Broadcasting Corp. (acq 5-18-98; $350,000). Natl. Network: USA, Westwood One, . Format: Hot country. News: 3 hrs wkly. Target aud: 25 plus. ◆Stephen Marks, pres; Mark Dodds, gen mgr, stn mgr, opns mgr, gen sls mgr, prom mgr, prom mgr, mus dir; Dave Bralley, news dir; Kelli Spragg, pub affrs dir; Tom Reynolds, chief of engrg.

Alberta

WWDW(FM)— 2001: 103.1 mhz; 2.2 kw. Ant 535 ft TL: N36 52 02 W77 53 31. Hrs open:
Rebroadcasts WSMY(AM) Weldon, NC 100%.
Box 910, Roanoke Rapids, NC, 27870. Phone: (252) 536-0209. Fax: (252) 538-0378.E-mail: info@wsmy1400.com Web Site:www.wsmy1400.com Licensee: First Media Radio LLC. (group owner; acq 12-3-2003; grpsl). Format: Gospel. ◆Alan Garrick, gen mgr.

Alexandria

WXTR(AM)—Licensed to Alexandria. See Washington DC

Altavista

WKDE(AM)— Apr 29, 1962: 1000 khz; 1 kw-D. TL: N37 07 20 W79 17 20. Hrs open: Sunrise-sunset Box 390, 200 Frazier Rd., 24517. Phone: (434) 369-5588. Fax: (434) 369-1632. Licensee: DJ Broadcasting Corp. (acq 1-13-92; $300,000 with co-located FM; 2-10-92). Population served: 250,000 Natl. Network: CNN Radio, . Rgnl. Network: Va. News Net. Format: News. News: one hr wkly. Target aud: General. Spec prog: Southern gospel 5 hrs wkly. ◆David Hoehne, pres, gen mgr; Elizabeth Clancy, chief of engrg & traf mgr.

WKDE-FM— June 30, 1969: 105.5 mhz; 6 kw. 328 ft TL: N37 09 37 W79 13 28. Stereo. Hrs open: 24 Box 390, 24517. Phone: (434) 369-1055. Fax: (434) 369-1632.E-mail: info@kdcountry.com Web Site:www.kdcountry.com Licensee: DJ Broadcasting Corp. Population served: 322,000 Natl. Network: AP Radio, . Format: C&W. News staff: one. Target aud: 25-54. Spec prog: Black gospel 5 hrs, bluegrass 10 hrs wkly. ◆David Hoehne, gen mgr; Lee Cameron, progmg dir & news dir; John Hart, chief of engrg; Elizabeth Haney, traf mgr.

Amherst

WAMV(AM)— Oct 1, 1976: 1420 khz; 2.2 kw-D, 17 w-N. TL: N37 34 29 W79 01 14. Hrs open: Box 1420, 24521. Secondary address: 132 School Rd. 24521. Phone: (434) 946-9000. Fax: (434) 946-2201.E-mail: wamvradio@aol.com Web Site:www.wamvradio.com Licensee: Community First Broadcasters Inc. (acq 4-1-88; $40,000). Population served: 120,000 Natl. Network: USA, . Format: Gospel. Target aud: 50+. ◆Robert Langstaff, pres, gen mgr, progmg dir, traf mgr, disc jockey; Mary Lu Gregg, disc jockey; Faron Tyree, sls.

WYYD(FM)— Jan 27, 1981: 107.9 mhz; 20.5 kw. 1,768 ft TL: N37 28 13 W79 22 30. Stereo. Hrs open: 24 3305 Old Forest Rd., Lynchburg, 24501. Phone: (434) 385-8298. Fax: (434) 385-8991.E-mail: joeldearing @clearchannel.com Web Site:www.wyyd.cc Licensee: Capstar TX L.P. Group owner: Clear Channel Communications Inc. (acq 8-30-00; grpsl). Population served: 337,500 Natl. Network: ABC, . Natl. Rep: McGavren Guild,. Format: Country. News staff: one. Target aud: 25-54; those with moderate high expendable income. ◆Dave Carwile, gen mgr; Barry Holston, gen sls mgr; Frank Smith, natl sls mgr; Barry Michaels, prom dir; Joel Dearing, progmg dir; Ed Kilbane, pub affrs dir; Jeff Parker, chief of engrg.

Appalachia

WAXM(FM)—See Big Stone Gap

Appomattox

WJJX(FM)— May 17, 1989: 102.7 mhz; 22 kw. Ant 745 ft TL: N37 28 07 W79 00 27. Stereo. Hrs open: 3305 Old Forest Rd., Lynchburg, 24501. Phone: (434) 385-8298. Fax: (434) 385-8991.E-mail: stevencross @clearchannel.com Web Site:www.wjjs.com Licensee: Capstar TX L.P. Group owner: Clear Channel Communications Inc. (acq 8-30-2000; grpsl). Format: CHR. Target aud: 35-54. ◆Chris Clendenen, gen mgr; Dave Carwile, gen sls mgr, adv mgr; Tom Sweat, natl sls mgr; Bobbi Crowder, prom dir; Ron Gaylor, adv VP; Sarah Macomber, adv dir; Bill Cahill, progmg VP; Steve Cross, progmg dir; Jeff Parker, chief of engrg.

WOWZ(AM)— June 1, 1974: 1280 khz; 1 kw-D. TL: N37 22 19 W78 50 06. (CP: COL Roanoke. 1290 khz; 10 kw-D, 17 w-N. TL: N37 16 06 W79 54 46). Hrs open: 6 AM-8 PM 1848 Clay St SE, Roanoke, 24013. Phone: (540) 343-7109. Fax: (540) 343-2306. Licensee: Perception Media Inc. (acq 1-28-2004; $150,000). Population served: 12,000 Rgnl. Network: Va. News Net. Format: News. ◆Ben Peyton, pres.

WTTX-FM— September 1976: 107.1 mhz; 1.7 kw. Ant 426 ft TL: N37 22 19 W78 50 06. Hrs open: Box 637, 24522. Phone: (434) 352-7607. Fax: (434) 352-2451.E-mail: mike@joyfm.org Web Site:www.joyfm.org Licensee: Positive Alternative Radio Inc. (acq 1-11-2006; $1.8 million). Population served: 600,000 Format: Southern gospel. ◆Edward A. Baker, pres; Brian Sanders, gen mgr.

Arlington

WAVA(AM)— Nov 7, 1946: 780 khz; 5 kw-D. TL: N38 53 44 W77 08 04. Hrs open: 7:30 AM-6PM 1901 N. Moore St., Suite 200, 22209. Phone: (703) 807-2266. Fax: (703) 807-2248.E-mail: comments@wava.com Web Site:www.wava.com Licensee: Salem Media of Virginia Inc. Group owner: Salem Communications Corp. (acq 1-10-2000). Population served: 6,000,000 Natl. Network: Salem Radio Network, . Natl. Rep: Salem,. Fletcher Heald & Hildreth. Format: Contemp Christian. News: 4 hrs wkly. Target aud: 25-54. ◆David Ruleman, gen mgr; Tom Moyer, stn mgr.

WAVA-FM—Licensed to Arlington. See Washington DC

WZHF(AM)— Apr 7, 1947: 1390 khz; 5 kw-U, DA-2. TL: N38 54 15 W77 09 54. Stereo. Hrs open: 13321 New Hampshire Ave, Silver Spring, MD, 20904. Phone: (301) 424-9292. Fax: (301) 424-8266. Licensee: Way Broadcasting Licensee LLC. Group owner: Multicultural Radio Broadcasting Inc. (acq 5-30-00; grpsl). Population served: 489,000 Format: Sp. ◆Bill Parris, gen mgr, progmg dir; Raoul Lopez Bastidas, sls dir; David Song, chief of engrg.

Ashland

WHAN(AM)— May 1, 1962: 1430 khz; 1 kw-D, 31 w-N. TL: N37 44 46 W77 29 44. (CP: COL Victoria. 650 khz; 50 kw-D, DA. TL: N37 22 27 W78 00 45). Hrs open: Sunrise-sunset Box 148, 23005. Secondary address: 11337 Ashcake Rd 23005. Phone: (804) 798-1010. Fax: (804) 798-7933.E-mail: Bill@WHAN1430.COM Web

Site:www.whan1430.com Licensee: Fifth Estate Communications LLC (acq 2-23-98). Population served: 2,934 Natl. Network: USA, Moody, . Format: Talk, Bluegrass. News: 7 hrs wkly. Target aud: 18-35; general. ♦William Roberts, pres, stn mgr, gen sls mgr & prom dir; Skip Andrews, progmg dir; Jim Grainger, chief of engrg; Arnold Meyer, traf mgr.

WYFJ(FM)— Dec 7, 1967: 100.1 mhz; 6 kw. Ant 321 ft TL: N37 44 46 W77 29 44. Stereo. Hrs open: 24 Box 7300, Charlotte, NC, 28241. Phone: (704) 523-5555. Web Site:www.bbnradio.org Licensee: Bible Broadcasting Network Inc. (group owner; acq 2-1-80). Natl. Network: Bible Bcstg Net, . Format: Relg, Christian. News: 9 hrs wkly. ♦Lowell Davey, pres; Randy Adams, gen mgr & stn mgr.

Bassett

WCBX(AM)— Oct 1, 1960: 900 khz; 1.1 kw-D, 180 w-N. TL: N36 42 36 W79 57 58. Hrs open: 24 Box 192, Martinsville, 24114. Secondary address: 1675 Grandview Dr., Martinsville 24112. Phone: (276) 638-5235. Fax: (276) 638-6089.E-mail: wcbxwodyfic@yahoo.com Web Site:thesportsaddictnetwork.com Licensee: Base Communications Inc. (acq 4-17-98). Population served: 750,000 Natl. Network: Fox Sports, . Format: Sports. News staff: one; News: 12 hrs wkly. Target aud: 35-55. ♦Edward A. Baker, pres, exec VP, gen mgr; Aaron Marks, stn mgr; Steven Kuszlyk, opns mgr & progmg dir.

Bayside

WBVA(AM)—Licensed to Bayside. See Virginia Beach

Bedford

WBLT(AM)— Feb 9, 1950: 1350 khz; 5 kw-D, 47 w-N. TL: N37 20 51 W79 31 25. Hrs open: Box 348, Forest, 24551. Phone: (434) 534-6100. Fax: (434) 534-6101.E-mail: wblt@inbox.com Web Site:www.espninva.com Licensee: 3 Daughters Media Inc. (acq 11-1-2005; $240,000). Natl. Network: ESPN Radio, . Format: Sports. ♦Gary E. Burns, pres; Devin Taylor, opns mgr.

WLEQ(FM)— Oct 20, 1992: 106.9 mhz; 290 w. Ant 1,276 ft TL: N37 19 14 W79 37 59. Stereo. Hrs open: 24 Box 11798, Lynchburg, 24506. Secondary address: 19-C Wadsworth St., Lynchburg 24501. Phone: (434) 845-3698. Phone: (866) 431-5253. Fax: (434) 845-2063. Web Site:www.rocktheplanet.fm Licensee: Centennial Broadcasting LLC. Group owner: Cumulus Media Inc. (acq 8-11-2005; $1.9 million). Natl. Network: ABC, Jones Radio Networks, . Natl. Rep: McGavren Guild,. Womble, Carlyle, Sandridge & Rice. Wire Svc: AP Format: Rock. News staff: 3; News: 14 hrs wkly. ♦Bob Abbott, opns mgr; Ron Gaylor, gen mgr & gen sls mgr; Kara Butterworth, traf mgr.

Berryville

WWRE(FM)— May 19, 1980: 105.5 mhz; 3 kw. Ant 300 ft TL: N39 07 03 W77 58 22. Stereo. Hrs open:
Simulcast with WWRT(FM) Strasburg 100%.
Box 3300, Winchester, 22604. Secondary address: 520 N. Pleasant Valley Rd., Winchester 22601. Phone: (540) 667-2224. Fax: (540) 722-3295. Web Site:www.everythingthatrocks.fm Licensee: Mid Atlantic Network Inc. Group owner: Mid Atlantic Network (acq 5-28-97; $850,000 with WWRT(FM) Strasburg). Population served: 280,000 Cole, Raywid & Braverman. Format: Rock. Target aud: 18 plus. ♦Allen Shaw, pres; Kathy Flerx, gen mgr, gen sls mgr; Jeff Adams, opns mgr; Ron Baker, progmg dir; Robert Allen, news dir; Archie McKay, chief of engrg.

Big Stone Gap

WAXM(FM)— Apr 8, 1975: 93.5 mhz; 2.45 kw. 1,883 ft TL: N36 54 50 W82 53 40. Stereo. Hrs open: 24 Prog sep from AM 724 Park Ave., Norton, 24273. Phone: (276) 679-1901. Fax: (276) 679-1198. Licensee: Valley Broadcasting Inc. Population served: 318,000 Natl. Network: CBS, . Format: Country. ♦Kim Swecker, prom dir; Tammy Robinson, traf mgr; David Stanley, disc jockey.

WLSD(AM)— Aug 20, 1953: 1220 khz; 1 kw-D, 45 w-N. TL: N36 50 26 W82 44 14. Stereo. Hrs open: Drawer W, 1600 Intermont Heights, 24219. Phone: (276) 523-1700. Phone: (276) 679-1901. Fax: (276) 679-1198.E-mail: 93.5@waxm.com Licensee: Valley Broadcasting and Communications Inc. (acq 5-1-80; $359,000; 5-12-80). Population served: 90,000 Natl. Network: CBS, . Jerry Miller. Format: Relg. Target aud: 19-60. ♦Greg Kress, pres; William Stanley, gen mgr, sls VP, gen sls mgr & rgnl sls mgr; Paul Miller, adv dir; Rick Phillips, progmg dir; Jack Starnes, chief of engrg.

Blacksburg

WBRW(FM)— December 1964: 105.3 mhz; 3.8 kw. 472 ft TL: N37 11 12 W80 28 54. (CP: 12 kw). Stereo. Hrs open: 24 7080 Lee Hwy., Rayford, 24141. Phone: (540) 633-5330. Fax: (540) 633-2998. Licensee: Cumulus Licensing LLC. Group owner: Cumulus Media Inc. (acq 3-31-2004; grpsl). Population served: 110,000 Format: Active Rock. News: 10 hrs wkly. Target aud: 18-49. ♦Scott Claytons, opns dir, gen sls mgr; Scott Stevens, opns mgr & sls dir; Courtney Quinn, progmg dir; Marty Gordon, news dir; Dave Dalesky, chief of engrg.

WFNR(AM)— 1973: 710 khz; 10 kw-D, DA. TL: N37 08 01 W80 21 17. Hrs open: 7080 Lee Hwy., Radford, 24141. Phone: (540) 633-5330. Fax: (540) 633-2998. Licensee: Cumulus Licensing LLC. Group owner: Cumulus Media Inc. (acq 3-31-2004; grpsl). Population served: 561,000 Rgnl. Network: Va. News Net. Va. News Net. Format: News/talk. Target aud: 25 plus; general. ♦Sarah Leftwich, gen mgr; Scott Stevens, opns mgr.

WKEX(AM)— July 10, 1969: 1430 khz; 1 kw-D, 62 w-N. TL: N37 13 57 W80 26 40. (CP: 5 kw-U, DA-2). Hrs open: 24 Box 889, 24063. Secondary address: 145 Jackson St 24060. Phone: (540) 951-9791. Fax: (540) 961-2021.E-mail: wkexam@yahoo.com Web Site:www.thesportsaddictnetwork.com Licensee: Base Communications Inc. Group owner: Baker Family Stations (acq 6-30-98; $60,000). Population served: 100,000 Natl. Network: ESPN Radio, . Format: Sports talk. Target aud: 35 plus; mature adults, all income levels. Spec prog: High School Sports, Redskins, MLB. ♦Amy Burnette, gen mgr; Alison Baker, traf mgr.

***WUVT-FM**— Oct 23, 1969: 90.7 mhz; 3 kw. 156 ft TL: N37 13 28 W80 24 30. Stereo. Hrs open: 24 350 Squires Student Ctr., 24061-0546. Phone: (540) 231-9880. Fax: (208) 692-5239.E-mail: wuvtamfm@vt.edu Web Site:www.wuvt.vt.edu Licensee: Educational Media Corporation at Virginia Tech. Population served: 29,400 Format: Div. Target aud: general; college students. Spec prog: American Indian 2 hrs, Greek 2 hrs, Chinese 2 hrs, Turkish 2 hrs, African 2 hrs, Latin 2 hrs wkly. ♦Jake Faber, gen mgr & opns mgr.

WWVT(AM)—See Christiansburg

Blackstone

WBBC-FM— Nov 17, 1975: 93.5 mhz; 17.5 kw. 394 ft TL: N37 03 14 W78 01 15. (CP: 17.5 kw). Stereo. Hrs open: 24 Box 300, 950 Kenbridge Rd., 23824. Phone: (434) 292-4146. Phone: (434) 292-7669.E-mail: wbbc@bobcatcountryradio.com Population served: 1000000 Natl. Network: Westwood One, . Format: Hot country. Target aud: 25-54; middle class, with two cars, homeowners.

WKLV(AM)— 1947: 1440 khz; 5 kw-D. TL: N37 03 14 W78 01 15. Stereo. Hrs open: Sunrise-sunset Box 300, 950 Kenbridge Rd., 23824. Phone: (434) 292-4146. Fax: (434) 292-7669.E-mail: wbbc@bobcatcountryradio.com Web Site:www.bobcatcountryradio.com Licensee: Denbar Communications Inc. (acq 7-26-91). Population served: 100,000 Natl. Network: ESPN Radio, . Format: Sports. Target aud: 25-54. ♦Dennis Royer, pres, progmg dir, chief of engrg; Dennis Royer Jr., gen sls mgr.

Bluefield

WBDY(AM)— Nov 17, 1980: Stn currently dark. 1190 khz; 10 kw-D, DA. TL: N37 16 19 W81 19 05. Hrs open: 900 Bluefield Ave., WV, 24701. Phone: (304) 327-7114. Fax: (304) 325-7850. Licensee: Monterey Licenses LLC. Group owner: Triad Broadcasting Co. LLC (acq 7-18-2000; grpsl). ♦Wm. Keith Bowman, gen mgr.

WHKX(FM)— December 1970: 106.3 mhz; 3 kw. 1,122 ft TL: N37 15 30 W81 10 36. Stereo. Hrs open: 24 Dups AM 98% 900 Bluefield Ave., 24701. Phone: (304) 327-7114. Fax: (304) 325-7850. Population served: 5,286 Natl. Network: Westwood One, . Format: Contemp country. News: 17 hrs wkly. ♦Dave Crosier, progmg dir.

Bon Air

WLES(AM)— September 1959: 580 khz; 201 w-D, 27 w-N. TL: N37 30 52 W77 30 28. (CP: 590 khz; 600 w-D, 58 w-N). Hrs open: 24
Rebroadcasts WTRU(AM) Kernersville, NC 95%.
2202 Jolliff Rd., Chesapeake, 23321. Secondary address: 1001 E Main St, Level M, richmond 23219. Phone: (804) 855-1524. Fax: (804) 855-1523.E-mail: info@1010wpmh.com Web Site:www.wtru.com Licensee: Chesapeake-Portsmouth Broadcasting Corp. (acq 7-19-2000). Population served: 18,000 Rgnl. Network: Va. News Net. Va. News Net. Format: Christian teaching. ♦Nancy Epperson, pres; Henry Hoot, VP, gen mgr.

Bowling Green

WWUZ(FM)— 1998: 96.9 mhz; 2.8 kw. 472 ft TL: N37 57 56 W77 22 19. Hrs open: 24 616 Armelia St., Fredericksburg, 22401. Phone: (540) 374-5500. Fax: (540) 374-5525.E-mail: info@classicrock969.com Web Site:www.classicrock969.com Licensee: The Free Lance-Star Publishing Co. of Fredericksburg, Virginia. Group owner: The Free Lance-Star Publishing Co. (acq 8-23-01; $2.15 million). Population served: 280,300 Natl. Network: AP Radio, . Rgnl rep: RMR Wire Svc: AP Format: Classic rock. News staff: one; News: 2.5 hours wkly. Target aud: 35 plus; male. ♦Josiah Rowe III, pres; John Moen, gen mgr; Jim Butler, sls dir; JoAnn Pope, prom dir; Paul Johnson, gen mgr & progmg dir; Frank Hammon, news dir, pub affrs dir; Chris Wilk, chief of engrg.

Bridgewater

WTGD(FM)— Mar 3, 1989: 105.1 mhz; 6 kw. Ant 328 ft TL: N38 27 08 W78 54 32. Stereo. Hrs open: 24 Box 752, Harrisonburg, 22803. Secondary address: 1820 Heritage Center Way, Harrisonburg 22801. Phone: (540) 434-0331. Web Site:www.1051online.com Licensee: M. Belmont VerStandig Inc. Group owner: VerStandig Broadcasting (acq 1993; $10,000 with WHBG(AM) Harrisonburg; 9-13-93). Natl. Network: La Gran D, . Format: Rgnl Mexican. News staff: 2. Target aud: 24-54. ♦Susanne Myers, gen mgr; Bill Phipps, progmg dir.

Bristol

WFHG(AM)— January 1947: 980 khz; 5 kw-D, 1 kw-N, DA-N. TL: N36 36 30 W82 09 36. Hrs open: 24 Box 1389, 24203. Secondary address: 901 E. Valley Dr. 24201. Phone: (276) 669-8112. Fax: (276) 669-0541.E-mail: bhagy@wxbq.com Web Site:www.supertalkwfhg.com Licensee: Bristol Broadcasting Inc. Group owner: Nininger Stations (acq 1972). Natl. Network: Fox Sports, . Natl. Rep: McGavren Guild,. Shaw Pittman. Format: Sports. ♦Lisa Hale, pres; Bill Hagy, gen mgr; Winnie Quaintance, gen sls mgr; Roger Bouldin, prom dir; Rick Perry, chief of engrg; Anna Honaker, traf mgr; George Grant, sports cmtr.

WIGN(AM)—See Bristol, TN

WQUT(FM)—See Johnson City, TN

WXBQ-FM—See Bristol, TN

WZAP(AM)— 1946: 690 khz; 10 kw-D, 14 w-N. TL: N36 37 51 W82 09 53. Hrs open: 6 AM-midnight Box 369, 24203. Secondary address: 11373 Wallace Pike 24202. Phone: (276) 669-6950. Phone: (276) 669-6900. Fax: (276) 669-0794.E-mail: wzapradio@aol.com Web Site:www.wzapradio.com Licensee: RAM Communications Inc. (acq 1-10-77; $375,000). Population served: 502,000 Natl. Network: USA, . Irwin, Campbell, & Tannenwald, P.C. Format: Relg. News: 8 hrs wkly. Target aud: General. ♦R.A. Morris, pres & gen mgr; Glen Harlow, mus dir, disc jockey; Al Morris, news dir; Joyce Boyd, pub affrs dir; Chuck Lawson, chief of engrg, disc jockey; Dave Ray, disc jockey.

Broadway

WJDV(FM)—Licensed to Broadway. See Broadway-Timberville

Broadway-Timberville

WBTX(AM)— May 18, 1972: 1470 khz; 5 kw-D, DA. TL: N38 37 24 W78 48 52. Hrs open: 6 AM-sunset P.O. Box 337, Broadway, 22815. Phone: (540) 896-8933. Fax: (540) 896-1448.E-mail: info@positive-radio.com Web Site:www.positive-radio.com Licensee: Massanutten Broadcasting Co. Inc. Population served: 150,000 Natl. Network: USA, . Natl. Rep: Salem,. Format: Southern gospel. News: 8 hrs wkly. Target aud: 35 plus. Spec prog: Farm one hr wkly. ♦David Eshleman, pres, gen mgr, disc jockey; Christine Pompeo, gen sls mgr; Jim Snavely, progmg dir, news dir; Bill Fawcett, chief of engrg; Judy Shafer, traf mgr.

WJDV(FM)—(Broadway, Dec 18, 1989: 96.1 mhz; 2.6 kw. Ant 1,010 ft TL: N38 33 50 W78 57 00. Stereo. Hrs open: 24 Box 752, Harrisonburg, 22803. Phone: (540) 434-0331. Fax: (540) 434-7084.E-mail: info@wjdv.com Web Site:www.valleyradio.com Licensee: HJV L.P. Group owner: VerStandig Broadcasting (acq 3-12-2001; swap with WLTK(FM) New Market). Population served: 150,000 Format: Lite rock. Target aud: 25-44. ♦Susanne Meyers, gen mgr; Bill Phipps, progmg dir.

WLTK(FM)—(New Market, 1997: 103.3 mhz; 2.1 kw. 544 ft TL: N38 36 31 W78 54 07. Stereo. Hrs open: 24 P.O. Box 337, Broadway, 22815. Phone: (540) 896-9585. Fax: (540) 896-1448.E-mail: info@positive-radio.com Web Site:www.positive-radio.com (Acq 8-8-2001; exchange for WJDV(FM)

Broadway plus $1.25 million). Population served: 150,000 Natl. Network: USA, . Natl. Rep: Salem,. Format: Contemp Christian. News: 9 hrs wkly. Target aud: 25-44. ♦David Eshelman, pres; David Eshleman, gen mgr; Christine Pompto, gen sls mgr; Greg Crabtree, progmg dir; Judy Shafer, traf mgr; Dave Wyant, disc jockey.

Brookneal

WODI(AM)— Feb. 1, 1997: 1230 khz; 1 kw-U. TL: N37 02 17 W78 56 30. Hrs open: 24 1230 Radio Rd., 24528-3141. Phone: (434) 376-1230. Fax: (434) 376-9634.E-mail: wodi@lynchburg.net Web Site:www.wodiradio.com Licensee: D & M Communications Inc. (acq 9-5-96; $47,000). Population served: 80,000 Natl. Network: USA, . Ferrot Imley & Booth. Format: Oldies. News staff: one; News: 6 hrs wkly. Target aud: 25-54; general. ♦David L. Marthouse, pres, gen mgr, progmg dir; Anthony R. DeNicola, VP, opns mgr, asst music dir; Anthony W. DeNicola, gen sls mgr, mktg mgr; Dianne D. DeNicola, prom mgr; Brian R. DeNicola, mus dir, mus critic; Bob O'Brien, pub affrs dir; John Gers, engrg dir; Dave Marthouse, disc jockey.

Buena Vista

WWZW(FM)— 1981: 96.7 mhz; 2 kw. Ant 1,135 ft TL: N37 43 37 W79 18 24. Stereo. Hrs open: Box 902, Lexington, 24450. Secondary address: 392 E Midland Trail, Lexington 24450. Phone: (540) 463-2161. Fax: (540) 463-9524. Web Site:www.firstmediava.com Licensee: First Media Radio LLC. (group owner; (acq 6-21-2004; $1.33 million with WREL(AM) Lexington). Population served: 60,000 Natl. Network: NBC Radio, . Format: Adult contemp. Target aud: 25-54. ♦Alex Kolobielski, pres; Debra Reed, sls dir; Steve Williams, sls dir & progmg dir.

Buffalo Gap

WBOP(FM)—Licensed to Buffalo Gap. See Staunton

Cape Charles

***WAZP(FM)**— 2000: 90.7 mhz; 13 kw. Ant 512 ft TL: N37 10 53 W75 57 47. Hrs open: 24 2351 Sunset Blvd., Suite 170-218, Rocklin, CA, 95765. Phone: (916) 251-1600. Fax: (916) 251-1650.E-mail: klove@klove.com Web Site:www.klove.com Licensee: Delmarva Educational Association. Natl. Network: K-Love, . Shaw Pittman. Format: Contemp Christian. News staff: 3. Target aud: 25-44; Judeo Christian, female. ♦Richard Jenkins, pres; Mike Novak, VP; Keith Whipple, dev dir; David Pierce, progmg mgr; Ed Lenane, news dir; Sam Wallington, engrg dir; Karen Johnson, news rptr.

Cedar Bluff

WHQX(FM)— 1989: 107.7 mhz; 550 w. 751 ft TL: N37 09 49 W81 46 06. Hrs open: 24 900 Bluefield Ave., Bluefield, WV, 24701. Phone: (304) 327-7114. Fax: (304) 325-7850. Web Site:www.kickscountry.com Licensee: Monterey Licenses LLC. Group owner: Triad Broadcasting Co. LLC (acq 7-18-00; grpsl). Format: Country. News staff: one. ♦John Halford, gen mgr, gen sls mgr; Dave Crouiser, progmg dir; Keith Bowman, chief of engrg.

WYRV(AM)— March 1985: 770 khz; 5 kw-D. TL: N37 05 05 W81 46 07. Hrs open: Sunrise-sunset Box 70, 24609. Secondary address: 504 Middlecreek Rd. 24609. Phone: (276) 964-9619. Phone: (276) 964-5167. Fax: (276) 964-9610.E-mail: brad@amen770.com Web Site:www.amen770.com Licensee: Faith Christian Music Broadcasting Ministries Inc. (acq 4-12-01). Population served: 285,000 Format: Positive Radio (contemp Christian/mainstream). News staff: one; News: 3 hrs wkly. Target aud: 30 plus. ♦Brad Ratliff, gen mgr, adv mgr, progmg dir; Greg Webb, mus dir; Acie T. Rasnake, chief of engrg.

Charles City

***WAUQ(FM)**— 2000: 89.7 mhz; 10 kw. Ant 351 ft TL: N37 25 58 W77 11 38. Hrs open: Box 3206, Tupelo, MS, 38803. Phone: (662) 844-8888. Fax: (662 842-6791. Web Site:www.afr.net Licensee: American Family Association. Group owner: American Family Radio Format: Christian, inspirational. ♦Marvin Sanders, gen mgr.

Charlottesville

WCHV(AM)— 1930: 1260 khz; 5 kw-D, 2.5 kw-N, DA-2. TL: N38 06 52 W78 27 18. Hrs open: 24 1150 Pepsi Pl., Suite 300, 22901. Phone: (434) 978-4408. Fax: (434) 978-0723. Web Site:www.wchv.com Licensee: Monticello Media LLC. (group owner; (acq 10-4-2007; grpsl). Population served: 136,000 Natl. Network: Fox News Radio, Wall Street, . Natl. Rep: Christal,. Format: News/talk. News staff: 4; News: 20 hrs wkly. Target aud: Adults 35+. ♦Dennis Mockler, gen mgr; Vinnie Kice, opns mgr; Karen Cote, gen sls mgr; Joe Thomas, progmg dir; Mellissa Neeley, news dir.

WCNR(FM)—(Keswick, Mar 2, 1991: 106.1 mhz; 600 w. Ant 1,023 ft TL: N37 59 06 W78 28 48. Stereo. Hrs open: 1140 Rose Hill Dr., 22903. Phone: (434) 220-2300. Fax: (434) 220-2304. Web Site:www.1061thecorner.com Licensee: Saga Communications of Charlottesville LLC. (group owner; (acq 11-2-2006; $2.9 million). Smithwick & Belendiuk, PC. Format: AAA. ♦Brad Savage, gen mgr, progmg dir; John Kappes, stn mgr; Rick Dainels, opns mgr.

WHTE-FM—(Ruckersville, Mar 29, 1990: 101.9 mhz; 6 kw. 228 ft TL: N38 13 06 W78 22 03. Hrs open: 24 1150 Pepsi Pl., Suite 300, 22901. Phone: (434) 978-4408. Fax: (434) 978-0723. Web Site:www.1019hot.com Licensee: Monticello Media LLC. Group owner: Clear Channel Communications Inc. (acq 10-4-2007; grpsl). Population served: 300,000 Natl. Rep: Christal,. Format: CHR. News: 5 hrs wkly. Target aud: 18-24. ♦Vinnie Kice, opns mgr; Karen Cote, gen sls mgr; P.J. Styles, progmg dir.

WINA(AM)— September 1949: 1070 khz; 5 kw-U, DA-N. TL: N38 05 22 W78 30 14. Hrs open: 24 1140 Rose Hill Dr., 22903. Phone: (434) 220-2300. Fax: (434) 220-2304. Web Site:www.wina.com Licensee: Saga Communications of Charlottesville LLC. (group owner; (acq 1-6-2005; grpsl). Population served: 150,000 Natl. Network: CBS, . Natl. Rep: Katz Radio,. Smithwick & Belendiuk. Format: News/talk, sports. News staff: 4; News: 20 hrs wkly. Target aud: General. ♦Dennis Mockler, VP, gen mgr, progmg dir; Rick Daniels, opns mgr; John Kappes, gen sls mgr; Jay James, progmg dir.

WKAV(AM)— October 1957: 1400 khz; 1 kw-U. TL: N38 01 49 W78 29 22. Hrs open: 24 1150 Pepsi Pl., Suite 300, 22901. Phone: (434) 978-4408. Fax: (434) 978-0723. Web Site:www.wkav.com Licensee: Monticello Media LLC. Group owner: Clear Channel Communications Inc. (acq 10-4-2007; grpsl). Population served: 150,000 Natl. Network: Fox Sports, . Natl. Rep: Christal,. Format: Sports. Target aud: 18 - 54; Men. ♦Dennis Mockler, gen mgr; Vinnie Kice, opns mgr; Karen Cote, gen sls mgr; Joe Thomas, progmg dir.

***WNRN(FM)**— September 1996: 91.9 mhz; 320 w. 1,066 ft TL: N37 58 55 W78 29 03. Hrs open: 24
Rebroadcasts WNRS-FM Sweetbriar 85%.
2250 Old Ivy Rd., Suite 2, 22903. Phone: (434) 971-4096. Fax: (434) 971-6562.E-mail: wnrn@wnrn.org Web Site:www.wnrn.org Licensee: Stu-Comm Inc. Population served: 500,000 Davis Wright Tremaine. Format: Alternative, AAA, urban contemp. Target aud: 18-49; educated, upscale young professionals and students. Spec prog: Folk 19 hrs, techno 6 hrs, industrial 2 hrs, punk 2 hrs wkly, urban 16 hrs wkly. ♦Mike Friend, gen mgr, dev dir, progmg dir, chief of engrg; Anne Williams, mktg dir; Mike Momson, mus dir; Steve Mendenhall, news dir.

WQMZ(FM)— Oct 1954: 95.1 mhz; 6 kw. Ant 144 ft TL: N38 02 54 W78 28 12. Stereo. Hrs open: 1140 Rose Hill Dr., 22903. Phone: (434) 220-2300. Fax: (434) 220-2304. Web Site:www.literockz951.com Licensee: Saga Communications of Charlottesville LLC. Population served: 150,000 Format: Adult contemp. ♦Les Sinclair, progmg dir.

***WTJU(FM)**— May 10, 1957: 91.1 mhz; 600 w. 1,066 ft TL: N37 58 55 W78 29 03. Stereo. Hrs open: 24 Box 400811, 22904-4811. Secondary address: 2464 Lambeth Commons, 2nd Floor 22904. Phone: (434) 924-0885. Fax: (434) 924-8996.E-mail: wtju@virginia.edu Web Site:wtju.net Licensee: Rector & Board of Visitors, University of Virginia. Population served: 330,000 Natl. Network: PRI, . Format: Var/div. News: 6 hrs wkly. Target aud: General; from rural population to college educated. Spec prog: Black 8 hrs, children 2 hrs, folk 20 hrs,gospel one hr Sp 2 hrs wkly. ♦Chuck Taylor, gen mgr & stn mgr.

WUVA(FM)— June 22, 1979: 92.7 mhz; 6 kw. 3,000 ft TL: N37 59 06 W78 28 51. Stereo. Hrs open: 24 1928 Arlington Blvd., Suite 312, 22903. Phone: (434) 817-6880. Fax: (434) 817-6884.E-mail: info@92.7kissfm.com Web Site:www.92.7kissfm.com Licensee: WUVA Inc. Population served: 118,500 Natl. Rep: Katz Radio,. Format: Adult urban contemp. News staff: 20; News: 20 hrs wkly. Target aud: 18-54. ♦Sharon Sant, gen mgr, sls, mktg, adv; Tanisha Thompson, opns mgr, progmg dir & progmg.

WVAX(AM)— April 2006: 1450 khz; 1 kw-U. TL: N38 02 54 W78 28 12. Hrs open: 24 1140 Rose Hill Dr., 22903. Phone: (434) 220-2300. Fax: (434) 220-2304. Web Site:www.wvax.com Licensee: Saga Communications of Charlottesville LLC. (acq 11-22-2005; $150,000 for CP). Natl. Network: CNN Radio, . Natl. Rep: Katz Radio,. Smithwick & Belendiuk, P.C. Format: Progsv talk. News staff: 4. Target aud: 25-54; adult. ♦John Kappes, gen sls mgr; Jay James, progmg dir; Rob Graham, news dir.

***WVTU(FM)**— Jan 8, 1991: 89.3 mhz; 195 w horiz, 160 w vert. 1,696 ft TL: N38 03 58 W78 47 54. (CP: 3.2 kw). Stereo. Hrs open:
Rebroadcasts WVTF(FM) Roanoke 100%.
3520 Kingsburg Ln., Roanoke, 24014. Phone: (540) 989-8900. Fax: (540) 776-2727.E-mail: info@wvtf.org Web Site:www.wvtf.org Licensee: Virginia Tech. Foundation Inc. Population served: 150,000 Natl. Network: NPR, PRI, . Rgnl. Network: Va. News Net. Va. News Net. Dow, Lohnes & Albertson. Format: Class, jazz, npr (simulcast @ wvtf). ♦Glenn Gleixner, gen mgr; Karen Dillon, dev dir; Seth Williamson, mus dir; Rick Mattioni, news dir; Paxton Durham, chief of engrg.

***WVTW(FM)**— 1997: 88.5 mhz; 120 w. 1,089 ft TL: N37 58 49 W78 29 21. Hrs open:
Rebroadcasts WVTF(FM) Roanoke 100%.
3520 Kingsburg Ln., Roanoke, 24014. Phone: (540) 989-8900. Fax: (540) 776-2727.E-mail: info@wvtf.org Web Site:www.wvtf.org Licensee: Virginia Tech Foundation Inc. Natl. Network: NPR, . Format: Class, jazz, NPR. ♦Glenn Gleixner, gen mgr; Karen Dillon, dev dir; Seth Williamson, mus dir; Rick Mattioni, news dir; Paxton Durham, chief of engrg.

WWTJ(FM)— 1995: 107.5 mhz; 210 w. Ant 1,109 ft TL: N37 59 05 W78 28 49. Hrs open: 1150 Pepsi Pl., Suite 300, 22901. Phone: (434) 978-4408. Phone: (434) 964-1075. Fax: (978) 978-1190.E-mail: info@1075tom.com Web Site:www.1075tom.com Licensee: Monticello Media LLC. (acq 10-4-2007; grpsl). Format: Rock, adult contemp, smooth jazz. ♦David Mitchel, gen mgr; Kevin McCabe, gen sls mgr; Kishore Persaud, engrg dir & chief of engrg.

WWWV(FM)— 1959: 97.5 mhz; 8.9 kw. Ant 1,132 ft TL: N37 59 05 W78 28 49. Stereo. Hrs open: 1140 Rose Hill Dr., 22903. Phone: (434) 220-2300. Fax: (434) 220-2304. Web Site:www.3wv.com Licensee: Saga Communications of Charlottesville LLC. (group owner; (acq 1-6-2005; grpsl). Population served: 136,000 Natl. Rep: Katz Radio,. Smithwick & Belendiuk. Format: Rock. Target aud: 18-49. ♦John Kappes, gen sls mgr; Rick Daniels, opns mgr & progmg dir.

WZGN(FM)—See Crozet

Chase City

WJYK(AM)— Jan 18, 1959: 980 khz; 500 w-D. TL: N36 48 22 W78 26 22. Hrs open: Box 8, 23924. Phone: (434) 372-0803.E-mail: wjyk@joyam980.com Web Site:www.joyam980.com Licensee: Stephen C. Battaglia Sr. & Janis G. Battaglia (acq 1-5-2006; $51,000). Format: Contemp Christian, inspirational. ♦Stephen C. Battaglia Sr., gen mgr.

***WMVE(FM)**— Oct 10, 2007: 90.1 mhz; 8 kw. Ant 371 ft TL: N36 46 29 W78 20 41. Stereo. Hrs open: 24
Rebroadcasts WCVE(FM) Richmond 100%.
23 Sesame St., Richmond, 23235. Phone: (804) 320-1301. Fax: (804) 320-8729. Web Site:www.ideastations.org/radio Licensee: Commonwealth Public Broadcasting Corp. Population served: 38,000 Natl. Network: NPR, PRI, . Wire Svc: AP Format: News/talk/classical. ♦Bill Miller, gen mgr.

Chatham

WKBY(AM)— June 8, 1966: 1080 khz; 1 kw-D. TL: N36 46 54 W79 23 29. Hrs open: 12932 U.S. Hwy. 29, 24531. Phone: (434) 432-8108. Fax: (434) 432-1523.E-mail: wkby1080@gamewood.net Licensee: William L. Bonner. (acq 11-15-90; $250,000; 12-3-90). Population served: 225,000 Format: Urban gospel. ♦William L. Bonner, pres; Van Jay, gen mgr; Lois Stephens, gen sls mgr, local news ed, reporter, relg ed, women's int ed, disc jockey; Rodney Harper, progmg dir, traf mgr; Tim Walker, chief of engrg, rsch dir; Dr. H.G. McGhee, min affrs dir; Everett C. Peace, political ed; Vickie Pritchett, disc jockey.

Cheriton

***WWIP(FM)**— 2005: 89.1 mhz; 20 kw. Ant 449 ft TL: N37 10 53 W75 57 47. Hrs open: 2202 Jolliff Rd., Chesapeake, 23321. Phone: (757) 465-1603. Fax: (757) 488-7761.E-mail: info@wwip.org Web Site:www.wwip.org Licensee: Delmarva Educational Association. Format: Christian music, edu. ♦Nancy A. Epperson, pres; Henry Hoot, gen mgr.

Chesapeake

WCDG(FM)—See Moyock, NC

WCPK(AM)— 1967: 1600 khz; 5 kw-D, 27 kw-N. TL: N36 48 10 W76 16 58. Hrs open: 24 645 Church St., Suite 400, Norfolk, 23501. Phone: (757) 622-4600. Fax: (757) 624-6515.E-mail:

willisbroadcasting@yahoo.com Web Site:www.wcpk.com Licensee: Christian Broadcasting of Chesapeake Inc. (acq 10-17-97; $200,000). Population served: 1,200,000 Winston & Strawn. Format: Gospel. News staff: one. Target aud: 45+; working class listeners. ♦Hortense Willis, pres; Walter Allen Brickhouse, gen mgr; Ernestine Willis, gen sls mgr; Julian Joyner, progmg dir; Christine Willis, news dir; Terry Love, chief of engrg.

***WFOS(FM)**— Sept 14, 1973: 88.7 mhz; 15 kw. 172 ft TL: N76 18 03 W36 43 18. Stereo. Hrs open: 1617 Cedar Rd., 23322-7111. Phone: (757) 547-1036. Phone: (757) 547-0134. Fax: (757) 547-0160. Web Site:www.cpschools.com Licensee: Chesapeake School Board. Population served: 30,000 Format: Big band, blues, oldies, class, educ. Target aud: High school. ♦W. Randolph Nichols, pres; Richie Babb, gen mgr.

WPYA(FM)— Nov 30, 1973: 93.7 mhz; 100 kw. 997 ft TL: N36 32 57 W76 11 21. Stereo. Hrs open: 24 500 Dominion Tower, 999 Waterside Dr., Norfolk, 23510. Phone: (757) 640-8500. Fax: (757) 640-8552. Web Site:bob-fm.com Licensee: Commonwealth Radio L.L.C. Group owner: Sinclair Communications Inc. (acq 1996; $8.1 million with WTAR(AM) Norfolk). Population served: 1,400,000 Natl. Rep: McGavren Guild, Interep,. Format: Adult hits. News staff: one; News: 2 hrs wkly. Target aud: 25-54. ♦Bob Sinclair, pres; Lisa Sinclair, gen mgr; Dave Morgan, stn mgr, opns mgr; Luciana Varvarude, gen sls mgr; Ginger Power, natl sls mgr; Donna Agresto, prom dir; Jay West, progmg dir.

Chester

WDYL(FM)— December 1968: 101.1 mhz; 4 kw. Ant 367 ft TL: N37 26 21 W77 25 57. Stereo. Hrs open: 812 Moorefield Park Dr., Suite 300, Richmond, 23236. Phone: (804) 330-5700. Fax: (804) 330-4079.E-mail: info@y101rocks.com Web Site:y101rocks.com Licensee: Cox Radio Inc. Group owner: Cox Communications Inc. (acq 2-1-2001; grpsl). Wire Svc: UPI Format: New rock/alternative rock. Target aud: 18-34. ♦Rene Clark, gen sls mgr; Mike Fisher, progmg dir; Gary Harrison, chief of engrg.

WGGM(AM)— September 1964: 820 khz; 10 kw-D, 1 kw-N, DA-2. TL: N37 22 58 W77 25 21. Hrs open: 24 4301 W. Hundred Rd., 23831. Phone: (804) 717-2000. Fax: (804) 717-2009. Web Site:www.amen820.com Licensee: Hoffman Communications Inc. (acq 10-76). Population served: 900,000 Steve Yelverton. Wire Svc: Metro Weather Service Inc. Format: Urban Gospel. Target aud: 25-49. ♦Hubert Hoffman, pres; Cavell Phillips, gen mgr; Paul Scott, VP & gen sls mgr.

Chincoteague

WCTG(FM)— 2004: 96.5 mhz; 5.3 kw. Ant 344 ft TL: N37 55 14 W75 23 07. Hrs open: 24 Sebago Broadcasting L.L.C., 6139 Franklin Park Rd., McLean, 22101. Phone: (703) 761-5013. Fax: (703) 761-5023. Licensee: Sebago Broadcasting Co. L.L.C. Gammon & Grange. Format: Classic rock. ♦A. Wray Fitch III, pres.

Christiansburg

WBRW(FM)—See Blacksburg

WFNR-FM— 1990: 100.7 mhz; 3 kw. 328 ft TL: N37 08 01 W80 21 17. (CP: Ant 453 ft.). Hrs open: 17 7080 Lee Hwy., Radford, 24141. Phone: (540) 633-5330. Fax: (540) 633-2998. Web Site:www.allthehitshot100.com Licensee: Cumulus Licensing LLC. Group owner: Cumulus Media Inc. (acq 3-31-2004; grpsl). Population served: 561000 Rgnl. Network: Va. News Net. Va. News Net. Format: Hot A/C. News: 7 hrs wkly. Target aud: 25 plus. ♦Sarah Leftwich, gen mgr; Scott Stevens, opns mgr; Don Walker, progmg dir; Sam Parks, chief of engrg.

***WWVT(AM)**— October 1954: 1260 khz; 2.8 kw-D, 28 w-N. TL: N37 09 11 W80 24 57. Hrs open: 6am-sunset
Rebroadcasts WWFC (FM) Ferrum 100%.
3520 Kingsbury Ln., Roanoke, 24014. Phone: (540) 989-8900. Fax: (540) 776-2727.E-mail: info@radioiq.org Web Site:www.radioiq.org Licensee: Virginia Tech Foundation Inc. (acq 5-22-98). Population served: 110,000 Natl. Network: NPR, PRI, . Format: BBC Talk, NPR. News: 60 hrs wkly. Target aud: 30-54; business professionals. ♦Glenn Gleixner, gen mgr; Rick Mattioni, progmg dir; Paxton Durham, chief of engrg.

Churchville

WNLR(AM)— Mar 9, 1962: 1150 khz; 2.5 kw-D, 30 w-N. TL: N38 12 39 W79 07 53. Hrs open: Box 400, 24421. Secondary address: Rt. 250 W. Phone: (540) 885-8600. Phone: (540) 885-1150. Fax: (540) 886-8624.E-mail: wnlr@nlministries.org Web Site:www.positive-radio.com Licensee: New Life Ministries Inc. (acq 12-8-93; $200,000; 1-3-94). Population served: 100,000 Natl. Network: Moody, USA, . Format: Relg, adult contemp. Target aud: 22-55; females with family size above average. ♦Bill Garvey, pres; Tom Watson, gen mgr; Russ Whitesell, opns mgr.

Claremont

WPMH(AM)— Aug 19, 1997: 670 khz; 20 kw-D, 3 w-N, DA-2. TL: N37 10 29 W76 53 49. Hrs open: Sunrise-sunset 2202 Jolliff Rd., Chesapeake, 23321. Phone: (757) 465-6700. Fax: (757) 488-7761.E-mail: info@wwip.org Web Site:www.wpmhradio.com Licensee: Chesapeake-Portsmouth Broadcasting Corp. (acq 3-2-2001; $950,000). Format: Conservative talk/news. ♦Henry Hoot, gen mgr & opns mgr.

Clarksville

WLUS-FM— Jan 1, 1984: 98.3 mhz; 17.5 kw. Ant 394 ft TL: N36 44 24 W78 44 49. Stereo. Hrs open: 24 Box 1603, Oxford, NC, 27565. Secondary address: 615 B Lewis St., Oxford, NC 27565. Phone: (919) 693-7900. Fax: (919) 693-9585. Web Site:www.bestcountryaround.com Licensee: Lakes Media Holding Company LLC. (group owner; (acq 2-1-2005; grpsl). Population served: 250,000 Natl. Network: ABC, . Format: Country. News staff: 3; News: 2 hrs wkly. Target aud: 25-54; male & female. ♦Thomas C. Birch, pres; Jerry E. Brown, VP, gen mgr; Mike Elliott, opns mgr, gen sls mgr; Melissa P. Wilkerson, gen sls mgr, news dir; John Hart, chief of engrg.

Clifton Forge

***KCFF(FM)**—Not on air, target date: unknown: 90.9 mhz; 17.5 kw. ant -410 ft TL: N37 46 59 W80 00 00. Hrs open: 282 Country Estate Dr., Springer, OK, 73458. Phone: (580) 653-2777. Licensee: Ron Elmore Ministries Inc. ♦Ron Elmore, pres.

WXCF(AM)— Oct 19, 1950: 1230 khz; 1 kw-U, DA-1. TL: N37 49 18 W79 48 46. Hrs open: 24 Box 710, 1047 Ingalls St., 24422. Phone: (540) 862-5751. Phone: (540) 962-1133. Fax: (540) 862-2120.E-mail: wkeywigo@aol.com Web Site:www.bigcountry101.com Licensee: Quorum Radio Partners of Virginia Inc. (acq 5-03; with co-located FM). Population served: 29,000 Format: Adult contemp. News: one hr wkly. Target aud: 40 & up. ♦Marcia Smith, gen sls mgr, prom dir; Michael Stone, pres, gen mgr, sls dir & progmg dir; Lawrence Mason, chief of engrg.

WXCF-FM— Nov 20, 1982: 103.9 mhz; 150 w. Ant 1,909 ft TL: N37 54 12 W79 52 15. Stereo. Hrs open: Box 710 1047 Ingalls st., 24422. Licensee: Quorum Radio Partners of Virginia Inc. Population served: 29,000 Format: Hits of the 70s, 80s & 90s. News staff: one. Target aud: 18-54; Targeting mostly women 25-54. ♦Dennis Royer Jr., disc jockey.

Clinchco

WDIC(AM)— May 1961: 1430 khz; 5 kw-D. TL: N37 08 42 W82 23 22. Stereo. Hrs open: 24 2298 Rose Ridge, Clintwood, 24228-7738. Phone: (276) 835-8626. Fax: (276) 835-8627.E-mail: wdic@wdicradio.com Licensee: Dickenson County Broadcasting Corp. Group owner: Richard W. Edwards (acq 1-84; $366,850;1-30-84). Population served: 17,000 Natl. Network: ABC, . Natl. Rep: Rgnl Reps,. Va. News Net. Rgnl rep: Rgnl Reps. Smithwick & Belendiuk. Format: Country. News staff: 3; News: 8 hrs wkly. Target aud: General. Spec prog: Trading Post - M-F 10:35 am. ♦Richard W. Edwards, pres; Rufus E. Nickles, gen mgr, adv mgr, adv; Betty N. Fleming, opns mgr, traf mgr; Tammy Hill, progmg mgr & progmg.

WDIC-FM— July 2, 1989: 92.1 mhz; 2.5 kw. Ant 505 ft TL: N37 08 42 W82 23 22. Stereo. Hrs open: 24 Prog sep from AM 2298 Rose Ridge, Clintwood, 24228. Phone: (276) 835-8626. Fax: (276) 835_8627.E-mail: wdic@wdicradio.com Web Site:www.wdicradio.com Population served: 35,000 Natl. Network: ABC, . Natl. Rep: Rgnl Reps,. Smithwick & Belendiuk. Format: Oldies, news, loc sports. News: 3 hrs wkly. Target aud: 25-55; baby boomers.

Coeburn

WGCK-FM— Apr 15, 1991: 99.7 mhz; 1.95 kw. Ant 1,168 ft TL: N37 03 15 W82 38 34. Stereo. Hrs open: Box 729, Whitesburg, KY, 41858. Secondary address: 32 Cowan St., Whitesburg 41858. Phone: (606) 633-9430. Fax: (606) 633-3314.E-mail: wvsg@msn.com Licensee: Letcher County Broadcasting Inc. (acq 11-22-2005; $250,000). Natl. Network: K-Love, . Miller & Neely. Format: Adult contemp. ♦Ernestine Kincer, pres; G.C. Kincer, gen mgr.

Collinsville

WFIC(AM)— Mar 1, 1970: 1530 khz; 1 kw-D, 250 w-CH. TL: N36 42 56 W79 55 15. Hrs open: Box 192, Martinsville, 24114. Secondary address: 1675 Grandview Dr., Martinsville 24112. Phone: (276) 638-5235. Fax: (276) 638-6089.E-mail: wcbxwodywfic@yahoo.com Licensee: BASE Communications Inc. Group owner: Baker Family Stations (acq 9-3-97; $60,000). Population served: 250,000 Natl. Network: USA, . Format: Southern gospel. Target aud: 35 plus; general. ♦Brian Sanders, gen mgr, stn mgr; Steven Kuszlyk, opns mgr, gen sls mgr; Wendell Minter, progmg dir.

Colonial Beach

WGRQ(FM)— May 3, 1986: 95.9 mhz; 2.4 kw. Ant 525 ft TL: N38 13 45 W77 07 10. Stereo. Hrs open: 24 4414 Lafayette Blvd. #100, Fredericksburg, 22408. Phone: (540) 891-9696. Fax: (540) 891-1656.E-mail: tcooper@959wgrq.com Web Site:www.959wgrq.com Licensee: Telemedia Broadcasting Inc. (acq 1-20-88). Natl. Network: ABC, . Natl. Rep: Roslin,. Format: Oldies. News staff: one; News: 3 hrs wkly. Target aud: 25 plus; baby boomers. ♦Carl W. Hurlebaus, pres; Thomas P. Cooper, gen mgr; Edwin Pardue, sls dir; Andi King, prom dir; Jerome Hruska, progmg dir; Cathy Sato, pub affrs dir, traf mgr; Paul Hayden, spec ev coord; Keefe Coble, news rptr.

Colonial Heights

WDZY(AM)—Licensed to Colonial Heights. See Richmond

WKHK(FM)—Licensed to Colonial Heights. See Richmond

***WKYV(FM)**—Not on air, target date: unknown: 90.1 mhz; 500 w vert. Ant 295 ft TL: N37 15 02 W77 18 23. Hrs open: 1951 28th Ave., Unit 29, Greeley, CO, 80634. Phone: (970) 352-3736. Licensee: JKJ Educational Foundation. ♦Kevin J. Youngers, pres.

Covington

WIQO-FM— October 1964: 100.9 mhz; 560 w. 1,059 ft TL: N37 47 36 W79 55 57. Hrs open: 24 Box 710, 24426. Phone: (540) 962-1133.E-mail: wkeywiqo@aol.com Web Site:www.bigcountry101.com Licensee: Quorum Radio Partners of Virginia Inc., debtor-in-possession Population served: 85,000 Format: Country. News staff: one; News: 10 hrs wkly. Target aud: 25-54; general. ♦Pat Pleasant, disc jockey.

WKEY(AM)— May 23, 1941: 1340 khz; 1 kw-U. TL: N37 46 09 W79 58 59. Hrs open: 24 Box 710, 508 W. Oak St., 24426. Phone: (540) 962-1133.E-mail: info@bigcountry101.com Web Site:www.bigcountry101.com Licensee: Quorum Radio Partners of Virginia Inc., debtor-in-possession Group owner: Quorum Radio Partners of Virginia Inc. (acq 4-20-2005; with co-located FM). Population served: 75,000 Fletcher, Heald & Hildreth. Format: Oldies. News staff: one; News: 12 hrs wkly. Target aud: 25 plus; younger country listeners. Spec prog: Black one hr, gospel 2 hrs wkly. ♦Marcia Smith, gen sls mgr; Michael Stone, pres, gen mgr & progmg dir; Dwight Rohr, news dir; Lawrence Mason, chief of engrg.

Crewe

WPZZ(FM)— June 9, 1949: 104.7 mhz; 100 kw horiz, 84 kw vert. Ant 981 ft TL: N37 10 15 W77 57 16. Stereo. Hrs open: 2809 Emerywood Pkwy., Suite 300, Richmond, 23294. Phone: (804) 672-9299. Fax: (804) 672-9316. Web Site:www.praise1047.com Licensee: Radio One Licenses LLC. Group owner: Radio One Inc. (acq 11-8-2001; grpsl). Population served: 1,725 Natl. Rep: Eastman Radio,. Hogan & Hartson. Format: Contemporary Gospel. Target aud: 25-54; adults. ♦Alfred Liggins, CFO; Linda Forem, VP & gen mgr; Jeff Anderson, opns mgr, progmg dir; Dennis Gettis, gen sls mgr; Bobby Walden, natl sls mgr; Dawna Covington, mktg dir, prom dir; Clovia Lawrence, pub affrs dir; Chris Lawless, chief of engrg.

WSVS(AM)— Apr 7, 1947: 800 khz; 5 kw-D, 275 w-N. TL: N37 11 43 W78 10 01. Hrs open: 24 Box 47, 1032 Melody Ln., 23930. Phone: (434) 645-7734. Phone: (434) 645-7735. Fax: (434) 645-1701.E-mail: wsvsam@wsvs.com Web Site:www.wsvs800am.com Licensee: Colonial Broadcasting of Crewe Inc. Population served: 2,200 Natl. Network: Family Radio, . Format: Classic Coountry, Bluegrass. News staff: one; News: 7 hrs wkly. Target aud: 35 plus. ♦Hope Epperson, CEO, CFO; John Hart, opns dir, chief of engrg; Steve Winn, progmg dir.

Crozet

*WMRY(FM)— May 1995: 103.5 mhz; 270 w. 1,515 ft TL: N37 57 00 W78 43 38. Stereo. Hrs open: 24 Rebroadcasts WMRA(FM) Harrisonburg 100%. 983 Reservoir St., Harrisonburg, 22801. Phone: (540) 568-6221. Web Site:www.wmra.org Licensee: James Madison University Board of Visitors. Population served: 235,000 Natl. Network: NPR, PRI, . Format: Public radio news, talk, variety. News staff: 2; News: 80 hrs wkly. Target aud: 35-64; well educated. Spec prog: Folk 8 hrs, blues 5 hrs wkly. ♦Thomas DuVal, gen mgr.

WZGN(FM)— September 1980: 102.3 mhz; 4.9 kw. Ant 360 ft TL: N38 04 47 W78 44 22. Stereo. Hrs open: 1150 Pepsi Pl., Ste 300, Charlottesville, 22901. Phone: (434) 978-4408. Fax: (434) 978-0723. Web Site:www.generations1023.com Licensee: Monticello Media LLC. Group owner: Clear Channel Communications Inc. (acq 10-4-2007; grpsl). Natl. Rep: Christal,. Format: Classic hits. News staff: one. Target aud: 25 - 54/35 - 54; general. ♦Karen Cote, gen sls mgr; Dennis Mockler, progmg dir.

Culpeper

*WARN(FM)— 1997: 91.5 mhz; 930 w. 121 ft TL: N38 27 15 W77 59 10. Hrs open: Box 3206, American Family Radio, Tupelo, MS, 38803. Phone: (662) 844-8888. Fax: (662) 842-6791. Web Site:www.afr.net Licensee: American Family Association. Group owner: American Family Radio Format: Christian, inspirational. ♦Marvin Sanders, gen mgr.

WCVA(AM)— February 1949: 1490 khz; 1 kw-U. TL: N38 29 04 W77 59 22. Hrs open: 24 Box 271, Orange, 22960. Phone: (540) 672-1000. Fax: (540) 672-0282.E-mail: advertising@wjmafm.com Licensee: Piedmont Communications Inc. (group owner; acq 11-21-2003; grpsl). Population served: 28,000 Natl. Network: Westwood One, ABC, . Rgnl. Network: Va. News Net. Format: Adult Standards. News staff: one; News: 10 hrs wkly. Target aud: 45 plus. ♦John Schick, pres & gen mgr.

WJMA-FM— Dec 4, 1971: 103.1 mhz; 600 w. Ant 1,027 ft TL: N38 18 38 W78 00 12. Stereo. Hrs open: Box 271, Orange, 22960. Phone: (540) 672-1000. Fax: (540) 672-0282.E-mail: advertising@wjmafm.com Web Site:www.wjmafm.com Licensee: Piedmont Communications Inc. 1993 Population served: 118,000 Wire Svc: AP Format: Country. News staff: one. Target aud: 25-54; male & female. ♦John Schick, pres.

*WPER(FM)— 1999: 89.9 mhz; 41 kw. Ant 417 ft TL: N38 40 42 W77 47 18. Hrs open: Box 113, Warrenton, 20188. Phone: (540) 347-4825. Fax: (540) 347-3562.E-mail: info@positivehits.org Web Site:www.positivehits.org Licensee: Positive Alternative Radio Inc. Group owner: Baker Family Stations (Positive Radio Group) Booth, Freret, Imlay & Tepper. Format: Contemp Christian. ♦Frankie Morea, gen mgr.

Danville

WAKG(FM)— June 3, 1968: 103.3 mhz; 100 kw. 630 ft TL: N36 44 28 W79 23 05. Stereo. Hrs open: 24 Prog sep from AM Box 1629, 24543. Phone: (434) 797-4290. Fax: (434) 797-3918. Web Site:www.wakg.com Population served: 250,000 Format: Modern country. Target aud: 18-54. ♦Alan Rowe, disc jockey.

WBTM(AM)— May 24, 1930: 1330 khz; 5 kw-D, 1 kw-N, DA-N. TL: N36 36 36 W79 25 47. Stereo. Hrs open: 24 Box 1629, 24543. Secondary address: 710 Grove St. 24541. Phone: (434) 793-4411. Fax: (434) 797-3918. Web Site:www.wbtm1330.com Licensee: Piedmont Broadcasting Corp. Population served: 150,000 Format: Oldies. News staff: 2; News: 5 hrs wkly. Target aud: 24 plus; young working adults. ♦Bob Ashby, CEO, chmn, pres, gen mgr; Mike Wimmer, natl sls mgr; Carol Metz, prom mgr; Alex Vardavas, progmg dir; Chuck Vipperman, news dir; Johnny Cole, chief of engrg.

WDVA(AM)— June 29, 1947: 1250 khz; 5 kw-U, DA-N. TL: N36 34 53 W79 26 33. Stereo. Hrs open: 24 One Radio Ln., 24541. Phone: (434) 797-1250. Phone: (434) 797-1266. Fax: (434) 797-1255.E-mail: mitchellcommunications1@veriz.net Licensee: Mitchell Communications Inc. (acq 6-28-93; 7-19-93). Population served: 1,900,000 Natl. Network: CBS, . Latham & Watkins. Format: Gospel. News: 12 hrs wkly. Target aud: 18 plus. ♦C.G. Hairston, pres & gen mgr.

WILA(AM)— Aug 25, 1957: 1580 khz; 1 kw-D. TL: N36 34 03 W79 22 50. Hrs open: Sunrise-sunset Box 3444, 24543. Secondary address: 865 Industrial Ave. 24541. Phone: (434) 792-2133. Fax: (434) 792-2134.E-mail: wilaradio@verizon.net Licensee: Tol-Tol Communications Inc. (acq 12-29-92; $250,000; 1-25-93). Population served: 100,000 Natl. Network: American Urban, . Format: Black, gospel, oldies. Target

aud: General; ethnic (Black) and citizens who enjoy div progmg. ♦Lawrence A. Toller, pres, gen mgr, sls dir, progmg dir & pub affrs dir.

*WOKD-FM— 1998: 91.1 mhz; 18 kw. Ant 466 ft TL: N36 44 30 W79 23 07. Hrs open: Rebroadcasts WPAR(FM) Salem 100%. Box 889, Blacksburg, 24063. Phone: (540) 961-2377. Fax: (540) 951-5282.E-mail: mail@spiritfm.com Web Site:www.spiritfm.com Licensee: Positive Alternative Radio Inc. Group owner: Baker Family Stations Format: Christian adult contemp. ♦Barry Armstrong, gen mgr.

Deltaville

WTYD(FM)— Jan 5, 1999: 92.3 mhz; 2.4 kw. Ant 525 ft TL: N37 29 37 W76 26 30. Hrs open: 24 5000 New Point Rd., Suite 2201, Williamsburg, 23188. Phone: (757) 565-1079. Fax: (757) 565-7094. Web Site:www.tideradio.com Licensee: Bullseye Broadcasting LLC (acq 3-3-2005). Wire Svc: AP Format: Triple A. News staff: one. ♦Tom Davis, pres & gen mgr; Derek Mason, gen sls mgr; Amy Miller, prom mgr, mus dir; Barbara Warren, traf mgr.

Dillwyn

WBNN-FM— July 2000: 105.3 mhz; 6 kw. Ant 328 ft TL: N37 34 50 W78 37 18. Stereo. Hrs open: 24 PO Box 7111, Charlottesville, 22906. Secondary address: 18498 N. Madison Hwy. 23936. Phone: (434) 983-6621. Fax: (434) 983-6772.E-mail: STUDIO@bigcountry1053.com Web Site:www.bigcountry1053.com Licensee: WKGM Inc. Group owner: Baker Family Stations Natl. Network: CNN Radio, Premiere Radio Networks, . Va. News Net. Booth, Freret, Imlay & Tepper P. Format: Country. Target aud: 18-49 and 25-54. Spec prog: Relg. ♦Vernon H. Baker, CEO; Brian Sanders, VP; Greg Breeden, gen mgr, progmg dir; Nancy McCaig, sls.

Dublin

WPIN(AM)— 1995: 810 khz; 4.2 kw-D. TL: N37 07 55 W80 37 07. Hrs open: Box 889, Blacksburg, 24063. Phone: (540) 951-9791. Fax: (540) 961-2021. Web Site:810wpin.com Licensee: Dublin Radio. Booth, Freret, Imlay & Tepper. Format: News/talk. ♦Amy Burnette, gen mgr.

*WPIN-FM— 1994: 91.5 mhz; 35 w horiz, 85 w vert. Ant 1,243 ft TL: N37 01 29 W80 44 46. Hrs open: Rebroadcasts WPAR(FM) Salem 100%. Box 889, Blacksburg, 24060. Phone: (540) 552-8073. Fax: (540) 951-5282. Web Site:www.spiritfm.com Licensee: Positive Alternative Radio Inc. Group owner: Baker Family Stations (Positive Radio Group) Population served: 100,000 Booth, Freret, Imlay & Tepper. Format: Christian adult contemp. ♦Barry Armstrong, CEO, gen mgr; Vernon H. Baker, chmn; Edward A. Baker, pres.

Dumfries-Triangle

WPWC(AM)— Dec 22, 1961: 1480 khz; 1 kw-D, 500 w-N, DA-2. TL: N38 34 06 W77 20 20. Hrs open: 14416 Jefferson Davis Hwy., Suite 20, Woodbridge, 22191. Phone: (703) 494-0100. Fax: (703) 490-1579.E-mail: radiofiesta1480@yahoo.com Web Site:www.wpwcam.com Licensee: JMK Communications Inc. (acq 1-19-00; $900,000). Population served: 550,000 Format: Sp. ♦Grant Chang, pres; Carlos Aragon, gen mgr; Clara Marshall, gen sls mgr; Emmanuel Szepeda, progmg dir; Dule Salinas, traf mgr.

Earlysville

WKTR(AM)— Feb 17, 1991: 840 khz; 8.2 kw-D, DA. TL: N38 15 57 W78 24 53. Hrs open: Daytime Box 7111, Charlottesville, 22906. Secondary address: 100 Business Park Circle, Quinque 22965. Phone: (434) 985-8585. Fax: (434) 985-7369.E-mail: aaron@espn840.com Web Site:www.espn840.com Licensee: Rural Radio Service. Group owner: Baker Family Stations Natl. Network: ESPN Radio, . Booth, Freret, Imlay & Tepper. Format: Sports, talk. ♦Edward A. Baker, pres; Brian Sanders, VP; Aaron Marks, gen mgr.

Edinburg

*WOTC(FM)— Apr 1, 1994: 88.3 mhz; 1 kw. 403 ft TL: N38 48 12 W78 41 23. Hrs open: WOTJ(FM) Morehead City, NC 80% 146 Parsons Point Lane, 22824. Phone: (540) 984-8998. Fax: (540) 984-8977.E-mail: wotcfm@shentel.net Web Site:www.valleybaptistchurch.net Licensee: Valley Baptist Church-Christian School. Natl. Network: USA, . Format: Educ, relg, news. Target aud: General; relg, children. ♦Karl Demay, gen mgr.

Elkton

WACL(FM)— Mar 6, 1989: 98.5 mhz; 900 w. Ant 1,607 ft TL: N38 23 36 W78 46 14. Stereo. Hrs open: 24 Box 1107, Harrisonburg, 22801. Secondary address: 207 University Blvd., Harrisonburg 22801. Phone: (540) 434-1777. Fax: (540) 432-9968.E-mail: ksdavis@clearchannel.com Web Site:www.98rockme.com Licensee: Capstar TX L.P. Group owner: Clear Channel Communications Inc. (acq 3-12-01; grpsl). Population served: 76,000 Format: Mainstream rock. News staff: one; News: one hr wkly. Target aud: 35-49. ♦Steve Davis, gen mgr.

Emory

*WEHC(FM)— Nov 15, 1994: 90.7 mhz; 500 w. Ant 95 ft TL: N36 46 19 W81 49 59. Hrs open: 24 Keller Box 947, Keller, Garnand Dr., 24327-0947. Phone: (276) 944-6822. Phone: (276) 944-6593. Fax: (276) 944-6934.E-mail: tdkeller@ehc.edu Web Site:www.ehcweb.ehc.edu/masscomm/wehc Licensee: Emory and Henry College. Format: Div, progsv. News: 3 hrs wkly. Target aud: College community. ♦Dr. Teresa Keller, gen mgr.

Emporia

WEVA(AM)— Nov 4, 1952: 860 khz; 1 kw-D. TL: N36 41 56 W77 32 55. Hrs open: 24 Box 1056, 705 Washington St., 23847. Secondary address: 705 Washington Street 23847. Phone: (434) 634-2133. Fax: (434) 634-5050.E-mail: info@wevaradio.com Web Site:www.wevaradio.com Licensee: Colonial Media Corp. Dec. 2001 Population served: 30,000 Natl. Network: CBS, Westwood One, . Va. News Net. Wilkinson, Barker, Knauer & Quinn. Format: Adult contemp, talk. News: 14 hrs wkly. Target aud: 25 plus; Adults 25-64. Spec prog: Gospel 3 hrs, garden 3 hrs, news 14 hrs wkly. ♦James Vavtrout, CEO; George A. Sperry, gen mgr, sls VP, prom mgr; Andy Lucy, progmg mgr, mus dir, disc jockey; Joseph Wetherbee, chief of engrg; Darrius Herring, local news ed, edit dir; Jim Wood, disc jockey.

*WJYA(FM)— January 1999: 89.3 mhz; 2 kw vert. Ant 443 ft TL: N36 46 04 W77 43 39. Stereo. Hrs open: 24 22226 Timberlake Rd., Lynchburg, 24502. Phone: (434) 237-9798. Fax: (434) 237-1025.E-mail: office@spiritfm.com Web Site:www.spiritfm.com Licensee: Positive Alternative Radio Inc. (group owner; (acq 12-30-2005; grpsl). Booth, Freret, Imlay & Tepper. Format: Contemp Christian. ♦Barry Armstrong, gen mgr.

WYTT(FM)— 2003: 99.5 mhz; 1.27 kw. Ant 501 ft TL: N36 39 20 W77 34 22. Hrs open: Box 910, Roanoke Rapids, NC, 27890. Phone: (252) 536-0597. Fax: (252)538-0378.E-mail: info@firstmediarr.com Web Site:www.firstmediarr.com Licensee: First Media Radio LLC. Group owner: The MainQuad Group. (acq 12-3-2003; grpsl). Format: Hits & Oldies. ♦Alan Garrick, gen mgr, progmg dir; Frank White, chief of engrg.

Ettrick

WLFV(FM)— 2001: 93.1 mhz; 5.2 kw. Ant 348 ft TL: N37 16 21 W77 33 59. Hrs open: 300 Arboretum Pl., Suite 590, Richmond, 23236. Phone: (804) 327-9902. Fax: (804) 327-9911.E-mail: info@thewolf.com Web Site:www.931thewolf.com Licensee: MLB-Richmond IV LLC. (acq 12-13-2005; grpsl). Format: Country. ♦Sandy Jimerson, gen sls mgr.

Exmore

WROX-FM—Licensed to Exmore. See Virginia Beach

Fairfax

WDCT(AM)— Sept 25, 1955: 1310 khz; 5 kw-D, 500 w-N, DA-2. TL: N38 51 08 W77 18 57. Hrs open: 6 AM-midnight 3251 Old Lee Hwy., Suite 506, 22030. Phone: (703) 273-4000. Fax: (703) 273-1015.E-mail: 1310@radiowashingtonnews.com Web Site:www.radiowashingtonnews.com Licensee: Family Radio Ltd. (acq 1995). Population served: 3,500,000 Natl. Network: Moody, . Format: Korean. Target aud: 25-54; 60% female, 40% male. ♦Kenneth Shin, gen mgr, sls dir, chief of engrg; Ronnie Shin, progmg dir.

Fairlawn

WKNV(AM)— 1998: 890 khz; 10 kw-D, DA. TL: N37 07 55 W80 37 07. Hrs open: Box 889, Blacksburg, 24063. Phone: (540) 951-9791. Fax: (540) 961-2021.E-mail: wknv@yahoo.com Licensee: Base Communications

Inc. Group owner: Baker Family Stations Format: Relg, Christian. ♦Amy Burnette, gen mgr; Alison Baker, progmg dir; Winston Hawkins, chief of engrg.

Falls Church

WFAX(AM)—Licensed to Falls Church. See Washington DC

Falmouth

WGRX(FM)— May 17, 2001: 104.5 mhz; 2.7 kw. Ant 492 ft TL: N38 16 31 W77 32 34. Stereo. Hrs open: 4414 Lafayette Blvd. #100, Fredericksburg, 22408. Phone: (540) 891-9696. Fax: (540) 891-1656.E-mail: wgrx@thunder1045.com Web Site:www.thunder1045.com Licensee: Telemedia Broadcasting Inc. (acq 4-17-01; $1.8 million for two-thirds). Population served: 220,000 Natl. Rep: Roslin,. Format: Country. News: 3 hrs wkly. Target aud: 18-49; male audience, working class. ♦Carl W. Hurlebaus, pres; Thomas P. Cooper, gen mgr; Edwin Pardue, sls dir; Jerome Hruska, progmg dir; Cathy Sato, pub affrs dir, traf mgr; Paul Hayden, spec ev coord; Keefe Coble, news rptr.

Farmville

WFLO(AM)— August 1947: 870 khz; 1 kw-D. TL: N37 19 35 W78 23 09. Hrs open: Sunrise-sunset Box 367, 1582 Cumberland Rd., 23901. Phone: (434) 392-4195. Fax: (434) 392-1823.E-mail: wflo@moonstar.com Web Site:www.wflo.net Licensee: Colonial Broadcasting Co. Inc. (acq 4-71). Population served: 100,000 Rgnl. Network: Va. News Net. Natl. Rep: Salem,. Va. News Net. Wire Svc: AP Format: C&W, news/talk. News staff: one; News: 4 hrs wkly. Target aud: 25 plus. Spec prog: Relg 10 hrs wkly. ♦John D. Wilson, pres; Henry Fulcher, VP; Francis E. Wood Jr., gen mgr; Chris Brochon, prom dir, traf mgr; Chris Wood, progmg dir; Elliott Irving, news dir, local news ed, news rptr.

WFLO-FM— May 1961: 95.7 mhz; 50 kw. 492 ft TL: N37 19 35 W78 23 09. Stereo. Hrs open: 24 Prog sep from AM Box 367, 1582 Cumberland Rd., 23901. Phone: (434) 392-4195. Fax: (434) 392-1823. Web Site:www.wflo.net Population served: 200,000 Natl. Network: Jones Radio Networks, AP Radio, . Rgnl. Network: Va. News Net. Va. News Net. Wire Svc: AP Format: Adult contemp. News staff: one; News: 4 hrs wkly. Target aud: 25 plus. ♦John Wilson, pres; Henry Fulcher, VP, disc jockey; Francis Wood, gen mgr; Polly Davis, gen sls mgr; Chris Brochon, traf mgr, disc jockey; Elliott Irving, news rptr; Chris Wood, disc jockey.

***WMLU(FM)**— 1988: 91.3 mhz; 1 w horiz, 150 w vert. Ant 72 ft TL: N37 17 50 W78 23 42. Hrs open: 24 Longwood University, 201 High St., 23909. Phone: (434) 395-2475. Phone: (434) 395-2792. Fax: (434) 395-2035 attn: WMLU.E-mail: wmlu@longwood.edu Web Site:www.wmlu.org Licensee: Longwood University. Population served: 5,000 Natl. Network: NPR, . Format: Div, progsv. Target aud: 18-23; div college students. ♦Valerie Hughs, gen mgr; James Campbell, progmg VP, progmg dir; Farris Campbell, mus dir, mus critic; Patrick Robins, news dir, news rptr; Gerry Martin, chief of engrg.

WPAK(AM)— June 15, 1978: 1490 khz; 1 kw-U. TL: N37 18 47 W78 23 41. Hrs open: 446 Plank Rd., 23901. Phone: (434) 392-8114. Fax: (434) 392-8115. Licensee: Great Virginia Venture Inc. (acq 5-11-98; $201,000). Population served: 100,000 Format: Relg. Spec prog: Farm one hr, gospel 12 hrs wkly. ♦George H. Granger, pres; Mark Neimand, gen mgr.

WVHL(FM)— Sept 1, 1997: 92.9 mhz; 6 kw. 328 ft TL: N37 17 06 W78 29 39. Hrs open: Drawer T, 116 North St., 23901. Secondary address: 116 North St. 23901. Phone: (434) 392-9393. Fax: (434) 392-6091.E-mail: v93@wvhl.net Web Site:www.wvhl.net Licensee: The Farmville Herald Inc. Natl. Network: ABC, . Format: Country. Target aud: General. ♦Steve Wall, gen mgr; Sherry Massaro, opns mgr.

Ferrum

***WFFC(FM)**— January 1989: 89.9 mhz; 1.1 kw. Ant 679 ft TL: N36 54 50 W79 57 07. Stereo. Hrs open: 16 WFFC Radio, 3520 Kingsbury Ln, Roanoke, 24014. Phone: (540) 989-8900. Fax: (540) 776-2727.E-mail: info@radioiq.org Web Site:www.radioiq.org Licensee: Virginia Tech Foundation Inc. (acq 1-23-2004; $10). Natl. Network: NPR, . Format: BBC Talk, NPR. ♦Glenn Gleixner, gen mgr & stn mgr.

Fieldale

WODY(AM)— July 1, 1993: 1160 khz; 5 kw-D, 250 w-N, DA-2. TL: N36 42 36 W79 57 58. Hrs open: 24 Box 192, Martinsville, 24114. Secondary address: 1675 Grandview Dr, Martinsville 24112. Phone: (276) 638-5235. Fax: (276) 638-6089.E-mail: wcbxwodywfic@yahoo.com Web Site:thesportsaddictnetwork.com Licensee: Base Communications Inc. Group owner: Baker Family Stations (acq 4-17-98). Population served: 250,000 Natl. Network: ESPN Radio, . Format: Sports, talk. Target aud: 25-54. ♦Vernon H. Baker, pres, CFO; Edward A. Baker, exec VP, gen mgr; Aaron Marks, stn mgr, sls dir; Steven Kuszlyk, opns mgr; Winston Hawkins, chief of engrg.

Floyd

WGFC(AM)— Apr 20, 1985: 1030 khz; 1 kw-D. TL: N36 55 53 W80 16 34. Hrs open: Sunrise-sunset PO Box 495, 24091. Secondary address: 401 Shooting Creek Rd. S.E. 24091. Phone: (540) 745-9811. Fax: (540) 745-9812.E-mail: wgfc@wgfcradio.com Web Site:www.wgfcradio.com Licensee: New Life Christian Communications Inc. (acq 7-1-02). Population served: 110,000 Format: Bluegrass, southern gospel. News staff: 2; News: 10 hrs wkly. Target aud: General; loc community interest. ♦Jackie Goad, VP, progmg dir; R. Leon Goad, CEO, pres & gen mgr; Leon Goad, chief of engrg.

Fort Lee

WKLR(FM)—Licensed to Fort Lee. See Richmond

Franklin

WLQM(AM)— Oct 13, 1956: 1250 khz; 1 kw-D. TL: N36 40 57 W76 55 43. Hrs open: 24 Box 735, 23851. Secondary address: 320 Franklin St. 23851. Phone: (757) 562-3135. Fax: (757) 562-2345.E-mail: wlqm@wlqmradio.com Web Site:www.wlqmradio.com Licensee: Franklin Broadcasting Corp. (acq 8-10-59). Natl. Network: American Urban, . Format: Urban gospel. News staff: 3. Target aud: 35-64. ♦Michael Clark, VP; Michael E. Clark, gen mgr; Louise Morings, rgnl sls mgr, progmg dir; Mickel Pruden, chief of engrg.

WLQM-FM— January 1988: 101.7 mhz; 6 kw. 469 ft TL: N36 41 17 W77 00 58. Hrs open: 320 N. Franklin St., P.O. Box 735, 23851. Phone: (757) 562-3135. Fax: (757) 562-2345.E-mail: wlqm@wlqmradio.com Web Site:www.wlqmradio.com Licensee: Franklin Broadcasting Corp. Natl. Network: Westwood One, . Pepper & Corazzini. Format: Contemp country. News staff: 9. Target aud: 35 plus; men & women. ♦Michael Clark, VP, gen mgr; Tim Parsons, news dir; Mickel Pruden, chief of engrg.

Fredericksburg

WBQB(FM)— May 15, 1960: 101.5 mhz; 50 kw. Ant 492 ft TL: N38 19 57 W77 23 41. Stereo. Hrs open: 24 Box 269, 22404. Secondary address: 1914 Mimosa St. 22405. Phone: (540) 373-7721. Fax: (540) 899-3879.E-mail: info@b1015.com Web Site:www.b1015.com Licensee: Mid Atlantic Network Inc. Population served: 500,000 Natl. Network: Westwood One, . Format: Adult contemp. News staff: 3; News: 8 hrs wkly. Target aud: 18-49. ♦Shawn Sloan, gen mgr; Chris Carmichael, opns mgr.

WFLS-FM— June 12, 1962: 93.3 mhz; 50 kw. 492 ft TL: N38 18 46 W77 26 20. Stereo. Hrs open: 24 616 Amelia St., 22401. Phone: (540) 373-1500. Fax: (540) 374-5525.E-mail: info@wfls.com Web Site:www.wfls.com Licensee: The Free Lance-Star Publishing Co. Population served: 225,000 Wire Svc: AP Format: Country. News staff: 4. Target aud: 25-54; adults. ♦Paul Johnson, opns dir & progmg mgr; Frank Hammon, news dir, pub affrs dir.

WFVA(AM)— Sept 8, 1939: 1230 khz; 1 kw-U. TL: N38 16 50 W77 26 11. Hrs open: 24 Box 269, 22404. Secondary address: 1914 Mimosa St. 22405. Phone: (540) 373-7721. Fax: (540) 899-3879.E-mail: info@newstalk1230.net Web Site:www.newstalk1230.net Licensee: Mid-Atlantic Network Inc. (group owner) Population served: 125,000 Rgnl. Network: Va. News Net. Cole, Raywid & Braverman. Format: News/talk. News staff: 3; News: 15 hrs wkly. Target aud: 35 plus. ♦John P. Lewis, pres; Shawn Sloan, gen mgr; Chris Carmichael, opns mgr; Maureen Posillico, prom dir; Mark Clifford, progmg dir; Ted Schubel, news dir; John Diamantis, chief of engrg.

WGRQ(FM)—See Colonial Beach

***WJYJ(FM)**— May 6, 1983: 90.5 mhz; 38 kw. Ant 500 ft TL: N38 11 48 W77 33 45. Stereo. Hrs open: 24
Simulcasts WPER(FM) Culpeper 100%.
Box 113, Warrenton, 20188. Phone: (540) 347-4825. Fax: (540) 347-3562.E-mail: info@positivehits.org Web Site:www.positivehits.org Licensee: Positive Alternative Radio Inc. (group owner; (acq 12-30-2005; grpsl). Format: Contemp Christian. ♦Frankie Morea, gen mgr & stn mgr.

WYSK(AM)— July 15, 1960: 1350 khz; 1 kw-D, 37 w-N. TL: N38 18 46 W77 26 20. Hrs open: 24 616 Amelia St., 22401. Phone: (540) 373-1500. Fax: (540) 374-5525.E-mail: info@wysk.com Web Site:www.wysk.com Licensee: The Free Lance-Star Publishing Co. (group owner). Population served: 85,000 Format: Latino. News staff: 3; News: 12 hrs wkly. Target aud: General. ♦John Moen, gen mgr; Jim Butler, sls dir; Jo Anne Pope, prom dir; Chris Wilk, chief of engrg; Sandy Ridgeway, traf mgr.

Front Royal

WFQX(FM)— Jan 17, 1973: 99.3 mhz; 3 kw. 295 ft TL: N39 00 11 W78 20 28. Stereo. Hrs open: 24 510 Pegasus Ct., Winchester, 22602-4596. Phone: (540) 662-5101. Fax: (540) 662-8610. Web Site:www.993thefox.com Licensee: Capstar TX L.P. Group owner: Clear Channel Communications Inc. (acq 8-30-00; grpsl). Population served: 127,000 Format: Rock/AOR. News staff: 3; News: one hr wkly. Target aud: 25-49; men. ♦Chuck Peterson, gen mgr; David Miller, opns mgr, progmg dir; Marcella Vance, sls dir; Justin Maglione, prom dir; Ben Gates, pub affrs dir; Mark Kesner, chief of engrg; Krissy Golden, traf mgr; Elwood King, disc jockey.

WFTR(AM)— Sept 19, 1948: 1450 khz; 1 kw-U. TL: N38 54 31 W78 10 37. Hrs open: 24 Box 192, 22630. Secondary address: 1106 Elm St. 22630. Phone: (540) 635-4121. Fax: (540) 635-9387.E-mail: sales@royalbroadcasting.net Web Site:www.realcountryonline.com Licensee: Royal Broadcasting Inc. (acq 8-15-00; $950,000 with co-located FM). Population served: 40,000 Natl. Network: ABC, . Rgnl rep: Commercial Media Sales. Format: Country. News staff: one; News: 20 hrs wkly. Target aud: 25-54. ♦Andrew Shearer, CEO; Lonnie Hill, opns mgr; Mike O'Dell, COO, gen mgr, gen sls mgr & progmg dir; Kathy Willis, traf mgr.

WZRV(FM)— 1981: 95.3 mhz; 6 kw. 300 ft TL: N38 58 29 W78 12 09. Stereo. Hrs open: 24 Box 192, 22630. Secondary address: 1106 Elm St. 22630. Phone: (540) 665-9595. Fax: (540) 635-9387. Web Site:www.oldiesradioonline.com Population served: 100,000 Natl. Network: ABC, . Format: Oldies. News staff: one. Target aud: 25-54. ♦Mike O'Dell, sls dir; Mario Retrosi, news dir; Kathy Willis, traf mgr; Randy Woodward, progmg mgr & disc jockey.

Galax

WBRF(FM)— Dec 15, 1961: 98.1 mhz; 100 kw. 1,756 ft TL: N36 34 50 W80 58 23. Stereo. Hrs open: 24 Box 838, 24333. Secondary address: 325 Poplar Knob Rd. 24333. Phone: (276) 236-9273. Fax: (276) 236-7198.E-mail: debby@blueridgecountry98.com Web Site:www.blueridgecountry98.com Licensee: Blue Ridge Radio Inc. (acq 4-19-85; 12-31-84). Natl. Network: CBS, Motor Racing Net, . Format: Country. Target aud: General. ♦Debby Sizer Stringer, gen mgr, gen sls mgr; Betty Liddle, progmg dir, traf mgr; Jason Blevins, mus dir; John Mullins, chief of engrg; Ray Bass, opns mgr & pub svc dir.

***WOKG(FM)**— 2005: 90.3 mhz; 2.7 kw. Ant 538 ft TL: N36 39 27 W80 54 22. Hrs open: Box 889, Blacksburg, 24063. Web Site:www.spiritfm.com Licensee: Positive Alternative Radio Inc. Group owner: Baker Family Stations. Format: Contemp Christian.

WWWJ(AM)— Feb 1, 1947: 1360 khz; 5 kw-D. TL: N36 39 48 W80 54 52. Hrs open: 6 AM-10 PM Box 270, 24333. Secondary address: 325 Poplar Knob Rd 24333. Phone: (276) 236-2921. Fax: (276) 236-2922. Licensee: Twin County Broadcasting Corp. (acq 4-19-85; $200,000; 4-8-85). Population served: 50,373 Natl. Network: CBS, . Rgnl. Network: Va. News Net. Va. News Net. Format: Gospel. News: one hr wkly. Target aud: 18 plus. Spec prog: Sp 20 hrs, farm one hr wkly. ♦Deborah E. Stringer, pres, gen mgr; J. Brice Parks, gen sls mgr; Carole Bonn, progmg dir, traf mgr; Anthony Phillips, mus dir, disc jockey; John Mullins, chief of engrg; Joel Bonn, disc jockey.

Gate City

WGAT(AM)— July 24, 1959: 1050 khz; 1 kw-D, 266 w-N. TL: N36 37 59 W82 34 56. Hrs open: 24 117 E. Jackson, Suite 2, 24251. Phone: (276) 386-7025. Fax: (276) 386-7025.E-mail: wgatradio@earthlink.com Licensee: Tri-Cities Broadcasting Corp. (acq 11-28-90; $70,000;12-17-90). Population served: 700,000 Natl. Network: Salem Radio Network, . Va. News Net. Dow, Lohnes & Albertson. Format: Sports, Southern Gospel Music. News staff: one; News: 10 hrs wkly. Target aud: 25 plus. ♦Alan Giles, pres; Mike Long, gen mgr.

Glade Spring

WFYE(FM)— 2008: 100.5 mhz; 6 kw. Ant -14 ft TL: N36 48 45.38 W81 33 20.38. Hrs open: 5835 Lawrence Dr., Indianapolis, IN, 46226. Phone: (317) 541-0417.E-mail: asradio@aol.com Licensee: ASRadio LLC. ♦Alan Sneed, gen mgr.

Glen Allen

WTOX(AM)— 2004: 1480 khz; 6.3 kw-D, 1.5 kw-N, DA-2. TL: N37 40 56 W77 33 49. Hrs open: 24 308 W. Broad St., Richmond, 23220. Phone: (804) 643-0990. Fax: (804) 474-5070. Web Site:www.radiorichmond.com Licensee: Davidson Media Station WTOX Licensee LLC. Group owner: 4M Communications Inc. (acq 5-13-2005; grpsl). Population served: 650,000 Format: Rgnl Mexican. Target aud: 25 plus; Hispanic. ♦Peter Davidson, pres; Jim Jacobs, gen mgr; Tim Hurley, opns dir; Carolyn Resendiz, gen sls mgr; Shalin Midence, progmg dir.

Gloucester

WXGM(AM)— Jan 20, 1957: 1420 khz; 740 w-D. TL: N37 24 36 W76 32 52. Stereo. Hrs open: 24 Dups FM 100% Box 634, 6267 Professional Dr., 23061. Phone: (804) 693-2105. Phone: (804) 693-9946. Fax: (804) 693-2182.E-mail: noair@xtra99.com Web Site:www.xtra99.com Licensee: WXGM Inc. (acq 7-91; 6-22-81). Population served: 200,000 Natl. Network: ABC, . Rgnl. Network: Agri-Net, Va. News Net. Va. News Net. Verner, Liipfert, Bernhard, McPherson & Hand. Format: Adult contemp. News staff: one; News: 7 hrs wkly. Target aud: 25-54. Spec prog: Farm 2 hrs, relg 2 hrs wkly. ♦Thomas W. Robinson, pres & gen mgr; Harvey King, opns mgr, progmg dir; Iris Lassister, gen sls mgr; Herman King, news dir; Bill Swartz, chief of engrg.

WXGM-FM— July 29, 1991: 99.1 mhz; 6 kw. 328 ft TL: N37 24 36 W76 32 52. Stereo. Hrs open: 24 Dups AM 100% Box 634 6267 Professional Dr., 23061. Web Site:www.xtra99.com Licensee: WXGM Inc. Format: Adult contemp.

Goochland

WZEZ(FM)— Apr 1, 2001: 100.5 mhz; 2.6 kw. Ant 509 ft TL: N37 47 37 W77 55 57. Stereo. Hrs open: 24 4301 W. Hundred Rd., Chester, 23831. Phone: (804) 717-2000. Fax: (804) 717-2009. Web Site:www.ezfmradio.com Licensee: Hubert N. Hoffman III, executor (acq 9-12-02). Natl. Network: CNN Radio, . Wire Svc: Metro Weather Service Inc. Format: Nostalgia. ♦Jay Hoffman, pres; Paul Scott, VP & gen mgr.

Gretna

WMNA(AM)— Aug 11, 1956: 730 khz; 1 kw-D, 28 w-N, DA. TL: N36 55 31 W79 19 50. Hrs open: 6 AM-10 PM
Rebroadcasts WLNI(FM) Lynchburg 80%.
Box 730, 677 Zion Rd., 24557. Phone: (434) 656-1234. Fax: (434) 847-5709. Web Site:www.wlni.com Licensee: 3 Daughters Media Inc. Group owner: Burns Media Strategies Inc. (acq 11-14-2002; $300,000 with co-located FM). Population served: 111,000 Rgnl. Network: Agri-Net. Agrinet Womble, Carlyle, Sandridge & Rice. Format: Country. News staff: one; News: 19 hrs wkly. Target aud: 18-55; family groups. Spec prog: Farm 8 hrs, Black 2 hrs, bluegrass 20 hrs, sports 10 hrs, gospel 15 hrs wkly. ♦Gary E. Burns, CEO, pres, gen mgr; Mike Slenski, gen mgr; Charlotte Wells, progmg dir, disc jockey; Dale Cook, chief of engrg; Melissa Eckhert, traf mgr; Bob Haynes, disc jockey.

WMNA-FM— Feb 28, 1959: 106.3 mhz; 6 kw. Ant 260 ft TL: N36 55 31 W79 19 50. Stereo. Hrs open: 5:30 AM-10 PM
Rebroadcasts WLNI(FM) Lynchburg 85%.
Box 730, 677 Zion Rd., 24557. Phone: (434) 656-1234. Fax: (434) 847-5709. Licensee: 3 Daughters Media Inc Rgnl. Network: Agri-Net. Agrinet Format: Talk. News: 10 hrs wkly. Target aud: 24-54; active & mature. ♦Melissa Eckhert, traf mgr; Brian Wegan, disc jockey.

Grundy

WMJD(FM)— June 21, 1965: 100.7 mhz; 2.3 kw. Ant 535 ft TL: N37 18 08 W82 07 04. Hrs open: 24 Box 2045, 24614. Phone: (276) 935-7227. Fax: (276) 935-2587.E-mail: wmjd.fm@gmail.com Web Site:www.wnrg-wmjd-tv7.com Licensee: Peggy Sue Broadcasting Media Corp. Population served: 50,000 Natl. Network: ABC, . Format: Classic country. News staff: 5. Target aud: 24-59. ♦Dirk Hall, stn mgr & gen sls mgr; Bink Rush, disc jockey.

***WNBV(FM)—** 2009: 88.1 mhz; 100 w vert. Ant 148 ft TL: N37 17 18 W82 05 09. Hrs open: Box 100, Bishop, 24604. Phone: (276) 979-9200. Web Site:www.newbeginningworldoutreach.net Licensee: New Beginning World Outreach Inc. ♦John Dash, pres; Harriett Dash, stn mgr.

WNRG(AM)— Nov 16, 1955: 940 khz; 5 kw-D, 14 w-N. TL: N37 18 08 W82 07 04. Hrs open: 1011 Radio Dr., 24614. Secondary address: Rt. 460 W. 24614. Phone: (276) 935-7227. Fax: (276) 935-2587.E-mail: wmjd.fm@gmail.com Licensee: Peggy Sue Broadcasting Media Corp. (group owner; (acq 3-31-2004; $200,000 with co-located FM). Population served: 40,000 Natl. Network: ABC, Salem Radio Network, . Format: Southern gospel. News staff: 2. Spec prog: Farm 5 hrs wkly. ♦Dirk Hall, gen mgr, opns mgr, gen sls mgr & progmg dir.

Hampden-Sydney

***WWHS-FM—** Oct 11, 1972: 92.1 mhz; 10 w. 140 ft TL: N37 14 19 W78 27 48. (CP: Ant 216 ft.). Stereo. Hrs open: 6 AM-2 AM Box 606, Hampden-Sydney College, 23943. Phone: (434) 223-6009. Fax: (434) 223-6009.E-mail: wwhs@wwhsfm.org Web Site:www.wwhsfm.org Licensee: President & Board of Trustees of Hampden-Sydney College. Population served: 3,700 Format: div, progsv. News: 5 hrs wkly. Target aud: 18-25; college community. Spec prog: Blues 2 hrs, class 2 hrs, jazz 6 hrs, reggae 4 hrs, funk 4 hrs wkly. ♦Vincent Sparzak, gen mgr.

Hampton

***WHOV(FM)—** Mar 5, 1964: 88.1 mhz; 2 kw horiz, 8 kw vert. 200 ft TL: N37 01 03 W76 20 13. Stereo. Hrs open: 17 Scripts Howard Sch Journalism, Hampton Univ., 23668. Phone: (757) 727-5407. Phone: (757) 727-5711. Fax: (757) 727-5084.E-mail: info@whovfm.com Licensee: Hampton University. Population served: 200,000 Format: Var/div. News: 2 hrs wkly. Target aud: 18-54. Spec prog: Sp 12 hrs, blues 3 hrs, reggae 4 hrs wkly. ♦Kevin Anderson, stn mgr, gen sls mgr; Alvin Delk, opns mgr; Robert Dixon, gen mgr & progmg dir.

WWDE-FM— June 1, 1962: 101.3 mhz; 50 kw. 499 ft TL: N36 49 41 W76 15 05. Stereo. Hrs open: 236 Clearfield Ave., Suite 206, Virginia Beach, 23462. Phone: (757) 497-2000. Fax: (757) 456-5458.E-mail: info@2wd.com Web Site:www.2wd.com Licensee: Entercom Norfolk License LLC. Group owner: Entercom Communications Corp. (acq 12-13-99; grpsl). Population served: 200,000 Natl. Rep: D & R Radio,. Bryan Cave. Format: Adult contemp. News: one hr wkly. ♦David J. Field, CEO, pres, opns dir; Steve Fisher, CFO, exec VP; Steve Godofsky, VP; Jeff Brown, gen mgr; Don London, opns mgr, progmg dir; Sandy Smith, gen sls mgr; Kym Wollman, traf mgr.

WXTG(AM)— July 1, 1948: 1490 khz; 970 w-U. TL: N37 01 50 W76 22 32. Hrs open: 24 232 Business Park Dr., Suite 120, Virginia Beach, 23462. Phone: (757) 747-1021. Fax: (757) 490-2755. Web Site:www.1021thegame.com racetalklive.com Licensee: Red Zebra Broadcasting Licensee (Norfolk) LLC. (acq 12-10-2007; $950,000). Population served: 1,000,000 Natl. Network: Fox Sports, . Wilmer Cutler Pickering Hale and Dorr LLP. Format: Sports. ♦Buck Albritton, gen mgr.

Harrisonburg

***WEMC(FM)—** 1955: 91.7 mhz; 1.85 kw. 190 ft TL: N38 28 20 W78 52 57. Stereo. Hrs open: 24 983 Reservoir St., 22801. Phone: (540) 568-3812. Web Site:www.wemcradio.org Licensee: Eastern Mennonite University. Population served: 250,000 Natl. Network: NPR, . Format: Classical music, news, variety. News staff: 2; News: 15 hrs wkly. Target aud: General. ♦Thomas DuVal, gen mgr.

WHBG(AM)— August 1956: 1360 khz; 5 kw-D, 9 w-N. TL: N38 27 04 W78 54 29. Stereo. Hrs open: 24 Box 752, 22803. Phone: (540) 434-0331. Web Site:www.valleyradio.com Licensee: M. Belmont VerStandig Inc. Group owner: VerStandig Broadcasting Population served: 120,779 Natl. Network: ESPN Radio, . Format: Sports. Target aud: 24-50. ♦Susanne Myers, gen mgr; Frank Wilt, progmg dir.

WKCY(AM)— May 11, 1967: 1300 khz; 5 kw-D. TL: N38 27 52 W78 50 53. Hrs open: Box 1107, 22801. Secondary address: 207 University Blvd. 22801. Phone: (540) 434-1777. Fax: (540) 432-9968. Web Site:www.goodradio.com Licensee: Capstar TX L.P. Group owner: Clear Channel Communications Inc. (acq 3-12-01; grpsl). Population served: 54,200 Natl. Network: USA, . Format: Talk. Target aud: 55 plus. Spec prog: Relg 2 hrs wkly. ♦Steve Davis, gen mgr; Susie Smith, gen sls mgr; Steve Knupp, progmg dir; David Burman, news dir; Jeff Caudell, chief of engrg.

WKCY-FM— November 1980: 104.3 mhz; 50 kw. 409 ft TL: N38 23 40 W79 08 26. Stereo. Hrs open: 24 Box 1107, 22801. Phone: (540) 434-1777. Fax: (540) 462-9968.E-mail: stevekeupp@clearchannel.com Web Site:www.goodradio.com Licensee: Capstar TX L.P. Format: Country. Target aud: 25-54. ♦Dennis Hughes, progmg dir.

***WMRA(FM)—** June 18, 1975: 90.7 mhz; 10.5 kw. 1,046 ft TL: N38 33 40 W78 56 56. Stereo. Hrs open: 24 983 Reservoir St., 22801. Phone: (540) 568-6221. Web Site:www.wmra.org Licensee: James Madison University Board of Visitors. Population served: 250,000 Natl. Network: PRI, . Format: Public radio news, talk, variety. News staff: 2; News: 80 hrs wkly. Target aud: 35-64; well-educated. Spec prog: Folk 8 hrs, blues 5 hrs wkly. ♦Thomas DuVal, gen mgr; Dan Easley, opns mgr; Diane Halke, dev dir; William Fawcett, chief of engrg.

WQPO(FM)— Dec 3, 1946: 100.7 mhz; 50 kw. Ant 492 ft TL: N38 27 08 W78 54 32. Stereo. Hrs open: 24 Prog sep from AM Box 752, 22803. Phone: (540) 434-0331. Web Site:q101online.com Population served: 36,500 Format: CHR. News staff: 3. ♦Susanne Myers, gen mgr; Dennis Burchill, gen sls mgr; Ryan O'Bryan, progmg dir.

WSVA(AM)— June 9, 1935: 550 khz; 5 kw-D, 1 kw-N, DA-N. TL: N38 27 04 W78 54 29. Hrs open: 24 Box 752, 22803. Phone: (540) 434-0331. Web Site:wsvaonline.com Licensee: M. Belmont VerStandig Inc. Group owner: VerStandig Broadcasting (acq 4-17-87). Population served: 100,000 Natl. Network: ABC, . Rgnl. Network: Va. News Net. Va. News Net. Format: News/talk. News staff: 5. Target aud: 35 plus. Spec prog: Farm 8 hrs wkly. ♦John D. VerStandig, pres; Susanne Myers, gen mgr; Dennis Burchill, sls dir; Frank Wilt, progmg dir.

***WXJM(FM)—** September 1990: 88.7 mhz; 390 w. 62 ft TL: N38 26 22 W78 52 21. Stereo. Hrs open: 6 AM-2 AM MSC 6803, James Madison Univ., 22807. Phone: (540) 568-6878. Phone: (540) 568-3425. Web Site:orgs.jmu.edu/wxjm Licensee: Board of Trustees of James Madison University. (acq 9-1-89). Format: Progsv. News: 7 hrs wkly. Target aud: General. Spec prog: Jazz 14 hrs, Sp 2 hrs wkly.

Heathsville

***WCNV(FM)—** 2007: 89.1 mhz; 3.8 kw. Ant 318 ft TL: N37 54 22 W76 29 09. Stereo. Hrs open: Community Idea Stations, 23 Sesame St., Richmond, 23235. Phone: (804) 320-1301. Fax: (804) 320-8729. Web Site:www.ideastations.org/radio Licensee: Commonwealth Public Broadcasting Corp. Population served: 25,000 Natl. Network: NPR, PRI, . Wire Svc: AP Format: News/talk. ♦Bill Miller, gen mgr.

Highland Springs

WCLM(AM)— May 18, 1959: 1450 khz; 960 w-U. TL: N37 32 39 W77 20 47. Hrs open: 24 3165 Hull St., Richmond, 23224. Phone: (804) 231-2186. Fax: (804) 231-2186. Web Site:www.wclmradio.com Licensee: World Media Broadcast Co. (acq 10-25-94; 11-14-94). Population served: 200,000 Format: Var/div. Target aud: 25-65. Spec prog: Gospel, blues 5 hrs wkly, country, Top 40. ♦George Lacey, dev dir; Kimberly Osacio, gen sls mgr; Jim Grainger, chief of engrg; Preston T. Brown, CEO, pres, VP, gen mgr, opns VP, progmg dir & rsch dir; Jean Trimble, traf mgr, disc jockey; Curtis Bowman, disc jockey.

***WHCE(FM)—** Sept 29, 1980: 91.1 mhz; 3 kw horiz. Ant 105 ft TL: N37 32 18 W77 19 27. Hrs open: Henrico County Schools, 100 Tech Dr., 23075. Phone: (804) 328-4079. Fax: (804) 328-4074.E-mail: mix91@mix91.com Web Site:www.mix91.com Licensee: Henrico County Schools. Format: CHR. Target aud: 12-20; teenagers, young adults. ♦Bob Kaufman, gen mgr.

Hillsville

WHHV(AM)— Sept 16, 1961: 1400 khz; 1 kw-U. TL: N36 45 00 W80 43 20. Hrs open: 6 AM-midnight Box 648, 24333. Secondary address: 343 Virginia St. 24343. Phone: (276) 728-9114. Fax: (276) 728-9968.E-mail: whhv@whhvradio.com Web Site:www.whhvradio.com Licensee: New Life Christian Communications Inc. (acq 4-2-01). Population served: 78,000 Format: Gospel. News: 20 hrs wkly. Target aud: General. Spec prog: Farm one hr wkly. ♦Leon Goad, pres, chief of engrg; Jackie Goad, VP, progmg dir, news dir; R. Leon Goad, gen mgr & adv dir.

Hopewell

WHAP(AM)— Jan 16, 1949: 1340 khz; 1 kw-U. TL: N37 17 46 W77 18 50. Hrs open: 24 150 S. Mesa Dr., 23860. Phone: (804) 452-4999. Web Site:whapradio.com Licensee: P.T. Brown Broadcast Company Inc. (acq 5-17-2007; $150,000). Population served: 150,000 Rgnl. Network: Va. News Net. Format: Gospel, oldies, var. Target aud: 25-65. ♦Preston Brown, CEO; Judy Brown, gen mgr.

Hot Springs

***WCHG(FM)**— September 1995: 107.1 mhz; 160 w. 1,407 ft TL: N38 01 53 W79 46 52. Stereo. Hrs open: 6 AM-10 PM
Rebroadcasts WVMR(AM) Frost, WV 50%.
Drawer G, 24445. Phone: (540) 839-5400. Fax: (540) 839-5403.E-mail: wchg@tds.net Web Site:www.alleghenymountainradio.org Licensee: Pocahontas Communications Cooperative Corp. (acq 11-23-93; $2,000; 12-13-93). Population served: 5,000 Rgnl. Network: Va. News Net. Va. News Net. Format: Variety. News: 15 hrs wkly. Target aud: General. ♦Cheryl Kinderman, gen mgr; Heather Niday, news dir; Chuck Niday, chief of engrg.

Jonesville

WJNV(FM)— 2000: 99.1 mhz; 4 kw. Ant 403 ft TL: N36 42 05 W83 10 14. Hrs open: Box 996, 24263. Phone: (276) 346-2000. Fax: (276) 346-2049.E-mail: wjnv-fm@verizon.net Web Site:www.wjnv.fm Licensee: Regina Kay Moore. Format: Country. ♦Regina Moore, gen mgr.

Keswick

WCNR(FM)—Licensed to Keswick. See Charlottesville

Kilmarnock

WKWI(FM)— Sept 1, 1975: 101.7 mhz; 3 kw. Ant 328 ft TL: N37 43 26 W76 23 27. Stereo. Hrs open: 24 Box 819, 22482. Secondary address: 101 Radio Rd 22482. Phone: (804) 435-1414. Phone: (804) 435-1313. Fax: (804) 435-0484.E-mail: charlielassitor@1017bayfm.com Licensee: Two Rivers Communications Inc. (acq 4-7-2004; $900,000). Population served: 40,000 Natl. Network: AP Network News, . Rgnl. Network: Va. News Net. Format: Adult contemp. Target aud: 25-64. Spec prog: Farm 2 hrs, Black 6 hrs, Gospel 5 hrs wkly. ♦William C. Sherard, pres; Charlie Lassitor, gen mgr; Syd Abel, sls dir; Tawne Hayes, mus dir.

Lawrenceville

WHFD(FM)— Sept 1, 1991: 105.5 mhz; 6 kw. 154 ft TL: N36 45 10 W77 51 49. Hrs open: Box 4, 23868. Secondary address: 2162 Plank Rd. 23868. Phone: (434) 848-9433. Fax: (434) 848-9434. Licensee: Willis Broadcasting Corp. (group owner; acq 4-27-99; $350,000 with co-located AM). Format: Gospel. ♦Katrina Chase, gen mgr.

Lebanon

WLRV(AM)— Oct 28, 1974: 1380 khz; 1 kw-D, 63 w-N. TL: N36 55 18 W82 06 16. Hrs open: 24 Box 939, 484 W. Main St., 24266. Phone: (276) 889-1380. Fax: (276) 889-1388.E-mail: wlrv@mounet.com Web Site:www.wlrv.com Licensee: Gary W. Ward Broadcasting Corp. (acq 12-13-99; $161,250). Population served: 32,000 Natl. Network: USA, . Format: Bluegrass, gospel,classic country, oldies rock. Target aud: 25 plus. ♦Gary W. Ward, pres, gen mgr; Mike Lowe, opns dir, prom dir, progmg dir, news dir; Gary Ward, gen sls mgr, adv dir, adv mgr; Rick Lang, chief of engrg.

WXLZ-FM— Feb 1, 1993: 107.3 mhz; 530 w. 774 ft TL: N36 50 38 W82 11 04. Stereo. Hrs open: 24 Box 1299, 24266. Secondary address: 265 WXLZ Dr 24266. Phone: (276) 889-1073. Fax: (276) 889-3677.E-mail: wxlz1073@verizon.net Web Site:www.wxlz.net Licensee: Yeary Broadcasting Inc. Population served: 231,000 Natl. Network: CBS, . Format: Modern country. News staff: 2; News: 3 hrs wkly. Target aud: 18 plus; students, farmers, miners, executives & rural residents. ♦Lannis Yeary, pres, gen mgr; Marshall Hendricks, progmg dir, spec ev coord; Richard Quillen, mus dir; Don Linkous, chief of engrg, local news ed; Anthony Stevens, sports cmtr; Ryland Sutherland, disc jockey.

Leesburg

WAGE(AM)— Mar 6, 1958: 1200 khz; 5 kw-D, 1 kw-N, DA-N. TL: N39 07 25 W77 37 31. Hrs open: 24
(CP: 1190 khz; 50 kw-D, DA. TL: N39 02 28 W77 26 42).
711 Wage Dr. S.W., 20175. Phone: (703) 777-1200. Fax: (703) 777-7431. Licensee: Potomac Radio LLC (acq 7-16-2008). Population served: 100,000 Rgnl. Network: Va. News Net. Leventhal, Senter & Lerman. ♦Grenville Emmet III, pres; Dene Hill, stn mgr.

Lexington

***WLUR(FM)**— Feb 27, 1967: 91.5 mhz; 175 w. Ant -75 ft TL: N37 47 17 W79 26 36. Stereo. Hrs open: 6:30 AM-2 AM WLUR, Washington and Lee Univ., 24450-0303. Phone: (540) 458-4017. Fax: (540) 458-4079.E-mail: wlur@wlu.edu Web Site:wlur.wlu.edu Licensee: Washington & Lee University. Population served: 12,000 Format: Div. News: 2 hrs wkly. Target aud: General; college students, city and county residents. ♦Tom Burish, pres; Jeremy Franklin, gen mgr; Angela Ernst, opns dir, prom dir; Amy McCamphill, mus dir.

***WMRL(FM)**— June 1992: 89.9 mhz; 100 w. 196 ft TL: N37 42 22 W79 26 11. Stereo. Hrs open: 24
Rebroadcasts WMRA(FM) Harrisonburg 100%.
983 Reservoir St., Harrisonburg, 22801. Phone: (540) 568-6221. Web Site:www.wmra.org Licensee: James Madison University Board of Visitors. Population served: 15,000 Natl. Network: NPR, PRI, . Format: Public radio news, talk, variety. News staff: 2; News: 80 hrs wkly. Target aud: 35-64; well-educated. Spec prog: Folk 8 hrs, blues 5 hrs wkly. ♦Thomas DuVal, gen mgr; Diane Halke, dev dir.

WREL(AM)— Nov 14, 1948: 1450 khz; 1 kw-U. TL: N37 46 00 W79 25 56. Hrs open: 24 Box 902, 24450. Secondary address: 392 E Midland Trail 24450. Phone: (540) 463-2161. Fax: (540) 463-9524. Web Site:www.firstmediava.com Licensee: First Media Radio LLC. (group owner; (acq 6-21-2004; $1.33 million with WWZW-FM Buena Vista). Population served: 30,280 Natl. Rep: Keystone (unwired net),. Format: News/talk, sports. News staff: one; News: 6 hrs wkly. Target aud: 35 plus. ♦Debra Reed, sls dir, mktg dir; Steve Williams, progmg dir; Jim Bresnahan, news dir; Wayne Boone, chief of engrg; Rebecca Rosson, traf mgr.

***WRIQ(FM)**—Not on air, target date: unknown: 88.7 mhz; 3.9 kw. Ant 220 ft TL: N37 53 17 W79 17 50. Hrs open: 3520 Kingsbury Ln., Roanoke, 24014. Phone: (540) 989-8900. Fax: (540) 776-2727. Web Site:www.wvtf.org Licensee: Virginia Tech Foundation Inc. ♦Glenn Gleixner, gen mgr.

Louisa

WOJL(FM)— July 10, 1980: 105.5 mhz; 6 kw. Ant 325 ft TL: N38 01 37 W78 01 05. Stereo. Hrs open: 24 Box 271, Orange, 22960. Phone: (540) 672-1000. Fax: (540) 672-0282.E-mail: advertising@1055samfm.com Web Site:www.1055samfm.com Licensee: Piedmont Communications Inc. (group owner; (acq 5-27-2004). Population served: 215,000 Natl. Network: Westwood One, . Format: Adult hits. News staff: one; News: 2 hrs wkly. Target aud: 25-54. ♦John Schick, pres.

Luray

WMXH-FM— Oct 16, 1979: 105.7 mhz; 440 w. 1,079 ft TL: N38 30 41 W78 29 15. Stereo. Hrs open: Prog sep from AM 130 University Blvd., Suite B, Harrisonburg, 22801. Phone: (540) 801-1057. Fax: (540) 633-6300. Web Site:www.stardust1057.com Rgnl. Network: Va. News Net. Va. News Net. Format: MOR, music of your life. Target aud: 18-54; working people with disposable income interested in mus, news & sports. Spec prog: Relg 5 hrs wkly.

WRAA(AM)— October 1962: 1330 khz; 1 kw-D, 40 w-N. TL: N38 39 34 W78 29 28. Hrs open: 130 University Blvd., Suite B, Harrisonburg, 22801. Phone: (540) 801-1057. Fax: (540) 564-2873.E-mail: production @easyradioinc.com Licensee: EZ Radio Inc. (acq 6-2-88; $585,000 with co-located FM). Population served: 50,000 Rgnl. Network: Va. News Net., Agri-Net. Natl. Rep: Keystone (unwired net),. Agrinet Tharrington, Smith & Hargrove. Format: Country. Target aud: 18-49; middle to upper income, mobile. Spec prog: Relg 7 hrs wkly. ♦Jason Cave, pres, gen sls mgr, progmg dir, chief of engrg; Joshua Cave, VP.

WYFT(FM)— October 1986: 103.9 mhz; 6 kw. Ant 302 ft TL: N38 38 17 W78 24 06. Stereo. Hrs open: Box 7300, Charlotte, NC, 28241. Phone: (704) 523-5555. Fax: (704) 522-1967.E-mail: wyft@bbnradio.org Web Site:www.bbnradio.org Licensee: Bible Broadcasting Network Inc. (group owner; (acq 12-22-86). Format: Relg. News: 13 hrs wkly. Target aud: General. ♦Lowell Davey, pres.

Lynchburg

WBRG(AM)— Sept 6, 1956: 1050 khz; 4000 w-D, 100 w-N. TL: N37 25 15 W79 06 55. Hrs open: 24 Box 1079, 24505. Secondary address: 239 Ragland Rd., Madison Heights 24572. Phone: (434) 845-5916.E-mail: wbrg@rev.net.com Licensee: Tri-County Broadcasting Inc. (acq 7-1-67). Population served: 670,000 Natl. Network: ABC, Westwood One, Motor Racing Net, . Rgnl. Network: Va. News Net Va. News Net. Format: News/talk, sports. News staff: 2; News: 12 hrs. wkly. Target aud: 25-54; College educated, professional/management, high household income, married with children. ♦Brent Epperson, gen mgr.

WKPA(AM)— July 7, 1988: 1390 khz; 4.7 kw-D, 34 w-N. TL: N37 27 52 W79 07 21. Hrs open:
Rebroadcasts WKBA (AM) Vinton 100%.
2043 10th St. NE, Roanoke, 24012. Phone: (540) 343-5597. Fax: (540) 345-4064.E-mail: ddurrett@radiowkba.com Web Site:www.radiowkba.com Licensee: Seven Hills Media Inc. Booth, Freret, Imlay & Tepper P. Format: Relg. Target aud: General. ♦Dorothy Durrett, gen mgr, opns dir, progmg dir, chief of engrg, traf mgr; Zeke Leonard, sls dir; Sharon M. Moran, prom mgr; Buddy Durrett, mus dir.

WLLL(AM)— Nov 1, 1963: 930 khz; 9 kw-D, 42 w-N. TL: N37 24 25 W79 13 57. Hrs open: Box 11375, 24506. Secondary address: 105 Whitehall Rd. 24501. Phone: (434) 385-9555. Fax: (434) 385-6073.E-mail: wlliam930@aol.com Web Site:www.wlllradio.com Licensee: Hubbards Advertising Agency Inc. (acq 1-28-02). Population served: 68,000 Format: Gospel. ♦Fletcher Hubbard, pres, gen mgr, sls dir, progmg dir; Savannah Hubbard, traf mgr.

WLNI(FM)— Feb 2, 1994: 105.9 mhz; 6 kw. Ant 266 ft TL: N37 25 37 W79 07 26. Hrs open: 24 Box 11798, 24506. Secondary address: 19-C Wadsworth St. 24501. Phone: (434) 845-5463. Fax: (434) 845-2063.E-mail: wlni@wlni.com Web Site:www.wlni.com Licensee: Centennial Broadcasting LLC. Group owner: Burns Media Strategies Inc. (acq 1-7-2005; grpsl). Natl. Network: ABC, Westwood One, Fox News Radio, Talk Radio Network, . Natl. Rep: McGavren Guild,. Womble, Carlyle, Sandridge & Rice. Wire Svc: AP Format: News/talk. News staff: 3; News: 20 hrs wkly. Target aud: 25-54. ♦Ron Gaylor, gen mgr; Bob Abbott, opns mgr; Sandi Conner, prom dir; Mari White, news dir, local news ed; Kara Butterworth, traf mgr.

WLVA(AM)— Apr 21, 1930: 590 khz; 5 kw-D, 1 kw-N, DA-2. TL: N37 25 39 W79 13 23. (CP: 580 khz; 250 w-D, 15 w-N. TL: N37 25 15 W79 06 55). Stereo. Hrs open: 24 230 Chelsea Dr., Forest, 24551. Phone: (434) 534-0400. Fax: (434) 534-0401.E-mail: news1280@msn.com Licensee: Chesapeake-Portsmouth Broadcasting Corp. (group owner; (acq 1-30-2009; $560,000). Population served: 250,000 Format: All news. Target aud: 25-54; upscale, decision makers & professionals. ♦Vic Bosiger, gen mgr & progmg dir.

***WRVL(FM)**— June 19, 1981: 88.3 mhz; 50 kw. 1,082 ft TL: N37 11 50 W79 21 07. Stereo. Hrs open: 24 1971 University Blvd., 24502-2269. Phone: (434) 582-3688. Fax: (434) 582-2994.E-mail: wrvl@liberty.edu Web Site:www.wrvlfm.com Licensee: Liberty University. Fletcher, Heald & Hildreth. Format: Educ, relg. News staff: one; News: 8 hrs wkly. Target aud: 25 plus. Spec prog: Liberty Univ. football & basketball. ♦David Young, sr VP; Jerry Edwards, gen mgr, stn mgr, mus dir; Mark Edwards, mus dir; Chris Wygal, pub affrs dir, chief of engrg; Rob Branch, engrg dir.

WSNZ(FM)— Aug 1, 1964: 101.7 mhz; 3.4 kw. Ant 300 ft TL: N37 25 37 W79 07 26. Stereo. Hrs open:
Simulcast with WSNV(FM) Salem 100%.
3807 Brandon Ave. S.W., Suite 2350, Roanoke, 24018. Phone: (540) 725-1220. Fax: (540) 725-1245.E-mail: sunny@mysunnyfm.com Web Site:www.mysunnyfm.com Licensee: Aloha Station Trust LLC (acq 7-30-2008; grpsl). Population served: 150,000 Format: Soft adult contemp. Target aud: 35-54. ♦Chris Clendenen, gen mgr; Steve Cross, progmg dir.

WVBE-FM— 1948: 100.1 mhz; 20 kw. 646 ft TL: N37 20 56 W79 10 06. (CP: Ant 328 ft. TL: N37 28 06 W79 05 50). Stereo. Hrs open: 24
Rebroadcasts WVBE(AM) Roanoke 90%.
Box 92, Roanoke, 24022. Secondary address: 3934 Electric Rd. S.W., Roanoke 24018. Phone: (540) 774-9200. Fax: (540) 774-5667.E-mail: info@vibe100.com Web Site:www.vibe100.com Licensee: Mel Wheeler Inc. (group owner; acq 3-12-97; $7.5 million with WXLK(FM) Roanoke). Population served: 200,000 Format: Urban contemp. News: one hr wkly. Target aud: 25-54; skew women, skew black. ♦Leonard Wheeler, CEO, pres & gen mgr; Kathy Rilee, rsch dir.

WVGM(AM)— Feb 22, 1962: 1320 khz; 1 kw-U. TL: N37 25 37 W79 07 26. Hrs open: 24 Box 348, Forest, 24551. Phone: (434) 534-6100. Fax: (434) 534-6101.E-mail: wblt@inbox.com Web Site:www.espninva.com Licensee: 3 Daughters Media Inc. Group owner: Clear Channel Communications Inc. (acq 6-22-2007; grpsl). Population served: 150,000 Natl. Network: ESPN Radio, . Natl. Rep: Katz Radio,. Format: Sports talk. News: 10 hrs wkly. ♦Devin Taylor, opns mgr.

***WWMC(FM)**— February 1993: 90.9 mhz; 100 w. 604 ft TL: N37 20 56 W79 10 05. Stereo. Hrs open: 24 1971 Univ. Blvd., 24502. Phone: (434) 582-3691. Fax: (434) 582-7461.E-mail: wwmcfm@liberty.edu Web Site:www.thelightonline.com Licensee: Liberty University Inc. Format: Christian, sports, var/div. News: 5 hrs wkly. Target aud: 12-45; high school, college & young adult. ♦Jamie Hall, stn mgr.

WYYD(FM)—See Amherst

WZZU(FM)— Sept 1, 1970: 97.9 mhz; 570 w. Ant 1,925 ft TL: N37 33 46 W79 11 38. Stereo. Hrs open: 24 Simulcasts WZZI(FM) Vinton 100%.
Box 11798, 24506. Secondary address: 19-C Wadsworth St. 24501. Phone: (434) 845-3698. Fax: (434) 845-2063.E-mail: babbott@centennialbroadcasting.com Web Site:www.rocktheplanet.fm Licensee: Centennial Broadcasting LLC. (group owner; (acq 11-23-2004; $4.15 million with WZZI(FM) Vinton). Natl. Network: Fox News Radio, . Natl. Rep: McGavren Guild,. Wire Svc: AP Format: Rock. News staff: 3. Spec prog: Relg one hr wkly. ◆Bob Abbott, opns mgr, progmg dir; Ron Gaylor, gen mgr, stn mgr & gen sls mgr; Kara Butterworth, traf mgr.

Manassas

WJFK-FM—Licensed to Manassas. See Washington DC

WKDV(AM)— Oct 1, 1957: 1460 khz; 5 kw-U, DA-2. TL: N38 45 00 W77 30 49. Hrs open: 24 9540 Godwin Dr., 20110. Phone: (703) 330-8244. Fax: (703) 331-4706.E-mail: metroradioinc@aol.com Web Site:www.metroradioinc.com Licensee: Metro Radio Inc. Group owner: Multicultural Radio Broadcasting Inc. (acq 8-1-2005; exchange for WFBR(AM) Glen Burnie, MD). Population served: 3,500,000 Format: Sp talk var. ◆David Houston, CEO, gen mgr; Kelly Koonce, COO; Bruce Houston, pres.

WWWT-FM— Mar 28, 1966: 107.7 mhz; 29 kw. Ant 646 ft TL: N38 44 30 W77 50 08. Stereo. Hrs open: 24 Rebroadcasts WTOP-FM Washington, DC 100%.
3400 Idaho Ave. N.W., Washington, DC, 20016. Phone: (202) 895-5000. Fax: (202) 895-5016.E-mail: info@wtop.com Web Site:www.wtop.com Licensee: Bonneville Holding Co. Group owner: Bonneville International Corp. (acq 4-27-98). Population served: 3,300,000 Natl. Network: CBS, . Rgnl. Network: Va. News Net. Natl. Rep: Katz Radio,. Va. News Net. Format: News. Target aud: 25-54. ◆Bruce Reese, CEO; Joel Oxley, sr VP; Jim Farley, gen mgr, progmg VP; Matt Mills, sls dir.

Marion

WITM(AM)— Apr 25, 1962: 1330 khz; 5 kw-D, 31 w-N. TL: N36 49 11 W81 28 12. Hrs open: Box 2061, Bristol, TN, 37621-2061. Phone: (423) 878-6279. Fax: (423) 878-6520. Licensee: Praise and Glory Ministries (acq 8-6-2009; donation). Population served: 78,158 ◆Maurice Gaines, pres; Kenneth C. Hill, gen mgr.

WMEV(AM)— Dec 12, 1948: 1010 khz; 1 kw-D, 30 w-N. TL: N36 51 23 W81 30 21. Hrs open: 24 1041 Radio Hill Rd., 24354. Phone: (276) 783-3151. Phone: (276) 783-9400 (STUDIO). Fax: (276) 783-3152.E-mail: fm94@smyth.net Web Site:www.fm94.com Licensee: Holston Valley Broadcasting Corp. Group owner: Glenwood Communications Corp. (acq 7-1-98; $1.65 million with co-located FM). Population served: 500,000 Natl. Network: Motor Racing Net, Salem Radio Network, . Rgnl rep: Rgnl Reps Format: Southern Gospel. News: 3 hrs wkly. Target aud: 18-54. Spec prog: Gospel 2 hrs, relg 8 hrs wkly. ◆George E. DeVault Jr., pres; Jim Mabe, opns dir, opns mgr, disc jockey; Anita Dixon, sls dir; N. David Widener, gen mgr & natl sls mgr; Lynn Rutledge, progmg dir, disc jockey; Duane Nelson, news dir; Evelyn Payne, traf mgr; Henry Thomas, disc jockey.

WMEV-FM— June 21, 1961: 93.9 mhz; 100 kw. 1,480 ft TL: N36 54 08 W81 32 33. Stereo. Hrs open: 1041 Radio Hill Rd., 24354. Phone: (276) 783-3151. Fax: (276) 783-3152.E-mail: fm94@smyth.net Licensee: Holston Valley Broadcasting Corp. Natl. Network: CNN Radio, . Wire Svc: AP Format: Hot country. Target aud: Persons 25-54. Spec prog: Nascar. ◆N. David Widener, exec VP; Anita Dixon, sls VP; Lyle Musser, chief of engrg; Everly Payne, traf mgr; Henry Thomas, disc jockey.

WOLD-FM— Mar 14, 1968: 102.5 mhz; 440 w. Ant 1,204 ft TL: N36 54 10 W81 32 27. Stereo. Hrs open: 24 Box 31, 24354. Phone: (276) 783-7100.E-mail: wold@netva.com Web Site:www.netva.com Licensee: T.E.C. 2 Broadcasting Inc. (acq 4-10-2008; $500,000). Population served: 185,000 Natl. Network: CNN Radio, . Format: Adult contemp. ◆Robert S. Dix, gen mgr; Patricia Ann Dix, stn mgr, opns mgr.

*WVTR(FM)— Nov 22, 1991: 91.9 mhz; 4.5 kw. 1,489 ft TL: N36 44 52 W81 18 15. Hrs open:
Rebroadcasts WVTF(FM) Roanoke 100%.
c/o WVTF, 3520 Kingsbury Ln., Roanoke, 24014. Phone: (540) 989-8900. Fax:(540) 776-2727.E-mail: info@wvtf.org Web Site:www.wvtf.org Licensee: Virginia Tech Foundation Inc. Natl. Network: NPR, . Format: Class, jazz. ◆Glenn Gleixner, gen mgr, stn mgr; Karen Dillon, dev dir.

WZVA(FM)— Sept 2, 1996: 103.5 mhz; 1.35 kw. -36 ft TL: N36 52 07 W81 26 07. Hrs open: 24 Box 85, 24354. Phone: (276) 783-4042. Fax: (276) 783-2120.E-mail: staff@z-103.com Web Site:www.z-103.com

Licensee: T.E.C.O. Broadcasting Inc. (acq 11-7-97; $125,000). Population served: 55,000 Format: CHR, adult contemp. Target aud: 18-49; women & men. ◆Tom Copenhaver, CEO; Blake Frazier, stn mgr.

Martinsville

WHEE(AM)— Aug 4, 1954: 1370 khz; 5 kw-D, 500 w-N. TL: N36 41 09 W79 54 14. Hrs open: Drawer 3551, 24112. Secondary address: 40 Franklin St. 24115. Phone: (276) 632-9811. Phone: (276) 632-5433. Fax: (276) 632-4500. Licensee: Martinsville Media Inc. (acq 1-5-98; $200,000 for stock). Population served: 125,000 Natl. Network: CBS, . Wilkinson, Barker, Knauer & Quinn. Format: Talk, Americana. Target aud: 17-60; agriculture & mfg area audience. ◆Bill Wyatt, pres, gen mgr, gen sls mgr, progmg dir, traf mgr, disc jockey; T.L. Walker, chief of engrg.

WMVA(AM)— December 1941: 1450 khz; 1 kw-U. TL: N36 42 00 W79 51 07. Hrs open: Box 3551, 24112-0545. Phone: (276) 632-2152. Fax: (276) 632-4500.E-mail: 93.5@waxm.com Web Site:www.martinsvillemedia.com Licensee: Martinsville Media Inc. Format: Talk. ◆Bill Wyatt, pres & gen mgr.

*WPIM(FM)— 1997: 90.5 mhz; 4 kw. Ant 387 ft TL: N36 42 16 W79 50 05. Hrs open: Box 929, Blacksburg, 24063. Phone: (540) 552-8073. Fax: (540) 951-5282.E-mail: mail@spiritfm.com Web Site:www.spiritfm.com Licensee: Positive Alternative Radio Inc. Group owner: Baker Family Stations (Positive Radio Group) Booth, Freret, Imlay & Tepper. Format: Christian adult contemp. ◆Vernon H. Baker, CEO & chmn; Edward A. Baker, pres, VP; Barry Armstrong, gen mgr, stn mgr.

WROV-FM— January 1950: 96.3 mhz; 13.8 kw. 2,076 ft TL: N36 43 00 W79 51 07. Stereo. Hrs open: 3807 Brandon Ave., Suite 2350, Roanoke, 24018. Phone: (540) 725-1220. Fax: (540) 725-1245. Web Site:www.wrov.cc Licensee: Capstar TX L.P. Group owner: Clear Channel Communications Inc. (acq 8-30-00; grpsl). Population served: 1,000,000 Natl. Rep: D & R Radio,. Format: AOR. Target aud: 18-49; general. ◆Dave Carwile, gen mgr; Tammy Cazad, gen sls mgr; Jay Prayter, progmg dir; Ed Kilbane, news dir; Jeff Parker, chief of engrg.

Mechanicsville

WCDX(FM)— Oct 7, 1985: 92.1 mhz; 4.5 kw. Ant 770 ft TL: N37 42 50 W77 30 23. Stereo. Hrs open: 2809 Emerywood Pkwy., Suite 300, Richmond, 23294. Phone: (804) 672-9299. Fax: (804) 672-9316. Web Site:www.power921jamz.com Licensee: Radio One Licenses LLC. Group owner: Radio One Inc. (acq 11-8-2001; grpsl). Natl. Rep: Eastman Radio,. Fletcher, Heald & Hildreth. Format: Urban contemp, HipHop. Target aud: Ages 18-44. ◆Linda Forem, VP, gen mgr; Al Payne, opns mgr; Brian Robertson, gen sls mgr; Bobby Walden, natl sls mgr; Dawna Covington, mktg dir, prom dir, prom mgr; Reggie Baker, progmg dir & mus dir; Clovia Lawrence, pub affrs dir; Chris Lawless, chief of engrg.

Midlothian

WOOK(AM)—Not on air, target date: unknown: 1410 khz; 350 w-U, DA-2. TL: N37 30 38 W77 39 50. Hrs open: 7993 Pelham Rd., Greenville, SC, 29615. Phone: (864) 918-4740. Licensee: Richmond 1410 LLC (acq 7-9-2009; $10,000 for CP). ◆J.R. McClure, gen mgr.

WWLB(FM)— Nov 22, 1971: 98.9 mhz; 4.8 kw. Ant 746 ft TL: N37 36 52 W77 30 56. Stereo. Hrs open: 5 AM-midnight 300 Arboretum Pl Suite 590, Richmond, 23236. Phone: (804) 327-9902. Fax: (804) 327-9911.E-mail: info@989liberty.com Web Site:www.989liberty.com Licensee: MLB-Richmond IV LLC. Group owner: The MainQuad Group (acq 12-13-2005; grpsl). Population served: 185,000 Format: Var. ◆Sandy Jimerson, gen sls mgr.

Moneta

WSLK(AM)— November 1991: 880 khz; 900 w-D. TL: N37 10 00 W70 37 50. Hrs open: 12 1848 Clay St. S.E., Roanoke, 24013. Phone: (540) 343-7109. Fax: (540) 343-2306. Web Site:www.wslk880.com Licensee: Smile Broadcasting LLC (group owner; (acq 4-7-2008; $125,000). Population served: 211,000 Format: Oldies. Target aud: 35 plus; mostly middle aged, affluent, cosmopolitan. ◆Frank Ernandes, pres; Ben Peyton, sls dir, progmg dir; Dale Cook, chief of engrg; Sharron Jeffrey, stn mgr & traf mgr; Martin Jeffrey, sls.

Monterey

*WVLS(FM)— September 1995: 89.7 mhz; 200 w. 1,460 ft TL: N38 20 39 W79 35 47. Stereo. Hrs open: 6 AM-10 PM
Rebroadcasts WVMR(AM) Frost, WV 60%.
R.R. 1 Box 139, Dunmore, WV, 24934. Phone: (304) 799-6004. Fax: (304) 799-7444.E-mail: wvls@htcnet.net Web Site:www.alleghenymountainradio.org Licensee: Pocahontas Communications Cooperative Corp. Population served: 2,500 Format: Var. Target aud: General. ◆Cheryl Kinderman, gen mgr; Chuck Niday, chief of engrg.

Mount Jackson

WSIG(FM)— October 1988: 96.9 mhz; 7 kw. Ant 558 ft TL: N38 36 31 W78 54 07. Hrs open: 24 1866 E. Market St., Suite 325, Harrisonburg, 22801. Phone: (540) 432-1063. Fax: (540) 433-9267.E-mail: wsig@shentel.net Licensee: Vox Communications Group LLC. (group owner; (acq 8-31-2005; $2 million). Population served: 70,000 Natl. Network: AP Radio, . Southmayd & Miller. Format: Classic country. Spec prog: Bluegrass 6 hrs, gospel 4 hrs wkly. ◆Tom Manley, gen mgr.

WSVG(AM)— Apr 23, 1954: 790 khz; 1 kw-D, 40 w-N. TL: N38 46 15 W78 37 17. Hrs open: Sunrise-sunset Box 425, 22842. Phone: (540) 477-4443. Fax: (540) 477-4407.E-mail: wsvg@chentil.net Licensee: Hometown Broadcasting of Mt. Jackson LLC (acq 2-25-2005). Population served: 35,000 Rgnl. Network: Agri-Net. Format: Talk. ◆Alan Arehart, gen mgr.

Narrows

WZFM(FM)— 1992: 101.3 mhz; 210 w. Ant 1,200 ft TL: N37 17 54 W80 48 36. Hrs open: Box 889, Blacksburg, 24063. Secondary address: 145 Jackson St., Blacksburg 24063. Phone: (540) 951-9791. Fax: (540) 961-2021. Licensee: WZFM LLC. (acq 5-19-2006; $600,000). Natl. Network: ABC, . Format: Oldies. Target aud: 30+. ◆Amy Burnette, gen mgr.

Narrows-Pearisburg

WNRV(AM)— August 1953: 990 khz; 5 kw-D, 10 w-N. TL: N37 20 39 W80 46 36. Hrs open: 24
Rebroadcast WWWR(AM) Roanoke 90%.
1848 Clay St. S.E., Roanoke, 24013. Phone: (540) 343-7109. Fax: (540) 343-2306. Licensee: Perception Media Group Inc. (group owner; (acq 6-2-99). Population served: 41,000 Format: Bluegrass. ◆Ben Peyton, pres.

Nassawadox

*WJCN(FM)— 2005: 90.1 mhz; 450 w vert. Ant 199 ft TL: N37 33 27 W75 49 44. Hrs open: 22226 Timberlake Rd., Lynchburg, 24502. Phone: (434) 237-9798. Fax: (434) 237-1025.E-mail: office@spiritfm.com Web Site:www.spiritfm.com Licensee: Positive Alternative Radio Inc. (group owner). (acq 12-30-2005; grpsl). Booth, Freret, Imlay & Tepper. Format: Contemp Christian. ◆Barry Armstrong, gen mgr.

New Market

WLTK(FM)—Licensed to New Market. See Broadway-Timberville

Newport News

WCMS(AM)— October 1928: 1310 khz; 5 kw-U, DA-N. TL: N36 57 47 W76 24 42. Hrs open: 24 Prog sep from FM 5589 Greenwich Rd., Virginia Beach, 23462. Phone: (757) 671-1000. Fax: (757) 671-1010.E-mail: info@espnradio.com Web Site:www.espnradio.com Licensee: MHR License LLC Format: Sports talk. Target aud: General. ◆Anthony Mercurio, mktg dir & progmg dir.

WGH-FM— November 1948: 97.3 mhz; 74 kw. 415 ft TL: N36 57 47 W76 24 42. Stereo. Hrs open: 5589 Greenwich Rd., Virginia Beach, 23462. Phone: (757) 671-1000. Fax: (757) 671-1010.E-mail: info@eagle97.com Web Site:www.eagle97.com Licensee: MHR License LLC Group owner: Barnstable Broadcasting Inc. (acq 3-24-2005; grpsl). Format: Country. Target aud: Adults 25-54. ◆Eric Mastel, pres, prom mgr; Vonneva Carter, gen mgr; John Shomby, progmg dir; Paul Campbell, chief of engrg.

WNVZ(FM)—See Norfolk

WTJZ(AM)— November 1947: 1270 khz; 1.5 kw-D, 900 w-N, DA-N. TL: N37 01 52 W76 22 00. Hrs open: 24 553 Michigan, Hampton, 23669. Phone: (757) 723-1270.E-mail: wtjz1270@aol.com Licensee: Chesapeake-Portsmouth Broadcasting Corp. (acq 1999; $380,000). Population served: 8,000 Format: Urban Gospel. ♦Martin Culpepper, gen mgr.

Norfolk

WCMS(AM)—See Newport News

WGH-FM—See Newport News

WGPL(AM)—See Portsmouth

***WHRO-FM**— 1990: 90.3 mhz; 23 kw. 630 ft TL: N36 48 32 W76 30 13. Stereo. Hrs open: 20 5200 Hampton Blvd., 23508. Phone: (757) 889-9400. Fax: (757) 489-0007.E-mail: info@whro.org Web Site:www.whro.org Licensee: Hampton Roads Educational Telecommunications Association Inc. Natl. Network: NPR, PRI, . Format: Class, fine arts. Target aud: 35 plus; well-educated, exec leaders. ♦Bert Schmidt, CEO, pres; Carol Vollbrecht, CFO; John Heimerl, VP, gen mgr; Heather Fleming Mazzoni, chief of opns, progmg dir; Virginia Thumm, dev dir. Co-owned TV: *WHRO-TV affil.

***WHRV(FM)**— 1974: 89.5 mhz; 8.8 kw. Ant 1,148 ft TL: N36 48 31 W76 30 13. Stereo. Hrs open: 24 5200 Hampton Blvd., 23508. Phone: (757) 889-9400. Fax: (757) 489-0007. Web Site:www.whro.org Licensee: Hampton Roads Educational Telecommunications Association, Inc. (acq 2-86). Population served: 1,600,000 Natl. Network: NPR, PRI, . Dow Lohnes. Wire Svc: AP Format: News/talk, jazz, alternative. News staff: one; News: 105 hrs wkly. Target aud: 35 plus. Spec prog: Progsv 14 hrs, folk 7 hrs wkly. ♦Regina Brayboy, COO; Carol Volbrecht, CFO; John Heimerl, gen mgr; Heather Mazzon, chief of opns, progmg mgr; Virginia Thumm, dev VP & dev dir. Co-owned TV: *WHRO-TV affil.

WJOI(AM)— 1949: 1230 khz; 1 kw-U. TL: N36 50 03 W76 16 12. Hrs open: 870 Greenbriar Cir., Suite 399, Chesapeake, 23320. Phone: (757) 366-9900. Fax: (757) 366-0022. Licensee: Tidewater Communications LLC. Group owner: Saga Communications Inc. (acq 9-15-86). Population served: 1,400,000 Natl. Rep: McGavren Guild,. Format: Adult Standards. ♦Dave Paulus, pres, VP, gen mgr; Don Crowder, chief of engrg.

WKUS(FM)—Licensed to Norfolk. See Portsmouth

WNIS(AM)— Sept 21, 1923: 790 khz; 5 kw-U, DA-1. TL: N37 04 23 W76 17 28. Stereo. Hrs open: 24 500 Dominion Tower, 999 Waterside Dr., 23510. Phone: (757) 640-8500. Fax: (757) 640-8552.E-mail: wnis@wnis.com Web Site:www.WNIS.com Licensee: Sinclair Communications Inc. (group owner). Population served: 1,400,000 Natl. Network: ABC, Westwood One, . Rgnl. Network: Va. News Net. Natl. Rep: McGavren Guild, Interep,. Va. News Net. Wire Svc: AP Format: News/talk. Target aud: 25-54. ♦Bob Sinclair, CEO, gen mgr; Lisa Sinclair, stn mgr; Dave Morgan, opns mgr; Juli Zobel, gen sls mgr; Ginger Power, natl sls mgr; Donna Agresto, prom dir; Jay West, progmg dir.

WNOR(FM)— 1961: 98.7 mhz; 46 kw. Ant 518 ft TL: N36 50 04 W76 16 11. Stereo. Hrs open: 870 Greenbriar Cir., Suite 399, Chesapeake, 23320. Phone: (757) 366-9900. Fax: (757) 366-0022.E-mail: info@fm99.com Web Site:www.fm99.com Licensee: Tidewater Communications LLC. Smithwick & Belendiuk. Format: Rock/AOR. ♦Harvey Najen, progmg dir.

***WNSB(FM)**— Mar 22, 1980: 91.1 mhz; 8.1 kw. 422 ft TL: N36 46 32 W76 23 11. (CP: 18 kw, ant 299 ft. TL: N36 45 23 W76 23 06). Stereo. Hrs open: 700 Park Ave., Suite 129, 23504-8015. Phone: (757) 823-9672. Fax: (757) 823-2385.E-mail: wnsb@nsu.edu Web Site:www.nsu.edu/wnsb/ Licensee: Norfolk State University Board of Visitors. Population served: 38,000 Natl. Network: NPR, . Format: Urban Contemp. Target aud: 18-24. ♦Wanda Brockington, gen mgr; Edward Turner, stn mgr.

WNVZ(FM)— July 1967: 104.5 mhz; 50 kw. 480 ft TL: N37 02 20 W76 18 30. Stereo. Hrs open: 236 Clearfield Ave., Suite 206, Virginia Beach, 23462. Phone: (757) 497-2000. Fax: (757) 497-7158.E-mail: tias@entercom.com Web Site:www.z104.com Licensee: Entercom Norfolk License LLC. Group owner: Entercom Communications Corp. (acq 12-13-99; grpsl). Population served: 983,800 Natl. Rep: D & R Radio,. Format: CHR. News staff: News progmg one hr wkly Target aud: 18-34; females.David J. Field, CEO, pres; Steve Fisher, CFO, exec VP; Steve Godofsky, VP; Jeff Brown, gen mgr; Don London, opns mgr; Hope Angelone, gen sls mgr; Cheri Pridgen, natl sls mgr; Chris Wilson, prom dir; Tias Schuster, progmg dir; Ernie Warinner, mus dir, chief of engrg; Tricia Harris, pub affrs dir, disc jockey; Cherrese Young, traf mgr; Nick Taylor, disc jockey

WOWI(FM)— June 1948: 102.9 mhz; 50 kw. 500 ft TL: N36 45 23 W76 23 06. Stereo. Hrs open: 1003 Norfolk Sq., 23502. Phone: (757) 466-0009. Fax: (757) 466-7043. Web Site:www.103jamz.com Licensee: CC Licenses LLC. Group owner: Clear Channel Communications Inc. (acq 1996; grpsl). Population served: 307,951 Natl. Rep: McGavren Guild,. Format: Urban contemp. Target aud: 18-34. ♦Lowery Mays, CEO, chmn, pres; Reggie Jordan, VP, gen mgr; Travis Dylan, opns mgr; Terry Ratliff, sls dir; Michael Mendelson, gen sls mgr; Toni Bailey Jones, prom mgr; D.J. Law, progmg dir, progmg mgr; D.J. Fountz, mus dir; Pavar Snipe, news dir; Doc Christian, pub affrs dir; Michael Bov-e, chief of engrg.

WPCE(AM)—See Portsmouth

WRJR(AM)—See Portsmouth

WTAR(AM)— September 1952: 850 khz; 50 kw-D, 25 kw-N, DA-2. TL: N36 51 39 W76 21 13. Hrs open: 24 500 Dominion Tower, 999 Waterside Dr., 23510. Phone: (757) 640-8500. Fax: (757) 640-8552. Web Site:www.wtar.com Licensee: Sinclair Communications Inc. (group owner; (acq 9-87; $725,000;9-21-87). Population served: 1,400,000 Natl. Rep: McGavren Guild, Interep,. Format: Sports. Target aud: 25-54. ♦Bob Sinclair, CEO, gen mgr; Lisa Sinclair, gen mgr & stn mgr; Juli Zobel, gen sls mgr; Ginger Power, natl sls mgr; Donna Agresto, prom dir; Jay West, progmg dir.

WTJZ(AM)—See Newport News

WVAB(AM)—(Virginia Beach, Dec 10, 1954: 1550 khz; 5 kw-D, 249 w-N. TL: N36 49 20 W76 05 30. Hrs open:
Simulcasts WWIP (FM) Cheriton 100%.
2202 Jolliss Rd, Chesapeake, 23321. Phone: (757) 488-1010. Fax: (757) 488-7761. Licensee: Ronald W. Cowan Jr. Natl. Network: CNN Radio, . Format: Christian, praise, worship. ♦Henry Hoot, gen mgr.

WVBW(FM)—See Suffolk

WVHT(FM)— Oct 1, 1962: 100.5 mhz; 50 kw. Ant 500 ft TL: N36 49 44 W76 12 26. Stereo. Hrs open: 24 5589 Greenwich Rd., Suite 200, Virginia Beach, 23462. Phone: (757) 671-1000. Fax: (757) 671-1010.E-mail: info@maxfm.fm Web Site:www.hot1005.com Licensee: MHR License LLC. (acq 3-24-2005; grpsl). Natl. Rep: Christal,. Format: Top-40. ♦Eric Martel, pres; Vonneva Carter, gen mgr.

WVKL(FM)— Sept 21, 1961: 95.7 mhz; 40 kw. Ant 881 ft TL: N36 48 56 W76 28 00. Stereo. Hrs open: 236 Clearfield Ave., Suite 206, Virginia Beach, 23462. Phone: (757) 497-2000. Fax: (757) 456-5458.E-mail: info@957rnb.com Web Site:www.957rnb.com Licensee: Entercom Norfolk License LLC. Group owner: Entercom Communications Corp. (acq 12-13-99; grpsl). Population served: 1,200,000 Format: Rhythm and blues. ♦David J. Field, CEO, pres; Steve Fisher, CFO, exec VP; Steve Godofsky, VP; Jeff Brown, gen mgr; Don London, opns mgr, progmg dir; Hope Angelone, gen sls mgr; Karen Parker-Chesson, news dir; Cherrese Young, traf mgr.

WVXX(AM)— July 1, 1954: 1050 khz; 5 kw-D, 358 w-N, DA-2. TL: N36 49 44 W76 12 26. Hrs open: Norfolk Plaza Hotel, 700 Monticello Ave., Suite 301, 23510. Phone: (757) 627-9899. Fax: (757) 627-0123. Web Site:www.wvxxselecta1050.com Licensee: Davidson Media Station WVXX Licensee LLC. Group owner: Barnstable Broadcasting Inc. (acq 2-10-2005; $975,000). Population served: 1,210,900 Format: Sp contemp. Target aud: 18-54; Hispanic adults. ♦Andy Hindlin, pres & gen mgr.

WWDE-FM—See Hampton

WXTG(AM)—See Hampton

WYFI(FM)— Oct 2, 1971: 99.7 mhz; 50 kw. 456 ft TL: N36 49 41 W76 15 05. Stereo. Hrs open: 11530 Carmel Commons Blvd., Charlotte, NC, 28226. Phone: (704) 523-5555. Fax: (704) 522-1967.E-mail: bbn@bbnradio.org Web Site:www.bbnradio.org Licensee: Bible Broadcasting Network Inc. (group owner; acq 12-24-70). Format: Relg. ♦Lowell Davey, pres; Dennis Gast, gen mgr.

WYRM(AM)— Apr 6, 1976: 1110 khz; 50 kw-D, DA. TL: N36 56 34 W76 31 56. Hrs open: day 700 Monticello Ave., Suite 305, 23510. Phone: (757) 622-9256. Fax: (757) 622-9253.E-mail: wyrm1110@hotmail.com Web Site:www.wyrmradio.com Licensee: Word Broadcasting Network Inc. (group owner; acq 7-29-2003; $1.25 million with WYMM(AM) Jacksonville, FL). Population served: 1,379,700 Format: Relg teaching. ♦Larry Cobb, gen mgr.

Norton

WNVA(AM)— March 1946: 1350 khz; 5 kw-D. TL: N36 57 58 W82 35 17. Hrs open: Sunrise-sunset Box 500, 24273. Phone: (276) 328-2244. Fax: (276) 328-0024.E-mail: wnva@mounet.com Licensee: Radio-Wise Inc. Population served: 60,000 Rgnl. Network: Rgnl reps. Rgnl rep: Regnl Reps Format: Adult contemp. News: 2 hrs wkly. Target aud: 25-65; adults & young adults. Spec prog: Gospel 15 hrs, relg 2 hrs wkly. ♦Willliam G. Stallard, VP; William G. Stallard, gen mgr; Deborah Baker, opns dir, sls dir; Gerald Hibbitts, chief of engrg.

WNVA-FM— July 25, 1969: 106.3 mhz; 1.65 kw. 613 ft TL: N36 57 58 W82 35 17. Stereo. Hrs open: 24 Prog sep from AM Box 500, 24273. Phone: (276) 328-2244. Fax: (276) 328-0024. Licensee: Radio-Wise Inc. Population served: 45,000 Natl. Network: Jones Radio Networks, . Rgnl rep: Regnl Reps Format: CHR country. News: 10 hrs wkly. Target aud: 18-45; young adults. ♦Debbie Baker, sls dir.

Onley-Onancock

WESR(AM)— Jan 23, 1958: 1330 khz; 5 kw-D, 51 w-N. TL: N37 43 02 W75 41 01. Hrs open: Box 100, Tasley, 23441. Secondary address: 22479 Front St., Accomac 23301. Phone: (757) 787-3852. Fax: (757) 787-3819. Web Site:www.west.net Licensee: Eastern Shore Radio Inc. (acq 1-23-97; $148,300 for stock with co-located FM). Population served: 6,000 Natl. Network: ABC, . Natl. Rep: Dome,. Format: Country classics, talk. ♦Charles Russell, gen mgr; Bill LeCato, progmg dir.

WESR-FM— 1968: 103.3 mhz; 50 kw. 320 ft TL: N37 43 02 W75 41 01. Stereo. Hrs open: Prog sep from AM Box 100, Tasley, 23441. Secondary address: 22479 Front St. 23301. Phone: (757) 787-3852. Fax: (757) 787- 3819. Web Site:www.wesr.net Population served: 46,000 Natl. Network: ABC, . Format: Adult contemp.

Orange

WVCV(AM)— Sept 10, 1949: 1340 khz; 1 kw-U. TL: N38 15 14 W78 07 15. Hrs open:
Simulcasts WCVA (AM) Culpeper 100%.
Box 271, 22960. Secondary address: 207 Spicers Mill Rd. 22960. Phone: (540) 672-1000. Fax: (540) 672-0282.E-mail: advertising@wjmafm.com Web Site:www.wjmafm.com Licensee: Piedmont Communications Inc. (group owner; acq 2-18-93; $30,000 with co-located FM;3-8-93). Population served: 162,400 Natl. Network: Westwood One, ABC, . Format: Adult standards. News staff: one. Target aud: 45 plus. Spec prog: Gospel 2 hrs, relg one hr, news 18 hrs wkly. ♦John Schick, pres & gen mgr.

Pamplin City

***WEQP(FM)**—Not on air, target date: unknown: 90.5 mhz; 1.8 kw. Ant 364 ft TL: N37 15 11 W78 40 45. Hrs open: 557 Wedgewood Way, Naples, FL, 34119. Phone: (434) 239-6388. Fax: (434) 239-6368. Licensee: Airwaves for Jesus Inc. ♦Art Ramos, pres.

Pearisburg

WNRV(AM)—See Narrows-Pearisburg

Pennington Gap

WSWV(AM)— June 1, 1959: 1570 khz; 2.3 kw-D, 191 w-N. TL: N36 44 02 W83 02 34. Hrs open: 24 Box 630, 203 W. Morgan Ave., 24277. Phone: (276) 546-2520. Fax: (276) 546-1356.E-mail: wswv@optidynamic.com Web Site:www.wswv.net Licensee: B C Broadcasting Co. Inc. (acq 6-6-2005; $105,000 with co-located FM). Population served: 26,000 Natl. Network: AP Network News, . Natl. Rep: Rgnl Reps,. Format: Southern gospel. Target aud: 24-54; young, working adults. ♦Robert Wright, gen mgr; Mike Cook, chief of engrg.

WSWV-FM— 1973: 105.5 mhz; 3.5 kw. 276 ft TL: N36 44 02 W83 02 34. Stereo. Hrs open: 24 Box 630, 203 W. Morgan Ave., 24277. Phone: (276) 546-2520. Fax: (276) 546-1356. Web Site:www.wswv.net Population served: 26,000 Format: Country. ♦Robert Wright, gen mgr.

Petersburg

WARV-FM— December 1992: 100.3 mhz; 4.7 kw. 328 ft TL: N37 08 57 W77 24 54. Hrs open:
Simulcast with WBBT-FM Powhatan 100%.
300 Arboretum Pl., Suite 590, Richmond, 23236. Phone: (804) 327-9902. Fax: (804) 327-9911.E-mail: info@1073bbt.com Web Site:www.1073bbt.com Licensee: MLB-Richmond IV LLC. (acq 12-13-2006;

grpsl). Format: Oldies 60's, 70's. ♦John Kolesa, gen sls mgr; Michelle Prosser, prom mgr; Mike Murphy, progmg dir, pub affrs dir; Rob Astleford, chief of engrg.

WKJM(FM)— Oct 1, 1966: 99.3 mhz; 6 kw. Ant 328 ft TL: N37 14 01 W77 22 36. Stereo. Hrs open: Prog sep from AM 2809 Emerywood Pkwy., Suite 300, Richmond, 23294. Phone: (804) 672-9299. Fax: (804) 672-9314.E-mail: info@yestokiss.com Web Site:www.yestokiss.com Population served: 700,000 Format: Urban adult contemp. Target aud: 25-54; Black adults. ♦Jeff Anderson, opns mgr; Dennis M. Gettis, gen sls mgr; Dawna Covington, mktg dir.

WTPS(AM)— May 7, 1945: 1240 khz; 1 kw-U. TL: N37 14 01 W77 22 36. Hrs open: 24 2809 Emerywood Pkwy., Suite 300, Richmond, 23294. Phone: (804) 672-9299. Fax: (804) 672-9314.E-mail: info@newstalk1240wtps.com Web Site:www.newstalk1240WTPS.com Licensee: Radio One Licenses LLC. Group owner: Radio One Inc. (acq 7-26-99; grpsl). Population served: 36,103 Natl. Rep: McGavren Guild,. Format: News/talk. Target aud: 25-54. ♦Linda Forem, gen mgr.

***WVST-FM**— July 12, 1987: 91.3 mhz; 2.2 kw vert. Ant 167 ft TL: N37 14 15 W77 24 55. Stereo. Hrs open: 19 Box 9067, 130 Harris Hall, Virginia State Univ., 23806. Phone: (804) 524-5000. Fax: (804) 524-5826. Web Site:www.vsu.edu/wvst Licensee: Virginia State University. Population served: 60,000,000 Va. News Net. Format: Div, jazz. Target aud: 25 plus; general. Spec prog: Gospel 13 hrs wkly. ♦Dr. Moadab, gen mgr; Yolie Thomas, stn mgr & opns mgr; Hugh Mannah, chief of opns.

Poquoson

WUSH(FM)— April 2001: 106.1 mhz; 2.6 kw. Ant 502 ft TL: N37 04 24 W76 17 33. Stereo. Hrs open: 24 500 Dominion Tower, 999 Waterside Dr., Norfolk, 23510. Phone: (757) 640-8500. Fax: (757) 640-8552. Web Site:www.us1061.com Licensee: Commonwealth Broadcasting L.L.C. (acq 8-24-2001; $1.883 million for CP). Population served: 1,400,000 Natl. Rep: McGavren Guild, Interep,. Format: Country. ♦Lisa Sinclair, gen mgr; Jeanett Xenakis, gen sls mgr; Ginger Power, natl sls mgr; Donna Agresto, prom dir; Jay Michaels, progmg dir.

Portsmouth

WGPL(AM)— January 1942: 1350 khz; 5 kw-U, DA-2. TL: N36 53 00 W76 22 22. Hrs open: 24 645 Church St., Suite 400, Norfolk, 23501. Phone: (757) 622-4600. Fax: (757) 624-6515.E-mail: willisbroadcasting@yahoo.com Web Site:www.wgpl1350.com Licensee: Christian Broadcasting of Norfolk Inc. Group owner: Willis Broadcasting Corp. Population served: 1,309,500 Format: Gospel. News staff: 2; News: 6 hrs wkly. Target aud: W25-54. ♦Hortense Willis, pres; Walter Allen Brickhouse, gen mgr; Ju Joyner, prom dir; Julian Joyner, progmg dir; Terry Love, chief of engrg.

WHKT(AM)— 1999: 1650 khz; 10 kw-D, 1 kw-N. TL: N36 48 10 W76 16 58. Hrs open: 5041 Corporate Woods Dr., Ste 165, Virginia Beach, 23462. Phone: (757) 519-9171. Fax: (757) 519-9147. Web Site:www.radiodisney.com Licensee: Radio Disney Group LLC. Group owner: ABC Inc. (acq 6-5-2002; $1.08 million with WRJR(AM) Portsmouth). Format: Radio Disney. ♦Monica Ward, opns mgr, gen sls mgr; Monica Rae Ward, mktg mgr, prom mgr, pub affrs dir; Tom Winslow, chief of engrg.

WKUS(FM)—(Norfolk, Aug 3, 1962: 105.3 mhz; 50 kw. 499 ft TL: N36 48 43 W76 27 49. Stereo. Hrs open: Clear Channel Communications, Inc., 1003 Norfolk Sq., Norfolk, 23502-4948. Phone: (757) 466-0009. Fax: (757) 466-4043.E-mail: info@1053kiss.com Web Site:www.1053kiss.com Licensee: CC Licenses LLC. Group owner: Clear Channel Communications Inc. (acq 1996; grpsl). Natl. Rep: Roslin,. Format: Adult urban. Target aud: 25-54. ♦Reggie Jordan, gen mgr; Joi Jamison, prom mgr, progmg dir.

WPCE(AM)— Jan 11, 1964: 1400 khz; 1 kw-U. TL: N36 49 45 W76 19 23. Hrs open: 24 645 Church St., Suite 400, Norfolk, 23501. Phone: (757) 622-4600. Fax: (757) 624-6515.E-mail: willisbroadcasting@yahoo.com Web Site:www.wpce1400.com Licensee: Christian Broadcasting of Portsmouth Inc. (group owner; (acq 3-4-92; grpsl; 3-23-92). Population served: 307,951 Format: Gospel. Target aud: W 35+. Spec prog: Block Programming. ♦Hortense Willis, pres; Walter Allen Brickhouse, gen mgr; L.E. Willis II, opns mgr; Julian Joyner, sls dir; Shaye Southall, progmg dir; Christine Willis, mus dir; Terry Love, chief of engrg.

WRJR(AM)— Jan 9, 1972: 1010 khz; 5 kw-D, 449 w-N, DA-2. TL: N36 49 20 W76 26 38. Hrs open: 2202 Jolliff Rd., Chesapeake, 23321. Phone: (757) 488-1010. Fax: (757) 488-7761.E-mail: info@wwip.org Web Site:www.wpmhradio.net Licensee: Radio Disney Group LLC. Group owner: ABC Inc. (acq 6-5-2002; $1.08 million with WHKT(AM) Portsmouth). Population served: 75,000 Format: Christian Teaching. ♦Henry W. Hoot, gen mgr.

Pound

WDXC(FM)— 1990: 102.3 mhz; 280 w. 992 ft TL: N37 09 07 W82 37 57. (CP: 35 kw, ant 1,315 ft.). Stereo. Hrs open: 24 12548 Orby Cantrell Hwy., 24279. Phone: (276) 796-5411. Fax: (276) 796-5412.E-mail: wdxc102fm@windstream.net Web Site:www.wdxcfm.com Licensee: WDXC Radio Inc. (acq 6-90; 6-4-90). Population served: 300,000 Format: Hot New Country. Target aud: General. ♦Howard Cornett, pres, gen mgr, sls VP; Jackie Cornett, exec VP; M.K. Combs, opns mgr.

Powhatan

WBBT-FM— 1999: 107.3 mhz; 1.4 kw. Ant 679 ft TL: N37 30 15 W77 42 14. Hrs open: 300 Arboretum Pl., Suite 590, Ricmond, 23236. Phone: (804) 327-9902. Fax: (804) 327-9911.E-mail: info@1073bbt.com Web Site:www.1073bbt.com Licensee: MLB-Richmond IV LLC. Group owner: The MainQuad Group (acq 12-13-2005; grpsl). Format: Oldies, 60's, 70's. ♦John Kolesa, gen sls mgr; Michelle Prosser, prom mgr; Mike Murphy, progmg dir, pub affrs dir; Rob Astleford, chief of engrg.

Pulaski

WPSK-FM— Dec 1, 1967: 107.1 mhz; 25 kw. 1,207 ft TL: N37 01 28 W80 44 47. Stereo. Hrs open: 24 7080 Lee Hwy., Radford, 24141. Phone: (540) 633-5330. Fax: (540) 633-2998. Web Site:www.wpsk107.com Licensee: Cumulus Licensing LLC. Group owner: Cumulus Media Inc. (acq 3-31-2004; grpsl). Population served: 163,000 Format: Country. News staff: one; News: 10 hrs wkly. Target aud: 25-54. ♦Sarah Leftwich, gen mgr; Scott Stevens, opns mgr & progmg dir; Sam Parks, chief of engrg.

Quantico

WPWC(AM)—See Dumfries-Triangle

WURA(AM)—Not on air, target date: unknown: 920 khz; 2 kw-D, 970 w-N, DA-2. TL: N38 34 05 W77 20 20. Hrs open: 1730 Rhode Island Ave. N.W., Suite 200, Washington, DC, 20036. Phone: (202) 728-0400. Fax: (202) 728-0354. Licensee: Prince William Broadcasting L.L.C. ♦Matthew H. McCormick, gen mgr.

Radford

WRAD(AM)— 1950: 1460 khz; 5 kw-D, 500 w-N, DA-N. TL: N37 08 35 W80 34 38. Stereo. Hrs open: 5 AM-11 PM Box 3788, 24143. Secondary address: 7080 Lee Hwy. 24141. Phone: (540) 633-5330. Fax: (540) 633-6300. Licensee: Cumulus Licensing LLC. Group owner: Cumulus Media Inc. (acq 3-31-2004; grpsl). Population served: 141,000 Format: Classic hits of the 60s, 70s & 80s, sports. Target aud: 25 plus. ♦Ron Walton, gen mgr; Scott Stevens, gen sls mgr; David Dalesky, chief of engrg.

***WVRU(FM)**— Oct 9, 1978: 89.9 mhz; 500 w. 15 ft TL: N37 08 26 W80 33 11. Stereo. Hrs open: 24 Box 6973, 24142. Secondary address: 236 Porterfield 24142. Phone: (540) 831-5171. Phone: (540) 831-6059. Fax: (540) 831-5893.E-mail: wvru@radford.edu Web Site:www.wvru.org Licensee: Radford University. Population served: 48,000 Natl. Network: PRI, . Format: Jazz, triple A, BBC, PRI. News: 6 hrs wkly. Target aud: General. Spec prog: Jazz 19 hrs, class 15 hrs, Black 6 hrs, folk one hr, blues 7 hrs, oldies 5 hrs, public affrs 6 hrs, new age 3 hrs wkly. ♦Ashlee B. Claud, gen mgr, dev VP, progmg VP; Jonathan Benfield, opns dir; Randy McCallister, engrg VP.

WWBU(FM)— 1965: 101.7 mhz; 3 kw. 66 ft TL: N37 08 33 W80 34 39. Stereo. Hrs open: 7080 Lee Hwy., Fairlawn, 24141. Phone: (540) 633-5330. Fax: (540) 633-6300. Population served: 50,000 Format: Talk. ♦Sarah Leftwich, gen mgr & gen sls mgr.

Richlands

WGTH(AM)— Oct 5, 1951: 540 khz; 1 kw-D, 97 w-N. TL: N37 05 01 W81 46 58. Hrs open: 24 Dups FM 70% Box 370, 24641. Phone: (276) 964-2502. Fax: (276) 964-4500. Licensee: High Knob Broadcasters Inc. (Acq 2-28-95; 5-22-95). Population served: 50,000 Natl. Network: Salem Radio Network, . News: 7 hrs wkly. Target aud: General. ♦Ron Brown, gen mgr.

WGTH-FM— Jan 3, 1977: 105.5 mhz; 450 w. 800 ft TL: N37 09 20 W81 46 11. Hrs open: 24 Box 370, 24641. Phone: (276) 964-2502. Fax: (276) 964-4500.E-mail: wgth@wgth.net Web Site:www.wgth.net Licensee: High Knob Broadcasters Inc. Natl. Network: Salem Radio Network, . Format: Relg, southern gospel. News: 6 hrs wkly. Target aud: General. ♦Eric Miller, opns dir; Charlene Pinkerton, gen sls mgr; Ron Brown, pres, gen mgr & mus dir; Mike Luttrel, chief of engrg.

WRIC-FM— November 1989: 97.7 mhz; 3.2 kw. Ant 751 ft TL: N37 09 04 W81 53 56. Stereo. Hrs open: 24
Rebroadcasts WSTG(FM) Princeton, WV 100%.
Box 5588, Princeton, WV, 24740. Phone: (276) 964-4066. Phone: (276) 963-4400. Fax: (276) 963-4927.E-mail: ronwitt@star95.com Web Site:www.star95.com Licensee: RR & WT Broadcasting Inc. (group owner; (acq 4-30-2009; $175,000). Population served: 50,000 Rgnl. Network: Va. News Net. Format: Adult top-40. ♦Ron Witt, gen mgr.

Richmond

WBTJ(FM)— May 1957: 106.5 mhz; 7.6 kw. Ant 1,233 ft TL: N37 30 14 W77 41 53. Stereo. Hrs open: 24 3245 Basie Rd, 23228. Phone: (804) 474-0000. Fax: (804) 474-0167.E-mail: sheilahbelle@clearchannel.com Web Site:www.1065thebeat.com Licensee: Capstar TX L.P. Group owner: Clear Channel Communications Inc. (acq 8-30-00; grpsl). Population served: 249,621 Natl. Rep: Christal,. Pepper & Corazzini. Format: Hip Hop, R&B. News staff: one; News: 5 hrs wkly. Target aud: 18-44. ♦Mark Mays, pres; Carrie Todd, sls dir; Ruth Jones, gen sls mgr, mktg mgr; Mynette Eady, prom dir; Aaron Maxwell, progmg dir; Mike Street, mus dir; Mike Flemming, chief of engrg; Kim Hutcheson, traf mgr; Sheilah Belle, news dir, pub affrs dir, min affrs dir & news rptr.

WBTK(AM)— September 1926: 1380 khz; 5 kw-U, DA-2. TL: N37 37 13 W77 26 57. Hrs open: 3600 W. Broad St., Ste 696, 23230. Phone: (804) 353-8544. Fax: (804) 353-8549. Licensee: Mount Rich Media LLC. Group owner: Salem Communications Corp. (acq 5-30-2006; $1.5 million). Population served: 556,200 Format: Sp Christian. Target aud: 35 plus; older, upscale. ♦Glenn Motto, opns mgr; Glen Motto, gen sls mgr, progmg dir, pub affrs dir.

WCDX(FM)—See Mechanicsville

WCLM(AM)—See Highland Springs

***WCVE(FM)**— May 6, 1988: 88.9 mhz; 17.5 kw. Ant 840 ft TL: N37 34 00 W77 28 36. Stereo. Hrs open: 23 Sesame St., 23235. Phone: (804) 320-1301. Fax: (804) 320-8729. Web Site:www.ideastations.org/radio Licensee: Commonwealth Public Broadcasting Corp. Population served: 1,000,000 Natl. Network: NPR, PRI, . Wire Svc: AP Format: News/talk/classical. News staff: one; News: 35 hrs wkly. Target aud: 35 plus. Spec prog: Folk 6 hrs, blues 3 hrs, jazz 18 hrs wkly. ♦Bill Miller, VP, stn mgr; Peter Solomon, opns mgr; Lisa Tait, dev VP, dev dir. Co-owned TV: *WCVE-TV affil.

***WDCE(FM)**— Sept 7, 1977: 90.1 mhz; 100 w. 118 ft TL: N37 34 48 W77 32 35. Stereo. Hrs open: 24 Univ. of Richmond, Box 85, 23173. Phone: (804) 289-8698. Fax: (804) 289-8996.E-mail: wdce@richmond.edu Web Site:www.wdce.org Licensee: University of Richmond. Population served: 300,000 Format: Progsv, div, new mus. News: 3 hrs wkly. Target aud: 15-30. Spec prog: Class 3 hrs, jazz 9 hrs, relg 3 hrs wkly. ♦Dan Inglis, gen mgr.

WDZY(AM)—(Colonial Heights, 1955: 1290 khz; 5 kw-D, 41 w-N. TL: N37 15 30 W77 23 40. (CP: 25 kw-D). Hrs open: 24 413 Stuart Cir., Suite 110, 23220. Phone: (804) 353-7200. Fax: (804) 353-2633.E-mail: info@wdzy.com Web Site:www.radiodisney.com/wdzy/1290 Licensee: Radio Disney Group LLC. Group owner: ABC Inc. (acq 8-22-00; grpsl). Format: Family progmg. News: 7 hrs wkly. Target aud: 2-12, 25-54; children & women. ♦Laura Haemker, stn mgr & gen sls mgr; Amy Garelick, prom mgr.

WFTH(AM)— June 16, 1964: 1590 khz; 5 kw-D, 19 w-N. TL: N37 30 02 W77 27 28. Hrs open: 227 E. Belt Blvd., 23224. Phone: (804) 233-0765. Fax: (804) 233-3725.E-mail: faithradio@verizon.net Web Site:www.faith1590.com Licensee: Tri-City Christian Radio Inc. (acq 3-22-90; $450,000; 4-16-90). Format: Gospel. ♦Jack Johnson, pres; Mary Johnson, VP; Shawn Nicholson, gen mgr & opns mgr.

WGGM(AM)—See Chester

WKHK(FM)—(Colonial Heights, Nov 17, 1972: 95.3 mhz; 17.5 kw. 393 ft TL: N37 26 21 W77 25 57. Stereo. Hrs open: 24 812 Morrefield Park Dr, Suite 300, 23236. Phone: (804) 330-5700. Fax: (804) 330-4079.E-mail: info@k95country.com Web Site:www.k95country.com Licensee: Cox Radio Inc. Group owner: Cox Broadcasting (acq 8-31-00; grpsl). Hogan & Hartson. Format: Country. News staff: one; News: 8 hrs wkly.

Target aud: 25-54. ♦Bob Willoughby, gen mgr; Laura Kibler, prom dir; Buddy VanArsdale, progmg dir; Gary Harrison, chief of engrg; Becky Wentworth, traf mgr.

WKJM(FM)—See Petersburg

WKJS(FM)— 1996: 99.3 mhz; 2.3 kw. Ant 531 ft TL: N37 30 52 W77 30 28. Hrs open:
100% simulcast 99.3& 105.7(WKJM).
2809 Emerywood Pkwy., Suite 300, 23294. Phone: (804) 672-9299. Fax: (804) 672-9314.E-mail: info@wkjs-fm.firstmediaworks.com Web Site:www.wkjs-fm.firstmediaworks.com Licensee: Radio One Licenses LLC. Group owner: Radio One Inc. (acq 11-8-2001; grpsl). Natl. Network: ABC, . Natl. Rep: Eastman Radio,. Fletcher, Heald & Hildreth. Format: Urban adult contemp. Target aud: 25-54; general. ♦Linda Forem, VP & gen mgr; Al Payne, opns mgr; Dennis Gettis, gen sls mgr; Bobby Walden, natl sls mgr; Dottie Brooks, mktg dir; Dawna Covington, prom dir; Clovia Lawrence, pub affrs dir; Chris Lawless, chief of engrg.

WKLR(FM)—(Fort Lee, July 29, 1963: 96.5 mhz; 50 kw. 453 ft TL: N37 20 22 W77 24 31. Stereo. Hrs open: 24 812 Moorefield Park Dr., Suite 300, 23236. Phone: (804) 330-5700. Fax: (320) 330-4079.E-mail: fisher@coxradio.com Web Site:www.965theplanet.com Licensee: Cox Radio Inc. Group owner: Cox Broadcasting (acq 8-31-00; grpsl). Population served: 800,000 Format: Classic rock. News staff: one; News: 5 hrs wkly. Target aud: 25-49. ♦James Kennedy, chmn; Bob Willoughby, gen mgr, sls dir; Rene Clark, gen sls mgr; David Koye, natl sls mgr; Paul Cannell, progmg dir, disc jockey; Gary Harrison, engrg dir, engrg mgr, chief of engrg; Sam Giles, disc jockey.

WLEE(AM)— May 4, 1951: 990 khz; 1 kw-D, 13 w-N. TL: N37 31 40 W77 22 48. Hrs open: 24 308 W. Broad St., 23220. Phone: (804) 643-0990. Fax: (804) 474-5070.E-mail: jjacobs@davidsonmediagroup.com Web Site:www.wlee990.am Licensee: Davidson Media Station WLEE Licensee LLC. Group owner: 4M Communications Inc. (acq 5-13-2005; grpsl). Population served: 925,000 Natl. Network: CNN Radio, . Format: News/Talk. Target aud: 25-64; white collar, upscale professionals. ♦Felix Perez, pres; Bryan Hill, exec VP, gen sls mgr; Jim Jacobs, gen mgr; Tim Hurley, opns dir, progmg dir & progmg mgr.

WMXB(FM)— Dec 23, 1961: 103.7 mhz; 18.5 kw. 750 ft TL: N37 30 31 W77 34 37. Stereo. Hrs open: 24 812 Moorefield Park Dr., Suite 300, 23236. Phone: (804) 330-5700. Fax: (804) 330-4079. Fax: (804) 323-1524 sls.E-mail: info@mix1037.com Web Site:www.mix1037.com Licensee: Cox Radio Inc. Group owner: Cox Broadcasting (acq 8-00; grpsl). Population served: 766,100 Natl. Network: ABC, . Natl. Rep: McGavren Guild,. Format: Best mix of 80's, 90's, today. News staff: one; News: 8 hrs wkly. Target aud: 25-54; predominately female. ♦James Kennedy, CEO & COO; Bob Willoughby, gen mgr; Amy DeVries, gen sls mgr; Fisher, progmg dir.

WREJ(AM)— May 8, 1964: 1540 khz; 10 kw-D, DA-D. TL: N37 37 08 W77 25 27. Hrs open: 24 308 W. Broad St., 23220. Phone: (804) 643-0990. Fax: (804) 474-5070.E-mail: jjacobs@davidsonmediagroup.com Web Site:www.rejoice1540.com Licensee: Davidson Media Station WREJ Licensee LLC. (acq 5-13-2005; grpsl). Population served: 925,000 Natl. Network: ABC, . Rgnl. Network: Va. News Net. Format: Urban inspirational. News staff: 1. Target aud: 35-64; African-American concerned about financial, civic & economic issues. ♦Felix Perez, pres; Jim Jacobs, gen mgr; Tim Hurley, opns dir; Bryan Hill, gen sls mgr; B.L. Westbrook, progmg dir.

***WRIH(FM)**— 2007: 88.1 mhz; 2 kw vert. Ant 410 ft TL: N37 43 00 W77 38 02. Hrs open:
Rebroadcasts WAFR(FM) Tupelo, MS 100%.
Drawer 2440, Tupelo, MS, 38803. Phone: (662) 844-8888. Fax: (662) 842-6791. Web Site:www.afr.net Licensee: American Family Association. Natl. Network: American Family Radio, . Format: Contemp Christian. ♦Marvin Sanders, gen mgr.

WRNL(AM)— Nov 15, 1937: 910 khz; 5 kw-U, DA-N. TL: N37 36 52 W77 30 49. Hrs open: 24 3245 Basie Rd., 23228. Phone: (804) 474-0000. Fax: (804) 474-0167.E-mail: info@sportsradio910.com Web Site:www.sportsradio910.com Licensee: CC Licenses LLC. Group owner: Clear Channel Communications Inc. (acq 8-10-93; $9.75 million with co-located FM; 8-30-93). Population served: 249,621 Rgnl. Network: Va. News Net. Va. News Net. Format: Sports. Target aud: 25-54; men. ♦Ruth Jones, VP & gen mgr; James Levy, gen sls mgr; Kirby Oliveras, prom dir; Mike Clifford, progmg dir.

WRVA(AM)— Nov 2, 1925: 1140 khz; 50 kw-U, DA-1. TL: N37 24 13 W77 18 59. Hrs open: 24 3245 Basie Rd., 23228. Phone: (804) 474-0000. Fax: (804) 474-0167.E-mail: jimmybarrett@clearchannel.com Web Site:www.wrva.com Licensee: CC Licenses LLC. (group owner: Clear Channel Communications Inc. (acq 6-26-92; grpsl; 7-20-92). Population served: 249,621 Natl. Network: ABC, . Natl. Rep: Clear Channel,. Format: News/talk. News staff: 10; News: 24 hrs wkly. Target aud: 35-54. Spec prog: Relg 10 hrs, computers 2 hrs, gardening 3 hrs, home care 2 hrs, legal one hr wkly. ♦Ruth Jones, gen mgr; Dan O'Shea, gen sls mgr; Jimmy Barrett, progmg dir, chief of engrg.

WRVQ(FM)— Aug 4, 1948: 94.5 mhz; 200 kw. Ant 455 ft TL: N37 24 13 W77 18 59. Stereo. Hrs open: 3245 Basie Rd., 23228. Phone: (804) 474-0167. Fax: (804) 474-0090.E-mail: billcahill@clearchannel.com Web Site:www.q94radio.com Licensee: CC Licenses LLC. Group owner: Clear Channel Communications Inc. Natl. Network: ABC, . Format: Mainstream. Target aud: 18-44; women. ♦Ruth Jones, gen mgr; Bill Cahill, opns mgr, traf mgr; Tracy Driskill, gen sls mgr; Christopher Layfield, progmg dir; Mike Fleming, chief of engrg.

WRXL(FM)— Mar 4, 1949: 102.1 mhz; 20 kw. Ant 790 ft TL: N37 36 52 W77 30 56. Stereo. Hrs open: 24 3245 Basie Rd., 23228. Phone: (804) 474-0167. Fax: (804) 474-0092. Web Site:www.1021thex.com Licensee: CC Licenses LLC. Format: AOR, oldies new rock. Target aud: 25-44. ♦Ruth Jones, gen mgr; Bill Cahill, opns mgr.

WTPS(AM)—See Petersburg

WTVR-FM— February 1946: 98.1 mhz; 50 kw. 1,004 ft TL: N37 34 00 W77 28 36. Stereo. Hrs open: 3245 Basie Rd., 23228. Phone: (804) 474-0000. Fax: (804) 474-0167.E-mail: billcahill@clearchannel.com Web Site:www.lite98.com Licensee: CC Licenses LLC. Group owner: Clear Channel Communications Inc. (acq 1996; $18 million with co-located AM). Natl. Rep: Clear Channel,. Format: Adult contemp. ♦Ruth Jones, gen mgr; Bill Cahill, opns mgr, progmg dir; Rhonda Reeser, gen sls mgr; Adam Stubbs, prom dir; Mike Fleming, chief of engrg.

WVNZ(AM)— September 1955: 1320 khz; 5 kw-D, DA. TL: N37 28 00 W77 27 08. Hrs open: 24 308 W. Broad St., 23220. Phone: (804) 643-0990. Fax: (804) 474-5070.E-mail: jjacobs@davidsonmediagroup.com Web Site:www.selecta1320.com Licensee: Davidson Media Station WVNZ Licensee LLC. Group owner: 4M Communications Inc. (acq 5-13-2005; grpsl). Population served: 925,000 Natl. Network: ABC, . Format: Sp. News staff: 3; News: 15 hrs wkly. Target aud: 25 plus; Hispanic population. ♦Felix Perez, pres; Jim Jacobs, gen mgr; Tim Hurley, opns dir & opns mgr; Carolyn Resendiz, gen sls mgr, progmg dir; Selvin Paredes, progmg dir.

WXGI(AM)— Oct 1, 1947: 950 khz; 5 kw-D, 64 w-N. TL: N37 30 52 W77 30 28. Hrs open: 5:30 AM-midnight 701 German School Rd., 23225. Phone: (804) 233-7666. Fax: (804) 233-7681.E-mail: info@espn950am.com Web Site:espn950am.com Licensee: Red Zebra Broadcasting Licensee (Richmond) LLC. (acq 9-27-2006; $1.4 million). Population served: 249,621 Natl. Network: ESPN Radio, . Format: All sports. Target aud: 30 plus. ♦Bruce Gilbert, CEO; Buck Albritton, gen mgr; Mitchell Bradley, progmg dir.

WYFJ(FM)—See Ashland

Roanoke

WFIR(AM)— June 20, 1924: 960 khz; 5 kw-U, DA-N. TL: N37 15 20 W79 57 20. Hrs open: 24 3934 Electric Rd., 24018. Secondary address: Box 92 24022. Phone: (540) 345-1511. Fax: (504) 342-2270. Web Site:www.960wfir.com Licensee: Mel Wheeler Inc. (group owner; acq 3-31-00; with co-located FM). Population served: 250,000 Natl. Network: ABC, Fox News Radio, . Natl. Rep: Katz Radio,. Format: News/talk. Target aud: 25-54; adult, skewed male 35-54. ♦Anne Booze, gen sls mgr; Jim Murphy, progmg dir; Becky Bruce, news dir.

WGMN(AM)— 1946: 1240 khz; 1 kw-U. TL: N37 16 12 W79 58 14. Hrs open: Box 348, Forest, 24551. Phone: (434) 534-6100. Fax: (434) 534-6101.E-mail: wblt@inbox.com Web Site:www.espninva.com Licensee: 3 Daughters Media Inc. Group owner: Clear Channel Communications Inc. (acq 6-22-2007; grpsl). Population served: 92,115 Natl. Network: ESPN Radio, . Rgnl. Network: Va. News Net. Natl. Rep: D & R Radio,. Va. News Net. Format: Sports. Target aud: 25-54. ♦Gary Burns, pres & gen mgr; Devin Taylor, opns mgr, progmg dir.

WJJS(FM)— November 1993: 104.9 mhz; 14.5 kw. Ant 925 ft TL: N37 22 23 W79 55 40. Hrs open: 24 3305 Old Forest Rd., Lynchburg, 24501. Phone: (434) 385-8298. Fax: (434) 385-8991.E-mail: joeldearing@clearchannel.com Web Site:www.wjjs.com Licensee: Capstar TX L.P. Group owner: Clear Channel Communications Inc. (acq 8-30-2000; grpsl). Format: CHR. News staff: 2. ♦Chris Clendenen, pres, gen mgr; Dave Carwile, sls dir, natl sls mgr; Joel Dearing, progmg dir.

WKBA(AM)—(Vinton, Oct 9, 1961: 1550 khz; 10 kw-D, DA. TL: N37 17 24 W79 55 22. Hrs open: 2043 10th St. N.E., 24012. Phone: (540) 343-5597. Fax: (540) 345-4064.E-mail: ddurrett@radiowkba.com Web Site:www.radiowkba.com Licensee: Tinker Creek Broadcasters Inc. (acq 2-1-83). Population served: 250,000 Booth, Freret, Imlay & Tepper P. Format: Relg. Target aud: General. Spec prog: Black 10 hrs wkly. ♦Dorothy Durrett, gen mgr & stn mgr; Dale Cook, chief of engrg.

WPAR(FM)—See Salem

WRIS(AM)— Feb 28, 1953: 1410 khz; 5 kw-D, 72 w-N. TL: N37 16 47 W79 59 29. Hrs open: 24 Box 6099, 24017. Secondary address: 219 Luckett St. N.W. 24017. Phone: (540) 342-1410. Phone: (540) 342-7811. Fax: (540) 342-5952.E-mail: info@wris.cc Web Site:www.wrisradio.com Licensee: WRIS L.L.C. (acq 1-15-98). Population served: 250,000 Rgnl. Network: Va. News Net. Va. News Net. Blair, Joyce & Silva. Format: Relg, inspirational. News staff: one. Target aud: 35-75. ♦Lloyd Gochenour, pres, gen mgr; Russ Brown, opns mgr.

WROV-FM—See Martinsville

***WRXT(FM)**— July 31, 1994: 90.3 mhz; 5.5 kw. Ant 1,112 ft TL: N37 23 09 W79 40 10. Hrs open: 22226 Timberlake Road, Lynchburg, 24502. Phone: (434) 237-9798. Fax: (434) 237-1025.E-mail: office@spiritfm.com Web Site:www.spiritfm.com Licensee: Positive Alternative Radio Inc. Group owner: Baker Family Stations (acq 4-15-2002). Format: Contemp Christian. ♦Barry Armstrong, gen mgr; Brian Sumner, mus dir.

WSLC-FM— November 1948: 94.9 mhz; 100 kw. Ant 1,979 ft TL: N37 11 41 W80 09 22. Stereo. Hrs open: 24 Prog sep from AM 3934 Electric Rd., 24018. Secondary address: Box 92 24022. Phone: (540) 774-0201. Fax: (540) 774-5667. Web Site:www.949starcountry.com Population served: 1,054,204 Natl. Rep: Katz Radio,. Format: Country. Target aud: 25-54. ♦Stan Reynolds, gen sls mgr; Rachel Rodes, prom dir; Brett Sharp, progmg dir.

WSLQ(FM)— Nov 1, 1947: 99.1 mhz; 200 kw. 1,985 ft TL: N37 11 42 W80 09 22. Stereo. Hrs open: 24 3934 Electric Rd., 24018. Secondary address: Box 92 24018. Phone: (540) 387-0234. Web Site:www.q99fm.com Licensee: Mel Wheeler Inc. Population served: 1,062,000 Natl. Rep: Katz Radio,. Format: Adult contemp. News: 1 hr wkly. Target aud: 25-54; skew female. ♦Leonard Wheeler, pres; Jim Murphy, progmg dir.

WSNV(FM)—See Salem

WVBE(AM)— Oct 1, 1940: 610 khz; 5 kw-D, 1 kw-N, DA-2. TL: N37 18 11 W80 02 33. Hrs open: 24
Rebroadcasts WVBE Lynchburg 100%.
3934 Electric Rd., 24018. Secondary address: Box 92 24022. Phone: (540) 774-9200. Fax: (540) 774-5667.E-mail: info@vibe100.com Web Site:www.vibe100.com Licensee: Mel Wheeler Inc. (group owner; (acq 10-1-76). Population served: 420,000 Natl. Rep: Katz Radio,. Format: Urban adult contemp. Target aud: Adult 25-54; skew female, skew black. ♦Leonard Wheeler, pres, gen mgr; Stan Reynolds, gen sls mgr; Walt Ford, progmg dir.

***WVTF(FM)**— Aug 1, 1973: 89.1 mhz; 100 kw. 1,970 ft TL: N37 11 56 W80 09 02. Stereo. Hrs open: 24 3520 Kingsbury Ln., 24014-1348. Phone: (540) 989-8900. Fax: (540) 776-2727.E-mail: info@wvtf.org Web Site:www.wvtf.org Licensee: Virginia Tech Foundation Inc. (acq 1-1-82). Population served: 850,000 Natl. Network: PRI, NPR, . Rgnl. Network: Va. News Net. Va. News Net. Dow, Lohnes & Albertson. Format: Class, jazz, NPR. News staff: 3; News: 39 hrs wkly. Target aud: General. ♦Glenn Gleixner, gen mgr; Karen Dillon, dev dir.

WWWR(AM)— April 1957: 910 khz; 1 kw-D, 84 w-N. TL: N37 16 06 W79 54 46. Hrs open: 24 1848 Clay St. S.E., 24013. Phone: (540) 343-7109. Fax: (540) 343-2306. Web Site:www.3wradio.com Licensee: Perception Media Group Inc. (group owner; (acq 4-25-91; $150,000; 5-13-91). Format: Talk. Target aud: 35-64. ♦Ben Peyton, pres; Sharron Jeffrey, stn mgr & opns mgr; Howie McKinney, mus dir; Dale Cook, chief of engrg; Martin Jeffrey, sls.

WXLK(FM)— Dec 17, 1960: 92.3 mhz; 93 kw. Ant 2,050 ft TL: N37 11 56 W80 09 01. Stereo. Hrs open: Box 92, 24022. Secondary address: 3934 Electric Rd. S.W. 24018. Phone: (540) 774-9200. Fax: (540) 774-5667. Web Site:www.k92radio.com Licensee: Mel Wheeler Inc. (group owner; acq 3-12-97; $7.5 million with WVBE-FM Lynchburg). Population served: 1,000,000 Format: CHR. Target aud: 18-44; women. ♦Leonard Wheeler, CEO, pres & gen mgr; Kathy Rilee, mktg dir.

Rocky Mount

WYTI(AM)— Mar 31, 1957: 1570 khz; 2.5 kw-D, 220 w-N. TL: N36 58 37 W79 53 45. Hrs open: 6 AM-9 PM Box430, 24151-0430. Secondary address: 275 Glenwood Dr 24151. Phone: (540) 483-9955. Phone: (540) 483-2166. Fax: (540) 483-7802.E-mail: wyti@wytiradio.com Web Site:www.wytiradio.com Licensee: WYTI Inc. Population served:

37,500 Natl. Network: ABC, . Format: Traditional country, bluegrass, gospel. Target aud: 30 plus; general. Spec prog: NASCAR races, relg 10 hrs wkly. ◆ Susan Mullins, exec VP, gen mgr; William E. Jefferson, pres & stn mgr; Don Mattingly, opns mgr.

Ruckersville

WHTE-FM—Licensed to Ruckersville. See Charlottesville

Rural Retreat

WLOY(AM)— May 15, 1985: 660 khz; 550 w-D. TL: N36 55 17 W81 14 34. Hrs open: Daytime Box 1247, 110 W. Spiller St., Wytheville, 24382. Phone: (276) 228-3185. Fax: (276) 228-9261.E-mail: wyve.wxbx@wiredog.com Licensee: Three Rivers Media Corp. (acq 10-16-2006; $125,000). Population served: 128,800 Rgnl. Network: Va. News Net. Natl. Rep: Rgnl Reps,. Brooks, Pierce, McClendon, Humphrey & Leonard. Format: Contemp Christian. News staff: one. Target aud: 25-54. ◆ Gary W. Hagerich, pres.

WXBX(FM)— June 11, 1992: 95.3 mhz; 6 kw. Ant 400 ft TL: N36 55 17 W81 14 34. Stereo. Hrs open: 24 Box 1247, 110 W. Spiller St., Wytheville, 24382. Phone: (276) 228-3185. Fax: (276) 228-9261.E-mail: wyve.wxbx@wiredog.com Web Site:www.3rivers.net Licensee: Three Rivers Media Corp. (acq 10-01-98; $200,000). Population served: 55,000 Natl. Network: AP Network News, Jones Radio Networks, . Rgnl rep: Rgnl Reps Brooks, Pierce, McLendon, Humphrey & Leonard. Format: Oldies. News staff: one; News: 12 hrs wkly. Target aud: 25 plus. ◆ Gary W. Hagerich, CEO, pres, gen mgr; Kristy Wrobel, traf mgr.

Rustburg

*WWEM(FM)—Not on air, target date: unknown: 91.7 mhz; 1.15 kw. Ant 748 ft TL: N37 17 07 W79 05 26. Hrs open: Box 905, Spotsylvania, 22553. Phone: (540) 582-9700. Web Site:www.wedfm.org Licensee: Educational Media Corp. ◆ Peter D. Stover, pres & gen mgr.

Saint Paul

WXLZ(AM)— Nov 3, 1981: 1140 khz; 2.5 kw-D. TL: N36 52 15 W82 18 21. Hrs open: Sunrise-sunset Rebroadcasts WXLZ-FM Lebanon 80%. Box 1299, Lebanon, 24266. Phone: (276) 762-5595. Phone: (276) 889-1073 (v). Fax: (276) 889-3677.E-mail: wxlz1073@mounet.com Web Site:www.wxlz.net Licensee: Yeary Broadcasting Inc. Population served: 108,000 Natl. Network: CBS, . Format: Relg, Modern Country. News staff: 3; News: 3 hrs wkly. Target aud: 25 plus; students, farmers, miners & rural area residents. Spec prog: Gospel 15 hrs wkly. ◆ Lannis Yeary, CEO; Marshall Hendrix, progmg dir & local news ed.

Salem

*WPAR(FM)— April 1994: 91.3 mhz; 3.3 kw. Ant 886 ft TL: N37 22 23 W79 55 37. Stereo. Hrs open: 24 Box 889, Blacksburg, 24063. Phone: (540) 961-2377. Fax: (540) 951-5282.E-mail: mail@spiritfm.com Web Site:www.spiritfm.com Licensee: Positive Alternative Radio Inc. Group owner: Baker Family Stations (acq 5-90; 5-21-90). Natl. Network: USA, . Booth, Freret, Imlay & Tepper. Format: Christian adult contemp. Target aud: 25-54; adults with families. ◆ Barry Armstrong, gen mgr.

WSNV(FM)— Mar 7, 1969: 93.5 mhz; 5.8 kw. Ant 98 ft TL: N37 16 47 W79 59 29. Stereo. Hrs open: 24 3807 Brandon Ave. S.W., Suite 2350, Roanoke, 24018. Phone: (540) 725-1220. Fax: (540) 725-1245.E-mail: stevencross@clearchannel.com Web Site:www.mysunnyfm.com Licensee: Aloha Station Trust LLC Group owner: Clear Channel Communications Inc. (acq 7-30-2008; grpsl). Population served: 200,000 Natl. Network: Westwood One, . Format: Soft adult contemp. News: one hr wkly. Target aud: 24 plus. ◆ Dave Carwile, gen mgr; Tammy Cazad, gen sls mgr; Steve Cross, progmg dir; Ed Kilbane, mus dir, news dir.

WTOY(AM)— Sept 7, 1956: 1480 khz; 5 kw-D. TL: N37 16 21 W80 04 52. Hrs open: 504 23rd St. NW, Roanoke, 24017. Phone: (540) 344-9869. Fax: (540) 344-0976.E-mail: wtoyradio@aol.com Licensee: Ward Broadcasting Corp. (acq 3-2-92). Population served: 220,000 Format: Adult urban contemp. ◆ Irving L. Ward Sr., pres & gen mgr.

Saltville

WXMY(AM)— Nov 5, 1981: 1600 khz; 5 kw-D. TL: N36 51 43 W81 43 29. Hrs open: 6 AM-sunset Box 5555, Chilhowie, 24319. Phone: (276) 685-1810. Fax: (641) 587-6242.E-mail: 1600wxmy@gmail.com Web

Site:www.1600wxmy.com Licensee: Continental Media Group LLC (acq 4-11-2001; $62,000). Format: Classic country, bluegrass, gospel. Target aud: 25-54. ◆ Wendy Raynor, gen mgr, stn mgr, gen sls mgr, progmg dir & traf mgr.

Smithfield

WKGM(AM)— Dec 18, 1974: 940 khz; 10 kw-D, 3.1 kw-N, DA-N. TL: N36 57 16 W76 37 48 (day), N37 05 51 W76 40 16 (night). Hrs open: 24 Box 339, 23431. Secondary address: 13379 Great Spring Rd. 23430. Phone: (757) 357-9546. Phone: (757) 622-9546. Fax: (757) 365-0412.E-mail: wkgm@hotmail.com Licensee: WKGM Inc. Group owner: Baker Family Stations Population served: 1,700,000 Format: Relg. News: one hr wkly. Target aud: 25 plus. Spec prog: Farm 2 hrs, Ger one hr, Sp one hr, gospel 5 hrs wkly. ◆ Vernon H. Baker, pres; T.R. Bumgardner, gen mgr.

South Boston

WAJL(AM)—Not on air, target date: unknown: 1400 khz; 1 kw-U. TL: N36 42 35 W78 52 28. Hrs open: Box 127, Semora, NC, 27343-0127. Phone: (336) 234-8416. Fax: (434) 572-9245.E-mail: wsbvgm@gcronline.com Licensee: Linda Waller-Barton. ◆ Linda Waller-Barton, gen mgr.

WHLF(FM)— Sept 1, 1992: 95.3 mhz; 6 kw. Ant 246 ft TL: N36 42 24 W78 55 28. Stereo. Hrs open: 24 Box 526, 24592. Secondary address: 1210 Porter Ln 24592. Phone: (434) 572-2988. Fax: (434) 572-1662.E-mail: whlf@whlf.com Web Site:www.whlf.com Licensee: JLC Properties Inc. (acq 4-1-93;4-19-93). Population served: 30,000 Natl. Network: ABC, . Wire Svc: AP Format: 80's, 90's and Today. News staff: one; News: 8 hrs wkly. Target aud: 25-54; those that have spendable income. ◆ Tom Birch, pres; Nick Long, gen mgr; Kelly Redd, progmg dir.

WQOK(FM)—Licensed to South Boston. See Raleigh NC

WSBV(AM)— 1980: 1560 khz; 2.5 kw-D, DA-1. TL: N36 42 24 W78 52 28. Hrs open: Box 778, 1180 Plywood Tr., 24592. Phone: (434) 572-4418. Fax: (434) 572-9245.E-mail: wsbvgm@gcronline.com Licensee: Linda Waller-Barton Format: Black Gospel. Target aud: 40 plus. Spec prog: Farm one hr wkly. ◆ Linda Waller-Barton, gen mgr; April Warf, stn mgr; James W. Barton, opns dir.

South Hill

WKSK-FM— Dec 23, 1966: 101.9 mhz; 6 kw. Ant 315 ft TL: N36 44 39 W78 09 42. Stereo. Hrs open: Prog sep from AM Box 216, 23970. Phone: (434) 447-8997. Phone: (434) 447-4007. Fax: (434) 447-4789.E-mail: wjws@yahoo.com Natl. Network: ABC, . Format: Country. News staff: one; News: 2 hrs wkly. Target aud: General; adults 25-54. ◆ Frank Malone, farm dir, women's int ed, disc jockey; Greg Thrift, disc jockey.

WSHV(AM)— Nov 1, 1953: 1370 khz; 5 kw-D. TL: N36 44 39 W78 09 42. Hrs open: 6 AM-6 PM Box 216, 23970. Phone: (434) 447-8997. Phone: (434) 447-4007. Fax: (434) 447-4789.E-mail: wshv@hotmail.com Licensee: Lakes Media Holding Company LLC. Group owner: Joyner Radio Inc. (acq 2-1-2005; grpsl). Population served: 30,650 Natl. Network: ABC, . Rgnl. Network: Tobacco. Format: Black. News staff: one. Target aud: General. ◆ Jerry E. Brown, sr VP; Greg Thrift, gen mgr; Robert Wilson, progmg mgr; Robby McMulian, news dir; John Hart, chief of engrg; Heather Skuggen, disc jockey.

Spotsylvania

WVBX(FM)— Mar 31, 1988: 99.3 mhz; 3 kw. Ant 295 ft TL: N38 08 31 W77 41 38. Hrs open: 24 616 Amelia St., Fredericksburg, 22401. Phone: (540) 582-2405. Phone: (540) 374-5500. Fax: (540) 374-5525.E-mail: info@993thevibe.com Web Site:www.993thevibe.com Licensee: The Free Lance-Star Publishing Co. (group owner) (acq 4-19-93; $200,000; 5-3-93). Population served: 90,000 Format: CHR. News staff: 3. Target aud: 25-49. ◆ Josiah P Rowe III, pres; John Moen, gen mgr; James T. Butler, sls dir, gen sls mgr; Joann Pope, prom dir; Paul Johnson, opns dir & progmg dir; Chris Wilk, chief of engrg.

*WWED(FM)— 2005: 89.5 mhz; 380 w vert. Ant 433 ft TL: N38 11 48 W77 33 45. Hrs open: Box 905, 22553. Phone: (540) 582-9700. Web Site:www.bluegrassfm.org Licensee: Educational Media Corp. Natl. Network: Moody, . Format: Bluegrass. ◆ Peter Stover, pres & gen mgr.

Stanleytown

WZBB(FM)— March 1989: 99.9 mhz; 3.6 kw. 722 ft TL: N36 54 50 W79 57 07. Stereo. Hrs open: 24 10899 Virginia Ave., Bassett, 24055. Phone: (540) 489-9999. Fax: (276) 629-8399.E-mail: kristib@wzbbfm.com Web Site:www.wzbbfm.com Licensee: WNLB Radio Inc. Rgnl. Network: Va. News Net. Va. News Net. Format: Country. Target aud: 21 plus. ◆ Donny Brook, pres; Glenn Lynch, VP; Kristi Banks, gen mgr; Amy Coleman, stn mgr; Craig Richards, progmg dir; Lisa Layne, news dir.

Staunton

WBOP(FM)—(Buffalo Gap, 1988: 95.5 mhz; 6 kw. Ant 308 ft TL: N38 10 55 W79 13 34. Stereo. Hrs open: 24 Box 2460, Harrisonburg, 22801. Secondary address: 639 N. Main St., Mt. Crawford 22841. Phone: (540) 432-1063. Fax: (540) 433-9267.E-mail: business@magic955fm.com Web Site:www.magic955fm.com Licensee: Vox Communications Group LLC. (acq 8-31-2005; $900,000). Population served: 150,000 Format: Oldies. ◆ Randy Thompson, gen mgr.

WCYK-FM— September 1984: 99.7 mhz; 3.3 kw. 1,692 ft TL: N38 03 52 W78 48 18. Stereo. Hrs open: 24 1150 Pepsi Pl., Suite 300, Charlottesville, 22901. Phone: (434) 978-4408. Fax: (434) 978-0723. Web Site:www.country997.com Licensee: Monticello Media LLC. Group owner: Clear Channel Communications Inc. (acq 10-4-2007; grpsl). Population served: 750,000 Natl. Rep: Clear Channel, Christal,. Format: Country. Target aud: 25-54. ◆ Karen Cote, gen sls mgr, chief of engrg; Dennis Mockler, natl sls mgr; Lisa Allen, progmg dir.

WKCI(AM)—See Waynesboro

WKDW(AM)— April 1954: 900 khz; 2.5 kw-D, 128 w-N. TL: N38 10 27 W79 04 12. Stereo. Hrs open: 24 Box 2189, 24401. Phone: (540) 886-2376. Fax: (540) 885-8662.E-mail: wkdw@ntelos.net Web Site:www.goodradio.com Licensee: CC Licenses LLC. Group owner: Clear Channel Communications Inc. (acq 11-15-2000; grpsl). Population served: 22,200 Holland & Knight. Format: Country. News staff: one; News: 15 hrs wkly. Target aud: 25-54. Spec prog: Farm one hr, blue grass one hr wkly. ◆ Steve Davis, gen mgr; Kris Losh, progmg dir; Jeff Caudell, chief of engrg.

WNLR(AM)—See Churchville

WSVO(FM)— May 29, 1959: 93.1 mhz; 2.8 kw. 338 ft TL: N38 10 27 W79 04 12. (CP: TL: N38 10 32 W79 04 12). Stereo. Hrs open: Prog sep from AM Box 2189, 24401. Phone: (540) 886-2376. Fax: (540) 885-8662.E-mail: info@goodradio.com Web Site:www.goodradio.com Licensee: CC Licenses LLC. Format: Oldies. News staff: one; News: 15 hrs wkly. Target aud: 35-54.

WTON(AM)— Mar 9, 1946: 1240 khz; 1 kw-U. TL: N38 08 30 W79 02 33. Hrs open: 24 Box 1085, 24402-1085. Secondary address: 304 W. Beverly St. 24401. Phone: (540) 885-5188. Fax: (540) 885-1240.E-mail: star94@ntelos.net Licensee: High Impact Communications Inc. (acq 3-1-96; $1 million). Population served: 120,200 Natl. Network: CBS, ESPN Radio, . Reddy & Begley. Format: All sports ESPN Network. News: one hr wkly. Target aud: 18-49. Spec prog: Virginia Tech Sports. ◆ Brenda Ratcliff, gen mgr; Cass Johnson, progmg dir.

WTON-FM— November 1990: 94.3 mhz; 330 w. 2,263 ft TL: N38 09 55 W79 18 51. Stereo. Hrs open: 24 Box 1085, 24402. Secondary address: 304 W. Beverly St. Phone: (540) 885-5188. Fax: (540) 885-1240.E-mail: star94@ntelos.net Population served: 360,000 Natl. Network: CBS, . Rgnl rep: Rgnl Reps Reddy & Begley. Format: Classic hits. News: 3 hrs wkly. Target aud: 18-49; 60% women, 40% men.

Stephens City

WKSI-FM— Aug 28, 1966: 98.3 mhz; 1.75 kw. Ant 617 ft TL: N39 10 38 W78 15 53. Stereo. Hrs open: 24 510 Pegasus Ct., Winchester, 22602-4596. Phone: (540) 662-5101. Fax: (540) 662-8610. Web Site:wxva.com Population served: 150,000 Format: CHR. Target aud: 25-54. ◆ Chuck Peterson, gen mgr.

Strasburg

WWRT(FM)— Jan 1, 1987: 104.9 mhz; 3 kw. Ant 219 ft TL: N39 01 22 W78 25 35. Stereo. Hrs open: 24 Simulcast with WWRE(FM) Berryville 100%. Box 3300, Winchester, 22604. Secondary address: 520 N. Pleasant Valley Rd., Winchester 22601. Phone: (540) 667-2224. Fax: (540) 722-3295. Web Site:www.everythingthatrocks.fm Licensee: Mid Atlantic Network Inc. Group owner: Mid Atlantic Network (acq 7-8-97; $850,000 with WWRE(FM) Berryville). Cole, Raywid & Braverman.

Format: Rock. Target aud: 18 plus. ♦Allen Shaw, pres; Kathie Flerx, gen mgr; Jeff Adams, opns mgr; Ron Baker, progmg dir; Robert Allen, news dir.

Stuart

WHEO(AM)— Oct 12, 1959: 1270 khz; 5 kw-D. TL: N36 37 25 W80 15 50. Hrs open: 6 AM-sunset 3824 Wayside Rd., 24171. Phone: (276) 694-3114. Fax: (276) 694-2241.E-mail: wheo@sitesstar.net Web Site:www.wheo.net Licensee: Mountain View Communications Inc. (acq 6-86). Population served: 75,000 Natl. Network: CNN Radio, . Rgnl. Network: Va. News Net. Va. News Net. Format: News/talk. News staff: one; News: 25 hrs wkly. Target aud: General. Spec prog: Farm 4 hrs, relg 10 hrs, loc news 10 hrs wkly. ♦Dean Goad, pres; Jamie Clark, VP, opns mgr, news dir, traf mgr; La Vergne Collins, gen sls mgr; Richard Rogers, progmg dir.

Suffolk

WAFX(FM)— Dec 12, 1983: 106.9 mhz; 100 kw. 984 ft TL: N36 48 16 W76 45 17. Stereo. Hrs open: 870 Greenbriar Cir., Suite 399, Chesapeake, 23320. Phone: (757) 366-9900. Fax: (757) 366-0022.E-mail: mbeck@tciradio.com Web Site:www.1069thefox.com Licensee: Tidewater Communications LLC. Group owner: Saga Communications Inc. (acq 3-15-94; $4 million;5-9-94). Natl. Rep: McGavren Guild,. Format: Classic rock. Target aud: 18-49. ♦Dave Paulus, gen mgr; Barry Haugh, gen sls mgr; Mike Beck, progmg dir; Leila Rice, news dir; Don Crowder, chief of engrg.

WVBW(FM)— December 1965: 92.9 mhz; 50 kw. 480 ft TL: N36 52 35 W76 23 28. Stereo. Hrs open: 24 5589 Greenwich Rd., Suite 200, Virginia Beach, 23462. Phone: (757) 671-1000. Fax: (757) 671-1010.E-mail: info@929thewave.com Web Site:www.929thewave.com Licensee: MHR License LLC. Group owner: Barnstable Broadcasting Inc. (acq 3-24-2005; grpsl). Population served: 1,200,000 Natl. Rep: Christal,. Format: Adult contemp. Target aud: 25-54; women. Spec prog: Relg 2 hrs, Sunday Morning Magazine one hr wkly. ♦Eric Mastel, pres; Michele Williams, opns mgr; Vonneva Carter, gen mgr & sls dir; Jim Long, prom dir, news dir; Mike Allen, progmg dir; Paul Campbell, chief of engrg.

Sweet Briar

*WNRS-FM— 1980: 89.9 mhz; 30 w. Ant 1,942 ft TL: N37 33 50 W79 11 34. Stereo. Hrs open: 24 Rebroadcasts WNRN(FM) Charlottesville. Box 143, 24595. Phone: (434) 381-6187. Fax: (434) 381-6173.E-mail: wnrs@sbc.edu Web Site:wnrs-fm.sbc.edu Licensee: Sweet Briar College. Population served: 75,000 Format: Modern rock. Target aud: General. ♦Victoria Nelson, gen mgr; Ashley Carroll, stn mgr; Allsion Bailey, mus dir.

Tappahannock

*WRAR(AM)— Nov 1, 1970: 1000 khz; 300 w-D. TL: N37 52 27 W76 43 37. Hrs open: PO Box 1393, 22560. Phone: (804) 443-6572. Licensee: A.C.T.I.O.N. Inc. (acq 7-19-2006). Population served: 15,000 Rgnl rep: Virginia Broadcast SolutionsRegnl Reps Format: Life talk. ♦Geoffrey Coleman, pres.

WRAR-FM— July 26, 1971: 105.5 mhz; 6 kw. Ant 328 ft TL: N37 52 27 W76 43 37. Stereo. Hrs open: 24 Box 1023, 22560. Secondary address: 156 Prince St. 22560. Phone: (804) 443-4321. Fax: (804) 443-1055.E-mail: rich@wrarfm.com Web Site:www.wrarfm.com Licensee: Real Media Inc. (acq 7-1-2006; $1.9 million). Natl. Network: ABC, . Natl. Rep: Rgnl Reps,. Wire Svc: AP Format: Adult contemp. ♦Billy Flynn, progmg dir; Tom Davis, news dir; Terry Brooks, traf mgr.

Tasley

WESR-FM—See Onley-Onancock

Tazewell

WKQY(FM)— Sept 1, 1968: 100.1 mhz; 4.2 kw. 395 ft TL: N37 08 00 W81 35 43. Stereo. Hrs open: 24 Dups AM 100% 900 Bluefield Ave., Bluefield, 24701. Phone: (304) 327-7144. Fax: (304) 325-7850. Format: Oldies. News staff: one. Target aud: 25 plus.

WTZE(AM)— Apr 22, 1966: 1470 khz; 5 kw-D. TL: N37 07 57 W81 33 21. Hrs open: 6 AM-sunset 900 Bluefield Ave., Bluefield, WV, 24701. Phone: (304) 327-7114. Fax: (304) 325-7850. Licensee: Monterey

Licenses LLC. Group owner: Triad Broadcasting Co. LLC (acq 7-18-00; grpsl). Population served: 85,000 Natl. Network: Motor Racing Net, . Format: News/talk. News: 5 hrs wkly. Target aud: 21-54. Spec prog: Gospel 5 hrs wkly. ♦John Halford, gen mgr; Dave Crosier, opns dir; Joseph Echoles, progmg dir; Keith Bowman, chief of engrg.

Vinton

WKBA(AM)—Licensed to Vinton. See Roanoke

WSFF(FM)— 1994: 106.1 mhz; 6 kw. Ant 95 ft TL: N37 17 03 W79 59 14. Hrs open: 3807 Brandon Ave. S.W., Suite 2350, Roanoke, 24018. Phone: (540) 725-1220. Fax: (540) 725-1245. Web Site:www.1061stevefm.com Licensee: Aloha Station Trust LLC Group owner: Clear Channel Communications Inc. (acq 7-30-2008; grpsl). Format: Adult hits. ♦Chris Clendenen, gen mgr; Ron Gaylor, gen sls mgr & rgnl sls mgr; David Lee Michaels, progmg dir; Ed Kilbane, news dir; Jeff Parker, chief of engrg.

WZZI(FM)— Dec 12, 1995: 101.5 mhz; 630 w. Ant 705 ft TL: N37 21 57 W79 52 01. Stereo. Hrs open: 24 Rebroadcasts WZZU(FM) Lynchburg 100%. 210 1st St., Suite 240, Roanoke, 24011. Phone: (540) 344-2800. Fax: (540) 344-4001.E-mail: info@rocktheplanet.fm Web Site:www.rocktheplanet.fm Licensee: Centennial Broadcasting LLC. (group owner; (acq 11-23-2004; $4.15 million with WZZU(FM) Lynchburg). Natl. Network: Fox News Radio, . Natl. Rep: McGavren Guild,. Womble, Carlyle, Sandridge & Rice. Format: Rock. News staff: one; News: 2 hrs wkly. ♦Allen B. Shaw, pres; Gary Kirtley, gen sls mgr; Dale Cook, chief of engrg.

Virginia Beach

WBVA(AM)—(Bayside, May 1999: 1450 khz; 1 kw-U. TL: N36 51 29 W76 09 28. Hrs open: WPMH. 2202 Jolliff Rd., Chesapeake, 23321. Phone: (757) 465-1603. Fax: (757) 488-7761. Licensee: Ronald W. Cowan Jr. (acq 5-21-2001). Format: News/Talk. ♦Ronald W. Cowan Jr., CEO & pres; Henry Hoot, gen mgr.

*WJLZ(FM)— Feb 12, 1989: 88.5 mhz; 1.2 kw. Ant 118 ft TL: N36 50 30.7 W76 05 37. Stereo. Hrs open: 24 W279AD 103.7, W280CX 103.9, W250AE 97.9. 3500 Virginia Beach Blvd., Suite 201, 23452. Phone: (757) 498-9632. Fax: (757) 498-8609.E-mail: info@currentfm.com Web Site:www.currentfm.com Licensee: Virginia Beach Educational Broadcasting Foundation Inc. Population served: 500,000 Format: Christian CHR. Target aud: General. ♦William M. Verebely Jr., pres; Anne Verebely, gen mgr.

WPTE(FM)— May 5, 1984: 94.9 mhz; 50 kw. 499 ft TL: N36 48 38 W76 16 57. Stereo. Hrs open: 24 236 Clearfield Ave., Suite 206, 23462. Phone: (757) 497-2000. Fax: (757) 456-5458.E-mail: info@pointradio.com Web Site:www.pointradio.com Licensee: Entercom Norfolk License LLC. Group owner: Entercom Communications Corp. (acq 12-13-99; grpsl). Population served: 1,200,000 Natl. D & R Radio,. Format: Modern adult comtemp rock. News: one hr wkly. Target aud: 18-49. ♦David J. Field, CEO; David J. Field, pres; Jeff Brown, gen mgr; Sandy Smith, gen sls mgr; Barry McKay, progmg dir; Kym Wollman, traf mgr.

WPYA(FM)—See Chesapeake

WROX-FM—(Exmore, 1986: 96.1 mhz; 23 kw. Ant 722 ft TL: N37 15 45 W76 00 45. Stereo. Hrs open: 24 500 Dominion Tower, 999 Waterside Dr., Norfolk, 23510. Phone: (757) 640-8500. Fax: (757) 640-8552. Web Site:www.96x.fm Licensee: Sinclair Telecable Inc. Group owner: Sinclair Communications Inc. (acq 9-28-93; $1.3 million;10-25-93). Population served: 1,400,000 Natl. Rep: McGavren Guild, Interep,. Format: Modern rock. News staff: one. Target aud: 18-34; men. ♦Bob Sinclair, pres; Lisa Sinclair, gen mgr; Dave Morgan, opns mgr; Jeanette Xenakis, gen sls mgr; Ginger Power, natl sls mgr; Donna Agresto, prom dir; Jay Michaels, progmg dir.

WVAB(AM)—Licensed to Virginia Beach. See Norfolk

WVHT(FM)—See Norfolk

WXTG-FM— 2002: 102.1 mhz; 6 kw. Ant 328 ft TL: N36 45 07 W76 08 57. Hrs open: 232 Business Park Dr., Suite 120, 23462. Phone: (757) 747-1021. Fax: (757) 490-2755. Web Site:www.1021fmthegame.com Licensee: Red Zebra Broadcasting Licensee (Norfolk) LLC. Group owner: On Top Communications Inc. (acq 12-4-2006; $4.25 million).

Natl. Network: Fox Sports, . Format: Sports/talk. ♦Buck Albriton, gen mgr; Gary Voss, gen sls mgr; Keith Bennett, progmg dir; Joe Weatherbee, chief of engrg.

Warrenton

WKCW(AM)— Dec 7, 1957: 1420 khz; 22 kw-D, 17 w-N. TL: N38 45 05 W77 44 38. Hrs open: 6 AM-sunset 9540 Godwin Dr, Manassas, 20110. Phone: (703) 330-8244. Fax: (703) 331-4706.E-mail: metroradioinc@aol.com Web Site:www.metroradioinc.com Licensee: Metro Radio Inc. (group owner; (acq 1-2-2004; $400,000). Population served: 48,471 Format: Sp programming. News staff: one; News: 2 hrs wkly. Target aud: 25-54; mature adults with discretionary income of $30,000 plus. Spec prog: Bluegrass, farm one hr, rel 6 hrs wkly. ♦David Houston, CEO, gen mgr, opns mgr; Kelly Koonce, COO; Bruce A. Houston, pres.

WKDL(AM)— Nov 21, 1957: 1250 khz; 8 kw-D, 32 w-N, DA-2. TL: N38 43 52 W77 46 42. Hrs open: 24 9540 Godwin Dr, Manassas, 20110. Phone: (703) 330-8244. Fax: (703) 331-4706.E-mail: metroradioinc@aol.com Web Site:www.1250classiccountry.com Licensee: Metro Radio Inc. (acq 10-4-2007; $1.1 million). Population served: 250,000 + Bentley Law Office. Format: Classic country. ♦David Houston, CEO, gen mgr; Kelly Koonce, COO; Bruce A. Houston, pres.

WWXX(FM)— Nov 2, 1978: 94.3 mhz; 3 kw. Ant 397 ft TL: N38 40 42 W77 47 18. Stereo. Hrs open: 24 8121 Georgia Ave., Suite 1050, Silver Spring, 20910. Phone: (301) 562-1045. Fax: (301) 562-5850. Web Site:www.espn980.com Licensee: Red Zebra Broadcasting Licensee LLC. Group owner: Mega Communications Inc. (acq 5-9-2006; grpsl). Population served: 58,000 Natl. Network: ESPN Radio, . Format: Sports. ♦Bruce Gilbert, CEO; Tod Castleberry, gen mgr.

Warsaw

WNNT-FM— Mar 1, 1967: 100.9 mhz; 3 kw. 305 ft TL: N37 56 39 W76 45 05. Stereo. Hrs open: Box 877, 22572. Secondary address: 194 Islington Rd. 22572. Phone: (804) 333-4900. Phone: (804) 333-3711. Fax: (804) 333-4531.E-mail: acwalker@rivercountry1009.com Web Site:www.rivercountry1009.com Licensee: Northern Neck & Tidewater Communications Inc. (acq 9-16-93; $400,000;10-11-93). Population served: 75,000 Format: Country. ♦Rich Morgan, gen mgr & gen sls mgr; A.C. Walker, progmg dir; Frank Miner, chief of engrg.

Waynesboro

WKCI(AM)— Mar 10, 1965: 970 khz; 5 kw-D, 1 kw-N, DA-2. TL: N38 05 12 W78 54 42. Hrs open: 24 Rebroadcasts WKCY(AM) Harrisonburg 100%. Box 1107, Harrisonburg, 22801. Secondary address: 207 University Blvd., Harrisonburg 22801. Phone: (540) 434-1777. Fax: (540) 432-9968. Web Site:www.shenandoahradio.com Licensee: CC Licenses LLC. Group owner: Clear Channel Communications Inc. (acq 11-16-2000; grpsl). Population served: 250,000 Rgnl. Network: Capitol Radio Net., Va. RFD. Format: News/talk. News staff: one; News: 2 hrs wkly. Target aud: 25-54. Spec prog: Black 3 hrs, farm 2 hrs wkly. ♦Steve Davis, gen mgr; Mike Chiumento, gen sls mgr; Steve Knupp, opns mgr & progmg dir; Mark Ness, chief of engrg.

*WPVA(FM)— 1999: 90.1 mhz; 2.5 kw. Ant 961 ft TL: N38 01 16 W78 52 38. Hrs open: 22226 Timberlake Rd., Lynchburg, 24502. Phone: (434) 237-9798. Fax: (434) 237-1025.E-mail: office@spiritfm.com Web Site:www.spiritfm.com Licensee: Positive Alternative Radio Inc. (group owner; (acq 12-30-2005; grpsl). Booth, Freret, Imlay & Tepper. Format: Contemp Christian. ♦Barry Armstrong, gen mgr.

Weber City

WVEK-FM— December 1994: 102.7 mhz; 1.65 kw. Ant 1,233 ft TL: N36 31 36 W82 35 13. Hrs open: 24 222 Commerce St., Kingsport, TN, 37660. Phone: (423) 246-9578. Fax: (423) 247-9836. Licensee: Holston Valley Broadcasting Corp. (acq 7-16-2008; $270,000). Population served: 150,000 ♦David Widener, gen mgr.

West Point

WBQK(FM)— July 1991: 107.9 mhz; 4 kw. Ant 328 ft TL: N37 27 00 W76 48 46. Stereo. Hrs open: 24 5000 New Point Rd., Suite 2201, Williamsburg, 23188. Phone: (757) 565-1079. Fax: (757) 565-7094. Web Site:www.wbach.net Licensee: Davis Media LLC (acq 6-17-2005; $1.13 million). Population served: 250,000 Format: Classical. ♦Thomas G. Davis, pres & gen mgr; Derek Mason, gen sls mgr; Amy Miller, prom mgr, mus dir; Barbara Warren, traf mgr.

White Stone

WIGO-FM— Sept 1, 1995: 104.9 mhz; 6 kw. Ant 282 ft TL: N37 43 26 W76 23 27. Hrs open: Box 819, Kilmarnock, 22482. Secondary address: 101 Radio Rd, Kilmarnock 22482. Phone: (804)435-9635. Fax: (804) 435-0484.E-mail: office@1049wigo.com Licensee: Two Rivers Communications Inc. (acq 3-31-2006; $700,000). Natl. Network: Westwood One, AP Radio, . Wire Svc: AP Format: Today's Country. News staff: one. Target aud: 25-54. ◆William C. Sherard, pres; Syd Abel, exec VP; Charlie Lassiter, gen mgr, gen sls mgr, engrg dir; Ron Jeffries, opns dir.

Williamsburg

*WCWM(FM)— Sept 28, 1959: 90.9 mhz; 13.5 kw. Ant 269 ft TL: N37 21 16 W76 59 58. Stereo. Hrs open: 24 Campus Ctr., College of Wiliam & Mary, Box 8793, 23186. Phone: (757) 221-3287.E-mail: wcwmxx@wm.edu Web Site:www.wcwm.org Licensee: College of William & Mary. Population served: 15,000 Natl. Network: Moody, . Format: Div, alternative new music, progsv. News: 3 hrs wkly. Target aud: General. Spec prog: Jazz 13 hrs, class 11 hrs, reggae 6 hrs, blues 3 hrs wkly. ◆Adam Burks, gen mgr & stn mgr.

WMBG(AM)— Jan 1, 1958: 740 khz; 500 w-D, 8 w-N. TL: N37 16 37 W76 45 07. Hrs open: 24 1005 Richmond Rd., 23185. Phone: (757) 229-7400. Fax: (757) 220-3074.E-mail: info@wmbgradio.com Web Site:www.wmbgradio.com Licensee: Williamsburg's Radio Station Inc. Population served: 12,000 Natl. Network: AP Radio, Jones Radio Networks, . Format: Adult Standards. News staff: one; News: one hr wkly. Target aud: 45 plus; wealthy & mature in Williamsburg. Spec prog: Gospel 5 hrs wkly. ◆Greg Granger, pres, gen mgr, stn mgr & opns mgr.

Winchester

WINC(AM)— June 15, 1941: 1400 khz; 1 kw-U. TL: N39 11 12 W78 09 06. Hrs open: 24 Box 3300, 22604. Secondary address: 520 N. Pleasant Valley Rd. 22601. Phone: (540) 667-2224. Fax: (540) 722-3295. Web Site:www.winc.fm Licensee: Mid-Atlantic Network Inc. (group owner) Population served: 75,000 Natl. Network: Westwood One, CBS, . Cole, Raywid & Braverman. Format: News/talk, sports. News staff: 3; News: 128 hrs wkly. Target aud: 25 plus; mid-to-upscale active adults. ◆John Lewis, pres; Chris Lewis, gen mgr, gen sls mgr; Jeff Adams, opns mgr, progmg dir; Steve Edwards, news dir; Archie McKay, chief of engrg; Pam Christian, traf mgr.

WINC-FM— October 1946: 92.5 mhz; 22 kw. Ant 1,424 ft TL: N38 57 21 W78 01 28. Stereo. Hrs open: 24 Box 3300, 22604. Secondary address: 520 N. Pleasant Valley Rd. 22601. Phone: (540) 667-2224. Fax: (540) 722-3295. Web Site:www.winc.fm Licensee: Mid-Atlantic Network Inc. Natl. Network: Westwood One, . Format: Hot adult contemp. News staff: 4; News: 6 hrs wkly. Target aud: 18-49; active, upscale listeners. ◆Pam Christian, mktg dir.

WLVE(AM)— Jan 27, 1961: Stn currently dark. 610 khz; 500 w-U, DA-2. TL: N39 11 53 W78 13 13. Hrs open: 24 510 Pegasus Ct., 22602. Phone: (540) 662-5101. Fax: (540) 662-8610. Licensee: Capstar TX L.P. Group owner: Clear Channel Communications Inc. (acq 8-30-2000; grpsl). Population served: 127,500 ◆Jim Shea, pres; Chuck Peterson, gen mgr.

*WTRM(FM)— July 1986: 91.3 mhz; 5.6 kw. Ant 1,401 ft TL: N39 11 02 W78 23 15. Stereo. Hrs open: 24 Box 3438, 22604. Phone: (540) 869-4997. Fax: (540) 869-7173.E-mail: wtrm@wtrm.org Web Site:www.wtrm.org Licensee: Timber Ridge Ministries Inc. Population served: 1,200,000 Natl. Network: USA, . Lauren A. Colby. Format: Southern gospel. Target aud: General. ◆Leona Choy, pres; Chris Petsko, gen mgr; Richard Choy, CEO, VP & chief of engrg.

WUSQ-FM— Dec 10, 1965: 102.5 mhz; 31 kw. 630 ft TL: N39 10 38 W78 15 53. Stereo. Hrs open: 24 510 Pegasus Ct., 22602. Phone: (540) 662-5101. Fax: (540) 662-8610. Web Site:www.wusq.com Population served: 127,000 Format: Country. News: one hr wkly. Target aud: 25-54; males. ◆Chuck Peterson, gen mgr.

Windsor

WJCD(FM)— May 1990: 107.7 mhz; 1.7 kw. Ant 620 ft TL: N36 48 32 W76 30 13. Stereo. Hrs open: 24 1003 Norfolk Sq., Norfolk, 23502-4948. Phone: (757) 466-0009. Fax: (757) 466-9523.E-mail: 1053smoothjazz@921.com Web Site:www.smoothjazz1077.com Licensee: CC Licenses LLC. Group owner: Clear Channel Communications Inc. (acq 9-10-96; grpsl). Natl. Network: CNN Radio, . Format: Smooth jazz. ◆Reggie Jordan, gen mgr; Terry Ratliff, sls dir; Travis Dylan, progmg dir; Michael Bov-e, chief of engrg.

Wise

*WISE-FM— Aug 1, 1999: 90.5 mhz; 220 w. 669 ft TL: N36 57 39 W82 30 56. Stereo. Hrs open: 24
Rebroadcasts WVTF(FM) Roanoke 100%.
3520 Kingsbury Ln, Roanoke, 24014-1348. Phone: (540) 989-8900. Fax: (540) 776-2727.E-mail: info@wvtf.org Web Site:www.wvtf.org Licensee: Clinch Valley College of the University of Virginia. Population served: 25,000 Natl. Network: NPR, PRI, . Rgnl. Network: Va. News Net. Va. News Net. Format: Class, jazz,NPR. News: 45 hrs wkly. Target aud: General. Spec prog: Jazz 9 hrs, Celtic 2 hrs wkly. ◆Glenn Gleixner, CEO & gen mgr.

WNVA-FM—See Norton

Woodbridge

WJZW(FM)—Licensed to Woodbridge. See Washington DC

Woodstock

WAMM(AM)— Oct 9, 1981: Stn currently dark. 1230 khz; 1 kw-U. TL: N38 51 11 W78 31 30. Hrs open: 24 Box 349, 22664. Phone: (540) 459-9595. Fax: (540) 459-3525.E-mail: jason@latino1230.com Web Site:www.latino1230.com Licensee: Jason M. Rodriguez (acq 1-5-2006; $300,000). Format: Sp, var, bi-lingual, Latino fusion. ◆Jason Rodriguez, gen mgr & progmg dir.

WAZR(FM)— Oct 18, 1985: 93.7 mhz; 8.5 kw. Ant 420 ft TL: N38 37 04 W78 42 39. Stereo. Hrs open: 24 Box 1107, Harrisonburg, 22801. Secondary address: 207 University Blvd., Harrisonburg 22801. Phone: (540) 434-1777. Fax: (540) 432-9968. Web Site:www.937kissfm.com Licensee: CC Licenses LLC. Group owner: Clear Channel Communications Inc. (acq 6-3-2002; $1.35 million including five-year noncompete agreement). Population served: 150,000 Natl. Network: Jones Radio Networks, . Format: CHR. ◆Steve Davis, gen mgr; Mike Chiumento, gen sls mgr; Steve Knupp, progmg dir; Mark Ness, chief of engrg.

Wytheville

WYVE(AM)— Sept 21, 1949: 1280 khz; 2.5 kw-D, 164 w-N. TL: N36 57 54 W81 04 55. Stereo. Hrs open: 24 Box 1247, 110 W.Spiller St., 24382. Phone: (276) 228-3185. Fax: (276) 228-9261.E-mail: trmedia@msn.com Web Site:www.wyve.com Licensee: Three Rivers Media Corp. (acq 10-1-98; $250,000). Population served: 37,700 Natl. Network: AP Network News, Jones Radio Networks, . Rgnl. Network: Va. News Net. Rgnl rep: Rgnl Reps Brooks, Pierce, McLendon, Humphrey & Leonard. Format: C&W, loc news, sports, info. News staff: one; News: 10 hrs wkly. Target aud: 25 plus; general. Spec prog: Gospel 4 hrs wkly. ◆Gary W. Hagerich, CEO, pres, stn mgr; Danny Gordon, opns dir; Teresa Kingl, traf mgr.

Yorktown

WXEZ(FM)— July 4, 1975: 94.1 mhz; 50 kw. 500 ft TL: N37 29 37 W76 26 30. (CP: 40 kw, ant 531 ft.). Stereo. Hrs open: 24 5589 Greenwich Rd., Suite 200, Virginia Beach, 23462. Phone: (757) 671-1000. Fax: (757) 518-9364.E-mail: dmurray@wxez941.com Web Site:www.wxez941.com Licensee: MHR License LLC. Group owner: Barnstable Broadcasting Inc. (acq 3-24-2005; grpsl). Natl. Rep: Christal,. Format: Urban adult contemp. News staff: 8. Target aud: 35-64. ◆Eric Martel, pres; Vonneva Carter, gen mgr; Cynthia Weatherspoon, gen sls mgr; Mary Stott, mktg dir; Dale Murray, progmg dir.

*WYCS(FM)— February 1966: 91.5 mhz; 1.3 kw horiz, 20 kw vert. Ant 371 ft TL: N37 12 17 W76 30 07. Stereo. Hrs open: 24 Box 1924, Tulsa, OK, 74101. Phone: (757) 886-7490. Phone: (918) 455-5693. Fax: (757) 886-7491.E-mail: mail@oasisnetwork.org Web Site:www.oasisnetwork.org Licensee: Creative Educational Media Corp. Inc. Format: Relg. Target aud: General. ◆David Ingles, pres; Greg Roth, gen mgr.

Washington

Aberdeen

KBKW(AM)— Aug 1, 1949: 1450 khz; 1 kw-U. TL: N46 56 59 W123 49 13. Hrs open: 24 Box 1198, 98520. Secondary address: 1520 Simpson Ave. 98520. Phone: (360) 533-3000. Fax: (360) 532-1456.E-mail: bossbill@jodesha.com Web Site:www.jodesha.com Licensee: Jodesha Broadcasting Inc. (group owner; acq 2-28-03; $750,000 with KSWW(FM) Montesano). Population served: 52,200 Natl. Network: ABC, . Wire Svc: AP Format: news/talk 24/7. News staff: one; News: 13. Target aud: 25-54. ◆Wm J. Wolfenbarger, pres; Bill Wolfenbarger, gen mgr; Gabrielle Jordan, opns dir; Sally Miller, gen sls mgr.

KDDS-FM—(Elma, 1981: 99.3 mhz; 41 kw. Ant 2,034 ft TL: N47 19 12 W123 20 41. Stereo. Hrs open: 1400 W. Main St., Auburn, 98001. Phone: (253) 735-9700. Fax: (253) 735-7424. Web Site:www.radiolagrand.com Licensee: Bustos Media of Seattle License LLC. (acq 9-28-2005; $20 million). Format: Rgnl Mexican. ◆Amador Bustos, pres; Jose Diaz, gen mgr; Cesar Valdiosera, progmg dir.

KDUX-FM—Listing follows KXRO(AM).

KWOK(AM)—See Hoquiam

KXRO(AM)— May 28, 1928: 1320 khz; 5 kw-D, 1 kw-N, DA-N. TL: N46 57 28 W123 48 26. Hrs open: 24 1308 Coolidge Rd., 98520. Phone: (360) 533-1320. Fax: (360) 532-0935.E-mail: info@kxro.com Web Site:www.kxro.com Licensee: Morris Communications Corp. Group owner: Morris Communications Inc. (acq 10-15-98; grpsl). Population served: 60,000 Natl. Network: CBS, . Natl. Rep: McGavren Guild,. Covington & Burling. Format: News/talk. News staff: 2; News: 6 hrs wkly. Target aud: 35-64. ◆Donna Rosi, gen mgr, gen sls mgr; Pat Anderson, opns dir, progmg dir; Liz Miller, news dir, pub affrs dir, news rptr; Jay White, chief of engrg; Lorrie Larson, traf mgr; Ian Cope, sports cmtr; James Michael Powers, disc jockey.

KXXK(FM)—See Olympia

Airway Heights

KXLX(AM)— October 1986: 700 khz; 10 kw-D, 600 w-N, DA-N. TL: N47 36 31 W117 22 25. Hrs open: 500 W. Boone Ave., Spokane, 99201. Phone: (509) 324-4000. Fax: (509) 324-8992. Licensee: QueenB Radio Inc. (acq 9-1-2005; $236,000). Natl. Network: ESPN Radio, . Natl. Rep: Katz Radio,. Format: Sports. ◆Stephen Herling, exec VP; Chris Garras, gen mgr; Teddi Gibbon, stn mgr; Roger Nelson, opns mgr, progmg mgr; Dick Brantley, rgnl sls mgr; Bud Nameck, progmg dir.

Anacortes

KWLE(AM)— Dec 18, 1957: 1340 khz; 1 kw-U. TL: N48 29 44 W122 36 15. Hrs open: 24 Box 96, 25th & Commercial Ave., 98221. Phone: (360) 293-3141. Fax: (360) 293-9463.E-mail: info@kwleam.com Web Site:www.1340thewhale.com Licensee: San Juan Communications Inc. (acq 6-29-2007; $760,000). Population served: 120,000 Natl. Network: Westwood One, CBS, ABC, . Format: Hot adult contemp. News staff: 3; News: 30 hrs wkly. Target aud: 25-60. Spec prog: SP 6 hrs, relg one hr wkly. ◆Jennifer Uteda, pres; William T. Berry, gen mgr; Lynn Mc Mullen, opns VP; Dedrick Allen, opns mgr; Glen Harris, progmg dir.

Asotin

KCLK(AM)—Licensed to Asotin. See Clarkston

KCLK-FM—See Clarkston

*KJCF(FM)— 2009: 89.3 mhz; 175 w. Ant -328 ft TL: N46 19 56 W117 02 34. Hrs open:
Rebroadcasts KAWZ(FM) Twin Falls, ID 100%.
Box 391, Twin Falls, ID, 83303. Phone: (208) 734-6633. Fax: (208) 736-1958. Web Site:www.csnradio.com Licensee: CSN International. Format: Christian praise & worship, bible teaching. ◆Michael Kestler, pres.

Auburn

*KGRG-FM— December 1974: 89.9 mhz; 250 w. Ant 367 ft TL: N47 15 23 W122 13 07. Stereo. Hrs open: 24 12401 S.E. 320th St., 98092-3699. Phone: (253) 833-9111. Fax: (253) 288-3439.E-mail: tkrause@greenriver.edu Web Site:www.kgrg.com Licensee: Green River Community College. Population served: 500,000 Format: Modern rock. News: 2 hrs wkly. Target aud: 16-34. Spec prog: Loc music 3 hrs, rap 3 hrs, metal 2 hrs, punk 4 hrs wkly. ◆Tom Evans Krause, gen mgr; J. Middleton, prom dir, progmg dir; Jon Kasprick, chief of engrg.

Auburn-Federal Way

KTBK(AM)— Aug 6, 1958: 1210 khz; 27.5 kw-D, 10 kw-N, DA-2. TL: N47 18 20 W122 14 53. Stereo. Hrs open: 24 1400 W. Main St., Auburn, 98001. Phone: (253) 735-9700. Fax: (253) 735-7424. Licensee: Bustos Media of Washington License LLC. Group owner: Entercom Communications Corp. (acq 1-21-2005; $6 million). Population served: 2,500,000 Natl. Network: Ke-Buena, . Format: Rgnl Mexican. ◆Amador Bustos, pres; Jose Diaz, gen mgr; Cesar Valdiosera, progmg dir.

Basin City

KOLW(FM)— February 1992: 97.5 mhz; 50 kw. Ant 620 ft TL: N46 17 23 W119 25 28. Stereo. Hrs open: 24 2621 West A St., Pasco, 99301. Phone: (509) 547-9791. Fax: (509) 547-8509.E-mail: info@kolw.com Web Site:www.975coolfm.com Licensee: GAP Broadcasting Tri-Cities License LLC. (acq 2-13-2008; grpsl). Population served: 225,000 Natl. Network: Jones Radio Networks, . Rgnl rep: Wheeler Broadcasting. Format: Classic hits. Target aud: 25-49; 60% male, 40% female. ◆Eric Van Winkle, gen mgr.

Bellevue

*KASB(FM)— Mar 22, 1971: 89.9 mhz; 60 w. Ant 59 ft TL: N47 36 17 W122 11 47. Hrs open: 10416 E. Wolverine Way, 98004-6698. Phone: (425) 456-7119. Fax: (425) 456-7110.E-mail: kasb89@hotmail.com Web Site:www.bsd405.org Licensee: Bellevue School District No. 405. Population served: 50,000 Format: Alternative, news. Spec prog: News magazine 3 hrs, sports 6 hrs wkly. ◆Wes Zujko, gen mgr.

*KBCS(FM)— Feb 3, 1973: 91.3 mhz; 7.9 kw. Ant 216 ft TL: N47 35 07 W122 08 39. Stereo. Hrs open: 24 3000 Landerholm Cir. S.E., 98007. Phone: (425) 564-2427. Fax: (425) 564-5697.E-mail: kbcs@ctc.edu Web Site:kbcs.fm Licensee: Bellevue Community College. Population served: 1,000,000 Format: Jazz, folk, world mus. News: 4 hrs wkly. Target aud: General. ◆Steve Ramsey, gen mgr; Bruce Wirth, opns dir, mus dir, pub affrs dir; Sabrina Roach, dev dir; Robert Jefferson, progmg dir; Sam Roffe, chief of engrg.

KQMV(FM)— November 1964: 92.5 mhz; 58 kw. Ant 2,342 ft TL: N47 30 14 W121 58 29. Stereo. Hrs open: 3650 131st Ave. S.E., Suite 550, 98006. Phone: (425) 653-9462. Fax: (425) 653-9464.E-mail: info@movin925.fm Web Site:www.movin925.fm Licensee: Bellevue Radio Inc. Group owner: Sandusky Radio Population served: 250,000 Natl. Rep: Christal,. Format: Rhythmic adult contemp. News: one hr wkly. Target aud: 25-49; working women & families. ◆Norman Rau, pres; Marc S. Kaye, VP, gen mgr; Lois Mares, sls dir, gen sls mgr; Annie O'Dell, rgnl sls mgr, prom mgr; Maynard Cohen, progmg dir.

KXPA(AM)— March 1958: 1540 mhz; 5 kw-U, DA-N. TL: N47 35 29 W122 10 56. Hrs open: 114 Lakeside Ave., Seattle, 98122-6542. Phone: (206) 292-7800. Fax: (206) 292-2140.E-mail: info@kxpa.com Web Site:www.kxpa.com Licensee: Multicultural Radio Broadcasting Licensee LLC. Group owner: Multicultural Radio Broadcasting Inc. (acq 2-13-98; grpsl). Format: Sp, ethnic, div. ◆Arthur Liu, pres; Lisa Shepherd, gen mgr; Dennis Hartley, opns mgr, progmg dir.

Bellingham

KAFE(FM)— July 2, 1965: 104.3 mhz; 60 kw. 2,310 ft TL: N48 40 48 W122 50 24. Stereo. Hrs open: 24 Prog sep from AM 2219 Yew Street Rd., 98226. Phone: (360) 734-9790, (360) 734-5233. Web Site:www.kafe.com Population served: 2,000,000 Format: Adult contemp. ◆Scotty Kvipers, prom dir; Don Hurley, progmg dir, chief of engrg; Bill Baker, news rptr; Jeff Nelson, disc jockey.

KARI(AM)— See Blaine

KBAI(AM)— Apr 4, 1958: 930 khz; 1 kw-D, 500 w-N, DA-N. TL: N48 47 53 W122 28 01. Hrs open: 24 2219 Yew Street Rd., 98229. Phone: (360) 734-9790. Fax: (360) 733-4551. Licensee: Saga Broadcasting LLC. Group owner: Saga Communications Inc. (acq 3-8-99; $1 million). Population served: 140,000 Natl. Rep: Tacher,. Garvey, Schubert & Barer. Format: Progressive talk. News staff: one; News: 5 hrs wkly. ◆Ed Christian, pres, local news ed; Rick Staeb, gen mgr.

KGMI(AM)— 1927: 790 khz; 5 kw-D, 1 kw-N, DA-N. TL: N48 41 09 W122 26 43. Hrs open: 2219 Yew Street Rd., 98229. Phone: (360) 734-9790. Web Site:www.kgmi.com Licensee: Saga Broadcasting LLC. Group owner: Saga Communications Inc. (acq 9-24-98; $8 million with co-located FM). Population served: 147,000 Natl. Rep: McGavren Guild,. Format: News/talk. Target aud: 35-64. ◆Ed Christian, pres; Rick Staeb, gen mgr, natl sls mgr; Krista Kay, prom dir, news dir; Brett Bonner, progmg dir; Will Vos, chief of engrg; Doug Lange, sports cmtr; Steve Ricci, women's int ed.

KISM(FM)— March 1960: 92.9 mhz; 50 kw. Ant 2,440 ft TL: N48 40 48 W122 50 24. Stereo. Hrs open: 2219 Yew Street Rd., 98229. Phone: (360) 734-9790. Web Site:www.kism.com Licensee: Saga Broadcasting LLC. Population served: 246,000 Format: Classic rock. Target aud: 25-44. ◆Carol Dooley, progmg dir & mus dir.

KPUG(AM)— Feb 29, 1948: 1170 khz; 10 kw-D, 5 kw-N, DA-N. TL: N40 45 34 W122 26 21. Hrs open: 24 2219 Yew Street Rd., 98226-8855. Phone: (360) 734-9790. Phone: (360) 734-5233. Web Site:www.1170kpug.com Licensee: Saga Broadcasting LLC. Group owner: Saga Communications Inc. (acq 10-30-98; $5,825,000 with co-located FM). Population served: 125,000 Natl. Rep: McGavren Guild,. Format: Sports/talk. News staff: 3; News: 24 hrs wkly. Target aud: 25-54. ◆Ed Chrtistian, pres, opns dir; Rick Staeb, gen mgr; Doug Lange, progmg dir; Will Vos, engrg dir & chief of engrg.

*KUGS(FM)— Jan 29, 1974: 89.3 mhz; 100 w. Ant 384 ft TL: N48 44 11 W122 28 47. (CP: 700 w, ant 482 ft). Stereo. Hrs open: 7 AM-12AM Western Wash. Univ., 700 Viking Union Bldg., 98225. Phone: (360) 650-4771. Phone: (360) 650-5847. Fax: (360) 650-2696. Web Site:www.kugs.org Licensee: Western Washington University. Population served: 150,000 Wire Svc: AP Format: Progsv, news/talk. News: 17 hrs wkly. Target aud: 18-34; college students & adults. Spec prog: Black 10 hrs, Hawaiian 2 hrs wkly. ◆Jamie Hoover, gen mgr; Juliana de Groot, opns dir; Sam Parker, progmg dir; Britt Barquist, mus dir; Jeff Emtman, news dir, pub affrs dir.

*KZAZ(FM)— Sept 1, 1991: 91.7 mhz; 120 w. 334 ft TL: N48 48 04 W122 27 40. Stereo. Hrs open: 24
Rebroadcasts KRFA-FM Pullman 95%.
Washington State University, Box 642530, Pullman, 99164. Phone: (509) 335-6500. Fax: (509) 335-6577.E-mail: nwpr@wsu.edu Web Site:www.nwpr.org Licensee: Washington State University. (acq 7-29-97). Population served: 60,000 Natl. Network: NPR, PRI, . Dow, Lohnes & Albertson. Format: Class, jazz, news. News: 40 hrs wkly. Target aud: 25-54; general. Spec prog: Folk 8 hrs, world music 7 hrs wkly. ◆Kerry Swanson, stn mgr; Robin Rilette, mus dir.

Benton City

KMMG(FM)— Aug 1, 1974: 96.7 mhz; 1.4 kw. Ant 692 ft TL: N46 15 33 W119 21 55. Stereo. Hrs open: 24 2730 West Lewis #B, Pasco, 99301. Phone: (509) 543-3334. Fax: (509) 452-0541.E-mail: zorro@radiozorro.com Licensee: Bustos Media of Eastern Washington License LLC. (acq 11-18-2004; grpsl). Population served: 45,000 Format: Rgnl Mexican. News staff: one; News: 22 hrs wkly. Target aud: 25 plus. ◆Bob Berry, gen mgr; Bob Berrt, gen sls mgr; Martin Ortiz, progmg dir; Keith Teske, chief of engrg.

Blaine

KAFE(FM)— See Bellingham

KARI(AM)— Feb 12, 1960: 550 khz; 5 kw-D, 2.5 kw-N, DA-2. TL: N48 57 15 W122 44 36. Hrs open: 24 4840 Lincoln Rd., 98230. Phone: (360) 371-5500. Phone: (604) 536-7733. Fax: (360) 371-7617.E-mail: kari@kari55.com Web Site:www.kari55.com Licensee: Way Broadcasting Licensee LLC (acq 7-20-00; $3 million with KVRI(AM) Blaine). Population served: 3,750,000 Format: Relg, news/talk. Target aud: 35 plus. Spec prog: Ger 2 hrs, Ukrainian one hr, Arabic one hr wkly. ◆Arthur Liu, pres; Yvonne Liu, VP; Gary Nawman, gen mgr, opns mgr.

KVRI(AM)— Jan 1, 2001: 1600 khz; 50 kw-D, 10 kw-N. TL: N48 57 15 W122 44 36. Hrs open: 4840 Lincoln Rd., 98230. Phone: (360) 371-5500. Fax: (360) 371-7617.E-mail: gary@kari55.com Web Site:www.kari55.com Licensee: Way Broadcasting Licensee LLC (acq 5-23-00; with KARI(AM) Blaine). Format: Punjabi. ◆Arthur Liu, pres; Yvonne Liu, VP; Gary Nawman, gen mgr, opns mgr.

Bremerton

KBRO(AM)— May 1947: 1490 khz; 1 kw-U. TL: N47 33 52 W122 39 26. Hrs open: 6 AM-midnight Box 348, Sedalia, CO, 80135. Phone: (303) 688-5162. Fax: (303) 660-4930. Licensee: Seattle Streaming Radio LLC. (acq 8-26-2005; $900,000 with KNTB(AM) Lakewood). Population served: 3,000,000 Format: Sp var. ◆Oscar Ibarra, gen mgr.

KRWM(FM)— Aug 22, 1964: 106.9 mhz; 49 kw. Ant 1,299 ft TL: N47 32 39 W122 06 29. Stereo. Hrs open: 24 3650 131 Ave. S.E., Suite 550, Bellevue, 98006. Phone: (425) 373-5545. Fax: (425) 653-1188. Web Site:www.warm1069.com Licensee: Seascape Radio Inc. Group owner: Sandusky Radio (acq 9-12-96; $29.25 million). Natl. Rep: Christal,. Format: Soft adult contemp. Target aud: 35-54; educated, upscale professionals, family oriented, white/blue collar. ◆Marc Kaye,

VP, gen mgr, chief of engrg; Susan huffman, gen sls mgr; Heather Gardner, prom dir; Laura Dane, progmg dir.

Brewster

*KEWR(FM)— Not on air, target date: unknown: 91.9 mhz; 1 kw. Ant 2,477 ft TL: N48 02 14 W119 59 07. Hrs open:
Rebroadcasts KPBX-FM Spokane 100%.
2319 N. Monroe St., Spokane, 99205. Phone: (509) 328-5729. Fax: (509) 328-5764.E-mail: kpbx@kpbx.org Web Site:www.kpbx.org Licensee: Spokane Public Radio Inc. Natl. Network: NPR, PRI, . ◆Richard Kunkel, gen mgr.

Burbank

KUJ-FM— 1997: 99.1 mhz; 52 kw. Ant 1,263 ft TL: N46 05 58 W119 07 40. Hrs open: 16 830 N. Columbia Center Blvd., Suite B-2, Kennewick, 99336. Phone: (509) 783-0783. Fax (509) 735-8627. Web Site:www.power991fm.com Licensee: New Northwest Broadcasters LLC (group owner; (acq 6-22-2004; $1.68 million). Format: Rhythmic CHR. Target aud: 18-34. ◆Don Morin, gen mgr; Curt Cartier, opns mgr.

KVAN(AM)— 2007: 1560 khz; 10 kw-D, 700 w-N, DA-2. TL: N46 10 11 W119 01 32. Hrs open: 3544 W. Ct., Pasco, 99301. Phone: (509) 882-4736.E-mail: info@kvanam.com Licensee: Compadres LC (acq 8-1-2007). ◆Angel Castaneda, gen mgr.

Burien-Seattle

KGNW(AM)— Oct 10, 1970: 820 khz; 50 kw-D, 5 kw-N, DA-2. TL: N47 26 00 W121 28 02. Hrs open: 24 2201 6th Ave., Ste 1500, Seattle, 98121. Phone: (206) 443-8200. Fax: (206) 777-1133.E-mail: webmaster@kgnw.com Web Site:www.kgnw.com Licensee: Inspiration Media Inc. Group owner: Salem Communications Corp. (acq 1984). Population served: 60,000 Natl. Rep: Salem,. Format: Relg, Christian talk. News: 3 hrs wkly. Target aud: 35 plus. Spec prog: Talk, women, loc affrs, health. ◆Stuart Epperson, chmn; Edward G. Atsinger III, pres; Tim Harper, gen mgr; Joshua Main, opns mgr; Dave Drui, progmg dir; Monte Passmore, chief of engrg.

Camas

KNRK(FM)— Licensed to Camas. See Portland OR

Cashmere

KWWX(FM)— 1993: 106.7 mhz; 6 kw. Ant 513 ft TL: N47 30 35 W120 31 24. Stereo. Hrs open: 231 N. Wenatchee Ave., Wenatchee, 98801. Phone: (509) 665-6565. Fax: (509) 663-1150. Web Site:www.therock1067.com Licensee: CCR-Wenatchee IV LLC. Group owner: Fisher Broadcasting Company (acq 10-31-2006; grpsl). Natl. Rep: McGavren Guild,. Fisher, Wayland, Cooper, Leader & Zaragoza. Format: Classic rock. Target aud: 25-54. ◆Jim Senst, gen mgr; Leona Frank, gen sls mgr; Dave Keefer, progmg dir.

KYSN(FM)— See Wenatchee

Castle Rock

KRQT(FM)— January 1994: 107.1 mhz; 800 w. Ant 1,715 ft TL: N46 20 18 W123 05 45. Hrs open: 1130 14th Ave., Longview, 98632. Phone: (360) 425-1500. Fax: (360) 425-1500. Web Site:www.theclassicrockexperience.com Licensee: Bicoastal Media Licenses IV LLC. Group owner: Entercom Communications Corp. (acq 3-31-2005; grpsl). Natl. Network: ABC, . Format: Classic rock & roll. News: One. ◆Julie Laird, stn mgr; Kevin Taylor, opns mgr; Sam Lee, gen sls mgr; Phil Blair, news dir; Dawn Crowe, traf mgr.

Centralia

KCED(FM)— Licensed to Centralia. See Centralia-Chehalis

KNBQ(FM)— Licensed to Centralia. See Centralia-Chehalis

Centralia-Chehalis

*KCED(FM)— (Centralia, Feb 17, 1975: 91.3 mhz; 1 kw. -72 ft TL: N46 42 54 W122 57 39. (CP: 1.2 kw, ant 131 ft.). Stereo. Hrs open: 600 W. Locust St., Centralia, 98531-4099. Phone: (360) 736-9391 x343.

Fax: (360) 330-7509. Fax: www.centralia.ctc.edu.E-mail: info@kcedfm.com Licensee: Board of Trustees, Centralia College. Population served: 50,000 Format: Variety/diversified, Sp. Spec prog: Sports 3 hrs wkly. ♦Wade Fisher, gen mgr & progmg dir.

KELA(AM)— Nov 1, 1937: 1470 khz; 5 kw-D, 1 kw-N. TL: N46 41 47 W122 57 23. Hrs open: 24 1635 S. Gold St., Centralia, 98531. Phone: (360) 736-3321. Phone: (360) 748-3321. Fax: (360) 736-0150.E-mail: johndimeoe@clearchannel.com Web Site:www.kelaam.com Licensee: Bicoastal Media Licenses IV LLC. Group owner: Clear Channel Communications Inc. (acq 12-1-2007; $4.175 milllion with KMNT(FM) Chehalis). Population served: 62,500 Natl. Network: Fox News Radio, . Natl. Rep: Tacher,. Format: News/talk/sports. News staff: 2; News: 28 hrs wkly. Target aud: 35 plus. Spec prog: Home Improvement. ♦John DiMeo Jr., gen mgr; Larry Miner, gen sls mgr; Steve Richert, progmg dir; Doug Adamson, news dir; Dan Smith, chief of engrg.

KITI(AM)—(Chehalis-Centralia, October 1954: 1420 khz; 5 kw-U, DA-2. TL: N46 42 08 W122 55 58. Hrs open: 24 1133 Kresky, Centralia, 98531. Phone: (360) 736-1355. Fax: (360) 736-4761.E-mail: mshannon@live95.com Licensee: Premier Broadcasters Inc. (acq 10-77). Population served: 60,000 Leventhal, Senter & Lerman. Format: Oldies. News staff: one; News: 15 hrs wkly. Target aud: 25-54. ♦Rod Etherton, pres & gen mgr.

KNBQ(FM)—(Centralia, Aug 24, 1965: 102.9 mhz; 70 kw. Ant 2,191 ft TL: N46 58 31 W123 08 16. Stereo. Hrs open: 24 351 Elliott Ave. W., Suite 300, Seattle, 98119. Phone: (206) 494-2000. Fax: (206) 286-2376.E-mail: info@qcountry1029.com Web Site:qcountry1029.com Licensee: Citicasters Licenses L.P. (acq 5-4-99; grpsl). Population served: 500,000 Format: Country. News staff: 2; News: 7 hrs wkly. Target aud: 18 plus. ♦Michele Grosenick, gen mgr.

Chehalis

***KACS(FM)**— Aug 18, 1993: 90.5 mhz; 6 kw. Ant 187 ft TL: N46 43 52 W123 01 28. Stereo. Hrs open: 24 2451 N.E. Kresky, Unit A, 98532. Phone: (360) 740-9436. Fax: (360) 740-9415.E-mail: manager@kacs.org Web Site:www.kacs.org Licensee: Chehalis Valley Educational Foundation. Population served: 350,000 Donald E. Martin. Format: Relg. News: 6 hrs wkly. Target aud: 45-54. ♦Kerry O'Connor, chmn; Cameron Beierle, gen mgr, stn mgr, progmg dir.

KITI(AM)—See Centralia-Chehalis

KMNT(FM)— 2005: 104.3 mhz; 2.35 kw. Ant 1,056 ft TL: N46 33 18 W123 03 27. Hrs open: 1635 S. Gold St., Centralia, 98531. Phone: (360) 330-0777. Fax: (360) 736-0150. Web Site:www.kmnt.com Licensee: Bicoastal Media Licenses IV LLC. (acq 12-1-2007; $4.175 million with KELA(AM) Centralia-Chehalis). Population served: 95,000 Natl. Rep: Tacher,. Rgnl rep: Tacher Format: Country. News staff: one; News: 60 minutes weekly. Spec prog: NFL Football. ♦John DiMeo Jr., gen mgr.

***KSWS(FM)**—Not on air, target date: unknown: 88.9 mhz; 50 w horiz, 1 kw vert. Ant 1,004 ft TL: N46 33 16 W123 03 26. Hrs open: Educational Telecommunications and Technology, Box 642530, Pullman, 99164-2530. Phone: (509) 335-6511.E-mail: wwpr@wsu.edu Licensee: Washington State University. ♦Dennis Haarsager, gen mgr.

Chehalis-Centralia

KITI(AM)—Licensed to Chehalis-Centralia. See Centralia-Chehalis

Chelan

KOZI(AM)— Mar 1, 1957: 1230 khz; 1 kw-U. TL: N47 51 00 W120 00 20. Hrs open: 24 Box 819, 98816. Secondary address: 123 E. Johnson 98816. Phone: (509) 682-4033. Fax: (509) 682-4035.E-mail: info@kozi.com Web Site:www.kozi.com Licensee: Icicle Broadcasting Co. (group owner; (acq 8-26-99; grpsl). Population served: 80,000 Natl. Rep: Target Broadcast Sales,. Haley, Bader & Potts. Format: Adult contemp, news/talk. News staff: 3; News: 32 hrs wkly. Target aud: General. Spec prog: Farm 3 hrs, Sp 5 hrs wkly. ♦Harriet Bullitt, pres; Gary Mathews, gen mgr; Joe Fiala, stn mgr; Steve Byquist, opns mgr, progmg dir; Vicky Chandler, gen sls mgr; Michael Dickes, mus dir, farm dir; Clint Strand, news dir.

KOZI-FM— Aug 26, 1981: 93.5 mhz; 590 w. Ant 1,040 ft TL: N47 51 07 W119 52 18. Stereo. Hrs open: Dups AM 100% Box 819, 98816. Secondary address: 123 E. Johnson 98816. Phone: (509) 682-4033. Fax: (509) 682-4035.E-mail: info@kozi.com Web Site:www.kozi.com Format: Adult contemp news/talk.

Cheney

***KEWU-FM**— Apr 3, 1964: 89.5 mhz; 10 kw. Ant 1,407 ft TL: N47 34 43 W117 17 50. Stereo. Hrs open: 6 AM-1 AM (M-F); 9 AM-1 AM (S, Su) Electronic Media & Film, 104 RTV Bldg., 99004-2495. Phone: (509) 359-2440. Fax: (509) 359-2850.E-mail: efarriss@mail.ewu.edu Licensee: Eastern Washington University Board of Trustees. Format: Jazz. ♦Marvin Smith, gen mgr; Elizabeth Farriss, progmg dir.

KEYF-FM— May 4, 1986: 101.1 mhz; 100 kw. 1,607 ft TL: N47 35 35 W117 17 46. Stereo. Hrs open: 24 1601 E. 57th, Spokane, 99223. Phone: (509) 448-1000. Phone: (509) 232-1011. Fax: (509) 448-7015. Web Site:www.oldies1011.com Licensee: Mapleton License of Spokane LLC. Group owner: Citadel Broadcasting Corp. (acq 12-3-2007; grpsl). Population served: 360,000 Format: Hits of the 60s & 70s. News: 15 hrs wkly. Target aud: 35-64. ♦Don Morin, gen mgr; Tim Cotter, progmg dir; Larry Weir, news dir; Dave Ratener, chief of engrg; Brenda Anderson, traf mgr.

Clarkston

KCLK(AM)—(Asotin, Mar 2, 1971: 1430 khz; 5 kw-D, 1 kw-N, DA-2. TL: N46 18 59 W117 02 24. Hrs open: 24 403 C St., Lewiston, 83501. Phone: (208) 743-6564. Fax: (208) 798-0110.E-mail: evanyeoman@pacempire.com Licensee: Bolland Enterprises LLC. (acq 9-12-2008; grpsl). Population served: 120,000 Format: Sports, talk. News staff: one. Target aud: 15 plus; sports interested. ♦Mark Bolland, gen mgr; Evan Yeoman, progmg dir; Leslie Gatherer, chief of engrg, traf mgr.

KCLK-FM— 1974: 94.1 mhz; 100 kw. 1,233 ft TL: N46 27 27 W117 06 03. Stereo. Hrs open: 24 403 C St., Lewiston, ID, 83501. Phone: (208) 743-6564. Fax: (208) 798-0110.E-mail: evanyeoman@pacempire.com Licensee: Bolland Enterprises LLC. Group owner: Pacific Empire Communications Corp. (acq 9-12-2008; grpsl). Population served: 120,000 Format: Classic Hits. Target aud: 25 plus. ♦Evan Yeoman, pres, progmg dir; Mark Bolland, pres, sls dir & gen sls mgr; Dave Forsman, chief of engrg.

***KNWV(FM)**— July 11, 1995: 90.5 mhz; 250 w. 1,063 ft TL: N46 27 26 W117 06 00. Hrs open: 24
Rebroadcasts KRFA-FM Moscow, ID 100%.
Box 642530, 382 Murrow Ctr., Pullman, 99164-2530. Phone: (509) 335-6500. Fax: (509) 335-3772.E-mail: nwpr@wsu.edu Web Site:www.nwpr.org Licensee: Washington State University. Dow, Lohnes & Albertson. Format: Class, news. News staff: one; News: 37 hrs wkly. ♦Karen Olstad, COO, gen mgr; Dennis Haarsager, gen mgr; Roger Johnson, stn mgr, sls dir; Scott Weatherly, opns mgr; Sarah McDaniel, dev dir; Mary Hawkins, progmg dir; Robin Rilette, mus dir; Ralph Hogan, engrg dir; Rachael McDonald, news rptr.

KQQQ(AM)—See Pullman

KRLC(AM)—See Lewiston, ID

***KUCC(FM)**—Not on air, target date: unknown: 88.1 mhz; 450 w. Ant 203 ft TL: N46 18 59 W117 02 24. Hrs open: Box 19039, Spokane, 99219-9039. Phone: (509) 838-2761. Fax: (509) 838-4882. Web Site:www.uccsda.org/communications Licensee: Upper Columbia Media Association.

KVAB(FM)— July 15, 1997: 102.9 mhz; 440 w. 1,171 ft TL: N46 27 27 W117 06 03. Hrs open: 24 403 C St., Lewiston, ID, 83501. Phone: (509) 758-3362. Fax: (509) 758-4986.E-mail: kvabfm@aol.com Web Site:kvabfm.com Licensee: Bolland Enterprises LLC. Group owner: Pacific Empire Communications Corp. (acq 9-12-2008; grpsl). Population served: 50,000 Natl. Network: Westwood One, . Natl. Rep: Tacher,. Format: Classic rock. Target aud: 25-55. ♦Mark Bolland, CEO, pres; Jay Mlazgar, gen mgr; Mark Bone, progmg dir.

Cle Elum

***KWSR(FM)**—Not on air, target date: unknown: 89.7 mhz; 750 w. Ant -459 ft TL: N47 10 06.78 W121 03 33.99. Hrs open: Box 642530, Pullman, 99164-2530. Phone: (509) 335-6500. Fax: (509) 335-6577.E-mail: nwpr@wsu.edu Web Site:www.nwpr.org Licensee: Washington State University. ♦Tony Wright, gen mgr.

KXAA(FM)— Nov., 2002: 93.7 mhz; 6 kw. Ant 95 ft TL: N47 09 06 W120 47 23. Stereo. Hrs open: 24 115 N Harris Ave., 98922. Phone: (509) 674-0937. Fax: (509) 674-4042.E-mail: kxaprod@aol.com Licensee: Wheeler Broadcasting Inc. (group owner; acq 5-28-2004; exercise of option). Population served: 22,000 Natl. Network: Jones Radio Networks, . Format: Classic Hits. ♦Jeri Trantham, opns dir; Mark Wheeler, gen mgr & gen sls mgr.

Colfax

KCLX(AM)— 1950: 1450 khz; 1 kw-U. TL: N46 52 17 W117 22 37. Hrs open: PO Box 8849, Moscow, ID, 83843. Phone: (509) 397-3441.E-mail: info@palousecountry.com Web Site:www.palousecountry.com Licensee: Inland Northwest Broadcasting LLC Natl. Rep: Farmakis,. Format: Classic country. Target aud: 25 plus; agricultural-urban. Spec prog: Farm 5 hrs, sports 7 hrs wkly. ♦Gary Cummings, gen mgr, stn mgr; Robert Hauser, opns mgr, rgnl sls mgr; Steve Grubbs, disc jockey.

KMAX(AM)— 1998: 840 khz; 10 kw-D, 280 w-N. TL: N46 54 50 W117 19 28. Hrs open: 24 Box 8849, Moscow, ID, 83843. Phone: (208) 882-2551. Fax: (208) 883-3571.E-mail: hauser@inlandradio.com Licensee: Inland Northwest Broadcasting LLC. (group owner). (acq 6-28-2005; grpsl). Natl. Network: Westwood One, . Format: Talk radio. News staff: 2; News: 15 hrs wkly. Target aud: 25-60; established professional aged people - young marrieds couples. ♦Gary Cummings, gen mgr; Ben Bonfield, gen sls mgr; Darin Sievert, progmg dir; Glen Vaagen, news dir; Steve Franko, chief of engrg.

KRAO-FM— Oct 10, 1994: 102.5 mhz; 2.2 kw. Ant 1,073 ft TL: N46 51 44 W117 10 20. Stereo. Hrs open: 24 Box 8849, 1114 N. Almon St., Moscow, 83843. Phone: (208) 882-2551. Fax: (208) 883-3571. Licensee: Inland Northwest Broadcasting LLC (group owner; (acq 6-28-2005; grpsl). Population served: 65,000 Format: Hot adult contemp. Target aud: 18-45. ♦Gary Cummings, gen mgr; Johnny Mann, progmg dir, spec ev coord; Steve Franco, chief of engrg & farm dir.

College Place

***KGTS(FM)**— Oct 5, 1963: 91.3 mhz; 7 kw. 1,250 ft TL: N45 59 20 W118 10 29. Stereo. Hrs open: 24 204 S. College Ave., 99324. Phone: (509) 527-2991. Fax: (509) 527-2611.E-mail: studio@plr.org Web Site:www.plr.org Licensee: Walla Walla College. Population served: 200,000 Format: Christian contemp. Target aud: 35-64. ♦Jon Dybdahl, pres; Kevin Krueger, gen mgr; Don Godman, opns dir; Elizabeth Nelson, progmg dir; Walter Cox, chief of engrg.

Colville

KCRK-FM— Oct 13, 1981: 92.1 mhz; 3 kw. Ant -790 ft TL: N48 31 15 W117 54 28. Stereo. Hrs open: 24 Prog sep from AM Box 111, 99114. Secondary address: 187 Mantz & Ricky Rd. 99114. Phone: (509) 684-5032. Fax: (509) 684-5034. Licensee: North Country Broadcasting. Natl. Network: Westwood One, . Format: Adult contemp.

KCVL(AM)— Nov 15, 1955: 1240 khz; 1 kw-U. TL: N48 31 15 W117 54 28. Hrs open: 24 Box 111, 187 Mantz & Ricky Rd., 99114. Phone: (509) 684-5031. Fax: (509) 684-5034.E-mail: info@kcvl.com Web Site:www.kcvl.com Licensee: North Country Broadcasting. (acq 1996). Population served: 16,000 Format: Country. ♦Eric Carpenter, pres, pres, gen mgr; Mike Eakins, sls dir.

Davenport

***KKRS(FM)**— 1998: 97.3 mhz; 5.1 kw. Ant 722 ft TL: N47 35 14 W117 53 26. Hrs open: 24 12720 W. Sunset Hwy., Suite C, Airway Heights, 99001. Phone: (509) 244-5577. Fax: (509) 244-2232.E-mail: kkrs@csnradio.com Licensee: CSN International. (group owner; acq 1999; $111,425). Format: Christian talk, educ, music. ♦Barney Dasovich, gen mgr.

Dayton

KZHR(FM)— August 1992: 92.5 mhz; 54 kw. Ant 1,243 ft TL: N46 19 14 W117 58 46. Hrs open: 24 Box 2623, Tri Cities, 99302. Secondary address: 2823 W. Lewis St., Pasco 99301. Phone: (509) 546-0313. Fax: (509) 546-2678.E-mail: gonzalo@kzhr.com Web Site:www.kzhr.com Licensee: CCR-Tri Cities IV LLC. Group owner: Cherry Creek Radio LLC (acq 12-19-2003; grpsl). Population served: 300,000 Natl. Rep: Interep, McGavren Guild,. Format: Mexican rgnl. News staff: one; News: 7 hrs wkly. Target aud: 25-54; adult. ♦Scott Smith, gen mgr; Gonzalo Cortez, stn mgr, progmg dir; Art Blum, chief of engrg; Daena Medina, traf mgr.

Deer Park

KAZZ(FM)— September 1983: 107.1 mhz; 25 kw. Ant 328 ft TL: N48 01 45 W117 35 57. Stereo. Hrs open: Box 1369, 99006. Phone: (509) 276-8816. Licensee: Nancy L. Isserlis, receiver for KAZZ (group owner; (acq 5-15-2009). ♦Christa McDonald, gen mgr.

Dishman

KEYF(AM)— Oct 3, 1984: 1050 khz; 5 kw-D, 260 w-N. TL: N47 36 27 W117 21 40. Hrs open: 24 1601 E. 57th Ave, Spokane, 99223. Phone: (509) 448-1000. Fax: (509) 448-7015. Licensee: Mapleton License of Spokane LLC. Group owner: Citadel Broadcasting Corp. (acq 12-3-2007; grpsl). Population served: 360,000 Format: Adult standards. News: 15 hrs wkly. Target aud: 54 plus. ◆Don Morin, gen mgr; Bob Castle, progmg dir; Larry Weir, news dir; Dave Ratener, chief of engrg; Brenda Anderson, traf mgr.

KSPO(FM)— 1996: 106.5 mhz; 6 kw. 328 ft TL: N47 41 39 W117 20 3. Hrs open:24 Box 31000, Spokane, 99223. Phone: (509) 443-1000.E-mail: acn@acn.cc Web Site:www.kspo.com Licensee: Thomas W. Read dba Classical Broadcasting. (acq 1996; $100,000). Population served: 1,000,000 Natl. Network: USA, Salem Radio Network, . Cohen & Marks. Format: Relg, talk. Target aud: 35 plus. ◆Melinda Read, sr VP; Thomas W. Read, pres & gen mgr.

East Wenatchee

*KLUW(FM)— 2008: 88.1 mhz; 600 w. Ant -131 ft TL: N47 22 52 W120 17 16. Hrs open:
Rebroadcasts KLVR(FM) Middletown, CA 100%.
2351 Sunset Blvd., Suite 170-218, Rocklin, CA, 95765. Phone: (916) 251-1600. Fax: (916) 251-1650. Web Site:www.klove.com Licensee: Educational Media Foundation. (acq 2-11-2008; $100,000 for CP). Natl. Network: K-Love, . Format: Contemp Christian. ◆Michael Novak, pres.

KYSN(FM)—Licensed to East Wenatchee. See Wenatchee

Eatonville

KFNK(FM)— 1995: 104.9 mhz; 17 kw. Ant 407 ft TL: N46 50 24 W122 15 27. Hrs open: 24 351 Elliott Ave. W., 3rd Fl., Seattle, 98119. Phone: (206) 494-2000. Fax: (206) 286-2376.E-mail: bobcase@clearchannel.com Web Site:www.funkymonkey1049.fm Licensee: Ackerley Broadcasting Operations LLC. Group owner: Clear Channel Communications Inc. (acq 2-12-2003; $4.5 million). Population served: 250000 Format: Alternative rock. ◆Michele Grosenick, gen mgr; Bob Case, opns mgr; Allison Hesse, gen sls mgr; Jay Kelly, progmg dir; Steven Kilbreath, news dir; Doug Irwin, chief of engrg.

Edmonds

KCIS(AM)— 1954: 630 khz; 5 kw-D, 2.5 kw-N, DA-N. TL: N47 46 06 W122 21 07. Hrs open: 24 19303 Fremont Ave. N., Seattle, 98133. Phone: (206) 546-7350. Fax: (206) 546-7372.E-mail: comments@kcisradio.com Web Site:www.kcisradio.com Licensee: CRISTA Ministries Group owner: Crista Broadcasting Population served: 50,000 Natl. Network: USA, Moody, AP Radio, . Fletcher, Heald & Hildreth. Wire Svc: AP Wire Svc: U.S. Newswire Format: Christian, inspirational. News staff: one; News: 40 hrs wkly. Target aud: 45-64. ◆Mark Holland, progmg dir.

KCMS(FM)— Mar 11, 1960: 105.3 mhz; 54 kw. Ant 1,263 ft TL: N47 32 40 W122 06 26. Stereo. Hrs open: 24 19303 Fremont Ave. N., Seattle, 98133. Phone: (206) 546-7350. Fax: (206) 546-7372.E-mail: comments@spirit1053.com Web Site:www.spirit1053.com Licensee: CRISTA Ministries Population served: 300,000 Fletcher, Heald & Hildretch. Wire Svc: AP Wire Svc: U.S. Newswire Format: Adult contemp, Christian music. News: one hr wkly. Target aud: 25-44. ◆Stan Mak, VP & gen mgr; Ann Marie Mulholland, sls dir; Amy Randolph, prom dir; Scott Valentine, progmg dir.

Ellensburg

*KCSH(FM)— 1998: 88.9 mhz; 380 w. 548 ft TL: N47 10 02 W120 45 50. Hrs open: 111 W. 6th Ave., Studio B, 98926. Phone: (509) 964-2061. Fax: (509) 964-2825.E-mail: info@kcshfm.com Web Site:www.lifetalk.net Licensee: Lifetalk Broadcasting Association. Format: Relg, inspirational. ◆Kermit Netteburg, pres; Don Zacharias, gen mgr.

*KCWU(FM)— Apr 30, 1999: 88.1 mhz; 500 w. Ant -194 ft TL: N47 00 21 W120 30 55. Stereo. Hrs open: 24 Central Washington Univ., 400 E. University Way, 98926-7594. Phone: (509) 963-2283, 2282. Fax: (509) 963-1688.E-mail: kcwu@cwu.edu Web Site:www.881theburg.com Licensee: Trustees of Central Washington University. Population served: 18,000 Morrison & Foerster. Format: Modern rock, alternative, div. News: 5 hrs wkly. Target aud: 15-49; 18-34 core. ◆Chris Hull, gen mgr & dev dir.

*KNWR(FM)— June 1992: 90.7 mhz; 5 kw. 2,552 ft TL: N47 15 48 W120 23 31. Hrs open: 24
Rebroadcasts KRFA-FM Moscow, ID 100%.
Box 642530, 382 Murrow Ctr., Pullman, 99164-2530. Phone: (509) 335-6500. Fax: (509) 335-3772.E-mail: nwpr@wsu.edu Web Site:www.nwpr.org Licensee: Washington State University. Natl. Network: NPR, PRI, . Format: Class, news. News staff: one; News: 37 hrs wkly. Target aud: General. Spec prog: Jazz, folk. ◆Karen Olstad, COO, gen mgr; Dennis Haarsager, gen mgr; Roger Johnson, stn mgr, sls dir; Scott Weatherly, opns mgr; Sarah McDaniel, dev dir; Mary Hawkins, progmg dir; Robin Rilette, mus dir; Ralph Hogan, engrg dir; Rachael McDonald, news rptr.

KXLE(AM)— 1946: 1240 khz; 1 kw-U. TL: N47 00 00 W120 31 40. Hrs open: 24 1311 Vantage Hwy., 98926. Phone: (509) 925-1488. Fax: (509) 962-7882.E-mail: kxle@fairpoint.net Licensee: KXLE Inc. (acq 6-82). Population served: 400,000 Natl. Network: CBS, . Natl. Rep: Tacher,. Bosari & Paxson. Wire Svc: AP Format: News/talk, sports. News staff: 4; News: 40 hrs wkly. Target aud: 25-54; adults. ◆Sol M. Tacher, pres; Brad Tacher, VP, gen mgr; Patti Burke, prom mgr; Dennis Leach, news dir; Kevin Whitaker, engrg dir; Frances Moen, traf mgr.

*KYKV(FM)— Nov 24, 1983: 103.1 mhz; 2 kw horiz. Ant 1,289 ft TL: N46 53 15 W120 26 29. Stereo. Hrs open:
Rebroadcasts KLVR(FM) Middletown, CA 100%.
2351 Sunset Blvd., Suite 170-218, Rocklin, CA, 95765. Phone: (916) 251-1600. Fax: (916) 251-1650. Web Site:www.klove.com Licensee: Educational Media Foundation. (acq 6-13-2008; $825,000). Natl. Network: K-Love, . Format: Contemp Christian. ◆Mike Novak, pres.

Elma

*KCFL(FM)—Not on air, target date: unknown: 91.3 mhz; 100 w. Ant -289 ft TL: N47 00 38 W123 22 59. Hrs open: 2200 Simpson Ave., Hoquiam, 98550. Phone: (360) 705-0619. Licensee: Northwest Indy Radio. ◆Stephen P. Lepisto, pres.

KDDS-FM—Licensed to Elma. See Aberdeen

Enumclaw

KGRG(AM)— Mar 1, 1992: 1330 khz; 500 w-D, 26 w-N. TL: N47 12 53 W121 58 19. Hrs open: 24 12401 S.E. 320 St., Auburn, 98092-3699. Phone: (253) 833-5004. Fax: (253) 288-3460.E-mail: programing@kgrg.com Web Site:www.kgrg1.com Licensee: Green River Foundation (acq 9-17-96; $40,000). Population served: 84,000 Format: Current alternative. ◆Tom Evans Krause, gen mgr.

Ephrata

KTAC(FM)— 1998: 93.9 mhz; 18 kw. 384 ft TL: N47 19 13 W119 34 22. Hrs open: 24
Simulcast with KTBI(AM) Ephrata.
Box 31000, Spokane, 99223. Phone: (509) 754-2000. Fax: (509) 448-3811.E-mail: ktac@ktac.com Web Site:www.ktac.com Licensee: TRMR Inc.

KTBI(AM)— Aug 17, 1950: 810 khz; 50 kw-D. TL: N47 21 22 W119 28 56. Hrs open: Sunrise-sunset
Simulcast with KTAC(FM) Ephrata.
Box 31000, Spokane, 99223. Phone: (509) 754-2000. Fax: (509) 448-3811.E-mail: ktbi@ktbi.com Web Site:www.ktbi.com Licensee: Tacoma Broadcasters Inc. Population served: 530,831 Pepper & Corazzini. Format: Relg, talk. Target aud: 35 plus. Spec prog: Farm 15 hrs wkly. ◆Melinda Read, VP; John Tillman, opns mgr; Thomas W. Read, pres, gen mgr & progmg dir; George Frese, engrg dir.

KULE(AM)— 1952: 730 khz; 1 kw-D, 29 w-N. TL: N47 19 01 W119 33 46. Hrs open: Box 2888, Yakima, 98907. Secondary address: 910 Basin S.W. 98823. Phone: (509) 457-1000. Fax: (509) 452-0541.E-mail: zorro@radiozorro.com Web Site:www.radiozorro.com Licensee: Bustos Media of Eastern Washington License LLC. (group owner; (acq 11-18-2004; grpsl). Natl. Network: Westwood One, CBS, . Timothy K. Brady. Format: News/talk, sports. News staff: one; News: 20 hrs wkly. Target aud: 25-54. Spec prog: Farm 1 hr wkly. ◆Amador S. Bustos, pres; Bob Berry, gen mgr; Keith Teske, opns mgr; Judith McInnis, prom dir; Martin Ortiz, progmg dir.

KULE-FM— Dec 25, 1982: 92.3 mhz; 26 kw. 460 ft TL: N47 19 14 W119 34 21. Stereo. Hrs open: Box 2888, Yakima, 98823. Secondary address: 910 Basin S.W. 98823. Phone: (509) 457-1000. Fax: (509) 754-4110.E-mail: kule@kule.com Web Site:www.radiozorro.com Population served: 200,000 Natl. Network: CBS, . Format: Country. ◆Bob Berry, gen mgr; Keith Teske, opns VP; Tom Vinup, news dir.

Everett

KRKO(AM)— Aug 1, 1920: 1380 khz; 5 kw-U, DA-N. TL: N47 55 32 W122 11 19. Stereo. Hrs open: 24 2707 Colby Ave. #1380, 98201. Phone: (425) 304-1381. Fax: (425) 304-1382.E-mail: andrew.skotdal@krko.com Web Site:www.krko.com Licensee: S - R Broadcasting Co., Inc. (acq 1987). Natl. Network: Westwood One, Fox Sports, . Cohn & Marks. Format: Talk, sports. News staff: one; News: 24 hrs wkly. Target aud: Men 25-54; residents of Northern Puget Sound. ◆Andrew P. Skotdal, pres, gen mgr; Andy Skotdal, opns mgr, progmg dir; Melene Thompson, gen sls mgr.

*KSER(FM)— Feb 9, 1991: 90.7 mhz; 5.8 kw. 302 ft TL: N48 01 28 W122 06 41. Stereo. Hrs open: 24 2623 Wetmore Ave, 98201. Phone: (425) 303-9070. Fax: (425) 303-9075.E-mail: info@kser.com Web Site:www.kser.org Licensee: KSER Foundation. (acq 1996). Population served: 140,000 Natl. Network: PRI, . Bechtel & Cole. Format: Div. News staff: one; News: 17 hrs wkly. Target aud: General; public radio. Spec prog: American Indian 2 hrs, folk 2 hrs, jazz 2 hrs, reggae 2 hrs, blues 6 hrs wkly. ◆Bruce Wirth, gen mgr.

KWYZ(AM)— July 21, 1957: 1230 khz; 1 kw-U. TL: N47 58 06 W122 10 24. Hrs open:
Rebroadcasts KSUH(AM) Puyallup.
807 S. 336 St., Federal Way, 98003. Phone: (253) 815-1212. Fax: (253) 815-1913. Web Site:www.radiohankook.com Licensee: Jean J. Suh dba Radio Hankook. (acq 1999; $480,000). Population served: 84,000 Natl. Rep: Roslin,. Format: Korean. ◆Sung Hong, gen mgr.

Ferndale

KRPI(AM)— May 1963: 1550 khz; 50 kw-D, 10 kw-N, DA-2. TL: N48 50 35 W122 36 05. Hrs open: 24 Box 3213, 98248. Secondary address: 5538 Imhoff Rd. 98248. Phone: (360) 384-5117. Fax: (360) 380-4202.E-mail: 1550radio@gmail.com Web Site:www.krpiradio.com Licensee: BBC Broadcasting Inc. (acq 4-19-02; $600,000). Population served: 2,000,000 Format: East Indian. News: 14 hrs wkly. Target aud: 35 plus; East Indian adults. ◆Suki Badh, gen mgr; Grace Phelan, stn mgr.

Forks

KBDB-FM— 1985: 103.9 mhz; 3 kw. -75 ft TL: N47 57 16 W124 23 20. Hrs open: Dups AM 100% Box 450, 98331. Phone: (360) 374-6233. Fax: (360) 374-6852. Licensee: First Broadcasting Investment Partners LLC Format: CHR.

KBIS(AM)— October 1967: 1490 khz; 1 kw-U. TL: N47 57 16 W124 23 20. Hrs open: 24 Box 450, 98331. Secondary address: 260 Cedar 9833331. Phone: (360) 374-6233. Fax: (360) 374-6852.E-mail: kllm@centurytel.net Web Site:www.ktbi.com Licensee: First Broadcasting Investment Partners LLC. (group owner; (acq 12-18-2003; $300,000 with co-located FM). Rgnl rep: Tacher. Format: Rock, CHR. News staff: 2; News: 2 hrs wkly. Target aud: 25-54; general. Spec prog: NFL, Sonics, college & high school football, Mariners 20 hrs, gospel 6.5 hrs wkly. ◆Gary Lawrence, pres; Al Monroe, gen mgr, progmg dir, chief of engrg; Marcia Nearhoff, gen sls mgr; Arthur W. George, min affrs dir.

*KNWU(FM)—Not on air, target date: unknown: 90.9 mhz; 2 kw. Ant -7 ft TL: N47 56 00 W124 23 41. Hrs open: Washington State University, Box 642530, Pullman, 99164-2530. Phone: (509) 335-6500. Fax: (509) 335-6577. Web Site:www.nwpr.org Licensee: Washington State University. ◆Tony Wright, gen mgr.

Friday Harbor

*KSJU(FM)—Not on air, target date: unknown: 91.9 mhz; 100 w. Ant 374 ft TL: N48 33 25 W123 01 29. Hrs open: Box 3215, 98250. Phone: (360) 378-3779. Licensee: San Juan Island Community Radio. ◆Michael H. Calhoun, pres.

Gig Harbor

*KGHP(FM)— Aug 30, 1988: 89.9 mhz; 1.5 kw. 190 ft TL: N47 14 29 W122 46 14. Stereo. Hrs open: 24 14105 62nd Ave. N.W., 98329. Phone: (253) 857-3513. Phone: (253) 857-3589. Fax: (253) 853-5841.E-mail: info@kghp.org Web Site:www.kghp.wednet.edu Licensee: Peninsula School District No. 401. Population served: 85,000 Format: AAA, eclectic, community info. News: 10 hrs wkly. Target aud: General; diverse community audience. ◆Leland Smith, gen mgr, news dir, pub affrs dir; Theresa Evans, progmg dir & asst music dir; Keith Stiles, chief of engrg.

Glenoma

*KRYA(FM)—Not on air, target date: unknown: 89.3 mhz; 10 w horiz, 1 kw vert. Ant -948 ft TL: N46 32 37 W122 03 36. Hrs open: 2708 Hampton Court S.E., Olympia, 98501. Phone: (360) 705-0619. Licensee: Northwest Indy Radio (acq 3-26-2009). ◆Stephen P. Lepisto, pres.

*KZFL(FM)—Not on air, target date: unknown: 90.1 mhz; 10 w horiz, 1 kw vert. Ant -958 ft TL: N46 32 37 W122 03 36. Hrs open: 2200 Simpson Ave., Hoquiam, 98550. Phone: (360) 705-0619. Licensee: Northwest Indy Radio. ◆Stephen P. Lepisto, pres.

Goldendale

KLCK(AM)— Sept 4, 1984: 1400 khz; 1 kw-U. TL: N45 49 14 W120 50 15. Hrs open: Box 305, 514 S. Columbus, 98620. Phone: (541) 296-9102. Fax: (541) 298-7775.E-mail: klck@gorge.net Web Site:www.klck1400.com Licensee: Klickitat Valley Broadcasting Services Inc. (acq 12-18-01; $400,000 with KYYT(FM) Goldendale). Format: Oldies. ◆Danny V. Manciu, pres, gen mgr; Jeanne Malcolm, gen sls mgr; Kevin Malcolm, progmg dir; Julian Notestine, news dir; Cole Malcolm, chief of engrg.

*KNWG(FM)—Not on air, target date: unknown: 90.5 mhz; 300 w. Ant 1,666 ft TL: N45 42 25 W121 05 28. Hrs open: Box 642530, Pullman, 99164-2530. Phone: (509) 335-6500. Fax: (509) 335-6577. Web Site:www.nwpr.org Licensee: Washington State University. Natl. Network: NPR, . ◆Tony Wright, gen mgr.

KYYT(FM)— Jan 6, 1992: 102.3 mhz; 1.8 kw. 574 ft TL: N45 48 02 W120 47 35. Hrs open: Box 1023, The Dalles, 97058. Secondary address: 620 E. 3rd St., The Dalles 97058. Phone: (541) 296-9102. Fax: (541) 298-7775.E-mail: kyyt@gorge.net Web Site:www.y102country.com Licensee: Haystack Broadcasting Inc. (acq 12-18-01; $400,000 with KLCK(AM) Goldendale). Format: Country. ◆Danny V. Manciu, pres, gen mgr; Betsy Hadden, gen sls mgr; Kevin B. Malcolm, progmg dir.

Grand Coulee

KEYG(AM)— 1979: 1490 khz; 1 kw-U. TL: N47 52 58 W118 58 20 (day), N47 56 02 W119 00 59 (night). (CP: 1 kw-D, 960 w-N. TL: N47 53 04 W118 58 20). Hrs open: 24 Drawer K, 99133. Phone: (509) 633-2020. Phone: (509) 633-1490. Fax: (509) 633-1014.E-mail: keygfm@nwi.net Web Site:www.keygfm.com Licensee: Wheeler Broadcasting Inc. (group owner; (acq 12-6-85). Population served: 75,000 Format: Country. News staff: one; News: 4 hrs wkly. Target aud: 25 plus. Spec prog: Class 4 hrs, mus to remember 4 hrs, big band 4 hrs wkly. ◆Verl D. Wheeler, CEO; Mark Wheeler, gen mgr, gen sls mgr, progmg dir; Mike Helgerson, chief of engrg.

KEYG-FM— Feb 10, 1984: 98.5 mhz; 100 kw horiz, 85 kw vert. 994 ft TL: N47 49 18 W118 55 59. Stereo. Hrs open: 24 Drawer K, 99133. Phone: (509) 633-2020. Phone: (509) 633-1490. Fax: (509) 633-1014.E-mail: keygfm@nwi.net Licensee: Wheeler Broadcasting Inc. Population served: 350,000 Format: Classic hits.

Grandview

KARY-FM— Aug 21, 1989: 100.9 mhz; 7.8 kw. Ant 1,210 ft TL: N46 29 12 W120 00 05. Stereo. Hrs open: 24 1200 Chesterly Dr., Suite 160, Yakima, 98902-7345. Phone: (509) 248-2900. Fax: (509) 452-9661.E-mail: info@cherryfm.com Web Site:cherryfm.com Licensee: New Northwest Broadcasters LLC (group owner; acq 10-20-98; grpsl). Population served: 140,000 Format: Oldies. Target aud: 25-54. Spec prog: Relg 8 hrs wkly. ◆Pete Benedetti, CEO; Joe Benedetti, pres, gen mgr; Dewey Boynton, sls dir, progmg dir; Kevin Miskimins, gen sls mgr, progmg dir.

Hamilton

*KSVU(FM)—Not on air, target date: unknown: 90.1 mhz; 330 w. Ant -522 ft TL: N48 33 16 W121 47 40. Hrs open: Skagit Valley College, 2405 E. College Way, Mount Vernon, 98273. Phone: (360) 416-7711. Fax: (360) 416-7822. Web Site:www.ksvr.org Licensee: Board of Trustees of Skagit Valley College. ◆Rip Robbins, gen mgr.

Hoquiam

KWOK(AM)— Nov 16, 1961: 1490 khz; 1 kw-U. TL: N46 58 22 W123 51 10. Stereo. Hrs open: 24 1308 Coolidge Rd., Aberdeen, 98520. Phone: (360) 533-1320. Fax: (360) 532-0935. Licensee: Morris Communications Corp. Group owner: Morris Communications Inc.

(acq 2-18-00; $650,000 with KXXK(FM) Hoquiam-Aberdeen). Population served: 68000 Format: Sports/talk-ESPN. Target aud: 26-65. ◆Donna Rosi, gen mgr; Donna Rosa, gen sls mgr; Pat Anderson, opns mgr & progmg dir; Harvey Brooks, chief of engrg.

Hoquiam-Aberdeen

KXXK(FM)—Licensed to Hoquiam-Aberdeen. See Olympia

Ilwaco

KVAS(FM)— 2000: 103.9 mhz; 10 kw. Ant 171 ft TL: N46 18 51 W124 03 07. Hrs open: 1006 W. Marine Dr., Astoria, OR, 97103. Phone: (503) 325-2911. Fax: (503) 325-5570.E-mail: kvas@newnw.com Web Site:www.kvasfm.com Licensee: New Northwest Broadcasters Inc (group owner; acq 8-25-99; $250,000 for CP). Format: Country. ◆Paul Mitchell, gen mgr; Brian Riffe, gen sls mgr; Tom Freel, opns mgr, progmg dir & news dir.

Kelso

KLOG(AM)— Oct 8, 1949: 1490 khz; 1 kw-U. TL: N46 07 00 W122 53 07. Stereo. Hrs open: 24 Box 90, 98626. Secondary address: 506 Cowlitz Way W. 98626. Phone: (360) 636-0110. Fax: (360) 577-6949.E-mail: info@klog.com Web Site:www.klog.com Licensee: Washington Interstate Broadcasting Co. Inc. (acq 6-5-02; with co-located FM). Population served: 40,296 Richard Hayes. Format: Adult contemp. News staff: 2. Target aud: 25-54. ◆Joel Hanson, gen mgr; Bill Dodd, progmg dir.

KLYK(FM)—Licensed to Kelso. See Longview

*KTJC(FM)— 2004: 91.1 mhz; 17 w horiz, 8 kw vert. Ant 620 ft TL: N46 19 46 W122 57 50. Hrs open: 803 Vandercook Way, Longview, 98632-4039. Phone: (360) 501-5852. Fax: (208) 736-1958.E-mail: ktjc@csnradio.com Web Site:csnradio.com Licensee: CSN International (group owner). Format: Christian. ◆Lee Flory, stn mgr & progmg dir.

KUKN(FM)—(Longview, July 7, 1962: 105.5 mhz; 700 w. Ant 859 ft TL: N46 09 52 W122 51 13. Stereo. Hrs open: 24 Prog sep from AM Box 90, 98626. Secondary address: 506 Cowlitz Way W., Longview 98626. Phone: (360) 633-0110. Fax: (360) 577-6949.E-mail: info@kukn.com Web Site:www.kukn.com (Acq 4-12-02; in exchange for KLYK(FM) Kelso.). Population served: 90,000 Format: Country. News staff: 2; News: 2 hrs wkly. ◆Joel Hanson, natl sls mgr, rgnl sls mgr; Jadd Curtis, prom dir, disc jockey; Beth Jensen, pub affrs dir; Ray Byers, news rptr; Kirc Rolland, sports cmtr; Bill Dodd, disc jockey.

Kennewick

*KBLD(FM)— 1998: 91.7 mhz; 800 w. 836 ft TL: N46 14 10 W119 19 15. Hrs open: 412 S. Vancouver St., 99336. Phone: (509) 586-8902. Fax: (509) 586-0521.E-mail: kbld@csnradio.com Web Site:www.kbld.com Licensee: CSN International (group owner; acq 6-12-97; $14,120). Format: Christian. ◆Marty Atkins, gen mgr & progmg dir.

KONA(AM)—Licensed to Kennewick. See Richland-Pasco-Kennewick

KONA-FM—Licensed to Kennewick. See Richland-Pasco-Kennewick

KTCR(AM)—Licensed to Kennewick. See Richland-Pasco-Kennewick

KTCV(FM)—Licensed to Kennewick. See Richland-Pasco-Kennewick

Kirkland

*KARR(AM)— 1964: 1460 khz; 5 kw-D, 2.5 kw-N, DA-2. TL: N47 40 24 W122 10 07. Hrs open: 24 290 Hegenberger Rd., Oakland, CA, 94621. Phone: (800) 543-1495.E-mail: farrradio@familyradio.com Web Site:www.familyradio.com Licensee: Family Stations Inc. (group owner; (acq 10-22-86; $50,000; 8-11-86). Format: Relg. News: 5 hrs wkly. Target aud: General; conservative Christians & evangelicals. ◆Harold Camping, pres.

KJAQ(FM)—See Seattle

Lacey

KBRD(AM)— June 1, 1986: 680 khz; 250 w-D. TL: N47 00 41 W122 49 53. Hrs open: 6 AM-6 PM Box 7034, Olympia, 98507. Secondary address: 642 Cougar SE 98503. Phone: (360) 491-6800. Web

Site:www.hezzie.com/kbrd/ Licensee: BJ & Skip's for the Music (acq 11-1-2005; with KLDY(AM) Lacey). Population served: 300,000 Natl. Network: AP Radio, . Format: Hits of the 20s, 30s, 40s & 50s. Target aud: General. Spec prog: Jazz one hr wkly. ◆Adrian DeBee, gen mgr.

KLDY(AM)— Sept 22, 1983: 1280 khz; 1 kw-D, 500 w-N. TL: N47 03 44 W122 49 49. Stereo. Hrs open: 24 Box 348, Sedalia, CO, 80135. Phone: (303) 688-5162. Fax: (303) 660-4930. Licensee: Seattle Streaming Radio LLC. (acq 4-25-2007; $300,000). Format: Sp. ◆Oscar Ibarra, gen mgr.

Lakewood

KLAY(AM)—Licensed to Lakewood. See Tacoma

KNTB(AM)—Licensed to Lakewood. See Tacoma

Leavenworth

KOHO-FM— 1998: 101.1 mhz; 6 kw. -872 ft TL: N47 35 32 W120 38 35. Hrs open: 7475 KOHO Pl., 98826. Phone: (509) 548-1011. Fax: (509) 548-3222.E-mail: esalmon@kohoradio.com Web Site:www.kohoradio.com Licensee: Icicle Broadcasting Inc. (group owner; acq 8-26-99; grpsl). Format: Bluegrass, jazz, classical. ◆Gary Mathews, gen mgr; Heather Winters, gen sls mgr; Michael Dickes, progmg dir; Ian Dunn, news dir; Traci Ellingson, traf mgr.

Long Beach

KJOX-FM— May 1987: 99.7 mhz; 6 kw. Ant 233 ft TL: N46 18 51 W124 03 07. Stereo. Hrs open: 24 1006 W. Marine Dr., Astoria, OR, 97103. Phone: (503) 325-2911. Fax: (503) 325-5570.E-mail: kaqx@newnw.com Web Site:www.997kjox.com Licensee: New Northwest Broadcasters LLC. (group owner; (acq 8-24-99; grpsl). Natl. Network: Fox Sports, . Natl. Rep: Tacher,. Format: Sports. ◆Paul Mitchell, gen mgr; Tom Freel, opns mgr; Bob Castle, progmg dir.

Longview

KBAM(AM)— Aug 15, 1955: 1270 khz; 5 kw-D, 83 w-N. TL: N46 10 58 W122 57 28. Hrs open: 1130 14th Ave., 98632. Phone: (360) 423-1210. Fax: (360) 423-1554.E-mail: dcrowe@entercom.com Web Site:www.realcountryonline.com Licensee: Bicoastal Media Licenses IV LLC. Group owner: Entercom Communications Corp. (acq 3-31-2005; grpsl). Population served: 80,000 Natl. Network: CBS, . Natl. Rep: McGavren Guild,. Format: Real country. ◆Julie Laird, gen mgr, gen sls mgr, progmg dir; Phil Blair, news dir; Doug Fisher, chief of engrg; Dawn Crowe, traf mgr.

KEDO(AM)— May 1938: 1400 khz; 1 kw-U. TL: N46 08 57 W122 58 29. Hrs open: 24 Broadcast Ctr., 1130 14th Ave., 98632. Phone: (360) 425-1500. Fax: (360) 423-1554. Web Site:www.oldiesradioonline.com Licensee: Bicoastal Media Licenses IV LLC. Group owner: Entercom Communications Corp. (acq 3-31-2005; grpsl). Population served: 86,000 Rgnl rep: Art Moore. Leventhal, Senter & Lerman. Format: News, oldies. News staff: one; News: 15 hrs wkly. Target aud: 25-54. Spec prog: Pub affrs 2 hrs wkly. ◆Gayle Kessinger, gen mgr, stn mgr, progmg mgr & news dir; Doug Fisher, chief of engrg.

*KJVH(FM)— 1988: 89.5 mhz; 100 w. 780 ft TL: N46 09 52 W122 51 13. Hrs open: 136 E. S. Temple, Suite 1630, Salt Lake City, UT, 84111. Phone: (801) 359-3147. Fax: (801) 359-8112.E-mail: info@familyradio.com Web Site:www.familyradio.com Licensee: Family Stations Inc. (group owner) Format: Christian relg. ◆Harold Camping, pres; Roger Crawford, gen mgr & stn mgr.

KLOG(AM)—See Kelso

KLYK(FM)—(Kelso, Aug 7, 1991: 94.5 mhz; 3 kw. Ant 476 ft TL: N46 16 49 W122 52 34. Stereo. Hrs open: 24 Broadcast Ctr., 1130 14th Ave., 98632. Phone: (360) 425-1500. Fax: (360) 423-1554. Web Site:www.todaysbesthits.com Licensee: Bicoastal Media Licenses IV LLC. (acq 3-31-2005; grpsl). Natl. Network: Westwood One, . Format: Hot adult contemp. News: 2 hrs wkly. Target aud: 18-49. ◆Gayle Kessinger, progmg dir.

KUKN(FM)—Licensed to Longview. See Kelso

*KWYQ(FM)— Oct 22, 1987: 90.3 mhz; 400 w vert. Ant 892 ft TL: N46 09 47 W122 51 14. Stereo. Hrs open: 24 Box 1000, Kelso, 98626. Secondary address: 3609 Columbia Heights Rd. 98632. Phone: (360) 578-1929. Fax: (360) 636-1357. Web Site:wayfm.com Licensee: WAY-FM Media Group Inc. (group owner; (acq 8-1-2003; with

KWYA(FM) Astoria, OR). Format: Contemp Christian. Target aud: 19-34. ◆Robert D. Augsburg, pres; Danny Houle, gen mgr.

Lynden

KWPZ(FM)— Nov 8, 1960: 106.5 mhz; 68 kw. Ant 2,332 ft TL: N48 40 45 W122 50 31. Stereo. Hrs open: 24 1843 Front St., Suite A, 98264. Phone: (360) 354-5596. Fax: (360) 354-7517.E-mail: comment@praise1065.com Web Site:www.praise1065.com Licensee: CRISTA Ministries Inc. Group owner: CRISTA Broadcasting (acq 12-80). Population served: 3,000,000 Format: Relg, Christian. Target aud: 25-54; female. ◆James Gwinn, pres; Melene Thompson, VP, gen mgr; Marvin Mickley, stn mgr, opns mgr; Jim Bouma, opns mgr; Roger Burke, sls dir & gen sls mgr; Lynette Schulz, prom mgr.

Mabton

KMNA(FM)— 1997: Stn currently dark. 98.7 mhz; 11.5 kw. Ant 874 ft TL: N46 28 33 W120 08 37. Hrs open: 424 E. Yakima Ave., Suite 100, Yakima, 98901. Phone: (509) 895-0000. Fax: (509) 895-0005. Licensee: MBProsser Licensee LLC. Group owner: Moon Broadcasting (acq 2-6-2004; $1.9 million). Format: Sp contemp. ◆Carol Crider, gen mgr.

Manson

*KPLK(FM)—Not on air, target date: unknown: 88.3 mhz; 380 w. Ant 499 ft TL: N47 51 16 W120 09 59. Hrs open: 12180 Park Ave. S., Tacoma, 98447-0885. Phone: (253) 535-7758. Fax: (253) 535-8332.E-mail: kplu@plu.edu Web Site:www.kplu.org Licensee: Pacific Lutheran University. ◆Paul Stankavich, gen mgr.

KZAL(FM)— 2007: 94.7 mhz; 10.3 kw. Ant 518 ft TL: N47 51 16 W120 09 59. Hrs open: 7475 KOHO Pl., Leavenworth, 98826. Phone: (509) 548-1011. Fax: (509) 548-3222.E-mail: koho@kohoradio.com Licensee: Icicle Broadcasting Inc. Format: Smooth jazz. ◆Harriet Bullitt, pres; Gary Mathews, gen mgr.

McCleary

KGY-FM— October 1992: 96.9 mhz; 2.33 kw. 1,056 ft TL: N47 05 08 W123 11 19. Hrs open: 24 Box 1249, Olympia, 98507. Phone: (360) 943-1240. Fax: (360) 352-1222.E-mail: kgysales@kgyradio.com Web Site:www.realcountryonline.com Licensee: KGY Inc. Population served: 500,000 Haley, Bader & Potts. Format: Country. News staff: 2. Target aud: 35 plus. ◆Dick Pust, gen mgr; Darlene Kemery, gen sls mgr; Tom Trotzer, chief of engrg; Jeanna Spain, traf mgr.

Medical Lake

KTSL(FM)— Mar 7, 1989: 101.9 mhz; 12 kw. Ant 495 ft TL: N47 41 30 W117 46 00. Stereo. Hrs open: 24 5700 W. Oaks Blvd., Rocklin, CA, 95765. Phone: (800) 434-8400. Fax: (800) 372-0888. Web Site:www.air1.com Licensee: Educational Media Foundation. Group owner: Pamplin Broadcasting (acq 5-23-2008; $2.15 million). Population served: 375,000 Davis Wright Tremaine LLP. Format: Contemp Christian. ◆Mike Novak, pres; Keith Whipple, gen mgr.

*KYRS(FM)—Not on air, target date: unknown: 88.1 mhz; 6.5 kw vert. Ant 2,854 ft TL: N48 10 50 W117 59 11. Hrs open: 35 W. Main, Suite 340, Spokane, 99201. Phone: (509) 747-3012.E-mail: lupito@kyrs.org Web Site:www.kyrs.org Licensee: Thin Air Community Radio. ◆Lupito Flores, stn mgr.

Mercer Island

*KMIH(FM)— February 1970: 88.9 mhz; 30 w. Ant 226 ft TL: N47 34 21 W122 13 05. Stereo. Hrs open: 24 4107 Factoria Blvd., 98007. Phone: (206) 236-3296. Fax: (206) 236-3342.E-mail: info@kmihfm.com Web Site:hotjamz.org Licensee: Mercer Island School District No. 400. Population served: 540,000 Womble, Carlyle, Sandridge & Rice. Format: CHR. Target aud: 18-34; Female. ◆Nick De Vogel, gen mgr; Chelsea Doran, gen sls mgr; Rich Brown, progmg dir & chief of engrg.

Mercer Island-Seattle

KIXI(AM)—Licensed to Mercer Island-Seattle. See Seattle

Montesano

KSWW(FM)— 1998: 102.1 mhz; 50 kw. Ant 440 ft TL: N46 56 30 W123 47 07. Stereo. Hrs open: 24 Box 1198, Aberdeen, 98520. Secondary address: 1520 Simpson Ave., Aberdeen 98520. Phone: (360) 533-3000. Fax: (360) 532-1456. Web Site:www.jodesha.com Licensee: Jodesha Broadcasting Inc. (group owner; acq 2-28-03; $750,000 with KBKW(AM) Aberdeen). Population served: 85,000 Natl. Network: ABC, . Rgnl rep: Tacher David Tillotson. Wire Svc: AP Format: Adult contemp. News staff: 1; News: 7 hrs wkly. Target aud: 25-54. ◆William J. Wolfenbarger, pres & gen mgr; Gabrielle Jordan, opns dir; Sally Miller, gen sls mgr.

Moses Lake

KBSN(AM)— November 1947: 1470 khz; 5 kw-D, 1 kw-N, DA-2. TL: N47 06 16 W119 17 32. Hrs open: 24 Drawer B, 98837. Secondary address: 2241 W. Main 98837. Phone: (509) 765-3441. Fax: (509) 766-0273.E-mail: jpl470@hotmail.com Licensee: KSEM Inc. Population served: 15,000 Natl. Network: ABC, . Natl. Rep: McGavren Guild,. Format: News/talk, sports, farm. News staff: 3. Target aud: General. Spec prog: Sp 9 hrs wkly. ◆Jim Davis, gen mgr, opns mgr, prom mgr; Stacey Lehman, gen sls mgr; Bill Ecret, progmg dir; Butch Bare, news dir; Will Vos, chief of engrg; Colleen Roth, traf mgr; Dennis Clay, outdoor ed; Dave Heaverlo, sports cmtr.

KDRM(FM)— Oct 1, 1980: 99.3 mhz; 3 kw. 275 ft TL: N47 05 54 W119 17 47. Stereo. Hrs open: 2241 W. Main, 98837. Phone: (509) 765-3441. Fax: (509) 766-0273. Licensee: KSEM Inc. Natl. Rep: McGavren Guild,. Format: Adult hits. News: 1. Target aud: 18-34. ◆Jim Davis, gen mgr, prom mgr; Stacey Lehman-Garcia, gen mgr & gen sls mgr; Colleen Roth, progmg dir, traf mgr; Butch Bare, news dir; Dale Roth, pub svc dir.

*KLWS(FM)— Apr 10, 1997: 91.5 mhz; 7.2 kw. Ant 686 ft TL: N47 18 50 W119 34 55. Hrs open: 24
Rebroadcasts KWSU(AM) Pullman 100%.
Box 642530, Murrow Communications Ctr., Washington State Univ., Rm. 382, Pullman, 99164-2530. Phone: (509) 335-6500. Fax: (509) 335-6577.E-mail: nwpr@wsu.edu Web Site:www.nwpr.org Licensee: Washington State University. Dow, Lohnes & Albertson. Format: News & views. ◆Dennis Haarsager, gen mgr; Roger Johnson, stn mgr; Scott Weatherly, opns mgr; Mary Hawkins, progmg dir; Robin Rilette, mus dir.

*KMLW(FM)— May 4, 1997: 88.3 mhz; 4 kw. 817 ft TL: N46 56 31 W119 25 41. Hrs open:
Rebroadcasts KMBI-FM Spokane 100%.
5408 N. Freya, Spokane, 99223. Secondary address: 820 N. LaSalle Blvd., Chicago, IL 60610. Phone: (509) 448-2555. Phone: (312) 329-4301. Fax: (509) 448-6855. Fax: (312) 329-4468.E-mail: kmbi@moody.edu Web Site:www.kmbi.fm Licensee: Moody Bible Institute of Chicago. (group owner) Format: Relg. Target aud: 35-54; Christians. Spec prog: Class one hr wkly. ◆Rich Monteith, gen mgr & stn mgr; Pete Fretwell, progmg dir; Gordon Canaday, chief of engrg.

KWIQ(AM)—(Moses Lake North, Feb 20, 1956: 1020 khz; 2 kw-D, 440 w-N, DA-D. TL: N47 09 48 W119 21 39. Hrs open: 24 Box 79, Wenatchee, 98807. Secondary address: 11768 Kittleson Rd. 98837. Phone: (509) 765-1761. Phone: (509) 663-5186. Fax: (509) 765-8901. Licensee: Morris Communications Corp. Group owner: Morris Communications Inc. (acq 10-15-98; grpsl). Population served: 85000 Natl. Network: ESPN Radio, . Natl. Rep: Katz Radio,. Format: Sports. News staff: one; News: 6 hrs wkly. Target aud: 18-49; men. ◆Gary Patrick, gen mgr; Jeff Dahlstrom, sls dir, gen sls mgr; John Windus, progmg dir; Jay White, chief of engrg.

KWIQ-FM— May 22, 1968: 100.3 mhz; 100 kw. Ant 167 ft TL: N47 06 09 W119 14 26. Stereo. Hrs open: 24 Box 79, Wenatchee, 98807. Secondary address: 11768 Kittleson Rd. 98837. Phone: (509) 765-1761. Phone: (509) 663-5186. Fax: (509) 765-8901.E-mail: info@kwiq.com Web Site:www.kwiq.com Population served: 105,000 Natl. Rep: Katz Radio,. Rgnl rep: Allied Radio Partners. Format: Country. News staff: one. ◆Jeff Dahlstrom, natl sls mgr.

Moses Lake North

KWIQ(AM)—Licensed to Moses Lake North. See Moses Lake

Mount Vernon

KAPS(AM)— Mar 17, 1963: 660 khz; 10 kw-D, 1 kw-N. TL: N48 26 22 W122 20 45. Hrs open: 24 2029 Freeway Dr., 98273. Phone: (360) 424-0660. Fax: (360) 424-1660.E-mail: country@kapsradio.com Web Site:www.kapsradio.com Licensee: Valley Broadcasters Inc. (acq 8-13-93; 8-30-93). Population served: 100,000 Rgnl rep: McGaven

Guild Format: Country. News staff: one; News: hourly. Target aud: General. ◆Jim Keane, pres; Jerry Keane, gen sls mgr; Mike Yeoman, progmg dir.

KBRC(AM)— Dec 11, 1946: 1430 khz; 5 kw-D, 1 kw-N, DA-N. TL: N48 25 22 W122 21 10. Stereo. Hrs open: 24 Box 250, 98273. Secondary address: 2029 Freeway Dr. 98273. Phone: (360) 424-4278. Phone: (360) 424-1430. Fax: (360) 424-1660.E-mail: oldies@kbrcradio.com Web Site:kbrcradio.com Licensee: Valley Broadcasting. (acq 1996; Population served: 154,000 Natl. Network: ABC, . Rgnl rep: Tacher. Covington & Burling. Format: Oldies. News staff: 2. Target aud: 25-54. Spec prog: Sp 3 hrs, farm 5 hrs wkly. ◆James Keane, pres, gen mgr; Jerry Keane, gen sls mgr; Mike Yoeman, progmg dir; Kirk Tollifson, news dir; Mike Gilbert, chief of engrg; Julia Rasmussen, traf mgr.

*KMWS(FM)— May 4, 1973: 89.7 mhz; 1.5 kw. Ant 118 ft TL: N48 32 30 W122 17 43. Hrs open: 24
Rebroadcasts KWSU(AM) Pullman 100%.
Northwest Public Radio, Box 642530, Pullman, 99164-2530. Phone: (509) 335-6536.E-mail: dahmen@wsu.edu Web Site:www.nwpr.org Licensee: Washington State University (acq 3-31-2003). Population served: 70,000 Format: News/talk. ◆Dennis Haahnsager, gen mgr.

*KSVR(FM)— 2002: 91.7 mhz; 170 w. Ant 669 ft TL: N48 23 49 W122 18 26. Hrs open: Skagit Valley College, 2405 E. College Way, 98273. Phone: (360) 416-7711. Fax: (360) 416-7822.E-mail: mail@ksvr.org Web Site:www.ksvr.org Licensee: Board of Trustees of Skagit Valley College (acq 4-19-2000). Format: Progsv, Sp, news/talk. ◆Rip Robbins, gen mgr, opns dir & progmg dir; Bill McCuskey, chief of engrg.

Naches

KQMY(FM)— November 2000: 99.3 mhz; 790 w. Ant 899 ft TL: N46 36 02 W120 52 06. Hrs open: 4010 Summitview Ave., Yakima, 98908. Phone: (509) 972-3461. Fax: (509) 972-3540.E-mail: my993@live.com Web Site:www.my993fm.com Licensee: GAP Broadcasting Yakima License LLC. Group owner: Clear Channel Communications Inc. (acq 2-13-2008; grpsl). ◆Larry Miner, gen mgr; Connie Johnston, gen sls mgr; Ron Harris, progmg dir; Lance Tormey, news dir; Bill Glenn, chief of engrg.

KZTA(FM)—Licensed to Naches. See Yakima

Newport

KPWL(AM)—Not on air, target date: unknown: 1370 khz; 50 kw-D, 350 w-N, DA-N. TL: N48 10 30 W117 01 27. Hrs open: 12272 Sarazen Pl., Granada Hills, CA, 91344. Phone: (213) 494-3377. Licensee: Scott Powell. ◆Scott Powell, gen mgr.

KQQB-FM— December 1989: Stn currently dark. 104.5 mhz; 87 kw hoirz. Ant 1,046 ft TL: N48 23 09 W117 14 15. Hrs open: 1600 Gray Lynn Dr., Walla Walla, 99362. Phone: (509) 252-1000. Licensee: Radio Station KMJY LLC (acq 9-10-2008). Target aud: 18-34. ◆Christa McDonald, gen mgr.

*KUBS(FM)— Sept 10, 1973: 91.5 mhz; 150 w horiz. Ant 735 ft TL: N48 10 42 W117 04 59. Hrs open: Box 70, Newport High School, 99156-0070. Phone: (509) 447-4931. Fax: (509) 447-4354.E-mail: info@kubsfm.com Licensee: Newport Consolidated School District #56415. Population served: 2,400 Format: Var radio.

Nile

*KSBC(FM)— 2003: Stn currently dark. 88.1 mhz; 200 w. Ant -1,145 ft TL: N46 50 02 W120 56 13. Stereo. Hrs open: 24 2351 Sunset Blvd., Suite 170-218, Rocklin, CA, 95765. Phone: (916) 251-1600. Fax: (916) 251-1650.E-mail: klove@klove.com Web Site:www.klove.com Licensee: Educational Media Foundation. Group owner: EMF Broadcasting (acq 10-2-2003; grpsl). Natl. Network: K-Love, . Shaw Pittman. Format: Contemp Christian. News staff: 3. Target aud: 25-44; Judeo Christian female. ◆Richard Jenkins, pres; Mike Novak, VP; Lloyd Parker, gen mgr; Ed Lenane, opns dir, news dir; Keith Whipple, dev dir; David Pierce, progmg mgr; Sam Wallington, engrg dir; Karen Johnson, news rptr.

Oak Harbor

KWDB(AM)— Dec 14, 1984: 1110 khz; 500 w-D. TL: N48 17 27 W122 42 28. (CP: 1520 khz, 1 kw-D. TL: N48 16 55 W122 42 26). Hrs open: 5:30 AM-6 PM Box 1455, 3170 D N. Heller Rd., 98277. Phone: (360) 675-7320. Phone: (360) 240-1520. Fax: (360) 675-0166.E-mail: kwdb@kwdb.com Web Site:www.kwdb.com Licensee: West Beach

Broadcasting Corp. (acq 3-20-00; $55,000). Population served: 68,500 Natl. Network: Fox News Radio, . Wire Svc: AP Format: Adult contemporary. News staff: 2; News: 6 hrs wkly. Target aud: 20-60. ♦Laura Noel, gen mgr.

Oakville

KOMO-FM— Oct 26, 1984: 97.7 mhz; 63 kw. Ant 2,388 ft TL: N47 18 46 W123 22 15. Stereo. Hrs open: 24 140 4th Ave. N., Seattle, 98109. Phone: (206) 404-4000. Fax: (206) 404-3646. Web Site:www.komonews.com Licensee: South Sound Broadcasting LLC (acq 3-1-2003; $2.28 million). Population served: 2,600,000 Format: News. ♦Jim Clayton, gen mgr; Dennis Kelly, progmg dir.

Ocean Park

***KLOP(FM)—** 2006: 88.1 mhz; 550 w. Ant 1,044 ft TL: 46 41 46 W123 46 17. Hrs open: 24
Rebroadcasts KLVR(FM) Santa Rosa, CA 100%.
2351 Sunset Blvd., Suite 170-218, Rocklin, CA, 95765. Phone: (916) 251-1600. Fax: (916) 251-1650.E-mail: klove@klove.com Web Site:www.klove.com Licensee: Educational Media Foundation. Group owner: EMF Broadcasting. Natl. Network: K-Love, . Shaw Pittman. Format: Contemp Christian. News staff: 3. Target aud: 25-44; Judeo Christian, female. ♦Richard Jenkins, pres; Mike Novak, VP, progmg dir; Lloyd Parker, gen mgr; Ed Lenane, opns dir, news dir; Keith Whipple, dev dir; Eric Allen, natl sls mgr; David Pierce, progmg mgr; Jon Rivers, mus dir; Sam Wallington, engrg dir; Arthur Vassar, traf mgr; Karen Johnson, news rptr.

Ocean Shores

KANY(FM)— 2008: 93.7 mhz; 14 kw. Ant 400 ft TL: N46 56 00 W123 43 57. Hrs open: Box 1198, Aberdeen, 98520. Phone: (360) 533-3000. Fax: (360) 532-1456. Web Site:www.jodesha.com Licensee: Jodesha Broadcasting Inc. (acq 3-16-2007; $600,000 for CP). Population served: 85,000 Natl. Network: Jones Radio Networks, . ♦Bill Wolfenbarger, gen mgr; Gabrielle Jordan, opns dir; Sally Miller, gen sls mgr.

Olympia

***KAOS(FM)—** Jan 1, 1973: 89.3 mhz; 1.5 kw. -19 ft TL: N47 04 22 W122 58 51. Stereo. Hrs open: 24 CAB 301, 98505. Phone: (360) 867-6895. Fax: (360) 866-6797.E-mail: kaos@evergreen.edu Web Site:www.kaosradio.org Licensee: Evergreen State College. Population served: 100,000 Natl. Network: PRI, . Format: Div. News: 5 hrs wkly. Target aud: 18-35. Spec prog: Folks 16 hrs, Asian 3 hrs, American Indian 3 hrs, Sp 6 hrs wkly. ♦Donna DiBianco, opns mgr; Jerry Drummond, gen mgr, dev dir & dev dir; Bryan Johnson, mus dir, pub affrs dir.

KGTK(AM)—Licensed to Olympia. See Tacoma

KGY(AM)— Apr 15, 1922: 1240 khz; 1 kw-U. TL: N47 03 31 W122 54 09. Hrs open: 24 Box 1249, 98507. Secondary address: 1700 Marine Dr. N.E. 98501. Phone: (360) 943-1240. Fax: (360) 352-1222.E-mail: kgysales@kgyradio.com Web Site:www.kgyradio.com Licensee: KGY Inc. (acq 1-15-39). Population served: 130,000 Natl. Network: CBS Radio, . Wire Svc: AP Format: Full service, adult contemp. News staff: 2. Target aud: General. ♦Dick Pust, gen mgr; Darlene Kemery, gen sls mgr; Kevin Huffer, progmg dir, progmg mgr; Jeanna Spain, mus dir, traf mgr; Steve George, news dir; Tom Trotzer, chief of engrg.

KLDY(AM)—See Lacey

***KPLI(FM)—** September 2006: 90.1 mhz; 100 w. Ant -59 ft TL: N47 02 20 W122 54 00. Hrs open:
Rebroadcasts KPLU-FM Tacoma 100%.
121st and Park Ave. S., Tacoma, 98447-0003. Phone: (253) 536-5009. Fax: (253) 535-8332. Licensee: Pacific Lutheran University Inc. (acq 9-27-2005; $400,000). Population served: 60,000 Natl. Network: NPR, PRI, . Dow, Lohnes & Albertson. Wire Svc: AP Format: News, jazz, blues. News staff: 7; News: 54 hrs wkly. ♦Paul Stankavich, gen mgr; Jeff Bauman, opns dir; Joey Cohn, progmg dir; Nick Francis, mus dir; Erin Hennessey, news dir; Lowell Kiesow, chief of engrg.

KXXK(FM)—(Hoquiam-Aberdeen, Sept 3, 1965: 95.3 mhz; 3 kw. 449 ft TL: N46 55 53 W123 44 02. (CP: 5 kw, ant 436 ft. TL: N46 56 30 W123 47 07). Stereo. Hrs open: 24 1308 Coolidge Rd., Aberdeen, 98520. Phone: (360) 533-1320. Fax: (360) 532-0935. Licensee: Morris Communications Corp. Group owner: Morris Communications Inc. (acq 2-18-00; $650,000 with KWOK(AM) Hoquiam). Population served: 69000 Format: Hot country. Target aud: 26-54. ♦Donna Rosi, gen mgr, gen sls mgr; Patrick Anderson, opns mgr & progmg dir; Ian Cope, news dir; Harvey Brooks, chief of engrg.

KXXO(FM)— Jan 16, 1990: 96.1 mhz; 85 kw. Ant 2,099 ft TL: N46 38 07 W122 28 01. Stereo. Hrs open: 24 Box 7937, 98507. Secondary address: Rockway/Leland Bldg., 119 N. Washington Ave. 98501. Phone: (360) 943-9937. Phone: (206) 624-3712. Fax: (360) 352-3643.E-mail: admin@mixx96.com Web Site:www.mixx96.com Licensee: 3 Cities Inc. Population served: 1,325,000 Format: Adult contemp. News staff: one; News: one hr wkly. Target aud: 25-54; general. ♦David Rauh, pres, gen mgr; Toni Holm, sr VP & stn mgr; Brian Butler, gen sls mgr; Alexis Murray, prom dir; John Foster, progmg dir; Tim Vik, chief of engrg; Deena Jacroux, traf mgr.

Omak

KNCW(FM)— Apr 10, 1978: 92.7 mhz; 4.1 kw. 941 ft TL: N48 19 12 W119 32 18. Stereo. Hrs open: 24 Box 151, 98841. Phone: (509) 826-0100. Fax: (509) 826-3929. Web Site:www.komw.net Population served: 25,000 Format: Country. Target aud: General.

***KOMQ(FM)—**Not on air, target date: unknown: 88.5 mhz; 100 w. Ant 2,549 ft TL: N48 27 15 W119 18 30. Hrs open:
Rebroadcasts KPBX-FM Spokane 100%.
2319 N. Monroe St., Spokane, 99205. Phone: (509) 328-5729. Fax: (509) 328-5764.E-mail: kpbx@kpbx.org Web Site:www.kpbx.org Licensee: Spokane Public Radio Inc. Natl. Network: NPR, PRI, . ♦Richard Kunkel, gen mgr.

KOMW(AM)— Sept 30, 1947: 680 khz; 5 kw-D. TL: N48 23 40 W119 32 00. Hrs open: Box 151, 98841. Secondary address: 320 Emery St. 98841. Phone: (509) 826-0100. Fax: (509) 826-3929. Web Site:www.komw.net Licensee: North Cascades Broadcasting Inc. (group owner; acq 7-90). Population served: 35,000 Natl. Network: ABC, . Format: Adult standards, talk. Target aud: 18-45. Spec prog: Farm 2 hrs, Sp 2 hrs wkly. ♦John P. Andrist, CEO, pres, gen mgr, prom dir, prom mgr; Rebecca L. Andrist, CFO, sr VP; Rick Duck, gen sls mgr; Chris Schmidt, progmg dir; Steve Hardy, news dir; Randy Gates, pub affrs dir; Jerry Robinson, chief of engrg.

***KQWS(FM)—** Jan 6, 1999: 90.1 mhz; 3 kw. Ant 2,457 ft TL: N48 44 37 W119 37 16. Hrs open: 24
Rebroadcasts KWSU(AM) Pullman 100%.
Box 642530, Murrow Communications Ctr., Washington State Univ., Pullman, 99164-2530. Phone: (509) 335-6500. Fax: (509)335-3772.E-mail: nwpr@wsu.edu Web Site:www.nwpr.org Licensee: Washington State University. Dow, Lohnes & Albertson. Format: News, class. News staff: one; News: 60 hrs wkly. ♦Dennis Haarsager, gen mgr; Roger Johnson, stn mgr; Scott Weatherly, opns mgr; Sarah McDaniel, dev dir; Mary Hawkins, progmg dir; Ralph Hogan, engrg dir, chief of engrg.

KZBE(FM)— June 22, 1998: 104.3 mhz; 3.5 kw. 981 ft TL: N48 19 12 W119 32 18. Hrs open: 24 Box 151, 98841. Phone: (509) 826-0100. Fax: (509) 826-3929.E-mail: news@komw.net Web Site:www.komw.net Licensee: North Cascades Broadcasting Inc. (group owner; acq 10-14-97; $47,606). Natl. Network: ABC, . Format: Contemp hit/Top-40. News staff: 2; News: 3 hrs wkly. Target aud: 18 plus. ♦John P. Andrist, CEO, pres, gen mgr; Rebecca L. Andrist, CFO, sr VP, news dir; Rick Duck, gen sls mgr; Chris Schmidt, progmg dir; Jerry Robinson, chief of engrg.

Opportunity

KIXZ-FM— Apr 1, 1961: 96.1 mhz; 56 kw. 2,378 ft TL: N47 34 11 W117 05 00. Stereo. Hrs open: 808 East Sprague, Spokane, 99202. Phone: (509) 242-2400. Fax: (509) 242-1160. Web Site:www.kix961.com Licensee: Capstar TX L.P. Group owner: Clear Channel Communications Inc. (acq 8-30-00; grpsl). Population served: 260,000 Shaw Pittman. Format: Country. Target aud: 25-54.

KTRW(AM)— November 1955: 630 khz; 530 w-D, 53 w-N. TL: N47 36 31 W117 22 25. Hrs open: 24 Box 31000, Spokane, 99223. Phone: (509) 443-1000.E-mail: ktw@fabulous.com Web Site:www.ktrw.com Licensee: Mutual Broadcasting System LLC Group owner: Morgan Murphy Stations (acq 9-1-2005; $375,000). Population served: 1,100,000 Natl. Network: Fox News Radio, Salem Radio Network, USA, . Cohn & Marks. Format: Nostalgia, big band, talk. ♦Thomas W. Read, gen mgr.

Oroville

***KWAN(FM)—**Not on air, target date: unknown: 90.9 mhz; 1 kw. Ant 15 ft TL: N48 46 59.1 W119 22 56.1. Hrs open:
Rebroadcasts KPBX-FM Spokane 100%.
2319 N. Monroe St., Spokane, 99205. Phone: (509) 328-5729. Fax: (509) 328-5764.E-mail: kpbx@kpbx.org Web Site:www.kpbx.org Licensee: Spokane Public Radio Inc. Natl. Network: NPR, PRI, . ♦Richard Kunkel, gen mgr.

Othello

KRSC(AM)— Sept 1, 1957: Stn currently dark. 1400 khz; 1 kw-U. TL: N46 49 29 W119 11 26. Hrs open: 128 S. 1st Ave., 99344. Phone: (509) 488-0606. Fax: (509) 488-0909. Licensee: Centro Familiar Cristiano (acq 4-1-2008; $250,000). Population served: 10,000 ♦Betsy Gomez, gen mgr.

Pacific

KZIZ(AM)— 1990: 1560 khz; 5 kw-D, 900 w-N, 3.3 kw-CH, DA-N. TL: N47 14 10 W122 13 44. Hrs open: 24 Box 22462, Seattle, 98122-0462. Secondary address: 2600 S. Jackson St., Seattle 98144. Phone: (206) 323-3070. Fax: (206) 322-6518.E-mail: ztwins@aol.com Web Site:www.ztwins.com Licensee: KRIS Bennett Broadcasting Inc. Population served: 3,000,000 Natl. Network: American Urban, . Format: Gospel. Target aud: 12 plus; African-American. Spec prog: Relg 18 hrs wkly. ♦Christopher H. Bennett, gen mgr; Gloria Bennett, stn mgr; Frank P. Barrow, chief of opns; Frank Barrow, progmg dir; Priscilla Hailey, chief of engrg.

Pasco

KEYW(FM)— June 30, 1986: 98.3 mhz; 3 kw. 197 ft TL: N46 08 48 W119 05 59. Stereo. Hrs open: 25 2621 W. A St., 99301. Phone: (509) 547-9791. Fax: (509) 547-8509. Web Site:www.keyw.com Licensee: GAP Broadcasting Tri-Cities License LLC. Group owner: Clear Channel Communications Inc. (acq 2-13-2008; grpsl). Format: Adult contemp. Target aud: 18-49. ♦Eric Van Winkle, gen mgr; Grant Linnen, gen sls mgr; Paul Drake, progmg dir & news dir; Bill Glenn, chief of engrg.

KFLD(AM)—Licensed to Pasco. See Richland-Pasco-Kennewick

KGDN(FM)—Licensed to Pasco. See Richland-Pasco-Kennewick

KGSG(FM)— Apr 1, 1997: Stn currently dark. 93.7 mhz; 600 w. Ant 958 ft TL: N46 04 59 W119 09 38. Hrs open: 24 Box 2852, 99302. Phone: (509) 547-5196. Fax: (509) 547-5203.E-mail: info@kgsg.com Web Site:www.kgsg.com Licensee: Gospel Music Broadcasting Corp. (acq 3-26-98). ♦Martin L. Gibbson, pres & gen mgr; Martin L. Gibbs, chief of engrg.

***KOLU(FM)—** Sept 1, 1971: 90.1 mhz; 3.99 kw. 93 ft TL: N46 14 59 W119 09 10. (CP: 7.5 kw, ant 1,000 ft.). Stereo. Hrs open: 4921 W. Wernett, 99301. Phone: (509) 547-2062. Fax: (509) 544-0340.E-mail: info@kolu.com Web Site:www.riverviewbaptist.org Licensee: Riverview Baptist Christian Schools. Format: Relg. ♦John Paisley, gen mgr.

Port Angeles

***KNWP(FM)—** Mar 23, 1998: 90.1 mhz; 1.6 kw. Ant 197 ft TL: N48 09 03 W123 40 09. Hrs open: 24
Rebroadcasts KRFA-FM Moscow, ID 100%.
Box 642530, 382 Murrow Ctr., Pullman, 99164-2530. Phone: (509) 335-6500. Fax: (509) 335-3772.E-mail: nwpr@wsu.edu Web Site:www.nwpr.org Licensee: Washington State University. Dow, Lohnes & Albertson. Format: Classical, news. News staff: one; News: 37 hrs wkly. ♦Dennis Haarsager, gen mgr; Roger Johnson, stn mgr; Scott Weatherly, opns mgr; Sarah McDaniel, dev dir; Mary Hawkins, progmg dir; Ralph Hogan, engrg dir, chief of engrg.

KONP(AM)— 1945: 1450 khz; 1 kw-U. TL: N48 07 19 W123 26 13. Hrs open: Box 1450, 313 W. First, 98362. Phone: (360) 457-1450. Fax: (360) 457-9114.E-mail: info@konp.com Web Site:www.konp.com Licensee: Radio Pacific Inc. (acq 2-12-02; $850,000). Population served: 38,736 Format: News/talk. Target aud: 28-54. ♦Brown Maloney, chmn; Stan Comeau, gen sls mgr; Todd Ortloff, gen mgr, opns mgr, progmg dir & chief of engrg.

***KVIX(FM)—** Mar 22, 2005: 89.3 mhz; 600 w. Ant 489 ft TL: N48 09 03 W123 40 09. Hrs open:
Rebroadcasts KPLU-FM Tacoma 100%.
c/o KPLU-FM, 121st and Park Ave., Tacoma, 98447. Phone: (253) 535-7758. Fax: (253) 535-8332.E-mail: info@kplu.org Web Site:www.kplu.org Licensee: Pacific Lutheran University Inc. Natl. Network: NPR, PRI, . Dow, Lohnes & Albertson. Wire Svc: AP Format: News, jazz, blues. ♦Paul Stankavich, gen mgr; Jeff Bauman, opns dir; Joey Cohn, progmg dir; Nick Francis, mus dir; Erin Hennessey, news dir; Lowell Kiesow, chief of engrg.

Port Townsend

***KPTZ(FM)**—Not on air, target date: unknown: 91.9 mhz; 2 kw. Ant 233 ft TL: N48 06 20 W122 51 47. Hrs open: 354 E St., 98368. Phone: (360) 379-8122.E-mail: radiopt@olympus.net Web Site:www.olympus.net/community/radiopt/ Licensee: Radio Port Townsend. ♦Sherry Jones, pres.

***KROH(FM)**—Not on air, target date: unknown: 91.1 mhz; 1 kw. Ant 1,551 ft TL: N48 00 58 W122 55 32. Hrs open: 331 Benton St., 98368-8141. Phone: (292) 929-2929. Licensee: Port Townsend Seventh-Day Adventist Church. ♦Glenn Gately, gen mgr.

Prosser

KLES(FM)— Sept 6, 1962: 101.7 mhz; 3.5 kw. Ant 865 ft TL: N46 11 12 W119 45 13. Stereo. Hrs open: 424 E. Yakima Ave., Suite 100, Yakima, 98901. Phone: (509) 895-0000. Fax: (509) 895-0005. Licensee: MBProsser Licensee LLC Group owner: Moon Broadcasting (acq 2-15-2000; $750,000). Population served: 8,000 Natl. Rep: Target Broadcast Sales,. Format: Sp contemp. Target aud: 18-49. ♦Carol Crider, gen mgr.

KZXR(AM)— Dec 14, 1956: 1310 khz; 5 kw-D, 66 w-N. TL: N46 14 03 W119 48 49. Hrs open: 424 E. Yakima Ave., Suite 100, Yakima, 98901. Phone: (509) 786-1310. Fax: (509) 786-6814.E-mail: info@kzxr.com Licensee: MBProsser Licensee LLC (Acq 2-24-2000; $500,000). Population served: 5,000 Format: Tejano. Target aud: 25-54. ♦Frank Allec, gen mgr.

Pullman

KHTR(FM)— 1967: 104.3 mhz; 24 kw. 1,669 ft TL: N46 48 40 W116 54 55. Stereo. Hrs open: Box 1, 99163. Secondary address: 801 Old Wawawai Rd. 99163. Phone: (509) 332-6551. Fax: (509) 332-5151.E-mail: info@border104.com Web Site:www.hot104.net Population served: 125,000 Format: CHR. News staff: one; News: 24 hrs wkly. Target aud: General. ♦Jeremy West, mus dir.

KQQQ(AM)— 1938: 1150 khz; 11 kw-D, 27 w-N. TL: N46 43 36 W117 12 23. Hrs open: 24 801 Old Wawawai Rd., 99163. Secondary address: Box 1 99163. Phone: (509) 332-6551. Fax: (509) 332-5151.E-mail: info@border104.com Web Site:www.hot104.net Licensee: Radio Palouse Inc. (group owner; acq 12-74). Population served: 49,000 Rgnl rep: Allied Radio Partners. David Tillotson. Format: News/talk. News staff: one; News: 28 hrs wkly. Target aud: General. Spec prog: Farm 3 hrs, loc news 10 hrs wkly. ♦Bill Weed, gen mgr; Larry Weir, opns mgr; Rod Schwartz, gen sls mgr; Evan Ellis, news dir; Steve Franko, chief of engrg.

KRFA-FM—See Moscow, ID

***KRLF(FM)**— July 1, 1991: 88.5 mhz; 420 w vert. 794 ft TL: N46 38 01 W117 05 13. Stereo. Hrs open: 24 345 S.W. Kimball, 99163. Phone: (509) 332-3545. Fax: (509) 332-5433.E-mail: krlf@lffmtc.org Web Site:www.krlf.org Licensee: Living Faith Fellowship Educational Ministries. Population served: 100,000 Natl. Network: Salem Radio Network, . Gammon & Grange. Format: Christian hot adult contemp. News: 18 hrs wkly. Target aud: 13-52. Spec prog: Alternative/CHR one hr, children 5 hrs—one hr weekday. ♦Phillip J. Vance, pres; Frank Younce, stn mgr, engrg mgr, chief of engrg; Ruth Younce, progmg dir.

KUUX(AM)—Not on air, target date: unknown: 650 khz; 3 kw-D, 250 w-N, DA-N. TL: N46 46 03 W117 11 03. Hrs open: Box 1, 99163. Phone: (509) 332-6551. Fax: (509) 332-5151. Licensee: Radio Palouse Inc. (group owner). ♦Bill Weed, gen mgr & progmg dir.

***KWSU(AM)**— June 1922: 1250 khz; 5 kw-U. TL: N46 41 47 W117 14 44. Hrs open: 24 Box 642530, Murrow Communications Ctr., Washington State Univ., Rm. 382, 99164-2530. Phone: (509) 335-6500. Fax: (509) 335-6577.E-mail: nwpr@wsu.edu Web Site:www.nwpr.org Licensee: Washington State University. Population served: 12,000 Natl. Network: NPR, . Dow, Lohnes & Albertson. Format: News, class. News staff: one; News: 60 hrs wkly. Target aud: General. Spec prog: Jazz 14 hrs wkly. ♦Karen Olstad, COO; Tony Wright, gen mgr; Warren Wright, stn mgr; Scott Weatherly, opns mgr; Sarah McDaniel, dev dir, dev mgr; Mary Hawkins, progmg dir, progmg mgr. Co-owned TV: *KWSU-TV affil.

***KZUU(FM)**— Sept 21, 1979: 90.7 mhz; 800 w. 105 ft TL: N46 43 51 W117 09 08. Stereo. Hrs open: 24 CUB Rm 311, Washington State Univ., 99164-7204. Phone: (509) 335-2208. Fax: (509) 335-3772. Licensee: Washington State University Board of Regents. Format: Rock, jazz, div. News staff: one; News: 5 hrs wkly. Target aud: 18-49; college students. Spec prog: Jazz 12 hrs, Black 12 hrs, folk 4 hrs, Sp 3 hrs, new mus 10 hrs, environmental protection 2 hrs wkly. ♦Mike Guay, gen mgr; Lori Stewart, prom dir; Jackie Kaiser, progmg dir.

KZZL-FM— Nov 1991: 99.5 mhz; 81.4 kw. 1,059 ft TL: N46 40 52 W116 58 19. Stereo. Hrs open: 24 1114 N. Almon St., Moscow, 83843. Phone: (208) 882-2551. Fax: (208) 883-3571. Licensee: Inland Northwest Broadcasting LLC. (group owner). (acq 6-28-2005; grpsl). Population served: 500,000 Dow, Lohnes & Albertson. Format: Country. News staff: one; News: 2 hrs wkly. Target aud: 25 plus. ♦Gary Cummings, gen mgr; Ben Bonfield, gen sls mgr; Ryan Chambers, progmg dir; Steve Franco, news dir & chief of engrg.

Puyallup

KSUH(AM)— Dec 1, 1951: 1450 khz; 1 kw-U. TL: N47 10 41 W122 16 24. (CP: 1440 khz; 5 kw-D, 2 kw-N, DA-2). Hrs open: 24 807 S. 336 St., Federal Way, 98003. Phone: (253) 815-1212. Fax: (253) 815-1913.E-mail: info@radiohankook.com Web Site:www.radiohankook.com Licensee: Jean J. Suh. (acq 4-4-97; $350,000). Population served: 84,000 Format: Korean, var/div. News staff: 2. Target aud: 25-65; working folks. ♦Sung Hong, gen mgr; Nancy Haan, stn mgr.

Quincy

KWNC(AM)— Sept 10, 1957: 1370 khz; 1 kw-D, 40 w-N. TL: N47 16 15 W119 51 13. Hrs open: 231 North Wenatchee Ave, Wenatchee, 98807. Phone: (509) 787-4461. Fax: (509) 664-6799.E-mail: info@cherrycreekradio.com Licensee: Wescoast Broadcasting Co. Inc. (acq 3-8-99). Population served: 11,370 Format: News, farm. News staff: 3; News: 168 hrs wkly. Target aud: 35 plus; farm-oriented. Spec prog: Farm 5 hrs wkly. ♦Jim Wallace Jr., pres, gen mgr; Debbie Capestrini, opns dir, progmg dir; Steve Hair, news dir.

KWWW-FM— Aug 29, 1985: 96.7 mhz; 440 w. 1,079 ft TL: N47 19 13 W199 48 00. Stereo. Hrs open: 24 231 N. Wenatchee Ave., Wenatchee, 98801. Phone: (509) 665-6565. Fax: (509) 663-1150. Web Site:www.kw3.com Licensee: CCR-Wenatchee IV LLC. Group owner: Fisher Broadcasting Company. (acq 10-31-2006; grpsl). Population served: 100,000 Natl. Rep: McGavren Guild,. Shaw Pittman. Format: CHR, 80s & 90s. Target aud: 18-49. ♦Jim Senst, gen mgr, adv mgr; Leona Frank, sls dir; Dave Herald, gen sls mgr, natl sls mgr; Dale Roth, prom mgr, progmg dir; Dave Bernstein, news dir; Lisa Rodriguez, pub affrs dir; Manuel Garcia, chief of engrg; Jennifer Busboug, rsch dir; Jose Luis High, spanish dir.

KZML(FM)— October 1998: 95.9 mhz; 2.51 kw. Ant 1,046 ft TL: N47 19 13 W119 47 59. Hrs open: 24
Rebroadcasts KZTA(FM) Naches 100%.
Box 2888, Yakima, 98907. Secondary address: 706 Butterfield Rd., Yakima 98901. Phone: (509) 457-1000. Fax: (509) 452-0541.E-mail: zorro@radiozorro.com Web Site:www.bustosmedia.com Licensee: Bustos Media of Eastern Washington License LLC. (group owner; (acq 11-18-2004; grpsl). Rgnl rep: Tacher Format: Mexican regional. News staff: one; News: 3 hrs wkly. Target aud: 18-35; Hispanic. ♦Bob Berry, gen mgr, gen sls mgr; Keith Teske, opns mgr, chief of engrg; Martin Ortiz, progmg dir; Judith McInnis, traf mgr.

Raymond

KJET(FM)— July 1999: 105.7 mhz; 58 kw. Ant 518 ft TL: N46 56 30 W123 47 07. Stereo. Hrs open: 24 Box 1198, Aberdeen, 98520. Secondary address: 1520 Simpson Ave., Aberdeen 98520. Phone: (360) 538-3000. Fax: (360) 532-1456.E-mail: info@jodesha.com Web Site:www.jodesha.com Licensee: Jodesha Broadcasting Inc. (group owner) Population served: 85,000 Natl. Network: ABC, . Natl. Rep: Tacher,. David Tillotson. Wire Svc: AP Format: Adult top-40. News staff: one; News: 7 hrs wkly. Target aud: 18-49. ♦William J. Wolfenbarger, pres & gen mgr; Gabrielle Jordan, opns dir, opns mgr; Sally Miller, gen sls mgr.

Renton

KRIZ(AM)— Feb 2, 1982: 1420 khz; 1 kw-D, 500 w-N, DA-2. TL: N47 26 25 W122 12 09. Hrs open: 24 2600 S. Jackson St., Seattle, 98144. Secondary address: Box 22462, Seattle 98122-0462. Phone: (206) 323-3070. Fax: (206) 322-6518.E-mail: ztwins@aol.com Web Site:www.ztwins.com Licensee: KRIZ Broadcasting Inc. (acq 2-84; $400,000; 3-5-84). Population served: 3,000,000 Natl. Network: American Urban, . Format: Black oldies, blues. Target aud: 18 plus. Spec prog: Relg 18 hrs wkly. ♦Christopher H. Bennett, pres, stn mgr; Gloria V. Bennett, VP; Frank P. Barrow, chief of opns; Frank Barrow, progmg dir.

KYIZ(AM)— 1998: 1620 khz; 10 kw-D, 1 kw-N. TL: N47 26 25 W122 12 09. Hrs open: 2600 S. Jackson St., Seattle, 98144. Secondary address: Box 22462, Seattle 98144. Phone: (206) 323-3070. Fax: (206) 322-6518.E-mail: ztwins@aol.com Web Site:www.ztwins.com Licensee: KRIZ Broadcasting Inc. Format: Urban contemp, rhythm & blues. ♦Christopher H. Bennett, pres, gen mgr; Gloria V. Bennett, VP, gen mgr, stn mgr; Frank P. Barrow, chief of opns; Frank Barrow, progmg dir; Priscilla Hailey, news dir.

Richland

KALE(AM)—Licensed to Richland. See Richland-Pasco-Kennewick

KEGX(FM)—Licensed to Richland. See Richland-Pasco-Kennewick

KFAE-FM—Licensed to Richland. See Richland-Pasco-Kennewick

KIOK(FM)—Licensed to Richland. See Richland-Pasco-Kennewick

KORD-FM—Licensed to Richland. See Richland-Pasco-Kennewick

Richland-Pasco-Kennewick

KALE(AM)—(Richland, Apr 1, 1950: 960 khz; 5 kw-D, 1 kw-N, DA-N. TL: N46 14 34 W119 10 48. Hrs open: 24 830 N. Columbia Center Blvd., Suite B-2, Kennewick, 99336. Phone: (509) 783-0783. Fax: (509) 735-8627.E-mail: info@am960.com Web Site:www.am960.com Licensee: New Northwest Broadcasters LLC (group owner; acq 12-10-99; grpsl). Population served: 157,000 Natl. Rep: D & R Radio,. Haley, Bader & Potts. Format: ESPN sports. News staff: one. Target aud: 25 plus; general. ♦Don Morin, gen mgr.

KEGX(FM)—(Richland, June 10, 1992: 106.5 mhz; 100 kw. Ant 1,392 ft TL: N46 05 58 W119 07 40. Stereo. Hrs open: 830 N. Columbia Ctr. Blvd., Suite B-2, Kennewick, 99336. Phone: (509) 783-0783. Fax: (509) 735-8627.E-mail: info@kegx.com Web Site:www.kegx.com Population served: 250,000 Format: Classic rock. Target aud: 25-54.

***KFAE-FM**—(Richland, July 1982: 89.1 mhz; 100 kw. 1,148 ft TL: N46 05 43 W119 11 41. Stereo. Hrs open: 24
Rebroadcasts KRFA-FM Moscow, ID 100%.
Box 642530, Murrow Communications Ctr., Washington State Univ., Rm 382, Pullman, 99164-2530. Secondary address: Washington State Univ. at Tri-Cities, 100 Sprout Rd., Richland 99164-2530. Phone: (509) 335-6500. Fax: (509) 335-3772.E-mail: nwpr@wsu.edu Web Site:www.nwpr.org Licensee: Washington State University. Population served: 243,000 Natl. Network: PRI, NPR, . Dow, Lohnes & Albertson. Format: Class, news. News staff: one; News: 37 hrs wkly. Target aud: General. Spec prog: Folk, jazz 15 hrs wkly. ♦Dennis Haarsager, gen mgr; Roger Johnson, stn mgr; Scott Weatherly, opns dir; Sarah McDaniel, dev dir; Mary Hawkins, progmg dir. Co-owned TV: *KTNW(TV) affil.

KFLD(AM)—(Pasco, July 28, 1956: 870 khz; 10 kw-U. TL: N46 13 41 W119 07 32. Hrs open: 24 Box 2485, Pasco, 99301. Secondary address: 2621 W.A. St., Pasco 99301. Phone: (509) 547-9791. Fax: (509) 547-8509. Web Site:www.newstalk870.am Licensee: GAP Broadcasting Tri-Cities License LLC. Group owner: Clear Channel Communications Inc. (acq 2-13-2008; grpsl). Population served: 285,400 Rgnl rep: Art Moore. Format: Sports. News staff: one; News: 3 hrs wkly. Target aud: 18-64. ♦Eric Van Winkle, gen mgr; Grant Linnen, gen sls mgr; Curt Cartier, progmg dir; Chuck Ince, chief of engrg.

KGDN(FM)—(Pasco, February 1992: 101.3 mhz; 2.75 kw. 1,000 ft TL: N46 05 47 W119 11 36. Hrs open: 24 Box 3258, Tri Cities, 99302. Secondary address: 830 N. Columbia Center Blvd., Suite B3, Pasco 99336. Phone: (509) 783-8600. Fax: (509) 448-3811.E-mail: kgdn@kgdn.com Web Site:www.kgdn.com Licensee: West Pasco Fine Arts Radio. Pepper & Corazzini. Format: Christian. Target aud: 35 plus. ♦Thomas W. Read, gen mgr; Bill Glenn, stn mgr, opns dir, engrg dir; Melinda Read, sls dir; Joseph Spinelli, progmg dir.

KIOK(FM)—(Richland, Oct 3, 1978: 94.9 mhz; 100 kw. 1,250 ft TL: N46 05 47 W119 11 36. Stereo. Hrs open: Prog sep from AM 830 N. Columbia Center Blvd., Suite B-2, Kennewick, 99336. Phone: (509) 783-0783. Fax: (509) 735-8627.E-mail: info@thundercountry949.com Web Site:www.thundercountry949.com Licensee: New Northwest Broadcasters LLC Population served: 250,000 Format: Country.

KONA(AM)—(Kennewick, January 1948: 610 khz; 5 kw-U, DA-2. TL: N46 13 41 W119 04 07. Stereo. Hrs open: 24 2823 W. Lewis, Pasco, 99301. Secondary address: Box 2623, Tri Cities 99302. Phone: (509) 547-1618. Fax: (509) 546-2678.E-mail: kona@konaradio.com Web Site:www.konaradio.com Licensee: CCR-Tri Cities IV LLC. (group owner; (acq 12-19-2003; grpsl). Population served: 200,000 Pepper & Corazzini. Format: News/talk. News staff: 2; News: 25 hrs wkly. Target

aud: 25-54. Spec prog: Farm 3 hrs, sports 8 hrs wkly. ♦Dennis W. Goodman, gen mgr; Scott Smith, gen sls mgr; Todd Nevard, prom dir, prom dir & progmg dir; Dennis Shannon, news dir; Art Blum, chief of engrg; Bob Martin, disc jockey.

KONA-FM—(Kennewick, Aug 1, 1969: 105.3 mhz; 100 kw. 1,180 ft TL: N46 05 48 W119 11 36. Stereo. Hrs open: 24 Prog sep from AM 2823 W. Lewis, Pasco, 99301. Secondary address: Box 2623, Tri Cities 99302. Phone: (509) 547-1618. Fax: (509) 546-2678.E-mail: kona@konaradio.com Web Site:www.konaradio.com Rgnl rep: Allied Radio Partners. Format: Light adult contemp. News staff: 2; News: 3 hrs wkly. ♦Dennis W. Goodman, COO, exec VP, stn mgr; Scott Smith, sls VP, sls dir; Todd Nevard, progmg VP, disc jockey; Linda Howard, traf mgr; Dennis Shannon, local news ed, news rptr; Willy Contretas, spanish dir; Mike McDonnal, sports cmtr; Bob Martin, disc jockey.

KORD-FM—(Richland, Oct 15, 1965: 102.7 mhz; 100 kw. Ant 1,100 ft TL: N46 05 47 W119 11 36. Stereo. Hrs open: P.O. Box 2485, Pasco, 99301. Secondary address: 2621 West A. St., Pasco 99301. Phone: (509) 547-9791. Fax: (509) 547-8509. Web Site:www.1027kord.com Licensee: GAP Broadcasting Tri-Cities License LLC. (acq 2-13-2008; grpsl). Format: Country. Target aud: 25-54. ♦Eric VanWinkle, gen mgr; Grant Linnen, gen sls mgr; Paul Drake, progmg dir.

KTCR(AM)—(Kennewick, August 1945: 1340 khz; 1 kw-U. TL: N46 13 16 W119 11 20. Hrs open: 830 N. Columbia Ctr. Blvd., Suite B-2, Kennewick, 99336. Phone: (509) 783-0783. Fax: (509) 735-8627.E-mail: info@ktcr.com Web Site:www.ktcr.com Licensee: New Northwest Broadcasters LLC (group owner; acq 12-10-99; grpsl). Population served: 125,000 Natl. Rep: Christal,. Format: News/talk. Target aud: 25-64. ♦Don Morin, gen mgr.

***KTCV(FM)**—(Kennewick, Dec 10, 1984: 88.1 mhz; 320 w. 92 ft TL: N46 13 05 W119 12 17. Stereo. Hrs open: 12 5929 W. Metaline, Kennewick, 99336. Phone: (509) 734-3621. Phone: (509) 734-3622. Fax: (509) 734-3609.E-mail: dailed@ksd.org Web Site:www.ktcv.net Licensee: Kennewick School District No. 17. Format: Alternative rock. ♦Ed Dailey, gen mgr.

Rock Island

KAAP(FM)— Sept 19, 1990: 99.5 mhz; 5 kw. 167 ft TL: N47 22 52 W120 17 15. (CP: 5.3 kw, ant -82 ft.). Stereo. Hrs open: 24 231 N. Wenatchee Ave., Wenatchee, 98801. Phone: (509) 665-6565. Fax: (509) 663-1150. Web Site:www.applefm.com Licensee: CCR-Wenatchee IV LLC. Group owner: Fisher Broadcasting Company (acq 10-31-2006; grpsl). Population served: 100,000 Natl. Rep: McGavren Guild,. Shaw Pittman. Format: Adult contemp. News staff: one. Target aud: 25-54. ♦Jim Senst, gen mgr, mktg dir; Leona Frank, gen sls mgr; Todd Johnson, prom mgr; Joe Bowers, engrg dir; Manuel Garcia, chief of engrg; Jennifer Busboug, rsch dir; Lisa Rodriguez, traf mgr; Jose Luis High, spanish dir.

Roy

***KWFJ(FM)**— September 1995: 89.7 mhz; 1 kw. 98 ft TL: N46 57 59 W122 32 56. Hrs open: Box 401, 9010 320 St. S., 98580. Phone: (800) 888-7077. Fax: (704) 522-1967. Web Site:www.bbnradio.org Licensee: Calvary Baptist Church. Natl. Network: Bible Bcstg Net, . Format: Christian. ♦Walt Stowe, gen mgr.

Royal City

KRCW(FM)— 1995: 96.3 mhz; 19.5 kw. 790 ft TL: N46 45 55 W119 16 51. Stereo. Hrs open: 24 508 W. Lewis St., Pasco, CA, 99301. Phone: (509) 545-0700. Fax: (509) 543-4100. Web Site:www.campesina.com Licensee: Farmworker Educational Radio Network. Population served: 250,000 Borsari & Paxson. Format: Rgnl Mexican. Target aud: 25-54; Hispanic market. ♦Anthony Chavez, pres, gen mgr; Paul Chavez, VP; Armando Ameta, stn mgr; Pepe Escavilla, opns dir & progmg dir; Cesar Chavez Jr., news dir; David Whitehead, chief of engrg.

KWDR(FM)—Not on air, target date: unknown: 93.5 mhz; 210 w. Ant 1,666 ft TL: N46 48 25 W119 33 20. Hrs open: 5331 Mt. Alifan Dr., San Diego, CA, 92111. Phone: (858) 277-4991. Fax: (858) 277-1365. Web Site:www.horizonsd.org/radio.asp Licensee: Horizon Christian Fellowship. ♦Mike MacIntosh, pres.

Seattle

***KBLE(AM)**— 1948: 1050 khz; 5 kw-D, 440 w-N. TL: N47 33 41 W122 21 34. Hrs open: 6 AM-midnight Box 2482, Kirkland, 98083. Phone: (425) 867-2340.E-mail: info@sacredheartradio.org Web Site:www.kble.com Licensee: Sacred Heart Radio Inc. (acq 1-11-01). Population served: 2,068,900 Pepper & Corazzini. Format: Relg. ♦Ron Belter, gen mgr & opns mgr.

KCMS(FM)—See Edmonds

***KEXP-FM**— 1972: 90.3 mhz; 3.3 kw. Ant 692 ft TL: N47 36 58 W122 18 28. Stereo. Hrs open: 24 113 Dexter Ave. N., 98109. Phone: (206) 520-KEXP. Fax: (206) 520-5899. Web Site:www.kexp.org Licensee: Regents of University of Washington. Population served: 2,000,000 Natl. Network: NPR, . Dow,Lohnes & Albertson. Format: Progsv, div, alternative. Target aud: 18-44; educated, culturally interested, active outdoors, prof/mngr/tech positions. ♦Tom Mara, gen mgr; Jack Walters, opns mgr; Courtney Miller, mktg dir; Kevin Cole, progmg dir; Mike McCormick, pub affrs dir; Jamie Alls, chief of engrg.

KGNW(AM)—See Burien-Seattle

KHHO(AM)—(Tacoma, August 1942: 850 khz; 10 kw-D, 1 kw-N, DA-2. TL: N47 13 56 W122 23 22. Stereo. Hrs open: 24 351 Elliott Ave. W., Suite 300, 98119. Phone: (206) 494-2000. Fax: (206) 286-2376.E-mail: info@khho-am.clearchannel.com Web Site:khho-am.clearchannel.com Licensee: Ackerley Broadcasting Operations LLC. Group owner: Clear Channel Communications Inc. (acq 6-14-2002; grpsl). Population served: 800,000 Format: Sports. Target aud: 25-55. ♦Michele Grosenick, pres, gen mgr; Sean Shannon, sls dir & gen sls mgr; Rich Moore, progmg dir; Doug Irwin, chief of engrg; Amy Spino, traf mgr.

KING-FM— 1947: 98.1 mhz; 58 kw. 2,342 ft TL: N47 30 55 W122 58 29. Stereo. Hrs open: 24 10 Harrison St., Suite 100, 98109. Phone: (206) 691-2981. Fax: (206) 691-2982.E-mail: web@king.org Web Site:www.king.org Licensee: Classic Radio Inc. (acq 2-92; $9.75 million with co-located AM). Natl. Rep: Katz Radio,. Format: Class music. News: 2 hrs wkly. ♦Jennifer Ridewood, gen mgr; Shawna Keen, prom mgr; Bob Goldfarb, progmg dir; Buzz Anderson, chief of engrg.

KIRO(AM)— 1927: 710 khz; 50 kw-U, DA-N. TL: N47 23 55 W122 26 01. Hrs open: 24 1820 Eastlake Ave. E., 98102-3711. Phone: (206) 726-7000. Fax: (206) 726-5446.E-mail: info@710kiro.com Web Site:www.mynorthwest.com Licensee: Bonneville Holding Co. Group owner: Entercom Communications Corp. (acq 3-14-2008; grpsl). Natl. Network: ESPN Radio, . Format: Sports. Target aud: 25-54. ♦David Pridemore, gen mgr; Dennis McCormick, gen sls mgr; Tom Lendening, progmg dir.

KIRO-FM—See Tacoma

KISW(FM)— 1950: 99.9 mhz; 100 kw. 1,150 ft TL: N47 32 41 W122 06 28. Stereo. Hrs open: 24 1100 Olive Way, Suite 1650, 98101. Phone: (206) 285-7625. Fax: (206) 215-9355.E-mail: rcastle@entercom.com Web Site:www.kisw.com Licensee: Entercom Seattle License LLC. Group owner: Entercom Communications Corp. (acq 1996). Population served: 2,844,400 Natl. Rep: D & R Radio,. Format: Rock/AOR. Target aud: 18-49; men. ♦David Field, pres; Amy Griesheimer, VP, gen mgr; Ron Steinman, gen sls mgr; Dave Richards, progmg dir; Dwight Small, engrg dir, chief of engrg; Joyce Jinka, traf mgr.

KIXI(AM)—(Mercer Island-Seattle, 1947: 880 khz; 50 kw-D, 10 kw-N, DA-2. TL: N47 34 59 W122 10 52. Hrs open: 24 3650 131st Ave. S.E., Suite 550, Bellevue, 98006. Phone: (425) 562-8964. Fax: (425) 653-1088.E-mail: danm@kixi.com Web Site:www.kixi.com Licensee: Bellevue Radio Inc. Group owner: Sandusky Radio (acq 11-15-91; $3.5 million; 12-3-91). Population served: 530,831 Natl. Network: Music of Your Life, . Natl. Rep: Christal,. Format: Adult standards. Target aud: 35 plus; mature active adults. ♦Marc S. Kaye, VP & gen mgr; Dan Murphy, opns mgr, progmg dir; Lois Mares, gen sls mgr, rgnl sls mgr; Julie Judge, natl sls mgr.

KJAQ(FM)— 1959: 96.5 mhz; 100 kw. 1,223 ft TL: N47 32 39 W122 06 32. Stereo. Hrs open: 24 1000 Dexter Ave. N., Suite 100, 98109. Phone: (206) 805-1100. Fax: (206) 805-0920. Web Site:www.965thepoint.com Licensee: Infinity Radio Holdings Inc. Group owner: Infinity Broadcasting Corp. (acq 11-13-98; grpsl). Target aud: 25-54. ♦Lisa McDonald, gen mgr; Nils Olsen, gen sls mgr; Jim Trapp, progmg dir; Tom McGinley, chief of engrg.

KJR(AM)— 1921: 950 khz; 5 kw-U, DA-N. TL: N47 34 57 W122 21 46. Hrs open: 351 Elliot Ave. W., Suite 300, 98119. Phone: (206) 285-2295. Fax: (206) 286-2376.E-mail: info@kjram.com Web Site:www.kjram.com Licensee: Ackerley Broadcasting Operations LLC. Group owner: Clear Channel Communications Inc. (acq 6-14-2002; grpsl). Population served: 2,800,000 Natl. Rep: D & R Radio,. Format: Sports. Target aud: 25-54. ♦Michelle Grosnick, VP, gen mgr; Sean Shannon, sls dir, adv mgr; Gus Swanson, mktg dir; Gina Gray, prom dir; Rich Moore, progmg dir; Tom Benton, pub affrs dir; Doug Irwin, chief of engrg; Amy Spino, traf mgr.

KJR-FM— May 25, 1960: 95.7 mhz; 100 kw. Ant 1,150 ft TL: N47 32 41 W122 06 28. Stereo. Hrs open: 351 Elliot Ave. W., Suite 300, 98119. Phone: (206) 494-2000. Fax: (206) 286-2376.E-mail: info@957kjrfm.com Web Site:www.957kjrfm.com Licensee: Ackerley Broadcasting Operations LLC. Format: Classic hits. Target aud: 30-44. ♦Rick Carter, gen sls mgr; Valerie Koch, prom dir; Bob Case, progmg dir, disc jockey; Stephen Kilbreath, mus dir, news dir; Amy Spino, traf mgr; Heidi May, disc jockey.

KKDZ(AM)— May 15 1993: 1250 khz; 5 kw-U, DA-N. TL: N47 33 41 W122 21 34. Hrs open: 24 200 First Ave. W., Suite 104, 98119. Phone: (206) 281-5300. Fax: (206) 281-8881.E-mail: info@kkdzam.com Web Site:www.radiodisney.com Licensee: WMAL Inc. Group owner: ABC Inc. (acq 1-21-98; $1.2 million). Population served: 530,831 Format: Children's. News staff: 5. Target aud: 6-14; Kids. ♦Bob Nordberg, gen mgr; Laura Dunham, prom mgr.

KKNW(AM)— 1926: 1150 khz; 10 kw-U, DA-N. TL: N47 35 11 W122 11 11. Hrs open: 24 Prog sep from FM 3650 131st Ave., Suite 550, Bellevue, 98006. Phone: (425) 373-5536. Fax: (425) 373-5507. Web Site:www.newschannel1150.com Licensee: Orca Radio Inc. Population served: 530,831 Format: News/talk. News staff: one; News: 10 hrs wkly. Target aud: 35-64; active, well educated adults with middle to upper income. Spec prog: Loc sports 15 hrs, Russian 5 hrs wkly. ♦Eric Burris, opns mgr, progmg dir; Erik Krema, stn mgr & gen sls mgr; Alan Hines, traf mgr.

KKOL(AM)— 1922: 1300 khz; 50 kw-D, 47 kw-N, DA-2. TL: N47 14 56 W122 24 18. Hrs open: 24 2201 6th Ave., Suite 1500, 98121. Phone: (206) 443-8200. Fax: (206) 777-1133.E-mail: tomc@1300kol.com Licensee: Inspiration Media Inc. Group owner: Salem Communications Corp. (acq 4-17-97; $2 million). Population served: 530,831 Natl. Rep: Salem,. Format: Business news. Target aud: 35 plus; men & women. ♦Tim Harper, gen mgr; Joshua Main, opns dir; Dave Drui, progmg dir, progmg mgr; Monte Passmore, chief of engrg.

KKWF(FM)— 1946: 100.7 mhz; 57 kw horiz, 52 kw vert. Ant 2,342 ft TL: N47 30 14 W121 58 29. Stereo. Hrs open: 24 1100 Olive Way, Suite 1650, 98101. Phone: (206) 285-7625. Fax: (206) 381-0997.E-mail: jemckenna@intercom.com Licensee: Entercom Seattle License LLC. Group owner: Entercom Communications Corp. Format: Country. News: 15 hrs wkly. ♦Steve Oshin, VP & gen mgr; Melissa Forrest, opns mgr; Ron Steinman, gen sls mgr; Lance Tidwell, progmg dir; Dwight Small, chief of engrg.

KLFE(AM)— Sept 10, 1956: 1590 khz; 5 kw-U, DA-N. TL: N47 39 19 W122 31 06. Hrs open: 24 2201 6th Ave., Suite 1500, 98121. Phone: (206) 443-8200. Fax: (206) 777-1133.E-mail: webmaster@kgnw.com Licensee: Inspiration Media Inc. Group owner: Salem Communications Corp. (acq 1994; $500,000). Population served: 530,831 Natl. Rep: Salem,. Format: Christian talk. Target aud: 25-54. Spec prog: Russian 12 hrs. ♦Tim Harper, gen mgr; Joshua Main, opns mgr.

KMPS-FM— July 8, 1961: 94.1 mhz; 57 kw. 2,342 ft TL: N47 30 14 W121 58 29. Stereo. Hrs open: Box 24888, 98124. Secondary address: 1000 Dexter Ave., N., Suite 100 98109. Phone: (206) 805-0941. Fax: (206) 805-0911.E-mail: email@kmps.com Web Site:www.kmps.com Licensee: Infinity Radio Holdings Inc. Group owner: Infinity Broadcasting Corp. (acq 11-13-98; grpsl). Format: Country. News: one. Target aud: General. ♦Dave McDonald, gen mgr; Becky Brenner, opns mgr, progmg dir; Rod Krebs, gen sls mgr; Don Riggs, news dir; Tom McGinley, chief of engrg.

KMTT(FM)—(Tacoma, June 2, 1958: 103.7 mhz; 58 kw. 2,343 ft TL: N47 30 14 W121 58 29. Stereo. Hrs open: 24 1100 Olive Way, Suite 1650, 98101-1827. Phone: (206) 233-1037. Fax: (206) 233-8979.E-mail: studio@kmtt.com Web Site:www.kmtt.com Licensee: Entercom Seattle License L.L.C. Group owner: Entercom Communications Corp. (acq 6-73; with co-located AM). Natl. Rep: D & R Radio,. Format: AAA. News staff: one; News: 3 hrs wkly. Target aud: 25-49. ♦David Field, pres; Steve Oshin, gen mgr; Traci Gregory, gen sls mgr; Jennifer Orr, prom dir; Shaun Stewart, progmg dir; Mike West, news dir; Dwight Smalls, chief of engrg; Joyce Jinka, traf mgr.

KNDD(FM)— Mar 9, 1985: 107.7 mhz; 100 kw. 1,194 ft TL: N47 32 35 W122 06 25. (CP: 57.3 kw, ant 2,342 ft.). Stereo. Hrs open: 24 1100 Olive Way, Suite 1650, 98101. Phone: (206) 622-3251. Fax: (206) 682-8349.E-mail: info@knddfm.com Web Site:www.1077theend.com Licensee: Entercom Seattle License L.L.C. Group owner: Entercom Communications Corp. (acq 1996). Natl. Rep: D & R Radio,. Format: Alternative. News staff: one. Target aud: 18-34; well educated active adults. ♦Amy Griesheimer, VP, gen mgr; Jennifer Wisbey, gen sls mgr; Phil Manning, progmg dir; Dwight Smalls, chief of engrg.

***KNHC(FM)**— Jan 25, 1971: 89.5 mhz; 8.5 kw. Ant 1,220 ft TL: N47 32 35 W122 06 25. Stereo. Hrs open: 24 10750 30th Ave. N.E., Suite 219, 98125. Phone: (206) 252-3800. Phone: (206) 421-8989. Fax: (206) 252-3805.E-mail: info@c895worldwide.com Web Site:www.c895worldwide.com Licensee: Seattle Public Schools. Population

served: 3,500,000 Wilmer, Cutler & Pickering. Wire Svc: AP Format: CHR, educ. News: 9 hrs wkly. Target aud: 18-34; male & female. Spec prog: Black, gospel 6 hrs, gothic/industrial 6 hrs wkly. ♦Gregg Neilson, gen mgr; Richard Dalton, opns mgr & gen sls mgr; Jon McDaniel, progmg dir.

KNTS(AM)— Mar 31, 2003: 1680 khz; 10 kw-D, 1 kw-N. TL: N47 39 20 W122 31 05. Hrs open: 24 2201 6th Ave., Suite 1500, 98121. Phone: (206) 443-8200. Fax: (206) 777-1133.E-mail: wilmerh@salemradioseattle.com Licensee: Inspiration Media Inc. Group owner: Salem Communications Corp. Format: Hispanic Christian talk. ♦Tim Harper, gen mgr; Joshua Main, opns dir.

KOMO(AM)— 1926: 1000 khz; 50 kw-U, DA-N. TL: N47 27 54 W122 26 27. Hrs open: 24 140 4th Ave. N., 98109. Phone: (206) 404-4000. Fax: (206) 404-3646.E-mail: comments@KOMO1000news.com Web Site:www.komonews.com Licensee: Fisher Broadcasting - Seattle Radio L.L.C. Group owner: Fisher Broadcasting Company Population served: 3,204,000 Natl. Network: ABC, . Pillsbury, Winthrop, Shaw & Pittman. Wire Svc: AP Format: News. News staff: 50; News: 168 hrs wkly. Target aud: 25-54. ♦Colleen Brown, CEO; Jim Clayton, gen mgr; Joe Heslet, gen sls mgr; Gary Greenberg, natl sls mgr; Charles Gouge, rgnl sls mgr; Jen Pivak, prom dir; Dennis Kelly, progmg dir, news dir; Brian Calvert, news dir; John Barrett, chief of engrg; Julie Ross, traf mgr. Co-owned TV: KOMO-TV affil.

KPLZ(FM)— Sept 1, 1959: 101.5 mhz; 99 kw. 1,263 ft TL: N47 32 40 W122 06 26. Stereo. Hrs open: 24 Fisher Plaza, 140 Fourth Ave. N., Suite 340, 98109. Phone: (206) 404-4000. Fax: (206) 404-3644.E-mail: jclayton@komotv.com Web Site:www.star1015.com Licensee: Fisher Broadcasting - Seattle Radio L.L.C. Group owner: Fisher Broadcasting Company (acq 5-5-94; with co-located AM). Population served: 3,700,000 Natl. Rep: Eastman Radio,. Pillsbury, Winthrop. Wire Svc: AP Format: Adult contemp. News staff: 2; News: one hr wkly. Target aud: 25-54; women. Spec prog: John Tesh at night. ♦Jim Clayton, gen mgr; Bryce Phillipy, gen sls mgr, natl sls mgr; Gary Greenberg, natl sls mgr; Jennifer Pirak, prom dir; Kent Phillips, progmg dir, disc jockey; John Barrett, chief of engrg; Sheri Blatman, traf mgr & disc jockey.

KPTK(AM)— 1927: 1090 khz; 50 kw-U, DA-2. TL: N47 23 38 W122 25 25. Hrs open: 24 1000 Dexter Ave. N., Suite 100, 98109. Phone: (206) 805-1090. Fax: (206) 805-0911. Web Site:www.am1090seattle.com Licensee: Infinity Radio Holdings Inc. Group owner: Infinity Broadcasting Corp. (acq 11-13-98; grpsl). Population served: 530,831 Format: Progressive talk. ♦Dave McDonald, gen mgr; Jim Trapp, progmg dir; Tom McGinley, chief of engrg; Missy Wise, traf mgr.

KQMV(FM)—See Bellevue

KTTH(AM)— 1925: 770 khz; 50 kw-D, 5 kw-N, DA-2. TL: N47 23 38 W122 25 25. Hrs open: 24 1820 Eastlake Ave. E., 98102-3711. Phone: (206) 726-7000. Fax: (206) 726-5446. Licensee: Bonneville Holding Co. Group owner: Entercom Communications Corp. (acq 3-14-2008; grpsl). Population served: 400,000 Wilkinson Barker Knauer LLP. Format: News. News staff: 6. Target aud: 25-54; adults. ♦David Pridemore, gen mgr; Ken Berry, stn mgr.

KUBE(FM)— May 6, 1964: 93.3 mhz; 100 kw. 1,291 ft TL: N47 32 39 W122 06 29. Stereo. Hrs open: 24 351 Elliott Ave. W. #300, 98119. Phone: (206) 285-2295. Fax: (206) 286-2376.E-mail: info@kube93.com Web Site:www.kube93.com Licensee: Ackerley Broadcasting Operations LLC. Group owner: Clear Channel Communications Inc. (acq 6-14-2002; grpsl). Population served: 1,750,000 Format: Rythmic dance, CHR. ♦Michele Grosenick, pres, gen mgr; Shellie Hart, opns mgr; Sean Shannon, gen sls mgr; Eric Powers, progmg dir; Doug Irwin, chief of engrg; Amy Spino, traf mgr.

***KUOW-FM**— Jan 16, 1952: 94.9 mhz; 100 kw. Ant 730 ft TL: N47 36 58 W122 18 28. Stereo. Hrs open: 24 4518 University Way N.E., Suite 310, 98105. Phone: (206) 543-2710. Fax: (206) 616-9125.E-mail: letters@kuow.org Web Site:www.kuow.org Licensee: University of Washington. Population served: 2,500,000 Natl. Network: NPR, PRI, . Ernest Sanchez. Format: News, info. News staff: 15; News: 60 hrs wkly. Target aud: 25-54; highly educated, influential,decision makers. Spec prog: Sp 2 hrs, jazz 5 hrs wkly. ♦Wayne Roth, gen mgr; Dane Johnson, opns dir; Marcia Scholl, dev dir; Jeff Hansen, progmg dir; Guy Nelson, news dir; Terry Denbrook, chief of engrg.

KVI(AM)— 1926: 570 khz; 5 kw-U. TL: N47 25 19 W122 25 44. Hrs open: 24 Fisher Plaza, 140 Fourth Ave. N., Suite 340, 98109. Phone: (206) 404-3050. Fax: (206) 404-3650.E-mail: dkelly@fisherradio.com Web Site:www.570kvi.com Licensee: Fisher Broadcasting - Seattle Radio L.L.C. Population served: 3,700,000 Natl. Network: Fox News Radio, . Natl. Rep: Eastman Radio,. Pillsbury, Winthrop & Shaw Pittman. Wire Svc: AP Format: Talk. News staff: 2; News: 20 hrs wkly. Target aud: 25-54. ♦Joe Heslet, gen sls mgr; Gary Greenberg, natl sls mgr; Jen Pirak, prom mgr; Dennis Kelley, progmg dir; Anna Johnson, traf mgr. Co-owned TV: KOMO-TV affil

KWJZ(FM)— Nov 1, 1954: 98.9 mhz; 100 kw. 1,110 ft TL: N47 32 41 W122 06 28. (CP: 58 kw, ant 2,342 ft. TL: N47 30 14 W121 58 29). Stereo. Hrs open: 24 3650 131st Ave. S.E., Suite 550, Bellevue, 98006. Phone: (425) 373-5536. Fax: (425) 653-1133. Web Site:www.kwjz.com Licensee: Orca Radio Inc. Group owner: Sandusky Radio (acq 1996; $26 million with co-located AM). Population served: 3,084,700 Natl. Network: Westwood One, . Natl. Rep: Christal,. Wiley, Rein & Fielding. Format: Smooth jazz, new adult contemp. News staff: 2; News: 9 hrs wkly. Target aud: 25-54; younger active, mid to upper income adults. ♦Marc Kaye, gen mgr; Susan Hoffman, sls dir; Ann Marie Mulholland, gen sls mgr; Cindy Gilsdorf, mktg dir, prom dir; Carol Handley, progmg mgr; Dianna Rose, mus dir; George Bisso, chief of engrg; Alan Hines, traf mgr.

KZOK-FM— December 1964: 102.5 mhz; 100 kw. 1,170 ft TL: N47 32 35 W122 06 25. (CP: 58 kw, ant 2,342 ft.). Stereo. Hrs open: 24 1000 Dexter Ave. N., Suite 100, 98109. Phone: (206) 805-1100. Fax: (206) 441-1411.E-mail: julie.warner@cbsradio.com Web Site:www.kzok.com Licensee: Infinity Radio Holdings Inc. Group owner: Infinity Broadcasting Corp. (acq 11-13-98; grpsl). Population served: 2,000,000 Format: Classic rock. Target aud: 25-49. ♦Carey Curelop, gen mgr, opns mgr.

Sedro-Woolley

***KPYU(FM)**—Not on air, target date: unknown: 88.9 mhz; 2.5 kw. Ant 95 ft TL: N48 32 30 W122 17 43. Hrs open: 12180 Park Ave. S., Tacoma, 98447-0885. Phone: (253) 535-7758. Fax: (253) 535-8332.E-mail: kplu@plu.edu Web Site:www.kplu.org Licensee: Pacific Lutheran University Inc. ♦Loren Anderson, pres; Paul Stankavich, gen mgr.

Selah

KBBO(AM)—Licensed to Selah. See Yakima

Sequim

***KSQM(FM)**— 2009: 91.5 mhz; 700 w. Ant -276 ft TL: N48 04 30 W123 11 32. Hrs open: Box 723, 98382. Phone: (360) 681-0000.E-mail: radio@ksqmfm.com Web Site:www.scbradio.com Licensee: Sequim Community Broadcasting. ♦Dennis "Rick" Perry, gen mgr; Pepper Fisher, progmg mgr; Steve Kellmeyer, mus dir.

Shelton

KMAS(AM)— Sept 21, 1962: 1030 khz; 10 kw-D, 1 kw-N. TL: N47 13 17 W123 04 46. Hrs open: 24 Box 760, 210 W. Cota St., 98584. Phone: (360) 426-1030. Fax: (360) 427-5268.E-mail: kmas1030@kmas.com Web Site:www.kmas.com Licensee: Olympic Broadcasting Inc. (acq 5-1-2006; $725,000). Population served: 320,000 Natl. Network: ABC, Jones Radio Networks, . Rgnl rep: Tacher. Wire Svc: AP Format: Oldies, full service. News staff: 3; News: 20 hrs wkly. Target aud: 35-64. Spec prog: Relg 3.5 hrs wkly. ♦Dale Hubbard, pres & gen mgr.

KRXY(FM)— October 1998: 94.5 mhz; 710 w. 954 ft TL: N47 08 18 W123 08 28. Stereo. Hrs open: 24 2124 Pacific Ave. S.E., Olympia, 98506-4753. Phone: (360) 236-1010. Fax: (360) 236-1133.E-mail: krxy@krxy.com Web Site:www.945roxy.com Licensee: Premier Broadcasters Inc. Group owner: Premier Group Leventhal, Senter, Lerman. Format: Top-40, Hits of the 80s & 90s. News staff: one. ♦Derek Shannon, gen mgr; Bob Hart, stn mgr; Jerry Farmer, sls dir; Paul Walker, news dir.

Silverdale

KITZ(AM)— Oct 26, 1948: 1400 khz; 1 kw-D, 890 w-N. TL: N47 37 45 W122 39 52. Hrs open: 1700 Mile Hill Dr., Suite 201A, Port Orchard, 98366. Phone: (360) 876-1400. Fax: (360) 876-7920.E-mail: info@kitz1400.com Web Site:kitz1400.com Licensee: KITZ Radio Inc. (acq 12-8-2000; $500,000 for 60%). Population served: 200,000 Natl. Network: Westwood One, . Pepper & Corazzini. Format: Megatalk. Target aud: 25 plus; adults. ♦Alan Gottlieb, chmn, pres; Paul Lyle, gen mgr; Kevin Corcoran, opns VP.

South Bend

***KACW(FM)**—Not on air, target date: unknown: 91.3 mhz; 225 w. Ant 889 ft TL: N46 41 44 W123 46 17. Hrs open: 2451 N.E. Kresky, Unit A, Chehalis, 98532. Phone: (360) 740-9436. Fax: (360) 740-9415. Licensee: Chehalis Valley Educational Foundation. ♦Kerry O'Connor, pres; Cameron Beierle, gen mgr.

KLSY(FM)— 2008: 107.9 mhz; 790 w. Ant 905 ft TL: N46 41 44 W123 46 17. Hrs open: 1803 State Ave. N.E., Olympia, 98506. Phone: (360) 918-9000. Fax: (360) 704-3146. Licensee: South Sound Broadcasting LLC. Format: Classic hits. ♦Bill Bradley, gen mgr.

Spokane

***KAGU(FM)**— Mar 16, 1988: 88.7 mhz; 100 w. -141 ft TL: N47 40 06 W117 24 05. Stereo. Hrs open: 502 E. Boone Ave., 99258. Phone: (509) 328-4220. Fax: (509) 324-5718.E-mail: info@gonzaga.edu/kagu.com Web Site:www.gonzaga.edu/kagu/ Licensee: Gonzaga University Telecommunications Association. (acq 12-4-91). Format: Adult contemp. Spec prog: Class 2 hrs, jazz 2 hrs, folk 2 hrs, drama 2 hrs wkly. ♦Fr. Robert Lyons, gen mgr; Matt Caputo, prom dir.

KBBD(FM)— 1988: 103.9 mhz; 5.5 kw. Ant 1,417 ft TL: N47 36 04 W117 17 53. Stereo. Hrs open: 24 1601 E. 57th, 99223. Phone: (509) 448-1000. Fax: (509) 448-7015. Web Site:www.1039bobfm.com Licensee: Mapleton License of Spokane LLC. Group owner: Citadel Broadcasting Corp. (acq 12-3-2007; grpsl). Natl. Network: ABC, . Pepper & Corazzini. Format: Hits of the 80s, 90s, & whatever. Target aud: 25-49. ♦Don Morin, gen mgr; Cary Rolfe, opns mgr; Larry Weir, news dir; Dave Ratener, chief of engrg; Brenda Anderson, traf mgr.

KCDA(FM)—(Post Falls, ID) June 29, 1979: 103.1 mhz; 9.4 kw. 2,450 ft TL: N47 34 14 W117 04 55. Stereo. Hrs open: 24 808 E. Sprague, 99202. Phone: (509) 242-2400. Fax: (509) 448-4043.E-mail: info@kcdafm.com Web Site:www.mix1031.com Licensee: Capstar TX L.P. Group owner: Clear Channel Communications Inc. (acq 10-18-00; $4.7 million). Population served: 480,000 Natl. Rep: Roslin,. Pepper & Corazzini. Format: Alternative music. News staff: 2; News: one hr wkly. Target aud: 25-54; active & affluent. ♦Kosta Panidis, gen mgr.

KDRK-FM— 1965: 93.7 mhz; 60 kw. Ant 2,424 ft TL: N47 34 14 W117 04 55. Stereo. Hrs open: 24 1601 E. 57th St., 99223-3000. Phone: (509) 448-1000. Fax: (509) 448-7015. Web Site:www.catcountry94.com Licensee: Mapleton License of Spokane LLC. (acq 12-3-2007; grpsl). Format: Country. Target aud: 25-54. ♦Cary Rolfe, progmg dir.

***KEEH(FM)**— July 1, 1991: 104.9 mhz; 10.5 kw. Ant 1,548 ft TL: N47 34 45 W117 17 51. Stereo. Hrs open: 24
Rebroadcasts KGTS(FM) College Place 100%.
Box 19039, 99219. Secondary address: 3715 S. Grove Rd. 99219. Phone: (509) 456-4870. Fax: (509) 838-4882.E-mail: keeh@plr.org Web Site:www.plr.org Licensee: Upper Columbia Media Association (acq 9-8-93; $148,000;10-4-93). Population served: 400,000 Natl. Network: USA, . Format: Christian. Target aud: General. ♦John Dolrymple, gen mgr.

KEYF-FM—See Cheney

KEZE(FM)— Dec 25, 1992: 96.9 mhz; 8.2 kw. Ant 1,197 ft TL: N47 43 33 W117 10 06. Hrs open: 24 500 W. Boone Ave., 99201. Phone: (509) 324-4000. Fax: (509) 324-8992. Web Site:www.coyotecountry969.com Licensee: QueenB Radio Inc. Group owner: Morgan Murphy Stations. Natl. Network: USA, . Natl. Rep: Katz Radio,. Format: Country. Target aud: 25 plus; general. ♦Elizabeth M. Burns, pres; Steve Herling, exec VP; Teddie Gibbon, stn mgr; Ken Hopkins, opns mgr; Maynard Cohen, progmg dir. Co-owned TV: KXLY-TV affil

KGA(AM)— 1926: 1510 khz; 50 kw-U, DA-N. TL: N47 35 44 W117 22 15. Hrs open: 24 1601 E. 57th St., 99223-3000. Phone: (509) 448-1000. Fax: (509) 448-7015. Web Site:www.1510kga.com Licensee: Mapleton License of Spokane LLC. Group owner: Citadel Broadcasting Corp. (acq 12-3-2007; grpsl). Population served: 170,516 Format: Sports talk. Target aud: 18-34. Spec prog: Farm one hr wkly. ♦Don Morin, gen mgr; Cary Rolfe, opns mgr; Regina Winkler, gen sls mgr & natl sls mgr; Bob Castle, progmg dir; Dave Ratener, chief of engrg.

KISC(FM)— May 1, 1966: 98.1 mhz; 94 kw. 2,030 ft TL: N47 34 53 W117 17 47. Stereo. Hrs open: Prog sep from AM 808 E. Spague Ave., 99202. Phone: (509) 242-3400. Fax: (509) 242-2581.E-mail: info@literockkiss.com Web Site:www.literockkiss.com Format: Adult contemp. ♦Rob Harder, progmg dir; Dawn Marcel, disc jockey.

KJRB(AM)— 1947: 790 khz; 5 kw-U, DA-N. TL: N47 36 16 W117 23 11. Hrs open: 24 E. 1601 57th, 99223. Phone: (509) 448-1000. Fax: (509) 448-7015. Licensee: Mapleton License of Spokane LLC. Group owner: Citadel Broadcasting Corp. (acq 12-3-2007; grpsl). Population served: 296,400 Format: News talk. Target aud: 25-54. ♦Don Morin, gen mgr; Cary Rolfe, opns mgr; Joe Via, sls dir & prom dir; Bob Castle, progmg dir; Dave Ratener, news dir, chief of engrg.

KKZX(FM)— Oct 10, 1975: 98.9 mhz; 100 kw. 1,614 ft TL: N47 35 35 W117 17 46. Stereo. Hrs open: 24 Prog sep from AM 808 E. Sprague Ave., 99202. Phone: (509) 242-2400. Fax: (509) 242-2482.E-mail: info@kkzx.com Web Site:www.kkzx.com Population served: 350,000

Format: Classic rock. News: one hr wkly. Target aud: 25-54. Spec prog: Blues 2 hrs wkly. ♦Jon McGann, progmg dir.

***KMBI(AM)**— July 12, 1959: 1330 khz; 5 kw-D. TL: N47 36 17 W117 21 27. Hrs open: 6 AM-sunset 5408 S. Freya St., 99223. Phone: (509) 448-2555. Fax: (509) 448-6855.E-mail: kmbi@moody.edu Licensee: Moody Bible Institute (Acq 6-74). Population served: 184,000 News: 6 hrs wkly. Target aud: 35-54; Christian men & women. ♦D. Gary Leonard, stn mgr; Steve Stewart, pub affrs dir.

***KMBI-FM**— July 1, 1974: 107.9 mhz; 64 kw. 2,380 ft TL: N47 34 15 W117 05 00. Stereo. Hrs open: 24 5408 S. Freya St., 99223. Phone: (509) 448-2555. Fax: (509) 448-6855.E-mail: kmbi@moody.edu Web Site:www.kmbi.org Licensee: Moody Bible Institute Group owner: The Moody Bible Institute of Chicago Population served: 300,000 Southmayd & Miller. Format: Relg. News: 9 hrs wkly. Target aud: 35-54; Christian men & women. ♦Rich Monteith, gen mgr, stn mgr, opns mgr; Gordon Canaday, chief of engrg; Bret Bremberg, disc jockey.

***KPBX-FM**— 1970: 91.1 mhz; 56 kw. 2,380 ft TL: N47 34 13 W117 05 00. Stereo. Hrs open: 24 2319 N. Monroe St., 99205. Phone: (509) 328-5729. Fax: (509) 328-5764.E-mail: rkunkel@kpbx.org Web Site:www.kpbx.org Licensee: Spokane Public Radio Inc. Population served: 700,000 Natl. Network: NPR, PRI, . Format: Class, news, jazz. News staff: 3; News: 50 hrs wkly. Target aud: General; educated. Spec prog: Jazz, folk, world mus, new age/space, new mus. ♦Richard Kunkel, CEO, pres & gen mgr; Brian Flick, opns dir, progmg dir; Kathy Sackett, dev dir, sls dir; John Vlahovich, news dir; Jerry Olson, chief of engrg.

***KPBZ(FM)**—Not on air, target date: unknown: 90.3 mhz; 500 w. Ant 1,102 ft TL: N47 48 48 W117 30 41. Hrs open: 2319 N. Monroe St., 99205. Phone: (509) 328-5729. Fax: (509) 328-5764. Licensee: Spokane Public Radio Inc. ♦Richard Kunkel, gen mgr.

KPTQ(AM)— 1965: 1280 khz; 5 kw-D, DA. TL: N47 36 27 W117 21 40. Hrs open: 6 AM-9 PM 808 E. Sprague Ave., 99202. Phone: (509) 242-2400. Fax: (509) 459-9850.E-mail: info@kaqq1280.com Web Site:www.kaqq1280.com Licensee: Capstar TX L.P. Group owner: Clear Channel Communications Inc. (acq 8-30-2000; grpsl). Population served: 510,000 Natl. Network: USA, . Natl. Rep: D & R Radio,. Rgnl rep: Tacher. Arent, Fox, Kintner, Plotkin & Kahn. Format: News/talk info. News: one hr wkly. Target aud: General. ♦Garth Trimble, gen sls mgr; Barry Watkins, progmg dir.

KQNT(AM)— 1922: 590 khz; 5 kw-U. TL: N47 36 59 W117 22 12. Hrs open: 808 E. Spague Ave., 99202. Phone: (509) 242-2400. Fax: (509) 242-1160.E-mail: info@newstalk590.com Web Site:www.newstalk590.com Licensee: Capstar TX L.P. Group owner: Clear Channel Communications Inc. (acq 8-30-00; grpsl). Population served: 170,516 Fisher, Wayland, Cooper, Leader & Zaragoza L.L.P. Wire Svc: Reuters Format: News/talk. Target aud: 35-64. ♦Kosta Panidis, gen mgr; Dean Allen, progmg dir; Kent Abendroth, chief of engrg.

KSBN(AM)— September 1921: 1230 khz; 1 kw-U. TL: N47 39 30 W117 25 08. Hrs open: 24 7 South Howard, Suite 430, 99201. Phone: (509) 838-4000. Fax: (509) 838-4800.E-mail: ksbn@ksbn.net Web Site:www.ksbn.net Licensee: KSBN Radio Inc. (acq 6-95). Population served: 400,000 Wire Svc: Bloomberg Financial Format: Business, financial, talk, news. News staff: one; News: 24 hrs wkly. Target aud: 30-65; upscale; business owners. ♦Alan Gottlieb, chmn; Brad Kemmer, gen mgr, progmg dir; Patrick Carey, gen sls mgr; Conrad Agate, chief of engrg.

***KSFC(FM)**— March 1973: 91.9 mhz; 100 w. 92 ft TL: N47 40 37 W117 27 31. Hrs open: 2319 N. Monroe St., 99205. Phone: (509) 328-5729. Fax: (509) 328-5764.E-mail: rkunkel@kpbx.org Web Site:www.ksfc.org Licensee: Spokane Public Radio Inc. Population served: 100,000 Format: News. Target aud: Curious. Spec prog: American Indian 5 hrs, black 2 hrs wkly. ♦Richard Kunkel, pres & gen mgr; Kathy Sackett, dev dir; Brian Flick, progmg dir; John Vlahovich, news dir; Jerry Olson, engrg dir, chief of engrg.

KTTO(AM)— 1947: 970 khz; 5 kw-D, 1 kw-N, DA-N. TL: N47 36 59 W117 21 55. Hrs open: 24 4419 N. Hawthorne St., 99205-1399. Phone: (509) 327-3695. Fax: (509) 327-5171. Web Site:www.spokanecatholicradio.com Licensee: Sacred Heart Radio Inc. (acq 9-29-2005;. $850,000). Population served: 700,900 Format: Catholic. ♦Sr. Patricia Proctor, gen mgr.

KXLY(AM)— October 1922: 920 khz; 5 kw-U. TL: N47 36 30 W117 22 25. Hrs open: 24 W. 500 Boone Ave., 99201. Phone: (509) 324-4000. Fax: (509) 324-8992.E-mail: kxly@kyly920.com Web Site:www.kxly.com Licensee: QueenB Radio Inc. Group owner: Morgan Murphy Stations (acq 3-21-62). Population served: 700,000 Natl. Network: CBS, Wall Street, . Natl. Rep: Katz Radio,. Format: News/talk. News staff: 25; News: 30 hrs wkly. Target aud: Adults 35 plus; upper end education & income levels. Spec prog: Sports talk 5 hrs, sports play-by-play 20 hrs, local talk 15 hrs wkly. ♦Stephen R. Herling, VP; Chris Garras, gen mgr; Teddie Gibbon, stn mgr; Roger Nelson, opns mgr, sls dir; Dick Brantley, rgnl sls mgr, mktg dir; Gina Mauro, prom dir.

KXLY-FM— September 1959: 99.9 mhz; 37 kw. Ant 2,998 ft TL: N47 55 18 W117 06 48. Stereo. Hrs open: 24 W. 500 Boone Ave., 99201. Phone: (509) 324-4000. Fax: (509) 324-8992.E-mail: classy@classy99.cox Web Site:www.classy99.com Natl. Network: Westwood One, Jones Radio Networks, . Natl. Rep: Katz Radio,. Format: Adult contemp. Target aud: 25-64; adults, upper end income & education levels. ♦Tery Garras, sls dir; Joe Via, rgnl sls mgr.

KZBD(FM)— Nov 8, 1965: 105.7 mhz; 100 kw. Ant 1,910 ft TL: N47 34 44 W117 17 46. Stereo. Hrs open: E. 1601 57th, 99223. Phone: (509) 448-1000. Fax: (509) 448-7015. Web Site:www.1057thebuzzard.com Licensee: Mapleton License of Spokane LLC. (acq 12-3-2007; grpsl). Population served: 706,000 Natl. Network: ABC, . Format: Alternative rock. Target aud: 18-49.

KZZU-FM— September 1955: 92.9 mhz; 81 kw. 2,080 ft TL: N47 35 42 W117 17 53. Stereo. Hrs open: 500 W. Boone Ave., 99201. Phone: (509) 324-4000. Fax: (509) 324-8992. Web Site:www.kzzu.com Licensee: QueenB Radio Inc. Group owner: Morgan Murphy Stations (acq 4-1-96; $1.75 million with co-located AM). Population served: 313,700 Natl. Rep: Katz Radio,. Format: Hot adult contemp. Target aud: 18-49. ♦Steve Herling, VP; Roger Nelson, gen mgr, mktg mgr; Teddie Gibbon, stn mgr; George Kessler, natl sls mgr, disc jockey; Maynard Cohen, progmg dir, mus dir; Tim Anderson, chief of engrg; Catherine Bruntlett, rsch dir; Jolene Longwill, traf mgr. Co-owned TV: KXLY-TV.

Sunnyside

***KAYB(FM)**— 1998: 88.1 mhz; 250 w. -190 ft TL: N46 19 53 W120 00 51. Hrs open: Box 3206, Tupelo, MS, 38803. Phone: (662) 844-8888. Fax: (662) 842-6791.E-mail: comments@afr.net Web Site:www.afr.net Licensee: American Family Association. Group owner: American Family Radio Format: Christian, inspirational. ♦Marvin Sanders, gen mgr.

KDYM(AM)— September 1950: 1230 khz; 700 w-U. TL: N46 19 49 W120 02 10. Hrs open: 24 Box 2888, Yakima, 98907. Secondary address: 706 Butterfield Rd., Yakima 98901. Phone: (509) 457-1000. Fax: (509) 452-0541.E-mail: zorro@radiozorro.com Web Site:www.bustosmedia.com Licensee: Bustos Media of Eastern Washington License LLC. (group owner; (acq 11-18-2004; grpsl). Population served: 100,000 Natl. Network: La Gran D, . Natl. Rep: Tacher,. Format: Rgnl Mexican. News staff: one. Target aud: 25-55; Hispanic. ♦Amador S. Bustos, pres; Bob Berry, gen mgr, gen sls mgr, news dir; Keith Teske, opns dir; Martin Ortiz, progmg dir; Lisa Gonzalez, traf mgr.

Tacoma

KBKS-FM— May 1959: 106.1 mhz; 55 kw. 699 ft TL: N47 18 15 W122 23 44. Stereo. Hrs open: 351 Elliott Ave. W., Suite 300, Seattle, 98119. Phone: (206) 494-2000. Fax: (206) 286-2376. Web Site:www.kissfmseattle.com Licensee: AMFM Texas Licenses L.P. Group owner: Infinity Broadcasting Corp. (acq 4-1-2009; grpsl). Population served: 400,000 Wiley Rein LLP. Format: CHR. Target aud: 25-54. ♦Michele Grosenick, gen mgr.

KGTK(AM)—(Olympia, October 1956: 920 khz; 3 kw-D, 7 w-N. TL: N47 03 44 W122 49 49. Stereo. Hrs open: 24
Rebroadcasts KITZ(AM) Silverdale 90%.
12500 N.E. Tenth Pl., Bellevue, 98005. Secondary address: 1700 Mile High Dr., Suite 201A, Port Orchard 98366. Phone: (360) 876-1400. Fax: (360) 876-7920.E-mail: info@kitz1400.com Web Site:www.kitz1400.com Licensee: KITZ Radio Inc. (acq 4-30-2004; $300,000). Population served: 150,000 Natl. Network: USA, Radio America, . Rgnl rep: Tacher Format: Talk. News: 7 hrs wkly. Target aud: 18-65; diversified adults. ♦Alan Gottlieb, pres; Julie Versnel, VP; Conn Williamson, gen mgr; Kevin Corcoran, opns mgr; Nichole Engelstad, gen sls mgr.

KHHO(AM)—Licensed to Tacoma. See Seattle

KIRO-FM— Oct 26, 1948: 97.3 mhz; 52 kw. Ant 2,391 ft TL: N47 30 14 W121 58 29. Stereo. Hrs open: 24 1820 Eastlake Ave. E., Seattle, 98102-3711. Phone: (206) 343-9700. Fax: (206) 623-7677.E-mail: kbsg@kbsg.com Web Site:www.mynorthwest.com Licensee: Bonneville Holding Co. Group owner: Entercom Communications Corp. (acq 3-14-2008; grpsl). Population served: 2,500,000 Natl. Rep: D & R Radio,. Format: News/talk, sports. Target aud: 25-54. ♦Bruce T. Reese, pres; Kevin McCarthy, VP; Gail Raisio, gen mgr, traf mgr; Jerry Riley, gen sls mgr; Brian Thomas, progmg dir; Tom Pierson, chief of engrg.

KKMO(AM)— 1922: 1360 khz; 5 kw-U. TL: N47 18 19 W122 26 33. Hrs open: 24 2201 6th Ave., Suite 1500, Seattle, 98121. Phone: (206) 443-8200. Fax: (206) 443-1561.E-mail: reception@inspirationradio.com Web Site:www.kgnw.com Licensee: Inspiration Media Inc. Group owner: Salem Communications Corp. (acq 8-12-98; $500,000). Population served: 2,137,800 Format: Rgnl Mexican. Target aud: 35 plus. ♦Tim Harper, gen mgr; Chuck Olmstead, opns dir, opns mgr, progmg dir, progmg mgr; Doug Rice, gen sls mgr; Juanita Jasso, prom dir; Monte Passmore, chief of engrg.

KLAY(AM)—(Lakewood, 1991: 1180 khz; 5 kw-D, 1 kw-N, DA-N. TL: N47 09 00 W122 24 38. Hrs open: 24 10025 Lakewood Dr. S.W., Suite B, 98499. Phone: (253) 581-0324. Fax: (253) 581-0326.E-mail: klay11800@blarg.net Web Site:www.klay1180.com Licensee: Clay Frank Huntington. Population served: 3,000,000 Natl. Network: Westwood One, . Format: Talk. News staff: 2; News: 11 hrs wkly. Target aud: 30-65. ♦Clay Frank Huntington, pres; Bruce Bond, opns dir, pub affrs dir; Bob McCluskey, sls VP; John Burton, progmg VP; Anna Winter, news dir; Nick Winter, engrg dir.

KMTT(FM)—Licensed to Tacoma. See Seattle

KNTB(AM)—(Lakewood, September 1978: 1480 khz; 1 kw-D, 111 w-N, DA-2. TL: N47 09 56 W122 34 32. Hrs open: 6 AM-sunset Box 348, Sedalia, CO, 80135. Phone: (303) 688-5162. Fax: (303) 660-4930. Licensee: Seattle Streaming Radio LLC. (acq 8-26-2005; $900,000 with KBRO(AM) Bremerton). Population served: 500,000 Format: Sp. ♦Oscar Ibarra, gen mgr.

***KPLU-FM**— November 1966: 88.5 mhz; 58 kw. 2,356 ft TL: N47 28 50 W122 31 58. Stereo. Hrs open: 24 12180 Park Ave. S., 98447-0885. Secondary address: 2601 4th Ave., Suite 150, Seattle 98121. Phone: (253) 535-7758. Fax: (253) 535-8332.E-mail: kplu@plu.edu Web Site:www.kplu.org Licensee: Pacific Lutheran University. Population served: 2,844,400 Natl. Network: NPR, PRI, . Dow, Lohnes & Albertson. Wire Svc: AP Format: NPR news, jazz, blues. News staff: 7; News: 54 hrs wkly. Target aud: 25-54; upscale, highly educated professionals. ♦Paul Stankavich, gen mgr; Jeff Bauman, opns dir; Brend Goldstein-Young, prom dir, traf mgr; Joey Cohn, progmg dir; Nick Francis, mus dir; Erin Hennessey, news dir; Lowell Kiesow, chief of engrg.

***KUPS(FM)**— Feb 28, 1978: 90.1 mhz; 100 w. 65 ft TL: N47 15 48 W122 28 37. Stereo. Hrs open: 24 1500 N. Warner, 98416. Phone: (253) 879-3288.E-mail: thesound@ups.edu Web Site:www.kups.net Licensee: University of Puget Sound. Population served: 75,000 Format: Progsv. Target aud: 18-45. Spec prog: Black 18 hrs, jazz 12 hrs, reggae 6 hrs, world mus 4 hrs, blues 6 hrs, metal 8 hrs wkly. ♦Brenden Goetz, gen mgr; Doug Herstad, chief of opns.

***KVTI(FM)**— Nov 15, 1955: 90.9 mhz; 51 kw. 364 ft TL: N47 09 39 W122 34 35. Stereo. Hrs open: 24 4500 Steilacoom Blvd. S.W., Lakewood, 98499-4098. Phone: (253) 589-5884. Fax: (253) 589-5797.E-mail: i-91fm@cptc.edu Web Site:www.i91.ctc.edu Licensee: Clover Park Technical College. Population served: 2,500,000 Garvey, Shubert & Barer. Wire Svc: AP Format: CHR, Top-40. News: 2 hrs wkly. Target aud: 12-34; young adults & teens. Spec prog: Live mus 3 hrs, talk 4 hrs wkly. ♦John L. Mangan, gen mgr & progmg dir; Beth Valiant, mus dir; Al Bednarczyk, chief of engrg.

***KXOT(FM)**— June 1, 1949: 91.7 mhz; 7.9 kw. Ant 553 ft TL: N47 18 15 W122 23 44. Stereo. Hrs open: 24 113 Dexter Ave. N., Seattle, 98109. Phone: (206) 520-5800. Fax: (206) 520-5899. Web Site:www.kxot.org Licensee: PRC Tacoma — I LLC (acq 1-31-2005; $5 million). Population served: 154,581 Natl. Network: NPR, . Format: News/talk. Target aud: . ♦Tom Mara, gen mgr; Gary Rubin, gen sls mgr; Kevin Cole, progmg dir. Co-owned TV: .

Toppenish

KDBL(FM)— Oct 31, 1977: 92.9 mhz; 17 kw. 843 ft TL: N46 30 15 W120 23 33. Stereo. Hrs open: 24 4010 Summitview, Yakima, 98908. Phone: (509) 972-3461. Fax: (509) 972-3542. Web Site:www.929thebull.com Licensee: GAP Broadcasting Yakima License LLC. Group owner: Clear Channel Communications Inc. (acq 2-13-2008; grpsl). Population served: 190,000 Natl. Rep: McGavren Guild,. Drinker Biddle & Reath LLP. Format: Country. News staff: 2. Target aud: 18-49. ♦Gary Donovan, pres, exec VP; Lzrry Miner, gen mgr; Ron Harris, opns mgr; Rick Michaels, progmg dir.

KYNR(AM)— May 16, 1954: 1490 khz; 1 kw-U. TL: N46 22 33 W120 19 18. Hrs open: 24 Box 151, 98948-0151. Secondary address: 711 King Ln. 98948. Phone: (509) 865-5363. Fax: (509) 865-2129.E-mail: kyn@yakama.com Web Site:www.kynr.com Licensee: Confederated Tribes and Bands of the Yakama Nation (acq 2-9-01; $300,000). Population served: 198,000 Format: Classic rock, Country, Diversified, Jazz, Oldies, News, Sports, Urban contemp. News: one hr wkly. Target

aud: 18-58. Spec prog: American Indian 20 hrs wkly. ♦Lenny Abrams, gen mgr; Reggie George, progmg dir.

Tumwater

KUOW(AM)— August 1987: 1340 khz; 1 kw-U. TL: N47 00 25 W122 55 07. Hrs open: 24
Rebroadcasts KUOW-FM Seattle 100%.
4518 University Way N.E., Suite 310, Seattle, 98105. Phone: (206) 543-2710. Fax: (206) 616-9125.E-mail: letters@kuow.org Web Site:www.kuow.org Licensee: KUOW/Puget Sound Public Radio (acq 5-18-2006; $500,000). Population served: 102,000 Natl. Network: NPR, PRI, . Format: News, info. ♦Wayne Roth, gen mgr & stn mgr.

Twisp

KCSY(FM)— June 1993: 106.3 mhz; 220 w. Ant 1,633 ft TL: N48 19 06 W120 06 46. Hrs open: Box 637, 98856. Phone: (509) 997-5857. Fax: (509) 997-5859.E-mail: sunnyfm@kcsyfm.com Web Site:kcsyfm.com Licensee: Resort Radio LLC (acq 11-15-2006;. $250,000). Format: Oldies. ♦Dave Bauer, gen mgr; Debbie Griggs, gen sls mgr; Lonnie England, chief of engrg.

***KTWP(FM)**—Not on air, target date: unknown: 91.1 mhz; 110 w. Ant 1,676 ft TL: N48 19 03 W120 06 53. Hrs open:
Rebroadcasts KPBX-FM Spokane 100%.
2319 N. Monroe St., Spokane, 99205. Phone: (509) 328-5729. Fax: (509) 328-5764.E-mail: kpbx@kpbx.org Web Site:www.kpbx.org Licensee: Spokane Public Radio Inc. Natl. Network: NPR, PRI, . ♦Richard Kunkel, gen mgr.

Union Gap

KDYK(AM)— Sept 13, 1983: 1020 khz; 4 kw-D, 400 w-N, DA-D. TL: N46 34 17 W120 27 15 (D), N46 34 14 W120 27 15 (N). Hrs open: 24 Box 2888, Yakima, 98907. Secondary address: 706 Butterfield Rd. 98907. Phone: (509) 457-1000. Fax: (509) 452-0541.E-mail: zorro@radiozorro.com Web Site:www.bustosmedia.com Licensee: Bustos Media of Eastern Washington License LLC. (group owner; (acq 11-18-2004; grpsl). Natl. Network: La Gran D, . Rgnl rep: Tacher. Format: Rgnl Mexican. Target aud: 25-49; Hispanic adults. ♦Bob Berry, gen mgr; Keith Teske, opns mgr; Martin Ortiz, progmg dir & news dir.

Vancouver

KBMS(AM)— 1955: 1480 khz; 1 kw-D, 2.5 kw-N, DA-N. TL: N45 36 06 W122 43 06. Hrs open: 24 601 Main St, Suite 400, 98660. Phone: (360) 699-1881. Phone: (360) 699-5370.E-mail: avjkbms@aol.com Licensee: Christopher H. Bennett Broadcasting Co. of WA Inc. Natl. Network: ABC, . Format: Urban contemp, talk. Target aud: 54; male & female. ♦Chris Bennett, gen mgr; Angela Jenkins, stn mgr.

KFBW(FM)— 2001: 105.9 mhz; 21 kw. Ant 1,542 ft TL: N45 31 21 W122 44 45. Stereo. Hrs open: Unlimited 4949 S.W. Macadam Ave., Portland, OR, 97239-3912. Phone: (503) 226-0100. Phone: (503) 323-6400. Fax: (503) 802-1640.E-mail: info@kqolfm.com Web Site:www.1059thebrew.com Licensee: Citicasters Licenses L.P. Group owner: Clear Channel Communications Inc. (acq 1999; grpsl). Format: Classic rock. ♦Robert Dove, gen mgr; Tony Coles, opns mgr.

KKAD(AM)— Aug 10, 1963: 1550 khz; 50 kw-D, 12 kw-N, DA-N. TL: N45 38 47 W122 30 51. Hrs open: 24 6605 S.E. Lake Rd., Portland, OR, 97222. Phone: (503) 223-4321. Fax: (503) 294-0074.E-mail: markail@kpam.com Web Site:www.sunny1550kkad.com Licensee: Pamplin Broadcasting-Washington Inc. Group owner: Pamplin Broadcasting (acq 11-20-98; $1.65 million). Natl. Network: AP Network News, . Natl. Rep: Tacher,. Rgnl rep: The Tacher Co., INc. Wire Svc: AP Format: Adult standards/music of your life. News staff: 2; News: 5.6 hrs wkly. Target aud: 35-64. Spec prog: Portland Beaver baseball 18 hrs wkly. ♦Paul Clithero, gen mgr; Mark L. Ail, stn mgr, opns dir; Margaret Evans, gen sls mgr; Jeanne Winters, natl sls mgr; Misty Osko, prom mgr; Paul Duckworth, progmg dir; Bill Gallagher, news dir; Dave Bischoff, chief of engrg; Paul Blanding, traf mgr.

KLPM(AM)—See Portland, OR

KTRO(AM)— Sept 1, 1946: 910 khz; 5 kw-U, DA-2. TL: N45 33 28 W122 30 09. Hrs open: 24 6400 S.E. Lake Rd., Suite 350, Portland, OR, 97222. Phone: (503) 786-0600. Fax: (503) 786-1551. Web Site:www.espndeportesradio.com Licensee: Entercom Portland License LLC. Group owner: Entercom (acq 4-23-98; grpsl). Population served: 230,600 Natl. Network: ESPN Deportes, . Natl. Rep: D & R Radio,. Format: Sp sports. ♦Dennis Hayes, gen mgr; Jordan Smith, mktg dir, prom dir; Justin Mansfield, progmg dir.

KYCH-FM—See Portland, OR

Walla Walla

KGDC(AM)— Dec 6, 1956: 1320 khz; 1 kw-D, 660 w-N. TL: N46 02 13 W118 21 07. Hrs open: 24 38 E. Main St., Suite 11, 99362. Phone: (509) 525-7878.E-mail: comments@kgdcradio.com Licensee: Two Hearts Communications LLC (acq 8-20-01). Population served: 23,619 Format: News/talk. News: 5 hrs wkly. Target aud: General. ♦Rod Fazzari, pres, stn mgr, progmg dir, chief of engrg & traf mgr.

KGTS(FM)—See College Place

KHSS(FM)— Nov 5, 1986: 100.7 mhz; 1.3 kw. 1,374 ft TL: N46 04 04 W118 20 21. (CP: Ant 1,414 ft. TL: N45 59 04 W118 10 08). Stereo. Hrs open: 24 38 E. Main St., 99362. Phone: (509) 525-7878. Fax: (509) 522-2046.E-mail: comments@khssradio.com Web Site:www.khssradui.com Licensee: Two Hearts Communications L.L.C. (acq 3-26-98; $160,000). Natl. Rep: Katz Radio,. Pepper & Corazzini. Format: Catholic talk. Target aud: 18-34. Spec prog: Relg 3 hrs wkly. ♦Rodney Fazzari, gen mgr, progmg dir; Todd Brandenburg, chief of engrg.

KKSR(FM)— Jan 1, 1980: 95.7 mhz; 100 kw. Ant 1,401 ft TL: N45 59 04 W118 10 08. Stereo. Hrs open: 830 N. Columbia Center Blvd., Suite B-2, Kennewick, 99336. Phone: (509) 783-0783. Fax: (509) 735-8627.E-mail: curt.cartier@nnbproduction.com Web Site:www.957starfm.com Licensee: New Northwest Broadcasters LLC. (group owner; (acq 1999). Natl. Rep: Christal,. Format: Adult contemp. Target aud: 25-54. ♦Cheryl Salomone, gen mgr; Rik Mikals, opns mgr; Lisa Perez, traf mgr.

***KRKL(FM)**— May 10, 1977: 93.3 mhz; 42 kw. Ant 1,378 ft TL: N45 59 19 W118 10 28. Stereo. Hrs open: 24 2351 Sunset Blvd., Suite 170-218, Rocklin, CA, 95765. Phone: (916) 251-1600. Fax: (916) 251-1650. Web Site:www.klove.com Licensee: Educational Media Foundation. Group owner: EMF Broadcasting (acq 4-1-02; $1 million). Population served: 80,000 Natl. Network: K-Love, . Shaw Pittman. Format: Contemp Christian. News staff: 3. Target aud: 25-44; Judeo Christian, female. ♦Richard Jenkins, pres; Mike Novak, VP; Keith Whipple, dev dir; David Pierce, progmg mgr; Ed Lenane, news dir; Sam Wallington, engrg dir; Karen Johnson, news rptr.

KTEL(AM)— October 1946: 1490 khz; 1 kw-U. TL: N46 20 33 W118 20 20. Hrs open: 24 13 1/2 E. Main St., Suite 202, 99362. Phone: (509) 522-1383. Fax: (509) 522-0211. Web Site:www.1490ktel.com Licensee: WW2 L.L.C. Group owner: Capps Broadcast Group (acq 6-2-03). Population served: 65,000 Natl. Network: Jones Radio Networks, ABC, . Rgnl rep: Tacher Format: Oldies. Target aud: 25 plus; general. Spec prog: Farm 5 hrs wkly. ♦Dave Capps, pres; Liz Halley, sls VP, sls dir; Randy McKone, VP, gen mgr, gen mgr & progmg dir.

KUJ(AM)— 1928: 1420 khz; 5 kw-U, DA-N. TL: N46 04 03 W118 24 08. Hrs open: 24 45 Campbell Rd., 99362. Phone: (509) 527-1000. Fax: (509) 529-5534.E-mail: kujam@bmi.net Licensee: Alexandra Communications Inc. (acq 4-13-2001). Population served: 56,000 Natl. Network: Westwood One, . Rgnl rep: Tacher. Taylor, Theimann & Aitken. Format: News/talk, sports. News staff: one; News: 15 hrs wkly. Target aud: 25 plus. ♦Cheryl Hodgins, exec VP; Tom Hodgins, CEO & gen mgr.

***KWCW(FM)**— 1971: 90.5 mhz; 160 w. Ant -52 ft TL: N46 04 11 W118 19 51. Stereo. Hrs open: 24 200 Boyer Ave., 99362. Phone: (509) 527-5285. Web Site:www.kwcw.net Licensee: The Associated Students of Whitman College Radio Committee. Population served: 40,000 Format: Var. News staff: one; News: 2.5 hrs wkly. ♦Brian Kilgore, gen mgr.

***KWWS(FM)**— Mar 6, 1997: 89.7 mhz; 3.2 kw. 1,345 ft TL: N45 59 04 W118 10 08. Hrs open:
Rebroadcasts KWSU(AM) Pullman 100%.
Box 642530, Murrow Communications Ctr., Washington State Univ., Pullman, 99164-2530. Phone: (509) 335-6500. Fax: (509) 335-6577.E-mail: nwpr@wsu.edu Web Site:www.nwpr.org Licensee: Washington State University. Dow, Lohnes & Albertson. Format: News/talk. ♦Karen Olstad, COO, gen mgr; Dennis Haarsager, gen mgr; Roger Johnson, stn mgr; Scott Weatherly, opns dir; Sarah McDaniel, dev dir; Mary Hawkins, progmg dir.

KXRX(FM)— August 1977: 97.1 mhz; 100 kw. Ant 1,328 ft TL: N45 59 04 W118 10 09. Stereo. Hrs open: 24 Box 2485, Pasco, 99302. Secondary address: 2621 West A. St. , Pasco 99301. Phone: (509) 547-9791. Fax: (509) 547-8509. Web Site:www.97rock.fm Licensee: GAP Broadcasting Tri-Cities License LLC. Group owner: Clear Channel Communications Inc. (acq 2-13-2008; grpsl). Population served: 216,000 Format: Rock. News staff: one; News: one hr wkly. Target aud: 25 plus; middle to upper income level listeners. ♦Eric Van Winkle, gen mgr; Grant Linnen, gen sls mgr; Scott Stele, progmg dir.

Wapato

***KSOH(FM)**— Mar 6, 1992: 89.5 mhz; 9.5 kw. 974 ft TL: N46 31 42 W120 31 16. Hrs open: Box 3006, Collegedale, 37315. Phone: (800) 775-4673. Fax: (615) 216-7266.E-mail: office@lifetalk.net Web Site:www.lifetalk.net Licensee: Life Talk Broadcasting Association. Format: Relg. Target aud: 25-50; families, singles needing courage, hope & answers to societal ills. ♦Steve Gallmore, gen mgr & stn mgr.

Wenatchee

KKRT(AM)— Nov 17, 1956: 900 khz; 1 kw-D, 78 w-N. TL: N47 27 45 W120 19 24. Hrs open: 24 Box 79, 32 N. Mission St., 2nd Fl., 98801. Phone: (509) 663-5186. Fax: (509) 663-8779.E-mail: info@kkrt.com Web Site:www.kkrt.com Licensee: Morris Communications Corp. Group owner: Morris Communications Inc. (acq 10-15-98; grpsl). Population served: 61,000 Natl. Network: ESPN Radio, . Natl. Rep: Katz Radio,. Format: Sports. Target aud: 18-54; men. ♦William Morris III, CEO; Michael Osterhont, exec VP; Gary Patrick, gen mgr; Jeff Dahlstrom, sls dir; John Windus, progmg dir; Jay White, chief of engrg.

KKRV(FM)— May 1, 1976: 104.7 mhz; 6.5 kw. Ant 1,322 ft TL: N47 28 44 W120 12 49. Stereo. Hrs open: 24 Box 79, 2nd Fl., 98801. Phone: (509) 663-5186. Fax: (509) 663- 8779.E-mail: info@kkrv.com Web Site:www.kkrv.com Licensee: Morris Communications Corp. Population served: 80,000 Format: Country. Target aud: 25-54; women. ♦Shari Alexander, traf mgr.

***KPLW(FM)**— 1996: 89.9 mhz; 6 kw. 1,222 ft TL: N47 19 10 W120 14 17. Hrs open: 24 606 N. Western Ave., 98801. Phone: (509) 665-6641. Fax: (509) 665-3126.E-mail: kplw@plr.org Web Site:www.plr.org Licensee: Growing Christian Foundation. Population served: 200,000 Format: Relg, Christian. News: 2 hrs wkly. Target aud: 35-54; female. ♦Kevin Krueger, chmn, pres; Sean Ruud, gen mgr.

KPQ(AM)— December 1929: 560 khz; 5 kw-U, DA-N. TL: N47 27 12 W120 19 43. Hrs open: 24 Box 159, 98807-0159. Secondary address: 231 North Wenatchee Ave 98801. Phone: (509) 663-5121. Fax: (509) 664-6799.E-mail: info@cherrycreekradio.com Web Site:www.kpq.com Licensee: Wescoast Broadcasting Co. Population served: 52,000 Natl. Rep: Tacher,. Davis Wright Tremaine. Format: News/talk. News: 165 hrs wkly. Target aud: 35 plus. Spec prog: Farm 3 hrs wkly. ♦Jim Wallace Jr., pres, gen mgr; Debi Campestrini, opns dir, opns mgr; Greg McEwen, gen sls mgr, mktg dir; Steve Hair, news dir; Pete Peterson, chief of engrg; Janette Morris, traf mgr; Tom Cashman, news rptr; Eric Granstrom, sports cmtr.

KPQ-FM— December 1967: 102.1 mhz; 35 kw. 2,655 ft TL: N47 16 28 W120 25 30. Stereo. Hrs open: 24 Prog sep from AM Box 159, 98807. Secondary address: 231 North Wenatchee Ave 98807.E-mail: info@cherrycreekradio.com Web Site:www.thequake1021.com Population served: 30,000 Format: Classic rock, CHR. News: one hr wkly. Target aud: 25 plus. ♦Kelly Hart, mus dir, local news ed; Janette Morris, traf mgr; Tom Cashman, news rptr; Eric Granstrom, sports cmtr.

KYSN(FM)—(East Wenatchee, Dec 25, 1980: 97.7 mhz; 7 kw. -150 ft TL: N47 22 52 W120 17 16. Stereo. Hrs open: 24 231 N. Wenatchee Ave., 98801. Phone: (509) 665-6565. Fax: (509) 663-1150.E-mail: production@nw-tel.net Web Site:www.kysn.com Licensee: CCR-Wenatchee IV LLC. Group owner: Fisher Broadcasting Company (acq 10-31-2006; grpsl). Format: Country. News staff: one; News: 20 hrs wkly. Target aud: 25-54. Spec prog: Farm one hr, relg one hr wkly. ♦Steven Miller, gen mgr; Leona Frank, gen sls mgr; John Ross, progmg dir; Dave Bernstein, news dir; Manuel Garcia, chief of engrg; Lisa Rodriguez, traf mgr.

KZNW(AM)— 1948: 1340 khz; 1 kw-U. TL: N47 23 50 W120 16 25. Hrs open: 24 231 N. Wenatchee Ave., 98801. Phone: (509) 665-6565. Fax: (509) 663-1150. Web Site:www.lasuperz.com Licensee: CCR-Wenatchee IV LLC. Group owner: Fisher Broadcasting Company (acq 10-31-2006; grpsl). Population served: 52,000 Natl. Rep: McGavren Guild,. Shaw Pittman. Format: Sp. News staff: one; News: 10 hrs wkly. Target aud: General; Hispanic. ♦Steve Miller, gen mgr; Leona Frank, gen sls mgr; Elsa Esparza, progmg dir; Manuel Garcia, chief of engrg.

West Clarkston

***KAUC(FM)**—Not on air, target date: unknown: 89.7 mhz; 500 w. Ant -607 ft TL: N46 26 20 W117 00 31. Hrs open: Box 19039, Spokane, 99219. Licensee: Upper Columbia Media Corp.

Westport

KABW(FM)—Not on air, target date: unknown: 101.3 mhz; 6 kw. Ant 226 ft TL: N46 53 04 W124 00 44. Hrs open: College Creek Media LLC, 980 N. Michigan Ave., Suite 1880, Chicago, IL, 60611. Phone: (312) 204-9900. Licensee: College Creek Media LLC. ♦Neal J. Robinson, pres.

***KEFL(FM)**—Not on air, target date: unknown: 91.7 mhz; 120 w. Ant 11 ft TL: N46 51 39 W124 06 31. Hrs open: 2200 Simpson Ave., Hoquiam, 98550. Phone: (360) 705-0619. Licensee: Northwest Indy Radio. ♦Stephen P. Lepisto, pres.

White Salmon

***KBNO-FM**— 2001: 89.3 mhz; 20 w vert. Ant 1,102 ft TL: N45 43 23 W121 26 42. Hrs open: 2650 Montello Ave., Hood River, OR, 97031. Phone: (541) 386-8810. Web Site:www.hcjb.org/wrn Licensee: World Radio Network Inc. Format: Relg, Sp. ♦John Estey, gen mgr.

Wilson Creek

KWLN(FM)— November 1994: 103.3 mhz; 25 kw. 243 ft TL: N47 16 40 W119 00 00. Hrs open: 24 Box 79, Wenatchee, 98807. Phone: (509) 663-5186. Fax: (509) 663-8779.E-mail: info@lanuevaradio.com Web Site:www.lanuevaradio.com Licensee: Morris Communications Corp. Group owner: Morris Communications Inc. (acq 10-15-98; grpsl). Natl. Rep: Katz Radio,. Wiley, Rein & Fielding. Format: Sp. Target aud: 15 plus. ♦Gary Patrick, gen mgr; Jeff Dahlstrom, gen sls mgr; Jose Luis High, progmg dir.

Winlock

KITI-FM— Aug 15, 1995: 95.1 mhz; 380 w. Ant 879 ft TL: N46 32 35 W123 01 14. Stereo. Hrs open: 24 1133 Kresky Rd., Centralia, 98531. Phone: (360) 736-1355. Fax: (360) 736-9108. Fax: (360) 736-4761.E-mail: live95@live95.com Web Site:www.live95.com Licensee: Premier Broadcasters Inc. Population served: 76,000 Rgnl rep: Allide Leventhal, Senter & Lerman. Format: Hot adult contemp. News staff: one. Target aud: 25-49. ♦Rod Etherton, pres; Rob Etherton, gen mgr; Andy West, opns mgr; Rick Petty, gen sls mgr, natl sls mgr; Matt Shannon, progmg dir; Harvey Brooks, engrg dir, chief of engrg.

Winthrop

KTRT(FM)— 2008: 97.5 mhz; 330 w. Ant 1,650 ft TL: N48 19 06 W120 06 47. Hrs open: Box 3008, 98862. Phone: (509) 341-4230. Licensee: Tin Can Communications LLC. Format: Americana. ♦Don Ashford, gen mgr.

Yakima

KATS(FM)— Dec 15, 1968: 94.5 mhz; 100 kw. Ant 850 ft TL: N46 31 59 W120 30 14. Stereo. Hrs open: 24 4010 Summitview Ave., 98908-2966. Phone: (509) 972-3461. Fax: (509) 972-3540. Fax: (509) 972-3542.E-mail: KATSFM@GMail.com Web Site:www.katsfm.com Licensee: GAP Broadcasting Yakima License LLC. (acq 2-13-2008; grpsl). Population served: 165,000 Format: Rock/AOR. News staff: one. Target aud: 20-45. ♦Ron Harris, mus dir; Lance Tormey, local news ed, news rptr.

KBBO(AM)—(Selah, 1955: 980 khz; 5 kw-D, 500 w-N, DA-N. TL: N46 36 46 W120 28 24. Hrs open: 24 1200 Chesterley Dr., #160, 98902. Phone: (509) 248-2900. Fax: (509) 452-9661. Licensee: New Northwest Broadcasters LLC (group owner; acq 12-1-98; grpsl). Population served: 193,000 Natl. Network: ABC, USA, . Rgnl rep: Allied Radio Partners. Dow, Lohnes & Albertson. Format: Talk, news, sports. News staff: one. Target aud: 35-64. ♦Pete Benedetti, CEO; Trila Bumstead, COO; Brent Phillipy, VP; Lou Barfelli, opns dir, progmg dir, pub affrs dir; Kit Osborne, sls dir; Ron King, natl sls mgr, rgnl sls mgr; Jenifer Wilde, prom dir; Tim Mauch, chief of engrg; Gail Dahl, traf mgr.

***KDNA(FM)**— Dec 19, 1979: 91.9 mhz; 18.5 kw. 920 ft TL: N46 31 42 W120 31 03. Stereo. Hrs open: 6 AM-midnight Box 800, 121 Sunnyside Ave., Granger, 98932. Phone: (509) 854-1900. Phone: (509) 854-1900. Fax: (509) 854-2223.E-mail: info@kdna.org Web Site:www.kdna.org Licensee: Northwest Communities Educational Center. Population served: 80,000 Format: Sp, informational. News staff: one; News: 8 hrs wkly. Target aud: General; Sp speaking farm workers. Spec prog: Relg 4 hrs, children 5 hrs, Sp 106 hrs wkly.

KDYK(AM)—See Union Gap

KFFM(FM)— Aug 31, 1970: 107.3 mhz; 100 kw. Ant 1,500 ft TL: N46 38 27 W120 23 42. Stereo. Hrs open: 24 4010 Summitview Ave., 98908. Phone: (509) 972-3461. Fax: (509) 972-3540.E-mail: jessicastuckel @gapbroadcasting.com Web Site:www.kffm.com Licensee: GAP Broadcasting Yakima License LLC. (acq 2-13-2008; grpsl). Population served: 35,000 Natl. Rep: McGavren Guild,. Drinker Biddle & Reath LLP. Format: CHR. News staff: one; News: one hr wkly. Target aud: 18-34. ♦Steve Rocha, progmg dir; Esther Johnson, traf mgr.

KHHK(FM)— Dec 1, 1984: 99.7 mhz; 7.6 kw. 584 ft TL: N46 31 53 W120 26 58. Stereo. Hrs open: 5 AM-midnight 1200 Chesterley Dr., Suite 160, 98902. Phone: (509) 248-2900. Fax: (509) 452-9661.E-mail: info@newhot997.com Web Site:newhot997.com Licensee: New Northwest Broadcasters LLC (group owner; acq 12-1-98; grpsl). Format: Urban contemp. Target aud: 18-34. ♦Pete Benedetti, CEO & pres; Don Morin, gen mgr; Dewey Boynton, opns mgr, progmg dir.

KIT(AM)— Apr 8, 1929: 1280 khz; 5 kw-D, 1 kw-N. TL: N46 34 19 W120 29 41. Stereo. Hrs open: 24 4010 Summitview Ave., 98908-2966. Phone: (509) 972-3461. Fax: (509) 972-3540. Fax: (509) 972-3542.E-mail: jessicastuckel@gapbroadcasting.com Web Site:www.1280kit.com Licensee: GAP Broadcasting Yakima License LLC. Group owner: Clear Channel Communications Inc. (acq 2-13-2008; grpsl). Population served: 190,000 Natl. Network: CBS, . Natl. Rep: McGavren Guild,. Drinker Biddle & Reath LLP. Format: News/talk. News staff: 2. Target aud: 25-64; professional, mature. Spec prog: Farm 6 hrs wkly. ♦Gary Donovan, exec VP; Cheryl Salomone, gen mgr; Ron Harris, opns mgr; Connie Johnston, sls dir; Dave Ettl, progmg dir; Lance Tormey, news dir; John Wilbanks, chief of engrg.

KJOX(AM)— 1947: 1390 khz; 5 kw-D, 500 w-N, DA-2. TL: N46 34 17 W120 27 15. (CP: 400 w-N). Hrs open: 24 1200 Chesterly Dr., Suite 160, 98902-7345. Phone: (509) 248-2990. Fax: (509) 452-9661. Licensee: New Northwest Broadcasters LLC. (group owner; (acq 10-20-98; grpsl). Population served: 140,000 Natl. Network: USA, . Format: Relg, Christian adult contemp. News staff: 2; News: 12 hrs wkly. Target aud: 35-64; family oriented. Spec prog: Black 2 hrs, gospel 2 hrs wkly. ♦Pete Benedetti, CEO; Trila Bumstead, COO, pres; Trila Houston, CFO; Brent Phillipy, VP; Kit Osborne, sls dir, traf mgr; Ron King, natl sls mgr, rgnl sls mgr; Jenifer Wilde, prom dir; Lou Bartelli, progmg dir, pub affrs dir; Tim Mauch, chief of engrg; Gail Dahl, traf mgr.

***KNWY(FM)**— Feb 20, 1993: 90.3 mhz; 5 kw. Ant 895 ft TL: N46 31 57 W120 30 37. Hrs open: 24
Rebroadcasts KFAE-FM Richland 100%.
Box 642530, 382 Murrow Ctr., Pullman, 99164-2530. Phone: (509) 335-6500. Fax: (509) 335-3772.E-mail: nwpr@wsu.edu Web Site:www.nwpr.org Licensee: Washington State University. Dow, Lohnes & Albertson. Format: News, class. News staff: one; News: 37 hrs wkly. ♦Karen Olstad, COO, gen mgr; Dennis Haarsager, gen mgr; Roger Johnson, stn mgr; Scott Weatherly, opns mgr; Sarah McDaniel, dev dir, dev mgr; Mary Hawkins, progmg dir.

KRSE(FM)— Aug 18, 1977: 105.7 mhz; 100 kw. Ant 584 ft TL: N46 42 45 W120 37 46. Stereo. Hrs open: 24 1200 Chesterly Dr., Suite 160, 98902-7345. Phone: (509) 248-2990. Fax: (509) 452-9661.E-mail: info@k105.com Web Site:k105.com Licensee: New Northwest Broadcasters LLC. Format: Adult contemp. Target aud: 25-64; upscale listener, primarily women. ♦Gail Dahl, prom dir, traf mgr; Kendall Weaver, opns mgr & progmg dir.

KUTI(AM)— Oct 19, 1944: 1460 khz; 5 kw-U, 3.7 kw-N, DA-N. TL: N46 33 29 W121 27 02. Hrs open: 24 4010 Summitview Ave., 98908-2966. Phone: (509) 972-3461. Fax: (509) 972-3540.E-mail: AM1460KUTI@yahoo.com Web Site:www.1460kuti.com Licensee: GAP Broadcasting Yakima License LLC. Group owner: Clear Channel Communications Inc. (acq 2-13-2008; grpsl). Population served: 10,000 Natl. Rep: McGavren Guild,. Drinker Biddle & Reath LLP. Format: Classic Country. News staff: one; News: 2 hrs wkly. Target aud: 35 plus. ♦Gary Donavan, exec VP; Cheryl Salomone, gen mgr; Ron Harris, opns mgr; Jack Balzer, progmg dir; Lance Tormey, news dir; John Wilbanks, chief of engrg; Lueta Bishop, traf mgr.

KXDD(FM)— July 1, 1971: 104.1 mhz; 61 kw. 781 ft TL: N46 30 48 W120 24 05. (CP: 100 kw, ant 1,128 ft. TL: N46 38 27 W120 23 42). Stereo. Hrs open: Prog sep from AM 1200 Chesterley Dr., #160, 98902. Phone: (509) 248-2900. Fax: (509) 452-9661. Licensee: New Northwest Broadcasters LLC Format: Country. Target aud: 18-54. ♦Dewey Boynton, opns mgr, mus dir; Stace Whitmire, prom mgr; Gail Dahl, traf mgr.

KYAK(AM)— Oct 17, 1962: 930 khz; 10 kw-D, 127 w-N. TL: N46 36 48 W120 28 51. Hrs open: 24 Box 31000, Spokane, 99223. Phone: (509) 452-5925.E-mail: kyak@kyak.com Web Site:kyak.com Licensee: Thomas W. Read dba Yakima Christian Broadcasting. (acq 6-1-98; $150,000). Natl. Network: Salem Radio Network, USA, . Cohen & Marks. Format: Christian. ♦Melinda Read, gen mgr; Bill Glenn, stn mgr.

***KYPL(FM)**— Oct 15, 1997: 91.1 mhz; 26 kw. Ant 797 ft TL: N46 30 48 W120 24 05. Stereo. Hrs open: 24
Rebroadcasts KGTS(FM) College Place 95%.
606 N. Western Ave., Wenatchee, 98801. Phone: (509) 527-2991. Fax: (509) 527-2611.E-mail: studio@plr.org Web Site:www.plr.org Licensee: Growing Christian Foundation. Population served: 225,000 Format: Christian contemp. News: 8 hrs wkly. Target aud: 35-64; family-oriented, Christian. ♦Kevin Krueger, chmn, gen mgr; Harry Watts, sls VP, gen sls mgr; Elizabeth Nelson, progmg dir; Walter Cox, engrg dir & chief of engrg.

***KYVT(FM)**— September 1980: 88.5 mhz; 3 kw. -254 ft TL: N46 35 06 W120 31 41. Stereo. Hrs open: 24 Yakima Valley Technical Ctr., 1116 S. 15th Ave., 98902. Phone: (509) 573-5013. Phone: (509) 573-5000. Fax: (509) 573-5023.E-mail: info@kyvt.com Web Site:yvtech.us Licensee: Yakima School District No. 7. Population served: 210000 Format: Alternative. News staff: one; News: 2 hrs wkly. Target aud: 18-25; student & working people. Spec prog: Urban alternative 3 hrs wkly. ♦John Schieche, pres; Randy Beckstead, gen mgr, chief of opns & dev dir; Andy Ward, prom dir.

KZTA(FM)—(Naches, Oct 25, 1988: 96.9 mhz; 14 kw. Ant 935 ft TL: N46 35 59 W120 52 08. Stereo. Hrs open: 24 Box 2888, 98901. Secondary address: 706 Butterfield Rd. 98901. Phone: (509) 457-1000. Fax: (509) 452-0541.E-mail: kteske@bustosmedia.com Web Site:www.bustosmedia.com Licensee: Bustos Media of Eastern Washington License LLC. (group owner; (acq 11-18-2004; grpsl). Natl. Rep: Tacher,. Format: Sp. News: 3 hrs wkly. Target aud: 18-35; Hispanic. ♦Amador S. Bustos, pres; Bob Berry, gen mgr; Keith Teske, opns mgr; Jesus Rosales, sls dir, news dir; Judith McInnes, progmg dir.

West Virginia

Barrackville

WFGM-FM— July 1993: 93.1 mhz; 2.6 kw. Ant 495 ft TL: N39 31 23 W80 12 00. Hrs open: 24
Rebroadcasts WBTQ-FM Buckhannon 100%.
Box 189, Buckhannon, 26201. Secondary address: WBUC Rd., Buckhannon 26201. Phone: (304) 472-1460. Fax: (304) 472-1528.E-mail: B93@verizon.net Licensee: Descendants Trust, Lauren M. Kelley, trustee Group owner: McGraw/Elliott Group Stations (acq 10-18-2005; $250,000). Population served: 400,000 Natl. Network: ABC, . Rgnl rep: Dome. Fisher, Wayland, Cooper, Leader & Zaragoza. Format: Oldies. News staff: one. Target aud: 25-54; active adults. ♦David Collett, gen sls mgr; Ryan Elliott, CFO, gen mgr, gen mgr & progmg dir; Brad Allen, news dir; Dick McGraw, chief of engrg.

Beckley

WCIR-FM— June 1971: 103.7 mhz; 5 kw. Ant 1,485 ft TL: N37 56 51 W81 18 32. Stereo. Hrs open: 24 306 S. Karawha St., 25801-5619. Phone: (304) 253-7000. Fax: (304) 255-1044.E-mail: 103cir@103cir.com Web Site:www.103cir.com Licensee: Southern Communications Corp. Population served: 194,000 Natl. Rep: Katz Radio,. Borsari & Paxson. Format: CHR. News staff: 2; News: 2 hrs wkly. Target aud: 25-54. ♦Rhonda Pritt, traf mgr.

WIWS(AM)— Nov 14, 1966: 1070 khz; 10 kw-D. TL: N37 45 18 W81 14 12. Hrs open: 306 S. Karawha St., 25801-5619. Phone: (304) 253-7000. Fax: (304) 255-1044. Licensee: Southern Communications Corp. (acq 1976). Population served: 70,000 Format: Oldies. Target aud: 18-54; traveling motorists. ♦Jay Quesenberry, gen mgr; Rennolt Madrazo, sls dir; Rick Pizer, prom dir & progmg dir; Randy Kerbawy, chief of engrg; Rhonda Pritt, traf mgr.

***WJJJ(FM)**— Oct 30, 2007: 88.1 mhz; 1 kw vert. Ant 1,059 ft TL: N37 35 20 W81 06 52. Hrs open: Box 12252, Charleston, 25302. Phone: (304) 382-0881.E-mail: wjjfm@soddenlinkmail,com Licensee: Shofar Broadcasting Corp. Format: Easy lstng, Christian. ♦James R. Jenkins, gen mgr.

WJLS(AM)— Mar 5, 1939: 560 khz; 4.5 kw-D, 470 w-N, DA-N. TL: N37 45 32 W81 11 12. Hrs open: 24 Prog sep from FM Box 5499, 25801. Secondary address: WJLS Bldg., 102 N. Kanawha St. 25801. Web Site:www.wjls.com Licensee: First Media Radio LLC Population served: 234,000 Natl. Network: CNN Radio, . Natl. Rep: Dome, Rgnl Reps,. Format: Relg, southern gospel. News staff: 5; News: 4 hrs wkly. Target aud: 25-54. Spec prog: Sports 3 hrs wkly. ♦Sandi Smith-Milam, progmg dir; Gary Hosey, mus dir.

WJLS-FM— Nov 6, 1946: 99.5 mhz; 34 kw. 1,050 ft TL: N37 35 23 W81 06 51. Stereo. Hrs open: 24 Box 5499, 25801. Secondary address: WJLS Bldg., 102 N. Kanawha St. 25801. Phone: (304)

253-7311. Fax: (304) 253-3466.E-mail: dawg@wjls.com Web Site:www.wjls.com Licensee: First Media Radio LLC (group owner; (acq 2-1-2002; $3.6 million with co-located AM). Population served: 349,000 Natl. Network: CNN Radio, . Rgnl rep: Dome, Rgnl Reps. Wire Svc: AP Format: Country. News staff: 15; News: 10 hrs wkly. Target aud: 25-54. ♦Mark Reid, gen mgr, sls dir & gen sls mgr; Darrell Ramsay, progmg dir; Bob Cannon, news dir; Charles Marlow, chief of engrg; Maria Marvin, traf mgr.

WOAY(AM)—See Oak Hill

***WVPB(FM)**— May 1, 1974: 91.7 mhz; 10.5 kw. 917 ft TL: N37 53 46 W80 59 21. Stereo. Hrs open: 24 600 Capitol St., Charleston, 25301. Phone: (304) 556-4900. Fax: (304) 556-4960.E-mail: feedback@wvpubcast.org Web Site:www.wvpubcast.org Licensee: West Virginia Educational Broadcasting Authority. Population served: 96,000 Natl. Network: NPR, PRI, . Format: News, class, jazz. ♦Marilyn DiVita, gen mgr, dev dir; James Muhammad, progmg dir; Greg Collard, news dir; Jack Wells, chief of engrg; Teresa Willis, traf mgr.

WWNR(AM)— Aug 9, 1946: 620 khz; 5 kw-D, 25 w-N. TL: N37 45 18 W81 14 12. Hrs open: 5 AM-midnight 306 S. Kanawha St., 25801. Phone: (304) 253-7000. Fax: (304) 255-1044.E-mail: wwnr@netphase.net Web Site:www.newstalk620.com Licensee: Southern Communications Corp. (group owner; acq 1-26-2004). Population served: 265,000 Natl. Network: CBS Radio, . Pepper & Corazzini. Format: News/talk. News staff: 2; News: 35 hrs wkly. Target aud: 25-54. ♦R. Shane Southern, pres; Jay Quesenberry, gen mgr, stn mgr, opns mgr; Rennold Madrazo, sls dir; Shane Sothern, gen sls mgr; Rick Rizer, prom dir, progmg dir; Warren Ellison, news dir; Randy Kerbawy, chief of engrg; Rhonda Pritt, traf mgr.

Berkeley Springs

WCST(AM)— Sept 7, 1958: 1010 khz; 250 w-D, 17 w-N. TL: N39 37 00 W78 13 03. Hrs open: 440 Radio Station Ln., 25411. Phone: (304) 258-1010. Fax: (304) 258-1976.E-mail: c929@comcast.net Licensee: Capper Broadcasting Co. Population served: 350,000 Format: News Talk. ♦Bonnie Rowbotham, CEO; Laura Haber, gen mgr, traf mgr; Shari Leadman, sls dir; Lee Bohrer, progmg dir; Mike Hurst, chief of engrg.

WDHC(FM)— December 1965: 92.9 mhz; 3.2 kw. Ant 456 ft TL: N39 37 00 W78 13 03. Stereo. Hrs open: Dups AM 100% 440 Radio Station Ln., 25411. Phone: (304) 258-1010. Fax: (304) 258-1976.E-mail: c929@comcast.net ♦Laura Haber, gen mgr, traf mgr; Lee Bohrer, progmg dir; Shari Leadman, sls.

Bethany

***WVBC(FM)**— Jan 1, 1967: 88.1 mhz; 1.1 kw. 410 ft TL: N40 12 58 W80 33 31. Stereo. Hrs open: Bethany House, Bethany College, 26032. Phone: (304) 829-7853. Licensee: Bethany College. Population served: 225,000 Natl. Network: AP Radio, . Wire Svc: AP Format: Div, educ, progsv. News: one hr wkly. Target aud: 18-34; high school & college students. Spec prog: Christian rock 4 hrs, folk 2 hrs, classic rock 8 hrs, class 2 hrs wkly. ♦Patrick Sutherland, gen mgr.

Bethlehem

WUKL(FM)— Feb 27, 2004: 105.5 mhz; 13.5 kw. Ant 312 ft TL: N40 03 17 W80 42 26. Stereo. Hrs open: 6 am-midnight Box 448, Bellaire, OH, 43906. Phone: (740) 676-5661. Fax: (740) 676-2742.E-mail: kool105@hotmail.com Web Site:oldiesradioonline.com Licensee: Keymarket Licenses LLC Group owner: Keymarket Communications LLC (acq 2-4-2004; $1.35 million). Population served: 44,369 Natl. Network: ABC, . Format: Oldies. News staff: one. Target aud: 35-54. ♦Gerald A. Getz, pres.

Blennerhassett

***WPJY(FM)**— 2008: 88.7 mhz; 10 kw. Ant 341 ft TL: N39 14 00 W81 53 26. Hrs open: Box 889, Blacksburg, VA, 24063. Phone: (540) 552-4252. Fax: (540) 951-5282. Web Site:www.joyfm.org Licensee: Positive Alternative Radio Inc. Format: Southern gospel. ♦Vernon H. Baker, pres.

Bluefield

WHAJ(FM)— Apr 23, 1963: 104.5 mhz; 100 kw. Ant 1,200 ft TL: N37 15 21 W81 10 55. Stereo. Hrs open: 900 Bluefield Ave., 24701. Phone: (304) 327-7114. Fax: (304) 325-7850. Web Site:www.1045.com Licensee: Monterey Licenses LLC. Population served: 151,000 Format: Adult contemp. Target aud: 25-54. ♦Dave Harris, progmg dir; Jackie White, traf mgr.

WHIS(AM)— June 27, 1929: 1440 khz; 5 kw-D, 500 w-N. TL: N37 16 33 W81 15 06. Stereo. Hrs open: 900 Bluefield Ave., 24701. Phone: (304) 327-7114. Fax: (304) 325-7850. Licensee: Monterey Licenses LLC. Group owner: Triad Broadcasting Co. LLC (acq 7-18-2000; grpsl). Population served: 26,200 Format: News/talk. Target aud: 35 plus; upper income, leaders of the community. ♦John Halford, gen mgr; Danny Clemons, sls dir; Joseph Echles, progmg dir; Keith Bowman, chief of engrg.

WKEZ(AM)— May 18, 1948: 1240 khz; 1 kw-U. TL: N37 15 57 W81 11 20. Hrs open: 24 900 Bluefield Ave., 24701. Phone: (304) 327-7114. Fax: (304) 325-7850. Licensee: Monterey Licenses LLC. Group owner: Triad Broadcasting Co. LLC (acq 7-18-2000; grpsl). Population served: 15,921 Format: Sports. Spec prog: Relg 5 hrs wkly. ♦David Benjamin, CEO, pres; John Halford, gen mgr, natl sls mgr, rgnl sls mgr; Danny Clemons, gen sls mgr; Ed Weiland, progmg dir; Keith Bowman, engrg mgr; Patty Davis, traf mgr.

***WPIB(FM)**— September 1995: 91.1 mhz; 12 kw. Ant 1,184 ft TL: N37 15 26 W81 10 43. Hrs open: Box 889, Blacksburg, VA, 24063. Fax: (540) 951-5282.E-mail: office@spiritfm.com Web Site:www.spiritfm.com Licensee: Positive Alternative Radio Inc. Group owner: Baker Family Stations (Positive Radio Group) (acq 4-22-92). Natl. Network: USA, . Format: Adult contemp, contemp Christian. ♦Edward A. Baker, pres & opns VP.

Bridgeport

WDCI(FM)— June 29, 1991: 104.1 mhz; 3 kw. 328 ft TL: N39 17 59 W80 17 30. (CP: 2.45 kw, ant 518 ft.). Stereo. Hrs open: 24 Box 360, 26330. Phone: (304) 842-8644. Fax: (304) 842-8653.E-mail: rtgresak@aol.com Licensee: WDCI Radio Inc. (acq 8-18-98; $405,000). Population served: 125,000 Natl. Network: Jones Radio Networks, . Rgnl rep: Dome. William D. Silva. Format: Soft adult contemp. Target aud: 25-54. ♦Bruce Wallace, pres, gen mgr; Tom Thompson, dev mgr, gen sls mgr, mktg mgr, prom mgr & adv mgr; Tina Grefak, progmg mgr; Hank Vest, chief of engrg.

Buckhannon

WBRB(FM)— June 16, 1990: 101.3 mhz; 50 kw. Ant 497 ft TL: N38 56 40 W80 10 46. Stereo. Hrs open: 24 Box 2377, WBUC Rd., Rt. 33, 26201. Phone: (304) 472-1460. Fax: (304) 472-1528. Licensee: West Virginia Radio Corp. of Buckhannon. (acq 10-18-2005; $4,267,900 with WBUC(AM) Buckhannon). Population served: 400000 Format: Country. News staff: one; News: 4 hrs wkly. Target aud: 25-54; upper middle class, white collar, craftsman. ♦Jan Harr, traf mgr.

WBTQ(FM)— 1984: 93.5 mhz; 16 kw. 417 ft TL: N38 58 11 W80 01 58. Stereo. Hrs open: 24 189 WBUC Rd., 26201. Phone: (304) 472-1400. Fax: (304) 472-1528. Licensee: West Virginia Radio Corp. of Elkins. Group owner: McGraw/Elliott Group Stations (acq 5-15-2008; $1.25 million). Population served: 110,000 Natl. Network: ABC, . Rgnl rep: Dome. Reddy, Begley & McCormick, LLP. Format: Adult contemp. News staff: one; News: 3 hrs wkly. Target aud: 18-49. ♦Brian Elliott, gen mgr, pub affrs dir, sls, prom; Richard McGraw, chief of engrg, engr; Wendy Dogas, traf mgr.

WBUC(AM)— Dec 13, 1959: 1460 khz; 5 kw-D, 87 w-N. TL: N39 00 07 W80 15 50. Stereo. Hrs open: Sunrise-sunset Box 2377, WBUC Rd., Rt. 33, 26201. Phone: (304) 472-1460. Fax: (304) 472-1528. Licensee: West Virginia Radio Corp. of Buckhannon. Group owner: McGraw/Elliott Group Stations (acq 10-18-2005; $4,267,900 with WBRB(FM) Buckhannon). Format: Talk. News staff: one. Target aud: General. Spec prog: Relg 7 hrs wkly. ♦Dale Miller, pres; Harry Elliott, CFO; Todd Elliott, gen mgr & opns VP; Brian Elliott, sls VP, gen sls mgr, adv VP; Ron Roth, prom VP, progmg VP; Tamara Cicogna, adv mgr; Nancy Boyce, news dir, pub affrs dir; Dick McGraw, chief of engrg; Jan Harr, traf mgr; Bill Austin, disc jockey.

***WVPW(FM)**— September 1968: 88.9 mhz; 14 kw. Ant 840 ft TL: N39 02 04 W80 33 47. Stereo. Hrs open: 24 600 Capitol St., Charleston, 25301. Phone: (304) 556-4900. Fax: (304) 556-4960.E-mail: feedback@wvpubcast.org Web Site:www.wvpubcast.org Licensee: West Virginia Education Broadcasting Authority. Natl. Network: NPR, PRI, . Format: News, class, jazz. ♦Marilyn DiVita, gen mgr, dev dir; James Muhammad, progmg dir; Greg Collard, news dir; Jack Wells, engrg dir; Teresa Wills, traf mgr.

***WVWC(FM)**— Sept 15, 1997: 92.1 mhz; 10 w. 85 ft TL: N38 59 24 W80 13 10. Hrs open: Box 167, 59 College Ave., 26201-2999. Phone: (304) 473-8292. Fax: (304) 472-2571.E-mail: c92@wvwc.edu Web Site:www.wvwc.edu/c92 Licensee: West Virginia Wesleyan College. Population served: 6,261 Format: Classic rock, progsv, div. Target aud: 12-25; high school & college audience. Spec prog: Black 4 hrs, class 2 hrs, jazz 8 hrs, relg 4 hrs, blues 2 hrs wkly. ♦Phillips B. Kolsun, gen mgr.

Charles Town

WMRE(AM)— May 28, 1962: 1550 khz; 5 kw-D, DA. TL: N39 16 23 W77 51 56. Hrs open: Sunrise-sunset 510 Pegasus Ct., Winchester, VA, 22602-4596. Phone: (540) 662-5101. Fax: (540) 662-8610. Web Site:www.sportstalk1550.com Licensee: AMFM Radio Licenses LLC. Group owner: Clear Channel Communications Inc. (acq 2-16-2001; $1.525 million with co-located FM). Natl. Network: Fox Sports, . Natl. Rep: Roslin,. Format: Sports. News staff: 2. ♦Chuck Peterson, gen mgr; David Miller, opns mgr; Marcella Vance, sls dir; Justin Maglione, prom dir; Maark Kesner, chief of engrg; Krissy Groves, traf mgr.

Charleston

WBES(AM)—(Dunbar, Nov 4, 1946: 1240 khz; 1 kw-U. TL: N38 23 08 W81 42 51. Hrs open: Box 871, 25323. Secondary address: 4250 Washington St. 25313. Phone: (304) 744-7020. Fax: (304) 744-8562. Licensee: Bristol Broadcasting Co. Inc. (group owner; acq 8-90; grpsl). Format: Talk, sports. Target aud: 18-49. ♦Mike Robinson, gen mgr; John Gush, natl sls mgr, rgnl sls mgr; Dan King, rgnl sls mgr.

WCHS(AM)— Sept 15, 1927: 580 khz; 5 kw-U, DA-N. TL: N38 21 49 W81 46 05. Hrs open: 1111 Virginia St. E., 25301. Phone: (304) 342-8131. Fax: (304) 344-4745.E-mail: 58live@wvradio.com Licensee: West Virginia Radio Corp. of Charleston. (acq 6-1-92; $1.74 million with co-located FM; 6-22-92). Natl. Network: CBS, . Natl. Rep: McGavren Guild,. Format: News/talk, sports. News staff: 2. Target aud: 25-54. ♦Dale Miller, pres, opns dir; Sean Banks, pres & gen mgr; Noel Richardson, opns VP, chief of engrg; Rick Johnson, opns dir, progmg dir; Sara Shingleyon, traf mgr.

WKAZ(AM)— 1946: 680 khz; 50 kw-D, 250 w-N, DA-2. TL: N38 19 15 W81 36 31. Hrs open: 24 1111 Virginia St. E., 25301. Phone: (304) 342-8131. Fax: (304) 344-4745. Licensee: West Virginia Radio Corp. of Charleston. (acq 7-14-93; $1.1 million with co-located FM; 8-9-93). Population served: 225,000 Natl. Network: ABC, . Format: Classic country. News staff: one. Target aud: 25-54. ♦Gregg Smith, progmg dir.

WKAZ-FM—See Miami

WKWS(FM)— Sept 16, 1969: 96.1 mhz; 50 kw. 360 ft TL: N38 21 24 W81 36 19. (CP: Ant 550 ft. TL: N38 21 51 W81 46 05). Stereo. Hrs open: Prog sep from AM 1111 Virginia St. E., 25301. Phone: (304) 342-8131. Fax: (304) 344-4745.E-mail: info@kick96.com Web Site:www.kick96.com Format: Hot country hits. ♦Rick Johnson, opns mgr, pub affrs dir; Christian Miller, gen sls mgr; John Anthony, progmg VP; Sara Shingleton, traf mgr.

WQBE-FM— Feb 16, 1957: 97.5 mhz; 50 kw. 500 ft TL: N38 24 22 W81 43 26. Hrs open: Prog sep from AM Box 871, 4250 Washington St. W., 25323. Phone: (304) 744-7020. Fax: (304) 744-8562.E-mail: info@wqbe.com Web Site:www.wqbe.com Format: Educ.

WSWW(AM)— 1939: 1490 khz; 1 kw-U. TL: N38 21 28 W81 37 00. Hrs open: 24 1111 Virginia St. E., 25301. Phone: (304) 342-8131. Fax: (304) 344-4745. Licensee: West Virginia Radio Corp. (group owner; (acq 6-5-97; $2.15 million with WKAZ-FM Miami). Population served: 250,000 Natl. Network: ESPN Radio, . Natl. Rep: D & R Radio,. Format: All sports/talk. ♦John Raese, chmn; Dale Miller, pres; Mike Buxser, gen mgr; Dave Harmon, opns dir, progmg dir; Vince Wardell, gen sls mgr; Noel Richardson, chief of engrg; Sarah Shingleton, traf mgr.

WVAF(FM)— Feb 1, 1965: 99.9 mhz; 50 kw. 490 ft TL: N38 19 15 W81 36 31. Stereo. Hrs open: Prog sep from AM 1111 Virginia St. E., 25301. Phone: (304) 342-8131. Fax: (304) 344-4745.E-mail: info@100radio.com Web Site:www.v100radio.com Licensee: West Virginia Radio Corp. of Charleston. Population served: 300,000 Format: Adult contemp. Target aud: Female skew. ♦Dale Miller, gen sls mgr; Greg Johnson, asst music dir; Nikki Walters, pub affrs dir; Doug Daniels, traf mgr, sports cmtr, sports cmtr, disc jockey; Denise Daniels, disc jockey.

***WVPN(FM)**— May 8, 1979: 88.5 mhz; 50 kw. Ant 299 ft TL: N38 22 32 W81 29 25. Stereo. Hrs open: 24 600 Capitol St., 25301. Phone: (304) 556-4900. Fax: (304) 556-4960.E-mail: feedback@wvpubcast.org Web Site:www.wvpubcast.org Licensee: West Virginia Educational Broadcasting Authority. Population served: 100,000 Natl. Network: NPR, PRI, . Format: News, class, jazz. ♦Rita Ray, gen mgr; Marilyn

DiVita, dev mgr; James Muhammad, progmg dir; Laura Harbert-Allen, mus dir; Greg Collard, news dir; Jack Wells, engrg dir; Teresa Wills, traf mgr.

WVSR-FM— September 1964: 102.7 mhz; 50 kw. Ant 403 ft TL: N38 21 26 W81 40 05. Stereo. Hrs open: Prog sep from AM Box 871, 25323. Secondary address: 4250 Washington St. 25313. Phone: (304) 744-7020. Fax: (304) 744-8562.E-mail: info@electric102.com Web Site:www.electric102.com Population served: 250,000 Format: CHR.

WVTS(AM)— Feb 16, 1957: 950 khz; 5 kw-D, 1 kw-N, DA-N. TL: N38 23 00 W81 42 52. Hrs open: Box 871, 4250 Washington St. W., 25323. Phone: (304) 744-7020. Fax: (304) 744-8562. Licensee: Bristol Broadcasting Co. Inc. (group owner; acq 5-1-64). Population served: 640,500 Natl. Rep: McGavren Guild,. Format: Talk. ♦Mike Robinson, gen mgr; John Gush, natl sls mgr, rgnl sls mgr; Dan King, rgnl sls mgr.

***WXAF(FM)—** 1994: 90.9 mhz; 800 w. Ant 623 ft TL: N38 16 25 W81 31 27. Hrs open: Box 7575, Huntington, 25777. Phone: (740) 867-5333. Licensee: Maranatha Broadcasting Inc. ♦Paul S. Warren, pres.

Clarksburg

***WCKU(FM)—** 1993: 90.1 mhz; 1.5 kw. Ant 597 ft TL: N39 19 09 W80 23 31. Hrs open: 2351 Sunset Blvd., Suite 170-218, Rocklin, CA, 95765. Phone: (916) 251-1600. Fax: (916) 251-1650. Web Site:www.klove.com Licensee: Educational Media Foundation. (acq 2-29-2008; $900,000 with WHKU(FM) Proctorville, OH). Natl. Network: K-Love, . Format: Contemp Christian. ♦Michael Novak, pres.

WGIE(FM)— 1975: 92.7 mhz; 620 w. 600 ft TL: N39 17 27 W80 18 56. Stereo. Hrs open: 24 Prog sep from AM
Rebroadcasts WGYE(FM) Fairmont 100%.
1489 Locust Ave. #C, Faimont, 26554-1402. Licensee: Burbach of DE LLC Population served: 250,000 Rgnl. Network: Metronews Radio Net. Format: Country. News: 3 hrs wkly. Target aud: 25-45; young professionals. ♦Dave Sturm, sports cmtr; Debbie Southrn, traf mgr & disc jockey.

***WKJL(FM)—** October 1992: 88.1 mhz; 23.5 kw. Ant 712 ft TL: N39 18 02 W80 20 37. Stereo. Hrs open: 19
Rebroadcasts WAIJ(FM) Grantsville, Md. 100%.
Box 540, Grantsville, MD, 21536-0540. Secondary address: He's Alive Corp. Offices, 34 Springs Rd., Grantsville 21536. Phone: (301) 895-3292. Fax: (301) 895-3293.E-mail: hesalive@hesalive.net Web Site:www.hesalive.net Licensee: He's Alive Inc. Natl. Network: USA, . Format: Gospel, Christian. Target aud: 18-35. ♦Sharon Johnson, pres; Melissa Flores, gen mgr, stn mgr; Tim Eutin, progmg dir; Hank Vest, chief of engrg; Brandon Hutzell, traf mgr.

WOBG(AM)— Apr 12, 1936: 1400 khz; 1 kw-U. TL: N39 17 46 W80 18 16. Hrs open: 24 1489 Locust Ave., #C, Fairmont, 26554-1337. Secondary address: Old Weatherservice Bldg., Old Rt. 50 E. 26301. Phone: (304) 624-1400. Fax: (304) 624-1402. Licensee: Clarksburg Radio Co. Group owner: Burbach Broadcasting Group (acq 1-11-99; $330,000 with WOBG-FM Salem). Rgnl rep: Commercial Media Sales. Format: Adult standards. Target aud: 35 plus. ♦Nicholas A. Galli, pres; David Bronham, gen mgr, gen sls mgr; Greg Bolyard, progmg dir; Larry Smith, chief of engrg.

WPDX(AM)— Aug 19, 1947: 750 khz; 1 kw-D. TL: N39 14 40 W80 23 05. Hrs open: 59 Mountain Park Dr., White Hall, 26554. Phone: (304) 363-3851. Fax: (304) 363-3852.E-mail: wpdx@iolinc.net Licensee: Tschudy Broadcasting Corp. Group owner: Tschudy Broadcast Group (acq 11-5-91; $405,000 with co-located FM; 12-2-91). Population served: 400,000 Natl. Network: AP Radio, . Rgnl rep: Commercial Media Sales Format: Classic country. Target aud: 35-54; blue collar.

WPDX-FM— Aug 19, 1974: 104.9 mhz; 7.4 kw. Ant 597 ft TL: N39 15 22 W80 06 46. Stereo. Hrs open: 24 7013 Mountains Park Dr., Fairmont, 26554. Phone: (304) 363-3851. Fax: (304) 363-3852. Licensee: Tschudy Broadcasting Corp. (acq 1992). Population served: 400,000 Natl. Network: AP Radio, . Rgnl rep: Commercial Media Sales Format: Classic country. News: 5 hrs wkly. Target aud: 35-54; blue collar.

WWLW(FM)— 1973: 106.5 mhz; 50 kw. 500 ft TL: N39 11 14 W80 32 45. Stereo. Hrs open: 24 1065 Radio Park Dr., Mt. Clare, 26408. Phone: (304) 623-6546. Fax: (304) 623-6547.E-mail: info@wvmagic.com Web Site:www.wvmagic.com Licensee: West Virginia Radio Corp. of Clarksburg. (acq 3-2-93; $1.2 million;3-22-93). Population served: 400,000 Format: Adult contemp. News staff: one; News: 2 hrs wkly. ♦Dale B. Miller, pres; Christian Miller, stn mgr; Chad Perry, opns VP, opns dir, progmg dir; Tim Brady, gen sls mgr & news dir; Steve Lough, chief of engrg; Donna Tubolino, traf mgr.

WXKX(AM)— Nov 28, 1946: 1340 khz; 1 kw-U. TL: N39 17 27 W80 18 56. Hrs open: 24 1489 Locust Ave., Suite C, Fairmont, 26554-1337. Phone: (304) 624-1400. Fax: (304) 624-1402. Licensee: Burbach of DE LLC. Group owner: Burbach Broadcasting Group (acq 11-2-00; $435,000 cash with co-located FM). Population served: 65,000 Natl. Network: ESPN Radio, . Natl. Rep: Roslin, Rgnl Reps,. Baraff, Koerner & Olender. Format: Sports. News: 14 hrs wkly. Target aud: 35 plus; office workers, retirees, upper income. Spec prog: Pittsburgh Pirates, Alderson-Broadus College basketball, high school football. ♦Nick Galli, pres; Dan Barham, gen mgr; David Branham, gen sls mgr; Greg Bolgard, prom dir; Larry Smith, chief of engrg; Debbie Southern, traf mgr.

Cowen

WKQV(FM)— Jan 1, 2007: 105.5 mhz; 3.5 kw. Ant 882 ft TL: N38 21 35 W80 38 51. Stereo. Hrs open: 24 180 Main St., Sutton, 26601. Phone: (304) 765-7373. Fax: (304) 765-7836.E-mail: info@105kqv.com Web Site:www.105kqv.com Licensee: Summit Media Broadcasting LLC. (acq 3-15-2006; $482,500 for CP). Natl. Network: CNN Radio, . Natl. Rep: Rgnl Reps,. Format: Classic rock. Target aud: 18-49. ♦Al Sergi, pres & gen mgr.

Craigsville

WSWW-FM— 2008: 95.7 mhz; 25 kw. Ant 325 ft TL: N38 24 56 W80 31 49. Hrs open: 812 Northside Dr., Suite 1, Summersville, 26651-2016. Phone: (304) 872-6403. Fax: (304) 872-6816. Licensee: West Virginia Radio Corp. of Charleston. (acq 9-11-2007). Format: Talk, light rock. ♦Dale B. Miller, pres.

Danville

WZAC-FM— Oct 9, 1989: 92.5 mhz; 610 w. 697 ft TL: N38 05 01 W81 48 17. Stereo. Hrs open: Box 87, 25053. Secondary address: 457 Main St., Madison 25130. Phone: (304) 369-5200. Phone: (304) 369-5201. Fax: (304) 369-5200. Licensee: Price Broadcasting Co. Format: Classic country. Target aud: General. ♦Wayne Price, gen mgr.

Dunbar

WBES(AM)—Licensed to Dunbar. See Charleston

WLUX(AM)—Not on air, target date: unknown: 1450 khz; 1 kw-U. TL: N38 23 08 W81 42 52. Hrs open: Box 3744, Charleston, 25337. Phone: (304) 345-2000. Fax: (304) 343-7999. Licensee: St. Paul Radio Co. ♦Mark A. Sadd, pres.

WZJO(FM)— Oct 13, 1988: 94.5 mhz; 9.6 kw. Ant 525 ft TL: N38 25 11 W81 43 24. Stereo. Hrs open: 24 Box 871, Charleston, 25323. Secondary address: 4250 Washington St., Charleston 25313. Phone: (304) 744-7020. Fax: (304) 744-8562.E-mail: info@mix945online.com Web Site:www.mix945online.com Licensee: Bristol Broadcasting Co. Inc. (group owner; acq 1996; grpsl). Natl. Network: Moody, Westwood One, . Natl. Rep: Dome, Rgnl Reps, Katz Radio,. Format: Adult contemp hits of the 80s. Spec prog: Class 2 hrs wkly. ♦Mike Robinson, gen mgr; Barrie Hamm, prom mgr; Dave Evans, progmg dir; Randy Justice, chief of engrg.

Elizabeth

WRZZ(FM)— 1986: 106.1 mhz; 3 kw. 469 ft TL: N39 09 48 W81 26 12. Stereo. Hrs open: 24 5 Rosemar Cir., Parkersburg, 26104. Phone: (304) 485-4565. Fax: (304) 424-6955.E-mail: info@classicrockz106.com Web Site:www.classicrockz106.com Licensee: Burbach of DE LLC. Group owner: Clear Channel Communications Inc. (acq 8-8-2005; $750,000). Population served: 200,000 Natl. Network: Westwood One, . Koerner & Olender. Format: Classic rock. Target aud: 25-54; baby boomer rock listeners. ♦Don Staats, gen mgr.

Elkins

***WBHZ(FM)—** 1999: 91.9 mhz; 280 w. 1,118 ft TL: N38 52 18 W79 55 39. Hrs open: Box 2440, Tupelo, MS, 38803. Phone: (662) 844-8888. Fax: (662) 842-6791. Web Site:www.afr.net Licensee: American Family Association. Group owner: American Family Radio Format: Christian. ♦Marvin Sanders, gen mgr.

WDNE(AM)— February 1948: 1240 khz; 1 kw-U. TL: N38 55 25 W79 51 33. Hrs open: 21 Box 1337, 26241. Phone: (304) 636-1300. Fax: (304) 636-2200.E-mail: wdne@wvradio.com Licensee: West Virginia Radio Corp. of Elkins. Group owner: West Virginia Radio Corp. (acq 6-17-97; $750,000 with co-located FM). Population served: 8,287 Format: Adult Standards. News staff: one. Target aud: 18 plus. ♦Rick Cooper, gen mgr, gen sls mgr; Howard Swick, prom dir; Roger Taylor, progmg dir; Joe Gaynor, mus dir; Noel Richardson, chief of engrg; Fay Cowgill, traf mgr.

WDNE-FM— June 15, 1985: 98.9 mhz; 3 kw. 328 ft TL: N38 51 53 W79 48 26. (CP: 5.1 kw, ant 725 ft. TL: N38 54 36 W79 47 18). Stereo. Hrs open: 21 Prog sep from AM Box 1337, 26241. Phone: (304) 636-1300. Fax: (304) 636-2200.E-mail: info@wdnefm.com Format: Country. ♦Fay Cowgill, traf mgr.

WELK(FM)— Oct 17, 1982: 94.7 mhz; 5 kw. 728 ft TL: N38 54 43 W79 47 19. Stereo. Hrs open: 24 228 Randolph Ave., 26241. Phone: (304) 636-1300. Fax: (304) 636-2200.E-mail: radiosales@3wlogic.net Licensee: West Virginia Radio Corp. of Elkins. Group owner: McGraw/Elliott Group Stations. (acq 5-15-2008; $1.05 million). Population served: 138,000 Natl. Network: CNN Radio, . Shaw Pittman. Format: Adult contemp, Top-40. News staff: one; News: 3 hrs wkly. Target aud: 18-49; female. ♦Dale Miller, pres; Harry Elliot, CFO; Todd Elliott, VP, gen mgr & opns dir; Brian Elliott, gen sls mgr; Brad Elliott, progmg dir; Jane Birdsong, news dir, pub affrs dir; Bill Davisson, chief of engrg; Connie Cade, traf mgr.

Fairmont

WKKW(FM)— October 1975: 97.9 mhz; 32 kw. 600 ft TL: N39 25 04 W80 03 44. Stereo. Hrs open: 1251 Earl L. Core Rd., Morgantown, 26505. Phone: (304) 296-0029. Fax: (304) 296-3876.E-mail: jshaffer@wvradio.com Web Site:www.wkkwfm.com Licensee: Descendants Trust, Lauren M. Kelley, trustee. (acq 9-13-00; $1.5 million). Population served: 280,000 Putbrese, Hunsaker & Trent. Format: Country. Target aud: 25-54; young professionals. ♦Dave Jecklin, gen mgr; Christian Miller, sls dir; John Thomas, progmg dir.

WMMN(AM)— Dec 22, 1928: 920 khz; 5 kw-U, DA-N. TL: N39 28 03 W80 12 20. (CP: 5 kw-D, 200 w-N, DA-N). Hrs open: Box 1549, 26555. Phone: (304) 366-3700. Fax: (304) 366-3706. Web Site:www.920wmmn.com Licensee: Fantasia Broadcasting Inc. Population served: 400,000 Natl. Network: Fox Sports, . Rgnl rep: Commercial Media Sales. Format: Sports. Target aud: 18 plus. ♦Nick L. Fantasia, pres & gen mgr; Bill Dunn, opns mgr.

WRLF(FM)— Aug 26, 1989: 94.3 mhz; 3.6 kw. Ant 249 ft TL: N39 28 03 W80 12 20. Stereo. Hrs open: 24 Box 1549, 26555. Secondary address: 450 Leonard Ave. 26554. Phone: (304) 366-3700. Fax: (304) 366-3706. Web Site:www.wrlf.com Licensee: Fairmont Broadcasting Co. Population served: 110,000 Rgnl. Network: Metronews Radio Net. Format: Classic rock. Target aud: 25-55; 60% male, 40% female. ♦Nick Fantasia, gen mgr; Bill Dunn, opns mgr, gen sls mgr.

WTCS(AM)— January 1948: 1490 khz; 1 kw-U. TL: N39 28 19 W80 08 27. Hrs open: 24 Box 1549, 26555. Secondary address: 450 Leonard Ave. 26554. Phone: (304) 366-3700. Fax: (304) 366-3706. Licensee: Fairmont Broadcasting Co. (acq 5-1-56). Population served: 26,093 Natl. Network: CNN Radio, . W. Va. MetroNews Network Rgnl rep: Commercial Media Sales. Putbrese, Hunsaker & Trent. Format: News/talk. Target aud: 35 plus. Spec prog: It 3 hrs wkly. ♦Nick Fantasia, gen mgr; Bill Dunn, opns mgr, gen sls mgr; Bob Ice, chief of engrg.

Fayetteville

WVBD(FM)— May 1, 2009: 100.7 mhz; 480 w. Ant 1,125 ft TL: N37 55 40.4 W80 58 11.5. Hrs open: 180 Main St., Sutton, 26601. Phone: (304) 765-3676.E-mail: info@wsgdfm.com Licensee: Summit Media South Inc. Format: Country. ♦Daniel W. Finch Jr., gen mgr.

Fisher

WELD(AM)— Aug 1, 1956: 690 khz; 2 kw-D. TL: N39 03 08 W79 00 21. Hrs open: 24 126 Kessel Rd., 26818. Phone: (304) 538-6062. Fax: (304) 538-7032.E-mail: WELD@hardynet.com Web Site:weldamfm.com Licensee: Thunder Associates LLC (acq 2-1-2004 $600,000 with WELD-FM Petersburg). Population served: 130,000 Natl. Network: ABC, . Natl. Rep: Dome,. W. Va. MetroNews Network Irwin, Campbell, Tannenwald. Format: Oldies. News: 3 hrs wkly. Target aud: 25+; 25+. Spec prog: Farm 3 hrs, relg 10 hrs wkly. ♦Curtis Durst, pres; Sandra Durst, exec VP; Alan Yokum, gen mgr.

WQWV(FM)— July 1998: 103.7 mhz; 310 w. 1,384 ft TL: N39 02 16 W79 05 23. Hrs open: 24 Box 55, Petersburg, 26847. Secondary address: 2 Alt Ave., Petersburg 26847. Phone: (304) 257-4432. Fax: (304) 257-9733.E-mail: V103@V103.NewCountry.com Web

Site:www.wqwv.com Licensee: McGuire Broadcasting L.L.C. (acq 5-20-99). Population served: 35,000 Natl. Network: CNN Radio, . Format: Contemp hit/Top-40, Variety/diverse. ♦Eric McGuire, gen mgr; Kevin Spencer, opns mgr; Angel Blizzard, gen sls mgr.

Fort Gay

***WFGH(FM)**— June 4, 1973: 90.7 mhz; 7.8 kw. 205 ft TL: N38 07 58 W82 35 37. Hrs open: 24 Box 410, 25514. Phone: (304) 648-5752. Fax: (304) 648-5447.E-mail: wfgh907@radio.com Web Site:www.tolisarebels.org/tech/broadcasting.htm Licensee: Wayne County Board of Education. Population served: 20,000 Wire Svc: AP Format: Oldies, country, gospel. News staff: 2; News: 15 hrs wkly. Target aud: General. Spec prog: Oldies. ♦Hazel B. Damron, progmg dir; Vernon R. Stanfill, gen mgr, opns dir & chief of engrg.

Franklin

***WVPC(FM)**—Not on air, target date: unknown: 91.1 mhz; 500 w. Ant -187 ft TL: N38 38 58 W79 20 28. Hrs open: Rt. 1, Box 139, Dunmore, 24934. Phone: (304) 799-6004. Fax: (304) 799-7444. Web Site:www.alleghenymountainradio.org Licensee: Pocahontas Communications Cooperative Corp. ♦Cheryl Kinderman, gen mgr.

Frost

***WVMR(AM)**— Aug 17, 1981: 1370 khz; 5 kw-D. TL: N38 17 25 W79 55 52. Hrs open: Box 139, Rte. 1, Dunmore, 24934. Phone: (304) 799-6004. Fax: (304) 799-7444.E-mail: amrinet@starband.net Web Site:www.alleghenymountainradio.org Licensee: Pocahontas Communications Cooperative Corp. Population served: 10,000 Format: Country. Target aud: General. Spec prog: Farm 5 hrs, relg 10 hrs, big band 3 hrs, bluegrass 5 hrs wkly. ♦Bill Ellenburg, pres.

Glenville

WVRW(FM)— 2008: 107.7 mhz; 1.7 kw. Ant 623 ft TL: N38 54 29 W80 49 48. Hrs open: 300 Harrison Ave., Weston, 26452. Phone: (304) 462-7771. Fax: (304) 269-4800.E-mail: info@wvrwfm.com Web Site:www.wvrwfm.com Licensee: Della Jane Woofter. Format: Oldies. ♦Stephen R. Peters, gen mgr.

Grafton

***WDKL(FM)**— Sept 10, 1979: 95.9 mhz; 3 kw. 150 ft TL: N39 21 16 W80 01 27. Stereo. Hrs open: 24 2351 Sunset Blvd., Suite 170-218, Rocklin, CA, 95765. Phone: (916) 251-1600. Fax: (916) 251-1650.E-mail: klove@klove.com Web Site:www.klove.com Licensee: Educational Media Foundation Group owner: EMF Broadcasting. (acq 5-28-02). Natl. Network: K-Love, . Shaw Pittman. Format: Contemp Christian. News staff: 3. Target aud: 25-44; female-Judeo Christian. ♦Richard Jenkins, pres; Mike Novak, VP; Keith Whipple, dev dir; David Pierce, progmg mgr; Ed Lenane, news dir; Sam Wallington, engrg dir; Karen Johnson, news rptr.

WVUS(AM)— January 1948: 1190 khz; 4.5 kw-D, 22 w-N. TL: N39 21 01 W80 02 40. Hrs open: 24 hrs Box 2, 26354. Phone: (304) 265-2200. Fax: (304) 265-0972.E-mail: wtbz@go.com Web Site:www.1190wvus.com Licensee: Appalachian Radio LLC (acq 8-12-2002). Reddy, Begley & McCormick LLP. Format: Adult contemp. News: 15 hrs wkly. Target aud: 18-65. ♦Melanie Tocco, gen mgr.

Green Valley

WAMN(AM)— January 1987: 1050 khz; 1.43 kw-D, 200 w-N. TL: N37 18 20 W81 07 30. Hrs open: Box 6350, Bluefield, 24701. Secondary address: 4415 Blue Prince Rd. 24701. Phone: (304) 327-9266. Phone: (304) 327-9140. Fax: (304) 325-8058.E-mail: espn1050@yahoo.com Web Site:www.thesportsaddictnetwork.com Licensee: WAMN Inc. Group owner: Baker Family Stations (acq 2-8-89). Natl. Network: ESPN Radio, . Format: Sports. ♦Vernon H. Baker, pres; Amy Burnette, gen mgr.

Hillsboro

***WVMR-FM**—Not on air, target date: unknown: 91.9 mhz; 700 w. Ant -1,023 ft TL: N38 11 15 W80 11 46. Hrs open: Rt. 1, Box 139, Dunmore, 24934-9712. Phone: (304) 799-6004. Fax: (304) 799-7444. Web Site:www.alleghenymountainradio.org Licensee: Pocahontas Communications Cooperative Corp. ♦Cheryl Kinderman, gen mgr.

Hinton

WMTD(AM)— Jan 11, 1963: 1380 khz; 1 kw-D. TL: N37 40 49 W80 54 24. Hrs open: 24
Rebroadcasts WAXS(FM) Oak Hill 75%.
306 S. Kanawha St., Beckley, 25801. Phone: (304) 253-7000. Fax: (304) 255-1044. Licensee: Southern Communications Corp. (group owner; (acq 4-19-2000; $107,000 with co-located FM). Population served: 38,000 Natl. Network: CBS, . Format: News/talk, oldies. News staff: 3; News: 9 hrs wkly. Target aud: General. ♦R. Shane Southern, pres; Jay Quesenberry, gen mgr; Rennold Madrazo, sls dir; Steve Coleman, rgnl sls mgr; Rick Rizer, progmg VP, chief of engrg; Randy Kerbawy, engrg VP; Rhonda Pritt, traf mgr.

WMTD-FM— Oct 1, 1985: 102.3 mhz; 160 w. 1,008 ft TL: N37 42 56 W80 56 55. (CP: 368 w, ant 1,273 ft.). Stereo. Hrs open: 24 306 S. Kanawha St., Beckley, 25801. Phone: (304) 253-7000. Fax: (304) 255-1044. Licensee: Southern Communications Corp. Population served: 38,000 News staff: one; News: 1 hr wkly. Target aud: Adults 18-49. ♦Rhonda Pritt, traf mgr.

Huntington

WAMX(FM)—(Milton, Oct 1, 1980: 106.3 mhz; 1.65 kw. Ant 1,109 ft TL: N38 30 21 W82 12 33. Stereo. Hrs open: 24 134 4th Ave., 25701. Phone: (304) 525-7788. Fax: (304) 525-6281.E-mail: x1063@x1063.com Web Site:www.x1063.com Licensee: Capstar TX L.P. Group owner: Clear Channel Communications Inc. (acq 8-30-00; grpsl). Population served: 350,000 Format: Active rock. News staff: one; News: 4 hrs wkly. Target aud: 25-49; males in their late teens to late '40s. ♦Judi Cornett, VP, chief of engrg; Judy Cornett, gen mgr; Kevin Beller, gen sls mgr; Erik Raines, progmg dir, progmg mgr; Robin Wilds, prom dir & news dir.

WCMI(AM)—See Ashland, KY

WDGG(FM)—See Ashland, KY

WEMM-FM— Sept 6, 1971: 107.9 mhz; 50 kw. 500 ft TL: N38 28 33 W82 15 00. Stereo. Hrs open: 24 703 3rd Ave., 25701. Phone: (304) 525-5141. Phone: (304) 525-9366. Fax: (304) 525-0748. Web Site:www.wemmfm.com Licensee: Mortenson Broadcasting Co. (group owner). Population served: 2,500,000 Natl. Network: USA, . Format: Christian, gospel. News: 4 hrs wkly. Target aud: 35 plus; responsive, loyal, family oriented. ♦Jack M. Mortenson, pres; Alicia Vance, gen mgr, opns mgr, traf mgr.

WHKU(FM)—See Proctorville, OH

WKEE-FM— November 1947: 100.5 mhz; 53 kw. Ant 561 ft TL: N38 23 35 W82 28 24. Stereo. Hrs open: Box 2288, 25724. Secondary address: 134 4th Ave. 25701. Phone: (304) 525-7788. Fax: (304) 525-6281. Web Site:www.wkee.com Licensee: Capstar TX L.P. (acq 8-30-2000; grpsl). Population served: 257,900 Format: CHR, pop. Target aud: 18-42. ♦Judy Cornett, VP & gen mgr; Gloria Ward, sls dir; Jim Davis, progmg dir; Gary Miller, mus dir.

***WMUL(FM)**— Nov 1, 1961: 88.1 mhz; 1.15 kw. -56 ft TL: N38 25 26 W82 25 39. Stereo. Hrs open: 6 AM-3 AM Comm. Bldg., One John Marshall Dr., 25755-2635. Phone: (304) 696-6640. Phone: (304) 696-6651. Fax: (304) 696-3232.E-mail: wmul@marshall.edu Web Site:www.marshall.edu/wmul Licensee: Marshall University Board of Governors (acq 8-7-01). Population served: 83,700 William D. Silva. Wire Svc: AP Format: Div. News: 7 hrs wkly. Target aud: General. ♦Dr. Stephen Kopp, pres; Dr. Chuck G. Bailey, gen mgr; Adam Cavalier, stn mgr; Michael Stanley, opns mgr; Chuck Cook, chief of opns, chief of engrg; Jason van Meter, prom dir; Jessie Kirk, mus dir; Leannda Carey, news dir; Ryan Epling, sports cmtr.

WRVC(AM)— Oct 23, 1923: 930 khz; 5 kw-D, 1 kw-N, DA-N. TL: N38 24 03 W82 29 42. Hrs open: 24 Box 1150, 25713. Secondary address: 401 11th St., Suite 200 25701. Phone: (304) 523-8401. Fax: (304) 523-4848.E-mail: wrvc@wrvc.com Web Site:www.wrvc.am Licensee: Fifth Avenue Broadcasting Co. Inc. Group owner: Kindred Communications Inc. (acq 6-1-70). Population served: 30,700 Natl. Network: ESPN Radio, ABC, CBS Radio, Motor Racing Net, Westwood One, . Natl. Rep: McGavren Guild,. W. Va. MetroNews Network Arent, Fox, Kintner, Plotkin & Kahn. Wire Svc: AP Wire Svc: Accu-Weather Wire Svc: ESPN/SportsTicker Format: Sports. News staff: one; News: 40 hrs wkly. Spec prog: Relg 3 hrs wkly. ♦Mike Kirtner, pres, gen mgr; Rae Ann Parsons, natl sls mgr; Rich Myhrwold, rgnl sls mgr; Cameron Smith, engrg dir.

WRWB(AM)— 1946: 1470 khz; 5 kw-D, 72 w-N. TL: N38 24 22 W82 29 04. Hrs open: 24 703 3rd Ave., 25701. Phone: (304) 525-5141. Fax: (304) 525-0748. Web Site:www.wrwbam.com Licensee: Mortenson Broadcasting Co. of West Virginia LLC. Group owner: Mortenson Broadcasting Co. (acq 1-30-2004; $200,000). Format: Southern gospel. Target aud: 25-50; general. ♦Jack Mortenson, pres; Alicia Vance, opns mgr.

WTCR(AM)—See Kenova

WTCR-FM— May 1, 1966: 103.3 mhz; 50 kw. 490 ft TL: N38 25 11 W82 24 06. Hrs open: 9801 Radio Park Rd., Catlettsburg, KY, 41129. Phone: (606) 739-8427. Fax: (606) 739-6009.E-mail: wtcr@clearchannel.com Web Site:wtcr.com Licensee: Capstar TX L.P. Group owner: Clear Channel Communications Inc. (acq 8-30-00; grpsl). Population served: 300,000 Natl. Network: ABC, . Natl. Rep: Rgnl Reps, Katz Radio,. Format: Country. ♦Judy Cornett, gen mgr.

WVHU(AM)— July 1947: 800 khz; 5 kw-D, 185 w-N. TL: N38 23 35 W82 28 24. Stereo. Hrs open: Box 2288, 25724. Secondary address: 134 4th Ave. 25701. Phone: (304) 525-7788. Fax: (304) 525-6281.E-mail: paulswann@clearchanneler Web Site:www.800wvhu.com Licensee: Capstar TX L.P. Group owner: Clear Channel Communications Inc. (acq 8-30-2000; grpsl). Population served: 257,000 Alan Campbell. Format: News/talk. Target aud: 25-54; older, professional, higher income. ♦Judy Cornett, gen mgr; Matt Tweel, sls dir; Kym Blake, natl sls mgr; Truezy Robinette, prom dir; Paul Swann, progmg dir; Bill Cornwell, news dir; Scott Hensley, chief of engrg.

***WVWV(FM)**— Nov 28, 1977: 89.9 mhz; 8.1 kw. 1,200 ft TL: N38 29 42 W82 12 03. Stereo. Hrs open: 24 600 Capitol St., Charleston, 25301. Phone: (304) 556-4900. Fax: (304) 556-4981.E-mail: feedback@wvpubcast.org Web Site:www.wvpubcast.org Licensee: West Virginia Educational Broadcasting Authority. Population served: 100,000 Natl. Network: NPR, PRI, . Format: News, class, jazz. ♦Marilyn DiVita, gen mgr, dev dir; Craig Lanham, progmg dir; Greg Collard, news dir; Jack Wells, chief of engrg; Teresa Willis, traf mgr.

Hurricane

WIHY(AM)— July 2, 1971: 1110 khz; 1 kw-D. TL: N38 26 41 W82 00 54. Hrs open: 10
Simulcast with WOKT(AM) Cannonsburg, KY 100%.
3006 Mt. Vernon Rd., Suite 1080, 25526. Phone: (304) 757-9661. Fax: (304) 757-9620.E-mail: info@i64country.com Web Site:www.i64country.com Licensee: Big River Radio Inc. Group owner: Baker Family Stations (acq 1996; $20,000). Population served: 800,000 Format: Classic country. ♦Vernon H. Baker, pres; Randy Parsons, gen mgr; Matt Curry, opns mgr, progmg dir, traf mgr; Winston Hawkins, chief of engrg.

***WPJW(FM)**— 2009: 91.5 mhz; 3 kw. Ant 302 ft TL: N38 26 41 W82 00 54. Hrs open: Box 889, Blacksburg, VA, 24063. Phone: (304) 757-9661. Web Site:www.joyfm.org Licensee: Positive Alternative Radio Inc. ♦Vernon H. Baker, pres.

Kenova

WMGA(FM)— 2006: 97.9 mhz; 3.5 kw. Ant 436 ft TL: N38 25 26 W82 32 08. Hrs open: Box 404, Huntington, 25708. Secondary address: 919 Fifth Ave., Suite 210, Huntington 25701. Phone: (304) 399-9603. Fax: (304) 399-9608. Web Site:www.magic979.com Licensee: Connoisseur Media LLC. Format: Adult contemp. ♦Newman Adkins, gen mgr.

WTCR(AM)— August 1954: 1420 khz; 5 kw-D, 500 w-N, DA-N. TL: N38 24 42 W82 36 13. Hrs open: 9801 Radio Park Rd., Catlettsburg, KY, 41129. Phone: (606) 739-8427. Fax: (606) 739-6009.E-mail: wtcr@clearchannel.com Licensee: Capstar TX L.P. Group owner: Clear Channel Communications Inc. (acq 8-30-2000; grpsl). Population served: 266,000 Natl. Network: Fox Sports, . Natl. Rep: Rgnl Reps, Katz Radio,. Format: Sports. Target aud: 35 plus. ♦Judy Cornett, VP & stn mgr.

Keyser

WCBC-FM— January 1990: 107.1 mhz; 530 w. 783 ft TL: N39 31 26 W78 51 44. Stereo. Hrs open: Box 1290, Cumberland, MD, 21501. Phone: (301) 724-5000. Fax: (301) 722-8336.E-mail: wcbc@1270am.com Licensee: Prosperitas Broadcasting System. (acq 9-7-89; $300,000; 9-25-89). Format: Oldies. ♦David Aydelotte, gen mgr; Mary Clites, gen sls mgr & progmg dir; Bryan Gowans, news dir; Martin White, chief of engrg.

WKLP(AM)— Aug 31, 1965: 1390 khz; 1 kw-D, 74 w-N. TL: N39 26 12 W78 57 21. Hrs open: 24 15 E. Industrial Blvd., Suite 3B, Cumberland, MD, 21502. Phone: (301) 759-1005. Fax: (301) 759-3124. Licensee: Starcast Systems Inc. (group owner; (acq 12-29-2006; with co-located FM). Population served: 100,000 Format: MOR. Target

aud: 35 plus. Spec prog: Big band. ◆Jerry Hannahs, gen mgr; Jack Mullen III, progmg dir; Mark Allen, mus dir; Pat Sullivan, news dir.

WQZK-FM— Sept 15, 1973: 94.1 mhz; 15 kw. Ant 801 ft TL: N39 25 08 W78 57 13. Stereo. Hrs open: 24 Prog sep from AM 15 E. Industrial Blvd., Suite 3B, Cumberland, MD, 21502. Phone: (304) 759-1005. Fax: (304) 759-3124. Web Site:www.941qzk.com Licensee: Starcast Systems Inc. Population served: 350,000 Format: Classic rock. Target aud: 18-49. ◆Jerry Hannahs, gen mgr.

Kingwood

WFSP(AM)— Aug 25, 1967: 1560 khz; 1 kw-D, 250 w-CH. TL: N39 20 01 W79 43 10. Hrs open: Box 567, 26537. Secondary address: Rt. 7, W. 26537. Phone: (304) 329-1780. Fax: (304) 329-1781.E-mail: wfsp@wvdsl.net Web Site:www.prestoncounty.com/wfsp Licensee: WFSP Inc. (acq 8-24-79). Population served: 50,000 Natl. Network: CBS, . Rgnl. Network: Metronews Radio Net. Natl. Rep: Dome,. Cohn & Marks LLP. Format: Christion, relg. News staff: one; News: 6 hrs wkly. Target aud: 20 plus. ◆Arthur W. George, pres, min affrs dir; Donna Nestor, opns mgr, women's int ed; Dave Wills, mus dir, mus critic, disc jockey; Kathy Casseday, news dir, pub affrs dir, spec ev coord, local news ed; Chuck Clemence, chief of engrg; Mike Barnett, disc jockey.

WFSP-FM— June 10, 1991: 107.7 mhz; 1.6 kw. 449 ft TL: N39 28 50 W79 43 11. Stereo. Hrs open: 24 Prog sep from AM Box 567, 26537. Secondary address: Rt. 7, W. 26537. Phone: (304) 329-1780. Fax: (304) 329-1781. Web Site:www.prestoncounty.com/wfsp Population served: 70,000 Natl. Network: Westwood One, . Natl. Rep: Dome,. Cohn & Marks LLP. Format: Oldies. News staff: one; News: 25 hrs wkly. Target aud: 18-45. ◆Arthur W. George, min affrs dir; Kathy Casseday, spec ev coord, local news ed; Donna Nestor, women's int ed; Dave Wills, disc jockey.

WKMM(FM)— Dec 1, 1986: 96.7 mhz; 300 w. 797 ft TL: N39 27 29 W79 35 18. Stereo. Hrs open: 24 106 E. Main St., 26537. Phone: (304) 329-0967. Fax: (304) 329-2131.E-mail: wkmmfm@yahoo.com Web Site:www.wkmmfm.com Licensee: MarPat Corp. (acq 8-1-93; $190,000; 8-23-93). Population served: 233,000 Natl. Network: Westwood One, CNN Radio, . Format: Country. Target aud: 25-55. ◆Neil Waldeck, gen mgr; Greg Bolyard, opns mgr; Tina Waldeck, traf mgr; Marty White, engr.

Lewisburg

WKCJ(FM)—See Ronceverte

WRON-FM— October 1981: 103.1 mhz; 25 kw. Ant 781 ft TL: N37 42 43 W80 30 20. Stereo. Hrs open: 24 Box 610, Rt. 60 W. Harts Run, White Sulphur Springs, 24986. Secondary address: 276 Seneca Trail, Ronceverte 24970. Phone: (304) 536-1310. Phone: (304) 645-1191. Fax: (304) 536-1311.E-mail: radio@wron.com Licensee: Michael J. Kidd dba Greenbrier Radio (group owner; (acq 1-7-2008; exchange for WKCJ(FM) Ronceverte). Population served: 50,000 Natl. Network: ABC, . Natl. Rep: Rgnl Reps,. Format: Modern & traditional country. News: 12 hrs wkly. Target aud: 25-55. Spec prog: Gospel 6 hrs, relg 4 hrs, farm 3 hrs wkly. ◆Joyce Tucker, gen mgr, sls dir; Chuck Harper, progmg dir, mus dir; Marcia Smith, gen sls mgr & chief of engrg.

Lindside

*WHFI(FM)— September 1990: 106.7 mhz; 3 kw. 303 ft TL: N37 28 56 W80 39 40. Hrs open: 24 Stn currently dark Box 97, Rt. 1, 24951. Phone: (304) 753-9971. Fax: (304) 753-9792. Web Site:www.whfi-fm.com Licensee: Monroe County Board of Education (acq 5-1-89). Format: MOR. ◆James W. Higginbotham, gen mgr.

Logan

WVOW(AM)— May 1954: 1290 khz; 5 kw-D, 1 kw-N, DA-N. TL: N37 51 22 W81 58 19. Hrs open: 24 Box 1776, 25601. Secondary address: 204 Main St. , Suite 201 25601. Phone: (304) 752-5080. Fax: (304) 752-5711.E-mail: amfmwvow@mountain.net Licensee: Logan Broadcasting Corp. Population served: 50,000 Format: Adult contemp. News staff: 2. Target aud: General. ◆Martha Jane Becker, pres, gen sls mgr, prom mgr; Larry Bevins, gen mgr; Rhonda Bryant, progmg dir, traf mgr; Bill France, mus dir; Bob Weisner, news dir; Terry Bucklew, chief of engrg.

WVOW-FM— August 1969: 101.9 mhz; 15 kw horiz, 13.5 kw vert. Ant 830 ft TL: N37 51 24 W81 58 18. Hrs open: 24 Dups AM 100% Box 1776, 25601. Secondary address: 204 Main St., Suite 201 25601. Phone: (304) 752-5080. Fax: (304) 752-5711.E-mail: wvow@verizon.net Population served: 3,311 Format: Adult contemp. ◆Rhonda Bryant, traf mgr & women's int ed.

Lost Creek

WOTR(FM)— Dec 9, 1991: 96.3 mhz; 6 kw horiz. 302 ft TL: N39 08 43 W80 19 40. Stereo. Hrs open: 8 AM-10 PM 300 Harrison Ave., Weston, 26452. Phone: (304) 269-5555. Fax: (304) 269-4800. Licensee: James W. Allman. Population served: 50,000 William D. Silva. Format: Inspirational country. Target aud: 25-99. ◆James W. Allman, CEO, chief of opns; Stephen R. Peters, gen mgr.

Mannington

WGYE(FM)— December 1992: 102.7 mhz; 3.2 kw. 453 ft TL: N39 32 18 W80 20 16. Hrs open: 24 1489 Locust Ave., Suite C, Fairmont, 26554. Phone: (304) 363-8888. Fax: (304) 367-1885.E-mail: david@froggycountry.net Web Site:www.froggcountry.net Licensee: Burbach of DE LLC. Group owner: Burbach Broadcasting Group (acq 6-20-2000; grpsl). Population served: 200,000 Format: Country. News staff: one; News: 4 hrs wkly. Target aud: 25-54. ◆Nicholas A. Galli, pres; David Bronham, gen mgr, gen sls mgr; Greg Bolyard, progmg dir, mus dir; Larry Smith, engrg mgr, chief of engrg.

Marlinton

*WNMP(FM)—Not on air, target date: unknown: 88.5 mhz; 1 kw. Ant -216 ft TL: N38 13 40 W80 04 40. Hrs open: Rt. 1, Box 139, Dunmore, 24934. Phone: (304) 799-6004. Fax: (304) 799-7444. Web Site:www.alleghenymountainradio.org Licensee: Pocahontas Communications Cooperative Corp. ◆Cheryl Kinderman, gen mgr.

Marmet

*WKVW(FM)— June 30, 1995: 93.3 mhz; 1.1 kw. Ant 771 ft TL: N38 16 32 W81 31 36. Hrs open: 24 2351 Sunset Blvd., Suite 170-218, Rocklin, CA, 95765-3719. Phone: (916) 251-1600. Fax: (916) 251-1650. Web Site:www.klove.com Licensee: Educational Media Foundation Group owner: EMF Broadcasting (acq 7-1-2002; $500,000). Natl. Network: K-Love, . Rgnl. Network: Metronews Radio Net. Shaw Pittman. Format: Contemp Christian. News staff: 3. Target aud: 25-44; Judeo Christian, female. ◆Richard Jenkins, pres; Mlke Novak, VP; Keith Whipple, dev dir; Eric Allen, natl sls mgr; Mike Novak, progmg dir; David Pierce, progmg mgr; Ed Lenane, news dir; Sam Wallington, engrg dir; Karen Johnson, news rptr.

Martinsburg

WEPM(AM)— Oct 13, 1946: 1340 khz; 1 kw-U. TL: N39 27 48 W77 59 11. Hrs open: 1606 W. King St., 25401. Phone: (304) 263-8868. Fax: (304) 263-8906. Licensee: Prettyman Broadcasting Co. (group owner; (acq 1-1-87; $2 million;11-10-86). Population served: 15,000 Natl. Network: CBS, . Natl. Rep: Katz Radio,. Format: News/talk, sports. Target aud: 35 plus. Spec prog: Relg 6 hrs wkly. ◆Yogi Yoder, gen mgr; Chuck Thornton, sls dir; Jay Young, progmg dir; Rodney Rockwell, chief of engrg; Susan Grissinger, traf mgr.

WLTF(FM)— 1949: 97.5 mhz; 11.4 kw. Ant 1,036 ft TL: N39 27 33 W78 03 48. Stereo. Hrs open: 24 Prog sep from AM 1606 W. King St., 25401. Phone: (304) 263-8868. Fax: (304) 263-8906. Web Site:www.lite975.com Format: Adult contemp. Target aud: 30-49. ◆Stacey Drake, progmg dir.

WRNR(AM)— Apr 16, 1976: 740 khz; 500 w-D, 21 w-N, DA-2. TL: N39 28 25 W77 55 57. Hrs open: 24 Box 709, 1762 Eagle School Rd., 25402. Phone: (304) 263-6586. Fax: (304) 263-3082.E-mail: info@talkradiowrnr.com Licensee: Shenandoah Communications Inc. Population served: 300,000 Natl. Network: Westwood One, CBS, CNN Radio, . Natl. Rep: Rgnl Reps,. Cohn & Marks, LLC. Format: News/talk, sports. News staff: 3; News: 28 hrs wkly. Target aud: 35 plus; middle to upper age & income. ◆Richard S. Wachtel, pres, gen mgr, gen sls mgr; Gregg M. Wachtel, exec VP; Matt Miller, opns dir; Tom Tucker, prom dir, progmg dir & news dir; Fran Little, chief of engrg.

*WVEP(FM)— Feb 11, 1987: 88.9 mhz; 3.6 kw. 1,623 ft TL: N39 08 38 W78 26 09. Stereo. Hrs open: 24 600 Capitol St., Charleston, 25301. Phone: (304) 556-4900. Fax: (304) 556-4981.E-mail: feedback@wvpubcast.org Web Site:www.wvpubcast.org Licensee: West Virginia Educational Broadcasting Authority. Population served: 100,000 Natl. Network: NPR, PRI, . Format: News, jazz, class. ◆Marilyn DiVita, gen mgr, dev dir; Greg Collard, news dir; Teresa Wills, traf mgr.

Matewan

WHJC(AM)— Dec 2, 1951: 1360 khz; 1 kw-D. TL: N37 37 02 W82 10 04. Hrs open: Box 68, 25678. Secondary address: 156 Radio Hill, McCarr, KY 41544. Phone: (606) 427-7261. Fax: (606) 427-7260.E-mail: pwr1067@bellsouth.net Licensee: Three States Broadcasting Co. Inc. Population served: 40,000 Format: Southern gospel. ◆George D. Warren, pres, news dir; Evelyn Warren, gen mgr, sls dir; Melissa White, gen sls mgr, progmg dir, traf mgr; Russell Laferty, chief of engrg.

WVKM(FM)— Aug 30, 1989: 106.7 mhz; 4.3 kw. Ant 751 ft TL: N37 36 49 W82 11 22. Stereo. Hrs open: 24 Box 68, 25678. Secondary address: 156 Radio Hill, McCarr, KY 41544.E-mail: kixx1067@yahoo.com Web Site:kixx1067.com Licensee: Three States Broadcasting Co. Inc. Population served: 160,000 Format: Classic rock. ◆Melissa White, traf mgr.

Miami

WKAZ-FM— November 1985: 107.3 mhz; 50 kw. Ant 600 ft TL: N38 16 25 W81 31 27. Stereo. Hrs open: 24 1111 Virginia St. E., Charleston, 25301. Phone: (304) 342-8131. Fax: (304) 344-4745. Licensee: West Virginia Radio Corp of Charleston. (group owner; (acq 6-5-97; $2.15 million with WCZR(AM) Charleston). Natl. Rep: D & R Radio,. Format: Oldies. Target aud: 25-54. ◆Sean Banks, gen mgr; Max Wulf, progmg dir; Noel Richardson, chief of engrg.

Middlebourne

*WRSG(FM)— 2001: 91.5 mhz; 900 w. Ant 157 ft TL: N39 30 59 W80 54 00. Hrs open: 24 1993 Silver Knight Dr., Sistersville, 26175. Phone: (304) 758-9007 (Studio). Phone: (304) 758-9000 (School Phone). Fax: (304) 758-9006.E-mail: wrsgfm@yahoo.com Web Site:tchs.tyle.k12.wv.us /ths/wrsg/wrsg.htm Licensee: Tyler County Board of Education. Format: Var.

Milton

WAMX(FM)—Licensed to Milton. See Huntington

WZZW(AM)— June 26, 1973: 1600 khz; 6 kw-D, 26 w-N. TL: N38 25 46 W82 06 21. Hrs open: 134 4th Ave., Huntington, 25701. Phone: (304) 525-7788. Fax: (304) 525-6281. Web Site:www.havejoy.com Licensee: Aloha Station Trust LLC Group owner: Clear Channel Communications Inc. (acq 7-30-2008; grpsl). Population served: 15,000 Format: Contemp Christian. Target aud: 25-44; adult, upscale baby boomers. ◆Judy Jennings, VP, gen mgr; Kym York-Blake, gen mgr, gen sls mgr & prom dir; Dixie McDavid, traf mgr.

Montgomery

WMON(AM)— July 14, 1946: 1340 khz; 1 kw-U. TL: N38 10 48 W81 20 06. Hrs open: 100 Kanawha Terr., St. Albans, 25177. Phone: (304) 722-3808. Fax: (304) 727-1300.E-mail: news@wklc.com Web Site:www.ccrronline.com Licensee: L.M. Communications of Kentucky LLC. Group owner: L.M. Communications Inc. (acq 4-1-03; grpsl). Population served: 40,000 Natl. Network: Salem Radio Network, . Format: Religious talk radio. Target aud: 25 plus. ◆Ron Walton, gen mgr; Chris Colagrosso, progmg dir; Fred Francis, chief of engrg; Emma Allen, traf mgr.

Moorefield

WELD-FM— Feb 6, 1987: 101.7 mhz; 285 w. Ant 1,492 ft TL: N38 58 58 W78 54 30. Stereo. Hrs open: 24 126 Kessel Rd., Fisher, 26818. Phone: (304) 538-6062. Fax: (304) 538-7032.E-mail: weld@hardynet.com Web Site:www.weldamfm.com Licensee: Thunder Associates LLC (acq 12-1-2003; $600,000 with WELD(AM) Fisher). Population served: 60,000 Natl. Network: ABC, . Natl. Rep: Dome, Keystone (unwired net),. Irwin, Campbell & Tammewald. Format: Country, relg, farm. News staff: one; News: 10 hrs wkly. Target aud: 25 plus. Spec prog: Gospel 3 hrs wkly/contemporary christian/talk 6hrs wkly. ◆Curtis Durst, pres; Sandra Durst, exec VP; Alan Yokum, gen mgr.

Morgantown

WAJR(AM)— Dec 7, 1940: 1440 khz; 5 kw-D, 500 w-N, DA-2. TL: N39 40 34 W80 00 12. Hrs open: 24 1251 Earl Core Rd., 26505. Phone: (304) 296-0029. Fax: (304) 296-3876. Web Site:www.wajr.com Licensee: West Virginia Radio Corp. Population served: 400,000 Natl. Network: ABC, . Fletcher, Heald & Hildreth. Format: News/talk. News staff: 7; News: 15 hrs wkly. Target aud: 25+. ◆Dale B. Miller, pres, gen mgr;

Harvey Kercheval, opns VP; Gary Mertins, sls dir; Tim Loughry, prom dir; Jim Stallings, progmg dir; Shawm Falkenstein, news dir; Kay Murray, pub affrs dir; Noel Richardson, engrg VP; Ralph Messer, chief of engrg; Donna Tubolino, traf mgr.

WCLG(AM)— December 1954: 1300 khz; 2.5 kw-D, 44 w-N. TL: N39 37 40 W79 58 11. Stereo. Hrs open: Box 885, 26507. Secondary address: 343 High St. 26505. Phone: (304) 292-2222. Fax: (304) 292-2224.E-mail: info@wclg.com Web Site:www.wclg.com Licensee: Bowers Broadcasting Corp. (acq 12-19-59). Population served: 29,431 Natl. Rep: Dome,. Format: Oldies. ♦Garry Bowers, pres, gen mgr; Rebecca Hunn, sls dir; Jeffrey Miller, progmg dir; Ken Tennant, chief of engrg; Lucinda Funk, traf mgr.

WCLG-FM— Sept 28, 1974: 100.1 mhz; 6 kw. 300 ft TL: N39 37 40 W79 58 11. Stereo. Hrs open: Box 885, 26507. Secondary address: 343 High St. 26505. Phone: (304) 292-2222. Fax: (304) 292-2224.E-mail: info@wclg.com Web Site:www.wclg.com Format: Classic rock. ♦Lucinda Funk, traf mgr.

***WLOL-FM**—Not on air, target date: unknown: 89.7 mhz; 100 w. Ant 213 ft TL: N39 39 44 W79 57 43. Hrs open: 132 Carubia Dr., Core, 26541. Phone: (304) 879-5752. Licensee: Light of Life Community Inc. Natl. Network: EWTN Radio, . ♦Robert Carubia, pres.

WVAQ(FM)— 1948: 101.9 mhz; 50 kw. 500 ft TL: N39 36 30 W79 59 07. Stereo. Hrs open: 24 Prog sep from AM 1251 Earl Core Rd., 26505. Phone: (304) 296-0029. Fax: (304) 296-3876. Web Site:www.wvaq.com Format: CHR. News staff: 2; News: one hr wkly. Target aud: 18-49. ♦Hoppy Kercheval, opns dir; Lacy Neff, progmg dir, disc jockey; Eric McGuire, disc jockey.

***WVPM(FM)**— May 27, 1981: 90.9 mhz; 5 kw. 1,440 ft TL: N39 41 45 W79 45 45. Stereo. Hrs open: 24 600 Capitol St., Charleston, 25301. Phone: (304) 556-4900. Fax: (304) 556-4960.E-mail: feedback@wvpubcast.org Web Site:www.wvpubcast.org Licensee: West Virginia Educational Broadcasting Authority. Population served: 96,000 Natl. Network: NPR, PRI, . Format: News, class, jazz. ♦Marilyn DiVita, gen mgr; James Muhammad, progmg dir.

***WWVU-FM**— Aug 20, 1982: 91.7 mhz; 2.6 kw. 180 ft TL: N39 38 09 W79 56 38. Stereo. Hrs open: 24 Box 6446, Mountainlair, West Virginia Univ., 26506-6446. Phone: (304) 293-3329. Fax: (304) 293-7363.E-mail: u92@mail.wvu.edu Web Site:u92.wvu.edu Licensee: West Virginia University Board of Governors (acq 8-10-01). William D. Silva. Format: Educ, div, progsv. News: 2 hrs wkly. Target aud: 18-35; mostly college & high school students. Spec prog: New age 6 hrs, reggae 4 hrs, metal 6 hrs, bluegrass one hr, oldies 8 hrs, big band 2 hrs wkly. ♦Alex Gavula, gen mgr & stn mgr.

WZST(FM)—See Westover

Moundsville

***WLVW(FM)**— Jan 15, 1990: 96.5 mhz; 1.9 kw. Ant 594 ft TL: N39 50 51 W80 45 23. Stereo. Hrs open: 24 2351 Sunset Blvd., Suite 170-218, Rocklin, CA, 95765. Phone: (916) 251-1600. Fax: (916) 251-1650. Web Site:www.klove.com Licensee: Educational Media Foundation. (acq 6-14-2007; $1 million). Natl. Network: K-Love, . Format: Contemp Christian. ♦Mike Novak, sr VP.

WVLY(AM)— Oct 1, 1950: 1370 khz; 5 kw-D, 20 w-N. TL: N39 54 20 W80 46 42. Hrs open: 24 1143 Main St., Suite 200, Wheeling, 26003. Phone: (304) 233-9859. Fax: (304) 214-9859.E-mail: wvlyradio@aol.com Web Site:www.talkradio1370.com Licensee: Monroe Communications LLC (acq 1-9-2004; $75,000). Population served: 185,000 Natl. Network: CNN Radio, . W. Va. MetroNews Network Format: News/talk. News: 14 hrs wkly. Target aud: 25-54; adults. ♦Howard Monroe, pres, gen mgr, gen sls mgr & progmg dir.

Mount Hope

WTNJ(FM)— June 1, 1980: 105.9 mhz; 4.4 kw. Ant 1,532 ft TL: N37 56 51 W81 18 29. Stereo. Hrs open: 24 306 S. Karawha St., Beckley, 25801-5619. Phone: (304) 253-7000. Fax: (304) 255-1044. Licensee: Southern Communications Group owner: Southern Communications Corp. (acq 3-12-01; $2.375 million). Population served: 295,300 Format: Country. News staff: one; News: 12 hrs wkly. Target aud: 25-54. Spec prog: NASCAR races, West Virginia Univ. sports. ♦Jay Quesenberry, gen mgr, gen sls mgr; Rick Reiser, opns mgr; Rick Peiser, progmg dir; Warren Ellison, news dir; Randy Kerbawy, chief of engrg; Bill Wise, traf mgr.

Mullens

WVJO(FM)— Sept 30, 1981: 92.7 mhz; 1.65 kw. 443 ft TL: N37 35 39 W81 23 49. Stereo. Hrs open: 213 Howard Ave., 25882. Phone: (304) 294-4405. Fax: (304) 294-5616.E-mail: ranny@c92.com Web Site:www.c92radio.com Licensee: West Virginia-Virginia Holding Co. LLC (acq 3-29-2006; $120,000). Natl. Network: ABC, . Format: Classic rock. ♦Ranny Parks, gen mgr; Debra Toler, gen sls mgr; Jeff Halsey, progmg dir.

New Martinsville

WETZ(AM)— May 25, 1953: 1330 khz; 1 kw-D, 60 w-N. TL: N39 39 27 W80 51 34. Hrs open: 24 Box 10, 26155. Secondary address: 325 N.Main St. 26155. Phone: (304) 455-1111. Fax: (304) 455-1170.E-mail: wetz@verizon.net Licensee: Dailey Corp. (group owner; (acq 2-1-2001; grpsl). Population served: 80,000 Natl. Network: ABC, . Reddy, Begley & McCormick. Format: Stardust Timeless Classic. News: 10 hrs wkly. Target aud: 25-64. ♦Calvin Dailey Jr., pres; Dennis Gage, gen mgr.

WETZ-FM— December 1977: 103.9 mhz; 2.5 kw. Ant 502 ft TL: N39 39 10 W80 54 47. Stereo. Hrs open: 24 Box 10, 26155. Secondary address: 325 N.Main St. 26155. Phone: (304) 455-1111. Fax: (304) 455-1170.E-mail: wetz@verizon.net Web Site:www.powercountry104.com Natl. Network: ABC, . News: 10 hrs wkly. Target aud: 25-54; country.

WXCR(FM)— 2002: 92.3 mhz; 3.2 kw. Ant 453 ft TL: N39 40 16 W80 53 04. Stereo. Hrs open: 24 Box 564, 26155. Secondary address: Box 374, Saints Marys 26170. Phone: (304) 684-3400. Fax: (304) 684-9241. Licensee: Seven Ranges Radio Co. Inc. Population served: 30,000 Reddy, Begley & McCormick. Format: Classic rock. Target aud: 25-54; 70% men, 30% women. ♦Sam Yoho, pres & gen mgr; Lou Petronio, opns mgr.

WYMJ(FM)— Dec 1, 2002: 99.5 mhz; 2.7 kw. Ant 482 ft TL: N39 39 10 W80 54 47. Stereo. Hrs open: 24 Box 10, 26155. Phone: (304) 455-1111. Fax: (304) 455-1170.E-mail: wetz@verizon.net Web Site:www.oldiesradioonline.com Licensee: Dailey Corp. (group owner; acq 2-6-2001; grpsl). Reddy, Begley & McCormick. Format: Adult contemp. News staff: 3. ♦Dex Gage, gen mgr, opns mgr, gen sls mgr; Ed Wilhelm, chief of engrg.

Oak Hill

WAXS(FM)— 1948: 94.1 mhz; 26 kw. 650 ft TL: N37 57 30 W81 09 03. Stereo. Hrs open: 24 306 S. Karawha St., Beckley, 25801. Phone: (304) 253-7000. Fax: (304) 255-1044. Licensee: Plateau Broadcasting Inc. Group owner: Southern Communications Corp. (acq 3-12-01; $875,000). Population served: 300,000 Natl. Network: ABC, . Format: Oldies. News staff: one; News: 2 hrs wkly. Target aud: General; baby boomers. ♦Jay Quesenberry, gen mgr, gen sls mgr; Rick Reiser, opns mgr, progmg dir; Warren Ellison, adv dir & news dir; Randy Kerbawy, chief of engrg.

WOAY(AM)— Feb 22, 1947: 860 khz; 10 kw-D, 11 w-N, 5 kw-CH. TL: N37 57 30 W81 09 03. Hrs open: 24 240 Central Ave., 25901-3006. Secondary address: 300 N. Kanawha St., Suite 100, Beckley 25801. Phone: (304) 252-9494.E-mail: info@woayradio.com Web Site:www.woayradio.com Licensee: Mountaineer Media Inc. (acq 12-31-2006; $250,000). Population served: 300,000 Format: Christian teaching/talk. Target aud: General. ♦Thomas H. Moffit Jr., pres; Vernon Drumheller, gen mgr; Robert Cook, opns mgr, chief of engrg.

WTNJ(FM)—See Mount Hope

Parkersburg

WADC(AM)— Apr 9, 1954: 1050 khz; 5 kw-D, 144 w-N. TL: N39 15 29 W81 33 49. Hrs open: 24 Box 4739, aParkersburg, 26104-4739. Phone: (304) 485-4565. Fax: (304) 424-6955. Licensee: Burbach of Delaware, LLC. Group owner: Burbach Broadcasting Group (acq 3-19-98; $1.775 million with co-located FM). Population served: 360,000 Natl. Network: CNN Radio, . Koerner & Olender. Format: Adult standards. News: 12 hrs wkly. Target aud: 35-64. Spec prog: Relg 3 hrs wkly. ♦Don Staats, gen mgr; Larry Smith, chief of engrg.

WGGE(FM)— Sept 1, 1965: 99.1 mhz; Sept 1, 1965. Sept 1, 1965 TL: Sept 1, 1965. Sept 1, 1965. Stereo. Prog sep from AM Box 4739, 26104. Phone: (304) 485-4565. Fax: (304) 424-6955.E-mail: info@froggy99.net Web Site:www.froggy99.net Population served: 500,000 Format: Mainstream country. Target aud: 25-54; loyal modern country listeners. Spec prog: Farm 2 hrs, NASCAR 5 hrs wkly.

WGGE(FM)— Sept 1, 1965: 99.1 mhz; 11.5 kw. 485 ft TL: N39 15 29 W81 33 49. Stereo. Hrs open: Prog sep from AM Box 4739, 26104. Phone: (304) 485-4565. Fax: (304) 424-6955.E-mail: info@froggy99.net Web Site:www.froggy99.net Population served: 500,000 Format: Mainstream country. Target aud: 25-54; loyal modern country listeners. Spec prog: Farm 2 hrs, NASCAR 5 hrs wkly.

WHBR-FM— March 1967: 103.1 mhz; 2.1 kw. Ant 561 ft TL: N39 21 00 W81 33 56. Stereo. Hrs open: 24 Prog sep from AM Box 4739, 26104. Phone: (304) 485-4565. Fax: (304) 424-6955. Population served: 299,890 Format: Active rock. News staff: one; News: 6 hrs wkly. Target aud: 18-49; active/modern rock listeners.

WHNK(AM)— July 12, 1935: 1450 khz; 1 kw-U. TL: N39 17 23 W81 31 36. Hrs open: 24 Box 5559, 6006 Grand Central Ave., Vienna, 26105. Phone: (304) 295-6070. Fax: (304) 295-4389.E-mail: johnchalfant@clearchannel.com Web Site:www.whnk.com Licensee: CC Licenses LLC. Group owner: Clear Channel Communications Inc. (acq 4-17-2001). Rgnl. Network: Ohio Radio Net. Natl. Rep: Clear Channel,. Format: Class country. News staff: one; News: 3 hrs wkly. Target aud: 25-54; middle-aged, middle to upper income. ♦Chuck Poet, gen mgr; John Chalfant, opns mgr; Kirk McCall, gen sls mgr; Rodney Ortiz, progmg dir; Doug Hess, news dir, pub affrs dir; Jerry Kuhn, chief of engrg; Belinda Marcinko, traf mgr.

WVNT(AM)— September 1947: 1230 khz; 1 kw-U. TL: N39 16 56 W81 33 17. Hrs open: 24 Box 4739, 26104-4739. Phone: (304) 485-4565. Fax: (304) 424-6955. Licensee: Burbach of Delaware, LLC. Group owner: Burbach Broadcasting Group (acq 1-1-97; grpsl). Population served: 44,208 Natl. Network: CNN Radio, . Natl. Rep: McGavren Guild,. Format: News/talk. News staff: one. Target aud: 30-50. Spec prog: Gospel 4 hrs wkly. ♦Don Staats, gen mgr.

***WVPG(FM)**— April 4, 1985: 90.3 mhz; 9 kw. 321 ft TL: N39 12 44 W81 35 30. Stereo. Hrs open: 24 600 Capitol St., Charleston, 25301. Phone: (304) 556-4900. Fax: (304) 556-4960.E-mail: feedback@wvpubcast.org Web Site:www.wvpubcast.org Licensee: West Virginia Educational Broadcasting Authority. Population served: 96,000 Natl. Network: NPR, PRI, . Format: News, class, jazz. News staff: 2. Spec prog: Mountain Stage 2 hrs, children one hr wkly. ♦Rita Ray, CEO; Marilyn DiVita, gen mgr; Peggy Dorsey, dev mgr; Beth Carenbauer, adv mgr; James Muhammad, progmg dir; Laura H. Allen, mus dir; Giles Snyder, news dir, pub affrs dir; David McClanahan, chief of engrg; Glenna Racer, traf mgr; Greg Callard, local news ed.

WXIL(FM)— Sept 1, 1975: 95.1 mhz; 50 kw. 500 ft TL: N39 14 47 W81 28 19. Stereo. Hrs open: 24 5 Rosemar Cir., 26104. Phone: (304) 485-7425. Phone: (304) 485-4565. Fax: (304) 424-6955.E-mail: productionparkersburg@resultsradiowv.com Web Site:www.95xil.net Licensee: PBBC Inc. Group owner: Burbach Broadcasting Group (acq 9-1-80; $1 million;7-7-80). Population served: 310,000 Natl. Rep: Katz Radio,. Format: Hot Adult Contemp. News staff: one; News: 6 hrs wkly. Target aud: 25-54; women. ♦Nicholas A. Galli, chmn & pres; Don Staats, VP, gen mgr; Brian Steel, opns dir, progmg dir; Larry Smith, news dir, chief of engrg.

Petersburg

***WAUA(FM)**— Dec 1, 1997: 89.5 mhz; 10 kw. Ant 1,056 ft TL: N39 12 07 W79 16 31. Stereo. Hrs open: 24 600 Capitol St., Charleston, 25301. Phone: (304) 556-4900. Fax: (304) 556-4981.E-mail: feedback@wvpubcast.org Web Site:www.wvpubcast.org Licensee: West Virginia Educational Broadcasting Authority. Population served: 56,404 Natl. Network: NPR, PRI, . Format: Class, news. ♦Rita Ray, gen mgr; Marilyn DeVita, dev dir, dev mgr; James Muhammad, progmg dir; Greg Collard, news dir; Jack Wells, chief of engrg; Teresa Wills, traf mgr.

Philippi

***WQAB(FM)**— October 1975: 91.3 mhz; 7.2 kw. 180 ft TL: N39 09 52 W80 02 57. Stereo. Hrs open: 8 AM-10 PM Box 2097, Withers-Brandon Hall, Alderson-Broaddus College, 26416. Phone: (304) 457-6281. Phone: (304) 457-2916. Fax: (304) 457-6239. Licensee: Alderson-Broaddus College. Population served: 50,000 Natl. Network: AP Radio, . Format: Div, CHR, adult contemp. News: 5 hrs wkly. Target aud: 15-40; college students. Spec prog: Jazz 4 hrs, Black 2 hrs, radio drama 2 hrs, children's 2 hrs wkly. ♦Harry Hancock, stn mgr; George Sommer, engrg VP.

Pineville

WWYO(AM)— 1949: 970 khz; 1 kw-D, 26 w-N. TL: N37 35 20 W81 32 25. Stereo. Hrs open: Box 647, Bluefield, 24701. Secondary address: Rt. 10, One Radio Rd. 24701. Phone: (304) 327-5651. Phone: (304) 732-8552. Fax: (304) 327-5651.E-mail: am970wwyo@citlink.net

Web Site:www.am970wwyo.bizland.com Licensee: MRJ Inc. (acq 4-20-90; $125,000). Population served: 75,000 Format: Southern gospel, country, MOR. Target aud: 25-65; housewives. Spec prog: Folk one hr, sports 18 hrs, educ 2 hrs, community 8 hrs wkly. ♦Rudolph D. Jennings, pres & gen mgr.

Pocatalico

WRVZ(FM)— 1995: 98.7 mhz; 63 w. 617 ft TL: N38 23 53 W81 41 06. Hrs open: 1111 Virginia St. E., Charleston, 25301. Phone: (304) 342-8131. Fax: (304) 344-4745.E-mail: mbuxser@wvradio.com Web Site:wvradioadvertising.com Licensee: West Virginia Radio Corp. of Charleston. Group owner: West Virginia Radio Corp. (acq 3-12-2001; $800,000). Format: CHR. ♦Dale Miller, pres; Mike Buxser, gen mgr; Courtney Patrick, prom dir; Woody Woods, opns dir & progmg dir; Jeff Jenkins, news dir; Noel Richardson, chief of engrg.

Point Pleasant

WBGS(AM)— 1994: 1030 khz; 10 kw-D, DA. TL: N38 48 42 W82 05 59. Hrs open: 303 8th St., VA, 25550. Phone: (304) 675-2763. Fax: (304) 675-2771. Licensee: Big River Radio Inc. Group owner: Baker Family Stations (Positive Radio Group) Booth, Freret, Imlay & Tepper. Format: News/talk. ♦Vernon H. Baker, CEO, chmn, pres; Edward A. Baker, VP; Kevin Nott, gen mgr, progmg dir; Shari Cochron, sls dir; Tom Payne, mus dir; Winston Hawkins, chief of engrg; Kathy Wise, traf mgr.

WBYG(FM)— 1994: 99.5 mhz; 4.7 kw. Ant 328 ft TL: N38 50 49 W82 07 50. Hrs open: 303 8th St., 25550. Phone: (304) 675-2763. Fax: (304) 675-2771. Web Site:www.wbyg.com (Acq 1-28-92). Format: Country. ♦Kathy Wise, gen mgr & traf mgr.

***WVRR(FM)**— Dec 21, 2000: 88.1 mhz; 3 kw. Ant 289 ft TL: N38 50 49 W82 07 50. Hrs open: 24 303 8th Street, 25550. Phone: (304) 675-2727. Fax: (304) 675-2771. Web Site:www.881theriver.org Licensee: Positive Alternative Radio Inc. Group owner: Baker Family Stations (Positive Radio Group) Booth, Freret, Imley & Tepper. Format: Contemp Christian. ♦Bryan K. Fowler, gen mgr.

Princeton

WAEY(AM)— December 1947: 1490 khz; 1 kw-U. TL: N37 23 23 W81 05 58. Hrs open: 24 Box 5588, 24740. Secondary address: Lilly Grove Addition, 1 Radio Ln. 24740. Phone: (304) 425-2151. Fax: (304) 487-2016.E-mail: progeam@star95.com Licensee: Princeton Broadcasting Inc. Population served: 65,000 Format: Gospel. News staff: one; News: 14 hrs wkly. Target aud: 25 plus; blue collar. ♦Linda Witt, pres; Pat Tolley, VP; Bob Spencer, gen mgr, gen sls mgr; Jason Reed, opns mgr, prom dir; Ron Witt, progmg dir; Wayne Boone, chief of engrg; Amy Mills, traf mgr; Patricia Tolley, min affrs dir.

WKOY-FM— April 1983: 100.9 mhz; 630 w. 641 ft TL: N37 18 20 W81 07 30. Stereo. Hrs open: 24 900 Bluefield Ave., Bluefield, 24701. Phone: (304) 327-7114. Fax: (304) 325-7850. Web Site:www.theeaglefm.com Licensee: Monterey Licenses LLC. Group owner: Triad Broadcasting Co. LLC (acq 7-18-00; grpsl). Natl. Network: ABC, . Natl. Rep: Katz Radio, Rgnl Reps,. Format: Classic Rock. News staff: one. Target aud: 25 plus. ♦John Halford, gen mgr; Ken Deitz, opns dir, progmg dir; Danny Clemmon, gen sls mgr; P.J. Toler, news dir; Keith Bowman, chief of engrg.

***WPWV(FM)**— September 2003: 90.1 mhz; 2.5 kw vert. Ant 1,040 ft TL: N37 30 35 W81 12 55. Hrs open: Box 3206, Tupelo, MS, 38801. Phone: (662) 844-8888. Fax: (662) 842-6791. Web Site:www.afr.net Licensee: American Family Association. Group owner: American Family Radio. Format: Christian. ♦Marvin Sanders, gen mgr.

WSTG(FM)— Apr 1, 1973: 95.9 mhz; 480 w. Ant 1,141 ft TL: N37 15 30 W81 10 37. Stereo. Hrs open: 24 Box 5588, 24740. Secondary address: Lilly Grove Addition, 1Radio Ln 24740. Phone: (304) 425-2151. Fax: (304) 487-2016.E-mail: program@star95.com Web Site:www.star95.com Licensee: L & P Broadcasting Inc. Format: Adult top-40s. News staff: one. ♦Amy Mills, traf mgr; Linda Witt, min affrs dir; Charlie Brown, local news ed; Jim Nelson, sports cmtr.

Rainelle

WRLB(FM)— February 1977: 95.3 mhz; 3.1 kw. 460 ft TL: N37 57 28 W80 45 45. (CP: 12.9 kw). Stereo. Hrs open: 24 Box 1727, Lewisburg, 24901. Phone: (304) 647-3606. Web Site:www.wrlb.com Licensee: Faith Communications Network Inc. (acq 10-25-01). Population served: 68,000 Format: Inspirational, Christian. Target aud: 25-54.

WRRL(AM)— 1973: 1130 khz; 1 kw-D. TL: N37 57 28 W80 45 45. Hrs open: H.C. 61, Box 383, Danese, 25831. Phone: (304) 438-8537 phone/fax.E-mail: wrrlam@mountain.net Licensee: Faith Mountain Communications Inc. (acq 2-8-01; $60,000). Population served: 45,000 Rgnl. Network: Metronews Radio Net. W. Va. MetroNews Network Format: Gospel, Christian, News/talk. Target aud: 35 plus. ♦Nancy Whitt, CEO; Allen R. Whitt, pres, gen mgr.

Ravenswood

WMOV(AM)— 1953: 1360 khz; 1 kw-U. TL: N38 57 52 W81 46 09. Hrs open: 6 AM-midnight 527 Gibbs St., 26164. Phone: (304) 273-2544. Fax: (304) 273-3020.E-mail: contact@wmov1360.com Licensee: Shay Hill, executor (acq 2-9-2004). Population served: 37,000 Natl. Network: USA, . Format: Full service. News staff: one; News: 14 hrs wkly. Target aud: 16 plus; emphasis on 25 plus. Spec prog: Talk 2 hrs, Pol one hr, folk 2 hrs, jazz 2 hrs, bluegrass 10 hrs wkly. ♦Burke Allen, pres; Greg Carter, gen mgr, opns VP & opns dir.

Richwood

WVAR(AM)— 1956: 600 khz; 1 kw-D. TL: N38 13 50 W80 32 49. Hrs open: 6 AM-sunset
Rebroadcasts WSGB(AM) Sutton 100%.
180 Main St., Sutton, 26601. Phone: (304) 765-7373. Fax: (304) 765-7836.E-mail: mail@wvaram.com Web Site:www.wvaram.com Licensee: Summit Media Inc. (group owner; (acq 3-8-2007; $1.24 million with WAFD(FM) Webster Springs). Population served: 3,717 Natl. Network: ABC, . Natl. Rep: Rgnl Reps,. W. Va. MetroNews Network Format: Classic hits. News: 5 hrs wkly. Target aud: 35-64; male and female. ♦Al Sergi, gen mgr.

Ridgeley

WDYK(FM)— 2006: 100.5 mhz; 4.6 kw. Ant 374 ft TL: N39 43 02.8 W78 42 42.5. Hrs open: 15 E. Industrial Blvd., Cumberland, MD, 21502. Phone: (301) 759-1005. Fax: (301) 759-3124. Web Site:www.cumberlandsmagic.com Licensee: Radioactive LLC. Population served: 40,000 Format: Adult contemp. ♦Dale Miller, pres; Jerry Hannahs, mktg mgr.

Ripley

WCEF(FM)— Feb 24, 1981: 98.3 mhz; 3 kw. Ant 300 ft TL: N38 46 04 W81 41 09. Stereo. Hrs open: 24 Box 798, 98 Cedar Lakes Rd., 25271. Phone: (304) 372-9800. Fax: (304) 372-9811.E-mail: shadow@c98.com Web Site:www.c98.com Licensee: Big River Radio Inc. Group owner: Baker Family Stations (acq 1-31-2003; $762,500). Natl. Network: ABC, . Format: Country. Target aud: 25-54. ♦Charmin McCarty, gen mgr, traf mgr; Rich Lacey, progmg dir; Larry Koenig, chief of engrg.

***WLKV(FM)**— Mar 26, 1994: 90.7 mhz; 3 kw. Ant 328 ft TL: N38 51 44 W81 41 27. Hrs open: 2351 Sunset Blvd., Suite 170-218, Rocklin, CA, 95765. Phone: (916) 251-1600. Fax: (916) 251-1650. Web Site:www.klove.com Licensee: Educational Media Foundation. (acq 3-31-2005; $700,000 with WLKP(FM) Belpre, OH). Natl. Network: K-Love, . Format: Christian. ♦Richard Jenkins, pres, gen mgr; Mike Novak, VP; Keith Whipple, dev dir; Eric Allen, natl sls mgr; David Pierce, progmg mgr; Ed Lenane, news dir; Sam Wallington, engrg dir; Karen Johnson, news rptr.

Romney

WDZN(FM)— Aug 29, 1988: 100.1 mhz; 480 w. 823 ft TL: N39 25 20 W78 47 25. Stereo. Hrs open: 24 Box 477, Cumberland, MD, 21501-0477. Phone: (301) 724-6000. Fax: (301) 724-0617. Web Site:www.radiodisney.com Licensee: Charter Equities Inc. Natl. Network: Jones Radio Networks, . Baraff, Koerner & Olender. Format: Disney. News staff: one; News: 15 hrs wkly. Target aud: 25-54; adult decision makers. ♦Warren Gregory, pres & gen mgr; Travis Medcalf, opns dir, sls dir; Rick Williams, chief of engrg.

***WVSB(FM)**— Mar 30, 1973: 104.1 mhz; 100 w. Ant 781 ft TL: N39 18 56 W78 43 04. Stereo. Hrs open: 24 301 E. Main St., 26757. Phone: (304) 822-4838. Fax: (304) 822-4896.E-mail: gpark@access.k12.wv.us Web Site:wvsdb.state.k12.wv.us/radio_station.htm Licensee: West Virginia Schools for the Deaf & Blind. Population served: 22000 Format: Classic country. Target aud: General. ♦Jane McBride, pres; Connie Newhouse, VP; George S. Park, gen mgr, chief of opns, progmg mgr.

Ronceverte

WKCJ(FM)— Dec 6, 1983: 97.7 mhz; 1 kw. Ant 800 ft TL: N37 47 54 W80 30 55. Stereo. Hrs open: 24 276 Seneca Trail N., 24970. Phone: (304) 645-1400. Fax: (304) 645-1327. Fax: (304) 647-4802. Web Site:www.wron.com Licensee: WVJT LLC (acq 1-7-2008; exchange for WRON-FM Lewisburg) Population served: 75,000 Natl. Network: CNN Radio, . Wire Svc: AP Format: Oldies. Target aud: 25-60. ♦Michael J. Kidd, dev mgr, local news ed, sports cmtr; Michael Kidd, mktg mgr; Roy Jarrell, progmg mgr; Larry Carver, engrg mgr, farm dir.

WRON(AM)— 1947: 1400 khz; 1 kw-U. TL: N37 45 36 W80 27 18. Hrs open: 24 276 Seneca Trail N., 24970. Phone: (304) 645-1400. Fax: (304) 645-1327. Fax: (304) 647-4802.E-mail: radio@wron.net Web Site:www.wron.com Licensee: Radio Greenbrier LLC. Population served: 35,604 Natl. Network: Premiere Radio Networks, Westwood One, Talk Radio Network, . Rgnl. Network: Metronews Radio Net. Natl. Rep: Dome, Rgnl Reps,. Wire Svc: AP Format: Talk, news. News: 21 hrs wkly. Target aud: 35; & under. Spec prog: Relg 2 hrs wkly. ♦Michael J. Kidd, gen mgr, stn mgr, news dir; Roy Jarrell, opns mgr, gen sls mgr, progmg dir & pub affrs dir; Larry Carver, chief of engrg; Jeff Campbell, sports cmtr.

Rupert

WYKM(AM)— Dec 9, 1981: 1250 khz; 5 kw-D, 32 w-N. TL: N37 59 35 W80 41 03. Hrs open: 6 AM-sunset Box 627, 25984. Secondary address: 714 Nicholas St. 25984. Phone: (304) 392-6003. Fax: (304) 392-5352.E-mail: wykm@frontier.net Licensee: Mountain State Broadcasting Co. Population served: 34,000 Natl. Network: CBS, . Format: Country, gospel. News: 7 hrs wkly. ♦Betty D. Crookshanks, pres, gen mgr, progmg dir; Donald Crookshanks, exec VP.

Saint Albans

WJYP(AM)— Jan 14, 1956: 1300 khz; 1 kw-D, 49 w-N. TL: N38 23 43 W81 51 00. Hrs open: 24 100 Kanawha Terr., 25177. Phone: (304) 722-3308. Fax: (304) 727-1300.E-mail: news@wklc.com Web Site:www.ccrnonline.com Licensee: WKLC Inc. Group owner: L.M. Communications Inc. (acq 2-23-80). Population served: 250,000 Leventhal, Senter & Lerman. Format: Relg talk radio. Target aud: 18-49. ♦Ron Walton, gen mgr; Chris Colagrosso, progmg dir; Fred Francis, chief of engrg; Emma Allen, traf mgr.

WKLC-FM— Jan 1, 1966: 105.1 mhz; 50 kw. 1,663 ft TL: N38 25 15 W81 55 27. Stereo. Hrs open: 24 Prog sep from AM 100 Kanawha Terr., 25177. Phone: (304) 722-3308. Fax: (304) 727-1300.E-mail: news@wkcl.com Web Site:www.wklc.com Population served: 1,123,200 Natl. Network: ABC, . Format: Rock/AOR. ♦Jay Nunley, progmg dir; Dawn Cox, mus dir.

Saint Marys

WJAW(AM)— October 1984: 630 khz; 1 kw-D. TL: N39 23 42 W81 13 49. Hrs open: 24 925 Lancaster St., Marietta, OH, 45750. Phone: (740) 373-1490. Fax: (740) 373-1717.E-mail: kwenzel@wmoa1490.com Web Site:www.wmoa1490.com Licensee: JAWCO Inc. (acq 2-26-2001; $25,000). Format: Sports. ♦John Wharff III, gen mgr, gen sls mgr; Jamey Styer, opns dir; Andy Rex, progmg dir; Ralph Matheny, chief of engrg.

WRRR-FM— Nov 16, 1983: 93.9 mhz; 17 kw. Ant 390 ft TL: N39 22 49 W81 11 36. Stereo. Hrs open: Box 374, 26170. Phone: (304) 684-3400. Fax: (304) 684-9241. Licensee: Seven Ranges Radio Co. Inc. Population served: 175,000 Irwin, Campbell & Tannenwald, P.C. Format: Adult contemp. News staff: one; News: 9 hrs wkly. Target aud: 25-49. ♦Sam Yoho, pres & gen mgr; Lou Petronio, opns mgr.

Salem

WAJR-FM— 1999: 103.3 mhz; 1.8 kw. Ant 589 ft TL: N39 15 44 W80 28 01. Hrs open: 1065 Radio Park Dr., Mount Clare, 26408-9516. Phone: (304) 623-6546. Fax: (304) 623-6547.E-mail: info@wajrfm.com Web Site:www.wajrfm.com Licensee: West Virginia Radio Corp. of Salem. Format: News/talk. ♦John Halford, gen mgr.

WOBG-FM— Nov 1, 1990: 105.7 mhz; 6 kw. 581 ft TL: N39 19 06 W80 26 18. Stereo. Hrs open: 24 1489 Locust Ave., Fairmont, 26554. Phone: (304) 624-1400. Fax: (304) 624-1402. Licensee: Burbach of DE LLC. Group owner: Burbach Broadcasting Group (acq 5-17-00; grpsl). Population served: 250,000 Rgnl rep: Commercial Media Sales. Format: Classic rock. Target aud: 25-54. ♦Nicholas A. Galli, pres; David Branham, gen mgr; Greg Bolyard, progmg dir; Jon Fox, news dir; Larry Smith, chief of engrg.

Shepherdstown

*WSHC(FM)— 1974: 89.7 mhz; 950 w. -10 ft TL: N39 25 53 W77 48 18. Stereo. Hrs open: 24 WSHC-FM, Shepherd College, King St., 25443. Phone: (304) 876-5134. Fax: (304) 876-5405.E-mail: wshc@shepherd.edu Web Site:www.897wshc.org Licensee: Shepherd College Board of Governors (acq 8-28-01). Population served: 3,500 Natl. Network: ABC, . Format: Alternative. News: 7 hrs wkly. Target aud: 18-24; college/young adult. ◆Buck Lam, gen mgr.

South Charleston

WMXE(FM)— July 29, 1985: 100.9 mhz; 3 kw. 285 ft TL: N38 22 34 W81 42 13. Stereo. Hrs open: 24 Prog sep from AM 100 Kanawha Terr., St. Albans, 25177. Fax: (304) 727-1300.E-mail: news@wklc.com Web Site:www.wmxe.com Format: Adult contemp, relg. Target aud: 25-54. ◆Mark Atkinson, progmg dir.

WSCW(AM)— Dec 13, 1963: 1410 khz; 5 kw-D. TL: N38 22 34 W81 42 13. Hrs open: 100 Kanawha Terr., St. Albans, 25177. Fax: (304) 727-1300.E-mail: news@wklc.com Web Site:www.ccrnonline.com Licensee: L.M. Communications of Kentucky LLC. Group owner: L.M. Communications Inc. (acq 4-1-03; grpsl). Population served: 252,000 Format: Relg talk radio. Target aud: 25-64. ◆Ron Walton, gen mgr; Chris Colagrasso, progmg dir, disc jockey; Fred Francis, chief of engrg; Emma Allen, traf mgr.

*WWLA(FM)—Not on air, target date: unknown: 89.3 mhz; 300 w. Ant 528 ft TL: N38 26 37 W81 36 08. Hrs open: 188 S. Bellevue, Suite 222, Memphis, TN, 38104. Phone: (901) 726-8970. Fax: (901) 375-0041.E-mail: mail@flinn.com Licensee: Broadcasting for the Challenged Inc. ◆George S. Flinn Jr., pres.

Spencer

WVRC(AM)— Sept 12, 1961: 1400 khz; 1 kw-U. TL: N38 48 23 W81 21 40. Hrs open: Box 622, 25276. Phone: (304) 927-3760. Fax: (304) 927-2877.E-mail: mail@wvrcradio.com Web Site:www.wvrcradio.com Licensee: Star Communications Inc. (acq 9-22-82; $40,000; 10-11-82). Population served: 15,000 Natl. Rep: Rgnl Reps,. Format: Gospel. ◆Larry Koenig, pres, chief of engrg; Bob Edwards, VP, gen mgr, gen sls mgr, progmg dir; Zachary Zdanek, news dir.

WVRC-FM— October 1992: 104.7 mhz; 3 kw. 328 ft TL: N38 47 40 W81 17 36. Hrs open: Box 622, 25276. Phone: (304) 927-3760. Fax: (304) 927-2877.E-mail: info@wcrvradio.com Web Site:www.wvrcradio.com (Acq 3-1-91; 3-25-91). Format: Country.

Summersville

WCWV(FM)— Mar 13, 1983: 92.9 mhz; 11 kw. 900 ft TL: N38 21 37 W80 38 49. Stereo. Hrs open: 24 713 Main St., 26651. Phone: (304) 872-5202. Fax: (304) 872-6904.E-mail: wcwv@wcwv92.9.com Web Site:www.c93net.com Licensee: R-S Broadcasting Co. Inc. Population served: 1,000,000 Natl. Network: Westwood One, . Natl. Rep: Dome,. Format: Adult contemp. News: 23 hrs wkly. Target aud: 18-54. Spec prog: Gospel 15 hrs, relg 18 hrs wkly. ◆Michael D. Brown, VP, gen mgr, chief of opns; Wes Brown, gen sls mgr, mktg dir & progmg dir; Fred Francis, engrg dir, chief of engrg; Cassy Holcomb, traf mgr.

WDBS(FM)—See Sutton

WKQV(FM)—See Cowen

*WMLJ(FM)— 1993: 90.5 mhz; 11 kw. Ant 1,033 ft TL: N38 06 42 W80 35 52. Hrs open: 24
Rebroadcasts WOTJ(FM) Morehead City, NC 90%.
Box 1014, 26651. Phone: (304) 872-4612. Licensee: Grace Missionary Baptist Church (acq 5-3-93; 5-24-93). Format: Gospel, children. Target aud: General. Spec prog: Sp one hr wkly. ◆Clyde I. Ebron, pres; Chris Brown, gen mgr; Mike Tyler, chief of engrg.

*WSJE(FM)—Not on air, target date: unknown: 91.3 mhz; 1 kw. Ant 892 ft TL: N38 21 37 W80 38 49. Hrs open: 330 Town Mountain Rd., 26651-1603. Phone: (304) 872-4968. Licensee: Kesan Inc. ◆Gary Criste, pres.

Sutton

WDBS(FM)— Apr 25, 1987: 97.1 mhz; 22 kw. Ant 751 ft TL: N38 27 05 W80 27 14. Stereo. Hrs open: 24 180 Main St., 26601. Phone: (304) 765-7373. Fax: (304) 765-7836.E-mail: mail@theboss97fm.com Web Site:theboss97fm.com Licensee: Summit Media Broadcasting

LLC. (acq 12-30-99). Population served: 200,000 Natl. Network: Jones Radio Networks, AP Radio, . Natl. Rep: Rgnl Reps,. W. Va. MetroNews Network Format: New country. News: 9 hrs wkly. Target aud: 18-49; young adults females/males. ◆Al Sergi, gen mgr.

WSGB(AM)— Jan 22, 1964: 1490 khz; 1 kw-U. TL: N38 39 11 W80 43 10. Hrs open: 24 180 Main St., 26601. Phone: (304) 765-7373. Fax: (304) 765-7836.E-mail: mail@wsgbam.com Web Site:www.wsgbam.com Licensee: Summit Media Broadcasting L.L.C. (acq 12-30-99; $250,000 with co-located FM). Population served: 12,000 Natl. Network: ABC, . Rgnl. Network: Metronews Radio Net. Natl. Rep: Rgnl Reps,. W. Va. MetroNews Network Rgnl rep: Dome, Regnl Reps Format: Classic Hits. News: News prgmg 5 hrs per week. Target aud: 35-64; male and female. ◆Al Sergi, pres, gen mgr; Daniel Finch, CFO.

Vienna

WDMX(FM)— May 22, 1989: 100.1 mhz; 1.65 kw. 440 ft TL: N39 20 18 W81 30 01. Stereo. Hrs open: 24 Box 5559, 6006 Grand Central Ave., 26105. Phone: (304) 295-6070. Phone: (304) 375-6558. Fax: (304) 295-4389.E-mail: oldies@radio1.netassoc.net Web Site:www.wdmx.com Licensee: CC Licenses LLC. Group owner: Clear Channel Communications Inc. (acq 4-17-2001; grpsl). Natl. Network: ABC, . Rgnl. Network: Ohio Radio Net. Natl. Rep: Clear Channel,. Format: Oldies. News staff: 2; News: 2 hrs wkly. Target aud: 25-54. ◆Chuck Poet, gen mgr; Jim Grywalsky, opns mgr; Kurt McCall, gen sls mgr; Jim Grywalsky, progmg dir; Doug Hess, news dir, pub affrs dir; Jerry Kuhn, chief of engrg; Belinda Marcinko, traf mgr.

Webster Springs

WAFD(FM)— Feb 1, 1996: 100.3 mhz; 32.2 kw. Ant 610 ft TL: N38 27 38.6 W80 25 12.7. Stereo. Hrs open: 24 180 Main St., Sutton, 26601. Phone: (304) 765-7373. Fax: (304) 765-7836. Web Site:www.wafdfm.com Licensee: Summit Media Inc. (group owner). (acq 3-8-2007; $1.24 million with WVAR(AM) Richwood). Population served: 200,000 Natl. Network: CNN Radio, . Natl. Rep: Rgnl Reps,. Format: Bright AC Mix. News: News prgrmg 3 hrs/week. Target aud: M-F/18-49. ◆Al Sergi, pres & gen mgr.

Weirton

WEIR(AM)— Sept 15, 1950: 1430 khz; 1 kw-U, DA-2. TL: N40 26 45 W80 37 36. Stereo. Hrs open: 24 2307 Pennsylvania Ave., 26062. Phone: (304) 723-1444. Fax: (304) 723-1688.E-mail: ckamr@frontiernet.net Web Site:www.unforgettablefavorites.com Licensee: Priority Communications Ohio L.L.C. Group owner: Priority Communications (acq 12-4-98; $475,000 with WCDK(FM) Cadiz, OH). Population served: 40,000 Natl. Network: Westwood One, . Rgnl rep: Dome Pepper & Corazzini. Format: Talk morning, adult standards. News staff: one; News: 25 hrs wkly. Target aud: General. Spec prog: It 3 hrs, Gr 1 hr wkly. ◆Jay Philippone, pres, gen mgr; Judy Vavrek, stn mgr; Tammie Beagle, opns mgr; Hank Siegle, chief of engrg.

Welch

WELA(AM)—Not on air, target date: unknown: 1340 khz; 1 kw-U. TL: N37 25 50 W81 35 33. Hrs open: 115 Farwood Dr., Moreland, OH, 44022. Phone: (216) 381-6037. Licensee: C. Douglas Thomas. ◆C. Douglas Thomas, gen mgr.

WELC(AM)— Aug 19, 1950: 1150 khz; 5 kw-D. TL: N37 25 01 W81 36 58. Hrs open: 6 AM- Sunset Box 949, 24801. Secondary address: U.S. Rt. 52 24801. Phone: (304) 436-2131. Fax: (304) 436-2132.E-mail: mail@welcamfm.com Web Site:www.welcamfm.com Licensee: Pocahontas Broadcasting Co. Population served: 35,000 Natl. Network: AP Radio, . Rgnl. Network: Metronews Radio Net. Rgnl rep: Rgnl Reps. William D. Silva. Wire Svc: AP Format: Adult contemp. News staff: 2. Target aud: 21-54. Spec prog: Relg 15 hrs wkly. ◆Bob Spencer, pres; Rick Lambert, gen mgr; Laura Green, opns mgr, gen sls mgr; Rod O'dell, prom mgr & sls.

WELC-FM— Feb 1, 1990: 102.9 mhz; 1.8 kw. Ant 423 ft TL: N37 25 01 W81 36 58. Stereo. Hrs open: 24 Dups AM 75% Box 949, 24801. Secondary address: U.S. Rt. 52 24801. Phone: (304) 436-2131. Fax: (304) 436-2132. Web Site:www.welcamfm.com Population served: 50,000 Wire Svc: AP News staff: 2. Target aud: 25-54. ◆Laura Green, opns mgr; Rod O'Dell, sls.

West Liberty

*WGLZ(FM)— Sept 4, 1990: 91.5 mhz; 150 w. Ant 213 ft TL: N40 09 49 W80 36 06. Hrs open: Box 13, West Liberty State College, 26074.

Phone: (304) 336-8045. Phone: (304) 336-8037. Fax: (304) 336-8286. Licensee: West Liberty State College. Format: Alternative/mix. ◆Christian H. Lee, stn mgr & chief of engrg.

West Union

*WVGV(FM)—Not on air, target date: unknown: 89.7 mhz; 4.7 kw. Ant 392 ft TL: N39 17 51 W80 46 02. Hrs open: Box 301, 26456. Phone: (304) 873-1049. Licensee: Araiza Revival Ministries Inc. ◆Oliver Araiza, pres.

Weston

WFBY(FM)— Aug 29, 1972: 102.3 mhz; 940 w. 489 ft TL: N39 04 15 W80 31 13. (CP: 10 kw, ant 509 ft.). Hrs open: 24 1065 Radio Park Dr., Mount Clare, 26408. Phone: (304) 623-6546. Fax: (304) 623-6547. Web Site:www.wfby.com Licensee: AJG Corporation (group owner; (acq 1994; $250,000). Population served: 25,000 Putbrese, Hunsaker & Trent. Format: Classic Rock. Target aud: 25-44. ◆Dale Miller, pres, gen mgr; Christian Miller, CFO, stn mgr; Harvey Kercheval, opns VP; Max Wurf, progmg dir; Mark Rogers, mus dir; Stan Fa, chief of engrg.

WHAW(AM)— Feb 14, 1948: 980 khz; 1 kw-D, 50 w-N. TL: N39 02 25 W80 27 16. Hrs open: 24 300 Harrison Ave., 26452. Phone: (304) 269-5555. Fax: (304) 269-4800.E-mail: whaw@aol.com Web Site:www.whawradio.com Licensee: Stephen R. Peters. (acq 4-16-98). Natl. Network: ABC, . Format: ABC True Oldies. News staff: one; News: 2 hrs wkly. Target aud: General. Spec prog: Bluegrass 8 hrs, folk 4 hrs, gospel 18 hrs wkly. ◆Stephen R. Peters, gen mgr.

Westover

WZST(FM)— Jan 5, 1983: 100.9 mhz; 3 kw. Ant 198 ft TL: N39 32 44 W79 55 58. Stereo. Hrs open: 7013 Mountain Park Dr., Fairmont, 26554. Phone: (304) 363-3851. Fax: (304) 363-3852.E-mail: star100radio@aol.com Licensee: Fantasia Broadcasting Inc. Group owner: Tschudy Broadcast Group (acq 7-19-2006; $750,000). Format: Hot adult contemp. Spec prog: Relg mus 2 hrs wkly. ◆Nick Fantasia, pres; Dick Yoder, gen mgr; Brian Dulaney, opns mgr; Judy King, gen sls mgr; Mike Donota, progmg dir.

Wheeling

WBBD(AM)— May 2, 1941: 1400 khz; 1 kw-U. TL: N40 05 49 W80 42 06. Hrs open: 24 1015 Main St., 26003. Phone: (304) 232-1170. Fax: (304) 234-0041. Licensee: Capstar TX L.P. Group owner: Clear Channel Communications Inc. (acq 8-30-00; grpsl). Population served: 60,000 Format: Big band, adult standards. Target aud: 35 plus. Spec prog: Pol 2 hrs wkly. ◆Scott Deel, gen sls mgr; Scott Miller, VP, gen mgr & mktg mgr; Minda Moticker, prom dir; Chad Tyson, progmg dir; Jack Reese, chief of engrg; Melissa Richie, traf mgr.

WEGW(FM)— October 1966: 107.5 mhz; 10.5 kw. 882 ft TL: N40 03 41 W80 45 08. Stereo. Hrs open: 24 1015 Main St., 26003. Phone: (304) 232-1170. Fax: (304) 234-0041. Web Site:www.wegw.com Licensee: Capstar TX L.P. Group owner: Clear Channel Communications Inc. (acq 8-30-00; grpsl). Population served: 50,000 Format: Rock/AOR. Target aud: 25-54. ◆Mark Mays, pres; Scott Miller, VP & gen mgr; Karen Hardy, sls dir, gen sls mgr; Minda Moticker, prom dir; Chad Tyson, progmg dir; Jonathan Nixon, news dir; Jack Rees, chief of engrg.

WKKX(AM)— Apr 7, 1963: 1600 khz; 5 kw-D, 33 w-N. TL: N40 05 26 W80 42 11. Hrs open: 24 Box 231, 26003. Phone: (304) 214-1610. Fax: (304) 232-8488.E-mail: tsanthony@stratuswave.net Web Site:www.espn1600.com Licensee: RCK 1 Group LLC (acq 7-19-2004; $400,000). Natl. Network: ESPN Radio, . Rgnl. Network: Metronews Radio Net. Natl. Rep: Christal,. Format: Sports talk. Target aud: 25-54; men. ◆Tom Anthony, gen mgr.

WKWK-FM— Mar 17, 1948: 97.3 mhz; 50 kw. 470 ft TL: N40 05 49 W80 42 06. Stereo. Hrs open: 24 Prog sep from AM 1015 Main St., 26003. Phone: (304) 232-1170. Fax: (304) 234-0041. Web Site:www.wk973.com Population served: 100,000 Format: Var/div. Target aud: 25-54. ◆Jim Connor, progmg dir; Steve Novotry, news dir.

WOVK(FM)— September 1947: 98.7 mhz; 50 kw. 390 ft TL: N40 04 58 W80 46 18. (CP: 15 kw, ant 906 ft., TL: N40 04 48 W80 46 06). Hrs open: 1015 Main St., 26003. Web Site:www.wovk.com Licensee: Capstar TX L.P. Format: Country. ◆Jim Elliott, progmg dir; Molly Kilgore, traf mgr & disc jockey.

*WPHP(FM)— Apr 4, 1977: 91.9 mhz; 1 kw. 259 ft TL: N40 04 07 W80 39 04. Hrs open: 1976 Parkview Rd., 26003. Phone: (304) 243-0400.

Fax: (304) 243-0449. Licensee: Ohio County Board of Education. Population served: 50,000 Format: Top-40. Spec prog: Black 4 hrs, jazz one hr wkly. ♦Carolyn Ihlenfeld, gen mgr.

***WVNP(FM)**— Oct 7, 1981: 89.9 mhz; 25 kw. Ant 499 ft TL: N40 12 58 W80 33 31. Stereo. Hrs open: 24 600 Capitol St., Charleston, 25301. Phone: (304) 556-4900. Fax: (304) 556-4960.E-mail: feedback@wvpubcast.org Web Site:www.wvpubcast.org Licensee: West Virginia Educational Broadcasting Authority. Population served: 100,000 Natl. Network: NPR, PRI, . Format: News, class, jazz. ♦Marilyn DiVita, gen mgr, dev dir; James Muhammad, progmg dir; Greg Callard, news dir; Jack Wells, engrg dir; Teresa Wills, traf mgr.

WWVA(AM)— December 1926: 1170 khz; 50 kw-U, DA-2. TL: N40 06 07 W80 52 02. Hrs open: 1015 Main St., 26003. Phone: (304) 232-1170. Fax: (304) 234-0041. Fax: (304) 234-0036. Web Site:www.wwva.com Licensee: Capstar TX L.P. Group owner: Clear Channel Communications Inc. (acq 8-30-00; grpsl). Population served: 48188 Natl. Rep: McGavren Guild,. Format: News/talk. Target aud: 25-54. Spec prog: Farm 2 hrs wkly. ♦Scott Miller, gen mgr; Scott Peel, natl sls mgr; Jim Harrington, progmg dir; Tammie Beagle, news dir; Barb Vaughn, traf mgr.

White Sulphur Springs

WSLW(AM)— 1971: 1310 khz; 5 kw-D. TL: N37 48 17 W80 21 03. Hrs open: 6 AM-sunset Box 610, 276 Seneca Tr., 24970. Secondary address: Rt. 60 W. Harts Run, Ronceverte 24986. Phone: (304) 536-1310. Fax: (304) 536-1311.E-mail: radio@wkcjwslw.com Licensee: Quorum Radio Partners of Virginia Inc., debtor-in-possession. (group owner; (acq 4-20-2005; grpsl). Population served: 150,000 Natl. Rep: Rgnl Reps,. Format: Adult standards. News: 8 hrs wkly. Target aud: 16-25 (60 plus). ♦Joyce Tucker, gen mgr.

Williamson

WBTH(AM)— Apr 19, 1939: 1400 khz; 1 kw-U. TL: N37 40 09 W82 16 09. Hrs open: Box 2200, Pikeville, KY, 25661. Phone: (606) 235-3600. Phone: (606) 437-4051. Fax: (606) 432-2809.E-mail: info@ekbradio.com Licensee: East Kentucky Radio Network Inc. (group owner; acq 4-4-00; $630,000 with co-located FM). Population served: 70,000 Rgnl. Network: Metronews Radio Net. Format: Adult contemp, oldies. Target aud: 25-54. ♦Keith Casebolt, gen mgr.

WXCC(FM)— Oct 27, 1978: 96.5 mhz; 50 kw. 500 ft TL: N37 40 09 W82 16 09. Hrs open: Prog sep from AM Box 2200, Pikeville, 25661. Phone: (606) 235-3600. Phone: (606) 437-4051. Fax: (606) 432-2809.E-mail: wxcc@mikrotec.com Web Site:www.wxccfm.com Population served: 350,000 Rgnl. Network: Ky. News Net, Metronews Radio Net. Ky. News Net Format: Contemp country. ♦Johnny Randolph, progmg dir.

Williamstown

WVVV(FM)— 2000: 96.9 mhz; 3.51 kw. 423 ft TL: N39 20 18 W81 30 01. Hrs open: Box 5559, Vienna, 26105. Phone: (304) 295-6070. Fax: (304) 295-4389.E-mail: info@z969radio.net Web Site:www.z969radio.net Licensee: Bennco Inc. (acq 11-2-01; $1.625 million). Format: Var/div. ♦Jack Horton, gen mgr.

Wisconsin

Adams

WDKM(FM)— Oct 8, 1993: 106.1 mhz; 6 kw. Ant 328 ft TL: N43 57 29 W89 49 43. Stereo. Hrs open: 24 1040 W. Center St., 53910. Phone: (608) 339-3221. Fax: (608) 339-2403.E-mail: info@wdkmfm.com Web Site:www.wdkmfm.com Licensee: Roche-A-Cri Broadcasting. Format: Adult Contemp. Spec prog: Polka 14 hrs wkly. ♦Glen Gardner, gen mgr; Izzy Jackson, stn mgr, opns mgr & progmg dir.

***WHAA(FM)**—Not on air, target date: unknown: 89.1 mhz; 28.5 kw. Ant 577 ft TL: N44 01 13 W89 33 29. Hrs open: 821 University Ave., Madison, 53706. Phone: (608) 263-3970. Fax: (608) 263-9763. Web Site:www.wpr.org Licensee: State of Wisconsin-Educational Communications Board. ♦Phil Corriveau, gen mgr.

Algoma

WBDK(FM)— Nov 12, 1986: 96.7 mhz; 8 kw. 538 ft TL: N44 42 26 W87 24 26. Stereo. Hrs open: 24 3030 Park Dr., Suite 3, Sturgeon Bay, 54235. Phone: (920) 746-9430. Fax: (920) 746-9433.E-mail: wbdk@itol.com Web Site:www.doorradio.com Licensee: Nicolet Broadcasting Inc. (group owner; acq 9-3-93; 9-27-93). Pepper & Corazzini. Format: Oldies of 50's & 60's. News staff: 3. Target aud: 34 plus. ♦Roger Utnehmer, pres; Paul Schmitt, sr VP; Miles Knuteson, gen mgr; Karen Leitzinger, opns mgr, progmg dir; Kathy Robinson, progmg dir, traf mgr; John Focke, news dir.

WRLU(FM)— Aug 1, 1999: 104.1 mhz; 6 kw. 328 ft TL: N44 40 02 W87 23 55. Hrs open: 3030 Park Dr., Suite 3, Sturgeon Bay, 54235. Phone: (920) 746-9430. Fax: (920) 746-9433.E-mail: info@doorradio.com Web Site:www.doorradio.com Licensee: Nicolet Broadcasting Inc. (group owner) Format: Country. News: 3 hrs wkly. ♦Roger Utnehmer, pres; Miles Knuteson, gen mgr, gen mgr, gen sls mgr; Karen Leitzinger, opns mgr, progmg dir; John Focke, news dir; Kathy Robinson, traf mgr.

Allouez

WZNN(FM)— 1996: 106.7 mhz; 25 kw. Ant 328 ft TL: N44 29 03 W87 56 12. Stereo. Hrs open: 24 810 Victoria St., Green Bay, 54302. Phone: (920) 468-4100. Fax: (920) 468-0250.E-mail: ted.bare@cumulus.com Web Site:www.1067thezone.com Licensee: WI Radio LLC, as trustee Group owner: Cumulus Media Inc. (acq 4-10-2009; with WWWX(FM) Oshkosh). Population served: 832,000 Natl. Network: Talk Radio Network, . Natl. Rep: Katz Radio,. Format: Alternative. News staff: one; News: 5 hrs wkly. Target aud: 18-49; educated, 65/35 male skew. ♦Greg Jessen, CEO, VP, mktg mgr; Jimmy Clark, CFO, opns mgr; Buck Hein, gen sls mgr; Ted Bare, progmg dir; Mark Heller, chief of engrg.

Altoona

WDVM(AM)—See Eau Claire

WISM-FM— Nov 15, 1991: 98.1 mhz; 25 kw. Ant 276 ft TL: N44 46 38 W91 28 29. Stereo. Hrs open: 24 619 Cameron St., Eau Claire, 54703. Phone: (715) 830-4000. Fax: (715) 835-9680. Web Site:www.themix981.com Licensee: Aloha Station Trust LLC, as Trustee Group owner: Clear Channel Communications Inc. (acq 7-30-2008). Population served: 200,000 Natl. Rep: Clear Channel,. Format: Adult contemp. News staff: 2. Target aud: 25-54. ♦Rick Hencley, VP, gen mgr; Jare Jordan, opns mgr; Steve Potter, gen sls mgr; Geri Feldhausen, prom dir; Jim Finn, progmg dir; Keith Edwards, news dir; Paul Orth, chief of engrg; Theresa Nelson, traf mgr.

Amery

WXCE(AM)— Jan 23, 1978: 1260 khz; 5 kw-U, DA-2. TL: N45 15 25 W92 22 00. Hrs open: 5 AM-noon Box 1260, 54001. Secondary address: 328 S. 100th St. 54001. Phone: (715) 268-7185. Fax: (715) 268-7187.E-mail: wxce@spacestar.net Web Site:www.wxce.com Licensee: Lake Country Broadcasting Corp. (acq 1-14-99). Population served: 200,000 Natl. Network: ABC, . Rgnl. Network: Tribune, Goetz Group, Wisconsin Radio Net. Wisconsin Radio Net. Format: News/talk. News staff: one; News: 20 hrs wkly. Target aud: 35 plus. ♦Darren Van Blaricom, gen mgr, gen sls mgr, rgnl sls mgr, progmg mgr; Greg Marsten, news dir, sports cmtr; Julie Measner, traf mgr.

Antigo

WACD(FM)— 1998: 106.1 mhz; 10 kw. 276 ft TL: N45 06 23 W89 09 09. Hrs open: N. 2237 US Hwy. 45 S., 54409. Phone: (715) 623-4124. Fax: (715) 627-4497.E-mail: info@wacd.com Web Site:cd106wacd.com Licensee: Results Broadcasting Inc. (group owner; (acq 4-29-2005; $500,000 with WATK(AM) Antigo). Format: Adult contemp. ♦Shaughn Novie, gen mgr; K.B. Butler, opns mgr.

WATK(AM)— Mar 15, 1948: 900 khz; 250 w-D, 196 w-N. TL: N45 06 50 W89 08 20. Hrs open: 24 Box 509, N. 2237 Hwy. 45 S., 54409. Phone: (715) 623-4124. Fax: (715) 627-4497.E-mail: wrlo@marathonmedianorth.net Web Site:www.wrlo1053.com Licensee: Results Broadcasting Inc. (group owner; (acq 4-29-2005; $500,000 with WACD(FM) Antigo). Population served: 25,900 Natl. Network: Jones Radio Networks, . Format: Adult standards. News staff: 2; News: 12 hrs wkly. Target aud: 25-59; two-income families. Spec prog: Gospel 2 hrs wkly. ♦Tom Hopfensperger, gen mgr; Duff Damos, opns dir, opns mgr; Shaughn Novy, gen sls mgr; Dave St. Peter, progmg dir, news dir; Cliff Groth, chief of engrg.

WRLO-FM— Nov 11, 1973: 105.3 mhz; 100 kw. Ant 541 ft TL: N45 22 04 W89 08 20. Stereo. Hrs open: 24 3616 Hwy. 47 N., Rhinelander, 54501-8819. Phone: (715) 362-1975. Fax: (715) 362-1973. Web Site:www.wrlo.com Licensee: NRG License Sub. LLC. (acq 10-31-2005; grpsl). Format: Classic rock. Target aud: 18-54. ♦Duff Damos, opns dir; Steve Albertson, gen sls mgr.

Appleton

WAPL(FM)— Dec 24, 1965: 105.7 mhz; 100 kw. 1,175 ft TL: N44 21 32 W87 59 07. Stereo. Hrs open: 24 Box 1519, 54912. Secondary address: 2800 E. College Ave. 54915. Phone: (920) 734-9226. Fax: (920) 733-3291.E-mail: wapl@wcinet.com Web Site:www.wapl.com Licensee: Woodward Communications Inc. (group owner; (acq 3-75). Population served: 305,000 Natl. Rep: McGavren Guild,. Hogan & Hartson. Wire Svc: AP Format: Mainstream rock. News: 2 hrs wkly. Target aud: 20-plus; professional & semi-profressional adults. ♦Greg Bell, gen mgr, stn mgr, opns mgr; Greg Lawrence, sls dir; Joe Calgaro, progmg dir, disc jockey; Steve Brown, chief of engrg; Kay Taylor, traf mgr; Elwood, disc jockey.

***WEMI(FM)**— 1994: 91.9 mhz; 3.1 kw. Ant 328 ft TL: N44 15 17 W88 26 13. Stereo. Hrs open: 24 1909 W. 2nd St., 54914. Phone: (920) 749-WEMI. Fax: (920) 749-0474. Web Site:christianfamilyradio.net Licensee: Evangel Ministries Inc. Population served: 300,000 Natl. Network: Moody, Salem Radio Network, . Leventhal, Senter & Lerman. Format: Family Friendly. News staff: 14; News: 10 hrs wkly. Target aud: 25-54; women. ♦Peggy Ament, chmn; Paul Cameron, gen mgr; Andy Kilgas, opns dir, sls dir; Heidi Prahl, dev dir.

***WOVM(FM)**— Mar 10, 1956: 91.1 mhz; 10.5 kw. Ant 120 ft TL: N44 15 42 W88 23 47. Stereo. Hrs open: 5 AM-midnight 2300 Riverside Dr., Green Bay, 54301. Phone: (920) 965-9696, ext 307. Fax: (920) 965-9697. Web Site:wovmfm.com Licensee: Starboard Media Foundation Inc. (acq 9-20-2005; $300,000). Population served: 300,000 Rgnl. Network: Wis. Pub. Format: Adult contemp. ♦Mike Watts, gen mgr.

WSCO(AM)— 1952: 1570 khz; 1 kw-D, 331 w-N. TL: N44 13 04 W88 24 33. Hrs open: 24 hrs PO Box 1519, 2800 E. College Ave., 54915. Phone: (920) 733-6639. Fax: (920) 739-0494. Licensee: Woodward Communications Inc. (group owner; acq 12-3-01; $450,000). Population served: 50,000 Natl. Network: Fox Sports, Sporting News Radio Network, . Format: Sports. Target aud: 25-54; Male. ♦Greg Bell, gen mgr; John Wanie, stn mgr; Mary Anne Drewer, gen sls mgr; Dave Edwards, progmg dir; Steve Brown, chief of engrg.

Ashland

WATW(AM)— May 1, 1940: 1400 khz; 1 kw-U. TL: N46 34 23 W90 51 56. (CP: 480 w-U. TL: N46 34 25 W90 51 56). Stereo. Hrs open: 24 2320 Ellis Ave., 54806. Phone: (715) 682-2727. Phone: (715) 682-2728. Fax: (715) 682-9338.E-mail: productionash@charter.net Web Site:www.watwam.com Licensee: Heartland Communications License LLC. (group owner; (acq 4-23-2004; grpsl). Population served: 50,000 Natl. Network: ABC, . Lauren A. Colby. Format: Hits of the 40s, 50s & 60s, news. News staff: one; News: 17 hrs wkly. Target aud: 40 plus; middle to upper income adults. Spec prog: Relg 5 hrs wkly. ♦Rich Cannata, VP, gen mgr, opns; Scott Jaeger, gen mgr; Skip Hunter, chief of engrg.

WBSZ(FM)— July 25, 1994: 93.3 mhz; 100 kw. 246 ft Stereo. Hrs open: 24 2320 Ellis Ave., 54806. Phone: (715) 682-2727. Fax: (715) 682-9338.E-mail: productionash@charter.net Web Site:www.wbszfm.com Licensee: Heartland Communications License LLC. (group owner; (acq 4-23-2004; grpsl). Population served: 250,000 Natl. Network: ABC, Westwood One, . Lauren A. Colby. Format: Hot country. Target aud: 18-49. ♦Scott Jaeger, gen mgr; Rich Canatta, opns VP; Skip Hunter, opns VP & progmg dir.

WEGZ(FM)—See Washburn

WJJH(FM)— Aug 1, 1970: 96.7 mhz; 50 kw. 246 ft TL: N46 34 25 W90 51 56. Stereo. Hrs open: 24 Prog sep from AM 2320 Ellis Ave., 54806. Phone: (715) 682-2727. Phone: (715) 682-2728. Fax: (715) 682-9338. Web Site:wjjhfm.com Population served: 250,000 Natl. Network: ABC, . Format: Classic rock. Target aud: 25-45. ♦Scott Jaeger, gen mgr; Rich Cannata, opns VP; Skip Hunter, progmg dir.

***WUWS(FM)**—Not on air, target date: unknown: 90.9 mhz; 23 kw. Ant 241 ft TL: N46 36 28 W90 50 13. Hrs open: Wisconsin Public Radio, 821 University Ave., Madison, 53706—1496. Phone: (608) 263-3970. Fax: (608) 263-9763. Web Site:www.wpr.org Licensee: Board of Regents of the University of Wisconsin System. ♦Phil Corriveau, gen mgr.

Auburndale

*WLBL(AM)— 1922: 930 khz; 5 kw-D. TL: N44 36 52 W90 02 08. Hrs open: Sunrise-sunset 518 S. 7th Ave., Wausau, 54401-5362. Phone: (715) 261-6298. Fax: (715) 848-28.E-mail: listener@wpr.org Web Site:www.wpr.org Licensee: State of Wisconsin, Education Communications Board. Natl. Network: NPR, PRI, . Format: News/talk, MOR. News staff: 4. ◆Phil Corriveau, gen mgr; Rick Reyer, stn mgr & dev dir.

Bailey's Harbor

WLGE(FM)— Apr 26, 2008: 106.9 mhz; 6 kw. Ant 184 ft TL: N45 03 14 W87 08 37. Hrs open: Box 106, Ephraim, 54211. Phone: (920) 854-3400. Fax: (800) 799-7143. Web Site:www.fm1069thelodge.com Licensee: Michael J. Mesic. Format: Rock. ◆Michael J. Mesic, gen mgr.

Balsam Lake

WLMX-FM— Feb 14, 1997: 104.9 mhz; 22 kw. Ant 348 ft TL: N45 25 07 W92 14 34. Stereo. Hrs open: Box 1260, 328 100th Street, Amery, 54001. Phone: (715) 268-7185. Fax: (715) 268-7187.E-mail: studio@mix105.ws Web Site:mix105.ws Licensee: Red Rock Radio Corp. (group owner; (acq 9-1-2006; grpsl). Natl. Network: ABC, . Rgnl. Network: Wisconsin Radio Net. Wisconsin Radio Net. Format: Classic country. News: 5 hrs wkly. Target aud: 18-49; adults. ◆Ron Revere, gen mgr.

Baraboo

WOLX-FM—Licensed to Baraboo. See Madison

WRPQ(AM)— June 1967: 740 khz; 250 w-D, 6.4 w-N. TL: N43 27 19 W89 45 13. Stereo. Hrs open: 24 Box 456, 53913. Secondary address: 407 Oak St. 53913. Phone: (608) 356-3974. Fax: (608) 355-9952.E-mail: jeffsmith@wrpq.com Web Site:www.wrpq.com Licensee: Baraboo Broadcasting Co. (acq 7-1-91; $125,000; 7-13-81). Population served: 14,000 Natl. Network: CNN Radio, . Rgnl. Network: Wisconsin Radio Net. Wisconsin Radio Net. Koerner & Olender. Format: Adult contemp. News staff: one; News: 8 hrs wkly. Target aud: 25-54. Spec prog: Relg 5 hrs wkly. ◆Gregory Buchwald, VP; Jeff Smith, pres & gen mgr; Annette Koberstein, sls dir, traf mgr.

Barron

WAQE-FM— 1999: 97.7 mhz; 15.5 kw. Ant 289 ft TL: N45 32 16 W91 45 50. Hrs open: Box 703, 1859 21st Ave., Rice Lake, 54868. Phone: (715) 234-9059. Fax: (715) 234-6942.E-mail: info@waqe.com Web Site:www.waqe.com Licensee: TKC Inc. Shaw Pittman. Format: Hits of the 80s, 90s & today. News staff: one; News: 5 hrs wkly. Target aud: 25-54; general. ◆Brian Schultz, gen mgr, stn mgr; Sondra Maanum, traf mgr.

Beaver Dam

WBEV(AM)— Mar 21, 1951: 1430 khz; 1 kw-U, DA-N. TL: N43 25 43 W88 53 33. Hrs open: 24 Box 902, 533916. Secondary address: 100 Stoddart St. 533916. Phone: (920) 885-4442. Fax: (920) 885-2152. Licensee: Good Karma Broadcasting L.L.C. (group owner; acq 12-2-97; grpsl). Population served: 80,000 Wire Svc: Wheeler News Service Format: Adult contemp, news/talk. News staff: 3; News: 20 hrs wkly. Target aud: 30 plus; general. Spec prog: Farm 8 hrs, sports 18 hrs wkly. ◆Craig Karmazin, pres, gen mgr; Rick Armon, chief of opns, progmg dir; John Moser, gen sls mgr, news dir; Warren Jorgenson, chief of engrg; Deb Iamers, traf mgr.

WXRO(FM)— July 15, 1968: 95.3 mhz; 6 kw. 328 ft TL: N43 28 09 W88 49 32. Stereo. Hrs open: 24 Prog sep from AM Box 902, 533916. Secondary address: 100 Stoddart St. 533916. Phone: (920) 885-4442. Fax: (920) 885-2152. Population served: 70,000 Wire Svc: Wheeler News Service Format: Modern country. News staff: 3; News: 10 hrs wkly. Target aud: 25-54; general. Spec prog: Farm 6 hrs wkly. ◆Craig Karmazin, chmn; John A. Moser, sls dir; John Kraft, farm dir; Rick Armon, prom dir & disc jockey.

Beloit

*WBCR-FM— Nov 30, 1965: 90.3 mhz; 100 w. 44 ft TL: N42 30 13 W89 01 55. (CP: 130 w). Hrs open: Beloit College, 700 College St., 53511. Phone: (608) 363-2402. Fax: (608) 363-2718.E-mail: wbcr@stubeloit.edu Web Site:www.beloit.edu/~wbcr/ Licensee: Beloit College. Population served: 100,000 Format: Educ, div. ◆Kyle McKenzie, gen mgr.

WGEZ(AM)— Sept 26, 1948: 1490 khz; 1 kw-U. TL: N42 29 45 W89 01 03. Hrs open: 24 Box 416, 53512. Secondary address: 622 Public Ave. 53511. Phone: (608) 365-8865. Fax: (608) 365-8867.E-mail: wgezam@hotmail.com Web Site:www.1490trueoldies.com Licensee: Alliance Communications Inc. (acq 2-18-2005; $325,000). Population served: 180,000 Natl. Network: AP Network News, . Brownfield Format: Oldies. News staff: one. Target aud: 25-54; baby boomers. ◆Alan Kearns, gen mgr, progmg dir, chief of engrg; Keith Salerno, gen sls mgr; Carla Cornell, traf mgr.

WTJK(AM)—(South Beloit, IL) May 18, 1948: 1380 khz; 5 kw-U, DA-N. TL: N42 27 34 W89 01 43. Stereo. Hrs open: 24 1 Parker Place, Suite 485, Janesville, 53545. Phone: (608) 758-9025. Fax: (608) 758-9550.E-mail: production@gkbradio.com Web Site:www.espn1380.com Licensee: Good Karma Broadcasting L.L.C. (group owner; acq 9-13-00; $235,000). Population served: 65,000 Natl. Network: ESPN Radio, . Natl. Rep: Interep,. Format: Sports, info. Target aud: 25-54; males. ◆Keith Williams, gen mgr; Kevin MacDougall, gen sls mgr; Kyle Jacob, progmg dir; Warren Jorgensen, chief of engrg.

Berlin

WBJZ(FM)— July 31, 1972: 104.7 mhz; 5.2 kw. Ant 351 ft TL: N43 53 57 W88 53 37. Hrs open: 24 112 Watson St., Ripon, 54971. Phone: (920) 748-9205. Fax: (920) 748-5530. Licensee: Caxambas Corp. Population served: 250,000 Format: Adult contemp. Target aud: 35-54; upscale, adults. ◆Mike Enfelt, gen mgr; Jason Mansmith, progmg dir.

WISS(AM)— June 28, 1971: 1100 khz; 1 kw-D. TL: N43 56 55 W88 59 09. Hrs open: Sunrise-sunset Box 71, 54923. Secondary address: 112 N. Pearl St. 54923. Phone: (920) 361-3551. Fax: (920) 361-3737.E-mail: production@hometownbroadcasting.com Web Site:www.wissradio.com Licensee: Hometown Broadcasting LLC (acq 12-1-99; $165,000). Population served: 250,000 Format: Country oldies. News staff: one; News: 10 hrs wkly. Target aud: 25-54; local community. ◆Tom Boyson, gen mgr; Margaret Corrente, sls dir; Bill Denkert, gen sls mgr; Bernie Phillips, progmg dir; Andrew Disterhaft, chief of engrg, traf mgr.

Birnamwood

WYNW(FM)— 2003: 92.9 mhz; 6 kw. Ant 328 ft TL: N44 59 50 W89 22 07. Hrs open: Starboard Network, 2300 Riverside Drive, Green Bay, 54301. Phone: (920) 469-3021. Fax: (920) 469-3023. Web Site:www.relevantradio.com Licensee: Starboard Media Foundation Inc. Group owner: Relevant Radio (acq 7-9-2002). Format: Catholic radio. ◆Mike Strub, stn mgr.

Black River Falls

WWIS(AM)— Aug 23, 1958: 1260 khz; 580 w-D. TL: N44 19 11 W90 53 31. Hrs open: 6 AM-sunset W11573 Town Creek Rd., 54615. Phone: (715) 284-4391. Fax: (715) 284-9740.E-mail: wwis@wwisradio.com Web Site:www.wwisradio.com Licensee: WWIS Radio Inc. (acq 5-1-68). Population served: 17,000 Natl. Network: CBS Radio, . Rgnl. Network: Brownfield. Brownfield Miller & Miller, P.C. Wire Svc: Wheeler News Service Format: Oldies. News: 6 hrs wkly. Target aud: General. ◆Nelson Lent, pres, VP; Robert A. Gabrielson, gen mgr.

WWIS-FM— Jan 21, 1991: 99.7 mhz; 25 kw. Ant 328 ft TL: N44 19 11 W90 53 31. Stereo. Hrs open: 24 W. 11573 Town Creek Rd., 54615. Phone: (715) 284-4391. Fax: (715) 284-9740.E-mail: wwis@cuttingedge.net Web Site:www.wwisradio.com Licensee: WWIS Radio Inc. Population served: 295,000 Natl. Network: CBS, . Wire Svc: Wheeler News Service Format: Adult contemp. News: 12 hrs wkly. Target aud: 25-55. ◆Robert Smith, pres; Nelson Lent, VP, gen mgr; Robert Gabrielson, gen mgr.

Bloomer

WQRB(FM)— 1993: 95.1 mhz; 25 kw. 430 ft TL: N45 01 59 W91 21 09. Stereo. Hrs open: 24 619 Cameron St., Eau Claire, 54703. Phone: (715) 830-4000. Fax: (715) 835-9680. Web Site:www.b95radio.com Licensee: Capstar TX L.P. Group owner: Clear Channel Communications Inc. (acq 2000; grpsl). Population served: 200,000 Natl. Rep: Clear Channel,. Format: Hot country. News staff: 2. Target aud: 25-54. ◆Rick Hencley, VP, gen mgr, mktg mgr; Jare Jordan, opns mgr; Steve Potter, gen sls mgr; Mike McKay, progmg dir; Keith Edwards, news dir; Paul Orth, chief of engrg; Trina Butak, traf mgr; Bobby Tripp, disc jockey.

Brillion

WDUZ-FM— March 1993: 107.5 mhz; 6 kw. 328 ft TL: N44 15 28 W88 11 43. (CP: 5 kw). Stereo. Hrs open: 24 810 Victoria St., Green Bay, 54302. Phone: (920) 468-4100. Fax: (920) 468-0250. Web Site:www.thefan1075.com Licensee: Jacor Broadcasting Corp. Group owner: Cumulus Media Inc. (acq 4-10-2009; grpsl). Population served: 832,000 Natl. Network: ABC, ESPN Radio, Premiere Radio Networks, . Wiley Rein LLP. Format: Sports/talk. Target aud: 18-49; educated, affluent, upper-income. ◆Greg Jessen, VP, gen mgr, mktg mgr; Jimmy Clark, opns mgr, sls dir, progmg dir; Buck Hein, gen sls mgr; Brian Stenzel, prom dir; Mark Heller, engrg mgr.

Brookfield

WJZX(FM)— Aug 18, 1995: 106.9 mhz; 4.4 kw. Ant 380 ft TL: N43 02 49 W87 58 52. Hrs open: 5407 W. McKinley Ave., Milwaukee, 53208. Phone: (414) 978-9000. Fax: (414) 978-9001. Web Site:smoothjazz1069.com Licensee: Saga Communications of Milwaukee LLC. Group owner: Saga Communications Inc. (acq 5-9-97; $5 million with WJMR-FM Menomonee Falls). Natl. Rep: Katz Radio,. Smithwick & Belendiuk. Format: Smooth jazz. News staff: one. Target aud: 35-64. ◆Thomas Joerres, pres, gen mgr; Traci Northrop, gen sls mgr; LaTonya Lucas, prom dir; Lauri Jones, progmg dir; Phil Longenecker, chief of engrg; Cris Ruid, traf mgr.

Brule

*WHSA(FM)— Sept 14, 1952: 89.9 mhz; 38 kw. 550 ft TL: N46 27 59 W91 33 56. Stereo. Hrs open: 24 P.O. Box 2000, Superior, 54880. Phone: (715) 394-8530. Fax: (715) 394-8404.E-mail: jmunson@uwsuper.edu Web Site:www.wpr.org Licensee: State of Wisconsin Educational Communications Board. Population served: 200,000 Natl. Network: NPR, . Rgnl. Network: Wis. Pub. Wis. Public Radio Format: Class, news/talk. News staff: one; News: 39 hrs wkly. Target aud: 34 plus. Spec prog: Folk 3 hrs, jazz 6 hrs wkly. ◆John A. Munson, gen mgr.

Burlington

*WBSD(FM)— Apr 7, 1975: 89.1 mhz; 300 w. 107 ft TL: N42 40 14 W88 16 18. Stereo. Hrs open: 24 400 McCanna prkwy, 53105. Phone: (262) 763-0195. Fax: (262) 763-0207.E-mail: wbsd@wbsdfm.com Web Site:www.wbsdfm.com Licensee: Burlington Area School District. Population served: 75,000 Format: Alternative, progsv rock. News: One. Target aud: 25-54. Spec prog: Jazz 8 hrs, reggae 3 hrs, ska/punk 2 hrs, metal one hr, blues 4 hrs, folk 5 hrs wkly. ◆Terry Havel, gen mgr; Kevin Fay, opns VP.

Chetek

WATQ(FM)— May 17, 1997: 106.7 mhz; 50 kw. 492 ft TL: N45 14 31 W91 44 43. Stereo. Hrs open: 24 619 Cameron St., Eau Claire, 54703. Phone: (715) 830-4000. Fax: (715) 835-9680.E-mail: rickhencley @clearchannel.com Web Site:www.moose106.com Licensee: Capstar TX L.P. Group owner: Clear Channel Communications Inc. (acq 2000; grpsl). Population served: 200,000 Natl. Network: CNN Radio, . Natl. Rep: Clear Channel,. Brownfield Format: Country. News staff: 2. Target aud: 35-64. ◆Rick Hencley, VP, gen mgr, mktg mgr; Jare Jordan, opns mgr; Steve Potter, gen sls mgr; Jay Moore, progmg dir; Keith Edwards, news dir; Paul Orth, chief of engrg; Theresa Nelson, traf mgr.

Chilton

WMBE(AM)— May 25, 1984: 1530 khz; 250 w-D. TL: N44 01 10 W88 09 32. Hrs open: Sunrise-sunset Box 1450, Fond du Lac, 54936. Secondary address: 354 Winnebago Dr., Fond du Lac 54935. Phone: (920) 921-1071. Fax: (920) 921-0757.E-mail: info@espnradio1530.com Web Site:www.espnradio1530.com Licensee: Maszka-Pacer Radio Inc. (acq 12-28-90; $4,469; 1-14-91). Natl. Network: USA, . Format: Sports. News staff: 2. Target aud: 18-54; male sports fans. ◆R.B. Hopper, gen mgr; Mark Kastein, gen sls mgr, prom mgr; Shawn A. Kiser, progmg dir; Stu Muck, engrg dir; Cindy Konen, traf mgr.

Chippewa Falls

WAXX(FM)—See Eau Claire

WCFW(FM)— Oct 20, 1968: 105.7 mhz; 25 kw. 305 ft TL: N44 52 18 W91 17 11. Stereo. Hrs open: 24 318 Well St., 54729. Phone: (715) 723-2257. Fax: (715) 723-8276.E-mail: wcfwradio@clearwire.net Licensee: Roland L. Bushland dba Bushland Radio/WCFW. Wire Svc: AP Format: Adult contemp. News: 8 hrs wkly. Target aud: 35 plus;

upscale. Spec prog: Relg 2 hrs wkly. ♦Patricia Bushland, gen sls mgr; Roland Bushland, gen mgr & progmg dir.

WEAQ(AM)— Sept 7, 1958: 1150 khz; 5 kw-D. TL: N45 53 05 W91 23 25. Hrs open: Box 1, Eau Claire, 54702. Secondary address: 944 Harlem St., Altoona 54720. Phone: (715) 832-1530. Fax: (715) 832-5329. Web Site:www.espn1150.com Licensee: Maverick Media of Eau Claire License LLC. Group owner: Maverick Media LLC (acq 6-13-2003; grpsl). Natl. Rep: Katz Radio,. Format: Sports/talk. Target aud: 40 plus; general. ♦Gary Rozynek, pres; George Roberts, VP; Bruce Butler, gen mgr; Dave Craig, stn mgr, opns dir; Bill Holden, chief of engrg.

Cleveland

WLKN(FM)— Apr 25, 1985: 98.1 mhz; 5.8 kw. Ant 292 ft TL: N43 59 03 W87 45 55. Stereo. Hrs open: 24 Box 26, 1050 Linden St., 53015. Phone: (920) 693-3103. Fax: (920) 693-3104.E-mail: manager@wlkn.com Web Site:www.wlkn.com Licensee: Radio K-T Inc. (acq 10-15-99; $980,000). Population served: 225,000 Vinson & Elkins. Wire Svc: AP Format: Adult contemp. News staff: one; News: 7 hrs wkly. Target aud: 25-54; active, upscale. ♦Jack Taddeo, CEO, pres, progmg dir, chief of engrg; David Jetzer, stn mgr, gen sls mgr, gen sls mgr, news dir; Wendy Dekker, traf mgr & farm dir.

Clintonville

WJMQ(FM)— Oct 27, 1986: 92.3 mhz; 6 kw. Ant 328 ft TL: N44 34 00 W88 44 36. Stereo. Hrs open: 24 1456 E. Green Bay St., Shawano, 54166. Phone: (715) 524-2194. Fax: (715) 524-9980. Licensee: Results Broadcasting Inc. Format: Country. News staff: one; News: 12 hrs wkly. Target aud: 12-plus. ♦Eric Voight, stn mgr.

WOTE(AM)— Feb 28, 1983: 1380 khz; 5 kw-D, 2.5 kw-N, DA-2. TL: N44 34 00 W88 44 36. Hrs open: 24 1456 E. Green Bay St., Shawano, 54166. Phone: (715) 524-2194. Fax: (715) 524-9980. Web Site:www.oldies1380.com Licensee: Results Broadcasting Inc. Group owner: Results Broadcasting (acq 1996). Natl. Network: ABC, . Wisconsin Radio Net. Miller & Miller, P.C. Format: Rock and roll oldies. News staff: one; News: 12 hrs wkly. Target aud: 25-54. Spec prog: Farm 8 hrs wkly. ♦Eric Voight, pres, gen mgr; Walt Baldwin, news dir & chief of engrg.

Columbus

WTLX(FM)— July 16, 1990: 100.5 mhz; 6 kw. Ant 328 ft TL: N43 20 04 W89 09 57. (CP: COL Monona. Ant 180 ft. TL: N43 08 04 W89 23 56). Stereo. Hrs open: 24 Box 902, Beaver Dam, 53916. Secondary address: 5315 Wall St., Suite 135, Madison 53718. Phone: (608) 245-9859. Fax: (608) 245-1720. Web Site:www.espnmadison.com Licensee: Good Karma Broadcasting L.L.C. (group owner; (acq 12-2-97; grpsl). Population served: 200,000 Natl. Network: ESPN Radio, . Format: Sports talk. Target aud: 25-54; males. ♦Craig Karmazin, pres; Ken Rovak, gen mgr.

WTTN(AM)— Apr 2, 1950: 1580 khz; 5 kw-D, 4 w-N, 800 w-CH, DA-D. TL: N43 20 05 W89 09 56 (day), N43 20 03 W89 09 57 (night, CH). Hrs open: 24 Box 509, 615 E. Main St., Watertown, 53094. Phone: (920) 261-1580. Fax: (920) 261-0624.E-mail: jmoser@gkbradio.com Licensee: Good Karma Broadcasting L.L.C. (group owner; (acq 8-26-99; $525,000). Population served: 100,000 Natl. Network: CNN Radio, . Rgnl. Network: Wisconsin Radio Net. Wire Svc: Wheeler News Service Format: Oldies. News staff: 2; News: 15 hrs wkly. Target aud: 25-64. Spec prog: Relg 4 hrs wkly. ♦Craig . Karmazin, CEO, pres; Scott M. Trentadue, gen mgr; Rick Armon, opns mgr; John Moser, gen sls mgr; Warren Jorgensen, chief of engrg.

Cornell

WDRK(FM)— 2001: 99.9 mhz; 25 kw. Ant 328 ft TL: N45 07 22 W91 24 23. Hrs open: 944 Harlem St., Altoona, 54720. Phone: (715) 832-1530. Fax: (715) 832-5329. Web Site:www.bobfm999.com Licensee: Maverick Media of Eau Claire License LLC. Group owner: Maverick Media LLC (acq 6-13-2003; grpsl). Population served: 150,000 Format: Adult hits. News staff: one; News: one hr wkly. ♦George Roberts, VP, gen mgr, mktg mgr; Al Shannon, opns mgr, mus dir; Lynn Bieritz, gen sls mgr; Dan Gainey, rgnl sls mgr; Kris Cooper, prom dir; Rick Roberts, stn mgr & progmg mgr; Dan Lea, news dir; Bill Holden, chief of engrg.

De Forest

WJQM(FM)— 2003: 93.1 mhz; 6 kw horiz, 5.4 kw vert. Ant 321 ft TL: N43 09 34 W89 12 55. Hrs open: Box 44408, Madison, 53744. Secondary address: 730 Rayovc Dr. 53711. Phone: (608) 273-1000. Fax: (608) 273-3588.E-mail: info@madisonjamz.com Web Site:www.madisonjams.com Licensee: Mid-West Management Inc. Group owner: The Mid-West Family Broadcast Group (acq 8-13-2002). Format: Rhythmic hits. ♦Tom Walker, gen mgr; Randy Hawke, opns mgr; Ted Waldbillig, gen sls mgr; J.D. Garfield, progmg dir.

De Pere

WKSZ(FM)—Licensed to De Pere. See Green Bay

Delafield

***WHAD(FM)**— May 30, 1948: 90.7 mhz; 72 kw. Ant 682 ft TL: N43 01 42 W88 23 32. Hrs open: 24
Rebroadcasts WHA(AM) Madison 60%.
111 E. Kilbourn Ave., Suite 2375, Milwaukee, 53202. Phone: (414) 227-2040. Fax: (414) 227-2043.E-mail: whad@wpr.org Web Site:www.wpr.org Licensee: State of Wisconsin Educational Communications Board. Population served: 1,100,000 Natl. Network: NPR, . Rgnl. Network: Wis. Pub. Format: Pub radio, news/talk. News staff: one; News: 11 hrs wkly. Target aud: 35-55; general. ♦Bill Estes, stn mgr; Shavonn Brown, gen sls mgr; Chuck Quirmbach, news dir.

Denmark

WPCK(FM)— Sept 1, 1969: 104.9 mhz; 10 kw. Ant 515 ft TL: N44 24 38 W87 34 20. Stereo. Hrs open: 24 810 Victoria St., Green Bay, 54302. Phone: (920) 468-4100. Fax: (920) 468-0250.E-mail: dylan.fletcher@cumulus.com Web Site:www.kicks1049.com Licensee: Citicasters Licenses Inc. Group owner: Cumulus Media Inc. (acq 4-10-2009; grpsl). Natl. Rep: Katz Radio,. Wiley Rein LLP. Format: Country. Target aud: 25-54; adults. ♦Greg Jessen, VP, gen mgr, mktg mgr; Chris Moreau, gen sls mgr; Dylan Fletcher, progmg dir; Mark Heller, chief of engrg.

Dickeyville

WVRE(FM)— 2/1/03: 101.1 mhz; 3.7 kw. Ant 423 ft TL: N42 31 43 W90 36 56. Stereo. Hrs open: 24 Box 659, Dubuque, IA, 52004. Phone: (563) 690-0800. Fax: (563) 588-5688. Licensee: Radio Dubuque Inc. (group owner; acq 8-1-01). Natl. Rep: International Media, Katz Radio,. Format: Country. News staff: one. Target aud: Adults; 25-54. ♦Thomas Parsley, gen mgr.

Dodgeville

WDMP(AM)— Nov 1, 1968: 810 khz; 250 w-D, 10 w-N. TL: N42 55 10 W90 08 06. Hrs open: 24 Box 9, 53533. Secondary address: 2163 Hwy. 151 S. 53523. Phone: (608) 935-2302. Fax: (608) 935-3464. Web Site:www.d99point3.com Licensee: Dodge-Point Broadcasting Co. Population served: 63250 Format: Country. News staff: one; News: 5 hrs wkly. Target aud: General. ♦Louise E. Hamlin, pres; Kurt Reinicke, gen mgr, gen sls mgr; Jennifer Mick, disc jockey.

WDMP-FM— Nov 1, 1968: 99.3 mhz; 1.55 kw. 459 ft TL: N42 55 10 W90 08 06. Stereo. Hrs open: 24 Dups AM 100%. Box 9, 53523. Secondary address: 2163 Hwy. 151 S. 53523. Phone: (608) 935-2302. Fax: (608) 935-3464.E-mail: mail@d99point3.com Web Site:www.d99point3.com Population served: 23,255 News staff: one. ♦Jennifer Mick, disc jockey.

Durand

WDMO(FM)— Oct 24, 1973: 95.9 mhz; 1.3 kw. Ant 498 ft TL: N44 34 53 W91 54 44. Stereo. Hrs open: 313 Main St., Menomonie, 54751. Phone: (715) 231-9500. Fax: (715) 231-9505. Web Site:www.thunder959.com Licensee: Zoe Communications Inc. (group owner; (acq 7-31-2001; with co-located AM). Population served: 89,673 Format: Country. ♦Bo Landry, opns mgr, progmg dir, news dir; Mike Oberg, chief of engrg; Wendy Oberg, gen mgr, gen sls mgr & traf mgr.

WQOQ(AM)— Nov 21, 1968: Stn currently dark. 1430 khz; 2 kw-D, 152 w-N. TL: N44 38 28 W91 55 22. Hrs open: 18 313 Main St., Menomonie, 54751. Phone: (715) 231-9500. Fax: (715) 231-9505. Licensee: Zoe Communications Inc. Population served: 2,103

Eagle River

WERL(AM)— May 23, 1961: 950 khz; 1 kw-D, 51 w-N. TL: N45 58 38 W89 14 52. Stereo. Hrs open: 24 Box 309, 909 Railroad St., 54521. Phone: (715) 479-4451. Fax: (715) 479-6511.E-mail: wrjo@wrjo.com Web Site:www.wrjo.com Licensee: Heartland Communications License LLC. (acq 12-7-2004; $2.2 million with co-located FM). Format: Adult standards. News staff: one; News: 7 hrs wkly. Target aud: General. ♦Mary Jo Berner, pres; Jeff Wagner, gen mgr, gen sls mgr; Jeff Litscher, prom dir, progmg dir; Chris Oatman, news dir; Del Dayton, chief of engrg; Lynn Weiland, traf mgr.

WRJO(FM)— July 31, 1971: 94.5 mhz; 50 kw. 492 ft TL: N45 58 38 W89 14 52. Stereo. Hrs open: 24 Prog sep from AM Box 309, 909 Railroad St., 54521. Phone: (715) 479-4451. Fax: (715) 479-6511.E-mail: info@wrjo.com Web Site:www.wrjo.com Format: Oldies, rock and roll.

Eau Claire

WAXX(FM)— February 1965: 104.5 mhz; 100 kw. 1,830 ft TL: N44 39 51 W90 57 41. Stereo. Hrs open: 24 944 Harlem, Altoona, 54720. Phone: (715) 832-1530. Fax: (715) 832-5329. Web Site:www.todayswaxx1045.com Licensee: Maverick Media of Eau Claire License LLC. Group owner: Maverick Media LLC (acq 6-13-2003; grpsl). Population served: 500,000 Format: Country. News staff: 4. Target aud: 25-54; metro & rgnl adults. Spec prog: Farm 15 hrs wkly. ♦Gary Rozynek, pres; George Roberts, gen mgr, mktg mgr; George House, stn mgr, opns mgr, progmg dir; Lynn Bieritz, sls dir; Dan Gainey, rgnl sls mgr; John Murphy, prom dir; Dan Lea, news dir; Bill Holden, chief of engrg.

WAYY(AM)— May 1937: 790 khz; 5 kw-U, DA-N. TL: N44 49 51 W91 26 58. Hrs open: 24 944 Harlem St., Altoona, 54720. Phone: (715) 832-1530. Fax: (715) 832-5329.E-mail: bruce@wayy790.com Web Site:www.wayy790.com Licensee: Maverick Media of Eau Claire License LLC. Group owner: Maverick Media LLC (acq 6-13-2003; grpsl). Population served: 250,000 Rgnl. Network: Wisconsin Radio Net. Wisconsin Radio Net. Pepper & Corazzini. Format: News/talk. News staff: one. Target aud: 35 plus; general. Spec prog: Farm 5 hrs wkly. ♦George Roberts, gen mgr; Dave Craig, opns mgr; Lynn Bieritz, gen sls mgr; John Murphy, prom dir; Bruce Butler, progmg dir; Dan Lea, news dir; Bill Holden, chief of engrg; Lorraine Diener, traf mgr.

WBIZ(AM)— Nov 11, 1947: 1400 khz; 1 kw-U. TL: N44 48 48 W91 31 15. Hrs open: 24 619 Cameron St., 54703. Phone: (715) 830-4000. Fax: (715) 835-9680. Web Site:www.sportsradio1400.com Licensee: Capstar TX L.P. Group owner: Clear Channel Communications Inc. (acq 2000; grpsl). Population served: 200,000 Natl. Network: CBS, . Natl. Rep: Clear Channel,. Format: All sports. Target aud: 25-54. ♦Rick Hencley, VP, gen mgr, mktg mgr; Jare Jordan, opns mgr; Steve Potter, gen sls mgr; Jimmie Kaska, progmg mgr; Keith Edwards, news dir; Paul Orth, chief of engrg; Theresa Nelson, traf mgr.

WBIZ-FM— December 1967: 100.7 mhz; 100 kw. 740 ft TL: N44 47 58 W91 27 59. Stereo. Hrs open: Prog sep from AM 619 Cameron St., 54703. Phone: (715) 830-4000. Fax: (715) 835-9680. Web Site:www.z100radio.com Licensee: Capstar Limited Partnership Population served: 250,000 Natl. Rep: Clear Channel,. Format: CHR. News: 2. Target aud: 18 - 49. ♦Rick Hencley, VP, gen sls mgr, mktg mgr; Jare Jordan, opns mgr; Jare E. Jordan, progmg dir, mus dir; Keith Edwards, news dir; Paul Orth, chief of engrg; Theresa Nelson, traf mgr.

***WDVM(AM)**— April 1948: 1050 khz; 1 kw-D, 500 w-N. TL: N44 46 36 W91 28 30. Stereo. Hrs open: Relevant Radio 1050 AM, WDVM, 1752 Bracket Ave., 54701. Phone: (715) 855-1439. Phone: (715) 577-0943. Fax: (715) 855-1471.E-mail: wdvm@relevantradio.com Web Site:www.relevantradio.com Licensee: Starboard Media Foundation Inc. Group owner: Relevant Radio (acq 7-6-2001). Population served: 75,000 Format: Talk, relg. News staff: one. Target aud: 35 plus; mature adults. ♦Mark Follett, CEO; Sherry Brownrigg, pres; Raymond P. Jay, stn mgr; Martin Jury, opns dir.

***WHEM(FM)**— Aug 22, 1995: 91.3 mhz; 350 w. Ant 216 ft TL: N44 45 50 W91 31 06. (CP: 300 w, ant 285 ft). Hrs open: 24 228 E. Lowes Creek Rd., 54701. Phone: (715) 838-9595.E-mail: whem@discover-net.net Web Site:www.whem.com Licensee: Fourth Dimension Inc. (acq 7-2-93; $2,810; 8-2-93). Format: Christian. ♦Harlan Reinders, gen mgr, chief of engrg; Phyllis Reinders, progmg dir.

WIAL(FM)— 1948: 94.1 mhz; 85 kw. 350 ft TL: N44 49 48 W91 26 48. Stereo. Hrs open: 24 944 Harlem St., Altoona, 54720. Phone: (715) 832-1530. Fax: (715) 832-5329. Web Site:www.i94online.com Format: Adult contemp. News staff: one. Target aud: 18-54. ♦Gary Rozynek, pres; George Roberts, gen mgr, opns mgr; Rick Roberts, stn mgr, progmg dir; Lynn Bieritz, sls dir; Luc Anthony, prom dir, disc jockey; Bill Holden, chief of engrg; Curt St ohn, disc jockey.

***WUEC(FM)**— Oct 27, 1975: 89.7 mhz; 5.2 kw. 630 ft TL: N44 47 58 W91 27 59. Stereo. Hrs open: 24 Wisconsin Public Radio, 1221 W. Clairemont Ave., 54701. Phone: (715) 839-3868. Fax: (715) 839-2939.E-mail: kallenbach@wpr.org Web Site:www.wpr.org Licensee: Board of Regents, University of Wisconsin. Population served: 168,000 Natl. Network: NPR, . Rgnl. Network: Wis. Pub. Wis. Public Radio Dow, Lohnes & Albertson. Format: Class, news, jazz. News: 24 hrs wkly. Target aud: General. Spec prog: Folk 3 hrs, blues 3 hrs wkly. ♦Dean Kallenbach, stn mgr; Marvin Spielman, dev dir, mktg dir; Mary Jo Wagner, news dir; Ron Viste, chief of engrg.

***WVCF(FM)**— 1997: 90.5 mhz; 980 w. 279 ft TL: N44 57 29 W91 28 58. Stereo. Hrs open: 24 VCY/America Inc., 3434 W. Kilbourn Ave., Milwaukee, 53208. Phone: (414) 935-3000. Fax: (414) 935-3015.E-mail: wvcf@vcyamerica.org Web Site:www.vcyamerica.org Licensee: VCY America Inc. (group owner) Natl. Network: USA, Moody, . Format: Relg, Christian. ♦Dr. Randall Melchert, pres; Victor Eliason, VP & gen mgr; Gordon Morris, opns mgr, mus dir, news dir; Jim Schneider, progmg dir.

Elk Mound

WECL(FM)— March 1, 2004: 92.9 mhz; 3.3 kw. 446 ft TL: N44 53 40 W91 35 40. Stereo. Hrs open: 24 944 Harlem St., Altoona, 54720. Phone: (715) 832-1530. Fax: (715) 832-5329. Web Site:www.929thebigcheese.com Licensee: Maverick Media of Eau Claire License LLC. Group owner: Maverick Media LLC (acq 6-13-2003; grpsl). Population served: 150,000 Pepper & Corazzini. Target aud: 35-54; adults. Spec prog: Flashback 4 hrs wkly. ♦Gary Rozynek, pres; George Roberts, gen mgr; Rick Roberts, stn mgr; Dan Lea, opns dir; Lynn Bieritz, sls dir; Dan Gainey, rgnl sls mgr; Bill Holden, chief of engrg.

Elm Grove

WGLB(AM)— Dec 6, 1963: 1560 khz; 185 w-D, 250 w-N, DA-2. TL: N43 00 32 W88 02 06. Hrs open: 24 5181 N. 35th St., Milwaukee, 53209. Phone: (414) 527-4365. Fax: (414) 527-4367.E-mail: wglb@wglbam1560.com Web Site:wglbam1560.com Licensee: Joel J. Kinlow (acq 7-25-95; with co-located FM;8-21-95). Population served: 600,000 Format: Gospel. African American. ♦Joel Kinlow, CEO; Joel Kinlow, pres, gen mgr; Willis H. Payne Jr., stn mgr & progmg dir.

Evansville

WWHG(FM)— Aug 17, 1989: 105.9 mhz; 1.7 kw. Ant 493 ft TL: N42 43 38 W89 15 02. Stereo. Hrs open: 24 One Parker Pl., Suite 485, Janesville, 53545. Phone: (608) 758-9025. Fax: (608) 758-9550.E-mail: production@gkbradio.com Web Site:hot1059.net Licensee: Good Karma Broadcasting L.L.C. (acq 10-2-97; $1.5 million). Format: Rock. News staff: one; News: 3 hrs wkly. ♦Craig Karmazin, CEO, pres; Keith Williams, gen mgr, stn mgr, gen sls mgr, prom dir; Rick Armon, opns dir, opns mgr; Dan Hunt, progmg dir; Kyle Jacob, news dir; Warren Jorgensen, engrg dir & chief of engrg; Deb Lamers, traf mgr.

Fond du Lac

KFIZ(AM)— July 6, 1922: 1450 khz; 1 kw-U. TL: N43 47 28 W88 28 16. Stereo. Hrs open: Box 1450, 54936-1450. Secondary address: 254 Winnebago Dr. 54935. Phone: (920) 921-1071. Fax: (920) 921-0757.E-mail: info@kfiz.com Web Site:www.kfiz.com Licensee: RBH Enterprises Inc. Group owner: Mountain Dog Media (acq 1-23-97; $1 plus assumption of liabilities with co-located FM). Population served: 135,515 Format: News/talk, sports. Target aud: 35-64; Men & Women. Spec prog: Farm 10 hrs wkly. ♦R.B. Hopper, pres & gen mgr.

***WDKV(FM)**— 2005: 91.7 mhz; 20 kw vert. Ant 357 ft TL: N43 39 35 W88 26 26. Hrs open: 2351 Sunset Blvd., Suite 170-218, Rocklin, CA, 95765. Phone: (916) 251-1600. Fax: (916) 251-1650. Licensee: Educational Media Foundation. (acq 2-21-2006; $350,000). Population served: 192,134 Format: Christian. ♦Richard Jenkins, pres; Keith Whipple, dev dir; David Pierce, progmg mgr; Ed Lenane, news dir; Sam Wallington, engrg dir; Karen Johnson, news rptr.

WFDL-FM—(Lomira, April 1993: 97.7 mhz; 17.5 kw. Ant 400 ft TL: N43 39 14 W88 26 25. Hrs open: 24 210 S. Main St., 54935. Phone: (920) 924-9697. Fax: (920) 929-8865.E-mail: info@sunny97-7.com Web Site:www.wfdl.com Licensee: Radio Plus of Fond du Lac Inc. (acq 4-96). Population served: 150,000 Haley, Bader & Potts. Format: Adult contemp. News staff: one. Target aud: 25-54. ♦Chris Bernier, pres; Terry Davis, VP, gen mgr, gen sls mgr; Mike Enfelt, opns mgr, chief of engrg; Todd Dehring, progmg dir; Greg Stensland, news dir; Kerry Longrie, traf mgr.

WFON(FM)— Oct 5, 1967: 107.1 mhz; 3 kw. Ant 312 ft TL: N43 50 22 W88 22 06. Stereo. Hrs open: 24 254 Winnebago Dr., 54935. Phone: (920) 921-1071. Fax: (920) 921-0757. Web Site:www.k107.com Licensee: RBH Enterprises Inc. Group owner: Mountain Dog Media (acq 1-23-97). Population served: 500,000 Format: Hot adult contemp. News staff: one; News: 1 hr wkly. Target aud: Women 25-54. ♦Randy Hopper, gen mgr.

WRPN(AM)—(Ripon, Sept 15, 1957: 1600 khz; 5 kw-U, DA-2. TL: N43 49 01 W88 50 49. Hrs open: 24 112 Watson St., Ripon, 54971. Phone: (920) 748-5111. Fax: (920) 748-5530.E-mail: wrpn@wrpnam.com Web Site:www.wrpnam.com Licensee: Radio Broadcasting L.P. Population served: 23247 Natl. Network: CBS, ABC, . Natl. Rep: Farmakis,. Haley, Bader & Potts. Wire Svc: Wheeler News Service Format: News/talk. News staff: 4; News: 25 hrs wkly. Target aud: 25 plus. ♦Mike Enfelt, gen mgr; Jason Marsmith, progmg dir.

WTCX(FM)—(Ripon, Feb 1, 1965: 96.1 mhz; 4 kw. Ant 403 ft TL: N43 49 10 W88 43 20. Stereo. Hrs open: 24 210 South Main St., Fon du Lac, 54935. Phone: (920) 924-9697. Fax: (920) 929-8865. Web Site:www.961themix.com Population served: 90,000 Format: Classic hits, new rock. News staff: one; News: 3 hrs wkly. Target aud: 25-54; women. ♦Mike Enfelt, opns mgr; Terry Davis, VP, gen mgr & gen sls mgr; Gregg Owens, progmg dir; Jean Hoffmann, chief of engrg, traf mgr.

***WVFL(FM)**— 2007: 89.9 mhz; 1 kw vert. Ant 384 ft TL: N43 48 09 W88 20 18. Hrs open:
Rebroadcasts WVCY-FM Milwaukee 100%.
3434 W. Kilbourn Ave., Milwaukee, 53208-3313. Phone: (414) 935-3000. Fax: (414) 935-3015.E-mail: vcy@vcyamerica.org Web Site:www.vcyamerica.org Licensee: VCY America Inc. Natl. Network: USA, . Format: Relg, Christian. ♦Vic Eliason, VP & gen mgr; Jim Schneider, progmg dir; Andy Eliason, chief of engrg.

Forestville

WRKU(FM)— Aug 1, 1999: 102.1 mhz; 6 kw. 328 ft TL: N44 46 58 W87 22 24. Hrs open: 3030 Park Dr., Suite 3, Sturgeon Bay, 54235. Phone: (920) 746-9430. Fax: (920) 746-9433.E-mail: info@doorradio.com Web Site:www.doorradio.com Licensee: Nicolet Broadcasting Inc. (group owner) Format: Oldies. News: 3 hrs wkly. ♦Roger Utnehmer, pres; Miles Knuteson, gen mgr, gen sls mgr, prom dir; Karen Leitzinger, opns mgr, progmg dir; John Focke, news dir; Kathy Robinson, traf mgr.

Fort Atkinson

WFAW(AM)— Jan 24, 1963: 940 khz; 500 w-D, 550 w-N, DA-2. TL: N42 54 24 W88 45 06. Hrs open: Box 94, 53538. Phone: (920) 563-9329. Fax: (920) 563-0315. Licensee: NRG License Sub. LLC. (group owner; (acq 10-31-2005; grpsl). Population served: 9,782 Natl. Rep: McGavren Guild,. Format: Sports, news/talk. News staff: one. ♦Mary Quass, CEO, VP; Chuck DuCoty, COO, stn mgr; Tami Gillmore, CFO; Jim Vriezen, gen mgr; Gary Douglas, opns dir, sports cmtr; Shane Sparks, sls VP, gen sls mgr, sports cmtr; Michael Clish, news dir, local news ed, news rptr; Ernie Swanson, chief of engrg; Lynette Furley, traf mgr; Jim Klug, sports cmtr; Jim King, disc jockey.

WSJY(FM)— Sept 4, 1959: 107.3 mhz; 26 kw. 676 ft TL: N42 50 48 W88 51 16. Stereo. Hrs open: 24 Prog sep from AM Box 2107, Janesville, 54547. Phone: (608) 756-0747. Fax: (608) 755-1252. Natl. Rep: McGavren Guild,. Format: Lite adult contemp. News staff: one. Target aud: 25-54. ♦Sonja Untz, traf mgr; Michael Clish, local news ed; Eric Stone, disc jockey.

Glenmore

WTAQ-FM— 2008: 97.5 mhz; 6 kw. Ant 328 ft TL: N44 24 35 W88 00 06. Hrs open: Box 23333, Green Bay, 54305-3333. Phone: (920) 435-3771. Fax: (920) 321-2300. Licensee: Midwest Communications Inc. (acq 7-28-2009; $1.725 million). ♦Duke Wright, pres.

Goodman

***WMVM(FM)**— May 3, 1993: Stn currently dark. 91.3 mhz; 422 w. Ant 118 ft TL: N45 37 36 W88 21 28. (CP: 90.7 mhz; 9 kw, ant 156 ft. TL: N45 46 27 W88 24 28). Hrs open: Box 212, Suring, 54174. Phone: (920) 842-2900. Fax: (920) 842-2704.E-mail: wrvm@wrvm.org Web Site:www.wrvm.org Licensee: WRVM Inc. (acq 9-11-02; $20,000). Format: Christian. ♦Michael A. Cornell, gen mgr; Bryan Hay, gen sls mgr; Dennis Jones, progmg dir; Alan Kilgore, chief of engrg.

Green Bay

WAPL(FM)—See Appleton

WDUZ(AM)— June 19, 1947: 1400 khz; 1 kw-U. TL: N44 29 36 W87 59 13. Hrs open: 24 810 Victoria St., 54302. Phone: (920) 468-4100. Fax: (920) 468-0250.E-mail: thefan@cumulus.com Web Site:www.thefan1075.com Licensee: Jacor Broadcasting Corp. Group owner: Cumulus Media Inc. (acq 4-10-2009; grpsl). Population served: 204,000 Natl. Network: ESPN Radio, ABC, Premiere Radio Networks, . Natl. Rep: Katz Radio,. Format: Sports. Target aud: 18-54; high income, male skew. ♦Greg Jessen, gen mgr; Jimmy Clark, opns mgr; Buck Hein, gen sls mgr, natl sls mgr; Bob Watts, progmg dir; Mark Heller, chief of engrg.

***WEMY(FM)**— Aug 26, 1974: 91.5 mhz; 710 w. 741 ft TL: N44 21 32 W87 59 07. Stereo. Hrs open: 24
Rebroadcasts WEMI(FM) Appleton 95%.
1909 W. 2nd St., Appleton, 54914. Phone: (920) 499-9957. Fax: (920) 749-0474. Web Site:www.christianfamilyradio.net Licensee: Evangel Ministries Inc. (group owner; acq 3-10-98). Population served: 200,000 Natl. Network: Salem Radio Network, USA, . Leventhal, Senter & Lerman. Format: Family Friendly. News: 10 hr wkly. Target aud: 25-54; women. ♦Peggy Ament, chmn; Paul Cameron, gen mgr; Andy Kilgas, opns dir, sls dir; Heidi Prahl, dev dir.

***WHID(FM)**— April 1997: 88.1 mhz; 17 kw. 1,023 ft TL: N44 21 32 W87 59 07. Stereo. Hrs open: 24 2420 Nicolet Drive, 54311. Phone: (920) 465-2444. Fax: (920) 465-2576.E-mail: nalbandian@wpr.org Web Site:www.wpr.org Licensee: Board of Regents of University of Wisconsin Systems. Population served: 300,000 Natl. Network: NPR, PRI, . Dow, Lohnes & Albertson. Format: Talk. News staff: one; News: 18 hrs wkly. Target aud: 35 plus; socially active, life-long learners. Spec prog: Hmong Public Radio, 2 hrs wkly. ♦Lisa Nalbandian, gen mgr.

WIXX(FM)— Nov 1, 1960: 101.1 mhz; 100 kw. 1,080 ft TL: N44 24 35 W88 00 05. Stereo. Hrs open: Box 23333, 54301. Secondary address: 115 South Jefferson St. 54301. Phone: (414) 435-3771. Fax: (414) 455-1155. Format: CHR. ♦Mary Kay Wright, gen sls mgr; Jeff McCarthy, progmg VP; Tony Wailckus, progmg dir.

WKSZ(FM)—(De Pere, Oct 1, 1984: 95.9 mhz; 4.5 kw. 774 ft TL: N44 21 32 W87 59 07. Stereo. Hrs open: 24 Box 1519, Appleton, 54912. Secondary address: 1263 main St., Suite #225 54301. Phone: (920) 431-0959. Fax: (920) 739-0494. Web Site:www.959kissfm.com Licensee: Woodward Communications Inc. (group owner; acq 1995). Population served: 192,200 Natl. Rep: McGavren Guild,. Hogan & Hartson. Format: Top-40. Target aud: 18-34; females. ♦Greg Bell, VP, gen mgr; Kelly Radandt, gen sls mgr; Dayton Kane, progmg dir; Steve Brown, chief of engrg.

WNFL(AM)— Dec 12, 1947: 1440 khz; 5 kw-D, 1 kw-N, DA-2. TL: N44 28 40 W88 00 00. Hrs open: 24 115 S. Jefferson St., 54301. Secondary address: Box 23333 54305. Phone: (920) 435-3771. Fax: (920) 444-1155. Licensee: Midwest Communications Inc. (group owner; acq 12-10-96; grpsl). Population served: 335,000 Natl. Network: Fox Sports, Westwood One, . Natl. Rep: Christal,. Miller & Neely. Wire Svc: AP Format: Sports. News staff: 4; News: 10 hrs wkly. Target aud: 35-64; people in upper-income level with above average education. ♦Duke Wright, pres, gen mgr; Gary Tesch, exec VP; Shelley Lukasik, gen sls mgr; Mark Daniels, progmg dir, progmg mgr; Jerry Bader, news dir; Tim Laes, chief of engrg.

***WORQ(FM)**— Feb 1, 1994: 90.1 mhz; 11 kw. Ant 646 ft TL: N44 21 32 W87 59 07. Hrs open: 24 1075 Brookwood Dr., 54304. Phone: (920) 494-9010. Fax: (920) 494-7602.E-mail: email@q90fm.com Web Site:www.q90fm.com Licensee: Lakeshore Communications Inc. Population served: 260,000 Natl. Network: USA, . Wiley, Rein & Fielding. Format: Christian. News: 7 hrs wkly. Target aud: 30; & under, rock and roll generation. ♦Mike LeMay, gen mgr; Jim Raider, gen sls mgr; Jim Kaider, progmg dir; Scott Grathen, chief of engrg; Jeff Rydell, traf mgr.

***WPNE(FM)**— Jan 15, 1973: 89.3 mhz; 100 kw. Ant 940 ft TL: N44 24 35 W88 00 05. Hrs open: 24 2420 Nicolet Dr., 54311-7001. Phone: (920) 465-2444. Fax: (920) 465-2576. Web Site:www.wpr.org Licensee: State of Wisconsin Educational Communications Board. Population served: 300,000 Natl. Network: NPR, PRI, . Rgnl. Network: Wis. Pub. Dow, Lohnes & Albertson. Format: Classical music, news. News staff: 2; News: 29 hrs wkly. Target aud: 35 plus; socially aware, artistically stimulated. Spec prog: Jazz 10 hrs, folk 3 hrs, Native American 2 hrs, blues 2 hrs, experimental 2 hrs, wkly. ♦Lisa Nalbandian, gen mgr & rgnl sls mgr.

WQLH(FM)— July 1, 1967: 98.5 mhz; 100 kw. 1,254 ft TL: N44 38 41 W88 08 13. Stereo. Hrs open: 810 Victoria St., 54302. Phone: (920) 468-4100. Fax: (920) 468-0250.E-mail: jimmy.clark@cumulus.com Web Site:www.star98.net Licensee: Citicasters Licenses Inc. Group

owner: Cumulus Media Inc. (acq 4-10-2009; grpsl). Population served: 681,000 Natl. Rep: Katz Radio,. Format: Hot AC. Target aud: Adults 25-54. ◆Jimmy Clark, pres, opns mgr, progmg dir; Greg Jessen, VP, gen mgr, mktg mgr; Buck Hein, gen sls mgr; Brian Stenzel, prom dir; Mark Heller, chief of engrg.

WTAQ(AM)— Apr 6, 1925: 1360 khz; 10 kw–D, 5 kw-N, DA-2. TL: N44 25 51 W88 04 51. Stereo. Hrs open: Box 23333, 54305. Secondary address: 1420 Bellevue St. 54311. Phone: (414) 435-3771. Fax: (414) 455-1155. Licensee: Midwest Communications Inc. (group owner; (acq 1975). Population served: 700,000 Natl. Network: CBS, . Natl. Rep: Christal,. Miller & Miller. Format: News/talk. News staff: 4. Target aud: 30 plus. Spec prog: Farm 5 hrs wkly. ◆D.E. Wright, pres, gen mgr; Gary Tesch, exec VP; Shelley LuKasik, gen sls mgr; Aaron Vorass, prom dir, prom mgr; Jerry Bader, progmg dir; Daniell Binna, news dir; Tim Laes, chief of engrg; Mike Austin, farm dir.

WZNN(FM)—See Allouez

Greenfield

WMCS(AM)—Licensed to Greenfield. See Milwaukee

Hallie

WOGO(AM)— June 1985: 680 khz; 2.5 kw-D, 500 w-N, DA-2. TL: N44 53 22 W91 23 03. Stereo. Hrs open: 24 2396 State Hwy. 53, Suite One, Chippewa Falls, 54729. Phone: (715) 723-1037. Fax: (715) 723-1348.E-mail: wwib@wwib.com Web Site:www.wwib.com Licensee: Stewards of Sound Inc. (Acq 10-29-93; with WWIB(FM) Ladysmith; 11-15-93). Population served: 200,000 Natl. Format: News/talk. News staff: one; News: 16 hrs wkly. Target aud: 25-54. ◆Greg Steward, sports cmtr.

WWIB(FM)— Dec 30, 1972: 103.7 mhz; 100 kw. 706 ft TL: N45 06 35 W91 09 43. Stereo. Hrs open: 24 2396 State Hwy. 53, Suite One, Chippewa Falls, 54729. Phone: (715) 723-1037. Fax: (715) 723-4626. Fax: (715) 723-1348.E-mail: wwib@wwib.com Web Site:www.wwib.com Licensee: Stewards of Sound Inc. (acq 10-29-93; with WOGO(AM) Hallie; 11-15-93). Population served: 980,000 Natl. Network: USA, . Format: Adult Christian contemp. News staff: one; News: 16 hrs wkly. Target aud: 25-54. ◆Terri Steward, gen mgr & stn mgr; Steven Slater, gen sls mgr; Greg Steward, progmg mgr; Mark Halvorsen, news dir.

Hartford

WTKM(AM)— 1951: 1540 khz; 500 w-D. TL: N43 16 48 W88 23 02. Hrs open: Sunrise-sunset Dups FM 100% Box 270216, 53027-0216. Secondary address: 27 N. Main St. 53027. Phone: (262) 673-3550. Phone: (262) 252-4567.E-mail: wtkm@inconnect.com Licensee: Kettle Moraine Broadcasting Co. Inc. Rgnl. Network: Agri-Net. Natl. Rep: Farmakis,. Agrinet

WTKM-FM— Oct 1, 1973: 104.9 mhz; 5.8 kw. Ant 300 ft TL: N43 16 48 W88 23 02. Stereo. Hrs open: 24 Box 270216, 53027-0216. Secondary address: 27 N. Main St. 53027. Phone: (262) 673-7800. Fax: (262) 673-5472.E-mail: wtkm@nconnect.net Web Site:www.wtkm.com Licensee: Kettle Moraine Broadcasting Co. Inc. (acq 3-12-90; grpsl;4-2-90). Population served: 1,500,000 Wire Svc: AP Format: Loc talk, classic country, polka. News staff: 2; News: 20 hrs wkly. Target aud: 35 plus. ◆Tom Shanahan, stn mgr.

Hayward

WHSM(AM)— Dec 21, 1957: 910 khz; 5 kw-D, 75 w-N. TL: N45 59 07 W91 32 21. Stereo. Hrs open: 24 16880 W. US Hwy. 63, 54843. Phone: (715) 634-4836. Phone: (800) 845-8984. Fax: (715) 634-8256.E-mail: radio@whsm.com Web Site:www.whsm.com Licensee: Red Rock Radio Corp. (acq 9-1-2006; grpsl). Population served: 40,000 Natl. Network: Jones Radio Networks, . Format: Adult Standards. News staff: one; News: 2 hrs wkly. Target aud: 34-70. ◆Ro Grignon, pres; Don Welch, exec VP, gen mgr, gen sls mgr; Bobi Hopp, opns mgr, progmg dir, traf mgr; Joe Lancello, news dir; Brent Christenson, chief of engrg.

WHSM-FM— June 21, 1980: 101.1 mhz; 1.45 kw. Ant 410 ft TL: N45 59 07 W91 32 23. Stereo. Hrs open: 24 16880 W. US Hwy. 63, 54843. Phone: (715) 634-4836. Phone: (800) 845-8984. Fax: (715) 634-8256.E-mail: radio@whsm.com Web Site:www.whsm.com Licensee: Red Rock Radio Corp. (acq 9-1-2006; grpsl). Natl. Network: Jones Radio Networks, . Format: Adult contemporary. News staff: one. Target aud: 24-60. ◆Ro Grignon, pres; Don Welch, VP, gen mgr; Bobi Hopp, opns mgr, traf mgr; Brent Christensen, chief of engrg.

WRLS-FM— Apr 16, 1968: 92.3 mhz; 6 kw. 321 ft TL: N46 01 17 W91 30 41. Stereo. Hrs open: 24 Box 1008, 10344 W. Radio Hill Rd., 54843. Phone: (715) 634-4871. Fax: (715) 634-3025.E-mail: wrls@cheqnet.net Web Site:www.wrlsfm.com Licensee: Vacationland Broadcasting Inc. (acq 12-9-92; 1-4-93). Population served: 25,000 Natl. Network: CNN Radio, AP Radio, . Wisconsin Radio Net. Wire Svc: AP Format: Adult contemp. News staff: one; News: news progrmg 10 hrs wkly. Target aud: 25 plus; general. ◆Tom Koser, pres; Robert Koser, VP; Steve Kaner, gen mgr; Grant Turpin, opns mgr.

Highland

*WHHI(FM)— Sept 14, 1952: 91.3 mhz; 100 kw. 560 ft TL: N43 02 58 W90 22 00. Hrs open: 24
Rebroadcasts WHA(AM) Madison 100%.
Wisconsin Public Radio, 821 University Ave., Madison, 53706-1496. Phone: (608) 263-3970. Fax: (608) 263-9763.E-mail: schnirring@wpr.org Web Site:www.wpr.org Licensee: State of Wisconsin Educational Communications Board. Natl. Network: NPR, PRI, . Dow, Lohnes & Albertson. Format: Educ, news/talk. News staff: 9. Target aud: 35-54; Skews female: issue oriented talk-variety of perspectives. ◆Phil Corriveau, gen mgr; Mary Kay Sherer, dev dir, prom dir; Steve Jorhnston, chief of engrg & traf mgr.

Holmen

WKBH(AM)— July 28, 1984: 1570 khz; 1 kw-D, 500 w-N. TL: N43 55 32 W91 16 02. Hrs open: 24 1407 2nd Ave. N., Onalaska, 54650. Phone: (608) 779-4418. Fax: (608) 779-4419.E-mail: WKBH@relevantradio.com Web Site:www.relevantradio.com Licensee: Starboard Media Foundation Inc. Group owner: Relevant Radio (acq 1-17-2003; $210,000). Smithwick & Belendiuk. Format: Catholic talk. News staff: one; News: 35 hrs wkly. Target aud: 40 plus; those interested in Catholic news, talk & opinion. ◆Jim DeSchepper, stn mgr; Mike Strub, opns mgr.

Hudson

WDGY(AM)— Dec 14, 1983: 740 khz; 1.1 kw-DA. TL: N44 58 05 W92 40 01. Hrs open: 6 AM-7 PM Box 25130, St. Paul, MN, 55125. Phone: (651) 436-4000. Fax: (651) 436-6770. Licensee: WRPX Inc. (acq 12-11-89; $300,000; 1-1-90). Format: Oldies. Target aud: 25-54. ◆Gregory Borgen, pres, gen mgr; Jeff Borgen, gen sls mgr; Tom Witschen, progmg dir; Paul Orth, chief of engrg.

WREY(AM)—Licensed to Hudson. See Minneapolis-St. Paul MN

Hurley

WHRY(AM)— Mar 1, 1985: 1450 khz; 1 kw-U. TL: N46 24 56 W90 09 34. Hrs open: Box 1450, 54534. Phone: (906) 932-5234. Fax: (906) 932-1548. Licensee: Big G Little O Inc. Format: Hits of the 50s, 60s & 70s. ◆Charles H. Gervasio, pres, gen mgr; Norma Rigoni, VP; Laura Keller, progmg dir.

Iron River

WNXR(FM)— November 1994: 107.3 mhz; 50 kw. 380 ft TL: N46 31 27 W91 16 18. Stereo. Hrs open: 24 2320 Ellis Ave., Ashland, 54806. Phone: (715) 372-5400. Fax: (715) 682-9338.E-mail: productionash@charter.net Web Site:www.wnxrfm.com Licensee: Heartland Communications License LLC. (group owner; (acq 4-23-2004; grpsl). Population served: 500,000 Natl. Network: Westwood One, . Format: Hits of the 50s, 60s & 70s. ◆Scott Jaeger, gen mgr; Rich Cannata, opns VP; Skip Hunter, progmg dir.

Jackson

WAUK(AM)— May 1, 1964: 540 khz; 400 w-U, DA-2. TL: N43 20 00 W88 09 11. Stereo. Hrs open: 24 770 N. Jefferson St., Milwaukee, 53202. Phone: (414) 273-3776. Fax: (414) 291-3776.E-mail: www.waukssportsradio@msn.com Web Site:www.espnmilwaukee.com Licensee: Good Karma Broadcasting LLC. Group owner: Salem Communications (acq 3-28-2008; $3.8 million). Population served: 1,500,000 Natl. Network: ESPN Radio, . Lance Riley. Format: Sports. ◆Craig Karmazin, gen mgr.

Janesville

WCLO(AM)— July 1930: 1230 khz; 1 kw-U. TL: N42 39 35 W89 02 32. Hrs open: 24 Box 5001, 53545. Secondary address: One S. Parker Dr. 53545. Phone: (608) 752-7895. Fax: (608) 752-4438.E-mail:

programming@wclo.com Web Site:www.wclo.com Licensee: Southern Wisconsin Broadcasting L.L.C. Group owner: Bliss Communications Inc. Population served: 136,000 Natl. Network: CNN Radio, Talk Radio Network, Premiere Radio Networks, Westwood One, . Wisconsin Radio Net. Dow, Lohnes & Albertson. Format: News/talk. News staff: 3; News: 9 hrs wkly. Target aud: General. ◆Robert Dailey, VP, gen mgr; Tim Bremel, progmg dir.

WJVL(FM)— October 1947: 99.9 mhz; 11 kw. 502 ft TL: N42 43 47 W89 10 10. Stereo. Hrs open: Prog sep from AM Box 5001, 5354. Secondary address: One S. Parker Dr. 53545. Phone: (608) 752-7895. Fax: (608) 752-4438. Web Site:www.wjvl.com Population served: 225,000 Format: country. Target aud: 25 plus. ◆Robert Dailey, exec VP, VP, gen mgr; Mike O'Brien, sls VP; Ken Scott, progmg dir; Stan Stricker, news dir.

WSJY(FM)—See Fort Atkinson

*WWJA(FM)—Not on air, target date: unknown: 91.5 mhz; 2.2 kw. Ant 387 ft TL: N42 43 47 W89 10 10. Hrs open: 4135 Northgate Blvd., Suite 1, Sacramento, CA, 95834-1226. Phone: (916) 641-8191. Fax: (916) 641-8238. Licensee: Family Stations Inc. ◆Peggy L. Renschler, gen mgr.

Kaukauna

WJOK(AM)— Sept 25, 1965: 1050 khz; 1 kw-D, 500 w-N, DA-2. TL: N44 14 51 W88 18 00. Hrs open: 24 1496 Bellevue St., Suite 202, Green Bay, 54311. Phone: (920) 469-3021. Fax: (920) 469-3023. Web Site:www.1050am.org Licensee: Starboard Media Foundation Inc. Group owner: Relevant Radio (acq 8-28-2001; $500,000). Population served: 867,000 Natl. Network: USA, Moody, . Leventhal, Senter & Lerman. Format: Catholic. Target aud: 35-54. Spec prog: Relg 2 hrs wkly. ◆Dave Nier, gen mgr.

WOGB(FM)— 1996: 103.1 mhz; 3.6 kw. 879 ft TL: N44 21 32 W87 59 07. Stereo. Hrs open: 24 810 Victoria St., Green Bay, 54302. Phone: (920) 468-4100. Fax: (920) 468-0250.E-mail: wogb@cumulus.com Web Site:www.wogb.fm Licensee: Jacor Broadcasting Corp. Group owner: Cumulus Media L.L.C. (acq 4-10-2009; grpsl). Natl. Rep: Katz Radio,. Wire Svc: AP Format: Greatest hits of the 70s. Target aud: 35-54; affluent baby-boomers, mid 40s. ◆Greg Jessen, VP, gen mgr, mktg mgr; Jimmy Clark, opns mgr; Buck Hein, sls dir, gen sls mgr; Dan Markus, progmg dir; Mark Heller, news dir & chief of engrg.

Kenosha

*WGTD(FM)— Dec 23, 1975: 91.1 mhz; 5 kw. 134 ft TL: N42 36 28 W87 50 55. Stereo. Hrs open: 3520 30th Ave., 53144. Phone: (262) 564-3800. Fax: (262) 564-3801.E-mail: coled@gtc.edu Web Site:wgtd.org Licensee: Gateway Technical College. Population served: 170,000 Natl. Network: NPR, . Wis. Public Radio Wire Svc: AP Format: News, classical music. News staff: 2. Target aud: General. Spec prog: Ger one hr wkly. ◆David Cole, gen mgr.

WIIL(FM)— 1961: 95.1 mhz; 50 kw. 384 ft TL: N42 33 10 W87 53 38. Stereo. Hrs open: Prog sep from AM 8500 Green Bay Rd., Pleasant Prairie, 53158. Phone: (262) 694-7800. Fax: (262) 694-7767.E-mail: info@95wiil.com Web Site:www.95wiil.com Licensee: NM Licensing LLC Format: Rock. Target aud: 18-54.

WLIP(AM)— May 11, 1947: 1050 khz; 250 w-U. TL: N42 33 10 W87 53 38. Hrs open: 24 8500 Green Bay Rd., Pleasant Prairie, 53158. Phone: (262) 694-7800. Fax: (262) 694-7767.E-mail: info@wlip.com Web Site:www.wlip.com Licensee: NM Licensing LLC. Group owner: NextMedia Group L.L.C. (acq 11-26-00; grpsl). Population served: 47,000 Rgnl. Network: Wisconsin Radio Net. Wisconsin Radio Net. Format: Talk. News staff: 2. Target aud: 35 plus. ◆Kara Lafond, gen mgr; John Perry, opns mgr, progmg dir; Rory Fraley, sls dir; Stewart Wattles, news dir; Lisa Sladek, traf mgr.

WWDV(FM)—See Zion, IL

Kewaunee

WAUN(FM)— 1973: 92.7 mhz; 6 kw. Ant 328 ft TL: N44 29 50 W87 35 12. Hrs open: 5 AM-10 PM 1021 N. Superior Ave., Suite 3, Tomah, 54660. Phone: (920) 388-9286. Fax: (920) 743-9183.E-mail: info@waun.com Licensee: Magnum Broadcasting Inc. (acq 12-2-98). Population served: 30,000 Wire Svc: AP Format: Smooth jazz. News staff: one; News: 15 hrs wkly. Target aud: 25-54. Spec prog: Czech one hr, farm 10 hrs, relg 3 hrs wkly. ◆Dave Magnum, pres; Frank Devillers, gen mgr, gen sls mgr; Rick Jensen, opns mgr, progmg dir & news dir; Debbie Doyle, traf mgr.

Kiel

***WSTM(FM)**—Not on air, target date: unknown: 91.3 mhz; 100 w hoirz, 1.25 kw vert. Ant 459 ft TL: N43 43 32 W88 03 07. Hrs open: Box 259, Plymouth, 53073. Phone: (920) 893-2661. Fax: (920) 892-2706.E-mail: wjub@excel.net Web Site:wjub.org Licensee: Jubilation Ministries Inc. Format: Christian. ♦Susan Noordyk, progmg dir.

Kimberly

WHBY(AM)— Dec 1, 1925: 1150 khz; 20 kw-D, 25 kw-N, DA-2. TL: N44 08 20 W88 32 46. Hrs open: 24 Box 1519, Appleton, 54912. Secondary address: 2800 E. College Ave., Appleton 54915. Phone: (920) 733-6639. Fax: (920) 739-0494.E-mail: whby@wcinet.com Web Site:www.whby.com Licensee: Woodward Communications Inc. (group owner; (acq 3-75). Population served: 305,000 Rgnl. Network: Wisconsin Radio Net. Natl. Rep: McGavren Guild,. Wisconsin Radio Net. Wire Svc: AP Format: News/talk. News staff: 3; News: 25 hrs wkly. Target aud: 35 plus; upper middle class, educated. ♦Greg Bell, gen mgr; John Wanie, stn mgr; Dave Edwards, progmg dir; Steve Brown, chief of engrg.

La Crosse

KQEG(FM)—(La Crescent, MN) Apr 5, 1989: 102.7 mhz; 4.3 kw. 863 ft TL: N43 44 53 W91 17 51. Stereo. Hrs open: 24 1407 Second Ave. N., Onalaska, 54650. Phone: (608) 782-8335. Fax: (608) 782-8340. Web Site:oldiesradioonline.net Licensee: White Eagle Broadcasting Inc. Group owner: La Crosse Radio Group (acq 2-4-2000; $2 million). Rgnl rep: O'Malley. Format: Oldies. News: 4 hrs wkly. Target aud: 25-54. ♦Pat Smith, gen mgr.

***WHLA(FM)**— Nov 21, 1950: 90.3 mhz; 100 kw. 1,010 ft TL: N43 48 17 W91 22 06. Stereo. Hrs open: 24
Rebroadcasts WHA(AM) Madison 95%.
Wisconsin Public Radio, 1725 State St, LaCrosse, 54601. Phone: (608) 785-8380. Fax: (608) 785-5005.E-mail: gaddo@wpr.org Web Site:www.wpr.org/whla Licensee: State of Wis. Educational Communications Board. Natl. Network: NPR, PRI, . Dow, Lohnes & Albertson. Wire Svc: AP Format: Educ, class, talk. News staff: 3. Target aud: 35-54; skews female: issue oriented talk-var of perspectives. ♦John Gaddo, gen mgr; Marv Spielman, dev dir; Steve Bauder, chief of engrg.

WIZM(AM)— Jan 2, 1923: 1410 khz; 5 kw-U, DA-N. TL: N43 50 48 W91 13 03. Hrs open: 24 Box 99, 201 State St., 54601. Phone: (608) 782-1230. Phone: (608) 796-2505. Fax: (608) 782-1170.E-mail: dickr@mwtbroadcasting.com Web Site:www.familybroadcasting.com Licensee: Family Radio Inc. Group owner: Mid-West Family Broadcast Group (acq 7-12-71; $500,000). Population served: 300,000 Natl. Network: Westwood One, CBS, . Natl. Rep: Christal,. Davis Wright Tremaine LLP. Wire Svc: AP Format: News/talk. News staff: 5; News: 18 hrs wkly. Target aud: 35 plus. Spec prog: Asian 2 hrs wkly. ♦Dick Record, pres, gen mgr; Howard Gloede, sls dir; Theresa Timm, gen sls mgr; Bill Black, rgnl sls mgr, reporter; Mike Hayes, prom mgr; Scott Robert Shaw, progmg dir, news dir; Keith Carr, pub affrs dir; Chris O'Hearn, chief of engrg; Peggy Schelbe, traf mgr; Brad Williams, news rptr; Mitch Reynolds, reporter; Bob Schmidt, sports cmtr.

WIZM-FM— 1966: 93.3 mhz; 100 kw. Ant 1,000 ft TL: N43 44 23 W91 22 04. Stereo. Hrs open: 24 Box 99, 54602-0099. Secondary address: 201 State St. 54601-3246. Phone: (608) 782-1230. Phone: (608) 796-2505. Fax: (608) 782-1170. Licensee: Family Radio Inc. (acq 6-15-76). Population served: 400,000 Wire Svc: AP Format: Top-40. News staff: 5; News: 2 hrs wkly. Target aud: 18-49. ♦Jen O'Brien, progmg dir, disc jockey; Mitch Reynolds, rsch dir, reporter; Peggy Schelbe, traf mgr; Scott Robert Shaw, local news ed; Brad Williams, news rptr; Brittany Styles, disc jockey.

WKBH-FM—(West Salem, Mar 15, 1982: 100.1 mhz; 3.6 kw. 426 ft TL: N43 51 02 W91 12 08. Stereo. Hrs open: 24 1407 2nd Ave., Onalaska, 54650. Phone: (608) 782-8335. Fax: (608) 782-8340. Licensee: Mississippi Valley Broadcasters LLC. Group owner: La Crosse Radio Group (acq 12-16-2000). Format: Classic rock. News staff: one. Target aud: 25-54. ♦Lee Norman, pres; Todd Wohlert, stn mgr.

WKTY(AM)— May 1948: 580 khz; 5 kw-D, 1 kw-N, DA-2. TL: N43 44 25 W91 12 21. Hrs open: 24 Box 99, 201 State St., 54601. Phone: (608) 782-1230. Fax: (608) 782-1170.E-mail: dickr@mwfbroadcasting.com Web Site:midwestfamilybroadcasting.com Licensee: Family Radio Inc. Group owner: The Mid-West Family Broadcast Group (acq 1996; $1.3 million). Population served: 500,000 Natl. Network: ABC, . Natl. Rep: Christal,. Davis Wright Tremaine LLP. Wire Svc: AP Format: Sports, talk. News staff: 5; News: 18 hrs wkly. Target aud: 25-54. Spec prog: Farm 5 hrs wkly. ♦Dick Record, pres, gen mgr; Howard Gloede, sls dir, gen sls mgr; Theresa Timm, gen sls mgr & rgnl sls mgr; Mike Kearns, prom dir, sports cmtr; Scott Robert Shaw, progmg dir, news dir; Keith Carr, pub affrs dir; Chris O'Hearn, chief of engrg; Peggy Schelbe, traf mgr; Brad Williams, news rptr; Pam Jahnke, farm dir.

WLFN(AM)— May 1947: 1490 khz; 1 kw-U. TL: N43 49 42 W91 14 27. Stereo. Hrs open: 24 Box 2017, 54602-2017. Secondary address: 1407 Second Ave. N., Onalaska 54650. Phone: (608) 782-8335. Fax: (608) 782-8340. Licensee: Mississippi Valley Broadcasters L.L.C. Group owner: La Crosse Radio Group. Population served: 96,500 Format: Original Hits. News staff: one; News: 5 hrs wkly. Target aud: 35 plus. ♦Pat Smith, gen mgr; Mike Schmitz, sls dir; Pete Schreier, progmg dir; Lucy Lemar, news dir; Patrick Delaney, chief of engrg; Laurie Lane, traf mgr.

***WLSU(FM)**— Jan 4, 1971: 88.9 mhz; 8.2 kw. Ant 928 ft TL: N43 48 17 W91 22 06. Stereo. Hrs open: 24 Wisconson Public Radio, 1725 State St., 54601. Phone: (608) 785-8380. Fax: (608) 785-5005.E-mail: gaddo@wpr.org Web Site:www.wpr.org/wlsu Licensee: University of Wisconsin System. Population served: 51,153 Natl. Network: NPR, PRI, . Rgnl. Network: Wis. Pub. Dow, Lohnes & Albertson. Wire Svc: AP Format: Class, jazz, news. News staff: 3; News: 40 hrs wkly. Target aud: General. ♦John Gaddo, gen mgr; Marvin Spielman, dev dir; John Davis, news dir.

WLXR-FM— March 1975: 104.9 mhz; 1.35 kw. 430 ft TL: N43 45 28 W91 17 26. (CP: 3.4 kw). Stereo. Hrs open: Box 2017, 54602. Secondary address: 1407 Second Ave. N. 54650. Phone: (608) 782-8335. Fax: (608) 782-8340. Web Site:www.wlxr.com Population served: 51,153 Format: Adult contemp. Target aud: 18-49. ♦Debbie Brague, progmg dir.

WQCC(FM)— Mar 31, 1994: 106.3 mhz; 12 kw. 476 ft Hrs open: 24 Box 2017, 54602-2017. Phone: (608) 782-1063. Phone: (608) 782-8335. Fax: (608) 779-5945.E-mail: wlxr/wqcc@aol.com Licensee: Mississippi Valley Broadcasters L.L.C. Group owner: La Crosse Radio Group (acq 12-31-96). Format: Country. ♦Pat Smith, gen mgr; Mike Schmitz, gen sls mgr; John Stevenson, progmg dir; Lucy Lemar, news dir; Patrick Delaney, chief of engrg.

WRQT(FM)— January 1972: 95.7 mhz; 50 kw. Ant 410 ft TL: N43 44 30 W91 18 14. Stereo. Hrs open: Box 99, 201 State St., 54602. Phone: (608) 782-1230. Fax: (608) 782-1170. Licensee: Family Radio Inc. (acq 1996). Population served: 350,000 Format: Active rock. News: 5 hrs wkly. Target aud: 18-49. ♦Jean Taylor, progmg dir; Scott Robert Shaw, news dir; Peggy Schelbe, traf mgr; Brad Williams, news rptr; Bill Black, reporter.

Ladysmith

WJBL(FM)— October 1984: 93.1 mhz; 4.9 kw. 358 ft TL: N45 27 59 W91 07 23. Stereo. Hrs open: 24 Box 351, 54848. Secondary address: W8746 Hwy. 8 54848. Phone: (715) 532-5588. Fax: (715) 532-7357.E-mail: wldy@centurytel.net Natl. Network: ABC, . Format: Oldies. News staff: one; News: 10 hrs wkly. Target aud: 25-54. ♦Tom Costello, local news ed; Robert Krejcarek, farm dir, sports cmtr, disc jockey; Sandy Zajec, women's int ed.

WLDY(AM)— September 1948: 1340 khz; 1 kw-U. TL: N45 27 52 W91 07 26. Hrs open: 24 Box 351, 54848-0351. Secondary address: W8746 Hwy. 8 54848. Phone: (715) 532-5588. Fax: (715) 532-7357.E-mail: wldy@centurytel.net Licensee: Roth Broadcasting Inc. (acq 1-9-2004; $924,722 with co-located FM). Population served: 100,000 Natl. Network: ABC, . Wire Svc: UPI Format: Country, news/talk. News staff: one; News: 15 hrs wkly. Target aud: 35 plus; mature audience. Spec prog: Polka 3 hrs wkly. ♦Sandra Roth, pres, gen mgr; David Roth, gen sls mgr, progmg dir; Jocelyn Kilmer, progmg dir; Del Dayton, chief of engrg; Judi Novak, traf mgr; Tom Costello, news dir & local news ed; Robert Krejcarek, farm dir, sports cmtr, disc jockey; Sandy Zajec, women's int ed.

Lake Geneva

WLKG(FM)— June 6, 1994: 96.1 mhz; 6 kw. 328 ft TL: N42 36 34 W88 26 36. Hrs open: 24 Box 996, 500 Interchange N., 53147. Phone: (262) 249-9600. Fax: (262) 249-9630.E-mail: lake96@wlkg.com Web Site:www.wlkg.com Licensee: CTJ Communications Ltd. Population served: 200,000 Shaw Pittman. Format: Hot adult contemp. News: 15 hrs wkly. Target aud: 25-54; mainly female. Spec prog: Hits of the 70s 10 hrs, sports 2 hrs wkly. ♦Tom Kwiatkowski, pres; Barb Kwiatkowski, VP; Nancy Douglass, gen mgr.

WZRK(AM)— May 15, 1964: Stn currently dark. 1550 khz; 1 kw-D, DA. TL: N42 35 40 W88 23 19. Hrs open: Box 272, Green Bay, 54305-0272. Secondary address: 2300 Riverside Dr., Green Bay 54301. Phone: (920) 271-1000. Fax: (920) 271-1010. Web Site:www.sovcity.com Licensee: Sovereign City Radio Services LLC Group owner: Relevant Radio (acq 11-17-2008; grpsl). Population served: 10,000 Rgnl. Network: Wis. Pub., Ill. Radio Net. Denise B. Moline. ♦Scott Krusinski, VP.

Lancaster

WGLR(AM)— Sept 9, 1977: 1280 khz; 500 w-D. TL: N42 50 22 W90 40 19. Hrs open: Box 587, 206 S. Sheridan St., 53813. Phone: (608) 723-7671. Fax: (608) 723-7674. Licensee: QueenB Radio Wisconsin Inc. Group owner: Morgan Murphy Stations (acq 3-18-98; $1.66 million with co-located FM). Format: C&W. Spec prog: Farm 10 hrs wkly. ♦Danny Sullivan, gen mgr; Doug Wagen, opns dir, news dir; Rick Sanson, sls dir, gen sls mgr; Rob Spangler, progmg dir.

WGLR-FM— Sept 9, 1982: 97.7 mhz; 11.5 kw. Ant 482 ft TL: N42 51 48 W90 42 11. Stereo. Hrs open: 24 51 Means Dr., Platteville, 53818. Phone: (608) 349-2000. Fax: (608) 349-2002.E-mail: wglrsales@queenbradio.com Web Site:www.wglr.com Licensee: QueenB Radio Wisconsin Inc. (acq 1998). Population served: 150,000 Natl. Network: ABC, Premiere Radio Networks, . Wisconsin Radio Net. Rgnl rep: Local Focus Format: Country. News: News prgmg 2 hrs per day. Target aud: 25-64. Spec prog: News, Sports and Agriculture. ♦Rob Spangler, progmg dir.

***WJTY(FM)**— Mar 12, 1983: 88.1 mhz; 7 kw horiz, 50 kw vert. Ant 476 ft TL: N42 57 08 W90 25 47. Stereo. Hrs open: 24 341 S. Washington, 53813. Phone: (608) 723-7888. Fax: (608) 723-4557.E-mail: info@wjty.org Web Site:www.wjty.org Licensee: Family Life Broadcasting Inc. (acq 5-23-2007; grpsl). Population served: 100,000 Natl. Network: Moody, USA, . Format: Relg, contemp, MOR. News staff: one; News: 11 hrs wkly. Target aud: 30-90; families. ♦Tom Bush, gen mgr & progmg dir; Dennis Baldridge, chief of engrg.

Lomira

WFDL-FM—Licensed to Lomira. See Fond du Lac

Madison

***WERN(FM)**— Mar 30, 1947: 88.7 mhz; 20.5 kw. Ant 990 ft TL: N43 03 18 W89 28 42. Stereo. Hrs open: 24 821 University Ave., 53706-1496. Phone: (608) 263-3970. Phone: (608) 263-4120. Fax: (608) 263-9763.E-mail: schnirring@wpr.org Web Site:www.wpr.org Licensee: State of Wisconsin Educational Communications Board. Natl. Network: NPR, PRI, . Rgnl. Network: Wis. Pub. Wis. Public Radio Format: News, classical. News staff: 9; News: 29 hrs wkly. Target aud: 25-64; persons seeking quality music & intellectual stimulation. ♦Phil Corriveau, gen mgr; Ben Spindler, dev dir; Anders Yokum, progmg dir; Vicki Nonn, mus dir & news dir.

***WHA(AM)**— 1922: 970 khz; 5 kw-D, 51 w-N. TL: N43 02 30 W89 24 31. Hrs open: 24 821 University Ave., 53706. Phone: (608) 263-3970. Fax: (608) 263-9763.E-mail: listener@wpr.org Web Site:www.wpr.org Licensee: Regents of University of Wisconsin System. Population served: 310,000 Natl. Network: NPR, PRI, . Rgnl. Network: Wis. Pub. Wis. Public Radio Wire Svc: NOAA Weather Format: Educ, talk, news. News staff: 9. Target aud: 35-54; male/female, educated, skews female: issue oriented talk-variety of perspectives. ♦Phil Corriveau, gen mgr; Tom Martin-Erickson, opns dir, opns mgr; Ben Spindler, dev dir, dev mgr; Anders Yokum, progmg dir; Vicki Nonn, mus dir. Co-owned TV: *WHA-TV affil

WHIT(AM)— Aug 14, 1964: 1550 khz; 5 kw-D, DA. TL: N43 00 08 W89 23 08. Hrs open: 24 Box 44408, 53744. Secondary address: 730 Rayovac Dr. 53711. Phone: (608) 273-1000. Fax: (608) 271-0400. Web Site:www.wtux.com Licensee: Mid-West Management Inc. Group owner: The Mid-West Family Broadcast Group (acq 8-12-97; $6.4 million with WWQM-FM Middleton). Population served: 173,258 Natl. Network: ABC, . Natl. Rep: McGavren Guild,. Format: Music from the 50s and 60s. Target aud: 25-54. ♦Tom Walker, pres & gen mgr; Ted Waldbillig, sls dir, chief of engrg; Amy Ziebel, progmg dir.

WIBA(AM)— Apr 2, 1925: 1310 khz; 5 kw-U, DA-N. TL: N42 59 53 W89 25 42. Stereo. Hrs open: 2651 S. Fish Hatchery Rd., 53711. Phone: (608) 274-5450. Fax: (608) 274-5521.E-mail: info@wiba.com Web Site:www.wiba.com Licensee: Capstar TX L.P. Group owner: Clear Channel Communications Inc. (acq 8-30-2000; grpsl). Population served: 176,258 Natl. Network: CBS, Wall Street, . Dow, Lohnes & Albertson. Format: News/talk. Target aud: 25-64. ♦Jeff Tyler, gen mgr, opns mgr; Kurt Peterson, sls dir; Tim Scott, progmg dir; Josh Wescott, news dir; Tim Wagner, chief of engrg; Marta Keller, traf mgr.

WIBA-FM— Mar 1947: 101.5 mhz; 12 kw. Ant 1,014 ft TL: N43 03 21 W89 32 06. Stereo. Hrs open: 2651 S. Fish Hatchery Rd., 53711. Phone: (608) 274-5450. Fax: (608) 274-5521.E-mail: info@wibafm.com

Web Site:www.wibafm.com Licensee: Capstar TX L.P. Format: Classic rock. ♦Mike Ferris, progmg dir; Jennie Hibbard, traf mgr.

WLMV(AM)— September 1948: 1480 khz; 5 kw-U, DA-N. TL: N43 01 30 W89 23 48. Stereo. Hrs open: 24 Box 2058, 53701. Secondary address: 2740 Ski Ln. 53713. Phone: (608) 273-1000. Fax: (608) 271-0400. Licensee: Mid-West Management Inc. Group owner: The Mid-West Family Broadcast Group. Population served: 50,000 Natl. Rep: McGavren Guild,. Shaw Pittman. Format: Sp. Target aud: General; Latino community. ♦Thomas A. Walker, pres & gen mgr; Ted Waldbillig, sls VP, gen sls mgr; Luis Montoto, progmg dir; Tara Arnold, news dir; John Bauer, chief of engrg.

WMAD(FM)—(Sauk City, Sept 18, 1964: 96.3 mhz; 5.1 kw. Ant 672 ft TL: N43 12 37 W89 35 57. Stereo. Hrs open: 24 2651 S. Fish Hatchery Rd., 53711. Phone: (608) 274-5450. Fax: (608) 274-5521.E-mail: info@wmad.com Web Site:www.wmad.com Licensee: Capstar TX L.P. Group owner: Clear Channel Communications Inc. (acq 8-30-2000; grpsl). Natl. Rep: Christal,. Leventhal, Senter & Lerman. Format: Alternative. News staff: one; News: one hr wkly. Target aud: 25-49. ♦Jeff Tyler, gen mgr; Hugh Garret, gen sls mgr; Brad Savage, progmg dir; Joshua Wescott, news dir; Cliff Groth, chief of engrg; Jacqueline Forney, traf mgr.

WMGN(FM)— September 1948: 98.1 mhz; 38 kw. 581 ft TL: N42 57 46 W89 22 46. Stereo. Hrs open: 24 Prog sep from AM 2740 Ski Ln., 53713. Phone: (608) 271-1000. Fax: (608) 271-8182.E-mail: info@magic98.com Web Site:www.magic98.com Licensee: Mid-West Management Inc. Population served: 50,000 Natl. Rep: McGavren Guild,. Shaw Pittman. Format: Adult contemp. Target aud: 25-54. ♦Tom Walker, gen mgr; Ted Waldbillig, sls dir; Pat O'Neill, progmg dir.

WNWC(AM)—See Sun Prairie

***WNWC-FM**— Apr 30, 1959: 102.5 mhz; 50 kw. 460 ft TL: N43 02 07 W89 30 25. Stereo. Hrs open: 5606 Medical Cir., 53719. Phone: (608) 271-1025. Fax: (608) 271-1150.E-mail: wnwc@nwc.edu Web Site:www.life1025.com Licensee: Northwestern College. Group owner: Northwestern College & Radio (acq 1-19-73). Population served: 173,258 Natl. Network: AP Radio, . Wire Svc: AP Format: Contemp Christian Music. News staff: one; News: 20 hrs wkly. Target aud: 35-45. ♦Greg Walters, gen mgr.

WOLX-FM—(Baraboo, Mar 3, 1946: 94.9 mhz; 37 kw. 1,299 ft TL: N43 25 40 W89 39 14. Stereo. Hrs open: 24 7601 Ganser Way, 53719. Phone: (608) 826-0077. Fax: (608) 826-1244.E-mail: info@wolx.com Web Site:www.wolx.com Licensee: Entercom Madison Licensee LLP. Group owner: Entercom Communications Corp. (acq 7-10-00; grpsl). Population served: 1,985,856 Natl. Rep: Christal,. Rosenman & Colin. Format: Oldies. News staff: 2; News: 2 hrs wkly. Target aud: 25-54. ♦David Field, pres; Ed Schulz, VP; Michael Weber, CFO & opns mgr; Lindsay Wood Davis, mktg mgr.

***WORT(FM)**— Dec 1, 1975: 89.9 mhz; 2 kw. 900 ft TL: N43 03 01 W89 29 15. Stereo. Hrs open: 24 118 S. Bedford St., 53703. Phone: (608) 256-2695/256-2001. Fax: (608) 256-3704.E-mail: wort@wort-fm.org Web Site:www.wort-fm.org Licensee: Back Porch Radio Broadcasting Inc. Population served: 350,000 Format: Div, class. News staff: one; News: 3 hrs wkly. Target aud: 25-34. Spec prog: Black 3 hrs, jazz 15 hrs wkly. ♦Norman Stockwell, opns dir; Rachel Pundsack, dev dir; Sybil Augustine, mus dir; Nathan Moore, news dir.

***WSUM(FM)**— 2003: 91.7 mhz; 5.5 kw. Ant 338 ft TL: N42 54 16 W89 33 20. Hrs open: 24 Box 260020, 53726-0020. Phone: (608) 262-1864. Web Site:www.wsum.org Licensee: Board of Regents of the University of Wisconsin. Format: Educ. ♦Dave Black, gen mgr.

WTDY(AM)— 1998: 1670 khz; 10 kw-D, 1 kw-N. TL: N43 01 30 W89 23 48. Hrs open: 24 Box 44408, 53744. Secondary address: 730 Rayovac Dr. 53711. Phone: (608) 273-1000. Fax: (608) 271-8182.E-mail: glen@wtdy.com Web Site:www.wtdy.com Licensee: Mid-West Management Inc. Group owner: The Mid-West Family Broadcast Group Natl. Rep: McGavren Guild,. Shaw Pittman. Format: News/talk. News staff: 5; News: 15 hrs wkly. Target aud: 25-54; young to middle aged males. ♦Tom Walker, pres & gen mgr; Ted Waldbillig, sls dir; Glen Gardner, progmg dir; Tara Arnold, news dir; John Bauer, chief of engrg.

WTSO(AM)— January 1948: 1070 khz; 10 kw-D, 5 kw-N, DA-2. TL: N42 59 45 W89 18 50. Hrs open: 24 2651 S. Fishhatchery Rd., 53711. Phone: (608) 274-5450. Fax: (608) 274-5521.E-mail: info@espn1070.com Web Site:www.espn1070.com Licensee: Capstar TX L.P. Group owner: Clear Channel Communications Inc. (acq 8-30-2000; grpsl). Population served: 731,900 Rgnl. Network: Wisconsin Radio Net. Wisconsin Radio Net. Dow, Lohnes & Albertson. Format: Sports. News staff: 6. Target aud: 25-54. Spec prog: Farm 20 hrs wkly. ♦Jeff Tyler, gen mgr, opns mgr; Kurt Peterson, sls dir; Tim Scott, progmg mgr; Tim Wagner, chief of engrg; Jennie Hibbard, traf mgr.

WWQM-FM—See Middleton

WXXM(FM)—See Sun Prairie

WZEE(FM)— 1948: 104.1 mhz; 9.4 kw. 1,119 ft TL: N43 03 09 W89 28 42. Stereo. Hrs open: 24 Prog sep from AM 2651 S. Fishhatchery Rd., 53711. Phone: (608) 274-5450. Fax: (608) 274-5521.E-mail: info@z104fm.com Web Site:www.z104fm.com Population served: 285,700 Format: Adult contemp, CHR. News staff: 2; News: one hr wkly. ♦Tommy Bodean, progmg dir.

Manitowoc

WCUB(AM)—(Two Rivers, November 1952: 980 khz; 5 kw-U, DA-2. TL: N44 03 50 W87 41 49. Hrs open: 24 Box 1990, 54221-1990. Secondary address: 1915 Mirro Dr. 54220. Phone: (920) 683-6800. Fax: (920)683-6807. Web Site:www.cubradio.com Licensee: Cub Radio Inc. (acq 1-1-61). Population served: 33,000 Natl. Rep: Katz Radio,. Format: C&W, farm. News staff: 2; News: 16 hrs wkly. Target aud: 35 plus. ♦Lee Davis, pres, gen mgr & gen sls mgr; Dean Lester, progmg dir; Bryan Lundberg, news dir.

WGBW(AM)—See Two Rivers

WLTU(FM)— Sept 1, 1966: 92.1 mhz; 3.7 kw. 420 ft TL: N44 07 31 W87 37 41. Stereo. Hrs open: 24 Box 1990, 54221. Secondary address: 1915 Mirro Dr. 54220. Phone: (920) 683-6800. Fax: (920) 683-6807. Web Site:www.cubradio.com Population served: 18,000 Natl. Rep: Katz Radio,. Format: Oldies. News staff: one. Target aud: 25-64. ♦Lee Davis, gen mgr & stn mgr.

WOMT(AM)— Nov 8, 1926: 1240 khz; 1 kw-U. TL: N44 07 31 W87 37 41. Hrs open: 24 Box 1385, 3730 Mangin St., 54221-1385. Phone: (920) 682-0351. Fax: (920) 682-1008.E-mail: info@womtradio.com Web Site:www.womtradio.com Licensee: Seehafer Broadcasting Corp. (acq 1-1-70). Population served: 150,000 Natl. Network: CBS, . Wisconsin Radio Net. Miller & Neely. Wire Svc: AP Format: Full service, adult contemp, MOR. News staff: 2; News: 45 hrs wkly. Target aud: 25-64; business executives, males/females. Spec prog: News 18 hrs wkly. ♦Don Seehafer, pres, gen mgr; Kent Reeves, stn mgr; Russ Matar, gen sls mgr; Scott Johnson, progmg dir; Joel Nelson, chief of engrg; Courtney Hermson, traf mgr; Brian Norton, local news ed.

WQTC-FM— Nov 19, 1965: 102.3 mhz; 3 kw. 328 ft TL: N44 07 31 W87 37 41. Stereo. Hrs open: 24 Prog sep from AM Box 1385, 3730 Mangin St., 54221-1385. Phone: (920) 682-0351. Fax: (920) 682-1008. Web Site:www.womtradio.com Licensee: Seehafer Broadcasting Corp. Population served: 150,000 Natl. Network: Jones Radio Networks, . Wisconsin Radio Net. Miller & Neely. Wire Svc: AP Format: Classic hits. News staff: 8; News: 8 hrs wkly. Target aud: 18-49. ♦Mark Seehafer, VP; Kent Reeves, stn mgr; Joel Nelson, chief of engrg; Courtney Hermson, traf mgr.

Marathon

WKQH(FM)— 1988: 104.9 mhz; 21 kw. Ant 358 ft TL: N44 50 13 W89 45 57. Stereo. Hrs open: 500 Division St., Stevens Point, 54481. Phone: (715) 341-9800. Fax: (715) 341-0000.E-mail: rmuzzy@1010wspt.com Web Site:www.b1049.com Licensee: RLM Communications Inc. Group owner: Muzzy Broadcasting L.L.C. (acq 1994; $150,000). Population served: 210,600 Format: Country. News staff: 3. Target aud: 25-54; adult. ♦Richard Muzzy, gen mgr; Rob West, progmg dir; Scott Krueger, news dir; Jim Zastnow, chief of engrg; Geri Butler, traf mgr.

Marinette

WAGN(AM)—See Menominee, MI

WHYB(FM)—See Menominee, MI

WLST(FM)— Sept 1, 1976: 95.1 mhz; 100 kw. Ant 436 ft TL: N45 03 48 W87 39 26. Stereo. Hrs open: 24 413 10th Ave., Menominee, 59859. Phone: (906) 863-5551. Fax: (906) 863-5679. Licensee: Armada Media - Menominee Inc. Population served: 450,000 Format: Country. Target aud: 35-64. ♦Joe Callow, gen mgr.

WMAM(AM)— Oct 8, 1939: 570 khz; 250 w-D, 100 w-N. TL: N45 06 02 W87 37 30. Hrs open: 24 N. 2880 Roosevelt Rd., 54143. Phone: (715) 735-6631. Fax: (715) 732-0125. Licensee: Armada Media - Menominee Inc. (group owner; (acq 12-19-2006; grpsl). Natl. Network: CBS, . Rgnl. Network: Wisconsin Radio Net., Goetz Group. Natl. Rep: Michigan Spot Sales,. Wisconsin Radio Net. Format: Talk, sports. News staff: one; News: 4 hrs wkly. Target aud: 25 plus; upscale. Spec prog: Milwaukee Brewers, Green Bay Packers, farm 3 hrs wkly. ♦Shawn Katzbeck, gen mgr & gen sls mgr; Jim Medley, progmg dir; Chuck Gennaro, chief of engrg; Lisa Bougie, traf mgr.

Marshall

***WJWD(FM)**— 2003: 90.3 mhz; 51 w horiz, 9.9 kw vert. Ant 312 ft TL: N43 20 40 W89 06 10. Hrs open: 152 McCrae Rd., Fall River, 53932. Phone: (920) 484-6220. Fax: (920) 484-3753.E-mail: wjwd@centurytel.net Licensee: CSN International (group owner). Format: Relg. ♦Patrick Lannoye, gen mgr & opns mgr.

Marshfield

WDLB(AM)— Feb 2, 1947: 1450 khz; 1 kw-U. TL: N44 41 49 W90 09 20. Hrs open: 24 1714 N. Central Ave., 54449. Phone: (715) 384-2191. Fax: (715) 387-3588. Web Site:wdlbwosq.com Licensee: Seehafer Broadcasting Corp. (group owner; (acq 6-1-2006; swap with WOSQ(FM) Spencer and WFHR(AM) Wisconsin Rapids for WBCV(FM) Wausau) Population served: 150,000 Natl. Network: ABC, Westwood One, . Rgnl. Network: Goetz Group. Brownfield Miller & Fields, P.C. Format: News/talk, sports, ac. News staff: 2. Target aud: 25-54. ♦Don Seehafer, pres; Kent Reeves, gen mgr, opns mgr; Arnie Peck, gen sls mgr, adv VP; Mike Warren, news dir; Chuck Gennaro, engrg dir.

WYTE(FM)— Dec 1, 1965: 106.5 mhz; 100 kw. Ant 800 ft TL: N44 38 41 W89 51 11. Stereo. Hrs open: 2301 Plover Rd., Plover, 54467. Phone: (715) 341-8838. Fax: (715) 341-9744.E-mail: info@wyte.com Web Site:www.wyte.com Licensee: NRG License Sub, LLC. (acq 10-31-2005; grpsl). Population served: 300,000 Natl. Rep: McGavren Guild,. Format: Country. Target aud: 25-54. ♦Benjamin D. Rosenthal, gen mgr; Mark Skibba, opns mgr; Bob Jung, rgnl sls mgr.

Mauston

WRJC(AM)— Jan 4, 1962: 1270 khz; 500 w-D. TL: N43 49 52 W90 04 51. Hrs open: 24 Box 200, Fairway Ln., 53948. Phone: (608) 847-6565. Fax: (608) 847-6249.E-mail: deb@wrjc.com Web Site:wrjc.com Licensee: WRJC Broadcasting Co. (acq 2-15-86; 12-23-85). Population served: 110,000 Natl. Network: CBS, . Natl. Rep: Rgnl Reps,. Womble, Carlyle, Sandridge & Rice. Wire Svc: AP Format: Oldies. News staff: one; News: 8 hrs wkly. Target aud: 35 plus; general. ♦Rick Charles, pres, gen mgr & gen sls mgr; Greg Lawrence, prom VP, mus dir; June Gill, news dir; Ken Ebneter, chief of engrg.

WRJC-FM— 1976: 92.1 mhz; 2 kw. Ant 571 ft TL: N43 47 16 W90 11 52. Stereo. Hrs open: 24 Prog sep from AM Box 200, Fairway Ln., 53948. Phone: (608) 847-6565. Fax: (608) 847-6249.E-mail: deb@wrjc.com Web Site:www.wrjc.com Licensee: WRJC Inc. Natl. Network: CBS Radio, . Wire Svc: AP Format: Adult contemp. News staff: one; News: 10 hrs wkly. Target aud: 18 plus; adults. ♦Rick Charles, CEO.

Mayville

WMDC(FM)— Oct 31, 1998: 98.7 mhz; 6 kw. 246 ft TL: N43 28 53 W88 28 45. Hrs open: 24 132 N. Main St., 53050. Phone: (920) 387-0000. Fax: (920) 387-2222.E-mail: bigsky@wmdcfm.com Web Site:www.great98.com Licensee: Radio Plus Inc. Format: Hits of the 60s & 70s. News staff: one. Target aud: 25-54. ♦Tom Biolo, gen mgr; Norm Grey, gen sls mgr.

Medford

WIGM(AM)— Oct 26, 1941: 1490 khz; 1 kw-U, DA-1. TL: N45 07 55 W90 19 54. Hrs open: 24 Box 59, 54451. Secondary address: 630 S. 8th 54451. Phone: (715) 748-2566.E-mail: k99@k99wigm.com Web Site:www.k99wigm.com Licensee: WIGM Inc. (acq 6-55). Population served: 175,000 Natl. Network: ESPN Radio, . Wire Svc: AP Format: Sports. News staff: one; News: 14 hrs wkly. Target aud: 21 plus. Spec prog: Farm 10 hrs wkly. ♦Brad Dahlvig, pres, gen mgr; Karen Dahlvig, sls dir; Paula Liske, news dir; Del Dayton, chief of engrg.

WKEB(FM)— September 1967: 99.3 mhz; 23 kw. Ant 342 ft TL: N45 07 55 W90 19 54. Stereo. Hrs open: 24 Box 59, 54451. Secondary address: 630 S. 8th 54451. Phone: (715) 748-2566.E-mail: k99@k99wigm.com Licensee: WIGM Inc. Population served: 300,000 Natl. Network: ABC, . Wire Svc: AP Format: Top-40. ♦Brad Dahlvig, CEO; Del Dayton, sls VP, engrg VP; Karen Dahlvig, sr VP, dev dir, sls VP & mktg dir.

Menomonee Falls

WJMR-FM— June 26, 1956: 98.3 mhz; 6 kw. 364 ft TL: N43 02 49 W88 07 25. (CP: Ant 292 ft.). Stereo. Hrs open: 24 5407 W. McKinley Ave., Milwaukee, 53208-2540. Phone: (414) 978-9000. Fax: (414) 978-9001. Web Site:www.wjmr.com Licensee: Lakefront Communications LLC. Group owner: Saga Communications Inc. (acq 4-24-97; $5 million with WJZX(FM) Brookfield). Population served: 1,600,000 Natl. Rep: Katz Radio,. Smithwick & Belendiuk. Format: Urban adult comtemp. News staff: one; News: 4 hrs wkly. Target aud: 25 plus. ♦Tom Joerres, pres, gen mgr; Traci Northrop, gen sls mgr; LaTonya Lucas, prom dir; Lauri Jones, progmg dir; Phil Longenecker, chief of engrg; Cris Ruid, traf mgr.

Menomonie

***WHWC(FM)**— June 28, 1950: 88.3 mhz; 70 kw. Ant 1,050 ft TL: N45 02 47 W91 51 42. Hrs open: 24
Rebroadcasts WHAD(FM) Delafield 90%.
1221 W. Clairemont Ave., Eau-Claire, 54701. Secondary address: 821 University Ave., Madison 53706-1496. Phone: (715) 839-3868. Fax: (715) 839-2939. Web Site:www.wpr.org Licensee: State of Wisconsin Educational Communications Board. Natl. Network: NPR, PRI, . Rgnl. Network: Wis. Pub. Wis. Public Radio Dow, Lohnes & Albertson. Format: Educ, talk. Target aud: 35-54. Spec prog: Folk 7 hrs wkly. ♦Dean Kallenbach, gen mgr, dev dir; Mary Jo Wagner, news dir.

WMEQ(AM)— May 1951: 880 khz; 10 kw-D, 210 w-N. TL: N44 48 48 W91 55 34. Stereo. Hrs open: 24 619 Cameron Street, Eau Claire, 54703. Phone: (715) 830-4000. Fax: (715) 835-9680. Web Site:www.wmeq.com Licensee: Capstar TX L.P. Group owner: Clear Channel Communications Inc. (acq 2000; grpsl). Population served: 100,000 Natl. Network: CBS Radio, . Natl. Rep: Clear Channel,. Format: News/talk, sports. News staff: 2. Target aud: 25 plus. ♦Rick Hencley, VP, gen mgr; Jare Jordan, opns mgr, progmg dir; Steve Potter, gen sls mgr; Paul Orth, chief of engrg; Trina Butak, traf mgr.

WMEQ-FM— July 19, 1967: 92.1 mhz; 50 kw. Ant 718 ft TL: N44 54 59 W91 41 55. Stereo. Hrs open: 24 Prog sep from AM 619 Cameron Street, Eau Claire, 54703. Phone: (715) 830-4000. Fax: (715) 835-9680. Web Site:www.rock921.com Licensee: Capstar TX LP Population served: 250,000 Natl. Rep: Clear Channel,. Format: Classic rock. News staff: 2. Target aud: 25-54. ♦Rick Hencley, VP, sls dir; Jare Jordan, opns dir, opns mgr, progmg dir; Steve Potter, gen sls mgr; Paul Orth, chief of engrg; Trina Butak, traf mgr.

***WVSS(FM)**— Apr 22, 1969: 90.7 mhz; 590 w. Ant 426 ft TL: N44 54 56 W92 04 34. Stereo. Hrs open: 24
Rebroadcasts WERN(FM) Madison 90%.
1221 W. Clairemont Ave., Eau-Claire, 54701. Phone: (715) 839-3868. Fax: (715) 839-2939. Licensee: Board of Regents, University of Wisconsin Systems. Population served: 11,275 Rgnl. Network: Wisconsin Radio Net. Wis. Public Radio Format: Class, news/talk. Target aud: 45-64. Spec prog: Folk 6 hrs, jazz 5 hrs wkly. ♦Dean Kallenbach, gen mgr.

Merrill

***WHJL(FM)**—Not on air, target date: unknown: 88.1 mhz; 63 kw. Ant 584 ft TL: N45 20 48.5 W89 38 53.5. Hrs open: Box 212, Suring, 54174-0212. Phone: (920) 842-2900. Fax: (920) 842-2704.E-mail: wrvm@wrvm.org Web Site:www.wrvm.org Licensee: WRVM Inc. ♦Elwood R. Anderson, pres; Michael A. Cornell, gen mgr.

WJMT(AM)— May 10, 1960: 730 khz; 1 kw-D, 127 w-N. TL: N45 10 45 W89 38 20. Hrs open: 24 120 S. Mill St., 54452-2508. Phone: (715) 536-6262. Fax: (715) 536-6208. Licensee: Quicksilver Broadcasting LLC. Group owner: Badger Communications L.L.C. Population served: 120,000 Natl. Rep: D & R Radio,. Format: Adult contemp, MOR, talk. News staff: one. Target aud: 35-59. Spec prog: Relg 3 hrs, farm 7 hrs, Pol 3 hrs wkly. ♦David Winters, pres; Steven Resnick, gen mgr; Christine Vorpagel, gen sls mgr; Nick Summers, progmg dir; Joe Weniger, news dir; Chuck Genarro, chief of engrg.

WMZK(FM)— Aug 25, 1968: 104.1 mhz; 24 kw. Ant 617 ft TL: N45 06 14 W89 43 05. Stereo. Hrs open: 24 120 S. Mill St., 54452-2508. Phone: (715) 536-6262. Fax: (715) 536-6208.E-mail: advertising@z104rocks.com Web Site:www.z104rocks.com Licensee: Quicksilver Broadcasting LLC. Population served: 350,000 Format: Rock/AOR. News staff: one. Target aud: 18-49.

Middleton

WHIT(AM)—See Madison

WWQM-FM— Oct 20, 1970: 106.3 mhz; 4.5 kw. Ant 374 ft TL: N43 03 03 W89 29 13. Stereo. Hrs open: 24 Box 2058, Madison, 53701. Phone: (608) 273-1000. Fax: (608) 271-8182. Web Site:www.q106.com Licensee: Mid-West Management Inc. Group owner: The Mid-West Family Broadcast Group (acq 8-15-97; $6.4 million with WHIT(AM) Madison). Population served: 173,258 Natl. Rep: McGavren Guild,. Shaw Pittman. Format: Country. Target aud: 25-54; general. ♦Thomas A. Walker, pres & gen mgr; Ted Waldbillig, gen sls mgr; Brad Austin, progmg dir, progmg mgr; John Bauer, chief of engrg.

Milladore

***WGNV(FM)**— Feb 13, 1986: 88.5 mhz; 50 kw. 584 ft TL: N44 38 37 W89 50 48. Stereo. Hrs open: 24
94.1 Antigo.
Box 88, Country Rd. N., 54454. Phone: (715) 457-2988. Fax: (715) 457-2987.E-mail: wgnv@christianfamilyradio.net Web Site:christianfamilyradio.net Licensee: Evangel Ministries Inc. Natl. Network: Moody, Salem Radio Network, . Leventhal, Senter & Leman. Format: Christian adult contemp. News: 10 hrs wkly. Target aud: Women; 35-49. Spec prog: Children 4 hrs wkly. ♦Paul Cameron, gen mgr; Karen Bencke, opns dir; Bill Schumacher, adv mgr, sls; Mark Bystrom, progmg dir; Todd Christopher, mus dir; Vicky Hofkens, engrg dir & traf mgr.

Milwaukee

WAUK(AM)—See Jackson

WHQG(FM)— October 1960: 102.9 mhz; 50 kw. Ant 440 ft TL: N43 02 49 W87 58 52. Stereo. Hrs open: 24 5407 W. McKinley Ave., 53208. Phone: (414) 978-9000. Fax: (414) 978-9001. Web Site:www.1029thehog.com Format: Active rock. ♦Annmarie Topel, sls dir; Scott Schubert, prom dir; Keith Hastings, progmg dir, disc jockey; Stacey Kolterjahn, traf mgr.

WISN(AM)— 1922: 1130 khz; 50 kw-D, 10 kw-N, DA-2. TL: N42 45 18 W88 04 53. Hrs open: 24 12100 W. Howard Ave., Greenfield, 53228. Phone: (414) 545-8900. Fax: (414) 327-3200.E-mail: info@newstalk1130.com Web Site:www.newstalk1130.com Licensee: Capstar TX L.P. Group owner: Clear Channel Communications Inc. (acq 8-30-2000; grpsl). Population served: 1,000,000 Natl. Network: Fox News Radio, Premiere Radio Networks, . Format: Talk, news. News staff: 4. Target aud: 25-54. ♦Cindy McDowell, gen mgr; Jay Daily, sls dir; Phil Kurth, gen sls mgr; Jerry Bott, progmg dir; Harold Mester, news dir; Al Hajny, chief of engrg; Shannon Lippert, traf mgr.

WJYI(AM)— 1955: 1340 khz; 1 kw-U. TL: N43 02 49 W87 58 52. Hrs open: 24 5407 W. McKinley Ave., 53208. Phone: (414) 978-9000. Fax: (414) 978-9001. Web Site:www.joy1340.com Licensee: Lakefront Communications LLC. Group owner: Saga Communications Inc. (acq 2-23-94; $7 million with co-located FM;3-14-94). Population served: 800,000 Natl. Network: CBS, . Format: Contemporary Christian. Target aud: 18-54. ♦Tom Joerres, pres & gen mgr; Ryan Salzer, opns mgr; Phil Longenecken, chief of engrg; Stacey Kolterjahn, traf mgr.

WKKV-FM—See Racine

WKLH(FM)— 1958: 96.5 mhz; 21.24 kw. 810 ft TL: N43 05 48 W87 54 19. Stereo. Hrs open: 24 5407 W. McKinley Ave., 53208. Phone: (414) 978-9000. Fax: (414) 978-9001. Web Site:www.wklh.com Licensee: Lakefront Communications LLC. Group owner: Saga Communications Inc. (acq 7-18-90). Population served: 500,000 Natl. Rep: Katz Radio,. Smith & Belendiuk. Format: Classic hits. News staff: one. Target aud: 35-54; baby boomers. ♦Tom Joerres, pres & gen mgr; Annmarie Topel, sls dir, gen sls mgr; Scott Schubert, prom dir; Bob Bellini, progmg dir; Carole Caine, news dir; Phil Longenecker, chief of engrg; Stacey Kolterjahn, traf mgr.

WLDB(FM)— June 1958: 93.3 mhz; 12.6 kw. Ant 992 ft TL: N43 05 15 W87 54 12. Stereo. Hrs open: 24 N72 W12922 Good Hope Rd., Menomonee Falls, 53051-4441. Phone: (414) 778-1933. Fax: (414) 771-3036.E-mail: info@b933fm.com Web Site:www.b933fm.com Licensee: Milwaukee Radio Alliance L.L.C. (group owner; (acq 9-23-97; grpsl). Format: Soft rock. Target aud: 25-54; general. ♦Willie D. Davis, chmn; William R. Lynett, pres; Bill Hurwitz, gen mgr; Traci Northrup, opns dir, gen sls mgr; Stan Atkinson, progmg dir, news dir; John Church, chief of engrg; Tiffany Dlugi, traf mgr.

WLUM-FM— September 1960: 102.1 mhz; 20 kw. Ant 761 ft TL: N43 05 48 W87 54 19. Stereo. Hrs open: N72 W12922 Good Hope Rd., Menomonee Falls, 53051-4441. Phone: (414) 771-1021. Fax: (414) 771-3036.E-mail: info@fm1021milwaukee.com Web Site:www.fm1021milwaukee.com Licensee: Milwaukee Radio Alliance LLC Population served: 275,000 Wire Svc: CBS Format: Rock. Target aud: 18-49; teens & adults. ♦Bill Hurwitz, gen mgr; Jerry Arndt, sls dir, natl sls mgr; Traci Northrop, gen sls mgr; Tommy Wilde, progmg dir; Stan Atkinson, news dir; John Church, chief of engrg; Tiffany Dlugi, traf mgr.

WLWK-FM— June 1959: 94.5 mhz; 15.5 kw. Ant 911 ft TL: N43 05 29 W87 54 07. Stereo. Hrs open: 24 720 E. Capitol Dr., 53212. Secondary address: Box 693 53201. Phone: (414) 332-9611. Fax: (414) 967-5266.E-mail: info@wkti.com Web Site:www.945lakefm.com Licensee: Journal Broadcast Corp. Population served: 305,800 Format: Adult hits. News staff: one. Target aud: 25-54. ♦Jon Schweitzer, stn mgr; Bob Walker, progmg dir; Lisa Letterman, mktg VP & rsch dir. Co-owned TV: WTMJ-TV affil

WMCS(AM)—(Greenfield, Apr 27, 1947: 1290 khz; 5 kw-U, DA-2. TL: N42 55 11 W87 59 17. Stereo. Hrs open: 24 4222 W. Capitol Dr., 53216. Secondary address: N72 W12922 Good Hope Road, Menomonee Falls 53051. Phone: (414) 444-1290. Fax: (414) 444-1409.E-mail: BHurwitz@Milwaukeeradio.com Web Site:www.1290wmcs.com Licensee: Milwaukee Radio Alliance L.L.C. (group owner; (acq 9-23-97; grpsl). Population served: 75,000 Format: Talk. News staff: one; News: 7 hrs wkly. Target aud: 25-54; upwardly mobile Blacks. Spec prog: Blues 6 hrs, gospel 5 hrs, Sp 5 hrs, church 3.25 hrs wkly. ♦Robbie Fulton, gen sls mgr; John Church, chief of engrg.

WMIL(FM)—See Waukesha

***WMSE(FM)**— Mar 14, 1981: 91.7 mhz; 1 kw. 125 ft TL: N43 02 43 W87 54 57. (CP: 3.2 kw, ant 128 ft.). Stereo. Hrs open: 24 1025 N. Broadway, 53202. Phone: (414) 277-7247. Fax: (414) 277-7149. Web Site:www.wmse.org Licensee: Milwaukee School of Engineering. Population served: 1,000,000 Format: Mix. Target aud: 18-35; young adults. Spec prog: Black 13 hrs, jazz 15 hrs, It 3 hrs, Sp 3 hrs, class 3 hrs wkly. ♦Tom Crawford, gen mgr.

***WMWK(FM)**— Dec 7, 1990: 88.1 mhz; 170 w. 955 ft TL: N43 05 24 W87 53 47. Stereo. Hrs open: 24 290 Hegenberger Rd., Oakland, CA, 94621. Secondary address: Box 11552, 1100 E. Capitol Dr., Shorewood 53211. Phone: (414) 964-9794. Phone: (800) 543-1495. Licensee: Family Stations Inc. (group owner) Format: Christian. ♦Harold Camping, pres; John Rorvik, gen mgr.

WMYX(FM)— Nov 1, 1962: 99.1 mhz; 50 kw. 450 ft TL: N42 56 44 W88 03 39. Stereo. Hrs open: Prog sep from AM 11800 W. Grange Ave., Hales Corners, 53130. Phone: (414) 529-1250. Fax: (414) 529-2122. Web Site:www.99wmyx.com Population served: 1,200,000 Natl. Network: Westwood One, . Natl. Rep: D & R Radio,. Format: Hot adult contemp. Target aud: 25-49; women. Spec prog: Relg one hr wkly. ♦Tom Gjerdrum, progmg mgr; Jane Matenaer, pub affrs dir.

WNOV(AM)— Aug 15, 1946: 860 khz; 250 w-D, 5 w-N. TL: N43 02 20 W87 54 17. (CP: TL: N43 04 20 W87 57 07). Hrs open: Box 06438, 3815 N. Teutonia Ave., 53206. Phone: (414) 449-9668. Fax: (414) 449-9945.E-mail: wnov860@yahoo.com Web Site:www.wnov.com Licensee: Courier Communications Corp. (acq 1-2-73). Population served: 717,099 Format: Urban contemp. ♦Jerrel W. Jones, CEO, pres; Sandra Robinson, gen mgr & opns mgr; Homer Blow, progmg dir; Amari Brown, news dir.

WOKY(AM)— 1947: 920 khz; 5 kw-D, 1 kw-N, DA-2. TL: N42 58 32 W88 03 56. Stereo. Hrs open: 24 12100 W. Howard Ave., Greenfield, 53228. Phone: (414) 545-8900. Fax: (414) 327-3200. Web Site:www.am920thewolf.com Licensee: Clear Channel Radio Licenses Inc. Group owner: Clear Channel Communications Inc. (acq 3-17-97; $40 million with WMIL(FM) Waukesha). Population served: 230,000 Natl. Network: CBS Radio, . Natl. Rep: Clear Channel,. Wire Svc: AP Format: Classic country. News staff: 3; News: 15 hrs wkly. Target aud: 35-64. ♦Cindy McDowell, VP, stn mgr; Jay Dailey, sls dir; Enid Parkinson, gen sls mgr, prom dir; Gregory Jon, progmg dir, mus dir; Terry James, progmg dir & news dir; Al Hajny, chief of engrg; Barb Fagnat, traf mgr.

WQBW(FM)— January 1961: 97.3 mhz; 15.5 kw. Ant 980 ft TL: N43 06 41 W87 55 38. Stereo. Hrs open: 24 12100 W. Howard Ave., Greenfield, 53228. Phone: (414) 545-8900. Fax: (414) 327-3200.E-mail: info@1973thebrew.com Web Site:www.l973thebrew.com Licensee: Capstar TX L.P. Population served: 717,099 Natl. Network: ABC, . ♦Randy Wanek, sls dir; Jeff Lynn, progmg dir.

WRIT-FM— May 10, 1961: 95.7 mhz; 34 kw. 610 ft TL: N43 05 25 W87 54 54. Stereo. Hrs open: 12100 W. Howard Ave., Greenfield, 53228-0920. Phone: (414) 944-5150. Fax: (414) 329-2587. Licensee: Clear Channel Radio Licenses Inc. Group owner: Clear Channel Communications Inc. (acq 10-97; $14.5 million). Population served: 633845 Natl. Rep: Clear Channel,. Format: Adult Hits. Target aud: 25-54; baby boomers. ♦Cindy McDowell, gen mgr; Jeff Lynn, stn mgr, progmg dir; Kerry Wolfe, opns mgr; Keith Bratel, gen sls mgr; Ken Kohl, prom dir; Harold Mester, news dir; Al Hajny, chief of engrg; Marvy Quesnell, traf mgr.

WSSP(AM)— Oct 14, 1935: 1250 khz; 5 kw-U, DA-2. TL: N42 56 44 W88 03 39. Hrs open: 24 11800 W. Grange Ave., Hales Corners, 53130. Phone: (414) 529-1250. Fax: (414) 529-2122. Licensee: Entercom Milwaukee License LLC. Group owner: Entercom Communications Corp. (acq 12-13-99; grpsl). Population served: 110,000 Akin, Gump, Strauss, Hauer & Feld. Format: Christian radio. Target aud: 25-49. Spec prog: Relg 3 hrs, Ger 8 hrs, Sp 3 hrs wkly. ♦Craig Hodgson, gen mgr; Alan Kirshbom, sls dir; Andrea Biebel, natl sls mgr; Jim Morales, prom dir; Glenn Redd, progmg dir, progmg mgr; Michael Clemens, news dir; Chris Tarr, chief of engrg.

WTMJ(AM)— July 25, 1927: 620 khz; 50 kw-D, 10 kw-N. TL: N43 01 56 W88 07 54. Stereo. Hrs open: 720 E. Capitol Dr., 53212. Secondary address: Box 693 53201. Phone: (414) 332-9611. Fax: (414) 967-5378.E-mail: info@620wtmj.com Web Site:www.620wtmj.com Licensee: Journal Broadcast Corp. Group owner: Journal Broadcast Group Inc. Population served: 1,820,000 Natl. Network: ABC, . Natl. Rep: Christal,. Hogan & Hartson. Format: News/talk, sports. Target aud: General. Spec prog: Relg 2 hrs wkly. ♦Doug Kiel, CEO; Jon Schweitzer, gen mgr, chief of engrg; Rick Belcher, opns VP, progmg dir; Jeff Kuether, sls VP; Diana Paul, mktg VP; Dan Shelley, news dir; Randy Price, engrg VP; Susan Petropoullis, traf mgr.

***WUWM(FM)**— Sept 24, 1964: 89.7 mhz; 15 kw. 871 ft TL: N43 05 24 W87 53 47. Stereo. Hrs open: 24 Milwaukee Public Radio, Box 413, 53201. Secondary address: John Plankinton Bldg., 161 W. Wisconsin Ave., Suite LL1000 53202. Phone: (414) 227-3355. Fax: (414) 270-1297.E-mail: wuwm@uwm.edu Web Site:www.wuwm.com Licensee: Board of Regents of University of Wisconsin. Natl. Network: PRI, NPR, . Format: News, AAA. News staff: 12. Target aud: General. ♦Dave Edwards, CEO, gen mgr; Noel Skarpmoen, dev dir; Bruce Winter, progmg dir; Tom May, chief of engrg.

***WVCY-FM**— 1961: 107.7 mhz; 43 kw. Ant 528 ft TL: N42 57 46 W88 04 23. Stereo. Hrs open: 24 3434 W. Kilbourn Ave., 53208. Phone: (414) 935-3000. Fax: (414) 935-3015.E-mail: wvcyfm@vcyamerica.org Web Site:www.vcyamerica.org Licensee: VCY/America Inc. (group owner; (acq 1-70). Natl. Network: USA, Moody, . Format: Relg, Christian. ♦Dr. Randall Melchert, pres; Victor Eliason, VP & gen mgr; Gordon Morris, opns mgr, news dir; Jim Schneider, progmg dir.

WXSS(FM)—See Wauwatosa

***WYMS(FM)**— Mar 5, 1973: 88.9 mhz; 1.5 kw. Ant 870 ft TL: N43 05 21 W87 53 47. Stereo. Hrs open: 24 5312 W. Vliet St., 53208. Phone: (414) 475-8890. Fax: (414) 475-8413.E-mail: info@radiomilwaukee.org Web Site:www.radioformilwaukee.org Licensee: Milwaukee Board of School Directors. Hogan & Hartson. Wire Svc: AP Format: AAA. Target aud: 20-40.

Minocqua

WLKD(AM)— Aug 1, 1978: 1570 khz; 5 kw-D, 500 w-N. TL: N45 49 13 W89 43 27. Stereo. Hrs open: 24 3616 Hwy. 47 N., Rhinelander, 54501. Phone: (715) 362-1975. Fax: (715) 362-1973. Web Site:www.am1570wlkd.com Licensee: Raven License Sub. LLC. Group owner: NewRadio Group LLC (acq 10-31-2005; grpsl). Population served: 40,000 Natl. Network: Fox News Radio, . Natl. Rep: Katz Radio,. Leventhal, Senter & Lerman. Wire Svc: Wheeler News Service Format: Music of your life. News staff: one. Target aud: 35 plus. ♦Duff Damos, opns mgr; Steve Albertson, stn mgr, gen sls mgr & rgnl sls mgr.

WMQA-FM— Apr 3, 1975: 95.9 mhz; 25 kw. Ant 289 ft TL: N45 52 14 W89 42 35. Stereo. Hrs open: 24 3613 Hwy. 47 N., Rhinelander, 54501. Phone: (715) 362-1975. Fax: (715) 362-2450.E-mail: wmqa@n5gnorthwoods.net Web Site:www.wmqa.com Licensee: Raven License Sub. LLC. Leventhal, Senter & Lerman. Wire Svc: Wheeler News Service Format: Oldies. News staff: one; News: 18 hrs wkly. Target aud: 25-54. ♦Duff Damos, opns dir; Steve Albertson, gen sls mgr; Dave Imlah, progmg dir.

Mishicot

WZOR(FM)— Dec 17, 1994: 94.7 mhz; 21.5 kw. Ant 354 ft TL: N44 20 30 W87 47 10. Hrs open: 24 Box 1519, Appleton, 54912. Secondary address: 2727 E. Radio Rd., Appleton 54915. Phone: (920) 734-9226. Fax: (920) 733-2391.E-mail: razor@wcinet.com Web Site:www.razor947.com Licensee: Woodward Communications Inc. (group owner; acq 1-27-00). Population served: 350000 Natl. Rep: McGavren Guild,. Hogan & Hartson. Format: Active rock. Target aud: 18-34; men. ♦Greg Bell, gen mgr; Kelly Radandt, gen sls mgr; Roxanne Steele, progmg dir.

Monroe

WEKZ(AM)— July 27, 1951: 1260 khz; 1 kw-D, 19 w-N. TL: N42 35 41 W89 35 35. Hrs open: 24 W4765 Radio Ln., 53566. Phone: (608) 325-2161. Fax: (608) 325-2164.E-mail: wekz@wekz.com Web Site:www.wekz.com Licensee: Green County Broadcasting Corp. (acq 4-96; $1,445,000). Population served: 225,000 Natl. Network: ABC, . Format: Country classic. News staff: 4; News: 16 hrs wkly. Target aud: 50 plus. Spec prog: Ger 3 hrs, Swiss 3 hrs wkly. ♦Kent McConnell, opns mgr, gen sls mgr; Wyatt Herrmann, progmg dir; Don Jacobson, news dir; Todd Hausser, chief of engrg; Becky Koester, traf mgr.

WEKZ-FM— June 1959: 93.7 mhz; 36 kw. 581 ft TL: N42 34 36 W89 41 34. Stereo. Hrs open: 24 Prog sep from AM W4765 Radio Ln., 53566. Phone: (608) 325-2161. Fax: (608) 325-2164. Web Site:www.bigradio.fm Licensee: Ronald M. Spielman, Scott A. Thompson dba Green County Broadcasting. (Acq 2-28-96). Population served: 720,000 Natl. Network: ABC, . Format: Adult contemp. News staff: 4; News: 10 hrs wkly. Target aud: 35-55. ♦Kent McConnell, opns mgr; Wyatt Herrmann, progmg dir; Don Jacobson, news dir; Todd Hausser, chief of engrg; Becky Koester, traf mgr.

Mosinee

WOFM(FM)— Oct 7, 1991: 94.7 mhz; 50 kw. Ant 492 ft TL: N44 59 18 W89 59 42. Stereo. Hrs open: 24
Simulcast with WIZD(FM) Rudolph 100%.
557 Scott St., Wausau, 54403. Phone: (715) 842-1672. Fax: (715) 848-3158.E-mail: info@947thepeak.com Web Site:www.lovethevalley.com Licensee: WRIG Inc. Group owner: Midwest Communications Inc. (acq 9-24-97; $35,000 for 70%). Population served: 212,000 Natl. Rep: Christal,. Format: Adult hits. News staff: one; News: 2 hrs wkly. Target aud: 25-54; upscale baby boomers. ♦Duke Wright, pres; Gary Tesch, exec VP; Brett Lucht, gen mgr; Jim Schroeder, gen sls mgr; Chad Edwards, progmg dir; Frank Zastrow, engrg VP, chief of engrg; Melanie Comeau, traf mgr.

Mount Horeb

WWQN(FM)— October 2004: 106.7 mhz; 2.9 kw. Ant 479 ft TL: N43 00 19 W89 52 25. Hrs open:
Simulcast with WWQM-FM Middleton 100%.
Box 2058, Madison, 53701. Phone: (608) 273-1000. Fax: (608) 271-8182. Web Site:www.q106.com Licensee: Mid-West Management Inc. (acq 3-20-2003; $2,166,000 for CP). Natl. Rep: McGavren Guild,. Format: Country. Target aud: 25-54; general. ♦Tom Walker, gen mgr; Ted Waldbillig, gen sls mgr; Brad Austin, progmg dir; John Bauer, chief of engrg.

Mukwonago

***WKMZ(FM)**— 2002: 105.3 mhz; 1.65 kw. Ant 633 ft TL: N42 58 05 W88 11 20. Hrs open: 24 2351 Sunset Blvd., Suite 170-218, Rocklin, CA, 95765. Phone: (916) 251-1600. Fax: (916) 251-1650. Web Site:www.klove.com Licensee: Educational Media Foundation. Group owner: Salem Communications Corp. (acq 5-30-2008; $8.05 million). Natl. Network: K-Love, . Format: Contemp Christian. ♦Mike Novak, pres.

Neenah-Menasha

WNAM(AM)— May 23, 1947: 1280 khz; 5 kw-U. TL: N44 09 36 W88 27 57. Stereo. Hrs open: 24 491 S. Washburn, Suite 400, Oshkosh, 54904. Phone: (920) 426-3239. Fax: (920) 231-0145.E-mail: info@1280wnam.com Web Site:www.1280wnam.com Licensee: Cumulus Broadcasting L.L.C. Group owner: Cumulus Media L.L.C. (acq 6-30-97; grpsl). Population served: 375,000 Rgnl. Network: Goetz Group. Format: Adult Standards. News staff: 3; News: 13 hrs wkly. Target aud: 35 plus. ♦Jeffrey A. Schmidt, gen mgr; Larry Phillip, sls dir.

WNCY-FM— Sept 9, 1977: 100.3 mhz; 45 kw. 489 ft TL: N44 15 27 W88 11 41. Stereo. Hrs open: 24 Box 23333, Green Bay, 54305. Secondary address: 115 S. Jefferson St., Green Bay 54301. Phone: (920) 435-3771. Fax: (920) 444-1155.E-mail: info@wncy.com Web Site:www.wncy.com Licensee: Midwest Communications Inc. (group owner; acq 12-10-96; grpsl). Population served: 820,000 Format: Country. ♦D.E. Wright, pres; Jeff McCarthy, VP; Craig Von Able, gen sls mgr; Dan Stone, progmg dir; Jerry Bader, news dir; Tim Laes, engrg dir & chief of engrg.

WROE(FM)— November 1971: 94.3 mhz; 13 kw. 459 ft TL: N44 09 30 W88 17 03. Stereo. Hrs open: Box 23333, Green Bay, 54305. Phone: (920) 435-3771. Fax: (920) 444-1155.E-mail: info@mci.fm Web Site:www.mci.fm Licensee: Midwest Communications Inc. (group owner; acq 12-10-96; grpsl). Population served: 27,600 Format: Soft adult contemp. Target aud: 25-54. ♦Duke Wright, CEO, gen mgr; David Fries, gen sls mgr; Jenny Lawrence, progmg dir; Jerry Bader, news dir, traf mgr; Tim Laes, chief of engrg.

WWWX(FM)—See Oshkosh

Neillsville

WCCN(AM)— Sept 22, 1957: 1370 khz; 5 kw-D, 42 w-N. TL: N44 34 18 W90 35 15. Hrs open: 24 Box 387, 1201 E. Division St., 54456. Phone: (715) 743-2222. Phone: (715) 743-3333. Fax: (715) 743-2288.E-mail: 1075therock@tds.net Web Site:memories1370.com Licensee: Central Wisconsin Broadcasting Inc. (group owner; acq 12-87;3-25-91). Population served: 380,400 Natl. Network: ABC, . Rgnl. Network: Wisconsin Radio Net. Wisconsin Radio Net. Miller & Neely P.C. Format: Big Band, nostalgia. News staff: one; News: 20 hrs wkly. Target aud: 45 plus. Spec prog: Farm 19 hrs, Polka 2 hrs wkly. ♦J. Kevin Grap, pres; Margaret L. Grap, VP.

WCCN-FM— July 1964: 107.5 mhz; 100 kw. Ant 577 ft TL: N44 35 30 W90 37 09. Stereo. Hrs open: 24 Prog sep from AM Box 387, 1201 E. Division St., 54456. Phone: (715) 743-2222. Fax: (715) 743-2288.E-mail: 1075therock@tds.net Web Site:www.1075therock.com Population served: 1,000,000 Format: Rock. News staff: one. Target aud: 25-40.

WPKG(FM)— February 2004: 92.7 mhz; 3.4 kw. Ant 440 ft TL: N44 35 30 W90 37 09. Hrs open: 24 Box 387, 54456. Phone: (715) 743-3333. Fax: (715) 743-2288. Web Site:927wpkg.com Licensee: Central Wisconsin Broadcasting Inc. (group owner). Natl. Network: ABC, . Format: Hot adult contemp. Target aud: 18+; Females. ♦J. Kevin Grap, gen mgr.

Nekoosa

WMMA(FM)— 2002: 93.9 mhz; 18 kw. Ant 367 ft TL: N44 13 23 W89 49 46. Hrs open: 24 Box 1103, Wisconsin Rapids, 54495. Secondary address: 645 25th Ave N, Wisconsin Rapids 54495. Phone: (715) 424-5050. Fax: (715) 424-5656.E-mail: wmma@relevantradio.com Web Site:www.relevantradio.com Licensee: Starboard Media Foundation Inc. Group owner: Relevant Radio (acq 12-20-2001; $2.3 million with WIBU(AM) Wisconsin Dells). Format: Relg. ♦Jack O'Keefe, gen mgr.

WRCW(FM)— 2003: 105.5 mhz; 6 kw. Ant 279 ft TL: N44 21 45 W90 03 58. Hrs open: 645 25th Ave. N., Wisconsin Rapids, 54495. Phone: (715) 424-1300. Fax: (715) 424-1347. Web Site:www.wrcwfm.com Licensee: Seehafer Broadcasting Corp. (acq 3-5-2008; $270,000). Format: Kool Gold. ♦Donald Seehafer, pres; Kent Reeves, opns mgr; Jeff Sigler, gen sls mgr.

New London

WOZZ(FM)— Oct 6, 1967: 93.5 mhz; 50 kw. 528 ft TL: N44 21 35 W88 42 46. (CP: Ant 492 ft.). Stereo. Hrs open: 24 1500 N. Casaloma Dr., Suite 307, Appleton, 54913-8220. Phone: (920) 733-4990. Fax: (920) 733-5507. Web Site:www.wozz.com Licensee: Midwest Communications of Iowa Inc. Group owner: Midwest Communications Inc. (acq 6-30-93; $1.85 million with WZBY(FM) Sturgeon Bay;7-26-93). Population served: 837,000 Format: Classic rock. News staff: 2; News: 8 hrs wkly. Target aud: 25-44. ♦David Fries, gen mgr, gen sls mgr, gen sls mgr; David Louis, progmg dir.

New Richmond

WIXK(AM)—Licensed to New Richmond. See Minneapolis-St. Paul MN

Oconto

WOCO(AM)— Mar 11, 1966: 1260 khz; 1 kw-D. TL: N45 53 31 W87 57 18. Hrs open: 3829 Hwy.22, 54153. Phone: (920) 834-3540. Fax: (920) 834-3532.E-mail: wocoamfm@bayland.net Licensee: Lamardo Inc. (acq 3-25-99; with co-located FM). Population served: 15,000 Format: C&W, var. Target aud: 29 plus. ♦Larry Kaszynski, gen sls mgr, adv mgr, mus dir, sports cmtr, disc jockey; Terri Kaszynski, rgnl sls mgr, prom mgr, news dir, spec ev coord, local news ed, disc jockey; Dorothy Kaszynski, progmg dir, women's int ed; Walter P. Kaszynski, pres, gen mgr, chief of engrg & farm dir; Walter Kaszynski, disc jockey.

WOCO-FM— Aug 1, 1968: 107.1 mhz; 3 kw. 210 ft TL: N44 53 31 W87 57 18. Hrs open: Dups AM 40% 3829 Hwy. 22, 54153. Phone: (920) 834-3540. Fax: (920) 834-3532.E-mail: wocoamfm@bayland.net Licensee: Lamardo Inc. Population served: 25,000 Format: Easy lstng.

♦Terri Kaszynski, spec ev coord, local news ed, disc jockey; Walter P. Kaszynski, farm dir; Larry Kaszynski, sports cmtr, disc jockey; Dorothy Kaszynski, women's int ed; Walter Kaszynski, disc jockey.

Omro

WPKR(FM)—Licensed to Omro. See Oshkosh

Oshkosh

WOSH(AM)— Dec 31, 1941: 1490 khz; 1 kw-U. TL: N44 02 46 W88 31 44. Hrs open: 491 S. Washburn St., Suite 400, 54904. Phone: (920) 426-3239. Fax: (920) 231-0145.E-mail: woshnews@cumulus.com Web Site:www.cumulus.com Licensee: Cumulus Broadcasting Inc. Group owner: Cumulus Media LLC. (acq 9-1-97; grpsl). Population served: 53,221 Rgnl. Network: Goetz Group. Natl. Rep: D & R Radio,. Format: News/talk, sports. Target aud: 25 plus. ♦Jeffrey Schmidt, gen mgr; Larry Phillip, gen sls mgr; John Stiloski, prom dir; Bob Burnell, progmg dir; Jonathan Krause, news dir; Steve Griesbach, chief of engrg; Alexandra Marohn, traf mgr.

WPKR(FM)—(Omro, July 12, 1990: 99.5 mhz; 50 kw. 420 ft TL: N43 50 51 W88 51 31. Stereo. Hrs open: 24 491 S. Washburn St., Suite 400, 54904. Phone: (920) 426-3239. Fax: (920) 231-0145.E-mail: info@wpkr.com Web Site:wpkr.com Licensee: Cumulus Licensing LLC. Group owner: Cumulus Media Inc. (acq 11-10-2003; $8.1 million with WPCK(FM) Denmark). Format: Country. News staff: one; News: 2 hrs wkly. Target aud: 25-54. Spec prog: Farm one hr wkly. ♦Jeff Schmidt, gen mgr.

***WRST-FM**— Apr 20, 1966: 90.3 mhz; 960 w. 125 ft TL: N44 01 45 W88 33 08. Stereo. Hrs open: 800 Algoma Blvd., 54901. Phone: (920) 424-3113. Phone: (920) 424-1234. Fax: (920) 424-1279. Licensee: Board of Regents, University of Wisconsin System. Population served: 60,000 Natl. Network: NPR, . Rgnl. Network: Wis. Pub. Wis. Public Radio Wire Svc: Wheeler News Service Format: Div. Target aud: General. ♦Ben Jarman, gen mgr; Kelly Bougneit, stn mgr.

WVBO(FM)—(Winneconne, Sept 1, 1966: 103.9 mhz; 25 kw. 318 ft TL: N44 02 47 W88 31 44. Stereo. Hrs open:
Rebroadcasts WOGB(FM) Kaukauna 80%.
491 S. Washburn St., Suite 400, 54904. Phone: (920) 426-3239. Fax: (920) 231-0145.E-mail: info@1039vbo.com Web Site:www.1039vbo.com Licensee: Cumulus Broadcasting Inc. Population served: 325,000 Natl. Network: Westwood One, . Format: Oldies. Target aud: 35-54. ♦Brian Roberts, progmg dir; Alexandra Marohn, traf mgr.

***WVCY(AM)**— July 1, 1969: 690 khz; 250 w-D, 77 w-N, DA-2. TL: N44 04 51 W88 33 53. Hrs open: 24 3434 W. Kilbourn Ave., Milwaukee, 53208. Phone: (414) 935-3000. Fax: (414) 935-3015.E-mail: wvcyam@vcyamerica.org Web Site:www.vcyamerica.org Licensee: VCY/America Inc. (group owner; acq 1-19-95). Population served: 500,000 Natl. Network: USA, . Format: Relg. ♦Dr. Randall Melchert, pres; Vic Eliason, VP & gen mgr.

WWWX(FM)— Jan 30, 1967: 96.9 mhz; 6 kw. 328 ft TL: N44 03 51 W88 31 44. Hrs open: 491 S. Washburn St., Suite 400, 54904. Phone: (920) 426-3239. Fax: (920) 231-0145.E-mail: info@fox969.com Web Site:www.fox969.com Licensee: WI Radio LLC, as trustee Group owner: Cumulus Media Inc. (acq 4-10-2009; with WZNN(FM) Allouez). Population served: 325,000 Natl. Network: ABC, . Rgnl. Network: Goetz Group. Wire Svc: UPI Format: Rock. Target aud: 25-54. ♦Jeff Schmidt, gen mgr.

Owen

***WVCS(FM)**—Not on air, target date: unknown: 90.1 mhz; 50 kw. Ant 131 ft TL: N44 56 58.7 W90 37 54.2. Hrs open: 3434 W. Kilbourn Ave., Milwaukee, 53208. Phone: (414) 935-3000. Fax: (414) 935-3015. Web Site:www.vcyamerica.org Licensee: VCY America Inc. (acq 12-30-2008; $7,000 for CP). ♦Vic Eliason, pres.

Park Falls

WCQM(FM)— Apr 13, 1968: 98.3 mhz; 57 kw. 233 ft TL: N45 55 04 W90 26 58. Hrs open: 24 Box 309, 54552. Phone: (715) 762-3221. Fax: (715) 762-2358.E-mail: wcqm@wcqm.com Web Site:www.wcqm.com Licensee: Heartland Communications License LLC Population served: 30,000 Natl. Network: ABC, . Format: Country. News staff: one; News: 6 hrs wkly. Target aud: 20-70. ♦Kirk Knoll, traf mgr.

***WHBM(FM)**— Nov 11, 1988: 90.3 mhz; 17.5 kw. 727 ft TL: N45 56 43 W90 16 28. Hrs open: 24
Rebroadcasts WHA (AM) Madison 100%.
518 S. 7th Ave., Wausau, 54401. Phone: (715) 261-6298. Fax: (715) 848-2890.E-mail: reyer@wpr.org Web Site:www.wpr.org Licensee: State of Wisconsin Educational Communications Board. Rgnl. Network: Wis. Pub. Wis. Public Radio Dow, Lohnes & Albertson. Format: News/talk. News staff: 9. Target aud: 35-54; skews female: Issue oriented talk-var of perspectives. ♦Wendy Wink, CEO; Ted Tobie, CFO; Phil Corriveau, gen mgr; Tom Martin-Erickson, opns dir, opns mgr; Rick Reyer, dev dir; Allen Rieland, engrg dir, chief of engrg.

WNBI(AM)— 1953: 980 khz; 1 kw-D, 105 w-N. TL: N45 55 04 W90 26 58. Hrs open: 24 Box 309, 54552. Secondary address: Hwy. 13 S. 54552. Phone: (715) 762-3221. Fax: (715) 762-2358.E-mail: wnbi@pctcnet.net Licensee: Heartland Comunications License LLC. (group owner; (acq 7-30-2002; $850,000 with co-located FM). Population served: 18,000 Natl. Network: ABC, . Format: Sports. News staff: 2; News: 12 hrs wkly. Target aud: 25-54; adults with disposable income. Spec prog: Relg one hr, loc community talk 5 hrs wkly. ♦James Gregori, gen mgr; Joel Karnick, opns dir, progmg dir, news dir; Darla Isham, gen sls mgr; Arthur Dunham, chief of engrg; Kirk Knoll, traf mgr.

Peshtigo

WSFQ(FM)— Aug 5, 1996: 96.3 mhz; 49 kw. 482 ft TL: N45 07 19 W87 51 07. Stereo. Hrs open: 24 N. 2880 Roosevelt Rd., Marinette, 54143. Phone: (715) 735-6631. Fax: (715) 732-0125. Web Site:www.badgerbbayarearadio.com Licensee: Armada Media - Menominee Inc. (group owner; (acq 12-19-2006; grpsl). Natl. Network: ABC, . Rgnl. Network: Wisconsin Radio Net. Wisconsin Radio Net. Format: Oldies. News staff: one. Target aud: 49; male. ♦Jim Coursolle, pres; Jim Medley, opns dir; Mike Wolfe, progmg dir.

Platteville

WPVL(AM)— Feb 22, 1955: 1590 khz; 1 kw-D, 500 w-N, DA-N. TL: N42 44 46 W90 28 28. Hrs open: 24 51 Means Dr., 53818. Phone: (608) 349-2000. Fax: (608) 349-2002.E-mail: info@wpvl.com Web Site:www.wpvl.com Licensee: QueenB Radio Wisconsin Inc. Group owner: Morgan Murphy Stations (acq 3-18-98; $825,000 with co-located FM). Population served: 50,000 Natl. Network: ABC, ESPN Radio, . Robert Olender. Format: All Sports. News staff: 2; News: 10 hrs wkly. Target aud: 35 plus. Spec prog: Farm 12 hrs, sports 15 hrs wkly. ♦Dan Sullivan, gen mgr.

WPVL-FM— Sept 1, 1966: 107.1 mhz; 4.1 kw. Ant 235 ft TL: N42 44 45 W90 38 27. Stereo. Hrs open: 24 51 Means Dr. , 53818. Phone: (608) 349-2000. Fax: (608) 349-2002.E-mail: info@wpvl.com Web Site:www.1071theedge.com Licensee: QueenB Radio Wisconsin Inc. Format: Top-40. News staff: one; News: 10 hrs wkly. Target aud: 30 plus; general adults. ♦Rick Samson, stn mgr.

***WSSW(FM)**— Feb 1, 2007: 89.1 mhz; 60 w. Ant 561 ft TL: N42 45 50.7 W90 24 19.7. Hrs open:
Rebroadcasts WERN(FM) Madison 100%.
Vilas Communications Hall, 821 University Ave., Madison, 53706-1496. Phone: (608) 263-3970. Fax: (608) 263-9763. Web Site:www.wpr.org Licensee: State of Wisconsin-Educational Communications Board. Natl. Network: NPR, . Wis. Public Radio Format: News, classical. ♦Phil Corniveau, gen mgr.

***WSUP(FM)**— Feb 25, 1964: 90.5 mhz; 1 kw. 146 ft TL: N42 43 57 W90 29 09. Stereo. Hrs open: 20 One Univ. Plaza, 42 Pioneer Tower, 53818. Phone: (608) 342-1165. Phone: (608) 342-1291. Fax: (608) 342-1290.E-mail: wsup@uwplatt.edu Web Site:ums.www.uwplatt.edu/~wsup/ Licensee: Board of Regents, University of Wisconsin System. Dow, Lohnes & Albertson. Format: AOR. News: 10 hrs wkly. Target aud: 18-24; college-age. Spec prog: Class 4 hrs, jazz 3 hrs, alternative 6 hrs, metal 6 hrs, dance 4 hrs wkly. ♦George E. Smith, gen mgr; Laura Lohfink, stn mgr.

Plymouth

WJUB(AM)— April 1954: 1420 khz; 500 w-D, 62 w-N. TL: N43 44 33 W87 56 21. Hrs open: 24 Box 259, N. 5569 State Hwy. 57, 53073-0259. Phone: (920) 893-2661. Phone: (920) 467-4891. Fax: (920) 892-2706.E-mail: 1420amthebreeze@jmiradio.org Web Site:www.1420thebreeze.com Licensee: Jubilation Ministries Inc. (acq 12-17-90; $185,000; 1-7-91). Population served: 62,620 Natl. Network: USA, . Format: Adult Standards. News: 11 hrs wkly. Target aud: 25-54. Spec prog: Farm 5 hrs wkly. ♦Gerry Krebsbach, pres; William Horsch, gen mgr; David Hendrickson, progmg dir.

WXER(FM)— Oct. 3, 2000: 104.5 mhz; 6 kw. 328 ft TL: N43 43 32 W88 03 07. Stereo. Hrs open: 24 2100 Washington Ave., Sheboygan Falls, 53081. Phone: (920) 458-2107. Fax: (920) 467-4300.E-mail: studio@wxerfm.com Web Site:www.1045thepoint.com Licensee: Midwest Communications Inc. Group owner: Mountain Dog Media (acq 11-1-2005; $2.3 million). Population served: 100,600 Format: Adult contemp. Target aud: 29-54. Spec prog: Ger 3 hrs wkly. ♦Duke E. Wright, pres; Randall B. Hopper, stn mgr; Steve Schouten, opns mgr, gen sls mgr; Patrick Pendergrast, mktg mgr; Dave Riley, progmg dir; Stewart Muck, chief of engrg; Karen Branch, traf mgr.

Port Washington

WPJP(FM)— October 1969: Stn currently dark. 100.1 mhz; 6 kw. Ant 318 ft TL: N43 25 14 W87 59 40. Stereo. Hrs open: 24 Box 10707, Green Bay, 54307. Phone: (920) 469-3021. Fax: (262) 784-2149. Licensee: Starboard Media Foundation Inc. Group owner: Relevant Radio (acq 5-15-2003; $900,000). Population served: 600,000 ♦Mark Follett, CEO, pres; Neil Robbins, stn mgr.

Portage

WBKY(FM)— 1998: 95.9 mhz; 5.4 kw. Ant 321 ft TL: N43 38 17 W89 34 16. Hrs open: 24 Box 360, 53901. Secondary address: 1420 E. Wisconsin St. 53901. Phone: (608) 635-7341. Fax: (608) 635-7343. Web Site:www.buckycountry959.com Licensee: Magnum Communications Inc. Natl. Network: AP Radio, . Fisher, Wayland, Cooper, Leader & Zaragoza. Format: Country. News staff: 2; News: 7 hrs wkly. ♦Dave Magnum, gen mgr; Rick Jensen, opns mgr; Doug Steele, gen sls mgr; Steve Paterson, progmg dir; Pete Holliday, news dir; Jon Zecherle, chief of engrg; Deb Doyle, traf mgr.

WDDC(FM)— Nov 8, 1966: 100.1 mhz; 3.3 kw. 300 ft TL: N43 31 40 W89 25 52. (CP: 1.84 kw. TL: N43 31 42 W89 26 01). Stereo. Hrs open: 24 Box 448, 53901. Secondary address: N6912 Hwy. 51 53901. Phone: (608) 742-1001. Fax: (608) 742-1688. Licensee: Zoe Communications Format: Country. News staff: 2. Target aud: 25-45; office workers, young adults. ♦Kevin Todryk, progmg dir.

WPDR(AM)— July 31, 1952: 1350 khz; 1 kw-D, 41 w-N. TL: N43 31 40 W89 25 52. Hrs open: 24 Box 448, 53901. Secondary address: N6912 Hwy. 51 53901. Phone: (608) 742-1001. Fax: (608) 742-1688.E-mail: wpdr@jvlnet.com Licensee: Zoe Communications Inc. (group owner; acq 2003; $1.1 million with co-located FM). Population served: 40,000 Format: News/talk, adult contemp. News staff: 2; News: 14 hrs wkly. Target aud: 35 plus. Spec prog: Farm 6 hrs wkly. ♦Mike Oberg, pres, gen mgr, chief of engrg; Lyric Klaske, gen mgr, traf mgr; Robert Hoffer, sls dir; Susann Gamble, progmg dir, news dir.

Poynette

WHFA(AM)— July 1925: 1240 khz; 1 kw-U. TL: N43 21 38 W89 24 08. Hrs open: 24 1496 Bellevue St., Suite 202, Green Bay, 54311. Phone: (920) 469-3021. Fax: (608) 833-7117.E-mail: whfa@relevantradio.com Web Site:www.relevantradio.com Licensee: Starboard Media Foundation Inc. Group owner: Relevant Radio (acq 6-28-2001; $1 million). Population served: 275,000 Natl. Network: ABC, . Rgnl. Network: Tribune, Wisconsin Radio Net. Wisconsin Radio Net. Format: Catholic. News: 3 hrs wkly. Target aud: 35-64. ♦Martin Jury, opns mgr & dev dir.

Prairie du Chien

WPRE(AM)— Dec 11, 1952: 980 khz; 1 kw-D. TL: N43 03 39 W91 09 26. Hrs open: 24 Box 90, 53821. Secondary address: 640 North Villa Louis Rd. 53821. Phone: (608) 326-2411. Fax: (608) 326-2412.E-mail: wqpcwpre@mwt.net Web Site:www.wpreradio.com Licensee: Robinson Corp. Group owner: Robinson Corporation (acq 1-7-98; with co-located FM). Population served: 89,164 Natl. Network: Westwood One, . Format: Oldies. News staff: one. ♦David Robinson, pres, gen mgr; Jeff Robinson, opns mgr.

WQPC(FM)— 1968: 94.3 mhz; 36 kw. 525 ft TL: N43 03 35 W91 06 02. Stereo. Hrs open: 24 Secondary address: 640 North Villa Louis Rd. 53821. Phone: (608) 326-2411. Fax: (608) 326-2412.E-mail: wqpcwpre@mwt.net Web Site:www.wqpcradio.com Licensee: Robinson Corp. Population served: 140,718 Rgnl. Network: Goetz Group. Format: Country.

Racine

WEZY(FM)— Aug 6, 1962: 92.1 mhz; 6 kw. 275 ft TL: N42 40 55 W87 50 59. (CP: 2.7 kw, ant 495 ft.). Stereo. Hrs open: 24 Prog sep from AM 4201 Victory Ave., 53405. Phone: (262) 634-3311. Fax: 92620 634-6515. Population served: 53,000 Format: Easy Listening. News staff: 2; News: 4 hrs wkly. Target aud: 25-54. ♦Don Rosen, mus dir; Curt Vollman, traf mgr.

WJTI(AM)— June 4, 1950: 1460 khz; 500 w-D, 62 w-N. TL: N42 45 06 W87 49 55. (CP: 350 w-D, 49 w-N. TL: N42 44 14 W87 56 20 (day), N43 04 20 W87 57 07 (night)). Hrs open: 24 1530 N Cass St., Suite A, Milwaukee, 53202. Phone: (414) 899-9902. Licensee: El Sol Broadcasting LLC (acq 1-30-2007; $467,500). Population served: 1,300,000 Format: Sp. News staff: 3. Sp all ages. ♦John Torres, gen mgr.

WKKV-FM— August 1948: 100.7 mhz; 50 kw. 500 ft TL: N42 48 18 W88 02 54. Stereo. Hrs open: 24 12100 W. Howard Ave., Greenfield, 53228. Phone: (414) 321-1007. Fax: (414) 327-3200.E-mail: info@v100.com Web Site:www.v100.com Licensee: Clear Channel Radio Licenses Inc. Group owner: Clear Channel Communications Inc. (acq 1996; grpsl). Natl. Network: Premiere Radio Networks, Superadio, . Natl. Rep: Clear Channel,. Format: Urban rhythm and blues. Target aud: 18-44; general. Spec prog: Gospel 6 hrs wkly. ♦L. Lowry Mays, CEO; Mark Mays, pres; Cindy McDowell, gen mgr; Kerry Wolfe, opns mgr; Randy Wanek, sls dir; Sean John, prom dir; Bailey Coleman, progmg dir, progmg mgr; Terry James, news dir; Al Hajny, chief of engrg; Karen Mason, traf mgr; Doug Banks, disc jockey.

WRJN(AM)— December 1926: 1400 khz; 1 kw-U. TL: N42 42 39 W87 49 48. Hrs open: 24 4201 Victory Ave., 53405. Phone: (262) 634-3311. Fax: (262) 634-6515.E-mail: wrjn@wi.net Licensee: Racine Broadcasting L.L.C. Group owner: Bliss Communications Inc. (acq 7-11-97; $5 million with co-located FM). Population served: 47,000 Natl. Rep: Christal,. Format: News/talk. News staff: 2; News: 40 hrs wkly. Target aud: 35 plus. Spec prog: Class 2 hrs, It 2.5, Serbian 2 hrs wkly. ♦Skip Bliss, pres; Rob Lisser, CFO; Bob Dailey, exec VP; Tim Etes, VP, gen mgr; Ron Richards, opns dir; Leo Edelstein, gen sls mgr, adv mgr; Lew Turner, prom dir; Don Rosen, progmg dir; Tom Karkow, news dir; Bill Lawrence, pub affrs dir; Bob Gorjance, chief of engrg; Curt Vollman, traf mgr.

Reedsburg

WBDL(FM)— 1997: 102.9 mhz; 3.6 kw. 423 ft TL: N43 35 32 W90 00 42. Hrs open: Box 349, 53959. Phone: (608) 356-3661. Fax: (608) 356-3561.E-mail: wbdl@baraboo.com Licensee: Magnum Communications Inc. (group owner; (acq 10-18-2007; grpsl). Natl. Network: ABC, . Format: Adult contemp. ♦Tommy Bychinski, gen mgr & gen sls mgr; Kevin Kellogg, progmg dir; David Stoeger, news dir.

WNFM(FM)— July 16, 1967: 104.9 mhz; 1.6 kw. 449 ft TL: N43 32 30 W90 02 05. (CP: 3.2 kw). Stereo. Hrs open: 24 Prog sep from AM Box 349 E, 53959. Phone: (608) 524-1400. Fax: (608) 524-2474. Format: C&W. News staff: one; News: 10 hrs wkly. Target aud: 25 plus.

WRDB(AM)— Feb 6, 1953: 1400 khz; 1 kw-U. TL: N43 32 30 W90 02 05. Hrs open: 24 Box 349 E., 53959. Phone: (608) 524-1400. Phone: (608) 524-1049. Fax: (608) 524-2474.E-mail: saukbroad@mwt.net Licensee: Magnum Communications Inc. (group owner; (acq 10-18-2007; grpsl). Population served: 5,038 Miller & Fields, P.C. Format: Oldies, farm, news. News staff: one; News: 14 hrs wkly. Target aud: 25-54. ♦Tommy Lee Bychinski, gen mgr; Amber Selje, traf mgr.

Reserve

***WOJB(FM)**— Apr 1, 1982: 88.9 mhz; 100 kw. 604 ft TL: N45 52 16 W91 20 56. Stereo. Hrs open: 13386 W. Trepania Rd., Hayward, 54843. Phone: (715) 634-2100. Fax: (715) 634-4070.E-mail: generalmanager@wojb.org Web Site:www.wojb.org Licensee: Lac Courte Oreilles Ojibwe Public Broadcasting Corp. Natl. Network: NPR, PRI, . Format: Div. Spec prog: Indian 15 hrs, country 15 hrs, jazz 10 hrs, bluegrass 2 hrs wkly. ♦Carolyn Nayquonabe, gen mgr.

Rhinelander

WHDG(FM)— Sept 1, 1994: 97.3 mhz; 100 kw. Ant 551 ft TL: N45 22 50 W89 11 22. Stereo. Hrs open: 24 3616 Hwy. 47 N., 54501. Phone: (715) 362-1975. Fax: (715) 362-1973.E-mail: whdg@whdg.com Web Site:www.whdg.com Licensee: Raven License Sub. LLC. Group owner: NewRadio Group LLC (acq 10-31-2005; grpsl). Leventhal, Senter & Lerman. Wire Svc: Wheeler News Service Format: Country. News staff: one; News: 10 hrs wkly. Target aud: 25-54. ♦Duff Damos, gen mgr, opns dir; Bill Mitchell, progmg dir; Al Johnson, chief of engrg; Mary Spatz, traf mgr; Steve Albertson, gen mgr, gen sls mgr & disc jockey.

WOBT(AM)— Mar 9, 1947: 1240 khz; 950 w-D, 1 kw-N. TL: N45 37 42 W89 23 38. Hrs open: 24 3616 Hwy. 47 N., 54501. Phone: (715) 362-1975. Fax: (715) 362-1973. Web Site:www.northwoodsespnsportszone.com Licensee: NRG License Sub. LLC. (group owner; (acq 10-31-2005; grpsl). Fisher, Wayland, Cooper, Leader & Zaragoza L.L.P. Format: ESPN sports. News staff: one; News: 10 hrs wkly. Target aud: 18+. ♦Duff Damos, opns dir, progmg dir; Steve Albertson, gen mgr & gen sls mgr; Al Johnson, chief of engrg; Mary Spartz, traf mgr.

WRHN(FM)— Jan 26, 1966: 100.1 mhz; 25 kw. 385 ft TL: N45 38 08 W89 22 42. (CP: 100 kw, ant 981 ft. TL: N45 24 03 W89 28 54). Stereo. Hrs open: 24 Prog sep from AM 3616 Hwy. 47 N., 54501. Phone: (715) 362-1975. Fax: (715) 362-1973. Web Site:www.wrhn.com Licensee: NRG License Sub. LLC. Format: Hot AC. Target aud: 18-49. ♦Duff Damos, opns dir; Steve Albertson, gen sls mgr.

***WXPR(FM)**— Apr 24, 1983: 91.7 mhz; 100 kw. 403 ft TL: N45 46 28 W89 14 54. Stereo. Hrs open: 5 AM-midnight 303 W. Prospect St., 54501. Phone: (715) 362-6000. Fax: (715) 362-6007.E-mail: wxpr@wxpr.org Web Site:www.wxpr.org Licensee: White Pine Community Broadcasting Inc. Population served: 70,000 Natl. Network: NPR, . Format: Div, class, folk. Spec prog: Jazz 8 hrs wkly. ♦Mick Fiocchi, pres, gen mgr; Walt Gander, opns mgr & opns mgr; Jessie Dick, dev dir; Ken Krall, news dir; Elmer Goetsch, chief of engrg.

Rice Lake

WAQE(AM)— Aug 6, 1979: 1090 khz; 5 kw-D. TL: N45 32 16 W91 45 50. Stereo. Hrs open: Box 703, 1859 21st Ave., 54868. Phone: (715) 234-9059. Fax: (715) 234-6942.E-mail: info@wage.com Web Site:www.waqe.com Licensee: TKC Inc. Group owner: Koser Radio Group (acq 1999). Population served: 187,000 Shaw Pittman. Format: Classic country. News staff: one; News: 5 hrs wkly. Target aud: 24-59; traditional country mus listeners. ♦Brian Schultz, gen mgr, stn mgr, sls dir; Dane Jensen, sls VP; Mike Bigner, progmg dir; Mike Murrey, chief of engrg; John Roberts, traf mgr.

WJMC(AM)— 1938: 1240 khz; 1 kw-U. TL: N45 30 27 W91 46 28. Hrs open: 24 Box 703, 1859 21st Ave., 54868. Phone: (715) 234-2131. Fax: (715) 234-6942.E-mail: info@wjmc.com Web Site:www.wjmcradio.com Licensee: TKC Inc. Group owner: Koser Radio Group (acq 1-1-89). Population served: 35,000 Rgnl. Network: Wisconsin Radio Net. Wisconsin Radio Net. Fisher, Wayland, Cooper, Leader & Zaragoza L.L.P. Format: Farm, news/talk, adult contemp. Target aud: 25-54. ♦Thomas A. Koser, pres & gen mgr; Dane Jensen, stn mgr, gen sls mgr; Mike Bigner, progmg dir; Ken DeNucci, news dir; Mike Murrey, chief of engrg; John Roberts, traf mgr, disc jockey.

WJMC-FM— 1947: 96.1 mhz; 50 kw. Ant 482 ft TL: N45 37 14 W91 44 44. Stereo. Hrs open: 24 Box 703, 54868. Secondary address: 1859 21st Ave. 54868. Phone: (715) 234-2131. Fax: (715) 234-6942. Web Site:www.wjmcradio.com Licensee: TKC Inc. Population served: 125,000 Format: Hot country. Target aud: 25-54. ♦Dane Jensen, stn mgr; Ken DeNucci, news rptr; Don Tobias, sports cmtr; Mike Bigner, disc jockey.

WKFX(FM)— Nov 20, 1980: 99.1 mhz; 44 kw. 522 ft TL: N45 22 23 W91 55 22. (CP: 44 kw, ant 522 ft. TL: N45 22 23 W91 55 22). Hrs open: 24 Box 352, 54868. Phone: (715) 234-9059. Fax: (715) 234-6942.E-mail: info@fox99.com Web Site:www.fox99.com Licensee: TKC Inc. Format: Classic hits. News staff: one; News: 3 hrs wkly. Target aud: 18-49; young, upscale adults. ♦Peter Neuser, stn mgr.

Richland Center

WRCO(AM)— Oct 18, 1949: 1450 khz; 1 kw-U. TL: N43 18 58 W90 22 31. Hrs open: 24 Box 529, 2111 Bohmann Dr., 53581-0529. Phone: (608) 647-2111. Fax: (608) 647-8025.E-mail: wrconews@wrco.com Web Site:www.wrco.com Licensee: Fruit Broadcasting LLC. (acq 1994). Population served: 100,000 Natl. Network: CBS, Westwood One, . Rgnl. Network: Wisconsin Radio Net. Wire Svc: AP Wire Svc: Wheeler News Service Format: Adult Standards. News staff: one; News: 20 hrs wkly. Target aud: 25-54; general. Spec prog: Farm 2.hrs wkly. ♦Ron Fruit, pres, gen mgr & opns mgr; Alice Schulte, gen sls mgr; Phil Nee, progmg dir; Aaron Joyce, news dir; Dennis Baldridge, chief of engrg; Amy Cook, traf mgr.

WRCO-FM— August 1965: 100.9 mhz; 6 kw. 240 ft TL: N43 20 14 W90 22 44. Stereo. Hrs open: 24 2111 Bohmann Dr., 53581. Phone: (608) 647-21111. Fax: (608) 647-8025.E-mail: wrconews@wrco.com Web Site:www.wrco.com Population served: 256,000 Natl. Network: CBS Radio, . Wisconsin Radio Net. Wire Svc: AP Wire Svc: Wheeler News Service Format: Country, news. News staff: 2; News: 45 hrs wkly. Target aud: General; adult. Spec prog: Farm 18 hrs, Gospel 6 hrs wkly. ♦Alice Schulte, sls dir; Phil Nee, progmg dir; Ron Fruit, pub affrs dir; Dennis Baldridge, chief of engrg; Adam Hess, disc jockey.

Ripon

WRPN(AM)—Licensed to Ripon. See Fond du Lac

***WRPN-FM**— Sept 15, 1957: 90.1 mhz; 231 w. 110 ft TL: N43 50 37 W88 50 31. Stereo. Hrs open: 24 Box 248, Harwood Memorial Union, 300 Seward St., 54971-0248. Phone: (920) 748-8147. Phone: (920) 748-8115 (college). Fax: (920) 748-7243.E-mail: wrpnfm@yahoo.com Web Site:www.homestead.com Licensee: Board of Trustees of Ripon College. Natl. Network: CBS, ABC, . Natl. Rep: Farmakis,. Haley, Bader & Potts. Wire Svc: Wheeler News Service Format: Classic rock, div, progsv. News staff: 4; News: 25 hrs wkly. Spec prog: Pol 2 hrs, sports 15 hrs wkly. ♦Guy McHendry, gen mgr; Joe Laedtke, opns dir.

WTCX(FM)—Licensed to Ripon. See Fond du Lac

River Falls

WEVR(AM)— Sept 14, 1969: 1550 khz; 1 kw-D. TL: N44 53 19 W92 39 04. Hrs open: 6 AM-sunset 178 Radio Rd., 54022. Phone: (715) 425-1111. Phone: (612) 381-1111. Licensee: Hanten Broadcasting Co. Inc. (acq 6-1-74). Population served: 250,000 Natl. Network: USA, . Wire Svc: Wheeler News Service Format: Lite adult contemp, sports. News: 5 hrs wkly. Target aud: General. Spec prog: Farm 18 hrs wkly. ♦Carol Hanten, pres & gen mgr.

WEVR-FM— Sept 30, 1970: 106.3 mhz; 6 kw. 328 ft TL: N44 53 19 W92 39 04. Stereo. Hrs open: 6 AM-11 PM 178 Radio Rd., 54022. Phone: (715) 425-1111. Fax: (715) 381-1111. Population served: 250,000 Wire Svc: Wheeler News Service Format: News, sports, lite adult contemp. News: 18 hrs wkly. Target aud: General.

***WRFW(FM)**— Nov 2, 1968: 88.7 mhz; 3 kw. 82 ft TL: N44 53 08 W92 39 20. Stereo. Hrs open: 24 Univ. of Wisconsin River Falls, 306 North Hall, 410 S. 3rd St., MN, 54022. Phone: (715) 425-3886/3887.E-mail: urfw@uwrf.edu Web Site:www.uwrf.edu/wrfw Licensee: University of Wisconsin System. Population served: 40,000 Natl. Network: NPR, . Rgnl rep: Wisconsin Public Radio Format: Var/div. Spec prog: Farm 10 hrs wkly. ♦Rick Burgsteiner, gen mgr; Nick Hassel, prom dir; Adam Lee, progmg dir; Paul Karklus, mus dir; Tara Sowle, news dir.

Rothschild

WDTX(FM)—Not on air, target date: unknown: 100.5 mhz; 25 kw. Ant 253 ft TL: N44 47 16 W89 45 40. Hrs open: 194 McGee Rd., Versailles, KY, 40383. Phone: (859) 879-0818. Licensee: JER Licenses LLC. ♦Jon E. Robinson, gen mgr.

Rudolph

WIZD(FM)— Sept 30, 1990: 99.9 mhz; 13 kw. Ant 453 ft TL: N44 20 19 W89 38 55. Stereo. Hrs open: 24
Simulcast with WOFM(FM) Mosinee 100%.
Box 850, 2460 Plover Rd., Plover, 54467. Phone: (715) 344-6050. Phone: (715) 421-4040. Fax: (715) 341-8070.E-mail: info@lovethevalley.com Web Site:www.lovethevalley.com Licensee: WRIG Inc. Group owner: Midwest Communications Inc. (acq 1999; $1.4 million). Natl. Network: Fox News Radio, . Natl. Rep: Christal,. Format: Adult hits. News staff: 3; News: 3 hrs wkly. Target aud: 35 plus; upper income. ♦Duke Wright, pres; Brett Lucht, gen mgr; Dawn Prudhomme, gen sls mgr; Bill Phillips, progmg dir; Frank Zastrow, chief of engrg; John Flesch, traf mgr.

Sarona

WPLT(FM)— 2003: 106.3 mhz; 3.4 kw. Ant 440 ft TL: N45 40 28 W91 58 52. Hrs open: 24 Box 190, Shell Lake, 54871. Phone: (715) 468-9500. Fax: (715) 468-9505.E-mail: spots@95gmo.com Web Site:www.king1063.com Licensee: Zoe Communications Inc. (group owner; acq 12-6-00; $439,000 for CP). Format: Country. ♦Wendy Oberg, gen mgr; Tasha Hagberg, gen sls mgr; Bo Landry, progmg dir; Mike Oberg, chief of engrg.

Sauk City

WMAD(FM)—Licensed to Sauk City. See Madison

Schofield

WRIG(AM)— Aug 1, 1958: 1390 khz; 10 kw-U, DA-2. TL: N44 52 42 W89 38 29. Hrs open: 24 Box 2048, Wausau, 54402-2048. Secondary address: 557 Scott St., Wausau 54403. Phone: (715) 842-1672. Fax: (715) 848-3158.E-mail: ken@bigwrig.com Web Site:www.bigwrig.com Licensee: WRIG Inc. Group owner: Midwest Communications Inc. Population served: 32,806 Natl. Network: Fox Sports, . Format: Sports. ♦D.E. Wright, pres; Gary Tesch, exec VP; Brett Lucht, gen

mgr; Samantha Milanowski, gen sls mgr; Ken Clark, progmg dir; Frank Zastrow, chief of engrg; John Flesch, traf mgr.

Seymour

WECB(FM)— May 1998: 104.3 mhz; 5.6 kw. Ant 341 ft TL: N44 31 26 W88 19 56. Hrs open: Box 1519, Appleton, 54912. Phone: (920) 734-9226. Fax: (920) 739-0494. Web Site:www.1043thebreeze.com Licensee: Woodward Communications Inc. (group owner; acq 6-23-2003; $1.75 million). Population served: 152,069 Hogan & Hartson. Format: Soft adult contemp hits of the 70s & 80s. ♦Greg Bell, gen mgr; Kelly Radandt, gen sls mgr; Dayton Kane, progmg dir; Steve Brown, chief of engrg.

Shawano

WOWN(FM)— December 1966: 99.3 mhz; 14 kw. Ant 440 ft TL: N44 45 14 W88 20 01. Stereo. Hrs open: 24 Dups AM 10% 1456 E. Green Bay St., 54166. Phone: (715) 524-2194. Fax: (715) 524-9980. Population served: 185,000 Natl. Network: ABC, . Format: Classic hits. News staff: one; News: 13 hrs wkly. Target aud: 20-45. ♦Bruce Grassman, CEO.

WTCH(AM)— Sept 3, 1948: 960 khz; 1 kw-U, DA-N. TL: N49 46 47 W88 37 53. Hrs open: 24 1456 E. Green Bay St., 54166. Phone: (715) 524-2194. Fax: (715) 524-9980.E-mail: info@wtcham960.com Web Site:www.wtcham960.com Licensee: Results Broadcasting Inc. Group owner: Results Broadcasting (acq 12-23-96; $2,704,670 for 50% of stock with co-located FM). Population served: 85,000 Natl. Network: CBS, . Format: Classic country. News staff: one; News: 25 hrs wkly. Target aud: 25-54; northeast Wisconsin adults. Spec prog: Farm 21 hrs wkly. ♦Bruce Grassman, chmn, pres, gen mgr; Trisha Peterson, VP.

Sheboygan

WBFM(FM)— Mar 1, 1977: 93.7 mhz; 6 kw. Ant 253 ft TL: N43 43 12 W87 44 04. Stereo. Hrs open: 920 Washinton Ave., 53081. Phone: (920) 458-2107. Fax: (920) 458-9775.E-mail: eddie@b93radio.com Web Site:wbfmb93radio.com Licensee: Midwest Communications Inc. Population served: 75,000 Natl. Network: ABC, . Rgnl rep: Rgnl Reps Format: Country. News staff: 2; News: 24 hrs wkly. Target aud: 25-54; adults in Sheboygan county/Northern Milwaukee metro area. ♦Eddie Ybarrna, progmg dir.

WCLB(AM)— January 1956: 950 khz; 500 w-D, DA. TL: N43 44 33 W87 49 00. Hrs open: 18 254 Winnebago Dr., Fond du Lac, 54935. Phone: (920) 921-1071. Fax: (920) 467-4300.E-mail: wbates@mdogmedia.com Web Site:www.sheboygansespn950.com Licensee: RBH Enterprises Inc. dba Yellow Dog Broadcasting. Group owner: Mountain Dog Media (acq 6-23-00; $700,000 with WXER(FM) Plymouth). Population served: 109,000 Natl. Network: Westwood One, . Holland & Knight. Format: Sports. News staff: 2; News: 8 hrs wkly. Target aud: 35-64. ♦Randy Hopper, gen mgr.

WHBL(AM)— Jan 1, 1926: 1330 khz; 5 kw-D, 1 kw-N, DA-2. TL: N43 43 14 W87 44 04. Hrs open: 24 Box 27, 53082. Secondary address: 2100 Washington Ave. 53081. Phone: (920) 458-2107. Fax: (920) 458-9775.E-mail: studio@whbl.com Licensee: Midwest Communications Inc. (group owner; (acq 8-8-2000; grpsl). Population served: 100,000 Natl. Network: ABC, . Rgnl. Network: Wisconsin Radio Net. Natl. Rep: Rgnl Reps,. Wisconsin Radio Net. Wire Svc: AP Format: News/talk. News staff: 2; News: 24 hrs wkly. Target aud: 35-64. Spec prog: Farm 10 hrs wkly. ♦Patrick Pendergast, gen mgr; Mark Smith, gen sls mgr; Nick Reed, progmg dir; Mike Kinzel, news dir; Tim Laes, chief of engrg.

***WSHS(FM)**— Nov 19, 1971: 91.7 mhz; 180 w. 82 ft TL: N43 46 37 W87 43 08. Stereo. Hrs open: 24 1042 School Ave., 53083. Phone: (920) 459-3610. Fax: (920) 803-7612.E-mail: wshs@sheboygan.kiz.wi.us Licensee: Sheboygan Area School District. Population served: 48,484 Natl. Network: NPR, . Wis. Public Radio Rgnl rep: Glenn Slatts Format: Adult contemp, AOR. Target aud: 18-45; young adults & teens. Spec prog: Hmong 3 hrs, Sp 3 hrs wkly. ♦Ron Rindfleish, pres; Jon Etter, gen mgr.

Sheboygan Falls

WHBZ(FM)— April 1997: 106.5 mhz; 6 kw. 239 ft TL: N43 43 16 W87 44 03. Hrs open: 2100 Washington Ave., Sheboygan, 53081. Phone: (920) 458-2107. Fax: (920) 458-9775.E-mail: thebuzz@whbz.fm Web Site:www.WHBZ.fm Licensee: Midwest Communications Inc. (group owner; acq 8-8-00; grpsl). Format: Rock. News staff: 2; News: 10 hrs wkly. Target aud: 18-49; males. ♦Matt Smith, gen mgr; Jennifer Weber, gen sls mgr, progmg dir; Ron Simonet, progmg dir; Mike Kinzel, news dir; Kevin Zimmerman, traf mgr.

Shell Lake

WCSW(AM)— Dec 30, 1967: 940 khz; 1 kw-D. TL: N45 41 36 W91 57 57. Hrs open: Box 190, 54871. Secondary address: 345 Hwy. 63 S. 54871. Phone: (715) 468-9500. Fax: (715) 468-9505.E-mail: info@wcsw.com Licensee: Zoe Communications Inc. (group owner; acq 1-1-00; with co-located FM). Population served: 50,000 Natl. Network: ABC, . Format: Talk. Target aud: General. Spec prog: Farm 3 hrs wkly. ♦Wendy Oberg, gen mgr; Loren Miller, gen sls mgr; Mike Oberg, progmg dir, news dir, chief of engrg; Stephanie Butenhoff, traf mgr.

WGMO(FM)— December 1974: 95.3 mhz; 7.1 kw. 512 ft TL: N45 40 28 W91 58 52. Stereo. Hrs open: 24 Dups AM 20% Box 190 , 54871. Secondary address: 345 Hwy. 63 S. 54871. Phone: (715) 468-9500. Fax: (715) 468-9505.E-mail: info@wgmo.com Web Site:www.95wgmo.com Natl. Network: Westwood One, . Rgnl. Network: Skylight. Format: Classic rock. News staff: one. ♦Donna Nelson, traf mgr.

Siren

WXCX(FM)— 2000: 105.7 mhz; 6 kw. Ant 328 ft TL: N45 52 21 W92 27 39. Stereo. Hrs open: 24 Box 179, Luck, 54853. Secondary address: 2547 Hwy. 35, Suite 3, Luck 54853. Phone: (715) 472-9569. Fax: (715) 472-6939. Web Site:oldies1057.ws Licensee: Red Rock Radio Corp. (group owner; (acq 9-1-2006; grpsl). Population served: 150,000 Natl. Network: Jones Radio Networks, . Natl. Rep: Midwest Radio,. Rgnl rep: MidwestRadio Format: Classic hits. News staff: one. Target aud: 35-64. ♦Ro Grignon, pres; Don Welch, VP; Ron Revere, gen mgr.

Sister Bay

***WHDI(FM)**— 2000: 91.9 mhz; 3.4 kw. Ant 476 ft TL: N45 14 19 W87 05 27. Hrs open: 3319 W. Beltline Hwy., Network HQ, Madison, 53713. Phone: (608) 264-9600. Fax: (608) 264-9664. Web Site:www.ecb.org Licensee: State of Wisconsin-Educational Communications Board. Natl. Network: NPR, . Wis. Public Radio Dow, Lohnes & Albertson. Format: Talk. ♦Gene Purcell, gen mgr; Phil Corriveau, stn mgr.

***WHND(FM)**— Sept. 16, 1999: 89.7 mhz; 3.4 kw. 538 ft TL: N45 14 19 W87 05 27. Hrs open: 24 2420 Nicolet Dr., Green Bay, 54311. Secondary address: 821 University Ave., Madison 53706. Phone: (920) 465-2444. Fax: (920) 465-2576. Web Site:www.wpr.org Licensee: State of Wisconsin Educational Communications Board. Population served: 50,000 Natl. Network: NPR, PRI, . Dow, Lohnes & Albertson. Format: News, classical music. News staff: one; News: 29 hrs wkly. Target aud: 35 plus; socially aware, educated & financially secure. Spec prog: Native American 2 hrs, blues 2 hrs, folk 2 hrs, jazz 10 hrs, experimental 2 hrs, wkly. ♦Lisa Nalbandian, rgnl sls mgr.

WSBW(FM)— 2007: 105.1 mhz; 3.1 kw. Ant 466 ft TL: N45 14 05 W87 05 27. Hrs open: 24 3030 Park Dr., Suite 3, Sturgeon, 54235. Phone: (920) 746-9430. Fax: (920) 746-9433.E-mail: info@dailynews.com Licensee: Nicolet Broadcasting Inc. Format: Oldies. News staff: 2; News: news prgmg 10 hrs wkly. ♦Roger Utnehmer, pres.

Soldiers Grove

WKPO(FM)— 2008: 105.9 mhz; 25 kw. Ant 328 ft TL: N43 34 26 W90 48 55. Hrs open: E7601A CTH SS, Viroqua, 54665. Phone: (608) 637-7200. Fax: (608) 637-7299. Licensee: Robinson Corp. (acq 6-5-2008; $250,000). Format: Adult hits. ♦David Robinson, pres & gen mgr.

Sparta

WCOW-FM— Mar 1, 1960: 97.1 mhz; 100 kw. 587 ft TL: N43 58 06 W90 51 35. Stereo. Hrs open: 24 113 W. Oak St., 54656-1712. Phone: (608) 269-3100. Fax: (608) 269-5170.E-mail: info@cow97.com Web Site:www.cow97.com Licensee: Sparta-Tomah Broadcasting Co. Inc. Population served: 139,300 Natl. Rep: Rgnl Reps,. Miller & Miller. Format: Contemp country. News: 15 hrs wkly. Target aud: 25 plus; rural & city residents. Spec prog: Green Bay Packers. ♦William Hoffman, gen mgr & gen sls mgr; Jake Preston, progmg dir; Arnie Andrews, mus dir; Clary Harris, news dir.

WKLJ(AM)— June 1951: 1290 khz; 5 kw-D, 59 w-N. TL: N43 58 06 W90 51 35. Hrs open: 6 AM-6 PM Prog sep from FM 113 W. Oak St., 54656-1712. Phone: (608) 269-3100. Fax: (608) 269-5170.E-mail: info@espnlacrosse.com Web Site:www.espnlacrosse.com Licensee: Sparta-Tomah Broadcasting Co. Inc. (Acq 1-19-89). Population served: 30,500 Natl. Network: ESPN Radio, . Natl. Rep: Rgnl Reps,. Format: Sports. ♦William Hoffman, gen mgr.

Spencer

WOSQ(FM)— Sept 20, 1984: 92.3 mhz; 6 kw. Ant 300 ft TL: N44 48 35 W90 21 51. Stereo. Hrs open: 24 1714 North Central Ave., Marshfield, 54449. Phone: (715) 384-2191. Fax: (715) 387-3588. Web Site:www.wdlbwosq.com Licensee: Seehafer Broadcasting Corp. (group owner; (acq 6-1-2006; swap with WDLB(AM) Marshfield and WFHR(AM) Wisconsin Rapids for WBCV(FM) Wausau) Natl. Network: ESPN Radio, . Rgnl. Network: Goetz Group. Brownfield Miller & Miller. Wire Svc: Wheeler News Service Format: Sports. News staff: 2; News: 7 hrs wkly. Target aud: 25-54. ♦Don Seehafer, pres, gen mgr; Kent Reeves, opns mgr; Mike Warren, news dir; Chuck Gennaro, chief of engrg.

Stevens Point

WSPT(AM)— 1948: 1010 khz; 1 kw-D. TL: N44 32 17 W89 35 43. Hrs open: 500 Division St., 54481. Phone: (715) 341-9800. Fax: (715) 341-0000.E-mail: rmuzzy@1010wspt.com Web Site:1010wspt.com Licensee: Americus Communications L.L.C. Group owner: Muzzy Broadcasting L.L.C. (acq 1996; $1.2 million with co-located FM). Population served: 23,631 Natl. Network: Fox News Radio, . Format: News/talk. Target aud: 25-54; upscale, male-orientated. Spec prog: Pol one hr wkly. ♦Richard L. Muzzy, pres & gen mgr.

WSPT-FM— May 1, 1961: 97.9 mhz; 100 kw. Ant 338 ft TL: N44 32 17 W89 35 43. Stereo. Hrs open: Prog sep from AM 500 Division St., 54481. Phone: (715) 341-9800. Fax: (715) 341-0000. Web Site:979jackfm.com Population served: 210,600 Format: Adult contemp. Target aud: 25-54; adult.

***WWSP(FM)**— Sept 28, 1968: 89.9 mhz; 11.5 kw. 325 ft TL: N44 28 55 W89 40 34. Stereo. Hrs open: 6 AM-2 AM 105 CAL, UWSP, Reserve St., 54481. Phone: (715) 346-3755. Fax: (715) 346-4012.E-mail: wwsp@uwsp.edu Web Site:www.uwsp.edu/stuorg/wwsp Licensee: Board of Regents, University of Wisconsin System. Dow, Lohnes & Albertson. Wire Svc: Wheeler News Service Wire Svc: UPI Format: Jazz, progsv. Target aud: College students. Spec prog: Hmong one hr, pub affrs 5 hrs, sports 3 hrs, blues 4 hrs wkly. ♦Mark Tolstedt, gen mgr; Courtney Sikorski, stn mgr; Cynthia Atchison, dev dir.

Sturgeon Bay

WDOR(AM)— Sept 8, 1951: 910 khz; 1 kw-D. TL: N44 49 38 W87 21 27. Hrs open: 6 AM-sunset Box 549, 800 S. 15th Ave., 54235. Phone: (920) 487-2822. Phone: (920) 743-4411. Fax: (920) 743-2334.E-mail: email@wdor.com Web Site:wdor.com Licensee: Door County Broadcasting Co. Inc. (acq 10-4-2007; with co-located FM). Population served: 50,000 Natl. Network: ABC, . Pillsbury, Winthrop, Shaw Pittman. Format: Adult contemp. News staff: one; News: 23 hrs wkly. Target aud: 21-50; general. ♦Edward Allen III, sls dir, pres, gen mgr, gen sls mgr; Edward Allen IV, progmg dir; Dan Allen, mus dir; Roger Levendusky, news dir, local news ed; Steve Konopka, engrg dir; Peggy Pfister, traf mgr; David Allen, relg ed; Chad Michaels, sports cmtr.

WDOR-FM— Dec 12, 1966: 93.9 mhz; 77 kw. Ant 640 ft TL: N44 54 23 W87 22 15. Stereo. Hrs open: 5 AM-midnight Box 549, 800 S. 15th Ave., 54235. Phone: (920) 487-2822. Phone: (920) 743-4411. Fax: (920) 743-2334.E-mail: info@wdor.com Web Site:wdor.com Licensee: Door County Broadcasting Co. Inc. Population served: 100,000 Natl. Network: ABC, . Pillsbury, Winthrop, Shaw Pittman. Wire Svc: Wheeler News Service Format: Sports. News: 25 hrs wkly. Target aud: 20-40; general. Spec prog: Farm 5 hrs wkly.

***WNLI(FM)**— July 1998: 88.5 mhz; 50 kw. Ant 518 ft TL: N44 54 14 W87 22 13. Hrs open: 24 Box 28, 54235. Secondary address: 1723 Michigan St. 54235. Phone: (920) 743-7443. Fax: (920) 743-7543.E-mail: wrgx@wrgx.com Web Site:www.wrgx.com Licensee: Bethesda Christian Broadcasting. (acq 12-31-2007; $1.7 million with WPFF(FM) Sturgeon Bay). Format: Christian; Rock/AOR. Target aud: 13-35; teens & generation x listeners. ♦Mark Pluimer, pres; Dr. Mark Schwarzbaur, gen mgr.

***WPFF(FM)**— August 1991: 90.5 mhz; 100 kw. 653 ft TL: N44 54 23 W87 22 15. Stereo. Hrs open: 24 Box 28, 1715 Michigan St., 54235. Phone: (920) 743-7443.E-mail: wpff@wpff.com Web Site:www.wpff.com Licensee: Bethesda Christian Broadcasting. (acq 12-31-2007; $1.7 million with WNLI(FM) Sturgeon Bay). Population served: 3,200,000

Natl. Network: USA, . Format: Christian, CHR. News: 12 hrs wkly. Target aud: 25-49; baby boomers. ♦Mark Schwarzbauer, gen mgr; Andy King, stn mgr.

WRQE(FM)— Mar 4, 1982: 99.7 mhz; 46 kw. Ant 512 ft TL: N44 38 08 W87 37 37. Stereo. Hrs open: 24 Box 23333, Green Bay, 54305. Secondary address: 115 S. Jefferson St., Green Bay 54301. Phone: (920) 435-3771. Fax: (920) 444-1155.E-mail: webmaster@997thebay.com Web Site:www.997thebay.com Licensee: Midwest Communications Inc. (group owner; (acq 6-18-93; $3.5 million with WOZZ(FM) New London;7-5-93). Population served: 867,000 Natl. Rep: Christal,. Miller & Miller. Format: Adult rock. News staff: 4; News: 3 hrs wkly. Target aud: 13-34; young, active, hip. ♦Duke Wright, pres, gen mgr; Jennifer Kalies, gen sls mgr; Jenny Lawrence, progmg dir; Jerry Bader, news dir; Tim Laes, chief of engrg.

WSRG(FM)— Apr 18, 1988: 97.7 mhz; 1.85 kw. Ant 597 ft TL: N44 54 14 W87 22 13. Stereo. Hrs open: 24 1009 Egg Harbor Rd., Suite 113, 54235. Phone: (920) 743-6677. Fax: (920) 743-9183.E-mail: info@wsrc.com Licensee: Al Johnson Broadcasting LLC (acq 5-1-2008; $712,500). Population served: 50,000 Natl. Network: Jones Radio Networks, . Format: Adult contemp. News staff: 2. Target aud: 25-54. ♦Dave Magnum, gen sls mgr, news dir; Rick Jensen, opns mgr & progmg dir.

Sturtevant

WDDW(FM)— June 18, 1993: 104.7 mhz; 4.2 kw. Ant 338 ft TL: N42 51 20 W87 50 41. Hrs open: 24 8500 Green Bay Rd., Pleasant Prairie, 53158. Phone: (262) 694-7800. Fax: (262) 694-7767. Licensee: Bustos Media Operating LLC. Group owner: NextMedia Group L.L.C. (acq 1-6-2006; $10.2 million). Population served: 920,000 Reddy, Begley & McCormick. Format: Rgnl Mexican. Target aud: 18-49. ♦Kira LaFond, gen mgr; John Perry, opns dir, opns mgr, progmg dir; Jerod Bast, gen sls mgr; Lisa Tyler, news dir; Mark Anthony, pub affrs dir & chief of engrg; Lisa Sladek, rsch dir, traf mgr.

Sun Prairie

***WNWC(AM)**— Jan 12, 1982: 1190 khz; 1 kw-D, DA. TL: N43 09 36 W89 12 41. Hrs open: Sunrise to sunset 5606 Medical Cir., Madison, 53719. Phone: (608) 271-1025. Fax: (608) 271-1150.E-mail: wnwc@nwc.edu Web Site:www.faith1190.com Licensee: Northwestern College. Group owner: Northwestern College & Radio (acq 12-19-96; $250,000). Population served: 697,500 Format: Relg, talk. ♦Greg Walters, gen mgr.

WXXM(FM)— Apr 12, 1972: 92.1 mhz; 3.7 kw. Ant 410 ft TL: N43 10 10 W89 15 38. Stereo. Hrs open: 2651 S. Fish Hatchery Rd., Madison, 53711. Phone: (608) 274-5450. Fax: (608) 274-5521.E-mail: info@themic921.com Web Site:www.themic921.com Licensee: Capstar TX L.P. Group owner: Clear Channel Communications Inc. (acq 8-30-2000; grpsl). Population served: 697,500 Natl. Network: Fox Sports, . Format: Progsv talk. ♦Jeff Tyler, gen mgr; Sue Garret, gen sls mgr; Ryan Turany, progmg dir; Josh Westscott, news dir; Cliff Groth, chief of engrg; Jacqueline Forney, traf mgr.

Superior

KHQG(FM)— Sept 9, 1979: 102.5 mhz; 100 kw. Ant 600 ft TL: N46 47 21 W92 07 09. Stereo. Hrs open: 24 715 E. Central Entrance, Duluth, 55811. Phone: (218) 722-4321. Fax: (218) 722-5423. Web Site:www.northlandsclassicrock.com Licensee: Midwest Communications Inc. Format: Classic rock. News: 3 hrs wkly. Target aud: 18-49. ♦Duke Wright, CEO; Jack Lawson, opns mgr, progmg dir; Mike Rasmusson, sls dir; John Talcott, chief of engrg.

KKCB(FM)—See Duluth, MN

KTCO(FM)—See Duluth, MN

***KUWS(FM)**— Jan 31, 1966: 91.3 mhz; 83 kw. 646 ft TL: N46 47 21 W92 06 51. Stereo. Hrs open: 24 Box 2000, 54880. Phone: (715) 394-8530. Fax: (715) 394-8404.E-mail: jmunson@facstaffuwsuper.edu Web Site:www.kuws.fm Licensee: Board of Regents, University of Wisconsin System. Population served: 150,000 Natl. Network: NPR, . Rgnl. Network: Wis. Pub. Wis. Public Radio Format: Div, news/talk, educ. News staff: one; News: 20 hrs wkly. Target aud: 12 plus; above average income & education. Spec prog: Alternative 16 hrs, Black 4 hrs, jazz 15 hrs, sports 6 hrs wkly. ♦John Munson, stn mgr.

WDSM(AM)— October 1939: 710 khz; 10 kw-D, 5 kw-N, DA-N. TL: N46 39 14 W92 08 51. Hrs open: 24 715 E. Central Entrance, Duluth, MN, 55811. Phone: (218) 722-4321. Fax: (218) 722-5423. Web Site:www.wdsm.am Licensee: Midwest Communications Inc. (group owner; (acq 8-1-2001; grpsl). Population served: 100,578 Natl. Network: ABC, Talk Radio Network, Salem Radio Network, Premiere Radio Networks, CNN Radio, . Wisconsin Radio Net. Rosenman & Colin. Wire Svc: AP Format: Talk. Target aud: 25-54. ♦Roxanne Charles, CEO; Jack Lawson, opns mgr; Mike Rasmusson, sls dir; Bruce Ciskie, progmg dir; John Talcott, chief of engrg.

WGEE(AM)— June 18, 1959: 970 khz; 1 kw-D, 27 w-N. TL: N46 43 28 W92 07 11. Hrs open: 24 715 E. Central Entrance, Midwest Communications, Duluth, MN, 55811. Phone: (218) 722-4321. Fax: (218) 722-5423.E-mail: fleisch@mwcradio.com Licensee: Midwest Communications Inc. (group owner; (acq 8-1-2001; grpsl). Natl. Network: Music of Your Life, . Rgnl rep: Hyett/Ramsland. Rosenman & Colin. Format: Adult standards. Target aud: 18-44. ♦Duke Wright, CEO, pres; Jack Lawson, opns mgr, progmg dir; Mike Rasmusson, sls dir; Bruce Ciskie, progmg dir, news dir; John Talcott, chief of engrg.

Suring

***WRVM(FM)**— Sept 17, 1967: 102.7 mhz; 100 kw. 980 ft TL: N44 59 50 W88 23 49. Stereo. Hrs open: 24 Box 212, 54174-0212. Secondary address: Hwy. 32 N. 54174. Phone: (920) 842-2839. Fax: (920) 842-2704.E-mail: wrvm@wrvm.org Web Site:www.wrvm.org Licensee: WRVM Inc. (acq 5-15-68). Population served: 1,500,000 Natl. Network: Moody, . Kenkel & Associates. Format: Christian. Target aud: General; family stn with children's programs. ♦Michael A. Cornell, gen mgr; Brian Hay, gen sls mgr; Dennis Jones, progmg dir; Alan Kilgore, chief of engrg.

Sussex

WKSH(AM)— November 2002: 1640 khz; 10 kw-D, 1 kw-N. TL: N43 04 38 W88 11 32. Hrs open: 24 W.223 N.3251 Shady Ln., Pewaukee, 53072. Phone: (262) 695-9500. Fax: (262) 691-2378.E-mail: debra.l.bratel@disney.com Web Site:www.radiodisney.com Licensee: Radio Disney Group LLC. Group owner: ABC Inc. (acq 9-26—02; $2.6 million). Population served: 1,000,000 Natl. Network: Radio Disney, . Natl. Rep: McGavren Guild,. Format: Family hits. Target aud: Kids 6-14 & Women 25-49. ♦Debra Bratel, gen mgr, stn mgr; Patricia Schultz, prom mgr; Melissa Schumacher, sls.

Three Lakes

WCYE(FM)— August 1994: 93.7 mhz; 100 kw. Ant 407 ft TL: N45 46 30 W89 14 55. Hrs open: 24 38 W. Davenport St., Rhinelander, 54501. Phone: (715) 369-9575. Fax: (715) 369-9475.E-mail: wcyeginger@nawnorth.net Web Site:www.mycoyoteradio.com Licensee: Results Broadcasting of Rhinelander Inc. Group owner: Results Broadcasting (acq 3-10-2000; $500,000). Format: Country. News staff: one; News: 4 hrs wkly. Target aud: 25-54. ♦Bruce Grassman, CEO; Trisha Peterson, VP & gen mgr.

Tomah

WBOG(AM)— Apr 19, 1959: 1460 khz; 1 kw-D, 42 w-N. TL: N43 58 07 W90 30 50. Hrs open: 24 1021 N. Superior Ave., Suite 5, 54660. Phone: (608) 372-9600. Fax: (608) 372-7566.E-mail: info@oldies1460.com Web Site:www.magnumradiogroup.net Licensee: Magnum Radio Inc. (group owner; acq 1994; $275,000 with co-located FM). Natl. Network: Jones Radio Networks, . Rgnl. Network: Wisconsin Radio Net. Wisconsin Radio Net. Format: Oldies. News staff: 2; News: 10 hrs wkly. Target aud: 35 plus. ♦Dave Magnum, pres; Brian Winnekins, opns dir, farm dir, sports cmtr; Diane Pergande, sls dir; Steve Peterson, gen mgr, prom dir & progmg mgr; Clary Harris, news dir; Darrell Sanders, chief of engrg.

WTMB(FM)— July 11, 1990: 94.5 mhz; 8.3 kw. Ant 564 ft TL: N43 53 56 W90 29 23. Stereo. Hrs open: 24 1021 N. Superior Ave., 54660. Phone: (608) 372-9420. Fax: (608) 372-7566.E-mail: info@buzzcountry.com Web Site:www.magnumradiogroup.net Format: Classic rock. News staff: 2; News: 6 hrs wkly.

***WVCX(FM)**— Jan 29, 1965: 98.9 mhz; 100 kw. 991 ft TL: N43 51 13 W90 27 28. Stereo. Hrs open: 24 3434 W. Kilbourn Ave., Milwaukee, 53208. Phone: (414) 935-3000. Fax: (414) 935-3015.E-mail: wvcx@vcyamerica.org Web Site:www.vcyamerica.org Licensee: VCY/America Inc. (group owner; acq 1984). Natl. Network: USA, Moody, . Format: Relg, talk, Christian. ♦Dr. Randall Melchert, pres; Victor Eliason, VP & gen mgr; Jim Schneider, progmg dir; Gordon Morris, news dir; Andy Eliason, chief of engrg.

WXYM(FM)— Mar 11, 1992: 96.1 mhz; 44 kw. 525 ft TL: N44 01 32 W90 48 58. Stereo. Hrs open: 24 1021 N. Superior Ave., Suite 5, 54660. Phone: (608) 372-9600. Fax: (608) 372-7566.E-mail: info@mixwxym.com Web Site:www.magnumradiogroup.net Licensee: Magnum Radio Inc. (acq 9-27-91; 10-14-91). Rgnl. Network: Wisconsin Radio Net. Wisconsin Radio Net. Format: Hot AC. News staff: 2; News: 6 hrs wkly. Target aud: 25-54. ♦Dave Magnum, pres; Steve Peterson, gen mgr; Debbie Doyle, opns mgr.

Tomahawk

WJJQ(AM)— August 1968: 810 khz; 980 w-D. TL: N45 29 27 W89 43 36. Hrs open: 24 Box 10, 54487. Secondary address: 81 E. Mohawk Dr. 54487. Phone: (715) 453-4482. Phone: (715) 457-4481. Fax: (715) 453-7169.E-mail: wjjq@wjjq.com Web Site:www.wjjq.com Licensee: Albert Broadcasting II LLC (acq 6-11-84). Population served: 25,000 Natl. Network: CBS, ESPN Radio, Westwood One, . Natl. Rep: Rgnl Reps,. Wisconsin Radio Net. Shaw Pittman. Wire Svc: AP Format: Sports, talk. News staff: one; News: 15 hrs wkly. Target aud: 25 plus. ♦Gregg Albert, pres, gen mgr; Margaruite Albert, VP; Tim Albert, prom mgr & progmg dir.

WJJQ-FM— Oct 15, 1984: 92.5 mhz; 25 kw. Ant 259 ft TL: N45 29 27 W89 43 36. Stereo. Hrs open: 24 Box 10, 54487. Secondary address: 81 E. Mohawk Dr. 54487. Phone: (715) 453-4482. Fax: (715) 453-7169.E-mail: galbert@wjjq.com Web Site:www.wjjq.com Licensee: Albert Broadcasting II LLC. Population served: 40,000 Natl. Network: CBS Radio, . Natl. Rep: Rgnl Reps,. Wisconsin Radio Net. Rgnl rep: Regional Reps Shaw Pittman. Wire Svc: AP Format: Lite hits, news, sports,oldies. News staff: one; News: 30 hrs wkly. Target aud: 25 plus. ♦Mary Lu Voermans, gen sls mgr; Gregg Albert, news rptr, disc jockey; Mark Everett, disc jockey.

Trempealeau

WFBZ(FM)— Nov 24, 1984: 105.5 mhz; 2.1 kw. Ant 531 ft TL: N43 56 33 W91 26 03. Stereo. Hrs open: 24 113 W. Oak St., Sparta, 54656. Phone: (608) 269-3100. Fax: (608) 269-5170.E-mail: info@espnlacrosse.com Web Site:www.espnlacrosse.com Licensee: Sparta-Tomah Broadcasting Co. Inc. Group owner: La Crosse Radio Group (acq 12-13-2006; $850,000). Natl. Network: ESPN Radio, . Natl. Rep: Rgnl Reps,. Wire Svc: ESPN/SportsTicker Format: ESPN. ♦Shelly Holen, pres; William Hoffman, gen mgr.

Two Rivers

WCUB(AM)—Licensed to Two Rivers. See Manitowoc

WGBW(AM)— Oct 29, 1951: 1590 khz; 1 kw-D, 33 w-N. TL: N44 10 23 W87 35 37. Denmark, WI (10Kw days). Hrs open: 24 1414 16th St., 54241-3031. Phone: (920) 794-1800. Fax: (920) 794-1800.E-mail: wgbw@lsol.net Web Site:wgbwradio.com Licensee: WTRW Inc. Population served: 70,000 Natl. Network: CNN Radio, Westwood One, . Thompson Hine LLC. Format: Oldies. News staff: one; News: 10 hrs wkly. Target aud: 35-54; baby boomers & professionals. ♦Mark Heller, pres.

WLTU(FM)—See Manitowoc

Verona

WMMM-FM— July 4, 1991: 105.5 mhz; 4.4 kw. 384 ft TL: N42 57 42 W89 29 32. Hrs open: 7601 Ganser Way, Madison, 53719. Phone: (608) 826-0077. Fax: (608) 826-1244.E-mail: info@wmmm.com Web Site:www.1055triplem.com Licensee: Entercom Madison Licensee LLP. Group owner: Entercom Communications Corp. (acq 7-10-00; grpsl). Format: AAA. Target aud: 25-44; upscale, college educated adults. ♦David Field, pres; Steve Fisher, CFO; Lindsay Wood Davis, mktg mgr.

Viroqua

***WDRT(FM)**—Not on air, target date: unknown: 91.9 mhz; 480 w. Ant 435 ft TL: N43 36 28 W90 53 24. Hrs open: 212 S. East Ave., 54665. Phone: (608) 627-2653.E-mail: headphones@radiodriftless.org Web Site:www.radiodriftless.org Licensee: Driftless Community Radio Inc. ♦Kreigh Rasikas, pres.

WVRQ(AM)— Feb 25, 1958: 1360 khz; 1 kw-D, 23 w-N. TL: N43 32 04 W90 52 23. Hrs open: 24 E7601A County Rd. SS, 54665. Phone: (608) 637-7200. Fax: (608) 637-7299.E-mail: wvrq@mwt.net Web Site:www.wvrq.com Licensee: Robinson Corp. Group owner: Robinson Corporation. Population served: 43,762 Natl. Network: ABC, . Rgnl. Network: Wisconsin Radio Net. Wisconsin Radio Net. Wire Svc: AP Format: Oldies/Full Service. News staff: one; News: 14 hrs wkly. Target aud: 25 plus. Spec prog: Farm one hr, relg 6 hrs, polka 6 hrs wkly. ♦David Robinson, pres; Jeff Robinson, gen mgr.

WVRQ-FM— Oct 6, 1967: 102.3 mhz; 3.3 kw. Ant 298 ft TL: N43 31 27 W90 51 51. Stereo. Hrs open: 24 E7601A County Rd. SS, 54665. Phone: (608) 637-7200. Fax: (608) 637-7299. Web Site:www.wvrq.com Licensee: Robinson Corp. Population served: 38,394 Rgnl. Network: Goetz Group. Wire Svc: AP Format: Country. News staff: one; News: 20 hrs wkly. Target aud: 25-54. Spec prog: Bluegrass 2 hrs, farm one hr wkly. ♦Jeff Robinson, gen sls mgr & progmg dir.

Washburn

***WEGZ(FM)—** Oct 5, 1981: 105.9 mhz; 98 kw. Ant 741 ft TL: N46 41 31 W90 59 27. Stereo. Hrs open: 24 3434 W. Kilbourn Ave., Milwaukee, 53208. Phone: (414) 935-3000. Fax: (414) 935-3015.E-mail: wegz@vcyamerica.org Web Site:www.vcyamerica.org Licensee: Keweenaw Bay Broadcasting Inc. Group owner: VCY/America Inc. (acq 4-19-2002). Population served: 225,000 Natl. Network: USA, . Format: Religious, Christian music, talk. ♦Dr. Randall Melchert, pres; Victor Eliason, VP & gen mgr; Gordon Morris, opns dir, news dir; Jim Schneider, progmg dir.

Watertown

WJJO(FM)— Aug 1, 1961: 94.1 mhz; 50 kw. 492 ft TL: N43 11 43 W88 45 17. Stereo. Hrs open: 24 Box 44408, Madison, 53744. Secondary address: 730 Rayovac Dr., Madison 53711. Phone: (608) 273-1000. Fax: (608) 271-8182. Web Site:www.wjjo.com Licensee: Mid-West Management Inc. Group owner: Mid-West Family Stations (acq 6-18-93; $1.6 million; 7-5-93). Population served: 450,000 Natl. Rep: McGavren Guild,. Format: Rock. Target aud: 21-49; male. ♦Ted Waldbillig, sls dir, prom mgr; Tom Walker, pres, gen mgr & gen sls mgr; Randy Hawke, progmg dir; Blake Patton, mus dir, pub affrs dir; John Bauer, chief of engrg.

Waukesha

***WCCX(FM)—** Sept 1, 1978: 104.5 mhz; 10 w. 50 ft TL: N43 00 16 W88 13 39. Hrs open: 24 100 N. E. Ave., 53186. Phone: (262) 524-7355. Fax: (262) 650-4950.E-mail: wccx@cc.edu Web Site:wccx.cc.edu Licensee: Trustees Carroll College. Format: Div. Target aud: General; high school & college students. Spec prog: Sp 8 hrs, metal 3 hrs, rap 3 hrs wkly.

WMIL(FM)— Jan 1, 1982: 106.1 mhz; 12 kw. Ant 997 ft TL: N43 05 46 W87 54 15. Stereo. Hrs open: 24 12100 W. Howard Ave., Greenfield, 53228. Phone: (414) 545-8900. Phone: (414) 545-5920. Fax: (414) 546-8058. Web Site:www.fm106.com Licensee: Clear Channel Broadcasting Inc. Group owner: Clear Channel Communications Inc. (acq 3-17-97; $40 million with WOKY(AM) Milwaukee). Population served: 1,400,000 Natl. Rep: Clear Channel,. Format: Country. News staff: 4; News: 1.5 hrs wkly. Target aud: 25-54; middle America. ♦L. Lowry Mays, CEO, chmn; Mark Mays, pres; Cindy McDowell, gen mgr; Keith Bratel, sls dir; Colleen Kurth, natl sls mgr, pub affrs dir; Enid Parkinson, prom dir; Kerry Wolfe, progmg dir; Mitch Morgan, mus dir.

WRRD(AM)— Mar 27, 1947: 1510 khz; 23 kw-D, 20 kw-CH, DA-2. TL: N43 01 02 W88 11 43. Stereo. Hrs open: 6 AM-8:30 PM 770 N. Jefferson St., Milwaukee, 53202. Phone: (414) 273-3776. Fax: (414) 291-3776.E-mail: www.wauksportsradio@msn.com Licensee: Good Karma Broadcasting L.L.C. (group owner; (acq 4-30-2004; $2 million). Population served: 1,000,000 Natl. Network: ESPN Deportes, . Hough & Cook. Format: Sp sports. ♦Craig Karmazin, pres, stn mgr, gen sls mgr; C.J. Knee, opns dir; Bill Johnson, progmg dir; Warren Jorgenson, traf mgr.

Waunakee

WCHY(FM)— Apr 20, 1992: 105.1 mhz; 6 kw. 328 ft TL: N43 13 20 W89 18 01. Stereo. Hrs open: 7601 Ganser Way, Madison, 53719. Phone: (608) 826-0077. Fax: (608) 826-1244.E-mail: info@wchy.com Web Site:www.y105.com Licensee: Entercom Madison Licensee LLP. Group owner: Entercom Communications Corp. (acq 7-10-2000; grpsl). Format: 70's & 80's. Target aud: 18-49. ♦David Field, pres; Steve Fisher, CFO; Ed Schulz, gen mgr.

Waupaca

WDUX(AM)— Apr 29, 1956: 800 khz; 5 kw-D, 500 w-N, DA-1. TL: N44 21 15 W89 03 29. Hrs open: 5 AM-midnight Box 247, 54981. Secondary address: 200 Tower Rd. 54981. Phone: (715) 258-5528. Fax: (715) 258-7711.E-mail: mail@wdux.net Web Site:www.wdux.net Licensee: Laird Broadcasting Co. (acq 12-30-99; grpsl). Natl. Network: ABC, Jones Radio Networks, . Rgnl. Network: Tribune, Goetz Group. Natl. Rep: Katz Radio,. Format: Classic country. News staff: one; News: 20 hrs wkly. Target aud: 35 plus. Spec prog: Farm 6 hrs wkly. ♦William L. Laird, pres; Tina Grenlie, stn mgr, gen sls mgr, prom mgr; Jack Barry, opns mgr, progmg dir, news dir, sports cmtr; Jan Calvey, traf mgr.

WDUX-FM— Jan 29, 1967: 92.7 mhz; 6 kw. 243 ft TL: N44 21 14 W89 03 44. Stereo. Hrs open: 24 Box 247, 54981. Secondary address: 200 Tower Rd. 54981. Phone: (715) 258-5528. Fax: (715) 258-7711. Web Site:www.wdux.net Natl. Network: ABC, Westwood One, . Format: Hot adult contemp. Target aud: 25-54. Spec prog: Sports 15 hrs wkly. ♦Rick Winters, progmg mgr; Jan Calvey, traf mgr.

Waupun

WFDL(AM)— May 26, 1966: 1170 khz; 1 kw-D. TL: N43 38 30 W88 43 22. Hrs open: Sunrise to sunset 609 Home Ave., 53963. Phone: (920) 324-4441. Fax: (920) 324-3139.E-mail: wmrh1170@yahoo.com Web Site:www.am1170.com Licensee: Radio Plus Inc. (acq 7-90; $170,000;7-2-90). Population served: 250,000 Natl. Network: CBS Radio, . Format: News/talk. Target aud: 35 plus; mature adults. Spec prog: Farm 5 hrs wkly. ♦Chris Bernier, pres; Terry Davis, gen mgr, gen sls mgr; Mike Enfelt, opns mgr, news dir, chief of engrg; Todd Dehring, progmg dir; Greg Stensland, news dir; Kerry Longrie, traf mgr.

Wausau

WBCV(FM)— Feb 1, 1985: 107.9 mhz; 100 kw. Ant 1,019 ft TL: N45 03 33 W89 26 10. Stereo. Hrs open: 2301 Plover Rd., Plover, 55467. Phone: (715) 341-8838. Fax: (715) 341-9744. Licensee: NRG License Sub, LLC. (acq 5-31-2006; swap for WDLB(AM) Marshfield, WOSQ(FM) Spencer and WFHR(AM) Wisconsin Rapids) Population served: 221,000 Natl. Rep: McGavren Guild,. Format: Rock hits. ♦Ben Rosenthal, gen mgr; Panama Jack, progmg dir.

***WCLQ(FM)—** May 23, 1988: 89.5 mhz; 8.5 kw. 328 ft TL: N44 58 58 W89 36 06. Stereo. Hrs open: 24 4111 Schofield Ave., Suite 10, Schofield, 54476. Phone: (715) 355-5151. Fax: (715) 359-3128.E-mail: 89q@89q,org Web Site:www.89q.org Licensee: Christian Life Communications Inc. Natl. Network: USA, . Format: Contemp hit/Top-40. News: 9 hrs wkly. Target aud: 18-35; Christian/young family. ♦Coy Sawyer, CFO, gen mgr, chief of opns; Scott Michaels, mus dir; Frank Zastrow, chief of engrg.

WDEZ(FM)— Mar 27, 1964: 101.9 mhz; 100 kw. 489 ft TL: N44 58 58 W89 36 06. (CP: 98 kw, ant 1,076 ft. TL: N44 55 14 W89 41 31). Stereo. Hrs open: 24 Box 2048, 54402-2048. Phone: (715) 842-1672. Fax: (715) 848-3158.E-mail: wdez@wdez.com Web Site:www.wdez.com Licensee: WRIG Inc. Group owner: Midwest Communications Inc. Population served: 212,000 Natl. Rep: Christal,. Wire Svc: Wheeler News Service Wire Svc: UPI Format: Country. News staff: one; News: 4 hrs wkly. Target aud: 25-54. Spec prog: Farm 4 hrs wkly. ♦D.E. Wright, pres; Gary Tesch, VP; Brett Lucht, gen mgr; Dave Weir, sls dir; Melissa Heise, prom dir; Chad Edwards, progmg dir; Vanessa Ryan, progmg dir & mus dir; Chris Conley, news dir; Frank Zastrow, chief of engrg; Mike Austin, farm dir.

***WHRM(FM)—** June 10, 1949: 90.9 mhz; 77kw. TL: N44 55 14 W89 41 31. Stereo. Hrs open: 24 518 S. 7th Ave., 54401. Phone: (715) 848-1978. Fax: (715) 848-2890.E-mail: rick.reyer@wpr.org Web Site:www.wpr.org Licensee: State of Wisconsin Educational Communications Board. Natl. Network: NPR, PRI, . Dow, Lohnes & Albertson. Format: Class, educ. News: 29 hrs wkly. Target aud: 25-64; male/female. ♦Wendy Wink, CEO; Ted Tobie, CFO; Phil Corriveau, gen mgr; Rick Reyer, stn mgr, dev dir; Maru Nonn, opns dir; Allen Rieland, engrg dir, chief of engrg.

WIFC(FM)— 1947: 95.5 mhz; 98 kw. 1,150 ft TL: N44 55 14 W89 41 31. Stereo. Hrs open: 24 Prog sep from AM Box 2048, 4402, 5. Secondary address: 557 Scott St. 54403. Phone: (715) 842-1672. Fax: (715) 848-3158.E-mail: wifc@wifc.com Web Site:www.wifc.com Population served: 411,000 Format: CHR. News staff: 2. Target aud: 18-49. ♦Brett Lucht, sls dir; Chris Pickett, progmg dir.

***WLBL-FM—** November 1995: 91.9 mhz; 560 w. 823 ft TL: N44 55 14 W89 41 31. Hrs open: 5 AM-midnight (M-F); 6 AM-midnight (S, Su) 518 S. 7th Ave., 54401. Phone: (715) 848-1978. Fax: (715) 848-2890.E-mail: rick.reyer@wpr.org Web Site:www.wpr.org Licensee: State of Wisconsin-Educational Communications Board. Population served: 70,000 Natl. Network: NPR, . Rgnl. Network: Wisconsin Radio Net. Wisconsin Radio Net. Format: Call-in talk. Spec prog: Folk 3 hrs wkly. ♦Wendy Wink, CEO; Phil Corriveau, gen mgr; Allen Rieland, news dir, chief of engrg.

WRIG(AM)—See Schofield

WSAU(AM)— Jan 30, 1937: 550 khz; 5 kw-U, DA-2. TL: N44 51 26 W89 35 13. Hrs open: 24 Box 2048, 54402-2048. Secondary address: 557 Scott St. 54403. Phone: (715) 842-1672. Fax: (715) 848-3158.E-mail: wsau@wsau.com Web Site:www.wsau.com Licensee: WRIG Inc. Group owner: Midwest Communications Inc. (acq 1996; $3.5 million with co-located FM). Population served: 113,000 Rgnl. Network: Goetz Group. Natl. Rep: Christal,. Format: News/talk. News staff: 2. Target aud: 35-64. Spec prog: Farm 5 hrs, Polish 3 hrs, religious 3 hrs wkly. ♦Brett Lucht, gen mgr; Patrick Snyder, opns mgr, progmg dir; Samantha Milanwwski, stn mgr & sls dir; Carrie Van Deraa, prom dir; Frank Zastrow, chief of engrg.

WXCO(AM)— Aug 1, 1953: 1230 khz; 1 kw-U. TL: N44 58 10 W89 36 25. Hrs open: 24 Box 778, 54402. Secondary address: 1110 E. Wausau Ave. 54403. Phone: (715) 845-8218. Fax: (715) 845-6582.E-mail: wxco@wxco.com Web Site:www.wxco.com Licensee: Seehafer Broadcasting Corp. Group owner: Badger Communications L.L.C. (acq 9-26-73). Population served: 100,000 Natl. Network: CBS, Westwood One, . Format: Sports talk. News staff: one. Target aud: 25 plus; professionals/business. ♦Ken Rajek, gen mgr, gen sls mgr; Chad Holmes, progmg dir; Charles Gennaro, chief of engrg; Pam Hilke, traf mgr.

***WXPW(FM)—** February 1996: 91.9 mhz; 560 w. 823 ft (ST WLBL-FM) TL: N44 55 14 W89 41 31. Hrs open:
Rebroadcasts WXPR(FM) Rhinelander.
303 W. Prospect St., Rhinelander, 54501. Phone: (715) 362-6000. Fax: (715) 362-6007.E-mail: wxpr@wxpr.org Web Site:www.wxpr.org Licensee: White Pine Community Broadcasting Inc. Format: NPR news, great music. ♦Mick Fiocchi, pres, gen mgr; Jessie Dick, dev dir; Walt Gander, opns mgr & progmg dir; Ken Krall, news dir; Elmer Goetsch, chief of engrg.

Wautoma

WAUH(FM)— 2001: 102.3 mhz; 5.3 kw. Ant 3,490 ft TL: N44 01 54 W89 09 07. Hrs open: Box 492, W7703 Johnson Court, 54982. Phone: (902) 787-0128. Fax: (902) 361-3737.E-mail: thebug@wauhradio.com Web Site:www.wauhradio.com Licensee: Hometown Broadcasting LLC (acq 8-9-02). Format: Classic hits. ♦Bill Denkert, gen sls mgr.

Wauwatosa

WXSS(FM)— Jan 1, 1961: 103.7 mhz; 19.5 kw. 840 ft TL: N43 05 48 W87 54 19. Stereo. Hrs open: 24 11800 W. Grange Ave., Hales Corners, 53130. Phone: (414) 529-1250. Fax: (414) 529-2122. Web Site:www.entercom.com Licensee: Entercom Milwaukee License LLC. Group owner: Entercom Communications Corp. (acq 12-13-99; grpsl). Population served: 717,099 Format: CHR. News staff: one. Target aud: 18-44; women. ♦Alan Kirshbon, sls dir; Andrea Biebel, natl sls mgr; Brian Kelly, progmg dir; Jane Matenaer, news dir; Chris Tarr, chief of engrg.

Wentworth

***WWEN(FM)—**Not on air, target date: unknown: 88.1 mhz; 31 kw vert. Ant 296 ft TL: N46 25 07 W91 55 12. Hrs open: Drawer 2440, Tupelo, MS, 38803-2440. Phone: (662) 844-5036. Fax: (662) 842-7798.E-mail: info@afa.net Web Site:www.afr.net Licensee: American Family Association. ♦Donald E. Wildmon, chmn.

West Bend

WBKV(AM)— November 1950: 1470 khz; 2.5 kw-U, DA-2. TL: N43 22 14 W88 09 58. Hrs open: 24 Box 933, 2410 South Main Street, Suite A, 53095. Secondary address: 2410 S. Main St., Suite A 53095. Phone: (262) 334-2344. Fax: (262) 334-1512.E-mail: jhodges@westbendradio.com Web Site:wbkvam.com Licensee: West Bend Broadcasting Inc. Group owner: Bliss Communications Inc. (acq 10-18-70). Population served: 50,000 Natl. Network: CNN Radio, . Rgnl. Network: Wisconsin Radio Net. Natl. Rep: Rgnl Reps,. Dow, Lohnes & Albertson. Format: Classic country. News staff: one; News: 20 hrs wkly. Target aud: 35-64; info-hungry adults interested in loc events & classic country music. ♦Skip Bliss, pres; Rob Lisser, CFO; James N. Hodges, VP, gen mgr, natl sls mgr; Bob Bonenfant, progmg dir; Mark Morris, news dir; Jason Mielke, chief of engrg.

WBWI-FM— September 1958: 92.5 mhz; 17.5 kw. 565 ft TL: N43 25 45 W88 17 53. Stereo. Hrs open: 24 Prog sep from AM Box 933, 53095. Secondary address: 2410 S. Main St., Suite A 53095. Phone: (262) 334-2344. Fax: (262) 334-1512.E-mail: jhodges@westbendradio.com Web Site:wbwifm.com Population served: 1,000,000 Natl. Rep: Rgnl Reps,. Format: Country. News staff: one; News: 2 hrs wkly. Target aud: 25-54; country music listeners with disposable income. ♦James Hodges, VP; Fuzz Martin, progmg dir.

West Salem

WKBH-FM—Licensed to West Salem. See La Crosse

Westby

WDSW(FM)—Not on air, target date: unknown: 103.9 mhz; 2.75 kw. Ant 477 ft TL: N43 37 36 W90 41 57. Hrs open: 5331 Mount Alifan Dr., San Diego, CA, 92111-2622. Phone: (858) 277-4991. Fax: (858) 277-1365. Licensee: Horizon Christian Fellowship. ◆ Michael MacIntosh, pres.

Whitehall

WHTL-FM— Sept 10, 1981: 102.3 mhz; 3 kw. 450 ft TL: N44 24 47 W91 17 03. Stereo. Hrs open: 24 Box 66, N35609 Hwy. 53, 54773. Phone: (715) 538-4341. Fax: (715) 538-4360.E-mail: whtl@centurytel.net Licensee: The WHTL Group L.L.C. (acq 11-9-2006) $200,000 for stock). Population served: 60,000 Natl. Network: Jones Radio Networks, . Rgnl. Network: Goetz Group. Wisconsin Radio Net. Bosari & Paxson. Format: Greatest hits. News staff: one; News: 24 hrs wkly. Target aud: 25 plus; adult fans who make household buying decisions. ◆Butch Halama, CFO, gen mgr, sls dir; Barb Semb, opns mgr, pub affrs dir; Mary Little, progmg mgr & mus dir; Marty Little, sports cmtr.

Whitewater

WKCH(FM)— Jan 2, 1998: 106.5 mhz; 6 kw. Ant 200 ft TL: N42 54 24 W88 45 06. Hrs open: Box 94, Fort Atkinson, 53538. Phone: (920) 563-9329. Fax: (920) 563-0315.E-mail: fortproduction@nrgmedia.com Licensee: NRG License Sub. LLC. (group owner; (acq 10-31-2005; grpsl). Format: Oldies. ◆ Mary Quass, CEO; Tami Billmore, CFO; James Vriezen, gen mgr; Gary Douglas, opns dir, progmg dir; Michael Clish, news dir; George Nicholas, chief of engrg; Jaimie Flom, traf mgr.

WSLD(FM)— Nov 16, 1992: 104.5 mhz; 6 kw. Ant 328 ft TL: N42 35 47 W88 43 16. Stereo. Hrs open: 24 Box 709, N. 6534 Hwy. 89, 53190. Phone: (608) 883-6677. Fax: (608) 883-2054.E-mail: wsld@starband.net Web Site:www.1045wsld.com Licensee: WPW Broadcasting Inc. (group owner; (acq 8-4-99; $700,000). Format: Country. News staff: one; News: 10 hrs wkly. Target aud: General. ◆Don Davis, CEO; Nora Karbash, gen mgr, gen sls mgr; Reggie Michaels, progmg dir; Ryan O'Brien, news dir; Aaron Winski, chief of engrg; Trish Donovan, traf mgr.

*WSUW(FM)— Jan 10, 1965: 91.7 mhz; 1.3 kw. 185 ft TL: N42 50 10 W88 44 36. Stereo. Hrs open: 6 AM-2 AM UW Whitewater, 1201 Anderson Library, 53190. Phone: (262) 472-1323. Phone: (262) 472-1314. Fax: (262) 472-5029.E-mail: wsuw@uww.edu Web Site:www.wsuw.org Licensee: Board of Regents University of Wisconsin System. Population served: 80,000 Format: Hip Hop, alternative. Target aud: 18-44. Spec prog: Heavy metal 14 hrs, jazz/world beat 6 hrs, urban contemp 14 hrs wkly. ◆ Wilfred Tremblay, gen mgr; Mark Neilsen, mktg dir; Kelly O'Brien, progmg dir.

Whiting

WLJY(FM)— Oct 21, 1985: 96.7 mhz; 50 kw. Ant 492 ft TL: N44 29 24 W89 32 54. Stereo. Hrs open: 24 2301 Plover Rd., Plover, 54467. Phone: (715) 341-8838. Fax: (715) 341-9744. Web Site:967wljy.com Licensee: NRG License Sub. LLC. (group owner; (acq 10-31-2005; grpsl). Population served: 300,000 Latham & Watkins. Format: Mainstream adult contemp. News: 2.5 hrs wkly. Target aud: 25-54. ◆Benjamin D. Rosenthal, gen mgr; Bob Jung, gen sls mgr; Bill Phillips, progmg dir.

Winneconne

WVBO(FM)—Licensed to Winneconne. See Oshkosh

Wisconsin Dells

WDLS(AM)— May 1969: 900 khz; 1 kw-D, 229 w-N. TL: N43 38 23 W89 43 14. Hrs open: 24 Box 360, Portage, 53901. Phone: (608) 254-2546. Fax: (608) 745-5771.E-mail: rick@magnumradiogroup.net Web Site:wdlsam.com Licensee: Magnum Communications Inc. Group owner: Magnum Radio Inc. (acq 2-10-99; $775,000 with co-located FM). Population served: 105,000 Natl. Network: Jones Radio Networks, AP Radio, . Format: Country. News staff: one; News: 6 hrs wlky. Spec prog: Medical 5 hrs wkly. ◆ Dave Magnum, chmn; Jim Coursole, gen mgr.

WNNO-FM— May 1974: 106.9 mhz; 6 kw. Ant 321 ft TL: N43 38 23 W89 43 14. Stereo. Hrs open: 24 Box 360, Portage, 53901. Phone: (608) 254-2546. Fax: (608) 745-5771.E-mail: rick@magnumradiogroup.net Web Site:mix106wnno.com Population served: 105,000 Format: Adult contemp. News staff: one; News: 7 hrs wkly. Target aud: 18-40.

Wisconsin Rapids

WFHR(AM)— Nov 5, 1940: 1320 khz; 5 kw-D, 500 w-N, DA-N. TL: N44 24 56 W89 50 06. Hrs open: Box 8022, 645 25th Ave. N., 54495-8022. Phone: (715) 424-1300. Fax: (715) 424-1347. Web Site:www.wfhrradio.com Licensee: Seehafer Broadcasting Corp. (group owner; (acq 6-1-2006); swap with WDLB(AM) Marshfield and WOSQ(FM) Spencer for WBCV(FM) Wausau). Population served: 100,000 Natl. Network: CBS, . Format: News/talk, info, full service. ◆Donald Seehafer, pres; Kent Reeves, gen mgr, opns mgr; Jeff Seigler, gen sls mgr; Mike Warren, news dir; Pam Hilke, traf mgr; Car Hilke, news rptr.

WGLX-FM— Aug 1, 1946: 103.3 mhz; 100 kw. Ant 331 ft TL: N44 24 56 W89 50 10. Stereo. Hrs open: 2301 Plover Road, Plover, 54467. Phone: (715) 341-8838. Fax: (715) 341-9744. Web Site:www.wglx.com Licensee: NRG License Sub, LLC. (acq 10-31-2005; grpsl). Population served: 275,000 Format: Classic rock. Target aud: 25-49. ◆ Benjamin D. Rosenthal, gen mgr; Panama Jack, progmg dir.

*WRAO(FM)—Not on air, target date: unknown: 91.9 mhz; 6.5 kw. Ant 174 ft TL: N44 28 50 W90 01 30. Hrs open: Box 95, 54495-0095. Secondary address: 611 24th St. N. 54494-5509. Phone: (715) 325-3486. Licensee: Wisconsin Rapids Seventh-Day Adventist Church. ◆ Fred Miller, gen mgr.

Wittenberg

*WVRN(FM)— Dec 27, 2007: 88.9 mhz; 25 kw. Ant 482 ft TL: N44 57 54 W89 00 18. Hrs open: 3434 W. Kilbourn Ave., Milwaukee, 53208-3313. Phone: (414) 935-3000. Fax: (414) 935-3015. Web Site:www.vcyamerica.org Licensee: VCY America Inc. Format: Relg, Christian. ◆ Vic Eliason, VP & gen mgr; Jim Schneider, progmg dir; Andy Eliason, chief of engrg.

Wyoming

Afton

KRSV(AM)— Aug 13, 1985: 1210 khz; 5 kw-D, 250 w-N. TL: N42 43 22 W110 57 39. Hrs open: Box 1210, Wyoming Hwy. 238, 83110. Phone: (307) 885-5778.E-mail: hansenjw@silverstar.com Licensee: Western Wyoming Radio Inc. Natl. Network: ABC, . Format: Modern country, loc news, sports. ◆Jerry Hansen, pres & gen mgr; Jennie Hansen, sls dir, progmg dir; Dan Dockstader, news dir.

KRSV-FM— Nov 13, 1985: 98.7 mhz; 3 kw. Ant -289 ft TL: N42 51 02 W110 58 46. Hrs open: Box 1210, Wyoming Hwy. 238, 83110. Phone: (307) 885-5778. Fax: (307) 885-3678. Format: Country. ◆Jerry Hansen, gen mgr.

*KUWA(FM)— July 1, 1998: 91.3 mhz; 400 w. -312 ft TL: N42 51 02 W110 58 46. Hrs open: 24 Rebroadcasts KUWR(FM) Laramie 100%. Box 3984, Laramie, 82071. Phone: (307) 766-4240. Fax: (307) 766-6184.E-mail: wpr@uwyo.edu Web Site:www.wyomingpublicradio.net Licensee: University of Wyoming. Natl. Network: NPR, PRI, . Wire Svc: AP Format: Progsv, news/talk, class. News: 4 hrs wkly. Target aud: 25-54 plus; demographic, high income, education. Spec prog: Folk 5 hrs, jazz 5 hrs wkly. ◆ Jon Schwartz, gen mgr; Hank Arnold, dev dir; Roger Adams, opns mgr & progmg dir; Bob Beck, news dir; Larry Dean, chief of engrg.

Albin

KKAW(FM)— 2001: 107.3 mhz; 9.3 kw. Ant 531 ft TL: N41 29 31 W104 05 07. Hrs open: Rebroadcasts KZDR(FM) Cheyenne 100%. 2109 E. 10th St., Cheyenne, 82001. Phone: (307) 638-8921. Fax: (307) 638-8922. Licensee: Chisholm Trail Broadcasting LLC Group owner: Northeast Broadcasting Company Inc. (acq 5-23-2005; $850,000 with KREO(FM) Pine Bluffs). Format: Country.

Basin

KBEN-FM—Not on air, target date: unknown: 103.3 mhz; 64 kw. Ant 2,375 ft TL: N44 48 38 W107 55 18. Hrs open: 288 S. River Rd., Bedford, NH, 03110. Phone: (603) 668-6400. Fax: (603) 668-6470. Licensee: White Park Broadcasting Inc. ◆ Steven A. Silberberg, pres.

KZMQ(AM)—See Greybull

Big Horn

KHNY(AM)—Not on air, target date: unknown: 1370 khz; 10 kw-D, 250 w-N, DA-N. TL: N44 41 17 W106 59 45 (day), N44 41 11 W106 59 46 (night). Hrs open: 813 Ventura Park, Irving, TX, 79605. Phone: (325) 518-6511. Licensee: Scott Powell. ◆Scott Powell, gen mgr.

Buffalo

KBBS(AM)— Apr 17, 1956: 1450 khz; 1 kw-U. TL: N44 20 33 W106 40 54. Hrs open: 24 1221 Fort St., 82834. Phone: (307) 684-7070. Fax: (307) 684-7676.E-mail: kbbs@vcn.com Licensee: Legend Communications of Wyoming L.L.C. Group owner: Legend Communications LLC (acq 9-1-2000; $1.05 million with KLGT(FM) Buffalo). Population served: 25,800 Natl. Rep: McGavren Guild,. Format: Oldies, News/talk, Sports. News: 10 hrs wkly. Target aud: 35-64; age group with the most money to spend. ◆ Larry Patrick, CEO; Larry Patrick, pres; Ed Cwiklin, gen mgr, progmg dir; Steve Lawrence, stn mgr & opns dir; Charles Dozier, chief of engrg.

*KBUW(FM)— 2000: 90.5 mhz; 430 w. Ant -197 ft TL: N44 20 50 W106 43 25. Hrs open: Box 3984, Laramie, 82071. Phone: (307) 766-4240. Fax: (307) 766-6184.E-mail: rgriscom@uwyo.edu Web Site:uwadmnweb.uwyo.edu/WPR Licensee: University of Wyoming. Format: News, AAA. ◆Jon Schwartz, gen mgr; Peg Arnold, dev dir; Bob Beck, news dir; Larry Dean, chief of engrg; Roger Adams, adv dir & traf mgr.

KLGT(FM)— Mar 7, 1983: 92.9 mhz; 100 kw. Ant 358 ft TL: N44 34 32 W106 52 23. Stereo. Hrs open: 24 1221 Fort St., 82834. Phone: (307) 684-5126. Phone: (307) 684-2584. Fax: (307) 684-7676.E-mail: klgt@vcn.com Licensee: Legend Communications of Wyoming L.L.C. Group owner: Legend Communications L.L.C. (acq 9-1-2000). Population served: 64,000 Natl. Network: Jones Radio Networks, . Natl. Rep: McGavren Guild,. Format: Country. News staff: one; News: 9 hrs wkly. Target aud: 24-54; those with spendable income. Spec prog: Relg one hr wkly. ◆ Larry Patrick, CEO, pres; Nicki Williams, CFO; Smokey Wildeman, gen mgr; Ed Cwiklin, opns mgr, progmg dir; Zach Morton, chief of engrg.

Burns

*KEZF(FM)— 2008: 88.9 mhz; 600 w. Ant 118 ft TL: N41 09 45 W104 30 16. Hrs open: 87 Jasper Lake Rd., Loveland, CO, 80537. Phone: (970) 669-9200. Fax: (970) 669-0800. Licensee: Cedar Cove Broadcasting Inc. ◆ Victor A. Michael Jr., pres.

KIGN(FM)— Sept 26, 1990: 101.9 mhz; 50 kw. 492 ft TL: N41 07 01 W104 40 07. Stereo. Hrs open: 24 101.9 KING FM, 1912 Capitol Ave., Suite 300, Cheyenne, 82001. Phone: (307) 632-4400. Fax: (307) 632-1818. Web Site:www.kingfm.com Licensee: GAP Broadcasting Cheyenne License LLC. Group owner: Clear Channel Communications Inc. (acq 2-13-2008; grpsl). Population served: 75,000 Format: Adult Rock. News staff: one; News: 3 hrs wkly. Target aud: 25-54. ◆ Craig Cochran, gen mgr, gen sls mgr; Rick Darcy, opns mgr; Geoff Gundy, progmg dir; Amy Richards, news dir, chief of engrg; Jim Mross, chief of engrg.

Casper

KASS(FM)— Oct 15, 1990: 106.9 mhz; 94 kw. Ant 1,765 ft TL: N42 44 37 W106 18 31. Stereo. Hrs open: 24 218 N. Wolcott St., 82602. Phone: (307) 265-1984. Fax: (307) 473-7461.E-mail: kass@wyomingradio.com Web Site:www.wyomingradio.com Licensee: Mount Rushmore Broadcasting Inc. (group owner; (acq 1995; $150,000). Population served: 60,000 Format: Classic rock. ◆Roger Arndt, gen mgr, gen sls mgr; Donny Rood, progmg dir; Steve Fritz, chief of engrg; Jenniey Lyman, traf mgr.

*KCSP-FM— 1992: 90.3 mhz; 100 kw. Ant 1,922 ft TL: N42 44 24 W106 18 23. Stereo. Hrs open: 24 6363 Hwy. 50 E., Carson City, 89701. Phone: (775) 883-5647. Fax: (775) 883-5704.E-mail: info@kcspfm.com Licensee: Western Inspirational Broadcasters Inc. (acq 10-3-90). Population served: 330,000 Natl. Network: AP Radio, . Wire Svc: AP Format: Contemp Christian. News: 16 hrs wkly. Target aud: General.

♦Tom Hesse, gen mgr; Tim Wwidemann, opns mgr; Bill Feltner, progmg dir; Janet Santana, mus dir; Paul Lierman, chief of engrg.

KHOC(FM)— 1998: 102.5 mhz; 100 kw. Ant 1,696 ft TL: N42 44 37 W106 18 31. Stereo. Hrs open: 24 218 N. Wolcott St., 82601. Phone: (307) 265-1984. Fax: (307) 266-3295.E-mail: mrbnews@wyoming.com Web Site:www.wyomingradio.com Licensee: Mount Rushmore Broadcasting Inc. (group owner; (acq 10-29-98; $300,000). Format: Hot adult contemp. News staff: 1. Target aud: M/f 18-45. ♦Kevin Gray, gen mgr; Glenna Hunter, progmg dir; Steve Fritz, engrg dir; Michelle Reynolds, traf mgr.

***KKRR(FM)**— 2008: 88.3 mhz; 500 w vert. Ant 1,725 ft TL: N42 44 26 W106 21 34. Hrs open: 2232 Dell Range Blvd., Suite 103, Cheyenne, 82009-4994. Phone: (307) 637-7777. Licensee: WCN Inc. Format: Oldies. ♦Robert R. Rule, pres.

KKTL(AM)— 1999: 1400 khz; 1 kw-U. TL: N42 51 22 W106 21 41. Hrs open: 150 N. Nichols Ave., 82601. Phone: (307) 266-5252. Fax: (307) 235-9143.E-mail: kktl@thegapbroadcasting.com Licensee: GAP Broadcasting Casper License LLC. Group owner: Clear Channel Communications Inc. (acq 2-13-2008; grpsl). Format: Sports. ♦Robert Price, gen mgr; Donovan Short, opns mgr, progmg dir; Walter Hawn, gen sls mgr; Dave Nutter, chief of engrg; Dave Borino, traf mgr.

***KLWC(FM)**— 2005: 89.1 mhz; 1.5 kw vert. Ant 1,848 ft TL: N42 44 03 W106 20 00. Hrs open:
Rebroadcasts KLVR(FM) Santa Rosa, CA).
2351 Sunset Blvd., Suite 170-218, Rocklin, CA, 95765. Phone: (916) 251-1600. Fax: (916) 251-1650. Web Site:www.klove.com Licensee: Educational Media Foundation. (acq 1-11-2005; $100,000 for CP with CP for KLRV(FM) Billings, MT). Natl. Network: K-Love, . Format: Christian. ♦Richard Jenkins, pres; Mike Novak, VP; Keith Whipple, dev dir; David Pierce, progmg mgr; Ed Lenane, news dir; Sam Wallington, engrg dir; Karen Johnson, news rptr.

KMGW(FM)— 1998: 96.7 mhz; 2.85 kw. Ant 1,771 ft TL: N42 44 37 W106 18 26. Hrs open: 150 N. Nichols Ave., 82601. Phone: (307) 266-5252. Fax: (307) 235-9143. Web Site:www.rock967online.com Licensee: GAP Broadcasting Casper License LLC. (acq 2-13-2008; grpsl). Format: Classic rock. ♦Bob Price, gen mgr; Donovan Short, opns mgr, progmg dir; Trisha Berry, prom dir.

KMLD(FM)— Oct 1, 1967: 94.5 mhz; 63 kw. Ant 1,909 ft TL: N42 44 03 W106 20 00. Stereo. Hrs open: 218 N. Wolcott St., 82601. Phone: (307) 265-1984. Fax: (307) 473-7461.E-mail: kmld@wyomingradio.com Web Site:www.wyomingradio.com Licensee: Mt. Rushmore Broadcasting Inc. Group owner: Mount Rushmore Broadcasting Inc. (acq 3-12-2001; grpsl). Format: Oldies. Target aud: 35-64. ♦Roger Arndt, gen mgr; Donny Rood, progmg dir; Steve Fritz, chief of engrg; Jenniey Lyman, traf mgr.

KQLT(FM)— Oct 7, 1983: 103.7 mhz; 97 kw. Ant 1,860 ft TL: N42 44 37 W106 18 31. Stereo. Hrs open: 24 218 N. Wolcott St., 82601. Phone: (307) 265-1984. Fax: (307) 473-7461.E-mail: kqlt@wyomingradio.com Web Site:www.wyomingradio.com Licensee: Mount Rushmore Broadcasting Inc. (group owner; (acq 8-17-94; $230,000;9-12-94). Natl. Rep: McGavren Guild,. Dow, Lohnes & Albertson. Format: Country. Target aud: General. ♦Jan Charles Gray, pres; Roger Arndt, gen mgr; Don Rood, opns mgr; Donny Rood, progmg dir; Steve Fritz, chief of engrg; Jenniey Lyman, traf mgr.

KTRS-FM— January 1997: 104.7 mhz; 18 w. 1,774 ft TL: N42 44 37 W106 18 26. Hrs open: 150 N. Nichols Ave., 82601. Phone: (307) 266-5252. Fax: (307) 235-9143.E-mail: ktrs@clearchannel.com Licensee: GAP Broadcasting Casper License LLC. Group owner: Clear Channel Communications Inc. (acq 2-13-2008; grpsl). Format: CHR. Target aud: 12-24. ♦Robert Price, gen mgr; Donovan Short, opns mgr, gen sls mgr, progmg dir; Walter Hawn, gen sls mgr & news dir; Dave Nutter, chief of engrg; Dave Borino, traf mgr.

KTWO(AM)— Jan 2, 1930: 1030 khz; 50 kw-U, DA-N. TL: N42 50 34 W106 13 07. Hrs open: 150 N. Nichols Ave., 82601. Phone: (307) 266-5252. Fax: (307) 235-9143.E-mail: ktwo@clearchanel.com Web Site:www.k2radio.com Licensee: GAP Broadcasting Casper License LLC. Group owner: Clear Channel Communications Inc. (acq 2-13-2008; grpsl). Population served: 159,361 Natl. Network: CBS, . Drinker Biddle & Reath LLP. Format: Talk. Target aud: 25-54. ♦Bob Price, gen mgr, opns mgr, gen sls mgr; Bob Davis, progmg dir; Vicki Daniels, news dir; David Nutter, chief of engrg; Dave Borino, traf mgr.

***KUWC(FM)**— 2000: 91.3 mhz; 530 w. Ant 1,784 ft TL: N42 44 26 W106 21 34. Hrs open: Box 3984, Laramie, 82071. Phone: (307) 766-4240. Fax: (307) 766-6184.E-mail: jbs@uwyo.edu Web Site:uwadmnweb.uwyo.edu Licensee: University of Wyoming. Format: News, AAA. ♦Jon Schwartz, gen mgr; Peg Arnold, prom dir; Roger Adams, progmg dir; Larry Dean, mus dir; Bob Beck, news dir.

KVOC(AM)— Sept 29, 1946: 1230 khz; 1 kw-U. TL: N42 50 05 W106 17 44. Hrs open: 218 N. Wolcott St., 82601. Phone: (307) 265-1984. Fax: (307) 473-7461.E-mail: mtrushmore@mrbradio.com Web Site:www.wyomingradio.com Licensee: Mount Rushmore Broadcasting Inc. (group owner; (acq 6-12-97; $105,000). Population served: 75,000 Natl. Network: ESPN Radio, . Format: Sports. ♦Jan Charles Gray, pres; Roger Arndt, gen mgr; Donny Rood, progmg dir; Steve Fritz, chief of engrg; Jenniey Lyman, traf mgr.

KWYX(FM)—Not on air, target date: unknown: 93.5 mhz; 15 kw. Ant 1,712 ft TL: N42 44 30 W106 18 29. Hrs open: Box 11060, Jackson, 83002. Licensee: Cochise Broadcasting LLC. ♦Ted Tucker, gen mgr.

Cheyenne

***KAIX(FM)**— 2006: 88.1 mhz; 1 kw. Ant 209 ft TL: N41 09 37 W104 42 13. Hrs open:
Rebroadcasts KLRD(FM) Yucaipa, CA 100%.
5700 West Oaks Blvd., Rocklin, CA, 95765. Phone: (916) 251-1600. Fax: (916) 251-1650. Web Site:www.air1.com Licensee: Educational Media Foundation. (acq 3-23-2007; grpsl). Natl. Network: Air 1, . Format: Alternative rock, div. ♦Richard Jenkins, pres.

KAZY(FM)— June 15, 2006: 93.7 mhz; 25 kw. Ant 115 ft TL: N41 08 04 W104 41 32. Hrs open: 2109 E. 10th St., 82001. Phone: (307) 638-8921. Fax: (307) 638-8922. Licensee: White Park Broadcasting Inc. Format: Active rock. ♦Steven A. Silberberg, pres; Roger Ingram, gen mgr.

KFBC(AM)— 1940: 1240 khz; 1 kw-U. TL: N41 07 17 W104 50 22. Hrs open: 24 1806 Capitol Ave., 82001. Phone: (307) 634-4461. Fax: (307) 632-8586.E-mail: info@kfbcam.com Licensee: Montgomery Broadcasting L.L.C. (acq 7-1-93; $250,000). Population served: 72,000 Natl. Network: ABC, . Format: Full service, news, sports. News staff: 5; News: 25 hrs wkly. Target aud: 35-54. ♦Dave Montgomery, pres, gen mgr; J.D. Harris, stn mgr.

KGAB(AM)—(Orchard Valley, 1952: 650 khz; 8.5 kw-D, 500 w-N, DA-N. TL: N41 03 11 W104 49 57. Hrs open: 24 1912 Capitol Ave., Suite 300, 82001. Phone: (307) 632-4400. Fax: (307) 632-1818. Web Site:www.kgab.com Licensee: GAP Broadcasting Cheyenne License LLC. Group owner: Clear Channel Communications Inc. (acq 2-13-2008; grpsl). Population served: 1,400,000 Format: News/talk. News staff: 3. Target aud: 25-64. ♦Craig Cochran, gen mgr; Dave Chaffin, opns mgr, progmg dir; Amy Richards, news dir; Jim Mross, chief of engrg.

KIGN(FM)—See Burns

KJUA(AM)— 1952: 1380 khz; 1 kw-D, 8 w-N. TL: N41 07 22 W104 48 07. Stereo. Hrs open: 24 110 East 17th St., Suite 205, 82001. Phone: (307) 635-8787. Fax: (307) 635-8788.E-mail: kjjl@kjjl.com Web Site:www.kjjl.com Licensee: Christus Broadcasting Inc. Population served: 70,000 Natl. Network: CNN Radio, . Booth, Freret, Imlay. Format: Adult contemp. News staff: 2; News: 22 hrs wkly. Target aud: 35 plus; mature adults. Spec prog: Gospel one hr wkly. ♦Paul Montoya, pres.

KKPL(FM)— 1997: 99.9 mhz; 50 kw. Ant 492 ft TL: N40 59 22 W105 03 47. Hrs open: 3201 E. Mulberry St., Unit H, Fort Collins, CO, 80524. Phone: (970) 674-2700. Phone: (970) 492-0999. Fax: (970) 407-0584.E-mail: info@999thepoint.com Web Site:www.999thepoint.com Licensee: Regent Broadcasting of Ft. Collins Inc. Group owner: Regent Communications Inc. (acq 11-15-2004; $7.75 million with KARS-FM Laramie). Format: Alternative. ♦Cal Hall, gen mgr; Mark Callaghan, opns mgr; Miles Schallert, sls dir; Mark Callagham, progmg dir; Susan Moore, news dir; Quin Morrison, chief of engrg.

KLEN(FM)— Sept 26, 1983: 106.3 mhz; 6 kw. Ant 325 ft TL: N41 03 09 W104 49 55. Stereo. Hrs open: 24 1912 Capitol Ave., Suite 300, 82001. Phone: (307) 632-4400. Fax: (307) 632-1818.E-mail: cheyenneaudio@clearchannel.com Web Site:www.1063klen.com Licensee: GAP Broadcasting Cheyenne License LLC. Group owner: Clear Channel Communications Inc. (acq 2-13-2008; grpsl). Population served: 60,000 Format: Country. News staff: 3. Target aud: 25-54. ♦Craig Cochran, gen mgr, gen sls mgr; Amy Richards, prom dir, news dir; Rick Darcy, opns mgr, gen sls mgr & progmg dir; Jim Mross, chief of engrg; Lesley Martin, traf mgr.

KOLZ(FM)— August 1961: 100.7 mhz; 100 kw. Ant 490 ft TL: N41 06 01 W105 00 23. Stereo. Hrs open: 1912 Capitol Ave., Suite 300, 82001. Phone: (307) 632-4400. Fax: (307) 632-1818. Web Site:www.kolz.com Licensee: Citicasters Licenses L.P. Population served: 135,000 Format: Country. ♦Jeff Brown, progmg dir.

KRAE(AM)— Apr 29, 1961: 1480 khz; 1 kw-D, 67 w-N. TL: N41 07 26 W104 49 10. Stereo. Hrs open: 2109 E. 10th St., 82001. Phone: (307) 638-8921. Fax: (307) 638-8922.E-mail: news@1049krrr.com Licensee: Brahmin Broadcasting Corp. Group owner: Northeast Broadcasting Company Inc. (acq 5-10-2004; grpsl). Population served: 200,000 Natl. Network: ESPN Radio, . Format: Sports. Spec prog: Sp 2 hrs wkly. ♦Larry Proietti, gen mgr; Jessica Cooper, sls dir; Larry Proeitti, progmg dir; R.J. Fox, news dir; Rob Thomas, chief of engrg; Sandra Cooper, traf mgr.

KRRR(FM)— 1997: 104.9 mhz; 25.5 kw. Ant 115 ft TL: N41 08 04 W104 41 32. Stereo. Hrs open: 2109 E. 10th St., 82001. Phone: (307) 638-8921. Fax: (307) 638-8922. Population served: 72,400 Format: Oldies. Target aud: 25-54. ♦Roger Ingram, gen mgr.

KXBG(FM)— Sept 1, 1968: 97.9 mhz; 100 kw. Ant 541 ft TL: N41 06 01 W105 00 23. Stereo. Hrs open: 24 4270 Byrd Dr, Loveland, CO, 80538. Phone: (970) 482-5991. Fax: (970) 482-5994. Licensee: Citicasters Licenses L.P. Group owner: Clear Channel Communications Inc. (acq 1999; grpsl). Population served: 350,000 Format: Country. News staff: 3; News: 2 hrs wkly. Target aud: 25-54. ♦Stu Haskell, gen mgr; Chris Kelly, opns mgr, progmg dir; Kathy Arias, gen sls mgr; Rich Bircumshaw, news dir; Cliff Mikkelson, chief of engrg; Karen Vissers, traf mgr.

Chugwater

***KLWV(FM)**— 2004: 90.9 mhz; 100 kw. Ant 1,183 ft TL: N41 18 39 W105 27 12. Hrs open: 24 2351 Sunset Blvd., Suite 170-218, Rocklin, CA, 95765. Phone: (916) 251-1600. Fax: (916) 251-1650.E-mail: klove@klove.com Web Site:www.klove.com Licensee: Educational Media Foundation. Group owner: EMF Broadcasting (acq 10-2-03; grpsl). Natl. Network: K-Love, . Shaw Pittman. Format: Contemp Christian. News staff: 3. Target aud: 25-44; Judeo Christian, female. ♦Richard Jenkins, pres; Mike Novak, VP; Ed Lenane, opns dir, news dir; Keith Whipple, dev dir; David Pierce, progmg mgr; Sam Wallington, engrg dir; Arthur Vassar, traf mgr; Karen Johnson, news rptr.

KMJY(FM)— 2007: 99.5 mhz; 9.6 kw. Ant 239 ft TL: N41 46 04 W104 49 00. Hrs open: 2109 E. 10th St., Cheyenne, 82001. Phone: (307) 638-8921. Fax: (307) 638-8922. Licensee: Brahmin Broadcasting Corp. Format: Oldies. ♦Steven A. Silberberg, pres; Roger Ingram, gen mgr.

Clearmont

KLQQ(FM)— 2006: 104.7 mhz; 2.1 kw. Ant 1,122 ft TL: N44 37 20 W107 06 57. Hrs open: Box 5086, Sheridan, 82801. Phone: (307) 672-7421. Fax: (307) 672-2933. Licensee: Lovcom Inc. Format: Top-40. ♦Kim Love, gen mgr.

Cody

***KNWT(FM)**—Not on air, target date: unknown: 89.1 mhz; 18.5 kw. Ant 1,794 ft TL: N44 29 46 W109 09 09. Hrs open: Northwest Community College, 231 W. Sixth St., Powell, 82435. Phone: (307) 754-6438.E-mail: dennis.davis@northwestcollege.edu Licensee: Northwest Community College, State of Wyoming. ♦Dennis Davis, gen mgr.

KODI(AM)— March 1947: 1400 khz; 1 kw-U. TL: N44 30 30 W109 04 05. Hrs open: 6 AM-midnight Box 1210, 1949 Mountain View Dr., 82414. Phone: (307) 578-5000. Fax: (307) 527-5045.E-mail: ckary@bhrnwy.com Web Site:www.bighornradio.com Licensee: Legend Communications of Wyoming LLC. Group owner: Legend Communications LLC (acq 6-29-99; $890,000 with co-located FM). Population served: 20,000 Wire Svc: NWS (National Weather Service) Format: News/talk, sports. News staff: one; News: 20 hrs wkly. Target aud: 35 plus. ♦Larry Patrick, pres; Roger Gelder, exec VP; Carol Kary, VP, gen mgr; Cory Ostermiller, gen sls mgr; Tom Morrison, progmg dir, pub affrs dir; Wendy Corr, news dir; Charles Dozier, chief of engrg.

***KOFG(FM)**— 2009: 91.1 mhz; 4 kw. Ant 1,801 ft TL: N44 29 46 W109 09 09. Hrs open: 1 Arrowhead Dr., 82414. Phone: (903) 503-0304. Web Site:www.oldfashiongospel.com Licensee: Tres Hermanas Educational Media Foundation of Texas Inc. Format: Gospel. ♦Lonnie M. Horton, pres.

KTAG(FM)— Nov 30, 1981: 97.9 mhz; 100 kw. 1,901 ft TL: N44 29 44 W109 09 13. Stereo. Hrs open: 6 AM-midnight Prog sep from AM Box 1210, 1949 Mountain View Dr., 82414. Phone: (307) 578-5000. Fax: (307) 527-5045.E-mail: ckary@bhrnwy.com Web Site:bighornradio.com Population served: 40,000 Format: Adult contemp. News: 6 hrs wkly. Target aud: 25-39; upper middle class, young families, suburban w/some college, 60% female. ♦Larry Patrick, CEO; Roger Gelder, COO; Carol Kary, gen mgr; Cory Ostermiller, gen sls mgr; Wendy Corr, news dir.

KWHO(FM)—Not on air, target date: unknown: 96.7 mhz; 2.4 kw. Ant 1,831 ft TL: N44 29 49 W109 09 19. Hrs open: 288 S. River Rd., Bedford, NH, 03110. Phone: (603) 668-6400. Fax: (603) 668-6470. Licensee: White Park Broadcasting Inc. ◆Steven A. Silberberg, pres.

Diamondville

KDWY(FM)— 2000: 105.3 mhz; 16 kw. Ant 886 ft TL: N41 50 18 W110 30 12. Hrs open: c/o Radio Station KMER(AM), Box 432, Kemmerer, 83101. Phone: (307) 877-4422. Fax: (307) 877-5537.E-mail: kmer@onewest.net Licensee: Simmons-SLC, LS LLC. Group owner: Simmons Media Group (acq 4-19-2004; grpsl). Population served: 80,000 Natl. Network: ABC, . Format: Country. News staff: one; News: one hr wkly. Target aud: 25-55. ◆Jim Carroll, gen mgr; Jim Thoeny, opns dir.

Douglas

KDAD(FM)— 2007: 92.5 mhz; 5.4 kw. Ant 3,188 ft TL: N42 16 05 W105 26 33. Hrs open: 2109 E. 10th St., Cheyenne, 82001. Phone: (307) 638-8921. Fax: (307) 638-8922. Licensee: White Park Broadcasting Inc. Format: Active rock. ◆Steven A. Silberberg, pres; Roger Ingram, gen mgr.

*KDUW(FM)— 2000: 91.7 mhz; 450 w. Ant -52 ft TL: N42 44 41 W105 20 09. Hrs open: Box 3984, Laramie, 82071. Phone: (307) 766-4240. Fax: (307) 766-6184.E-mail: hgriscom@uwyo.edu Web Site:www.wyomingpublicradio.org Licensee: University of Wyoming. Format: News, progsv, class. ◆Jon Schwartz, gen mgr; Peg Arnold, progmg dir; Larry Dean, chief of engrg.

KKTY(AM)— June 22, 1957: 1470 khz; 1 kw-D, 500 w-N. TL: N42 45 48 W105 23 32. Hrs open: 24 Box 135, 247 Russell Ave., 82633. Phone: (307) 358-3636. Fax: (307) 358-4010.E-mail: kkty@netcommander.com Web Site:www.kktyonline.com Licensee: Douglas Broadcasting Inc. (acq 2-11-93; $120,000 with co-located FM; 3-8-93). Population served: 12,000 Natl. Network: Westwood One, CNN Radio, . Rgnl rep: Regnl Reps Wire Svc: AP Format: Oldies. News: 28 hrs wkly. Target aud: General. ◆Dennis Switzer, pres & gen mgr.

KKTY-FM— Dec 6, 1982: 99.3 mhz; 813 w. 530 ft TL: N42 43 42 W105 31 46. Stereo. Hrs open: 24 Box 135, 247 Russell Ave., 82633. Phone: (307) 358-3636 . Fax: (307) 358-4010.E-mail: kkty@netcommander.com Web Site:www.kktyonline.com Natl. Network: Jones Radio Networks, CNN Radio, . Format: Country. News staff: one; News: 28 hrs wkly. Target aud: General. ◆Becky Heidt, traf mgr.

*KKWY(FM)—Not on air, target date: unknown: 88.7 mhz; 7 kw. Ant 239 ft TL: N42 51 29 W105 14 03. Hrs open: 5944 Kenosha St., Cheyenne, 82001. Phone: (307) 460-4224. Licensee: Wren Communications Inc. ◆Tara D. Parker, pres.

Dubois

KLEP(FM)—Not on air, target date: unknown: 104.7 mhz; 5.5 kw horiz. Ant 1,407 ft TL: N43 40 26 W110 01 49. Hrs open: Box 11060, Jackson, 83002. Licensee: Cochise Media Licenses LLC (acq 2-19-2009; $165,000 for CP). ◆Ted Tucker, gen mgr.

Elk Mountain

*KGCV(FM)—Not on air, target date: unknown: 88.1 mhz; 100 w. Ant 3,428 ft TL: N41 38 00 W106 31 33. Hrs open: 6139 Franklin Park Rd., McLean, VA, 22101-4214. Phone: (703) 761-5013. Licensee: Ocean Side Broadcasting Inc. ◆A. Wray Fitch III, pres.

Esterbrook

*KGCY(FM)—Not on air, target date: unknown: 89.5 mhz; 900 w vert. Ant 3,165 ft TL: N42 16 06 W105 26 31. Hrs open: 87 Jasper Lake Rd., Loveland, CO, 80537. Phone: (970) 669-9200. Licensee: Cedar Cove Broadcasting Inc. ◆Victor A. Michael, pres.

Ethete

*KWRR(FM)— 2000: 89.5 mhz; 85 kw. Ant 1,820 ft TL: N43 27 30 W108 11 39. Hrs open: Box 327, Kinnear, 82516. Phone: (307) 335-8659. Phone: (307) 335-8658. Fax: (307) 335-8740.E-mail: rproductions@hotmail.com Licensee: Business Council of the Northern

Arapaho Tribe. (acq 8-11-98). Format: Var, Native American. ◆Steven White, gen mgr; Jason Foskey, progmg dir; Lincoln Scott, chief of engrg.

Evanston

KADQ-FM— 2008: 98.3 mhz; 1.2 kw. Ant 1,489 ft TL: N41 21 10 W110 54 31. Hrs open: College Creek Media LLC, 980 N. Michigan Ave., Suite 1880, Chicago, IL, 60611. Phone: (312) 204-9900. Licensee: College Creek Media LLC. ◆David Stout, gen mgr.

KBMG(FM)— June 1982: 106.1 mhz; 89 kw horiz. Ant 2,122 ft TL: N40 52 16 W110 59 43. Stereo. Hrs open: 2722 S. Redwood Rd., Suite 1, Salt Lake City, UT, 84119. Phone: (801) 908-8777. Fax: (801) 908-8782 . Licensee: Bustos Media of Utah License LLC. Group owner: Bustos Media Holdings (acq 7-1-2004; $3 million). Format: Sp. ◆Edward Distel, gen mgr.

*KCWW(FM)—Not on air, target date: unknown: 88.1 mhz; 92 w. Ant 1,348 ft TL: N41 21 10 W110 54 29. Hrs open: Box 1372, Park City, UT, 84060-1372. Phone: (435) 649-9004. Fax: (435) 645-9063. Licensee: Community Wireless of Park City Inc. ◆Blair Feulner, gen mgr.

KEVA(AM)— June 27, 1953: 1240 khz; 1 kw-U. TL: N41 15 29 W111 00 51. Hrs open: 24 Box 190, 568 Airport Rd., 82931. Phone: (307) 789-9101. Phone: (307) 789-9102. Fax: (307) 789-8521.E-mail: keva@vcn.com Web Site:1240keva,com Licensee: Sagebrush Broadcasting Co. Inc. Group owner: Jimmy Ray Carroll Stns (acq 1-23-2001). Population served: 25,000 Format: Country. Target aud: 25-54. ◆Linda Burris, gen mgr, prom mgr; Linda Burns, gen sls mgr; Bill Smith, prom dir, progmg dir; J.C. Jewett, news dir; Michael Richard, progmg mgr & chief of engrg.

Evansville

KTED(FM)— 2008: 100.5 mhz; 10 kw. Ant 1,433 ft TL: N42 45 30 W106 19 23. Hrs open: 288 S. River Rd., Bedford, NH, 03110. Phone: (603) 668-6470. Licensee: White Park Broadcasting Inc. ◆Steven A. Silberberg, pres.

KUYO(AM)— Aug 23, 1985: 830 khz; 25 kw-D. TL: N42 52 13 W106 12 12. Hrs open: Sunrise-sunset Box 50607, Casper, 82605-0607. Secondary address: 1423 S. Beverly, Casper 82609. Phone: (307) 577-5896. Fax: (307) 577-0850.E-mail: info@kuyo.com Web Site:www.kuyo.com Licensee: Wyoming Christian Broadcasting Co. (acq 6-1-99; $75,000). Format: Classic Christian, talk. Target aud: 35-65; general. ◆Aaron Remington, VP; Steve Stumbo, pres & gen mgr.

Fort Bridger

KNYN(FM)— 2001: 99.1 mhz; 27.5 kw. Ant 1,604 ft TL: N41 21 10 W110 54 26. Hrs open: Box 190, Evanston, 83931. Phone: (307) 789-9101. Fax: (307) 789-8521.E-mail: info@keva.com Licensee: M. Kent Frandsen. (acq 6-22-99; $125,000). Format: Adult contemp. ◆Linda Burris, gen mgr, gen sls mgr; Bill Smith, progmg dir; J.C. Jewett, news dir; Michael Richard, chief of engrg.

Fort Washakie

*KFTW(FM)—Not on air, target date: unknown: 90.9 mhz; 8 kw. Ant 499 ft TL: N42 54 27 W108 44 50. Hrs open: 90 Ethete Rd., 82514. Phone: (307) 332-5983. Fax: (307) 332-7267. Licensee: Fremont County School District #21. ◆Gregory Cox, gen mgr.

Fox Farm

KRND(AM)— 1998: 1630 khz; 10 kw-D, 1 kw-N. TL: N41 07 22 W104 48 07. Hrs open: 24 110 E. 17th St., Suite 205, Cheyenne, 82001. Phone: (307) 635-8787. Fax: (307) 635-8788.E-mail: kwy@kwyradio.com Web Site:www.kwyradio.com Licensee: Christus Broadcasting Inc. Population served: 170,000 Natl. Network: AP Network News, . Booth, Freret & Imlay. Format: Classic country. News staff: one; News: 22 hrs wkly. Target aud: 35 plus; mature adults. ◆Paul Montoya, pres, gen mgr & chief of opns.

Gillette

KAML-FM— May 1976: 96.9 mhz; 100 kw. Ant 456 ft TL: N44 18 10 W105 27 00. Stereo. Hrs open: 24 Box 1179, 82717. Phone: (307) 686-2242. Fax: (307) 686-7736. Web Site:www.basinsradio.com Licensee:

Legend Communications of Wyoming LLC. (acq 1-16-2007; $300,000 with KIML(AM) Gillette). Population served: 30,000 Format: Top 40. News staff: one; News: one hr wkly. Target aud: 25-54. ◆Don Clonch, gen mgr; Terry Michael, progmg mgr.

*KAXG(FM)— Mar 27, 2003: 89.7 mhz; 400 w vert. Ant 449 ft TL: N44 12 34 W105 28 04. Hrs open: 24 Rebroadcasts KXEI(FM) Havre, MT 100%. Box 2426, Havre, MT, 59501-2426. Phone: (406) 265-5845. Fax: (406) 265-8860.E-mail: ynop@ynopradio.org Web Site:www.ynopradio.org Licensee: Hi-Line Radio Fellowship Inc. (acq 3-25-2003; $65,000). Natl. Network: Salem Radio Network, . Wire Svc: AP Format: Christian inspirational. Target aud: General; those looking for inprirational Christian music & progmg. ◆Roger Lonnquist, gen mgr; Brenda Boyum, stn mgr; Brian Jackson, progmg dir.

KGCC(FM)— 2004: 103.9 mhz; 50 kw. Ant 392 ft TL: N44 13 50 W105 27 45. Hrs open: Box 2230, 82717. Phone: (307) 687-1003. Fax: (307) 687-1006.E-mail: koaal1039@collinscom.net Licensee: Keyhole Broadcasting LLC. Format: Classic rock. ◆Deborah Semple, gen mgr, gen sls mgr; Rob Olsen, progmg dir.

*KGLL(FM)—Not on air, target date: unknown: 88.1 mhz; 200 w vert. Ant 279 ft TL: N44 13 50 W105 27 45. Hrs open: Drawer 2440, Tupelo, MS, 38803. Phone: (662) 844-8888. Licensee: Solid Rock Broadcasting Inc. ◆Barbara Coggin, pres.

KGWY(FM)— Jan 5, 1983: 100.7 mhz; 100 kw. Ant 635 ft TL: N44 14 35 W105 32 19. Stereo. Hrs open: 24 Box 1179, 82717. Secondary address: 2810 Southern Dr. 82718. Phone: (307) 686-2242. Fax: (307) 686-7736.E-mail: thefox@basinsradio.com Web Site:www.basinsradio.com Licensee: Legend Communications of Wyoming LLC. Group owner: Legend Communications L.L.C. (acq 5-29-2001; $1.9 million). Format: Country. News staff: one. Target aud: 20-45. ◆Larry Patrick, pres; Don Clonch, gen mgr; Terry Michael, opns mgr.

KIML(AM)— Sept 13, 1957: 1270 khz; 5 kw-D, 1 kw-N, DA-N. TL: N44 18 12 W015 59 52. Stereo. Hrs open: 24 Box 1179, 82717. Phone: (307) 686-2242. Fax: (307) 686-7736. Web Site:www.basinsradio.com Licensee: Legend Communications of Wyoming LLC. (acq 1-16-2007; $300,000 with KAML-FM Gillette). Population served: 50,000 Natl. Network: Fox News Radio, Fox Sports, . Wire Svc: AP Format: News/talk, sports. News staff: one; News: 40 hrs wkly. Target aud: 25 plus. ◆Don Clonch, gen mgr; Terry Michael, opns mgr & gen sls mgr.

*KLOF(FM)— 2000: 88.9 mhz; 430 w. Ant 440 ft TL: N44 12 34 W105 28 04. Hrs open: 5700 West Oaks Blvd., Rocklin, CA, 95765. Phone: (916) 251-1600. Fax: (916) 251-1650. Licensee: Educational Media Foundation. (acq 3-29-2007; $55,000). Format: Christian. ◆Mike Novak, sr VP.

*KLWD(FM)— 2001: 91.9 mhz; 1 kw. Ant 226 ft TL: N44 17 00 W105 31 00. Stereo. Hrs open: 24 Box 1492, 82717. Phone: (307) 682-9553. Fax: (307) 682-8509.E-mail: calvarycom@vcn.com Web Site:klwd.vcn.com Licensee: CSN International (group owner; acq 5-8-00; $10,000 for CP). Population served: 50,000 Format: Christian. ◆Don Wight, pres, gen mgr & progmg dir.

*KUWG(FM)— 1997: 90.9 mhz; 450 w. 459 ft TL: N44 12 33 W105 28 05. Hrs open: Rebroadcasts KUWR(FM) Laramie 100%. Box 3984, Univ. Station, Laramie, 82071. Phone: (307) 766-4240. Fax: (307) 766-6184.E-mail: wpr@uwyo.edu Web Site:uwadmnweb.uwyo.edu Licensee: University of Wyoming. Format: News, progsv, class. ◆Jon Schwartz, gen mgr; Hank Arnold, dev dir; Roger Adams, progmg dir; Bob Beck, news dir; Larry Dean, chief of engrg.

Glendo

KYOD(FM)— July 10, 1999: 100.1 mhz; 100 kw. Ant 456 ft TL: N42 46 13 W105 13 21. Stereo. Hrs open: 24 1837 Madora Ave., Suite B, Douglas, 82633. Phone: (307) 358-6177. Fax: (307) 358-0978.E-mail: kyod@netcommander.com Web Site:www.kyod.com Licensee: Canned Ham Communications LLC (acq 5-23-00; $150,000 for CP). Population served: 50,000 Natl. Network: Westwood One, . Natl. Rep: Interep,. Womble, Carlyle, Sandridge & Rice, PLLC. Format: Talk/Music variety. News staff: one; News: one hr wkly. Target aud: 25-54. Spec prog: Hard rock 2 hrs wkly; Religious, 2hrs wkly. ◆Darrell Woolsey, gen mgr; Mary Woolsey, stn mgr.

Glenrock

KGRK(FM)— 2007: 98.3 mhz; 200 w. Ant -249 ft TL: N42 51 49 W105 52 15. Hrs open: 87 Jasper Lake Rd., Loveland, CO, 80537. Phone: (307) 778-9318. Licensee: Michael Radio Group LLC. ◆Victor A. Michael Jr., gen mgr.

Green River

KFRZ(FM)— Sept 23, 1999: 92.1 mhz; 90 kw. 1,138 ft TL: N41 29 47 W109 20 44. Hrs open: 24 Box 970 , 82935. Secondary address: 40 Shoshone Ave. 82935. Phone: (307) 875-6666. Fax: (307) 875-5847.E-mail: mail@theradionetwork.net Web Site:www.theradionetwork.net Population served: 60,000 Natl. Network: Westwood One, . Format: Country. News staff: one; News: 3 hrs wkly. Target aud: General. ♦Teresa Warren, traf mgr.

KSIT(FM)—See Rock Springs

KUGR(AM)— June 18, 1976: 1490 khz; 1 kw-U. TL: N41 30 56 W109 26 11. Hrs open: 24 Box 970, 82935. Secondary address: 40 Shoshone Ave. 82935. Phone: (307) 875-6666. Fax: (307) 875-5847.E-mail: mail@theradionetwork.net Web Site:www.theradionetwork.net Licensee: Wagon Wheel Communications Corp. (acq 1-1-79). Population served: 40,000 Natl. Network: CBS, Westwood One, . Format: Soft adult contemp. News staff: one; News: 4 hrs wkly. Target aud: 30 plus. Spec prog: Sp 5 hrs wkly. ♦Al Harris, CEO, pres, chief of engrg; Steve Core, gen mgr, opns dir; Jeff Driggs, gen sls mgr; Jasmine Weaver, progmg dir, chief of engrg; Jon Schade, news dir; Teresa Warren, traf mgr.

KZWB(FM)— 2005: 97.9 mhz; 10.5 kw. Ant 1,073 ft TL: N41 29 47 W109 20 44. Stereo. Hrs open: 24 40 Shoshone Ave., 82935. Phone: (307) 875-6666. Fax: (307) 875-5847.E-mail: mail@theradionetwork.net Web Site:theradionetwork.net Licensee: Wagonwheel Communications Corp. Population served: 50,000 Format: Classic hits. News staff: one. ♦Alan W. Harris, pres; Steve Core, gen mgr.

Greybull

KZMQ(AM)— May 20, 1979: 1140 khz; 10 kw-D. TL: N44 27 01 W108 02 56. Hrs open: Box 1210, 1949 Mountain View Dr., Cody, 82414. Phone: (307) 578-5000. Fax: (307) 527-5045.E-mail: rgelder@bhmway.com Web Site:www.bighornradio.com Licensee: Legend Communications of Wyoming L.L.C. Group owner: Legend Communications LLC (acq 1-27-98; $1.5 million with co-located FM). Population served: 50,000 Format: Real country. Target aud: 25-49. ♦Larry Patrick, pres; Roger Gelder, exec VP & gen mgr; Carol Kary, stn mgr, gen sls mgr; Rita Conners, opns dir, opns mgr; Barbara Greene, sls VP, sls dir; Jerry Dunning, progmg dir; Mack Frost, news dir; Charlie Dozier, chief of engrg.

KZMQ-FM— Feb 21, 1986: 100.3 mhz; 56 kw. 2,443 ft TL: N44 48 41 W107 55 06. Stereo. Hrs open: Box 1210, 1949 Mountain View Dr., Cody, 82414. Phone: (307) 578-5000. Fax: (307) 527-5045.E-mail: ckary@bhrnwy.com Format: Country. ♦Carol Kary, gen mgr.

Guernsey

KANT(FM)— 2008: 104.1 mhz; 36 kw. Ant 564 ft TL: N42 20 46.6 W105 02 03.9. Hrs open: 2109 E. 10th St., Cheyenne, 82001. Phone: (307) 638-8921. Fax: (307) 638-8922. Web Site:1049krrr.com Licensee: Brahmin Broadcasting Corp. Format: Oldies. ♦Steven A. Silberberg, pres; Roger Ingram, gen mgr.

Hanna

KBDY(FM)— 2009: 102.1 mhz; 630 w. Ant 3,444 ft TL: N41 38 00.9 W106 31 32.1. Hrs open: 213 W. 2nd Ave., Cheyenne, 82001-1207. Phone: (307) 638-6054. Licensee: Toga Radio LLC (acq 5-13-2008; $150,000 for CP). ♦Don Day Jr., gen mgr.

Hudson

KTUG(FM)—Not on air, target date: unknown: 105.1 mhz; 6 kw. Ant 13 ft TL: N42 53 49 W108 34 59. Hrs open: 288 S. River Rd., Bedford, NH, 03110. Phone: (603) 668-6400. Fax: (603) 668-6470. Licensee: White Park Broadcasting Inc. ♦Steven A. Silberberg, pres.

KXWY(FM)— 2009: 102.9 mhz; 9.6 kw. Ant 1,988 ft TL: N43 26 16 W107 59 46. Hrs open: Box 36148, Tucson, AZ, 85740. Phone: (520) 797-4434.E-mail: ttucker@skywestmedia.com Licensee: SkyWest Media LLC. ♦Ted Tucker, gen mgr.

Jackson

***KHOL(FM)**— Apr 4, 2008: 89.1 mhz; 2.2 kw. Ant 1,102 ft TL: N43 27 40 W110 45 09. Hrs open: Box 8639, 83002. Phone: (307) 733-4030.E-mail: info@jhcr.org Web Site:www.jhcr.org Licensee: Jackson Hole Community Radio Inc. (acq 3-29-2007; $18,000 for CP). Format: Var. ♦Jim Tallichet, gen mgr.

KJAX(FM)— 2000: 93.3 mhz; 100 kw. Ant 1,069 ft TL: N43 27 40 W110 45 09. Hrs open: c/o KSGT(AM) and KMTN(FM), Box 100, 83001. Phone: (307) 733-2120. Fax: (307) 733-4760. Licensee: Chaparral Broadcasting Inc. Group owner: Chaparral Communications (acq 3-29-2000; $393,787 for stock). Format: Country. ♦Scott Anderson, gen mgr.

***KMLT(FM)**— 2008: 88.3 mhz; 150 w horiz, 15 w vert. Ant 938 ft TL: N43 27 43 W110 45 12. Hrs open:
Rebroadcasts KLVR(FM) Middletown, CA 100%.
2351 Sunset Blvd., Suite 170-218, Rocklin, CA, 95765. Phone: (916) 251-1600. Fax: (916) 251-1650. Web Site:www.klove.com Licensee: Educational Media Foundation. (acq 7-23-2007; grpsl). Natl. Network: K-Love, . Format: Contemp Christian. ♦Mike Novak, pres.

KMTN(FM)— Dec 16, 1974: 96.9 mhz; 48 kw. 940 ft TL: N43 27 42 W110 45 10. Stereo. Hrs open: Prog sep from AM Box 100, 83001. Secondary address: 645 S. Cache St. 83001. Phone: (307) 733-2120. Fax: (307) 733-4760. Web Site:www.jacksonholeradio.com Population served: 16,000 Natl. Network: ABC, . Format: AOR. Target aud: 18-54. ♦Mark Fishman, progmg dir; Lynda John, traf mgr.

***KMWY(FM)**—Not on air, target date: unknown: 91.1 mhz; 350 w. Ant 1,023 ft TL: N43 27 40 W110 45 09. Hrs open: 820 N. LaSalle Blvd., Chicago, IL, 60610-3214. Phone: (312) 329-4438.E-mail: info@mbn.org Licensee: The Moody Bible Institute of Chicago. ♦Robert C. Neff, VP.

KSGT(AM)— July 20, 1962: 1340 khz; 1 kw-U. TL: N43 30 22 W110 45 16. Hrs open: Box 100, 83001. Secondary address: 645 S. Cache St. 83001. Phone: (307) 733-2120. Fax: (307) 733-4760. Web Site:www.jacksonholeradio.com Licensee: Chaparral Broadcasting Inc. (group owner; (acq 11-30-92; $215,000 with KMER(AM) Kemmerer; 12-21-92). Population served: 8,000 Keck, Mahin & Cate. Format: Country. Target aud: 25 plus. ♦Del Ray, progmg dir; Scott Anderson, gen mgr, opns VP, gen sls mgr, prom VP & chief of engrg; Lynda John, traf mgr.

***KUWJ(FM)**— November 1992: 90.3 mhz; 3 kw. 1,105 ft TL: N43 27 40 W110 45 09. Stereo. Hrs open: 5 AM-midnight
Rebroadcasts KUWR(FM) Laramie 100%.
Department 3984, 1000 E. University Ave., Laramie, 82071. Phone: (307) 766-4240. Fax: (307) 766-6184.E-mail: wpr@uwyo.edu Web Site:www.wyomingpublicradio.net Licensee: University of Wyoming. Population served: 15,000 Natl. Network: NPR, PRI, . Format: News, class, progsv. News staff: 3; News: 42 hrs wkly. Target aud: 25-54; educated, upper-income professionals. Spec prog: Folk 10 hrs, jazz 6 hrs, state news 3 hrs wkly. ♦Jon B. Schwartz, gen mgr; Hank Arnold, dev dir; Roger Adams, progmg dir; Bob Beck, news dir; Larry Dean, engrg dir, chief of engrg.

KZJH(FM)— July 13, 1989: 95.3 mhz; 100 kw. 1,056 ft TL: N43 27 40 W110 45 09. Hrs open: 24 Box 2620, 83001. Phone: (307) 733-1770. Fax: (307) 733-4760.E-mail: kz95@blissnet.com Licensee: Chaparral Broadcasting Co. Group owner: Chaparral Communications (acq 8-25-00; $1.1 million). Natl. Network: ABC, . Format: Classic rock. News staff: one. Target aud: 18-55. ♦Patricia Karnik, prom dir; Jay Martin, progmg dir; Dee Dee Dudley, news dir; Scott Anderson, gen mgr & chief of engrg.

Kaycee

KCYA(FM)—Not on air, target date: unknown: 97.7 mhz; 51 kw horiz. Ant -10 ft TL: N43 43 12 W106 39 02. Hrs open: Box 36148, Tucson, AZ, 85740. Phone: (520) 797-4434.E-mail: ttucker@skywestmedia.com Licensee: Skywest Media LLC. ♦Ted Tucker, gen mgr.

Kemmerer

KAOX(FM)— Oct. 1, 1999: 107.3 mhz; 13.5 kw. Ant 948 ft TL: N41 50 18 W110 30 11. Stereo. Hrs open: 24 Box 432, c/o KMER (AM), 83101. Secondary address: 436 Fossil Butte 83101. Phone: (307) 877-4422. Fax: (307) 877-5537.E-mail: kmer@onewest.net Licensee: Simmons-SLC, LS LLC. Group owner: Simmons Media Group (acq 4-19-2004; grpsl). Population served: 80,000 Natl. Network: CBS, . Format: Adult standards. News staff: one; News: 2 hrs wkly. Target aud: 35 plus; male / female. ♦Jim Carroll, gen mgr; Jim Thoeny, chief of opns.

KMER(AM)— Dec 7, 1962: 940 khz; 240 w-D, 150 w-N. TL: N41 47 57 W110 32 44. Hrs open: Box 432, 83101. Secondary address: 436 Fossil Butte Dr. 83101. Phone: (307) 877-4422. Fax: (307) 877-5537.E-mail: kmer@onewest.net Licensee: Simmons-SLC, LS LLC. Group owner: Simmons Media Group (acq 5-20-2004; grpsl). Population served: 70,000 Format: Oldies. News staff: one; News: one hr wkly. Target aud: 25-54. Spec prog: News/talk 7 hrs, farm 3 hrs wkly. ♦Jim Carroll, gen mgr; Jim Thoeny, opns dir.

Kirby

***KKBY(FM)**—Not on air, target date: unknown: 90.5 mhz; 3 kw vert. Ant 249 ft TL: N43 39 07 W108 15 07. Hrs open: Box 94, Stonewall, OK, 74872. Phone: (580) 265-9475. Licensee: Union Valley Baptist Church Inc. ♦Steve Vandegrift, pres.

Lander

KDLY(FM)— 1975: 97.5 mhz; 62 kw. Ant 420 ft TL: N42 49 20 W108 45 48. Stereo. Hrs open: 24 1530 Main St., 82520. Phone: (307) 332-5683. Fax: (307) 332-5548.E-mail: radio1@wyoming.com Web Site:www.kdlykove.com Licensee: Fremont Broadcasting Inc. Natl. Network: Fox News Radio, . Natl. Rep: Commercial Media Sales,. Wire Svc: AP Format: Rock classics. News staff: one; News: 5 hrs wkly. Target aud: 18-49; general. ♦Joe Kenney, pres.

KOVE(AM)— 1947: 1330 khz; 5 kw-D, 1 kw-N, DA-N. TL: N42 50 35 W108 44 38. Hrs open: 1530 Main St., 82520. Phone: (307) 332-5683. Fax: (307) 332-5548.E-mail: radio1@wyoming.com Web Site:www.kdlykove.com Licensee: Fremont Broadcasting Inc. Population served: 40,000 Natl. Network: Fox News Radio, . Natl. Rep: Commercial Media Sales,. Wire Svc: AP Format: C&W. News: one. Target aud: 25 plus. Spec prog: Talk 15 hrs wkly. ♦Joe Kenney, pres, gen mgr, gen sls mgr; Glenn Lemons, news dir; Lincoln Scott, chief of engrg; Krista Perez, traf mgr.

Laramie

***KAIW(FM)**— 2006: 88.9 mhz; 400 w. Ant 645 ft TL: N41 17 46 W105 53 30. Hrs open:
Rebroadcasts KLVR(FM) Santa Rosa, CA 100%.
2351 Sunset Blvd., Suite 170-218, Rocklin, CA, 95765. Phone: (916) 251-1600. Fax: (916) 251-1650. Web Site:www.klove.com Licensee: Educational Media Foundation. Natl. Network: K-Love, . Format: Contemp Christian. ♦Richard Jenkins, pres; Mike Novak, VP; Keith Whipple, dev dir; David Pierce, progmg mgr; Ed Lenane, news dir; Sam Wallington, engrg dir; Karen Johnson, news rptr.

KARS-FM— Sept 23, 1974: 102.9 mhz; 100 kw. Ant 1,220 ft TL: N41 18 39 W105 27 12. Stereo. Hrs open: 3201 E. Mulberry St., Unit H, Fort Collins, CO, 80524. Phone: (970) 674-2700. Phone: (970) 492-0999. Fax: (970) 407-0584. Web Site:www.rock1029.com Licensee: Regent Broadcasting of Ft. Collins Inc. Group owner: Regent Communications Inc. (acq 11-15-2004; $7.75 million with KKPL(FM) Cheyenne). Population served: 80,000 Wire Svc: CBS Format: Classic rock. Target aud: 18-44. ♦Cal Hall, gen mgr, progmg dir; Miles Schallert, sls dir, sports cmtr; Bill Cody, progmg dir, disc jockey; Susan Moore, news dir; Quin Morrison, chief of engrg.

KCGY(FM)— Nov 7, 1983: 95.1 mhz; 100 kw. 1,070 ft TL: N41 18 34 W105 27 11. Stereo. Hrs open: 24 Box 1290, 82073. Secondary address: 3525 Soldier Springs Rd. 82070. Phone: (307) 745-4888. Fax: (307) 742-4576.E-mail: andyhoefer@gapbroadcasting.com Web Site:www.y95country.com Licensee: GAP Broadcasting Laramie License LLC. Group owner: Clear Channel Communications Inc. (acq 2-13-2008; grpsl). Population served: 100,000 Natl. Network: Jones Radio Networks, . Natl. Rep: Katz Radio,. Wire Svc: AP Format: Mainstream country. Target aud: 25-54. ♦Andrew W. Hoefer, gen mgr; Eric Henderson, gen sls mgr; Dave Shannon, progmg dir; Jim Mross, chief of engrg.

KHAT(AM)— Feb 27, 1962: 1210 khz; 10 kw-D, 1 kw-N, DA-N. TL: N41 15 19 W105 33 01. Stereo. Hrs open: 302 S. 2rd St., Suite 204, 82070. Phone: (307) 745-5208. Fax: (307) 745-8570.E-mail: mix967@fiberpipe.net Licensee: Appaloosa Broadcasting Co. Group owner: Northeast Broadcasting Company Inc. (acq 3-2-2004; $160,000). Population served: 26,972 Natl. Network: ESPN Radio, . Format: Sports. Spec prog: Farm one hr wkly. ♦Mike Schutta, gen mgr.

KIMX(FM)— 2002: 96.7 mhz; 6.5 kw. Ant 932 ft TL: N41 17 07 W105 26 41. Hrs open: 302 S. 2nd St., Suite 204, 82070. Phone: (307) 745-5208. Fax: (307) 745-8570.E-mail: mix967@fiberpipe.net Licensee: Appaloosa Broadcasting Co. Inc. Group owner: Northeast Broadcasting Company Inc. (acq 11-12-2003; $775,000). Format: Adult contemp. ♦Jim O'Reilly, gen mgr.

KOWB(AM)— Feb 20, 1948: 1290 khz; 5 kw-D, 1 kw-N, DA-2. TL: N41 17 02 W105 34 51. Hrs open: 24 Box 1290, 82073. Secondary address: 3525 Soldier Springs Rd. 82070. Phone: (307) 745-4888.

Fax: (307) 742-4576.E-mail: andyhoefer@gapbroadcasting.com Web Site:www.kowb1290.com Licensee: GAP Broadcasting Laramie License LLC. Group owner: Clear Channel Communications Inc. (acq 2-13-2008; grpsl). Population served: 35,000 Natl. Network: Fox News Radio, . Natl. Rep: Katz Radio,. Wire Svc: AP Format: News/talk, sports. News staff: one; News: 7 hrs wkly. Target aud: 25-54. ◆Andrew W. Hoefer, gen mgr; David Settle, opns mgr, progmg mgr; Eric Henderson, gen sls mgr; Jim Mross, chief of engrg.

KRQU(FM)— 2006: 98.7 mhz; 110 w. Ant 1,073 ft TL: N41 18 39 W105 27 12. Hrs open: 302 S. 2nd St., Suite 204, 82070. Phone: (307) 745-5208. Fax: (307) 745-8570.E-mail: mix967@fiberpipe.net Licensee: Murray Grey Broadcasting Inc. (acq 12-21-2005; $750,000 with KVUW(FM) Wendover, NV). Format: Classic rock. ◆Steven A. Silberberg, pres; Jim O'Reilly, gen mgr.

*****KTDX(FM)**— 2008: 89.3 mhz; 450 w. Ant 1,138 ft TL: N41 18 39 W105 27 12. Hrs open:
Rebroadcasts KTLF(FM) Colorado Springs, CO 100%.
1665 Briargate Blvd., Suite 100, Colorado Springs, CO, 80920. Phone: (719) 593-0600. Fax: (719) 593-2399. Web Site:www.ktlf.org Licensee: Educational Communications of Colorado Springs Inc. Format: Christian music. ◆Ron Johnson, chmn.

KUSZ(FM)— 2000: 93.9 mhz; 800 w. Ant -85 ft TL: N41 20 20 W105 35 31. Hrs open: 302 S. 2nd St., Suite 204, 82070. Phone: (307) 745-5208. Fax: (307) 745-8570.E-mail: mix967@fiberpipe.net Licensee: Laramie Mountain Broadcasting LLC. Group owner: Kona Coast Radio LLC (acq 6-20-2002). Population served: 389,300 Format: Oldies. ◆Jim O'Reilly, gen mgr.

*****KUWL(FM)**— 2008: 90.1 mhz; 110 w. Ant 968 ft TL: N41 18 36 W105 27 17. Hrs open: 24 Wyoming Public Radio, Dept. 3984, 1000 E. University Ave., 82071. Phone: (307) 766-4240. Fax: (307) 766-6184. Licensee: University of Wyoming. Wyoming Public Radio Format: Jazz. ◆Jon Schwartz, gen mgr.

*****KUWR(FM)**— Sept 10, 1966: 91.9 mhz; 100 kw. Ant 1,128 ft TL: N41 18 39 W105 27 12. Stereo. Hrs open: 5 AM-midnight Department 3984, 1000 E. University Ave., 82071. Phone: (307) 766-4240. Fax: (307) 766-6184.E-mail: wpr@uwyo.edu Web Site:www.wyomingpublicradio.net Licensee: University of Wyoming. Population served: 325,000 Natl. Network: NPR, PRI, . Format: News, progsv, class. News staff: 3; News: 42 hrs wkly. Target aud: 25-54; educated, college graduates, professionals, upper income. Spec prog: Folk 10 hrs, jazz 6 hrs, state news 3 hrs wkly. ◆Jon Schwartz, gen mgr; Don Woods, dev VP, mus dir; Peg Arnold, dev dir, sls dir, adv dir; Bob Beck, news dir; Larry Dean, chief of engrg; Roger Adams, prom mgr, progmg dir & traf mgr; Jim Morgan, local news ed, news rptr; Aaron Alpern, news rptr; Pat Gabriel, disc jockey.

*****KUWY(FM)**— 2008: 88.5 mhz; 134 w. Ant 977 ft TL: N41 18 36 W105 27 17. Hrs open: 24 Wyoming Public Radio, Dept. 3984, 1000 E. University Ave., 82071. Phone: (307) 766-4240. Fax: (307) 766-6184. Licensee: University of Wyoming. Wyoming Public Radio Format: Classical. ◆Jon Schwartz, gen mgr.

Lingle

*****KUWV(FM)**—Not on air, target date: unknown: 90.7 mhz; 100 kw. Ant 200 ft TL: N42 35 05 W104 23 13. Hrs open: 1000 E. University Ave., Dept. 3984, Laramie, 82071. Phone: (307) 766-4240. Fax: (307) 766-6184. Web Site:www.wyomingpublicradio.net Licensee: University of Wyoming (acq 5-12-2009; $32,000 for CP). ◆Jon Schwartz, gen mgr.

Lost Cabin

KWYW(FM)— 2001: 99.1 mhz; 50 kw. Ant 1,896 ft TL: N43 26 18 W107 59 37. Hrs open: 320 Senior Ave., Thermopolis, 82443. Phone: (307) 864-2119. Fax: (307) 864-3937.E-mail: kthe@directairnet.com Web Site:www.mykwyw.com Licensee: Jimmy Ray Carroll. Group owner: Jimmy Ray Carroll Stns (acq 6-25-2001; $30,000 for CP). Format: Country. ◆Jimmy Carroll, pres; Cheerie Dorris, gen mgr; Amanda Plant, prom dir; Jeremy James, progmg dir; Mike St. Clair, news dir.

Lovell

KROW(FM)—Not on air, target date: unknown: 107.1 mhz; 64 kw. Ant 2,375 ft TL: N44 48 38 W107 55 18. Hrs open: 288 S. River Rd., Bedford, NH, 03110. Phone: (603) 668-6470. Licensee: White Park Broadcasting Inc. ◆Steven A. Silberberg, pres & gen mgr.

Lusk

KQWY(FM)—Not on air, target date: unknown: 96.3 mhz; 100 kw. Ant 1,958 ft TL: N42 41 05 W104 39 53. Hrs open: 1282 Smallwood Dr., Suite 372, Waldorf, MD, 20603. Phone: (202) 251-7589. Licensee: Alma Corp. ◆Dennis Wallace, pres.

Lyman

KYLZ(FM)— July 1, 1983: 104.7 mhz; 89 kw horiz. Ant 2,122 ft TL: N40 52 16 W110 59 43. Stereo. Hrs open: 24 Box 3369, Logan, 84321. Phone: (435) 752-1390. Fax: (435) 752-1392. Licensee: 3 Point Media - Utah LLC, debtor-in-possession (acq 11-28-2001; $1.73 million). Population served: 300,000 Natl. Network: CBS, . Dan J. Alpert. Format: Classic rock. Target aud: 35-54. ◆Kent Frandsen, pres; Jay Eubanks, gen mgr, stn mgr; Lori Gill, gen sls mgr, traf mgr; Paul Anderson, chief of engrg.

Manville

KOUZ(FM)—Not on air, target date: unknown: 98.9 mhz; 100 kw. Ant 977 ft TL: N42 41 56 W104 35 18. Hrs open: 1282 Smallwood Dr., Suite 372, Waldorf, MD, 20603. Licensee: Alma Corp. ◆Dennis Wallace, pres.

Marbleton

KFMR(FM)—Not on air, target date: unknown: 95.7 mhz; 7 kw. Ant 1,394 ft TL: N42 19 28 W110 19 12. Hrs open: Box 36148, Tucson, AZ, 85740. Phone: (520) 797-4434. Licensee: Skywest Media L.L.C. ◆Ted Tucker, gen mgr.

Midwest

KWYY(FM)— Nov 30, 1981: 95.5 mhz; 100 kw. Ant 1,938 ft TL: N42 44 37 W106 18 24. Stereo. Hrs open: 150 Nichols Ave., Casper, 82601. Phone: (307) 266-5252. Fax: (307) 235-9143.E-mail: kwyy@clearchannel.com Licensee: GAP Broadcasting Casper License LLC. Group owner: Clear Channel Communications Inc. (acq 2-13-2008; grpsl). Format: Country. Target aud: 25-54. ◆Robert Price, gen mgr; Donovan Short, opns mgr, progmg dir; Walter Hawn, gen sls mgr; Dave Nutter, chief of engrg; Dave Borino, traf mgr.

Mills

KZQL(FM)— 2008: 105.5 mhz; 2.75 kw. Ant 1,781 ft TL: N42 44 03 W106 20 00. Hrs open: 288 S. River Rd., Bedford, NH, 03110. Phone: (603) 668-6470. Licensee: White Park Broadcasting Inc. Format: Adult hits. ◆Steven A. Silberberg, pres & gen mgr.

Moorcroft

KXXL(FM)— 2008: 106.1 mhz; 100 kw. Ant 392 ft TL: N44 13 50 W105 27 45. Hrs open: Box 2230, Gillette, 82717. Phone: (307) 687-1003. Fax: (307) 687-1006. Licensee: Keyhole Broadcasting LLC (acq 4-29-2009; exchange for KLSX(FM) Rozet). Format: Classic rock. ◆Debora Semple, gen mgr.

Newcastle

KASL(AM)— July 10, 1953: 1240 khz; 1 kw-U. TL: N43 50 47 W104 12 45. Hrs open: 24 933 W. Main St., 82701. Phone: (307) 746-4433.E-mail: kasl@vcn.com Web Site:www.kaslradio.com Licensee: Val Rasmuson Cook (acq 4-9-2007; $76,000). Population served: 7,800 Smithwick & Belendiuk. Format: C&W. News staff: one; News: 35 hrs wkly. Target aud: General; town & county residents, children through adults. Spec prog: Farm 5 hrs, relg 2 hrs wkly. ◆Val Cook, CEO, gen mgr, opns mgr & gen sls mgr; Ed Schlup, progmg dir.

KRKI(FM)— 2003: 99.5 mhz; 100 kw horiz. Ant 735 ft TL: N43 51 24 W103 45 50. Hrs open: Box 969, 82701. Secondary address: 1711 W. Main St., Rapid City 57702. Phone: (605) 721-9005. Fax: (605) 721-9007. Web Site:www.995espn.com Licensee: Michael Radio Group. Natl. Network: ESPN Radio, . Format: Sports. ◆Lonnie Glasford, gen mgr, gen sls mgr; Scott McCormick, opns mgr & progmg dir.

*****KUWN(FM)**— 1998: 90.5 mhz; 400 w. 203 ft TL: N43 49 57 W104 13 08. Hrs open:
Rebroadcasts KUWR(FM) Laramie 100%.
Department 3984, 1000 E. University Ave., Laramie, 82071. Phone:

(307) 766-4240. Fax: (307) 766-6184.E-mail: wpr@uwyo.edu Web Site:www.wyomingpublicradio.net Licensee: University of Wyoming. Format: News, progsv, class. ◆Jon Schwartz, gen mgr; Peg Arnold, dev dir, sls dir, adv dir; Don Woods, mus dir; Bob Beck, news dir; Larry Dean, chief of engrg; Roger Adams, progmg dir & traf mgr.

Orchard Valley

KGAB(AM)—Licensed to Orchard Valley. See Cheyenne

*****KWYC(FM)**— 2005: 90.3 mhz; 20 kw. Ant 425 ft TL: N41 13 01 W104 26 53. Stereo. Hrs open: 24 CSN International, 4002 N. 3300 E., Twin Falls, ID, 83301. Phone: (208) 734-6633. Fax: (208) 736-1958. Web Site:www.csnradio.com Licensee: CSN International. (group owner; (acq 1-9-2004; $1 for CP). Format: Contemp Chrisitan talk. ◆Mike Kestler, pres; Mike Stockland, gen mgr; Don Mills, progmg dir.

Pine Bluffs

KREO(FM)— December 2000: 105.3 mhz; 400 w. Ant 157 ft TL: N41 09 55 W104 04 31. (CP: 6 kw, ant 249 ft. TL: N41 17 17 W104 00 21). Stereo. Hrs open: 24
Simulcast with KRRR(FM) Cheyenne.
2109 E. 10th St., Cheyenne, 82001. Phone: (307) 638-8921. Fax: (307) 638-8922.E-mail: news@1049krrr.com Web Site:www.1049krrr.com Licensee: Chisholm Trail Broadcasting LLC Group owner: Northeast Broadcasting Company Inc. (acq 5-23-2005; $850,000 with KKAW(FM) Albin). Population served: 50,000 Format: Oldies. Target aud: 25-54. ◆Larry Proietti, gen mgr, progmg dir; Dan Conway, gen sls mgr; Ron Krob, chief of engrg.

Pinedale

KPIN(FM)— December 1997: 101.1 mhz; 211 w. Ant -180 ft TL: N42 51 59 W109 52 08. Hrs open: Box 2000, 82941. Phone: (307) 367-2000. Fax: (307) 367-3300.E-mail: kpin@wyoming.com Licensee: Robert R. Rule dba Rule Communications. Format: Country, oldies. ◆Robert R. Rule, gen mgr.

*****KUWX(FM)**— 2000: 90.9 mhz; 450 w. Ant 440 ft TL: N42 50 40 W109 55 24. Hrs open: Department 3984, 1000 E. Wyoming Ave., Laramie, 82071. Phone: (307) 766-4240. Fax: (307) 766-6184.E-mail: wpr@uwyo.edu Web Site:www.wyomingpublicradio.net Licensee: University of Wyoming. Format: News, progsv, class. ◆Jon Schwartz, gen mgr; Peg Arnold, dev dir, sls dir, adv dir; Don Woods, mus dir; Bob Beck, news dir; Larry Dean, chief of engrg; Roger Adams, progmg dir & traf mgr.

Powell

KCGL(FM)— Nov 26, 2001: 104.1 mhz; 100 kw. Ant 1,942 TL: N44 29 46 W109 09 16. Hrs open: 24 Box 1210, Cody, 82414. Secondary address: 1949 Mountain View Dr., Cody 82414. Phone: (307) 578-5000. Fax: (307) 527-5045.E-mail: rgelder@bhrnwy.com Web Site:www.thecornradio.com Licensee: Legend Communications of Wyoming LLC. Group owner: Legend Communications L.L.C. (acq 4-3-02; $450,000). Format: Classic rock. ◆Larry Patrick, pres; Roger Gelder, exec VP; Carol Kary, VP, gen mgr, gen sls mgr; Tom Morrison, progmg dir; Tom Huge, news dir; Charles Dozier, chief of engrg; Karla McMillen, traf mgr.

*****KFGR(FM)**—Not on air, target date: unknown: 88.1 mhz; 600 w. Ant 1,578 ft TL: N44 35 07 W108 51 01. Hrs open: 507 N. Clark St., 82435. Phone: (307) 754-2660. Web Site:tbcwyoming.com/radio-log Licensee: Trinity Bible Church. ◆Donald Thomas, pres.

KPOW(AM)— Mar 30, 1941: 1260 khz; 5 kw-D, 1 kw-N, DA-N. TL: N44 42 00 W108 46 00. Hrs open: 6 AM-1 AM Box 968, 82435. Secondary address: 912 Ln. 11 1/2 82435. Phone: (307) 754-5183. Phone: (307) 527-5949. Fax: (307) 754-9667.E-mail: kpow@tritel.net Licensee: Chaparral Broadcasting Inc. Group owner: Chaparral Communications (acq 11-30-92; $215,000 with co-located FM; 12-21-92). Population served: 40,000 Keck, Mahin & Cate. Format: News, Talk. News: 38 hrs wkly. Target aud: 29-64. Spec prog: Farm 19 hrs wkly. ◆Scott Anderson, gen mgr, progmg mgr, chief of engrg; Scott Mangold, sls dir, news dir & traf mgr.

*****KUWP(FM)**— 2000: 90.1 mhz; 430 w. Ant 1,624 ft TL: N44 35 14 W108 51 08. Hrs open: Department 3984, 1000 E. Wyoming Ave., Laramie, 82071. Phone: (307) 766-4240. Fax: (307) 766-6184(.E-mail: wpr@uwyo.edu Web Site:www.wyomingpublicradio.net Licensee: University of Wyoming. Format: News, progsv, class. ◆Jon Schwartz, gen mgr; Peg Arnold, dev dir, sls dir, adv dir; Don Woods, mus dir; Bob Beck, news dir; Larry Dean, chief of engrg; Roger Adams, progmg dir & traf mgr.

Rawlins

KIQZ(FM)— Nov 12, 1981: 92.7 mhz; 3 kw. Ant 298 ft TL: N41 46 16 W107 14 15. Stereo. Hrs open: 2346 W. Spruce, 82301. Phone: (307) 324-3315. Fax: (307) 324-3509. Web Site:www.kiqz-kral.com Population served: 10,000

KRAL(AM)— February 1947: 1240 khz; 1 kw-U. TL: N41 46 55 W107 15 40. Hrs open: 24 2346 W. Spruce, 82301. Phone: (307) 324-3315. Fax: (307) 324-3509.E-mail: jackmorgan@vcn.com Web Site:www.kiqz-kral.com Licensee: Mount Rushmore Broadcasting Inc. (group owner; (acq 8-6-93; $80,000 with co-located FM;8-23-93). Population served: 15,123 Natl. Network: ABC, . Rgnl. Network: Jones Satellite Audio. Wire Svc: UPI Format: Adult contemp. Target aud: 14 plus. ♦Jack Morgan, progmg dir & news dir.

***KRWY(FM)**—Not on air, target date: unknown: 89.3 mhz; 100 kw vert. Ant 52 ft TL: N42 00 41 W107 26 29. Hrs open: Box 217, Gainesville, TX, 76241. Phone: (940) 668-7971. Licensee: 1 A Chord Inc. ♦Mary Fay Jackson, gen mgr.

***KUWI(FM)**— 2009: 89.9 mhz; 2 kw. Ant 986 ft TL: N41 40 46 W107 14 08. Hrs open: University of Wyoming, 1000 E. University Ave., Dept. 3984, Laramie, 82071. Phone: (307) 766-4240. Fax: (307) 766-6184. Web Site:www.wyomingpublicradio.net Licensee: University of Wyoming. Wyoming Public Radio ♦Jon Schwartz, gen mgr.

Reliance

KWXR(FM)—Not on air, target date: unknown: 98.7 mhz; 8 kw. Ant 551 ft TL: N41 39 24 W109 09 32. Hrs open: Box 11060, Jackson, 83002. Licensee: Cochise Broadcasting LLC. ♦Ted Tucker, gen mgr.

***KZUW(FM)**—Not on air, target date: unknown: 88.5 mhz; 4 kw. Ant -295 ft TL: N41 34 51 W109 12 26. Hrs open:
Rebroadcasts KUWYFM) Laramie 100%.
Wyoming Public Radio, Dept. 3984, 1000 E. University Ave., Laramie, 82071. Phone: (307) 766-4240. Fax: (307) 766-6184. Web Site:www.wyomingpublicradio.org Licensee: University of Wyoming. ♦Jon Schwartz, gen mgr.

Riverton

***KCWC-FM**— March 1974: 88.1 mhz; 3 kw. 1,449 ft TL: N42 34 59 W108 42 36. Stereo. Hrs open: 24 2660 Peck Ave., 82501. Phone: (307) 855-2121. Phone: (307) 855-2268. Fax: (307) 856-3893.E-mail: jgabriel@cwc.edu Licensee: Central Wyoming College. Format: Jazz, new age, progsv. ♦JoAnne McFarland, pres; Dale Smith, stn mgr.

KTAK(FM)— Dec 15, 1976: 93.9 mhz; 50 kw. 951 ft TL: N42 43 10 W108 08 45. Stereo. Hrs open: 603 E. Pershing Ave., 82501. Phone: (307) 856-2251. Fax: (307) 856-0252.E-mail: edward@rivertonradio.com Web Site:www.ktakradio.com Format: Country.

KTRZ(FM)— Dec 4, 1984: 93.1 mhz; 100 kw. 884 ft TL: N42 43 10 W108 08 41. Stereo. Hrs open: 24 Box 808, 82501. Secondary address: 1002 N. 8th West 82501. Phone: (307) 856-2922. Fax: (307) 856-7552.E-mail: ktrz@tcinc.net Web Site:www.ktrzfm.com Licensee: Jimmy Ray Carroll. Group owner: Jimmy Ray Carroll Stns (acq 4-1-02). Population served: 55,000 Natl. Network: AP Network News, . Pepper & Corazzini. Wire Svc: AP Format: Adult contemp. News staff: one; News: 2 hrs wkly. Target aud: 25 plus; rgnl/loc tourists, agribusiness, core population. ♦Jim Carroll, CEO; Jim Hockett, gen mgr, stn mgr & gen sls mgr.

KVOW(AM)— July 2, 1948: 1450 khz; 1 kw-U. TL: N43 01 35 W108 20 45. Hrs open: 603 E. Pershing Ave., 82501. Phone: (307) 856-2251. Fax: (307) 856-0252.E-mail: edward@rivertonradio.com Web Site:www.kvowradio.com Licensee: Edwards Communications L.C. (group owner; (acq 6-22-99; $875,000 with co-located FM). Population served: 12,000 Format: Info, oldies. Spec prog: Farm 5 hrs wkly. ♦Larry Cross, gen mgr, gen sls mgr; Jeff Kehl, progmg dir, news dir; Lonnie Fairfield, chief of engrg; Tracy Coston, traf mgr; John Gabrielsen, sports cmtr.

Rock River

KLMI(FM)— 2008: 106.5 mhz; 25 kw. Ant 171 ft TL: N41 29 05 W106 03 06. Hrs open: 1020 9th St., Suite 201, Greeley, CO, 80631. Phone: (970) 356-1452. Fax: (970) 356-8522. Licensee: Greeley Broadcasting Corp. (acq 4-18-2008; $250,000 for CP). Format: Rgnl Mexican. ♦Ricardo Salazar, gen mgr.

Rock Springs

KQSW(FM)— January 1977: 96.5 mhz; 100 kw. Ant 1,680 ft TL: N41 25 54 W109 07 01. Hrs open: Box 2128 , 82902. Secondary address: 2717 Yellowstone Rd. 82902. Phone: (307) 362-3793. Fax: (307) 362-8727.E-mail: wyoradio@wyoradio.com Licensee: Big Thicket Broadcasting Co. of Wyoming Inc. Population served: 28,000 Format: Country.

KRKK(AM)— 1938: 1360 khz; 5 kw-D, 1 kw-N, DA-N. TL: N41 37 12 W109 14 20. Hrs open: Box 2128, 82902. Secondary address: 2717 Yellowstone Rd. 82901. Phone: (307) 362-3793. Fax: (307) 362-8727.E-mail: wyoradio@wyoradio.com Web Site:www.wyoradio.com Licensee: Big Thicket Broadcasting Co. of Wyoming Inc. (acq 12-2-2005; grpsl). Population served: 11,657 Format: Oldies. ♦Bill Luzmoor, pres, pres, progmg dir; Jon Collins, gen mgr, chief of engrg; Tom Ellis, gen sls mgr; Doug Randall, news dir; Tim Walker, traf mgr.

KSIT(FM)— October 1981: 104.5 mhz; 100 kw. Ant 1,630 ft TL: N41 26 00 W109 07 02. Stereo. Hrs open: 24 Box 2128, 82902. Secondary address: 2717 Yellowstone Rd. 82902. Phone: (307) 362-7034. Phone: (307) 362-3793. Fax: (307) 362-8727.E-mail: wyoradio@wyoradio.com Web Site:www.wyoradio.com Licensee: Big Thicket Broadcasting Co. of Wyoming Inc. (acq 12-2-2005; grpsl). Population served: 40000 Arent, Fox, Kintner, Plotkin & Kahn. Format: Classic rock. News staff: one; News: 10 hrs wkly. Target aud: 18-45; general. ♦Bill Luzmoor, pres; Jon Collins, gen mgr, opns mgr, chief of engrg; Tom Ellis, gen sls mgr; John Collins, progmg dir; Doug Randall, news dir; Kim Walker, traf mgr.

***KUWZ(FM)**— November 1994: 90.5 mhz; 35 kw. Ant 1,679 ft TL: N41 25 39 W109 07 17. Stereo. Hrs open: Sunrise-sunset
Rebroadcasts KUWR(FM) Laramie 100%.
Department 3984, 1000E. Wyoming Ave., Laramie, 82071. Phone: (307) 766-4240. Fax: (307) 766-6184.E-mail: wpr@uwyo.edu Web Site:www.wyomingpublicradio.net Licensee: University of Wyoming. (group owner) Population served: 50,000 Natl. Network: NPR, PRI, . Format: Class, progsv, news. News staff: 3; News: 52 hrs wkly. Target aud: 25-54; college graduates, professionals, mgrs, upper income. Spec prog: Folk 10 hrs, jazz 6 hrs, state news 3 hrs wkly. ♦Jon Schwartz, gen mgr; Peg Arnold, dev dir, sls dir, adv dir; Don Woods, mus dir; Bob Beck, news dir; Larry Dean, engrg dir, chief of engrg; Roger Adams, progmg dir & traf mgr.

KYCS(FM)— Oct 1, 1986: 95.1 mhz; 100 kw. 1,635 ft TL: N41 29 50 W109 20 36. Stereo. Hrs open: 24 40 Shoshone Ave., Green River, 82902. Phone: (307) 362-6746. Fax: (307) 875-5847.E-mail: mail@theradionetwork.net Web Site:www.theradionetwork.net Licensee: Faith Broadcasting Corporation. Population served: 50,000 Format: Top-40. News staff: one. ♦Faith Harris, pres; Steve Core, gen mgr; Jeff Driggs, gen sls mgr; Jasmine Weaver, progmg dir, mus dir; Ron Krob, chief of engrg.

Rozet

KLSX(FM)—Not on air, target date: unknown: 99.1 mhz; 16.5 kw. Ant 413 ft TL: N44 18 10 W105 27 00. Hrs open: 535 W. Edgemont Ave., Phoenix, AZ, 85003. Phone: (602) 248-9116. Licensee: Family Voice Communications LLC (acq 4-29-2009; exchange for KXXL(FM) Moorcroft). ♦Robert M. Olson Jr., gen mgr.

Saratoga

KTGA(FM)— 2008: 99.3 mhz; 18 kw. Ant 1,063 ft TL: N41 40 46 W107 14 08. Hrs open: 24 Box 990, 82331. Secondary address: 106 N. First St. 82331. Phone: (307) 326-8642. Fax: (307) 326-8340.E-mail: bigfoot@bigfoot99.com Web Site:www.bigfoot99.com Licensee: Toga Radio LLC (acq 8-31-2007; $140,000 for CP). Format: Rock 'n Country. News staff: 3. ♦Jim O'Reilly, gen mgr.

Sheridan

***KOHR(FM)**— 2004: 88.9 mhz; 425 w vert. Ant 72 ft TL: N44 47 54 W106 55 51. Hrs open: 24
Rebroadcasts KXEI(FM) Havre, MT 100%.
Box 2426, Hevre, MT, 59501. Phone: (406) 265-5845. Fax: (406) 265-8860. Licensee: Hi-Line Radio Fellowship Inc. (acq 7-31-2003; $10,000 for CP). Wire Svc: AP Format: Christian inspirational. ♦Ed Matter, gen mgr; Brenda Boyum, opns mgr; Roger Lonnquist, dev dir; Brian Jackson, progmg dir.

***KPRQ(FM)**— 2006: 88.1 mhz; 450 w. Ant 1,118 ft TL: N44 37 26 W107 07 02. Hrs open: Yellowstone Public Radio, 1500 University Dr., Billings, MT, 59101-0298. Phone: (406) 657-2941. Fax: (406) 657-2977. Web Site:www.yellowstonepublicradio.org Licensee: Montana State University-Billings. Natl. Network: NPR, . Format: News, classical, jazz. ♦Lois Bent, gen mgr.

KROE(AM)— Mar 18, 1961: 930 khz; 5 kw-D, 117 w-N. TL: N44 47 54 W106 55 51. Hrs open: 24 Box 5086, 82801. Secondary address: 1716 KROE Ln. 82801. Phone: (307) 672-7421. Fax: (307) 672-2933.E-mail: kimlove@sheridanmedia.com Web Site:www.sheridanmedia.com Licensee: Lovcom Inc. (group owner). Population served: 30,000 Natl. Network: CBS, . Pepper & Corazzini. Wire Svc: AP Format: News/talk. News staff: 3. Target aud: 25-54; general. ♦Kim Love, pres, gen mgr; Steve Sisson, opns dir, chief of engrg, engr; Jim Schellinger, gen sls mgr; Russ Davidson, progmg dir; Mary Jo Johnson, news dir; Liz Reynolds, traf mgr; Trevor Jackson, sports cmtr.

***KSUW(FM)**— 1998: 91.3 mhz; 450 w. 1,161 ft TL: N44 56 09 W106 55 51. Hrs open:
Rebroadcasts KUWR(FM) Laramie 100%.
Department 3984, 1000 E. Wyoming Ave., Laramie, 82071. Phone: (307) 766-4240. Fax: (307) 766-6184.E-mail: wpr@uwyo.edu Web Site:www.wyomingpublicradio.net Licensee: University of Wyoming. Format: News, progsv, class. ♦Jon Schwartz, gen mgr; Peg Arnold, dev dir, adv dir; Don Woods, mus dir; Bob Beck, news dir; Larry Dean, chief of engrg; Roger Adams, progmg dir & traf mgr.

***KVLZ(FM)**— 2009: 89.9 mhz; 150 w. Ant -138 ft TL: N44 47 54 W106 55 51. Hrs open:
Rebroadcasts KLVR(FM) Middletown, CA 100&.
2351 Sunset Blvd., Suite 170-218, Rocklin, CA, 95765. Phone: (916) 251-1600. Fax: (916) 251-1650. Web Site:www.klove.com Licensee: Educational Media Foundation. (acq 3-23-2007; grpsl). Natl. Network: K-Love, . Format: Contemp Christian. ♦Mike Novak, pres.

***KWCF(FM)**— 2005: 88.9 mhz; 1 kw. Ant 961 ft TL: N44 36 10 W106 55 42. Hrs open: Box 1492, Gillette, 82717. Secondary address: CSN International, 3232 W. MacArthur Blvd. , Santa Ana, CA 92704-6802. Phone: (307) 682-9553. Fax: (307) 682-8509.E-mail: calvarycomm@vcn.com Licensee: CSN International (group owner). Format: Relg.

KWYO(AM)— July 9, 1934: 1410 khz; 5 kw-D, 500 w-N. TL: N44 46 15 W106 55 37. Hrs open: 24 Box 5086, 82801-1387. Secondary address: 1716 Kroe Ln 82801. Phone: (307) 672-0701. Fax: (307) 672-2933.E-mail: info@sheridanmedia.com Web Site:www.sheridanmedia.com Licensee: Lovcom Inc. (group owner; acq 9-11-03). Population served: 40,000 Pepper & Corazzini. Format: adult standards. News staff: one; News: 20 hrs wkly. Target aud: 25-54. ♦Kim Love, gen mgr; Steve Sisson, opns mgr; Jim Schellinger, gen sls mgr; Russ Davidson, progmg dir; Ace Young, news dir; Tony Questa, chief of engrg.

KYTI(FM)— September 1978: 93.7 mhz; 75 kw. 1,207 ft TL: N44 37 20 W107 06 57. Stereo. Hrs open: 24 Box 5086, 1716 KROE Ln., 82801. Phone: (307) 672-7421. Fax: (307) 672-2933. Web Site:www.sheridanmedia.com Licensee: Lovcom Inc. (group owner; acq 5-15-97). Population served: 30,000 Natl. Network: ABC, . Format: Country. News: 4 hrs wkly. Target aud: 25-50. ♦Kim Love, gen mgr; Steve Sisson, opns mgr; Jim Schellinger, gen sls mgr; Russ Davidson, progmg dir; Ace Young, news dir; Tony Questa, chief of engrg.

KZWY(FM)— December 1977: 94.9 mhz; 75 kw. 1,207 ft TL: N44 37 20 W107 06 57. Stereo. Hrs open: 24 Prog sep from AM Box 5086, 82801. Secondary address: 1716 KROE Ln. 82801. Phone: (307) 672-7421. Fax: (307) 672-2933.E-mail: info@sheridanmedia.com Web Site:www.sheridanmedia.com Format: Classic rock. Target aud: 18-49; general. ♦Steve Sisson, chief of opns; Liz Reynolds, traf mgr; Trevor Jackson, sports cmtr.

Shoshoni

KTWY(FM)— 2009: 97.1 mhz; 2.2 kw. Ant 1,988 ft TL: N43 26 16 W107 59 46. Hrs open: Box 11060, Jackson, 83002. Licensee: Cochise Broadcasting LLC. ♦Ted Tucker, gen mgr.

KWWY(FM)— 2009: 106.3 mhz; 2.2 kw. Ant 1,988 ft TL: N43 26 16 W107 59 46. Hrs open: Box 11060, Jackson, 83002. Licensee: Cochise Broadcasting LLC. ♦Ted Tucker, gen mgr.

Sinclair

KXJW(FM)—Not on air, target date: unknown: 101.3 mhz; 51 kw. Ant 820 ft TL: N41 48 46 W107 19 00. Hrs open: Box 11060, Jackson, 83002. Licensee: Cochise Broadcasting LLC. ♦Ted Tucker, gen mgr.

Sleepy Hollow

KQOL(FM)—Not on air, target date: unknown: 105.3 mhz; 100 kw. Ant 269 ft TL: N44 18 10 W105 27 00. Hrs open: 202 Ross Ave., Gillette, 82716. Phone: (307) 687-1003. Fax: (307) 687-1006. Licensee: Keyhole Broadcasting LLC (acq 4-30-2009; $150,000 for CP). ◆Kevin Clements, gen mgr.

South Greeley

*KDNR(FM)— Dec 23, 2003: 88.7 mhz; 500 w. Ant 423 ft TL: N41 06 02 W105 01 29.1. Stereo. Hrs open: 24 Box 21888, Carson City, NV, 89721. Phone: (775) 883-5647.E-mail: info@pilgrimradio.com Web Site:www.pilgrimradio.com Licensee: Cedar Cove Broadcasting Inc. Group owner: EMF Broadcasting. (acq 2-21-2006; $200,000). Population served: 100,000 Gammon & Grange. Format: Christian. News staff: 3. ◆Robert T. Hesse, gen mgr.

South Park

KJXN(FM)— 2008: Stn currently dark. 105.1 mhz; 11 kw. Ant 1,050 ft TL: N43 27 39 W110 45 09. Hrs open: Box 11060, Jackson, 83002. Licensee: Cochise Media Licenses LLC (acq 12-23-2008; $470,000). ◆Ted Tucker, gen mgr.

Story

KZZS(FM)— Nov 13, 2003: 98.3 mhz; 100 kw. Ant 272 ft TL: N44 34 32 W106 52 23. Stereo. Hrs open: 24 1221 Fort St., Buffalo, 82834. Secondary address: 610 Illinois St., Buffalo 82834. Phone: (307) 684-7070. Fax: (307) 684-7676.E-mail: kbbs@vcn.com Licensee: Legend Communications of Wyoming L.L.C. Group owner: Legend Communications LLC. (acq 5-31-00; $200,000 for CP). Population served: 64,000 Format: Hot adult hits. News staff: one; News: 6 hrs wkly. Target aud: 18-35. ◆Larry Patrick, CEO, pres; Smokey Wildeman, gen mgr; Ed Cwik, opns mgr, progmg dir; Charles Dozier, chief of engrg; Rita Conners, traf mgr.

Sundance

*KUWD(FM)— 2000: 91.5 mhz; 430 w. Ant 1,591 ft TL: N44 28 35 W104 26 54. Hrs open: Department 3984, 1000 E. Wyoming Ave., Laramie, 82071. Phone: (307) 766-4240. Fax: (307) 766-6184.E-mail: wpr@uwyo.edu Web Site:www.wyomingpublicradio.net Licensee: University of Wyoming. Format: News, progsv, class. ◆Jon Schwartz, gen mgr; Peg Arnold, dev dir, sls dir, adv dir; Don Woods, mus dir; Bob Beck, news dir; Larry Dean, chief of engrg; Roger Adams, progmg dir & traf mgr.

KYDT(FM)— November 1997: 103.1 mhz; 25.2 kw. 1,650 ft TL: N44 28 35 W104 26 54. Stereo. Hrs open: 24 Rebroadcasts KBFS(AM) Belle Fourche 99.9%. Box 787, Belle Fourche, SD, 57717. Phone: (605) 892-2571. Fax: (605) 892-2573.E-mail: wyodak@hotmail.com Web Site:www.kydt.com Licensee: Ultimate Caps Inc. Population served: 150,000 Natl. Network: ESPN Radio, Westwood One, AP Network News, . Rgnl. Network: Jones Satellite Audio. Wire Svc: AP Format: Country, sports, news, talk. News: 25 hrs wkly. Target aud: General; rural, suburban, country mus, sports fans. ◆Cynthia Grimmelmann, pres; Karl Grimmelmann, exec VP, gen mgr & opns VP.

Superior

KMRZ-FM— July 15, 2008: 106.7 mhz; 7 kw. Ant 1,581 ft TL: N41 25 28 W109 07 54. Hrs open: Box 2128, Rock Springs, 82902. Phone: (307) 362-3793. Fax: (307) 362-8727. Web Site:www.wyoradio.com Licensee: Big Thicket Broadcasting Co. of Wyoming Inc. (acq 8-1-2008; $400,000). Format: Rgnl Mexican. ◆Wiliam Luzmoor III, pres; Jon Collins, gen mgr.

Ten Sleep

KYTS(FM)—Not on air, target date: unknown: 105.1 mhz; 25 kw. Ant -82 ft TL: N44 01 39 W107 21 04. Hrs open: c/o Patrick Communications, LLC, 6805 Douglas Legum Dr., Suite 100, Elkridge, MD, 21075. Phone: (410) 799-1740. Licensee: Legend Communications of Wyoming LLC. ◆W. Lawrence Patrick, pres.

Thayne

*KTYN(FM)—Not on air, target date: unknown: 91.9 mhz; 77 w. Ant 2,329 ft TL: N43 06 18 W111 07 17. Hrs open: Box 1065, 83127-1065. Phone: (801) 580-4339. Licensee: Intermountain Public Radio. ◆Carolyn E. Ashauer, pres.

Thermopolis

KDNO(FM)— Aug 30, 2001: 101.7 mhz; 16.25 kw. Ant 1,901 ft TL: N43 26 18 W107 59 37. Hrs open: Box 591, 82443-0501. Secondary address: 420 Arapahoe 82443. Phone: (307) 864-2119. Fax: (307) 864-3937.E-mail: kthe@directairnet.com Licensee: Carjim LLC. Group owner: Jimmy Ray Carroll Stns (acq 9-13-2001; $20,000 for CP). Format: Classic country. ◆Jim Carroll, pres; Dick Howe, gen mgr, gen sls mgr, progmg dir; Dennis Silver, chief of engrg.

KTHE(AM)— April 1957: 1240 khz; 1 kw-U. TL: N43 38 42 W108 12 15. Hrs open: Box 591, 82443-0591. Secondary address: 420 Arapahoe 82443. Phone: (307) 864-2119. Fax: (307) 864-3937.E-mail: kthe@directairnet.com Licensee: Carjim LLC. Group owner: Jimmy Ray Carroll Stns (acq 5-7-2002). Population served: 3,800 Format: Adult contemp, oldies. Target aud: 25-54; varied. ◆Jim Carroll, pres; Dick Howe, gen mgr, gen sls mgr, gen sls mgr, progmg dir.

KUWT(FM)— 2001: 91.3 mhz; 2 kw. Ant 1,961 ft TL: N43 26 16 W107 59 48. Hrs open: Rebroadcasts KUWR(FM) Laramie 100%. Department 3984, 1000 E. Wyoming Ave., Laramie, 82071. Phone: (307) 766-4240. Fax: 307 766-6184.E-mail: wpr@uwyo.edu Web Site:www.wyomingpublicradio.net Licensee: University of Wyoming. Format: News, progsv, class. ◆Jon Schwartz, gen mgr.

Torrington

KERM(FM)— Dec 15, 1976: 98.3 mhz; 3 kw. Ant 300 ft TL: N41 59 41 W104 12 05. Stereo. Hrs open: 760 Radio Rd., 82240. Phone: (307) 532-2158. Fax: (307) 532-2641. Licensee: Mount Rushmore Broadcasting Inc. Population served: 30,000 Format: Country.

KGOS(AM)— May 15, 1950: 1490 khz; 1 kw-U. TL: N42 04 20 W104 13 40. Hrs open: 5:30 AM-10:15 PM 760 Radio Rd., 82240. Phone: (307) 532-2158. Fax: (307) 532-2641. Licensee: Mount Rushmore Broadcasting Inc. (group owner) Population served: 30,000 Rgnl rep: Art Moore. Format: Country. Target aud: 20 plus; general. ◆Grant Kath, gen mgr.

Upton

KHAD(FM)—Not on air, target date: unknown: 104.5 mhz; 100 kw. Ant 682 ft TL: N44 25 17 W104 26 57. Hrs open: 288 S. River Rd., Bedford, NH, 03110. Phone: (603) 668-6400. Fax: (603) 668-6470. Licensee: White Park Broadcasting Inc. ◆Steven A. Silberberg, pres.

KWDU(FM)—Not on air, target date: unknown: 93.5 mhz; 2 kw. Ant 26 ft TL: N44 06 41 W104 37 40. Hrs open: 5331 Mount Alifan Dr., San Diego, CA, 92111-2622. Phone: (858) 277-4991. Fax: (858) 277-1365. Licensee: Horizon Christian Fellowship. ◆Tom Phillips, COO.

Vista West

KRVK(FM)— 2001: 107.9 mhz; 15.5 kw. Ant 1,938 ft TL: N42 44 37 W106 18 24. Hrs open: 150 N. Nichols, Casper, 82601. Phone: (307) 266-5252. Fax: (307) 235-9143.E-mail: krvk@clearchannel.com Web Site:theriver1079.com Licensee: GAP Broadcasting Casper License LLC. Group owner: Clear Channel Communications Inc. (acq 2-13-2008; grpsl). Format: Classic rock. ◆Robert Price, gen mgr; Walter Hawn, gen sls mgr; Donovan Short, progmg dir; Dave Nutter, chief of engrg; Dave Borino, traf mgr.

Wamsutter

KHNA(FM)— 2009: 94.7 mhz; 120 w. Ant 52 ft TL: N41 39 56 W107 58 11. Hrs open: 288 S. River Rd., Bedford, NH, 03110. Phone: (603) 668-6400. Fax: (603) 668-6470. Licensee: White Park Broadcasting Inc. ◆Steven A. Silberberg, pres.

KYPT(FM)—Not on air, target date: unknown: 104.3 mhz; 100 kw. Ant 606 ft TL: N41 33 46 W108 16 56. Hrs open: c/o Sciarrino & Shubert, PLLC, 5425 Tree Line Dr., Centreville, VA, 20120. Phone: (202) 350-9658. Licensee: Martin Dirst (acq 12-21-2007). ◆Martin Dirst, gen mgr.

Warren AFB

KOLT-FM— Aug 4, 1978: 92.9 mhz; 33 kw. Ant 607 ft TL: N41 04 35 W105 12 10. Stereo. Hrs open: 24 29 S. 4th Ave., Brighton, CO, 80601. Phone: (720) 685-0757. Fax: (720) 685-0756. Web Site:www.lapantera929.com Licensee: Tracy Broadcasting Corp. Group owner: Tracy Broadcasting Corp. Population served: 125,000 Format: Rgnl Mexican. ◆Rob Quinn, gen mgr & stn mgr; Beto Gaytan, progmg dir.

KRAN(FM)— 2009: 103.3 mhz; 37 kw. Ant 256 ft TL: N41 09 34 W104 43 19. Hrs open: 288 S. River Rd., Bedford, NH, 03110. Phone: (603) 668-6400. Licensee: Freisland Broadcasting Corp. ◆Steven A. Silberberg, pres.

West Laramie

*KRWT(FM)—Not on air, target date: unknown: 89.9 mhz; 100 kw vert. Ant 571 ft TL: N41 54 19 W106 32 37. Hrs open: CSN International, 4002 N. 3300 E., Twin Falls, ID, 83301. Phone: (208) 734-6633. Fax: (208) 736-1958. Web Site:www.csnradio.com Licensee: CSN International (group owner). Format: Contemp Christian talk. ◆Mike Stocklin, gen mgr; Don Mills, progmg dir; Kelly Carlson, chief of engrg.

Wheatland

KMQS(FM)—Not on air, target date: unknown: 106.1 mhz; 30 kw. Ant 423 ft TL: N41 56 13 W104 55 50. Hrs open: 911 Colonial Dr., Cheyenne, 82001-7415. Phone: (307) 638-1345. Licensee: Lorenz E. Proietti. ◆Lorenz E. Proietti, gen mgr.

KPAD(FM)— 2009: 107.5 mhz; 530 w. Ant 1,092 ft TL: N41 49 00 W105 03 48. Hrs open: 288 S. River Rd., Bedford, NH, 03110. Phone: (603) 668-6400. Licensee: Brahmin Broadcasting Corp. ◆Steven A. Silberberg, pres.

KYCN(AM)— Nov 16, 1960: 1340 khz; 250 w-U. TL: N42 02 44 W104 56 47. Hrs open: 24 Box 248, 82201. Secondary address: 450 E. Cole 82201. Phone: (307) 322-5926. Phone: (307) 322-9300.E-mail: info@kycn-kzew.com Web Site:www.kycn-kzew.com Licensee: Smith Broadcasting Inc. (acq 12-6-91; with co-located FM). Population served: 12,000 Natl. Network: ABC, . Natl. Rep: Target Broadcast Sales,. Bryan Cave. Format: Country. News staff: one; News: 14 hrs wkly. Target aud: General. Spec prog: Farm 7 hrs wkly. ◆Catherine Smith, gen sls mgr, mktg mgr, prom mgr, adv mgr; Derek Barton, news dir; Kent G. Smith, pres, gen mgr, mus dir, chief of engrg & traf mgr.

KZEW(FM)— February 1985: 101.7 mhz; 3 kw. 156 ft TL: N42 02 44 W104 56 47. Stereo. Hrs open: 24 Box 248, 82201. Secondary address: 450 E. Cole 82201. Phone: (307) 322-5926. Phone: (307) 322-5927. Fax: (307) 322-9300. Web Site:www.kycn-kzew.com Natl. Network: Jones Radio Networks, . Format: Adult contemp. ◆Kent G. Smith, chief of opns, progmg dir, pub affrs dir & disc jockey.

Worland

KKLX(FM)— Dec 1, 1980: 96.1 mhz; 50 kw. 400 ft TL: N44 04 06 W107 51 57. Stereo. Hrs open: Prog sep from AM 1340 Radio Dr., 82401. Phone: (307) 347-3231. Fax: (307) 347-4880. Population served: 45,000 Format: Mus of the 80s & 90s & today. ◆Nancy Harrington, traf mgr.

KWOR(AM)— Mar 7, 1946: 1340 khz; 1 kw-U. TL: N44 01 01 W107 58 14. Hrs open: 1340 Radio Dr., 82401. Phone: (307) 347-3231. Fax: (307) 347-4880.E-mail: kwor@rtconnect.net Web Site:www.kworkklx.com Licensee: Legend Communications of Wyoming LLC. (acq 12-31-2007; $750,000 with co-located FM). Population served: 30,000 Eugene T. Smith. Format: Oldies. Target aud: General. ◆Bill Harrington, gen mgr, progmg dir, progmg dir; Tony Cuesta, chief of engrg; Nancy Harrington, traf mgr.

Wright

KDDV-FM— 2008: 101.5 mhz; 100 kw. Ant 1,098 ft TL: N43 59 57 W105 15 15. Hrs open: Box 1179, Gillette, 82717-1179. Phone: (307) 686-2242. Fax: (307) 686-7736. Web Site:www.basinradio.com Licensee: Legend Communications of Wyoming LLC. Format: Classic hits. ◆Don Clonch, gen mgr.

KHRW(FM)—Not on air, target date: unknown: 92.7 mhz; 6 kw. Ant 328 ft TL: N43 44 32 W105 28 14. Hrs open: 5331 Mt. Alifan Dr., San

Diego, CA, 92111. Phone: (858) 277-4991. Fax: (858) 277-1365. Web Site:www.horizonsd.org/radio.asp Licensee: Horizon Christian Fellowship. ♦ Mike MacIntosh, pres.

American Samoa

Fagaitua

WVUV-FM— 2008: 103.1 mhz; 1.3 kw. Ant 1,591 ft TL: S14 19 21 W170 45 47. Hrs open: Box 6008, Pago Pago, 96799. Phone: (684) 258-9393. Web Site:www.wvuv.com Licensee: Horizon Christian Fellowship. (acq 2-9-2006; grpsl). ♦ Shannon J. Cummings, gen mgr.

Leone

KKHJ(AM)—Not on air, target date: unknown: 900 khz; 5 kw-D, 3 kw-N. TL: S14 20 24 W170 46 22. Hrs open: Box 1787, Cleveland, 38732. Phone: (662) 846-1787. Licensee: South Seas Broadcasting Inc. ♦ Larry G. Fuss, pres; Joey Cummings, gen mgr.

KNWJ(FM)— 2001: 104.7 mhz; 280 w. Ant 1,499 ft TL: N14 19 21 W170 45 47. Stereo. Hrs open: 24 Box 997777, Pago Pago, 96799. Phone: (684) 699 8127. Fax: (684) 699-8126.E-mail: info@fm104.org Web Site:www.fm104.org Licensee: Showers of Blessings Radio (acq 5-26-00; $70,000 for CP). Population served: 30000 Format: Today's Christian hits. ♦ Dan Dalle, gen mgr.

WVUV(AM)— Apr 16, 1975: 648 khz; 10 kw-U. TL: S14 21 28 W170 46 36. Hrs open: Box 6758, Pago Pago, 96799. Phone: (684) 633-7793. Fax: (684) 633-4493. Licensee: South Seas Broadcasting Inc. Format: Hot adult contemp. ♦ Joey Cummings, gen mgr.

Mapusaga

*KPPO(FM)—Not on air, target date: unknown: 90.5 mhz; 750 w. Ant 1,614 ft TL: S14 19 03 W170 45 51. Hrs open: 655 Cedar Ave., Long Beach, CA, 90802-1222. Phone: (562) 628-9282. Licensee: Second Samoan Congregational Church of Long Beach. ♦ Misipouena S. Tagaloa, gen mgr.

Nu'uuli

*KMOA(FM)—Not on air, target date: unknown: 89.7 mhz; 1.5 kw. Ant 1,463 ft TL: S14 16 12 W170 41 10. Hrs open: Box 6008, Pago Pago, 96799. Phone: (684) 258-9393. Licensee: Society of Pure Truth Ministries Inc. ♦ Shannon J. Cummings, pres.

Pago Pago

KKHJ-FM— May 1, 2000: 93.1 mhz; 420 w. Ant 1,489 ft TL: N14 16 12 W170 41 10. Stereo. Hrs open: 24 Box 6758, 96799. Secondary address: 9408 Grand Gate St., Las Vegas 89143. Phone: (684) 633-7793. Licensee: South Seas Broadcasting. Group owner: Contemporary Communications. Population served: 55,000 Wood, Maines & Brown, Chartered. Format: Hot adult contemp. Target aud: General. ♦ Larry G. Fuss, pres; Joey Cummings, gen mgr.

KSBS-FM— Apr 14, 1988: 92.1 mhz; 3 kw. -135 ft TL: S14 17 41 W170 39 44. (CP: 15 kw, ant -92 ft.). Stereo. Hrs open: 6:00am-Midnight Box 793, 96799-0793. Phone: (684) 633-7000. Fax: (684) 633-5727.E-mail: prescott.esther@ksbsfm.com Web Site:www.ksbsfm.com Licensee: Samoa Technologies Inc. Format: Adult contemp. Target aud: Working adults. ♦ Barney Sene, pres; Esther Prescott, gen mgr.

Tafuna

KJAL(AM)— 2005: 585 khz; 5 kw-U. TL: S14 21 28 W170 46 36. Hrs open: Box 218, Pago Pago, 96799. Phone: (684) 699-2253. Licensee: District Council of the Assemblies of God in AS. Format: Contemp Christian. ♦ Viliamu Paaga, gen mgr.

Guam

Agat

*KSDA-FM— Nov 22, 1990: 91.9 mhz; 3.8 kw. 1,000 ft TL: N13 25 53 W144 42 36. Stereo. Hrs open: 24 290 Chalan Palasyo, Agana Heights, 96910. Phone: (671) 472-5732. Fax: (671) 477-4678.E-mail: mail@joy92.net Licensee: Good News Broadcasting Corp. (acq 8-9-01; charitable contribution). Population served: 180,000 Format: Inspirational, Christian. News: 7 hrs wkly. Target aud: 25-54. ♦ Robert Gibbons, chmn & pres; Matt Dodd, gen mgr, stn mgr.

Barrigada

*KHMG(FM)— Mar 26, 1996: 88.1 mhz; 8 kw. 472 ft TL: N13 29 17 W144 49 53. Stereo. Hrs open: 24 Box 23189, 170C Machaute St., 96921. Phone: (671) 477-6341. Fax: (671) 477-7136.E-mail: khmg@harvestministries.net Web Site:www.harvestministries.net Licensee: Harvest Christian Academy. Population served: 140,000 Garvey, Schubert & Barer. Format: Relg, Christian. News: 5 hrs wkly. Target aud: General; Christian, church and school families. Spec prog: Children 2 hrs wkly. ♦ Dr. Marty Herron, pres; John Collier, stn mgr & progmg dir.

Dededo

KGUM-FM— Feb 28, 1999: 105.1 mhz; 12 kw. Ant 502 ft TL: N13 29 17 W144 49 30. Hrs open: 111 W. Santo Papa, Suite 800, Hagatna, 96910. Phone: (671) 477-5700. Fax: (671) 477-3982. Web Site:www.105therock.com Licensee: Sorensen Pacific Broadcasting Inc. (group owner; acq 6-23-03; grpsl). Format: Rock. ♦ Jon Anderson, pres; Rex W. Sorensen, CEO, chmn & gen mgr; Albert Juan, stn mgr.

Hagatna

KGUM(AM)— February 1975: 567 khz; 10 kw-U, DA-1. TL: N13 23 21 E144 45 34. Hrs open: 24 111 W. Chalan Santo Papa, Suite 800, 96910. Phone: (671) 477-5700. Fax: (671) 477-3982. Web Site:www.radiopacific.com Licensee: Sorensen Pacific Broadcasting Inc. (group owner; (acq 6-23-2003); grpsl). Population served: 165,000 Natl. Network: CBS, Westwood One, . Format: News/talk. News staff: 5; News: 20 hrs wkly. Target aud: 35 plus; adults with high income & education. Spec prog: Educ one hr, computer 3 hrs, police one hr, health & fitness one hr, environmental one hr, drug recovery one hr wkly. ♦ Rex Sorensen, VP & gen mgr; Ray Gibson, opns mgr.

KISH(FM)— 2003: 102.9 mhz; 25 kw. Ant 535 ft TL: N13 29 17 W144 49 53. Stereo. Hrs open: 24 Inter-Island Communications Inc., 1868 Halsey Dr., Piti, 96915. Phone: (671) 477-9448. Phone: (671) 477-5474. Fax: (671) 477-6411. Licensee: Inter-Island Communications Inc. (group owner). Population served: 160,000 Format: Chamorro music-language of Guam and Marianas Islands. News staff: one; News: 15 hrs wkly. Target aud: General; indeginous residents of Marianas Islands. ♦ Edward H. Poppe Jr., pres; Frances W. Poppe, CFO; Edward H. Poppe III, exec VP; Joe Tighe, opns mgr; Rosalin Koss, progmg dir.

KOKU(FM)— Apr 28, 1984: 100.3 mhz; 5 kw. 190 ft TL: N13 26 28 W144 42 40. Stereo. Hrs open: 24 424 W. O'Brien Dr., 107 Julace Ctr., 96910. Fax: (671) 477-5658.E-mail: marketing@hitradio.com Web Site:www.hitradio100.com Licensee: Moy Communications Inc. (acq 4-29-2004; $350,000). Population served: 149,000 Dow, Lohnes & Albertson. Format: Top-40. Target aud: 18-34; females. ♦ Kurt S. Moylan, pres; Rick Nauta, progmg dir, chief of engrg; Vince R. Limuaco, gen mgr, sls & mktg.

*KPRG(FM)— Jan 27, 1994: 89.3 mhz; 2.8 kw. 485 ft TL: N13 29 17 W144 49 30. Stereo. Hrs open: 24 KPRG, UoG Stn., Mangilao, 96923. Phone: (671) 734-8930. Fax: (671) 734-2958.E-mail: kprg@kprg.org Web Site:www.kprg.org Licensee: Guam Educational Radio Foundation. Natl. Network: NPR, . Format: News, div, class. ♦ Denise Mendiola, gen mgr; Olympia Terral, dev dir; Lydia Taleu, progmg dir, disc jockey.

KSTO(FM)— September 1973: 95.5 mhz; 25 kw. 530 ft TL: N13 29 17 E144 49 53. Stereo. Hrs open: 24 1868 Halsey Dr., Piti, 96915. Phone: (671) 477-7108. Phone: (671) 477-5786. Fax: (671) 477-6411.E-mail: ksto@ite.net Licensee: Inter-Island Communications Inc. (group owner; acq 11-77). Population served: 160,000 Format: Adult contemp. News staff: one; News: 14 hrs wkly. Target aud: 25-54. Spec prog: Country 12 hrs, gospel 6 hrs wkly. ♦ Edward H. Poppe Jr., pres; Frances Poppe, CFO; Edward H. Poppe III, exec VP; Joe Tighe, opns mgr; Rosalin Koss, progmg dir.

KTKB-FM— 2003: 101.9 mhz; 50 kw. Ant 492 ft TL: N13 29 16 W144 49 36. Hrs open: KM Broadcasting of Guam L.L.C., 3654 W. Jarvis Ave., Skokie, IL, 60076. Phone: (847) 674-0864. Phone: (671) 647-1019. Fax: (847) 674-9188. Fax: (671) 648-1019. Web Site:www.ktkb.com Licensee: KM Broadcasting of Guam L.L.C. Group owner: KM Communications Inc. Format: Filipino. ♦ Myoung Bae, pres; Kevin Bae, gen mgr; Rolly Manumtag, progmg dir.

KTWG(AM)— August 1975: 801 khz; 10 kw-U. TL: N13 27 07 W144 42 32. Hrs open: 24 Simulcasts KCNM(AM) Saipan, Northern Mariana Islands. 1868 Halsey Dr., Piti, 96915. Phone: (671) 477-5894. Fax: (671) 477-6411.E-mail: ktwg@ktwg.com Web Site:www.ktwg.com Licensee: Edward H. Poppe Jr. and Frances W. Poppe. Group owner: Inter-Island Communications Inc. (acq 2-20-2002). Population served: 160,000 Format: Relg. News staff: one; News: 5 hrs wkly. Target aud: 25-49; Christian. ♦ K. Leilani S. Dahilig, stn mgr.

KUAM(AM)— Mar 14, 1954: 630 khz; 10 kw-U. TL: N13 26 53 E144 45 22. Hrs open: 600 Harmon Loop Rd., Suite 102, Dededo, 96912. Phone: (671) 637-5826. Fax: (671) 637-9865. Web Site:www.kuam.com/i94 Licensee: Pacific Telestations Inc. (acq 9-27-77). Natl. Network: CBS, . Format: MOR. ♦ Joey Calvo, gen mgr.

KUAM-FM— Sept 1, 1966: 93.9 mhz; 2 kw. 950 ft TL: N13 25 53 E144 42 36. (CP: 5.2 kw, ant 948 ft.). Hrs open: 600 Harmon Loop Rd., Suite 102, Dededo, 96912. Phone: (671) 637-0094. Fax: (671) 637-9865. Web Site:www.kuam.com/i94 Format: CHR. ♦ Joey Calvo, gen mgr.

KVOG(AM)—Not on air, target date: unknown: 1530 khz; 250 w-U. TL: N13 27 24 W144 40 20. Hrs open: 1100 Alakea, Suite 1800, Honolulu, HI, 96813-2839. Phone: (808) 521-4711. Fax: (808) 538-3269. Licensee: Guam Power II Inc. ♦ Wagdy Guirguis, pres.

KZGZ(FM)— December 1986: 97.5 mhz; 40 kw. Ant 538 ft TL: N13 29 17 W144 49 30. Stereo. Hrs open: 24 111 W. Chalan Santo Papa, Suite 800, 96910. Phone: (671) 477-5700. Fax: (671) 477-3982. Licensee: Sorensen Pacific Broadcasting Inc. Population served: 150,000 Format: Hip hop. News: 15 hrs wkly. Target aud: 18-34; young affluent adults.

Tamuning

KTKB(AM)—Not on air, target date: unknown: 675 khz; 10 kw-U. TL: N13 34 22 W144 51 47. Hrs open: KM Broadcasting of Guam L.L.C., 3654 W. Jarvis Ave., Skokie, IL, 60076. Phone: (847) 674-0864. Fax: (671) 648-1019. Licensee: KM Broadcasting of Guam L.L.C. ♦ Myoung Bae, pres; Kevin Bae, gen mgr.

Tumon

KIJI(FM)— 2006: 104.3 mhz; 12.5 kw. Ant 292 ft TL: N13 30 07 E144 47 21. Hrs open: La Casa de Colina, 3rd Fl., 200 Chichirica St., Tamuning, 96913-4217. Phone: (671) 648-1043. Fax: (671) 648-0104. Web Site:www.kijifm104.com Licensee: Guam Broadcast Services Inc. (acq 3-2-2009). Format: Favorite hits from the 70s and 80s. ♦ Yasunori Kawauchi, pres; Kevin H. Yamazaki, VP.

Puerto Rico

Adjuntas

WOQI(AM)— 1997: 1020 khz; 1 kw-D, 280 w-N. TL: N18 09 04 W66 42 48. Hrs open: Box 7243, Ponce, 00732. Phone: (787) 829-1453. Fax: (787) 840-7077.E-mail: administracion@wpabradio.com Licensee: WPAB Inc. (acq. 6-23-01; $450,000). Population served: 35,000 Format: Sp, var/div. News staff: one; News: 3 hrs wkly. Target aud: General; General Public. ♦ Alfonso Gimenez-Lucchetti, gen mgr.

Aguada

WFDT(FM)— 1975: 105.5 mhz; 3 kw. 1,036 ft TL: N18 18 57 W67 10 54. Stereo. Hrs open: 24 Box 363222, San Juan, 00936. Phone: (787) 758-1300. Fax: (787) 754-1395. Web Site:www.fidelitypr.com Licensee: Arso Radio Corp. Group owner: Uno Radio Group (acq 4-19-01; $3.2 million). Format: Adult contemp, easy lstng. News staff: 4. Target aud: 25-49; middle class. ♦ Luis Soto, pres.

Aguadilla

WABA(AM)— Nov 15, 1951: 850 khz; 5 kw-D, 1 kw-N. TL: N18 24 02 W67 09 27. Hrs open: Box 188, 00605. Phone: (787) 891-1230. Fax: (787) 882-2282.E-mail: radiowaba@gmail.com Web Site:www.waba850.com Licensee: Aquadilla Radio & TV Corp. Inc. (acq 9-11-2007). Format: Adult contemp, Talk. ♦Eridania Sucana, pres; Luis Rosario, gen mgr; Mereida Nieves, gen sls mgr, news dir, traf mgr; Tito R. Areicaga, adv dir & progmg dir; Max Perez, chief of engrg.

WIVA-FM— Apr 16, 1964: 100.3 mhz; 22 kw. Ant 2,014 ft TL: N18 09 07 W66 59 15. Stereo. Hrs open: 24 Box 3822, Mayaguez, 00681. Phone: (787) 834-2320. Fax: (787) 831-7969.E-mail: www.@unoradio.com Web Site:www.salsoul.com Licensee: Arso Radio Corp. Group owner: Uno Radio Group (acq 3-85). Format: Salsa. News staff: one; News: 5 hrs wkly. Target aud: 12 plus. ♦Jesus M. Soto, CEO, pres; Luis A. Soto, pres, chief of engrg; Maida Bedaya, gen mgr; Raymond Totti, gen sls mgr; Anthony Soto, progmg dir.

WTPM(FM)— May 27, 1971: 92.9 mhz; 50 kw. 1,223 ft TL: N18 18 52 W67 10 58. Stereo. Hrs open: 18 Box 1629, Mayaguez, 00681. Phone: (787) 831-9200. Phone: (787) 834-6340. Fax: (787) 831-9292.E-mail: baraiso@radiotv.com Web Site:www.wtpm.com Licensee: Corp. of the 7th Day Adventists of West Puerto Rico (acq 2-80; $125,000). Population served: 300,000 Format: Sp adult contemp. News: 11 hrs wkly. Target aud: General; traditional Christian groups. Spec prog: English one hr, class 7 hrs wkly. ♦Daniel Ponce, gen mgr & opns dir.

WWNA(AM)— 1956: 1340 khz; 950 w-U. TL: N18 24 00 W67 09 48. Hrs open: Box 7, Moca, 00676. Secondary address: Rd. 111, Aquadilla 00605. Phone: (787) 252-1730. Fax: (787) 868-1340. Licensee: Dominga Barreto Santiago (acq 1-25-2005; $500,000). Format: Sp var. Target aud: 20-55. Spec prog: Jazz 3 hrs wkly. ♦Aureo Matos, gen mgr, gen sls mgr, progmg dir; Ron Cushing, chief of engrg; Felix Gonzalez, disc jockey.

Arecibo

WCMN(AM)— June 24, 1947: 1280 khz; 5 kw-D, 1 kw-N. TL: N18 28 52 W66 41 16. Hrs open: 24 Box 436, 00613. Secondary address: 55 Gonzalo Marin St. 00612. Phone: (787) 878-0070. Phone: (787) 781-6303. Fax: (787) 880-1112.E-mail: unoarecivo.aruba@gmail.com Licensee: Caribbean Broadcasting Corp. Group owner: Uno Radio Group (acq 4-7-2004; $5.75 million for stock with co-located FM). Population served: 450,000 Fisher, Wayland, Cooper, Leader & Zaragoza L.L.P. Format: Sp, news/talk. News staff: 3; News: 50 hrs wkly. Target aud: 30 plus. ♦Byron Mitchell, VP, gen mgr; Maria M. Mitchell, sls dir, prom dir & progmg dir; Juan Rivera, chief of engrg; Jacquelyn Rames, traf mgr.

WCMN-FM— Jan 1, 1967: 107.3 mhz; 50 kw. Ant 3,000 ft TL: N18 14 52 W66 48 43. Stereo. Hrs open: 24 Box 363222, San Juan, 00936-3222. Phone: (787) 474-0630.E-mail: info@wcmn.com Web Site:www.tocadeto.com Licensee: Caribbean Broadcasting Corp. Population served: 1,000,000 Format: Sp, Top-40. Target aud: 18-42; young adults.

WMIA(AM)— Feb 21, 1957: 1070 khz; 500 w-D, 2.5 kw-N. TL: N18 27 33 W66 45 20. Hrs open: 19 Box 1055, 00613-1055. Secondary address: 1168 Miramar Ave. 00612. Phone: (787) 878-1275. Phone: (787) 878-2727. Fax: 787-878-1275.E-mail: epifanioro@gmail.com Licensee: Abacoa Radio Corp. Population served: 1,250,000 Booth, Freret, Imlay & Tepper. Format: Sp talk, tropical. Target aud: 25 plus; the buying power in the area. ♦Epifanio Rodriguez-Velez, gen mgr & chief of opns.

WNIK(AM)— 1957: 1230 khz; 1 kw-U. TL: N18 27 20 W66 44 24. Hrs open: Box 142041, 00614. Phone: (787) 880-2461. Fax: (787) 879-1011. Licensee: Unik Broadcasting System Corp. (acq 12-10-2004; $335,000). Format: Div, Sp. Target aud: General. ♦Manuel Santiago, gen mgr.

WNIK-FM— July 17, 1965: 106.5 mhz; 25 kw. Ant 20 ft TL: N18 27 20 W66 44 24. Stereo. Hrs open: Box 556, 00613. Phone: (787) 880-2613. Fax: (787) 879-1011. Licensee: Kelly Broadcasting System Inc. (acq 4-87). Format: Ballads. ♦Raul Santiago, gen mgr.

Barceloneta-Manati

WBQN(AM)— Mar 1, 1975: 1160 khz; 5 kw-D, 2.5 kw-N, DA-D. TL: N18 26 23 W66 33 07. Hrs open: Box 1625, Manati, 00674. Phone: (787) 854-2450. Phone: (787) 854-3738. Fax: (787) 854-3738.E-mail: riveraolmo@hotmail.com Licensee: Radio Borinquen Inc. Format: Top-40 CHR, Sp. Target aud: General. ♦Angel M. Rivera, pres; Luis R. Rivera Jr., gen mgr.

Barranquitas

WOLA(AM)— March 1986: 1380 khz; 1 kw-U. TL: N18 11 01 W66 18 24. Hrs open: Box 669, Carr 719 KMo1 Bo Halechal, 00794. Phone: (787) 857-1380. Fax: (787) 857-1381.E-mail: info@radioprocer.com Licensee: Torrecillas Broadcasting Corp. Format: Sp/tropical. Target aud: General. Spec prog: Jazz 5 hrs wkly. ♦Edwin Aponte, gen mgr; Jose A. Rojas, progmg dir; Jacqueline Pagan, chief of engrg.

Bayamon

WLUZ(AM)— 1966: Stn currently dark. 1600 khz; 5 kw-U. TL: N18 21 38 W66 09 30. Hrs open: 18 Box 9394, San Juan, 00908-0394. Secondary address: 403 Del Parque, 15 th Fl., Santurce 00912-3709. Phone: (787) 785-1600. Phone: (787) 729-1600. Fax: (787) 785-2094. Fax: (787) 723-8685.E-mail: ttrelles@yahoo.com Licensee: Marketing Promotion Network Inc. (acq 11-1-98; $1.6 million plus $800,000 penthouse). Population served: 2,000,000. Fletcher, Heald & Hildreth, P. L. C. ♦Tony Trelles, pres; Martha Villanueva, opns dir.

WODA(FM)— Dec 3, 1959: 94.7 mhz; 31 kw. Ant 1,837 ft TL: N18 16 44 W65 51 12. Stereo. Hrs open: 24 Box 949, Guayanbo, 00970-0949. Secondary address: Amelia Industrial Park, Calle Frances 42, Guaynabo 00968. Phone: (787) 622-9700. Fax: (787) 622-9478.E-mail: info@onda94.com Web Site:www.onda94.com Licensee: WLDI Inc. Group owner: Spanish Broadcasting System Inc. (acq 11-29-99; grpsl). Booth, Freret, Imlay & Tepper. Format: Sp, Top-40. Target aud: 12-24; males & females, middle/upper socio-economic. ♦Raul Alarcon, pres; Ismael Nieves, gen mgr; Marie Elena Martinez, gen sls mgr; Luis Enrique Rivera, prom VP; Jose Nelson Diaz, progmg dir; Alejandro Luciano, chief of engrg; Demare Ramirez, traf mgr.

WRSJ(AM)— 1947: 1560 khz; 5 kw-D, 750 w-N. TL: N18 24 05 W66 07 14. Hrs open: 1554 Bori St., San Juan, 00927-6113. Phone: (787) 274-1800. Fax: (787) 281-9758. Licensee: International Broadcasting Corp. (group owner; (acq 7-6-2004; $1.45 million with WCHQ(AM) Quebradillas). Format: Sp. ♦Pedro Roman Collazo, pres; Margarita Nazario, gen mgr.

WXYX(FM)— Feb 1, 1979: 100.7 mhz; 50 kw. 1,092 ft TL: N18 16 58 W66 10 47. Stereo. Hrs open: 24 HC67 Box 15390, 00956-9535. Secondary address: Rd 174, KM 5.0 Bo. Guaraguao 00956-9535. Phone: (787) 785-9390. Phone: (787) 785-9100. Fax: (787) 785-9377.E-mail: info@lax.fm Web Site:www.lax.fm Licensee: RAAD Broadcasting Corp. Population served: 1,700,000 Format: Top 40 pop. Target aud: 12-34; young teens, adults. ♦Roberto Davila, pres, gen mgr & opns mgr; Eduardo Cora, gen sls mgr; Michelle Torres, prom dir; Herman Davila, progmg dir; Juan Rivera, chief of engrg; Edwardo Carrasguillo, traf mgr.

Cabo Rojo

WMIO(FM)— Jan 10, 1988: 102.3 mhz; 3 kw. Ant 680 ft TL: N17 59 37 W67 10 27. Stereo. Hrs open: 6 AM-midnight Box 9023916, San Juan, 00902. Phone: (787) 798-7878. Fax: (787) 620-0720. Licensee: Arso Radio Corp. (acq 3-26-2007; $3.25 million). Reddy, Begley & McCormick. Format: Adult contemp. Target aud: 18-45; general. ♦Alan Mejia, gen mgr.

WYAC(AM)— Jan 9, 1970: 930 khz; 2.5 kw-U. TL: N18 06 05 W67 09 17. Hrs open: 21 Box 489, Mayaguez, 00681. Secondary address: Radio Centre, Post & Bosgue Sts., Mayaguez 00684. Phone: (787) 620-9898.E-mail: info@wyac.com Web Site:www.radiopr740.com Licensee: Bestov Broadcasting Inc. (acq 4-14-99; $3.65 million with co-located FM). Population served: 650,000 Reddy, Begley & McCormick. Format: News/talk, Sp. Target aud: General; Mayaguez county residents. ♦Luis Majia, pres; Francisco Acosta, gen mgr.

Caguas

WNEL(AM)— July 21, 1947: 1430 khz; 5 kw-U. TL: N18 14 53 W66 01 25. Stereo. Hrs open: 24 Box 487, 00726-0487. Phone: (787) 744-3131. Fax: (787) 743-0252.E-mail: leon@unoradio.com Licensee: Turabo Radio Corp. Group owner: Uno Radio Group (acq 4-1-73). John P. Bankson Jr. Format: Latin Oldies. News: 15. Target aud: 24 plus. ♦Jesus M. Soto, CEO, chmn; Luis M. Soto, pres; Luis Gonzales, CFO; Elba Esmirria, VP; Luis Leon, gen mgr, gen sls mgr, progmg dir; Tanya Ramos, mktg dir; Jaime Soto, progmg VP; Alberto Pereira, chief of engrg.

WNVM(FM)—See Cidra

WPRM-FM—See San Juan

WVJP(AM)— Nov 24, 1947: 1110 khz; 2.5 kw-D, 500 w-N. TL: N18 13 25 W66 01 11. Hrs open: 24 Box 207, 00726. Secondary address: Tomas de Castro #2 00626. Phone: (787) 743-5790. Fax: (787) 746-6996. Licensee: Borinquen Broadcasting Co. Inc. (acq 7-7-99; $700,000 for 12). Format: Adult contemp, btfl mus, Sp. ♦Jancel Pereira, CEO; Bienvenido Rodriguez, gen mgr; Norma Rodriquez-Trinidad, progmg dir; Jesus R. Gomez, chief of engrg.

WVJP-FM— October 1968: 103.3 mhz; 28 kw. 1,906 ft TL: N18 16 41 W65 51 09. Stereo. Hrs open: Prog sep from AM Box 207, 00726. Secondary address: Tomas de Castro #2 00626. Phone: (787) 743-5790. Fax: (787) 746-6996. Format: Sp, romantic.

Camuy

WDIN(FM)— Aug 15, 1968: 102.9 mhz; 50 kw. 303 ft TL: N18 28 49 W66 51 14. Hrs open: Box 780, 00627. Phone: (787) 743-5790. Fax: (787) 746-6996. Web Site:www.dimension.fm Licensee: HQ 103 Inc. (acq 5-28-86). Format: Sp variety. ♦Bienvenido Rodriguez, gen mgr, progmg dir; Maggie Lopez, progmg dir.

Canovanas

WGIT(AM)— 2001: 1660 khz; 10 kw-D, 1 kw-N. TL: N18 23 09 W65 55 16. Hrs open: 1554 Calle Bori, San Juan, 00927. Phone: (787) 274-1800. Fax: (787) 281-9758. Licensee: International Broadcasting Corp. (group owner; acq 5-29-03; $1.3 million). Format: Sp, sports, music. ♦Pedro Roman-Collazo, gen mgr; Margarita Nazario, stn mgr.

Carolina

WIDA(AM)— Mar 16, 1964: 1400 khz; 1 kw-U. TL: N18 23 49 W65 56 06. Hrs open: Box 188, 00986. Secondary address: Ignacio Arzuaga 203-7 00987. Phone: (787) 757-1414. Phone: (787) 757-1717. Fax: (787) 769-4103.E-mail: radiovida@cadenaradiovida.com Web Site:www.cadenaradiovida.com Licensee: Radio Vida Inc. Format: Sp. ♦Yexica Rosario, gen mgr; Hilda Dumont, progmg dir; Alberto Periera, chief of engrg.

***WIDA-FM**— August 1983: 90.5 mhz; 25 kw. Ant 1,900 ft TL: N18 06 48 W66 03 07. Hrs open: Box 188, 00986. Secondary address: Ignacio Arzuaga 203-7 00987. Phone: (787) 757-1414. Phone: (787) 757-1717. Fax: (787) 769-4103. Web Site:www.cadenaradiovida.com Licensee: Radio Vida Inc. Format: Educ.

WVOZ-FM— Mar 3, 1967: 107.7 mhz; 50 kw. 1,636 ft TL: N18 24 10 W66 03 21. (CP: 12 kw, ant 2,758 ft.). Stereo. Hrs open: 1554 Calle Bori, Rio Piedras, 00927. Phone: (787) 274-1800. Fax: (787) 281-9758. Licensee: International Broadcasting Corp. (group owner). Format: Adult contemp. ♦Pedro Roman-Collazo, pres; Margarita Nazario, gen mgr, progmg dir.

Cayey

WLEY(AM)— Dec 3, 1965: 1080 khz; 250 w-U. TL: N18 06 55 W66 08 28. Hrs open: 19
WSKN 1320 Radio Isla.
100 Gran Bulevar Paseo, Suite 403A, San Juan, 00926. Phone: (787) 292-1700. Fax: (787) 292-1717.E-mail: noticias@radioisla1320.com Licensee: Media Power Group Inc. (group owner; (acq 9-30-2003; grpsl). Population served: 179,000 Natl. Network: CNN Radio, . Format: Talk/News. News staff: 40; News: 24 hrs wkly. Target aud: 35 plus. ♦Eduardo Rivero, pres; Ismael Nieves, VP, gen mgr; Nora Plaza, gen sls mgr; Luis Penchi, progmg VP; Orlando Morales, opns; Fernando Vazquez, prom, adv.

Ceiba

WFAB(AM)— 1993: 890 khz; 250 w-U. TL: N18 12 16 W65 42 40. Hrs open: Box 318, Rio Blanco, 00744. Phone: (787) 874-0890. Fax: (787) 874-0190. Web Site:www.lanaveprdc.net Licensee: Daniel Rosario Diaz. (acq 12-18-98). Format: Relg. ♦Daniel Rosario Diaz, pres, gen mgr; Jose N. Garcia, stn mgr.

Cidra

WNVM(FM)— Mar 1, 1972: 97.7 mhz; 5 kw. Ant 876 ft TL: N18 13 30 W66 05 53. Stereo. Hrs open: 24 Box 6715, Caguas, 00726-9297. Phone: (787) 745-9700. Phone: (787) 745-9770. Fax: (787) 745-9777.E-mail: nuevavida@nuevavidafm.net Web Site:www.nuevavidafm.net Licensee: New Life Broadcasting Inc. (acq 3-20-2001; $3.6 million). Lee J. Peltzman, Shainis & Peltzman. Format: Sp, Contemp Christian. News

staff: one; News: one hr wkly. Target aud: 25-54; women. ◆Juan Carlos Matos, pres; Orlando Mercado, gen mgr & progmg dir.

Coamo

WCPR(AM)— 1967: 1450 khz; 1 kw-U. TL: N18 05 29 W66 22 15. Hrs open: 16 Box 1863, 00769. Phone: (787) 825-7061. Fax: (787) 825-1905. Licensee: Coamo Broadcasting Corp. Format: Adult contemp. News: 9 hrs wkly. Target aud: General. ◆Jose David Soler, pres & gen mgr.

Corozal

WORO(FM)— July 1968: 92.5 mhz; 50 kw. 1,197 ft TL: N18 15 09 W66 19 58. Hrs open: 415 Carbonell St., San Juan, 00918. Secondary address: Box 9021967, San Juan 00902. Phone: (787) 751-1380. Fax: (787) 758-9967. Licensee: Catholic Apostolic & Roman Church San Juan Archdiocese. (acq 1981; $1 million; 3-2-81). Format: Btfl mus. ◆Roberto Octavio Gonzalez, pres; Allan Corales, gen mgr; Elsa Feernandez, sls dir; Carlos Rodriguiz, progmg dir; Jesus Gomez, chief of engrg.

Culebra

*WJVP(FM)— 1998: 89.3 mhz; 30 kw vert. 577 ft TL: N18 19 37 W65 18 21. Hrs open: Box 40000, Bayamon, 00958. Secondary address: An 167 Calle Granada AM Alahambra, Bayamon 00956. Phone: (787) 288-4336. Phone: (787) 288-4332. Fax: (787) 740-7104. Web Site:www.clamorpr.org Licensee: Clamor Broadcasting Network Inc. Format: Relg, civic, cultural. ◆Jorde Raschke, gen mgr.

WNVE(FM)— December 1996: 98.7 mhz; 6 kw. Ant 584 ft TL: N18 19 19 W65 17 59. Stereo. Hrs open: 24 Box 1047, Fajardo, 00738. Phone: (787) 860-1065. Fax: (787) 860-1055. Licensee: Western New Life Inc (acq 5-30-2005; $1.8 million). Population served: 100,000 Scott C. Cinnanmon LLC. Format: Sp, Christian, tropical music. News staff: 4. Target aud: 25-54. ◆Aureo Matos, gen mgr.

Fajardo

WIOA(FM)—See San Juan

WMDD(AM)— May 31, 1947: 1480 khz; 5 kw-U. TL: N18 21 46 W65 38 24. Hrs open: 24 Box 948, 00738. Phone: (787) 863-0202. Phone: (787) 793-0669. Fax: (787) 863-0166. Licensee: Pan Caribbean Broadcasting de P.R. Inc. (acq 3-19-03; with WZIN(FM) Charlotte Amalie, VI). Format: Tropical. Target aud: 25-49. ◆Rita Friedman, pres & opns mgr.

WRXD(FM)— Feb 15, 1969: 96.5 mhz; 11.5 kw. Ant 2,795 ft TL: N18 18 36 W65 47 41. Hrs open: 24 Box 949, Guaynabo, 00970-0949. Secondary address: Amelia Industrial Park , Calle Frances #42, Guaynabo 00968. Phone: (787) 622-9700. Fax: (787) 622-9478. Web Site:www.spanishbroadcastingsystem.com Licensee: WCMA Licensing Inc. Group owner: Spanish Broadcasting System Inc. (acq 8-4-98; $8.25 million). Format: Sp news. ◆Falex Bonnet, gen mgr.

WYAS(FM)—See Vieques

Guayama

*WCRP(FM)— 1991: 88.1 mhz; 27 kw. 1,889 ft TL: N18 06 47 W66 03 08. Hrs open: Box 344, 00655. Phone: (787) 653-0880. Fax: (787) 653-1988. Licensee: Ministerio Radial Cristo Viene Pronto Inc. Format: Sp relg. ◆Carmita Rodriguez, pres & gen mgr.

WIBS(AM)— Mar 1, 1981: 1540 khz; 1 kw-D. TL: N17 59 44 W66 04 39. Hrs open: Calle Bori 1554, San Juan, 00927. Phone: (787) 274-1800. Fax: (787) 281-9758. Licensee: International Broadcasting Corp. (group owner; acq 12-3-01; $300,000). Format: Sp, tropical. ◆Pedro Roman-Collazo, CEO; Margarita Nazario, gen mgr, progmg dir.

WMEG(FM)— November 1966: 106.9 mhz; 25 kw. 1,994 ft TL: N18 06 48 W66 03 07. Stereo. Hrs open: Box 949, Guaynabo, 00970-0949. Secondary address: Amelia Industrial Park, Calle Frances 42, Guaynabo 00968. Phone: (787) 622-9700. Fax: (787) 622-9478.E-mail: info@broadcastingsystem.com Web Site:www.broadcastingsystem.com Licensee: WMEG Licensing Inc. Group owner: Spanish Broadcasting System Inc. (acq 3-15-99; $16 million with WZET(FM) Hormigueros). Format: Rock, English. ◆Falex Bonnet, gen mgr & gen sls mgr.

WXRF(AM)— July 1948: 1590 khz; 1 kw-U. TL: N17 57 40 W66 08 20. Hrs open: Calle Bori 1554, San Juan, 00927. Phone: (787) 274-1800. Fax: (787) 281-9758. Licensee: International Broadcasting Corp. (acq 10-8-2004; $1,382,961 with WVEO(TV) Aguadilla). Format: Sports, music. ◆Pedro Roman-Collazo, pres; Margarita Nazario, gen mgr, gen sls mgr, progmg dir.

Guayanilla

WOIZ(AM)— Oct 1, 1986: 1130 khz; 200 w-D, 700 w-N. TL: N18 01 03 W66 46 22. Hrs open: 5 AM-10 PM Box 561130, 00656. Secondary address: 383 Road klmo.4, Bo Magas Arriba 00656. Phone: (787) 835-1130. Phone: (787) 835-3130. Fax: (787) 835-3130.E-mail: radioantillas@yahoo.com Web Site:www.radioantillas.4t.com Licensee: Radio Antillas of Harriet Broadcasters. Population served: 250,000 Format: Adult contemp, oldies, news/talk. Target aud: 35 plus. ◆Luis A. Rodriguez III, pres, gen mgr, opns mgr, gen sls mgr; Maria de los Angeles Rivera, VP.

Hatillo

WMSW(AM)— 1980: 1120 khz; 5 kw-U. TL: N18 28 15 W66 50 24. Hrs open: Box 140961, Arecibo, 00614. Phone: (787) 879-4094. Fax: (787) 880-0441. Licensee: Aurora Broadcasting Corp. (acq 11-23-2004). Format: News/talk, music. ◆Manuel Santiago Santos, pres, progmg dir; Hector Santiago Santos, VP; Lloyd Santiago Santos, gen sls mgr; Ronald Cushing, chief of engrg.

Hormigueros

WRRH(FM)— 1998: 106.1 mhz; 800 w. Ant 1,932 ft TL: N18 08 33 W66 58 56. Hrs open: Box 1061, 00660. Phone: (787) 849-1061. Fax: (787) 849-6106.E-mail: renacer1061@yahoo.com Web Site:www.renacer1061.com Licensee: Renacer Broadcasters Corp. Format: Contemp Christian music. ◆Larry W. Ramos, gen mgr & gen sls mgr; Kehmuel Ramos, progmg dir.

WZET(FM)— Oct 12, 1980: 92.1 mhz; 3 kw. 581 ft TL: N18 11 15 W67 07 04. (CP: 2 kw, ant 1,105 ft.). Stereo. Hrs open: Box 949, Gauynabo, 00970-0949. Secondary address: Amelia Industrial Park, Calle Frances 42, Guaynabo 00968. Phone: (787) 622-9700. Fax: (787) 622-9478.E-mail: info@spanishbroadcastingsystem.com Web Site:www.spanishbroadcastingsystem.com Licensee: WSMA Licensing Inc. Group owner: Spanish Broadcasting System Inc. (acq 3-15-99; $16 million with WMEG(FM) Guayama). Format: Sp, tropical. ◆Falex Bonnet, gen mgr.

Humacao

WALO(AM)— Feb 11, 1958: 1240 khz; 1 kw-U. TL: N18 08 49 W65 48 49. Hrs open: 19 Box 9230, 00792. Phone: (787) 852-1240. Fax: (787) 852-1280.E-mail: wlo@prtc.net Licensee: Ochoa Broadcasting Corp. (acq 4-70; $400,000). Fletcher, Heald & Hildreth. Wire Svc: CNN Format: Sp, news/talk, music, sports, MOR. News staff: 2; News: 60 hrs wkly. Target aud: 18-54; general. Spec prog: Relg 2 hrs wkly. ◆Efrain Archilla-Roig, CEO, chmn, pres; Beatriz Archilla, gen mgr; Maribel Ortiz-Del Valle, opns dir; Ken Allen, dev dir.

Isabela

WISA(AM)— Oct 19, 1961: 1390 khz; 1 kw-U. TL: N18 30 08 W67 01 38. Hrs open: Box 750, 00662. Phone: (787) 872-0100. Phone: (787) 872-2030. Fax: (787) 872-0802. Licensee: Isabela Broadcasting Inc. (acq 4-87). Format: MOR. ◆David Marda, gen mgr; Edwin Nieves, progmg dir.

WKSA-FM— 1987: 101.5 mhz; 42 kw. Ant -26 ft TL: N18 26 36 W67 08 50. Hrs open: Box 9023916, San Juan, 00902-3916. Phone: (787) 620-9898. Web Site:www.sistema102.com Licensee: Isabela Broadcasting Inc. Format: Ballads. ◆Luis A. Mejia, CEO & pres.

Juana Diaz

WCGB(AM)— Nov 23, 1967: 1060 khz; 5 kw-D, 500 w-N. TL: N17 59 28 W66 28 32. Hrs open: 5 AM-midnight Box 1414, 00795. Secondary address: Carretera Hwy. 1, KM 112.0 00795. Phone: (787) 837-1060. Fax: (787) 260-1060.E-mail: wcgb@therockradio.org Licensee: Calvary Evangelistic Mission Inc. (acq 12-3-2004; $500,000). Format: Relg, var/div, Sp. News: 10 hrs wkly. Target aud: Adult. ◆Lawrence Trumbower, gen mgr & opns dir.

Juncos

WRRE(AM)— 1971: 1460 khz; 500 w-U, DA-2. TL: N18 12 54 W65 54 33. Hrs open: 24 Box 1460, Las Piedras, 00771. Phone: (787) 561-1460. Phone: (888) 561-1460. Fax: (787) 716-0808.E-mail: sonidosantidad@hotmail.com Web Site:www.sonidosantidad.com Licensee: Hacienda San Eladio Inc. (acq 4-16-03; $625,000). Format: Sp relg. Target aud: All. ◆Miguel A. Medina, pres & gen mgr.

Lajas

WBSG(AM)— 1986: 1510 khz; 1 kw-U, DA-1. TL: N18 02 11 W67 04 58. (CP: COL San German. 1 kw-U, DA-2). Hrs open: 16 Box 1689, 00667. Phone: (787) 899-5724. Fax: (787) 899-5475. Licensee: Perry Broadcasting Systems (acq 4-1-2002; $535,500). Format: Sp news/talk. ◆Oscar Vega, gen mgr.

WXLX(FM)— Jan 5, 1994: 103.7 mhz; 50 kw. 456 ft TL: N17 59 37 W67 11 09. Stereo. Hrs open: 24 Rebroadcasts WXYX(FM) Bayamon 100%. HC 67, Bayamon, 00956-9535. Phone: (787) 255-2325. Phone: (787) 785-9390. Fax: (787) 785-9377. Licensee: Radio X Broadcasting Corp. (acq 1-20-98; $3 million). Population served: 600,000 Format: CHR. ◆Roberto Davila, pres, gen mgr; Roberto Davila Rios, opns mgr.

Lares

WGDL(AM)— February 1983: 1200 khz; 250 w-D. TL: N18 17 40 W66 53 50. Hrs open: 12 Box 872, 00669. Phone: (787) 897-1200. Phone: (787) 897-3889. Fax: (787) 897-7821.E-mail: wgdl1200@yahoo.com Licensee: Lares Broadcasting Corp. John P. Bankson Jr. Format: Tropical, Sp. News staff: one; News: 20 hrs wkly. Target aud: General. ◆Pedro Hernandez, pres; Julia Bello, gen mgr, gen sls mgr, traf mgr; Angel Perez, progmg dir.

Levittown

*WPLI(FM)— Oct 1, 1986: 88.5 mhz; 100 w vert. Ant 69 ft TL: N18 26 55 W66 10 26. Hrs open: Box 371177, Cayey, 00737. Phone: (787) 798-8850. Fax: (787) 798-8851.E-mail: info@plenitudfm.com Web Site:www.plenitudfm.com Licensee: La Gigante Siembra Inc. (acq 5-5-2007; $1 million). Format: Relg. ◆Shay Garcya, stn mgr.

Luquillo

WZOL(FM)— 1976: 92.1 mhz; 6.9 kw. Ant 915 ft TL: N18 19 54 W65 41 11. Hrs open: 24 Box 29027, Rio Piedras, 00929. Phone: (787) 767-1005. Fax: (787) 758-1055.E-mail: wzol@radiosol.org Web Site:www.radiosol.org Licensee: Radio Sol 92, WZOL Inc. Format: Relg. ◆Pedro M. Canales, pres; William H. Irizarry, gen mgr; Maria Navarro, progmg dir, traf mgr; Raymond Hernandez, chief of engrg.

Manati

WBQN(AM)—See Barceloneta-Manati

WMNT(AM)— Dec 59: 1500 khz; 1 kw-D, 250 w-N. TL: N18 26 06 W66 29 54. Hrs open: 16 Box 6, 00674. Secondary address: Delta St. #1305 Caparra Terr., San Juan 00920. Phone: (787) 854-2223. Fax: (787) 781-7647. Fax: (787) 854-2713.E-mail: radio@atenas.com Web Site:www.radioatenas.com Licensee: Manati Radio Corp. (acq 9-4-97; $200,000 for 100%). Population served: 350,000 Shaw Pittman. Format: News/talk, sports, Sp. News staff: 2; News: 25 hrs wkly. Target aud: 25 plus; men & women. Spec prog: NBA, World Series in Sp. ◆Jose Ariras Dominicci, CEO; Jose A. Ribas-Dominicci, pres; Freddy Ribas, VP, gen mgr, sls dir; Maria Elena Rodriguez, stn mgr.

WNRT(FM)— 1973: 96.9 mhz; 50 kw. Ant 882 ft TL: N18 15 41 W66 32 19. Hrs open: 24 hours Box 13324, San Juan, 00908. Phone: (787) 758-8562. Fax: (787) 758-8833. Web Site:www.radiotriunfo.com Licensee: La Voz Evangelica de Puerto Rico Inc. Format: Christian. ◆Luis Barajas, pres; Mosses Flores, gen mgr; Moises Flores, opns mgr, dev mgr; Virgen Perez, sls VP; Carlos Vazquez Flecha, progmg dir; Jorge Figueroa, engrg dir.

Maricao

WAEL-FM— July 1970: 96.1 mhz; 24.2 kw. 2,011 ft TL: N18 09 07 W66 49 15. Stereo. Hrs open: 24 Box 1370, Mayaguez, 00681-1370. Secondary address: 600 Ramirez Pabon St., Guanajibo Homes, Mayaguez 00681. Phone: (787) 832-4560/ 832-0600. Fax: (787)

792-3140.E-mail: waeline@prte.net Web Site:www.waelfm96.com Licensee: WAEL Inc. Booth, Freret, Imlay & Tepper. Format: Sp, CHR. Target aud: 12-24. ♦Luis Pirallo, opns mgr, progmg dir; Maria del Pilar-Pirallo, pres & gen sls mgr; Ivan Feliu, chief of engrg; Lydia Vargas, traf mgr.

WYEL(AM)—See Mayaguez

Mayaguez

WAEL-FM—See Maricao

WEGM(FM)—See San German

WIOB(FM)— Oct 12, 1947: 97.5 mhz; 25 kw. 990 ft TL: N18 19 33 W67 10 13. (CP: 50 kw). Hrs open:
Rebroadcasts WIOA(FM) San Juan 80%.
Box 949, Guaynabo, 00970-0949. Secondary address: Amelia Industrial Park, Calle Frances 42, Guaynabo 00968. Phone: (787) 622-9700. Fax: (787) 622-9478.E-mail: info@spanishbroadcastingsystem.com Web Site:www.spanishbroadcastingsystem.com Licensee: Cadena Estereotempo Inc. Group owner: Spanish Broadcasting System Inc. (acq 11-29-99; grpsl). Population served: 500,000 Hogan & Hartson. Format: Sp, ballads. Target aud: 30-50; women. ♦Falex Bonnet, gen mgr.

WIVA-FM—See Aguadilla

WKJB(AM)— Dec 6, 1946: 710 khz; 10 kw-D, 750 w-N. TL: N18 10 08 W67 09 03. Hrs open: Box 1293, 00681. Phone: (787) 834-6666. Fax: (787) 831-6925. Licensee: WKJB-AM Inc. Format: News/talk. Spec prog: Sp 1 hr wkly. ♦Dennis Bechara, pres; Jose A. Bechara Jr., exec VP, gen mgr; Ada Ramos, gen sls mgr; Eric Graniela, progmg dir; Rafy Aviles, news dir; Pedro Velez Jr., chief of engrg; Johhny Flores, sports cmtr.

WNOD(FM)— 1960: 94.1 mhz; 25 kw. 2,967 ft TL: N18 09 05 W66 59 20. Stereo. Hrs open: 24
Rebroadcasts WCOM(FM) San Juan 80%.
Box 949, Guaynabo, 00970-0949. Phone: (787) 265-9494. Fax: (787) 622-9700. Web Site:www.lamega.fm Licensee: WOYE Inc. Group owner: Spanish Broadcasting System Inc. (acq 11-29-99; grpsl). Population served: 1,000,000 Hogan & Hartson. Format: Top-40. News staff: one; News: 10 hrs wkly. Target aud: 18-49; young adults. ♦Raul Alarcon, chmn; Ismael Nieves, gen mgr; Marie Elena Martinez, gen sls mgr, rgnl sls mgr; Luis Enriquez Rivera, mktg dir; Pedro Arroyo, progmg dir; Alejandro Luciano, chief of engrg.

WORA(AM)— May 12, 1947: 760 khz; 5 kw-U, DA-1. TL: N18 11 30 W67 09 28. Hrs open: Box 363222, San Juan, 00936-3222. Phone: (787) 758-1300. Fax: (787) 751-2319.E-mail: noticias@notiuno.com Web Site:www.notiuno.com Licensee: Arso Radio Corp. Group owner: Uno Radio Group (acq 5-10-01; grpsl). Format: News. ♦Luis Soto, pres; Elba Esmurria, sls VP; Tanya Ramos, mktg dir; Ray Cruz, progmg dir; Alberto Pereira, chief of engrg.

WPRA(AM)— Oct 16, 1937: 990 khz; 1 kw-U. TL: N18 10 52 W67 10 07. Stereo. Hrs open: 18 Box 1293, 00681. Phone: (787) 834-6666. Fax: (787) 831-6925. Licensee: WPRA Inc. (acq 1996). Population served: 110,000 Natl. Network: AP Radio, . Shainis & Peltzman, Chartead. Format: Top-40, Sp, talk. Target aud: General. ♦Dennis Bechara, pres; Jose A. Bechara, VP & gen mgr.

***WRUO(FM)**— December 1998: 88.3 mhz; 2 kw. 1,004 ft TL: N18 19 31 W67 10 13. Hrs open: Box 21305, San Juan, 00931-1305. Phone: (787) 751-8640. Fax: (787) 763-5205.E-mail: lluna@wrtu.pr Web Site:www.wrtu.PR Licensee: University of Puerto Rico. Format: Sp var. ♦Yolanda Zabala, gen mgr.

WTIL(AM)— November 1950: 1300 khz; 1 kw-U. TL: N18 11 00 W67 10 04. Hrs open: 261 Castilla St., Sultana Park, Naywest, 00680. Secondary address: Post & Bosque Sts. 00680. Phone: (787) 652-0633. Fax: (787) 652-1292.E-mail: info@wtil.com Licensee: International Broadcasting Corp. (group owner; acq 5-12-2004; $700,000). Population served: 600,000 Format: Talk, oldies, Sp, adult contemp. Target aud: 35 plus. ♦Jose Ramiez, gen mgr.

WTPM(FM)—See Aguadilla

WUKQ-FM— Jan 15, 1963: 99.1 mhz; 50 kw. 1,963 ft TL: N18 09 05 W66 59 19. Stereo. Hrs open: Box 364668, San Juan, 00936. Phone: (787) 833-9910. Fax: (787) 833-9911. Licensee: El Mundo Broadcasting Corp. Group owner: Univision Radio (acq 8-1-2003; grpsl). Format: Top 40. Spec prog: Jazz 6 hrs wkly. ♦Jaime Bauza, VP, gen mgr; Edgardo Aubray, sls dir, gen sls mgr; Miguel Rodriguez, gen sls mgr, rgnl sls mgr; Betty Enriquez, mktg mgr, chief of engrg; Carlos Gonzalez, progmg dir; Nestor Perez, engrg mgr.

WYEL(AM)— 1949: 600 khz; 5 kw, DA-1. TL: N18 10 46 W67 10 14. (CP: 5 kw). Hrs open: 4:30 AM-midnight Box 1370, 00681-1370. Secondary address: 600 Ramirez Pabon , Guanajibo Homes 00680. Phone: (787) 832-0600. Phone: (787) 832-4560. Fax: (787) 792-3140.E-mail: mgmt@waelfm96.com Web Site:www.waelfm96.com Licensee: Univision Radio Puerto Rico Inc. (acq 11-17-2006; $2 million). Booth, Freret, Imlay & Tepper P. Format: Oldies, sports. Target aud: 25 plus. ♦Luis Pirallo, opns mgr, progmg dir, engrg dir; Maria Pirallo, gen sls mgr; Ivan Seliu, engrg dir.

Moca

WZNA(AM)— December 1983: 1040 khz; 5 kw-D, 245 w-N, DA-1. TL: N18 16 38 W67 10 01. Stereo. Hrs open: Box 6715, Caguas, 00725. Phone: (787) 745-9770. Fax: (787) 745-9777.E-mail: nuevavuda@nuevavidafm.com Web Site:www.nuevavidafm.com Licensee: Western New Life Inc. (acq 8-9-2004; $950,000). Format: Contemp Christian. ♦Juan Carlos Matos Barreto, pres; Orlando Mercede, gen mgr & opns mgr.

Morovis

WEKO(AM)— December 1981: 1580 khz; 5 kw-D, 2.5 kw-N, DA-D. TL: N18 20 32 W66 25 08. Hrs open: Calle Bori 1554, San Juan, 00927. Phone: (787) 274-1800. Fax: (787) 281-9758. Licensee: International Broadcasting Corp. (group owner; acq 9-29-98; $315,000). Fletcher, Heald & Hildreth. Format: Pop Latin & American mus, news. Target aud: 30 plus. ♦Pedro Roman-Collazo, pres; Margarita Nazario, gen mgr, progmg dir.

Naguabo

WYQE(FM)— December 1994: 92.9 mhz; 3.9 kw. 853 ft TL: N18 16 49 W65 40 12. Stereo. Hrs open: 24 Box 9300, 00718. Secondary address: Apt. 2-A 00718. Phone: (809) 847-9300. Phone: (809) 874-9300. Fax: (809) 874-9290.E-mail: wyqe@yunque93.com Web Site:www.yunque93.com Licensee: Fajardo Broadcasting Co. Inc. (acq 12-29-99). Population served: 500,000 Format: Sp tropical. News staff: 2; News: 20 hrs wkly. Target aud: 18 plus; general. ♦Efrain Archilla-Diez, pres, gen mgr, chief of engrg; Raul Rivera, VP, opns mgr, prom dir, progmg mgr, mus dir; Edwin Glass, sls dir; Vanessa Jimenez, natl sls mgr; Victor Cordero, news rptr; Jose Carrion, sports cmtr.

Pastillo

***WJDZ(FM)**— 2006: 90.1 mhz; 200 w. Ant -121 ft TL: N17 59 40 W66 27 33. Hrs open: Box 8072, Ponce, 00732. Licensee: Siembra Fertil P.R. Inc. (acq 5-13-2008; $800,000 with WNNV(FM) San German).

Patillas

WEXS(AM)— 1991: 610 khz; 250 w-D, 1 kw-N, DA-D. TL: N18 00 36 W66 01 28. Hrs open: 5:30 AM-10 PM Box 640, 00723. Phone: (787) 839-0610. Fax: (787) 839-0960. Licensee: Community Broadcasting Inc. Population served: 100,000 Format: Adult contemp, CHR, news. Target aud: 18-55. Spec prog: Relg 2 hrs, sports 6 hrs wkly. ♦Enrique Garcia, gen mgr.

Penuelas

WENA(AM)—See Yauco

WPPC(AM)— May 25, 1976: 1570 khz; 1 kw-D, 126 w-N. TL: N18 03 47 W66 43 04. Hrs open: 12 Box 9064, Pompanos Stn., Ponce, 00732-9064. Phone: (809) 836-1570. Phone: (809) 848-4670. Fax: (787) 848-4670.E-mail: radiofelicidad@yahoo.com Web Site:www.wppc1570am.org Licensee: Radio Felicidad Inc. (acq 6-18-81; $125,000; 7-13-81). Format: MOR, relg, Sp. Target aud: General. ♦Julio Valazquez, pres; Rafael Acosta, chief of engrg.

Ponce

WDEP(AM)— Feb 1, 1973: 1490 khz; 5 kw-D, 1 kw-N. TL: N17 58 52 W66 36 51. Stereo. Hrs open: 24 100 Gran Bulevar Paseo, Suite 403A, San Juan, 00926. Phone: (787) 292-1700. Fax: (787) 292-1717.E-mail: noticias@radioisla1320.com Licensee: Media Power Group Inc. (group owner; (acq 9-30-2003; grpsl). Population served: 421,000 Natl. Network: CNN Radio, . Fletcher, Heald & Hildreth, P.L.C. Format: Sp, news/talk, var. News: 24 hrs wkly. Target aud: 35 plus. ♦Eduardo Rivero, pres; Ismaez Nieves, VP, gen mgr; Nora Plaza, gen sls mgr; Luis Penchi, progmg VP; Orlado Moraless, opns; Fernando Vazquez, prom.

WIOC(FM)— January 1970: 105.1 mhz; 47 kw. Ant -200 ft TL: N17 59 27 W66 37 45. Hrs open: 24
Rebroadcasts WIOA(FM) San Juan 80%.
Box 949, Guaynabo, 00970-0949. Secondary address: Amelia Industrial Park, Calle Frances 42, Guaynabo 00978. Phone: (787) 622-9700. Fax: (787) 622-9478.E-mail: info@lamega.fm Web Site:www.lamega.fm Licensee: Cadena Estereotempo Inc. Group owner: Spanish Broadcasting System Inc. (acq 11-29-99; grpsl). Population served: 500,000 Hogan & Hartson. Format: Adult contemp. News staff: one; News: one hr wkly. Target aud: 30-50; women. ♦Raul Alarcon, pres; Ismael Nieves, gen mgr; Marie Elena Martinez, gen sls mgr; Luis Enrique Rivera, prom dir; Pedro Arroyo, progmg dir; Alejandro Luciano, chief of engrg; Demare Ramirez, traf mgr.

WISO(AM)— Sept 15, 1953: 1260 khz; 1 kw-U. TL: N17 59 22 W66 37 11. Hrs open: 16 134 Domenech Ave., Hato Rey, 00918-3502. Phone: (787) 763-1066. Fax: (787) 763-4195.E-mail: jblanco25@hotmail.com Web Site:www.waparadio.net Licensee: Wilfredo G. Blanco Pi. (acq 1996; $500,000). Population served: 500,000 Format: News/talk. News: 26 hrs wkly. Target aud: Adults. ♦Wilfredo G. Blanco, pres & gen mgr; Jorge Blanco, opns mgr, prom mgr, progmg dir, news dir, chief of engrg; Carmen Blanco, gen sls mgr, traf mgr.

WLEO(AM)— Nov 3, 1956: 1170 khz; 250 w-U. TL: N17 58 52 W66 36 51. Hrs open: 24 Box 7213, 00732. Secondary address: WLEO/WZAR, 46 Sector Purto Viejo, Playa De Ponce 00732. Phone: (787) 842-0048. Phone: (787) 841-1011. Fax: (787) 840-0049. Licensee: Uno Radio of Ponce Inc. Group owner: Uno Radio Group (acq 2-18-00; grpsl). Population served: 225,000 Borsari & Paxson. Format: Oldies. News staff: 2; News: 50 hrs wkly. Target aud: 25 plus; mature, blue-collar & professionals. Spec prog: Sports. ♦Jose Juan Santiago, stn mgr; Carlos Conesa, rgnl sls mgr; Ray Cruz, progmg mgr & news dir; Oscar Vega, chief of engrg; Carmen Reyes, traf mgr; Luis Torres, news rptr; Adam Asencio, disc jockey.

WPAB(AM)— Aug 14, 1940: 550 khz; 5 kw-U. TL: N17 59 27 W66 37 46. Hrs open: 24 Box 7243, 00732-7243. Secondary address: 1643 Ave. Eduardo Ruberte 00716. Phone: (787) 840-5550. Fax: (787) 840-7077. Licensee: WPAB Inc. (acq 8-21-97; $3 million for stock with co-located FM). Population served: 524,675 Natl. Network: CNN Radio, . Rgnl rep: Sayda Ortiz Booth, Freret, Imlay & Tepper PC. Wire Svc: AP Format: Sp, news/talk. News staff: 4; News: news progrmg 15 hrs wkly. Target aud: 25 plus; concerned adults. ♦Alfonso Gimenez-Porrata, CEO, pres; Alfonso Gimenez-Lucchetti, VP, gen mgr; Maria Luisa Gimenez-Lucchetti, opns VP; Sayda Ortiz, sls VP & gen sls mgr.

WPRP(AM)— 1936: 910 khz; 5 kw-U. TL: N17 59 49 W66 37 31. Hrs open: Box 7213, 00732. Secondary address: WLEO/WZAR Bldg., Sector Puerto Viejo, Paseo Sauri, Playa de Ponce 00732. Phone: (787) 842-0048. Fax: (787) 840-0049.E-mail: jsantiago@unoradio.com Web Site:www.unoradio.com Licensee: Arso Radio Corp. Group owner: Uno Radio Group (acq 5-8-01; grpsl). Format: News/talk, Sp. Target aud: 35 plus. ♦Jose Juan Santiago, pres, gen mgr, opns VP; Carlos Conesa, sls dir, gen sls mgr; Glerys Rivera, prom dir; Ray Cruz, progmg dir & pub affrs dir; Oscar Vega, engrg dir.

***WPUC-FM**— May 17, 1984: 88.9 mhz; 10.8 kw. 2,912 ft TL: N18 10 27 W66 35 32. Stereo. Hrs open: 4 AM-midnight 2250 Ave. Las Americas, Suite 529, 00717-9997. Phone: (787) 651-2000 ext. 2600. Phone: (787) 844-8809. Fax: (787) 651-2022.E-mail: info@catolicaradiopr.com Web Site:www.catolicaradiopr.com Licensee: Pontifical Catholic University of Puerto Rico Service Association Inc. Format: Adult contemp. News staff: 2; News: 30 hrs wkly. Target aud: 25-39/40-45; professional young adults, retirees-middle & upper class. ♦Julio Feliu Ramirez, gen mgr; Jose R Leon, stn mgr; Rolando Mendez, mktg mgr; Ediel Montalvo, progmg dir; Rey Moreira, chief of engrg.

WRIO(FM)— 1986: 101.1 mhz; 34 kw. 1,768 ft TL: N18 09 15 W66 33 15. Hrs open: 24 Box 7213, 00732. Phone: (787) 842-0048. Fax: (787) 840-0049. Web Site:www.salsoul.com Licensee: Arso Radio Corp. Group owner: Uno Radio Group. Format: Sp Salsa. ♦Jose Santiago, gen mgr; Vicente Veldodere, sls dir; Vicente Bergodere, gen sls mgr; Donny Cruz, progmg dir; Alberto Pereira, chief of engrg; Marianna Colon, traf mgr.

WUKQ(AM)— May 1, 1957: 1420 khz; 1 kw-U. TL: N17 59 23 W66 37 21. Hrs open: 24
Rebroadcasts WKAQ(AM) San Juan 99%.
PO Box 364668, San Juan, 00936-4668. Phone: (787) 758-5800. Fax: (787) 763-1854. Web Site:www.univision.com Licensee: El Mundo Broadcasting Corp. Group owner: Univision Radio (acq 8-1-2003; grpsl). Format: News/talk info. Target aud: 25-55; young professionals, retirees, middle & upper income. ♦Jaime Bauza, gen mgr.

WZAR(FM)— Mar 17, 1966: 101.9 mhz; 14 kw. 2,580 ft TL: N18 01 40 W66 39 14. Stereo. Hrs open: 24 Prog sep from AM Box 7213, 00732. Secondary address: 46 Sector Purto Viejo, Playa De Ponce 00732. Phone: (787) 842-0048. Fax: (787) 840-0049. Population served: 1,700,000 Format: Adult contemp, Sp. News: 12 hrs wkly. Target aud: 18-49; blue & white collar, adults, professionals. Spec prog: Talk show 15 hrs wkly. ♦Jose Juan Santiago, opns mgr; Pedro Gonzales, progmg mgr; Rafael Acosta, engrg mgr; Carmen Reyes, traf mgr.

WZMT(FM)— May 1969: 93.3 mhz; 14.5 kw. -225 ft TL: N17 59 26 W66 37 43. Stereo. Hrs open: 20
Rebroadcasts WZNT(FM) San Juan 100%.
Box 949, Guaynabo, 00970-0949. Secondary address: Amelia Industrial Park, Calle Frances 42, Guaynabo 00968. Phone: (787) 622-9700. Fax: (787) 622-9478.E-mail: info@lamega.fm Web Site:www.lamega.fm Licensee: Potorican American Broadcasting Inc. Group owner: Spanish Broadcasting System Inc. (acq 2000; grpsl). Population served: 250,000 Latham & Watkins. Format: Modern, tropical, Sp. News staff: one; News: 6 hrs wkly. Target aud: 18-49; affluent young adults. ♦Raul Alarcon, pres; Ismael Nieves, gen mgr; Maria Elena Martinez, gen sls mgr, rgnl sls mgr; Luis Enrique Rivera, prom dir; Pedro Arroyo, progmg dir; Alejandro Luciano, chief of engrg; Demare Ramirez, traf mgr.

Quebradillas

WCHQ(AM)— February 1998: 960 khz; 1 kw-D, 1.7 kw-N, DA-2. TL: N18 26 38 W66 57 43. Hrs open:
Rebroadcasts WZNA(AM) Moca 100%.
Box 4039, Carolina, 00984. Phone: (787) 750-4090. Fax: (787) 750-6440. Licensee: International Broadcasting Corp. (group owner; (acq 7-6-2004; $1.45 million with WRSJ(AM) Bayamon). Format: Sp, relg. ♦Luis Rosado, pres; Josue Salgado, progmg dir.

WIDI(FM)— Nov 17, 1974: 98.3 mhz; 3 kw. Ant 1,000 ft TL: N18 23 33 W66 59 46. Stereo. Hrs open: 24 Box 1553, 00678. Phone: (787) 895-2725. Phone: (787) 895-0000. Fax: (787) 895-4198.E-mail: magic973@prtc.net Licensee: Jose J. Arzuaga. (acq 7-10-79). Population served: 754,130 Format: Tropical, oldies, Sp. News: 2 hrs wkly. Target aud: General. ♦Jose J. Arzuaga, pres, exec VP; Idalia Arzuaga, sr VP; Joshua Arzuaga, gen mgr, dev VP; Idalia Arrieta, opns VP; Rosidalia Villafane, dev dir.

Rio Grande

WOYE(FM)— 2003: 97.3 mhz; 800 w. Ant 1,906 ft TL: N18 16 46 W65 51 12. Hrs open: Box 1553, Quebradillas, 00678. Phone: (787) 895-0000. Fax: (787) 895-4198.E-mail: magic973@prtc.net Web Site:www.magic973.com Licensee: Jose J. Arzuaga (acq 3-14-2007; $2.89 million). Irwin, Campbell & Tannenwald. Format: Oldies. ♦Tommy Carrasquillo, gen mgr; Idalia Arzuaga, opns dir; Eva Cordero, dev dir; Roberto Toledo, sls dir; Arlene Perez, adv dir; Joshua Arzuaga, progmg dir; Rafael Brito, news dir; Nitza Mercado, pub affrs dir; Jose Arzuaga, engrg dir.

Rio Piedras

WFID(FM)— Nov 17, 1958: 95.7 mhz; 50 kw. 941 ft TL: N18 16 00 W66 05 05. Stereo. Hrs open: Box 363222, San Juan, 00936-3222. Secondary address: 1581 Ponce DeLeon St. 00926. Phone: (787) 758-1300. Fax: (787) 754-1395. Web Site:www.unoradiogroup.com Licensee: Madifide Inc. Group owner: Uno Radio Group (acq 3-26-98; $11,537,500). Wiley, Rein & Fielding. Format: Easy lstng, adult contemp. Target aud: 25-49; middle & upper income. ♦Luis Soto, pres; Elba Esmurria, sls VP; Tanya Ramos, mktg VP; Ray Cruz, progmg VP.

WSKN(AM)—See San Juan

WVOZ(AM)—See San Juan

Sabana

WJIT(AM)— Mar. 31, 2000: 1250 khz; 1 kw-N, 250 w-D. TL: N18 25 28 W66 20 17. Hrs open: 16 Box 878, Vega Alta, 00692. Secondary address: Road #2 km 30.5, Vega Alta 00769. Phone: (787) 449-9304. Fax: (787) 825-1905. Licensee: WJIT Broadcasting Corp. Format: Var. ♦Olga Fernandez, pres; Jose David Soler, progmg dir, chief of engrg; Carlos Ortiz, local news ed.

Sabana Grande

WYKO(AM)— 1990: Stn currently dark. 880 khz; 1 kw-D, 500 w-N. TL: N18 04 21 W66 57 06. Hrs open: 34 Doctor Felix Tio St., 00637. Fax: (787) 873-5795. Licensee: Juan Galiano Rivera (acq 8-3-90; $450,000;8-6-90). ♦Juan Galiano Rivera, pres & gen mgr.

Salinas

WHOY(AM)— Apr 6, 1967: 1210 khz; 5 kw-U, DA-2. TL: N17 58 38 W66 18 14. Hrs open: Box 1148, 00751. Phone: (787) 824-2755. Fax: (787) 824-8054.E-mail: whoyam@coquinet.com Licensee: Colon Radio Corp. (acq 1-31-97; $700,000). Fletcher, Heald & Hildreth. Format: Sp. ♦Martin Colon, gen mgr, gen sls mgr, prom mgr, progmg dir, news dir; Rafael Pagan, chief of engrg.

San German

WEGM(FM)— Feb 1, 1969: 95.1 mhz; 25 kw. 1,970 ft TL: N18 08 55 W66 58 54. Hrs open: 24 Box 949, Guaynabo, 00970-0949. Secondary address: Amelia Industrial Park , Calle Frances 42, Guaynabo 00968. Phone: (787) 622-9700. Fax: (787) 622-9478.E-mail: info@lamega.fm Web Site:www.lamega.fm Licensee: WRPC Inc. Group owner: Spanish Broadcasting System Inc. (acq 11-29-99; grpsl). Format: CHR-English. Target aud: 18-49; men. ♦Raul Alarcon, pres; Ismael Nieves, gen mgr; Marie Elena Martinez, gen sls mgr, progmg VP; Luis Enriquez Rivera, prom dir; Pedro Arroyo, progmg dir; Roque Gallart, progmg mgr; Alejandro Luciano, chief of engrg; Demare Ramirez, traf mgr.

***WNNV(FM)**— Nov 14, 1996: 91.7 mhz; 5 kw. 436 ft TL: N18 04 08 W67 02 54. Hrs open: 24 Box 847, Mayaguez, 00681. Phone: (787) 883-7100. Fax: (787) 833-7940. Licensee: Siembra Fertil P.R. Inc. (acq 5-13-2008; $800,000 with WJDZ(FM) Pastillo). Population served: 283,016 Format: Contemp Christian. Target aud: 25-49. ♦Miguel Marquez, progmg dir.

WPRA(AM)—See Mayaguez

WSOL(AM)— 1955: 1090 khz; 250 w-D, 730 w-N. TL: N18 04 44 W67 01 18. (CP: TL: N18 08 18 W67 07 43). Stereo. Hrs open: Ave. Atleticos de San German, 00683. Phone: (787) 892-2216. Phone: (787) 892-2975. Fax: (787) 264-1090.E-mail: w1090sol@yahoo.com Licensee: San German Broadcasters Group. Roy F. Perkins. Format: Tropical, Sp, news. Target aud: Adults. Spec prog: Farm 2 hrs wkly. ♦Alfredo Cardona, pres; Luz Maria Rivera, gen mgr; Gloria Silva, stn mgr, opns mgr; Lucy Rivera, opns dir.

San Juan

WAPA(AM)— Jan 15, 1947: 680 khz; 10 kw-U, DA-N. TL: N18 24 17 W65 56 55. Hrs open: 134 Domenech Ave., Hato Rey, 00918-3502. Phone: (787) 763-1066. Fax: (787) 763-4195.E-mail: jblanco25@hotmail.com Web Site:www.waparadio.net Licensee: Wifredo G. Blanco Pi (acq 2-25-91). Format: Sp, news/talk. ♦Wilfredo G. Blanco, gen mgr; Jorge Blanco, opns mgr.

WBMJ(AM)— July 19, 1968: 1190 khz; 10 kw-D, 5 kw-N, DA-2. TL: N18 21 00 W66 06 50. Hrs open: 24 Box 367000, 00936-7000. Phone: (787) 724-1190. Phone: (787) 724-2727. Fax: (787) 722-5395. Fax: (787) 723-9633.E-mail: radio@vrockradio.org Licensee: Calvary Evangelistic Mission Inc. (acq 11-85). Population served: 2,200,000 Natl. Network: Moody, USA, Salem Radio Network, . Format: Relg, talk, MOR (English). News: 7 hrs wkly. Target aud: General; relg community of central Puerto Rico. ♦Janet Luttrell, CEO & VP.

WCAD(FM)— Mar 5, 1968: 105.7 mhz; 50 kw. 1,100 ft TL: N18 16 54 W66 06 46. Stereo. Hrs open: Box 9024188, 00902-4188. Secondary address: 1667 Fernandez Juncos Ave., San Turce 00910. Phone: (787) 726-6144. Fax: (787) 268-3313.E-mail: alfa@alfarock.com Web Site:www.alfarock.com Licensee: Broadcasting & Programming Systems of Puerto Rico Inc. Format: Rock/AOR. ♦Ralph Perez, gen mgr; Felipe Diaz, sls dir; Pedro Davila, progmg dir; Ada Cox, pub affrs dir; T. Morales, engrg dir.

WFID(FM)—See Rio Piedras

WIAC(AM)— 1947: 740 khz; 10 kw-U, DA-1. TL: N18 25 25 W66 08 20. Hrs open: 24 Box 9023916, 00902-3916. Phone: (787) 620-9898. Fax: (787) 620-0730.E-mail: tcarrasquillo@radiopr740.com Web Site:www.radiopr740.com Licensee: Bestov Broadcasting Inc. (acq 1954). John P. Bankson Jr. Format: News,politics. Target aud: General. ♦Luis A. Mejia, pres; Valerie Majia, VP & gen mgr; Luis Penchi, news dir; Rey Moraira, chief of engrg; Johnny Men, traf mgr.

WIAC-FM— Mar 1, 1961: 102.5 mhz; 50 kw. Ant 1,139 ft TL: N18 25 25 W66 08 20. Stereo. Hrs open: Box 9023916, 00902-3916. Phone: (787) 620-9898. Fax: (787) 620-0730.E-mail: losorio@sistem102.net Web Site:www.sistema102.com Licensee: MSG Radio Inc. (acq 8-5-2008; $4 million). Format: Pop, soft music. ♦Danny Gonzalez, chief of opns; Glenn Valares, sls dir; Valerie Mejia, progmg dir.

WIOA(FM)— Mar 1, 1961: 99.9 mhz; 31 kw. Ant 1,837 ft TL: N18 16 44 W65 51 12. Stereo. Hrs open: Box 949, Guaynabo, 00970-0949. Secondary address: Amelia Industrial Park, Calle Frances 42, Guaynabo 00968. Phone: (787) 622-9700. Fax: (787) 622-9478.E-mail: info@lamega.fm Web Site:www.lamega.fm Licensee: Cadena Estereotempo Inc. Group owner: Spanish Broadcasting System Inc. (acq 11-29-99; grpsl). Format: Adult contemp, ballads, Sp. Target aud: 18-49; predominantly women. ♦Raul Alarcon, pres; Ismael Nieves, gen mgr; Maria Elena Martinez, gen sls mgr; Luis Enrique Rivera, prom dir; Fernando de Hostas, progmg mgr; Alejandro Luciano, chief of engrg; Demare Ramirez, traf mgr.

***WIPR(AM)**— Jan 26, 1948: 940 khz; 10 kw-U, DA-1. TL: N18 25 36 W66 08 29. Hrs open: 24 Box 190909, 00919. Phone: (787) 766-0505. Fax: (787) 250-7694. Web Site:tutv.puertorico.pr Licensee: Puerto Rico Corp. for Public Broadcasting. Population served: 3,000,000 Natl. Network: NPR, . Format: Newstalk. News staff: 7; News: 7 hrs wkly. ♦Luis Agrait, chmn; Linda Hernandez, pres; Yolanda Zavala, exec VP; Raul Carbonell, gen mgr, progmg dir, progmg mgr; Vilma Reyes, stn mgr; Susan Marte, opns VP; Ileana Rivera, dev dir; Luis Santiago, sls dir, mktg VP; Jorge Gonzalez, engrg dir, chief of engrg; Osvaldo Torres, chief of engrg.

***WIPR-FM**— June 3, 1960: 91.3 mhz; 125 kw. Ant 2,719 ft TL: N18 06 42 W66 03 05. (CP: 105 kw, ant 2,706 ft.). Hrs open: 24 Box 190909, 00919. Phone: (787) 766-0505. Fax: (787) 250-7694. Web Site:tutv.puertorico.pr Licensee: Puerto Rico Corp. for Public Broadcasting. (acq 8-87). Format: Class.

WKAQ(AM)— Dec 3, 1922: 580 khz; 10 kw-U, DA-1. TL: N18 25 55 W66 08 07. Hrs open: 24 PO Box 364668, 00936-4668. Secondary address: 383 F.D. Roosevelt Ave., Third Floor, Hato Rey 00918. Phone: (787) 758-5800. Fax: (787) 763-1854. Licensee: El Mundo Broadcasting Corp. Group owner: Univision Radio (acq 8-1-2003; grpsl). Format: News/talk. News staff: 22. Target aud: General. ♦Jamie Bauza, gen mgr; Javier Cosme, news dir; Nestor Perez, chief of engrg.

WKAQ-FM— Oct 8, 1958: 104.7 mhz; 50 kw. 1,220 ft TL: N18 16 51 W66 06 38. Stereo. Hrs open: Prog sep from AM Box 364668, 00936. Secondary address: 383 F.D. Roosevelt Ave. 00918. Phone: (787)758-5800. Fax: (787) 756-5220. Web Site:www.kq105fm.com Format: Top-40. ♦Huberto E. Biaggi, exec VP; Raul Muxo, gen sls mgr; Carlos Gonzalez, progmg dir.

WKVM(AM)— 1951: 810 khz; 50 kw-U, DA-1. TL: N18 21 47 W66 08 13. Hrs open: 415 Carbonell St., Hato Rey, 00918. Secondary address: c/o Arquidiocesis de San Juan, Apartado 1967 00901-1967. Phone: (787) 751-1018. Fax: (787) 758-9967. Licensee: Catholic, Apostolic & Roman Church, San Juan Archdiocese. (acq 3-4-82; $1.01 million; 1-18-82). Format: Oldies (daytime), relg Catholic (evenings). ♦Roberto Gonzalez, pres; Allan Corales, stn mgr; Mrs. Elsa Fernandez, sls VP; Jose Antonio Cruz, progmg dir; Jose Gomez, chief of engrg; Placido Padilla, traf mgr; Mrs. Judith Felicie Rivera, local news ed; Reverend Efrain Rodriguez, relg ed; Enrigue Liboy, sports cmtr.

WNEL(AM)—See Caguas

WODA(FM)—See Bayamon

WORO(FM)—See Corozal

WOSO(AM)— Nov 21, 1977: 1030 khz; 10 kw-U, DA-1. TL: N18 22 07 W66 15 17. Hrs open: 24 Box 11487, 00910-2587. Phone: (787) 724-4242. Fax: (787) 723-9676. Web Site:www.woso.com Licensee: Sherman Broadcasting Corp. Natl. Network: Wall Street, CBS, . Format: News/talk. News staff: 2; News: 6 hrs wkly. Target aud: 25-49. ♦Sherman Wildman, pres; Sergio Fernandez, gen mgr; Mariano Calderon, opns dir; Sherman Wildmon, progmg dir; Gary Tuominen, news dir; Rodolfo Rivas, chief of engrg; Danette Hudoba, traf mgr.

WPRM-FM— April 1959: 98.5 mhz; 25 kw. Ant 1,904 ft TL: N18 06 47 W66 03 06. Stereo. Hrs open: 24 Box 487, Caguas, 00726-0487. Phone: (787) 744-3131. Fax: (787) 743-0252. Web Site:www.salsoul.com Licensee: Arso Radio Corp. Group owner: Uno Radio Group (acq 4-1-73). Population served: 2,500,000 Drinker Biddle & Reath. Format: Salsoul. News staff: one; News: 3 hrs wkly. Target aud: 18-49. ♦Jesus M. Soto, CEO, chmn; Luis A. Soto, pres; Luis A. Gonzalez, CFO; Maida Bedaya, gen mgr; Raymond Totti, gen sls mgr; Anthony Soto, progmg dir.

WQBS(AM)— Nov 1, 1954: 870 khz; 10 kw-U, DA-1. TL: N18 22 17 W66 12 17. Hrs open: 1508 Calle Bori, 00927-6116. Phone: (787) 758-8700. Fax: (787) 765-2965.E-mail: angel@aercobroadcasting.com Licensee: Aerco Broadcasting Corp. (acq 1-11-2005). Format: Div, Sp. ♦Luz Alvarez, gen mgr. Co-owned TV: WSJU-TV

WQII(AM)— 1947: 1140 khz; 10 kw-U, DA-1. TL: N18 21 30 W66 08 05. Hrs open: Cobians Plaza GM01, 1607 Ponce de Leon Ave., Stop 24, Santurce, 00909. Secondary address: Box 906 6590 00906-6590. Phone: (787) 723-4848. Fax: (787) 723-4035.E-mail: postmaster@1140qpr.com Licensee: Communications Council Group Inc. Format: Talk shows (women's). ♦Nieves Gonzalez Avreu, pres; Jorge Rudolfo Marquina, gen mgr; William Padilla, sls dir; Danny Gonzalez, progmg dir; Raymond Hernandez, chief of engrg.

WRSJ(AM)—See Bayamon

***WRTU(FM)**— Feb 8, 1980: 89.7 mhz; 50 kw. 796 ft TL: N18 16 00 W66 05 05. Stereo. Hrs open: 24 Box 21305, 00931-1305. Secondary address: Mariana Bracetti St., Ponce de Leon Ave. 00931. Phone: (787) 763-4699. Phone: (787) 751-8640. Fax: (787) 763-5205.E-mail: lluna@wrtu.pr Web Site:www.wrtu.pr Licensee: University of Puerto Rico. Dow, Lohnes & Albertson. Format: Sp var. News staff: 8. Target aud: General. ♦Yolanda Zabala, gen mgr.

WRXD(FM)—See Fajardo

WSKN(AM)— Oct 15, 1949: 1320 khz; 5 kw-D, 2.3 kw-N. TL: N18 23 00 W66 04 01. Hrs open: 24 100 Gran Bulevar Paseo, Suite 403A, 00926. Phone: (787) 292-1700. Fax: (787) 292-1717.E-mail: noticias@radioisla1320.com Web Site:www.radioisla1320.com Licensee: Media Power Group Inc. (group owner; (acq 9-30-2003; grpsl). Natl. Network: CNN Radio, . Fletcher, Heald & Hildreth P.L.C. Format: Sp, news/talk. News staff: 40; News: 24 hrs wkly. Target aud: 35 plus. ♦Eduardo Rivero, pres; Ismael Nieves, VP, gen mgr; Nora Plaza, gen sls mgr; Luis Penchi, progmg VP; Orlando Morales, opns; Fernando Vazquez, prom, adv.

WUNO(AM)— Jan 11, 1960: 630 khz; 5 kw-U, DA-2. TL: N18 26 00 W66 07 29. Hrs open: 24 Box 363222, 00936-3222. Secondary address: 1581 Ponce de Leon St., Rio Peidras 00926. Phone: (787) 758-1300. Fax: (787) 754-1395.E-mail: info@notiuno.com Web Site:www.notiuno.com Licensee: Madifide Inc. Group owner: Uno Radio Group (acq 5-8-01; grpsl). Format: News/talk. News staff: 22. Target aud: 25 plus. ♦Jesus M. Soto, CEO; Luis Soto, pres; Tanya Ramus, mktg VP; Ray Cruz, progmg VP.

WVOZ(AM)— July 4, 1949: 1520 khz; 25 kw-U, DA-2. TL: N18 21 11 W66 12 09. Hrs open: 16 1554 Calle Bori, 00927. Phone: (787) 764-1077. Phone: (787) 274-1800. Fax: (787) 281-9758. Licensee: Pedro Roman Collazo. Freret & Imlay. Format: Tropical, sports. Target aud: 35 plus; medium & low income individuals. Spec prog: Puerto Rican & Latin hits 15 hrs wkly. ♦Pedro Roman-Collazo, pres; Margarita Nazario, gen mgr.

WZNT(FM)— 1959: 93.7 mhz; 50 kw. 280 ft TL: N18 22 42 W66 07 04. Stereo. Hrs open: 24 Box 949, Guaynabo, 00970-0949. Secondary address: Amelia Industrial Park, Calle Frances 42, Guaynabo 00968. Phone: (787) 622-9700. Fax: (787) 622-9478.E-mail: info@lamega.fm Web Site:www.lamega.fm Licensee: WZNT Inc. Group owner: Spanish Broadcasting System Inc. (acq 2000; grpsl). Population served: 920,900 Fletcher, Heald & Hildreth. Format: Tropical, salsa & merengue. Target aud: 18-49; male. ♦Raul Alarcon, pres; Ismael Nieves, gen mgr, stn mgr; Marie Elena Martinez, sls VP, gen sls mgr; Luis Enrique Rivera, prom dir; Billie Fourquet, progmg VP; Pedro Arroyo, progmg dir; Nestor Rodriguez, progmg mgr; Alejandro Luciano, chief of engrg; Demare Ramirez, traf mgr.

San Sebastian

WLRP(AM)— Feb 15, 1965: 1460 khz; 500 w-U. TL: N18 20 50 W66 59 56. (CP: 2.5 kw). Hrs open: 19 Box 1670, 00685. Phone: (787) 896-1460. Fax: (787) 896-8100.E-mail: radioraices@prtc.net Web Site:www.radioracies.net Licensee: Las Raices Pepinianas Inc. Format: Adult contemp. News staff: one. ♦Ramon Colon Pratts, pres; Susan Munoz, gen mgr; Alfredo Perez, gen sls mgr; Ramon E. Pratts, prom mgr; Hilda Serrano, mus dir; Juan Felin, chief of engrg.

WNOD(FM)—See Mayaguez

WRSS(AM)— April 1984: 1410 khz; 1 kw-U, DA-1. TL: N18 19 14 W66 58 45. Hrs open: Box 1410, 00685. Secondary address: Segundo Ruez # 52 St. 00685. Phone: (787) 896-2121. Fax: (787) 896-5753.E-mail: tunuevafamilia@hotmail.com Licensee: Angel Vera-Maury (acq 2-9-03; $250,000). Format: Talk, oldies, Sp. News staff: 6; News: 30 hrs wkly. Target aud: 30 plus. ♦Angel Vera, pres; Cesar Vera, gen mgr; Arturo Soto, gen sls mgr; Nestor Gonzalez, progmg VP & progmg dir.

Utuado

WUPR(AM)— Apr 18, 1964: 1530 khz; 1 kw-D, 250 w-N. TL: N18 16 02 W66 42 38. Hrs open: 17 Box 868, 00641. Phone: (787) 894-2460. Fax: (787) 894-4955.E-mail: info@coqui.net Web Site:www.coqui.net Licensee: Central Broadcasting Corp. Format: Sp, news/talk. News staff: 2; News: 11 hrs wkly. Target aud: 18-49; middle income adults. ♦Jose A. Martinez, pres, gen mgr, gen sls mgr, progmg dir; Manuel E. Andujar, mus dir; Manuel B. Martinez, news dir; Epifanio Rodriguez Velez, chief of engrg.

Vega Alta

WERR(FM)— Feb 1, 1970: 104.1 mhz; 50 kw. Ant 987 ft TL: N18 17 29 W66 39 39. Stereo. Hrs open: 24 Box 29404, San Juan, 00929. Secondary address: San Felipe # 205, Arecibo 00612. Phone: (787) 751-6318. Phone: (787) 751-1310. Fax: (787) 751-6854.E-mail: jrivera@redentor104fm.com Web Site:www.redentor104fm.com Licensee: Radio Redentor Inc. (acq 6-75). Population served: 2,000,000 Fletcher, Heald & Hildreth. Format: Adult contemp, Sp, Christian. News staff: 4; News: one hr wkly. Target aud: General. ♦Rev. Miguel Cintron, pres; Jesus M. Rivera, gen mgr; Brenda Lis Gines, mktg dir, mktg mgr; Ramon Rivera, engrg dir; Elizabeth Bosques, traf mgr; Omayra Martinez, spec ev coord; Shirley Lopresti, women's cmtr.

Vega Baja

WEGA(AM)— October 1971: 1350 khz; 2.5 kw-U, DA-2. TL: N18 28 38 W66 23 43. Hrs open: Box 1488, 00694-1488. Phone: (787) 858-0386. Fax: (787) 855-0916.E-mail: info@wega.com Licensee: A Radio Company Inc. (acq 9-1-2004; $850,000). Format: Var/div. ♦Gerardo Angulo, pres; Carmelo Santiago, gen mgr; Hector Santiago, sls VP, progmg dir; Lloyd Santiago, mktg VP; Ronald Cushing, chief of engrg.

Vieques

WIVV(AM)— Dec 8, 1956: 1370 khz; 5 kw-D, 1 kw-N. TL: N18 06 19 W65 28 03. Hrs open: 24
Rebroadcasting WBMJ(AM) San Juan 100%.
Box 367000, San Juan, 00936-7000. Phone: (787) 724-1190. Phone: (787) 741-8717. Fax: (787) 722-5395. Fax: (787) 741-8717.E-mail: radio@vrockradio.org Licensee: Calvary Evangelistic Mission Inc. Population served: 1,340,504 Natl. Network: Salem Radio Network, . Format: Relg, talk, MOR, Sp. News: 7 hrs wkly. Target aud: General; eastern Puerto Rico & the Leeward Islands. Spec prog: News 7 hrs wkly. ♦Janet L. Luttrell, CEO & VP.

WVIS(FM)— June 10, 1973: Stn currently dark. 106.1 mhz; 9 kw. Ant 892 ft TL: N17 44 51 W64 50 11. (CP: 32 kw, ant 485 ft. TL: N18 19 19 W65 17 59). Hrs open: c/o Michael Bahr, Calle Guajataca #153, San Juan, 00926. Phone: (787) 756-5914. Licensee: V.I. Stereo Communications Corporation (PR) (acq 8-14-2007). ♦Michael Gregory Bahr, pres.

WYAS(FM)— Nov 4, 1978: 98.9 mhz; 50 kw. Ant 751 ft TL: N18 19 39 W65 18 05. Stereo. Hrs open: Box 1047, Fajardo, 00738. Phone: (787) 860-1065. Fax: (787) 860-1055. Licensee: La Mas Z Radio Inc. (acq 7-6-2004; $1.99 million). Format: Jazz.

Yabucoa

WXEW(AM)— Jan 1, 1978: 840 khz; 5 kw-D, 1 kw-N, DA-N. TL: N18 02 58 W65 52 07. (CP: 5 kw-U). Hrs open: 19 203 Font Martelo Ave., Humacao, 00971. Secondary address: Box 100 00767. Phone: (787) 893-3065. Phone: (787) 850-0840. Fax: (787) 850-4055.E-mail: victor@victoria840.com Web Site:www.victoria840.com Licensee: Radio Victoria Inc. (acq 9-19-83). Format: MOR, Sp, talk. ♦Victoria Vargas, pres; Victor M. Calderon, VP, gen mgr; Caly Burmudez, gen sls mgr; Brenda Calderon, mktg dir; Jose Calderon, prom mgr, mus dir; Luis Calderon, progmg dir; Angel Bena, news dir; Alberto Pereira, chief of engrg.

Yauco

WENA(AM)— Nov 11, 1978: 1330 khz; 2 kw-D, 1.4 kw-N, DA-1. TL: N18 02 04 W66 51 48. Stereo. Hrs open: 24 Box 1338, 25 DeJullo St., Condominio Torres Navel Bldg., 00698. Phone: (787) 267-1330. Phone: (787) 856-1330. Fax: (787) 267-1340.E-mail: wena@cogui.net Web Site:www.yaucoweb.com/wena/ Licensee: Southern Broadcasting Corp. Population served: 55,000 Roy F. Perkins. Format: Adult contemp, CHR, news/talk. News staff: 5; News: 28 hrs wkly. Target aud: 25 plus; young adults & women. ♦Nephtali Rodriguez, pres, gen mgr, traf mgr; Israel Rodriguez, VP, opns VP; Ramon Ramos, dev mgr; Pedro Gregory, sls dir, disc jockey; Juan Diaz, adv mgr; Guillermo Valls, progmg dir, disc jockey; Isaac Pagan, engrg dir; Ronald Cushing, engrg mgr; Israel Muniz, local news ed; Hector Rios, disc jockey.

WKFE(AM)— Nov 3, 1961: 1550 khz; 250 w-U. TL: N18 01 24 W66 52 02. Hrs open: 24
Rebroadcasts WSKN(AM) San Juan 70%.
100 Gran Bulevar Paseo, Suite 403A, San Juan, 00926. Phone: (787) 292-1700. Fax: (787) 292-1717.E-mail: noticias@radioisla1320.com Licensee: Media Power Group Inc. (group owner; (acq 9-30-2003; grpsl). Population served: 100,000 Fletcher, Heald & Hildreth. Format: Sp news/talk. News staff: 2; News: 40 hrs wkly. Target aud: P35-64 P35+. ♦Eduardo Rivero, pres; Jose Pagan, gen mgr; Orlando Morales, progmg dir.

Virgin Islands

Charlotte Amalie

WGOD(AM)— 1992: 1090 khz; 250 w-D. TL: N18 18 57 W64 53 02. Hrs open: Box 305012, St. Thomas, 00803. Phone: (340) 774-4498. Fax: (340) 777-9978. Licensee: Three Angels Broadcasting Corp. Inc. (acq 7-5-89). Format: Gospel. ♦Charles Saunders, pres & gen mgr.

***WIUJ(FM)**— Oct 5, 1979: 102.9 mhz; 1.5 kw. 1,427 ft TL: N18 21 26 W64 56 50. Stereo. Hrs open: Box 2477, St. Thomas, 00803. Phone: (340) 776-1029. Phone: (340) 777-9485. Fax: (340) 774-0004. Web Site:www.wiuj.com Licensee: Virgin Islands Youth Development Radio. (acq 8-6-90). Format: Adult contemp, btfl music, big band. News staff: one. Target aud: General. Spec prog: Class 5 hrs, jazz 6 hrs, Fr 4 hrs, Sp 4 hrs wkly. ♦Leo Morone, gen mgr; F. Ottley, opns mgr; Greg Cyntje, progmg dir; Ron Hall, chief of engrg.

WIVI(FM)— Apr 26, 1992: 96.1 mhz; 2.4 kw. 1,500 ft TL: N18 21 33 W64 58 18. Stereo. Hrs open: 24 Box 302179, St. Thomas, 00803-4383. Phone: (340) 774-1972. Phone: (340) 776-9696. Fax: (340) 776-7060. Web Site:www.pirateradiovi.com Licensee: Rox Radio Enterprises Inc. (acq 11-20-98; $30,000 for 60% of stock). Population served: 115,000 Format: AAA, classic rock. News: one hr wkly. Target aud: 25-54; general. ♦Lou Lambert, gen mgr; Dorene Carle, gen sls mgr.

WSTA(AM)— Aug 1, 1950: 1340 khz; 1 kw-U. TL: N18 20 10 W64 57 17. Hrs open: 24 Box 1340, # 121 Subbase, St. Thomas, 00804. Secondary address: 121 Sub Base, St. Thomas 00802. Phone: (340) 774-1340. Phone: (340) 777-4500. Fax: (340) 776-1316.E-mail: addie@wsta.com Web Site:www.WSTA.com or www.lucky13wsta.com Licensee: Ottley Communications Corp. (acq 12-1-84). Population served: 110,000 Natl. Network: ABC, CNN Radio, . Miller & Neely, P.C. Format: Div, oldies, adult urban contemp. News staff: 3; News: 20 hrs wkly. Target aud: General. ♦Athneil Ottley, pres; Jean Forde, gen mgr.

WVGN(FM)— 2002: 107.3 mhz; 1.4 kw. Ant 1,565 ft TL: N18 21 31 W64 58 20. Hrs open: 714 Nisky Mail Box, PMB PP-105, St. Thomas, 00802. Phone: (340) 774-2012. Fax: (340) 776-5362.E-mail: npr@wvgn.org Web Site:www.wvgn.org Licensee: LKK Group Corp. (acq 6-27-02; $290,000). Natl. Network: NPR, . Format: News/talk. ♦Patricia Bourne, VP, gen mgr, stn mgr; Victoria Squires, gen sls mgr.

WVJZ(FM)— Mar 15, 1986: 105.3 mhz; 7.7 kw. 1,490 ft TL: N18 21 33 W64 58 18. Stereo. Hrs open: 24 Box 305678, 13 Crown Bay Fill, St. Thomas, 00803-5678. Secondary address: Box 8209, Bluebeards's Castle, Suite 255, St. Thomas 00801. Phone: (340) 776-5260. Phone: (340) 776-5260. Fax: (340) 776-5357. Fax: (340) 776-5357.E-mail: contact@kasvi.net Web Site:www.wvjz.net Licensee: Gark LLC. Group owner: Knight Quality Stations (acq 6-4-98). Population served: 100,000 Pepper & Corazzini. Format: Urban contemp. News staff: 2. Target aud: 18-34; young adults, business professionals & college students. ♦Randolph H. Knight, pres; Mark P. Bastin, gen mgr, progmg dir; Jean Greaux Jr., opns dir.

WVWI(AM)— Nov 19, 1962: 1000 khz; 5 kw-D, 1 kw-N. TL: N18 20 11 W64 41 38. Hrs open: 24 Box 305678, 13 Crown Bay Fill, St. Thomas, 00803-5678. Phone: (340) 776-1000. Fax: (340) 776-5357.E-mail: contact@kqsvi.net Web Site:www.wvwi.net Licensee: Knight Communications of the Virgin Islands Inc. Group owner: Knight Quality Stations (acq 1996; $250,000). Population served: 100,000 Natl. Network: CBS, Westwood One, . Pepper & Corazzini. Format: Sports, news/talk. News staff: 2; News: 25 hrs wkly. Target aud: 25-54; middle/upper income professionals. Spec prog: Relg 6 hrs, West Indian one hr, East Indian one hr wkly. ♦Randolph H. Knight, pres; Mark P. Bastin, gen mgr; Jean Greaux Jr., opns dir.

WZIN(FM)— Nov 2, 1976: 104.3 mhz; 44 kw. Ant 1,617 ft TL: N18 21 35 W64 58 19. Stereo. Hrs open: P.O. Box 306117, St. Thomas, 00803. Phone: (340) 776-1043. Fax: (340) 775-3446.E-mail: info@buzzrocks.com Web Site:www.buzzrocks.com Licensee: Pan Caribbean Broadcasting de P.R. Inc. (acq 7-11-02; $1 million). Population served: 4,000,000 Arter & Hadden. Format: Alternative rock. Target aud: 18-34. ◆Alan Friedman, VP & gen mgr.

Christiansted

*WIVH(FM)— July 1993: 90.1 mhz; 1 kw. 731 ft TL: N17 44 10 W64 42 04. Hrs open: 24 2457 Rt. 118, Hunlock Creek, PA, 18621. Secondary address: 5007 Estate Mt. Washington 00820-4565. Phone: (570) 477-3688. Phone: (340) 778-2852. Fax: (340) 719-3076.E-mail: wrgn@epix.net Web Site:www.wrgn.org/wivh.htm Licensee: Gospel Media Institute Inc. Format: Relg. Target aud: General. ◆Burl F. Updyke, pres, gen mgr; Shirley J. Updyke, progmg dir.

WJKC(FM)— Oct 29, 1983: 95.1 mhz; 50 kw. 886 ft TL: N17 44 07 W64 40 46. (CP: Ant 791 ft.). Stereo. Hrs open: Box 25680, St.Croix, 00824-1680. Phone: (340) 773-0995. Fax: (340) 773-9093. Web Site:www.viradio.com Licensee: Radio 95 Inc. Rosenman & Colin. Format: Reggae, urban hip-hop. Target aud: General. ◆Jonathan K. Cohen, pres, gen mgr; Collin Hodge, gen sls mgr; Tom Yarborough, progmg dir; Alvin Gee, news dir.

WMNG(FM)— 1997: 104.9 mhz; 6 kw. 699 ft TL: N17 44 08 W64 40 47. Hrs open: Box 25680, St. Croix, 00824-1680. Phone: (340) 773-0995. Fax: (340) 773-9093.E-mail: jkc95@aol.com Web Site:www.viradio.com Licensee: Clara Communications Corp. Format: Classic hits. ◆Jonathan K. Cohen, gen mgr; Amanda Cohen, gen sls mgr; Tom Yarbaugh, progmg dir; Herb Schoenbahm, chief of engrg; Celia Jean, traf mgr.

WSTX(AM)— 1952: 970 khz; 5 kw-D, 1 kw-N. TL: N17 45 23 W64 41 38. Hrs open: Box 3279, 00822. Phone: (340) 773-0390. Fax: (340) 773-8515.E-mail: wstx@vitelcom.net Web Site:vipn.vitelcom.net/herbs/ Licensee: Family Broadcasting Inc. Format: Carribean. ◆Kevin Rames, gen mgr.

WVIQ(FM)— May 17, 1965: 99.5 mhz; 10.5 kw. 1,080 ft TL: N17 45 20 W64 47 55. Stereo. Hrs open: Box 25680, St. Croix, 00824-1680. Phone: (340) 773-1180. Fax: (340) 773-9093.E-mail: jkc95@aol.com Web Site:www.viradio.com Licensee: JKC Communications of the Virgin Islands Inc. (acq 1999; $590,000). Format: Adult contemp. ◆Jonathan Cohen, gen mgr, gen sls mgr; Tom Yarborough, progmg dir; Alvin Gee, news dir.

WVVI-FM— Feb 26, 1989: 93.5 mhz; 11.5 kw. Ant 735 ft TL: N17 44 08 W64 40 47. Stereo. Hrs open: 24 Box 25868, 00824. Secondary address: 5027 Anchor Way 00820. Phone: (340) 773-3693. Fax: (340) 719-1800.E-mail: paradise935fm@yahoo.com Web Site:www.paradise935fm.com Licensee: The Rain Broadcasting Inc. (acq 12-20-2007; $375,000). Format: Adult contemp. News: one hr wkly. Target aud: General; affluent young adult permanent residents. Spec prog: Relg 3 hrs wkly. ◆Roger Morgan, pres, gen mgr & progmg dir; Herb Schoenbohm, chief of engrg.

*WXZT(FM)— Not on air, target date: unknown: 90.9 mhz; 10 kw. Ant 777 ft TL: N17 44 07 W64 40 46. Hrs open: 573 State Mon Bijou, 00082. Phone: (340) 277-7821.E-mail: crucianedu@yahoo.com Licensee: Crucian Educational Nonprofit Group Inc. ◆Jose J. Martnez, pres.

Cruz Bay

WWKS(FM)— Feb 3, 1997: 101.3 mhz; 48 kw. 1,302 ft TL: N18 20 17 W64 43 40. Stereo. Hrs open: 24 Box 305678, St. Thomas, 00803-5678. Secondary address: Box 8209, Bluebeard's Castle, St. Thomas 00801. Phone: (340) 776-4585. Phone: (340) 776-1013. Fax: (340) 776-5357. Fax: (340) 774-4455. Web Site:www.wwks.net Licensee: Knight V.I. Radio Corp. Group owner: Knight Quality Stations (acq 1996; $225,000). Population served: 100,000 Natl. Network: ABC, . Pepper & Corazzini. Format: Urban contemp. News staff: 2; News: 2 hrs wkly. Target aud: 25-54; middle/upper income professionals. Spec prog: West Indian/calypso 25 hrs wkly. ◆Randolph H. Knight, pres; Mark P. Bastin, gen mgr; Jean Greaux Jr., opns dir.

Frederiksted

WAXJ(FM)— 1999: 103.5 mhz; 6 kw. Ant -33 ft TL: N17 43 28 W64 53 03. Hrs open: 24
Rebroadcasts WDHP (AM) Frederiksted 50%.
79-A Castle Coakley, Christiansted, 00820. Phone: (340) 719-1620. Fax: (340) 778-1686.E-mail: wrra@islands.vi Web

WDHP(AM)— May 1999: 1620 khz; 10 kw-D, 1 kw-N. TL: N17 43 28 W64 53 03. Hrs open: 79A Castle Coakley, Christiansted, VA, 00820. Phone: (340) 719-1620. Fax: (340) 778-1686.E-mail: wrra@islands.vi Web Site:www.reefbroadcasting.com Licensee: Reef Broadcasting Inc. Format: Div, bilingual. ◆Beverley Meyers, gen sls mgr; Hugh Pemberton, gen mgr, progmg dir & chief of engrg.

WEVI(FM)— 2003: 101.7 mhz; 900 w. Ant 790 ft TL: N17 43 15 W64 51 26. Hrs open: Box 892, Christiansted, 00821. Phone: (340) 719-1400. Fax: (340) 719-8783.E-mail: info@frontlinemissions.org Web Site:www.frontlinemissions.org Licensee: Frontline Missions International Inc. (acq 3-12-02). Format: Christian Carribbean music, bible teachings. ◆Antony Whitehead, gen mgr & progmg dir.

WMYP(FM)— 2002: 98.3 mhz; 1.9 kw. Ant 915 ft TL: N17 44 51 W64 50 11. Hrs open: 24 Box 8294, Christiansted, 00823. Phone: (340) 772-0098. Fax: (340) 772-9852.E-mail: latino98@viaccess.net Licensee: Amanda Friedman (acq 7-28-2006; $350,000). Format: Sp, tropical/pop. Target aud: 18-49. ◆Jose Martinez, gen mgr.

WRRA(AM)— 1976: 1290 khz; 500 w-D, 250 w-N. TL: N17 43 28 W64 53 03. Hrs open: 24
Rebroadcasts WDH (AM) Frederiksted 100%.
79A Castle Coakley, Christiansted, 00820. Phone: (340) 719-1620. Phone: (340) 778-1290. Fax: (340) 778-1686.E-mail: wrra@islands.vi Web Site:www.reefbroadcasting.com Licensee: Reef Broadcasting Inc. Roy F. Perkins. Format: Div music, bilingual. News staff: 2; News: 25 hrs wkly. Target aud: 18-56. Spec prog: Jazz 6 hrs, gospel 12 hrs, relg 10 hrs wkly. ◆Beverley Meyers, gen sls mgr; Hugh Pemberton, gen mgr, progmg dir & chief of engrg.

St. Thomas

WYAS(FM)— See Vieques, PR

Mexico

Tijuana

XETRA(AM)— Licensed to Tijuana. See San Diego CA

XETRA-FM— Licensed to Tijuana. See San Diego CA

XHRM-FM— Licensed to Tijuana. See San Diego CA

Federated States of Micronesia

Pohnpei

V6AH(AM)— 1964: 1449 khz; 10 kw-U. Hrs open: 18 Box 1086, Kolonia Pohnpei, 96941. Phone: (691) 320-2296. Fax: (691) 320-5212.E-mail: v6ah_radio@mail.fm Web Site:www.fm/ppbc Licensee: Oltrick D. Santos. Format: CHR. News: 20 hrs wkly. Target aud: General. Spec prog: Farm 20 hrs, folk 20 hrs, gospel 2 hrs, relg 2 hrs wkly. ◆Oltrick D. Santos, gen mgr.

Truk

V6AK(AM)— 1962: 1593 khz; 5 kw-U, DA-1. Hrs open: Midnight-6 AM Box 2222, Weno, Chuuk, 96942. Phone: (691) 330-2596. Web Site:www.fm/chuuk/radio.htm Licensee: FSM Telecommunications Corp. Format: News. Target aud: General. ◆Johnny Esa, gen mgr.

Yap

*V6AI(AM)— June 9, 1965: 1494 khz; 10 kw-U. Hrs open: 6 AM-midnight Box 117, Colonia YAP State Western Caroline Islands, 96943. Phone: (691) 350-2174. Fax: (691) 350-4426.E-mail: s-tamagken@yahoo.com Web Site:www.fm/yap/radio.htm Licensee: Yap State Government. Population served: 10,000 Format: CHR, country, news. News staff: 2; News: 20 hrs wkly. Target aud: General. Spec prog: Yapese 10 hrs, Micronesian 10 hrs, Japanese 5 hrs, Filipino 5 hrs wkly. ◆Sebastian Tamagken, gen mgr; John Gilmatam, progmg dir; Anthony Taveg Jr., mus dir; Jovencio David, chief of engrg; John Hasmai, news rptr; Benjamin Fithingmen, disc jockey. Co-owned TV: *WAAB-TV affil

Northern Mariana Islands

Chalan Kanoa-Saipan

*KRNM(FM)— Feb 28, 1998: 88.1 mhz; 1.8 kw. Ant 125 ft TL: N15 09 05 E145 43 11. Stereo. Hrs open: 24 Box 501250, Northern Marianas College, Saipan, 96950. Phone: (670) 234-5766. Fax: (670) 235-0915.E-mail: carlp@nmcnet.edu Web Site:www.krnm.org Licensee: Northern Marianas College. Population served: 75,000 Natl. Network: NPR, PRI, . Thomas Crowe. Format: Classical, jazz, news/talk. News: 65 hrs wkly. Spec prog: Chamorro 2 hrs, Korean one hrs, Chinese one hr wkly. ◆Carl Pogue, gen mgr; Joe Servino, engr.

Garapan-Saipan

KCNM(AM)— October 1984: 1080 khz; 5 kw-U. TL: N15 09 00 W145 42 52. Hrs open: 24 Box 500914, Saipan, 96950. Phone: (670) 234-7239. Fax: (670) 234-0447.E-mail: kzmi-fm@vzpavifica.net Licensee: Choice Broadcasting Co. LLC. (group owner; (acq 5-1-2009; grpsl). Population served: 60,000 Natl. Network: AP Network News, . Format: Relg teaching. News staff: one; News: 168 hrs wkly. Target aud: General. ◆Harry B. Blalock, gen mgr.

KCNM-FM— 1999: 101.1 mhz; 3.2 kw. Ant 827 ft TL: N15 11 00 W145 44 06. Hrs open: 125 Tun Jesus Cristostomo St., Suite 308, Tamuning, GU, 96931. Phone: (671) 648-4262. Licensee: Choice Broadcasting Co. LLC. (group owner). (acq 5-1-2009; grpsl). Population served: 65,000 Format: Ethnic. News staff: one; News: 16 hrs wkly. ◆Robert F. Kelley Jr., gen mgr.

*KORU(FM)— Not on air, target date: unknown: 89.9 mhz; 5.2 kw. Ant 1,442 ft TL: N15 11 06 E145 44 30. Hrs open: 290 Chalan Palasyo, Agana Heights, GU, 96910. Phone: (671) 472-5732. Fax: (671) 477-4678. Licensee: Good News Broadcasting Corp. ◆Robert J. Gibbons, pres; Matt Dodd, gen mgr.

KPXP(FM)— Nov 5, 1992: 99.5 mhz; 6.5 kw. 1,492 ft TL: N15 11 10 W145 44 25. Stereo. Hrs open: 24 111 W. Chalan Santo Papa St., Hagatna, GU, 96910. Phone: (670) 235-7996. Phone: (670) 235-7997. Fax: (670) 235-7998.E-mail: rex@spbguam.com Web Site:www.power99.com Licensee: Sorensen Pacific Broadcasting Inc. (group owner; acq 6-23-03; grpsl). Population served: 40,000 Kaye, Scholer, Fierman, Hays & Handler. Format: CHR. News staff: one; News: 14 hrs wkly. Target aud: 14-39; affluent adults. ◆Jon A. Anderson, pres; Rex W. Sorensen, CEO, chmn & CFO; Curtis Dancoe, stn mgr, sls dir, gen sls mgr; Laurence Bejerana, prom mgr; Raymond Gibson, progmg dir; Marvin Palmer, chief of engrg.

KRSI(FM)— July 1992: 97.9 mhz; 4.5 kw. Ant 1,519 ft TL: N15 11 09 E145 44 29. Stereo. Hrs open: 24 111 W. Chalan Santo Papa St., Hagatna, GU, 96910. Phone: (670) 235-7996. Fax: (670) 235-7998.E-mail: rex@spbguam.com Web Site:www.radiopacific.com Licensee: Sorensen Pacific Broadcasting Inc. (group owner; acq 6-23-03; grpsl). Coin & Marks. Format: Classic rock, div, rock. News: one hr wkly. Target aud: 25-49. Spec prog: Blues 6 hrs, reggae 19 hrs, Hawaiian 2 hrs, Chamdru 4 hrs, jazz one hr wkly. ◆Rex Sorensen, CEO & pres; Curtis Dancoe, gen mgr, gen sls mgr, disc jockey; Laurence Bejerana, prom mgr; Raymond Gibson, progmg dir; Marvin Palmer, chief of engrg.

KWAW(FM)— 1999: 100.3 mhz; 1.1 kw. Ant 1,512 ft TL: N15 11 05 W145 44 26. Hrs open: 24 Box 7094, Box 504651, Tamuning, GU, 96931. Secondary address: Box 504651, Saipan 96950. Phone: (671) 646-7197. Fax: (670) 234-2262. Web Site:www.magic100radio.com Licensee: Leon Padilla Ganacias (acq 8-13-98; $25,615). News: 30 hrs wkly. ◆Victoria Ganacias Borja, gen mgr.

KZMI(FM)— 1997: 103.9 mhz; 3.2 kw. Ant 827 ft TL: N15 11 00 E145 44 06. Stereo. Hrs open: 24 Box 500914 , Saipan , 96950. Phone: (670) 234-7239. Fax: (670) 234-0447. Web Site:www.itecrmi.com Licensee: Choice Broadcasting Co. LLC. (group owner). (acq 5-1-2009; grpsl). Population served: 65,000 Format: Adult contemp. News staff: one; News: 16 hrs wkly. ◆Harry Blalock, gen mgr.

Directory of Radio Stations in Canada

Alberta

Airdrie

CFIT-FM— Apr 12, 2007: 106.1 mhz; 3.6 kw. TL: N51 17 35 W113 59 30. Hrs open: 159 B East Lake Blvd., T4A 2G2. Phone: (403) 945-3772. Fax: (403) 945-0277.E-mail: contactus@therangeonline.ca Web Site:www.therangeonline.ca Licensee: Tiessen Media Inc. Format: Eclectic adult contemp. Target aud: 25-54. ◆Jamie Tiessen, gen mgr; Bruce Daniels, opns mgr, progmg dir; Carol Close, gen sls mgr.

Athabasca

CKBA-FM— 2009: 94.1 mhz; 9 kw. Hrs open: #1, 4902 49 St., T9S 1C2. Phone: (780) 675-5301. Fax: (780) 675-4938.E-mail: wbetts@newcap.ca Web Site:www.fox850.ca Licensee: Newcap Inc. Format: Classic hits. Target aud: 25-54. ◆Wray Betts, stn mgr.

Blairmore

CJPR-FM— 2004: 94.9 mhz; 760 w. TL: N49 38 02 W114 29 30. Hrs open: Box 840, T0K 0E0. Phone: (403) 562-2806. Fax: (403) 562-8114. Licensee: Newcap Inc. Format: Full country. ◆Linda Huze, stn mgr; Darryl Ferguson, progmg dir.

Bonnyville

CFNA-FM— 2007: 99.7 mhz; 50 kw. TL: N54 10 55 W110 51 59. Hrs open: 5316 54th Ave., Suite 102, T9N 2C9. Phone: (780) 573-1745. Fax: (780) 573-1746. Web Site:thegoatrocks.com Licensee: Vista Radio Ltd. (acq 11-21-2008; C$7.3 million with CKLM-FM Lloydminster). Format: Rock. ◆J. Stewart Dent, gen mgr.

CJEG-FM— May 23, 2006: 101.3 mhz; 27 kw. Hrs open: Box 8251, T9N 2J5. Phone: (780) 812-3058.E-mail: info@cjegfm.com Web Site:www.1013koolfm.com Licensee: NewCap Inc. Format: CHR. ◆Lise Lacombe, stn mgr, gen sls mgr; R.C. Ryder, progmg mgr, mus dir; Cash Kaye, mus dir; Robb Hunter, news dir; Raymond Green, chief of engrg.

Brooks

CIBQ(AM)— Apr 15, 1973: 1340 khz; 1 kw-U, DA-1. Hrs open: 24 Unit 8-403 2nd Ave., West Brooks, T1R 1S3. Phone: (403) 362-3418. Phone: (403) 362-6000 (NEWS). Fax: (403) 362-8168.E-mail: Q13@newcap.ca Web Site:www.eidnet.org/local/Q13 Licensee: Newcap Inc. Group owner: NewCap Broadcasting Ltd. (acq 4-19-2002; grpsl). Population served: 13,000 Format: Contemp country. News staff: one; News: 12 hrs wkly. Target aud: 25-54. ◆Ron Thompson, gen mgr; John Petrie, stn mgr, gen sls mgr; Brent Young, progmg dir; Sue Stevens, news dir.

CIXF-FM— Oct 11, 2005: 101.1 mhz; 2.2 kw. Hrs open: Unit 8-403 2nd Ave., West Brooks, T1R 1S3. Phone: (403) 362-3418. Fax: (403) 362-8168.E-mail: 1011thefox@mewcap.ca Licensee: Newcap Inc. Format: Adult contemp.

Calgary

CBCX-FM— 2003: 89.7 mhz; 10 kw. Hrs open: 1724 Westmount Blvd. N.W., T2N 3G7. Phone: (403) 521-6000. Web Site:www.cbc.ca Licensee: CBC. Natl. Network: Espace Musique, . Format: Fr. ◆Don Orchard, gen mgr; Henk VanLeeuwen, progmg dir.

*CBR(AM)— Oct 1, 1964: 1010 khz; 50 kw-U, DA-2. Hrs open: 20 Box 2640, T2P 2M7. Secondary address: 1724 Westmount Blvd. N.W. T2N 3G7. Phone: (403) 521-6000. Fax: (403) 521-6271.E-mail: info@cbc.ca Web Site:www.cbc.ca Licensee: CBC. Format: Info, div, news/talk. News: 24 hrs wkly. ◆Dan Orchard, gen mgr; Randy Winczira, opns mgr; Harry Wagter, mktg mgr; David Perlich, progmg dir; Helen Henderson, progmg mgr; Donna McElligott, news dir.

CBRF-FM— 2002: 103.7 mhz; 22 kw. Hrs open: Rebroadcasts CHFA(AM) Edmonton 100%.

Box 555, Edmonton, T5J 2P4. Secondary address: 1724 Westmount Blvd. N.W. T2N 3G7. Phone: (780) 468-7500. Fax: (780) 468-7849. Web Site:radio-canada.ca/regions/alberta/index.shtml Licensee: Canadian Broadcasting Corp. Natl. Network: Premiere Chaine, . Format: Fr. ◆Francois Pageau, gen mgr.

*CBR-FM— Sept 29, 1975: 102.1 mhz; 100 kw. 788 ft Stereo. Hrs open: Box 2640, T2N 3G7. Phone: (403) 521-6000. Fax: (403) 521-6271.E-mail: info@cbc.ca Licensee: CBC. Natl. Network: CBC Radio Two, . Format: Class, blues.

CFAC(AM)— May 1922: 960 khz; 50 kw-U. Stereo. Hrs open: 24 2723 37th Ave. N.E., T1Y 5R8. Phone: (403) 291-0000. Fax: (403) 291-4368. Licensee: Rogers Broadcasting Ltd. (acq 12-89). Population served: 850,000 Format: All sports. News staff: 3; News: 15 hrs wkly. Target aud: 55 plus. Spec prog: Agriculture, rural 10 hrs wkly. ◆Tony Viner, pres; Gary Miles, exec VP; Kevin McKenna, VP, gen mgr, opns VP; Jim Dunlop, gen sls mgr; Paul Williams, adv dir; Kelly Kirch, progmg dir.

CFEX-FM— Jan 1, 2007: 92.9 mhz; 45 kw. Hrs open: 24 255 17th Ave. S.W., Suite 400, T2S 2T8. Phone: (403) 670-0210. Fax: (403) 212-1399. Web Site:www.x929.ca Licensee: Harvard Broadcasting Inc. Format: New alternative rock. ◆Cam Cowie, gen mgr; Christian Hall, opns mgr, progmg dir; Gary Brasil, gen sls mgr; Ginette Sowerby, mktg dir; James Callsen, news dir.

CFFR(AM)— Jan 10, 1984: 660 khz; 50 kw-U, DA-2. Stereo. Hrs open: 24 2723 37 Ave. N.E., T1Y 5R8. Phone: (403) 291-0000. Fax: (403) 291-5342. Licensee: Rogers (Alberta) Ltd. Group owner: Rogers Broadcasting Ltd. (acq 9-10-99; grpsl). Format: All news. News staff: 5; News: 10 hrs wkly. Target aud: 25-49. Spec prog: Sports 15 hrs wkly. ◆Kevin McKenna, gen mgr; Karen Parsons, prom dir, progmg dir, news dir; Shannon Kotylak, prom dir & progmg dir.

CFGQ-FM— Apr 15, 1982: 107.3 mhz; 100 kw. Ant 638 ft TL: N51 03 54 W114 12 47. Stereo. Hrs open: 630 3rd Ave. S.W., Suite 105, T2P 4L4. Phone: (403) 716-6500. Fax: (403) 716-2111. Web Site:www.q107fm.ca Licensee: CKIK-FM Ltd. Group owner: Corus Entertainment Inc. (acq 7-6-2000; grpsl). Population served: 760,000 Format: Classic rock. Target aud: 25-44. ◆Garry McKenzie, gen mgr; Doug Young, gen sls mgr; Christian Hall, progmg dir; Natasha Rapchuk, news dir; Wade Wensink, chief of engrg; Judy Rickleton, traf mgr.

CFUL-FM— Mar 12, 2007: 90.3 mhz; 100 kw. Ant 1,122 ft TL: N51 03 37 W114 10 13. Hrs open: 1110 Centre St. N.E., Suite 100, T2E 2R2. Phone: (403) 278-6772.E-mail: youshouldplaythis @fuelcalgary.com Web Site:www.ampradiocalgary.com Licensee: Newcap Inc. Format: Top-40/pop. ◆Murray Brookshaw, opns mgr, progmg dir; Stephen Peck, gen mgr & gen sls mgr; Michael Godfrey, mktg dir, prom dir.

CFXL-FM— Aug 30, 2002: 103.1 mhz; 100 kw. Ant 1,122 ft TL: N51 03 54 W114 12 51. Stereo. Hrs open: 1110 Centre St. N.E., Suite 100, T2E 2R2. Phone: (403) 271-6366. Fax: (403) 278-6772.E-mail: feedback@xl103Calgary.com Web Site:www.xl103calgary.com Licensee: Newcap Inc. Group owner: NewCap Broadcasting Ltd. (acq 4-19-2002; grpsl). Population served: 900,000 Wire Svc: BN Wire Format: Greatest hits from the 60s, 70s and 80s. News staff: one; News: 35 hrs wkly. Target aud: 35-54. ◆Vinka Dubroja, gen mgr; Murray Brookshaw, opns mgr; Hal Gardiner, news dir; Mike Gratton, chief of engrg.

CHFM-FM— Aug 29, 1962: 95.9 mhz; 48 kw. Ant 480 ft TL: N51 03 37 W114 10 13. Stereo. Hrs open: 24 Prog sep from AM 2723 37th Ave. N.E., T1Y 5R8. Phone: (403) 291-0000. Fax: (403) 291-4368.E-mail: info@chfm.com Web Site:www.chfm.com Licensee: Rogers Broadcasting Ltd. Natl. Rep: Canadian Broadcast Sales,. Format: Adult contemp. News staff: one. Target aud: 35-54; females. ◆Tony Viner, CEO; Kevin McKenna, stn mgr; Jennifer Enns, prom dir; Vince Cownden, progmg dir; Darren Robson, mus dir; David Spence, news dir; Tanya Berner, pub affrs dir.

CHKF-FM— Nov 14, 1998: 94.7 mhz; 53 kw. Hrs open: 24 2723-37 Ave. N.E. #109, T1Y 5R4. Phone: (403) 717-1940. Fax: (403) 717-1945.E-mail: general @fm947.com Web Site:www.fm947.com Licensee: Fairchild Radio (Calgary FM) Ltd. Population served: 150,000 Format: Ethnic. News staff: 2; News: 21 hrs wkly. Target aud: General. ◆Christine Leung, gen mgr, mktg dir; Perry Chan, progmg dir.

CHQR(AM)— November 1964: 770 khz; 50 kw-U, DA-2. Stereo. Hrs open: 24 630 3rd Ave. S.W., Suite 105, T2P 4L4. Phone: (403) 716-6500. Fax: (403) 716-2111. Web Site:www.qr77.com Licensee: CKIK-FM Ltd. (Acq 4-15-70). Natl. Rep: Canadian Broadcast Sales, Dora-Clayton,. Format: News/talk, sports. News staff: 11; News: 17 hrs wkly. Target aud: 35 plus. ◆Phil Kallsen, progmg dir; Bill Powers, sports cmtr. Co-owned TV: CICT-TV affil

CIBK-FM— Sept 6, 2002: 98.5 mhz; 100 kw. Hrs open: Suite 300, 1110 Cernter St. N., T2E 2R2. Phone: (403) 240-5800. Fax: (403) 240-5801. Web Site:www.vibe985.com Licensee: Astral Media Radio G.P. Group owner: Standard Broadcasting Corp. (acq 10-29-2007; grpsl). Format: CHR. ◆Tom Peacock, gen mgr; Stew Meyers, opns mgr, progmg dir; Vinka Dubroja, gen sls mgr; Gillian Storey, prom dir.

CIGY-FM— Mar 6, 2008: 97.7 mhz; 100 kw. TL: N51 04 24 W114 15 38. Hrs open: 6807 Railway St. S.E., Suite 110, T2H 2V6. Phone: (403) 385-4000. Fax: (403) 385-4001.E-mail: win@977CalgaryFM.com Web Site:www.977CalgaryFM.com Licensee: Rawlco Radio Ltd. Natl. Rep: Canadian Broadcast Sales,. Format: Var. News staff: 27. ◆Kent Newson, VP, gen mgr, progmg dir; Marianne Vibert, opns mgr; Maranne Vibert, mktg dir.

CJAQ-FM— June 3, 1996: 96.9 mhz; 48 kw. Ant 686 ft TL: N51 02 18 W114 13 28. Hrs open: 2723 37th Ave. N.E., T1Y 5R8. Phone: (403) 250-9797. Fax: (403) 291-4368. Web Site:www.jackfm.ca Licensee: Rogers (Alberta) Ltd. Format: Classic rock. ◆Kevin McKanna, gen mgr; Gavin Tucker, progmg dir; K. Kirch, mus dir; Jerry Pendree, engrg VP, chief of engrg.

CJAY-FM— June 1, 1977: 92.1 mhz; 100 kw. Ant 979 ft TL: N51 03 37 W114 10 13. Stereo. Hrs open: 24 Prog sep from AM Box 2750 Broadcast House, T2P 4P8. Phone: (403) 242-6956. Web Site:www.cjay92.com Licensee: Astral Media Radio G.P. Format: Rock. ◆Ryan Dryden, mktg dir; Bob Harris, progmg dir; Ben Jeffery, mus dir; Ken Pasolli, engrg dir.

CJSI-FM— December 1997: 88.9 mhz; 100 kw. Ant 979 ft TL: N51 03 54 W114 12 47. Hrs open: Suite 100, 4510 Macleod Trail S., T2G 0A4. Phone: (403) 276-1111. Fax: (403) 276-1114.E-mail: cameron.harris@shinefm.com Web Site:www.cjsi.ca Licensee: Touch Canada Broadcasting LP. Natl. Rep: Target Broadcast Sales,. Format: Contemp Christian. Target aud: 25-54; adults. ◆Mark Imbach, opns mgr; Mike Kelly, gen mgr & progmg dir.

*CJSW-FM— Jan 15, 1985: 90.9 mhz; 4 kw. Stereo. Hrs open: 24 Rm. 127- MacEwan Hall, 2500 University Dr. N.W., T2N 1N4. Phone: (403) 220-3904. Fax: (403) 289-8212. Web Site:www.cjsw.com Licensee: The University of Calgary Student Radio Society. Population served: 1,000,000 Format: Alternative, jazz, community. News: 5 hrs wkly. Target aud: General; young, trendy & well-heeled. Spec prog: Fr one hr, Ger 2 hrs, It one, Sp one hr wkly. ◆Chad Saunders, gen mgr.

CKAV-FM-3—Not on air, target date: unknown: 88.1 mhz; 33 kw. Ant 1,040 ft TL: N51 03 54 W114 12 47. Hrs open: 366 Adelaide St. E., Suite 323, Toronto, ON, M5A 3X9. Phone: (416) 703-1287. Fax: (416) 703-4328. Web Site:aboriginalvoices.com Licensee: Aboriginal Voices Radio Inc. ◆Roy Hennessy, opns mgr; Patrice Mousseau, progmg dir.

CKCE-FM— Mar 22, 2007: 101.5 mhz; 48 kw. TL: N51 03 37 W114 10 13. Hrs open: 535 7th Ave. S.W., T2P 0Y4. Phone: (403) 508-2222. Fax: (403) 508-2224. Web Site:www.calgary1015.com Licensee: CTV Ltd. (acq 6-22-2007; grpsl). Format: Hot adult contemp. ◆James Stuart, gen mgr; Gavin Mortimer, gen sls mgr; Khazma Tichon, mktg dir, prom dir; Rob Mise, progmg dir.

CKMX(AM)— May 18, 1922: 1060 khz; 50 kw-U, DA-N. TL: N50 54 02 W26 113 52. Stereo. Hrs open: 24 Box 2750, Broadcast House, T2P 4P8. Phone: (403) 240-5800. Fax: (403) 240-5801. Web Site:www.cjay92.com Licensee: Astral Media Radio G.P. Group owner: Standard Broadcasting Corp. (acq 10-29-2007; grpsl). Population served: 750,000 Format: Adult contemp. News staff: one. Target aud: 45 plus. Spec prog: Jazz 5 hrs wkly. ◆Tom Peacock, gen mgr; Sandi Leonard, gen sls mgr; Ken Rigel, progmg dir.

CKRY-FM— July 9, 1982: 105.1 mhz; 100 kw. Ant 400 ft Stereo. Hrs open: 24 630 3rd Ave. S.W., Suite 105, T2P 4L4. Phone: (403) 716-2105. Fax: (403) 716-2111. Web Site:www.country105.com Licensee: Corus Entertainment Inc. (group owner) Population served: 800,000 Natl. Rep: Canadian Broadcast Sales,. Format: Country. News staff: 6; News: 7 hrs wkly. Target aud: 25-54. ◆Garry McKenzie, gen mgr & stn mgr.

Camrose

CFCW(AM)— Nov 2, 1954: 840 khz; 50 kw-U, DA-2. TL: N52 57 37 W112 57 33. Stereo. Hrs open: 24 2394 W. Edmonton Mall, 8882 170th St., Edmonton, T5T 4M2. Secondary address: 5708-48 Avenue T4V 0K1. Phone: (780) 437-4996. Fax: (780) 436-9803. Web Site:www.cfcw.com Licensee: Newcap Inc. Group owner: NewCap Inc. Population served: 900,000 Natl. Rep: imsradio,. Format: Country. News: 11 hrs wkly. Target aud: 25-54; country music, sports & hockey listeners in Edmonton rgn. Spec prog: Farm 5 hrs wkly. ♦Randy Lemay, gen mgr; Patrick Cardinal, opns mgr; Ross Hawse, gen sls mgr; Jackie Rae-Greening, progmg dir.

CFCW-FM— Oct 1, 2005: 98.1 mhz; 50 kw. Stereo. Hrs open: 5708 48th Ave., T4V 0K1. Phone: (780) 672-9822. Fax: (780) 672-4678. Web Site:www.981camfm.com Licensee: Newcap Inc. Wire Svc: BN Wire Format: Classic Hits.

Canmore

CHMN-FM— February 1998: 106.5 mhz; 510 w. Hrs open: Peschl's Corner, 749 Railway Ave., T1W 1P2. Phone: (403) 678-2222. Phone: (403) 678-2223. Fax: (403) 678-6844. Licensee: Rogers Broadcasting Ltd. (group owner). Natl. Rep: Canadian Broadcast Sales,. Format: Hot adult contemp. ♦Kevin McKenna, gen mgr; Paul Williams, gen sls mgr; Vince Camden, progmg dir; Jeff Hubbard, mus dir.

Cold Lake

CJXK-FM— Sept 3, 2004: 95.3 mhz; 100 kw. TL: N54 17 26 W110 28 57. Hrs open: B5412 55th St., T9M 1R5. Phone: (780) 594-2459. Fax: (780) 594-3001.E-mail: requests@k-rock953.com Web Site:www.953krock.com Licensee: Newcap Inc. Population served: 40,000 Format: Classic rock. ♦Carla Loffler, stn mgr.

Drayton Valley

CIBW-FM— 1994: 92.9 mhz; 7.4 kw. Stereo. Hrs open: 24 Postal Bag 929, T7A 1V3. Phone: (780) 542-9290. Fax: (780) 542-9319.E-mail: bwc929@bigwestcountry.ca Web Site:www.bigwestcountry.ca Licensee: Jim Pattison Broadcast Group Ltd. (the general partner) and Jim Pattison Industries Ltd. (the limited partner) carrying on business as Jim Pattison Broadcast Group L.P. Group owner: The Jim Pattison Broadcast Group (acq 9-7-95). Population served: 100,000 Natl. Rep: Canadian Broadcast Sales, Target Broadcast Sales,. Wire Svc: BN Wire Format: Country. News staff: one; News: 16 hrs wkly. Target aud: General. ♦Paul Mason, gen mgr; Bryn James, gen sls mgr; Trevor Grinde, progmg dir.

Drumheller

CHOO-FM— 2009: 99.5 mhz; 3.6 kw. TL: N51 27 01 W112 44 10. Hrs open: 105 S. Railway Ave. Ss 6, T0J 0Y6. Phone: (403) 823-9936. Web Site:www.995drumfm.com Licensee: Golden West Broadcasting Ltd. Format: Adult contemp. Target aud: 25-50. ♦Ron Zuke, stn mgr.

CKDQ(AM)— 1958: 910 khz; 50 kw-U, DA-2. TL: Strathmore. Stereo. Hrs open: 24 Box 1480, T0J 0Y0. Secondary address: 515 Hwy. 10 E. T0J 0Y0. Phone: (403) 823-3384. Fax: (403) 823-7241.E-mail: bbrown@ab.ncc.ca Licensee: Newcap Inc. Group owner: NewCap Broadcasting Ltd. (acq 4-19-2002; grpsl). Population served: 365000 Natl. Rep: CBS Radio,. Format: Country. News staff: 2; News: 11 hrs wkly. Target aud: 25-54. Spec prog: Farm 8 hrs, relg 2 hrs wkly. ♦Rick Walters, gen mgr.

Edmonton

CBX(AM)— 1948: 740 khz; 50 kw-U, DA-2. Hrs open: 24 Box 555, T5J 2P4. Secondary address: Edmonton City Ctr., 10062-102 Ave., Suite 123, Alberta T5J 24G. Phone: (780) 468-7500. Fax: (780) 468-7419.E-mail: cbx_edmonton@cbc.ca Web Site:www.edmonton.cbc.ca Licensee: CBC. Natl. Network: CBC Radio One, . Format: Info, news/talk. Target aud: 35 plus; college educated. ♦Mike Linden, VP; Judy Piercey, progmg dir.

CBX-FM—Not on air, target date: unknown: 90.9 mhz; 100 kw. Ant 633 ft Stereo. Hrs open: Box 555, T5J 2P4. Phone: (780) 468-7500. Fax: (780) 468-7419. Web Site:www.edmonton.cdc.ca Licensee: CBC Natl. Network: CBC Radio Two, . Format: Btfl mus, class, news.

CFBR-FM— Apr 25, 1951: 100.3 mhz; 100 kw. 482 ft Stereo. Hrs open: Prog sep from AM 18520 Stony Plain Rd., Suite 100, T5S 2E2. Phone: (780) 486-2800. Fax: (780) 489-6927.E-mail: info@thebearrocks.com Web Site:www.thebearrocks.com Licensee: Astral media Radio G.P. Format: Rock, classic rock. ♦Susan Reade, gen sls mgr; Ryan Zimmerman, progmg dir; Park Warden, mus dir; Bob Hunter, chief of engrg.

CFCW(AM)—See Camrose

CFRN(AM)— 1934: 1260 khz; 50 kw-U, DA-N. Hrs open: 18520 Stony Plain Rd., Suite 100, T5S 2E2. Phone: (780) 486-2800. Fax: (780) 489-6927.E-mail: info@cfrn.com Web Site:www.cfrn.com Licensee: Astral Media Radio G.P. Group owner: Standard Broadcasting Corp. (acq 10-29-2007; grpsl). Format: Sports. Target aud: 45 plus. ♦Stewart Meyers, gen mgr; Ryan Zimmerman, progmg dir.

CFWE-FM-4— 1990: 98.5 mhz; 9.3 kw. TL: N53 38 45 W114 00 14. Hrs open: 24 13245 146th St., T5L 4S8. Phone: (780) 447-2393. Fax: (780) 454-2820.E-mail: info@cfweradio.ca Web Site:www.cfweradio.ca Licensee: Aboriginal Multi-Media Society of Alberta. Format: Country/aboriginal. Target aud: General; Cree, Blackfoot, Stoney, Dene & English language listeners. ♦Bert Crowfoot, CEO & gen mgr; Alan Standerwick, stn mgr.

CHBN-FM— Feb 17, 2005: 91.7 mhz; 100 kw. Hrs open: 10212 Jasper Ave. N.W., T5J 5A3. Phone: (780) 424-2222. Fax: (780) 401-1600. Web Site:www.thebounce.ca Licensee: Edmonton Urban Partnership. Natl. Rep: CHUM Radio Sales,. Format: Rhythmic CHR. Target aud: 15-39. ♦James Stuart, gen mgr; Giselle Sowa, gen sls mgr; Dan Tucek, progmg dir; Lamya Asiff, news dir; Trevor Stuart, chief of engrg.

CHDI-FM— May 9, 2005: 102.9 mhz; 100 kw. Hrs open: 24 5915 Gateway Blvd., T6H 2H3. Phone: (780) 423-2005. Fax: (780) 437-5129.E-mail: al.ford@rci.rogers.com Web Site:www.radiosonic.fm Licensee: Rogers Broadcasting Ltd. (acq 11-29-2006; grpsl). Format: Modern rock. News staff: one. ♦Tom Bedore, gen mgr; Stephen Crane, opns mgr; Shelley Ruis, gen sls mgr; Brent Shelton, prom dir; Al Ford, progmg dir; Kory Read, news dir.

CHED(AM)— Mar 3, 1954: 630 khz; 50 kw-U, DA-N. Stereo. Hrs open: 5204-84 St., T6E 5N8. Phone: (780) 440-6300. Fax: (780) 468-6739. Fax: (780) 469-5937.E-mail: info@630ched.com Web Site:www.630ched.com Licensee: Corus Premium Television Ltd. Group owner: Corus Entertainment Inc. (acq 7-6-00; grpsl). Format: Sports, talk. ♦Doug Rutherford, gen mgr; Tanya Laughren, prom dir; Syd Smith, progmg dir; Tom Davies, chief of engrg.

***CHFA(AM)—** Nov 20, 1949: 680 khz; 10 kw-U, DA-1. Hrs open: 24 Box 555, T5J 2P4. Secondary address: 123 Edmonton City Center T5J 2P4. Phone: (780) 468-7800. Fax: (780) 468-7849. Licensee: CBC. (acq 4-1-74). Format: Div, MOR, news/talk. News staff: 8; News: 8 hrs wkly. Target aud: 20-60; Fr speaking. ♦Francois Pageau, gen mgr; Jack Tyler, chief of engrg.

CHMC-FM— Dec 8, 2005: 99.3 mhz; 100 kw. Hrs open: 5241 Calgary Tr., Suite 700, Centre 104, T6H 5G8. Phone: (780) 433-7877. Fax: (780) 438-8484.E-mail: thofer@rawlco.com Web Site:www.magic99.ca Licensee: Rawlco Radio Ltd. Format: Vocal jazz, blues and soft rock. ♦Kelly Walter, gen sls mgr; Kurt Leavins, gen mgr, progmg dir & mus dir.

CHQT(AM)— Aug 19, 1965: 880 khz; 50 kw-U, DA-N. Hrs open: 5204 84th St., T6E 5N8. Phone: (780) 440-6300. Fax: (780) 469-5937. Web Site:www.inews880.com Licensee: Corus Radio Co. Format: All news. ♦Tanya Laughren, prom dir; Syd Smith, progmg dir; Danielle Mattiello, traf mgr.

CIRK-FM— 1949: 97.3 mhz; 100 kw. Stereo. Hrs open: 2394 W. Edmonton Mall, 8882 170th St., T5T 4M2. Phone: (780) 437-4996. Fax: (780) 436-9803. Web Site:www.k-rock973.com Licensee: NewCap Inc. Group owner: NewCap Broadcasting Ltd. (acq 2-17-99; C$10 million). Natl. Rep: imsradio,. Format: Classic rock. Target aud: 18-54; mobile adults. ♦Randy Lemey, gen mgr; Patrick Cardinal, opns mgr; Ross House, gen sls mgr; James Gushnowski, progmg dir.

CISN-FM— June 5, 1982: 103.9 mhz; 100 kw. 757 ft Stereo. Hrs open: 5204 84th St., T6E 5N8. Phone: (780) 428-1104. Fax: (780) 469-5937.E-mail: info@cisnfm.com Web Site:www.cisnfm.com Licensee: Corus Radio Co. Group owner: Corus Entertainment Inc. (acq 7-6-00; grpsl). Format: Contemp country. ♦Doug Rutherford, gen mgr, stn mgr; Neil Cunningham, gen sls mgr; Danielle L'hirrondelle, prom dir; Chris Scheetz, progmg dir; Bob Layton, news dir; Tom Davies, chief of engrg; Danielle Mattiello, traf mgr; Bryan Hall, sports cmtr.

CJCA(AM)— May 22, 1922: 930 khz; 50 kw-U, DA-N. Hrs open: 24 531 Calgary Tr., T6H 4JB. Phone: (780) 466-4930. Fax: (780) 469-5335. Web Site:www.cjca.ca Licensee: Touch Canada Broadcasting LP. (acq 4-12-94). Population served: 1,000,000 Format: Contemp Christian. News: 6 hrs wkly. Target aud: 25-54. ♦Jamie Moffat, gen sls mgr, disc jockey; Topher Braithwaite, prom dir; Malcolm Hunt, progmg dir; Gord Craig, news dir; Len Dehek, disc jockey.

CJRY-FM— 2004: 105.9 mhz; 100 kw. Ant 633 ft Hrs open: 531 Calgary Tr., T6H 4JB. Phone: (780) 466-4930. Fax: (780) 469-5335. Web Site:www.cjry.ca/cms Licensee: Touch Canada Broadcasting L.P. Format: Contemp Christian music.

***CJSR-FM—** 1984: 88.5 mhz; 900 w. Stereo. Hrs open: 24 Room 0-09, Students' Union Bldg., Univ. of Alberta, T6G 2J7. Phone: (780) 492-2577. Fax: (780) 492-3121.E-mail: admin@cjsr.com Web Site:www.cjsr.com Licensee: The First Alberta Campus Radio Association. Population served: 1,500,000 Format: Alternative progmg. News staff: 1; News: 8 hrs wkly. Anyone tired with commercial radio. Spec prog: American Indian 2 hrs, Black 7 hrs, class 2 hrs, folk 16 hrs, Fr one hr, Metal 4 hrs, Electronic 4 hrs, Pol 2 hrs, Sp 2 hrs wkly. ♦Aaron Levin, mus dir; Sam Power, news dir.

CKAV-FM-4— 2007: 89.3 mhz; 100 kw. TL: N53 30 53 W113 17 07. Hrs open: 366 Adelaide St. E., Suite 323, Toronto, ON, M5A 3X9. Phone: (416) 703-1287. Fax: (416) 703-4328.E-mail: info@aboriginalvoices.com Web Site:aboriginalvoices.com Licensee: Aboriginal Voices Radio Inc.

CKER-FM— 1996: 101.7 mhz; 100 kw. Stereo. Hrs open: 24 5915 Gateway Blvd., T6H 2H3. Phone: (780) 702-1188. Fax: (780) 437-5129.E-mail: feedback@worldfm.ca Web Site:www.worldfm.ca Licensee: Rogers Broadcasting Ltd. (acq 11-29-2006; grpsl). Population served: 1,000,000 Format: Ethnic, Chinese. News staff: 2; News: 14 hrs wkly. Target aud: General; ethnic audience (24 languages) & Christian. Spec prog: It 3 hrs, Sp 8 hrs, Por 2 hrs, Ukrainian 10 hrs, Dutch 3 hrs, Pol 6 hrs, E. Indian 7 hrs wkly. ♦Tom Bedore, gen mgr; Stephen Crane, opns mgr; Shelley Ruis, gen sls mgr; Roman Brytan, progmg dir.

CKNG-FM— Aug 11, 1982: 92.5 mhz; 100 kw. 900 ft Stereo. Hrs open: 5204-84 St., T6E 5N8. Phone: (780) 440-6300. Fax: (780) 468-6739.E-mail: info@power92.com Licensee: Corus Premium Television Ltd. Format: Top-40. ♦Julie James, progmg dir; Greg Cooper, prom.

CKRA-FM— Nov 15, 1979: 96.3 mhz; 100 kw. Ant 757 ft Stereo. Hrs open: 24 2394 W. Edmonton Mall, 8882 170th St., T5T 4M2. Phone: (780) 437-4996. Fax: (780) 436-9803. Web Site:www.963capitalfm.com Licensee: NewCap Inc. Group owner: NewCap Broadcasting Ltd. Population served: 800,000 Natl. Rep: imsradio,. Format: Hits of the 60s, 70s, & 80s. Target aud: 25-54; urban young adults. ♦Randy Lemay, gen mgr; Patrick Cardinal, opns mgr, progmg dir; Ross Hawse, gen sls mgr.

CKUA(AM)— Nov 21, 1927: 580 khz; 10 kw-U, DA-2. TL: N53 20 34 W113 27 27. Hrs open: 24 Dups FM 100% 10526 Jasper Ave., 4th Fl., T5J 1Z7. Phone: (780) 428-7595. Fax: (780) 428-7624.E-mail: radio@ckua.com Web Site:www.ckua.com Licensee: CKUA Radio Foundation Format: Diversified.

***CKUA-FM—** June 28, 1948: 94.9 mhz; 100 kw. 400 ft Stereo. Hrs open: 24 hrs 4th Fl., 10526 Jasper Ave., T5J 1Z7. Phone: (780) 428-7595. Fax: (780) 428-7624.E-mail: radio@ckua.com Web Site:www.ckua.com Licensee: CKUA Radio Foundation. (acq 5-29-95). Population served: 3,000,000 Format: Div, class, jazz. News staff: 4; News: 6 hrs wkly. Target aud: General; Alberta population. ♦Ken Regan, gen mgr, opns mgr; Andrea Louie, gen sls mgr; Brian Dunsmore, progmg dir; Peter North, mus dir; Neil Lutes, chief of engrg; Sharon Cross, traf mgr.

Edson

CFXE-FM— 2007: 94.3 mhz; 11 kw. TL: N53 38 47 W116 32 26. Hrs open: 24 Box 7800, Edson Alberta, T7E 1V8. Secondary address: 422 50th St. T7E 1T1. Phone: (780) 723-4461. Fax: (780) 723-3765.E-mail: dschuck@fox-radio.ca Web Site:www.thefoxradio.ca Licensee: Newcap Inc. Natl. Rep: imsradio,. Wire Svc: Canadian Press Format: Adult contemp, CHR. News staff: 3. Target aud: 18-55. Spec prog: Farm 2 hrs wkly. ♦Al Anderson, VP; Dave Schuck, gen mgr, stn mgr; Rob Alexander, progmg dir; Steve Bethge, news dir.

Falher

***CKRP-FM—** Nov 2, 1996: 95.7 mhz; 671 w. TL: N55 44 07 W117 11 34. Stereo. Hrs open:
Rebroadcasts CITE-FM Montreal 65%.
Box 718, Association Canadienne-Francaise de l'Alberta, Regionale de Riviere-la-Paix, T0H 1M0. Phone: (780) 837-2346. Fax: (780) 837-2092.E-mail: ckrp_fm@yahoo.ca Licensee: Association

canadienne-francaise de l'Alberta-Regionale de Riviere-la-Paix. Format: Fr, adult contemp, community svc. Fr population. ♦Julie Cadieux, pres.

Fort McMurray

CFVR-FM— 2008: 103.7 mhz; 20 kw. TL: N56 48 29 W111 26 55. Hrs open: 9904 Franklin Ave., T9H 2K5. Phone: (780) 791-0103. Fax: (780) 791-1448. Web Site:www.mix1037fm.com Licensee: Harvard Broadcasting Inc. Format: Adult contemp. Target aud: 18-54; women. ♦Jason Huschi, gen mgr; Craig Picton, progmg dir.

CHFT-FM— June 16, 2008: 100.5 mhz; 20 kw. TL: N56 44 00 W111 23 04. Hrs open: 9904 Franklin Ave., T9H 2K5. Phone: (780) 791-0810. Fax: (780) 791-0811. Web Site:www.krock.fm Licensee: Newcap Inc. Format: Classic Rock. ♦Rick Colliou, gen mgr; Jay Lawrence, progmg dir; Brad MacLauchlan, mus dir.

CJOK-FM— 2003: 93.3 mhz; 40 kw. TL: N56 41 16 W111 19 55. Hrs open: 24 9912 Franklin Ave., T9H 2K5. Phone: (780) 743-2246. Fax: (780) 791-7250. Web Site:mymcmurray.com Licensee: Rogers Broadcasting Ltd. (acq 11-29-2006; grpsl). Population served: 60,000 Format: Today's hot country. News staff: 3; News: 4 hrs wkly. Target aud: 25-44. ♦Jim Schneider, gen mgr & gen sls mgr.

CKOS-FM— 2007: 91.1 mhz; 35 w. TL: N56 40 11 W111 19 57. Hrs open: 10014 Main St., T9H 2G5. Phone: (780) 791-5911 . Web Site:kaos911.com Licensee: King's Kids Promotions Outreach Ministries Inc. Format: Christian CHR, hot adult cotemp. Target aud: 18-34. ♦Rick Kirschner, gen mgr; Jill Edwards, gen sls mgr; Murray Jordan, progmg dir.

CKYX-FM— March 1985: 97.9 mhz; 40 kw. Stereo. Hrs open: 24 9912 Franklin Ave., T9H 2K5. Phone: (780) 743-2246. Fax: (780) 791-7250. Web Site:mymcmurray.com Licensee: Rogers Broadcasting Ltd. (acq 11-29-2006; grpsl). Population served: 60,000 Format: Classic rock. News staff: 3; News: 5 hrs wkly. Target aud: 18-44. ♦Jim Schneider, gen mgr & gen sls mgr.

Fort Vermilion

CIAM-FM— Jan 27, 2003: 92.7 mhz; 30 w. Hrs open: 24 Box 609, T0H 1N0. Secondary address: 4709 River Rd. T0H 1N0. Phone: (780)-927-2426. Fax: (780) 927-2427.E-mail: ciam@telus.net Web Site:www.ciamradio.com Licensee: Care Radio Broadcasting Association. Format: Var/div/multingual. ♦Michael Sandstrom, gen mgr; Kevin Wiebe, news dir; Phil Peters, progmg dir & chief of engrg.

Grande Prairie

CFGP-FM— June 20, 1996: 97.7 mhz; 70 kw. TL: N55 27 57 W118 45 32. Stereo. Hrs open: 24 Suite 200, 9835 101st Ave., T8V 5V4. Phone: (780) 539-9700. Fax: (780) 532-1600. Fax: (780) 539-0367 (news). Web Site:www.sunfm.com Licensee: Rogers Broadcasting Ltd. (acq 11-29-2006; grpsl). Format: Hot CHR-top 40. News staff: 4; News: 4 hrs wkly. Target aud: 25-55. ♦Dave Reid, gen mgr, opns mgr, gen sls mgr; Lisa Kirby, prom dir; Kevin Becker, progmg dir; Daryl Major, news dir; Sam Lowe, chief of engrg.

CFRI-FM— Mar 30, 2007: 104.7 mhz; 100 kw. Hrs open: #1 11002 104th Ave., T8V 7W5. Phone: (780) 357-3733. Fax: (780) 830-7815. Web Site:www.1047freefm.com Licensee: Vista Radio Ltd. Format: Hit classic rock, new country rock. News staff: 3. ♦Gordon Gauvin, gen mgr; Pete Montana, progmg dir.

CIKT-FM— Apr 9, 2007: 98.9 mhz; 100 kw. Ant 842 ft TL: N55 28 44 W118 45 04. Hrs open: 8716 108th St., Suite 104, T8V 4C7. Phone: (780) 882-6612. Fax: (780) 882-6708. Web Site:www.q99live.com Licensee: Bear Creek Broadcasting Ltd. Natl. Rep: Target Broadcast Sales,. Rgnl rep: WTR Media Format: Var. Target aud: 35-54. ♦Ken Truhn, gen mgr & gen sls mgr; Jen Baron, prom dir; Dave Sawchuk, progmg dir.

CJGY-FM— Dec 3, 2007: 96.3 mhz; 100 kw. TL: N55 29 20 W118 44 50. Hrs open: #111, 10530 117 Ave., T8V 7N7. Phone: (780) 830-7640. Fax: (780) 830-7636.E-mail: 96.3@shinefm.com Web Site:www.cjcy.ca Licensee: Grande Prairie Radio Ltd. Format: Christian music. ♦Allan Hunsperger, gen mgr.

CJXX-FM— Nov 1, 2000: 93.1 mhz; 100 kw. TL: N55 03 08 W118 51 59. Hrs open: 24 9817 101st Ave., Suite 202, Grand Prairie, T8V 0X6. Phone: (780) 532-0840. Fax: (780) 538-1266. Fax: (780) 539-6397.E-mail: general@bigcountryxx.com Web Site:www.bigcountryxx.com Licensee: Jim Pattison Broadcast Group Ltd. (the general partner) and Jim Pattison Industries Ltd. (the limited partner) carrying on business as Jim Pattison Broadcast Group L.P. Group owner: The Jim Pattison Broadcast Group (acq 12-21-2000; grpsl). Population served: 200,000 Wire Svc: BN Wire Format: C&W. News staff: 5; News: 14 hrs wkly. Target aud: 25-49; adults who love country music. ♦Rick Arnish, pres; Ken Norman, gen mgr, progmg dir; Anne Graham, gen sls mgr; Barbara Shannon, prom dir.

High Level

CKHL-FM— July 1999: 102.1 mhz; 8.765 kw. Hrs open: Box 3759, T0H 1Z0. Phone: (780) 926-4531. Fax: (780) 926-4564. Web Site:www.ylcountry.com Licensee: 912038 Alberta Ltd. Format: Country. ♦Terry Babiy, gen mgr & sls dir; Chris Black, gen sls mgr; Don Jennings, progmg dir; Karin Koppitz, news dir.

High Prairie

CKVH(AM)— 1990: 1020 khz; 1 kw-D, 400 w-N. Hrs open: Box 2219, T0G 1E0. Phone: (780) 523-5111. Fax: (780) 523-3360. Web Site:www.ncc.ca Licensee: Newcap Inc. Group owner: NewCap Broadcasting Ltd. (acq 4-19-2002; grpsl). Format: Country. ♦Ron Gendron, gen mgr & gen sls mgr; Rob Alexander, progmg dir.

High River

CHRB(AM)— Dec 5, 1977: 1140 khz; 50 kw-D, 46 kw-N, DA-2. TL: N50 55 25 W113 49 58. Hrs open: 24 11 5th Ave. S.E., TIV 1G2. Phone: (403) 652-2472. Fax: (403) 652-7861.E-mail: am1140@am1140radio.com Web Site:www.am1140radio.com Licensee: Golden West Broadcasting Ltd. (group owner). Population served: 50,000 Natl. Rep: Canadian Broadcast Sales,. Format: C&W, relg. News staff: 2; News: 10 hrs wkly. Target aud: General. Spec prog: Farm 5 hrs hrs wkly. ♦Elmer Hildebrand, CEO; Lyndon Friesen, sr VP; Keith Leask, stn mgr, gen sls mgr, prom dir, progmg dir; Menno Friesen, sls VP; Don McCracken, news dir; Vern Moores, chief of engrg.

CKUV-FM—(High River-Okotoks, 2003: 100.9 mhz; 100 kw. Hrs open: 11 5th Ave, S.E., T1V 1G2. Phone: (403) 652-2472. Fax: (403) 652-7861. Licensee: Golden West Broadcasting Ltd.

High River-Okotoks

CFXO-FM— Oct 30, 2007: 99.7 mhz; 18 kw. TL: N50 40 01 W113 58 27. Hrs open: 11 5th Ave. S.E., High River, T1V 1G2. Phone: (403) 652-2472. Fax: (403) 652-7861.E-mail: info@sun99radio.com Web Site:sun99radio.com Licensee: Golden West Broadcasting Ltd. Format: Country. ♦Jeff Young, stn mgr.

CKUV-FM—Licensed to High River-Okotoks. See High River

Hinton

CFXH-FM— July 2004: 97.5 mhz; 1.2 kw. Hrs open: P.O. Box 7800, Edson, T7E 1V8. Phone: (780) 723-4461. Fax: (780) 723-3765. Web Site:www.thefoxradio.ca Licensee: Newcap Inc. Format: Classic hits. Target aud: 18-54. ♦Dave Schuck, gen mgr; Rob Alexander, progmg dir; Steve Bethge, news dir.

Lacombe

CJUV-FM— June 28, 2006: 94.1 mhz; 27 kw. Hrs open: 4725 49B Ave, T4L 1K1. Phone: (403) 786-0194. Fax: (403) 786-0199.E-mail: sonia@laradiogroup.com Web Site:www.sunny94.com Licensee: L.A. Radio Group Inc. Population served: 216,000 Format: Classic Hits. Target aud: 35-54. ♦Troy Stevens, pres; Sonia Sawyer, gen sls mgr, opns.

Lethbridge

CFRV-FM— 1979: 107.7 mhz; 100 kw. 600 ft TL: N49 42 23 W112 43 11. Stereo. Hrs open: 24 1015 3rd Ave S., T1J 0J3. Phone: (403) 328-1077. Fax: (403) 380-1539.E-mail: info@1077theriver.ca Web Site:www.1077theriver.ca Licensee: Rogers Broadcasting Ltd. (group owner) Population served: 200,000 Format: Adult contemp, classic rock, CHR. News staff: one; News: 2 hrs wkly. Target aud: 18-49; males. ♦Terry Voth, gen mgr; Tanya Wolford, prom dir; Robin Haggar, progmg dir; Erin Lucas, mus dir.

CHLB-FM— 1997: 95.5 mhz; 100 kw. Stereo. Hrs open: 24 401 Mayor Magrath Dr. S., T1J 3L8. Phone: (403) 329-0955. Fax: (403) 329-0195.E-mail: rbye@country95.fm Web Site:www.country95.fm Licensee: Jim Pattison Broadcast Group Ltd. (the general partner) and Jim Pattison Industries Ltd. (the limited partner) carrying on business as Jim Pattison Broadcast Group L.P. Group owner: The Jim Pattison Broadcast Group (acq 12-21-2000; grpsl). Format: Country. News staff: 5. Target aud: 25-54.

CJOC-FM— June 2007: 94.1 mhz; 100 kw. Ant 433 ft TL: N49 43 59 W112 57 36. Hrs open: 220 Third Ave. S., Suite 400, T1J 0G9. Phone: (403) 388-2910. Fax: (866) 841-7971.E-mail: info@loungeradio.ca Web Site:www.loungeradio.ca Licensee: Clear Sky Radio Inc. Format: Adult standards. ♦Paul Larsen, pres & gen mgr.

CJRX-FM— Nov 3, 2000: 106.7 mhz; 100 kw. 600 ft. TL: N49 42 23 W112 43 11. Stereo. Hrs open: 1015 3rd Ave S., T1K 0J3. Phone: (403) 320-1220. Fax: (403) 380-1539.E-mail: info@rock106.ca Web Site:www.rock106.ca Licensee: Rogers Broadcasting Ltd. (group owner) Population served: 200,000 Format: Rock. News staff: one; News: 2 hrs wkly. Target aud: 25-44; female. ♦Terry Voth, gen mgr & progmg dir; Scott McGregor, mus dir.

CKVN-FM— 2001: 98.1 mhz; 20 kw. Hrs open: 24 1277 3rd Ave. S., T1J 0K3. Phone: (403) 327-0981. Fax: (403) 328-0095. Web Site:ckvnradio.com Licensee: Golden West Broadcasting Ltd. (acq 8-2-2006). Natl. Rep: Canadian Broadcast Sales,. Format: Contemp Christian. News staff: 2; News: 6 hrs wkly. ♦Keith Leask, gen mgr.

CKXU-FM— Apr 8, 2004: 88.3 mhz; 125 w. Stereo. Hrs open: 24 SU 164, 4401 University Dr. W., T1K 3M4. Phone: (403) 329-2180. Fax: (403) 329-2224.E-mail: manager@ckxu.com Web Site:www.ckxu.com Licensee: CKXU Radio Society. Population served: 75,000 Format: Var, Fr. ♦Nicholas Baingo, stn mgr; Alan Gillespie, progmg dir; John Pantherbone, mus dir.

Lloydminster

CKLM-FM— May 18, 2001: 106.1 mhz; 100 kw. Stereo. Hrs open: 24 Box 21 Atrium Ctr., T9V 0K2. Secondary address: 5012 49th St. T9V 0K2. Phone: (780) 875-5400. Fax: (780) 875-4628.E-mail: admin@boarderrock.com Web Site:www.borderrock.com Licensee: Vista Radio Ltd. (acq 11-21-2008; C$7.3 million with CFNA-FM Bonnyville). Population served: 125,000 Format: Rock/AOR. News staff: 3. Target aud: 12-54; male. ♦Anita B. Dent, VP; Doug Zackodnik, gen sls mgr; James Gushnowski, progmg dir.

CKSA-FM— Aug 29, 2003: 95.9 mhz; 100 kw. Hrs open: 5026 50th St., T9V 1P3. Phone: (780) 875-3321. Fax: (780) 875-4704.E-mail: blabrie@newcap.ca Licensee: NewCap Inc. Group owner: Midwest Broadcasting. (acq 12-22-2004; C$6,246,000 with CILR-FM Lloydminster). Format: Country's best mix. ♦Mike Keller, gen mgr; Brian Labrie, stn mgr.

Medicine Hat

CFMY-FM— Feb 1, 1999: 96.1 mhz; 100 kw. Hrs open: Division of the Jim Pattison Broadcast Group, Box 1270, T1A 7H5. Secondary address: Division to the Jim Pattison Broadcast Group, 10 Boundary Rd. S.E. T0J 2P0. Phone: (403) 548-8282. Fax: (403) 548-8270.E-mail: myfm@jpbg.com Web Site:www.my96fm.com Licensee: Jim Pattison Broadcast Group Ltd. (the general partner) and Jim Pattison Industries Ltd. (the limited partner) carrying on business as Jim Pattison Broadcast Group L.P. Group owner: The Jim Pattison Broadcast Group (acq 12-21-2000; grpsl). Format: Adult contemp. ♦Rick Arnish, pres; Dwaine Dietrich, gen mgr; Ed Lundberg, gen sls mgr; Michael Thibbau, progmg dir; Adrian Bateman, news dir; Carey Downs, chief of engrg.

CHAT-FM— Jan 9, 2006: 94.5 mhz; 100 kw. Hrs open: 24 Division of the Jim Pattison Broadcast Group, Box 1270, T1A 7H5. Secondary address: Division of the Jim Pattison Broadcast Group, 10 Boundary Rd. S.E. T0J 2P0. Phone: (403) 548-8282. Fax: (403) 548-8270.E-mail: info@chat945.com Web Site:www.chat945.com Licensee: Jim Pattison Broadcast Group Ltd. (the general partner) and Jim Pattison Industries Ltd. (the limited partner) carrying on business as Jim Pattison Broadcast Group Ltd. Natl. Rep: Canadian Broadcast Sales,. Format: Country. News staff: 4; News: 14 hrs wkly. Target aud: General. ♦Rick Arnish, pres; Dwaine Dietrich, gen mgr. Co-owned TV: CHAT-TV affil

CJCY-FM— May 23, 2008: 102.1 mhz; 100 kw. Ant 686 ft TL: N50 02 46 W110 37 08. Hrs open: 1865 Dunmore Rd. S.E., Suite 104, T1A 1Z8. Phone: (403) 528-2827. Fax: (403) 488-4678.E-mail: info@clearskyradio.com Web Site:cjcy.loungeradio.ca Licensee: Clear Sky Radio Inc. Format: Adult contemp. ♦Jason Todd, gen sls mgr, mktg mgr; Joe McFarland, news dir.

CJLT-FM— April 2003: 93.7 mhz; 2.3 kw. TL: N50 02 46 W110 37 11. Hrs open: 1201 Kingsway Ave. S.E., Suite 101, T1A 2Y2. Phone: (403) 529-9599. Fax: (403) 529-9282.E-mail: rachel@power937.com Web Site:www.power937.com Licensee: Lighthouse Broadcasting Ltd. Format: Christian adult contemp, CHR. ◆Pat Lough, pres; Darcee Grange, mus dir; John Enns, sls.

CKMH-FM— Feb 25, 2008: 105.3 mhz; 77.9 kw. TL: N50 02 46 W110 37 11. Hrs open: 1741 Dunmore Rd. S.E., Suite 206, T1A 1Z8. Phone: (403) 548-7581. Web Site:www.rock1053.ca Licensee: Rogers Broadcasting Ltd. Format: Rock. Target aud: 25-54. ◆Tony Marsh, gen mgr.

Okotoks

CFXO-FM—See High River-Okotoks

CKUV-FM—See High River

Olds

CKJX-FM— June 2, 2008: 104.5 mhz; 12 kw. TL: N51 45 30 W114 05 39. Hrs open: 4526 49 Ave.#6, T4H 1A4. Phone: (403) 556-2628. Phone: (403) 556-2206. Fax: (403) 556-2637.E-mail: info@rock104.ca Web Site:www.rock104.ca Licensee: CAB-K Broadcasting Ltd. Format: Classic rock. ◆Brian Hepp, gen mgr.

CKLJ-FM— Feb 2, 2004: 96.5 mhz; 35 kw. Hrs open: #6, 4526 49th Ave., T4H 1A4. Phone: (403) 556-2628. Fax: (403) 556-2637.E-mail: cklj@telus.net Licensee: CAB-K Broadcasting Ltd. Format: Country. ◆Brian Hepp, gen mgr.

Peace River

CKKX-FM— July 1997: 106.1 mhz; 990 w. Hrs open: Bag Service No. 300, T8S 1T5. Secondary address: 9807 100th Ave T8S 1T5. Phone: (780) 624-2535. Fax: (780) 624-5424.E-mail: reception@ylcountry.com Web Site:www.kix106.net Licensee: Peace River Broadcasting, LTD. Format: Hot adult contemp. ◆Cynthia Babiy, VP; Terry Babiy, pres & gen mgr.

CKYL(AM)— Nov 1, 1954: 610 khz; 10 kw-U, DA-2. Hrs open: Bag Service No. 300, T8S 1T5. Phone: (780) 624-2535. Fax: (780) 624-5424. Web Site:www.ylcountry.com Licensee: Peace River Broadcasting Ltd. (acq 12-15-95). Natl. Rep: Target Broadcast Sales,. Format: Country. ◆Terry Babiy, gen mgr.

Red Deer

CFDV-FM— Nov 8, 2004: 106.7 mhz; 100 kw. Hrs open: 2840 Bremner Ave., T4R 1M9. Phone: (403) 343-7105. Fax: (403) 343-2573.E-mail: onair@1067thedrive.fm Web Site:www.1067thedrive.fm Licensee: Jim Pattison Broadcast Group Ltd. (the general partner) and Jim Pattison Industries Ltd. (the limited partner) carrying on business as Jim Pattison Broadcast Group L.P. Population served: 250,000 Natl. Rep: Target Broadcast Sales,. Rgnl rep: WTR Media sales Wire Svc: BN Wire Format: Classic rock. News staff: 0. Target aud: 25-54; adults, primary demo-males. ◆Jim Pattison, CEO; Rick Arnish, pres; Paul Mason, gen mgr; Bryn James, gen sls mgr; Jim Hall, progmg dir.

CHUB-FM— 1949: 105.5 mhz; 100 kw. Hrs open: 24 2840 Bremner Ave., T4R 1M9. Phone: (403) 343-7105. Fax: (403) 343-2573. Licensee: Jim Pattison Broadcast Group Ltd. (the general partner) and Jim Pattison Industries Ltd. (the limited partner) carrying on business as Jim Pattison Broadcast Group L.P. Group owner: The Jim Pattison Broadcast Group (acq 12-21-2000; grpsl). Population served: 250,000 Natl. Rep: Target Broadcast Sales,. Rgnl rep: WTR Media Sales Wire Svc: BN Wire Format: Hot adult contemp. News staff: 0. Target aud: Adults 25-49; primary demo-females. ◆Jim Pattison, CEO; Rick Arnish, pres; Paul Mason, gen mgr; Bryn James, gen sls mgr; Jim Hall, progmg dir.

CIZZ-FM— Nov 1, 1987: 98.9 mhz; 100 kw. Ant 800 ft Stereo. Hrs open: 24 Box 5339, T4N 6W1. Secondary address: 4920 59th St. T4N 2N1. Phone: (403) 343-1303. Fax: (403) 346-1230.E-mail: zedfm@cnewcap.ca Web Site:www.zedfm.com Licensee: Newcap Inc. Group owner: Corus Entertainment Inc. (acq 8-10-2005; C$8,392,714 with CKGY-FM Red Deer). Population served: 110,000 Wire Svc: BN Wire Format: Adult contemp, CHR. News staff: 6. Target aud: 18-49; male 55%, female 45%. ◆R.C. (Ron) Thompson, gen mgr, stn mgr, gen sls mgr; Sue Stevenson, news dir; Brent Young, progmg.

CKGY-FM— April 2001: 95.5 mhz; 100 kw. Ant 800 ft. Stereo. Hrs open: 24 Bag 5339, T4N 6W1. Secondary address: 4920 59th St. T4N 2N1. Phone: (403) 348-0955. Fax: (403) 346-1230.E-mail: kgcountry@newcap.ca Web Site:www.ckgy.com Licensee: Newcap Inc. Group owner: Corus Entertainment Inc. (acq 8-10-2005; C$8,392,714 with CIZZ-FM Red Deer). Population served: 120,000 Natl. Rep: Canadian Broadcast Sales,. Wire Svc: BN Wire Format: Today's hottest country. News staff: 6. Target aud: 25-54; 50% male, 50% female. ◆R.C. (Ron) Thompson, gen mgr & gen sls mgr.

CKIK-FM— 2009: 101.3 mhz; 26 kw. TL: N52 18 43 W113 57 32. Hrs open: 6751 52 Ave. #103, T4N 4K8. Phone: (403) 358-3100. Fax: (403) 309-8311.E-mail: danielle@kraze1013.com Web Site:www.kraze1013.com Licensee: L.A. Radio Group Inc. Format: New hit music. Target aud: 18-44. ◆Troy Stevens, gen mgr; Sonia Sawyer, opns mgr; Dennis Allan, progmg mgr; Mark Crichton, chief of engrg.

Rocky Mountain House

CHBW-FM— 1997: 94.5 mhz; 720 w. Hrs open: 4814B 49th St., T4T 1S8. Phone: (403) 844-9450. Fax: (403) 844-4770.E-mail: bigshow@telus.net Licensee: Jim Pattison Broadcast Group Ltd. (the general partner) and Jim Pattison Industries Ltd. (the limited partner) carrying on business as Jim Pattison Broadcast Group L.P. Group owner: The Jim Pattison Broadcast Group. Format: Country. ◆Paul Mason, gen mgr; Barry Simon, stn mgr.

Saint Albert

CFMG-FM— Aug 29, 1994: 104.9 mhz; 100 kw. Hrs open: 24 18520 Stony Plain Rd., Suite 100, Edmonton, T5S 2E2. Phone: (780) 486-2800. Fax: (780) 489-6927.E-mail: cfmg@radio.astral.com Web Site:www.ezrock1049.com Licensee: Astral Media Radio G.P. Group owner: Standard Broadcasting Corp. (acq 10-29-2007; grpsl). Population served: 870,000 Format: Adult contemp. News staff: 2; News: 4 hrs wkly. Target aud: 25-54; middle to upper income families. ◆Stewart Meyers, VP, gen sls mgr; Stewart Myers, gen mgr; Susan Reade, gen sls mgr; Karen Paulguaard, prom dir; Rob Vavrek, progmg dir; Bob Hunter, engrg dir, chief of engrg.

Saint Paul

CHLW(AM)— 1975: 1310 khz; 10 kw-U, DA-2. Hrs open: 24 201-4341 50th Ave., St. Paul, T0A 3A3. Phone: (780) 645-4425. Fax: (780) 645-2383.E-mail: dwhite@newcap.ca Web Site:www.1310chlw.com Licensee: Newcap Inc. Group owner: NewCap Broadcasting Ltd. (acq 4-19-2002; grpsl). Population served: 50,000 Format: New country. News staff: one; News: 4 hrs wkly. Target aud: 25-54. Spec prog: Farm 5 hrs, relg 5 hrs wkly. ◆Mike Keller, gen mgr; Danny White, stn mgr; Jeff Murray, progmg dir.

Siksika

CHDH-FM— 2002: 97.7 mhz; 50 w. Hrs open: Box 1490, T0J 3W0. Phone: (403) 734-5339. Fax: (403) 734-5497.E-mail: siksikamedia @siksikanation.com Licensee: Siksika Communications Society. Format: News/talk, education, native music. ◆Paul Melting Tallow, gen mgr.

Slave Lake

CHSL-FM— Sept 8, 2006: 92.7 mhz; 5.7 kw. TL: N55 28 18 W114 47 05. Stereo. Hrs open: 221 3rd Ave. N.W., T0G 2A1. Phone: (780) 849-2569. Fax: (780) 849-4833.E-mail: wbetts@newcap.ca Web Site:www.927thefox.ca Licensee: Newcap Inc. Format: Classic hits.

Spruce Grove

CFWE-FM-4—See Edmonton

Stettler

CKSQ(AM)— Dec 15, 1975: 1400 khz; 1 kw-U, DA-2. Hrs open: 24 Box 2050, 4812A - 50 th Street, T0C 2L0. Phone: (403) 742-1400. Fax: (403) 742-0660.E-mail: cksq@newcap.ca. Licensee: Newcap Inc. Group owner: NewCap Broadcasting Ltd. (acq 4-19-2002; grpsl). Population served: 10,000 Format: Country. News staff: one; News: 7 hrs wkly. Target aud: 25-54; 55% female, 45% male. ◆Vicki Leuck, gen mgr, stn mgr & gen sls mgr; Brent Young, progmg dir; Tim Day, news dir; Cliff Wheeler, chief of engrg.

Taber

CJBZ-FM— 2000: 93.3 mhz; 50 kw. Hrs open: 401 Mayor Magrath Dr., Lethbridge, T1J 3L8. Phone: (403) 394-9300. Fax: (403) 329-0195.E-mail: info@b93.fm Web Site:www.b93.fm Licensee: Jim Pattison Broadcast Group Ltd. (the general partner) and Jim Pattison Industries Ltd. (the limited partner) carrying on business as Jim Pattison Broadcast Group L.P. Group owner: The Jim Pattison Broadcast Group (acq 12-21-2000; grpsl). Format: CHR/adult contemp. News staff: 4. Target aud: 18-44; adults. ◆Rick Arnish, pres; Rod Schween, gen sls mgr; Jarod Neithercut, prom dir; Reid Morgan, progmg dir; Dori Modney, news dir.

Wainwright

CKKY(AM)— February 1984: 830 khz; 10 kw-D, 3.5 kw-N. Hrs open: 24 1037 2nd Ave., 2nd fl, T9W 1K7. Phone: (780) 842-4311. Fax: (780) 842-4636.E-mail: ckky@ab.ncc.ca Licensee: Newcap Inc. Group owner: NewCap Broadcasting Ltd. (acq 5-20-2002; grpsl). Population served: 100,000 Format: C&W. News staff: 2; News: 14 hrs wkly. Target aud: 20-45; agriculture-related working class. Spec prog: Farm 10 hrs wkly. ◆Ron Prochner, gen mgr & progmg dir.

CKWY-FM— 2005: 93.7 mhz; 100 kw. Hrs open: 1037 2nd Ave., 2nd Fl., Wainright, T9W 1K7. Phone: (780) 842-4311. Fax: (780) 842-4636. Web Site:wayneradio.com Licensee: Newcap Inc. Format: Adult contemp. ◆Paul O'Neil, progmg dir.

Westlock

CFOK(AM)— Aug 19, 1975: 1370 khz; 10 kw-U, DA-2. Hrs open: 24 10030-106 St., Suite 17, T7P 2K4. Phone: (780) 349-4421. Fax: (780) 349-6259.E-mail: wbetts@newcap.ca Web Site:www.1370thefox.ca Licensee: Newcap Inc. Group owner: NewCap Broadcasting Ltd. (acq 4-19-2002; grpsl). Population served: 35,000 Natl. Rep: Canadian Broadcast Sales,. Format: The Fox. News staff: one; News: 15 hrs wkly. Target aud: 25-54. ◆Dave Schuck, gen mgr; Rob Alexander, stn mgr, progmg dir; Wray Betts, stn mgr & opns VP; Steve Bethge, news dir.

Wetaskiwin

CIHS-FM— December 2000: 93.5 mhz; 5.12 kw. Ant 365 ft Hrs open: 24 5222 50th Ave., T9A 0S8. Phone: (780) 361-0245. Fax: (866) 409-2797.E-mail: mail@cihsfm.net Web Site:www.cihsfm.net Licensee: 902890 Alberta Ltd. Format: Classic country, country gospel & world music. Target aud: 0-100. ◆Dave Dhillon, CEO, chmn, pres, gen mgr; Paula Osha, stn mgr.

CKJR(AM)— 1971: 1440 khz; 10 kw-U, DA-2. Hrs open: 5214 A-50th Ave., T9A-0S8. Phone: (780) 352-0144. Fax: (780) 352-0606. Web Site:www.1440.com Licensee: Newcap Inc. Group owner: NewCap Broadcasting Ltd. (acq 4-19-2002; grpsl). Format: Hot new country. Spec prog: Greek 2 hrs wkly. ◆David Gilmore, gen sls mgr; Nick Addams, progmg dir.

Whitecourt

CFXW-FM— July 1, 2005: 96.7 mhz; 9 kw. Hrs open: Box 2288, T7S 1A2. Secondary address: 5118 50th St. T7S 1A1. Phone: (780) 778-5101. Fax: (780) 778-5137.E-mail: info@therig.ca Web Site:www.therig.ca Licensee: Newcap Inc. Format: Classic rock. ◆Dave Schuck, gen mgr; Randy Turner, gen sls mgr; Rob Alexander, progmg dir; Jeremy Lye, news dir.

CIXM-FM— 2006: 105.3 mhz; 42.3 kw. Hrs open: Box 1050, T7S 1N9. Secondary address: 4912A 50th Ave. T7S 1N9. Phone: (780) 706-1053. Fax: (780) 706-1017. Web Site:www.xm105.com Licensee: 1097282 Alberta Ltd. (acq 5-11-2006). Natl. Rep: Target Broadcast Sales,. Format: Country. ◆Gene Fabro, pres; Neil Shewchuk, stn mgr, gen sls mgr; Ken Singer, opns VP, natl sls mgr; Sarah Ryan, prom dir; Andrew Joseph, progmg dir; Bayne Opseth, chief of engrg.

British Columbia

100 Mile House

CKBX(AM)— July 30, 1971: 840 khz; 1 kw-D, 250 w-N, DA-1. Hrs open: Box 939, V0K 2E0. Phone: (250) 395-3848. Fax: (250) 395-4147.E-mail: spence@ckbx.ca Web Site:www.thewolfpack.ca Licensee:

Vista Radio Ltd. Group owner: Cariboo Central Interior Radio Inc. (acq 1981). Format: Modern country, southern rock. Spec prog: Class one hr wkly. ◆Paul Mann, gen mgr; Tracey Gard, stn mgr.

Abbotsford

CIVL-FM— September 2007: Stn currently dark. 88.5 mhz; 92 w. Stereo. Hrs open: 24 33844 King Rd., V2S 7M8. Phone: (604) 851-6306.E-mail: Bob@civl.ca Web Site:www.civl.ca Licensee: UCFV Campus and Community Radio Society. Format: Var. Target aud: 18 plus; campus & community radio. ◆Bob Simpson, stn mgr; Swinder Singh, progmg mgr.

CKQC-FM— September 2001: 107.1 mhz; 215 w. Stereo. Hrs open: #520-45715 Hocking Ave., Chilliwack, V2P 6Z6. Phone: (604) 859-5277. Fax: (604) 702-3212.E-mail: A carrie.crooks@rsi.rogers.com Licensee: Rogers Radio (British Columbia) Ltd. Group owner: Rogers Broadcasting Ltd. Format: Country. ◆Ken Geiger, gen mgr; Janis Correia, gen sls mgr; Murray Olfert, prom dir.

Boston Bar

CKGO-FM-1— July 4, 1980: 106.1 mhz; 91 w. -2,871 ft Hrs open: #520-45715 Hocking Ave., Chilliwack, V2P 6Z6. Phone: (604) 795-5711. Fax: (604) 702-3212. Web Site:www.starfm.ca Licensee: Rogers Broadcasting Ltd. (group owner; acq 9-10-99; grpsl). Format: Hot adult contemp. News staff: 3. ◆Ken Geiger, gen mgr, stn mgr, progmg dir; Janis Correia, gen sls mgr; Murray Olfert, prom mgr.

Burnaby

CFML-FM— 2006: 107.9 mhz; 12 w. Hrs open: Bldg. SE 10, 3700 Willingdon Ave., V5G 3H2. Phone: (604) 432-8934. Phone: (604) 432-8545(sales). Fax: (604) 432-1792.E-mail: allofus@evolution1079.com Web Site:www.evolution1079.com Licensee: B.C.I.T. Radio Society. Format: AAA, news, feature programs. ◆Brian Antonson, pres & gen mgr.

*CJSF-FM— Feb 6, 2003: 90.1 mhz; 450 w. Hrs open: 7 AM-2AM CJSF Radio, TC 216, Simon Fraser University, V5A 1S6. Phone: (604) 291-3727. Fax: (604) 291-3695. Web Site:www.cjsf.ca Licensee: Simon Fraser Campus Radio Society. Population served: 1,500,000 Format: Diversified. Spec prog: Persian 2 hrs, Portugese 2 hrs, Sp 4 hrs wkly. ◆Magnus Thyvold, stn mgr; Charlotte Bourne, progmg dir; Ed Blake, mus dir; Frieda Werden, pub affrs dir.

Burns Lake

CFLD(AM)— November 1965: 760 khz; 1 kw-U. Hrs open: Box 355, Smithers, V0J 2N0. Phone: (250) 692-3414. Fax: (250) 847-9411.E-mail: thepeak@bulkley.net Licensee: Vista Radio Ltd. (group owner) Format: Adult contemp. ◆J.C. Brown, gen mgr.

Campbell River

CIQC-FM— 2008: 99.7 mhz; 6 kw. TL: N50 03 15 W125 19 30. Hrs open: 470 13th Ave., V9W 7J4. Phone: (250) 287-7106. Fax: (250) 287-7170. Web Site:www.997fm.ca Licensee: Vista Radio Ltd. Natl. Rep: Target Broadcast Sales,. Format: Adult contemp. ◆Raymond Henderson, gen mgr.

Castlegar

CKQR-FM— 1998: 99.3 mhz; 333 w. TL: N 49 18 54 W117 37 27. Hrs open: 24 1101 A 4th St., V1N 2A8. Phone: (250) 365-7600. Fax: (250) 365-8480.E-mail: rudy@mountainfm.net Web Site:www.mountainfm.com Licensee: Vista Radio Ltd. Natl. Rep: Canadian Broadcast Sales,. Format: Classic rock. News staff: one; News: 6 hrs wkly. Target aud: 18-49; median target demo. ◆Rudy Parachoniak, gen mgr & progmg dir.

Chase

CFCH-FM— Jan 10,2005: 103.5 mhz; 4.7 w. Hrs open: 8am - 8pm Box 1197, V0E 1M0. Phone: (250) 679-8622. Fax: (250) 679-3231.E-mail: cfchradio@cablelan.net Web Site:www.cablelan.net/ronfair/CFCH.html Licensee: Chase and District Community Radio Society (acq 5-10-2007). Format: Community radio. ◆Ron Fairhurst, gen mgr.

Chetwynd

CHET-FM— 1997: 94.5 mhz; 25 w. Hrs open: 4612 N. Access Rd., V0C 1J0. Phone: (250) 788-9452. Fax: (250) 788-9402.E-mail: info@peacefm.ca Web Site:www.peacefm.ca Licensee: Chetwynd Communications Society. Format: Hits of the 80s thru today, MOR, div. ◆Leo Sabulsky, gen mgr.

Chilliwack

CHWK-FM— Feb 20, 2009: 89.5 mhz; 380 w. Ant 619 ft TL: N49 06 35 W121 50 52. Hrs open: Box 589, V2P 7V5. Phone: (604) 795-2429. Fax: (604) 795-9472.E-mail: info@895thehawk.com Web Site:www.895thehawk.com Licensee: Radio CJVR Ltd. Natl. Rep: Target Broadcast Sales,. Format: Diversified rock. Target aud: 25-54. ◆Kevin Gemmell, gen mgr & gen sls mgr.

CKCL-FM— Sept 29, 1986: 107.5 mhz; 303 w. TL: N49 06 35 W121 50 52. Stereo. Hrs open: 24 2440 Ash St., Vancouver, V5Z 4J6. Phone: (604) 877-6357. Fax: (604) 877-4443. Web Site:1049greatesthits.com Licensee: Rogers Radio (British Columbia) Ltd. Group owner: Rogers Broadcasting Ltd. (acq 9-10-99; grpsl). Format: Oldies. News: 6 hrs wkly. Target aud: 35 plus. ◆Paul Fisher, VP; David Larsen, progmg dir.

CKSR-FM— Aug 31, 2001: 98.3 mhz; 2.34 kw. Stereo. Hrs open: 24 45715 Hocking Ave., Suite 520, V2P 6Z6. Phone: (604) 795-5711. Web Site:www.starfm.ca Licensee: Rogers Radio (British Columbia) Ltd. Group owner: Rogers Broadcasting Ltd. Natl. Rep: Canadian Broadcast Sales,. Format: Light rock. News staff: 3. Target aud: 25-54; general. Spec prog: Farm 2 hrs wkly. ◆Ken Geiger, gen mgr.

Courtenay

CFCP-FM— 1959: 98.9 mhz; 2.685 kw. Stereo. Hrs open: 24 1625-A McPhee Ave., V9N 3A6. Phone: (250) 334-2421. Fax: (250) 334-1977. Web Site:www.jetfm.ca Licensee: CFCP Radio Ltd. Wire Svc: BN Wire Format: Classic rock, classic hits. News staff: 4; News: 16 hrs wkly. Target aud: 25-54; women. ◆Raymond Henderson, pres & gen sls mgr.

CKLR-FM— 1998: 97.3 mhz; 4.7 kw. Stereo. Hrs open: 24 801B 29th St., V9N 7Z5. Phone: (250) 703-2200. Fax: (250) 703-9611.E-mail: info@973theeagle.com Web Site:www.islandradio.bc.ca Licensee: Jim Pattison Broadcast Group Ltd. (the general partner) and Jim Pattison Industries Ltd. (the limited partner), carrying on business as Jim Pattison Broadcast Group L.P. (acq 6-27-2006; grpsl). Population served: 90,000 Natl. Rep: Canadian Broadcast Sales,. Format: Classic hits. News staff: 2. Target aud: 25-54; adult. ◆Richard Skinner, opns mgr, rgnl sls mgr; Ryan Mennie, mktg dir; Robyn Nicholson, prom dir, prom mgr; Steve Power, progmg dir; Bill Nation, news dir; Pam Doherty, traf mgr.

Cranbrook

CHBZ-FM— Oct 1, 1995: 104.7 mhz; 1.26 kw. Hrs open: 24 19 9th Ave. S. , V1C 2L9. Phone: (250) 426-2224. Fax: (250) 426-5520.E-mail: info@b104.ca Web Site:www.b104.ca Licensee: Jim Pattison Broadcast Group Ltd. (the general partner) and Jim Pattison Industries Ltd. (the limited partner) carrying on business as Jim Pattison Broadcast Group L.P. Group owner: The Jim Pattison Broadcast Group (acq 2-1-2001; grpsl). Population served: 65,000 Natl. Rep: Target Broadcast Sales,. Format: Country. News staff: 3. Target aud: 18-54. ◆Rick Arnish, pres; Rod Schween, gen mgr; Bruce Davis, sls VP; Derek Kortschaga, progmg dir.

CHDR-FM— 2002: 102.9 mhz; 1.6 kw. Hrs open: 24 19 9th Ave. S., V1C 2L9. Phone: (250) 426-2224. Fax: (250) 426-5520.E-mail: info@thedrivefm.ca Web Site:www.thedrivefm.ca Licensee: Jim Pattison Broadcast Group Ltd. (the general partner) and Jim Pattison Industries Ltd. (the limited partner) carrying on business as Jim Pattison Broadcast Group L.P. Group owner: The Jim Pattison Broadcast Group. Natl. Rep: Target Broadcast Sales,. Format: Adult rock. News staff: 3. Target aud: 25-54. ◆Rick Arnish, pres; Rod Schween, gen mgr; Bruce Davis, sls VP; Dave Walker, gen sls mgr; Derek Kortschaga, progmg dir.

Crawford Bay

CBTE-FM— 1988: 89.9 mhz; 135 kw. TL: N49 38 54 W116 50 53. Hrs open:
Rebroadcasts CBTK-FM Kelowna 100%.
c/o CBTK-FM, 243 Lawrence Ave., Kelowna, V1Y 6L2. Phone: (250) 861-3781. Fax: (250) 861-6644.E-mail: kelowna@cbc.ca Web

Site:www.vancouver.cbc.ca/daybreaksouth Licensee: Canadian Broadcasting Corp. Format: News, pub affrs, entertainment. ◆Charlie Cheffins, opns mgr.

Creston

CFKC(AM)— Sept 21, 1968: 1340 khz; 250 w-U, DA-1. Hrs open: 24 1560 2nd Ave., Trail, V1R 1M4. Secondary address: 138-10 Ave. N. V0B 1G0. Phone: (250) 368-5510. Fax: (250) 368-8471.E-mail: kbs@radio.astral.com Licensee: Astral Media Radio G.P. Group owner: Standard Broadcasting Corp. (acq 10-29-2007; grpsl). Population served: 11,400 Format: Adult Contemporary. ◆Lea Wilman, progmg dir; David Ford, engr.

CIDO-FM—Not on air, target date: unknown: 97.7 mhz; 20 w. Ant 1,092 ft TL: N49 05 25 W116 22 45. Hrs open: Box 8, V0B 1G0. Phone: (250) 402-6772.E-mail: info@crestonradio.ca Web Site:www.crestonradio.ca Licensee: Creston Community Radio Society. Format: Var. ◆Bernie LeFrancois, pres.

Dawson Creek

CHAD-FM— 2003: 104.1 mhz; 50 w. Hrs open:
Rebroadcasts CHET-FM Chetwynd 100%.
c/o CHET-FM, Box 214, Chetwynd, V0C 1J0. Phone: (250) 784-1880. Fax: (250) 782-7566.E-mail: info@chetchad.com Web Site:www.chetchad.com Licensee: Chetwynd Communications Society. Format: MOR, div, oldies. ◆Leo Sabulsky, gen mgr; Mike Sabulsky, chief of engrg.

CJDC(AM)— Dec 15, 1947: 890 khz; 10 kw-U. Hrs open: 24 901-102 Ave., V1G 2B6. Phone: (250) 782-3341. Fax: (250) 782-3154. Licensee: Astral Media Radio G.P. Group owner: Standard Broadcasting Corp. (acq 10-29-2007; grpsl). Population served: 56,000 Format: Country. News staff: 3. Target aud: General. ◆Terry Shepherd, gen mgr; J. Terrence, opns mgr, chief of engrg.

Duncan

CJSU-FM— August 2000: 89.7 mhz; 1.862 kw. Hrs open: 24 130 Trans Canada Highway, V9L 3P7. Phone: (250) 746-0897. Fax: (250) 748-1517. Web Site:www.897sunfm.ca Licensee: Vista Radio Ltd. Natl. Rep: Target Broadcast Sales, Canadian Broadcast Sales,. Format: Adult contemp. News staff: 2; News: 12 hrs wkly. Target aud: 35-54. Spec prog: Oldies 8 hrs wkly. ◆Keith James, gen mgr; Jim Jackson, progmg dir; Andy Beeley, mus dir; Ric Rathburn, news dir; Julie Winter, traf mgr.

Egmont

CIEG-FM— July 1985: 107.5 mhz; 50 w. 300 ft Hrs open: 24
Rebroadcasts CISQ-FM Squamish 100%.
Box 1068, Squamish, V0N 3G0. Phone: (604) 892-1021. Fax: (604) 892-6383.E-mail: mountainfm@mountainfm.com Web Site:www.mountainfm.com Licensee: Rogers Broadcasting. Natl. Rep: Canadian Broadcast Sales,. Format: Adult contemp. News staff: 3; News: 16 hrs wkly. Target aud: 25-44. ◆Gary Miles, pres; Paul Fisher, VP; Ken Geiger, gen mgr; Janis Correia, gen sls mgr, prom dir.

Fernie

CJDR-FM— Aug 30, 2002: 99.1 mhz; 470 w. Hrs open: 24
Rebroadcasts CHOR-FM Cranbrook 66%.
19 9th Ave. S., Cranbrook, V1C 2L9. Phone: (250) 426-2224. Fax: (250) 426-5520.E-mail: info@thedrivefm.ca Web Site:www.thedrivefm.ca Licensee: Jim Pattison Broadcast Group Ltd. (the general partner) and Jim Pattison Industries Ltd. (the limited partner) carrying on business as Jim Pattison Broadcast Group L.P. Group owner: The Jim Pattison Broadcast Group. Natl. Rep: Target Broadcast Sales,. Format: Adult rock. News staff: 3. ◆Rick Arnish, pres; Rod Schween, gen mgr; Bruce Davis, sls VP; Dave Walker, gen sls mgr; Derek Korschaga, progmg dir.

Fort Nelson

CKRX-FM— 1998: 102.3 mhz; 1.8 kw. Hrs open: Box 880, V0C 1R0. Secondary address: 5152 Liard St. V0C 1R0. Phone: (250) 774-2525. Fax: (250) 774-2577.E-mail: kjohnson@sri.ca Licensee: Astral Media Radio G.P. Group owner: Standard Broadcasting Corp. (acq 10-29-2007; grpsl). Format: CHR. ◆Terry Shepard, gen mgr; Kevin Larkin, progmg dir, progmg mgr.

Fort St. John

CHRX-FM—Not on air, target date: unknown: 98.5 mhz; 50 kw. Hrs open: 10532 Alaska Rd., V1J 1B3. Phone: (250) 785-6634. Fax: (250) 785-4544. Licensee: Astral Media Radio G.P. Group owner: Standard Broadcasting Corp. (acq 10-29-2007; grpsl). Format: Rock. ◆ Terry Shepard, opns mgr.

CKFU-FM— Sept 1, 2003: 100.1 mhz; Stereo. Hrs open: 24 10423 101st Ave., V1J 2B7. Phone: (250) 787-7100. Fax: (250) 263-9749.E-mail: reception@moosefm.ca Web Site:www.moosefm.ca Licensee: 663975 B.C. Ltd. Population served: 30,000 Natl. Rep: Canadian Broadcast Sales,. Wire Svc: BN Wire Format: Country. News staff: 3; News: 5 hours wkly. Target aud: 24-45; female. ◆ Russ Beerlling, pres; Adam Reaburn, prom mgr, progmg mgr.

CKNL-FM— 2003: 101.5 mhz; 40 kw. Hrs open: 10532 Alaska Rd., V1J 1B3 . Phone: (250) 785-6634. Fax: (250) 785-4544. Licensee: Astral Media Radio G.P. Group owner: Standard Broadcasting Corp. (acq 10-29-2007; grpsl). Format: Classic rock. ◆ Angie Cloury, opns mgr.

Gibsons

CISC-FM— October 1984: 107.5 mhz; 820 w. Ant 1,000 ft Hrs open: 24
Rebroadcasts CISQ-FM Squamish.
Box 1068, Squamish, V0N 3G0. Phone: (604) 892-1021. Fax: (604) 892-6383.E-mail: mountainfm@mountainfm.com Web Site:www.mountainfm.com Licensee: Rogers Broadcasting. Format: Hot adult contemp. News staff: 3; News: 16 hrs wkly. Target aud: 25-44. Spec prog: Magazine show 3 hrs wkly. ◆ Gary Miles, pres; Paul Fisher, VP; Ken Geiger, gen mgr, opns mgr; Janis Correia, opns mgr.

Golden

CKGR(AM)— 1973: 1400 khz; 1 kw-D, DA-1. Hrs open: Box 1403, V0A 1H0. Phone: (250) 832-2161. Phone: (250) 344-7177. Fax: (250) 344-7233.E-mail: info@myezrock.com Web Site:www.myezrock.com Licensee: Astral Media Radio G.P. Group owner: Standard Broadcasting Corp. (acq 10-29-2007; grpsl). Natl. Rep: Target Broadcast Sales,. Format: Easy rock. ◆ Ron Langridge, gen mgr.

Greenwood

CKGF-FM-2— 2003: 96.7 mhz; 40 w horiz. Ant 1,886 ft TL: N49 05 29 W118 36 36. Hrs open: 1101 A 4th St., Castlegar, V1N 2A8. Phone: (250) 365-7600. Fax: (250) 365-8480.E-mail: rudy@mountainfm.net Web Site:www.mountainfm.net Licensee: Boundary Broadcasting Ltd. Format: Classic rock. Target aud: 25-54. ◆ Rudy Parachoniak, gen mgr; Rudy Parachoiak, progmg dir.

Hope

CFSR-FM— 2001: 100.5 mhz; 157 w. Hrs open: 46167 Yale Rd., Suite 309, Chilliwack, V2P 2P2. Phone: (604) 869-9313. Fax: (604) 702-3212.E-mail: A carrie.crooks@rsi.rogers.com Web Site:www.starfm.com Licensee: Rogers Radio (British Columbia) Ltd. Group owner: Rogers Broadcasting Ltd. Format: Adult contemp. ◆ Ken Geiger, gen mgr; Janis Correia, gen sls mgr; Murray Olfert, prom mgr.

Invermere

CKIR(AM)— December 1989: 870 khz; 1 kw-U. Hrs open:
Rebroadcasts CKGR(AM) Golden.
Box 69 Stn Main, Salmon Arm, V1E 4N2. Phone: (250) 832-2161. Fax: (250) 344-7233.E-mail: ckir@rockies.net Web Site:www.myezrock.com Licensee: Astral Media Radio G.P. Group owner: Standard Broadcasting Corp. (acq 10-29-2007; grpsl). Format: Easy rock. ◆ Ron Langridge, gen mgr.

Kamloops

CFBX-FM— Apr 2, 2001: 92.5 mhz; 420 w. Hrs open: 900 McGill Rd., House 8, V2C 5N3. Phone: (250) 377-3988. Fax: (250) 852-6350.E-mail: radio@tru.ca Web Site:www.thex.ca Licensee: The Kamloops Campus/Community Radio Society. Population served: 88,000 Format: Div. ◆Brant Zwicker, stn mgr; Steve Marlow, progmg dir.

CHNL(AM)— May 1, 1970: 610 khz; 25 kw-D, 5 kw-N, DA-N. Hrs open: 24 611 Lansdowne St., V2C 1Y6. Phone: (250) 372-2292. Phone: (250) 372-2197. Fax: (250) 372-2293.E-mail: info@radionl.com

Web Site:www.radionl.com Licensee: NL Broadcasting Ltd. Population served: 160,000 Natl. Rep: CHUM Radio Sales,. CRN Rgnl rep: CHUM Radio Sales Wire Svc: Canadian Press Format: News- Talk-Sports. News staff: 8; News: 15.5 hrs wkly. Target aud: 25-54; family oriented, middle-upper class income. ◆ Robbie Dunn, pres, gen mgr; Jim Reynolds, opns mgr, progmg dir; Peter Angle; gen sls mgr; Crystal Lilly, prom dir; Frieda Whitehall, adv mgr; Paul Graham, mus dir; Jim Harrison, news dir; Dave Coulter, chief of engrg; Shaunda Willis, traf mgr.

CIFM-FM— 1961: 98.3 mhz; 4.3 kw. Stereo. Hrs open: 460 Pemberton Terr., V2C 1T5. Phone: (250) 372-3322. Fax: (250) 374-0445.E-mail: info@98.3cifm.com Web Site:www.98.3cifm.com Licensee: Jim Pattison Broadcast Group Ltd. (the general partner) and Jim Pattison Industries Ltd. (the limited partner) carrying on business as Jim Pattison Broadcast Group L.P. Group owner: The Jim Pattison Broadcast Group (acq 1987). Population served: 170,000 Format: Adult rock. News staff: 6; News: 9 hrs wkly. Target aud: 30-40; baby boomers with disposable income. ◆ Rick Arnish, pres, gen mgr & stn mgr; Doug Collins, chief of opns; Bruce Uptigrove, gen sls mgr. Co-owned TV: CFJC-TV affil.

CJKC-FM— 2006: 103.1 mhz; 5 kw. Stereo. Hrs open: 24 611 Lansdowne St., V2C 1Y6. Phone: (250) 571-1031. Fax: (250) 372-2293.E-mail: info@country103.ca Web Site:www.country103.ca Licensee: NL Broadcasting Ltd. Natl. Rep: CHUM Radio Sales,. Rgnl rep: CHUM Radio Sales Format: Country. News staff: one; News: 10 hrs wkly. Target aud: 25-54. ◆ Robbie Dunn, pres, gen mgr; Crystal Lilly, prom dir; Kelly Moore, progmg dir; Tim Tyler, mus dir; Dave Coulter, chief of engrg; Cheryl Austin, traf mgr.

CKBZ-FM— 2001: 100.1 mhz; 3.5 kw. Stereo. Hrs open: 460 Pemberton Terr., V2C 1T5. Phone: (250) 372-3322. Fax: (250) 374-0445.E-mail: info@b100.ca Web Site:www.b100.ca Licensee: Jim Pattison Broadcast Group Ltd. (the general partner) and Jim Pattison Industries Ltd. (the limited partner) carrying on business as Jim Pattison Broadcast Group L.P. Group owner: The Jim Pattison Broadcast Group. Population served: 170,000 Format: Adult contemp. News staff: 6; News: 10 hrs wkly. Target aud: 25-44; large, loyal audience with disposable income. ◆ Rick Arnish, pres & gen mgr; Doug Collins, opns mgr; Bruce Uptigrove, gen sls mgr. Co-owned TV: CFJC-TV affil.

CKRV-FM— Jan 28, 1984: 97.5 mhz; 5 kw. Stereo. Hrs open: 24 611 Lansdowne St., V2C 1Y6. Phone: (250) 372-2197. Fax: (250) 372-2293.E-mail: info@ckrv.com Web Site:www.ckrv.com Licensee: NL Broadcasting Ltd. (Acq 6-10-93; $925,000.). Population served: 80,000 Natl. Rep: CHUM Radio Sales,. Rgnl rep: CHUM Radio Sales Format: Hot adult contemp/Top 40. News staff: one; News: 5 hrs wkly. Target aud: 25-54; professionals, office personnel. ◆Robbie Dunn, pres, gen mgr; Jim Reynolds, opns mgr; Peter Angle, gen sls mgr; Crystal Lilly, prom dir; Tim Tyler, mus dir; Dave Coulter, chief of engrg; Cheryl Austin, traf mgr.

Kelowna

*CBTK-FM— November 1987: 88.9 mhz; 4.7 kw. 1,676 ft Hrs open: 243 Lawrence Ave., V1Y 6L2. Phone: (250) 861-3781. Fax: (250) 861-6644.E-mail: kelowna@cbc.ca Web Site:www.vancouver.cbc.ca/daybreaksouth Licensee: Canadian Broadcasting Corp. Natl. Network: CBC Radio One, . Format: News, pub affrs, entertainment. ◆Charlie Cheffins, opns mgr & progmg dir.

CHSU-FM— Sept 21, 1995: 99.9 mhz; 13 kw. Hrs open: Prog sep from AM 435 Bernard Ave., V1Y 6N8. Phone: (250) 860-8600. Fax: (250) 860-8856.E-mail: info@thesun.net Web Site:www.thesun.net Licensee: Astral Media Radio G.P. Format: Adult comtemp. News staff: 3. ◆Roy McKenzie, gen sls mgr; Mark Burley, progmg dir; Howard Alexander, news dir.

CILK-FM— June 21, 1985: 101.5 mhz; 11 kw. 1,246 ft (CP: 10.3 kw.). Stereo. Hrs open: 24 1598 Pandosy St., V1Y 1P4. Phone: (250) 860-1010. Fax: (250) 860-5754.E-mail: info@silk.fm Web Site:www.silk.fm Licensee: Astral Media Radio G.P. (acq 10-29-2007; grpsl). Format: Adult contemp 80s & 90s. News staff: 2; News: 2 hrs wkly. Target aud: 25-54; women. Spec prog: Gospel 3 hrs wkly. ◆ Rick Dyer, gen mgr & gen sls mgr.

CJUI-FM— Sept 29, 2008: 103.9 mhz; 5.2 kw. TL: N49 58 00 W119 31 40. Hrs open: 1729 Gordon Dr., V1Y 3H3. Phone: (250) 980-9009. Fax: (250) 980-1038. Web Site:www.1039thejuice.com Licensee: Vista Radio Ltd. Format: Classic hits. ◆Jason Mann, gen mgr; Carla Leinemann, prom dir.

CKFR(AM)— Nov 8, 1971: 1150 khz; 10 kw-U, DA-N. Hrs open: 435 Bernard Ave., V1Y 6N8. Phone: (250) 860-8600. Fax: (250) 860-8856.E-mail: info@am1150.ca Web Site:www.am1150.ca Licensee: Astral Media Radio G.P. Group owner: Standard Broadcasting Corp. (acq 10-29-2007;

grpsl). Population served: 150,000 Format: News/talk, sports. News staff: 3. Target aud: 25-54. Spec prog: Home improvements 2 hrs, American gold 4 hrs wkly. ◆Don Shafer, gen mgr; Darren Robertson, gen sls mgr, progmg dir; Andrew Quinn-Young, progmg dir; Howard Alexander, news dir.

CKKO-FM— 2008: 96.3 mhz; 7.1 kw. TL: N49 46 47 W119 30 26. Hrs open: 1601 Bertram St., V1Y 2G5. Phone: (250) 861-5963. Web Site:www.k963.fm Licensee: Sun Country Radio Ltd. Format: Classic rock. ◆Dallas Gray, gen mgr, gen sls mgr; Garry Barker, prom mgr & progmg mgr.

CKLZ-FM— 1964: 104.7 mhz; 3.8 kw. Ant 1,611 ft TL: N49 46 06 W119 29 59. Stereo. Hrs open: 24 3805 Lakeshore Rd., V1W 3K6. Phone: (250) 763-1047. Fax: (250) 762-2141.E-mail: power104@power104.fm Web Site:www.power104.fm Licensee: Jim Pattison Broadcast Group Ltd. (the general partner) and Jim Pattison Industries Ltd. (the limited partner), carrying on business as Jim Pattison Broadcast Group L.P. (acq 6-30-98). Format: Best rock. News staff: 2; News: 4 hrs wkly. Target aud: 25-49. ◆Rick Arnish, pres; Bruce Davis, gen mgr; Don Huculak, gen sls mgr; Dan McFarland, prom mgr; Bob Miller, progmg mgr; Jasmin Doobay, news dir; Craig Foster, chief of engrg.

CKOV-FM— Aug 17, 2007: 103.1 mhz; 11 kw. TL: N49 46 06 W119 29 59. Hrs open: 3805 Lakeshore Rd., V1W 3K6. Phone: (250) 762-3331. Fax: (250) 762-2141. Web Site:www.b103.ca Licensee: Jim Pattison Broadcast Group Ltd. (the general partner) and Jim Pattison Industries Ltd. (the limited partner), carrying on business as Jim Pattison Broadcast Group L.P. Format: Country. ◆Rick Arnish, pres; Bruce Davis, gen mgr; Don Huculak, gen sls mgr; Dan McFarland, prom mgr; Bob Miller, progmg mgr; Jasmin Doobay, news dir; Craig Foster, chief of engrg.

Kitimat

CKTK-FM— 2004: 97.7 mhz; 170 w. Hrs open: 4625 Lazelle Ave., Terrace, V8G 1S4. Phone: (250) 635-6316. Fax: (250) 638-6320. Licensee: Astral Media Radio G.P. Group owner: Standard Broadcasting Corp. (acq 10-29-2007; grpsl). Format: CHR. ◆Brian Langston, gen mgr & gen sls mgr.

Lillooet

CHLS-FM— 2001: 100.5 mhz; 5 w. TL: lillooet. Hrs open: 24 Box 1545, V0K 1V0. Phone: (250) 256-2113. Fax: (250) 256-2113.E-mail: station@radiolillooet.ca Licensee: Radio Lillooet Society. Population served: 5,000 Format: Var/div. News: 5 hrs wkly. All ages; community of Lillooet. Spec prog: First nations 16 hrs wkly.

MacKenzie

CHMM-FM— Oct 27, 2003: 103.5 mhz; 900 w. Stereo. Hrs open: 86 Centennial Ave., Box 547, V0J 2C0. Phone: (250) 997-6277. Fax: (250) 997-6222.E-mail: jd@chmm.ca Web Site:www.chmm.ca Licensee: MacKenzie and Area Community Radio Society. Format: Var. ◆J.D. MacKenzie, stn mgr; Bryan Bezo, gen sls mgr.

Merritt

CJNL(AM)— 1970: 1230 khz; 1 kw-D, 250 w-N. TL: N50 06 29 W120 46 06. Hrs open:
Rebroadcasts CHNL(AM) Kamloops 60%.
Box 1630, V1K 1B8. Secondary address: 2196 Quilchena Ave., Unit 201 V1K 1B8. Phone: (250) 378-4288. Fax: (250) 378-6979.E-mail: news@cjnl.com Licensee: Merritt Broadcasting Ltd. (acq 1-30-95; C$214,800). Population served: 10,000 Natl. Rep: Target Broadcast Sales,. CRN Wire Svc: Canadian Press Format: Adult contemp, oldies, news. News staff: one; News: 2 hrs wkly. Target aud: General; working family all ages. ◆Elizabeth Laird, gen mgr; Brian Wiebe, opns dir, progmg mgr; Jamie McDerment, mus dir; Al Clarke, news dir.

Nanaimo

CHLY-FM— Sept 21, 2001: 101.7 mhz; 1.3 kw. Ant 312 ft TL: N49 13 20 W124 00 07. Hrs open: #2-34 Victoria Crescent, V9R 5B8. Phone: (250) 716-3410. Fax: (250) 716-1082.E-mail: music@chly.ca Web Site:www.chly.ca Licensee: Radio Malaspina Society. Format: Div. ◆James Booker, progmg dir.

CHWF-FM— Oct 1, 2001: 106.9 mhz; 1.6 kw. TL: Nanaimo. Stereo. Hrs open: 24 hrs 4550 Wellington Rd., V9T H3. Phone: (250) 758-1131. Fax: (250) 758-4644.E-mail: info@1069thewolf.com Web

Site:www.1069thewolf.com Licensee: Jim Pattison Broadcast Group Ltd. (the general partner) and Jim Pattison Industries Ltd. (the limited partner), carrying on business as Jim Pattison Broadcast Group L.P. (acq 6-27-2006; grpsl). Population served: 125,000 Natl. Rep: Canadian Broadcast Sales,. Format: Rock. News staff: 2. Target aud: 25-54; general. ◆Chris Barron, prom dir; Kent Wilson, mus dir; Heather Mousseau, news dir; Barry Mandziak, chief of engrg; Pam Dogherty, traf mgr; Rob Bye, sls.

CKWV-FM— Jan 2, 1995: 102.3 mhz; 1.3 kw. TL: Nanaimo, sc. Stereo. Hrs open: 24 4550 Wellington Rd., V9T 2H3. Phone: (250) 758-1131. Fax: (250) 758-4644.E-mail: info@1023thewave.com Web Site:www.1023thewave.com Licensee: Jim Pattison Broadcast Group Ltd. (the general partner) and Jim Pattison Industries Ltd. (the limited partner), carrying on business as Jim Pattison Broadcast Group L.P. (acq 6-27-2006; grpsl). Population served: 125,000 Natl. Rep: Canadian Broadcast Sales,. Format: Adult contemp. News staff: 2. Target aud: 25-54; general. ◆ Rob Bye, gen mgr; Chris Barron, prom dir; Heather Mousseau, news dir; Barry Mandziak, chief of engrg; Pam Dogherty, traf mgr.

Nelson

CHNV-FM— Apr 18, 2006: 103.5 mhz; 1.1 kw. Ant 1,233 ft Hrs open: 312 Hall St., V1L 1Y8. Phone: (250) 352-1902. Fax: (250) 352-0301.E-mail: info@chnvfm.com Web Site:www.mountainfm.net Licensee: Vista Radio Ltd. Format: Rock. ◆ Paul Mann, gen mgr; Rudy Parachoniak, progmg dir.

*CJLY-FM— 2002: 93.5 mhz; 70 w. Hrs open: 308a Hall St., Box 767, V1L 5R4. Phone: (250) 352-9600. Fax: (250) 352-9653.E-mail: kcr@kootenaycoopradio.com Web Site:www.kootenaycoopradio.com Licensee: Kootenay Co-operative Radio. Format: Div. ◆ Bill Metcalfe, opns mgr; Terry Brennan, progmg dir.

CKKC-FM— 2006: 106.9 mhz; 920 w. TL: N49 31 50 W117 17 58. Hrs open: 1560 Second Ave., Trail, V1R 1M4. Phone: (250) 368-5510. Fax: (250) 368-8471.E-mail: kbs@sri.ca Web Site:www.nelson.kbsradio.ca Licensee: Astral Media Radio G.P. (acq 10-29-2007; grpsl). Natl. Rep: Target Broadcast Sales,. Format: Adult contemp. ◆ Kavin Einarson, opns mgr; Kevin Einarson, gen sls mgr; Chris Kuchar, progmg dir.

New Denver

CKZX-FM— October 1981: 93.5 mhz; 100 w. TL: N49 59 10 W117 22 38. Hrs open: Rebroadcasts CKKC(AM) Nelson 100%. c/o Radio Station CKKC(AM), 1560 2nd Ave., Trail, V1R 1M4. Phone: (250) 368-5510. Fax: (250) 368-8471.E-mail: kbs@sri.ca Web Site:www.kbsradio.ca Licensee: Astral Media Radio G.P. Group owner: Standard Broadcasting Corp. (acq 10-29-2007; grpsl). Format: Adult Contemp. ◆ Kevin Einarson, gen sls mgr; Larry King, chief of engrg.

New Westminster

CFMI-FM—Licensed to New Westminster. See Vancouver

CKNW(AM)—Licensed to New Westminster. See Vancouver

Osoyoos

CJOR(AM)— December 1966: 1240 khz; 1 kw-U, DA-1. Hrs open: 33 Carmi Ave., Penticton, V2A 364. Phone: (250) 492-2800. Fax: (250) 493-0370. Licensee: Astral Media Radio G.P. Group owner: Standard Broadcasting Corp. (acq 10-29-2007; grpsl). Natl. Rep: Canadian Broadcast Sales,. Format: Adult contemp. News staff: one. Target aud: 25-49. Spec prog: Por 3 hrs wkly. ◆ Janet Burley, gen mgr.

Parksville

CHPQ-FM— Feb 11, 2005: 99.9 mhz; 1.1 kw. Stereo. Hrs open: 24 Box 1370, V9P 2H3. Phone: (250) 248-4211. Fax: (250) 248-4210.E-mail: info@thelounge999.com Web Site:www.thelounge999.com Licensee: Jim Pattison Broadcast Group Ltd. (the general partner) and Jim Pattison Industries Ltd. (the limited partner), carrying on business as Jim Pattison Broadcast Group L.P. (acq 6-27-2006; grpsl). Population served: 45,000 Natl. Rep: Canadian Broadcast Sales,. Format: Adult standards. News staff: one. Target aud: 45 plus; adults. ◆ Rob Bye, gen mgr; Marlow Weldon, news dir; Pam Doherty, traf mgr.

CIBH-FM— 1999: 88.5 mhz; 960 w. TL: Parksville, BC. Hrs open: 24 Box 1370, V9P 2H3. Phone: (250) 248-4211. Fax: (250) 248-4210.E-mail: info@885thebeach.com   info@885thebeach.com   Web

Site:www.885thebeach.com Licensee: Jim Pattison Broadcast Group Ltrd. (the general partner) and Jim Pattison Industries Ltd. (the limited partner), carrying on business as Jim Pattison Broadcast Group L.P. (acq 6-27-2006; grpsl). Population served: 45,000 Format: Adult contemp, oldies soft rock. News staff: 2. Target aud: 25-54; Adults. ◆ Marlow Weldon, news dir; Pam Dogherty, traf mgr.

Pemberton

CFPV-FM—Not on air, target date: unknown: 98.9 mhz; 420 w. Hrs open: McBride Communications & Media Inc., 10760 Fundy Dr., Richmond, V7E 5K7. Phone: (604) 220-8393. Fax: (604) 677-6316.E-mail: info@cimmfm.com Licensee: 0749943 BC Ltd. (Matthew G. McBride). ◆ Matthew G. McBride, pres.

CISP-FM— Oct 5, 1982: 104.5 mhz; 400 w. 1,000 ft Hrs open: 24 Rebroadcasts CISQ-FM Squamish 100%. Box 1068, Squamish, V0N 3G0. Phone: (604) 892-1021. Fax: (604) 892-6383.E-mail: mountainfm@mountainfm.com   Web Site:www.mountainfm.com Licensee: Rogers Broadcasting Ltd. (group owner) Format: Hot adult contemp. News staff: 3; News: 16 hrs wkly. Target aud: 25-45. ◆ Gary Miles, pres; Paul Fisher, VP; Ken Geiger, gen mgr; Janis Correia, opns mgr.

Pender Harbour

CIPN-FM— October 1984: 104.7 mhz; 750 w. 1,500 ft Hrs open: 24 Rebroadcasts CISQ-FM Squamish. Box 1068, Squamish, V0N 3G0. Phone: (604) 892-1021. Phone: (604) 683-8060. Fax: (604) 892-6383.E-mail: mountainfm@mountainfm.com Web Site:www.mountainfm.com Licensee: Rogers Broadcasting. Format: Hot adult contemp. News staff: 3; News: 16 hrs wkly. ◆ Gary Miles, pres; Paul Fisher, VP; Ken Geiger, gen mgr; Janis Correia, opns mgr.

Penticton

CIGV-FM— Oct 18, 1981: 100.7 mhz; 6.3 kw. Ant 2,486 ft TL: N49 42 46 W119 36 26. Stereo. Hrs open: 24 125 Nanaimo Ave. W., V2A 1N2. Phone: (250) 493-6767. Fax: (250) 493-0098.E-mail: info@giantfm.ca Web Site:www.giantfm.ca Licensee: Great Valleys Radio Ltd. Population served: 242,323 Natl. Rep: Target Broadcast Sales,. Wire Svc: Broadcast News Ltd. Format: Country, adult contemp. News staff: 3; News: 16 hrs wkly. Target aud: 18 plus. Spec prog: Class 2 hrs, farm one hr wkly. ◆ James Robinson, CEO, pres & gen mgr; Greg Masson, gen sls mgr; Harry Shaw, chief of engrg.

CJMG-FM— June 1, 1965: 97.1 mhz; 1.8 kw. 755 ft Stereo. Hrs open: Prog sep from AM 33 Carmi Ave., V2A 3G4. Phone: (250) 492-2800. Fax: (250) 493-0370. Licensee: Astral Media Radio G.P. Format: AOR.

CKOR(AM)— September 1948: 800 khz; 10 kw-D, 500 w-N. Hrs open: 33 Carmi Ave., V2A 3G4. Phone: (250) 492-2800. Fax: (250) 493-0370. Licensee: Astral Media Radio G.P. Group owner: Standard Broadcasting Corp. (acq 10-29-2007; grpsl). Format: EZRock. ◆ Janet Burley, gen mgr.

Port Alberni

CJAV-FM— Sept 2, 2005: 93.3 mhz; 6 kw. Hrs open: 24 3296 Third Ave., V9Y 4E1. Phone: (250) 723-2455. Fax: (250) 723-0797.E-mail: info@933thepeak.com Web Site:www.933thepeak.com Licensee: Jim Pattison Broadcast Group Ltd. (the general partner) and Jim Pattison Industries Ltd. (the limited partner), carrying on business as Jim Pattison Broadcast Group L.P. (acq 6-27-2006; grpsl). Population served: 30,000 Format: Classic Hits. Target aud: 25-54; Adults. ◆ Chris Talbot, opns mgr, sls; Rob Bye, gen mgr & gen sls mgr; Pam Doherty, traf mgr.

Port Hardy

CFNI(AM)— Sept 1, 1979: 1240 khz; 1 kw-U, DA-1. Hrs open: Box 1000, V0N 2P0. Phone: (250) 949-6500. Phone: (250) 334-2421. Fax: (250) 949-6580.E-mail: cfniradio@cablerocket.com Licensee: CFCP Radio Ltd. Format: Adult contemp, rock mix. News staff: one. Target aud: General. ◆ Paul Mann, CEO.

Powell River

CFPW-FM— Aug 27, 2008: 95.7 mhz; 1.2 kw. TL: N49 41 54 W124 26 05. Hrs open: 4675 Marine Dr., Suite 103, V8A 2L2. Phone: (604) 485-4207. Fax: (604) 485-4210.E-mail: onair@957sunfm.ca Web

Site:www.957sunfm.ca Licensee: Vista Radio Ltd. Format: Adult contemp. ◆ Raymond Henderson, gen mgr.

CJMP-FM— 2006: 90.1 mhz; 3.6 w. Hrs open: 4476 A Marine Ave., V8A 2K2. Phone: (604) 485-2688. Fax: (604) 485-2683.E-mail: modelcommunity@prcn.org;   modelcommunity@shaw.ca   Web Site:www.jumpradiopr.com Licensee: Powell River Model Community Project for Persons with Disabilities. Format: Var, diverse.

Prince George

CBYG-FM— 91.5 mhz; 100 kw. Hrs open: 890 Victoria St., Unit 1, V2L 5P1. Phone: (250) 562-6701. Fax: (250) 562-4777.E-mail: daybreaknorth@cbc.ca Web Site:www.vancouver.cbc.ca/daybreaknorth Licensee: CBC. Natl. Network: CBC Radio One, . Format: Current affrs. ◆ Faydra Aldridge, gen mgr.

CFIS-FM— July 3, 2007: 93.1 mhz; 5 w. TL: N53 54 37 W122 46 34. Hrs open: 2880 15th Ave. #109, V2M 1T1. Phone: (250) 563-2347.E-mail: cfisfm@yahoo.ca Licensee: Prince George Community Radio Society. Format: Pre-80s hits. ◆ Reg Feyer, opns mgr.

*CFUR-FM— 2002: 88.7 mhz; 510 w. Hrs open: 3333 University Way, V2N 4Z9. Phone: (250) 960-7664. Fax: (250) 960-5995.E-mail: info@cfur.ca Web Site:www.cfur.ca Licensee: Education Alternative Radio Society. Population served: 80,000 Format: Div. Target aud: Community of Prince George. ◆ Christopher Earl, stn mgr; Joshua Laurin, progmg dir; Bryndis Ogmundson, mus dir; Glen Yakemchuk, engrg dir.

CIRX-FM— Oct 1, 1983: 94.3 mhz; 3.5 kw. Ant 1,145 ft Stereo. Hrs open: 1940 3rd Ave., V2M 1G7. Phone: (250) 564-2524. Fax: (250) 562-6611.E-mail: info@94xfm.com Web Site:www.94xfm.com Licensee: Vista Radio Ltd. (group owner). Format: Rock. Target aud: 18-34. ◆ Gary Russell, gen mgr; Sandy Whitwhan, gen sls mgr; Brad Bregani, progmg mgr; Bill Fox, news dir; Chris Terpsma, chief of engrg.

CJCI-FM— Aug 5, 2003: 97.3 mhz; 12 kw. Hrs open: 24 The Wolf, 1940 3rd Ave., V2M 1G7. Phone: (250) 564-2524. Fax: (250) 562-6611.E-mail: thewolf@97fm.ca Web Site:www.97fm.ca Licensee: Vista Radio Ltd. (group owner). Format: Modern country, southern rock. News staff: 3. Target aud: 25-54. ◆ Gary Russell, gen mgr; Sandy Whitwhan, gen sls mgr; Bill Fee, news dir; Chris Terpsma, chief of engrg.

CKDV-FM— 2003: 99.3 mhz; 9.3 kw. Hrs open: 24 1810 3rd Ave., 2nd Fl, V2M 1G4. Phone: (250) 564-8861. Fax: (250) 562-8768.E-mail: ckpgmail@ckpg.bc.ca Web Site:www.993thedrive.com Licensee: Jim Pattison Broadcast Group Ltd. (the general partner) and Jim Pattison Industries Ltd. (the limited partner) carrying on business as Jim Pattison Broadcast Group L.P. Group owner: The Jim Pattison Broadcast Group. Format: Classic rock. ◆ Ken Kilcullen, gen mgr; Randy Seabrook, gen sls mgr; Ron Polillo, progmg dir; Mike Woodworth, news dir.

CKKN-FM— Mar 1, 1981: 101.3 mhz; 10 kw. Ant 1,000 ft Stereo. Hrs open: 2nd Fl. 1810 3rd Ave., V2M 1G4. Phone: (250) 564-8861. Fax: (250) 562-8768. Fax: (250) 562-7681.E-mail: ckpgmail@ckpg.bc.ca Web Site:www.1013theriver.com Licensee: Jim Pattison Broadcast Group Ltd. (the general partner) and Jim Pattison Industries Ltd. (the limited partner) carrying on business as Jim Pattison Broadcast Group L.P. Group owner: The Jim Pattison Broadcast Group (acq 12-21-2000; grpsl). Format: Hot adult contmep. ◆ Rick Arnish, pres; Ken Kilcullen, gen mgr; Ron Polillo, progmg mgr; Mike Woodworth, news dir. Co-owned TV: CKPG-TV affil.

Prince Rupert

*CFPR(AM)— 1936: 860 khz; 10 kw-D, DA-1. Hrs open: 24 222 Third Ave. W., Suite 1, V8J 1L1. Phone: (250) 624-2161. Fax: (250) 627-8594.E-mail: daybreaknorth@vancouver.cbc.ca Web Site:www.cbc.ca/daybreaknorth Licensee: CBC. (acq 1953). Natl. Network: CBC Radio One, . Format: Current affairs, news. Target aud: General. Spec prog: Current affrs. ◆ Faydra Aldridge, gen mgr.

CHTK(AM)— 1965: 560 khz; 1 kw-D, 250 w-N. Hrs open: 215 Cowbay Rd., Unit 212, V8J 1A2. Phone: (250) 627-8255. Fax: (250) 624-3100.E-mail: gsimpson@sri.ca Licensee: Astral Media Radio G.P. Group owner: Standard Broadcasting Corp. (acq 10-29-2007; grpsl). Format: CHR. ◆ Mike Lunn, gen mgr.

CIAJ-FM— 2000: 100.7 mhz; 26.5 w. Hrs open: Box 1, 531 6th Ave. W., V8J 3P4. E-mail: cfirm@citytel.net Licensee: Aboriginal Christian Voice Network. Format: Christian. ◆ Prescott Sandhu, gen mgr.

Princeton

CIOR(AM)— June 1972: 1400 khz; 1 kw-U, DA-1. TL: N49 26 50 W120 30 42. Hrs open: 6 AM-6 PM Box 539, 203 8309 Main St., Osoyoos, V0H 1V0. Phone: (250) 492-2800. Fax: (250) 495-7228. Licensee: Astral Media Radio G.P. (acq 10-29-2007; grpsl). Population served: 5,000 Natl. Rep: Canadian Broadcast Sales,. Format: Adult contemp. ◆Lee Sterry, gen mgr & stn mgr.

Qualicum

CIBH-FM—See Parksville

Quesnel

CKCQ-FM— 2004: 100.3 mhz; 1.8 kw. Stereo. Hrs open: 502-410 Kinchant St., V2J 7J5. Phone: (250) 992-7046. Fax: (250) 992-2354. Licensee: Vista Radio Ltd. Format: Modern country, southern rock. News staff: 4. ◆Tracey Gard, gen mgr; Tom Tompkins, opns mgr; George Henderson, news rptr.

Revelstoke

CKCR(AM)— Nov 21, 1965: 1340 khz; 1 kw-D, 250 w-N. Hrs open: Box 1420, V0E 2S0. Secondary address: 208 E. 1st. St. V0E 2S0. Phone: (250) 837-2149. Fax: (250) 837-5577.E-mail: ckcr@rctvonline.net Web Site:www.myezrock.com Licensee: Astral Media Radio G.P. Group owner: Standard Broadcasting Corp. (acq 10-29-2007; grpsl). Format: Easy rock. ◆Ron Langridge, pres & gen mgr.

Richmond

CISL(AM)— May 1, 1980: 650 khz; 10 kw-U, DA-2. TL: N49 08 38 W123 03 41. (Digital radio: 1465.024 mhz; 3.381 kw). Hrs open: No. 20, 11151 Horseshoe Way, V7A 4S5. Phone: (604) 272-6500. Fax: (604) 272-0917. Web Site:www.am650radio.com Licensee: Astral Media Radio G.P. Group owner: Standard Broadcasting Corp. (acq 10-29-2007; grpsl). Format: Adult standards. ◆Brad Phillips, VP & gen mgr.

CJVB(AM)— June 18, 1972: 1470 khz; 50 kw-U, DA-2. TL: N49 11 36 W123 01 17. Hrs open: 24 2090 -4151 Hazelbridge Way, V6X 4J7. Phone: (604) 295-1234. Fax: (604) 295-1201.E-mail: general@am1470.com Web Site:www.am1470.com Licensee: Fairchild Radio Group Ltd. Population served: 1,300,000 Natl. Rep: Target Broadcast Sales,. Rgnl rep: In House Format: Ethnic, Chinese. News staff: 10; News: 23 hrs wkly. Target aud: General. ◆Thomas Fung, chmn & pres; Brenda Lo, sr VP, dev VP; Alan Kwok, opns mgr; Pearl Kwan, sls VP; Pearl Kwan, mktg VP.

Rossland

CHLI-FM— Jan 1, 2009: 101.1 mhz; 5 w. TL: N49 04 47 W117 47 54. Hrs open: Box 408, V0G 1Y0. Phone: (250) 362-0080. Web Site:www.rosslandradio.com Licensee: Rossland Radio Cooperative.

Salmo

CFAD-FM— Oct 11, 2008: 92.1 mhz; 5 w. TL: N49 11 45 W117 16 51. Hrs open: Box 549, V0G 1Z0. Phone: (250) 357-2299.E-mail: info@salmofm.info Web Site:www.salmofm.info Licensee: Salmo FM Radio Society.

Salmon Arm

CKXR-FM— June 5, 2006: 91.5 mhz; 400 w. Stereo. Hrs open: 24 Box 69, V1E 4N2. Secondary address: 360 Ross St. V1E 4N2. Phone: (250) 832-2161. Fax: (250) 832-2240. Web Site:www.salmonarm.myezrock.com Licensee: Astral Media Radio G.P. (acq 10-29-2007; grpsl). Format: Soft rock. News staff: 3. Target aud: 25-54. ◆Ron Langridge, gen mgr.

Sechelt

CKAY-FM— May 20, 2006: 91.7 mhz; 600 w. TL: Mount Benson-Van. Island. Stereo. Hrs open: 24 1-1877 Field Rd., V0N 3A1. Phone: (604) 741-9170. Fax: (604) 741-9172.E-mail: info@ckay.ca Web Site:www.ckay.ca Licensee: Westwave Broadcasting Inc. Natl. Rep: imsradio,. Rgnl rep: IMS Wire Svc: BN Wire Format: Gold based adult contemp. News

staff: 3; News: 8 hrs wkly. Target aud: 35 plus; adults. ◆Bob Morris, pres, gen mgr; Paul Nattal, sls VP; Sean Eckford, news dir.

CKKS-FM— July 1985: 104.7 mhz; 750 w. 2,000 ft Hrs open: 24 Rebroadcasts CISQ-FM Squamish. Box 1068, Squamish, V0N 3G0. Phone: (604) 892-1021. Fax: (604) 892-6383.E-mail: mountainfm@mountainfm.com Web Site:www.mountainfm.com Licensee: Rogers Broadcasting Ltd. (group owner). Natl. Rep: Canadian Broadcast Sales,. Format: Hits of the 80s & 90s. News staff: 3; News: 16 hrs wkly. Target aud: 25-45. Spec prog: Magazine show 3 hrs wkly. ◆Gary Miles, pres; Ken Geiger, gen mgr, opns mgr, progmg dir; Janis Correia, opns mgr; Paul Fisher, gen sls mgr; janis Correia, sls.

Smithers

CFBV(AM)— Oct 25, 1963: 870 khz; 1 kw-D, 250 w-N. Hrs open: Box 335, V0J 2N0. Secondary address: 1139 Queen St. V0J 2N0. Phone: (250) 847-2521. Fax: (250) 847-9411. Licensee: Vista Radio Ltd. (group owner) Format: The best of the 70s, 80s, 90s & now. ◆Al Collison, gen mgr.

Squamish

CISQ-FM— Nov 30, 1981: 107.1 mhz; 12.48 kw. Ant 800 ft Hrs open: 24 Box 1068, V0N 3G0. Phone: (604) 892-1021. Fax: (604) 892-6383.E-mail: mountainfm@mountainfm.com Web Site:www.mountainfm.com Licensee: Rogers Broadcasting. Natl. Rep: Canadian Broadcast Sales,. Format: Hot adult contemp. News staff: 3; News: 5 hrs wkly. Target aud: 18-54. Spec prog: Talk 5 hrs wkly. ◆Ken Geiger, gen mgr; Janis Correia, opns mgr.

Summerland

CHOR(AM)— 1972: 1450 khz; 1 kw-U, DA-1. Hrs open: 24 Rebroadcasts CHOR(AM) Summerland 70%. Box 1170, V0H 1Z0. Phone: (250) 494-0333. Fax: (250) 493-0370.E-mail: info@thesun.net Web Site:www.am1450.com Licensee: Astral Media Radio G.P. (acq 10-29-2007; grpsl). Natl. Rep: Canadian Broadcast Sales,. Format: EZRock. News staff: 3. Spec prog: Class 3 hrs. ◆Janet Burley, gen mgr.

Terrace

CFNR-FM— 1995: 92.1 mhz; 43 w. Hrs open: 24 4562 B Queensway Dr., V8G 3X6. Phone: (250) 638-8137. Fax: (250) 638-8027.E-mail: info@mycfnr.com Web Site:www.mycfnr.com Starchoice Ch. 851 Licensee: Northern Native Broadcasting (Terrace, B.C.). Population served: 50,000+ Format: Classic rock. News: 10 hrs wkly. Target aud: General; 35+. Spec prog: First nations 9 hrs. ◆Barry Wall, gen mgr, progmg dir; Ron Bartlett, mktg mgr; D.C. Cara, prom.

CFTK(AM)— 1960: 590 khz; 1 kw-U, DA-1. Hrs open: 4625 Lazelle Ave., V8G 1S4. Phone: (250) 635-6316. Fax: (250) 638-6320. Licensee: Astral Media Radio G.P. Group owner: Standard Broadcasting Corp. (acq 10-29-2007; grpsl). Format: MOR. ◆Brian Langston, gen mgr & gen sls mgr.

CJFW-FM— December 1983: 103.1 mhz; Hrs open: Phone: (250) 635-6316. Fax: (250) 638-6320. Licensee: Astral Media Radio G.P. Format: Contemp country. ◆Brian Langston, gen mgr; Steve Hart, progmg mgr; John Crawford, news dir. Co-owned TV: CFTK-TV affil.

Tofino

CHMZ-FM— 2005: 90.1 mhz; 170 w. Hrs open: Box 1092, V0R 2Z0. Phone: (250) 725-4411. Fax: (250) 725-4411.E-mail: info@chmzfm.com Web Site:www.chmzfm.com Licensee: West Island Radio Enterprises General Partnership. Format: Pop-rock, country. ◆Matthew McBride, gen mgr.

Trail

CJAT-FM— 1996: 95.7 mhz; 13.5 kw. Hrs open: 1560 2nd Ave., V1R 1M4. Phone: (250) 368-5510. Fax: (250) 368-8471. Web Site:www.kbsradio.ca Licensee: Astral Media Radio G.P. Group owner: Standard Broadcasting Corp. (acq 10-29-2007; grpsl). Format: Adult contemp. ◆Janet Burley, gen mgr; Lea Wilman, progmg dir; David Ford, engr.

Ucluelet

CIMM-FM— Sept 1, 2006: 99.5 mhz; 180 w. Hrs open: 10760 Fundy Dr., Richmond, V7E 5K7. Phone: (604) 220-8393. Fax: (604) 677-6316.E-mail: info@cimmfm.com Web Site:www.cimmfm.com Licensee: CIMM-FM Radio Ltd. Format: Var. ◆Matthew McBride, gen mgr.

Vancouver

*CBU(AM)— 1925: 690 khz; 50 kw-U, DA-1. (Digital radio: 1459.792 mhz). Hrs open: 24 Box 4600, 700 Hamilton St., V6B 4A2. Phone: (604) 662-6000. Fax: (604) 662-6088.E-mail: info@cbc.ca/bc Web Site:www.cbc.ca/bc Licensee: Canadian Broadcasting Corp. Format: News/talk, var. ◆Joan Anderson, gen mgr; Joan Athey, prom dir; Brett Ballah, news dir; Dave Newbury, engrg dir; Terry Donnelly, news rptr.

CBUF-FM— Dec 1, 1967: 97.7 mhz; 50 kw. Ant 1,823 ft (Digital radio: 1459.792 mhz). Stereo. Hrs open: 700 Hamilton St., V6B 4A2. Secondary address: Box 4600 V6B 4A2. Phone: (604) 662-6169. Fax: (604) 662-6161. Web Site:www.radio-canada.ca/c-b Licensee: CBC. Natl. Network: Premiere Chaine, . Format: Div. ◆Stephane Boisjoly, gen mgr; Mario Deschamps, progmg dir.

CBU-FM— 1947: 105.7 mhz; 100 kw. 1,823 ft (Digital radio: 1459.792 mhz). Stereo. Hrs open: 24 Prog sep from AM Box 4600, 700 Hamilton St., V6B 4A2. Phone: (604) 662-6000. Fax: (604) 662-6088.E-mail: info@cbc.ca/bc Web Site:www.cbc.ca/bc Licensee: Canadian Broadcasting Corp Format: Music. ◆Tod Elvidge, mus dir.

CBUX-FM— Sept 22, 2002: 90.9 mhz; 1.28 kw. Hrs open: 700 Hamilton St., V6B 4A2. Phone: (604) 662-6000. Fax: (604) 662-6335. Web Site:www.radio-canada.ca/c-b Licensee: Canadian Broadcasting Corp. Natl. Network: Espace Musique, . Format: Var, Fr. ◆Stephane Boisjoly, gen mgr; Mario Deschamps, progmg dir.

CFBT-FM— February 2002: 94.5 mhz; 46 kw. Hrs open: 24 #A301 - 770 Pacific Blvd., Plaza of Nations, V6B 5E7. Phone: (604) 699-2328. Fax: (604) 484-4912.E-mail: info@thebeat.com Web Site:www.thebeat.com Licensee: CTV Ltd. (acq 10-12-2007; C$46,006,717). Format: Rythmic CHR, Top 40. News staff: one; News: 2 hrs wkly. ◆Jennifer Smith, VP & gen sls mgr; Chris Myers, progmg dir.

CFMI-FM—(New Westminster, Mar 22, 1970: 101.1 mhz; 100 kw. 3,500 ft Stereo. Hrs open: Prog sep from AM 700 W. Georgia St., Suite 2000, V7Y 1K9. Phone: (604) 331-2808. Fax: (604) 331-2727.E-mail: rock101@rock101.com Web Site:www.rock101.com Licensee: Corus Premium Television Ltd. Format: Classic rock. Target aud: 25-49.

CFOX-FM— October 1964: 99.3 mhz; 100 kw. 2,243 ft Stereo. Hrs open: Prog sep from AM 700 W. Georgia St., Suite 2000, V7Y 1K9. Phone: (604) 684-7221. Fax: (604) 331-2722.E-mail: info@cfox.com Licensee: Corus Radio Co. Format: AOR. ◆Bob Mills, progrng dir.

*CFRO-FM— Apr 22, 1975: 102.7 mhz; 5.5 kw. 1,005 ft Hrs open: 110-360 Columbia St., V6A 4J1. Phone: (604) 684-8494.E-mail: program@coopradio.org Web Site:www.coopradio.org Licensee: Vancouver Co-Op Radio. Format: Community, news/talk, alternative pub affrs. Target aud: General; alternative community. Spec prog: Black 14 hrs, Chinese 2 hrs, Greek one hr, hip hop 17 hrs, jazz 16 hrs, Latin American 7 hrs, Pol 5 hrs wkly. ◆Leela Chinniah, progmg mgr; Rob Gauvin, mus dir; Danjel van Tijn, engrg dir.

CFUN(AM)— Apr 20, 1922: 1410 khz; 50 kw-U, DA-2. (Digital radio: 1463.280 mhz). Hrs open: 24 Prog sep from FM 380 W. 2nd Ave. Suite 300, V5Y 1C8. Phone: (604) 871-9000. Fax: (604) 871-2901.E-mail: info@cfun.com Web Site:www.cfun.com Licensee: CTV Ltd. Format: Talk. Target aud: 25-49; upscale, well-educated females.

CHHR-FM— June 1, 2009: 104.3 mhz; 5.2 kw. Ant 1,968 ft TL: N49 21 16 W122 57 30. Hrs open: 225 W. 8th Ave., 3rd Fl., V5Y 1N3. Phone: (604) 628-1041. Fax: (778) 331-0320.E-mail: info@shore104.com Web Site:www.shore104.com Licensee: Shore Media Group Inc. Format: Adult album alternative. Target aud: 25-54. ◆Roy Hennessy, pres, gen mgr; Sherri Pierce, sls VP.

CHKG-FM— Sept 6, 1997: 96.1 mhz; 46 kw. TL: N49 21 12 W122 57 18. Hrs open: 24 2090-4151 Hazelbridge Way, Richmond, V6X 4J7. Phone: (604) 295-1234. Fax: (604) 295-1201.E-mail: general@fm961.com Web Site:www.fm961.com Licensee: Fairchild Radio (Vancouver CHF) Ltd. Population served: 1,300,000 Natl. Rep: Target Broadcast Sales,. Format: Ethnic. News staff: 10; News: 10 hrs wky. Target aud: General. ◆Brenda Lo, sr VP, dev VP; Thomas Fung, chmn & VP; Alan Kwok, opns mgr; Pearl Kwan, sls VP; Pearl Kwan, mktg VP.

CHMB(AM)— Dec 10, 1959: 1320 khz; 50 kw-U, DA-2. TL: N49 09 55 W123 02 28. Hrs open: 24 1200 W. 73rd Ave., Suite 100, V6P 6G5. Phone: (604) 263-1320. Fax: (604) 261-0310.E-mail: info@am1320.com Web Site:www.am1320.com Licensee: Mainstream Broadcasting Corp. (acq 12-14-93; C$1.8 million). Population served: 600,000 Natl. Rep: Canadian Broadcast Sales,. Format: Chinese, multicultural. News staff: 8; News: 30 hrs wkly. Target aud: 18-65; multilingual, mainly Chinese. Spec prog: American Indian one hr, Japanese 1 hr, Vietnamese 1 hr wkly, Ukranian one hr, Portuguese one hr, Scandinavian one hour, Greek 1/2 hr, Tamil 1/2 hr. ♦James Ho, chmn, pres; George Feng, dev VP, sls VP; Trix Chan, news dir.

CHMJ(AM)— June 1954: 730 khz; 50 kw-U, DA-2. Stereo. Hrs open: 700 W. Georgia St., Suite 2000, V7Y 1K9. Phone: (604) 681-7511. Fax: (604) 331-2722.E-mail: info@chmj.com Licensee: Corus Radio Co. Group owner: Corus Entertainment Inc. (acq 7-6-2000; grpsl). Format: Drive time traffic, talk. ♦J.J. Johnston, gen mgr; Shari Wong, gen sls mgr; Ian Koenigsfest, progmg dir.

CHQM-FM— Aug 10, 1960: 103.5 mhz; 53 kw. Ant 2,026 ft (Digital radio: 1463.280 mhz). Stereo. Hrs open: 24 380 W. 2nd Ave., Suite 300, V5Y 1C8. Phone: (604) 871-9000. Fax: (604) 871-2901.E-mail: info@chqm.com Web Site:www.qmfm.com Licensee: CTV Ltd. Group owner: CHUM Ltd. (acq 6-22-2007; grpsl). Format: Adult contemp. News staff: 5; News: 2 hrs wkly. Target aud: 25-54. ♦Barry O'Donnell, gen sls mgr; Carl LeGrice, prom dir; Neil Gallagher, gen mgr & progmg mgr; Clara Carotenuto, mus dir; Dave Youell, chief of engrg.

***CITR-FM**— Apr 1, 1982: 101.9 mhz; 1.8 kw. 170 ft Stereo. Hrs open: 7:30 AM-4 AM Univ. of British Columbia, 233-6138 Sub Blvd., V6T 1Z1. Phone: (604) 822-3017. Fax: (604) 822-9364.E-mail: citrmgr@ams.ubc.ca Web Site:www.citr.ca Licensee: Student Radio Society of University of British Columbia. Population served: 2,000,000 Format: Div. News: 5 hrs wkly. Target aud: General; campus/community. ♦Brenda Grunau, stn mgr; Bryce Dunn, chief of opns; Luke Meat, mus dir.

CJJR-FM— July 1, 1986: 93.7 mhz; 75 kw. 2,250 ft Stereo. Hrs open: 24 Prog sep from AM 300-1401 W. 8th Ave., V6H 1C9. Phone: (604) 731-7772. Fax: (604) 731-1329.E-mail: cjjr@jrfm.com Web Site:www.jrfm.com Licensee: Jim Pattison Broadcast Group Ltd. Format: Contemp country. News staff: 2. Target aud: 25-54. ♦Mark Rogers, gen sls mgr; Brian Pritchard, natl sls mgr; Tamsin Carling, prom dir; Gordon Eno, progmg dir; Mark Patric, mus dir; David Linder, engr.

CJRJ(AM)— November 2006: 1200 khz; 25 kw-U, DA-2. TL: N49 09 55 W123 02 28. Hrs open: 110-3060 Norland Ave., Unit 110, Burnaby, V5B 3A6. Phone: (604) 299-8863. Fax: (604) 299-3088.E-mail: info@rj1200.com Web Site:www.rj1200.com Licensee: I.T. Productions Ltd. Format: Ethnic, Hindustani, Punjabi. ♦Shushma Datt, CEO; Sudhir Datta, gen mgr.

CKAV-FM-2— 2007: 106.3 mhz; 9 kw. Ant 1,968 ft TL: N49 21 17 W122 57 25. Hrs open: 366 Adelaide St. E., Suite 323, Toronto, ON, M5A 3X9. Phone: (416) 703-1287. Fax: (416) 703-4328. Web Site:aboriginalvoices.com Licensee: Aboriginal Voices Radio Inc. Format: Aboriginal music. ♦Roy Hennessy, opns mgr; Patrice Mousseau, progmg dir.

CKLG-FM— Mar 1, 1980: 96.9 mhz; 100 kw. 2,500 ft TL: N49 21 29 W122 57 09. Stereo. Hrs open: 24 2440 Ash St., V5Z 4J6. Phone: (604) 877-4488. Fax: (604) 877-4494. Web Site:www.969jackfm.com Licensee: Rogers Broadcasting Ltd. Format: Adult contemp. ♦Barry Taylor, mus dir; Rick dal Farra, engrg mgr.

CKNW(AM)—(New Westminster, Sept 1, 1944: 980 khz; 50 kw-U, DA-2. Stereo. Hrs open: 24 700 W. Georgia St., Suite 2000, V7Y 1K9. Phone: (604) 331-2711. Fax: (604) 331-2722.E-mail: info@cknw.com Web Site:www.cknw.com Licensee: Corus Premium Television Ltd. Group owner: Corus Entertainment Inc. (acq 7-6-2000; grpsl). Natl. Rep: Canadian Broadcast Sales,. Format: News/talk, sports. News staff: 20; News: 14 hrs wkly. Target aud: General. ♦J.J. Johnson, gen mgr.

CKPK-FM— Nov 13, 2008: 100.5 mhz; 2.6 kw. Ant 1,932 ft TL: N49 21 16 W122 57 30. Hrs open: 1401 W. 8th Ave., Suite 300, V6H 1C9. Phone: (604) 731-6111. Fax: (604) 731-0493. Web Site:www.thepeak.fm Licensee: Jim Pattison Broadcast Group Ltd. (the general partner) and Jim Pattison Industries Ltd. (the limited partner), carrying on business as Jim Pattison Broadcast Group L.P. Natl. Rep: Canadian Broadcast Sales,. Format: Adult album alternative. Target aud: 25-49; adults. ♦Gerry Siemens, gen mgr.

CKST(AM)— Jan 19, 1963: 1040 khz; 50 kw-U, DA-2. Stereo. Hrs open: 24 300-380 W. 2nd Ave., Suite 300, V5Y 1C8. Phone: (604) 871-9000. Fax: (604) 871-2901.E-mail: info@ckst.com Web Site:www.team1040.ca Licensee: CTV Ltd. (group owner; acq 6-22-2007;. grpsl). Population served: 2,000,000 Natl. Rep: Canadian Broadcast Sales,. Format: All sports. News staff: 4; News: 8 hrs wkly. Target aud: 40 plus; intelligent, socially conscious, older demographic. ♦Neil Gallagher, gen mgr.

CKWX(AM)— Apr 1, 1923: 1130 khz; 50 kw-U, DA-N. TL: N49 09 22 W123 04 00. Hrs open: 2440 Ash St., V5Z 4J6. Phone: (604) 877-4488. Phone: (604) 872-2557. Fax: (604) 877-4494. Web Site:www.news1130.com Licensee: Rogers Broadcasting Ltd. (group owner; acq 1989). Population served: 2,000,000 Natl. Rep: CBS Radio,. Format: All news. News staff: 45; News: 168 hrs wkly. Target aud: 35-54; men. ♦Ted Rogers, CEO, chmn; Tony Viner, pres; Gary Miles, exec VP; Paul Fisher, gen mgr, opns mgr; Kattie Bull, prom mgr; Jacquie Donaldson, progmg dir, news dir; Rick Dal Farra, chief of engrg.

CKYE-FM— Feb 1, 2006: 93.1 mhz; 4.2 kw. TL: N49 21 17 W122 57 25. Hrs open: 8383A 128th St. #201, Surrey, V3W 4G1. Phone: (604) 598-9311.E-mail: info@redfm.ca Web Site:redfm.ca Licensee: South Asian Broadcasting Corp. Inc. Format: Ethnic. ♦Bijoy Samuel, gen mgr.

CKZZ-FM— May 1991: 95.3 mhz; 75 kw. (Digital radio: 1465.024 mhz; 2.774 kw). Hrs open: #20, 11151 Horseshoe Way, Richmond, V7A 4S5. Phone: (604) 241-0953. Fax: (604) 272-0917.E-mail: info@virginradio.ca Web Site:www.virginradio.ca Licensee: Astral Media Radio G.P. Group owner: Standard Broadcasting Corp. (acq 10-29-2007; grpsl). Format: Hot adult contemp. ♦Brad Phillips, VP & gen mgr.

Vanderhoof

CIVH(AM)— November 1973: 1340 khz; 1 kw-D, 500 w-N, DA-1. TL: N54 01 00 W123 59 00. Hrs open: 6-10 AM Box 1370, V0J 3A0. Phone: (250) 567-4914. Fax: (250) 567-4982.E-mail: thewolf@hwy16.com Licensee: Vista Radio Ltd. (group owner) Natl. Rep: Target Broadcast Sales,. Format: Modern country & best southern rock. Target aud: General. Spec prog: Relg 5 hrs wkly. ♦Gary Russell, gen mgr; Sandy Whitwham, gen sls mgr; Jacqui Ryks, mus dir; Bill Fee, news dir; Karen Fridleifson, sls.

Vernon

CICF-FM— 2001: 105.7 mhz; 46 kw. Hrs open: 8:30 AM-5 PM 2800 31st St., V1T 5H4. Phone: (250) 545-9222. Fax: (250) 542-2083.E-mail: reception@thesunonline.ca Web Site:www.thesunonline.ca Licensee: Astral Media Radio G.P. Group owner: Standard Broadcasting Corp. (acq 10-29-2007; grpsl). Format: Hot adult contemp. News staff: 2. ♦Gord Leighton, gen mgr; Larry King, chief of engrg.

CKIZ-FM— Nov 8, 2001: 107.5 mhz; 46 kw. Hrs open: 3313 32nd Ave., V1T 2M7. Phone: (250) 545-2141. Fax: (250) 545-9008.E-mail: kissfm@1075kiss.com Web Site:www.1075kiss.com Licensee: Jim Pattison Broadcast Group Ltd. (the general partner) and Jim Pattison Industries Ltd. (the limited partner), carrying on business as Jim Pattison Broadcast Group L.P. (group owner). (acq 10-31-2008; C$4 million). Natl. Rep: Canadian Broadcast Sales,. Format: News, lite favorites of yesterday & today. ♦Gord Wiens, gen sls mgr; Patrick Nicol, VP, gen mgr & progmg dir; Duane Schindel, chief of engrg.

Victoria

***CBCV-FM**— Sept 28, 1998: 90.5 mhz; 3 kw. Hrs open: 1025 Pandora Ave., V8V 3P6. Phone: (250) 360-2227. Fax: (250) 360-2600.E-mail: victoria@cbc.ca Web Site:www.vancouver.cbc.ca/ontheisland Licensee: CBC. Natl. Network: CBC Radio One, . Format: Current Affairs. News staff: 11; News: 23 hrs wkly. ♦Peter Hutchinson, stn mgr & progmg mgr.

CFAX(AM)— Sept 4, 1959: 1070 khz; 10 kw-U, DA-1. TL: N48 23 50 W123 18 20. Stereo. Hrs open: 24 Mellor Bldg., 825 Broughton St., V8W 1E5. Phone: (250) 920-4602. Fax: (250) 386-5775.E-mail: tspence@cfax1070.com Web Site:www.cfax1070.com Licensee: CTV Ltd. (acq 10-1-2004;. C$7.5 million with co-located FM). Population served: 350,000 Natl. Rep: Target Broadcast Sales,. Wire Svc: BN Wire Format: News/talk. News staff: 7; News: 21 hrs wkly. Target aud: 45 plus; 50% males, 50% females. ♦Kevin Bell, sls dir; Shannon Kowalko, prom dir, adv dir; Al Ferraby, news dir, disc jockey; Bud Goes, chief of engrg; Frank Stanford, news rptr.

***CFUV-FM**— Dec 17, 1984: 101.9 mhz; 2.29 kw. 265 ft Stereo. Hrs open: 24 Box 3035, University of Victoria, V8W 3P3. Phone: (250) 721-8702. Web Site:www.cfuv.uvic.ca Licensee: University of Victoria Student Radio Society. Format: Div. News: 8.5 hrs wkly. Target aud: General; people tired of coml radio, on campus & in the community. Spec prog: It 2 hrs, American Indian one hrs; Fr 2 hrs, Pol one hr, Sp 3 hrs wkly. ♦Randy Gelling, stn mgr; Jana Grazley, progmg dir; Justin Lanoue, mus dir.

CHBE-FM— Aug 23, 2002: 107.3 mhz; 20 kw. TL: N48 25 06 W123 30 35. Hrs open: Mellor Bldg., 825 Broughton St., V8W 1E5. Phone: (250) 382-1073. Fax: (250) 386-5775.E-mail: curtis@1073kool.fm Web Site:www.b1073kool.fm Licensee: CTV Ltd Format: Hot adult contemp. News: 2 hrs wkly. Target aud: 35-49. ♦Curtis Strange, progmg dir.

CHTT-FM— September 2000: 103.1 mhz; 50 w. TL: N48 26 52 W123 19 19. Stereo. Hrs open: 9 AM-9 PM 817 Fort St., V8W 1H6. Phone: (250) 382-0900. Fax: (250) 382-4358. Web Site:www.1031jackfm.ca Licensee: Rogers Broadcasting Ltd. (group owner) Population served: 200,000. Natl. Rep: Canadian Broadcast Sales,. Format: Classic hits. News: 5 hrs wkly. ♦Gorde Edlund, gen mgr, progmg dir; Tony Marsh, gen sls mgr.

CILS-FM— Nov 7, 2007: 107.9 mhz; 250 w. TL: N48 25 26 W123 20 10. Hrs open: 200-535 Yates St., V8W 2Z6. Phone: (250) 220-4139. Fax: (250) 388-6280.E-mail: radio@francocentre.com Web Site:www.cilsfm.ca Licensee: Societe radio communautaire Victoria. Format: French. ♦Jacques P. Vallee, pres; Jules Desjarlais, progmg dir.

CIOC-FM— Mar 18, 1965: 98.5 mhz; 100 kw. 567 ft Stereo. Hrs open: 24 817 Fort St., V8W 1H6. Phone: (250) 382-0900. Fax: (250) 382-4358. Web Site:www.ocean985.com Licensee: Rogers Broadcasting Ltd. (group owner) Population served: 300,000 Format: Lite rock, adult contemp. News staff: one; News: 2 hrs wkly. Target aud: 35-54; female. ♦Kim Hesketh, VP, gen mgr, stn mgr; Tony Marsh, gen sls mgr; Dawn Kaysoe, progmg dir; Dean Fox, chief of engrg.

CJZN-FM— May 2000: 91.3 mhz; 1.766 kw. (Digital radio: 1,472.000 mhz; 2 kw). Stereo. Hrs open: Top Floor, 2750 Quadra St., V8T 4E8. Phone: (250) 475-6611. Fax: (250) 475-3299.E-mail: modernrock@thezone.fm Web Site:www.thezone.fm Licensee: Jim Pattison Broadcast Group Ltd. (the general partner) and Jim Pattison Industries Ltd. (the limited partner), carrying on business as Jim Pattison Broadcast Group L.P. (acq 11-24-2006; C$15.75 million with CKKQ-FM Victoria). Format: Modern rock. Target aud: 25-64. ♦Dan McAllister, gen mgr, natl sls mgr; John Shields, opns mgr; Brian Blackburn, sls VP.

CKKQ-FM— Dec 12, 1987: 100.3 mhz; 100 kw. Ant 1,620 ft TL: N48 35 41 W123 32 37. (Digital radio: 1,472.000 mhz; 2 kw). Stereo. Hrs open: 24 Top Floor, 2750 Quadra St., V8T 4E8. Phone: (250) 475-0100. Fax: (250) 475-3299.E-mail: thecrew@theQ.fm Web Site:www.theq.fm Licensee: Jim Pattison Broadcast Group Ltd. (the general partner) and Jim Pattison Industries Ltd. (the limited partner), carrying on business as Jim Pattison Broadcast Group L.P. (acq 11-24-2006; C$15.75 million with CJZN-FM Victoria). Natl. Rep: Canadian Broadcast Sales,. Format: Classic Rock. News staff: 2; News: 4 hrs wkly. Target aud: 25-49. ♦Dan McAllister, gen mgr, natl sls mgr; John Shields, opns mgr; Brian Blackburn, sls VP.

***CKMO(AM)**— Sept 4, 2000: 900 khz; 10 kw-U, DA-1. Stereo. Hrs open: 3100 Foul Bay Rd., V8P 5J2. Phone: (250) 370-3658. Fax: (250) 370-3679.E-mail: info@village900.ca Web Site:www.village900.ca Licensee: CKMO Radio Society. Format: Educ. News: 5 hrs wkly. Spec prog: Portugese 3 hrs, news/talk 3 hrs wkly. ♦Brad Edwards, gen mgr.

Whistler

CISW-FM— Feb 25, 1982: 102.1 mhz; 586 w. 2,250 ft Hrs open: Rebroadcasts CISQ-FM Squamish.
Box 1068, Squamish, V0N 1B4. Phone: (604) 892-1021. Fax: (604) 892-6383.E-mail: mountainfm@mountainfm.com Web Site:www.mountainfm.com Licensee: Rogers Broadcasting Ltd. (group owner). Format: Hot adult contemp. ♦Gary Miles, pres; Paul Fisher, VP; Ken Geiger, gen mgr; Janis Correia, opns mgr.

Williams Lake

CFFM-FM— Aug 31, 1987: 97.5 mhz; Stereo. Hrs open: 24 Dups AM 50% 83 S. First Ave., V2G 1H4. Phone: (250) 398-2336. Fax: (250) 392-4142.E-mail: info@cffmthemax.com Web Site:www.cffmthemax.com Licensee: Vista Radio Ltd. (Acq 2006). Natl. Rep: Target Broadcast Sales, Canadian Broadcast Sales,. Format: Rock and pop. News staff: 2. Target aud: 18-44.

CKWL(AM)— Feb 25, 1960: 570 khz; 1 kw-U, DA-2. Hrs open: 24 83 S. First Ave., V2G 1H4. Phone: (250) 392-6551. Fax: (250) 392-4142. Web Site:www.thewolfpack.ca Licensee: Vista Radio Ltd. Group

owner: Cariboo Central Interior Radio Inc. Natl. Rep: Canadian Broadcast Sales, Target Broadcast Sales,. Format: Modern country, southern rock. News staff: one. Target aud: 25-54 plus. ◆ Terry Coles, pres, gen sls mgr; Paul Mann, exec VP, stn mgr; Tracey Gard, gen sls mgr; Jason Mann, progmg.

Manitoba

Altona

CFAM(AM)— Mar 13, 1957: 950 khz; 10 kw-U, DA-2. Hrs open: 24 Box 950, 201-125 Centre Avenue, R0G 0B0. Phone: (204) 324-6464. Fax: (204) 324-8918.E-mail: cfam@goldenwestradio.com Web Site:www.cfamradio.com Licensee: Golden West Broadcasting Ltd. (group owner) Natl. Rep: Canadian Broadcast Sales,. Format: Agriculture, MOR. News staff: 8; News: 12 hrs wkly. Target aud: General. Spec prog: Class 15 hrs wkly. ◆ Elmer Hildebrand, CEO & pres; Ang Enns, stn mgr.

Boissevain

CJRB(AM)— 1973: 1220 khz; 10 kw-U. Hrs open: 24 Box 1220, R0K 0E0. Phone: (204) 324-6464. Fax: (204) 324-8918. Licensee: Golden West Broadcasting Ltd. (group owner) Wire Svc: BN Wire Format: Easy lstng, inspirational, agriculture. News staff: one. Target aud: General. ◆ E. Hildebrand, pres; Lyndon Friesen, exec VP; Menno Friesen, sls VP & gen sls mgr; Al Friesen, progmg mgr; Laverne Siemens, engrg dir.

Brandon

CJJJ-FM— May 2003: 106.5 mhz; 930 w. Hrs open: Assiniboine Community College, 1430 Victoria Ave. E., Rm 223, R7A 2A9. Phone: (204) 571-3900. Fax: (204) 726-7014.E-mail: campusradio@assiniboine.net Web Site:www.mediaproacc.ca Licensee: Assiniboine Campus-Community Radio Society Inc. Format: Var. ◆ Jill Ferguson, stn mgr.

CKLF-FM— June 1, 2000: 94.7 mhz; 100 kw. Stereo. Hrs open: 24 624 14th St. E., R7A 7E1. Phone: (204) 726-8888. Fax: (204) 726-1270.E-mail: qcountry@cklffm.ca Web Site:www.starfmradio.com Licensee: Riding Mountain Broadcasting Ltd. Format: Adult contemp. News staff: 7. Target aud: 25-54; adults. ◆ Cam Clark, gen mgr.

CKLQ(AM)— October 1977: 880 khz; 10 kw-U, DA-2. Hrs open: 24 624 14th St. E., R7A 7E1. Phone: (204) 726-8888. Fax: (204) 726-1270.E-mail: qcountry@cklq.mb.ca Web Site:www.cklq.com Licensee: Riding Mountain Broadcasting Ltd. Natl. Rep: Target Broadcast Sales,. Format: Country. News staff: 7. Target aud: 35 plus. Spec prog: Farm 18 hrs wkly. ◆ Cam Clark, gen mgr.

CKXA-FM— February 2000: 101.1 mhz; 100 kw. Hrs open: 2940 Victoria Ave., R7B 3Y3. Phone: (204) 728-1150. Fax: (204) 725-3794.E-mail: dsmith@kx96online.com Web Site:www.1011thefarm.com Licensee: Astral Media Radio G.P. Group owner: Standard Broadcasting Corp. (acq 10-29-2007; grpsl). Format: Country. ◆ Sharon Taylor, VP, gen mgr; Janet Trecarten, opns mgr; Tim Black, progmg dir.

CKX-FM— Dec 16, 1963: 96.1 mhz; 100 kw. 1,042 ft Stereo. Hrs open: Prog sep from AM 2940 Victoria Ave., R7B 3Y3. Phone: (204) 728-1150. Fax: (204) 725-3794.E-mail: dsmith@kx96online.com Web Site:www.kx96online.com Licensee: Astral Media Radio G.P. Group owner: Standard Broadcasting Corp. (acq 10-29-2007; grpsl). Format: Classic rock. ◆ Sharon Taylor, gen mgr; Janet Trecarten, opns mgr, progmg dir; Gyl Tosheck, gen sls mgr; Norine Mitchell, rgnl sls mgr; Donna Smith, prom dir; Angela Greig, asst music dir; Bob Bruce, news dir.

Cross Lake

CFNC(AM)— 1990: 1490 khz; 50 w. Hrs open: Box 129, R0B 0J0. Phone: (204) 676-2331. Phone: (204) 676-2248. Fax: (204) 676-2911. Licensee: Native Communications Inc. Format: Community. ◆ Dina Monias, pres; Joyce Halcrow, gen mgr.

Dauphin

CKDM(AM)— Jan 6, 1951: 730 khz; 10 kw-D, 5 kw-N, DA-N. Hrs open: 24 27 3rd Ave. N.E., R7N 0Y5. Phone: (204) 638-3230. Fax: (204) 638-8257/8891.E-mail: 730ckdm@mts.net Web Site:www.730ckdm.com Licensee: Dauphin Broadcasting Co. Ltd. (acq 11-23-93). Format: Country. News staff: 3. ◆ Allan Truman, gen mgr.

Flin Flon

CFAR(AM)— Nov 14, 1937: 590 khz; 10 kw-D, 1 kw-N, DA-2. Hrs open: 24 316 Green St., R8A 0H2. Phone: (204) 687-3469. Phone: (204) 687-8300. Fax: (204) 687-6786.E-mail: cfar@arcticradio.ca Web Site:www.arcticradio.ca Licensee: Arctic Radio (1982) Ltd. (acq 9-1-82). Format: Adult contemp. News staff: 2; News: 15 hrs wkly. Target aud: General. ◆ Tom O'Brien, pres & gen mgr; Maureen Kozar, stn mgr.

Portage la Prairie

CFRY(AM)— Oct 18, 1956: 920 khz; 25 kw-D, 15 kw-N, DA-2. Hrs open: 350 River Rd., R1N 0N6. Phone: (204) 239-5111. Fax: (204) 857-3456. Licensee: Golden West Broadcasting Ltd. Group owner: Golden West Broadcasting Ltd. (acq 7-26-2000; with co-located FM). Format: C&W. Spec prog: Farm 4 hrs wkly. ◆ Warren Neufeld, stn mgr.

CFRY-FM— 1996: 93.1 mhz; 27 kw. Hrs open: Dups AM 100% 350 River Rd., R1N 0N6. Phone: (204) 239-5111. Fax: (204) 857-3456. Licensee: Golden West Broadcasting Ltd.

CJPG-FM— May 4, 2004: 96.5 mhz; 24 kw. Hrs open: Box 920, R1N 0N6. Secondary address: 350 River Rd. R1N 0N6. Phone: (204) 239-5111. Fax: (204) 857-3456. Web Site:www.mix965fm.com Licensee: Golden West Broadcasting Ltd. Format: CHR. ◆ Warren Neufeld, stn mgr.

Pukatawagan

CFPX-FM— Sept 19, 1971: 98.3 mhz; 34.8 w. Hrs open: Missinnippi River Native, Communications Inc., R0B 1G0. Phone: (204) 553-2155. Fax: (204) 553-2158. Licensee: Missinnippi River Native Communications Inc. Format: Country, rock. ◆ Rosie Colomb, gen mgr.

Saint Boniface

*CKSB(AM)— May 27, 1946: 1050 khz; 10 kw-U. Hrs open: 24 607 Langevin St., R2H 2W2. Phone: (204) 788-3236. Fax: (204) 788-3245. Web Site:www.radiocanada.ca/radio/manitoba Licensee: Societe Radio Canada. (acq 4-1-73). Format: Div, Fr. Target aud: General. ◆ Robert Rabinovitch, CEO; Huguette Le Gall, mktg mgr; Rene Fontaine, progmg dir; Gilles Frechette, progmg mgr; Marc Babin, news dir.

CKXL-FM— October 1991: 91.1 mhz; 61 kw. Hrs open: 24 340 Provencher Blvd., Winnipeg, R2H 0G7. Phone: (204) 233-4243. Phone: (204) 231-3691. Fax: (204) 233-3646.E-mail: info@envol91.mb.ca Web Site:www.envol91.mb.ca Licensee: La Radio Communautaire du Manitoba Inc. Population served: 600,000. Rgnl rep: Target Media, George McKringan Format: Soft rock, div, Fr. Target aud: 20-50; Francophone. Spec prog: Folk 2 hrs, jazz 4 hrs, Sp 2 hrs, blues 2 hrs, reggae 2 hrs wkly. ◆ Rokhaya Soumbounou, sls.

Selkirk

CFQX-FM— Nov 9, 1981: 104.1 mhz; 100 kw. 500 ft (CP: 95.3 mhz.). Stereo. Hrs open: 24 177 Lombard Ave., 3rd Fl., Winnipeg, R3B 0W5. Phone: (204) 944-1031. Fax: (204) 943-7687.E-mail: jtrecarten@qx104fm.com Web Site:www.qx104fm.com Licensee: Astral Media Radio G.P. Group owner: Standard Broadcasting Corp. (acq 10-29-2007; grpsl). Format: Country. News staff: 2. Target aud: 25-54. ◆ Sharon Taylor, VP, gen mgr & gen mgr; Gyl Tosheck, gen sls mgr, natl sls mgr; Janet Trecarten, progmg dir; Karen Black, mus dir.

CICY-FM— 2000: 105.5 mhz; 100 kw. Stereo. Hrs open: 1507 Inkster Blvd., Winnipeg, R2X 1R2. Phone: (204) 772-8255. Fax: (204) 779-5628.E-mail: info@ncifm.com Web Site:www.ncifm.com Licensee: Native Communication Inc. Format: Div in English, Cree, Saulteaux, Ojibiway languages; CHR, country. News staff: 2. Target aud: 25 and up; aboriginal. ◆ Dave McLeod, CEO; Rita Ducharme, pres.

Steinbach

CHSM(AM)— Mar 19, 1964: 1250 khz; 10 kw-U, DA-2. Hrs open: 24 105-32 Brandt St., R5G 2J7. Phone: (204) 326-3737. Fax: (204) 326-2299. Web Site:www.am1250online.com Licensee: Golden West Broadcasting Ltd. (group owner) Natl. Rep: Canadian Broadcast Sales,. Format: MOR. News staff: 3; News: 12 hrs wkly. Target aud:

General. ◆ Elmer Hildebrand, pres; Richard Kroeker, gen mgr; Al Friesen, progmg dir; Laverne Siemens, engrg dir, chief of engrg.

CILT-FM— Sept 29, 1998: 96.7 mhz; 50 kw. Hrs open: 24 105-32 Brandt St., R5G 2J7. Phone: (204) 346-0000. Fax: (204) 326-2299. Web Site:www.lite967online.com Licensee: Golden West Broadcasting Ltd. Format: Light adult contemp. ◆ Trev Schellenberg, progmg dir.

Swan River

CJSB-FM— July 1, 2006: 104.5 mhz; 210 w. TL: N52 06 18 W101 16 10. Stereo. Hrs open: 24 Box 1268, R0L 1Z0. Phone: (204) 734-6484. Fax: (204) 734-5897.E-mail: onair@cj104radio.com Web Site:www.cj104radio.ca Licensee: Stillwater Broadcasting Ltd. Natl. Rep: Target Broadcast Sales,. Wire Svc: Canadian Press Format: Var. News staff: 2; News: 20 hrs/week. ◆ Bill Gade, gen mgr.

The Pas

CJAR(AM)— 1974: 1240 khz; 1 kw-U, DA-1. Hrs open: Box 2980, R9A 1R7. Phone: (204) 623-5307. Fax: (204) 623-5337.E-mail: cjar@articradio.ca Web Site:www.articradio.ca Licensee: Arctic Radio Corp. Ltd. Format: Adult contemp, AOR, C&W. Spec prog: Aboriginal 5 hrs wkly. ◆ Tom O'Brien, chmn & pres; Jeremy Wachal, gen mgr.

Thompson

*CBWK-FM— 1980: 100.9 mhz; 9.4 kw. Hrs open: 7 AM-5 PM 7 Selkirk Ave., R8N 0M4. Phone: (204) 677-1680. Fax: (204) 677-9517.E-mail: north@winnwpeg.cbc.ca Web Site:www.winnipeg.cbc.ca Licensee: CBC. Population served: 50,000 Natl. Network: CBC Radio One, . Format: Div, talk. ◆ Mark Sislo, gen mgr, progmg dir & news dir; Doug MacPherson, chief of engrg.

CHTM(AM)— Mar 29, 1964: 610 khz; 1 kw-U. Hrs open: 24 103 Cree, R8N 0B9. Phone: (204) 778-7361. Fax: (204) 778-5252.E-mail: chtm@arcticradio.ca Web Site:www.arcticradio.ca Licensee: Arctic Radio (1982) Ltd. Population served: 60,000 Format: Adult contemp, classic rock, country. News staff: 2; News: 15 hrs wkly. Target aud: General. Spec prog: Relg 12 hrs, Cree (American Indian) 10 hrs wkly. ◆ Tom O'Brien, pres; Sue O'Brien, gen mgr, opns mgr; Dave Moore, gen sls mgr; Tony Taylor, progmg dir; Don Barkman, mus dir, local news ed.

CINC-FM— 1994: 96.3 mhz; 86 w. Hrs open: rebroadcasts CICY-FM Winnipeg 80%. 76 Severn Crescent, R8N 1M6. Phone: (204) 778-8343. Fax: (204) 778-6559.E-mail: info@ncifm.com Web Site:www.ncifm.com Licensee: Native Communications Inc. Format: Div in English, Cree, Saulteaux, Ojibiway languages, CHR Country. ◆ Dave McLeod, CEO; Rosanne Ferguson, progmg dir.

Winkler

CJEL-FM— Oct 4, 2000: 93.5 mhz; 100 kw. Hrs open: 24 Box 399, R6W 4A6. Secondary address: 201-295 Main St. R6W 4A6. Phone: (204) 331-9300. Fax: (204) 325-2206.E-mail: info@eagle935fm.com Web Site:www.eagle935fm.com Licensee: Golden West Broadcasting Ltd. (group owner) Format: Adult contemp. ◆ Elmer Hildebrand, CEO, chmn & pres; Bill Hildebrand, stn mgr.

Winkler-Morden

CKMW(AM)— Aug 1, 1980: 1570 khz; 10 kw-U, DA-2. Hrs open: 24 Box 399 201-295 Main St., Winkler, R6W 4AG. Phone: (204) 325-9506. Fax: (204) 325-2206.E-mail: country1570@goldenwestradio.com Web Site:www.ckmwradio.com Licensee: Golden West Broadcasting Ltd. (group owner) Natl. Rep: Canadian Broadcast Sales,. Format: Country. News staff: 2. Target aud: General. ◆ Bill Hildebrand, gen mgr, stn mgr; Elmer Hildebrand, CEO, pres & engrg dir.

Winnipeg

CBW(AM)— Sept 3, 1948: 990 khz; 50 kw-D, 46 kw-N. Hrs open: Box 160, R3C 2H1. Phone: (204) 788-3222. Fax: (204) 788-3227. Web Site:www.cbc.ca Licensee: Canadian Broadcasting Corp. Natl. Network: CBC Radio One, . Format: Div. Spec prog: Farm 6 hrs, class 8 hrs, C&W one hr wkly. ◆ John Bertrand, gen mgr.

CBW-FM— Oct 11, 1965: 98.3 mhz; 354 kw. Stereo. Hrs open: Dups AM 50% Box 160, R3C 2H1. Phone: (204) 788-3222. Fax: (204)

788-3227. Licensee: Canadian Broadcasting Corp Natl. Network: CBC Radio Two, . Co-owned TV: CBWT(TV) affil

CFEQ-FM— 2003: 107.1 mhz; 920 w. Hrs open: 1-741 St. Mary's Rd., R2M 3N5. Phone: (204) 452-9602. Fax: (204) 478-6735. Web Site:www.ignite107.com Licensee: Golden West Broadcasting Ltd. (acq 6-27-2008; C$725,000). Format: Christian rock. ♦Tom Hiebert, gen mgr; Wayne Yaskew, mktg dir; Gordo Fry, progmg dir.

CFRW(AM)— Nov 1, 1963: 1290 khz; 10 kw-U, DA-2. Stereo. Hrs open: 1445 Pembina Hwy., R3T 5C2. Phone: (204) 477-5120. Fax: (204) 453-0815. Licensee: CTV Ltd. (group owner; (acq 6-22-2007; grpsl). Format: Oldies. ♦Jim Blundell, gen mgr; Corey Mospanchuk, gen sls mgr; Ryan Ghidoni, progmg mgr.

CFWM-FM— June 13, 1996: 99.9 mhz; 100 kw. Hrs open: 24 1445 Pembina Hwy., R3T 5C2. Phone: (204) 477-5120. Fax: (204) 453-0815.E-mail: info@999bobfm.com Web Site:www.999bobfm.com Licensee: CTV Ltd. (group owner; (acq 6-22-2007; grpsl). Population served: 672,000 Format: Adult contemp. News staff: one; News: 5 hrs wkly. Target aud: 25-54. ♦Jim Blundell, gen mgr; Chris Brook, progmg dir.

CHIQ-FM— Nov 1, 1963: 94.3 mhz; 100 kw. Ant 450 ft TL: N49 47 58 W97 16 30. Stereo. Hrs open: 1445 Pembina Hwy., R3T 5C2. Phone: (204) 477-5120. Fax: (204) 453-0815.E-mail: info@q94fm.com Web Site:www.curve94.com Licensee: CTV Ltd. Format: Pop alternative. ♦Andrew Long, progmg mgr.

CHNK-FM— Dec 7, 2002: 100.7 mhz; 60.9 kw. Ant 578 ft Hrs open: 24 520 Corydon Ave., R3L 0P1. Phone: (204) 477-1221.E-mail: info@hank.fm Web Site:www.hank.fm Licensee: Newcap Inc. (acq 12-5-2005; C$1,790,000 for stock). Format: Country. News staff: one. ♦Randy Skulsky, gen mgr; Michelle Pereira, gen sls mgr; Ami Freeman, prom dir; Abbey White, progmg dir.

CHVN-FM— Sept 14, 2000: 95.1 mhz; 100 kw. TL: N49 46 15 W97 30 35. Stereo. Hrs open: 24 741 St. Mary's Rd., R2M 3N5. Phone: (204) 452-9602. Fax: (204)478-6735.E-mail: chvn@goldenwestradio.com Web Site:www.chvnradio.com Licensee: Golden West Broadcasting Ltd. (acq 2004). Natl. Network: Salem Radio Network, . Format: Contemp Christian music. Target aud: 18-49; families. Spec prog: Children one hr, gospel 4 hrs, teens 6 hrs wkly. ♦Elmer Hildebrand, CEO; Richard Kroeker, gen mgr; Trev Schellenbert, progmg dir.

CITI-FM— 1962: 92.1 mhz; 100 kw. Ant 700 ft Stereo. Hrs open: 166 Osborne St., Unit 4, R3L 1Y8. Phone: (204) 788-3400. Fax: (204) 788-3401.E-mail: crais@letaawskywinnipegradio.rogers.com Web Site:www.92citifm.ca Licensee: Rogers Broadcasting Ltd. (group owner; acq 8-20-92). Format: Classic rock. ♦Geoff Poulton, gen mgr; Gayle Zarbatany, progmg dir; Frank Andrews, mus dir.

CJGV-FM— March 2003: 99.1 mhz; 63.7 kw. TL: N49 45 20 W97 07 52. Stereo. Hrs open: 30th Fl. CanWest Global Pl., 201 Portage Ave., R3B 3K6. Phone: (204) 253-2665. Fax: (204) 926-1674. Licensee: Corus Premium Television Ltd. Group owner: CanWest Global Communications Corp. (acq 7-6-2007; C$14.5 million with CKBT-FM Kitchener-Waterloo, ON). Format: Smooth jazz. News staff: one. Target aud: 35-45. ♦Brian Wortley, opns mgr, gen sls mgr; Jay Thomas, prom dir; Barry Horne, progmg dir.

CJKR-FM— March 1948: 97.5 mhz; 310 kw. 228 ft Stereo. Hrs open: 930 Portage Ave., R3G 0P8. Fax: (204) 780-9750. Web Site:www.power97.com Licensee: Corus Premuim Television Ltd. Format: Winnipeg best rock. Target aud: 25-44; males. ♦Matt Cundill, progmg dir; Casey Norman, mus dir.

CJNU-FM— December 2006: 104.7 mhz; 40 w. Hrs open: Box 2282, Stn Main, R3C 4A6. Phone: (204) 942-2568.E-mail: cjnu@mts.net Web Site:www.nostalgiawinnipeg.com Licensee: Nostalgia Broadcasting Cooperative. Format: Nostalgia. ♦Bill Stewart, pres.

CJOB(AM)— 1946: 680 khz; 50 kw-U, DA-N. Hrs open: 24 930 Portage Ave., R3G 0P8. Phone: (204) 786-2471. Fax: (204) 783-4512. Web Site:www.cjob.com Licensee: Corus Premium Television Ltd. Group owner: Corus Entertainment Inc. (acq 7-6-2000; grpsl). Population served: 600,000 Natl. Rep: Canadian Broadcast Sales,. Format: News/talk. News staff: 25; News: 56 hrs wkly. Target aud: 25-54. ♦Garth Buchko, pres, gen mgr, mktg mgr; Sherrie Johnston, opns mgr; Steve Dubois, gen sls mgr; Colin Lougheed, prom dir; Paul Graham, mus dir; Vic Grant, progmg dir & news dir; Jack Hoeppner, chief of engrg.

CJUM-FM— Sept 4, 1998: 101.5 mhz; 1.2 kw. Stereo. Hrs open: 24 UMFM, 308 University Center, University of Manitoba, R3T 2N2. Phone: (204) 474-7027. Fax: (204) 269-1299.E-mail: station.manager@umfm.com Web Site:www.umfm.com Licensee: The University of Manitoba Students' Union. Population served: 650,000 Format: Div. News: 12 hrs wkly. Target aud: 18-58; all genders, all ages who prefer non-coml music & culture. ♦Jared McKetiak, stn mgr; Michael Elves, progmg dir.

CKIC-FM— March 2004: 92.9 mhz; 201 w. Hrs open: W302-160 Princess St., R3B 1K9. Phone: (204) 949-8480. Fax: (204) 949-0057.E-mail: rick@kick.fm Licensee: Red River College Radio. Format: Adult alternative. ♦Rick Everett, stn mgr.

CKJS(AM)— Mar 25, 1975: 810 khz; 10 kw-U, DA-1. Hrs open: 520 Corydon Ave., R3L 0P1. Phone: (204) 477-1221. Fax: (204) 453-8244.E-mail: info@ckjs.com Web Site:www.ckjs.com Licensee: Newcap Inc. (acq 4-30-2006; C$2.3 million). Rgnl rep: Direct. Format: Ethnic, Christian. Target aud: General. Spec prog: Ger 6 hrs, It 5 hrs, Pol 7 hrs, Sp 3 hrs, Por 8 hrs, Greek one hr, Filipino 20 hrs wkly. ♦Randy Skulsky, gen mgr; Michelle Pereira, gen sls mgr; Ami Freeman, prom dir; Gido Gigliotti, progmg dir.

CKMM-FM— Feb 14, 1980: 103.1 mhz; 70 kw. Ant 676 ft Stereo. Hrs open: 177 Lombard Ave., 3rd. Fl., R3B 0W5. Phone: (204) 944-1031. Fax: (204) 943-7687.E-mail: ace@hot103live.com Web Site:www.hot103live.com Licensee: Astral Media Radio G.P. Group owner: Standard Broadcasting Corp. (acq 10-29-2007; grpsl). Format: CHR. ♦Sharon Taylor, gen mgr; Ace Burpee, progmg dir; Chris Love, mus dir.

***CKUW-FM—** May 1, 1999: 95.9 mhz; 450 w. TL: N49 52 51 W97 08 56. Stereo. Hrs open: 24 515 Portage Ave., Rm. 4C M11, R3B 2E9. Phone: (204) 786-9782. Fax: (204) 783-7080.E-mail: ckuw@uwinnipeg.ca Web Site:www.ckuw.ca Licensee: The Winnipeg Campus/Community Radio Society. Population served: 660,000 Format: Urban contemp, rock/AOR, news/talk. News: 5 hrs wkly. Target aud: General; Our community. Spec prog: Children 2 hrs, class 4 hrs, folk 2 hrs, jazz 8 hrs wkly. ♦Rob Schmidt, stn mgr; Robin Eriksson, progmg dir; Don Baily, mus dir.

CKY-FM— Jan 21, 2004: 102.3 mhz; 70 kw. Hrs open: 166 Osborne St., Unit 4, R3L 1Y8. Phone: (204) 788-3400. Fax: (204) 788-3401.E-mail: crais.letawksy@winnipegradio.rogers.com Web Site:www.102clearfm.com Licensee: Rogers Broadcasting Ltd. (group owner). Format: Adult contemp. ♦Geoff Poulton, VP & gen mgr; Gayle Zarbatany, progmg dir; Craig Pfeifer, mus dir.

New Brunswick

Balmoral

CIMS-FM— 1994: 103.9 mhz; 7.295 kw. Hrs open: 1991 Ave. CP2561, des Pionniers, E8E 2W7. Phone: (506) 826-1040. Fax: (506) 826-2400.E-mail: cimsfm@nbnet.nb.ca Web Site:www.cimsfm.ca Licensee: Cooperative Radio Restigouche Ltee. Format: Var. ♦Pierre Morais, gen mgr; Camille Deschenes, rgnl sls mgr.

Bathurst

CKBC-FM— Jan 22, 2004: 104.9 mhz; 20 kw. Stereo. Hrs open: 24 176 Main St., E2A 1A4. Phone: (506) 547-1360. Fax: (506) 547-1367.E-mail: maxfm@theradioatl.ca Licensee: Astral Media Radio Atlantic Inc. Group owner: Astral Media Inc. Population served: 107,000 Natl. Rep: Canadian Broadcast Sales,. Format: Adult contemp. News staff: 3; News: 9 hrs wkly. Target aud: 25-49. Spec prog: Fr 9 hrs wkly. ♦Jacques Parisien, pres; John Eddy, exec VP; Jamie Robichaud, gen mgr; Pat Brenan, sls VP.

CKLE-FM— Mar 29, 1990: 92.9 mhz; 100 kw. Stereo. Hrs open: 24 195 Main St., E2A 1A7. Phone: (506) 546-4600. Phone: (506) 546-1122. Fax: (506) 546-6611.E-mail: ckleadmin@mb.aibn.com Licensee: Radio De LaBaie Ltd. Format: CHR. Spec prog: Jazz 2 hrs wkly. ♦Armand Roussy, gen mgr, gen sls mgr & progmg dir.

Blackville

CJFY-FM— 2004: 107.7 mhz; 45 w. Hrs open: 401 Main St., E9B 1T3. Phone: (506) 843-2208. Fax: (506) 843-2603.E-mail: staff@liferadio.ca Web Site:www.life1075.com Licensee: Miramichi Fellowship Center Inc. Format: Christian music. ♦John D. Stewart, CEO; Shaun Mackenzie, gen mgr.

Campbellton

CKNB(AM)— 1939: 950 khz; 10 kw-D, 1 kw-N, DA-2. Hrs open: 24 Box 340, 74 Water Street, E3N 3G7. Phone: (506) 753-4415. Fax: (506) 789-9505.E-mail: cknb@nb.sympatico.ca Licensee: Maritime Broadcasting System Ltd. Format: Adult contemp, country, CHR. News: 10 hrs wkly. Target aud: General. Spec prog: Fr 18 hrs wkly. ♦Merv Russell, pres; David Montgomery, gen mgr.

Caraquet

CJVA(AM)— Sept 15, 1977: 810 khz; 10 kw-U, DA-2. Hrs open: 18 195 Main St., Bathurst, E2A 1A7. Phone: (506) 727-4605. Fax: (506) 727-6611. Licensee: Radio Acadie Ltd. Natl. Rep: Canadian Broadcast Sales,. Format: Div, adult contemp, MOR. Target aud: 25 plus. Spec prog: C&W 15 hrs wkly. ♦Rufino Landry, pres; Armand Roussy, gen mgr.

Edmundston

CFAI-FM— Jan 15, 1991: 101.1 mhz; 4 kw. TL: N47 23 25 W68 18 59. Stereo. Hrs open: 24 165 Blvd. Hebert, E3V 2S8. Phone: (506) 737-5060. Fax: (506) 737-5084.E-mail: radio@cfai.fm Web Site:www.cfai.fm Licensee: La Cooperative des Montagnes Ltee. Population served: 45,000 Format: Top-40, soft rock. News staff: one; News: 6 hrs wkly. Target aud: 12-50. ♦Louis G. Plourde, pres; Eric Morneault, gen mgr; Sheila Desroches, gen sls mgr.

CJEM-FM— July 1998: 92.7 mhz; 40.75 kw. TL: N47 21 47 W68 17 21. Stereo. Hrs open: 24 174 Church St., E3V 1K2. Phone: (506) 735-3351. Fax: (506) 739-5803.E-mail: cjem@nbnet.nb.ca Licensee: Radio Edmundston Inc. Population served: 50,000 Natl. Rep: Canadian Broadcast Sales,. Format: Hot adult contemp, CHR. News staff: 2; News: 6 hrs wkly. Target aud: 25-54. ♦Jean Marc Michaud, pres; Murillo Soucy, gen mgr.

Fredericton

CBZF-FM— 2004: 99.5 mhz; 3.2 kw. Hrs open: Box 2200, E3B 5G4. Secondary address: 1160 Regent St. E3B 5G4. Phone: (506) 451-4000. Fax: (506) 451-4170. Web Site:www.cbc.ca Licensee: Canadian Broadcasting Corp. Natl. Network: CBC Radio One, . Format: Div.

***CBZ-FM—** January 1978: 101.5 mhz; 100 kw. Stereo. Hrs open: Rebroadcasts CBH-FM Halifax, NS 100%.
Box 2200, E3B 5G4. Secondary address: 1160 Regent St. E3B 5G4. Phone: (506) 451-4000. Fax: (506) 451-4170. Web Site:www.cbc.ca Licensee: Canadian Broadcasting Corp. Natl. Network: CBC Radio Two, . Format: Classics & beyond, news/talk. ♦Gary Arsenault, gen mgr.

CFRK-FM— 2005: 92.3 mhz; 93 kw. Hrs open: 77 Westmoreland St., Frederickton, E3B 6Z3. Phone: (506) 455-0923. Fax: (506) 455-3602. Web Site:www.fredfm.ca Licensee: Newcap Inc. Format: Greatest hits of 60s, 70s & 80s. ♦Hilary Montbourquette, gen mgr; Brad Muir, opns dir, progmg dir.

CFXY-FM— July 15, 1983: 105.3 mhz; 78 kw. 800 ft Stereo. Hrs open: 206 Rookwood Ave., E3B 2M2. Phone: (506) 451-9111. Fax: (506) 452-2345. Licensee: Astral Media Radio Atlantic Inc. Format: C&W, rock.

CHSR-FM— Jan 24, 1961: 97.9 mhz; 250 w. Ant 157 ft Stereo. Hrs open: 7 AM-3 AM Box 4400, Student Union Bldg., Univ. of New Brunswick, E3B 5A3. Phone: (506) 453-4985. Fax: (506) 453-4999.E-mail: chsr@unb.ca Web Site:www.unb.ca/chsr Licensee: CHSR Broadcasting Inc. Format: Alternative, div. News: 6 hrs wkly. Target aud: General. Spec prog: Fr 2 hrs, ethnic 5 hrs, American Indian one hr, class 6 hrs, jazz 6 hrs, Chinese 3 hrs wkly. ♦Tristis Ward, stn mgr; Linda Pelletier, dev mgr.

CIBX-FM— June 11, 1996: 106.9 mhz; 100 kw. (CP: 78 kw.). Hrs open: 24 206 Rookwood Ave., E3B 2M2. Phone: (506) 455-1069. Fax: (506) 452-2345. Licensee: Astral Media Radio Atlantic Inc. Group owner: Astral Media Inc. (acq 4-19-2002; grpsl). Natl. Rep: Canadian Broadcast Sales,. Format: Lite rock. News staff: 4; News: 8 hrs wkly. Target aud: 25-54. ♦John Eddy, pres; Pat Brennan, gen mgr.

CIXN-FM— Apr 8, 2001: 96.5 mhz; 27 w. Hrs open: JoyFM, 1010 Hanwell Rd., Suite 10, E3B 6A4. Phone: (506) 454-9600. Fax: (506) 443-0991.E-mail: welcome@joyfm.ca Web Site:www.joyfm.ca Licensee: The Joy FM Network Inc. Format: Christian. ♦Doug Boyd, gen mgr; Jonathan Ramirez, progmg dir.

*CJPN-FM— August 1997: 90.5 mhz; 1.56 kw. Stereo. Hrs open: 715 Priestman St., E3B 5W7. Phone: (506) 454-2576. Fax: (506) 453-3958.E-mail: cjpn@nbnet.nb.ca Web Site:www.cjpn.ca Licensee: Radio Fredericton Inc. Format: Adult contemp. ◆Pierre Dumas, gen mgr.

CJRI-FM— May 18, 2005: 104.5 mhz; 50 w. TL: N45 56 14 W66 39 19. Hrs open: 151 Main St., E3A 1C6. Phone: (506) 472-0947. Fax: (506) 459-8194.E-mail: gospel@cjri.fm Web Site:www.cjri.fm Licensee: Faithway Communications Inc. Format: Southern gospel, country gospel, praise music. ◆Ross Ingram, pres.

CKHJ(AM)— Aug 19, 1977: 1260 khz; 10 kw-U, DA-N. Hrs open: 206 Rookwood Ave., E3B 2M2. Phone: (506) 451-9111. Fax: (506) 452-2345. Licensee: Astral Media Radio Atlantic Inc. Group owner: Astral Media Inc. Format: Country. Spec prog: Fr one hr wkly. ◆John Eddy, gen mgr; Pat Brennan, gen sls mgr.

Fredericton Centre

CKTP-FM— 2002: 95.7 mhz; 50 w. Hrs open: Kchikhusis Commercial Center, 150 Cliffe St., Box R13, Fredericton, E3A 0A1. Fax: (506) 459-4404.E-mail: info@cktpradio.com Web Site:www.cktpradio.com Licensee: Maliseet Nation Radio Inc. Format: All hits. ◆Conrad Mead, stn mgr.

Grand Falls

CIKX-FM— 2001: 93.5 mhz; 5.3 kw. Hrs open: 399 Broadway Blvd., E3Z 2K5. Phone: (506) 473-9393. Fax: (506) 473-3893.E-mail: k93@radioatl.ca Web Site:www.k93.ca Licensee: Astral Media Radio Atlantic Inc. Group owner: Astral Media Inc. (acq 2003; grpsl). Format: Hot adult contemp. ◆Pat Brennan, gen mgr; Jacques Lafrance, gen sls mgr; Rick McGuire, progmg dir; Todd Vinotte, news dir.

CKMV-FM— August 2000: 95.1 mhz; 975 w. Stereo. Hrs open: 24 Rebroadcasts CJEM-FM Edmundston 100%. 174 Church St., Edmundston, E3V 1K2. Phone: (506) 735-3351. Fax: (506) 739-5803.E-mail: cjem@nbnet.nb.ca Licensee: Radio Edmundston Inc. Natl. Rep: Canadian Broadcast Sales,. Format: Hot adult contemp, CHR. Target aud: 25-54. ◆Jean-Marc Michaud, pres; Murillo Soucy, gen mgr, gen sls mgr; Paul Clavette, progmg dir.

Kedgwick

*CFJU-FM— 1991: 90.1 mhz; 3 kw. TL: N47 35 05 W67 21 47. Stereo. Hrs open: 24 C.P. 1043, E8B 1Z9. Phone: (506) 235-9000. Fax: (506) 235-9001.E-mail: cfjufm@nbnet.nb.ca Licensee: La Radio Communautaire des Hauts-Plateaux Inc. Population served: 7,000 Format: Div, Fr. News: 8 hrs wkly. Target aud: 25-55. Spec prog: Country 12 hrs wkly. ◆M. Victor St- Pierre, pres; Lucille Theriault, gen mgr.

Miramichi

CKMA-FM—Not on air, target date: unknown: 93.7 mhz; 11 kw. TL: N47 00 37 W65 35 14. Hrs open: 300 chemin Beaverbrook, E1V 1A1. Phone: (506) 627-4125. Fax: (506) 627-4592.E-mail: radio.miracadie@nb.aibn.com Web Site:www.radio-miracadie.ca Licensee: Radio MirAcadie Inc. Format: Fr.

Miramichi City

CFAN-FM— Jan 10, 2003: 99.3 mhz; 17.8 kw. Hrs open: 24 396 Pleasant Dr., E1V 1X3. Phone: (506) 622-3311. Fax: (506) 627-0335.E-mail: cfan@nb.sympatico.ca Web Site:www.993theriver.com Licensee: Maritime Broadcasting System Ltd. Group owner: Maritime Broadcasting. Population served: 50,000 Format: Adult contemp. News staff: one; News: 8 hrs wkly. Target aud: General. Spec prog: Relg 4 hrs, folk 2 hrs wkly. ◆Brent Preston, gen mgr.

Moncton

*CBAF-FM— 1982: 88.5 mhz; 50 kw. Hrs open: Box 950, 250 University Ave, E1C 8N8. Phone: (506) 853-6666. Fax: (506) 853-6400. Web Site:www.cbc.ca/nb Licensee: Radio Canada. Natl. Network: Radio Canada, . Format: News, Current Affairs, French. ◆Susan Mitton, gen mgr.

CBA-FM— March 1982: 95.5 mhz; 68 kw. Hrs open: Rebroadcasts CBH-FM Halifax, NS 100%. Box 950, 250 University Ave., E1C 8N8. Phone: (506) 853-6666. Fax:

(506) 853-6400.E-mail: infomorning@moncton.cbc.com Web Site:www.cbc.ca Licensee: CBC Natl. Network: CBC Radio Two, . Format: Class.

*CBAL-FM— 1983: 98.3 mhz; 67.6 kw. Ant 577 ft TL: N46 08 41 W64 54 14. Stereo. Hrs open: Box 950, E1C 8N8. Phone: (506) 853-6666. Fax: (506) 853-6739. Web Site:www.cbc.radio-canada.ca Licensee: Societe Radio Canada. Natl. Network: Espace Musique, . Format: Music. ◆Louise Imbeault, gen mgr; Claire Hendy, opns mgr, progmg dir.

CBAM-FM— Jan 8, 2008: 106.1 mhz; 69.5 kw. TL: N46 08 41 W64 54 11. Hrs open: 250 University Ave. E1C 8N8. Phone: (506) 853-6666. Fax: (506) 853-6400. Web Site:www.cbc.ca Licensee: CBC. Natl. Network: CBC Radio One, . Format: News, current affrs. ◆Jonna Brewer, gen mgr.

CFBO-FM— 2008: 90.7 mhz; 30 kw. TL: N46 11 04 W64 52 52. Hrs open: 96 rue Providence, Shediac, E4P 2M9. Phone: (506) 532-0100. Fax: (506) 532-0120.E-mail: cjse@cjse.ca Web Site:www.cfbo.ca Licensee: Radio Beausejour Inc. Format: Fr adult contemp. ◆Serge Parent, gen mgr.

CFQM-FM— 1976: 103.9 mhz; 25 kw. Hrs open: 1000 St. George Blvd., E1E 4M7. Phone: (506) 858-1220. Fax: (506) 858-1209.E-mail: magic104@radiomoncton.com Web Site:www.radiomoncton.com Licensee: Maritime Broadcasting System Ltd. Format: Adult contemp. ◆Scott Clements, gen mgr.

CHOY-FM— Feb 19, 2001: 99.9 mhz; 9.5 kw. Hrs open: 1000 St. George Blvd., E1E 4M7. Phone: (506) 858-1220. Fax: (506) 858-1209.E-mail: magic104@radiomoncton.com Web Site:www.radiomoncton.com Licensee: CHOY-FM Ltee. Group owner: Maritime Broadcasting. (acq 12-19-2005). Format: Fr. ◆Scott Clements, gen mgr.

CITA-FM— January 2001: 105.1 mhz; 880 w. Hrs open: 101 Ilsley Ave., Unit 3, Dartmouth, NS, B3B 1S8. Phone: 9024688854. Fax: 9024688851.E-mail: info@cjlufm.com Web Site:www.citafm.com Licensee: International Harvesters for Christ Evangelistic Association Inc. Format: Christian music. ◆Jeff Lutes, pres.

CJMO-FM— June 19, 1987: 103.1 mhz; 46.8 kw. Stereo. Hrs open: 24 27 Arsenault Ct., E1E 4J8. Phone: (506) 858-5525. Fax: (506) 858-5539.E-mail: c103@c103.com Web Site:www.c103.com Licensee: Newcap Inc. Natl. Rep: Canadian Broadcast Sales,. Format: Classic rock. News staff: 4; News: 5 hrs wkly. Target aud: 25-54; adults. Spec prog: Jazz 2 hrs wkly. ◆Mark Maheu, pres; David Murray, CFO, opns VP; Hilary Montbourquette, gen mgr.

CJXL-FM— November 2000: 96.9 mhz; 100 kw. Hrs open: 24 27 Arsenault Ct., E1E 4J8. Phone: (506) 858-5525. Fax: (506) 858-5539.E-mail: xl96@xl96.com Web Site:www.xl96.com Licensee: Newcap Inc. Population served: 150,000 Format: Today's best country. Target aud: 25-54; adults. ◆Mark Maheu, pres; Hilary Montbourquette, gen mgr; Dave Murray, opns VP.

CKCW-FM— January 2001: 94.5 mhz; 19 kw. Hrs open: 1000 St. George Blvd., E1E 4M7. Phone: (506) 858-1220. Fax: (506) 858-1209.E-mail: magic104@radiomoncton.com Web Site:www.radiomoncton.com Licensee: Maritime Broadcasting System Ltd. Format: Today's newest music. Target aud: 18-44; adults. ◆Scott Clements, gen mgr.

CKNI-FM— Oct 11, 2005: 91.9 mhz; 70 kw. Hrs open: 70 Assomption Blvd., E1C 1A1. Phone: (506) 872-5678. Licensee: Rogers Broadcasting Ltd. Format: News/talk. ◆Rael Merson, pres; Jim Hamm, gen mgr.

CKOE-FM— November 2000: 107.3 mhz; 50 w. Ant 82 ft Hrs open: 3030 Mountain Rd., E1G 2W8. Phone: (506) 384-1009. Fax: (506) 383-9699.E-mail: x101fm@radiochristian.com Web Site:www.radiochristian.com Licensee: Houssen Broadcasting Ltd. Format: Christian hit radio. ◆James Houssen, gen mgr, progmg dir; Don Houssen, gen sls mgr; Steve Raye, news dir.

CKUM-FM— 1982: 93.5 mhz; 250 w. 98 ft TL: N46 06 16 W64 46 57. Stereo. Hrs open: 24 Universite de Moncton, Centre etudiant, 2e etage, E1A 3E9. Phone: (506) 858-3750. Fax: (506) 858-4524.E-mail: routierm@umoncton.ca Web Site:www.radioj935.com Licensee: Les Medias Acadiens Universitaires Inc. Population served: 100,000 Format: Var/div, Fr. News: one hr wkly. Target aud: 15-30. Spec prog: Jazz 4 hrs wkly. ◆Brian Gallant, pres; Justin Robichaud, VP; Michele Routier, gen mgr; Mylene Dugas, VP & gen sls mgr.

Pokemouche

CKRO-FM— 1988: 97.1 mhz; 50 kw. Hrs open: Radio Peninsule Inc., 142 Rt. 113, E8P 1K7. Phone: (506) 336-9706. Fax: (506) 336-9058.E-mail: info@ckro.ca Licensee: Radio Peninsule Inc. Format: Fr., MOR. Target aud: General. ◆Rachel Savoie, VP; Donald Noel, gen mgr, gen sls mgr; Marilyne McLaughlin, natl sls mgr, prom mgr.

Sackville

*CHMA-FM— 1985: 106.9 mhz; 50 w. Stereo. Hrs open: Suite 303, 152A Main St., E4L 1B4. Phone: (506) 364-2221. Fax: (506) 536-4230.E-mail: chma@mta.ca Web Site:www.mta.ca/chma Licensee: Attic Broadcasting Ltd. (acq 8-24-00). Population served: 15,000 Format: Div. ◆Pierre Malloy, gen mgr & stn mgr.

Saint John

CBD-FM— April 1981: 91.3 mhz; 80 kw. Hrs open: Box 2358, E2L 3V6. Phone: (506) 632-7744. Fax: (506) 632-7761. Web Site:www.nb.cbc.ca Licensee: Canadian Broadcasting Corp. Natl. Network: CBC Radio One, . Format: Talk, info.

CFBC(AM)— Nov 21, 1946: 930 khz; 50 kw-U, DA-2. TL: N45 13 55 W66 06 15. Stereo. Hrs open: 24 226 Union St., E2L 1B1. Phone: (506) 658-5100. Fax: (506) 658-5116.E-mail: mailbag@k100.ca Licensee: Maritime Broadcasting System Ltd. Group owner: Maritime Broadcasting (acq 9-29-98; C$2 million with co-located FM). Population served: 85,000 Format: Oldies. ◆Kelly O'Neill, gen sls mgr; Donnie Robertson, progmg dir; Brian McLain, news dir.

CFMH-FM— January 2001: 107.3 mhz; 250 w. Hrs open: c/o Student Services, PO Box 5050, UNB Saint John, Box 5050, E2L 4L5. Phone: (506) 648-5667. Fax: (506) 648-5541.E-mail: cfmh@unbsj.ca Web Site:www.unb.ca/cfmh Licensee: Campus Radio Saint John Inc. Format: Var. ◆Linda Pelletier, stn mgr.

CHNI-FM— Oct 11, 2005: 88.9 mhz; 79 kw. Hrs open: 55 Waterloo St., E2L 4V9. Phone: (506) 646-5161. Licensee: Rogers Broadcasting Ltd. Format: News/talk. ◆Rael Merson, pres; Jim Hamm, gen mgr.

CHQC-FM— 2006: 105.7 mhz; 1.85 kw. Hrs open: 24 67 Chemin Ragged Point, E2K 5C3. Phone: (506) 643-6996. Fax: (506) 658-3984.E-mail: info@chqc.ca Licensee: Cooperative radiophonique - La Brise de la Baie Ltee. Format: French variety. ◆Steve Pilotte, pres; Nay Saade, gen mgr, sls, mktg.

CHSJ-FM— Jan 7, 1998: 94.1 mhz; 50.4 kw. Hrs open: 24 Box 2000, 58 King St., E2L 3T4. Phone: (506) 633-3323. Fax: (506) 644-3485.E-mail: chsj@radioabl.ca Web Site:www.country94.ca Licensee: Acadia Broadcasting Ltd. (group owner). Natl. Network: CBS Radio, . Format: C&W. Target aud: 25-54. ◆Jim MacMullin, gen mgr.

CHWV-FM— 2001: 97.3 mhz; 55 kw. Hrs open: 24 Box 2000 58 King St., E2L 1G4. Phone: (506) 633-3323. Fax: (506) 644-3485.E-mail: chsj@radioabl.ca Web Site:www.thewave.ca Licensee: Acadia Broadcasting Ltd. (group owner). Format: Adult contemp. ◆Jim MacMullin, VP.

CINB-FM— Nov 16, 2000: 96.1 mhz; 50 w. Hrs open: NewSong FM, Box 96, E2L 3X1. Phone: (506) 657-9600. Fax: (506) 657-7664.E-mail: staff@newsongfm.com Web Site:www.newsongfm.com Licensee: New Song Communications Ministries Ltd. (acq 10-18-2005). Format: Contemp Christian. ◆Don Mabee, stn mgr.

CIOK-FM— Aug 10, 1987: 100.5 mhz; 100 kw. 1,650 ft Hrs open: 24 226 Union St., E2L 1B1. Phone: (506) 658-5100. Fax: (506) 658-5116.E-mail: mailbag@k100.ca Web Site:www.k100.ca Licensee: Maritime Broadcasting System Ltd. Group owner: Maritime Broadcasting Format: Adult contemp. News staff: 0; News: 7 hrs wkly. Target aud: 25-49; housewives, families, professionals. Spec prog: Real radio 4 hrs wkly. ◆Scott Clements, gen mgr & progmg dir.

CJRP-FM— Oct 20, 2003: 103.5 mhz; 49.6 w. Ant 200 ft TL: N45 16 31 W65 04 25. (CP: Ant 102 ft). Hrs open: 24 87 Landsdowne Ave., E2K 3A1. Phone: (506) 657-2533. Fax: (506) 642-7408.E-mail: OnAir@saintjohnfm.ca Web Site:www.saintjohnfm.ca Licensee: TFG Communications Inc. Format: Comedy, urban, rock. Target aud: 18-34. ◆Geoffrey Rivett, CEO; Gary Stackhouse, gen mgr, progmg dir; John Kierstead, gen sls mgr; Mark Henwood, mus dir; Kathy Stackhouse, traf mgr.

CJYC-FM— Mar 12, 1965: 98.9 mhz; 12 kw. 350 ft TL: N45 18 49 W66 04 43. Hrs open: 24 Prog sep from AM 266 Union St., E2L 1B1. Phone: (506) 658-5100. Fax: (506) 658-5116.E-mail:

mailbag@989bigjohnfm.com Web Site:www.989bigjohnfm.com Licensee: Maritime Broadcasting System Ltd. Format: Classic rock. Target aud: 25-34; young, upwardly, mobile, family oriented. ◆Paul Jensen, progmg dir.

Saint Stephen

CHTD-FM— May 31, 2001: 98.1 mhz; 40 kw. Stereo. Hrs open: 24 112 Milltown Blvd., St. Stephen, E3L 1G6. Phone: (506) 466-1000. Fax: (506) 466-4500.E-mail: mail@thetide.ca Web Site:www.thetide.ca Licensee: Acadia Broadcasting Ltd. (group owner) Population served: 61,000 Format: Country. News staff: 2. Target aud: 25-54. ◆Jim MacMullin, gen mgr; John Higgins, stn mgr.

Shediac

CJSE-FM— July 26, 1994: 89.5 mhz; 20.445 kw. TL: N46 11 04 W64 52 52. Hrs open: 24 96 Rue Providence, E4P2M9. Phone: (506) 532-0080. Fax: (506) 532-0120.E-mail: patricia@cjse.ca Web Site:www.cjse.ca Licensee: Radio Beausejour Inc. Format: Country. ◆Patricia Bourque-Chevarie, gen mgr.

Sussex

CJCW(AM)— June 1975: 590 khz; 1 kw-D, 250 w-N, DA-2. Hrs open: Box 5900, E4E 4N3. Phone: (506) 432-2529. Fax: (506) 433-4900.E-mail: cjcw@nbnet.nb.ca Web Site:www.favorites590.com Licensee: Maritime Broadcasting System Ltd. Group owner: Maritime Broadcasting Format: Adult contemp. Target aud: General. Spec prog: Relg 4 hrs wkly. ◆Robert Pace, CEO; Merv Russell, pres; Louis McNamara, gen mgr; James Keirstead, news dir.

Woodstock

CJCJ-FM— June 1, 2001: 104.1 mhz; 10 kw. Hrs open: Unit Two, 131 Queen St., E7M 2M8. Phone: (506) 325-3030. Fax: (506) 325-3031.E-mail: cj104@radioatl.ca Web Site:www.cj104.com Licensee: Astral Media Radio Atlantic Inc. Group owner: Astral Media Inc. (acq 4-19-2002; grpsl). Format: Adult contemp. ◆Pat Brennan, gen mgr.

Newfoundland

Argentia

CFOZ-FM— 1980: 100.3 mhz; 5 kw. Hrs open: 24 Rebroadcasts CHOZ-FM St. John's. c/o CHOZ-FM, Box 2020, 446 Logy Bay Rd., St. John's, A1C 5S2. Phone: (709) 726-2922. Fax: (709) 726-3300. Web Site:www.ozfm.com Licensee: Newfoundland Broadcasting Co. Ltd. Population served: 500,000 Natl. Rep: Canadian Broadcast Sales,. Format: CHR, adult contemp, classic rock. News staff: 2. Target aud: 18-49. ◆Geoff Stirling, chmn; Frank Collins, CFO; Doug Neal, gen mgr, chief of opns, chief of engrg; Lorraine Pope, sls dir, gen sls mgr, progmg dir; Jesse Stirling, mktg VP, mktg dir; Scott G. Stirling, CEO, pres & progmg dir; Maurice Fitzgerald, mus dir; Larry Davis, news dir.

Baie Verte

CKIM(AM)— 1979: 1240 khz; 1 kw-D, 500 w-N. Hrs open: Box 620, Grenfell Heights, A2A 2K2. Phone: (709) 489-2192. Fax: (709) 489-8626. Web Site:www.vocm.com Licensee: NewCap Inc. Group owner: NewCap Broadcasting Ltd. (acq 6-00; grpsl). Format: News/talk, country. ◆Dave Hillier, gen mgr; Denn Dillion, gen sls mgr; Richard King, progmg dir; Roger Barnett, news dir; Harold Steele, chief of engrg.

Bonavista Bay

CBGY(AM)— Aug 25, 1977: 750 khz; 10 kw-U, DA-2. Hrs open: Rebroadcasts CBG(AM) Gander. c/o Radio Stn CBG, Box 369, Gander, A1V 1W7. Secondary address: 98 Sullivan Ave., Gander A1V 1W7. Phone: (709) 256-4311. Fax: (709) 651-2021. Web Site:www.cbc.ca/nl/ Licensee: CBC. Format: News, current affrs. ◆Robert Rabinowitz, CEO; Michael Aucoin, stn mgr.

CJOZ-FM— 1979: 92.1 mhz; 50 kw. Hrs open: 24 Rebroadcasts CHOZ-FM, St John's. c/o CHOZ-FM, 446 Logy Bay Rd., Box 2020, St. John's, A1C 5S2.

Phone: (709) 726-2922. Fax: (709) 726-3300. Web Site:www.ozfm.com Licensee: Newfoundland Broadcasting Co. (group owner) Population served: 500,000 Natl. Rep: Canadian Broadcast Sales,. Format: CHR, adult contemp, classic rock. News staff: 2. Target aud: 18-49. ◆Geoff Stirling, chmn; Scott Stirling, CEO & pres; Frank Collins, CFO; Doug Neal, gen mgr, chief of opns, chief of engrg; Jesse Stirling, gen sls mgr, mktg dir; Maurice Fitzgerald, mus dir; Larry Davis, news dir.

Burnt Islands

CHBI-FM— 2007: 95.7 mhz; 50 w. TL: N47 36 18 W58 52 06. Hrs open: Box 101, A0M 1B0. Phone: (709) 698-3100. Fax: (709) 698-3100.E-mail: chbi95.7fm@hotmail.com Licensee: Burnt Islands Economic Development Board. Format: Var. ◆Holly Keeping, gen mgr.

Carbonear

CHVO-FM— Jan 7, 2008: 103.9 mhz; 14 kw. TL: N47 43 13 W53 12 50. Hrs open: One CHVO Dr., A1Y 1A2. Phone: (709) 596-1560. Fax: (709) 596-8626.E-mail: chvo@vocm.com Web Site:www.kixxcountry.ca Licensee: Newcap Inc. Format: Country. Target aud: 25-54; adults. ◆John Steele, pres; John Murphy, gen mgr; Aiden Hibbs, stn mgr; Ron Ryan, gen sls mgr; Mike Campbell, progmg dir; Gerry Phalen, news dir; Harold Steele, chief of engrg.

Churchill Falls

CFLC-FM— 1974: 97.9 mhz; 8 w. 50 ft Hrs open: c/o CFCB(AM), Box 570, Corner Brook, A2H 6H5. Phone: (709) 634-3111. Fax: (709) 634-4081. Licensee: NewCap Inc. Group owner: NewCap Broadcasting Ltd. (acq 4-2-01; grpsl). Format: Country, adult contemp. ◆Michael Murphy, gen mgr & stn mgr; Ken Ash, progmg dir, progmg mgr.

Clarenville

CJKK-FM— 1988: 105.3 mhz; 2.07 kw. Hrs open: 24 c/o CHOZ-FM, 446 Logy Bay Rd., St. John's, A1C 5R6. Phone: (709) 726-2922. Fax: (709) 726-3300. Web Site:www.ozfm.com Licensee: Newfoundland Broadcasting Co. (group owner) Population served: 500,000 Natl. Rep: Canadian Broadcast Sales,. Format: CHR, adult contemp, classic rock. News staff: 2. Target aud: 18-49. ◆Geoff Stirling, chmn; Scott Stirling, CEO & pres; Frank Collins, CFO; Doug Neal, gen mgr, opns mgr, chief of opns.

CKVO(AM)— Nov 15, 1974: 710 khz; 10 kw-U. Hrs open: Rebroadcasts VOCM(AM) St. John's except 9 AM-5 PM (loc progmg). c/o VOCM(AM), Box 8590, Stn. A, 391 Kenmount Rd., St. John's, A1B 3P5. Phone: (709) 726-4633. Fax: (709) 726-8626/726-4633.E-mail: feedback@vocm.com Web Site:www.vocm.com Licensee: NewCap Inc. Group owner: NewCap Broadcasting Ltd. (acq 6-00; grpsl). Format: Contemp country. ◆John Murphy, gen mgr; Ken Ash, opns mgr; Dennis Dillon, gen sls mgr; Paul Raynes, progmg dir; Gerry Phelan, news dir; Harold Steele, chief of engrg.

Corner Brook

*CBY(AM)— Apr 1, 1949: 990 khz; 10 kw-U, DA-1. Hrs open: Rebroadcasts CBT(AM) Grand Falls-Windsor. Box 610, A2H 6G1. Phone: (709) 637-1151. Fax: (709) 634-8506. Web Site:www.cbc.ca/nl/ Licensee: CBC. Natl. Network: CBC Radio One, . Format: News/talk, var. Target aud: 30 plus; mature. ◆Robert Rabinowitz, CEO; Gordon Lannon, gen mgr.

CFCB(AM)— Oct 3, 1960: 570 khz; 1 kw-D. Hrs open: 24 Box 570, A2H 6H5. Phone: (709) 634-4570. Fax: (709) 726-4633. Web Site:www.vocm.com Licensee: Newcap Inc. Group owner: NewCap Broadcasting Ltd. (acq 4-2-01; grpsl). Population served: 40,000 Natl. Rep: Canadian Broadcast Sales,. Format: Country. ◆Harry Steele, pres; J. Steele, VP; Michael Murphy, gen mgr; Darryl Stevens, opns mgr, progmg dir.

CKOZ-FM— 1979: 92.3 mhz; 50 kw. Hrs open: 24 Rebroadcasts CHOZ-FM St. John's. c/o CHOZ-FM, 446 Logy Bay Rd., Box 2020, St. John's, A1C 5S2. Phone: (709) 726-2922. Fax: (709) 726-3300. Web Site:www.ozfm.com Licensee: Newfoundland Broadcasting Co. (group owner) Population served: 500,000 Natl. Rep: Canadian Broadcast Sales,. Format: CHR, adult contemp, classic rock. News staff: 2. Target aud: 18-49. ◆Geoff Stirling, chmn; Scott Stirling, CEO & pres; Frank Collins, CFO; Doug Neal, gen mgr, chief of opns, chief of engrg; Lorraine Pope, gen sls mgr, progmg dir; Jesse Stirling, mktg dir; Maurice Fitzgerald, mus dir; Larry Davis, news dir.

CKXX-FM— June 20, 1997: 103.9 mhz; 40 kw. Stereo. Hrs open: 24 P.O. Box570, 345 O'Connell Dr., Corner Brook, NL, A2H6H5. Phone: (709) 634-4570. Fax: (709) 634-4081. Web Site:k-rock1039.com Licensee: NewCap Inc. (acq 8-29-90). Population served: 40,000 Natl. Rep: Canadian Broadcast Sales,. Format: Rock. News staff: 2. Target aud: 25-54. Spec prog: Oldies 3 hrs wkly. ◆Michael Murphy, gen mgr; Daryl Stevens, opns mgr.

Gander

*CBG(AM)— 1949: 1400 khz; 4 kw-U. Hrs open: Box 369, A1V 1W7. Secondary address: 98 Sullivan Ave. A1V 1W7. Phone: (709) 256-4311. Fax: (709) 651-2021.E-mail: gandernews@cbc.ca Web Site:www.cbc.ca/nl/ Licensee: CBC. Format: Info. ◆Robert Rabinowitz, CEO; Michael Aucion, gen mgr.

CKGA(AM)— 1969: 650 khz; 5 kw-U, DA-2. Hrs open: Box 650, A1V 1X2. Phone: (709) 651-3650. Fax: (709) 651-2542. Web Site:www.vocm.com Licensee: NewCap Inc. Group owner: NewCap Broadcasting Ltd. (acq 6-00; grpsl). Format: Country, news, talk. ◆Dave Hillier, gen mgr; Dennis Dillon, gen sls mgr; Dean Clarke, progmg dir; Robet Tuck, news dir; Harold Steele, chief of engrg.

CKXD-FM— November 2000: 98.7 mhz; 6 kw. Hrs open: Box 650, A1V 1X2. Phone: (709) 651-3650. Fax: (709) 651-2542.E-mail: ckxd.ckga.psa@vocm.com Web Site:www.vocm.com Licensee: Newcap Inc. Group owner: NewCap Broadcasting Ltd. Format: Classic rock. Spec prog: Newfoundland & Irish 12 hrs wkly. ◆John Murphy, gen mgr; Dennis Dillon, gen sls mgr; Ken Ash, progmg dir; Harold Steele, chief of engrg; Connie Pasher, traf mgr.

Goose Bay

CFGB-FM—See Happy Valley

CFLN(AM)— Aug 1, 1974: 1230 khz; 1 kw-D, 250 w-N, DA-1. Hrs open: Box 160, Station C, Happy Valley Goose Bay. Phone: (709) 896-2968. Fax: (709) 896-8708. Web Site:www.vocm.com Licensee: NewCap Inc. Group owner: NewCap Broadcasting Ltd. (acq 4-2-01; grpsl). Format: Adult contemp. ◆Harry Steele, chmn; Robert G. Steele, pres.

Grand Falls

CKCM(AM)— October 1962: 620 khz; 10 kw-U, DA-1. Hrs open: Box 620, Grand Falls-Windsor, A22 2K2. Secondary address: 35 A Grenfell Heights, Grand Falls-Windsor A2A 2K2. Phone: (709) 489-2192. Fax: (709) 489-8626. Web Site:www.vocm.com Licensee: NewCap Inc. Group owner: NewCap Broadcasting Ltd. (acq 6-00; grpsl). Format: Contemp country. ◆Dave Hillier, gen mgr; Dennis Dillon, gen sls mgr; Richard King, progmg dir; Roger Barnett, news dir; Harold Steele, chief of engrg.

Grand Falls-Windsor

CBT(AM)— July 1, 1949: 540 khz; 10 kw-U. Hrs open: 2 Harris Ave., A2A 2Y4. Phone: (709) 489-2102. Fax: (709) 489-1055. Web Site:www.cbc.ca/nl/ Licensee: CBC. Format: Info. ◆Robert Rabinowitz, CEO; Diane Humber, gen mgr; Chris Norman, stn mgr.

CKXG-FM— 2001: 102.3 mhz; 20 kw. Hrs open: 24 Box 620, A2A 2K2. Phone: (709) 489-2192. Fax: (709) 489-8626.E-mail: vocm.krock.psa@vocm.com Web Site:www.vocm.com Licensee: NewCap Broadcasting Ltd. Group owner: NewCap Broadcasting Ltd. Format: Classic rock. ◆Dave Hillier, gen mgr; Dennis Dillon, gen sls mgr; Richard King, progmg dir; Harold Steele, chief of engrg; Margot pitcher-Hamlyn, traf mgr.

Happy Valley

*CFGB-FM— Feb 23, 1959: 89.5 mhz; 1 kw-w. Hrs open: Box 1029, Stn C, 12 Loring Dr., Happy Valley-Goose Bay, A0P 1CO. Phone: (709) 896-2911. Fax: (709) 896-8900.E-mail: labmorning@stjohns.cbc.ca Web Site:www.cbc.ca/nl/ Licensee: CBC. Natl. Network: CBC Radio One, . Format: Info. ◆Diane Humber, gen mgr; Cynthia Wall, progmg mgr; Lorne Burry, engrg mgr; Conrad Lutes, news rptr.

Labrador City

CBDQ-FM— 1997: 96.3 mhz; 255 w. Hrs open: Rebroadcasts CFGB-FM Happy Valley.

Box 576, A2V 2L3. Phone: (709) 944-3616. Fax: (709) 944-5472. Web Site:www.cbc.ca/nl/ Licensee: CBC. Format: Talk, info. ◆Diane Humber, gen mgr.

CJRM-FM— Sept 23, 1992: 97.3 mhz; 500 w. 1,998 ft TL: N52 57 01 W66 55 01. Stereo. Hrs open: C.P. 453, 308 Hudson Dr., A2V 2K7. Phone: (709) 944-7600. Phone: (709) 944-2973. Fax: (709) 944-5125.E-mail: cjrm@crrstv.net Licensee: Radio Communautaire du Labrador Inc. (acq 9-4-92). Population served: 17,000 Format: Fr, English, div. Target aud: General; English & Fr speaking audience in Labrador West. ◆Norman Gillespie, pres; Dean Baker, exec VP, mus dir; linda McLean, stn mgr.

Lewisporte

CIFX-FM— 2002: 93.7 mhz; 50 w. Stereo. Hrs open: 24 Box 601, 37 George Street, A0G 3A0. Secondary address: 37 George Street A0G 3AO. Phone: (709) 535-6000. Phone: (709) 535-2546. Fax: (709) 535-6600.E-mail: mixfm@nf.sympatico.ca Licensee: Mix FM Inc. Population served: 25,000 Format: CHR/hot adult contemp/rock-talk. News staff: 2. Target aud: 18-52. ◆Todd Foss, stn mgr, mus dir, progmg; Vicki Fudge, pub affrs dir; Koren Hurley, sls; Angela Brenton, prom; Peter Ginn, engr.

Marystown

CHCM(AM)— 1961: 740 khz; 10 kw-U, DA-N. Hrs open: Box 560, A0E 2M0. Phone: (709) 279-2560. Phone: (709) 279-2426. Fax: (709) 279-3538. Fax: (709) 279-2800.E-mail: chem.frontdesk@vocm.com Web Site:www.vocm.com Licensee: NewCap Inc. Group owner: NewCap Broadcasting Ltd. (acq 5-4-00; grpsl). Format: Country. ◆Russell Murphy, gen mgr, opns mgr & gen sls mgr; Harry Myles, progmg dir; Bob Tower, news dir; Harold Steele, chief of engrg.

CIOZ-FM— 1979: 96.3 mhz; 25 kw. Hrs open: 24 Rebroadcasts CHOZ-FM St. John's. c/o CHOZ-FM, 446 Logy Bay Rd., Box 2020, St. John's, A1C 5S2. Phone: (709) 726-2922. Fax: (709) 726-3300. Web Site:www.ozfm.com Licensee: Newfoundland Broadcasting Co. (group owner) Population served: 500,000 Natl. Rep: Canadian Broadcast Sales,. Format: CHR, adult contemp, classic rock. News staff: 2. Target aud: 18-49. ◆Geoff Stirling, chmn; Scott Stirling, CEO & pres; Frank Collins, CFO; Doug Neal, gen mgr, chief of opns, chief of engrg; Lorraine Pope, gen sls mgr, progmg dir; Jesse Stirling, mktg VP, mktg dir, prom VP; Maurice Fitzgerald, mus dir, asst music dir; Larry Davis, news dir.

Mount Pearl

*VOAR(AM)— 1930: 1210 khz; 10 kw, DA-1. TL: N47 32 01 W52 49 01. Hrs open: 24 1041 Topsail Rd., A1N 5E9. Phone: (709) 745-VOAR. Fax: (709)745-1600.E-mail: voar@voar.org Web Site:www.voar.org Licensee: Seventh-Day Adventist Church in Newfoundland. Population served: 350,000 Format: Relg, gospel. News: 12 hrs wkly. Target aud: 25-44; individuals interested in family life & traditional values. ◆Gary Hodder, pres; Sherry Griffin, stn mgr & opns mgr.

Port au Choix

CFNW(AM)— 1960: 790 khz; 1 kw-U, DA-1. Hrs open: 24 c/o CFCB(AM), 345 O'Connell Dr., Corner Brook, A2H 6H5. Phone: (709) 634-4570. Fax: (709) 634-4081. Licensee: Newcap Inc. Group owner: NewCap Broadcasting Ltd. (acq 4-2-01; grpsl). Population served: 22,000 Format: Country. ◆Harry Steele, pres; Michael Murphy, gen mgr; Darryl Stevens, opns mgr.

Rattling Brook

CHOS-FM— 1979: 95.9 mhz; 50 kw. Hrs open: 24 Rebroadcasts CHOZ-FM St. John's. c/o CHOZ-FM, 446 Logy Bay Rd., Box 2020, St. John's, A1C 5S2. Phone: (709) 726-2922. Fax: (709) 726-3300. Web Site:www.ozfm.com Licensee: Newfoundland Broadcasting Co. (group owner) Population served: 500,000 Natl. Rep: Canadian Broadcast Sales,. Format: CHR, adult contemp, classic rock. News staff: 2. Target aud: 18-49. ◆Geoff Stirling, chmn; Scott G. Sterling, CEO & pres; Frank Collins, CFO; Doug Neal, gen mgr, chief of opns.

Red Rocks

CKSS-FM— 1994: 96.9 mhz; 520 w. Hrs open: 24 Rebroadcasts CHOZ-FM St. John's 100%. c/o CHOZ-FM, 466 Logy Bay Rd., Box 2020, St. John's, A1C 5S2. Phone: (709) 726-2922. Phone: (709) 722-5015. Fax: (709) 726-3300.

Fax: (709) 726-5107. Web Site:www.ozfm.com Licensee: Newfoundland Broadcasting Co. (group owner) Population served: 500,000 Natl. Rep: Canadian Broadcast Sales,. Format: CHR, adult contemp, classic rock. News staff: 2. Target aud: 18-49. ◆Geoff Stirling, chmn; Scott Stirling, CEO & pres; Frank Collins, CFO; Doug Neal, chief of opns, chief of engrg; Lorraine Pope, gen sls mgr, progmg dir; Jesse Stirling, mktg dir; Larry Davis, news dir.

Saint Andrews

CFCV-FM— 1974: 97.7 mhz; Hrs open: Rebroadcasts CFGN(AM) Port-aux-Basques. 60 West St., Stephenville, A2N 1C6. Secondary address: C/o CFGN(AM), Port-aux-Basques A0M 1C0. Phone: (709) 695-2183. Fax: (709) 695-9614.E-mail: cfsx@vocm.com Web Site:www.vocm.com Licensee: NewCap Inc. Group owner: NewCap Broadcasting Ltd. Format: Country, oldies. ◆Michael Murphy, gen mgr; Gerry Murphy, gen sls mgr; Larry Bennett, progmg dir; Harold Steele, chief of engrg.

Saint John's

*CBN(AM)— Apr 1, 1949: 640 khz; 10 kw-U. Hrs open: 19 Box 12010, Stn A, 342-44 Duckworth St., A1B 3T8. Phone: (709) 576-5000. Fax: (709) 576-5205. Web Site:www.cbc.ca Licensee: CBC. Natl. Network: CBC Radio One, . Format: Div. News staff: 6; News: 10 hrs wkly. Target aud: General. Spec prog: Fisheries 3 hrs wkly. ◆Diane Humber, gen mgr, news dir; Larry O'Brien, opns dir; Lori Wheeler, prom mgr; Liz Lacey, mus dir.

*CBN-FM— July 1, 1975: 106.9 mhz; 100 kw. 300 ft Stereo. Hrs open: Box 12010, Stn A, A1B 3T8. Phone: (709) 576-5000. Fax: (709) 576-5205. Licensee: CBC Natl. Network: CBC Radio Two, . Format: Class, news/talk. Co-owned TV: *CBNT-TV affil

*CHMR-FM— January 1986: 93.5 mhz; 50 w. -10 ft Stereo. Hrs open: 24 Memorial University, MUNSU, South Annex, Rm 2009, A1C 5S7. Phone: (709) 737-4777. Phone: (709) 737-4778. Fax: (709) 737-7688.E-mail: chmr@mun.ca Web Site:www.chmr.ca/ Licensee: Memorial University of Newfoundland Radio Society Inc. Population served: 200,000 Format: Div, alternative. News: 7 hrs wkly. Target aud: General. Spec prog: Fr 2 hrs, jazz 6 hrs, relg 4 hrs, blues 6 hrs, rap 2 hrs, reggae 2 hrs, Indian one hr wkly.Kathy Rowe, gen mgr, opns mgr, dev mgr, rgnl sls mgr, adv mgr, mus dir, traf mgr, edit dir, edit mgr, women's cmtr; Ernst Rollmann, progmg dir, asst music dir, rsch dir, local news ed, mus critic, political ed, relg ed; Nancy Earle, mktg mgr, prom mgr, progmg dir, asst music dir & news dir; Craig Peterman, chief of engrg; Jay Healey, min affrs dir; Mike Rossiter, news rptr, sports cmtr; Erin McKee, women's int ed

CHOZ-FM— June 15, 1977: 94.7 mhz; 100 kw. 821 ft TL: NN47 31 36 W52 42 50. Stereo. Hrs open: 24 Box 2050, 446 Logy Bay Rd., A1C 5R6. Phone: (709) 722-5015. Fax: (709) 726-3300.E-mail: ntvsales@ntv.ca Web Site:www.ozfm.com Licensee: Newfoundland Broadcasting Co. Ltd. Group owner: Newfoundland Broadcasting Co. Population served: 500,000 Natl. Rep: Canadian Broadcast Sales,. Format: CHR, adult contemp, classic rock. News staff: 2. Target aud: 18-49. ◆Geoff Stirling, chmn; Scott G. Stirling, CEO & pres; Frank Collins, CFO; Jesse Stirling, VP, sls dir, mktg VP, mktg dir, prom mgr; Doug Neal, gen mgr, opns mgr, chief of opns, engrg dir, chief of engrg; Dave Lawrence, stn mgr; Lorraine Pope, natl sls mgr, mus dir; Paul Kinsman, progmg dir; Larry Davis, news dir. Co-owned TV: CJON-TV affil.

CJYQ(AM)— 1951: 930 khz; 25 kw-U. Hrs open: Box 8590 Station A., St. John's, A1B 3P5. Phone: (709) 726-5590. Fax: (709) 726-4633. Licensee: Newcap Inc. Format: Country.

CKIX-FM— Oct 15, 1983: 99.1 mhz; 100 kw. Ant 930 ft Stereo. Hrs open: Box 8590, Station A, St. John's, A1B 3P5. Phone: (709) 726-5590. Fax: (709) 726-4633. Web Site:www.991hitsfm.com Licensee: Newcap Inc. Group owner: NewCap Broadcasting Ltd. (acq 1-17-83). Format: CHR. ◆John Murphey, gen mgr; Randy Snow, progmg dir; Brad Michaels, mus dir.

CKSJ-FM— 2004: 101.1 mhz; 20 kw. Hrs open: Box 28106, A1B 4J8. Phone: (709) 754-6748. Fax: (709) 754-6749.E-mail: onair@coast1011.com Web Site:www.coast1011.com Licensee: Coast Broadcasting Ltd. Format: Adult contemp. ◆Andrew Newman, gen mgr.

VOCM(AM)— Oct 19, 1936: 590 khz; 20 kw-U, DA-2. Stereo. Hrs open: 24 391 Kenmount Rd., A1B 3P5. Phone: (709) 726-5590. Fax: (709) 726-4633.E-mail: feedback@vocm.com Web Site:www.vocm.com Licensee: NewCap Inc. Group owner: NewCap Broadcasting Ltd. (acq 6-00; grpsl). Natl. Rep: Canadian Broadcast Sales,. Format: Adult contemp, country, news/talk. News staff: 16. Target aud: 25 plus.

◆John Steele, pres; John Murphy, gen mgr; Ken Ash, opns mgr; Ron Ryan, sls VP; Paul Magee, progmg dir; Gerry Phelan, news dir; Harold Steele, engrg dir; Cathy Ridgely-Ryan, traf mgr.

VOCM-FM— September 1982: 97.5 mhz; 100 kw. Stereo. Hrs open: 24 Prog sep from AM 391 Kenmount Rd., A1B 3P5. Phone: (709) 726-5590. Fax: (709) 726-4633. Web Site:www.k-rock975.com Format: Classic rock. News: 7 hrs wkly. Target aud: Adults 25-54. ◆Ron Ryan, stn mgr.

*VOWR(AM)— June 20, 1924: 800 khz; 10 kw-D, 2.5 kw-N, DA-1. TL: N47 34 16 W52 45 13. Hrs open: 24 Box 7430, Patrick St., St. John's, A1E 3Y5. Phone: (709) 579-9233. Fax: (709) 579-9232.E-mail: vowr@vowr.org Web Site:www.vowr.org Licensee: Wesley United Church Radio Board. Population served: 200,000 Format: Div, oldies, folk. Target aud: 40 plus. Spec prog: Relg 10 hrs, folk 15 hrs wkly. ◆Marvin Barnes, chmn; John Tessier, gen mgr, opns mgr.

Stephenville

CFSX(AM)— Nov 14, 1964: 870 khz; 500 w-U. Hrs open: 24 60 West St., A2N 1C6. Phone: (709) 643-2191. Fax: (709) 643-5025. Web Site:www.vocm.com Licensee: NewCap Inc. Group owner: NewCap Broadcasting Ltd. (acq 2001; grpsl). Population served: 33,000 Format: Country. News staff: 2. Target aud: General. Spec prog: Relg one hr wkly. ◆Harry Steele, chmn; Robert G. Steele, pres; John Murphy, gen mgr; Gerry Murphy, stn mgr.

CIOS-FM— 1979: 98.5 mhz; 10 kw. Hrs open: 24 Rebroadcasts CHOZ-FM St. John's. c/o CHOZ-FM, 446 Logy Bay Rd., Box 2020, St. John's, A1C 5S2. Phone: (709) 726-2922. Fax: (709) 726-3300. Web Site:www.ozfm.com Licensee: Newfoundland Broadcasting Co. (group owner) Population served: 500,000 Format: CHR, adult contemp, classic rock. News staff: 2. Target aud: 18-49. ◆Geoff Stirling, chmn; Scott Stirling, CEO & pres; Frank Collins, CFO; Doug Neal, gen mgr, opns mgr, chief of opns.

Wabush

CFLW(AM)— 1971: 1340 khz; 250 w-U, DA-1. Hrs open: Rebroadcasts CFCB(AM) Corner Brooks 99%. Box 6000, 4 Grenfell Dr., A0R 1B0. Phone: (709) 282-3602. Phone: (709) 282-3601. Fax: (709) 282-5543. Licensee: Newcap Inc. Group owner: NewCap Broadcasting Ltd. (acq 4-2-01; grpsl). Format: Country. Target aud: General. ◆Harry Steele, chmn; Robert G. Steele, pres; Mike Murphy, gen mgr.

Northwest Territories

Hay River

CJCD-FM-1— Sept 15, 1986: 100.1 mhz; 300 w. 175 ft Stereo. Hrs open: Rebroadcasts CJCD(FM) Yellowknife. Box 218, Yellowknife, X1A 2N2. Phone: (867) 920-4636. Fax: (867) 920-4033.E-mail: info@cjcd.ca Web Site:www.cjcd.ca Licensee: CJCD Radio Ltd. (acq 3-8-00). Natl. Rep: Canadian Broadcast Sales,. Format: Hot adult contemp. Target aud: 25-49. ◆Eileen Dent, pres, gen mgr; Tim Jaworski, gen sls mgr; Joanne McKenzie, progmg dir, news dir; Kirby Marshall, chief of engrg; Mandy Church, traf mgr.

CKHR-FM— January 1979: 107.3 mhz; 32 w. 185 ft Hrs open: Box 4394, X0E 1G3. Phone: (867) 874-2547.E-mail: ckhr@northwestel.nt Licensee: Hay River Broadcasting Society. Format: MOR, var. ◆Al Erickson, pres; Ray Lawson, stn mgr.

Inuvik

*CHAK(AM)— Nov 26, 1960: 860 khz; 1 kw-D, DA-1. Hrs open: Bag 8, X0E 0T0. Phone: (867) 777-7600. Fax: (867) 777-7640. Licensee: CBC. Format: News/talk. Target aud: General. Spec prog: Inuvialuktun 9 hrs, Gwich'in 9 hrs wkly. ◆Peter Skinner, gen mgr.

Tuktoyaktuk

CFCT(AM)— 1971: 600 khz; 1 kw-U. Hrs open: c/o Radio Station CHAK, Bag 8, Inuvik, X0E 0T0. Phone: (867) 777-7600. Fax: (867)

777-7640. Licensee: CBC. (acq 1982). Natl. Network: CBC Radio One, . Format: Div. Spec prog: Eskimo 5 hrs wkly. ◆ Peter Skinner, gen mgr.

Yellowknife

*CFYK(AM)— Dec 13, 1958: 1340 khz; 2.5 kw-U. Hrs open: Box 160, X1A 2N2. Phone: (867) 920-5400. Fax: (867) 920-5410 (ADMIN). Fax: (867) 920-5440 PROG. Licensee: CBC. Format: Div, news/talk. Target aud: General. Spec prog: Slavey 8 hrs, Dogrib 4 hrs, Chipewayan 4 hrs wkly. ◆ Peter Skinner, gen mgr; David McNaughton, opns mgr.

CIVR-FM— 2001: 103.5 mhz; 164 w. Hrs open: Rebroadcasts RFA Ottawa 60%.
Box 1586, X1A 2P2. Phone: (867) 873-3292. E-mail: civr@franco-nord.com Web Site:www.radiotaiga.ca Licensee: L'Association franco-culturelle de Yellowknife. Format: Fr. News: 2 hrs wkly. Spec prog: Worldbeat 3 hrs, jazz 4 hrs wkly. ◆ Jeff Hipfner, pres.

CJCD-FM— 1998: 100.1 mhz; 400 w. TL: N62 27 00 W114 19 00. Hrs open: Box 218, X1A 2N2. Phone: (867) 920-4636. Fax: (867) 920-4033. E-mail: info@cjcd.ca Web Site:www.cjcd.ca Licensee: CJCD Radio Ltd. (acq 3-8-00). Natl. Rep: Canadian Broadcast Sales,. Format: Hot Adult contemp. Target aud: 25-54. ◆ Eileen Dent, pres, gen mgr; Joanne McKenzie, progmg dir & news dir.

CKLB-FM— Dec 11, 1985: 101.9 mhz; 130 w. 162 ft Stereo. Hrs open: 7 AM-10 PM (M-F); 11 AM-9 PM (S)
Rebroadcasts CFWE-FM Lac La Biche, Alberta News.
4 Lessard Drive, X1A 2G5. Phone: (867) 920-2277. Fax: (867) 920-4205. E-mail: ncs@internorth.com Web Site:www.ncfnwt.com Licensee: Native Communications Society of the Western N.W.T. Population served: 30,000 Format: C&W. News staff: 3. Spec prog: Black one hr wkly. ◆ Dane Gibson, gen mgr; William Greenland, progmg dir; Jasmine Netsena, news dir.

Nova Scotia

Amherst

CKDH(AM)— Oct 25, 1957: 900 khz; 1 kw-U, DA-N. Hrs open: Box 670, B4H 4B8. Phone: (902) 667-3875. Fax: (902) 667-4490. E-mail: ckdh@ckdh.net Web Site:www.ckdh.net Licensee: Maritime Broadcasting System Ltd. (acq 1989). Natl. Rep: Canadian Broadcast Sales,. Format: Light rock. Target aud: 18-49; general. Spec prog: C&W 11 hrs, farm 2 hrs wkly. ◆ Dave March, gen mgr, progmg dir; Dennis Landriault, gen mgr & gen sls mgr.

Antigonish

CFXU-FM— 2006: 93.3 mhz; 50 w. TL: N45 37 10 W61 59 40. Hrs open: Box 948, St. Francis Xavier University, B2G 2X1. Phone: (902) 867-3941. E-mail: thefox@stfx.ca Web Site:www.theu.ca/comm/cfxu Licensee: Radio CFXU Club. Format: Var. ◆ Caitlin Van Horne, stn mgr; Rose Murphy, progmg mgr; Cameron Brioux, mus dir; John Best, news dir.

CJFX-FM— 2003: 98.9 mhz; 75.39 kw. Stereo. Hrs open: 24 Box 5800, B2G 2R9. Secondary address: 85 Kirk St. B2G 2R9. Phone: (902) 863-4580. Fax: (902) 863-6300. E-mail: cjfx@cjfx.ca Web Site:www.cjfx.ca Licensee: Atlantic Broadcasters Ltd. Natl. Rep: Canadian Broadcast Sales,. Rgnl rep: Canadian Broadcast Sales Format: CHR, maritime. News staff: 3; News: 24 hrs wkly. Target aud: 18 plus. ◆ Ken Farrell, gen mgr; Neil Scribner, gen sls mgr; Barry Mackinnon, progmg dir; Ken Kingston, news dir.

Barrington

CJLS-FM-1— 1982: 96.3 mhz; 5.5 kw. Hrs open: Rebroadcasts CJLS-FM Yarmouth.
c/o CJLS(AM), 328 Main St., Suite 201, Yarmouth, B5A 1E4. Phone: (902) 742-7175. Fax: (902) 742-3143. E-mail: cjls@cjls.com Web Site:www.cjls.com Licensee: Radio CJLS Ltd. (acq 7-1-98). Format: Adult contemp. ◆ Chris Perry, VP, progmg mgr; Ray Zinck, pres & gen mgr; Dave Hall, gen sls mgr; Gary Nickerson, news dir; Jim Harris, engrg dir.

Bedford

CHSB-FM— 2007: 99.3 mhz; 50 w. TL: N44 44 13 W63 39 13. Hrs open: Box 44073, B4A 3X5. Phone: (902) 835-5966. Web Site:www.bedfordbaptist.ca Licensee: Bedford Baptist Church. Format: Religious services from the Bedford Baptist Church. ◆ Kevin Haggarty, gen mgr.

Bridgewater

CKBW-FM— February 2002: 98.1 mhz; 32 kw. Stereo. Hrs open: 24 215 Dominion St., B4V 2G8. Phone: (902) 543-2401. Fax: (902) 543-1208. E-mail: ckbw@ckbw.com Web Site:www.ckbw.ca Licensee: Acadia Broadcasting Ltd. (group owner). Population served: 80,000 Natl. Rep: Canadian Broadcast Sales,. Rgnl rep: Canadian Broadcast Sales Format: Hot adult contemp. News staff: 15; News: 11 hrs wkly. Target aud: General; rural & small town urban. ◆ John Wiles, gen mgr, opns mgr, progmg dir; Chris Pearson, gen sls mgr, natl sls mgr; Brian Tepper, prom dir; Frank Grayney, chief of engrg; Pamela Smith, traf mgr; Jonathan Crouse, spec ev coord, disc jockey; Sheldon MacLeod, news dir, pub affrs dir & local news ed; Greg Lowe, sports cmtr; Leitha Haysom, disc jockey.

Cheticamp

*CKJM-FM— June 10, 1995: 106.1 mhz; 3 kw. TL: N46 36 55 W61 02 52. Stereo. Hrs open: 24
Rebroadcasts CFIM-FM Iles-De-La Madeleine, PQ 5%.
Box 699, Les Trois Pignons, Main Rd., B0E 1H0. Phone: (902) 224-1242. Fax: (902) 224-1770. E-mail: info@ckjm.ca Web Site:www.ckjm.ca Licensee: La Cooperative Radio Cheticamp Ltee. Population served: 5,000 Format: Country, Folklore and Variety. Target aud: General. Spec prog: Gaelic one hr, jazz 3 hrs wkly. ◆ Normand Poirier, pres; Angus Lefort, gen mgr, opns mgr, mktg dir, engrg dir; Carole Aucoin, natl sls mgr, adv dir; Ginette Chiasson, progmg dir.

Comeauville

*CIFA-FM— Sept 28, 1990: 104.1 mhz; 39.3 w. 475 ft Stereo. Hrs open: 6am to 10pm Box 8, Saulnierville, B0W 2Z0. Phone: (902) 769-2432. Fax: (902) 769-3101. E-mail: info@cifafm.ca Web Site:www.cifa.fm Licensee: Association Radio Clare. Population served: 60,000 Format: Div, community news. News staff: 1/2. Target aud: General. ◆ Albert Geddry, pres; Dave LeBlau, gen mgr; Paul Lomberd, gen sls mgr; Emile Blinn, progmg dir, engrg mgr.

Dartmouth

CFLT-FM— 2009: 92.9 mhz; 63 kw. TL: N44 39 03 W63 39 25. Hrs open: 6080 Young St., Halifax, B3K 5L2. Phone: (902) 493-7200. Licensee: Rogers Broadcasting Ltd. Format: Light rock.

CFRQ-FM— Nov 28, 1983: 104.3 mhz; 100 kw. Ant 400 ft TL: N44 38 47 W63 39 37. Stereo. Hrs open: 3770 Kempt Rd., Suite 200, Halifax, B2X 4X8. Phone: (902) 453-4004. Fax: (902) 453-3120. E-mail: jcdouglas@newcap.ca Web Site:www.q104.ca Licensee: Newcap Inc. Format: Classic rock & current rock. ◆ Ted Hyland, gen mgr & gen sls mgr; JC Douglas, progmg dir; Rich Horner, news dir; Steve Lunn, engrg dir.

Digby

CKDY(AM)— Feb 2, 1970: 1420 khz; 1 kw-U, DA-1. Hrs open: Rebroadcasts CKEN(AM) Kentville and CKAD(AM) Middleton.
29 Oakdene Ave., P.O. Box 310, Kentville, B4N 1H5. Phone: (902) 245-2111. Fax: (902) 678-9720. E-mail: programming@avrnetwork.com Web Site:www.avrnetwork.com Licensee: Maritime Broadcasting System Ltd. (group owner; acq 8-79). Format: Contemp country. Spec prog: Farm 7 hrs wkly. ◆ Dianne Best, gen mgr; Mike Mitchell, opns mgr; Karen Corey, gen sls mgr; Amanda Misner, progmg dir; Dave Chaulk, news dir; Matthew Povah, chief of engrg.

Eastern Passage

*CFEP-FM— 2002: 105.9 mhz; 1.36 kw. Ant 161 ft TL: N44 36 46 W63 29 40. Hrs open: 24 Seaside-FM, Box 196, B3G 1M5. Phone: (902) 469-9231. Fax: (902) 469-1935. E-mail: seasidefm@ns.sympatico.ca Web Site:www.seasidefm.com Licensee: Seaside Broadcasting Organization. Population served: 25,000 Format: Easy lstng, big band, adult standards. News staff: 4; News: 50 hrs wkly. ◆ Jim Mason Coe, gen sls mgr; Wayne Harrett, gen mgr & progmg mgr.

Eskasoni Indian Reserve

CICU-FM— 1994: 94.1 mhz; 1 w. Hrs open: Box 7100, Eskasoni, B1W 1A1. Secondary address: 130 Anslum Rd., Eskasoni Indian Reserve, Eskasoni B1W 1A1. Phone: (902) 379-2955. Fax: (902) 379-2966. E-mail: greguj@ns.sympatico.ca Licensee: Greg Johnson. Format: Micmac-language (32and English-language (75%) progmg. ◆ Greg Johnson, gen mgr, chief of engrg; Linda Johnson, progmg dir.

Glace Bay

CKOA-FM— Dec 3, 2007: 89.7 mhz; 6.0 kw. TL: N46 11 59 W59 58 46. Stereo. Hrs open: 24 106 Reserve St., B1A 4W5. Phone: (902) 849-4301. Fax: (902) 849-1272. E-mail: info@coastalradio.ca Web Site:www.coastalradio.ca Licensee: Coastal Community Radio Cooperative Ltd. Population served: 110,000 Natl. Rep: Target Broadcast Sales,. Format: Variety/diversified. News staff: 2; News: 105 hrs wkly. Target aud: 40-65; prime demographic. ◆ Bill MacNeil, gen mgr, progmg dir; Dennis Chipman, mus dir; Jennifer Ludlow, news dir; Rose MacNeil, prom mgr & traf mgr.

Halifax

CBAX-FM— September 2003: 91.5 mhz; 77.5 kw. TL: N44 39 03 W63 39 28. Hrs open: c/o CBAL-FM, 250 University Ave., Moncton, NB, E1C 5K3. Phone: (506) 853-6666. Fax: (506) 867-8000. Licensee: Societe Radio-Canada. Format: Fr classical, jazz, world music. ◆ Benoit Quennecille, gen mgr; Andree Girard, progmg dir.

CBHA-FM— 1989: 90.5 mhz; 91 kw. 711 ft Hrs open: Box 3000, B3J 3E9. Phone: (902) 420-8311. Fax: (902) 420-4357. Fax: (902) 420-4429. E-mail: mainstreet@halifax.cbc.ca Web Site:www.cbc.ca Licensee: CBC. Natl. Network: CBC Radio One, . Format: News, jazz, div. ◆ Susan Mitton, opns dir; Nicole Vautour, progmg dir.

*CBH-FM— June 1, 1976: 102.7 mhz; 81 kw. 711 ft Stereo. Hrs open: 24 Box 3000, B3J 3E9. Phone: (902) 420-8311. Fax: (902) 420-4429. Fax: (902) 420-4089. E-mail: weekender@halifax.cbc.ca Web Site:www.cbc.ca Licensee: CBC. Natl. Network: CBC Radio One, . Format: Div, class. Target aud: General. ◆ Susan Mitton, opns dir; Nicole Vautour, progmg dir.

CHFX-FM— Feb 9, 1970: 101.9 mhz; 100 kw. Ant 546 ft Stereo. Hrs open: 24 Box 400, B3J 2R2. Phone: (902) 422-1651. Fax: (902) 422-5330. E-mail: rpace@mdradio.com Licensee: Maritime Broadcasting System Ltd. (acq 6-94). Population served: 300,000 Wire Svc: Broadcast News Ltd. Format: Country. News staff: 5; News: 6 hrs wkly. Target aud: 25-44. ◆ Allan Gidyk, opns dir, progmg dir; Ian Kent, gen sls mgr; Robert Pace, CEO, gen mgr & mus dir.

CHNS-FM— July 19, 2006: 89.9 mhz; 100 kw. Hrs open: 5121 Sackville St., 3rd Fl., B3J 1K1. Phone: (902) 425-1225. Fax: (902) 422-5330. E-mail: rpace@mradio.com Web Site:www.899HALFM.com Licensee: Maritime Broadcasting System Ltd. Format: Classic rock. Target aud: 25-54; adults. ◆ Robert Pace, CEO & gen mgr; Allan Gidyk, opns mgr; Ian Kent, gen sls mgr.

CIOO-FM— November 1977: 100.1 mhz; 100 kw. 770 ft TL: N44 39 05 W63 39 51. Stereo. Hrs open: 24 Prog sep from AM 2900 Agricola St., B3K 6B2. Phone: (902) 453-2524. Fax: (902) 453-3120. Web Site:www.c100.net Licensee: CTV Ltd. Format: Adult contemp. ◆ Trent McGrath, prom dir; Rob Davidson, traf mgr.

CJCH-FM— May 30, 2008: 101.3 mhz; 100 kw. TL: N44 38 47 W63 39 37. Hrs open: 24 2900 Agricola St., B3K 6B2. Phone: (902) 453-2524. Fax: (902) 453-3120. Fax: (902) 453-3132. Web Site:www.1013thebounce.com Licensee: CTV Ltd. Format: Top-40. ◆ Bob Basile, progmg dir.

CJNI-FM— Oct 11, 2005: 95.7 mhz; 65 kw. Hrs open: 6080 Young St., B3K 5L2. Phone: (902) 493-7200. Web Site:www.news957.com Licensee: Rogers Broadcasting Ltd. Format: News/talk. ◆ Scott Parsons, gen mgr.

*CKDU-FM— February 1985: 97.5 mhz; 3.2 kw. Ant 300 ft Hrs open: 24 Dalhousie SUB, 6136 University Ave., B3H 4J2. Phone: (902) 494-6479. E-mail: ckdu@ckdu.ca Web Site:www.ckdu.ca Licensee: CKDU-FM Society Ltd. Population served: 250,000 Format: Div. News staff: one; News: 4 hrs wkly. Target aud: General. ◆ Michael Catano, stn mgr.

CKHZ-FM— Sept 1, 2006: 103.5 mhz; 78 kw. TL: N44 38 47 W63 39 40. Stereo. Hrs open: 24 Evanov Radio Group, 5302 Dundas St. W.,

Toronto, ON, M9B 1B2. Phone: (416) 213-1035. Fax: (416) 233-8617.E-mail: info@z103halifax.com Web Site:z103halifax.com Licensee: HFX Broadcasting Inc. Format: Top 40.

CKRH-FM— Sept 25, 2007: 98.5 mhz; 2.35 kw. TL: N44 39 03 W63 39 28. Hrs open: 5527 Cogswell St., B3J 1R2. Phone: (902) 490-2574. Fax: (902) 429-2574.E-mail: info@ckrhfm.com Web Site:www.ckrhfm.com Licensee: Cooperative Radio-Halifax-Metro limitee. Format: Fr var. News staff: 3. ◆Nay Marie Saade, gen mgr.

CKUL-FM— August 1990: 96.5 mhz; 100 kw. Hrs open: 24 3770 Kempt Rd., Suite 200, B2X 4X8. Phone: (902) 453-4004. Fax: (902) 453-3120.E-mail: thyland@newcap.ca Web Site:www.kool1965fm.ca Licensee: Newcap Inc. Group owner: NewCap Broadcasting Ltd. (acq 12-17-2001). Natl. Rep: Canadian Broadcast Sales,. Format: Classic hits 60s & 70s & 80s. News staff: 3; News: 3 hrs wkly. Target aud: 35-54. ◆Ted Hyland, sls VP; Rob Johnson, progmg dir, progmg mgr; Rich Horner, news dir, pub affrs dir; Steve Lunn, chief of engrg.

Kentville

CIJK-FM— 9.9 kw: 89.3 mhz; TL: N45 12 12 W64 24 03. Hrs open: 8794 Commercial St., Suite 3, New Minas, B4N 3C5. Phone: (902) 365-8930. Fax: (902) 365-3566.E-mail: info@k-rock893.com Web Site:www.k-rock893.com Licensee: Newcap Inc. Format: Rock. Target aud: 24-54. ◆Ken Geddes, gen mgr; Tina McAuley, prom dir; Gary Tredwell, progmg dir, mus dir; Vicki Winger, traf mgr.

CKEN-FM— Mar 14, 1965: 97.7 mhz; 18 kw. Ant 680 ft Stereo. Hrs open: Box 310, B4N 1H5. Secondary address: 29 Oakdene Ave. B4N 1H5. Phone: (902) 678-2111. Fax: (902) 678-9894.E-mail: avr@avrnetwork.com Web Site:www.avrnetwork.com Licensee: Maritime Broadcasting System Ltd. Group owner: Maritime Broadcasting (acq 1998; grpsl). Natl. Rep: Canadian Broadcast Sales,. Format: Country. News staff: 5. Target aud: 18-49. Spec prog: Farm 5 hrs wkly. ◆Dianne Best, gen mgr; Mike Mitchell, opns mgr; Karen Corey, gen sls mgr; Amanda Misner, progmg dir; Matthew Povah, chief of engrg.

CKWM-FM— 2003: 94.9 mhz; 100 kw. Hrs open: Box 310, B4N 1H5. Secondary address: 29 Oakdene Ave. B4N 1H5. Phone: (902) 678-2111. Fax: (902) 678-9894.E-mail: magic949@magic949.ca Web Site:www.magic949.ca Licensee: Maritime Broadcasting System Ltd. Group owner: Maritime Broadcasting. Format: Adult contemp. ◆Dianne Best, gen mgr; Mike Mitchell, opns mgr; Karen Corey, gen sls mgr; Matthew Povah, chief of engrg.

Liverpool

CKBW-FM-1— Sept 15, 1980: 94.5 mhz; 8.7 kw. Ant 250 ft Stereo. Hrs open: 24
Rebroadcasts CKBW-FM Bridgewater 100%.
c/o CKBW, 215 Dominion St., Bridgewater, B4V 2G8. Phone: (902) 543-2401. Fax: (902) 543-1208.E-mail: ckbw@ckbw.com Web Site:www.ckbw.ca Licensee: Acadia Broadcasting Ltd. (group owner; acq 8-31-89). Natl. Rep: Canadian Broadcast Sales,. Rgnl rep: Canadian Broadcast Sales. Wire Svc: Broadcast News Ltd. Format: Hot AC. News staff: 2.5; News: 11 hrs wkly. Target aud: General; rural & small town urban.John Wiles, gen mgr, opns mgr, progmg dir; Chris Pearson, gen sls mgr, natl sls mgr; Brian Tepper, prom dir; Leitha Haysom, mus dir, disc jockey; Frank Grayney, chief of engrg; Pamela Smith, traf mgr; Jonathan Crouse, spec ev coord, disc jockey; Sheldon MacLeod, news dir, pub affrs dir & local news ed; Joan Fillmore, news rptr; Greg Lowe, sports cmtr; Mike Richards, disc jockey

Middleton

CKAD(AM)— 1962: 1350 khz; 1 kw-U, DA-1. Hrs open: 29 Oakdene Ave., P.O. Box 310, Kentville, B4N 1H5. Phone: (902) 825-3429. Fax: (902) 678-9894.E-mail: programming@avrnetwork.com Licensee: Maritime Broadcasting. (group owner; acq 6-26-79). Format: Country. Spec prog: Farm 3 hrs wkly. ◆Dianne Best, gen mgr; Mike Mitchell, opns mgr; Karen Corey, gen sls mgr; Amanda Misner, progmg dir, progmg mgr; Dave Chaulk, news dir; Matthew Povah, chief of engrg.

New Glasgow

CKEC-FM— Dec 11, 2007: 94.1 mhz; 36.68 kw. TL: N45 32 24 W62 56 44. Hrs open: 24 Box 519, B2H 5E7. Secondary address: 84 Provost St. B2H 5E7. Phone: (902) 752-4200. Phone: (902) 755-1320. Fax: (902) 755-2468. Fax: (902) 928-1320.E-mail: info@ckecradio.ca Web Site:ckec941.ca Licensee: Hector Broadcasting Co. Ltd. Natl. Rep: Canadian Broadcast Sales,. Format: Adult contemp. News staff: 3; News: 15 hrs wkly. Target aud: General. Spec prog: Scottish. ◆D.B. Freeman, CEO; M.D. Freeman, exec VP & gen mgr.

New Tusket

CJLS-FM-2— 1982: 93.5 mhz; 3 kw. Hrs open:
Rebroadcasts CJLS-FM Yarmouth.
c/o Radio Station CJLS(AM), 328 Main St., Suite 201, Yarmouth, B5A 1E4. Phone: (902) 742-7175. Fax: (902) 742-3143.E-mail: cjls@cjls.com Web Site:www.cjls.com Licensee: Radio CJLS Ltd. Format: Adult contemp. ◆Chris Perry, VP, progmg mgr; Ray Zinck, pres & gen mgr; Dave Hall, gen sls mgr; Gary Nickerson, news dir; Jim Harris, engrg dir.

Port Hawkesbury

CIGO-FM— 2000: 101.5 mhz; 19 kw. TL: N45 39 00 W61 28 00. Hrs open: 609 Church St., Ste 201, B9A 2X4. Phone: (902) 625-1220. Phone: (902) 625-1015. Fax: (902) 625-2664. Fax: (902) 625-6397.E-mail: 1015thehawk@1015thehawk.com Web Site:www.1015thehawk.com Licensee: MacEachern Broadcasting Ltd. Population served: 45,000 Wire Svc: BN Wire Format: Adult contemp. News staff: 2; News: 4 hrs wkly. Target aud: 18-49; blue collar, high school education, married. Spec prog: East Coast 3 hrs, Scottish 1 hrs, Irish one hr wkly. ◆Bob MacEachern, pres, stn mgr; Kelly Atchison, progmg mgr; Kevin MacEachern, sls.

Shelburne

CKBW-FM-2— Sept 15, 1980: 93.1 mhz; 8.6 kw. Stereo. Hrs open:
Rebroadcasts CKBW-FM Bridgewater 100%.
c/o CKBW, 215 Dominion St., Bridgewater, B4V 2G8. Phone: (902) 543-2401. Fax: (902) 543-1208.E-mail: ckbw@ckbw.com Web Site:www.ckbw.ca Licensee: Acadia Broadcasting Ltd. (group owner; acq 8-31-89). Natl. Rep: Canadian Broadcast Sales,. Rgnl rep: Canadian Broadcast Sales. Wire Svc: Broadcast News Ltd. Format: Hot adult contemp. News staff: 2.5. Target aud: General; rural & small town urban. ◆John Wiles, gen mgr, opns mgr, progmg dir, mus dir; Barry Smith, gen sls mgr, natl sls mgr; Brian Tepper, prom dir; Frank Grayney, chief of engrg; Pamela Smith, traf mgr; Greg Lowe, spec ev coord, sports cmtr; Sheldon MacLeod, news dir, pub affrs dir & local news ed; Jonathan Crouse, disc jockey.

Sydney

CBI(AM)— Nov 1, 1948: 1140 khz; 10 kw-U, DA-2. Hrs open: 285 Alexandra St., B1S 2E8. Phone: (902) 539-5050. Fax: (902) 539-1562. Web Site:www.cbc.ca/ns Licensee: CBC. Natl. Network: CBC Radio One, . Format: Info. ◆Kathy Large, progmg mgr.

CBI-FM— July 1977: 105.1 mhz; 20 kw. 400 ft Stereo. Hrs open: Prog sep from AM 285 Alexandra St., B1S 2E8. Phone: (902) 539-5050. Fax: (902) 539-1562. Web Site:www.cbc.ca/ns Licensee: CBC Natl. Network: CBC Radio Two, . Format: Classics, lite classics. ◆Kathy Large, progmg dir.

CHER-FM— 2007: 98.3 mhz; 100 kw. Stereo. Hrs open: 318 Charlotte St., B1P 1C5. Phone: (902) 564-5596. Fax: (902) 564-1873.E-mail: info@cherfm.com Web Site:www.capebretonradio.com Licensee: Maritime Broadcasting System Ltd. Natl. Rep: Canadian Broadcast Sales,. Format: Classic hits. News staff: 3. ◆Alan Peddle, gen mgr, gen sls mgr; Fred Denney, opns mgr; Phil Thompson, progmg dir; Gary Andrea, news dir; Roy MacIntosh, chief of engrg.

CHRK-FM— May 27, 2008: 101.9 mhz; 57 kw. TL: N46 05 40 W60 08 52. Hrs open: 5 Dethridge Dr., Sydney River, B1L 1B8. Phone: (902) 270-1019. Fax: (902) 270-3566. Web Site:www.giant1019.com Licensee: Newcap Inc. Format: Top-40/pop. ◆Dave Newbury, gen mgr, gen sls mgr; Daryl Stevens, opns mgr, progmg dir; Scott Boyd, news dir.

CJCB(AM)— Feb 14, 1929: 1270 khz; 10 kw-U, DA-N. Stereo. Hrs open: 24 Radio Bldg., 318 Charlotte St., B1P 1C8. Phone: (902) 564-5596. Fax: (902) 564-1057.E-mail: info@cjcb.com Web Site:www.capebretonradio.com Licensee: Maritime Broadcasting System Ltd. Population served: 109,000 Format: Today's country. News staff: 3. Target aud: General. ◆Rod Deviller, opns mgr; Alan Peddle, gen sls mgr; Phil Thompson, prom mgr; Roy MacIntosh, engrg mgr & chief of engrg.

CJIJ-FM— June 2, 2003: 99.9 mhz; 50 w. TL: N46 07 01 W60 11 40. Hrs open: Membertou Radio, 111 Membertou St., Membertou, B1S 2M9. Secondary address: 1969 Upper Water St., Suite 1703, Tower II, Purdy's Wharf, Halifax B3J 3R7. Phone: (902) 562-0009. Fax: (902) 539-6645.E-mail: c99@membertou.ca Licensee: Membertou Radio Association Inc. Format: Classic hits, classic rock. ◆Dawn Wells, gen mgr.

CKCH-FM— June 20, 2008: 103.5 mhz; 26.5 kw. TL: N46 05 55 W60 18 41. Hrs open: 5 Dethridge Dr., Sydney River, B1L 1B8. Phone: (902) 563-1035. Fax: (902) 270-3566. Web Site:www.eagle1035.com Licensee: 3221809 Nova Scotia Ltd. Format: Country. ◆Dave Newbury, gen mgr.

CKPE-FM— September 1962: 94.9 mhz; 61 kw. 210 ft Stereo. Hrs open: 24 Prog sep from AM Radio Bldg., 318 Charlotte St., B1P 1C8. Phone: (902) 564-5596. Fax: (902) 564-1057.E-mail: info@ckpe.com Web Site:www.capebretonradio.com Licensee: Maritime Broadcasting System Ltd. Population served: 109,000 Format: Todays best music. News staff: 3. ◆Phil Thompson, prom dir, prom mgr; Joe Purdy, mus dir; Roy MacIntosh, chief of engrg.

Truro

CINU-FM— 2004: 98.5 mhz; 50 w. Hrs open: Box 25012, B2N 7B8. Secondary address: 883 Prince St. B2N 1H2. Phone: (902) 843-4673. Fax: (902) 662-2879.E-mail: hopefmministries@eastlink.ca Licensee: Hope FM Ministries Ltd. Format: Christian music. ◆Barry Reid, pres & gen mgr.

CKTO-FM— 1965: 100.9 mhz; 50 kw. Ant 189 ft Stereo. Hrs open: 24 187 Industrial Ave., B2N 6V3. Phone: (902) 893-6060. Fax: (902) 893-7771.E-mail: turreception@radioatl.ca Web Site:www.bigdog1009.ca Licensee: Astral Media Radio Atlantic Inc. Group owner: Astral Media Inc. (acq 4-19-2002; grpsl). Natl. Rep: Canadian Broadcast Sales,. Format: Adult contemp, rock. News staff: 3; News: 6 hrs wkly. Target aud: 25-49. ◆John Eddy, exec VP; Mike Worsley, stn mgr, gen mgr; Chris Van Tassel, progmg dir; James Cormier, mus dir; Tim Tucker, news dir; Victor Deveau, chief of engrg.

CKTY-FM— 2001: 99.5 mhz; 16.75 kw. Hrs open: 187 Industrial Ave., B2N 6V3. Phone: (902) 893-6060. Fax: (902) 893-7771.E-mail: turreception@radioatl.ca Web Site:www.catcountry995.ca Licensee: Astral Media Radio Atlantic Inc. Group owner: Astral Media Inc. (acq 4-19-2002; grpsl). Natl. Rep: Canadian Broadcast Sales,. Format: Country. ◆John Eddy, exec VP; Mike Worsley, gen sls mgr; Chris Van Tassel, progmg dir; Rob De Viller, mus dir.

Windsor

CFAB(AM)— 1945: 1450 khz; 1 kw-U. Hrs open: 24 ARV, 29 Oakdene Ave., Box 310, Kensville, B4N 1H5. Phone: (902) 798-2111. Fax: (902) 798-8140.E-mail: avr@avrnetwork.com Web Site:www.avrnetwork.com Licensee: Maritime Broadcasting System Ltd. Group owner: Maritime Broadcasting. Format: Country. News staff: 5; News: 9 hrs wkly. Target aud: 25-54. ◆Dianne Best, gen mgr; Mike Mitchell, opns mgr; Karen Corey, gen sls mgr; Amanda Misner, progmg dir; Dave Chaulk, news dir; Matthew Povah, engrg dir, chief of engrg.

Yarmouth

CJLS-FM— 2003: 95.5 mhz; 18 kw. Stereo. Hrs open: 24 328 Main St., Suite 201, B5A 1E4. Phone: (902) 742-7175. Fax: (902) 742-3143.E-mail: CJLS@cjls.com Web Site:www.cjls.com Licensee: Radio CJLS Ltd. Format: Adult contemp. ◆Ray Zinck, gen mgr; Dave Hall, gen sls mgr; Chris Perry, progmg dir; Jim Harris, chief of engrg.

Nunavut

Baker Lake

CKQN-FM— 1973: 99.3 mhz; 60 w. -50 ft Hrs open: Box 13, X0C 0A0. Phone: (867) 793-2962. Fax: (867-793-2726). Web Site:www.tvradioworld.com Licensee: Qamani'tuap Naalautaa Society. Natl. Network: CBC Radio One, . Format: Eskimo, Inuit. ◆Eva Elytuk, pres & gen mgr.

Iqaluit

CFFB(AM)— Feb 6, 1961: 1230 khz; 1 kw-U, DA-1. Hrs open: 24 Box 490, X0A 0H0. Phone: (867) 979-6100. Fax: (867) 979-6147.E-mail: nunavut@cbc.ca Web Site:cbc.ca/north Licensee: CBC. Natl. Network: CBC Radio One, . Format: News/talk, Inuktitut language. News staff: 9. ◆Patrick Nagle, gen mgr; Fiona Christensen, news dir.

CFRT-FM— 1994: 107.3 mhz; 27 w. Hrs open: C.P. 880, X0A 0H0. Phone: (867) 979-4606. Fax: (867) 979-0800. E-mail: cfrt@nunafranc.ca

Web Site:www.franconunavut.ca Licensee: Association des francophones de Nunavut. Format: Fr. ◆Daniel Cuerrier, gen mgr; Sabrina Bertrand, progmg dir.

CKIQ-FM— May 26, 2003: 99.9 mhz; 537 w. Hrs open: Box 417, X0A 0H0. Secondary address: 1036 Airport Rd. X0A 0H0. Phone: (867) 975-2547. Fax: (867) 975-2598.E-mail: 99.9@ckiq.com Web Site:www.ckiq.ca Licensee: Northern Lights Entertainment Inc. (acq 3-2-2009; C$185,000 plus 75% of the good accounts receivable at closing) Natl. Rep: Target Broadcast Sales,. Format: Classic rock. ◆Terri Chegwyn, gen mgr.

Rankin Inlet

CBQR-FM— 1988: 105.1 mhz; 87 w. Hrs open: 24 Box 130, X0C 0G0. Phone: (867) 645-2244. Fax: (867) 645-2820. Web Site:www.north.cbc.ca Licensee: CBC Radio. Natl. Network: CBC Radio One, . Format: Adult contemp, talk, div. Spec prog: Inuktitut 10 hrs wkly. ◆Patrick Nagle, gen mgr; Fiona Christensen, news dir.

Ontario

Ajax

CJKX-FM— 1994: 95.9 mhz; 19.94 kw. Ant 330 ft Stereo. Hrs open: 24 1200 Airport Blvd., Suite 207, Oshawa, L1J 8P5. Phone: (905) 428-9600. Fax: (905) 571-1150.E-mail: kx96@kx96.fm Web Site:www.kx96.fm Licensee: Durham Radio Inc. (group owner). Population served: 2,500,000 Format: New country. News staff: 3; News: 1.5 hrs wkly. Target aud: 25-54; . ◆Douglas E. Kirk, pres, gen mgr; Steve Kassay, opns VP, opns mgr; Steve Macaulay, sls VP & gen sls mgr; Stacey Garfield, traf mgr.

Akwesasne

CKON-FM— Oct 1, 1984: 97.3 mhz; 150 w. 150 ft Hrs open: Box 140, Rooseveltown, NY, 13683. Secondary address: Box 1496 K6H 5V5. Phone: (613) 575-2100. Phone: (518) 358-3426 (US). Fax: (613) 575-2566.E-mail: ckon@ckonfm.com Web Site:www.ckonfm.com Licensee: Mohawk Nation Council. Group owner: Akwesasne Communication Society Format: Div. Target aud: General. Spec prog: Mohawk. ◆Judy Laffin, gen mgr; Larry Edwards, gen mgr & progmg dir.

Alexandria

CHOD-FM—See Cornwall

Alliston

CFAO-FM— 2009: 94.7 mhz; 50 w. TL: N44 08 57 W79 52 33. Hrs open: 27 Victoria St. E., Suite 208, L9R 1T3. Phone: (705) 435-3399. Fax: (705) 435-3383. Web Site:cfao947.com Licensee: Frank Rogers, on behalf of a corporation to be incorporated. Format: Adult contemp. ◆Frank Rogers, gen mgr.

Apsley

CFSH-FM—Not on air, target date: unknown: 92.9 mhz; 50 w. TL: N44 45 54 W78 05 27. Hrs open: Attn: John Trotter, 299 McFadden Rd., K0L 1A0. Phone: (705) 656-1510. Fax: (705) 656-1510. Licensee: Apsley Community Chapel. Format: Christian music.

Aylmer

CHPD-FM— September 2003: 105.9 mhz; 250 w. TL: N42 45 40 W80 56 03. Hrs open: 7 AM- 8 AM; 5 PM- 8 PM 16 Talbot St., N5H 1H4. Phone: (519) 765-3028. Fax: (519) 773-8606.E-mail: radio @debrigj.org Licensee: Mennonite Community Services. Population served: 15,000 Format: Low German. News staff: one; News: one hr wkly. Target aud: 5-70; Low German newcomers. ◆Abe Harms, CEO; Peter Bergen, chmn & pres; Abe Harder, VP; Jake Wall, stn mgr.

Bancroft

CHMS-FM— May 2001: 97.7 mhz; 50 w. Hrs open: 24 Box 1240, K0L 1C0. Phone: (613) 332-1423. Fax: (613) 332-0841.E-mail: moose977@hbgradio.com Web Site:www.moosefm.com Licensee:

The Haliburton Broadcasting Group Inc. Group owner: Haliburton Broadcasting Group Inc. Population served: 30,000 Format: The best of whatever. Target aud: General. ◆Wendy Gray, opns mgr.

Barrie

CFJB-FM— Oct 7, 1988: 95.7 mhz; 41 kw. Ant 500 ft Hrs open: 24 Phone: (705) 725-7304. Fax: (705) 792-7858.E-mail: dbingley@rock95.com Web Site:www.rock95.com Licensee: Rock 95 Broadcasting (Barrie-Orillia) Ltd. (acq 2-7-94). Population served: 280,000 Format: Classic rock, new rock, 80s rock. News staff: 3; News: 4 hrs wkly. Target aud: 18-49; broad-based, well-educated, above-average income. ◆Doug Bingley, CEO, pres, gen mgr; Tom Manton, gen sls mgr; Todd Palmer, prom dir; Dave Carr, progmg dir.

CHAY-FM— May 21, 1977: 93.1 mhz; 100 kw. Ant 1,000 ft Stereo. Hrs open: 24 Box 937, L4M 4Y6. Phone: (705) 737-3511. Fax: (705) 737-0603.E-mail: knoel@corusent.com Web Site:www.fm93.ca/home/ Licensee: Corus Radio Co. Group owner: Corus Entertainment Inc. Population served: 350,000 Format: Adult contemp. News staff: 3; News: 13 hrs wkly. Target aud: 25-64; general. ◆John Hayes, pres; Kim Noel, gen mgr; Frank Allinson, gen sls mgr; Dave Pinder, prom mgr; Derrick Scott, progmg dir.

CIQB-FM— November 1994: 101.1 mhz; 4.3 kw. Hrs open: 24 Box 101, L4M 4S9. Secondary address: 1125 Bayfield St. N. L4M 4S9. Phone: (705) 726-1011. Fax: (705) 726-0022.E-mail: knoel@corusent.com Web Site:www.b101fm.com Licensee: Corus Entertainment, Inc. Group owner: Corus Entertainment Inc. (acq 3-24-2000; grpsl). Format: Hot adult contemp. News staff: 3; News: 11 hrs wkly. Target aud: 25-54; women 35-49 & 25-54 & at work people. ◆John Hayes, pres, VP; Kim Noel, gen mgr; Dave Pinder, mktg dir, prom; Derrick Scott, progmg dir.

CJLF-FM— Aug 15, 1999: 100.3 mhz; 18.7 kw. Hrs open: 115 Bell Farm Rd, Unit 111, L4M 5G1. Phone: (705) 735-3370. Fax: (705) 735-3301. Web Site:www.lifeonline.fm Licensee: Trust Communications Ministries. Format: Christian music. ◆Scott Jackson, stn mgr; Jen Taylor, prom dir.

CKMB-FM— 1/1/2006: 107.5 mhz; 20 kw. Hrs open: 24 431 Huronia Rd., Unit 10, L4M 9B3. Phone: (705) 725-7304. Fax: (705) 792-7858. Web Site:www.koolfm1075.com Licensee: Rock 95 Broadcasting (Barrie-Orillia) Ltd. Format: Top 40/contemp hits. ◆Doug Bingley, CEO, pres, gen mgr; Tom Manton, gen sls mgr; Helen Mathers, prom dir; Dave Carr, progmg mgr.

Belleville

CHCQ-FM— 2001: 100.1 mhz; 21 kw. Stereo. Hrs open: 24 354 Pinnacle St., K8N 3B4. Phone: (613) 966-0955. Fax: (613) 967-2565.E-mail: news@classichits955.fm Web Site:www.cool100.fm Licensee: Starboard Communications Ltd. (acq 7-26-02; C$541,351). Population served: 105,000 Natl. Rep: CHUM Radio Sales,. Format: Country. News staff: 4. Target aud: 25-54; adults. ◆John Sherratt, pres, gen mgr; Darren Matassa, gen sls mgr; Mark Philbin, progmg dir.

CIGL-FM— August 1962: 97.1 mhz; 50 kw. Hrs open: 24 Prog sep from AM Secondary address: Box 488 K8N 5B2. Phone: (613) 969-5555. Fax: (613) 969-8122. Web Site:www.mix97.com Licensee: Quinte Broadcasting, LTD Format: Hot adult contemp. ◆Jody Brooker, gen sls mgr; Sean Kelly, progmg dir.

CJBQ(AM)— Aug 12, 1946: 800 khz; 10 kw-U, DA-2. Hrs open: 24 Box 488, K8N 5B2. Secondary address: 10 S. Front St. K8N2Y3. Phone: (613) 969-5555. Fax: (613) 969-8122.E-mail: quinte@broadcasting.com Web Site:www.cjbq.com Licensee: Quinte Broadcasting Ltd. (group owner). Format: Country/Talk. Spec prog: Farm 3 hrs wkly. ◆Bill Morton, gen mgr; Jody Brooker, gen sls mgr; Sean Kelly, progmg dir.

CJLX-FM— October 1992: 91.3 mhz; 3.4 kw. Ant 300 ft TL: N44 09 50 W77 23 24. Stereo. Hrs open: 24 Box 4200, Loyalist College, Wallbridge-Loyalist Rd., K8N 5B9. Phone: (613) 966-0923. Fax: (613) 966-1993.E-mail: contact@91x.fm Web Site:www.91x.fm Licensee: Loyalist College Radio Inc. (acq 11-13-90). Population served: 177,000 Natl. Rep: Target Broadcast Sales,. Wire Svc: BN Wire Format: Rock, community svc. News staff: 15; News: 6 hrs wkly. Target aud: 18-34; primary, ages 50 plus secondary. Spec prog: Folk one hr, jazz 3 hrs, Greek one hr, class 2 hr, blues one hr, educ 4 hrs, big band 2 hrs, reggae one hr wkly. ◆Greg Schatzmann, CEO, gen mgr; Sandi Ramsey, sls dir, gen sls mgr; Len Arminio, news dir; Tim Rorabeck, chief of engrg.

CJOJ-FM— Dec 1, 1993: 95.5 mhz; 42 kw. Stereo. Hrs open: 24 354 Pinnacle St., K8N 3B4. Phone:(613) 966-0955.E-mail: news@classichits955.fm Web Site:www.classichits955.fm Licensee:

Starboard Communications Ltd. (acq 7-26-02; C$1,456,610). Population served: 105,000 Natl. Rep: CHUM Radio Sales,. Format: CHR, adult contemp. Target aud: 25-54; adults-skewed females 60%, males 40%. ◆John Sherratt, pres, stn mgr; Darron Matassa, gen sls mgr; Mark Philbin, progmg dir.

CKJJ-FM— Oct 18, 2003: 102.3 mhz; 45 kw. Hrs open: Box 23095, K8P 5J3. Secondary address: 214 Pinnacle St. K8P 3A6. Phone: (613) 966-4822. Fax: (613) 966-3211.E-mail: info@ucbcanada.com Web Site:www.ucbcanada.com Licensee: United Christian Broadcasters Canada. Format: Christian music. ◆James Hunt, CEO.

Bolton

CJFB-FM— Mar 21, 2008: 105.5 mhz; 50 w. TL: N43 52 46 W79 44 18. Hrs open: Box 27, Caledon East, L7C 3L8. Phone: (905) 951-2899.E-mail: info@radiocaledon.com Web Site:caledononline.com Licensee: Rick Sargent. Format: Eclectic adult contemp. ◆Rick Sargent, gen mgr.

Bracebridge

CFBG-FM— May 1988: 99.5 mhz; 12 kw. Hrs open: Box 960, Haliburton, K0M 1S0. Phone: (705) 645-2218. Fax: (705) 645-6957.E-mail: moose995@hbgradio.com Web Site:www.hbgradio.com Licensee: The Haliburton Broadcasting Group Inc. Group owner: Haliburton Broadcasting Group Inc. (acq 12-10-97; C$295,000). Format: Hot adult contemp. Target aud: 34-45; older adult contemporary. Spec prog: Jazz 2 hrs, big band one hr, loc magazine one hr wkly. ◆Christopher Grossman, pres, gen mgr; Kimberley Ward, VP; Wendy Gray, opns mgr; Sean Connon, gen sls mgr.

Brampton

CIAO(AM)— Dec 23, 1953: 530 khz; 1 kw-D, 250 w-N, DA-2. (Digital radio: 1466.768 mhz; 5.084 kw). Hrs open: 24 5302 Dundas S. W., Toronto, M9B-1B2. Phone: (416) 213-1035. Fax: (416) 233-8617.E-mail: info@am530.ca Web Site:www.am530.ca Licensee: CKMW Radio Ltd. Group owner: Evanov Radio Group (acq 9-26-83). Natl. Rep: Target Broadcast Sales,. Format: Ethnic, multilingual. ◆Bill Evanov, pres; Paul Evanov, exec VP.

Brantford

CFWC-FM— 2002: 93.9 mhz; 250 w. Hrs open: 271 Greenwich St., N3S 2X9. Phone: (519) 759-2339. Fax: (519) 753-1157.E-mail: vicki@power93.ca Web Site:www.power93.ca Licensee: 1486781 Ontario Ltd. Format: Christian music. ◆Vicki Schleifer, stn mgr; Luke Schleifer, progmg dir.

CKPC(AM)— December 1923: 1380 khz; 25 kw-U, DA-2. TL: N43 03 05 W80 18 50. Hrs open: 24 571 West St., N3T 5P8. Phone: (519) 759-1000. Fax: (519) 753-1470.E-mail: salesmgr@ckpc.on.ca Web Site:www.ckpc.on.ca Licensee: Telephone City Broadcast Ltd. Population served: 115,652 Natl. Rep: Target Broadcast Sales,. Format: Classic hits. News staff: 7; News: 9 hrs wkly. Target aud: 35-64. ◆Peter Jackman, sls VP & gen sls mgr.

CKPC-FM— May 1949: 92.1 mhz; 80 kw. Ant 750 ft Stereo. Hrs open: 24 Prog sep from AM 571 West St., N3T 5P8. Phone: (519) 759-1000. Fax:(519) 753-1470.E-mail: salesmgr@ckpc.on.ca Web Site:www.ckpc.on.ca Licensee: Telephone City Broadcast Ltd. Population served: 500,000 Natl. Rep: Target Broadcast Sales,. Format: Adult contemp. News staff: 7; News: 7 hrs wkly. Target aud: 25-49.

Brockville

CFJR-FM— 2003: 104.9 mhz; 5.6 kw. Hrs open: 24 601 Stewart Blvd., K6V 5V9. Phone: (613) 345-1666. Fax: (613) 342-2438.E-mail: comments@hometownradio.ca Web Site:www.hometownradio.ca Licensee: CTV Ltd. (group owner). (acq 6-22-2007; grpsl). Format: Adult contemp. News staff: 3; News: 5 hrs wkly. Target aud: 35-54; female slant. ◆Greg Hinton, gen mgr; Rick Moran, gen sls mgr; Dan Wylie, progmg dir; Warren Davies, chief of engrg.

CJPT-FM— July 28, 1988: 103.7 mhz; 100 kw. Ant 495 ft TL: N44 23 58 W75 58 21. Hrs open: 24 601 Stewart Blvd., K6V 5V9. Phone: (613) 345-1666. Fax: (613) 342-2438.E-mail: info@bob.fm Web Site:www.bob.fm Licensee: CTV Ltd. (group owner). (acq 6-22-2007; grpsl). Format: Hits of the 80s. News staff: 3. Target aud: 18-44; male. ◆Paul Ski, exec VP; Greg Hinton, gen mgr; Rick Moran, rgnl sls mgr; Greg Zehr, prom dir; Dan Wylie, progmg dir.

Burlington

CIWV-FM—See Hamilton

CJXY-FM— Sept 23, 1976: 107.9 mhz; 26.4 kw. Ant 672 ft TL: N43 23 12 W79 52 34. Stereo. Hrs open: 24 875 Main St. West, Hamilton, L8S 4R1. Phone: (905) 521-9900. Fax: (905) 540-2452. Web Site:www.y108.ca Licensee: Corus Radio Co. Group owner: Corus Entertainment Inc. Format: Mainstream rock. News staff: one; News: 2 hrs wkly. Target aud: 25-39. ◆Suzanne Carpenter, gen mgr.

Cambridge

CJDV-FM— 1998: 107.5 mhz; 2.5 kw. Stereo. Hrs open: 24 1315 Bishop St. N., Unit 100, N1R 6Z2. Phone: (519) 621-7510. Fax: (519) 621-0165.E-mail: lars@davefm.com Web Site:www.davefm.com Licensee: 591989 B.C. Ltd. Group owner: Corus Entertainment Inc. (acq 4-2000; grpsl). Population served: 400,000 Format: 80's; 90's & current. News staff: 2. Target aud: 18-49. Spec prog: Por 2 hrs wkly. ◆Lars Wunsche, gen mgr; Scott Turner, progmg dir; Brian Clemens, engrg VP, chief of engrg.

Campbellford

CKOL-FM— 7/1/1993: 93.7 mhz; 500 w. Hrs open: 8 am-9 pm Box 551, K0L 1L0. Secondary address: 15 Ragland St. S. K0L 1L0. Phone: (705) 653-1089.E-mail: ckol-radio@excite.com Web Site:www.ckolradio.ca Licensee: Campbellford Area Radio Association. Format: Div. Spec prog: Gospel 3 hrs, bluegrass 3 hrs wkly. ◆Dave Lockwood, gen mgr.

Cape Croker (Neyaashiinigmiing)

CHFN-FM— 2003: 100.1 mhz; 72 w. Hrs open: 24 RR 5, Wiarton, N0H 2T0. Phone: (519) 534-1003. Fax: (519) 534-4916.E-mail: chfnradio_station@yahoo.ca Web Site:www.nawash.ca/chfn Licensee: Jessica Nadjiwon, on behalf of a non-profit corporation to be incorporated. Population served: 1,200 Format: Aboriginal news & programs relevant to the Ojibway people. News: 12 hrs wkly. Target aud: 18-65; progmg is div. ◆Jake Linklater, pres; Peter Akiwenzie, VP; Jessica Nadjiwon, gen mgr; Beedahsega Elliott, mktg mgr; Johnathan Pedoniquotte, progmg mgr.

Chatham

CFCO(AM)— 1926: 630 khz; 10 kw-D, 6 kw-N, DA-2. TL: N42 20 03 W82 16 53. (Note: CFCO(AM) is rebroadcast on transmitter CFCO-1-FM Chatham on 92.9 mhz). Stereo. Hrs open: 24 Box 100, N7M 5K1. Secondary address: 117 Keil Dr. S. N7M 5K1. Phone: (519) 354-2853. Fax: (519) 354-2880.E-mail: info@630cfco.com Web Site:www.630cfco.com Licensee: Blackburn Groupe, Inc (acq 3-20-97). Population served: 130,000 Rgnl rep: Rgnl Reps Format: Country. News staff: 6; News: 6 hrs wkly. Target aud: 35 plus. Spec prog: Farm 3 hrs, gospel 2 hrs wkly. ◆Carl Veroba, CEO, pres, gen mgr; Doug Kirk, VP; Walter Ploegman, opns mgr; Jenna Herdman, mktg dir.

CKGW-FM— 2007: 89.3 mhz; 16.7 kw. Ant 436 ft TL: N42 26 14 W82 06 23. Hrs open: 40 Centre St., N7M 5W3. Phone: (613) 966-4822. Fax: (613) 966-3211.E-mail: info@ucbcanada.com Web Site:www.ucbchathamkent.com Licensee: United Christian Broadcasters Canada. Format: Christian music. ◆Garry Quinn, gen mgr.

CKSY-FM— 7/1/1986: 94.3 mhz; 50 kw. Ant 495 ft TL: N42 26 14 W82 06 23. Hrs open: 24 Box 100, N7M 5K1. Secondary address: 117 Keil Dr. S. N7M 5K1. Phone: (519) 354-2200. Phone: (519) 354-0311. Fax: (519) 354-2880.E-mail: info@630cfco.com Web Site:www.cksyfm.com Licensee: Blackburn Group, Inc. Population served: 130,000 Format: Adult contemp. News staff: 5; News: 5 hrs wkly. Target aud: 18-54. Spec prog: Gospel 2 hrs wkly. ◆Doug Kirk, VP; Carl Veroba, gen mgr; Walter Ploegman, opns mgr; Phil Ceccacci, gen sls mgr; Jenna Herdman, mktg dir; Shannon Snoes, prom dir; Jay Poole, progmg mgr.

CKUE-FM— July 1, 1986: 95.1 mhz; 36.4 kw. Ant 495 ft TL: N42 26 14 W82 06 23. Stereo. Hrs open: 24 Box 100, N7M 5K1. Secondary address: 117 Keil Dr. S. N7M 5K1. Phone: (519) 354-2853. Fax: (519) 354-2880.E-mail: info@therock951.com Web Site:www.therock951.com Licensee: Blackburn Group, Inc Population served: 130,000 Format: AOR. News staff: 2. Target aud: 18-49. ◆Carl Veroba, CEO, pres, gen mgr; Doug Kirk, VP; Jenna Herdman, mktg dir; Justin Oliphant, prom dir; Walter Ploegman, progmg dir; Ron Wilken, chief of engrg.

Christian Island

CKUN-FM— 2003: 101.3 mhz; 900 w. Ant 156 ft TL: N44 49 16 W80 10 24. Hrs open: 24 Beausoleil First Nation Band Council no. 30 & 30A, Administration Office, 1 O'Gema St., L0K 1C0. Phone: (705) 247-2456. Phone: (705) 247-2051. Fax: (705) 247-2239.E-mail: rasuth@email.com Web Site:www.chimnissing.ca/xtras/radio.html Licensee: Chimnissing Communications. Format: Div music. News staff: 2. ◆Edna King, gen mgr; Richard Sutherland, progmg dir, engrg mgr & disc jockey.

Cobourg

CFMX-FM— 2008: 103.1 mhz; 86.7 kw. Ant 825 ft TL: N01 44 04 W01 78 09. (Digital radio: 1466.768 mhz; 5.084 kw). Stereo. Hrs open: 24 550 Queen St. E., Suite 205, Toronto, M5A 1VZ. Secondary address: Box 1031, One Queen St. K9A 1M8. Phone: (905) 367-5353. Fax: (905) 367-1742.E-mail: info@classical963fmx.com Web Site:www.classical963fm.com Licensee: MZ Media Inc. (acq 8-31-2006; C$12 million with CFMZ-FM Toronto). Population served: 630,000 Natl. Rep: imsradio,. Robson Broadcast Consultants. Format: Classical. News staff: 3; News: 4 hrs wkly. Target aud: 35 plus; well-educated, upscale, owners/managers/professionals. ◆Truus Rosenthal, VP; John van Driel, gen mgr, mus dir; Roberta Hunt, opns mgr; Al Kingdon, rgnl sls mgr; Marissa Colalillo, prom dir; David Franco, news dir; Wassim Saikali, chief of engrg; Ann Pospischil, traf mgr.

CHUC-FM— August 2006: 107.9 mhz; 6.3 kw. Stereo. Hrs open: 24 P.O. Box 520, K9A 4L3. Secondary address: 7805 Telephone Rd. K9A 4J7. Phone: (905) 372-5401. Fax: (905) 372-6280.E-mail: don.conway @1079thebreeze.com Web Site:www.1079thebreeze.com Licensee: Pineridge Broadcasting Inc. Natl. Rep: Canadian Broadcast Sales,. Wire Svc: Canadian Press Format: Adult Contemp. News staff: 3; News: news prgmg 3.5 hrs per week. ◆Don Conway, pres.

CKSG-FM— July 18, 2002: 93.3 mhz; 4 kw. Stereo. Hrs open: 24 P.O. Box 520, K9A 4L3. Secondary address: 7805 Telephone Rd. K9A 4J7. Phone: (905) 372-5401. Fax: (905) 372-6280.E-mail: info@star933.com Web Site:www.star933.com Licensee: Pineridge Broadcasting Inc. Population served: 210,000 Natl. Rep: Canadian Broadcast Sales,. Format: Hot Adult contemp. News staff: 3; News: one hr wkly. Target aud: 25-54; predominately female. ◆Don Conway, pres & gen mgr.

Cochrane

CFDY-FM— 2008: 104.7 mhz; 5 w. TL: N49 03 35 W81 01 51. Hrs open: Box 855, P0L 1C0. Phone: (705) 272-4623. Fax: (705) 272-2783. Licensee: Cochrane Polar Bear Radio Club. Format: Div. Spec prog: Fr 5 hrs wkly. ◆Douglas W. Young, gen mgr.

CHPB-FM— 2004: 98.1 mhz; 50 w. Hrs open: 24 49 Cedar St. South, Timmins, P4N 2Q5. Phone: (705) 267-6070. Fax: (705) 267-6095.E-mail: moose981@hbgradio.com Licensee: The Haliburton Broadcasting Group Inc. Group owner: Haliburton Broadcasting Group Inc. (acq 11-19-2003; with CFIF-FM Iroquois Falls). Format: Adult contemp. News staff: one; News: 1.5 hrs wkly. Target aud: 18-65. ◆Kimberly Ward, VP; Christopher Grossman, gen mgr; Mike Fry, progmg dir; Kent Matheson, mus dir; Wendy Gray, news dir; Penny Proulx, traf mgr; Donna Todd, sls.

Collingwood

CKCB-FM— Mar 29, 1996: 95.1 mhz; 350 w. Hrs open: 24 1400 Hwy. 26 E., L9Y 4W2. Phone: (705) 446-9510. Fax: (705) 444-6776.E-mail: jeaton@thepeakfm.com Web Site:www.thepeakfm.com Licensee: 591989 B.C. Ltd. Group owner: Corus Entertainment Inc. (acq 3-24-00; grpsl). Format: Adult contemp. News staff: one; News: 11 hrs wkly. Target aud: 25-54. ◆John Eaton, gen mgr; John Nichols, opns mgr, gen sls mgr, progmg dir; Matt McLean, prom mgr; Dale West, news dir.

Cornwall

CFLG-FM— 1973: 104.5 mhz; 15 kw. 300 ft TL: N45 03 30 W74 44 45. Stereo. Hrs open: 24 709 Cotton Mill Street, K6H 5V1. Secondary address: P.O. 969 K6H 5V1. Phone: (613) 932-5180. Fax: (613) 938-0355.E-mail: scott@seawayvalley.com Web Site:www.variety104.com Licensee: Corus Entertainment Inc. Group owner: Corus Entertainment Inc. (acq 11-19-01; grpsl). Population served: 104,300 Natl. Rep: Canadian Broadcast Sales,. Format: Adult contemp. News staff: 4; News: 5 hrs wkly. Target aud: 25-54; predominantly female professionals & housewives. ◆Scott Armstrong, gen mgr; Angie Baker, gen sls mgr, traf mgr; Meghan Kyer, prom dir.

CHOD-FM— May 1, 1994: 92.1 mhz; 19.2 kw. Stereo. Hrs open: 24 1111 Montreal Rd., Suite 202, K6H 1E1. Phone: (613) 936-2463. Fax: (613) 936-2568.E-mail: chodfm921@fastmail.fm Licensee: Radio Communautaire Cornwall-Alexandria Inc. Population served: 45,000 Format: Adult pop, French. News staff: one; News: 10 hrs wkly. Target aud: 25-54. Spec prog: Class 4 hrs, jazz 4 hrs wkly. ◆Norman Couture, pres; Marc Charbonneau, gen mgr.

CJSS-FM— 2/1/2007: 101.9 mhz; 1.42 kw. TL: N45 03 30 W74 44 45. Hrs open: 24 709 Cotton Mill Street, PO Box 969, K6H 5V1. Phone: (613) 932-5180. Fax: (613) 938-0355. Web Site:www.rock1019.com Licensee: Corus Entertainment, Inc. Group owner: Corus Entertainment Inc. (acq 11-19-01; grpsl). Natl. Rep: Canadian Broadcast Sales,. Format: Rock. News staff: 4; News: 2 hrs wkly. Target aud: 35 -54; males. Spec prog: Relg one hr wkly. ◆Scott Armstrong, gen mgr; Angie Baker, gen sls mgr; Rob Seguin, prom mgr, progmg dir.

CJUL(AM)— Nov 24, 2000: 1220 khz; 1 kw-U. Hrs open: 24 709 Cotton Mill St., P.O. Box 969, K6H 5V1. Phone: (613) 932-5180. Fax: (613) 938-0355.E-mail: news@am1220.ca Web Site:www.am1220.ca Licensee: Corus Radio Co. Natl. Rep: Canadian Broadcast Sales,. Wire Svc: BN Wire Format: News/talk, super hits 60's & 70's. News staff: 4; News: 4 hrs wkly. Target aud: 35-54 adults. ◆Scott Armstrong, gen mgr; Angie Baker, gen sls mgr; Meghan Kyer, prom mgr; Lorne Wiebe, progmg dir, news dir.

Dryden

*CJIV-FM— March 2003: 97.3 mhz; 50 w. Hrs open: 24 Box 112, P8N 2Y7. Phone: (807) 937-9731. Fax: (807) 937-6490.E-mail: cjivradio@yahoo.ca Web Site:www.cjiv973.net Licensee: Way of Life Broadcasting. Format: Christian. News: 2 hrs wkly. Target aud: All ages; interested in Christian radio bcsts. ◆Gordon Robinson, gen mgr; Jake Letkeman, progmg mgr.

CKDR-FM— Nov 9, 2005: 92.7 mhz; 36.8 kw. Hrs open: Box 580, P8N 2Z3. Phone: (807) 223-2355. Fax: (807) 223-5090.E-mail: mail@ckdr.net Web Site:www.ckdr.net Licensee: Northwoods Broadcasting Ltd. (acq 5-1-2007; grpsl). Format: Adult contemp. Target aud: 25 plus. ◆Bruce Walchuk, gen mgr; Richard McCarthy, opns dir; Mike Ebbeling, news dir.

Elliot Lake

CKNR-FM— Mar 3, 1997: 94.1 mhz; 90 kw. Stereo. Hrs open: 144 Ontario Ave, P5A-1Y3. Phone: (705) 848-3608. Fax: (705) 848-1378.E-mail: moose941@moosefm.com Web Site:www.moosefm.com Licensee: The Haliburton Broadcasting Group Inc. Group owner: Haliburton Broadcasting Group Inc. (acq 3-12-2004; C$625,000). Format: Light Rock. News staff: one. Target aud: 35-54. ◆Christopher Grossman, pres, gen mgr; Kimberly Ward, VP; Erika MacLellan, opns mgr, sls; Bob Alexander, prom dir; Kyle Duggan, news rptr; Chris Waschuk, sls.

Englehart

CJBB-FM— January 2000: 103.1 mhz; 1.6 kw. Stereo. Hrs open: 24 Box 665, 50 Third St., P0J 1H0. Phone: (705) 544-1121. Fax: (705) 544-2286.E-mail: cjbb@nt.net Licensee: 1353151 Ontario Inc. Population served: 39,000 Natl. Rep: Target Broadcast Sales,. Format: Adult contemp, rock. News staff: one; News: 5 hrs wkly. Target aud: 18-54; male & female. ◆Boyd Woods, CEO; Rick Stow, stn mgr; Pat Ferris, traf mgr.

Erin

CHES-FM— 2006: 101.5 mhz; 50 w. Stereo. Hrs open: 24 Box 881, N0B 1T0. Secondary address: 106 Main St. N0B 1T0. Phone: (519) 833-1155.E-mail: info@erinradio.ca Web Site:www.erinradio.ca Licensee: Erin Community Radio. Population served: 11,000 Format: Var. ◆Jay Mowat, chmn.

Espanola

CJJM-FM—Not on air, target date: unknown: 99.3 mhz; 794 w. TL: N46 14 16 W81 46 34. Hrs open: 12006 Hwy. 17, Unit 8, Sturgeon Falls, P2B 3K8. Phone: (705) 753-6776. Fax: (705) 753-6776.E-mail: joco993@yahoo.ca Web Site:www.joco.ca/Espanola/993home.htm Licensee: JOCO Communications Inc. Format: Classic hits. ◆Joe Cormier, pres.

Fort Erie

CKEY-FM— May 19, 1991: 101.1 mhz; 19.7 kw. TL: N42 53 52 W78 57 27. Stereo. Hrs open: 24 4668 St. Clair Ave., Niagara Falls, L2E 6X7. Phone: (905) 356-6710. Fax: (905) 356-0696.E-mail: robwhite@niagara.com Web Site:www.z101.com Licensee: Niagara Radio Group Inc. (acq 5-1-2009; with CFLZ-FM Niagara Falls). Population served: 1,385,000 Format: Top-40, CHR. Target aud: 18-44; upper income adults. ◆Elizabeth Lewis, gen mgr; Andrew Bilous, gen sls mgr; Dana Hussman, prom dir; Dave Universal, progmg dir; Mike Ridley, chief of engrg.

Fort Frances

CFOB-FM— June 4, 2002: 93.1 mhz; 21 kw. Hrs open: 24 242 Scott St., P9A 1G7. Phone: (807) 275-5341. Fax: (807) 274-2033.E-mail: alad@b93.ca Licensee: Northwoods Broadcasting Ltd. (group owner). (acq 5-1-2007; grpsl). Population served: 30,000 Natl. Rep: TeleRep,. Format: Adult contemp. News staff: 2. Target aud: 25-54; International Falls/N. Central MN. ◆Ala Dulas, gen mgr.

Georgina Island

CFGI-FM— 2004: 102.7 mhz; 250 w. Hrs open: 102.7 Nish Radio, Box N-13, Sutton West, L0E 1R0. Phone: (705) 437-3748. Fax: (705) 437-3748.E-mail: nish_cfgi@hotmail.com Licensee: Georgina Island First Nations Communications. Format: Var. ◆Sally Charles, gen mgr.

Goderich

CHWC-FM— Oct 15, 2007: 104.9 mhz; 5.33 kw. TL: N43 40 42 W81 42 31. Stereo. Hrs open: 24 300 Suncoast Dr., Unit E, N7A 4N7. Phone: (519) 612-1149. Fax: (519) 612-1050.E-mail: thebeach@1049thebeach.ca Web Site:www.1049thebeach.ca Licensee: Bayshore Broadcasting Corp. Format: Classic adult contemp. Target aud: 35-64. ◆Ross Kentner, gen mgr; Rob Brignell, stn mgr; Don Vail, progmg dir.

Guelph

*CFRU-FM— Jan 28, 1980: 93.3 mhz; 250 w. 1,085 ft TL: N43 32 07 W80 13 25. Stereo. Hrs open: 24
BBC World Service Overnight.
Level 2 CFRU-FM 93.3, Univ. of Guelph, N1G 2W1. Phone: (519) 824-4120, Ext. 5352. Fax: (519) 763-9603.E-mail: info@cfru.ca Web Site:www.cfru.ca Licensee: University of Guelph Radio-Radio Gryphon. Population served: 200,000 Format: Multicultural, Div. News staff: one; News: 12 hrs wkly. Target aud: General. Spec prog: It one hr, relg one hr, Sp. ◆Barry Rooke, opns mgr; Vish Khanna, progmg dir; Peter Bradley, mus dir.

CIMJ-FM— 1969: 106.1 mhz; 50 kw. 249 ft Stereo. Hrs open: 24 Prog sep from AM 75 Speedvale Ave. E., N1E 6M3. Fax: (519) 824-7000.E-mail: kkelly@magic106.com Web Site:www.magic106.com Licensee: 591989 B.C., Ltd Population served: 101,000 Format: Adult contemp. News: 6 hrs wkly. Target aud: 18-49. ◆Guus Hazelaar, gen mgr; Kevin Kelly, progmg dir.

CJOY(AM)— June 14, 1948: 1460 khz; 10 kw-U. Stereo. Hrs open: 24 75 Speedvale Ave. E., N1E 6M3. Phone: (519) 824-7000. Fax: (519) 824-4118.E-mail: cjoy@cjoy.com Web Site:www.cjoy.com Licensee: 591989 B.C. Ltd. Group owner: Corus Entertainment Inc. (acq 3-24-00; grpsl). Format: Oldies. News staff: 4; News: 8 hrs wkly. Target aud: 25-54. ◆Guus Hazelaar, gen mgr; Larry Mellott, progmg mgr; Mike Stevens, engrg VP.

Haldimand County

CKJN-FM— May 15, 2006: 92.9 mhz; 3.3 kw. Ant 358 ft TL: N42 56 29 W79 50 45. Hrs open: 282 Argyle St. S., Unit 4, Caledonia, N3W 1K7. Phone: (289) 284-1070. Fax: (289) 284-1072. Web Site:www.moosefm.com Licensee: Bel-Roc Communications Inc. (acq 4-18-2007). Natl. Rep: imsradio,. Format: Lt rock. News staff: two.

Haliburton

CFZN-FM— Mar13, 2006: 93.5 mhz; 6 kw. Hrs open: Box 960, K0M 1S0. Secondary address: 153 Highland St., Upper Level K0M 1S0. Phone: (705) 457-3897. Fax: (705) 457-3827.E-mail: moose935@hbgradio.com Web Site:www.moosehbgradio.com Licensee: The Haliburton Broadcasting Group Inc. Format: Classic rock. ◆Christopher Grossman, pres; Wendy Gray, opns mgr.

CKHA-FM— July 2003: 100.9 mhz; 3.4 kw. Hrs open: Box 1125, K0M 1S0. Phone: (705) 457-9603. Fax: (705) 457-9522.E-mail: canoefmadmin@bellnet.ca Web Site:www.canoefm.com Licensee: Haliburton County Community Radio Association. Format: Var. Target aud: 50 plus. ◆Sue Black, stn mgr.

Hamilton

*CFMU-FM— Jan 13, 1978: 93.3 mhz; 166 w. 300 ft TL: N47 14 41 W79 54 58. Stereo. Hrs open: 24 McMaster Univ. Student Center, Rm. B119, L8S 4S4. Phone: (905) 525-9140, Ext 27208. Fax: (905) 529-3208.E-mail: cfmumsu@msumcmaster.ca Web Site:cfmu.mcmaster.ca Licensee: CFMU Radio Inc. (acq 1978). Population served: 400,000 Format: Div, pub affrs, multicultural. News: 15 hrs wkly. Target aud: General; univ students, people with an adventurous outlook towards life. Spec prog: Class 5 hrs, Sp one hr, blues 5 hrs, Canadian Indian one hr, Fr one hr, It one hr wkly. ◆Sandeep Bhandari, stn mgr; James Tennant, progmg dir; Rachel Palmieri, mus dir.

CHAM(AM)— November 1959: 820 khz; 50 kw-U, DA-2. Stereo. Hrs open: 24 883 Upper WentWorth, Suite 401, L9A 4Y6. Phone: (905) 574-1150. Fax: (905) 575-6429.E-mail: info@820cham.com Web Site:www.820cham.com Licensee: Astral Media Radio G.P. Group owner: Standard Broadcasting Corp. (acq 10-29-2007; grpsl). Wire Svc: BN Wire Format: Talk. News staff: 4; News: 26 hrs wkly. Target aud: 25-54. ◆Ian Greenberg, pres; Tom Cooke, VP & gen mgr.

CHML(AM)— May 27, 1927: 900 khz; 50 kw-U, DA-1. Stereo. Hrs open: 24 875 Main St. W., L8S 4R1. Phone: (905) 521-9900. Fax: (905) 521-2306. Licensee: Corus Premium Television Ltd. Group owner: Corus Entertainment Inc. (acq 7-6-2000; grpsl). Natl. Rep: Canadian Broadcast Sales,. Format: News/talk, sports. Target aud: 35 plus. ◆Suzanne Carpenter, gen mgr; Greg Hinton, progmg dir; Mike Rose, mus dir.

CING-FM— Sept 14, 1964: 95.3 mhz; 100 kw. Ant 1,000 ft Stereo. Hrs open: 24 Prog sep from AM 64 Jefferson Ave., Unit 18, Toronto, M6K 3H4. Secondary address: 875 Main St. W., Suite 900 L8S 4R1. Phone: (416) 534-1191. Phone: (905) 521-9900. Fax: (905) 583-4133. Fax: (905) 540-2453. Web Site:www.country953.com Licensee: Corus Premium Television Ltd. Natl. Rep: Canadian Broadcast Sales,. Format: Country. Target aud: 25-54; female. ◆Ginny Townson Sedik, gen sls mgr; Nadia Cerelli-Fiore, prom dir; Steve Parsons, progmg dir; Rick Walters, mus dir; Ted Townsend, engrg dir.

*CIOI-FM— 1998: 101.5 mhz; 240 w. TL: N43 14 12 W79 53 13. Stereo. Hrs open: 24 Mohawk College, Ste G108, 135 Fennell Ave. W., L8N 3T2. Phone: (905) 575-2175. Fax: (905) 575-2385.E-mail: lespalango@mohawkcollege.ca Web Site:http://c101.mohawkcollege.ca Licensee: The Mohawk College Radio Corp. Population served: 400,000 Format: College alternative. News: 6 hrs wkly. Target aud: 17-24; college students & the div communities they represent. ◆Les Palango, gen mgr & stn mgr; Jamie Smith, progmg dir; Jeff Cudahy, engrg dir.

CIWV-FM— Sept 1, 2000: 94.7 mhz; 40 kw. Ant 446 ft TL: N43 12 21 W79 43 50. Stereo. Hrs open: 24 589 Upper Wellington St., L9A 3P8. Phone: (905) 388-8911. Fax: (905) 388-7947.E-mail: smoothjazz@wave947.fm Web Site:www.wave947.fm Licensee: Durham Radio Inc. (acq 8-31-2007). Population served: 3,638,000 Natl. Rep: Target Broadcast Sales,. Wire Svc: Broadcast News Ltd. Format: Smooth jazz. News staff: 2. Target aud: 35-64. ◆Douglas E. Kirk, chmn, pres, gen mgr; Thomas A. Pippy, CFO; Steve Kassay, opns VP; Simon Constam, gen sls mgr; Cathy Philippo, traf mgr.

CKLH-FM— Oct 7, 1986: 102.9 mhz; 40.3 kw. TL: N43 20 12 W79 52 07. Stereo. Hrs open: Prog sep from AM 883 Upper Wentworth St., Ste 401, L9A 4Y6. Phone: (905) 574-1150. Fax: (905) 575-6429.E-mail: info@k-litefm.com Web Site:www.k-litefm.com Licensee: SR L.P. Format: Adult contemp. Target aud: 25-54; working women, owners, mgrs, professionals. ◆Tom Cooke, gen mgr; Randy Redden, gen sls mgr; Michelle Williams, prom dir.

CKOC(AM)— May 20, 1922: 1150 khz; 50 kw-U, DA-2. TL: N43 03 04 W79 48 42. Stereo. Hrs open: 24 883 Upper Wentworth St., Suite 401, L9A 4Y6. Phone: (905) 574-1150. Fax: (905) 575-6429.E-mail: info@oldies1150.com Web Site:www.oldies1150.com Licensee: Astral Media Radio G.P. Group owner: Standard Broadcasting Corp. (acq 10-29-2007; grpsl). Population served: 572,000 Natl. Rep: Canadian Broadcast Sales,. Wire Svc: Broadcast News Ltd. Format: Oldies. News staff: 4; News: 3 hrs wkly. Target aud: 25-54. ◆Tom Cooke, gen mgr; Randy Redden, gen sls mgr; Wendy Rose, prom dir & prom mgr; Ted Yates, asst music dir.

Hanover

CFBW-FM— Dec 31, 2001: 91.3 mhz; 250 w. Ant 290 ft TL: N44 08 31 W81 01 47. Stereo. Hrs open: 24 267 10th St., N4N 1P1. Phone: (519) 364-0200. Fax: (519) 364-5175.E-mail: bluewaterradio@on.aibn Web Site:www.bluewaterradio.ca Licensee: Bluewater Community Radio Inc. Format: Div. Target aud: 12-75; Ontario audience rural agricultural/urban. Spec prog: Blues 2 hrs, gospel 6 hrs, Scottish 2 hrs wkly. ◆Andrew McBride, stn mgr; Carole Plunkett, adv.

Hawkesbury

CHPR-FM— February 1986: 102.1 mhz; 789 w. 70 ft TL: N45 35 01 N45 35 01. Hrs open: 24 115 Principale E., Suite 101, K6A 1A1. Phone: (613) 632-1000. Fax: (613) 632-1110.E-mail: infocouleurfmm@radionord.vom Web Site:www.radionord.com Licensee: RNC MEDIA Inc. Group owner: Radio Nord Inc. (acq 8-22-89). Format: Easy listening. News staff: one. Target aud: 25 plus. ◆Pierre R. Brosseau, pres & gen mgr; M Yves Trottier, progmg dir.

CKHK-FM— Apr 2, 2008: 107.7 mhz; 875 w. TL: N45 39 24 W74 39 43. Hrs open: 1320 Main St. E., K6A 1C5. Phone: (613) 872-1077. Fax: (613) 632-4022.E-mail: info@1077thejewel.com Web Site:www.jewelradio.com Licensee: Ottawa Media Inc. Format: Pop standards/instrumental easy lstng.

Hearst

CHYK-FM-3— 1996: 92.9 mhz; 140 w. Hrs open: 24 Rebroadcasts CHYK-FM Timmins.
49 Cedar St. S., Timmins, P4N 2G5. Phone: (705) 267-6070. Fax: (705) 267-6095.E-mail: chycfm@nbgradio.com Web Site:www.chycfm.com Licensee: LE5 Communications Inc. (group owner; (acq 10-31-2008; C$425,000 with CHYC-FM Sudbury and CHYK-FM Timmins). Natl. Rep: Canadian Broadcast Sales,. Format: Hot adult contemp, Fr, English. News staff: one; News: one hrs wkly. Target aud: 18-65. ◆Kimberley Grossman, VP; Christopher Grossman, gen mgr; Sylvain Boucher, progmg dir, mus dir; Gilles Lafortune, news dir; Penny Proulx, traf mgr; Sylvie Beaulieu, sls.

*CINN-FM— 1988: 91.1 mhz; 5.5 kw. 298 ft TL: N49 38 50 W83 30 50. Hrs open: 6 AM-9 PM Box 2648, 1004, rue Prince, P0L 1N0. Phone: (705) 372-1011. Fax: (705) 362-7411.E-mail: cinnfm@cinnfm.com Web Site:www.cinnfm.com Licensee: Radio de l'Epinette Noire Inc. Format: Adult contemp. News staff: 2. Target aud: 0-75. ◆Isabelle Lacroix-Breton, pres; Gaitane Morrissette, gen mgr.

Huntsville

CFBK-FM— September 1957: 105.5 mhz; 43.4 kw. Ant 482 ft TL: N45 19 44 W78 57 55. Hrs open: 24 Unit 2, 15 Main St. E., P1H 2C6. Phone: (705) 789-4461. Fax: (705) 789-1269. Licensee: Muskoka-Parry Sound Broadcasting Ltd. (acq 11-7-2007). Population served: 30,000 Natl. Network: CHUM Radio Network, . Wire Svc: BN Wire Format: Adult contemp. News staff: 3. Target aud: 21 plus. ◆Margaret Byers, opns mgr & progmg mgr.

Iroquois Falls

CFIF-FM— Dec 8, 1998: 101.1 mhz; 50 w. Hrs open: 24 49 Cedar St. S., Timmins, P4N 2G5. Phone: (705) 267-6070. Fax: (705) 267-6095.E-mail: moose1011@hbgradio.com Web Site:www.hbgradio.com no Licensee: The Haliburton Broadcasting Group Inc. Group owner: Haliburton Broadcasting Group Inc. (acq 11-19-2003; with CHPB-FM Cochrane). Population served: 2,500 Format: Classic hits. News staff: one; News: 1.5 hrs wkly. Target aud: 25-54. ◆Christopher Grossman, pres, gen mgr; Mike Fry, progmg dir; Kent Matheson, mus dir; Wendy Gray, news dir; Penny Proulx, traf mgr; Shawn McArthur, sls.

Kaministiquia

CFQK-FM— 2002: 104.5 mhz; 50 w. TL: N48 30 27 W89 27 28. Hrs open: 87 Hill St. N., Thunder Bay, P7A 5V6. Phone: (807) 346-2600. Fax: (807) 345-9923.E-mail: thunder@thethunder.ca Web Site:www.thethunder.ca Licensee: Northwest Broadcasting Inc. Format: Country. ◆Bill Malcolm, progmg dir.

Kapuskasing

CKAP-FM— September 2001: 100.9 mhz; 12 kw. Hrs open: Box 960, Haliburton, K0M 1S0. Phone: (705) 335-2379. Fax: (705) 337-6391. Web Site:www.hbgradio.com Licensee: The Haliburton Broadcasting

Group Inc. Group owner: Haliburton Broadcasting Group Inc. Format: CHR. News staff: 2. Target aud: General. ◆Christopher Grossman, pres; Brent Lecour, opns mgr.

CKGN-FM— October 1993: 89.7 mhz; 3 kw. Hrs open: 24 77 chemin Brunelle Nd., P5N 2M1. Phone: (705) 335-5915. Fax: (705) 335-3508.E-mail: ckgnfm@nt.net Web Site:www.ckgn.ca Licensee: Radio communautaire KapNord Inc. Population served: 20,000 Format: Fr, var/div, mixed music. News staff: one. Target aud: General. ◆Claude Chabot, gen mgr.

Kenora

CBQX-FM— Mar 28, 1978: 98.7 mhz; 38 kw. Hrs open: Rebroadcasts CBW(AM) Winnipeg, Man. & CBQT-FM Thunder Bay. 213 Miles St. E., Thunder Bay, P7C 1J5. Phone: (807) 625-5000/(416) 205-3700. Fax: (416) 205-3111. Web Site:www.nwo.cbc.ca Licensee: CBC. Natl. Network: CBC Radio One, . Format: Info. ◆Kelly McInnes, gen mgr & stn mgr.

CJRL-FM— 2004: 89.5 mhz; 40 kw. TL: N49 46 45 W94 27 25. Hrs open: 128 Main St. S., P9N 1S9. Phone: (807) 468-3181. Fax: (807) 468-4188.E-mail: cjrl@cjrl.ca Web Site:www.cjrl.ca Licensee: Northwoods Broadcasting Ltd. (acq 5-1-2007; grpsl). Format: Hot adult contemp. News staff: 2. Target aud: 25-54. ◆Jim MacMullin, VP; Brent Preston, stn mgr.

Kettle Point

CKTI-FM— Apr 26, 2004: 107.7 mhz; 420 w. Hrs open: 24 9111 W. Ipperwash Rd., Unit 6, R.R. 2, Forest, N0N 1J0. Phone: (519) 786-3883. Fax: (519) 786-2834.E-mail: info@eaglecountry.ca Web Site:www.eaglecountry.ca Licensee: Point Eagle Radio Inc. Format: Country, classic rock. ◆Jermey Henry, opns dir.

Killaloe

CHCR-FM— 1998: 102.9 mhz; 33 w. Hrs open: Box 195, K0J 2A0. Secondary address: 14 Lake St., 2nd Fl. K0J 2A0. Phone: (613) 757-0657. Fax: (613) 757-0818.E-mail: stationmanager@chcr.org Web Site:www.chcr.org Licensee: Homegrown Community Radio. Format: Div. Spec prog: Canadian fiddle 8 hrs, Fr 8 hrs, Pol one hr, traditional bluegrass 6 hrs wkly. ◆Daryl Andermann, gen mgr; Peter Benner, stn mgr.

Kincardine

CIYN-FM— March 2006: 95.5 mhz; 5.66 kw. Hrs open: 24 807 Queen St., N2Z 2Y2. Phone: (519) 396-7770. Fax: (519) 396-7771.E-mail: info@thecoastfm.ca Web Site:www.thecoastfm.ca Licensee: 2079966 Ontario Ltd. (acq 5-13-2009; C$1,126,520 for stock). Population served: 20,000 Format: Adult classic hits. News staff: one. ◆Mike Brough, gen mgr; Lynda Cooper, news dir; Steve Howard, sls.

Kingston

CBBK-FM— May 21, 1979: 92.9 mhz; 1.6 kw. 395 ft TL: N44 17 32 W76 28 50. Stereo. Hrs open: 24 Box 500, Station A, Toronto, M5W 1E6. Phone: (416) 205-3700. Fax: (416) 205-6063.E-mail: info@cbbk.com Web Site:www.cbc.ca Licensee: Canadian Broadcasting Corp. Natl. Network: CBC Radio Two, . Format: Public radio. ◆Robert Raeinobitch, CFO & progmg dir.

CFFX-FM— 2007: 104.3 mhz; 4 kw. Ant 813 ft TL: N44 10 02 W76 25 40. Hrs open: 170 Queen St., K7K 1B2. Phone: (613) 544-2340. Fax: (613) 544-5508. Web Site:www.lite1043.ca Licensee: 591989 B.C. Ltd. Format: Easy lstng, light rock. News staff: one; News: 3 hrs wkly. Target aud: 35-64; female. Spec prog: Kingston, Frontenacs Hockey Club. ◆Mike Ferguson, gen mgr; Brad Gibb, progmg dir. Co-owned TV: CKWS-TV affil

CFLY-FM— 1963: 98.3 mhz; 100 kw. 400 ft Stereo. Hrs open: 24 993 Princess St., Suite 10, K7L 1H3. Phone: (613) 544-1380. Fax: (613) 546-9751.E-mail: flyfm@flyfmkingston.com Web Site:www.flyfmkingston.com Licensee: CTV Ltd. (acq 6-22-2007; grpsl). Format: Adult contemp. News staff: 2; News: 5 hrs wkly. Target aud: 25-44. ◆Gary Perrin, gen mgr.

CFMK-FM— Aug 31, 1942: 96.3 mhz; 14 kw. Ant 500 ft Stereo. Hrs open: 24 170 Queen St., K7K 1B2. Phone: (613) 544-2340. Fax: (613) 544-5508.E-mail: lite1043@ca.com Web Site:www.fm96.ca Licensee: 591989 B.C. Ltd. (acq 3-24-2000; grpsl). Format: Classic Rock. News

staff: one; News: new progmg 2 hrs wkly. Target aud: 35-64; Male. ◆Mike Ferguson, gen mgr; Brad Gibb, prom dir. Co-owned TV: CKWS-TV affil.

*CFRC-FM— January 1953: 101.9 mhz; 3 kw. 295 ft TL: N44 17 24 W77 25 55. Stereo. Hrs open: 24 Queens Univ., Lower Carruthers Hall, K7L 3N6. Phone: (613) 533-2121. Fax: (613) 533-6049.E-mail: cfrcops@ams.queensu.ca Web Site:www.cfrc.ca Licensee: Radio Queen's University. Population served: 130,000 Format: Div. News: 15 hrs wkly. Target aud: General. ◆Eric Beers, stn mgr.

CIKR-FM— Feb 19, 2001: 105.7 mhz; 24 kw. Stereo. Hrs open: 24 863 Princess St., Suite 301, K7L 5N4. Phone: (613) 549-1057. Fax: (613) 549-5302. Web Site:www.krock1057.ca Licensee: Rogers Broadcasting Ltd. (acq 5-4-2009; with CKXC-FM Kingston). Population served: 150,000 Format: Rock. News staff: 2; News: 2 hrs wkly. Target aud: 25-54; adults. ◆John P. Wright, gen mgr; Doug Elliot, opns mgr; Andrew Revelle, prom.

CKLC-FM— 2007: 98.9 mhz; 8.7 kw. Ant 433 ft TL: N44 12 36 W76 25 05. Hrs open: 993 Princess St., Suite 10, K7L 1H3. Phone: (613) 544-1380. Fax: (613) 546-9751. Web Site:www.989.fm Licensee: CTV Ltd. Format: Alternative. News staff: 4; News: 3 hrs wkly. ◆Gary Perrin, gen mgr.

*CKVI-FM— 1997: 91.9 mhz; 6.5 w. Hrs open: 235 Frontenac St., K7L 3S7. Phone: (613) 544-7864. Fax: (613) 544-8795.E-mail: ckvi@limestone.on.ca Web Site:www.thecave.ca Licensee: KCVI Educational Radio Station Inc. Format: Div. ◆Max Lienhard, gen mgr, progmg dir & chief of engrg.

CKXC-FM— 2007: 93.5 mhz; 3.23 kw. Ant 371 ft TL: N44 17 22 W76 28 50. Hrs open: 863 Princess St., Suite 301, K7L 5N4. Phone: (613) 549-1057. Fax: (613) 549-5302 .E-mail: info@1027.com Web Site:kix935.com Licensee: Rogers Broadcasting Ltd. (acq 5-4-2009; with CIKR-FM Kingston). Format: Country. Target aud: 35-64. ◆John Wright, gen mgr; James Ligthart, prom dir; Jacquie Beckett, mus dir.

Kirkland Lake

CJKL-FM— 1934: 101.5 mhz; 23 kw. Stereo. Hrs open: 24 Box 430, P2N 3J4. Phone: (705) 567-3366. Fax: (705) 567-6101.E-mail: cjkl@cjklfm.com Web Site:www.cjklfm.com Licensee: Connelly Communications Corp. Natl. Rep: Canadian Broadcast Sales,. Format: Hot Adult contemp. News staff: 2. ◆Ann Connelly, gen sls mgr; Rob Connelly, pres, stn mgr & progmg dir; Elesha Teskey, news dir; Don Elvidge, engrg dir.

Kitchener

CFCA-FM—Licensed to Kitchener. See Waterloo

CHYM-FM— 1949: 96.7 mhz; 25 kw. Ant 658 ft (CP: 100 kw). Stereo. Hrs open: 24 305 King St. W., N2G 4E4. Secondary address: Box 936 N2G 4E4. Phone: (519) 743-2611. Fax: (519) 743-7510.E-mail: chymckgl@kitchenerradio.rogers.com Web Site:www.570news.com Licensee: Rogers Broadcasting, Ltd Population served: 500,000 Format: Lite rock. ◆Mike Collins, gen mgr; Wendy Duff, progmg dir; Neil Beaumont, mus dir; Mike McCabe, engrg mgr.

CKGL(AM)— 1929: 570 khz; 10 kw-U, DA-1. Hrs open: 24 305 King St. W., N2G 4E4. Phone: (519) 743-2611. Fax: (519) 743-7510.E-mail: chymckgl@kitchenerradio.rogers.com Web Site:www.570news.com Licensee: Rogers Broadcasting Ltd. Natl. Network: CBS, . Format: News/talk, sports. Target aud: 35 plus. ◆Mike Collins, gen mgr.

CKKW-FM— January 2009: 99.5 mhz; 2.1 kw. Ant 335 ft TL: N43 24 13 W80 31 54. Hrs open: 255 King St. N., Suite 207, Waterloo, N2J 4V2. Phone: (519) 884-4470. Fax: (519) 884-6482. Web Site:www.kfun995.com Licensee: CTV Ltd. Format: Oldies. ◆Paul Cugliari, gen mgr; John Yost, gen sls mgr; Jay Nijhuis, prom mgr; Dave Schneider, progmg dir.

CKWR-FM—Licensed to Kitchener. See Waterloo

Kitchener/Paris

CJIQ-FM— Jan 8, 2001: 88.3 mhz; 4 kw. Hrs open: 24 Rm 3B15, Conestoga College, 299 Doon Valley Dr., Kitchener, N2G 4M4. Phone: (519) 748-5220 Ext 3223.E-mail: cjiqinfo@cjiq.fm Web Site:www.cjiq.fm Licensee: Conestoga College Communications Corp. Format: Div. ◆Mark Burley, stn mgr; Mike Thurnell, progmg dir.

Kitchener-Waterloo

CIKZ-FM— Feb 6, 2004: 106.7 mhz; 1.7 kw. Ant 657 ft Hrs open: 305 King St. W., Kitchener, N2G 4E4. Phone: (519) 743-2611. Fax: (519) 743-7510.E-mail: plarche@kicxfm.com Web Site:www.kix106online.com Licensee: Rogers Broadcasting Ltd. (acq 12-24-2007; exchange for CICX-FM Orillia). Format: New country. ◆Mike Collins, gen mgr; Jordan Cooledge, gen sls mgr; Derm Carnduff, progmg dir.

CJTW-FM— February 2004: 94.3 mhz; 50 w. Stereo. Hrs open: 24 Faith FM 94.3, Box 1433, Unit 202, Kitchener, N2G 4H6. Secondary address: 659 King St. E., Kitchener N2G 2M4. Phone: (519) 575-9090. Fax: (519) 575-9119.E-mail: info@faithfm.org Web Site:www.faithfm.org Licensee: Sound of Faith Broadcasting. Format: Christian. Target aud: A25-54. ◆Dave MacDonald, gen mgr; Brad Loveday, progmg dir; Joy Cooper, mus dir.

CKBT-FM— January 2004: 91.5 mhz; 3.6 kw. Stereo. Hrs open: 24 235 King St. E., Ste 120, Kitchener, N2G 4N5. Phone: (519) 741-9915. Fax: (519) 568-6390. Web Site:www.915thebeat.com Licensee: Corus Premium Television Ltd. Group owner: CanWest Global Communications Corp. (acq 7-6-2007; C$14.5 million with CJZZ-FM Winnipeg, MB). Format: Rhythmic CHR. Target aud: 18-34. ◆Lars Wunsche, gen mgr; Scott Wilkie, prom mgr; Brian Clemens, chief of engrg; Adelia Dias, sls.

Leamington

CHYR-FM— Aug 23, 1993: 96.7 mhz; 10.65 kw. Hrs open: 24 100 Talbot St. E., N8H 1L3. Phone: (519) 326-6171. Fax: (519) 322-1110.E-mail: 96.7@chyr.com Web Site:www.chyr.com Licensee: Blackburn Radio Inc. Group owner: Blackburn Group Inc. (acq 12-19-94; grpsl). Format: Hot adult contemp. Target aud: 25-54. ◆Terry Regier, gen mgr; Tim O'Neil, gen sls mgr, sls, adv; Tina Delciancio, mktg dir; Corey Robertson, progmg dir; Kevin Black, news dir.

CJSP-FM—Not on air, target date: unknown: 92.7 mhz; 960 w. Ant 474 ft TL: N42 00 35 W82 33 45. Hrs open: 100 Talbot St. E., N8H 1L3. Phone: (519) 326-6171. Fax: (519) 322-1110.E-mail: 96.7@chyr.com Licensee: Blackburn Radio Inc. Format: Country. Target aud: 25-64. ◆Terry Regier, gen mgr.

Lindsay (city of Kawartha Lakes)

CKLY-FM— May 16, 1998: 91.9 mhz; 5.27 kw. Hrs open: 24 249 Kent St. W., Lindsay, K9V 2Z3. Phone: (705) 742-8844. Fax: (705) 324-4149.E-mail: y92@y92.net Web Site:www.919bobfm.com Licensee: CTV Ltd. (group owner; acq 6-22-2007; grpsl). Population served: 70,000 Natl. Rep: Canadian Broadcast Sales,. Format: Adult contemp. News staff: 2; News: 14 hrs wkly. Target aud: 30-65. ◆Steve Fawcett, gen mgr; Dave Illman, progmg dir, disc jockey; Harvey Spry, engrg mgr, sls.

Little Current

CFRM-FM— September 2002: 100.7 mhz; 27.5 kw. Ant 508 ft TL: N45 57 14 W81 56 50. Stereo. Hrs open: 24 10 Campbell St. E., P0P 1K0. Phone: (705) 368-1419. Fax: (705) 368-1080.E-mail: radio@manitoulin.net Web Site:www.theislandfm.com Licensee: Manitoulin Radio Communication Inc. Population served: 3,000 Format: Country. News staff: 2. Target aud: General; baby boomer. ◆Craig Timmermans, CEO & pres.

London

CBBL-FM— Oct 1, 1978: 100.5 mhz; 22.5 kw. TL: N42 57 20 W81 21 20. Stereo. Hrs open: 24
Rebroadcasts CBL-FM Toronto.
Box 500, Station A, Toronto, M5W 1E6. Phone: (416) 205-3700. Fax: (416) 205-6063.E-mail: info@cbbk.com Web Site:www.cbc.ca Licensee: Canadian Broadcasting Corp. Natl. Network: CBC Radio Two, . Format: Public radio. ◆Robert Raeinobitch, CFO & chief of engrg.

CBCL-FM— June 1998: 93.5 mhz; 69.3 kw. Hrs open: 4 am-6 pm 208 Piccadilly St., Unit 4, N6A 1S1. Phone: (519) 667-1990. Fax: (519) 667-1557. Web Site:www.cbc.ca Licensee: Canadian Broadcasting Corp. Natl. Network: CBC Radio One, . Format: Public radio. Spec prog: News 10 hrs wkly. ◆Hubert T. Lacroix, pres.

CFHK-FM—See St. Thomas

CFPL(AM)— September 1922: 980 khz; 10 kw-D, 5 kw-N, DA-2. TL: N42 53 29 W81 12 02. Stereo. Hrs open: 24 380 Wellington St., Rm. 222, N6A 5B5. Phone: (519) 931-6000. Fax: (519) 438-2415. Web

Site:www.am980.net Licensee: Corus Radio Co. Group owner: Corus Entertainment Inc. Population served: 450,000 Format: Sports, adult contemp, news/talk. News staff: 5; News: 10 hrs wkly. Target aud: 35-54. ◆Dave Farough, gen mgr; Dave Hopkins, rgnl sls mgr; Rob Chiaramida, gen sls mgr & prom dir; Kevin Bernard, progmg dir; Andy Bingle, engrg dir.

CFPL-FM— 1948: 95.9 mhz; 179 kw. 885 ft TL: N42 57 15 W81 15 58. Stereo. Hrs open: 24 Prog sep from AM 380 Wellington St., Rm.222, N6A 5B5. Phone: (519) 931-6000. Fax: (519) 438-2415. Web Site:www.fm96.com Licensee: Corus Radio Co. Population served: 788,000 Format: Adult contemp. Target aud: 25-49. ◆Dave Farough, gen mgr; Rob Chiaramida, gen sls mgr; Dave Hopkins, rgnl sls mgr; Kevin Bernard, progmg dir; Andy Bingle, engrg dir.

CHJX-FM— 2003: 105.9 mhz; 10 w. Hrs open: 24 100 Fullarton St., N6A 1K1. Phone: (519) 679-9882. Fax: (519) 679-2459.E-mail: gracefm_administration@skynet.ca Web Site:www.gracefm.ca Licensee: Sound of Faith Broadcasting. Format: Contemp Christian music. ◆Dale Elliott, stn mgr.

*CHRW-FM— Sept. 2, 1980: 94.9 mhz; 3.5 kw. Ant 128 ft TL: N43 00 30 W81 16 36. Hrs open: 24 250 Univ. Community Ctr., Univ. of Western Ontario, Room 250, N6A 3K7. Phone: (519) 661-3601. Fax: (519) 661-3372.E-mail: chrwgm@uwo.ca Web Site:www.chrwradiio.com Licensee: Radio Western Inc. Population served: 350,000 Format: Alternative, multicultural, jazz,blues,metal. News staff: one; News: 5 hrs wkly. ◆Grant Stein, stn mgr, progmg VP; Alicks Girowski, prom dir, mus dir; Michael Brown, adv mgr & progmg dir.

CHST-FM— Sept 1, 2000: 102.3 mhz; 4.77 kw. Stereo. Hrs open: 24 102.3 Bob FM, 1 Communication Rd., N6J 4Z1. Phone: (519) 690-0102. Fax: (519) 686-5942.E-mail: whatever@1023bob.com Web Site:www.1023bob.com Licensee: CTV Ltd. (group owner) (acq 6-22-2007; grpsl). Natl. Network: CHUM Radio Network, . Wire Svc: BN Wire Format: Best of the 80s; 90s & whatever. News staff: one; News: weekday mornings. Target aud: 25-54; adults. ◆Don Mumford, gen mgr; Ann LaRocque, gen sls mgr; David Jones, progmg dir. Co-owned TV: CFPL-TV.

CIQM-FM— June 1, 1986: 97.5 mhz; 50 kw. 300 ft Stereo. Hrs open: 24 743 Wellington Rd. S., N6C 4R5. Phone: (519) 686-2525. Fax: (519) 686-3658. Web Site:www.975sri.ca Licensee: Astral Media Radio G.P. Group owner: Standard Broadcasting Corp. (acq 10-29-2007; grpsl). Wire Svc: BN Wire Format: Adult contemp. Target aud: 25-54; female. ◆Braden Doerr, exec VP, VP, gen mgr; Barry Smith, opns mgr, progmg dir; Dan MacGillivray, gen sls mgr.

*CIXX-FM— Oct 31, 1978: 106.9 mhz; 3 kw. Ant 150 ft Stereo. Hrs open: 24 1460 Oxford St. E., N5V 1W2. Phone: (519) 453-2810. Fax: (519) 452-4153.E-mail: contact106.9thex@qmail.com Web Site:www.1069fm.ca Licensee: Radio Fanshawe Inc. Population served: 350,000 Format: Urban contemp. News staff: 2. Target aud: 12-34; primarily college, univ., high school. Spec prog: Christian 3 hrs, educ 4 hrs hrs wkly. ◆Steve Andruiak, gen mgr; Barry Sutherland, opns mgr, gen sls mgr, prom mgr; Michael Stoparczyk, progmg.

CJBC-FM-4— Sept 3, 1978: 99.3 mhz; 22.5 kw. 91 ft TL: N42 57 20 W81 21 20. Hrs open:
Rebroadcasts CJBC(AM) Toronto.
Box 500, Stn A, Toronto, M5W 1E6. Phone: (416) 205-3311. Fax: (416) 205-7795. Web Site:www.torontocbc.ca Licensee: Canadian Broadcasting Corp. Natl. Network: Premiere Chaine, . Format: Div, Fr. ◆Claire Margetti, gen mgr & progmg dir.

CJBK(AM)— Jan 25, 1967: 1290 khz; 10 kw-U, DA-2. TL: N42 52 08 W81 13 58. Stereo. Hrs open: 24 743 Wellington Rd. S., N6C 4R5. Phone: (519) 686-2525. Fax: (519) 686-3658.E-mail: mailbag@cjbk.com Web Site:www.cjbk.com Licensee: Astral Media Radio G.P. Group owner: Standard Broadcasting Corp. (acq 10-29-2007; grpsl). Population served: 330,000 Format: News/talk. News staff: 4. Target aud: 35-54. ◆Braden Doerr, pres, gen mgr; Barry Smith, opns mgr; Dan MacGillvrey, gen sls mgr.

CJBX-FM— Mar 3, 1980: 92.7 mhz; 50 kw. 400 ft Stereo. Hrs open: 24 Prog sep from AM 743 Wellington Rd. S., N6C 4R5. Phone: (519) 686-2525. Fax: (519) 686-3658.E-mail: mailbag@bx93.com Web Site:www.bx93.com Licensee: Astral Media Radio G.P. Population served: 330,000 Format: Country. ◆Braden Doerr, gen mgr; Barry Smith, opns mgr; Dan MacGillivray, gen sls mgr.

CKSL(AM)— June 1956: 1410 khz; 10 kw-U, DA-2. Stereo. Hrs open: 24 743 Wellington St. S., N6C4R5. Phone: (519) 686-2525. Fax: (519) 686-3658.E-mail: comments@oldies1410.com Web Site:www.am1410.ca Licensee: Astral Media Radio G.P. Group owner: Standard Broadcasting Corp. (acq 10-29-2007; grpsl). Wire Svc: BN Wire Format: Adult standards. News staff: one; News: one hr wkly.

Target aud: 35-54; adults. ◆Braden Doerr, gen mgr; Barry Smith, opns mgr; Dan MacGillivray, gen sls mgr.

Marathon

CFNO-FM— July 17, 1982: 93.1 mhz; 50 kw. 879 ft Stereo. Hrs open: 24 Box 1000, P0T 2E0. Secondary address: 93 Evergreen Dr. P0T 2E0. Phone: (807) 229-1010. Fax: (807) 229-1686.E-mail: sales@cfno.fm Web Site:www.cfno.fm Licensee: North Superior Broadcasting Ltd. (acq 1982). Format: Adult contemp. Spec prog: C&W 12 hrs wkly. ◆Ian Popple, gen mgr; Vince Natomagan, progmg dir.

Midland

CICZ-FM— September 1993: 104.1 mhz; 9.354 kw. Hrs open: Box 609, 355 Cranston Crescent, L4R 4L3. Phone: (705) 526-2268. Fax: (705) 526-3060.E-mail: paul.larche@larchecom.com Web Site:www.thedockfm.com Licensee: Larche Communications Inc. Format: Greatest Rock & Roll of All Time. ◆Paul Larche, pres, gen mgr; Mora Austin, VP, gen sls mgr; Ted Roop, progmg dir; Glen Prinz, chief of engrg.

Mississauga

CINA(AM)— Dec 22, 2008: 1650 khz; 1 kw-D, 680 w-N. TL: N43 37 32 W79 37 52. Hrs open: 1515 Britannia Rd. E., Suite 315, L4W 4K1. Phone: (416) 777-1650. Fax: (905) 795-9030.E-mail: cinaradio@gmail.com Web Site:www.cinaradio.com Licensee: Neeti Prakash. Format: Ethnic. ◆Neeti P. Ray, pres.

Moosonee

*CHMO(AM)— Feb 29, 1976: 1450 khz; 50 w. TL: N51 16 39 W80 38 40. Hrs open: 6 AM-11 PM Box 400, P0L 1Y0. Secondary address: 24 First St. P0L 1Y0. Phone: (705) 336-2466. Fax: (705) 336-2186.E-mail: jbbtcorp@owlink.net Licensee: James Bay Broadcasting Corp. Population served: 5,000 Format: Div, country. News staff: one; News: 10 hrs wkly. Target aud: General. Spec prog: Cree Indian 5 hrs wkly. ◆John Kirk, pres; Ernest Hunter, stn mgr, prom mgr; Jack Williams, mus dir; George Witham, chief of engrg.

Napanee

CKYM-FM— 2007: 88.7 mhz; 5 kw. TL: N44 08 30 W77 04 33. Hrs open: 20 Market Sq., K7R 1J3. Phone: (613) 354-4554. Fax: (613) 354-3661.E-mail: napanee@myfmradio.ca Web Site:www.myfmradio.ca/887/ Licensee: My Broadcasting Corp. Format: Variety. ◆Pam Oliver, gen mgr & gen sls mgr.

New Liskeard

CJTT-FM— June 26, 1998: 104.5 mhz; 10 kw. Hrs open: PO Box 1058, P0J 1P0. Secondary address: 55 Whitewood Ave. P0J 1P0. Phone: (705) 647-7334. Fax: (705) 647-8660.E-mail: cjtt@cjttfm.com Web Site:www.cjttfm.com Licensee: Connelly Communications Corp. (acq 9-79). Natl. Rep: Canadian Broadcast Sales,. Format: Mix. News staff: one. ◆Gail Moore, gen mgr.

Newmarket

*CHOP-FM— Sept 28, 2007: 102.7 mhz; 5 w. TL: N44 02 49 W79 27 08. Hrs open: Pickering College, 16945 Bayview Ave., L3Y 4X2. Phone: (905) 895-1700. Fax: (905) 895-9076. Web Site:www.pickeringcollege.on.ca Licensee: Pickering College. Format: Var. ◆Peter Sturrup, gen mgr.

CKDX-FM— September 1994: 88.5 mhz; 11.3 kw. Hrs open: 5302 Dundas St. W., Etobicoke, M9B 1B2. Phone: (416) 213-1035. Fax: (416) 233-8617.E-mail: gracep@885thejewel.com Web Site:www.885thejewel.com Licensee: CKDX Radio Ltd. Group owner: Evanov Radio Group (acq 12-21-2000). Format: Adult favorites. ◆Bill Evanov, pres; Bruce Campbell, progmg dir, sls; Gary Gamble, progmg mgr; Grace Pascucci, prom.

Niagara Falls

CFLZ-FM— 1996: 105.1 mhz; 4 kw. Hrs open: 24/7 Box 710, L2E 6X7. Secondary address: 4668 St. Clair Ave. L2E 3S8. Phone: (905) 356-6710. Fax: (905) 356-0644.E-mail: robwhite@niagara.com Web Site:www.river.fm Licensee: Niagara Radio Group Inc. (acq 5-1-2009;

with CKEY-FM Fort Erie). Natl. Rep: Target Broadcast Sales,. Format: Modern adult contemp. News staff: 3; News: 5 hrs wkly. Target aud: 25-54. ◆Elizabeth Lewis, gen mgr; Andrew Bilous, gen sls mgr; Mike Ryan, progmg dir.

North Bay

CFXN-FM— 2006: 106.3 mhz; 10 kw. TL: N46 18 10 W79 24 39. Hrs open: 9am-5pm 118 Main St. E., P1B 1A8. Phone: (705) 475-9991. Fax: (705) 475-9058.E-mail: moose1063@hbgradio.com Web Site:www.hbgradio.com Licensee: The Haliburton Broadcasting Group Inc. Format: Adult classic hits. News staff: 2. ◆Sean Connon, sls dir; Amanda Butler, prom mgr; Mike Fry, progmg dir; Mike Monaghan, progmg mgr; Kent Matheson, mus dir; Rocco Frangione, news dir; Dave Belanger, chief of engrg.

CHUR-FM— 1996: 100.5 mhz; 100 kw. Stereo. Hrs open: Box 3000, P1B 8K8. Phone: (705) 474-2000. Fax: (705) 474-7761.E-mail: andy.wilson@northbayradio.rogers.com Web Site:www.ezrocknorthbay.com Licensee: Rogers Broadcasting Ltd. (group owner; acq 4-19-2002; grpsl). Format: Adult contemp, soft rock. Target aud: 25-54. ◆Ted Rogers, CEO & pres; Peter Mckeown, gen mgr, stn mgr.

CKAT(AM)— Mar 3, 1931: 600 khz; 10 kw-D, 5 kw-N, DA-1. Hrs open: 24 Box 3000, P1B 8K8. Phone: (705) 474-2000. Fax: (705) 474-7761.E-mail: mitch.belanger@northbayradio.rogers.com Web Site:www.600ckat.com Licensee: Rogers Broadcasting Ltd. (group owner; acq 4-19-02; grpsl). Population served: 56,000 Format: Country. News staff: 5; News: 6 hrs wkly. Target aud: 25-54. ◆Peter McKeown, gen mgr; James Dahlke, gen sls mgr; Kevin O'Schefski, prom dir; Dean Belanger, progmg dir, asst music dir; Richard Coffin, news dir; Csaba Senyi, engrg dir.

CKFX-FM— Jan 19, 1967: 101.9 mhz; 100 kw. Ant 350 ft Stereo. Hrs open: 24 743 Main St. E., P1B 1C2. Secondary address: Box 3000 P1B 8K8. Phone: (705) 472-2000. Fax: (705) 474-7761.E-mail: dean.belanger@northbayradio.rogers.com Web Site:www.taxradio.ca Licensee: Rogers Broadcasting Ltd. Format: Rock. ◆Kevin Ochefski, prom dir; Mike Belanger, progmg dir.

North York

CILQ-FM—Licensed to North York. See Toronto

Oakville

CJMR(AM)— June 17, 1974: 1320 khz; 20 kw-U. (Digital radio: 1466.768 mhz; 5.084 kw). Hrs open: 24 Broadcasting Ctr., 284 Church St., L6J 7N2. Phone: (905) 845-2821. Fax: (905) 842-1250.E-mail: hmcdonald@whiteoaksgroup.ca Licensee: Trafalgar Broadcasting Ltd. Natl. Rep: Target Broadcast Sales,. Format: Ethnic. ◆Harry H. McDonald, gen mgr, sls VP, sls dir; Michael Caine, pres & progmg dir.

CJYE(AM)— Nov 17, 1956: 1250 khz; 10 kw-D, 5 kw-N, DA-2. Hrs open: 24 Broadcasting Ctr., 284 Church St., L6J 7N2. Phone: (905) 845-2821. Phone: (905) 271-1320. Fax: (905) 842-1250.E-mail: dmillar@joy1250.ca Web Site:www.christianradio.ca/station/cjye Licensee: Trafalgar Broadcasting Ltd. Natl. Rep: Western Regional Broadcast Sales,. Format: Contemp Christian music. ◆Michael Caine, pres; Harry McDonald, gen mgr.

Ohsweken

*CKRZ-FM— 1991: 100.3 mhz; 250 w. Stereo. Hrs open: 6 AM-11 PM Box 189, N0A 1M0. Secondary address: 1721 Chiefswood Rd., Oashweken Phone: (519) 445-4140. Fax: (519) 445-0177.E-mail: ckrzinfo@ckrz.com Web Site:www.ckrz.com Licensee: Southern Onkwehon: We Nishinabec Indigenous Communications Society. Format: Div, country, classic contemp rock, blues. News staff: one; News: 4.5 hrs wkly. Target aud: General. ◆Loreen Harris, sls.

Orangeville

CIDC-FM— May 1, 1987: 103.5 mhz; 30.7 kw. Stereo. Hrs open: 24 5302 Dundas St., W., Etobicoke, M9B 1B2. Phone: (416) 213-1035. Fax: (416) 233-8617.E-mail: info@z1035.com Web Site:www.z1035.com Licensee: Dufferin Communications Inc. Group owner: Evanov Radio Group (acq 9-28-94). Natl. Rep: Canadian Broadcast Sales,. Format: Dance, Top-40. News staff: one. Target aud: 18-44. ◆Bill Evanov, pres; Bruce Campbell, gen mgr; Paul Evanov, progmg dir.

Orillia

CICX-FM— Sept 7, 1943: 105.9 mhz; 10.6 kw. Stereo. Hrs open: 24 7 Progress Dr., Box 550, L3V 6K2. Phone: (705) 326-3511. Fax: (705) 326-1816. Web Site:www.kicx106.com Licensee: Larche Communications Inc. (group owner; (acq 1-28-2008; exchange for CIKZ-FM Kitchener-Waterloo). Format: Country. News staff: 2; News: 2 hrs wkly. ♦Paul Larche, pres; Mora Austin, VP, gen mgr; Linda Young, gen sls mgr; Martin Vanderwoude, news dir.

Oshawa

CKDO(AM)— 1946: 1580 khz; 10 kw-U, DA-2. Stereo. Hrs open: 24 1200 Airport Blvd., Suite 207, L1J 8P5. Phone: (905) 571-0949. Fax: (905) 571-1150.E-mail: info@ckdo.ca Web Site:www.ckdo.ca Licensee: Durham Radio Inc. (group owner; (acq 4-23-2003; C$3.9 million with co-located FM). Format: Classic Hits. News staff: 4; News: 9 hrs wkly. Target aud: 45 plus. Spec prog: Relg one hr wkly. ♦Doug Kirk, gen mgr; Steve Kassay, opns VP, progmg VP; Steve Macaulay, sls VP.

CKGE-FM— Sept 12, 1957: 94.9 mhz; 50 kw. 474 ft TL: N43 57 15 W78 48 24. Stereo. Hrs open: 24 1200 Airport Blvd., Ste 207, L1J 8P5. Phone: (905) 571-0949. Fax: (905) 571-1150.E-mail: therock@therock.fm Web Site:www.therock.fm Licensee: Durham Radio Inc. Format: Classic rock, new rock. News staff: 4; News: 5 hrs wkly. Target aud: 35-54. ♦Doug Kirk, gen mgr.

Ottawa

***CBOF-FM—** Sept 12, 1974: 90.7 mhz; (Digital radio: 1482.464 mhz). Stereo. Hrs open: Box 3220, Station C, K1Y 1E4. Phone: (613) 724-1200. Phone: (613) 562-8521. Fax: (613) 562-8520. Web Site:www.cbc.radio-canada.ca/regions/ottawa Licensee: Societe Radio-Canada. Natl. Network: Radio Canada, . Format: Var/div.

***CBO-FM—** Jan 7, 1991: 91.5 mhz; 20 kw. (Digital radio: 1482.464 mhz). Hrs open: Box 3220, Station C, K1Y 1E4. Secondary address: Ottawa Broadcast Centre, 181 Queen St. K1P 1K9. Phone: (613) 288-6000. Fax: (613) 288-6495. Web Site:www.ottawa.cbc.ca Licensee: CBC. Natl. Network: CBC Radio One, . Format: Var/div. ♦Hubert Lacroix, CEO & pres.

***CBOQ-FM—** Feb 18, 1947: 103.3 mhz; 70 kw. (Digital radio: 1482.464 mhz). Stereo. Hrs open: Box 3220, Station C, K1Y 1E4. Phone: (613) 724-1200. Phone: (613) 562-8422. Fax: (613) 562-8430. Fax: (613) 562-8408. Web Site:www.ottawa.cbc.ca Licensee: CBC. Natl. Network: CBC Radio Two, . Format: Div, class. ♦Robert Rabinovitch, CEO & pres; Miriam Fry, gen mgr; Gilles R. Tessier, opns dir.

***CBOX-FM—** 1990: 102.5 mhz; 70 kw. Ant 1,077 ft (Digital radio: 1482.464 mhz). Stereo. Hrs open: Box 3220, Station C, K1Y 1E4. Phone: (613) 724-1200. Phone: (613) 562-8521. Fax: (613) 562-8520. Web Site:www.radio-canada.ca/regions/ottawa Licensee: Societe Radio-Canada. Natl. Network: Radio Canada, . Format: Div, class.

CFGO(AM)— June 7, 1964: 1200 khz; 50 kw-U, DA-2. (Digital radio: 1487.696 mhz). Stereo. Hrs open: 24 Team 1200, 87 George St., K1N 9H7. Phone: (613) 789-2486. Fax: (613) 738-2881. Web Site:www.team1200.com Licensee: CHUM (Ottawa) Ltd. Group owner: CHUM Ltd. (acq 9-10-99; for 87.5%). Population served: 1,000,000 Format: Sports, talk. News staff: 5. Target aud: 18-34; men. ♦Allan Waters, CEO; Jack Derouin, rgnl sls mgr, gen sls mgr; Don Holtby, sls VP; Brad Boechler, natl sls mgr; Al Macartney, mktg dir; J. R. Ello, prom dir, prom mgr; Dave Mitchell, progmg dir; Steve Winogron, news dir; Harrie Jones, engrg dir, chief of engrg.

CFRA(AM)— May 3, 1947: 580 khz; 50 kw-D, 10 kw-N, DA-2. (Digital radio: 1487.696 mhz). Hrs open: 24 87 George St., K1N 9H7. Phone: (613) 789-2486. Fax: (613) 523-6423. Fax: (613) 738-5024. Web Site:www.cfra.com Licensee: CTV Ltd. (group owner). Natl. Network: ABC, . Format: News/talk. News: 24 hrs wkly. Target aud: 35-54. ♦Jack Derouin, rgnl sls mgr; Al Macartney, mktg dir; Dave Mitchell, progmg mgr; Steve Winogron, news dir; Linda Ulmer, pub affrs dir, traf mgr; Harrie Jones, engrg mgr, chief of engrg; Daniel Proussalidis, news rptr.

CHEZ-FM— Mar 25, 1977: 106.1 mhz; 100 kw. Ant 998 ft (Digital radio: 1484.208 mhz). Stereo. Hrs open: 24 2001 Thurston Dr., K1G 6C9. Phone: (613) 736-2001. Fax: (613) 736-2002. Web Site:www.chez106.com Licensee: Rogers Broadcasting Ltd. (acq 7-2-99; grpsl). Format: Classic rock. News staff: 3; News: 2 hrs wkly. Target aud: 25-54; males. ♦Scott Parsons, chmn, pres, VP & gen mgr.

CHLX-FM—See Gatineau, PQ

CHRI-FM— Mar 6, 1997: 99.1 mhz; 25.3 kw. 551 ft TL: N45 13 01 W75 37 51. Stereo. Hrs open: 24 1010 Thomas Spratt Pl., Suite 3, K1G 5L5. Phone: (613) 247-1440. Phone: (613) 247-1886. Fax: (613) 247-7128.E-mail: chri@chri.ca Web Site:www.chri.ca Licensee: Christian Hit Radio Inc. Population served: 1,300,000 Format: Contemp Christian music. News staff: one; News: 2 hrs wkly. Target aud: 18-44. Spec prog: Children 4 hrs wkly. ♦Ethel Mahoney, pres; Bill Stevens, gen mgr; Brock Tozer, progmg dir.

***CHUO-FM—** May 31, 1991: 89.1 mhz; 18.2 kw. TL: N45 30 11 W75 51 02. Stereo. Hrs open: 24 65 University PVT., Suite 0038, K1N 9A5. Phone: (613) 562-5965. Fax: (613) 562-5969.E-mail: info@chuo.fm Web Site:www.chuo.fm Licensee: Radio Ottawa Inc. Population served: 900,000 Format: English/French. Target aud: General. Spec prog: Ger 2 hrs, jazz 5 hrs, relg 2 hrs, Sp 3 hrs, Chinese 2 hrs, Haitian 2 hrs, African 4 hrs wkly. ♦Marc Gill, gen mgr.

CIHT-FM— February 2003: 89.9 mhz; 27 kw. Hrs open: 6 Antores Dr., Phase 1, Unit 100, K2E 8A9. Phone: (613) 723-8990. Fax: (613) 723-7016.E-mail: sbroderick@newcap.ca Web Site:www.hot899.com Licensee: NewCap Inc. Group owner: NewCap Broadcasting Ltd. Format: CHR, Top-40. Target aud: 25-34; females. ♦Scott Broderick, gen mgr; Josie Geller, stn mgr.

CILV-FM— Dec 26, 2005: 88.5 mhz; 2.3 kw. Hrs open: 6 Antares Dr., Phase 1, Unit 100, K2E 8A9. Phone: (613) 688-8888. Fax: (613) 723-7016.E-mail: sbroderick@newcap.ca Web Site:www.livelifelive.fm Licensee: NewCap Inc. Format: Alternative Rock. ♦Scott Broderick, gen mgr; Dan Youngs, progmg dir; Noah Sabourin, mus dir.

CIMF-FM—See Gatineau, PQ

CISS-FM— Oct 29, 1969: 105.3 mhz; 100 kw. Ant 1,077 ft (Digital radio: 1484.208 mhz). Stereo. Hrs open: Prog sep from AM 2001 Thurston Dr., K1G 6C9. Phone: (613) 736-2001. Fax: (613) 736-2002. Web Site:www.1053kissfm.com Licensee: Rogers Media Format: Adult contemp, top-40. ♦Danny Kingsbury, progmg dir.

CIWW(AM)— June 1, 1949: 1310 khz; 50 kw-U, DA-2. (Digital radio: 1484.208 mhz). Hrs open: 24 2001 Thurston Dr., K1G 6C9. Phone: (613) 736-2001. Fax: (613) 736-2002. Web Site:www.oldies1310.com Licensee: Rogers Media. Format: Oldies. ♦Scott Anderson, gen mgr.

CJLL-FM— 2003: 97.9 mhz; 6.77 kw. Stereo. Hrs open: 24 CHIN Radio Ottawa, 30 Murray St., Suite 100, K1N 5M4. Phone: (613) 244-0979. Fax: (613) 244-3858.E-mail: chinottawa@chinradio.com Web Site:www.chinradioottawa.com Licensee: Radio 1540 Ltd. Population served: 1,150,000 Format: Multicultural, Ethnic. News staff: 2; News: 12. Target aud: Ethnic 12 plus; mutlicultural. ♦Francesco DiCandia, VP, gen mgr, gen sls mgr; Gary Michaels, progmg dir.

CJMJ-FM— Aug 13, 1991: 100.3 mhz; 100 kw. (Digital radio: 1487.696 mhz). Stereo. Hrs open: 24 Prog sep from AM Team 1200, 87 George St., K1N 9H7. Fax: (613) 750-0100. Web Site:www.majic100.fm Licensee: CHUM (Ottawa) Ltd. Population served: 1,000,000 Format: Adult contemp, oldies. Target aud: 25-44; female. ♦Jack Derouin, rgnl sls mgr; Al Macartney, prom mgr; Kent Newson, progmg mgr; Codi Jeffreys, mus dir.

CJRC-FM—(Gatineau, PQ) Apr 16, 2007: 104.7 mhz; 36 kw. Ant 136 ft TL: N45 25 09 W75 42 18. (Digital radio: 1463.280 mhz). Hrs open: 150, rue d'Edmonton, Gatineau, PQ, J8Y 3S6. Phone: (819) 561-8801. Fax: (819) 561-9439. Web Site:www.1047cjrc.ca Licensee: 591991 B.C. Ltd. Population served: 200,000 Format: Greatest hits. ♦Kathleen Michaud, sls dir; Sylvie Charette, gen mgr & progmg dir; Sebastien Lavoie, mus dir.

CJWL-FM— February 2006: 98.5 mhz; 485 w. Hrs open: 127 York St., K1N 5T4. Phone: (613) 241-9850. Fax: (613) 241-9852.E-mail: info@985thejewel.com Web Site:www.985thejewel.com Licensee: Ottawa Media Inc. Format: Adult standards, lite adult contemp. Target aud: 45 plus. ♦Doug Large, gen mgr; Ted Silver, mus dir.

CKAV-FM-9— 2007: 95.7 mhz; 6 kw. Hrs open: 366 Adelaide St. E., Suite 323, Toronto, M5A 3X9. Phone: (416) 703-1287. Fax: (416) 703-4328. Web Site:aboriginalvoices.com Licensee: Aboriginal Voices Radio Inc. Format: Div. ♦Roy Hennessy, opns mgr; Patrice Mousseau, progmg dir.

CKCU-FM— Nov 15, 1975: 93.1 mhz; 12 kw. 853 ft TL: N45 30 11 W75 51 02. Stereo. Hrs open: 24 517 Unicentre, 1125 Colonel By Dr., K1S 5B6. Phone: (613) 520-2898. Fax: (613) 520-4060.E-mail: info@ckcufm.com Web Site:www.ckcufm.com Licensee: Radio Carleton Inc. Population served: 2,000,000 Format: Progsv, div, community, campus. News staff: 2; News: 25 hrs wkly. Target aud: General; alternative rock, spoken word, ethnic audience. Spec prog: Jazz 15 hrs, Black 12 hrs, Fr 2 hrs, Pol one hr, Vietnamese one hr, Canadian Indian 2 hrs, folk 12 hrs, It 1 hr, relg 3 hrs wkly. ♦Matthew Crosier, stn mgr.

***CKDJ-FM—** Oct 3, 1994: 107.9 mhz; 100 w. Hrs open: 1385 Woodroffe Ave., Algonquin College, Rm. N 101, K2G 1V8. Phone: (613) 727-4723, ext. 5523. Fax: (613) 727-7689. Web Site:www.ckdj.net Licensee: CKDJ-FM Algonquin Radio. Population served: 300,000 Format: Hip Hop / Alternative. Target aud: 17-24; collegel students. ♦Don Crockford, gen mgr; Ryan Lindsay, stn mgr.

CKKL-FM— 1959: 93.9 mhz; 95 kw. Ant 1,077 ft (Digital radio: 1487.696 mhz). Stereo. Hrs open: 24 Prog sep from AM 87 George St., K1N 9H7. Fax: (613) 739-4040. Web Site:www.939bobfm.com Licensee: CTV Ltd. Natl. Network: ABC, . Format: Hits of the 80s & 90s. News staff: 2; News: one hr wkly. Target aud: 18-34. ♦Al Macartney, mktg mgr, prom dir, prom mgr, disc jockey; Steve Winogron, asst music dir & news dir; Harrie Jones, engrg mgr, local news ed; Louise Seguin, traf mgr; J.R. Rodenburg, disc jockey.

CKQB-FM— Sept 1, 1994: 106.9 mhz; 84 kw. (Digital radio: 1487.696 mhz). Stereo. Hrs open: 24 1504 Merivale Rd., K2E 6Z5. Phone: (613) 225-1069. Fax: (613) 226-3381.E-mail: bearinfo@thebear.fm Web Site:www.thebear.fm Licensee: Astral Media Radio G.P. (acq 10-29-2007; grpsl). Format: Mainstream rock. News staff: 3; News: one hr wkly. Target aud: 18-34; professionals. ♦Eric Stafford, VP, gen mgr; Gary Perrin, gen sls mgr; Gord Taylor, progmg dir.

Owen Sound

CFOS(AM)— Mar 1, 1940: 560 khz; 7.5 kw-D, 1 kw-N. TL: N44 32 40 W80 54 08. Hrs open: 24 Box 280, N4K 5P5. Phone: (519) 376-2030. Fax: (519) 371-4242.E-mail: bayshore@bayshorebroadcasting.ca Web Site:www.560cfos.ca Licensee: Bayshore Broadcasting Corp. Natl. Rep: Target Broadcast Sales,. Wire Svc: BN Wire Format: News/talk, oldies. News staff: 7; News: 12 hrs wkly. Target aud: 35 plus. ♦Ross Kentner, gen mgr; J.D. Moffat, opns mgr; Manny Paiva, news dir.

CIXK-FM— Jan 3, 1989: 106.5 mhz; 100 kw. 555 ft TL: N44 44 37 W80 54 16. Stereo. Hrs open: 24 Prog sep from AM Box 280, N4K 5P5. Phone: (519) 376-2030. Fax: (519) 371-4242. Web Site:www.mix106.ca Licensee: Bayshore Broadcasting Corp. Natl. Rep: Target Broadcast Sales,. Wire Svc: BN Wire Format: Hot AC. News staff: 7. Target aud: 18-40. ♦Ross Kentner, gen mgr; Rob Brignell, mktg dir; J.D. Moffatt, progmg dir; Manny Paiva, news dir.

CKYC-FM— Sept 4, 2001: 93.7 mhz; 31.6 kw. Hrs open: 24 270 9th St. E., N4K 5P5. Phone: (519) 376-2030. Fax: (519) 371-4242.E-mail: bayshore@radioowensound.com Web Site:www.radioowensound.com Licensee: Bayshore Broadcasting Corp. Natl. Rep: Target Broadcast Sales,. Format: New country. Target aud: 25-54; adult. ♦Deb Shaw, gen mgr; Kevin Brown, gen sls mgr.

Parry Sound

CKLP-FM— July 1986: 103.3 mhz; 50 kw. 400 ft (CP: 46.6 kw.). Stereo. Hrs open: 24 60 James St., Suite 301, P2A 1T5. Phone: (705) 746-2163. Fax: (705) 746-4292.E-mail: moose1033@hbgradio.com Web Site:www.moosefm.com/cklp Licensee: The Haliburton Broadcasting Group Inc. Group owner: Haliburton Broadcasting Group Inc. (acq 11-9-01; C$2,025,000). Population served: 60,000 Natl. Rep: imsradio,. Format: Adult contemp. News staff: 2; News: 12 hrs wkly. Target aud: General. Spec prog: Canadian First Nation 1 hr feature. ♦Sean Connon, gen mgr.

Pembroke

CHVR-FM— May 6, 1996: 96.7 mhz; 100 kw. Stereo. Hrs open: 595 Pembroke St. E., K8A 3L7. Phone: (613) 735-9670. Fax: (613) 735-7748.E-mail: music@star96.ca Web Site:www.star96.ca Licensee: Astral Media Radio G.P. Group owner: Standard Broadcasting Corp. (acq 10-29-2007; grpsl). Population served: 500,000 Format: Country. Target aud: 25-54. ♦Al Kennedy, gen mgr, gen sls mgr; Rick Johnston, progmg dir.

CIMY-FM— September 2005: 104.9 mhz; 1.62 kw. Hrs open: 84 Isabella St., 2nd Fl, K8A 5S5. Phone: (613) 735-6936. Fax: (613) 732-4054.E-mail: info@myfmradio.ca Web Site:www.myfmradio.ca/1049/index.htm Licensee: My Broadcasting Corp. Format: Adult contemp. ♦Andrew Dickson, gen mgr; Jon Pole, progmg dir.

Penetanguishene

*CFRH-FM— Sept 24, 1999: 88.1 mhz; 8.6 kw. TL: N44 46 10 W79 59 25. Hrs open: 24 C.P. 5099, L9M 2G3. Secondary address: 63 rue Main L9M 2G3. Phone: (705) 549-3116. Fax: (705) 549-6463.E-mail: cfrh@lacle.ca Web Site:www.lacle.ca Licensee: La Cle d'la Baie en Huronie - Association culturelle francophone. (acq 2-17-99). Population served: 15,000 Rgnl rep: Richard Lebrun Format: Fr. Target aud: Francophone; francophone minority in mid-southern Ontario. ◆Peter Hominuk, CEO; Michelle Laurin, opns mgr, mktg VP; Steve Lapierre, sls dir, progmg dir; Leslie Tran, mus dir; Suzanne Roy, gen sls mgr & mktg.

Perth

CHLK-FM— July 2007: 88.1 mhz; 700 w. TL: N44 54 34 W76 16 51. Hrs open: 43 Wilson St. W., K7H 2N3. Phone: (613) 264-8811. Fax: (613) 264-1119.E-mail: communityradio@perth.igs.net Web Site:www.lake88.ca Licensee: Perth FM Radio Inc. Format: Adult contemp. ◆Norm Wright, gen mgr.

Peterborough

CFFF-FM— 1969: 92.7 mhz; 700 w. Hrs open: 715 George St., N., K9H 3T2. Phone: (705) 741-4011.E-mail: info@trentradio.ca Web Site:www.trentu.ca/trentradio Licensee: Trent Radio. Population served: 40,000 Format: Div. Target aud: General. ◆John Muir, gen mgr.

CKKK-FM— Nov 24, 2004: 90.5 mhz; 230 w. Hrs open: 24 993 Talwood Dr., Second Floor, K9J 7R8. Phone: (705) 876-0404. Fax: (705) 755-0688.E-mail: info@kaosradio.com Web Site:www.kaosradio.com Licensee: Andy McNabb, on behalf of a corporation to be incorporated (acq 6-26-2009; C$190,000). Population served: 112,000 Format: Non classic religious music. News staff: 5. Target aud: 18-40. ◆Rick Kirschner, gen mgr.

CKPT-FM— Sept 10, 2007: 99.7 mhz; 17 kw. Ant 301 ft TL: N44 17 36 W78 21 20. Stereo. Hrs open: 24 59 George St. N., K9J 6Y8. Phone: (705) 742-8844. Fax: (705) 742-1417.E-mail: energy997@chumradio.com Web Site:www.energy997.ca Licensee: CTV Ltd. Format: Hot adult contemp. News staff: 3; News: 2 hrs wkly. Target aud: 18-54; 60% women. ◆Ivan Secan, pres; Steve Fawcett, gen mgr; Wanda Bergshoeff, gen sls mgr; Mel Hannah, prom dir; Brian Young, progmg dir; George Gall, news dir; Ed Crompton, engrg dir.

CKQM-FM— Sept 16, 1977: 105.1 mhz; 7.5 kw. Ant 910 ft TL: N44 17 36 W78 21 20. Stereo. Hrs open: 24 Box 177, K9J 6Y8. Phone: (705) 742-8844. Fax: (705) 742-1417.E-mail: country105@chumradio.com Web Site:www.country105.fm Licensee: CTV Ltd. (acq 6-22-2007; grpsl). Format: Country. News staff: 3; News: 4 hrs wkly. Target aud: 25-64. ◆Ivan Fecan, pres; Steve Fawcett, gen mgr; Wanda Bergshoeff, gen sls mgr; Brian Young, progmg dir; Ray Hebert, mus dir; Ed Crompton, engrg dir; Mel Hannah, prom.

CKRU(AM)— Mar 21, 1942: 980 khz; 10 kw-D, 7.5 kw-D, DA-2. Hrs open: 24 159 King St., K9J 2R8. Phone: (705) 748-6101. Fax: (705) 742-7708. Web Site:www.980kruz.net Licensee: 591989 B.C. Ltd. Group owner: Corus Entertainment Inc. (acq 3-24-00; grpsl). Format: Oldies. News staff: 2. ◆Chris Pandof, gen mgr; Brian Ellis, progmg dir.

CKWF-FM— July 24, 1968: 101.5 mhz; 15.2 kw. Ant 896 ft Stereo. Hrs open: 24 Prog sep from AM 159 King St., K9J 2R8. Phone: (705) 748-6101. Fax: (705) 742-7708.E-mail: info@thewolf.com Web Site:www.thewolf.ca Licensee: 591989 B.C. Ltd. Format: Rock. News staff: 2. ◆Chris Pandof, gen mgr; Brian Ellis, progmg dir.

Pickle Lake

CJTL-FM— 2009: 96.5 mhz; 50 w. TL: N51 28 14 W90 10 11. Hrs open: Box 4096, Redwood Postal Outlet, Winnipeg, MB, R2W 5K8. Phone: (204) 669-7389. Fax: (204) 661-3982.E-mail: email@nefc.ca Web Site:www.nefc.ca Licensee: Native Evangelical Fellowship of Canada. Format: Christian.

Port Elgin

CFPS-FM— 2005: 97.9 mhz; 3.8 kw. Stereo. Hrs open: 24 382 Goderich St., N0H 2C0. Phone: (519) 832-9800. Fax: (519) 371-4242. Web Site:www.98thebeach.ca Licensee: Bayshore Broadcasting Corp. Natl. Rep: Target Broadcast Sales,. Format: Adult contemp. Target aud: 18-54. ◆Ross Kentner, gen mgr; Rob Brignell, dev dir, mktg dir; Don Vail, progmg dir; John Divinski, news dir.

Port Hope

CKSG-FM—See Cobourg

Quinte West

CJTN-FM— 2004: 107.1 mhz; 3.64 kw. Hrs open: 24 31 Quinte St., K8V 3S7. Phone: (613) 392-1237. Fax: (613) 394-6430.E-mail: billmorton@mix97.com Web Site:www.rock107.ca Licensee: Quinte Broadcasting Co. Ltd. Format: Classic rock. ◆Bill Morton, pres; Bob Rowbotham, gen mgr, gen sls mgr; Lorne Brooker, prom.

Red Lake

CKDR-FM-5— 2008: 97.1 mhz; 420 w. TL: N51 01 12 W93 49 51. Hrs open:
Rebroadcasts CKDR-FM Dryden 99%.
Box 580, Dryden, P8N 2Z3. Secondary address: 122 King St., Dryden P8N 2Z3. Phone: (807) 223-2355. Fax: (807) 223-5090.E-mail: mail@ckdr.net Web Site:www.ckdr.net Licensee: Northwoods Broadcasting Ltd. (acq 5-1-2007; grpsl). Format: Contemp hits/top-40. ◆Bruce Walchuk, gen mgr.

Renfrew

CHMY-FM— August 2004: 96.1 mhz; 1.66 kw. Hrs open: Box 961, K7V 1R6. Secondary address: 321-B Raglan St. S. K7V 4H4. Phone: (613) 432-6936. Fax: (613) 432-1086. Web Site:www.myfmradio.ca Licensee: My Broadcasting Corp. Format: Adult contemp. ◆Andrew Dickson, gen mgr.

CJHR-FM— Dec 11, 2006: 98.7 mhz; 14 kw. Hrs open: Box 945, K7V 4H4. Phone: (613) 432-9873. Fax: (613) 432-3686.E-mail: info@valleyheritageradio.com Web Site:www.valleyheritageradio.ca Licensee: Valley Heritage Radio. Format: Country and easy lstng. ◆Vic Garbutt, gen mgr.

Saint Catharines

CFBU-FM— 1997: 103.7 mhz; 250 w. Stereo. Hrs open: 24 % Brock University, 500 Glenridge Ave., St. Catharines, L2S 3A1. Phone: (905) 346-2644.E-mail: pd@cfbu.ca Web Site:www.cfbu.ca Licensee: Brock University Student Radio. Format: Var. Spec prog: American Indian one hr, jazz 4 hrs, Sp 4 hrs, Por 2 hrs, Mandarin 2 hrs, blues 2 hrs, classical one hr wkly. ◆Deborah Cartmer, progmg dir; Jordy Yack, mus dir.

CHRE-FM— Mar 1, 1967: 105.7 mhz; 50 kw. 438 ft Stereo. Hrs open: 24 12 Yates St., L2R 5R2. Phone: (905) 688-1057. Fax: (905) 684-4800.E-mail: info@1057ezrock.com Web Site:www.1057ezrock.com Licensee: Astral Media Radio G.P. Group owner: Standard Broadcasting Corp. (acq 10-29-2007; grpsl). Format: Soft rock. News staff: 4. Target aud: 25-54. ◆Madelyn Hamilton, gen mgr; Laurie Graham, gen sls mgr; Michelle Williams, prom mgr; Sarah Cummings, progmg dir; Mark Munroe, mus dir; Bonnie Heslop, news dir; Joe Gurney, engr.

CHSC(AM)— Mar 20, 1967: 1220 khz; 10 kw-U, DA-2. Hrs open: 36 Queenston St., L2R 2Y9. Phone: (905) 682-6692. Fax: (905) 682-9434.E-mail: pssa@1220chsc.ca Web Site:www.1220chsc.ca Licensee: Pellpropco Inc. (acq 6-19-02; C$725,000). Natl. Rep: Canadian Broadcast Sales,. Format: Adult contemp, news. Target aud: 25-54; female. ◆Domick Pellgrino, gen mgr.

CHTZ-FM— February 1949: 97.7 mhz; 50 kw. 414 ft Stereo. Hrs open: 12 Yates Street, L2R 5R2. Phone: (905) 688-0977. Fax: (905) 684-4800.E-mail: info@htzfm.com Web Site:www.htzfm.com Licensee: Astral Media Radio G.P. Format: Rock/AOR. ◆Madelyn Hamilton, gen mgr; Laurie Graham, gen sls mgr; Michelle Williams, prom mgr; Paul Morris, mus dir; Joe Gurney, engr.

CKTB(AM)— 1930: 610 khz; 10 kw-D, 5 kw-N, DA-1. Hrs open: 12 Yates Street, L2R 5R2. Phone: (905) 984-6610. Fax: (905) 684-4800.E-mail: newsroom@610cktb.com Web Site:www.610cktb.com Licensee: Astral Media Radio G.P. Group owner: Standard Broadcasting Corp. (acq 10-29-2007; grpsl). Format: News/talk. Target aud: 35-65. ◆Madelyn Hamilton, gen mgr, gen sls mgr; Laurie Graham, gen sls mgr; Michelle Williams, prom mgr; Sarah Cummings, progmg dir; Joe Gurney, chief of engrg, engr.

Sarnia

CBEG-FM— Nov 27, 1977: 90.3 mhz; 50 kw. 375 ft Hrs open: Rebroadcasts CBE(AM) Windsor.
Box 500 Stn A, Toronto, M5W 1E6. Phone: (519) 255-3411. Fax: (519) 255-3443.E-mail: earlyshift@cbc.ca Web Site:www.windsor.cbc.ca Licensee: CBC. Natl. Network: CBC Radio One, . Format: Info. ◆Janice Stein, stn mgr.

CFGX-FM— Sept 14, 1981: 99.9 mhz; 27 kw. TL: N42 52 12 W82 23 50. Stereo. Hrs open: 24 1415 London Rd., N7S 1P6. Phone: (519) 542-5500. Fax: (519) 542-1520.E-mail: info@foxfm.com Web Site:www.foxfm.com Licensee: Blackburn Radio Inc. Group owner: Blackburn Group Inc. (acq 12-19-94; grpsl). Format: Adult contemp. Target aud: 25-54; females in the workplace. Spec prog: New age 7 hrs wkly. ◆Terry Regier, gen mgr; Ron Dann, opns mgr, mktg mgr; George Hayes, progmg dir; Larry Gordon, news dir.

CHKS-FM— 1999: 106.3 mhz; 35 kw. Hrs open: 1415 London Rd., N7S 1P6. Phone: (519) 542-5500. Fax: (519) 542-1520.E-mail: rock@k106fm.com Web Site:www.k106fm.com Licensee: Blackburn Radio Inc. Group owner: Blackburn Group Inc. Format: Rock. ◆Terry Regier, gen mgr; Ron Dann, opns mgr, mktg mgr; George Hayes, progmg dir; Larry Gordon, news dir.

CHOK(AM)— July 26, 1946: 1070 khz; 10 kw-U, DA-2. TL: N42 53 30 W82 19 20. Stereo. Hrs open: 24 1415 London Rd., N7S 1P6. Phone: (519) 542-5500. Fax: (519) 542-1520.E-mail: radio@chok.com Web Site:www.chok.com Licensee: Sarnia Broadcasters (1993) Ltd. Group owner: Blackburn Group Inc. (acq 12-18-98; C$902,600). Population served: 118,000 Natl. Rep: Canadian Broadcast Sales,. Format: Country. News staff: 3; News: 11 hrs wkly. Target aud: 25-54. Spec prog: Toronto Blue Jays baseball, Toronto Maple Leaf hockey, Jr. "A" Sting hockey. ◆Ron Dann, gen mgr; Martin Vrolyk, gen sls mgr; Jeff Teolis, mktg mgr; Larry Gordon, prom dir, news dir; Sue Storr, progmg dir.

CKCI-FM— 2008: 103.3 mhz; 3.4 kw. Ant 218 ft TL: N42 54 31 W82 20 19. Hrs open:
Rebroadcasts CKTI-FM Kettle Point 94%.
9111 W. Ipperwash Rd., Unit 6, R.R. 2, Forest, N0N 1J0. Phone: (519) 542-8001. Fax: (519) 786-2834. Web Site:www.eaglecountry.ca Licensee: Points Eagle Radio Inc.

Sault Ste. Marie

CHAS-FM— May 15, 1964: 100.5 mhz; 13.9 kw. 103 ft TL: N46 35 40 W84 21 00. Stereo. Hrs open: 642 Great Northern Rd., P6B 4Z9. Phone: (705) 759-9200. Fax: (705) 946-3575. Web Site:www.ezrocksoo.com Licensee: Rogers Broadcasting Ltd. (group owner; acq 4-19-2002; grpsl). Format: Adult contemp. News staff: 3. Target aud: 25-54; adults. Spec prog: Class 5 hrs, jazz 2 hrs, lt 2 hrs wkly. ◆Scott Sexsmith, gen mgr.

CJQM-FM— May 13, 1964: 104.3 mhz; 100 kw. Ant 1,000 ft Stereo. Hrs open: 642 Great Northern Rd., P6B 4Z9. Phone: (705) 759-9200. Fax: (705) 946-3575. Web Site:www.qcountry.ca Licensee: Rogers Broadcasting Ltd. (group owner; acq 4-19-2002; grpsl). Format: Country. News: 3 hrs wkly. Target aud: 25-54; adults. Spec prog: lt 4 hrs wkly. ◆Scott Sexsmith, gen mgr.

Savant Lake

CBQL-FM— January 1977: 104.9 mhz; 78 w. 287 ft Hrs open: Rebroadcasts CBQT-FM Thunder Bay.
213 Miles St. E., Thunder Bay, P7C 1J5. Phone: (807) 625-5000. Phone: (416) 205-3700. Fax: (807) 625-5035. Fax: (416) 205-3311. Licensee: CBC. Natl. Network: CBC Radio One, . Format: Info. ◆Tom Grand, stn mgr.

Simcoe

CHCD-FM— 1997: 98.9 mhz; 14.37 kw. Ant 500 Ft Stereo. Hrs open: 24 Box 98, N3Y 4K8. Secondary address: 55 Park Rd. N3Y 4K8. Phone: (519) 426-7700. Fax: (519) 426-8574. Web Site:www.cd989.com Licensee: CHCD Inc. (acq 2-26-01; C$1.05 million). Population served: 50,000 Natl. Rep: Canadian Broadcast Sales,. Format: Adult contemp. News staff: 3. Target aud: Women; 25-54. ◆Jim MacLeod, pres; Blair Daggett, gen mgr; Gerry Hamill, prom mgr; Kate Buick, news dir.

Sioux Lookout

CKDR-FM-2— 2008: 97.1 mhz; 560 w. TL: N50 06 07 W91 55 17. Hrs open: 24
Rebroadcasts CKDR-FM Dryden 99%.
Box 580, Dryden, P8N 2Z3. Phone: (807) 223-2355. Fax: (807) 223-5090.E-mail: mail@ckdr.net Web Site:www.ckdr.net Licensee: Northwoods Broadcasting Ltd. (acq 5-1-2007; grpsl). Format: Contemp hits of the 60s, 70s, 80s & 90s. News staff: one. Target aud: 25-54. ◆Bruce Walchuk, gen mgr; Richard McCarthy, opns dir.

CKWT-FM— 2007: 89.9 mhz; 224 w. TL: N50 05 55 W91 55 08. Hrs open: Box 1180, P8T 1B7. Secondary address: 16 5th Ave. P8T 1B7. Phone: (807) 737-2951. Fax: (807) 737-3224. Web Site:www.wawataynews.ca Licensee: Wawatay Native Communications Society. ◆Adrienne Fox-Keesic, gen mgr.

Sioux Narrows

CBQS-FM— May 1977: 95.7 mhz; 1.3 kw. 134 ft Hrs open: Rebroadcasts CBQT-FM Thunder Bay 100%.
c/o CBC Radio, 213 Miles St. E., Thunder Bay, P7C 1J5. Phone: (807) 625-5000, EXT. 5021. Fax: (807) 625-5035. Web Site:www.cbc.ca/ottawa Licensee: CBC. Format: Public radio. Spec prog: Canadian Indian one hr wkly. ◆Tom Grand, gen mgr & stn mgr.

Smiths Falls

CJET-FM— November 2000: 92.3 mhz; 9.3 kw. Hrs open: Box 630, K7A 2B1. Phone: (613) 283-4630. Fax: (613) 283-7243.E-mail: webmaster@923jackfm.com Web Site:www.923jackfm.com Licensee: Rogers Broadcasting Ltd., on behalf of CHEZ-FM Inc. Format: Hits from 80s to present. ◆Scott Parsons, gen mgr.

CKBY-FM— Jan 29, 1969: 101.1 mhz; 100 kw. Ant 500 ft Stereo. Hrs open: 24 2001 Thurston Dr, Ottawa, K1G 6C9. Phone: (613) 736-2001. Fax: (613) 736-2002. Web Site:www.y101.fm Licensee: Rogers Broadcasting, Ltd. Group owner: Rogers Broadcasting Ltd. (acq 7-2-99; grpsl). Format: Country. News staff: 2; News: 6 hrs wkly. Target aud: 35-54; female. ◆Scott Parsons, chmn, pres & gen mgr.

St. Thomas

CFHK-FM— June 20, 1994: 103.1 mhz; 50 kw. 492 ft TL: N42 50 57 W81 08 52. Stereo. Hrs open: 24 380 Wellington St.,Ste. 222, London, N6A 5B5. Phone: (519) 931-6000. Fax: (519) 679-1967.E-mail: jeff@energy103.ca Web Site:www.energy103.ca Licensee: Corus Radio Co. Group owner: Corus Entertainment Inc. (acq 8-23-99; grpsl). Population served: 600,000 Format: Top 40. Target aud: 18-39. ◆Dave Farough, gen mgr; Bob Fisher, gen sls mgr, natl sls mgr; Andy Bingle, progmg mgr, engr.

Stella

CJAI-FM— Apr 1, 2006: 92.1 mhz; 250 w. TL: N44 10 15 W76 42 11. Hrs open: 5830 Front Rd., K0H 2S0. Phone: (613) 384-8282.E-mail: air@cjai.ca Web Site:www.cjai.ca Licensee: Amherst Island Radio Broadcasting Inc. Format: Var. ◆Rosemary Richmond, stn mgr.

Stratford

CHGK-FM— Sept 2, 2003: 107.7 mhz; 2.805 kw. Hrs open: 376 Romeo St. S., N5A 4T9. Phone: (519) 271-2450. Fax: (519) 271-3102.E-mail: crae@cjcsradio.com Licensee: Raedio Inc. Format: Adult contemp. ◆Steve Rae, pres; Carolyn Rae, gen mgr; Eddie Matthews, progmg dir; Kirk Dickson, news dir; Bill Tofflemire, chief of engrg.

CJCS(AM)— 1924: 1240 khz; 1 kw-U, DA-1. Hrs open: 376 Romeo St. S., N5A 4T9. Phone: (519) 271-2450. Fax: (519) 271-3102.E-mail: cray@cjcsradio.com Web Site:www.cjcsradio.com Licensee: Raedio Inc. Format: Oldies. Target aud: 25-54. ◆Steve Rae, pres, gen mgr & sls dir; Jim Fewer, prom dir; Eddie Matthews, progmg mgr; Kirk Dickson, news dir; Bill Tofflemire, chief of engrg.

Strathroy

CJMI-FM— Feb 6, 2007: 105.7 mhz; 1.75 kw. Hrs open: 125 Metcalfe St., N7G 1M9. Phone: (519) 246-6936. Fax: (519) 245-6670. Web Site:www.myfmradio.ca/1057/index.php Licensee: My Broadcasting Corp. Format: Adult contemp/MOR. ◆Jeff Degraw, gen mgr.

Sturgeon Falls

CFSF-FM— Apr 4, 2003: 99.3 mhz; 1.35 kw. Hrs open: 12006 Hwy. 17, Unit 8, P2B 3K8. Phone: (705) 753-6776. Fax: (705) 753-6776.E-mail: joco@bellnet.ca Web Site:www.joco.ca Licensee: JOCO Communications Inc. Format: Top-40, adult contemp, Fr (20%). News staff: 4. ◆Joseph Cormier, pres.

Sudbury

CBBS-FM— Mar 29, 2001: 90.1 mhz; 50 kw. Hrs open: CBC Radio, 15 MacKenzie St., P3C 4Y1. Phone: (705) 688-3200. Fax: (705) 688-3220. Web Site:www.sudbury.cbc.ca Licensee: Canadian Broadcasting Corp. Natl. Network: CBC Radio Two, . Format: Classical jazz. ◆Kelly McInnes, gen mgr.

CBBX-FM— Mar 29, 2001: 90.9 mhz; 50 kw. Hrs open: c/o CBFX-FM, Box 6000, Montreal, PQ, H3C 3A8. Phone: (514) 597-6000.E-mail: auditoire@radio-canada.ca Web Site:www.cbc.radio-canada.ca Licensee: Canadian Broadcasting Corp. Natl. Network: Espace Musique, . Format: Var. ◆Sylvain LaFrance, VP.

CBCS-FM— June 17, 1978: 99.9 mhz; 50 kw. 250 ft Hrs open: 24 15 Mackenzie St., P3C 4Y1. Phone: (705) 688-3200. Fax: (705) 688-3220. Web Site:www.sudbury.cbc.ca Licensee: Radio-Canada/CBC. Population served: 550,000 Natl. Network: CBC Radio One, . Format: Info, news/talk. News staff: 4; News: 3 hrs wkly. Target aud: 30 plus; College/university educated/professional. ◆Kelly McInnes, progmg mgr.

CBON-FM— June 19, 1978: 98.1 mhz; 50 kw. 800 ft Stereo. Hrs open: 15 Mackenzie St., P3C 4Y1. Phone: (705) 688-3200. Fax: (705) 688-3220. Web Site:www.radio-canada.ca Licensee: Radio-Canada/CBC. Natl. Network: CBC Radio One, . Format: Fr var. ◆Gui Babineau, gen mgr.

CHNO-FM— February 2000: 103.9 mhz; 100 kw. Ant 493 ft TL: N46 30 14 W80 58 03. Stereo. Hrs open: 24 493-B Barrydowne Rd., P3A 3T4. Phone: (705) 560-8323. Fax: (705) 560-7765.E-mail: wwatson@bigdaddy1039.ca Web Site:www.bigdaddy1039.ca Licensee: NewCap Inc. Group owner: NewCap Broadcasting Ltd. (acq 11-9-2001; C$2,843,000). Population served: 160,000 Natl. Rep: CBS Radio,. Format: Classic hits. News staff: 2.5; News: 4 hrs wkly. Target aud: 25-54; middle-income. ◆Rob Steele, CEO, pres; Dave Murray, COO; Wendy Watson, gen mgr.

CHYC-FM— 2000: 98.9 mhz; 1 kw. Hrs open: 493-B Barrydowne Rd., P3A 3T4. Phone: (705) 560-8323. Fax: (705) 560-2492.E-mail: sbncher@nbgradio.com Web Site:www.chycfm.com Licensee: LE5 Communications Inc. Group owner: Haliburton Broadcasting Group Inc. (acq 10-31-2008; C$425,000 with CHYK-FM Timmins). Format: CHR, adult contemp. Target aud: General. ◆Christopher Grossman, gen mgr.

CICS-FM— Aug 18, 2008: 91.7 mhz; 50 kw. TL: N46 30 14 W80 58 03. Hrs open: 60 Elm St., P3C 1R8. Phone: (705) 671-7330. Fax: (705) 671-7320. Web Site:www.kicx917.com Licensee: Larche Communications Inc. Format: New country. Target aud: 35-64. ◆Paul Larche, pres; Mick Weaver, gen mgr; Beth Warren, mktg dir; Ted Roop, progmg dir; Shannon Dowling, news dir.

CIGM-FM— 2009: 93.5 mhz; 100 kw. TL: N46 30 03 W81 01 12. Hrs open: 493-B Barrydowne Rd., P3A 3T4. Phone: (705) 560-8323. Fax: (705) 560-7765. Licensee: Newcap Inc. ◆Wendy Watson, gen mgr.

CJMX-FM— 1980: 105.3 mhz; 100 kw. Ant 780 ft TL: N46 30 02 W81 01 16. Stereo. Hrs open: 24 880 Lasalle Blvd., P3A 1X5. Phone: (705) 566-4480. Fax: (705) 560-7232. Web Site:www.ezrocksudbury.com Licensee: Rogers Broadcasting Ltd. (group owner; (acq 4-19-2002; grpsl). Population served: 165,000 Natl. Rep: Canadian Broadcast Sales,. Format: Adult contemp, soft rock. News staff: 6; News: 1 hr wkly. Target aud: Females 35-44. ◆Mike Allard, pres & progmg dir.

CJRQ-FM— September 1965: 92.7 mhz; 100 kw. 889 ft Stereo. Hrs open: 24 880 LaSalle Blvd., P3A 1X5. Phone: (705) 566-4480. Fax: (705) 560-7232.E-mail: q92@q92rocks.com Web Site:www.q92rocks.com Licensee: Rogers Broadcasting Ltd. Format: Rock. News staff: 5; News: one hr wkly. ◆Terry Callaghan, progmg dir; Kevin Britton, mus dir.

CJTK-FM— 1998: 95.5 mhz; 1.4 kw. Stereo. Hrs open: 24 417 Notre Dame Ave., P3C 5K6. Phone: (705) 674-2585. Fax: (705) 688-1081.E-mail: mail@cjtk.com Web Site:cjtk.com Licensee: Eternacom Inc. Population served: 240,000 Format: Relg, Christian. News staff: one; News: 2 hrs wkly. Target aud: General. ◆Curtis Belcher, CEO, chmn, pres; Louis Depatie, chief of opns.

CKLU-FM— Apr 30, 1997: 96.7 mhz; 1.3 kw. TL: N46 25 29 W81 00 54. Stereo. Hrs open: 7:30 AM-2:30 AM 935 Ramsey Lake Rd., P3E 2C6. Phone: (705) 673-6538. Phone: (705) 675-1151. Fax: (705) 675-4878.E-mail: chef@ckfu.ujyf.ca Licensee: Laurentian Student and Community Radio Corp. Population served: 150,000 Format: News/talk, div, jazz. News: 3 hrs wkly. Target aud: General. Spec prog: It one hr, Pol one hr, Fr 19 hrs, Sp one hr, Ger one hr wkly. ◆Dan Welch, pres; Lindsey Chrysler, VP; Carl Jorgensen, opns mgr.

CKSO-FM— 2002: 101.1 mhz; 50 w. TL: N46 27 59 W80 58 23. Hrs open: 24 Box 536, South Porcupine, P0N 1H0. Phone: (866) 799-3072. Fax: (705) 235-3921.E-mail: cksofm@vianet.ca Web Site:www.cksofm.netfirms.com Licensee: David Jackson, on behalf of a corporation to be incorporated. Format: Christian. ◆David Jackson, gen mgr; Sarah Jackson, mus dir.

Thunder Bay

CBQ-FM— July 5, 1984: 101.7 mhz; 23.5 kw. 900 ft Stereo. Hrs open: 24 213 Miles St. E., P7C 1J5. Phone: (807) 625-5000. Fax: (807) 625-5035. Web Site:www.cbc.ca Licensee: CBC. Natl. Network: CBC Radio One, . Format: Talk/news, public radio. ◆Robert Rabinovitch, pres, stn mgr; Tom Grand, gen mgr.

CBQT-FM— August 1990: 88.3 mhz; 23.5 kw. Hrs open: 19 213 Miles St. E., P7C 1J5. Phone: (807) 625-5000. Fax: (807) 625-5035. Web Site:www.cbc.ca Licensee: CBC. Natl. Network: CBC Radio One, . Format: News, current affairs. Target aud: General; northwestern Ontario residents. Spec prog: Canadian Indian one hr wkly. ◆Robert Rabinovitch, CEO, progmg mgr; Tom Grand, gen mgr.

CILU-FM— Mar 1, 2005: 102.7 mhz; 100 w. TL: N48 25 14 W89 15 37. Stereo. Hrs open: 24 955 Oliver Rd., P7B 5E1. Secondary address: 707 Oliver Rd. P7B 2H8. Phone: (807) 343-8881.E-mail: manager@luradio.ca Web Site:www.luradio.ca Licensee: LU Campus Radio Inc. Population served: 113,000 Format: Var. ◆Jason Wellwood, stn mgr; David Ivany, mus dir.

CJOA-FM— Dec 20, 1998: 95.1 mhz; 50 w. Stereo. Hrs open: 24 63 Carrie St., Rm 42, P7A 4J2. Phone: (807) 344-9525. Fax: (807) 344-9525.E-mail: info@cjoa.org Web Site:www.cjoa.org Licensee: Thunder Bay Christian Radio. Population served: 130,000 Format: Christian music. All ages. ◆Ray Gauthier, pres; Bonnie Gauthier, gen mgr.

CJSD-FM— October 1948: 94.3 mhz; 93 kw. Ant 1,009 ft Stereo. Hrs open: 24 87 N. Hill St., P7A 5V6. Phone: (807) 346-2600. Fax: (807) 345-9923.E-mail: rock@rock94.fm Web Site:rock94.com Licensee: C.J.S.D. Inc. (acq 5-25-92). Population served: 113,000 Natl. Rep: Target Broadcast Sales,. Format: Adult rock. Target aud: 18-44. ◆H.F. Dougall, pres.

CJUK-FM— August 2001: 99.9 mhz; 37 w. Hrs open: 180 Park Ave., Suite 200, P7B6J4. Phone: (807) 344-2000. Fax: (807) 345-9939.E-mail: magicmail@magic999.fm Web Site:www.magic999.fm Licensee: Newcap Inc. (acq 5-10-2005; C$2.3 million). Format: Soft rock, adult contemp. ◆Dennis Landriault, pres & gen mgr.

CKPR-FM— June 4, 2007: 91.5 mhz; 100 kw. TL: N48 31 27 W89 06 53. Hrs open: 24 87 N. Hill St., P7A 5V6. Phone: (807) 346-2600. Fax: (807) 345-9923. Web Site:ckpr.com Licensee: C.J.S.D. Inc. Natl. Rep: Target Broadcast Sales,. Format: Adult contemp. Target aud: 25-54; families & office workers. Spec prog: News/talk 10 hrs wkly. ◆H.F. Dougall, pres.

CKTG-FM— March 1996: 105.3 mhz; 100 kw. Hrs open: 24 180 Park Ave., Suite 200, 7V5 6J4. Phone: (807) 346-2006. Fax: (807) 345-9923.E-mail: hits@hot105.fm Web Site:www.thenewhot105.com Licensee: NewCap Broadcasting Ltd. (group owner) Natl. Rep: Canadian Broadcast Sales,. Format: Classic rock. News staff: 5; News: 4 hrs wkly. Target aud: 25 plus. Spec prog: It, relg, Finnish one hr wkly. ◆Bob Templeton, pres; K. Klein, VP, gen mgr & gen mgr.

Tillsonburg

CJDL-FM— Aug 1, 2007: 107.3 mhz; 4.5 kw. Ant 538 ft TL: N43 00 44 W80 50 10. Hrs open: Box 10, N4G 4H3. Secondary address: 77 Broadway N4G 4H3. Phone: (519) 842-4281. Fax: (519) 842-4284.E-mail: jlamers@easy101.com Licensee: Tillsonburg Broadcasting Co. Ltd. Natl. Rep: Target Broadcast Sales,. Format: Country. News staff: 5; News: 7 hrs wkly. Target aud: 18-50; general. Spec prog: Ger one hr, Hungarian one hr, Belgian one hr, Dutch one hr wkly. ◆John Lamers, pres, gen mgr; Robin Henry, sls VP.

CKOT(AM)— Apr 30, 1955: 1510 khz; 10 kw-D, DA-D. TL: N42 44 08 W80 39 19. Hrs open: Sunrise-sunset Dups FM 100% Box 10, N4G 4H3. Secondary address: 77 Broadway N4G 4H3. Phone: (519) 842-4281. Fax: (519) 842-4284.E-mail: jlamers@easy101.com Licensee: Tillsonburg Broadcasting Co. Ltd. Population served: 200,000

CKOT-FM— Dec 1, 1965: 101.3 mhz; 26 kw. Ant 454 ft TL: N43 00 44 W80 50 10. Stereo. Hrs open: 24 Box 10, N4G 4H3. Secondary address: 77 Broadway N4G 4H3. Phone: (519) 842-4281. Fax: (519) 842-4284.E-mail: jlamers@easy101.com Licensee: Tillsonburg Broadcasting Co. Ltd. Natl. Rep: Target Broadcast Sales,. Format: Easy lstng. Target aud: 30 plus; general. Spec prog: Gospel one hr wkly. ♦John Lamers, pres, gen mgr; Robin Henry, sls VP.

Timmins

***CHIM-FM**— 1996: 102.3 mhz; 84 w. Hrs open: 226 Delnite Rd., P4N 7C2. Phone: (705) 264-2150.E-mail: chimfm@vianet.ca Web Site:www.chimfm.com Licensee: 1158556 Ontario Ltd. Format: Christian music. ♦Roger de Brabant, chmn; Karen Turner, stn mgr.

CHMT-FM— July 12, 2001: 93.1 mhz; 3.6 kw. Hrs open: 24 49 Cedar St. S, P4N 2G5. Phone: (705) 267-6070. Fax: (705) 267-6095.E-mail: moose931@hbgradio.com Web Site:www.hbgradio.com Licensee: The Haliburton Broadcasting Group Inc. Group owner: Haliburton Broadcasting Group Inc. Natl. Network: CBS Radio, . Format: Classic hits. News staff: 2; News: 1.5 hrs wkly. Target aud: 25-54. ♦Christopher Grossman, pres, gen mgr; Kimberly Ward, VP; Penny Proulx, opns mgr; Mike Fry, progmg dir; Kent Matheson, mus dir; Wendy Gray, news dir; Shawn McArthur, sls.

CHYK-FM— 2000: 104.1 mhz; 3.5 kw. Hrs open: 24 49 Cedar St. S, P4N 2Gs. Phone: (705) 267-6070. Fax: (705) 267-6095.E-mail: chykfm@hbgradio.com Licensee: LE5 Communications Inc. (group owner). (acq 10-31-2008; C$425,000 with CHYC-FM Sudbury). Population served: 45,000 Natl. Rep: Canadian Broadcast Sales,. Format: Hot adult contemp, Fr, English. News staff: one; News: one hr wkly. Target aud: 18-65. ♦Christopher Grossman, gen mgr; Kimberly Ward, opns VP; Sean Connon, gen sls mgr; Jim Whealan, natl sls mgr; Sylvain Boucher, progmg dir, mus dir; Gilles Lafortune, news dir; Penny Proulx, traf mgr; Sylvie Bealieu, sls.

CJQQ-FM— Sept 6, 1976: 92.1 mhz; 40 kw. Ant 400 ft Stereo. Hrs open: 24 260 2nd Ave., P4N 8A4. Phone: (705) 264-2351. Fax: (705) 264-2984. Web Site:www.q92timmis.com Licensee: Rogers Broadcasting Ltd. (group owner; acq 4-19-02;. grpsl). Format: AOR. Target aud: 18-44. ♦Art Pultz, opns mgr; Angelo Lia, gen sls mgr.

CKGB-FM— August 2001: 99.3 mhz; 40 kw. Hrs open: 260 2nd Ave., P4N 8A4. Phone: (705) 264-2351. Fax: (705) 264-2984. Web Site:www.ezrocktimmins.com Licensee: Rogers Broadcasting Ltd. (group owner; (acq 4-19-2002; grpsl). Format: Easy rock. News staff: 2; News: 4 hrs wkly. Target aud: 35-55. ♦Al Campagnola, gen mgr; Dave Novak, gen sls mgr.

Toronto

CBLA-FM— Apr 19, 1998: 99.1 mhz; 55.1 kw. (Digital radio: Dec 3, 1998: 1461.536 mhz; 5.084 kw). Hrs open: Box 500, Station A, M5W 1E6. Phone: (416) 205-7400. Fax: (416) 205-6336. Web Site:www.cbc.ca Licensee: CBC. Natl. Network: CBC Radio One, . Format: Talk, public radio. ♦Robert Rabinovitch, CEO, pres; Tom Grand, gen mgr.

CBL-FM— 1946: 94.1 mhz; 55.7 kw. 389 ft (Digital radio: Dec 3, 1998: 1461.536 mhz; 5.084 kw). Hrs open: Box 500, Station A., M5W 1E6. Secondary address: Box 3220, Station C., Ottawa K1Y 1E4. Phone: (416) 205-7400. Fax: (416) 205-6336. Web Site:www.cbc.ca Licensee: CBC. Natl. Network: CBC Radio Two, . Format: Class, public radio. ♦Robert Rabinovitch, CEO, pres; Tom Grand, gen mgr.

CFMJ(AM)— July 1, 1957: 640 khz; 50 kw-U, DA-2. (Digital radio: Dec 3, 1998: 1465.024 mhz; 5.084 kw). Stereo. Hrs open: 24 One Dundas St. W., Suite 1600, 5G123. Phone: (416) 221-6400. Fax: (416) 847-3300. Web Site:www.am640toronto.com Licensee: Corus Premium Corp. Group owner: Corus Entertainment Inc. (acq 7-6-00; grpsl). Natl. Rep: Canadian Broadcast Sales,. Format: News/talk. News staff: 12. Target aud: 35-64; upscale, mature, male. Spec prog: Sports/NHL hockey. ♦John Cassidy, CEO; John Hayes, pres; Chris Sisam, gen mgr; Darren Wasylyk, prom dir; Gord Harris, progmg dir; Stephanie Smyth, news dir.

CFMZ-FM— 1988: 96.3 mhz; 24.5 kw. Ant 930 ft TL: N56 43 38 W55 79 22. Stereo. Hrs open: 24 550 Queen St. E., Suite 205, M5A 1V2. Phone: (416) 367-5353. Fax: (416) 367-1742.E-mail: info@classical1963.com Web Site:www.classical963fm.com Licensee: MZ Media Inc. (acq 8-31-2006; C$12 million with CFMX-FM Cobourg). Population served: 4,800,000 Natl. Network: BN Audio, . Natl. Rep: imsradio,. Wire Svc: Standard Broadcast News Format: Classical. News staff: 3; News: 4 hrs wkly. Target aud: 35 plus; well educated, upscale, owners/managers/professionals. ♦George Grant, CEO; John Van Driel, gen mgr & progmg VP.

CFNY-FM— Aug 8, 1960: 102.1 mhz; 35 kw. Ant 1,378 ft TL: N43 38 33 W79 23 15. (Digital radio: Dec 3, 1998: 1465.024 mhz; 5.084 kw). Stereo. Hrs open: 24 One Dundas St. W., Suite 1600, M5G 1Z3. Phone: (416) 408-3343. Fax: (416) 847-3300. Web Site:www.edge.ca Licensee: Corus Radio Co. Group owner: Corus Entertainment Inc. (acq 1995; C$16.75 million). Population served: 5,000,000 Natl. Rep: Canadian Broadcast Sales,. Format: Modern rock, progsv. News staff: 2; News: 3 hrs wkly. Target aud: 18-34; self motivated, mus loving, active, young at heart people. ♦John Cassaday, CEO, pres; Heather Shaw, chmn; Tom Peddie, CFO; Chris Sisam, gen mgr; Alan Cross, progmg dir.

CFRB(AM)— Feb 19, 1927: 1010 khz; 50 kw-U, DA-2. (Digital radio: Dec 3, 1998: 1458.048 mhz; 5.084 kw). Stereo. Hrs open: 24 2nd Fl., 2 St. Clair Ave. W., M4V 1L6. Phone: (416) 924-5711. Fax: (416) 872-8683.E-mail: comments@cfrb.com Web Site:www.cfrb.com Licensee: Astral Media Radio G.P. Group owner: Standard Broadcasting Corp. (acq 10-29-2007; grpsl). Format: News/talk. News staff: 10; News: 40 hrs wkly. Target aud: 25-64; general. Spec prog: Class 7 hrs, farm 2 hrs wkly. ♦Pat Holiday, gen mgr; Bill Herz, sls dir; G. Scott Johns, rgnl sls mgr; Nancy Ceneviva, mktg dir, prom dir, pub affrs dir; Steve Kowch, opns mgr & progmg dir; Dave Trafford, news dir; Dave Simon, engrg VP; Gail Prentice, rsch dir, traf mgr; Scott Ferguson, sports cmtr.

CFTR(AM)— Aug 8, 1962: 680 khz; 50 kw-U. TL: N43 12 50 W79 36 29. (Digital radio: Dec 3, 1998: 1456.304 mhz; 5.084 kw). Stereo. Hrs open: 24 777 Jarvis St., M4Y 3B7. Phone: (416) 935-8468. Fax: (416) 935-8480. Web Site:www.680news.com Licensee: Rogers Broadcasting Ltd. Population served: 6,000,000 Natl. Network: ABC, . Natl. Rep: Canadian Broadcast Sales,. Wire Svc: BN Wire Wire Svc: Bloomberg News Format: News. News staff: 50; News: 168 hrs wkly. Target aud: 25-54; owners, managers, professionals. ♦John Hinnen, gen mgr.

CFXJ-FM— Feb 9, 2001: 93.5 mhz; 1.058 kw. Ant 980 ft (Digital radio: 1454.56 mhz; 5.084 kw). Hrs open: 9 AM-5:30 PM 211 Yonge St., Suite 400, M5B 1M4. Phone: (416) 214-5000. Fax: (416) 214-0660.E-mail: info@flow935.com Web Site:www.flow935.com Licensee: Milestone Radio Inc. Wire Svc: BN Wire Format: Urban. News staff: one. Target aud: 18-35. ♦Denham Jolly, CEO, pres; Nicole Jolly, opns VP; Vanessa Santos, prom mgr; Wayne Williams, progmg dir; Scott Palmateer, chief of engrg.

CFZM(AM)— Jan 8, 2001: 740 khz; 50 kw-U. TL: N43 34 30 W79 49 02. (Digital radio: 1454.56 mhz; 5.084 kw). Hrs open: 24 Box 740, Station A, M5W 4K6. Secondary address: Broadcasting Ctr., 284 Church St., Oakville L6J 7N2. Phone: (905) 845-2821. Phone: (416) 544-0740. Fax: (905) 842-1250. Web Site:www.am740.ca Licensee: MZ Media Inc. (acq 3-31-2008; C$7,320,433). Population served: 4,000,000 Format: Adult standard. News: 9 hrs wkly. Target aud: 50 plus. Spec prog: Scottish 2hrs, British 1hr, Irish 1hr. ♦George Grant, CEO; Michael Caine, gen mgr; Jacqui Gerrard, opns mgr.

CHFI-FM— Feb 8, 1957: 98.1 mhz; 44 kw. 1,815 ft (Digital radio: Dec 3, 1998: 1456.304 mhz; 5.084 kw). Stereo. Hrs open: 24 777 Jarvis St., M4Y 3B7. Phone: (416) 935-8298. Fax: (416) 935-8480.E-mail: 680news@earthci.rodgers.com Licensee: Rogers Broadcasting Ltd. Format: Soft adult contemp. Target aud: 25-54. ♦Julie Adam, VP, gen mgr, progmg VP, progmg dir; Victor Dann, gen sls mgr; Vicky Belfiore, prom dir, adv dir; Drew Keith, mus dir; Phyllis Antoniandis, traf mgr; John Hinnen, local news ed; Jim Morris, news rptr; Bill Cole, sports cmtr.

CHHA(AM)— Nov 21, 2004: 1610 khz; 10 kw-D, 1 kw-N. TL: N43 42 40 W79 27 11. Hrs open: 30 22 Wenderly Dr., M6B 2N9. Phone: (416) 782-2953, ext 225. Fax: (416) 782-1219.E-mail: sanlorenzo@rogers.com Web Site:www.torontohispano.com Licensee: San Lorenzo Latin American Community Centre. Format: Sp, ethnic. News: 10 hrs wkly. ♦Herman Astudillo, gen mgr.

CHIN(AM)— 1966: 1540 khz; 50 kw-D, 30 kw-N, DA-2. TL: N43 35 32 W79 39 22. Stereo. Hrs open: 24 622 College St., M6G 1B6. Phone: (416) 531-9991. Fax: (416) 531-5274.E-mail: sales@chinradio.com Web Site:www.chinradio.com ANIK e-z, KUBAND (digital) Licensee: Radio 1540 Ltd. Format: Ethnic, multilingual (21 languages). News staff: 4; News: 9 hrs wkly. Target aud: 30 plus; immigrants in the Toronto census metropolitan area. ♦Johnny Lombardi, CEO; Lenny Lombardi, pres, exec VP; Theresa Lombardi, sr VP; Joe Mulvihill, gen mgr; Donina Lombardi, pub affrs dir; Michael Evans, engrg dir.

CHIN-FM— 1967: 100.7 mhz; 8.5 kw. 1,700 ft TL: N48 38 33 W79 23 15. (Digital radio: Dec 3, 1998: 1465.024 mhz; 5.084 kw). Stereo. Hrs open: 24 Dups AM 100% 622 College St., M6G 1B6. Phone: (416) 531-9991. Fax: (416) 531-5274. Licensee: Radio 1540 Ltd. News: 10 hrs wkly. Target aud: 30 plus; multi-ethnic, first & second generation immigrants.

CHKT(AM)— Feb 21, 1951: 1430 khz; 50 kw-U, DA-2. Hrs open: 24 135 East Beaver Creek Rd., Units 7 & 8, Richmond Hill, L4B 1E2. Phone: (905) 763-3360. Fax: (905) 889-9828. Web Site:www.fairchildradio.com Licensee: Fairchild Radio Group Ltd. (acq 10-3-96; C$1.8 million). Format: Multicultural, Chinese. Chinese and other ethnic groups. ♦Cyril Lai, gen mgr; Maureen Tang, sls dir, mktg dir; River Lee, progmg dir; Louisa Lam, news dir, pub affrs dir.

CHOQ-FM— 2005: 105.1 mhz; 1 kw. Hrs open: 24 425 W. Adelaide St., # 302, M5V 3C1. Phone: (416) 599-2666. Fax: (416) 599-7639.E-mail: info@choqfm.ca Web Site:www.choqfm.com Licensee: La Cooperative radiophonique de Toronto inc. Format: Fr variety. ♦Tonia Mori, gen mgr.

CHRY-FM— 1987: 105.5 mhz; 158 w. Hrs open: 24 413 Student Ctr., York University, 4700 Keele St., M3J 1P3. Phone: (416) 736-5293. Fax: (416) 650-8052.E-mail: chry@yorku.ca Web Site:www.yorku.ca/chry Licensee: CHRY Community Radio Inc. Format: Black, alternative, div. News staff: 4; News: 10 hrs wkly. Target aud: General; campus community. Spec prog: Afghan, African, Black, Chinese, environment, Fr, gospel, jazz, Sp, Hebrew. ♦Susy Glass, gen mgr & stn mgr; Anderson Rouse, opns mgr; Neil Armstrong, progmg dir.

CHTO(AM)— 1690 khz; 1 kw-U. TL: N43 43 26 W79 16 41. Hrs open: 437 Danforth Ave., Suite 204, M4K 1P1. Phone: (416) 465-1112. Fax: (416) 465-6592.E-mail: info@am1960.ca Web Site:www.am1690.ca Licensee: Canadian Hellenic Toronto Radio Inc. Format: Greek, ethnic.

CHUM(AM)— October 1944: 1050 khz; 50 kw-U, DA-2. (Digital radio: Dec 3, 1998: 1456.304 mhz; 5.084 kw). Stereo. Hrs open: 1331 Yonge St., M4T 1Y1. Phone: (416) 925-6666. Fax: (416) 926-4026.E-mail: info@1050chum.com Web Site:www.cp24.com Licensee: CTV Ltd. (group owner) (acq 6-22-2007; grpsl). Format: News. News staff: 6. ♦Paul Ski, pres; Bob McLaughlin, gen mgr; Larry Keats, chief of engrg.

CHUM-FM— Sept 15, 1963: 104.5 mhz; 40 kw. 1,380 ft (Digital radio: Dec 3, 1998: 1456.304 mhz; 5.084 kw). Stereo. Hrs open: 1331 Yonge St., M4T 1Y1. Phone: (416) 925-6666. Fax: (416) 926-4026. Web Site:www.chumfm.com Licensee: CTV Ltd. Format: Adult contemp. News: 6 hrs wkly. ♦Loretta Tate, prom dir; David Corey, progmg dir.

CIAO(AM)—See Brampton

CILQ-FM—(North York, May 22, 1977: 107.1 mhz; 40 kw. 1,380 ft (Digital radio: Dec 3, 1998: 1465.024 mhz; 5.084 kw). Stereo. Hrs open: 24 1 Dundas St., Suite 1600, M5G 1Z3. Phone: (416) 221-0107. Fax: (416) 847-3300. Web Site:www.q107.com Licensee: Corus Premium Television Ltd. Group owner: Corus Entertainment Inc. (acq 7-2000; grpsl). Format: Classic rock. News staff: 5; News: 15 hrs wkly. Target aud: 18-44. ♦John Cassaday, CEO; John P Hayes Jr., pres; Chris Sisam, gen mgr; Blair Bartrem, progmg dir.

CIRR-FM— Apr 16, 2007: 103.9 mhz; 50 w. Ant 433 ft TL: N43 42 20 W79 23 44. Hrs open: 65 Wellesley St. E., Suite 201, M4Y 1G7. Phone: (416) 922-1039. Fax: (416) 922-3692.E-mail: info@proudfm.com Web Site:www.proudfm.com Licensee: Dufferin Communications Inc. Format: Top-40, talk. ♦Carmela Laurignano, pres; Rob Basile, progmg dir; Sean Moreman, news dir.

CIRV-FM— 1986: 88.9 mhz; 1.88 kw. (Digital radio: 1466.768 mhz; 5.084 kw). Hrs open: 24 1087 Dundas St. W., M6J 1W9. Phone: (416) 537-1088. Phone: (416) 588-2472. Fax: (416) 537-2463.E-mail: info@cirvfm.com Web Site:www.cirvfm.com Licensee: CIRC Radio Inc. Format: Multicultural/ethnic. News staff: 5. ♦Alberto Elmir, VP; Frank Alvarez, CEO, pres & gen mgr.

***CIUT-FM**— 1986: 89.5 mhz; 15 kw. Stereo. Hrs open: 24 91 St. George St., M5S 2E8. Phone: (416) 978-0909. Fax: (416) 946-7004.E-mail: b.burchell@ciut.fm Web Site:www.ciut.fm Licensee: University of Toronto Community Radio Inc. Population served: 8,800,000 Wire Svc: Canadian Press Format: Var/div. News: 3 hrs wkly. Target aud: General. Spec prog: Fr 2 hrs, Sp 4 , Punjabi 5 hrs hrs wkly. ♦Brian Burchell, stn mgr; Ken Stowar, progmg dir.

CJBC(AM)— 1947: 860 khz; 50 kw-U. (Digital radio: Dec 3, 1998: 1461.536 mhz; 5.084 kw). Hrs open: Box 500, Station A, M5W 1E6. Phone: (416) 205-3311. Fax: (416) 205-5622. Web Site:www.cbc.ca Licensee: CBC. Format: Educ, cultural, var. ♦Alain Dorion, gen mgr.

CJBC-FM— 1993: 90.3 mhz; 5.73 kw. 1,414 ft TL: N43 38 33 W79 23 15. (Digital radio: Dec 3, 1998: 1461.536 mhz; 5.084 kw). Stereo. Hrs open: Box 500, Station A, M5W 1E6. Phone: (416) 205-2522. Fax: (416) 205-7660. Licensee: CBC Natl. Network: Radio Canada, . Format: Class. ◆Manon Cote, gen mgr.

CJCL(AM)— 1944: 590 khz; 50 kw-U, DA-1. (Digital radio: Dec 3, 1998: 1458.048 mhz; 5.084 kw). Stereo. Hrs open: 24 777 Jarvis St., M4Y 3B7. Phone: (416) 935-0590. Fax: (416) 413-4116.E-mail: contact@fan590.com Web Site:www.fan590.com Licensee: Rogers Broadcasting Ltd. (group owner; acq 4-19-02; grpsl). Population served: 4,000,000 Format: Sports, talk. Target aud: 25-54; men. ◆Nelson Millmen, stn mgr.

CJEZ-FM— May 24, 1987: 97.3 mhz; 28.9 kw. Ant 1,500 ft (Digital radio: Dec 3, 1998: 1458.048 mhz; 5.084 kw). Hrs open: 2 St. Clair Ave. W., 2nd Fl., M4V 1L6. Phone: (416) 482-0973. Fax: (416) 486-5696.E-mail: info@ezrock.com Web Site:www.ezrock.com Astral Media Radio G.P. Group owner: Standard Broadcasting Corp. (acq 10-29-2007; grpsl). Population served: 3,000,000 Format: Adult contemp. Target aud: 35-54. ◆Pat Holiday, gen mgr.

CJMR(AM)—See Oakville

*CJRT-FM— 1949: 91.1 mhz; 100 kw. 1,300 ft (Digital radio: Dec 3, 1998: 1458.048 mhz; 5.084 kw). Stereo. Hrs open: 24 4 Pardee Ave., Unit 100, M6K 3H5. Phone: (416) 595-0404. Fax: (416) 595-9413.E-mail: info@jazz.fm Web Site:www.jazz.fm Licensee: CJRT-FM Inc. (acq 1974). Population served: 6,000,000 Wire Svc: Broadcast News Ltd. Format: Jazz. Target aud: 35 plus. ◆Ross Porter, CEO; B. Webber, chmn; Brad Barker, opns dir; Vince De Lilla, sls dir; Stacy MacKenzie, traf mgr; Donnie Tong, engr.

CJSA-FM— 2004: 101.3 mhz; 373 w. Hrs open: Canadian Multicultural Radio, 306 Rexdale Rd., Unit 7, M9W 1R6. Phone: (416) 292-4059. Fax: (416) 292-4574.E-mail: info@cmr24.com Web Site:www.cmr24.com Licensee: 3885275 Canada Inc. Format: Ethnic. ◆Sivakumaran Sivapaphafundaram, gen mgr.

CKAV-FM— Dec 13, 2002: 106.5 mhz; 1.1 kw. Hrs open: 366 Adelaide St., Suite 323, M5A 3X9. Phone: (416) 703-1287. Fax: (416) 703-4328.E-mail: info@aboriginalvoices.com Web Site:aboriginalvoices.com Licensee: Aboriginal Voices Radio Inc. Format: Canadian aboriginal and world aboriginal. ◆Mark MacLeod, opns mgr; Patrice Mousseau, progmg dir.

CKFM-FM— July 1, 1961: 99.9 mhz; 40 kw. Ant 1,550 ft TL: N43 38 33 W79 23 15. (Digital radio: Dec 3, 1998: 1458.048 mhz; 5.084 kw). Stereo. Hrs open: 2 St. Clair Ave. W., 2nd Fl., M4V 1L6. Phone: (416) 922-9999. Fax: (416) 872-8683.E-mail: info@virginradio999.com Web Site:www.virginradio999.com Licensee: Astral Media Radio G.P. Format: Hit adult contemp. Target aud: 25-49. ◆Pat Holiday, gen mgr; Lorie Russell, gen sls mgr; David Lindores, mktg dir, prom dir; Martin Tremblay, prom dir, progmg dir; Wayne Webster, mus dir.

CKHC-FM— 2007: 96.9 mhz; 60 w. TL: N43 43 43 W79 36 30. Stereo. Hrs open: 24 Radio Humber 96.9fm, 205 Humber College Blvd., M5W 5L7. Phone: (416) 675-6622, ext 4913. Fax: (416) 675-9730.E-mail: radiohumber@humber.ca Web Site:http://radio.humber.ca Licensee: Humber Communications Community Corp. Natl. Rep: Target Broadcast Sales,. Wire Svc: Canadian Press Format: All Canadian. College students.

CKIS-FM— Jan 26, 1993: 92.5 mhz; 9.1 kw. (Digital radio: Dec 3, 1998: 1456.304 mhz; 5.084 kw). Hrs open: 24 777 Jarvis St., M4Y 3B7. Phone: (416) 935-8392. Fax: (416) 935-8410. Web Site:www.kiss925.ca Licensee: Rogers (Toronto) Ltd. Group owner: Rogers Broadcasting Ltd. (acq 9-10-99; grpsl). Population served: 4,000,000 Format: All hits. News staff: 4; News: 6 hrs wkly. Target aud: 25-54. ◆Gary L. Miles, CEO; Rael Merson, pres; Laura Nixon, CFO; Pat Cardinal, gen mgr.

*CKLN-FM— July 1983: 88.1 mhz; 250 w. Hrs open: c/o CKLN Radio Inc., 380 Victoria St., M5B 1W7. Phone: (416) 595-1477. Fax: (416) 595-0226.E-mail: stationmanager@ckln.fm Web Site:www.ckln.fm Licensee: CKLN Radio Inc. Format: Alternative. ◆Tim May, progmg dir.

Vermillion Bay

CKQV-FM— June 2004: 103.3 mhz; 1.6 kw. Hrs open: Box 459, P0V 2V0. Secondary address: 78 Spruce St. P0V 2V0. Phone: (807) 227-9988. Fax: (807) 227-9985.E-mail: info@q104.ca Web Site:www.q104fm.ca Licensee: Norwesto Communications Ltd. Format: Hot adult contemp. ◆Rick Doucet, gen mgr; Ken O'Neil, progmg dir.

Wahta Mohawk Territory near Bala

CFWP-FM— 2003: 98.3 mhz; 1.06 kw. Ant 96 ft Hrs open: 24 Phone: (705) 762-1274. Fax: (705) 762-2045.E-mail: hawk98@mohawknationradio.ca Web Site:www.mohawkradionation.ca Licensee: Wahta Communications Society. Population served: 1,000 Format: Var. ◆Cal White, gen mgr.

Wasaga Beach

CHGB-FM— Apr 30, 2007: 97.7 mhz; 200 w. Hrs open: 1383 Mosley St., L9Z 2C5. Phone: (705) 422-0970.E-mail: info@977thebeach.ca Web Site:www.977thebeach.ca Licensee: Bayshore Broadcasting Corp. Format: Classic adult contemp. ◆Ross Kentner, gen mgr; Rick Ringer, opns mgr.

Waterloo

CFCA-FM—(Kitchener, Apr 3, 1967: 105.3 mhz; 100 kw. 820 ft TL: N43 24 15 W80 38 05. Stereo. Hrs open: 24 Dups AM 16% 255 King St. N., Suite 207, N2J 4V2. E-mail: info@koolfm.com Web Site:www.koolfm.com Licensee: CTV Ltd. Format: Classic rock.

CIKZ-FM—See Kitchener-Waterloo

*CKMS-FM— Oct 16, 1977: 100.3 mhz; 250 w. Ant 110 ft Stereo. Hrs open: 6 AM-midnight 200 University Ave. W., N2L 3G1. Phone: (519) 886-2567. Fax: (519) 884-3530.E-mail: ckmsfm@web.ca Web Site:www.ckmsfm.uwaterloo.ca Licensee: Radio Waterloo Inc. Population served: 300,000 Format: Div, campus. News staff: one. Target aud: General. ◆Steve Krysak, pres; Mark Green, progmg.

CKWR-FM—(Kitchener, Mar 23, 1974: 98.5 mhz; 15.2 kw. Ant 576 ft Stereo. Hrs open: 24 375 University Ave. E., N2k 3M7. Phone: (519) 886-9870. Fax: (519) 886-0090.E-mail: general@ckwr.com Web Site:www.ckwr.com Licensee: Wired World Inc. Population served: 1,000,000 Natl. Rep: CHUM Radio Sales,. Wire Svc: BN Wire Format: Adult contemp; speciality & multicultural. News staff: 2; News: 8 hrs wkly. Target aud: 35-64; mature audience. Spec prog: Romanian 2 hrs, Ger 3 hrs, Greek 2 hrs, Serbian 2 hrs, Pol 4 hrs, Por 5 hrs, Sp 4 hrs wkly. ◆Scott Jensen, pres; Clyde Ross, stn mgr, gen sls mgr.

Wawa

CJWA-FM— 1996: 107.1 mhz; 210 w. Hrs open: 55 Broadway Ave., P0S 1K0. Phone: (705) 856-4555. Fax: (705) 856-1520. Licensee: Labbe Media Inc. (acq 9-1-2002). Natl. Rep: Canadian Broadcast Sales,. Format: Adult contemp. Target aud: 25-54. ◆Rick Labbe, pres, gen mgr, sls dir, progmg dir; Mark Capeless, progmg dir, news dir; Vern Valois, chief of engrg.

Welland

CIXL-FM— May 20, 1999: 91.7 mhz; 50 kw. TL: N52 42 56 W19 79 16. Stereo. Hrs open: 24 860 Forks Road West, L3B 5R6. Phone: (905) 732-4433. Fax: (905) 732-4780.E-mail: info@giantfm.com Web Site:www.giantfm.com Licensee: R.B. Communications, LTD. Population served: 500,000 Natl. Rep: Canadian Broadcast Sales,. Format: Classic rock. News staff: 20; News: 6 hrs wkly. Target aud: 25-54; adults. ◆Pat St. John, pres; Peter Morena, opns mgr, chief of opns; Brian Salmon, mus dir; Susan Honsberger, traf mgr.

Whitchurch-Stouffville

CIWS-FM—Not on air, target date: unknown: 102.7 mhz; 50 w. Hrs open: Box 59, Stouffville, L4A 7Z4. Secondary address: 6379 Main St., Stouffville L4A 7Z4. Phone: (905) 640-6429 .E-mail: jim@whistleradio.com Web Site:www.whistleradio.com Licensee: WhiStle Community Radio. Format: Var. ◆Jim Priebe, CEO.

Windsor

*CBE(AM)— July 1, 1950: 1550 khz; 10 kw-U, DA-1. (Digital radio: 1484.208 mhz; 4.369 kw). Hrs open: 825 Riverside Dr. W., N9A 5K9. Phone: (519) 255-3411. Fax: (519) 255-3443.E-mail: earlyshift@cbc.ca Web Site:www.cbc.ca/windsor Licensee: CBC. Natl. Network: CBC Radio One, . Format: Div, news/talk. Spec prog: Class 4 hrs, jazz 2 hrs wkly.

*CBEF(AM)— May 1970: 540 khz; 2.5 kw-D, 5 kw-N, DA-1. Hrs open: 24 825 Riverside Dr. W., Box 1609, N9A 1k7. Phone: (519) 255-3572. Fax: (519) 255-3573. Licensee: CBC. Natl. Network: CBC Radio One, . Format: Div. News: 3. ◆Benoit Quenneville, gen mgr.

*CBE-FM— Oct 15, 1978: 89.9 mhz; 100 kw. 538 ft (Digital radio: 1484.208 mhz; 4.369 kw). Stereo. Hrs open: 825 Riverside Dr. W., N9A 5K9. Phone: (519) 255-3411. Fax: (519) 255-3443.E-mail: earlyshift@cbc.ca Web Site:www.cbc.ca Licensee: CBC Natl. Network: CBC Radio Two, . Format: Class, div.

CIDR-FM— 1949: 93.9 mhz; 100 kw. Ant 700 ft (Digital radio: 1484.208 mhz; 4.369 kw). Hrs open: 24 Prog sep from AM 30100 Telegraph Rd., Suite 460, Bingham Farms, 48025. Phone: (313) 961-9811. Fax: (313) 961-1603.E-mail: feedback@93.9fmradio.com Web Site:www.93.9fmradio.com Licensee: CTV Ltd. Natl. Rep: McGavren Guild,. Format: Adult contemp. ◆Christine Copeland, prom dir; Murray Brookshaw, progmg dir.

CIMX-FM— July 10, 1967: 88.7 mhz; 100 kw. 577 ft (Digital radio: 1484.208 mhz; 4.369 kw). Stereo. Hrs open: Prog sep from AM 1640 Ouellette Ave., N8X L1. Phone: 519-258-8888/313-961-9811. Fax: 519-258-0182/313-961-1603. Licensee: CTV Ltd. Format: Modern rock. Target aud: 18-34. ◆Cal Cagno, prom mgr; Dave Hunter, progmg dir.

*CJAM-FM— November 1983: 99.1 mhz; 456 w. TL: N42 18 19 W83 04 05. Hrs open: 401 Sunset Ave., N9B 3P4. Phone: (519) 971-3606. Fax: (519) 971-3605.E-mail: news@cjam.ca Web Site:www.cjam.ca Licensee: Student Media, University of Windsor. Population served: 2,500,000 Format: Progsv, info, ethnic. Target aud: General; listeners in Windsor/Detroit area. Spec prog: Black 10 hrs, class 4 hrs, folk 4 hrs, jazz 6 hrs, Pol one hr, Sp one hr wkly. ◆Armondo Correia, pres; Christien Gagnier, stn mgr & progmg dir.

CKLW(AM)— June 1, 1932: 800 khz; 50 kw-U, DA-2. (Digital radio: 1484.208 mhz; 4.369 kw). Hrs open: 24 1640 Ouellette Ave., N8X 1L1. Phone: (519) 258-8888. Fax: (519) 258-0182.E-mail: info@am800cklw.com Web Site:www.am800cklw.com Licensee: CTV Ltd. (group owner; acq 6-22-2007; grpsl). Natl. Rep: McGavren Guild,. Format: News/talk. Target aud: 25-54. ◆Eric Proksch, gen mgr; Heidi Baiden, prom dir; Keith Chinnery, progmg dir; Jason Moore, news dir; Jim Valvasori, engrg dir, chief of engrg.

CKWW(AM)— Mar 29, 1964: 580 khz; 500 w-U, DA-1. (Digital radio: 1484.208 mhz; 4.369 kw). Hrs open: 1640 Ouellette Ave., N8X 1L1. Secondary address: 30100 Telegraph Rd., Suite 460, Bingham Farms, MI 48025. Phone: (519) 258-8888. Phone: (313) 961-9811. Fax: (519) 258-0182. Fax: (313) 961-1603.E-mail: info@am580radio.com Web Site:www.am580radio.com Licensee: CTV Ltd. Group owner: CHUM Ltd. (acq 6-22-2007; grpsl). Natl. Rep: McGavren Guild,. Format: Soft adult contemp. News: 2 hrs wkly. Target aud: 45 plus. ◆Eric Proksch, gen mgr; Charlie O'Brien, progmg dir.

Wingham

CIBU-FM— Apr 1, 2005: 94.5 mhz; 75 kw. Ant 705 ft TL: N44 05 26 W81 12 25. Hrs open: 215 Carling Terr., N0G 2W0. Phone: (519) 357-1310. Fax: (519) 357-1897. Web Site:www.945thebull.ca Licensee: Blackburn Radio Inc. Format: Adult rock. ◆John Weese, gen mgr.

CKNX(AM)— Feb 20, 1926: 920 khz; 10 kw-D, 1 kw-N, DA-2. Hrs open: 24 215 Carling Terr., N0G 2W0. Phone: (519) 357-1310. Fax: (519) 357-1897.E-mail: news@cknxradio.com Licensee: Blackburn Radio Inc. Group owner: Blackburn Group Inc. Format: Country. News staff: 7; News: 10 hrs wkly. Target aud: 35-54. Spec prog: Relg 6 hrs wkly. ◆John Weese, gen mgr.

CKNX-FM— Apr 17, 1977: 101.7 mhz; 100 kw. Ant 705 ft TL: N44 05 26 W81 12 25. Stereo. Hrs open: 24 215 Carling Terr., N0G 2W0. Phone: (519) 357-1310. Fax: (519) 357-1897. Licensee: Blackburn Radio Inc. Format: Adult contemp. Target aud: 25-49. Co-owned TV: CKNX-TV affil.

Woodstock

CIHR-FM— Apr 10, 2006: 104.7 mhz; 7.096 kw. Ant 326 ft TL: N43 06 07 W80 46 18. Hrs open: 24 233 Norwich Ave., N4S 3V8. Phone: (519) 537-8400. Fax: (519)537-8600.E-mail: info@ByrnesMedia.com Web Site:1047.ca Licensee: Byrnes Communications Inc. Population served: 100,000 Natl. Rep: Target Broadcast Sales,. Format: Adult contemp. News staff: 3. Target aud: 25-54; adults. ◆Chris Byrnes, pres; Michael Jones, gen mgr & gen sls mgr; Dan Henry, progmg dir; Adam Nyp, news dir.

CJFH-FM— 2004: 94.3 mhz; 37 w. Hrs open: 24 Phone: (519) 539-2304. Fax: (519) 539-2011.E-mail: info@hopefm.ca Web Site:www.hopefm.ca Licensed: Sound of Faith Broadcasting. Format: Christian. ◆ Gary Hill, gen mgr.

CKDK-FM— July 1, 1987: 103.9 mhz; 52 kw. 400 ft Stereo. Hrs open: 24 290 Dundas St., N4S 1B2. Phone: (519) 539-1040. Fax: (519) 539-7479.E-mail: dave.farough@corusent.com Web Site:www.thehawk.ca Licensed: Corus Radio Group owner: Corus Entertainment Inc. (acq 1991). Population served: 100,000 Natl. Rep: Canadian Broadcast Sales,. Format: Classic rock. News staff: 3; News: 9 hrs wkly. Target aud: 25-54. ◆ John Cassaday, CEO; John Hayes, pres; Dave Farough, gen mgr; Gord Harris, progmg dir.

Prince Edward Island

Charlottetown

*CBCT-FM— 1972: 96.1 mhz; 93.5 kw. 540 ft Hrs open: 24 Box 2230, 430 University Ave., C1A 4N6. Phone: (902) 629-6400. Fax: (902) 629-6518. Web Site:www.cbc.ca/pei Licensed: CBC. Population served: 140,000 Natl. Network: CBC Radio One, . Format: Talk. News: 11 hrs wkly.

CFCY-FM— 2006: 95.1 mhz; 100 kw. Hrs open: Box 1060, C1A 7M4. Secondary address: 5 Prince St. C1A 4P4. Phone: (902) 892-1066. Fax: (902) 566-1338.E-mail: requests@cfcy.pe.ca Web Site:www.951fmcfcy.com Licensed: Maritime Broadcasting System Ltd. Population served: 140,000 Format: Country. ◆ Robert Pace, chmn; Paul Alan, opns mgr.

CHLQ-FM— March 1982: 93.1 mhz; 25 kw. Stereo. Hrs open: Box 1066, C1A 7M4. Secondary address: 5 Prince St. C1A 4P4. Phone: (902) 892-1066. Fax: (902) 566-1338.E-mail: requests@magic93.pe.ca Web Site:www.magic93.fm.ca Licensed: Maritime Broadcasting System Ltd. Population served: 140,000 Format: Hot adult contemp. ◆ Robert Pace, chmn; Paul Alan, opns mgr.

CHTN-FM— 2006: 100.3 mhz; 33 kw. TL: N46 11 22 W63 09 54. Hrs open: 90 University Ave., Suite 320, Atlantic Technology Centre, C1A 4K9. Phone: (902) 569-1003. Fax: (902) 569-8693. Web Site:www.ocean100.com Licensed: Newcap Inc. Population served: 130,000 Natl. Rep: Canadian Broadcast Sales,. Format: Classic hits. News staff: 2; News: 17 hrs wkly. Target aud: 25-54. ◆ Jennifer Evans, gen mgr, gen sls mgr; Mandy Dennis, prom dir; Gerard Murphy, progmg dir; Scott Chapman, news dir.

CKQK-FM— July 25, 2006: 105.5 mhz; 33 kw. TL: N46 12 44 W63 20 32. Hrs open: 90 University Ave., Suite 320, Atlantic Technology Centre, C1A 4K9. Phone: (902) 569-1003. Fax: (902) 569-8693. Web Site:www.krock1055.com Licensed: Newcap Inc. Format: Classic rock. Target aud: 25-44; male. ◆ Jennifer Evans, gen mgr.

Summerside

CJRW-FM— 2000: 102.1 mhz; 11 kw. Hrs open: 5:57 AM-12:15 AM 763 Water St. E., C1N 4J3. Phone: (902) 436-2201. Fax: (902) 436-8573.E-mail: spud@mbsradio.com Web Site:www.1021spvdfm.com Licensed: Maritime Broadcasting System Ltd. Group owner: Maritime Broadcasting (acq 8-10-2000; C$650,000 for approximately 92.9% of the common shares). Format: Everything classic. News staff: one. Target aud: General. ◆ Lois E. Schurman, chmn; Paul M. Schurman, pres; Brent Schurman, VP; Don Smith, gen mgr, gen sls mgr; Heather MacCauley, prom dir; Todd MacEwen, progmg dir; Chris Pride, mus dir.

Quebec

Acton Vale

CFID-FM— 2004: 103.7 mhz; 2.647 kw. TL: N45 39 03 W72 33 54. Hrs open: 24 C.P. 130, J0H 1A0. Phone: (450) 546-1037. Fax: (450) 546-7521.E-mail: info@radio-acton.com Web Site:www.radio-acton.com Licensed: Radio-Acton inc. Format: Fr, var. ◆ Gaetan Chevanelle, gen mgr.

Alma

CFGT(AM)— October 1953: 1270 khz; 10 kw-D, 5 kw-N, DA-2. Hrs open: 460 Sacre- Coeur W., Suite 200, G8B 1L9. Phone: (418) 662-6673. Fax: (418) 662-6070.E-mail: vdionne@mcmedia.com Licensed: Groupe Radio Antenne 6 Inc. Group owner: Group Radio Antenne 6 Inc. (acq 8-18-94). Format: Talk AC some country. ◆ Marc-Andre Levesque, gen mgr; Lewis Gagnon, sls dir, mus dir; Louis Arcand, progmg dir.

CKYK-FM— 1993: 95.7 mhz; 100 kw. TL: N48 24 05 W72 05 23. Hrs open: 460 Sacre-Coeur W., Suite 200, G8B 1L9. Phone: (418) 662-6888. Phone: (418) 543-8912. Fax: (418) 662-6070.E-mail: vdionne@rncmedia.com Web Site:kykf.com Licensed: Groupe Radio Antenne 6 Inc. Format: Rock of the 80's. ◆ Marc-Andre Levesque, pres.

Amos

CHOW-FM— Not on air, target date: unknown: 105.3 mhz; 5.376 kw. TL: N48 34 25 W78 09 44. Hrs open: 401 1re rue ouest, Bureau 100, J9T 2M3. Phone: (819) 732-4415. Fax: (819) 732-4008.E-mail: infos@radioboreale.com Web Site:www.radioboreale.com Licensed: Radio Boreale. Format: Var. ◆ Donald Perron, pres.

Amqui

CFVM-FM— 2003: 99.9 mhz; 23.8 kw. Hrs open: 111 rue de l'Hopital, G5J 2K1. Phone: (418) 629-2025. Fax: (418) 629-2599.E-mail: cfvm@globetrotter.net Web Site:www.lamatapedia.com/cfvm Licensed: Astral Media Radio inc. Group owner: Corus Entertainment Inc. (acq 5-30-2005; grpsl). Format: Adult contemp, classic rock, CHR. News staff: 2; News: 6 hrs wkly. Target aud: 18 plus. ◆ Adalbert Levesque, gen mgr, sls dir; Jean Lemay, progmg dir; Jean Fournier, engrg mgr; Jennifer Gravel, news rptr; Alain Revard, disc jockey.

Asbestos

CJAN-FM— AM 1972;FM 2001: 99.3 mhz; 11.1 kw. Stereo. Hrs open: 185 du Roi, PE, J1T 1S4. Phone: (819) 879-5439. Phone: (819) 879-5430. Fax: (819) 879-7922.E-mail: info@fm993.ca Web Site:www.fm993.ca Licensed: Radio Plus B.M.D. inc. Natl. Rep: Target Broadcast Sales,. Format: Adult contemp, MOR. News staff: one. Target aud: 35-75; general. ◆ Marie-Paule Drouin, pres.

Baie Comeau

CBMI-FM— May 28, 1974: 93.7 mhz; 3 kw. Hrs open: Rebroadcasts CBVE-FM Quebec 100%. c/o CBVE-FM, 888 Saint-Jean St., Quebec, G1R 5H6. Phone: (418) 691-3613. Fax: (418) 691-3610. Licensed: Canadian Broadcasting Corp. Natl. Network: CBC Radio One, . Format: Pub affrs, info. ◆ David Kyle, gen mgr.

CHLC-FM— 1996: 97.1 mhz; 4.21 kw. Stereo. Hrs open: 907 Rue de Puyjalon, G5C 1N3. Phone: (418) 589-3771. Fax: (418) 589-9086.E-mail: info@chlc.com Web Site:www.chlc.com Licensed: 9022-6242 Quebec Inc. (acq 4-29-96). Format: Adult contemp, MOR. Target aud: General. ◆ Yvon Savoes, pres; Francois Morache, VP; George Daviault, gen mgr, sls dir, news dir; Mike Mainville, progmg dir; Mark Andre Halle, news dir.

Becancour and Nicolet

CKBN-FM— 2008: 90.5 mhz; 34 kw. Ant 118 ft TL: N46 17 04 W72 32 01. Hrs open: 10275 Leblanc, Suite 127, Becancour, G0X 1B0. Phone: (819) 294-2526. Fax: (819) 294-2527. Web Site:www.ckbn.ca Licensed: Cooperative de solidarite radio communautaire Nicolet-Yamaska/Becancour. ◆ Marie-Helene Roy, gen mgr.

Carleton

CIEU-FM— 1983: 94.9 mhz; 25 kw. 1,466 ft TL: N48 08 27 W66 06 32. Hrs open: 24 1645 Perron Est., G0C 1J0. Phone: (418) 364-7094. Fax: (418) 364-3150.E-mail: cieufm@cieufm.com Web Site:www.cieufm.com Licensed: Diffusion Communautaire Baie des Chaleurs Inc. Format: CHR, adult contemp. News staff: 2; News: 7 hrs wkly. Target aud: General. Spec prog: Blues 5 hrs, class 3 hrs, folk 3 hrs, jazz 3 hrs wkly. ◆ Jacques Veillette, pres; Louis St-Laurent, gen mgr; Carol Boudreau, mus dir; Yues Sigouin, traf mgr; Claude Roy, local news ed.

Chandler

CFMV-FM— June 8, 2005: 96.3 mhz; 5.716 kw. Hrs open: C.P. 99, G0C 1K0. Secondary address: 141 rue Commerciale Ouest G0C 1K0. Phone: (418) 689-4921. Fax: (418) 689-3852.E-mail: cfmv@fm92-1.com Web Site:www.fm92-1.com Licensed: Radio du Golfe inc. Format: French, rock. ◆ Jacques Vallee, gen mgr.

Charlesbourg

CIMI-FM— Aug 10, 2001: 103.7 mhz; 20 w. Hrs open: 4500, Blvd. Henri-Bairassa bur. 103, G1H 3A5. Phone: (418) 841-4445. Phone: (418) 624-0700. Fax: (418) 623-2538. Web Site:www.cimifm.com Format: Alternative. ◆ Francois Beaule, opns mgr; Gerald St. Arnaud, pres & sls dir; Eric Veilleux, progmg dir.

Chateauguay

CHAI-FM— 1980: 101.9 mhz; 100 w. Stereo. Hrs open: 25 boul. St. Francis, J6J 1Y2. Phone: (450) 698-3131. Fax: (450) 698-3339.E-mail: chai@videotrom.ca Web Site:www.101fm.net Licensed: Radio Communautaires de Chateauguay Inc. Population served: 75,000 Format: Adult contemp, CHR. News staff: 2; News: 4 hrs wkly. Target aud: General; all ages. ◆ Christian Laberge, pres; Sylvain Poirier, opns dir & progmg dir.

Chibougamau

CJMD(AM)— Nov 21, 1969: 1240 khz; 1 kw-U. TL: N49 54 35 W74 22 08. Hrs open: 24 c/o CHRL, 568 Boul. St. Joseph, Roberval, G8H 2K6. Secondary address: 539 Zieme Rue G8P 1N8. Phone: (418) 275-1831. Phone: (418) 748-3931. Fax: (418) 275-2475. Fax: (418) 748-3931.E-mail: contact@antenne6.com Licensed: Groupe Radio Antenne 6 inc. Group owner: Group Radio Antenne 6 Inc. (acq 1-6-93). Format: Pop music. News staff: one; News: 20 hrs wkly. Target aud: General; mainly adults. ◆ Marc-Andre Levesque, pres; Louis Arcand, opns dir.

CKXO-FM— 2007: 93.5 mhz; 19.8 kw. TL: N49 56 46 W74 20 57. Hrs open: 171-A rue Jean-Proulx, Gatineau, J8Z 1W5. Phone: (819) 770-9650. Web Site:www.tagradio.fm Licensed: Groupe Radio Antenne 6 Inc. Format: CHR. ◆ Robert H. Parent, VP & gen mgr.

Chicoutimi

CBJE-FM— 1976: 102.7 mhz; 30 kw. Ant 294 ft TL: N48 25 29 W71 06 32. Hrs open: Rebroadcasts CBM(AM) Montreal. Weekdays 6 AM-9 AM rebroadcasts CBVE-FM Quebec City. CP 6000, c/o CBM(AM), Montreal, H3C 3A8. Phone: (514) 597-4444. Fax: (514) 597-4416.E-mail: info@cbc.ca/montreal Licensed: CBC. Format: Talk radio. ◆ Patricia Pleszczynska, gen mgr; Judith Bleier, opns mgr; Kate Arthur, prom mgr; Sally Caudwell, news dir.

CBJ-FM— 2001: 93.7 mhz; 50 kw. Ant 1,719 ft TL: N48 36 04 W70 49 46. Hrs open: 24 Rebroadcasts CBF-FM Montreal, 70%. 500 rue Des Sagueneens, G7H 6N4. Phone: (418) 696-6600. Fax: (418) 696-6689. Licensed: Canadian Broadcasting Corp. Population served: 295,000 Natl. Network: Premiere Chaine, . Format: Var, talk, adlult contemp. News staff: 7. Target aud: 35 plus; adlut, news-oriented. ◆ Patrick Boie, gen mgr, prom dir & news dir.

*CBJX-FM— Sept 20, 1933: 100.9 mhz; 98 kw. Ant 294 ft TL: N48 25 29 W71 06 32. Hrs open: 24 Rebroadcasts CBF-FM Montreal 95%. 500 rue Des Sagueneens, G7H 6N4. Phone: (418) 696-6600. Fax: (418) 696-6689. Licensed: Canadian Broadcasting Corp. Population served: 150,000 Natl. Network: Espace Musique, . Format: Classical. ◆ Patrick Boie, opns mgr.

CFIX-FM— July 31, 1987: 96.9 mhz; 43.8 kw. Hrs open: 24 267 est, rue Racine, G7H 5K3. Phone: (418) 543-9797. Fax: (418) 543-7968.E-mail: cfix@rock-detente.com Web Site:www.rock-detente.com Licensed: Astral Media Radio inc. Group owner: Radio Nord (acq 4-19-2002; grpsl). Format: Adult contemp, MOR. ◆ Richard Durcotte, gen mgr.

Degelis

CFVD-FM— 1995: 95.5 mhz; 12.47 kw. 300 ft TL: N47 33 02 W68 43 48. Stereo. Hrs open: 24 654 6ieme rue est, Ville Degelis, G5T 1Y1. Phone: (418) 853-2370. Phone: (418) 853-3370. Fax: (418) 853-3321.E-mail: cfvd@fm95.ca Web Site:www.fm95.ca Licensed: Radio Degelis Inc.

Population served: 30,000. Format: CHR, country, adult contemp. News staff: 10. Target aud: General. ◆Gilles Caron, pres & gen mgr.

Dolbeau-Mistassini

CHVD-FM— 2003: 100.3 mhz; 21.4 kw. Hrs open: 24 1975 Boul Wallberg, Dolbeau, G8L 1J5. Phone: (418) 276-3333. Fax: (418) 276-6755. Licensee: Groupe Radio Antenne 6 Inc. Group owner: Radio Nord (acq 5-2004). Format: MOR. ◆Pierre Broseau, pres; Marc Andre Levesque, opns mgr, sls dir; Louis Arcand, progmg dir, news dir.

CKII-FM— 2004: 101.3 mhz; 250 w. Hrs open: 1709 boul. Wallberg, G8L 1H6. Phone: (418) 239-2544. Fax: (418) 239-0842. Licensee: L'Alliance Laurentienne des metis et indiens sans statut, Local 30 Mistassini inc. Format: Fr. ◆Michel Bouchard, gen mgr.

Donnacona

CHXX-FM— 1997: 100.9 mhz; 1.585 kw. Hrs open: 274 rue Notre-Dame, G0A 1T0. Phone: (418) 285-2568. Fax: (418) 285-5483. Licensee: RNC MEDIA Inc. (acq 12-23-2005). Format: News/talk. ◆Patrice Denerse, opns mgr.

Drummondville

CHRD-FM— 1997: 105.3 mhz; 2.9 kw. Stereo. Hrs open: 24 2070 rue St. Georges, J2C 5G6. Phone: (819) 475-1480. Fax: (819) 478-0099. Fax: (819) 475-5180.E-mail: chrd@hy.cgocable.ca Licensee: Astral Media Radio Inc. Group owner: Astral Media Inc. (acq 8-13-2001). Format: Adult contemp, MOR, news. News staff: 3; News: 15 hrs wkly. Target aud: 18 plus; general. Spec prog: Relg one hr wkly. ◆Joel Rioux, pres, gen mgr, opns dir, sls dir, prom dir; Martin Tremblay, progmg dir; David Rivet, news dir; Michel Cournoyer, chief of engrg; Robert Veilleux, spec ev coord & mus critic; Julie Brisson, women's int ed.

CJDM-FM— Aug 15, 1987: 92.1 mhz; 3 kw. 300 ft Stereo. Hrs open: 24 207 Rue St-Georges, BC, J2C 5G6. Phone: (819) 474-1892. Fax: (819) 474-6610.E-mail: cjdm@cgocable.ca Web Site:www.cjdm.fm Licensee: Astral Media Radio inc. Group owner: Corus Entertainment Inc. (acq 5-30-2005; grpsl). Population served: 65,000 Natl. Rep: Canadian Broadcast Sales,. Format: Adult contemp, Fr. News staff: 2; News: 5 hrs wkly. Target aud: 18-44. ◆Joel Rioux, gen mgr, sls dir, gen sls mgr; Martine Pichette, prom dir; Claude Rene Piette, progmg dir; Alain Rivard, mus dir; Claude Boucher, news dir; Daniel Pelletier, engrg dir.

CJRD-FM— Dec 27, 2007: 88.9 mhz; 710 w. TL: N45 53 00 W72 29 19. Hrs open: 161 rue Marchand, J2B 4N3. Phone: (819) 474-2573. Fax: (819) 474-0296. Web Site:www.cjrd.fm Licensee: Radio Drummond. Format: Var. ◆Georges Masse, pres; Jean-Pierre Charbonneau, gen mgr.

Fermont

CBMR-FM— 1982: 105.1 mhz; 16 w. Hrs open: 1400 Rene Levesque E., c/o CBM(AM) - A 4, Montreal, H2L 8M2. Phone: (514) 597-4444. Fax: (514) 597-4416.E-mail: info@cbc.ca/montreal Licensee: Canadian Broadcasting Corp. ◆Patricia Pleszczynska, opns dir; Judith Bleier, opns mgr.

CFMF-FM— 1980: 103.1 mhz; 50 w. 100 ft Stereo. Hrs open: Box 280, G0G 1J0. Phone: (418) 287-5147. Fax: (418) 287-5776.E-mail: cfmf103_1@diffusionfermont.com Web Site:www.cfmf.ca Licensee: Radio Communautaire de Fermont Inc. Format: Div, Fr, Top 40, Pop Rock. Target aud: 7-55. Spec prog: Jazz one hr, C&W 4 hrs wkly. ◆Nadia Larrizee, pres; Marc Poulin, sr VP; Nadia Larrivee, gen mgr; Karl Gagne-Cote, progmg mgr; Genevieve Richard, mus dir; Carl Champagne, news dir.

Forestville

CFRP(AM)— 1977: 620 khz; 1 kw-U. Hrs open: 907 Rue de Puyjalon, Baie Cameau, G5C 1N3. Phone: (418) 589-3771. Fax: (418) 589-9086. Licensee: 9022-6242 Quebec Inc. (acq 3-29-96). Format: Adult contemp, MOR. ◆Yvon Savoie, pres; George Baviauet, gen mgr; Lynn Martin, traf mgr.

Fort Coulonge

CHIP-FM— May 2, 1981: 101.7 mhz; 10 kw. 299 ft TL: N45 45 41 W76 35 01. Stereo. Hrs open: 24 Box 820, La Radio du Pontiac, 33 Romain St., J0X 1V0. Secondary address: 138 Principal St. J0X 1V0. Phone: (819) 683-3155. Fax: (819) 683-3211.E-mail: radiopontiac@chipfm.com Web Site:www.chipfm.com Licensee: La Radio du Pontiac Inc. Population served: 105,000 Format: Country in Fr & English. News: 5 hrs wkly. Target aud: 35 yrs & up; rural people. farming communities, small towns. Spec prog: Oldies, rock, gospel 7 hrs, class 2 hrs wkly. ◆Chantele Legault, gen mgr.

Gaspe

CJRG-FM— December 1978: 94.5 mhz; 3.8 kw. Ant 1,150 ft Stereo. Hrs open: 162 Jacques Cartier, G4X 1M9. Phone: (418) 368-3511. Fax: (418) 368-1663. Licensee: Radio Gaspesie Inc. Format: MOR. Spec prog: Class 2 hrs, jazz 2 hrs wkly. ◆Jacques Chartier, gen mgr, progmg dir; Paul Minville, gen sls mgr; Richard O'Leary, news dir; Yvan DuPuis, engrg dir.

Gatineau

CFTX-FM— 2006: 96.5 mhz; 1.75 kw. Hrs open: 171-A rue Jean-Proulx, J8Z 1W5. Phone: (819) 770-9650. Web Site:www.tagradio.fm Licensee: RNC MEDIA Inc. Format: Fr CHR. ◆Robert H. Parent, VP & gen mgr; Eric Brousseau, prom dir; Benoit Vanasse, mus dir.

CHLX-FM— Sept 23, 2002: 97.1 mhz; 12.6 kw. Hrs open: 125 rue Jean-Proulx, J8Z 1T4. Phone: (819) 770-9710. Fax: (819) 770-9740.E-mail: classique@radionord.com Web Site:www.radionord.com/radio-classic/index.html Licensee: RNC MEDIA Inc. Group owner: Radio Nord Communications Inc. (acq 8-25-2004). Format: Fr, classical, jazz. ◆Jean-Pierre Major, gen mgr; Diane Pelletier, sls dir; Yurs Trottier, progmg dir.

CIMF-FM— Jan 1, 1970: 94.9 mhz; 84 kw horiz. Ant 1,059 ft TL: N45 30 11 W75 51 02. (Digital radio: 1463.280 mhz). Stereo. Hrs open: 15 Taschereau, J8Y 2V6. Phone: (819) 770-2463. Fax: (819) 770-9338.E-mail: cimf@rockdetente Web Site:www.rockdetente.com Licensee: Astral Media Radio Inc. Group owner: Astral Media Inc. (acq 10-28-2002; grpsl). Format: Soft rock. News staff: 2; News: 3 hrs wkly. ◆Ian Greenberg, pres; Carmen Rodrigue, gen mgr; Claude Raymond, sls dir, gen sls mgr; Eric St-Louis, prom mgr; Patrice Croteau, progmg mgr; Jean-Guy Faucher, mus dir; Mano Aube, news dir; Pierre Sylvestre, chief of engrg.

CJLL-FM—See Ottawa, ON

CJRC-FM—Licensed to Gatineau. See Ottawa ON

CKTF-FM— Mar 11, 1988: 104.1 mhz; 19 kw. Ant 1,077 ft TL: N45 30 11 W75 51 02. (Digital radio: 1463.280 mhz). Stereo. Hrs open: 24 15 rue Taschereau, J8Y 2V6. Phone: (819) 243-5555. Fax: (819) 243-6816. Web Site:www.radioenergie.com Licensee: Astral Media Radio Inc. Group owner: Astral Media Inc. Format: Dance, top-40, AOR. ◆Carmen Rodrigue, gen mgr; Vincent Pons, sls dir; Melany Gauvin, prom mgr; Astral Musique, mus dir; Pierre Sylvestre, engrg dir.

Granby

CFXM-FM— 1997: 104.9 mhz; 1.184 kw. Ant 1,168 ft TL: N45 21 48 W72 37 32. Hrs open: 135 rue Principale, Bureau 35, J2G 2V1. Phone: (450) 372-5105. Fax: (450) 372-3105. Web Site:www.m105.ca Licensee: Cooperative de travail de la radio de Granby. Format: Adult contemp. ◆Stephan Roy, gen mgr; Luc Normandin, sls dir; Guy Laporte, mktg dir, prom dir, mus dir.

Harrington Harbour

*CFTH-FM-1— Oct 30, 1991: 97.7 mhz; 180 w. TL: N50 29 36 W59 28 50. Stereo. Hrs open: Box 88, Harrington Harbour, Duplessis, G0G 1N0. Phone: (418) 795-3349. Fax: (418) 795-3200.E-mail: cfth@globetrotter.qc.ca Licensee: Radio Communautaire de Harrington Harbour. Format: Adult contemp, country, oldies. Target aud: General; five fishing villages. ◆Lana Shattler, gen mgr; Quenton Lessard, progmg dir; Betty Strickland, news dir.

Havre-Saint-Pierre

CILE-FM— 1987: 95.1 mhz; 1.496 kw. Ant 201 ft Hrs open: 24 992 Rue du Bouleau, G0G 1P0. Phone: (418) 538-2453. Phone: (418) 538-2451. Fax: (418) 538-3870.E-mail: cilemf@globetrotter.net Web Site:www.cilemf.com Licensee: Radio & Television Communautaire Havre-St. Pierre. Format: MOR. ◆Berchmens Boudreau, gen mgr, progmg dir; Catherine Ramoisy, news dir; Gerald Gallant, engrg mgr.

Iles-de-la-Madeleine

CFIM-FM— Nov 15, 1981: 92.7 mhz; 6.3 kw. Stereo. Hrs open: 24 C.P. 8192, 1172 Chemin Laverniere, Cap-aux-Meules, G4T 1R3. Phone: (418) 986-5233. Fax: (418) 986-5319.E-mail: pub@cfim.ca Web Site:www.cfim.ca Licensee: Diffusion Communautaire des Iles Inc. Diffusion Communautaire des Iles Format: Div, news/talk, community radio. Target aud: General. ◆Charles Eugene Cyr, gen mgr; Linda Noel, mktg VP; Helen Fauteux, news dir; Paul Turbide, engrg dir.

Joliette

CJLM-FM— 1996: 103.5 mhz; 3 kw. TL: N45 59 0 W73 25 52. Stereo. Hrs open: 24 540 St. Thomas, J6E 3R4. Phone: (450) 756-1035. Fax: (450) 756-8097.E-mail: radio@m1035fm.com Web Site:www.m1035fm.com Licensee: Cooperative de Radiodiffusion MF 103.5 de Lanaudiere. Cooperative de Radiodiffusion MF 103.5 de Lanaudiere Format: MOR. News staff: 4. Target aud: 25-49. Spec prog: Oldies 6 hrs wkly. ◆Marie Josee Demera, prom VP; Benoit Simard, progmg mgr, news dir; Martin Beaucage, mus dir; Normand Masse, gen mgr, sls dir & engrg dir.

Jonquiere

CKAJ-FM— Apr 11, 1977: 92.5 mhz; 14.164 kw. Stereo. Hrs open: 6 AM-midnight C.P. 872, G7X 7M8. Secondary address: Pavillon Manicouagan, 3791, De La Fabrique G7X 7W8. Phone: (418) 546-2525. Phone: (418) 546-2526. Fax: (418) 546-2528.E-mail: informations@ckaj.org Web Site:www.ckaj.org Licensee: Radio Communautaire du Saguenay Inc. Format: Div, country, retro. News staff: one; News: 6 hrs wkly. Target aud: 25-54. ◆Johanne Tremblay, pres; Pierre Boivin, progmg dir; Henri Girard, chief of engrg.

Kahnawake

*CKRK-FM— Mar 30, 1981: 103.7 mhz; 250 w. 75 ft Stereo. Hrs open: 24 Box 1050, J0L 1B0. Phone: (450) 638-1313. Fax: (450) 638-4009.E-mail: programming@k103radio.com Web Site:www.k103radio.com Licensee: Mohawk Radio Kahnawake Association. (acq 8-4-94). Format: Adult contemp, C&W, contemp hit. News staff: 2; News: 3 hrs wkly. Native community in Kahawake; general audience Montreal region. Spec prog: Mohawk 10 wkly. ◆Lois Williams, gen sls mgr; Dino Sisto, news dir, sports cmtr; Marsha Dailleboust, traf mgr, sports cmtr; Thomasina Phillips, news rptr; Don Garrett, disc jockey.

Kuujjuaq

CKUJ-FM— 1992: 97.3 mhz; 394 w. Hrs open: 10am-12pm; 2-5pm Box 1082, J0M 1C0. Phone: (819) 964-2921. Fax: (819) 964-2229. Licensee: Minister Council of Kuujjuaq. Format: Inuit. ◆Larry Watt, pres; Mary Gordon, opns dir & news dir.

La Malbaie

*CBV-FM-6— Sept 20, 1979: 99.3 mhz; 820 w. Ant 108 ft TL: N47 41 02 W70 08 06. Hrs open: 24
Rebroadcasts CBV-FM Quebec 100%.
888 Saint-Jean St., Quebec, G1R 5H6. Phone: (418) 654-1341. Fax: (418) 656-8842. Licensee: CBC. Natl. Network: Premiere Chaine, . Format: Current Affairs/News. ◆Susan Campbell, gen mgr; Claude-Saindon, opns mgr; Sally Caldwell, news dir; Gaston LeBlanc, engrg mgr.

La Pocatiere

CHOX-FM— Apr 23, 1992: 97.5 mhz; 25 kw. Stereo. Hrs open: 601 First St., Suite 20, G0R1Z0. Phone: (418) 856-1310. Fax: (418) 856-3747.E-mail: chox@chox97.com Web Site:www.chox97.com Licensee: CHOX-FM Inc. Format: Hot AC. ◆Guy Simard, pres; Gilles Gosselin, opns mgr, progmg VP; Diane Bouchard, dev VP; Georgette Charent, sls VP; Renee Giard, mktg VP; Gabriel Hudon, prom VP; Maxima Parabas, mus dir; Jacques Dufour, news dir; Clement Lavoie, engrg VP.

La Tabatiere

CFTH-FM-2— 1991: 98.5 mhz; 70 w. Hrs open: Box 88, Harrington Harbour, G0G 1N0. Phone: (418) 795-3349. Fax: (418) 795-3200. Licensee: Radio communautaire de Harrington Harbour. Format: Var.

La Tuque

CFLM(AM)— Oct 3, 1959: 1240 khz; 1 kw-U, DA-2. Hrs open: 24 C.P. 850, 529 St. Louis, G9X 3P6. Phone: (819) 523-4575. Fax: (819) 676-8000.E-mail: radio.h-m@sympatico.ca Licensee: Radio Haute Mauricle Inc. (acq 1982). Format: Var; adult contemp; CHR. News staff: one. Target aud: General. ◆Rejean LeClerc, pres, gen mgr & opns dir.

Lac Megantic

CJIT-FM— 2002: 106.7 mhz; 4.25 kw. Hrs open: 24 4766 rue Laval, G6B 1C7. Phone: (819) 583-0663. Fax: (819) 583-0665.E-mail: info@cjitfm.com Web Site:www.cjitfm.com Licensee: Les Productions du temps perdu inc. (acq 3-12-2007; C$200,000). Natl. Rep: Target Broadcast Sales,. Format: Top-40, MOR. ◆Louis Longchamps, opns mgr, gen sls mgr, progmg dir, news dir; Normand Blondeau, engrg dir.

Lac-Brome

CIDI-FM— Sept 20, 2007: 99.1 mhz; 1.45 kw. Ant 165 ft TL: N45 11 10 W72 35 20. Stereo. Hrs open: Box 3611, 305B Knowlton Rd., Knowlton, J0E 1V0. Phone: (450) 243-6285. Fax: (450) 243-1041.E-mail: deweydurrell@axion.ca Web Site:www.sunnymead.org/cidi Licensee: Radio Communautaire Missisquoi. Population served: 138,000 Format: Music, talk. News staff: 3; News: 21 hrs wkly. Target aud: 18-60.

Lac-Etchemin

***CFIN-FM**— Mar 27, 1992: 100.5 mhz; 6.7 kw. 676 ft TL: N46 24 41 W70 35 44. Stereo. Hrs open: 24 201 Claude-Bilodeau St., G0R 1S0. Phone: (418) 625-3737. Fax: (418) 625-3730.E-mail: cfinfm@sogetel.net Web Site:www.cfinfm.com Licensee: Radio Bellechasse. Population served: 50,000 Rgnl rep: Target. Format: MOR, country, flashback. News staff: 2; News: 30 hrs wkly. Target aud: 35-60. Spec prog: Class 4 hrs, jazz 6 hrs, relg one hr, country 6 hrs wkly. ◆Marcel Asselin, pres; Raymond Boutin, pres & stn mgr; Isabelle Giasson, progmg dir; Norman Poulin, mus dir, news dir, pub affrs dir.

Lachute

CJLA-FM— Dec 1, 1974: 104.9 mhz; 3 kw. Stereo. Hrs open: 24 11 Argenteuil, J8H 1X8. Phone: (450) 562-3733.E-mail: fusionfm@citenet.net Licensee: RNC MEDIA Inc. (group owner; (acq 8-22-89). Format: Adult contemp. News staff: one; News: 8 hrs wkly. Target aud: 25-59. ◆Pierre Brosseau, pres; Jean-Pierre Major, gen mgr; Marc Dubois, opns mgr, progmg dir; Yves Trottier, gen sls mgr; Olivier Proulx, news dir; Gaston Tousignant, chief of engrg.

Lac-Simon (Louvicourt)

CHUT-FM— 2000: 95.3 mhz; 97.9 w. Hrs open: 1016 rue Wabanonik, Lac-Simon, J0Y 3M0. Phone: (819) 736-4501. Fax: (819) 736-2333. Licensee: Radio communautaire MF Lac Simon inc. Format: Community/aboriginal. ◆Alain Flamand, gen mgr.

Laval

CFAV(AM)— January 2004: 1570 khz; 10 kw-U. Hrs open: Radio Nostalgie, 2040 Autoroute Laval, H7S 2M9. Phone: (450) 680-1570.E-mail: avidtoire@nostalgie1570.com Web Site:www.nostalgie1570.com Licensee: Gilles Lajoie and Colette Chabot, on behalf of a corporation to be incorporated. Format: Nostalgia. ◆Colette Chabot, gen mgr.

CFGL-FM— September 1968: 105.7 mhz; 41 kw. TL: N45 30 20 W73 35 32. (Digital radio: 1454.56 mhz; 1.594 kw at Laval, 1.4 kw at Montreal). Stereo. Hrs open: 24 2830 Boul. St. Martin E., H7E 5A1. Phone: (450) 664-1500. Phone: (514) 381-5903. Fax: (450) 664-4138. Fax: (450) 664-1651. Web Site:www.rythmefm.com Licensee: Cogeco Diffusion inc. Group owner: Cogeco Inc. Format: Adult contemp. News staff: 2; News: 2 hrs wkly. Target aud: 25-54; those preferring soft & easy lstng hits. ◆Richard LaChance, gen mgr; Sylvain Venne, chief of opns; Daniel Brouilette, prom dir; Andre St-Amand, progmg dir; Lilianne Randall, mus dir; Jean Arcand, engrg dir.

Les Escoumins

CHME-FM— 1994: 94.9 mhz; 5kw. Hrs open: 24 34 rue de la Reserve, G0T 1K0. Phone: (418) 233-2700. Fax: (418) 233-3326.E-mail: chme@b2b2c.ca Licensee: Radio Essipit Haute Cote-Nord inc. Population served: 25,000 Format: Fr. ◆Claudine Roussel, gen mgr.

Levis

CFOM-FM— 1992: 102.9 mhz; 16.8 kw. Stereo. Hrs open: 2136 chemin Ste-Foy, 3e etage, Quebec, G1V 1R8. Phone: (418) 694-1029. Fax: (418) 682-8430. Web Site:www.1029cfom.ca Licensee: 591991 B.C. Ltd. Group owner: Astral Media Inc. (acq 1-21-2005; grpsl). Format: Hits of the 60s, 70s, 80s & 90s. Target aud: 25 plus. ◆Hermann Charest, gen mgr; Jean-Pier Poulin, sls dir; Annie Anglehart, prom dir; Richard Blondin, progmg dir.

Listuguj

CFIC-FM— 2000: 105.1 mhz; 425 w. Hrs open: Box 304, G0C 2R0. Secondary address: 44A Riverside E. G0C 2R0. Phone: (418) 788-5166. Fax: (418) 788-3524.E-mail: info@105hotcountry.com Web Site:www.105hotcountry.com Licensee: Societe d'Art, de Culture et d'Histoire Micmacs. Format: Country. ◆Gerald Dedam, pres; Chris Dedam, gen mgr, engrg dir; Linda Gilbert, sls dir & news dir.

Longueuil

CHAA-FM— 1987: 103.3 mhz; 64 w. Stereo. Hrs open: 24 91 St. Jean, J4H 2W8. Phone: (450) 646-6800. Fax: (450) 646-7378.E-mail: admin@fm1033.ca Web Site:www.fm1033.ca Licensee: Radio Communautaire de la Rive-Sud Inc. Population served: 500,000 Natl. Rep: Target Broadcast Sales,. Format: Adult contemp. News staff: 2; News: 5 hrs wkly. Target aud: 24-54; general. Spec prog: Fr 18 hrs, retro oldies 9 hrs, Greek 5 hrs, Vietnamese 4 hrs, Sp 3 hrs wkly. ◆Eric Tetreault, chmn, gen mgr; Richard Boileau, sls dir & mktg dir; France Dube, progmg dir.

CHMP-FM— Apr 9, 1977: 98.5 mhz; 40.8 kw. Ant 623 ft Stereo. Hrs open: 211 avenue Gordon, Verdun, H4G 2R2. Phone: (514) 767-2435. Fax: (514) 761-0985. Web Site:www.fm985.ca Licensee: Diffusion Metromedia CMR Inc. Group owner: Corus Entertainment Inc. (acq 1-26-2001; grpsl). Natl. Rep: Canadian Broadcast Sales,. Format: Talk. News: 5 hrs wkly. Target aud: 18-44. ◆Pierre Beland, pres; Pierre Accand, VP; Jacques Papin, gen mgr; David Therrien, sls dir; Michel Lacroix, gen sls mgr; Maurice Tietolman, natl sls mgr; Pierre Tremblay, prom mgr; Denis Fortin, progmg dir; Michel Belleau, mus dir; Real Terrault, chief of engrg.

Louiseville

CHHO-FM— Jan 22, 2007: 103.1 mhz; 1.52 kw. Hrs open: 50-A de la Fabrique, J0K 2W0. Phone: (819) 228-1001. Fax: (819) 228-0330.E-mail: info@ch2ofm.ca Web Site:www.ch2ofm.ca Licensee: Coop de solidarite radio communautaire de la MRC de Maskinonge. Format: Fr var. ◆Stephane Carbonneau, gen mgr.

Lourdes-de-Blanc-Sablon

CFBS-FM— 1989: 89.9 mhz; 178 w. Hrs open: 7 AM-5 PM C.P. 8, G0G 1W0. Phone: (418) 461-2445. Fax: (418) 461-2425.E-mail: cfbs@globetrotter.qc.ca Licensee: Radio Blanc-Sablon inc. Format: Current affrs. ◆Vicki Driscoll, pres.

Magog

CIMO-FM— 1979: 106.1 mhz; 50 kw. Stereo. Hrs open: 6 AM-8 PM 1845 King W., #200, Sherbrooke, J1J 2E4. Phone: (819) 347-1414. Fax: (819) 347-1061. Web Site:www.radioenergie.com Licensee: Astral Media Radio Inc. Group owner: Astral Media Inc. Format: Top 40. Target aud: 18-34. ◆Nathalie Johnson, gen mgr; Isabelle Gagnon, sls dir; Anne-Marie Bercier, prom dir, progmg dir; Marc Toussaint, news dir; J.P. Maheu, chief of engrg.

Maliotenam

CKAU-FM— 1993: 104.5 mhz; 50 w. Hrs open: C.P. 338, Succ Bureau-chef, Sept-Iles, G4R 4K6. Phone: (418) 927-2909. Fax: (418) 927-2800.E-mail: dels@globetrotter.net Web Site:www.ckau.com Licensee: Corporation de Radio Kushapetsheken Apetuamiss Uashat. Format: Var. ◆Yves Rock, gen mgr; Reginald Thomas, adv dir; Mathieu McKenzie, engrg mgr.

Maniwaki

CBOF-1(AM)— Oct 22, 1973: 990 khz; 40 w, DA-1. Hrs open: Rebroadcasts CBOF-FM Ottawa.
Box 3220, Stn C, Ottawa, ON, K1Y 1E4. Phone: (613) 288-6000. Fax: (613) 288-6560. Web Site:cbc.ca Licensee: Canadian Broadcasting Corp. Format: Div. ◆Robert Rabinowitz, CEO; Denis Simard, gen mgr.

CFOR-FM— August 1994: 99.3 mhz; 2.4 kw. Hrs open: 24 139 Principale Sud., J9E 1Z8. Phone: (819) 441-0993. Fax: (819) 441-3488.E-mail: cfor993@b2b2c.ca Licensee: 9116-1299 Quebec Inc. (acq 4-22-02). Format: Rock music. News staff: 3. Target aud: 15-45. ◆Laure Voilquin, gen sls mgr; Rock Lepine, pres, gen mgr & progmg dir.

CHGA-FM— Nov 1980: 97.3 mhz; 2.8 kw. Hrs open: 24 163 Laurier Maniwaki, J9E 2K6. Phone: (819) 449-3959. Phone: (819) 449-5590. Fax: (819) 449-7331.E-mail: chga@bellnet.ca Web Site:www.chga.qc.ca Licensee: Radio Communautaire Type B. Format: Div, adult contemp. News staff: one; News: 15 hrs wkly. Spec prog: Class one hr, jazz 3 hrs, country 8 hrs, folk 5 hrs wkly. ◆Hubert Tremblay, pres; Lise Morissette, gen mgr; Lise Morisette, opns dir; Gaitam Bussiere, dev dir, gen sls mgr, mktg dir, progmg dir; Linda Lemieux, rgnl sls mgr; Kim Lacaille, mus dir; Georges Vasiloff, engrg dir; Michel Riel, news rptr.

Maniwaki (Kitigan Zibi Anishinabeg Reserve)

CKWE-FM— 1987: 103.9 mhz; 50 w. Hrs open: River Desert Indian Band, Box 309, Maniwaki, J9E 3C9. Phone: (819) 449-5170. Phone: (819) 449-5097. Fax: (819) 449-5673.E-mail: anita.tenasco@kza.qc.ca Licensee: Jean-Guy Whiteduck. Format: Talk, var, community news. ◆Anita Penasco, gen mgr, sls dir; Eleanor Whiteduck, opns mgr; Anita Tenasco, progmg dir.

Maria (Reserve)

CHRG-FM— 1991: 101.7 mhz; 10 w. Hrs open: 24 Box 118, G0C 1Y0. Secondary address: 120 School St. G0C 1Y0. Phone: (418) 759-8196. Fax: (418) 759-8196.E-mail: radio@globetrotter.net Web Site:www.chrgfm.com Licensee: Douglas Martin. Format: Country, oldies, var/div. ◆Douglas Martin, gen mgr, gen sls mgr; Wes Jones, progmg dir & news dir.

Mashteuiatsh (Pointe-Bleue)

CHUK-FM— 1996: 107.3 mhz; 50 w. Hrs open: 24 1491 rue Ouiatchouan, Mashteuiatsh, G0W 2H0. Phone: (418) 275-4684. Fax: (418) 275-7964.E-mail: chuk@chukfm.ca Web Site:www.chukfm.ca Licensee: Corporation Mediatique Teuehikan. Format: Montagnais, Fr. ◆Karl Clary, gen mgr; Jean Denis Gill, progmg dir.

Matagami

CHEF-FM— 2001: 99.9 mhz; 36 w. Hrs open: 110 boulevard Matagami, C.P. 39, J0Y 2A0. Phone: (819) 739-9990. Fax: (819) 739-6003. Licensee: Radio Matagami. Format: Fr, MOR. ◆M. Jean-Claude Constantineau, pres; Marie-Eve C. Gallant, gen mgr; Daniel Cliche, dev mgr; David Chabot, news dir.

Matane

CBGA-FM— 2004: 102.1 mhz; 42.93 kw. Hrs open: 5:30 AM-midnight 155 rue Saint-Sacrement, G4W 1Y9. Phone: (418) 562-0290. Phone: (418) 566-2322. Fax: (418) 562-3555.E-mail: communications_matane@radiocanada.ca Web Site:radio-canada.ca/gaspesie Licensee: CBC. Natl. Network: Premiere Chaine, . Format: CHR, div, news/talk. News staff: 5; News: 3 hrs wkly. Target aud: General. ◆Louis Pelletier, gen mgr; Johanne LaBrie, prom mgr; Richard Morisset, mus dir.

CHOE-FM— May 1991: 95.3 mhz; 30 kw. Stereo. Hrs open: 24 800 Ouest du Phare, G4W 1V7. Phone: (418) 562-8181. Fax: (418) 562-0778.E-mail: choe.routage@globetrotter.net Licensee: Les Communications Matane Inc. Population served: 20,000 Format: Light rock. Target aud: 18-34; young workers. ◆Kenneth Gagne, pres; Kenneth Gagne Jr., gen mgr, chief of opns, progmg dir; Michel Desrosiers, sls dir; Carol St-Pierre, news dir; Jacques Tremblay, chief of engrg.

CHRM-FM— April 2001: 105.3 mhz; 30 kw. Hrs open: 24 800 avenue du Phare Ouest, G4W 1V7. Phone: (418) 562-4141. Fax: (418) 562-0778. Licensee: Les Communications Matane inc. Format: MOR. ◆Kenneth Gagne, pres; Kenneth Gagne Jr., gen mgr, chief of opns, progmg dir; Michel Desrosiers, sls dir; Carol St-Pierre, news dir.

Mont-Laurier

CFLO-FM— 1995: 104.7 mhz; 10.98 kw. Stereo. Hrs open: Rebroadcasts CFLO FM-1 L'Annonciation 100%.
332 de la Madone, J9L 1R9. Phone: (819) 623-5610. Phone: (819) 623-6610. Fax: (819) 623-7406.E-mail: cflofm@cflo.ca Web Site:www.cflo.ca Licensee: Soneme Inc. Soneme Inc. (acq 1988). Format: Adult contemp, Fr. News: 3 hrs wkly. Target aud: 24-54. ♦Sylvain Lacasse, pres, gen mgr & stn mgr; Dominic Bell, progmg dir.

Montmagny

CFEL-FM— 1987: 102.1 mhz; 25.7 kw. Ant 443 ft TL: N46 56 21 W70 30 29. Stereo. Hrs open: 24 191 Chemen des Poirier, G5V 4L2. Secondary address: 5245 Boulevard De La Rive-Sud Levis, Levis G6V4ZA. Phone: (418) 248-1122. Fax: (418) 248-1951.E-mail: cfel@globetrotter.net Licensee: 5191991 B.C. Ltd. Group owner: Corus Entertainment Inc. (acq 3-24-2000; grpsl). Population served: 30,000 Format: Adult contemp. News staff: one. Target aud: 25-49. ♦Michel Montminy, gen mgr, opns VP; Rene' Nadeau, sls VP & progmg dir.

Montreal

CBF-FM— 1947: 95.1 mhz; 100 kw. 823 ft (Digital radio: 1458.048 mhz; 11.724 kw). Stereo. Hrs open: Box 6000, Quebec, H3C 3A8. Phone: (514) 597-6000.E-mail: auditore@radio-canada.ca Web Site:www.cbc.radio-canada.ca Licensee: CBC. Format: Class. ♦Sylvain LaFrance, VP; Bertrand Emond, gen mgr. Co-owned TV: CBFT(TV) affil.

CBFX-FM— 1998: 100.7 mhz; 100 kw. (Digital radio: 1458.048 mhz; 11.724 kw). Hrs open: Box 6000, H3C 3A8. Phone: (514) 597-6000. Fax: (416) 205-3714. Web Site:www.cbc.radio-canada.ca Licensee: CBC. Natl. Network: Espace Musique, . Format: Var. ♦Sylvain LaFrance, VP; Bertrand Emond, stn mgr, progmg dir; Alain Saulnier, news dir.

CBME-FM— 1998: 88.5 mhz; 16.9 kw. (Digital radio: 1458.048 mhz; 11.724 kw). Hrs open: 24 Box 6000, H3C 3A8. Phone: (514) 597-4444. Fax: (514) 597-4142. Web Site:www.radio-canada.ca Licensee: Canadian Broadcasting Corp. Natl. Network: CBC Radio One, . Format: News, current affrs. ♦Patricia Pleszczynska, stn mgr; Judith Bleier, opns mgr; Sally Caldwell, progmg dir & news dir.

CBM-FM— 1947: 93.5 mhz; 24.6 kw. 823 ft (Digital radio: 1458.048 mhz; 11.724 kw). Stereo. Hrs open: Box 6000, H3C 3A8. Phone: (514) 597-6000. Fax: (514) 597-4416.E-mail: info@cbc.ca/montreal Licensee: Canadian Broadcasting Corp. Format: Class. ♦Patricia Pleszczynska, stn mgr; Judith Bleier, opns mgr; Patricia Plesczynska, progmg dir. Co-owned TV: CBMT(TV) affil.

CFMB(AM)— Dec 21, 1962: 1280 khz; 50 kw-U, DA-2. TL: N45 19 31 W73 32 55. Hrs open: 24 35 York St., Westmount, H3Z 2Z5. Phone: (514) 483-2362. Fax: (514) 483-1362.E-mail: admin@cfmb.ca Web Site:www.cfmb.ca Licensee: CFMB Ltee. Population served: 4,000,000 Rgnl rep: Direct Format: Ethnic. News staff: 7; News: 35 hrs wkly.Andrew Mielewczyk, pres, gen sls mgr; A.M. St. Germain-Stanczykowski, exec VP; Luigi Valente, stn mgr, chief of engrg; Marcello Silveri, rgnl sls mgr; Ivana Bombardieri, prom mgr, pub affrs dir, women's int ed; Walter Centa, natl sls mgr & progmg dir; Tony Ferrara, mus dir; Nino Di Stefano, news dir, sports cmtr; Silvana Di Flavio, spec ev coord; Rinaldo Giordano, local news ed; Luigi Di Vito, reporter; Denise Agiman, disc jockey

CFQR-FM— November 1966: 92.5 mhz; 41.4 kw. Ant 979 ft Stereo. Hrs open: 24 Place Bonaventure, 800 de la Gauchetiere West, Suite 1100, H5A 1M1. Phone: (514) 767-9250. Web Site:www.925theq.com Licensee: Metromedia CMR Broadcasting Inc. Format: Adult contemp. Target aud: 25-54. ♦Mark Dickie, gen mgr; Kimberly Kieran, prom mgr; Brian DePoe, progmg dir.

CFZZ-FM—(Saint Jean-Iberville, 1992: 104.1 mhz; 1.35 kw. Hrs open: 24 104 rue Richelieu, St. Jean-Sur-Richelieu, J3B 6X3. Phone: (450) 346-0104. Fax: (450) 348-2274.E-mail: lstemarie@boomfm.astral.com Web Site:www.boomfm.com Licensee: Astral Media Radio inc. Group owner: Corus Entertainment Inc. (acq 5-30-2005; grpsl). Format: Oldies. ♦Leopold Stemarie, gen mgr; Luc Lalonde, mktg dir; Ghislaine Plourde, progmg dir, news dir.

CHOM-FM— July 16, 1963: 97.7 mhz; 47.1 kw. Ant 979 ft TL: N45 30 20 W73 35 32. (Digital radio: 1452.816 mhz; 11.724 kw). Stereo. Hrs open: 24 1411 Du Fort, 3rd Fl., H3H 2R1. Phone: (514) 989-2523. Fax: (514) 989-3868. Web Site:www.chom.com Licensee: Astral Media Radio G.P. Group owner: Standard Broadcasting Corp. (acq 10-29-2007; grpsl). Format: Classic Rock. ♦Bob Harris, opns mgr; Jacques Bolduc, gen sls mgr; Ray Scott, mus dir; Mike Bendixen, news dir; Mark Kavanagh, engrg dir.

CHOU(AM)— 2007: 1450 khz; 2 kw-U. TL: N45 29 45 W73 44 38. Hrs open: 24 11876 rue de Meulles, H4J 2E6. Phone: (514) 790-0002. Fax: (514) 745-3475.E-mail: info@crmo.ca Web Site:www.1450am.ca Licensee: 9015-2018 Quebec inc. Format: Ethnic, Arabic. ♦Antoine Karam, pres, gen mgr; Zeina Karam, progmg dir.

***CIBL-FM—** Apr 26, 1980: 101.5 mhz; 315 w. Stereo. Hrs open: 24 2nd Fl., 1691 Boul. Pie IX, H1V 2C3. Phone: (514) 526-2581. Fax: (514) 526-3583.E-mail: administration@cibl1015.com Web Site:www.cibl1015.com Licensee: Radio Communautaire Francophone de Montreal Inc. Population served: 2,500,000 Format: Music/talk. News staff: 4; News: 14 hrs wkly. Target aud: General. Spec prog: Black 13 hrs, class 4 hrs, jazz 14 hrs, reggae 4 hrs, world beat 8 hrs wkly. ♦Eric Lefebvre, gen mgr; Genevieve Dore, gen mgr & sls dir.

CINF(AM)—(Verdun, Nov 3, 1946: 690 khz; 50 kw-U, DA-2. Hrs open: 215 Jacques, Bureau 333, H2Y 1M6. Phone: (514) 849-1690. Fax: (514) 849-0733.E-mail: info@info690.com Web Site:www.info690.com Licensee: Metromedia CMR Montreal Inc. Group owner: Corus Entertainment Inc. (acq 1-26-01; grpsl). Format: News. ♦Pierre Arcand, pres; Maurice Tietolman, gen mgr; Christian Chalifour, sls dir; Marie Claude Baribault, prom dir; Yvon Vadnais, progmg dir; Kim Bickerdike, chief of engrg.

CINQ-FM— Jan 27, 1975: 102.3 mhz; 1.29 kw. Ant 180 ft Stereo. Hrs open: 24 5212 Boul. St. Laurent, H2T 1S1. Phone: (514) 495-2597. Fax: (514) 495-2429. Web Site:www.radiocentreville.com Licensee: Radio Centre-Ville Saint Louis Inc. Format: Multilingual, Fr, world music. News staff: one. Target aud: 25-54; Fr & multilingual. Spec prog: Sp 16, Portugese 13 hrs, Greek 13 hrs, Chinese 5 hrs, Haitian 6 hrs, Creole 12, English 16 hrs wkly. ♦Nadi Mobarak, pres; Evan Kapetanakis, stn mgr; Daniel Moreau, gen sls mgr, adv mgr; Miguel Greco (English), progmg mgr; Robert Laplante, news dir; Marc Provencher, chief of engrg.

CINW(AM)— November 1999: 940 khz; 50 kw-U. Hrs open: 24 215 St. Jacques, Suite 333, H2Y 1M6. Phone: (514) 849-0940. Fax: (514) 849-0733.E-mail: news@940news.com Web Site:www.940montreal.com Licensee: Metromedia CMR Broadcasting Inc. Group owner: Corus Entertainment Inc. (acq 1-26-2001; grpsl). Natl. Rep: Canadian Broadcast Sales,. Format: Oldies. Target aud: 35-54. ♦Pierre Beland, pres; Pierre Arcand, exec VP; Maurice Tietolman, gen mgr; George Weiss, sls VP, sls dir; Marie Claude Baribault, prom dir, prom mgr; Yven G. Vadnais, progmg dir & progmg mgr; Kim Bickerdike, chief of engrg.

CIRA-FM— 1994: 91.3 mhz; 36.2 kw. Hrs open: 24 4020 Rue St-Ambroise, #199, H4C 2C7. Phone: (514) 382-3913. Fax: (514) 858-0965.E-mail: cira@radiovm.com Web Site:www.radiovm.com Licensee: Radio Ville-Marie. Format: Relg, div music. News staff: 15. ♦Jean-Guy Roy, gen mgr; Gaston Pearson, sls dir, progmg dir; Renaude Gregoire, progmg dir; Mario Bard, news dir; Joe Pacheco, engrg mgr; Roger Landry, chief of engrg.

***CISM-FM—** March 1991: 89.3 mhz; 10 kw. Hrs open: Box 6128, C-1509, 2332 Edouard Montpetit, H3C 3J7. Phone: (514) 343-7511. Fax: (514) 343-2418. Web Site:www.cism893.ca Licensee: Communications du Versant Nord. Format: Alternative. ♦Jules Hedert, gen mgr; Patrick Gelinas, prom dir; Guillaume Vincenot, progmg dir; Martin Roussy, mus dir; Catherine Valois, engrg dir.

CITE-FM— May 20, 1977: 107.3 mhz; 42.9 kw. 700 ft (Digital radio: 1452.816 mhz; 11.724 kw). Stereo. Hrs open: 24 1717 Rene Levesque Est, H2L 4T9. Phone: (514) 845-2483. Fax: (514) 288-1073.E-mail: cite@rock-detente.com Web Site:www.rock-detente.com Licensee: Astral Media Radio Inc. Group owner: Astral Media Inc. (acq 4-19-2002; grpsl). Format: Adult contemp. Target aud: 25-49. ♦Jacques Parisien, pres; Sylvain Langlois, VP; Luc Tremblay, gen mgr.

CJAD(AM)— Dec 8, 1945: 800 khz; 50 kw-D, 10 kw-N, DA-2. (Digital radio: 1454.56 mhz; 1.4 kw in Montreal, 1.594 kw in Laval). Stereo. Hrs open: 24 1411 Rue du Fort, H3H 2R1. Phone: (514) 989-2523. Fax: (514) 989-3868. Web Site:www.cjad.com Licensee: Astral Media Radio G.P. Group owner: Standard Broadcasting Corp. (acq 10-29-2007; grpsl). Format: News/talk, info. News staff: 15; News: 14 hrs wkly. ♦Rob Braide, VP & gen mgr; Bob Harris, opns mgr; Jacques Bolduc, gen sls mgr; Lisa Faoco, prom mgr; Mike Bendixen, progmg mgr; Derek Conlon, news dir; Mark Kavanagh, engrg dir.

CJFM-FM— Oct 1, 1962: 95.9 mhz; 41.2 kw. 979 ft (Digital radio: 1454.56 mhz; 1.4 kw in Montreal, 1.594 kw in Laval). Stereo. Hrs open: 1411 Rue du Fort, H3H 2R1. Phone: (514) 989-2536. Fax: (514) 989-2554. Web Site:www.themix.com Licensee: Astral Media Radio G.P. Format: Adult contemp. ♦Matthew Wood, prom mgr; Bob Harris, progmg mgr; Ray Scott, mus dir; Mark Kavanagh, chief of engrg.

CJLO(AM)— 2007: 1690 khz; 1 kw-U. TL: N45 26 51 W73 37 57. Hrs open: 7141 Sherbrooke St. Ouest, Suite CC-430, H4B 1R6. Fax: (514) 848-7450. Web Site:www.cjlo.com Licensee: Concordia Student Broadcasting Corp. Format: Var. ♦Chris Quinnell, stn mgr; Amrew Weekes, gen sls mgr; Katie Seline, prom dir, progmg dir; Omar Husain, mus dir; Jessica Hemmerich, news dir.

CJPX-FM— June 25, 1998: 99.5 mhz; Stereo. Hrs open: Radio Classique Montreal Inc., Iles Notre Dame, Parc Jean-Drapeau, H3C 1A9. Phone: (514) 871-0995. Fax: (514) 871-0990. Web Site:www.radioclassique.ca Licensee: Radio Classique Montreal Inc. Format: Classical music. ♦Jean-Pierre Coallier, CEO; Pierre Barbeau, VP; Francois Pare, gen mgr; Sebastian Beaulieu, sls dir.

CJRS(AM)— 2007: 1650 khz; 1 kw-U. Hrs open: 4835 Cote St., Catherine Suite 2, H3W 1M4. Phone: (514) 738-4100. Web Site:www.radio-shalom.ca Licensee: Radio Chalom. Format: Relg. ♦Robert Levy, pres; Greg McLachlan, sls dir.

CJWI(AM)— 2002: 1610 khz; 1 kw-U. Hrs open: 3733 Jarry St. E., H1Z 2G1. Phone: (514) 287-1288. Fax: (514) 287-3299. Licensee: CPAM Radio Union.com inc. Format: Ethnic. ♦Jean Ernest Pierre, gen mgr.

CKAC(AM)— Sept 22, 1922: 730 khz; 50 kw-U, DA-1. (Digital radio: 1452.816 mhz; 11.724 kw). Hrs open: 24 1411 Peel St., BUR. 400, H3A 3L5. Phone: (514) 845-5151. Fax: (514) 845-2229. Web Site:www.ckac.com Licensee: 591991 B.C. Ltd. Group owner: Astral Media Inc. (acq 1-21-2005; grpsl). Format: Sports. News: 20 hrs wkly. Target aud: 35-54. ♦Sylvain Chamberland, gen mgr; Julie Gagnon, opns dir.

CKDG-FM— Apr 18, 2004: 105.1 mhz; 224 w. Ant 722 ft TL: N45 30 10 W73 35 46. Hrs open: 24 5899 Park Ave., H2V 4H4. Phone: (514) 273-2481. Fax: (514) 273-3707.E-mail: info@mikefm.ca Web Site:www.mikefm.ca Licensee: Canadian Hellenic Cable Radio Ltd. Wire Svc: Catholic News Service Format: English mainstream-ethnic. News staff: 3. Target aud: 25-54; mostly trilingual. ♦John Daperis, pres; Marie Griffiths, gen mgr, progmg dir; Chris Nucgaud, mus dir; Tony Choundalas, news dir; Jean Frechette, engrg mgr; Pota Gotsis, traf mgr.

CKGM(AM)— Dec 7, 1959: 990 khz; 50 kw-U. TL: N45 17 43 W73 43 20. (Digital radio: 1452.816 mhz; 11.724 kw). Hrs open: 1310 Greene Ave., H3Z 2B5. Phone: (514) 931-4487. Fax: (514) 931-4079. Web Site:www.team990.com Licensee: CTV Ltd. (group owner; (acq 6-22-2007; grpsl). Format: Sports. ♦Lee Hambleton, gen mgr; Wayne Bews, sls dir & natl sls mgr.

CKLX-FM— Dec 14, 2004: 91.9 mhz; 1.9 kw. Ant 633 ft TL: N45 30 12 W73 35 49. Hrs open: 200 avenue Laurier Ouest, Bureau 250, H2T 2N8. Phone: (514) 871-0919. Fax: (514) 871-8884. Web Site:www.planetjazz.ca Licensee: RNC MEDIA Inc. Group owner: Radio Nord Communications Inc. Format: Jazz and blues. Target aud: 35-64. ♦Raynald Briere, pres; Marc Giguere, VP; Rene Menard, sls dir; Dominic Plamondon, progmg dir; Annie Belanger, mus dir.

CKMF-FM— May 11, 1964: 94.3 mhz; 41.4 kw. 979 ft (Digital radio: 1452.816 mhz; 11.724 kw). Stereo. Hrs open: 24 1717 Rene Levesque E., H2L 4T9. Phone: (514) 529-3229. Fax: (514) 529-9308.E-mail: Lsabbatini@radio.astral.com Web Site:www.radioenergie.com Licensee: Astral Media Radio Inc. Group owner: Astral Media Inc. (acq 1-12-2000; grpsl). Natl. Network: Radiomutuel, . Format: CHR. News: one hr wkly. Target aud: 18-34. Spec prog: Disco. ♦Ian Greenburg, CEO; Jacques Parisien, chmn, pres; Luc Sabbatini, exec VP, opns mgr; Charles Benoit, VP; Luc Tremblay, gen mgr; Robert Latreille, stn mgr, engrg dir; Marie Josee Lefelbvre, natl sls mgr; Michel Tartif, rgnl sls mgr; Andre Allara, mktg dir; Johanne Cloutier, mktg mgr; Sylvain Legare, prom dir; Sylvain Simard, progmg dir.

CKOI-FM—(Verdun, 1953: 96.9 mhz; 307 kw. 712 ft Stereo. Hrs open: Prog sep from AM Phone: (514) 849-1690. Fax: (514) 849-0733.E-mail: info@info690.com Web Site:www.info690.com Licensee: Metromedia CMR Montreal Inc. Format: CHR. ♦Andre St. Amard, progmg dir.

***CKUT-FM—** November 1987: 90.3 mhz; Stereo. Hrs open: 24 3647 University, H3A 2B3. Phone: (514) 448-4041. Fax: (514) 398-8261.E-mail: admin@ckut.ca Web Site:www.ckut.ca Licensee: Radio McGill Inc. Population served: 3,500,000 Format: Div. News staff: one; News: 6 hrs wkly. Spec prog: Black 20 hrs, Fr 9 hrs, Sp 6 hrs, folk 3 hrs, gospel 2 hrs wkly. ♦Louise Burns, sls VP, mktg dir; Juliet Lammers, prom dir; Kristiana Clemmens, mus dir; Gretchen King, news dir; Marc Montanchez, chief of engrg.

Montreal (zone LaSalle)

CKVL-FM— Jan 8, 2008: 100.1 mhz; 250 w. TL: N45 25 51 W73 35 37. Hrs open: 24 7644 rue Edouard, Local 204, LaSalle, H8P 1T3. Phone: (514) 367-6338. Fax: (514) 367-4471.E-mail: info@radiolasalle.com Web Site:www.100-1fm.com Licensee: La radio communautaire de LaSalle. Format: Div. ♦Patrick Coutu, gen mgr.

Natashquan

CKNA-FM— Jan 30, 1983: 104.1 mhz; 6.56 kw. Hrs open: 29 chemin d'en Haut, G0G 2E0. Phone: (418) 726-3284. Phone: (418) 726-3240. Fax: (418) 726-3572.E-mail: ckna@globetrotter.net Web Site:pages.globetrotter.net/ckna/ Licensee: La Radio Communautaire CKNA Inc. Format: MOR. ♦Jean Jaques Landry, gen mgr, sls dir; Renee Lapierre, prom mgr, progmg VP & mus dir.

New Carlisle

CHNC-FM— Dec 23, 2008: 107.1 mhz; 3.8 kw. TL: N48 08 27 W65 14 35. Stereo. Hrs open: 24
Carleton, Chandler, Perce, Gaspe.
153 boulevard Gerard-D.-Levesque, G0C 1Z0. Secondary address: 153 boulevard Gerard-D.-Levesque G0C 1Z0. Phone: (418) 752-2215. Fax: (418) 752-6939.E-mail: radiochnc@globetrotter.net Web Site:www.radiohnc.com Licensee: Cooperative des travailleurs CHNC. Population served: 70,000 Format: Classic rock, country. News staff: 15. Target aud: General; adult. ♦Francis Remillard, gen mgr; Michel Morin, news dir.

Pikogan

CKAG-FM— 1993: 100.1 mhz; 3.738 kw. Ant 126 ft TL: N48 35 48 W78 07 05. Hrs open: 30 rue David Kistabish, J9T 3A3. Phone: (819) 727-3237. Fax: (819) 727-4432.E-mail: ckagfm@cableamos.com Licensee: Societe de Communication Ikito Pikogan Ltee. Format: Div. ♦Brenda Rankin, opns mgr; Brenda Rankin, gen sls mgr, prom dir; Brenda Rankin, progmg dir.

Plessisville

CKYQ-FM— 1996: 95.7 mhz; 1 kw. Hrs open: 24 Box 142, G6L 2Y6. Phone: (819) 362-3737. Fax: (819) 362-3414.E-mail: ckyq-fm@ivic.qc.ca Web Site:www.kyqfm.com Licensee: Societe CKYQ Radio Media Enr. Format: MOR. ♦Sebastian Doyon, news dir; Stephane Dion, pres, stn mgr, mktg dir, progmg dir & chief of engrg.

Pohenegamook

CFVD-FM-2— Sept 10, 1983: 92.1 mhz; 294 w. Stereo. Hrs open: Rebroadcasts CFVD-FM Degelis.
654 6th St. E., Degelis, G5T 1Y1. Phone: (418) 853-3370. Phone: (418) 853-2370. Fax: (418) 853-3321.E-mail: cfvd@fm95.ca Web Site:www.fm95.ca Licensee: Radio Degelis Inc. Format: Div, CHR. News staff: 10. Target aud: General. ♦Gilles Caron, pres, gen mgr & dev dir.

Port-Cartier

CIPC-FM— 1995: 99.1 mhz; 13 kw. Stereo. Hrs open: 24 52 Elie Roche Fort, G5B 1N2. Phone: (418) 766-6868. Fax: (418) 766-6870.E-mail: cipc991@globetrotter.net Web Site:www.laradioactive.com Licensee: Radio Port-Cartier Inc. Format: Top-40. ♦Yvan Beaulieu, gen mgr; Luc Boucher, gen sls mgr; Matthieu Pineau, progmg dir, progmg mgr; Elizabeth Chevalier, mus dir; Jean-Hugo Savard, news dir.

Port-Menier

CJBE-FM— Jan 1, 1988: 90.5 mhz; 88 w. Hrs open: C.P. 15, Port-Menier (Ile d'Anticosti), G0G 2Y0. Phone: (418) 535-0292. Fax: (418) 535-0292.E-mail: radioanticosti@hotmail.com Licensee: Radio Anticosti Inc. Format: Var. News staff: one. ♦Francine Ross, pres; Julie Lavallee, gen mgr & progmg dir.

Quebec

CBVE-FM— March 1979: 104.7 mhz; 100 kw. 411 ft Hrs open: 5:30-8:30 AM; 4-6 PM 888 Saint-Jean St., G1R 5H6. Phone: (418) 691-3613. Fax: (418) 691-3610.E-mail: quebecam@cbc.ca Web Site:www.cbc.ca Licensee: Canadian Broadcasting Corp. Natl. Network: CBC Radio One, . Format: News/talk, div. ♦Claude Saindon, gen mgr, progmg dir; Judith Bleier, opns dir; Peter Black, news rptr.

***CBV-FM—** 1974: 106.3 mhz; 100 kw. Ant 541 ft TL: N46 51 40 W71 04 46. Hrs open: 24 888 Rue Saint-Jean, GIR 5H6. Phone: (418) 656-8235. Fax: (418) 656-8842. Web Site:www.cbc.ca Licensee: Societe Radio Canada. Population served: 500,000 Natl. Network: Premiere Chaine, . Format: Div, news/talk. News: 15 hrs wkly. Target aud: General. ♦Robert Rabinovitch, pres & gen mgr; Norman LaCombe, news dir; Robert Jacques, engrg mgr. Co-owned TV: *CBVT-TV affil.

***CBVX-FM—** 1998: 95.3 mhz; 100 kw. 541 ft TL: N46 51 40 W71 04 46. Stereo. Hrs open: 888 Saint-Jean St., G1R 5H6. Phone: (418) 654-1341. Fax: (418) 656-8212. Web Site:www.cbc.ca Licensee: Societe Radio Canada. Natl. Network: Radio Canada, . Format: Class. Target aud: General. Spec prog: Jazz 16 hrs, news 7 hrs wkly. ♦Marleine Simard, gen mgr, progmg dir; Real Jean, opns mgr; Clodine Dorval, traf mgr.

CHIK-FM— Aug 1, 1982: 98.9 mhz; 41 kw. 1,355 ft TL: N46 49 22 W71 29 43. Hrs open: 900 d'Youville St., 1st Floor, G1R 3P7. Phone: (418) 687-9900. Fax: (418) 687-3106.E-mail: info@radioenergie.com Web Site:www.radioenergie.com Licensee: Astral Media Radio Inc. Group owner: Astral Media Inc. Format: Adult contemp. ♦Daniel Tremblay, gen mgr; Real Marcotte, sls dir; Julie Durand, prom dir; Jean Alexandre, progmg dir; Rejean Bergeron, news dir; Michel Duval, engrg dir.

CHOI-FM— Nov 1, 1949: 98.1 mhz; 40 kw. Ant 250 ft TL: N46 49 17 W71 29 48. Hrs open: 1134 Grande-Allee Ouest, Bureau 300, G1S 1E5. Phone: (418) 687-9810. Fax: (418) 682-8427. Web Site:www.choiradiox.com Licensee: RNC MEDIA Inc. Format: Fr alternative rock music. Target aud: 18-34; young adults.

CHRC(AM)— Apr 1, 1926: 800 khz; 50 kw-U, DA-1. Hrs open: 24 2136 Chemin Sainte-Foy, Sainte.-Foy, G1V 1R8. Phone: (418) 688-8080. Fax: (418) 670-1234. Web Site:www.chrc.com Licensee: 9183-9084 Quebec Inc. Group owner: Astral Media Inc. (acq 6-26-2008; C$282,177). Format: Sports. Target aud: 35 plus. Spec prog: French.

***CION-FM—** Sept 19, 1995: 90.9 mhz; 5.69 kw. 1,364 ft TL: N46 49 17 W71 29 48. Stereo. Hrs open: 8 (M-S); 16 (Su) 2511 Chemin Ste-Foy, Suite 200, G1V 1T7. Phone: (418) 659-9090. Phone: (418) 650-1572. Fax: (418) 650-3306.E-mail: cionfm@radiogalilee.qc.ca Licensee: Radio Galilee. Format: Relg, adult contemp, btfl mus. Target aud: General. ♦Alexandre St. Hilaire, pres, rsch dir; Denis Veilleux, gen mgr, progmg dir; Mario Blouin, mus dir; Jacques Fortin, news dir; Daniel Coulombe, engrg mgr.

CITF-FM— July 22, 1982: 107.5 mhz; 37.8 kw. 500 ft Stereo. Hrs open: 24 900 Dyouville St., 1st Fl., G1R 3P7. Phone: (418) 527-3232. Fax: (418) 687-3106.E-mail: info@rockdetente.com Web Site:www.rockdetente.com Licensee: Astral Media Radio Inc. Group owner: Astral Media Inc. (acq 4-19-2002; grpsl). Rgnl rep: Radio Plus. Format: Adult contemp. News staff: 2. Target aud: 25-54. ♦Michel Duval, CEO, chief of engrg; Daniel Tremblay, gen mgr; Suzie Baronet, sls dir; Julie Durand, prom dir; Marc Tanguay, progmg dir.

CJEC-FM— August 2003: 91.9 mhz; 14.45 kw. Hrs open: 1305 Chemin Ste-Foy, 4e etage, G1S 4Y5. Phone: (418) 688-0919. Fax: (418) 527-0919. Web Site:www.rythmefm.com Licensee: Cogeco Diffusion Inc. Group owner: Cogeco Radio-Television Inc. Format: Adult contemp. ♦Louis Audet, pres; Jean-Paul Lemire, gen mgr; Carole Vezina, sls dir; Daniel Plante, mktg dir, prom dir, progmg dir; Lilianne Randall, mus dir; Martin Perkins, engrg dir.

CJMF-FM— Sept 15, 1979: 93.3 mhz; 32.96 kw. Ant 1,275 ft Stereo. Hrs open: 24 1305 Chemin Ste-Foy, 4e etage, G1S 4Y5. Phone: (418) 687-9330. Fax: (418) 687-0211.E-mail: commentaire@cjmf.com Web Site:www.le933.com Licensee: Cogeco Diffusion Inc. Group owner: Cogeco Radio-Television Inc. (acq 11-87; $8 million). Format: Talk, classic rock. News staff: 0; News: 5 hrs wkly. Target aud: 25-54; mostly males. ♦Louis Audet, pres; Jean-Paul Lemire, gen mgr.

CJSQ-FM— July 25, 2007: 92.7 mhz; 2.1 kw. TL: N46 49 22 W71 29 41. Stereo. Hrs open: Radio-Classique Quebec, 2525 BLVD Laurier, G1V 2L2. Phone: (418) 650-9270. Fax: (418) 650-5735. Web Site:www.radioclassique.ca Licensee: 9147-2605 Quebec inc. Format: Classical music. ♦Pierre Barbeau, gen mgr.

CKIA-FM— Oct 31, 1984: 88.3 mhz; 350 w. 700 ft TL: N46 48 28 W71 12 57. Hrs open: 24 600 Cote d'Abraham, G1R 1A1. Phone: (418) 529-9026. Fax: (418) 529-4156.E-mail: ckiafm@meduse.org Web Site:www.ckiafm.org Licensee: Radio Basse-Ville Inc. Format: Classic rock, country, div, world music. News staff: one; News: 2 hrs wkly. Target aud: 18-35; general. Spec prog: Class 3 hrs, jazz 4 hrs, Sp 4 hrs, Haitian 2 hrs, African one hr wkly. ♦Ernst Caze, gen mgr; Max Raneau, gen sls mgr; Bryan St. Louis, progmg dir, news dir; Denis Roberge, chief of engrg.

***CKRL-FM—** Feb 15, 1973: 89.1 mhz; 1.4 kw. 700 ft TL: N46 48 27 W71 13 02. Stereo. Hrs open: 24 405 3rd Ave., G1L 2W2. Phone: (418) 640-2575. Fax: (418) 640-1588.E-mail: ckrl@ckrl.qc.ca Web Site:www.ckrl.qc.ca Licensee: CKRL MF 89.1 Inc. Format: Adult contemp, jazz, class, rock. News staff: one. Spec prog: Sp 2 hrs, It 2 hrs, Black 6 hrs, Arab 3 hrs wkly. ♦Dany Fortin, gen mgr & sls dir; Daniel Deslauriers, mktg dir; Bastien Gagnon La France, progmg dir; Daniel Marcoux, mus dir.

Radisson

CIAU-FM— 1996: 103.1 mhz; 17 w. Hrs open: Box 285, J0Y 2X0. Secondary address: 143 rue Jolliet J0Y 2X0. Phone: (819) 638-7033. Phone: (819) 638-1031. Fax: (819) 638-7033.E-mail: ciaufm@lino.com Web Site:www.ciaufm.com Licensee: Radio communautaire de Radisson (acq 4-23-2004). Population served: 1,000 Format: Var. News staff: one; News: 3 hrs wkly. Spec prog: Fr 8 hrs, Jazz 3 hrs wkly. ♦Eric Hamel, pres, dev dir, sls dir; Patrice Maltais, stn mgr, opns dir, prom dir, adv dir & progmg dir.

Restigouche

CHRQ-FM— 1991: 106.9 mhz; 31 w. Hrs open: Box 180, G0C 2R0. Phone: (418) 788-2449. Fax: (418) 788-2653.E-mail: chrq1069@globetrotter.net Licensee: Gespegewag Communications Society. Format: English-language & Micmac-language community radio. News staff: 5; News: one hr wkly. Community members all ages. ♦Sandra Bulmer, stn mgr; Chad Gedeon, rgnl sls mgr; Karen Duguay, prom mgr; Steve Clement, progmg mgr.

Rimouski

***CBRX-FM—** Feb 28, 1959: 101.5 mhz; 50 kw. 931 ft Stereo. Hrs open: 273 rue St-Jean Baptiste Ouest, G5L 4J8. Phone: (418) 723-2217. Fax: (418) 723-6126.E-mail: nouvelles_rimouski@canada.ca Licensee: Canadian Broadcasting Corp. Natl. Network: Espace Musique, . Format: Class, jazz, talk. ♦Bernard Labarge, pres, news dir; Bernard Lebarge, gen mgr; Bernard Labarbe, progmg dir.

CFYX-FM— October 2007: 93.3 mhz; 18.197 kw. TL: N48 27 53 W68 12 32. Hrs open: 158 Saint-Germain Ouest, G5L 4B7. Phone: (418) 722-2848.E-mail: direction@cfyx93.com Web Site:www.cfyx93.com Licensee: Radio Rimouski Inc. (acq 12-20-2006). Format: Classic rock. ♦Pierre-Yves Renaud, gen mgr; Rene Girard, sls dir.

CIKI-FM— Feb 14, 1988: 98.7 mhz; 76 kw. Stereo. Hrs open: 24 Prog sep from AM 875 Boul. St. Germain Ouest, G5L 3T9. Phone: (418) 723-2323. Fax: (418) 722-7508.E-mail: ciki@pqm.net Web Site:www.ciki.fm Licensee: Astral Media Radio Inc. Group owner: Corus Entertainment Inc. (acq 5-30-2005; grpsl). Format: AOR. ♦Bertrand Bellavance, gen mgr; Jean Fournier, opns mgr, chief of engrg; Ghislain Desgardins, sls dir; Francois La Fond, progmg dir; Alain Rivard, mus dir; Martin Bressard, news dir.

CJBR-FM— 2000: 89.1 mhz; 19.4 kw. Hrs open: 273 rue St-Jean Baptiste Ouest, G5L 4J8. Phone: (418) 723-2217. Fax: (418) 723-6126.E-mail: nouvelles_rimouski@radiocanada.ca Licensee: Canadian Broadcasting Corp. Format: MOR, adult contemp, news/talk. Spec prog: Fr. ♦Bernard Labarge, gen mgr & news dir.

CJOI-FM— Oct 22, 2000: 102.9 mhz;; 33.6 kw. Hrs open: 24 875 Boul. St. Germain Ouest, G5L 3T9. Phone: (418) 723-2323. Fax: (418) 722-7508.E-mail: cjoi@pqm.net Web Site:www.cjoi.fm Licensee: Astral Media Radio inc. Group owner: Corus Entertainment Inc. (acq 5-30-2005; grpsl). Format: MOR. ♦Bertrand Bellavance, gen mgr; Jean Fournier, opns mgr, chief of engrg; Francois La Fond, progmg dir; Martin Bressard, news dir.

Rimouski-Mont Joli

CKMN-FM— June 4, 1990: 96.5 mhz; 6.4 kw. TL: N48 22 32 W68 35 43. Stereo. Hrs open: 24 323 Montee Industrielle, Rimouski, G5M 1A7. Phone: (418) 722-2566. Fax: (418) 724-7815.E-mail: ckmn-fm@cgocable.ca Licensee: La Radio Communautaire du Comte. Wire Svc: CNW Broadcast Format: Adult contemp, CHR, country. News staff: 5. Target aud: 25-55; general. Spec prog: Oldies 3 hrs, classical 3 hrs wkly. ♦Daniel Menard, pres; Gabriel Dumont, exec VP; Reynald LaPierre, mktg dir; Renie Langlois, prom dir, progmg dir; Michel Vallee, chief of engrg.

Riviere au Renard

CJRE-FM— 1979: 97.9 mhz; 56 w. 594 ft Hrs open: 24 162 Jacques Cartier, Gaspe, G4X 1M9. Phone: (418) 368-3511. Fax: (418) 368-1663. Licensee: Radio Gaspesie Inc. Format: MOR. ♦Jacques Chartier, gen mgr; Paul Mainville, sls dir; Richard O'Leary, news dir; Yvan Dupuis, engrg dir.

Riviere du Loup

CIBM-FM— 1966: 107.1 mhz; 100 kw. Ant 244 ft Hrs open: 24 64 Hotel de Ville, G5R 1L5. Phone: (418) 867-1071. Fax: (418) 862-7704. Web Site:www.cibm107.com Licensee: CIBM Mont-Bleu. Natl. Network: Radiomedia, . Format: Pop rock. ♦Guy Simard, gen mgr; Renee Giard, gen sls mgr, prom dir; Daniel St. Pierre, progmg dir; Stephane Gemdrom, news dir; Clement LaVoie, engrg dir.

CIEL-FM— Dec 15, 1994: 103.7 mhz; 60 kw. Ant 1,050 ft TL: N47 34 53 W69 22 20. Hrs open: 64 Hotel-de-Ville, G5R 1L5. Phone: (418) 862-8241. Fax: (418) 862-7704. Web Site:www.ciel103.com Licensee: Radio CJFP (1986) Ltee. Format: Adult contemp. ♦Guy Simard, pres, gen mgr; Renee Giard, sls dir, natl sls mgr, rgnl sls mgr, mktg dir; Christian Duchesne, prom dir; Daniel St. Pierre, progmg dir, mus dir, asst music dir; Stephane Gemdrom, news dir; Clement LaVoie, engrg dir.

Roberval

CHRL-FM— March 1, 2002: 99.5 mhz; 15.031 kw. Ant 490 ft TL: N48 26 25 W72 06 47. Hrs open: 24 568 Blvd. St. Joseph, G8H 2K6. Phone: (418) 275-1831. Fax: (418) 275-2475.E-mail: chrl@antenne6.com Licensee: Groupe Radio Antenne 6 inc. Group owner: Group Radio Antenne 6 Inc. Format: Div, info, music. News staff: one; News: 20 hrs wkly. Target aud: General; mainly adults. ♦Marc Andre' Levesque, gen mgr; Lewis Gagnon, sls dir; Louis Arcand, progmg dir, news dir.

Rouyn-Noranda

CHIC-FM— 2003: 88.7 mhz; 300 w. Hrs open: C.P. 2185, J9X 5A6. Phone: (819) 797-4242. Fax: (819) 797-3803. Licensee: Communications CHIC (C.H.I.C.). Format: Fr, Christian music. ♦Andre Curadeau, gen mgr; Vic Cimon, stn mgr & opns dir; Jocelyn Cote, sls dir, progmg dir.

CHOA-FM— Sept 21, 1990: 96.5 mhz; 55 kw. 600 ft Stereo. Hrs open: 380 Ave. Murdoch, J9X 1G5. Phone: (819) 762-0741. Fax: (819) 762-2280. Licensee: RNC MEDIA Inc. (group owner). Format: Adult contemp. Target aud: 25-54. ♦Pierre R. Brosseau, CEO; Raynald Briere, pres; Andre Houle, gen mgr; Nancy Deschenes, gen sls mgr; Robert Ashby, progmg dir; Gerald Landry, chief of engrg. Co-owned TV: CFEM-TV, CKRN-TV affils.

CHUN-FM— 2005: 98.3 mhz; 490 w. TL: N48 18 05 W79 03 08. Hrs open: 1016 rue Wabanonic, Lac Simon, J0Y 3M0. Phone: (819) 736-2555. Phone: (819) 797-5316 (studio).E-mail: chun98.3@tlb.sympatico.ca Web Site:www.chunfm.ca Licensee: Radio communautaire MF Lac Simon Inc. Format: Country rock. ♦Noe Mitchell, gen mgr.

CJMM-FM— June 17, 1988: 99.1 mhz; 3.5 kw. Ant 200 ft Stereo. Hrs open: 24 191, avenue Murdoch, J9X 1E3. Phone: (819) 797-2566. Fax: (819) 797-1664.E-mail: mtrottier@radioenergie.astral.com Web Site:www.radioenergie.com Licensee: Astral Media Radio Inc. Group owner: Astral Media Inc. (acq 1-12-2000; grpsl). Format: CHR. News staff: one; News: 5 hrs wkly. Target aud: 18-44. ♦Marlene Trottier, gen mgr; Chantel Massicotte, sls dir; Ian Clermont, prom dir, prom mgr, progmg dir, mus dir; Fanny-Garance Carrier, news dir; Mathieu Barrette, engrg mgr.

Saguenay

CJAB-FM— May 25, 1979: 94.5 mhz; 44.2 kw. Stereo. Hrs open: 24 267 rue Racine Est., 2ieme etage, Chicoutimi, G7H 1S5. Phone: (418) 545-9450. Fax: (418) 543-7968. Web Site:www.radioenergie.com Licensee: Astral Media Radio Inc. Group owner: Astral Media Inc. (acq 8-21-92). Natl. Network: Radiomutuel, . Format: Pop. ♦Richard Turcotte, gen mgr; Carol Tremblay, sls dir; Katia Boivin, progmg dir; Jean-Francois Cote, news dir; Stephane Villeneuve, engrg mgr.

CKRS-FM— 2007: 98.3 mhz; 51 kw. TL: N48 22 15 W71 10 20. Stereo. Hrs open: 121 rue Racine Est, Chicoutimi, G7H 5G4. Phone: (418) 545-2577. Fax: (418) 545-9186. Web Site:www.ckrs.ca Licensee: 591991 B.C. Ltd. Format: Talk. News staff: six. Target aud: 25-54. ♦Daniel Larocque, gen mgr.

Saguenay (zone La Baie)

CKGS-FM— Mar 19, 2009: 105.5 mhz; 6 kw. TL: N48 21 08 W70 53 56. Hrs open: 169 6th St., Saguenay, G7B 0A3. Phone: (418) 544-2105.E-mail: info@ckgsfm.com Web Site:www.ckgsfm.com Licensee: Carl Gilbert. Format: Pop rock. ♦Carl Gilbert, gen mgr.

Saint Augustin

CJAS-FM— 1992: 93.5 mhz; 100 w. Hrs open: Rebroadcasts VOCM(AM) St. John's, NF weekends. Box 100, 558 rue Principal, St. Augustine, QC, G0G 2R0. Phone: (418) 947-2239. Fax: (418) 947-2664.E-mail: cjasradio@gmail.com Web Site:www.cjasradio.piczo.com Licensee: La Radio Communautaire de Riviere St-Augustin Inc. Format: Adult contemp. ♦Laurette Gallibois, gen mgr, sls dir, mktg dir; Maria Shattler, progmg dir; Lindsey Durepos, mus dir; Rachel Bilodeau, news dir.

Saint Constant

CJMS(AM)— May 1999: 1040 khz; 10 kw-D, 5 kw-N. Hrs open: 24 143 rue St-Pierre, J5A 2G9. Phone: (514) 990-2567. Fax: (450) 632-0528.E-mail: cjms@videotron.ca Web Site:www.cjms10.com Licensee: 3553230 Canada Inc. (acq 3-29-01). Natl. Network: Radio Unica, . Format: Country. News staff: 2. ♦Alex Azoulay, pres.

Saint Gabriel-de-Brandon

CFNJ-FM— Aug 10, 1985: Stn currently dark. 99.1 mhz; 9.75 kw. Ant 1,400 ft TL: N46 20 56 W73 29 49. Hrs open: 24 245 Beauvilliers, J0K 2N0. Phone: (450) 835-3437. Phone: (450) 835-3438. Fax: (450) 835-3581.E-mail: droch@intermonde.net Web Site:www.cfnj.net Licensee: Radio Nord-Joli Inc. Format: MOR. News staff: 2; News: 14 hrs wkly. Spec prog: Black one hr, class 2 hrs, C&W 4 hrs, jazz 2 hrs. ♦Denis Roch, gen mgr.

Saint Georges

CHJM-FM— June 22, 1987: 99.7 mhz; 100 kw. 350 ft Stereo. Hrs open: 24 C.P. 100, Saint Georges-de-Beauce, G5Y 5C4. Secondary address: 11760 Third Ave, Saint Georges-de-Beauce G5Y 5C4. Phone: (418) 227-0997. Phone: (418) 228-5535. Fax: (418) 228-0096.E-mail: adminrb@cgocable.ca Web Site:www.mix997.com Licensee: Radio Beauce Inc. (acq 10-24-02; C$432,000 with CKRB-FM Saint Georges-de-Beauce). Format: Rock. News staff: one; News: 4 hrs wkly. Target aud: 18-35. ♦Guy Simard, pres; Claude Girard, sls dir; Jacques Goulet, natl sls mgr; Maurice Marcotte, gen mgr & prom mgr; Marcel Rancourt, mus dir; Gaston Guay, chief of engrg.

Saint Georges-de-Beauce

CKRB-FM— October 1953: 103.5 mhz; 17 kw. Stereo. Hrs open: 24 C.P. 100, G5Y 5C4. Secondary address: 11760 Third Ave. G5Y 5C4. Phone: (418) 228-1460. Phone: (418) 228-5535. Fax: (418) 228-0096.E-mail: adminrb@cgocable.ca Web Site:www.coolfm.biz Licensee: Radio Beauce Inc. (acq 10-24-02; C$432,000 with CHJM-FM Saint Georges). Format: Adult contemp. News staff: 2; News: 11 hrs wkly. Target aud: 35 plus. ♦Guy Simard, pres; Maurice Marcotte, gen mgr, prom mgr; Claude Girard, sls dir; Jacques Goulet, natl sls mgr; Marcel Rancourt, mus dir; Suzanne Bougie, news dir; Gaston Guay, chief of engrg.

Saint Hilarion

CIHO-FM— Oct 10, 1986: 96.3 mhz; Hrs open: 24 315 Cartier Nord, G0A 3V0. Phone: (418) 457-3333. Fax: (418) 457-3518.E-mail: ciho@charlevoix.net Licensee: Radio MF Charlevoix Inc. Format: MOR. Spec prog: Class 2 hrs, jazz 2 hrs wkly. ♦Gervais Desbiens, gen mgr; Rene Belanger, adv dir; Pierre Beauchesne, progmg dir, engrg mgr; Dave Kid, news dir.

Saint Hyacinthe

CFEI-FM— 1988: 106.5 mhz; 3 kw. Hrs open: 24 855 rue Ste. Marie, J2S 4R9. Phone: (450) 774-6486. Fax: (450) 774-7785.E-mail: jhebert@boomfm.astral.com Web Site:www.boomfm.com Licensee: Astral Media Radio Inc. Group owner: Astral Media Inc. (acq 8-13-2001). Format: 60s, 70s, Oldies, news. ♦Jacques Parisien, pres; Pierre Demondehare, gen mgr & opns mgr; Leopold St. Marie, sls dir; Jean-Francois Hebert, progmg dir; Andre Lalier, mus dir.

Saint Jean-Iberville

CFZZ-FM—Licensed to Saint Jean-Iberville. See Montreal

Saint Jerome

CFND-FM— Dec 29, 2008: 101.9 mhz; 49 w. Ant 78 ft TL: N45 47 04 W73 59 21. Hrs open: Ecole Notre-Dame, 581 rue Ouimet, J5Z 1R3. Phone: (450) 432-4472. Fax: (450) 432-8694.E-mail: radionotredame @edu.csrdn.qc.ca Licensee: Amie du Quartier. Format: Talk. ♦Marc Bourcier, gen mgr.

CIME-FM— Mar 25, 1977: 103.9 mhz; 39.3 kw. Stereo. Hrs open: 24 120 Delagare St., J7Z 2C2. Phone: (450) 431-2463. Fax: (450) 565-9755.E-mail: ventes@cime.fm Licensee: Diffusion Metromedia CMR Inc. Group owner: Corus Entertainment Inc. (acq 1-26-01; grpsl). Format: Adult contemp. News staff: 2. Target aud: 25-54; Adult. ♦John Cassidy, pres; Gilbert Cerat, gen mgr; Etienne Gregoire, mktg dir; Ghislaiu Plourde, progmg dir; Jean Francois Rousseau, news dir.

Saint Pamphile

CJDS-FM— Dec 7, 2001: 94.7 mhz; 24 w. Hrs open: 109 Rue de l'Eglise, G0R 3X0. Phone: (418) 356-1303. Fax: (418) 356-2586.E-mail: cjdsradio@globetrotter.net Licensee: 3819914 Canada inc. Format: MOR. ♦Jean-Claude Dignard, pres & gen mgr; Claire Soulieres, opns mgr, sls dir; Ann Dignard, dev dir, progmg dir; J. C. Dignard, pub affrs dir.

Saint Remi

*CHOC-FM— 1999: 104.9 mhz; 250 w. Hrs open: 93 Ruelachapelle Est, J0L 2L0. Phone: (450) 454-5500. Fax: (450) 454-9435.E-mail: studio@chocfm.com Web Site:www.chocfm.com Licensee: Radio Communautaire Intergeneration Jardin du Quebec. Format: Community radio. News staff: one; News: 10 hrs wkly. ♦Sylvain Remillard, pres; Richard Vegneault, gen mgr.

Sainte Anne des Monts

CBGN(AM)— 1972: 1340 khz; 1 kw-D, 250 w-N. Hrs open: 155 St. Sacrament St., Matane, G4W 1Y9. Phone: (418) 562-0290. Fax: (418) 566-6068. Licensee: CBC. (acq 9-1-72). Format: Talk, news. ♦Louis Pelletier, gen mgr.

CJMC-FM— March 1996: 100.3 mhz; 2.51 kw. Hrs open: 24 170 Boul. Ste. Anne, G4V 1N1. Phone: (418) 763-5523. Fax: (418) 763-7211. Web Site:cjmc@quebectel.com Licensee: Radio du Golfe Inc. Format: MOR. Spec prog: Class 2 hrs, western 2 hrs wkly. ♦Jacques Vallee, pres, opns dir, sls dir, mktg dir; Olivier Vallee, prom dir; Stephane Cyr, progmg dir, mus dir, news dir & chief of engrg.

Sainte Foy

*CHYZ-FM— Jan 29, 1997: 94.3 mhz; 6 kw. Stereo. Hrs open: 24 Local 0236, Pavillon Pollack, Cite Universitaire, Suite 023, G1K 7P4. Phone: (418) 656-2131 ext. 4595. Phone: (418) 656-7007. Fax: (418) 656-3660.E-mail: chyz@public.ulaval.ca Web Site:www.chyz.ca Licensee: Radio Campus Laval. Population served: 600,000 Format: Fr, div, techno/electronica. News staff: 4; News: 10 hrs wkly. Target aud: 18-30; univ students. Spec prog: Hip-hop/rap 15 hrs wkly. ♦Jean-Philippe Lessard, gen mgr.

Sainte-Marie-de-Beauce

CHEQ-FM— Nov 29, 1998: 101.5 mhz; 26 kw. Ant 214 ft TL: N46 23 24 W70 59 03. Hrs open: 1068 boul. Vachon N., Suite 101, G6E 1M6. Phone: (418) 387-1013. Fax: (418) 387-3757.E-mail: info@cheqfm.qc.ca Web Site:www.cheqfm.qc.ca Licensee: 9174-8004 Quebec Inc. (acq 8-16-2000). Format: MOR, adult contemp. ♦Michel Lambert, pres; Mario Paquin, gen mgr, opns mgr.

Senneterre

CIBO-FM— 1982: 100.5 mhz; Hrs open: 24 C.P. 1150, J0Y 2M0. Phone: (819) 737-2222. Fax: (819) 737-8599.E-mail: cibofm@yahoo.ca Licensee: Radio communautaire M.F. de Senneterre Inc. Population served: 5,600 Format: Community. ♦Guy Bilodeau, pres & gen mgr.

Sept-Iles

*CBSI-FM— Nov 1, 1982: 98.1 mhz; 96.7 kw. 350 ft Hrs open: 24 350 rue Smith, bur. 30, G4R 3X2. Phone: (418) 968-0720. Phone: (800) 463-1731. Fax: (418) 968-9219. Fax: (418) 962-1344.E-mail: cbsi@radio-canada.ca Web Site:www.radio-canada.ca/cote-nord Licensee: CBC. Population served: 8,000 Format: Div, educ, talk. Target aud: Over 30. ◆Pierre Lafreniere, stn mgr.

CKCN-FM— December 1998: 94.1 mhz; 4.88 kw. Hrs open: 437 Arnaud St., G4R 3B3. Phone: (418) 962-3838. Fax: (418) 968-6662.E-mail: dyr@globetrotter.net Web Site:www.ckcnfm.com Licensee: Radio Sept-Iles Inc. Format: Adult contemp, news/talk. News: 16 hrs wkly. Target aud: 25-54. Spec prog: Country 8 hrs wkly. ◆Pierre Bergeron, pres & gen mgr; Dominique Marquis, stn mgr.

Shawinigan

CFUT-FM— Feb 7, 2005: 91.1 mhz; 5 w. Hrs open: 540 Broadway Ave., G9N 1M3. Phone: (819) 537-0911.E-mail: info@radioshawinigan.com Web Site:www.radio911.ca Licensee: La radio campus communautaire francophone de Shawinigan inc. Format: Fr var. ◆Pierre-Yves Rousselle, progmg dir.

CKSM(AM)— Apr 30, 1951: 1220 khz; 10 kw-D, 2.5 kw-N, DA-2. Hrs open:
Rebroadcasts CHLN(AM) Trois Rivieres 100%.
Phone: (819) 378-1023. Fax: (819) 378-1360. Licensee: Astral Media Radio Inc. Group owner: Astral Media Inc. Format: Adult contemp, news/talk, sports. Target aud: 40-55. ◆Jean Martin, gen mgr.

Sherbrooke

CFAK-FM— 2003: 88.3 mhz; 490 w. Hrs open: Radio CFAK, 2500 boul. de Universite, local 116, J1K 2R1. Phone: (819) 821-8000 ext 2693. Fax: (819) 821-7930.E-mail: dq@cfak.qc.ca Web Site:www.cfak.qc.ca Licensee: Comite de la radio etudiante universitaire de Sherbrooke (CREUS). Format: Fr. ◆Steve Bazinet, gen mgr.

CFGE-FM— July 2004: 93.7 mhz; 3.8 kw. TL: Fleurimont. Hrs open: 3720 boulevard Industriel, J1L 1Z9. Phone: (819) 822-0937. Fax: (819) 822-2112. Web Site:www.rythmefm.com/estrie Licensee: Cogeco Diffusion inc. Format: Adult contemp. News staff: one. Target aud: 25-54. ◆Michel Cloutier, gen mgr; Marc Fabi, gen sls mgr; Dominc D'Anjou, progmg dir.

CFLX-FM— 1984: 95.5 mhz; 1 kw. TL: N45 22 50 W71 54 51. Stereo. Hrs open: 24 67 N Wellington St., J1H 5A9. Phone: (819) 566-2787. Fax: (819) 566-7331.E-mail: commentaire@cflx.qc.ca Web Site:www.cflx.qc.ca Licensee: Radio communautaire de l'Estrie. Population served: 100,000 Format: News/talk, div, Fr. News staff: 1; News: 10 hrs wkly. Target aud: 18-35; college degree. Spec prog: Class 7 hrs, jazz 8 hrs, Sp 3 hrs wkly. ◆Jean Comtois, pres; Bruno Guillemette, gen mgr.

CHLT-FM— 2008: 107.7 mhz; 24 kw. Ant 298 ft TL: N45 26 28 W72 00 35. Hrs open: 4020 boul. de Portland, J1L 2V6. Phone: (819) 563-6363. Fax: (819) 566-4222. Licensee: 591991 B.C. Ltd. Format: Talk. ◆Jocelyn Proulx, gen mgr.

CIMO-FM—See Magog

CITE-FM-1— September 1962: 102.7 mhz; 92.8 kw. Ant 1,851 ft Stereo. Hrs open: 1845 King West, Suite 200, J1J 2E4. Phone: (819) 566-6655. Fax: (819) 566-1011. Licensee: Astral Media Radio Inc. (acq 4-19-2002; grpsl). Format: Adult contemp. ◆Natalie Johnson, gen mgr.

CJMQ-FM— 2004: 88.9 mhz; 1.67 kw. Stereo. Hrs open: 6am-12am 2600 College St, J1M 0C8. Phone: (819) 822-9600, EXT. 2689. Phone: (819) 822-9600. Fax: (819) 822-9682.E-mail: cjmqnews@yahoo.ca Web Site:www.cjmq.fm Licensee: Radio Bishop's Inc. Population served: 170,000 Format: Community. News: 5 hrs wkly. Target aud: General; campus & community. ◆David Teasdale, stn mgr; Joel Heath, prom dir; Maureen Teasdale, progmg dir; Zaheed Bardai, mus dir; David Humble, engrg dir; Wayne Stacey, chief of engrg.

CKOY-FM— 2004: 104.5 mhz; 1.3 kw. TL: N45 23 48 W71 49 52. Hrs open: 4020 Boul. Portland, J1L 2V6. Phone: (819) 829-1045. Fax: (819) 829-1315.E-mail: info@grock.fm Web Site:ckoy.ca Licensee: 591991 B.C. Ltd. Format: Fr, rock. ◆Jocelyn Proulx, gen mgr.

Sorel

CJSO-FM— Sept 27, 1989: 101.7 mhz; 3.5 kw. 327 ft Hrs open: 24 100 boul. Couillard Despres, Sorel-Tracy, J3P 5C1. Phone: (450) 743-2772. Fax: (450) 743-0293.E-mail: cjso@cjso.qc.ca Web Site:www.cjso.qc.ca Licensee: Radio Diffusion Sorel-Tracy Inc. (acq 4-21-95). Format: Soft rock. News staff: 2; News: 5 hrs wkly. Spec prog: Class 2 hrs wkly. ◆Claude St. Germain, gen mgr; Jean Lemay, progmg dir; Valerie Ferland, mus dir; Jean-Marc Lebeau, news dir; Marie-Theresee Thibeault, traf mgr; Yanick Levesque, sports cmtr; Andre Champagne, disc jockey.

Tete-a-la-Baleine

CJTB-FM— 2003: 93.1 mhz; 49 w. TL: N50 42 12 W59 19 30. Hrs open: C.P. 138, G0G 2W0. Phone: (418) 242-2974. Licensee: Radio Communautaire Tete-a-la-Baleine. Format: Fr. ◆Bertha Monger, pres; Mireille Monger, gen mgr.

Thetford Mines

CFJO-FM— July 15, 1989: 97.3 mhz; 100 kw. Ant 270 ft Hrs open: 24 55 St. Jean Baptiste, Victoriaville, G6P 6T3. Secondary address: 327 Rue Labbe G6G 5S3. Phone: (418) 338-1009. Phone: (819) 752-2785. Fax: (418) 338-0386. Fax: (819) 752-3182. Web Site:www.o973.com Licensee: Reseau des Appalaches (FM) Ltee. Group owner: Gestion Appalaches inc. Population served: 87,913 Natl. Rep: Target Broadcast Sales,. Format: Classic rock, AOR. News staff: 15. Target aud: 18-40. ◆Annie Labbe, pres.

CKLD-FM— 1950: 105.5 mhz; 6 kw. Stereo. Hrs open: 24 55 Street, St-Jean Baptiste, G6G 4E1. Phone: (418) 335-7533. Fax: (418) 335-9009. Web Site:www.passionrock.com Licensee: Radio Megantic Ltee. Group owner: Gestion Appalaches inc. Population served: 40,384 Natl. Rep: Target Broadcast Sales,. Format: Hot adult contemp. News staff: 5. Target aud: 35-64. ◆Annie Labbe, gen mgr & opns dir.

Trois Rivieres

CBF-FM-1— July 21, 1977: 104.3 mhz; 100 kw. 1,000 ft TL: N46 29 27 W72 39 00. Stereo. Hrs open: Box 6000, Montreal, H3C 3A8. Phone: (514) 597-6000. Fax: (514) 597-4510. Web Site:www.cbc.radio-canada.ca Licensee: CBC French. Natl. Network: Radio Canada, . Format: Class, cultural, drama. ◆Sylvain La France, gen mgr; Louise Carriere, progmg dir.

CFOU-FM— Sept 7, 1997: 89.1 mhz; 3 kw. TL: Trois Rivieres, Quebec, Canada. Stereo. Hrs open: 24 Universite du Quebec a Trois-Rivieres, 1002 Pavillon Neree-Beauchemin, 3351 boulevard des Forges, G9A 5H7. Phone: (819) 376-5184. Fax: (819) 376-5239.E-mail: dgcfou@uqtr.uqtr.ca Web Site:www.cfou.ca Licensee: Radio campus des etudiants de l"Universite du Quebec a Trois-Rivieres. Natl. Network: CBC Radio One, . Format: Div. News: one hr wkly. Target aud: 18-35. ◆Marc Periard, gen mgr; Francois Marchand, mktg.

CHEY-FM— Aug 22, 1990: 94.7 mhz; 100 kw. Hrs open: RockDetente 94.7, 1500 rue Royale, Bur 260, G9A 6J4. Phone: (819) 376-0947. Fax: (819) 373-5555. Web Site:www.rockdetente.com Licensee: Astral Media Radio Inc. (acq 4-19-2002; grpsl). Format: Soft rock. Target aud: 30-40; women. ◆Jean Martin, gen mgr; Rene Rivard, sls dir; Damien Miville-Deschenes, prom dir; Eric Lachapelle, progmg dir.

CHLN-FM— Aug 20, 2007: 106.9 mhz; 60 kw. Ant 285 ft TL: N46 14 21 W72 35 26. Hrs open: 1350 rue Royale, Bureau 1200, G9A 4J4. Phone: (819) 374-3556. Fax: (819) 374-3222. Web Site:www.1069fm.net Licensee: 591991 B.C. Ltd. Format: Talk. ◆Pierre Gaudreau, gen mgr & sls dir; Denis Pratte, prom dir, adv dir, progmg dir.

CIGB-FM— Aug 27, 1979: 102.3 mhz; 5.8 kw. Stereo. Hrs open: 24 1500 Royale, Bureau 260, G9A 6J4. Phone: (819) 378-1023. Fax: (819) 378-1360. Web Site:www.radioenergie.com Licensee: Astral Media Radio Inc. Group owner: Astral Media Inc. (acq 8-24-90). Population served: 150,000 Format: CHR. News staff: 3; News: 3 hrs wkly. Target aud: 18-30. ◆Jean Martin, gen mgr; Mr. Damien Miville-Deschenes, prom dir; Mr. Danny Champagne, progmg dir.

CJEB-FM— June 8, 2004: 100.1 mhz; 30.61 kw. Ant 1,177 ft Hrs open: 4141 boul. St. Jean, G9B 2M8. Phone: (819) 691-1001. Fax: (819) 691-1002. Web Site:www.rythmefm.com/maur Licensee: Cogeco Diffusion inc. Format: Fr adult contemp. ◆Sylvie Caliberte, gen mgr.

Val d'Or

CHGO-FM— 2000: 104.3 mhz; 100 kw. Hrs open: 1729 3e Ave., J9X 1G5. Phone: (819) 825-0010. Fax: (819) 825-7313. Web Site:www.gofm.net Licensee: RNC MEDIA Inc. (group owner). Natl. Network: Radiomedia, . Format: Classic rock. ◆Pierre R. Brosseau, CEO & pres; Jean-Pierre Major, gen mgr; Ghislain Beaulieu, opns mgr.

CJMV-FM— June 17, 1989: 102.7 mhz; 65 kw. 200 ft Hrs open: 24 173 Perreault St., J9P 2H3. Phone: (819) 825-2568. Fax: (819) 825-2840. Web Site:www.radioenergie.com Licensee: Astral Media Radio Inc. Group owner: Astral Media Inc. (acq 1-12-2000; grpsl). Population served: 50,000 Format: Top-40. Target aud: 18-49. ◆Ian Greenberg, pres; Marlene Trottier, gen mgr & opns dir.

Valleyfield

CKOD-FM— June 6, 1994: 103.1 mhz; 3 kw. 167 ft TL: N45 16 08 W74 05 50. (CP: 103.1 mhz). Stereo. Hrs open: 24 249 Victoria St., J6T 1A9. Phone: (450) 373-0103. Phone: (450) 452-0103. Fax: (450) 373-4297.E-mail: fm103@ckod.qc.ca Web Site:www.ckod.qc.ca Licensee: Radio Express Inc. Natl. Rep: Target Broadcast Sales,. Format: Adult contemp. News staff: one; News: 7 hrs wkly. Target aud: 18-54; general. ◆Robert Brunet, pres & gen mgr; Martin Leblanc, opns dir, progmg dir; Dean Nevins, sls dir.

Vaudreuil-Dorion

CJVD-FM— Sept 29, 2008: 100.1 mhz; 550 w. TL: N45 24 55 W74 02 45. Hrs open: 2555 rue Dutrisac, Local RC-08 A, J7V 7E6. Phone: (514) 790-1001.E-mail: info@cjvd.ca Web Site:cjvd.ca Licensee: Yves Sauve. Format: Fr, music from the 70s, 80s & 90s. ◆Yves Sauve, pres.

Verdun

CINF(AM)—Licensed to Verdun. See Montreal

CKOI-FM—Licensed to Verdun. See Montreal

Victoriaville

CFDA-FM— 1999: 101.9 mhz; 1.35 kw. Hrs open: 24 Box 490, G6P 6T3. Secondary address: 55 St. Jean Baptiste St. G6P 6T3. Phone: (819) 752-5545. Fax: (819) 752-7552. Web Site:www.passionrock.com Licensee: Radio Victoriaville Ltee. Group owner: Gestion Appalaches inc. Natl. Rep: Target Broadcast Sales,. Format: Adult contemp. News staff: 7. Target aud: 35-65. Spec prog: Country 3 hrs, retro/oldies 3 hrs wkly. ◆Annie Labbe, gen mgr.

Ville-Marie

CKVM-FM— 2004: 93.1 mhz; 18.4 kw. TL: N47 19 57 W79 25 38. Stereo. Hrs open: 24 62 Suite Anne, J9V 2B7. Secondary address: 62 Ste. Anne J9V 2B7. Phone: (819) 629-2710. Fax: (819) 622-0716.E-mail: ckvm@ckvm.qc.ca Web Site:www.ckvm.qc.ca Licensee: Radio Temiscamingue Inc. Format: Adult contemp. News staff: one; News: 11 hrs wkly. Target aud: General. ◆Jacquelin Bastien, pres; Patrick Guilbault, VP; Claude Gagnon, gen mgr; Serge Lalonde, stn mgr.

Westmount

CKGM(AM)—See Montreal

Windsor

CIAX-FM— 2000: 98.3 mhz; 426 w. Hrs open: 49 Sixth Ave., J1S 1T2. Phone: (819) 845-5900. Phone: (819) 845-2692. Fax: (819) 845-2692.E-mail: unite@qc.aira.ca Licensee: La Radio communautaire de Windsor et region inc. Format: Div. ◆Patrick Levesque, pres & gen mgr; Julie Lupien, progmg dir.

Saskatchewan

Blucher

CFAQ-FM— 2006: 100.3 mhz; 36 w. Hrs open: 2127 St. Andrews Ave., Saskatoon, S7M 0M2. Phone: (306) 290-7222.E-mail: free@radiofree.ca Web Site:www.saskatoonchristianradio.com Licensee: Bertor Communications Ltd. Format: Christian music. ♦Robert Orr, gen mgr.

Cumberland House

CJCF-FM— 1990: 89.9 mhz; 30.5 w. Hrs open: Box 100, S0E 0S0. Phone: (306) 888-2176. Phone: (306) 888-4444. Fax: (306) 888-2103. Licensee: Cumberland House Radio & Television Committee Inc. Format: Ethnic. ♦Rachel Fiddler, gen mgr.

Estevan

CHSN-FM— 2001: 102.3 mhz; 100 kw. Hrs open: 200-1236 Fifth St., S4A 0Z6. Phone: (306) 634-1280. Fax: (306) 634-6364. Licensee: Golden West Broadcasting Ltd. Format: Light rock.

CJSL(AM)— August 1959: 1280 khz; 10 kw-U, DA-N. Hrs open: 24 200-1236 Fifth St., S4A 0Z6. Phone: (306) 634-1280. Fax: (306) 634-6364. Licensee: Golden West Broadcasting Ltd. (group owner; acq 3-95). Natl. Rep: Canadian Broadcast Sales,. Wire Svc: BN Wire Format: Contemp country. Target aud: General. Spec prog: Farm 4 hrs, relg 10 hrs wkly. ♦Elmer Hilderbrand, CEO, pres; Laverne Pappel, stn mgr & gen sls mgr.

Gravelbourg

CBKF-1(AM)— 1952: 540 khz; 5 kw-U, DA-2. Hrs open: 2440 Broad St., Regina, S4P 4A1. Phone: (306) 347-9540. Fax: (306) 347-9635. Web Site:www.cbc.ca Licensee: CBC French. Format: Div. ♦Rikki Bote, gen mgr; Robert Rabinowitz, CEO & progmg dir.

CFRG-FM— 2003: 93.1 mhz; 48 w. Hrs open: C.P. 176, S0H 1X0. Phone: (306) 648-2374. Fax: (306) 648-3258.E-mail: info@cfrg.ca Licensee: Association communautaire fransaskoise de Gravelbourg Inc. Format: Fr & En. ♦Robert Dumont, stn mgr.

Hudson Bay

CFMQ-FM— Sept 15, 1994: 98.1 mhz; 38.2 w. TL: N52 54 03 W102 23 31. Stereo. Hrs open: 24 Box 1272, S0E 0Y0. Phone: (306) 865-3065. Fax: (306) 865-2227.E-mail: cfmq@sk.sympatico.ca Licensee: HB Communications Inc. Population served: 6,000 Format: Easy lstng, div, country. News: one hr wkly. Target aud: General. ♦Mark Brann, pres; Dan Brann, gen mgr, sls VP, progmg mgr, news dir, engrg mgr.

Kindersley

CFYM(AM)— July 29, 1987: 1210 khz; 1 kw-U. Hrs open: Rebroadcasts CJYM(AM) Rosetown 95%.
Box 490, Rosetown, S0L 2V0. Phone: (306) 463-4411. Fax: (306) 882-3037.E-mail: cjmnnews@goldenwestradio.com Web Site:www.cjym.ca Licensee: Golden West Broadcasting Ltd. Group owner: Golden West Broadcasting Ltd. (acq 10-21-99). Natl. Rep: Target Broadcast Sales,. Format: Hit Gold, adult contemp. ♦Elmer Hildebrand, pres.

CKVX-FM—Not on air, target date: unknown: 104.9 mhz; 50 w. Hrs open: Box 490, Rosetown, S0L 2V0. Phone: (306) 463-4411. Fax: (306) 882-3037.E-mail: cjmnnews@goldenwestradio.com Format: Contemp country.

La Ronge

CBKA-FM— September 1979: 105.9 mhz; 80 w. Hrs open: Box 959, S0J 1L0. Phone: (306) 347-9540. Fax: (306) 425-2270. Web Site:www.sask.cbc.ca Licensee: CBC. Natl. Network: CBC Radio One, . Format: Rgnl current affrs. Spec prog: Cree & Dene 20 hrs wkly. ♦David Kyle, gen mgr.

CJLR-FM— 1990: 89.9 mhz; 216 w. Ant 151 ft Hrs open: 24 Box 1529, S0J 1L0. Phone: (306) 425-4003. Fax: (306) 425-3123.E-mail: mbcradio@mbcradio.com Web Site:www.mbcradio.com Licensee: Natotawin

Broadcasting Inc. (acq 9-2-93). Population served: 50,000 Format: Ethnic, country, div. Target aud: General. Spec prog: Cree & Dene languages. ♦Deborah Charles, CEO, gen mgr; William Dumais, pres; Keith Kratchmer, CFO; Teddy Clark, VP; Dallas Hicks, stn mgr, progmg dir.

Meadow Lake

CFDM-FM— 2001: 105.7 mhz; 46.5 w. Hrs open: Box 8168, Flying Dust First Nation, S9X 1T8. Phone: (306) 236-1445. Fax: (306) 236-2861.E-mail: cfdmradio@hotmail.com Licensee: FDB Broadcasting Inc. Format: Country, top-40. ♦Duwayne Derocher, stn mgr.

CJNS(AM)— Nov 1, 1977: 1240 khz; 1 kw-U, DA-1. Hrs open: Box 1460, North Battleford, S9A 2Z5. Phone: (306) 236-6494. Fax: (306) 236-6141. Licensee: Northwestern Radio Partnership Group owner: Rawlco Radio Ltd. (acq 1-7-2003; grpsl). Format: Contemp country. ♦David Dekker, gen mgr.

CJNS-FM—Not on air, target date: unknown: 102.3 mhz; 45 kw. Hrs open: Box 1460, North Battleford, S9A 2Z5. Phone: (306) 236-6494. Fax: (306) 236-6141. Licensee: Northwestern Radio Partnership

Melfort

CJVR-FM— March 1, 2002: 105.1 mhz; 100 kw. Hrs open: Box 750, 611 Main St., S0E 1A0. Phone: (306) 752-2587. Fax: (306) 752-5932. Licensee: Radio CJVR Ltd. Format: Country.

CKJH(AM)— Oct 8, 1966: 750 khz; 25 kw-U, DA-N. TL: N52 47 57 W104 35 25. Stereo. Hrs open: 24 Box 750, 611 Main St., S0E 1A0. Phone: (306) 752-2587. Fax: (306) 752-5932. Fax: (306) 752-6339.E-mail: cjvr@cjvr.com Web Site:www.cjvr.com Licensee: Radio CJVR Ltd. (acq 9-27-90). Natl. Rep: Target Broadcast Sales,. Format: Just the hits. News staff: 4; News: 15 hrs wkly. Target aud: General. Spec prog: Relg 9 hrs wkly. ♦Eugene Fabro Sr., chmn; Eugene W. Fabro, pres; Gary Fitz, VP, gen mgr, natl sls mgr; Karen Anderson, prom dir; Bill Wood, progmg dir; Cal Gratton, mus dir; Neil Shewchuk, news dir; Bayne Opseth, chief of engrg.

Moose Jaw

CHAB(AM)— Apr 22, 1922: 800 khz; 10 kw-U, DA-N. TL: N50 22 38 W105 23 35. Stereo. Hrs open: 24 1704 Main St. N., S6J 1L4. Phone: (306) 694-0800. Fax: (306) 692-8880.E-mail: greatesthits @goldenwestradio.com Licensee: Golden West Broadcasting Ltd. (group owner; (acq 8-20-92). Natl. Rep: Canadian Broadcast Sales,. Format: Greatest hits. News staff: 3. Target aud: 25-54. ♦Elmer Hildebrand, CEO, pres; Barry Vice, stn mgr, progmg dir; Abbey White, prom mgr; Rob Carnie, news dir.

CILG-FM— 2002: 100.7 mhz; 100 kw. Hrs open: 1704 Main St. N., S6J 1L4. Phone: (306) 692-1007. Fax: (306) 692-8880.E-mail: country100@goldenwestradio.com Licensee: Golden West Broadcasting Ltd. Format: Country.

CJAW-FM— Apr 22, 2008: 103.9 mhz; 100 kw. TL: N50 35 44 W105 04 09. Hrs open: 1704 Main St. N., S6J 1L4. Phone: (306) 694-0800. Fax: (306) 692-8880.E-mail: mixmorningshow@goldenwestradio.com Web Site:www.mix1039fm.com Licensee: Golden West Broadcasting Ltd. Format: Adult contemp. ♦Darryl Pisio, stn mgr; Craig Hemingway, progmg dir.

Nipawin

CIOT-FM— January 2005: 104.1 mhz; 200 w. Stereo. Hrs open: 24 Box 1240, S0E 1E0. Phone: (306) 862-2468. Fax: (306) 862-2660.E-mail: info@lighthousefm.ca Web Site:www.lighthousefm.ca Licensee: Wilderness Ministries Inc. Population served: 14,000 Format: Christian. News staff: one. Target aud: 20-55. ♦Rod Petersen, progmg dir; Andrew Hildebrandt, mus dir; Angela Petersen, news rptr; Andrew Clark, progmg.

CJNE-FM— June 2002: 94.7 mhz; 14.8 kw. Stereo. Hrs open: Box 220, S0E 1E0. Phone: (306) 862-9478. Fax: (306) 862-2334.E-mail: sales@cjnefm.com Web Site:www.cjnefm.com Licensee: CJNE FM Radio Inc. Format: Classic rock, golden oldies. News staff: one. Target aud: 18-50. ♦Norm Rudock, gen mgr, gen sls mgr; Treana Rudock, stn mgr; Les Blair, prom mgr.

North Battleford

CJCQ-FM— September 2001: 97.9 mhz; 100 kw. Hrs open: Prog sep from AM Box 1460, S9A 2Z5. Phone: (3060) 445-2477. Fax: (306) 445-4599. Licensee: Northwestern Radio Partnership Format: Pop rock.

CJHD-FM— 2008: 93.3 mhz; 100 kw. TL: N52 48 15 W108 35 18. Hrs open: Box 1460, S9A 2Z5. Phone: (306) 445-2477. Fax: (306) 445-4599. Licensee: Northwestern Radio Partnership. Format: Rock. ♦David Dekker, gen mgr.

CJNB(AM)— Jan 28, 1947: 1050 khz; 10 kw-U, DA-1. Hrs open: Box 1460, S9A 2Z5. Phone: (306) 445-2477. Fax: (306) 445-4599. Licensee: Northwestern Radio Partnership. Group owner: Rawlco Radio Ltd. (acq 1-7-2003;. grpsl). Natl. Rep: Canadian Broadcast Sales,. Format: Country. Spec prog: Farm 7 hrs, relg 10 hrs wkly. ♦Gord Rawlinson, pres; David Dekker, gen mgr, gen sls mgr; Harry M. Dekker, prom mgr; Doug Harrison, progmg dir; Dave Senft, chief of engrg.

Okanese Indian Reserve

CHXL-FM— June 2003: 95.3 mhz; 50 kw. TL: N50 56 34 W103 23 51. Hrs open: Box 940, Balcarres, S0G 0C0. Phone: (306) 334-3331. Fax: (306) 334-2545.E-mail: info@chxlfm.com Licensee: O.K. Creek Radio Station Inc. Format: Var. ♦William Yuzicapi, stn mgr.

Pinehouse Lake

CFNK-FM— 1996: 89.9 mhz; 7 w. Hrs open: General Delivery, Box 370, S0J 2B0. Phone: (306) 884-2011. Phone: (306) 884-2016. Fax: (306) 884-2365. Web Site:www.cfnk.radiok.sympatico.ca Licensee: Pinehouse Communications Society Inc. Format: Cree language, adult contemp, oldies. ♦Peter Smith, gen mgr; Vince Natomagan, progmg dir.

Prince Albert

CFMM-FM— Jan 30, 1982: 99.1 mhz; 100 kw. 606 ft Stereo. Hrs open: Prog sep from AM Box 900, S6V 7R4. Phone: (306) 763-7421. Fax: (306) 764-1850.E-mail: power99fm@rawlco.com Licensee: Rawlco Radio Ltd. Format: Classic rock mix 101, contemp hit, news. ♦Garth Kalin, progmg mgr.

CHQX-FM— June 18, 2001: 101.5 mhz; 100 kw. Ant 606 ft Stereo. Hrs open: 24 Box 900, S6V 7R4. Phone: (306) 763-7421. Fax: (306) 764-1850.E-mail: mix101fm@rawlco.com Licensee: Rawlco Radio Ltd. (group owner). Format: Adult rock. ♦Jim Scarrow, gen mgr, opns mgr; Karl Johnson, gen sls mgr.

CKBI(AM)— 1934: 900 khz; 10 kw-U, DA-N. Hrs open: Box 900, S6V 7R4. Phone: (306) 763-7421. Fax: (306) 764-1850.E-mail: 900ckbi@rawlco.com Licensee: Rawlco Radio Ltd. (group owner; acq 1946). Natl. Rep: Canadian Broadcast Sales,. Format: Adult contemp, MOR, oldies. Target aud: 34 plus; working women. Spec prog: Farm 2 hrs wkly. ♦Jim Scarrow, gen mgr; Dave Hryhor, rgnl sls mgr; Neil Headrick, progmg mgr; Jeff White, news dir; Dale Zimmerman, engrg mgr.

Regina

CBK(AM)— July 29, 1939: 540 khz; 50 kw-D, DA. Hrs open: 24 Box 540, 2440 Broad St., S4P 4A1. Phone: (306) 347-9540. Fax: (306) 347-9524.E-mail: kyled@cbc.ca Licensee: CBC. Natl. Network: CBC Radio One, . Format: Div, news, talk. Spec prog: Farm 5 hrs wkly. ♦Debbie Carpentier, gen mgr, opns dir; David Kyle, stn mgr, news dir; Nigel Simms, stn mgr & news dir.

CBKF-FM— Sept 1, 1973: 97.7 mhz; 13.7 kw. 501 ft Hrs open: 24 Box 540, S4P 4A1. Secondary address: 2440 Broad St. S4P-3Z4. Phone: (306) 347-9540. Fax: (306) 347-9493. Web Site:www.cbc.ca Licensee: Radio Canada. Natl. Network: CBC Radio Two, . Format: Div. ♦Rene Fontaine, gen mgr; Anne Brochu, progmg dir, news dir; Steve Tomchuk, engrg mgr. Co-owned TV: CBKF(TV) affil.

CBK-FM— May 1, 1977: 96.9 mhz; 100 kw. Ant 501 ft Stereo. Hrs open: 2440 Broad St., S4P 4A1. Phone: (360) 956-7400. Fax: (306) 956-7417. Web Site:www.cbc.ca/sask/ Licensee: CBC Natl. Network: CBC Radio Two, . Format: Var/div, jazz, classical. ♦David Kyle, gen mgr. Co-owned TV: *CBKT(TV) affil

CFWF-FM— Apr 15, 1982: 104.9 mhz; 100 kw. 400 ft Stereo. Hrs open: Prog sep from AM 190 Rose St., S4P 0A9. Phone: (306) 546-6200. Fax: (306) 781-7338.E-mail: info@cwfw.com Web Site:www.620ckrm.com Licensee: Harvard Broadcasting Inc. (Acq 8-25-95). Natl. Rep: Canadian Broadcast Sales,. Format: Classic rock.

CHBD-FM— Feb 20, 2008: 92.7 mhz; 100 kw. TL: N50 28 58 W104 30 20. Hrs open: 4303 Albert St., Suite 100 (main floor), S4S 3R6. Phone: (306) 337-2850. Fax: (306) 359-0931.E-mail: mshannon@bigdog927.com Web Site:www.bigdog927.com Licensee: Astral Media Radio G.P. (acq 9-28-2007; grpsl). Format: New country. Target aud: 25-64. ◆Mike Shannon, gen mgr; Gary Wilson, gen sls mgr; Tia Daniels, prom dir; Paul O'Neil, progmg mgr.

CHMX-FM— Feb 4, 1966: 92.1 mhz; 100 kw. 499 ft Stereo. Hrs open: 24 1900 Rose St., S4P 0A9. Phone: (306) 546-6200. Fax: (306) 781-7338. Web Site:www.lite92fm.com Licensee: Harvard Broadcasting Inc. (acq 3-1-81). Format: Adult Contemp. ◆Les Schuster, opns dir & gen sls mgr.

CIZL-FM— June 1982: 98.9 mhz; 100 kw. 435 ft Stereo. Hrs open: Prog sep from AM 2401 Saskatchewan Ave., S4P 4H8. Phone: (306) 525-0000. Fax: (306) 347-8557. Licensee: Rawlco Radio Ltd. (Acq 4-67). Format: AOR, classic hits, adult contemp. Target aud: 18-49. ◆Craig Romanyk, rgnl sls mgr; Marci Watsen, prom mgr; Tom Newton, progmg dir.

CJME(AM)— July 27, 1926: 980 khz; 10 kw-D, 5 kw-N, DA-2. Hrs open: 24 2401 Saskatchewan Dr., Suite 210, S4P 4H8. Phone: (306) 525-0000. Fax: (306) 347-8557. Licensee: Rawlco Radio Ltd. (group owner; acq 11-30-2001). Format: News/talk. ◆Tom Newton, gen mgr; Keith Black, rgnl sls mgr; Marcie Watson, prom dir; Don Kollins, progmg dir; Murray Wood, news dir.

*CJTR-FM— Nov 1, 2001: 91.3 mhz; 480 w. TL: N50 27 18 W104 36 30. Stereo. Hrs open: 24 Box 334, Station Main, S4P 3A1. Phone: (306) 525-7274. Fax: (306) 525-9741.E-mail: radius@cjtr.ca Web Site:www.cjtr.ca Licensee: Radius Communications Inc. Population served: 250,000 Format: Div. News: 10 hrs wkly. Spec prog: American Indian 4 hrs, Black 2 hrs, Chinese one hr, It one hr, Portugese one hr wkly. ◆Rick August, pres; Dave Kuzenko, VP; Keith Colhoun, gen mgr.

CKCK-FM— Aug 9, 2002: 94.5 mhz; 100 kw. Hrs open: 24 2401 Saskatchewan Dr., Suite 210, S4P 4H8. Phone: (306) 525-0000. Fax: (306) 347-8557. Licensee: Rawlco Radio Ltd. (group owner). Format: Classic rock. ◆Gord Rawlinson, pres; Ralph Bird, gen sls mgr; Tom Newton, gen mgr & progmg dir; Michael Zaplitny, news dir; Gord Stankey, engrg mgr; Karen Mains, traf mgr.

CKRM(AM)— July 29, 1922: 620 khz; 10 kw-U, DA-2. Hrs open: 1900 Rose St., S4P 0A9. Phone: (306) 546-6200. Fax: (306) 781-7338.E-mail: info@ckrm.com Web Site:www.620ckrm.com Licensee: Harvard Broadcasting Inc. (acq 11-30-2001; C$4.2 million with co-located FM). Format: C&W, farm. ◆Mike Olstrom, stn mgr.

Rosetown

CJYM(AM)— Aug 8, 1966: 1330 khz; 10 kw-U, DA-1. Hrs open: 24 Box 490, S0L 2V0. Secondary address: 208 Hwy.4 S0L 2V0. Phone: (306) 882-2686. Fax: (306) 882-3037.E-mail: cjmmnews@goldenwestradio.com Web Site:www.cjym.com Licensee: Dace Broadcasting Corp. Group owner: Golden West Broadcasting Ltd. (acq 10-21-99). Natl. Rep: Target Broadcast Sales,. Format: Classic hits. News staff: 2. Target aud: General. ◆Barb Bell, gen mgr.

Saskatoon

CBKF-2(AM)— Nov 6, 1952: 860 khz; 10 kw-U, DA-2. Hrs open: 144 2nd Ave., S7K 1K5. Phone: (306) 956-7400. Fax: (306) 956-7476. Web Site:www.sask.cbc.ca Licensee: CBC French. Format: Div. Target aud: General. ◆David Kyle, gen mgr; Robert Rabinowitz, progmg dir.

*CBKS-FM— July 1, 1978: 105.5 mhz; 98 kw. Ant 586 ft Stereo. Hrs open: 24
Rebroadcasts CBK-FM Regina.
144 2nd Ave. S., S7K 1K5. Phone: (306) 956-7400. Fax: (306) 956-7417. Web Site:www.cbc.ca/sask/ Licensee: CBC. Natl. Network: CBC Radio Two, . Format: Div, jazz, classical. ◆David Kyle, stn mgr.

CFCR-FM— 1991: 90.5 mhz; 1.48 kw. Stereo. Hrs open: 6 AM-1 AM Box 7544, 103 3rd Ave. N., S7K 4L4. Phone: (306) 664-6678.E-mail: cfcr@quadrant.net Web Site:www.cfcr.ca Licensee: Community Radio Society of Saskatoon Inc. Population served: 200,000 Format: Var.

News: one hr wkly. Target aud: General. Spec prog: Fr one hr, Ger 2 hrs, It one hr, Pol one hr, Sp 2 hrs wkly. ◆Dianne Deminchuk, pres; Ron Spizziri, gen mgr; Bill Jones, sls dir; Theo Kivol, progmg VP & traf mgr.

CFMC-FM— Dec 12, 1965: 95.1 mhz; 100 kw. Ant 110 ft Stereo. Hrs open: 715 Saskatchewan Crescent W., S7M 5V7. Phone: (306) 934-2222. Fax: (306) 477-0002. Web Site:www.c95.com Licensee: Rawlco Radio Ltd. Format: Saskatoon's #1 Hit Music Station. ◆Jamie Wall, gen mgr.

CFWD-FM— 2008: 96.3 mhz; 96 kw. TL: N52 10 28 W106 26 04. Hrs open: 105 21st St. E., Suite 200, S7K 0B3. Phone: (306) 653-9630.E-mail: info@cfwd.com Web Site:www.wired963.com Licensee: Harvard Broadcasting Inc. Natl. Rep: CHUM Radio Sales,. Format: Rhythmic top-40. ◆Carley Caverly, gen mgr, gen sls mgr; Karen Broderick, natl sls mgr; Stacie Driedger, prom dir; Chris Myers, progmg dir.

CJDJ-FM— June 1990: 102.1 mhz; 100 kw. Hrs open: 24 715 Saskatchewan Crescent West, S7M 5V7. Phone: (306) 934-2222. Fax: (306) 477-0002. Web Site:www.rock102rocks.com Licensee: Rawlco Radio Ltd. (group owner; (acq 12-21-2000; C$870,000 for all the issued and outstanding shares). Population served: 200,000 Format: Saskatoon's Rock Station. News staff: 3; News: 4 hrs wkly. Target aud: 25-49; well educated, well paid professionals. Spec prog: Relg 6 hrs wkly. ◆Pam Leyland, pres & gen mgr.

CJMK-FM— May 2001: 98.3 mhz; 100 kw. Hrs open: 24 366 3rd Ave. S., S7K 1M5. Phone: (306) 244-1975. Fax: (306) 665-5501. Web Site:www.magic983.fm Licensee: 629112 Saskatchewan Ltd. (group owner). Format: Adult gold contemp. ◆Elmer Hildebrand, pres; Vic Dubois, gen mgr; Ken McFarlane, gen sls mgr; Steve Chisholm, progmg dir; Matt Bradley, mus dir; Eldon Duchscher, news dir; Kurtis Krowchuk, chief of engrg.

CJWW(AM)— January 1976: 600 khz; 25 kw-D, 8 kw-N, DA-N. Stereo. Hrs open: 24 366 3rd Ave. S., S7K 1M5. Phone: (306) 244-1975. Fax: (306) 665-7730. Fax: (306) 665-5501. Web Site:www.cjwwradio.com Licensee: 629112 Saskatchewan Ltd. (group owner; (acq 12-21-2000; C$7,450,000). Population served: 350,000 Natl. Rep: Canadian Broadcast Sales,. Format: Country, info. News staff: 7. Target aud: 35-64; central. Spec prog: Gospel 3 hrs wkly. ◆Elmer Hildebrand, chmn, pres; Dawn Mann, CFO; V. Dubois, gen mgr; Ken McFarlane, gen sls mgr; Rod Kitter, progmg dir; Jay Richards, mus dir; E. Duchscher, news dir; Steve Shannon, pub affrs dir; Kurtis Krwochuk, chief of engrg.

CKBL-FM— Feb 6, 1995: 92.9 mhz; 100 kw. Hrs open: 366 3rd Ave. S., S7K 1M5. Phone: (306) 244-1975. Fax: (306) 665-7730.E-mail: cjww.radio@sasktel.com Licensee: 629112 Saskatchewan Ltd. Natl. Rep: Canadian Broadcast Sales,. Format: New country. News staff: 2. Target aud: General.

CKOM(AM)— June 8, 1951: 650 khz; 10 kw-U, DA-2. Hrs open: 715 Saskatchewan Crescent W., S7M 5V7. Phone: (306) 934-2222. Fax: (306) 477-0002. Web Site:www.newstalk650.com Licensee: Rawlco Radio Ltd. (group owner). Format: News/Talk. News: 10. ◆Jamie Wall, gen mgr.

Shaunavon

CJSN(AM)— Dec 6, 1966: 1490 khz; 1 kw-U. Hrs open: 407 Centre St., S0N 2M0. Phone: (306) 297-2671. Fax: (306) 297-3051. Web Site:www.swiftcurrentonline.com Licensee: Frontier City Broadcasting. Group owner: Golden West Broadcasting Ltd. (acq 1973). Population served: 1,200,000 Format: C&W, MOR. ◆Deborah Gauger, gen mgr & opns mgr; Darwin Gooding, progmg dir.

Swift Current

CIMG-FM— Oct 20, 1979: 94.1 mhz; 100 kw. 400 ft Stereo. Hrs open: 24 134 Central Ave. N., S9H 0L1. Phone: (306) 773-4605. Fax: (306) 773-6390.E-mail: eaglecontrol@goldenwestradio.com Web Site:www.eagle94.com Licensee: Golden West Broadcasting Ltd. (group owner; (acq 11-8-95; C$97,500). Population served: 48,500 Natl. Rep: Canadian Broadcast Sales,. Format: Classic hits. News staff: 3; News: 4 hrs wkly. Target aud: 18-35. ◆Deborah Gauger, stn mgr, gen sls mgr; Ryan Switzer, progmg dir.

CKFI-FM— Nov 5, 2005: 97.1 mhz; 100 kw. Stereo. Hrs open: 134 Central Ave. N., S9H 0L1. Phone: (306) 773-4605. Fax: (306) 773-6390. Licensee: Golden West Broadcasting Ltd. Format: Adult contemp. ◆Deborah Gauger, gen mgr, stn mgr; Ryan Switzer, progmg dir.

CKSW(AM)— June 1, 1956: 570 khz; 10 kw-U, DA-2. Hrs open: 24 134 Central Ave., S9H 0L1. Phone: (306) 773-4605. Fax: (306) 773-6390. Web Site:www.swiftcurrentonline.com Licensee: Golden West Broadcasting Ltd. Group owner: Golden West Broadcasting Ltd. Natl. Rep: Canadian Broadcast Sales,. Format: Country, regl. News staff: 5; News: 9 hrs wkly. Target aud: 25-54. Spec prog: Farm 5 hrs, Ger one hr wkly. ◆Deborah Granger, rgnl sls mgr; Ryan Switzer, progmg dir; Dave Funk, chief of engrg.

Weyburn

CFSL(AM)— Aug 16, 1957: 1190 khz; 10 kw-D, 5 kw-N, DA-N. Hrs open: 24 305 Souris Ave., S4H 2K2. Phone: (306) 848-1190. Fax: (306) 842-2720.E-mail: am1190@coldwestradio.com Licensee: Golden West Broadcasting Ltd. (acq 2-16-95). Natl. Rep: Canadian Broadcast Sales,. Wire Svc: BN Wire Format: C&W. News staff: 3. Target aud: 25 plus. Spec prog: Farm 3 hrs, relg 9 hrs wkly. ◆Elmer Hildenbrand, CEO; Cameron Birnie, stn mgr, news dir.

CKRC-FM—Not on air, target date: unknown: 103.5 mhz; 100 kw. Hrs open: 305 Souris Ave., S4H 2K2. Phone: (306) 848-1190. Fax: (306) 842-2720. Licensee: Golden West Broadcasting Ltd. Format: Rock.

White Bear Lake Resort

CIDD-FM— 2002: 97.7 mhz; 46.5 w. Hrs open: Box 875, Kenosee Lake, S0C 2S0. Phone: (306) 577-2450. Fax: (306) 577-4313. Licensee: White Bear Children's Charity Inc. Format: Div. ◆Lana Littlechief, gen mgr.

Yorkton

CFGW-FM— July 1, 2001: 94.1 mhz; 100 kw. Hrs open: 120 Smith St. E., S3N 3V3. Phone: (306) 782-2256. Fax: (3006) 783-4994.E-mail: gx94.reception@sasktel.net Licensee: Yorkton Broadcasting Ltd. Format: Hot adult contemp.

CJGX(AM)— Aug 19, 1927: 940 khz; 50 kw-D, 10 kw-N. Hrs open: 120 Smith St. E., S3N 3V3. Phone: (306) 782-2256. Fax: (306) 783-4994. Licensee: Yorkton Broadcasting Ltd. and Walsh Investments Inc., partners of GX Radio, a gen partnership. (acq 2-15-89). Natl. Rep: CHUM Radio Sales, Target Broadcast Sales,. Format: Country. ◆Lyle Walsh, pres & gen mgr; Bryan Mireau, engrg dir.

CJJC-FM— Jan 2, 2006: 100.5 mhz; 44.8 w. Hrs open: 395 Riverview Rd., S3N 3V6. Phone: (306) 786-7625. Fax: (306) 782-4437.E-mail: rocktalk@1005therock.com Web Site:www.1005therock.ca Licensee: Dennis M. Dyck, on behalf of a corporation to be incorporated. Format: Christian music. ◆Dennis Dyck, stn mgr; Scott Fitzsimmons, progmg dir.

Zenon Park

CKZP-FM— January 2002: 102.7 mhz; 5.4 w. Hrs open: Box 100, S0E 1W0. Phone: (306) 767-2451. Fax: (306) 767-2548.E-mail: legeru@tsd53.ca Web Site:www.thinkfast.ca/tsd/tsdpromo2/zpradio.htm Licensee: Radio Zenon Park Inc. Format: Var (English and French progmg). ◆J. Ulysse Leger, gen mgr.

Yukon Territory

Dawson City

CFYT-FM— October 2006: 106.9 mhz; 5 w. TL: N64 03 27 W139 24 36. Hrs open:
Rebroadcasts CKRW-FM Whitehorse 86%.
Box 689, Y0B 1G0. Phone: (867) 993-5152. Fax: (867) 993-6834.E-mail: cfytradio@hotmail.com Web Site:www.cfyt.ca Licensee: Dawson City Community Radio Society. Format: Var. ◆Ashley Doiron, pres.

Tagish

CFET-FM— June 1, 2003: 106.7 mhz; 50 w. Hrs open: Mile 234, Y0B 1T0. Phone: (867) 667-6397. Fax: (867) 668-2633.E-mail: cfet@tagishtel.ca Web Site:www.tagishtel.ca/radio Licensee: Robert G. Hopkins. Format: Variety/classic rock. ◆Robert G. Hopkins, gen mgr.

Whitehorse

*CFWH(AM)— 1958: 570 khz; 5 kw-U, DA-1. Hrs open: 24 3103 Third Ave., Y1A 1E5. Phone: (867) 668-8400. Fax: (867) 668-8408. Licensee: CBC. Natl. Network: CBC Radio One, . Format: Talk, info. Spec prog: Fr one hr wkly. ◆Frank Fry, opns dir, opns mgr & progmg dir.

CHON-FM— Feb 1, 1985: 98.1 mhz; 4.261 kw. 250 ft Stereo. Hrs open: 4230 A 4th Ave., Suite 6, Y1A 1K1. Phone: (867) 668-6629. Fax: (867) 668-6612.E-mail: nnby@nnby.net Web Site:www.nnby.net Licensee: Northern Native Broadcasting. Format: C&W, classic rock. Spec prog: Yukon native language 15 hrs wkly. ◆Shirley Adamson, gen mgr; Christine Genier, gen sls mgr; Denis Gerard, engrg dir.

CIAY-FM— 2003: 100.7 mhz; 50 w. Hrs open: 24 91806 Alaska Hwy., Y1A 5B7. Phone: (867) 393-2429. Fax: (867) 393-2439.E-mail: stnmgr@newlifefmyukon.ca Web Site:www.newlifefmyukon.ca Licensee: Bethany Pentecostal Tabernacle. Population served: 20,000 Format: Christian. ◆Rod Carby, stn mgr; Theresa Aitcheson, gen sls mgr; Ian McDonald, progmg dir.

CKRW(AM)— November 1969: 610 khz; 1 kw-U, DA-1. Hrs open: 203-4103 4th Ave., Suite 203, Y1A 1H6. Phone: (867) 668-6100. Fax: (867) 668-4209.E-mail: marketing@ckrw.com Web Site:www.ckrw.com Licensee: Klondike Broadcasting Co. Ltd. Natl. Rep: Canadian Broadcast Sales,. Format: CHR. ◆Rolf Hougen, CEO; Jennifer Johnstone, gen mgr; Eva Bidrman, gen sls mgr; Ron McFadyen, news dir; Alan Dailey, chief of engrg.

Michigan

Detroit

CIDR-FM—See Windsor, ON

CKLW(AM)—See Windsor, ON

Miscellaneous Radio Services

American Forces Radio & Television Service (AFRTS), Department of Defense, American Forces Info Service, 601 N. Fairfax St., Alexandria, VA, 22314. Phone: (703) 428-0616. Fax: (703) 428-0624. E-mail: afrtdir@hq.afis.osd.mil Web Site:www.afrts.osd.mil

Melvin W. Russell, dir; Andreas I. Friedrich, deputy dir.

March Air Reserve BaseCA . AFRTS Broadcast Center, 1363 Z St, Bldg. 2730. Phone:

AFRTS has radio & TV svc 177 countries & on bd U.S. Navy ships. AFRTS stns operate in 15 countries providing rgnl & loc info to large concentrations of U.S. forces. All of the entertainment progmg, U.S sporting events, & natl. & international news is provided to the outlets either directly via international satellites from the AFRTS Broadcast Center at March Air Reserve Base, CA., or through the AFRTS operated stns which insert their rgnl & loc radio drive-time programs & radio & TV news & spot announcements. A rgnl AFRTS svc in Europe delivers the AFRTS fed progmg & rgnl news & info via EUTELSAT to affils located in seven nations as well as directly to cable head-ends, remote transmitters, homes throughout Europe & the Middle East. The worldwide AFRTS-TV progmg consists of: an entertainment svc time shifted for the various parts of the globe & providing the best of U.S. net TV progmg; a news svc providing natl & international news from CNN, Fox News, MSNB, major U.S. networks; a sports ch providing sports news & sporting events from ESPN, ESPN2 & the major U.S. nets & a fourth svc devoted to alternative entertainment progmg primarily oriented on family-type programs from PBS & from U.S.cable TV chs. A fifth & sixth svc were added in 2005 for family entertainmnet & full-time movies. A seventh svc began in 2006 providing additional sporting events. Finally, the Pentagon Channel is also carried by AFRTS. AFRTS-Radio satellite progmg consists of two continuous news info & sporting events svcs, a NPR svc & entertainment svcs with music for practically all tastes & likes of AFRTS' authorized audience which is all active duty military & Department of Defense civilian personnel & their families stationed overseas. Access to the AFRTS worldwide satellite svcs is restricted through the use of the Scientific Atlanta Power-Vu MPEG-2 digital compression encoding system.

Radio Free Asia

Radio Free Asia, 2025 M St. N.W., Suite 300, Washington, DC, 20036. Phone: (202) 530-4900. Fax: (202) 530-7797.E-mail: contact@rfa.org Web Site:www.rfa.org

Richard Richter, pres; Patrick Taylor, CFO; Daniel Southerland, VP progmg/exec editor; Sarah Jackson-Han, dir of communications.

Provides info, news & commentary about events in the respective countries of Asia & elsewhere. The svc is intended to be a forum for a var of opinions & voices from within Asian nations whose people do not fully enjoy freedom of expression.

Radio Free Europe/Radio Liberty

Radio Free Europe/Radio Liberty, (RFE/RL Inc.). 1201 Connecticut Ave. N.W., Suite 400, Washington, DC, 20036. Phone: (202) 457-6900. Fax: (202) 457-6992. Web Site:www.ferl.org

Through bcsts in 28 languages to 20 countries, RFE/RL provides news, info, responsible dicussion of domestic & international issues to countries where free & ind media are not permitted, or not yet fully established.

Broadcasting Board of Governors, 330 Independence Ave. S.W., Rm. 3360, Washington, DC, 20237. Phone: (202) 203-4545. Fax: (202) 203-4585. Web Site:www.bbg.gov/

The bd makes & supervises grants to Radio Free Europe, Radio Liberty, & Radio Free Asia, the Middle East Bcstg Networks & assures that funds are applied consistently with the broad foreign policy objectives of the U.S. govt. The BBG serves as the governing body for all non-military U.S. bcstg including VOA, OCB, RFE/RL, RFA, & MBN.

U.S. International Radio

Adventist World Radio, 12501 Old Columbia Pike, Silver Spring, MD, 20904-6600. Phone: (301) 680-6304. Fax: (301) 680-6303.E-mail: info@awr.org Web Site:www.awr.org

Benjamin D. Schoun, pres.

AWR has 70 production studios bcstg worldwide in over 75 languages thousands of hours daily via AM/FM, shortwave & internet.

Blue Ridge Communications Inc., Shortwave Radio Station WWRB, c/o Airline Transport Communications, Box 7, Manchester, TN, 37349-0007. Phone: (931) 841-0492. Phone: (931) 728-6087. Web Site:www.wwrb.org

WWRB Manchester, TN. Worldwide bcstg utilizing 5 shortwave transmitters & 6 major antenna systems (azimuths); more than 10 years of well established global audience.

EWTN Global Catholic Network, 5817 Old Leeds Rd., Irondale, AL, 35210-2164. Phone: (205) 271-2900. Fax: (205) 271-2926.E-mail: radio@ewtn.com Web Site:www.ewtn.com

Michael Warsaw, pres; Frank Leurck, gen mgr; Thom Price, progmg dir; Doug Keck, VP progmg; Willaim Stelemeier, chmn; John Pepe, mktg mgr.

Global Catholic Radio Networks available in English & Sp 24 hours a day, satellite delivered, free of charge.

Family Stations Inc., 10400 N.W. 240th St., Okeechobee, FL, 34972. Phone: (863) 763-0281. Fax: (863) 763-8867.E-mail: fsiyfr@okeechobee.com Web Site:www.familyradio.com

Harold Camping, pres; Dan Elyea, engrg mgr; David Hoff, mgr International department.

WYFR Okeechobee, Fla. Twelve 100 kw transmitters & two 50 kw transmitters in Florida. Bcstg on various frequencies, in English to Europe, Africa & the Americas (including Caribbean area), in German to Europe, in Russian to East Europe, in Arabic to West Africa, in French to Europe, North Africa & the Americas & in Sp to Southern Europe, Central & South America, in Portuguese to Europe, South America & West Africa, in It to Europe. Format: Relg.

Far East Broadcasting Co. Inc., Box 1, La Mirada, CA, 90637. Phone: (562) 947-4651. Fax: (310) 943-0160.E-mail: febc@febc.org Web Site:www.febc.org

Dr. Robert S. Fortner, chmn; Gregg J. Harris, pres.

Broadcasts 560 hrs of progmg in 150 languages, to a potential audience of more than 2.5 billion people. FEBC's broadcasts are heard in many countries with limited access to Christian ministry, or where there is tremendous political and cultural opposition to the gospel.

Fundamental Broadcasting Network, c/o Grace Missionary Baptist Church, 520 Roberts Rd., Newport, NC, 28570. Phone: (252) 223-4600. Fax: (252) 223-2201.E-mail: fbn@fbnradio.com Web Site:www.fbnradio.com

WBOH Newport, NC, Broadcasts on 5.920 mhz 24 hrs a day. WTJC Newport, NC, Broadcasts on 9.370 mhz 24 hrs a day.

Good News World Outreach, WRNO Worldwide, Box 895, Fort Worth, TX, 76101-0895. Phone: (817) 850-9990. Fax: (817) 850-9994.E-mail: wrnoradio@mailup.net Web Site:www.wrnoworldwide.org

Dr. Robert E. Mawire, CEO.

WRNO New Orleans. 50 kw shortwave transmitter reaching North America, Central America, Europe, & Far East. Format: news, talk (educational, Christian), sports, music.

Hill Radio International, 5920 Oak Manor Dr., Milton, FL, 32570-7704.

CP for New International HF Broadcast Station in Mllton, FL.

International Fellowship of Churches Inc., dba IMF World Missions. Radio Station KIMF, 9746 6th St., Rancho Cucamonga, CA, 91730. Phone: (909) 466-4793.E-mail: james@plancktech.com

Broadcasts on 5.835 mhz and 11.885 mhz with two 50 kw transmitters.

La Voz de Restauracion Broadcasting Inc., Box 56320, Los Angeles, CA, 90056. Phone: (323) 766-2454. Fax: (323) 766-2458.E-mail: info@restauracion.com Web Site:www.restauracion.com

Rene F. Molina, dir.

KVOH Rancho Simi, CA Format: Sp.

Leap of Faith Inc., 661 Ormond Dr., Nashville, TN, 37205.

New international HF broadcast stn in Lebanon, TN.

Radio Miami International, 175 Fontainebleau Blvd., Suite 1N4, Miami, FL, 33172. Phone: (305) 559-9764. Fax: (305) 559-8186.E-mail: info@wrmi.net Web Site:www.wrmi.net

Jeff White, gen mgr .

WRMI Miami. Stn sells block airtime for $1/minute to organizations wanting to reach any part of the Americas in any language. 7,385 & 9,955 & 15,725 khz shortwave, 50 kw power.

Trans World Radio, Box 8700, Cary, NC, 27512-8700. Phone: (919) 460-3700. Fax: (919) 460-3702.E-mail: info@twr.org Web Site:www.twr.org

Thomas Lowell, CEO.

KTWR Agana, Guam. Guam E-mail: twrguamk@twr.hafa.net.gu Four 100-kw shortwave transmitters to bcst to Australia, Bali, China, the eastern & central part of the Commonwealth of Independent States, Far East, India, Indonesia, Japan, Korea, Myanmar, Southeast Asia. Format: Relg (more than 30 languages).

Trinity Broadcasting Network, Attn Superpower KTBN Radio QSL Mgr., Tustin, CA, 92780. Phone: (801) 250-4111 (office). Web Site:www.tbn.org

Johnny Mitchell, gen mgr .

TBN, is the worlds largest religious net offering 24 hours commerical-free inspiration progmg that appeals to a wind variety of denominations.

Two If By Sea Broadcasting Corp., 1784 W. Northfield Blvd., Suite 305, Murfreesboro, TN, 37129-1702. E-mail: studio@kaij.us Web Site:kaij.us

George McClintock, gen mgr; John McClintock, progmg dir; Ted Randall, mktg dir.

KAIJ Dallas, TX.

United Nations, Audio-Visual Promotion & Distribution. 405 E. 42nd St., Rm. S-805, HQ-Secretariat Bldg.," INT'L ORG", New York, NY, 10017. Phone: (212) 963-6982. Phone: (212) 963-7318. Fax: (212) 963-6869.E-mail: audio-visual@un.org Web Site:www.unmultimedia.org

Caroline Petit, chief/prom/distribution unit news/media div; Antonio Carlos Da Silva, chief/multimedia resources unit news/media div.

TV coverage of UN meetings events, the production, prom & distribution of UN TV radio progmg, photo & footage. All major UN events are also recorded on audio for radio distribution. Offices in 63 countries of 192 member countries.

The Voice of the OAS, 17th & Constitution N.W., Washington, DC, 20006. Phone: (202) 458-3000. Fax: (202) 458-3930.E-mail: informacion-publica@oas.org Web Site:www.oas.org

Von Martin, producer; Claudio Lessa, producer.

Radio programs with news, interviews, info & music from Latin America. Concentrating on the acitivities of the Organization of American States.

WBCQ Radio, 274 Britton Rd., Monticello, ME, 04760-3110. Phone: (207) 538-9180.E-mail: wbcq@wbcq.com Web Site:www.wbcq.com

Allan H. Weiner, gen mgr .

WBCQ Monticello, Me. International bcst shortwave stn. Lease & program time available. 5.105 mhz, 7.415 mhz, 9.330 mhz & 17.495 mhz. Serves North, Central, South America & the Carribean.

WJIE International Shortwave, Box 197309, Louisville, KY, 40259. Phone: (502) 968-1220. Fax: (502) 964-3304.E-mail: wjiesw@hotmail.com Web Site:www.wjiesw.com

Robert W. Rodgers, pres; Greg Holt, VP; Doug Rumsey, dir.

WJIE Millerstown, Ky. On two sw frequencies operating 24 hours daily. Target areas: Europe & Asia. Also operates WJIE-FM on 88.5 mhz with 24.5 kw horiz, 18.5 kw vert in Okolona, Ky.

WMLK Radio, Assemblies of Yahweh, Box C, Bethel, PA, 19507. Phone: (717) 933-4518. Phone: (800) 523-3827. Web Site:www.assembliesofyahweh.com

Elder Jacob O. Meyer, pres.

Branch offices in Metro-Manila, Phillippines; San Juan, Port of Spain, Trinidad & Tobago; Leeds, England. WMLK Bethel, PA. Bcstg to Europe & the Middle East 5 hours, five days a week, Mon-Fri, with relg instruction content.

WNQM Inc., Group owner: F.W. Robbert Broadcasting Inc. 1300 WWCR Ave., Nashville, TN, 37218. Phone: (615) 255-1300. Phone: (800) 238-5576. Fax: (615) 255-1311.E-mail: wwcr@wwcr.com Web Site:www.wwcr.com

Eric Westenberger, CEO.

WWCR Nashville. Frequencies: 3.210 mhz, 5.070 mhz,

5.935 mhz, 7.465 mhz, 9.475 mhz, 12.160 mhz, 15.825 mhz.

World Christian Broadcasting Corp., Operations Center, 605 Bradley Court, Franklin, TN, 37067-8200. Phone: (615) 371-8707. Fax: (615) 371-8791. E-mail: gcrowe@worldchristian.org Web Site:www.knls.org

Charles Caudill, CEO.

KNLS Anchor Point, Alaska (transmission facilities): Relg & secular progmg beamed to Asia, eastern Europe & the Pacific Rim on the international shortwave bands.

Anchor PointAK . KNLS, Box 473. Phone:

World Harvest Radio International, 61300 Ironwood Rd., South Bend, IN, 46614. Phone: (574) 291-8200. Fax: (574) 291-9043.E-mail: whr@lesea.com Web Site:www.whr.org

Pete Sumarall, pres; Joe Hill, sls, opns mgr; Douglas Garlinger, chief engr.

WHRI Indianapolis. Two 100 kw transmitters serving Europe, Russia, North, Central & South America. **KWHR Naalehu, Hawaii.** Two 100 kw transmitters serving primarily Asia, & also Oceania & Australia/New Zealand. **WHRA Greenbush, Me.** One 250 kw transmitter serving Africa & the Middle East. Shortwave transmitters are available for lease (time sls).

World International Broadcasters Inc., Box 88, Red Lion, PA, 17356. Phone: (717) 246-1681, EXT. 140. Fax: (717) 244-9316.E-mail: businessoffice@wgctv.com Web Site:www.wgcbtv.com

John H. Norris, pres; Patricia Norris-Slaughter, sec; John C. Norris, dir; Mary Norris-Michel, dir; Fred Wise, dir.

WINB Red Lion, Pa. Shortwave progmg of programs to Western Europe, the Mediterranean, North Africa, Mexico, Philippines, Guam, Formosa & Australia. Format: Relg.

U.S. International Radio

Voice of America, 330 Independence Ave. S.W., Washington, DC, 20237. Phone: (202) 203-4959. Fax: (202) 203-4960.E-mail: publicrelations@voanews.com Web Site:www.voanews.com

Danforth W. Austin, dir.

Went on the air in 1942, is a multimedia international bcstg svc funded by the U.S govt through Bcstg Bd of Governors. Bcsts more than 1,000 hrs of news, info, educ, & cultural progmg every week to an estimated worldwide audience of more than 138 million people. Programs are produced in 45 languages. AM/FM & shortwave transmitters are located at over 30 transmitting sites world-wide.

Satellite Services

SIRIUS Satellite Radio

A division of Sirius XM Radio. Inc.

1221 Avenue of the Americas, 49th St., New York, NY 10020. Phone: (888) 539-7474. Website: www.sirius.com.

Management: Sirius XM Radio Inc., Gary Parsons, chmn; Mel Karmazin, CEO; Scott Greenstein, pres, chief officer content; James E. Meyer, pres, opns & sls; Patrick L. Donnelly, exec VP & gen counsel; David J. Frear, exec VP & CFO; Dara Altman, exec VP, chief admin officer.

SIRIUS bcsts over 130, digital-quality channels, including 69 channels of 100

commercial-free music, plus channels of sports, news, talk, entertainment, weather & data. SIRIUS also bcsts live play-by-play games of the NFL, NBA & NHL. It is the only radio outlet to provide listeners with every NFL game.

You can install SIRIUS radios yourself or visit an authorize retailer to have it professionally installed. The service can be used in cars, trucks, RVs, homes, offices, stores, & even outdoors. Boaters around the country & up to miles offshore can also tune into SIRIUS.

The receiver product line starts with transportable plug & play radios & continues to high-end receivers with motorized touch-control display screens, as well as radios that are found in new cars & trucks.

SIRIUS radios are currently offered in vehicles from Audi, BMW, Chrysler, Dodge, Ford, Infiniti, Jaguar, Jeep, Land Rover, Lexus, Lincoln, Mazda, Maybach, Mercedes-Benz, Mercury, MINI, Mitsubish Motors, Nissan, Porsche, Subaru, Scion, Toyota, Volkswagen & Volvo.

XM Satellite Radio Inc.

Headquarters, 1255 23rd St N.W., Washington, DC 20037. Phone: (202) 969-7050.

XM Innovation Center 3161 S.W. 10th St., Deerfield Beach, FL 33442. Phone: (954) 571-4300; Fax: (954) 360-2521. Website: www.xmradio.com. Contact: XM Satellite Radio (866) 962-2557.

OEM Liason Office 39810 Grand River, Suite 180, Novi, MI 48375-2138. Phone: (248) 478-6500; Fax: 248-427-9958.

Japan Office XM Satellite Radio, c/o Eugene Moosa-Mikami, Bellhouse B, 27-18 Honmoku Wada, Nakaku, Yokohama, 231-0827. Phone/Fax: 81-45-621-4519.

XM Studios-New York Economist Building, 111 W. 57th St., New York, NY 10019. Phone: (212) 956-5656.

XM Studios-Nashville Country Music Hall of Fame & Museum, 222 5th Ave. S., Nashville, TN 37203.

XM Satellite Radio Inc. is a wholly owned subsidiary of the publicly traded XM Satellite Radio Holdings Inc. (Nasdaq: XMSR).

Management: Gary Parsons, chmn.

Director & Member: Nathaniel A. Davis.

XM Satellite Radio Programming: Authoritative news & talk: NPR, CNN, FOX News, BBC, World Service, CNBC & others. Entertainment & comedy: Laugh Attack, High Voltage, Fox News Talk, Radio Disney & many more. sports Coverage: Play-by-play of the NHL, Nascar, MLB & more. Music: New hits, Old favorites, Classical, Country, Broadway, Jazz & more, 100

commercial-free.

U.S. AM Stations by Call Letters

KAAA Kingman, AZ
KAAB Batesville, AR
KAAM(AM) Garland, TX
KAAN Bethany, MO
KAAY Little Rock, AR
KABC Los Angeles, CA
KABI Abilene, KS
KABQ Albuquerque, NM
*KABR Alamo Community, NM
KACE(AM) Bishop, CA
KACH Preston, ID
KACI The Dalles, OR
KACT Andrews, TX
KADA Ada, OK
KADI(AM) Springfield, MO
KADR Elkader, IA
KADS Elk City, OK
KAFF Flagstaff, AZ
KAFY(AM) Bakersfield, CA
KAGC Bryan, TX
KAGE Winona, MN
KAGH Crossett, AR
*KAGI Grants Pass, OR
KAGO Klamath Falls, OR
KAGV(AM) Big Lake, AK
KAGY Port Sulphur, LA
KAHI Auburn, CA
KAHL(AM) San Antonio, TX
KAHS(AM) El Dorado, KS
KAHZ(AM) Pomona, CA
KAIR Atchison, KS
KAJO(AM) Grants Pass, OR
KAKC(AM) Tulsa, OK
KAKK(AM) Walker, MN
KALE Richland, WA
KALI West Covina, CA
KALL(AM) North Salt Lake City, UT
KALM Thayer, MO
KALV Alva, OK
KALY Los Ranchos de Albuquerque, NM
KAMA El Paso, TX
*KAMI(AM) Cozad, NE
KAML Kenedy-Karnes City, TX
KAMQ Carlsbad, NM
KANA(AM) Anaconda, MT
KAND Corsicana, TX
KANE New Iberia, LA
KANI Wharton, TX
*KANN Roy, UT
KAOI(AM) Kihei, HI
KAOK Lake Charles, LA
KAOL Carrollton, MO
KAPE Cape Girardeau, MO
*KAPL(AM) Phoenix, OR
KAPR Douglas, AZ
KAPS Mount Vernon, WA
KAPZ Bald Knob, AR
KARI Blaine, WA
KARN Little Rock, AR
*KARR Kirkland, WA
KARS Belen, NM
KART Jerome, ID
KARV Russellville, AR
KASA Phoenix, AZ
KASI Ames, IA
KASL Newcastle, WY
KASM Albany, MN
KASO Minden, LA
KAST Astoria, OR
KATA Arcata, CA
KATD Pittsburg, CA
KATE Albert Lea, MN
KATH(AM) Frisco, TX
KATK Carlsbad, NM
KATL(AM) Miles City, MT
KATO Safford, AZ
KATQ Plentywood, MT
KATZ(AM) Saint Louis, MO
KAUS Austin, MN
KAVA Pueblo, CO

KAVL Lancaster, CA
KAVP(AM) Colona, CO
*KAWC Yuma, AZ
KAWL York, NE
KAWW(AM) Heber Springs, AR
KAYL Storm Lake, IA
KAYS Hays, KS
KAZA(AM) Gilroy, CA
KAZG(AM) Scottsdale, AZ
KAZM(AM) Sedona, AZ
KAZN Pasadena, CA
KBAD Las Vegas, NV
KBAI(AM) Bellingham, WA
KBAM Longview, WA
KBAR Burley, ID
*KBBI Homer, AK
KBBO(AM) Selah, WA
KBBR(AM) North Bend, OR
KBBS Buffalo, WY
KBBW Waco, TX
KBCH Lincoln City, OR
KBCK(AM) Deer Lodge, MT
KBCL(AM) Bossier City, LA
KBCQ(AM) Roswell, NM
KBCR Steamboat Springs, CO
KBCV(AM) Hollister, MO
KBDB(AM) Sparks, NV
KBEC(AM) Waxahachie, TX
KBED(AM) Nederland, TX
KBEN Carrizo Springs, TX
KBET(AM) Winchester, NV
KBEW Blue Earth, MN
KBFI(AM) Bonners Ferry, ID
KBFL(AM) Springfield, MO
KBFP(AM) Bakersfield, CA
KBFS Belle Fourche, SD
KBGG(AM) Des Moines, IA
KBGN Caldwell, ID
KBHB Sturgis, SD
KBHC Nashville, AR
KBHS(AM) Hot Springs, AR
*KBIB Marion, TX
KBIF Fresno, CA
KBIM Roswell, NM
KBIS(AM) Forks, WA
KBIX Muskogee, OK
KBIZ Ottumwa, IA
KBJA(AM) Sandy, UT
KBJD Denver, CO
KBJM Lemmon, SD
KBJT Fordyce, AR
KBKB Fort Madison, IA
KBKR Baker City, OR
KBKW Aberdeen, WA
KBLA Santa Monica, CA
*KBLE(AM) Seattle, WA
KBLF Red Bluff, CA
KBLG Billings, MT
KBLI(AM) Blackfoot, ID
KBLJ(AM) La Junta, CO
KBLL Helena, MT
KBLU Yuma, AZ
KBLY(AM) Idaho Falls, ID
KBME Houston, TX
KBMO(AM) Benson, MN
KBMR Bismarck, ND
KBMS Vancouver, WA
KBMW Breckenridge, MN
KBND Bend, OR
KBNN Lebanon, MO
KBNO(AM) Denver, CO
KBNP Portland, OR
KBNW(AM) Bend, OR
KBOA Kennett, MO
KBOE Oskaloosa, IA
KBOI Boise, ID
KBOK(AM) Malvern, AR
KBOV(AM) Bishop, CA
KBOW Butte, MT
KBOZ Bozeman, MT

KBPO(AM) Port Neches, TX
*KBPS Portland, OR
KBQX(AM) Big Spring, TX
KBRB Ainsworth, NE
KBRC(AM) Mount Vernon, WA
KBRD Lacey, WA
KBRF Fergus Falls, MN
KBRH Baton Rouge, LA
KBRI Brinkley, AR
KBRK Brookings, SD
KBRL McCook, NE
KBRN Boerne, TX
KBRO Bremerton, WA
KBRT Avalon, CA
KBRV Soda Springs, ID
*KBRW(AM) Barrow, AK
KBRX O'Neill, NE
KBRZ(AM) Missouri City, TX
KBSF Springhill, LA
KBSN Moses Lake, WA
KBSR Laurel, MT
KBST Big Spring, TX
*KBSU Boise, ID
KBSZ Wickenburg, AZ
KBTA Batesville, AR
KBTC Houston, TX
KBTM(AM) Jonesboro, AR
KBTN(AM) Neosho, MO
KBUF(AM) Holcomb, KS
KBUL Billings, MT
KBUN Bemidji, MN
KBUR Burlington, IA
KBUY Ruidoso, NM
KBWD Brownwood, TX
KBYG Big Spring, TX
KBYO Tallulah, LA
KBYR(AM) Anchorage, AK
KBZO Lubbock, TX
KBZY Salem, OR
KBZZ(AM) Sparks, NV
KCAA(AM) Loma Linda, CA
KCAB Dardanelle, AR
KCAL Redlands, CA
KCAM Glennallen, AK
KCAP Helena, MT
KCAR Clarksville, TX
*KCAT Pine Bluff, AR
KCBC Riverbank, CA
KCBF Fairbanks, AK
KCBL Fresno, CA
KCBQ San Diego, CA
KCBR Monument, CO
KCBS San Francisco, CA
KCCB Corning, AR
KCCC Carlsbad, NM
KCCR Pierre, SD
KCCT Corpus Christi, TX
KCCV Overland Park, KS
KCEE(AM) Tucson, AZ
KCEO Vista, CA
KCFC(AM) Boulder, CO
KCFJ(AM) Alturas, CA
KCFM(AM) Florence, OR
KCFO Tulsa, OK
*KCFR(AM) Denver, CO
KCGS Marshall, AR
KCHA Charles City, IA
KCHE(AM) Cherokee, IA
KCHI Chillicothe, MO
KCHJ Delano, CA
KCHK New Prague, MN
KCHL San Antonio, TX
KCHN(AM) Brookshire, TX
KCHR Charleston, MO
KCHS Truth or Consequences, NM
*KCHU(AM) Valdez, AK
KCID(AM) Caldwell, ID
KCII(AM) Washington, IA
KCIK(AM) Blue Lake, CA
KCIM Carroll, IA

KCIS(AM) Edmonds, WA
KCJB Minot, ND
KCJJ(AM) Iowa City, IA
KCKK(AM) Littleton, CO
KCKM(AM) Monahans, TX
KCKN(AM) Roswell, NM
KCKX Stayton, OR
KCKY Coolidge, AZ
KCLA Pine Bluff, AR
KCLE(AM) Burleson, TX
KCLF(AM) New Roads, LA
KCLI Clinton, OK
KCLK Asotin, WA
KCLN Clinton, IA
KCLR Ralls, TX
KCLU(AM) Santa Barbara, CA
KCLV(AM) Clovis, NM
KCLW Hamilton, TX
KCLX Colfax, WA
KCMC Texarkana, TX
KCMD(AM) Portland, OR
KCMN Colorado Springs, CO
KCMO Kansas City, MO
KCMW(AM) Boise, ID
KCMX Phoenix, OR
KCMY(AM) Carson City, NV
KCNI Broken Bow, NE
KCNM(AM) Garapan-Saipan, NP
KCNN East Grand Forks, MN
KCNR(AM) Shasta, CA
KCNW(AM) Fairway, KS
KCNZ(AM) Cedar Falls, IA
KCOB Newton, IA
KCOG Centerville, IA
KCOH Houston, TX
KCOL(AM) Wellington, CO
KCOM Comanche, TX
KCOR(AM) San Antonio, TX
KCOW Alliance, NE
KCOX(AM) Jasper, TX
KCPS Burlington, IA
KCPX(AM) Spanish Valley, UT
KCQL Aztec, NM
KCRC Enid, OK
KCRN San Angelo, TX
KCRO Omaha, NE
KCRS(AM) Midland, TX
KCRT Trinidad, CO
KCRV Caruthersville, MO
KCRX Roswell, NM
KCSF(AM) Colorado Springs, CO
KCSJ Pueblo, CO
KCSP(AM) Kansas City, MO
KCSR Chadron, NE
KCTA Corpus Christi, TX
KCTC(AM) West Sacramento, CA
KCTE Independence, MO
KCTI(AM) Gonzales, TX
KCTO(AM) Cleveland, MO
KCTX(AM) Childress, TX
KCUB Tucson, AZ
KCUE Red Wing, MN
KCUL Marshall, TX
KCUP(AM) Toledo, OR
KCUZ Clifton, AZ
KCVL Colville, WA
KCVR Lodi, CA
KCWJ(AM) Blue Springs, MO
KCWM Hondo, TX
KCXL Liberty, MO
KCYL Lampasas, TX
KCZZ(AM) Mission, KS
KDAC Fort Bragg, CA
KDAE Sinton, TX
KDAK Carrington, ND
KDAL Duluth, MN
KDAN(AM) Beatty, NV
KDAO Marshalltown, IA
KDAP Douglas, AZ
KDAV Lubbock, TX

KDAZ(AM) Albuquerque, NM
KDBM Dillon, MT
KDBS Alexandria, LA
KDBV(AM) Salinas, CA
KDCC Dodge City, KS
KDCE(AM) Espanola, NM
KDDD Dumas, TX
KDDR Oakes, ND
KDDZ Arvada, CO
KDEC Decorah, IA
KDEF Albuquerque, NM
*KDEI(AM) Port Arthur, TX
KDET Center, TX
KDEX Dexter, MO
KDFN Doniphan, MO
KDFT Ferris, TX
KDGO Durango, CO
KDHL Faribault, MN
KDHN Dimmitt, TX
KDIA Vallejo, CA
KDIF Riverside, CA
KDIL(AM) Dillon, MT
KDIO Ortonville, MN
KDIS(AM) Pasadena, CA
KDIX Dickinson, ND
KDIZ Golden Valley, MN
KDJI Holbrook, AZ
KDJQ(AM) Meridian, ID
KDJS Willmar, MN
KDJW(AM) Amarillo, TX
KDKA Pittsburgh, PA
KDKD Clinton, MO
KDKT(AM) Beulah, ND
KDLA De Ridder, LA
*KDLG Dillingham, AK
KDLM Detroit Lakes, MN
KDLR Devils Lake, ND
KDLS Perry, IA
KDMA Montevideo, MN
KDMO Carthage, MO
KDMS El Dorado, AR
KDNZ(AM) Cedar Falls, IA
KDOK(AM) Kilgore, TX
KDOM Windom, MN
KDOW(AM) Palo Alto, CA
KDOX Henderson, NV
KDQN De Queen, AR
KDRO Sedalia, MO
KDRS Paragould, AR
KDRY Alamo Heights, TX
KDSJ Deadwood, SD
KDSN(AM) Denison, IA
KDTA Delta, CO
KDTD(AM) Kansas City, KS
KDTH Dubuque, IA
KDUN(AM) Reedsport, OR
KDUS Tempe, AZ
KDUZ Hutchinson, MN
KDWA Hastings, MN
KDWN Las Vegas, NV
KDXE(AM) North Little Rock, AR
KDXU Saint George, UT
KDYA Vallejo, CA
KDYK(AM) Union Gap, WA
KDYL(AM) South Salt Lake, UT
KDYM(AM) Sunnyside, WA
KDYN Ozark, AR
KDZA(AM) Pueblo, CO
KDZR(AM) Lake Oswego, OR
KEAR(AM) San Francisco, CA
KEAS Eastland, TX
KEBC(AM) Midwest City, OK
KEBE Jacksonville, TX
*KEBR Rocklin, CA
*KECR El Cajon, CA
KEDA San Antonio, TX
KEDO Longview, WA
KEEL(AM) Shreveport, LA
KEES Gladewater, TX
KEHT(AM) Eads, CO

KEIN Great Falls, MT
KEIP(AM) Las Vegas, NV
KEJO Corvallis, OR
KELA Centralia-Chehalis, WA
KELD El Dorado, AR
KELE Mountain Grove, MO
KELG(AM) Manor, TX
KELK Elko, NV
KELO Sioux Falls, SD
KELP El Paso, TX
KELY Ely, NV
KENA(AM) Mena, AR
KENI Anchorage, AK
KENN Farmington, NM
KENO Las Vegas, NV
KENT(AM) Parowan, UT
KEOR(AM) Catoosa, OK
KEPL(AM) Estes Park, CO
KEPN(AM) Lakewood, CO
KEPS Eagle Pass, TX
KERB Kermit, TX
KERI(AM) Bakersfield, CA
KERN(AM) Wasco-Greenacres, CA
KERR Polson, MT
KERV Kerrville, TX
KESJ(AM) Saint Joseph, MO
KESM El Dorado Springs, MO
KESP(AM) Modesto, CA
KESQ Indio, CA
KEST San Francisco, CA
KETX Livingston, TX
KEUN Eunice, LA
KEVA Evanston, WY
KEVT(AM) Sahuarita, AZ
KEWA(AM) Ewa Beach, HI
KEWE(AM) Oroville, CA
KEWI(AM) Benton, AR
KEX Portland, OR
KEXO Grand Junction, CO
*KEXS(AM) Excelsior Springs, MO
KEYE Perryton, TX
KEYF(AM) Dishman, WA
KEYG Grand Coulee, WA
KEYH Houston, TX
KEYL Long Prairie, MN
*KEYQ Fresno, CA
KEYS(AM) Corpus Christi, TX
*KEYY(AM) Provo, UT
KEYZ Williston, ND
*KEZJ Twin Falls, ID
KEZL(AM) Visalia, CA
KEZM Sulphur, LA
KEZW Aurora, CO
*KEZX(AM) Medford, OR
KEZY San Bernardino, CA
KFAB Omaha, NE
KFAL Fulton, MO
KFAN Minneapolis, MN
KFAQ(AM) Tulsa, OK
KFAR Fairbanks, AK
KFAX San Francisco, CA
KFAY Farmington, AR
KFBC Cheyenne, WY
KFBK Sacramento, CA
KFBX(AM) Fairbanks, AK
KFCD(AM) Farmersville, TX
KFCR Custer, SD
KFEL Pueblo, CO
KFEQ(AM) Saint Joseph, MO
KFFA Helena, AR
KFFF(AM) Boone, IA
KFFK(AM) Rogers, AR
KFFN Tucson, AZ
KFGO Fargo, ND
KFH(AM) Wichita, KS
KFI Los Angeles, CA
KFIA Carmichael, CA
KFIG Fresno, CA
KFIL Preston, MN
KFIR Sweet Home, OR
KFIT-EX San Antonio, TX
KFIT Lockhart, TX
KFIV Modesto, CA
KFIZ Fond du Lac, WI
KFJB Marshalltown, IA
KFJL(AM) Central Point, OR

KFJZ Fort Worth, TX
KFKA(AM) Greeley, CO
*KFLB(AM) Odessa, TX
KFLC(AM) Fort Worth, TX
KFLD Pasco, WA
KFLG(AM) Bullhead City, AZ
KFLN Baker, MT
KFLP(AM) Floydada, TX
KFLS Klamath Falls, OR
*KFLT Tucson, AZ
KFMB San Diego, CA
KFMO Park Hills, MO
KFMZ(AM) Brookfield, MO
KFNN Mesa, AZ
KFNS(AM) Wood River, IL
*KFNW(AM) West Fargo, ND
KFNX Cave Creek, AZ
KFNZ Salt Lake City, UT
KFON Austin, TX
KFOR(AM) Lincoln, NE
KFOX(AM) Torrance, CA
KFOY(AM) Sparks, NV
KFPT(AM) Clovis, CA
KFPW Fort Smith, AR
KFQD Anchorage, AK
KFRA Franklin, LA
KFRC(AM) San Francisco, CA
KFRM(AM) Salina, KS
*KFRN Long Beach, CA
KFRO Longview, TX
KFRU Columbia, MO
KFSA Fort Smith, AR
KFSD(AM) Escondido, CA
KFSG(AM) Roseville, CA
KFST Fort Stockton, TX
KFTA(AM) Rupert, ID
KFTI(AM) Wichita, KS
KFTM Fort Morgan, CO
KFUN Las Vegas, NM
*KFUO(AM) Clayton, MO
KFUT(AM) Thousand Palms, CA
KFVR Crescent City, CA
KFWB Los Angeles, CA
KFXD(AM) Boise, ID
KFXN Minneapolis, MN
KFXR(AM) Dallas, TX
KFXX(AM) Portland, OR
KFXY(AM) Enid, OK
KFXZ(AM) Lafayette, LA
KFYI(AM) Phoenix, AZ
KFYN Bonham, TX
KFYO Lubbock, TX
KFYR Bismarck, ND
KGA Spokane, WA
KGAB Orchard Valley, WY
KGAF Gainesville, TX
KGAK Gallup, NM
KGAL(AM) Lebanon, OR
KGAM Palm Springs, CA
KGAS Carthage, TX
KGAY(AM) Ashland, OR
KGBA(AM) Calexico, CA
KGBC Galveston, TX
KGBT Harlingen, TX
KGDC Walla Walla, WA
KGDD(AM) Oregon City, OR
KGDP(AM) Oildale, CA
KGED(AM) Fresno, CA
KGEM(AM) Boise, ID
KGEN Tulare, CA
KGEO Bakersfield, CA
KGEZ Kalispell, MT
KGFF Shawnee, OK
KGFL Clinton, AR
KGFW(AM) Kearney, NE
KGFX Pierre, SD
KGGF Coffeyville, KS
KGGN Gladstone, MO
KGGR Dallas, TX
KGGS(AM) Garden City, KS
KGHL Billings, MT
KGHS International Falls, MN
KGIL(AM) Beverly Hills, CA
KGIM Aberdeen, SD
KGIR Cape Girardeau, MO
KGIW Alamosa, CO

KGKL San Angelo, TX
KGLA Gretna, LA
KGLB(AM) Saint Peter, MN
KGLD Tyler, TX
KGLE Glendive, MT
KGLN Glenwood Springs, CO
KGLO(AM) Mason City, IA
KGME(AM) Phoenix, AZ
KGMI Bellingham, WA
KGMS(AM) Tucson, AZ
KGMT Fairbury, NE
KGMY Springfield, MO
KGNB New Braunfels, TX
KGNC Amarillo, TX
KGND(AM) Vinita, OK
KGNM Saint Joseph, MO
KGNO Dodge City, KS
*KGNU(AM) Denver, CO
KGNW Burien-Seattle, WA
KGO San Francisco, CA
KGOE Eureka, CA
KGOL Humble, TX
KGOS Torrington, WY
KGOW(AM) Bellaire, TX
KGRE Greeley, CO
KGRG(AM) Enumclaw, WA
KGRN Grinnell, IA
KGRO Pampa, TX
KGRV Winston, OR
KGRZ Missoula, MT
KGSO(AM) Wichita, KS
KGST Fresno, CA
KGTK(AM) Olympia, WA
KGTL Homer, AK
KGTO Tulsa, OK
KGU Honolulu, HI
KGUM(AM) Hagatna, GU
KGVL Greenville, TX
KGVO Missoula, MT
KGVW Belgrade, MT
KGVY(AM) Green Valley, AZ
KGWA(AM) Enid, OK
KGY Olympia, WA
KGYM(AM) Cedar Rapids, IA
KGYN Guymon, OK
KHAC Tse Bonito, NM
KHAR Anchorage, AK
KHAS Hastings, NE
KHAT(AM) Laramie, WY
KHBM Monticello, AR
KHBR Hillsboro, TX
KHBZ(AM) Honolulu, HI
*KHCB Galveston, TX
*KHCH(AM) Huntsville, TX
KHCM(AM) Honolulu, HI
KHDN(AM) Hardin, MT
KHEY(AM) El Paso, TX
KHFT(AM) Chugiak, AK
KHFX(AM) Cleburne, TX
KHGG(AM) Van Buren, AR
KHHO Tacoma, WA
KHIL Willcox, AZ
KHIT Reno, NV
KHJ(AM) Los Angeles, CA
KHLO Hilo, HI
KHLT(AM) Hallettsville, TX
KHMO Hannibal, MO
KHNC Johnstown, CO
KHND Harvey, ND
KHNR(AM) Honolulu, HI
KHNU(AM) Hilo, HI
KHNY(AM) Big Horn, WY
KHOB Hobbs, NM
KHOJ(AM) Saint Charles, MO
KHOT Madera, CA
KHOW Denver, CO
KHOZ Harrison, AR
KHPI(AM) Moreno Valley, CA
KHPP(AM) Waukon, IA
KHPY(AM) Moreno Valley, CA
KHQN Spanish Fork, UT
KHRA(AM) Honolulu, HI
KHRJ(AM) Del Norte, CO
KHRO(AM) El Paso, TX
KHRT Minot, ND
KHRX(AM) Marathon, TX

KHSE(AM) Wylie, TX
KHSN(AM) Coos Bay, OR
KHTK Sacramento, CA
KHTS(AM) Canyon Country, CA
KHTW(AM) Langtry, TX
KHTY(AM) Bakersfield, CA
KHUA(AM) Presidio, TX
KHUB Fremont, NE
KHVH Honolulu, HI
KHVL(AM) Huntsville, TX
KHVN Fort Worth, TX
KHWG(AM) Fallon, NV
KIAM Nenana, AK
KIBL Beeville, TX
KICA Clovis, NM
KICD Spencer, IA
KICE(AM) Bend, OR
KICS Hastings, NE
KICY Nome, AK
KID Idaho Falls, ID
KIDD Monterey, CA
KIDO(AM) Nampa, ID
KIDR Phoenix, AZ
KIEV(AM) Culver City, CA
KIFG Iowa Falls, IA
KIFO(AM) Hawthorne, NV
KIFW Sitka, AK
KIGO(AM) Saint Anthony, ID
KIGS Hanford, CA
KIHH(AM) Eureka, CA
*KIHM(AM) Reno, NV
KIHN Hugo, OK
KIHR Hood River, OR
KIHU(AM) Tooele, UT
KIID(AM) Sacramento, CA
KIIX(AM) Fort Collins, CO
KIJN Farwell, TX
KIJV Huron, SD
KIKC(AM) Forsyth, MT
KIKK Pasadena, TX
KIKO Miami, AZ
KIKR Beaumont, TX
KIKZ Seminole, TX
KILE(AM) Hilo, HI
KILJ Mount Pleasant, IA
KILR Estherville, IA
KILT Houston, TX
KIMB Kimball, NE
KIML Gillette, WY
KIMM Rapid City, SD
KIMP(AM) Mount Pleasant, TX
KINA Salina, KS
KIND Independence, KS
KINE Kingsville, TX
KINN Alamogordo, NM
KINO Winslow, AZ
KINS Eureka, CA
KINY Juneau, AK
KIOL(AM) Iola, KS
KION(AM) Salinas, CA
KIOU Shreveport, LA
KIOV Payette, ID
KIPA(AM) Hilo, HI
KIQI San Francisco, CA
KIQQ Barstow, CA
KIQS Willows, CA
KIRN(AM) Simi Valley, CA
KIRO Seattle, WA
KIRT Mission, TX
KIRV Fresno, CA
KIRX Kirksville, MO
KIST(AM) Santa Barbara, CA
KIT Yakima, WA
KITI Chehalis-Centralia, WA
KITZ Silverdale, WA
KIUL Garden City, KS
KIUN Pecos, TX
KIUP Durango, CO
KIVA(AM) Albuquerque, NM
KIVY Crockett, TX
KIWA Sheldon, IA
KIXI Mercer Island-Seattle, WA
KIXK(AM) Dalhart, TX
KIXL(AM) Del Valle, TX
KIXW(AM) Apple Valley, CA
KIXZ Amarillo, TX

KIYU Galena, AK
KJAA Globe, AZ
KJAL(AM) Tafuna, AS
KJAM(AM) Madison, SD
KJAN(AM) Atlantic, IA
KJAY Sacramento, CA
KJBN Little Rock, AR
KJCB Lafayette, LA
KJCE Rollingwood, TX
KJCK(AM) Junction City, KS
KJDJ San Luis Obispo, CA
KJDL(AM) Lubbock, TX
KJDY John Day, OR
KJEF(AM) Jennings, LA
KJFF(AM) Festus, MO
KJFK(AM) Reno, NV
KJIM Sherman, TX
KJIN(AM) Houma, LA
KJJD(AM) Windsor, CO
KJJK Fergus Falls, MN
KJJQ Volga, SD
KJJR Whitefish, MT
KJLL South Tucson, AZ
*KJLT North Platte, NE
KJMJ(AM) Alexandria, LA
KJML(AM) Desert Hot Springs, CA
KJMP(AM) Pierce, CO
KJMU(AM) Sand Springs, OK
KJNO(AM) Juneau, AK
*KJNP(AM) North Pole, AK
*KJNT(AM) Jackson, WY
KJOC Davenport, IA
KJOJ Conroe, TX
KJOK(AM) Yuma, AZ
KJOL(AM) Grand Junction, CO
KJON(AM) Carrollton, TX
KJOP Lemoore, CA
KJOX(AM) Yakima, WA
KJPG(AM) Frazier Park, CA
KJPR(AM) Shasta Lake City, CA
KJPW Waynesville, MO
KJQS(AM) Murray, UT
KJR Seattle, WA
KJRB Spokane, WA
KJRG Newton, KS
KJSA Mineral Wells, TX
KJSK(AM) Columbus, NE
KJSL Saint Louis, MO
KJTV(AM) Lubbock, TX
KJUA(AM) Cheyenne, WY
KJUG Tulare, CA
KJXX(AM) Jackson, MO
*KKAA(AM) Aberdeen, SD
KKAD(AM) Vancouver, WA
KKAM Lubbock, TX
KKAN Phillipsburg, KS
KKAQ Thief River Falls, MN
KKAR Omaha, NE
KKAT(AM) Salt Lake City, UT
KKAY White Castle, LA
KKBJ(AM) Bemidji, MN
KKCQ Fosston, MN
KKDA Grand Prairie, TX
KKDD San Bernardino, CA
KKDZ Seattle, WA
KKEA(AM) Honolulu, HI
KKEE(AM) Astoria, OR
KKGM(AM) Fort Worth, TX
KKGN(AM) Oakland, CA
KKGR East Helena, MT
KKHJ(AM) Leone, AS
KKIM Albuquerque, NM
KKIN Aitkin, MN
KKJL San Luis Obispo, CA
KKKK(AM) Colorado Springs, CO
KKLE(AM) Winfield, KS
KKLF(AM) Richardson, TX
KKLL(AM) Carthage-, MO
KKLO Leavenworth, KS
KKLS Rapid City, SD
KKMC Gonzales, CA
KKMO Tacoma, WA
KKMS Richfield, MN
KKNE(AM) Waipahu, HI
KKNO Gretna, LA
KKNS(AM) Corrales, NM

KKNT(AM) Phoenix, AZ
KKNW(AM) Seattle, WA
KKNX Eugene, OR
KKOB-EX Santa Fe, NM
KKOB(AM) Albuquerque, NM
KKOH Reno, NV
KKOJ Jackson, MN
KKOL Seattle, WA
KKON(AM) Kealakekua, HI
KKOW Pittsburg, KS
KKOY Chanute, KS
KKOZ Ava, MO
KKPC Pueblo, CO
KKPZ(AM) Portland, OR
KKRT Wenatchee, WA
KKRX Lawton, OK
KKSA San Angelo, TX
*KKSM Oceanside, CA
KKTK(AM) Texarkana, TX
KKTL Casper, WY
KKTX(AM) Corpus Christi, TX
KKTY Douglas, WY
KKUB Brownfield, TX
KKVV(AM) Las Vegas, NV
KKXL Grand Forks, ND
KKXX Paradise, CA
KKYX San Antonio, TX
KKZN(AM) Thornton, CO
KKZZ(AM) Santa Paula, CA
KLAA(AM) Orange, CA
KLAC Los Angeles, CA
KLAD(AM) Klamath Falls, OR
KLAM Cordova, AK
KLAR Laredo, TX
KLAT Houston, TX
KLAV(AM) Las Vegas, NV
KLAY(AM) Lakewood, WA
KLBB(AM) Stillwater, MN
KLBJ Austin, TX
KLBM La Grande, OR
KLBS Los Banos, CA
KLBW(AM) New Boston, TX
KLCB Libby, MT
KLCK Goldendale, WA
KLCL Lake Charles, LA
KLCN Blytheville, AR
KLDC(AM) Denver, CO
KLDS Falfurrias, TX
KLDY Lacey, WA
KLEA Lovington, NM
KLEB Golden Meadow, LA
KLEE Ottumwa, IA
KLEM(AM) Le Mars, IA
KLER Orofino, ID
KLEX Lexington, MO
KLEY(AM) Wellington, KS
KLFD Litchfield, MN
KLFE Seattle, WA
KLFF(AM) Arroyo Grande, CA
KLFJ Springfield, MO
KLGA Algona, IA
KLGN Logan, UT
KLGR Redwood Falls, MN
KLHC(AM) Bakersfield, CA
KLHT Honolulu, HI
KLIB(AM) Roseville, CA
KLIC(AM) Monroe, LA
KLID Poplar Bluff, MO
KLIF(AM) Dallas, TX
KLIK(AM) Jefferson City, MO
KLIM Limon, CO
KLIN Lincoln, NE
KLIV San Jose, CA
KLIX Twin Falls, ID
KLIZ(AM) Brainerd, MN
KLKC(AM) Parsons, KS
KLLA Leesville, LA
KLLB West Jordan, UT
KLLK Willits, CA
KLLV(AM) Breen, CO
KLMR Lamar, CO
KLMS(AM) Lincoln, NE
KLMX Clayton, NM
KLNG(AM) Council Bluffs, IA
KLNT Laredo, TX
KLO Ogden, UT

KLOA Ridgecrest, CA
KLOC(AM) Turlock, CA
KLOE Goodland, KS
KLOG Kelso, WA
KLOH Pipestone, MN
KLOK San Jose, CA
KLOO Corvallis, OR
KLPF(AM) Midland, TX
KLPL Lake Providence, LA
KLPM(AM) Portland, OR
KLPW(AM) Union, MO
KLPZ Parker, AZ
KLRG(AM) Sheridan, AR
KLSD(AM) San Diego, CA
KLSQ(AM) Whitney, NV
KLTC Dickinson, ND
KLTF Little Falls, MN
KLTI Macon, MO
KLTK(AM) Centerton, AR
KLTT Commerce City, CO
KLTX Long Beach, CA
KLTZ Glasgow, MT
KLUP(AM) Terrell Hills, TX
KLVI Beaumont, TX
KLVL Pasadena, TX
KLVQ(AM) Athens, TX
KLVT Levelland, TX
KLVZ(AM) Brighton, CO
KLWN(AM) Lawrence, KS
KLWT Lebanon, MO
KLXR(AM) Redding, CA
KLXX Bismarck-Mandan, ND
KLYC(AM) McMinnville, OR
KLYQ Hamilton, MT
KLYR Clarksville, AR
KLZ Denver, CO
KLZS(AM) Eugene, OR
KMA Shenandoah, IA
KMAD Madill, OK
KMAJ Topeka, KS
KMAL(AM) Malden, MO
KMAM(AM) Butler, MO
KMAN Manhattan, KS
KMAQ Maquoketa, IA
KMAS(AM) Shelton, WA
KMAX Colfax, WA
KMBD Tillamook, OR
*KMBI Spokane, WA
KMBL Junction, TX
KMBQ(AM) Wasilla, AK
KMBS West Monroe, LA
KMBX(AM) Soledad, CA
KMBZ Kansas City, MO
KMCD Fairfield, IA
KMCL(AM) Donnelly, ID
KMDO Fort Scott, KS
KMED Medford, OR
KMER Kemmerer, WY
KMET Banning, CA
KMFS(AM) Guthrie, OK
KMFX Wabasha, MN
KMHI Mountain Home, ID
KMHL Marshall, MN
KMHS Coos Bay, OR
KMHT Marshall, TX
KMIA(AM) Black Canyon City, AZ
KMIC(AM) Houston, TX
KMIK Tempe, AZ
KMIN Grants, NM
KMIS Portageville, MO
KMJ Fresno, CA
KMJC Mount Shasta, CA
KMJM(AM) Cedar Rapids, IA
KMKI Plano, TX
KMKY Oakland, CA
KMLB(AM) Monroe, LA
KMMJ Grand Island, NE
KMMM(AM) Pratt, KS
KMMO Marshall, MO
KMMQ(AM) Plattsmouth, NE
KMMS(AM) Bozeman, MT
KMND Midland, TX
KMNQ(AM) Brooklyn Park, MN
KMNS Sioux City, IA
KMNV(AM) Saint Paul, MN
KMNY(AM) Hurst, TX

KMOG Payson, AZ
KMON Great Falls, MT
KMOX Saint Louis, MO
KMOZ Rolla, MO
KMPC(AM) Los Angeles, CA
KMPG Hollister, CA
KMPH(AM) Modesto, CA
KMPT(AM) East Missoula, MT
KMRB San Gabriel, CA
KMRC Morgan City, LA
KMRF Marshfield, MO
KMRI West Valley City, UT
KMRN Cameron, MO
KMRS Morris, MN
KMRY Cedar Rapids, IA
KMSD Milbank, SD
KMSR(AM) Mayville, ND
KMTA Miles City, MT
KMTI Manti, UT
KMTL Sherwood, AR
KMTX Helena, MT
KMUL(AM) Farwell, TX
KMUS(AM) Sperry, OK
KMVI(AM) Wailuku, HI
KMVL Madisonville, TX
KMVP Phoenix, AZ
KMXA Aurora, CO
KMXO(AM) Merkel, TX
KMYC(AM) Marysville, CA
KMZK Billings, MT
KMZQ(AM) Las Vegas, NV
KNAB Burlington, CO
KNAF Fredericksburg, TX
KNAK Delta, UT
KNAL(AM) Victoria, TX
KNAM(AM) Silt, CO
KNAX(AM) McCook, NE
KNBR San Francisco, CA
KNBY Newport, AR
KNCB Vivian, LA
KNCK Concordia, KS
KNCO(AM) Grass Valley, CA
KNCR Fortuna, CA
KNCY Nebraska City, NE
KNDC Hettinger, ND
KNDI Honolulu, HI
KNDK Langdon, ND
KNDN Farmington, NM
KNDY Marysville, KS
KNEA(AM) Jonesboro, AR
KNEB Scottsbluff, NE
KNED McAlester, OK
KNEK Washington, LA
KNEL Brady, TX
KNEM Nevada, MO
KNET Palestine, TX
KNEU Roosevelt, UT
KNEW Oakland, CA
KNFL(AM) Tremonton, UT
KNFT Bayard, NM
KNGL McPherson, KS
*KNGN McCook, NE
KNGR(AM) Daingerfield, TX
KNHD Camden, AR
KNIA Knoxville, IA
KNIM(AM) Maryville, MO
KNIR New Iberia, LA
KNIT(AM) Dallas, TX
KNIW(AM) Wink, TX
KNJY(AM) Boise, ID
KNLV Ord, NE
KNML(AM) Albuquerque, NM
KNMX Las Vegas, NM
KNND Cottage Grove, OR
KNNS Larned, KS
KNOC Natchitoches, LA
*KNOM Nome, AK
KNOT(AM) Prescott, AZ
KNOX Grand Forks, ND
KNPT Newport, OR
KNRO(AM) Redding, CA
KNRS Salt Lake City, UT
KNRV(AM) Englewood, CO
KNRY Monterey, CA
KNSA Unalakleet, AK
KNSI Saint Cloud, MN

KNSN(AM) San Diego, CA
KNSP(AM) Staples, MN
KNSS(AM) Wichita, KS
KNST Tucson, AZ
KNTB Lakewood, WA
KNTH(AM) Houston, TX
KNTR(AM) Lake Havasu City, AZ
KNTS(AM) Seattle, WA
KNTX(AM) Bowie, TX
KNUI Kahului, HI
KNUJ(AM) New Ulm, MN
KNUS Denver, CO
KNUU(AM) Paradise, NV
KNUV(AM) Tolleson, AZ
KNUZ Bellville, TX
KNWA Bellefonte, AR
*KNWC(AM) Sioux Falls, SD
KNWH(AM) Twentynine Palms, CA
KNWQ(AM) Palm Springs, CA
*KNWS Waterloo, IA
KNWZ(AM) Coachella, CA
KNX Los Angeles, CA
KNXN Sierra Vista, AZ
KNZR Bakersfield, CA
KNZZ(AM) Grand Junction, CO
KOA Denver, CO
*KOAC Corvallis, OR
KOAH(AM) Comstock, TX
KOAI(AM) Van Buren, AR
KOAK Red Oak, IA
KOAL Price, UT
KOAN(AM) Eagle River, AK
KOAQ Terrytown, NE
KOBB Bozeman, MT
KOBE Las Cruces, NM
KOBO Yuba City, CA
KOBY(AM) Cedar City, UT
KOCY(AM) Del City, OK
KODI Cody, WY
KODL The Dalles, OR
KODY North Platte, NE
KOEL(AM) Oelwein, IA
KOFC Fayetteville, AR
KOFE Saint Maries, ID
KOFI Kalispell, MT
KOFO Ottawa, KS
KOGA Ogallala, NE
KOGN(AM) Ogden, UT
KOGO(AM) San Diego, CA
KOGT Orange, TX
KOHI(AM) Saint Helens, OR
KOHU Hermiston, OR
KOIL(AM) Bellevue, NE
KOJM Havre, MT
KOKA Shreveport, LA
KOKB Blackwell, OK
KOKC(AM) Oklahoma City, OK
KOKE Pflugerville, TX
KOKK Huron, SD
KOKL(AM) Okmulgee, OK
KOKO Warrensburg, MO
KOKP Perry, OK
KOKX Keokuk, IA
KOLE Port Arthur, TX
KOLJ(AM) Quanah, TX
KOLM(AM) Rochester, MN
KOLT Scottsbluff, NE
KOLY Mobridge, SD
KOMC Branson, MO
KOMJ(AM) Omaha, NE
KOMO(AM) Seattle, WA
KOMW Omak, WA
KOMY(AM) La Selva Beach, CA
KONA Kennewick, WA
KONO San Antonio, TX
KONP Port Angeles, WA
KOOQ(AM) North Platte, NE
KOOR(AM) Milwaukie, OR
KOPB(AM) Eugene, OR
KOPY Alice, TX
KORC Waldport, OR
KORE Springfield-Eugene, OR
KORL(AM) Honolulu, HI
KORN Mitchell, SD
KORT Grangeville, ID

KOSE Wilson, AR
KOSS(AM) Lancaster, CA
KOSY Texarkana, AR
KOTA Rapid City, SD
KOTC Kennett, MO
KOTK(AM) Omaha, NE
KOTN Pine Bluff, AR
KOTS Deming, NM
*KOTZ Kotzebue, AK
KOUU(AM) Pocatello, ID
KOVC Valley City, ND
KOVE Lander, WY
KOVO Provo, UT
KOWB(AM) Laramie, WY
KOWL(AM) South Lake Tahoe, CA
KOWZ(AM) Waseca, MN
KOXR Oxnard, CA
KOY Phoenix, AZ
KOZA Odessa, TX
KOZE Lewiston, ID
KOZI Chelan, WA
KOZN(AM) Bellevue, NE
KOZQ Waynesville, MO
KOZY Grand Rapids, MN
KPAM Troutdale, OR
KPAN(AM) Hereford, TX
KPAY Chico, CA
KPBL Hemphill, TX
KPCO Quincy, CA
KPDQ Portland, OR
KPEL Lafayette, LA
KPET Lamesa, TX
KPGE Page, AZ
KPGM(AM) Pawhuska, OK
KPHI(AM) Honolulu, HI
KPHN Kansas City, MO
KPHX Phoenix, AZ
KPIG(AM) Piedmont, CA
KPIO(AM) Loveland, CO
KPIR(AM) Granbury, TX
KPJC(AM) Salem, OR
KPKE(AM) Gunnison, CO
KPLT Paris, TX
KPLY(AM) Reno, NV
*KPMO(AM) Mendocino, CA
KPNP(AM) Watertown, MN
KPNS(AM) Duncan, OK
KPNW Eugene, OR
KPOC(AM) Pocahontas, AR
KPOD Crescent City, CA
*KPOF Denver, CO
KPOJ(AM) Portland, OR
KPOK Bowman, ND
KPOW Powell, WY
KPQ(AM) Wenatchee, WA
KPRC Houston, TX
KPRK Livingston, MT
KPRL Paso Robles, CA
KPRM Park Rapids, MN
KPRO Riverside, CA
KPRT Kansas City, MO
KPRV Poteau, OK
KPRZ San Marcos-Poway, CA
KPSI Palm Springs, CA
KPSZ(AM) Des Moines, IA
KPTK(AM) Seattle, WA
KPTO(AM) Pocatello, ID
KPTQ(AM) Spokane, WA
KPTR(AM) Cathedral City, CA
KPUA Hilo, HI
KPUG Bellingham, WA
KPUR Amarillo, TX
KPWB Piedmont, MO
KPWL(AM) Newport, WA
KPXQ(AM) Glendale, AZ
KPYK(AM) Terrell, TX
KPYN(AM) Atlanta, TX
KPZK(AM) Little Rock, AR
KQAB Lake Isabella, CA
KQAD(AM) Luverne, MN
KQAM Wichita, KS
KQAQ(AM) Austin, MN
KQBU(AM) El Paso, TX
KQCV Oklahoma City, OK
KQDE(AM) Columbia Falls, MT
KQDI Great Falls, MT

KQDJ Jamestown, ND
KQDS Duluth, MN
KQEN(AM) Roseburg, OR
KQEQ Fowler, CA
KQIK Lakeview, OR
KQJZ(AM) Evergreen, MT
*KQKD(AM) Redfield, SD
KQLO(AM) Sun Valley, NV
KQLX Lisbon, ND
KQMG Independence, IA
KQMS Redding, CA
KQNA(AM) Prescott Valley, AZ
KQNG Lihue, HI
KQNK Norton, KS
KQNM(AM) Milan, NM
KQNT Spokane, WA
KQPN(AM) West Memphis, AR
KQQQ Pullman, WA
KQSP(AM) Shakopee, MN
KQTY Borger, TX
KQUE Houston, TX
KQV Pittsburgh, PA
KQWB(AM) West Fargo, ND
KQWC Webster City, IA
KQYX(AM) Galena, KS
KRAE Cheyenne, WY
KRAI(AM) Craig, CO
KRAK(AM) Hesperia, CA
KRAL Rawlins, WY
KRAM West Klamath, OR
KRBA(AM) Lufkin, TX
KRBT Eveleth, MN
KRCM Beaumont, TX
KRCN(AM) Longmont, CO
KRCO(AM) Prineville, OR
KRDD Roswell, NM
KRDH(AM) Canton, TX
KRDM(AM) Redmond, OR
KRDO(AM) Colorado Springs, CO
KRDU Dinuba, CA
KRDY(AM) San Antonio, TX
KRDZ Wray, CO
KREA(AM) Honolulu, HI
KREB(AM) Bentonville-Bella Vista, AR
KREF(AM) Norman, OK
KREH Pecan Grove, TX
KREI Farmington, MO
KREW(AM) Plainview, TX
KRFE Lubbock, TX
KRFO Owatonna, MN
KRFS Superior, NE
KRFT(AM) De Soto, MO
KRGE Weslaco, TX
KRGI Grand Island, NE
KRGS(AM) Rifle, CO
KRHC(AM) Burnet, TX
KRHW Sikeston, MO
KRIB(AM) Mason City, IA
KRIL Odessa, TX
KRIO(AM) McAllen, TX
KRIZ Renton, WA
KRJO(AM) Monroe, LA
KRJY(AM) Sacramento, CA
KRKC(AM) King City, CA
KRKE(AM) Albuquerque, NM
KRKK Rock Springs, WY
KRKO(AM) Everett, WA
KRKS Denver, CO
KRKY(AM) Granby, CO
KRLA(AM) Glendale, CA
KRLC Lewiston, ID
KRLD Dallas, TX
KRLL(AM) California, MO
KRLN(AM) Canon City, CO
KRLV Las Vegas, NV
KRLW Walnut Ridge, AR
KRMD Shreveport, LA
KRMG Tulsa, OK
KRML Carmel, CA
KRMO(AM) Cassville, MO
KRMP(AM) Oklahoma City, OK
KRMS Osage Beach, MO
KRMY Killeen, TX
KRND(AM) Fox Farm, WY
*KRNI(AM) Mason City, IA
KRNT Des Moines, IA

KROB(AM) Robstown, TX
KROC(AM) Rochester, MN
KROD El Paso, TX
KROE(AM) Sheridan, WY
KROF Abbeville, LA
KROO(AM) Breckenridge, TX
KROP(AM) Brawley, CA
KROS Clinton, IA
KROX Crookston, MN
KRPI(AM) Ferndale, WA
KRPL Moscow, ID
KRQX Mexia, TX
KRRP(AM) Coushatta, LA
KRRS Santa Rosa, CA
KRRZ Minot, ND
KRSA Petersburg, AK
KRSC Othello, WA
KRSL Russell, KS
KRSN(AM) Los Alamos, NM
KRSV Afton, WY
KRSX(AM) Victorville, CA
KRSY(AM) Alamogordo, NM
KRTA Medford, OR
KRTK Chubbuck, ID
KRTN Raton, NM
KRTR(AM) Honolulu, HI
KRTX Rosenberg-Richmond, TX
KRUI Ruidoso Downs, NM
KRUN Ballinger, TX
KRUS Ruston, LA
KRVA Cockrell Hill, TX
*KRVM(AM) Eugene, OR
KRVN Lexington, NE
KRVT(AM) Claremore, OK
KRVZ(AM) Springerville, AZ
KRWB Roseau, MN
KRWC Buffalo, MN
KRWZ(AM) Denver, CO
KRXA(AM) Carmel Valley, CA
KRXK(AM) Rexburg, ID
KRXR Gooding, ID
KRZE Farmington, NM
KRZI(AM) Waco, TX
KRZY(AM) Albuquerque, NM
KSAH(AM) Universal City, TX
KSAL(AM) Salina, KS
KSAM(AM) Whitefish, MT
KSAZ(AM) Marana, AZ
KSBN Spokane, WA
KSBQ Santa Maria, CA
KSCB Liberal, KS
KSCJ Sioux City, IA
KSCO Santa Cruz, CA
KSCR(AM) Eugene, OR
KSDN Aberdeen, SD
KSDO San Diego, CA
*KSDP Sand Point, AK
KSDR Watertown, SD
KSDT Hemet, CA
KSEI Pocatello, ID
KSEK Pittsburg, KS
KSEL Portales, NM
KSEN Shelby, MT
KSEO Durant, OK
KSET(AM) Silsbee, TX
KSEV(AM) Tomball, TX
KSEW(AM) Seward, AK
KSEY Seymour, TX
KSFA(AM) Nacogdoches, TX
KSFB(AM) San Francisco, CA
KSFO San Francisco, CA
KSGF(AM) Springfield, MO
KSGL Wichita, KS
KSGM(AM) Chester, IL
KSGT Jackson, WY
KSHO(AM) Lebanon, OR
KSHP North Las Vegas, NV
KSIB Creston, IA
KSID Sidney, NE
KSIG Crowley, LA
KSIM(AM) Sikeston, MO
KSIR Brush, CO
KSIS(AM) Sedalia, MO
KSIV(AM) Clayton, MO
KSIW Woodward, OK
KSIX Corpus Christi, TX

KSJB Jamestown, ND
*KSJK Talent, OR
KSJX(AM) San Jose, CA
KSKE(AM) Buena Vista, CO
KSKR(AM) Roseburg, OR
KSKY(AM) Balch Springs, TX
KSL Salt Lake City, UT
KSLD(AM) Soldotna, AK
KSLG(AM) Saint Louis, MO
KSLI(AM) Abilene, TX
KSLL(AM) Price, UT
KSLO(AM) Opelousas, LA
KSLR San Antonio, TX
KSLV(AM) Monte Vista, CO
KSMA(AM) Lompoc, CA
KSMH(AM) West Sacramento, CA
KSML Diboll, TX
KSMM(AM) Liberal, KS
KSMO Salem, MO
KSMX(AM) Santa Maria, CA
KSNM(AM) Las Cruces, NM
KSNY Snyder, TX
KSOK(AM) Arkansas City, KS
KSOO(AM) Sioux Falls, SD
KSOP South Salt Lake, UT
KSOU Sioux Center, IA
KSOX Raymondville, TX
KSPA(AM) Ontario, CA
KSPD Boise, ID
KSPI Stillwater, OK
KSPN(AM) Los Angeles, CA
KSPT(AM) Sandpoint, ID
KSPZ(AM) Ammon, ID
KSQB(AM) Sioux Falls, SD
KSRA Salmon, ID
KSRM Soldotna, AK
KSRO Santa Rosa, CA
KSRR(AM) Provo, UT
KSRV Ontario, OR
KSSK(AM) Honolulu, HI
KSSR Santa Rosa, NM
KSST Sulphur Springs, TX
KSTA Coleman, TX
KSTC Sterling, CO
KSTE Rancho Cordova, CA
KSTL Saint Louis, MO
KSTN Stockton, CA
KSTP(AM) Saint Paul, MN
KSTV Stephenville, TX
KSUB Cedar City, UT
KSUE Susanville, CA
KSUH Puyallup, WA
KSUM Fairmont, MN
KSUN Phoenix, AZ
KSVA(AM) Albuquerque, NM
KSVC Richfield, UT
KSVE(AM) El Paso, TX
KSVN Ogden, UT
KSVP Artesia, NM
KSWA(AM) Graham, TX
KSWB Seaside, OR
KSWM Aurora, MO
KSWV(AM) Santa Fe, NM
KSYB(AM) Shreveport, LA
*KSYC(AM) Yreka, CA
KSYL Alexandria, LA
KSZL Barstow, CA
KSZN(AM) Gresham, OR
KTAE(AM) Cameron, TX
KTAM(AM) Bryan, TX
KTAN(AM) Sierra Vista, AZ
KTAP Santa Maria, CA
KTAR(AM) Phoenix, AZ
KTAT Frederick, OK
KTBA Tuba City, AZ
KTBB Tyler, TX
KTBI Ephrata, WA
KTBK(AM) Auburn-Federal Way, WA
KTBL(AM) Los Ranchos de Albuquerque, NM
*KTBR(AM) Roseburg, OR
KTBZ(AM) Tulsa, OK
KTCH Wayne, NE
KTCK Dallas, TX
KTCR Kennewick, WA
KTCS Fort Smith, AR

KTCT San Mateo, CA
KTDD(AM) San Bernardino, CA
KTEK Alvin, TX
KTEL Walla Walla, WA
KTEM Temple, TX
KTFI Twin Falls, ID
KTFJ Dakota City, NE
KTFS(AM) Texarkana, TX
KTGE Salinas, CA
*KTGG Spring Arbor, MI
KTGO Tioga, ND
KTGR Columbia, MO
KTHE Thermopolis, WY
KTHH(AM) Albany, OR
KTHO(AM) South Lake Tahoe, CA
KTHS Berryville, AR
KTIB Thibodaux, LA
KTIC West Point, NE
KTIE(AM) San Bernardino, CA
KTIK Nampa, ID
KTIP Porterville, CA
KTIQ(AM) Merced, CA
KTIS Minneapolis, MN
KTIX Pendleton, OR
KTJK Del Rio, TX
KTJS Hobart, OK
KTKB(AM) Tamuning, GU
KTKK Sandy, UT
KTKN Ketchikan, AK
KTKR San Antonio, TX
KTKT Tucson, AZ
KTKZ Sacramento, CA
KTLK(AM) Los Angeles, CA
KTLO Mountain Home, AR
KTLQ Tahlequah, OK
KTLR(AM) Oklahoma City, OK
KTLU Rusk, TX
KTLV(AM) Midwest City, OK
KTMC McAlester, OK
KTMM(AM) Grand Junction, CO
KTMR(AM) Converse, TX
KTMS Santa Barbara, CA
KTNC Falls City, NE
KTNF(AM) Saint Louis Park, MN
KTNM Tucumcari, NM
KTNN Window Rock, AZ
KTNO(AM) University Park, TX
KTNP(AM) Tonopah, NV
KTNQ Los Angeles, CA
KTNS Oakhurst, CA
KTNZ Amarillo, TX
KTOB(AM) Petaluma, CA
KTOE(AM) Mankato, MN
KTOK(AM) Oklahoma City, OK
KTON Belton, TX
KTOP Topeka, KS
KTOQ Rapid City, SD
KTOX Needles, CA
KTPA Prescott, AR
KTPI(AM) Mojave, CA
KTRB(AM) San Francisco, CA
KTRC(AM) Santa Fe, NM
KTRF Thief River Falls, MN
KTRH Houston, TX
KTRO(AM) Vancouver, WA
KTRP(AM) Mount Angel, OR
KTRS Saint Louis, MO
KTRW(AM) Opportunity, WA
KTSA San Antonio, TX
KTSM(AM) El Paso, TX
KTSN Elko, NV
KTTH(AM) Seattle, WA
KTTN Trenton, MO
KTTO Spokane, WA
KTTP(AM) Pineville, LA
KTTR Rolla, MO
KTTT Columbus, NE
KTUB(AM) Centerville, UT
KTUC Tucson, AZ
KTUE Tulia, TX
KTUI Sullivan, MO
KTUV(AM) Little Rock, AR
KTWG(AM) Hagatna, GU
KTWO Casper, WY
KTXV(AM) Mabank, TX
KTXW(AM) Manor, TX

KTXZ West Lake Hills, TX
KTYM Inglewood, CA
KTZN Anchorage, AK
KUAI Eleele, HI
KUAM(AM) Hagatna, GU
KUAU Haiku, HI
*KUAZ(AM) Tucson, AZ
KUBA(AM) Yuba City, CA
KUBC(AM) Montrose, CO
KUBR San Juan, TX
KUCU(AM) Farmington, NM
KUDO(AM) Anchorage, AK
KUGN Eugene, OR
KUGR Green River, WY
KUHL(AM) Santa Maria, CA
KUIK(AM) Hillsboro, OR
KUJ Walla Walla, WA
KUKI Ukiah, CA
KUKU(AM) Willow Springs, MO
KULE Ephrata, WA
KULP El Campo, TX
KULY Ulysses, KS
KUMA Pendleton, OR
KUMU Honolulu, HI
KUNF(AM) Washington, UT
KUNO Corpus Christi, TX
KUNX(AM) Ventura, CA
KUOA(AM) Siloam Springs, AR
KUOL San Marcos, TX
*KUOM(AM) Minneapolis, MN
KUOW(AM) Tumwater, WA
KUPA Pearl City, HI
KURL Billings, MT
KURM Rogers, AR
KURS San Diego, CA
KURV Edinburg, TX
KURY Brookings, OR
KUSH(AM) Cushing, OK
KUTI(AM) Yakima, WA
KUTR Taylorsville, UT
KUTY Palmdale, CA
KUUX(AM) Pullman, WA
KUVR Holdrege, NE
KUYO Evansville, WY
KUZZ Bakersfield, CA
KVAK(AM) Valdez, AK
KVAN(AM) Burbank, WA
KVBR Brainerd, MN
KVCE(AM) Highland Park, TX
KVCK(AM) Wolf Point, MT
KVCL Winnfield, LA
KVCU Boulder, CO
KVDW(AM) England, AR
KVEC San Luis Obispo, CA
KVEL Vernal, UT
KVEN Ventura, CA
KVET Austin, TX
KVFC Cortez, CO
KVFD(AM) Fort Dodge, IA
KVGB Great Bend, KS
KVI(AM) Seattle, WA
KVIN(AM) Ceres, CA
*KVIP Redding, CA
KVIS Miami, OK
KVIV El Paso, TX
KVJY Pharr, TX
KVKK(AM) Verndale, MN
KVLE(AM) Vail, CO
KVLF Alpine, TX
KVLG La Grange, TX
KVLH(AM) Pauls Valley, OK
KVLV(AM) Fallon, NV
KVMA(AM) Magnolia, AR
KVMC Colorado City, TX
KVML(AM) Sonora, CA
KVNA(AM) Flagstaff, AZ
KVNI Coeur d'Alene, ID
KVNN(AM) Victoria, TX
KVNR Santa Ana, CA
KVNS(AM) Brownsville, TX
KVNU Logan, UT
KVOC Casper, WY
KVOE(AM) Emporia, KS
KVOG(AM) Hagatna, GU
KVOI(AM) Cortaro, AZ
KVOK(AM) Kodiak, AK

U.S. AM Stations by Call Letters

KVOL Lafayette, LA
KVOM Morrilton, AR
KVON Napa, CA
KVOP(AM) Plainview, TX
KVOR Colorado Springs, CO
KVOT(AM) Taos, NM
KVOU Uvalde, TX
KVOW Riverton, WY
KVOX(AM) Fargo, ND
KVOZ Del Mar Hills, TX
KVPI Ville Platte, LA
KVRC Arkadelphia, AR
KVRH Salida, CO
KVRI(AM) Blaine, WA
KVRP Stamford, TX
KVSA McGehee, AR
KVSF(AM) Santa Fe, NM
KVSH Valentine, NE
KVSI Montpelier, ID
KVSL Show Low, AZ
KVSO Ardmore, OK
KVSV Beloit, KS
KVTA Port Hueneme, CA
KVTK(AM) Vermillion, SD
KVTO Berkeley, CA
KVVN Santa Clara, CA
KVWC Vernon, TX
KVWG(AM) Pearsall, TX
KVWM(AM) Show Low, AZ
KVXR(AM) Moorhead, MN
KWAC Bakersfield, CA
KWAD Wadena, MN
KWAI Honolulu, HI
KWAK Stuttgart, AR
KWAL Wallace, ID
KWAM Memphis, TN
KWAT Watertown, SD
KWAY Waverly, IA
KWBC Navasota, TX
KWBE Beatrice, NE
KWBG Boone, IA
KWBW Hutchinson, KS
KWBY Woodburn, OR
KWCK Searcy, AR
KWDB(AM) Oak Harbor, WA
KWDF Ball, LA
KWDJ(AM) Ridgecrest, CA
KWDZ(AM) Salt Lake City, UT
KWEB(AM) Rochester, MN
KWED(AM) Seguin, TX
KWEI(AM) Weiser, ID
KWEL Midland, TX
KWES(AM) Ruidoso, NM
KWEY Weatherford, OK
KWFA(AM) Tye, TX
KWFM(AM) Tucson, AZ
KWFS Wichita Falls, TX
*KWG(AM) Stockton, CA
KWHI Brenham, TX
KWHN(AM) Fort Smith, AR
KWHW Altus, OK
KWIK Pocatello, ID
KWIL Albany, OR
KWIP Dallas, OR
KWIQ(AM) Moses Lake North, WA
KWIX Moberly, MO
KWKA Clovis, NM
KWKC(AM) Abilene, TX
KWKH(AM) Shreveport, LA
KWKU(AM) Pomona, CA
KWKW Los Angeles, CA
KWKY Des Moines, IA
KWLA Many, LA
*KWLC Decorah, IA
KWLE(AM) Anacortes, WA
KWLM Willmar, MN
KWLO(AM) Waterloo, IA
KWLW(AM) Keystone, CO
KWMC Del Rio, TX
*KWMF(AM) Pleasanton, TX
KWMO Washington, MO
KWMT Fort Dodge, IA
KWNA(AM) Winnemucca, NV
KWNC Quincy, WA
KWNO Winona, MN
KWNX(AM) Taylor, TX

KWOA Worthington, MN
KWOC Poplar Bluff, MO
KWOD(AM) Salem, OR
KWOK(AM) Hoquiam, WA
KWON Bartlesville, OK
KWOR Worland, WY
KWOS(AM) Jefferson City, MO
KWPC Muscatine, IA
KWPM West Plains, MO
KWRD Henderson, TX
KWRE(AM) Warrenton, MO
KWRF Warren, AR
KWRM Corona, CA
KWRN Apple Valley, CA
KWRO Coquille, OR
KWRP(AM) Pueblo, CO
KWRT(AM) Boonville, MO
KWRU(AM) Fresno, CA
KWSH Wewoka, OK
KWSL Sioux City, IA
KWSN(AM) Sioux Falls, SD
KWST(AM) El Centro, CA
*KWSU Pullman, WA
KWSW Eureka, CA
KWSX(AM) Stockton, CA
*KWTL(AM) Grand Forks, ND
KWTO Springfield, MO
KWTX Waco, TX
KWUD(AM) Woodville, TX
KWUF(AM) Pagosa Springs, CO
KWVR Enterprise, OR
KWWJ Baytown, TX
KWWN(AM) Las Vegas, NV
KWXI Glenwood, AR
KWXT Dardanelle, AR
KWYN Wynne, AR
KWYO Sheridan, WY
KWYR(AM) Winner, SD
KWYS West Yellowstone, MT
KWYZ Everett, WA
KXAM Mesa, AZ
KXAR Hope, AR
KXBX Lakeport, CA
KXCA(AM) Lawton, OK
KXEG(AM) Phoenix, AZ
KXEL Waterloo, IA
KXEN(AM) Saint Louis, MO
KXEO Mexico, MO
KXEQ Reno, NV
KXEW South Tucson, AZ
KXEX Fresno, CA
KXGF Great Falls, MT
KXGM(AM) Waterloo, IA
KXGN Glendive, MT
KXIC Iowa City, IA
KXJK Forrest City, AR
KXKS(AM) Albuquerque, NM
KXL Portland, OR
KXLE Ellensburg, WA
KXLJ(AM) Juneau, AK
KXLO Lewistown, MT
KXLQ Indianola, IA
KXLX(AM) Airway Heights, WA
KXLY Spokane, WA
KXMR Bismarck, ND
KXMX(AM) Anaheim, CA
KXNO(AM) Des Moines, IA
KXNT North Las Vegas, NV
KXO(AM) El Centro, CA
KXOI Crane, TX
KXOL Brigham City, UT
KXOR(AM) Junction City, OR
KXOX Sweetwater, TX
KXPA Bellevue, WA
*KXPD(AM) Tigard, OR
*KXPL(AM) El Paso, TX
KXPN(AM) Kearney, NE
KXPO Grafton, ND
KXPS(AM) Thousand Palms, CA
KXRA Alexandria, MN
KXRB(AM) Sioux Falls, SD
KXRE(AM) Manitou Springs, CO
KXRO Aberdeen, WA
KXSP(AM) Omaha, NE
KXSS(AM) Waite Park, MN
KXTD Wagoner, OK

KXTK(AM) Arroyo Grande, CA
KXTL Butte, MT
KXTO Reno, NV
KXTR(AM) Kansas City, KS
KXXA(AM) Conway, AR
KXXT(AM) Tolleson, AZ
KXXX Colby, KS
KXYL(AM) Brownwood, TX
KXYZ Houston, TX
KXZZ Lake Charles, LA
KYAA(AM) Soquel, CA
KYAK Yakima, WA
KYAL(AM) Sapulpa, OK
KYBC(AM) Cottonwood, AZ
KYCA(AM) Prescott, AZ
KYCN Wheatland, WY
KYCR Golden Valley, MN
KYDZ(AM) North Las Vegas, NV
KYES(AM) Rockville, MN
KYET Williams, AZ
*KYFR Shenandoah, IA
KYHN(AM) Fort Smith, AR
KYHR(AM) Richfield, UT
KYIZ Renton, WA
KYKK(AM) Hobbs, NM
KYKN Keizer, OR
KYLS Fredericktown, MO
KYLT Missoula, MT
KYLW(AM) Lockwood, MT
KYMN Northfield, MN
KYMO East Prairie, MO
KYND Cypress, TX
KYNG(AM) Springdale, AR
KYNN(AM) Cameron, AZ
KYNO Fresno, CA
KYNR(AM) Toppenish, WA
KYNS(AM) San Luis Obispo, CA
KYNT Yankton, SD
KYOK(AM) Conroe, TX
KYOO Bolivar, MO
KYOS Merced, CA
KYPA Los Angeles, CA
KYRO Potosi, MO
KYSM(AM) Mankato, MN
KYST Texas City, TX
KYTY(AM) Somerset, TX
*KYUK Bethel, AK
KYUL(AM) Scott City, KS
KYVA(AM) Gallup, NM
KYW Philadelphia, PA
KYYS(AM) Kansas City, KS
KYYW(AM) Abilene, TX
KYZS Tyler, TX
KZDC San Antonio, TX
KZEE Weatherford, TX
KZER(AM) Santa Barbara, CA
KZEY Tyler, TX
KZHN(AM) Paris, TX
KZHS(AM) Hot Springs, AR
KZIM Cape Girardeau, MO
KZIP Amarillo, TX
KZIZ(AM) Pacific, WA
KZLI(AM) Catoosa, OK
KZMP(AM) University Park, TX
KZMQ Greybull, WY
KZMX Hot Springs, SD
KZNE(AM) College Station, TX
KZNG Hot Springs, AR
KZNS(AM) Salt Lake City, UT
KZNT(AM) Colorado Springs, CO
KZNU(AM) Saint George, UT
KZNW(AM) Wenatchee, WA
KZNX(AM) Creedmoor, TX
KZOO Honolulu, HI
*KZPA(AM) Fort Yukon, AK
KZQQ(AM) Abilene, TX
KZQZ(AM) Saint Louis, MO
KZRG(AM) Joplin, MO
KZRK(AM) Canyon, TX
KZSB(AM) Santa Barbara, CA
KZSF San Jose, CA
KZSJ(AM) San Martin, CA
KZTD(AM) Cabot, AR
KZUE El Reno, OK
KZXR Prosser, WA
KZYM(AM) Joplin, MO

KZZB Beaumont, TX
KZZJ Rugby, ND
KZZN Littlefield, TX
KZZR(AM) Burns, OR
KZZZ(AM) Bullhead City, AZ
V6AH Pohnpei, FM
*V6AI Yap, FM
V6AK Truk, FM
WAAM Ann Arbor, MI
WAAV Leland, NC
WAAX Gadsden, AL
WABA Aguadilla, PR
WABB Mobile, AL
WABC(AM) New York, NY
WABF(AM) Fairhope, AL
WABG Greenwood, MS
WABH Bath, NY
WABJ Adrian, MI
WABL Amite, LA
WABN Abingdon, VA
WABO Waynesboro, MS
WABQ(AM) Painesville, OH
WABV(AM) Abbeville, SC
WABY(AM) Mechanicville, NY
WACA Wheaton, MD
WACB Taylorsville, NC
WACC Hialeah, FL
WACE Chicopee, MA
WACK(AM) Newark, NY
WACM West Springfield, MA
WACQ(AM) Carrville, AL
WACT(AM) Tuscaloosa, AL
WACV Montgomery, AL
WADA Shelby, NC
WADB(AM) Asbury Park, NJ
WADC Parkersburg, WV
WADE Wadesboro, NC
WADK Newport, RI
WADM(AM) Decatur, IN
WADO New York, NY
WADR Remsen, NY
WADS Ansonia, CT
WADV Lebanon, PA
WAEB Allentown, PA
WAEC Atlanta, GA
WAEI(AM) Bangor, ME
WAEW Crossville, TN
WAEY Princeton, WV
WAFC Clewiston, FL
WAFS(AM) Atlanta, GA
WAFZ(AM) Immokalee, FL
WAGE Leesburg, VA
WAGF Dothan, AL
WAGG(AM) Birmingham, AL
WAGL(AM) Lancaster, SC
WAGN Menominee, MI
WAGR Lumberton, NC
WAGS Bishopville, SC
WAGY(AM) Forest City, NC
WAHT Clemson, SC
WAIA(AM) Beaver Dam, KY
WAIK Galesburg, IL
WAIM Anderson, SC
WAIN Columbia, KY
WAIS Buchtel, OH
WAIT(AM) Crystal Lake, IL
WAIZ(AM) Hickory, NC
WAJD Gainesville, FL
WAJL(AM) South Boston, VA
WAJQ Alma, GA
WAJR Morgantown, WV
WAKE Valparaiso, IN
WAKI McMinnville, TN
WAKK McComb, MS
WAKM Franklin, TN
WAKO Lawrenceville, IL
WAKR Akron, OH
WAKV Otsego, MI
WALD(AM) Johnsonville, SC
WALE Greenville, RI
WALG Albany, GA
WALH Mountain City, GA
WALK(AM) East Patchogue, NY
WALL Middletown, NY
WALO(AM) Humacao, PR
WALR Atlanta, GA

WALT Meridian, MS
WAMA Tampa, FL
WAMB(AM) Nashville, TN
*WAMC(AM) Albany, NY
WAMD Aberdeen, MD
WAME(AM) Statesville, NC
WAMF(AM) Fulton, NY
WAMG(AM) Dedham, MA
WAMI Opp, AL
WAML Laurel, MS
WAMM Woodstock, VA
WAMN Green Valley, WV
WAMO(AM) Millvale, PA
WAMT Pine Castle-Sky Lake, FL
WAMV Amherst, VA
WAMW(AM) Washington, IN
WAMY Amory, MS
WANB(AM) Waynesburg, PA
WANG Havelock, NC
WANI Opelika, AL
WANO Pineville, KY
WANR Warren, OH
WANS Anderson, SC
WANY Albany, KY
WAOC(AM) Saint Augustine, FL
WAOK Atlanta, GA
WAOS(AM) Austell, GA
WAOV Vincennes, IN
WAPA San Juan, PR
WAPF(AM) McComb, MS
WAPI Birmingham, AL
WAPZ Wetumpka, AL
WAQE Rice Lake, WI
WAQI Miami, FL
WARD(AM) Petoskey, MI
WARE(AM) Ware, MA
WARF(AM) Akron, OH
WARK Hagerstown, MD
WARL(AM) Attleboro, MA
WARM Scranton, PA
WARR Warrenton, NC
WARU Peru, IN
WARV Warwick, RI
WASB Brockport, NY
WASC Spartanburg, SC
WASG(AM) Daphne, AL
WASK Lafayette, IN
WASN(AM) Youngstown, OH
WASO Covington, LA
WASP Brownsville, PA
WASR Wolfeboro, NH
WATA Boone, NC
WATB Decatur, GA
WATH Athens, OH
WATK Antigo, WI
WATN Watertown, NY
WATO Oak Ridge, TN
WATR(AM) Waterbury, CT
WATS Sayre, PA
WATT Cadillac, MI
WATV(AM) Birmingham, AL
WATW Ashland, WI
WATX Algood, TN
WATZ Alpena, MI
WAUB Auburn, NY
WAUC Wauchula, FL
WAUD Auburn, AL
WAUG New Hope, NC
WAUK(AM) Jackson, WI
WAUR Sandwich, IL
WAVA(AM) Arlington, VA
WAVL Apollo, PA
WAVN Southaven, MS
WAVO Rock Hill, SC
WAVQ(AM) Jacksonville, NC
WAVS Davie, FL
WAVU(AM) Albertville, AL
WAVZ New Haven, CT
WAWK Kendallville, IN
WAXO Lewisburg, TN
WAXY South Miami, FL
WAYE Birmingham, AL
WAYN Rockingham, NC
*WAYR Orange Park, FL
WAYS(AM) Macon, GA
WAYX(AM) Waycross, GA

WAYY(AM) Eau Claire, WI
WAZL Hazleton, PA
WAZN(AM) Watertown, MA
WAZS(AM) Summerville, SC
WAZX Smyrna, GA
WAZZ(AM) Fayetteville, NC
*WBAA(AM) West Lafayette, IN
WBAC(AM) Cleveland, TN
WBAE Portland, ME
WBAF Barnesville, GA
WBAG Burlington-Graham, NC
WBAJ Blythwood, SC
WBAL Baltimore, MD
WBAP Fort Worth, TX
WBAT Marion, IN
WBAX Wilkes-Barre, PA
WBBD Wheeling, WV
WBBF(AM) Buffalo, NY
WBBK Blakely, GA
WBBM(AM) Chicago, IL
WBBP Memphis, TN
WBBR New York, NY
WBBT Lyons, GA
WBBW Youngstown, OH
WBBX Kingston, TN
WBBZ Ponca City, OK
WBCB Levittown-Fairless Hills, PA
WBCE Wickliffe, KY
WBCF(AM) Florence, AL
WBCH Hastings, MI
WBCK Battle Creek, MI
WBCN(AM) Charlotte, NC
WBCO(AM) Bucyrus, OH
WBCP Urbana, IL
WBCR Alcoa, TN
WBCU Union, SC
WBDY Bluefield, VA
WBEC Pittsfield, MA
WBEJ(AM) Elizabethton, TN
WBEN Buffalo, NY
WBES(AM) Dunbar, WV
WBEV Beaver Dam, WI
WBEX Chillicothe, OH
WBFC Stanton, KY
WBFD(AM) Bedford, PA
WBFJ Winston-Salem, NC
WBFN(AM) Battle Creek, MI
WBGC Chipley, FL
WBGG(AM) Pittsburgh, PA
WBGN(AM) Bowling Green, KY
WBGR Baltimore, MD
WBGS Point Pleasant, WV
WBGX(AM) Harvey, IL
WBGZ Alton, IL
WBHB Fitzgerald, GA
WBHF(AM) Cartersville, GA
WBHN Bryson City, NC
WBHP Huntsville, AL
WBHR Sauk Rapids, MN
WBHV(AM) Somerset, PA
WBHY Mobile, AL
WBIB Centreville, AL
WBIG Aurora, IL
WBIL Tuskegee, AL
WBIN Benton, TN
WBIP Booneville, MS
WBIS(AM) Annapolis, MD
WBIW Bedford, IN
WBIX(AM) Natick, MA
WBIZ Eau Claire, WI
WBKK(AM) Wilton, MN
WBKV(AM) West Bend, WI
WBLA Elizabethtown, NC
WBLC Lenoir City, TN
WBLF Bellefonte, PA
WBLJ(AM) Dalton, GA
WBLL Bellefontaine, OH
WBLO(AM) Thomasville, NC
WBLR Batesburg, SC
WBLT(AM) Bedford, VA
WBMC McMinnville, TN
WBMD Baltimore, MD
WBMJ San Juan, PR
WBML Macon, GA
WBMQ Savannah, GA
WBNC Conway, NH

WBNL(AM) Boonville, IN
WBNM(AM) Alexander City, AL
WBNR Beacon, NY
WBNS Columbus, OH
WBNW Concord, MA
WBOB(AM) Jacksonville, FL
WBOG(AM) Tomah, WI
WBOK New Orleans, LA
WBOL Bolivar, TN
WBOW(AM) Terre Haute, IN
WBOX Bogalusa, LA
WBPZ Lock Haven, PA
WBQN(AM) Barceloneta-Manati, PR
WBRD Palmetto, FL
WBRG Lynchburg, VA
WBRI(AM) Indianapolis, IN
WBRK Pittsfield, MA
WBRM Marion, NC
WBRN Big Rapids, MI
WBRT Bardstown, KY
WBRV Boonville, NY
WBRY Woodbury, TN
WBSA Boaz, AL
WBSC Bennettsville, SC
WBSG(AM) Lajas, PR
WBSM New Bedford, MA
WBSR Pensacola, FL
WBT Charlotte, NC
WBTA Batavia, NY
WBTC Uhrichsville, OH
WBTE Windsor, NC
WBTG Sheffield, AL
WBTH Williamson, WV
WBTK(AM) Richmond, VA
WBTM Danville, VA
WBTN Bennington, VT
WBTO Linton, IN
WBTX Broadway-Timberville, VA
WBUC Buckhannon, WV
*WBUR(AM) West Yarmouth, MA
WBUT Butler, PA
WBVA(AM) Bayside, VA
WBVP(AM) Beaver Falls, PA
WBWL Jacksonville, FL
WBXR(AM) Hazel Green, AL
WBYE Calera, AL
WBYN(AM) Lehighton, PA
WBYS(AM) Canton, IL
WBYU New Orleans, LA
WBZ Boston, MA
WBZI Xenia, OH
WBZK York, SC
WBZQ Huntington, IN
WBZT(AM) West Palm Beach, FL
WBZU(AM) Scranton, PA
WCAB(AM) Rutherfordton, NC
WCAM Camden, SC
WCAO Baltimore, MD
WCAP(AM) Lowell, MA
WCAR Livonia, MI
WCAT(AM) Burlington, VT
WCAZ Carthage, IL
WCBA Corning, NY
WCBC Cumberland, MD
WCBG(AM) Waynesboro, PA
WCBL Benton, KY
WCBM Baltimore, MD
WCBQ Oxford, NC
WCBR Richmond, KY
WCBS New York, NY
WCBT Roanoke Rapids, NC
WCBX(AM) Bassett, VA
WCBY Cheboygan, MI
WCCC(AM) West Hartford, CT
WCCD(AM) Parma, OH
WCCF(AM) Punta Gorda, FL
WCCM(AM) Salem, NH
WCCN Neillsville, WI
WCCO Minneapolis, MN
WCCS Homer City, PA
WCCW(AM) Traverse City, MI
WCCY Houghton, MI
WCDL(AM) Carbondale, PA
WCDO Sidney, NY
WCDS(AM) Glasgow, KY
WCDT Winchester, TN

WCEC(AM) Haverhill, MA
WCED DuBois, PA
WCEH Hawkinsville, GA
WCEM Cambridge, MD
WCEO(AM) Columbia, SC
WCER Canton, OH
WCEV Cicero, IL
WCFJ Chicago Heights, IL
WCFO(AM) East Point, GA
WCFR(AM) Springfield, VT
WCGA Woodbine, GA
WCGB Juana Diaz, PR
WCGC Belmont, NC
WCGL Jacksonville, FL
WCGO(AM) Evanston, IL
WCGR Canandaigua, NY
WCGW Nicholasville, KY
WCHA Chambersburg, PA
WCHB Taylor, MI
WCHE West Chester, PA
WCHI Chillicothe, OH
WCHJ Brookhaven, MS
WCHK Canton, GA
WCHL Chapel Hill, NC
WCHM Clarkesville, GA
WCHN Norwich, NY
WCHO(AM) Washington Court House, OH
WCHP Champlain, NY
WCHQ(AM) Quebradillas, PR
WCHR(AM) Trenton, NJ
WCHS Charleston, WV
WCHT Escanaba, MI
WCHV Charlottesville, VA
WCIL Carbondale, IL
WCIN Cincinnati, OH
WCIS Morganton, NC
WCIT(AM) Lima, OH
WCJU Columbia, MS
WCJW(AM) Warsaw, NY
WCKA(AM) Jacksonville, AL
WCKB Dunn, NC
WCKI Greer, SC
WCKL Catskill, NY
*WCKW(AM) Garyville, LA
WCKY(AM) Cincinnati, OH
WCLA(AM) Claxton, GA
WCLB(AM) Sheboygan, WI
WCLC Jamestown, TN
WCLD Cleveland, MS
WCLE Cleveland, TN
WCLG Morgantown, WV
WCLM Highland Springs, VA
WCLN(AM) Clinton, NC
WCLO Janesville, WI
WCLT(AM) Newark, OH
WCLU Glasgow, KY
WCLW Eden, NC
WCLY Raleigh, NC
WCMA(AM) Daleville, AL
WCMC(AM) Wildwood, NJ
WCMD(AM) Cumberland, MD
WCME(AM) Brunswick, ME
WCMI Ashland, KY
WCMN Arecibo, PR
WCMP Pine City, MN
WCMR(AM) Elkhart, IN
WCMS(AM) Newport News, VA
WCMT(AM) Martin, TN
WCMX Leominster, MA
WCMY(AM) Ottawa, IL
WCNC(AM) Elizabeth City, NC
WCND Shelbyville, KY
WCNL(AM) Newport, NH
WCNN North Atlanta, GA
WCNS Latrobe, PA
WCNW Fairfield, OH
WCNX(AM) Hope Valley, RI
*WCNZ(AM) Marco Island, FL
WCOA Pensacola, FL
WCOC(AM) Dora, AL
WCOG Greensboro, NC
WCOH Newnan, GA
WCOJ(AM) Coatesville, PA
WCOK Sparta, NC
WCON Cornelia, GA

WCOR(AM) Lebanon, TN
WCOS Columbia, SC
WCPA Clearfield, PA
WCPC Houston, MS
WCPH Etowah, TN
WCPK Chesapeake, VA
WCPM Cumberland, KY
WCPR Coamo, PR
WCPS(AM) Tarboro, NC
WCPT(AM) Willow Springs, IL
WCRA Effingham, IL
WCRE Cheraw, SC
WCRK(AM) Morristown, TN
WCRL Oneonta, AL
WCRM Fort Myers, FL
WCRN Worcester, MA
WCRO Johnstown, PA
WCRS Greenwood, SC
WCRT(AM) Donelson, TN
WCRU(AM) Dallas, NC
WCRV Collierville, TN
WCRW(AM) Pocomoke City, MD
WCSA Ripley, MS
WCSI(AM) Columbus, IN
WCSJ(AM) Morris, IL
WCSL Cherryville, NC
WCSM Celina, OH
WCSR Hillsdale, MI
WCSS Amsterdam, NY
WCST Berkeley Springs, WV
WCSV(AM) Crossville, TN
WCSW Shell Lake, WI
WCSY(AM) South Haven, MI
WCSZ(AM) Sans Souci, SC
WCTA Alamo, TN
WCTC(AM) New Brunswick, NJ
*WCTF Vernon, CT
WCTN Potomac-Cabin John, MD
WCTR(AM) Chestertown, MD
WCTS(AM) Maplewood, MN
WCTT Corbin, KY
WCUB(AM) Two Rivers, WI
*WCUE Cuyahoga Falls, OH
WCUG Cuthbert, GA
WCUM Bridgeport, CT
WCVA Culpeper, VA
WCVC Tallahassee, FL
WCVG Covington, KY
WCVL Crawfordsville, IN
WCVP Murphy, NC
WCVX(AM) Cincinnati, OH
WCWA Toledo, OH
*WCWC(AM) Williamsburg, KY
WCXI(AM) Fenton, MI
WCXJ(AM) Kearsarge, PA
WCXN Claremont, NC
WCXZ(AM) Harrogate, TN
WCYN Cynthiana, KY
WCZZ(AM) Greenwood, SC
WDAD Indiana, PA
WDAE(AM) Saint Petersburg, FL
WDAK Columbus, GA
WDAL Dalton, GA
WDAN(AM) Danville, IL
WDAO Dayton, OH
WDAY Fargo, ND
WDBC Escanaba, MI
WDBL(AM) Springfield, TN
WDBO Orlando, FL
WDBQ Dubuque, IA
WDBZ(AM) Cincinnati, OH
WDCD(AM) Albany, NY
WDCF Dade City, FL
WDCO(AM) Cochran, GA
WDCR(AM) Hanover, NH
WDCT Fairfax, VA
WDCX(AM) Rochester, NY
WDCY Douglasville, GA
WDDD Johnston City, IL
WDDO Macon, GA
WDDV(AM) Venice, FL
WDDY(AM) Albany, NY
WDDZ(AM) Pawtucket, RI
WDEA Ellsworth, ME
WDEB Jamestown, TN
WDEF Chattanooga, TN

WDEH Sweetwater, TN
WDEL Wilmington, DE
WDEO(AM) Ypsilanti, MI
WDEP(AM) Ponce, PR
WDER(AM) Derry, NH
WDEV Waterbury, VT
WDEX Monroe, NC
WDFB Junction City, KY
WDFN Detroit, MI
WDGR Dahlonega, GA
WDGY(AM) Hudson, WI
WDHP Frederiksted, VI
WDIA Memphis, TN
WDIC(AM) Clinchco, VA
WDIG Steubenville, OH
WDIS Norfolk, MA
WDIZ Panama City, FL
WDJA(AM) Delray Beach, FL
WDJL Huntsville, AL
WDJS Mount Olive, NC
WDJZ Bridgeport, CT
WDKD Kingstree, SC
WDKN Dickson, TN
WDLA Walton, NY
WDLB Marshfield, WI
WDLC Port Jervis, NY
WDLK Dadeville, AL
*WDLM East Moline, IL
WDLR(AM) Delaware, OH
WDLS(AM) Wisconsin Dells, WI
WDLW Lorain, OH
WDLX Washington, NC
WDMC(AM) Melbourne, FL
WDMG Douglas, GA
WDMJ Marquette, MI
WDMP(AM) Dodgeville, WI
WDMV(AM) Walkersville, MD
WDNC(AM) Durham, NC
WDND(AM) South Bend, IN
WDNE Elkins, WV
WDNG Anniston, AL
WDNT(AM) Dayton, TN
WDNY(AM) Dansville, NY
WDOC Prestonsburg, KY
WDOD Chattanooga, TN
WDOE Dunkirk, NY
WDOG Allendale, SC
WDOR Sturgeon Bay, WI
WDOS Oneonta, NY
WDOV Dover, DE
WDOW Dowagiac, MI
WDOX(AM) Raleigh, NC
WDPC Dallas, GA
WDPN Alliance, OH
WDPT(AM) Decatur, AL
*WDPZ(AM) Dover, DE
WDQN Du Quoin, IL
WDRC(AM) Hartford, CT
WDRD(AM) Newburg, KY
WDRF(AM) Woodruff, SC
WDRJ(AM) Inkster, MI
WDRU(AM) Wake Forest, NC
WDSC Dillon, SC
WDSK Cleveland, MS
WDSL Mocksville, NC
WDSM Superior, WI
WDSP(AM) De Funiak Springs, FL
WDSR(AM) Lake City, FL
WDTK Detroit, MI
WDTM Selmer, TN
WDTW(AM) Dearborn, MI
WDUN Gainesville, GA
WDUR Durham, NC
WDUX(AM) Waupaca, WI
WDUZ(AM) Green Bay, WI
WDVA Danville, VA
WDVH(AM) Gainesville, FL
*WDVM(AM) Eau Claire, WI
WDWD Atlanta, GA
WDWR(AM) Pensacola, FL
WDWS(AM) Champaign, IL
WDXE Lawrenceburg, TN
WDXI Jackson, TN
WDXL Lexington, TN
WDXR Paducah, KY
WDXY Sumter, SC

WDYT(AM) Kings Mountain, NC
WDYZ(AM) Orlando, FL
WDZ(AM) Decatur, IL
WDZK Bloomfield, CT
WDZY Colonial Heights, VA
WEAE Pittsburgh, PA
WEAF(AM) Camden, SC
WEAL Greensboro, NC
WEAM Columbus, GA
WEAQ Chippewa Falls, WI
WEAV Plattsburgh, NY
WEBC Duluth, MN
WEBJ Brewton, AL
WEBO Owego, NY
WEBQ Harrisburg, IL
WEBS(AM) Calhoun, GA
WEBY(AM) Milton, FL
WECK Cheektowaga, NY
WECM Milton, FL
WECO Wartburg, TN
WECR Newland, NC
WECU(AM) Winterville, NC
WECZ Punxsutawney, PA
WEDI(AM) Eaton, OH
WEDO McKeesport, PA
WEEB Southern Pines, NC
WEED(AM) Rocky Mount, NC
WEEF Highland Park, IL
WEEI Boston, MA
WEEL(AM) Dothan, AL
WEEN(AM) Lafayette, TN
WEEO(AM) Shippensburg, PA
WEEU Reading, PA
WEEX Easton, PA
WEFL(AM) Tequesta, FL
WEGA Vega Baja, PR
WEGG Rose Hill, NC
WEGI(AM) Fort Campbell, KY
WEGO Concord, NC
WEGP Presque Isle, ME
WEHH Elmira Heights-Horseheads, NY
WEIC Charleston, IL
WEIR Weirton, WV
WEIS Centre, AL
WEJL Scranton, PA
WEKB(AM) Elkhorn City, KY
WEKC Williamsburg, KY
WEKG Jackson, KY
WEKO(AM) Morovis, PR
WEKR Fayetteville, TN
WEKT Elkton, KY
WEKY Richmond, KY
WEKZ Monroe, WI
WELA(AM) Welch, WV
WELB Elba, AL
WELC Welch, WV
WELD(AM) Fisher, WV
WELE Ormond Beach, FL
WELG(AM) Ellenville, NY
WELI New Haven, CT
WELM Elmira, NY
WELO Tupelo, MS
WELP(AM) Easley, SC
WELR Roanoke, AL
WELS Kinston, NC
WELW Willoughby-Eastlake, OH
WELY Ely, MN
WELZ Belzoni, MS
WEMB Erwin, TN
WEMD(AM) Easton, MD
WEMG(AM) Camden, NJ
WEMJ Laconia, NH
WENA Yauco, PR
WENC Whiteville, NC
WENE(AM) Endicott, NY
WENG Englewood, FL
WENI(AM) Corning, NY
WENJ(AM) Atlantic City, NJ
WENK Union City, TN
WENN(AM) Birmingham, AL
WENO Nashville, TN
WENR Englewood, TN
WENT Gloversville, NY
WENU(AM) South Glens Falls, NY
WENY Elmira, NY
WEOA Evansville, IN

WEOK Poughkeepsie, NY
WEOL Elyria, OH
WEPG South Pittsburg, TN
WEPM Martinsburg, WV
WEPN(AM) New York, NY
WERC Birmingham, AL
WERE(AM) Cleveland Heights, OH
WERH Hamilton, AL
WERL Eagle River, WI
WERT Van Wert, OH
WESB(AM) Bradford, PA
WESO Southbridge, MA
WESR Onley-Onancock, VA
WEST Easton, PA
WESX Salem, MA
WESY Leland, MS
WETB Johnson City, TN
WETC Wendell-Zebulon, NC
WETR(AM) Knoxville, TN
WETZ New Martinsville, WV
WEUP(AM) Huntsville, AL
WEUS(AM) Orlovista, FL
WEUV(AM) Moulton, AL
WEVA(AM) Emporia, VA
WEVR River Falls, WI
WEW Saint Louis, MO
WEWC(AM) Callahan, FL
WEWO Laurinburg, NC
WEXL Royal Oak, MI
WEXS Patillas, PR
WEXY Wilton Manors, FL
WEZE Boston, MA
WEZR(AM) Lewiston, ME
WEZS Laconia, NH
WEZZ(AM) Monroeville, AL
WFAB Ceiba, PR
WFAD Middlebury, VT
WFAI(AM) Salem, NJ
WFAM(AM) Augusta, GA
WFAN New York, NY
WFAS(AM) White Plains, NY
WFAU Gardiner, ME
WFAW Fort Atkinson, WI
WFAX Falls Church, VA
WFAY(AM) Fayetteville, NC
WFBG Altoona, PA
WFBL(AM) Syracuse, NY
WFBR(AM) Glen Burnie, MD
WFBS(AM) Berwick, PA
WFBX(AM) Spring Lake, NC
*WFCM Smyrna, TN
WFCV Fort Wayne, IN
WFDF(AM) Farmington Hills, MI
WFDL(AM) Waupun, WI
WFDR Manchester, GA
WFEA Manchester, NH
WFEB Sylacauga, AL
WFED(AM) Washington, DC
WFFF Columbia, MS
WFFG(AM) Marathon, FL
WFFX(AM) East St. Louis, IL
WFGI(AM) Charleroi, PA
WFGL Fitchburg, MA
WFGM(AM) Sandy Springs, GA
WFGN Gaffney, SC
WFGO(AM) Orono, ME
WFGW Black Mountain, NC
WFHG(AM) Bristol, VA
WFHK Pell City, AL
WFHR Wisconsin Rapids, WI
WFHT(AM) Avon Park, FL
WFIA Louisville, KY
WFIC(AM) Collinsville, VA
WFIF Milford, CT
WFIL(AM) Philadelphia, PA
WFIN Findlay, OH
WFIR(AM) Roanoke, VA
WFIS Fountain Inn, SC
WFIW(AM) Fairfield, IL
WFJS(AM) Trenton, NJ
*WFKJ Cashtown, PA
WFKN Franklin, KY
WFLA(AM) Tampa, FL
WFLE Flemingsburg, KY
WFLF(AM) Pine Hills, FL
WFLI Lookout Mountain, TN

WFLL(AM) Fort Lauderdale, FL
WFLN(AM) Arcadia, FL
WFLO Farmville, VA
WFLR Dundee, NY
WFLT Flint, MI
WFLW Monticello, KY
WFMB(AM) Springfield, IL
WFMC(AM) Goldsboro, NC
WFMD(AM) Frederick, MD
WFMH(AM) Cullman, AL
WFMO Fairmont, NC
WFMW Madisonville, KY
WFNC Fayetteville, NC
WFNI(AM) Indianapolis, IN
WFNN(AM) Erie, PA
WFNO Norco, LA
WFNR Blacksburg, VA
WFNS(AM) Blackshear, GA
WFNT Flint, MI
WFNW(AM) Naugatuck, CT
WFNY(AM) Gloversville, NY
WFNZ Charlotte, NC
WFOB(AM) Fostoria, OH
WFOM Marietta, GA
WFOR Hattiesburg, MS
WFOY Saint Augustine, FL
WFPA(AM) Fort Payne, AL
WFPB Orleans, MA
WFPR Hammond, LA
WFRA Franklin, PA
WFRB Frostburg, MD
*WFRF(AM) Tallahassee, FL
WFRL Freeport, IL
WFRM Coudersport, PA
WFRX West Frankfort, IL
WFSC Franklin, NC
WFSH(AM) Valparaiso-Niceville, FL
WFSM(AM) Dry Branch, GA
WFSP Kingwood, WV
WFSR Harlan, KY
*WFST(AM) Caribou, ME
WFTD Marietta, GA
WFTG London, KY
WFTH Richmond, VA
WFTL(AM) West Palm Beach, FL
WFTM Maysville, KY
WFTN Franklin, NH
WFTR Front Royal, VA
WFTU(AM) Riverhead, NY
WFTW Fort Walton Beach, FL
WFUL(AM) Fulton, KY
WFUN Ashtabula, OH
WFUR Grand Rapids, MI
WFVA(AM) Fredericksburg, VA
WFWL(AM) Camden, TN
WFXH(AM) Hilton Head Island, SC
WFXJ(AM) Jacksonville, FL
WFXN(AM) Moline, IL
WFXY Middlesboro, KY
WFYC(AM) Alma, MI
WFYL(AM) King of Prussia, PA
WGAB Newburgh, IN
WGAC Augusta, GA
WGAD(AM) Rainbow City, AL
WGAI(AM) Elizabeth City, NC
WGAM(AM) Manchester, NH
WGAN(AM) Portland, ME
WGAP Maryville, TN
*WGAS South Gastonia, NC
WGAT Gate City, VA
WGAU(AM) Athens, GA
WGAW Gardner, MA
WGBB Freeport, NY
WGBF Evansville, IN
WGBN New Kensington, PA
WGBR Goldsboro, NC
WGBW(AM) Two Rivers, WI
WGCD Chester, SC
WGCH(AM) Greenwich, CT
WGCK(AM) Neon, KY
WGCL Bloomington, IN
WGCM Gulfport, MS
WGCR(AM) Pisgah Forest, NC
WGCV(AM) Cayce, SC
WGDJ(AM) Rensselaer, NY
WGDL Lares, PR

WGDN Gladwin, MI
WGEA Geneva, AL
WGEE(AM) Superior, WI
WGEM Quincy, IL
WGEN Geneseo, IL
WGES(AM) Saint Petersburg, FL
WGET Gettysburg, PA
WGEZ(AM) Beloit, WI
WGFA(AM) Watseka, IL
WGFC Floyd, VA
WGFP Webster, MA
WGFS Covington, GA
WGFT(AM) Campbell, OH
WGFY Charlotte, NC
WGGA(AM) Gainesville, GA
WGGG Gainesville, FL
WGGH Marion, IL
WGGM Chester, VA
WGGO Salamanca, NY
WGGQ(AM) Newport, TN
WGHB Farmville, NC
WGHC(AM) Clayton, GA
WGHM(AM) Nashua, NH
WGHN Grand Haven, MI
WGHQ Kingston, NY
WGHT Pompton Lakes, NJ
WGIG(AM) Brunswick, GA
WGIL Galesburg, IL
WGIN Rochester, NH
WGIR Manchester, NH
WGIT(AM) Canovanas, PR
WGIV(AM) Pineville, NC
WGJK(AM) Rome, GA
WGKA(AM) Atlanta, GA
WGL Fort Wayne, IN
WGLB(AM) Elm Grove, WI
WGLD(AM) Red Lion, PA
WGLL Auburn, IN
WGLM(AM) Greenville, MI
WGLR Lancaster, WI
WGMA Spindale, NC
WGMF(AM) Tunkhannock, PA
WGMI Bremen, GA
WGML Hinesville, GA
WGMN Roanoke, VA
WGN(AM) Chicago, IL
WGNC Gastonia, NC
WGNQ(AM) Bridgeport, AL
*WGNR Anderson, IN
WGNS Murfreesboro, TN
WGNU(AM) Granite City, IL
WGNY Newburgh, NY
WGNZ Fairborn, OH
WGOC(AM) Kingsport, TN
WGOD Charlotte Amalie, VI
WGOH Grayson, KY
WGOK Mobile, AL
WGOL Russellville, AL
WGOP(AM) Pocomoke City, MD
WGOS High Point, NC
WGOV(AM) Valdosta, GA
WGOW Chattanooga, TN
WGPA(AM) Bethlehem, PA
WGPC Albany, GA
WGPL Portsmouth, VA
WGR Buffalo, NY
WGRA Cairo, GA
WGRB(AM) Chicago, IL
WGRK(AM) Greensburg, KY
WGRM Greenwood, MS
WGRO Lake City, FL
WGRP Greenville, PA
WGRV Greeneville, TN
WGRY Grayling, MI
WGSB Mebane, NC
WGSF(AM) Memphis, TN
WGSO New Orleans, LA
WGSP Charlotte, NC
WGST Atlanta, GA
WGSV Guntersville, AL
WGTA Summerville, GA
WGTH Richlands, VA
WGTJ(AM) Murrayville, GA
WGTK(AM) Louisville, KY
WGTM Wilson, NC
WGTN Georgetown, SC

WGTO Cassopolis, MI
WGUL(AM) Dunedin, FL
WGUN Atlanta, GA
WGUS(AM) Augusta, GA
WGUY(AM) Newport, ME
WGVA Geneva, NY
WGVL Greenville, SC
WGVM Greenville, MS
WGVN(AM) Georgetown, KY
WGVS(AM) Muskegon, MI
*WGVU Kentwood, MI
WGWM London, KY
WGY Schenectady, NY
WGYM(AM) Hammonton, NJ
WGYV Greenville, AL
*WHA Madison, WI
WHAG Halfway, MD
WHAK Rogers City, MI
WHAL(AM) Phenix City, AL
WHAM Rochester, NY
WHAN Ashland, VA
WHAP Hopewell, VA
WHAS Louisville, KY
WHAT Philadelphia, PA
WHAW Weston, WV
WHAZ Troy, NY
WHB Kansas City, MO
WHBB Selma, AL
WHBC Canton, OH
WHBG Harrisonburg, VA
WHBK Marshall, NC
WHBL(AM) Sheboygan, WI
WHBN(AM) Harrodsburg, KY
WHBO(AM) Pinellas Park, FL
WHBQ Memphis, TN
WHBS(AM) Moultrie, GA
WHBT(AM) Tallahassee, FL
WHBU Anderson, IN
WHBY(AM) Kimberly, WI
WHCG Metter, GA
WHCO(AM) Sparta, IL
WHCU Ithaca, NY
WHDD(AM) Sharon, CT
WHDL Olean, NY
WHDM McKenzie, TN
WHEE Martinsville, VA
WHEN Syracuse, NY
WHEO Stuart, VA
WHEP Foley, AL
WHEW(AM) Franklin, TN
WHFA(AM) Poynette, WI
WHFB(AM) Benton Harbor-St. Joseph, MI
WHFS(AM) Morningside, MD
WHGB(AM) Harrisburg, PA
WHGG(AM) Kingsport, TN
WHGH Thomasville, GA
WHGS(AM) Hampton, SC
WHGT(AM) Chambersburg, PA
WHHO Hornell, NY
WHHV Hillsville, VA
WHIC(AM) Rochester, NY
WHIE Griffin, GA
WHIM Apopka, FL
WHIN Gallatin, TN
WHIO Dayton, OH
WHIP Mooresville, NC
WHIR(AM) Danville, KY
WHIS Bluefield, WV
WHIT(AM) Madison, WI
WHIY(AM) Huntsville, AL
WHIZ Zanesville, OH
WHJA(AM) Laurel, MS
WHJB(AM) Bedford, PA
WHJC Matewan, WV
WHJJ Providence, RI
WHK Cleveland, OH
WHKP(AM) Hendersonville, NC
WHKT Portsmouth, VA
WHKW(AM) Cleveland, OH
WHKY(AM) Hickory, NC
WHKZ(AM) Warren, OH
WHLD Niagara Falls, NY
WHLI Hempstead, NY
WHLL(AM) Springfield, MA
WHLM(AM) Bloomsburg, PA

WHLN Harlan, KY
WHLO Akron, OH
WHLS Port Huron, MI
WHLX(AM) Marine City, MI
WHLY(AM) South Bend, IN
WHMA Anniston, AL
WHMP Northampton, MA
WHMQ(AM) Greenfield, MA
WHNC Henderson, NC
WHNK(AM) Parkersburg, WV
WHNP(AM) East Longmeadow, MA
WHNR Cypress Gardens, FL
WHNY McComb, MS
WHNZ(AM) Tampa, FL
WHO(AM) Des Moines, IA
WHOA(AM) Saraland, AL
WHOC Philadelphia, MS
WHOG Hobson City, AL
WHOL Allentown, PA
WHON Centerville, IN
WHOO(AM) Kissimmee, FL
WHOP(AM) Hopkinsville, KY
WHOS Decatur, AL
WHOW Clinton, IL
WHOY Salinas, PR
WHP Harrisburg, PA
WHPY Clayton, NC
WHRY Hurley, WI
WHSC Hartsville, SC
WHSM Hayward, WI
WHSR Pompano Beach, FL
WHSY(AM) Hattiesburg, MS
WHTB Fall River, MA
WHTC(AM) Holland, MI
WHTG Eatontown, NJ
WHTH Heath, OH
WHTK Rochester, NY
WHUB Cookeville, TN
WHUC Hudson, NY
WHUN Huntingdon, PA
WHVN Charlotte, NC
WHVO(AM) Hopkinsville, KY
WHVR Hanover, PA
WHVW Hyde Park, NY
WHWH Princeton, NJ
WHYL Carlisle, PA
WHYM(AM) Lake City, SC
WHYN Springfield, MA
WIAC San Juan, PR
WIAM Williamston, NC
WIAN Ishpeming, MI
WIBA Madison, WI
WIBB(AM) Macon, GA
WIBG Ocean City, NJ
WIBH Anna, IL
WIBM Jackson, MI
WIBR Baton Rouge, LA
WIBS Guayama, PR
WIBW Topeka, KS
WIBX Utica, NY
WICC Bridgeport, CT
WICH(AM) Norwich, CT
WICK Scranton, PA
WICO(AM) Salisbury, MD
WICY Malone, NY
WIDA Carolina, PR
WIDG Saint Ignace, MI
WIDS Russell Springs, KY
WIDU(AM) Fayetteville, NC
WIEL Elizabethtown, KY
WIEZ Lewistown, PA
WIFA(AM) Knoxville, TN
WIFE(AM) Connersville, IN
WIFI Florence, NJ
WIGG Wiggins, MS
WIGM Medford, WI
WIGN(AM) Bristol, TN
WIGO(AM) Morrow, GA
*WIHM Taylorville, IL
WIHY(AM) Hurricane, WV
WIIN Ridgeland, MS
WIJD(AM) Prichard, AL
WIJR(AM) Highland, IL
WIKB Iron River, MI
WIKC Bogalusa, LA
WIKE Newport, VT

WILA Danville, VA
WILB(AM) Canton, OH
WILC Laurel, MD
WILD Boston, MA
WILE Cambridge, OH
WILI(AM) Willimantic, CT
WILK Wilkes-Barre, PA
*WILL(AM) Urbana, IL
WILM Wilmington, DE
WILO Frankfort, IN
WILS Lansing, MI
WILY Centralia, IL
WIMA Lima, OH
WIMG Ewing, NJ
WIMO Winder, GA
WIMS Michigan City, IN
WINA Charlottesville, VA
WINC Winchester, VA
WIND Chicago, IL
WINE Brookfield, CT
WING Dayton, OH
WINI(AM) Murphysboro, IL
WINK(AM) Fort Myers, FL
WINR Binghamton, NY
WINS New York, NY
WINT(AM) Melbourne, FL
WINU(AM) Shelbyville, IL
WINV(AM) Beverly Hills, FL
WINW Canton, OH
WINY Putnam, CT
WINZ(AM) Miami, FL
WIOD Miami, FL
WIOI New Boston, OH
WION(AM) Ionia, MI
WIOO Carlisle, PA
WIOS Tawas City, MI
WIOU Kokomo, IN
WIOV Reading, PA
WIOZ Pinehurst, NC
WIP Philadelphia, PA
WIPC(AM) Lake Wales, FL
*WIPR(AM) San Juan, PR
WIPS Ticonderoga, NY
WIQB(AM) Conway, SC
WIQR Prattville, AL
WIRA Fort Pierce, FL
WIRB(AM) Level Plains, AL
WIRD Lake Placid, NY
WIRJ Humboldt, TN
WIRL(AM) Peoria, IL
WIRO Ironton, OH
WIRV Irvine, KY
WIRY Plattsburgh, NY
WISA Isabela, PR
WISE Asheville, NC
WISK Americus, GA
WISN Milwaukee, WI
WISO Ponce, PR
WISP Doylestown, PA
WISR Butler, PA
WISS Berlin, WI
WIST(AM) New Orleans, LA
WISW Columbia, SC
WITA Knoxville, TN
WITK(AM) Pittston, PA
WITM(AM) Marion, VA
WITS(AM) Sebring, FL
WITY(AM) Danville, IL
WITZ Jasper, IN
WIVV Vieques, PR
WIWA(AM) Saint Cloud, FL
WIWS Beckley, WV
WIXC(AM) Titusville, FL
WIXE(AM) Monroe, NC
WIXI(AM) Jasper, AL
WIXK(AM) New Richmond, WI
WIXN Dixon, IL
WIXT(AM) Little Falls, NY
WIYD Palatka, FL
WIZE Springfield, OH
WIZK(AM) Bay Springs, MS
WIZM La Crosse, WI
WIZR Johnstown, NY
WIZS(AM) Henderson, NC
WIZZ(AM) Greenfield, MA
WJAG(AM) Norfolk, NE

WJAK Jackson, TN
WJAM(AM) Selma, AL
WJAS Pittsburgh, PA
WJAT Swainsboro, GA
WJAW(AM) Saint Marys, WV
WJAX Jacksonville, FL
WJAY Mullins, SC
WJBB Haleyville, AL
WJBC Bloomington, IL
WJBD Salem, IL
WJBI Batesville, MS
WJBM Jerseyville, IL
WJBO Baton Rouge, LA
WJBS Holly Hill, SC
WJBW(AM) Jupiter, FL
WJBY(AM) Gadsden, AL
WJCM(AM) Sebring, FL
WJCP(AM) North Vernon, IN
WJCV Jacksonville, NC
WJCW Johnson City, TN
WJDA Quincy, MA
WJDB Thomasville, AL
WJDJ(AM) Hartsville, SC
WJDM Elizabeth, NJ
WJDX Jackson, MS
WJDY(AM) Salisbury, MD
WJEH Gallipolis, OH
WJEJ Hagerstown, MD
WJEM(AM) Valdosta, GA
WJER Dover-New Philadelphia, OH
WJES(AM) Saluda, SC
WJET(AM) Erie, PA
WJFA(AM) Hilliard, FL
WJFC Jefferson City, TN
WJFJ Tryon, NC
WJFN(AM) Brandon, MS
WJGK(AM) Highland, NY
WJHX(AM) Lexington, AL
WJIB Cambridge, MA
WJIG Tullahoma, TN
WJIL Jacksonville, IL
WJIM(AM) Lansing, MI
WJIT Sabana, PR
WJJC Commerce, GA
WJJG Elmhurst, IL
WJJL Niagara Falls, NY
WJJM Lewisburg, TN
WJJQ Tomahawk, WI
WJJT Jellico, TN
WJKB(AM) Moncks Corner, SC
*WJKN(AM) Jackson, MI
WJKY Jamestown, KY
WJLD Fairfield, AL
WJLE Smithville, TN
WJLG Savannah, GA
WJLS Beckley, WV
WJLX(AM) Jasper, AL
WJMC Rice Lake, WI
WJML(AM) Petoskey, MI
WJMO(AM) Cleveland, OH
WJMP Kent, OH
WJMS Ironwood, MI
WJMT Merrill, WI
WJMX Florence, SC
WJNC Jacksonville, NC
WJNL(AM) Kingsley, MI
WJNO(AM) West Palm Beach, FL
WJNT Pearl, MS
WJNX(AM) Fort Pierce, FL
WJNZ(AM) Kentwood, MI
WJOB Hammond, IN
WJOC Chattanooga, TN
WJOE(AM) Orange-Athol, MA
WJOI Norfolk, VA
WJOK Kaukauna, WI
WJOL Joliet, IL
WJON Saint Cloud, MN
WJOT Wabash, IN
WJOY(AM) Burlington, VT
WJPA Washington, PA
WJPF Herrin, IL
WJPI(AM) Plymouth, NC
WJQS(AM) Jackson, MS
WJR Detroit, MI
WJRD(AM) Tuscaloosa, AL
WJRI Lenoir, NC

WJRM Troy, NC
WJRW(AM) Grand Rapids, MI
WJSA Jersey Shore, PA
WJSB Crestview, FL
WJSS(AM) Havre de Grace, MD
WJST(AM) New Castle, PA
WJTB North Ridgeville, OH
WJTH Calhoun, GA
WJTI(AM) Racine, WI
WJTN Jamestown, NY
WJTO Bath, ME
WJTP(AM) Walhalla, SC
WJUB(AM) Plymouth, WI
WJUN Mexico, PA
WJUS Marion, AL
WJWB(AM) Gibsonia, FL
WJWF(AM) Columbus, MS
WJWK Seaford, DE
WJWL Georgetown, DE
WJXL(AM) Jacksonville Beach, FL
WJYI Milwaukee, WI
WJYK(AM) Chase City, VA
WJYM Bowling Green, OH
WJYP(AM) Saint Albans, WV
WJYZ Albany, GA
WJZ(AM) Baltimore, MD
WJZD(AM) Bay St. Louis, MS
WJZM Clarksville, TN
WJZN(AM) Augusta, ME
WKAC Athens, AL
WKAJ(AM) Little Falls, NY
WKAM Goshen, IN
WKAN Kankakee, IL
WKAQ San Juan, PR
*WKAR East Lansing, MI
WKAT North Miami, FL
WKAV Charlottesville, VA
WKAX Russellville, AL
WKAZ(AM) Charleston, WV
WKBA Vinton, VA
WKBC North Wilkesboro, NC
WKBF Rock Island, IL
WKBH Holmen, WI
WKBI Saint Marys, PA
WKBK(AM) Keene, NH
WKBL(AM) Covington, TN
WKBN Youngstown, OH
WKBO Harrisburg, PA
WKBR(AM) Lancaster, NH
WKBV(AM) Richmond, IN
WKBY Chatham, VA
WKBZ(AM) Muskegon, MI
WKCB Hindman, KY
WKCE Maryville, TN
WKCI(AM) Waynesboro, VA
WKCM Hawesville, KY
WKCT(AM) Bowling Green, KY
WKCU Corinth, MS
WKCW Warrenton, VA
WKCY Harrisonburg, VA
WKDA(AM) Lebanon, TN
WKDE Altavista, VA
WKDI Denton, MD
WKDK Newberry, SC
WKDL(AM) Warrenton, VA
WKDM(AM) New York, NY
WKDO Liberty, KY
WKDP Corbin, KY
WKDR(AM) Berlin, NH
WKDV Manassas, VA
WKDW Staunton, VA
WKDX Hamlet, NC
WKDZ Cadiz, KY
WKEI(AM) Kewanee, IL
WKEU Griffin, GA
WKEW Greensboro, NC
WKEX Blacksburg, VA
WKEY Covington, VA
WKEZ Bluefield, WV
WKFB(AM) Jeannette, PA
WKFD(AM) Charlestown, RI
WKFE Yauco, PR
WKFI(AM) Wilmington, OH
WKFL Bushnell, FL
WKFN(AM) Clarksville, TN
WKFO(AM) Corbin, KY

*WKGC Panama City Beach, FL
WKGE(AM) Johnstown, PA
WKGM Smithfield, VA
WKGN Knoxville, TN
WKGX Lenoir, NC
WKHB(AM) Irwin, PA
WKHM(AM) Jackson, MI
WKHZ(AM) Ocean City, MD
WKIC Hazard, KY
WKII(AM) Solana, FL
WKIK La Plata, MD
WKIP Poughkeepsie, NY
WKIQ Eustis, FL
WKIZ Key West, FL
WKJB Mayaguez, PR
WKJG(AM) Fort Wayne, IN
WKJK(AM) Louisville, KY
WKJQ Parsons, TN
WKJR(AM) Rantoul, IL
WKKP McDonough, GA
WKKS Vanceburg, KY
WKKX(AM) Wheeling, WV
WKLA Ludington, MI
WKLB Manchester, KY
WKLJ Sparta, WI
WKLK Cloquet, MN
WKLP Keyser, WV
WKLQ(AM) Whitehall, MI
WKLV Blackstone, VA
WKLY Hartwell, GA
WKMB Stirling, NJ
WKMC Roaring Spring, PA
WKMG Newberry, SC
WKMI Kalamazoo, MI
WKMQ(AM) Tupelo, MS
WKND(AM) Windsor, CT
WKNG Tallapoosa, GA
WKNR(AM) Cleveland, OH
WKNV Fairlawn, VA
WKNW Sault Ste. Marie, MI
WKNY Kingston, NY
WKOK Sunbury, PA
WKOR(AM) Starkville, MS
WKOX Framingham, MA
WKOZ Kosciusko, MS
WKPA Lynchburg, VA
WKPR Kalamazoo, MI
WKPT Kingsport, TN
WKQW Oil City, PA
WKRA Holly Springs, MS
WKRC Cincinnati, OH
WKRD(AM) Louisville, KY
WKRK Murphy, NC
WKRM(AM) Columbia, TN
WKRO Cairo, IL
WKRS Waukegan, IL
WKSC Kershaw, SC
WKSH(AM) Sussex, WI
WKSK(AM) West Jefferson, NC
WKSN Jamestown, NY
WKSR Pulaski, TN
WKST(AM) New Castle, PA
WKTA Evanston, IL
WKTE King, NC
WKTF(AM) Vienna, GA
WKTI(AM) Powell, TN
WKTP Jonesborough, TN
WKTQ South Paris, ME
WKTR Earlysville, VA
WKTX Cortland, OH
WKTY(AM) La Crosse, WI
WKUN(AM) Bostwick, GA
WKVA Lewistown, PA
WKVG Jenkins, KY
WKVI Knox, IN
WKVL(AM) Knoxville, TN
WKVM San Juan, PR
WKVQ Eatonton, GA
WKVT Brattleboro, VT
WKVX Wooster, OH
WKWF(AM) Key West, FL
WKWL Florala, AL
WKWN Trenton, GA
WKXG Greenwood, MS
WKXL(AM) Concord, NH
WKXM Winfield, AL

WKXO Berea, KY
WKXR Asheboro, NC
WKXV Knoxville, TN
WKY Oklahoma City, OK
WKYH(AM) Paintsville, KY
WKYK Burnsville, NC
WKYO Caro, MI
WKYW(AM) Frankfort, KY
WKYX(AM) Paducah, KY
WKZD(AM) Priceville, AL
WKZI Casey, IL
WKZK North Augusta, SC
WKZN(AM) West Hazleton, PA
WKZO(AM) Kalamazoo, MI
WKZV Washington, PA
WLAA(AM) Winter Garden, FL
WLAC Nashville, TN
WLAD Danbury, CT
WLAF La Follette, TN
WLAG La Grange, GA
WLAM(AM) Lewiston, ME
WLAN Lancaster, PA
WLAP Lexington, KY
WLAQ Rome, GA
WLAR Athens, TN
WLAT(AM) New Britain, CT
WLAY Muscle Shoals, AL
WLBA Gainesville, GA
WLBB(AM) Carrollton, GA
WLBE Leesburg, FL
WLBG Laurens, SC
WLBH Mattoon, IL
WLBK(AM) De Kalb, IL
*WLBL Auburndale, WI
WLBN Lebanon, KY
WLBQ Morgantown, KY
WLBR Lebanon, PA
WLBY(AM) Saline, MI
WLCC Brandon, FL
WLCK(AM) Scottsville, KY
WLCM(AM) Holt, MI
WLCO(AM) Lapeer, MI
WLCR(AM) Mt. Washington, KY
WLDS Jacksonville, IL
WLDX Fayette, AL
WLDY Ladysmith, WI
WLEA Hornell, NY
WLEC Sandusky, OH
WLEE(AM) Richmond, VA
WLEM Emporium, PA
WLEO(AM) Ponce, PR
WLES(AM) Bon Air, VA
WLET Toccoa, GA
WLEW Bad Axe, MI
WLEY Cayey, PR
WLFJ(AM) Greenville, SC
WLFN La Crosse, WI
WLFP(AM) Braddock, PA
WLGC Greenup, KY
WLGN Logan, OH
WLIB New York, NY
WLIE(AM) Islip, NY
WLIJ Shelbyville, TN
WLIK Newport, TN
WLIL(AM) Lenoir City, TN
WLIM Patchogue, NY
WLIP Kenosha, WI
WLIQ(AM) Quincy, IL
WLIS Old Saybrook, CT
WLIV Livingston, TN
*WLJN Elmwood Township, MI
WLJW(AM) Cadillac, MI
WLKD Minocqua, WI
WLKF(AM) Lakeland, FL
WLKR(AM) Norwalk, OH
WLKS West Liberty, KY
WLKW(AM) West Warwick, RI
WLLH Lowell, MA
WLLI(AM) Humboldt, TN
WLLL Lynchburg, VA
WLLM(AM) Lincoln, IL
*WLLN Lillington, NC
WLLQ(AM) Chapel Hill, NC
WLLV Louisville, KY
WLLY Wilson, NC
WLMC Georgetown, SC

WLMR(AM) Chattanooga, TN
WLMV(AM) Madison, WI
WLNA(AM) Peekskill, NY
WLNC Laurinburg, NC
WLNL Horseheads, NY
WLNO New Orleans, LA
WLNR Kinston, NC
WLOA(AM) Farrell, PA
WLOB Portland, ME
WLOC(AM) Munfordville, KY
WLOD Loudon, TN
WLOE Eden, NC
WLOH Lancaster, OH
WLOI La Porte, IN
WLOK Memphis, TN
WLOL(AM) Minneapolis, MN
WLON Lincolnton, NC
WLOP Jesup, GA
WLOR Huntsville, AL
WLOU Louisville, KY
WLOV Washington, GA
WLOY(AM) Rural Retreat, VA
WLPA Lancaster, PA
WLPO La Salle, IL
WLPR Prichard, AL
WLQH Chiefland, FL
WLQM Franklin, VA
WLQR Toledo, OH
WLQV Detroit, MI
WLQY Hollywood, FL
WLRB Macomb, IL
WLRC Walnut, MS
WLRM(AM) Millington, TN
WLRP San Sebastian, PR
WLRT(AM) Nicholasville, KY
WLRV Lebanon, VA
WLS Chicago, IL
WLSB Copperhill, TN
WLSC Loris, SC
WLSD Big Stone Gap, VA
WLSG(AM) Wilmington, NC
WLSH Lansford, PA
WLSI Pikeville, KY
WLSS(AM) Sarasota, FL
WLSV Wellsville, NY
WLTA Alpharetta, GA
WLTG Panama City, FL
WLTH Gary, IN
WLTN Littleton, NH
WLTP(AM) Marietta, OH
WLTQ(AM) Charleston, SC
WLUV Loves Park, IL
WLUX(AM) Dunbar, WV
WLUZ(AM) Bayamon, PR
WLVA Lynchburg, VA
WLVE(AM) Winchester, VA
WLVF Haines City, FL
WLVJ(AM) Boynton Beach, FL
WLVL Lockport, NY
WLVP(AM) Gorham, ME
WLVV Mobile, AL
WLW Cincinnati, OH
WLWI(AM) Montgomery, AL
WLWL Rockingham, NC
WLXE(AM) Rockville, MD
WLXG Lexington, KY
WLXN Lexington, NC
WLYC Williamsport, PA
WLYJ(AM) Centre, AL
WLYN Lynn, MA
WLYV Fort Wayne, IN
WMAC Macon, GA
WMAF Madison, FL
WMAL Washington, DC
WMAM Marinette, WI
WMAN Mansfield, OH
WMAX Bay City, MI
WMAY(AM) Springfield, IL
WMBA Ambridge, PA
WMBD Peoria, IL
WMBE Chilton, WI
WMBG Williamsburg, VA
WMBH(AM) Joplin, MO
*WMBI(AM) Chicago, IL
WMBM Miami Beach, FL
WMBN(AM) Petoskey, MI

WMBS Uniontown, PA
WMC(AM) Memphis, TN
WMCA New York, NY
WMCH Church Hill, TN
WMCJ(AM) Cullman, AL
WMCL McLeansboro, IL
WMCP Columbia, TN
WMCR Oneida, NY
WMCS Greenfield, WI
WMCT Mountain City, TN
WMCU(AM) Coral Gables, FL
WMCW(AM) Harvard, IL
WMDB(AM) Nashville, TN
WMDD Fajardo, PR
WMDH New Castle, IN
*WMDR Augusta, ME
WMEL(AM) Cocoa Beach, FL
WMEN(AM) Royal Palm Beach, FL
WMEQ(AM) Menomonie, WI
WMER Meridian, MS
WMET Gaithersburg, MD
WMEV Marion, VA
WMFA(AM) Raeford, NC
WMFC Monroeville, AL
WMFD Wilmington, NC
WMFG Hibbing, MN
WMFJ Daytona Beach, FL
WMFN Zeeland, MI
WMFR High Point, NC
WMFS(AM) Memphis, TN
WMGC Murfreesboro, TN
WMGG(AM) Dunedin, FL
WMGJ Gadsden, AL
WMGO Canton, MS
WMGR Bainbridge, GA
WMGW Meadville, PA
WMGY Montgomery, AL
WMIA Arecibo, PR
WMIC(AM) Sandusky, MI
WMID(AM) Atlantic City, NJ
WMIK Middlesboro, KY
WMIN(AM) Sauk Rapids, MN
WMIQ Iron Mountain, MI
WMIR Atlantic Beach, SC
WMIS Natchez, MS
WMIX Mount Vernon, IL
WMIZ Vineland, NJ
WMJH Rockford, MI
WMJL Marion, KY
WMJQ(AM) Ontario, NY
WMJR Winchester, KY
WMKI(AM) Boston, MA
WMKT(AM) Charlevoix, MI
WMLB(AM) Avondale Estates, GA
WMLC(AM) Monticello, MS
WMLM Saint Louis, MI
WMLP(AM) Milton, PA
WMLR Hohenwald, TN
WMLT(AM) Dublin, GA
WMMB Melbourne, FL
WMMG Brandenburg, KY
WMMI Shepherd, MI
WMML Glens Falls, NY
WMMN Fairmont, WV
WMMV Cocoa, FL
WMMW Meriden, CT
WMNA Gretna, VA
WMNC Morganton, NC
WMNE(AM) Riviera Beach, FL
WMNI Columbus, OH
WMNT(AM) Manati, PR
WMNY(AM) McKeesport, PA
WMNZ Montezuma, GA
WMOA Marietta, OH
WMOB Mobile, AL
WMOG Brunswick, GA
WMOH Hamilton, OH
WMOK Metropolis, IL
WMON Montgomery, WV
WMOP Ocala, FL
WMOR Morehead, KY
WMOU Berlin, NH
WMOV Ravenswood, WV
WMOX Meridian, MS
*WMPC(AM) Lapeer, MI
WMPL Hancock, MI

WMPM Smithfield, NC
WMPO Middleport-Pomeroy, OH
WMPS(AM) Bartlett, TN
WMPX Midland, MI
WMQM(AM) Lakeland, TN
WMRB Columbia, TN
WMRC Milford, MA
WMRD(AM) Middletown, CT
WMRE Charles Town, WV
WMRI(AM) Marion, IN
WMRN Marion, OH
WMRO(AM) Gallatin, TN
WMSA Massena, NY
WMSG Oakland, MD
WMSH Sturgis, MI
WMSK(AM) Morganfield, KY
WMSP Montgomery, AL
WMSR Manchester, TN
WMST(AM) Mt. Sterling, KY
WMSW Hatillo, PR
WMSX Brockton, MA
WMT Cedar Rapids, IA
WMTA(AM) Central City, KY
WMTC Vancleve, KY
WMTD Hinton, WV
WMTE Manistee, MI
WMTL Leitchfield, KY
WMTM Moultrie, GA
WMTN Morristown, TN
WMTR(AM) Morristown, NJ
WMTY(AM) Farragut, TN
WMUF Paris, TN
WMVA(AM) Martinsville, VA
WMVB Millville, NJ
WMVG Milledgeville, GA
WMVO(AM) Mount Vernon, OH
WMVP Chicago, IL
WMXF(AM) Waynesville, NC
WMYF Portsmouth, NH
WMYJ(AM) Martinsville, IN
WMYM(AM) Miami, FL
WMYN Mayodan, NC
WMYR Fort Myers, FL
WMYT Carolina Beach, NC
WNAE Warren, PA
WNAH Nashville, TN
WNAK Nanticoke, PA
WNAM Neenah-Menasha, WI
WNAP Norristown, PA
WNAT Natchez, MS
WNAU New Albany, MS
WNAV(AM) Annapolis, MD
WNAW North Adams, MA
WNAX(AM) Yankton, SD
WNBF Binghamton, NY
WNBH New Bedford, MA
WNBI Park Falls, WI
WNBN(AM) Meridian, MS
WNBP(AM) Newburyport, MA
WNBS Murray, KY
WNBT Wellsboro, PA
WNBY Newberry, MI
WNBZ Saranac Lake, NY
WNCA Siler City, NC
WNCC(AM) Northern Cambria, PA
WNCO Ashland, OH
WNCT Greenville, NC
WNDA(AM) New Albany, IN
WNDB Daytona Beach, FL
WNDE Indianapolis, IN
WNDI Sullivan, IN
WNDZ Portage, IN
WNEA Newnan, GA
WNEB Worcester, MA
*WNED Buffalo, NY
WNEG(AM) Toccoa, GA
WNEL Caguas, PR
WNEM(AM) Bridgeport, MI
WNER(AM) Watertown, NY
WNES Central City, KY
WNEX Macon, GA
WNEZ(AM) Manchester, CT
WNFL Green Bay, WI
WNFO Ridgeland, SC
WNFS(AM) White Springs, FL
WNGM(AM) Hiawassee, GA

WNGO(AM) Mayfield, KY
WNHV White River Junction, VT
WNIK Arecibo, PR
WNIL Niles, MI
WNIO(AM) Youngstown, OH
WNIS Norfolk, VA
WNIV Atlanta, GA
WNIX(AM) Greenville, MS
WNJC Washington Township, NJ
WNJE(AM) Flemington, NJ
WNKX Centerville, TN
WNLA Indianola, MS
WNLK(AM) Norwalk, CT
WNLR Churchville, VA
WNLS Tallahassee, FL
WNMA Miami Springs, FL
WNMB(AM) North Myrtle Beach, SC
WNML(AM) Knoxville, TN
WNMT Nashwauk, MN
WNNC Newton, NC
WNNG(AM) Warner Robins, GA
WNNR(AM) Jacksonville, FL
WNNW(AM) Lawrence, MA
WNNZ Westfield, MA
WNOG Naples, FL
WNOO(AM) Chattanooga, TN
WNOP Newport, KY
WNOS New Bern, NC
WNOV Milwaukee, WI
WNOW Mint Hill, NC
WNPL(AM) Golden Gate, FL
WNPV Lansdale, PA
WNPZ(AM) Knoxville, TN
WNQM Nashville, TN
WNRG Grundy, VA
WNRI Woonsocket, RI
WNRP(AM) Gulf Breeze, FL
WNRR(AM) Augusta, GA
WNRS Herkimer, NY
WNRV(AM) Narrows-Pearisburg, VA
WNSH Beverly, MA
WNSI(AM) Robertsdale, AL
WNSR Brentwood, TN
WNSS(AM) Syracuse, NY
WNST Towson, MD
WNSW Newark, NJ
WNTA Rockford, IL
WNTD Chicago, IL
WNTF Bithlo, FL
WNTJ(AM) Johnstown, PA
WNTM(AM) Mobile, AL
WNTN Newton, MA
WNTP(AM) Philadelphia, PA
WNTS Beech Grove, IN
WNTT Tazewell, TN
WNTW(AM) Somerset, PA
WNUZ Talladega, AL
WNVA Norton, VA
WNVL(AM) Nashville, TN
WNVR Vernon Hills, IL
WNVY Cantonment, FL
*WNWC(AM) Sun Prairie, WI
WNWF(AM) Destin, FL
WNWI Oak Lawn, IL
WNWK(AM) Newark, DE
WNWN Portage, MI
WNWR Philadelphia, PA
WNWS Brownsville, TN
WNWT(AM) Rossford, OH
WNWZ Grand Rapids, MI
WNXT Portsmouth, OH
*WNYC New York, NY
WNYG Babylon, NY
WNYH(AM) Huntington, NY
WNYM(AM) Hackensack, NJ
WNYY(AM) Ithaca, NY
WNZF(AM) Bunnell, FL
WNZK Dearborn Heights, MI
WNZS(AM) Veazie, ME
WNZZ Montgomery, AL
WOAD Jackson, MS
WOAI San Antonio, TX
WOAM(AM) Peoria, IL
WOAP Owosso, MI
WOAY Oak Hill, WV
WOBG Clarksburg, WV

WOBL Oberlin, OH
WOBM(AM) Lakewood, NJ
WOBT(AM) Rhinelander, WI
WOBX(AM) Wanchese, NC
WOC Davenport, IA
WOCA Ocala, FL
WOCC Corydon, IN
WOCN Miami, FL
WOCO Oconto, WI
WOCV Oneida, TN
WODI Brookneal, VA
WODT New Orleans, LA
WODY Fieldale, VA
WOEG Hazlehurst, MS
WOEN(AM) Olean, NY
WOF(AM) Andover, NJ
WOFC(AM) Murray, KY
WOFX(AM) Troy, NY
WOGO Hallie, WI
WOGR Charlotte, NC
WOHI East Liverpool, OH
WOHS Shelby, NC
*WOI Ames, IA
WOIC(AM) Columbia, SC
WOIR Homestead, FL
WOIZ Guayanilla, PR
WOKA(AM) Douglas, GA
WOKB(AM) Winter Garden, FL
WOKC Okeechobee, FL
WOKS Columbus, GA
WOKV Jacksonville, FL
WOKY Milwaukee, WI
WOL Washington, DC
WOLA Barranquitas, PR
WOLB(AM) Baltimore, MD
WOLF Syracuse, NY
WOLH(AM) Florence, SC
WOLI(AM) Spartanburg, SC
WOMI(AM) Owensboro, KY
WOMN(AM) Franklinton, LA
WOMP Bellaire, OH
WOMT(AM) Manitowoc, WI
WONA Winona, MS
WOND(AM) Pleasantville, NJ
WONE Dayton, OH
WONG Canton, MS
WONN(AM) Lakeland, FL
WONQ Oviedo, FL
WONW Defiance, OH
WOOD Grand Rapids, MI
WOOF Dothan, AL
WOOK(AM) Midlothian, VA
WOON(AM) Woonsocket, RI
WOPI Bristol, TN
WOPP Opp, AL
WOQI(AM) Adjuntas, PR
WOR New York, NY
WORA Mayaguez, PR
WORC Worcester, MA
WORD(AM) Spartanburg, SC
WORL(AM) Altamonte Springs, FL
WORM Savannah, TN
WORV Hattiesburg, MS
WOSH Oshkosh, WI
WOSO San Juan, PR
*WOSU Columbus, OH
WOTE(AM) Clintonville, WI
WOTS Kissimmee, FL
*WOUB Athens, OH
WOWO Fort Wayne, IN
WOWW Germantown, TN
WOWZ(AM) Appomattox, VA
WOYK York, PA
WOYL Oil City, PA
WOZK Ozark, AL
WPAB Ponce, PR
WPAD Paducah, KY
WPAK Farmville, VA
WPAM Pottsville, PA
WPAQ Mount Airy, NC
WPAT Paterson, NJ
WPAX Thomasville, GA
WPAY Portsmouth, OH
WPAZ Pottstown, PA
WPBC Decatur, GA
WPBQ(AM) Flowood, MS

WPBR Lantana, FL
WPBS(AM) Conyers, GA
WPCC Clinton, SC
WPCE Portsmouth, VA
WPCF(AM) Panama City Beach, FL
WPCI Greenville, SC
WPCM Burlington, NC
WPDC Elizabethtown, PA
WPDM Potsdam, NY
WPDR Portage, WI
WPDX(AM) Clarksburg, WV
WPEH Louisville, GA
WPEK(AM) Fairview, NC
*WPEL Montrose, PA
WPEN Philadelphia, PA
WPEO Peoria, IL
WPET Greensboro, NC
WPFB Middletown, OH
WPFC Port Allen, LA
WPFD Fairview, TN
WPFJ Franklin, NC
WPFR(AM) Terre Haute, IN
WPGA Perry, GA
WPGG(AM) Evergreen, AL
*WPGM Danville, PA
WPGR(AM) Monroeville, PA
WPGS Mims, FL
WPGW Portland, IN
WPGY(AM) Ellijay, GA
WPHB Philipsburg, PA
WPHE Phoenixville, PA
WPHM Port Huron, MI
WPHT Philadelphia, PA
WPHX(AM) Sanford, ME
WPIC Sharon, PA
WPID Piedmont, AL
WPIE Trumansburg, NY
WPIN Dublin, VA
WPIP Winston-Salem, NC
WPIT Pittsburgh, PA
WPJF(AM) Greenville, SC
WPJK Orangeburg, SC
WPJL Raleigh, NC
WPJM Greer, SC
WPJS Conway, SC
WPJX(AM) Zion, IL
WPKE Pikeville, KY
WPKY Princeton, KY
WPKZ(AM) Fitchburg, MA
WPLK Palatka, FL
WPLM Plymouth, MA
WPLN(AM) Madison, TN
WPLO Grayson, GA
WPLV West Point, GA
*WPLX(AM) Turrell, AR
WPLY(AM) Mount Pocono, PA
WPMB Vandalia, IL
WPMH(AM) Claremont, VA
WPMP(AM) Pascagoula-Moss Point, MS
WPMZ Providence, RI
WPNA Oak Park, IL
WPNH Plymouth, NH
WPNI(AM) Amherst, MA
WPNN(AM) Pensacola, FL
WPNT(AM) South Bend, IN
WPNW(AM) Zeeland, MI
WPOG(AM) Saint Matthews, SC
WPOL Winston-Salem, NC
WPON Walled Lake, MI
WPOP Hartford, CT
WPPA Pottsville, PA
WPPC Penuelas, PR
WPPI(AM) Sauk Rapids, MN
WPRA Mayaguez, PR
WPRD Winter Park, FL
WPRE(AM) Prairie du Chien, WI
WPRN Butler, AL
WPRO Providence, RI
WPRP Ponce, PR
WPRR(AM) Ada, MI
WPRS Paris, IL
WPRT Prestonsburg, KY
WPRV(AM) Providence, RI
WPRX(AM) Bristol, CT
WPRY Perry, FL

WPSE Erie, PA
WPSL(AM) Port St. Lucie, FL
WPSN Honesdale, PA
WPSO New Port Richey, FL
WPSP Royal Palm Beach, FL
WPTB(AM) Statesboro, GA
WPTF Raleigh, NC
WPTK(AM) Pine Island Center, FL
WPTL Canton, NC
WPTN Cookeville, TN
WPTW(AM) Piqua, OH
WPTX(AM) Lexington Park, MD
WPUL South Daytona, FL
WPUT(AM) Brewster, NY
WPVL Platteville, WI
WPWA Chester, PA
WPWC Dumfries-Triangle, VA
WPWT(AM) Colonial Heights, TN
WPYB Benson, NC
WPYR(AM) Baton Rouge, LA
WPYT(AM) Wilkinsburg, PA
WQAM Miami, FL
WQBA Miami, FL
WQBC Vicksburg, MS
WQBN Temple Terrace, FL
WQBQ Leesburg, FL
WQBS San Juan, PR
WQCD(AM) Milford, PA
WQCH La Fayette, GA
WQCR(AM) Alabaster, AL
WQCT Bryan, OH
WQEW New York, NY
WQFX Gulfport, MS
WQHC(AM) Hanceville, AL
WQHL(AM) Live Oak, FL
WQII San Juan, PR
WQIZ Saint George, SC
WQKC(AM) Jeffersonville, IN
WQKR(AM) Portland, TN
WQLA(AM) La Follette, TN
WQLR(AM) Kalamazoo, MI
WQLS Ozark, AL
WQMS(AM) Quitman, MS
WQMV(AM) Waverly, TN
WQNT(AM) Charleston, SC
WQNX Aberdeen, NC
WQOH(AM) Irondale, AL
WQOP Atlantic Beach, FL
WQOQ(AM) Durand, WI
WQOR(AM) Olyphant, PA
WQPM Princeton, MN
WQQT(AM) Brooklet, GA
WQRT(AM) Florence, KY
WQRX Valley Head, AL
WQSC Charleston, SC
WQSE White Bluff, TN
WQST Forest, MS
WQSV Ashland City, TN
WQTW Latrobe, PA
WQUN(AM) Hamden, CT
WQVA(AM) Lexington, SC
WQWK(AM) State College, PA
WQXI Atlanta, GA
WQXL Columbia, SC
WQXM(AM) Bartow, FL
WQXO Munising, MI
WQXY Hazard, KY
WQYK(AM) Seffner, FL
WQZQ(AM) Clarksville, TN
WRAA Luray, VA
WRAB Arab, AL
WRAD Radford, VA
WRAK Williamsport, PA
WRAM Monmouth, IL
*WRAR(AM) Tappahannock, VA
WRAW(AM) Reading, PA
WRAY Princeton, IN
WRBE Lucedale, MS
WRBS(AM) Baltimore, MD
WRBZ Raleigh, NC
WRCA Waltham, MA
WRCE(AM) Watkins Glen, NY
WRCG Columbus, GA
WRCI(AM) Three Rivers, MI
WRCO Richland Center, WI
WRCR(AM) Spring Valley, NY

WRCS Ahoskie, NC
WRCY(AM) Mount Vernon, IN
WRDB Reedsburg, WI
WRDD Ebensburg, PA
WRDT(AM) Monroe, MI
WRDW(AM) Augusta, GA
WRDZ La Grange, IL
WREC(AM) Memphis, TN
WRED(AM) Westbrook, ME
WREF(AM) Ridgefield, CT
WREJ(AM) Richmond, VA
WREL Lexington, VA
WREN(AM) Carrollton, AL
WREV Reidsville, NC
WREY(AM) Hudson, WI
WRFC Athens, GA
WRFD(AM) Columbus-Worthington, OH
WRFM(AM) Muncie, IN
WRFV(AM) Valdosta, GA
WRGA Rome, GA
WRGC(AM) Sylva, NC
WRGM Ontario, OH
WRGS Rogersville, TN
WRHC Coral Gables, FL
WRHI(AM) Rock Hill, SC
WRHL Rochelle, IL
WRIE Erie, PA
WRIG Schofield, WI
WRIN Rensselaer, IN
WRIS Roanoke, VA
WRIV Riverhead, NY
WRIX Homeland Park, SC
WRJC Mauston, WI
WRJD(AM) Durham, NC
WRJN Racine, WI
WRJR(AM) Portsmouth, VA
WRJW Picayune, MS
WRJX(AM) Jackson, AL
WRJZ Knoxville, TN
WRKB Kannapolis, NC
WRKD Rockland, ME
WRKK Hughesville, PA
WRKL New City, NY
WRKM Carthage, TN
WRKO Boston, MA
WRKQ Madisonville, TN
WRLA(AM) West Point, GA
WRLL(AM) Cicero, IL
WRLV Salyersville, KY
WRLZ Eatonville, FL
WRME(AM) Hampden, ME
WRMG Red Bay, AL
WRMN Elgin, IL
WRMQ Orlando, FL
WRMS Beardstown, IL
WRMT(AM) Rocky Mount, NC
WRNA China Grove, NC
WRNE(AM) Gulf Breeze, FL
WRNI(AM) Providence, RI
WRNJ(AM) Hackettstown, NJ
WRNL Richmond, VA
WRNN(AM) Myrtle Beach, SC
WRNR Martinsburg, WV
WRNS Kinston, NC
WRNY Rome, NY
WROA Gulfport, MS
WROB(AM) West Point, MS
WROC(AM) Rochester, NY
WROD Daytona Beach, FL
WROK Rockford, IL
WROL Boston, MA
WROM Rome, GA
WRON Ronceverte, WV
WROP(AM) Belton, SC
WROS Jacksonville, FL
WROW(AM) Albany, NY
WROX Clarksdale, MS
WROY Carmi, IL
WRPM Poplarville, MS
WRPN(AM) Ripon, WI
WRPQ(AM) Baraboo, WI
WRRA Frederiksted, VI
WRRD(AM) Waukesha, WI
WRRE Juncos, PR
WRRL Rainelle, WV
WRRZ Clinton, NC

WRSA(AM) Saint Albans, VT
WRSB Canandaigua, NY
WRSC State College, PA
WRSJ(AM) Bayamon, PR
WRSM Sumiton, AL
WRSS San Sebastian, PR
WRSW Warsaw, IN
WRTA Altoona, PA
WRTG Garner, NC
WRTK(AM) Niles, OH
WRTO(AM) Chicago, IL
WRUF Gainesville, FL
*WRUN(AM) Utica, NY
WRUS Russellville, KY
WRVA Richmond, VA
WRVC Huntington, WV
WRVK(AM) Mt. Vernon, KY
WRVP(AM) Mount Kisco, NY
WRWB(AM) Huntington, WV
WRWH Cleveland, GA
WRXB Saint Petersburg Beach, FL
WRXO(AM) Roxboro, NC
WRYM(AM) New Britain, CT
*WRYT(AM) Edwardsville, IL
WRZN Hernando, FL
WSAI(AM) Cincinnati, OH
WSAL Logansport, IN
WSAM Saginaw, MI
WSAN(AM) Allentown, PA
WSAO Senatobia, MS
WSAR Fall River, MA
WSAT Salisbury, NC
WSAU Wausau, WI
WSB Atlanta, GA
WSBA York, PA
WSBB New Smyrna Beach, FL
WSBC(AM) Chicago, IL
WSBI Static, TN
WSBM(AM) Florence, AL
WSBR Boca Raton, FL
WSBS Great Barrington, MA
WSBT South Bend, IN
WSBV South Boston, VA
WSBX(AM) Ochlocknee, GA
WSCO(AM) Appleton, WI
WSCP Sandy Creek-Pulaski, NY
WSCR(AM) Chicago, IL
WSCW South Charleston, WV
WSDE(AM) Cobleskill, NY
WSDO(AM) Sanford, FL
WSDQ Dunlap, TN
WSDR Sterling, IL
WSDS Salem Township, MI
WSDT Soddy-Daisy, TN
WSDV(AM) Sarasota, FL
WSDX(AM) Brazil, IN
WSDZ Belleville, IL
WSEG(AM) Savannah, GA
WSEL Pontotoc, MS
WSEM Donalsonville, GA
WSEN(AM) Baldwinsville, NY
WSEV Sevierville, TN
WSEZ Paoli, IN
WSFB Quitman, GA
WSFC Somerset, KY
WSFE(AM) Burnside, KY
WSFN Brunswick, GA
WSFW Seneca Falls, NY
WSFZ(AM) Jackson, MS
WSGB(AM) Sutton, WV
WSGC(AM) Elberton, GA
WSGF(AM) Augusta, GA
WSGH Lewisville, NC
WSGI Springfield, TN
WSGO Oswego, NY
WSGW Saginaw, MI
WSHE(AM) Columbus, GA
WSHN Fremont, MI
WSHO New Orleans, LA
*WSHU(AM) Westport, CT
WSHV(AM) South Hill, VA
WSHY(AM) Lafayette, IN
WSIC Statesville, NC
WSIP Paintsville, KY
WSIR Winter Haven, FL
WSIV East Syracuse, NY

WSJC Magee, MS
WSJM Saint Joseph, MI
WSJS Winston-Salem, NC
WSKI Montpelier, VT
WSKN(AM) San Juan, PR
WSKR Denham Springs, LA
WSKW Skowhegan, ME
WSKY(AM) Asheville, NC
WSLA Slidell, LA
WSLB Ogdensburg, NY
WSLK(AM) Moneta, VA
WSLM Salem, IN
WSLW White Sulphur Springs, WV
WSM Nashville, TN
WSME(AM) Camp Lejeune, NC
WSMG Greeneville, TN
WSMI Litchfield, IL
WSML Graham, NC
WSMN Nashua, NH
WSMT Sparta, TN
WSMX Winston-Salem, NC
WSMY Weldon, NC
WSNG Torrington, CT
WSNJ Bridgeton, NJ
WSNL(AM) Flint, MI
WSNO Barre, VT
WSNR(AM) Jersey City, NJ
WSNT Sandersville, GA
WSNW(AM) Seneca, SC
WSOK Savannah, GA
WSOL San German, PR
WSOM Salem, OH
WSON Henderson, KY
WSOO Sault Ste. Marie, MI
WSOS(AM) Saint Augustine Beach, FL
WSOY(AM) Decatur, IL
WSPC Albemarle, NC
WSPD Toledo, OH
WSPG(AM) Spartanburg, SC
WSPL(AM) Streator, IL
WSPO(AM) Charleston, SC
WSPQ(AM) Springville, NY
WSPR Springfield, MA
WSPT Stevens Point, WI
WSPY(AM) Geneva, IL
WSPZ(AM) Birmingham, AL
WSQL Brevard, NC
WSQR Sycamore, IL
WSRA(AM) Albany, GA
WSRF Fort Lauderdale, FL
WSRO(AM) Ashland, MA
WSRP(AM) Jacksonville, NC
WSRQ(AM) Sarasota, FL
WSRW Hillsboro, OH
WSRY(AM) Elkton, MD
WSSC Sumter, SC
WSSG(AM) Goldsboro, NC
WSSO Starkville, MS
WSSP(AM) Milwaukee, WI
WSTA(AM) Charlotte Amalie, VI
WSTC(AM) Stamford, CT
WSTJ Saint Johnsbury, VT
WSTL(AM) Providence, RI
WSTN Somerville, TN
WSTP(AM) Salisbury, NC
WSTT Thomasville, GA
WSTU(AM) Stuart, FL
WSTV Steubenville, OH
WSTX(AM) Christiansted, VI
WSUA Miami, FL
WSUB Groton, CT
*WSUI Iowa City, IA
WSVA Harrisonburg, VA
WSVG(AM) Mount Jackson, VA
WSVM(AM) Valdese, NC
WSVS Crewe, VA
WSVU(AM) North Palm Beach, FL
WSVX(AM) Shelbyville, IN
*WSWI Evansville, IN
WSWN Belle Glade, FL
WSWV Pennington Gap, VA
WSWW Charleston, WV
WSYA(AM) Anniston, AL
WSYB Rutland, VT
WSYD Mount Airy, NC
WSYL Sylvania, GA

WSYR Syracuse, NY
WSYW Indianapolis, IN
WSYY(AM) Millinocket, ME
WTAA(AM) Pleasantville, NJ
WTAB Tabor City, NC
WTAD Quincy, IL
WTAG Worcester, MA
WTAL Tallahassee, FL
WTAM Cleveland, OH
WTAN(AM) Clearwater, FL
WTAQ(AM) Green Bay, WI
WTAR(AM) Norfolk, VA
WTAW(AM) College Station, TX
WTAX(AM) Springfield, IL
WTAY Robinson, IL
WTBC Tuscaloosa, AL
WTBF Troy, AL
WTBI Pickens, SC
WTBN(AM) Pinellas Park, FL
WTBO Cumberland, MD
WTBQ Warwick, NY
WTCA Plymouth, IN
WTCG(AM) Mount Holly, NC
WTCH Shawano, WI
WTCJ Tell City, IN
WTCL Chattahoochee, FL
WTCM(AM) Traverse City, MI
WTCO Campbellsville, KY
WTCR Kenova, WV
WTCS Fairmont, WV
WTCW Whitesburg, KY
WTDY Madison, WI
WTEL(AM) Red Springs, NC
WTEM Washington, DC
WTGA Thomaston, GA
WTGM Salisbury, MD
WTHB Augusta, GA
WTHE(AM) Mineola, NY
WTHQ(AM) Brookport, IL
WTHU(AM) Thurmont, MD
WTHV(AM) Hahira, GA
WTIC Hartford, CT
WTIF Tifton, GA
WTIG Massillon, OH
WTIK Durham, NC
WTIL Mayaguez, PR
WTIQ Manistique, MI
WTIS Tampa, FL
WTIV Titusville, PA
WTIX(AM) Winston-Salem, NC
WTJH East Point, GA
WTJK South Beloit, IL
WTJS Jackson, TN
WTJV(AM) De Land, FL
WTJZ Newport News, VA
WTKA Ann Arbor, MI
WTKG Grand Rapids, MI
WTKI(AM) Huntsville, AL
WTKM(AM) Hartford, WI
WTKN(AM) Corinth, MS
WTKS(AM) Savannah, GA
WTKT(AM) Harrisburg, PA
WTKY(AM) Tompkinsville, KY
WTKZ Allentown, PA
WTLA North Syracuse, NY
WTLB Utica, NY
WTLC Indianapolis, IN
WTLK Taylorsville, NC
WTLM Opelika, AL
WTLN(AM) Orlando, FL
WTLO Somerset, KY
WTLS Tallassee, AL
WTMA Charleston, SC
WTMC(AM) Wilmington, DE
WTME(AM) Rumford, ME
WTMJ Milwaukee, WI
WTMN(AM) Gainesville, FL
WTMP Egypt Lake, FL
WTMR Camden, NJ
WTMY Sarasota, FL
WTMZ Dorchester Terrace-Brentwood, SC
WTNE Trenton, TN
WTNI(AM) Biloxi, MS
WTNK(AM) Hartsville, TN
WTNL Reidsville, GA

WTNS Coshocton, OH
WTNT(AM) Bethesda, MD
WTNY Watertown, NY
WTOB Winston-Salem, NC
WTOC(AM) Newton, NJ
WTOD Toledo, OH
WTOE Spruce Pine, NC
WTOF(AM) Bay Minette, AL
WTON Staunton, VA
WTOR Youngstown, NY
WTOT Marianna, FL
WTOX(AM) Glen Allen, VA
WTOY Salem, VA
WTPR(AM) Paris, TN
WTPS(AM) Petersburg, VA
WTQS(AM) Cameron, SC
WTRB Ripley, TN
WTRC Elkhart, IN
WTRE Greensburg, IN
WTRI Brunswick, MD
WTRN Tyrone, PA
WTRO Dyersburg, TN
WTRP La Grange, GA
WTRU(AM) Kernersville, NC
WTRX Flint, MI
WTSA Brattleboro, VT
WTSB(AM) Selma, NC
WTSJ(AM) Randolph, VT
WTSK(AM) Tuscaloosa, AL
WTSL(AM) Hanover, NH
WTSN Dover, NH
WTSO Madison, WI
WTSV Claremont, NH
WTSZ(AM) Eminence, KY
WTTB Vero Beach, FL
WTTC Towanda, PA
WTTF Tiffin, OH
WTTI(AM) Dalton, GA
WTTL Madisonville, KY
WTTM(AM) Lindenwold, NJ
WTTN(AM) Columbus, WI
WTTR(AM) Westminster, MD
WTUP Tupelo, MS
WTUV(AM) Louisville, KY
WTVB(AM) Coldwater, MI
WTVL(AM) Waterville, ME
WTVN(AM) Columbus, OH
WTWA Thomson, GA
WTWB Auburndale, FL
WTWD(AM) Plant City, FL
WTWG(AM) Columbus, MS
WTWK(AM) Plattsburgh, NY
WTWN Wells River, VT
WTWZ Clinton, MS
WTXY Whiteville, NC
WTYL Tylertown, MS
WTYM Kittanning, PA
WTYS Marianna, FL
WTZE Tazewell, VA
WTZN(AM) Troy, PA
WTZQ(AM) Hendersonville, NC
WTZX Sparta, TN
WUAM(AM) Watervliet, NY
WUAT Pikeville, TN
WUBA(AM) Philadelphia, PA
WUBR(AM) Baton Rouge, LA
WUCN(AM) Smithville, GA
WUCO(AM) Marysville, OH
WUFE Baxley, GA
WUFF Eastman, GA
*WUFL Sterling Heights, MI
WUFO Amherst, NY
WUKQ(AM) Ponce, PR
WULA Eufaula, AL
WULM(AM) Springfield, OH
WUMP Madison, AL
WUNA Ocoee, FL
*WUNN(AM) Mason, MI
WUNO(AM) San Juan, PR
WUNR Brookline, MA
WUPE(AM) Pittsfield, MA
WUPR Utuado, PR
WURA(AM) Quantico, VA
WURD(AM) Philadelphia, PA
WURL Moody, AL
WURN(AM) Kendall, FL

WUST Washington, DC
WUTQ Utica, NY
WUUS(AM) Rossville, GA
WUVR(AM) Lebanon, NH
WVAA(AM) Palm Springs, FL
WVAB Virginia Beach, VA
WVAE(AM) Biddeford, ME
WVAL Sauk Rapids, MN
WVAM Altoona, PA
WVAR Richwood, WV
WVAX(AM) Charlottesville, VA
WVBE(AM) Roanoke, VA
WVBF(AM) Middleborough Center, MA
WVBG(AM) Vicksburg, MS
WVBS Burgaw, NC
WVCB Shallotte, NC
WVCC(AM) Hogansville, GA
WVCD(AM) Bamberg-Denmark, SC
WVCH Chester, PA
WVCV Orange, VA
*WVCY Oshkosh, WI
WVEI(AM) Worcester, MA
WVEL Pekin, IL
WVFN(AM) East Lansing, MI
WVGB Beaufort, SC
WVGM Lynchburg, VA
WVHI Evansville, IN
WVHU(AM) Huntington, WV
WVIE(AM) Pikesville, MD
WVJP Caguas, PR
WVJS(AM) Owensboro, KY
WVKO Columbus, OH
WVKZ Schenectady, NY
WVLD(AM) Valdosta, GA
WVLG(AM) Wildwood, FL
WVLK Lexington, KY
WVLN Olney, IL
WVLY(AM) Moundsville, WV
WVLZ(AM) Knoxville, TN
WVMC Mount Carmel, IL
*WVMR Frost, WV
WVMT Burlington, VT
WVNA Tuscumbia, AL
WVNC(AM) Masonboro, NC
WVNE(AM) Leicester, MA
WVNJ(AM) Oakland, NJ
WVNN Athens, AL
WVNR Poultney, VT
WVNT(AM) Parkersburg, WV
WVNZ(AM) Richmond, VA
WVOA(AM) Dewitt, NY
WVOC Columbia, SC
WVOE Chadbourn, NC
WVOG New Orleans, LA
WVOH Hazlehurst, GA
WVOI(AM) Marco Island, FL
WVOJ(AM) Fernandina Beach, FL
WVOK(AM) Oxford, AL
WVOL Berry Hill, TN
WVON(AM) Berwyn, IL
WVOP Vidalia, GA
WVOS Liberty, NY
WVOT(AM) Wilson, NC
WVOW Logan, WV
WVOX New Rochelle, NY
WVOZ San Juan, PR
WVPO Stroudsburg, PA
WVRC Spencer, WV
WVRQ(AM) Viroqua, WI
WVSA Vernon, AL
WVSM Rainsville, AL
WVTJ(AM) Pensacola, FL
WVTL(AM) Amsterdam, NY
WVTS(AM) Charleston, WV
WVUS(AM) Grafton, WV
WVUV(AM) Leone, AS
WVVT(AM) Essex Junction, VT
WVWI Charlotte Amalie, VI
WVXX(AM) Norfolk, VA
WVZN Columbia, PA
WWAB Lakeland, FL
WWAM Jasper, TN
WWBA(AM) Largo, FL
WWBC Cocoa, FL
WWBF Bartow, FL
WWBG Greensboro, NC

WWBJ(AM) Martinsburg, PA
WWCA Gary, IN
WWCB Corry, PA
WWCH Clarion, PA
WWCK Flint, MI
WWCL Lehigh Acres, FL
WWCN North Fort Myers, FL
WWCO(AM) Waterbury, CT
WWCS Canonsburg, PA
WWDB(AM) Philadelphia, PA
WWDJ(AM) Boston, MA
WWDR(AM) Murfreesboro, NC
WWDX(AM) Huntingdon, TN
WWFD(AM) Frederick, MD
WWFE(AM) Miami, FL
*WWFJ(FM) East Fayetteville, NC
WWFL Clermont, FL
WWGB Indian Head, MD
WWGC(AM) Albertville, AL
WWGE(AM) Loretto, PA
WWGK(AM) Cleveland, OH
WWGP(AM) Sanford, NC
WWHM(AM) Sumter, SC
WWHN Joliet, IL
WWIC Scottsboro, AL
WWII Shiremanstown, PA
WWIL Wilmington, NC
WWIN Baltimore, MD
WWIO(AM) Saint Mary's, GA
WWIS Black River Falls, WI
WWJ Detroit, MI
WWJB(AM) Brooksville, FL
WWJC Duluth, MN
WWJZ Mount Holly, NJ
WWKB Buffalo, NY
WWKO(AM) Fair Bluff, NC
WWKU(AM) Glasgow, KY
WWL(AM) New Orleans, LA
WWLE Cornwall, NY
WWLF(AM) Auburn, NY
WWLK Eddyville, KY
WWLS(AM) Moore, OK
WWLX Lawrenceburg, TN
WWLZ Horseheads, NY
WWMI Saint Petersburg, FL
WWMK Cleveland, OH
WWNA(AM) Aguadilla, PR
WWNB New Bern, NC
WWNC Asheville, NC
WWNH Madbury, NH
WWNL Pittsburgh, PA
WWNN Pompano Beach, FL
WWNR Beckley, WV
WWNS Statesboro, GA
WWNT Dothan, AL
WWNZ(AM) Veazie, ME
WWOL Forest City, NC
WWON(AM) Waynesboro, TN
WWOW Conneaut, OH
WWPA Williamsport, PA
WWPG Tuscaloosa, AL
WWPR Bradenton, FL
WWRC(AM) Washington, DC
WWRF(AM) Lake Worth, FL
WWRK(AM) Darlington, SC
WWRL(AM) New York, NY
WWRU(AM) Jersey City, NJ
*WWRV New York, NY
WWSC Glens Falls, NY
WWSD Quincy, FL
WWSJ Saint Johns, MI
WWSM Annville-Cleona, PA
WWTC Minneapolis, MN
WWTK(AM) Lake Placid, FL
WWTM(AM) Decatur, AL
WWTR(AM) Bridgewater, NJ
WWTX(AM) Wilmington, DE
WWVA(AM) Wheeling, WV
*WWVT(AM) Christiansburg, VA
WWWC(AM) Wilkesboro, NC
WWWE(AM) Hapeville, GA
WWWI(AM) Baxter, MN
WWWJ Galax, VA
WWWL(AM) New Orleans, LA
WWWR Roanoke, VA
WWWS Buffalo, NY

WWXL Manchester, KY
WWYO Pineville, WV
WWZN(AM) Boston, MA
WWZQ Aberdeen, MS
WXAG Athens, GA
WXAL Demopolis, AL
WXAM(AM) Buffalo, KY
WXBD Biloxi, MS
WXBR(AM) Brockton, MA
WXCE Amery, WI
WXCF Clifton Forge, VA
WXCO Wausau, WI
WXCT(AM) Southington, CT
WXEM Buford, GA
WXEW Yabucoa, PR
WXEX(AM) Exeter, NH
WXFN Muncie, IN
WXFO(AM) Royston, GA
WXGI Richmond, VA
WXGM Gloucester, VA
WXGO Madison, IN
WXIC Waverly, OH
WXIT Blowing Rock, NC
WXJC(AM) Birmingham, AL
WXJO(AM) Douglasville, GA
WXKL Sanford, NC
WXKO Fort Valley, GA
WXKS Everett, MA
WXKX(AM) Clarksburg, WV
WXLA Dimondale, MI
WXLI Dublin, GA
WXLW Indianapolis, IN
WXLZ Saint Paul, VA
WXMC Parsippany-Troy Hills, NJ

WXME(AM) Monticello, ME
WXMY Saltville, VA
WXNC(AM) Monroe, NC
WXNH(AM) Jaffrey, NH
WXNI(AM) Westerly, RI
WXNT(AM) Indianapolis, IN
WXOK Baton Rouge, LA
WXOZ(AM) Highland, IL
WXQK(AM) Spring City, TN
WXQW(AM) Fairhope, AL
WXRF Guayama, PR
WXRL Lancaster, NY
WXRQ(AM) Mount Pleasant, TN
WXRS Swainsboro, GA
WXSM(AM) Blountville, TN
WXTG(AM) Hampton, VA
WXTN Lexington, MS
WXTR(AM) Alexandria, VA
WXVI Montgomery, AL
*WXXI(AM) Rochester, NY
WXYB Indian Rocks Beach, FL
WXYT Detroit, MI
WYAC(AM) Cabo Rojo, PR
WYAL Scotland Neck, NC
WYAM(AM) Hartselle, AL
WYBC New Haven, CT
WYBG Massena, NY
WYBT Blountstown, FL
WYBY(AM) Cortland, NY
WYCB Washington, DC
WYCK Plains, PA
WYCV Granite Falls, NC
WYDE(AM) Birmingham, AL
WYEA Sylacauga, AL

WYEL(AM) Mayaguez, PR
WYFN Nashville, TN
*WYFQ(AM) Charlotte, NC
WYFY Rome, NY
WYGH Paris, KY
WYGL Selinsgrove, PA
WYGM(AM) Orlando, FL
WYHG(AM) Young Harris, GA
WYHL(AM) Meridian, MS
WYHM(AM) Rockwood, TN
WYHY(AM) Cannonsburg, KY
WYIS McRae, GA
WYJK(AM) Connellsville, PA
WYKC Grenada, MS
WYKM Rupert, WV
WYKO Sabana Grande, PR
WYLD New Orleans, LA
WYLF(AM) Penn Yan, NY
WYLL(AM) Chicago, IL
WYLS(AM) York, AL
WYMB Manning, SC
WYMC Mayfield, KY
WYMM(AM) Jacksonville, FL
WYNC Yanceyville, NC
WYND De Land, FL
WYNE(AM) North East, PA
WYNF(AM) North Augusta, SC
WYNN Florence, SC
WYNY(AM) Middletown, NY
WYOS(AM) Binghamton, NY
WYPC Wellston, OH
WYRD Greenville, SC
WYRE(AM) Annapolis, MD

WYRM(AM) Norfolk, VA
WYRN(AM) Louisburg, NC
WYRV Cedar Bluff, VA
WYSE(AM) Canton, NC
WYSH Clinton, TN
WYSK Fredericksburg, VA
WYSL(AM) Avon, NY
WYSR(AM) High Point, NC
WYTH(AM) Madison, GA
WYTI Rocky Mount, VA
WYTS(AM) Columbus, OH
WYUS Milford, DE
WYVE Wytheville, VA
WYWY Barbourville, KY
WYXC(AM) Cartersville, GA
WYXE Gallatin, TN
WYXI Athens, TN
WYYC(AM) York, PA
WYYZ Jasper, GA
WYZD Dobson, NC
WYZE Atlanta, GA
WZAA(AM) Silver Spring, MD
WZAB(AM) Sweetwater, FL
WZAM Ishpeming, MI
WZAN Portland, ME
WZAP(AM) Bristol, VA
WZAZ Jacksonville, FL
WZBK(AM) Keene, NH
WZBO(AM) Edenton, NC
WZCC(AM) Cross City, FL
WZCT Scottsboro, AL
WZEP(AM) De Funiak Springs, FL
WZFG(AM) Dilworth, MN
WZFN(AM) Fort Walton Beach, FL

WZGM(AM) Black Mountain, NC
WZGX(AM) Bessemer, AL
WZHF Arlington, VA
WZHR(AM) Zephyrhills, FL
WZJY(AM) Mt. Pleasant, SC
WZKY Albemarle, NC
WZME(AM) Richmond, ME
WZMG Pepperell, AL
WZNA(AM) Moca, PR
WZNG Shelbyville, TN
WZNH(AM) Fitzwilliam Depot, NH
WZNZ Jacksonville, FL
WZOB Fort Payne, AL
WZOE Princeton, IL
WZON Bangor, ME
WZOO(AM) Asheboro, NC
WZOT Rockmart, GA
WZQZ(AM) Trion, GA
WZRC New York, NY
WZRK(AM) Lake Geneva, WI
WZRX Jackson, MS
WZSK(AM) Everett, PA
WZTA(AM) Vero Beach, FL
WZUM Carnegie, PA
WZYX(AM) Cowan, TN
WZZA(AM) Tuscumbia, AL
WZZB Seymour, IN
WZZQ(AM) Gaffney, SC
WZZW Milton, WV
WZZX Lineville, AL
XETRA Tijuana, MEX

U.S. FM Stations by Call Letters

*KAAI(FM) Palisade, CO
KAAK(FM) Great Falls, MT
KAAN-FM Bethany, MO
KAAP(FM) Rock Island, WA
KAAQ(FM) Alliance, NE
KAAR(FM) Butte, MT
KAAT(FM) Oakhurst, CA
*KAAX(FM) Avenal, CA
KABD(FM) Ipswich, SD
*KABF(FM) Little Rock, AR
KABG(FM) Los Alamos, NM
*KABN-FM Kasilof, AK
KABQ-FM Bosque Farms, NM
*KABR-FM Alamo, NM
KABU(FM) Fort Totten, ND
KABW(FM) Westport, WA
KABX-FM Merced, CA
KABZ(FM) Little Rock, AR
*KACC(FM) Alvin, TX
KACI-FM The Dalles, OR
KACL(FM) Bismarck, ND
KACO(FM) Apache, OK
KACQ(FM) Lometa, TX
*KACS(FM) Chehalis, WA
KACT-FM Andrews, TX
*KACU(FM) Abilene, TX
*KACV-FM Amarillo, TX
KACW(FM) South Bend, WA
KACY(FM) Arkansas City, KS
KACZ(FM) Riley, KS
KADA-FM Ada, OK
KADD(FM) Logandale, NV
*KADE(FM) Salida, CO
KADI-FM Republic, MO
KADL(FM) Imperial, NE
KADQ-FM Evanston, WY
*KADU(FM) Hibbing, MN
*KADV(FM) Modesto, CA
KAEH(FM) Beaumont, CA
*KAER(FM) Saint George, UT
*KAFC(FM) Anchorage, AK
KAFE(FM) Bellingham, WA
KAFF-FM Flagstaff, AZ
*KAFH(FM) Great Falls, MT
*KAFM(FM) Grand Junction, CO
KAFN(FM) Gould, AR
*KAFR(FM) Conroe, TX
KAFX-FM Diboll, TX
KAGB(FM) Waimea, HI
KAGE-FM Winona, MN
KAGG(FM) Madisonville, TX
KAGH-FM Crossett, AR
*KAGJ(FM) Ephraim, UT
KAGL(FM) El Dorado, AR
KAGM(FM) Los Lunas, NM
KAGO-FM Klamath Falls, OR
*KAGT(FM) Abilene, TX
*KAGU(FM) Spokane, WA
KAGZ(FM) Lufkin, TX
KAHA(FM) Olney, TX
KAHE(FM) Dodge City, KS
KAHM(FM) Prescott, AZ
KAHR(FM) Poplar Bluff, MO
*KAHU(FM) Pahala, HI
*KAIA(FM) Blytheville, AR
*KAIB(FM) Shafter, CA
*KAIC(FM) Tucson, AZ
*KAIG(FM) Dodge City, KS
*KAIH(FM) Lake Havasu City, AZ
*KAIK(FM) Tillamook, OR
KAIM-FM Honolulu, HI
*KAIO(FM) Idaho Falls, ID
*KAIP(FM) Wapello, IA
KAIQ(FM) Wolfforth, TX
KAIR-FM Horton, KS
*KAIS(FM) Juneau, AK
*KAIW(FM) Laramie, WY
*KAIX(FM) Cheyenne, WY
*KAIZ(FM) Mesquite, NV
*KAJA(FM) San Antonio, TX

*KAJC(FM) Salem, OR
*KAJF(FM) Ipswich, SD
KAJL(FM) Adelanto, CA
KAJM(FM) Camp Verde, AZ
KAJN-FM Crowley, LA
KAJP(FM) Carrizo Springs, TX
KAJR(FM) Indian Wells, CA
*KAJT(FM) Ada, OK
*KAJX(FM) Aspen, CO
KAJZ(FM) Llano, TX
*KAKA(FM) Salina, KS
KAKJ(FM) Marianna, AR
*KAKL(FM) Anchorage, AK
KAKN(FM) Naknek, AK
*KAKO(FM) Ada, OK
KAKQ-FM Fairbanks, AK
KAKS(FM) Huntsville, AR
KAKT(FM) Phoenix, AZ
*KAKV(FM) El Dorado, AR
*KAKX(FM) Mendocino, CA
*KALA(FM) Davenport, IA
KALC(FM) Denver, CO
*KALD(FM) Caldwell, TX
KALF(FM) Red Bluff, CA
*KALG(FM) Kaltag, AK
KALI-FM Santa Ana, CA
KALK(FM) Winfield, TX
KALN(FM) Dexter, NM
KALP(FM) Alpine, TX
KALQ-FM Alamosa, CO
*KALR(FM) Hot Springs, AR
KALS(FM) Kalispell, MT
KALT-FM Alturas, CA
*KALU(FM) Langston, OK
*KALW(FM) San Francisco, CA
*KALX(FM) Berkeley, CA
KALZ(FM) Fowler, CA
KAMA-FM Missouri City, TX
*KAMB(FM) Merced, CA
KAMD-FM Camden, AR
*KAMF(FM) Tulare, SD
KAMJ-FM Gosnell, AR
KAML-FM Gillette, WY
KAMO-FM Rogers, AR
KAMP-FM Los Angeles, CA
KAMS(FM) Mammoth Spring, AR
*KAMU-FM College Station, TX
KAMX(FM) Luling, TX
*KAMY(FM) Lubbock, TX
KAMZ(FM) Tahoka, TX
*KANC(FM) Baker City, OR
*KANH(FM) Emporia, KS
*KANJ(FM) Giddings, TX
*KANL(FM) Baker City, OR
KANM(FM) Magdalena, NM
*KANO(FM) Hilo, HI
KANR(FM) Belle Plaine, KS
KANS(FM) Emporia, KS
KANT(FM) Guernsey, WY
*KANU(FM) Lawrence, KS
*KANV(FM) Olsburg, KS
*KANW(FM) Albuquerque, NM
*KANX(FM) Sheridan, AR
KANY(FM) Ocean Shores, WA
*KANZ(FM) Garden City, KS
KAOC(FM) Cavalier, ND
KAOD(FM) Babbitt, MN
*KAOG(FM) Jonesboro, AR
KAOI-FM Wailuku, HI
*KAOR(FM) Vermillion, SD
*KAOS(FM) Olympia, WA
*KAOW(FM) Fort Smith, AR
KAOX(FM) Kemmerer, WY
KAOY(FM) Kealakekua, HI
KAPA(FM) Hilo, HI
KAPB-FM Marksville, LA
*KAPC(FM) Butte, MT
*KAPG(FM) Bentonville, AR
*KAPI(FM) Ruston, LA
*KAPK(FM) Grants Pass, OR

*KAPM(FM) Alexandria, LA
KAPN(FM) Caldwell, TX
KAPW(FM) Cotton Plant, AR
*KAQA(FM) Kilauea, HI
*KAQD(FM) Abilene, TX
*KAQF(FM) Clovis, NM
*KARA(FM) Williams, CA
KARB(FM) Price, UT
*KARF(FM) Independence, KS
*KARG(FM) Poteau, OK
*KARH(FM) Forrest City, AR
*KARJ(FM) Kuna, ID
KARL(FM) Tracy, MN
*KARM(FM) Visalia, CA
*KARO(FM) Nyssa, OR
KARP-FM Dassel, MN
*KARQ(FM) East Sonora, CA
KARS-FM Laramie, WY
*KARU(FM) Cache, OK
KARV-FM Ola, AR
KARX(FM) Claude, TX
KARY-FM Grandview, WA
KARZ(FM) Marshall, MN
*KASB(FM) Bellevue, WA
*KASD(FM) Rapid City, SD
KASE-FM Austin, TX
*KASF(FM) Alamosa, CO
KASH-FM Anchorage, AK
*KASK(FM) Fairfield, CA
KASR(FM) Conway, AR
KASS(FM) Casper, WY
*KASU Jonesboro, AR
*KASV(FM) Borger, TX
*KATB(FM) Anchorage, AK
KATC-FM Colorado Springs, CO
KATF(FM) Dubuque, IA
*KATG(FM) Athens, TX
KATI(FM) California, MO
KATJ-FM George, CA
KATK-FM Carlsbad, NM
KATM(FM) Modesto, CA
KATO-FM New Ulm, MN
KATP(FM) Amarillo, TX
KATQ-FM Plentywood, MT
KATR-FM Otis, CO
KATS-FM Yakima, WA
KATT-FM Oklahoma City, OK
*KATW(FM) Lewiston, ID
KATX(FM) Eastland, TX
KATY-FM Idyllwild, CA
KATZ-FM Alton, IL
*KAUC(FM) West Clarkston, WA
*KAUD(FM) Mexico, MO
*KAUF(FM) Kennett, MO
*KAUG(FM) Anchorage, AK
KAUJ(FM) Grafton, ND
KAUL(FM) Ellington, MO
KAUM(FM) Colorado City, TX
*KAUR(FM) Sioux Falls, SD
KAUS-FM Austin, MN
KAUU(FM) Manti, UT
KAVB(FM) Hawthorne, NV
KAVD(FM) Limon, CO
*KAVE(FM) Oakridge, OR
KAVH(FM) Eudora, AR
*KAVK(FM) Many, LA
*KAVO(FM) Pampa, TX
KAVV(FM) Benson, AZ
*KAVW(FM) Amarillo, TX
*KAVX(FM) Lufkin, TX
KAWC-FM Yuma, AZ
KAWK(FM) Custer, SD
*KAWN(FM) Winslow, AZ
KAWO(FM) Boise, ID
*KAWS(FM) Marsing, ID
*KAWZ(FM) Twin Falls, ID
*KAXE(FM) Grand Rapids, MN
*KAXG(FM) Gillette, WY
*KAXL(FM) Green Acres, CA

*KAXR(FM) Arkansas City, KS
*KAXV(FM) Bastrop, LA
*KAYA(FM) Hubbard, NE
*KAYB(FM) Sunnyside, WA
*KAYC(FM) Durant, OK
KAYD-FM Silsbee, TX
*KAYE-FM Tonkawa, OK
KAYF(FM) Bayfield, CO
KAYG(FM) Camp Wood, TX
*KAYH(FM) Fayetteville, AR
*KAYK(FM) Victoria, TX
KAYL-FM Storm Lake, IA
*KAYM(FM) Weatherford, OK
*KAYO(FM) Wasilla, AK
*KAYP(FM) Burlington, IA
KAYQ(FM) Warsaw, MO
*KAYT(FM) Jena, LA
KAYW(FM) Meeker, CO
*KAYX(FM) Richmond, MO
*KAZC(FM) Healdton, OK
KAZE(FM) Ore City, TX
*KAZF(FM) Hebronville, TX
*KAZI-FM Austin, TX
*KAZR(FM) Pella, IA
KAZX(FM) Kirtland, NM
KAZY(FM) Cheyenne, WY
KAZZ(FM) Deer Park, WA
*KBAA(FM) Grass Valley, CA
KBAC(FM) Las Vegas, NM
*KBAH(FM) Plainview, TX
*KBAJ(FM) Deer River, MN
KBAL-FM San Saba, TX
*KBAN(FM) De Ridder, LA
*KBAQ-FM Phoenix, AZ
KBAR-FM Victoria, TX
KBAT(FM) Monahans, TX
KBAW(FM) Zapata, TX
KBAY(FM) Gilroy, CA
KBAZ(FM) Hamilton, MT
KBBB(FM) Billings, MT
KBBD(FM) Spokane, WA
KBBE(FM) McPherson, KS
*KBBF(FM) Calistoga, CA
*KBBG(FM) Waterloo, IA
KBBK(FM) Lincoln, NE
KBBM(FM) Jefferson City, MO
KBBN-FM Broken Bow, NE
KBBO-FM Houston, AK
KBBQ-FM Van Buren, AR
KBBT(FM) Schertz, TX
KBBU(FM) Modesto, CA
KBBX-FM Nebraska City, NE
KBBY-FM Ventura, CA
KBBZ(FM) Kalispell, MT
KBCE(FM) Boyce, LA
*KBCM(FM) Blytheville, AR
KBCN-FM Marshall, AR
KBCO(FM) Boulder, CO
KBCQ-FM Roswell, NM
KBCR-FM Steamboat Springs, CO
*KBCS(FM) Bellevue, WA
KBCT-FM Waco, TX
*KBCU(FM) North Newton, KS
*KBCW-FM McAlester, OK
*KBCX(FM) Big Spring, TX
KBCY(FM) Tye, TX
*KBDA(FM) Great Bend, KS
KBDB-FM Forks, WA
*KBDC(FM) Mason City, IA
*KBDD(FM) Winfield, KS
*KBDE(FM) Temple, TX
*KBDG(FM) Turlock, CA
*KBDH(FM) San Ardo, CA
KBDK(FM) Leakey, TX
*KBDN(FM) Bandon, OR
*KBDO(FM) Des Arc, MO
KBDR(FM) Mirando City, TX
KBDS(FM) Taft, CA
KBDV(FM) Leesville, LA

*KBDW(FM) Wheeler, TX
KBDX(FM) Blanding, UT
KBDY(FM) Hanna, WY
KBDZ(FM) Perryville, MO
KBEA-FM Muscatine, IA
*KBEE(FM) Salt Lake City, UT
KBEF(FM) Gibsland, LA
KBEK(FM) Mora, MN
KBEL-FM Idabel, OK
*KBEM-FM Minneapolis, MN
KBEN-FM Basin, WY
KBEQ(FM) Kansas City, MO
KBER(FM) Ogden, UT
*KBES(FM) Ceres, CA
KBEV-FM Dillon, MT
KBEW-FM Blue Earth, MN
KBEY(FM) Burnet, TX
KBEZ(FM) Tulsa, OK
KBFB(FM) Dallas, TX
KBFC(FM) Forrest City, AR
KBFL-FM Buffalo, MO
KBFM(FM) Edinburg, TX
KBFO(FM) Aberdeen, SD
KBFP-FM Delano, CA
*KBFR(FM) Bismarck, ND
KBFX(FM) Anchorage, AK
*KBGA(FM) Missoula, MT
KBGL(FM) Larned, KS
*KBGM(FM) Park Hills, MO
KBGO(FM) Waco, TX
KBGX(FM) Keaau, HI
KBGY(FM) Faribault, MN
*KBHE-FM Rapid City, SD
*KBHG(FM) Alexandria, MN
KBHH(FM) Kerman, CA
KBHI(FM) Miner, MO
*KBHK(FM) Thompson Falls, MT
KBHL(FM) Osakis, MN
*KBHN(FM) Booneville, AR
KBHP(FM) Bemidji, MN
KBHR(FM) Big Bear City, CA
KBHT(FM) Crockett, TX
*KBHU-FM Spearfish, SD
*KBHW(FM) International Falls, MN
*KBHZ(FM) Willmar, MN
*KBIA(FM) Columbia, MO
KBIC(FM) Raymondville, TX
KBIG-FM Los Angeles, CA
KBIJ(FM) Guymon, OK
*KBIL(FM) Park City, MT
KBIM-FM Roswell, NM
*KBIO(FM) Natchitoches, LA
KBIQ(FM) Manitou Springs, CO
KBIU(FM) Lake Charles, LA
*KBIY(FM) Van Buren, MO
*KBJF(FM) Nephi, UT
*KBJQ(FM) Bronson, KS
*KBJS(FM) Jacksonville, TX
*KBJX(FM) Shelley, ID
KBKB-FM Fort Madison, IA
*KBKC(FM) Moberly, MO
KBKG(FM) Corning, AR
KBKK(FM) Ball, LA
*KBKL(FM) Grand Junction, CO
*KBKN(FM) Lamesa, TX
KBKS-FM Tacoma, WA
KBKY(FM) Merced, CA
*KBKZ(FM) Raton, NM
KBLB(FM) Nisswa, MN
*KBLC(FM) Fredericksburg, TX
*KBLD(FM) Kennewick, WA
KBLL-FM Helena, MT
KBLO(FM) Corcoran, CA
*KBLP(FM) Lindsay, OK
KBLQ-FM Logan, UT
KBLR-FM Blair, NE
*KBLS(FM) North Fort Riley, KS
*KBLT(FM) Leakey, TX
*KBLV(FM) Tehachapi, CA
*KBLW(FM) Billings, MT

KBLX-FM Berkeley, CA
KBLZ(FM) Winona, TX
KBMB(FM) Sacramento, CA
*KBMC(FM) Bozeman, MT
*KBMD(FM) Marble Falls, TX
KBMG(FM) Evanston, WY
*KBMH(FM) Holbrook, AZ
KBMI(FM) Roma, TX
*KBMJ(FM) Heber Springs, AR
*KBMK(FM) Bismarck, ND
*KBMM(FM) Odessa, TX
*KBMP(FM) Enterprise, KS
*KBMQ(FM) Monroe, LA
KBMV-FM Birch Tree, MO
KBMX(FM) Proctor, MN
KBNA-FM El Paso, TX
KBNG(FM) Ridgway, CO
*KBNJ(FM) Corpus Christi, TX
*KBNL(FM) Laredo, TX
*KBNO-FM White Salmon, WA
*KBNR(FM) Brownsville, TX
KBNU(FM) Uvalde, TX
*KBNV(FM) Fayetteville, AR
KBOA-FM Piggott, AR
KBOB-FM De Witt, IA
KBOC(FM) Bridgeport, TX
KBOE-FM Oskaloosa, IA
*KBOJ(FM) Worthington, MN
*KBOM(FM) Socorro, NM
KBON(FM) Mamou, LA
*KBOO(FM) Portland, OR
KBOQ(FM) Seaside, CA
KBOS-FM Tulare, CA
KBOQ(FM) Pelican Rapids, MN
KBOX(FM) Lompoc, CA
KBOY-FM Medford, OR
KBOZ-FM Bozeman, MT
KBPA(FM) San Marcos, TX
*KBPB(FM) Harrison, AR
*KBPG(FM) Montevideo, MN
KBPI(FM) Denver, CO
*KBPK(FM) Buena Park, CA
*KBPN(FM) Brainerd, MN
*KBPR(FM) Brainerd, MN
*KBPU(FM) De Queen, AR
*KBPW(FM) Hampton, AR
KBQB(FM) Chico, CA
*KBQC(FM) Independence, KS
KBQF(FM) McFarland, CA
*KBQI(FM) Albuquerque, NM
KBQL(FM) Las Vegas, NM
KBQQ(FM) Pinesdale, MT
KBRA(FM) Freer, TX
KBRB-FM Ainsworth, NE
KBRE(FM) Atwater, CA
KBRG(FM) San Jose, CA
KBRJ(FM) Anchorage, AK
KBRK-FM Brookings, SD
KBRQ(FM) Hillsboro, TX
*KBRW-FM Barrow, AK
KBRX-FM O'Neill, NE
*KBSA(FM) El Dorado, AR
*KBSB(FM) Bemidji, MN
*KBSJ(FM) Jackpot, NV
*KBSK(FM) McCall, ID
*KBSM(FM) McCall, ID
*KBSO(FM) Corpus Christi, TX
*KBSQ(FM) McCall, ID
*KBSS(FM) Sun Valley, ID
KBST-FM Big Spring, TX
*KBSU-FM Boise, ID
*KBSW(FM) Twin Falls, ID
*KBSX(FM) Boise, ID
*KBSY(FM) Burley, ID
KBTA-FM Batesville, AR
KBTE(FM) Tulia, TX
*KBTK(FM) Grand Island, NE
*KBTL(FM) El Dorado, KS
KBTN-FM Neosho, MO
KBTO(FM) Bottineau, ND
KBTQ(FM) Harlingen, TX
KBTS(FM) Big Spring, TX
KBTT(FM) Haughton, LA
KBTW(FM) Lenwood, CA
KBTY(FM) Benjamin, TX
KBUA(FM) San Fernando, CA

*KBUB(FM) Brownwood, TX
KBUC(FM) Raymondville, TX
KBUD(FM) Sardis, MS
KBUE(FM) Long Beach, CA
*KBUG(FM) Malin, OR
KKBUK(FM) La Grange, TX
KBUL-FM Carson City, NV
KBUS(FM) Paris, TX
*KKBUT(FM) Crested Butte, CO
*KBUW(FM) Buffalo, WY
KBUX(FM) Quartzsite, AZ
*KBUZ(FM) Topeka, KS
KBVA(FM) Bella Vista, AR
KBVB(FM) Barnesville, MN
KBVC(FM) Buena Vista, CO
*KBVM(FM) Portland, OR
*KBVR(FM) Corvallis, OR
KBVU-FM Alta, IA
*KBWA(FM) Brush, CO
*KBWC(FM) Marshall, TX
KBWF(FM) San Francisco, CA
KBWM(FM) Breckenridge, TX
KBWS-FM Sisseton, SD
KBWT(FM) Santa Anna, TX
*KBWW(FM) Broken Bow, OK
*KBWY(FM) Pryor, MT
KBXB(FM) Sikeston, MO
*KBXE(FM) Bagley, MN
KBXJ(FM) Los Ybanez, TX
KBXL(FM) Caldwell, ID
KBXR(FM) Columbia, MO
KBXT(FM) Franklin, TX
KBXX(FM) Houston, TX
KBYB(FM) Hope, AR
*KBYI(FM) Rexburg, ID
KBYN(FM) Arnold, CA
KBYO-FM Farmerville, LA
*KBYR-FM Rexburg, ID
*KBYU-FM Provo, UT
KBYZ(FM) Bismarck, ND
KBZB(FM) Hurricane, UT
KBZC(FM) Sacramento, CA
KBZD(FM) Amarillo, TX
KBZE(FM) Berwick, LA
KBZI(FM) Columbus, KS
KBZM(FM) Big Sky, MT
KBZN(FM) Ogden, UT
KBZQ(FM) Lawton, OK
KBZS(FM) Wichita Falls, TX
KBZT(FM) San Diego, CA
KBZU(FM) Albuquerque, NM
*KCAC(FM) Camden, AR
KCAD(FM) Dickinson, ND
*KCAI(FM) Kingman, AZ
KCAJ-FM Roseau, MN
KCAL-FM Redlands, CA
KCAQ(FM) Oxnard, CA
KCAR-FM Baxter Springs, KS
*KCAS(FM) McCook, TX
*KCAV(FM) Marshall, AR
*KCAW(FM) Sitka, AK
*KCBG(FM) Broadus, MT
*KCBI(FM) Dallas, TX
KCBS-FM Los Angeles, CA
*KCBX(FM) San Luis Obispo, CA
KCBZ(FM) Cannon Beach, OR
*KCCD(FM) Moorhead, MN
*KCCK-FM Cedar Rapids, IA
KCCL(FM) Placerville, CA
*KCCM-FM Moorhead, MN
KCCN-FM Honolulu, HI
KCCQ(FM) Ames, IA
*KCCS(FM) Starkville, CO
*KCCU(FM) Lawton, OK
KCCV-FM Olathe, KS
KCCY(FM) Pueblo, CO
KCDA(FM) Post Falls, ID
KCDC(FM) Milford, UT
KCDD(FM) Hamlin, TX
KCDG(FM) Madison, MO
KCDL(FM) Cordell, OK
KCDQ(FM) Douglas, AZ
*KCDS(FM) Deadhorse, AK
KCDU(FM) Carmel, CA
KCDV(FM) Cordova, AK
KCDX(FM) Florence, AZ

KCDY(FM) Carlsbad, NM
KCDZ(FM) Twentynine Palms, CA
*KCEA(FM) Atherton, CA
KCEC-FM Wellton, AZ
*KCED(FM) Centralia, WA
KCEL(FM) Mojave, CA
*KCEP(FM) Las Vegas, NV
*KCEU(FM) Price, UT
KCEZ(FM) Los Molinos, CA
*KCFA(FM) Arnold, CA
*KCFB(FM) Saint Cloud, MN
*KCFD(FM) Crawford, NE
*KCFE(FM) Hoven, SD
*KCFF(FM) Clifton Forge, VA
*KCFL(FM) Elma, WA
*KCFN(FM) Wichita, KS
*KCFP(FM) Pueblo, CO
KCFR-FM Denver, CO
*KCFS(FM) Sioux Falls, SD
*KCFV(FM) Ferguson, MO
KCFX(FM) Harrisonville, MO
*KCFY(FM) Yuma, AZ
KCGB-FM Hood River, OR
KCGC(FM) Coarsegold, CA
KCGL(FM) Powell, WY
*KCGM(FM) Scobey, MT
KCGN-FM Ortonville, MN
KCGQ-FM Gordonville, MO
*KCGR(FM) Oran, MO
KCGY(FM) Laramie, WY
KCHA-FM Charles City, IA
*KCHB(FM) Kaibito, AZ
KCHC(FM) Willows, CA
KCHE-FM Cherokee, IA
*KCHG(FM) Cedar City, UT
KCHI-FM Chillicothe, MO
*KCHO(FM) Chico, CA
*KCHQ(FM) Driggs, ID
*KCHT(FM) Childress, TX
KCHX(FM) Midland, TX
KCHZ(FM) Ottawa, KS
*KCIC(FM) Grand Junction, CO
*KCIE(FM) Dulce, NM
*KCIF(FM) Hilo, HI
KCII-FM Washington, IA
KCIJ(FM) Atlanta, LA
KCIL(FM) Houma, LA
KCIN(FM) Cedar City, UT
*KCIR(FM) Twin Falls, ID
KCIV(FM) Mount Bullion, CA
KCIX(FM) Garden City, ID
KCJC(FM) Dardanelle, AR
*KCJF(FM) Earle, AR
*KCJH(FM) Livingston, CA
KCJK(FM) Garden City, MO
*KCJX(FM) Carbondale, CO
*KCKC(FM) Kansas City, MO
*KCKE(FM) Chillicothe, MO
*KCKL(FM) Malakoff, TX
*KCKR(FM) Church Point, LA
KCKS(FM) Concordia, KS
*KCKT(FM) Crockett, TX
*KCKV(FM) Kirksville, MO
KCLB-FM Coachella, CA
*KCLC(FM) Saint Charles, MO
KCLD-FM Saint Cloud, MN
KCLH(FM) Caledonia, MN
KCLK-FM Clarkston, WA
KCLL(FM) San Angelo, TX
KCLQ(FM) Lebanon, MO
KCLR-FM Boonville, MO
KCLS(FM) Ely, NV
KCLT(FM) West Helena, AR
*KCLU-FM Thousand Oaks, CA
KCLV(FM) Clovis, NM
KCLY(FM) Clay Center, KS
KCMB(FM) Baker City, MO
*KCME(FM) Manitou Springs, CO
*KCMF(FM) Fergus Falls, MN
*KCMH(FM) Mountain Home, AR
KCMI(FM) Terrytown, NE
KCML(FM) Saint Joseph, MN
KCMM(FM) Belgrade, MT
KCMO-FM Kansas City, MO
*KCMP(FM) Northfield, MN
KCMQ(FM) Columbia, MO

*KCMR(FM) Mason City, IA
KCMS(FM) Edmonds, WA
KCMT(FM) Oro Valley, AZ
KCMX-FM Ashland, OR
*KCNA-FM Cave Junction, OR
*KCNB(FM) Chadron, NE
*KCND(FM) Bismarck, ND
*KCNE-FM Chadron, NE
*KCNJ(FM) Oskaloosa, IA
KCNL(FM) Sunnyvale, CA
KCNM-FM Garapan-Saipan, NP
*KCNO(FM) Alturas, CA
*KCNP(FM) Ada, OK
KCNQ(FM) Kernville, CA
*KCNT(FM) Hastings, NE
*KCNV(FM) Las Vegas, NV
KCNY(FM) Bald Knob, AR
KCOB-FM Newton, IA
*KCOI(FM) Clovis, NM
KCOL-FM Groves, TX
KCOO(FM) Dunkerton, IA
*KCOU(FM) Columbia, MO
*KCOZ(FM) Point Lookout, MO
*KCPB-FM Warrenton, OR
*KCPC(FM) Sealy, TX
KCPI(FM) Albert Lea, MN
*KCPK(FM) Paola, KS
*KCPR(FM) San Luis Obispo, CA
*KCPW-FM Salt Lake City, UT
*KCQQ(FM) Davenport, IA
*KCRB-FM Bemidji, MN
KCRE-FM Crescent City, CA
KCRF-FM Lincoln City, OR
*KCRH(FM) Hayward, CA
*KCRI(FM) Indio, CA
KCRK-FM Colville, WA
*KCRL(FM) Sunrise Beach, MO
KCRN-FM San Angelo, TX
*KCRR(FM) Grundy Center, IA
KCRS-FM Midland, TX
KCRT-FM Trinidad, CO
*KCRU(FM) Oxnard, CA
KCRV-FM Caruthersville, MO
*KCRW(FM) Santa Monica, CA
KCRX-FM Seaside, OR
*KCRY(FM) Mojave, CA
KCRZ(FM) Tipton, CA
*KCSB-FM Santa Barbara, CA
*KCSC(FM) Edmond, OK
*KCSD(FM) Sioux Falls, SD
*KCSH(FM) Ellensburg, WA
KCSI(FM) Red Oak, IA
*KCSM(FM) San Mateo, CA
*KCSN(FM) Northridge, CA
*KCSP-FM Casper, WY
*KCSS(FM) Turlock, CA
KCST-FM Florence, OR
*KCSU-FM Fort Collins, CO
KCSY(FM) Twisp, WA
KCTN(FM) Garnavillo, IA
KCTR-FM Billings, MT
KCTT-FM Yellville, AR
KCTX-FM Childress, TX
KCTY(FM) Wayne, NE
KCUA(FM) Naples, UT
KCUB-FM Ranger, TX
*KCUF(FM) El Jebel, CO
*KCUK(FM) Chevak, AK
KCUL-FM Marshall, TX
*KCUR-FM Kansas City, MO
KCUV(FM) Greenwood Village, CO
KCVD(FM) New England, ND
KCVF(FM) Sarles, ND
KCVG(FM) Medina, ND
KCVI(FM) Blackfoot, ID
*KCVJ(FM) Osceola, MO
*KCVK(FM) Otterville, MO
KCVM(FM) Hudson, IA
KCVN(FM) Cozad, NE
*KCVO-FM Camdenton, MO
*KCVQ(FM) Knob Noster, MO
KCVR-FM Columbia, CA
*KCVS(FM) Salina, KS
*KCVT(FM) Silver Lake, KS
KCVW(FM) Kingman, KS
*KCVX(FM) Salem, MO

*KCVY(FM) Cabool, MO
*KCVZ(FM) Dixon, MO
*KCWC-FM Riverton, WY
KCWD(FM) Harrison, AR
KCWN(FM) New Sharon, IA
KCWR(FM) Bakersfield, CA
*KCWU(FM) Ellensburg, WA
*KCWW(FM) Evanston, WY
KCXR(FM) Taft, OK
KCXX(FM) Lake Arrowhead, CA
*KCXY(FM) East Camden, AR
KCYA(FM) Kaycee, WY
KCYE(FM) Boulder City, NV
KCYN(FM) Moab, UT
KCYQ(FM) Elsinore, UT
KCYS(FM) Seaside, OR
KCYY(FM) San Antonio, TX
KCZE(FM) New Hampton, IA
KCZO(FM) Carrizo Springs, TX
KCZQ(FM) Cresco, IA
KDAA(FM) Rolla, MO
*KDAB(FM) Central City, CO
KDAD(FM) Douglas, WY
KDAG(FM) Farmington, NM
*KDAI(FM) Scottsbluff, NE
KDAL-FM Duluth, MN
KDAO-FM Eldora, IA
KDAP-FM Douglas, AZ
*KDAQ(FM) Shreveport, LA
KDAR(FM) Oxnard, CA
KDAT(FM) Cedar Rapids, IA
KDAY(FM) Redondo Beach, CA
KDB(FM) Santa Barbara, CA
KDBB(FM) Bonne Terre, MO
KDBH(FM) Natchitoches, LA
KDBI(FM) Emmett, ID
KDBL(FM) Toppenish, WA
KDBN(FM) Haltom City, TX
*KDBQ(FM) Rattan, OK
KDBR(FM) Kalispell, MT
KDBX(FM) Clear Lake, SD
KDBZ(FM) Anchorage, AK
KDCD(FM) San Angelo, TX
KDCQ(FM) Coos Bay, OR
*KDCR(FM) Sioux Center, IA
*KDCV-FM Blair, NE
KDDB(FM) Waipahu, HI
KDDD-FM Dumas, TX
KDDG(FM) Albany, MN
KDDK(FM) Franklin, LA
KDDL(FM) Chino Valley, AZ
KDDQ(FM) Comanche, OK
KDDS-FM Elma, WA
KDDV-FM Wright, WY
KDDX(FM) Spearfish, SD
KDEC-FM Decorah, IA
KDEL-FM Arkadelphia, AR
KDEM(FM) Deming, NM
KDEP(FM) Garibaldi, OR
KDES-FM Palm Springs, CA
KDEW-FM De Witt, AR
KDEX-FM Dexter, MO
KDEZ(FM) Brandon, SD
KDFC-FM San Francisco, CA
KDFM(FM) Falfurrias, TX
KDFO(FM) Delano, CA
*KDFR(FM) Des Moines, IA
KDGE(FM) Fort Worth-Dallas, TX
KDGL(FM) Yucca Valley, CA
KDGS(FM) Andover, KS
KDHT(FM) Cedar Park, TX
*KDHX(FM) Saint Louis, MO
*KDIM(FM) Coweta, OK
KDIS-FM Little Rock, AR
*KDJC(FM) Baker City, OR
KDJE(FM) Jacksonville, AR
KDJF(FM) Ester, AK
KDJK(FM) Mariposa, CA
KDJM(FM) Lindsborg, KS
KDJR(FM) De Soto, MO
KDJS-FM Willmar, MN
KDKB(FM) Mesa, AZ
KDKD-FM Clinton, MO
KDKK(FM) Park Rapids, MN
*KDKL(FM) Coalinga, CA
*KDKO(FM) Lake Andes, SD

*KDKR(FM) Decatur, TX
KDKS-FM Blanchard, LA
*KDLD(FM) Santa Monica, CA
KDLE(FM) Newport Beach, CA
*KDLG-FM Dillingham, AK
*KDLI(FM) Del Rio, TX
KDLK-FM Del Rio, TX
*KDLL(FM) Kenai, AK
KDLO-FM Watertown, SD
KDLS-FM Perry, IA
*KDLW(FM) Belen, NM
KDLX(FM) Makawao, HI
KDLY(FM) Lander, WY
KDMG(FM) Burlington, IA
*KDMR(FM) Mitchellville, IA
KDMX(FM) Dallas, TX
*KDNA(FM) Yakima, WA
KDND(FM) Sacramento, CA
*KDNE(FM) Crete, NE
KDNG(FM) Durango, CO
*KDNI(FM) Duluth, MN
*KDNK(FM) Glenwood Springs, CO
KDNN(FM) Honolulu, HI
KDNO(FM) Thermopolis, WY
*KDNR(FM) South Greeley, WY
KDNS(FM) Downs, KS
*KDNV(FM) Winnemucca, NV
*KDNW(FM) Duluth, MN
KDOE(FM) Antlers, OK
KDOG(FM) North Mankato, MN
KDOM-FM Windom, MN
KDON-FM Salinas, CA
*KDOO(FM) Goodland, KS
KDOT-FM Reno, NV
*KDOV-FM Medford, OR
KDPM(FM) Cottage Grove, OR
*KDPR(FM) Dickinson, ND
KDQN-FM De Queen, AR
KDRB(FM) Des Moines, IA
*KDRE(FM) Sterling, CO
KDRF(FM) Albuquerque, NM
*KDRG(FM) Breckenridge, TX
*KDRH(FM) King City, CA
KDRK-FM Spokane, WA
KDRM-FM Moses Lake, WA
KDRS-FM Paragould, AR
KDRW(FM) Hewitt, TX
KDRX(FM) Rocksprings, TX
*KDSC(FM) Thousand Oaks, CA
*KDSD-FM Pierpont, SD
KDSK(FM) Grants, NM
KDSN-FM Denison, IA
*KDSO(FM) Cascade, IA
KDSR-FM Williston, ND
KDSS-FM Ely, NV
KDST-FM Dyersville, IA
*KDSU-FM Fargo, ND
KDTR(FM) Florence, MT
*KDUB(FM) Dubuque, IA
KDUC-FM Barstow, CA
KDUK-FM Florence, OR
*KDUP(FM) Cedarville, CA
KDUQ-FM Ludlow, CA
*KDUR-FM Durango, CO
KDUT(FM) Randolph, UT
*KDUV-FM Visalia, CA
*KDUW(FM) Douglas, WY
KDUX-FM Aberdeen, WA
KDVA(FM) Buckeye, AZ
KDVB(FM) Effingham, KS
KDVC(FM) Dove Creek, CO
KDVE(FM) Pittsburg, TX
*KDVI(FM) Devils Lake, ND
KDVL-FM Devils Lake, ND
*KDVO(FM) Mason City, IA
*KDVS-FM Davis, CA
KDVV-FM Topeka, KS
KDWB-FM Richfield, MN
*KDWG(FM) Dillon, MT
*KDWI(FM) Ottumwa, IA
*KDWT(FM) Perry, IA
KDWY(FM) Diamondville, WY
*KDXL-FM Saint Louis Park, MN
KDXN(FM) South Heart, ND
KDXT(FM) Lolo, MT
KDXX(FM) Benbrook, TX

KDXY(FM) Lake City, AR
KDYN-FM Ozark, AR
KDZA-FM Pueblo, CO
KDZN-FM Glendive, MT
KDZY-FM McCall, ID
KDZZ(FM) Saint Charles, MN
*KEAF(FM) Fort Smith, AR
KEAG-FM Anchorage, AK
KEAL(FM) Taft, CA
KEAN-FM Abilene, TX
*KEAR-FM Sacramento, CA
KEAU(FM) Fairfield, MT
KEAZ(FM) Heber Springs, AR
KEBG(FM) Spring Creek, NV
KEBN(FM) Garden Grove, CA
KEBT(FM) Lost Hills, CA
*KECC(FM) La Junta, CA
*KECG(FM) El Cerrito, CA
KECH-FM Sun Valley, ID
KECK(FM) Eckley, CO
KECO(FM) Elk City, OK
*KECU(FM) Kaibito, AZ
KEDB(FM) Chariton, IA
KEDC(FM) Hearne, TX
KEDG-FM Alexandria, LA
KEDJ(FM) Gilbert, AZ
*KEDM-FM Monroe, LA
KEDP-FM Las Vegas, NM
*KEDR(FM) Bay City, TX
*KEDT-FM Corpus Christi, TX
*KEEA(FM) Aberdeen, SD
KEEC(FM) Teec Nos Pos, AZ
*KEEH(FM) Spokane, WA
KEEI(FM) Hanapepe, HI
KEEP-FM Bandera, TX
KEEY-FM Saint Paul, MN
KEEZ-FM Mankato, MN
KEFH-FM Clarendon, TX
*KEFL(FM) Westport, WA
*KEFR-FM Le Grand, CA
*KEFS(FM) North Powder, OR
*KEFX-FM Twin Falls, ID
KEGA-FM Oakley, UT
KEGE(FM) Pocatello, ID
KEGH(FM) Brigham City, UT
KEGI(FM) Jonesboro, AR
KEGK(FM) Wahpeton, ND
KEGL-FM Fort Worth, TX
*KEGR(FM) Fort Dodge, IA
KEGX(FM) Richland, WA
KEHD(FM) Fernley, NV
KEHK-FM Brownsville, OR
*KEIS(FM) York, NE
*KEJA(FM) Cale, AR
KEJJ(FM) Gunnison, CO
KEJL(FM) Eunice, NM
KEJS-FM Lubbock, TX
KEJY(FM) Blue Lake, CA
KEKA-FM Eureka, CA
KEKB-FM Fruita, CO
*KEKL(FM) Mesquite, NV
KEKO-FM Hebronville, TX
KEKS(FM) Olpe, KS
*KELC(FM) Hawthorne, NV
KELD-FM Hampton, AR
KELE-FM Mountain Grove, MO
KELI-FM San Angelo, TX
KELN-FM North Platte, NE
KELO-FM Sioux Falls, SD
*KELP-FM Mesquite, NM
KELU(FM) Clovis, NM
KEMA(FM) Three Rivers, TX
*KEMC-FM Billings, MT
KEMR(FM) Castle Dale, UT
KEMX-FM Locust Grove, OK
KENA-FM Mena, AR
KEND-FM Roswell, NM
KENG(FM) Parachute, CO
*KENM(FM) Tucumcari, NM
KENR(FM) Superior, MT
*KENU(FM) Des Moines, NM
*KENW-FM Portales, NM
KENZ(FM) Ogden, UT
KEOJ-FM Caney, KS
KEOK-FM Tahlequah, OK
*KEOL-FM La Grande, OR

*KEOM-FM Mesquite, TX
*KEOS(FM) College Station, TX
*KEPC(FM) Colorado Springs, CO
KEPD(FM) Ridgecrest, CA
*KEPI-FM Eagle Pass, TX
*KEPX-FM Eagle Pass, TX
*KEQS(FM) Quartzsite, AZ
*KEQX(FM) Stephenville, TX
*KERA-FM Dallas, TX
KERB-FM Kermit, TX
KERM-FM Torrington, WY
KERP(FM) Ingalls, KS
KERT(FM) Alberton, MT
KERX(FM) Paris, AR
KESA(FM) Eureka Springs, AR
*KESC(FM) Morro Bay, CA
*KESD-FM Brookings, SD
*KESG(FM) Sayre, OK
KESM-FM El Dorado Springs, MO
KESN(FM) Allen, TX
KESO-FM South Padre Island, TX
KESR(FM) Shasta Lake City, CA
KESS-FM Lewisville, TX
KESY(FM) Cuba, MO
KESZ-FM Phoenix, AZ
*KETP(FM) Enterprise, OR
*KETR-FM Commerce, TX
KETT(FM) Mitchell, NE
KETX-FM Livingston, TX
KEUG(FM) Veneta, OR
*KEUL-FM Girdwood, AK
KEUN-FM Eunice, LA
KEWB-FM Anderson, CA
KEWL-FM New Boston, TX
*KEWR(FM) Brewster, WA
*KEWU-FM Cheney, WA
KEXA(FM) King City, CA
KEXL-FM Norfolk, NE
*KEXP-FM Seattle, WA
KEXS-FM Ravenwood, MO
*KEYA-FM Belcourt, ND
*KEYB-FM Altus, OK
*KEYD(FM) Delta, UT
KEYE-FM Perryton, TX
KEYF-FM Cheney, WA
KEYG-FM Grand Coulee, WA
KEYJ-FM Abilene, TX
KEYN-FM Wichita, KS
*KEYP(FM) Price, UT
*KEYR(FM) Richfield, UT
*KEYV(FM) Vernal, UT
KEYW-FM Pasco, WA
KEZA-FM Fayetteville, AR
*KEZB(FM) Beaver, UT
*KEZC(FM) Red Feather Lakes, CO
*KEZD(FM) Estes Park, CO
KEZE-FM Spokane, WA
*KEZF(FM) Burns, WY
KEZJ-FM Twin Falls, ID
KEZK-FM Saint Louis, MO
KEZN-FM Palm Desert, CA
KEZO-FM Omaha, NE
KEZP-FM Bunkie, LA
KEZQ-FM West Yellowstone, MT
KEZR(FM) San Jose, CA
KEZS-FM Cape Girardeau, MO
KEZZ(FM) Walden, CO
*KFAE-FM Richland, WA
*KFAI-FM Minneapolis, MN
KFAN-FM Johnson City, TX
KFAT(FM) Anchorage, AK
KFAV-FM Warrenton, MO
KFBD-FM Waynesville, MO
*KFBN-FM Fargo, ND
*KFBW-FM Vancouver, WA
KFBZ(FM) Haysville, KS
*KFCF-FM Fresno, CA
*KFCH(FM) Childress, TX
KFCM-FM Cherokee Village, AR
*KFDC(FM) Shiprock, NM
KFDI-FM Wichita, KS
KFEB(FM) Campbell, MO
*KFEG(FM) Klamath Falls, OR
*KFER-FM Santa Cruz, CA
KFFA-FM Helena, AR
*KFFB-FM Fairfield Bay, AR

KFFF-FM Boone, IA
KFFG-FM Los Altos, CA
KFFM-FM Yakima, WA
KFFX-FM Emporia, KS
KFGE-FM Milford, NE
KFGI(FM) Crosby, MN
KFGL(FM) Abilene, TX
*KFGR(FM) Powell, WY
KFGY-FM Healdsburg, CA
*KFHC(FM) Ponca, NE
*KFHL(FM) Wasco, CA
KFIL-FM Preston, MN
KFIN(FM) Jonesboro, AR
KFIS(FM) Scappoose, OR
KFIX-FM Plainville, KS
*KFJC-FM Los Altos, CA
*KFJM-FM Grand Forks, ND
*KFKB(FM) Girard, KS
KFKF-FM Kansas City, KS
*KFKX-FM Hastings, NE
*KFLB-FM Stanton, TX
*KFLF(FM) Somers, MT
KFLG-FM Big River, CA
KFLI(FM) Des Arc, AR
*KFLO-FM Blanchard, LA
KFLP-FM Floydada, TX
*KFLQ-FM Albuquerque, NM
*KFLR-FM Phoenix, AZ
KFLS-FM Tulelake, CA
*KFLT-FM Tucson, AZ
*KFLV(FM) Wilber, NE
KFLW-FM Saint Robert, MO
*KFLX-FM Kachina Village, AZ
*KFLY-FM Corvallis, OR
KFMA-FM Green Valley, AZ
KFMB-FM San Diego, CA
KFMC-FM Fairmont, MN
KFMF-FM Chico, CA
*KFMH(FM) Belle Fourche, SD
KFMI-FM Eureka, CA
*KFMJ-FM Ketchikan, AK
*KFMK-FM Round Rock, TX
KFML-FM Little Falls, MN
KFMM-FM Thatcher, AZ
*KFMN(FM) Lihue, HI
KFMQ-FM Gallup, NM
*KFMR(FM) Marbleton, WY
KFMT-FM Fremont, NE
*KFMU-FM Oak Creek, CO
KFMW-FM Waterloo, IA
KFMX-FM Lubbock, TX
KFNC(FM) Beaumont, TX
KFNF-FM Oberlin, KS
KFNK(FM) Eatonville, WA
*KFNL(FM) Kindred, ND
*KFNO-FM Fresno, CA
KFNS-FM Troy, MO
KFNV-FM Ferriday, LA
*KFNW-FM Fargo, ND
KFOG-FM San Francisco, CA
KFPR-FM Redding, CA
KFPW-FM Barling, AR
*KFRB-FM Bakersfield, CA
KFRC-FM San Francisco, CA
*KFRD(FM) Butte, MT
*KFRG-FM San Bernardino, CA
*KFRH(FM) North Las Vegas, NV
*KFRI(FM) West Odessa, TX
*KFRJ(FM) China Lake, CA
KFRO-FM Gilmer, TX
*KFRP(FM) Coalinga, CA
KFRQ-FM Harlingen, TX
KFRR-FM Woodlake, CA
*KFRS-FM Soledad, CA
*KFRT(FM) Butte, MT
*KFRW(FM) Great Falls, MT
KFRX-FM Lincoln, NE
*KFRY(FM) Pueblo, CO
KFRZ-FM Green River, WY
KFSE-FM Kasilof, AK
KFSH-FM Anaheim, CA
*KFSI(FM) Rochester, MN
*KFSK(FM) Petersburg, AK
KFSO-FM Visalia, CA
*KFSR-FM Fresno, CA

*KFST-FM Fort Stockton, TX
*KFSZ(FM) Munds Park, AZ
KFTE-FM Breaux Bridge, LA
*KFTG-FM Pasadena, TX
KFTI-FM Newton, KS
KFTK(FM) Florissant, MO
KFTT(FM) Bagdad, AZ
*KFTW(FM) Fort Washakie, WY
KFTX-FM Kingsville, TX
KFTZ-FM Idaho Falls, ID
KFUO-FM Clayton, MO
KFVR-FM La Junta, CO
*KFWR(FM) Mineral Wells, TX
*KFXH-FM Marlow, OK
KFXI-FM Marlow, OK
KFXJ-FM Augusta, KS
KFXR-FM Chinle, AZ
KFXS-FM Rapid City, SD
*KFXT-FM Sulphur, OK
*KFXU(FM) Chickasha, OK
*KFXV(FM) Kensett, AR
KFXX-FM Hugoton, KS
KFXZ-FM Opelousas, LA
KFYV-FM Ojai, CA
*KFYX(FM) Texarkana, AR
KFZO(FM) Denton, TX
KFZX-FM Gardendale, TX
*KGAC(FM) Saint Peter, MN
KGAP-FM Clarksville, TX
KGAS-FM Carthage, TX
KGBA-FM Holtville, CA
KGBB(FM) Edwards, CA
KGB-FM San Diego, CA
*KGBI-FM Omaha, NE
KGBM(FM) Randsburg, CA
KGBR-FM Gold Beach, OR
KGBT-FM McAllen, TX
KGBX-FM Nixa, MO
KGBY-FM Sacramento, CA
*KGCB-FM Prescott, AZ
*KGCC-FM Gillette, WY
*KGCD(FM) Lincoln, ND
KGCE(FM) Post, TX
*KGCF-FM Juneau, AK
*KGCL-FM Jordan Valley, OR
*KGCM(FM) Belgrade, MT
*KGCN-FM Roswell, NM
*KGCO(FM) Fort Collins, CO
*KGCQ(FM) Kimball, NE
*KGCR(FM) Goodland, KS
*KGCU(FM) Port Alsworth, AK
*KGCV(FM) Elk Mountain, WY
KGCX-FM Sidney, MT
*KGCY(FM) Esterbrook, WY
KGDN-FM Pasco, WA
*KGDP-FM Santa Maria, CA
KGEE-FM Pecos, TX
KGEN-FM Hanford, CA
*KGFA(FM) Great Falls, MT
*KGFC-FM Great Falls, MT
*KGFJ(FM) Belt, MT
KGFM-FM Bakersfield, CA
KGFT-FM Pueblo, CO
KGFX-FM Pierre, SD
KGFY-FM Stillwater, OK
*KGGA(FM) Gallup, NM
KGGB(FM) Yorktown, TX
KGGF-FM Fredonia, KS
*KGGG(FM) Pacific Junction, IA
KGGI-FM Riverside, CA
*KGGL-FM Missoula, MT
*KGGM-FM Delhi, LA
KGGO-FM Des Moines, IA
*KGGY(FM) Stratton, CO
KGHL-FM Billings, MT
*KGHP-FM Gig Harbor, WA
*KGHR(FM) Tuba City, AZ
*KGHY(FM) Beaumont, TX
KGIM-FM Redfield, SD
*KGIO(FM) Astoria, OR
KGKL-FM San Angelo, TX
KGKS-FM Scott City, MO
*KGLC-FM Miami, OK
*KGLF(FM) Doss, TX
KGLI-FM Sioux City, IA
*KGLK(FM) Lake Jackson, TX

*KGLL(FM) Gillette, WY
KGLM-FM Anaconda, MT
*KGLP-FM Gallup, NM
*KGLT(FM) Bozeman, MT
*KGLU(FM) Gideon, MO
*KGLV(FM) Manhattan, KS
*KGLX(FM) Gallup, NM
*KGLY-FM Tyler, TX
KGMG-FM Oracle, AZ
KGMN-FM Kingman, AZ
KGMO(FM) Cape Girardeau, MO
KGMX-FM Lancaster, CA
*KGNA-FM Arnold, NE
KGNC-FM Amarillo, TX
*KGNN-FM Cuba, MO
KGNT(FM) Smithfield, UT
*KGNU-FM Boulder, CO
*KGNV(FM) Washington, MO
*KGNY(FM) Dixon, MO
*KGNZ-FM Abilene, TX
KGON-FM Portland, OR
KGOR-FM Omaha, NE
KGOT-FM Anchorage, AK
*KGOU-FM Norman, OK
KGOZ-FM Gallatin, MO
KGPQ-FM Monticello, AR
*KGPR-FM Great Falls, MT
KGPZ-FM Coleraine, MN
*KGQD(FM) Fraser, CO
KGRA-FM Jefferson, IA
KGRC-FM Hannibal, MO
*KGRD-FM Orchard, NE
*KGRG-FM Auburn, WA
*KGRI(FM) Lebanon, OR
KGRK(FM) Glenrock, WY
*KGRM-FM Grambling, LA
*KGRP(FM) Cazadero, CA
KGRR-FM Epworth, IA
KGRS-FM Burlington, IA
KGRT-FM Las Cruces, NM
KGRW-FM Friona, TX
*KGSF(FM) Green Forest, AR
KGSG-FM Pasco, WA
*KGSP-FM Parkville, MO
KGSR-FM Bastrop, TX
KGSX(FM) Comfort, TX
KGTM(FM) Rexburg, ID
*KGTR(FM) Albany, MO
*KGTS-FM College Place, WA
KGTW-FM Ketchikan, AK
*KGUA(FM) Gualala, CA
*KGUD(FM) Longmont, CO
KGUM-FM Dededo, GU
*KGVA-FM Fort Belknap Agency, MT
*KGVB(FM) Holliday, TX
KGVE-FM Grove, OK
*KGWB(FM) Snyder, TX
*KGWP(FM) Pittsburg, TX
KGWT(FM) George West, TX
KGWY-FM Gillette, WY
KGXL(FM) Winters, TX
KGY-FM McCleary, WA
*KGZO(FM) Shafter, CA
*KHAA(FM) Orleans, CA
KHAD(FM) Upton, WY
*KHAI(FM) Wahiawa, HI
KHAK(FM) Cedar Rapids, IA
KHAM(FM) Britt, IA
*KHAP(FM) Chico, CA
KHAQ(FM) Maxwell, NE
KHAY-FM Ventura, CA
KHAZ-FM Hays, KS
KHBC(FM) Hilo, HI
KHBM-FM Monticello, AR
KHBT-FM Humboldt, IA
*KHBW(FM) Brownwood, TX
KHBZ-FM Oklahoma City, OK
KHCA(FM) Wamego, KS
*KHCB-FM Houston, TX
*KHCC-FM Hutchinson, KS
*KHCD-FM Salina, KS
*KHCJ(FM) Jefferson, TX
KHCK-FM Robinson, TX
KHCL(FM) Arcadia, LA
KHCM-FM Honolulu, HI
*KHCO(FM) Hayden, CO

*KHCP(FM) Paris, TX
KHCR(FM) Bismarck, MO
*KHCS-FM Palm Desert, CA
*KHCT-FM Great Bend, KS
*KHCX(FM) Soda Springs, ID
*KHDC-FM Chualar, CA
KHDK(FM) New London, IA
KHDR(FM) Lenwood, CA
KHDV(FM) Darby, MT
*KHDX(FM) Conway, AR
*KHEB(FM) Granite, OK
*KHEC(FM) Crescent City, CA
*KHED(FM) Arkadelphia, AR
KHEI-FM Kihei, HI
KHER-FM Crystal City, TX
KHES(FM) Rocksprings, TX
*KHEV(FM) Fairview, OK
*KHEW(FM) Rocky Boy's Reservation, MT
KHEY-FM El Paso, TX
KHFI-FM Georgetown, TX
KHFM(FM) Santa Fe, NM
*KHFR-FM Santa Maria, CA
KHGE(FM) Fresno, CA
KHGG-FM Waldron, AR
*KHGN-FM Kirksville, MO
*KHGO(FM) Homer, AK
*KHGQ(FM) Quincy, CA
*KHHC(FM) Canadian, TX
KHHK-FM Yakima, WA
KHHL(FM) Leander, TX
*KHHT(FM) Los Angeles, CA
KHHZ(FM) Gridley, CA
*KHIB(FM) Bastrop, TX
*KHID(FM) McAllen, TX
KHIH(FM) Hugo, CO
*KHII(FM) Cloudcroft, NM
KHIJ(FM) Mesquite, NV
*KHIM-FM Mangum, OK
KHIP(FM) Gonzales, CA
KHIT-FM Madera, CA
KHIX-FM Carlin, NV
*KHJC(FM) Lihue, HI
*KHJJ(FM) Shaniko, OR
KHJK-FM La Porte, TX
KHJL(FM) Thousand Oaks, CA
KHKC-FM Atoka, OK
*KHKE-FM Cedar Falls, IA
KHKI-FM Des Moines, IA
KHKK-FM Modesto, CA
*KHKL(FM) Laytonville, CA
KHKN(FM) Benton, AR
KHKR-FM East Helena, MT
KHKS-FM Denton, TX
*KHKV(FM) Kerrville, TX
KHKX(FM) Odessa, TX
*KHKY(FM) Akiachak, AK
KHKZ(FM) Mercedes, TX
KHLA-FM Jennings, LA
KHLB-FM Mason, TX
KHLE-FM Kempner, TX
KHLL-FM Richwood, LA
KHLN(FM) Montana City, MT
KHLR-FM Maumelle, AR
KHLS-FM Blytheville, AR
*KHLV(FM) Helena, MT
KHLX(FM) Pollock Pines, CA
KHMB-FM Hamburg, AR
KHMC(FM) Goliad, TX
*KHMD-FM Mansfield, LA
KHME-FM Winona, MN
*KHMG-FM Barrigada, GU
*KHML(FM) Madisonville, TX
KHMR(FM) Lovelady, TX
*KHMS-FM Victorville, CA
KHMX-FM Houston, TX
KHMY(FM) Pratt, KS
KHNA(FM) Wamsutter, WY
*KHNE-FM Hastings, NE
KHNK(FM) Columbia Falls, MT
*KHNS-FM Haines, AK
KHOC-FM Casper, WY
KHOD(FM) Des Moines, NM
*KHOE(FM) Fairfield, IA
*KHOI(FM) Story City, IA
KHOK-FM Hoisington, KS

*KHOL(FM) Jackson, WY
KHOM(FM) Salem, AR
KHOP-FM Oakdale, CA
KHOS-FM Sonora, TX
*KHOT-FM Paradise Valley, AZ
KHOV-FM Wickenburg, AZ
*KHOY-FM Laredo, TX
KHOZ-FM Harrison, AR
KHPA-FM Hope, AR
KHPE-FM Albany, OR
*KHPO(FM) Port O'Connor, TX
KHPQ-FM Clinton, AR
*KHPR-FM Honolulu, HI
*KHPS(FM) Camp Wood, TX
KHPT-FM Conroe, TX
*KHQG-FM Superior, WI
*KHQT(FM) Las Cruces, NM
KHRD-FM Weaverville, CA
*KHRI(FM) Hollister, CA
KHRQ-FM Baker, CA
KHRS(FM) Winthrop, MN
KHRT-FM Minot, ND
KHRU-FM Beulah, ND
*KHRV(FM) Hood River, OR
KHRW(FM) Wright, WY
KHSK(FM) Allen, NE
KHSL-FM Paradise, CA
*KHSR-FM Crescent City, CA
KHSS-FM Walla Walla, WA
KHST-FM Lamar, MO
*KHSU-FM Arcata, CA
*KHTA(FM) Wake Village, TX
KHTB(FM) Provo, UT
KHTE-FM England, AR
KHTN-FM Planada, CA
KHTQ-FM Hayden, ID
KHTR-FM Pullman, WA
KHTS-FM El Cajon, CA
KHTT-FM Muskogee, OK
KHTZ(FM) Ganado, TX
KHUI(FM) Honolulu, HI
KHUM(FM) Garberville, CA
KHUN(FM) Huntington, UT
*KHUS(FM) Huslia, AK
KHUT-FM Hutchinson, KS
*KHVT(FM) Bloomington, TX
*KHWD(FM) Wiggins, CO
KHWG-FM Crystal, NV
KHWI(FM) Holualoa, HI
KHWK-FM Tonopah, NV
KHWY-FM Essex, CA
KHWZ-FM Ludlow, CA
KHXS-FM Merkel, TX
KHYI-FM Howe, TX
KHYL-FM Auburn, CA
*KHYM-FM Copeland, KS
KHYS(FM) Hays, KS
KHYT-FM Tucson, AZ
KHYY-FM Minatare, NE
KHYZ-FM Mountain Pass, CA
KHZA(FM) Bunker, MO
*KHZK(FM) Kotzebue, AK
KHZR-FM Potosi, MO
KHZS(FM) Georgetown, TX
KHZX(FM) Yakutat, AK
KHZY(FM) Overton, NE
KHZZ(FM) Sargent, NE
*KIAD(FM) Dubuque, IA
KIAI(FM) Mason City, IA
KIAK-FM Fairbanks, AK
*KIAM-FM North Nenana, AK
KIAQ-FM Clarion, IA
KIBB(FM) Haven, KS
*KIBC-FM Burney, CA
KIBG-FM Bigfork, MT
KIBR(FM) Sandpoint, ID
KIBS(FM) Bishop, CA
KIBT(FM) Fountain, CO
*KIBX(FM) Bonners Ferry, ID
KIBZ(FM) Crete, NE
KICA-FM Farwell, TX
*KICB-FM Fort Dodge, IA
KICD-FM Spencer, IA
KICK-FM Palmyra, MO
KICM(FM) Healdton, OK
*KICO(FM) Rico, CO

*KICR(FM) Coeur d'Alene, ID
KICT-FM Wichita, KS
KICX-FM McCook, NE
KICY-FM Nome, AK
*KIDE-FM Hoopa, CA
KIDI-FM Lompoc, CA
KIDN-FM Hayden, CO
*KIDS(FM) Grants, NM
KIDX(FM) Ruidoso, NM
KIFG-FM Iowa Falls, IA
KIFM-FM San Diego, CA
*KIFR(FM) Alice, TX
KIFS(FM) Ashland, OR
KIFX-FM Roosevelt, UT
*KIGC-FM Oskaloosa, IA
KIGL(FM) Seligman, MO
KIGN(FM) Burns, WY
KIHK-FM Rock Valley, IA
*KIHS(FM) Adel, IA
KIHT-FM Saint Louis, MO
KIIC(FM) Albia, IA
KIIK-FM Waynesville, MO
KIIM-FM Tucson, AZ
KIIS-FM Los Angeles, CA
KIIZ-FM Killeen, TX
KIJI(FM) Tumon, GU
KIJN-FM Farwell, TX
KIKC-FM Forsyth, MT
KIKD-FM Lake City, IA
KIKF-FM Cascade, MT
*KIKG(FM) Licking, MO
KIKI-FM Honolulu, HI
*KIKL(FM) Lafayette, LA
KIKN-FM Salem, SD
KIKO-FM Claypool, AZ
KIKS-FM Iola, KS
KIKT-FM Greenville, TX
KIKV-FM Sauk Centre, MN
KIKX-FM Ketchum, ID
*KILE-FM Woodland Park, CO
*KILI(FM) Porcupine, SD
KILJ-FM Mount Pleasant, IA
KILO-FM Colorado Springs, CO
KILR-FM Estherville, IA
KILT-FM Houston, TX
*KILV(FM) Castana, IA
KILX(FM) Hatfield, AR
KIMN-FM Denver, CO
KIMX(FM) Laramie, WY
KIMY-FM Watonga, OK
KINB(FM) Kingfisher, OK
KIND-FM Independence, KS
KINE-FM Honolulu, HI
KING-FM Seattle, WA
*KINI(FM) Crookston, NE
KINK-FM Portland, OR
KINL-FM Eagle Pass, TX
KINT-FM El Paso, TX
*KINU(FM) Kotzebue, AK
KINV(FM) Enderlin, ND
KINX(FM) Great Falls, MT
KINZ-FM Humboldt, KS
KIOA-FM Des Moines, IA
KIOC-FM Orange, TX
KIOD(FM) McCook, NE
KIOI-FM San Francisco, CA
KIOK-FM Richland, WA
KIOO-FM Porterville, CA
*KIOS-FM Omaha, NE
KIOT-FM Los Lunas, NM
KIOW-FM Forest City, IA
KIOX-FM Edna, TX
KIOZ-FM San Diego, CA
*KIPO(FM) Honolulu, HI
KIPR-FM Pine Bluff, AR
KIQK-FM Rapid City, SD
KIQN(FM) Pueblo, CO
KIQO-FM Atascadero, CA
*KIQQ-FM Newberry Springs, CA
KIQX(FM) Durango, CO
KIQZ(FM) Rawlins, WY
KIRC-FM Seminole, TX
KIRK-FM Macon, MO
*KIRL(FM) Osage Beach, MO
KIRO-FM Tacoma, WA

*KIRQ(FM) Twin Falls, ID
KISC-FM Spokane, WA
KISD-FM Pipestone, MN
KISF-FM Las Vegas, NV
*KISH(FM) Hagatna, GU
*KISL(FM) Avalon, CA
KISM-FM Bellingham, WA
KISN(FM) Belgrade, MT
*KISQ-FM San Francisco, CA
KISR-FM Fort Smith, AR
KISS-FM San Antonio, TX
KIST-FM Santa Barbara, CA
*KISU-FM Pocatello, ID
KISV(FM) Bakersfield, CA
KISW-FM Seattle, WA
KISX-FM Whitehouse, TX
KISZ-FM Cortez, CO
*KITA(FM) Iota, LA
KITE(FM) Port Lavaca, TX
*KITF(FM) International Falls, MN
*KITG(FM) Sarcoxie, MO
KITH(FM) Kapaa, HI
KITI-FM Winlock, WA
KITN-FM Worthington, MN
KITO-FM Vinita, OK
KITS-FM San Francisco, CA
KITT(FM) Soda Springs, ID
KITX(FM) Hugo, OK
KITY(FM) Llano, TX
KIVY-FM Crockett, TX
KIWA-FM Sheldon, IA
KIWI(FM) McFarland, CA
*KIWR-FM Council Bluffs, IA
KIXA-FM Lucerne Valley, CA
KIXB-FM El Dorado, TX
KIXC(FM) Bearden, AR
KIXF-FM Baker, CA
KIXN-FM Hobbs, NM
KIXO-FM Sulphur, OK
KIXQ-FM Joplin, MO
KIXR-FM Ponca City, OK
KIXS-FM Victoria, TX
KIXT-FM Bay City, TX
KIXW-FM Lenwood, CA
KIXX-FM Watertown, SD
KIXY-FM San Angelo, TX
KIXZ-FM Opportunity, WA
KIYS-FM Jonesboro, AR
*KIYU-FM Galena, AK
KIYX-FM Sageville, IA
KIZN-FM Boise, ID
KIZS-FM Collinsville, OK
KIZZ-FM Minot, ND
*KJAB-FM Mexico, MO
KJAC(FM) Timnath, CO
KJAE-FM Leesville, LA
KJAK-FM Slaton, TX
KJAM-FM Madison, SD
KJAQ(FM) Seattle, WA
*KJAR(FM) Susanville, CA
KJAS-FM Jasper, TX
KJAV-FM Alamo, TX
KJAX(FM) Jackson, WY
KJAZ-FM Point Comfort, TX
*KJBB(FM) Watertown, SD
KJBI(FM) Fort Pierre, SD
KJBL(FM) Julesburg, CO
KJBR-FM Marked Tree, AR
KJBX-FM Trumann, AR
KJBZ-FM Laredo, TX
*KJCC(FM) Carnegie, OK
KJCD(FM) Fort Benton, MT
*KJCF(FM) Asotin, WA
*KJCG(FM) Missoula, MT
*KJCH(FM) Coos Bay, OR
KJCK-FM Junction City, KS
*KJCM-FM Snyder, OK
KJCQ(FM) Westwood, CA
*KJCR(FM) Keene, TX
*KJCS(FM) Nacogdoches, TX
*KJCU(FM) Fort Bragg, CA
*KJCV(FM) Country Club, MO
KJCY(FM) Saint Ansgar, IA
KJDL(FM) Levelland, TX
KJDX(FM) Susanville, CA
KJDY-FM Canyon City, OR

KJEB(FM) New Castle, CO
KJEE-FM Montecito, CA
KJEL-FM Lebanon, MO
KJET(FM) Raymond, WA
KJEZ-FM Poplar Bluff, MO
KJFA(FM) Santa Fe, NM
KJFM-FM Louisiana, MO
*KJFT(FM) Arlee, MT
KJFX-FM Fresno, CA
*KJHA-FM Houston, AK
*KJHK(FM) Lawrence, KS
*KJHL(FM) Boise City, OK
KJIA(FM) Spirit Lake, ID
KJIK(FM) Duncan, AZ
*KJIL-FM Copeland, KS
*KJIR(FM) Hannibal, MO
*KJIV(FM) Reno, NV
KJIW-FM Helena, AR
KJJJ-FM Lake Havasu City, AZ
KJJK-FM Fergus Falls, MN
KJJM-FM Baker, MT
*KJJP(FM) Amarillo, TX
KJJS(FM) Zapata, TX
KJJY(FM) West Des Moines, IA
KJJZ-FM Indio, CA
KJKB-FM Jacksboro, TX
KJKJ-FM Grand Forks, ND
KJKK(FM) Dallas, TX
*KJKL(FM) Selma, OR
KJKS(FM) Kahului, HI
*KJKT(FM) Spearfish, SD
*KJLC(FM) Susanville, CA
*KJLF(FM) Butte, MT
*KJLG(FM) Guymon, OK
KJLH-FM Compton, CA
*KJLI(FM) La Junta, CO
*KJLJ(FM) Scott City, KS
KJLL-FM Fountain Valley, CA
KJLN(FM) Sac City, IA
KJLO-FM Monroe, LA
*KJLP(FM) Palmer, AK
KJLS-FM Hays, KS
*KJLT-FM North Platte, NE
*KJLU(FM) Jefferson City, MO
KJLV(FM) Hoxie, AR
KJLY-FM Blue Earth, MN
*KJMA(FM) Floresville, TX
KJMB-FM Blythe, CA
*KJMC(FM) Des Moines, IA
KJMD(FM) Pukalani, HI
KJMG-FM Bastrop, LA
KJMH(FM) Lake Arthur, LA
KJMK-FM Webb City, MO
KJMM-FM Bixby, OK
KJMN-FM Castle Rock, CO
KJMO(FM) Linn, MO
KJMQ(FM) Lihue, HI
KJMS(FM) Olive Branch, MS
KJMT(FM) Calico Rock, AR
KJMX(FM) Reedsport, OR
KJMY(FM) Bountiful, UT
KJMZ(FM) Cache, OK
KJNA-FM Jena, LA
*KJND-FM Williston, ND
*KJNP-FM North Pole, AK
KJNY(FM) Ferndale, CA
KJNZ(FM) Hereford, TX
KJOE-FM Slayton, MN
*KJOG(FM) Cleveland, OK
KJOJ-FM Freeport, TX
*KJOL-FM Montrose, CO
KJOR(FM) Windsor, CA
KJOT(FM) Boise, ID
*KJOV-FM Woodward, OK
KJOX-FM Long Beach, WA
KJOY-FM Stockton, CA
KJQN(FM) Coalville, UT
KJQY(FM) La Veta, CO
*KJRF(FM) Lawton, OK
KJR-FM Seattle, WA
*KJRL(FM) Herington, KS
*KJRT-FM Amarillo, TX
KJRV-FM Wessington Springs, SD
*KJSB(FM) Jonesboro, AR
*KJSM-FM Augusta, AR
KJSN-FM Modesto, CA

KJSR-FM Tulsa, OK
*KJTA-FM Flagstaff, AZ
*KJTH(FM) Ponca City, OK
*KJTW(FM) Jamestown, ND
KJTX(FM) Jefferson, TX
*KJTY-FM Topeka, KS
KJUG-FM Tulare, CA
KJUL(FM) Moapa Valley, NV
KJVC-FM Mansfield, LA
*KJVH(FM) Longview, WA
*KJVL(FM) Chanute, KS
*KJWA(FM) Rye, CO
KJWL-FM Fresno, CA
*KJWR(FM) Windom, MN
KJXJ(FM) Cameron, TX
KJXK(FM) San Antonio, TX
KJXN(FM) South Haven, MO
KJYE-FM Grand Junction, CO
*KJYL-FM Eagle Grove, IA
KJYO-FM Oklahoma City, OK
*KJZA(FM) Drake, AZ
*KJZK(FM) Kingman, AZ
KJZN(FM) San Joaquin, CA
*KJZP(FM) Prescott, AZ
KJZS(FM) Sparks, NV
KJZY-FM Sebastopol, CA
*KJZZ(FM) Phoenix, AZ
KKAC(FM) Vandalia, MO
*KKAG(FM) Grangeville, ID
KKAJ-FM Ardmore, OK
KKAL(FM) Paso Robles, CA
KKAT-FM Orem, UT
KKAW-FM Albin, WY
*KKBA(FM) Kingsville, TX
KKBB-FM Bakersfield, CA
KKBC-FM Baker City, OR
KKBD(FM) Sallisaw, OK
KKBG-FM Hilo, HI
KKBI-FM Broken Bow, OK
KKBJ-FM Bemidji, MN
KKBL-FM Monett, MO
KKBN(FM) Twain Harte, CA
KKBO(FM) Flasher, ND
KKBQ-FM Pasadena, TX
KKBR-FM Billings, MT
KKBS-FM Guymon, OK
*KKBY(FM) Kirby, WY
KKBZ(FM) Auberry, CA
KKCA-FM Fulton, MO
KKCB-FM Duluth, MN
KKCD-FM Omaha, NE
KKCH(FM) Glenwood Springs, CO
KKCI-FM Goodland, KS
*KKCJ(FM) Cannon AFB, NM
KKCK-FM Marshall, MN
KKCL-FM Lorenzo, TX
KKCN-FM Ballinger, TX
KKCQ-FM Bagley, MN
*KKCR-FM Hanalei, HI
KKCT-FM Bismarck, ND
KKCV(FM) Rozel, KS
KKCW-FM Beaverton, OR
KKCY-FM Colusa, CA
KKDA-FM Dallas, TX
KKDC(FM) Dolores, CO
KKDL(FM) Dilley, TX
KKDM-FM Des Moines, IA
KKDQ(FM) Thief River Falls, MN
KKDT(FM) Burdett, KS
KKDV(FM) Walnut Creek, CA
KKDY-FM West Plains, MO
KKED-FM Fairbanks, AK
KKEG(FM) Bentonville, AR
KKEN(FM) Duncan, OK
KKEQ-FM Fosston, MN
*KKER(FM) Kerrville, TX
KKEV(FM) Centerville, TX
KKEX(FM) Preston, ID
KKEZ-FM Fort Dodge, IA
*KKFC(FM) Hart, TX
KKFD-FM Fairfield, IA
KKFG-FM Bloomfield, NM
*KKFI-FM Kansas City, MO
KKFM-FM Colorado Springs, CO
KKFN(FM) Longmont, CO
*KKFR(FM) Mayer, AZ

KKFS(FM) Lincoln, CA
KKFT(FM) Gardnerville-Minden, NV
KKGB-FM Sulphur, LA
KKGL-FM Nampa, ID
KKGO(FM) Los Angeles, CA
KKHA-FM Markham, TX
KKHB-FM Eureka, CA
KKHH(FM) Houston, TX
KKHI(FM) Centennial, CO
KKHJ-FM Pago Pago, AS
KKHK(FM) Carmel, CA
KKHN(FM) Calhan, CO
KKHQ-FM Oelwein, IA
KKHR-FM Abilene, TX
KKHT-FM Winnie, TX
KKIA-FM Ida Grove, IA
KKID-FM Salem, MO
KKIK(FM) Horseshoe Bend, AR
KKIM-FM Santa Fe, NM
KKIN-FM Aitkin, MN
KKIQ-FM Livermore, CA
KKIS-FM Soldotna, AK
KKIT(FM) Taos, NM
KKIX-FM Fayetteville, AR
*KKJA(FM) Redmond, OR
KKJG-FM San Luis Obispo, CA
KKJJ(FM) Henderson, NV
KKJK(FM) Ravenna, NE
KKJM(FM) Saint Joseph, MN
KKJO-FM Saint Joseph, MO
KKJQ-FM Garden City, KS
KKJW-FM Stanton, TX
KKJY(FM) Santa Rosa, NM
*KKJZ(FM) Long Beach, CA
KKKJ(FM) Merrill, OR
KKLA-FM Los Angeles, CA
KKLB(FM) Madisonville, TX
*KKLC(FM) Mount Shasta, CA
KKLD(FM) Cottonwood, AZ
*KKLG(FM) Newton, IA
KKLH(FM) Marshfield, MO
*KKLI-FM Widefield, CO
*KKLJ(FM) Klamath Falls, OR
*KKLM(FM) Corpus Christi, TX
KKLN-FM Atwater, MN
*KKLP(FM) La Pine, OR
KKLQ(FM) Harwood, ND
KKLR-FM Poplar Bluff, MO
KKLS-FM Sioux Falls, SD
*KKLT(FM) Texarkana, AR
*KKLU(FM) Lubbock, TX
KKLV(FM) Turrell, AR
*KKLW(FM) Willmar, MN
KKLX-FM Worland, WY
*KKLY(FM) El Paso, TX
KKLZ-FM Las Vegas, NV
KKMA(FM) Le Mars, IA
KKMG-FM Pueblo, CO
KKMI-FM Burlington, IA
KKMJ-FM Austin, TX
KKMK-FM Rapid City, SD
KKMR(FM) Arizona City, AZ
KKMT(FM) Pablo, MT
KKMV(FM) Rupert, ID
KKMX(FM) Tri City, OR
KKMY-FM Orange, TX
KKND(FM) Belle Chasse, LA
KKNG-FM Newcastle, OK
KKNI(FM) Seward, AK
*KKNL(FM) Valentine, NE
KKNM(FM) Bovina, TX
KKNN-FM Delta, CO
KKNU(FM) Springfield-Eugene, OR
KKOA(FM) Volcano, HI
KKOB-FM Albuquerque, NM
KKOK-FM Morris, MN
KKOL-FM Aiea, HI
KKOO(FM) Rayne, LA
KKOR(FM) Gallup, NM
KKOT-FM Columbus, NE
KKOW-FM Pittsburg, KS
KKOY-FM Chanute, KS
KKOZ-FM Ava, MO
KKPK(FM) Colorado Springs, CO
KKPL(FM) Cheyenne, WY
KKPN(FM) Rockport, TX

KKPR-FM Kearney, NE
KKPS-FM Brownsville, TX
KKPT-FM Little Rock, AR
KKQQ-FM Volga, SD
KKQX(FM) Manhattan, MT
KKQY-FM Hill City, KS
KKRB-FM Klamath Falls, OR
KKRC-FM Granite Falls, MN
*KKRD(FM) Enid, OK
KKRE(FM) Hollis, OK
KKRF-FM Stuart, IA
KKRG(FM) Albuquerque, NM
*KKRH(FM) Grangeville, ID
*KKRI(FM) Pocola, OK
KKRK(FM) Coffeyville, KS
KKRL-FM Carroll, IA
*KKRN(FM) Bella Vista, CA
KKRO(FM) Redding, CA
KKRQ-FM Iowa City, IA
*KKRR(FM) Casper, WY
*KKRS(FM) Davenport, WA
KKRV-FM Wenatchee, WA
KKRW-FM Houston, TX
*KKRY(FM) Kearny, AZ
KKRZ-FM Portland, OR
KKSD-FM Milbank, SD
KKSF-FM San Francisco, CA
KKSI-FM Eddyville, IA
KKSN(FM) Kansas City, MO
KKSP(FM) Bryant, AR
KKSR-FM Walla Walla, WA
KKSS-FM Santa Fe, NM
KKST-FM Oakdale, LA
KKSY-FM Anamosa, IA
KKTC(FM) Angel Fire, NM
*KKTO-FM Tahoe City, CA
*KKTR(FM) Kirksville, MO
KKTX-FM Kilgore, TX
KKTY-FM Douglas, WY
KKTZ(FM) Lakeview, AR
*KKUA-FM Wailuku, HI
KKUL-FM Groveton, TX
*KKUP-FM Cupertino, CA
KKUS(FM) Tyler, TX
KKUU(FM) Indio, CA
*KKVI(FM) Overland, MO
KKVO-FM Altus, OK
KKVR(FM) Kerrville, TX
KKVS(FM) Truth or Consequences, NM
KKVU(FM) Stevensville, MT
KKWB(FM) Kelliher, MN
KKWD(FM) Bethany, OK
KKWF(FM) Seattle, WA
KKWK(FM) Cameron, MO
KKWQ(FM) Warroad, MN
KKWS(FM) Wadena, MN
*KKWV(FM) Aransas Pass, TX
*KKWY(FM) Douglas, WY
KKXK(FM) Montrose, CO
KKXL-FM Grand Forks, ND
KKXS(FM) Shingletown, CA
KKXX-FM Shafter, CA
KKYA-FM Yankton, SD
KKYC-FM Clovis, NM
KKYN-FM Plainview, TX
KKYR-FM Texarkana, TX
KKYS(FM) Bryan, TX
KKYY(FM) Whiting, IA
KKYZ-FM Sierra Vista, AZ
KKZQ(FM) Tehachapi, CA
KKZX-FM Spokane, WA
KKZY-FM Bemidji, MN

KLBL(FM) Pearcy, AR
KLBN(FM) Fresno, CA
KLBQ(FM) El Dorado, AR
*KLBR(FM) Bend, OR
*KLBT(FM) Beaumont, TX
*KLBU(FM) Pecos, NM
*KLBV(FM) Steamboat Springs, CO
*KLBZ(FM) Bozeman, MT
KLCA-FM Tahoe City, CA
*KLCC-FM Eugene, OR
*KLCD-FM Decorah, IA
KLCE-FM Blackfoot, ID
*KLCH(FM) Lake City, MN
*KLCI(FM) Elk River, MN
KLCM-FM Lewistown, MT
*KLCO-FM Newport, OR
*KLCR-FM Lakeview, OR
*KLCU-FM Ardmore, OK
KLCX-FM Eyota, MN
*KLCY-FM Vernal, UT
*KLCZ(FM) Lewiston, ID
KLDD(FM) McCloud, CA
KLDE-FM Eldorado, TX
KLDG-FM Liberal, KS
KLDJ-FM Duluth, MN
*KLDN-FM Lufkin, TX
KLDR(FM) Harbeck-Fruitdale, OR
*KLDV(FM) Morrison, CO
KLDZ(FM) Medford, OR
KLEA-FM Lovington, NM
*KLEF-FM Anchorage, AK
KLEN-FM Cheyenne, WY
KLEO(FM) Kahaluu, HI
KLEP(FM) Dubois, WY
KLER-FM Orofino, ID
KLES(FM) Prosser, WA
*KLEU(FM) Lewistown, MT
KLEY-FM Jourdanton, TX
KLEZ(FM) Malvern, AR
*KLFC(FM) Branson, MO
*KLFF-FM San Luis Obispo, CA
*KLFH-FM Ojai, CA
KLFM-FM Great Falls, MT
KLFN(FM) Sunburg, MN
*KLFO-FM Florence, OR
*KLFR(FM) Reedsport, OR
*KLFS(FM) Van Buren, AR
*KLFV(FM) Grand Junction, CO
KLFX-FM Nolanville, TX
KLGA-FM Algona, IA
KLGD-FM Stamford, TX
*KLGG(FM) Kellogg, ID
KLGL(FM) Richfield, UT
*KLGO-FM Thorndale, TX
*KLGQ(FM) Grants, NM
KLGR-FM Redwood Falls, MN
*KLGS(FM) College Station, TX
*KLGT-FM Buffalo, WY
KLHB(FM) Odem, TX
KLHI-FM Kahului, HI
*KLHK(FM) Hobbs, NM
*KLHV(FM) Cotton Valley, LA
KLIL-FM Moreauville, LA
KLIP-FM Monroe, LA
KLIQ(FM) Hastings, NE
KLIR-FM Columbus, NE
KLIX-FM Twin Falls, ID
KLIZ-FM Brainerd, MN
*KLJC-FM Kansas City, MO
*KLJH(FM) Bayfield, CO
KLJR-FM Santa Paula, CA
KLJT-FM Jacksonville, TX
*KLJV(FM) Scottsbluff, NE
KLJZ(FM) Yuma, AZ
*KLKA(FM) Globe, AZ
KLKC-FM Parsons, KS
KLKK(FM) Clear Lake, IA
KLKL(FM) Minden, LA
*KLKM(FM) Kalispell, MT
KLKO(FM) Elko, NV
*KLKR(FM) Elko, NV
KLKS-FM Breezy Point, MN
KLKX-FM Rosamond, CA
KLKY(FM) Stanfield, OR
KLLC-FM San Francisco, CA

KLLE(FM) North Fork, CA
KLLL-FM Lubbock, TX
*KLLN-FM Newark, AR
KLLP-FM Chubbuck, ID
*KLLR(FM) Dripping Springs, TX
KLLT(FM) Spencer, IA
*KLLU(FM) Gallup, NM
KLLY-FM Oildale, CA
KLLZ-FM Walker, MN
KLMA-FM Hobbs, NM
*KLMB(FM) Roundup, MT
*KLMF(FM) Klamath Falls, OR
KLMG(FM) Esparto, CA
KLMI(FM) Rock River, WY
*KLMJ(FM) Hampton, IA
*KLMK(FM) Marvell, AR
KLMM(FM) Morro Bay, CA
KLMO-FM Dilley, TX
*KLMP(FM) Rapid City, SD
KLMR-FM Lamar, CO
*KLMT(FM) Billings, MT
*KLNB(FM) Grand Island, NE
KLNC(FM) Lincoln, NE
*KLND-FM Little Eagle, SD
*KLNE-FM Lexington, NE
*KLNI(FM) Decorah, IA
KLNN(FM) Questa, NM
KLNO(FM) Fort Worth, TX
KLNR(FM) Panaca, NV
KLNV-FM San Diego, CA
KLNZ-FM Glendale, AZ
KLOB-FM Thousand Palms, CA
*KLOF(FM) Gillette, WY
*KLOJ(FM) Glennallen, AK
KLOK-FM Greenfield, CA
KLOL-FM Houston, TX
*KLON(FM) Rockaway Beach, OR
KLOO-FM Corvallis, OR
*KLOP(FM) Ocean Park, WA
KLOQ-FM Winton, CA
KLOR-FM Ponca City, OK
KLOS-FM Los Angeles, CA
KLOU(FM) Saint Louis, MO
*KLOV(FM) Winchester, OR
KLOW(FM) Reno, TX
*KLOX(FM) Creston, IA
*KLOY(FM) Astoria, OR
KLOZ-FM Eldon, MO
*KLPI-FM Ruston, LA
KLPL-FM Lake Providence, LA
*KLPR(FM) Kearney, NE
KLPW-FM Elsberry, MO
KLPX-FM Tucson, AZ
KLQB(FM) Taylor, TX
*KLQL(FM) Luverne, MN
KLQP-FM Madison, MN
KLQQ(FM) Clearmont, WY
KLQV-FM San Diego, CA
*KLRB(FM) Stuart, OK
*KLRC(FM) Siloam Springs, AR
*KLRD(FM) Yucaipa, CA
*KLRE-FM Little Rock, AR
*KLRF-FM Milton-Freewater, OR
KLRH(FM) Sparks, NV
*KLRI(FM) Rigby, ID
KLRJ(FM) Aberdeen, SD
KLRK(FM) Marlin, TX
*KLRM(FM) Melbourne, AR
KLRO(FM) Hot Springs, AR
*KLRQ(FM) Clinton, MO
KLRR-FM Redmond, OR
*KLRS(FM) Lodi, CA
*KLRV(FM) Billings, MT
*KLRW(FM) Byrne, TX
KLRX(FM) Lee's Summit, MO
*KLRY(FM) Gypsum, CO
KLRZ-FM Larose, LA
*KLSA-FM Alexandria, LA
KLSC-FM Malden, MO
*KLSE-FM Rochester, MN
*KLSF(FM) Juneau, AK
*KLSI(FM) Moss Beach, CA
KLSK(FM) Great Falls, MT
KLSM(FM) Tallulah, LA
*KLSN(FM) Four Corners, MT
*KLSP(FM) Angola, LA

KLSR-FM Memphis, TX
*KLSS-FM Mason City, IA
*KLSU-FM Baton Rouge, LA
KLSX(FM) Rozet, WY
KLSY-FM South Bend, WA
KLSZ-FM Fort Smith, AR
*KLTA(FM) Breckenridge, MN
*KLTB(FM) Palestine, TX
KLTD-FM Temple, TX
KLTE-FM Kirksville, MO
KLTG-FM Corpus Christi, TX
KLTH(FM) Lake Oswego, OR
KLTI-FM Ames, IA
KLTN(FM) Houston, TX
KLTO-FM McQueeney, TX
*KLTP(FM) San Angelo, TX
*KLTR(FM) Brenham, TX
*KLTU(FM) Mammoth, AZ
KLTW-FM Prineville, OR
KLTY(FM) Arlington, TX
KLUA(FM) Kailua-Kona, HI
KLUB-FM Bloomington, TX
KLUC-FM Las Vegas, NV
KLUE(FM) Poplar Bluff, MO
*KLUH-FM Poplar Bluff, MO
KLUK(FM) Needles, CA
KLUN(FM) Paso Robles, CA
KLUR-FM Wichita Falls, TX
*KLUU(FM) Jamestown, ND
KLUV(FM) Dallas, TX
*KLUW(FM) East Wenatchee, WA
*KLUX-FM Robstown, TX
*KLVA(FM) Casa Grande, AZ
*KLVB(FM) Red Bluff, CA
*KLVC-FM Magalia, CA
KLVE-FM Los Angeles, CA
KLVF-FM Las Vegas, NM
*KLVG(FM) Garberville, CA
*KLVH(FM) San Luis Obispo, CA
*KLVJ-FM Julian, CA
*KLVK(FM) Fountain Hills, AZ
*KLVM-FM Prunedale, CA
*KLVN(FM) Livingston, CA
KLVO(FM) Los Alamos, NM
*KLVP(FM) Sandy, OR
*KLVR(FM) Middletown, CA
*KLVS(FM) Citrus Heights, CA
*KLVU-FM Sweet Home, OR
*KLVV-FM Ponca City, OK
*KLVW(FM) Odessa, TX
*KLVY(FM) Fairmead, CA
*KLWC(FM) Casper, WY
*KLWD(FM) Gillette, WY
*KLWG(FM) Lompoc, CA
*KLWS-FM Moses Lake, WA
*KLWV(FM) Chugwater, WY
*KLXA-FM Alexandria, LA
*KLXD(FM) Springfield, CO
KLXK(FM) Breckenridge, TX
*KLXL(FM) Wheeler, TX
*KLXM(FM) Clayton, NM
*KLXN(FM) Stratford, TX
KLXO(FM) Beaver, OK
KLXQ(FM) Mountain Pine, AR
KLXS-FM Pierre, SD
*KLXV(FM) Glenwood Springs, CO
KLYD(FM) Snyder, TX
KLYK(FM) Kelso, WA
KLYR-FM Clarksville, AR
*KLYT-FM Albuquerque, NM
KLYV-FM Dubuque, IA
KLYY(FM) Riverside, CA
KLZA-FM Falls City, NE
*KLZK-FM New Deal, TX
KLZN(FM) Susanville, CA
KLZR(FM) Lawrence, KS
*KLZV(FM) Sterling, CO
KLZX(FM) Weston, ID
KLZY(FM) Honokaa, HI
KLZZ-FM Waite Park, MN
KMAC-FM Gainesville, MO
KMAD-FM Whitesboro, TX
KMA-FM Clarinda, IA
KMAG-FM Fort Smith, AR
KMAJ-FM Topeka, KS
*KMAK(FM) Orange Cove, CA

KMAP(FM) Arriba, CO
KMAQ-FM Maquoketa, IA
KMAR-FM Winnsboro, LA
KMAT(FM) Seadrift, TX
KMAV-FM Mayville, ND
KMAX-FM Wellington, CO
*KMBH-FM Harlingen, TX
*KMBI-FM Spokane, WA
*KMBM(FM) Polson, MT
*KMBN(FM) Las Cruces, NM
KMBQ-FM Wasilla, AK
KMBR-FM Butte, MT
*KMBT(FM) Tecumseh, NE
*KMBV(FM) Valentine, NE
*KMCG(FM) McGrath, AK
KMCH-FM Manchester, IA
KMCJ(FM) Colstrip, MT
KMCK-FM Siloam Springs, AR
KMCM-FM Odessa, TX
KMCN(FM) Clinton, IA
KMCO(FM) Wilburton, OK
KMCQ-FM The Dalles, OR
KMCR-FM Montgomery City, MO
KMCS-FM Muscatine, IA
*KMCU(FM) Wichita Falls, TX
*KMCV(FM) High Point, MO
KMCX-FM Ogallala, NE
KMDL-FM Kaplan, LA
KMDR(FM) McKinleyville, CA
KMDX-FM San Angelo, TX
*KMDY-FM Keokuk, IA
KMDZ(FM) Las Vegas, NM
KMEL-FM San Francisco, CA
KMEM-FM Memphis, MO
KMEN(FM) Mendota, CA
*KMEO(FM) Mertzon, TX
KMEZ(FM) Port Sulphur, LA
*KMFA-FM Austin, TX
KMFB-FM Mendocino, CA
KMFC(FM) Centralia, MO
KMFG(FM) Nashwauk, MN
KMFM-FM Premont, TX
KMFR(FM) Hondo, TX
KMFX-FM Lake City, MN
KMFY-FM Grand Rapids, MN
KMGA-FM Albuquerque, NM
KMGC-FM Camden, AR
KMGE-FM Eugene, OR
KMGI-FM Pocatello, ID
KMGJ(FM) Grand Junction, CO
KMGK(FM) Glenwood, MN
KMGL-FM Oklahoma City, OK
KMGM-FM Montevideo, MN
KMGN-FM Flagstaff, AZ
KMGO-FM Centerville, IA
KMGQ(FM) Goleta, CA
KMGR-FM Delta, UT
*KMGT(FM) Circle, MT
KMGV-FM Fresno, CA
KMGW(FM) Casper, WY
KMGX(FM) Bend, OR
KMGZ-FM Lawton, OK
*KMHA-FM Four Bears, ND
*KMHB(FM) Seward, NE
*KMHD(FM) Gresham, OR
KMHK(FM) Hardin, MT
KMHM-FM Lutesville, MO
KMHO(FM) Mountain Home, TX
*KMHS-FM Coos Bay, OR
KMHT-FM Marshall, TX
KMHX(FM) Rohnert Park, CA
*KMIH(FM) Mercer Island, WA
KMIL(FM) Cameron, TX
KMIQ-FM Robstown, TX
*KMIT-FM Mitchell, SD
KMIX-FM Tracy, CA
KMJE-FM Gridley, CA
KMJ-FM Fresno, CA
*KMJG(FM) Homer, AK
KMJI(FM) Ashdown, AR
KMJJ-FM Shreveport, LA
KMJK(FM) Lexington, MO
KMJM-FM Columbia, IL
KMJO(FM) Hope, ND
KMJQ-FM Houston, TX
KMJR(FM) Portland, TX

KMJV(FM) Soledad, CA
KMJX-FM Conway, AR
KMJY(FM) Chugwater, WY
KMKF-FM Manhattan, KS
KMKK-FM Kaunakakai, HI
*KMKL(FM) North Branch, MN
*KMKR(FM) Oakridge, OR
KMKS-FM Bay City, TX
KMKT-FM Bells, TX
KMKX-FM Willits, CA
KMLA-FM El Rio, CA
KMLD(FM) Casper, WY
*KMLE-FM Chandler, AZ
*KMLK-FM El Dorado, AR
*KMLL(FM) Marysville, KS
KMLO-FM Lowry, SD
*KMLR(FM) Gonzales, TX
*KMLT(FM) Jackson, WY
*KMLU(FM) Brownfield, TX
*KMLV(FM) Ralston, NE
KMLW-FM Moses Lake, WA
KMMG(FM) Benton City, WA
*KMML(FM) Cimarron, KS
KMMO-FM Marshall, MO
KMMR-FM Malta, MT
KMMS-FM Bozeman, MT
KMMT-FM Mammoth Lakes, CA
*KMMX(FM) Tahoka, TX
KMMY(FM) Soper, OK
KMMZ(FM) Crane, TX
KMNA(FM) Mabton, WA
*KMNE-FM Bassett, NE
*KMNR(FM) Rolla, MO
KMNT(FM) Chehalis, WA
*KMOA(FM) Nu'uuli, AS
*KMOC(FM) Wichita Falls, TX
KMOD-FM Tulsa, OK
KMOE-FM Butler, MO
*KMOJ-FM Minneapolis, MN
KMOK(FM) Lewiston, ID
KMOM(FM) Roscoe, SD
KMON-FM Great Falls, MT
KMOO-FM Mineola, TX
KMOQ(FM) Columbus, KS
KMOR(FM) Gering, NE
KMOU(FM) Roswell, NM
KMOZ-FM Grand Junction, CO
*KMPB(FM) Frisco, CO
*KMPO-FM Modesto, CA
*KMPQ(FM) Roseburg, OR
*KMPR-FM Minot, ND
KMPS-FM Seattle, WA
*KMPZ(FM) Salida, CO
KMQA-FM East Porterville, CA
KMQS(FM) Wheatland, WY
*KMQX(FM) Weatherford, TX
KMRJ-FM Rancho Mirage, CA
KMRK-FM Odessa, TX
*KMRL-FM Buras, LA
*KMRO-FM Camarillo, CA
KMRQ(FM) Manteca, CA
KMRR(FM) Rexburg, ID
KMRX(FM) El Dorado, AR
KMRZ-FM Superior, WY
*KMSA-FM Grand Junction, CO
*KMSC-FM Sioux City, IA
*KMSE(FM) Rochester, MN
*KMSI(FM) Moore, OK
KMSK-FM Austin, MN
KMSL(FM) Mansfield, LA
*KMSM-FM Butte, MT
KMSO-FM Missoula, MT
*KMST(FM) Rolla, MO
*KMSU(FM) Mankato, MN
*KMSW(FM) The Dalles, OR
KMTB-FM Murfreesboro, AR
*KMTC-FM Russellville, AR
*KMTG(FM) San Jose, CA
*KMTH-FM Maljamar, NM
KMTK(FM) Bend, OR
KMTN-FM Jackson, WY
KMTS-FM Glenwood Springs, CO
KMTT-FM Tacoma, WA
KMTX-FM Helena, MT
KMTY-FM Holdrege, NE
KMTZ(FM) Three Forks, MT

KMUD-FM Garberville, CA
*KMUE-FM Eureka, CA
KMUL-FM Muleshoe, TX
*KMUN-FM Astoria, OR
*KMUW-FM Wichita, KS
*KMUZ(FM) Turner, OR
KMVA-FM Dewey-Humboldt, AZ
*KMVC-FM Marshall, MO
KMVE(FM) California City, CA
KMVK(FM) Fort Worth, TX
KMVL-FM Madisonville, TX
KMVQ-FM San Francisco, CA
KMVR(FM) Mesilla Park, NM
KMVV(FM) Sterling, AK
KMVX-FM Jerome, ID
KMWB(FM) Captain Cook, HI
*KMWR(FM) Brookings, OR
*KMWS(FM) Mount Vernon, WA
*KMWY(FM) Jackson, WY
KMXA-FM Minot, ND
*KMXB(FM) Henderson, NV
KMXC-FM Sioux Falls, SD
KMXD(FM) Monroe, UT
KMXE-FM Red Lodge, MT
KMXF(FM) Lowell, AR
*KMXG(FM) Clinton, IA
KMXH(FM) Alexandria, LA
KMXI-FM Chico, CA
*KMXJ-FM Amarillo, TX
KMXK-FM Cold Spring, MN
KMXL-FM Carthage, MO
*KMXN(FM) Osage City, KS
*KMXP-FM Phoenix, AZ
*KMXQ(FM) Socorro, NM
KMXR-FM Corpus Christi, TX
KMXS-FM Anchorage, AK
*KMXT-FM Kodiak, AK
KMXV-FM Kansas City, MO
KMXX-FM Imperial, CA
*KMXY-FM Grand Junction, CO
KMXZ-FM Tucson, AZ
*KMYI(FM) San Diego, CA
*KMYK(FM) Osage Beach, MO
KMYO-FM Morgan City, LA
KMYT-FM Temecula, CA
KMYX-FM Arvin, CA
KMYY(FM) Rayville, LA
KMYZ-FM Pryor, OK
KMZA-FM Seneca, KS
KMZE(FM) Woodward, OK
*KMZL-FM Missoula, MT
*KMZO(FM) Hamilton, MT
KMZQ-FM Payson, AZ
KMZU-FM Carrollton, MO
*KMZZ(FM) Bishop, TX
*KNAA-FM Show Low, AZ
KNAB-FM Burlington, CO
KNAC-FM Earlimart, CA
*KNAD-FM Page, AZ
*KNAF-FM Fredericksburg, TX
*KNAG(FM) Grand Canyon, AZ
KNAH(FM) Merced, CA
*KNAI(FM) Phoenix, AZ
KNAN-FM Nanakuli, HI
*KNAQ(FM) Prescott, AZ
*KNAR(FM) San Angelo, TX
KNAS-FM Nashville, AR
*KNAU(FM) Flagstaff, AZ
*KNBA-FM Anchorage, AK
KNBB(FM) Dubach, LA
*KNBE(FM) Beatrice, NE
*KNBJ-FM Bemidji, MN
KNBQ(FM) Centralia, WA
KNBT-FM New Braunfels, TX
*KNBU-FM Baldwin City, KS
KNBZ-FM Redfield, SD
*KNCA-FM Burney, CA
KNCB-FM Vivian, LA
*KNCC-FM Elko, NV
*KNCH-FM Somerville, TX
KNCI-FM Sacramento, CA
*KNCM-FM Appleton, MN
*KNCN-FM Sinton, TX
KNCO-FM Grass Valley, CA
KNCQ-FM Redding, CA
*KNCT-FM Killeen, TX

KNCU(FM) Newport, OR
KNCW-FM Omak, WA
KNCY-FM Auburn, NE
KNDA(FM) Alice, TX
KNDD-FM Seattle, WA
KNDE(FM) College Station, TX
KNDH(FM) Hettinger, ND
KNDK-FM Langdon, ND
*KNDL-FM Angwin, CA
KNDR(FM) Mandan, ND
*KNDW(FM) Williston, ND
KNDY-FM Marysville, KS
*KNDZ(FM) McKinleyville, CA
KNEB-FM Scottsbluff, NE
KNEC-FM Yuma, CO
*KNEF(FM) Franklin, NE
KNEI-FM Waukon, IA
KNEK-FM Washington, LA
KNEL-FM Brady, TX
KNEN-FM Norfolk, NE
*KNEO(FM) Neosho, MO
KNES-FM Fairfield, TX
KNEV-FM Reno, NV
KNEX-FM Laredo, TX
*KNFA(FM) Grand Island, NE
KNFM-FM Midland, TX
KNFO-FM Basalt, CO
KNFT-FM Bayard, NM
KNFX-FM Bryan, TX
*KNGA(FM) Saint Peter, MN
*KNGM-FM Emporia, KS
KNGS-FM Coalinga, CA
KNGT-FM Lake Charles, LA
*KNGW(FM) Juneau, AK
KNGY(FM) Alameda, CA
*KNHC(FM) Seattle, WA
*KNHM(FM) Bayside, CA
*KNHS(FM) Hastings, NE
*KNHT(FM) Rio Dell, CA
*KNHU(FM) Humboldt, NE
KNID(FM) North Enid, OK
KNIK-FM Anchorage, AK
KNIM-FM Maryville, MO
KNIN-FM Wichita Falls, TX
*KNIS(FM) Carson City, NV
KNIX-FM Phoenix, AZ
*KNIZ(FM) Gallup, NM
*KNJT(FM) Coldwater, KS
KNKI(FM) Pinetop, AZ
KNKK(FM) Needles, CA
*KNKL(FM) North Ogden, UT
KNKT(FM) Armijo, Albuquerque, NM
*KNLB-FM Lake Havasu City, AZ
*KNLE-FM Round Rock, TX
KNLF(FM) Quincy, CA
*KNLG-FM New Bloomfield, MO
*KNLH-FM Cedar Hill, MO
*KNLK(FM) Santa Rosa, NM
*KNLL-FM Nashville, AR
*KNLM-FM Marshfield, MO
*KNLN(FM) Vienna, MO
*KNLP-FM Potosi, MO
*KNLQ(FM) Cuba, MO
KNLR-FM Bend, OR
KNLV-FM Ord, NE
KNLX-FM Prineville, OR
*KNMA(FM) Tularosa, NM
KNMB(FM) Cloudcroft, NM
*KNMC-FM Havre, MT
*KNMI-FM Farmington, NM
KNMO-FM Nevada, MO
KNMZ-FM Alamogordo, NM
*KNNB-FM Whiteriver, AZ
KNNG(FM) Sterling, CO
KNNK-FM Dimmitt, TX
KNNN(FM) Shasta Lake City, CA
KNOB(FM) Healdsburg, CA
KNOD-FM Harlan, IA
KNOE-FM Monroe, LA
KNOF-FM Saint Paul, MN
*KNOG(FM) Nogales, AZ
*KNOM-FM Nome, AK
*KNON-FM Dallas, TX
KNOR-FM Krum, TX
KNOS(FM) Albany, TX
KNOU(FM) Empire, LA

*KNOW-FM Minneapolis-St. Paul, MN
KNOX-FM Grand Forks, ND
*KNPE(FM) Hyannis, NE
KNPQ(FM) Hershey, NE
*KNPR(FM) Las Vegas, NV
KNRB(FM) Atlanta, TX
KNRG-FM New Ulm, TX
*KNRI(FM) Bismarck, ND
KNRJ(FM) Payson, AZ
KNRK-FM Camas, WA
KNRQ-FM Eugene, OR
KNRS-FM Centerville, UT
KNRX(FM) Sterling City, TX
*KNSE(FM) Austin, MN
KNSG-FM Springfield, MN
*KNSQ-FM Mount Shasta, CA
*KNSR-FM Collegeville, MN
*KNSU-FM Thibodaux, LA
*KNSW(FM) Worthington-Marshall, MN
KNTE-FM El Campo, TX
KNTI-FM Lakeport, CA
KNTK(FM) Weed, CA
*KNTN-FM Thief River Falls, MN
KNTO(FM) Chowchilla, CA
*KNTU(FM) McKinney, TX
KNTY(FM) Shingle Springs, CA
KNUE(FM) Tyler, TX
KNUJ-FM Sleepy Eye, MN
*KNUL(FM) Nulato, AK
KNUQ-FM Paauilo, HI
KNUW-FM Santa Clara, NM
KNVO-FM Port Isabel, TX
KNWB-FM Hilo, HI
*KNWC-FM Sioux Falls, SD
*KNWD-FM Natchitoches, LA
*KNWF-FM Fergus Falls, MN
*KNWG(FM) Goldendale, WA
*KNWI(FM) Osceola, IA
KNWJ(FM) Leone, AS
*KNWM(FM) Madrid, IA
*KNWO-FM Cottonwood, ID
*KNWP-FM Port Angeles, WA
*KNWR-FM Ellensburg, WA
*KNWS-FM Waterloo, IA
*KNWT(FM) Cody, WY
*KNWU(FM) Forks, WA
*KNWV-FM Clarkston, WA
*KNWY-FM Yakima, WA
KNXR(FM) Rochester, MN
KNXX(FM) Donaldsonville, LA
*KNYD-FM Broken Arrow, OK
KNYE(FM) Pahrump, NV
KNYN-FM Fort Bridger, WY
*KNYR(FM) Yreka, CA
KNZA-FM Hiawatha, KS
KNZS(FM) Arlington, KS
*KOAB-FM Bend, OR
*KOAP(FM) Lakeview, OR
*KOAR(FM) Beebe, AR
KOAS(FM) Dolan Springs, AZ
KOBB-FM Bozeman, MT
*KOBC-FM Joplin, MO
*KOBH(FM) Hobbs, NM
*KOBK(FM) Baker City, OR
*KOBN(FM) Burns, OR
KOCD(FM) Wilburton, OK
KOCK-FM Walsenburg, CO
KOCN-FM Pacific Grove, CA
KOCP(FM) Camarillo, CA
*KOCU(FM) Altus, OK
*KOCV-FM Odessa, TX
KODA-FM Houston, TX
KODJ-FM Salt Lake City, UT
KODM-FM Odessa, TX
*KODS-FM Carnelian Bay, CA
*KODV(FM) Barstow, CA
KODZ-FM Eugene, OR
KOEA-FM Doniphan, MO
*KOEC(FM) O'Neill, NE
KOEL-FM Cedar Falls, IA
*KOFG(FM) Cody, WY
KOFH-FM Nogales, AZ
KOFM(FM) Enid, OK
KOFX-FM El Paso, TX
KOGA-FM Ogallala, NE
*KOGB(FM) McGrath, AK

*KOGL(FM) Gleneden Beach, OR
KOGM-FM Opelousas, LA
*KOGR(FM) Rosedale, CA
*KOHL-FM Fremont, CA
*KOHM-FM Lubbock, TX
*KOHN(FM) Sells, AZ
*KOHP(FM) Riley, OR
*KOHR(FM) Sheridan, WY
*KOHS-FM Orem, UT
KOHT-FM Marana, AZ
*KOIA(FM) Storm Lake, IA
KOIR-FM Edinburg, TX
KOIT-FM San Francisco, CA
*KOJB(FM) Cass Lake, MN
*KOJD(FM) John Day, OR
*KOJI(FM) Okoboji, IA
KOJK(FM) Blanchard, OK
KOJO-FM Lake Charles, LA
KOJY(FM) Bloomfield, IA
*KOKF-FM Edmond, OK
*KOKN(FM) Oketo, KS
KOKO-FM Kerman, CA
KOKR(FM) Newport, AR
*KOKS-FM Poplar Bluff, MO
KOKU(FM) Hagatna, GU
KOKX-FM Keokuk, IA
KOKY-FM Sherwood, AR
KOKZ(FM) Waterloo, IA
KOLA-FM San Bernardino, CA
KOLB(FM) Firth, NE
*KOLI-FM Electra, TX
*KOLJ-FM Warroad, MN
KOLL-FM Lonoke, AR
KOLT-FM Warren AFB, WY
*KOLU-FM Pasco, WA
KOLV-FM Olivia, MN
KOLW-FM Basin City, WA
KOLY-FM Mobridge, SD
KOLZ-FM Cheyenne, WY
KOMA(FM) Oklahoma City, OK
KOMB-FM Fort Scott, KS
KOMC-FM Kimberling City, MO
KOME-FM Meridian, TX
KOMG(FM) Ozark, MO
*KOMH(FM) Marshall, MN
KOMO-FM Oakville, WA
KOMP-FM Las Vegas, NV
*KOMQ(FM) Omak, WA
KOMR(FM) Sun City, AZ
KOMS-FM Poteau, OK
KOMT(FM) Mountain Home, AR
KOMX-FM Pampa, TX
KONA-FM Kennewick, WA
KOND-FM Clovis, CA
KONE(FM) Lubbock, TX
KONI-FM Lanai City, HI
KONN-FM Bennett, CO
KONO-FM Helotes, TX
*KONQ-FM Dodge City, KS
KONV(FM) Overton, NV
KONY(FM) Saint George, UT
*KONZ(FM) Riley, KS
KOOC(FM) Belton, TX
KOOI-FM Jacksonville, TX
KOOK-FM Junction, TX
KOOL-FM Phoenix, AZ
KOOO(FM) Lincoln, NE
*KOOP-FM Hornsby, TX
KOOS(FM) North Bend, OR
*KOOT(FM) Hurley, NM
KOOU-FM Hardy, AR
*KOOW(FM) Crook, CO
*KOOZ(FM) Myrtle Point, OR
*KOPA(FM) Pala, CA
*KOPB-FM Portland, OR
*KOPD(FM) Pescadero, CA
*KOPJ(FM) Sebeka, MN
*KOPN-FM Columbia, MO
KOPR-FM Butte, MT
KOPW(FM) Plattsmouth, NE
KOPY-FM Alice, TX
KOQL-FM Ashland, MO
KORA-FM Bryan, TX
*KORB(FM) Hopland, CA
KORD-FM Richland, WA
KORL-FM Waianae, HI

KORQ(FM) Baird, TX
KORR-FM American Falls, ID
KORT-FM Grangeville, ID
*KORU(FM) Garapan-Saipan, NP
*KORV(FM) Ashland, OR
KOSB-FM Perry, OK
KOSG(FM) Pawhuska, OK
KOSI-FM Denver, CO
*KOSK(FM) Oskaloosa, IA
*KOSN(FM) Ketchum, ID
KOSO-FM Patterson, CA
KOSP(FM) Willard, MO
*KOSR(FM) Stillwater, OK
KOST-FM Los Angeles, CA
*KOSU(FM) Stillwater, OK
KOSY-FM Spanish Fork, UT
*KOTD(FM) The Dalles, OR
KOTE-FM Eureka, KS
*KOTO-FM Telluride, CO
KOTY(FM) Mason, TX
*KOUI(FM) Louisville, MS
KOUL-FM Sinton, TX
KOUT-FM Rapid City, SD
KOUZ(FM) Manville, WY
*KOVA(FM) Bovina, TX
KOVE-FM Galveston, TX
*KOWI(FM) Lamoni, IA
KOWZ-FM Blooming Prairie, MN
KOXE-FM Brownwood, TX
*KOYA(FM) Rosebud, SD
KOYE(FM) Frankston, TX
KOYN-FM Paris, TX
KOYT(FM) Elko, NV
*KOYU(FM) Koyukuk, AK
*KOZB(FM) Livingston, MT
KOZE-FM Lewiston, ID
KOZI-FM Chelan, WA
*KOZO-FM Branson, MO
KOZT-FM Fort Bragg, CA
KOZX-FM Cabool, MO
KOZY-FM Bridgeport, NE
KOZZ-FM Reno, NV
*KPAC(FM) San Antonio, TX
KPAD(FM) Wheatland, WY
*KPAE-FM Erwinville, LA
KPAK(FM) Alva, OK
KPAN-FM Hereford, TX
*KPAQ(FM) Plaquemine, LA
KPAS-FM Fabens, TX
KPAT-FM Orcutt, CA
KPAU(FM) Center, CO
KPAW-FM Fort Collins, CO
*KPBB-FM Brownfield, TX
*KPBD(FM) Big Spring, TX
*KPBE-FM Brownwood, TX
*KPBJ(FM) Midland, TX
KPBM-FM McCamey, TX
*KPBN(FM) Freer, TX
KPBQ-FM Pine Bluff, AR
*KPBR(FM) Joliet, MT
*KPBS-FM San Diego, CA
*KPBX-FM Spokane, WA
*KPBZ(FM) Spokane, WA
*KPCC(FM) Pasadena, CA
KPCH(FM) Ruston, LA
*KPCJ(FM) Yankton, SD
KPCL-FM Farmington, NM
*KPCP(FM) New Roads, LA
*KPCR(FM) Burlington, CO
*KPCS(FM) Princeton, CA
*KPCV(FM) Coachella, CA
*KPCW(FM) Park City, UT
KPDA(FM) Gooding, ID
KPDB(FM) Big Lake, TX
*KPDO(FM) Pescadero, CA
KPDQ-FM Portland, OR
*KPDR(FM) Wheeler, TX
KPEK-FM Albuquerque, NM
KPEL-FM Abbeville, LA
KPEN-FM Soldotna, AK
KPER(FM) Hobbs, NM
KPEZ-FM Austin, TX
*KPFA-FM Berkeley, CA
*KPFB-FM Berkeley, CA
*KPFC-FM Callisburg, TX

*KPFK-FM Los Angeles, CA
KPFM-FM Mountain Home, AR
*KPFR(FM) Pine Grove, OR
*KPFT-FM Houston, TX
KPFX(FM) Fargo, ND
*KPFZ-FM Lakeport, CA
*KPGA(FM) Morton, TX
*KPGB(FM) Pryor, MT
KPGG(FM) Ashdown, AR
*KPGR-FM Pleasant Grove, UT
*KPGS(FM) Pagosa Springs, CO
KPHD(FM) Elko, NV
*KPHF-FM Phoenix, AZ
*KPHL(FM) Pahala, HI
KPHR-FM Ortonville, MN
*KPHS-FM Plains, TX
KPHT(FM) Rocky Ford, CO
KPHW(FM) Kaneohe, HI
KPIG-FM Freedom, CA
*KPIJ(FM) Junction City, OR
KPIN-FM Pinedale, WY
KPIO-FM Pleasanton, KS
*KPIP(FM) Mount Pleasant, TX
*KPIT(FM) Pittsburg, TX
*KPJH(FM) Polson, MT
*KPJP-FM Greenville, CA
*KPKJ(FM) Mentmore, NM
KPKK(FM) Amargosa Valley, NV
*KPKN(FM) Pitkin, CO
*KPKO(FM) Pecos, TX
*KPKP(FM) Harts Bluff, TX
KPKR(FM) Parker, AZ
KPKX(FM) Phoenix, AZ
KPKY-FM Pocatello, ID
KPLA(FM) Columbia, MO
KPLD(FM) Kanab, UT
*KPLG-FM Plains, MT
*KPLI(FM) Olympia, WA
*KPLK(FM) Manson, WA
KPLM-FM Palm Springs, CA
KPLN(FM) Lockwood, MT
KPLO-FM Reliance, SD
KPLT-FM Paris, TX
*KPLU-FM Tacoma, WA
KPLV-FM Las Vegas, NV
*KPLW-FM Wenatchee, WA
*KPLX(FM) Fort Worth, TX
KPLZ-FM Seattle, WA
*KPMB(FM) Plainview, TX
KPMW-FM Haliimaile, HI
*KPMX(FM) Sterling, CO
*KPMZ(FM) Flower Mound, TX
KPNC(FM) Ponca City, OK
KPND(FM) Sandpoint, ID
*KPNE-FM North Platte, NE
*KPNO-FM Norfolk, NE
KPNT-FM Sainte Genevieve, MO
KPNY-FM Alliance, NE
KPOA-FM Lahaina, HI
KPOC-FM Pocahontas, AR
KPOD-FM Crescent City, CA
KPOI-FM Honolulu, HI
*KPOO-FM San Francisco, CA
*KPOR-FM Emporia, KS
*KPOS(FM) Fouke, AR
KPOW-FM La Monte, MO
*KPPD(FM) Devils Lake, ND
KPPK(FM) Rainier, OR
KPPL(FM) Poplar Bluff, MO
*KPPO(FM) Mapusaga, AS
*KPPR(FM) Williston, ND
KPPT-FM Toledo, OR
KPPV(FM) Prescott Valley, AZ
KPQ-FM Wenatchee, WA
KPQX(FM) Havre, MT
*KPRA-FM Ukiah, CA
KPRB-FM Brush, CO
KPRC-FM Salinas, CA
*KPRD-FM Hays, KS
*KPRE-FM Vail, CO
*KPRF(FM) Amarillo, TX
*KPRG-FM Hagatna, GU
*KPRH-FM Montrose, CO
KPRI(FM) Encinitas, CA
*KPRJ(FM) Jamestown, ND
*KPRN-FM Grand Junction, CO

*KPRQ(FM) Sheridan, WY
KPRR-FM El Paso, TX
*KPRS-FM Kansas City, MO
*KPRU(FM) Delta, CO
KPRV-FM Heavener, OK
KPRW(FM) Perham, MN
*KPRX-FM Bakersfield, CA
KPSA-FM Lordsburg, NM
*KPSC-FM Palm Springs, CA
KPSD-FM Faith, SD
*KPSH(FM) Coachella, CA
KPSI-FM Palm Springs, CA
KPSL-FM Bakersfield, CA
KPSM(FM) Brownwood, TX
KPSO-FM Falfurrias, TX
*KPSS(FM) Broken Bow, NE
*KPSU-FM Goodwell, OK
KPTE-FM Durango, CO
KPTL(FM) Ankeny, IA
KPTT(FM) Denver, CO
KPTX-FM Pecos, TX
KPTY(FM) Winnie, TX
*KPTZ(FM) Port Townsend, WA
*KPUB(FM) Flagstaff, AZ
KPUL(FM) Winterset, IA
KPUR-FM Canyon, TX
KPUS(FM) Gregory, TX
*KPVL(FM) Postville, IA
KPVR(FM) Bowling Green, MO
KPVS-FM Hilo, HI
*KPVU-FM Prairie View, TX
KPVW(FM) Aspen, CO
KPWB-FM Piedmont, MO
KPWR-FM Los Angeles, CA
KPWT(FM) Terrell Hills, TX
KPWW-FM Hooks, TX
KPXI-FM Overton, TX
KPXP(FM) Garapan-Saipan, NP
KPYG(FM) Cayucos, CA
*KPYR(FM) Craig, CO
*KPYU(FM) Sedro-Woolley, WA
KPZA-FM Jal, NM
KPZE-FM Carlsbad, NM
KPZK-FM Cabot, AR
*KQAC(FM) Portland, OR
*KQAI(FM) Roswell, NM
KQAK(FM) Bend, OR
*KQAL(FM) Winona, MN
KQAY-FM Tucumcari, NM
KQAZ(FM) Springerville, AZ
KQBA(FM) Los Alamos, NM
KQBB(FM) Center, TX
KQBK(FM) Booneville, AR
KQBL(FM) Billings, MT
KQBO-FM Rio Grande City, TX
KQBR(FM) Lubbock, TX
KQBU-FM Port Arthur, TX
KQBW(FM) Omaha, NE
KQBZ(FM) Coleman, TX
KQCH(FM) Omaha, NE
KQCL-FM Faribault, MN
KQCM(FM) Joshua Tree, CA
KQCR-FM Parkersburg, IA
KQCS(FM) Bettendorf, IA
KQCV-FM Shawnee, OK
KQDI-FM Great Falls, MT
KQDJ-FM Valley City, ND
*KQDL(FM) The Dalles, OR
KQDR-FM Savoy, TX
KQDS-FM Duluth, MN
KQDY-FM Bismarck, ND
*KQED-FM San Francisco, CA
KQEG-FM La Crescent, MN
*KQEI-FM North Highlands, CA
KQEL-FM Alamogordo, NM
KQEO(FM) Idaho Falls, ID
KQEW-FM Fordyce, AR
KQFC-FM Boise, ID
*KQFE-FM Springfield, OR
*KQFM-FM Hermiston, OR
*KQFR(FM) Rapid City, SD
KQFX-FM Borger, TX
*KQGC(FM) Belen, NM
KQHC-FM Burns, OR
KQHK-FM McCook, NE
KQHN(FM) Waskom, TX

*KQHR(FM) Hood River, OR
KQHT-FM Crookston, MN
KQIB-FM Idabel, OK
KQIC-FM Willmar, MN
KQID-FM Alexandria, LA
KQIK-FM Lakeview, OR
KQIS-FM Basile, LA
KQIZ-FM Amarillo, TX
KQJK(FM) Roseville, CA
KQKI-FM Bayou Vista, LA
KQKK(FM) Walker, MN
*KQKL(FM) Selma, CA
KQKQ-FM Council Bluffs, IA
KQKS-FM Lakewood, CO
KQKY(FM) Kearney, NE
KQLA-FM Ogden, KS
KQLB-FM Los Banos, CA
KQLK(FM) De Ridder, LA
KQLL-FM Owasso, OK
KQLM-FM Odessa, TX
*KQLN(FM) Alamo, NV
KQLP(FM) Gallup, NM
*KQLQ(FM) Columbia, LA
*KQLR(FM) Whitehall, MT
KQLT-FM Casper, WY
*KQLV(FM) Santa Fe, NM
KQLX-FM Lisbon, ND
*KQLZ(FM) Mountain Home, ID
KQMA-FM Phillipsburg, KS
KQMB(FM) Levan, UT
*KQMC(FM) Hawthorne, NV
KQMG-FM Independence, IA
KQMJ(FM) Osceola, AR
*KQMN-FM Thief River Falls, MN
KQMO-FM Shell Knob, MO
KQMQ-FM Honolulu, HI
KQMR(FM) Globe, AZ
KQMT(FM) Denver, CO
KQMV(FM) Bellevue, WA
KQMX(FM) Lost Hills, CA
KQMY(FM) Naches, WA
*KQNC(FM) Quincy, CA
KQNG-FM Lihue, HI
KQNK-FM Norton, KS
KQNO(FM) Coalinga, CA
*KQNV(FM) Fallon, NV
*KQNY(FM) Quincy, CA
*KQOB(FM) Enid, OK
*KQOC(FM) Gleneden Beach, OR
KQOD-FM Stockton, CA
KQOL(FM) Sleepy Hollow, WY
KQOR(FM) Mena, AR
*KQPD(FM) Ardmore, OK
KQPI(FM) Aberdeen, ID
KQPM-FM Ukiah, CA
KQPR-FM Albert Lea, MN
KQPT(FM) Colusa, CA
KQQB-FM Newport, WA
KQQK(FM) Beaumont, TX
KQQL-FM Anoka, MN
KQQX(FM) Hermann, MO
KQRA(FM) Brookline, MO
KQRB(FM) Windom, MN
KQRC-FM Leavenworth, KS
*KQRI(FM) Bosque Farms, NM
KQRK-FM Ronan, MT
KQRN(FM) Mitchell, SD
KQRQ(FM) Rapid City, SD
KQRS-FM Golden Valley, MN
KQRT-FM Las Vegas, NV
KQRV-FM Deer Lodge, MT
KQRX-FM Midland, TX
*KQSC(FM) Santa Barbara, CA
*KQSD-FM Lowry, SD
KQSE-FM Gypsum, CO
KQSI(FM) San Augustine, TX
KQSK(FM) Chadron, NE
KQSM-FM Fayetteville, AR
KQSR(FM) Belleville, IL
KQSS-FM Miami, AZ
KQST-FM Sedona, AZ
KQSW-FM Rock Springs, WY
KQTA(FM) Homedale, ID
KQTH(FM) Tucson, AZ
*KQTM(FM) Rio Rancho, NM
KQTP-FM Saint Marys, KS

KQTY-FM Borger, TX
KQTZ-FM Hobart, OK
KQUL-FM Lake Ozark, MO
KQUR(FM) Laredo, TX
KQUS-FM Hot Springs, AR
*KQVO(FM) Calexico, CA
KQVT-FM Victoria, TX
KQWB-FM Moorhead, MN
KQWC-FM Webster City, IA
*KQWS-FM Omak, WA
KQWY(FM) Lusk, WY
KQXC-FM Wichita Falls, TX
*KQXE(FM) Eastland, TX
KQXL-FM New Roads, LA
KQXR-FM Payette, ID
*KQXS(FM) Stephenville, TX
KQXT-FM San Antonio, TX
KQXX-FM Mission, TX
KQXY-FM Beaumont, TX
KQYB-FM Spring Grove, MN
KQYK(FM) Lake Crystal, MN
KQZB(FM) Troy, ID
KQZQ(FM) Kiowa, KS
KQZR(FM) Hayden, CO
KQZT-FM Covelo, CA
KQZZ-FM Devils Lake, ND
KRAB-FM Green Acres, CA
*KRAF(FM) Fort Stockton, TX
KRAI-FM Craig, CO
KRAJ(FM) Johannesburg, CA
KRAN(FM) Warren AFB, WY
KRAO-FM Colfax, WA
KRAQ(FM) Jackson, MN
*KRAR(FM) Espanola, NM
KRAT-FM Altamont, OR
KRAV-FM Tulsa, OK
*KRAW(FM) Sterling, AK
KRAY-FM Salinas, CA
KRAZ-FM Santa Ynez, CA
KRBB-FM Wichita, KS
*KRBD-FM Ketchikan, AK
KRBE-FM Houston, TX
*KRBG(FM) Hereford, TX
KRBI-FM Saint Peter, MN
KRBL-FM Idalou, TX
*KRBM-FM Pendleton, OR
KRBW-FM Ottawa, KS
*KRBY(FM) Ruby, AK
KRBZ(FM) Kansas City, MO
*KRCB-FM Santa Rosa, CA
KRCC-FM Colorado Springs, CO
KRCD(FM) Inglewood, CA
KRCH(FM) Rochester, MN
*KRCI(FM) Pinetop-Lakeside, AZ
KRCK-FM Mecca, CA
*KRCL-FM Salt Lake City, UT
KRCQ-FM Detroit Lakes, MN
KRCS-FM Sturgis, SD
*KRCU(FM) Cape Girardeau, MO
KRCV(FM) West Covina, CA
KRCW(FM) Royal City, WA
KRCX-FM Marysville, CA
KRCY-FM Lake Havasu City, AZ
KRDA(FM) Hanford, CA
*KRDC(FM) Many Farms, AZ
KRDE(FM) Globe, AZ
KRDG-FM Shingletown, CA
KRDJ(FM) New Iberia, LA
KRDO-FM Security, CO
KRDQ(FM) Colby, KS
*KRDR-FM Red River, NM
KRDS-FM New Prague, MN
KRDX(FM) Vail, AZ
KREC(FM) Brian Head, UT
KRED-FM Eureka, CA
KREJ-FM Medicine Lodge, KS
KREK-FM Bristow, OK
KREO(FM) Pine Bluffs, WY
KREP-FM Belleville, IL
KRER-FM Hamilton City, CA
KRES-FM Moberly, MO
KREU-FM Roland, OK
KREZ-FM Chaffee, MO
*KRFA-FM Moscow, ID
*KRFC(FM) Fort Collins, CO
KRFD-FM Merino, CO

*KRFG(FM) Glenwood, MN
*KRFH(FM) Marshalltown, IA
*KRFI(FM) Redwood Falls, MN
KRFM-FM Show Low, AZ
*KRFO-FM Owatonna, MN
KRFS-FM Superior, NE
*KRFW(FM) Watertown, SD
KRFX-FM Denver, CO
KRGI-FM Grand Island, NE
*KRGM(FM) Marshall, MN
KRGN-FM Amarillo, TX
*KRGO-FM Alton, IA
KRGT-FM Indian Springs, NV
KRGX(FM) Rio Grande City, TX
KRGY-FM Aurora, NE
*KRHS-FM Overland, MO
KRHV-FM Big Pine, CA
KRIA(FM) Plainview, TX
KRID(FM) Ashton, ID
KRIG-FM Nowata, OK
KRIK(FM) Perry, FL
KRIO-FM Pearsall, TX
KRIT(FM) Parker, AZ
KRJB-FM Ada, MN
KRJC-FM Elko, NV
KRJM(FM) Mahnomen, MN
KRJT(FM) Elgin, OR
KRKA(FM) Erath, LA
KRKC-FM King City, CA
KRKD(FM) Dermott, AR
*KRKH(FM) Wailea-Makena, HI
KRKI(FM) Newcastle, WY
*KRKL(FM) Walla Walla, WA
*KRKM(FM) Breckenridge, CO
KRKN-FM Eldon, MO
KRKP(FM) Leakey, TX
KRKQ(FM) Mountain Village, CO
KRKR(FM) Valley, NE
KRKS-FM Boulder, CO
KRKT-FM Albany, OR
KRKV(FM) Las Animas, CO
KRKX(FM) Billings, MT
KRKY-FM Estes Park, CO
KRKZ-FM Altus, OK
KRLD-FM Dallas, TX
*KRLE(FM) Oberlin, KS
*KRLF(FM) Pullman, WA
*KRLH(FM) Hereford, TX
KRLI-FM Malta Bend, MO
*KRLP(FM) Windom, MN
KRLQ(FM) Hodge, LA
*KRLR(FM) Sulphur, LA
*KRLS(FM) Knoxville, IA
KRLT-FM South Lake Tahoe, CA
*KRLU(FM) Roswell, NM
KRLW-FM Walnut Ridge, AR
*KRLX-FM Northfield, MN
*KRMB-FM Bisbee, AZ
*KRMC-FM Douglas, AZ
KRMD-FM Shreveport, LA
KRMG-FM Sand Springs, OK
*KRMH-FM Red Mesa, AZ
KRMQ-FM Clovis, NM
KRMR-FM Hays, KS
KRNA(FM) Iowa City, IA
KRNB-FM Decatur, TX
*KRNC(FM) Steamboat Springs, CO
*KRNE-FM Merriman, NE
*KRNF(FM) Montezuma, IA
KRNG(FM) Fallon, NV
KRNH(FM) Kerrville, TX
*KRNL(FM) Mount Vernon, IA
*KRNM(FM) Chalan Kanoa-Saipan, NP
KRNN(FM) Juneau, AK
KRNO(FM) Incline Village, NV
KRNP(FM) Sutherland, NE
KRNQ(FM) Keokuk, IA
*KRNR(FM) Butte City, CA
*KRNU-FM Lincoln, NE
KRNV-FM Reno, NV
*KRNW(FM) Chillicothe, MO
KRNY(FM) Kearney, NE
*KROA(FM) Grand Island, NE
KROC-FM Rochester, MN
KROG-FM Grants Pass, OR
*KROH(FM) Port Townsend, WA

KROI(FM) Seabrook, TX
KROK(FM) South Fort Polk, LA
KROM(FM) San Antonio, TX
KROQ-FM Pasadena, CA
KROR(FM) Hastings, NE
*KROU(FM) Spencer, OK
KROW(FM) Lovell, WY
KROX-FM Buda, TX
KROY(FM) Palacios, TX
KRPH(FM) Yarnell, AZ
KRPM(FM) Billings, MT
*KRPR(FM) Rochester, MN
*KRPS-FM Pittsburg, KS
KRPT-FM Devine, TX
KRPX-FM Wellington, UT
KRQB-FM San Jacinto, CA
KRQK-FM Lompoc, CA
KRQN-FM Vinton, IA
KRQQ-FM Tucson, AZ
KRQR-FM Orland, CA
KRQT-FM Castle Rock, WA
KRQU-FM Laramie, WY
KRQX-FM Mexia, TX
*KRQZ(FM) Lompoc, CA
*KRRA(FM) Paragonah, UT
*KRRC-FM Portland, OR
*KRRE(FM) Las Vegas, NM
KRRG-FM Laredo, TX
*KRRK-FM Lake Havasu City, AZ
KRRM-FM Rogue River, OR
KRRN(FM) Kingman, AZ
KRRO-FM Sioux Falls, SD
KRRQ-FM Lafayette, LA
KRRR(FM) Cheyenne, WY
*KRRT(FM) Arroyo Seco, NM
KRRV-FM Alexandria, LA
KRRW(FM) Saint James, MN
KRRX-FM Burney, CA
KRRY(FM) Canton, MO
KRSB-FM Roseburg, OR
*KRSC-FM Claremore, OK
*KRSD(FM) Sioux Falls, SD
KRSE-FM Yakima, WA
*KRSF(FM) Ridgecrest, CA
KRSH(FM) Healdsburg, CA
KRSI-FM Garapan-Saipan, NP
KRSJ-FM Durango, CO
KRSK(FM) Molalla, OR
KRSL-FM Russell, KS
*KRSP-FM Salt Lake City, UT
KRSQ-FM Laurel, MT
KRSR-FM Ingleside, TX
*KRSS(FM) Tarkio, MO
*KRST-FM Albuquerque, NM
*KRSU-FM Appleton, MN
KRSV-FM Afton, WY
*KRSW(FM) Worthington, MN
KRSX-FM Yermo, CA
KRSY-FM La Luz, NM
KRTH-FM Los Angeles, CA
KRTI(FM) Grinnell, IA
*KRTM-FM Temecula, CA
KRTN-FM Raton, NM
KRTO-FM Guadalupe, CA
KRTR-FM Kailua, HI
KRTS(FM) Marfa, TX
*KRTT(FM) Great Bend, KS
*KRTU-FM San Antonio, TX
KRTY-FM Los Gatos, CA
KRTZ-FM Cortez, CO
*KRUA-FM Anchorage, AK
*KRUC-FM Las Cruces, NM
KRUE-FM Waseca, MN
*KRUF-FM Shreveport, LA
*KRUI-FM Iowa City, IA
*KRUK-FM Happy Camp, CA
KRUP-FM Dillingham, AK
*KRUX-FM Las Cruces, NM
KRUZ(FM) Santa Barbara, CA
KRVA-FM Campbell, TX
KRVB(FM) Nampa, ID
KRVC(FM) Hornbrook, CA
KRVE-FM Brusly, LA
KRVF(FM) Kerens, TX
KRVG(FM) Glenwood Springs, CO
*KRVH-FM Rio Vista, CA

KRVK(FM) Vista West, WY
KRVL(FM) Kerrville, TX
*KRVM-FM Eugene, OR
KRVN-FM Lexington, NE
KRVO(FM) Columbia Falls, MT
KRVQ(FM) Victor, ID
KRVR-FM Copperopolis, CA
*KRVS-FM Lafayette, LA
KRVV-FM Bastrop, LA
KRVX(FM) Wimbledon, ND
KRVY-FM Starbuck, MN
*KRWA(FM) Rye, CO
*KRWG-FM Las Cruces, NM
KRWK(FM) Fargo, ND
KRWM-FM Bremerton, WA
KRWN-FM Farmington, NM
KRWP(FM) Stockton, MO
KRWQ-FM Gold Hill, OR
*KRWT(FM) West Laramie, WY
*KRWY(FM) Rawlins, WY
KRXB(FM) Beeville, TX
KRXF(FM) Sunriver, OR
KRXL(FM) Kirksville, MO
KRXO-FM Oklahoma City, OK
KRXP(FM) Pueblo West, CO
KRXQ-FM Sacramento, CA
KRXT-FM Rockdale, TX
KRXV-FM Yermo, CA
*KRXW(FM) Roseau, MN
KRXX-FM Kodiak, AK
KRXY-FM Shelton, WA
*KRYA(FM) Glenoma, WA
KRYD(FM) Norwood, CO
KRYE(FM) Rye, CO
KRYK(FM) Chinook, MT
KRYP(FM) Gladstone, OR
KRYS-FM Corpus Christi, TX
*KRZA-FM Alamosa, CO
KRZK-FM Branson, MO
KRZN(FM) Billings, MT
KRZQ-FM Sparks, NV
KRZR-FM Hanford, CA
KRZS(FM) Hunt, TX
KRZX(FM) Monticello, UT
KRZY-FM Santa Fe, NM
KRZZ(FM) San Francisco, CA
KSAB-FM Robstown, TX
KSAC-FM Dunnigan, CA
KSAG(FM) Pearsall, TX
KSAJ-FM Abilene, KS
*KSAK-FM Walnut, CA
KSAL-FM Salina, KS
KSAM-FM Huntsville, TX
KSAN-FM San Mateo, CA
KSAQ(FM) Charlotte, TX
KSAR(FM) Thayer, MO
KSAS-FM Caldwell, ID
*KSAU(FM) Nacogdoches, TX
KSAY(FM) Fort Bragg, CA
*KSBA-FM Coos Bay, OR
*KSBC(FM) Nile, WA
KSBH(FM) Coushatta, LA
*KSBJ-FM Humble, TX
KSBL-FM Carpinteria, CA
*KSBR-FM Mission Viejo, CA
KSBS-FM Pago Pago, AS
KSBV(FM) Salida, CO
*KSBX(FM) Santa Barbara, CA
KSBZ-FM Sitka, AK
KSCA-FM Glendale, CA
KSCB-FM Liberal, KS
KSCF(FM) San Diego, CA
KSCH-FM Sulphur Springs, TX
*KSCL-FM Shreveport, LA
KSCN(FM) Pittsburg, TX
KSCQ-FM Silver City, NM
KSCR-FM Benson, MN
KSCS-FM Fort Worth, TX
*KSCU-FM Santa Clara, CA
*KSCV(FM) Springfield, MO
KSCY(FM) Four Corners, MT
KSD(FM) Saint Louis, MO
*KSDA-FM Agat, GU
*KSDB-FM Manhattan, KS
*KSDJ-FM Brookings, SD
KSDL-FM Sedalia, MO

KSDM-FM International Falls, MN
KSDN-FM Aberdeen, SD
*KSDQ(FM) Moberly, MO
KSDR-FM Watertown, SD
*KSDS-FM San Diego, CA
KSDZ(FM) Gordon, NE
KSEA(FM) Greenfield, CA
KSEC(FM) Bentonville, AR
KSED-FM Sedona, AZ
*KSEF(FM) Farmington, MO
KSEG-FM Sacramento, CA
KSEH(FM) Brawley, CA
KSEK-FM Girard, KS
KSEL-FM Portales, NM
KSEM-FM Seminole, TX
KSEQ-FM Visalia, CA
*KSER-FM Everett, WA
KSES-FM Seaside, CA
KSEY-FM Seymour, TX
KSEZ-FM Sioux City, IA
*KSFC-FM Spokane, WA
*KSFH-FM Mountain View, CA
KSFI-FM Salt Lake City, UT
KSFM-FM Woodland, CA
*KSFR(FM) White Rock, NM
*KSFS-FM Sioux Falls, SD
KSFT-FM South Sioux City, NE
KSFX(FM) Roswell, NM
KSGC-FM Tusayan, AZ
KSGF-FM Ash Grove, MO
*KSGN-FM Riverside, CA
*KSGR(FM) Portland, TX
*KSGU(FM) Saint George, UT
KSHA-FM Redding, CA
KSHE(FM) Crestwood, MO
*KSHI-FM Zuni, NM
KSHK-FM Kekaha, HI
KSHL-FM Gleneden Beach, OR
KSHN-FM Liberty, TX
KSHR-FM Coquille, OR
*KSHU-FM Huntsville, TX
KSIB-FM Creston, IA
KSID-FM Sidney, NE
*KSIH(FM) Belcourt, ND
KSII-FM El Paso, TX
KSIL(FM) Hurley, NM
KSIQ-FM Brawley, CA
KSIT(FM) Rock Springs, WY
*KSIV-FM Saint Louis, MO
*KSJD-FM Cortez, CO
*KSJE(FM) Farmington, NM
*KSJI(FM) Saint Joseph, MO
KSJJ-FM Redmond, OR
*KSJL(FM) Strasburg, CO
*KSJN-FM Minneapolis, MN
KSJO-FM San Jose, CA
KSJQ(FM) Savannah, MO
*KSJR-FM Collegeville, MN
*KSJS-FM San Jose, CA
KSJT-FM San Angelo, TX
*KSJU(FM) Friday Harbor, WA
*KSJV-FM Fresno, CA
*KSJY(FM) Saint Martinville, LA
KSJZ-FM Jamestown, ND
*KSKA-FM Anchorage, AK
KSKB-FM Brooklyn, IA
*KSKD-FM Livingston, CA
KSKE-FM Vail, CO
*KSKF-FM Klamath Falls, OR
KSKG-FM Salina, KS
*KSKI-FM Sun Valley, ID
KSKK-FM Staples, MN
KSKL-FM Scott City, KS
KSKR-FM Sutherlin, OR
KSKS-FM Fresno, CA
KSKU(FM) Sterling, KS
*KSKX(FM) Chemult, OR
KSKZ(FM) Copeland, KS
*KSLC-FM McMinnville, OR
KSLE(FM) Wewoka, OK
KSL-FM Midvale, UT
KSLG-FM Hydesville, CA
KSLK-FM Visalia, CA
KSLQ-FM Washington, MO
KSLT-FM Spearfish, SD
*KSLU-FM Hammond, LA

KSLV-FM Del Norte, CA
KSLX-FM Scottsdale, AZ
KSLY-FM San Luis Obispo, CA
KSLZ(FM) Saint Louis, MO
KSMA-FM Osage, IA
KSMB-FM Lafayette, LA
*KSMC-FM Moraga, CA
KSMD(FM) Pangburn, AR
KSME(FM) Greeley, CO
*KSMF-FM Ashland, OR
KSMG(FM) Seguin, TX
KSMJ(FM) Shafter, CA
KSML-FM Huntington, TX
KSMM-FM Liberal, KS
*KSMR-FM Winona, MN
*KSMS-FM Point Lookout, MO
KSMT-FM Breckenridge, CO
*KSMU-FM Springfield, MO
*KSMW(FM) West Plains, MO
KSMX-FM Clovis, NM
KSMY(FM) Lompoc, CA
KSMZ(FM) Viola, AR
KSNA(FM) Rexburg, ID
*KSNB(FM) Norton, KS
KSND-FM Monmouth, OR
KSNE-FM Las Vegas, NV
KSNI-FM Santa Maria, CA
KSNN-FM Saint George, UT
KSNO-FM Snowmass Village, CO
KSNP(FM) Burlington, KS
KSNQ(FM) Twin Falls, ID
KSNR-FM Thief River Falls, MN
*KSNS-FM Medicine Lodge, KS
KSNX-FM Show Low, AZ
KSNY-FM Snyder, TX
KSOB(FM) Larned, KS
KSOC(FM) Gainesville, TX
KSOF-FM Dinuba, CA
*KSOH-FM Wapato, WA
KSOK-FM Winfield, KS
KSOL(FM) San Francisco, CA
KSOM(FM) Audubon, IA
KSON(FM) San Diego, CA
KSOO-FM Lennox, SD
KSOP-FM Salt Lake City, UT
KSOQ-FM Escondido, CA
*KSOR-FM Ashland, OR
*KSOS(FM) Las Vegas, NV
KSOU-FM Sioux Center, IA
*KSPB-FM Pebble Beach, CA
*KSPC(FM) Claremont, CA
KSPE-FM Ellwood, CA
KSPI-FM Stillwater, OK
KSPK(FM) Walsenburg, CO
*KSPL-FM Kalispell, MT
*KSPM(FM) Sand Point, AK
KSPN-FM Aspen, CO
KSPO(FM) Dishman, WA
KSPQ-FM West Plains, MO
KSPW(FM) Sparta, MO
KSQB-FM Dell Rapids, SD
KSQL(FM) Santa Cruz, CA
*KSQM(FM) Sequim, WA
KSQQ-FM Morgan Hill, CA
*KSQS(FM) Ririe, ID
KSQX(FM) Springtown, TX
KSQY-FM Deadwood, SD
KSRA-FM Salmon, ID
*KSRC(FM) Loup City, NE
*KSRD(FM) Saint Joseph, MO
KSRF-FM Poipu, HI
*KSRG-FM Ashland, OR
*KSRH-FM San Rafael, CA
*KSRI(FM) Santa Cruz, CA
*KSRJ(FM) Arlington, SD
KSRN(FM) Kings Beach, CA
*KSRQ(FM) Thief River Falls, MN
*KSRS-FM Roseburg, OR
KSRT(FM) Cloverdale, CA
KSRV-FM Ontario, OR
KSRW(FM) Independence, CA
KSRX(FM) Sterling, CO
KSRY(FM) Tehachapi, CA
KSRZ-FM Omaha, NE
KSSA-FM Ingalls, KS
KSSB-FM Calipatria, CA

KSSC(FM) Ventura, CA
KSSD(FM) Fallbrook, CA
KSSE(FM) Arcadia, CA
*KSSH(FM) Shubert, NE
KSSI-FM China Lake, CA
KSSJ-FM Fair Oaks, CA
KSSK-FM Waipahu, HI
KSSM(FM) Copperas Cove, TX
KSSN-FM Little Rock, AR
*KSSO(FM) Norman, OK
KSSS-FM Bismarck, ND
*KSSU-FM Durant, OK
KSSW(FM) Nashville, AR
KSSZ(FM) Fayette, MO
KSTB-FM Crystal Beach, TX
KSTH(FM) Holyoke, CO
*KSTJ(FM) Norfolk, NE
KSTK(FM) Wrangell, AK
*KSTM-FM Indianola, IA
KSTN-FM Stockton, CA
KSTO(FM) Hagatna, GU
KSTP-FM Saint Paul, MN
KSTR-FM Montrose, CO
*KSTT-FM Los Osos-Baywood Park, CA
KSTV-FM Dublin, TX
KSTX(FM) San Antonio, TX
KSTY(FM) Canon City, CO
KSTZ(FM) Des Moines, IA
*KSUA-FM Fairbanks, AK
*KSUI-FM Iowa City, IA
*KSUL(FM) Port Sulphur, LA
KSUP-FM Juneau, AK
*KSUR(FM) Mart, TX
*KSUT-FM Ignacio, CO
*KSUU-FM Cedar City, UT
*KSUW-FM Sheridan, WY
KSUX(FM) Winnebago, NE
KSVL-FM Smith, NV
*KSVR(FM) Mount Vernon, WA
*KSVU(FM) Hamilton, WA
*KSVY(FM) Sonoma, CA
*KSWC-FM Winfield, KS
KSWD(FM) Los Angeles, CA
KSWF(FM) Aurora, MO
KSWG-FM Wickenburg, AZ
*KSWH-FM Arkadelphia, AR
KSWI(FM) Atlantic, IA
KSWN-FM McCook, NE
*KSWP-FM Lufkin, TX
*KSWS(FM) Chehalis, WA
KSWW-FM Montesano, WA
KSXY(FM) Calistoga, CA
KSYC-FM Yreka, CA
*KSYD(FM) Reedsport, OR
*KSYE(FM) Frederick, OK
*KSYM-FM San Antonio, TX
KSYN-FM Joplin, MO
KSYR(FM) Benton, LA
KSYU-FM Corrales, NM
KSYV-FM Solvang, CA
KSYY(FM) Ingram, TX
KSYZ-FM Grand Island, NE
KSZR(FM) Oro Valley, AZ
*KTAA(FM) Big Sandy, TX
KTAC-FM Ephrata, WA
*KTAD(FM) Sterling, CO
KTAG-FM Cody, WY
*KTAI-FM Kingsville, TX
KTAK-FM Riverton, WY
KTAL-FM Texarkana, TX
KTAO-FM Taos, NM
KTAR-FM Glendale, AZ
*KTAW(FM) Walsenburg, CO
KTBB-FM Tyler, TX
*KTBG(FM) Warrensburg, MO
KTBH-FM Kurtistown, HI
*KTBJ(FM) Festus, MO
KTBQ(FM) Nacogdoches, TX
KTBT(FM) Broken Arrow, OK
KTBX(FM) Tubac, AZ
KTBZ-FM Houston, TX
*KTCB(FM) Tillamook, OR
*KTCC-FM Colby, KS
KTCE-FM Payson, UT
*KTCF(FM) Dolores, CO
KTCL(FM) Wheat Ridge, CO

KTCO-FM Duluth, MN
KTCS-FM Fort Smith, AR
*KTCU-FM Fort Worth, TX
*KTCV-FM Kennewick, WA
KTCX-FM Beaumont, TX
KTCY(FM) Azle, TX
KTCZ-FM Minneapolis, MN
*KTDA(FM) Dalhart, TX
*KTDB-FM Ramah, NM
KTDE(FM) Gualala, CA
KTDK(FM) Sanger, TX
*KTDL(FM) Trinidad, CO
KTDR-FM Del Rio, TX
*KTDU(FM) Durango, CO
*KTDV(FM) State Center, IA
*KTDX(FM) Laramie, WY
*KTDY-FM Lafayette, LA
KTDZ(FM) College, AK
*KTEA(FM) Cambria, CA
*KTEC-FM Klamath Falls, OR
*KTED(FM) Evansville, WY
KTEE-FM North Bend, OR
*KTEG-FM Santa Fe, NM
*KTEI(FM) Placerville, CO
*KTEP-FM El Paso, TX
*KTER(FM) Rudolph, TX
KTEX-FM Mercedes, TX
*KTEZ-FM Zwolle, LA
KTFC-FM Sioux City, IA
KTFG-FM Sioux Rapids, IA
KTFM(FM) Floresville, TX
KTFR-FM Chelsea, OK
KTFW-FM Glen Rose, TX
KTFX-FM Warner, OK
*KTFY(FM) Buhl, ID
KTGA(FM) Saratoga, WY
KTGL-FM Beatrice, NE
*KTGS(FM) Tishomingo, OK
KTGV(FM) Jonesville, LA
*KTGW(FM) Fruitland, NM
KTHC-FM Sidney, MT
*KTHF(FM) Hammon, OK
KTHI(FM) Caldwell, ID
KTHK(FM) Idaho Falls, ID
*KTHL(FM) Altus, OK
*KTHM(FM) Red Bluff, CA
KTHN(FM) La Junta, CO
KTHP-FM Hemphill, TX
KTHQ-FM Eagar, AZ
KTHR(FM) Wichita, KS
KTHS-FM Berryville, AR
KTHT(FM) Cleveland, TX
KTHU(FM) Corning, CA
KTHX-FM Dayton, NV
KTIC-FM West Point, NE
KTIG(FM) Pequot Lakes, MN
KTIJ-FM Elk City, OK
KTIL-FM Tillamook, OR
*KTIS-FM Minneapolis, MN
*KTJC(FM) Kelso, WA
KTJJ-FM Farmington, MO
KTJM-FM Port Arthur, TX
*KTJO-FM Ottawa, KS
KTJZ(FM) Tallulah, LA
KTKB-FM Hagatna, GU
KTKC-FM Springhill, LA
KTKE(FM) Truckee, CA
*KTKL(FM) Stigler, OK
KTKO-FM Beeville, TX
KTKS(FM) Versailles, MO
KTKU-FM Juneau, AK
KTKY-FM Refugio, TX
KTLB-FM Twin Lakes, IA
*KTLC-FM Canon City, CO
*KTLF-FM Colorado Springs, CO
*KTLI(FM) El Dorado, KS
KTLK-FM Minneapolis, MN
*KTLN-FM Thibodaux, LA
KTLO-FM Mountain Home, AR
KTLS-FM Holdenville, OK
*KTLT(FM) Anson, TX
*KTLW-FM Lancaster, CA
*KTLX-FM Columbus, NE
*KTLZ-FM Cuero, TX
KTMC-FM McAlester, OK
KTMG(FM) Prescott, AZ

*KTMH(FM) Colona, CO
*KTMK(FM) Tillamook, OR
*KTML(FM) South Fork, CO
KTMO(FM) New Madrid, MO
KTMQ(FM) Temecula, CA
KTMT-FM Medford, OR
*KTMU(FM) Muenster, TX
KTMX-FM York, NE
*KTNA(FM) Talkeetna, AK
KTNE-FM Alliance, NE
KTNI-FM Strasburg, CO
*KTNR(FM) Kenedy, TX
KTNX(FM) Arcadia, MO
KTNY(FM) Libby, MT
*KTOC-FM Jonesboro, LA
KTOH(FM) Kalaheo, HI
*KTOL(FM) Leadville, CO
KTOM-FM Marina, CA
*KTOO-FM Juneau, AK
KTOR(FM) Westwood, CA
*KTOT(FM) Spearman, TX
KTOY(FM) Texarkana, AR
KTOZ-FM Pleasant Hope, MO
*KTPF(FM) Salida, CO
*KTPH-FM Tonopah, NV
KTPI-FM Mojave, CA
*KTPK-FM Topeka, KS
*KTPL(FM) Pueblo, CO
*KTPM(FM) Falfurrias, TX
KTPO(FM) Kootenai, ID
*KTPR-FM Fort Dodge, IA
*KTPS(FM) Pagosa Springs, CO
*KTPT(FM) Rapid City, SD
KTPZ(FM) Hazelton, ID
KTQM-FM Clovis, NM
*KTQX-FM Bakersfield, CA
KTRA-FM Farmington, NM
KTRI-FM Mansfield, MO
*KTRL(FM) Stephenville, TX
*KTRM-FM Kirksville, MO
KTRN-FM White Hall, AR
KTRQ(FM) Colt, AR
KTRR-FM Loveland, CO
KTRS-FM Casper, WY
KTRT(FM) Winthrop, WA
*KTRU-FM Houston, TX
KTRX(FM) Dickson, OK
KTRZ-FM Riverton, WY
*KTSC-FM Pueblo, CO
*KTSD-FM Reliance, SD
KTSE-FM Patterson, CA
*KTSG(FM) Steamboat Springs, CO
KTSL-FM Medical Lake, WA
KTSM-FM El Paso, TX
KTSO(FM) Glenpool, OK
KTSR(FM) De Quincy, LA
KTST-FM Oklahoma City, OK
*KTSU-FM Houston, TX
*KTSW-FM San Marcos, TX
KTSX(FM) Knox City, TX
*KTSY-FM Caldwell, ID
*KTTA(FM) Jackson, CA
*KTTB(FM) Glencoe, MN
KTTG-FM Mena, AR
KTTI-FM Yuma, AZ
*KTTK(FM) Lebanon, MO
KTTN-FM Trenton, MO
KTTQ(FM) Turkey, TX
KTTR-FM Saint James, MO
KTTS-FM Springfield, MO
*KTTU-FM Brownfield, TX
KTTX-FM Brenham, TX
KTTY(FM) New Boston, TX
KTUF-FM Kirksville, MO
KTUG(FM) Hudson, WY
*KTUH-FM Honolulu, HI
KTUI-FM Sullivan, MO
KTUM(FM) Tatum, NM
KTUN-FM Eagle, CO
*KTUT(FM) Frankfort, SD
KTUX-FM Carthage, TX
KTUZ-FM Okarche, OK
*KTVR-FM La Grande, OR
KTWA-FM Ottumwa, IA
KTWB(FM) Sioux Falls, SD

*KTWD(FM) Wallace, ID
KTWI(FM) Bennington, NE
*KTWL(FM) Hempstead, TX
*KTWP(FM) Twisp, WA
KTWS(FM) Bend, OR
KTWV-FM Los Angeles, CA
*KTWY(FM) Shoshoni, WY
*KTXB-FM Beaumont, TX
KTXC-FM Lamesa, TX
*KTXG(FM) Greenville, TX
*KTXI(FM) Ingram, TX
KTXJ-FM Jasper, TX
*KTXK-FM Texarkana, TX
KTXM-FM Hallettsville, TX
KTXN-FM Victoria, TX
KTXO(FM) Goldsmith, TX
*KTXP(FM) Bushland, TX
KTXR-FM Springfield, MO
*KTXT-FM Lubbock, TX
KTXX(FM) Karnes City, TX
KTXY-FM Jefferson City, MO
*KTYD-FM Santa Barbara, CA
KTYL-FM Tyler, TX
*KTYN(FM) Thayne, WY
*KTYY(FM) Middleton, ID
KTZA(FM) Artesia, NM
KTZR-FM Green Valley, AZ
KTZU(FM) Velva, ND
KTZZ(FM) Conrad, MT
*KUAC-FM Fairbanks, AK
KUAD-FM Windsor, CO
*KUAF-FM Fayetteville, AR
KUAL-FM Brainerd, MN
KUAM-FM Hagatna, GU
*KUAP-FM Pine Bluff, AR
*KUAR-FM Little Rock, AR
KUAT-FM Tucson, AZ
*KUAZ-FM Tucson, AZ
KUBB-FM Mariposa, CA
KUBE-FM Seattle, WA
*KUBJ-FM Brenham, TX
KUBL-FM Salt Lake City, UT
*KUBO-FM Calexico, CA
KUBQ-FM La Grande, OR
*KUBS-FM Newport, WA
*KUBU(FM) Coggon, IA
*KUCA-FM Conway, AR
*KUCB(FM) Unalaska, AK
*KUCC(FM) Clarkston, WA
KUCD(FM) Pearl City, HI
*KUCI-FM Irvine, CA
*KUCR-FM Riverside, CA
*KUCV-FM Lincoln, NE
KUDD(FM) Roy, UT
KUDE(FM) Nephi, UT
*KUDI(FM) Choteau, MT
KUDL-FM Kansas City, KS
*KUDU-FM Tok, AK
KUEL-FM Fort Dodge, IA
*KUER-FM Salt Lake City, UT
*KUFL(FM) Libby, MT
*KUFM-FM Missoula, MT
*KUFN-FM Hamilton, MT
KUFO-FM Portland, OR
*KUFR-FM Salt Lake City, UT
KUFX-FM San Jose, CA
*KUGS-FM Bellingham, WA
*KUHB-FM Saint Paul, AK
*KUHF-FM Houston, TX
KUHI(FM) Haiku, HI
*KUHM-FM Helena, MT
*KUHN(FM) Golden Meadow, LA
KUIC-FM Vacaville, CA
KUJ-FM Burbank, WA
KUJJ(FM) Weston, OR
KUJZ(FM) Creswell, OR
KUKA-FM San Diego, TX
KUKI-FM Ukiah, CA
*KUKL-FM Kalispell, MT
KUKN(FM) Longview, WA
KUKU-FM Willow Springs, MO
KUKY(FM) Wellton, AZ
KULE-FM Ephrata, WA
*KULH(FM) Wheeling, MO
KULL-FM Abilene, TX
*KULM-FM Columbus, TX

KULO(FM) Alexandria, MN
*KULV(FM) Ukiah, CA
KUMA-FM Pendleton, OR
*KUMD-FM Duluth, MN
*KUMM-FM Morris, MN
KUMR(FM) Doolittle, MO
KUMU-FM Honolulu, HI
*KUMX(FM) North Fort Polk, LA
*KUNA-FM La Quinta, CA
*KUNC(FM) Greeley, CO
*KUND-FM Grand Forks, ND
*KUNE(FM) Ottumwa, IA
*KUNI-FM Cedar Falls, IA
*KUNJ(FM) Fairfield, IA
*KUNM-FM Albuquerque, NM
KUNQ(FM) Houston, MO
*KUNR-FM Reno, NV
*KUNV-FM Las Vegas, NV
*KUNY(FM) Mason City, IA
*KUNZ(FM) Ottumwa, IA
*KUOI-FM Moscow, ID
*KUOM-FM Saint Louis Park, MN
KUOO-FM Spirit Lake, IA
*KUOP-FM Stockton, CA
*KUOR-FM Redlands, CA
KUPD-FM Tempe, AZ
KUPH-FM Mountain View, MO
KUPI-FM Idaho Falls, ID
KUPL-FM Portland, OR
*KUPR-FM Alamogordo, NM
*KUPS-FM Tacoma, WA
*KUQL(FM) Wessington Springs, SD
KUQQ-FM Milford, IA
KURB-FM Little Rock, AR
*KURE-FM Ames, IA
KURK(FM) Reno, NV
*KURM-FM Gravette, AR
KURQ(FM) Grover Beach, CA
KURR(FM) Hurricane, UT
KURY-FM Brookings, OR
KUSB(FM) Hazelton, ND
*KUSC-FM Los Angeles, CA
*KUSD-FM Vermillion, SD
*KUSF-FM San Francisco, CA
KUSJ(FM) Harker Heights, TX
*KUSL-FM Richfield, UT
KUSN-FM Dearing, KS
KUSO-FM Albion, NE
*KUSP(FM) Santa Cruz, CA
*KUSQ(FM) Sibley, IA
*KUSR-FM Logan, UT
KUSS(FM) Carlsbad, CA
*KUSU-FM Logan, UT
*KUSW(FM) Flora Vista, NM
KUSZ(FM) Laramie, WY
*KUT-FM Austin, TX
*KUTE-FM Ignacio, CO
*KUTN(FM) Utica, NE
KUTT-FM Fairbury, NE
*KUTX-FM San Angelo, TX
KUUB(FM) Sun Valley, NV
*KUUL(FM) East Moline, IL
KUUR(FM) Carbondale, CO
KUUS(FM) Vaughn, MT
*KUUT(FM) Farmington, NM
KUUU(FM) South Jordan, UT
KUUZ-FM Lake Village, AR
KUVA-FM Uvalde, TX
*KUVO-FM Denver, CO
*KUWA-FM Afton, WY
*KUWC-FM Casper, WY
*KUWD(FM) Sundance, WY
*KUWG-FM Gillette, WY
*KUWI(FM) Rawlins, WY
*KUWJ-FM Jackson, WY
*KUWL-FM Laramie, WY
*KUWN-FM Newcastle, WY
*KUWP-FM Powell, WY
*KUWR-FM Laramie, WY
*KUWS-FM Superior, WI
KUWT-FM Thermopolis, WY
*KUWV-FM Lingle, WY
*KUWX-FM Pinedale, WY
*KUWY(FM) Laramie, WY
*KUWZ-FM Rock Springs, WY

KUYI-FM Hotevilla, AZ
*KUYY(FM) Emmetsburg, IA
KUZN(FM) Centerville, TX
KUZZ-FM Bakersfield, CA
*KVAB(FM) Clarkston, WA
*KVAK-FM Valdez, AK
KVAL(FM) Cal-Nev-Ari, NV
KVAN-FM Pilot Rock, OR
*KVAR(FM) Pine Ridge, SD
KVAS(FM) Ilwaco, WA
KVAY(FM) Lamar, CO
*KVAZ-FM Henryetta, OK
KVBE(FM) Moapa, NV
*KVCF(FM) Freeman, SD
*KVCH(FM) Huron, SD
KVCK-FM Wolf Point, MT
*KVCL-FM Winnfield, LA
*KVCM-FM Helena, MT
*KVCO-FM Concordia, KS
*KVCR-FM San Bernardino, CA
*KVCS(FM) Spring Valley, MN
*KVCX-FM Gregory, SD
*KVCY-FM Fort Scott, KS
*KVDC(FM) Dodge City, KS
*KVDG-FM Midland, TX
*KVDP-FM Dry Prong, LA
KVEG-FM Mesquite, NV
*KVER-FM El Paso, TX
KVET-FM Austin, TX
*KVFG(FM) Victorville, CA
*KVFL(FM) Pierre, SD
*KVFM-FM Beeville, TX
KVFX-FM Logan, UT
*KVGB-FM Great Bend, KS
KVGG(FM) Salome, AZ
KVGO-FM Spring Valley, MN
KVGQ(FM) Snowflake, AZ
KVGS-FM Laughlin, NV
*KVHR(FM) Van Horn, TX
*KVHS(FM) Concord, CA
KVHT-FM Vermillion, SD
*KVHU(FM) Judsonia, AR
KVIB(FM) Sun City West, AZ
KVIC(FM) Victoria, TX
*KVIJ(FM) Tucumcari, NM
*KVIL-FM Highland Park-Dallas, TX
*KVIP-FM Redding, CA
*KVIR(FM) Bullhead City, AZ
*KVIX(FM) Port Angeles, WA
*KVJC(FM) Globe, AZ
*KVJM-FM Hearne, TX
*KVJZ(FM) Vail, CO
KVKI-FM Shreveport, LA
*KVKL(FM) Las Vegas, NV
*KVKR(FM) Pine Ridge, SD
*KVLB(FM) Bend, OR
KVLC(FM) Hatch, NM
*KVLD(FM) Atkins, AR
*KVLE-FM Gunnison, CO
*KVLI-FM Lake Isabella, CA
*KVLK(FM) Socorro, NM
KVLL-FM Wells, TX
*KVLO(FM) Humnoke, AR
*KVLP-FM Tucumcari, NM
*KVLT(FM) Temple, TX
*KVLU-FM Beaumont, TX
KVLV-FM Fallon, NV
*KVLW(FM) Waco, TX
KVLY-FM Edinburg, TX
*KVLZ(FM) Sheridan, WY
KVMA-FM Shreveport, LA
KVMI(FM) Arthur, ND
*KVMN(FM) Cave City, AR
*KVMR(FM) Nevada City, CA
*KVMT-FM Montrose, CO
KVMV-FM McAllen, TX
*KVMX(FM) Bakersfield, CA
KVMZ(FM) Waldo, AR
KVNA-FM Flagstaff, AZ
*KVNE-FM Tyler, TX
*KVNF-FM Paonia, CO
*KVNO(FM) Omaha, NE
KVOB(FM) Lindsborg, KS
*KVOD(FM) Lakewood, CO
KVOE-FM Emporia, KS
*KVOM-FM Morrilton, AR

KVOO-FM Tulsa, OK
KVOU-FM Uvalde, TX
*KVOV(FM) Carbondale, CO
KVOX-FM Moorhead, MN
*KVPI-FM Ville Platte, LA
*KVPR-FM Fresno, CA
KVPW(FM) Kingsburg, CA
*KVRA(FM) Sisters, OR
*KVRD-FM Cottonwood, AZ
*KVRE-FM Hot Springs Village, AR
KVRG(FM) Victor, ID
*KVRH-FM Salida, CO
*KVRK(FM) Sanger, CA
KVRM(FM) Glennallen, AK
KVRO-FM Stillwater, OK
*KVRP-FM Haskell, TX
*KVRS-FM Lawton, OK
*KVRT-FM Victoria, TX
KVRV-FM Monte Rio, CA
KVRW-FM Lawton, OK
*KVRX-FM Austin, TX
*KVRZ(FM) Libby, MT
*KVSC-FM Saint Cloud, MN
*KVSD(FM) Wasta, SD
KVSF-FM Pecos, NM
*KVSP-FM Oklahoma City, OK
KVSS(FM) Lincoln, NE
*KVST(FM) Willis, TX
KVSV-FM Beloit, KS
*KVTI-FM Tacoma, WA
*KVTT-FM Dallas, TX
KVTY-FM Lewiston, ID
*KVUH(FM) Laytonville, CA
KVUU-FM Pueblo, CO
*KVUW(FM) Wendover, NV
*KVVA-FM Apache Junction, AZ
*KVVF(FM) Santa Clara, CA
*KVVP(FM) Leesville, LA
KVVR(FM) Dutton, MT
*KVVS(FM) Rosamond, CA
*KVVZ(FM) San Rafael, CA
KVWC-FM Vernon, TX
*KVWE(FM) Frenchtown, MT
KVWF(FM) Augusta, KS
KVWG-FM Dilley, TX
*KVYB(FM) Santa Barbara, CA
*KVYL(FM) Mohave Valley, AZ
KVYN-FM Saint Helena, CA
KWAK-FM Stuttgart, AR
*KWAN(FM) Oroville, WA
*KWAR(FM) Waverly, IA
KWAV-FM Monterey, CA
KWAW-FM Garapan-Saipan, NP
*KWAX-FM Eugene, OR
KWAY-FM Waverly, IA
KWBF-FM North Little Rock, AR
*KWBI(FM) Great Bend, KS
*KWBU-FM Waco, TX
*KWBX(FM) Salem, OR
*KWBZ(FM) Monroe City, MO
*KWCA(FM) Weaverville, CA
*KWCB(FM) Graford, TX
*KWCD-FM Bisbee, AZ
*KWCF(FM) Sheridan, WY
KWCK-FM Searcy, AR
*KWCL-FM Oak Grove, LA
*KWCO-FM Chickasha, OK
KWCQ(FM) Condon, OR
*KWCR-FM Ogden, UT
*KWCW-FM Walla Walla, WA
KWCX-FM Willcox, AZ
KWDC-FM Coahoma, TX
KWDI(FM) Idalia, CO
*KWDM-FM West Des Moines, IA
KWDN-FM Newell, IA
KWDQ-FM Woodward, OK
KWDR(FM) Royal City, WA
*KWDS(FM) Kettleman City, CA
KWDU(FM) Upton, WY
KWDV(FM) Valier, MT
*KWEH(FM) Weatherford, OK
KWEI-FM Fruitland, ID
KWEN-FM Tulsa, OK
KWES-FM Ruidoso, NM
KWEY-FM Clinton, OK
KWFB(FM) Quanah, TX

*KWFC(FM) Springfield, MO
*KWFH(FM) Parker, AZ
*KWFJ-FM Roy, WA
*KWFL-FM Roswell, NM
KWFR-FM San Angelo, TX
KWFS-FM Wichita Falls, TX
KWFX-FM Woodward, OK
KWGB-FM Colby, KS
KWGL(FM) Ouray, CO
KWGO-FM Burlington, ND
*KWGS-FM Tulsa, OK
*KWGT(FM) Goltry, OK
KWHF(FM) Harrisburg, AR
KWHK(FM) Hutchinson, KS
KWHL-FM Anchorage, AK
KWHO(FM) Cody, WY
KWHQ-FM Kenai, AK
KWHT-FM Pendleton, OR
KWIC-FM Topeka, KS
KWID(FM) Las Vegas, NV
KWIE(FM) Ontario, CA
KWIM-FM Window Rock, AZ
KWIN-FM Lodi, CA
KWIQ-FM Moses Lake, WA
*KWIS(FM) Plummer, ID
*KWIT-FM Sioux City, IA
KWIZ-FM Santa Ana, CA
*KWJC(FM) Liberty, MO
*KWJG(FM) Kasilof, AK
KWJJ-FM Portland, OR
KWJK(FM) Boonville, MO
KWJZ(FM) Seattle, WA
KWKJ(FM) Windsor, MO
KWKK-FM Russellville, AR
*KWKL(FM) Grandfield, OK
KWKM-FM Saint Johns, AZ
KWKQ(FM) Graham, TX
KWKR(FM) Leoti, KS
KWKZ-FM Charleston, MO
*KWLD-FM Plainview, TX
KWLF-FM Fairbanks, AK
*KWLH(FM) Beatty, NV
KWLN(FM) Wilson Creek, WA
KWLR-FM Maumelle, AR
KWLS(FM) Winfield, KS
*KWLT-FM North Crossett, AR
KWLU(FM) Chester, CA
KWLV-FM Many, LA
KWLZ-FM Warm Springs, OR
*KWMB(FM) Fairbanks, AK
*KWMD(FM) Kasilof, AK
KWME-FM Wellington, KS
*KWMR-FM Point Reyes Station, CA
KWMT-FM Tucson, AZ
*KWMU-FM Saint Louis, MO
KWMW-FM Maljamar, NM
KWMX-FM Williams, AZ
KWMY(FM) Park City, MT
KWNA-FM Winnemucca, NV
*KWND-FM Springfield, MO
KWNE-FM Ukiah, CA
KWNG-FM Red Wing, MN
*KWNJ(FM) Bettendorf, IA
*KWNM(FM) Winnemucca, NV
KWNN-FM Turlock, CA
KWNO-FM Rushford, MN
KWNR-FM Henderson, NV
KWNS-FM Winnsboro, TX
KWNZ(FM) Sun Valley, NV
KWOA-FM Worthington, MN
KWOF(FM) Broomfield, CO
*KWOI(FM) Carroll, IA
KWOL-FM Whitefish, MT
KWOW-FM Clifton, TX
KWOX(FM) Woodward, OK
KWOZ-FM Mountain View, AR
KWPK-FM Sisters, OR
*KWPR(FM) Lund, NV
KWPT(FM) Fortuna, CA
KWPZ(FM) Lynden, WA
KWQW(FM) Boone, IA
*KWRB-FM Bisbee, AZ
*KWRC(FM) Hermosa, SD
KWRD-FM Highland Village, TX
KWRF-FM Warren, AR
*KWRI(FM) Bartlesville, OK

KWRK-FM Window Rock, AZ
KWRL-FM La Grande, OR
KWRQ-FM Clifton, AZ
*KWRR-FM Ethete, WY
*KWRV-FM Sun Valley, ID
KWRW-FM Rusk, TX
*KWRX(FM) Redmond, OR
KWSA(FM) Price, UT
*KWSB-FM Gunnison, CO
*KWSC-FM Wayne, NE
*KWSO-FM Warm Springs, OR
*KWSR(FM) Cle Elum, WA
*KWTD(FM) Ridgecrest, CA
KWTG(FM) Amarillo, TX
KWTH(FM) Vidalia, LA
*KWTH(FM) Barstow, CA
*KWTM(FM) June Lake, CA
KWTO-FM Springfield, MO
KWTR-FM Big Lake, TX
*KWTS-FM Canyon, TX
*KWTU(FM) Tulsa, OK
*KWTW(FM) Bishop, CA
KWTX-FM Waco, TX
KWTY-FM Cartago, CA
KWUF-FM Pagosa Springs, CO
KWUP-FM Navasota, TX
*KWUR-FM Clayton, MO
KWUZ(FM) Poncha Springs, CO
*KWVA(FM) Eugene, OR
KWVE(FM) San Clemente, CA
*KWVI-FM Waverly, IA
KWVR-FM Enterprise, OR
KWVV-FM Homer, AK
*KWVZ-FM Florence, OR
*KWWC-FM Columbia, MO
KWWK-FM Rochester, MN
KWWR-FM Mexico, MO
*KWWS-FM Walla Walla, WA
KWWV(FM) Santa Margarita, CA
KWWW-FM Quincy, WA
KWWX(FM) Cashmere, WA
KWWY(FM) Shoshoni, WY
*KWXC(FM) Grove, OK
KWXD-FM Asbury, MO
KWXR(FM) Reliance, WY
KWXX-FM Hilo, HI
KWXY-FM Cathedral City, CA
*KWYA(FM) Astoria, OR
*KWYC(FM) Orchard Valley, WY
KWYD(FM) Parma, ID
KWYE(FM) Fresno, CA
KWYI-FM Kawaihae, HI
KWYK-FM Aztec, NM
KWYL(FM) South Lake Tahoe, CA
KWYN-FM Wynne, AR
*KWYQ(FM) Longview, WA
KWYR-FM Winner, SD
KWYS-FM Island Park, ID
KWYW(FM) Lost Cabin, WY
KWYX(FM) Casper, WY
KWYY(FM) Midwest, WY
KXAA(FM) Cle Elum, WA
KXAC-FM Saint James, MN
KXAL-FM Tatum, TX
KXAZ-FM Page, AZ
KXBA(FM) Nikiski, AK
*KXBC(FM) Garberville, CA
KXBG(FM) Cheyenne, WY
*KXBJ-FM Victoria, TX
KXBL(FM) Henryetta, OK
KXBN(FM) Cedar City, UT
*KXBR(FM) International Falls, MN
KXBT(FM) Dripping Springs, TX
KXBX-FM Lakeport, CA
KXBZ-FM Manhattan, KS
*KXCI-FM Tucson, AZ
KXCL(FM) Westcliffe, CO
*KXCM(FM) Twentynine Palms, CA
*KXCV-FM Maryville, MO
KXDD-FM Yakima, WA
KXDG-FM Webb City, MO
KXDJ(FM) Spearman, TX
KXDL-FM Browerville, MN
KXDR-FM Hamilton, MT
*KXDS(FM) Saint George, UT
KXDZ(FM) Templeton, CA
*KXEI-FM Havre, MT

KXEZ-FM Farmersville, TX
KXFC(FM) Coalgate, OK
KXFE-FM Dumas, AR
*KXFF(FM) Colorado City, AZ
KXFG-FM Sun City, CA
KXFM-FM Santa Maria, CA
*KXFR(FM) Socorro, NM
*KXFT(FM) Manson, IA
KXFX-FM Santa Rosa, CA
*KXGA(FM) Glennallen, AK
KXGE-FM Dubuque, IA
KXGJ-FM Bay City, TX
KXGL(FM) Amarillo, TX
*KXGM-FM Hiawatha, IA
KXGO-FM Arcata, CA
KXGT(FM) Carrington, ND
KXHT-FM Marion, AR
KXIA-FM Marshalltown, IA
KXIO-FM Clarksville, AR
KXIT(FM) Dalhart, TX
KXIX(FM) Bend, OR
*KXJH(FM) Linton, IN
KXJM(FM) Banks, OR
KXJO(FM) Saint Maries, ID
*KXJS(FM) Sutter, CA
KXJW-FM Sinclair, WY
*KXJZ(FM) Sacramento, CA
KXKC(FM) New Iberia, LA
KXKK-FM Park Rapids, MN
KXKL-FM Denver, CO
*KXKM-FM McCarthy, AK
KXKQ-FM Safford, AZ
KXKS-FM Shreveport, LA
KXKT(FM) Glenwood, IA
KXKU-FM Lyons, KS
KXKW(FM) Simmesport, LA
KXKX-FM Knob Noster, MO
KXKZ-FM Ruston, LA
KXLB(FM) Livingston, MT
*KXLC-FM La Crescent, MN
KXLE-FM Ellensburg, WA
KXLG(FM) Milbank, SD
*KXLL(FM) Juneau, AK
KXLM-FM Oxnard, CA
*KXLP-FM Eagle Lake, MN
KXLR-FM Fairbanks, AK
KXLS(FM) Lahoma, OK
KXLT-FM Eagle, ID
*KXLU(FM) Los Angeles, CA
*KXLV(FM) Amarillo, TX
KXLW-FM Houston, AK
KXLY-FM Spokane, WA
KXME(FM) Wellington, TX
KXML(FM) Salmon, ID
KXMO-FM Owensville, MO
*KXMS-FM Joplin, MO
KXMT(FM) Taos, NM
KXMZ(FM) Box Elder, SD
*KXNA(FM) Springdale, AR
KXNC(FM) Ness City, KS
*KXNE-FM Norfolk, NE
KXNM(FM) Encino, NM
KXNP-FM North Platte, NE
KXO-FM El Centro, CA
KXOJ-FM Sapulpa, OK
KXOL-FM Los Angeles, CA
KXOO-FM Elk City, OK
KXOQ-FM Kennett, MO
KXOR-FM Thibodaux, LA
KXOS(FM) Los Angeles, CA
*KXOT(FM) Tacoma, WA
KXOW-FM Eldorado, OK
KXOX-FM Sweetwater, TX
KXPC-FM Lebanon, OR
KXPK-FM Evergreen, CO
*KXPR(FM) Sacramento, CA
KXPT-FM Las Vegas, NV
KXPZ(FM) Las Cruces, NM
KXQL-FM Flandreau, SD
KXRA-FM Alexandria, MN
*KXRD(FM) Victorville, CA
*KXRI(FM) Amarillo, TX
*KXRJ-FM Russellville, AR
KXRK-FM Provo, UT
KXRL(FM) Cherry Valley, AR
KXRQ(FM) Roosevelt, UT

KXRR(FM) Monroe, LA
KXRS(FM) Hemet, CA
*KXRT(FM) Idabel, OK
KXRV(FM) Cannon Ball, ND
KXRX-FM Walla Walla, WA
KXRZ(FM) Alexandria, MN
KXSA-FM Dermott, AR
KXSB-FM Big Bear Lake, CA
*KXSE(FM) Davis, CA
KXSM(FM) Hollister, CA
*KXSR(FM) Groveland, CA
KXSS-FM Amarillo, TX
KXTC-FM Thoreau, NM
KXTE-FM Pahrump, NV
KXTG(FM) Portland, OR
*KXTH(FM) Seminole, OK
KXTN-FM San Antonio, TX
KXTQ-FM Lubbock, TX
KXTS(FM) Geyserville, CA
KXTT(FM) Maricopa, CA
KXTZ-FM Pismo Beach, CA
*KXUA(FM) Fayetteville, AR
*KXUL(FM) Monroe, LA
KXUS-FM Springfield, MO
*KXWA(FM) Loveland, CO
KXWY(FM) Hudson, WY
KXXI-FM Gallup, NM
KXXK(FM) Hoquiam-Aberdeen, WA
*KXXL(FM) Moorcroft, WY
KXXM-FM San Antonio, TX
KXXN-FM Iowa Park, TX
KXXO-FM Olympia, WA
*KXXQ(FM) Milan, NM
KXXR(FM) Minneapolis, MN
KXXS(FM) Elgin, TX
KXXY-FM Oklahoma City, OK
KXXZ-FM Barstow, CA
KXYL-FM Brownwood, TX
KXZK(FM) Vail, AZ
KXZM(FM) Felton, CA
KXZS(FM) Wall, SD
KXZT(FM) Newell, SD
*KYAF(FM) Firebaugh, CA
*KYAH(FM) Manhattan, KS
KYAL-FM Muskogee, OK
*KYAR(FM) Gatesville, TX
KYBA-FM Stewartville, MN
KYBB(FM) Canton, SD
KYBE-FM Frederick, OK
KYBI(FM) Lufkin, TX
*KYBJ-FM Lake Jackson, TX
KYBR-FM Espanola, NM
*KYCC(FM) Stockton, CA
KYCH-FM Portland, OR
*KYCI(FM) Firebaugh, CA
*KYCJ(FM) Camino, CA
KYCK-FM Crookston, MN
*KYCM(FM) Alamogordo, NM
*KYCO(FM) Limon, CO
KYCS(FM) Rock Springs, WY
*KYCT(FM) Ruidoso, NM
*KYCU(FM) Clinton, OK
*KYCV(FM) Lovington, NM
KYDL(FM) Hot Springs, AR
KYDN(FM) Monte Vista, CO
*KYDS(FM) Sacramento, CA
KYDT-FM Sundance, WY
KYEE-FM Alamogordo, NM
KYEL(FM) Danville, AR
KYEN(FM) Severance, CO
KYEZ(FM) Salina, KS
*KYFB(FM) Denison, TX
*KYFG(FM) Omaha, NE
*KYFL-FM Monroe, LA
KYFM-FM Bartlesville, OK
*KYFO-FM Ogden, UT
*KYFP(FM) Palestine, TX
*KYFS(FM) San Antonio, TX
*KYFW-FM Wichita, KS
KYGL-FM Texarkana, AR
KYGO-FM Denver, CO
KYIS(FM) Oklahoma City, OK
KYIX-FM South Oroville, CA
*KYJC(FM) Commerce, TX
KYJK(FM) Missoula, MT
KYKC-FM Byng, OK

KYKD-FM Bethel, AK
*KYKL(FM) Tracy, CA
KYKM-FM Yoakum, TX
KYKR-FM Beaumont, TX
*KYKS(FM) Lufkin, TX
*KYKV(FM) Ellensburg, WA
KYKX-FM Longview, TX
KYKY-FM Saint Louis, MO
KYKZ-FM Lake Charles, LA
KYLA-FM Homer, AK
*KYLC-FM Lake Charles, LA
KYLD-FM San Francisco, CA
*KYLR(FM) Hutto, TX
KYLS-FM Ironton, MO
*KYLV-FM Oklahoma City, OK
KYLZ(FM) Lyman, WY
*KYMC-FM Ballwin, MO
KYME(FM) Rockford, IA
KYMG-FM Anchorage, AK
KYMK-FM Maurice, LA
KYMO-FM East Prairie, MO
*KYMS(FM) Rathdrum, ID
KYMV(FM) Woodruff, UT
KYMX-FM Sacramento, CA
KYNF(FM) Prairie Grove, AR
KYNU(FM) Jamestown, ND
KYNZ(FM) Lone Grove, OK
KYOD(FM) Glendo, WY
KYOE(FM) Point Arena, CA
KYOO-FM Halfway, MO
*KYOR(FM) Newport, OR
KYOT-FM Phoenix, AZ
KYOX(FM) Comanche, TX
KYOY(FM) Kimball, NE
*KYPB(FM) Big Timber, MT
*KYPC(FM) Colstrip, MT
*KYPF(FM) Stanford, MT
*KYPL-FM Yakima, WA
*KYPM(FM) Livingston, MT
*KYPR(FM) Miles City, MT
KYPT(FM) Wamsutter, WY
*KYPW(FM) Wolf Point, MT
KYQQ(FM) Arkansas City, KS
*KYQX(FM) Weatherford, TX
KYRK(FM) Houma, LA
*KYRM(FM) Yuma, AZ
KYRN(FM) Socorro, NM
*KYRQ(FM) Natalia, TX
*KYRS(FM) Medical Lake, WA
KYRT(FM) Mason, TX
*KYRV-FM Concordia, MO
KYRX-FM Marble Hill, MO
KYSC-FM Fairbanks, AK
KYSE(FM) El Paso, TX
KYSF-FM Bonanza, OR
KYSJ(FM) Coos Bay, OR
KYSL-FM Frisco, CO
KYSM-FM Mankato, MN
KYSN-FM East Wenatchee, WA
KYSR-FM Los Angeles, CA
KYSS-FM Missoula, MT
KYTC-FM Northwood, IA
KYTE-FM Newport, OR
KYTI-FM Sheridan, WY
KYTM(FM) Corrigan, TX
KYTS(FM) Ten Sleep, WY
KYTT-FM Coos Bay, OR
KYTZ(FM) Walhalla, ND
KYUN(FM) Hailey, ID
KYUS-FM Miles City, MT
KYVA-FM Churchrock, NM
*KYVT(FM) Yakima, WA
*KYWA(FM) Wichita, KS
*KYWH(FM) Lockwood, MT
KYXK(FM) Gurdon, AR
KYXX(FM) Ozona, TX
KYXY-FM San Diego, CA
KYYA-FM Billings, MT
KYYI-FM Burkburnett, TX
*KYYK(FM) Palestine, TX
KYYT-FM Goldendale, WA
KYYX-FM Minot, ND
KYYY-FM Bismarck, ND
KYYZ-FM Williston, ND
KYZK(FM) Sun Valley, ID
KYZQ(FM) Sulphur Bluff, TX

KYZZ(FM) Salinas, CA
*KZAI(FM) Coolidge, AZ
*KZAL(FM) Manson, WA
KZAM(FM) Pleasant Valley, TX
*KZAN(FM) Hays, KS
KZAP-FM Paradise, CA
*KZAR(FM) Gonzales, TX
*KZAT-FM Belle Plaine, IA
*KZAZ-FM Bellingham, WA
KZBB-FM Poteau, OK
KZBD(FM) Spokane, WA
KZBE-FM Omak, WA
KZBG(FM) Lapwai, ID
*KZBJ(FM) Bay City, TX
KZBK(FM) Brookfield, MO
KZBL-FM Natchitoches, LA
KZBQ(FM) Pocatello, ID
KZBR(FM) La Jara, CO
KZBS(FM) Granite, OK
KZBT(FM) Midland, TX
KZCC(FM) Trinidad, CA
KZCD(FM) Lawton, OK
KZCH(FM) Derby, KS
*KZCL(FM) Logan, UT
KZCR(FM) Fergus Falls, MN
KZCU(FM) Woodward, OK
KZDX-FM Burley, ID
KZDY-FM Cawker City, KS
KZEL(FM) Eugene, OR
KZEN-FM Central City, NE
KZEP-FM San Antonio, TX
*KZET(FM) Cortez, CO
KZEW-FM Wheatland, WY
*KZFL(FM) Glenoma, WA
KZFM(FM) Corpus Christi, TX
KZFN-FM Moscow, ID
*KZFR(FM) Chico, CA
*KZFT(FM) Fannett, TX
KZGL(FM) Flagstaff, AZ
*KZGM(FM) Cabool, MO
KZGZ(FM) Hagatna, GU
KZHD(FM) Lovelock, NV
KZHE-FM Stamps, AR
KZHK-FM Saint George, UT
KZHR(FM) Dayton, WA
KZHT(FM) Salt Lake City, UT
KZIA-FM Cedar Rapids, IA
KZID(FM) Orofino, ID
KZII-FM Lubbock, TX
KZIN-FM Shelby, MT
KZIO-FM Two Harbors, MN
KZIQ-FM Ridgecrest, CA
*KZJB(FM) Pocatello, ID
KZJF(FM) Jefferson City, MO
KZJH-FM Jackson, WY
*KZJK(FM) Saint Louis Park, MN
KZJZ(FM) Saint Regis, MT
KZKE-FM Seligman, AZ
KZKK-FM Huron, SD
*KZKL(FM) Wichita Falls, TX
KZKS(FM) Rifle, CO
KZKX-FM Seward, NE
KZKZ-FM Greenwood, AR
KZLA(FM) Huron, CA
KZLE-FM Batesville, AR
KZLG(FM) Mansura, LA
KZLK-FM Rapid City, SD
*KZLO-FM Kilgore, TX
KZLS(FM) Mustang, OK
KZLT-FM East Grand Forks, MN
*KZLU(FM) Inyokern, CA
*KZLV(FM) Lytle, TX
KZLZ-FM Kearny, AZ
KZMA(FM) Naylor, MO
KZMC(FM) McCook, NE
*KZME(FM) Brightwood, OR
KZMG(FM) New Plymouth, ID
KZMI(FM) Garapan-Saipan, NP
KZMK(FM) Sierra Vista, AZ
KZML(FM) Quincy, WA
KZMN(FM) Kalispell, MT
KZMP-FM Pilot Point, TX
KZMQ(FM) Greybull, WY
KZMT-FM Helena, MT
*KZMU-FM Moab, UT
KZMV(FM) Kremmling, CO

KZMX-FM Hot Springs, SD
KZMY(FM) Bozeman, MT
KZMZ-FM Alexandria, LA
*KZNA-FM Hill City, KS
KZND-FM Houston, AK
*KZNJ(FM) Marion, IA
KZNN-FM Rolla, MO
KZNO(FM) Seymour, TX
KZOH(FM) Heber, AZ
KZOK-FM Seattle, WA
KZON(FM) Phoenix, AZ
KZOQ(FM) Missoula, MT
KZOR-FM Hobbs, NM
KZOZ-FM San Luis Obispo, CA
KZPE-FM Ford City, CA
*KZPI(FM) Deming, NM
KZPK-FM Paynesville, MN
KZPR-FM Minot, ND
KZPS-FM Dallas, TX
KZQD-FM Liberal, KS
KZQL(FM) Mills, WY
KZRB-FM New Boston, TX
KZRC(FM) Bennington, OK
KZRD(FM) Dodge City, KS
*KZRI(FM) Welches, OR
KZRK-FM Canyon, TX
KZRM(FM) Chama, NM
KZRO(FM) Dunsmuir, CA
*KZRP(FM) Hope, ID
KZRQ-FM Mount Vernon, MO
KZRR-FM Albuquerque, NM
KZRS(FM) Great Bend, KS
KZRV(FM) Sartell, MN
KZRX-FM Dickinson, ND
KZRZ(FM) West Monroe, LA
*KZSC-FM Santa Cruz, CA
*KZSD-FM Martin, SD
*KZSE(FM) Rochester, MN
KZSN(FM) Hutchinson, KS
KZSP-FM South Padre Island, TX
KZSQ-FM Sonora, CA
KZSR(FM) Onawa, IA
KZST-FM Santa Rosa, CA
*KZSU-FM Stanford, CA
KZTA-FM Naches, WA
KZTB(FM) Milton-Freewater, OR
*KZTH(FM) Piedmont, OK
KZTK-FM White Oak, TX
*KZTL(FM) Paxton, NE
KZTQ(FM) Carson City, NV
KZUA-FM Holbrook, AZ
KZUH(FM) Minneapolis, KS
KZUL-FM Lake Havasu City, AZ
*KZUM-FM Lincoln, NE
KZUS-FM Highwood, MT
*KZUU-FM Pullman, WA
*KZUW(FM) Reliance, WY
KZWA(FM) Moss Bluff, LA
KZWB-FM Green River, WY
*KZWD(FM) Bennett, CO
KZWF(FM) Patterson, IA
KZWU(FM) Pleasantville, IA
KZWV(FM) Eldon, MO
KZWY-FM Sheridan, WY
KZXK-FM Doney Park, AZ
KZXL(FM) Hudson, TX
KZXQ(FM) Reserve, NM
KZXT-FM Eureka, MT
KZXY-FM Apple Valley, CA
*KZXZ(FM) Wyola, MT
KZYP-FM Pine Bluff, AR
KZYQ-FM Lake Village, AR
KZYR-FM Avon, CO
*KZYX-FM Philo, CA
*KZYZ-FM Willits, CA
KZZA(FM) Muenster, TX
KZZD(FM) Fallon, NV
KZZE-FM Eagle Point, OR
KZZI(FM) Belle Fourche, SD
KZZK-FM New London, MO
KZZL-FM Pullman, WA
KZZO-FM Sacramento, CA
KZZP-FM Mesa, AZ
*KZZQ-FM Coalville, UT
KZZS(FM) Story, WY
KZZT-FM Moberly, MO

KZZU-FM Spokane, WA
KZZX(FM) Alamogordo, NM
KZZY-FM Devils Lake, ND
WAAC(FM) Valdosta, GA
*WAAE-FM New Bern, NC
WAAF(FM) Westborough, MA
WAAG-FM Galesburg, IL
WAAI(FM) Hurlock, MD
*WAAJ-FM Benton, KY
WAAL-FM Binghamton, NY
WAAO-FM Andalusia, AL
WAAW-FM Williston, SC
WAAZ-FM Crestview, FL
WABB-FM Mobile, AL
*WABE-FM Atlanta, GA
WABK-FM Gardiner, ME
WABO-FM Waynesboro, MS
*WABR(FM) Tifton, GA
*WABT(FM) Fairland, IN
WABX-FM Evansville, IN
WABZ(FM) Sherman, IL
WACD-FM Antigo, WI
WACF(FM) Young Harris, GA
*WACG-FM Augusta, GA
WACL-FM Elkton, VA
WACO-FM Waco, TX
WACR-FM Columbus AFB, MS
WADI-FM Corinth, MS
WAEB-FM Allentown, PA
*WAEF-FM Cordele, GA
WAEG-FM Evans, GA
WAEI-FM Bangor, ME
WAEL-FM Maricao, PR
*WAER-FM Syracuse, NY
*WAES-FM Lincolnshire, IL
WAEV-FM Savannah, GA
WAEZ(FM) Greeneville, TN
WAFC-FM Clewiston, FL
WAFD(FM) Webster Springs, WV
*WAFG(FM) Fort Lauderdale, FL
*WAFJ(FM) Belvedere, SC
WAFL-FM Milford, DE
WAFM-FM Amory, MS
WAFN-FM Arab, AL
*WAFR-FM Tupelo, MS
WAFT(FM) Valdosta, GA
WAFX-FM Suffolk, VA
WAFY-FM Middletown, MD
WAFZ-FM Immokalee, FL
WAGF-FM Dothan, AL
WAGH(FM) Smiths, AL
*WAGO-FM Snow Hill, NC
*WAGP-FM Beaufort, SC
WAGR-FM Lexington, MS
WAGX-FM Manchester, OH
WAHR-FM Huntsville, AL
*WAHS-FM Auburn Hills, MI
WAIB-FM Tallahassee, FL
*WAIC-FM Springfield, MA
WAID-FM Clarksdale, MS
*WAIH-FM Potsdam, NY
*WAII-FM Hattiesburg, MS
*WAIJ-FM Grantsville, MD
WAIL-FM Key West, FL
WAIN-FM Columbia, KY
*WAIR(FM) Lake City, MI
WAIV(FM) Cape May, NJ
*WAJC(FM) Zebulon, NC
WAJI-FM Fort Wayne, IN
*WAJJ(FM) McKenzie, TN
WAJK-FM La Salle, IL
WAJM-FM Atlantic City, NJ
WAJQ-FM Alma, GA
WAJR-FM Salem, WV
*WAJS-FM Tupelo, MS
WAJV-FM Brooksville, MS
WAJZ(FM) Voorheesville, NY
WAKB(FM) Waynesboro, GA
WAKD-FM Sheffield, AL
WAKG-FM Danville, VA
WAKH-FM McComb, MS
*WAKJ(FM) De Funiak Springs, FL
*WAKL(FM) Flint, MI
WAKO-FM Lawrenceville, IL
*WAKP(FM) Smithboro, GA
WAKQ-FM Paris, TN

WAKS(FM) Akron, OH
WAKT-FM Callaway, FL
WAKU-FM Crawfordville, FL
WAKW-FM Cincinnati, OH
WAKY(FM) Radcliff, KY
WAKZ(FM) Sharpsville, PA
WALC-FM Charleston, SC
*WALF-FM Alfred, NY
WALI-FM Walterboro, SC
WALK-FM Patchogue, NY
*WALN-FM Carrollton, AL
WALR-FM La Grange, GA
WALS-FM Oglesby, IL
WALV-FM Lakesite, TN
WALX(FM) Orrville, AL
WALY-FM Bellwood, PA
WALZ-FM Machias, ME
*WAMC-FM Albany, NY
*WAMH-FM Amherst, MA
WAMI-FM Opp, AL
*WAMJ(FM) Roswell, GA
*WAMK-FM Kingston, NY
WAMO-FM Beaver Falls, PA
*WAMP-FM Jackson, TN
*WAMQ-FM Great Barrington, MA
WAMR-FM Miami, FL
*WAMU-FM Washington, DC
WAMW-FM Washington, IN
WAMX-FM Milton, WV
WAMZ(FM) Louisville, KY
*WANC-FM Ticonderoga, NY
*WANH(FM) Meredith, NH
*WANM-FM Tallahassee, FL
WANT-FM Lebanon, TN
WANV(FM) Annville, KY
WANY-FM Albany, KY
WAOA-FM Melbourne, FL
WAOL-FM Ripley, OH
WAOQ-FM Brantley, AL
WAOR-FM Niles, MI
WAOX-FM Staunton, IL
*WAOY-FM Gulfport, MS
*WAPB(FM) Madison, FL
WAPD-FM Campbellsville, KY
WAPE-FM Jacksonville, FL
*WAPJ-FM Torrington, CT
WAPL-FM Appleton, WI
*WAPN-FM Holly Hill, FL
WAPO-FM Mount Vernon, IL
WAPR-FM Selma, AL
*WAPS-FM Akron, OH
*WAPX-FM Clarksville, TN
*WAQB-FM Tupelo, MS
WAQE-FM Barron, WI
*WAQG-FM Ozark, AL
*WAQL-FM McComb, MS
*WAQQ(FM) Onsted, MI
*WAQU-FM Selma, AL
*WAQV-FM Crystal River, FL
WAQX-FM Manlius, NY
WAQY-FM Springfield, MA
*WARA(FM) New Washington, IN
*WARC-FM Meadville, PA
*WARG-FM Summit, IL
WARH(FM) Granite City, IL
WARM-FM York, PA
*WARN-FM Culpeper, VA
WARO-FM Naples, FL
WARQ(FM) Columbia, SC
WARU-FM Roann, IN
WARV-FM Petersburg, VA
*WARW(FM) Dorsey, IL
*WARX(FM) Lewiston, ME
*WARY(FM) Valhalla, NY
WASH-FM Washington, DC
WASJ(FM) Panama City Beach, FL
WASK-FM Battle Ground, IN
WASL-FM Dyersburg, TN
*WASM-FM Natchez, MS
*WASU-FM Boone, NC
*WASW-FM Waycross, GA
WATD-FM Marshfield, MA
WATG-FM Trion, GA
*WATI-FM Vincennes, IN
*WATP-FM Laurel, MS
WATQ(FM) Chetek, WI

*WATU-FM Port Gibson, MS
*WATY-FM Folkston, GA
WATZ-FM Alpena, MI
*WAUA-FM Petersburg, WV
WAUH-FM Wautoma, WI
*WAUI-FM Shelby, OH
*WAUM-FM Duck Hill, MS
WAUN-FM Kewaunee, WI
*WAUO-FM Hohenwald, TN
*WAUQ-FM Charles City, VA
*WAUS(FM) Berrien Springs, MI
*WAUT-FM Tullahoma, TN
*WAUV-FM Ripley, OH
*WAUZ-FM Greensburg, IN
WAVA-FM Arlington, VA
WAVC-FM Mio, MI
WAVF(FM) Hanahan, SC
WAVH-FM Daphne, AL
WAVI-FM Oxford, MS
WAVJ-FM Princeton, KY
WAVK(FM) Marathon, FL
WAVM-FM Maynard, MA
WAVR-FM Waverly, NY
WAVT-FM Pottsville, PA
WAVV(FM) Naples Park, FL
WAVW(FM) Stuart, FL
WAWC-FM Syracuse, IN
*WAWF-FM Kankakee, IL
*WAWH-FM Dublin, GA
*WAWI-FM Lawrenceburg, TN
*WAWJ(FM) Marion, IL
*WAWN-FM Franklin, PA
WAWZ(FM) Zarephath, NJ
*WAXG-FM Mt. Sterling, KY
WAXI-FM Rockville, IN
WAXJ-FM Frederiksted, VI
WAXL-FM Santa Claus, IN
WAXM-FM Big Stone Gap, VA
WAXQ-FM New York, NY
*WAXR-FM Geneseo, IL
WAXS-FM Oak Hill, WV
WAXU-FM Troy, AL
WAXX-FM Eau Claire, WI
WAYA(FM) Decatur, TN
WAYB-FM Graysville, TN
WAYC-FM Bedford, PA
WAYD(FM) Auburn, KY
*WAYF(FM) West Palm Beach, FL
*WAYG(FM) Grand Rapids, MI
*WAYH(FM) Harvest, AL
WAYI(FM) Charlestown, IN
*WAYJ-FM Fort Myers, FL
*WAYK-FM Kalamazoo, MI
*WAYL(FM) Saint Augustine, FL
*WAYM(FM) Columbia, TN
*WAYO-FM Benton Harbor, MI
*WAYP(FM) Marianna, FL
WAYQ(FM) Clarksville, TN
*WAYR-FM Brunswick, GA
*WAYT(FM) Thomasville, GA
WAYU(FM) Steele, AL
WAYV(FM) Atlantic City, NJ
*WAYW(FM) New Johnsonville, TN
WAYZ(FM) Hagerstown, MD
WAZA-FM Liberty, MS
*WAZD-FM Savannah, TN
WAZO-FM Southport, NC
*WAZP-FM Cape Charles, VA
*WAZQ(FM) Islamorada, FL
WAZR-FM Woodstock, VA
*WAZU(FM) Peoria, IL
WAZX-FM Cleveland, GA
WAZY-FM Lafayette, IN
*WBAA-FM West Lafayette, IN
WBAB-FM Babylon, NY
WBAD-FM Leland, MS
*WBAI-FM New York, NY
WBAM-FM Montgomery, AL
WBAQ-FM Greenville, MS
WBAR-FM Lake Luzerne, NY
WBAV-FM Gastonia, NC
WBAW-FM Pembroke, GA
WBAZ(FM) Bridgehampton, NY
WBBA-FM Pittsfield, IL
WBBB-FM Raleigh, NC
WBBC-FM Blackstone, VA

WBBE(FM) Heyworth, IL
WBBG(FM) Niles, OH
WBBI(FM) Endwell, NY
WBBK-FM Blakely, GA
WBBL-FM Greenville, MI
WBBM-FM Chicago, IL
WBBN(FM) Taylorsville, MS
WBBO(FM) Bass River Township, NJ
WBBQ-FM Augusta, GA
WBBS-FM Fulton, NY
WBBT-FM Powhatan, VA
WBBV-FM Vicksburg, MS
WBCG(FM) Murdock, FL
WBCH-FM Hastings, MI
WBCI-FM Bath, ME
*WBCJ-FM Spencerville, OH
WBCK-FM Battle Creek, MI
*WBCL-FM Fort Wayne, IN
WBCM(FM) Boyne City, MI
WBCQ-FM Monticello, ME
*WBCR-FM Beloit, WI
WBCT-FM Grand Rapids, MI
WBCV(FM) Wausau, WI
*WBCX(FM) Gainesville, GA
*WBCY-FM Archbold, OH
WBDC(FM) Huntingburg, IN
*WBDG-FM Indianapolis, IN
WBDK-FM Algoma, WI
WBDL-FM Reedsburg, WI
WBDR(FM) Copenhagen, NY
WBDX-FM Trenton, GA
WBEA(FM) Southold, NY
WBEB-FM Philadelphia, PA
WBEC-FM Pittsfield, MA
WBEE-FM Rochester, NY
WBEI(FM) Reform, AL
*WBEL-FM Cairo, IL
WBEN-FM Philadelphia, PA
*WBEQ(FM) Morris, IL
*WBER-FM Rochester, NY
*WBEW(FM) Chesterton, IN
WBEY-FM Crisfield, MD
*WBEZ-FM Chicago, IL
WBFA(FM) Fort Mitchell, AL
WBFB-FM Belfast, ME
WBFG-FM Parker's Crossroads, TN
*WBFH-FM Bloomfield Hills, MI
*WBFI-FM McDaniels, KY
*WBFJ-FM Winston-Salem, NC
WBFM(FM) Sheboygan, WI
*WBFO-FM Buffalo, NY
*WBFR-FM Birmingham, AL
WBFX(FM) Grand Rapids, MI
*WBFY-FM Pinehurst, NC
WBFZ-FM Selma, AL
WBGA(FM) Saint Simons Island, GA
*WBGD-FM Brick Township, NJ
WBGE(FM) Bainbridge, GA
WBGF-FM Belle Glade, FL
WBGG-FM Fort Lauderdale, FL
WBGK(FM) Newport Village, NY
*WBGL-FM Champaign, IL
*WBGM-FM New Berlin, PA
*WBGO-FM Newark, NJ
WBGQ(FM) Bulls Gap, TN
*WBGU-FM Bowling Green, OH
WBGV-FM Marlette, MI
*WBGW-FM Fort Branch, IN
*WBGY-FM Naples, FL
WBHB-FM Waynesboro, PA
WBHC-FM Hampton, SC
WBHD(FM) Olyphant, PA
WBHJ(FM) Midfield, AL
WBHK-FM Warrior, AL
*WBHM-FM Birmingham, AL
WBHQ(FM) Beverly Beach, FL
WBHT-FM Mountain Top, PA
WBHV-FM State College, PA
*WBHW-FM Loogootee, IN
WBHX-FM Tuckerton, NJ
*WBHY-FM Mobile, AL
*WBHZ-FM Elkins, WV
*WBIA-FM Shelbyville, TN
*WBIB-FM Forsyth, GA
*WBIE-FM Delphos, OH
WBIG-FM Washington, DC

WBIK-FM Pleasant City, OH
*WBIM-FM Bridgewater, MA
WBIO(FM) Philpot, KY
*WBIY-FM La Belle, FL
WBIZ-FM Eau Claire, WI
*WBJB-FM Lincroft, NJ
*WBJC-FM Baltimore, MD
*WBJD-FM Atlantic Beach, NC
WBJI-FM Blackduck, MN
*WBJV-FM Steubenville, OH
*WBJW-FM Albion, IL
*WBJY-FM Americus, GA
WBJZ-FM Berlin, WI
*WBKE-FM North Manchester, IN
*WBKG-FM Macon, GA
*WBKL(FM) Clinton, LA
WBKN-FM Brookhaven, MS
WBKR(FM) Owensboro, KY
WBKS(FM) Ironton, OH
WBKT-FM Norwich, NY
*WBKU-FM Ahoskie, NC
*WBKW(FM) Beekman, NY
WBKX(FM) Fredonia, NY
*WBKY(FM) Portage, WI
*WBLD-FM Orchard Lake, MI
WBLE-FM Batesville, MS
WBLH(FM) Black River, NY
*WBLI-FM Patchogue, NY
WBLJ-FM Shamokin, PA
WBLK-FM Depew, NY
WBLM-FM Portland, ME
WBLS-FM New York, NY
*WBLU-FM Grand Rapids, MI
*WBLV-FM Twin Lake, MI
*WBLW(FM) Gaylord, MI
WBLX-FM Mobile, AL
WBLZ(FM) Greenwood, MS
*WBMF-FM Crete, IL
WBMH(FM) Grove Hill, AL
WBMI-FM West Branch, MI
*WBMK-FM Morehead, KY
*WBMR-FM Telford, PA
*WBMT-FM Boxford, MA
*WBMV-FM Mount Vernon, IL
WBMW-FM Ledyard, CT
*WBMX(FM) Boston, MA
WBMZ-FM Metter, GA
*WBNB(FM) Equality, AL
WBNE(FM) Shallotte, NC
*WBNH-FM Pekin, IL
*WBNI-FM Roanoke, IN
*WBNJ(FM) Barnegat, NJ
WBNK(FM) Pine Knoll Shores, NC
WBNN-FM Dillwyn, VA
WBNO-FM Bryan, OH
WBNQ-FM Bloomington, IL
WBNS-FM Columbus, OH
WBNT-FM Oneida, TN
WBNV-FM Barnesville, OH
*WBNY(FM) Buffalo, NY
WBNZ(FM) Beulah, MI
WBOB-FM Enfield, NC
*WBOI(FM) Fort Wayne, IN
WBOJ(FM) Cusseta, GA
WBON(FM) Westhampton, NY
*WBOO(FM) Morganfield, KY
WBOP(FM) Buffalo Gap, VA
WBOQ-FM Gloucester, MA
*WBOR-FM Brunswick, ME
WBOS-FM Brookline, MA
WBOW-FM Terre Haute, IN
WBOX-FM Varnado, LA
WBOZ(FM) Woodbury, TN
WBPC(FM) Ebro, FL
WBPE(FM) Brookston, IN
WBPM-FM Saugerties, NY
*WBPR-FM Worcester, MA
WBPT(FM) Homewood, AL
*WBPW(FM) Presque Isle, ME
WBQB(FM) Fredericksburg, VA
WBQI(FM) Bar Harbor, ME
WBQK(FM) West Point, VA
WBQQ-FM Kennebunk, ME
*WBQW(FM) Kennebunkport, ME
WBQX-FM Thomaston, ME
WBRB-FM Buckhannon, WV

WBRF(FM) Galax, VA
*WBRH-FM Baton Rouge, LA
WBRK-FM Pittsfield, MA
*WBRO(FM) Marengo, IN
*WBRQ(FM) La Grange, GA
WBRR-FM Bradford, PA
*WBRS-FM Waltham, MA
WBRU-FM Providence, RI
WBRV-FM Boonville, NY
WBRW-FM Blacksburg, VA
WBRX(FM) Cresson, PA
*WBSB-FM Anderson, IN
*WBSD(FM) Burlington, WI
*WBSH-FM Hagerstown, IN
*WBSJ-FM Portland, IN
*WBSL-FM Sheffield, MA
WBSN-FM New Orleans, LA
WBSS-FM Mount Union, PA
*WBST-FM Muncie, IN
*WBSU-FM Brockport, NY
*WBSW-FM Marion, IN
WBSX-FM Hazleton, PA
WBSZ(FM) Ashland, WI
*WBTB(FM) Young Harris, GA
WBTF-FM Midway, KY
WBT-FM Chester, SC
WBTG-FM Sheffield, AL
WBTI-FM Lexington, MI
WBTJ(FM) Richmond, VA
WBTN-FM Bennington, VT
WBTO-FM Petersburg, IN
WBTP(FM) Clearwater, FL
WBTQ(FM) Buckhannon, WV
WBTR-FM Carrollton, GA
WBTS-FM Doraville, GA
WBTT(FM) Naples Park, FL
WBTU-FM Kendallville, IN
WBTY-FM Homerville, GA
WBTZ-FM Plattsburgh, NY
WBUF-FM Buffalo, NY
WBUG-FM Fort Plain, NY
WBUK(FM) Ottawa, OH
WBUL-FM Lexington, KY
*WBUQ-FM Bloomsburg, PA
*WBUR-FM Boston, MA
WBUS(FM) Boalsburg, PA
WBUV(FM) Moss Point, MS
*WBUX(FM) Buxton, NC
WBUZ(FM) La Vergne, TN
WBVB-FM Coal Grove, OH
*WBVC-FM Pomfret, CT
WBVD-FM Melbourne, FL
WBVE(FM) Bedford, PA
WBVI-FM Fostoria, OH
*WBVM-FM Tampa, FL
*WBVN-FM Carrier Mills, IL
WBVR-FM Auburn, KY
WBVV(FM) Guntown, MS
WBVX(FM) Carlisle, KY
WBWB-FM Bloomington, IN
*WBWC-FM Berea, OH
WBWI-FM West Bend, WI
WBWN-FM Le Roy, IL
WBWR-FM Hilliard, OH
WBWZ-FM New Paltz, NY
WBXB(FM) Edenton, NC
*WBXE-FM Baxter, TN
*WBXL-FM Baldwinsville, NY
WBXQ(FM) Patton, PA
WBXX(FM) Marshall, MI
WBXY-FM La Crosse, FL
WBOX-FM Varnado, LA
WBYA(FM) Islesboro, ME
WBYB(FM) Portville, NY
WBYG-FM Point Pleasant, WV
*WBYH(FM) Hawley, PA
*WBYK(FM) Kulpmont, PA
WBYL(FM) Salladasburg, PA
WBYN-FM Boyertown, PA
*WBYO(FM) Sellersville, PA
WBYP-FM Belzoni, MS
WBYR-FM Van Wert, OH
WBYT-FM Elkhart, IN
*WBYX-FM Stroudsburg, PA
WBYY-FM Somersworth, NH
WBYZ-FM Baxley, GA
WBZA(FM) Rochester, NY

*WBZC-FM Pemberton, NJ
WBZD-FM Muncy, PA
WBZE-FM Tallahassee, FL
WBZF-FM Hartsville, SC
WBZ-FM Boston, MA
WBZG(FM) Peru, IL
WBZN-FM Old Town, ME
WBZO-FM Bay Shore, NY
WBZT-FM Mauldin, SC
WBZV(FM) Hudson, MI
WBZW-FM Pittsburgh, PA
WBZX(FM) Hancock, NY
WBZY(FM) Bowdon, GA
WBZZ(FM) Malta, NY
WCAA-FM Newark, NJ
WCAD-FM San Juan, PR
*WCAI-FM Woods Hole, MA
*WCAL(FM) California, PA
*WCAN-FM Canajoharie, NY
WCAT-FM Carlisle, PA
WCBC-FM Keyser, WV
*WCBE-FM Columbus, OH
WCBH-FM Casey, IL
WCBJ-FM Campton, KY
WCBK-FM Martinsville, IN
*WCBL-FM Benton, KY
*WCBN-FM Ann Arbor, MI
WCBS-FM New York, NY
*WCBU(FM) Peoria, IL
*WCBW-FM East St. Louis, IL
WCCC-FM Hartford, CT
*WCCE(FM) Buie's Creek, NC
WCCG-FM Hope Mills, NC
*WCCH-FM Holyoke, MA
WCCI-FM Savanna, IL
WCCK-FM Calvert City, KY
WCCL(FM) Central City, PA
*WCCN-FM Neillsville, WI
WCCP-FM Clemson, SC
WCCQ-FM Crest Hill, IL
WCCR-FM Clarion, PA
*WCCT-FM Harwich, MA
*WCCV-FM Cartersville, GA
WCCW-FM Traverse City, MI
*WCCX-FM Waukesha, WI
*WCDA-FM Versailles, KY
*WCDB-FM Albany, NY
WCDD(FM) Canton, IL
WCDG(FM) Moyock, NC
WCDK-FM Cadiz, OH
WCDO-FM Sidney, NY
WCDQ-FM Crawfordsville, IN
*WCDR-FM Cedarville, OH
WCDV-FM Hammond, LA
WCDW(FM) Susquehanna, PA
WCDX-FM Mechanicsville, VA
WCDZ(FM) Dresden, TN
WCEF-FM Ripley, WV
WCEI-FM Easton, MD
*WCEL-FM Plattsburgh, NY
WCEM-FM Cambridge, MD
WCEN-FM Hemlock, MI
WCEZ(FM) Carthage, IL
WCFB-FM Daytona Beach, FL
WCFF-FM Urbana, IL
*WCFG(FM) Springfield, MI
*WCFL-FM Morris, IL
*WCFM-FM Williamstown, MA
WCFS-FM Elmwood Park, IL
WCFW-FM Chippewa Falls, WI
WCFX(FM) Clare, MI
*WCGN(FM) Calhoun, GA
WCGQ-FM Columbus, GA
*WCHC-FM Worcester, MA
*WCHG-FM Hot Springs, VA
WCHH-FM Baltimore, MD
WCHO-FM Washington Court House, OH
WCHR-FM Manahawkin, NJ
*WCHW-FM Bay City, MI
WCHX-FM Lewistown, PA
WCHY(FM) Waunakee, WI
WCHZ-FM Harlem, GA
WCIB-FM Falmouth, MA
*WCIC-FM Pekin, IL
*WCID-FM Friendship, NY

*WCIE(FM) New Port Richey, FL
WCIF-FM Melbourne, FL
WCIG-FM Dallas, PA
*WCIH-FM Elmira, NY
*WCII-FM Spencer, NY
*WCIJ-FM Laporte, PA
*WCIK-FM Bath, NY
WCIL-FM Carbondale, IL
*WCIM(FM) Shenandoah, PA
WCIR-FM Beckley, WV
*WCIT-FM Trout Run, PA
*WCIX(FM) Versailles, IN
*WCIY-FM Canandaigua, NY
WCIZ-FM Watertown, NY
WCJC-FM Van Buren, IN
WCJK(FM) Murfreesboro, TN
*WCJL(FM) Morgantown, IN
WCJM-FM West Point, GA
WCJO-FM Jackson, OH
WCJU-FM Prentiss, MS
WCJX-FM Five Points, FL
WCKC-FM Cadillac, MI
WCKF(FM) Ashland, AL
*WCKJ-FM Saint Johnsbury, VT
WCKK-FM Carthage, MS
WCKM-FM Lake George, NY
WCKQ-FM Campbellsville, KY
WCKR-FM Hornell, NY
WCKS(FM) Fruithurst, AL
*WCKT-FM Lehigh Acres, FL
*WCKU(FM) Clarksburg, WV
WCKX-FM Columbus, OH
WCKY-FM Tiffin, OH
*WCKZ(FM) Orland, IN
WCLC-FM Jamestown, TN
WCLD-FM Cleveland, MS
WCLE-FM Calhoun, TN
*WCLG-FM Morgantown, WV
*WCLH(FM) Wilkes-Barre, PA
*WCLK-FM Atlanta, GA
WCLN-FM Clinton, NC
*WCLQ-FM Wausau, WI
*WCLR(FM) Arlington Heights, IL
WCLS(FM) Spencer, IN
WCLT-FM Newark, OH
*WCLU-FM Munfordville, KY
WCLV(FM) Lorain, OH
*WCLX(FM) Westport, NY
WCLZ-FM Brunswick, ME
*WCMB-FM Oscoda, MI
WCMC-FM Creedmoor, NC
*WCMD-FM Barre, VT
WCMF-FM Rochester, NY
WCMG-FM Latta, SC
*WCMI-FM Catlettsburg, KY
*WCMJ-FM Cambridge, OH
WCMK(FM) Putney, VT
*WCML-FM Alpena, MI
*WCMM-FM Gulliver, MI
WCMN-FM Arecibo, PR
*WCMO-FM Marietta, OH
WCMP-FM Pine City, MN
WCMQ-FM Hialeah, FL
WCMR-FM Bruce, MS
WCMS-FM Hatteras, NC
WCMT-FM South Fulton, TN
*WCMU-FM Mount Pleasant, MI
*WCMW-FM Harbor Springs, MI
WCMZ-FM Sault Ste. Marie, MI
WCNA-FM Potts Camp, MS
WCNB(FM) Lebanon, IN
WCNG-FM Murphy, NC
*WCNI-FM New London, CT
WCNK-FM Key West, FL
*WCNO-FM Palm City, FL
WCNR(FM) Keswick, VA
*WCNV-FM Heathsville, VA
*WCNY-FM Syracuse, NY
*WCOD-FM Hyannis, MA
*WCOE-FM La Porte, IN
*WCOF(FM) Arcade, NY
*WCOG-FM Galeton, PA
WCOH-FM DuBois, PA
WCOL-FM Columbus, OH
*WCOM-FM Belfast, NY
WCON-FM Cornelia, GA

WCOO(FM) Kiawah Island, SC
WCOP(FM) Farmington Township, PA
*WCOQ(FM) Colquitt, GA
WCOS-FM Columbia, SC
*WCOT-FM Jamestown, NY
*WCOU-FM Warsaw, NY
*WCOV-FM Clyde, NY
WCOY(FM) Quincy, IL
*WCOZ(FM) Laceyville, PA
*WCPE-FM Raleigh, NC
*WCPI-FM McMinnville, TN
*WCPN(FM) Cleveland, OH
*WCPQ(FM) Park Forest, IL
WCPR-FM D'Iberville, MS
WCPT-FM Arlington Heights, IL
WCPV-FM Essex, NY
WCPY(FM) De Kalb, IL
WCPZ(FM) Sandusky, OH
WCQL(FM) Queensbury, NY
WCQM-FM Park Falls, WI
*WCQR-FM Kingsport, TN
*WCQS-FM Asheville, NC
WCRB(FM) Lowell, MA
WCRC-FM Effingham, IL
*WCRF-FM Cleveland, OH
*WCRG-FM Williamsport, PA
*WCRH-FM Williamsport, MD
WCRI(FM) Block Island, RI
*WCRJ(FM) Jacksonville, FL
*WCRP(FM) Guayama, PR
WCRQ-FM Dennysville, ME
*WCRT-FM Terre Haute, IN
*WCRX-FM Chicago, IL
WCRZ-FM Flint, MI
*WCSB-FM Cleveland, OH
*WCSF-FM Joliet, IL
*WCSG(FM) Grand Rapids, MI
WCSJ-FM Morris, IL
*WCSK-FM Kingsport, TN
WCSM-FM Celina, OH
WCSN-FM Orange Beach, AL
*WCSO-FM Columbus, MS
*WCSP-FM Washington, DC
WCSR-FM Hillsdale, MI
*WCSU-FM Wilberforce, OH
WCSX-FM Birmingham, MI
WCSY-FM South Haven, MI
WCTB-FM Fairfield, ME
WCTG(FM) Chincoteague, VA
WCTH(FM) Plantation Key, FL
WCTK(FM) New Bedford, MA
WCTL-FM Union City, PA
WCTO-FM Easton, PA
*WCTP(FM) Gagetown, MI
WCTQ(FM) Sarasota, FL
WCTT-FM Corbin, KY
WCTW-FM Catskill, NY
WCTY(FM) Norwich, CT
WCTZ(FM) Stamford, CT
*WCUC-FM Clarion, PA
WCUP(FM) L'Anse, MI
*WCUR-FM West Chester, PA
*WCUW-FM Worcester, MA
WCUZ(FM) Bear Lake, MI
*WCVE-FM Richmond, VA
*WCVF-FM Fredonia, NY
*WCVH(FM) Flemington, NJ
*WCVJ-FM Jefferson, OH
*WCVK(FM) Bowling Green, KY
*WCVM-FM Bronson, MI
*WCVO-FM Gahanna, OH
WCVP-FM Robbinsville, NC
WCVQ-FM Fort Campbell, KY
WCVR-FM Randolph, VT
WCVS-FM Virden, IL
WCVT-FM Stowe, VT
WCVU(FM) Solana, FL
*WCVV-FM Belpre, OH
*WCVY-FM Coventry, RI
*WCVZ-FM South Zanesville, OH
*WCWB(FM) Coldwater, MI
*WCWM-FM Williamsburg, VA
WCWP-FM Brookville, NY
*WCWS(FM) Wooster, OH
*WCWT-FM Centerville, OH

WCWV-FM Summersville, WV
WCXL(FM) Kill Devil Hills, NC
WCXO(FM) Carlyle, IL
WCXR(FM) Lewisburg, PA
WCXT-FM Hartford, MI
WCXU-FM Caribou, ME
WCXV(FM) Van Buren, ME
WCXX-FM Madawaska, ME
WCYE(FM) Three Lakes, WI
*WCYJ-FM Waynesburg, PA
WCYK-FM Staunton, VA
WCYN-FM Cynthiana, KY
WCYO-FM Irvine, KY
WCYQ(FM) Karns, TN
*WCYT-FM Lafayette Township, IN
WCYY-FM Biddeford, ME
WCZE(FM) Harbor Beach, MI
WCZQ-FM Monticello, IL
WCZR(FM) Vero Beach, FL
WCZT(FM) Villas, NJ
WCZW(FM) Charlevoix, MI
WCZX-FM Hyde Park, NY
WCZY-FM Mount Pleasant, MI
WDAC-FM Lancaster, PA
WDAF-FM Liberty, MO
WDAI-FM Pawley's Island, SC
WDAQ(FM) Danbury, CT
WDAR-FM Darlington, SC
WDAS-FM Philadelphia, PA
*WDAV-FM Davidson, NC
WDAY-FM Fargo, ND
*WDBK-FM Blackwood, NJ
*WDBM-FM East Lansing, MI
WDBN-FM Wrightsville, GA
WDBQ-FM Galena, IL
WDBR(FM) Springfield, IL
WDBS(FM) Sutton, WV
WDBT(FM) Headland, AL
*WDBX-FM Carbondale, IL
WDBY(FM) Patterson, NY
*WDCB-FM Glen Ellyn, IL
*WDCC(FM) Sanford, NC
*WDCE-FM Richmond, VA
WDCG-FM Durham, NC
*WDCI-FM Bridgeport, WV
*WDCL-FM Somerset, KY
*WDCV-FM Carlisle, PA
WDCX-FM Buffalo, NY
WDDC-FM Portage, WI
WDDD-FM Johnston City, IL
*WDDH(FM) Saint Marys, PA
WDDJ(FM) Paducah, KY
WDDK-FM Greensboro, GA
*WDDM(FM) Hazlet, NJ
WDDQ-FM Adel, GA
WDDW(FM) Sturtevant, WI
WDEB-FM Jamestown, TN
WDEC-FM Americus, GA
*WDEE-FM Reed City, MI
WDEF-FM Chattanooga, TN
WDEN-FM Macon, GA
WDEO-FM San Carlos Park, FL
*WDEQ-FM De Graff, OH
*WDET-FM Detroit, MI
WDEV-FM Warren, VT
WDEZ-FM Wausau, WI
*WDFB-FM Danville, KY
*WDFH-FM Ossining, NY
WDFM-FM Defiance, OH
WDFX-FM Cleveland, MS
*WDGC-FM Downers Grove, IL
WDGG-FM Ashland, KY
WDGL-FM Baton Rouge, LA
WDGM(FM) Greensboro, AL
WDHA-FM Dover, NJ
WDHC-FM Berkeley Springs, WV
WDHI-FM Delhi, NY
WDHR-FM Pikeville, KY
WDHT(FM) Springfield, OH
WDIC-FM Clinchco, VA
*WDIH-FM Salisbury, MD
WDIN-FM Camuy, PR
*WDIY-FM Allentown, PA
WDJC-FM Birmingham, AL
*WDJM-FM Framingham, MA
WDJQ-FM Alliance, OH

WDJR(FM) Enterprise, AL
*WDJW-FM Somers, CT
WDJX-FM Louisville, KY
WDKB-FM De Kalb, IL
WDKC(FM) Covington, PA
WDKF(FM) Englewood, OH
*WDKL(FM) Grafton, WV
WDKM-FM Adams, WI
WDKR(FM) Maroa, IL
WDKS-FM Newburgh, IN
*WDKV(FM) Fond du Lac, WI
WDKX-FM Rochester, NY
WDKZ(FM) Salisbury, MD
WDLA-FM Walton, NY
WDLD(FM) Halfway, MD
*WDLF(FM) Maynardville, TN
*WDLG(FM) Thomasville, AL
*WDLJ(FM) Breese, IL
*WDLL(FM) Dillon, SC
*WDLM(FM) East Moline, IL
WDLT-FM Chickasaw, AL
WDLZ-FM Murfreesboro, NC
WDME-FM Dover Foxcroft, ME
WDMG-FM Ambrose, GA
WDMK(FM) Detroit, MI
WDML(FM) Woodlawn, IL
WDMO(FM) Durand, WI
WDMP-FM Dodgeville, WI
WDMS-FM Greenville, MS
WDMT(FM) Pittston, PA
WDMX-FM Vienna, WV
*WDMY(FM) Stockbridge, MA
*WDNA-FM Miami, FL
WDNB(FM) Jeffersonville, NY
WDNE-FM Elkins, WV
WDNH-FM Honesdale, PA
*WDNJ(FM) Hopatcong, NJ
WDNL-FM Danville, IL
*WDNR-FM Chester, PA
WDNS(FM) Bowling Green, KY
*WDNX-FM Olive Hill, TN
WDNY-FM Dansville, NY
WDOD-FM Chattanooga, TN
WDOG-FM Allendale, SC
WDOH-FM Delphos, OH
WDOK-FM Cleveland, OH
*WDOM-FM Providence, RI
WDOR-FM Sturgeon Bay, WI
WDOT(FM) Danville, VT
*WDPG-FM Greenville, OH
*WDPR(FM) Dayton, OH
*WDPS-FM Dayton, OH
*WDPW(FM) Greenville, MI
WDQN-FM Du Quoin, IL
WDQX(FM) Morton, IL
WDQZ(FM) Lexington, IL
WDRC-FM Hartford, CT
WDRE(FM) Calverton-Roanoke, NY
WDRK(FM) Cornell, WI
WDRM-FM Decatur, AL
WDRQ(FM) Detroit, MI
WDRR(FM) Martinez, GA
*WDRT(FM) Viroqua, WI
WDRV(FM) Chicago, IL
WDSD(FM) Dover, DE
WDSJ(FM) Greenville, OH
WDSN-FM Reynoldsville, PA
*WDSO(FM) Chesterton, IN
WDST-FM Woodstock, NY
*WDSV(FM) Greenville, MS
WDSW(FM) Westby, WI
WDSY-FM Pittsburgh, PA
WDTL-FM Cleveland, MS
*WDTR(FM) Monroe, MI
WDTW-FM Detroit, MI
WDTX(FM) Rothschild, WI
*WDUB-FM Granville, OH
*WDUK-FM Havana, IL
*WDUQ-FM Pittsburgh, PA
WDUV-FM New Port Richey, FL
WDUX-FM Waupaca, WI
WDUZ-FM Brillion, WI
WDVD(FM) Detroit, MI
WDVE-FM Pittsburgh, PA
WDVH-FM Trenton, FL
WDVI(FM) Rochester, NY

*WDVL(FM) Danville, IN
*WDVR-FM Delaware Township, NJ
WDVT(FM) Rutland, VT
*WDVV-FM Wilmington, NC
WDVW(FM) La Place, LA
*WDVX-FM Clinton, TN
WDWG-FM Rocky Mount, NC
*WDWN(FM) Auburn, NY
*WDXB(FM) Jasper, AL
WDXC-FM Pound, VA
WDXE-FM Lawrenceburg, TN
WDXO-FM Hazlehurst, MS
*WDXQ-FM Cochran, GA
WDXX-FM Selma, AL
*WDYF(FM) Dothan, AL
WDYK-FM Ridgeley, WV
WDYL-FM Chester, VA
*WDYN-FM Chattanooga, TN
WDZN(FM) Romney, WV
WDZQ-FM Decatur, IL
WDZZ-FM Flint, MI
*WEAA(FM) Baltimore, MD
WEAI(FM) Lynnville, IL
WEAM-FM Buena Vista, GA
WEAN-FM Wakefield-Peacedale, RI
WEAS-FM Springfield, GA
WEAT-FM West Palm Beach, FL
*WEAX-FM Angola, IN
*WEAZ(FM) Holly Hill, FL
WEBB-FM Waterville, ME
WEBE-FM Westport, CT
*WEBH(FM) Cuthbert, GA
*WEBK(FM) Society Hill, SC
WEBN(FM) Cincinnati, OH
WEBQ-FM Eldorado, IL
*WEBT-FM Valley, AL
WEBX-FM Tuscola, IL
WEBZ(FM) Mexico Beach, FL
WECB(FM) Seymour, WI
*WECC-FM Folkston, GA
*WECI(FM) Richmond, IN
WECL-FM Elk Mound, WI
WECO-FM Wartburg, TN
WECR-FM Beech Mountain, NC
*WECS-FM Willimantic, CT
*WECW-FM Elmira, NY
WEDB(FM) East Dublin, GA
WEDG-FM Buffalo, NY
WEDJ(FM) Danville, IN
*WEDM-FM Indianapolis, IN
WEDR-FM Miami, FL
*WEDW-FM Stamford, CT
*WEEC-FM Springfield, OH
WEEI-FM Westerly, RI
*WEEM-FM Pendleton, IN
WEEO-FM McConnellsburg, PA
*WEER(FM) Easthampton, Village, NY
WEEY(FM) Springfield, VT
*WEFG-FM Whitehall, MI
*WEFI(FM) Effingham, IL
WEFM(FM) Michigan City, IN
*WEFR-FM Erie, PA
*WEFT-FM Champaign, IL
WEFX-FM Henderson, KY
*WEGB(FM) Napeague, NY
WEGC-FM Sasser, GA
WEGE(FM) Lima, OH
WEGH(FM) Northumberland, PA
WEGI-FM Oak Grove, KY
*WEGL-FM Auburn, AL
WEGM(FM) San German, PR
*WEGN(FM) Kankakee, IL
WEGR(FM) Memphis, TN
*WEGS-FM Milton, FL
WEGT(FM) Lafayette, FL
WEGW-FM Wheeling, WV
WEGX-FM Dillon, SC
*WEGZ(FM) Washburn, WI
*WEHA(FM) Port Republic, NJ
*WEHC-FM Emory, VA
WEHM-FM Southampton, NY
WEHN(FM) East Hampton, NY
WEIB-FM Northampton, MA
WEII(FM) Dennis, MA
*WEIU-FM Charleston, IL

*WEJF-FM Palm Bay, FL
WEJK(FM) Boonville, IN
WEJT-FM Shelbyville, IL
WEJZ(FM) Jacksonville, FL
*WEKF(FM) Corbin, KY
*WEKH-FM Hazard, KY
WEKL(FM) Augusta, GA
WEKS(FM) Zebulon, GA
*WEKU(FM) Richmond, KY
*WEKV(FM) South Webster, OH
WEKX(FM) Jellico, TN
WEKZ-FM Monroe, WI
WELC-FM Welch, WV
WELD-FM Moorefield, WV
*WELH-FM Providence, RI
*WELJ(FM) Brewton, AL
WELK-FM Elkins, WV
*WELL-FM Dadeville, AL
WELR-FM Roanoke, AL
WELS-FM Kinston, NC
WELY-FM Ely, MN
*WEMC(FM) Harrisonburg, VA
WEMI(FM) Appleton, WI
WEMM-FM Huntington, WV
*WEMR(FM) Dushore, PA
*WEMU(FM) Ypsilanti, MI
WEMX-FM Kentwood, LA
*WEMY-FM Green Bay, WI
WEND-FM Salisbury, NC
WENI-FM Big Flats, NY
WENJ-FM Millville, NJ
*WENS(FM) Wadesville, IN
WENY-FM Elmira, NY
WENZ-FM Cleveland, OH
WEOS-FM Geneva, NY
WEOW(FM) Key West, FL
*WEPC-FM Belton, SC
*WEPR-FM Greenville, SC
*WEPS-FM Elgin, IL
*WEQP(FM) Pamplin City, VA
WEQR(FM) Walnut Creek, NC
WEQX-FM Manchester, VT
*WERB-FM Berlin, CT
WERC-FM Hoover, AL
*WERG(FM) Erie, PA
WERH-FM Hamilton, AL
WERK-FM Muncie, IN
*WERN-FM Madison, WI
WERO(FM) Washington, NC
WERQ-FM Baltimore, MD
WERR(FM) Vega Alta, PR
*WERS-FM Boston, MA
*WERU-FM Blue Hill, ME
WERV-FM Aurora, IL
WERX-FM Columbia, NC
WERZ-FM Exeter, NH
WESC-FM Greenville, SC
WESE-FM Baldwyn, MS
*WESM-FM Princess Anne, MD
*WESN-FM Bloomington, IL
WESP-FM Dothan, AL
WESR-FM Onley-Onancock, VA
*WESS-FM East Stroudsburg, PA
*WESU-FM Middletown, CT
*WETA-FM Washington, DC
*WETD-FM Alfred, NY
*WETL-FM South Bend, IN
*WETN-FM Wheaton, IL
*WETS-FM Johnson City, TN
WETZ-FM New Martinsville, WV
*WEUC(FM) Morganfield, KY
*WEUL-FM Kingsford, MI
WEUP-FM Moulton, AL
WEUZ(FM) Minor Hill, TN
*WEVC(FM) Gorham, NH
WEVE-FM Eveleth, MN
WEVH-FM Hanover, NH
WEVI(FM) Frederiksted, VI
*WEVJ(FM) Jackson, NH
*WEVL-FM Memphis, TN
*WEVN-FM Keene, NH
*WEVO-FM Concord, NH
*WEVP(FM) Laporte, PA
WEVR-FM River Falls, WI
*WEVS(FM) Nashua, NH

*WEWH(FM) Washington Court House, OH
WEXC-FM Greenville, PA
WEXP-FM Brandon, VT
WEXT(FM) Amsterdam, NY
WEYE(FM) Surgoinsville, TN
*WEYY(FM) Tallapoosa, GA
WEZB-FM New Orleans, LA
WEZC(FM) Clinton, IL
WEZF-FM Burlington, VT
*WEZG(FM) Tignall, GA
WEZJ-FM Williamsburg, KY
WEZL-FM Charleston, SC
WEZN-FM Bridgeport, CT
WEZQ-FM Bangor, ME
WEZV(FM) North Myrtle Beach, SC
WEZW(FM) Wildwood Crest, NJ
WEZX-FM Scranton, PA
WEZY-FM Racine, WI
*WFAE-FM Charlotte, NC
WFAF(FM) Mount Kisco, NY
*WFAR-FM Danbury, CT
WFAS-FM Bronxville, NY
WFAV(FM) Gilman, IL
WFBC-FM Greenville, SC
WFBE-FM Flint, MI
*WFBF-FM Buffalo, NY
*WFBK(FM) Fort Mill, SC
WFBQ-FM Indianapolis, IN
WFBY(FM) Weston, WV
WFBZ-FM Trempealeau, WI
WFCA-FM Ackerman, MS
WFCC-FM Chatham, MA
*WFCF(FM) Saint Augustine, FL
WFCG(FM) Tylertown, MS
*WFCH-FM Charleston, SC
*WFCI-FM Franklin, IN
WFCJ(FM) Miamisburg, OH
*WFCM-FM Murfreesboro, TN
*WFCO(FM) Lancaster, OH
*WFCR-FM Amherst, MA
*WFCS-FM New Britain, CT
WFCT(FM) Apalachicola, FL
WFCX(FM) Leland, MI
*WFDD-FM Winston-Salem, NC
WFDL-FM Lomira, WI
WFDM(FM) Franklin, IN
WFDR-FM Woodbury, GA
WFDT(FM) Aguada, PR
*WFDU-FM Teaneck, NJ
WFDX(FM) Atlanta, MI
WFDZ(FM) Perry, FL
*WFEN-FM Rockford, IL
WFEX(FM) Peterborough, NH
*WFFC-FM Ferrum, VA
WFFF-FM Columbia, MS
WFFG-FM Corinth, NY
WFFH(FM) Smyrna, TN
WFFI(FM) Kingston Springs, TN
*WFFL(FM) Panama City, FL
*WFFM(FM) Ashburn, GA
WFFN-FM Cordova, AL
WFFY(FM) Destin, FL
WFGA-FM Hicksville, OH
*WFGB-FM Kingston, NY
WFGE(FM) Tyrone, PA
WFGF(FM) Wapakoneta, OH
*WFGH-FM Fort Gay, WV
WFGI-FM Johnstown, PA
WFGM-FM Barrackville, WV
*WFGP(FM) Greene, ME
WFGR-FM Grand Rapids, MI
WFGS(FM) Murray, KY
WFGY-FM Altoona, PA
WFGZ-FM Lobelville, TN
*WFHB-FM Bloomington, IN
*WFHE-FM Hickory, NC
WFHG-FM Abingdon, VA
*WFHL(FM) New Bedford, MA
WFHM-FM Cleveland, OH
WFHN-FM Fairhaven, MA
*WFHU(FM) Henderson, TN
WFIA-FM New Albany, IN
WFID-FM Rio Piedras, PR
*WFIT-FM Melbourne, FL
*WFIU-FM Bloomington, IN

WFIV-FM Loudon, TN
WFIW-FM Fairfield, IL
*WFIX(FM) Florence, AL
WFIZ(FM) Odessa, NY
WFJA-FM Sanford, NC
WFJO-FM Folkston, GA
*WFKL(FM) Fairport, NY
WFKS(FM) Neptune Beach, FL
WFKX(FM) Henderson, TN
WFKY(FM) Frankfort, KY
WFKZ(FM) Plantation Key, FL
WFLA-FM Midway, FL
WFLB-FM Laurinburg, NC
WFLC-FM Miami, FL
WFLE-FM Flemingsburg, KY
WFLF-FM Parker, FL
*WFLJ(FM) Frostproof, FL
WFLK-FM Geneva, NY
WFLM-FM White City, FL
WFLO-FM Farmville, VA
WFLQ(FM) French Lick, IN
WFLS-FM Fredericksburg, VA
WFLY-FM Troy, NY
WFLZ-FM Tampa, FL
WFMB-FM Springfield, IL
*WFME-FM Newark, NJ
WFMF(FM) Baton Rouge, LA
WFMH-FM Hackleburg, AL
WFMI-FM Southern Shores, NC
WFMK(FM) East Lansing, MI
WFML(FM) Vincennes, IN
WFMM-FM Sumrall, MS
WFMN-FM Flora, MS
WFMP(FM) Coon Rapids, MN
*WFMQ-FM Lebanon, TN
*WFMR(FM) Orleans, MA
WFMS-FM Indianapolis, IN
WFMT-FM Chicago, IL
*WFMU-FM East Orange, NJ
WFMV(FM) South Congaree, SC
WFMX-FM Skowhegan, ME
WFMZ(FM) Hertford, NC
WFNK(FM) Lewiston, ME
*WFNM-FM Lancaster, PA
*WFNP-FM Rosendale, NY
WFNQ(FM) Nashua, NH
WFNR-FM Christiansburg, VA
WFNX(FM) Lynn, MA
WFOF-FM Covington, IN
WFON(FM) Fond du Lac, WI
*WFOS-FM Chesapeake, VA
*WFOT(FM) Lexington, OH
WFOX-FM Norwalk, CT
*WFPB-FM Falmouth, MA
WFPG-FM Atlantic City, NJ
*WFPK-FM Louisville, KY
*WFPL-FM Louisville, KY
WFPS-FM Freeport, IL
WFQR(FM) Harwich Port, MA
*WFQS-FM Franklin, NC
WFQX-FM Front Royal, VA
WFRB-FM Frostburg, MD
*WFRC-FM Columbus, GA
WFRD(FM) Hanover, NH
WFRE-FM Frederick, MD
*WFRF-FM Monticello, FL
WFRG-FM Utica, NY
*WFRH-FM Kingston, NY
WFRI-FM Winamac, IN
*WFRJ-FM Johnstown, PA
WFRN-FM Elkhart, IN
WFRO-FM Fremont, OH
*WFRP(FM) Americus, GA
WFRQ(FM) Mashpee, MA
WFRR(FM) Walton, IN
*WFRS-FM Smithtown, NY
WFRU(FM) Quincy, FL
*WFRW-FM Webster, NY
WFRY-FM Watertown, NY
*WFSE-FM Edinboro, PA
WFSH-FM Athens, GA
*WFSI-FM Annapolis, MD
*WFSK-FM Nashville, TN
*WFSL(FM) Thomasville, GA
*WFSO(FM) Olivebridge, NY

WFSP-FM Kingwood, WV
*WFSQ-FM Tallahassee, FL
*WFSS-FM Fayetteville, NC
*WFSU-FM Tallahassee, FL
*WFSW-FM Panama City, FL
WFSY-FM Panama City, FL
WFTA-FM Fulton, MS
*WFTE(FM) Mount Cobb, PA
*WFTF(FM) Rutland, VT
*WFTI-FM Saint Petersburg, FL
WFTK(FM) Lebanon, OH
WFTM-FM Maysville, KY
WFTN-FM Franklin, NH
WFTZ-FM Manchester, TN
*WFUM-FM Flint, MI
WFUN-FM Bethalto, IL
WFUR-FM Grand Rapids, MI
*WFUS(FM) Gulfport, FL
*WFUV(FM) New York, NY
*WFUZ(FM) Carbondale, PA
WFVL(FM) Lumberton, NC
WFWI-FM Fort Wayne, IN
*WFWM-FM Frostburg, MD
*WFWO(FM) Medina, NY
*WFWR(FM) Attica, IN
WFXA-FM Augusta, GA
WFXC-FM Durham, NC
WFXD-FM Marquette, MI
WFXE-FM Columbus, GA
*WFXF(FM) Honeoye Falls, NY
WFXH-FM Hilton Head Island, SC
WFXJ-FM North Kingsville, OH
WFXK-FM Tarboro, NC
*WFXM-FM Gordon, GA
WFXN-FM Galion, OH
WFXO(FM) Centre, AL
WFXX-FM Georgiana, AL
*WFYB(FM) Fryeburg, ME
WFYE(FM) Glade Spring, VA
*WFYI-FM Indianapolis, IN
WFYR-FM Elmwood, IL
WFYV-FM Atlantic Beach, FL
WFYX(FM) Walpole, NH
WFYY(FM) Bloomsburg, PA
WGAC-FM Warrenton, GA
*WGAJ-FM Deerfield, MA
*WGAO-FM Franklin, MA
WGAR-FM Cleveland, OH
*WGBE-FM Bryan, OH
WGBF-FM Henderson, KY
WGBG-FM Seaford, DE
*WGBH-FM Boston, MA
WGBJ(FM) Auburn, IN
*WGBK(FM) Glenview, IL
*WGBQ(FM) Lynchburg, TN
WGBT(FM) Eden, NC
*WGCA-FM Quincy, IL
*WGCC-FM Batavia, NY
*WGCF(FM) Paducah, KY
WGCI-FM Chicago, IL
WGCK-FM Coeburn, VA
WGCM-FM Gulfport, MS
*WGCN(FM) Nashville, GA
WGCO-FM Midway, GA
*WGCP(FM) Cadillac, MI
*WGCQ(FM) Hayti, MO
*WGCS(FM) Goshen, IN
*WGCU-FM Fort Myers, FL
WGCY-FM Gibson City, IL
*WGDE-FM Defiance, OH
WGDN-FM Gladwin, MI
WGDQ(FM) Sumrall, MS
*WGDR-FM Plainfield, VT
WGEL-FM Greenville, IL
WGEM-FM Quincy, IL
WGER(FM) Saginaw, MI
*WGES-FM Key Largo, FL
WGFA-FM Watseka, IL
WGFB(FM) Rockton, IL
WGFG-FM Branchville, SC
WGFM(FM) Cheboygan, MI
WGFN(FM) Glen Arbor, MI
*WGFR-FM Glens Falls, NY
WGFX-FM Gallatin, TN
WGGC(FM) Bowling Green, KY
WGGE(FM) Parkersburg, WV

WGGI-FM Benton, PA
*WGGL-FM Houghton, MI
WGGN-FM Castalia, OH
WGGY-FM Scranton, PA
*WGH-FM Newport News, VA
WGHN-FM Grand Haven, MI
*WGHW(FM) Lockwoods Folly Town, NC
*WGIA(FM) Damascus, GA
*WGIB-FM Birmingham, AL
WGIC-FM Cookeville, TN
WGIE(FM) Clarksburg, WV
WGIR-FM Manchester, NH
*WGIW(FM) Pilot Mountain, NC
WGIX-FM Gouverneur, NY
*WGJU(FM) Tawas City, MI
WGKC-FM Mahomet, IL
WGKL-FM Gladstone, MI
*WGKR-FM Grand Gorge, NY
WGKS-FM Paris, KY
*WGKV(FM) Pulaski, NY
WGKX-FM Memphis, TN
WGKY-FM Wickliffe, KY
WGLC-FM Mendota, IL
*WGLE-FM Lima, OH
WGLF(FM) Tallahassee, FL
WGL-FM Huntington, IN
WGLI(FM) Hancock, MI
WGLM-FM Lakeview, MI
WGLO-FM Pekin, IL
WGLQ-FM Escanaba, MI
WGLR-FM Lancaster, WI
*WGLS-FM Glassboro, NJ
*WGLT(FM) Normal, IL
*WGLV-FM Woodstock, VT
WGLX-FM Wisconsin Rapids, WI
*WGLY-FM Bolton, VT
*WGLZ-FM West Liberty, WV
*WGMC(FM) Greece, NY
WGMD-FM Rehoboth Beach, DE
WGMG-FM Crawford, GA
*WGMK-FM Donalsonville, GA
WGMM-FM Corning, NY
WGMO-FM Shell Lake, WI
*WGMR(FM) Effingham, IL
*WGMS(FM) Hagerstown, MD
WGMT-FM Lyndon, VT
WGMX(FM) Marathon, FL
WGMZ-FM Glencoe, AL
WGNA-FM Albany, NY
*WGNB(FM) Zeeland, MI
WGNE-FM Palatka, FL
WGNG-FM Tchula, MS
WGNI-FM Wilmington, NC
*WGNJ(FM) Saint Joseph, IL
*WGNK(FM) Pennsuco, FL
WGNL-FM Greenwood, MS
*WGNN-FM Fisher, IL
*WGNR-FM Anderson, IN
*WGNV(FM) Milladore, WI
WGNX(FM) Colchester, IL
WGNY-FM Newburgh, NY
*WGOD-FM Charlotte Amalie, VI
WGOG-FM Walhalla, SC
*WGOJ(FM) Conneaut, OH
*WGOR(FM) Minerva, NY
*WGOW-FM Soddy-Daisy, TN
*WGPB(FM) Rome, GA
*WGPH(FM) Vidalia, GA
*WGPO(FM) Grand Portage, MN
WGPR-FM Detroit, MI
*WGPS(FM) Elizabeth City, NC
WGQR-FM Elizabethtown, NC
*WGRC-FM Lewisburg, PA
WGRD-FM Grand Rapids, MI
*WGRE-FM Greencastle, IN
WGRF-FM Buffalo, NY
WGRH(FM) Hinckley, MN
WGRK-FM Greensburg, KY
*WGRL-FM Frederic, MI
WGRM-FM Greenwood, MS
WGRQ-FM Colonial Beach, VA
WGRR-FM Hamilton, OH
*WGRS-FM Guilford, CT
WGRT-FM Port Huron, MI
*WGRW-FM Anniston, AL

WGRX(FM) Falmouth, VA
WGRY-FM Grayling, MI
*WGSG-FM Mayo, FL
*WGSK-FM South Kent, CT
*WGSL-FM Loves Park, IL
WGSM(FM) Greensburg, PA
WGSN-FM Newport, TN
WGSP-FM Pageland, SC
WGSQ-FM Cookeville, TN
*WGSS(FM) Copiague, NY
WGSU-FM Geneseo, NY
WGSY-FM Phenix City, AL
WGTD-FM Kenosha, WI
WGTE-FM Toledo, OH
WGTF-FM Dothan, AL
WGTH-FM Richlands, VA
WGTI(FM) Windsor, NC
WGTN-FM Andrews, SC
WGTR-FM Bucksport, SC
*WGTS-FM Takoma Park, MD
*WGTT(FM) Emeralda, FL
WGTX(FM) Truro, MA
WGTY-FM Gettysburg, PA
WGTZ-FM Eaton, OH
*WGUC(FM) Cincinnati, OH
WGUF-FM Marco, FL
*WGUR-FM Milledgeville, GA
*WGUS-FM New Ellenton, SC
*WGVE-FM Gary, IN
WGVS-FM Whitehall, MI
*WGVU-FM Allendale, MI
WGVX(FM) Lakeville, MN
WGVY(FM) Cambridge, MN
WGVZ(FM) Eden Prairie, MN
WGWD-FM Gretna, FL
*WGWG-FM Boiling Springs, NC
*WGWR-FM Liberty, NY
*WGWS(FM) Saint Mary's City, MD
*WGXC(FM) Acra, NY
WGXL-FM Hanover, NH
WGYE(FM) Mannington, WV
WGYI-FM Oil City, PA
*WGYL-FM Vero Beach, FL
WGYY-FM Meadville, PA
WGZB-FM Lanesville, IN
WGZO-FM Parris Island, SC
*WGZR(FM) Bluffton, SC
*WGZS(FM) Cloquet, MN
WGZZ(FM) Dadeville, AL
*WHAA(FM) Adams, WI
*WHAB-FM Acton, MA
*WHAD-FM Delafield, WI
WHAI(FM) Greenfield, MA
WHAJ-FM Bluefield, WV
WHAK-FM Rogers City, MI
WHAL-FM Horn Lake, MS
WHAY-FM Whitley City, KY
WHAZ-FM Hoosick Falls, NY
WHBC-FM Canton, OH
WHBM(FM) Park Falls, WI
*WHBP(FM) Harbor Springs, MI
WHBQ-FM Germantown, TN
WHBR-FM Parkersburg, WV
WHBX(FM) Tallahassee, FL
WHBZ(FM) Sheboygan Falls, WI
*WHCB-FM Bristol, TN
WHCC-FM Ellettsville, IN
*WHCE(FM) Highland Springs, VA
*WHCF(FM) Bangor, ME
*WHCI(FM) Hartford City, IN
*WHCJ-FM Savannah, GA
*WHCL-FM Clinton, NY
*WHCM(FM) Palatine, IL
*WHCN-FM Hartford, CT
*WHCR-FM New York, NY
*WHCY-FM Blairstown, NJ
*WHDD-FM Sharon, CT
WHDG-FM Rhinelander, WI
*WHDI-FM Sister Bay, WI
WHDQ-FM Claremont, NH
WHDR-FM Miami, FL
*WHDX(FM) Buxton, NC
WHDZ(FM) Buxton, NC
WHEB-FM Portsmouth, NH
*WHEM-FM Eau Claire, WI
WHER-FM Heidelberg, MS

WHET(FM) West Frankfort, IL
*WHEY(FM) North Muskegon, MI
WHFB-FM Benton Harbor, MI
*WHFC(FM) Bel Air, MD
WHFD-FM Lawrenceville, VA
*WHFG(FM) Broussard, LA
WHFH-FM Flossmoor, IL
WHFI-FM Lindside, WV
WHFM-FM Southampton, NY
WHFR-FM Dearborn, MI
WHFX-FM Darien, GA
WHGL-FM Canton, PA
*WHGN-FM Crystal River, FL
WHGO(FM) Pascagoula, MS
*WHHB-FM Holliston, MA
WHHD(FM) Clearwater, SC
WHHH-FM Indianapolis, IN
WHHI-FM Highland, WI
WHHL(FM) Jerseyville, IL
WHHM-FM Henderson, TN
*WHHN(FM) Hollidaysburg, PA
WHHR(FM) Vienna, WV
*WHHS-FM Havertown, PA
WHHT(FM) Horse Cave, KY
WHHY-FM Montgomery, AL
WHHZ(FM) Newberry, FL
*WHID-FM Green Bay, WI
*WHIF-FM Palatka, FL
*WHIJ-FM Ocala, FL
*WHIL-FM Mobile, AL
WHIO-FM Piqua, OH
WHIZ-FM Zanesville, OH
*WHJE-FM Carmel, IN
*WHJH(FM) Kincaid, IL
*WHJL(FM) Merrill, WI
*WHJM(FM) Anna, OH
WHJT-FM Clinton, MS
WHJX(FM) Baldwin, FL
WHJY-FM Providence, RI
WHKB(FM) Houghton, MI
*WHKC(FM) Columbus, OH
WHKF(FM) Harrisburg, PA
WHKL-FM Crenshaw, MS
WHKN-FM Millen, GA
WHKO-FM Dayton, OH
WHKR-FM Rockledge, FL
WHKS-FM Port Allegany, PA
*WHKU(FM) Proctorville, OH
*WHKV(FM) Sylvester, GA
WHKX-FM Bluefield, VA
*WHLA-FM La Crosse, WI
WHLC(FM) Highlands, NC
WHLF(FM) South Boston, VA
WHLG(FM) Port St. Lucie, FL
WHLH(FM) Jackson, MS
WHLJ(FM) Statenville, GA
WHLM-FM Berwick, PA
*WHLP(FM) Hanna, IN
WHLW(FM) Luverne, AL
WHLZ(FM) Marion, SC
WHMA-FM Hobson City, AL
*WHMC-FM Conway, SC
WHMD(FM) Hammond, LA
WHME-FM South Bend, IN
*WHMF(FM) Marianna, FL
WHMH-FM Sauk Rapids, MN
WHMI-FM Howell, MI
WHMJ(FM) Franklin, PA
*WHMO(FM) Madison, IN
*WHMR(FM) Ledbetter, KY
WHMS-FM Champaign, IL
*WHMX-FM Lincoln, ME
*WHND-FM Sister Bay, WI
WHNN-FM Bay City, MI
WHOD(FM) Jackson, AL
WHOF-FM North Canton, OH
WHOG-FM Ormond-by-the-Sea, FL
*WHOJ(FM) Terre Haute, IN
WHOK-FM Lancaster, OH
WHOM-FM Mt. Washington, NH
WHOP-FM Hopkinsville, KY
WHOT-FM Youngstown, OH
WHOU-FM Houlton, ME
*WHOV-FM Hampton, VA
WHPA(FM) Gallitzin, PA
*WHPC-FM Garden City, NY

WHPD(FM) Dowagiac, MI
*WHPE-FM High Point, NC
*WHPF(FM) Pittston Farm, ME
*WHPH(FM) Jemison, AL
*WHPI(FM) Glasford, IL
*WHPK-FM Chicago, IL
*WHPL-FM West Lafayette, IN
WHPO-FM Hoopeston, IL
*WHPR(FM) Highland Park, MI
WHPT(FM) Sarasota, FL
WHPZ-FM Bremen, IN
WHQG(FM) Milwaukee, WI
*WHQQ(FM) Neoga, IL
*WHQR(FM) Wilmington, NC
WHQT-FM Coral Gables, FL
*WHQX-FM Cedar Bluff, VA
WHRB-FM Cambridge, MA
WHRK-FM Memphis, TN
WHRL-FM Albany, NY
*WHRM-FM Wausau, WI
*WHRO-FM Norfolk, VA
WHRP-FM Gurley, AL
*WHRQ(FM) Sandusky, OH
*WHRS-FM Cookeville, TN
*WHRV-FM Norfolk, VA
*WHRW-FM Binghamton, NY
*WHSA-FM Brule, WI
WHSB-FM Alpena, MI
*WHSD-FM Hinsdale, IL
WHSM-FM Hayward, WI
*WHSN-FM Bangor, ME
*WHSS-FM Hamilton, OH
*WHST(FM) Tawas City, MI
WHSX-FM Edmonton, KY
WHTA(FM) Hampton, GA
WHTD(FM) Mount Clemens, MI
WHTE-FM Ruckersville, VA
WHTF-FM Havana, FL
WHTG-FM Eatontown, NJ
WHTL-FM Whitehall, WI
WHTO(FM) Iron Mountain, MI
WHTQ-FM Orlando, FL
WHTS(FM) Coopersville, MI
WHTT-FM Buffalo, NY
WHTU(FM) Newton, MS
WHTZ-FM Newark, NJ
WHUD-FM Peekskill, NY
WHUG(FM) Jamestown, NY
WHUR-FM Washington, DC
*WHUS(FM) Storrs, CT
WHVE-FM Russell Springs, KY
*WHVM(FM) Owego, NY
*WHVP-FM Hudson, NY
*WHVT-FM Clyde, PA
*WHVY(FM) Coshocton, OH
*WHWC-FM Menomonie, WI
*WHWE(FM) Howe, IN
*WHWG-FM Trout Lake, MI
WHWK-FM Binghamton, NY
*WHWL-FM Marquette, MI
*WHWN(FM) Painesville, OH
WHWT(FM) New Hope, AL
WHXQ(FM) Scarborough, ME
WHXR(FM) North Windham, ME
WHXT-FM Orangeburg, SC
WHYB-FM Menominee, MI
*WHYC-FM Swanquarter, NC
WHYI-FM Fort Lauderdale, FL
WHYN-FM Springfield, MA
*WHYT(FM) Goodland Township, MI
*WHYY-FM Philadelphia, PA
*WHYZ(FM) Palm Coast, FL
*WHZN(FM) New Whiteland, IN
WHZR-FM Royal Center, IN
WHZT(FM) Seneca, SC
WHZZ-FM Lansing, MI
*WIAA(FM) Interlochen, MI
*WIAB(FM) Mackinaw City, MI
WIAC-FM San Juan, PR
WIAL-FM Eau Claire, WI
WIBA-FM Madison, WI
WIBB-FM Fort Valley, GA
WIBC(FM) Indianapolis, IN
WIBG-FM Avalon, NJ
*WIBI-FM Carlinville, IL
WIBL(FM) Augusta, GA

WIBN-FM Earl Park, IN
WIBQ-FM Paris, IL
WIBT(FM) Shelby, NC
WIBV(FM) Mount Vernon, IL
WIBW-FM Topeka, KS
WIBZ-FM Wedgefield, SC
*WICA(FM) Traverse City, MI
*WICB(FM) Ithaca, NY
WICL(FM) Williamsport, MD
*WICN-FM Worcester, MA
WICO-FM Pocomoke City, MD
*WICR(FM) Indianapolis, IN
*WICV(FM) East Jordan, MI
*WIDA-FM Carolina, PR
WIDI(FM) Quebradillas, PR
WIDL-FM Caro, MI
*WIDR-FM Kalamazoo, MI
WIFC-FM Wausau, WI
WIFE-FM Rushville, IN
*WIFF(FM) Binghamton, NY
*WIFL-FM Inglis, FL
WIFM-FM Elkin, NC
WIFN(FM) Macon, GA
WIFO-FM Jesup, GA
WIFX-FM Jenkins, KY
*WIGH-FM Lexington, TN
WIGL(FM) Saint Matthews, SC
WIGO-FM White Stone, VA
*WIGW(FM) Eustis, FL
WIGY-FM Madison, ME
WIHB-FM Moncks Corner, SC
WIHC-FM Newberry, MI
WIHG(FM) Rockwood, TN
WIHN-FM Normal, IL
*WIHS(FM) Middletown, CT
WIHT(FM) Washington, DC
WIII(FM) Cortland, NY
WIIL-FM Kenosha, WI
WIIS(FM) Key West, FL
*WIIT(FM) Chicago, IL
WIIZ-FM Blackville, SC
WIJV(FM) Harriman, TN
WIKB-FM Iron River, MI
WIKI-FM Carrollton, KY
WIKK-FM Newton, IL
*WIKL(FM) Greencastle, IN
WIKQ(FM) Tusculum, TN
WIKS-FM New Bern, NC
*WIKV(FM) Plymouth, IN
WIKX-FM Charlotte Harbor, FL
WIKY-FM Evansville, IN
WIKZ-FM Chambersburg, PA
WILE-FM Byesville, OH
*WILF(FM) Monroeville, AL
WIL-FM Saint Louis, MO
WILI-FM Willimantic, CT
WILK-FM Avoca, PA
*WILL-FM Urbana, IL
WILN-FM Panama City, FL
WILQ-FM Williamsport, PA
WILT(FM) Wilmington, NC
WILV(FM) Chicago, IL
WILZ-FM Saginaw, MI
WIMC(FM) Crawfordsville, IN
WIMI-FM Ironwood, MI
WIMK-FM Iron Mountain, MI
WIMT(FM) Lima, OH
WIMX-FM Gibsonburg, OH
WIMZ-FM Knoxville, TN
WINC-FM Winchester, VA
WINK-FM Fort Myers, FL
WINL-FM Linden, AL
WINN(FM) Columbus, IN
*WINO(FM) Odessa, NY
WINQ(FM) Winchester, NH
WINX-FM Saint Michaels, MD
WIOA(FM) San Juan, PR
WIOB-FM Mayaguez, PR
WIOC-FM Ponce, PR
WIOG(FM) Bay City, MI
WIOK-FM Falmouth, KY
WIOL(FM) Greenville, GA
WIOP(FM) Isle of Palms, SC
WIOQ-FM Philadelphia, PA
WIOT(FM) Toledo, OH
WIOV-FM Ephrata, PA

WIOX(FM) Roxbury, NY
WIOZ-FM Southern Pines, NC
*WIPA-FM Pittsfield, IL
*WIPR-FM San Juan, PR
*WIQH-FM Concord, MA
WIQO-FM Covington, VA
WIQQ-FM Leland, MS
*WIRC(FM) Ely, MN
*WIRE-FM Lebanon, IN
WIRK-FM West Palm Beach, FL
*WIRN-FM Buhl, MN
*WIRQ-FM Rochester, NY
*WIRR-FM Virginia-Hibbing, MN
WIRX-FM Saint Joseph, MI
*WISE-FM Wise, VA
*WISG(FM) Clifford, IN
WISH-FM Galatia, IL
WISK-FM Americus, GA
WISM-FM Altoona, WI
WIST-FM Thomasville, NC
*WISU-FM Terre Haute, IN
WISX(FM) Philadelphia, PA
*WITC-FM Cazenovia, NY
*WITF-FM Harrisburg, PA
*WITH(FM) Ithaca, NY
WITL-FM Lansing, MI
*WITR-FM Henrietta, NY
*WITT(FM) Zionsville, IN
*WITX-FM Beaver Falls, PA
WITZ-FM Jasper, IN
*WIUJ-FM Charlotte Amalie, VI
*WIUM-FM Macomb, IL
*WIUP-FM Indiana, PA
*WIUS-FM Macomb, IL
*WIUV-FM Castleton, VT
*WIUW-FM Warsaw, IL
WIVA-FM Aguadilla, PR
WIVG(FM) Tunica, MS
*WIVH-FM Christiansted, VI
WIVI-FM Charlotte Amalie, VI
WIVK-FM Knoxville, TN
*WIVL(FM) Jasper, GA
WIVQ(FM) Spring Valley, IL
WIVR(FM) Kentland, IN
WIVY(FM) Morehead, KY
*WIWC-FM Kokomo, IN
WIWF(FM) Charleston, SC
WIXO(FM) Peoria, IL
*WIXQ(FM) Millersville, PA
WIXV-FM Savannah, GA
WIXX-FM Green Bay, WI
WIXY-FM Champaign, IL
WIYN-FM Deposit, NY
WIYY-FM Baltimore, MD
WIZB-FM Abbeville, AL
WIZD-FM Rudolph, WI
WIZF-FM Erlanger, KY
WIZM-FM La Crosse, WI
WIZN-FM Vergennes, VT
WJAA-FM Austin, IN
*WJAB-FM Huntsville, AL
WJAD-FM Leesburg, GA
WJAQ-FM Marianna, FL
*WJAU-FM Lincoln, AL
WJAW-FM McConnelsville, OH
*WJAZ-FM Summerdale, PA
WJBB-FM Haleyville, AL
*WJBC-FM Fernandina Beach, FL
*WJBD-FM Salem, IL
*WJBE(FM) Five Points, AL
WJBL-FM Ladysmith, WI
*WJBP-FM Red Bank, TN
WJBQ-FM Portland, ME
WJBR-FM Wilmington, DE
WJBT(FM) Callahan, FL
WJBX-FM Fort Myers Beach, FL
WJBZ-FM Seymour, TN
*WJCA(FM) Albion, NY
*WJCB(FM) Clewiston, FL
WJCD(FM) Windsor, VA
*WJCE(FM) Elkton, MI
*WJCF(FM) Morristown, IN
*WJCG(FM) Sunbright, TN
*WJCH-FM Joliet, IL
*WJCI(FM) Baptist Village, MA
*WJCJ(FM) Ladoga, IN

WJCK-FM Piedmont, AL
*WJCL-FM Savannah, GA
*WJCN(FM) Nassawadox, VA
*WJCO(FM) Montpelier, IN
*WJCR-FM Upton, KY
*WJCS-FM Allentown, PA
*WJCT-FM Jacksonville, FL
*WJCU-FM University Heights, OH
WJCX-FM Pittsfield, ME
*WJCY-FM Cicero, IN
*WJCZ(FM) Milford, IL
WJDB-FM Thomasville, AL
*WJDD-FM Carrollton, OH
WJDF-FM Orange, MA
WJDK-FM Seneca, IL
WJDQ(FM) Marion, MS
WJDR-FM Prentiss, MS
*WJDS(FM) Sparta, GA
WJDT-FM Rogersville, TN
*WJDV(FM) Broadway, VA
*WJDZ(FM) Pastillo, PR
WJEC-FM Vernon, AL
*WJED-FM Dogwood Lakes Estate, FL
*WJEF(FM) Lafayette, IN
*WJEL-FM Indianapolis, IN
*WJEN(FM) Killington, VT
*WJEP(FM) Cusseta, GA
WJEQ(FM) Macomb, IL
WJEZ(FM) Dwight, IL
WJFD-FM New Bedford, MA
*WJFF(FM) Jeffersonville, NY
*WJFH(FM) Sebring, FL
WJFK-FM Manassas, VA
*WJFL-FM Tennille, GA
*WJFM-FM Baton Rouge, LA
*WJFP-FM Fort Pierce, FL
*WJFR-FM Jacksonville, FL
WJFX-FM New Haven, IN
WJGA-FM Jackson, GA
WJGL(FM) Jacksonville, FL
WJGO-FM Tice, FL
*WJHD-FM Portsmouth, RI
WJHM-FM Daytona Beach, FL
*WJHO(FM) Alexander City, AL
*WJHS-FM Columbia City, IN
WJHT(FM) Johnstown, PA
*WJIA-FM Guntersville, AL
*WJIC-FM Zanesville, OH
*WJIE-FM Okolona, KY
*WJIF-FM Opp, AL
*WJIJ(FM) Norlina, NC
*WJIK(FM) Monroeville, AL
WJIM-FM Lansing, MI
*WJIR-FM Key West, FL
*WJIS-FM Bradenton, FL
WJIV-FM Cherry Valley, NY
WJIW(FM) Greenville, MS
WJIZ-FM Albany, GA
*WJJB-FM Gary, MS
*WJJE-FM Delaware, OH
WJJH-FM Ashland, WI
*WJJJ(FM) Beckley, WV
WJJK(FM) Noblesville, IN
WJJM-FM Lewisburg, TN
WJJN-FM Columbia, AL
WJJO-FM Watertown, WI
WJJQ-FM Tomahawk, WI
WJJR-FM Rutland, VT
WJJS(FM) Roanoke, VA
*WJJW-FM North Adams, MA
WJJX(FM) Appomattox, VA
WJJY-FM Brainerd, MN
*WJKA(FM) Jacksonville, NC
WJKC-FM Christiansted, VI
*WJKD(FM) Vero Beach, FL
*WJKI(FM) Bethany Beach, DE
*WJKK-FM Vicksburg, MS
*WJKL(FM) Glendale Heights, IL
*WJKN-FM Spring Arbor, MI
*WJKQ(FM) Jackson, MI
WJKS-FM Canton, NJ
WJKW-FM Athens, OH
WJKX-FM Ellisville, MS
*WJKZ(FM) Hanover, MI
WJLB-FM Detroit, MI
WJLE-FM Smithville, TN

*WJLF-FM Gainesville, FL
*WJLH-FM Flagler Beach, FL
WJLK(FM) Asbury Park, NJ
WJLQ(FM) Pensacola, FL
*WJLR-FM Seymour, IN
WJLS-FM Beckley, WV
WJLT(FM) Evansville, IN
*WJLU(FM) New Smyrna Beach, FL
*WJLY(FM) Ramsey, IL
*WJLZ(FM) Virginia Beach, VA
WJMA-FM Culpeper, VA
WJMC-FM Rice Lake, WI
WJMD-FM Hazard, KY
*WJMF-FM Smithfield, RI
WJMG(FM) Hattiesburg, MS
WJMH-FM Reidsville, NC
WJMI-FM Jackson, MS
*WJMJ-FM Hartford, CT
WJMK-FM Chicago, IL
WJMM-FM Keene, KY
WJMN-FM Boston, MA
WJMQ(FM) Clintonville, WI
WJMR-FM Menomonee Falls, WI
*WJMU(FM) Decatur, IL
WJMX-FM Cheraw, SC
WJMZ-FM Anderson, SC
*WJNF(FM) Dalton, MA
WJNG-FM Johnsonburg, PA
WJNI(FM) Ladson, SC
WJNR-FM Iron Mountain, MI
WJNS-FM Yazoo City, MS
WJNV-FM Jonesville, VA
*WJNY-FM Watertown, NY
WJOD-FM Asbury, IA
*WJOG(FM) Good Hart, MI
*WJOH(FM) Raco, MI
*WJOJ(FM) Harrisville, MI
*WJOM(FM) Eagle, MI
WJOT-FM Wabash, IN
*WJOU(FM) Huntsville, AL
WJOW(FM) Philipsburg, PA
WJOX(FM) Birmingham, AL
WJPA-FM Washington, PA
WJPD-FM Ishpeming, MI
*WJPG(FM) Cape May Court House, NJ
*WJPH-FM Woodbine, NJ
WJPK(FM) Barton, VT
*WJPR(FM) Jasper, IN
WJPT(FM) Fort Myers Villas, FL
*WJPZ-FM Syracuse, NY
WJQB(FM) Spring Hill, FL
WJQK-FM Zeeland, MI
WJQM(FM) De Forest, WI
WJQZ-FM Wellsville, NY
*WJRC(FM) Lewistown, PA
WJRE(FM) Galva, IL
*WJRF(FM) Duluth, MN
*WJRH-FM Easton, PA
WJRL-FM Ozark, AL
WJRR-FM Cocoa Beach, FL
WJRS-FM Jamestown, KY
WJRV(FM) Oliver Springs, TN
WJRZ-FM Manahawkin, NJ
WJSA-FM Jersey Shore, PA
*WJSC-FM Johnson, VT
WJSE-FM Petersburg, NJ
WJSG-FM Hamlet, NC
WJSH(FM) Folsom, LA
WJSJ-FM Fernandina Beach, FL
*WJSL-FM Houghton, NY
WJSM-FM Martinsburg, PA
WJSN-FM Jackson, KY
*WJSO-FM Pikeville, KY
*WJSP-FM Warm Springs, GA
WJSQ-FM Athens, TN
*WJSR(FM) Birmingham, AL
*WJSU(FM) Jackson, MS
*WJSV-FM Morristown, NJ
WJSZ-FM Ashley, MI
*WJTF-FM Panama City, FL
*WJTG(FM) Fort Valley, GA
*WJTJ(FM) Cameron, MO
WJTK(FM) Columbia City, FL
*WJTL-FM Lancaster, PA
WJTT-FM Red Bank, TN

*WJTY-FM Lancaster, WI
WJUC-FM Swanton, OH
*WJUF-FM Inverness, FL
WJUN-FM Mexico, PA
WJUX(FM) Monticello, NY
*WJVH(FM) Belfast, ME
*WJVK(FM) Owensboro, KY
WJVL(FM) Janesville, WI
WJVO-FM South Jacksonville, IL
*WJVP(FM) Culebra, PR
*WJVS-FM Cincinnati, OH
*WJWD(FM) Marshall, WI
*WJWJ-FM Beaufort, SC
*WJWR(FM) Bloomington, IL
*WJWT(FM) Gardner, MA
*WJWV(FM) Fort Gaines, GA
WJWZ-FM Wetumpka, AL
WJXA-FM Nashville, TN
WJXB-FM Knoxville, TN
WJXM(FM) De Kalb, MS
WJXN-FM Utica, MS
WJXQ-FM Jackson, MI
WJXR-FM Macclenny, FL
WJXY-FM Conway, SC
*WJYA-FM Emporia, VA
WJYD(FM) London, OH
WJYE-FM Buffalo, NY
*WJYJ-FM Fredericksburg, VA
*WJYO-FM Fort Myers, FL
*WJYW-FM Union City, IN
WJYY-FM Concord, NH
*WJZA(FM) Pickerington, OH
*WJZB(FM) Starkville, MS
WJZD-FM Long Beach, MS
WJZE-FM Oak Harbor, OH
WJZ-FM Catonsville, MD
*WJZJ(FM) Glen Arbor, MI
WJZL(FM) Charlotte, MI
WJZQ(FM) Cadillac, MI
WJZR-FM Rochester, NY
WJZS(FM) Block Island, RI
WJZT-FM Woodville, FL
WJZW-FM Woodbridge, VA
WJZX(FM) Brookfield, WI
*WJZZ(FM) North Salem, NY
WKAA(FM) Willacoochee, GA
WKAD(FM) Harrietta, MI
WKAF(FM) Brockton, MA
WKAI-FM Macomb, IL
WKAK-FM Albany, GA
*WKAO(FM) Ashland, KY
WKAQ-FM San Juan, PR
*WKAR-FM East Lansing, MI
WKAY(FM) Knoxville, IL
WKAZ-FM Miami, WV
WKBB(FM) West Point, MS
WKBC-FM North Wilkesboro, NC
WKBE-FM Warrensburg, NY
WKBH-FM West Salem, WI
WKBI-FM Saint Marys, PA
*WKBM-FM Wallace, NC
WKBQ(FM) Covington, TN
WKBU-FM New Orleans, LA
WKBX-FM Kingsland, GA
WKCA(FM) Salt Lick, KY
WKCB-FM Hindman, KY
*WKCC(FM) Kankakee, IL
WKCH-FM Whitewater, WI
WKCI-FM Hamden, CT
WKCJ(FM) Ronceverte, WV
*WKCL-FM Ladson, SC
WKCN-FM Lumpkin, GA
*WKCO-FM Gambier, OH
*WKCP(FM) Miami, FL
WKCQ-FM Saginaw, MI
*WKCR-FM New York, NY
*WKCS-FM Knoxville, TN
*WKCX(FM) Crittenden, KY
WKCY-FM Harrisonburg, VA
WKDB(FM) Laurel, DE
WKDD-FM Canton, OH
WKDE-FM Altavista, VA
WKDF-FM Nashville, TN
*WKDJ-FM Clarksdale, MS
*WKDL-FM Brockport, NY
*WKDN-FM Camden, NJ

WKDO-FM Liberty, KY
WKDP-FM Corbin, KY
WKDQ-FM Henderson, KY
*WKDS-FM Kalamazoo, MI
*WKDU-FM Philadelphia, PA
WKDZ-FM Cadiz, KY
WKEA-FM Scottsboro, AL
WKEB-FM Medford, WI
*WKEE-FM Huntington, WV
*WKEL(FM) Confluence, PA
WKEQ(FM) Somerset, KY
*WKES-FM Lakeland, FL
*WKET-FM Kettering, OH
WKEU-FM The Rock, GA
WKEY-FM Key West, FL
WKEZ-FM Tavenier, FL
*WKFA(FM) Saint Catherine, FL
WKFC(FM) North Corbin, KY
WKFM-FM Huron, OH
WKFP(FM) Navarre, FL
WKFR-FM Battle Creek, MI
WKFS-FM Milford, OH
WKFX(FM) Rice Lake, WI
WKGA(FM) Goodwater, AL
WKGB-FM Conklin, NY
*WKGC-FM Panama City, FL
WKGL-FM Loves Park, IL
WKGO-FM Cumberland, MD
WKGR-FM Fort Pierce, FL
WKGS-FM Irondequoit, NY
*WKGV(FM) Swansboro, NC
WKHG-FM Leitchfield, KY
WKHI(FM) Fruitland, MD
*WKHJ(FM) Mountain Lake Park, MD
WKHK-FM Colonial Heights, VA
*WKHL(FM) West Lafayette, IN
WKHM-FM Brooklyn, MI
WKHQ-FM Charlevoix, MI
*WKHR-FM Bainbridge, OH
*WKHS-FM Worton, MD
WKHT(FM) Knoxville, TN
WKHX-FM Marietta, GA
WKHY-FM Lafayette, IN
WKIB(FM) Anna, IL
WKID-FM Vevay, IN
WKIF-FM Kankakee, IL
WKIK-FM California, MD
WKIM(FM) Munford, TN
WKIS-FM Boca Raton, FL
WKIT-FM Brewer, ME
*WKIV(FM) Westerly, RI
WKIX(FM) Goldsboro, NC
*WKJA(FM) Brunswick, OH
WKJC-FM Tawas City, MI
*WKJD(FM) Columbus, IN
*WKJL-FM Clarksburg, WV
WKJM(FM) Petersburg, VA
WKJN(FM) Centreville, MS
WKJQ-FM Parsons, TN
WKJS(FM) Richmond, VA
WKJT-FM Teutopolis, IL
WKJX(FM) Elizabeth City, NC
WKJY-FM Hempstead, NY
WKJZ-FM Hillman, MI
WKKB(FM) Middletown, RI
*WKKC-FM Chicago, IL
WKKF(FM) Ballston Spa, NY
WKKG-FM Columbus, IN
WKKI(FM) Celina, OH
WKKJ(FM) Chillicothe, OH
*WKKL-FM West Barnstable, MA
*WKKM(FM) Harrison, MI
WKKN(FM) Westminster, VT
WKKO-FM Toledo, OH
WKKQ(FM) Barbourville, KY
WKKR-FM Auburn, AL
WKKS-FM Vanceburg, KY
WKKT-FM Statesville, NC
WKKV-FM Racine, WI
WKKW-FM Fairmont, WV
WKKY-FM Geneva, OH
WKKZ-FM Dublin, GA
WKLA-FM Ludington, MI
WKLB-FM Waltham, MA
WKLC-FM Saint Albans, WV
WKLD-FM Oneonta, AL

WKLG-FM Rock Harbor, FL
WKLH-FM Milwaukee, WI
WKLI-FM Albany, NY
WKLK-FM Cloquet, MN
WKLL-FM Frankfort, NY
WKLM-FM Millersburg, OH
WKLN(FM) Wilmington, OH
WKLO(FM) Hardinsburg, IN
WKLR-FM Fort Lee, VA
WKLS(FM) Atlanta, GA
WKLT(FM) Kalkaska, MI
WKLU-FM Brownsburg, IN
WKLW-FM Paintsville, KY
WKLX(FM) Brownsville, KY
WKLZ-FM Petoskey, MI
*WKMD(FM) Madisonville, KY
WKMJ-FM Hancock, MI
WKMK(FM) Ocean Acres, NJ
WKML-FM Lumberton, NC
WKMM-FM Kingwood, WV
*WKMO(FM) Lebanon Junction, KY
*WKMS-FM Murray, KY
*WKMT(FM) Fulton, KY
*WKMV(FM) Muncie, IN
WKMX-FM Enterprise, AL
*WKMY(FM) Winchendon, MA
*WKMZ(FM) Mukwonago, WI
WKNA(FM) Logan, OH
WKNB-FM Clarendon, PA
*WKNC-FM Raleigh, NC
WKNE(FM) Keene, NH
*WKNG-FM Heflin, AL
*WKNH-FM Keene, NH
*WKNJ-FM Union Township, NJ
WKNL(FM) New London, CT
WKNN-FM Pascagoula, MS
*WKNO-FM Memphis, TN
*WKNP-FM Jackson, TN
WKNS-FM Kinston, NC
WKNU-FM Brewton, AL
*WKNZ(FM) Harrington, DE
WKOA-FM Lafayette, IN
WKOE(FM) North Cape May, NJ
WKOL-FM Plattsburgh, NY
WKOM(FM) Columbia, TN
WKOR-FM Columbus, MS
WKOS-FM Kingsport, TN
WKOT-FM Marseilles, IL
WKOV-FM Wellston, OH
WKOY-FM Princeton, WV
WKPB-FM Henderson, KY
WKPE-FM South Yarmouth, MA
*WKPK(FM) Michigamme, MI
WKPL-FM Ellwood City, PA
WKPO(FM) Soldiers Grove, WI
WKPQ-FM Hornell, NY
*WKPS-FM State College, PA
*WKPW(FM) Knightstown, IN
WKPX-FM Sunrise, FL
WKQC(FM) Charlotte, NC
WKQH(FM) Marathon, WI
WKQI-FM Detroit, MI
WKQK(FM) Germantown, TN
WKQL-FM Brookville, PA
WKQQ-FM Winchester, KY
WKQS-FM Negaunee, MI
WKQV(FM) Cowen, WV
WKQW-FM Oil City, PA
WKQX-FM Chicago, IL
WKQY-FM Tazewell, VA
WKQZ-FM Midland, MI
WKRA-FM Holly Springs, MS
*WKRB-FM Brooklyn, NY
WKRD-FM Shelbyville, KY
*WKRE(FM) Argo, AL
WKRF(FM) Tobyhanna, PA
WKRH-FM Minetto, NY
*WKRI(FM) Cokesbury, SC
*WKRJ-FM New Philadelphia, OH
WKRK-FM Cleveland Heights, OH
WKRL-FM North Syracuse, NY
WKRO-FM Edgewater, FL
WKRQ-FM Cincinnati, OH
WKRR-FM Asheboro, NC
WKRV-FM Vandalia, IL
*WKRW-FM Wooster, OH

*WKRX-FM Roxboro, NC
*WKRY(FM) Versailles, IN
WKRZ-FM Wilkes-Barre, PA
WKSA-FM Isabela, PR
WKSB-FM Williamsport, PA
WKSC-FM Chicago, IL
WKSD-FM Paulding, OH
WKSE-FM Niagara Falls, NY
WKSF-FM Asheville, NC
*WKSG-FM Cedar Creek, FL
WKSI-FM Stephens City, VA
WKSJ-FM Mobile, AL
WKSK-FM South Hill, VA
WKSL-FM Cary, NC
WKSM-FM Fort Walton Beach, FL
WKSO(FM) Natchez, MS
WKSP(FM) Aiken, SC
WKSQ-FM Ellsworth, ME
WKSR-FM Loretto, TN
WKSS-FM Hartford, CT
WKST-FM Pittsburgh, PA
*WKSU-FM Kent, OH
*WKSV(FM) Thompson, OH
WKSW-FM Urbana, OH
WKSX-FM Johnston, SC
WKSZ-FM De Pere, WI
WKTG-FM Madisonville, KY
WKTJ-FM Farmington, ME
WKTK-FM Crystal River, FL
*WKTL-FM Struthers, OH
WKTM-FM Soperton, GA
*WKTN(FM) Kenton, OH
*WKTO-FM Edgewater, FL
*WKTS(FM) Kingston, TN
WKTT(FM) Salisbury, MD
WKTU-FM Lake Success, NY
*WKTZ-FM Jacksonville, FL
WKUB(FM) Blackshear/Waycross, GA
*WKUE-FM Elizabethtown, KY
WKUL-FM Cullman, AL
WKUS(FM) Norfolk, VA
WKUZ(FM) Wabash, IN
WKVB(FM) Port Matilda, PA
*WKVC(FM) North Myrtle Beach, SC
WKVE(FM) Mount Pleasant, PA
*WKVF(FM) Byhalia, MS
*WKVH(FM) Monticello, FL
*WKVI-FM Knox, IN
*WKVJ(FM) Dannemora, NY
*WKVK(FM) Semora, NC
*WKVN(FM) Morganfield, KY
*WKVP(FM) Cherry Hill, NJ
*WKVR-FM Huntingdon, PA
WKVS-FM Lenoir, NC
WKVT-FM Brattleboro, VT
*WKVU(FM) Utica, NY
WKVV(FM) Searsport, ME
*WKVW(FM) Marmet, WV
*WKVY(FM) Somerset, KY
*WKVZ(FM) Dexter, ME
*WKWC(FM) Owensboro, KY
*WKWH(FM) Liberty, IN
WKWI-FM Kilmarnock, VA
WKWK-FM Wheeling, WV
*WKWM(FM) Marathon, FL
*WKWR(FM) Key West, FL
*WKWS-FM Charleston, WV
*WKWV(FM) Watertown, NY
WKWX(FM) Savannah, TN
WKWY(FM) Tompkinsville, KY
*WKWZ-FM Syosset, NY
WKXA-FM Findlay, OH
WKXB-FM Burgaw, NC
WKXC-FM Aiken, SC
WKXD-FM Monterey, TN
WKXH-FM Saint Johnsbury, VT
WKXI-FM Magee, MS
WKXK(FM) Pine Hill, AL
WKXM-FM Winfield, AL
WKXN-FM Greenville, AL
WKXP(FM) Kingston, NY
WKXQ-FM Rushville, IL
WKXS-FM Leland, NC
WKXU(FM) Louisburg, NC
WKXW(FM) Trenton, NJ
WKXX-FM Attalla, AL

WKXY(FM) Merigold, MS
WKXZ-FM Norwich, NY
WKYA-FM Greenville, KY
WKYB(FM) Burgin, KY
WKYE(FM) Johnstown, PA
*WKYJ(FM) Rouses Point, NY
WKYL-FM Lawrenceburg, KY
WKYM-FM Monticello, KY
WKYN(FM) Owingsville, KY
WKYQ-FM Paducah, KY
WKYR-FM Burkesville, KY
WKYS-FM Washington, DC
*WKYU-FM Bowling Green, KY
*WKYV(FM) Colonial Heights, VA
WKYX-FM Golconda, IL
WKYZ(FM) Key Colony Beach, FL
WKZA(FM) Lakewood, NY
WKZB(FM) Stonewall, MS
WKZC-FM Scottville, MI
WKZE-FM Salisbury, CT
*WKZG(FM) Key West, FL
WKZJ(FM) Eufaula, AL
WKZL-FM Winston-Salem, NC
*WKZM-FM Sarasota, FL
WKZQ-FM Forestbrook, SC
WKZR-FM Milledgeville, GA
WKZS-FM Covington, IN
WKZU(FM) Iuka, MS
WKZW-FM Bay Springs, MS
WKZX-FM Lenoir City, TN
WKZY(FM) Cross City, FL
WKZZ-FM Tifton, GA
*WLAB(FM) Fort Wayne, IN
*WLAI(FM) Danville, KY
WLAK-FM Huntingdon, PA
WLAN-FM Lancaster, PA
WLAV-FM Grand Rapids, MI
WLAW(FM) Newaygo, MI
WLAY-FM Littleville, AL
*WLAZ(FM) Kissimmee, FL
WLBC-FM Muncie, IN
*WLBF-FM Montgomery, AL
WLBH-FM Mattoon, IL
*WLBL-FM Wausau, WI
*WLBS(FM) Bristol, PA
WLBW-FM Fenwick Island, DE
*WLCA-FM Godfrey, IL
WLCE(FM) Petersburg, IL
*WLCH-FM Lancaster, PA
WLCL(FM) Sellersville, IN
WLCN(FM) Atlanta, IL
WLCS-FM North Muskegon, MI
WLCT(FM) Lafayette, TN
*WLCU(FM) Campbellsville, KY
WLCY-FM Blairsville, PA
WLDA(FM) Slocomb, AL
WLDB(FM) Milwaukee, WI
WLDE-FM Fort Wayne, IN
WLDI-FM Fort Pierce, FL
WLDR-FM Traverse City, MI
WLEG(FM) Ligonier, IN
WLEK(FM) Gouldsboro, ME
WLEL(FM) Ellaville, GA
WLEN-FM Adrian, MI
WLEQ(FM) Bedford, VA
WLER-FM Butler, PA
WLEV-FM Allentown, PA
WLEW-FM Bad Axe, MI
WLEY-FM Aurora, IL
*WLFA-FM Asheville, NC
*WLFC-FM Findlay, OH
WLFE-FM Saint Albans, VT
WLFF(FM) Georgetown, SC
WLFH-FM Rantoul, IL
*WLFJ-FM Greenville, SC
*WLFR-FM Pomona, NJ
*WLFS-FM Port Wentworth, GA
WLFV(FM) Ettrick, VA
WLFW-FM Chandler, IN
WLFX(FM) Berea, KY
WLGC-FM Greenup, KY
WLGD(FM) Jacksonville, NC
WLGE(FM) Bailey's Harbor, WI
*WLGH-FM Leroy Township, MI
*WLGI-FM Hemingway, SC
WLGL-FM Riverside, PA

*WLGO(FM) Ashtabula, OH
WLGP-FM Harkers Island, NC
WLGT(FM) Washington, NC
WLGZ-FM Webster, NY
WLHC(FM) Robbins, NC
WLHK(FM) Shelbyville, IN
WLHM-FM Logansport, IN
WLHR-FM Lavonia, GA
*WLHS-FM West Chester, OH
WLHT-FM Grand Rapids, MI
*WLHW(FM) Casey, IL
*WLIC-FM Frostburg, MD
WLIF-FM Baltimore, MD
WLIH-FM Whitneyville, PA
WLIN-FM Durant, MS
WLIR-FM Hampton Bays, NY
WLIT-FM Chicago, IL
*WLIU(FM) Southampton, NY
WLIV-FM Monterey, TN
WLJA-FM Ellijay, GA
WLJC-FM Beattyville, KY
WLJE-FM Valparaiso, IN
*WLJH-FM Glens Falls, NY
WLJI-FM Summerton, SC
*WLJK-FM Aiken, SC
*WLJN-FM Traverse City, MI
*WLJP-FM Monroe, NY
*WLJR-FM Birmingham, AL
*WLJS-FM Jacksonville, AL
WLJY(FM) Whiting, WI
WLJZ(FM) Mackinaw City, MI
*WLKA(FM) Tafton, PA
*WLKB(FM) Bay City, MI
WLKC-FM Campton, NH
WLKE-FM Bar Harbor, ME
WLKG-FM Lake Geneva, WI
WLKH(FM) Somerset, PA
WLKI-FM Angola, IN
WLKJ(FM) Portage, PA
WLKK(FM) Wethersfield Township, NY
*WLKL(FM) Mattoon, IL
WLKM-FM Three Rivers, MI
WLKN(FM) Cleveland, WI
*WLKO(FM) Quitman, MS
*WLKP(FM) Belpre, OH
WLKQ-FM Buford, GA
WLKR-FM Norwalk, OH
WLKS-FM West Liberty, KY
WLKT-FM Lexington-Fayette, KY
WLKU(FM) Rock Island, IL
*WLKV(FM) Ripley, WV
WLKX-FM Forest Lake, MN
WLKZ-FM Wolfeboro, NH
WLLD(FM) Lakeland, FL
WLLE(FM) Clinton, NY
WLLF-FM Mercer, PA
WLLG-FM Lowville, NY
WLLJ(FM) Etowah, TN
WLLK-FM Somerset, KY
WLLR-FM Davenport, IA
WLLT-FM Polo, IL
WLLW(FM) Seneca Falls, NY
WLLX-FM Lawrenceburg, TN
WLMD-FM Bushnell, IL
WLME(FM) Lewisport, IN
WLMG(FM) New Orleans, LA
*WLMH-FM Morrow, OH
WLMI-FM Kane, PA
*WLMN(FM) Manistee, MI
*WLMS-FM Lecanto, FL
*WLMU-FM Harrogate, TN
*WLMW-FM Manchester, NH
WLMX-FM Balsam Lake, WI
WLMY(FM) Williamsport, PA
*WLNB(FM) Wartburg, TN
WLND-FM Signal Mountain, TN
*WLNF(FM) Rapids, NY
WLNG-FM Sag Harbor, NY
WLNH-FM Laconia, NH
WLNI-FM Lynchburg, VA
*WLNJ(FM) Lakehurst, NJ
WLNK-FM Charlotte, NC
WLNP-FM Carbondale, PA
*WLNQ-FM Spring City, TN
*WLNX-FM Lincoln, IL
*WLNZ-FM Lansing, MI

WLOB-FM Topsham, ME
WLOD-FM Sweetwater, TN
WLOF-FM Attica, NY
*WLOG(FM) Markleysburg, PA
*WLOL-FM Morgantown, WV
WLOQ-FM Winter Park, FL
WLOW-FM Port Royal, SC
*WLPE(FM) Augusta, GA
WLPF-FM Ocilla, GA
*WLPG-FM Florence, SC
*WLPR-FM Lowell, IN
*WLPS-FM Lumberton, NC
*WLPT(FM) Jesup, GA
WLPW-FM Lake Placid, NY
WLQB(FM) Ocean Isle Beach, NC
WLQI-FM Rensselaer, IN
WLQK(FM) Livingston, NY
WLQM-FM Franklin, VA
WLQR-FM Delta, OH
WLQT-FM Kettering, OH
*WLRA-FM Lockport, IL
WLRD(FM) Willard, OH
*WLRH-FM Huntsville, AL
*WLRK(FM) Greenville, MS
*WLRN-FM Miami, FL
WLRQ-FM Cocoa, FL
WLRR-FM Milledgeville, GA
WLRS(FM) Shepherdsville, KY
WLRW-FM Champaign, IL
*WLRY(FM) Rushville, OH
WLS-FM Chicago, IL
WLSK-FM Lebanon, KY
WLSM-FM Louisville, MS
*WLSN(FM) Grand Marais, MN
WLSO-FM Sault Ste. Marie, MI
WLSQ(FM) Byrdstown, TN
WLSR(FM) Galesburg, IL
WLST-FM Marinette, WI
*WLSU-FM La Crosse, WI
WLSW-FM Scottdale, PA
*WLSZ(FM) Key West, FL
WLTB(FM) Johnson City, NY
WLTE-FM Minneapolis, MN
WLTF-FM Martinsburg, WV
WLTI(FM) Syracuse, NY
WLTJ-FM Pittsburgh, PA
WLTK-FM New Market, VA
*WLTL-FM La Grange, IL
WLTN-FM Lisbon, NH
WLTO-FM Nicholasville, KY
WLTQ-FM Venice, FL
*WLTR-FM Columbia, SC
WLTT(FM) Shallotte, NC
WLTU(FM) Manitowoc, WI
WLTW-FM New York, NY
WLTY-FM Cayce, SC
WLUE(FM) Louisville, KY
*WLUJ(FM) Springfield, IL
WLUM-FM Milwaukee, WI
WLUN(FM) Pinconning, MI
WLUP-FM Chicago, IL
*WLUR-FM Lexington, VA
WLUS-FM Clarksville, VA
*WLUW-FM Chicago, IL
*WLVB-FM Morrisville, VT
*WLVF-FM Haines City, FL
WLVG-FM Center Moriches, NY
WLVH-FM Hardeeville, SC
WLVK-FM Fort Knox, KY
*WLVM(FM) Ironwood, MI
WLVQ(FM) Columbus, OH
*WLVR-FM Bethlehem, PA
WLVS-FM Clifton, TN
*WLVU(FM) Halifax, PA
*WLVW(FM) Moundsville, WV
WLVY-FM Elmira, NY
*WLVZ(FM) Collins, MS
WLWD-FM Columbus Grove, OH
WLWI-FM Montgomery, AL
*WLWJ(FM) Petersburg, IL
WLWK-FM Milwaukee, WI
*WLWM(FM) Macomb, IL
WLXC-FM Columbia, SC
WLXO(FM) Stamping Ground, KY
*WLXP(FM) Savannah, GA
WLXR-FM La Crosse, WI

WLXT(FM) Petoskey, MI
WLXV-FM Cadillac, MI
WLXX(FM) Lexington, KY
WLYE-FM Glasgow, KY
WLYF(FM) Miami, FL
WLYK(FM) Cape Vincent, NY
WLYT-FM Hickory, NC
WLYU-FM Lyons, GA
WLYX(FM) Valdosta, GA
WLZA(FM) Eupora, MS
WLZK-FM Paris, TN
WLZL(FM) Annapolis, MD
WLZN(FM) Macon, GA
WLZS(FM) Beaver Springs, PA
WLZT(FM) Chillicothe, OH
WLZW-FM Utica, NY
WLZX(FM) Northampton, MA
WLZZ(FM) Montpelier, OH
*WMAB-FM Mississippi State, MS
WMAD(FM) Sauk City, WI
*WMAE-FM Booneville, MS
WMAG(FM) High Point, NC
*WMAH-FM Biloxi, MS
WMAJ-FM Centre Hall, PA
*WMAO-FM Greenwood, MS
WMAS-FM Springfield, MA
*WMAU-FM Bude, MS
*WMAV-FM Oxford, MS
*WMAW-FM Meridian, MS
WMAX-FM Holland, MI
*WMBI-FM Chicago, IL
*WMBJ(FM) Murrell's Inlet, SC
*WMBL(FM) Mitchell, IN
*WMBR-FM Cambridge, MA
*WMBU-FM Forest, MS
*WMBV-FM Dixons Mills, AL
*WMBW-FM Chattanooga, TN
WMBX-FM Jensen Beach, FL
WMCD(FM) Claxton, GA
*WMCE-FM Erie, PA
WMC-FM Memphis, TN
WMCG-FM Milan, GA
WMCI-FM Mattoon, IL
WMCM-FM Rockland, ME
*WMCN-FM Saint Paul, MN
*WMCO-FM New Concord, OH
*WMCQ(FM) Muskegon, MI
WMCR-FM Oneida, NY
*WMCX-FM West Long Branch, NJ
WMDC-FM Mayville, WI
WMDH-FM New Castle, IN
WMDJ-FM Allen, KY
WMDM-FM Lexington Park, MD
*WMDR-FM Oakland, ME
*WMEA-FM Portland, ME
WMEB-FM Orono, ME
*WMED-FM Calais, ME
WMEE-FM Fort Wayne, IN
*WMEF-FM Fort Kent, ME
WMEG-FM Guayama, PR
*WMEH-FM Bangor, ME
*WMEM-FM Presque Isle, ME
*WMEP(FM) Camden, ME
WMEQ-FM Menomonie, WI
WMEV-FM Marion, VA
*WMEW-FM Waterville, ME
*WMEX(FM) Edgartown, MA
WMEZ-FM Pensacola, FL
WMFC-FM Monroeville, AL
WMFE-FM Orlando, FL
WMFG-FM Hibbing, MN
*WMFL-FM Florida City, FL
WMFM(FM) Key West, FL
WMFO-FM Medford, MA
WMFQ-FM Ocala, FL
WMFS-FM Bartlett, TN
*WMFT(FM) Tuscaloosa, AL
*WMFU(FM) Mount Hope, NY
WMFX(FM) Saint Andrews, SC
WMGA(FM) Kenova, WV
WMGB-FM Montezuma, GA
WMGC-FM Detroit, MI
WMGE-FM Miami Beach, FL
WMGF-FM Mount Dora, FL
WMGH-FM Tamaqua, PA
WMGI-FM Terre Haute, IN

WMGK-FM Philadelphia, PA
WMGL-FM Ravenel, SC
WMGM(FM) Atlantic City, NJ
WMGN-FM Madison, WI
WMGP(FM) Hogansville, GA
*WMGQ-FM New Brunswick, NJ
WMGS-FM Wilkes-Barre, PA
*WMGU-FM Southern Pines, NC
WMGV-FM Newport, NC
WMGX-FM Portland, ME
WMGZ-FM Eatonton, GA
*WMHB-FM Waterville, ME
*WMHC-FM South Hadley, MA
*WMHD-FM Terre Haute, IN
*WMHI-FM Cape Vincent, NY
*WMHK-FM Columbia, SC
*WMHN-FM Webster, NY
*WMHQ(FM) Malone, NY
*WMHR-FM Syracuse, NY
*WMHS(FM) Pike Creek, DE
*WMHT-FM Schenectady, NY
*WMHW-FM Mount Pleasant, MI
WMHX(FM) Hershey, PA
WMIA-FM Miami Beach, FL
WMIB(FM) Fort Lauderdale, FL
*WMIE-FM Cocoa, FL
WMIK-FM Middlesboro, KY
WMIL-FM Waukesha, WI
WMIO(FM) Cabo Rojo, PR
*WMIS-FM Blackduck, MN
*WMIT-FM Black Mountain, NC
WMIX-FM Mount Vernon, IL
WMJC(FM) Smithtown, NY
WMJD-FM Grundy, VA
WMJE-FM Clarkesville, GA
WMJI-FM Cleveland, OH
WMJJ-FM Birmingham, AL
WMJK(FM) Clyde, OH
WMJL-FM Marion, KY
WMJM-FM Jeffersontown, KY
WMJO(FM) Essexville, MI
WMJT(FM) McMillan, MI
WMJU-FM Bude, MS
WMJW-FM Cleveland, MS
WMJX-FM Boston, MA
WMJY-FM Biloxi, MS
WMJZ-FM Gaylord, MI
WMKB-FM Earlville, IL
WMKC(FM) Saint Ignace, MI
WMKD(FM) Pickford, MI
WMKJ(FM) Mt. Sterling, KY
WMKK-FM Lawrence, MA
*WMKL-FM Key Largo, FL
*WMKO-FM Marco, FL
WMKR(FM) Pana, IL
WMKS(FM) Clemmons, NC
*WMKV(FM) Reading, OH
*WMKW-FM Crossville, TN
WMKX-FM Brookville, PA
*WMKY-FM Morehead, KY
WMKZ-FM Monticello, KY
WMLF(FM) Watseka, IL
*WMLJ-FM Summersville, WV
WMLL(FM) Bedford, NH
*WMLN-FM Milton, MA
WMLQ(FM) Manistee, MI
*WMLS(FM) Grand Marais, MN
*WMLU-FM Farmville, VA
WMLV(FM) Butler, AL
WMLX-FM Saint Mary's, OH
*WMMA-FM Nekoosa, WI
WMMC-FM Marshall, IL
WMME-FM Augusta, ME
WMMG-FM Brandenburg, KY
WMMJ-FM Bethesda, MD
WMMM-FM Verona, WI
WMMO-FM Orlando, FL
WMMQ-FM East Lansing, MI
WMMR-FM Philadelphia, PA
WMMS-FM Cleveland, OH
*WMMT-FM Whitesburg, KY
WMMX-FM Dayton, OH
WMMY(FM) Jefferson, NC
WMNA-FM Gretna, VA
WMNC-FM Morganton, NC
*WMNF-FM Tampa, FL

WMNG-FM Christiansted, VI
*WMNJ-FM Madison, NJ
*WMNR-FM Monroe, CT
WMNV-FM Rupert, VT
WMNX-FM Wilmington, NC
*WMOC-FM Lumber City, GA
WMOD-FM Bolivar, TN
WMOI-FM Monmouth, IL
WMOJ-FM Connersville, IN
WMOM-FM Pentwater, MI
WMOO-FM Derby Center, VT
WMOQ-FM Bostwick, GA
WMOR-FM Morehead, KY
WMOS(FM) Stonington, CT
*WMOT-FM Murfreesboro, TN
WMOZ(FM) Moose Lake, MN
*WMPG-FM Gorham, ME
*WMPH-FM Wilmington, DE
WMPI-FM Scottsburg, IN
*WMPN-FM Jackson, MS
*WMPR-FM Jackson, MS
WMPZ-FM Ringgold, GA
WMQA-FM Minocqua, WI
WMQT-FM Ishpeming, MI
WMQX(FM) Alexandria, IN
WMQZ-FM Colchester, IL
*WMRA-FM Harrisonburg, VA
WMRF-FM Lewistown, PA
WMRK-FM Shorter, AL
*WMRL-FM Lexington, KY
WMRN-FM Marion, OH
WMRQ-FM Waterbury, CT
WMRR-FM Muskegon Heights, MI
WMRS(FM) Monticello, IN
*WMRT-FM Marietta, OH
WMRV-FM Endicott, NY
WMRX-FM Beaverton, MI
*WMRY(FM) Crozet, VA
WMRZ(FM) Dawson, GA
*WMSB(FM) Senatobia, MS
*WMSC-FM Upper Montclair, NJ
*WMSD(FM) Rose Township, MI
*WMSE-FM Milwaukee, WI
WMSH-FM Sturgis, MI
WMSI-FM Jackson, MS
*WMSJ-FM Freeport, ME
WMSK-FM Sturgis, KY
*WMSL(FM) Athens, GA
WMSO(FM) Meridian, MS
*WMSQ(FM) Marlette, MI
WMSR-FM Collinwood, TN
*WMSS-FM Middletown, PA
WMSU(FM) Starkville, MS
*WMSV(FM) Starkville, MS
*WMTB-FM Emmittsburg, MD
WMTC-FM Vancleve, KY
WMTD-FM Hinton, WV
WMTE-FM Manistee, MI
WMT-FM Cedar Rapids, IA
*WMTH-FM Park Ridge, IL
WMTI(FM) Picayune, MS
WMTK-FM Littleton, NH
WMTM-FM Moultrie, GA
*WMTP(FM) Kennebunkport, ME
WMTR-FM Archbold, OH
*WMTS-FM Murfreesboro, TN
WMTT(FM) Tioga, PA
*WMTU-FM Houghton, MI
WMTX(FM) Tampa, FL
*WMUA-FM Amherst, MA
*WMUB(FM) Oxford, OH
*WMUC-FM College Park, MD
WMUF-FM Henry, TN
*WMUH(FM) Allentown, PA
*WMUI(FM) Rushville, IN
*WMUK-FM Kalamazoo, MI
*WMUL-FM Huntington, WV
WMUM-FM Cochran, GA
*WMUO(FM) Greenville, OH
WMUP(FM) Carney, MI
WMUS(FM) Muskegon, MI
WMUT(FM) Grenada, MS
WMUU-FM Greenville, SC
WMUV(FM) Brunswick, GA
*WMUW(FM) Columbus, MS
WMUZ-FM Detroit, MI

*WMVE(FM) Chase City, VA
WMVL-FM Linesville, PA
*WMVM(FM) Goodman, WI
*WMVR-FM Sidney, OH
*WMVV-FM Griffin, GA
*WMVW(FM) Peachtree City, GA
WMVX-FM Cleveland, OH
WMVY-FM Tisbury, MA
*WMWI(FM) Demopolis, AL
*WMWK-FM Milwaukee, WI
*WMWM-FM Salem, MA
*WMWR(FM) Lincoln, ME
WMWV-FM Conway, NH
*WMWX(FM) Miamitown, OH
WMXA(FM) Opelika, AL
WMXB-FM Richmond, VA
WMXC-FM Mobile, AL
WMXD-FM Detroit, MI
WMXE(FM) South Charleston, WV
WMXG(FM) Stephenson, MI
WMXH-FM Luray, VA
WMXI(FM) Laurel, MS
WMXJ-FM Pompano Beach, FL
WMXK-FM Morristown, TN
WMXL-FM Lexington, KY
*WMXM-FM Lake Forest, IL
WMXN-FM Stevenson, AL
WMXO-FM Olean, NY
WMXQ(FM) Hartford City, IN
WMXR-FM Woodstock, VT
WMXS-FM Montgomery, AL
WMXT-FM Pamplico, SC
WMXU-FM Starkville, MS
WMXV(FM) Saint Joseph, TN
WMXW-FM Vestal, NY
WMXX-FM Jackson, TN
WMXY(FM) Youngstown, OH
WMXZ(FM) De Funiak Springs, FL
WMYB(FM) Myrtle Beach, SC
*WMYE(FM) Fort Myers, FL
WMYI(FM) Hendersonville, NC
*WMYJ-FM Oolitic, IN
WMYK-FM Peru, IN
WMYL(FM) Halls Crossroads, TN
WMYP(FM) Fredriksted, VI
WMYQ(FM) South Whitley, IN
WMYX-FM Milwaukee, WI
WMYY-FM Schoharie, NY
*WMYZ(FM) Clermont, FL
WMZK-FM Merrill, WI
WMZQ-FM Washington, DC
*WNAA-FM Greensboro, NC
WNAE-FM Clarendon, PA
*WNAN-FM Nantucket, MA
*WNAS-FM New Albany, IN
WNAX-FM Yankton, SD
*WNAZ-FM Nashville, TN
WNBB(FM) Bayboro, NC
*WNBK(FM) Whitmire, SC
WNBQ-FM Mansfield, PA
WNBR-FM Bethel, NC
*WNBT-FM Wellsboro, PA
WNBU-FM Oriental, NC
*WNBV(FM) Grundy, VA
WNBY-FM Newberry, MI
WNCB(FM) Gardendale, AL
WNCC-FM Franklin, NC
WNCD(FM) Youngstown, OH
*WNCH(FM) Norwich, VT
WNCI-FM Columbus, OH
*WNCK(FM) Nantucket, MA
WNCL(FM) Milford, DE
WNCM(FM) Sharpsburg, NC
WNCO-FM Ashland, OH
WNCQ-FM Canton, NY
WNCS-FM Montpelier, VT
WNCT-FM Greenville, NC
*WNCU-FM Durham, NC
WNCV(FM) Shalimar, FL
*WNCW-FM Spindale, NC
WNCX(FM) Cleveland, OH
WNCY-FM Neenah-Menasha, WI
WNDD-FM Silver Springs, FL
WNDH-FM Napoleon, OH
WNDI-FM Sullivan, IN
WNDN(FM) Chiefland, FL

WNDT(FM) Alachua, FL
WNDV-FM South Bend, IN
*WNDY-FM Crawfordsville, IN
*WNEC-FM Henniker, NH
*WNED-FM Buffalo, NY
*WNEE-FM Patterson, GA
*WNEF-FM Newburyport, MA
*WNEK-FM Springfield, MA
WNEV(FM) Friar's Point, MS
WNEW-FM Jupiter, FL
*WNFA-FM Port Huron, MI
WNFB-FM Lake City, FL
*WNFC(FM) Paducah, KY
WNFK-FM Perry, FL
WNFM-FM Reedsburg, WI
WNFN(FM) Millersville, TN
*WNFR-FM Sandusky, MI
WNFZ-FM Oak Ridge, TN
WNGA(FM) Helen, GA
*WNGB(FM) Petersham, MA
WNGC-FM Toccoa, GA
WNGE-FM Negaunee, MI
*WNGF(FM) Swanton, VT
*WNGG(FM) Gloversville, NY
*WNGH-FM Chatsworth, GA
WNGN-FM Argyle, NY
*WNGU-FM Dahlonega, GA
WNGZ-FM Montour Falls, NY
*WNHI(FM) Farmington, NH
WNHT(FM) Churubusco, IN
*WNHU-FM West Haven, CT
WNHW(FM) Belmont, NH
WNIC-FM Dearborn, MI
*WNIE-FM Freeport, IL
*WNIJ-FM De Kalb, IL
WNIK-FM Arecibo, PR
*WNIN-FM Evansville, IN
*WNIQ-FM Sterling, IL
WNIR-FM Kent, OH
*WNIU-FM Rockford, IL
*WNIW-FM La Salle, IL
*WNJA-FM Jamestown, NY
*WNJB-FM Bridgeton, NJ
*WNJM-FM Manahawkin, NJ
*WNJN-FM Atlantic City, NJ
*WNJO(FM) Toms River, NJ
*WNJP-FM Sussex, NJ
*WNJR-FM Washington, PA
*WNJS-FM Berlin, NJ
*WNJT-FM Trenton, NJ
*WNJY(FM) Netcong, NJ
*WNJZ-FM Cape May Court House, NJ
WNKI-FM Corning, NY
*WNKJ(FM) Hopkinsville, KY
WNKK(FM) Circleville, OH
*WNKL(FM) Wauseon, OH
WNKO-FM Newark, OH
WNKR(FM) Williamstown, KY
WNKS-FM Charlotte, NC
WNKT(FM) Eastover, SC
*WNKU-FM Highland Heights, KY
*WNKV(FM) Norco, LA
WNKX-FM Centerville, TN
WNKZ(FM) Laporte, PA
WNLA-FM Indianola, MS
WNLC-FM East Lyme, CT
WNLF(FM) Macomb, IL
*WNLI(FM) Sturgeon Bay, WI
WNLT-FM Harrison, OH
*WNMC-FM Traverse City, MI
*WNMH-FM Northfield, MA
WNML-FM Loudon, TN
*WNMP(FM) Marlinton, WV
WNMQ(FM) Columbus, MS
WNMR-FM Dannemora, NY
*WNMU-FM Marquette, MI
WNNF(FM) Cincinnati, OH
WNNG-FM Unadilla, GA
WNNH-FM Henniker, NH
WNNJ(FM) Newton, NJ
WNNK-FM Harrisburg, PA
WNNL-FM Fuquay-Varina, NC
WNNO-FM Wisconsin Dells, WI
WNNS(FM) Springfield, IL
WNNT-FM Warsaw, VA

*WNNV(FM) San German, PR
WNNX(FM) College Park, GA
*WNOC(FM) Bowling Green, OH
WNOD-FM Mayaguez, PR
WNOE-FM New Orleans, LA
WNOI-FM Flora, IL
*WNOK-FM Columbia, SC
*WNON(FM) Warfield, KY
WNOR(FM) Norfolk, VA
WNOU-FM Speedway, IN
WNOW-FM Gaffney, SC
WNOX(FM) Oak Ridge, TN
WNPC-FM Newport, TN
WNPQ-FM New Philadelphia, OH
*WNPR-FM Norwich, CT
WNPT-FM Marion, AL
*WNRE(FM) Enoree, SC
*WNRK(FM) Norwalk, OH
*WNRN(FM) Charlottesville, VA
WNRQ-FM Nashville, TN
*WNRS-FM Sweet Briar, VA
WNRT-FM Manati, PR
*WNRX(FM) Jefferson City, TN
*WNRZ-FM Dickson, TN
*WNSB-FM Norfolk, VA
*WNSC-FM Rock Hill, SC
WNSI-FM Atmore, AL
WNSL-FM Laurel, MS
WNSN-FM South Bend, IN
*WNSP-FM Bay Minette, AL
WNSV-FM Nashville, IL
WNSX(FM) Winter Harbor, ME
WNSY-FM Talking Rock, GA
WNTB(FM) Wrightsville Beach, NC
WNTC-FM Drakesboro, KY
*WNTE-FM Mansfield, PA
*WNTH-FM Winnetka, IL
*WNTI(FM) Hackettstown, NJ
WNTK-FM New London, NH
WNTO(FM) Racine, OH
WNTQ(FM) Syracuse, NY
WNTR(FM) Indianapolis, IN
WNTY-FM Estero, FL
WNUA-FM Chicago, IL
*WNUB-FM Northfield, VT
WNUE-FM Titusville, FL
WNUQ(FM) Sylvester, GA
*WNUR-FM Evanston, IL
WNUS-FM Belpre, OH
WNUW(FM) Burlington, NJ
WNUY(FM) Bluffton, IN
WNVA-FM Norton, VA
WNVE(FM) Culebra, PR
WNVM(FM) Cidra, PR
WNVZ-FM Norfolk, VA
*WNWC-FM Madison, WI
WNWN-FM Coldwater, MI
WNWS-FM Jackson, TN
WNWV-FM Elyria, OH
*WNXR(FM) Iron River, WI
WNXT-FM Portsmouth, OH
WNXX(FM) Jackson, LA
*WNYC-FM New York, NY
*WNYE(FM) New York, NY
*WNYK-FM Nyack, NY
WNYN-FM Whitefield, NH
*WNYO-FM Oswego, NY
WNYQ(FM) Hudson Falls, NY
WNYR-FM Waterloo, NY
*WNYU-FM New York, NY
WNYV-FM Whitehall, NY
*WNYX(FM) Montgomery, NY
*WNZN-FM Lorain, OH
*WNZR(FM) Mount Vernon, OH
WOAB-FM Ozark, AL
WOAH(FM) Glennville, GA
*WOAK-FM La Grange, GA
*WOAR-FM South Vienna, OH
*WOAS(FM) Ontonagon, MI
WOBB-FM Tifton, GA
*WOBC-FM Oberlin, OH
WOBE-FM Crystal Falls, MI
WOBG-FM Salem, WV
*WOBH(FM) Lindenhurst, NY
WOBM-FM Toms River, NJ
*WOBN-FM Westerville, OH

*WOBO-FM Batavia, OH
WOBR-FM Wanchese, NC
WOBX-FM Manteo, NC
WOCE(FM) Ringgold, GA
*WOCL-FM De Land, FL
WOCM(FM) Selbyville, DE
WOCN-FM Orleans, MA
WOCO-FM Oconto, WI
WOCQ-FM Berlin, MD
*WOCR-FM Olivet, MI
*WOCS(FM) Lerose, KY
*WOCU(FM) Sinking Spring, OH
WOCY-FM Carrabelle, FL
WODA-FM Bayamon, PR
WODB(FM) Richwood, OH
WODE-FM Easton, PA
WODR-FM Fair Bluff, NC
WODS-FM Boston, MA
WODZ-FM Rome, NY
*WOEL-FM Elkton, MD
*WOES-FM Ovid-Elsie, MI
WOFM-FM Mosinee, WI
*WOFN(FM) Beach City, OH
*WOFR(FM) Schoolcraft, MI
WOFX-FM Cincinnati, OH
WOGB-FM Kaukauna, WI
*WOGF(FM) East Liverpool, OH
WOGG(FM) Oliver, PA
WOGH(FM) Burgettstown, PA
WOGI(FM) Charleroi, PA
WOGK-FM Ocala, FL
WOGL(FM) Philadelphia, PA
WOGR-FM Salisbury, NC
WOGT-FM East Ridge, TN
WOGY-FM Jackson, TN
*WOHC-FM Chillicothe, OH
WOHF-FM Bellevue, OH
*WOHP-FM Portsmouth, OH
WOHT(FM) Grenada, MS
*WOI-FM Ames, IA
*WOJB-FM Reserve, WI
*WOJC(FM) Crothersville, IN
WOJG-FM Bolivar, TN
WOJL(FM) Louisa, VA
WOJO-FM Evanston, IL
WOKA-FM Douglas, GA
*WOKD-FM Danville, VA
WOKE-FM Garrison, KY
*WOKG(FM) Galax, VA
*WOKI(FM) Oliver Springs, TN
WOKK-FM Meridian, MS
*WOKL(FM) Troy, OH
WOKN-FM Southport, NY
WOKO-FM Burlington, VT
WOKQ-FM Dover, NH
WOKR(FM) Remsen, NY
WOKV-FM Ponte Vedra Beach, FL
WOKW-FM Curwensville, PA
WOKZ(FM) Fairfield, IL
WOLC-FM Princess Anne, MD
WOLD-FM Marion, VA
WOLF-FM Oswego, NY
*WOLG-FM Carlinville, IL
WOLI-FM Easley, SC
WOLL-FM Hobe Sound, FL
*WOLN-FM Olean, NY
*WOLR-FM Lake City, FL
WOLS(FM) Waxhaw, NC
WOLT-FM Greer, SC
WOLV-FM Houghton, MI
*WOLW-FM Cadillac, MI
WOLX-FM Baraboo, WI
WOLZ-FM Fort Myers, FL
*WOMB(FM) Ellettsville, IN
WOMC-FM Detroit, MI
WOMG-FM Lexington, SC
*WOMR-FM Provincetown, MA
WOMX-FM Orlando, FL
WONA-FM Winona, MS
*WONB(FM) Ada, OH
*WONC(FM) Naperville, IL
WONE-FM Akron, OH
*WONU-FM Kankakee, IL
*WONY-FM Oneonta, NY
WOOD-FM Grand Rapids, MI
WOOF-FM Dothan, AL

WOOZ-FM Harrisburg, IL
*WOPG(FM) Esperance, NY
WORC-FM Webster, MA
WORD-FM Pittsburgh, PA
WORG-FM Elloree, SC
*WORI(FM) Delhi Hills, OH
WORK-FM Barre, VT
WORM-FM Savannah, TN
WORO-FM Corozal, PR
*WORQ-FM Green Bay, WI
*WORT-FM Madison, WI
*WORW-FM Port Huron, MI
WORX-FM Madison, IN
*WOSB-FM Marion, OH
WOSC-FM Bethany Beach, DE
*WOSE-FM Coshocton, OH
WOSM-FM Ocean Springs, MS
WOSN-FM Indian River Shores, FL
WOSP-FM Portsmouth, OH
WOSQ-FM Spencer, WI
*WOSR-FM Middletown, NY
*WOSS-FM Ossining, NY
*WOSU-FM Columbus, OH
*WOSV-FM Mansfield, OH
*WOTC-FM Edinburg, VA
*WOTJ-FM Morehead City, NC
*WOTL-FM Toledo, OH
WOTR-FM Lost Creek, WV
WOTT(FM) Calcium, NY
*WOTW(FM) Monee, IL
WOTX(FM) Lunenburg, VT
*WOUB-FM Athens, OH
*WOUC-FM Cambridge, OH
WOUF-FM Frankfort, MI
*WOUH-FM Chillicothe, OH
*WOUL-FM Ironton, OH
WOUR-FM Utica, NY
*WOUZ-FM Zanesville, OH
*WOVI-FM Novi, MI
WOVK-FM Wheeling, WV
*WOVM(FM) Appleton, WI
WOVO(FM) Glasgow, KY
*WOVV(FM) Ocracoke, NC
WOWC-FM Morrison, TN
WOWE-FM Vassar, MI
WOWF-FM Crossville, TN
WOWI-FM Norfolk, VA
*WOWL(FM) Burnsville, MS
WOWN-FM Shawano, WI
WOWQ(FM) DuBois, PA
*WOWY-FM University Park, PA
WOXD-FM Oxford, MS
WOXL-FM Biltmore Forest, NC
*WOXM(FM) Middlebury, VT
WOXO-FM Norway, ME
*WOXR(FM) Schuyler Falls, NY
WOXY-FM Oxford, OH
WOYE(FM) Rio Grande, PR
WOYS-FM Apalachicola, FL
WOZI(FM) Presque Isle, ME
*WOZQ-FM Northampton, MA
WOZZ-FM New London, WI
WPAC-FM Ogdensburg, NY
*WPAE-FM Centreville, MS
WPAL-FM Ridgeville, SC
WPAP-FM Panama City, FL
*WPAR-FM Salem, VA
*WPAS-FM Pascagoula, MS
WPAT-FM Paterson, NJ
WPAW-FM Winston-Salem, NC
WPAY-FM Portsmouth, OH
WPBG-FM Peoria, IL
WPBH(FM) Port St. Joe, FL
WPBK(FM) Crab Orchard, KY
WPBX(FM) Crossville, TN
WPBZ-FM Indiantown, FL
*WPCD-FM Champaign, IL
WPCH(FM) Gray, GA
*WPCJ-FM Pittsford, MI
WPCK(FM) Denmark, WI
WPCL(FM) Northern Cambria, PA
*WPCR-FM Plymouth, NH
*WPCS(FM) Pensacola, FL
WPCV(FM) Winter Haven, FL
WPDA-FM Jeffersonville, NY
WPDH-FM Poughkeepsie, NY

*WPDJ(FM) Trailtown, FL
WPDT-FM Johnsonville, SC
WPDX-FM Clarksburg, WV
*WPEA-FM Exeter, NH
*WPEB-FM Philadelphia, PA
*WPEF(FM) Kentwood, LA
WPEG-FM Concord, NC
WPEH-FM Louisville, GA
WPEI(FM) Saco, ME
*WPEL-FM Montrose, PA
*WPER-FM Culpeper, VA
WPEZ(FM) Jeffersonville, GA
WPFB-FM Middletown, OH
*WPFF(FM) Sturgeon Bay, WI
*WPFG(FM) Carlisle, PA
WPFL-FM Century, FL
WPFM-FM Panama City, FL
*WPFR-FM Clinton, IN
WPFT(FM) Pigeon Forge, TN
*WPFW-FM Washington, DC
WPFX-FM North Baltimore, OH
WPGA-FM Perry, GA
WPGB-FM Pittsburgh, PA
WPGC-FM Morningside, MD
WPGI-FM Horseheads, NY
*WPGL-FM Pattersonville, NY
*WPGM-FM Danville, PA
*WPGT(FM) Roanoke Rapids, NC
WPGU-FM Urbana, IL
WPGW-FM Portland, IN
WPHD-FM South Waverly, PA
*WPHH(FM) Conway, NH
WPHI-FM Media, PA
WPHK-FM Blountstown, FL
*WPHN-FM Gaylord, MI
*WPHP-FM Wheeling, WV
WPHR-FM Auburn, NY
*WPHS-FM Warren, MI
WPHX-FM Sanford, ME
WPHZ(FM) Mitchell, IN
WPIA(FM) Eureka, IL
*WPIB-FM Bluefield, WV
WPIG-FM Olean, NY
WPIK-FM Summerland Key, FL
*WPIL(FM) Heflin, AL
WPIM-FM Martinsville, VA
*WPIN-FM Dublin, VA
WPIO-FM Titusville, FL
WPIQ(FM) Manistique, MI
*WPIR-FM Hickory, NC
*WPJC(FM) Pontiac, IL
WPJP(FM) Port Washington, WI
*WPJW(FM) Hurricane, WV
*WPJY(FM) Blennerhassett, WV
WPKE-FM Coal Run, KY
WPKF(FM) Poughkeepsie, NY
WPKG(FM) Neillsville, WI
WPKL(FM) Uniontown, PA
*WPKM(FM) Montauk, NY
WPKN-FM Bridgeport, CT
WPKO-FM Bellefontaine, OH
WPKQ(FM) North Conway, NH
WPKR-FM Omro, WI
*WPKT-FM Meriden, CT
*WPKV(FM) Nanty Glo, PA
WPKX-FM Enfield, CT
WPLA(FM) Jacksonville, FL
*WPLH-FM Tifton, GA
*WPLI-FM Levittown, PR
WPLJ-FM New York, NY
WPLM-FM Plymouth, MA
*WPLN-FM Nashville, TN
WPLR-FM New Haven, CT
WPLT-FM Sarona, WI
WPLZ-FM Ooltewah, TN
WPMA(FM) Buckhead, GA
WPMJ(FM) Chillicothe, IL
*WPMW(FM) Bayview, MA
WPMX-FM Statesboro, GA
WPNC-FM Plymouth, NC
*WPNE(FM) Green Bay, WI
WPNG-FM Pearson, GA
WPNH-FM Plymouth, NH
*WPNR-FM Utica, NY
*WPOB-FM Plainview, NY
WPOC-FM Baltimore, MD

WPOI(FM) Saint Petersburg, FL
WPOR(FM) Portland, ME
WPOS-FM Holland, OH
WPOW-FM Miami, FL
*WPOZ-FM Union Park, FL
WPPG(FM) Repton, AL
WPPL(FM) Blue Ridge, GA
WPPN(FM) Des Plaines, IL
*WPPR-FM Demorest, GA
WPPT(FM) Mercersburg, PA
WPPZ-FM Jenkintown, PA
WPRB-FM Princeton, NJ
*WPRC-FM Princeton, IL
WPRF(FM) Reserve, LA
*WPRG(FM) Columbia, MS
WPRH(FM) Paris, TN
*WPRJ-FM Coleman, MI
*WPRK-FM Winter Park, FL
*WPRL-FM Lorman, MS
WPRM-FM San Juan, PR
WPRN-FM Lisman, AL
WPRO-FM Providence, RI
WPRS-FM Waldorf, MD
WPRT-FM Pegram, TN
WPRW-FM Martinez, GA
*WPRZ-FM Fredonia, KY
WPSA-FM Paul Smiths, NY
*WPSC-FM Wayne, NJ
*WPSF(FM) Clewiston, FL
WPSK-FM Pulaski, VA
WPSM-FM Fort Walton Beach, FL
*WPSR-FM Evansville, IN
WPST(FM) Trenton, NJ
*WPSU-FM State College, PA
*WPSX(FM) Kane, PA
*WPTC-FM Williamsport, PA
WPTE-FM Virginia Beach, VA
*WPTH-FM Olney, IL
*WPTJ(FM) Paris, KY
WPTM-FM Roanoke Rapids, NC
WPTQ(FM) Cave City, KY
WPTR(FM) Clifton Park, NY
*WPTS-FM Pittsburgh, PA
WPUB-FM Camden, SC
*WPUC-FM Ponce, PR
*WPUM(FM) Rensselaer, IN
WPUP(FM) Watkinsville, GA
WPUR-FM Atlantic City, NJ
*WPVA-FM Waynesboro, VA
*WPVH(FM) Plymouth, NH
*WPVL-FM Platteville, WI
WPVQ(FM) Greenfield, MA
*WPWB(FM) Byron, GA
WPWQ(FM) Mount Sterling, IL
*WPWV(FM) Princeton, WV
WPWX(FM) Hammond, IN
WPWZ(FM) Pinetops, NC
WPXC-FM Hyannis, MA
WPXN-FM Paxton, IL
WPXY-FM Rochester, NY
WPXZ-FM Punxsutawney, PA
WPYA(FM) Chesapeake, VA
WPYO-FM Maitland, FL
WPYX-FM Albany, NY
WPZE-FM Mableton, GA
WPZS(FM) Albemarle, NC
WPZX(FM) Pocono Pines, PA
WPZZ(FM) Crewe, VA
*WQAB-FM Philippi, WV
*WQAC-FM Alma, MI
WQAH-FM Addison, AL
*WQAI(FM) Thomson, GA
WQAK(FM) Union City, TN
WQAL-FM Cleveland, OH
*WQAQ-FM Hamden, CT
WQAR-FM Stillwater, NY
WQBE-FM Charleston, WV
WQBJ-FM Cobleskill, NY
WQBK-FM Rensselaer, NY
WQBR-FM Avis, PA
WQBT-FM Savannah, GA
WQBU-FM Garden City, NY
WQBW-FM Milwaukee, WI
WQBX(FM) Alma, MI
WQBZ-FM Fort Valley, GA
WQCB-FM Brewer, ME

WQCC-FM La Crosse, WI
WQCM(FM) Greencastle, PA
*WQCS-FM Fort Pierce, FL
WQCY(FM) Quincy, IL
WQDK-FM Ahoskie, NC
WQDR-FM Raleigh, NC
WQDY-FM Calais, ME
*WQED-FM Pittsburgh, PA
*WQEJ-FM Johnstown, PA
WQEL-FM Bucyrus, OH
WQEM(FM) Columbiana, AL
WQEN(FM) Trussville, AL
*WQFL-FM Rockford, IL
WQFM-FM Nanticoke, PA
WQFN(FM) Forest City, PA
*WQFS-FM Greensboro, NC
WQFX-FM Russell, PA
WQGN-FM Groton, CT
WQHH-FM Dewitt, MI
WQHK-FM Decatur, IN
WQHL-FM Live Oak, FL
WQHQ-FM Ocean City-Salisbury, MD
WQHR-FM Presque Isle, ME
WQHT-FM New York, NY
WQHY-FM Prestonsburg, KY
WQHZ(FM) Erie, PA
WQIC-FM Lebanon, PA
WQIK-FM Jacksonville, FL
WQIL-FM Chauncey, GA
WQIO-FM Mount Vernon, OH
WQJB(FM) State College, MS
WQJK(FM) Maryville, TN
WQJQ-FM Kosciusko, MS
*WQJU-FM Mifflintown, PA
WQJZ-FM Ocean Pines, MD
*WQKE-FM Plattsburgh, NY
WQKI-FM Orangeburg, SC
WQKL-FM Ann Arbor, MI
*WQKO-FM Howe, IN
WQKQ(FM) Carthage, IL
WQKS-FM Montgomery, AL
*WQKT-FM Wooster, OH
*WQKV(FM) Rochester, IN
WQKX(FM) Sunbury, PA
WQKY-FM Emporium, PA
WQKZ-FM Ferdinand, IN
WQLB-FM Tawas City, MI
WQLC-FM Watertown, FL
WQLF(FM) Lena, IL
WQLH-FM Green Bay, WI
WQLI-FM Meigs, GA
WQLJ-FM Oxford, MS
WQLK-FM Richmond, IN
*WQLN-FM Erie, PA
WQLT-FM Florence, AL
WQLV-FM Millersburg, PA
WQLZ-FM Taylorville, IL
WQME-FM Anderson, IN
*WQMF-FM Jeffersonville, IN
WQMG-FM Greensboro, NC
*WQMI(FM) Grand Marais, MI
WQMJ(FM) Forsyth, GA
WQMR(FM) Snow Hill, MD
WQMU-FM Indiana, PA
WQMX-FM Medina, OH
WQMZ(FM) Charlottesville, VA
*WQNA(FM) Springfield, IL
WQNC(FM) Harrisburg, NC
WQNQ(FM) Fletcher, NC
WQNR-FM Tallassee, AL
WQNS-FM Waynesville, NC
WQNU-FM Lyndon, KY
WQNY-FM Ithaca, NY
WQNZ-FM Natchez, MS
WQOK-FM South Boston, VA
WQOL-FM Vero Beach, FL
WQON-FM Roscommon, MI
*WQOX-FM Memphis, TN
WQPC-FM Prairie du Chien, WI
WQPO-FM Harrisonburg, VA
*WQPR-FM Muscle Shoals, AL
WQPW-FM Valdosta, GA
WQQB-FM Rantoul, IL
WQQK-FM Hendersonville, TN
WQQL(FM) Springfield, IL
WQQQ(FM) Sharon, CT

WQQR(FM) Mayfield, KY
WQRB-FM Bloomer, WI
WQRC-FM Barnstable, MA
*WQRI-FM Bristol, RI
WQRK-FM Bedford, IN
WQRL-FM Benton, IL
*WQRN(FM) Cook, MN
*WQRP-FM Dayton, OH
WQRS-FM Salamanca, NY
WQRV-FM Tuscumbia, AL
WQRW-FM Wellsville, NY
WQSB-FM Albertville, AL
*WQSG(FM) Lafayette, IN
WQSI-FM Union Springs, AL
WQSL-FM Jacksonville, NC
WQSM-FM Fayetteville, NC
WQSO-FM Rochester, NH
WQSR(FM) Baltimore, MD
WQSS-FM Camden, ME
WQST-FM Forest, MS
*WQSU(FM) Selinsgrove, PA
WQTC-FM Manitowoc, WI
WQTE-FM Adrian, MI
WQTK(FM) Ogdensburg, NY
WQTL(FM) Tallahassee, FL
*WQTQ-FM Hartford, CT
WQTU-FM Rome, GA
WQTX(FM) Saint Johns, MI
WQTY-FM Linton, IN
WQUA-FM Citronelle, AL
*WQUB(FM) Quincy, IL
WQUE-FM New Orleans, LA
WQUS(FM) Lapeer, MI
WQUT-FM Johnson City, TN
WQVE-FM Albany, GA
*WQVI(FM) Forest, MS
WQWV(FM) Fisher, WV
WQXA-FM York, PA
WQXB-FM Grenada, MS
WQXC-FM Otsego, MI
WQXE-FM Elizabethtown, KY
*WQXJ-FM Blackduck, MN
WQXK-FM Salem, OH
WQXQ(FM) Central City, KY
WQXR-FM New York, NY
WQXZ(FM) Hawkinsville, GA
WQYK-FM Saint Petersburg, FL
WQYX-FM Clearfield, PA
WQYZ-FM Ocean Springs, MS
WQZK-FM Keyser, WV
WQZL(FM) Belhaven, NC
WQZS-FM Meyersdale, PA
WQZX-FM Greenville, AL
WQZY-FM Dublin, GA
WQZZ-FM Eutaw, AL
WRAC-FM West Union, OH
*WRAE(FM) Raeford, NC
*WRAF-FM Toccoa Falls, GA
WRAK-FM Bainbridge, GA
WRAL(FM) Raleigh, NC
WRAN(FM) Tower Hill, IL
*WRAO(FM) Wisconsin Rapids, WI
WRAR-FM Tappahannock, VA
*WRAS-FM Atlanta, GA
WRAT(FM) Point Pleasant, NJ
*WRAU(FM) Ocean City, MD
WRAX(FM) Walhalla, MI
WRAY-FM Princeton, IN
WRAZ-FM Leisure City, FL
WRBA(FM) Springfield, FL
*WRBB-FM Boston, MA
*WRBC-FM Lewiston, ME
WRBE-FM Lucedale, MS
WRBF(FM) Plainville, GA
*WRBH-FM New Orleans, LA
WRBI-FM Batesville, IN
WRBJ-FM Brandon, MS
*WRBK-FM Richburg, SC
WRBN-FM Clayton, GA
WRBO-FM Como, MS
WRBP-FM Hubbard, OH
WRBQ-FM Tampa, FL
WRBR-FM South Bend, IN
WRBS-FM Baltimore, MD
WRBT-FM Harrisburg, PA
WRBV-FM Warner Robins, GA

WRBX-FM Reidsville, GA
*WRCC(FM) Dibrell, TN
WRCD-FM Canton, NY
WRCH-FM New Britain, CT
*WRCJ-FM Detroit, MI
WRCK-FM Utica, NY
WRCL(FM) Frankenmuth, MI
*WRCM-FM Wingate, NC
WRCN-FM Riverhead, NY
WRCO-FM Richland Center, WI
WRCQ-FM Dunn, NC
*WRCT-FM Pittsburgh, PA
*WRCU-FM Hamilton, NY
WRCV(FM) Dixon, IL
WRCW-FM Nekoosa, WI
*WRDK(FM) Bladenboro, NC
*WRDL-FM Ashland, OH
WRDO-FM Fitzgerald, GA
*WRDR(FM) Freehold Township, NJ
WRDU-FM Wilson, NC
*WRDV-FM Warminster, PA
WRDW-FM Philadelphia, PA
WRDX(FM) Smyrna, DE
WRDZ-FM Plainfield, IN
WREB-FM Greencastle, IN
*WREE(FM) Fargo, GA
*WREH(FM) Cypress Quarters, FL
*WREI(FM) Kings Bay, GA
*WREK-FM Atlanta, GA
WREO-FM Ashtabula, OH
WREQ-FM Ridgebury, PA
WREW(FM) Fairfield, OH
WREZ-FM Metropolis, IL
*WRFE(FM) Chesterfield, SC
WRFF(FM) Philadelphia, PA
*WRFG-FM Atlanta, GA
*WRFI(FM) Watkins Glen, NY
*WRFL-FM Lexington, KY
WRFQ-FM Mt. Pleasant, SC
*WRFR(FM) Grand Rapids, MN
*WRFT-FM Indianapolis, IN
*WRFW-FM River Falls, WI
WRFX(FM) Kannapolis, NC
WRFY-FM Reading, PA
*WRGC-FM Milledgeville, GA
*WRGF-FM Greenfield, IN
*WRGN-FM Sweet Valley, PA
WRGO-FM Cedar Key, FL
*WRGP(FM) Homestead, FL
WRGR-FM Tupper Lake, NY
*WRGY-FM Rangeley, ME
WRGZ(FM) Rogers City, MI
WRHD(FM) Williamston, NC
WRHK-FM Danville, IL
WRHL-FM Rochelle, IL
WRHM(FM) Lancaster, SC
WRHN-FM Rhinelander, WI
*WRHO-FM Oneonta, NY
WRHQ-FM Richmond Hill, GA
WRHT-FM Morehead City, NC
WRHU-FM Hempstead, NY
*WRHV-FM Poughkeepsie, NY
WRIC-FM Richlands, VA
WRIF(FM) Detroit, MI
*WRIH(FM) Richmond, VA
*WRIJ(FM) Masontown, PA
WRIK-FM Metropolis, IL
WRIL-FM Pineville, KY
WRIO-FM Ponce, PR
WRIP-FM Windham, NY
*WRIQ(FM) Lexington, VA
WRIT-FM Milwaukee, WI
*WRIU-FM Kingston, RI
WRIX-FM Honea Path, SC
*WRJA-FM Sumter, SC
WRJB-FM Camden, TN
WRJC-FM Mauston, WI
*WRJI(FM) East Greenwich, RI
WRJJ(FM) La Center, KY
WRJK(FM) Norris, TN
WRJL-FM Eva, AL
WRJO-FM Eagle River, WI
WRJT-FM Royalton, VT
WRJY(FM) Brunswick, GA
*WRKA(FM) Louisville, KY
*WRKC-FM Wilkes-Barre, PA

*WRKF-FM Baton Rouge, LA
WRKG-FM Drew, MS
WRKH-FM Mobile, AL
WRKI-FM Brookfield, CT
*WRKJ(FM) Westbrook, ME
WRKN-FM Niceville, FL
WRKR-FM Portage, MI
WRKS(FM) New York, NY
WRKT-FM North East, PA
WRKU-FM Forestville, WI
WRKW(FM) Ebensburg, PA
WRKX(FM) Ottawa, IL
*WRKY-FM Hollidaysburg, PA
WRKZ(FM) Columbus, OH
WRLB-FM Rainelle, WV
*WRLC-FM Williamsport, PA
WRLD-FM Valley, AL
WRLF-FM Fairmont, WV
*WRLI-FM Southampton, NY
WRLO-FM Antigo, WI
WRLS-FM Hayward, WI
WRLT-FM Franklin, TN
WRLU-FM Algoma, WI
WRLV-FM Salyersville, KY
WRLX-FM West Palm Beach, FL
WRMA-FM Fort Lauderdale, FL
*WRMB-FM Boynton Beach, FL
*WRMC-FM Middlebury, VT
WRMF(FM) Palm Beach, FL
WRMJ-FM Aledo, IL
WRMM-FM Rochester, NY
WRMO(FM) Milbridge, ME
WRMS-FM Beardstown, IL
*WRMU-FM Alliance, OH
WRNB-FM Pennsauken, NJ
*WRNF(FM) Selma, AL
WRNH(FM) Groveton, NH
WRNI-FM Narragansett Pier, RI
*WRNM(FM) Ellsworth, ME
WRNN-FM Socastee, SC
WRNO-FM New Orleans, LA
WRNQ-FM Poughkeepsie, NY
WRNR-FM Grasonville, MD
WRNS-FM Kinston, NC
WRNX-FM Amherst, MA
WRNZ(FM) Lancaster, KY
WROE-FM Neenah-Menasha, WI
WROG-FM Cumberland, MD
*WROI-FM Rochester, IN
WRON-FM Lewisburg, WV
WROO(FM) South Bristol Township, NY
WROQ-FM Anderson, SC
WROR-FM Framingham, MA
WROU-FM West Carrollton, OH
WROV-FM Martinsville, VA
WROX-FM Exmore, VA
WROZ-FM Lancaster, PA
*WRPB(FM) Benedicta, ME
*WRPI-FM Troy, NY
*WRPJ-FM Port Jervis, NY
*WRPN-FM Ripon, WI
*WRPR-FM Mahwah, NJ
*WRPS-FM Rockland, MA
WRPW(FM) Colfax, IL
*WRQC(FM) East Tawas, MI
WRQE-FM Sturgeon Bay, WI
WRQK-FM Canton, OH
*WRQM-FM Rocky Mount, NC
WRQN-FM Bowling Green, OH
WRQO-FM Monticello, MS
WRQQ-FM Goodlettsville, TN
WRQT(FM) La Crosse, WI
WRQX-FM Washington, DC
WRR(FM) Dallas, TX
WRRB(FM) Arlington, NY
*WRRC-FM Lawrenceville, NJ
*WRRG-FM River Grove, IL
WRRH(FM) Hormigueros, PR
*WRRI(FM) Brownsville, TN
WRRK(FM) Braddock, PA
WRRM-FM Cincinnati, OH
WRRN-FM Warren, PA
WRRQ(FM) Windsor, NY
WRRR-FM Saint Marys, WV
WRRV-FM Middletown, NY

*WRRX(FM) Gulf Breeze, FL
WRSA-FM Holly Pond, AL
WRSC-FM State College, PA
*WRSD-FM Folsom, PA
*WRSE(FM) Elmhurst, IL
WRSF-FM Columbia, NC
*WRSG(FM) Middlebourne, WV
*WRSH-FM Rockingham, NC
WRSI-FM Turners Falls, MA
*WRSN-FM Lebanon, TN
WRSR-FM Owosso, MI
*WRST-FM Oshkosh, WI
*WRSU-FM New Brunswick, NJ
WRSV-FM Rocky Mount, NC
WRSW-FM Warsaw, IN
WRSY(FM) Marlboro, VT
WRTB(FM) Winnebago, IL
*WRTC-FM Hartford, CT
*WRTE-FM Chicago, IL
*WRTH(FM) Layton, FL
*WRTI-FM Philadelphia, PA
*WRTJ(FM) Coatesville, PA
*WRTL(FM) Ephrata, PA
WRTM-FM Port Gibson, MS
WRTO-FM Goulds, FL
*WRTP(FM) Roanoke Rapids, NC
*WRTQ-FM Ocean City, NJ
WRTR(FM) Brookwood, AL
WRTS-FM Erie, PA
WRTT-FM Huntsville, AL
*WRTU-FM San Juan, PR
*WRTW(FM) Crown Point, IN
*WRTX-FM Dover, DE
*WRTY-FM Jackson Township, PA
WRUC-FM Schenectady, NY
WRUF-FM Gainesville, FL
WRUL-FM Carmi, IL
WRUM(FM) Orlando, FL
*WRUN-FM Remsen, NY
WRUO(FM) Mayaguez, PR
WRUP(FM) Munising, MI
*WRUR-FM Rochester, NY
*WRUV-FM Burlington, VT
*WRUW-FM Cleveland, OH
WRVA-FM Rocky Mount, NC
WRVB-FM Marietta, OH
*WRVD(FM) Syracuse, NY
WRVE-FM Schenectady, NY
WRVF(FM) Toledo, OH
*WRVG(FM) Georgetown, KY
WRVI-FM Valley Station, KY
*WRVJ(FM) Watertown, NY
*WRVL-FM Lynchburg, VA
*WRVM-FM Suring, WI
*WRVN(FM) Utica, NY
*WRVO-FM Oswego, NY
WRVQ-FM Richmond, VA
WRVR(FM) Memphis, TN
WRVS-FM Elizabeth City, NC
*WRVT-FM Rutland, VT
*WRVU-FM Nashville, TN
WRVV-FM Harrisburg, PA
WRVW-FM Lebanon, TN
WRVX(FM) Eufaula, AL
WRVY-FM Henry, IL
WRVZ-FM Pocatalico, WV
*WRWA-FM Dothan, AL
WRWC-FM Ellenville, NY
WRWD-FM Highland, NY
*WRWJ(FM) Murrysville, PA
WRWM(FM) Lawrence, IN
*WRWV(FM) Saint Marys, PA
*WRXC-FM Shelton, CT
WRXD(FM) Fajardo, PR
WRXK-FM Bonita Springs, FL
WRXL-FM Richmond, VA
WRXP(FM) New York, NY
WRXQ(FM) Coal City, IL
WRXR-FM Rossville, GA
WRXS(FM) Dublin, MN
*WRXT-FM Roanoke, VA
*WRXV(FM) State College, PA
WRXW(FM) Pearl, MS
WRXX-FM Centralia, IL
WRXZ(FM) Briarcliff Acres, SC
*WRYN(FM) Hickory, NC

*WRYP(FM) Wellfleet, MA
*WRYS(FM) Grayson, KY
*WRYV(FM) Milroy, PA
*WRYZ(FM) Palm Bay, FL
WRZE-FM Kingstree, SC
WRZI-FM Vine Grove, KY
WRZK-FM Colonial Heights, TN
WRZQ-FM Greensburg, IN
WRZR-FM Loogootee, IN
WRZX-FM Indianapolis, IN
WRZZ(FM) Elizabeth, WV
*WSAA(FM) Benton, TN
*WSAE-FM Spring Arbor, MI
WSAG-FM Linwood, MI
*WSAJ-FM Grove City, PA
WSAK(FM) Hampton, NH
WSAQ-FM Port Huron, MI
*WSBF-FM Clemson, SC
WSB-FM Atlanta, GA
WSBG-FM Stroudsburg, PA
*WSBH(FM) Satellite Beach, FL
*WSBU-FM Saint Bonaventure, NY
WSBW(FM) Sister Bay, WI
WSBY-FM Salisbury, MD
WSBZ-FM Miramar Beach, FL
*WSCB-FM Springfield, MA
WSCC-FM Goose Creek, SC
*WSCD-FM Duluth, MN
*WSCF-FM Vero Beach, FL
WSCH-FM Aurora, IN
*WSCI-FM Charleston, SC
*WSCL-FM Salisbury, MD
WSCN-FM Cloquet, MN
*WSCS(FM) New London, NH
*WSCT(FM) Springfield, IL
WSCY-FM Moultonborough, NH
*WSDH-FM Sandwich, MA
*WSDL-FM Ocean City, MD
WSDM-FM Brazil, IN
*WSDP-FM Plymouth, MI
WSEA(FM) Atlantic Beach, SC
*WSEB-FM Englewood, FL
*WSEH(FM) South Elgin, IL
WSEI-FM Olney, IL
WSEK(FM) Burnside, KY
WSEL-FM Pontotoc, MS
WSEN-FM Baldwinsville, NY
WSEO-FM Nelsonville, OH
WSEV-FM Gatlinburg, TN
*WSEW-FM Sanford, ME
*WSEY(FM) Oregon, IL
WSFF(FM) Vinton, VA
WSFL-FM New Bern, NC
*WSFM(FM) Oak Island, NC
*WSFP(FM) Rust Township, MI
WSFQ-FM Peshtigo, WI
WSFR-FM Corydon, IN
*WSFX-FM Nanticoke, PA
WSGA(FM) Hinesville, GA
WSGC-FM Elberton, GA
*WSGE-FM Dallas, NC
*WSGG(FM) Norfolk, CT
WSGL-FM Naples, FL
WSGM-FM Coalmont, TN
*WSGN-FM Gadsden, AL
*WSGP(FM) Glasgow, KY
*WSGR-FM Port Huron, MI
WSGS-FM Hazard, KY
WSGW-FM Carrollton, MI
*WSHA-FM Raleigh, NC
*WSHB(FM) Willard, OH
*WSHC-FM Shepherdstown, WV
*WSHD-FM Eastport, ME
WSHH-FM Pittsburgh, PA
*WSHJ-FM Southfield, MI
WSHK(FM) Kittery, ME
*WSHL-FM Easton, MA
*WSHM(FM) Wixom, MI
WSHP(FM) Attica, IN
*WSHR-FM Lake Ronkonkoma, NY
*WSHS-FM Sheboygan, WI
*WSHU-FM Fairfield, CT
WSHW-FM Frankfort, IN
WSHZ(FM) Muskegon, MI
*WSIA-FM Staten Island, NY
WSIB-FM Selmer, TN

*WSIE-FM Edwardsville, IL
WSIF-FM Wilkesboro, NC
WSIG(FM) Mount Jackson, VA
WSIM(FM) Lamar, SC
WSIP-FM Paintsville, KY
*WSIS-FM Riverside, MI
*WSIU(FM) Carbondale, IL
WSIX-FM Nashville, TN
WSIZ-FM Jacksonville, GA
WSJD-FM Princeton, IN
*WSJE(FM) Summersville, WV
*WSJL(FM) Northport, AL
WSJM-FM Benton Harbor, MI
*WSJO(FM) Egg Harbor City, NJ
WSJR-FM Dallas, PA
WSJT-FM Holmes Beach, FL
WSJW-FM Starview, PA
*WSJY-FM Fort Atkinson, WI
WSJZ-FM Sebastian, FL
*WSKB-FM Westfield, MA
WSKE-FM Everett, PA
*WSKG-FM Binghamton, NY
WSKK(FM) Ripley, MS
*WSKL-FM Veedersburg, IN
WSKQ-FM New York, NY
WSKS-FM Whitesboro, NY
WSKU-FM Little Falls, NY
WSKV-FM Stanton, KY
WSKX(FM) York Center, ME
WSKY-FM Micanopy, FL
WSKZ-FM Chattanooga, TN
*WSLC-FM Roanoke, VA
WSLD-FM Whitewater, WI
*WSLE-FM Salem, IL
*WSLG-FM Gouverneur, NY
*WSLI(FM) Belding, MI
*WSLJ-FM Watertown, NY
*WSLL-FM Saranac Lake, NY
WSLM-FM Salem, IN
*WSLN-FM Delaware, OH
*WSLO-FM Malone, NY
*WSLP-FM Saranac Lake, NY
WSLQ-FM Roanoke, VA
*WSLT(FM) Statesboro, GA
*WSLU-FM Canton, NY
*WSLX-FM New Canaan, CT
*WSLY-FM York, AL
*WSLZ-FM Cape Vincent, NY
*WSMA(FM) Scituate, MA
*WSMC-FM Collegedale, TN
WSMD-FM Mechanicsville, MD
WSM-FM Nashville, TN
WSMI-FM Litchfield, IL
*WSMJ-FM Wilkinson, IN
WSMK-FM Buchanan, MI
*WSMM(FM) New Carlisle, IN
WSMP-FM New Hebron, MS
*WSMR-FM Sarasota, FL
WSMS-FM Artesia, MS
WSMW(FM) Greensboro, NC
*WSNC-FM Winston-Salem, NC
*WSND-FM Notre Dame, IN
WSNE-FM Taunton, MA
WSNI(FM) Swanzey, NH
WSNN-FM Potsdam, NY
WSNQ(FM) Cape May Court House, NJ
WSNT-FM Sandersville, GA
WSNU-FM Lock Haven, PA
WSNV(FM) Salem, VA
WSNX-FM Muskegon, MI
WSNY-FM Columbus, OH
WSNZ(FM) Lynchburg, VA
WSOC-FM Charlotte, NC
*WSOE(FM) Elon, NC
*WSOF-FM Madisonville, KY
*WSOG(FM) Spring Valley, IL
WSOL-FM Brunswick, GA
*WSOR-FM Naples, FL
WSOS-FM Saint Augustine, FL
*WSOU-FM South Orange, NJ
WSOX-FM Red Lion, PA
WSOY-FM Decatur, IL
WSPA-FM Spartanburg, SC
*WSPI(FM) Ellsworth, IL

*WSPK-FM Poughkeepsie, NY
*WSPM(FM) Cloverdale, IN
*WSPN(FM) Saratoga Springs, NY
*WSPS-FM Concord, NH
*WSPT-FM Stevens Point, WI
*WSPX-FM Bowman, SC
*WSPY-FM Plano, IL
*WSQA-FM Hornell, NY
*WSQC-FM Oneonta, NY
*WSQE(FM) Corning, NY
*WSQG-FM Ithaca, NY
*WSQH(FM) Forest, MS
*WSQX-FM Binghamton, NY
*WSRB(FM) Lansing, IL
*WSRG-FM Sturgeon Bay, WI
*WSRI(FM) Sugar Grove, IL
*WSRJ(FM) Honor, MI
*WSRK(FM) Oneonta, NY
*WSRM(FM) Coosa, GA
*WSRN-FM Swarthmore, PA
*WSRS-FM Worcester, MA
*WSRT(FM) Gaylord, MI
*WSRU(FM) Slippery Rock, PA
*WSRV(FM) Gainesville, GA
*WSRW-FM Hillsboro, OH
*WSRX-FM Naples, FL
*WSRZ-FM Coral Cove, FL
*WSSB-FM Orangeburg, SC
*WSSD-FM Chicago, IL
*WSSJ(FM) Rincon, GA
*WSSK-FM Saratoga Springs, NY
*WSSL-FM Gray Court, SC
*WSSM(FM) Havelock, NC
*WSSQ-FM Sterling, IL
*WSSR(FM) Joliet, IL
*WSSW(FM) Platteville, WI
*WSSX-FM Charleston, SC
*WSSY(FM) Pinehurst, GA
*WSTB-FM Streetsboro, OH
*WSTF-FM Andalusia, AL
*WSTG-FM Princeton, WV
*WSTH-FM Alexander City, AL
*WSTI-FM Quitman, GA
*WSTK(FM) Aurora, NC
*WSTM(FM) Kiel, WI
*WSTO-FM Owensboro, KY
*WSTQ(FM) Streator, IL
*WSTR-FM Smyrna, GA
*WSTS-FM Fairmont, NC
*WSTV-FM Frankfort, KY
*WSTW-FM Wilmington, DE
*WSTX-FM Christiansted, VI
*WSTZ-FM Vicksburg, MS
*WSUC-FM Cortland, NY
*WSUE-FM Sault Ste. Marie, MI
*WSUF-FM Noyack, NY
*WSUL(FM) Monticello, NY
*WSUM-FM Madison, WI
*WSUN-FM Holiday, FL
*WSUP-FM Platteville, WI
*WSUS-FM Franklin, NJ
*WSUW-FM Whitewater, WI
*WSVH-FM Savannah, GA
*WSVO-FM Staunton, VA
*WSVP(FM) Connellsville, PA
*WSWR-FM Shelby, OH
*WSWT-FM Peoria, IL
*WSWV-FM Pennington Gap, VA
*WSWW-FM Craigsville, WV
*WSYC-FM Shippensburg, PA
*WSYE-FM Houston, MS
*WSYN-FM Surfside Beach, SC
*WSYR-FM Gifford, FL
*WSYY-FM Millinocket, ME
*WTAC(FM) Burton, MI
*WTAI(FM) Union City, TN
*WTAK-FM Hartselle, AL
*WTAO-FM Herrin, IL
*WTAQ-FM Glenmore, WI
*WTBB-FM Gadsden, AL
*WTBD-FM Delhi, NY
*WTBF-FM Brundidge, AL
WTBG-FM Brownsville, TN
WTBI-FM Greenville, SC
*WTBJ-FM Oxford, AL
WTBK-FM Manchester, KY

*WTBM(FM) Mexico, ME
*WTBP(FM) Bath, ME
WTBX-FM Hibbing, MN
WTCB-FM Orangeburg, SC
*WTCC-FM Springfield, MA
*WTCD(FM) Indianola, MS
*WTCJ-FM Tell City, IN
*WTCK(FM) Charlevoix, MI
WTCM-FM Traverse City, MI
WTCQ-FM Vidalia, GA
WTCR-FM Huntington, WV
WTCX(FM) Ripon, WI
*WTDA(FM) Westerville, OH
*WTDK-FM Federalsburg, MD
*WTDR(FM) Talladega, AL
*WTEB-FM New Bern, NC
*WTFH(FM) Helen, GA
WTFM-FM Kingsport, TN
WTFX-FM Clarksville, IN
WTGA-FM Thomaston, GA
WTGB-FM Bethesda, MD
WTGD(FM) Bridgewater, VA
WTGE(FM) Baker, LA
WTGG-FM Amite, LA
*WTGN-FM Lima, OH
WTGR-FM Union City, OH
WTGV-FM Sandusky, MI
WTGY-FM Charleston, MS
WTGZ(FM) Tuskegee, AL
WTHB-FM Wrens, GA
WTHD-FM Lagrange, IN
WTHG(FM) Hinesville, GA
WTHI-FM Terre Haute, IN
WTHK(FM) Wilmington, VT
*WTHL-FM Somerset, KY
*WTHN(FM) Sault Ste. Marie, MI
WTHO-FM Thomson, GA
WTHP(FM) Gibson, GA
*WTHS-FM Holland, MI
WTHT(FM) Auburn, ME
WTHX(FM) Hodgenville, KY
WTHZ(FM) Lexington, KY
WTIB(FM) Farmville, NC
WTIC-FM Hartford, CT
WTID(FM) Thomaston, AL
WTIF-FM Omega, GA
WTIM-FM Taylorville, IL
*WTIP-FM Grand Marais, MN
WTIX-FM Galliano, LA
*WTJB-FM Columbus, GA
WTJJ(FM) Dyer, TN
*WTJM(FM) South Webster, OH
*WTJT-FM Baker, FL
*WTJU-FM Charlottesville, VA
WTJW(FM) Humboldt, TN
*WTJY-FM Asheboro, NC
*WTKB-FM Atwood, TN
*WTKC(FM) Findlay, OH
WTKE-FM Holt, FL
WTKF-FM Atlantic, NC
WTKK(FM) Boston, MA
*WTKL(FM) North Dartmouth, MA
WTKM-FM Hartford, WI
WTKS-FM Cocoa Beach, FL
WTKU-FM Ocean City, NJ
WTKV-FM Oswego, NY
WTKW-FM Bridgeport, NY
WTKX-FM Pensacola, FL
WTKY-FM Tompkinsville, KY
WTLC-FM Greenwood, IN
*WTLD(FM) Jesup, GA
*WTLG-FM Starke, FL
*WTLI-FM Bear Creek Township, MI
WTLP(FM) Braddock Heights, MD
WTLQ-FM Punta Rassa, FL
WTLR-FM State College, PA
WTLT-FM Naples, FL
WTLX(FM) Columbus, WI
WTLY(FM) Thomasville, GA
WTLZ-FM Saginaw, MI
*WTMB(FM) Tomah, WI
*WTMD(FM) Towson, MD
WTMG-FM Williston, FL
*WTMH-FM Smithboro, IL
*WTMI(FM) Fleming, NY
*WTMK(FM) Lowell, IN

*WTML(FM) Tullahoma, TN
WTMM-FM Mechanicville, NY
WTMP-FM Dade City, FL
*WTMQ(FM) Lumpkin, GA
*WTMT(FM) Weaverville, NC
*WTMV-FM Youngsville, PA
*WTMW(FM) North Judson, IN
WTMX-FM Skokie, IL
WTNE-FM Trenton, TN
WTNJ-FM Mount Hope, WV
WTNM(FM) Water Valley, MS
WTNN(FM) Bristol, VT
*WTNP(FM) Richland, MI
WTNQ(FM) La Follette, TN
WTNR-FM Holland, MI
WTNS-FM Coshocton, OH
WTNT-FM Tallahassee, FL
WTNV(FM) Tiptonville, TN
WTOJ(FM) Carthage, NY
WTON-FM Staunton, VA
WTOP-FM Washington, DC
WTOS-FM Skowhegan, ME
WTOT-FM Graceville, FL
WTPA-FM Mechanicsburg, PA
*WTPG(FM) Weston, OH
*WTPL(FM) Hillsboro, NH
WTPM-FM Aguadilla, PR
WTPO(FM) New Albany, MS
WTPR-FM McKinnon, TN
WTPT-FM Forest City, NC
WTQR-FM Winston-Salem, NC
WTQX(FM) Boothbay Harbor, ME
WTRG-FM Gaston, NC
*WTRH(FM) Ramsey, NJ
*WTRK-FM Freeland, MI
*WTRM-FM Winchester, VA
WTRS(FM) Dunnellon, FL
*WTRT-FM Benton, KY
WTRV-FM Walker, MI
WTRX-FM Pontiac, IL
WTRY-FM Rotterdam, NY
*WTRZ(FM) Spencer, TN
*WTSA-FM Brattleboro, VT
*WTSC-FM Potsdam, NY
*WTSE(FM) Benton, TN
*WTSG-FM Carlinville, IL
*WTSH-FM Rockmart, GA
*WTSR-FM Trenton, NJ
WTSS(FM) Buffalo, NY
*WTSU(FM) Montgomery-Troy, AL
WTSX-FM Port Jervis, NY
WTTC-FM Towanda, PA
WTTH(FM) Margate City, NJ
WTTS-FM Bloomington, IN
WTTT(FM) Stratford, NH
*WTTU(FM) Cookeville, TN
WTTX-FM Appomattox, VA
WTUA-FM Saint Stephen, SC
WTUE-FM Dayton, OH
WTUF-FM Boston, GA
WTUG-FM Northport, AL
WTUK-FM Harlan, KY
*WTUL-FM New Orleans, LA
WTUR-FM Upland, IN
WTUV-FM Eminence, KY
WTUZ-FM Uhrichsville, OH
WTVR-FM Richmond, VA
WTVY-FM Dothan, AL
WTWF-FM Fairview, PA
WTWR-FM Luna Pier, MI
WTWS(FM) Harrison, MI
*WTWT(FM) Bradford, PA
WTWX-FM Guntersville, AL
*WTXN(FM) Goodwater, AL
WTXO(FM) Ashland, AL
*WTXR(FM) Toccoa Falls, GA
WTXT-FM Fayette, AL
WTYB(FM) Tybee Island, GA
WTYD(FM) Deltaville, VA
WTYE-FM Robinson, IL
*WTYG-FM Sparr, FL
WTYJ-FM Fayette, MS
WTYL-FM Tylertown, MS
WTYS-FM Marianna, FL
WTZB(FM) Englewood, FL
*WTZI(FM) Rosemont, IL

*WTZR(FM) Elizabethton, TN
WUAG-FM Greensboro, NC
WUAL-FM Tuscaloosa, AL
WUAW-FM Erwin, NC
WUBE-FM Cincinnati, OH
WUBJ-FM Jamestown, NY
WUBL(FM) Atlanta, GA
*WUBS-FM South Bend, IN
WUBT-FM Russellville, KY
WUBU-FM South Bend, IN
*WUCF-FM Orlando, FL
*WUCL(FM) Meridian, MS
*WUCX-FM Bay City, MI
WUCZ(FM) Carthage, TN
WUDR(FM) Dayton, OH
WUEC-FM Eau Claire, WI
*WUEV-FM Evansville, IN
WUEZ(FM) Carterville, IL
WUFF-FM Eastman, GA
*WUFM(FM) Columbus, OH
*WUFN(FM) Albion, MI
*WUFR(FM) Bedford, PA
*WUFT-FM Gainesville, FL
*WUGA-FM Athens, GA
*WUGN(FM) Midland, MI
WUGO-FM Grayson, KY
WUHT(FM) Birmingham, AL
*WUHU(FM) Smiths Grove, KY
WUIL(FM) Arcola, IL
WUIN(FM) Carolina Beach, NC
*WUIS-FM Springfield, IL
*WUJC(FM) Saint Marks, FL
WUJM(FM) Gulfport, MS
WUKL(FM) Bethlehem, WV
WUKQ-FM Mayaguez, PR
WUKS(FM) Saint Pauls, NC
*WUKY-FM Lexington, KY
WULF-FM Hardinsburg, KY
WULS-FM Broxton, GA
*WUMB-FM Boston, MA
*WUMC-FM Elizabethton, TN
*WUMD(FM) North Dartmouth, MA
WUME-FM Paoli, IN
*WUMF-FM Farmington, ME
*WUMI(FM) Newberry, MI
WUMJ-FM Fayetteville, GA
*WUML(FM) Lowell, MA
*WUMM-FM Machias, ME
WUMR-FM Memphis, TN
WUMS-FM University, MS
WUMX(FM) Rome, NY
*WUNC(FM) Chapel Hill, NC
*WUND-FM Manteo, NC
*WUNH-FM Durham, NH
*WUNV-FM Albany, GA
*WUNY-FM Utica, NY
*WUOG-FM Athens, GA
*WUOL-FM Louisville, KY
*WUOM-FM Ann Arbor, MI
*WUOT-FM Knoxville, TN
WUPE-FM North Adams, MA
*WUPF(FM) Powers, MI
WUPG(FM) Republic, MI
*WUPI-FM Presque Isle, ME
WUPK-FM Marquette, MI
WUPM-FM Ironwood, MI
WUPN(FM) Paradise, MI
WUPS-FM Houghton Lake, MI
WUPT(FM) Gwinn, MI
*WUPX-FM Marquette, MI
WUPY-FM Ontonagon, MI
WUPZ(FM) Crystal Falls, MI
*WURC-FM Holly Springs, MS
*WURI(FM) Manteo, NC
WURK-FM Elwood, IN
WURV(FM) Walden, TN
*WUSB-FM Stony Brook, NY
*WUSC-FM Columbia, SC
WUSD-FM Geneva, AL
*WUSF(FM) Tampa, FL
WUSH-FM Poquoson, VA
*WUSI(FM) Olney, IL
WUSJ(FM) Madison, MS
WUSL-FM Philadelphia, PA
*WUSM-FM Hattiesburg, MS
*WUSN-FM Chicago, IL

*WUSO-FM Springfield, OH
*WUSQ-FM Winchester, VA
*WUSR-FM Scranton, PA
WUSW-FM Hattiesburg, MS
WUSX-FM Addison, VT
WUSY-FM Cleveland, TN
WUSZ-FM Virginia, MN
*WUTC(FM) Chattanooga, TN
*WUTK-FM Knoxville, TN
*WUTM-FM Martin, TN
*WUTS-FM Sewanee, TN
WUUF-FM Sodus, NY
*WUUQ(FM) South Pittsburg, TN
*WUUU(FM) Franklinton, LA
*WUUZ(FM) Cooperstown, NY
WUVA-FM Charlottesville, VA
*WUVT-FM Blacksburg, VA
*WUWF-FM Pensacola, FL
*WUWG(FM) Carrollton, GA
*WUWM(FM) Milwaukee, WI
*WUWS(FM) Ashland, WI
WUZR-FM Bicknell, IN
*WUZZ(FM) Saegertown, PA
*WVAC-FM Adrian, MI
WVAF-FM Charleston, WV
WVAQ-FM Morgantown, WV
*WVAS-FM Montgomery, AL
WVAZ-FM Oak Park, IL
WVBB(FM) Columbia City, IN
*WVBC-FM Bethany, WV
WVBD-FM Fayetteville, WV
WVBE-FM Lynchburg, VA
WVBG-FM Redwood, MS
*WVBH(FM) Beach Haven West, NJ
WVBO-FM Winneconne, WI
WVBR-FM Ithaca, NY
*WVBU-FM Lewisburg, PA
*WVBV(FM) Medford Lakes, NJ
WVBW(FM) Suffolk, VA
WVBX(FM) Spotsylvania, VA
WVBZ(FM) High Point, NC
*WVCF-FM Eau Claire, WI
*WVCM(FM) Iron Mountain, MI
*WVCN(FM) Baraga, MI
WVCO-FM Loris, SC
*WVCP-FM Gallatin, TN
*WVCR-FM Loudonville, NY
*WVCS(FM) Owen, WI
*WVCT-FM Keavy, KY
*WVCX(FM) Tomah, WI
*WVCY-FM Milwaukee, WI
*WVDA(FM) Valdosta, GA
WVEE-FM Atlanta, GA
WVEI-FM Easthampton, MA
*WVEK-FM Weber City, VA
*WVEP-FM Martinsburg, WV
WVES-FM Accomac, VA
*WVEZ(FM) Louisville, KY
*WVFA(FM) Lebanon, NH
WVFB-FM Celina, TN
WVFJ-FM Manchester, GA
*WVFL(FM) Fond du Lac, WI
WVFM(FM) Kalamazoo, MI
*WVFS(FM) Tallahassee, FL
WVGA(FM) Lakeland, GA
WVGC-FM Pendleton, SC
*WVGN-FM Charlotte Amalie, VI
*WVGR-FM Grand Rapids, MI
*WVGS-FM Statesboro, GA
*WVGV(FM) West Union, WV
*WVHC-FM Herkimer, NY
*WVHL-FM Farmville, VA
*WVHM-FM Benton, KY
WVHR-FM Huntingdon, TN
WVHT-FM Norfolk, VA
*WVIA-FM Scranton, PA
WVIB(FM) Holton, MI
WVIC-FM Jackson, MI
*WVIJ-FM Port Charlotte, FL
*WVIK-FM Rock Island, IL
WVIL(FM) Virginia, IL
WVIM-FM Coldwater, MS
WVIN-FM Bath, NY
WVIP-FM New Rochelle, NY
WVIQ-FM Christiansted, VI
WVIS(FM) Vieques, PR

WVIV-FM Highland Park, IL
WVIX(FM) Joliet, IL
*WVJC(FM) Mount Carmel, IL
WVJO(FM) Mullens, WV
WVJP-FM Caguas, PR
WVJZ-FM Charlotte Amalie, VI
*WVKC-FM Galesburg, IL
WVKF(FM) Shadyside, OH
WVKL-FM Norfolk, VA
WVKM-FM Matewan, WV
WVKO-FM Johnstown, OH
*WVKR-FM Poughkeepsie, NY
WVKS-FM Toledo, OH
WVKV(FM) Nashville, GA
WVKX-FM Irwinton, GA
WVLC-FM Mannsville, KY
WVLE(FM) Scottsville, KY
WVLF(FM) Norwood, NY
WVLI-FM Kankakee, IL
WVLK-FM Richmond, KY
*WVLS-FM Monterey, VA
WVLT-FM Vineland, NJ
WVLY-FM Milton, PA
*WVMC-FM Mansfield, OH
WVMD(FM) Midland, MD
*WVME(FM) Meadville, PA
WVMG(FM) Normal, IL
WVMJ(FM) Conway, NH
*WVML(FM) Millersburg, OH
*WVMM(FM) Grantham, PA
*WVMN-FM New Castle, PA
*WVMR-FM Hillsboro, WV
*WVMS-FM Sandusky, OH
WVMV-FM Detroit, MI
*WVMW-FM Scranton, PA
WVMX(FM) Delaware, OH
WVNA-FM Muscle Shoals, AL
*WVNG(FM) Tallulah Falls, GA
*WVNH-FM Concord, NH
WVNI-FM Nashville, IN
*WVNK(FM) Manchester, VT
*WVNL(FM) Vandalia, IL
WVNN-FM Trinity, AL
WVNO-FM Mansfield, OH
*WVNP-FM Wheeling, WV
WVNU(FM) Greenfield, OH
WVNV-FM Malone, NY
WVNW-FM Burnham, PA
WVOA-FM DeRuyter, NY
*WVOB-FM Dothan, AL
WVOD-FM Manteo, NC
*WVOF-FM Fairfield, CT
WVOH-FM Hazlehurst, GA
WVOK-FM Oxford, AL
WVOM-FM Howland, ME
WVOR(FM) Canandaigua, NY
WVOS-FM Liberty, NY
WVOU-FM Mexico, NY
WVOW-FM Logan, WV
WVOZ-FM Carolina, PR
*WVPA-FM Saint Johnsbury, VT
*WVPB-FM Beckley, WV
*WVPC(FM) Franklin, WV
*WVPE-FM Elkhart, IN
*WVPG-FM Parkersburg, WV
*WVPH-FM Piscataway, NJ
*WVPM-FM Morgantown, WV
*WVPN-FM Charleston, WV
*WVPR-FM Windsor, VT
*WVPS-FM Burlington, VT
*WVPW-FM Buckhannon, WV
WVQM-FM Augusta, ME
WVRB-FM Wilmore, KY
WVRC-FM Spencer, WV
WVRE(FM) Dickeyville, WI
WVRK-FM Columbus, GA
*WVRN(FM) Wittenberg, WI
WVRQ-FM Viroqua, WI
*WVRR(FM) Point Pleasant, WV
WVRT(FM) Mill Hall, PA
*WVRU-FM Radford, VA
WVRV-FM Pine Level, AL
WVRW-FM Glenville, WV
WVRY-FM Waverly, TN
WVRZ(FM) Mount Carmel, PA
*WVSB(FM) Romney, WV

*WVSD-FM Itta Bena, MS
*WVSH-FM Huntington, IN
*WVSI(FM) Mount Vernon, IL
WVSR-FM Charleston, WV
*WVSS-FM Menomonie, WI
*WVST-FM Petersburg, VA
*WVSU-FM Birmingham, AL
WVSZ-FM Chesterfield, SC
*WVTC-FM Randolph Center, VT
*WVTF-FM Roanoke, VA
WVTI(FM) Brighton, VT
WVTK(FM) Port Henry, NY
*WVTQ(FM) Sunderland, VT
*WVTR-FM Marion, VA
*WVTU-FM Charlottesville, VA
*WVTW-FM Charlottesville, VA
*WVUA-FM Tuscaloosa, AL
*WVUB-FM Vincennes, IN
*WVUD-FM Newark, DE
*WVUM-FM Coral Gables, FL
*WVUR-FM Valparaiso, IN
WVUV-FM Fagaitua, AS
*WVVC-FM Dolgeville, NY
WVVE(FM) Panama City Beach, FL
*WVVI-FM Christiansted, VI
*WVVL(FM) Elba, AL
WVVR(FM) Hopkinsville, KY
*WVVS-FM Valdosta, GA
WVVV(FM) Williamstown, WV
*WVWA(FM) Auburn, NY
*WVWC-FM Buckhannon, WV
*WVWV-FM Huntington, WV
WVXG(FM) Mount Gilead, OH
*WVXI(FM) Cole, IN
*WVXU-FM Cincinnati, OH
*WVYA(FM) Williamsport, PA
WVYB-FM Holly Hill, FL
*WVYC-FM York, PA
*WVYN(FM) Bluford, IL
WVZA(FM) Murphysboro, IL
WWAG(FM) McKee, KY
WWAV-FM Santa Rosa Beach, FL
WWAX-FM Hermantown, MN
WWBB-FM Providence, RI
WWBD(FM) Sumter, SC
WWBE-FM Mifflinburg, PA
WWBL-FM Washington, IN
*WWBM(FM) Yates, GA
WWBN-FM Tuscola, MI
WWBR(FM) Big Rapids, MI
WWBU-FM Radford, VA
WWCD-FM Grove City, OH
*WWCF-FM McConnellsburg, PA
*WWCJ-FM Cape May, NJ
WWCK-FM Flint, MI
WWCM-FM Standish, MI
WWCT(FM) Bartonville, IL
*WWCU-FM Cullowhee, NC
WWDC-FM Washington, DC
WWDE-FM Hampton, VA
*WWDL-FM Lebanon, IN
WWDM(FM) Sumter, SC
*WWDS-FM Muncie, IN
WWDV(FM) Zion, IL
WWDW(FM) Alberta, VA
WWEB-FM Wallingford, CT
*WWEC-FM Elizabethtown, PA
*WWED(FM) Spotsylvania, VA
WWEG(FM) Hagerstown, MD
WWEL-FM London, KY
WWEM(FM) Rustburg, VA
WWEN(FM) Wentworth, WI
WWES(FM) Mount Kisco, NY
*WWET(FM) Valdosta, GA
*WWEV-FM Cumming, GA
WWFA(FM) Saint Florian, AL
WWFF-FM New Market, AL
WWFG-FM Ocean City, MD
*WWFM(FM) Trenton, NJ
WWFN-FM Lake City, SC
*WWFP(FM) Brigantine, NJ
*WWFR-FM Stuart, FL
WWFS(FM) New York, NY
WWFX(FM) Southbridge, MA
*WWFY(FM) Berlin, VT
WWGF-FM Donalsonville, GA

*WWGM(FM) Alamo, TN
*WWGN-FM Ottawa, IL
WWGO-FM Charleston, IL
WWGR-FM Fort Myers, FL
*WWGV(FM) Grove City, OH
WWGY(FM) Grove City, PA
WWHC-FM Oakland, MD
WWHG(FM) Evansville, WI
*WWHI-FM Muncie, IN
WWHK-FM Concord, NH
WWHP-FM Farmer City, IL
WWHQ(FM) Meredith, NH
*WWHR(FM) Bowling Green, KY
*WWHS-FM Hampden-Sydney, VA
WWHT-FM Syracuse, NY
WWHV(FM) Lynn Haven, FL
WWIB-FM Hallie, WI
WWIK(FM) McClellanville, SC
*WWIL-FM Wilmington, NC
WWIN-FM Glen Burnie, MD
WWIO-FM Brunswick, GA
*WWIP(FM) Cheriton, VA
WWIS-FM Black River Falls, WI
WWIZ-FM Mercer, PA
*WWJA(FM) Janesville, WI
WWJD-FM Pippa Passes, KY
WWJK-FM Jackson, MS
WWJM-FM New Lexington, OH
WWJN(FM) Ridgeland, SC
WWJO-FM Saint Cloud, MN
WWKA-FM Orlando, FL
WWKC-FM Caldwell, OH
WWKF-FM Fulton, KY
WWKI-FM Kokomo, IN
WWKL-FM Palmyra, PA
*WWKM(FM) Imlay City, MI
WWKN(FM) Morgantown, KY
WWKR(FM) Hart, MI
WWKS-FM Cruz Bay, VI
WWKT-FM Kingstree, SC
WWKX-FM Woonsocket, RI
WWKY(FM) Providence, KY
WWKZ(FM) Columbus, MS
*WWLA(FM) South Charleston, WV
WWLB(FM) Midlothian, VA
*WWLC(FM) Cross City, FL
WWLD(FM) Cairo, GA
WWLF-FM Sylvan Beach, NY
WWL-FM Kenner, LA
WWLG(FM) Peachtree City, GA
WWLI-FM Providence, RI
WWLL(FM) Sebring, FL
*WWLN(FM) Lincoln, ME
*WWLR-FM Lyndonville, VT
WWLS-FM Edmond, OK
WWLT-FM Manchester, KY
*WWLU(FM) Lincoln University, PA
WWLW(FM) Clarksburg, WV
*WWMC-FM Lynchburg, VA
WWMG(FM) Millbrook, AL
WWMJ-FM Ellsworth, ME
WWMM-FM Northport, AL
WWMP(FM) Waterbury, VT
WWMR(FM) Saltillo, MS
WWMS-FM Oxford, MS
WWMX-FM Baltimore, MD
WWMY-FM Raleigh, NC
*WWNJ-FM Dover Township, NJ
*WWNO-FM New Orleans, LA
WWNQ(FM) Forest Acres, SC
WWNU(FM) Irmo, SC
*WWNW(FM) New Wilmington, PA
WWOD(FM) Hartford, VT
*WWOG-FM Cookeville, TN
WWOJ(FM) Avon Park, FL
WWOT(FM) Altoona, PA
*WWOZ-FM New Orleans, LA
*WWPH-FM Princeton Junction, NJ
*WWPJ(FM) Pen Argyl, PA
WWPN-FM Westernport, MD
WWPR-FM New York, NY
*WWPT-FM Westport, CT
*WWPV-FM Colchester, VT
WWQM-FM Middleton, WI
WWQN(FM) Mount Horeb, WI
WWQQ-FM Wilmington, NC

WWRA(FM) Clinton, LA
WWRE(FM) Berryville, VA
WWRM(FM) Tampa, FL
*WWRN(FM) Rockport, MA
WWRQ-FM Valdosta, GA
WWRR(FM) Scranton, PA
WWRT(FM) Strasburg, VA
WWRX(FM) Pawcatuck, CT
WWRZ-FM Fort Meade, FL
WWSE-FM Jamestown, NY
WWSH(FM) Pleasant Gap, PA
WWSL-FM Philadelphia, MS
WWSN-FM Waycross, GA
WWSP-FM Stevens Point, WI
WWSR(FM) Lima, OH
WWST(FM) Sevierville, TN
*WWSU-FM Dayton, OH
WWSW-FM Pittsburgh, PA
WWSY(FM) Seelyville, IN
*WWTA-FM Marion, MA
*WWTG(FM) Carpentersville, IL
WWTH(FM) Oscoda, MI
WWTJ(FM) Charlottesville, VA
WWTN-FM Manchester, TN
*WWTP(FM) Augusta, ME
*WWTS(FM) Logansport, IN
WWUF-FM Waycross, GA
*WWUH-FM West Hartford, CT
WWUN-FM Friar's Point, MS
WWUS(FM) Big Pine Key, FL
WWUZ(FM) Bowling Green, VA
WWVA-FM Canton, GA
*WWVO(FM) Albany, GA
WWVR-FM West Terre Haute, IN
*WWVU-FM Morgantown, WV
*WWVY(FM) Waverly, OH
*WWWA(FM) Winslow, ME
WWWD(FM) Bolingbroke, GA
WWWI-FM Pillager, MN
WWWK(FM) Islamorada, FL
WWWM-FM Sylvania, OH
WWWQ(FM) Atlanta, GA
WWWT-FM Manassas, VA
WWWV-FM Charlottesville, VA
WWWW-FM Ann Arbor, MI
WWWX-FM Oshkosh, WI
WWWY(FM) North Vernon, IN
WWWZ-FM Summerville, SC
WWXM(FM) Garden City, SC
WWXT(FM) Prince Frederick, MD
WWXX(FM) Warrenton, VA
WWYL(FM) Chenango Bridge, NY
WWYN(FM) McKenzie, TN
WWYW(FM) Dundee, IL
WWYY-FM Belvidere, NJ
WWYZ-FM Waterbury, CT
WWZD-FM New Albany, MS
WWZW-FM Buena Vista, VA
WWZY-FM Long Branch, NJ
WXAB-FM McLain, MS
*WXAC-FM Reading, PA
*WXAF(FM) Charleston, WV
WXAJ(FM) Hillsboro, IL
WXAN-FM Ava, IL
*WXBA(FM) Brentwood, NY
WXBB(FM) Erie, PA
WXBC-FM Hardinsburg, KY
*WXBE(FM) Beaufort, NC
WXBM-FM Milton, FL
WXBQ-FM Bristol, TN
WXBT(FM) West Columbia, SC
WXBW(FM) Gallipolis, OH
WXBX(FM) Rural Retreat, VA
WXCC-FM Williamson, WV
WXCF-FM Clifton Forge, VA
WXCH(FM) Hope, IN
*WXCI-FM Danbury, CT
WXCL(FM) Pekin, IL
WXCM(FM) Whitesville, KY
WXCR(FM) New Martinsville, WV
WXCV-FM Homosassa Springs, FL
WXCX(FM) Siren, WI
WXCY(FM) Havre de Grace, MD
WXDJ-FM North Miami Beach, FL
*WXDU-FM Durham, NC
WXDX-FM Pittsburgh, PA

WXEF-FM Effingham, IL
WXEG-FM Beavercreek, OH
*WXEL-FM West Palm Beach, FL
WXER-FM Plymouth, WI
WXEZ-FM Yorktown, VA
WXFL-FM Florence, AL
WXFM-FM Mount Zion, IL
*WXFR(FM) State College, PA
WXFX(FM) Montgomery, AL
WXGL(FM) Saint Petersburg, FL
WXGM-FM Gloucester, VA
*WXGN-FM Egg Harbor Township, NJ
WXHB(FM) Richton, MS
WXHC-FM Homer, NY
*WXHL-FM Christiana, DE
*WXHM(FM) Middletown, DE
WXHT(FM) Madison, FL
*WXHZ(FM) Bridgeport, OH
WXIL-FM Parkersburg, WV
WXIS-FM Erwin, TN
*WXIV(FM) Lumpkin, GA
WXIZ-FM Waverly, OH
WXJC-FM Cordova, AL
*WXJM-FM Harrisonburg, VA
WXJY-FM Georgetown, SC
*WXJZ(FM) Gainesville, FL
WXKB-FM Cape Coral, FL
WXKC-FM Erie, PA
WXKE-FM Fort Wayne, IN
WXKQ-FM Whitesburg, KY
WXKR-FM Port Clinton, OH
WXKS-FM Medford, MA
WXKT-FM Royston, GA
*WXKU-FM Austin, IN
*WXKV-FM Selmer, TN
WXKY-FM Stanford, KY
WXKZ-FM Prestonsburg, KY
*WXLB-FM Boonville, NY
WXLC-FM Waukegan, IL
*WXLE(FM) Canton, NY
WXLF(FM) White River Junction, VT
*WXLG-FM North Creek, NY
*WXLH-FM Blue Mountain Lake, NY
WXLK-FM Roanoke, VA
WXLM(FM) Montauk, NY
WXLO-FM Fitchburg, MA
*WXLP-FM Moline, IL
*WXLQ(FM) Bristol, VT
WXLR-FM Harold, KY
*WXLS(FM) Tupper Lake, NY
WXLT(FM) Christopher, IL
*WXLU-FM Peru, NY
*WXLV-FM Schnecksville, PA
WXLX-FM Lajas, PR
WXLY-FM North Charleston, SC
WXLZ-FM Lebanon, VA
WXMA(FM) Louisville, KY
*WXMF(FM) Marion, OH
WXMG-FM Upper Arlington, OH
WXMJ(FM) Cambridge Springs, PA
WXMK-FM Dock Junction, GA
*WXML(FM) Upper Sandusky, OH
WXMR(FM) Minerva, KY
WXMT(FM) Smethport, PA
WXMX(FM) Millington, TN
WXMZ-FM Hartford, KY
WXNR-FM Grifton, NC
WXNU(FM) Saint Anne, IL
WXOF-FM Yankeetown, FL
WXOQ-FM Selmer, TN
*WXOS(FM) East St. Louis, IL
*WXOU-FM Auburn Hills, MI
*WXPH(FM) Middletown, PA
WXPK(FM) Briarcliff Manor, NY
*WXPL-FM Fitchburg, MA
*WXPN-FM Philadelphia, PA
*WXPR-FM Rhinelander, WI
*WXPW-FM Wausau, WI
*WXPZ(FM) Clyde Township, MI
WXQR-FM Jacksonville, NC
*WXRA(FM) Inglis, FL
*WXRB(FM) Dudley, MA
WXRC-FM Hickory, NC
WXRD-FM Crown Point, IN
*WXRG(FM) Athol, MA
*WXRI-FM Winston-Salem, NC

WXRK(FM) New York, NY
*WXRN(FM) Warren, CT
WXRO-FM Beaver Dam, WI
WXRR-FM Hattiesburg, MS
WXRS-FM Swainsboro, GA
WXRT-FM Chicago, IL
WXRV(FM) Andover, MA
WXRX-FM Belvidere, IL
WXRZ(FM) Corinth, MS
WXSH(FM) Pocomoke City, MD
WXSR-FM Quincy, FL
WXSS-FM Wauwatosa, WI
WXST(FM) Hollywood, SC
WXTA-FM Edinboro, PA
WXTB-FM Clearwater, FL
WXTG-FM Virginia Beach, VA
WXTK-FM West Yarmouth, MA
WXTQ(FM) Athens, OH
*WXTS-FM Toledo, OH
WXTT(FM) Danville, IL
WXTU-FM Philadelphia, PA
WXUR-FM Herkimer, NY
*WXUT-FM Toledo, OH
*WXVS-FM Waycross, GA
*WXVU-FM Villanova, PA
*WXVW(FM) Veedersburg, IN
WXWX(FM) Marietta, MS
WXXB(FM) Delphi, IN
WXXC(FM) Marion, IN
*WXXE-FM Fenner, NY
WXXF(FM) Loudonville, OH
*WXXI-FM Rochester, NY
WXXJ(FM) Jacksonville, FL
WXXK-FM Lebanon, NH
WXXL-FM Tavares, FL
WXXM(FM) Sun Prairie, WI
WXXQ(FM) Freeport, IL
WXXR(FM) Fredericktown, OH
WXXS-FM Lancaster, NH
WXXX-FM South Burlington, VT
WXXZ-FM Grand Marais, MN
*WXYC Chapel Hill, NC
WXYK-FM Gulfport, MS
WXYM(FM) Tomah, WI
*WXYP(FM) Ludington, MI
WXYT-FM Detroit, MI
WXYX-FM Bayamon, PR
WXZO(FM) Willsboro, NY
WXZQ-FM Piketon, OH
*WXZT(FM) Christiansted, VI
WXZZ-FM Georgetown, KY
WYAB(FM) Flora, MS
*WYAD(FM) Benton, MS
*WYAI(FM) Scotia, NY
*WYAJ-FM Sudbury, MA
WYAR-FM Yarmouth, ME
WYAS(FM) Vieques, PR
WYAV-FM Myrtle Beach, SC
WYAY-FM Gainesville, GA
*WYAZ(FM) Yazoo City, MS
WYBB-FM Folly Beach, SC
WYBC-FM New Haven, CT
*WYBF-FM Radnor Township, PA
*WYBH(FM) Fayetteville, NC
*WYBJ(FM) Newton Grove, NC
WYBL(FM) Ashtabula, OH
WYBR-FM Big Rapids, MI
*WYBV(FM) Wakarusa, IN
WYBZ-FM Crooksville, OH
WYCA(FM) Crete, IL
WYCD-FM Detroit, MI
*WYCE-FM Wyoming, MI
WYCL-FM Pensacola, FL
*WYCM(FM) Charlton, MA

WYCR-FM York-Hanover, PA
*WYCS(FM) Yorktown, VA
WYCT(FM) Pensacola, FL
WYCY-FM Hawley, PA
WYDE-FM Cullman, AL
WYDL(FM) Middleton, TN
*WYDM(FM) Monroe, MI
WYDS(FM) Decatur, IL
WYEC(FM) Cambridge, IL
*WYEP-FM Pittsburgh, PA
*WYER(FM) Carmi, IL
WYEZ(FM) Murrell's Inlet, SC
*WYFA-FM Waynesboro, GA
*WYFB-FM Gainesville, FL
*WYFC-FM Clinton, TN
*WYFD-FM Decatur, AL
*WYFE-FM Tarpon Springs, FL
*WYFG-FM Gaffney, SC
*WYFH-FM North Charleston, SC
WYFI-FM Norfolk, VA
WYFJ-FM Ashland, VA
*WYFK-FM Columbus, GA
WYFL-FM Henderson, NC
WYFM-FM Sharon, PA
*WYFO-FM Lakeland, FL
*WYFP-FM Harpswell, ME
*WYFQ-FM Wadesboro, NC
*WYFS-FM Savannah, GA
*WYFT-FM Luray, VA
*WYFU-FM Masontown, PA
*WYFV-FM Cayce, SC
*WYFW-FM Winder, GA
WYFX(FM) Mount Vernon, IN
*WYFZ(FM) Belleview, FL
WYGB-FM Edinburgh, IN
WYGC(FM) High Springs, FL
WYGE(FM) London, KY
*WYGG-FM Asbury Park, NJ
WYGL-FM Elizabethville, PA
WYGO-FM Madisonville, TN
WYGS(FM) Columbus, IN
*WYGY(FM) Fort Thomas, KY
WYHT-FM Mansfield, OH
WYJB(FM) Albany, NY
*WYJC(FM) Greenville, FL
WYJK-FM Bellaire, OH
*WYJZ(FM) Fearsville, KY
*WYKL(FM) Crestline, OH
WYKR-FM Haverhill, NH
WYKS-FM Gainesville, FL
WYKT-FM Wilmington, IL
*WYKV(FM) Ravena, NY
WYKX-FM Escanaba, MI
*WYKY(FM) Science Hill, KY
WYKZ(FM) Beaufort, SC
*WYLC(FM) Jackson, KY
WYLD-FM New Orleans, LA
WYLK(FM) Lacombe, LA
*WYLV-FM Alcoa, TN
WYME(FM) Au Sable, MI
WYMG(FM) Jacksonville, IL
WYMJ-FM New Martinsville, WV
*WYMS(FM) Milwaukee, WI
WYMV(FM) Madisonville, KY
WYMX-FM Greenwood, MS
WYMY(FM) Goldsboro, NC
WYNA-FM Calabash, NC
WYND-FM Hatteras, NC
WYNG(FM) Mount Carmel, IL
*WYNJ(FM) Blackduck, MN
WYNK-FM Baton Rouge, LA
WYNN-FM Florence, SC
WYNR(FM) Waycross, GA
*WYNS(FM) Waynesville, OH

WYNT(FM) Caledonia, OH
WYNU-FM Milan, TN
WYNW(FM) Birnamwood, WI
WYNZ-FM Westbrook, ME
WYOK-FM Atmore, AL
WYOO-FM Springfield, FL
WYOR(FM) Cross Hill, SC
WYOY-FM Gluckstadt, MS
*WYPF(FM) Frederick, MD
*WYPL-FM Memphis, TN
*WYPO(FM) Ocean City, MD
*WYPR(FM) Baltimore, MD
WYPW(FM) Nappanee, IN
*WYPY(FM) Baton Rouge, LA
WYQE(FM) Naguabo, PR
*WYQS(FM) Mars Hill, NC
WYRB(FM) Genoa, IL
WYRD-FM Simpsonville, SC
WYRK-FM Buffalo, NY
WYRO(FM) McArthur, OH
WYRQ-FM Little Falls, MN
*WYRR(FM) Lakewood, NY
*WYRS-FM Manahawkin, NJ
WYRY-FM Hinsdale, NH
*WYSA-FM Wauseon, OH
WYSB(FM) Springfield, KY
WYSC-FM McRae, GA
*WYSM(FM) Lima, OH
*WYSO-FM Yellow Springs, OH
WYSP-FM Philadelphia, PA
WYSS-FM Sault Ste. Marie, MI
WYST(FM) Fairbury, IL
*WYSU(FM) Youngstown, OH
WYSX-FM Morristown, NY
*WYSZ-FM Maumee, OH
WYTE(FM) Marshfield, WI
*WYTF(FM) Indianola, MS
*WYTJ(FM) Linton, IN
WYTK(FM) Rogersville, AL
*WYTL(FM) Wyomissing, PA
WYTM-FM Fayetteville, TN
*WYTN-FM Youngstown, OH
WYTT(FM) Emporia, VA
WYTZ-FM Bridgman, MI
WYUL-FM Chateaugay, NY
WYUM-FM Mount Vernon, GA
WYUR(FM) Midland, MD
WYUU(FM) Safety Harbor, FL
WYVK-FM Middleport, OH
WYVN(FM) Saugatuck, MI
WYVY-FM Union City, TN
WYXB(FM) Indianapolis, IN
WYXL-FM Ithaca, NY
WYYD-FM Amherst, VA
WYYS(FM) Streator, IL
WYYU-FM Dalton, GA
WYYX-FM Bonifay, FL
WYYY-FM Syracuse, NY
WYZB(FM) Mary Esther, FL
WYZO(FM) Portage, MI
WYZY(FM) Saranac Lake, NY
WZAC-FM Danville, WV
WZAD-FM Wurtsboro, NY
*WZAE(FM) Wadley, GA
WZAI(FM) Brewster, MA
WZAK-FM Cleveland, OH
WZAQ(FM) Louisa, KY
WZAR-FM Ponce, PR
WZAT-FM Savannah, GA
WZAX(FM) Nashville, NC
WZBA(FM) Westminster, MD
WZBB-FM Stanleytown, VA
*WZBC-FM Newton, MA
WZBD-FM Berne, IN

WZBG-FM Litchfield, CT
WZBH-FM Georgetown, DE
WZBN(FM) Camilla, GA
WZBQ-FM Carrollton, AL
*WZBT-FM Gettysburg, PA
WZBX-FM Sylvania, GA
WZBZ(FM) Pleasantville, NJ
WZCH(FM) Warner Robins, GA
*WZCP(FM) Chillicothe, OH
WZCR(FM) Hudson, NY
WZDB(FM) Sykesville, PA
*WZDG(FM) Scotts Hill, NC
WZDM-FM Vincennes, IN
WZDQ(FM) Humboldt, TN
WZEB(FM) Ocean View, DE
WZEE-FM Madison, WI
WZET(FM) Hormigueros, PR
WZEW-FM Fairhope, AL
WZEZ(FM) Goochland, VA
WZFJ(FM) Pequot Lakes, MN
WZFM(FM) Narrows, VA
WZFX-FM Whiteville, NC
*WZGC(FM) Atlanta, GA
*WZGL(FM) Charleston, IL
WZGN(FM) Crozet, VA
*WZGO(FM) Aurora, NC
WZHL(FM) New Augusta, MS
WZHT-FM Troy, AL
WZID(FM) Manchester, NH
WZIN(FM) Charlotte Amalie, VI
*WZIP-FM Akron, OH
WZIQ-FM Smithville, GA
WZJO-FM Dunbar, WV
WZJS-FM Banner Elk, NC
WZJZ(FM) Port Charlotte, FL
WZKB-FM Wallace, NC
WZKF(FM) Salem, IN
*WZKL(FM) Woodstock, IL
*WZKM(FM) Waynesboro, MS
WZKR(FM) Decatur, MS
WZKS-FM Union, MS
WZKT(FM) Lewes, DE
*WZKV(FM) Dyersburg, TN
WZKX(FM) Bay St. Louis, MS
WZKZ-FM Alfred, NY
WZLA-FM Abbeville, SC
WZLD(FM) Petal, MS
WZLK-FM Virgie, KY
*WZLM(FM) Jemison, AL
WZLQ-FM Tupelo, MS
WZLR(FM) Xenia, OH
WZLT-FM Lexington, TN
WZLX-FM Boston, MA
*WZLY-FM Wellesley, MA
*WZMB-FM Greenville, NC
*WZMI(FM) Reed City, MI
WZMJ-FM Batesburg, SC
WZMR-FM Altamont, NY
WZMT-FM Ponce, PR
WZMX-FM Hartford, CT
*WZNB(FM) New Bern, NC
WZNE-FM Brighton, NY
WZNF-FM Lumberton, NC
WZNJ-FM Demopolis, AL
WZNL-FM Norway, MI
WZNN(FM) Allouez, WI
WZNO(FM) Pickens, MS
*WZNP(FM) Newark, OH
WZNS-FM Fort Walton Beach, FL
WZNT-FM San Juan, PR
WZNX(FM) Sullivan, IL
WZOC-FM Plymouth, IN
WZOE-FM Princeton, IL

WZOK-FM Rockford, IL
WZOL(FM) Luquillo, PR
WZOM-FM Defiance, OH
WZOO-FM Edgewood, OH
WZOR(FM) Mishicot, WI
WZOW(FM) Goshen, IN
WZOZ-FM Oneonta, NY
*WZPE(FM) Bath, NC
WZPL-FM Greenfield, IN
WZPN(FM) Farmington, IL
WZPR(FM) Nags Head, NC
WZPT-FM New Kensington, PA
WZPW(FM) Peoria, IL
WZQQ-FM Hyden, KY
*WZRD-FM Chicago, IL
*WZRI(FM) Spring Lake, NC
*WZRN(FM) Norlina, NC
*WZRP-FM Richmond, IN
WZRR-FM Birmingham, AL
*WZRS(FM) Pana, IL
WZRT-FM Rutland, VT
*WZRU(FM) Roanoke Rapids, NC
WZRV(FM) Front Royal, VA
WZRX-FM Fort Shawnee, OH
WZSN-FM Greenwood, SC
*WZSP(FM) Nocatee, FL
WZSR-FM Woodstock, IL
WZST-FM Westover, WV
WZTF(FM) Scranton, SC
*WZTH(FM) Tusculum, TN
WZTK-FM Burlington, NC
WZTR-FM Dahlonega, GA
WZUN(FM) Phoenix, NY
WZUP(FM) La Grange, NC
WZUS(FM) Macon, IL
WZUU-FM Allegan, MI
WZVA-FM Marion, VA
WZVN-FM Lowell, IN
*WZWP(FM) West Union, OH
WZWW-FM Bellefonte, PA
WZWZ-FM Kokomo, IN
*WZXE(FM) East Nottingham, PA
*WZXF-FM Hustontown, PA
*WZXH(FM) Hagerstown, MD
WZXL(FM) Wildwood, NJ
*WZXM(FM) Harrisburg, PA
*WZXQ(FM) Chambersburg, PA
WZXR-FM South Williamsport, PA
WZXV-FM Palmyra, NY
*WZXX(FM) Lawrenceburg, TN
WZYP-FM Athens, AL
WZYQ-FM Mound Bayou, MS
WZYY-FM Renovo, PA
*WZYZ(FM) Spencer, TN
*WZZD(FM) Warwick, PA
*WZZE-FM Glen Mills, PA
*WZZG(FM) Toomsboro, GA
*WZZH(FM) Honesdale, PA
WZZI-FM Vinton, VA
WZZK-FM Birmingham, AL
WZZL-FM Reidland, KY
WZZO-FM Bethlehem, PA
WZZP-FM Hopkinsville, KY
WZZR-FM Riviera Beach, FL
WZZS(FM) Zolfo Springs, FL
WZZT-FM Morrison, IL
WZZU-FM Lynchburg, VA
WZZY-FM Winchester, IN
WZZZ-FM Portsmouth, OH
XETRA-FM Tijuana, MEX
XHRM-FM Tijuana, MEX

Canadian AM Stations by Call Letters

*CBE Windsor, ON
*CBEF(AM) Windsor, ON
*CBG Gander, NF
CBGN Sainte Anne des Monts, PQ
CBGY Bonavista Bay, NF
CBI Sydney, NS
*CBK Regina, SK
*CBKF-1 Gravelbourg, SK
CBKF-2 Saskatoon, SK
*CBN Saint John's, NF
CBOF-1 Maniwaki, PQ
*CBR Calgary, AB
CBT Grand Falls-Windsor, NF
*CBU Vancouver, BC
CBW Winnipeg, MB
CBX Edmonton, AB
*CBY Corner Brook, NF
CFAB Windsor, NS
CFAC(AM) Calgary, AB
CFAM Altona, MB
CFAR Flin Flon, MB
CFAV(AM) Laval, PQ
CFAX Victoria, BC
CFBC Saint John, NB
CFBV Smithers, BC
CFCB Corner Brook, NF
CFCO Chatham, ON
CFCT Tuktoyaktuk, NT
CFCW Camrose, AB
CFFB(AM) Iqaluit, NU
CFFR Calgary, AB
CFGO Ottawa, ON
CFGT Alma, PQ
CFKC Creston, BC
CFLD Burns Lake, BC
CFLM La Tuque, PQ
CFLN Goose Bay, NF
CFLW Wabush, NF
CFMB Montreal, PQ

CFMJ(AM) Toronto, ON
CFNC Cross Lake, MB
CFNI Port Hardy, BC
CFNW Port au Choix, NF
CFOK(AM) Westlock, AB
CFOS(AM) Owen Sound, ON
CFPL London, ON
*CFPR Prince Rupert, BC
CFRA Ottawa, ON
CFRB Toronto, ON
CFRN Edmonton, AB
CFRP Forestville, PQ
CFRW(AM) Winnipeg, MB
CFRY Portage la Prairie, MB
CFSL Weyburn, SK
CFSX Stephenville, NF
CFTK Terrace, BC
CFTR Toronto, ON
CFUN Vancouver, BC
*CFWH Whitehorse, YT
*CFYK Yellowknife, NT
CFYM Kindersley, SK
CFZM(AM) Toronto, ON
CHAB Moose Jaw, SK
*CHAK Inuvik, NT
CHAM Hamilton, ON
CHCM Marystown, NF
CHED Edmonton, AB
*CHFA Edmonton, AB
CHHA(AM) Toronto, ON
CHIN Toronto, ON
CHKT(AM) Toronto, ON
CHLW(AM) Saint Paul, AB
CHMB Vancouver, BC
CHMJ(AM) Vancouver, BC
CHML Hamilton, ON
*CHMO(AM) Moosonee, ON
CHNL(AM) Kamloops, BC
CHOK Sarnia, ON

CHOR Summerland, BC
CHOU(AM) Montreal, PQ
CHQR Calgary, AB
CHQT Edmonton, AB
CHRB High River, AB
CHRC Quebec, PQ
CHSC Saint Catharines, ON
CHSM Steinbach, MB
CHTK Prince Rupert, BC
CHTM Thompson, MB
CHTO(AM) Toronto, ON
CHUM Toronto, ON
CIAO Brampton, ON
CIBQ Brooks, AB
CINA(AM) Mississauga, ON
CINF(AM) Verdun, PQ
CINW(AM) Montreal, PQ
CIOR Princeton, BC
CISL Richmond, BC
CIVH Vanderhoof, BC
CIWW Ottawa, ON
CJAD Montreal, PQ
CJAR The Pas, MB
CJBC Toronto, ON
CJBK(AM) London, ON
CJBQ Belleville, ON
CJCA Edmonton, AB
CJCB(AM) Sydney, NS
CJCL Toronto, ON
CJCS Stratford, ON
CJCW Sussex, NB
CJDC Dawson Creek, BC
CJGX Yorkton, SK
CJLO(AM) Montreal, PQ
CJMD Chibougamau, PQ
CJME(AM) Regina, SK
CJMR(AM) Oakville, ON
CJMS Saint Constant, PQ
CJNB North Battleford, SK

CJNL Merritt, BC
CJNS Meadow Lake, SK
CJOB Winnipeg, MB
CJOR Osoyoos, BC
CJOY Guelph, ON
CJRB Boissevain, MB
CJRJ(AM) Vancouver, BC
CJRS(AM) Montreal, PQ
CJSL Estevan, SK
CJSN Shaunavon, SK
CJUL(AM) Cornwall, ON
CJVA Caraquet, NB
CJVB(AM) Richmond, BC
CJWI(AM) Montreal, PQ
CJWW Saskatoon, SK
CJYE(AM) Oakville, ON
CJYM Rosetown, SK
CJYQ Saint John's, NF
CKAC Montreal, PQ
CKAD Middleton, NS
CKAT(AM) North Bay, ON
CKBI Prince Albert, SK
CKBX 100 Mile House, BC
CKCM Grand Falls, NF
CKCR Revelstoke, BC
CKDH Amherst, NS
CKDM Dauphin, MB
CKDO Oshawa, ON
CKDQ Drumheller, AB
CKDY Digby, NS
CKFR(AM) Kelowna, BC
CKGA Gander, NF
CKGL Kitchener, ON
CKGM Montreal, PQ
CKGR Golden, BC
CKHJ(AM) Fredericton, NB
CKIM Baie Verte, NF
CKIR Invermere, BC
CKJH(AM) Melfort, SK

CKJR Wetaskiwin, AB
CKJS Winnipeg, MB
CKKY Wainwright, AB
CKLQ Brandon, MB
CKLW Windsor, ON
*CKMO(AM) Victoria, BC
CKMW Winkler-Morden, MB
CKMX Calgary, AB
CKNB Campbellton, NB
CKNW New Westminster, BC
CKNX Wingham, ON
CKOC Hamilton, ON
CKOM(AM) Saskatoon, SK
CKOR Penticton, BC
CKOT(AM) Tillsonburg, ON
CKPC(AM) Brantford, ON
CKRM(AM) Regina, SK
CKRU Peterborough, ON
CKRW Whitehorse, YT
*CKSB Saint Boniface, MB
CKSL London, ON
CKSM Shawinigan, PQ
CKSQ(AM) Stettler, AB
CKST Vancouver, BC
CKSW Swift Current, SK
CKTB Saint Catharines, ON
CKUA Edmonton, AB
CKVH High Prairie, AB
CKVO Clarenville, NF
CKWL Williams Lake, BC
CKWW Windsor, ON
CKWX Vancouver, BC
CKYL Peace River, AB
*VOAR Mount Pearl, NF
VOCM(AM) Saint John's, NF
*VOWR Saint John's, NF

Canadian FM Stations by Call Letters

*CBAF-FM Moncton, NB
CBA-FM Moncton, NB
*CBAL-FM Moncton, NB
CBAM-FM Moncton, NB
CBAX-FM Halifax, NS
CBBK-FM Kingston, ON
CBBL-FM London, ON
CBBS-FM Sudbury, ON
CBBX-FM Sudbury, ON
CBCL-FM London, ON
*CBCS-FM Sudbury, ON
*CBCT-FM Charlottetown, PE
*CBCV-FM Victoria, BC
CBCX-FM Calgary, AB
CBD-FM Saint John, NB
CBDQ-FM Labrador City, NF
*CBE-FM Windsor, ON
CBEG-FM Sarnia, ON
CBF-FM Montreal, PQ
CBF-FM-1 Trois Rivieres, PQ
CBFX-FM Montreal, PQ
CBGA-FM Matane, PQ
CBHA-FM Halifax, NS
*CBH-FM Halifax, NS
CBI-FM Sydney, NS
CBJE-FM Chicoutimi, PQ
CBJ-FM Chicoutimi, PQ
*CBJX-FM Chicoutimi, PQ
*CBKA-FM La Ronge, SK
CBKF-FM Regina, SK
*CBK-FM Regina, SK
CBKS-FM Saskatoon, SK
CBLA-FM Toronto, ON
CBL-FM Toronto, ON
CBME-FM Montreal, PQ
CBM-FM Montreal, PQ
CBMI-FM Baie Comeau, PQ
CBMR-FM Fermont, PQ
*CBN-FM Saint John's, NF
CBOF-FM Ottawa, ON
*CBO-FM Ottawa, ON
*CBON-FM Sudbury, ON
*CBOQ-FM Ottawa, ON
*CBOX-FM Ottawa, ON
*CBQ-FM Thunder Bay, ON
CBQL-FM Savant Lake, ON
CBQR-FM Rankin Inlet, NU
CBQS-FM Sioux Narrows, ON
*CBQT-FM Thunder Bay, ON
CBQX-FM Kenora, ON
CBRF-FM Calgary, AB
CBR-FM Calgary, AB
*CBRX-FM Rimouski, PQ
*CBSI-FM Sept-Iles, PQ
CBTE-FM Crawford Bay, BC
*CBTK-FM Kelowna, BC
CBUF-FM Vancouver, BC
CBU-FM Vancouver, BC
CBUX-FM Vancouver, BC
CBVE-FM Quebec, PQ
*CBV-FM Quebec, PQ
*CBV-FM-6 La Malbaie, PQ
*CBVX-FM Quebec, PQ
CBW-FM Winnipeg, MB
*CBWK-FM Thompson, MB
CBX-FM Edmonton, AB
CBYG-FM Prince George, BC
CBZF-FM Fredericton, NB
*CBZ-FM Fredericton, NB
CFAD-FM Salmo, BC
CFAI-FM Edmundston, NB
CFAK-FM Sherbrooke, PQ
CFAN-FM Miramichi City, NB
CFAO-FM Alliston, ON
CFAQ-FM Blucher, SK
CFBG-FM Bracebridge, ON
CFBK-FM Huntsville, ON
CFBO-FM Moncton, NB
CFBR-FM Edmonton, AB
CFBS-FM Lourdes-de-Blanc-Sablon, PQ

CFBT-FM Vancouver, BC
CFBU-FM Saint Catharines, ON
CFBW-FM Hanover, ON
CFBX-FM Kamloops, BC
CFCA-FM Kitchener, ON
CFCH-FM Chase, BC
CFCP-FM Courtenay, BC
CFCR-FM Saskatoon, SK
CFCV-FM Saint Andrews, NF
CFCW-FM Camrose, AB
CFCY-FM Charlottetown, PE
CFDA-FM Victoriaville, PQ
CFDM-FM Meadow Lake, SK
CFDV-FM Red Deer, AB
CFDY-FM Cochrane, ON
CFEI-FM Saint Hyacinthe, PQ
CFEL-FM Montmagny, PQ
*CFEP-FM Eastern Passage, NS
CFEQ-FM Winnipeg, MB
CFET-FM Tagish, YT
CFEX-FM Calgary, AB
CFFF-FM Peterborough, ON
CFFM-FM Williams Lake, BC
CFFX-FM Kingston, ON
*CFGB-FM Happy Valley, NF
CFGE-FM Sherbrooke, PQ
CFGI-FM Georgina Island, ON
CFGL-FM Laval, PQ
CFGP-FM Grande Prairie, AB
CFGQ-FM Calgary, AB
CFGW-FM Yorkton, SK
CFGX-FM Sarnia, ON
CFHK-FM St. Thomas, ON
CFIC-FM Listuguj, PQ
CFID-FM Acton Vale, PQ
CFIF-FM Iroquois Falls, ON
CFIM-FM Iles-de-la-Madeleine, PQ
*CFIN-FM Lac-Etchemin, PQ
CFIS-FM Prince George, BC
CFIT-FM Airdrie, AB
CFIX-FM Chicoutimi, PQ
CFJB-FM Barrie, ON
CFJO-FM Thetford Mines, PQ
CFJR-FM Brockville, ON
*CFJU-FM Kedgwick, NB
CFLC-FM Churchill Falls, NF
CFLG-FM Cornwall, ON
CFLO-FM Mont-Laurier, PQ
CFLT-FM Dartmouth, NS
CFLX-FM Sherbrooke, PQ
CFLY-FM Kingston, ON
CFLZ-FM Niagara Falls, ON
CFMC-FM Saskatoon, SK
CFMF-FM Fermont, PQ
CFMG-FM Saint Albert, AB
CFMH-FM Saint John, NB
CFMI-FM New Westminster, BC
CFMK-FM Kingston, ON
CFML-FM Burnaby, BC
CFMM-FM Prince Albert, SK
CFMQ-FM Hudson Bay, SK
*CFMU-FM Hamilton, ON
CFMV-FM Chandler, PQ
CFMX-FM Cobourg, ON
CFMY-FM Medicine Hat, AB
CFMZ-FM Toronto, ON
CFNA-FM Bonnyville, AB
CFND-FM Saint Jerome, PQ
CFNJ-FM Saint Gabriel-de-Brandon, PQ
CFNK-FM Pinehouse Lake, SK
CFNO-FM Marathon, ON
CFNR-FM Terrace, BC
CFNY-FM Toronto, ON
CFOB-FM Fort Frances, ON
CFOM-FM Levis, PQ
CFOR-FM Maniwaki, PQ
CFOU-FM Trois Rivieres, PQ
CFOX-FM Vancouver, BC
CFOZ-FM Argentia, NF
CFPL-FM London, ON

CFPS-FM Port Elgin, ON
CFPV-FM Pemberton, BC
CFPW-FM Powell River, BC
CFPX-FM Pukatawagan, MB
CFQK-FM Kaministiquia, ON
CFQM-FM Moncton, NB
CFQR-FM Montreal, PQ
CFQX-FM Selkirk, MB
*CFRC-FM Kingston, ON
CFRG-FM Gravelbourg, SK
*CFRH-FM Penetanguishene, ON
CFRI-FM Grande Prairie, AB
CFRK-FM Fredericton, NB
CFRM-FM Little Current, ON
*CFRO-FM Vancouver, BC
CFRQ-FM Dartmouth, NS
CFRT-FM Iqaluit, NU
*CFRU-FM Guelph, ON
CFRV-FM Lethbridge, AB
CFRY-FM Portage la Prairie, MB
CFSF-FM Sturgeon Falls, ON
CFSH-FM Apsley, ON
CFSR-FM Hope, BC
*CFTH-FM-1 Harrington Harbour, PQ
CFTH-FM-2 La Tabatiere, PQ
CFTX-FM Gatineau, PQ
CFUL-FM Calgary, AB
*CFUR-FM Prince George, BC
CFUT-FM Shawinigan, PQ
*CFUV-FM Victoria, BC
CFVD-FM Degelis, PQ
CFVD-FM-2 Pohenegamook, PQ
CFVM-FM Amqui, PQ
CFVR-FM Fort McMurray, AB
CFWC-FM Brantford, ON
CFWD-FM Saskatoon, SK
CFWE-FM-4 Edmonton, AB
CFWF-FM Regina, SK
CFWM-FM Winnipeg, MB
CFWP-FM Wahta Mohawk Territory near Bala, ON
CFXE-FM Edson, AB
CFXH-FM Hinton, AB
CFXJ-FM Toronto, ON
CFXL-FM Calgary, AB
CFXM-FM Granby, PQ
CFXN-FM North Bay, ON
CFXO-FM High River-Okotoks, AB
CFXU-FM Antigonish, NS
CFXW-FM Whitecourt, AB
CFXY-FM Fredericton, NB
CFYT-FM Dawson City, YT
CFYX-FM Rimouski, PQ
CFZN-FM Haliburton, ON
CFZZ-FM Saint Jean-Iberville, PQ
CHAA-FM Longueuil, PQ
CHAD-FM Dawson Creek, BC
CHAI-FM Chateauguay, PQ
CHAS-FM Sault Ste. Marie, ON
CHAT-FM Medicine Hat, AB
CHAY-FM Barrie, ON
CHBD-FM Regina, SK
CHBE-FM Victoria, BC
CHBI-FM Burnt Islands, NF
CHBN-FM Edmonton, AB
CHBW-FM Rocky Mountain House, AB
CHBZ-FM Cranbrook, BC
CHCD-FM Simcoe, ON
CHCQ-FM Belleville, ON
CHCR-FM Killaloe, ON
CHDH-FM Siksika, AB
CHDI-FM Edmonton, AB
CHDR-FM Cranbrook, BC
CHEF-FM Matagami, PQ
CHEQ-FM Sainte-Marie-de-Beauce, PQ
CHER-FM Sydney, NS
CHES-FM Erin, ON
CHET-FM Chetwynd, BC
CHEY-FM Trois Rivieres, PQ
CHEZ-FM Ottawa, ON

CHFI-FM Toronto, ON
CHFM-FM Calgary, AB
CHFN-FM Cape Croker (Neyaashiinigmiing), ON
CHFT-FM Fort McMurray, AB
CHFX-FM Halifax, NS
CHGA-FM Maniwaki, PQ
CHGB-FM Wasaga Beach, ON
CHGK-FM Stratford, ON
CHGO-FM Val d'Or, PQ
CHHO-FM Louiseville, PQ
CHHR-FM Vancouver, BC
CHIC-FM Rouyn-Noranda, PQ
CHIK-FM Quebec, PQ
*CHIM-FM Timmins, ON
CHIN-FM Toronto, ON
CHIP-FM Fort Coulonge, PQ
CHIQ-FM Winnipeg, MB
CHJM-FM Saint Georges, PQ
CHJX-FM London, ON
CHKF-FM Calgary, AB
CHKG-FM Vancouver, BC
CHKS-FM Sarnia, ON
CHLB-FM Lethbridge, AB
CHLC-FM Baie Comeau, PQ
CHLI-FM Rossland, BC
CHLK-FM Perth, ON
CHLN-FM Trois Rivieres, PQ
CHLQ-FM Charlottetown, PE
CHLS-FM Lillooet, BC
CHLT-FM Sherbrooke, PQ
CHLX-FM Gatineau, PQ
CHLY-FM Nanaimo, BC
*CHMA-FM Sackville, NB
CHMC-FM Edmonton, AB
CHME-FM Les Escoumins, PQ
CHMM-FM MacKenzie, BC
CHMN-FM Canmore, AB
CHMP-FM Longueuil, PQ
*CHMR-FM Saint John's, NF
CHMS-FM Bancroft, ON
CHMT-FM Timmins, ON
CHMX-FM Regina, SK
CHMY-FM Renfrew, ON
CHMZ-FM Tofino, BC
CHNC-FM New Carlisle, PQ
CHNI-FM Saint John, NB
CHNK-FM Winnipeg, MB
CHNO-FM Sudbury, ON
CHNS-FM Halifax, NS
CHNV-FM Nelson, BC
CHOA-FM Rouyn-Noranda, PQ
*CHOC-FM Saint Remi, PQ
CHOD-FM Cornwall, ON
CHOE-FM Matane, PQ
CHOI-FM Quebec, PQ
CHOM-FM Montreal, PQ
CHON-FM Whitehorse, YT
CHOO-FM Drumheller, AB
*CHOP-FM Newmarket, ON
CHOQ-FM Toronto, ON
CHOS-FM Rattling Brook, NF
CHOW-FM Amos, PQ
CHOX-FM La Pocatiere, PQ
CHOY-FM Moncton, NB
CHOZ-FM Saint John's, NF
CHPB-FM Cochrane, ON
CHPD-FM Aylmer, ON
CHPQ-FM Parksville, BC
CHPR-FM Hawkesbury, ON
CHQC-FM Saint John, NB
CHQM-FM Vancouver, BC
CHQX-FM Prince Albert, SK
CHRD-FM Drummondville, PQ
CHRE-FM Saint Catharines, ON
CHRG-FM Maria (Reserve), PQ
CHRI-FM Ottawa, ON
CHRK-FM Sydney, NS
CHRL-FM Roberval, PQ
CHRM-FM Matane, PQ
CHRQ-FM Restigouche, PQ

*CHRW-FM London, ON
CHRX-FM Fort St. John, BC
CHRY-FM Toronto, ON
CHSB-FM Bedford, NS
CHSJ-FM Saint John, NB
CHSL-FM Slave Lake, AB
CHSN-FM Estevan, SK
CHSR-FM Fredericton, NB
CHST-FM London, ON
CHSU-FM Kelowna, BC
CHTD-FM Saint Stephen, NB
CHTN-FM Charlottetown, PE
CHTT-FM Victoria, BC
CHTZ-FM Saint Catharines, ON
CHUB-FM Red Deer, AB
CHUC-FM Cobourg, ON
CHUK-FM Mashteuiatsh (Pointe-Bleue), PQ
CHUM-FM Toronto, ON
CHUN-FM Rouyn-Noranda, PQ
*CHUO-FM Ottawa, ON
CHUR-FM North Bay, ON
CHUT-FM Lac-Simon (Louvicourt), PQ
CHVD-FM Dolbeau-Mistassini, PQ
CHVN-FM Winnipeg, MB
CHVO-FM Carbonear, NF
CHVR-FM Pembroke, ON
CHWC-FM Goderich, ON
CHWF-FM Nanaimo, BC
CHWK-FM Chilliwack, BC
CHWV-FM Saint John, NB
CHXL-FM Okanese Indian Reserve, SK
CHXX-FM Donnacona, PQ
CHYC-FM Sudbury, ON
CHYK-FM Timmins, ON
CHYK-FM-3 Hearst, ON
CHYM-FM Kitchener, ON
CHYR-FM Leamington, ON
*CHYZ-FM Sainte Foy, PQ
CIAJ-FM Prince Rupert, BC
CIAM-FM Fort Vermilion, AB
CIAU-FM Radisson, PQ
CIAX-FM Windsor, PQ
CIAY-FM Whitehorse, YT
CIBH-FM Parksville, BC
CIBK-FM Calgary, AB
*CIBL-FM Montreal, PQ
CIBM-FM Riviere du Loup, PQ
CIBO-FM Senneterre, PQ
CIBU-FM Wingham, ON
CIBW-FM Drayton Valley, AB
CIBX-FM Fredericton, NB
CICF-FM Vernon, BC
CICS-FM Sudbury, ON
CICU-FM Eskasoni Indian Reserve, NS
CICX-FM Orillia, ON
CICY-FM Selkirk, MB
CICZ-FM Midland, ON
CIDC-FM Orangeville, ON
CIDD-FM White Bear Lake Resort, SK
CIDI-FM Lac-Brome, PQ
CIDO-FM Creston, BC
CIDR-FM Windsor, ON
CIEG-FM Egmont, BC
CIEL-FM Riviere du Loup, PQ
CIEU-FM Carleton, PQ
*CIFA-FM Comeauville, NS
CIFM-FM Kamloops, BC
CIFX-FM Lewisporte, NF
CIGB-FM Trois Rivieres, PQ
CIGL-FM Belleville, ON
CIGM-FM Sudbury, ON
CIGO-FM Port Hawkesbury, NS
CIGV-FM Penticton, BC
CIGY-FM Calgary, AB
CIHO-FM Saint Hilarion, PQ
CIHR-FM Woodstock, ON
CIHS-FM Wetaskiwin, AB
CIHT-FM Ottawa, ON
CIJK-FM Kentville, NS

CIKI-FM Rimouski, PQ
CIKR-FM Kingston, ON
CIKT-FM Grande Prairie, AB
CIKX-FM Grand Falls, NB
CIKZ-FM Kitchener-Waterloo, ON
CILE-FM Havre-Saint-Pierre, PQ
CILG-FM Moose Jaw, SK
CILK-FM Kelowna, BC
CILQ-FM North York, ON
CILS-FM Victoria, BC
CILT-FM Steinbach, MB
CILU-FM Thunder Bay, ON
CILV-FM Ottawa, ON
CIME-FM Saint Jerome, PQ
CIMF-FM Gatineau, PQ
CIMG-FM Swift Current, SK
CIMI-FM Charlesbourg, PQ
CIMJ-FM Guelph, ON
CIMM-FM Ucluelet, BC
CIMO-FM Magog, PQ
CIMS-FM Balmoral, NB
CIMX-FM Windsor, ON
CIMY-FM Pembroke, ON
CINB-FM Saint John, NB
CINC-FM Thompson, MB
CING-FM Hamilton, ON
*CINN-FM Hearst, ON
CINQ-FM Montreal, PQ
CINU-FM Truro, NS
CIOC-FM Victoria, BC
*CIOI-FM Hamilton, ON
CIOK-FM Saint John, NB
*CION-FM Quebec, PQ
CIOO-FM Halifax, NS
CIOS-FM Stephenville, NF
CIOT-FM Nipawin, SK
CIOZ-FM Marystown, NF
CIPC-FM Port-Cartier, PQ
CIPN-FM Pender Harbour, BC
CIQB-FM Barrie, ON
CIQC-FM Campbell River, BC
CIQM-FM London, ON
CIRA-FM Montreal, PQ
CIRK-FM Edmonton, AB
CIRR-FM Toronto, ON
CIRV-FM Toronto, ON
CIRX-FM Prince George, BC
CISC-FM Gibsons, BC
*CISM-FM Montreal, PQ
CISN-FM Edmonton, AB
CISP-FM Pemberton, BC
CISQ-FM Squamish, BC
CISS-FM Ottawa, ON
CISW-FM Whistler, BC
CITA-FM Moncton, NB
CITE-FM Montreal, PQ
CITE-FM-1 Sherbrooke, PQ
CITF-FM Quebec, PQ
CITI-FM Winnipeg, MB
*CITR-FM Vancouver, BC
*CIUT-FM Toronto, ON
CIVL-FM Abbotsford, BC
CIVR-FM Yellowknife, NT
CIWS-FM Whitchurch-Stouffville, ON
CIWV-FM Hamilton, ON
CIXF-FM Brooks, AB
CIXK-FM Owen Sound, ON
CIXL-FM Welland, ON
CIXM-FM Whitecourt, AB
CIXN-FM Fredericton, NB
*CIXX-FM London, ON
CIYN-FM Kincardine, ON
CIZL-FM Regina, SK
CIZZ-FM Red Deer, AB
CJAB-FM Saguenay, PQ
CJAI-FM Stella, ON
*CJAM-FM Windsor, ON
CJAN-FM Asbestos, PQ
CJAQ-FM Calgary, AB
CJAS-FM Saint Augustin, PQ
CJAT-FM Trail, BC
CJAV-FM Port Alberni, BC
CJAW-FM Moose Jaw, SK
CJAY-FM Calgary, AB
CJBB-FM Englehart, ON
CJBC-FM Toronto, ON

CJBC-FM-4 London, ON
CJBE-FM Port-Menier, PQ
CJBR-FM Rimouski, PQ
CJBX-FM London, ON
CJBZ-FM Taber, AB
CJCD-FM Yellowknife, NT
CJCD-FM-1 Hay River, NT
CJCF-FM Cumberland House, SK
CJCH-FM Halifax, NS
CJCI-FM Prince George, BC
CJCJ-FM Woodstock, NB
CJCQ-FM North Battleford, SK
CJCY-FM Medicine Hat, AB
CJDJ-FM Saskatoon, SK
CJDL-FM Tillsonburg, ON
CJDM-FM Drummondville, PQ
CJDR-FM Fernie, BC
CJDS-FM Saint Pamphile, PQ
CJDV-FM Cambridge, ON
CJEB-FM Trois Rivieres, PQ
CJEC-FM Quebec, PQ
CJEG-FM Bonnyville, AB
CJEL-FM Winkler, MB
CJEM-FM Edmundston, NB
CJET-FM Smiths Falls, ON
CJEZ-FM Toronto, ON
CJFB-FM Bolton, ON
CJFH-FM Woodstock, ON
CJFM-FM Montreal, PQ
CJFW-FM Terrace, BC
CJFX-FM Antigonish, NS
CJFY-FM Blackville, NB
CJGV-FM Winnipeg, MB
CJGY-FM Grande Prairie, AB
CJHD-FM North Battleford, SK
CJHR-FM Renfrew, ON
CJIJ-FM Sydney, NS
CJIQ-FM Kitchener/Paris, ON
CJIT-FM Lac Megantic, PQ
*CJIV-FM Dryden, ON
CJJC-FM Yorkton, SK
CJJJ-FM Brandon, MB
CJJM-FM Espanola, ON
CJJR-FM Vancouver, BC
CJKC-FM Kamloops, BC
CJKK-FM Clarenville, NF
CJKL-FM Kirkland Lake, ON
CJKR-FM Winnipeg, MB
CJKX-FM Ajax, ON
CJLA-FM Lachute, PQ
CJLF-FM Barrie, ON
CJLL-FM Ottawa, ON
CJLM-FM Joliette, PQ
CJLR-FM La Ronge, SK
CJLS-FM Yarmouth, NS
CJLS-FM-1 Barrington, NS
CJLS-FM-2 New Tusket, NS
CJLT-FM Medicine Hat, AB
CJLU-FM Halifax, NS
CJLX-FM Belleville, ON
*CJLY-FM Nelson, BC
CJMC-FM Sainte Anne des Monts, PQ
CJMF-FM Quebec, PQ
CJMG-FM Penticton, BC
CJMI-FM Strathroy, ON
CJMJ-FM Ottawa, ON
CJMK-FM Saskatoon, SK
CJMM-FM Rouyn-Noranda, PQ
CJMO-FM Moncton, NB
CJMP-FM Powell River, BC
CJMQ-FM Sherbrooke, PQ
CJMV-FM Val d'Or, PQ
CJMX-FM Sudbury, ON
CJNE-FM Nipawin, SK
CJNI-FM Halifax, NS
CJNS-FM Meadow Lake, SK
CJNU-FM Winnipeg, MB
*CJOA-FM Thunder Bay, ON
CJOC-FM Lethbridge, AB
CJOI-FM Rimouski, PQ
CJOJ-FM Belleville, ON
CJOK-FM Fort McMurray, AB
CJOZ-FM Bonavista Bay, NF
CJPG-FM Portage la Prairie, MB
*CJPN-FM Fredericton, NB
CJPR-FM Blairmore, AB

CJPT-FM Brockville, ON
CJPX-FM Montreal, PQ
CJQM-FM Sault Ste. Marie, ON
CJQQ-FM Timmins, ON
CJRC-FM Gatineau, PQ
CJRD-FM Drummondville, PQ
CJRE-FM Riviere au Renard, PQ
CJRG-FM Gaspe, PQ
CJRI-FM Fredericton, NB
CJRL-FM Kenora, ON
CJRM-FM Labrador City, NF
CJRP-FM Saint John, NB
CJRQ-FM Sudbury, ON
*CJRT-FM Toronto, ON
CJRW-FM Summerside, PE
CJRX-FM Lethbridge, AB
CJRY-FM Edmonton, AB
CJSA-FM Toronto, ON
CJSB-FM Swan River, MB
CJSD-FM Thunder Bay, ON
CJSE-FM Shediac, NB
*CJSF-FM Burnaby, BC
CJSI-FM Calgary, AB
CJSO-FM Sorel, PQ
CJSP-FM Leamington, ON
CJSQ-FM Quebec, PQ
*CJSR-FM Edmonton, AB
CJSS-FM Cornwall, ON
CJSU-FM Duncan, BC
*CJSW-FM Calgary, AB
CJTB-FM Tete-a-la-Baleine, PQ
CJTK-FM Sudbury, ON
CJTL-FM Pickle Lake, ON
CJTN-FM Quinte West, ON
*CJTR-FM Regina, SK
CJTT-FM New Liskeard, ON
CJTW-FM Kitchener-Waterloo, ON
CJUI-FM Kelowna, BC
CJUK-FM Thunder Bay, ON
CJUM-FM Winnipeg, MB
CJUV-FM Lacombe, AB
CJVD-FM Vaudreuil-Dorion, PQ
CJVR-FM Melfort, SK
CJWA-FM Wawa, ON
CJWL-FM Ottawa, ON
CJXK-FM Cold Lake, AB
CJXL-FM Moncton, NB
CJXX-FM Grande Prairie, AB
CJXY-FM Burlington, ON
CJYC-FM Saint John, NB
CJZN-FM Victoria, BC
CKAG-FM Pikogan, PQ
CKAJ-FM Jonquiere, PQ
CKAP-FM Kapuskasing, ON
CKAU-FM Maliotenam, PQ
CKAV-FM Toronto, ON
CKAV-FM-2 Vancouver, BC
CKAV-FM-3 Calgary, AB
CKAV-FM-4 Edmonton, AB
CKAV-FM-9 Ottawa, ON
CKAY-FM Sechelt, BC
CKBA-FM Athabasca, AB
CKBC-FM Bathurst, NB
CKBL-FM Saskatoon, SK
CKBN-FM Becancour and Nicolet, PQ
CKBT-FM Kitchener-Waterloo, ON
CKBW-FM Bridgewater, NS
CKBW-FM-1 Liverpool, NS
CKBW-FM-2 Shelburne, NS
CKBY-FM Smiths Falls, ON
CKBZ-FM Kamloops, BC
CKCB-FM Collingwood, ON
CKCE-FM Calgary, AB
CKCH-FM Sydney, NS
CKCI-FM Sarnia, ON
CKCK-FM Regina, SK
CKCL-FM Chilliwack, BC
CKCN-FM Sept-Iles, PQ
CKCQ-FM Quesnel, BC
CKCU-FM Ottawa, ON
CKCW-FM Moncton, NB
CKDG-FM Montreal, PQ
*CKDJ-FM Ottawa, ON
CKDK-FM Woodstock, ON
CKDR-FM Dryden, ON
CKDR-FM-2 Sioux Lookout, ON

CKDR-FM-5 Red Lake, ON
*CKDU-FM Halifax, NS
CKDV-FM Prince George, BC
CKDX-FM Newmarket, ON
CKEC-FM New Glasgow, NS
CKEN-FM Kentville, NS
CKER-FM Edmonton, AB
CKEY-FM Fort Erie, ON
CKFI-FM Swift Current, SK
CKFM-FM Toronto, ON
CKFU-FM Fort St. John, BC
CKFX-FM North Bay, ON
CKGB-FM Timmins, ON
CKGE-FM Oshawa, ON
CKGF-FM-2 Greenwood, BC
CKGN-FM Kapuskasing, ON
CKGO-FM-1 Boston Bar, BC
CKGS-FM Saguenay (zone La Baie), PQ
CKGW-FM Chatham, ON
CKGY-FM Red Deer, AB
CKHA-FM Haliburton, ON
CKHC-FM Toronto, ON
CKHK-FM Hawkesbury, ON
CKHL-FM High Level, AB
CKHR-FM Hay River, NT
CKHZ-FM Halifax, NS
CKIA-FM Quebec, PQ
CKIC-FM Winnipeg, MB
CKII-FM Dolbeau-Mistassini, PQ
CKIK-FM Red Deer, AB
CKIQ-FM Iqaluit, NU
CKIS-FM Toronto, ON
CKIX-FM Saint John's, NF
CKIZ-FM Vernon, BC
CKJJ-FM Belleville, ON
*CKJM-FM Cheticamp, NS
CKJN-FM Haldimand County, ON
CKJX-FM Olds, AB
CKKC-FM Nelson, BC
CKKK-FM Peterborough, ON
CKKL-FM Ottawa, ON
CKKN-FM Prince George, BC
CKKO-FM Kelowna, BC
CKKS-FM Sechelt, BC
CKKW-FM Kitchener, ON
CKKX-FM Peace River, AB
CKLB-FM Yellowknife, NT
CKLC-FM Kingston, ON
CKLD-FM Thetford Mines, PQ
CKLE-FM Bathurst, NB
CKLF-FM Brandon, MB
CKLG-FM Vancouver, BC
CKLH-FM Hamilton, ON
CKLJ-FM Olds, AB
CKLM-FM Lloydminster, AB
*CKLN-FM Toronto, ON
CKLP-FM Parry Sound, ON
CKLR-FM Courtenay, BC
*CKLU-FM Sudbury, ON
CKLX-FM Montreal, PQ
CKLY-FM Lindsay (city of Kawartha Lakes), ON
CKLZ-FM Kelowna, BC
CKMA-FM Miramichi, NB
CKMB-FM Barrie, ON
CKMF-FM Montreal, PQ
CKMH-FM Medicine Hat, AB
CKMM-FM Winnipeg, MB
CKMN-FM Rimouski-Mont Joli, PQ
*CKMS-FM Waterloo, ON
CKMV-FM Grand Falls, NB
CKNA-FM Natashquan, PQ
CKNI-FM Moncton, NB
CKNL-FM Fort St. John, BC
CKNR-FM Elliot Lake, ON
CKNX-FM Wingham, ON
CKOA-FM Glace Bay, NS
CKOD-FM Valleyfield, PQ
CKOE-FM Moncton, NB
CKOI-FM Verdun, PQ
CKOL-FM Campbellford, ON
CKON-FM Akwesasne, ON
CKOS-FM Fort McMurray, OS
CKOT-FM Tillsonburg, ON

CKOV-FM Kelowna, BC
CKOY-FM Sherbrooke, PQ
CKOZ-FM Corner Brook, NF
CKPC-FM Brantford, ON
CKPE-FM Sydney, NS
CKPK-FM Vancouver, BC
CKPR-FM Thunder Bay, ON
CKPT-FM Peterborough, ON
CKQB-FM Ottawa, ON
CKQC-FM Abbotsford, BC
CKQK-FM Charlottetown, PE
CKQM-FM Peterborough, ON
CKQN-FM Baker Lake, NU
CKQR-FM Castlegar, BC
CKQV-FM Vermillion Bay, ON
CKRA-FM Edmonton, AB
CKRB-FM Saint Georges-de-Beauce, PQ
CKRC-FM Weyburn, SK
CKRH-FM Halifax, NS
*CKRK-FM Kahnawake, PQ
*CKRL-FM Quebec, PQ
CKRO-FM Pokemouche, NB
*CKRP-FM Falher, AB
CKRS-FM Saguenay, PQ
CKRV-FM Kamloops, BC
CKRX-FM Fort Nelson, BC
CKRY-FM Calgary, AB
*CKRZ-FM Ohsweken, ON
CKSA-FM Lloydminster, AB
CKSG-FM Cobourg, ON
CKSJ-FM Saint John's, NF
CKSO-FM Sudbury, ON
CKSR-FM Chilliwack, BC
CKSS-FM Red Rocks, NF
CKSY-FM Chatham, ON
CKTF-FM Gatineau, PQ
CKTG-FM Thunder Bay, ON
CKTI-FM Kettle Point, ON
CKTK-FM Kitimat, BC
CKTO-FM Truro, NS
CKTP-FM Fredericton Centre, NB
CKTY-FM Truro, NS
*CKUA-FM Edmonton, AB
CKUE-FM Chatham, ON
CKUJ-FM Kuujjuaq, PQ
CKUL-FM Halifax, NS
CKUM-FM Moncton, NB
CKUN-FM Christian Island, ON
*CKUT-FM Montreal, PQ
CKUV-FM High River-Okotoks, AB
CKUW-FM Winnipeg, MB
*CKVI-FM Kingston, ON
CKVL-FM Montreal (zone LaSalle), PQ
CKVM-FM Ville-Marie, PQ
CKVN-FM Lethbridge, AB
CKVX-FM Kindersley, SK
CKWE-FM Maniwaki (Kitigan Zibi Anishinabeg Reserve), PQ
CKWF-FM Peterborough, ON
CKWM-FM Kentville, NS
CKWR-FM Kitchener, ON
CKWT-FM Sioux Lookout, ON
CKWV-FM Nanaimo, BC
CKWY-FM Wainwright, AB
CKXA-FM Brandon, MB
CKXC-FM Kingston, ON
CKXD-FM Gander, NF
CKX-FM Brandon, MB
CKXG-FM Grand Falls-Windsor, NF
CKXL-FM Saint Boniface, MB
CKXO-FM Chibougamau, PQ
CKXR-FM Salmon Arm, BC
CKXU-FM Lethbridge, AB
CKXX-FM Corner Brook, NF
CKYC-FM Owen Sound, ON
CKYE-FM Vancouver, BC
CKY-FM Winnipeg, MB
CKYK-FM Alma, PQ
CKYM-FM Napanee, ON
CKYQ-FM Plessisville, PQ
CKYX-FM Fort McMurray, AB
CKZP-FM Zenon Park, SK
CKZX-FM New Denver, BC
CKZZ-FM Vancouver, BC
VOCM-FM Saint John's, NF

U.S. AM Stations by Frequency

88.1 mhz
*WWFJ(FM) East Fayetteville, NC

540 khz
KRXA(AM) Carmel Valley, CA
*KVIP(AM) Redding, CA
WFLF(AM) Pine Hills, FL
WDAK(AM) Columbus, GA
KWMT(AM) Fort Dodge, IA
KMLB(AM) Monroe, LA
WGOP(AM) Pocomoke City, MD
WPPI(AM) Sauk Rapids, MN
WETC(AM) Wendell-Zebulon, NC
WXNH(AM) Jaffrey, NH
KNMX(AM) Las Vegas, NM
WLIE(AM) Islip, NY
WWCS(AM) Canonsburg, PA
WYNN(AM) Florence, SC
WKFN(AM) Clarksville, TN
KDFT(AM) Ferris, TX
KNAK(AM) Delta, UT
WGTH(AM) Richlands, VA
WAUK(AM) Jackson, WI

550 khz
KTZN(AM) Anchorage, AK
WASG(AM) Daphne, AL
KFYI(AM) Phoenix, AZ
KUZZ(AM) Bakersfield, CA
KLLV(AM) Breen, CO
KRAI(AM) Craig, CO
*WAYR(AM) Orange Park, FL
WDUN(AM) Gainesville, GA
KMVI(AM) Wailuku, HI
KFRM(AM) Salina, KS
KTRS(AM) Saint Louis, MO
KBOW(AM) Butte, MT
WIOZ(AM) Pinehurst, NC
WAME(AM) Statesville, NC
KFYR(AM) Bismarck, ND
WGR(AM) Buffalo, NY
WKRC(AM) Cincinnati, OH
*KOAC(AM) Corvallis, OR
WPAB(AM) Ponce, PR
WDDZ(AM) Pawtucket, RI
KCRS(AM) Midland, TX
KTSA(AM) San Antonio, TX
WSVA(AM) Harrisonburg, VA
WDEV(AM) Waterbury, VT
KARI(AM) Blaine, WA
WSAU(AM) Wausau, WI

560 khz
KVOK(AM) Kodiak, AK
WOOF(AM) Dothan, AL
KBLU(AM) Yuma, AZ
KSFO(AM) San Francisco, CA
KLZ(AM) Denver, CO
WQAM(AM) Miami, FL
WIND(AM) Chicago, IL
WMIK(AM) Middlesboro, KY
WHYN(AM) Springfield, MA
WFRB(AM) Frostburg, MD
WGAN(AM) Portland, ME
WRDT(AM) Monroe, MI
WEBC(AM) Duluth, MN
KWTO(AM) Springfield, MO
KMON(AM) Great Falls, MT
WGAI(AM) Elizabeth City, NC
WCKL(AM) Catskill, NY
WFIL(AM) Philadelphia, PA
WVOC(AM) Columbia, SC
WNSR(AM) Brentwood, TN
WHBQ(AM) Memphis, TN
KLVI(AM) Beaumont, TX
KPQ(AM) Wenatchee, WA
WJLS(AM) Beckley, WV

567 khz
KGUM(AM) Hagatna, GU

570 khz
WAAX(AM) Gadsden, AL
KCFJ(AM) Alturas, CA
KLAC(AM) Los Angeles, CA
WTBN(AM) Pinellas Park, FL
KQNG(AM) Lihue, HI
WKYX(AM) Paducah, KY
WIDS(AM) Russell Springs, KY
WTNT(AM) Bethesda, MD
WWNC(AM) Asheville, NC
WDOX(AM) Raleigh, NC
KSNM(AM) Las Cruces, NM
WMCA(AM) New York, NY
WSYR(AM) Syracuse, NY
WKBN(AM) Youngstown, OH
WNAX(AM) Yankton, SD
KLIF(AM) Dallas, TX
KACP(AM) Salt Lake City, UT
KVI(AM) Seattle, WA
WMAM(AM) Marinette, WI

580 khz
KRSA(AM) Petersburg, AK
WBIL(AM) Tuskegee, AL
KSAZ(AM) Marana, AZ
KMJ(AM) Fresno, CA
KUBC(AM) Montrose, CO
WDBO(AM) Orlando, FL
WGAC(AM) Augusta, GA
KIDO(AM) Nampa, ID
*WILL(AM) Urbana, IL
WIBW(AM) Topeka, KS
KMJJ(AM) Alexandria, LA
WTAG(AM) Worcester, MA
WTCM(AM) Traverse City, MI
WELO(AM) Tupelo, MS
KANA(AM) Anaconda, MT
WKSK(AM) West Jefferson, NC
KGAY(AM) Ashland, OR
WHP(AM) Harrisburg, PA
WKAQ(AM) San Juan, PR
KZMX(AM) Hot Springs, SD
WYHM(AM) Rockwood, TN
KRFE(AM) Lubbock, TX
WLES(AM) Bon Air, VA
WKTY(AM) La Crosse, WI
WCHS(AM) Charleston, WV

585 khz
KJAL(AM) Tafuna, AS

590 khz
KHAR(AM) Anchorage, AK
WREN(AM) Carrollton, AL
KZHS(AM) Hot Springs, AR
KTIE(AM) San Bernardino, CA
KTHO(AM) South Lake Tahoe, CA
KCSJ(AM) Pueblo, CO
WAFC(AM) Clewiston, FL
WDIZ(AM) Panama City, FL
WDWD(AM) Atlanta, GA
KSSK(AM) Honolulu, HI
KID(AM) Idaho Falls, ID
KFNS(AM) Wood River, IL
WVLK(AM) Lexington, KY
WEZE(AM) Boston, MA
WJMS(AM) Ironwood, MI
WKZO(AM) Kalamazoo, MI
KGLE(AM) Glendive, MT
WCAB(AM) Rutherfordton, NC
WGTM(AM) Wilson, NC
KXSP(AM) Omaha, NE
WROW(AM) Albany, NY
KUGN(AM) Eugene, OR
WARM(AM) Scranton, PA
WMBS(AM) Uniontown, PA
WWLX(AM) Lawrenceburg, TN
KLBJ(AM) Austin, TX
KSUB(AM) Cedar City, UT
WLVA(AM) Lynchburg, VA
KQNT(AM) Spokane, WA

600 khz
KVNA(AM) Flagstaff, AZ
KOGO(AM) San Diego, CA
KCOL(AM) Wellington, CO
WICC(AM) Bridgeport, CT
WBWL(AM) Jacksonville, FL
WMT(AM) Cedar Rapids, IA
WKYH(AM) Paintsville, KY
WVOG(AM) New Orleans, LA
WCAO(AM) Baltimore, MD
*WFST(AM) Caribou, ME
WCHT(AM) Escanaba, MI
WSNL(AM) Flint, MI
WCVP(AM) Murphy, NC
WSJS(AM) Winston-Salem, NC
KSJB(AM) Jamestown, ND
WSOM(AM) Salem, OH
WFRM(AM) Coudersport, PA
WYEL(AM) Mayaguez, PR
WREC(AM) Memphis, TN
KROD(AM) El Paso, TX
KERB(AM) Kermit, TX
KTBB(AM) Tyler, TX
WVAR(AM) Richwood, WV

610 khz
WAGG(AM) Birmingham, AL
KARV(AM) Russellville, AR
KAVL(AM) Lancaster, CA
KEAR(AM) San Francisco, CA
KVLE(AM) Vail, CO
WSNG(AM) Torrington, CT
WIOD(AM) Miami, FL
WVTJ(AM) Pensacola, FL
WPLO(AM) Grayson, GA
WCEH(AM) Hawkinsville, GA
WRUS(AM) Russellville, KY
KDAL(AM) Duluth, MN
KCSP(AM) Kansas City, MO
KOJM(AM) Havre, MT
WFNZ(AM) Charlotte, NC
KCSR(AM) Chadron, NE
WGIR(AM) Manchester, NH
KNML(AM) Albuquerque, NM
WTVN(AM) Columbus, OH
KRTA(AM) Medford, OR
WIP(AM) Philadelphia, PA
WEXS(AM) Patillas, PR
KILT(AM) Houston, TX
KVNU(AM) Logan, UT
WVBE(AM) Roanoke, VA
WLVE(AM) Winchester, VA
KONA(AM) Kennewick, WA

620 khz
KGTL(AM) Homer, AK
WJHX(AM) Lexington, AL
KTAR(AM) Phoenix, AZ
KIGS(AM) Hanford, CA
KMJC(AM) Mount Shasta, CA
KJOL(AM) Grand Junction, CO
WDAE(AM) Saint Petersburg, FL
WTRP(AM) La Grange, GA
KHNU(AM) Hilo, HI
KMNS(AM) Sioux City, IA
KWAL(AM) Wallace, ID
WTUV(AM) Louisville, KY
WZON(AM) Bangor, ME
WJDX(AM) Jackson, MS
WDNC(AM) Durham, NC
WSNR(AM) Jersey City, NJ
WHEN(AM) Syracuse, NY
KPOJ(AM) Portland, OR
WKHB(AM) Irwin, PA
WGCV(AM) Cayce, SC
WRJZ(AM) Knoxville, TN
KMKI(AM) Plano, TX
WVMT(AM) Burlington, VT
WTMJ(AM) Milwaukee, WI
WWNR(AM) Beckley, WV

630 khz
KJNO(AM) Juneau, AK
KIAM(AM) Nenana, AK
WAVU(AM) Albertville, AL
WJDB(AM) Thomasville, AL
KVMA(AM) Magnolia, AR
KIDD(AM) Monterey, CA
KHOW(AM) Denver, CO
WMAL(AM) Washington, DC
WBMQ(AM) Savannah, GA
WNEG(AM) Toccoa, GA
KUAM(AM) Hagatna, GU
KFXD(AM) Boise, ID
WLAP(AM) Lexington, KY
KJSL(AM) Saint Louis, MO
WAIZ(AM) Hickory, NC
WMFD(AM) Wilmington, NC
KLEA(AM) Lovington, NM
KPLY(AM) Reno, NV
KWRO(AM) Coquille, OR
WEJL(AM) Scranton, PA
WUNO(AM) San Juan, PR
WPRO(AM) Providence, RI
KSLR(AM) San Antonio, TX
KTKK(AM) Sandy, UT
KCIS(AM) Edmonds, WA
KTRW(AM) Opportunity, WA
WREY(AM) Hudson, WI
WJAW(AM) Saint Marys, WV

640 khz
*KYUK(AM) Bethel, AK
KFI(AM) Los Angeles, CA
WMEN(AM) Royal Palm Beach, FL
WVLG(AM) Wildwood, FL
WGST(AM) Atlanta, GA
*WOI(AM) Ames, IA
KTIB(AM) Thibodaux, LA
WNNZ(AM) Westfield, MA
WMFN(AM) Zeeland, MI
KGVW(AM) Belgrade, MT
WFNC(AM) Fayetteville, NC
WWJZ(AM) Mount Holly, NJ
WHLO(AM) Akron, OH
WWLS(AM) Moore, OK
WXSM(AM) Blountville, TN
WCRV(AM) Collierville, TN

648 khz
WVUV(AM) Leone, AS

650 khz
KENI(AM) Anchorage, AK
KSTE(AM) Rancho Cordova, CA
KRTR(AM) Honolulu, HI
WSRO(AM) Ashland, MA
WNMT(AM) Nashwauk, MN
WSM(AM) Nashville, TN
KIKK(AM) Pasadena, TX
KMTI(AM) Manti, UT
KUUX(AM) Pullman, WA
KGAB(AM) Orchard Valley, WY

660 khz
KFAR(AM) Fairbanks, AK
WXQW(AM) Fairhope, AL
KTNN(AM) Window Rock, AZ
KGDP(AM) Oildale, CA
WORL(AM) Altamonte Springs, FL
WNFS(AM) White Springs, FL
WMIC(AM) Sandusky, MI
WBHR(AM) Sauk Rapids, MN
KEYZ(AM) Williston, ND
KCRO(AM) Omaha, NE
WFAN(AM) New York, NY
WXIC(AM) Waverly, OH
KXOR(AM) Junction City, OR
WPYT(AM) Wilkinsburg, PA
WLFJ(AM) Greenville, SC
KSKY(AM) Balch Springs, TX
WLOY(AM) Rural Retreat, VA
KAPS(AM) Mount Vernon, WA

670 khz
*KDLG(AM) Dillingham, AK
WYLS(AM) York, AL
KWXI(AM) Glenwood, AR
KIRN(AM) Simi Valley, CA
KLTT(AM) Commerce City, CO
WWFE(AM) Miami, FL
KPUA(AM) Hilo, HI
KBOI(AM) Boise, ID
WSCR(AM) Chicago, IL
KMZQ(AM) Las Vegas, NV
WIEZ(AM) Lewistown, PA
WMTY(AM) Farragut, TN
WPMH(AM) Claremont, VA
WVVT(AM) Essex Junction, VT

675 khz
KTKB(AM) Tamuning, GU

680 khz
*KBRW(AM) Barrow, AK
KNBR(AM) San Francisco, CA
WGES(AM) Saint Petersburg, FL
WCNN(AM) North Atlanta, GA
WCTT(AM) Corbin, KY
WDRD(AM) Newburg, KY
WRKO(AM) Boston, MA
WCBM(AM) Baltimore, MD
WDBC(AM) Escanaba, MI
KFEQ(AM) Saint Joseph, MO
KKGR(AM) East Helena, MT
WPTF(AM) Raleigh, NC
WRGC(AM) Sylva, NC
KWKA(AM) Clovis, NM
WINR(AM) Binghamton, NY
WISR(AM) Butler, PA
WAPA(AM) San Juan, PR
WMFS(AM) Memphis, TN
KKYX(AM) San Antonio, TX
KBRD(AM) Lacey, WA
KOMW(AM) Omak, WA
WOGO(AM) Hallie, WI
WKAZ(AM) Charleston, WV

690 khz
WSPZ(AM) Birmingham, AL
KEWI(AM) Benton, AR
KCEE(AM) Tucson, AZ
KWRP(AM) Pueblo, CO
KRGS(AM) Rifle, CO
WADS(AM) Ansonia, CT
WOKV(AM) Jacksonville, FL
KHNR(AM) Honolulu, HI
KBLI(AM) Blackfoot, ID
KGGF(AM) Coffeyville, KS
WIST(AM) New Orleans, LA
XETRA(AM) Tijuana, MEX
KFXN(AM) Minneapolis, MN
KSTL(AM) Saint Louis, MO
KOAQ(AM) Terrytown, NE
KRCO(AM) Prineville, OR
WPHE(AM) Phoenixville, PA
KTSM(AM) El Paso, TX
KPET(AM) Lamesa, TX
KZEY(AM) Tyler, TX
WZAP(AM) Bristol, VA
*WVCY(AM) Oshkosh, WI
WELD(AM) Fisher, WV

700 khz
KBYR(AM) Anchorage, AK
WEEL(AM) Dothan, AL
KMBX(AM) Soledad, CA
WJWB(AM) Gibsonia, FL
WVBB(AM) Orange-Athol, MA
WDMV(AM) Walkersville, MD
KNAX(AM) McCook, NE
WLW(AM) Cincinnati, OH
KGRV(AM) Winston, OR
KSEV(AM) Tomball, TX
KHSE(AM) Wylie, TX
KALL(AM) North Salt Lake City, UT

KXLX(AM) Airway Heights, WA

710 khz
WNTM(AM) Mobile, AL
KAPZ(AM) Bald Knob, AR
KMIA(AM) Black Canyon City, AZ
KFIA(AM) Carmichael, CA
KSPN(AM) Los Angeles, CA
KNUS(AM) Denver, CO
WAQI(AM) Miami, FL
WUFF(AM) Eastman, GA
WROM(AM) Rome, GA
WEKC(AM) Williamsburg, KY
KEEL(AM) Shreveport, LA
KCMO(AM) Kansas City, MO
WZOO(AM) Asheboro, NC
WEGG(AM) Rose Hill, NC
KXMR(AM) Bismarck, ND
WOR(AM) New York, NY
WKJB(AM) Mayaguez, PR
WPOG(AM) Saint Matthews, SC
WTPR(AM) Paris, TN
*WFCM(AM) Smyrna, TN
KGNC(AM) Amarillo, TX
KURV(AM) Edinburg, TX
WFNR(AM) Blacksburg, VA
KIRO(AM) Seattle, WA
WDSM(AM) Superior, WI

720 khz
*KOTZ(AM) Kotzebue, AK
WRZN(AM) Hernando, FL
WVCC(AM) Hogansville, GA
KUAI(AM) Eleele, HI
WGN(AM) Chicago, IL
WGCR(AM) Pisgah Forest, NC
KDWN(AM) Las Vegas, NV
WVOA(AM) Dewitt, NY
KFIR(AM) Sweet Home, OR
WWII(AM) Shiremanstown, PA
KSAH(AM) Universal City, TX

730 khz
WUMP(AM) Madison, AL
KQPN(AM) West Memphis, AR
WWTK(AM) Lake Placid, FL
WSTT(AM) Thomasville, GA
*KBSU(AM) Boise, ID
KLOE(AM) Goodland, KS
WFMW(AM) Madisonville, KY
WMTC(AM) Vancleve, KY
WASO(AM) Covington, LA
WACE(AM) Chicopee, MA
WJTO(AM) Bath, ME
WVFN(AM) East Lansing, MI
KWOA(AM) Worthington, MN
KWRE(AM) Warrenton, MO
KURL(AM) Billings, MT
WFMC(AM) Goldsboro, NC
WOHS(AM) Shelby, NC
KDAZ(AM) Albuquerque, NM
WDOS(AM) Oneonta, NY
WJYM(AM) Bowling Green, OH
*KEZX(AM) Medford, OR
WNAK(AM) Nanticoke, PA
WPIT(AM) Pittsburgh, PA
WLTQ(AM) Charleston, SC
WLIL(AM) Lenoir City, TN
KBQX(AM) Big Spring, TX
KKDA(AM) Grand Prairie, TX
KSVN(AM) Ogden, UT
WXTR(AM) Alexandria, VA
WMNA(AM) Gretna, VA
KULE(AM) Ephrata, WA
WJMT(AM) Merrill, WI

740 khz
WMSP(AM) Montgomery, AL
KIDR(AM) Phoenix, AZ
KBRT(AM) Avalon, CA
KCBS(AM) San Francisco, CA
KVOR(AM) Colorado Springs, CO
KVFC(AM) Cortez, CO
WSBR(AM) Boca Raton, FL
WYGM(AM) Orlando, FL
KBOE(AM) Oskaloosa, IA
WVLN(AM) Olney, IL

WNOP(AM) Newport, KY
WJIB(AM) Cambridge, MA
WPAQ(AM) Mount Airy, NC
KVOX(AM) Fargo, ND
KATK(AM) Carlsbad, NM
WNYH(AM) Huntington, NY
KRMG(AM) Tulsa, OK
WVCH(AM) Chester, PA
WIAC(AM) San Juan, PR
WCXZ(AM) Harrogate, TN
WIRJ(AM) Humboldt, TN
WJIG(AM) Tullahoma, TN
KTRH(AM) Houston, TX
KCMC(AM) Texarkana, TX
WMBG(AM) Williamsburg, VA
WRPQ(AM) Baraboo, WI
WDGY(AM) Hudson, WI
WRNR(AM) Martinsburg, WV

750 khz
KFQD(AM) Anchorage, AK
WSB(AM) Atlanta, GA
WTHQ(AM) Brookport, IL
WNDZ(AM) Portage, IN
KKNO(AM) Gretna, LA
WBMD(AM) Baltimore, MD
WRME(AM) Hampden, ME
WARD(AM) Petoskey, MI
KBNN(AM) Lebanon, MO
KERR(AM) Polson, MT
WAUG(AM) New Hope, NC
KMMJ(AM) Grand Island, NE
KHWG(AM) Fallon, NV
KSEO(AM) Durant, OK
KXL(AM) Portland, OR
WQOR(AM) Olyphant, PA
KAMA(AM) El Paso, TX
KOAL(AM) Price, UT
WPDX(AM) Clarksburg, WV

760 khz
WURL(AM) Moody, AL
KMTL(AM) Sherwood, AR
KFMB(AM) San Diego, CA
KKZN(AM) Thornton, CO
WLCC(AM) Brandon, FL
WEFL(AM) Tequesta, FL
KGU(AM) Honolulu, HI
KCCV(AM) Overland Park, KS
WVNE(AM) Leicester, MA
WJR(AM) Detroit, MI
WCIS(AM) Morganton, NC
WCPS(AM) Tarboro, NC
KEIP(AM) Las Vegas, NV
WCHP(AM) Champlain, NY
WORA(AM) Mayaguez, PR
WETR(AM) Knoxville, TN
WENO(AM) Nashville, TN
KTKR(AM) San Antonio, TX

770 khz
*KCHU(AM) Valdez, AK
WVNN(AM) Athens, AL
WHOA(AM) Saraland, AL
KCBC(AM) Riverbank, CA
WWCN(AM) North Fort Myers, FL
WYHG(AM) Young Harris, GA
WCGW(AM) Nicholasville, KY
KJCB(AM) Lafayette, LA
*KUOM(AM) Minneapolis, MN
WEW(AM) Saint Louis, MO
KATL(AM) Miles City, MT
WLWL(AM) Rockingham, NC
KKOB(AM) Albuquerque, NM
KKOB Exp Stn Santa Fe, NM
WABC(AM) New York, NY
WTOR(AM) Youngstown, NY
WAIS(AM) Buchtel, OH
WKFB(AM) Jeannette, PA
KAAM(AM) Garland, TX
WYRV(AM) Cedar Bluff, VA
KTTH(AM) Seattle, WA

780 khz
*KNOM(AM) Nome, AK
WZZX(AM) Lineville, AL
KAZM(AM) Sedona, AZ

WBBM(AM) Chicago, IL
WXME(AM) Monticello, ME
WTME(AM) Rumford, ME
WIIN(AM) Ridgeland, MS
WCKB(AM) Dunn, NC
WWOL(AM) Forest City, NC
WJAG(AM) Norfolk, NE
KKOH(AM) Reno, NV
KSPI(AM) Stillwater, OK
WPTN(AM) Cookeville, TN
WAVA(AM) Arlington, VA

790 khz
KCAM(AM) Glennallen, AK
WTSK(AM) Tuscaloosa, AL
KURM(AM) Rogers, AR
KOSY(AM) Texarkana, AR
KNST(AM) Tucson, AZ
KFPT(AM) Clovis, CA
KWSW(AM) Eureka, CA
KABC(AM) Los Angeles, CA
WLBE(AM) Leesburg, FL
WPNN(AM) Pensacola, FL
WAXY(AM) South Miami, FL
WQXI(AM) Atlanta, GA
WSFN(AM) Brunswick, GA
WGRA(AM) Cairo, GA
KKON(AM) Kealakekua, HI
KSPD(AM) Boise, ID
KBRV(AM) Soda Springs, ID
WRMS(AM) Beardstown, IL
KXXX(AM) Colby, KS
WKRD(AM) Louisville, KY
WSGW(AM) Saginaw, MI
KGHL(AM) Billings, MT
WBLO(AM) Thomasville, NC
KFGO(AM) Fargo, ND
KBET(AM) Winchester, NV
WTNY(AM) Watertown, NY
WLSV(AM) Wellsville, NY
WHTH(AM) Heath, OH
KWIL(AM) Albany, OR
WAEB(AM) Allentown, PA
WPIC(AM) Sharon, PA
WPRV(AM) Providence, RI
WVCD(AM) Bamberg-Denmark, SC
WQSV(AM) Ashland City, TN
WETB(AM) Johnson City, TN
WMC(AM) Memphis, TN
KBME(AM) Houston, TX
KFYO(AM) Lubbock, TX
WSVG(AM) Mount Jackson, VA
WNIS(AM) Norfolk, VA
KGMI(AM) Bellingham, WA
KJRB(AM) Spokane, WA
WAYY(AM) Eau Claire, WI

800 khz
KINY(AM) Juneau, AK
WHOS(AM) Decatur, AL
WMGY(AM) Montgomery, AL
KAGH(AM) Crossett, AR
KVOM(AM) Morrilton, AR
KBFP(AM) Bakersfield, CA
WLAD(AM) Danbury, CT
WPLK(AM) Palatka, FL
WJAT(AM) Swainsboro, GA
KXIC(AM) Iowa City, IA
WKZI(AM) Casey, IL
WSHO(AM) New Orleans, LA
WNNW(AM) Lawrence, MA
KQAD(AM) Luverne, MN
WVAL(AM) Sauk Rapids, MN
KREI(AM) Farmington, MO
WKBC(AM) North Wilkesboro, NC
WTMR(AM) Camden, NJ
KQCV(AM) Oklahoma City, OK
KPDQ(AM) Portland, OR
WCHA(AM) Chambersburg, PA
WDSC(AM) Dillon, SC
WPJM(AM) Greer, SC
WDEH(AM) Sweetwater, TN
KDDD(AM) Dumas, TX
WSVS(AM) Crewe, VA
WDUX(AM) Waupaca, WI
WVHU(AM) Huntington, WV

801 khz
KTWG(AM) Hagatna, GU

810 khz
WCKA(AM) Jacksonville, AL
KGO(AM) San Francisco, CA
KLVZ(AM) Brighton, CO
WEUS(AM) Orlovista, FL
WTHV(AM) Hahira, GA
WXFO(AM) Royston, GA
WDDD(AM) Johnston City, IL
WSYW(AM) Indianapolis, IN
WEKG(AM) Jackson, KY
WYRE(AM) Annapolis, MD
WMJH(AM) Rockford, MI
WHB(AM) Kansas City, MO
WSJC(AM) Magee, MS
KSWV(AM) Santa Fe, NM
WGY(AM) Schenectady, NY
WEDO(AM) McKeesport, PA
WKVM(AM) San Juan, PR
WQIZ(AM) Saint George, SC
KBHB(AM) Sturgis, SD
WCTA(AM) Alamo, TN
WMGC(AM) Murfreesboro, TN
KXOI(AM) Crane, TX
KYTY(AM) Somerset, TX
WPIN(AM) Dublin, VA
KTBI(AM) Ephrata, WA
WDMP(AM) Dodgeville, WI
WJJQ(AM) Tomahawk, WI

820 khz
KCBF(AM) Fairbanks, AK
WWBA(AM) Largo, FL
WCPT(AM) Willow Springs, IL
*WSWI(AM) Evansville, IN
WWFD(AM) Frederick, MD
WBKK(AM) Wilton, MN
WVNC(AM) Masonboro, NC
WWLZ(AM) Horseheads, NY
*WNYC(AM) New York, NY
*WOSU(AM) Columbus, OH
KORC(AM) Waldport, OR
WWAM(AM) Jasper, TN
WBAP(AM) Fort Worth, TX
KUTR(AM) Taylorsville, UT
WGGM(AM) Chester, VA
KGNW(AM) Burien-Seattle, WA

830 khz
*KSDP(AM) Sand Point, AK
*KFLT(AM) Tucson, AZ
KNCO(AM) Grass Valley, CA
KLAA(AM) Orange, CA
WACC(AM) Hialeah, FL
WJFA(AM) Hilliard, FL
WFGM(AM) Sandy Springs, GA
KHVH(AM) Honolulu, HI
WFNO(AM) Norco, LA
WCRN(AM) Worcester, MA
WMMI(AM) Shepherd, MI
WCCO(AM) Minneapolis, MN
KOTC(AM) Kennett, MO
WTRU(AM) Kernersville, NC
WKTX(AM) Cortland, OH
WEEU(AM) Reading, PA
KMUL(AM) Farwell, TX
KUYO(AM) Evansville, WY

840 khz
WBHY(AM) Mobile, AL
KMPH(AM) Modesto, CA
WRYM(AM) New Britain, CT
WPGS(AM) Mims, FL
WHGH(AM) Thomasville, GA
WHAS(AM) Louisville, KY
KWDF(AM) Ball, LA
WKDI(AM) Denton, MD
KTIC(AM) West Point, NE
KXNT(AM) North Las Vegas, NV
KKNX(AM) Eugene, OR
KSWB(AM) Seaside, OR
WVPO(AM) Stroudsburg, PA
WXEW(AM) Yabucoa, PR
WCEO(AM) Columbia, SC
KVJY(AM) Pharr, TX
WKTR(AM) Earlysville, VA

KMAX(AM) Colfax, WA

850 khz
KICY(AM) Nome, AK
WXJC(AM) Birmingham, AL
KOA(AM) Denver, CO
WREF(AM) Ridgefield, CT
WRUF(AM) Gainesville, FL
WFTL(AM) West Palm Beach, FL
WCUG(AM) Cuthbert, GA
WPTB(AM) Statesboro, GA
KHLO(AM) Hilo, HI
KXGM(AM) Waterloo, IA
WAIT(AM) Crystal Lake, IL
WEEI(AM) Boston, MA
WGVS(AM) Muskegon, MI
WWJC(AM) Duluth, MN
*KFUO(AM) Clayton, MO
WQST(AM) Forest, MS
WLRC(AM) Walnut, MS
WRBZ(AM) Raleigh, NC
WYLF(AM) Penn Yan, NY
WKNR(AM) Cleveland, OH
WKGE(AM) Johnstown, PA
WABA(AM) Aguadilla, PR
WPFD(AM) Fairview, TN
WKVL(AM) Knoxville, TN
KJON(AM) Carrollton, TX
KEYH(AM) Houston, TX
WTAR(AM) Norfolk, VA
KHHO(AM) Tacoma, WA

860 khz
WAMI(AM) Opp, AL
KWRF(AM) Warren, AR
KOSE(AM) Wilson, AR
KMVP(AM) Phoenix, AZ
KTRB(AM) San Francisco, CA
WGUL(AM) Dunedin, FL
WAEC(AM) Atlanta, GA
WDMG(AM) Douglas, GA
KWPC(AM) Muscatine, IA
WMRI(AM) Marion, IN
KKOW(AM) Pittsburg, KS
WSON(AM) Henderson, KY
WSBS(AM) Great Barrington, MA
WBGR(AM) Baltimore, MD
KNUJ(AM) New Ulm, MN
WFMO(AM) Fairmont, NC
WACB(AM) Taylorsville, NC
KARS(AM) Belen, NM
KPAM(AM) Troutdale, OR
WAMO(AM) Millvale, PA
WWDB(AM) Philadelphia, PA
WLBG(AM) Laurens, SC
WTZX(AM) Sparta, TN
KFST(AM) Fort Stockton, TX
KPAN(AM) Hereford, TX
KSFA(AM) Nacogdoches, TX
KONO(AM) San Antonio, TX
KKAT(AM) Salt Lake City, UT
WEVA(AM) Emporia, VA
WNOV(AM) Milwaukee, WI
WOAY(AM) Oak Hill, WV

870 khz
WQRX(AM) Valley Head, AL
KRLA(AM) Glendale, CA
KJMP(AM) Pierce, CO
WINU(AM) Shelbyville, IL
WMTL(AM) Leitchfield, KY
WWL(AM) New Orleans, LA
WLVP(AM) Gorham, ME
*WKAR(AM) East Lansing, MI
KPRM(AM) Park Rapids, MN
KAAN(AM) Bethany, MO
WTCG(AM) Mount Holly, NC
WZNH(AM) Fitzwilliam Depot, NH
KLSQ(AM) Whitney, NV
WHCU(AM) Ithaca, NY
WQBS(AM) San Juan, PR
WPWT(AM) Colonial Heights, TN
KFJZ(AM) Fort Worth, TX
WFLO(AM) Farmville, VA
KFLD(AM) Pasco, WA

880 khz

KLRG(AM) Sheridan, AR
KKMC(AM) Gonzales, CA
WZAB(AM) Sweetwater, FL
KHCM(AM) Honolulu, HI
WIJR(AM) Highland, IL
KJJR(AM) Whitefish, MT
WRRZ(AM) Clinton, NC
WPEK(AM) Fairview, NC
WPIP(AM) Winston-Salem, NC
KRVN(AM) Lexington, NE
KHAC(AM) Tse Bonito, NM
WCBS(AM) New York, NY
WRFD(AM) Columbus-Worthington, OH
KWIP(AM) Dallas, OR
KCMX(AM) Phoenix, OR
WYKO(AM) Sabana Grande, PR
WMDB(AM) Nashville, TN
KJOJ(AM) Conroe, TX
WSLK(AM) Moneta, VA
KIXI(AM) Mercer Island-Seattle, WA
WMEQ(AM) Menomonie, WI

890 khz

*KBBI(AM) Homer, AK
WYAM(AM) Hartselle, AL
KLFF(AM) Arroyo Grande, CA
KDJQ(AM) Meridian, ID
WLS(AM) Chicago, IL
WAMG(AM) Dedham, MA
KGGN(AM) Gladstone, MO
WHJA(AM) Laurel, MS
WHNC(AM) Henderson, NC
KQLX(AM) Lisbon, ND
KTLR(AM) Oklahoma City, OK
*WFKJ(AM) Cashtown, PA
WFAB(AM) Ceiba, PR
WBAJ(AM) Blythwood, SC
KVOZ(AM) Del Mar Hills, TX
KTXV(AM) Mabank, TX
KDXU(AM) Saint George, UT
WKNV(AM) Fairlawn, VA

900 khz

*KZPA(AM) Fort Yukon, AK
WATV(AM) Birmingham, AL
WGOK(AM) Mobile, AL
WOZK(AM) Ozark, AL
KHOZ(AM) Harrison, AR
KKHJ(AM) Leone, AS
KBIF(AM) Fresno, CA
KALI(AM) West Covina, CA
WJWL(AM) Georgetown, DE
WSWN(AM) Belle Glade, FL
WMOP(AM) Ocala, FL
WJTH(AM) Calhoun, GA
WBML(AM) Macon, GA
WJLG(AM) Savannah, GA
KNUI(AM) Kahului, HI
KSGL(AM) Wichita, KS
WWLK(AM) Eddyville, KY
WFIA(AM) Louisville, KY
WLSI(AM) Pikeville, KY
WILC(AM) Laurel, MD
WCME(AM) Brunswick, ME
*KTIS(AM) Minneapolis, MN
KFAL(AM) Fulton, MO
WYCV(AM) Granite Falls, NC
WAYN(AM) Rockingham, NC
WIAM(AM) Williamston, NC
KJSK(AM) Columbus, NE
WGHM(AM) Nashua, NH
WBRV(AM) Boonville, NY
WUAM(AM) Watervliet, NY
WCER(AM) Canton, OH
WCPA(AM) Clearfield, PA
WURD(AM) Philadelphia, PA
WNMB(AM) North Myrtle Beach, SC
WKXV(AM) Knoxville, TN
WKDA(AM) Lebanon, TN
KPYN(AM) Atlanta, TX
KFLP(AM) Floydada, TX
KCLW(AM) Hamilton, TX
KREH(AM) Pecan Grove, TX
WCBX(AM) Bassett, VA
WKDW(AM) Staunton, VA
KKRT(AM) Wenatchee, WA

WATK(AM) Antigo, WI
WDLS(AM) Wisconsin Dells, WI

910 khz

*KIYU(AM) Galena, AK
WZMG(AM) Pepperell, AL
KLCN(AM) Blytheville, AR
KGME(AM) Phoenix, AZ
*KECR(AM) El Cajon, CA
KRAK(AM) Hesperia, CA
KNEW(AM) Oakland, CA
KOXR(AM) Oxnard, CA
*KPOF(AM) Denver, CO
WLAT(AM) New Britain, CT
WTWD(AM) Plant City, FL
WRFV(AM) Valdosta, GA
*WSUI(AM) Iowa City, IA
WAKO(AM) Lawrenceville, IL
KINA(AM) Salina, KS
WSFE(AM) Burnside, KY
WUBR(AM) Baton Rouge, LA
WAEI(AM) Bangor, ME
WGTO(AM) Cassopolis, MI
WFDF(AM) Farmington Hills, MI
WALT(AM) Meridian, MS
WSRP(AM) Jacksonville, NC
KCJB(AM) Minot, ND
KBIM(AM) Roswell, NM
WRKL(AM) New City, NY
WLTP(AM) Marietta, OH
WPFB(AM) Middletown, OH
KVIS(AM) Miami, OK
KURY(AM) Brookings, OR
WAVL(AM) Apollo, PA
WBZU(AM) Scranton, PA
WSBA(AM) York, PA
WPRP(AM) Ponce, PR
WTMZ(AM) Dorchester Terrace-Brentwood, SC
WOLI(AM) Spartanburg, SC
KJJQ(AM) Volga, SD
WMRB(AM) Columbia, TN
WJCW(AM) Johnson City, TN
WEPG(AM) South Pittsburg, TN
KNAF(AM) Fredericksburg, TX
KATH(AM) Frisco, TX
KRIO(AM) McAllen, TX
KWDZ(AM) Salt Lake City, UT
WRNL(AM) Richmond, VA
WWWR(AM) Roanoke, VA
WNHV(AM) White River Junction, VT
KTRO(AM) Vancouver, WA
WHSM(AM) Hayward, WI
WDOR(AM) Sturgeon Bay, WI

920 khz

KSRM(AM) Soldotna, AK
WGOL(AM) Russellville, AL
KARN(AM) Little Rock, AR
KVIN(AM) Ceres, CA
KPSI(AM) Palm Springs, CA
KVEC(AM) San Luis Obispo, CA
KLMR(AM) Lamar, CO
WDMC(AM) Melbourne, FL
WGKA(AM) Atlanta, GA
WVOH(AM) Hazlehurst, GA
*KYFR(AM) Shenandoah, IA
WGNU(AM) Granite City, IL
WMOK(AM) Metropolis, IL
*WBAA(AM) West Lafayette, IN
WTCW(AM) Whitesburg, KY
WBOX(AM) Bogalusa, LA
WMPL(AM) Hancock, MI
KDHL(AM) Faribault, MN
KWAD(AM) Wadena, MN
KWYS(AM) West Yellowstone, MT
WPCM(AM) Burlington, NC
WPTL(AM) Canton, NC
WCHR(AM) Trenton, NJ
KSVA(AM) Albuquerque, NM
KBAD(AM) Las Vegas, NV
*KIHM(AM) Reno, NV
WYBY(AM) Cortland, NY
WGHQ(AM) Kingston, NY
WIRD(AM) Lake Placid, NY
WMNI(AM) Columbus, OH

KSHO(AM) Lebanon, OR
WKVA(AM) Lewistown, PA
WHJJ(AM) Providence, RI
WYMB(AM) Manning, SC
KKLS(AM) Rapid City, SD
WLIV(AM) Livingston, TN
KQBU(AM) El Paso, TX
*KFLB(AM) Odessa, TX
KYST(AM) Texas City, TX
KVEL(AM) Vernal, UT
WURA(AM) Quantico, VA
KGTK(AM) Olympia, WA
KXLY(AM) Spokane, WA
WOKY(AM) Milwaukee, WI
WMMN(AM) Fairmont, WV

930 khz

KTKN(AM) Ketchikan, AK
KNSA(AM) Unalakleet, AK
WEZZ(AM) Monroeville, AL
WGAD(AM) Rainbow City, AL
KAPR(AM) Douglas, AZ
KAFF(AM) Flagstaff, AZ
KHJ(AM) Los Angeles, CA
KKXX(AM) Paradise, CA
KIUP(AM) Durango, CO
KRKY(AM) Granby, CO
WYUS(AM) Milford, DE
WLVF(AM) Haines City, FL
WFXJ(AM) Jacksonville, FL
WLSS(AM) Sarasota, FL
WMGR(AM) Bainbridge, GA
KSEI(AM) Pocatello, ID
WTAD(AM) Quincy, IL
WAUR(AM) Sandwich, IL
WHON(AM) Centerville, IN
WKCT(AM) Bowling Green, KY
WFMD(AM) Frederick, MD
WBCK(AM) Battle Creek, MI
KKIN(AM) Aitkin, MN
KWOC(AM) Poplar Bluff, MO
WSFZ(AM) Jackson, MS
KMPT(AM) East Missoula, MT
*WYFQ(AM) Charlotte, NC
WDLX(AM) Washington, NC
KOGA(AM) Ogallala, NE
WGIN(AM) Rochester, NH
WPAT(AM) Paterson, NJ
KCCC(AM) Carlsbad, NM
WBEN(AM) Buffalo, NY
WIZR(AM) Johnstown, NY
WEOL(AM) Elyria, OH
WKY(AM) Oklahoma City, OK
*KAGI(AM) Grants Pass, OR
WHLM(AM) Bloomsburg, PA
WYAC(AM) Cabo Rojo, PR
KSDN(AM) Aberdeen, SD
WSEV(AM) Sevierville, TN
WWON(AM) Waynesboro, TN
KDET(AM) Center, TX
KLUP(AM) Terrell Hills, TX
WLLL(AM) Lynchburg, VA
KBAI(AM) Bellingham, WA
KYAK(AM) Yakima, WA
*WLBL(AM) Auburndale, WI
WRVC(AM) Huntington, WV
KROE(AM) Sheridan, WY

940 khz

KGMS(AM) Tucson, AZ
KWRU(AM) Fresno, CA
WINE(AM) Brookfield, CT
WLQH(AM) Chiefland, FL
WINZ(AM) Miami, FL
WMAC(AM) Macon, GA
KKNE(AM) Waipahu, HI
KPSZ(AM) Des Moines, IA
WMIX(AM) Mount Vernon, IL
WCND(AM) Shelbyville, KY
WYLD(AM) New Orleans, LA
WGFP(AM) Webster, MA
WIDG(AM) Saint Ignace, MI
WCSY(AM) South Haven, MI
KSWM(AM) Aurora, MO
WCPC(AM) Houston, MS
KDIL(AM) Dillon, MT
WKYK(AM) Burnsville, NC

KVSH(AM) Valentine, NE
WCIT(AM) Lima, OH
KICE(AM) Bend, OR
KWBY(AM) Woodburn, OR
WFGI(AM) Charleroi, PA
WGRP(AM) Greenville, PA
WADV(AM) Lebanon, PA
*WIPR(AM) San Juan, PR
WECO(AM) Wartburg, TN
KIXZ(AM) Amarillo, TX
KTON(AM) Belton, TX
KTFS(AM) Texarkana, TX
KOBY(AM) Cedar City, UT
WNRG(AM) Grundy, VA
WKGM(AM) Smithfield, VA
WFAW(AM) Fort Atkinson, WI
WCSW(AM) Shell Lake, WI
KMER(AM) Kemmerer, WY

950 khz

KSEW(AM) Seward, AK
WNZZ(AM) Montgomery, AL
KXJK(AM) Forrest City, AR
KFSA(AM) Fort Smith, AR
KAHI(AM) Auburn, CA
KRWZ(AM) Denver, CO
WTLN(AM) Orlando, FL
WGTA(AM) Summerville, GA
WGOV(AM) Valdosta, GA
KOEL(AM) Oelwein, IA
KNJY(AM) Boise, ID
KOZE(AM) Lewiston, ID
WNTD(AM) Chicago, IL
WXLW(AM) Indianapolis, IN
KJRG(AM) Newton, KS
WYWY(AM) Barbourville, KY
KRRP(AM) Coushatta, LA
WROL(AM) Boston, MA
WCTN(AM) Potomac-Cabin John, MD
WWJ(AM) Detroit, MI
KTNF(AM) Saint Louis Park, MN
KWOS(AM) Jefferson City, MO
WHSY(AM) Hattiesburg, MS
KMTX(AM) Helena, MT
WPET(AM) Greensboro, NC
KNFT(AM) Bayard, NM
KDCE(AM) Espanola, NM
WHVW(AM) Hyde Park, NY
WROC(AM) Rochester, NY
WIBX(AM) Utica, NY
WDIG(AM) Steubenville, OH
*KTBR(AM) Roseburg, OR
WNCC(AM) Northern Cambria, PA
WPEN(AM) Philadelphia, PA
WJKB(AM) Moncks Corner, SC
WORD(AM) Spartanburg, SC
KWAT(AM) Watertown, SD
WAKM(AM) Franklin, TN
KPRC(AM) Houston, TX
KJTV(AM) Lubbock, TX
WXGI(AM) Richmond, VA
KJR(AM) Seattle, WA
WERL(AM) Eagle River, WI
WCLB(AM) Sheboygan, WI
WVTS(AM) Charleston, WV

960 khz

WERC(AM) Birmingham, AL
WLPR(AM) Prichard, AL
KCGS(AM) Marshall, AR
KKNT(AM) Phoenix, AZ
KIXW(AM) Apple Valley, CA
KKGN(AM) Oakland, CA
WELI(AM) New Haven, CT
WGRO(AM) Lake City, FL
WSVU(AM) North Palm Beach, FL
WJYZ(AM) Albany, GA
WRFC(AM) Athens, GA
KMA(AM) Shenandoah, IA
KSRA(AM) Salmon, ID
*WDLM(AM) East Moline, IL
WSBT(AM) South Bend, IN
WPRT(AM) Prestonsburg, KY
KROF(AM) Abbeville, LA
WFGL(AM) Fitchburg, MA
WTGM(AM) Salisbury, MD
WHAK(AM) Rogers City, MI

KLTF(AM) Little Falls, MN
KZIM(AM) Cape Girardeau, MO
WABG(AM) Greenwood, MS
KFLN(AM) Baker, MT
WCRU(AM) Dallas, NC
WRNS(AM) Kinston, NC
KNEB(AM) Scottsbluff, NE
KNDN(AM) Farmington, NM
WEAV(AM) Plattsburgh, NY
WKVX(AM) Wooster, OH
KGWA(AM) Enid, OK
KLAD(AM) Klamath Falls, OR
WHYL(AM) Carlisle, PA
WPLY(AM) Mount Pocono, PA
WATS(AM) Sayre, PA
WCHQ(AM) Quebradillas, PR
WQLA(AM) La Follette, TN
WBMC(AM) McMinnville, TN
KIMP(AM) Mount Pleasant, TX
KGKL(AM) San Angelo, TX
KOVO(AM) Provo, UT
WFIR(AM) Roanoke, VA
KALE(AM) Richland, WA
WTCH(AM) Shawano, WI

970 khz

KFBX(AM) Fairbanks, AK
WERH(AM) Hamilton, AL
WTBF(AM) Troy, AL
KNEA(AM) Jonesboro, AR
KVWM(AM) Show Low, AZ
KHTY(AM) Bakersfield, CA
KNWZ(AM) Coachella, CA
KESP(AM) Modesto, CA
KFEL(AM) Pueblo, CO
WNNR(AM) Jacksonville, FL
WFLA(AM) Tampa, FL
WNIV(AM) Atlanta, GA
WVOP(AM) Vidalia, GA
KFTA(AM) Rupert, ID
WMAY(AM) Springfield, IL
WFSR(AM) Harlan, KY
WGTK(AM) Louisville, KY
KSYL(AM) Alexandria, LA
WESO(AM) Southbridge, MA
WAMD(AM) Aberdeen, MD
WZAN(AM) Portland, ME
WZAM(AM) Ishpeming, MI
WKHM(AM) Jackson, MI
KQAQ(AM) Austin, MN
WJFN(AM) Brandon, MS
KBUL(AM) Billings, MT
WRCS(AM) Ahoskie, NC
WYSE(AM) Canton, NC
WDAY(AM) Fargo, ND
*KJLT(AM) North Platte, NE
WNYM(AM) Hackensack, NJ
KNUU(AM) Paradise, NV
*WNED(AM) Buffalo, NY
WCHN(AM) Norwich, NY
WFUN(AM) Ashtabula, OH
WATH(AM) Athens, OH
KCFO(AM) Tulsa, OK
KCMD(AM) Portland, OR
WBLF(AM) Bellefonte, PA
WBGG(AM) Pittsburgh, PA
WJMX(AM) Florence, SC
WXQK(AM) Spring City, TN
KIXL(AM) Del Valle, TX
WHVN(AM) Fort Worth, TX
WKCI(AM) Waynesboro, VA
WSTX(AM) Christiansted, VI
KTTO(AM) Spokane, WA
*WHA(AM) Madison, WI
WGEE(AM) Superior, WI
WWYO(AM) Pineville, WV

980 khz

KCAB(AM) Dardanelle, AR
KNTR(AM) Lake Havasu City, AZ
KINS(AM) Eureka, CA
*KEYQ(AM) Fresno, CA
KFWB(AM) Los Angeles, CA
KDBV(AM) Salinas, CA
KGLN(AM) Glenwood Springs, CO
WSUB(AM) Groton, CT
WTEM(AM) Washington, DC

WDVH(AM) Gainesville, FL
WRNE(AM) Gulf Breeze, FL
WTOT(AM) Marianna, FL
WHSR(AM) Pompano Beach, FL
WKLY(AM) Hartwell, GA
WPGA(AM) Perry, GA
WUUS(AM) Rossville, GA
KSPZ(AM) Ammon, ID
KSGM(AM) Chester, IL
WITY(AM) Danville, IL
WGWM(AM) London, KY
KOKA(AM) Shreveport, LA
WCAP(AM) Lowell, MA
WAKV(AM) Otsego, MI
KKMS(AM) Richfield, MN
KMBZ(AM) Kansas City, MO
WAKK(AM) McComb, MS
WKOR(AM) Starkville, MS
WAAV(AM) Leland, NC
WTIX(AM) Winston-Salem, NC
KICA(AM) Clovis, NM
KMIN(AM) Grants, NM
KVLV(AM) Fallon, NV
WOFX(AM) Troy, NY
WONE(AM) Dayton, OH
WILK(AM) Wilkes-Barre, PA
WAZS(AM) Summerville, SC
WBZK(AM) York, SC
KDSJ(AM) Deadwood, SD
WYFN(AM) Nashville, TN
KRTX(AM) Rosenberg-Richmond, TX
KSVC(AM) Richfield, UT
WFHG(AM) Bristol, VA
WJYK(AM) Chase City, VA
KBBO(AM) Selah, WA
WNBI(AM) Park Falls, WI
WPRE(AM) Prairie du Chien, WI
WCUB(AM) Two Rivers, WI
WHAW(AM) Weston, WV

990 khz
WEIS(AM) Centre, AL
WLDX(AM) Fayette, AL
KTKT(AM) Tucson, AZ
KATD(AM) Pittsburg, CA
KTMS(AM) Santa Barbara, CA
KRKS(AM) Denver, CO
WXCT(AM) Southington, CT
WMYM(AM) Miami, FL
WDYZ(AM) Orlando, FL
WGML(AM) Hinesville, GA
KHBZ(AM) Honolulu, HI
KAYL(AM) Storm Lake, IA
WCAZ(AM) Carthage, IL
WITZ(AM) Jasper, IN
WRFM(AM) Muncie, IN
KRSL(AM) Russell, KS
WGSO(AM) New Orleans, LA
WDEO(AM) Ypsilanti, MI
KRMO(AM) Cassville, MO
WABO(AM) Waynesboro, MS
WEEB(AM) Southern Pines, NC
WBTE(AM) Windsor, NC
KSVP(AM) Artesia, NM
WDCX(AM) Rochester, NY
WJEH(AM) Gallipolis, OH
WTIG(AM) Massillon, OH
KTHH(AM) Albany, OR
WNTP(AM) Philadelphia, PA
WNTW(AM) Somerset, PA
WPRA(AM) Mayaguez, PR
WALE(AM) Greenville, RI
WNML(AM) Knoxville, TN
KWAM(AM) Memphis, TN
KZZB(AM) Beaumont, TX
KFCD(AM) Farmersville, TX
KAML(AM) Kenedy-Karnes City, TX
WNRV(AM) Narrows-Pearisburg, VA
WLEE(AM) Richmond, VA

1000 khz
WDJL(AM) Huntsville, AL
WNSI(AM) Robertsdale, AL
KFLG(AM) Bullhead City, AZ
KCEO(AM) Vista, CA
WYBT(AM) Blountstown, FL
WJBW(AM) Jupiter, FL

WMVP(AM) Chicago, IL
WKVG(AM) Jenkins, KY
WCMX(AM) Leominster, MA
WXTN(AM) Lexington, MS
WRTG(AM) Garner, NC
WOF(AM) Andover, NJ
KKIM(AM) Albuquerque, NM
WLNL(AM) Horseheads, NY
WCCD(AM) Parma, OH
KTOK(AM) Oklahoma City, OK
WIOO(AM) Carlisle, PA
WJTP(AM) Walhalla, SC
KXRB(AM) Sioux Falls, SD
WMUF(AM) Paris, TN
KSTA(AM) Coleman, TX
*KBIB(AM) Marion, TX
WKDE(AM) Altavista, VA
*WRAR(AM) Tappahannock, VA
WVWI(AM) Charlotte Amalie, VI
KOMO(AM) Seattle, WA

1010 khz
WCOC(AM) Dora, AL
KXXT(AM) Tolleson, AZ
KCHJ(AM) Delano, CA
KIQI(AM) San Francisco, CA
KXPS(AM) Thousand Palms, CA
KSIR(AM) Brush, CO
WJXL(AM) Jacksonville Beach, FL
WQYK(AM) Seffner, FL
WGUN(AM) Atlanta, GA
*KRNI(AM) Mason City, IA
WCSI(AM) Columbus, IN
KIND(AM) Independence, KS
KDLA(AM) De Ridder, LA
*WCKW(AM) Garyville, LA
WOLB(AM) Baltimore, MD
WMIN(AM) Sauk Rapids, MN
KCHI(AM) Chillicothe, MO
KXEN(AM) Saint Louis, MO
WMOX(AM) Meridian, MS
WSPC(AM) Albemarle, NC
WFGW(AM) Black Mountain, NC
WELS(AM) Kinston, NC
WCNL(AM) Newport, NH
WINS(AM) New York, NY
WIOI(AM) New Boston, OH
KOOR(AM) Milwaukie, OR
WHIN(AM) Gallatin, TN
WORM(AM) Savannah, TN
KTNZ(AM) Amarillo, TX
KLAT(AM) Houston, TX
KBBW(AM) Waco, TX
KIHU(AM) Tooele, UT
WMEV(AM) Marion, VA
WRJR(AM) Portsmouth, VA
WSPT(AM) Stevens Point, WI
WCST(AM) Berkeley Springs, WV

1020 khz
KOAN(AM) Eagle River, AK
KTNQ(AM) Los Angeles, CA
WHDD(AM) Sharon, CT
WURN(AM) Kendall, FL
WSBX(AM) Ochlocknee, GA
WCIL(AM) Carbondale, IL
WPEO(AM) Peoria, IL
KJJK(AM) Fergus Falls, MN
KMMQ(AM) Plattsmouth, NE
WIBG(AM) Ocean City, NJ
KCKN(AM) Roswell, NM
KOKP(AM) Perry, OK
KDKA(AM) Pittsburgh, PA
WOQI(AM) Adjuntas, PR
WRIX(AM) Homeland Park, SC
KWIQ(AM) Moses Lake North, WA
KDYK(AM) Union Gap, WA

1030 khz
KFAY(AM) Farmington, AR
KVOI(AM) Cortaro, AZ
KJDJ(AM) San Luis Obispo, CA
WONQ(AM) Oviedo, FL
WEBS(AM) Calhoun, GA
WNVR(AM) Vernon Hills, IL
KBUF(AM) Holcomb, KS
WBZ(AM) Boston, MA

WWGB(AM) Indian Head, MD
*WUFL(AM) Sterling Heights, MI
WCTS(AM) Maplewood, MN
KCWJ(AM) Blue Springs, MO
WNOW(AM) Mint Hill, NC
WDRU(AM) Wake Forest, NC
KDUN(AM) Reedsport, OR
WOSO(AM) San Juan, PR
WGSF(AM) Memphis, TN
WQSE(AM) White Bluff, TN
KCTA(AM) Corpus Christi, TX
KWFA(AM) Tye, TX
WGFC(AM) Floyd, VA
KMAS(AM) Shelton, WA
WBGS(AM) Point Pleasant, WV
KTWO(AM) Casper, WY

1040 khz
KURS(AM) San Diego, CA
KCBR(AM) Monument, CO
WLVJ(AM) Boynton Beach, FL
WHBO(AM) Pinellas Park, FL
WPBS(AM) Conyers, GA
KLHT(AM) Honolulu, HI
WHO(AM) Des Moines, IA
WLCR(AM) Mt. Washington, KY
WSGH(AM) Lewisville, NC
WNJE(AM) Flemington, NJ
WYSL(AM) Avon, NY
WJTB(AM) North Ridgeville, OH
*KXPD(AM) Tigard, OR
WZSK(AM) Everett, PA
WZNA(AM) Moca, PR
WKTI(AM) Powell, TN
KGGR(AM) Dallas, TX

1050 khz
WBNM(AM) Alexander City, AL
WWIC(AM) Scottsboro, AL
KJBN(AM) Little Rock, AR
KTBA(AM) Tuba City, AZ
KJPG(AM) Frazier Park, CA
KCAA(AM) Loma Linda, CA
KTCT(AM) San Mateo, CA
WJSB(AM) Crestview, FL
WROS(AM) Jacksonville, FL
WJCM(AM) Sebring, FL
WFAM(AM) Augusta, GA
WMNZ(AM) Montezuma, GA
WDZ(AM) Decatur, IL
WTCA(AM) Plymouth, IN
WNES(AM) Central City, KY
KLPL(AM) Lake Providence, LA
KVPI(AM) Ville Platte, LA
WMSG(AM) Oakland, MD
WZAA(AM) Silver Spring, MD
WTKA(AM) Ann Arbor, MI
KLOH(AM) Pipestone, MN
KMIS(AM) Portageville, MO
KSIS(AM) Sedalia, MO
WTWG(AM) Columbus, MS
KMTA(AM) Miles City, MT
WFSC(AM) Franklin, NC
WLON(AM) Lincolnton, NC
WWGP(AM) Sanford, NC
WBNC(AM) Conway, NH
KTBL(AM) Los Ranchos de Albuquerque, NM
WSEN(AM) Baldwinsville, NY
WYBG(AM) Massena, NY
WEPN(AM) New York, NY
WCVX(AM) Cincinnati, OH
KKRX(AM) Lawton, OK
KGTO(AM) Tulsa, OK
KORE(AM) Springfield-Eugene, OR
WBUT(AM) Butler, PA
WLYC(AM) Williamsport, PA
WIQB(AM) Conway, SC
WSMT(AM) Sparta, TN
KCHN(AM) Brookshire, TX
KRMY(AM) Killeen, TX
WGAT(AM) Gate City, VA
WBRG(AM) Lynchburg, VA
WVXX(AM) Norfolk, VA
KEYF(AM) Dishman, WA
*KBLE(AM) Seattle, WA
*WDVM(AM) Eau Claire, WI

WJOK(AM) Kaukauna, WI
WLIP(AM) Kenosha, WI
WAMN(AM) Green Valley, WV
WADC(AM) Parkersburg, WV

1060 khz
KOAI(AM) Van Buren, AR
KDUS(AM) Tempe, AZ
KTNS(AM) Oakhurst, CA
KRCN(AM) Longmont, CO
WIXC(AM) Titusville, FL
WKNG(AM) Tallapoosa, GA
KIPA(AM) Hilo, HI
KBGN(AM) Caldwell, ID
WMCL(AM) McLeansboro, IL
WRHL(AM) Rochelle, IL
WFLE(AM) Flemingsburg, KY
WJKY(AM) Jamestown, KY
WLNO(AM) New Orleans, LA
WBIX(AM) Natick, MA
WHFB(AM) Benton Harbor-St. Joseph, MI
KFIL(AM) Preston, MN
KBFL(AM) Springfield, MO
WKMQ(AM) Tupelo, MS
WGSB(AM) Mebane, NC
WXNC(AM) Monroe, NC
WCOK(AM) Sparta, NC
KNLV(AM) Ord, NE
KUCU(AM) Farmington, NM
KKVV(AM) Las Vegas, NV
KFOY(AM) Sparks, NV
WILB(AM) Canton, OH
KYW(AM) Philadelphia, PA
WCGB(AM) Juana Diaz, PR
KGFX(AM) Pierre, SD
WGGQ(AM) Newport, TN
WQMV(AM) Waverly, TN
KXPL(AM) El Paso, TX
KIJN(AM) Farwell, TX
KFIT(AM) Lockhart, TX
KFIT EXP STN San Antonio, TX
KDYL(AM) South Salt Lake, UT

1070 khz
WAPI(AM) Birmingham, AL
KNX(AM) Los Angeles, CA
WKII(AM) Solana, FL
*WFRF(AM) Tallahassee, FL
KILR(AM) Estherville, IA
WFNI(AM) Indianapolis, IN
KFTI(AM) Wichita, KS
WEKT(AM) Elkton, KY
KBCL(AM) Bossier City, LA
WCRW(AM) Pocomoke City, MD
KVKK(AM) Verndale, MN
KHMO(AM) Hannibal, MO
KATQ(AM) Plentywood, MT
WNCT(AM) Greenville, NC
WGOS(AM) High Point, NC
WKMB(AM) Stirling, NJ
WTWK(AM) Plattsburgh, NY
WSCP(AM) Sandy Creek-Pulaski, NY
KRAM(AM) West Klamath, OR
WKOK(AM) Sunbury, PA
WMIA(AM) Arecibo, PR
WCSZ(AM) Sans Souci, SC
WFLI(AM) Lookout Mountain, TN
WDIA(AM) Memphis, TN
KOPY(AM) Alice, TX
KNTH(AM) Houston, TX
KWEL(AM) Midland, TX
WINA(AM) Charlottesville, VA
WTSO(AM) Madison, WI
WIWS(AM) Beckley, WV

1080 khz
KUDO(AM) Anchorage, AK
WKAC(AM) Athens, AL
KGVY(AM) Green Valley, AZ
KSCO(AM) Santa Cruz, CA
WTIC(AM) Hartford, CT
WMCU(AM) Coral Gables, FL
WHOO(AM) Kissimmee, FL
WFTD(AM) Marietta, FL
KWAI(AM) Honolulu, HI
KOAK(AM) Red Oak, IA

KVNI(AM) Coeur d'Alene, ID
*WRYT(AM) Edwardsville, IL
WNWI(AM) Oak Lawn, IL
WYHY(AM) Cannonsburg, KY
WKJK(AM) Louisville, KY
WOAP(AM) Owosso, MI
KYMN(AM) Northfield, MN
KYMO(AM) East Prairie, MO
WKGX(AM) Lenoir, NC
WWDR(AM) Murfreesboro, NC
KNDK(AM) Langdon, ND
KCNM(AM) Garapan-Saipan, NP
WUFO(AM) Amherst, NY
KFXX(AM) Portland, OR
WWNL(AM) Pittsburgh, PA
WLEY(AM) Cayey, PR
WALD(AM) Johnsonville, SC
KRLD(AM) Dallas, TX
KSLL(AM) Price, UT
WKBY(AM) Chatham, VA

1090 khz
WWGC(AM) Albertville, AL
KAAY(AM) Little Rock, AR
KNCR(AM) Fortuna, CA
KMXA(AM) Aurora, CO
WNVY(AM) Cantonment, FL
WBAF(AM) Barnesville, GA
KSOU(AM) Sioux Center, IA
*KNWS(AM) Waterloo, IA
WCRA(AM) Effingham, IL
WFCV(AM) Fort Wayne, IN
WILD(AM) Boston, MA
WBAL(AM) Baltimore, MD
WCAR(AM) Livonia, MI
WKBZ(AM) Muskegon, MI
*KEXS(AM) Excelsior Springs, MO
KBOZ(AM) Bozeman, MT
WKTE(AM) King, NC
WTSB(AM) Selma, NC
KTGO(AM) Tioga, ND
WKFI(AM) Wilmington, OH
WSOL(AM) San German, PR
WCZZ(AM) Greenwood, SC
WENR(AM) Englewood, TN
WTNK(AM) Hartsville, TN
WHGG(AM) Kingsport, TN
KNUZ(AM) Bellville, TX
KVOP(AM) Plainview, TX
WGOD(AM) Charlotte Amalie, VI
KPTK(AM) Seattle, WA
WAQE(AM) Rice Lake, WI

1100 khz
KFNX(AM) Cave Creek, AZ
KAFY(AM) Bakersfield, CA
KFAX(AM) San Francisco, CA
KNZZ(AM) Grand Junction, CO
WWWE(AM) Hapeville, GA
WCGA(AM) Woodbine, GA
WZFG(AM) Dilworth, MN
KKLL(AM) Carthage-, MO
KQNM(AM) Milan, NM
KWWN(AM) Las Vegas, NV
WHLI(AM) Hempstead, NY
WTAM(AM) Cleveland, OH
WGPA(AM) Bethlehem, PA
WSGI(AM) Springfield, TN
KDRY(AM) Alamo Heights, TX
WTWN(AM) Wells River, VT
WISS(AM) Berlin, WI

1110 khz
KAGV(AM) Big Lake, AK
WTOF(AM) Bay Minette, AL
WBIB(AM) Centreville, AL
KGFL(AM) Clinton, AR
KDIS(AM) Pasadena, CA
KLIB(AM) Roseville, CA
WTIS(AM) Tampa, FL
KAOI(AM) Kihei, HI
*WMBI(AM) Chicago, IL
WKDZ(AM) Cadiz, KY
WCBR(AM) Richmond, KY
WOMN(AM) Franklinton, LA
KTTP(AM) Pineville, LA
WUPE(AM) Pittsfield, MA

*WUNN(AM) Mason, MI
WJML(AM) Petoskey, MI
WKRA(AM) Holly Springs, MS
WBT(AM) Charlotte, NC
KFAB(AM) Omaha, NE
WCCM(AM) Salem, NH
KYKK(AM) Hobbs, NM
WSFW(AM) Seneca Falls, NY
WTBQ(AM) Warwick, NY
WGNZ(AM) Fairborn, OH
KBND(AM) Bend, OR
WWBJ(AM) Martinsburg, PA
WNAP(AM) Norristown, PA
WKZV(AM) Washington, PA
WVJP(AM) Caguas, PR
WPMZ(AM) Providence, RI
WUAT(AM) Pikeville, TN
KTEK(AM) Alvin, TX
KJSA(AM) Mineral Wells, TX
WYRM(AM) Norfolk, VA
KWDB(AM) Oak Harbor, WA
WIHY(AM) Hurricane, WV

1120 khz
WHOG(AM) Hobson City, AL
KZSJ(AM) San Martin, CA
KLIM(AM) Limon, CO
WPRX(AM) Bristol, CT
WUST(AM) Washington, DC
WNWF(AM) Destin, FL
WXJO(AM) Douglasville, GA
WBNW(AM) Concord, MA
WZME(AM) Richmond, ME
KMOX(AM) Saint Louis, MO
WTWZ(AM) Clinton, MS
WSME(AM) Camp Lejeune, NC
WBBF(AM) Buffalo, NY
WKAJ(AM) Little Falls, NY
KEOR(AM) Catoosa, OK
KPNW(AM) Eugene, OR
WKQW(AM) Oil City, PA
WMSW(AM) Hatillo, PR
WKCE(AM) Maryville, TN
KTXW(AM) Manor, TX
*KANN(AM) Roy, UT

1130 khz
WACQ(AM) Carrville, AL
KAAB(AM) Batesville, AR
KQNA(AM) Prescott Valley, AZ
KRDU(AM) Dinuba, CA
KSDO(AM) San Diego, CA
WWBF(AM) Bartow, FL
WLBA(AM) Gainesville, GA
KPHI(AM) Honolulu, HI
KILJ(AM) Mount Pleasant, IA
WSDX(AM) Brazil, IN
KLEY(AM) Wellington, KS
WOFC(AM) Murray, KY
KWKH(AM) Shreveport, LA
WDFN(AM) Detroit, MI
KFAN(AM) Minneapolis, MN
WQFX(AM) Gulfport, MS
WPYB(AM) Benson, NC
WCLW(AM) Eden, NC
WECR(AM) Newland, NC
KBMR(AM) Bismarck, ND
WBBR(AM) New York, NY
WEDI(AM) Eaton, OH
KTRP(AM) Mount Angel, OR
WASP(AM) Brownsville, PA
WOIZ(AM) Guayanilla, PR
WEAF(AM) Camden, SC
WFXH(AM) Hilton Head Island, SC
WYXE(AM) Gallatin, TN
KTMR(AM) Converse, TX
WISN(AM) Milwaukee, WI
WRRL(AM) Rainelle, WV

1140 khz
KSLD(AM) Soldotna, AK
WBXR(AM) Hazel Green, AL
KLTK(AM) Centerton, AR
KQAB(AM) Lake Isabella, CA
KNWQ(AM) Palm Springs, CA
KHTK(AM) Sacramento, CA
KNAB(AM) Burlington, CO

WQBA(AM) Miami, FL
WRMQ(AM) Orlando, FL
KGEM(AM) Boise, ID
WVEL(AM) Pekin, IL
WAWK(AM) Kendallville, IN
WMMG(AM) Brandenburg, KY
WRLV(AM) Salyersville, KY
WJNZ(AM) Kentwood, MI
KCXL(AM) Liberty, MO
KPWB(AM) Piedmont, MO
WAPF(AM) McComb, MS
WSAO(AM) Senatobia, MS
WRNA(AM) China Grove, NC
KYDZ(AM) North Las Vegas, NV
WCJW(AM) Warsaw, NY
KRMP(AM) Oklahoma City, OK
WQII(AM) San Juan, PR
KSOO(AM) Sioux Falls, SD
WLOD(AM) Loudon, TN
KHFX(AM) Cleburne, TX
KYOK(AM) Conroe, TX
WRVA(AM) Richmond, VA
WXLZ(AM) Saint Paul, VA
KZMQ(AM) Greybull, WY

1150 khz
WGEA(AM) Geneva, AL
WJRD(AM) Tuscaloosa, AL
KCKY(AM) Coolidge, AZ
KTLK(AM) Los Angeles, CA
KNRV(AM) Englewood, CO
WMRD(AM) Middletown, CT
WDEL(AM) Wilmington, DE
WNDB(AM) Daytona Beach, FL
WTMP(AM) Egypt Lake, FL
WXKO(AM) Fort Valley, GA
WJEM(AM) Valdosta, GA
KCPS(AM) Burlington, IA
KWKY(AM) Des Moines, IA
WGGH(AM) Marion, IL
KSAL(AM) Salina, KS
WMST(AM) Mt. Sterling, KY
WLOC(AM) Munfordville, KY
WJBO(AM) Baton Rouge, LA
WWDJ(AM) Boston, MA
KASM(AM) Albany, MN
KRMS(AM) Osage Beach, MO
WONG(AM) Canton, MS
KSEN(AM) Shelby, MT
WBAG(AM) Burlington-Graham, NC
WGBR(AM) Goldsboro, NC
KDEF(AM) Albuquerque, NM
*WRUN(AM) Utica, NY
*WCUE(AM) Cuyahoga Falls, OH
WIMA(AM) Lima, OH
KNED(AM) McAlester, OK
KAGO(AM) Klamath Falls, OR
KLPM(AM) Portland, OR
WHUN(AM) Huntingdon, PA
WGBN(AM) New Kensington, PA
WAVO(AM) Rock Hill, SC
WSNW(AM) Seneca, SC
KIMM(AM) Rapid City, SD
WGOW(AM) Chattanooga, TN
WCRK(AM) Morristown, TN
WDTM(AM) Selmer, TN
KZNE(AM) College Station, TX
KCCT(AM) Corpus Christi, TX
KHRO(AM) El Paso, TX
KLPF(AM) Midland, TX
KBPO(AM) Port Neches, TX
KOLJ(AM) Quanah, TX
WNLR(AM) Churchville, VA
KQQQ(AM) Pullman, WA
KKNW(AM) Seattle, WA
WEAQ(AM) Chippewa Falls, WI
WHBY(AM) Kimberly, WI
WELC(AM) Welch, WV

1160 khz
KHFT(AM) Chugiak, AK
WEWC(AM) Callahan, FL
WIWA(AM) Saint Cloud, FL
WCFO(AM) East Point, GA
KHPP(AM) Waukon, IA
WYLL(AM) Chicago, IL
WQRT(AM) Florence, KY

WKCM(AM) Hawesville, KY
WMET(AM) Gaithersburg, MD
WSKW(AM) Skowhegan, ME
WCXI(AM) Fenton, MI
KCTO(AM) Cleveland, MO
WTEL(AM) Red Springs, NC
WJFJ(AM) Tryon, NC
WOBM(AM) Lakewood, NJ
WVNJ(AM) Oakland, NJ
WABY(AM) Mechanicville, NY
WPIE(AM) Trumansburg, NY
WCCS(AM) Homer City, PA
WBYN(AM) Lehighton, PA
WBQN(AM) Barceloneta-Manati, PR
WCRT(AM) Donelson, TN
KVCE(AM) Highland Park, TX
KRDY(AM) San Antonio, TX
KSL(AM) Salt Lake City, UT
WODY(AM) Fieldale, VA

1170 khz
*KJNP(AM) North Pole, AK
WQHC(AM) Hanceville, AL
WACV(AM) Montgomery, AL
KCBQ(AM) San Diego, CA
KLOK(AM) San Jose, CA
KJJD(AM) Windsor, CO
*WCTF(AM) Vernon, CT
WKFL(AM) Bushnell, FL
WAVS(AM) Davie, FL
WSOS(AM) Saint Augustine Beach, FL
KJOC(AM) Davenport, IA
WLBH(AM) Mattoon, IL
WDFB(AM) Junction City, KY
WDIS(AM) Norfolk, MA
WFPB(AM) Orleans, MA
KOWZ(AM) Waseca, MN
KJXX(AM) Jackson, MO
WCXN(AM) Claremont, NC
WCLN(AM) Clinton, NC
WWTR(AM) Bridgewater, NJ
WWLE(AM) Cornwall, NY
KFAQ(AM) Tulsa, OK
WLEO(AM) Ponce, PR
WQVA(AM) Lexington, SC
KPUG(AM) Bellingham, WA
WFDL(AM) Waupun, WI
WWVA(AM) Wheeling, WV

1180 khz
*WPLX(AM) Turrell, AR
KYET(AM) Williams, AZ
KERN(AM) Wasco-Greenacres, CA
WZQZ(AM) Trion, GA
KORL(AM) Honolulu, HI
WLDS(AM) Jacksonville, IL
WSQR(AM) Sycamore, IL
WGAB(AM) Newburgh, IN
WXLA(AM) Dimondale, MI
KYES(AM) Rockville, MN
WJNT(AM) Pearl, MS
KOFI(AM) Kalispell, MT
WMYT(AM) Carolina Beach, NC
KOIL(AM) Bellevue, NE
WHAM(AM) Rochester, NY
WFYL(AM) King of Prussia, PA
WCNX(AM) Hope Valley, RI
WFGN(AM) Gaffney, SC
WVLZ(AM) Knoxville, TN
KGOL(AM) Humble, TX
KLAY(AM) Lakewood, WA

1190 khz
WEUV(AM) Moulton, AL
KREB(AM) Bentonville-Bella Vista, AR
KNUV(AM) Tolleson, AZ
KXMX(AM) Anaheim, CA
KDYA(AM) Vallejo, CA
KVCU(AM) Boulder, CO
WAMT(AM) Pine Castle-Sky Lake, FL
WPSP(AM) Royal Palm Beach, FL
WAFS(AM) Atlanta, GA
WWIO(AM) Saint Mary's, GA
KDAO(AM) Marshalltown, IA
WOWO(AM) Fort Wayne, IN
KVSV(AM) Beloit, KS
KNEK(AM) Washington, LA

WBIS(AM) Annapolis, MD
KKOJ(AM) Jackson, MN
KMFX(AM) Wabasha, MN
KRFT(AM) De Soto, MO
KPHN(AM) Kansas City, MO
WJZD(AM) Bay St. Louis, MS
WIXE(AM) Monroe, NC
KXKS(AM) Albuquerque, NM
WSDE(AM) Cobleskill, NY
WLIB(AM) New York, NY
KEX(AM) Portland, OR
WBMJ(AM) San Juan, PR
WJES(AM) Saluda, SC
WSDQ(AM) Dunlap, TN
WLLI(AM) Humboldt, TN
KFXR(AM) Dallas, TX
WBDY(AM) Bluefield, VA
*WNWC(AM) Sun Prairie, WI
WVUS(AM) Grafton, WV

1200 khz
KYAA(AM) Soquel, CA
WPTK(AM) Pine Island Center, FL
WRTO(AM) Chicago, IL
WBCE(AM) Wickliffe, KY
WKOX(AM) Framingham, MA
WCHB(AM) Taylor, MI
KYOO(AM) Bolivar, MO
WXIT(AM) Blowing Rock, NC
WSML(AM) Graham, NC
*KFNW(AM) West Fargo, ND
WJGK(AM) Highland, NY
WTLA(AM) North Syracuse, NY
WRKK(AM) Hughesville, PA
WKST(AM) New Castle, PA
WGDL(AM) Lares, PR
WMIR(AM) Atlantic Beach, SC
WAMB(AM) Nashville, TN
WOAI(AM) San Antonio, TX
WAGE(AM) Leesburg, VA

1210 khz
WQLS(AM) Ozark, AL
KEVT(AM) Sahuarita, AZ
KQEQ(AM) Fowler, CA
*KEBR(AM) Rocklin, CA
KPRZ(AM) San Marcos-Poway, CA
WNMA(AM) Miami Springs, FL
WDGR(AM) Dahlonega, GA
KZOO(AM) Honolulu, HI
WILY(AM) Centralia, IL
WSKR(AM) Denham Springs, LA
WJNL(AM) Kingsley, MI
WDAO(AM) Dayton, OH
KGYN(AM) Guymon, OK
WPHT(AM) Philadelphia, PA
WHOY(AM) Salinas, PR
KOKK(AM) Huron, SD
WMPS(AM) Bartlett, TN
WSBI(AM) Static, TN
KUBR(AM) San Juan, TX
KUNF(AM) Washington, UT
KTBK(AM) Auburn-Federal Way, WA
KRSV(AM) Afton, WY
KHAT(AM) Laramie, WY

1220 khz
WAYE(AM) Birmingham, AL
WABF(AM) Fairhope, AL
KVSA(AM) McGehee, AR
KHTS(AM) Canyon Country, CA
KJML(AM) Desert Hot Springs, CA
KDOW(AM) Palo Alto, CA
KWKU(AM) Pomona, CA
KLDC(AM) Denver, CO
WQUN(AM) Hamden, CT
WJAX(AM) Jacksonville, FL
WOTS(AM) Kissimmee, FL
WSRQ(AM) Sarasota, FL
WZOT(AM) Rockmart, GA
KJAN(AM) Atlantic, IA
KQMG(AM) Independence, IA
WLPO(AM) La Salle, IL
WKRS(AM) Waukegan, IL
WSLM(AM) Salem, IN
KOFO(AM) Ottawa, KS
WFKN(AM) Franklin, KY

WPHX(AM) Sanford, ME
WBCH(AM) Hastings, MI
KLBB(AM) Stillwater, MN
KOMC(AM) Branson, MO
KGIR(AM) Cape Girardeau, MO
KLPW(AM) Union, MO
WOEG(AM) Hazlehurst, MS
WDYT(AM) Kings Mountain, NC
WREV(AM) Reidsville, NC
WENC(AM) Whiteville, NC
KDDR(AM) Oakes, ND
WZBK(AM) Keene, NH
WGNY(AM) Newburgh, NY
WHKW(AM) Cleveland, OH
WERT(AM) Van Wert, OH
KTLV(AM) Midwest City, OK
KPJC(AM) Salem, OR
WJUN(AM) Mexico, PA
WSTL(AM) Providence, RI
WFWL(AM) Camden, TN
WCPH(AM) Etowah, TN
WAXO(AM) Lewisburg, TN
KMVL(AM) Madisonville, TX
KZEE(AM) Weatherford, TX
WLSD(AM) Big Stone Gap, VA
WFAX(AM) Falls Church, VA

1230 khz
KIFW(AM) Sitka, AK
KVAK(AM) Valdez, AK
WAUD(AM) Auburn, AL
WKWL(AM) Florala, AL
WJBB(AM) Haleyville, AL
WBHP(AM) Huntsville, AL
WRJX(AM) Jackson, AL
WNUZ(AM) Talladega, AL
WTBC(AM) Tuscaloosa, AL
KFPW(AM) Fort Smith, AR
KBTM(AM) Jonesboro, AR
KAAA(AM) Kingman, AZ
KOY(AM) Phoenix, AZ
KATO(AM) Safford, AZ
KINO(AM) Winslow, AZ
KGEO(AM) Bakersfield, CA
KSZL(AM) Barstow, CA
KBOV(AM) Bishop, CA
KXO(AM) El Centro, CA
KDAC(AM) Fort Bragg, CA
KYPA(AM) Los Angeles, CA
KPRL(AM) Paso Robles, CA
KLXR(AM) Redding, CA
*KWG(AM) Stockton, CA
KEXO(AM) Grand Junction, CO
KKPC(AM) Pueblo, CO
KBCR(AM) Steamboat Springs, CO
KSTC(AM) Sterling, CO
WNEZ(AM) Manchester, CT
WGGG(AM) Gainesville, FL
WONN(AM) Lakeland, FL
WMAF(AM) Madison, FL
WSBB(AM) New Smyrna Beach, FL
WDWR(AM) Pensacola, FL
WWSD(AM) Quincy, FL
WBZT(AM) West Palm Beach, FL
WNRR(AM) Augusta, GA
WBLJ(AM) Dalton, GA
WXLI(AM) Dublin, GA
WNGM(AM) Hiawassee, GA
WFOM(AM) Marietta, GA
WSOK(AM) Savannah, GA
WUCN(AM) Smithville, GA
WAYX(AM) Waycross, GA
KFJB(AM) Marshalltown, IA
KBAR(AM) Burley, ID
KORT(AM) Grangeville, ID
KRXK(AM) Rexburg, ID
WJBC(AM) Bloomington, IL
WFXN(AM) Moline, IL
WHCO(AM) Sparta, IL
WJOB(AM) Hammond, IN
WSAL(AM) Logansport, IN
WTCJ(AM) Tell City, IN
WHIR(AM) Danville, KY
WCDS(AM) Glasgow, KY
WHOP(AM) Hopkinsville, KY
WANO(AM) Pineville, KY

KLIC(AM) Monroe, LA
WBOK(AM) New Orleans, LA
KSLO(AM) Opelousas, LA
WNAW(AM) North Adams, MA
WESX(AM) Salem, MA
WNEB(AM) Worcester, MA
WRBS(AM) Baltimore, MD
WCMD(AM) Cumberland, MD
WGUY(AM) Newport, ME
WTKG(AM) Grand Rapids, MI
WGRY(AM) Grayling, MI
WIKB(AM) Iron River, MI
*WMPC(AM) Lapeer, MI
WSOO(AM) Sault Ste. Marie, MI
WMSH(AM) Sturgis, MI
WKLK(AM) Cloquet, MN
KGHS(AM) International Falls, MN
KYSM(AM) Mankato, MN
KMRS(AM) Morris, MN
KTRF(AM) Thief River Falls, MN
KWNO(AM) Winona, MN
KZYM(AM) Joplin, MO
KLWT(AM) Lebanon, MO
KWIX(AM) Moberly, MO
WTKN(AM) Corinth, MS
WSSO(AM) Starkville, MS
KOBB(AM) Bozeman, MT
KHDN(AM) Hardin, MT
KXLO(AM) Lewistown, MT
KLCB(AM) Libby, MT
WSKY(AM) Asheville, NC
WFAY(AM) Fayetteville, NC
WMFR(AM) High Point, NC
WLNR(AM) Kinston, NC
WNNC(AM) Newton, NC
WCBT(AM) Roanoke Rapids, NC
KDIX(AM) Dickinson, ND
KTNC(AM) Falls City, NE
KHAS(AM) Hastings, NE
WMOU(AM) Berlin, NH
WTSV(AM) Claremont, NH
WCMC(AM) Wildwood, NJ
KRSY(AM) Alamogordo, NM
KOTS(AM) Deming, NM
KYVA(AM) Gallup, NM
KFUN(AM) Las Vegas, NM
KBCQ(AM) Roswell, NM
KELY(AM) Ely, NV
KLAV(AM) Las Vegas, NV
KJFK(AM) Reno, NV
WECK(AM) Cheektowaga, NY
WENY(AM) Elmira, NY
WMML(AM) Glens Falls, NY
WHUC(AM) Hudson, NY
WIXT(AM) Little Falls, NY
WFAS(AM) White Plains, NY
WDBZ(AM) Cincinnati, OH
WYTS(AM) Columbus, OH
WIRO(AM) Ironton, OH
WCWA(AM) Toledo, OH
KADA(AM) Ada, OK
WBBZ(AM) Ponca City, OK
KKEE(AM) Astoria, OR
KZZR(AM) Burns, OR
KHSN(AM) Coos Bay, OR
KSZN(AM) Gresham, OR
KQIK(AM) Lakeview, OR
*KSJK(AM) Talent, OR
KCUP(AM) Toledo, OR
WBVP(AM) Beaver Falls, PA
WEEX(AM) Easton, PA
WKBO(AM) Harrisburg, PA
WCRO(AM) Johnstown, PA
WBPZ(AM) Lock Haven, PA
WTIV(AM) Titusville, PA
WNIK(AM) Arecibo, PR
WXNI(AM) Westerly, RI
WAIM(AM) Anderson, SC
WOIC(AM) Columbia, SC
WOLH(AM) Florence, SC
KWSN(AM) Sioux Falls, SD
WMLR(AM) Hohenwald, TN
WAKI(AM) McMinnville, TN
KSIX(AM) Corpus Christi, TX
KTJK(AM) Del Rio, TX
KQUE(AM) Houston, TX

KERV(AM) Kerrville, TX
KLVT(AM) Levelland, TX
KOZA(AM) Odessa, TX
KGRO(AM) Pampa, TX
KHUA(AM) Presidio, TX
KSEY(AM) Seymour, TX
KSST(AM) Sulphur Springs, TX
KWTX(AM) Waco, TX
KJQS(AM) Murray, UT
WABN(AM) Abingdon, VA
WODI(AM) Brookneal, VA
WXCF(AM) Clifton Forge, VA
WFVA(AM) Fredericksburg, VA
WJOI(AM) Norfolk, VA
WAMM(AM) Woodstock, VA
WJOY(AM) Burlington, VT
KOZI(AM) Chelan, WA
KWYZ(AM) Everett, WA
KSBN(AM) Spokane, WA
KDYM(AM) Sunnyside, WA
WCLO(AM) Janesville, WI
WXCO(AM) Wausau, WI
WVNT(AM) Parkersburg, WV
KVOC(AM) Casper, WY

1240 khz
WEBJ(AM) Brewton, AL
WULA(AM) Eufaula, AL
WBCF(AM) Florence, AL
WMGJ(AM) Gadsden, AL
WJLX(AM) Jasper, AL
KVRC(AM) Arkadelphia, AR
KTLO(AM) Mountain Home, AR
KWAK(AM) Stuttgart, AR
KJAA(AM) Globe, AZ
KPOD(AM) Crescent City, CA
KJOP(AM) Lemoore, CA
KNRY(AM) Monterey, CA
KLOA(AM) Ridgecrest, CA
KRJY(AM) Sacramento, CA
KEZY(AM) San Bernardino, CA
KNSN(AM) San Diego, CA
KSMX(AM) Santa Maria, CA
KSUE(AM) Susanville, CA
KRDO(AM) Colorado Springs, CO
KDGO(AM) Durango, CO
KSLV(AM) Monte Vista, CO
KCRT(AM) Trinidad, CO
WWCO(AM) Waterbury, CT
WBGC(AM) Chipley, FL
WZCC(AM) Cross City, FL
WKIQ(AM) Eustis, FL
WINK(AM) Fort Myers, FL
WMMB(AM) Melbourne, FL
WFOY(AM) Saint Augustine, FL
WBHB(AM) Fitzgerald, GA
WGGA(AM) Gainesville, GA
WLAG(AM) La Grange, GA
WDDO(AM) Macon, GA
WWNS(AM) Statesboro, GA
WPAX(AM) Thomasville, GA
WTWA(AM) Thomson, GA
KDEC(AM) Decorah, IA
*KWLC(AM) Decorah, IA
KBIZ(AM) Ottumwa, IA
KICD(AM) Spencer, IA
KMCL(AM) Donnelly, ID
KMHI(AM) Mountain Home, ID
KWIK(AM) Pocatello, ID
KOFE(AM) Saint Maries, ID
WSBC(AM) Chicago, IL
WEBQ(AM) Harrisburg, IL
WTAX(AM) Springfield, IL
WSDR(AM) Sterling, IL
WHBU(AM) Anderson, IN
KIUL(AM) Garden City, KS
KFH(AM) Wichita, KS
WLLV(AM) Louisville, KY
WFTM(AM) Maysville, KY
WPKE(AM) Pikeville, KY
WSFC(AM) Somerset, KY
KASO(AM) Minden, LA
KANE(AM) New Iberia, LA
WHMQ(AM) Greenfield, MA
*WBUR(AM) West Yarmouth, MA
WCEM(AM) Cambridge, MD

WJEJ(AM) Hagerstown, MD
WEZR(AM) Lewiston, ME
WSYY(AM) Millinocket, ME
WATT(AM) Cadillac, MI
WCBY(AM) Cheboygan, MI
WIAN(AM) Ishpeming, MI
WJIM(AM) Lansing, MI
WMFG(AM) Hibbing, MN
WJON(AM) Saint Cloud, MN
KLIK(AM) Jefferson City, MO
KNEM(AM) Nevada, MO
KFMO(AM) Park Hills, MO
WWZQ(AM) Aberdeen, MS
WPBQ(AM) Flowood, MS
WGRM(AM) Greenwood, MS
WGCM(AM) Gulfport, MS
WMIS(AM) Natchez, MS
WAVN(AM) Southaven, MS
KMZK(AM) Billings, MT
KLTZ(AM) Glasgow, MT
KLYQ(AM) Hamilton, MT
KBLL(AM) Helena, MT
KSAM(AM) Whitefish, MT
WSQL(AM) Brevard, NC
WHVN(AM) Charlotte, NC
WCNC(AM) Elizabeth City, NC
WJNC(AM) Jacksonville, NC
WPJL(AM) Raleigh, NC
WWWC(AM) Wilkesboro, NC
KDLR(AM) Devils Lake, ND
KFOR(AM) Lincoln, NE
KODY(AM) North Platte, NE
WFTN(AM) Franklin, NH
WSNJ(AM) Bridgeton, NJ
KAMQ(AM) Carlsbad, NM
KCLV(AM) Clovis, NM
KALY(AM) Los Ranchos de
    Albuquerque, NM
KDAN(AM) Beatty, NV
KELK(AM) Elko, NV
WGBB(AM) Freeport, NY
WGVA(AM) Geneva, NY
WJTN(AM) Jamestown, NY
WVOS(AM) Liberty, NY
WNBZ(AM) Saranac Lake, NY
WVKZ(AM) Schenectady, NY
WATN(AM) Watertown, NY
WBBW(AM) Youngstown, OH
WHIZ(AM) Zanesville, OH
KVSO(AM) Ardmore, OK
KADS(AM) Elk City, OK
KOKL(AM) Okmulgee, OK
KEJO(AM) Corvallis, OR
KTIX(AM) Pendleton, OR
KRDM(AM) Redmond, OR
KQEN(AM) Roseburg, OR
WRTA(AM) Altoona, PA
WIOV(AM) Reading, PA
WYGL(AM) Selinsgrove, PA
WBAX(AM) Wilkes-Barre, PA
WALO(AM) Humacao, PR
WOON(AM) Woonsocket, RI
WLSC(AM) Loris, SC
WKDK(AM) Newberry, SC
WDXY(AM) Sumter, SC
KCCR(AM) Pierre, SD
WBEJ(AM) Elizabethton, TN
WEKR(AM) Fayetteville, TN
WIFA(AM) Knoxville, TN
WNVL(AM) Nashville, TN
WSDT(AM) Soddy-Daisy, TN
WENK(AM) Union City, TN
KVLF(AM) Alpine, TX
KXYL(AM) Brownwood, TX
KTAM(AM) Bryan, TX
KIXK(AM) Dalhart, TX
KPBL(AM) Hemphill, TX
KDOK(AM) Kilgore, TX
KSOX(AM) Raymondville, TX
KXOX(AM) Sweetwater, TX
WTPS(AM) Petersburg, VA
WGMN(AM) Roanoke, VA
WTON(AM) Staunton, VA
WSKI(AM) Montpelier, VT
KCVL(AM) Colville, WA
KXLE(AM) Ellensburg, WA

KGY(AM) Olympia, WA
WOMT(AM) Manitowoc, WI
WHFA(AM) Poynette, WI
WOBT(AM) Rhinelander, WI
WJMC(AM) Rice Lake, WI
WKEZ(AM) Bluefield, WV
WBES(AM) Dunbar, WV
WDNE(AM) Elkins, WV
KFBC(AM) Cheyenne, WY
KEVA(AM) Evanston, WY
KASL(AM) Newcastle, WY
KRAL(AM) Rawlins, WY
KTHE(AM) Thermopolis, WY

1250 khz
WZOB(AM) Fort Payne, AL
WAPZ(AM) Wetumpka, AL
KOFC(AM) Fayetteville, AR
KPZK(AM) Little Rock, AR
KBSZ(AM) Wickenburg, AZ
KHIL(AM) Willcox, AZ
KZER(AM) Santa Barbara, CA
KNWH(AM) Twentynine Palms, CA
KLLK(AM) Willits, CA
KDCO(AM) Johnstown, CO
WQHL(AM) Live Oak, FL
WHNZ(AM) Tampa, FL
WSRA(AM) Albany, GA
WYTH(AM) Madison, GA
KDNZ(AM) Cedar Falls, IA
WSPL(AM) Streator, IL
WGL(AM) Fort Wayne, IN
WRAY(AM) Princeton, IN
KYYS(AM) Kansas City, KS
WLRT(AM) Nicholasville, KY
WLCK(AM) Scottsville, KY
WARE(AM) Ware, MA
WNEM(AM) Bridgeport, MI
KBRF(AM) Fergus Falls, MN
KCUE(AM) Red Wing, MN
KBTC(AM) Houston, MO
WHNY(AM) McComb, MS
KIKC(AM) Forsyth, MT
WGHB(AM) Farmville, NC
WKDX(AM) Hamlet, NC
WBRM(AM) Marion, NC
KTFJ(AM) Dakota City, NE
WGAM(AM) Manchester, NH
WMTR(AM) Morristown, NJ
WIPS(AM) Ticonderoga, NY
WCHO(AM) Washington Court House,
    OH
KCFM(AM) Florence, OR
WLEM(AM) Emporium, PA
*WPEL(AM) Montrose, PA
WEAE(AM) Pittsburgh, PA
WYYC(AM) York, PA
WJIT(AM) Sabana, PR
WTMA(AM) Charleston, SC
WKBL(AM) Covington, TN
WRKQ(AM) Madisonville, TN
WNTT(AM) Tazewell, TN
KZHN(AM) Paris, TX
*KDEI(AM) Port Arthur, TX
KZDC(AM) San Antonio, TX
KIKZ(AM) Seminole, TX
KNEU(AM) Roosevelt, UT
WDVA(AM) Danville, VA
WLQM(AM) Franklin, VA
WKDL(AM) Warrenton, VA
*KWSU(AM) Pullman, WA
KKDZ(AM) Seattle, WA
WSSP(AM) Milwaukee, WI
WYKM(AM) Rupert, WV

1260 khz
WYDE(AM) Birmingham, AL
KCCB(AM) Corning, AR
KBHC(AM) Nashville, AR
KGIL(AM) Beverly Hills, CA
KSFB(AM) San Francisco, CA
*WSHU(AM) Westport, CT
WWRC(AM) Washington, DC
WNWK(AM) Newark, DE
WFTW(AM) Fort Walton Beach, FL
WSUA(AM) Miami, FL

WIYD(AM) Palatka, FL
WUFE(AM) Baxley, GA
WBBK(AM) Blakely, GA
WTJH(AM) East Point, GA
KFFF(AM) Boone, IA
KBLY(AM) Idaho Falls, ID
KWEI(AM) Weiser, ID
WSDZ(AM) Belleville, IL
WNDE(AM) Indianapolis, IN
KBRH(AM) Baton Rouge, LA
WMKI(AM) Boston, MA
WPNW(AM) Zeeland, MI
KROX(AM) Crookston, MN
KDUZ(AM) Hutchinson, MN
KSGF(AM) Springfield, MO
WGVM(AM) Greenville, MS
WCSA(AM) Ripley, MS
WKXR(AM) Asheboro, NC
WZBO(AM) Edenton, NC
KIMB(AM) Kimball, NE
WFJS(AM) Trenton, NJ
KTRC(AM) Santa Fe, NM
WBNR(AM) Beacon, NY
WNSS(AM) Syracuse, NY
WWMK(AM) Cleveland, OH
WNXT(AM) Portsmouth, OH
KWSH(AM) Wewoka, OK
KLYC(AM) McMinnville, OR
WRIE(AM) Erie, PA
WPHB(AM) Philipsburg, PA
WISO(AM) Ponce, PR
WPJF(AM) Greenville, SC
WHYM(AM) Lake City, SC
KWYR(AM) Winner, SD
WNOO(AM) Chattanooga, TN
WMCH(AM) Church Hill, TN
WDKN(AM) Dickson, TN
WCLC(AM) Jamestown, TN
KSML(AM) Diboll, TX
KLDS(AM) Falfurrias, TX
KKSA(AM) San Angelo, TX
KWNX(AM) Taylor, TX
KTUE(AM) Tulia, TX
WCHV(AM) Charlottesville, VA
*WWVT(AM) Christiansburg, VA
WXCE(AM) Amery, WI
WWIS(AM) Black River Falls, WI
WEKZ(AM) Monroe, WI
WOCO(AM) Oconto, WI
KPOW(AM) Powell, WY

1270 khz
WGSV(AM) Guntersville, AL
WIJD(AM) Prichard, AL
KDJI(AM) Holbrook, AZ
KXBX(AM) Lakeport, CA
KFUT(AM) Thousand Palms, CA
KJUG(AM) Tulare, CA
WRLZ(AM) Eatonville, FL
WNOG(AM) Naples, FL
WNLS(AM) Tallahassee, FL
WYXC(AM) Cartersville, GA
WSHE(AM) Columbus, GA
WJJC(AM) Commerce, GA
KNDI(AM) Honolulu, HI
KTFI(AM) Twin Falls, ID
WEIC(AM) Charleston, IL
WKBF(AM) Rock Island, IL
WCMR(AM) Elkhart, IN
WWCA(AM) Gary, IN
WXGO(AM) Madison, IN
KSCB(AM) Liberal, KS
WAIN(AM) Columbia, KY
WFUL(AM) Fulton, KY
KVCL(AM) Winnfield, LA
WSPR(AM) Springfield, MA
WCBC(AM) Cumberland, MD
WMKT(AM) Charlevoix, MI
WXYT(AM) Detroit, MI
WWWI(AM) Baxter, MN
KWEB(AM) Rochester, MN
KGNM(AM) Saint Joseph, MO
KOZQ(AM) Waynesville, MO
WMLC(AM) Monticello, MS
WCGC(AM) Belmont, NC
WMPM(AM) Smithfield, NC

KLXX(AM) Bismarck-Mandan, ND
WTSN(AM) Dover, NH
WMIZ(AM) Vineland, NJ
KINN(AM) Alamogordo, NM
KBZZ(AM) Sparks, NV
WHLD(AM) Niagara Falls, NY
WDLA(AM) Walton, NY
WILE(AM) Cambridge, OH
WUCO(AM) Marysville, OH
KRVT(AM) Claremore, OK
KAJO(AM) Grants Pass, OR
WLBR(AM) Lebanon, PA
WHGS(AM) Hampton, SC
*KNWC(AM) Sioux Falls, SD
WLIK(AM) Newport, TN
WQKR(AM) Portland, TN
KEPS(AM) Eagle Pass, TX
KFLC(AM) Fort Worth, TX
WTJZ(AM) Newport News, VA
WHEO(AM) Stuart, VA
KBAM(AM) Longview, WA
WRJC(AM) Mauston, WI
KIML(AM) Gillette, WY

1280 khl
WCPM(AM) Cumberland, KY

1290 khz
WOPP(AM) Opp, AL
WBTG(AM) Sheffield, AL
WYEA(AM) Sylacauga, AL
KDMS(AM) El Dorado, AR
KUOA(AM) Siloam Springs, AR
KCUB(AM) Tucson, AZ
KPAY(AM) Chico, CA
KAZA(AM) Gilroy, CA
KKDD(AM) San Bernardino, CA
KZSB(AM) Santa Barbara, CA
WCCC(AM) West Hartford, CT
WWTX(AM) Wilmington, DE
WPCF(AM) Panama City Beach, FL
WJNO(AM) West Palm Beach, FL
WCHK(AM) Canton, GA
WTKS(AM) Savannah, GA
KOUU(AM) Pocatello, ID
WIRL(AM) Peoria, IL
KMMM(AM) Pratt, KS
WCBL(AM) Benton, KY
WKLB(AM) Manchester, KY
KJEF(AM) Jennings, LA
WNIL(AM) Niles, MI
WLBY(AM) Saline, MI
KBMO(AM) Benson, MN
KALM(AM) Thayer, MO
WJBI(AM) Batesville, MS
WNBN(AM) Meridian, MS
WTYL(AM) Tylertown, MS
KGVO(AM) Missoula, MT
WHKY(AM) Hickory, NC
WJCV(AM) Jacksonville, NC
WXKL(AM) Sanford, NC
KKAR(AM) Omaha, NE
WKBK(AM) Keene, NH
WNBF(AM) Binghamton, NY
WOMP(AM) Bellaire, OH
WHIO(AM) Dayton, OH
KUMA(AM) Pendleton, OR
WFBG(AM) Altoona, PA
WRNI(AM) Providence, RI
WWHM(AM) Sumter, SC
WATO(AM) Oak Ridge, TN
KIVY(AM) Crockett, TX
KRGE(AM) Weslaco, TX
KWFS(AM) Wichita Falls, TX
WDZY(AM) Colonial Heights, VA
WRRA(AM) Frederiksted, VI
WMCS(AM) Greenfield, WI
WKLJ(AM) Sparta, WI
WVOW(AM) Logan, WV
KOWB(AM) Laramie, WY

1300 khz
WBSA(AM) Boaz, AL
WTLS(AM) Tallassee, AL
WKXM(AM) Winfield, AL
KWCK(AM) Searcy, AR
KROP(AM) Brawley, CA

KYNO(AM) Fresno, CA
*KPMO(AM) Mendocino, CA
KAZN(AM) Pasadena, CA
KCSF(AM) Colorado Springs, CO
WAVZ(AM) New Haven, CT
WMEL(AM) Cocoa Beach, FL
WFFG(AM) Marathon, FL
WQBN(AM) Temple Terrace, FL
WMTM(AM) Moultrie, GA
WNEA(AM) Newnan, GA
WIMO(AM) Winder, GA
KGLO(AM) Mason City, IA
KLER(AM) Orofino, ID
WRDZ(AM) La Grange, IL
WFRX(AM) West Frankfort, IL
WBZQ(AM) Huntington, IN
WBOW(AM) Terre Haute, IN
WLXG(AM) Lexington, KY
WIBR(AM) Baton Rouge, LA
KSYB(AM) Shreveport, LA
WJDA(AM) Quincy, MA
WJZ(AM) Baltimore, MD
WOOD(AM) Grand Rapids, MI
WQPM(AM) Princeton, MN
KMMO(AM) Marshall, MO
WOAD(AM) Jackson, MS
WSSG(AM) Goldsboro, NC
WLNC(AM) Laurinburg, NC
WSYD(AM) Mount Airy, NC
KBRL(AM) McCook, NE
WPNH(AM) Plymouth, NH
WIMG(AM) Ewing, NJ
KCMY(AM) Carson City, NV
WAMF(AM) Fulton, NY
WXRL(AM) Lancaster, NY
WGDJ(AM) Rensselaer, NY
WRCR(AM) Spring Valley, NY
WJMO(AM) Cleveland, OH
WMVO(AM) Mount Vernon, OH
KAKC(AM) Tulsa, OK
*KAPL(AM) Phoenix, OR
KACI(AM) The Dalles, OR
WWCH(AM) Clarion, PA
WKZN(AM) West Hazleton, PA
WTIL(AM) Mayaguez, PR
WCKI(AM) Greer, SC
WKSC(AM) Kershaw, SC
KOLY(AM) Mobridge, SD
WMTN(AM) Morristown, TN
WNQM(AM) Nashville, TN
KVET(AM) Austin, TX
KKUB(AM) Brownfield, TX
KLAR(AM) Laredo, TX
KSET(AM) Silsbee, TX
WKCY(AM) Harrisonburg, VA
KKOL(AM) Seattle, WA
WCLG(AM) Morgantown, WV
WJYP(AM) Saint Albans, WV

1310 khz
WHEP(AM) Foley, AL
WJUS(AM) Marion, AL
WKZD(AM) Priceville, AL
KBOK(AM) Malvern, AR
KXAM(AM) Mesa, AZ
KIQQ(AM) Barstow, CA
KFVR(AM) Crescent City, CA
KMKY(AM) Oakland, CA
KFKA(AM) Greeley, CO
WICH(AM) Norwich, CT
WYND(AM) De Land, FL
WAUC(AM) Wauchula, FL
WPBC(AM) Decatur, GA
WOKA(AM) Douglas, GA
WPLV(AM) West Point, GA
KOKX(AM) Keokuk, IA
KDLS(AM) Perry, IA
KLIX(AM) Twin Falls, ID
WTLC(AM) Indianapolis, IN
KYUL(AM) Scott City, KS
WTTL(AM) Madisonville, KY
WDOC(AM) Prestonsburg, KY
KEZM(AM) Sulphur, LA
KMBS(AM) West Monroe, LA
WORC(AM) Worcester, MA
WLOB(AM) Portland, ME

WDTW(AM) Dearborn, MI
WCCW(AM) Traverse City, MI
KGLB(AM) Saint Peter, MN
KZRG(AM) Joplin, MO
KEIN(AM) Great Falls, MT
WISE(AM) Asheville, NC
WGSP(AM) Charlotte, NC
WTIK(AM) Durham, NC
KNOX(AM) Grand Forks, ND
KGMT(AM) Fairbury, NE
WADB(AM) Asbury Park, NJ
WEMG(AM) Camden, NJ
WXMC(AM) Parsippany-Troy Hills, NJ
KKNS(AM) Corrales, NM
WRSB(AM) Canandaigua, NY
WRVP(AM) Mount Kisco, NY
WTLB(AM) Utica, NY
WDPN(AM) Alliance, OH
KNPT(AM) Newport, OR
WBFD(AM) Bedford, PA
WTZN(AM) Troy, PA
WNAE(AM) Warren, PA
WDKD(AM) Kingstree, SC
WDOD(AM) Chattanooga, TN
WDXI(AM) Jackson, TN
WOCV(AM) Oneida, TN
KZIP(AM) Amarillo, TX
KTCK(AM) Dallas, TX
KAHL(AM) San Antonio, TX
WDCT(AM) Fairfax, VA
WCMS(AM) Newport News, VA
KZXR(AM) Prosser, WA
WIBA(AM) Madison, WI
WSLW(AM) White Sulphur Springs, WV

1320 khz
WENN(AM) Birmingham, AL
WAGF(AM) Dothan, AL
KWHN(AM) Fort Smith, AR
KRLW(AM) Walnut Ridge, AR
*KAWC(AM) Yuma, AZ
KSDT(AM) Hemet, CA
*KKSM(AM) Oceanside, CA
KCTC(AM) West Sacramento, CA
KWLW(AM) Keystone, CO
WATR(AM) Waterbury, CT
WLQY(AM) Hollywood, FL
WBOB(AM) Jacksonville, FL
WDDV(AM) Venice, FL
WHIE(AM) Griffin, GA
KEWA(AM) Ewa Beach, HI
KNIA(AM) Knoxville, IA
KMAQ(AM) Maquoketa, IA
WKAN(AM) Kankakee, IL
KLWN(AM) Lawrence, KS
WBRT(AM) Bardstown, KY
WCVG(AM) Covington, KY
WNGO(AM) Mayfield, KY
KNCB(AM) Vivian, LA
WARL(AM) Attleboro, MA
WICO(AM) Salisbury, MD
WILS(AM) Lansing, MI
WDMJ(AM) Marquette, MI
KOZY(AM) Grand Rapids, MN
KSIV(AM) Clayton, MO
WRJW(AM) Picayune, MS
WAGY(AM) Forest City, NC
WCOG(AM) Greensboro, NC
WKRK(AM) Murphy, NC
KHRT(AM) Minot, ND
KOLT(AM) Scottsbluff, NE
WDER(AM) Derry, NH
KRDD(AM) Roswell, NM
WHHO(AM) Hornell, NY
WLOH(AM) Lancaster, OH
WOBL(AM) Oberlin, OH
KCLI(AM) Clinton, OK
KSCR(AM) Eugene, OR
WTKZ(AM) Allentown, PA
WGET(AM) Gettysburg, PA
WJAS(AM) Pittsburgh, PA
WSKN(AM) San Juan, PR
WISW(AM) Columbia, SC
KELO(AM) Sioux Falls, SD
WGOC(AM) Kingsport, TN

WMSR(AM) Manchester, TN
KVMC(AM) Colorado City, TX
KXYZ(AM) Houston, TX
KFNZ(AM) Salt Lake City, UT
WVGM(AM) Lynchburg, VA
WVNZ(AM) Richmond, VA
WTSJ(AM) Randolph, VT
KXRO(AM) Aberdeen, WA
KGDC(AM) Walla Walla, WA
WFHR(AM) Wisconsin Rapids, WI

1330 khz
KXLJ(AM) Juneau, AK
WPRN(AM) Butler, AL
WZCT(AM) Scottsboro, AL
KXXA(AM) Conway, AR
KJLL(AM) South Tucson, AZ
KWKW(AM) Los Angeles, CA
KLBS(AM) Los Banos, CA
KJPR(AM) Shasta Lake City, CA
WJNX(AM) Fort Pierce, FL
WWAB(AM) Lakeland, FL
WEBY(AM) Milton, FL
WCVC(AM) Tallahassee, FL
WLBB(AM) Carrollton, GA
WMLT(AM) Dublin, GA
WGTJ(AM) Murrayville, GA
KWLO(AM) Waterloo, IA
WKTA(AM) Evanston, IL
WRAM(AM) Monmouth, IL
WNTA(AM) Rockford, IL
WVHI(AM) Evansville, IN
WTRE(AM) Greensburg, IN
KNSS(AM) Wichita, KS
WKDP(AM) Corbin, KY
WMOR(AM) Morehead, KY
KVOL(AM) Lafayette, LA
WRCA(AM) Waltham, MA
WJSS(AM) Havre de Grace, MD
WTRX(AM) Flint, MI
WLOL(AM) Minneapolis, MN
KUKU(AM) Willow Springs, MO
WNIX(AM) Greenville, MS
WANG(AM) Havelock, NC
KGAK(AM) Gallup, NM
*WWRV(AM) New York, NY
WMJQ(AM) Ontario, NY
WEBO(AM) Owego, NY
WSPQ(AM) Springville, NY
WHAZ(AM) Troy, NY
WGFT(AM) Campbell, OH
WFIN(AM) Findlay, OH
WYPC(AM) Wellston, OH
WELW(AM) Willoughby-Eastlake, OH
KKPZ(AM) Portland, OR
WFNN(AM) Erie, PA
WBHV(AM) Somerset, PA
WENA(AM) Yauco, PR
WPJS(AM) Conway, SC
WYRD(AM) Greenville, SC
WAEW(AM) Crossville, TN
KTAE(AM) Cameron, TX
KSWA(AM) Graham, TX
KINE(AM) Kingsville, TX
KCKM(AM) Monahans, TX
KGLD(AM) Tyler, TX
WBTM(AM) Danville, VA
WRAA(AM) Luray, VA
WITM(AM) Marion, VA
WESR(AM) Onley-Onancock, VA
KGRG(AM) Enumclaw, WA
*KMBI(AM) Spokane, WA
WHBL(AM) Sheboygan, WI
WETZ(AM) New Martinsville, WV
KOVE(AM) Lander, WY

1340 khz
WFMH(AM) Cullman, AL
WSBM(AM) Florence, AL
WJAM(AM) Selma, AL
WFEB(AM) Sylacauga, AL
KBTA(AM) Batesville, AR
KZNG(AM) Hot Springs, AR
*KCAT(AM) Pine Bluff, AR
KIKO(AM) Miami, AZ
KPGE(AM) Page, AZ
KATA(AM) Arcata, CA

KACE(AM) Bishop, CA
KPTR(AM) Cathedral City, CA
KCBL(AM) Fresno, CA
KOMY(AM) La Selva Beach, CA
KTPI(AM) Mojave, CA
KTOX(AM) Needles, CA
KEWE(AM) Oroville, CA
KYNS(AM) San Luis Obispo, CA
KCLU(AM) Santa Barbara, CA
*KCFR(AM) Denver, CO
KTMM(AM) Grand Junction, CO
KVRH(AM) Salida, CO
WYBC(AM) New Haven, CT
WYCB(AM) Washington, DC
WTAN(AM) Clearwater, FL
WWFL(AM) Clermont, FL
WROD(AM) Daytona Beach, FL
WDSR(AM) Lake City, FL
WPBR(AM) Lantana, FL
WTYS(AM) Marianna, FL
WITS(AM) Sebring, FL
WFSH(AM) Valparaiso-Niceville, FL
WGAU(AM) Athens, GA
WALR(AM) Atlanta, GA
WSGF(AM) Augusta, GA
WOKS(AM) Columbus, GA
WBBT(AM) Lyons, GA
WALH(AM) Mountain City, GA
WTIF(AM) Tifton, GA
KROS(AM) Clinton, IA
KACH(AM) Preston, ID
WSOY(AM) Decatur, IL
WJPF(AM) Herrin, IL
WJOL(AM) Joliet, IL
WBIW(AM) Bedford, IN
WTRC(AM) Elkhart, IN
WXFN(AM) Muncie, IN
KGGS(AM) Garden City, KS
KDTD(AM) Kansas City, KS
KSEK(AM) Pittsburg, KS
WCMI(AM) Ashland, KY
WBGN(AM) Bowling Green, KY
WKCB(AM) Hindman, KY
WNBS(AM) Murray, KY
WEKY(AM) Richmond, KY
KRMD(AM) Shreveport, LA
WGAW(AM) Gardner, MA
WNBH(AM) New Bedford, MA
WBRK(AM) Pittsfield, MA
*WMDR(AM) Augusta, ME
WNZS(AM) Veazie, ME
WLEW(AM) Bad Axe, MI
WJRW(AM) Grand Rapids, MI
WCSR(AM) Hillsdale, MI
WMTE(AM) Manistee, MI
WAGN(AM) Menominee, MI
WMBN(AM) Petoskey, MI
WEXL(AM) Royal Oak, MI
KVBR(AM) Brainerd, MN
KDLM(AM) Detroit Lakes, MN
KRBT(AM) Eveleth, MN
KROC(AM) Rochester, MN
KWLM(AM) Willmar, MN
KXEO(AM) Mexico, MO
KLID(AM) Poplar Bluff, MO
KSMO(AM) Salem, MO
KADI(AM) Springfield, MO
WKOZ(AM) Kosciusko, MS
WAML(AM) Laurel, MS
KQJZ(AM) Evergreen, MT
KCAP(AM) Helena, MT
KPRK(AM) Livingston, MT
KYLT(AM) Missoula, MT
WJRI(AM) Lenoir, NC
WAGR(AM) Lumberton, NC
WCBQ(AM) Oxford, NC
WADE(AM) Wadesboro, NC
WLSG(AM) Wilmington, NC
WPOL(AM) Winston-Salem, NC
KPOK(AM) Bowman, ND
KXPO(AM) Grafton, ND
KHUB(AM) Fremont, NE
KGFW(AM) Kearney, NE
KSID(AM) Sidney, NE
WDCR(AM) Hanover, NH
WWNH(AM) Madbury, NH

WMID(AM) Atlantic City, NJ
KCQL(AM) Aztec, NM
KSSR(AM) Santa Rosa, NM
KVOT(AM) Taos, NM
KTSN(AM) Elko, NV
KRLV(AM) Las Vegas, NV
KXEQ(AM) Reno, NV
WWLF(AM) Auburn, NY
WENT(AM) Gloversville, NY
WKSN(AM) Jamestown, NY
WLVL(AM) Lockport, NY
WMSA(AM) Massena, NY
WALL(AM) Middletown, NY
WIRY(AM) Plattsburgh, NY
WNCO(AM) Ashland, OH
*WOUB(AM) Athens, OH
WIZE(AM) Springfield, OH
WSTV(AM) Steubenville, OH
KIHN(AM) Hugo, OK
KEBC(AM) Midwest City, OK
KJMU(AM) Sand Springs, OK
KBNW(AM) Bend, OR
KLOO(AM) Corvallis, OR
KWVR(AM) Enterprise, OR
KIHR(AM) Hood River, OR
KBBR(AM) North Bend, OR
WYJK(AM) Connellsville, PA
WOYL(AM) Oil City, PA
WHAT(AM) Philadelphia, PA
WYCK(AM) Plains, PA
WRAW(AM) Reading, PA
WTRN(AM) Tyrone, PA
WWPA(AM) Williamsport, PA
WWNA(AM) Aguadilla, PR
WQSC(AM) Charleston, SC
WRHI(AM) Rock Hill, SC
WSSC(AM) Sumter, SC
KIJV(AM) Huron, SD
KTOQ(AM) Rapid City, SD
WBAC(AM) Cleveland, TN
WKRM(AM) Columbia, TN
WGRV(AM) Greeneville, TN
WKGN(AM) Knoxville, TN
WLOK(AM) Memphis, TN
WCDT(AM) Winchester, TN
KWKC(AM) Abilene, TX
KRHC(AM) Burnet, TX
KAND(AM) Corsicana, TX
KVIV(AM) El Paso, TX
KKAM(AM) Lubbock, TX
KRBA(AM) Lufkin, TX
KOLE(AM) Port Arthur, TX
KCRN(AM) San Angelo, TX
KVNN(AM) Victoria, TX
WKEY(AM) Covington, VA
WHAP(AM) Hopewell, VA
WVCV(AM) Orange, VA
WSTA(AM) Charlotte Amalie, VI
WVNR(AM) Poultney, VT
WSTJ(AM) Saint Johnsbury, VT
KWLE(AM) Anacortes, WA
KTCR(AM) Kennewick, WA
KUOW(AM) Tumwater, WA
KZNW(AM) Wenatchee, WA
WLDY(AM) Ladysmith, WI
WJYI(AM) Milwaukee, WI
WXKX(AM) Clarksburg, WV
WEPM(AM) Martinsburg, WV
WMON(AM) Montgomery, WV
WELA(AM) Welch, WV
KSGT(AM) Jackson, WY
KYCN(AM) Wheatland, WY
KWOR(AM) Worland, WY

1350 khz
WELB(AM) Elba, AL
WJBY(AM) Gadsden, AL
KZTD(AM) Cabot, AR
KLHC(AM) Bakersfield, CA
KTDD(AM) San Bernardino, CA
KSRO(AM) Santa Rosa, CA
KDZA(AM) Pueblo, CO
WNLK(AM) Norwalk, CT
WINY(AM) Putnam, CT
WMMV(AM) Cocoa, FL
WDCF(AM) Dade City, FL

WCRM(AM) Fort Myers, FL
WFNS(AM) Blackshear, GA
WRWH(AM) Cleveland, GA
WNNG(AM) Warner Robins, GA
KRNT(AM) Des Moines, IA
KRLC(AM) Lewiston, ID
KTIK(AM) Nampa, ID
WOAM(AM) Peoria, IL
WJBD(AM) Salem, IL
WIOU(AM) Kokomo, IN
KMAN(AM) Manhattan, KS
WLOU(AM) Louisville, KY
WWWL(AM) New Orleans, LA
WGDN(AM) Gladwin, MI
KCHK(AM) New Prague, MN
KDIO(AM) Ortonville, MN
WCMP(AM) Pine City, MN
KCHR(AM) Charleston, MO
KWMO(AM) Washington, MO
WKCU(AM) Corinth, MS
WQNX(AM) Aberdeen, NC
WZGM(AM) Black Mountain, NC
WHIP(AM) Mooresville, NC
WLLY(AM) Wilson, NC
KBRX(AM) O'Neill, NE
WEZS(AM) Laconia, NH
WHWH(AM) Princeton, NJ
KABQ(AM) Albuquerque, NM
WCBA(AM) Corning, NY
WRNY(AM) Rome, NY
WARF(AM) Akron, OH
WCSM(AM) Celina, OH
WCHI(AM) Chillicothe, OH
KPNS(AM) Duncan, OK
KTLQ(AM) Tahlequah, OK
WOYK(AM) York, PA
WEGA(AM) Vega Baja, PR
WRKM(AM) Carthage, TN
KCAR(AM) Clarksville, TX
KCOX(AM) Jasper, TX
KCOR(AM) San Antonio, TX
WBLT(AM) Bedford, VA
WYSK(AM) Fredericksburg, VA
WNVA(AM) Norton, VA
WGPL(AM) Portsmouth, VA
WPDR(AM) Portage, WI

1360 khz
WIXI(AM) Jasper, AL
WMOB(AM) Mobile, AL
WMFC(AM) Monroeville, AL
WELR(AM) Roanoke, AL
KLYR(AM) Clarksville, AR
KFFA(AM) Helena, AR
KPXQ(AM) Glendale, AZ
KFIV(AM) Modesto, CA
KWDJ(AM) Ridgecrest, CA
KLSD(AM) San Diego, CA
KHNC(AM) Johnstown, CO
WDRC(AM) Hartford, CT
WHNR(AM) Cypress Gardens, FL
WCGL(AM) Jacksonville, FL
WKAT(AM) North Miami, FL
WHCG(AM) Metter, GA
WGJK(AM) Rome, GA
KMJM(AM) Cedar Rapids, IA
KBKB(AM) Fort Madison, IA
KSCJ(AM) Sioux City, IA
WLBK(AM) De Kalb, IL
WVMC(AM) Mount Carmel, IL
WGFA(AM) Watseka, IL
KAHS(AM) El Dorado, KS
WFLW(AM) Monticello, KY
KNIR(AM) New Iberia, LA
KBYO(AM) Tallulah, LA
WLYN(AM) Lynn, MA
WKYO(AM) Caro, MI
WKMI(AM) Kalamazoo, MI
KKBJ(AM) Bemidji, MN
KRWC(AM) Buffalo, MN
KMRN(AM) Cameron, MO
KELE(AM) Mountain Grove, MO
WFFF(AM) Columbia, MS
WCHL(AM) Chapel Hill, NC
*KNGN(AM) McCook, NE
WTOC(AM) Newton, NJ

WNJC(AM) Washington Township, NJ
KBUY(AM) Ruidoso, NM
WYOS(AM) Binghamton, NY
WOEN(AM) Olean, NY
WSAI(AM) Cincinnati, OH
WWOW(AM) Conneaut, OH
KOHU(AM) Hermiston, OR
KUIK(AM) Hillsboro, OR
WMNY(AM) McKeesport, PA
WPPA(AM) Pottsville, PA
WELP(AM) Easley, SC
WBLC(AM) Lenoir City, TN
WNAH(AM) Nashville, TN
KDJW(AM) Amarillo, TX
KACT(AM) Andrews, TX
KWWJ(AM) Baytown, TX
KKTX(AM) Corpus Christi, TX
KMNY(AM) Hurst, TX
WWWJ(AM) Galax, VA
WHBG(AM) Harrisonburg, VA
KKMO(AM) Tacoma, WA
WTAQ(AM) Green Bay, WI
WVRQ(AM) Viroqua, WI
WHJC(AM) Matewan, WV
WMOV(AM) Ravenswood, WV
KRKK(AM) Rock Springs, WY

1370 khz
WBYE(AM) Calera, AL
KAWW(AM) Heber Springs, AR
KTPA(AM) Prescott, AR
KWRM(AM) Corona, CA
KRAC(AM) Quincy, CA
KZSF(AM) San Jose, CA
KGEN(AM) Tulare, CA
WOCA(AM) Ocala, FL
WCOA(AM) Pensacola, FL
WZTA(AM) Vero Beach, FL
WLOP(AM) Jesup, GA
WFDR(AM) Manchester, GA
WLOV(AM) Washington, GA
KUPA(AM) Pearl City, HI
KDTH(AM) Dubuque, IA
WLLM(AM) Lincoln, IL
WGCL(AM) Bloomington, IN
WLTH(AM) Gary, IN
KGNO(AM) Dodge City, KS
KIOL(AM) Iola, KS
WEGI(AM) Fort Campbell, KY
WGOH(AM) Grayson, KY
WTKY(AM) Tompkinsville, KY
WVIE(AM) Pikesville, MD
WDEA(AM) Ellsworth, ME
WLJW(AM) Cadillac, MI
WGHN(AM) Grand Haven, MI
KSUM(AM) Fairmont, MN
KWRT(AM) Boonville, MO
KCRV(AM) Caruthersville, MO
WMGO(AM) Canton, MS
KXTL(AM) Butte, MT
*WLLN(AM) Lillington, NC
WGIV(AM) Pineville, NC
WTAB(AM) Tabor City, NC
*KWTL(AM) Grand Forks, ND
KAWL(AM) York, NE
WFEA(AM) Manchester, NH
WALK(AM) East Patchogue, NY
WELG(AM) Ellenville, NY
*WXXI(AM) Rochester, NY
WSPD(AM) Toledo, OH
KAST(AM) Astoria, OR
WWCB(AM) Corry, PA
WPAZ(AM) Pottstown, PA
WKMC(AM) Roaring Spring, PA
WIVV(AM) Vieques, PR
WKFD(AM) Charlestown, RI
WDEF(AM) Chattanooga, TN
WDXE(AM) Lawrenceburg, TN
WRGS(AM) Rogersville, TN
KFRO(AM) Longview, TX
KJCE(AM) Rollingwood, TX
KSOP(AM) South Salt Lake, UT
WHEE(AM) Martinsville, VA
WSHV(AM) South Hill, VA
WBTN(AM) Bennington, VT
KPWL(AM) Newport, WA

KWNC(AM) Quincy, WA
WCCN(AM) Neillsville, WI
*WVMR(AM) Frost, WV
WVLY(AM) Moundsville, WV
KHNY(AM) Big Horn, WY

1380 khz
WRAB(AM) Arab, AL
WGYV(AM) Greenville, AL
WVSA(AM) Vernon, AL
KDXE(AM) North Little Rock, AR
KLPZ(AM) Parker, AZ
KOSS(AM) Lancaster, CA
KTKZ(AM) Sacramento, CA
WFNW(AM) Naugatuck, CT
WTMC(AM) Wilmington, DE
WWRF(AM) Lake Worth, FL
WELE(AM) Ormond Beach, FL
WWMI(AM) Saint Petersburg, FL
WAOK(AM) Atlanta, GA
KCIM(AM) Carroll, IA
KCII(AM) Washington, IA
WTJK(AM) South Beloit, IL
WKJG(AM) Fort Wayne, IN
KCNW(AM) Fairway, KS
WMTA(AM) Central City, KY
WMJR(AM) Winchester, KY
WPYR(AM) Baton Rouge, LA
WGLM(AM) Greenville, MI
WPHM(AM) Port Huron, MI
KLIZ(AM) Brainerd, MN
KAGE(AM) Winona, MN
KSLG(AM) Saint Louis, MO
WNLA(AM) Indianola, MS
WTOB(AM) Winston-Salem, NC
KUVR(AM) Holdrege, NE
WMYF(AM) Portsmouth, NH
WABH(AM) Bath, NY
WKDM(AM) New York, NY
WDLW(AM) Lorain, OH
KXCA(AM) Lawton, OK
KMUS(AM) Sperry, OK
KSRV(AM) Ontario, OR
WTYM(AM) Kittanning, PA
WMLP(AM) Milton, PA
WCBG(AM) Waynesboro, PA
WOLA(AM) Barranquitas, PR
WNRI(AM) Woonsocket, RI
WAGS(AM) Bishopville, SC
WYNF(AM) North Augusta, SC
KOTA(AM) Rapid City, SD
*KQKD(AM) Redfield, SD
WYSH(AM) Clinton, TN
WHEW(AM) Franklin, TN
WLRM(AM) Millington, TN
KRCM(AM) Beaumont, TX
KBWD(AM) Brownwood, TX
KHEY(AM) El Paso, TX
*KWMF(AM) Pleasanton, TX
WLRV(AM) Lebanon, VA
WBTK(AM) Richmond, VA
WSYB(AM) Rutland, VT
KRKO(AM) Everett, WA
WOTE(AM) Clintonville, WI
WMTD(AM) Hinton, WV
KJUA(AM) Cheyenne, WY

1390 khz
WHMA(AM) Anniston, AL
KDQN(AM) De Queen, AR
KFFK(AM) Rogers, AR
KLTX(AM) Long Beach, CA
KLOC(AM) Turlock, CA
*KGNU(AM) Denver, CO
WFHT(AM) Avon Park, FL
WAJD(AM) Gainesville, FL
WISK(AM) Americus, GA
WTNL(AM) Reidsville, GA
KCLN(AM) Clinton, IA
WGRB(AM) Chicago, IL
WFIW(AM) Fairfield, IL
WZZB(AM) Seymour, IN
KNCK(AM) Concordia, KS
WANY(AM) Albany, KY
WZQQ(AM) Hazard, KY
KFRA(AM) Franklin, LA
WPLM(AM) Plymouth, MA

WEGP(AM) Presque Isle, ME
WLCM(AM) Holt, MI
KRFO(AM) Owatonna, MN
KXSS(AM) Waite Park, MN
KJPW(AM) Waynesville, MO
WROA(AM) Gulfport, MS
WMER(AM) Meridian, MS
WEED(AM) Rocky Mount, NC
WADA(AM) Shelby, NC
WJRM(AM) Troy, NC
KRRZ(AM) Minot, ND
KENN(AM) Farmington, NM
KHOB(AM) Hobbs, NM
WEOK(AM) Poughkeepsie, NY
WRIV(AM) Riverhead, NY
WFBL(AM) Syracuse, NY
WBLL(AM) Bellefontaine, OH
WMPO(AM) Middleport-Pomeroy, OH
WNIO(AM) Youngstown, OH
KCRC(AM) Enid, OK
KWOD(AM) Salem, OR
WLAN(AM) Lancaster, PA
WRSC(AM) State College, PA
WISA(AM) Isabela, PR
WROP(AM) Belton, SC
WSPO(AM) Charleston, SC
KJAM(AM) Madison, SD
WYXI(AM) Athens, TN
WTJS(AM) Jackson, TN
WMCT(AM) Mountain City, TN
KULP(AM) El Campo, TX
KBEC(AM) Waxahachie, TX
KLGN(AM) Logan, UT
WZHF(AM) Arlington, VA
WKPA(AM) Lynchburg, VA
WCAT(AM) Burlington, VT
KJOX(AM) Yakima, WA
WRIG(AM) Schofield, WI
WKLP(AM) Keyser, WV

1400 khz
WWTM(AM) Decatur, AL
WXAL(AM) Demopolis, AL
WJLD(AM) Fairfield, AL
WFPA(AM) Fort Payne, AL
WANI(AM) Opelika, AL
KELD(AM) El Dorado, AR
KCLA(AM) Pine Bluff, AR
KWYN(AM) Wynne, AR
KSUN(AM) Phoenix, AZ
KRVZ(AM) Springerville, AZ
KTUC(AM) Tucson, AZ
KJOK(AM) Yuma, AZ
KVTO(AM) Berkeley, CA
KIHH(AM) Eureka, CA
KESQ(AM) Indio, CA
KQMS(AM) Redding, CA
KKJL(AM) San Luis Obispo, CA
KKZZ(AM) Santa Paula, CA
KUKI(AM) Ukiah, CA
KEZL(AM) Visalia, CA
KRLN(AM) Canon City, CO
KDTA(AM) Delta, CO
KFTM(AM) Fort Morgan, CO
KBLJ(AM) La Junta, CO
KWUF(AM) Pagosa Springs, CO
WSTC(AM) Stamford, CT
WILI(AM) Willimantic, CT
WFLL(AM) Fort Lauderdale, FL
WIRA(AM) Fort Pierce, FL
WZFN(AM) Fort Walton Beach, FL
WZAZ(AM) Jacksonville, FL
WPRY(AM) Perry, FL
WSDO(AM) Sanford, FL
WZHR(AM) Zephyrhills, FL
WAJQ(AM) Alma, GA
WLTA(AM) Alpharetta, GA
WGHC(AM) Clayton, GA
WSGC(AM) Elberton, GA
WNEX(AM) Macon, GA
WHBS(AM) Moultrie, GA
WCOH(AM) Newnan, GA
WSEG(AM) Savannah, GA
KCOG(AM) Centerville, IA
KADR(AM) Elkader, IA
KVFD(AM) Fort Dodge, IA

KART(AM) Jerome, ID
KRPL(AM) Moscow, ID
KSPT(AM) Sandpoint, ID
WDWS(AM) Champaign, IL
WGIL(AM) Galesburg, IL
WEOA(AM) Evansville, IN
WBAT(AM) Marion, IN
KVOE(AM) Emporia, KS
KAYS(AM) Hays, KS
WCYN(AM) Cynthiana, KY
WIEL(AM) Elizabethtown, KY
WFTG(AM) London, KY
WFPR(AM) Hammond, LA
KAOK(AM) Lake Charles, LA
KWLA(AM) Many, LA
WHTB(AM) Fall River, MA
WLLH(AM) Lowell, MA
WHMP(AM) Northampton, MA
WWIN(AM) Baltimore, MD
WJZN(AM) Augusta, ME
WVAE(AM) Biddeford, ME
WWNZ(AM) Veazie, ME
WBFN(AM) Battle Creek, MI
WDTK(AM) Detroit, MI
*WLJN(AM) Elmwood Township, MI
WCCY(AM) Houghton, MI
WQXO(AM) Munising, MI
WSAM(AM) Saginaw, MI
WSJM(AM) Saint Joseph, MI
WKNW(AM) Sault Ste. Marie, MI
KEYL(AM) Long Prairie, MN
KMHL(AM) Marshall, MN
KMNV(AM) Saint Paul, MN
KFRU(AM) Columbia, MO
KJFF(AM) Festus, MO
KSIM(AM) Sikeston, MO
KGMY(AM) Springfield, MO
WBIP(AM) Booneville, MS
WJWF(AM) Columbus, MS
WYKC(AM) Grenada, MS
WFOR(AM) Hattiesburg, MS
WJQS(AM) Jackson, MS
KQDE(AM) Columbia Falls, MT
KBCK(AM) Deer Lodge, MT
KXGN(AM) Glendive, MT
KXGF(AM) Great Falls, MT
WKEW(AM) Greensboro, NC
WAVQ(AM) Jacksonville, NC
WMFA(AM) Raeford, NC
WSIC(AM) Statesville, NC
WMXF(AM) Waynesville, NC
WSMY(AM) Weldon, NC
KQDJ(AM) Jamestown, ND
KBRB(AM) Ainsworth, NE
KCOW(AM) Alliance, NE
KLIN(AM) Lincoln, NE
WTSL(AM) Hanover, NH
WLTN(AM) Littleton, NH
WOND(AM) Pleasantville, NJ
KVSF(AM) Santa Fe, NM
KCHS(AM) Truth or Consequences, NM
KTNM(AM) Tucumcari, NM
KSHP(AM) North Las Vegas, NV
KBDB(AM) Sparks, NV
KTNP(AM) Tonopah, NV
KWNA(AM) Winnemucca, NV
*WAMC(AM) Albany, NY
WWWS(AM) Buffalo, NY
WDNY(AM) Dansville, NY
WYNY(AM) Middletown, NY
WSLB(AM) Ogdensburg, NY
WMAN(AM) Mansfield, OH
WPAY(AM) Portsmouth, OH
KWON(AM) Bartlesville, OK
KTMC(AM) McAlester, OK
KREF(AM) Norman, OK
KFJL(AM) Central Point, OR
KNND(AM) Cottage Grove, OR
KJDY(AM) John Day, OR
KBCH(AM) Lincoln City, OR
WEST(AM) Easton, PA
WJET(AM) Erie, PA
WHGB(AM) Harrisburg, PA
WWGE(AM) Loretto, PA
WKBI(AM) Saint Marys, PA

WICK(AM) Scranton, PA
WRAK(AM) Williamsport, PA
WIDA(AM) Carolina, PR
WCOS(AM) Columbia, SC
WWRK(AM) Darlington, SC
WGTN(AM) Georgetown, SC
WSPG(AM) Spartanburg, SC
KBJM(AM) Lemmon, SD
WJZM(AM) Clarksville, TN
WHUB(AM) Cookeville, TN
WLSB(AM) Copperhill, TN
WKPT(AM) Kingsport, TN
WGAP(AM) Maryville, TN
WZNG(AM) Shelbyville, TN
KRUN(AM) Ballinger, TX
KBYG(AM) Big Spring, TX
KUNO(AM) Corpus Christi, TX
*KHCB(AM) Galveston, TX
KGVL(AM) Greenville, TX
KEBE(AM) Jacksonville, TX
KHTW(AM) Langtry, TX
KIUN(AM) Pecos, TX
KEYE(AM) Perryton, TX
KREW(AM) Plainview, TX
KVRP(AM) Stamford, TX
KTEM(AM) Temple, TX
KKTK(AM) Texarkana, TX
KVOU(AM) Uvalde, TX
KENT(AM) Parowan, UT
KSRR(AM) Provo, UT
WKAV(AM) Charlottesville, VA
WHHV(AM) Hillsville, VA
WPCE(AM) Portsmouth, VA
WAJL(AM) South Boston, VA
WINC(AM) Winchester, VA
KLCK(AM) Goldendale, WA
KEDO(AM) Longview, WA
KRSC(AM) Othello, WA
KITZ(AM) Silverdale, WA
WATW(AM) Ashland, WI
WBIZ(AM) Eau Claire, WI
WDUZ(AM) Green Bay, WI
WRJN(AM) Racine, WI
WRDB(AM) Reedsburg, WI
WOBG(AM) Clarksburg, WV
WRON(AM) Ronceverte, WV
WVRC(AM) Spencer, WV
WBBD(AM) Wheeling, WV
WBTH(AM) Williamson, WV
KKTL(AM) Casper, WY
KODI(AM) Cody, WY

1410 khz
WLVV(AM) Mobile, AL
WIQR(AM) Prattville, AL
WZZA(AM) Tuscumbia, AL
KTCS(AM) Fort Smith, AR
KERI(AM) Bakersfield, CA
KRML(AM) Carmel, CA
KSMA(AM) Lompoc, CA
KMYC(AM) Marysville, CA
KCAL(AM) Redlands, CA
KIIX(AM) Fort Collins, CO
WPOP(AM) Hartford, CT
WDOV(AM) Dover, DE
WMYR(AM) Fort Myers, FL
WRHB(AM) Leesburg, FL
WHBT(AM) Tallahassee, FL
WKKP(AM) McDonough, GA
WYIS(AM) McRae, GA
WLAQ(AM) Rome, GA
KGRN(AM) Grinnell, IA
KLEM(AM) Le Mars, IA
WRMN(AM) Elgin, IL
*WIHM(AM) Taylorville, IL
WSHY(AM) Lafayette, IN
KKLO(AM) Leavenworth, KS
KGSO(AM) Wichita, KS
WHLN(AM) Harlan, KY
KDBS(AM) Alexandria, LA
WMSX(AM) Brockton, MA
WHAG(AM) Halfway, MD
WNWZ(AM) Grand Rapids, MI
KLFD(AM) Litchfield, MN
KRWB(AM) Roseau, MN
WDSK(AM) Cleveland, MS

WEGO(AM) Concord, NC
WRJD(AM) Durham, NC
WVCB(AM) Shallotte, NC
KDKT(AM) Beulah, ND
KOOQ(AM) North Platte, NE
WHTG(AM) Eatontown, NJ
WDOE(AM) Dunkirk, NY
WELM(AM) Elmira, NY
WENU(AM) South Glens Falls, NY
WNER(AM) Watertown, NY
WING(AM) Dayton, OH
KBNP(AM) Portland, OR
WLSH(AM) Lansford, PA
KQV(AM) Pittsburgh, PA
WRSS(AM) San Sebastian, PR
WPCC(AM) Clinton, SC
WBBX(AM) Kingston, TN
WCMT(AM) Martin, TN
WSTN(AM) Somerville, TN
KLVQ(AM) Athens, TX
KNTX(AM) Bowie, TX
*KHCH(AM) Huntsville, TX
KCUL(AM) Marshall, TX
KRIL(AM) Odessa, TX
KNVR(AM) San Saba, TX
KNAL(AM) Victoria, TX
WOOK(AM) Midlothian, VA
WRIS(AM) Roanoke, VA
WIZM(AM) La Crosse, WI
WSCW(AM) South Charleston, WV
KWYO(AM) Sheridan, WY

1420 khz
WACT(AM) Tuscaloosa, AL
KBHS(AM) Hot Springs, AR
KPOC(AM) Pocahontas, AR
KMOG(AM) Payson, AZ
KTAN(AM) Sierra Vista, AZ
KSTN(AM) Stockton, CA
WLIS(AM) Old Saybrook, CT
WDJA(AM) Delray Beach, FL
WBRD(AM) Palmetto, FL
WAOC(AM) Saint Augustine, FL
WRCG(AM) Columbus, GA
WATB(AM) Decatur, GA
WPEH(AM) Louisville, GA
WLET(AM) Toccoa, GA
WKWN(AM) Trenton, GA
KKEA(AM) Honolulu, HI
WOC(AM) Davenport, IA
KIGO(AM) Saint Anthony, ID
WINI(AM) Murphysboro, IL
WIMS(AM) Michigan City, IN
KJCK(AM) Junction City, KS
KULY(AM) Ulysses, KS
WHBN(AM) Harrodsburg, KY
WVJS(AM) Owensboro, KY
KPEL(AM) Lafayette, LA
WBSM(AM) New Bedford, MA
WBEC(AM) Pittsfield, MA
WFLT(AM) Flint, MI
WKPR(AM) Kalamazoo, MI
KTOE(AM) Mankato, MN
KRLL(AM) California, MO
KBTN(AM) Neosho, MO
WQBC(AM) Vicksburg, MS
WIGG(AM) Wiggins, MS
WMYN(AM) Mayodan, NC
*WGAS(AM) South Gastonia, NC
WVOT(AM) Wilson, NC
KOTK(AM) Omaha, NE
WASR(AM) Wolfeboro, NH
WNRS(AM) Herkimer, NY
WACK(AM) Newark, NY
WLNA(AM) Peekskill, NY
WHK(AM) Cleveland, OH
KTJS(AM) Hobart, OK
KMHS(AM) Coos Bay, OR
WCOJ(AM) Coatesville, PA
WCED(AM) DuBois, PA
WUKQ(AM) Ponce, PR
WCRE(AM) Cheraw, SC
KGIM(AM) Aberdeen, SD
WEMB(AM) Erwin, TN
WKSR(AM) Pulaski, TN
KFYN(AM) Bonham, TX

KPIR(AM) Granbury, TX
KJDL(AM) Lubbock, TX
KGNB(AM) New Braunfels, TX
WAMV(AM) Amherst, VA
WXGM(AM) Gloucester, VA
WKCW(AM) Warrenton, VA
WRSA(AM) Saint Albans, VT
KITI(AM) Chehalis-Centralia, WA
KRIZ(AM) Renton, WA
KUJ(AM) Walla Walla, WA
WJUB(AM) Plymouth, WI
WTCR(AM) Kenova, WV

1430 khz
KMBQ(AM) Wasilla, AK
WFHK(AM) Pell City, AL
WRMG(AM) Red Bay, AL
KHBM(AM) Monticello, AR
KWST(AM) El Centro, CA
KFIG(AM) Fresno, CA
KJAY(AM) Sacramento, CA
KMRB(AM) San Gabriel, CA
KVVN(AM) Santa Clara, CA
KEZW(AM) Aurora, CO
WTMN(AM) Gainesville, FL
WOIR(AM) Homestead, FL
WLKF(AM) Lakeland, FL
WLTG(AM) Panama City, FL
WGFS(AM) Covington, GA
WDAL(AM) Dalton, GA
KASI(AM) Ames, IA
KCMW(AM) Boise, ID
WEEF(AM) Highland Park, IL
WCMY(AM) Ottawa, IL
WXNT(AM) Indianapolis, IN
WXAM(AM) Buffalo, KY
WYMC(AM) Mayfield, KY
KMRC(AM) Morgan City, LA
WPNI(AM) Amherst, MA
WXKS(AM) Everett, MA
WNAV(AM) Annapolis, MD
WION(AM) Ionia, MI
KNSP(AM) Staples, MN
KKOZ(AM) Ava, MO
KAOL(AM) Carrollton, MO
KZQZ(AM) Saint Louis, MO
WDEX(AM) Monroe, NC
WMNC(AM) Morganton, NC
WDJS(AM) Mount Olive, NC
WRXO(AM) Roxboro, NC
KRGI(AM) Grand Island, NE
WNSW(AM) Newark, NJ
KCRX(AM) Roswell, NM
WENE(AM) Endicott, NY
WFOB(AM) Fostoria, OH
WCLT(AM) Newark, OH
KALV(AM) Alva, OK
KTBZ(AM) Tulsa, OK
KYKN(AM) Keizer, OR
WVAM(AM) Altoona, PA
WNEL(AM) Caguas, PR
WBLR(AM) Batesburg, SC
WNFO(AM) Ridgeland, SC
KBRK(AM) Brookings, SD
WOWW(AM) Germantown, TN
WPLN(AM) Madison, TN
KROO(AM) Breckenridge, TX
KEES(AM) Gladewater, TX
KCOH(AM) Houston, TX
KLO(AM) Ogden, UT
WHAN(AM) Ashland, VA
WKEX(AM) Blacksburg, VA
WDIC(AM) Clinchco, VA
KCLK(AM) Asotin, WA
KBRC(AM) Mount Vernon, WA
WBEV(AM) Beaver Dam, WI
WQOQ(AM) Durand, WI
WEIR(AM) Weirton, WV

1440 khz
WLWI(AM) Montgomery, AL
KTUV(AM) Little Rock, AR
KAZG(AM) Scottsdale, AZ
KVON(AM) Napa, CA
KDIF(AM) Riverside, CA
KUHL(AM) Santa Maria, CA
KRDZ(AM) Wray, CO

WWCL(AM) Lehigh Acres, FL
WPRD(AM) Winter Park, FL
WGMI(AM) Bremen, GA
WGIG(AM) Brunswick, GA
WDCO(AM) Cochran, GA
KCHE(AM) Cherokee, IA
KPTO(AM) Pocatello, ID
WIBH(AM) Anna, IL
WPRS(AM) Paris, IL
WGEM(AM) Quincy, IL
WROK(AM) Rockford, IL
WPGW(AM) Portland, IN
KMAJ(AM) Topeka, KS
WWKU(AM) Glasgow, KY
WYGH(AM) Paris, KY
*WCWC(AM) Williamsburg, KY
WVEI(AM) Worcester, MA
WRED(AM) Westbrook, ME
WMAX(AM) Bay City, MI
WDOW(AM) Dowagiac, MI
WDRJ(AM) Inkster, MI
KDIZ(AM) Golden Valley, MN
WRBE(AM) Lucedale, MS
WSEL(AM) Pontotoc, MS
WBLA(AM) Elizabethtown, NC
WLXN(AM) Lexington, NC
KKXL(AM) Grand Forks, ND
WMVB(AM) Millville, NJ
WNYG(AM) Babylon, NY
WFNY(AM) Gloversville, NY
WJJL(AM) Niagara Falls, NY
WSGO(AM) Oswego, NY
WRGM(AM) Ontario, OH
WHKZ(AM) Warren, OH
KMED(AM) Medford, OR
KODL(AM) The Dalles, OR
WCDL(AM) Carbondale, PA
WNPV(AM) Lansdale, PA
WGLD(AM) Red Lion, PA
WGVL(AM) Greenville, SC
WJBS(AM) Holly Hill, SC
WZYX(AM) Cowan, TN
WHDM(AM) McKenzie, TN
KPUR(AM) Amarillo, TX
KEYS(AM) Corpus Christi, TX
KETX(AM) Livingston, TX
KELG(AM) Manor, TX
KTNO(AM) University Park, TX
WKLV(AM) Blackstone, VA
WNFL(AM) Green Bay, WI
WHIS(AM) Bluefield, WV
WAJR(AM) Morgantown, WV

1449 khz
V6AH(AM) Pohnpei, FM

1450 khz
KLAM(AM) Cordova, AK
WDNG(AM) Anniston, AL
WZGX(AM) Bessemer, AL
WDLK(AM) Dadeville, AL
WWNT(AM) Dothan, AL
WTKI(AM) Huntsville, AL
WLAY(AM) Muscle Shoals, AL
KNHD(AM) Camden, AR
KENA(AM) Mena, AR
KYNN(AM) Cameron, AZ
KDAP(AM) Douglas, AZ
KNOT(AM) Prescott, AZ
KVSL(AM) Show Low, AZ
KWFM(AM) Tucson, AZ
KCIK(AM) Blue Lake, CA
KFSD(AM) Escondido, CA
KGAM(AM) Palm Springs, CA
KTIP(AM) Porterville, CA
KEST(AM) San Francisco, CA
KVML(AM) Sonora, CA
KVEN(AM) Ventura, CA
KOBO(AM) Yuba City, CA
KGIW(AM) Alamosa, CO
KSKE(AM) Buena Vista, CO
KAVP(AM) Colona, CO
KEHT(AM) Eads, CO
KGRE(AM) Greeley, CO
WCUM(AM) Bridgeport, CT
WOL(AM) Washington, DC
WILM(AM) Wilmington, DE

WWJB(AM) Brooksville, FL
WMFJ(AM) Daytona Beach, FL
WOCN(AM) Miami, FL
WBSR(AM) Pensacola, FL
WSDV(AM) Sarasota, FL
WSTU(AM) Stuart, FL
WTAL(AM) Tallahassee, FL
WGPC(AM) Albany, GA
WQQT(AM) Brooklet, GA
WBHF(AM) Cartersville, GA
WCON(AM) Cornelia, GA
WKEU(AM) Griffin, GA
WMVG(AM) Milledgeville, GA
WVLD(AM) Valdosta, GA
KMRY(AM) Cedar Rapids, IA
KBFI(AM) Bonners Ferry, ID
KVSI(AM) Montpelier, ID
KIOV(AM) Payette, ID
*KEZJ(AM) Twin Falls, ID
WCEV(AM) Cicero, IL
WRLL(AM) Cicero, IL
WKEI(AM) Kewanee, IL
WFMB(AM) Springfield, IL
WLYV(AM) Fort Wayne, IN
WQKC(AM) Jeffersonville, IN
WASK(AM) Lafayette, IN
WAOV(AM) Vincennes, IN
KQYX(AM) Galena, KS
KWBW(AM) Hutchinson, KS
WTCO(AM) Campbellsville, KY
WWXL(AM) Manchester, KY
WDXR(AM) Paducah, KY
WLKS(AM) West Liberty, KY
KSIG(AM) Crowley, LA
KNOC(AM) Natchitoches, LA
WBYU(AM) New Orleans, LA
WNBP(AM) Newburyport, MA
WHLL(AM) Springfield, MA
WTBO(AM) Cumberland, MD
WTHU(AM) Thurmont, MD
WRKD(AM) Rockland, ME
WKTQ(AM) South Paris, ME
WATZ(AM) Alpena, MI
WHTC(AM) Holland, MI
WMIQ(AM) Iron Mountain, MI
WIBM(AM) Jackson, MI
WKLA(AM) Ludington, MI
WNBY(AM) Newberry, MI
WHLS(AM) Port Huron, MI
KATE(AM) Albert Lea, MN
KBUN(AM) Bemidji, MN
KBMW(AM) Breckenridge, MN
WELY(AM) Ely, MN
KNSI(AM) Saint Cloud, MN
KYLS(AM) Fredericktown, MO
KIRX(AM) Kirksville, MO
KOKO(AM) Warrensburg, MO
KWPM(AM) West Plains, MO
WROX(AM) Clarksdale, MS
WCJU(AM) Columbia, MS
WYHL(AM) Meridian, MS
WNAT(AM) Natchez, MS
WROB(AM) West Point, MS
KMMS(AM) Bozeman, MT
KQDI(AM) Great Falls, MT
KYLW(AM) Lockwood, MT
KGRZ(AM) Missoula, MT
KVCK(AM) Wolf Point, MT
WATA(AM) Boone, NC
WGNC(AM) Gastonia, NC
WIZS(AM) Henderson, NC
WHKP(AM) Hendersonville, NC
WNOS(AM) New Bern, NC
WFBX(AM) Spring Lake, NC
KZZJ(AM) Rugby, ND
KWBE(AM) Beatrice, NE
WKXL(AM) Concord, NH
WKBR(AM) Lancaster, NH
WENJ(AM) Atlantic City, NJ
WCTC(AM) New Brunswick, NJ
KRZY(AM) Albuquerque, NM
KLMX(AM) Clayton, NM
KOBE(AM) Las Cruces, NM
KSEL(AM) Portales, NM
KWES(AM) Ruidoso, NM
KIFO(AM) Hawthorne, NV

KHIT(AM) Reno, NV
WENI(AM) Corning, NY
WWSC(AM) Glens Falls, NY
WHDL(AM) Olean, NY
WKIP(AM) Poughkeepsie, NY
WYFY(AM) Rome, NY
WJER(AM) Dover-New Philadelphia, OH
WMOH(AM) Hamilton, OH
WLEC(AM) Sandusky, OH
KWHW(AM) Altus, OK
KGFF(AM) Shawnee, OK
KSIW(AM) Woodward, OK
KLZS(AM) Eugene, OR
KFLS(AM) Klamath Falls, OR
KLBM(AM) La Grande, OR
*KBPS(AM) Portland, OR
WPSE(AM) Erie, PA
WFRA(AM) Franklin, PA
WDAD(AM) Indiana, PA
WQCD(AM) Milford, PA
WPAM(AM) Pottsville, PA
WQWK(AM) State College, PA
WJPA(AM) Washington, PA
WCPR(AM) Coamo, PR
WLKW(AM) West Warwick, RI
WQNT(AM) Charleston, SC
WCRS(AM) Greenwood, SC
WHSC(AM) Hartsville, SC
WRNN(AM) Myrtle Beach, SC
KBFS(AM) Belle Fourche, SD
KYNT(AM) Yankton, SD
WLAR(AM) Athens, TN
WLMR(AM) Chattanooga, TN
WTRO(AM) Dyersburg, TN
WSMG(AM) Greeneville, TN
WLAF(AM) La Follette, TN
WGNS(AM) Murfreesboro, TN
KIKR(AM) Beaumont, TX
KBEN(AM) Carrizo Springs, TX
KOAH(AM) Comstock, TX
KCTI(AM) Gonzales, TX
KMBL(AM) Junction, TX
KCYL(AM) Lampasas, TX
KMHT(AM) Marshall, TX
KNET(AM) Palestine, TX
KSNY(AM) Snyder, TX
*KEYY(AM) Provo, UT
KZNU(AM) Saint George, UT
WBVA(AM) Bayside, VA
WVAX(AM) Charlottesville, VA
WFTR(AM) Front Royal, VA
WCLM(AM) Highland Springs, VA
WREL(AM) Lexington, VA
WMVA(AM) Martinsville, VA
WSNO(AM) Barre, VT
WTSA(AM) Brattleboro, VT
KBKW(AM) Aberdeen, WA
KCLX(AM) Colfax, WA
KONP(AM) Port Angeles, WA
KSUH(AM) Puyallup, WA
KFIZ(AM) Fond du Lac, WI
WHRY(AM) Hurley, WI
WDLB(AM) Marshfield, WI
WRCO(AM) Richland Center, WI
WLUX(AM) Dunbar, WV
WHNK(AM) Parkersburg, WV
KBBS(AM) Buffalo, WY
KVOW(AM) Riverton, WY

1460 khz
WMCJ(AM) Cullman, AL
WHAL(AM) Phenix City, AL
KTYM(AM) Inglewood, CA
KION(AM) Salinas, CA
KRRS(AM) Santa Rosa, CA
KCNR(AM) Shasta, CA
KZNT(AM) Colorado Springs, CO
WQXM(AM) Bartow, FL
WZEP(AM) De Funiak Springs, FL
WNPL(AM) Golden Gate, FL
WZNZ(AM) Jacksonville, FL
WXEM(AM) Buford, GA
KHRA(AM) Honolulu, HI
KXNO(AM) Des Moines, IA
WROY(AM) Carmi, IL

WIXN(AM) Dixon, IL
WKJR(AM) Rantoul, IL
WKAM(AM) Goshen, IN
WJCP(AM) North Vernon, IN
KKOY(AM) Chanute, KS
WEKB(AM) Elkhorn City, KY
WRVK(AM) Mt. Vernon, KY
WXOK(AM) Baton Rouge, LA
KBSF(AM) Springhill, LA
WXBR(AM) Brockton, MA
WEMD(AM) Easton, MD
WBRN(AM) Big Rapids, MI
WPON(AM) Walled Lake, MI
KDWA(AM) Hastings, MN
KDMA(AM) Montevideo, MN
KKAQ(AM) Thief River Falls, MN
KHOJ(AM) Saint Charles, MO
WELZ(AM) Belzoni, MS
WRKB(AM) Kannapolis, NC
WEWO(AM) Laurinburg, NC
WHBK(AM) Marshall, NC
KLTC(AM) Dickinson, ND
KXPN(AM) Kearney, NE
WIFI(AM) Florence, NJ
KENO(AM) Las Vegas, NV
WDDY(AM) Albany, NY
WVOX(AM) New Rochelle, NY
WHIC(AM) Rochester, NY
WBNS(AM) Columbus, OH
WABQ(AM) Painesville, OH
KZUE(AM) El Reno, OK
KCKX(AM) Stayton, OR
WMBA(AM) Ambridge, PA
WTKT(AM) Harrisburg, PA
WGMF(AM) Tunkhannock, PA
WRRE(AM) Juncos, PR
WLRP(AM) San Sebastian, PR
WDOG(AM) Allendale, SC
WBCU(AM) Union, SC
WJAK(AM) Jackson, TN
WEEN(AM) Lafayette, TN
WXRQ(AM) Mount Pleasant, TN
KCLE(AM) Burleson, TX
KCWM(AM) Hondo, TX
KBZO(AM) Lubbock, TX
KBRZ(AM) Missouri City, TX
WKDV(AM) Manassas, VA
WRAD(AM) Radford, VA
*KARR(AM) Kirkland, WA
KUTI(AM) Yakima, WA
WJTI(AM) Racine, WI
WBOG(AM) Tomah, WI
WBUC(AM) Buckhannon, WV

1470 khz
WPGG(AM) Evergreen, AL
KNXN(AM) Sierra Vista, AZ
KUTY(AM) Palmdale, CA
KIID(AM) Sacramento, CA
KEPL(AM) Estes Park, CO
WMMW(AM) Meriden, CT
WMGG(AM) Dunedin, FL
WWNN(AM) Pompano Beach, FL
WXAG(AM) Athens, GA
WCLA(AM) Claxton, GA
WRGA(AM) Rome, GA
KWSL(AM) Sioux City, IA
KWAY(AM) Waverly, IA
WCFJ(AM) Chicago Heights, IL
WMBD(AM) Peoria, IL
*WGNR(AM) Anderson, IN
KAIR(AM) Atchison, KS
KSMM(AM) Liberal, KS
WBFC(AM) Stanton, KY
KLCL(AM) Lake Charles, LA
WAZN(AM) Watertown, MA
WJDY(AM) Salisbury, MD
WTTR(AM) Westminster, MD
WLAM(AM) Lewiston, ME
WFNT(AM) Flint, MI
KMNQ(AM) Brooklyn Park, MN
KFMZ(AM) Brookfield, MO
KMAL(AM) Malden, MO
WCHJ(AM) Brookhaven, MS
WNAU(AM) New Albany, MS
WVBS(AM) Burgaw, NC

WWBG(AM) Greensboro, NC
WJPI(AM) Plymouth, NC
WTOE(AM) Spruce Pine, NC
KHND(AM) Harvey, ND
WNYY(AM) Ithaca, NY
WPDM(AM) Potsdam, NY
WLQR(AM) Toledo, OH
KVLH(AM) Pauls Valley, OK
KGND(AM) Vinita, OK
WSAN(AM) Allentown, PA
WLOA(AM) Farrell, PA
WQXL(AM) Columbia, SC
WLMC(AM) Georgetown, SC
WBCR(AM) Alcoa, TN
WVOL(AM) Berry Hill, TN
KYYW(AM) Abilene, TX
KDHN(AM) Dimmitt, TX
KWRD(AM) Henderson, TX
KHRX(AM) Marathon, TX
KUOL(AM) San Marcos, TX
KNFL(AM) Tremonton, UT
WBTX(AM) Broadway-Timberville, VA
WTZE(AM) Tazewell, VA
KELA(AM) Centralia-Chehalis, WA
KBSN(AM) Moses Lake, WA
WBKV(AM) West Bend, WI
WRWB(AM) Huntington, WV
KKTY(AM) Douglas, WY

1480 khz
WGNQ(AM) Bridgeport, AL
WQOH(AM) Irondale, AL
WABB(AM) Mobile, AL
KTHS(AM) Berryville, AR
KPHX(AM) Phoenix, AZ
KGOE(AM) Eureka, CA
KYOS(AM) Merced, CA
KVNR(AM) Santa Ana, CA
KSBQ(AM) Santa Maria, CA
KAVA(AM) Pueblo, CO
WKND(AM) Windsor, CT
WFLN(AM) Arcadia, FL
WVOI(AM) Marco Island, FL
WUNA(AM) Ocoee, FL
*WKGC(AM) Panama City Beach, FL
WYZE(AM) Atlanta, GA
WGUS(AM) Augusta, GA
KLEE(AM) Ottumwa, IA
KRXR(AM) Gooding, ID
WSPY(AM) Geneva, IL
WJBM(AM) Jerseyville, IL
WPFR(AM) Terre Haute, IN
WRSW(AM) Warsaw, IN
KCZZ(AM) Mission, KS
KQAM(AM) Wichita, KS
WHVO(AM) Hopkinsville, KY
WGCK(AM) Neon, KY
WTLO(AM) Somerset, KY
KIOU(AM) Shreveport, LA
WSAR(AM) Fall River, MA
*WGVU(AM) Kentwood, MI
WSDS(AM) Salem Township, MI
WIOS(AM) Tawas City, MI
KAUS(AM) Austin, MN
KKCQ(AM) Fosston, MN
WGFY(AM) Charlotte, NC
WWKO(AM) Fair Bluff, NC
WPFJ(AM) Franklin, NC
WYRN(AM) Louisburg, NC
KLMS(AM) Lincoln, NE
WLEA(AM) Hornell, NY
WZRC(AM) New York, NY
WADR(AM) Remsen, NY
WHBC(AM) Canton, OH
WCIN(AM) Cincinnati, OH
WCNS(AM) Latrobe, PA
WUBA(AM) Philadelphia, PA
WEEO(AM) Shippensburg, PA
WMDD(AM) Fajardo, PR
WZJY(AM) Mt. Pleasant, SC
KSDR(AM) Watertown, SD
WJFC(AM) Jefferson City, TN
WBBP(AM) Memphis, TN
WJLE(AM) Smithville, TN
KNIT(AM) Dallas, TX
KLVL(AM) Pasadena, TX

KCHL(AM) San Antonio, TX
KNIW(AM) Wink, TX
KHQN(AM) Spanish Fork, UT
WPWC(AM) Dumfries-Triangle, VA
WTOX(AM) Glen Allen, VA
WTOY(AM) Salem, VA
WCFR(AM) Springfield, VT
KNTB(AM) Lakewood, WA
KBMS(AM) Vancouver, WA
WLMV(AM) Madison, WI
KRAE(AM) Cheyenne, WY

1490 khz
WSYA(AM) Anniston, AL
WDPT(AM) Decatur, AL
WIRB(AM) Level Plains, AL
WHBB(AM) Selma, AL
KWXT(AM) Dardanelle, AR
KXAR(AM) Hope, AR
KDRS(AM) Paragould, AR
KOTN(AM) Pine Bluff, AR
KZZZ(AM) Bullhead City, AZ
KCUZ(AM) Clifton, AZ
KYCA(AM) Prescott, AZ
KFFN(AM) Tucson, AZ
KWAC(AM) Bakersfield, CA
KMET(AM) Banning, CA
KGBA(AM) Calexico, CA
KRKC(AM) King City, CA
KTOB(AM) Petaluma, CA
KBLF(AM) Red Bluff, CA
KIST(AM) Santa Barbara, CA
KOWL(AM) South Lake Tahoe, CA
*KSYC(AM) Yreka, CA
KCFC(AM) Boulder, CO
KHRJ(AM) Del Norte, CO
KPKE(AM) Gunnison, CO
KXRE(AM) Manitou Springs, CO
KNAM(AM) Silt, CO
WGCH(AM) Greenwich, CT
WWPR(AM) Bradenton, FL
WTJV(AM) De Land, FL
WAFZ(AM) Immokalee, FL
WMBM(AM) Miami Beach, FL
WECM(AM) Milton, FL
WTTB(AM) Vero Beach, FL
WSIR(AM) Winter Haven, FL
WKUN(AM) Bostwick, GA
WMOG(AM) Brunswick, GA
WCHM(AM) Clarkesville, GA
WYYZ(AM) Jasper, GA
WSFB(AM) Quitman, GA
WSNT(AM) Sandersville, GA
WSYL(AM) Sylvania, GA
WRLA(AM) West Point, GA
KBUR(AM) Burlington, IA
WDBQ(AM) Dubuque, IA
KXLQ(AM) Indianola, IA
KRIB(AM) Mason City, IA
KCID(AM) Caldwell, ID
KRTK(AM) Chubbuck, ID
WKRO(AM) Cairo, IL
WDAN(AM) Danville, IL
WFFX(AM) East St. Louis, IL
WPNA(AM) Oak Park, IL
WZOE(AM) Princeton, IL
WKBV(AM) Richmond, IN
WPNT(AM) South Bend, IN
KKAN(AM) Phillipsburg, KS
KTOP(AM) Topeka, KS
WKYW(AM) Frankfort, KY
WCLU(AM) Glasgow, KY
WFXY(AM) Middlesboro, KY
WOMI(AM) Owensboro, KY
WSIP(AM) Paintsville, KY
WIKC(AM) Bogalusa, LA
KEUN(AM) Eunice, LA
KJIN(AM) Houma, LA
KRUS(AM) Ruston, LA
WCEC(AM) Haverhill, MA
WMRC(AM) Milford, MA
WACM(AM) West Springfield, MA
WARK(AM) Hagerstown, MD
WBAE(AM) Portland, ME
WTVL(AM) Waterville, ME
WABJ(AM) Adrian, MI

WTIQ(AM) Manistique, MI
WMPX(AM) Midland, MI
WKLQ(AM) Whitehall, MI
KXRA(AM) Alexandria, MN
KQDS(AM) Duluth, MN
KLGR(AM) Redwood Falls, MN
KDMO(AM) Carthage, MO
KTTR(AM) Rolla, MO
KDRO(AM) Sedalia, MO
WXBD(AM) Biloxi, MS
WCLD(AM) Cleveland, MS
WHOC(AM) Philadelphia, MS
WTUP(AM) Tupelo, MS
WVBG(AM) Vicksburg, MS
KDBM(AM) Dillon, MT
KBSR(AM) Laurel, MT
WDUR(AM) Durham, NC
WLOE(AM) Eden, NC
WAZZ(AM) Fayetteville, NC
WWNB(AM) New Bern, NC
WRMT(AM) Rocky Mount, NC
WSTP(AM) Salisbury, NC
WSVM(AM) Valdese, NC
WWIL(AM) Wilmington, NC
KNDC(AM) Hettinger, ND
KOVC(AM) Valley City, ND
KOMJ(AM) Omaha, NE
WKDR(AM) Berlin, NH
WEMJ(AM) Laconia, NH
WUVR(AM) Lebanon, NH
WTAA(AM) Pleasantville, NJ
KRSN(AM) Los Alamos, NM
KRTN(AM) Raton, NM
KRUI(AM) Ruidoso Downs, NM
WCSS(AM) Amsterdam, NY
WBTA(AM) Batavia, NY
WKNY(AM) Kingston, NY
WICY(AM) Malone, NY
WDLC(AM) Port Jervis, NY
WCDO(AM) Sidney, NY
WOLF(AM) Syracuse, NY
WRCE(AM) Watkins Glen, NY
WBEX(AM) Chillicothe, OH
WERE(AM) Cleveland Heights, OH
WOHI(AM) East Liverpool, OH
WMOA(AM) Marietta, OH
WMRN(AM) Marion, OH
KMFS(AM) Guthrie, OK
KBIX(AM) Muskogee, OK
KBKR(AM) Baker City, OR
KSKR(AM) Roseburg, OR
KBZY(AM) Salem, OR
WESB(AM) Bradford, PA
WAZL(AM) Hazleton, PA
WNTJ(AM) Johnstown, PA
WLPA(AM) Lancaster, PA
WBCB(AM) Levittown-Fairless Hills, PA
WMGW(AM) Meadville, PA
WNBT(AM) Wellsboro, PA
WDEP(AM) Ponce, PR
WVGB(AM) Beaufort, SC
WTQS(AM) Cameron, SC
WGCD(AM) Chester, SC
WPCI(AM) Greenville, SC
WJDJ(AM) Hartsville, SC
KFCR(AM) Custer, SD
KORN(AM) Mitchell, SD
WOPI(AM) Bristol, TN
WJOC(AM) Chattanooga, TN
WCSV(AM) Crossville, TN
WITA(AM) Knoxville, TN
WCOR(AM) Lebanon, TN
WJJM(AM) Lewisburg, TN
WDXL(AM) Lexington, TN
KFON(AM) Austin, TX
KIBL(AM) Beeville, TX
KBST(AM) Big Spring, TX
KQTY(AM) Borger, TX
KNEL(AM) Brady, TX
KWMC(AM) Del Rio, TX
KHVL(AM) Huntsville, TX
KLNT(AM) Laredo, TX
KZZN(AM) Littlefield, TX
KPLT(AM) Paris, TX
KYZS(AM) Tyler, TX
KVWC(AM) Vernon, TX

KWUD(AM) Woodville, TX
KOGN(AM) Ogden, UT
KYHR(AM) Richfield, UT
KCPX(AM) Spanish Valley, UT
WCVA(AM) Culpeper, VA
WPAK(AM) Farmville, VA
WXTG(AM) Hampton, VA
WKVT(AM) Brattleboro, VT
WFAD(AM) Middlebury, VT
WIKE(AM) Newport, VT
KBRO(AM) Bremerton, WA
KBIS(AM) Forks, WA
KEYG(AM) Grand Coulee, WA
KWOK(AM) Hoquiam, WA
KLOG(AM) Kelso, WA
KYNR(AM) Toppenish, WA
KTEL(AM) Walla Walla, WA
WGEZ(AM) Beloit, WI
WLFN(AM) La Crosse, WI
WIGM(AM) Medford, WI
WOSH(AM) Oshkosh, WI
WSWW(AM) Charleston, WV
WTCS(AM) Fairmont, WV
WAEY(AM) Princeton, WV
WSGB(AM) Sutton, WV
KUGR(AM) Green River, WY
*KJNT(AM) Jackson, WY
KGOS(AM) Torrington, WY

1494 khz
*V6AI(AM) Yap, FM

1500 khz
WQCR(AM) Alabaster, AL
WVSM(AM) Rainsville, AL
WKAX(AM) Russellville, AL
KIEV(AM) Culver City, CA
KSJX(AM) San Jose, CA
WFIF(AM) Milford, CT
WFED(AM) Washington, DC
WKIZ(AM) Key West, FL
WPSO(AM) New Port Richey, FL
WVAA(AM) Palm Springs, FL
WDPC(AM) Dallas, GA
WSEM(AM) Donalsonville, GA
WAYS(AM) Macon, GA
KUMU(AM) Honolulu, HI
WGEN(AM) Geneseo, IL
WPMB(AM) Vandalia, IL
WPJX(AM) Zion, IL
WBRI(AM) Indianapolis, IN
WAKE(AM) Valparaiso, IN
WKXO(AM) Berea, KY
WMJL(AM) Marion, KY
KCLF(AM) New Roads, LA
WLQV(AM) Detroit, MI
KSTP(AM) Saint Paul, MN
KDFN(AM) Doniphan, MO
WQMS(AM) Quitman, MS
WSMX(AM) Winston-Salem, NC
WGHT(AM) Pompton Lakes, NJ
*KABR(AM) Alamo Community, NM
WBZI(AM) Xenia, OH
WASN(AM) Youngstown, OH
KPGM(AM) Pawhuska, OK
WMNT(AM) Manati, PR
WZZQ(AM) Gaffney, SC
WDEB(AM) Jamestown, TN
WTNE(AM) Trenton, TN
KBRN(AM) Boerne, TX
KMXO(AM) Merkel, TX
KJIM(AM) Sherman, TX
KANI(AM) Wharton, TX

1510 khz
KFNN(AM) Mesa, AZ
KIRV(AM) Fresno, CA
KSPA(AM) Ontario, CA
KPIG(AM) Piedmont, CA
KCKK(AM) Littleton, CO
WWBC(AM) Cocoa, FL
KIFG(AM) Iowa Falls, IA
WXOZ(AM) Highland, IL
WWHN(AM) Joliet, IL
*WLRB(AM) Macomb, IL
WJOT(AM) Wabash, IN
KNNS(AM) Larned, KS

KAGY(AM) Port Sulphur, LA
WWZN(AM) Boston, MA
*WJKN(AM) Jackson, MI
KCTE(AM) Independence, MO
KMRF(AM) Marshfield, MO
WEAL(AM) Greensboro, NC
KTTT(AM) Columbus, NE
WRNJ(AM) Hackettstown, NJ
WFAI(AM) Salem, NJ
WPUT(AM) Brewster, NY
WLGN(AM) Logan, OH
WLKR(AM) Norwalk, OH
WWSM(AM) Annville-Cleona, PA
WPGR(AM) Monroeville, PA
WBSG(AM) Lajas, PR
WDRF(AM) Woodruff, SC
KMSD(AM) Milbank, SD
WLAC(AM) Nashville, TN
KAGC(AM) Bryan, TX
KRDH(AM) Canton, TX
KCTX(AM) Childress, TX
KMND(AM) Midland, TX
KBED(AM) Nederland, TX
KROB(AM) Robstown, TX
KSTV(AM) Stephenville, TX
KLLB(AM) West Jordan, UT
KGA(AM) Spokane, WA
WRRD(AM) Waukesha, WI

1520 khz
WTLM(AM) Opelika, AL
KMPG(AM) Hollister, CA
KVTA(AM) Port Hueneme, CA
WHIM(AM) Apopka, FL
WXYB(AM) Indian Rocks Beach, FL
WEXY(AM) Wilton Manors, FL
WDCY(AM) Douglasville, GA
WKVQ(AM) Eatonton, GA
KSIB(AM) Creston, IA
WHOW(AM) Clinton, IL
WLUV(AM) Loves Park, IL
WKVI(AM) Knox, IN
WSVX(AM) Shelbyville, IN
WLGC(AM) Greenup, KY
KFXZ(AM) Lafayette, LA
WIZZ(AM) Greenfield, MA
WTRI(AM) Brunswick, MD
WMLM(AM) Saint Louis, MI
WRCI(AM) Three Rivers, MI
KOLM(AM) Rochester, MN
KRHW(AM) Sikeston, MO
WDSL(AM) Mocksville, NC
WGMA(AM) Spindale, NC
WARR(AM) Warrenton, NC
KMSR(AM) Mayville, ND
WWKB(AM) Buffalo, NY
WTHE(AM) Mineola, NY
WQCT(AM) Bryan, OH
WINW(AM) Canton, OH
WJMP(AM) Kent, OH
WNNT(AM) Rossford, OH
KOKC(AM) Oklahoma City, OK
KGDD(AM) Oregon City, OR
WCHE(AM) West Chester, PA
WVOZ(AM) San Juan, PR
WKMG(AM) Newberry, SC
KSQB(AM) Sioux Falls, SD
WNWS(AM) Brownsville, TN
KYND(AM) Cypress, TX
KHLT(AM) Hallettsville, TX

1530 khz
KVDW(AM) England, AR
KHPI(AM) Moreno Valley, CA
KFBK(AM) Sacramento, CA
KCMN(AM) Colorado Springs, CO
WDJZ(AM) Bridgeport, CT
WENG(AM) Englewood, FL
WYMM(AM) Jacksonville, FL
WTTI(AM) Dalton, GA
KVOG(AM) Hagatna, GU
KDSN(AM) Denison, IA
WJJG(AM) Elmhurst, IL
WLIQ(AM) Quincy, IL
KQNK(AM) Norton, KS
WVBF(AM) Middleborough Center, MA
WCTR(AM) Chestertown, MD

WFGO(AM) Orono, ME
WLCO(AM) Lapeer, MI
WYGR(AM) Wyoming, MI
KQSP(AM) Shakopee, MN
KMAM(AM) Butler, MO
WRPM(AM) Poplarville, MS
WLLQ(AM) Chapel Hill, NC
WOBX(AM) Wanchese, NC
WJDM(AM) Elizabeth, NJ
WCKY(AM) Cincinnati, OH
KXTD(AM) Wagoner, OK
WYNE(AM) North East, PA
WUPR(AM) Utuado, PR
WASC(AM) Spartanburg, SC
WWDX(AM) Huntingdon, TN
KZNX(AM) Creedmoor, TX
KGBT(AM) Harlingen, TX
KLBW(AM) New Boston, TX
KCLR(AM) Ralls, TX
WFIC(AM) Collinsville, VA
WMBE(AM) Chilton, WI

1540 khz
WKDG(AM) Sumiton, AL
KDYN(AM) Ozark, AR
KASA(AM) Phoenix, AZ
KMPC(AM) Los Angeles, CA
KREA(AM) Honolulu, HI
KXEL(AM) Waterloo, IA
WSMI(AM) Litchfield, IL
WBNL(AM) Boonville, IN
WADM(AM) Decatur, IN
WLOI(AM) La Porte, IN
WMYJ(AM) Martinsville, IN
KNGL(AM) McPherson, KS
KLKC(AM) Parsons, KS
WGRK(AM) Greensburg, KY
KGLA(AM) Gretna, LA
WACA(AM) Wheaton, MD
*KTGG(AM) Spring Arbor, MI
KBOA(AM) Kennett, MO
WKXG(AM) Greenwood, MS
WOGR(AM) Charlotte, NC
WTXY(AM) Whiteville, NC
WYNC(AM) Yanceyville, NC
WXEX(AM) Exeter, NH
WDCD(AM) Albany, NY
WSIV(AM) East Syracuse, NY
WBCO(AM) Bucyrus, OH
WWGK(AM) Cleveland, OH
WRTK(AM) Niles, OH
WBTC(AM) Uhrichsville, OH
WNWR(AM) Philadelphia, PA
WECZ(AM) Punxsutawney, PA
WIBS(AM) Guayama, PR
WADK(AM) Newport, RI
WTBI(AM) Pickens, SC
WBIN(AM) Benton, TN
WJJT(AM) Jellico, TN
WBRY(AM) Woodbury, TN
KGBC(AM) Galveston, TX
KEDA(AM) San Antonio, TX
KZMP(AM) University Park, TX
WREJ(AM) Richmond, VA
WTKM(AM) Hartford, WI

1550 khz
WLOR(AM) Huntsville, AL
*KUAZ(AM) Tucson, AZ
KWRN(AM) Apple Valley, CA
KXEX(AM) Fresno, CA
KFRC(AM) San Francisco, CA
WDZK(AM) Bloomfield, CT
WNZF(AM) Bunnell, FL
WRHC(AM) Coral Gables, FL
WAMA(AM) Tampa, FL
WTHB(AM) Augusta, GA
WAZX(AM) Smyrna, GA
WKTF(AM) Vienna, GA
KIWA(AM) Sheldon, IA
WJIL(AM) Jacksonville, IL
WCSJ(AM) Morris, IL
WOCC(AM) Corydon, IN
WCVL(AM) Crawfordsville, IN
WMDH(AM) New Castle, IN
WNDI(AM) Sullivan, IN
KDCC(AM) Dodge City, KS

KKLE(AM) Winfield, KS
WIRV(AM) Irvine, KY
WMSK(AM) Morganfield, KY
WPFC(AM) Port Allen, LA
WNTN(AM) Newton, MA
WSRY(AM) Elkton, MD
WSHN(AM) Fremont, MI
KAPE(AM) Cape Girardeau, MO
KESJ(AM) Saint Joseph, MO
KLFJ(AM) Springfield, MO
WCLY(AM) Raleigh, NC
WBFJ(AM) Winston-Salem, NC
KICS(AM) Hastings, NE
KIVA(AM) Albuquerque, NM
KXTO(AM) Reno, NV
WCGR(AM) Canandaigua, NY
WUTQ(AM) Utica, NY
WDLR(AM) Delaware, OH
KMAD(AM) Madill, OK
KYAL(AM) Sapulpa, OK
WLFP(AM) Braddock, PA
WITK(AM) Pittston, PA
WTTC(AM) Towanda, PA
WKFE(AM) Yauco, PR
WBSC(AM) Bennettsville, SC
WIGN(AM) Bristol, TN
WQZQ(AM) Clarksville, TN
WKJQ(AM) Parsons, TN
KZRK(AM) Canyon, TX
KCOM(AM) Comanche, TX
KWBC(AM) Navasota, TX
KMRI(AM) West Valley City, UT
WKBA(AM) Vinton, VA
WVAB(AM) Virginia Beach, VA
KRPI(AM) Ferndale, WA
KKAD(AM) Vancouver, WA
WZRK(AM) Lake Geneva, WI
WHIT(AM) Madison, WI
WEVR(AM) River Falls, WI
WMRE(AM) Charles Town, WV

1560 khz
WLYJ(AM) Centre, AL
WCMA(AM) Daleville, AL
KNZR(AM) Bakersfield, CA
KIQS(AM) Willows, CA
WINV(AM) Beverly Hills, FL
WINT(AM) Melbourne, FL
WPGY(AM) Ellijay, GA
KLNG(AM) Council Bluffs, IA
WBYS(AM) Canton, IL
WSEZ(AM) Paoli, IN
WRIN(AM) Rensselaer, IN
KABI(AM) Abilene, KS
WQXY(AM) Hazard, KY
WKDO(AM) Liberty, KY
WPAD(AM) Paducah, KY
WSLA(AM) Slidell, LA
WKIK(AM) La Plata, MD
WNWN(AM) Portage, MI
KBEW(AM) Blue Earth, MN
WMBH(AM) Joplin, MO
KLTI(AM) Macon, MO
KTUI(AM) Sullivan, MO
WYZD(AM) Dobson, NC
WQEW(AM) New York, NY
WTNS(AM) Coshocton, OH
WCNW(AM) Fairfield, OH
WTOD(AM) Toledo, OH
KOCY(AM) Del City, OK
WRSJ(AM) Bayamon, PR
WAHT(AM) Clemson, SC
WAGL(AM) Lancaster, SC
*KKAA(AM) Aberdeen, SD
WBOL(AM) Bolivar, TN
WMRO(AM) Gallatin, TN
KZQQ(AM) Abilene, TX
KGOW(AM) Bellaire, TX
KNGR(AM) Daingerfield, TX
KHBR(AM) Hillsboro, TX
KTXZ(AM) West Lake Hills, TX
WSBV(AM) South Boston, VA
KVAN(AM) Burbank, WA
KZIZ(AM) Pacific, WA
WGLB(AM) Elm Grove, WI
WFSP(AM) Kingwood, WV

1570 khz
WCRL(AM) Oneonta, AL
KBRI(AM) Brinkley, AR
KCVR(AM) Lodi, CA
KPRO(AM) Riverside, CA
KTGE(AM) Salinas, CA
KPIO(AM) Loveland, CO
WTWB(AM) Auburndale, FL
WVOJ(AM) Fernandina Beach, FL
WOKC(AM) Okeechobee, FL
WIGO(AM) Morrow, GA
KUAU(AM) Haiku, HI
KMCD(AM) Fairfield, IA
KQWC(AM) Webster City, IA
WBGZ(AM) Alton, IL
WFRL(AM) Freeport, IL
WBGX(AM) Harvey, IL
WTAY(AM) Robinson, IL
WGLL(AM) Auburn, IN
WILO(AM) Frankfort, IN
WNDA(AM) New Albany, IN
KNDY(AM) Marysville, KS
WLBQ(AM) Morgantown, KY
WKKS(AM) Vanceburg, KY
WABL(AM) Amite, LA
KLLA(AM) Leesville, LA
WNSH(AM) Beverly, MA
WNST(AM) Towson, MD
WWCK(AM) Flint, MI
WFUR(AM) Grand Rapids, MI
KYCR(AM) Golden Valley, MN
KAKK(AM) Walker, MN
KBCV(AM) Hollister, MO
KLEX(AM) Lexington, MO
WIZK(AM) Bay Springs, MS
WONA(AM) Winona, MS
WNCA(AM) Siler City, NC
WTLK(AM) Taylorsville, NC
WECU(AM) Winterville, NC
WVTL(AM) Amsterdam, NY
WFLR(AM) Dundee, NY
WFTU(AM) Riverhead, NY
WPTW(AM) Piqua, OH
WANR(AM) Warren, OH
KZLI(AM) Catoosa, OK
KTAT(AM) Frederick, OK
*WPGM(AM) Danville, PA
WISP(AM) Doylestown, PA
WQTW(AM) Latrobe, PA
WPPC(AM) Penuelas, PR
KVTK(AM) Vermillion, SD
WNKX(AM) Centerville, TN
WCLE(AM) Cleveland, TN
WTRB(AM) Ripley, TN
KVLG(AM) La Grange, TX
KPYK(AM) Terrell, TX
WSWV(AM) Pennington Gap, VA
WYTI(AM) Rocky Mount, VA
WSCO(AM) Appleton, WI
WKBH(AM) Holmen, WI
WLKD(AM) Minocqua, WI

1580 khz
WVOK(AM) Oxford, AL
KHGG(AM) Van Buren, AR
KMIK(AM) Tempe, AZ

KBLA(AM) Santa Monica, CA
KKKK(AM) Colorado Springs, CO
WNTF(AM) Bithlo, FL
WTCL(AM) Chattahoochee, FL
WSRF(AM) Fort Lauderdale, FL
WCCF(AM) Punta Gorda, FL
WEAM(AM) Columbus, GA
KCHA(AM) Charles City, IA
WDQN(AM) Du Quoin, IL
WBCP(AM) Urbana, IL
WIFE(AM) Connersville, IN
WHLY(AM) South Bend, IN
WAMW(AM) Washington, IN
WGVN(AM) Georgetown, KY
WPKY(AM) Princeton, KY
KXZZ(AM) Lake Charles, LA
WHFS(AM) Morningside, MD
WWSJ(AM) Saint Johns, MI
KDOM(AM) Windom, MN
KTGR(AM) Columbia, MO
KESM(AM) El Dorado Springs, MO
KNIM(AM) Maryville, MO
WAMY(AM) Amory, MS
WORV(AM) Hattiesburg, MS
WESY(AM) Leland, MS
WPMP(AM) Pascagoula-Moss Point, MS
WZKY(AM) Albemarle, NC
*KAMI(AM) Cozad, NE
WGYM(AM) Hammonton, NJ
WLIM(AM) Patchogue, NY
WVKO(AM) Columbus, OH
KOKB(AM) Blackwell, OK
KGAL(AM) Lebanon, OR
WVZN(AM) Columbia, PA
WRDD(AM) Ebensburg, PA
WANB(AM) Waynesburg, PA
WEKO(AM) Morovis, PR
WPJK(AM) Orangeburg, SC
WNPZ(AM) Knoxville, TN
WLIJ(AM) Shelbyville, TN
KGAF(AM) Gainesville, TX
KIRT(AM) Mission, TX
KTLU(AM) Rusk, TX
KWED(AM) Seguin, TX
WILA(AM) Danville, VA
WTTN(AM) Columbus, WI

1590 khz
WVNA(AM) Tuscumbia, AL
KBJT(AM) Fordyce, AR
KYNG(AM) Springdale, AR
KLIV(AM) San Jose, CA
KUNX(AM) Ventura, CA
KRSX(AM) Victorville, CA
WPSL(AM) Port St. Lucie, FL
WRXB(AM) Saint Petersburg Beach, FL
WPUL(AM) South Daytona, FL
WALG(AM) Albany, GA
WQCH(AM) La Fayette, GA
WXRS(AM) Swainsboro, GA
WTGA(AM) Thomaston, GA
KILE(AM) Hilo, HI
KWBG(AM) Boone, IA
WCGO(AM) Evanston, IL

WAIK(AM) Galesburg, IL
WNTS(AM) Beech Grove, IN
WRCY(AM) Mount Vernon, IN
KVGB(AM) Great Bend, KS
WLBN(AM) Lebanon, KY
KKAY(AM) White Castle, LA
WFBR(AM) Glen Burnie, MD
WKHZ(AM) Ocean City, MD
WTVB(AM) Coldwater, MI
WHLX(AM) Marine City, MI
KCNN(AM) East Grand Forks, MN
KDJS(AM) Willmar, MN
KDEX(AM) Dexter, MO
KPRT(AM) Kansas City, MO
KMOZ(AM) Rolla, MO
WZRX(AM) Jackson, MS
WBHN(AM) Bryson City, NC
WVOE(AM) Chadbourn, NC
WCSL(AM) Cherryville, NC
WHPY(AM) Clayton, NC
WYSR(AM) High Point, NC
KTCH(AM) Wayne, NE
WSMN(AM) Nashua, NH
KQLO(AM) Sun Valley, NV
WAUB(AM) Auburn, NY
WASB(AM) Brockport, NY
WGGO(AM) Salamanca, NY
WAKR(AM) Akron, OH
WSRW(AM) Hillsboro, OH
KWEY(AM) Weatherford, OK
KMBD(AM) Tillamook, OR
WHGT(AM) Chambersburg, PA
WPWA(AM) Chester, PA
WPSN(AM) Honesdale, PA
WCXJ(AM) Kearsarge, PA
WXRF(AM) Guayama, PR
WARV(AM) Warwick, RI
WABV(AM) Abbeville, SC
WCAM(AM) Camden, SC
WATX(AM) Algood, TN
WKTP(AM) Jonesborough, TN
WDBL(AM) Springfield, TN
KGAS(AM) Carthage, TX
KEAS(AM) Eastland, TX
KELP(AM) El Paso, TX
KMIC(AM) Houston, TX
KDAV(AM) Lubbock, TX
KRQX(AM) Mexia, TX
KDAE(AM) Sinton, TX
WFTH(AM) Richmond, VA
KLFE(AM) Seattle, WA
WIXK(AM) New Richmond, WI
WPVL(AM) Platteville, WI
WGBW(AM) Two Rivers, WI

1593 khz
V6AK(AM) Truk, FM

1600 khz
WHIY(AM) Huntsville, AL
WXVI(AM) Montgomery, AL
KNWA(AM) Bellefonte, AR
KYBC(AM) Cottonwood, AZ
KXEW(AM) South Tucson, AZ
KGST(AM) Fresno, CA

KAHZ(AM) Pomona, CA
KTAP(AM) Santa Maria, CA
KUBA(AM) Yuba City, CA
KEPN(AM) Lakewood, CO
*WAMS(AM) Dover, DE
WQOP(AM) Atlantic Beach, FL
WKWF(AM) Key West, FL
WMNE(AM) Riviera Beach, FL
WLAA(AM) Winter Garden, FL
WAOS(AM) Austell, GA
KLGA(AM) Algona, IA
KGYM(AM) Cedar Rapids, IA
WMCW(AM) Harvard, IL
WBTO(AM) Linton, IN
WARU(AM) Peru, IN
KMDO(AM) Fort Scott, KS
WAIA(AM) Beaver Dam, KY
WKFO(AM) Corbin, KY
WTSZ(AM) Eminence, KY
KLEB(AM) Golden Meadow, LA
WUNR(AM) Brookline, MA
WHNP(AM) East Longmeadow, MA
WLXE(AM) Rockville, MD
WAAM(AM) Ann Arbor, MI
KPNP(AM) Watertown, MN
KATZ(AM) Saint Louis, MO
KTTN(AM) Trenton, MO
WIDU(AM) Fayetteville, NC
WTZQ(AM) Hendersonville, NC
KDAK(AM) Carrington, ND
KNCY(AM) Nebraska City, NE
KRFS(AM) Superior, NE
KRKE(AM) Albuquerque, NM
WEHH(AM) Elmira Heights-Horseheads, NY
WWRL(AM) New York, NY
WMCR(AM) Oneida, NY
WULM(AM) Springfield, OH
WTTF(AM) Tiffin, OH
KUSH(AM) Cushing, OK
KOPB(AM) Eugene, OR
KOHI(AM) Saint Helens, OR
WHOL(AM) Allentown, PA
WHJB(AM) Bedford, PA
WPDC(AM) Elizabethtown, PA
WJSA(AM) Jersey Shore, PA
WLUZ(AM) Bayamon, PR
WFIS(AM) Fountain Inn, SC
WKZK(AM) North Augusta, SC
WMQM(AM) Lakeland, TN
KRVA(AM) Cockrell Hill, TX
KOGT(AM) Orange, TX
KOKE(AM) Pflugerville, TX
KTUB(AM) Centerville, UT
WCPK(AM) Chesapeake, VA
WXMY(AM) Saltville, VA
KVRI(AM) Blaine, WA
WRPN(AM) Ripon, WI
WZZW(AM) Milton, WV
WKKX(AM) Wheeling, WV

1620 khz
KSMH(AM) West Sacramento, CA
WNRP(AM) Gulf Breeze, FL
WDND(AM) South Bend, IN
KOZN(AM) Bellevue, NE

WTAW(AM) College Station, TX
WDHP(AM) Frederiksted, VI
KYIZ(AM) Renton, WA

1630 khz
WRDW(AM) Augusta, GA
KCJJ(AM) Iowa City, IA
KKGM(AM) Fort Worth, TX
KRND(AM) Fox Farm, WY

1640 khz
KDIA(AM) Vallejo, CA
WTNI(AM) Biloxi, MS
KFXY(AM) Enid, OK
KDZR(AM) Lake Oswego, OR
KBJA(AM) Sandy, UT
WKSH(AM) Sussex, WI

1650 khz
KYHN(AM) Fort Smith, AR
KFOX(AM) Torrance, CA
KBJD(AM) Denver, CO
KCNZ(AM) Cedar Falls, IA
KSVE(AM) El Paso, TX
WHKT(AM) Portsmouth, VA

1660 khz
KTIQ(AM) Merced, CA
*WCNZ(AM) Marco Island, FL
KXTR(AM) Kansas City, KS
WQLR(AM) Kalamazoo, MI
WBCN(AM) Charlotte, NC
KQWB(AM) West Fargo, ND
WWRU(AM) Jersey City, NJ
WGIT(AM) Canovanas, PR
KRZI(AM) Waco, TX
KXOL(AM) Brigham City, UT

1670 khz
KHPY(AM) Moreno Valley, CA
KNRO(AM) Redding, CA
WFSM(AM) Dry Branch, GA
WTDY(AM) Madison, WI

1680 khz
KGED(AM) Fresno, CA
WOKB(AM) Winter Garden, FL
KRJO(AM) Monroe, LA
WPRR(AM) Ada, MI
WTTM(AM) Lindenwold, NJ
KNTS(AM) Seattle, WA

1690 khz
KFSG(AM) Roseville, CA
KDDZ(AM) Arvada, CO
WMLB(AM) Avondale Estates, GA
WVON(AM) Berwyn, IL
WPTX(AM) Lexington Park, MD

1700 khz
WEUP(AM) Huntsville, AL
KBGG(AM) Des Moines, IA
KVNS(AM) Brownsville, TX
KKLF(AM) Richardson, TX

U.S. FM Stations by Frequency

87.9 mhz
*KSFH(FM) Mountain View, CA

88.1 mhz
*KRUA(FM) Anchorage, AK
*KCUK(FM) Chevak, AK
*KAIS(FM) Juneau, AK
*WKRE(FM) Argo, AL
*WAYH(FM) Harvest, AL
*WSJL(FM) Northport, AL
*KAPG(FM) Bentonville, AR
*KARH(FM) Forrest City, AR
*KBPW(FM) Hampton, AR
*KUYI(FM) Hotevilla, AZ
*KLTU(FM) Mammoth, AZ
*KNNB(FM) Whiteriver, AZ
*KCFY(FM) Yuma, AZ
*KDUP(FM) Cedarville, CA
*KECG(FM) El Cerrito, CA
*KFCF(FM) Fresno, CA
*KPFZ(FM) Lakeport, CA
*KLWG(FM) Lompoc, CA
*KKJZ(FM) Long Beach, CA
*KCRY(FM) Mojave, CA
*KNSQ(FM) Mount Shasta, CA
*KQNC(FM) Quincy, CA
*KEAR-FM Sacramento, CA
*KSRH(FM) San Rafael, CA
*KZSC(FM) Santa Cruz, CA
*KOOW(FM) Crook, CO
*KDNK(FM) Glenwood Springs, CO
*KAFM(FM) Grand Junction, CO
*KVOD(FM) Lakewood, CO
*KPGS(FM) Pagosa Springs, CO
*KMPZ(FM) Salida, CO
*WESU(FM) Middletown, CT
*WMNR(FM) Monroe, CT
*WMHS(FM) Pike Creek, DE
*WJIS(FM) Bradenton, FL
*WEAZ(FM) Holly Hill, FL
*WRGP(FM) Homestead, FL
*WCRJ(FM) Jacksonville, FL
*WBGY(FM) Naples, FL
*WHIJ(FM) Ocala, FL
*WUWF(FM) Pensacola, FL
*WAYF(FM) West Palm Beach, FL
*WNEE(FM) Patterson, GA
*WLXP(FM) Savannah, GA
*WAYT(FM) Thomasville, GA
*WJSP-FM Warm Springs, GA
*KHMG(FM) Barrigada, GU
*KHPR(FM) Honolulu, HI
*KUNJ(FM) Fairfield, IA
*KICB(FM) Fort Dodge, IA
*KOIA(FM) Storm Lake, IA
*KBBG(FM) Waterloo, IA
*KTFY(FM) Buhl, ID
*WESN(FM) Bloomington, IL
*WWTG(FM) Carpentersville, IL
*WZGL(FM) Charleston, IL
*WCRX(FM) Chicago, IL
*WSSD(FM) Chicago, IL
*WBMF(FM) Crete, IL
*WAXR(FM) Geneseo, IL
*WLTL(FM) La Grange, IL
*WAES(FM) Lincolnshire, IL
*WLRA(FM) Lockport, IL
*WPTH(FM) Olney, IL
*WLWJ(FM) Petersburg, IL
*WTZI(FM) Rosemont, IL
*WSOG(FM) Spring Valley, IL
*WETN(FM) Wheaton, IL
*WNTH(FM) Winnetka, IL
*WVXI(FM) Cole, IN
*WDVL(FM) Danville, IN
*WVPE(FM) Elkhart, IN
*WHCI(FM) Hartford City, IN
*WMBL(FM) Mitchell, IN
*WJCF(FM) Morristown, IN
*WNAS(FM) New Albany, IN
*WKRY(FM) Versailles, IN

*KBTL(FM) El Dorado, KS
*KRTT(FM) Great Bend, KS
*KBCU(FM) North Newton, KS
*KJTY(FM) Topeka, KS
*WAYD(FM) Auburn, KY
*WTRT(FM) Benton, KY
*WDFB-FM Danville, KY
*WRFL(FM) Lexington, KY
*WAXG(FM) Mt. Sterling, KY
*WKVY(FM) Somerset, KY
*KAYT(FM) Jena, LA
*KPAQ(FM) Plaquemine, LA
*WMBR(FM) Cambridge, MA
*WMEX(FM) Edgartown, MA
*WFHL(FM) New Bedford, MA
*WCHC(FM) Worcester, MA
*WYPR(FM) Baltimore, MD
*WMUC-FM College Park, MD
*WYPF(FM) Frederick, MD
*WGWS(FM) Saint Mary's City, MD
*WHPF(FM) Pittston Farm, ME
*WBFH(FM) Bloomfield Hills, MI
*WBLW(FM) Gaylord, MI
*WHYT(FM) Goodland Township, MI
*WHPR(FM) Highland Park, MI
*WLGH(FM) Leroy Township, MI
*WDTR(FM) Monroe, MI
*WSDP(FM) Plymouth, MI
*WYCE(FM) Wyoming, MI
*WRFR(FM) Grand Rapids, MN
*KRLX(FM) Northfield, MN
*KRFI(FM) Redwood Falls, MN
*KVSC(FM) Saint Cloud, MN
*KRLP(FM) Windom, MN
*KBOJ(FM) Worthington, MN
*KLFC(FM) Branson, MO
*KZGM(FM) Cabool, MO
*KCOU(FM) Columbia, MO
*KYRV(FM) Concordia, MO
*KDHX(FM) Saint Louis, MO
*WURC(FM) Holly Springs, MS
*WMAW-FM Meridian, MS
*KGFJ(FM) Belt, MT
*KFRT(FM) Butte, MT
*KGVA(FM) Fort Belknap Agency, MT
*WCQS(FM) Asheville, NC
*WPIR(FM) Hickory, NC
*WGHW(FM) Lockwoods Folly Town, NC
*WKNC-FM Raleigh, NC
*KCFD(FM) Crawford, NE
*KCNT(FM) Hastings, NE
*KSRC(FM) Loup City, NE
*KFHC(FM) Ponca, NE
*KMLV(FM) Ralston, NE
*WYGG(FM) Asbury Park, NJ
*WNJS-FM Berlin, NJ
*WJPG(FM) Cape May Court House, NJ
*WDNJ(FM) Hopatcong, NJ
*WNJT-FM Trenton, NJ
*KABR-FM Alamo, NM
*KCOI(FM) Clovis, NM
*KUSW(FM) Flora Vista, NM
*KGGA(FM) Gallup, NM
*KIDS(FM) Grants, NM
*KOOT(FM) Hurley, NM
*KNMA(FM) Tularosa, NM
*KRNM(FM) Chalan Kanoa-Saipan, NP
*KCEP(FM) Las Vegas, NV
*WXBA(FM) Brentwood, NY
*WCWP(FM) Brookville, NY
*WSLZ(FM) Cape Vincent, NY
*WUBJ(FM) Jamestown, NY
*WGWR(FM) Liberty, NY
*WGOR(FM) Minerva, NY
*WNYX(FM) Montgomery, NY
*WXLU(FM) Peru, NY
*WARY(FM) Valhalla, NY
*WFRW(FM) Webster, NY
*WZIP(FM) Akron, OH

*WBGU(FM) Bowling Green, OH
*WDPR(FM) Dayton, OH
*WWGV(FM) Grove City, OH
*WHRQ(FM) Sandusky, OH
*WBCJ(FM) Spencerville, OH
*KDIM(FM) Coweta, OK
*KMSI(FM) Moore, OK
*KKRI(FM) Pocola, OK
*KDJC(FM) Baker City, OR
*KLBR(FM) Bend, OR
*KWVA(FM) Eugene, OR
*KLFO(FM) Florence, OR
*KQOC(FM) Gleneden Beach, OR
*KHRV(FM) Hood River, OR
*KGRI(FM) Lebanon, OR
*KMPQ(FM) Roseburg, OR
*KQDL(FM) The Dalles, OR
*WDIY(FM) Allentown, PA
*WEFR(FM) Erie, PA
*WZXM(FM) Harrisburg, PA
*WHHN(FM) Hollidaysburg, PA
*WRWJ(FM) Murrysville, PA
*WBGM(FM) New Berlin, PA
*WPEB(FM) Philadelphia, PA
*WSRU(FM) Slippery Rock, PA
*WRGN(FM) Sweet Valley, PA
*WZZD(FM) Warwick, PA
*WPTC(FM) Williamsport, PA
*WCRP(FM) Guayama, PR
*WELH(FM) Providence, RI
*WKIV(FM) Westerly, RI
*WSBF-FM Clemson, SC
*WNRE(FM) Enoree, SC
*WRJA-FM Sumter, SC
*KOYA(FM) Rosebud, SD
*KRSD(FM) Sioux Falls, SD
*WUTC(FM) Chattanooga, TN
*WAMP(FM) Jackson, TN
*WRSN(FM) Lebanon, TN
*WFSK-FM Nashville, TN
*WAZD(FM) Savannah, TN
*KGNZ(FM) Abilene, TX
*KKWV(FM) Aransas Pass, TX
*KVJS(FM) Arroyo, TX
*KATG(FM) Athens, TX
*KEDR(FM) Bay City, TX
*KLBT(FM) Beaumont, TX
*KGLF(FM) Doss, TX
*KTPM(FM) Falfurrias, TX
*KZAR(FM) Gonzales, TX
*KHOY(FM) Laredo, TX
*KTXT-FM Lubbock, TX
*KHID(FM) McAllen, TX
*KNTU(FM) McKinney, TX
*KFTG(FM) Pasadena, TX
*KNLE-FM Round Rock, TX
*KNCH(FM) Somerville, TX
*KFLB-FM Stanton, TX
*KVLW(FM) Waco, TX
*KWCR-FM Ogden, UT
*KPGR(FM) Pleasant Grove, UT
*WNBV(FM) Grundy, VA
*WHOV(FM) Hampton, VA
*WRIH(FM) Richmond, VA
*WNCH(FM) Norwich, VT
*KUCC(FM) Clarkston, WA
*KLUW(FM) East Wenatchee, WA
*KCWU(FM) Ellensburg, WA
*KTCV(FM) Kennewick, WA
*KYRS(FM) Medical Lake, WA
*KSBC(FM) Nile, WA
*KLOP(FM) Ocean Park, WA
*KAYB(FM) Sunnyside, WA
*WHID(FM) Green Bay, WI
*WJTY(FM) Lancaster, WI
*WHJL(FM) Merrill, WI
*WMWK(FM) Milwaukee, WI
*WWEN(FM) Wentworth, WI
*WJJJ(FM) Beckley, WV
*WVBC(FM) Bethany, WV

*WKJL(FM) Clarksburg, WV
*WMUL(FM) Huntington, WV
*WVRR(FM) Point Pleasant, WV
*KAIX(FM) Cheyenne, WY
*KGCV(FM) Elk Mountain, WY
*KCWW(FM) Evanston, WY
*KGLL(FM) Gillette, WY
*KFGR(FM) Powell, WY
*KCWC-FM Riverton, WY
*KPRQ(FM) Sheridan, WY

88.3 mhz
*WJCK(FM) Piedmont, AL
*WAPR(FM) Selma, AL
*KBCM(FM) Blytheville, AR
*KXUA(FM) Fayetteville, AR
*KJSB(FM) Jonesboro, AR
*KABF(FM) Little Rock, AR
*KNAI(FM) Phoenix, AZ
*KPHF(FM) Phoenix, AZ
*KYCJ(FM) Camino, CA
*KDKL(FM) Coalinga, CA
*KMUE(FM) Eureka, CA
*KAXL(FM) Green Acres, CA
*KGUA(FM) Gualala, CA
*KLVN(FM) Livingston, CA
*KLVC(FM) Magalia, CA
*KUCR(FM) Riverside, CA
*KSDS(FM) San Diego, CA
*KCLU-FM Thousand Oaks, CA
*KPYR(FM) Craig, CO
*KGCO(FM) Fort Collins, CO
*KPRH(FM) Montrose, CO
*KTPL(FM) Pueblo, CO
*WKZG(FM) Key West, FL
*WBIY(FM) La Belle, FL
*WLMS(FM) Lecanto, FL
*WAYP(FM) Marianna, FL
*WGNK(FM) Pennsuco, FL
*WTLG(FM) Starke, FL
*WPOZ(FM) Union Park, FL
*WPPR(FM) Demorest, GA
*WAWH(FM) Dublin, GA
*WIVL(FM) Jasper, GA
*WLPT(FM) Jesup, GA
*WRGC-FM Milledgeville, GA
*KCCK-FM Cedar Rapids, IA
*KKLG(FM) Newton, IA
*KUNE(FM) Ottumwa, IA
*KMSC(FM) Sioux City, IA
*KHOI(FM) Story City, IA
*KKRH(FM) Grangeville, ID
*KARJ(FM) Kuna, ID
*KWIS(FM) Plummer, ID
*WCLR(FM) Arlington Heights, IL
*WZRD(FM) Chicago, IL
*WDGC-FM Downers Grove, IL
*WAWF(FM) Kankakee, IL
*WIUS(FM) Macomb, IL
*WHCM(FM) Palatine, IL
*WPJC(FM) Pontiac, IL
*WPRC(FM) Princeton, IL
*WJLY(FM) Ramsey, IL
*WFEN(FM) Rockford, IL
*WQNA(FM) Springfield, IL
*WEAX(FM) Angola, IN
*WDSO(FM) Chesterton, IN
*WNIN-FM Evansville, IN
*WLAB(FM) Fort Wayne, IN
*WKMV(FM) Muncie, IN
*WARA(FM) New Washington, IN
*WHZN(FM) New Whiteland, IN
*KBJQ(FM) Bronson, KS
*KVCO(FM) Concordia, KS
*KDOO(FM) Goodland, KS
*KYFW(FM) Wichita, KS
*WSGP(FM) Glasgow, KY
*WOCS(FM) Lerose, KY
*WRBH(FM) New Orleans, LA
*KPCP(FM) New Roads, LA
*KAPI(FM) Ruston, LA

*WBMT(FM) Boxford, MA
*WIQH(FM) Concord, MA
*WGAO(FM) Franklin, MA
*WRPS(FM) Rockland, MA
*WYUR(FM) Midland, MD
*WRAU(FM) Ocean City, MD
*WMTP(FM) Kennebunkport, ME
*WYAR(FM) Yarmouth, ME
*WCBN-FM Ann Arbor, MI
*WXOU(FM) Auburn Hills, MI
*WLVM(FM) Ironwood, MI
*WAYK(FM) Kalamazoo, MI
*WKPK(FM) Michigamme, MI
*WAQQ(FM) Onsted, MI
*WNFA(FM) Port Huron, MI
*WSHJ(FM) Southfield, MI
*WEJC(FM) White Star, MI
*WSHM(FM) Wixom, MI
*KBPN(FM) Brainerd, MN
*WQRN(FM) Cook, MN
*KITF(FM) International Falls, MN
*KJAB-FM Mexico, MO
*KWND(FM) Springfield, MO
*WYAD(FM) Benton, MS
*WAFR(FM) Tupelo, MS
*KJCG(FM) Missoula, MT
*KPGB(FM) Pryor, MT
*KLMB(FM) Roundup, MT
*KYPW(FM) Wolf Point, MT
*WGWG(FM) Boiling Springs, NC
*WGPS(FM) Elizabeth City, NC
*WUAW(FM) Erwin, NC
*KBMK(FM) Bismarck, ND
*KLNB(FM) Grand Island, NE
*KGCQ(FM) Kimball, NE
*KLJV(FM) Scottsbluff, NE
*WEVS(FM) Nashua, NH
*WVBH(FM) Beach Haven West, NJ
*WBGO(FM) Newark, NJ
*KLYT(FM) Albuquerque, NM
*KLRH(FM) Sparks, NV
*WBKW(FM) Beekman, NY
*WVCR-FM Loudonville, NY
*WFSO(FM) Olivebridge, NY
*WSBU(FM) Saint Bonaventure, NY
*WLIU(FM) Southampton, NY
*WAER(FM) Syracuse, NY
*WXLS(FM) Tupper Lake, NY
*WCOU(FM) Warsaw, NY
*WBWC(FM) Berea, OH
*WJVS(FM) Cincinnati, OH
*WLFC(FM) Findlay, OH
*WMRT(FM) Marietta, OH
*WHWN(FM) Painesville, OH
*WOHP(FM) Portsmouth, OH
*WAUI(FM) Shelby, OH
*WOAR(FM) South Vienna, OH
*WXTS-FM Toledo, OH
*WXUT(FM) Toledo, OH
*KBWW(FM) Broken Bow, OK
*KIOP(FM) Prague, OK
*KOSR(FM) Stillwater, OK
*KTGS(FM) Tishomingo, OK
*KOEG(FM) Walters, OK
*KSRG(FM) Ashland, OR
*KBVM(FM) Portland, OR
*WDCV-FM Carlisle, PA
*WZXQ(FM) Chambersburg, PA
*WZXE(FM) East Nottingham, PA
*WWEC(FM) Elizabethtown, PA
*WRCT(FM) Pittsburgh, PA
*WXFR(FM) State College, PA
*WLKA(FM) Tafton, PA
*WRUO(FM) Mayaguez, PR
*WQRI(FM) Bristol, RI
*WAFJ(FM) Belvedere, SC
*WMBJ(FM) Murrell's Inlet, SC
*KESD(FM) Brookings, SD
*KCFE(FM) Hoven, SD
*KVKR(FM) Pine Ridge, SD

*KLMP(FM) Rapid City, SD
*WRRI(FM) Brownsville, TN
*WAYQ(FM) Clarksville, TN
*WRCC(FM) Dibrell, TN
*WCQR-FM Kingsport, TN
*WDLF(FM) Maynardville, TN
*WMTS-FM Murfreesboro, TN
*WBIA(FM) Shelbyville, TN
*KIFR(FM) Alice, TX
*KJRT(FM) Amarillo, TX
*KBNR(FM) Brownsville, TX
*KAFR(FM) Conroe, TX
*KRAF(FM) Fort Stockton, TX
*KJCR(FM) Keene, TX
*KPIP(FM) Mount Pleasant, TX
*KPAC(FM) San Antonio, TX
*KLXL(FM) Wheeler, TX
*KCPW-FM Salt Lake City, UT
*WOTC(FM) Edinburg, VA
*WRVL(FM) Lynchburg, VA
*WNUB-FM Northfield, VT
*KPLK(FM) Manson, WA
*KMLW(FM) Moses Lake, WA
*WHWC(FM) Menomonie, WI
*KKRR(FM) Casper, WY
*KMLT(FM) Jackson, WY

88.5 mhz

*KAKL(FM) Anchorage, AK
*WLJR(FM) Birmingham, AL
*WJBE(FM) Five Points, AL
*WJIA(FM) Guntersville, AL
*WBHY-FM Mobile, AL
*KLKA(FM) Globe, AZ
*KECU(FM) Kaibito, AZ
*KFLT-FM Tucson, AZ
*KKRN(FM) Bella Vista, CA
*KWTW(FM) Bishop, CA
*KZLU(FM) Inyokern, CA
*KVUH(FM) Laytonville, CA
*KSBR(FM) Mission Viejo, CA
*KCSN(FM) Northridge, CA
*KPSC(FM) Palm Springs, CA
*KQED-FM San Francisco, CA
*KLVH(FM) San Luis Obispo, CA
*KQKL(FM) Selma, CA
*KHMS(FM) Victorville, CA
*KJCQ(FM) Westwood, CA
*KGNU-FM Boulder, CO
*KTDU(FM) Durango, CO
*KCIC(FM) Grand Junction, CO
*KRNC(FM) Steamboat Springs, CO
*KVJZ(FM) Vail, CO
*WVOF(FM) Fairfield, CT
*WEDW-FM Stamford, CT
*WAMU(FM) Washington, DC
*WJCB(FM) Clewiston, FL
*WWLC(FM) Cross City, FL
*WMFL(FM) Florida City, FL
*WRYZ(FM) Palm Bay, FL
*WFCF(FM) Saint Augustine, FL
*WKPX(FM) Sunrise, FL
*WMNF(FM) Tampa, FL
*WRAS(FM) Atlanta, GA
*WREI(FM) Kings Bay, GA
*WTMQ(FM) Lumpkin, GA
*WSLT(FM) Statesboro, GA
*WVDA(FM) Valdosta, GA
*KURE(FM) Ames, IA
*KALA(FM) Davenport, IA
*KIAD(FM) Dubuque, IA
*KBDC(FM) Mason City, IA
*KDCR(FM) Sioux Center, IA
*KBSY(FM) Burley, ID
*WBEL(FM) Cairo, IL
*WHPK-FM Chicago, IL
*WHFH(FM) Flossmoor, IL
*WGBK(FM) Glenview, IL
*WHSD(FM) Hinsdale, IL
*WBNH(FM) Pekin, IL
*WGCA-FM Quincy, IL
*WSEH(FM) South Elgin, IL
*WTMK(FM) Lowell, IN
*WQKV(FM) Rochester, IN
*WCRT-FM Terre Haute, IN
*WXVW(FM) Veedersburg, IN

*KBQC(FM) Independence, KS
*KAKA(FM) Salina, KS
*KJLJ(FM) Scott City, KS
*WEKF(FM) Corbin, KY
*WBMK(FM) Morehead, KY
*WJIE-FM Okolona, KY
*WJFM(FM) Baton Rouge, LA
*KLHV(FM) Cotton Valley, LA
*WFCR(FM) Amherst, MA
*WPMW(FM) Bayview, MA
*WWTA(FM) Marion, MA
*WHCF(FM) Bangor, ME
*WSEW(FM) Sanford, ME
*WRKJ(FM) Westbrook, ME
*WGVU-FM Allendale, MI
*WJOM(FM) Eagle, MI
*WCTP(FM) Gagetown, MI
*WJKQ(FM) Jackson, MI
*WIAB(FM) Mackinaw City, MI
*WOAS(FM) Ontonagon, MI
*WSFP(FM) Rust Township, MI
*KNCM(FM) Appleton, MN
*KCRB-FM Bemidji, MN
WGRH(FM) Hinckley, MN
*KBEM-FM Minneapolis, MN
*KLJC(FM) Kansas City, MO
*KMST(FM) Rolla, MO
*WMUW(FM) Columbus, MS
*WUSM-FM Hattiesburg, MS
*WJSU(FM) Jackson, MS
*KHEW(FM) Rocky Boy's Reservation, MT
*KBHK(FM) Thompson Falls, MT
*WXBE(FM) Beaufort, NC
*WZNB(FM) New Bern, NC
*WRTP(FM) Roanoke Rapids, NC
*WZDG(FM) Scotts Hill, NC
*WHYC(FM) Swanquarter, NC
*WFDD-FM Winston-Salem, NC
*KEYA(FM) Belcourt, ND
*KLCV(FM) Lincoln, NE
*WNJP(FM) Sussex, NJ
*KENU(FM) Des Moines, NM
*KPKJ(FM) Mentmore, NM
*KEKL(FM) Mesquite, NV
*WVVC-FM Dolgeville, NY
*WPOB-FM Plainview, NY
*WRUR-FM Rochester, NY
*WCII(FM) Spencer, NY
*WKWZ(FM) Syosset, NY
*WMUB(FM) Oxford, OH
*WYSA(FM) Wauseon, OH
*WWVY(FM) Waverly, OH
*WYSU(FM) Youngstown, OH
*KZTH(FM) Piedmont, OK
*KTKL(FM) Stigler, OK
*KSBA(FM) Coos Bay, OR
*KPIJ(FM) Junction City, OR
*KLMF(FM) Klamath Falls, OR
*KLRF(FM) Milton-Freewater, OR
*KAVE(FM) Oakridge, OR
*KWRX(FM) Redmond, OR
*KAIK(FM) Tillamook, OR
*KMUZ(FM) Turner, OR
*WMCE(FM) Erie, PA
*WLVU(FM) Halifax, PA
*WYFU(FM) Masontown, PA
*WXPN(FM) Philadelphia, PA
*WRKC(FM) Wilkes-Barre, PA
*WTMV(FM) Youngsville, PA
*WPLI(FM) Levittown, PR
*WEPC(FM) Belton, SC
*WYFV(FM) Cayce, SC
*WFCH(FM) Charleston, SC
*KAJF(FM) Ipswich, SD
*WTTU(FM) Cookeville, TN
*WVCP(FM) Gallatin, TN
*WZXX(FM) Lawrenceburg, TN
*WQOX(FM) Memphis, TN
*WLNQ(FM) Spring City, TN
*WAUT-FM Tullahoma, TN
*KHIB(FM) Bastrop, TX
*KGHY(FM) Beaumont, TX
*KPBB(FM) Brownfield, TX
*KLRW(FM) Byrne, TX
*KCKT(FM) Crockett, TX

*KOIR(FM) Edinburg, TX
*KTEP(FM) El Paso, TX
*KEDC(FM) Hearne, TX
*KBMD(FM) Marble Falls, TX
*KEOM(FM) Mesquite, TX
*KPMB(FM) Plainview, TX
*KVLT(FM) Temple, TX
*KAYK(FM) Victoria, TX
*WVTW(FM) Charlottesville, VA
*WJLZ(FM) Virginia Beach, VA
*WVPA(FM) Saint Johnsbury, VT
*KOMQ(FM) Omak, WA
*KRLF(FM) Pullman, WA
*KPLU-FM Tacoma, WA
*KYVT(FM) Yakima, WA
*WGNV(FM) Milladore, WI
*WNLI(FM) Sturgeon Bay, WI
*WVPN(FM) Charleston, WV
*WNMP(FM) Marlinton, WV
*KUWY(FM) Laramie, WY
*KZUW(FM) Reliance, WY

88.7 mhz

KVRM(FM) Glennallen, AK
*KJHA(FM) Houston, AK
*WELL-FM Dadeville, AL
*WMMI(FM) Demopolis, AL
*WRWA(FM) Dothan, AL
*WQPR(FM) Muscle Shoals, AL
*KBPU(FM) De Queen, AR
*KGSF(FM) Green Forest, AR
*KNAU(FM) Flagstaff, AZ
*KISL(FM) Avalon, CA
*KUBO(FM) Calexico, CA
*KSPC(FM) Claremont, CA
*KORB(FM) Hopland, CA
*KMPO(FM) Modesto, CA
*KQSC(FM) Santa Barbara, CA
*KXJS(FM) Sutter, CA
*KBLV(FM) Tehachapi, CA
*KRZA(FM) Alamosa, CO
*KRKM(FM) Breckenridge, CO
*KCME(FM) Manitou Springs, CO
*KEZC(FM) Red Feather Lakes, CO
*WNHU(FM) West Haven, CT
*WKNZ(FM) Harrington, DE
*WMYZ(FM) Clermont, FL
*WKTO(FM) Edgewater, FL
*WAYJ(FM) Fort Myers, FL
*WJFR(FM) Jacksonville, FL
*WFRP(FM) Americus, GA
*WMOC(FM) Lumber City, GA
*WJDS(FM) Sparta, GA
*WEYY(FM) Tallapoosa, GA
*KUBU(FM) Coggon, IA
*KLNI(FM) Decorah, IA
*KRFH(FM) Marshalltown, IA
*KIGC(FM) Oskaloosa, IA
*KWDM(FM) West Des Moines, IA
*KTYY(FM) Middleton, ID
*WPCD(FM) Champaign, IL
*WLUW(FM) Chicago, IL
*WSIE(FM) Edwardsville, IL
*WRSE(FM) Elmhurst, IL
*WCSF(FM) Joliet, IL
*WEGN(FM) Kankakee, IL
*WSRI(FM) Sugar Grove, IL
*WGVE(FM) Gary, IN
*WICR(FM) Indianapolis, IN
*WBHW(FM) Loogootee, IN
*KVDC(FM) Dodge City, KS
*KOKN(FM) Oketo, KS
*WLCU(FM) Campbellsville, KY
*WEUC(FM) Morganfield, KY
*WMMT(FM) Whitesburg, KY
*KRVS(FM) Lafayette, LA
*KBMQ(FM) Monroe, LA
*WIAA(FM) Interlochen, MI
*WSIS(FM) Riverside, MI
*WMLS(FM) Grand Marais, MN
*KMSE(FM) Rochester, MN
*KXMS(FM) Joplin, MO
*KTRM(FM) Kirksville, MO
*KSDQ(FM) Moberly, MO
*WYTF(FM) Indianola, MS
*WJZB(FM) Starkville, MS

*KUDI(FM) Choteau, MT
*KLKM(FM) Kalispell, MT
*WXDU(FM) Durham, NC
*WRAE(FM) Raeford, NC
*WAGO(FM) Snow Hill, NC
*WNCW(FM) Spindale, NC
*KFBN(FM) Fargo, ND
*KLNE-FM Lexington, NE
*WRSU-FM New Brunswick, NJ
*WEHA(FM) Port Republic, NJ
*WPSC-FM Wayne, NJ
KXNM(FM) Encino, NM
*KBOM(FM) Socorro, NM
*KWPR(FM) Lund, NV
*KUNR(FM) Reno, NV
*WBFO(FM) Buffalo, NY
*WXLE(FM) Canton, NY
*WHCL-FM Clinton, NY
*WTMI(FM) Fleming, NY
*WRHU(FM) Hempstead, NY
*WSQA(FM) Hornell, NY
*WPKM(FM) Montauk, NY
*WNYK(FM) Nyack, NY
*WRHV(FM) Poughkeepsie, NY
*WFNP(FM) Rosendale, NY
*WKYJ(FM) Rouses Point, NY
*WHJM(FM) Anna, OH
*WOBO(FM) Batavia, OH
*WOFN(FM) Beach City, OH
*WUFM(FM) Columbus, OH
*WJCU(FM) University Heights, OH
*KAJT(FM) Ada, OK
*KFXH(FM) Marlow, OK
*KLVV(FM) Ponca City, OK
*KESG(FM) Sayre, OK
*KWTU(FM) Tulsa, OK
*KLOY(FM) Astoria, OR
*KBVR(FM) Corvallis, OR
*KETP(FM) Enterprise, OR
*KOAP(FM) Lakeview, OR
*KLVP(FM) Sandy, OR
*KJKL(FM) Selma, OR
*WSVP(FM) Connellsville, PA
*WEMR(FM) Dushore, PA
*WWLU(FM) Lincoln University, PA
*WWCF(FM) McConnellsburg, PA
*WXPH(FM) Middletown, PA
*WRYV(FM) Milroy, PA
*WSYC-FM Shippensburg, PA
*WBYX(FM) Stroudsburg, PA
*WCYJ-FM Waynesburg, PA
*WJMF(FM) Smithfield, RI
*WAGP(FM) Beaufort, SC
*KVCH(FM) Huron, SD
*WAYM(FM) Columbia, TN
*WIGH(FM) Lexington, TN
*KAZI-FM Austin, TX
*KASV(FM) Borger, TX
*KKLM(FM) Corpus Christi, TX
*KEPI(FM) Eagle Pass, TX
*KTCU-FM Fort Worth, TX
*KRBG(FM) Hereford, TX
*KUHF(FM) Houston, TX
*KKER(FM) Kerrville, TX
*KZLO(FM) Kilgore, TX
*KTMU(FM) Muenster, TX
*KFRI(FM) West Odessa, TX
*KMCU(FM) Wichita Falls, TX
*KNKL(FM) North Ogden, UT
*WFOS(FM) Chesapeake, VA
*WXJM(FM) Harrisonburg, VA
*WRIQ(FM) Lexington, VA
*WWPV-FM Colchester, VT
*WRVT(FM) Rutland, VT
*KAGU(FM) Spokane, WA
*WERN(FM) Madison, WI
*WRFW(FM) River Falls, WI
*WPJY(FM) Blennerhassett, WV
*KKWY(FM) Douglas, WY
*KDNR(FM) South Greeley, WY

88.9 mhz

*KEUL(FM) Girdwood, AK
*KMJG(FM) Homer, AK
*KNGW(FM) Juneau, AK
*KJLP(FM) Palmer, AK

*KTNA(FM) Talkeetna, AK
*WILF(FM) Monroeville, AL
*WMFT(FM) Tuscaloosa, AL
*KAKV(FM) El Dorado, AR
*KAOW(FM) Fort Smith, AR
*KAIC(FM) Tucson, AZ
*KAWC-FM Yuma, AZ
*KUCI(FM) Irvine, CA
*KTLW(FM) Lancaster, CA
*KXLU(FM) Los Angeles, CA
*KFPR(FM) Redding, CA
*KOGR(FM) Rosedale, CA
*KXPR(FM) Sacramento, CA
*KUSP(FM) Santa Cruz, CA
*KRTM(FM) Temecula, CA
*KDUV(FM) Visalia, CA
*KCJX(FM) Carbondale, CO
*KDAB(FM) Central City, CO
*KRFC(FM) Fort Collins, CO
*WJMJ(FM) Hartford, CT
*WQCS(FM) Fort Pierce, FL
*WDNA(FM) Miami, FL
*WFSU-FM Tallahassee, FL
*WYFE(FM) Tarpon Springs, FL
*WMSL(FM) Athens, GA
*WWIO-FM Brunswick, GA
*WBKG(FM) Macon, GA
*WGUR(FM) Milledgeville, GA
*WKEU-FM The Rock, GA
*KHJC(FM) Lihue, HI
*KIHS(FM) Adel, IA
*KDSO(FM) Cascade, IA
*KSTM(FM) Indianola, IA
*KDMR(FM) Mitchellville, IA
*KJIA(FM) Spirit Lake, IA
*KAIP(FM) Wapello, IA
*KWVI(FM) Waverly, IA
*KLCZ(FM) Lewiston, ID
*KHCX(FM) Soda Springs, ID
*KEFX(FM) Twin Falls, ID
*WEIU(FM) Charleston, IL
*WIIT(FM) Chicago, IL
*WEPS(FM) Elgin, IL
*WMXM(FM) Lake Forest, IL
*WLNX(FM) Lincoln, IL
*WOTW(FM) Monee, IL
*WVSI(FM) Mount Vernon, IL
*WWGN(FM) Ottawa, IL
*WRRG(FM) River Grove, IL
*WARG(FM) Summit, IL
*WJCJ(FM) Ladoga, IN
*WSND-FM Notre Dame, IN
*WMYJ-FM Oolitic, IN
*WJYW(FM) Union City, IN
*KPRD(FM) Hays, KS
*KGLV(FM) Manhattan, KS
*KTJO-FM Ottawa, KS
*WKYU-FM Bowling Green, KY
*WEKU(FM) Richmond, KY
*WERS(FM) Boston, MA
*WEAA(FM) Baltimore, MD
*WMDR-FM Oakland, ME
*WDBM(FM) East Lansing, MI
*WJCE(FM) Elkton, MI
*WAKL(FM) Flint, MI
*WBLU-FM Grand Rapids, MI
*WHEY(FM) North Muskegon, MI
*WGJU(FM) Tawas City, MI
*KNSR(FM) Collegeville, MN
*KRNW(FM) Chillicothe, MO
*KSEF(FM) Farmington, MO
*KJLU(FM) Jefferson City, MO
*WMAU-FM Bude, MS
*WMSB(FM) Senatobia, MS
*KFRD(FM) Butte, MT
*KGFC(FM) Great Falls, MT
*KVRZ(FM) Libby, MT
*KYWH(FM) Lockwood, MT
*WUND-FM Manteo, NC
*WSHA(FM) Raleigh, NC
*KLUU(FM) Jamestown, ND
*KMPR(FM) Minot, ND
*KNBE(FM) Beatrice, NE
*KYFG(FM) Omaha, NE
WAJM(FM) Atlantic City, NJ
*WMNJ(FM) Madison, NJ

*WBZC(FM) Pemberton, NJ
*WMCX(FM) West Long Branch, NJ
*KHII(FM) Cloudcroft, NM
*KNMI(FM) Farmington, NM
*KLLU(FM) Gallup, NM
*KRUC(FM) Las Cruces, NM
*KNPR(FM) Las Vegas, NV
*WCIY(FM) Canandaigua, NY
*WITC(FM) Cazenovia, NY
*WCVF-FM Fredonia, NY
*WYRR(FM) Lakewood, NY
WWES(FM) Mount Kisco, NY
*WNYO(FM) Oswego, NY
*WRPJ(FM) Port Jervis, NY
*WFRS(FM) Smithtown, NY
*WSIA(FM) Staten Island, NY
*WSLJ(FM) Watertown, NY
*WRDL(FM) Ashland, OH
*WMWX(FM) Miamitown, OH
*WLRY(FM) Rushville, OH
*WBJV(FM) Steubenville, OH
*WSTB(FM) Streetsboro, OH
*WTPG(FM) Weston, OH
*WCSU-FM Wilberforce, OH
*KARU(FM) Cache, OK
*KWXC(FM) Grove, OK
*KJLG(FM) Guymon, OK
*KYLV(FM) Oklahoma City, OK
*KOBK(FM) Baker City, OR
*KKLJ(FM) Klamath Falls, OR
*KYOR(FM) Newport, OR
*KQFE(FM) Springfield, OR
*WFSE(FM) Edinboro, PA
*WFRJ(FM) Johnstown, PA
*WWNW(FM) New Wilmington, PA
*WQSU(FM) Selinsgrove, PA
*WBYO(FM) Sellersville, PA
*WPUC-FM Ponce, PR
*WKVC(FM) North Myrtle Beach, SC
*WNSC-FM Rock Hill, SC
*KVSD(FM) Wasta, SD
*WMBW(FM) Chattanooga, TN
*WTAI(FM) Union City, TN
*KETR(FM) Commerce, TX
*KMBH-FM Harlingen, TX
*KLDN(FM) Lufkin, TX
*KSUR(FM) Mart, TX
*KCHG(FM) Cedar City, UT
*WCVE(FM) Richmond, VA
*KSWS(FM) Chehalis, WA
*KCSH(FM) Ellensburg, WA
*KMIH(FM) Mercer Island, WA
*KPYU(FM) Sedro-Woolley, WA
*WLSU(FM) La Crosse, WI
*WYMS(FM) Milwaukee, WI
*WOJB(FM) Reserve, WI
*WVRN(FM) Wittenberg, WI
*WVPW(FM) Buckhannon, WV
*WVEP(FM) Martinsburg, WV
*KEZF(FM) Burns, WY
*KLOF(FM) Gillette, WY
*KAIW(FM) Laramie, WY
*KOHR(FM) Sheridan, WY
*KWCF(FM) Sheridan, WY

89.1 mhz
*WKNG-FM Heflin, AL
*WLBF(FM) Montgomery, AL
*KUAR(FM) Little Rock, AR
*KLVK(FM) Fountain Hills, AZ
*KUAZ-FM Tucson, AZ
*KCEA(FM) Atherton, CA
*KPRX(FM) Bakersfield, CA
*KODV(FM) Barstow, CA
*KBBF(FM) Calistoga, CA
*KHAP(FM) Chico, CA
*KXBC(FM) Garberville, CA
*KCJH(FM) Livingston, CA
*KCRU(FM) Oxnard, CA
*KUOR-FM Redlands, CA
*KBWA(FM) Brush, CO
*KTLC(FM) Canon City, CO
*KGQD(FM) Fraser, CO
*KECC(FM) La Junta, CO
*KYCO(FM) Limon, CO
*KVMT(FM) Montrose, CO

*WNPR(FM) Norwich, CT
*WXHL-FM Christiana, DE
*WUFT-FM Gainesville, FL
*WLSZ(FM) Key West, FL
*WLAZ(FM) Kissimmee, FL
*WFSW(FM) Panama City, FL
*WSMR(FM) Sarasota, FL
*WBIB-FM Forsyth, GA
*WBCX(FM) Gainesville, GA
*WAKP(FM) Smithboro, GA
*KXGM(FM) Hiawatha, IA
*KDWI(FM) Ottumwa, IA
*KPVL(FM) Postville, IA
*KAWS(FM) Marsing, ID
*WNIE(FM) Freeport, IL
*WHJH(FM) Kincaid, IL
*WVJC(FM) Mount Carmel, IL
*WONC(FM) Naperville, IL
*WGLT(FM) Normal, IL
*WSPM(FM) Cloverdale, IN
*WBOI(FM) Fort Wayne, IN
*WAUZ(FM) Greensburg, IN
*WLPR-FM Lowell, IN
*WSMJ(FM) Wilkinson, IN
*KMUW(FM) Wichita, KS
*WKCX(FM) Crittenden, KY
*KFLO-FM Blanchard, LA
*KVDP(FM) Dry Prong, LA
*WBSN-FM New Orleans, LA
*KLPI-FM Ruston, LA
*KRLR(FM) Sulphur, LA
*WHAB(FM) Acton, MA
*WGMS(FM) Hagerstown, MD
*WLKB(FM) Bay City, MI
*WWKM(FM) Imlay City, MI
*WIDR(FM) Kalamazoo, MI
*WPHS(FM) Warren, MI
*WEMU(FM) Ypsilanti, MI
*WGZS(FM) Cloquet, MN
*KVCS(FM) Spring Valley, MN
*KCLC(FM) Saint Charles, MO
*KWFC(FM) Springfield, MO
*WMBU(FM) Forest, MS
*WPAS(FM) Pascagoula, MS
*KYPH(FM) East Helena, MT
*KUFM(FM) Missoula, MT
*WRYN(FM) Hickory, NC
*KGCD(FM) Lincoln, ND
*KHNE-FM Hastings, NE
*KDAI(FM) Scottsbluff, NE
*WEVO(FM) Concord, NH
*WWCJ(FM) Cape May, NJ
*WFDU(FM) Teaneck, NJ
*WWFM(FM) Trenton, NJ
*KANW(FM) Albuquerque, NM
*KQAI(FM) Roswell, NM
*WDWN(FM) Auburn, NY
*WBSU(FM) Brockport, NY
*WCID(FM) Friendship, NY
*WNYU-FM New York, NY
*WMHT-FM Schenectady, NY
*WJPZ-FM Syracuse, NY
*WOUC-FM Cambridge, OH
*WJJE(FM) Delaware, OH
*WOUL-FM Ironton, OH
*WNZN(FM) Lorain, OH
*WLMH(FM) Morrow, OH
*WUSO(FM) Springfield, OH
*WKSV(FM) Thompson, OH
*KWRI(FM) Bartlesville, OK
*KYCU(FM) Clinton, OK
*KXTH(FM) Seminole, OK
*KSMF(FM) Ashland, OR
*KMHD(FM) Gresham, OR
*KLFR(FM) Reedsport, OR
*KOHP(FM) Riley, OR
*WBYH(FM) Hawley, PA
*WFNM(FM) Lancaster, PA
*WLOG(FM) Markleysburg, PA
*WSFX(FM) Nanticoke, PA
*WYBF(FM) Radnor Township, PA
*WRXV(FM) State College, PA
*WXVU(FM) Villanova, PA
*WLJK(FM) Aiken, SC
*KVFL(FM) Pierre, SD
*KAUR(FM) Sioux Falls, SD

*KBHU-FM Spearfish, SD
*KJBB(FM) Watertown, SD
*WYLV(FM) Alcoa, TN
*WNAZ-FM Nashville, TN
*WDNX(FM) Olive Hill, TN
*KXLV(FM) Amarillo, TX
*KEOS(FM) College Station, TX
*KPKP(FM) Harts Bluff, TX
*KOHM(FM) Lubbock, TX
*KYFP(FM) Palestine, TX
*KSTX(FM) San Antonio, TX
*KSQX(FM) Springtown, TX
*KQXS(FM) Stephenville, TX
*KBYU-FM Provo, UT
*WWIP(FM) Cheriton, VA
*WCNV(FM) Heathsville, VA
*WVTF(FM) Roanoke, VA
*KFAE-FM Richland, WA
*WHAA(FM) Adams, WI
*WBSD(FM) Burlington, WI
*WSSW(FM) Platteville, WI
*KLWC(FM) Casper, WY
*KNWT(FM) Cody, WY
*KHOL(FM) Jackson, WY

89.3 mhz
*KATB(FM) Anchorage, AK
*WALN(FM) Carrollton, AL
*WLRH(FM) Huntsville, AL
*WZLM(FM) Jemison, AL
*WJIK(FM) Monroeville, AL
*KAYH(FM) Fayetteville, AR
*KKLT(FM) Texarkana, AR
*KAIH(FM) Lake Havasu City, AZ
*KNAQ(FM) Prescott, AZ
*KPFB(FM) Berkeley, CA
*KOHL(FM) Fremont, CA
*KVPR(FM) Fresno, CA
*KPJP(FM) Greenville, CA
*KCRI(FM) Indio, CA
*KNDZ(FM) McKinleyville, CA
*KAKX(FM) Mendocino, CA
*KLSI(FM) Moss Beach, CA
*KQEI-FM North Highlands, CA
*KPCC(FM) Pasadena, CA
*KPDO(FM) Pescadero, CA
*KRSF(FM) Ridgecrest, CA
*KMTG(FM) San Jose, CA
*KLFF-FM San Luis Obispo, CA
*KUVO(FM) Denver, CO
*KDNG(FM) Durango, CO
*KLBV(FM) Steamboat Springs, CO
*KTAW(FM) Walsenburg, CO
*WRTC-FM Hartford, CT
*WSGG(FM) Norfolk, CT
*WPFW(FM) Washington, DC
*WRMB(FM) Boynton Beach, FL
*WFLJ(FM) Frostproof, FL
*WAZQ(FM) Islamorada, FL
*WKFA(FM) Saint Catherine, FL
*WPIO(FM) Titusville, FL
*WBJY(FM) Americus, GA
*WRFG(FM) Atlanta, GA
*WECC-FM Folkston, GA
*KPRG(FM) Hagatna, GU
*KIPO(FM) Honolulu, HI
*KJMC(FM) Des Moines, IA
*KLGG(FM) Kellogg, ID
*KUOI-FM Moscow, ID
*WKKC(FM) Chicago, IL
*WDLM-FM East Moline, IL
*WNUR-FM Evanston, IL
*WZRS(FM) Pana, IL
*WIPA(FM) Pittsfield, IL
*WGNJ(FM) Saint Joseph, IL
*WJEL(FM) Indianapolis, IN
*WYTJ(FM) Linton, IN
*WIKV(FM) Plymouth, IN
*WZRP(FM) Richmond, IN
*WNKJ(FM) Hopkinsville, KY
*WFPL(FM) Louisville, KY
*WGCF(FM) Paducah, KY
*WRKF(FM) Baton Rouge, LA
*KUHN(FM) Golden Meadow, LA
*WAMH(FM) Amherst, MA
*WUMD(FM) North Dartmouth, MA

*WHSN(FM) Bangor, ME
*WRPB(FM) Benedicta, ME
*WMSJ(FM) Freeport, ME
*WTLI(FM) Bear Creek Township, MI
*WHFR(FM) Dearborn, MI
*WMSQ(FM) Marlette, MI
*WBLD(FM) Orchard Lake, MI
*WJKN-FM Spring Arbor, MI
*WGNB(FM) Zeeland, MI
*WIRC(FM) Ely, MN
*KCMP(FM) Northfield, MN
*KOPJ(FM) Sebeka, MN
*KRSW(FM) Worthington, MN
*KGNY(FM) Dixon, MO
*KTBJ(FM) Festus, MO
*KCUR-FM Kansas City, MO
*KIRL(FM) Osage Beach, MO
*WAII(FM) Hattiesburg, MS
*WATU(FM) Port Gibson, MS
*KYPB(FM) Big Timber, MT
*KLMT(FM) Billings, MT
*KLBZ(FM) Bozeman, MT
*WXYC(FM) Chapel Hill, NC
*WSOE(FM) Elon, NC
*WTEB(FM) New Bern, NC
*WZRI(FM) Spring Lake, NC
*WBFJ-FM Winston-Salem, NC
*KUND-FM Grand Forks, ND
*KZUM(FM) Lincoln, NE
*KXNE-FM Norfolk, NE
*KKNL(FM) Valentine, NE
*WNJB(FM) Bridgeton, NJ
*WSFS(FM) Freehold, NJ
*WDDM(FM) Hazlet, NJ
*WNJY(FM) Netcong, NJ
*KELP-FM Mesquite, NM
*KENM(FM) Tucumcari, NM
*KLKR(FM) Elko, NV
*WSKG-FM Binghamton, NY
*WRVH(FM) Clayton, NY
*WGSS(FM) Copiague, NY
*WGSU(FM) Geneseo, NY
*WLJP(FM) Monroe, NY
*WMHN(FM) Webster, NY
*WZCP(FM) Chillicothe, OH
*WCSB(FM) Cleveland, OH
*WYSM(FM) Lima, OH
*WYSZ(FM) Maumee, OH
*WZNP(FM) Newark, OH
*WMKV(FM) Reading, OH
*WYNS(FM) Waynesville, OH
*WKRW(FM) Wooster, OH
*KTHL(FM) Altus, OK
*KAZC(FM) Healdton, OK
*KALU(FM) Langston, OK
*KCCU(FM) Lawton, OK
*KSSO(FM) Norman, OK
*KLRB(FM) Stuart, OK
*KOGL(FM) Gleneden Beach, OR
*KVRA(FM) Sisters, OR
*KLOV(FM) Winchester, OR
*WJCS(FM) Allentown, PA
*WRTJ(FM) Coatesville, PA
*WQED-FM Pittsburgh, PA
*WRDV(FM) Warminster, PA
*WJVP(FM) Culebra, PR
*WSCI(FM) Charleston, SC
*WRFE(FM) Chesterfield, SC
*WLFJ-FM Greenville, SC
*KBHE-FM Rapid City, SD
*WMKW(FM) Crossville, TN
*WAJJ(FM) McKenzie, TN
*WYPL(FM) Memphis, TN
*KPBD(FM) Big Spring, TX
*KPBE(FM) Brownwood, TX
*KNON(FM) Dallas, TX
*KKFC(FM) Hart, TX
*KHCP(FM) Paris, TX
*KNAR(FM) San Angelo, TX
*KXBJ(FM) Victoria, TX
*KUSL(FM) Richfield, UT
*WVTU(FM) Charlottesville, VA
*WJYA(FM) Emporia, VA
*KJCF(FM) Asotin, WA
*KUGS(FM) Bellingham, WA

*KRYA(FM) Glenoma, WA
*KAOS(FM) Olympia, WA
*KVIX(FM) Port Angeles, WA
*KBNO-FM White Salmon, WA
*WPNE(FM) Green Bay, WI
*WWLA(FM) South Charleston, WV
*KTDX(FM) Laramie, WY
*KRWY(FM) Rawlins, WY

89.5 mhz
*KABN-FM Kasilof, AK
*WBFR(FM) Birmingham, AL
*WGTF(FM) Dothan, AL
*WJAU(FM) Lincoln, AL
*WRNF(FM) Selma, AL
*KCAC(FM) Camden, AR
*KBMJ(FM) Heber Springs, AR
*KJZA(FM) Drake, AZ
*KBAQ-FM Phoenix, AZ
*KRCI(FM) Pinetop-Lakeside, AZ
*KBES(FM) Ceres, CA
*KARQ(FM) East Sonora, CA
*KSMC(FM) Moraga, CA
*KVMR(FM) Nevada City, CA
*KLFH(FM) Ojai, CA
*KHAA(FM) Orleans, CA
*KPBS-FM San Diego, CA
*KPOO(FM) San Francisco, CA
*KSBX(FM) Santa Barbara, CA
*KAIB(FM) Shafter, CA
*KPRA(FM) Ukiah, CA
*KXRD(FM) Victorville, CA
*KTCF(FM) Dolores, CO
*KPRN(FM) Grand Junction, CO
*KTSC-FM Pueblo, CO
*KICO(FM) Rico, CO
*KILE-FM Woodland Park, CO
*WPKN(FM) Bridgeport, CT
*WKSG(FM) Cedar Creek, FL
*WGSG(FM) Mayo, FL
*WFIT(FM) Melbourne, FL
*WSRX(FM) Naples, FL
*WPCS(FM) Pensacola, FL
*WYFK(FM) Columbus, GA
*WNGU(FM) Dahlonega, GA
*WYFS(FM) Savannah, GA
*WQAI(FM) Thomson, GA
*WYFW(FM) Winder, GA
*WHKE(FM) Cedar Falls, IA
*KLCD(FM) Decorah, IA
*KEGR(FM) Fort Dodge, IA
*KCNJ(FM) Oskaloosa, IA
*KTSY(FM) Caldwell, ID
*KLRI(FM) Rigby, ID
*WNIJ(FM) De Kalb, IL
*WJMU(FM) Decatur, IL
*WARW(FM) Dorsey, IL
*WEFI(FM) Effingham, IL
*WSPI(FM) Ellsworth, IL
*WIUW(FM) Warsaw, IL
*WBSB(FM) Anderson, IN
*WBEW(FM) Chesterton, IN
*WFCI(FM) Franklin, IN
*WWTS(FM) Logansport, IN
*WBKE-FM North Manchester, IN
*WCIX(FM) Versailles, IN
*KHCD(FM) Salina, KS
*WKMT(FM) Fulton, KY
*WKPB(FM) Henderson, KY
*KITA(FM) Iota, LA
*KYFL(FM) Monroe, LA
*WJCI(FM) Baptist Village, MA
*WNCK(FM) Nantucket, MA
*WSKB(FM) Westfield, MA
*WSCL(FM) Salisbury, MD
*WWTP(FM) Augusta, ME
*WMWR(FM) Lincoln, ME
*WAHS(FM) Auburn Hills, MI
*WCMU-FM Mount Pleasant, MI
*WOVI(FM) Novi, MI
*WOFR(FM) Schoolcraft, MI
*KBHG(FM) Alexandria, MN
*WYNJ(FM) Blackduck, MN
*WJRF(FM) Duluth, MN
*KBPG(FM) Montevideo, MN
*KQAL(FM) Winona, MN

*KNLH(FM) Cedar Hill, MO
*KOPN(FM) Columbia, MO
*KCFV(FM) Ferguson, MO
*KOKS(FM) Poplar Bluff, MO
*KITG(FM) Sarcoxie, MO
*WMAE-FM Booneville, MS
*WPRG(FM) Columbia, MS
*WYAZ(FM) Yazoo City, MS
*KPJH(FM) Polson, MT
*KYPF(FM) Stanford, MT
*WTJY(FM) Asheboro, NC
*WLPS-FM Lumberton, NC
*WKBM-FM Wallace, NC
*KPPR(FM) Williston, ND
*KMHB(FM) Seward, NE
*WKVP(FM) Cherry Hill, NJ
*WSOU(FM) South Orange, NJ
*KENW-FM Portales, NM
*KVLK(FM) Socorro, NM
*KWLH(FM) Beatty, NV
*KLAP(FM) Gerlach, NV
*KCNV(FM) Las Vegas, NV
*KJIV(FM) Reno, NV
*WCOF(FM) Arcade, NY
*WSLU(FM) Canton, NY
*WSLL(FM) Saranac Lake, NY
*WUNY(FM) Utica, NY
*WBCY(FM) Archbold, OH
*WCVV(FM) Belpre, OH
*WHVY(FM) Coshocton, OH
*WDPS(FM) Dayton, OH
*WQRP(FM) Dayton, OH
*WHSS(FM) Hamilton, OH
*WFOT(FM) Lexington, OH
*WVMS(FM) Sandusky, OH
*WZWP(FM) West Union, OH
*KCNP(FM) Ada, OK
*KJCC(FM) Carnegie, OK
*KWGS(FM) Tulsa, OK
*KORV(FM) Ashland, OR
*KSKX(FM) Chemult, OR
*KTEC(FM) Klamath Falls, OR
*KEFS(FM) North Powder, OR
*KPFR(FM) Pine Grove, OR
*KTCB(FM) Tillamook, OR
*WDNR(FM) Chester, PA
*WAWN(FM) Franklin, PA
*WITF-FM Harrisburg, PA
*WNTE(FM) Mansfield, PA
*WWPJ(FM) Pen Argyl, PA
*KTUT(FM) Frankfort, SD
*KDKO(FM) Lake Andes, SD
*KLND(FM) Little Eagle, SD
*WETS(FM) Johnson City, TN
*WMOT(FM) Murfreesboro, TN
*KMFA(FM) Austin, TX
*KZBJ(FM) Bay City, TX
*KFCH(FM) Childress, TX
*KEPX(FM) Eagle Pass, TX
*KKLY(FM) El Paso, TX
*KBMM(FM) Odessa, TX
*KLUX(FM) Robstown, TX
*KTOT(FM) Spearman, TX
*KVNE(FM) Tyler, TX
*KYQX(FM) Weatherford, TX
*KMOC(FM) Wichita Falls, TX
*KAGJ(FM) Ephraim, UT
*KUSR(FM) Logan, UT
*KAER(FM) Saint George, UT
*WHRV(FM) Norfolk, VA
*WWED(FM) Spotsylvania, VA
*WVPR(FM) Windsor, VT
*KEWU-FM Cheney, WA
*KJVH(FM) Longview, WA
*KNHC(FM) Seattle, WA
*KSOH(FM) Wapato, WA
*WCLQ(FM) Wausau, WI
*WAUA(FM) Petersburg, WV
*KGCY(FM) Esterbrook, WY
*KWRR(FM) Ethete, WY

89.7 mhz
*KGCF(FM) Juneau, AK
*KXKM(FM) McCarthy, AK
*KUCB(FM) Unalaska, AK
*WJHO(FM) Alexander City, AL

*KBHN(FM) Booneville, AR
*KUAP(FM) Pine Bluff, AR
*KMOA(FM) Nu'uuli, AS
*KRMH(FM) Red Mesa, AZ
*KNCA(FM) Burney, CA
*KLRS(FM) Lodi, CA
*KFJC(FM) Los Altos, CA
*KLVM(FM) Prunedale, CA
*KGBM(FM) Randsburg, CA
*KSGN(FM) Riverside, CA
*KHFR(FM) Santa Maria, CA
*KARM(FM) Visalia, CA
*KEPC(FM) Colorado Springs, CO
*KXWA(FM) Loveland, CO
*KTPS(FM) Pagosa Springs, CO
*KJWA(FM) Rye, CO
*KADE(FM) Salida, CO
*WDJW(FM) Somers, CT
*WKCP(FM) Miami, FL
*WJLU(FM) New Smyrna Beach, FL
*WVFS(FM) Tallahassee, FL
*WUSF(FM) Tampa, FL
*WMUM-FM Cochran, GA
*WGIA(FM) Damascus, GA
*WTXR(FM) Toccoa Falls, GA
*WWBM(FM) Yates, GA
*KIWR(FM) Council Bluffs, IA
*KDUB(FM) Dubuque, IA
*KRUI-FM Iowa City, IA
*KRNF(FM) Montezuma, IA
*KRNL-FM Mount Vernon, IA
*WCBW-FM East St. Louis, IL
*WONU(FM) Kankakee, IL
*WLWM(FM) Macomb, IL
*WBMV(FM) Mount Vernon, IL
*WLUJ(FM) Springfield, IL
*WRGF(FM) Greenfield, IN
*WHWE(FM) Howe, IN
*WKWH(FM) Liberty, IN
*WUBS(FM) South Bend, IN
*WISU(FM) Terre Haute, IN
*WTUR(FM) Upland, IN
*KNBU(FM) Baldwin City, KS
*KANH(FM) Emporia, KS
*KBDA(FM) Great Bend, KS
*KHYS(FM) Hays, KS
*KCPK(FM) Paola, KS
*WAAJ(FM) Benton, KY
*WNKU(FM) Highland Heights, KY
*WYLC(FM) Jackson, KY
*WDCL-FM Somerset, KY
*KAVK(FM) Many, LA
*KBIO(FM) Natchitoches, LA
*WGBH(FM) Boston, MA
*WTMD(FM) Towson, MD
*WTBP(FM) Bath, ME
*WMED(FM) Calais, ME
*WMHB(FM) Waterville, ME
*WTAC(FM) Burton, MI
*WJOJ(FM) Harrisville, MI
*WLNZ(FM) Lansing, MI
*WLMN(FM) Manistee, MI
*WOCR(FM) Olivet, MI
*KBSB(FM) Bemidji, MN
*KCMF(FM) Fergus Falls, MN
*WLSN(FM) Grand Marais, MN
*KMSU(FM) Mankato, MN
*KUMM(FM) Morris, MN
*KPCS(FM) Princeton, MN
*KGNX(FM) Ballwin, MO
*KOZO(FM) Branson, MO
*KJCV(FM) Country Club, MO
*KKTR(FM) Kirksville, MO
*KCVQ(FM) Knob Noster, MO
*KNLP(FM) Potosi, MO
*KMNR(FM) Rolla, MO
*WPAE(FM) Centreville, MS
*WZKM(FM) Waynesboro, MS
*KBIL(FM) Park City, MT
*KQLR(FM) Whitehall, MT
*WGIW(FM) Pilot Mountain, NC
*WCPE(FM) Raleigh, NC
*WDVV(FM) Wilmington, NC
*KNRI(FM) Bismarck, ND
*WNJN-FM Atlantic City, NJ
*WDVR(FM) Delaware Township, NJ

*WRDR(FM) Freehold Township, NJ
*WGLS-FM Glassboro, NJ
*KUUT(FM) Farmington, NM
*KMBN(FM) Las Cruces, NM
*KTDB(FM) Ramah, NM
*KWNM(FM) Winnemucca, NV
*WALF(FM) Alfred, NY
*WKVJ(FM) Dannemora, NY
*WEOS(FM) Geneva, NY
*WITR(FM) Henrietta, NY
*WNJA(FM) Jamestown, NY
*WFGB(FM) Kingston, NY
*WOBH(FM) Lindenhurst, NY
*WFWO(FM) Medina, NY
*WRHO(FM) Oneonta, NY
*WSSK(FM) Saratoga Springs, NY
*WRUC(FM) Schenectady, NY
*WNOC(FM) Bowling Green, OH
*WOSU-FM Columbus, OH
*WTKC(FM) Findlay, OH
*WKSU-FM Kent, OH
*KJTH(FM) Ponca City, OK
*KDBQ(FM) Rattan, OK
*KWYA(FM) Astoria, OR
*KLCC(FM) Eugene, OR
*KOJD(FM) John Day, OR
*KOTD(FM) The Dalles, OR
*WQEJ(FM) Johnstown, PA
*WVYA(FM) Williamsport, PA
*WRTU(FM) San Juan, PR
*WMHK(FM) Columbia, SC
*KUSD(FM) Vermillion, SD
*WDYN-FM Chattanooga, TN
*WAWI(FM) Lawrenceburg, TN
*WAUV(FM) Ripley, TN
*KACU(FM) Abilene, TX
*KACC(FM) Alvin, TX
*KTXB(FM) Beaumont, TX
*KUBJ(FM) Brenham, TX
*KHPS(FM) Camp Wood, TX
*KJMA(FM) Floresville, TX
*KVRK(FM) Sanger, TX
*KEQX(FM) Stephenville, TX
*WAUQ(FM) Charles City, VA
*WVLS(FM) Monterey, VA
*KWSR(FM) Cle Elum, WA
*KMWS(FM) Mount Vernon, WA
*KWFJ(FM) Roy, WA
*KWWS(FM) Walla Walla, WA
*KAUC(FM) West Clarkston, WA
*WUEC(FM) Eau Claire, WI
*WUWM(FM) Milwaukee, WI
*WHND(FM) Sister Bay, WI
*WLOL-FM Morgantown, WV
*WSHC(FM) Shepherdstown, WV
*WVGV(FM) West Union, WV
*KAXG(FM) Gillette, WY

89.9 mhz
*KAUG(FM) Anchorage, AK
*KDLG-FM Dillingham, AK
*KUAC(FM) Fairbanks, AK
*KHGO(FM) Homer, AK
*KINU(FM) Kotzebue, AK
*WTBB(FM) Gadsden, AL
*WTSU(FM) Montgomery-Troy, AL
*WAKD(FM) Sheffield, AL
*KVMN(FM) Cave City, AR
*KVIR(FM) Bullhead City, AZ
*KZAI(FM) Coolidge, AZ
*KJTA(FM) Flagstaff, AZ
*KNDL(FM) Angwin, CA
*KJCU(FM) Fort Bragg, CA
*KCRH(FM) Hayward, CA
*KWDS(FM) Kettleman City, CA
*KEFR(FM) Le Grand, CA
*KFER(FM) Santa Cruz, CA
*KCRW(FM) Santa Monica, CA
*KFRS(FM) Soledad, CA
*KTMH(FM) Colona, CO
*KFRY(FM) Pueblo, CO
*KTAD(FM) Sterling, CO
*KPRE(FM) Vail, CO
*WQTQ(FM) Hartford, CT
*WAPJ(FM) Torrington, CT
*WWEB(FM) Wallingford, CT

*WJCT-FM Jacksonville, FL
*WUCF-FM Orlando, FL
*WCNO(FM) Palm City, FL
*WJTF(FM) Panama City, FL
*WTFH(FM) Helen, GA
*KAYP(FM) Burlington, IA
*KZNJ(FM) Marion, IA
*KWAR(FM) Waverly, IA
*KBSK(FM) McCall, ID
*KYMS(FM) Rathdrum, ID
*KMRR(FM) Rexburg, ID
*KAWZ(FM) Twin Falls, ID
*WLCA(FM) Godfrey, IL
*WLKL(FM) Mattoon, IL
*WCBU(FM) Peoria, IL
*WTMH(FM) Smithboro, IL
*WISG(FM) Clifford, IN
*WOJC(FM) Crothersville, IN
*WOMB(FM) Ellettsville, IN
*WHLP(FM) Hanna, IN
*WBRO(FM) Marengo, IN
*WATI(FM) Vincennes, IN
*WYBV(FM) Wakarusa, IN
*WHPL(FM) West Lafayette, IN
*KAIG(FM) Dodge City, KS
*KYAH(FM) Manhattan, KS
*KRPS(FM) Pittsburg, KS
*WRVG(FM) Georgetown, KY
*WSOF-FM Madisonville, KY
*KLXA-FM Alexandria, LA
*WWNO(FM) New Orleans, LA
*KSJY(FM) Saint Martinville, LA
*KDAQ(FM) Shreveport, LA
*WSCB(FM) Springfield, MA
*WOEL-FM Elkton, MD
*WMTB-FM Emmittsburg, MD
*WERU-FM Blue Hill, ME
*WAYO-FM Benton Harbor, MI
*WAYG(FM) Grand Rapids, MI
*WTHS(FM) Holland, MI
*WKDS(FM) Kalamazoo, MI
*WLJN-FM Traverse City, MI
*WHWG(FM) Trout Lake, MI
*KRGM(FM) Marshall, MN
*KMOJ(FM) Minneapolis, MN
*KRPR(FM) Rochester, MN
*KQRB(FM) Windom, MN
*KGTR(FM) Albany, MO
*KGNA-FM Arnold, MO
*KCVY(FM) Cabool, MO
*KMCV(FM) High Point, MO
*KAUF(FM) Kennett, MO
*KGNV(FM) Washington, MO
*WMAB-FM Mississippi State, MS
*KYPC(FM) Colstrip, MT
*KGPR(FM) Great Falls, MT
*KUKL(FM) Kalispell, MT
*KBGA(FM) Missoula, MT
*WDAV(FM) Davidson, NC
*WRVS-FM Elizabeth City, NC
*KDVI(FM) Devils Lake, ND
*KDPR(FM) Dickinson, ND
*KJTW(FM) Jamestown, ND
*KNHU(FM) Humboldt, NE
*KFLV(FM) Wilber, NE
*WNJM(FM) Manahawkin, NJ
*WJPH(FM) Woodbine, NJ
*KYCM(FM) Alamogordo, NM
*KUNM(FM) Albuquerque, NM
*KNIZ(FM) Gallup, NM
*KORU(FM) Garapan-Saipan, NP
*KQNV(FM) Fallon, NV
*WFBF(FM) Buffalo, NY
*WOPG(FM) Esperance, NY
*WKCR-FM New York, NY
*WXLG(FM) North Creek, NY
*WSUF(FM) Noyack, NY
*WINO(FM) Odessa, NY
*WRVO(FM) Oswego, NY
*WDPG(FM) Greenville, OH
*WLHS(FM) West Chester, OH
*KWKL(FM) Grandfield, OK
*KTHF(FM) Hammon, OK
*KANC(FM) Baker City, OR
*KQAC(FM) Portland, OR
*KKJA(FM) Redmond, OR

*WVIA-FM Scranton, PA
*WTLR(FM) State College, PA
*WJWJ-FM Beaufort, SC
*KSRJ(FM) Arlington, SD
*KQFR(FM) Rapid City, SD
*WDVX(FM) Clinton, TN
*WEVL(FM) Memphis, TN
*WAYW(FM) New Johnsonville, TN
*KACV-FM Amarillo, TX
*KDRG(FM) Breckenridge, TX
*KLGS(FM) College Station, TX
*KTLZ(FM) Cuero, TX
*KDLI(FM) Del Rio, TX
*KBNL(FM) Laredo, TX
*KKVI(FM) Overland, TX
*KTSW(FM) San Marcos, TX
*KBDE(FM) Temple, TX
*KCEU(FM) Price, UT
*WPER(FM) Culpeper, VA
*WFFC(FM) Ferrum, VA
*WMRL(FM) Lexington, VA
*WVRU(FM) Radford, VA
*WNRS-FM Sweet Briar, VA
*WCMD-FM Barre, VT
*WNGF(FM) Swanton, VT
*KGRG-FM Auburn, WA
*KASB(FM) Bellevue, WA
*KGHP(FM) Gig Harbor, WA
*KPLW(FM) Wenatchee, WA
*WHSA(FM) Brule, WI
*WVFL(FM) Fond du Lac, WI
*WORT(FM) Madison, WI
*WWSP(FM) Stevens Point, WI
*WVWV(FM) Huntington, WV
*WVNP(FM) Wheeling, WV
*KUWI(FM) Rawlins, WY
*KVLZ(FM) Sheridan, WY
*KRWT(FM) West Laramie, WY

90.1 mhz
*KRAW(FM) Sterling, AK
*WJOU(FM) Huntsville, AL
*WDLG(FM) Thomasville, AL
KXRL(FM) Cherry Valley, AR
*KBNV(FM) Fayetteville, AR
*KLRO(FM) Hot Springs, AR
*KRMB(FM) Bisbee, AZ
*KCHB(FM) Kaibito, AZ
*KWFH(FM) Parker, AZ
*KJZP(FM) Prescott, AZ
*KTQX(FM) Bakersfield, CA
*KBPK(FM) Buena Park, CA
*KZFR(FM) Chico, CA
*KCBX(FM) San Luis Obispo, CA
*KZSU(FM) Stanford, CA
*KYCC(FM) Stockton, CA
*KSAK(FM) Walnut, CA
*KLRD(FM) Yucaipa, CA
*KCFR-FM Denver, CO
*KHCO(FM) Hayden, CO
*KUTE(FM) Ignacio, CO
*KJLI(FM) La Junta, CO
*KPKN(FM) Pitkin, CO
*WRXC(FM) Shelton, CT
*WGSK(FM) South Kent, CT
*WECS(FM) Willimantic, CT
*WCSP-FM Washington, DC
*WTJT(FM) Baker, FL
*WGCU-FM Fort Myers, FL
*WJUF(FM) Inverness, FL
*WKWR(FM) Key West, FL
*WFRU(FM) Quincy, FL
*WABE(FM) Atlanta, GA
*WXIV(FM) Lumpkin, GA
*WXVS(FM) Waycross, GA
*WOI-FM Ames, IA
*KNWO(FM) Cottonwood, ID
*WTSG(FM) Carlinville, IL
*WEFT(FM) Champaign, IL
*WMBI-FM Chicago, IL
*WAWJ(FM) Marion, IL
*WFYI-FM Indianapolis, IN
*KXJH(FM) Linton, IN
*WENS(FM) Wadesville, IN
*KHCC-FM Hutchinson, KS
*WHMR(FM) Ledbetter, KY

*WJSO(FM) Pikeville, KY
*WJCR-FM Upton, KY
*WYCM(FM) Charlton, MA
*WRYP(FM) Wellfleet, MA
*WCAI(FM) Woods Hole, MA
*WMEA(FM) Portland, ME
*WUCX-FM Bay City, MI
*WXPZ(FM) Clyde Township, MI
*WCWB(FM) Coldwater, MI
*WHBP(FM) Harbor Springs, MI
*WNMU-FM Marquette, MI
*WLSO(FM) Sault Ste. Marie, MI
*KNSE(FM) Austin, MN
*KOJB(FM) Cass Lake, MN
*KSJR-FM Collegeville, MN
*WGPO(FM) Grand Portage, MN
*KADU(FM) Hibbing, MN
*KSRQ(FM) Thief River Falls, MN
*KKFI(FM) Kansas City, MO
*KBKC(FM) Moberly, MO
*KRHS(FM) Overland, MO
*KSCV(FM) Springfield, MO
*WMPR(FM) Jackson, MS
*KBLW(FM) Billings, MT
*KNMC(FM) Havre, MT
*KHLV(FM) Helena, MT
*KYPM(FM) Livingston, MT
*WZPE(FM) Bath, NC
*WCCE(FM) Buie's Creek, NC
*WNAA(FM) Greensboro, NC
*WJKA(FM) Jacksonville, NC
*WOVV(FM) Ocracoke, NC
*WZRU(FM) Roanoke Rapids, NC
*KSIH(FM) Belcourt, ND
*KNEF(FM) Franklin, NE
*KFKX(FM) Hastings, NE
*KRDR(FM) Red River, NM
*KRLU(FM) Roswell, NM
*KQMC(FM) Hawthorne, NV
*WIFF(FM) Binghamton, NY
*WGMC(FM) Greece, NY
*WRCU-FM Hamilton, NY
*WITH(FM) Ithaca, NY
*WMHQ(FM) Malone, NY
*WMFU(FM) Mount Hope, NY
*WJZZ(FM) North Salem, NY
*WUSB(FM) Stony Brook, NY
*WKWV(FM) Watertown, NY
*WOHC(FM) Chillicothe, OH
*WORI(FM) Delhi Hills, OH
*WXML(FM) Upper Sandusky, OH
*WOUZ(FM) Zanesville, OH
*KOCU(FM) Altus, OK
*KCSC(FM) Edmond, OK
*KSOR(FM) Ashland, OR
*KOBN(FM) Burns, OR
*KQHR(FM) Hood River, OR
*KKLP(FM) La Pine, OR
*KAJC(FM) Salem, OR
*WIUP-FM Indiana, PA
*WPSX(FM) Kane, PA
*WVMN(FM) New Castle, PA
*WRTI(FM) Philadelphia, PA
*WCIT-FM Trout Run, PA
*WJDZ(FM) Pastillo, PR
*WHMC-FM Conway, SC
*WEPR(FM) Greenville, SC
*KEEA(FM) Aberdeen, SD
*KILI(FM) Porcupine, SD
*KSFS(FM) Sioux Falls, SD
*WKNP(FM) Jackson, TN
*WKTS(FM) Kingston, TN
*WZYZ(FM) Spencer, TN
*KERA(FM) Dallas, TX
*KPFT(FM) Houston, TX
*KTXI(FM) Ingram, TX
*KAMY(FM) Lubbock, TX
*KPBJ(FM) Midland, TX
*KSAU(FM) Nacogdoches, TX
*KUTX(FM) San Angelo, TX
*KSYM-FM San Antonio, TX
*KZMU(FM) Moab, UT
*KUER(FM) Salt Lake City, UT
*WMVE(FM) Chase City, VA
*WKYV(FM) Colonial Heights, VA
*WJCN(FM) Nassawadox, VA

*WDCE(FM) Richmond, VA
*WPVA(FM) Waynesboro, VA
*WIVH(FM) Christiansted, VI
*WRUV(FM) Burlington, VT
*WOXM(FM) Middlebury, VT
*KZFL(FM) Glenoma, WA
*KSVU(FM) Hamilton, WA
*KPLI(FM) Olympia, WA
*KQWS(FM) Omak, WA
*KOLU(FM) Pasco, WA
*KNWP(FM) Port Angeles, WA
*KUPS(FM) Tacoma, WA
*WORQ(FM) Green Bay, WI
*WVCS(FM) Owen, WI
*WRPN-FM Ripon, WI
*WCKU(FM) Clarksburg, WV
*WPWV(FM) Princeton, WV
*KUWL(FM) Laramie, WY
*KUWP(FM) Powell, WY

90.3 mhz
*KNBA(FM) Anchorage, AK
*KMCG(FM) McGrath, AK
*KGCU(FM) Port Alsworth, AK
*KSPM(FM) Sand Point, AK
*WBHM(FM) Birmingham, AL
*WDYF(FM) Dothan, AL
*KCAV(FM) Marshall, AR
*KLFS(FM) Van Buren, AR
*KNAG(FM) Grand Canyon, AZ
*KBMH(FM) Holbrook, AZ
*KFLR-FM Phoenix, AZ
*KMRO(FM) Camarillo, CA
*KPCV(FM) Coachella, CA
*KDVS(FM) Davis, CA
*KFNO(FM) Fresno, CA
*KLAI(FM) Laytonville, CA
*KAZU(FM) Pacific Grove, CA
*KUSF(FM) San Francisco, CA
*KZET(FM) Cortez, CO
*KBUT(FM) Crested Butte, CO
*KMPB(FM) Frisco, CO
*KLFV(FM) Grand Junction, CO
*WWPT(FM) Westport, CT
*WIGW(FM) Eustis, FL
*WJLH(FM) Flagler Beach, FL
*WAFG(FM) Fort Lauderdale, FL
*WYJC(FM) Greenville, FL
*WLVF-FM Haines City, FL
*WEJF(FM) Palm Bay, FL
*WAEF(FM) Cordele, GA
*WHCJ(FM) Savannah, GA
*WEZG(FM) Tignall, GA
*WBTB(FM) Young Harris, GA
*KCIF(FM) Hilo, HI
*KTUH(FM) Honolulu, HI
*KWIT(FM) Sioux City, IA
*KBSU-FM Boise, ID
*KZJB(FM) Pocatello, ID
*WJWR(FM) Bloomington, IL
*WUSI(FM) Olney, IL
*WQUB(FM) Quincy, IL
*WVIK(FM) Rock Island, IL
*WKJD(FM) Columbus, IN
*WFOF(FM) Covington, IN
*WBCL(FM) Fort Wayne, IN
*KJVL(FM) Chanute, KS
*KNJT(FM) Coldwater, KS
*KBUZ(FM) Topeka, KS
*WMKY(FM) Morehead, KY
*WBOO(FM) Morganfield, KY
*WKWC(FM) Owensboro, KY
*WBRH(FM) Baton Rouge, LA
*KYLC(FM) Lake Charles, LA
*KEDM(FM) Monroe, LA
*WCCT-FM Harwich, MA
*WZBC(FM) Newton, MA
*WAIJ(FM) Grantsville, MD
*WDIH(FM) Salisbury, MD
*WUMI(FM) Newberry, MI
*WBLV(FM) Twin Lake, MI
*KFAI(FM) Minneapolis, MN
*KCCD(FM) Moorhead, MN
*KMKL(FM) North Branch, MN
*KCKE(FM) Chillicothe, MO
*KWUR(FM) Clayton, MO

*KGNN-FM Cuba, MO
*KNLG(FM) New Bloomfield, MO
*KGSP(FM) Parkville, MO
*KLUH(FM) Poplar Bluff, MO
*KCRL(FM) Sunrise Beach, MO
*WMAH-FM Biloxi, MS
*WMAV-FM Oxford, MS
*KJFT(FM) Arlee, MT
*KMGT(FM) Circle, MT
*KLSN(FM) Four Corners, MT
*KMZO(FM) Hamilton, MT
*WFHE(FM) Hickory, NC
*WKNS(FM) Kinston, NC
*WBFY(FM) Pinehurst, NC
*KMNE-FM Bassett, NE
*KRNU(FM) Lincoln, NE
*KEIS(FM) York, NE
*WNJZ(FM) Cape May Court House, NJ
*WRPR(FM) Mahwah, NJ
*WVPH(FM) Piscataway, NJ
*WNJO(FM) Toms River, NJ
*WKNJ-FM Union Township, NJ
*WMSC(FM) Upper Montclair, NJ
*KELU(FM) Clovis, NM
*KLGQ(FM) Grants, NM
*WAMC-FM Albany, NY
*WVVA(FM) Auburn, NY
*WKRB(FM) Brooklyn, NY
*WCIH(FM) Elmira, NY
*WHPC(FM) Garden City, NY
*WJSL(FM) Houghton, NY
*WHCR-FM New York, NY
*WDFH(FM) Ossining, NY
*WAIH(FM) Potsdam, NY
*WRUN-FM Remsen, NY
*WRVD(FM) Syracuse, NY
*WCDR-FM Cedarville, OH
*WCPN(FM) Cleveland, OH
*WOTL(FM) Toledo, OH
*KLCU(FM) Ardmore, OK
*KHEV(FM) Fairview, OK
*KVRS(FM) Lawton, OK
*KTVR-FM La Grande, OR
*KSLC(FM) McMinnville, OR
*KLON(FM) Rockaway Beach, OR
*KWBX(FM) Salem, OR
*KZRI(FM) Welches, OR
*WESS(FM) East Stroudsburg, PA
*WJTL(FM) Lancaster, PA
*WARC(FM) Meadville, PA
*WFTE(FM) Mount Cobb, PA
*WXLV(FM) Schnecksville, PA
*WRIU(FM) Kingston, RI
*WSSB-FM Orangeburg, SC
*WRBK(FM) Richburg, SC
*KASD(FM) Rapid City, SD
*WCSK(FM) Kingsport, TN
*WUTK-FM Knoxville, TN
*WUTM(FM) Martin, TN
*WPLN-FM Nashville, TN
*WLNB(FM) Wartburg, TN
*KBUB(FM) Brownwood, TX
*KEDT-FM Corpus Christi, TX
*KWCB(FM) Graford, TX
*KBJS(FM) Jacksonville, TX
*KYRQ(FM) Natalia, TX
*KPHS(FM) Plains, TX
*KSGU(FM) Saint George, UT
*WOKG(FM) Galax, VA
*WHRO-FM Norfolk, VA
*WRXT(FM) Roanoke, VA
*KWYQ(FM) Longview, WA
*KEXP-FM Seattle, WA
*KPBZ(FM) Spokane, WA
*KNWY(FM) Yakima, WA
*WBCR-FM Beloit, WI
*WHLA(FM) La Crosse, WI
*WJWD(FM) Marshall, WI
*WRST-FM Oshkosh, WI
*WHBM(FM) Park Falls, WI
*WVPG(FM) Parkersburg, WV
*KCSP-FM Casper, WY
*KUWJ(FM) Jackson, WY
*KWYC(FM) Orchard Valley, WY

90.5 mhz
*KXGA(FM) Glennallen, AK
*KLSF(FM) Juneau, AK
*KWMD(FM) Kasilof, AK
*KAOG(FM) Jonesboro, AR
*KLRE-FM Little Rock, AR
*KNLL(FM) Nashville, AR
*KPPO(FM) Mapusaga, AS
*KUAT-FM Tucson, AZ
*KHSU-FM Arcata, CA
*KIBC(FM) Burney, CA
*KVHS(FM) Concord, CA
*KYCI(FM) Firebaugh, CA
*KADV(FM) Modesto, CA
*KWMR(FM) Point Reyes Station, CA
*KSJS(FM) San Jose, CA
*KGDP-FM Santa Maria, CA
*KKTO(FM) Tahoe City, CA
*KVOV(FM) Carbondale, CO
*KTLF(FM) Colorado Springs, CO
*KCSU-FM Fort Collins, CO
*WPKT(FM) Meriden, CT
*WVUM(FM) Coral Gables, FL
*WREH(FM) Cypress Quarters, FL
*WYFB(FM) Gainesville, FL
*WANM(FM) Tallahassee, FL
*WBVM(FM) Tampa, FL
*WUOG(FM) Athens, GA
*WPWB(FM) Byron, GA
*WCOQ(FM) Colquitt, GA
*WFRC(FM) Columbus, GA
*WTLD(FM) Jesup, GA
*WGCN(FM) Nashville, GA
*KPHL(FM) Pahala, HI
*KHOE(FM) Fairfield, IA
*KOSK(FM) Oskaloosa, IA
*KAIO(FM) Idaho Falls, ID
*WYER(FM) Carmi, IL
*WRTE(FM) Chicago, IL
*WAPO(FM) Mount Vernon, IL
*WMTH(FM) Park Ridge, IL
*WNIU(FM) Rockford, IL
*WSCT(FM) Springfield, IL
*WRTW(FM) Crown Point, IN
*WIKL(FM) Greencastle, IN
*WWDS(FM) Muncie, IN
*WPUM(FM) Rensselaer, IN
*KBMP(FM) Enterprise, KS
*KZNA(FM) Hill City, KS
*KRBW(FM) Ottawa, KS
*WVHM(FM) Benton, KY
*WUOL(FM) Louisville, KY
*WTHL(FM) Somerset, KY
*KTLN(FM) Thibodaux, LA
*WSMA(FM) Scituate, MA
*WICN(FM) Worcester, MA
*WCRH(FM) Williamsport, MD
*WKHS(FM) Worton, MD
*WMEP(FM) Camden, ME
*WWLN(FM) Lincoln, ME
*WRGY(FM) Rangeley, ME
*WKAR-FM East Lansing, MI
*WPHN(FM) Gaylord, MI
*KBXE(FM) Bagley, MN
*KDNI(FM) Duluth, MN
*KRFG(FM) Glenwood, MN
*KGAC(FM) Saint Peter, MN
*KWWC-FM Columbia, MO
*KXCV(FM) Maryville, MO
*KAUD(FM) Mexico, MO
*KCGR(FM) Oran, MO
*KSMS-FM Point Lookout, MO
*WCSO(FM) Columbus, MS
*WQVI(FM) Forest, MS
*WAQL(FM) McComb, MS
*KJLF(FM) Butte, MT
*KUFL(FM) Libby, MT
*KBWY(FM) Pryor, MT
*WASU-FM Boone, NC
*WBUX(FM) Buxton, NC
*WWCU(FM) Cullowhee, NC
*WYQS(FM) Mars Hill, NC
*WZRN(FM) Norlina, NC
*WDCC(FM) Sanford, NC
*WWIL-FM Wilmington, NC
*WSNC(FM) Winston-Salem, NC

*WAJC(FM) Zebulon, NC
*KCND(FM) Bismarck, ND
*WSPS(FM) Concord, NH
*WPEA(FM) Exeter, NH
*WVFA(FM) Lebanon, NH
*WWFP(FM) Brigantine, NJ
*WXGN(FM) Egg Harbor Township, NJ
*WCVH(FM) Flemington, NJ
*WBJB-FM Lincroft, NJ
*WVBV(FM) Medford Lakes, NJ
*WJSV(FM) Morristown, NJ
*KLXM(FM) Clayton, NM
*KCIE(FM) Dulce, NM
*KFDC(FM) Shiprock, NM
*KSOS(FM) Las Vegas, NV
*WBXL(FM) Baldwinsville, NY
*WHRW(FM) Binghamton, NY
*WSUC-FM Cortland, NY
*WXXE(FM) Fenner, NY
*WSLG(FM) Gouverneur, NY
*WJFF(FM) Jeffersonville, NY
*WLNF(FM) Rapids, NY
*WBER(FM) Rochester, NY
*WHVT(FM) Clyde, OH
*WCBE(FM) Columbus, OH
*WVML(FM) Millersburg, OH
*KNYD(FM) Broken Arrow, OK
*KFXU(FM) Chickasha, OK
*KWGT(FM) Goltry, OK
*KAYM(FM) Weatherford, OK
*KGIO(FM) Astoria, OR
*KVLB(FM) Bend, OR
*KLCO(FM) Newport, OR
*WTWT(FM) Bradford, PA
*WERG(FM) Erie, PA
*WCOZ(FM) Laceyville, PA
*WVBU-FM Lewisburg, PA
*WDUQ(FM) Pittsburgh, PA
*WIDA-FM Carolina, PR
*WUSC-FM Columbia, SC
*WDLL(FM) Dillon, SC
*WKVCF(FM) Freeman, SD
*WSMC-FM Collegedale, TN
*WUMC(FM) Elizabethton, TN
*WXKV(FM) Selmer, TN
*KAGT(FM) Abilene, TX
*KUT(FM) Austin, TX
*KZFT(FM) Fannett, TX
*KTXG(FM) Greenville, TX
*KSHU(FM) Huntsville, TX
*KLVW(FM) Odessa, TX
*KBAH(FM) Plainview, TX
*KTRL(FM) Stephenville, TX
*KPDR(FM) Wheeler, TX
*KZKL(FM) Wichita Falls, TX
*KZCL(FM) Logan, UT
*KBJF(FM) Nephi, UT
*WJYJ(FM) Fredericksburg, VA
*WPIM(FM) Martinsville, VA
*WEQP(FM) Pamplin City, VA
*WISE-FM Wise, VA
*WXLQ(FM) Bristol, VT
*WFTF(FM) Rutland, VT
*WCKJ(FM) Saint Johnsbury, VT
*KACS(FM) Chehalis, WA
*KNWV(FM) Clarkston, WA
*KNWG(FM) Goldendale, WA
*KWCW(FM) Walla Walla, WA
*WVCF(FM) Eau Claire, WI
*WSUP(FM) Platteville, WI
*WPFF(FM) Sturgeon Bay, WI
*WMLJ(FM) Summersville, WV
*KBUW(FM) Buffalo, WY
*KKBY(FM) Kirby, WY
*KUWN(FM) Newcastle, WY
*KUWZ(FM) Rock Springs, WY

90.7 mhz
*KWMB(FM) Fairbanks, AK
*WGRW(FM) Anniston, AL
*WVAS(FM) Montgomery, AL
*WVUA-FM Tuscaloosa, AL
*KEAF(FM) Fort Smith, AR
*KLMK(FM) Marvell, AR
*KLRM(FM) Melbourne, AR
*KJZK(FM) Kingman, AZ

*KNAA(FM) Show Low, AZ
*KALX(FM) Berkeley, CA
*KFRP(FM) Coalinga, CA
*KFSR(FM) Fresno, CA
*KRUK(FM) Happy Camp, CA
*KHRI(FM) Hollister, CA
*KPFK(FM) Los Angeles, CA
*KZYX(FM) Philo, CA
*KTHM(FM) Red Bluff, CA
*KSRI(FM) Santa Cruz, CA
*KYKL(FM) Tracy, CA
*KEZD(FM) Estes Park, CO
*KGUD(FM) Longmont, CO
*KTEI(FM) Placerville, CO
*KDRE(FM) Sterling, CO
*KTDL(FM) Trinidad, CO
*KHWD(FM) Wiggins, CO
*WMFE-FM Orlando, FL
*WKGC-FM Panama City, FL
*WXEL(FM) West Palm Beach, FL
*WWVO(FM) Albany, GA
*WACG-FM Augusta, GA
*WAYR-FM Brunswick, GA
*WUWG(FM) Carrollton, GA
*WMVV(FM) Griffin, GA
*WFSL(FM) Thomasville, GA
*KKUA(FM) Wailuku, HI
*KWOI(FM) Carroll, IA
*KDVO(FM) Mason City, IA
*KOJI(FM) Okoboji, IA
*KZRP(FM) Hope, ID
*KBSQ(FM) McCall, ID
*KCIR(FM) Twin Falls, ID
*WVKC(FM) Galesburg, IL
*WBEQ(FM) Morris, IL
*WAZU(FM) Peoria, IL
*WPSR(FM) Evansville, IN
*WKPW(FM) Knightstown, IN
*WQSG(FM) Lafayette, IN
*WMHD-FM Terre Haute, IN
*KPOR(FM) Emporia, KS
*KJHK(FM) Lawrence, KS
*KYWA(FM) Wichita, KS
*WCVK(FM) Bowling Green, KY
*WPTJ(FM) Paris, KY
*KLSA(FM) Alexandria, LA
*WWOZ(FM) New Orleans, LA
*WTCC(FM) Springfield, MA
*WKKL(FM) West Barnstable, MA
*WSDL(FM) Ocean City, MD
*WAUS(FM) Berrien Springs, MI
*WKKM(FM) Harrison, MI
*WNFR(FM) Sandusky, MI
*WNMC-FM Traverse City, MI
*KBPR(FM) Brainerd, MN
*WTIP(FM) Grand Marais, MN
*KOMH(FM) Marshall, MN
*KZSE(FM) Rochester, MN
*KOBC(FM) Joplin, MO
*KHGN(FM) Kirksville, MO
*KTTK(FM) Lebanon, MO
*KWMU(FM) Saint Louis, MO
*WATP(FM) Laurel, MS
*KOUI(FM) Louisville, MS
*KGFA(FM) Great Falls, MT
*KYPR(FM) Miles City, MT
*KMBM(FM) Polson, MT
*WRDK(FM) Bladenboro, NC
*WFAE(FM) Charlotte, NC
*WNCU(FM) Durham, NC
*WOTJ(FM) Morehead City, NC
*WYBJ(FM) Newton Grove, NC
*KABU(FM) Fort Totten, ND
*KFJM(FM) Grand Forks, ND
*KJND-FM Williston, ND
*KNFA(FM) Grand Island, NE
*KVNO(FM) Omaha, NE
*KMBV(FM) Valentine, NE
*WEVN(FM) Keene, NH
*WLMW(FM) Manchester, NH
*WPVH(FM) Plymouth, NH
*WYRS(FM) Manahawkin, NJ
*KQGC(FM) Belen, NM
*KKCJ(FM) Cannon AFB, NM
*KRWG(FM) Las Cruces, NM
*KQLV(FM) Santa Fe, NM

*WGXC(FM) Acra, NY
*WETD(FM) Alfred, NY
*WGCC-FM Batavia, NY
*WEER(FM) Easthampton, Village, NY
*WEGB(FM) Napeague, NY
*WFUV(FM) New York, NY
*WPGL(FM) Pattersonville, NY
*WPNR(FM) Utica, NY
*WGLE(FM) Lima, OH
*WVMC-FM Mansfield, OH
*WMCO(FM) New Concord, OH
*WNRK(FM) Norwalk, OH
*WOCU(FM) Sinking Spring, OH
*WKTL(FM) Struthers, OH
*KFXT(FM) Sulphur, OK
*KAYE-FM Tonkawa, OK
*KJOV(FM) Woodward, OK
*KANL(FM) Baker City, OR
*KMWR(FM) Brookings, OR
*KBOO(FM) Portland, OR
*WRTL(FM) Ephrata, PA
*WVMM(FM) Grantham, PA
*WPKV(FM) Nanty Glo, PA
*WKPS(FM) State College, PA
*WCLH(FM) Wilkes-Barre, PA
*WCRG(FM) Williamsport, PA
*WJHD(FM) Portsmouth, RI
*WYFH(FM) North Charleston, SC
*KSDJ(FM) Brookings, SD
*KJKT(FM) Spearfish, SD
*WZKV(FM) Dyersburg, TN
*WAUO(FM) Hohenwald, TN
*WGSN(FM) Newport, TN
*KAVW(FM) Amarillo, TX
*KTAA(FM) Big Sandy, TX
*KMLU(FM) Brownfield, TX
*KPBN(FM) Freer, TX
*KTER(FM) Rudolph, TX
*KCPC(FM) Sealy, TX
*KVRT(FM) Victoria, TX
*KEZB(FM) Beaver, UT
*WUVT-FM Blacksburg, VA
*WAZP(FM) Cape Charles, VA
*WEHC(FM) Emory, VA
*WMRA(FM) Harrisonburg, VA
*WJSC-FM Johnson, VT
*WVTC(FM) Randolph Center, VT
*KNWR(FM) Ellensburg, WA
*KSER(FM) Everett, WA
*KZUU(FM) Pullman, WA
*WHAD(FM) Delafield, WI
*WVSS(FM) Menomonie, WI
*WFGH(FM) Fort Gay, WV
*WLKV(FM) Ripley, WV
*KUWV(FM) Lingle, WY

90.9 mhz
*WELJ(FM) Brewton, AL
*WJAB(FM) Huntsville, AL
*KBSA(FM) El Dorado, AR
*KLLN(FM) Newark, AR
*KWRB(FM) Bisbee, AZ
*KKRY(FM) Kearny, AZ
*KGCB(FM) Prescott, AZ
*KHDC(FM) Chualar, CA
*KPSH(FM) Coachella, CA
*KWTM(FM) June Lake, CA
*KXJZ(FM) Sacramento, CA
*KGZO(FM) Shafter, CA
*KJLC(FM) Susanville, CA
*KBDG(FM) Turlock, CA
*KASF(FM) Alamosa, CO
*KTOL(FM) Leadville, CO
*KVNF(FM) Paonia, CO
*KRWA(FM) Rye, CO
*WCNI(FM) New London, CT
*WETA(FM) Washington, DC
*WAQV(FM) Crystal River, FL
*WKTZ-FM Jacksonville, FL
*WGES-FM Key Largo, FL
*WJIR(FM) Key West, FL
*WSOR(FM) Naples, FL
*WJWV(FM) Fort Gaines, GA
*WOAK(FM) La Grange, GA
*WRAF-FM Toccoa Falls, GA
*WVVS(FM) Valdosta, GA

*KKCR(FM) Hanalei, HI
*KUNI(FM) Cedar Falls, IA
*KLOX(FM) Creston, IA
*KMDY(FM) Keokuk, IA
*KKAG(FM) Grangeville, ID
*WVYN(FM) Bluford, IL
*WDCB(FM) Glen Ellyn, IL
*WILL-FM Urbana, IL
*WABT(FM) Fairland, IN
*WBDG(FM) Indianapolis, IN
*WBSW(FM) Marion, IN
*WCJL(FM) Morgantown, IN
*KHCT(FM) Great Bend, KS
*KONZ(FM) Riley, KS
*WKUE(FM) Elizabethtown, KY
*WEKH(FM) Hazard, KY
*WKMD(FM) Madisonville, KY
*KSLU(FM) Hammond, LA
*KIKL(FM) Lafayette, LA
*WBUR-FM Boston, MA
*WMEH(FM) Bangor, ME
*WMPG(FM) Gorham, ME
*WQAC-FM Alma, MI
*WSLI(FM) Belding, MI
*WTCK(FM) Charlevoix, MI
*WRCJ-FM Detroit, MI
*WTRK(FM) Freeland, MI
*WJKZ(FM) Hanover, MI
*WMSD(FM) Rose Township, MI
*WCFG(FM) Springfield, MI
*WIRR(FM) Virginia-Hibbing, MN
*KKLW(FM) Willmar, MN
*KJWR(FM) Windom, MN
*KRCU(FM) Cape Girardeau, MO
*KNLN(FM) Vienna, MO
*KTBG(FM) Warrensburg, MO
*KSMW(FM) West Plains, MO
*WMAO-FM Greenwood, MS
*WAQB(FM) Tupelo, MS
*KGCM(FM) Belgrade, MT
*KLRV(FM) Billings, MT
*KDWG(FM) Dillon, MT
*KSPL(FM) Kalispell, MT
*KZXZ(FM) Wyola, MT
*WQFS(FM) Greensboro, NC
*WURI(FM) Manteo, NC
*WRQM(FM) Rocky Mount, NC
*WSIF(FM) Wilkesboro, NC
*KPNO(FM) Norfolk, NE
*WSCS(FM) New London, NH
*KRRT(FM) Arroyo Seco, NM
*KSJE(FM) Farmington, NM
*KLHK(FM) Hobbs, NM
*KVIJ(FM) Tucumcari, NM
*KSHI(FM) Zuni, NM
*WCDB(FM) Albany, NY
*WLJH(FM) Glens Falls, NY
*WNGG(FM) Gloversville, NY
*WSQG-FM Ithaca, NY
*WCOT(FM) Jamestown, NY
*WAMK(FM) Kingston, NY
*WSLO(FM) Malone, NY
*WONY(FM) Oneonta, NY
*WOXR(FM) Schuyler Falls, NY
*WJNY(FM) Watertown, NY
*WGBE(FM) Bryan, OH
*WJDD(FM) Carrollton, OH
*WGUC(FM) Cincinnati, OH
*WCVJ(FM) Jefferson, OH
*WFCO(FM) Lancaster, OH
*WNZR(FM) Mount Vernon, OH
*WTJM(FM) South Webster, OH
*WSHB(FM) Willard, OH
*WCWS(FM) Wooster, OH
*KKVO(FM) Altus, OK
*KJHL(FM) Boise City, OK
*KOKF(FM) Edmond, OK
*KXRT(FM) Idabel, OK
*KJCH(FM) Coos Bay, OR
*KGCL(FM) Jordan Valley, OR
*KSKF(FM) Klamath Falls, OR
*KRBM(FM) Pendleton, OR
*KHJJ(FM) Shaniko, OR
*KCPB-FM Warrenton, OR
*WITX(FM) Beaver Falls, PA
*WZZH(FM) Honesdale, PA

*WCIJ(FM) Laporte, PA
*WJRC(FM) Lewistown, PA
*WHYY-FM Philadelphia, PA
*WLGI(FM) Hemingway, SC
*WNBK(FM) Whitmire, SC
*KWRC(FM) Hermosa, SD
*KDSD-FM Pierpont, SD
*KCSD(FM) Sioux Falls, SD
*WWOG(FM) Cookeville, TN
*WPRH(FM) Paris, TN
*KOVA(FM) Bovina, TX
*KAMU-FM College Station, TX
*KCBI(FM) Dallas, TX
*KRLH(FM) Hereford, TX
*KGVB(FM) Holliday, TX
*KTSU(FM) Houston, TX
*KKLU(FM) Lubbock, TX
*KSWP(FM) Lufkin, TX
*KVDG(FM) Midland, TX
*KAVO(FM) Pampa, TX
*KLTP(FM) San Angelo, TX
*KYFS(FM) San Antonio, TX
*KRCL(FM) Salt Lake City, UT
*KCFF(FM) Clifton Forge, VA
*WWMC(FM) Lynchburg, VA
*WCWM(FM) Williamsburg, VA
*WXZT(FM) Christiansted, VI
*KNWU(FM) Forks, WA
*KWAN(FM) Oroville, WA
*KVTI(FM) Tacoma, WA
*WUWS(FM) Ashland, WI
*WHRM(FM) Wausau, WI
*WXAF(FM) Charleston, WV
*WVPM(FM) Morgantown, WV
*KLWV(FM) Chugwater, WY
*KFTW(FM) Fort Washakie, WY
*KUWG(FM) Gillette, WY
*KUWX(FM) Pinedale, WY

91.1 mhz
*KSKA(FM) Anchorage, AK
*WEGL(FM) Auburn, AL
*WJSR(FM) Birmingham, AL
*WVSU-FM Birmingham, AL
*WTXN(FM) Goodwater, AL
*WAQU(FM) Selma, AL
*WAYU(FM) Steele, AL
*WAXU(FM) Troy, AL
*KMTC(FM) Russellville, AR
*KANX(FM) Sheridan, AR
*KNLB(FM) Lake Havasu City, AZ
*KNOG(FM) Nogales, AZ
*KFRJ(FM) China Lake, CA
*KHEC(FM) Crescent City, CA
*KLVY(FM) Fairmead, CA
*KMUD(FM) Garberville, CA
*KCSM(FM) San Mateo, CA
*KRCB-FM Santa Rosa, CA
*KDSC(FM) Thousand Oaks, CA
*KWSB-FM Gunnison, CO
*KLDV(FM) Morrison, CO
*WSHU(FM) Fairfield, CT
*WBVC(FM) Pomfret, CT
*WJED(FM) Dogwood Lakes Estate, FL
*WJFP(FM) Fort Pierce, FL
*WPSM(FM) Fort Walton Beach, FL
*WKES(FM) Lakeland, FL
*WHMF(FM) Marianna, FL
*WHYZ(FM) Palm Coast, FL
*WUJC(FM) Saint Marks, FL
*WREK(FM) Atlanta, GA
*WJEP(FM) Cusseta, GA
*WREE(FM) Fargo, GA
*WSVH(FM) Savannah, GA
*WABR(FM) Tifton, GA
*KANO(FM) Hilo, HI
*KWNJ(FM) Bettendorf, IA
*KTPR(FM) Fort Dodge, IA
*KUNZ(FM) Ottumwa, IA
*KISU-FM Pocatello, ID
*KBSS(FM) Sun Valley, ID
*WDBX(FM) Carbondale, IL
*WIBI(FM) Carlinville, IL
*WKCC(FM) Kankakee, IL
*WGSL(FM) Loves Park, IL

*WYGS(FM) Columbus, IN
*WGCS(FM) Goshen, IN
*WBSH(FM) Hagerstown, IN
*WEDM(FM) Indianapolis, IN
*WCYT(FM) Lafayette Township, IN
*WIRE(FM) Lebanon, IN
*WHMO(FM) Madison, IN
*WVUB(FM) Vincennes, IN
*KANZ(FM) Garden City, KS
*KCFN(FM) Wichita, KS
*WKAO(FM) Ashland, KY
*KLSU(FM) Baton Rouge, LA
*KOJO(FM) Lake Charles, LA
*KXUL(FM) Monroe, LA
*WNKV(FM) Norco, LA
*WMUA(FM) Amherst, MA
*WNAN(FM) Nantucket, MA
*WJJW(FM) North Adams, MA
*WTKL(FM) North Dartmouth, MA
*WKMY(FM) Winchendon, MA
*WHFC(FM) Bel Air, MD
*WBOR(FM) Brunswick, ME
*WFGP(FM) Greene, ME
*XETRA-FM Tijuana, MEX
*WOLW(FM) Cadillac, MI
*WFUM-FM Flint, MI
*WGGL-FM Houghton, MI
*WPCJ(FM) Pittsford, MI
*KXLC(FM) La Crescent, MN
*KNOW-FM Minneapolis-St. Paul, MN
*KCCM-FM Moorhead, MN
*KIKG(FM) Licking, MO
*KBGM(FM) Park Hills, MO
*KSJI(FM) Saint Joseph, MO
*KSMU(FM) Springfield, MO
*WASM(FM) Natchez, MS
*WMSV(FM) Starkville, MS
*KCBG(FM) Broadus, MT
*KLEU(FM) Lewistown, MT
*KMZL(FM) Missoula, MT
*WZGO(FM) Aurora, NC
*WYBH(FM) Fayetteville, NC
*WPGT(FM) Roanoke Rapids, NC
*WRSH(FM) Rockingham, NC
*KTNE-FM Alliance, NE
*KDCV-FM Blair, NE
*KUCV(FM) Lincoln, NE
*WVNH(FM) Concord, NH
*WPHH(FM) Conway, NH
*WWNJ(FM) Dover Township, NJ
*WFMU(FM) East Orange, NJ
*KAQF(FM) Clovis, NM
*KEDP(FM) Las Vegas, NM
*KVKL(FM) Las Vegas, NV
*KAIZ(FM) Mesquite, NV
*KDNV(FM) Winnemucca, NV
*WSQE(FM) Corning, NY
*WHVP(FM) Hudson, NY
*WOSS(FM) Ossining, NY
*WTSC-FM Potsdam, NY
*WSPN(FM) Saratoga Springs, NY
*WRMU(FM) Alliance, OH
*WXHZ(FM) Bridgeport, OH
*WRUW-FM Cleveland, OH
*WOSE(FM) Coshocton, OH
*WDUB(FM) Granville, OH
*WOSB(FM) Marion, OH
*WEWH(FM) Washington Court House, OH
*KQPD(FM) Ardmore, OK
*KJOG(FM) Cleveland, OK
*KAYC(FM) Durant, OK
*KKRD(FM) Enid, OK
*KJRF(FM) Lawton, OK
*KZME(FM) Brightwood, OR
*KWAX(FM) Eugene, OR
*KAPK(FM) Grants Pass, OR
*KTMK(FM) Tillamook, OR
*WUFR(FM) Bedford, PA
*WBUQ(FM) Bloomsburg, PA
*WZBT(FM) Gettysburg, PA
*WSAJ-FM Grove City, PA
*WRTY(FM) Jackson Township, PA
*WMSS(FM) Middletown, PA
*WRWV(FM) Saint Marys, PA
*WYFG(FM) Gaffney, SC

*WEBK(FM) Society Hill, SC
*KTSD-FM Reliance, SD
*KAOR(FM) Vermillion, SD
*WTSE(FM) Benton, TN
*WKCS(FM) Knoxville, TN
*WKNO-FM Memphis, TN
*WRVU(FM) Nashville, TN
*WZTH(FM) Tusculum, TN
*KHHC(FM) Canadian, TX
*KWTS(FM) Canyon, TX
*KQXE(FM) Eastland, TX
*KVER(FM) El Paso, TX
*KANJ(FM) Giddings, TX
*KHKV(FM) Kerrville, TX
*KTAI(FM) Kingsville, TX
*KYBJ(FM) Lake Jackson, TX
*KBWC(FM) Marshall, TX
*KLTB(FM) Palestine, TX
*KGWP(FM) Pittsburg, TX
*KSGR(FM) Portland, TX
*KGWB(FM) Snyder, TX
*KLXN(FM) Stratford, TX
*KSUU(FM) Cedar City, UT
*WTJU(FM) Charlottesville, VA
*WOKD-FM Danville, VA
*WHCE(FM) Highland Springs, VA
*WNSB(FM) Norfolk, VA
*WVNK(FM) Manchester, VT
*WRMC-FM Middlebury, VT
*WGDR(FM) Plainfield, VT
*KTJC(FM) Kelso, WA
*KROH(FM) Port Townsend, WA
*KPBX-FM Spokane, WA
*KTWP(FM) Twisp, WA
*KYPL(FM) Yakima, WA
*WOVM(FM) Appleton, WI
*WGTD(FM) Kenosha, WI
*WPIB(FM) Bluefield, WV
*WVPC(FM) Franklin, WV
*KOFG(FM) Cody, WY
*KMWY(FM) Jackson, WY

91.3 mhz
*KLOJ(FM) Glennallen, AK
*KOGB(FM) McGrath, AK
*WVOB(FM) Equality, AL
*WBNB(FM) Equality, AL
*WFIX(FM) Florence, AL
*WHIL-FM Mobile, AL
*WTBJ(FM) Oxford, AL
*KUCA(FM) Conway, AR
*KUAF(FM) Fayetteville, AR
*KGHR(FM) Tuba City, AZ
*KXCI(FM) Tucson, AZ
*KAWN(FM) Winslow, AZ
*KFRB(FM) Bakersfield, CA
*KWTH(FM) Barstow, CA
*KRNR(FM) Butte City, CA
*KIDE(FM) Hoopa, CA
*KDRH(FM) King City, CA
*KOPA(FM) Pala, CA
*KCPR(FM) San Luis Obispo, CA
*KSVY(FM) Sonoma, CA
*KUOP(FM) Stockton, CA
*KNYR(FM) Yreka, CA
*KMSA(FM) Grand Junction, CO
*KLRY(FM) Gypsum, CO
*KSUT(FM) Ignacio, CO
*KTPF(FM) Salida, CO
*KLZV(FM) Sterling, CO
*WWUH(FM) West Hartford, CT
*WVUD(FM) Newark, DE
*WYFZ(FM) Belleview, FL
*WAKJ(FM) De Funiak Springs, FL
*WSEB(FM) Englewood, FL
*WOLR(FM) Lake City, FL
*WLRN-FM Miami, FL
*WHIF(FM) Palatka, FL
*WCGN(FM) Calhoun, GA
*WATY(FM) Folkston, GA
*WJTG(FM) Fort Valley, GA
*KDFR(FM) Des Moines, IA
*WGMR(FM) Effingham, IL
*WNIW(FM) La Salle, IL
*WIUM(FM) Macomb, IL
*WJCZ(FM) Milford, IL

*WSLE(FM) Salem, IL
*WFHB(FM) Bloomington, IN
*WHJE(FM) Carmel, IN
*WNDY(FM) Crawfordsville, IN
*WJCO(FM) Montpelier, IN
*WWHI(FM) Muncie, IN
*WTMW(FM) North Judson, IN
*WCKZ(FM) Orland, IN
*KAXR(FM) Arkansas City, KS
*KRLE(FM) Oberlin, KS
*KANV(FM) Olsburg, KS
*WUKY(FM) Lexington, KY
*WKMS-FM Murray, KY
*WNON(FM) Warfield, KY
*WHFG(FM) Broussard, LA
*KSCL(FM) Shreveport, LA
*WSHL-FM Easton, MA
*WXPL(FM) Fitchburg, MA
*WDJM-FM Framingham, MA
*WFMR(FM) Orleans, MA
*WNGB(FM) Petersham, MA
*WCUW(FM) Worcester, MA
*WESM(FM) Princess Anne, MD
*WMEW(FM) Waterville, ME
*WCHW-FM Bay City, MI
*WRQC(FM) East Tawas, MI
*WJOG(FM) Good Hart, MI
*WCSG(FM) Grand Rapids, MI
*WOES(FM) Ovid-Elsie, MI
*WSGR-FM Port Huron, MI
*KRSU(FM) Appleton, MN
*KMSK(FM) Austin, MN
*KNBJ(FM) Bemidji, MN
*KBIA(FM) Columbia, MO
*KBIY(FM) Van Buren, MO
*WMPN-FM Jackson, MS
*KAPC(FM) Butte, MT
*KFLF(FM) Somers, MT
*WLFA(FM) Asheville, NC
*WFQS(FM) Franklin, NC
*WZMB(FM) Greenville, NC
*WHQR(FM) Wilmington, NC
*WXRI(FM) Winston-Salem, NC
*KMHA(FM) Four Bears, ND
*KPSS(FM) Broken Bow, NE
*KAYA(FM) Hubbard, NE
*KLPR(FM) Kearney, NE
*KSSH(FM) Shubert, NE
*WUNH(FM) Durham, NH
*WEVH(FM) Hanover, NH
*WKNH(FM) Keene, NH
*WRTQ(FM) Ocean City, NJ
*WTSR(FM) Trenton, NJ
*KYCV(FM) Lovington, NM
*KYCT(FM) Ruidoso, NM
*KQLN(FM) Alamo, NV
*KNIS(FM) Carson City, NV
*KBSJ(FM) Jackpot, NV
*WXLH(FM) Blue Mountain Lake, NY
*WBNY(FM) Buffalo, NY
*WOLN(FM) Olean, NY
*WVKR-FM Poughkeepsie, NY
*WIOX(FM) Roxbury, NY
*WRLI-FM Southampton, NY
*WCNY-FM Syracuse, NY
*WAPS(FM) Akron, OH
*WOUB-FM Athens, OH
*WGTE-FM Toledo, OH
*WYSO(FM) Yellow Springs, OH
*KAKO(FM) Ada, OK
*KRSC-FM Claremore, OK
*KWEH(FM) Weatherford, OK
*KOAB-FM Bend, OR
*KMHS-FM Coos Bay, OR
*WLVR(FM) Bethlehem, PA
*WFUZ(FM) Carbondale, PA
*WPFG(FM) Carlisle, PA
*WQLN-FM Erie, PA
*WLCH(FM) Lancaster, PA
*WGRC(FM) Lewisburg, PA
*WYEP-FM Pittsburgh, PA
*WXAC(FM) Reading, PA
*WIPR-FM San Juan, PR
*WDOM(FM) Providence, RI
*WLTR(FM) Columbia, SC
*WLMU(FM) Harrogate, TN

*WCPI(FM) McMinnville, TN
*WUTS(FM) Sewanee, TN
*KAQD(FM) Abilene, TX
*KVLU(FM) Beaumont, TX
*KVFM(FM) Beeville, TX
*KYJC(FM) Commerce, TX
*KDKR(FM) Decatur, TX
*KNCT-FM Killeen, TX
*KBKN(FM) Lamesa, TX
*KZLV(FM) Lytle, TX
*KOCV(FM) Odessa, TX
*KPKO(FM) Pecos, TX
*KPVU(FM) Prairie View, TX
*KGLY(FM) Tyler, TX
*KBDW(FM) Wheeler, TX
*KRRA(FM) Paragonah, UT
*KXDS(FM) Saint George, UT
*WMLU(FM) Farmville, VA
*WVST-FM Petersburg, VA
*WPAR(FM) Salem, VA
*WTRM(FM) Winchester, VA
*WIUV(FM) Castleton, VT
*KBCS(FM) Bellevue, WA
*KCED(FM) Centralia, WA
*KGTS(FM) College Place, WA
*KCFL(FM) Elma, WA
*KACW(FM) South Bend, WA
*WHEM(FM) Eau Claire, WI
*WMVM(FM) Goodman, WI
*WHHI(FM) Highland, WI
*WSTM(FM) Kiel, WI
*KUWS(FM) Superior, WI
*WQAB(FM) Philippi, WV
*WSJE(FM) Summersville, WV
*KUWA(FM) Afton, WY
*KUWC(FM) Casper, WY
*KSUW(FM) Sheridan, WY
*KUWT(FM) Thermopolis, WY

91.5 mhz
*KSUA(FM) Fairbanks, AK
*KWJG(FM) Kasilof, AK
*WSTF(FM) Andalusia, AL
*WSGN(FM) Gadsden, AL
*WUAL-FM Tuscaloosa, AL
*WEBT(FM) Valley, AL
*KAIA(FM) Blytheville, AR
*KALR(FM) Hot Springs, AR
*KCMH(FM) Mountain Home, AR
*KJZZ(FM) Phoenix, AZ
*KNHM(FM) Bayside, CA
*KKUP(FM) Cupertino, CA
*KASK(FM) Fairfield, CA
*KSJV(FM) Fresno, CA
*KRQZ(FM) Lompoc, CA
*KUSC(FM) Los Angeles, CA
*KKRO(FM) Redding, CA
*KYDS(FM) Sacramento, CA
*KZYZ(FM) Willits, CA
*KAJX(FM) Aspen, CO
*KRCC(FM) Colorado Springs, CO
*KSJD(FM) Cortez, CO
*KUNC(FM) Greeley, CO
*KTML(FM) South Fork, CO
*WGRS(FM) Guilford, CT
*WXRN(FM) Warren, CT
*WPSF(FM) Clewiston, FL
*WMIE(FM) Cocoa, FL
*WGTT(FM) Emeralda, FL
*WJYO(FM) Fort Myers, FL
*WAPN(FM) Holly Hill, FL
*WKWM(FM) Marathon, FL
*WCIE(FM) New Port Richey, FL
*WJFH(FM) Sebring, FL
*WTYG(FM) Sparr, FL
*WFSQ(FM) Tallahassee, FL
*WPDJ(FM) Trailtown, FL
*WPRK(FM) Winter Park, FL
*WWEV-FM Cumming, GA
*WGPH(FM) Vidalia, GA
*KRGO-FM Alton, IA
*KUNY(FM) Mason City, IA
*KBSX(FM) Boise, ID
*KBYR-FM Rexburg, ID
*WLHW(FM) Casey, IL
*WBEZ(FM) Chicago, IL

*WCIC(FM) Pekin, IL
*WNIQ(FM) Sterling, IL
*WFWR(FM) Attica, IN
*WJCY(FM) Cicero, IN
*WJHS(FM) Columbia City, IN
*WUEV(FM) Evansville, IN
*WGRE(FM) Greencastle, IN
*WRFT(FM) Indianapolis, IN
*WCNB(FM) Lebanon, IN
*WWDL(FM) Lebanon, IN
*WECI(FM) Richmond, IN
*WJLR(FM) Seymour, IN
*KANU(FM) Lawrence, KS
*KSNS(FM) Medicine Lodge, KS
*KSNB(FM) Norton, KS
*WVCT(FM) Keavy, KY
*WBFI(FM) McDaniels, KY
*KBAN(FM) De Ridder, LA
*KPAE(FM) Erwinville, LA
*KGRM(FM) Grambling, LA
*WPEF(FM) Kentwood, LA
*WTUL(FM) New Orleans, LA
*KSUL(FM) Port Sulphur, LA
*KNSU(FM) Thibodaux, LA
*WBIM-FM Bridgewater, MA
*WUML(FM) Lowell, MA
*WMFO(FM) Medford, MA
*WMLN-FM Milton, MA
*WNMH(FM) Northfield, MA
*WWRN(FM) Rockport, MA
*WSDH(FM) Sandwich, MA
*WMHC(FM) South Hadley, MA
*WZLY(FM) Wellesley, MA
*WBJC(FM) Baltimore, MD
*WJVH(FM) Belfast, ME
*WFYB(FM) Fryeburg, ME
*WRBC(FM) Lewiston, ME
*WVCM(FM) Iron Mountain, MI
*WXYP(FM) Ludington, MI
*WUPX(FM) Marquette, MI
*WMHW-FM Mount Pleasant, MI
*WJOH(FM) Raco, MI
*WICA(FM) Traverse City, MI
*KNWF(FM) Fergus Falls, MN
*KCFB(FM) Saint Cloud, MN
*KNGA(FM) Saint Peter, MN
*KQMN(FM) Thief River Falls, MN
*KSIV-FM Saint Louis, MO
*WLRK(FM) Greenville, MS
*WAVI(FM) Oxford, MS
*KAFH(FM) Great Falls, MT
*KPLG(FM) Plains, MT
*WBJD(FM) Atlantic Beach, NC
*WUNC(FM) Chapel Hill, NC
*KPRJ(FM) Jamestown, ND
*KBTK(FM) Grand Island, NE
*KRNE-FM Merriman, NE
*KIOS-FM Omaha, NE
*KOEC(FM) O'Neill, NE
*WANH(FM) Meredith, NH
*WDBK(FM) Blackwood, NJ
*KFLQ(FM) Albuquerque, NM
*KRUX(FM) Las Cruces, NM
*KNCC(FM) Elko, NV
*KUNV(FM) Las Vegas, NV
*WSQX-FM Binghamton, NY
*WVHC(FM) Herkimer, NY
*WNYE(FM) New York, NY
*WXXI-FM Rochester, NY
*WRPI(FM) Troy, NY
*WKHR(FM) Bainbridge, OH
*WHKC(FM) Columbus, OH
*WBIE(FM) Delphos, OH
*WKRJ(FM) New Philadelphia, OH
*WOBC-FM Oberlin, OH
*WOSP(FM) Portsmouth, OH
*KSYE(FM) Frederick, OK
*KVAZ(FM) Henryetta, OK
*KWVZ(FM) Florence, OR
*KOPB-FM Portland, OR
*KSRS(FM) Roseburg, OR
*WCIM(FM) Shenandoah, PA
*WPSU(FM) State College, PA
*WSRN-FM Swarthmore, PA
*WCVY(FM) Coventry, RI
*WRJI(FM) East Greenwich, RI

*WFBK(FM) Fort Mill, SC
*WKCL(FM) Ladson, SC
*WHCB(FM) Bristol, TN
*WNRZ(FM) Dickson, TN
*WFHU(FM) Henderson, TN
*WFMQ(FM) Lebanon, TN
*WJBP(FM) Red Bank, TN
*WJCG(FM) Sunbright, TN
*WTML(FM) Tullahoma, TN
*KBCX(FM) Big Spring, TX
*KHVT(FM) Bloomington, TX
*KTXP(FM) Bushland, TX
*KYFB(FM) Denison, TX
*KBLC(FM) Fredericksburg, TX
*KHML(FM) Madisonville, TX
*KCAS(FM) McCook, TX
*KWLD(FM) Plainview, TX
*KTXK(FM) Texarkana, TX
*KVHR(FM) Van Horn, TX
*KUSU-FM Logan, UT
*WARN(FM) Culpeper, VA
*WPIN-FM Dublin, VA
*WLUR(FM) Lexington, VA
*WYCS(FM) Yorktown, VA
*WGLY-FM Bolton, VT
*WWLR(FM) Lyndonville, VT
*KLWS(FM) Moses Lake, WA
*KUBS(FM) Newport, WA
*KSQM(FM) Sequim, WA
*WEMY(FM) Green Bay, WI
*WWJA(FM) Janesville, WI
*WPJW(FM) Hurricane, WV
*WRSG(FM) Middlebourne, WV
*WGLZ(FM) West Liberty, WV
*KUWD(FM) Sundance, WY

91.7 mhz
*KIBH-FM Seward, AK
*WYFD(FM) Decatur, AL
*WPIL(FM) Heflin, AL
*WAQG(FM) Ozark, AL
*KEJA(FM) Cale, AR
*KBDO(FM) Des Arc, AR
*KRMC(FM) Douglas, AZ
*KPUB(FM) Flagstaff, AZ
*KNAD(FM) Page, AZ
*KEQS(FM) Quartzsite, AZ
*KCHO(FM) Chico, CA
*KXSR(FM) Groveland, CA
*KHCS(FM) Palm Desert, CA
*KBDH(FM) San Ardo, CA
*KALW(FM) San Francisco, CA
*KFHL(FM) Wasco, CA
*KZWD(FM) Bennett, CO
*KLXD(FM) Springfield, CO
*KCCS(FM) Starkville, CO
*KTSG(FM) Steamboat Springs, CO
*KOTO(FM) Telluride, CO
*WXCI(FM) Danbury, CT
*WHUS(FM) Storrs, CT
*WRTX(FM) Dover, DE
*WMPH(FM) Wilmington, DE
*WJBC-FM Fernandina Beach, FL
*WJLF(FM) Gainesville, FL
*WAPB(FM) Madison, FL
*WMKO(FM) Marco, FL
*WEGS(FM) Milton, FL
*WFFL(FM) Panama City, FL
*WVIJ(FM) Port Charlotte, FL
*WFTI-FM Saint Petersburg, FL
*WWFR(FM) Stuart, FL
*WUNV(FM) Albany, GA
*WUGA(FM) Athens, GA
*WLPE(FM) Augusta, GA
*WCCV(FM) Cartersville, GA
*WTJB(FM) Columbus, GA
*WMVW(FM) Peachtree City, GA
*WVNG(FM) Tallulah Falls, GA
*WWET(FM) Valdosta, GA
*KAHU(FM) Pahala, HI
*KSUI(FM) Iowa City, IA
*KDWT(FM) Perry, IA
*KBSM(FM) McCall, ID
*KRFA-FM Moscow, ID
*KSQS(FM) Ririe, ID
*KBSW(FM) Twin Falls, ID

*WBJW(FM) Albion, IL
*WBGL(FM) Champaign, IL
*WVNL(FM) Vandalia, IL
*WZKL(FM) Woodstock, IL
*WJPR(FM) Jasper, IN
*WIWC(FM) Kokomo, IN
*WEEM-FM Pendleton, IN
*WBSJ(FM) Portland, IN
*WETL(FM) South Bend, IN
*KZAN(FM) Hays, KS
*KMLL(FM) Marysville, KS
*KCVS(FM) Salina, KS
*WWHR(FM) Bowling Green, KY
*WAPD(FM) Campbellsville, KY
*WYJZ(FM) Fearsville, KY
*WRYS(FM) Grayson, KY
*WJVK(FM) Owensboro, KY
*WNFC(FM) Paducah, KY
*WWJD(FM) Pippa Passes, KY
*KAPM(FM) Alexandria, LA
*KLSP(FM) Angola, LA
*KMSL(FM) Mansfield, LA
*KNWD(FM) Natchitoches, LA
*WJNF(FM) Dalton, MA
*WGAJ(FM) Deerfield, MA
*WJWT(FM) Gardner, MA
*WAVM(FM) Maynard, MA
*WNEF(FM) Newburyport, MA
*WMWM(FM) Salem, MA
*WBSL-FM Sheffield, MA
*WZXH(FM) Hagerstown, MD
*WSHD(FM) Eastport, ME
*WRNM(FM) Ellsworth, ME
*WUMM(FM) Machias, ME
*WCML-FM Alpena, MI
*WUOM(FM) Ann Arbor, MI
*WQMI(FM) Grand Marais, MI
*WMCQ(FM) Muskegon, MI
*KAXE(FM) Grand Rapids, MN
*KLSE-FM Rochester, MN
*WMCN(FM) Saint Paul, MN
*KOLJ-FM Warroad, MN
*KNSW(FM) Worthington-Marshall, MN
*KCVO-FM Camdenton, MO
*WJTJ(FM) Cameron, MO
*KJIR(FM) Hannibal, MO
*KMVC(FM) Marshall, MO
*KNEO(FM) Neosho, MO
*KCOZ(FM) Point Lookout, MO
*KCVX(FM) Salem, MO
*WSQH(FM) Forest, MS
*WAOY(FM) Gulfport, MS
*WVSD(FM) Itta Bena, MS
*WPRL(FM) Lorman, MS
*WAJS(FM) Tupelo, MS
*KEMC(FM) Billings, MT
*KUHM(FM) Helena, MT
*WBKU(FM) Ahoskie, NC
*WSGE(FM) Dallas, NC
*KBFR(FM) Bismarck, ND
*KPPD(FM) Devils Lake, ND
*KNDW(FM) Williston, ND
*KNHS(FM) Hastings, NE
*KSTJ(FM) Norfolk, NE
*KPNE-FM North Platte, NE
*KMBT(FM) Tecumseh, NE
*KUTN(FM) Utica, NE
*WNEC-FM Henniker, NH
*WPCR-FM Plymouth, NH
*WLNJ(FM) Lakehurst, NJ
*WLFR(FM) Pomona, NJ
*KUPR(FM) Alamogordo, NM
*KZPI(FM) Deming, NM
*KTGW(FM) Fruitland, NM
*KGLP(FM) Gallup, NM
*KOBH(FM) Hobbs, NM
*KGCN(FM) Roswell, NM
*KVLP(FM) Tucumcari, NM
*KLNR(FM) Panaca, NV
*KTPH(FM) Tonopah, NV
*WCOM-FM Belfast, NY
*WXLB(FM) Boonville, NY
*WICB(FM) Ithaca, NY
*WFRH(FM) Kingston, NY
*WOSR(FM) Middletown, NY
*WSQC-FM Oneonta, NY

*WRVJ(FM) Watertown, NY
*WLGO(FM) Ashtabula, OH
*WVXU(FM) Cincinnati, OH
*WOSV(FM) Mansfield, OH
*WYTN(FM) Youngstown, OH
*WJIC(FM) Zanesville, OH
*KPSU(FM) Goodwell, OK
*KARG(FM) Poteau, OK
*KOSU(FM) Stillwater, OK
*KEOL(FM) La Grande, OR
*KDOV(FM) Medford, OR
*WMUH(FM) Allentown, PA
*WLBS(FM) Bristol, PA
*WCUC-FM Clarion, PA
*WZXF(FM) Hustontown, PA
*WEVP(FM) Laporte, PA
*WIXQ(FM) Millersville, PA
*WKDU(FM) Philadelphia, PA
*WVMW-FM Scranton, PA
*WJAZ(FM) Summerdale, PA
*WBMR(FM) Telford, PA
*WNJR(FM) Washington, PA
*WCUR(FM) West Chester, PA
*WRLC(FM) Williamsport, PA
*WYTL(FM) Wyomissing, PA
*WNNV(FM) San German, PR
*WLPG(FM) Florence, SC
*WTBI-FM Greenville, SC
*KAMF(FM) Tulare, SD
*WHRS(FM) Cookeville, TN
*WUMR(FM) Memphis, TN
*WFCM-FM Murfreesboro, TN
*KVRX(FM) Austin, TX
*KHBW(FM) Brownwood, TX
*KBNJ(FM) Corpus Christi, TX
*KTDA(FM) Dalhart, TX
*KVTT(FM) Dallas, TX
*KOOP(FM) Hornsby, TX
*KTRU(FM) Houston, TX
*KPIT(FM) Pittsburg, TX
*KRTU(FM) San Antonio, TX
*KOHS(FM) Orem, UT
*KEYR(FM) Richfield, UT
*KUFR(FM) Salt Lake City, UT
*KEYV(FM) Vernal, UT
*WEMC(FM) Harrisonburg, VA
*WWEM(FM) Rustburg, VA
*WGLV(FM) Woodstock, VT
*KZAZ(FM) Bellingham, WA
*KBLD(FM) Kennewick, WA
*KSVR(FM) Mount Vernon, WA
*KXOT(FM) Tacoma, WA
*KEFL(FM) Westport, WA
*WDKV(FM) Fond du Lac, WI
*WSUM(FM) Madison, WI
*WMSE(FM) Milwaukee, WI
*WXPR(FM) Rhinelander, WI
*WSHS(FM) Sheboygan, WI
*WSUW(FM) Whitewater, WI
*WVPB(FM) Beckley, WV
*WWVU-FM Morgantown, WV
*KDUW(FM) Douglas, WY

91.9 mhz
*KBRW-FM Barrow, AK
*KDLL(FM) Kenai, AK
*KIAM-FM North Nenana, AK
*KUHB-FM Saint Paul, AK
*KUDU(FM) Tok, AK
*WGIB(FM) Birmingham, AL
*WMBV(FM) Dixons Mills, AL
*WLJS-FM Jacksonville, AL
*WJIF(FM) Opp, AL
*KHED(FM) Arkadelphia, AR
*KBPB(FM) Harrison, AR
*KASU Jonesboro, AR
*KXRJ(FM) Russellville, AR
*KVJC(FM) Globe, AZ
*KCAI(FM) Kingman, AZ
*KRDC(FM) Many Farms, AZ
*KOHN(FM) Sells, AZ
*KYRM(FM) Yuma, AZ
*KHSR(FM) Crescent City, CA
*KHKL(FM) Laytonville, CA
*KLDD(FM) McCloud, CA
*KLVR(FM) Middletown, CA

*KSPB(FM) Pebble Beach, CA
*KQNY(FM) Quincy, CA
*KWTD(FM) Ridgecrest, CA
*KVCR(FM) San Bernardino, CA
*KCSB-FM Santa Barbara, CA
*KCSS(FM) Turlock, CA
*KDUR(FM) Durango, CO
*KLXV(FM) Glenwood Springs, CO
*KJOL-FM Montrose, CO
*KCFP(FM) Pueblo, CO
*WSLX(FM) New Canaan, CT
*WHDD-FM Sharon, CT
*WXHM(FM) Middletown, DE
*WHGN(FM) Crystal River, FL
*WMYE(FM) Fort Myers, FL
*WMKL(FM) Key Largo, FL
*WYFO(FM) Lakeland, FL
*WKVH(FM) Monticello, FL
*WAYL(FM) Saint Augustine, FL
*WSCF-FM Vero Beach, FL
*WCLK(FM) Atlanta, GA
*WEBH(FM) Cuthbert, GA
*WBRQ(FM) La Grange, GA
*WLFS(FM) Port Wentworth, GA
*WVGS(FM) Statesboro, GA
*WZZG(FM) Toomsboro, GA
*WASW(FM) Waycross, GA
*KSDA-FM Agat, GU
*KAQA(FM) Kilauea, HI
*KTDV(FM) State Center, IA
*KWRV(FM) Sun Valley, ID
*WSIU(FM) Carbondale, IL
*WJCH(FM) Joliet, IL
*WUIS(FM) Springfield, IL
*WQKO(FM) Howe, IN
*WVSH(FM) Huntington, IN
*WJEF(FM) Lafayette, IN
*WMUI(FM) Rushville, IN
*WHOJ(FM) Terre Haute, IN
*WITT(FM) Zionsville, IN
*KTCC(FM) Colby, KS
*KONQ(FM) Dodge City, KS
*KNGM(FM) Emporia, KS
*KFKB(FM) Girard, KS
*KWBI(FM) Great Bend, KS
*KARF(FM) Independence, KS
*KSDB-FM Manhattan, KS
*KBDD(FM) Winfield, KS
*WFPK(FM) Louisville, KY
*KAXV(FM) Bastrop, LA
*KMRL(FM) Buras, LA
*KCKR(FM) Church Point, LA
*WWRA(FM) Clinton, LA
*WUMB-FM Boston, MA
*WFPB-FM Falmouth, MA
*WOZQ(FM) Northampton, MA
*WAIC(FM) Springfield, MA
*WDMY(FM) Stockbridge, MA
*WCFM(FM) Williamstown, MA
*WBPR(FM) Worcester, MA
*WFWM(FM) Frostburg, MD
*WGTS(FM) Takoma Park, MD
*WYFP(FM) Harpswell, ME
*WMEB-FM Orono, ME
*WGCP(FM) Cadillac, MI
*WDPW(FM) Greenville, MI
*WMTU-FM Houghton, MI
*WORW(FM) Port Huron, MI
*WZMI(FM) Reed City, MI
*WTNP(FM) Richland, MI
*KXBR(FM) International Falls, MN
*KBHZ(FM) Willmar, MN
*KNLQ(FM) Cuba, MO
*KCKV(FM) Kirksville, MO
*KWJC(FM) Liberty, MO
*KNLM(FM) Marshfield, MO
*KSRD(FM) Saint Joseph, MO
*WOWL(FM) Burnsville, MS
*WAUM(FM) Duck Hill, MS
*WDSV(FM) Greenville, MS
*WSMP(FM) New Hebron, MS
*KGLT(FM) Bozeman, MT
*KFRW(FM) Great Falls, MT
*KUFN(FM) Hamilton, MT
*WFSS(FM) Fayetteville, NC
*WAAE(FM) New Bern, NC

*WRCM(FM) Wingate, NC
*KDSU(FM) Fargo, ND
*KCNE-FM Chadron, NE
*KTLX(FM) Columbus, NE
*KDNE(FM) Crete, NE
*KWSC(FM) Wayne, NE
*WBNJ(FM) Barnegat, NJ
*WBGD(FM) Brick Township, NJ
*WNTI(FM) Hackettstown, NJ
*KRAR(FM) Espanola, NM
*KRRE(FM) Las Vegas, NM
*KNLK(FM) Santa Rosa, NM
*KXFR(FM) Socorro, NM
*KELC(FM) Hawthorne, NV
*WNGN(FM) Argyle, NY
*WSHR(FM) Lake Ronkonkoma, NY
*WHVM(FM) Owego, NY
*WCEL(FM) Plattsburgh, NY
*WRVN(FM) Utica, NY
*WRFI(FM) Watkins Glen, NY
*WLKP(FM) Belpre, OH
*WKJA(FM) Brunswick, OH
*WOUH-FM Chillicothe, OH
*WGDE(FM) Defiance, OH
*WKCO(FM) Gambier, OH
*WMUO(FM) Greenville, OH
*WXMF(FM) Marion, OH
*WHKU(FM) Proctorville, OH
*KLXO(FM) Beaver, OK
*KSSU(FM) Durant, OK
*KHEB(FM) Granite, OK
*KBCW-FM McAlester, OK
*KMUN(FM) Astoria, OR
*KRVM-FM Eugene, OR
*KWSO(FM) Warm Springs, OR
*WCAL(FM) California, PA
*WBYK(FM) Kulpmont, PA
*WVME(FM) Meadville, PA
*WKRI(FM) Cokesbury, SC
*KQSD-FM Lowry, SD
*KRFW(FM) Watertown, SD
*KPCJ(FM) Yankton, SD
*WAPX-FM Clarksville, TN
*WUOT(FM) Knoxville, TN
*WGBQ(FM) Lynchburg, TN
*KXRI(FM) Amarillo, TX
*KALD(FM) Caldwell, TX
*KPFC(FM) Callisburg, TX
*KLLR(FM) Dripping Springs, TX
*KAZF(FM) Hebronville, TX
*KHCJ(FM) Jefferson, TX
*KAVX(FM) Lufkin, TX
*KMEO(FM) Mertzon, TX
*KPGA(FM) Morton, TX
*KHPO(FM) Port O'Connor, TX
*KEYD(FM) Delta, UT
*KPCW-FM Park City, UT
*KEYP(FM) Price, UT
*WNRN(FM) Charlottesville, VA
*WVTR(FM) Marion, VA
*WCMK(FM) Putney, VT
*KEWR(FM) Brewster, WA
*KSJU(FM) Friday Harbor, WA
*KPTZ(FM) Port Townsend, WA
*KSFC(FM) Spokane, WA
*KDNA(FM) Yakima, WA
*WEMI(FM) Appleton, WI
*WHDI(FM) Sister Bay, WI
*WDRT(FM) Viroqua, WI
*WLBL-FM Wausau, WI
*WXPW(FM) Wausau, WI
*WRAO(FM) Wisconsin Rapids, WI
*WBHZ(FM) Elkins, WV
*WVMR-FM Hillsboro, WV
*WPHP(FM) Wheeling, WV
*KLWD(FM) Gillette, WY
*KUWR(FM) Laramie, WY
*KTYN(FM) Thayne, WY

92.1 mhz
KBBO-FM Houston, AK
WJJN(FM) Columbia, AL
WKUL(FM) Cullman, AL
WZEW(FM) Fairhope, AL
WERH-FM Hamilton, AL
KHPQ(FM) Clinton, AR

KDQN-FM De Queen, AR
KQSM-FM Fayetteville, AR
KSBS-FM Pago Pago, AS
KFMA(FM) Green Valley, AZ
KZUA(FM) Holbrook, AZ
KSGC(FM) Tusayan, AZ
KPSL-FM Bakersfield, CA
KOND(FM) Clovis, CA
KSOQ-FM Escondido, CA
KQCM(FM) Joshua Tree, CA
KCCL(FM) Placerville, CA
KKDV(FM) Walnut Creek, CA
KJMN(FM) Castle Rock, CO
KTHN(FM) La Junta, CO
WLBW(FM) Fenwick Island, DE
WFFY(FM) Destin, FL
WAFZ-FM Immokalee, FL
WJXR(FM) Macclenny, FL
WNFK(FM) Perry, FL
WLTQ-FM Venice, FL
WRLX(FM) West Palm Beach, FL
WDDQ(FM) Adel, GA
WBTR-FM Carrollton, GA
WJGA-FM Jackson, GA
WLHR-FM Lavonia, GA
WPEH-FM Louisville, GA
WHHR(FM) Vienna, GA
KHWI(FM) Holualoa, HI
KCHE-FM Cherokee, IA
KUEL(FM) Fort Dodge, IA
KRLS(FM) Knoxville, IA
*KIBX(FM) Bonners Ferry, ID
KEGE(FM) Pocatello, ID
KXJO(FM) Saint Maries, ID
WQKQ(FM) Carthage, IL
WWGO(FM) Charleston, IL
WFPS(FM) Freeport, IL
*WBST(FM) Muncie, IN
WROI(FM) Rochester, IN
WZDM(FM) Vincennes, IN
KREP(FM) Belleville, KS
KMZA(FM) Seneca, KS
WBVX(FM) Carlisle, KY
*WPRZ-FM Fredonia, KY
WTKY-FM Tompkinsville, KY
KSYR(FM) Benton, LA
KTSR(FM) De Quincy, LA
KLIL(FM) Moreauville, LA
KVCL-FM Winnfield, LA
*WOMR(FM) Provincetown, MA
*WUPI(FM) Presque Isle, ME
WPHX-FM Sanford, ME
WIDL(FM) Caro, MI
WHPD(FM) Dowagiac, MI
WGHN-FM Grand Haven, MI
WTWS(FM) Harrison, MI
WCSR-FM Hillsdale, MI
WQTX(FM) Saint Johns, MI
WMIS-FM Blackduck, MN
WWAX(FM) Hermantown, MN
WYRQ(FM) Little Falls, MN
KLQP(FM) Madison, MN
KRUE(FM) Waseca, MN
KKOZ-FM Ava, MO
KMOE(FM) Butler, MO
KMFC(FM) Centralia, MO
KCVZ(FM) Dixon, MO
KSDL(FM) Sedalia, MO
WBKN(FM) Brookhaven, MS
WJMG(FM) Hattiesburg, MS
WKKY(FM) Merigold, MS
WMSU(FM) Starkville, MS
WUMS(FM) University, MS
WJNS-FM Yazoo City, MS
WMNC-FM Morganton, NC
WCDG(FM) Moyock, NC
WRSV(FM) Rocky Mount, NC
KZRX(FM) Dickinson, ND
KHZZ(FM) Sargent, NE
WFEX(FM) Peterborough, NH
WVLT(FM) Vineland, NJ
KATK-FM Carlsbad, NM
KJZS(FM) Sparks, NV
WSEN-FM Baldwinsville, NY
WCKR(FM) Hornell, NY
WVTK(FM) Port Henry, NY

WRNQ(FM) Poughkeepsie, NY
WLNG(FM) Sag Harbor, NY
WDLA-FM Walton, NY
WOHF(FM) Bellevue, OH
WYVK(FM) Middleport, OH
WBIK(FM) Pleasant City, OH
WFGF(FM) Wapakoneta, OH
WROU-FM West Carrollton, OH
KTBT(FM) Broken Arrow, OK
KFXI(FM) Marlow, OK
KMZE(FM) Woodward, OK
KWVR-FM Enterprise, OR
*KMKR(FM) Oakridge, OR
KVAN-FM Pilot Rock, OR
*KSYD(FM) Reedsport, OR
WKPL(FM) Ellwood City, PA
WJHT(FM) Johnstown, PA
WSNU(FM) Lock Haven, PA
WPPT(FM) Mercersburg, PA
WQFM(FM) Nanticoke, PA
WWKL(FM) Palmyra, PA
*WPTS(FM) Pittsburgh, PA
WZET(FM) Hormigueros, PR
WZOL(FM) Luquillo, PR
WBHC-FM Hampton, SC
WWNU(FM) Irmo, SC
WMYB(FM) Myrtle Beach, SC
WQQK(FM) Hendersonville, TN
WEUZ(FM) Minor Hill, TN
KOPY-FM Alice, TX
KCZO(FM) Carrizo Springs, TX
KXEZ(FM) Farmersville, TX
KTFW-FM Glen Rose, TX
*KYLR(FM) Hutto, TX
*KTNR(FM) Kenedy, TX
KNBT(FM) New Braunfels, TX
KROI(FM) Seabrook, TX
KHOS-FM Sonora, TX
KTBB-FM Tyler, TX
KTCE(FM) Payson, UT
WDIC-FM Clinchco, VA
*WWHS(FM) Hampden-Sydney, VA
WCDX(FM) Mechanicsville, VA
WMOO(FM) Derby Center, VT
KCRK-FM Colville, WA
WLTU(FM) Manitowoc, WI
WRJC-FM Mauston, WI
WMEQ-FM Menomonie, WI
WEZY(FM) Racine, WI
WXXM(FM) Sun Prairie, WI
*WVWC(FM) Buckhannon, WV
KFRZ(FM) Green River, WY

92.3 mhz
WLWI-FM Montgomery, AL
KIPR(FM) Pine Bluff, AR
KWCD(FM) Bisbee, AZ
KTAR-FM Glendale, AZ
KRED-FM Eureka, CA
KHHT(FM) Los Angeles, CA
KSJO(FM) San Jose, CA
KJYE(FM) Grand Junction, CO
KSTH(FM) Holyoke, CO
KHIH(FM) Hugo, CO
KVRH-FM Salida, CO
WCMQ-FM Hialeah, FL
WWKA(FM) Orlando, FL
WMOQ(FM) Bostwick, GA
WAEG(FM) Evans, GA
WSGA(FM) Hinesville, GA
WLZN(FM) Macon, GA
WQLI(FM) Meigs, GA
KSSK-FM Waipahu, HI
KKHQ-FM Oelwein, IA
KIZN(FM) Boise, ID
KRVQ(FM) Victor, ID
WZPW(FM) Peoria, IL
WTTS(FM) Bloomington, IN
WFWI(FM) Fort Wayne, IN
WPWX(FM) Hammond, IN
KFTI-FM Newton, KS
KCCV-FM Olathe, KS
WYGE(FM) London, KY
WZAQ(FM) Louisa, KY
WDVW(FM) La Place, LA
KMYY(FM) Rayville, LA

WERQ-FM Baltimore, MD
WWHC(FM) Oakland, MD
WMME-FM Augusta, ME
WZUU(FM) Allegan, MI
WBNZ(FM) Beulah, MI
WMXD(FM) Detroit, MI
WJPD(FM) Ishpeming, MI
KXRA-FM Alexandria, MN
WIL-FM Saint Louis, MO
KSAR(FM) Thayer, MO
KTTN-FM Trenton, MO
WOHT(FM) Grenada, MS
KYUS-FM Miles City, MT
KQRK(FM) Ronan, MT
WKRR(FM) Asheboro, NC
WQSL(FM) Jacksonville, NC
WZPR(FM) Nags Head, NC
KCVG(FM) Medina, ND
KEZO-FM Omaha, NE
WGXL(FM) Hanover, NH
KRST(FM) Albuquerque, NM
KOMP(FM) Las Vegas, NV
KSVL(FM) Smith, NV
WXRK(FM) New York, NY
WFLY(FM) Troy, NY
WKRK-FM Cleveland Heights, OH
WCOL-FM Columbus, OH
KREU(FM) Roland, OK
KGON(FM) Portland, OR
*WKVR-FM Huntingdon, PA
WNBQ(FM) Mansfield, PA
WLGL(FM) Riverside, PA
WRRN(FM) Warren, PA
WPRO-FM Providence, RI
KQRQ(FM) Rapid City, SD
WDEF-FM Chattanooga, TN
WYNU(FM) Milan, TN
KOFX(FM) El Paso, TX
KIJN-FM Farwell, TX
KRNH(FM) Kerrville, TX
KIIZ-FM Killeen, TX
KETX-FM Livingston, TX
KCUL-FM Marshall, TX
KNFM(FM) Midland, TX
KNRG(FM) New Ulm, TX
KZNO(FM) Seymour, TX
KQVT(FM) Victoria, TX
WTYD(FM) Deltaville, VA
WXLK(FM) Roanoke, VA
KULE-FM Ephrata, WA
WJMQ(FM) Clintonville, WI
WRLS-FM Hayward, WI
WOSQ(FM) Spencer, WI
WXCR(FM) New Martinsville, WV

92.5 mhz
WXJC-FM Cordova, AL
WVNN-FM Trinity, AL
KWYN-FM Wynne, AR
KTHQ(FM) Eagar, AZ
KMYX-FM Arvin, CA
KBRE(FM) Atwater, CA
KSRW(FM) Independence, CA
KKAL(FM) Paso Robles, CA
KGBY(FM) Sacramento, CA
KAYF(FM) Bayfield, CO
KWOF(FM) Broomfield, CO
KCRT-FM Trinidad, CO
WWYZ(FM) Waterbury, CT
WNDT(FM) Alachua, FL
WNTY(FM) Estero, FL
WPAP-FM Panama City, FL
WYUU(FM) Safety Harbor, FL
WFJO(FM) Folkston, GA
WKZZ(FM) Tifton, GA
WEKS(FM) Zebulon, GA
KLHI-FM Kahului, HI
KJJY(FM) West Des Moines, IA
WCPY(FM) De Kalb, IL
WKXQ(FM) Rushville, IL
WCFF(FM) Urbana, IL
WZWZ(FM) Kokomo, IN
KQMA-FM Phillipsburg, KS
KCVT(FM) Silver Lake, KS
WBKR(FM) Owensboro, KY
*KHCL(FM) Arcadia, LA

KVPI-FM Ville Platte, LA
WXRV(FM) Andover, MA
WICO-FM Pocomoke City, MD
XHRM-FM Tijuana, MEX
WJSZ(FM) Ashley, MI
WFDX(FM) Atlanta, MI
WBGV(FM) Marlette, MI
WLAW(FM) Newaygo, MI
*WIRN(FM) Buhl, MN
KQRS-FM Golden Valley, MN
KXKK(FM) Park Rapids, MN
KKWQ(FM) Warroad, MN
*KSMR(FM) Winona, MN
KSYN(FM) Joplin, MO
KELE-FM Mountain Grove, MO
KPPL(FM) Poplar Bluff, MO
KAYX(FM) Richmond, MO
WESE(FM) Baldwyn, MS
WQST-FM Forest, MS
WQYZ(FM) Ocean Springs, MS
KAAR(FM) Butte, MT
KPQX(FM) Havre, MT
KWMY(FM) Park City, MT
WYFL(FM) Henderson, NC
WBLH(FM) Black River, NY
WKGB-FM Conklin, NY
WBEE-FM Rochester, NY
WDJQ(FM) Alliance, OH
WOFX-FM Cincinnati, OH
WVKS(FM) Toledo, OH
KPRV-FM Heavener, OK
KKRE(FM) Hollis, OK
KOMA(FM) Oklahoma City, OK
KLAD-FM Klamath Falls, OR
WQMU(FM) Indiana, PA
WJUN-FM Mexico, PA
WXTU(FM) Philadelphia, PA
WORO(FM) Corozal, PR
WESC-FM Greenville, SC
WIHB(FM) Moncks Corner, SC
KELO-FM Sioux Falls, SD
KULL(FM) Abilene, TX
KBEY(FM) Burnet, TX
KZPS(FM) Dallas, TX
KRPT(FM) Devine, TX
KXXS(FM) Elgin, TX
KCOL-FM Groves, TX
KKHA(FM) Markham, TX
KWUP(FM) Navasota, TX
KHES(FM) Rocksprings, TX
KQSI(FM) San Augustine, TX
*KHTA(FM) Wake Village, TX
KYKM(FM) Yoakum, TX
KXBN(FM) Cedar City, UT
KCUA(FM) Naples, UT
KUUU(FM) South Jordan, UT
WINC-FM Winchester, VA
KQMV(FM) Bellevue, WA
KZHR(FM) Dayton, WA
WJJQ-FM Tomahawk, WI
WBWI-FM West Bend, WI
WZAC-FM Danville, WV
KDAD(FM) Douglas, WY

92.7 mhz
*KHKY(FM) Akiachak, AK
WAFN-FM Arab, AL
WKZJ(FM) Eufaula, AL
WJBB-FM Haleyville, AL
WTDR(FM) Talladega, AL
KIXC(FM) Bearden, AR
KLYR-FM Clarksville, AR
KASR(FM) Conway, AR
KRRN(FM) Kingman, AZ
KAJL(FM) Adelanto, CA
KNGY(FM) Alameda, CA
KBQB(FM) Chico, CA
KJLL(FM) Fountain Valley, CA
KKUU(FM) Indio, CA
KTOM-FM Marina, CA
KMFB(FM) Mendocino, CA
KZIQ-FM Ridgecrest, CA
KZSQ-FM Sonora, CA
KHJL(FM) Thousand Oaks, CA
KKCH(FM) Glenwood Springs, CO
WGMD(FM) Rehoboth Beach, DE

WBHQ(FM) Beverly Beach, FL
WEOW(FM) Key West, FL
WAVW(FM) Stuart, FL
WKKZ(FM) Dublin, GA
WBGA(FM) Saint Simons Island, GA
KHBC(FM) Hilo, HI
KLGA-FM Algona, IA
KTWA(FM) Ottumwa, IA
KORT-FM Grangeville, ID
KSRA-FM Salmon, ID
WCPT-FM Arlington Heights, IL
WLSR(FM) Galesburg, IL
WTAO-FM Herrin, IL
WKIF(FM) Kankakee, IL
WQLZ(FM) Taylorville, IL
WXKU-FM Austin, IN
WZBD(FM) Berne, IN
WSDM-FM Brazil, IN
KANR(FM) Belle Plaine, KS
KZUH(FM) Minneapolis, KS
WCMI-FM Catlettsburg, KY
WMIK-FM Middlesboro, KY
WHVE(FM) Russell Springs, KY
*WBKL(FM) Clinton, LA
KBYO-FM Farmerville, LA
KLPL-FM Lake Providence, LA
KBDV(FM) Leesville, LA
KJVC(FM) Mansfield, LA
WMVY(FM) Tisbury, MA
WWXT(FM) Prince Frederick, MD
WQDY-FM Calais, ME
WOXO-FM Norway, ME
WJZL(FM) Charlotte, MI
WDZZ-FM Flint, MI
WYVN(FM) Saugatuck, MI
KLOZ(FM) Eldon, MO
KSJQ(FM) Savannah, MO
WKRA-FM Holly Springs, MS
KVCK-FM Wolf Point, MT
WQNC(FM) Harrisburg, NC
WBNK(FM) Pine Knoll Shores, NC
*KFNL(FM) Kindred, ND
KBRB-FM Ainsworth, NE
KUSO(FM) Albion, NE
WOBM-FM Toms River, NJ
KDSK(FM) Grants, NM
KRSY-FM La Luz, NM
KBQL(FM) Las Vegas, NM
KQAY-FM Tucumcari, NM
KDSS(FM) Ely, NV
KHWK(FM) Tonopah, NV
KWNA-FM Winnemucca, NV
WENY-FM Elmira, NY
WQBU-FM Garden City, NY
*WGFR(FM) Glens Falls, NY
WXUR(FM) Herkimer, NY
WRRV(FM) Middletown, NY
WQTK(FM) Ogdensburg, NY
WQEL(FM) Bucyrus, OH
*WCVZ(FM) South Zanesville, OH
KTRX(FM) Dickson, OK
KKBS(FM) Guymon, OK
KQHC(FM) Burns, OR
KGBR(FM) Gold Beach, OR
KNCU(FM) Newport, OR
KRXF(FM) Sunriver, OR
KMSW(FM) The Dalles, OR
WCCR(FM) Clarion, PA
WJSM-FM Martinsburg, PA
WSJW(FM) Starview, PA
WKSX-FM Johnston, SC
KGFX-FM Pierre, SD
WIJV(FM) Harriman, TN
KALP(FM) Alpine, TX
KIVY-FM Crockett, TX
KINL(FM) Eagle Pass, TX
KKBA(FM) Kingsville, TX
KJBZ(FM) Laredo, TX
KJAK(FM) Slaton, TX
KESO(FM) South Padre Island, TX
KBDX(FM) Blanding, UT
WFHG-FM Abingdon, VA
WUVA(FM) Charlottesville, VA
WKVT-FM Brattleboro, VT
KNCW(FM) Omak, WA
WAUN(FM) Kewaunee, WI

WPKG(FM) Neillsville, WI
WDUX-FM Waupaca, WI
WGIE(FM) Clarksburg, WV
WVJO(FM) Mullens, WV
KIQZ(FM) Rawlins, WY
KHRW(FM) Wright, WY

92.9 mhz
KFAT(FM) Anchorage, AK
WBLX-FM Mobile, AL
WTUG-FM Northport, AL
KVRE-FM Hot Springs Village, AR
KAFF-FM Flagstaff, AZ
KWMT-FM Tucson, AZ
KFGY(FM) Healdsburg, CA
KJEE(FM) Montecito, CA
KOSO(FM) Patterson, CA
KXFG(FM) Sun City, CA
KFSO-FM Visalia, CA
KKPK(FM) Colorado Springs, CO
WRDX(FM) Smyrna, DE
WIKX(FM) Charlotte Harbor, FL
WMFQ(FM) Ocala, FL
WZGC(FM) Atlanta, GA
WAAC(FM) Valdosta, GA
KATF(FM) Dubuque, IA
KKIA(FM) Ida Grove, IA
KYME(FM) Rockford, IA
WRPW(FM) Colfax, IL
WSEI(FM) Olney, IL
WNDV-FM South Bend, IN
WSKL(FM) Veedersburg, IN
KMML(FM) Cimarron, KS
KMXN(FM) Osage City, KS
WLXX(FM) Lexington, KY
KHLA(FM) Jennings, LA
KTKC(FM) Springhill, LA
WBOX-FM Varnado, LA
WBOS(FM) Brookline, MA
WEZQ(FM) Bangor, ME
WJZQ(FM) Cadillac, MI
*WSCD-FM Duluth, MN
*KFSI(FM) Rochester, MN
KKJM(FM) Saint Joseph, MN
KGRC(FM) Hannibal, MO
KLSC(FM) Malden, MO
KOMG(FM) Ozark, MO
KKID(FM) Salem, MO
WDTL-FM Cleveland, MS
WDXO(FM) Hazlehurst, MS
KLFM(FM) Great Falls, MT
KEZQ(FM) West Yellowstone, MT
KYYY(FM) Bismarck, ND
KKXL-FM Grand Forks, ND
KTGL(FM) Beatrice, NE
KTZA(FM) Artesia, NM
KYBR(FM) Espanola, NM
KRWN(FM) Farmington, NM
KSCQ(FM) Silver City, NM
KMXQ(FM) Socorro, NM
KURK(FM) Reno, NV
WBUF(FM) Buffalo, NY
WBPM(FM) Saugerties, NY
WEHM(FM) Southampton, NY
WGTZ(FM) Eaton, OH
KBEZ(FM) Tulsa, OK
KDCQ(FM) Coos Bay, OR
WLTJ(FM) Pittsburgh, PA
WMGS(FM) Wilkes-Barre, PA
WTPM(FM) Aguadilla, PR
WYQE(FM) Naguabo, PR
WZLA-FM Abbeville, SC
WEGX(FM) Dillon, SC
KSDR-FM Watertown, SD
WMFS-FM Bartlett, TN
WJXA(FM) Nashville, TN
WNPC-FM Newport, TN
KLRK(FM) Marlin, TX
KKBQ-FM Pasadena, TX
KDCD(FM) San Angelo, TX
KROM(FM) San Antonio, TX
*KMQX(FM) Weatherford, TX
KNIN-FM Wichita Falls, TX
KBLQ(FM) Logan, UT
WVHL(FM) Farmville, VA
WVBW(FM) Suffolk, VA

WEZF(FM) Burlington, VT
KISM(FM) Bellingham, WA
KZZU-FM Spokane, WA
KDBL(FM) Toppenish, WA
WYNW(FM) Birnamwood, WI
WECL(FM) Elk Mound, WI
WDHC(FM) Berkeley Springs, WV
WCWV(FM) Summersville, WV
KLGT(FM) Buffalo, WY
KOLT-FM Warren AFB, WY

93.1 mhz

WGMZ(FM) Glencoe, AL
KZLE(FM) Batesville, AR
*KHDX(FM) Conway, AR
KKHJ-FM Pago Pago, AS
KLJZ(FM) Yuma, AZ
KXGO(FM) Arcata, CA
KCBS-FM Los Angeles, CA
KHLX(FM) Pollock Pines, CA
KKXX-FM Shafter, CA
KMGJ(FM) Grand Junction, CO
WKRO-FM Edgewater, FL
WHDR(FM) Miami, FL
WBBK-FM Blakely, GA
WEAS-FM Springfield, GA
WGAC-FM Warrenton, GA
KMWB(FM) Captain Cook, HI
KQMQ-FM Honolulu, HI
KMCS(FM) Muscatine, IA
KZMG(FM) New Plymouth, ID
WXRT-FM Chicago, IL
WYDS(FM) Decatur, IL
WTFX-FM Clarksville, IN
WIBC(FM) Indianapolis, IN
KHMY(FM) Pratt, KS
WMKZ(FM) Monticello, KY
WDHR(FM) Pikeville, KY
KQID(FM) Alexandria, LA
WHYN-FM Springfield, MA
WPOC(FM) Baltimore, MD
WMGX(FM) Portland, ME
WDRQ(FM) Detroit, MI
WIMK(FM) Iron Mountain, MI
KATO-FM New Ulm, MN
KWJK(FM) Boonville, MO
KBDZ(FM) Perryville, MO
WGDQ(FM) Sumrall, MS
KGCX(FM) Sidney, MT
WPAW(FM) Winston-Salem, NC
KRVN-FM Lexington, NE
WPAT-FM Paterson, NJ
WEZW(FM) Wildwood Crest, NJ
KPLV(FM) Las Vegas, NV
WNTQ(FM) Syracuse, NY
WZAK(FM) Cleveland, OH
WWSR(FM) Lima, OH
WNTO(FM) Racine, OH
KRYP(FM) Gladstone, OR
WQYX(FM) Clearfield, PA
WZMJ(FM) Batesburg, SC
KRCS(FM) Sturgis, SD
KKYA(FM) Yankton, SD
WWGM(FM) Alamo, TN
WSAA(FM) Benton, TN
WCYQ(FM) Karns, TN
KQIZ-FM Amarillo, TX
KMKT(FM) Bells, TX
KSTV-FM Dublin, TX
KSII(FM) El Paso, TX
KBDK(FM) Leakey, TX
KTYL-FM Tyler, TX
WLFV(FM) Ettrick, VA
WSVO(FM) Staunton, VA
WJQM(FM) De Forest, WI
WJBL(FM) Ladysmith, WI
WFGM-FM Barrackville, WV
KTRZ(FM) Riverton, WY

93.3 mhz

KXBA(FM) Nikiski, AK
KVAK-FM Valdez, AK
WWFF-FM New Market, AL
KMJI(FM) Ashdown, AR
KKSP(FM) Bryant, AR
KAGL(FM) El Dorado, AR
KDKB(FM) Mesa, AZ

KXAZ(FM) Page, AZ
KBHR(FM) Big Bear City, CA
KRHV(FM) Big Pine, CA
KNTO(FM) Chowchilla, CA
KHTS-FM El Cajon, CA
KRZZ(FM) San Francisco, CA
KZOZ(FM) San Luis Obispo, CA
KJDX(FM) Susanville, CA
KKDC(FM) Dolores, CO
KLMR-FM Lamar, CO
KTCL(FM) Wheat Ridge, CO
*WFAR(FM) Danbury, CT
WJBT(FM) Callahan, FL
WGWD(FM) Gretna, FL
WNCV(FM) Shalimar, FL
WFLZ-FM Tampa, FL
WVFJ-FM Manchester, GA
*WZAE(FM) Wadley, GA
KIOA(FM) Des Moines, IA
WPBG(FM) Peoria, IL
WTRH(FM) Ramsey, IL
WBTU(FM) Kendallville, IN
WQTY(FM) Linton, IN
WDNS(FM) Bowling Green, KY
WKYQ(FM) Paducah, KY
WQUE-FM New Orleans, LA
WSNE-FM Taunton, MA
WKQZ(FM) Midland, MI
KBLB(FM) Nisswa, MN
KQQX(FM) Hermann, MO
KMXV(FM) Kansas City, MO
KIGL(FM) Seligman, MO
WSYE(FM) Houston, MS
KYYA-FM Billings, MT
KGGL(FM) Missoula, MT
WTPT(FM) Forest City, NC
*WOGR-FM Salisbury, NC
WERO(FM) Washington, NC
KSJZ(FM) Jamestown, ND
KTWI(FM) Bennington, NE
KMOR(FM) Gering, NE
WNHW(FM) Belmont, NH
KKOB-FM Albuquerque, NM
*WCAN(FM) Canajoharie, NY
WFKL(FM) Fairport, NY
WWSE(FM) Jamestown, NY
WBWZ(FM) New Paltz, NY
WSLP(FM) Saranac Lake, NY
WCIZ-FM Watertown, NY
WLZT(FM) Chillicothe, OH
WAKW(FM) Cincinnati, OH
WNCD(FM) Youngstown, OH
KKNG-FM Newcastle, OK
KKNU(FM) Springfield-Eugene, OR
WQZS(FM) Meyersdale, PA
WBZD-FM Muncy, PA
WMMR(FM) Philadelphia, PA
WZMT(FM) Ponce, PR
WWWZ(FM) Summerville, SC
KJRV(FM) Wessington Springs, SD
KDHT(FM) Cedar Park, TX
KLIF-FM Haltom City, TX
KZBT(FM) Midland, TX
KQBU-FM Port Arthur, TX
KITE(FM) Port Lavaca, TX
KUBL-FM Salt Lake City, UT
WFLS-FM Fredericksburg, VA
KUBE(FM) Seattle, WA
*KRKL(FM) Walla Walla, WA
WBSZ(FM) Ashland, WI
WIZM-FM La Crosse, WI
WLDB(FM) Milwaukee, WI
*WKVW(FM) Marmet, WV
KJAX(FM) Jackson, WY

93.5 mhz

KDJF(FM) Ester, AK
WMLV(FM) Butler, AL
KBKG(FM) Corning, AR
KBFC(FM) Forrest City, AR
KKTZ(FM) Lakeview, AR
KSNX(FM) Show Low, AZ
KNAC(FM) Earlimart, CA
KXSM(FM) Hollister, CA
KWIE(FM) Ontario, CA
KDAY(FM) Redondo Beach, CA

KLKX(FM) Rosamond, CA
KKBN(FM) Twain Harte, CA
KMKX(FM) Willits, CA
KALQ-FM Alamosa, CO
KVVQ(FM) Aspen, CO
WZBH(FM) Georgetown, DE
WBGF(FM) Belle Glade, FL
WKEY-FM Key West, FL
WFDZ(FM) Perry, FL
WPBH(FM) Port St. Joe, FL
WSRM(FM) Coosa, GA
WLJA-FM Ellijay, GA
WVOH-FM Hazlehurst, GA
KPOA(FM) Lahaina, HI
KQNG-FM Lihue, HI
KQCS(FM) Bettendorf, IA
KKMI(FM) Burlington, IA
WVIX(FM) Joliet, IL
WEBX(FM) Tuscola, IL
WLFW(FM) Chandler, IN
WMXQ(FM) Hartford City, IN
WKHY(FM) Lafayette, IN
KKDT(FM) Burdett, KS
KOTE(FM) Eureka, KS
KLKC-FM Parsons, KS
KWME(FM) Wellington, KS
WMMG-FM Brandenburg, KY
WAIN-FM Columbia, KY
KGGM(FM) Delhi, LA
KJAE(FM) Leesville, LA
WFQR(FM) Harwich Port, MA
WCTB(FM) Fairfield, ME
WBCM(FM) Boyne City, MI
WKMJ-FM Hancock, MI
WHMI-FM Howell, MI
KSCR(FM) Benson, MN
KITN(FM) Worthington, MN
KMYK(FM) Osage Beach, MO
*KRSS(FM) Tarkio, MO
WHJT(FM) Clinton, MS
KZXT(FM) Eureka, MT
KLAN(FM) Glasgow, MT
WLQB(FM) Ocean Isle Beach, NC
*WYFQ-FM Wadesboro, NC
KNDH(FM) Hettinger, ND
KKOT(FM) Columbus, NE
KZTL(FM) Paxton, NE
WMWV(FM) Conway, NH
KWES(FM) Ruidoso, NM
KADD(FM) Logandale, NV
WZCR(FM) Hudson, NY
WVBR-FM Ithaca, NY
WVIP(FM) New Rochelle, NY
WOKR(FM) Remsen, NY
WQRW(FM) Wellsville, NY
WBNV(FM) Barnesville, OH
WRQN(FM) Bowling Green, OH
KRKZ(FM) Altus, OK
KWCQ(FM) Condon, OR
KQIK-FM Lakeview, OR
WHPA(FM) Gallitzin, PA
WTPA(FM) Mechanicsburg, PA
WSBG(FM) Stroudsburg, PA
WDOG-FM Allendale, SC
WARQ(FM) Columbia, SC
WKBQ(FM) Covington, TN
WKZX-FM Lenoir City, TN
WKWX(FM) Savannah, TN
KLXK(FM) Breckenridge, TX
KAJP(FM) Carrizo Springs, TX
KBHT(FM) Crockett, TX
KGWT(FM) George West, TX
KIKT(FM) Greenville, TX
KOOK(FM) Junction, TX
KRTS(FM) Marfa, TX
KBAW(FM) Zapata, TX
KSNN(FM) Saint George, UT
WAXM(FM) Big Stone Gap, VA
WBBC-FM Blackstone, VA
WSNV(FM) Salem, VA
WVVI-FM Christiansted, VI
WEEY(FM) Springfield, VT
KOZI-FM Chelan, WA
KWDR(FM) Royal City, WA
WOZZ(FM) New London, WI
WBTQ(FM) Buckhannon, WV

KWYX(FM) Casper, WY
KWDU(FM) Upton, WY

93.7 mhz

KAFC(FM) Anchorage, AK
WDJC-FM Birmingham, AL
WUSD(FM) Geneva, AL
KISR(FM) Fort Smith, AR
KJBR(FM) Marked Tree, AR
KHBM-FM Monticello, AR
KVYL(FM) Mohave Valley, AZ
KRQQ(FM) Tucson, AZ
KCLB-FM Coachella, CA
KXZM(FM) Felton, CA
KSKS(FM) Fresno, CA
KQJK(FM) Roseville, CA
KDB(FM) Santa Barbara, CA
KJZY(FM) Sebastopol, CA
KRAI-FM Craig, CO
KSBV(FM) Salida, CO
WZMX(FM) Hartford, CT
WSTW(FM) Wilmington, DE
WTLT(FM) Naples, FL
WOGK(FM) Ocala, FL
WGYL(FM) Vero Beach, FL
WPEZ(FM) Jeffersonville, GA
WMPZ(FM) Ringgold, GA
KKRL(FM) Carroll, IA
KZBQ(FM) Pocatello, ID
WTRX-FM Pontiac, IL
WFRR(FM) Walton, IN
KAIR-FM Horton, KS
KPIO-FM Pleasanton, KS
KYEZ(FM) Salina, KS
WDGG(FM) Ashland, KY
KRDJ(FM) New Iberia, LA
KXKS-FM Shreveport, LA
WMKK(FM) Lawrence, MA
WRMO(FM) Milbridge, ME
WRCL(FM) Frankenmuth, MI
WBCT(FM) Grand Rapids, MI
WKAD(FM) Harrietta, MI
KXXR(FM) Minneapolis, MN
KTUF(FM) Kirksville, MO
KSD(FM) Saint Louis, MO
WMJY(FM) Biloxi, MS
WQLJ(FM) Oxford, MS
KOBB-FM Bozeman, MT
KTZZ(FM) Conrad, MT
WNTB(FM) Wrightsville Beach, NC
WDAY-FM Fargo, ND
KIZZ(FM) Minot, ND
KOLB(FM) Firth, NE
KXXI(FM) Gallup, NM
KLKO(FM) Elko, NV
KWNZ(FM) Sun Valley, NV
*WCOV-FM Clyde, NY
WBLK(FM) Depew, NY
*WYAI(FM) Scotia, NY
WFCJ(FM) Miamisburg, OH
WQIO(FM) Mount Vernon, OH
KSPI-FM Stillwater, OK
KTMT-FM Medford, OR
WBUS(FM) Boalsburg, PA
WSJR(FM) Dallas, PA
WBZW-FM Pittsburgh, PA
WZNT(FM) San Juan, PR
WXJY(FM) Georgetown, SC
WFBC-FM Greenville, SC
WSIM(FM) Lamar, SC
WALI(FM) Walterboro, SC
KBRK-FM Brookings, SD
KVAR(FM) Pine Ridge, SD
KWYR-FM Winner, SD
WTKB-FM Atwood, TN
WBXE(FM) Baxter, TN
WFFI(FM) Kingston Springs, TN
KLBJ-FM Austin, TX
KKDL(FM) Dilley, TX
KKRW(FM) Houston, TX
KNOR(FM) Krum, TX
KXTQ-FM Lubbock, TX
KLGL(FM) Richfield, UT
WPYA(FM) Chesapeake, VA
WAZR(FM) Woodstock, VA
WUSX(FM) Addison, VT

WOTX(FM) Lunenburg, VT
KXAA(FM) Cle Elum, WA
KANY(FM) Ocean Shores, WA
KGSG(FM) Pasco, WA
KDRK-FM Spokane, WA
WEKZ-FM Monroe, WI
WBFM(FM) Sheboygan, WI
WCYE(FM) Three Lakes, WI
KAZY(FM) Cheyenne, WY
KYTI(FM) Sheridan, WY

93.9 mhz

WYTK(FM) Rogersville, AL
WQSI(FM) Union Springs, AL
KAMJ-FM Gosnell, AR
KMGN(FM) Flagstaff, AZ
KRIT(FM) Parker, AZ
KFMF(FM) Chico, CA
KEXA(FM) King City, CA
KXOS(FM) Los Angeles, CA
KBBU(FM) Modesto, CA
KRLT(FM) South Lake Tahoe, CA
KYSL(FM) Frisco, CO
WKYS(FM) Washington, DC
WMIA-FM Miami Beach, FL
WDRR(FM) Martinez, GA
WMTM-FM Moultrie, GA
KUAM-FM Hagatna, GU
KIKI-FM Honolulu, HI
KLUA(FM) Kailua-Kona, HI
KIAI(FM) Mason City, IA
KSOU-FM Sioux Center, IA
WYEC(FM) Cambridge, IL
WCEZ(FM) Carthage, IL
WLIT-FM Chicago, IL
WABZ(FM) Sherman, IL
*WPFR-FM Clinton, IN
WRWM(FM) Marion, IN
WLCL(FM) Sellersville, IN
KDGS(FM) Andover, KS
KZRD(FM) Dodge City, KS
WSEK(FM) Burnside, KY
WKTG(FM) Madisonville, KY
KMXH(FM) Alexandria, LA
WRSI(FM) Turners Falls, MA
*WARX(FM) Lewiston, ME
WAVC(FM) Mio, MI
WNBY-FM Newberry, MI
KKRC(FM) Granite Falls, MN
WTBX(FM) Hibbing, MN
KSSZ(FM) Fayette, MO
KGKS(FM) Scott City, MO
KJMK(FM) Webb City, MO
KSPQ(FM) West Plains, MO
WGRM-FM Greenwood, MS
WRXW(FM) Pearl, MS
WKSL(FM) Cary, NC
KSWN(FM) McCook, NE
KRTN-FM Raton, NM
WDNY-FM Dansville, NY
*WNYC-FM New York, NY
WKXZ(FM) Norwich, NY
*WQKE(FM) Plattsburgh, NY
WLWD(FM) Columbus Grove, OH
KIMY(FM) Watonga, OK
KPDQ-FM Portland, OR
WTWF(FM) Fairview, PA
WKBI-FM Saint Marys, PA
WJXY-FM Conway, SC
WIGL(FM) Saint Matthews, SC
KKMK(FM) Rapid City, SD
WAYA(FM) Decatur, TN
WSIB(FM) Selmer, TN
KMXR(FM) Corpus Christi, TX
KINT-FM El Paso, TX
KAGZ(FM) Lufkin, TX
KOYN(FM) Paris, TX
KCRN-FM San Angelo, TX
KBNU(FM) Uvalde, TX
WMEV-FM Marion, VA
WLVB(FM) Morrisville, VT
WMXR(FM) Woodstock, VT
KTAC(FM) Ephrata, WA
WMMA(FM) Nekoosa, WI
WDOR-FM Sturgeon Bay, WI
WRRR(FM) Saint Marys, WV

KUSZ(FM) Laramie, WY
KTAK(FM) Riverton, WY

94.1 mhz
WZBQ(FM) Carrollton, AL
WHRP(FM) Gurley, AL
KKPT(FM) Little Rock, AR
KRDE(FM) Globe, AZ
KXKQ(FM) Safford, AZ
KISV(FM) Bakersfield, CA
*KPFA(FM) Berkeley, CA
KNCO-FM Grass Valley, CA
KSLG-FM Hydesville, CA
KBKY(FM) Merced, CA
KLMM(FM) Morro Bay, CA
KMYI(FM) San Diego, CA
KWDI(FM) Idalia, CO
KKXK(FM) Montrose, CO
KEZZ(FM) Walden, CO
WAKU(FM) Crawfordville, FL
WLLD(FM) Lakeland, FL
WTYS-FM Marianna, FL
WMEZ(FM) Pensacola, FL
WSOS-FM Saint Augustine, FL
WQBT(FM) Savannah, GA
WSTR(FM) Smyrna, GA
KRNA(FM) Iowa City, IA
KBXL(FM) Caldwell, ID
WMIX-FM Mount Vernon, IL
WGFA-FM Watseka, IL
*WBNI-FM Roanoke, IN
KDNS(FM) Downs, KS
KFKF-FM Kansas City, KS
WLYE-FM Glasgow, KY
KRLQ(FM) Hodge, LA
WEMX(FM) Kentwood, LA
WWKR(FM) Hart, MI
WVIC(FM) Jackson, MI
WUPK(FM) Marquette, MI
KKLN(FM) Atwater, MN
KXLP(FM) Eagle Lake, MN
KFML(FM) Little Falls, MN
KPVR(FM) Bowling Green, MO
KRKX(FM) Billings, MT
KOPR(FM) Butte, MT
WTHZ(FM) Lexington, NC
WNBU(FM) Oriental, NC
KQCH(FM) Omaha, NE
KNEB-FM Scottsbluff, NE
WFTN-FM Franklin, NH
KZRR(FM) Albuquerque, NM
KZOR(FM) Hobbs, NM
KMXB(FM) Henderson, NV
WZNE(FM) Brighton, NY
WOTT(FM) Calcium, NY
WNYV(FM) Whitehall, NY
WHBC-FM Canton, OH
WNNF(FM) Cincinnati, OH
KTSO(FM) Glenpool, OK
KZCD(FM) Lawton, OK
KXIX(FM) Bend, OR
*KOOZ(FM) Myrtle Point, OR
WYSP(FM) Philadelphia, PA
WQKX(FM) Sunbury, PA
WNOD(FM) Mayaguez, PR
WHJY(FM) Providence, RI
WYOR(FM) Cross Hill, SC
WRZE(FM) Kingstree, SC
KSDN-FM Aberdeen, SD
WKQK(FM) Germantown, TN
WMXK(FM) Morristown, TN
WLZK(FM) Paris, TN
WFFH(FM) Smyrna, TN
KMXJ-FM Amarillo, TX
KQXY-FM Beaumont, TX
KLTR(FM) Brenham, TX
KDLK-FM Del Rio, TX
KTFM(FM) Floresville, TX
KLNO(FM) Fort Worth, TX
KJAZ(FM) Point Comfort, TX
KODJ(FM) Salt Lake City, UT
WXEZ(FM) Yorktown, VA
KCLK-FM Clarkston, WA
KMPS-FM Seattle, WA
WIAL(FM) Eau Claire, WI
WJJO(FM) Watertown, WI

WQZK-FM Keyser, WV
WAXS-FM Oak Hill, WV

94.3 mhz
WIZB(FM) Abbeville, AL
WQZX(FM) Greenville, AL
KAMO-FM Rogers, AR
KSMZ(FM) Viola, AR
KDDL(FM) Chino Valley, AZ
KBUX(FM) Quartzsite, AZ
KDUC(FM) Barstow, CA
KCRE-FM Crescent City, CA
KEBN(FM) Garden Grove, CA
KTTA(FM) Jackson, CA
KOKO(FM) Kerman, CA
KBUA(FM) San Fernando, CA
KILO(FM) Colorado Springs, CO
KMAX-FM Wellington, CO
WYBC-FM New Haven, CT
WNFB(FM) Lake City, FL
WGMX(FM) Marathon, FL
WZZR(FM) Riviera Beach, FL
WLEL(FM) Ellaville, GA
WTHP(FM) Gibson, GA
KEEI(FM) Hanapepe, HI
KDLX(FM) Makawao, HI
KTPZ(FM) Hazelton, ID
KSNA(FM) Rexburg, ID
WRMS-FM Beardstown, IL
WPMJ(FM) Chillicothe, IL
WJKL(FM) Glendale Heights, IL
WKYX-FM Golconda, IL
WMKR(FM) Pana, IL
WSSQ(FM) Sterling, IL
WREB(FM) Greencastle, IN
WZOC(FM) Plymouth, IN
WIFE-FM Rushville, IN
KCVW(FM) Kingman, KS
WULF(FM) Hardinsburg, KY
WIFX-FM Jenkins, KY
WEGI-FM Oak Grove, KY
WTIX-FM Galliano, LA
WZAI(FM) Brewster, MA
WINX-FM Saint Michaels, MD
WCYY(FM) Biddeford, ME
WFCX(FM) Leland, MI
WZNL(FM) Norway, MI
KKIN-FM Aitkin, MN
KULO(FM) Alexandria, MN
KDOM-FM Windom, MN
KATI(FM) California, MO
WKZW(FM) Bay Springs, MS
WXRZ(FM) Corinth, MS
WBAD(FM) Leland, MS
WTIB(FM) Farmville, NC
*WJIJ(FM) Norlina, NC
WZKB(FM) Wallace, NC
WJLK(FM) Asbury Park, NJ
WIBG-FM Avalon, NJ
KYEE(FM) Alamogordo, NM
KDEM(FM) Deming, NM
WLVY(FM) Elmira, NY
WKXP(FM) Kingston, NY
WMJC(FM) Smithtown, NY
WKKI(FM) Celina, OH
WKKJ(FM) Chillicothe, OH
WMRN-FM Marion, OH
KXOO(FM) Elk City, OK
KTIL-FM Tillamook, OR
WLNP(FM) Carbondale, PA
WQCM(FM) Greencastle, PA
WBXQ(FM) Patton, PA
WUZZ(FM) Saegertown, PA
WWNQ(FM) Forest Acres, SC
WSCC-FM Goose Creek, SC
WCMG(FM) Latta, SC
WTJJ(FM) Dyer, TN
WJJM-FM Lewisburg, TN
WNFZ(FM) Oak Ridge, TN
WJTT(FM) Red Bank, TN
KBTS(FM) Big Spring, TX
KYOX(FM) Comanche, TX
KHER(FM) Crystal City, TX
KFST-FM Fort Stockton, TX
KRVL(FM) Kerrville, TX
KYXX(FM) Ozona, TX

KSEY-FM Seymour, TX
KXRQ(FM) Roosevelt, UT
WTON-FM Staunton, VA
WWXX(FM) Warrenton, VA
WBTN-FM Bennington, VT
WROE(FM) Neenah-Menasha, WI
WQPC(FM) Prairie du Chien, WI
WRLF(FM) Fairmont, WV

94.5 mhz
WJOX(FM) Birmingham, AL
WHOD(FM) Jackson, AL
KFPW-FM Barling, AR
KJIW-FM Helena, AR
KOOL-FM Phoenix, AZ
KCNO(FM) Alturas, CA
KSEH(FM) Brawley, CA
KWTY(FM) Cartago, CA
KCGC(FM) Coarsegold, CA
KSPE-FM Ellwood, CA
KBAY(FM) Gilroy, CA
KGEN-FM Hanford, CA
KMYT(FM) Temecula, CA
KWNE(FM) Ukiah, CA
KRFD(FM) Merino, CO
KJEB(FM) New Castle, CO
*WERB(FM) Berlin, CT
WCFB(FM) Daytona Beach, FL
WARO(FM) Naples, FL
WFLF-FM Parker, FL
WBYZ(FM) Baxley, GA
WFDR-FM Woodbury, GA
KKEZ(FM) Fort Dodge, IA
KHTQ(FM) Hayden, ID
WLRW(FM) Champaign, IL
WRZR(FM) Loogootee, IN
KSKL(FM) Scott City, KS
WIBW-FM Topeka, KS
WMXL(FM) Lexington, KY
KSMB(FM) Lafayette, LA
KRUF(FM) Shreveport, LA
WJMN(FM) Boston, MA
WKSQ(FM) Ellsworth, ME
WCEN-FM Hemlock, MI
WTNR(FM) Holland, MI
WLJZ(FM) Mackinaw City, MI
WELY-FM Ely, MN
KSTP-FM Saint Paul, MN
KRXL(FM) Kirksville, MO
KKLR(FM) Poplar Bluff, MO
WCMR-FM Bruce, MS
WJZD-FM Long Beach, MS
KMON-FM Great Falls, MT
WGBT(FM) Eden, NC
WCMS-FM Hatteras, NC
WKXS-FM Leland, NC
KQDY(FM) Bismarck, ND
KLIQ(FM) Hastings, NE
WPST(FM) Trenton, NJ
KKOR(FM) Gallup, NM
KOYT(FM) Elko, NV
KVBE(FM) Moapa, NV
KUUB(FM) Sun Valley, NV
*WNED-FM Buffalo, NY
*WYKV(FM) Ravena, NY
WYYY(FM) Syracuse, NY
WDKF(FM) Englewood, OH
WXKR(FM) Port Clinton, OH
KEMX(FM) Locust Grove, OK
KJDY-FM Canyon City, OR
KMGE(FM) Eugene, OR
WDAC(FM) Lancaster, PA
WWSW-FM Pittsburgh, PA
WBHV-FM State College, PA
WSPX(FM) Bowman, SC
WMUU-FM Greenville, SC
WYEZ(FM) Murrell's Inlet, SC
KPLO-FM Reliance, SD
*KCFS(FM) Sioux Falls, SD
WFGZ(FM) Lobelville, TN
KSOC(FM) Gainesville, TX
KFRQ(FM) Harlingen, TX
KTBZ-FM Houston, TX
KFMX-FM Lubbock, TX
KEMA(FM) Three Rivers, TX
KBCT-FM Waco, TX

KVFX(FM) Logan, UT
WRVQ(FM) Richmond, VA
WDVT(FM) Rutland, VT
KLYK(FM) Kelso, WA
KRXY(FM) Shelton, WA
KATS(FM) Yakima, WA
WRJO(FM) Eagle River, WI
WLWK-FM Milwaukee, WI
WTMB(FM) Tomah, WI
WZJO(FM) Dunbar, WV
KMLD(FM) Casper, WY

94.7 mhz
KZND(FM) Houston, AK
WTBF-FM Brundidge, AL
KKLV(FM) Turrell, AR
KEWB(FM) Anderson, CA
KFLG-FM Big River, CA
KSSJ(FM) Fair Oaks, CA
*KYAF(FM) Firebaugh, CA
KTWV(FM) Los Angeles, CA
KLOB(FM) Thousand Palms, CA
KRKS-FM Boulder, CO
WDSD(FM) Dover, DE
WSYR-FM Gifford, FL
WDEC-FM Americus, GA
KWXX-FM Hilo, HI
KUMU-FM Honolulu, HI
KMCN(FM) Clinton, IA
KMCH(FM) Manchester, IA
WLS-FM Chicago, IL
WFBQ(FM) Indianapolis, IN
WFIA-FM New Albany, IN
KSKU(FM) Sterling, KS
WQQR(FM) Mayfield, KY
WKLW-FM Paintsville, KY
WBIO(FM) Philpot, KY
WYLK(FM) Lacombe, LA
WMAS-FM Springfield, MA
WTGB-FM Bethesda, MD
WBCQ-FM Monticello, ME
WCSX(FM) Birmingham, MI
*WCVM(FM) Bronson, MI
WUPN(FM) Paradise, MI
KCLH(FM) Caledonia, MN
KNSG(FM) Springfield, MN
KSKK(FM) Staples, MN
KSHE(FM) Crestwood, MO
KTTS-FM Springfield, MO
WWJK(FM) Jackson, MS
WQDR(FM) Raleigh, NC
KNOX-FM Grand Forks, ND
KCNB(FM) Chadron, NE
KNEN(FM) Norfolk, NE
*WFME(FM) Newark, NJ
KKIM-FM Santa Fe, NM
*WMHI(FM) Cape Vincent, NY
WYUL(FM) Chateaugay, NY
WIYN(FM) Deposit, NY
WBAR-FM Lake Luzerne, NY
WSNY(FM) Columbus, OH
KHBZ-FM Oklahoma City, OK
KRRM(FM) Rogue River, OR
WBRX(FM) Cresson, PA
WXBB(FM) Erie, PA
WMTT(FM) Tioga, PA
WODA(FM) Bayamon, PR
WWBD(FM) Sumter, SC
WAAW(FM) Williston, SC
WOJG(FM) Bolivar, TN
WGSQ(FM) Cookeville, TN
KBSO(FM) Corpus Christi, TX
KYSE(FM) El Paso, TX
KGRW(FM) Friona, TX
KTXO(FM) Goldsmith, TX
KWKQ(FM) Graham, TX
KAMX(FM) Luling, TX
KIXY-FM San Angelo, TX
KVLL-FM Wells, TX
KNRK(FM) Camas, WA
KZAL(FM) Manson, WA
WZOR(FM) Mishicot, WI
WOFM(FM) Mosinee, WI
WELK(FM) Elkins, WV
KHNA(FM) Wamsutter, WY

94.9 mhz
WKSJ-FM Mobile, AL
KHLR(FM) Maumelle, AR
KYNF(FM) Prairie Grove, AR
KMXZ-FM Tucson, AZ
KHRQ(FM) Baker, CA
KPYG(FM) Cayucos, CA
KXTT(FM) Maricopa, CA
KBZT(FM) San Diego, CA
KYLD(FM) San Francisco, CA
KBOS-FM Tulare, CA
WMGE(FM) Miami Beach, FL
WTNT-FM Tallahassee, FL
WWRM(FM) Tampa, FL
WUBL(FM) Atlanta, GA
WHKN(FM) Millen, GA
KGGO(FM) Des Moines, IA
KRVB(FM) Nampa, ID
KPKY(FM) Pocatello, ID
WRHK(FM) Danville, IL
WDKB(FM) De Kalb, IL
WAAG(FM) Galesburg, IL
WYNG(FM) Mount Carmel, IL
KCKS(FM) Concordia, KS
KSBH(FM) Coushatta, LA
WPRF(FM) Reserve, LA
WSYY(FM) Millinocket, ME
WSJM-FM Benton Harbor, MI
WUPZ(FM) Crystal Falls, MI
WMMQ(FM) East Lansing, MI
WKJZ(FM) Hillman, MI
WKZC(FM) Scottville, MI
KCPI(FM) Albert Lea, MN
KMXK(FM) Cold Spring, MN
KQDS-FM Duluth, MN
KLCH(FM) Lake City, MN
*WGCQ(FM) Hayti, MO
KCMO-FM Kansas City, MO
*WKVF(FM) Byhalia, MS
WKOR-FM Columbus, MS
KYSS-FM Missoula, MT
KTZU(FM) Velva, ND
*KJLT-FM North Platte, NE
KRKR(FM) Valley, NE
WHOM(FM) Mt. Washington, NH
KWYK-FM Aztec, NM
KBIM-FM Roswell, NM
WKLL(FM) Frankfort, NY
*WONB(FM) Ada, OH
WREW(FM) Fairfield, OH
WQMX(FM) Medina, OH
*WEKV(FM) South Webster, OH
KCBZ(FM) Cannon Beach, OR
KTEE(FM) North Bend, OR
*WRSD(FM) Folsom, PA
WRBT(FM) Harrisburg, PA
WOGG(FM) Oliver, PA
WHKS(FM) Port Allegany, PA
WVCO(FM) Loris, SC
KLRJ(FM) Aberdeen, SD
WMSR-FM Collinwood, TN
WAEZ(FM) Greeneville, TN
KLTY(FM) Arlington, TX
*KOLI(FM) Electra, TX
KQUR(FM) Laredo, TX
KCIN(FM) Cedar City, UT
KHTB(FM) Provo, UT
WSLC-FM Roanoke, VA
WPTE(FM) Virginia Beach, VA
KIOK(FM) Richland, WA
*KUOW-FM Seattle, WA
WOLX-FM Baraboo, WI
KZWY(FM) Sheridan, WY

95.1 mhz
WRTT-FM Huntsville, AL
WXFX(FM) Montgomery, AL
KAMS(FM) Mammoth Spring, AR
KVIB(FM) Sun City West, AZ
KTTI(FM) Yuma, AZ
*KAAX(FM) Avenal, CA
KMXI(FM) Chico, CA
KMDR(FM) McKinleyville, CA
KHOP(FM) Oakdale, CA
KFRG(FM) San Bernardino, CA
KBBY-FM Ventura, CA
KATC-FM Colorado Springs, CO

KKNN(FM) Delta, CO
WRKI(FM) Brookfield, CT
WBPC(FM) Ebro, FL
WAPE-FM Jacksonville, FL
WBVD(FM) Melbourne, FL
WCHZ(FM) Harlem, GA
WMGB(FM) Montezuma, GA
WACF(FM) Young Harris, GA
KAOI-FM Wailuku, HI
KMAQ-FM Maquoketa, IA
KCZE(FM) New Hampton, IA
KLER-FM Orofino, ID
WUEZ(FM) Carterville, IL
WDZQ(FM) Decatur, IL
WVLI(FM) Kankakee, IL
WAJI(FM) Fort Wayne, IN
WVNI(FM) Nashville, IN
*WVUR-FM Valparaiso, IN
KICT-FM Wichita, KS
WGGC(FM) Bowling Green, KY
WFLE-FM Flemingsburg, KY
*WXRB(FM) Dudley, MA
WXTK(FM) West Yarmouth, MA
WRBS-FM Baltimore, MD
WFBE(FM) Flint, MI
KBVB(FM) Barnesville, MN
KWOA-FM Worthington, MN
KMXL(FM) Carthage, MO
KTKS(FM) Versailles, MO
WJDQ(FM) Marion, MS
WQNZ(FM) Natchez, MS
WONA-FM Winona, MS
KMMS-FM Bozeman, MT
*KXEI(FM) Havre, MT
KTHC(FM) Sidney, MT
WNKS(FM) Charlotte, NC
WRNS-FM Kinston, NC
WAYV(FM) Atlantic City, NJ
KSYU(FM) Corrales, NM
KNUW(FM) Santa Clara, NM
KNYE(FM) Pahrump, NV
WFXF(FM) Honeoye Falls, NY
WVXG(FM) Mount Gilead, OH
KQCV(FM) Shawnee, OK
KSND(FM) Monmouth, OR
KLTW-FM Prineville, OR
WZZO(FM) Bethlehem, PA
WIKZ(FM) Chambersburg, PA
WWGY(FM) Grove City, PA
WEGM(FM) San German, PR
WSSX-FM Charleston, SC
KSQY(FM) Deadwood, SD
WCDZ(FM) Dresden, TN
KORQ(FM) Baird, TX
KYKR(FM) Beaumont, TX
KNDE(FM) College Station, TX
KGSX(FM) Comfort, TX
KQRX(FM) Midland, TX
KEWL-FM New Boston, TX
KRGX(FM) Rio Grande City, TX
KVIC(FM) Victoria, TX
WQMZ(FM) Charlottesville, VA
WJKC(FM) Christiansted, VI
*WVTQ(FM) Sunderland, VT
KITI-FM Winlock, WA
WQRB(FM) Bloomer, WI
WIIL(FM) Kenosha, WI
WLST(FM) Marinette, WI
WXIL(FM) Parkersburg, WV
KCGY(FM) Laramie, WY
KYCS(FM) Rock Springs, WY

95.3 mhz
WFFN(FM) Cordova, AL
WRLD-FM Valley, AL
KCXY(FM) East Camden, AR
KVHU(FM) Judsonia, AR
KERX(FM) Paris, AR
KCDQ(FM) Douglas, AZ
KEEC(FM) Teec Nos Pos, AZ
KOZT(FM) Fort Bragg, CA
KBHH(FM) Kerman, CA
KRTY(FM) Los Gatos, CA
KLLY(FM) Oildale, CA
KXTZ(FM) Pismo Beach, CA
KUIC(FM) Vacaville, CA

KECK(FM) Eckley, CO
KYDN(FM) Monte Vista, CO
WKDB(FM) Laurel, DE
WOLZ(FM) Fort Myers, FL
WXCV(FM) Homosassa Springs, FL
WPYO(FM) Maitland, FL
WVKV(FM) Nashville, GA
KQMG-FM Independence, IA
KIFG-FM Iowa Falls, IA
KOKX-FM Keokuk, IA
KCSI(FM) Red Oak, IA
KPND(FM) Sandpoint, ID
KECH-FM Sun Valley, ID
WRXX(FM) Centralia, IL
WRKX(FM) Ottawa, IL
WLFH(FM) Rantoul, IL
WRTB(FM) Winnebago, IL
WBPE(FM) Brookston, IN
WUME-FM Paoli, IN
WNDI-FM Sullivan, IN
KINZ(FM) Humboldt, KS
KHCA(FM) Wamego, KS
WIKI(FM) Carrollton, KY
*WKVN(FM) Morganfield, KY
WVRB(FM) Wilmore, KY
KQKI(FM) Bayou Vista, LA
WHRB(FM) Cambridge, MA
WPVQ(FM) Greenfield, MA
WALZ-FM Machias, ME
*WWWA(FM) Winslow, ME
WSKX(FM) York Center, ME
WQTE(FM) Adrian, MI
WBCK-FM Battle Creek, MI
WCFX(FM) Clare, MI
WGRL(FM) Frederic, MI
WAOR(FM) Niles, MI
WGVS-FM Whitehall, MI
WXXZ(FM) Grand Marais, MN
KNOF(FM) Saint Paul, MN
KDJS-FM Willmar, MN
KAGE-FM Winona, MN
KDKD-FM Clinton, MO
KXMO-FM Owensville, MO
WAFM(FM) Amory, MS
WVIM-FM Coldwater, MS
WADI(FM) Corinth, MS
WRKG(FM) Drew, MS
WZNF(FM) Lumberton, MS
WOBR-FM Wanchese, NC
KSEL-FM Portales, NM
KRJC(FM) Elko, NV
WGIX-FM Gouverneur, NY
WBKT(FM) Norwich, NY
WHFM(FM) Southampton, NY
WKTN(FM) Kenton, OH
WKLM(FM) Millersburg, OH
WLKR-FM Norwalk, OH
WZLR(FM) Xenia, OH
KMGZ(FM) Lawton, OK
KKBC-FM Baker City, OR
KURY-FM Brookings, OR
KUJZ(FM) Creswell, OR
KLCR(FM) Lakeview, OR
WZWW(FM) Bellefonte, PA
WDNH-FM Honesdale, PA
WBLJ-FM Shamokin, PA
WTTC-FM Towanda, PA
WJPA-FM Washington, PA
WFMV(FM) South Congaree, SC
KLXS-FM Pierre, SD
WTBG(FM) Brownsville, TN
*WYFC(FM) Clinton, TN
WPLZ(FM) Ooltewah, TN
KBTY(FM) Benjamin, TX
KNEL-FM Brady, TX
KVWG-FM Dilley, TX
KDDD-FM Dumas, TX
KFRO-FM Gilmer, TX
KHYI(FM) Howe, TX
KPBM(FM) McCamey, TX
KOME-FM Meridian, TX
KZSP(FM) South Padre Island, TX
KRPX(FM) Wellington, UT
WKHK(FM) Colonial Heights, VA
WZRV(FM) Front Royal, VA
WXBX(FM) Rural Retreat, VA

WHLF(FM) South Boston, VA
WXLF(FM) White River Junction, VT
KXLE-FM Ellensburg, WA
KXXK(FM) Hoquiam-Aberdeen, WA
WXRO(FM) Beaver Dam, WI
WGMO(FM) Shell Lake, WI
WRLB(FM) Rainelle, WV
KZJH(FM) Jackson, WY

95.5 mhz
WTVY-FM Dothan, AL
WFMH-FM Hackleburg, AL
WHMA-FM Hobson City, AL
WJDB-FM Thomasville, AL
KYOT-FM Phoenix, AZ
KKHK(FM) Carmel, CA
KLOS(FM) Los Angeles, CA
KZCC(FM) Trinidad, CA
KRVG(FM) Glenwood Springs, CO
KRKQ(FM) Mountain Village, CO
KPHT(FM) Rocky Ford, CO
WLDI(FM) Fort Pierce, FL
WNDD(FM) Silver Springs, FL
WBTS(FM) Doraville, GA
WIXV(FM) Savannah, GA
KSTO(FM) Hagatna, GU
KAIM-FM Honolulu, HI
KZAT(FM) Belle Plaine, IA
KJCY(FM) Saint Ansgar, IA
KGLI(FM) Sioux City, IA
WFUN-FM Bethalto, IL
WNUA(FM) Chicago, IL
WGLO(FM) Pekin, IL
WFMS(FM) Indianapolis, IN
KAHE(FM) Dodge City, KS
KVOB(FM) Lindsborg, KS
KNDY-FM Marysville, KS
WQHY(FM) Prestonsburg, KY
KRRQ(FM) Lafayette, LA
WPGC(FM) Morningside, MD
WLOB-FM Topsham, ME
WKQI(FM) Detroit, MI
WJZJ(FM) Glen Arbor, MI
KKZY(FM) Bemidji, MN
KBEK(FM) Mora, MN
KRDS-FM New Prague, MN
KAAN-FM Bethany, MO
KTOZ-FM Pleasant Hope, MO
KJEZ(FM) Poplar Bluff, MO
WHLH(FM) Jackson, MS
WOXD(FM) Oxford, MS
KMBR(FM) Butte, MT
KMHK(FM) Hardin, MT
*WHPE-FM High Point, NC
WPWZ(FM) Pinetops, NC
KYNU(FM) Jamestown, ND
KSDZ(FM) Gordon, NE
KHFM(FM) Santa Fe, NM
KWNR(FM) Henderson, NV
KNEV(FM) Reno, NV
WYJB(FM) Albany, NY
WPLJ(FM) New York, NY
WFIZ(FM) Odessa, NY
WFHM-FM Cleveland, OH
WHOK-FM Lancaster, OH
KWEY(FM) Clinton, OK
KITX(FM) Hugo, OK
KWEN(FM) Tulsa, OK
KXTG(FM) Portland, OR
WFGI-FM Johnstown, PA
WBYL(FM) Salladasburg, PA
WBRU(FM) Providence, RI
WIBZ(FM) Wedgefield, SC
WSM-FM Nashville, TN
KKMJ-FM Austin, TX
KZFM(FM) Corpus Christi, TX
KAFX-FM Diboll, TX
KLAQ(FM) El Paso, TX
KJKB(FM) Jacksboro, TX
KAIQ(FM) Wolfforth, TX
*KYFO-FM Ogden, UT
WBOP(FM) Buffalo Gap, VA
WXXX(FM) South Burlington, VT
WIFC(FM) Wausau, WI
KWYY(FM) Midwest, WY

95.7 mhz
WBHJ(FM) Midfield, AL
KSEC(FM) Bentonville, AR
KSSN(FM) Little Rock, AR
KWKM(FM) Saint Johns, AZ
KUSS(FM) Carlsbad, CA
KJFX(FM) Fresno, CA
KPAT(FM) Orcutt, CA
KALF(FM) Red Bluff, CA
KBWF(FM) San Francisco, CA
KPTT(FM) Denver, CO
WKSS(FM) Hartford, CT
WBTP(FM) Clearwater, FL
WKFP(FM) Navarre, FL
WXDJ(FM) North Miami Beach, FL
WHOG-FM Ormond-by-the-Sea, FL
WIOL(FM) Greenville, GA
WATG(FM) Trion, GA
WQPW(FM) Valdosta, GA
KKSY(FM) Anamosa, IA
KSWI(FM) Atlantic, IA
KQWC-FM Webster City, IA
KEZJ-FM Twin Falls, ID
WCRC(FM) Effingham, IL
WSEY(FM) Oregon, IL
WJDK-FM Seneca, IL
WSHP(FM) Attica, IN
WQMF(FM) Jeffersonville, IN
WYPW(FM) Nappanee, IN
KCHZ(FM) Ottawa, KS
WCCK(FM) Calvert City, KY
KLKL(FM) Minden, LA
WKBU(FM) New Orleans, LA
KROK(FM) South Fort Polk, LA
WWMJ(FM) Ellsworth, ME
WLHT-FM Grand Rapids, MI
*WHWL(FM) Marquette, MI
*WCMB-FM Oscoda, MI
KDAL-FM Duluth, MN
KQYK(FM) Lake Crystal, MN
KKOK(FM) Morris, MN
KWWR(FM) Mexico, MO
WTGY(FM) Charleston, MS
WHAL-FM Horn Lake, MS
KCGM(FM) Scobey, MT
WXRC(FM) Hickory, NC
WKML(FM) Lumberton, NC
KNDK-FM Langdon, ND
KCVD(FM) New England, ND
*KROA(FM) Grand Island, NE
WZID(FM) Manchester, NH
KPCL(FM) Farmington, NM
KPER(FM) Hobbs, NM
WAQX-FM Manlius, NY
WPIG(FM) Olean, NY
WIMX(FM) Gibsonburg, OH
WHIO-FM Piqua, OH
WVKF(FM) Shadyside, OH
KKAJ-FM Ardmore, OK
KXLS(FM) Lahoma, OK
KBOY-FM Medford, OR
WMRF-FM Lewistown, PA
WBHD(FM) Olyphant, PA
WBEN-FM Philadelphia, PA
WFID(FM) Rio Piedras, PR
KSQB-FM Dell Rapids, SD
WAYB-FM Graysville, TN
WFKX(FM) Henderson, TN
WQJK(FM) Maryville, TN
KBST-FM Big Spring, TX
KARX(FM) Claude, TX
KKHH(FM) Houston, TX
KLEY(FM) Jourdanton, TX
KOTY(FM) Mason, TX
KBGO(FM) Waco, TX
WFLO-FM Farmville, VA
WVKL(FM) Norfolk, VA
WDOT(FM) Danville, VT
KJR-FM Seattle, WA
KKSR(FM) Walla Walla, WA
WRQT(FM) La Crosse, WI
WRIT-FM Milwaukee, WI
WSWW-FM Craigsville, WV
KFMR(FM) Marbleton, WY

95.9 mhz
KXLR(FM) Fairbanks, AK
WKXN(FM) Greenville, AL
WTWX-FM Guntersville, AL
WTGZ(FM) Tuskegee, AL
KWHF(FM) Harrisburg, AR
KUUZ(FM) Lake Village, AR
KKLD(FM) Cottonwood, AZ
KUKY(FM) Wellton, AZ
KFSH-FM Anaheim, CA
KBYN(FM) Arnold, CA
KXXZ(FM) Barstow, CA
KOCP(FM) Camarillo, CA
KRSH(FM) Healdsburg, CA
KAJR(FM) Indian Wells, CA
KSKD(FM) Livingston, CA
KNLF(FM) Quincy, CA
KMAP(FM) Arriba, CO
KIDN-FM Hayden, CO
WFOX(FM) Norwalk, CT
WOSC(FM) Bethany Beach, DE
WSJZ-FM Sebastian, FL
WRBA(FM) Springfield, FL
WQZY(FM) Dublin, GA
KPVS(FM) Hilo, HI
KSRF(FM) Poipu, HI
KCHA-FM Charles City, IA
KILR-FM Estherville, IA
KKFD-FM Fairfield, IA
KCOB-FM Newton, IA
KLZX(FM) Weston, ID
WERV-FM Aurora, IL
*WOLG(FM) Carlinville, IL
WEZC(FM) Clinton, IL
WDQN-FM Du Quoin, IL
WNLF(FM) Macomb, IL
WMLF(FM) Watseka, IL
WFDM(FM) Franklin, IN
WEFM(FM) Michigan City, IN
WWSY(FM) Seelyville, IN
WKID(FM) Vevay, IN
WKUZ(FM) Wabash, IN
KWHK(FM) Hutchinson, KS
KRSL-FM Russell, KS
KSOK(FM) Winfield, KS
WFTM-FM Maysville, KY
WGKY(FM) Wickliffe, KY
KZLG(FM) Mansura, LA
KMAR-FM Winnsboro, LA
WATD-FM Marshfield, MA
WBEC-FM Pittsfield, MA
WWIN-FM Glen Burnie, MD
WICL(FM) Williamsport, MD
WPEI(FM) Saco, ME
WLKM-FM Three Rivers, MI
KQCL(FM) Faribault, MN
WLKX-FM Forest Lake, MN
WWWI-FM Pillager, MN
KYLS-FM Ironton, MO
KTRI-FM Mansfield, MO
KKBL(FM) Monett, MO
WCNA(FM) Potts Camp, MS
WBBN(FM) Taylorsville, MS
HHNK(FM) Columbia Falls, MT
KJCD(FM) Fort Benton, MT
KLCM(FM) Lewistown, MT
WPNC-FM Plymouth, NC
WCVP-FM Robbinsville, NC
WRAT(FM) Point Pleasant, NJ
KZRM(FM) Chama, NM
KANM(FM) Magdalena, NM
KKJY(FM) Santa Rosa, NM
KKIT(FM) Taos, NM
WVOS-FM Liberty, NY
WCQL(FM) Queensbury, NY
WJKW(FM) Athens, OH
WYNT(FM) Caledonia, OH
WNPQ(FM) New Philadelphia, OH
KYBE(FM) Frederick, OK
KBBD(FM) Sallisaw, OK
KZCU(FM) Woodward, OK
KIXT(FM) Bay City, OR
WGGI(FM) Benton, PA
WAKZ(FM) Sharpsville, PA
WZDB(FM) Sykesville, PA
WCRI(FM) Block Island, RI

WIOP(FM) Isle of Palms, SC
WVGC(FM) Pendleton, SC
KZZI(FM) Belle Fourche, SD
WRZK(FM) Colonial Heights, TN
WLQK(FM) Livingston, TN
KBRA(FM) Freer, TX
KHMC(FM) Goliad, TX
KPWW(FM) Hooks, TX
KCKL(FM) Malakoff, TX
KFWR(FM) Mineral Wells, TX
KSCH(FM) Sulphur Springs, TX
KMGR(FM) Delta, UT
KZHK(FM) Saint George, UT
WGRQ(FM) Colonial Beach, VA
KZML(FM) Quincy, WA
WKSZ(FM) De Pere, WI
WDMO(FM) Durand, WI
WMQA-FM Minocqua, WI
WBKY(FM) Portage, WI
*WDKL(FM) Grafton, WV
WSTG(FM) Princeton, WV

96.1 mhz
*KNOM-FM Nome, AK
WXFL(FM) Florence, AL
WRKH(FM) Mobile, AL
WQKS-FM Montgomery, AL
KMRX(FM) El Dorado, AR
KCWD(FM) Harrison, AR
KLPX(FM) Tucson, AZ
KWRK(FM) Window Rock, AZ
KSIQ(FM) Brawley, CA
KCEL(FM) Mojave, CA
KSQQ(FM) Morgan Hill, CA
KYMX(FM) Sacramento, CA
KRQB(FM) San Jacinto, CA
KSLY-FM San Luis Obispo, CA
KKXS(FM) Shingletown, CA
KSLK(FM) Visalia, CA
KIBT(FM) Fountain, CO
KSME(FM) Greeley, CO
KSTR-FM Montrose, CO
WRXK-FM Bonita Springs, FL
WTMP-FM Dade City, FL
WEJZ(FM) Jacksonville, FL
WHBX(FM) Tallahassee, FL
WKLS(FM) Atlanta, GA
KMXG(FM) Clinton, IA
KCVM(FM) Hudson, IA
KNWM(FM) Madrid, IA
KID-FM Idaho Falls, ID
WQQB(FM) Rantoul, IL
WQLK(FM) Richmond, IN
KANS(FM) Emporia, KS
WKKQ(FM) Barbourville, KY
WSTO(FM) Owensboro, KY
WLXO(FM) Stamping Ground, KY
KRVE(FM) Brusly, LA
KYKZ(FM) Lake Charles, LA
WSRS(FM) Worcester, MA
WQHR(FM) Presque Isle, ME
WHNN(FM) Bay City, MI
WMAX-FM Holland, MI
KQPR-FM Albert Lea, MN
KGPZ(FM) Coleraine, MN
KQHT(FM) Crookston, MN
*KLRQ(FM) Clinton, MO
WLZA(FM) Eupora, MS
WIVG(FM) Tunica, MS
WBBB(FM) Raleigh, NC
WIBT(FM) Shelby, NC
KYYZ(FM) Williston, ND
*KINI(FM) Crookston, NE
KICX-FM McCook, NE
KQBW(FM) Omaha, NE
WTTH(FM) Margate City, NJ
KALN(FM) Dexter, NM
WJYE(FM) Buffalo, NY
WLVG(FM) Center Moriches, NY
WVLF(FM) Norwood, NY
WPKF(FM) Poughkeepsie, NY
WODZ-FM Rome, NY
WMTR(FM) Archbold, OH
WKFM(FM) Huron, OH
KXXY-FM Oklahoma City, OK
KITO-FM Vinita, OK

KZEL-FM Eugene, OR
KSRV-FM Ontario, OR
KLKY(FM) Stanfield, OR
WCTO(FM) Easton, PA
WKST-FM Pittsburgh, PA
WSOX(FM) Red Lion, PA
WPHD(FM) South Waverly, PA
WAEL-FM Maricao, PR
WKZQ-FM Forestbrook, SC
KIXX(FM) Watertown, SD
KCTX-FM Childress, TX
KIOX-FM Edna, TX
KBTQ(FM) Harlingen, TX
KKTX-FM Kilgore, TX
KAGG(FM) Madisonville, TX
KMRK-FM Odessa, TX
KEYE-FM Perryton, TX
KXXM(FM) San Antonio, TX
KGXL(FM) Winters, TX
WJDV(FM) Broadway, VA
WROX-FM Exmore, VA
WIVI(FM) Charlotte Amalie, VI
WDEV-FM Warren, VT
KXXO(FM) Olympia, WA
KIXZ-FM Opportunity, WA
WLKG(FM) Lake Geneva, WI
WJMC-FM Rice Lake, WI
WTCX(FM) Ripon, WI
WXYM(FM) Tomah, WI
WKWS(FM) Charleston, WV
KKLX(FM) Worland, WY

96.3 mhz
KXLW(FM) Houston, AK
KHLS(FM) Blytheville, AR
KTTG(FM) Mena, AR
KSWG(FM) Wickenburg, AZ
KFMI(FM) Eureka, CA
KXOL-FM Los Angeles, CA
KUBB(FM) Mariposa, CA
KLZN(FM) Susanville, CA
KXCM(FM) Twentynine Palms, CA
WHUR-FM Washington, DC
WXOF(FM) Yankeetown, FL
WJIZ-FM Albany, GA
KRTR-FM Kailua, HI
KRNQ(FM) Keokuk, IA
KZWU(FM) Pleasantville, IA
WLCN(FM) Atlanta, IL
WBBM-FM Chicago, IL
WJAA(FM) Austin, IN
WNHT(FM) Churubusco, IN
WHHH(FM) Indianapolis, IN
KZDY(FM) Cawker City, KS
KZCH(FM) Derby, KS
KERP(FM) Ingalls, KS
KACZ(FM) Riley, KS
WIVY(FM) Morehead, KY
WXKY-FM Stanford, KY
WEII(FM) Dennis, MA
WJJB-FM Gary, ME
WDVD(FM) Detroit, MI
WLXT(FM) Petoskey, MI
KTTB(FM) Glencoe, MN
KIHT(FM) Saint Louis, MO
WUSJ(FM) Madison, MS
WXWX(FM) Marietta, MS
KRZN(FM) Billings, MT
KBAZ(FM) Hamilton, MT
WRHT(FM) Morehead City, NC
WFYX(FM) Walpole, NH
KBZU(FM) Albuquerque, NM
KKLZ(FM) Las Vegas, NV
WQXR-FM New York, NY
WAJZ(FM) Voorheesville, NY
WLVQ(FM) Columbus, OH
WJSA-FM Jersey Shore, PA
WKQW-FM Oil City, PA
WKSP(FM) Aiken, SC
WGOG(FM) Walhalla, SC
WCJK(FM) Murfreesboro, TN
WJBZ-FM Seymour, TN
KXIT(FM) Dalhart, TX
KTDR(FM) Del Rio, TX
KHEY-FM El Paso, TX
KSCS(FM) Fort Worth, TX

KZXL(FM) Hudson, TX
KXXN(FM) Iowa Park, TX
KAJZ(FM) Llano, TX
KLLL-FM Lubbock, TX
KGGB(FM) Yorktown, TX
KXRK(FM) Provo, UT
WROV-FM Martinsville, VA
KRCW(FM) Royal City, WA
WSFQ(FM) Peshtigo, WI
WMAD(FM) Sauk City, WI
WOTR(FM) Lost Creek, WV
KQWY(FM) Lusk, WY

96.5 mhz
KKIS-FM Soldotna, AK
WMJJ(FM) Birmingham, AL
KHTE-FM England, AR
KDAP-FM Douglas, AZ
KRFM(FM) Show Low, AZ
KVMX(FM) Bakersfield, CA
KSLV-FM Del Norte, CA
KYXY(FM) San Diego, CA
KOIT-FM San Francisco, CA
KLCA(FM) Tahoe City, CA
KFLS-FM Tulelake, CA
KXPK(FM) Evergreen, CO
KJBL(FM) Julesburg, CO
WTIC-FM Hartford, CT
WJTK(FM) Columbia City, FL
WZNS(FM) Fort Walton Beach, FL
WPOW(FM) Miami, FL
WHTQ(FM) Orlando, FL
WPCH(FM) Gray, GA
WJCL-FM Savannah, GA
KSOM(FM) Audubon, IA
WMT-FM Cedar Rapids, IA
KRID(FM) Ashton, ID
KOZE-FM Lewiston, ID
KLIX-FM Twin Falls, ID
WKIB(FM) Anna, IL
WZPN(FM) Farmington, IL
WKOT(FM) Marseilles, IL
WAZY-FM Lafayette, IN
WGZB-FM Lanesville, IN
WTGG(FM) Amite, LA
KFTE(FM) Breaux Bridge, LA
KVKI-FM Shreveport, LA
WQHH(FM) Dewitt, MI
WYZO(FM) Portage, MI
WKLK-FM Cloquet, MN
KJJK-FM Fergus Falls, MN
KWWK(FM) Rochester, MN
KRBZ(FM) Kansas City, MO
KSPW(FM) Sparta, MO
WKDJ-FM Clarksdale, MS
WXHB(FM) Richton, MS
KDZN(FM) Glendive, MT
WOXL-FM Biltmore Forest, NC
WFLB(FM) Laurinburg, NC
KBYZ(FM) Bismarck, ND
KRGI-FM Grand Island, NE
WMLL(FM) Bedford, NH
KLMA(FM) Hobbs, NM
KBKZ(FM) Raton, NM
WBKX(FM) Fredonia, NY
WVNV(FM) Malone, NY
WCMF-FM Rochester, NY
WAKS(FM) Akron, OH
WFTK(FM) Lebanon, OH
KECO(FM) Elk City, OK
KMMY(FM) Soper, OK
KRAV(FM) Tulsa, OK
KBDN(FM) Bandon, OR
KWLZ-FM Warm Springs, OR
WKYE(FM) Johnstown, PA
*WPEL-FM Montrose, PA
WRDW-FM Philadelphia, PA
WRXD(FM) Fajardo, PR
*KNWC-FM Sioux Falls, SD
WDOD-FM Chattanooga, TN
WBFG(FM) Parker's Crossroads, TN
KKNM(FM) Bovina, TX
KLTG(FM) Corpus Christi, TX
KHMX(FM) Houston, TX
KSYY(FM) Ingram, TX
KNRX(FM) Sterling City, TX

WCTG(FM) Chincoteague, VA
WKLR(FM) Fort Lee, VA
KJAQ(FM) Seattle, WA
WKLH(FM) Milwaukee, WI
*WLVW(FM) Moundsville, WV
WXCC(FM) Williamson, WV
KQSW(FM) Rock Springs, WY

96.7 mhz
WMXA(FM) Opelika, AL
WKXK(FM) Pine Hill, AL
KYDL(FM) Hot Springs, AR
KOKR(FM) Newport, AR
KDYN-FM Ozark, AR
KRCY-FM Lake Havasu City, AZ
KWMX(FM) Williams, AZ
KALZ(FM) Fowler, CA
KNOB(FM) Healdsburg, CA
KUNA-FM La Quinta, CA
KMRQ(FM) Manteca, CA
KZAP(FM) Paradise, CA
KCAL-FM Redlands, CA
KWIZ(FM) Santa Ana, CA
KLJR-FM Santa Paula, CA
KSYV(FM) Solvang, CA
KUUR(FM) Carbondale, CO
WCTZ(FM) Stamford, CT
WDXQ-FM Cochran, GA
WWLG(FM) Peachtree City, GA
WLYX(FM) Valdosta, GA
KIIC(FM) Albia, IA
KKEX(FM) Preston, ID
WCXO(FM) Carlyle, IL
WGNX(FM) Colchester, IL
WSSR(FM) Joliet, IL
WKGL-FM Loves Park, IL
WIHN(FM) Normal, IL
WCVS-FM Virden, IL
WMQX(FM) Alexandria, IN
WBWB(FM) Bloomington, IN
WCOE(FM) La Porte, IN
WORX-FM Madison, IN
WFML(FM) Vincennes, IN
KSOB(FM) Larned, KS
KBBE(FM) McPherson, KS
WANV(FM) Annville, KY
WBVR(FM) Auburn, KY
KMYO-FM Morgan City, LA
KWCL-FM Oak Grove, LA
WCEI-FM Easton, MD
WDLD(FM) Halfway, MD
WTQX(FM) Boothbay Harbor, ME
*WUFN(FM) Albion, MI
WLXV(FM) Cadillac, MI
WMJT(FM) McMillan, MI
WUPG(FM) Republic, MI
WRGZ(FM) Rogers City, MI
KKCQ-FM Bagley, MN
KDOG(FM) North Mankato, MN
KZRV(FM) Sartell, MN
KCMQ(FM) Columbia, MO
KAHR(FM) Poplar Bluff, MO
WFFF-FM Columbia, MS
WUJM(FM) Gulfport, MS
WSEL-FM Pontotoc, MS
KISN(FM) Belgrade, MT
KZIN-FM Shelby, MT
WKJX(FM) Elizabeth City, NC
WNCC-FM Franklin, NC
WKRX(FM) Roxboro, NC
KQZZ(FM) Devils Lake, ND
WLTN-FM Lisbon, NH
WQSO(FM) Rochester, NH
KNMB(FM) Cloudcroft, NM
KMDZ(FM) Las Vegas, NM
KHIX(FM) Carlin, NV
KHIJ(FM) Mesquite, NV
WPTR(FM) Clifton Park, NY
WYSX(FM) Morristown, NY
WMVN(FM) Oswego, NY
WTSX(FM) Port Jervis, NY
WBYB(FM) Portville, NY
WXZO(FM) Willsboro, NY
WCMJ(FM) Cambridge, OH
WCSM-FM Celina, OH
WBVI(FM) Fostoria, OH

WKOV-FM Wellston, OH
KBEL(FM) Idabel, OK
KCRF-FM Lincoln City, OR
WVNW(FM) Burnham, PA
*WPGM-FM Danville, PA
WLLF(FM) Mercer, PA
WLTY(FM) Cayce, SC
WBZT(FM) Mauldin, SC
KZMX-FM Hot Springs, SD
WMOD(FM) Bolivar, TN
WNKX-FM Centerville, TN
WMYL(FM) Halls Crossroads, TN
KPMZ(FM) Flower Mound, TX
KOYE(FM) Frankston, TX
KHFI-FM Georgetown, TX
KXOX-FM Sweetwater, TX
KQMB(FM) Levan, UT
WWZW(FM) Buena Vista, VA
WTSA-FM Brattleboro, VT
KMMG(FM) Benton City, WA
KWWW-FM Quincy, WA
WBDK(FM) Algoma, WI
WJJH(FM) Ashland, WI
WLJY(FM) Whiting, WI
WKMM(FM) Kingwood, WV
KRNK(FM) Casper, WY
KWHO(FM) Cody, WY
KIMX(FM) Laramie, WY

96.9 mhz
KYSC(FM) Fairbanks, AK
WDJR(FM) Enterprise, AL
WRSA-FM Holly Pond, AL
KWLR(FM) Maumelle, AR
KSSW(FM) Nashville, AR
KMXP(FM) Phoenix, AZ
KQZT(FM) Covelo, CA
KHDR(FM) Lenwood, CA
KEBT(FM) Lost Hills, CA
KWAV(FM) Monterey, CA
KSEG(FM) Sacramento, CA
KCCY(FM) Pueblo, CO
KBCR-FM Steamboat Springs, CO
WINK-FM Fort Myers, FL
WJGL(FM) Jacksonville, FL
WKEZ-FM Tavenier, FL
WRDO(FM) Fitzgerald, GA
WTHB-FM Wrens, GA
KFMN(FM) Lihue, HI
KIAQ(FM) Clarion, IA
KKGL(FM) Nampa, ID
WLBH-FM Mattoon, IL
WXLP(FM) Moline, IL
WWDV(FM) Zion, IL
WHPZ(FM) Bremen, IN
WKLO(FM) Hardinsburg, IN
KDVB(FM) Effingham, KS
KKOW-FM Pittsburg, KS
KFIX(FM) Plainville, KS
WDDJ(FM) Paducah, KY
WGKS(FM) Paris, KY
KZMZ(FM) Alexandria, LA
WTKK(FM) Boston, MA
WBPW(FM) Presque Isle, ME
WLAV-FM Grand Rapids, MI
WBTI(FM) Lexington, MI
WWCM(FM) Standish, MI
KMFY(FM) Grand Rapids, MN
KZBK(FM) Brookfield, MO
KUPH(FM) Mountain View, MO
WTCD(FM) Indianola, MS
WXAB(FM) McLain, MS
KQRV(FM) Deer Lodge, MT
WYMY(FM) Goldsboro, NC
WKKT(FM) Statesville, NC
KZKX(FM) Seward, NE
KCMI(FM) Terrytown, NE
WFPG(FM) Atlantic City, NJ
KDAG(FM) Farmington, NM
WRRB(FM) Arlington, NY
WGRF(FM) Buffalo, NY
WEHN(FM) East Hampton, NY
WOUR(FM) Utica, NY
*WOKL(FM) Troy, OH
*WNKL(FM) Wauseon, OH
WLRD(FM) Willard, OH

KXOW(FM) Eldorado, OK
KQOB(FM) Enid, OK
KROG(FM) Grants Pass, OR
WRRK(FM) Braddock, PA
WLAN-FM Lancaster, PA
WREQ(FM) Ridgebury, PA
WNRT(FM) Manati, PR
WIWF(FM) Charleston, SC
KDLO-FM Watertown, SD
WXBQ-FM Bristol, TN
KXSS-FM Amarillo, TX
KXYL-FM Brownwood, TX
KNTE-FM El Campo, TX
KVMV(FM) McAllen, TX
KMCM(FM) Odessa, TX
KSCN(FM) Pittsburg, TX
WWUZ(FM) Bowling Green, VA
WSIG(FM) Mount Jackson, VA
KGY-FM McCleary, WA
KZTA(FM) Naches, WA
KEZE(FM) Spokane, WA
WWWX(FM) Oshkosh, WI
WVVV(FM) Williamstown, WV
KAML-FM Gillette, WY
KMTN(FM) Jackson, WY

97.1 mhz
*KIYU-FM Galena, AK
WWMG(FM) Millbrook, AL
KJMT(FM) Calico Rock, AR
KAMD-FM Camden, AR
KTZR-FM Green Valley, AZ
KAMP-FM Los Angeles, CA
KTSE-FM Patterson, CA
*KULV(FM) Ukiah, CA
KSEQ(FM) Visalia, CA
KZBR(FM) La Jara, CO
KGGY(FM) Stratton, CO
WASH(FM) Washington, DC
WSUN-FM Holiday, FL
WOSN(FM) Indian River Shores, FL
WSRV(FM) Gainesville, GA
KNWB(FM) Hilo, HI
WDRV(FM) Chicago, IL
WLHK(FM) Shelbyville, IN
KIBB(FM) Haven, KS
WKEQ(FM) Somerset, KY
WXCM(FM) Whitesville, KY
WEZB(FM) New Orleans, LA
*WLIC(FM) Frostburg, MD
WQJZ(FM) Ocean Pines, MD
WAEI-FM Bangor, ME
WXYT-FM Detroit, MI
WGLQ(FM) Escanaba, MI
KYCK(FM) Crookston, MN
KTCZ-FM Minneapolis, MN
KFTK(FM) Florissant, MO
KNIM-FM Maryville, MO
KAYQ(FM) Warsaw, MO
WOKK(FM) Meridian, MS
KKBR(FM) Billings, MT
KALS(FM) Kalispell, MT
WQMG(FM) Greensboro, NC
WYND-FM Hatteras, NC
KYYX(FM) Minot, ND
KELN(FM) North Platte, NE
KBCQ-FM Roswell, NM
KXPT(FM) Las Vegas, NV
WQHT(FM) New York, NY
WREO-FM Ashtabula, OH
WBVB(FM) Coal Grove, OH
WBNS-FM Columbus, OH
KYAL-FM Muskogee, OK
KYCH-FM Portland, OR
WBHT(FM) Mountain Top, PA
WOWY(FM) University Park, PA
KPSD(FM) Faith, SD
WRQQ(FM) Goodlettsville, TN
WHRK(FM) Memphis, TN
KTHT-FM Cleveland, TX
KEGL(FM) Fort Worth, TX
KVRP-FM Haskell, TX
KCYN(FM) Moab, UT
KZHT(FM) Salt Lake City, UT
WZRT(FM) Rutland, VT
KXRX(FM) Walla Walla, WA

WCOW-FM Sparta, WI
WDBS(FM) Sutton, WV
KTWY(FM) Shoshoni, WY

97.3 mhz
KEAG(FM) Anchorage, AK
WNCB(FM) Gardendale, AL
KDEW-FM De Witt, AR
KPKR(FM) Parker, AZ
KQNO(FM) Coalinga, CA
KNCQ(FM) Redding, CA
KSON(FM) San Diego, CA
KLLC(FM) San Francisco, CA
KBCO(FM) Boulder, CO
WZBG(FM) Litchfield, CT
WFLC(FM) Miami, FL
WSKY-FM Micanopy, FL
WRAK-FM Bainbridge, GA
WAEV(FM) Savannah, GA
KRKH(FM) Wailea-Makena, HI
KHKI(FM) Des Moines, IA
KGRR(FM) Epworth, IA
KHDK(FM) New London, IA
KLCE(FM) Blackfoot, ID
WRUL(FM) Carmi, IL
WFYR(FM) Elmwood, IL
WTIM-FM Taylorville, IL
WMEE(FM) Fort Wayne, IN
KKJQ(FM) Garden City, KS
WYGY(FM) Fort Thomas, KY
WJSN-FM Jackson, KY
KJMG(FM) Bastrop, LA
KMDL(FM) Kaplan, LA
KDBH(FM) Natchitoches, LA
WJFD-FM New Bedford, MA
WJDF(FM) Orange, MA
WMJO(FM) Essexville, MI
WDEE-FM Reed City, MI
*KDNW(FM) Duluth, MN
KRVY(FM) Starbuck, MN
KLRX(FM) Lee's Summit, MO
KCDG(FM) Madison, MO
KYRX(FM) Marble Hill, MO
KXUS(FM) Springfield, MO
WFMN(FM) Flora, MS
WKSO(FM) Natchez, MS
WFMM(FM) Sumrall, MS
WKBC-FM North Wilkesboro, NC
WMNX(FM) Wilmington, NC
KRGY(FM) Aurora, NE
KBLR-FM Blair, NE
WENJ-FM Millville, NJ
KKSS(FM) Santa Fe, NM
KZTQ(FM) Carson City, NV
WYXL(FM) Ithaca, NY
WMYY(FM) Schoharie, NY
WZAD(FM) Wurtsboro, NY
WJZE(FM) Oak Harbor, OH
KOJK(FM) Blanchard, OK
*WZZE(FM) Glen Mills, PA
WRVV(FM) Harrisburg, PA
WPCL(FM) Northern Cambria, PA
WOYE(FM) Rio Grande, PR
KMXC(FM) Sioux Falls, SD
WKJQ-FM Parsons, TN
WUUQ(FM) South Pittsburg, TN
WTNV(FM) Tiptonville, TN
KLZK(FM) New Deal, TX
KGEE(FM) Pecos, TX
KAJA(FM) San Antonio, TX
KQHN(FM) Waskom, TX
WGH-FM Newport News, VA
*KKRS(FM) Davenport, WA
KIRO-FM Tacoma, WA
WQBW(FM) Milwaukee, WI
WHDG(FM) Rhinelander, WI
WKWK-FM Wheeling, WV

97.5 mhz
WKGA(FM) Goodwater, AL
WABB-FM Mobile, AL
WVRV(FM) Pine Level, AL
KQUS-FM Hot Springs, AR
KMVA(FM) Dewey-Humboldt, AZ
KSZR(FM) Oro Valley, AZ
KABX-FM Merced, CA

KLYY(FM) Riverside, CA
KRUZ(FM) Santa Barbara, CA
KWUZ(FM) Poncha Springs, CO
KSRX(FM) Sterling, CO
WPCV(FM) Winter Haven, FL
WUFF-FM Eastman, GA
WUMJ(FM) Fayetteville, GA
WHLJ(FM) Statenville, GA
KZGZ(FM) Hagatna, GU
KHCM(FM) Honolulu, HI
KBVU-FM Alta, IA
*KTWD(FM) Wallace, ID
WDLJ(FM) Breese, IL
WHMS-FM Champaign, IL
WBBA-FM Pittsfield, IL
WZOK(FM) Rockford, IL
KJCK-FM Junction City, KS
WZZP(FM) Hopkinsville, KY
WAMZ(FM) Louisville, KY
KTJZ(FM) Tallulah, LA
WKTT(FM) Salisbury, MD
WIGY(FM) Madison, ME
WYTZ(FM) Bridgman, MI
WKLT(FM) Kalkaska, MI
WJIM-FM Lansing, MI
*WYDM(FM) Monroe, MI
WEFG-FM Whitehall, MI
KDKK-FM Park Rapids, MN
KNXR(FM) Rochester, MN
KOEA(FM) Doniphan, MO
KJMO(FM) Linn, MO
KNMO(FM) Nevada, MO
WWMS(FM) Oxford, MS
KOZB(FM) Livingston, MT
KKCT(FM) Bismarck, ND
KQSK(FM) Chadron, NE
WOKQ(FM) Dover, NH
WNUW(FM) Burlington, NJ
KPHD(FM) Elko, NV
KVEG(FM) Mesquite, NV
WTBD-FM Delhi, NY
WHAZ-FM Hoosick Falls, NY
WALK-FM Patchogue, NY
WFRY-FM Watertown, NY
WONE-FM Akron, OH
WVNU(FM) Greenfield, OH
WTGR(FM) Union City, OH
*WOBN(FM) Westerville, OH
KPAK(FM) Alva, OK
KMOD-FM Tulsa, OK
KNLR(FM) Bend, OR
KSHL(FM) Gleneden Beach, OR
WDDH(FM) Saint Marys, PA
WIOB(FM) Mayaguez, PR
WCOS-FM Columbia, SC
WJXB-FM Knoxville, TN
WLLX(FM) Lawrenceburg, TN
KFNC(FM) Beaumont, TX
KBNA-FM El Paso, TX
KFTX(FM) Kingsville, TX
KGKL-FM San Angelo, TX
KLAK(FM) Tom Bean, TX
KWTX-FM Waco, TX
KZZQ(FM) Coalville, UT
WWWV(FM) Charlottesville, VA
WQOK(FM) South Boston, VA
WTNN(FM) Bristol, VT
KOLW(FM) Basin City, WA
KTRT(FM) Winthrop, WA
WTAQ-FM Glenmore, WI
WQBE-FM Charleston, WV
WLTF(FM) Martinsburg, WV
KDLY(FM) Lander, WY

97.7 mhz
WKKR(FM) Auburn, AL
WHPH(FM) Jemison, AL
WZZN(FM) Oneonta, AL
WKXM-FM Winfield, AL
*KJSM-FM Augusta, AR
KAVV(FM) Benson, AZ
*KQVO(FM) Calexico, CA
KHHZ(FM) Gridley, CA
KWIN(FM) Lodi, CA
KFFG(FM) Los Altos, CA
KRCK-FM Mecca, CA

KTPI-FM Mojave, CA
KVRV(FM) Monte Rio, CA
KSMJ(FM) Shafter, CA
KZYR(FM) Avon, CO
*KSJL(FM) Strasburg, CO
WCTY(FM) Norwich, CT
WAFL(FM) Milford, DE
WYYX(FM) Bonifay, FL
WAVK(FM) Marathon, FL
WTLQ-FM Punta Rassa, FL
WMGZ(FM) Eatonton, GA
*WGPB(FM) Rome, GA
WTCQ(FM) Vidalia, GA
WWUF(FM) Waycross, GA
KCRR(FM) Grundy Center, IA
KHBT(FM) Humboldt, IA
KOTM-FM Ottumwa, IA
KZBG(FM) Lapwai, ID
WMOI(FM) Monmouth, IL
WLCE(FM) Petersburg, IL
WSTQ(FM) Streator, IL
WHET(FM) West Frankfort, IL
WZOW(FM) Goshen, IN
WLQI(FM) Rensselaer, IN
WCLS(FM) Spencer, IN
KSNP(FM) Burlington, KS
WWKY(FM) Providence, KY
WKCA(FM) Salt Lick, KY
KNBB(FM) Dubach, LA
KAPB-FM Marksville, LA
WKAF(FM) Brockton, MA
*WYAJ(FM) Sudbury, MA
WMDM-FM Lexington Park, MD
WCXU(FM) Caribou, ME
WNSX(FM) Winter Harbor, ME
WMRX-FM Beaverton, MI
WOLV(FM) Houghton, MI
WMLQ(FM) Manistee, MI
WTGV-FM Sandusky, MI
KLGR-FM Redwood Falls, MN
KPOW-FM La Monte, MO
KHZR(FM) Potosi, MO
KQMO(FM) Shell Knob, MO
WRBJ-FM Brandon, MS
WTYJ(FM) Fayette, MS
WTYL-FM Tylertown, MS
KGLM-FM Anaconda, MT
WEQR(FM) Walnut Creek, NC
WGTI(FM) Windsor, NC
KMTY(FM) Holdrege, NE
KBBX-FM Nebraska City, NE
WSNI(FM) Swanzey, NH
KDLW(FM) Belen, NM
KPSA-FM Lordsburg, NM
WEXT(FM) Amsterdam, NY
WENI-FM Big Flats, NY
WCZX(FM) Hyde Park, NY
WILE-FM Byesville, OH
WGGN(FM) Castalia, OH
WCJO(FM) Jackson, OH
*WTGN(FM) Lima, OH
WOXY(FM) Oxford, OH
KICM(FM) Healdton, OK
*KHIM(FM) Mangum, OK
KRAT(FM) Altamont, OR
KACI-FM The Dalles, OR
WLER-FM Butler, PA
WVRT(FM) Mill Hall, PA
WLKH(FM) Somerset, PA
WNVM(FM) Cidra, PR
WWXM(FM) Garden City, SC
KNBZ(FM) Redfield, SD
WTNE-FM Trenton, TN
KATX(FM) Eastland, TX
KLTO-FM McQueeney, TX
KBMI(FM) Roma, TX
KWRW(FM) Rusk, TX
KALK(FM) Winfield, TX
KCYQ(FM) Elsinore, UT
WRIC-FM Richlands, VA
WGMT(FM) Lyndon, VT
KYSN(FM) East Wenatchee, WA
KOMO-FM Oakville, WA
WAQE-FM Barron, WI
WGLR-FM Lancaster, WI
WFDL-FM Lomira, WI

WSRG(FM) Sturgeon Bay, WI
WKCJ(FM) Ronceverte, WV
KCYA(FM) Kaycee, WY

97.9 mhz
WRVX(FM) Eufaula, AL
WVOK-FM Oxford, AL
WJWZ(FM) Wetumpka, AL
KTLO-FM Mountain Home, AR
KZXK(FM) Doney Park, AZ
KUPD-FM Tempe, AZ
KPOD-FM Crescent City, CA
KLAX-FM East Los Angeles, CA
KLMG(FM) Esparto, CA
KMGV(FM) Fresno, CA
KLUK(FM) Needles, CA
KYZZ(FM) Salinas, CA
KISZ-FM Cortez, CO
WPKX(FM) Enfield, CT
WXTB(FM) Clearwater, FL
WFKS(FM) Neptune Beach, FL
WRMF(FM) Palm Beach, FL
WJZT(FM) Woodville, FL
WDMG-FM Ambrose, GA
WIBB-FM Fort Valley, GA
KKBG(FM) Hilo, HI
*KOWI(FM) Lamoni, IA
*KCMR(FM) Mason City, IA
KSEZ(FM) Sioux City, IA
KQFC(FM) Boise, ID
WLUP-FM Chicago, IL
WXEF(FM) Effingham, IL
WBBE(FM) Heyworth, IL
*WGNR-FM Anderson, IN
WSLM-FM Salem, IN
KWGB(FM) Colby, KS
KRBB(FM) Wichita, KS
WKIC(FM) Hyden, KY
KQLK(FM) De Ridder, LA
WIYY(FM) Baltimore, MD
WBEY-FM Crisfield, MD
WJBQ(FM) Portland, ME
WJLB(FM) Detroit, MI
WGRD-FM Grand Rapids, MI
WIHC(FM) Newberry, MI
WEVE-FM Eveleth, MN
KICK-FM Palmyra, MO
KBXB(FM) Sikeston, MO
KFBD-FM Waynesville, MO
KXDG(FM) Webb City, MO
WCPR-FM D'Iberville, MS
WBAQ(FM) Greenville, MS
WHTU(FM) Newton, MS
KVVR(FM) Dutton, MT
KDXT(FM) Lolo, MT
WNBB(FM) Bayboro, NC
WPEG(FM) Concord, NC
WTRG(FM) Gaston, NC
KHRU(FM) Beulah, ND
*KFNW-FM Fargo, ND
KNPE(FM) Hyannis, NE
KRSI(FM) Garapan-Saipan, NP
WYME(FM) Au Sable, NY
WSKQ-FM New York, NY
WPXY-FM Rochester, NY
WSKS(FM) Whitesboro, NY
WRIP(FM) Windham, NY
WNCI(FM) Columbus, OH
KJMZ(FM) Cache, OK
WWLS-FM Edmond, OK
KZBB(FM) Poteau, OK
KNRQ(FM) Eugene, OR
KZTB(FM) Milton-Freewater, OR
*KRRC(FM) Portland, OR
WXTA(FM) Edinboro, PA
WBSX(FM) Hazleton, PA
WIIZ(FM) Blackville, SC
KTPT(FM) Rapid City, SD
WSIX-FM Nashville, TN
KGNC-FM Amarillo, TX
KBFB(FM) Dallas, TX
KBXX(FM) Houston, TX
KODM(FM) Odessa, TX
KBZN(FM) Ogden, UT
WZZU(FM) Lynchburg, VA
WGOD-FM Charlotte Amalie, VI

WSPT-FM Stevens Point, WI
WKKW(FM) Fairmont, WV
WMGA(FM) Kenova, WV
KXBG(FM) Cheyenne, WY
KTAG(FM) Cody, WY
KZWB(FM) Green River, WY

98.1 mhz

KLEF(FM) Anchorage, AK
KWLF(FM) Fairbanks, AK
*KHUS(FM) Huslia, AK
*KALG(FM) Kaltag, AK
*KOYU(FM) Koyukuk, AK
*KRBY(FM) Ruby, AK
WTXT(FM) Fayette, AL
KTBX(FM) Tubac, AZ
*KVIP-FM Redding, CA
KIFM(FM) San Diego, CA
KISQ(FM) San Francisco, CA
KKJG(FM) San Luis Obispo, CA
KRXV(FM) Yermo, CA
KKFM(FM) Colorado Springs, CO
KAYW(FM) Meeker, CO
*WQAQ(FM) Hamden, CT
WKZE-FM Salisbury, CT
WOCM(FM) Selbyville, DE
WTKE-FM Holt, FL
WQHL-FM Live Oak, FL
WNUE-FM Titusville, FL
WMRZ(FM) Dawson, GA
WEDB(FM) East Dublin, GA
WMGP(FM) Hogansville, GA
KJMQ(FM) Lihue, HI
KHAK(FM) Cedar Rapids, IA
KGTM(FM) Rexburg, ID
WZOE-FM Princeton, IL
WIBN(FM) Earl Park, IN
WRAY-FM Princeton, IN
KSKZ(FM) Copeland, KS
KUSN(FM) Dearing, KS
KUDL(FM) Kansas City, KS
WBUL-FM Lexington, KY
WDGL(FM) Baton Rouge, LA
WCTK(FM) New Bedford, MA
WCXV(FM) Van Buren, ME
WGFN(FM) Glen Arbor, MI
*WEUL(FM) Kingsford, MI
WKCQ(FM) Saginaw, MI
KBEW-FM Blue Earth, MN
WWJO(FM) Saint Cloud, MN
KOZX(FM) Cabool, MO
KYKY(FM) Saint Louis, MO
WMXI(FM) Laurel, MS
WQSM(FM) Fayetteville, NC
WOBX-FM Manteo, NC
KFGE(FM) Milford, NE
KBAC(FM) Las Vegas, NM
KBUL-FM Carson City, NV
WHWK(FM) Binghamton, NY
WKDD(FM) Canton, OH
*WUDR(FM) Dayton, OH
WDFM(FM) Defiance, OH
KZRC(FM) Bennington, OK
KCYS(FM) Seaside, OR
WFGY(FM) Altoona, PA
WOGL(FM) Philadelphia, PA
WYBB(FM) Folly Beach, SC
WHZT(FM) Seneca, SC
WXMX(FM) Millington, TN
WLND(FM) Signal Mountain, TN
KTLT(FM) Anson, TX
KVET-FM Austin, TX
KKUL-FM Groveton, TX
KRRG(FM) Laredo, TX
KKCL(FM) Lorenzo, TX
KTAL-FM Texarkana, TX
KREC(FM) Brian Head, UT
WBRF(FM) Galax, VA
WTVR-FM Richmond, VA
WJJR(FM) Rutland, VT
KING-FM Seattle, WA
KISC(FM) Spokane, WA
WISM-FM Altoona, WI
WLKN(FM) Cleveland, WI
WMGN(FM) Madison, WI

98.3 mhz

WTXO(FM) Ashland, AL
WDLT-FM Chickasaw, AL
WBFA(FM) Fort Mitchell, AL
WKEA-FM Scottsboro, AL
KKEG(FM) Bentonville, AR
KFCM(FM) Cherokee Village, AR
KOHT(FM) Marana, AZ
KKFR(FM) Mayer, AZ
KQSS(FM) Miami, AZ
KZLA(FM) Huron, CA
KXBX-FM Lakeport, CA
KDAR(FM) Oxnard, CA
KWNN(FM) Turlock, CA
KRCV(FM) West Covina, CA
KEJJ(FM) Gunnison, CO
KATR-FM Otis, CO
WDAQ(FM) Danbury, CT
WILI-FM Willimantic, CT
WWRZ(FM) Fort Meade, FL
WRTO-FM Goulds, FL
WGCO(FM) Midway, GA
WSSY(FM) Pinehurst, GA
KJMD(FM) Pukalani, HI
KWQW(FM) Boone, IA
KDZY(FM) McCall, ID
KSNQ(FM) Twin Falls, ID
WCCQ(FM) Crest Hill, IL
WWHP(FM) Farmer City, IL
WRIK-FM Metropolis, IL
WRAN(FM) Tower Hill, IL
WRDZ-FM Plainfield, IN
WZZY(FM) Winchester, IN
KQZQ(FM) Kiowa, KS
WQXE(FM) Elizabethtown, KY
WOKE(FM) Garrison, KY
WHAY(FM) Whitley City, KY
KZRZ(FM) West Monroe, LA
WHAI(FM) Greenfield, MA
WSMD-FM Mechanicsville, MD
WCXT(FM) Hartford, MI
WTWR-FM Luna Pier, MI
WRUP(FM) Munising, MI
WLCS(FM) North Muskegon, MI
*WCMZ-FM Sault Ste. Marie, MI
WBJI(FM) Blackduck, MN
KQYB(FM) Spring Grove, MN
WCKK(FM) Carthage, MS
WDFX(FM) Cleveland, MS
WJDR(FM) Prentiss, MS
KBEV-FM Dillon, MT
WDLZ(FM) Murfreesboro, NC
WSFM(FM) Oak Island, NC
WIST-FM Thomasville, NC
WLGT(FM) Washington, NC
KXGT(FM) Carrington, ND
KBBN-FM Broken Bow, NE
WLNH-FM Laconia, NH
WMGQ(FM) New Brunswick, NJ
WTKU-FM Ocean City, NJ
WVIN-FM Bath, NY
WKJY(FM) Hempstead, NY
WSUL(FM) Monticello, NY
*WPSA(FM) Paul Smiths, NY
WTRY-FM Rotterdam, NY
WQRS(FM) Salamanca, NY
WYBL(FM) Ashtabula, OH
WPKO-FM Bellefontaine, OH
WXXR(FM) Fredericktown, OH
*WKET(FM) Kettering, OH
WKNA(FM) Logan, OH
KTWS(FM) Bend, OR
KLDR(FM) Harbeck-Fruitdale, OR
KPPK(FM) Rainier, OR
WOGF(FM) Duquesne, PA
WWBE(FM) Mifflinburg, PA
WIDI(FM) Quebradillas, PR
WHHD(FM) Clearwater, SC
WLJI(FM) Summerton, SC
KUQL(FM) Wessington Springs, SD
WRJB(FM) Camden, TN
WKSR-FM Loretto, TN
WLOD-FM Sweetwater, TN
KPDB(FM) Big Lake, TX
KBOC(FM) Bridgeport, TX
KORA-FM Bryan, TX

KULM-FM Columbus, TX
KICA-FM Farwell, TX
*KYAR(FM) Gatesville, TX
KLHB(FM) Odem, TX
KYYK(FM) Palestine, TX
KPTX(FM) Pecos, TX
KXDJ(FM) Spearman, TX
KARB(FM) Price, UT
WLUS-FM Clarksville, VA
WKSI-FM Stephens City, VA
WMYP(FM) Frederiksted, VI
KEYW(FM) Pasco, WA
WJMR-FM Menomonee Falls, WI
WCQM(FM) Park Falls, WI
WCEF(FM) Ripley, WV
KADQ-FM Evanston, WY
KGRK(FM) Glenrock, WY
KZZS(FM) Story, WY
KERM(FM) Torrington, WY

98.5 mhz

WINL(FM) Linden, AL
KURB(FM) Little Rock, AR
KRDX(FM) Vail, AZ
KWXY-FM Cathedral City, CA
KDFO(FM) Delano, CA
KSAY(FM) Fort Bragg, CA
KRXQ(FM) Sacramento, CA
KUFX(FM) San Jose, CA
KYGO-FM Denver, CO
*KAAI(FM) Palisade, CO
WGBG(FM) Seaford, DE
WKTK(FM) Crystal River, FL
WFSY(FM) Panama City, FL
WDEO-FM San Carlos Park, FL
WSBH(FM) Satellite Beach, FL
WSB-FM Atlanta, GA
WLPF(FM) Ocilla, GA
KDNN(FM) Honolulu, HI
KOEL-FM Cedar Falls, IA
KQKQ-FM Council Bluffs, IA
KLLP(FM) Chubbuck, ID
KZID(FM) Orofino, ID
WPIA(FM) Eureka, IL
WXXQ(FM) Freeport, IL
WIBQ(FM) Paris, IL
WQKZ(FM) Ferdinand, IN
WMYK(FM) Peru, IN
KSAJ-FM Abilene, KS
WYLD-FM New Orleans, LA
WBZ-FM Boston, MA
WEBB(FM) Waterville, ME
WNWN-FM Coldwater, MI
WUPS(FM) Houghton Lake, MI
*KTIS-FM Minneapolis, MN
KTJJ(FM) Farmington, MO
KWKJ(FM) Windsor, MO
WZLQ(FM) Tupelo, MS
KGHL-FM Billings, MT
KBBZ(FM) Kalispell, MT
KHLN(FM) Montana City, MT
WDWG(FM) Rocky Mount, NC
KHAQ(FM) Maxwell, NE
WKMK(FM) Ocean Acres, NJ
KABG(FM) Los Alamos, NM
KLUC-FM Las Vegas, NV
WCTW(FM) Catskill, NY
WCKM-FM Lake George, NY
WKSE(FM) Niagara Falls, NY
WNYR-FM Waterloo, NY
WBON(FM) Westhampton, NY
WRRM(FM) Cincinnati, OH
WNCX(FM) Cleveland, OH
*WCMO(FM) Marietta, OH
KACO(FM) Apache, OK
KVOO-FM Tulsa, OK
*WKEL(FM) Confluence, PA
WGYI(FM) Oil City, PA
WKRZ(FM) Wilkes-Barre, PA
WYCR(FM) York-Hanover, PA
WPRM-FM San Juan, PR
WBZF(FM) Hartsville, SC
WOMG(FM) Lexington, SC
WDAI(FM) Pawley's Island, SC
WGIC(FM) Cookeville, TN
WTFM(FM) Kingsport, TN

KGAP(FM) Clarksville, TX
KBXJ(FM) Los Ybanez, TX
KGBT-FM McAllen, TX
KTJM(FM) Port Arthur, TX
KCUB-FM Ranger, TX
KRXT(FM) Rockdale, TX
KBBT(FM) Schertz, TX
KXME(FM) Wellington, TX
KCDC(FM) Milford, UT
KIFX(FM) Roosevelt, UT
WACL(FM) Elkton, VA
KEYG-FM Grand Coulee, WA
WQLH(FM) Green Bay, WI

98.7 mhz

WBHK(FM) Warrior, AL
KLBQ(FM) El Dorado, AR
KPKX(FM) Phoenix, AZ
KXTS(FM) Geyserville, CA
KYSR(FM) Los Angeles, CA
KLOQ-FM Winton, CA
KRTZ(FM) Cortez, CO
WNLC(FM) East Lyme, CT
WMZQ-FM Washington, DC
WKGR(FM) Fort Pierce, FL
WSJT(FM) Holmes Beach, FL
WCNK(FM) Key West, FL
WYCT(FM) Pensacola, FL
WISK-FM Americus, GA
WBTY(FM) Homerville, GA
KMGO(FM) Centerville, IA
KSMA-FM Osage, IA
WFMT(FM) Chicago, IL
WNNS(FM) Springfield, IL
WQME(FM) Anderson, IN
WASK-FM Battle Ground, IN
KFH-FM Clearwater, KS
WHOP-FM Hopkinsville, KY
WKDO-FM Liberty, KY
KKST(FM) Oakdale, LA
WVMV(FM) Detroit, MI
WFGR(FM) Grand Rapids, MI
WGLI(FM) Hancock, MI
KQWB-FM Moorhead, MN
KISD(FM) Pipestone, MN
KWTO-FM Springfield, MO
WNEV(FM) Friar's Point, MS
WJKK(FM) Vicksburg, MS
KXDR(FM) Hamilton, MT
WSMW(FM) Greensboro, NC
WLGD(FM) Jacksonville, NC
KACL(FM) Bismarck, ND
KSID-FM Sidney, NE
WBYY(FM) Somersworth, NH
WINQ(FM) Winchester, NH
WCZT(FM) Villas, NJ
*KMTH(FM) Maljamar, NM
KKVS(FM) Truth or Consequences, NM
KAVB(FM) Hawthorne, NV
WGMM(FM) Corning, NY
WRKS(FM) New York, NY
WPAC(FM) Ogdensburg, NY
WLZW(FM) Utica, NY
*WYKL(FM) Crestline, OH
*WSLN(FM) Delaware, OH
WYRO(FM) McArthur, OH
KYTT-FM Coos Bay, OR
KUBQ(FM) La Grande, OR
*KARO(FM) Nyssa, OR
KUPL-FM Portland, OR
WWSH(FM) Pleasant Gap, PA
WNVE(FM) Culebra, PR
WYKZ(FM) Beaufort, SC
KOUT(FM) Rapid City, SD
WOKI(FM) Oliver Springs, TN
KPRF(FM) Amarillo, TX
KLUV(FM) Dallas, TX
KZAM(FM) Pleasant Valley, TX
KELI(FM) San Angelo, TX
KTXN-FM Victoria, TX
KBEE(FM) Salt Lake City, UT
WNOR(FM) Norfolk, VA
KMNA(FM) Mabton, WA
WMDC(FM) Mayville, WI
WRVZ(FM) Pocatalico, WV

WOVK(FM) Wheeling, WV
KRSV-FM Afton, WY
KRQU(FM) Laramie, WY
KWXR(FM) Reliance, WY

98.9 mhz

KYMG(FM) Anchorage, AK
WBAM-FM Montgomery, AL
KWLU(FM) Chester, CA
KCVR-FM Columbia, CA
KSOF(FM) Dinuba, CA
KHWY(FM) Essex, CA
KRVC(FM) Hornbrook, CA
KSOL(FM) San Francisco, CA
KKMG(FM) Pueblo, CO
WGUF(FM) Marco, FL
WBCG(FM) Murdock, FL
WMMO(FM) Orlando, FL
WBZE(FM) Tallahassee, FL
*WNGH-FM Chatsworth, GA
KITH(FM) Kapaa, HI
KGRA(FM) Jefferson, IA
KQCR-FM Parkersburg, IA
WJEZ(FM) Dwight, IL
WISH-FM Galatia, IL
WHQQ(FM) Neoga, IL
WLKU(FM) Rock Island, IL
WZKF(FM) Salem, IN
KKRK(FM) Coffeyville, KS
KQRC-FM Leavenworth, KS
WSIP-FM Paintsville, KY
WUUU(FM) Franklinton, LA
WORC-FM Webster, MA
WSBY-FM Salisbury, MD
WCLZ(FM) Brunswick, ME
WKLZ-FM Petoskey, MI
WOWE(FM) Vassar, MI
WRAX(FM) Walhalla, MI
KTCO(FM) Duluth, MN
KZPK(FM) Paynesville, MN
KFLW(FM) Saint Robert, MO
WAJV(FM) Brooksville, MS
*WLKO(FM) Quitman, MS
KAAK(FM) Great Falls, MT
WNBR-FM Bethel, NC
KKPR-FM Kearney, NE
WBZA(FM) Rochester, NY
WXMG(FM) Upper Arlington, OH
WBYR(FM) Van Wert, OH
WMXY(FM) Youngstown, OH
KYIS(FM) Oklahoma City, OK
WQKY(FM) Emporium, PA
WQLV(FM) Millersburg, PA
WUSL(FM) Philadelphia, PA
WYAS(FM) Vieques, PR
WWIK(FM) McClellanville, SC
WSPA-FM Spartanburg, SC
WLSQ(FM) Byrdstown, TN
WANT(FM) Lebanon, TN
WKIM(FM) Munford, TN
KNOS(FM) Albany, TX
KTUX(FM) Carthage, TX
KLMO-FM Dilley, TX
KHHL(FM) Leander, TX
KLOW(FM) Reno, TX
KLYD(FM) Snyder, TX
KBZB(FM) Hurricane, UT
WWLB(FM) Midlothian, VA
WOKO(FM) Burlington, VT
KWJZ(FM) Seattle, WA
KKZX(FM) Spokane, WA
*WVCX(FM) Tomah, WI
WDNE-FM Elkins, WV
KOUZ(FM) Manville, WY

99.1 mhz

KRUP(FM) Dillingham, AK
*KNUL(FM) Nulato, AK
WDGM(FM) Greensboro, AL
WAHR(FM) Huntsville, AL
KMAG(FM) Fort Smith, AR
KSMD(FM) Pangburn, AR
KVMZ(FM) Waldo, AR
KOFH(FM) Nogales, AZ
KTMG(FM) Prescott, AZ
KFMM(FM) Thatcher, AZ
KJNY(FM) Ferndale, CA

KGGI(FM) Riverside, CA
KSQL(FM) Santa Cruz, CA
KXFM(FM) Santa Maria, CA
*KARA(FM) Williams, CA
KMTS(FM) Glenwood Springs, CO
KUAD-FM Windsor, CO
WPLR(FM) New Haven, CT
WWOJ(FM) Avon Park, FL
WQIK-FM Jacksonville, FL
WEDR(FM) Miami, FL
WDEN(FM) Macon, GA
KAGB(FM) Waimea, HI
KSKB(FM) Brooklyn, IA
KUPI-FM Idaho Falls, ID
KQLZ(FM) Mountain Home, ID
WXTT(FM) Danville, IL
*KJIL(FM) Copeland, KS
*KTLI(FM) El Dorado, KS
KSEK-FM Girard, KS
WCBL-FM Benton, KY
WHSX(FM) Edmonton, KY
WJMM-FM Keene, KY
WWKN(FM) Morgantown, KY
KXKC(FM) New Iberia, LA
WPLM-FM Plymouth, MA
WLZL(FM) Annapolis, MD
WLKE(FM) Bar Harbor, ME
WSMK(FM) Buchanan, MI
WFMK(FM) East Lansing, MI
WIKB-FM Iron River, MI
KEEZ-FM Mankato, MN
KLLZ(FM) Walker, MN
KFUO-FM Clayton, MO
KYOO-FM Halfway, MO
WYMX(FM) Greenwood, MS
WKNN-FM Pascagoula, MS
KCMM(FM) Belgrade, MT
KZJZ(FM) Saint Regis, MT
WVOD(FM) Manteo, NC
WZFX(FM) Whiteville, NC
KCAD(FM) Dickinson, ND
WNNH(FM) Henniker, NH
WNYN-FM Whitefield, NH
WAWZ(FM) Zarephath, NJ
KCLV-FM Clovis, NM
KGLX(FM) Gallup, NM
KXMT(FM) Taos, NM
KKFT(FM) Gardnerville-Minden, NV
WAAL(FM) Binghamton, NY
WHKO(FM) Dayton, OH
WFRO-FM Fremont, OH
KODZ(FM) Eugene, OR
WRKW(FM) Ebensburg, PA
WUKQ-FM Mayaguez, PR
KSOO-FM Lennox, SD
KXLG(FM) Milbank, SD
WNML-FM Loudon, TN
KAYG(FM) Camp Wood, TX
KRYS-FM Corpus Christi, TX
KFZO(FM) Denton, TX
KNES(FM) Fairfield, TX
KODA(FM) Houston, TX
KHKX(FM) Odessa, TX
WXGM-FM Gloucester, VA
WJNV(FM) Jonesville, VA
WSLQ(FM) Roanoke, VA
KUJ-FM Burbank, WA
WMYX(FM) Milwaukee, WI
WKFX(FM) Rice Lake, WI
WGGE(FM) Parkersburg, WV
KNYN(FM) Fort Bridger, WY
KWYW(FM) Lost Cabin, WY
KLSX(FM) Rozet, WY

99.3 mhz

WMFC-FM Monroeville, AL
KVLD(FM) Atkins, AR
KAPW(FM) Cotton Plant, AR
KZYP(FM) Pine Bluff, AR
KMZQ-FM Payson, AZ
KKBB(FM) Bakersfield, CA
KJWL(FM) Fresno, CA
KMXX(FM) Imperial, CA
KVYN(FM) Saint Helena, CA
KNNN(FM) Shasta Lake City, CA
KJOY(FM) Stockton, CA

KPCR(FM) Burlington, CO
WLRQ-FM Cocoa, FL
WJBX(FM) Fort Myers Beach, FL
WXRA(FM) Inglis, FL
WEBZ(FM) Mexico Beach, FL
WCON-FM Cornelia, GA
WKCN(FM) Lumpkin, GA
WBAW-FM Pembroke, GA
KFFF-FM Boone, IA
KMA-FM Clarinda, IA
KDST(FM) Dyersville, IA
KWAY-FM Waverly, IA
WDUK(FM) Havana, IL
WAJK(FM) La Salle, IL
WXFM(FM) Mount Zion, IL
WSCH(FM) Aurora, IN
WKVI-FM Knox, IN
WCJC(FM) Van Buren, IN
KWIC(FM) Topeka, KS
WWKF(FM) Fulton, KY
WKMO(FM) Lebanon Junction, KY
WVLE(FM) Scottsville, KY
KPCH(FM) Ruston, LA
WLZX(FM) Northampton, MA
WKTJ-FM Farmington, ME
WBQQ(FM) Kennebunk, ME
WATZ-FM Alpena, MI
WOUF(FM) Frankfort, MI
WMSH-FM Sturgis, MI
WJQK(FM) Zeeland, MI
KXRZ(FM) Alexandria, MN
KWNO-FM Rushford, MN
KKDQ(FM) Thief River Falls, MN
KCLR-FM Boonville, MO
KCGQ-FM Gordonville, MO
KUNQ(FM) Houston, MO
WBVV(FM) Guntown, MS
WHER(FM) Heidelberg, MS
KMXE-FM Red Lodge, MT
WQDK(FM) Ahoskie, NC
WZAX(FM) Nashville, NC
KETT(FM) Mitchell, NE
KHZY(FM) Overton, NE
WFRD(FM) Hanover, NH
WZBZ(FM) Pleasantville, NJ
*KWFL(FM) Roswell, NM
KVLV-FM Fallon, NV
KRGT(FM) Indian Springs, NV
WRWC(FM) Ellenville, NY
WLLG(FM) Lowville, NY
WSNN(FM) Potsdam, NY
WLLW(FM) Seneca Falls, NY
WTNS-FM Coshocton, OH
WNXT-FM Portsmouth, OH
KADA-FM Ada, OK
KCDL(FM) Cordell, OK
KGVE(FM) Grove, OK
KLOR-FM Ponca City, OK
WHMJ(FM) Franklin, PA
WHKF(FM) Harrisburg, PA
WZXR(FM) South Williamsport, PA
WPKL(FM) Uniontown, PA
WJZS(FM) Block Island, RI
WBT-FM Chester, SC
WWKT-FM Kingstree, SC
WPBX(FM) Crossville, TN
WTZR(FM) Elizabethton, TN
WNRX(FM) Jefferson City, TN
WZLT(FM) Lexington, TN
KPSM(FM) Brownwood, TX
KEFH(FM) Clarendon, TX
KYTM(FM) Corrigan, TX
KLGO(FM) Thorndale, TX
KZTK(FM) White Oak, TX
WVES(FM) Accomac, VA
WFQX(FM) Front Royal, VA
WKJM(FM) Petersburg, VA
WKJS(FM) Richmond, VA
WVBX(FM) Spotsylvania, VA
KDDS(FM) Elma, WA
KDRM(FM) Moses Lake, WA
KQMY(FM) Naches, WA
WDMP-FM Dodgeville, WI
WKEB(FM) Medford, WI
WOWN(FM) Shawano, WI
KKTY-FM Douglas, WY

KTGA(FM) Saratoga, WY

99.5 mhz

WZRR(FM) Birmingham, AL
KBTA-FM Batesville, AR
KHMB(FM) Hamburg, AR
KAKS(FM) Huntsville, AR
KDIS-FM Little Rock, AR
KMTB(FM) Murfreesboro, AR
KIIM-FM Tucson, AZ
KRPH(FM) Yarnell, AZ
*KLVS(FM) Citrus Heights, CA
KLOK-FM Greenfield, CA
KNTI(FM) Lakeport, CA
KKLA-FM Los Angeles, CA
KHYZ(FM) Mountain Pass, CA
KMRJ(FM) Rancho Mirage, CA
KQMT(FM) Denver, CO
WIHT(FM) Washington, DC
WJBR-FM Wilmington, DE
WAFC-FM Clewiston, FL
WKSM(FM) Fort Walton Beach, FL
WAIL(FM) Key West, FL
WBXY(FM) La Crosse, FL
WQYK-FM Saint Petersburg, FL
WKAA(FM) Willacoochee, GA
KHUI(FM) Honolulu, HI
KHAM(FM) Britt, IA
KDAO-FM Eldora, IA
KKMA(FM) Le Mars, IA
KPUL(FM) Winterset, IA
KQPI(FM) Aberdeen, ID
KWEI-FM Fruitland, ID
WUSN(FM) Chicago, IL
WDQZ(FM) Lexington, IL
WCOY(FM) Quincy, IL
WZPL(FM) Greenfield, IN
KHAZ(FM) Hays, KS
WKDP-FM Corbin, KY
WKDQ(FM) Henderson, KY
KNGT(FM) Lake Charles, LA
WRNO-FM New Orleans, LA
WCRB(FM) Lowell, MA
WVMD(FM) Midland, MD
WJCX(FM) Pittsfield, ME
WYCD(FM) Detroit, MI
WNGE(FM) Negaunee, MI
WYSS(FM) Sault Ste. Marie, MI
*KBHW(FM) International Falls, MN
*KSJN(FM) Minneapolis, MN
KPRW(FM) Perham, MN
KHCR(FM) Bismarck, MO
KADI-FM Republic, MO
KMCJ(FM) Colstrip, MT
KBLL-FM Helena, MT
WXNR(FM) Grifton, NC
WMAG(FM) High Point, NC
KUTT(FM) Fairbury, NE
WEVJ(FM) Jackson, NH
KMGA(FM) Albuquerque, NM
KXPZ(FM) Las Cruces, NM
KPXP(FM) Garapan-Saipan, NP
WTKW(FM) Bridgeport, NY
WDCX-FM Buffalo, NY
*WBAI(FM) New York, NY
WRVE(FM) Schenectady, NY
WOKN(FM) Southport, NY
WGAR-FM Cleveland, OH
WAOL(FM) Ripley, OH
KBIJ(FM) Guymon, OK
KXBL(FM) Henryetta, OK
KBZQ(FM) Lawton, OK
KAGO-FM Klamath Falls, OR
KWJJ-FM Portland, OR
KJMX(FM) Reedsport, OR
WMAJ-FM Centre Hall, PA
*WUSR(FM) Scranton, PA
WKXC-FM Aiken, SC
WRNN-FM Socastee, SC
KOLY-FM Mobridge, SD
WYGO(FM) Madisonville, TN
KKPS(FM) Brownsville, TX
KNFX-FM Bryan, TX
KPLX(FM) Fort Worth, TX
KQBR(FM) Lubbock, TX
KISS-FM San Antonio, TX

KJMY(FM) Bountiful, UT
WYTT(FM) Emporia, VA
WVIQ(FM) Christiansted, VI
KZZL-FM Pullman, WA
KAAP(FM) Rock Island, WA
WPKR(FM) Omro, WI
WJLS-FM Beckley, WV
WYMJ(FM) New Martinsville, WV
WBYG(FM) Point Pleasant, WV
KMJY(FM) Chugwater, WY
KRKI(FM) Newcastle, WY

99.7 mhz

KMBQ-FM Wasilla, AK
WOOF-FM Dothan, AL
KVGQ(FM) Snowflake, AZ
*KESC(FM) Morro Bay, CA
KIOO(FM) Porterville, CA
KMVQ-FM San Francisco, CA
KTOR(FM) Westwood, CA
KPTE(FM) Durango, CO
WJKD(FM) Vero Beach, FL
WWWQ(FM) Atlanta, GA
KXFT(FM) Manson, IA
KBEA-FM Muscatine, IA
WXAJ(FM) Hillsboro, IL
WSHW(FM) Frankfort, IN
WDJX(FM) Louisville, KY
KMJJ-FM Shreveport, LA
WIMI(FM) Ironwood, MI
*WUGN(FM) Midland, MI
KXDL(FM) Browerville, MN
KKCK(FM) Marshall, MN
KMAC(FM) Gainesville, MO
KKSN(FM) Kansas City, MO
KBTN-FM Neosho, MO
KTTR-FM Saint James, MO
WJMI(FM) Jackson, MS
KKMT(FM) Pablo, MT
WRFX(FM) Kannapolis, NC
KOGA-FM Ogallala, NE
WNTK-FM New London, NH
WBHX(FM) Tuckerton, NJ
WJUX(FM) Monticello, NY
WBGK(FM) Newport Village, NY
WZXV(FM) Palmyra, NY
WRKZ(FM) Columbus, OH
WKSD(FM) Paulding, OH
KZLS(FM) Mustang, OK
KMTK(FM) Bend, OR
WVRZ(FM) Mount Carmel, PA
WSHH(FM) Pittsburgh, PA
*WVYC(FM) York, PA
WEAN-FM Wakefield-Peacedale, RI
WXST(FM) Hollywood, SC
WWTN(FM) Manchester, TN
WMC-FM Memphis, TN
KBZD(FM) Amarillo, TX
KYRT(FM) Mason, TX
KROY(FM) Palacios, TX
KRBR(FM) Sulphur Bluff, TX
KBCY(FM) Tye, TX
KVST(FM) Willis, TX
WGCK-FM Coeburn, VA
WYFI(FM) Norfolk, VA
WCYK-FM Staunton, VA
KJOX-FM Long Beach, WA
KHHK(FM) Yakima, WA
WWIS-FM Black River Falls, WI
WRQE(FM) Sturgeon Bay, WI

99.9 mhz

KFMJ(FM) Ketchikan, AK
WRJL-FM Eva, AL
WMXC(FM) Mobile, AL
WQNR(FM) Tallassee, AL
*KSWH(FM) Arkadelphia, AR
KTCS-FM Fort Smith, AR
KGPQ(FM) Monticello, AR
KWCK(FM) Searcy, AR
KESZ(FM) Phoenix, AZ
KRCX-FM Marysville, CA
KCIV(FM) Mount Bullion, CA
KOLA(FM) San Bernardino, CA
KTYD(FM) Santa Barbara, CA
KEKB(FM) Fruita, CO
KVUU(FM) Pueblo, CO

WEZN-FM Bridgeport, CT
WKIS(FM) Boca Raton, FL
WEGT(FM) Lafayette, FL
WGNE-FM Palatka, FL
WSNT-FM Sandersville, GA
WNNG-FM Unadilla, GA
KJKS(FM) Kahului, HI
KTOH(FM) Kalaheo, HI
KCWN(FM) New Sharon, IA
KZDX(FM) Burley, ID
KXML(FM) Salmon, ID
WWCT(FM) Bartonville, IL
WOOZ-FM Harrisburg, IL
WCPQ(FM) Park Forest, IL
WTHI-FM Terre Haute, IN
KWKR(FM) Leoti, KS
KSKG(FM) Salina, KS
WVLC(FM) Mannsville, KY
WMTC-FM Vancleve, KY
KTDY(FM) Lafayette, LA
KTEZ(FM) Zwolle, LA
WXRG(FM) Athol, MA
WQRC(FM) Barnstable, MA
*WHHB(FM) Holliston, MA
WFRE(FM) Frederick, MD
WWFG(FM) Ocean City, MD
WTHT(FM) Auburn, ME
WHFB-FM Benton Harbor, MI
WMUP(FM) Carney, MI
WPIQ(FM) Manistique, MI
WHAK-FM Rogers City, MI
KAUS-FM Austin, MN
KVOX-FM Moorhead, MN
KCML(FM) Saint Joseph, MN
WUSZ(FM) Virginia, MN
KBFL-FM Buffalo, MO
KIRK(FM) Macon, MO
KZMA-FM Naylor, MO
KFAV(FM) Warrenton, MO
WSMS(FM) Artesia, MS
KBOZ-FM Bozeman, MT
WKSF(FM) Asheville, NC
WKXB(FM) Burgaw, NC
WHDX(FM) Buxton, NC
WCMC-FM Creedmoor, NC
KMXA-FM Minot, ND
KGOR(FM) Omaha, NE
KKTC(FM) Angel Fire, NM
KTQM-FM Clovis, NM
KXTC(FM) Thoreau, NM
WIII(FM) Cortland, NY
WBTZ(FM) Plattsburgh, NY
WLQT(FM) Kettering, OH
WKKO(FM) Toledo, OH
WTUZ(FM) Uhrichsville, OH
KRKT-FM Albany, OR
KWRL(FM) La Grande, OR
WQBR(FM) Avis, PA
WODE-FM Easton, PA
WXKC(FM) Erie, PA
WIOA(FM) San Juan, PR
KTSM-FM El Paso, TX
KTXM(FM) Hallettsville, TX
KRZS(FM) Hunt, TX
KSHN-FM Liberty, TX
KMOO-FM Mineola, TX
KBAT(FM) Monahans, TX
KSAB(FM) Robstown, TX
WACO-FM Waco, TX
KLUR(FM) Wichita Falls, TX
KONY(FM) Saint George, UT
WZBB(FM) Stanleytown, VA
KISW(FM) Seattle, WA
KXLY-FM Spokane, WA
WDRK(FM) Cornell, WI
WJVL(FM) Janesville, WI
WSAU-FM Rudolph, WI
WVAF(FM) Charleston, WV
KKPL(FM) Cheyenne, WY

100.1 mhz

KYKD(FM) Bethel, AK
KWHQ-FM Kenai, AK
*KMXT(FM) Kodiak, AK
WGSY(FM) Phenix City, AL
WDXX(FM) Selma, AL

KVNA-FM Flagstaff, AZ
KGMN(FM) Kingman, AZ
KNGS(FM) Coalinga, CA
KZRO(FM) Dunsmuir, CA
KGBA-FM Holtville, CA
*KLVJ(FM) Julian, CA
KHWZ(FM) Ludlow, CA
KZST(FM) Santa Rosa, CA
KQOD(FM) Stockton, CA
KKZQ(FM) Tehachapi, CA
WVVE(FM) Panama City Beach, FL
WZJZ(FM) Port Charlotte, FL
WQMJ(FM) Forsyth, GA
WSSJ(FM) Rincon, GA
WNSY(FM) Talking Rock, GA
WPUP(FM) Watkinsville, GA
KUYY(FM) Emmetsburg, IA
KCTN(FM) Garnavillo, IA
KITT(FM) Soda Springs, ID
WKAI(FM) Macomb, IL
WGLC-FM Mendota, IL
WJBD-FM Salem, IL
WNUY(FM) Bluffton, IN
WFLQ(FM) French Lick, IN
WFRI(FM) Winamac, IN
WMDJ-FM Allen, KY
WKQQ(FM) Winchester, KY
KRVV(FM) Bastrop, LA
WUPE-FM North Adams, MA
WWFX(FM) Southbridge, MA
*WBRS(FM) Waltham, MA
*WUMF-FM Farmington, ME
WHOU-FM Houlton, ME
WCUZ(FM) Bear Lake, MI
WBCH-FM Hastings, MI
WVIB(FM) Holton, MI
KOLV(FM) Olivia, MN
WZFJ(FM) Pequot Lakes, MN
KKWK(FM) Cameron, MO
KDJR(FM) De Soto, MO
KBBM(FM) Jefferson City, MO
KOMC-FM Kimberling City, MO
WQXB(FM) Grenada, MS
KMMR(FM) Malta, MT
KZOQ-FM Missoula, MT
KATQ(FM) Plentywood, MT
WBXB(FM) Edenton, NC
KYOY(FM) Kimball, NE
WPNH-FM Plymouth, NH
WJRZ-FM Manahawkin, NJ
KHWG-FM Crystal, NV
KTHX-FM Dayton, NV
WDST(FM) Woodstock, NY
WNIR(FM) Kent, OH
WXZQ(FM) Piketon, OH
WSWR(FM) Shelby, OH
KYFM(FM) Bartlesville, OK
KYKC(FM) Byng, OK
KWFX(FM) Woodward, OK
WWOT(FM) Altoona, PA
WBRR(FM) Bradford, PA
WQFN(FM) Forest City, PA
WQIC(FM) Lebanon, PA
WWFN-FM Lake City, SC
WXBT(FM) West Columbia, SC
KDEZ(FM) Brandon, SD
KJBI(FM) Fort Pierre, SD
WASL(FM) Dyersburg, TN
WRLT(FM) Franklin, TN
KNRB(FM) Atlanta, TX
KBWM(FM) Breckenridge, TX
KYBI(FM) Lufkin, TX
KCLL(FM) San Angelo, TX
WYFJ(FM) Ashland, VA
WVBE-FM Lynchburg, VA
WKQV(FM) Tazewell, VA
WPJP(FM) Port Washington, WI
WDDC(FM) Portage, WI
WRHN(FM) Rhinelander, WI
WKBH-FM West Salem, WI
WCLG-FM Morgantown, WV
WDZN(FM) Romney, WV
WDMX(FM) Vienna, WV
KYOD(FM) Glendo, WY

100.3 mhz
KICY-FM Nome, AK
*KJNP-FM North Pole, AK
WAOQ(FM) Brantley, AL
WGZZ(FM) Dadeville, AL
WQRV(FM) Tuscumbia, AL
KURM-FM Gravette, AR
KDJE(FM) Jacksonville, AR
KQMR(FM) Globe, AZ
KJMB(FM) Blythe, CA
KWPT(FM) Fortuna, CA
KRQK(FM) Lompoc, CA
KSWD(FM) Los Angeles, CA
KMAK(FM) Orange Cove, CA
KHGQ(FM) Quincy, CA
KBRG(FM) San Jose, CA
KIMN(FM) Denver, CO
WBIG-FM Washington, DC
WRKN(FM) Niceville, FL
WRUM(FM) Orlando, FL
WCTH(FM) Plantation Key, FL
WOBB(FM) Tifton, FL
KOKU(FM) Hagatna, GU
KAPA(FM) Hilo, HI
KCCN(FM) Honolulu, HI
KDRB(FM) Des Moines, IA
KQXR(FM) Payette, ID
KATZ-FM Alton, IL
WIXY(FM) Champaign, IL
WILV(FM) Chicago, IL
WCCI(FM) Savanna, IL
WLKI(FM) Angola, IN
WMOJ(FM) Connersville, IN
WYGB(FM) Edinburgh, IN
KNZS(FM) Arlington, KS
KRDQ(FM) Colby, KS
KDVV(FM) Topeka, KS
*KSWC(FM) Winfield, KS
WVVR(FM) Hopkinsville, KY
KRRV-FM Alexandria, LA
KLRZ(FM) Larose, LA
WKIT-FM Brewer, ME
WNIC(FM) Dearborn, MI
WGRY-FM Grayling, MI
WUPT(FM) Gwinn, MI
KTLK-FM Minneapolis, MN
KSNR(FM) Thief River Falls, MN
*KCVJ(FM) Osceola, MO
KUKU-FM Willow Springs, MO
WNSL(FM) Laurel, MS
KLSK(FM) Great Falls, MT
WLGP(FM) Harkers Island, NC
WVBZ(FM) High Point, NC
KZEN(FM) Central City, NE
WHEB(FM) Portsmouth, NH
WHTZ(FM) Newark, NJ
KPEK(FM) Albuquerque, NM
KWAW(FM) Garapan-Saipan, NP
WDHI(FM) Delhi, NY
WMVU(FM) Sylvan Beach, NY
WKBE(FM) Warrensburg, NY
WCLT-FM Newark, OH
*KJCM(FM) Snyder, OK
KCXR(FM) Taft, OK
KRWQ(FM) Gold Hill, OR
KKRZ(FM) Portland, OR
WHGL-FM Canton, PA
WGYY(FM) Meadville, PA
WPHI-FM Media, PA
WIVA-FM Aguadilla, PR
WKKB(FM) Middletown, RI
WSEA(FM) Atlantic Beach, SC
WORG(FM) Elloree, SC
KFXS(FM) Rapid City, SD
WNOX(FM) Oak Ridge, TN
KJKK(FM) Dallas, TX
KILT-FM Houston, TX
KTEX(FM) Mercedes, TX
KOMX(FM) Pampa, TX
KCYY(FM) San Antonio, TX
KMMX(FM) Tahoka, TX
KXAL-FM Tatum, TX
KSFI(FM) Salt Lake City, UT
WARV-FM Petersburg, VA
WSTX-FM Christiansted, VI
WJPK(FM) Barton, VT

KWIQ-FM Moses Lake, WA
WNCY-FM Neenah-Menasha, WI
WAFD(FM) Webster Springs, WV
KZMQ-FM Greybull, WY

100.5 mhz
KBFX(FM) Anchorage, AK
WWMM(FM) Northport, AL
WLDA(FM) Slocomb, AL
KEGI(FM) Jonesboro, AR
KZHE(FM) Stamps, AR
KMQA(FM) East Porterville, CA
KTDE(FM) Gualala, CA
KMEN(FM) Mendota, CA
KPSI-FM Palm Springs, CA
KZZO(FM) Sacramento, CA
KXDZ(FM) Templeton, CA
KRSJ(FM) Durango, CO
KCUF(FM) El Jebel, CO
WRCH(FM) New Britain, CT
WOYS(FM) Apalachicola, FL
WHHZ(FM) Newberry, FL
WNNX(FM) College Park, GA
WXRS-FM Swainsboro, GA
KDEC-FM Decorah, IA
*KBYI(FM) Rexburg, ID
KQZB(FM) Troy, ID
WRVY-FM Henry, IL
WYMG(FM) Jacksonville, IL
WWKI(FM) Kokomo, IN
WSJD(FM) Princeton, IN
KVWF(FM) Augusta, KS
WLGX(FM) Louisville, KY
WSGW-FM Carrollton, MI
WTRV(FM) Walker, MI
*WSCN(FM) Cloquet, MN
KXAC(FM) Saint James, MN
KSWF(FM) Aurora, MO
KKCA(FM) Fulton, MO
KMEM-FM Memphis, MO
WBLE(FM) Batesville, MS
WRTM-FM Port Gibson, MS
KJJM(FM) Baker, MT
WXXK(FM) Lebanon, NH
KSFX(FM) Roswell, NM
KKJJ(FM) Henderson, NV
WDVI(FM) Rochester, NY
WYJK-FM Bellaire, OH
WKXA-FM Findlay, OH
KATT-FM Oklahoma City, OK
KDPM(FM) Cottage Grove, OR
KQFM(FM) Hermiston, OR
WYGL-FM Elizabethville, PA
WJNG(FM) Johnsonburg, PA
WCDW(FM) Susquehanna, PA
WALC(FM) Charleston, SC
WSSL-FM Gray Court, SC
WHLZ(FM) Marion, SC
KIKN-FM Salem, SD
KQBB(FM) Center, TX
KNNK(FM) Dimmitt, TX
KMVL-FM Madisonville, TX
KBDR(FM) Mirando City, TX
KMXD(FM) Monroe, UT
WFYE(FM) Glade Spring, VA
WZEZ(FM) Goochland, VA
WVHT(FM) Norfolk, VA
WTLX(FM) Columbus, WI
WDTX(FM) Rothschild, WI
WKEE-FM Huntington, WV
WDYK(FM) Ridgeley, WV
KTED(FM) Evansville, WY

100.7 mhz
*KXLL(FM) Juneau, AK
WCKF(FM) Ashland, AL
KLSZ-FM Fort Smith, AR
KEAZ(FM) Heber Springs, AR
KJIK(FM) Duncan, AZ
KSLX-FM Scottsdale, AZ
KIBS(FM) Bishop, CA
KTHU(FM) Corning, CA
KATJ-FM George, CA
KPRC-FM Salinas, CA
KFMB-FM San Diego, CA
KVVZ(FM) San Rafael, CA
KHAY(FM) Ventura, CA

KMOZ-FM Grand Junction, CO
KGFT(FM) Pueblo, CO
WHYI-FM Fort Lauderdale, FL
WFLA-FM Midway, FL
WJLQ(FM) Pensacola, FL
WMTX(FM) Tampa, FL
WMUV(FM) Brunswick, GA
WEAM-FM Buena Vista, GA
WLRR(FM) Milledgeville, GA
*KJYL(FM) Eagle Grove, IA
KKRQ(FM) Iowa City, IA
KPDA(FM) Gooding, ID
WRXQ(FM) Coal City, IL
WVMG(FM) Normal, IL
WBYT(FM) Elkhart, IN
WMGI(FM) Terre Haute, IN
KHOK(FM) Hoisington, KS
WKLX(FM) Brownsville, KY
WCYO(FM) Irvine, KY
WYPY(FM) Baton Rouge, LA
KZBL(FM) Natchitoches, LA
WZLX(FM) Boston, MA
WZBA(FM) Westminster, MD
WTBM(FM) Mexico, ME
WOBE(FM) Crystal Falls, MI
WSRJ(FM) Honor, MI
WITL-FM Lansing, MI
WWTH(FM) Oscoda, MI
KIKV-FM Sauk Centre, MN
KGMO(FM) Cape Girardeau, MO
KMZU(FM) Carrollton, MO
KFNS-FM Troy, MO
WDMS(FM) Greenville, MS
KIBG(FM) Bigfork, MT
KXLB(FM) Livingston, MT
WZJS(FM) Banner Elk, NC
WRVA-FM Rocky Mount, NC
KKLQ(FM) Harwood, ND
*KGBI-FM Omaha, NE
KRNP(FM) Sutherland, NE
WZXL(FM) Wildwood, NJ
KLVF(FM) Las Vegas, NM
*KXXQ(FM) Milan, NM
WEFX(FM) Henderson, NY
WXMR(FM) Minerva, NY
WHUD(FM) Peekskill, NY
*WKVU(FM) Utica, NY
WMMS(FM) Cleveland, OH
*WEEC(FM) Springfield, OH
KTFR(FM) Chelsea, OK
KPNC(FM) Ponca City, OK
KMGX(FM) Bend, OR
KPPT-FM Toledo, OR
WLEV(FM) Allentown, PA
*WCOG-FM Galeton, PA
WZPT(FM) New Kensington, PA
WXYX(FM) Bayamon, PR
WGTN-FM Andrews, SC
KMLO(FM) Lowry, SD
WBGQ(FM) Bulls Gap, TN
WUSY(FM) Cleveland, TN
WYDL(FM) Middleton, TN
KFGL(FM) Abilene, TX
KASE-FM Austin, TX
KWRD-FM Highland Village, TX
KPXI(FM) Overton, TX
KKHT-FM Winnie, TX
KYMV(FM) Woodruff, UT
WFNR-FM Christiansburg, VA
WMJD(FM) Grundy, VA
WQPO(FM) Harrisonburg, VA
WTHK(FM) Wilmington, VT
KKWF(FM) Seattle, WA
KHSS(FM) Walla Walla, WA
WBIZ-FM Eau Claire, WI
WKKV-FM Racine, WI
WVBD(FM) Fayetteville, WV
KOLZ(FM) Cheyenne, WY
KGWY(FM) Gillette, WY

100.9 mhz
KCDV(FM) Cordova, AK
KAKN(FM) Naknek, AK
*KFSK(FM) Petersburg, AK
KAYO(FM) Wasilla, AK
WALX(FM) Orrville, AL

KDEL-FM Arkadelphia, AR
KESA(FM) Eureka Springs, AR
KWKK(FM) Russellville, AR
KHOM(FM) Salem, AR
KZMK(FM) Sierra Vista, AZ
KQSR(FM) Yuma, AZ
KAEH(FM) Beaumont, CA
KSSB(FM) Calipatria, CA
KSXY(FM) Calistoga, CA
KRAJ(FM) Johannesburg, CA
KMIX(FM) Tracy, CA
KNEC(FM) Yuma, CO
WKNL(FM) New London, CT
WXJZ(FM) Gainesville, FL
WJAQ(FM) Marianna, FL
WLYU(FM) Lyons, GA
WPGA-FM Perry, GA
WAKB(FM) Waynesboro, GA
WCJM-FM West Point, GA
KWDN(FM) Newell, IA
WHPO(FM) Hoopeston, IL
WZUS(FM) Macon, IL
WBZG(FM) Peru, IL
WQFL(FM) Rockford, IL
WBDC(FM) Huntingburg, IN
WPGW-FM Portland, IN
WNOU(FM) Speedway, IN
KCLY(FM) Clay Center, KS
WLSK(FM) Lebanon, KY
KHLL(FM) Richwood, LA
WRNX(FM) Amherst, MA
WAAI(FM) Hurlock, MD
WYNZ(FM) Westbrook, ME
WWBR(FM) Big Rapids, MI
*WICV(FM) East Jordan, MI
WQXC-FM Otsego, MI
WLUN(FM) Pinconning, MI
KOWZ-FM Blooming Prairie, MN
WCMP-FM Pine City, MN
KRRY(FM) Canton, MO
WJXN-FM Utica, MS
WKBB(FM) West Point, MS
WPZS(FM) Albemarle, NC
WIFM-FM Elkin, NC
WSTS(FM) Fairmont, NC
WFMI(FM) Southern Shores, NC
KAUJ(FM) Grafton, ND
KHSK(FM) Allen, NE
KEJL(FM) Eunice, NM
KRZQ-FM Sparks, NV
WKLI-FM Albany, NY
WPGI(FM) Horseheads, NY
WKRL-FM North Syracuse, NY
WCDO-FM Sidney, NY
WBNO-FM Bryan, OH
WMJK(FM) Clyde, OH
WJAW-FM McConnelsville, OH
WXIZ(FM) Waverly, OH
KGLC(FM) Miami, OK
KXOJ-FM Sapulpa, OK
*KBUG(FM) Malin, OR
WAYC(FM) Bedford, PA
WVLY-FM Milton, PA
WRKT(FM) North East, PA
WPAL-FM Ridgeville, SC
WEIO(FM) Huntingdon, TN
KXGL(FM) Amarillo, TX
KWFB(FM) Quanah, TX
KBAR(FM) Victoria, TX
KWSA(FM) Price, UT
WIQO-FM Covington, VA
WDYL(FM) Lakeside, VA
WNNT-FM Warsaw, VA
WWFY(FM) Berlin, VT
KARY-FM Grandview, WA
WRCO-FM Richland Center, WI
WKOY-FM Princeton, WV
WMXE(FM) South Charleston, WV
WZST(FM) Westover, WV

101.1 mhz
KAKQ-FM Fairbanks, AK
KRXX(FM) Kodiak, AK
WYDE-FM Cullman, AL
WVVL(FM) Elba, AL
WPPG(FM) Repton, AL

KWBF-FM North Little Rock, AR
*KLRC(FM) Siloam Springs, AR
KRRK(FM) Lake Havasu City, AZ
KNRJ(FM) Payson, AZ
KHYL(FM) Auburn, CA
KWYE(FM) Fresno, CA
KRTH(FM) Los Angeles, CA
KWCA(FM) Weaverville, CA
KOSI(FM) Denver, CO
KDBN(FM) Parachute, CO
WWDC-FM Washington, DC
WJRR(FM) Cocoa Beach, FL
WAVV(FM) Naples Park, FL
WYOO(FM) Springfield, FL
WTGA-FM Thomaston, GA
WAFT(FM) Valdosta, GA
KORL-FM Waianae, HI
KXIA(FM) Marshalltown, IA
KWYD(FM) Parma, ID
WKQX(FM) Chicago, IL
WXOS(FM) East St. Louis, IL
WHPI(FM) Glasford, IL
WMYQ(FM) South Whitley, IN
KEOJ(FM) Caney, KS
KFNF(FM) Oberlin, KS
WIZF(FM) Erlanger, KY
WSGS(FM) Hazard, KY
WUBT(FM) Russellville, KY
KBON(FM) Mamou, LA
WNOE-FM New Orleans, LA
KRMD-FM Shreveport, LA
WFRQ(FM) Mashpee, MA
WQMR(FM) Snow Hill, MD
WWPN(FM) Westernport, MD
WLEK(FM) Gouldsboro, ME
WRIF(FM) Detroit, MI
WUPY(FM) Ontonagon, MI
WQON(FM) Roscommon, MI
KBHP(FM) Bemidji, MN
KLQL(FM) Luverne, MN
KHME(FM) Winona, MN
KCFX(FM) Harrisonville, MO
WLIN-FM Durant, MS
KJMS(FM) Olive Branch, MS
KZMT(FM) Helena, MT
WQZL(FM) Belhaven, NC
WZTK(FM) Burlington, NC
KQDJ-FM Valley City, ND
KDSR(FM) Williston, ND
KLIR(FM) Columbus, NE
WGIR-FM Manchester, NH
KVLC(FM) Hatch, NM
KSFR(FM) White Rock, NM
KCNM-FM Garapan-Saipan, NP
KPKK(FM) Amargosa Valley, NV
WBUG-FM Fort Plain, NY
WCBS-FM New York, NY
WWCD(FM) Grove City, OH
WHOT-FM Youngstown, OH
KVRO(FM) Stillwater, OK
KWOX(FM) Woodward, OK
KUFO-FM Portland, OR
KSKR-FM Sutherlin, OR
WBEB(FM) Philadelphia, PA
WFGE(FM) Tyrone, PA
WRIO(FM) Ponce, PR
WROQ(FM) Anderson, SC
WLVH(FM) Hardeeville, SC
KDDX(FM) Spearfish, SD
WRR(FM) Dallas, TX
KONO-FM Helotes, TX
KLOL(FM) Houston, TX
KONE(FM) Lubbock, TX
KNVO-FM Port Isabel, TX
KPLD(FM) Kanab, UT
KBER(FM) Ogden, UT
KEYF-FM Cheney, WA
KOHO-FM Leavenworth, WA
WVRE(FM) Dickeyville, WI
WIXX(FM) Green Bay, WI
WHSM-FM Hayward, WI
KPIN(FM) Pinedale, WY

101.3 mhz
KGOT(FM) Anchorage, AK
WAGF-FM Dothan, AL

WAGH(FM) Smiths, AL
KARV-FM Ola, AR
KPBQ-FM Pine Bluff, AR
KATY-FM Idyllwild, CA
KSTT-FM Los Osos-Baywood Park, CA
KIOI(FM) San Francisco, CA
KIQX(FM) Durango, CO
KOCK(FM) Walsenburg, CO
WKCI-FM Hamden, CT
WNCL(FM) Milford, DE
WHLG(FM) Port St. Lucie, FL
WTMG(FM) Williston, FL
WQIL(FM) Chauncey, GA
KSIB-FM Creston, IA
KKYY(FM) Whiting, IA
KUUL(FM) East Moline, IL
WMCI(FM) Mattoon, IL
WVIL(FM) Virginia, IL
WFMG(FM) Richmond, IN
*WBAA-FM West Lafayette, IN
KFDI-FM Wichita, KS
WMJM(FM) Jeffersontown, KY
WMSK-FM Sturgis, KY
KKGB(FM) Sulphur, LA
WVQM(FM) Augusta, ME
WBFX(FM) Grand Rapids, MI
WSUE(FM) Sault Ste. Marie, MI
KDWB-FM Richfield, MN
KTXR(FM) Springfield, MO
WMUT(FM) Grenada, MS
WMSO(FM) Meridian, MS
WBBV(FM) Vicksburg, MS
KRYK(FM) Chinook, MT
KIKC-FM Forsyth, MT
WWQQ-FM Wilmington, NC
KOZY-FM Bridgeport, NE
KLZA(FM) Falls City, NE
WYKR-FM Haverhill, NH
KKRG(FM) Albuquerque, NM
KRNG(FM) Fallon, NV
WBRV-FM Boonville, NY
WCPV(FM) Essex, NY
WRMM-FM Rochester, NY
WQAR(FM) Stillwater, NY
WNCO-FM Ashland, OH
WAGX(FM) Manchester, OH
KLAW(FM) Lawton, OK
KMCO(FM) Wilburton, OK
WROZ(FM) Lancaster, PA
WGGY(FM) Scranton, PA
WWDM(FM) Sumter, SC
WCMT-FM South Fulton, TN
WECO-FM Wartburg, TN
KOXE(FM) Brownwood, TX
KMMZ(FM) Crane, TX
KKLB(FM) Madisonville, TX
KNCN(FM) Sinton, TX
WWDE-FM Hampton, VA
WZFM(FM) Narrows, VA
WWKS(FM) Cruz Bay, VI
KGDN(FM) Pasco, WA
KABW(FM) Westport, WA
WBRB(FM) Buckhannon, WV
KXJW(FM) Sinclair, WY

101.5 mhz
WQEM(FM) Columbiana, AL
*KOAR(FM) Beebe, AR
KMLK(FM) El Dorado, AR
KAVH(FM) Eudora, AR
KLEZ(FM) Malvern, AR
KZON(FM) Phoenix, AZ
KIXF(FM) Baker, CA
KGFM(FM) Bakersfield, CA
KEKA-FM Eureka, CA
KMJE(FM) Gridley, CA
*KAMB(FM) Merced, CA
*KRVH(FM) Rio Vista, CA
KGB-FM San Diego, CA
KTKE(FM) Truckee, CA
KTNI-FM Strasburg, CO
WLYF(FM) Miami, FL
WTKX-FM Pensacola, FL
WXSR(FM) Quincy, FL
WPOI(FM) Saint Petersburg, FL
WSOL-FM Brunswick, GA

WKHX-FM Marietta, GA
KAOY(FM) Kealakekua, HI
KKSI(FM) Eddyville, IA
KCVI(FM) Blackfoot, ID
KATW(FM) Lewiston, ID
WBNQ(FM) Bloomington, IL
WCIL-FM Carbondale, IL
WKKG(FM) Columbus, IN
*WBGW(FM) Fort Branch, IN
WNSN(FM) South Bend, IN
KIKS-FM Iola, KS
KSMM-FM Liberal, KS
KMKF(FM) Manhattan, KS
WVLK-FM Richmond, KY
WTHX(FM) Vine Grove, KY
WYNK-FM Baton Rouge, LA
WMJZ-FM Gaylord, MI
WJNR-FM Iron Mountain, MI
WMTE-FM Manistee, MI
WWBN(FM) Tuscola, MI
KFGI(FM) Crosby, MN
KRJM(FM) Mahnomen, MN
KCGN-FM Ortonville, MN
KRRW(FM) Saint James, MN
KPLA(FM) Columbia, MO
WWUN-FM Friar's Point, MS
WTPO-FM New Albany, MS
KVWE(FM) Frenchtown, MT
WHDZ(FM) Buxton, NC
WRAL(FM) Raleigh, NC
KSSS(FM) Bismarck, ND
KROR(FM) Hastings, NE
WRNH(FM) Groveton, NH
WWHQ(FM) Meredith, NH
WKXW(FM) Trenton, NJ
KRMQ-FM Clovis, NM
KQLP(FM) Gallup, NM
KVSF-FM Pecos, NM
KIDX(FM) Ruidoso, NM
WRCD(FM) Canton, NY
WXHC(FM) Homer, NY
WMXO(FM) Olean, NY
WPDH(FM) Poughkeepsie, NY
*WCWT-FM Centerville, OH
WXBW(FM) Gallipolis, OH
WRVF(FM) Toledo, OH
KIZS(FM) Collinsville, OK
KFLY(FM) Corvallis, OR
WDKC(FM) Covington, PA
WORD-FM Pittsburgh, PA
WBHB-FM Waynesboro, PA
WKSA-FM Isabela, PR
WWBB(FM) Providence, RI
*KVCX(FM) Gregory, SD
WVFB(FM) Celina, TN
WNWS-FM Jackson, TN
WQUT(FM) Johnson City, TN
WFTZ(FM) Manchester, TN
WMXV(FM) Saint Joseph, TN
KROX-FM Buda, TX
KSTB(FM) Crystal Beach, TX
KSNY-FM Snyder, TX
KNUE(FM) Tyler, TX
KEGA(FM) Oakley, UT
WBQB(FM) Fredericksburg, VA
WZZI(FM) Vinton, VA
WEXP(FM) Brandon, VT
WRSY(FM) Marlboro, VT
KPLZ(FM) Seattle, WA
WIBA-FM Madison, WI
KDDV-FM Wright, WY

101.7 mhz
KPEN-FM Soldotna, AK
*KSTK(FM) Wrangell, AK
WBEI(FM) Reform, AL
WMXN-FM Stevenson, AL
KBYB(FM) Hope, AR
KVLO(FM) Humnoke, AR
KVOM-FM Morrilton, AR
KCTT-FM Yellville, AR
KKYZ(FM) Sierra Vista, AZ
KQAZ(FM) Springerville, AZ
KXSB(FM) Big Bear Lake, CA
KCDU(FM) Carmel, CA
KSBL(FM) Carpinteria, CA

KRER(FM) Hamilton City, CA
KKIQ(FM) Livermore, CA
KXFX(FM) Santa Rosa, CA
KTUN(FM) Eagle, CO
KXCL(FM) Westcliffe, CO
WZEB(FM) Ocean View, DE
WTOT-FM Graceville, FL
WKYZ(FM) Key Colony Beach, FL
WDVH-FM Trenton, FL
WCZR(FM) Vero Beach, FL
WQVE(FM) Albany, GA
WYUM(FM) Mount Vernon, GA
WTHO-FM Thomson, GA
WRBV(FM) Warner Robins, GA
KBKB-FM Fort Madison, IA
KAYL-FM Storm Lake, IA
WRCV(FM) Dixon, IL
WGEL(FM) Greenville, IL
WTYE(FM) Robinson, IL
WURK(FM) Elwood, IN
WLDE(FM) Fort Wayne, IN
WIVR(FM) Kentland, IN
KVOE-FM Emporia, KS
KDJM(FM) Lindsborg, KS
KREJ(FM) Medicine Lodge, KS
WKYM(FM) Monticello, KY
WKRD(FM) Shelbyville, KY
WFNX(FM) Lynn, MA
WBRK-FM Pittsfield, MA
*WKVV(FM) Searsport, ME
*WPRJ(FM) Coleman, MI
WHZZ(FM) Lansing, MI
WMRR(FM) Muskegon Heights, MI
KLDJ(FM) Duluth, MN
KRCH(FM) Rochester, MN
WHMH-FM Sauk Rapids, MN
KLPW-FM Elsberry, MO
KGOZ(FM) Gallatin, MO
KHST(FM) Lamar, MO
WYOY(FM) Gluckstadt, MS
WZHL(FM) New Augusta, MS
KZUS(FM) Highwood, MT
KTNY(FM) Libby, MT
WJKS(FM) Canton, NJ
KLEA-FM Lovington, NM
KQTM(FM) Rio Rancho, NM
KCLS(FM) Ely, NV
WLOF(FM) Attica, NY
WFLK(FM) Geneva, NY
WNYQ(FM) Hudson Falls, NY
WLTB(FM) Johnson City, NY
*WGKV(FM) Pulaski, NY
WBEA(FM) Southold, NY
WNKO(FM) Newark, OH
WHOF(FM) North Canton, OH
WKSW(FM) Urbana, OH
KKZU(FM) Sayre, OK
KTFX-FM Warner, OK
KLRR(FM) Redmond, OR
WCCL(FM) Central City, PA
WMVL(FM) Linesville, PA
WAVF(FM) Hanahan, SC
WMGL(FM) Ravenel, SC
WJSQ(FM) Athens, TN
WKOM(FM) Columbia, TN
WTPR-FM McKinnon, TN
WORM-FM Savannah, TN
WJLE-FM Smithville, TN
KTCY(FM) Azle, TX
KXGJ(FM) Bay City, TX
KEKO(FM) Hebronville, TX
KSAM-FM Huntsville, TX
KAYD-FM Silsbee, TX
KLTD(FM) Temple, TX
WLQM-FM Franklin, VA
WKWI(FM) Kilmarnock, VA
WSNZ(FM) Lynchburg, VA
WWBU(FM) Radford, VA
WEVI(FM) Frederiksted, VI
WCVT(FM) Stowe, VT
KLES(FM) Prosser, WA
WELD-FM Moorefield, WV
KDNO(FM) Thermopolis, WY
KZEW(FM) Wheatland, WY

101.9 mhz
WHHY-FM Montgomery, AL
KIYS-FM Jonesboro, AR
KMXF(FM) Lowell, AR
KLXQ(FM) Mountain Pine, AR
KVGG(FM) Salome, AZ
KLBN(FM) Fresno, CA
KSCA(FM) Glendale, CA
KNTY(FM) Shingle Springs, CA
KKHI(FM) Centennial, CO
WJHM(FM) Daytona Beach, FL
WWGR(FM) Fort Myers, FL
WBGE(FM) Bainbridge, GA
WAZX-FM Cleveland, GA
WPNG(FM) Pearson, GA
WOCE(FM) Ringgold, GA
WJFL(FM) Tennille, GA
KTKB-FM Hagatna, GU
KUCD(FM) Pearl City, HI
*KNWS-FM Waterloo, IA
KDBI(FM) Emmett, ID
WTMX(FM) Skokie, IL
WQQL(FM) Springfield, IL
WKLU(FM) Brownsburg, IN
WARU-FM Roann, IN
KKQY(FM) Hill City, KS
WQXQ(FM) Central City, KY
WKFC(FM) North Corbin, KY
KNOE-FM Monroe, LA
WLMG(FM) New Orleans, LA
WCIB(FM) Falmouth, MA
WLIF(FM) Baltimore, MD
WPOR(FM) Portland, ME
WOZI(FM) Presque Isle, ME
*WDET-FM Detroit, MI
WKQS-FM Negaunee, MI
WLDR-FM Traverse City, MI
KQKK(FM) Walker, MN
KZWV(FM) Eldon, MO
WFTA-FM Fulton, MS
WZYQ(FM) Mound Bayou, MS
KRSQ(FM) Laurel, MT
WBAV-FM Gastonia, NC
WIKS(FM) New Bern, NC
KBTO(FM) Bottineau, ND
KRWK(FM) Fargo, ND
KOOO(FM) Lincoln, NE
KTAO(FM) Taos, NM
KWID(FM) Las Vegas, NV
WKZF(FM) Alfred, NY
WJIV(FM) Cherry Valley, NY
WHUG(FM) Jamestown, NY
WRXP(FM) New York, NY
WKRQ(FM) Cincinnati, OH
WRBP(FM) Hubbard, OH
KTST(FM) Oklahoma City, OK
KCMX-FM Ashland, OR
KINK(FM) Portland, OR
KUJJ(FM) Weston, OR
WAVT-FM Pottsville, PA
WZAR(FM) Ponce, PR
KTWB(FM) Sioux Falls, SD
KATP(FM) Amarillo, TX
KBXT(FM) Franklin, TX
KSML-FM Huntington, TX
KACQ(FM) Lometa, TX
KBUS(FM) Paris, TX
KWFR(FM) San Angelo, TX
KQXT(FM) San Antonio, TX
KENZ(FM) Ogden, UT
WHTE-FM Ruckersville, VA
WKSK-FM South Hill, VA
WKKN(FM) Westminster, VT
KTSL(FM) Medical Lake, WA
WDEZ(FM) Wausau, WI
WVOW-FM Logan, WV
WVAQ(FM) Morgantown, WV
KIGN(FM) Burns, WY

102.1 mhz
KDBZ(FM) Anchorage, AK
WQUA(FM) Citronelle, AL
WDRM(FM) Decatur, AL
KENA-FM Mena, AR
KOKY(FM) Sherwood, AR
KCMT(FM) Oro Valley, AZ
KAHM(FM) Prescott, AZ

KPRI(FM) Encinitas, CA
KZPE(FM) Ford City, CA
KRKC-FM King City, CA
KCEZ(FM) Los Molinos, CA
KDFC-FM San Francisco, CA
KRKY-FM Estes Park, CO
WKLG(FM) Rock Harbor, FL
WWAV-FM Santa Rosa Beach, FL
WQLC(FM) Watertown, FL
WWWD(FM) Bolingbroke, GA
WGMG(FM) Crawford, GA
WZAT(FM) Savannah, GA
WNUQ(FM) Sylvester, GA
KTBH-FM Kurtistown, HI
KUQQ(FM) Milford, IA
KCHQ(FM) Driggs, ID
KIRQ(FM) Twin Falls, ID
WDNL(FM) Danville, IL
WQLF(FM) Lena, IL
WIBV(FM) Mount Vernon, IL
WALS(FM) Oglesby, IL
KZSN(FM) Hutchinson, KS
WLJC(FM) Beattyville, KY
WLLE(FM) Clinton, KY
WKYL(FM) Lawrenceburg, KY
KQIS(FM) Basile, LA
KDKS-FM Blanchard, LA
WAQY(FM) Springfield, MA
*WKVZ(FM) Dexter, ME
WLEW-FM Bad Axe, MI
*WMUK(FM) Kalamazoo, MI
KCAJ-FM Roseau, MN
KEEY-FM Saint Paul, MN
KQRA(FM) Brookline, MO
KCKC(FM) Kansas City, MO
KJFM(FM) Louisiana, MO
KTUI-FM Sullivan, MO
WUCL(FM) Meridian, MS
WRQO(FM) Monticello, MS
KBUD(FM) Sardis, MS
*KBMC(FM) Bozeman, MT
WJMH(FM) Reidsville, NC
KPNY(FM) Alliance, NE
KZMC(FM) McCook, NE
WSAK(FM) Hampton, NH
KTRA-FM Farmington, NM
KYRN(FM) Socorro, NM
KRNV-FM Reno, NV
*WJCA(FM) Albion, NY
WDNB(FM) Jeffersonville, NY
WZUN(FM) Phoenix, NY
WRGR(FM) Tupper Lake, NY
WAVR(FM) Waverly, NY
WDOK(FM) Cleveland, OH
WIMT(FM) Lima, OH
WRVB(FM) Marietta, OH
KHKC-FM Atoka, OK
KEOK(FM) Tahlequah, OK
WOWQ(FM) DuBois, PA
WIOQ(FM) Philadelphia, PA
WMXT(FM) Pamplico, SC
KFMH(FM) Belle Fourche, SD
WLCT(FM) Lafayette, TN
WWST(FM) Sevierville, TN
KPRR(FM) El Paso, TX
KDGE(FM) Fort Worth-Dallas, TX
KFZX(FM) Gardendale, TX
KMJQ(FM) Houston, TX
KMHO(FM) Mountain Home, TX
KBUC(FM) Raymondville, TX
KEMR(FM) Castle Dale, UT
WRXL(FM) Richmond, VA
WXTG-FM Virginia Beach, VA
WCVR-FM Randolph, VT
KSWW(FM) Montesano, WA
KPQ-FM Wenatchee, WA
WRKU(FM) Forestville, WI
WLUM-FM Milwaukee, WI
KBDY(FM) Hanna, WY

102.3 mhz

*KHNS(FM) Haines, AK
WAMI-FM Opp, AL
WELR-FM Roanoke, AL
KTRQ(FM) Colt, AR
KCJC(FM) Dardanelle, AR

KQEW(FM) Fordyce, AR
KWRQ(FM) Clifton, AZ
KJJJ(FM) Lake Havasu City, AZ
KZXY-FM Apple Valley, CA
KJLH-FM Compton, CA
KBLO(FM) Corcoran, CA
KJJZ(FM) Indio, CA
KJSN(FM) Modesto, CA
KYOE(FM) Point Arena, CA
KNTK(FM) Weed, CA
KSMT(FM) Breckenridge, CO
KCUV(FM) Greenwood Village, CO
KVLE-FM Gunnison, CO
KSPK(FM) Walsenburg, CO
WMOS(FM) Stonington, CT
WTRS(FM) Dunnellon, FL
WMBX(FM) Jensen Beach, FL
WIBL(FM) Augusta, GA
WLKQ-FM Buford, GA
WWLD(FM) Cairo, GA
WSIZ-FM Jacksonville, GA
WKZR(FM) Milledgeville, GA
WQTU(FM) Rome, GA
KMKK-FM Kaunakakai, HI
KCZQ(FM) Cresco, IA
KXGE(FM) Dubuque, IA
KZSR(FM) Onawa, IA
KICR-FM Coeur d'Alene, ID
WRMJ(FM) Aledo, IL
WYCA(FM) Crete, IL
WEBQ-FM Eldorado, IL
WDQX(FM) Morton, IL
WRHL(FM) Rochelle, IL
WKJT(FM) Teutopolis, IL
WXLC(FM) Waukegan, IL
WGBJ(FM) Auburn, IN
WLHM(FM) Logansport, IN
WCBK-FM Martinsville, IN
WSMM(FM) New Carlisle, IN
WBTO-FM Petersburg, IN
WUGO(FM) Grayson, KY
WXMA(FM) Louisville, KY
WCLU-FM Munfordville, KY
WLLK-FM Somerset, KY
KBCE(FM) Boyce, LA
WGTX(FM) Truro, MA
WMMJ(FM) Bethesda, MD
WCXX(FM) Madawaska, ME
WYBR(FM) Big Rapids, MI
WHKB(FM) Houghton, MI
WGRT(FM) Port Huron, MI
*WTHN(FM) Sault Ste. Marie, MI
KRCQ(FM) Detroit Lakes, MN
KBXR(FM) Columbia, MO
KDEX-FM Dexter, MO
KIIK-FM Waynesville, MO
WGCM-FM Gulfport, MS
WIQQ(FM) Leland, MS
WWSL(FM) Philadelphia, MS
WSKK(FM) Ripley, MS
WECR-FM Beech Mountain, NC
WKIX(FM) Goldsboro, NC
WFVL(FM) Lumberton, NC
WPTM(FM) Roanoke Rapids, NC
KRNY(FM) Kearney, NE
WWHK(FM) Concord, NH
WXXS(FM) Lancaster, NH
WAIV(FM) Cape May, NJ
WSUS(FM) Franklin, NJ
KKYC(FM) Clovis, NM
KVUW(FM) Wendover, NV
WBAB(FM) Babylon, NY
WKKF(FM) Ballston Spa, NY
WVOR(FM) Canandaigua, NY
WFXN-FM Galion, OH
WPOS-FM Holland, OH
WKLN(FM) Wilmington, OH
KDOE(FM) Antlers, OK
KKEN(FM) Duncan, OK
KRMG-FM Sand Springs, OK
KWDQ(FM) Woodward, OK
KEHK(FM) Brownsville, OR
KCRX-FM Seaside, OR
WCAT-FM Carlisle, PA
WQHZ(FM) Erie, PA
WDMT(FM) Pittston, PA

WMIO(FM) Cabo Rojo, PR
WGSP-FM Pageland, SC
WMFX(FM) Saint Andrews, SC
KKQQ(FM) Volga, SD
WZDQ(FM) Humboldt, TN
WGOW-FM Soddy-Daisy, TN
KPEZ(FM) Austin, TX
KSAQ(FM) Charlotte, TX
KQBZ(FM) Coleman, TX
KLJT(FM) Jacksonville, TX
KKPN(FM) Rockport, TX
KUVA(FM) Uvalde, TX
KWFS-FM Wichita Falls, TX
KDUT(FM) Randolph, UT
WZGN(FM) Crozet, VA
WDXC(FM) Pound, VA
WLFE-FM Saint Albans, VT
KYYT(FM) Goldendale, WA
WQTC-FM Manitowoc, WI
WVRQ-FM Viroqua, WI
WAUH(FM) Wautoma, WI
WHTL-FM Whitehall, WI
WMTD-FM Hinton, WV
WFBY(FM) Weston, WV

102.5 mhz
KIAK-FM Fairbanks, AK
WESP(FM) Dothan, AL
WDXB(FM) Jasper, AL
KPZK-FM Cabot, AR
KAFN(FM) Gould, AR
KNIX-FM Phoenix, AZ
KCNQ(FM) Kernville, CA
KDUQ(FM) Ludlow, CA
KDON-FM Salinas, CA
KSNI-FM Santa Maria, CA
KSFM(FM) Woodland, CA
KDVC(FM) Dove Creek, CO
KQSE(FM) Gypsum, CO
KTRR(FM) Loveland, CO
WHPT(FM) Sarasota, FL
WPIK(FM) Summerland Key, FL
WPZE(FM) Mableton, GA
WZCH(FM) Warner Robins, GA
WYNR(FM) Waycross, GA
KSTZ(FM) Des Moines, IA
KMGI(FM) Pocatello, ID
KIBR(FM) Sandpoint, ID
*WGNN(FM) Fisher, IL
WJRE(FM) Galva, IL
WPHZ(FM) Mitchell, IN
WMDH-FM New Castle, IN
KACY(FM) Arkansas City, KS
KKCI(FM) Goodland, KS
KBLS-FM North Fort Riley, KS
KKCV(FM) Rozel, KS
WCYN-FM Cynthiana, KY
WLTO(FM) Nicholasville, KY
WFMF(FM) Baton Rouge, LA
WKLB-FM Waltham, MA
WOLC(FM) Princess Anne, MD
WQSS(FM) Camden, ME
WIOG(FM) Bay City, MI
WCMM(FM) Gulliver, MI
WBZV(FM) Hudson, MI
KKWB(FM) Kelliher, MN
KMFX-FM Lake City, MN
KQIC(FM) Willmar, MN
KIXQ(FM) Joplin, MO
KEZK-FM Saint Louis, MO
KKDY(FM) West Plains, MO
WJKX(FM) Ellisville, MS
WAGR-FM Lexington, MS
KMSO(FM) Missoula, MT
WERX-FM Columbia, NC
WMYI(FM) Hendersonville, NC
WKXU(FM) Louisburg, NC
WIOZ-FM Southern Pines, NC
KDVL(FM) Devils Lake, ND
KIOT(FM) Los Lunas, NM
WBAZ(FM) Bridgehampton, NY
WTSS(FM) Buffalo, NY
WUMX(FM) Rome, NY
WZOO(FM) Edgewood, OH
WHIZ-FM Zanesville, OH
KTNT(FM) Eufaula, OK

WDVE(FM) Pittsburgh, PA
WRFY-FM Reading, PA
WIAC-FM San Juan, PR
WXLY(FM) North Charleston, SC
*KZSD-FM Martin, SD
WOWF(FM) Crossville, TN
WPRT-FM Pegram, TN
KMKS(FM) Bay City, TX
KTCX(FM) Beaumont, TX
KBRQ(FM) Hillsboro, TX
KZII-FM Lubbock, TX
KHLB(FM) Mason, TX
KKYR-FM Texarkana, TX
KMAD(FM) Whitesboro, TX
WOLD-FM Marion, VA
WUSQ-FM Winchester, VA
KRAO-FM Colfax, WA
KZOK-FM Seattle, WA
*WNWC-FM Madison, WI
KHQG(FM) Superior, WI
KHOC(FM) Casper, WY

102.7 mhz
*KRNN(FM) Juneau, AK
WCKS(FM) Fruithurst, AL
WWFA(FM) Saint Florian, AL
KWLT(FM) North Crossett, AR
KBBQ-FM Van Buren, AR
KSSI(FM) China Lake, CA
KHGE(FM) Fresno, CA
KIIS-FM Los Angeles, CA
*KLVB(FM) Red Bluff, CA
KBIQ(FM) Manitou Springs, CO
WPHK(FM) Blountstown, FL
WRGO(FM) Cedar Key, FL
WXHT(FM) Madison, FL
WXBM-FM Milton, FL
WMXJ(FM) Pompano Beach, FL
WHKR(FM) Rockledge, FL
WPMA(FM) Buckhead, GA
WYSC(FM) McRae, GA
WBDX(FM) Trenton, GA
KDDB(FM) Waipahu, HI
KYTC(FM) Northwood, IA
WJEQ(FM) Macomb, IL
WZZT(FM) Morrison, IL
WVAZ(FM) Oak Park, IL
WLEG(FM) Ligonier, IN
WBOW-FM Terre Haute, IN
KLDG(FM) Liberal, KS
WMJL(FM) Marion, KY
WYSB(FM) Springfield, KY
WKWY(FM) Tompkinsville, KY
KJNA-FM Jena, LA
WQSR(FM) Baltimore, MD
WHTD(FM) Mount Clemens, MI
WMOM(FM) Pentwater, MI
KQEG(FM) La Crescent, MN
KTIG(FM) Pequot Lakes, MN
*KNTN(FM) Thief River Falls, MN
KQUL(FM) Lake Ozark, MO
KEAU(FM) Fairfield, MT
WCNG(FM) Murphy, NC
WGNI(FM) Wilmington, NC
KVSS(FM) Lincoln, NE
WJSE(FM) Petersburg, NJ
KCYE(FM) Boulder City, NV
WLYK(FM) Cape Vincent, NY
WWFS(FM) New York, NY
WLGZ-FM Webster, NY
WEBN(FM) Cincinnati, OH
WCPZ(FM) Sandusky, OH
KJYO(FM) Oklahoma City, OK
KCNA-FM Cave Junction, OR
KYTE(FM) Newport, OR
WNAE-FM Clarendon, PA
WKSB(FM) Williamsport, PA
WRNI-FM Narragansett Pier, RI
WPUB-FM Camden, SC
WGUS-FM New Ellenton, SC
KXMZ(FM) Box Elder, SD
KYBB(FM) Canton, SD
WEKX(FM) Jellico, TN
WEGR(FM) Memphis, TN
KTXJ-FM Jasper, TX
KHXS(FM) Merkel, TX

KJXK(FM) San Antonio, TX
KBLZ(FM) Winona, TX
KSL-FM Midvale, UT
WJJX(FM) Appomattox, VA
WVEK-FM Weber City, VA
WEQX(FM) Manchester, VT
KORD-FM Richland, WA
*WRVM(FM) Suring, WI
WVSR-FM Charleston, WV
WGYE(FM) Mannington, WV

102.9 mhz
WKXX(FM) Attalla, AL
WNPT-FM Marion, AL
KHOZ-FM Harrison, AR
KARN-FM Sheridan, AR
KQST(FM) Sedona, AZ
KBLX-FM Berkeley, CA
KIWI(FM) McFarland, CA
KXLM(FM) Oxnard, CA
KLQV(FM) San Diego, CA
KWYL(FM) South Lake Tahoe, CA
WDRC-FM Hartford, CT
WXXJ(FM) Jacksonville, FL
WJGO(FM) Tice, FL
WMJE(FM) Clarkesville, GA
WVRK(FM) Columbus, GA
WPMX(FM) Statesboro, GA
KISH(FM) Hagatna, GU
KLZY(FM) Honokaa, HI
KZIA(FM) Cedar Rapids, IA
KTFG(FM) Sioux Rapids, IA
KWYS-FM Island Park, ID
KMVX(FM) Jerome, ID
WSOY-FM Decatur, IL
WMKB(FM) Earlville, IL
WXXB(FM) Delphi, IN
WXCH(FM) Hope, IN
WGL-FM Huntington, IN
WLME(FM) Lewisport, IN
KHUT(FM) Hutchinson, KS
KIND-FM Independence, KS
KQTP(FM) Saint Marys, KS
WPBK(FM) Crab Orchard, KY
WLKS-FM West Liberty, KY
KKND(FM) Belle Chasse, LA
KAJN-FM Crowley, LA
KVMA-FM Shreveport, LA
WPXC(FM) Hyannis, MA
WKIK-FM California, MD
WROG(FM) Cumberland, MD
WCRQ(FM) Dennysville, ME
WBLM(FM) Portland, ME
WWWW-FM Ann Arbor, MI
WFUR-FM Grand Rapids, MI
WMKC(FM) Saint Ignace, MI
WLTE(FM) Minneapolis, MN
KMFG(FM) Nashwauk, MN
KEZS-FM Cape Girardeau, MO
KMMO-FM Marshall, MO
WMSI(FM) Jackson, MS
WWMR(FM) Saltillo, MS
KCTR-FM Billings, MT
WLYT(FM) Hickory, NC
WELS-FM Kinston, NC
WWMY(FM) Raleigh, NC
KWGO(FM) Burlington, ND
KADL(FM) Imperial, NE
KBRX-FM O'Neill, NE
KNFT-FM Bayard, NM
KIXN(FM) Hobbs, NM
KAZX(FM) Kirtland, NM
KLBU(FM) Pecos, NM
WNCQ-FM Canton, NY
*WMHR(FM) Syracuse, NY
WCLX(FM) Westport, NY
WDHT(FM) Springfield, OH
KQIB(FM) Idabel, OK
KYSF(FM) Bonanza, OR
KSJJ(FM) Redmond, OR
WOKW(FM) Curwensville, PA
WMGK(FM) Philadelphia, PA
WYFM(FM) Sharon, PA
WDIN(FM) Camuy, PR
WQKI-FM Orangeburg, SC
WZTF(FM) Scranton, SC

KBWS-FM Sisseton, SD
WBUZ(FM) La Vergne, TN
KNDA(FM) Alice, TX
KDMX(FM) Dallas, TX
KLTN(FM) Houston, TX
KITY(FM) Llano, TX
WOWI(FM) Norfolk, VA
*WIUJ(FM) Charlotte Amalie, VI
KNBQ(FM) Centralia, WA
KVAB(FM) Clarkston, WA
WHQG(FM) Milwaukee, WI
WBDL(FM) Reedsburg, WI
WELC-FM Welch, WV
KXWY(FM) Hudson, WY
KARS-FM Laramie, WY

103.1 mhz
KMXS(FM) Anchorage, AK
KSBZ(FM) Sitka, AK
WEUP-FM Moulton, AL
KXSA-FM Dermott, AR
KFFA-FM Helena, AR
KHGG-FM Waldron, AR
WVUV-FM Fagaitua, AS
KFTT(FM) Bagdad, AZ
KCDX(FM) Florence, AZ
KKCY(FM) Colusa, CA
KDLE(FM) Newport Beach, CA
KAAT(FM) Oakhurst, CA
KEZN(FM) Palm Desert, CA
KLUN(FM) Paso Robles, CA
KDLD(FM) Santa Monica, CA
KSRY(FM) Tehachapi, CA
KVFG(FM) Victorville, CA
KHRD(FM) Weaverville, CA
KSPN-FM Aspen, CO
KAVD(FM) Limon, CO
WMMXZ(FM) De Funiak Springs, FL
WPBZ(FM) Indiantown, FL
WFKZ(FM) Plantation Key, FL
WAIB(FM) Tallahassee, FL
WLOQ(FM) Winter Park, FL
WFXA-FM Augusta, GA
*WPLH(FM) Tifton, GA
KDMG(FM) Burlington, IA
KCDA(FM) Post Falls, ID
WVIV-FM Highland Park, IL
WAKO-FM Lawrenceville, IL
WCSJ-FM Morris, IL
WGFB(FM) Rockton, IL
WKZS(FM) Covington, IN
WHME(FM) South Bend, IN
KEKS(FM) Olpe, KS
WPKE-FM Coal Run, KY
WGRK-FM Greensburg, KY
WGBF-FM Henderson, KY
WQNU(FM) Lyndon, KY
WWLT(FM) Manchester, KY
KQLQ(FM) Columbia, LA
WRNR-FM Grasonville, MD
WAFY(FM) Middletown, MD
WZON-FM Dover Foxcroft, ME
WGDN-FM Gladwin, MI
WQUS(FM) Lapeer, MI
KFIL-FM Preston, MN
KDAA(FM) Rolla, MO
WNMQ(FM) Columbus, MS
WOSM(FM) Ocean Springs, MS
KRVO(FM) Columbia Falls, MT
*KVCM(FM) Helena, MT
*WUAG(FM) Greensboro, NC
WLHC(FM) Robbins, NC
WNCM(FM) Sharpsburg, NC
KRVX(FM) Wimbledon, ND
KNCY-FM Auburn, NE
KKJK(FM) Ravenna, NE
KHQT(FM) Las Cruces, NM
WHRL(FM) Albany, NY
*WCIK(FM) Bath, NY
WBZO(FM) Bay Shore, NY
WTOJ(FM) Carthage, NY
WGNY-FM Newburgh, NY
WZOZ(FM) Oneonta, NY
WVKO-FM Johnstown, OH
WNDH(FM) Napoleon, OH
WRAC(FM) West Union, OH

KOFM(FM) Enid, OK
KRSB-FM Roseburg, OR
WILK-FM Avoca, PA
WKVE-FM Mount Pleasant, PA
WQFX-FM Russell, PA
WRSC-FM State College, PA
WLXC(FM) Columbia, SC
WRIX-FM Honea Path, SC
WGZO(FM) Parris Island, SC
WSYN(FM) Surfside Beach, SC
KJAM-FM Madison, SD
WLLJ(FM) Etowah, TN
WMXX-FM Jackson, TN
WIKQ(FM) Tusculum, TN
KRGN(FM) Amarillo, TX
KKCN(FM) Ballinger, TX
KEEP(FM) Bandera, TX
KSSM(FM) Copperas Cove, TX
KPAS(FM) Fabens, TX
KVJM(FM) Hearne, TX
KTXX(FM) Karnes City, TX
KMUL-FM Muleshoe, TX
KDVE(FM) Pittsburg, TX
KVWC-FM Vernon, TX
KJQN(FM) Coalville, UT
KURR(FM) Hurricane, UT
WWDW(FM) Alberta, VA
WJMA-FM Culpeper, VA
WRJT(FM) Royalton, VT
*KYKV(FM) Ellensburg, WA
WOGB(FM) Kaukauna, WI
WRON-FM Lewisburg, WV
WHBR-FM Parkersburg, WV
KYDT(FM) Sundance, WY

103.3 mhz
WMXS(FM) Montgomery, AL
KIXB(FM) El Dorado, AR
KWOZ(FM) Mountain View, AR
KZKE(FM) Seligman, AZ
KBAA(FM) Grass Valley, CA
KATM(FM) Modesto, CA
KVYB(FM) Santa Barbara, CA
*KSCU(FM) Santa Clara, CA
KTMQ(FM) Temecula, CA
KUKI-FM Ukiah, CA
*KPRU(FM) Delta, CO
KJQY(FM) La Veta, CO
WQQQ(FM) Sharon, CT
WVYB(FM) Holly Hill, FL
WVEE(FM) Atlanta, GA
WWSN(FM) Waycross, GA
KSHK(FM) Kekaha, HI
WJOD(FM) Asbury, IA
KAZR(FM) Pella, IA
KTFC(FM) Sioux City, IA
KSAS-FM Caldwell, ID
KFTZ(FM) Idaho Falls, ID
WIVQ(FM) Spring Valley, IL
WRZX(FM) Indianapolis, IN
WAXL(FM) Santa Claus, IN
KJLS(FM) Hays, KS
WXZZ(FM) Georgetown, KY
WCDV(FM) Hammond, LA
KBIU(FM) Lake Charles, LA
WODS(FM) Boston, MA
WMCM(FM) Rockland, ME
WKFR-FM Battle Creek, MI
WFXD(FM) Marquette, MI
WQLB(FM) Tawas City, MI
*KUMD-FM Duluth, MN
KZCR(FM) Fergus Falls, MN
KPRS(FM) Kansas City, MO
KLOU(FM) Saint Louis, MO
WZKR(FM) Decatur, MS
WBLZ(FM) Greenwood, MS
KDTR(FM) Florence, MT
WKVS(FM) Lenoir, NC
WMGV(FM) Newport, NC
KUSB(FM) Hazelton, ND
WPRB(FM) Princeton, NJ
KDRF(FM) Albuquerque, NM
WEDG(FM) Buffalo, NY
WMXW(FM) Vestal, NY
*WCRF(FM) Cleveland, OH
*WDEQ-FM De Graff, OH

WMLX(FM) Saint Mary's, OH
KJSR(FM) Tulsa, OK
KKCW(FM) Beaverton, OR
WKQL(FM) Brookville, PA
WARM-FM York, PA
WVJP-FM Caguas, PR
WJMX-FM Cheraw, SC
WOLT(FM) Greer, SC
WKDF(FM) Nashville, TN
KESN(FM) Allen, TX
KDFM(FM) Falfurrias, TX
KJOJ-FM Freeport, TX
KCRS-FM Midland, TX
KJCS(FM) Nacogdoches, TX
KSAG(FM) Pearsall, TX
WAKG(FM) Danville, VA
WLTK(FM) New Market, VA
WESR-FM Onley-Onancock, VA
WWMP(FM) Waterbury, VT
KWLN(FM) Wilson Creek, WA
WGLX-FM Wisconsin Rapids, WI
WTCR-FM Huntington, WV
WAJR-FM Salem, WV
KBEN-FM Basin, WY
KRAN(FM) Warren AFB, WY

103.5 mhz
KWVV-FM Homer, AK
WLAY-FM Littleville, AL
WHWT(FM) New Hope, AL
KZYQ(FM) Lake Village, AR
KLNZ(FM) Glendale, AZ
KTEA(FM) Cambria, CA
KOST(FM) Los Angeles, CA
KHSL-FM Paradise, CA
KBMB(FM) Sacramento, CA
KRAY-FM Salinas, CA
KRFX(FM) Denver, CO
WTOP-FM Washington, DC
WJKI(FM) Bethany Beach, DE
WAKT-FM Callaway, FL
WMIB(FM) Fort Lauderdale, FL
WFUS(FM) Gulfport, FL
WJAD(FM) Leesburg, GA
*KHAI(FM) Wahiawa, HI
KNEI-FM Waukon, IA
WKSC-FM Chicago, IL
WXLT(FM) Christopher, IL
WIKK(FM) Newton, IL
WAWC(FM) Syracuse, IN
KQLA(FM) Ogden, KS
WAKY(FM) Radcliff, KY
KLAA-FM Tioga, LA
*WCCH(FM) Holyoke, MA
WMUZ(FM) Detroit, MI
WTCM-FM Traverse City, MI
KUAL-FM Brainerd, MN
KYSM-FM Mankato, MN
*KRXW(FM) Roseau, MN
KWXD(FM) Asbury, MO
KLUE(FM) Poplar Bluff, MO
WRBO(FM) Como, MS
KZMY(FM) Bozeman, MT
WRCQ(FM) Dunn, NC
KZZY(FM) Devils Lake, ND
KXNP(FM) North Platte, NE
KISF(FM) Las Vegas, NV
WQBJ(FM) Cobleskill, NY
WKTU(FM) Lake Success, NY
WUUF(FM) Sodus, NY
WJQZ(FM) Wellsville, NY
WGRR(FM) Hamilton, OH
WJZA(FM) Pickerington, OH
KVSP(FM) Oklahoma City, OK
KLDZ(FM) Medford, OR
KWHT(FM) Pendleton, OR
WHLM-FM Berwick, PA
WOGH(FM) Burgettstown, PA
WLAK(FM) Huntingdon, PA
WEZL(FM) Charleston, SC
WZSN(FM) Greenwood, SC
WIMZ-FM Knoxville, TN
KKEV(FM) Centerville, TX
KJNZ(FM) Hereford, TX
KZRB(FM) New Boston, TX
KBPA(FM) San Marcos, TX

KAMZ(FM) Tahoka, TX
KRSP-FM Salt Lake City, UT
*WMRY(FM) Crozet, VA
WZVA(FM) Marion, VA
WAXJ(FM) Frederiksted, VI

103.7 mhz
WAAO-FM Andalusia, AL
WQEN(FM) Trussville, AL
KABZ(FM) Little Rock, AR
KZGL(FM) Flagstaff, AZ
KXZK(FM) Vail, AZ
KODS(FM) Carnelian Bay, CA
KMLA(FM) El Rio, CA
*KLVG(FM) Garberville, CA
KRZR(FM) Hanford, CA
KIQQ-FM Newberry Springs, CA
KSCF(FM) San Diego, CA
KKSF(FM) San Francisco, CA
KBNG(FM) Ridgway, CO
WRUF-FM Gainesville, FL
WQOL(FM) Vero Beach, FL
WULS(FM) Broxton, GA
WBOJ(FM) Cusseta, GA
WVKX(FM) Irwinton, GA
WBMZ(FM) Metter, GA
WXKT(FM) Royston, GA
KNUQ(FM) Paauilo, HI
KLKK(FM) Clear Lake, IA
WLLR-FM Davenport, IA
KXKT(FM) Glenwood, IA
KSKI-FM Sun Valley, ID
KVRG(FM) Victor, ID
WFAV(FM) Gilman, IL
WDBR(FM) Springfield, IL
*WFIU(FM) Bloomington, IN
WHZR(FM) Royal Center, IN
KEYN-FM Wichita, KS
WCBJ(FM) Campton, KY
WPTQ(FM) Cave City, KY
WSTV-FM Frankfort, KY
WFGS(FM) Murray, KY
KBTT(FM) Haughton, LA
WXCY(FM) Havre de Grace, MD
WCZE(FM) Harbor Beach, MI
WHYB(FM) Menominee, MI
WCSY-FM South Haven, MI
KKBJ-FM Bemidji, MN
KLZZ(FM) Waite Park, MN
KJEL(FM) Lebanon, MO
WUSW(FM) Hattiesburg, MS
KBBB(FM) Billings, MT
WSOC-FM Charlotte, NC
WBNE(FM) Shallotte, NC
WRHD(FM) Williamston, NC
WKNE(FM) Keene, NH
WPKQ(FM) North Conway, NH
WMGM(FM) Atlantic City, NJ
WNNJ(FM) Newton, NJ
KNMZ(FM) Alamogordo, NM
KYVA-FM Churchrock, NM
KPZA-FM Jal, NM
KLNN(FM) Questa, NM
WQNY(FM) Ithaca, NY
WCKY-FM Tiffin, OH
KOCD(FM) Wilburton, OK
KXPC(FM) Lebanon, OR
WRTS(FM) Erie, PA
WCXR(FM) Lewisburg, PA
WEEO-FM McConnellsburg, PA
WXLX(FM) Lajas, PR
WEEI-FM Westerly, RI
KXZT(FM) Newell, SD
KGIM-FM Redfield, SD
KRRO(FM) Sioux Falls, SD
WURV(FM) Walden, TN
KCDD(FM) Hamlin, TX
KVIL(FM) Highland Park-Dallas, TX
KHJK(FM) La Porte, TX
KOUL(FM) Sinton, TX
WMXB(FM) Richmond, VA
KMTT(FM) Tacoma, WA
WWIB(FM) Hallie, WI
WXSS(FM) Wauwatosa, WI
WCIR-FM Beckley, WV
WQWV(FM) Fisher, WV

KQLT(FM) Casper, WY

103.9 mhz
KTDZ(FM) College, AK
*KHZK(FM) Kotzebue, AK
KHZX(FM) Yakutat, AK
WJRL-FM Ozark, AL
WTID(FM) Thomaston, AL
KPGG(FM) Ashdown, AR
KCJF(FM) Earle, AR
KKIX(FM) Fayetteville, AR
KEDJ(FM) Gilbert, AZ
KGBB(FM) Edwards, CA
KRCD(FM) Inglewood, CA
KCXX(FM) Lake Arrowhead, CA
KKFS(FM) Lincoln, CA
KDJK(FM) Mariposa, CA
KBOQ(FM) Seaside, CA
KBDS(FM) Taft, CA
KSYC-FM Yreka, CA
KRXP(FM) Pueblo West, CO
KYEN(FM) Severance, CO
KSNO-FM Snowmass Village, CO
WXKB(FM) Cape Coral, FL
WPPL(FM) Blue Ridge, GA
WDDK(FM) Greensboro, GA
WQXZ(FM) Hawkinsville, GA
WTYB(FM) Tybee Island, GA
KCOO(FM) Dunkerton, IA
KUOO(FM) Spirit Lake, IA
WXAN(FM) Ava, IL
WWYW(FM) Dundee, IL
WNOI(FM) Flora, IL
WQCY(FM) Quincy, IL
WRBI(FM) Batesville, IN
WIMC(FM) Crawfordsville, IN
WXRD(FM) Crown Point, IN
WXKE(FM) Fort Wayne, IN
WRBR-FM South Bend, IN
*KHYM(FM) Copeland, KS
KOMB(FM) Fort Scott, KS
KNZA(FM) Hiawatha, KS
WNTC(FM) Drakesboro, KY
WWEL(FM) London, KY
WRKA(FM) Louisville, KY
WXKQ(FM) Whitesburg, KY
WKPE(FM) South Yarmouth, MA
WOCQ(FM) Berlin, MD
WTLP(FM) Braddock Heights, MD
WVOM(FM) Howland, ME
WLEN(FM) Adrian, MI
*WCMW-FM Harbor Springs, MI
WRSR(FM) Owosso, MI
KLCX(FM) Eyota, MN
KBHL(FM) Osakis, MN
KTNX(FM) Arcadia, MO
KCHI-FM Chillicothe, MO
KGLU(FM) Gideon, MO
KRLI(FM) Malta Bend, MO
KMCR(FM) Montgomery City, MO
WCLD-FM Cleveland, MS
WWKZ(FM) Columbus, MS
WYAB(FM) Flora, MS
KZMN(FM) Kalispell, MT
KUUS(FM) Vaughn, MT
WNNL(FM) Fuquay-Varina, NC
KVMI(FM) Arthur, ND
KQHK(FM) McCook, NE
KNLV-FM Ord, NE
KRFS-FM Superior, NE
KGRT-FM Las Cruces, NM
KZMI(FM) Garapan-Saipan, NP
KEBG(FM) Spring Creek, NV
WFAS-FM Bronxville, NY
WVOA-FM Mexico, NY
WSRK(FM) Oneonta, NY
WQBK(FM) Rensselaer, NY
WRCN-FM Riverhead, NY
WDKX(FM) Rochester, NY
*WANC(FM) Ticonderoga, NY
WXEG(FM) Beavercreek, OH
WTDA(FM) Westerville, OH
KOSG(FM) Pawhuska, OK
WALY(FM) Bellwood, PA
WPPZ-FM Jenkintown, PA
WLMI(FM) Kane, PA

WNKZ(FM) Laporte, PA
WWIZ(FM) Mercer, PA
WLSW(FM) Scottdale, PA
WOLI-FM Easley, SC
WHXT(FM) Orangeburg, SC
WXIS(FM) Erwin, TN
WDEB-FM Jamestown, TN
KJXJ(FM) Cameron, TX
KMHT-FM Marshall, TX
KQXC-FM Wichita Falls, TX
KJJS(FM) Zapata, TX
KUDE(FM) Nephi, UT
KGNT(FM) Smithfield, UT
WXCF-FM Clifton Forge, VA
WYFT(FM) Luray, VA
KBDB-FM Forks, WA
KVAS(FM) Ilwaco, WA
KBBD(FM) Spokane, WA
WDSW(FM) Westby, WI
WVBO(FM) Winneconne, WI
WETZ-FM New Martinsville, WV
KGCC(FM) Gillette, WY

104.1 mhz
KBRJ(FM) Anchorage, AK
WYOK(FM) Atmore, AL
KILX(FM) Hatfield, AR
KPOC-FM Pocahontas, AR
KQTH(FM) Tucson, AZ
KBOX(FM) Lompoc, CA
KHHK(FM) Modesto, CA
KJOR(FM) Windsor, CA
KFRR(FM) Woodlake, CA
KBVC(FM) Buena Vista, CO
KNAB-FM Burlington, CO
KFMU-FM Oak Creek, CO
WMRQ-FM Waterbury, CT
WWUS(FM) Big Pine Key, FL
WTKS-FM Cocoa Beach, FL
WGLF(FM) Tallahassee, FL
WRJY(FM) Brunswick, GA
WRBN(FM) Clayton, GA
WALR-FM La Grange, GA
WRBX(FM) Reidsville, GA
KLTI-FM Ames, IA
KORR(FM) American Falls, ID
WMQZ(FM) Colchester, IL
WHHL(FM) Jerseyville, IL
WBWN(FM) Le Roy, IL
WIKY-FM Evansville, IN
WLBC-FM Muncie, IN
KGGF-FM Fredonia, KS
WCKQ(FM) Campbellsville, KY
KYRK(FM) Houma, LA
KJLO-FM Monroe, LA
WBMX(FM) Boston, MA
WPRS-FM Waldorf, MD
*WVGR(FM) Grand Rapids, MI
WSAG(FM) Linwood, MI
KSDM(FM) International Falls, MN
KBOT(FM) Pelican Rapids, MN
KZJK(FM) Saint Louis Park, MN
KSGF-FM Ash Grove, MO
KZJF(FM) Jefferson City, MO
KMHM(FM) Lutesville, MO
WZKS(FM) Union, MS
KHKR-FM East Helena, MT
WCXL(FM) Kill Devil Hills, NC
*WKGV(FM) Swansboro, NC
WTQR(FM) Winston-Salem, NC
KIBZ(FM) Crete, NE
KCDY(FM) Carlsbad, NM
KTEG(FM) Santa Fe, NM
KZZD(FM) Fallon, NV
WHTT-FM Buffalo, NY
WWYL(FM) Chenango Bridge, NY
WQAL(FM) Cleveland, OH
WPAY-FM Portsmouth, OH
KMGL(FM) Oklahoma City, OK
KFIS(FM) Scappoose, OR
KWPK-FM Sisters, OR
WAEB-FM Allentown, PA
WNNK-FM Harrisburg, PA
WPXZ-FM Punxsutawney, PA
WERR(FM) Vega Alta, PR
WYAV-FM Myrtle Beach, SC

KIQK(FM) Rapid City, SD
WNAX-FM Yankton, SD
WCLE-FM Calhoun, TN
WUCZ(FM) Carthage, TN
WOGY(FM) Jackson, TN
KWTR(FM) Big Lake, TX
KCHT(FM) Childress, TX
KWOW(FM) Clifton, TX
KBFM(FM) Edinburg, TX
KRBE(FM) Houston, TX
KRIO-FM Pearsall, TX
KTDK(FM) Sanger, TX
KKUS(FM) Tyler, TX
WMNV(FM) Rupert, VT
KXDD(FM) Yakima, WA
WRLU(FM) Algoma, WI
WZEE(FM) Madison, WI
WMZK(FM) Merrill, WI
WDCI(FM) Bridgeport, WV
*WVSB(FM) Romney, WV
KANT(FM) Guernsey, WY
KCGL(FM) Powell, WY

104.3 mhz
*KTOO(FM) Juneau, AK
WZYP(FM) Athens, AL
WQZZ(FM) Eutaw, AL
WHLW(FM) Luverne, AL
*KPOS(FM) Fouke, AR
KBCN-FM Marshall, AR
KAJM(FM) Camp Verde, AZ
KXSE(FM) Davis, CA
KHIP(FM) Gonzales, CA
KBIG-FM Los Angeles, CA
KBQF(FM) McFarland, CA
KSHA(FM) Redding, CA
KMXY(FM) Grand Junction, CO
KKFN(FM) Longmont, CO
WIFL(FM) Inglis, FL
WWHV(FM) Lynn Haven, FL
*WKZM(FM) Sarasota, FL
WEAT-FM West Palm Beach, FL
WAJQ-FM Alma, GA
WBBQ-FM Augusta, GA
WZTR(FM) Dahlonega, GA
KIJI(FM) Tumon, GU
KPHW(FM) Kaneohe, HI
KRKN(FM) Eldon, IA
KUSQ(FM) Sibley, IA
KAWO(FM) Boise, ID
WCBH(FM) Casey, IL
WJMK(FM) Chicago, IL
WAYI(FM) Charlestown, IN
KCAR-FM Baxter Springs, KS
KVGB-FM Great Bend, KS
WXBC(FM) Hardinsburg, KY
WRJJ(FM) La Center, KY
WEZJ-FM Williamsburg, KY
KEZP(FM) Bunkie, LA
WCHH(FM) Baltimore, MD
WABK-FM Gardiner, ME
*WVCN(FM) Baraga, MI
WOMC(FM) Detroit, MI
WCZY-FM Mount Pleasant, MI
KLKS(FM) Breezy Point, MN
KZLT-FM East Grand Forks, MN
KVGO(FM) Spring Valley, MN
KZIO(FM) Two Harbors, MN
KDBB(FM) Bonne Terre, MO
KBEQ-FM Kansas City, MO
KXOQ(FM) Kennett, MO
KKAC(FM) Vandalia, MO
WMJU(FM) Bude, MS
WGNL(FM) Greenwood, MS
WQNQ(FM) Fletcher, NC
WJSG(FM) Hamlet, NC
WFXK(FM) Tarboro, NC
KFRH(FM) North Las Vegas, NV
WAXQ(FM) New York, NY
WFRG-FM Utica, NY
WNLT(FM) Harrison, OH
WODB(FM) Richwood, OH
KZBS(FM) Granite, OK
KKMX(FM) Tri City, OR
WKNB(FM) Clarendon, PA
WSKE(FM) Everett, PA

WOGI(FM) Moon Township, PA
KKSD(FM) Milbank, SD
WEYE(FM) Surgoinsville, TN
KQFX(FM) Borger, TX
KTTU-FM Brownfield, TX
KGAS-FM Carthage, TX
KBLT(FM) Leakey, TX
KHMR(FM) Lovelady, TX
KAHA(FM) Olney, TX
KLQB(FM) Taylor, TX
KSOP-FM Salt Lake City, UT
WKCY-FM Harrisonburg, VA
WZIN(FM) Charlotte Amalie, VI
WWOD(FM) Hartford, VT
KAFE(FM) Bellingham, WA
KMNT(FM) Chehalis, WA
KZBE(FM) Omak, WA
KHTR(FM) Pullman, WA
WECB(FM) Seymour, WI
KYPT(FM) Wamsutter, WY

104.5 mhz
KMGC(FM) Camden, AR
KLBL(FM) Pearcy, AR
KTRN(FM) White Hall, AR
KZUL-FM Lake Havasu City, AZ
KCEC-FM Wellton, AZ
KIQO(FM) Atascadero, CA
KVLI-FM Lake Isabella, CA
KBTW(FM) Lenwood, CA
KFOG(FM) San Francisco, CA
KSTY(FM) Canon City, CO
WFYV-FM Atlantic Beach, FL
WKAK(FM) Albany, GA
WYYU(FM) Dalton, GA
KDAT(FM) Cedar Rapids, IA
*WBVN(FM) Carrier Mills, IL
WFMB-FM Springfield, IL
WJJK(FM) Noblesville, IN
KFXJ(FM) Augusta, KS
WLKT(FM) Lexington-Fayette, KY
KNOU(FM) Empire, LA
KBEF(FM) Gibsland, LA
WNXX(FM) Jackson, LA
KLSM(FM) Tallulah, LA
WXLO(FM) Fitchburg, MA
WKHJ(FM) Mountain Lake Park, MD
WSNX-FM Muskegon, MI
WILZ(FM) Saginaw, MI
WQXJ(FM) Blackduck, MN
KJLY(FM) Blue Earth, MN
KUMR(FM) Doolittle, MO
KSLQ-FM Washington, MO
WXRR(FM) Hattiesburg, MS
WQJB(FM) State College, MS
KKVU(FM) Stevensville, MT
WSTK(FM) Aurora, NC
WHLC(FM) Highlands, NC
WCCG(FM) Hope Mills, NC
WILT(FM) Wilmington, NC
*KCVN(FM) Cozad, NE
KSRZ(FM) Omaha, NE
WVMJ(FM) Conway, NH
KKFG(FM) Bloomfield, NM
KZXQ(FM) Reserve, NM
KDOT(FM) Reno, NV
WTMM-FM Mechanicville, NY
WLZZ(FM) Montpelier, OH
WQKT(FM) Wooster, OH
KMYZ-FM Pryor, OK
KMCQ(FM) The Dalles, OR
WXMJ(FM) Cambridge Springs, PA
WRFF(FM) Philadelphia, PA
WNBT-FM Wellsboro, PA
WRFQ(FM) Mt. Pleasant, SC
WGFX(FM) Gallatin, TN
WKHT(FM) Knoxville, TN
WRVR(FM) Memphis, TN
KKDA-FM Dallas, TX
KPUS(FM) Gregory, TX
KJTX(FM) Jefferson, TX
KKMY(FM) Orange, TX
KZEP-FM San Antonio, TX
WGRX(FM) Falmouth, VA
WNVZ(FM) Norfolk, VA
KQQB-FM Newport, WA

WAXX(FM) Eau Claire, WI
WXER(FM) Plymouth, WI
*WCCX(FM) Waukesha, WI
WSLD(FM) Whitewater, WI
WHAJ(FM) Bluefield, WV
KSIT(FM) Rock Springs, WY
KHAD(FM) Upton, WY

104.7 mhz
KKED(FM) Fairbanks, AK
*KCAW(FM) Sitka, AK
WZZK-FM Birmingham, AL
KQBK(FM) Booneville, AR
KFLI(FM) Des Arc, AR
KOOU(FM) Hardy, AR
KTOY(FM) Texarkana, AR
KNWJ(FM) Leone, AS
KZZP(FM) Mesa, AZ
KHUM(FM) Garberville, CA
KCAQ(FM) Oxnard, CA
KDES-FM Palm Springs, CA
KHTN(FM) Planada, CA
KKHN(FM) Calhan, CO
KNNG(FM) Sterling, CO
KSKE-FM Vail, CO
WAAZ-FM Crestview, FL
WSGL(FM) Naples, FL
WRBQ-FM Tampa, FL
WFLM(FM) White City, FL
WFSH-FM Athens, GA
WTHG(FM) Hinesville, GA
KONI(FM) Lanai City, HI
KJLN(FM) Sac City, IA
KIKX(FM) Ketchum, ID
WLMD(FM) Bushnell, IL
*WCFL(FM) Morris, IL
WNSV(FM) Nashville, IL
WFRN-FM Elkhart, IN
WITZ-FM Jasper, IN
*KVCY(FM) Fort Scott, KS
KXBZ(FM) Manhattan, KS
KXNC(FM) Ness City, KS
WJMD(FM) Hazard, KY
WJSH(FM) Folsom, LA
*KHMD(FM) Mansfield, LA
KWTG(FM) Vidalia, LA
KNEK-FM Washington, LA
WOCN-FM Orleans, MA
WAYZ(FM) Hagerstown, MD
WQHQ(FM) Ocean City-Salisbury, MD
WBFB(FM) Belfast, ME
WBQW(FM) Kennebunkport, ME
WYKX(FM) Escanaba, MI
WKJC(FM) Tawas City, MI
KCLD-FM Saint Cloud, MN
KREZ(FM) Chaffee, MO
KKLH(FM) Marshfield, MO
KRES(FM) Moberly, MO
WJIW(FM) Greenville, MS
KBZM(FM) Big Sky, MT
WKQC(FM) Charlotte, NC
WZUP(FM) La Grange, NC
KMJO(FM) Hope, ND
KNDR(FM) Mandan, ND
KABQ-FM Bosque Farms, NM
KMOU(FM) Roswell, NM
KJUL(FM) Moapa Valley, NV
WBBS(FM) Fulton, NY
WXLM(FM) Montauk, NY
WSPK(FM) Poughkeepsie, NY
*WIRQ(FM) Rochester, NY
WTUE(FM) Dayton, OH
WKKY(FM) Geneva, OH
WIOT(FM) Toledo, OH
KIXR(FM) Ponca City, OK
KSLE(FM) Wewoka, OK
KCMB(FM) Baker City, OR
KDUK-FM Florence, OR
KFEG(FM) Klamath Falls, OR
WPGB(FM) Pittsburgh, PA
WKAQ-FM San Juan, PR
WNOK(FM) Columbia, SC
KKLS-FM Sioux Falls, SD
WSGM(FM) Coalmont, TN
WMUF-FM Henry, TN
WLIV-FM Monterey, TN

KKYS(FM) Bryan, TX
KYYI(FM) Burkburnett, TX
KHTZ(FM) Ganado, TX
KTXC(FM) Lamesa, TX
KWNS(FM) Winnsboro, TX
WPZZ(FM) Crewe, VA
WNCS(FM) Montpelier, VT
KDUX-FM Aberdeen, WA
KKRV(FM) Wenatchee, WA
WBJZ(FM) Berlin, WI
WDDW(FM) Sturtevant, WI
WVRC-FM Spencer, WV
KTRS-FM Casper, WY
KLQQ(FM) Clearmont, WY
KLEP(FM) Dubois, WY
KYLZ(FM) Lyman, WY

104.9 mhz
KMVV(FM) Sterling, AK
WOAB(FM) Ozark, AL
WSLY(FM) York, AL
KAGH-FM Crossett, AR
KHPA(FM) Hope, AR
KDXY(FM) Lake City, AR
KXNA(FM) Springdale, AR
KCLT(FM) West Helena, AR
KWCX-FM Willcox, AZ
KWIM(FM) Window Rock, AZ
KEPD(FM) Ridgecrest, CA
KMHX(FM) Rohnert Park, CA
KYIX(FM) South Oroville, CA
KCNL(FM) Sunnyvale, CA
KCRZ(FM) Tipton, CA
KRYD(FM) Norwood, CO
KRYE(FM) Rye, CO
*WIHS(FM) Middletown, CT
WHTF(FM) Havana, FL
WYGC(FM) High Springs, FL
WCVU(FM) Solana, FL
WFXE(FM) Columbus, GA
WMCG(FM) Milan, GA
WRBF(FM) Plainville, GA
KBOB-FM De Witt, IA
KLMJ(FM) Hampton, IA
KBOE-FM Oskaloosa, IA
KLLT(FM) Spencer, IA
WXRX(FM) Belvidere, IL
KMJM-FM Columbia, IL
WFIW-FM Fairfield, IL
WPXN(FM) Paxton, IL
WXCL(FM) Pekin, IL
WINN(FM) Columbus, IN
WERK(FM) Muncie, IN
WAXI(FM) Rockville, IN
KFFX(FM) Emporia, KS
KSAL-FM Salina, KS
WFKY(FM) Frankfort, KY
WXLR(FM) Harold, KY
WJRS(FM) Jamestown, KY
WKHG(FM) Leitchfield, KY
WAVJ(FM) Princeton, KY
WSKV(FM) Stanton, KY
WKKS-FM Vanceburg, KY
KNXX(FM) Donaldsonville, LA
*KTOC-FM Jonesboro, LA
KZWA(FM) Moss Bluff, LA
*WRBB(FM) Boston, MA
WBOQ(FM) Gloucester, MA
WQBX(FM) Alma, MI
*WAIR(FM) Lake City, MI
WBXX(FM) Marshall, MI
KRFO-FM Owatonna, MN
KPWB-FM Piedmont, MO
WKJN(FM) Centreville, MS
WKZU(FM) Iuka, MS
WBUV(FM) Moss Point, MS
WCJU-FM Prentiss, MS
KIKF(FM) Cascade, MT
WYNA(FM) Calabash, NC
WFMZ(FM) Hertford, NC
WQNS(FM) Waynesville, NC
KCTY(FM) Wayne, NE
KTMX(FM) York, NE
WYRY(FM) Hinsdale, NH
WLKZ(FM) Wolfeboro, NH
WSJO(FM) Egg Harbor City, NJ

KMVR(FM) Mesilla Park, NM
KVAL(FM) Cal-Nev-Ari, NV
WZMR(FM) Altamont, NY
*WKDL-FM Brockport, NY
WNGZ(FM) Montour Falls, NY
WWKC(FM) Caldwell, OH
*WCVO(FM) Gahanna, OH
WEGE(FM) Lima, OH
WCLV(FM) Lorain, OH
KKWD(FM) Bethany, OK
KREK(FM) Bristow, OK
KRIG-FM Nowata, OK
KNLX(FM) Prineville, OR
*WJRH(FM) Easton, PA
WRKY-FM Hollidaysburg, PA
WWRR(FM) Scranton, PA
WCCP-FM Clemson, SC
WWJN(FM) Ridgeland, SC
WKOS(FM) Kingsport, TN
WTNQ(FM) La Follette, TN
WYVY(FM) Union City, TN
WBOZ(FM) Woodbury, TN
KJAV(FM) Alamo, TX
KXBT(FM) Dripping Springs, TX
KLDE(FM) Eldorado, TX
KBUK(FM) La Grange, TX
KRQX-FM Mexia, TX
KAMA-FM Missouri City, TX
KZMP-FM Pilot Point, TX
KMFM(FM) Premont, TX
KMIQ(FM) Robstown, TX
KBTE(FM) Tulia, TX
KVOU-FM Uvalde, TX
WJJS(FM) Roanoke, VA
WWRT(FM) Strasburg, VA
WIGO-FM White Stone, VA
WMNG(FM) Christiansted, VI
KFNK(FM) Eatonville, WA
*KEEH(FM) Spokane, WA
WLMX-FM Balsam Lake, WI
WPCK(FM) Denmark, WI
WTKM-FM Hartford, WI
WLXR-FM La Crosse, WI
WKQH(FM) Marathon, WI
WNFM(FM) Reedsburg, WI
WPDX-FM Clarksburg, WV
KRRR(FM) Cheyenne, WY

105.1 mhz

KTKU(FM) Juneau, AK
WQSB(FM) Albertville, AL
KMJX(FM) Conway, AR
KFLX(FM) Kachina Village, AZ
KKBZ(FM) Auberry, CA
KIDI-FM Lompoc, CA
KKGO(FM) Los Angeles, CA
KOCN(FM) Pacific Grove, CA
KNCI(FM) Sacramento, CA
KXKL-FM Denver, CO
WPFL(FM) Century, FL
WHQT(FM) Coral Gables, FL
WOMX-FM Orlando, FL
WASJ(FM) Panama City Beach, FL
WKUB(FM) Blackshear/Waycross, GA
WSGC-FM Elberton, GA
WNGA(FM) Helen, GA
KGUM-FM Dededo, GU
KINE-FM Honolulu, HI
KCCQ(FM) Ames, IA
KJOT(FM) Boise, ID
KVTY(FM) Lewiston, ID
WOJO(FM) Evanston, IL
WVZA(FM) Murphysboro, IL
WGEM-FM Quincy, IL
WEJT(FM) Shelbyville, IL
WQHK-FM Decatur, IN
WHCC(FM) Ellettsville, IN
KZQD(FM) Liberal, KS
WTUK(FM) Harlan, KY
WRNZ(FM) Lancaster, KY
WLRS(FM) Shepherdsville, KY
KPEL-FM Abbeville, LA
KTGV(FM) Jonesville, LA
*WAMQ(FM) Great Barrington, MA
*WNEK-FM Springfield, MA
WTOS-FM Skowhegan, ME

WGFM(FM) Cheboygan, MI
WMGC-FM Detroit, MI
KLTA(FM) Breckenridge, MN
KKCB(FM) Duluth, MN
WGVX(FM) Lakeville, MN
KARL(FM) Tracy, MN
KCRV-FM Caruthersville, MO
KCJK(FM) Garden City, MO
KOSP(FM) Willard, MO
WQJQ(FM) Kosciusko, MS
KQBL(FM) Billings, MT
KWOL-FM Whitefish, MT
WDCG(FM) Durham, NC
WSSM(FM) Havelock, NC
KAOC(FM) Cavalier, ND
KWMW(FM) Maljamar, NM
KJFA(FM) Santa Fe, NM
KQRT(FM) Las Vegas, NV
WOLF-FM DeRuyter, NY
WWPR-FM New York, NY
WKOL(FM) Plattsburgh, NY
WUBE-FM Cincinnati, OH
WQXK(FM) Salem, OH
KBLP(FM) Lindsay, OK
KTMC-FM McAlester, OK
KOSB(FM) Perry, OK
KRSK(FM) Molalla, OR
KAKT(FM) Phoenix, OR
WIOV-FM Ephrata, PA
WILQ(FM) Williamsport, PA
WIOC(FM) Ponce, PR
WWLI(FM) Providence, RI
WGFG(FM) Branchville, SC
WPDT(FM) Johnsonville, SC
KAWK(FM) Custer, SD
KZKK(FM) Huron, SD
WCLC-FM Jamestown, TN
WALV-FM Lakesite, TN
WVRY(FM) Waverly, TN
KEAN-FM Abilene, TX
KMIL(FM) Cameron, TX
KYKS(FM) Lufkin, TX
KTTY(FM) New Boston, TX
KMAT(FM) Seadrift, TX
KAUU(FM) Manti, UT
WAVA-FM Arlington, VA
WTGD(FM) Bridgewater, VA
WSBW(FM) Sister Bay, WI
WCHY(FM) Waunakee, WI
WKLC-FM Saint Albans, WV
KTUG(FM) Hudson, WY
KJXN(FM) South Park, WY
KYTS(FM) Ten Sleep, WY

105.3 mhz

*KRBD(FM) Ketchikan, AK
WDBT(FM) Headland, AL
WBFZ(FM) Selma, AL
KJLV(FM) Hoxie, AR
KAKJ(FM) Marianna, AR
KQOR(FM) Mena, AR
KZLZ(FM) Kearny, AZ
KHOV-FM Wickenburg, AZ
KBFP-FM Delano, CA
KIOZ(FM) San Diego, CA
KITS(FM) San Francisco, CA
KRDG(FM) Shingletown, CA
KRSX-FM Yermo, CA
KPAU(FM) Center, CO
KZKS(FM) Rifle, CO
WJSJ(FM) Fernandina Beach, FL
WYKS(FM) Gainesville, FL
WZSP(FM) Nocatee, FL
WBZY(FM) Bowdon, GA
WSTI-FM Quitman, GA
WRHQ(FM) Richmond Hill, GA
KBGX(FM) Keaau, HI
KEDB(FM) Chariton, IA
KLYV(FM) Dubuque, IA
KNOD(FM) Harlan, IA
KIWA-FM Sheldon, IA
WKAY(FM) Knoxville, IL
WAOX(FM) Staunton, IL
WJLT(FM) Evansville, IN
WKOA(FM) Lafayette, IN
WMPI(FM) Scottsburg, IN

KMOQ(FM) Columbus, KS
KFBZ(FM) Haysville, KS
WOVO(FM) Glasgow, KY
WXKZ-FM Prestonsburg, KY
WWL-FM Kenner, LA
KLIP(FM) Monroe, LA
KXKW(FM) Simmesport, LA
KNCB-FM Vivian, LA
WFRB-FM Frostburg, MD
WSHK(FM) Kittery, ME
WKHM-FM Brooklyn, MI
WHTS(FM) Coopersville, MI
WGVY(FM) Cambridge, MN
KYBA(FM) Stewartville, MN
KYMO-FM East Prairie, MO
KZNN(FM) Rolla, MO
WACR-FM Columbus AFB, MS
KMTX-FM Helena, MT
WODR(FM) Fair Bluff, NC
KZPR(FM) Minot, ND
KLNC(FM) Lincoln, NE
KIOD(FM) McCook, NE
*KGRD(FM) Orchard, NE
KZZX(FM) Alamogordo, NM
KHOD(FM) Des Moines, NM
WDRE(FM) Calverton-Roanoke, NY
*WGKR(FM) Grand Gorge, NY
WKPQ(FM) Hornell, NY
WYHT(FM) Mansfield, OH
KJMM(FM) Bixby, OK
KDDQ(FM) Comanche, OK
KINB(FM) Kingfisher, OK
WYCY(FM) Hawley, PA
WDAS-FM Philadelphia, PA
WNOW-FM Gaffney, SC
WTJW(FM) Humboldt, TN
WFIV-FM Loudon, TN
WOWC(FM) Morrison, TN
KRLD-FM Dallas, TX
KTWL(FM) Hempstead, TX
KJDL-FM Levelland, TX
KLSR-FM Memphis, TX
KSMG(FM) Seguin, TX
KPTY(FM) Winnie, TX
WBRW(FM) Blacksburg, VA
WBNN-FM Dillwyn, VA
WKUS(FM) Norfolk, VA
WVJZ(FM) Charlotte Amalie, VI
WJEN(FM) Killington, VT
KCMS(FM) Edmonds, WA
KONA-FM Kennewick, WA
WRLO-FM Antigo, WI
*WKMZ(FM) Mukwonago, WI
KDWY(FM) Diamondville, WY
KREO(FM) Pine Bluffs, WY
KQOL(FM) Sleepy Hollow, WY

105.5 mhz

WNSP(FM) Bay Minette, AL
WERC-FM Hoover, AL
WVNA-FM Muscle Shoals, AL
KYEL(FM) Danville, AR
KPFM(FM) Mountain Home, AR
KNAS(FM) Nashville, AR
KBOA-FM Piggott, AR
KWAK-FM Stuttgart, AR
KWRF-FM Warren, AR
*KLVA(FM) Casa Grande, AZ
KZOH(FM) Heber, AZ
KRVR(FM) Copperopolis, CA
KSAC-FM Dunnigan, CA
KKHB(FM) Eureka, CA
KRTO(FM) Guadalupe, CA
KBUE(FM) Long Beach, CA
KFYV(FM) Ojai, CA
KVVS(FM) Rosamond, CA
KJZN(FM) San Joaquin, CA
KRDO-FM Security, CO
KJAC(FM) Timnath, CO
WQGN-FM Groton, CT
WFCT(FM) Apalachicola, FL
WOLL(FM) Hobe Sound, FL
WWWK(FM) Islamorada, FL
WYZB(FM) Mary Esther, FL
WBTT(FM) Naples Park, FL
WDUV(FM) New Port Richey, FL

WSJF(FM) Saint Augustine Beach, FL
WZBN(FM) Camilla, GA
WIFO-FM Jesup, GA
WROK-FM Macon, GA
WRXR-FM Rossville, GA
KPMW(FM) Haliimaile, HI
KILJ-FM Mount Pleasant, IA
KDLS-FM Perry, IA
KTHK(FM) Idaho Falls, ID
WREZ(FM) Metropolis, IL
WCZQ(FM) Monticello, IL
WJVO(FM) South Jacksonville, IL
WYKT(FM) Wilmington, IL
WZSR(FM) Woodstock, IL
WQRK(FM) Bedford, IN
WTHD(FM) Lagrange, IN
WLJE(FM) Valparaiso, IN
WWVR(FM) West Terre Haute, IN
KVSV-FM Beloit, KS
KKOY-FM Chanute, KS
WLVK(FM) Fort Knox, KY
WKYA(FM) Greenville, KY
WMKJ(FM) Mt. Sterling, KY
KBKK(FM) Ball, LA
KEUN-FM Eunice, LA
KDDK(FM) Franklin, LA
WVEI-FM Easthampton, MA
WDKZ(FM) Salisbury, MD
WBYA(FM) Islesboro, ME
WWCK-FM Flint, MI
WGKL(FM) Gladstone, MI
WMKD(FM) Pickford, MI
WBMI(FM) West Branch, MI
KDDG(FM) Albany, MN
KBAJ(FM) Deer River, MN
KMGM(FM) Montevideo, MN
KRBI-FM Saint Peter, MN
KESM-FM El Dorado Springs, MO
KZZT(FM) Moberly, MO
KKJO(FM) Saint Joseph, MO
WNLA-FM Indianola, MS
WVBG-FM Redwood, MS
WTNM(FM) Water Valley, MS
WABO-FM Waynesboro, MS
KERT(FM) Alberton, MT
WXQR(FM) Jacksonville, NC
WFJA(FM) Sanford, NC
KMAV-FM Mayville, ND
KFMT-FM Fremont, NE
WJYY(FM) Concord, NH
WSNQ(FM) Cape May Court House, NJ
WDHA-FM Dover, NJ
*KQRI(FM) Bosque Farms, NM
KSIL(FM) Hurley, NM
WLPW(FM) Lake Placid, NY
WSKU(FM) Little Falls, NY
WTKV(FM) Oswego, NY
WDBY(FM) Patterson, NY
WXTQ(FM) Athens, OH
*WGOJ(FM) Conneaut, OH
WMVR-FM Sidney, OH
WWWM-FM Sylvania, OH
WCHO-FM Washington Court House, OH
KWCO-FM Chickasha, OK
KXFC(FM) Coalgate, OK
KGFY(FM) Stillwater, OK
KDEP(FM) Garibaldi, OR
KCGB-FM Hood River, OR
KKKJ(FM) Merrill, OR
KEUG(FM) Veneta, OR
WMKX(FM) Brookville, PA
WCHX(FM) Lewistown, PA
WMGH-FM Tamaqua, PA
WFDT(FM) Aguada, PR
WDAR-FM Darlington, SC
WCOO(FM) Kiawah Island, SC
KMOM(FM) Roscoe, SD
WYTM-FM Fayetteville, TN
WSEV-FM Gatlinburg, TN
WBNT-FM Oneida, TN
WAKQ(FM) Paris, TN
WXOQ(FM) Selmer, TN
KACT-FM Andrews, TX
KWDC(FM) Coahoma, TX

KUSJ(FM) Harker Heights, TX
KQXX-FM Mission, TX
KMJR(FM) Portland, TX
KBWT(FM) Santa Anna, TX
KLCY(FM) Vernal, UT
WKDE-FM Altavista, VA
WWRE(FM) Berryville, VA
WHFD(FM) Lawrenceville, VA
WOJL(FM) Louisa, VA
WSWV-FM Pennington Gap, VA
WGTH-FM Richlands, VA
WRAR-FM Tappahannock, VA
WKXH(FM) Saint Johnsbury, VT
KUKN(FM) Longview, WA
WRCW(FM) Nekoosa, WI
WFBZ(FM) Trempealeau, WI
WMMM-FM Verona, WI
WUKL(FM) Bethlehem, WV
WKQV(FM) Cowen, WV
KZQL(FM) Mills, WY

105.7 mhz

KNIK-FM Anchorage, AK
WQAH(FM) Addison, AL
WCSN-FM Orange Beach, AL
WZHT(FM) Troy, AL
KRKD(FM) Dermott, AR
KFXV(FM) Kensett, AR
KMCK(FM) Siloam Springs, AR
KVRD-FM Cottonwood, AZ
KOAS(FM) Dolan Springs, AZ
KXRS(FM) Hemet, CA
KQMX(FM) Lost Hills, CA
KVVF(FM) Santa Clara, CA
KVAY(FM) Lamar, CO
KWGL(FM) Ouray, CO
KPMX(FM) Sterling, CO
WHJX(FM) Baldwin, FL
*WFRF-FM Monticello, FL
WWLL(FM) Sebring, FL
*WFFM(FM) Ashburn, GA
WEKL(FM) Augusta, GA
WWVA-FM Canton, GA
KOKZ(FM) Waterloo, IA
WIXO(FM) Peoria, IL
WUZR(FM) Bicknell, IN
WYXB(FM) Indianapolis, IN
WTCJ-FM Tell City, IN
KRMR(FM) Hays, KS
*KJRL(FM) Herington, KS
WTUV-FM Eminence, KY
WLGC-FM Greenup, KY
WTBK(FM) Manchester, KY
KVVP(FM) Leesville, LA
WROR-FM Framingham, MA
WJZ-FM Catonsville, MD
*WHMX(FM) Lincoln, ME
WOOD-FM Grand Rapids, MI
WCUP(FM) L'Anse, MI
WGVZ(FM) Eden Prairie, MN
KRAQ(FM) Jackson, MN
KXKX(FM) Knob Noster, MO
KPNT(FM) Sainte Genevieve, MO
WJXM(FM) De Kalb, MS
WAKH(FM) McComb, MS
KKQX(FM) Manhattan, MT
KWDV(FM) Valier, MT
WMKS(FM) Clemmons, NC
WRSF(FM) Columbia, NC
WGQR(FM) Elizabethtown, NC
KDXN(FM) South Heart, ND
KSUX(FM) Winnebago, NE
WLKC(FM) Campton, NH
WCHR-FM Manahawkin, NJ
KOZZ-FM Reno, NV
WMRV-FM Endicott, NY
WBZZ(FM) Malta, NY
WMJI(FM) Cleveland, OH
WZOM(FM) Defiance, OH
WBWR(FM) Hilliard, OH
*KROU(FM) Spencer, OK
KQAK(FM) Bend, OR
WLKJ(FM) Portage, PA
WQXA-FM York, PA
WCAD(FM) San Juan, PR
WIHG(FM) Rockwood, TN

WQAK(FM) Union City, TN
*KJJP(FM) Amarillo, TX
KTKO(FM) Beeville, TX
KRNB(FM) Decatur, TX
KNAF-FM Fredericksburg, TX
*KHCB-FM Houston, TX
KRBL(FM) Idalou, TX
KYKX(FM) Longview, TX
KBIC(FM) Raymondville, TX
KNRS-FM Centerville, UT
WMXH-FM Luray, VA
KJET(FM) Raymond, WA
KZBD(FM) Spokane, WA
KRSE(FM) Yakima, WA
WAPL(FM) Appleton, WI
WCFW(FM) Chippewa Falls, WI
WXCX(FM) Siren, WI
WOBG-FM Salem, WV

105.9 mhz
KKNI(FM) Seward, AK
WNSI(FM) Atmore, AL
WRTR(FM) Brookwood, AL
WFXO(FM) Centre, AL
KLAZ(FM) Hot Springs, AR
KHOT-FM Paradise Valley, AZ
KMJ-FM Fresno, CA
KPWR(FM) Los Angeles, CA
KRAZ(FM) Santa Ynez, CA
KQPM(FM) Ukiah, CA
KALC(FM) Denver, CO
WHCN(FM) Hartford, CT
WZKT(FM) Lewes, DE
WOCL(FM) De Land, FL
WTZB(FM) Englewood, FL
WBGG-FM Fort Lauderdale, FL
WILN(FM) Panama City, FL
WXMK(FM) Dock Junction, GA
WVGA(FM) Lakeland, GA
KPOI-FM Honolulu, HI
KZWF(FM) Patterson, IA
KTLB(FM) Twin Lakes, IA
KCIX(FM) Garden City, ID
WCFS-FM Elmwood Park, IL
WOKZ(FM) Fairfield, IL
WGKC(FM) Mahomet, IL
WMMC(FM) Marshall, IL
WJOT-FM Wabash, IN
KSSA(FM) Ingalls, KS
KLZR(FM) Lawrence, KS
WKYB(FM) Burgin, KY
WRVI(FM) Valley Station, KY
KBZE(FM) Berwick, LA
KFXZ-FM Opelousas, LA
WBCI(FM) Bath, ME
WKHQ-FM Charlevoix, MI
WDMK(FM) Detroit, MI
KWNG(FM) Red Wing, MN
KKWS(FM) Wadena, MN
KHRS(FM) Winthrop, MN
KZZK(FM) New London, MO
KGBX-FM Nixa, MO
KULH(FM) Wheeling, MO
WHGO(FM) Pascagoula, MS
WZNO(FM) Pickens, MS
KPBR(FM) Joliet, MT
KYJK(FM) Missoula, MT
WTMT(FM) Weaverville, NC
KKBO(FM) Flasher, ND
KCVF(FM) Sarles, ND
KAAQ(FM) Alliance, NE
KQKY(FM) Kearney, NE
KKCD(FM) Omaha, NE
WCAA(FM) Newark, NJ
KRZY-FM Santa Fe, NM
WJZR(FM) Rochester, NY
WLTI(FM) Syracuse, NY
WPFB-FM Middletown, OH
WWJM(FM) New Lexington, OH
KQTZ(FM) Hobart, OK
KIRC(FM) Seminole, OK
KYSJ(FM) Coos Bay, OR
KRJT(FM) Elgin, OR
WJOW(FM) Philipsburg, PA
WXDX-FM Pittsburgh, PA
WPZX(FM) Pocono Pines, PA

WEZV(FM) North Myrtle Beach, SC
KMIT(FM) Mitchell, SD
WGKX(FM) Memphis, TN
WNRQ(FM) Nashville, TN
KUZN(FM) Centerville, TX
KMFR(FM) Hondo, TX
KFMK(FM) Round Rock, TX
KUKA(FM) San Diego, TX
KKJW(FM) Stanton, TX
WLNI(FM) Lynchburg, VA
WJZW(FM) Woodbridge, VA
KFBW(FM) Vancouver, WA
WWHG(FM) Evansville, WI
WKPO(FM) Soldiers Grove, WI
*WEGZ(FM) Washburn, WI
WTNJ(FM) Mount Hope, WV

106.1 mhz
WSTH-FM Alexander City, AL
WBMH(FM) Grove Hill, AL
WTAK-FM Hartselle, AL
KFFB(FM) Fairfield Bay, AR
KIKO-FM Claypool, AZ
KFSZ(FM) Munds Park, AZ
*KCFA(FM) Arnold, CA
KRRX(FM) Burney, CA
KRAB(FM) Green Acres, CA
KPLM(FM) Palm Springs, CA
KMEL(FM) San Francisco, CA
KWWV(FM) Santa Margarita, CA
KNFO(FM) Basalt, CO
WRRX(FM) Gulf Breeze, FL
WQTL(FM) Tallahassee, FL
WKTM(FM) Soperton, GA
*WHKV(FM) Sylvester, GA
WNGC(FM) Toccoa, GA
KLEO(FM) Kahaluu, HI
KLSS-FM Mason City, IA
KIYX(FM) Sageville, IA
KCII(FM) Washington, IA
KZFN(FM) Moscow, ID
KKMV(FM) Rupert, ID
WSMI-FM Litchfield, IL
WYYS(FM) Streator, IL
WDKS(FM) Newburgh, IN
WWWY(FM) North Vernon, IN
KXKU(FM) Lyons, KS
WMOR-FM Morehead, KY
WYKY(FM) Science Hill, KY
KXRR(FM) Monroe, LA
WCOD-FM Hyannis, MA
WKGO(FM) Cumberland, MD
WXSH(FM) Pocomoke City, MD
*WMEM(FM) Presque Isle, ME
WJXQ(FM) Jackson, MI
*WHST(FM) Tawas City, MI
KLCI(FM) Elk River, MN
KJOE(FM) Slayton, MN
KOQL(FM) Ashland, MO
KWKZ(FM) Charleston, MO
*KEXS-FM Ravenwood, MO
WMTI(FM) Picayune, MS
WMXU(FM) Starkville, MS
KQDI-FM Great Falls, MT
WMMY(FM) Jefferson, NC
WOLS(FM) Waxhaw, NC
WRDU(FM) Wilson, NC
KQLX-FM Lisbon, ND
WHDQ(FM) Claremont, NH
KPZE-FM Carlsbad, NM
KFMQ(FM) Gallup, NM
WNKI(FM) Corning, NY
WPDA(FM) Jeffersonville, NY
WBLI(FM) Patchogue, NY
WVNO-FM Mansfield, OH
WBBG(FM) Niles, OH
KKBI(FM) Broken Bow, OK
KQLL(FM) Owasso, OK
KIXO(FM) Sulphur, OK
KLOO-FM Corvallis, OR
WLZS(FM) Beaver Springs, PA
WCOP(FM) Farmington Township, PA
WISX(FM) Philadelphia, PA
WRRH(FM) Hormigueros, PR
WVIS(FM) Vieques, PR
WFXH-FM Hilton Head Island, SC

WTUA(FM) Saint Stephen, SC
WJRV(FM) Oliver Springs, TN
KTTX(FM) Brenham, TX
WHHKS(FM) Denton, TX
KFLP-FM Floydada, TX
KKVR(FM) Kerrville, TX
KNEX(FM) Laredo, TX
KIOC(FM) Orange, TX
KTKY(FM) Refugio, TX
KMDX(FM) San Angelo, TX
KBAL-FM San Saba, TX
KRZX(FM) Monticello, UT
WCNR(FM) Keswick, VA
WUSH(FM) Poquoson, VA
WSFF(FM) Vinton, VA
KBKS-FM Tacoma, WA
WDKM(FM) Adams, WI
WACD(FM) Antigo, WI
WMIL(FM) Waukesha, WI
WRZZ(FM) Elizabeth, WV
KBMG(FM) Evanston, WY
KXXL(FM) Moorcroft, WY
KMQS(FM) Wheatland, WY

106.3 mhz
KSUP(FM) Juneau, AK
WKNU(FM) Brewton, AL
WBTG-FM Sheffield, AL
KZKZ-FM Greenwood, AR
KOLL(FM) Lonoke, AR
KYGL(FM) Texarkana, AR
KRLW-FM Walnut Ridge, AR
KGMG(FM) Oracle, AZ
KOMR(FM) Sun City, AZ
KEJY(FM) Blue Lake, CA
KGRP(FM) Cazadero, CA
KMGQ(FM) Goleta, CA
KVPW(FM) Kingsburg, CA
KGMX(FM) Lancaster, CA
KNAH(FM) Merced, CA
KALI-FM Santa Ana, CA
KMJV(FM) Soledad, CA
KCHC(FM) Willows, CA
KPRB(FM) Brush, CO
KZMV(FM) Kremmling, CO
KWUF-FM Pagosa Springs, CO
KKLI(FM) Widefield, CO
WJPT(FM) Fort Myers Villas, FL
WNEW(FM) Jupiter, FL
WRAZ-FM Leisure City, FL
WCIF(FM) Melbourne, FL
WSBZ(FM) Miramar Beach, FL
WJQB(FM) Spring Hill, FL
WTUF(FM) Boston, GA
WGMK(FM) Donalsonville, GA
WQBZ(FM) Fort Valley, GA
WOAH(FM) Glennville, GA
WKBX(FM) Kingsland, GA
KPTL(FM) Ankeny, IA
KQTA(FM) Homedale, ID
KBJX(FM) Shelley, ID
WQRL(FM) Benton, IL
WYRB(FM) Genoa, IL
WGCY(FM) Gibson City, IL
WSRB(FM) Lansing, IL
WJOE(FM) Columbia City, IN
WCDQ(FM) Crawfordsville, IN
WUBU(FM) South Bend, IN
WANY-FM Albany, KY
WXMZ(FM) Hartford, KY
WRIL(FM) Pineville, KY
WCDA(FM) Versailles, KY
KYMK-FM Maurice, LA
KXOR-FM Thibodaux, LA
WEIB(FM) Northampton, MA
WCEM-FM Cambridge, MD
WHXQ(FM) Scarborough, ME
WGLM-FM Lakeview, MI
WKLA-FM Ludington, MI
WGER(FM) Saginaw, MI
WMXG(FM) Stephenson, MI
KRJB(FM) Ada, MN
WMFG-FM Hibbing, MN
KPHR(FM) Ortonville, MN
KRZK(FM) Branson, MO
KHZA(FM) Bunker, MO

WZLD(FM) Petal, MS
WGNG(FM) Tchula, MS
KDBR(FM) Kalispell, MT
WLTT(FM) Shallotte, NC
KFRX(FM) Lincoln, NE
WMTK(FM) Littleton, NH
WFNQ(FM) Nashua, NH
WHCY(FM) Blairstown, NJ
WHTG-FM Eatontown, NJ
KAGM(FM) Los Lunas, NM
KZHD(FM) Lovelock, NV
WFAF(FM) Mount Kisco, NY
WMCR-FM Oneida, NY
WYZY(FM) Saranac Lake, NY
WCDK(FM) Cadiz, OH
WJYD(FM) London, OH
WBUK(FM) Ottawa, OH
KLBC(FM) Durant, OK
*KGOU(FM) Norman, OK
KZZE(FM) Eagle Point, OR
WLCY(FM) Blairsville, PA
WBSS(FM) Mount Union, PA
WXMT(FM) Smethport, PA
WCTL(FM) Union City, PA
WWKX(FM) Woonsocket, RI
WYNN-FM Florence, SC
WJNI(FM) Ladson, SC
WYRD-FM Simpsonville, SC
KZLK(FM) Rapid City, SD
KVHT(FM) Vermillion, SD
WPFT(FM) Pigeon Forge, TN
KKHR(FM) Abilene, TX
KOOC(FM) Belton, TX
KPSO-FM Falfurrias, TX
*KMLR(FM) Gonzales, TX
KPAN-FM Hereford, TX
KERB-FM Kermit, TX
KHKZ(FM) Mercedes, TX
KSEM-FM Seminole, TX
KBZS(FM) Wichita Falls, TX
WHKX(FM) Bluefield, VA
WMNA-FM Gretna, VA
WNVA-FM Norton, VA
KCSY(FM) Twisp, WA
WQCC(FM) La Crosse, WI
WWQM-FM Middleton, WI
WEVR-FM River Falls, WI
WPLT(FM) Sarona, WI
WAMX(FM) Milton, WV
KLEN(FM) Cheyenne, WY
KWWY(FM) Shoshoni, WY

106.5 mhz
KWHL(FM) Anchorage, AK
WAVH(FM) Daphne, AL
WZNJ(FM) Demopolis, AL
WJEC(FM) Vernon, AL
KBVA(FM) Bella Vista, AR
KELD-FM Hampton, AR
KKIK(FM) Horseshoe Bend, AR
KKMR(FM) Arizona City, AZ
KALT-FM Alturas, CA
KIXA(FM) Lucerne Valley, CA
KMMT(FM) Mammoth Lakes, CA
KBZC(FM) Sacramento, CA
KLNV(FM) San Diego, CA
KEZR(FM) San Jose, CA
KEAL(FM) Taft, CA
KFVR-FM La Junta, CO
WBMW(FM) Ledyard, CT
WOCY(FM) Carrabelle, FL
WCJX(FM) Five Points, FL
WOKV-FM Ponte Vedra Beach, FL
WCTQ(FM) Sarasota, FL
WZIQ(FM) Smithville, GA
WZBX(FM) Sylvania, GA
KRYL(FM) Haiku, HI
KCQQ(FM) Davenport, IA
WARH(FM) Granite City, IL
WXNU(FM) Saint Anne, IL
WWBL(FM) Washington, IN
KYQQ(FM) Arkansas City, KS
WKDZ-FM Cadiz, KY
WRLV-FM Salyersville, KY
KCIJ(FM) Atlanta, LA
KQXL-FM New Roads, LA

WWMX(FM) Baltimore, MD
WQCB(FM) Brewer, ME
*WMEF(FM) Fort Kent, ME
WVFM(FM) Kalamazoo, MI
KFMC(FM) Fairmont, MN
*KDXL(FM) Saint Louis Park, MN
*KUOM-FM Saint Louis Park, MN
KLFN(FM) Sunburg, MN
WDAF-FM Liberty, MO
KTMO(FM) New Madrid, MO
WAID(FM) Clarksdale, MS
WSFL-FM New Bern, NC
WEND(FM) Salisbury, NC
KMCX(FM) Ogallala, NE
*WNHI(FM) Farmington, NH
WBBO(FM) Bass River Township, NJ
KEND(FM) Roswell, NM
KSNE-FM Las Vegas, NV
WPYX(FM) Albany, NY
WYRK(FM) Buffalo, NY
WKRH(FM) Minetto, NY
WMVX(FM) Cleveland, OH
WLQR-FM Delta, OH
WDSJ(FM) Greenville, OH
KTLS-FM Holdenville, OK
WFYY(FM) Bloomsburg, PA
WDSN(FM) Reynoldsville, PA
WNIK-FM Arecibo, PR
WLFF(FM) Georgetown, SC
WSKZ(FM) Chattanooga, TN
WLVS-FM Clifton, TN
WJDT(FM) Rogersville, TN
KOVE-FM Galveston, TX
KOOI-FM Jacksonville, TX
KEJS(FM) Lubbock, TX
KOSY-FM Spanish Fork, UT
WBTJ(FM) Richmond, VA
KSPO(FM) Dishman, WA
KWPZ(FM) Lynden, WA
KEGX(FM) Richland, WA
WYTE(FM) Marshfield, WI
WHBZ(FM) Sheboygan Falls, WI
WKCH(FM) Whitewater, WI
WWLW(FM) Clarksburg, WV
KLMI(FM) Rock River, WY

106.7 mhz
KGTW(FM) Ketchikan, AK
WKMX(FM) Enterprise, AL
WHKN(FM) Benton, AR
KJBX(FM) Trumann, AR
KNKI(FM) Pinetop, AZ
KPPV(FM) Prescott Valley, AZ
KSMY(FM) Lompoc, CA
KRQR(FM) Orland, CA
KROQ-FM Pasadena, CA
KJUG-FM Tulare, CA
KBPI(FM) Denver, CO
WRMA(FM) Fort Lauderdale, FL
WXXL(FM) Tavares, FL
WOKA-FM Douglas, GA
WYAY(FM) Gainesville, GA
KNAN(FM) Nanakuli, HI
KRTI(FM) Grinnell, IA
KIKD(FM) Lake City, IA
KYUN(FM) Hailey, ID
KTPO(FM) Kootenai, ID
WPPN(FM) Des Plaines, IL
WPWQ(FM) Mount Sterling, IL
WZNX(FM) Sullivan, IL
WTLC-FM Greenwood, IN
WYFX(FM) Mount Vernon, IN
*WKHL(FM) West Lafayette, IN
KFXX-FM Hugoton, KS
KQNK-FM Norton, KS
WLFX(FM) Berea, KY
WHHT(FM) Horse Cave, KY
WZZL(FM) Reidland, KY
WNKR(FM) Williamstown, KY
KYLA(FM) Homer, LA
KUMX(FM) North Fort Polk, LA
KMEZ(FM) Port Sulphur, LA
KKOO(FM) Rayne, LA
WMJX(FM) Boston, MA
WHXR(FM) North Windham, ME
WDTW-FM Detroit, MI

U.S. FM Stations by Frequency

WSRT(FM) Gaylord, MI
WHTO(FM) Iron Mountain, MI
KAOD(FM) Babbitt, MN
WJJY-FM Brainerd, MN
KAUL(FM) Ellington, MO
KZRQ-FM Mount Vernon, MO
WWZD-FM New Albany, MS
WSTZ-FM Vicksburg, MS
KPLN(FM) Lockwood, MT
KBQQ(FM) Pinesdale, MT
WUIN(FM) Carolina Beach, NC
WKVK(FM) Semora, NC
KYTZ(FM) Walhalla, ND
KEXL(FM) Norfolk, NE
WKOE(FM) North Cape May, NJ
KLVO(FM) Los Alamos, NM
WBDR(FM) Copenhagen, NY
WKGS(FM) Irondequoit, NY
WLTW(FM) New York, NY
WRRQ(FM) Windsor, NY
WRXS(FM) Dublin, OH
WFGA(FM) Hicksville, OH
WSRW-FM Hillsboro, OH
KTUZ-FM Okarche, OK
KLTH(FM) Lake Oswego, OR
WAMO-FM Beaver Falls, PA
WMHX(FM) Hershey, PA
WTCB(FM) Orangeburg, SC
KBFO(FM) Aberdeen, SD
WDXE-FM Lawrenceburg, TN
WNFN(FM) Millersville, TN
WRJK(FM) Norris, TN
KQTY-FM Borger, TX
KDRW(FM) Hewitt, TX
KCHX(FM) Midland, TX
KZZA(FM) Muenster, TX
KPWT(FM) Terrell Hills, TX
WJFK-FM Manassas, VA
WIZN(FM) Vergennes, VT
KWWX(FM) Cashmere, WA
WZNN(FM) Allouez, WI
WATQ(FM) Chetek, WI
WWQN(FM) Mount Horeb, WI
*WHFI(FM) Lindside, WV
WVKM(FM) Matewan, WV
KMRZ-FM Superior, WY

106.9 mhz
KFSE(FM) Kasilof, AK
WBPT(FM) Homewood, AL
KXIO(FM) Clarksville, AR
KXFE(FM) Dumas, AR
KYXK(FM) Gurdon, AR
KDVA(FM) Buckeye, AZ
KMVE(FM) California City, CA
KQLB(FM) Los Banos, CA
KFRC-FM San Francisco, CA
KDGL(FM) Yucca Valley, CA
KIQN(FM) Pueblo, CO
WCCC-FM Hartford, CT
WKZY(FM) Cross City, FL
WZZS(FM) Zolfo Springs, FL
KWYI(FM) Kawaihae, HI
KOJY(FM) Bloomfield, IA
KIHK(FM) Rock Valley, IA
KMOK(FM) Lewiston, ID
WSWT(FM) Peoria, IL
WDML(FM) Woodlawn, IL
WXXC(FM) Marion, IN
KBGL(FM) Larned, KS
KTPK(FM) Topeka, KS
WVEZ(FM) Louisville, KY
WYMV(FM) Madisonville, KY
KEDG(FM) Alexandria, LA
WWEG(FM) Hagerstown, MD
*WYPO(FM) Ocean City, MD
WBQX(FM) Thomaston, ME
WUPM(FM) Ironwood, MI
WMUS(FM) Muskegon, MI
*WSAE(FM) Spring Arbor, MI
KARP-FM Dassel, MN
WMOZ(FM) Moose Lake, MN
KROC-FM Rochester, MN
KTXY(FM) Jefferson City, MO
WHKL(FM) Crenshaw, MS
WRBE-FM Lucedale, MS

WKZB(FM) Stonewall, MS
*KMSM-FM Butte, MT
KSCY(FM) Four Corners, MT
WMIT(FM) Black Mountain, NC
WMGU(FM) Southern Pines, NC
KHRT-FM Minot, ND
KEGK(FM) Wahpeton, ND
KHYY(FM) Minatare, NE
KOPW(FM) Plattsmouth, NE
WSCY(FM) Moultonborough, NH
*WKDN-FM Camden, NJ
KRNO(FM) Incline Village, NV
KONV(FM) Overton, NV
WKZA(FM) Lakewood, NY
WPHR-FM Solvay, NY
WRQK(FM) Canton, OH
*WWSU(FM) Dayton, OH
KTIJ(FM) Elk City, OK
KHTT(FM) Muskogee, OK
KCST-FM Florence, OR
KKRB(FM) Klamath Falls, OR
*WRIJ(FM) Masontown, PA
WZYY(FM) Renovo, PA
WEZX(FM) Scranton, PA
WMEG(FM) Guayama, PR
WGZR(FM) Bluffton, SC
WWYN(FM) McKenzie, TN
WKXD(FM) Monterey, TN
KMZZ(FM) Bishop, TX
KLUB(FM) Bloomington, TX
KHPT(FM) Conroe, TX
KHLE(FM) Kempner, TX
KRVF(FM) Kerens, TX
KAZE(FM) Ore City, TX
KKYN-FM Plainview, TX
KRIA(FM) Plainview, TX
KDRX(FM) Rocksprings, TX
KLGD(FM) Stamford, TX
KEGH(FM) Brigham City, UT
WLEQ(FM) Bedford, VA
WAFX(FM) Suffolk, VA
WVTI(FM) Brighton, VT
KRWM(FM) Bremerton, WA
WLGE(FM) Bailey's Harbor, WI
WJZX(FM) Brookfield, WI
WNNO-FM Wisconsin Dells, WI
KASS(FM) Casper, WY

107.1 mhz
KCNY(FM) Bald Knob, AR
KTHS-FM Berryville, AR
KXHT(FM) Marion, AR
KDRS-FM Paragould, AR
KFYX(FM) Texarkana, AR
KVVA-FM Apache Junction, AZ
KSSE(FM) Arcadia, CA
KCWR(FM) Bakersfield, CA
KSRT(FM) Cloverdale, CA
KSSD(FM) Fallbrook, CA
KHIT-FM Madera, CA
KNKK(FM) Needles, CA
KSES-FM Seaside, CA
KESR(FM) Shasta Lake City, CA
KSSC(FM) Ventura, CA
KPVW(FM) Aspen, CO
KLJH(FM) Bayfield, CO
KONN-FM Bennett, CO
WIIS(FM) Key West, FL
WCKT(FM) Lehigh Acres, FL
WAOA-FM Melbourne, FL
WFXM(FM) Gordon, GA
WTSH-FM Rockmart, GA
WTLY(FM) Thomasville, GA
WYFA(FM) Waynesboro, GA
KDSN-FM Denison, IA
*KNWI(FM) Osceola, IA
KRQN(FM) Vinton, IA
KTHI(FM) Caldwell, ID
KQEO(FM) Idaho Falls, ID
WEAI(FM) Lynnville, IL
WSPY-FM Plano, IL
WPGU(FM) Urbana, IL
WKRV(FM) Vandalia, IL
WEJK(FM) Boonville, IN
WEDJ(FM) Danville, IN
WZVN(FM) Lowell, IN

KBZI(FM) Columbus, KS
*WLAI(FM) Danville, KY
WKCB(FM) Hindman, KY
WUHU(FM) Smiths Grove, KY
KFNV-FM Ferriday, LA
WHMD(FM) Hammond, LA
KWLV(FM) Many, LA
KOGM(FM) Opelousas, LA
WFHN(FM) Fairhaven, MA
WTDK(FM) Federalsburg, MD
WQKL(FM) Ann Arbor, MI
WCKC(FM) Cadillac, MI
WSAQ(FM) Port Huron, MI
WTLZ(FM) Saginaw, MI
WIRX(FM) Saint Joseph, MI
WFMP(FM) Coon Rapids, MN
KKEQ(FM) Fosston, MN
KMGK(FM) Glenwood, MN
KBMV-FM Birch Tree, MO
KBHI(FM) Miner, MO
WBYP(FM) Belzoni, MS
*WLVZ(FM) Collins, MS
WXYK(FM) Gulfport, MS
WLSM-FM Louisville, MS
WFXC(FM) Durham, NC
KSFT-FM South Sioux City, NE
WERZ(FM) Exeter, NH
*WEVC(FM) Gorham, NH
WWYY(FM) Belvidere, NJ
WWZY(FM) Long Branch, NJ
KNKT(FM) Armijo, Albuquerque, NM
KTUM(FM) Tatum, NM
WXPK(FM) Briarcliff Manor, NY
WFFG-FM Corinth, NY
WNMR(FM) Dannemora, NY
WLIR-FM Hampton Bays, NY
WBZX(FM) Hancock, NY
WNUS(FM) Belpre, OH
WNKK(FM) Circleville, OH
WDOH(FM) Delphos, OH
WBKS(FM) Ironton, OH
WKFS(FM) Milford, OH
KYNZ(FM) Lone Grove, OK
KNID(FM) North Enid, OK
*KLVU(FM) Sweet Home, OR
WGSM(FM) Greensburg, PA
WEXC(FM) Greenville, PA
*WQJU(FM) Mifflintown, PA
WLIH(FM) Whitneyville, PA
WRXZ(FM) Briarcliff Acres, SC
WRHM(FM) Lancaster, SC
KDBX(FM) Clear Lake, SD
KGSR(FM) Bastrop, TX
KRXB(FM) Beeville, TX
KDXX(FM) Benbrook, TX
KRVA-FM Campbell, TX
KPUR-FM Canyon, TX
KAUM(FM) Colorado City, TX
*KWBU-FM Waco, TX
KHUN(FM) Huntington, UT
WTTX-FM Appomattox, VA
*WCHG(FM) Hot Springs, VA
WPSK-FM Pulaski, VA
WORK(FM) Barre, VT
WZLF(FM) Bellows Falls, VT
KRQT(FM) Castle Rock, WA
KAZZ(FM) Deer Park, WA
WFON(FM) Fond du Lac, WI
WOCO-FM Oconto, WI
WPVL-FM Platteville, WI
WCBC-FM Keyser, WV
KROW(FM) Lovell, WY

107.3 mhz
WQLT-FM Florence, AL
KQXF(FM) Osceola, AR
KFXR-FM Chinle, AZ
KXFF(FM) Colorado City, AZ
KURQ(FM) Grover Beach, CA
KIXW-FM Lenwood, CA
*KNHT(FM) Rio Dell, CA
KSTN-FM Stockton, CA
KQZR(FM) Hayden, CO
KRKV(FM) Las Animas, CO
WRQX(FM) Washington, DC
WPLA(FM) Jacksonville, FL

WYCL(FM) Pensacola, FL
WXGL(FM) Saint Petersburg, FL
WMCD(FM) Claxton, GA
WCGQ(FM) Columbus, GA
KGRS(FM) Burlington, IA
KIOW(FM) Forest City, IA
WDDD-FM Johnston City, IL
WRZQ-FM Greensburg, IN
WRSW-FM Warsaw, IN
KTHR(FM) Wichita, KS
WCTT-FM Corbin, KY
WRZI(FM) Hodgenville, KY
WTGE(FM) Baker, LA
WAAF(FM) Westborough, MA
WBZN(FM) Old Town, ME
WBBL-FM Greenville, MI
WUPF(FM) Powers, MI
KNUJ-FM Sleepy Eye, MN
KESY(FM) Cuba, MO
KMJK(FM) Lexington, MO
WFCG(FM) Tylertown, MS
KINX(FM) Great Falls, MT
WTKF(FM) Atlantic, NC
WCLN-FM Clinton, NC
WBOB-FM Enfield, NC
KINV(FM) Enderlin, ND
KNPQ(FM) Hershey, NE
KBBK(FM) Lincoln, NE
WPUR(FM) Atlantic City, NJ
KEHD(FM) Fernley, NV
WRWD-FM Highland, NY
WROO(FM) South Bristol Township, NY
WRCK(FM) Utica, NY
WYBZ(FM) Crooksville, OH
WNWV(FM) Elyria, OH
WJUC(FM) Swanton, OH
KVRW(FM) Lawton, OK
KOMS(FM) Poteau, OK
KOOS(FM) North Bend, OR
WCOH-FM DuBois, PA
WEGH(FM) Northumberland, PA
WCMN-FM Arecibo, PR
WJMZ-FM Anderson, SC
WVSZ(FM) Chesterfield, SC
KQRN(FM) Mitchell, SD
KSLT(FM) Spearfish, SD
WTRZ(FM) Spencer, TN
KAPN(FM) Caldwell, TX
KRSR(FM) Ingleside, TX
KJAS(FM) Jasper, TX
KTSX(FM) Knox City, TX
KLFX(FM) Nolanville, TX
KGCE(FM) Post, TX
KQDR(FM) Savoy, TX
KISX(FM) Whitehouse, TX
WXLZ-FM Lebanon, VA
WBBT-FM Powhatan, VA
WVGN(FM) Charlotte Amalie, VI
KFFM(FM) Yakima, WA
WSJY(FM) Fort Atkinson, WI
WNXR(FM) Iron River, WI
WKAZ-FM Miami, WV
KKAW(FM) Albin, WY
KAOX(FM) Kemmerer, WY

107.5 mhz
KASH-FM Anchorage, AK
KOMT(FM) Mountain Home, AR
KSED(FM) Sedona, AZ
KHYT(FM) Tucson, AZ
KQPT(FM) Colusa, CA
KXO-FM El Centro, CA
KPIG-FM Freedom, CA
KRDA(FM) Hanford, CA
KLVE(FM) Los Angeles, CA
KQKS(FM) Lakewood, CO
WAMR-FM Miami, FL
WWGF(FM) Donalsonville, GA
WTIF-FM Omega, GA
WAMJ(FM) Roswell, GA
WDBN(FM) Wrightsville, GA
KHEI-FM Kihei, HI
*KILV(FM) Castana, IA
KKDM(FM) Des Moines, IA

KYZK(FM) Sun Valley, ID
WGCI-FM Chicago, IL
WDBQ-FM Galena, IL
WABX(FM) Evansville, IN
KSCB-FM Liberal, KS
WIOK(FM) Falmouth, KY
WZLK(FM) Virgie, KY
KCIL(FM) Houma, LA
KJMH(FM) Lake Arthur, LA
KXKZ(FM) Ruston, LA
WFCC-FM Chatham, MA
WFNK(FM) Lewiston, ME
WGPR(FM) Detroit, MI
WCCW-FM Traverse City, MI
KLIZ-FM Brainerd, MN
KBGY(FM) Faribault, MN
KARZ(FM) Marshall, MN
KFEB(FM) Campbell, MO
KWBZ(FM) Monroe City, MO
WMJW(FM) Cleveland, MS
WKXI-FM Magee, MS
KENR(FM) Superior, MT
WAZO(FM) Southport, NC
WKZL(FM) Winston-Salem, NC
KXRV(FM) Cannon Ball, ND
KJKJ(FM) Grand Forks, ND
KSMX-FM Clovis, NM
KQBA(FM) Los Alamos, NM
KXTE(FM) Pahrump, NV
WBBI(FM) Endwell, NY
WBLS(FM) New York, NY
WCKX(FM) Columbus, OH
WZRX-FM Fort Shawnee, OH
WFXJ-FM North Kingsville, OH
WZZZ(FM) Portsmouth, OH
*KOSN(FM) Ketchum, OK
KIFS(FM) Ashland, OR
KXJM(FM) Banks, OR
WBVE(FM) Bedford, PA
WBYN-FM Boyertown, PA
WNKT(FM) Eastover, SC
KXZS(FM) Wall, SD
WHBQ-FM Germantown, TN
WRVW(FM) Lebanon, TN
KMVK(FM) Fort Worth, TX
KGLK(FM) Lake Jackson, TX
KQBO(FM) Rio Grande City, TX
KSJT-FM San Angelo, TX
KXTN-FM San Antonio, TX
KTTQ(FM) Turkey, TX
KKAT-FM Orem, UT
WWTJ(FM) Charlottesville, VA
WDUZ-FM Brillion, WI
WCCN-FM Neillsville, WI
WEGW(FM) Wheeling, WV
KPAD(FM) Wheatland, WY

107.7 mhz
WUHT(FM) Birmingham, AL
WFXX(FM) Georgiana, AL
WPRN-FM Lisman, AL
KLAL(FM) Wrightsville, AR
KSRN(FM) Kings Beach, CA
KSAN(FM) San Mateo, CA
KIST-FM Santa Barbara, CA
KCDZ(FM) Twentynine Palms, CA
*WFCS(FM) New Britain, CT
WWRX(FM) Pawcatuck, CT
WMGF(FM) Mount Dora, FL
WAJP(FM) Perry, FL
WHFX(FM) Darien, GA
WPRW-FM Martinez, GA
WEGC(FM) Sasser, GA
KKOA(FM) Volcano, HI
KGGG(FM) Pacific Junction, IA
KICD-FM Spencer, IA
WYST(FM) Fairbury, IL
WLLT(FM) Polo, IL
WSFR(FM) Corydon, IN
WMRS(FM) Monticello, IN
*KGCR(FM) Goodland, KS
KMAJ-FM Topeka, KS
WKYN(FM) Owingsville, KY
WKHI(FM) Fruitland, MD
WBQI(FM) Bar Harbor, ME
WHSB(FM) Alpena, MI

D-734

WMQT(FM) Ishpeming, MI
WRKR(FM) Portage, MI
KBMX(FM) Proctor, MN
KDZZ(FM) Saint Charles, MN
*KCVK(FM) Otterville, MO
KSLZ(FM) Saint Louis, MO
KRWP(FM) Stockton, MO
WAZA(FM) Liberty, MS
KMTZ(FM) Three Forks, MT
WUKS(FM) Saint Pauls, NC
KSYZ-FM Grand Island, NE
WTPL(FM) Hillsboro, NH
*WRRC(FM) Lawrenceville, NJ
*WECW(FM) Elmira, NY
WLKK(FM) Wethersfield Township, NY
WMMX(FM) Dayton, OH
WXXF(FM) Loudonville, OH
WSEO(FM) Nelsonville, OH
WPFX-FM North Baltimore, OH
KRXO(FM) Oklahoma City, OK
KUMA-FM Pendleton, OR
WUUZ(FM) Cooperstown, PA
WCIG(FM) Dallas, PA
WGTY(FM) Gettysburg, PA
WVOZ-FM Carolina, PR
KABD(FM) Ipswich, SD

WHHM-FM Henderson, TN
WIVK-FM Knoxville, TN
KHZS(FM) Georgetown, TX
KRKP(FM) Leakey, TX
KTBQ(FM) Nacogdoches, TX
KPLT-FM Paris, TX
WHQX(FM) Cedar Bluff, VA
WWWT-FM Manassas, VA
WJCD(FM) Windsor, VA
KNDD(FM) Seattle, WA
*WVCY-FM Milwaukee, WI
WVRW(FM) Glenville, WV
WFSP-FM Kingwood, WV

107.9 mhz
WMRK-FM Shorter, AL
KEZA(FM) Fayetteville, AR
KFIN(FM) Jonesboro, AR
KMLE(FM) Chandler, AZ
KUZZ-FM Bakersfield, CA
KSEA(FM) Greenfield, CA
*KKLC(FM) Mount Shasta, CA
KLLE(FM) North Fork, CA
KDND(FM) Sacramento, CA
KWVE(FM) San Clemente, CA
KPAW(FM) Fort Collins, CO
KBKL(FM) Grand Junction, CO

KDZA-FM Pueblo, CO
WEBE(FM) Westport, CT
WNDN(FM) Chiefland, FL
WSRZ-FM Coral Cove, FL
WMFM(FM) Key West, FL
WPFM-FM Panama City, FL
WIRK-FM West Palm Beach, FL
WHTA(FM) Hampton, GA
WWRQ-FM Valdosta, GA
KKOL-FM Aiea, HI
KKRF(FM) Stuart, IA
KFMW(FM) Waterloo, IA
KXLT-FM Eagle, ID
WUIL(FM) Arcola, IL
WLEY-FM Aurora, IL
WCDD(FM) Canton, IL
WNTR(FM) Indianapolis, IN
WJFX(FM) New Haven, IN
WAMW-FM Washington, IN
KZRS(FM) Great Bend, KS
KWLS(FM) Winfield, KS
WKYR-FM Burkesville, KY
WCVQ(FM) Fort Campbell, KY
WWAG(FM) McKee, KY
WBTF(FM) Midway, KY
KRKA(FM) Erath, LA
WXKS-FM Medford, MA

*WFSI(FM) Annapolis, MD
WFMX(FM) Skowhegan, ME
*WVAC-FM Adrian, MI
WCZW(FM) Charlevoix, MI
WCRZ(FM) Flint, MI
WSHZ(FM) Muskegon, MI
KQQL(FM) Anoka, MN
KLTE(FM) Kirksville, MO
KCLQ(FM) Lebanon, MO
WFCA(FM) Ackerman, MS
WZKX(FM) Bay St. Louis, MS
KHDV(FM) Darby, MT
WLNK(FM) Charlotte, NC
WNCT-FM Greenville, NC
KPFX(FM) Fargo, ND
KTIC-FM West Point, NE
WRNB(FM) Pennsauken, NJ
*WWPH(FM) Princeton Junction, NJ
KQEL(FM) Alamogordo, NM
KBQI(FM) Albuquerque, NM
KVGS(FM) Laughlin, NV
WWHT(FM) Syracuse, NY
WENZ(FM) Cleveland, OH
WVMX(FM) Delaware, OH
KEYB(FM) Altus, OK
KHPE(FM) Albany, OR
*WHHS(FM) Havertown, PA

WDSY-FM Pittsburgh, PA
WKVB(FM) Port Matilda, PA
WKRF(FM) Tobyhanna, PA
WLMY(FM) Williamsport, PA
WGTR(FM) Bucksport, SC
WLOW(FM) Port Royal, SC
KXQL(FM) Flandreau, SD
WOGT(FM) East Ridge, TN
KEYJ-FM Abilene, TX
KQQK(FM) Beaumont, TX
KZRK-FM Canyon, TX
KVLY(FM) Edinburg, TX
KFAN-FM Johnson City, TX
KESS-FM Lewisville, TX
KQLM(FM) Odessa, TX
KHCK-FM Robinson, TX
KIXS(FM) Victoria, TX
KUDD(FM) Roy, UT
WYYD(FM) Amherst, VA
WBQK(FM) West Point, VA
*WVPS(FM) Burlington, VT
KLSY(FM) South Bend, WA
*KMBI-FM Spokane, WA
WBCV(FM) Wausau, WI
WEMM-FM Huntington, WV
KRVK(FM) Vista West, WY

Canadian AM Stations by Frequency

530 khz
CIAO(AM) Brampton, ON

540 khz
CBT(AM) Grand Falls-Windsor, NF
*CBEF(AM) Windsor, ON
*CBKF-1(AM) Gravelbourg, SK
*CBK(AM) Regina, SK

560 khz
CHTK(AM) Prince Rupert, BC
CFOS(AM) Owen Sound, ON

570 khz
CKWL(AM) Williams Lake, BC
CFCB(AM) Corner Brook, NF
CKGL(AM) Kitchener, ON
CKSW(AM) Swift Current, SK
*CFWH(AM) Whitehorse, YT

580 khz
CKUA(AM) Edmonton, AB
CFRA(AM) Ottawa, ON
CKWW(AM) Windsor, ON

590 khz
CFTK(AM) Terrace, BC
CFAR(AM) Flin Flon, MB
CJCW(AM) Sussex, NB
VOCM(AM) Saint John's, NF
CJCL(AM) Toronto, ON

600 khz
CFCT(AM) Tuktoyaktuk, NT
CKAT(AM) North Bay, ON
CJWW(AM) Saskatoon, SK

610 khz
CKYL(AM) Peace River, AB
CHNL(AM) Kamloops, BC
CHTM(AM) Thompson, MB
CKTB(AM) Saint Catharines, ON
CKRW(AM) Whitehorse, YT

620 khz
CKCM(AM) Grand Falls, NF
CFRP(AM) Forestville, PQ
CKRM(AM) Regina, SK

630 khz
CHED(AM) Edmonton, AB
CFCO(AM) Chatham, ON

640 khz
*CBN(AM) Saint John's, NF
CFMJ(AM) Toronto, ON

650 khz
CISL(AM) Richmond, BC
CKGA(AM) Gander, NF
CKOM(AM) Saskatoon, SK

660 khz
CFFR(AM) Calgary, AB

680 khz
*CHFA(AM) Edmonton, AB
CJOB(AM) Winnipeg, MB
CFTR(AM) Toronto, ON

690 khz
*CBU(AM) Vancouver, BC
CINF(AM) Verdun, PQ

710 khz
CKVO(AM) Clarenville, NF

730 khz
CHMJ(AM) Vancouver, BC
CKDM(AM) Dauphin, MB
CKAC(AM) Montreal, PQ

740 khz
CBX(AM) Edmonton, AB
CHCM(AM) Marystown, NF
CFZM(AM) Toronto, ON

750 khz
CBGY(AM) Bonavista Bay, NF
CKJH(AM) Melfort, SK

760 khz
CFLD(AM) Burns Lake, BC

770 khz
CHQR(AM) Calgary, AB

790 khz
CFNW(AM) Port au Choix, NF

800 khz
CKOR(AM) Penticton, BC
*VOWR(AM) Saint John's, NF
CJBQ(AM) Belleville, ON
CKLW(AM) Windsor, ON
CJAD(AM) Montreal, PQ
CHRC(AM) Quebec, PQ
CHAB(AM) Moose Jaw, SK

810 khz
CKJS(AM) Winnipeg, MB
CJVA(AM) Caraquet, NB

820 khz
CHAM(AM) Hamilton, ON

830 khz
CKKY(AM) Wainwright, AB

840 khz
CFCW(AM) Camrose, AB
CKBX(AM) 100 Mile House, BC

860 khz
*CFPR(AM) Prince Rupert, BC
*CHAK(AM) Inuvik, NT
CJBC(AM) Toronto, ON
CBKF-2(AM) Saskatoon, SK

870 khz
CKIR(AM) Invermere, BC
CFBV(AM) Smithers, BC
CFSX(AM) Stephenville, NF

880 khz
CHQT(AM) Edmonton, AB
CKLQ(AM) Brandon, MB

890 khz
CJDC(AM) Dawson Creek, BC

900 khz
*CKMO(AM) Victoria, BC
CKDH(AM) Amherst, NS
CHML(AM) Hamilton, ON

CKBI(AM) Prince Albert, SK

910 khz
CKDQ(AM) Drumheller, AB

920 khz
CFRY(AM) Portage la Prairie, MB
CKNX(AM) Wingham, ON

930 khz
CJCA(AM) Edmonton, AB
CFBC(AM) Saint John, NB
CJYQ(AM) Saint John's, NF

940 khz
CINW(AM) Montreal, PQ
CJGX(AM) Yorkton, SK

950 khz
CFAM(AM) Altona, MB
CKNB(AM) Campbellton, NB

960 khz
CFAC(AM) Calgary, AB

980 khz
CKNW(AM) New Westminster, BC
CFPL(AM) London, ON
CJME(AM) Regina, SK

990 khz
CBW(AM) Winnipeg, MB
*CBY(AM) Corner Brook, NF
CBOF-1(AM) Maniwaki, PQ
CKGM(AM) Montreal, PQ

1010 khz
*CBR(AM) Calgary, AB
CFRB(AM) Toronto, ON

1020 khz
CKVH(AM) High Prairie, AB

1040 khz
CKST(AM) Vancouver, BC
CJMS(AM) Saint Constant, PQ

1050 khz
*CKSB(AM) Saint Boniface, MB
CHUM(AM) Toronto, ON
CJNB(AM) North Battleford, SK

1060 khz
CKMX(AM) Calgary, AB

1070 khz
CFAX(AM) Victoria, BC
CHOK(AM) Sarnia, ON

1130 khz
CKWX(AM) Vancouver, BC

1140 khz
CHRB(AM) High River, AB
CBI(AM) Sydney, NS

1150 khz
CKFR(AM) Kelowna, BC
CKOC(AM) Hamilton, ON

1190 khz
CFSL(AM) Weyburn, SK

1200 khz
CJRJ(AM) Vancouver, BC
CFGO(AM) Ottawa, ON

1210 khz
*VOAR(AM) Mount Pearl, NF
CFYM(AM) Kindersley, SK

1220 khz
CJRB(AM) Boissevain, MB
CJUL(AM) Cornwall, ON
CHSC(AM) Saint Catharines, ON
CKSM(AM) Shawinigan, PQ

1230 khz
CFLN(AM) Goose Bay, NF
CFFB(AM) Iqaluit, NU

1240 khz
CJOR(AM) Osoyoos, BC
CFNI(AM) Port Hardy, BC
CJAR(AM) The Pas, MB
CKIM(AM) Baie Verte, NF
CJCS(AM) Stratford, ON
CJMD(AM) Chibougamau, PQ
CFLM(AM) La Tuque, PQ
CJNS(AM) Meadow Lake, SK

1250 khz
CHSM(AM) Steinbach, MB
CJYE(AM) Oakville, ON

1260 khz
CFRN(AM) Edmonton, AB
CKHJ(AM) Fredericton, NB

1270 khz
CJCB(AM) Sydney, NS
CFGT(AM) Alma, PQ

1280 khz
CFMB(AM) Montreal, PQ
CJSL(AM) Estevan, SK

1290 khz
CFRW(AM) Winnipeg, MB
CJBK(AM) London, ON

1310 khz
CHLW(AM) Saint Paul, AB
CIWW(AM) Ottawa, ON

1320 khz
CHMB(AM) Vancouver, BC
CJMR(AM) Oakville, ON

1330 khz
CJYM(AM) Rosetown, SK

1340 khz
CIBQ(AM) Brooks, AB
CFKC(AM) Creston, BC
CKCR(AM) Revelstoke, BC
CIVH(AM) Vanderhoof, BC
CFLW(AM) Wabush, NF
*CFYK(AM) Yellowknife, NT
CBGN(AM) Sainte Anne des Monts, PQ

1350 khz
CKAD(AM) Middleton, NS

1370 khz
CFOK(AM) Westlock, AB

1380 khz
CKPC(AM) Brantford, ON

1400 khz
CKSQ(AM) Stettler, AB
CKGR(AM) Golden, BC
CIOR(AM) Princeton, BC
*CBG(AM) Gander, NF

1410 khz
CFUN(AM) Vancouver, BC
CKSL(AM) London, ON

1420 khz
CKDY(AM) Digby, NS

1430 khz
CHKT(AM) Toronto, ON

1440 khz
CKJR(AM) Wetaskiwin, AB

1450 khz
CHOR(AM) Summerland, BC
CFAB(AM) Windsor, NS
*CHMO(AM) Moosonee, ON
CHOU(AM) Montreal, PQ

1460 khz
CJOY(AM) Guelph, ON

1470 khz
CJVB(AM) Richmond, BC

1490 khz
CFNC(AM) Cross Lake, MB
CJSN(AM) Shaunavon, SK

1510 khz
CKOT(AM) Tillsonburg, ON

1540 khz
CHIN(AM) Toronto, ON

1550 khz
*CBE(AM) Windsor, ON

1570 khz
CKMW(AM) Winkler-Morden, MB
CFAV(AM) Laval, PQ

1580 khz
CKDO(AM) Oshawa, ON

1610 khz
CHHA(AM) Toronto, ON
CJWI(AM) Montreal, PQ

1650 khz
CINA(AM) Mississauga, ON
CJRS(AM) Montreal, PQ

1690 khz
CHTO(AM) Toronto, ON
CJLO(AM) Montreal, PQ

Canadian FM Stations by Frequency

88.1 mhz
CKAV-FM-3 Calgary, AB
*CFRH-FM Penetanguishene, ON
CHLK-FM Perth, ON
*CKLN-FM Toronto, ON

88.3 mhz
CKXU-FM Lethbridge, AB
CJIQ-FM Kitchener/Paris, ON
*CBQT-FM Thunder Bay, ON
CKIA-FM Quebec, PQ
CFAK-FM Sherbrooke, PQ

88.5 mhz
*CJSR-FM Edmonton, AB
CIVL-FM Abbotsford, BC
CIBH-FM Parksville, BC
*CBAF-FM Moncton, NB
CKDX-FM Newmarket, ON
CILV-FM Ottawa, ON
CBME-FM Montreal, PQ

88.7 mhz
*CFUR-FM Prince George, BC
CKYM-FM Napanee, ON
CIMX-FM Windsor, ON
CHIC-FM Rouyn-Noranda, PQ

88.9 mhz
CJSI-FM Calgary, AB
*CBTK-FM Kelowna, BC
CHNI-FM Saint John, NB
CIRV-FM Toronto, ON
CJRD-FM Drummondville, PQ
CJMQ-FM Sherbrooke, PQ

89.1 mhz
CISO-FM Orillia, ON
*CHUO-FM Ottawa, ON
*CKRL-FM Quebec, PQ
CJBR-FM Rimouski, PQ
CFOU-FM Trois Rivieres, PQ

89.3 mhz
CKAV-FM-4 Edmonton, AB
CIJK-FM Kentville, NS
CKGW-FM Chatham, ON
*CISM-FM Montreal, PQ

89.5 mhz
CHWK-FM Chilliwack, BC
CJSE-FM Shediac, NB
*CFGB-FM Happy Valley, NF
CJRL-FM Kenora, ON
*CIUT-FM Toronto, ON

89.7 mhz
CBCX-FM Calgary, AB
CJSU-FM Duncan, BC
CKOA-FM Glace Bay, NS
CKGN-FM Kapuskasing, ON

89.9 mhz
CBTE-FM Crawford Bay, BC
CHNS-FM Halifax, NS
CIHT-FM Ottawa, ON
CKWT-FM Sioux Lookout, ON
*CBE-FM Windsor, ON
CFBS-FM Lourdes-de-Blanc-Sablon, PQ
CJCF-FM Cumberland House, SK
CJLR-FM La Ronge, SK
CFNK-FM Pinehouse Lake, SK

90.1 mhz
*CJSF-FM Burnaby, BC
CJMP-FM Powell River, BC
CHMZ-FM Tofino, BC
*CFJU-FM Kedgwick, NB
CBBS-FM Sudbury, ON

90.3 mhz
CFUL-FM Calgary, AB
CBEG-FM Sarnia, ON
CJBC-FM Toronto, ON

*CKUT-FM Montreal, PQ

90.5 mhz
*CBCV-FM Victoria, BC
*CJPN-FM Fredericton, NB
CBHA-FM Halifax, NS
CKKK-FM Peterborough, ON
CKBN-FM Becancour and Nicolet, PQ
CJBE-FM Port-Menier, PQ
CFCR-FM Saskatoon, SK

90.7 mhz
CFBO-FM Moncton, NB
*CBOF-FM Ottawa, ON

90.9 mhz
*CJSW-FM Calgary, AB
CBX-FM Edmonton, AB
CBUX-FM Vancouver, BC
CBBX-FM Sudbury, ON
*CION-FM Quebec, PQ

91.1 mhz
CKOS-FM Fort McMurray, AB
CKXL-FM Saint Boniface, MB
*CINN-FM Hearst, ON
*CJRT-FM Toronto, ON
CFUT-FM Shawinigan, PQ

91.3 mhz
CJZN-FM Victoria, BC
CBD-FM Saint John, NB
CJLX-FM Belleville, ON
CFBW-FM Hanover, ON
CIRA-FM Montreal, PQ
*CJTR-FM Regina, SK

91.5 mhz
CBYG-FM Prince George, BC
CKXR-FM Salmon Arm, BC
CBAX-FM Halifax, NS
CKBT-FM Kitchener-Waterloo, ON
*CBO-FM Ottawa, ON
CKPR-FM Thunder Bay, ON

91.7 mhz
CHBN-FM Edmonton, AB
CKAY-FM Sechelt, BC
CICS-FM Sudbury, ON
CIXL-FM Welland, ON

91.9 mhz
CKNI-FM Moncton, NB
*CKVI-FM Kingston, ON
CKLY-FM Lindsay (city of Kawartha Lakes), ON
CKLX-FM Montreal, PQ
CJEC-FM Quebec, PQ

92.1 mhz
CJAY-FM Calgary, AB
CFAD-FM Salmo, BC
CFNR-FM Terrace, BC
CITI-FM Winnipeg, MB
CJOZ-FM Bonavista Bay, NF
CKPC-FM Brantford, ON
CHOD-FM Cornwall, ON
CJAI-FM Stella, ON
CJQQ-FM Timmins, ON
CJDM-FM Drummondville, PQ
CFVD-FM-2 Pohenegamook, PQ
CHMX-FM Regina, SK

92.3 mhz
CFRK-FM Fredericton, NB
CKOZ-FM Corner Brook, NF
CJET-FM Smiths Falls, ON

92.5 mhz
CKNG-FM Edmonton, AB
CFBX-FM Kamloops, BC
CKIS-FM Toronto, ON
CKAJ-FM Jonquiere, PQ
CFQR-FM Montreal, PQ

92.7 mhz
CIAM-FM Fort Vermilion, AB
CHSL-FM Slave Lake, AB
CJEM-FM Edmundston, NB
CKDR-FM Dryden, ON
CJSP-FM Leamington, ON
CJBX-FM London, ON
CFFF-FM Peterborough, ON
CJRQ-FM Sudbury, ON
CFIM-FM Iles-de-la-Madeleine, PQ
CJSQ-FM Quebec, PQ
CHBD-FM Regina, SK

92.9 mhz
CFEX-FM Calgary, AB
CIBW-FM Drayton Valley, AB
CKIC-FM Winnipeg, MB
CKLE-FM Bathurst, NB
CFLT-FM Dartmouth, NS
CFSH-FM Apsley, ON
CKJN-FM Haldimand County, ON
CHYK-FM-3 Hearst, ON
CBBK-FM Kingston, ON
CKBL-FM Saskatoon, SK

93.1 mhz
CJXX-FM Grande Prairie, AB
CFIS-FM Prince George, BC
CKYE-FM Vancouver, BC
CFRY-FM Portage la Prairie, MB
CKBW-FM-2 Shelburne, NS
CHAY-FM Barrie, ON
CFOB-FM Fort Frances, ON
CFNO-FM Marathon, ON
CKCU-FM Ottawa, ON
CHMT-FM Timmins, ON
CHLQ-FM Charlottetown, PE
CJTB-FM Tete-a-la-Baleine, PQ
CKVM-FM Ville-Marie, PQ
CFRG-FM Gravelbourg, SK

93.3 mhz
CJOK-FM Fort McMurray, AB
CJBZ-FM Taber, AB
CJAV-FM Port Alberni, BC
CFXU-FM Antigonish, NS
CKSG-FM Cobourg, ON
*CFRU-FM Guelph, ON
*CFMU-FM Hamilton, ON
CJMF-FM Quebec, PQ
CFYX-FM Rimouski, PQ
CJHD-FM North Battleford, SK

93.5 mhz
CIHS-FM Wetaskiwin, AB
*CJLY-FM Nelson, BC
CKZX-FM New Denver, BC
CJEL-FM Winkler, MB
CIKX-FM Grand Falls, NB
CKUM-FM Moncton, NB
*CHMR-FM Saint John's, NF
CJLS-FM-2 New Tusket, NS
CFZN-FM Haliburton, ON
CKXC-FM Kingston, ON
CBCL-FM London, ON
CIGM-FM Sudbury, ON
CFXJ-FM Toronto, ON
CKXO-FM Chibougamau, PQ
CBM-FM Montreal, PQ
CJAS-FM Saint Augustin, PQ

93.7 mhz
CJLT-FM Medicine Hat, AB
CKWY-FM Wainwright, AB
CJJR-FM Vancouver, BC
CKMA-FM Miramichi, NB
CIFX-FM Lewisporte, NF
CKOL-FM Campbellford, ON
CKYC-FM Owen Sound, ON
CBMI-FM Baie Comeau, PQ
CBJ-FM Chicoutimi, PQ
CFGE-FM Sherbrooke, PQ

93.9 mhz
CJLU-FM Halifax, NS
CFWC-FM Brantford, ON
CKKL-FM Ottawa, ON
CIDR-FM Windsor, ON

94.1 mhz
CKBA-FM Athabasca, AB
CJUV-FM Lacombe, AB
CJOC-FM Lethbridge, AB
CHSJ-FM Saint John, NB
CICU-FM Eskasoni Indian Reserve, NS
CKEC-FM New Glasgow, NS
CKNR-FM Elliot Lake, ON
CBL-FM Toronto, ON
CKCN-FM Sept-Iles, PQ
CIMG-FM Swift Current, SK
CFGW-FM Yorkton, SK

94.3 mhz
CFXE-FM Edson, AB
CIRX-FM Prince George, BC
CHIQ-FM Winnipeg, MB
CKSY-FM Chatham, ON
CJTW-FM Kitchener-Waterloo, ON
CJSD-FM Thunder Bay, ON
CJFH-FM Woodstock, ON
CKMF-FM Montreal, PQ
*CHYZ-FM Sainte Foy, PQ

94.5 mhz
CHAT-FM Medicine Hat, AB
CHBW-FM Rocky Mountain House, AB
CHET-FM Chetwynd, BC
CFBT-FM Vancouver, BC
CKCW-FM Moncton, NB
CKBW-FM-1 Liverpool, NS
CIBU-FM Wingham, ON
CJRG-FM Gaspe, PQ
CJAB-FM Saguenay, PQ
CKCK-FM Regina, SK

94.7 mhz
CHKF-FM Calgary, AB
CKLF-FM Brandon, MB
CHOZ-FM Saint John's, NF
CFAO-FM Alliston, ON
CIWV-FM Hamilton, ON
CJDS-FM Saint Pamphile, PQ
CHEY-FM Trois Rivieres, PQ
CJNE-FM Nipawin, SK

94.9 mhz
CJPR-FM Blairmore, AB
*CKUA-FM Edmonton, AB
CKWM-FM Kentville, NS
CKPE-FM Sydney, NS
*CHRW-FM London, ON
CKGE-FM Oshawa, ON
CIEU-FM Carleton, PQ
CIMF-FM Gatineau, PQ
CHME-FM Les Escoumins, PQ

95.1 mhz
CHVN-FM Winnipeg, MB
CKMV-FM Grand Falls, NB
CKUE-FM Chatham, ON
CKCB-FM Collingwood, ON
*CJOA-FM Thunder Bay, ON
CFCY-FM Charlottetown, PE
CILE-FM Havre-Saint-Pierre, PQ
CBF-FM Montreal, PQ
CFMC-FM Saskatoon, SK

95.3 mhz
CJXK-FM Cold Lake, AB
CKZZ-FM Vancouver, BC
CING-FM Hamilton, ON
CHUT-FM Lac-Simon (Louvicourt), PQ
CHOE-FM Matane, PQ
*CBVX-FM Quebec, PQ
CHXL-FM Okanese Indian Reserve, SK

95.5 mhz
CHLB-FM Lethbridge, AB
CKGY-FM Red Deer, AB
CBA-FM Moncton, NB
CJLS-FM Yarmouth, NS
CJOJ-FM Belleville, ON
CIYN-FM Kincardine, ON
CJTK-FM Sudbury, ON
CFVD-FM Degelis, PQ
CFLX-FM Sherbrooke, PQ

95.7 mhz
*CKRP-FM Falher, AB
CFPW-FM Powell River, BC
CJAT-FM Trail, BC
CKTP-FM Fredericton Centre, NB
CHBI-FM Burnt Islands, NF
CJNI-FM Halifax, NS
CFJB-FM Barrie, ON
CKAV-FM-9 Ottawa, ON
CBQS-FM Sioux Narrows, ON
CKYK-FM Alma, PQ
CKYQ-FM Plessisville, PQ

95.9 mhz
CHFM-FM Calgary, AB
CKSA-FM Lloydminster, AB
*CKUW-FM Winnipeg, MB
CHOS-FM Rattling Brook, NF
CJKX-FM Ajax, ON
CFPL-FM London, ON
CJFM-FM Montreal, PQ

96.1 mhz
CFMY-FM Medicine Hat, AB
CHKG-FM Vancouver, BC
CKX-FM Brandon, MB
CINB-FM Saint John, NB
CHMY-FM Renfrew, ON
*CBCT-FM Charlottetown, PE

96.3 mhz
CKRA-FM Edmonton, AB
CJGY-FM Grande Prairie, AB
CKKO-FM Kelowna, BC
CINC-FM Thompson, MB
CBDQ-FM Labrador City, NF
CIOZ-FM Marystown, NF
CJLS-FM-1 Barrington, NS
CFMK-FM Kingston, ON
CFMZ-FM Toronto, ON
CFMV-FM Chandler, PQ
CIHO-FM Saint Hilarion, PQ
CFWD-FM Saskatoon, SK

96.5 mhz
CKLJ-FM Olds, AB
CJPG-FM Portage la Prairie, MB
CIXN-FM Fredericton, NB
CKUL-FM Halifax, NS
CJTL-FM Pickle Lake, ON
CFTX-FM Gatineau, PQ
CKMN-FM Rimouski-Mont Joli, PQ
CHOA-FM Rouyn-Noranda, PQ

96.7 mhz
CFXW-FM Whitecourt, AB
CKGF-FM-2 Greenwood, BC
CILT-FM Steinbach, MB
CHYM-FM Kitchener, ON
CHYR-FM Leamington, ON
CHVR-FM Pembroke, ON
*CKLU-FM Sudbury, ON

96.9 mhz
CJAQ-FM Calgary, AB
CKLG-FM Vancouver, BC
CJXL-FM Moncton, NB
CKSS-FM Red Rocks, NF
CKHC-FM Toronto, ON
CFIX-FM Chicoutimi, PQ
CKOI-FM Verdun, PQ
*CBK-FM Regina, SK

97.1 mhz
CJMG-FM Penticton, BC
CKRO-FM Pokemouche, NB
CIGL-FM Belleville, ON
CKDR-FM-5 Red Lake, ON
CKDR-FM-2 Sioux Lookout, ON
CHLC-FM Baie Comeau, PQ
CHLX-FM Gatineau, PQ
CKFI-FM Swift Current, SK

97.3 mhz
CIRK-FM Edmonton, AB
CKLR-FM Courtenay, BC
CJCI-FM Prince George, BC
CHWV-FM Saint John, NB
CJRM-FM Labrador City, NF
CKON-FM Akwesasne, ON
*CJIV-FM Dryden, ON
CJEZ-FM Toronto, ON
CKUJ-FM Kuujjuaq, PQ
CHGA-FM Maniwaki, PQ
CFJO-FM Thetford Mines, PQ

97.5 mhz
CFXH-FM Hinton, AB
CKRV-FM Kamloops, BC
CFFM-FM Williams Lake, BC
CJKR-FM Winnipeg, MB
VOCM-FM Saint John's, NF
*CKDU-FM Halifax, NS
CIQM-FM London, ON
CHOX-FM La Pocatiere, PQ

97.7 mhz
CIGY-FM Calgary, AB
CFGP-FM Grande Prairie, AB
CHDH-FM Siksika, AB
CIDO-FM Creston, BC
CKTK-FM Kitimat, BC
CBUF-FM Vancouver, BC
CFCV-FM Saint Andrews, NF
CKEN-FM Kentville, NS
CHMS-FM Bancroft, ON
CHTZ-FM Saint Catharines, ON
CHGB-FM Wasaga Beach, ON
*CFTH-FM-1 Harrington Harbour, PQ
CHOM-FM Montreal, PQ
CBKF-FM Regina, SK
CIDD-FM White Bear Lake Resort, SK

97.9 mhz
CKYX-FM Fort McMurray, AB
CHSR-FM Fredericton, NB
CFLC-FM Churchill Falls, NF
CJLL-FM Ottawa, ON
CFPS-FM Port Elgin, ON
CJRE-FM Riviere au Renard, PQ
CJCQ-FM North Battleford, SK

98.1 mhz
CFCW-FM Camrose, AB
CKVN-FM Lethbridge, AB
CHTD-FM Saint Stephen, NB
CKBW-FM Bridgewater, NS
CHPB-FM Cochrane, ON
*CBON-FM Sudbury, ON
CHFI-FM Toronto, ON
CHOI-FM Quebec, PQ
*CBSI-FM Sept-Iles, PQ
CFMQ-FM Hudson Bay, SK
CHON-FM Whitehorse, YT

98.3 mhz
CKSR-FM Chilliwack, BC
CIFM-FM Kamloops, BC
CFPX-FM Pukatawagan, MB
CBW-FM Winnipeg, MB
*CBAL-FM Moncton, NB
CHER-FM Sydney, NS
CFLY-FM Kingston, ON
CFWP-FM Wahta Mohawk Territory
   near Bala, ON
CHUN-FM Rouyn-Noranda, PQ
CKRS-FM Sagueñay, PQ
CIAX-FM Windsor, PQ
CJMK-FM Saskatoon, SK

98.5 mhz
CIBK-FM Calgary, AB
CFWE-FM-4 Edmonton, AB
CHRX-FM Fort St. John, BC
CIOC-FM Victoria, BC
CIOS-FM Stephenville, NF
CKRH-FM Halifax, NS
CKWR-FM Kitchener, ON
CJWL-FM Ottawa, ON
CFTH-FM-2 La Tabatiere, PQ
CHMP-FM Longueuil, PQ

98.7 mhz
CKXD-FM Gander, NF
CBQX-FM Kenora, ON
CJHR-FM Renfrew, ON
CIKI-FM Rimouski, PQ

98.9 mhz
CIKT-FM Grande Prairie, AB
CIZZ-FM Red Deer, AB
CFCP-FM Courtenay, BC
CFPV-FM Pemberton, BC
CJYC-FM Saint John, NB
CJFX-FM Antigonish, NS
CKLC-FM Kingston, ON
CHCD-FM Simcoe, ON
CHYC-FM Sudbury, ON
CHIK-FM Quebec, PQ
CIZL-FM Regina, SK

99.1 mhz
CJDR-FM Fernie, BC
CJGV-FM Winnipeg, MB
CKIX-FM Saint John's, NF
CHRI-FM Ottawa, ON
CBLA-FM Toronto, ON
*CJAM-FM Windsor, ON
CIDI-FM Lac-Brome, PQ
CIPC-FM Port-Cartier, PQ
CJMM-FM Rouyn-Noranda, PQ
CFNJ-FM Saint Gabriel-de-Brandon,
   PQ
CFMM-FM Prince Albert, SK

99.3 mhz
CHMC-FM Edmonton, AB
CKQR-FM Castlegar, BC
CKDV-FM Prince George, BC
CFOX-FM Vancouver, BC
CFAN-FM Miramichi City, NB
CHSB-FM Bedford, NS
CKQN-FM Baker Lake, NU
CJJM-FM Espanola, ON
CJBC-FM-4 London, ON
CFSF-FM Sturgeon Falls, ON
CKGB-FM Timmins, ON
CJAN-FM Asbestos, PQ
*CBV-FM-6 La Malbaie, PQ
CFOR-FM Maniwaki, PQ

99.5 mhz
CHOO-FM Drumheller, AB
CIMM-FM Ucluelet, BC
CBZF-FM Fredericton, NB
CKTY-FM Truro, NS
CFBG-FM Bracebridge, ON
CKKW-FM Kitchener, ON
CJPX-FM Montreal, PQ
CHRL-FM Roberval, PQ

99.7 mhz
CFNA-FM Bonnyville, AB
CFXO-FM High River-Okotoks, AB
CIQC-FM Campbell River, BC
CKPT-FM Peterborough, ON
CHJM-FM Saint Georges, PQ

99.9 mhz
CHSU-FM Kelowna, BC
CHPQ-FM Parksville, BC
CFWM-FM Winnipeg, MB
CHOY-FM Moncton, NB
CJIJ-FM Sydney, NS
CKIQ-FM Iqaluit, NU
CFGX-FM Sarnia, ON
*CBCS-FM Sudbury, ON
CJUK-FM Thunder Bay, ON
CKFM-FM Toronto, ON

CFVM-FM Amqui, PQ
CHEF-FM Matagami, PQ

100.1 mhz
CKFU-FM Fort St. John, BC
CKBZ-FM Kamloops, BC
CIOO-FM Halifax, NS
CJCD-FM-1 Hay River, NT
CJCD-FM Yellowknife, NT
CHCQ-FM Belleville, ON
CHFN-FM Cape Croker
   (Neyaashiinigmiing), ON
CKVL-FM Montreal (zone LaSalle), PQ
CKAG-FM Pikogan, PQ
CJEB-FM Trois Rivieres, PQ
CJVD-FM Vaudreuil-Dorion, PQ

100.3 mhz
CFBR-FM Edmonton, AB
CKCQ-FM Quesnel, BC
CKKQ-FM Victoria, BC
CFOZ-FM Argentia, NF
CJLF-FM Barrie, ON
*CKRZ-FM Ohsweken, ON
CJMJ-FM Ottawa, ON
*CKMS-FM Waterloo, ON
CHTN-FM Charlottetown, PE
CHVD-FM Dolbeau-Mistassini, PQ
CJMC-FM Sainte Anne des Monts, PQ
CFAQ-FM Blucher, SK

100.5 mhz
CHFT-FM Fort McMurray, AB
CFSR-FM Hope, BC
CHLS-FM Lillooet, BC
CKPK-FM Vancouver, BC
CIOK-FM Saint John, NB
CBBL-FM London, ON
CHUR-FM North Bay, ON
CKRU-FM Peterborough, ON
CHAS-FM Sault Ste. Marie, ON
*CFIN-FM Lac-Etchemin, PQ
CIBO-FM Senneterre, PQ
CJJC-FM Yorkton, SK

100.7 mhz
CIGV-FM Penticton, BC
CIAJ-FM Prince Rupert, BC
CHNK-FM Winnipeg, MB
CFRM-FM Little Current, ON
CHIN-FM Toronto, ON
CBFX-FM Montreal, PQ
CILG-FM Moose Jaw, SK
CIAY-FM Whitehorse, YT

100.9 mhz
CKUV-FM High River-Okotoks, AB
*CBWK-FM Thompson, MB
CKTO-FM Truro, NS
CKHA-FM Haliburton, ON
CKAP-FM Kapuskasing, ON
*CBJX-FM Chicoutimi, PQ
CHXX-FM Donnacona, PQ

101.1 mhz
CIXF-FM Brooks, AB
CKMQ-FM Merritt, BC
CFMI-FM New Westminster, BC
CHLI-FM Rossland, BC
CKXA-FM Brandon, MB
CFAI-FM Edmundston, NB
CKSJ-FM Saint John's, NF
CIQB-FM Barrie, ON
CKEY-FM Fort Erie, ON
CFIF-FM Iroquois Falls, ON
CKBY-FM Smiths Falls, ON
CKSO-FM Sudbury, ON

101.3 mhz
CJEG-FM Bonnyville, AB
CKIK-FM Red Deer, AB
CKKN-FM Prince George, BC
CJCH-FM Halifax, NS
CKUN-FM Christian Island, ON
CKOT-FM Tillsonburg, ON
CJSA-FM Toronto, ON
CKII-FM Dolbeau-Mistassini, PQ

101.5 mhz
CKCE-FM Calgary, AB
CKNL-FM Fort St. John, BC
CILK-FM Kelowna, BC
CJUM-FM Winnipeg, MB
*CBZ-FM Fredericton, NB
CIGO-FM Port Hawkesbury, NS
CHES-FM Erin, ON
*CIOI-FM Hamilton, ON
CJKL-FM Kirkland Lake, ON
CKWF-FM Peterborough, ON
*CIBL-FM Montreal, PQ
*CBRX-FM Rimouski, PQ
CHEQ-FM Sainte-Marie-de-Beauce,
   PQ
CHQX-FM Prince Albert, SK

101.7 mhz
CKER-FM Edmonton, AB
CHLY-FM Nanaimo, BC
*CBQ-FM Thunder Bay, ON
CKNX-FM Wingham, ON
CHIP-FM Fort Coulonge, PQ
CHRG-FM Maria (Reserve), PQ
CJSO-FM Sorel, PQ

101.9 mhz
*CITR-FM Vancouver, BC
*CFUV-FM Victoria, BC
CHFX-FM Halifax, NS
CHRK-FM Sydney, NS
CKLB-FM Yellowknife, NT
CJSS-FM Cornwall, ON
*CFRC-FM Kingston, ON
CKFX-FM North Bay, ON
CHAI-FM Chateauguay, PQ
CFND-FM Saint Jerome, PQ
CFDA-FM Victoriaville, PQ

102.1 mhz
*CBR-FM Calgary, AB
CKHL-FM High Level, AB
CJCY-FM Medicine Hat, AB
CISW-FM Whistler, BC
CHPR-FM Hawkesbury, ON
CFNY-FM Toronto, ON
CJRW-FM Summerside, PE
CBGA-FM Matane, PQ
CFEL-FM Montmagny, PQ
CJDJ-FM Saskatoon, SK

102.3 mhz
CKRX-FM Fort Nelson, BC
CKWV-FM Nanaimo, BC
CKY-FM Winnipeg, MB
CKXG-FM Grand Falls-Windsor, NF
CKJJ-FM Belleville, ON
CHST-FM London, ON
*CHIM-FM Timmins, ON
CINQ-FM Montreal, PQ
CIGB-FM Trois Rivieres, PQ
CHSN-FM Estevan, SK
CJNS-FM Meadow Lake, SK

102.5 mhz
*CBOX-FM Ottawa, ON

102.7 mhz
*CFRO-FM Vancouver, BC
*CBH-FM Halifax, NS
CFGI-FM Georgina Island, ON
*CHOP-FM Newmarket, ON
CILU-FM Thunder Bay, ON
CIWS-FM Whitchurch-Stouffville, ON
CBJE-FM Chicoutimi, PQ
CITE-FM-1 Sherbrooke, PQ
CJMV-FM Val d'Or, PQ
CKZP-FM Zenon Park, SK

102.9 mhz
CHDI-FM Edmonton, AB
CHDR-FM Cranbrook, BC
CKLH-FM Hamilton, ON
CHCR-FM Killaloe, ON
CFOM-FM Levis, PQ

103.1 mhz
CFXL-FM Calgary, AB
CJKC-FM Kamloops, BC

CKOV-FM Kelowna, BC
CJFW-FM Terrace, BC
CHTT-FM Victoria, BC
CKMM-FM Winnipeg, MB
CJMO-FM Moncton, NB
CFMX-FM Cobourg, ON
CJBB-FM Englehart, ON
CFHK-FM St. Thomas, ON
CFMF-FM Fermont, PQ
CHHO-FM Louiseville, PQ
CIAU-FM Radisson, PQ
CKOD-FM Valleyfield, PQ

103.3 mhz
*CBOQ-FM Ottawa, ON
CKLP-FM Parry Sound, ON
CKCI-FM Sarnia, ON
CKQV-FM Vermillion Bay, ON
CHAA-FM Longueuil, PQ

103.5 mhz
CFCH-FM Chase, BC
CHMM-FM MacKenzie, BC
CHNV-FM Nelson, BC
CHQM-FM Vancouver, BC
CJRP-FM Saint John, NB
CKHZ-FM Halifax, NS
CKCH-FM Sydney, NS
CIVR-FM Yellowknife, NT
CIDC-FM Orangeville, ON
CJLM-FM Joliette, PQ
CKRB-FM Saint Georges-de-Beauce,
   PQ
CKRC-FM Weyburn, SK

103.7 mhz
CBRF-FM Calgary, AB
CFVR-FM Fort McMurray, AB
CJPT-FM Brockville, ON
CFBU-FM Saint Catharines, ON
CFID-FM Acton Vale, PQ
CIMI-FM Charlesbourg, PQ
*CKRK-FM Kahnawake, PQ
CIEL-FM Riviere du Loup, PQ

103.9 mhz
CISN-FM Edmonton, AB
CJUI-FM Kelowna, BC
CIMS-FM Balmoral, NB
CFQM-FM Moncton, NB
CHVO-FM Carbonear, NF
CKXX-FM Corner Brook, NF
CHNO-FM Sudbury, ON
CIRR-FM Toronto, ON
CKDK-FM Woodstock, ON
CKWE-FM Maniwaki (Kitigan Zibi
   Anishinabeg Reserve), PQ
CIME-FM Saint Jerome, PQ
CJAW-FM Moose Jaw, SK

104.1 mhz
CHAD-FM Dawson Creek, BC
CFQX-FM Selkirk, MB
CJCJ-FM Woodstock, NB
*CIFA-FM Comeauville, NS
CICZ-FM Midland, ON
CHYK-FM Timmins, ON
CKTF-FM Gatineau, PQ
CKNA-FM Natashquan, PQ
CFZZ-FM Saint Jean-Iberville, PQ
CIOT-FM Nipawin, SK

104.3 mhz
CHHR-FM Vancouver, BC
CFRQ-FM Dartmouth, NS
CFFX-FM Kingston, ON
CJQM-FM Sault Ste. Marie, ON
CBF-FM-1 Trois Rivieres, PQ
CHGO-FM Val d'Or, PQ

104.5 mhz
CKJX-FM Olds, AB
CISP-FM Pemberton, BC
CJSB-FM Swan River, MB
CJRI-FM Fredericton, NB
CFLG-FM Cornwall, ON
CFQK-FM Kaministiquia, ON
CJTT-FM New Liskeard, ON
CHUM-FM Toronto, ON

CKAU-FM Maliotenam, PQ
CKOY-FM Sherbrooke, PQ

104.7 mhz
CFRI-FM Grande Prairie, AB
CHBZ-FM Cranbrook, BC
CKLZ-FM Kelowna, BC
CIPN-FM Pender Harbour, BC
CKKS-FM Sechelt, BC
CJNU-FM Winnipeg, MB
CFDY-FM Cochrane, ON
CIHR-FM Woodstock, ON
CJRC-FM Gatineau, PQ
CFLO-FM Mont-Laurier, PQ
CBVE-FM Quebec, PQ

104.9 mhz
CFMG-FM Saint Albert, AB
CKBC-FM Bathurst, NB
CFJR-FM Brockville, ON
CHWC-FM Goderich, ON
CIMY-FM Pembroke, ON
CBQL-FM Savant Lake, ON
CFXM-FM Granby, PQ
CJLA-FM Lachute, PQ
*CHOC-FM Saint Remi, PQ
CKVX-FM Kindersley, SK
CFWF-FM Regina, SK

105.1 mhz
CKRY-FM Calgary, AB
CITA-FM Moncton, NB
CBI-FM Sydney, NS
CBQR-FM Rankin Inlet, NU

CFLZ-FM Niagara Falls, ON
CKQM-FM Peterborough, ON
CHOQ-FM Toronto, ON
CBMR-FM Fermont, PQ
CFIC-FM Listuguj, PQ
CKDG-FM Montreal, PQ
CJVR-FM Melfort, SK

105.3 mhz
CKMH-FM Medicine Hat, AB
CIXM-FM Whitecourt, AB
CFXY-FM Fredericton, NB
CJKK-FM Clarenville, NF
CFCA-FM Kitchener, ON
CISS-FM Ottawa, ON
CJMX-FM Sudbury, ON
CKTG-FM Thunder Bay, ON
CHOW-FM Amos, PQ
CHRD-FM Drummondville, PQ
CHRM-FM Matane, PQ

105.5 mhz
CHUB-FM Red Deer, AB
CICY-FM Selkirk, MB
CJFB-FM Bolton, ON
CFBK-FM Huntsville, ON
CHRY-FM Toronto, ON
CKQK-FM Charlottetown, PE
CKGS-FM Saguenay (zone La Baie), PQ
CKLD-FM Thetford Mines, PQ
*CBKS-FM Saskatoon, SK

105.7 mhz
CBU-FM Vancouver, BC
CICF-FM Vernon, BC
CHQC-FM Saint John, NB
CIKR-FM Kingston, ON
CHRE-FM Saint Catharines, ON
CJMI-FM Strathroy, ON
CFGL-FM Laval, PQ
CFDM-FM Meadow Lake, SK

105.9 mhz
CJRY-FM Edmonton, AB
*CFEP-FM Eastern Passage, NS
CHPD-FM Aylmer, ON
CHJX-FM London, ON
CICX-FM Orillia, ON
*CBKA-FM La Ronge, SK

106.1 mhz
CFIT-FM Airdrie, AB
CKLM-FM Lloydminster, AB
CKKX-FM Peace River, AB
CKGO-FM-1 Boston Bar, BC
CBAM-FM Moncton, NB
*CKJM-FM Cheticamp, NS
CIMJ-FM Guelph, ON
CHEZ-FM Ottawa, ON
CIMO-FM Magog, PQ

106.3 mhz
CKAV-FM-2 Vancouver, BC
CINU-FM Truro, NS
CFXN-FM North Bay, ON
CHKS-FM Sarnia, ON
*CBV-FM Quebec, PQ

106.5 mhz
CHMN-FM Canmore, AB
CJJJ-FM Brandon, MB
CIXK-FM Owen Sound, ON
CKAV-FM Toronto, ON
CFEI-FM Saint Hyacinthe, PQ

106.7 mhz
CJRX-FM Lethbridge, AB
CFDV-FM Red Deer, AB
CIKZ-FM Kitchener-Waterloo, ON
CJIT-FM Lac Megantic, PQ
CFET-FM Tagish, YT

106.9 mhz
CHWF-FM Nanaimo, BC
CKKC-FM Nelson, BC
CIBX-FM Fredericton, NB
*CHMA-FM Sackville, NB
*CBN-FM Saint John's, NF
*CIXX-FM London, ON
CKQB-FM Ottawa, ON
CHRQ-FM Restigouche, PQ
CHLN-FM Trois Rivieres, PQ
CFYT-FM Dawson City, YT

107.1 mhz
CKQC-FM Abbotsford, BC
CISQ-FM Squamish, BC
CFEQ-FM Winnipeg, MB
CILQ-FM North York, ON
CJTN-FM Quinte West, ON
CJWA-FM Wawa, ON
CHNC-FM New Carlisle, PQ
CIBM-FM Riviere du Loup, PQ

107.3 mhz
CFGQ-FM Calgary, AB
CHBE-FM Victoria, BC
CKOE-FM Moncton, NB
CFMH-FM Saint John, NB
CKHR-FM Hay River, NT
CFRT-FM Iqaluit, NU
CJDL-FM Tillsonburg, ON
CHUK-FM Mashteuiatsh (Pointe-Bleue), PQ
CITE-FM Montreal, PQ

107.5 mhz
CKCL-FM Chilliwack, BC
CIEG-FM Egmont, BC
CISC-FM Gibsons, BC
CKIZ-FM Vernon, BC
CKMB-FM Barrie, ON
CJDV-FM Cambridge, ON
CITF-FM Quebec, PQ

107.7 mhz
CFRV-FM Lethbridge, AB
CJFY-FM Blackville, NB
CKHK-FM Hawkesbury, ON
CKTI-FM Kettle Point, ON
CHGK-FM Stratford, ON
CHLT-FM Sherbrooke, PQ

107.9 mhz
CFML-FM Burnaby, BC
CILS-FM Victoria, BC
CJXY-FM Burlington, ON
CHUC-FM Cobourg, ON
*CKDJ-FM Ottawa, ON

Radio Formats Defined

AAA (or Triple A)—Adult Album Alternative. Eclectic choice of music ranging from hard rock to folk music.

Adult Contemporary—Recent popular songs, with a few oldies. The songs tend to be upbeat and soft. News and talk segments are prominent during rush hour "drive times." Also known as **Light Rock**.

Agriculture & Farm—News, weather and features of interest to farmers and others involved in agriculture.

Albanian.

Album-Oriented Rock—Popular rock music from past and present rock albums. Also see **Rock/AOR**.

Alternative—Rock music first popularized in the late 80s and early 90s. Also known as **Progressive**.

American Indian—Programming for North American Indians; includes native language (i.e. Navajo) broadcasts.

Arabic.

Armenian.

Beautiful Music—Uninterrupted, instrumental soft music. There is usually very little talk and few commercials. Also known as **Easy Listening**.

Big Band—Popular music from the 30s and 40s. Primarily instrumental works by bands such as Glen Miller's Orchestra and Tommy Dorsey. Also see **Nostalgia**.

Black—Music, talk and news targeted at Black listeners. Music at these stations is similar to **Urban Contemporary** stations, but this format caters more directly to the interests and tastes of Black audiences.

Bluegrass—Related formats are **Country** and **Folk**.

Blues—Some **Jazz** and **Progressive** stations also program blues music.

Children—Programming for children, usually for educational purposes. Includes music, informational programming, and news presented for young people.

Chinese.

Christian.

Classic Rock—Popular rock music of the 60s, 70s and 80s. Also see **Rock/AOR**.

Classical—Classical music, often long pieces played without interruption. Announcers provide extended commentary and criticism on the pieces. Special features, such as live concerts, are common. Primarily a noncommercial FM format.

Comedy—Recorded stand-up comics and/or old radio comedy series. A rare format.

Contemporary Hit/Top-40—Current hot selling records. Usually a playlist of 20 to 40 songs continuously played throughout the day. DJs are often upbeat "personalities." News and information are given light coverage.

Country—Country music, ranging from older traditional country and western to today's "Hit Country" sounds. The amount of news and talk on country stations varies widely from station to station.

Croatian.

Czech.

Disco—High-energy dance music first popular in the 70s. Also see **Black** and **Urban Contemporary**.

Discussion.

Diversified—See **Variety/Diverse**.

Drama/Literature—Dramatic readings, poetry, and broadcasts of live dramatic performances. A rare format in the U.S. and Canada.

Easy Listening—Similar to **Beautiful Music**, but may include some soft rock.

Educational—Informative and instructional programming, such as over-the-air college courses. Primarily a noncommercial format.

Eskimo.

Ethnic—Programming for ethnic minorities, mostly in foreign languages.

Farsi.

Filipino.

Finnish.

Folk—Played full-time on very few stations, American folk music is also heard on noncommercial **Variety** stations. Also see **Bluegrass**.

Foreign Language/Ethnic—In addition to the specific language categories (i.e. French, German), this format denotes multilingual stations and others catering to ethnic minorities.

French.

Full Service—Mixture of music, news and talk with a general target audience.

German.

Golden Oldies—Hit songs of the 50s. Also see **Oldies**.

Gospel—Especially popular in the South, evangelical music is programmed on many **Religious** format stations.

Greek.

Hardcore.

Hebrew.

Hindi.

Hungarian.

Inspirational.

Irish.

Italian.

Japanese.

Jazz—Primarily a noncommercial FM format. Some Classical stations program jazz music features.

Jewish.

Korean.

Light Rock—See **Adult Contemporary**.

Lithuanian.

MOR (Middle-of-the-Road)—Traditional AM format featuring a balanced mix of music, news and talk. Songs are usually popular standards. Announcers are often personalities who try to keep the listener interested and informed. News, both local and national, plays an important role at most MOR stations; coverage of sporting events and other features of interest to the community is common.

Native American.

New Age—Soft "fusion" (a form mixing elements of jazz and rock), often played as background entertainment. As the name implies, this format is a recent development.

New Wave—A type of rock music which gained popularity in the early 80s, often performed by United Kingdom musicians.

News—Continous coverage of local, national and international news, including sports, weather forecasts and features.

News/Talk—Combination of news and talk formats. One of these elements may receive more emphasis. Also see **News** and **Talk**.

Nostalgia—Popular tunes from the 30s, 40s and 50s. Nostalgia stations often feature on-air personalities, and usually have heavy news and information coverage.

Oldies—Hit songs from the 50s, 60s and 70s. Usually played by upbeat DJs, with news, talk and special features (chart countdowns, trivia contests, etc.) playing an important role.

Other—Programming which falls outside the categories listed here.

Polish.

Polka—Music for the traditional dance. Most polka format stations are located in Wisconsin.

Portuguese.

Progressive—Progressive stations play many types of music, often including avant-garde music not played on conventional stations. Primarily a noncommercial format, common among college radio stations. Also known as **Alternative**.

Public Affairs—Community interest programming (ie: broadcasts of city council meetings.) Many noncommercial, **News**, and **Talk** stations cover local issues on news features or talk shows.

Reggae—Jamaican music. Often played on **Progressive** stations.

Religious—Inspirational/spiritual talk and music. Most religious stations air Christian sermons or songs. Also see **Gospel**.

Rock/AOR—Rock music from the 60s to the present. Album-oriented rock features music "sweeps" or uninterrrupted sets. News plays a secondary role. Also see **Classic Rock**.

Russian.

Sacred.

Scottish.

Serbian.

Slovak.

Slovenian.

Spanish.

Sports— Play-by-play and taped coverage, sports news, interviews, discussion.

Talk—Topical programs on various subjects. Includes health, finance, and community issues. Listener call-in and interview shows are common, and the host's personality tends to be an important element. Many talk stations air national satellite-delivered talk programs. News, sports and weather are usually emphasized during "drive times." Also see **News** and **News/Talk**.

Tejano—Bicultural programming including Spanish programming, popular in Texas, particularly near the Mexican border. Interest surged in this type of Spanish music during the early 90s.

Ukranian.

Top-40—See **Contemporary Hit/Top-40**.

Underground—The opposite of mainstream, this music is produced and appreciated by those outside the establishment.

Urban Contemporary—Dance music, often from a variety of genres (i.e. rhythm & blues, rap). Most Urban Contemporary stations emphasize music by Black artists. Also see **Black** and **Disco**.

Variety/Diverse—A station listing four or more formats. Typical of noncommerical stations.

Vietnamese.

Women—Programming for women. Emphasis on news and information, pertaining to women's issues.

U.S. and Canada Radio Programming Formats

Format	United States					Canada				
	Total	AM	FM	Com	Non	Total	AM	FM	Com	Non
Adult Contemp	1718	230	1488	1602	116	247	26	221	239	8
Agriculture	53	41	12	53	0	3	3	0	3	0
Albanian	0	0	0	0	0	0	0	0	0	0
Album-Oriented Rock	76	0	76	64	12	6	1	5	6	0
Alternative	238	3	235	86	152	16	0	16	8	8
American Indian	5	2	3	2	3	3	0	3	3	0
Arabic	1	1	0	1	0	1	1	0	1	0
Armenian	0	0	0	0	0	0	0	0	0	0
Beautiful Music	44	14	30	29	15	2	0	2	1	1
Big Band	40	23	17	30	10	1	0	1	0	1
Black	67	40	27	54	13	1	0	1	1	0
Bluegrass	36	25	11	27	9	0	0	0	0	0
Blues	78	24	54	53	25	5	0	5	2	3
Children	40	37	3	38	2	0	0	0	0	0
Chinese	6	6	0	6	0	4	3	1	4	0
Christian	1453	302	1151	497	956	38	3	35	35	3
Classic Rock	641	22	619	608	33	83	2	81	82	1
Classical	488	8	480	39	449	28	2	26	13	15
Comedy	1	0	1	1	0	1	0	1	1	0
Contemporary Hit/Top-40	567	25	542	488	79	77	8	69	76	1
Country	2109	583	1526	2082	27	147	57	90	140	7
Croation	0	0	0	0	0	0	0	0	0	0
Czech	0	0	0	0	0	0	0	0	0	0
Disco	1	0	1	1	0	0	0	0	0	0
Discussion	0	0	0	0	0	0	0	0	0	0
Diversified	258	22	236	25	233	90	17	73	52	38
Drama/Literature	0	0	0	0	0	1	0	1	1	0
Easy Listening	39	12	27	31	8	10	3	7	9	1
Educational	237	19	218	20	217	8	3	5	3	5
Eskimo	0	0	0	0	0	1	0	1	1	0
Ethnic	80	51	29	68	12	25	11	14	22	3
Farsi	1	1	0	1	0	0	0	0	0	0
Filipino	2	1	1	2	0	1	0	1	1	0
Finnish	0	0	0	0	0	0	0	0	0	0
Folk	21	1	20	1	20	2	1	1	0	2
Foreign/Ethnic	47	23	24	43	4	8	3	5	8	0
French	1	1	0	1	0	56	1	55	49	7
Full Service	59	47	12	55	4	1	0	1	1	0
German	0	0	0	0	0	1	0	1	1	0
Golden Oldies	21	11	10	20	1	2	1	1	2	0
Gospel	612	427	185	519	93	3	1	2	2	1
Greek	3	3	0	3	0	1	1	0	1	0
Hardcore	0	0	0	0	0	0	0	0	0	0
Hebrew	0	0	0	0	0	0	0	0	0	0
Hindi	0	0	0	0	0	1	0	1	1	0
Hungarian	0	0	0	0	0	0	0	0	0	0
Inspirational	100	13	87	23	77	1	1	0	1	0
Irish	0	0	0	0	0	0	0	0	0	0
Italian	1	1	0	1	0	0	0	0	0	0

U.S. and Canada Radio Programming Formats

Format	United States Total	AM	FM	Com	Non	Canada Total	AM	FM	Com	Non
Japanese	1	1	0	1	0	0	0	0	0	0
Jazz	317	11	306	29	288	17	1	16	7	10
Jewish	0	0	0	0	0	1	1	0	1	0
Korean	11	11	0	11	0	0	0	0	0	0
Light Rock	46	4	42	43	3	12	1	11	12	0
Lithuanian	0	0	0	0	0	0	0	0	0	0
MOR	186	139	47	167	19	38	10	28	36	2
Native American	10	2	8	2	8	4	0	4	4	0
New Age	16	1	15	3	13	0	0	0	0	0
New Wave	0	0	0	0	0	0	0	0	0	0
News	729	245	484	300	429	34	12	22	26	8
News/talk	1284	999	285	1072	212	55	35	20	39	16
Nostalgia	70	50	20	62	8	3	1	2	2	1
Oldies	1023	432	591	990	33	39	16	23	37	2
Other	251	99	152	194	57	26	3	23	20	6
Polish	4	4	0	4	0	0	0	0	0	0
Polka	6	3	3	4	2	0	0	0	0	0
Portugese	3	1	2	1	2	0	0	0	0	0
Progressive	128	6	122	14	114	3	0	3	2	1
Public Affairs	59	16	43	14	45	21	3	18	13	8
Reggae	3	1	2	3	0	0	0	0	0	0
Religious	803	349	454	399	404	9	4	5	7	2
Rock/AOR	510	11	499	392	118	75	7	68	73	2
Russian	3	3	0	3	0	0	0	0	0	0
Sacred	0	0	0	0	0	0	0	0	0	0
Scottish	0	0	0	0	0	0	0	0	0	0
Serbian	0	0	0	0	0	0	0	0	0	0
Slovak	0	0	0	0	0	0	0	0	0	0
Slovenian	0	0	0	0	0	0	0	0	0	0
Smooth Jazz	45	3	42	39	6	3	0	3	3	0
Soul	11	3	8	11	0	0	0	0	0	0
Spanish	779	404	375	711	68	1	1	0	1	0
Sports	1087	922	165	1073	14	17	17	0	17	0
Talk	780	606	174	699	81	32	11	21	24	8
Tejano	21	5	16	21	0	0	0	0	0	0
Top-40	96	9	87	91	5	18	0	18	18	0
Triple A	120	3	117	62	58	3	0	3	3	0
Ukranian	0	0	0	0	0	0	0	0	0	0
Underground	0	0	0	0	0	0	0	0	0	0
Urban Contemporary	364	60	304	305	59	5	0	5	3	2
Variety/Diverse	345	62	283	100	245	72	5	67	59	13
Vietnamese	6	6	0	6	0	0	0	0	0	0
Women	1	1	0	1	0	0	0	0	0	0

Programming on Radio Stations in the U.S.

Adult Contemp

KDBZ(FM) Anchorage AK
KMXS(FM) Anchorage AK
KYMG(FM) Anchorage AK
*KBRW-FM Barrow AK
KTDZ(FM) College AK
KCDV(FM) Cordova AK
*KDLG(AM) Dillingham AK
KYSC(FM) Fairbanks AK
*KEUL(FM) Girdwood AK
KWVV-FM Homer AK
KINY(AM) Juneau AK
KTKN(AM) Ketchikan AK
KAKN(FM) Naknek AK
KIFW(AM) Sitka AK
KKIS-FM Soldotna AK
KMVV(FM) Sterling AK
KVAK-FM Valdez AK
KMBQ-FM Wasilla AK
WSYA(AM) Anniston AL
WYOK(FM) Atmore AL
WKXX(FM) Attalla AL
WMJJ(FM) Birmingham AL
WYDE(AM) Birmingham AL
WMLV(FM) Butler AL
WDLT-FM Chickasaw AL
WYDE-FM Cullman AL
WAGF-FM Dothan AL
WOOF-FM Dothan AL
WKZJ(FM) Eufaula AL
WABF(AM) Fairhope AL
WQLT-FM Florence AL
WFPA(AM) Fort Payne AL
WCKS(FM) Fruithurst AL
WFXX(FM) Georgiana AL
WRSA-FM Holly Pond AL
WAHR(FM) Huntsville AL
WHOD(FM) Jackson AL
WWMG(FM) Millbrook AL
*WBHY-FM Mobile AL
WMXC(FM) Mobile AL
WMXS(FM) Montgomery AL
WMXA(FM) Opelika AL
WCSN-FM Orange Beach AL
WALX(FM) Orrville AL
WVOK-FM Oxford AL
WOAB(FM) Ozark AL
WGSY(FM) Phenix City AL
WPID(AM) Piedmont AL
WBEI(FM) Reform AL
WLDA(FM) Slocomb AL
KMJI(FM) Ashdown AR
KCNY(FM) Bald Knob AR
KBTA-FM Batesville AR
KZLE(FM) Batesville AR
KAMD-FM Camden AR
*KUCA(FM) Conway AR
KBKG(FM) Corning AR
KDMS(AM) El Dorado AR
KLBQ(FM) El Dorado AR
KMRX(FM) El Dorado AR
KESA(FM) Eureka Springs AR
KEZA(FM) Fayetteville AR
KHMB(FM) Hamburg AR
KHOZ(AM) Harrison AR
KILX(FM) Hatfield AR
KEAZ(FM) Heber Springs AR
KFFA-FM Helena AR
KBHS(AM) Hot Springs AR
KLAZ(FM) Hot Springs AR
KYDL(FM) Hot Springs AR
KVHU(FM) Judsonia AR
KFXV(FM) Kensett AR
KKTZ(FM) Lakeview AR
KURB(FM) Little Rock AR
KHLR(FM) Maumelle AR
KGPQ(FM) Monticello AR
KOMT(FM) Mountain Home AR
KNAS(FM) Nashville AR
KDRS-FM Paragould AR

KBOA-FM Piggott AR
KOTN(AM) Pine Bluff AR
KPOC(AM) Pocahontas AR
KPOC-FM Pocahontas AR
KYNF(FM) Prairie Grove AR
KWKK(FM) Russellville AR
KOKY(FM) Sherwood AR
KJBX(FM) Trumann AR
KSMZ(FM) Viola AR
KLAL(FM) Wrightsville AR
WVUV(AM) Leone AS
KKHJ-FM Pago Pago AS
KSBS-FM Pago Pago AS
KDVA(FM) Buckeye AZ
KIKO-FM Claypool AZ
KWRQ(FM) Clifton AZ
KMVA(FM) Dewey-Humboldt AZ
KJIK(FM) Duncan AZ
KVNA-FM Flagstaff AZ
KFLX(FM) Kachina Village AZ
KZUL-FM Lake Havasu City AZ
KESZ(FM) Phoenix AZ
KMXP(FM) Phoenix AZ
KPKX(FM) Phoenix AZ
KSUN(AM) Phoenix AZ
*KGCB(FM) Prescott AZ
KTMG(FM) Prescott AZ
KPPV(FM) Prescott Valley AZ
KWKM(FM) Saint Johns AZ
KQST(FM) Sedona AZ
KRFM(FM) Show Low AZ
KZMK(FM) Sierra Vista AZ
KOMR(FM) Sun City AZ
KTBA(AM) Tuba City AZ
KMXZ-FM Tucson AZ
KSGC(FM) Tusayan AZ
KWIM(FM) Window Rock AZ
KLJZ(FM) Yuma AZ
KQSR(FM) Yuma AZ
KAJL(FM) Adelanto CA
KCFJ(AM) Alturas CA
KZXY-FM Apple Valley CA
KHYL(FM) Auburn CA
KGFM(FM) Bakersfield CA
KBLX-FM Berkeley CA
KJMB(FM) Blythe CA
*KBPK(FM) Buena Park CA
KSXY(FM) Calistoga CA
*KYCJ(FM) Camino CA
KCDU(FM) Carmel CA
KSBL(FM) Carpinteria CA
KBQB(FM) Chico CA
KMXI(FM) Chico CA
KQPT(FM) Colusa CA
KCRE-FM Crescent City CA
KXSE(FM) Davis CA
KGBB(FM) Edwards CA
KXO-FM El Centro CA
KFSD(AM) Escondido CA
KHWY(FM) Essex CA
KFMI(FM) Eureka CA
KSAY(FM) Fort Bragg CA
KJLL-FM Fountain Valley CA
KALZ(FM) Fowler CA
KHGE(FM) Fresno CA
KJWL(FM) Fresno CA
KMGQ(FM) Goleta CA
KNCO-FM Grass Valley CA
KMJE(FM) Gridley CA
KTDE(FM) Gualala CA
KNOB(FM) Healdsburg CA
KATY-FM Idyllwild CA
KSRW(FM) Independence CA
KAJR(FM) Indian Wells CA
KRCD(FM) Inglewood CA
KEXA(FM) King City CA
KRKC-FM King City CA
KXBX-FM Lakeport CA
KGMX(FM) Lancaster CA
KKIQ(FM) Livermore CA

*KCJH(FM) Livingston CA
KSKD(FM) Livingston CA
KBIG-FM Los Angeles CA
KCBS-FM Los Angeles CA
KLVE(FM) Los Angeles CA
KOST(FM) Los Angeles CA
KYSR(FM) Los Angeles CA
KSTT-FM Los Osos-Baywood Park CA
KMMT(FM) Mammoth Lakes CA
KBKY(FM) Merced CA
KJSN(FM) Modesto CA
KWAV(FM) Monterey CA
KLMM(FM) Morro Bay CA
*KLSI(FM) Moss Beach CA
KHYZ(FM) Mountain Pass CA
KTNS(AM) Oakhurst CA
KLLY(FM) Oildale CA
KFYV(FM) Ojai CA
KSPA(AM) Ontario CA
KXLM(FM) Oxnard CA
KEZN(FM) Palm Desert CA
KKAL(FM) Paso Robles CA
KLUN(FM) Paso Robles CA
KOSO(FM) Patterson CA
*KLVM(FM) Prunedale CA
KSHA(FM) Redding CA
KMHX(FM) Rohnert Park CA
KQJK(FM) Roseville CA
KBZC(FM) Sacramento CA
KGBY(FM) Sacramento CA
KYMX(FM) Sacramento CA
KZZO(FM) Sacramento CA
KVYN(FM) Saint Helena CA
KFMB-FM San Diego CA
KMYI(FM) San Diego CA
KSCF(FM) San Diego CA
KIOI(FM) San Francisco CA
KLLC(FM) San Francisco CA
KMVQ-FM San Francisco CA
KOIT-FM San Francisco CA
KEZR(FM) San Jose CA
KSBQ(AM) Santa Maria CA
KLJR-FM Santa Paula CA
KZST(FM) Santa Rosa CA
KESR(FM) Shasta Lake City CA
KSYV(FM) Solvang CA
KZSQ-FM Sonora CA
KRLT(FM) South Lake Tahoe CA
KJOY(FM) Stockton CA
*KYCC(FM) Stockton CA
KLZN(FM) Susanville CA
KLCA(FM) Tahoe City CA
KHJL(FM) Thousand Oaks CA
KLOB(FM) Thousand Palms CA
KCRZ(FM) Tipton CA
KCDZ(FM) Twentynine Palms CA
KWNE(FM) Ukiah CA
KUIC(FM) Vacaville CA
KBBY-FM Ventura CA
*KHMS(FM) Victorville CA
KKDV(FM) Walnut Creek CA
KRXV(FM) Yermo CA
KGIW(AM) Alamosa CO
KPRB(FM) Brush CO
KKPK(FM) Colorado Springs CO
KRTZ(FM) Cortez CO
KRAI-FM Craig CO
KALC(FM) Denver CO
KIMN(FM) Denver CO
KOSI(FM) Denver CO
KPTT(FM) Denver CO
KIQX(FM) Durango CO
KPTE(FM) Durango CO
KFTM(AM) Fort Morgan CO
KJYE(FM) Grand Junction CO
KMXY(FM) Grand Junction CO
KSTH(FM) Holyoke CO
KTRR(FM) Loveland CO
KBIQ(FM) Manitou Springs CO
KWUF-FM Pagosa Springs CO

KVUU(FM) Pueblo CO
KBNG(FM) Ridgway CO
KZKS(FM) Rifle CO
KPHT(FM) Rocky Ford CO
KVRH-FM Salida CO
KPMX(FM) Sterling CO
KKLI(FM) Widefield CO
KNEC(FM) Yuma CO
WEZN-FM Bridgeport CT
WDAQ(FM) Danbury CT
WTIC-FM Hartford CT
WBMW(FM) Ledyard CT
WZBG(FM) Litchfield CT
WRCH(FM) New Britain CT
WINY(AM) Putnam CT
WQQQ(FM) Sharon CT
WCTZ(FM) Stamford CT
WEBE(FM) Westport CT
WILI(AM) Willimantic CT
WASH(FM) Washington DC
WRQX(FM) Washington DC
*WXHL-FM Christiana DE
WKDB(FM) Laurel DE
WAFL(FM) Milford DE
WZEB(FM) Ocean View DE
WJBR-FM Wilmington DE
WSTW(FM) Wilmington DE
WOYS(FM) Apalachicola FL
WBHQ(FM) Beverly Beach FL
*WJIS(FM) Bradenton FL
*WKSG(FM) Cedar Creek FL
WBTP(FM) Clearwater FL
WHQT(FM) Coral Gables FL
WKZY(FM) Cross City FL
*WAQV(FM) Crystal River FL
WKTK(FM) Crystal River FL
WCFB(FM) Daytona Beach FL
WMXZ(FM) De Funiak Springs FL
WOCL(FM) De Land FL
WJSJ(FM) Fernandina Beach FL
WWRZ(FM) Fort Meade FL
WINK-FM Fort Myers FL
WJPT(FM) Fort Myers Villas FL
WSYR-FM Gifford FL
WCMQ-FM Hialeah FL
WVYB(FM) Holly Hill FL
WIFL(FM) Inglis FL
*WAZQ(FM) Islamorada FL
WEJZ(FM) Jacksonville FL
WMBX(FM) Jensen Beach FL
WKEY-FM Key West FL
WNFB(FM) Lake City FL
WAVK(FM) Marathon FL
WGMX(FM) Marathon FL
WTOT(AM) Marianna FL
WMMB(AM) Melbourne FL
WAMR-FM Miami FL
WLYF(FM) Miami FL
WMIA-FM Miami Beach FL
WSBZ(FM) Miramar Beach FL
WMGF(FM) Mount Dora FL
WBCG(FM) Murdock FL
WSGL(FM) Naples FL
WTLT(FM) Naples FL
WAVV(FM) Naples Park FL
*WCIE(FM) New Port Richey FL
WDUV(FM) New Port Richey FL
*WHIJ(FM) Ocala FL
WMMO(FM) Orlando FL
WOMX-FM Orlando FL
*WHIF(FM) Palatka FL
*WEJF(FM) Palm Bay FL
WRMF(FM) Palm Beach FL
*WCNO(FM) Palm City FL
WFSY(FM) Panama City FL
WVVE(FM) Panama City Beach FL
WBSR(AM) Pensacola FL
WJLQ(FM) Pensacola FL
WZJZ(FM) Port Charlotte FL
WHLG(FM) Port St. Lucie FL

WKLG(FM) Rock Harbor FL
WSOS-FM Saint Augustine FL
WRXB(AM) Saint Petersburg Beach FL
WWAV-FM Santa Rosa Beach FL
WSDV(AM) Sarasota FL
WLLL(FM) Sebring FL
WNCV(FM) Shalimar FL
WCVU(FM) Solana FL
WBZE(FM) Tallahassee FL
WMTX(FM) Tampa FL
WWRM(FM) Tampa FL
WJGO(FM) Tice FL
WDDV(AM) Venice FL
WGYL(FM) Vero Beach FL
WJKD(FM) Vero Beach FL
WEAT-FM West Palm Beach FL
WDEC-FM Americus GA
WSB-FM Atlanta GA
WBBQ-FM Augusta GA
WBGE(FM) Bainbridge GA
WRAK-FM Bainbridge GA
WSOL-FM Brunswick GA
WMCD(FM) Claxton GA
WRBN(FM) Clayton GA
WGMG(FM) Crawford GA
WYYU(FM) Dalton GA
WXMK(FM) Dock Junction GA
WGMK(FM) Donalsonville GA
WMGZ(FM) Eatonton GA
WRDO(FM) Fitzgerald GA
WSGA(FM) Hinesville GA
WJGA-FM Jackson GA
WALR-FM La Grange GA
*WBKG(FM) Macon GA
WQLI(FM) Meigs GA
WPNG(FM) Pearson GA
WPGA-FM Perry GA
WSTI-FM Quitman GA
WRHQ(FM) Richmond Hill GA
WQTU(FM) Rome GA
WEGC(FM) Sasser GA
WPMX(FM) Statesboro GA
WTLY(FM) Thomasville GA
WTWA(AM) Thomson GA
WKZZ(FM) Tifton GA
WBDX(FM) Trenton GA
WNNG-FM Unadilla GA
WQPW(FM) Valdosta GA
WTCQ(FM) Vidalia GA
WWSN(FM) Waycross GA
KSTO(FM) Hagatna GU
KUAI(AM) Eleele HI
KKBG(FM) Hilo HI
KPVS(FM) Hilo HI
KWXX-FM Hilo HI
KINE-FM Honolulu HI
KSSK(AM) Honolulu HI
KUMU-FM Honolulu HI
KLEO(FM) Kahaluu HI
KJKS(FM) Kahului HI
KRTR-FM Kailua HI
KLUA(FM) Kailua-Kona HI
KWYI(FM) Kawaihae HI
KAOY(FM) Kealakekua HI
KTBH-FM Kurtistown HI
KFMN(FM) Lihue HI
KQNG-FM Lihue HI
KAOI-FM Wailuku HI
KSSK-FM Waipahu HI
KLGA(AM) Algona IA
KLGA-FM Algona IA
KLTI-FM Ames IA
KJAN(AM) Atlantic IA
KSKB(FM) Brooklyn IA
KBUR(AM) Burlington IA
KGRS(FM) Burlington IA
KKMI(FM) Burlington IA
KKRL(FM) Carroll IA
KMRY(AM) Cedar Rapids IA
WMT-FM Cedar Rapids IA

KCHA-FM Charles City IA	WAJK(FM) La Salle IL	*WVUB(FM) Vincennes IN	KLSM(FM) Tallulah LA	WOOD-FM Grand Rapids MI
KCHE-FM Cherokee IA	WAKO(AM) Lawrenceville IL	WZDM(FM) Vincennes IN	KNEK-FM Washington LA	WKMJ-FM Hancock MI
KMA-FM Clarinda IA	WAKO-FM Lawrenceville IL	WKUZ(FM) Wabash IN	KZRZ(FM) West Monroe LA	WCXT(FM) Hartford MI
KMCN(FM) Clinton IA	WKAI(FM) Macomb IL	WAMW(AM) Washington IN	KTEZ(FM) Zwolle LA	WCSR(AM) Hillsdale MI
KMXG(FM) Clinton IA	WMMC(FM) Marshall IL	WAMW-FM Washington IN	WXRV(FM) Andover MA	WCSR-FM Hillsdale MI
KQKQ-FM Council Bluffs IA	WLBH-FM Mattoon IL	WZZY(FM) Winchester IN	WQRC(FM) Barnstable MA	WIKB-FM Iron River MI
KCZQ(FM) Cresco IA	WREZ(FM) Metropolis IL	KVSV(AM) Beloit KS	WBMX(FM) Boston MA	WIMI(FM) Ironwood MI
*KLOX(FM) Creston IA	WRIK-FM Metropolis IL	KZDY(FM) Cawker City KS	WMJX(FM) Boston MA	WUPM(FM) Ironwood MI
KDSN(AM) Denison IA	WMOI(FM) Monmouth IL	KKOY-FM Chanute KS	WJIB(AM) Cambridge MA	WMQT(FM) Ishpeming MI
KDSN-FM Denison IA	*WCFL(FM) Morris IL	KCLY(FM) Clay Center KS	WXLO(FM) Fitchburg MA	WVFM(FM) Kalamazoo MI
KDRB(FM) Des Moines IA	WYNG(FM) Mount Carmel IL	KRDQ(FM) Colby KS	WSBS(AM) Great Barrington MA	WBTI(FM) Lexington MI
KSTZ(FM) Des Moines IA	*WBMV(FM) Mount Vernon IL	KCKS(FM) Concordia KS	WHAI(FM) Greenfield MA	WKLA-FM Ludington MI
KATF(FM) Dubuque IA	WXFM(FM) Mount Zion IL	KSKZ(FM) Copeland KS	WFQR(FM) Harwich Port MA	WMLQ(FM) Manistee MI
KDAO-FM Eldora IA	WNSV(FM) Nashville IL	*KTLI(FM) El Dorado KS	WCOD-FM Hyannis MA	WBXX(FM) Marshall MI
KADR(AM) Elkader IA	WVMG(FM) Normal IL	KANS(FM) Emporia KS	WATD-FM Marshfield MA	WMJT(FM) McMillan MI
KUYY(FM) Emmetsburg IA	WVAZ(FM) Oak Park IL	KFFX(FM) Emporia KS	WFRQ(FM) Mashpee MA	WMPX(AM) Midland MI
KKFD-FM Fairfield IA	WCMY(AM) Ottawa IL	KVOE(FM) Emporia KS	WMRC(AM) Milford MA	WHTD(FM) Mount Clemens MI
KIOW(FM) Forest City IA	WRKX(FM) Ottawa IL	KKJQ(FM) Garden City KS	*WMLN-FM Milton MA	WCZY-FM Mount Pleasant MI
KKEZ(FM) Fort Dodge IA	*WCIC(FM) Pekin IL	KKCI(FM) Goodland KS	WNAW(AM) North Adams MA	WSHZ(FM) Muskegon MI
KGRN(AM) Grinnell IA	WSWT(FM) Peoria IL	KZRS(FM) Great Bend KS	WJDF(FM) Orange MA	WKQS-FM Negaunee MI
KLMJ(FM) Hampton IA	WLLT(FM) Polo IL	KIBB(FM) Haven KS	WBEC-FM Pittsfield MA	WZNL(FM) Norway MI
KCVM(FM) Hudson IA	*WGCA-FM Quincy IL	KJLS(FM) Hays KS	WBRK-FM Pittsfield MA	WWTH(FM) Oscoda MI
KHBT(FM) Humboldt IA	WLIQ(AM) Quincy IL	KFBZ(FM) Haysville KS	WPLM(AM) Plymouth MA	WMOM(FM) Pentwater MI
KQMG(AM) Independence IA	WTAY(AM) Robinson IL	KIND-FM Independence KS	WPLM-FM Plymouth MA	WLXT(FM) Petoskey MI
KQMG-FM Independence IA	WTYE(FM) Robinson IL	KIKS-FM Iola KS	*WRPS(FM) Rockland MA	WMBN(AM) Petoskey MI
KIFG(AM) Iowa Falls IA	WRHL-FM Rochelle IL	KUDL(FM) Kansas City KS	WHYN-FM Springfield MA	WGRT(FM) Port Huron MI
KOKX(AM) Keokuk IA	WGFB(FM) Rockton IL	KSCB-FM Liberal KS	WMAS-FM Springfield MA	WQON(FM) Roscommon MI
KRLS(FM) Knoxville IA	WJBD-FM Salem IL	KVOB(FM) Lindsborg KS	WSNE(FM) Taunton MA	WGER(FM) Saginaw MI
KLEM(AM) Le Mars IA	WJDK-FM Seneca IL	KBLS(FM) North Fort Riley KS	WSRS(FM) Worcester MA	WTGV-FM Sandusky MI
KMCH(FM) Manchester IA	WABZ(FM) Sherman IL	KQNK(AM) Norton KS	WNAV(AM) Annapolis MD	WSOO(AM) Sault Ste. Marie MI
*KBDC(FM) Mason City IA	WTMX(FM) Skokie IL	KQNK-FM Norton KS	WLIF(FM) Baltimore MD	*WCFG(FM) Springfield MI
KLSS-FM Mason City IA	WIVQ(FM) Spring Valley IL	KQLA(FM) Ogden KS	WWMX(FM) Baltimore MD	WTRV(FM) Walker MI
KCWN(FM) New Sharon IA	WNNS(FM) Springfield IL	KLKC-FM Parsons KS	WMMJ(FM) Bethesda MD	KDDG(FM) Albany MN
KSMA-FM Osage IA	WAOX(FM) Staunton IL	KHMY(FM) Pratt KS	WTGB-FM Bethesda MD	KCPI(FM) Albert Lea MN
KTWA(FM) Ottumwa IA	WSSQ(FM) Sterling IL	KMAJ-FM Topeka KS	WCEM-FM Cambridge MD	KAUS(AM) Austin MN
KQCR-FM Parkersburg IA	WRAN(FM) Tower Hill IL	KHCA(FM) Wamego KS	WCMD(AM) Cumberland MD	KKBJ-FM Bemidji MN
KSOU-FM Sioux Center IA	WKRV(FM) Vandalia IL	KRBB(FM) Wichita KS	WCEI-FM Easton MD	KKZY(FM) Bemidji MN
KGLI(FM) Sioux City IA	WPMB(AM) Vandalia IL	WKKQ(FM) Barbourville KY	*WLIC(FM) Frostburg MD	KBMO(AM) Benson MN
KUOO(FM) Spirit Lake IA	WGFA-FM Watseka IL	WLJC(FM) Beattyville KY	WWEG(FM) Hagerstown MD	KOWZ-FM Blooming Prairie MN
KAYL-FM Storm Lake IA	WXLC(FM) Waukegan IL	*WTRT(FM) Benton KY	WILC(FM) Laurel MD	WJJY-FM Brainerd MN
KCII(AM) Washington IA	WRTB(FM) Winnebago IL	*WCVK(FM) Bowling Green KY	WSMD-FM Mechanicsville MD	KLTA(FM) Breckenridge MN
*KNWS-FM Waterloo IA	WZSR(FM) Woodstock IL	WKLX(FM) Brownsville KY	WAFY(FM) Middletown MD	KLKS(FM) Breezy Point MN
KWAY-FM Waverly IA	WQME(FM) Anderson IN	WCKQ(FM) Campbellsville KY	WKHJ(FM) Mountain Lake Park MD	KXDL(FM) Browerville MN
KQWC-FM Webster City IA	*WEAX(FM) Angola IN	WQXQ(FM) Central City KY	WMSG(AM) Oakland MD	KRWC(AM) Buffalo MN
KORR(FM) American Falls ID	WLKI(FM) Angola IN	WCTT-FM Corbin KY	WQHQ(FM) Ocean City-Salisbury MD	WKLK-FM Cloquet MN
KLCE(FM) Blackfoot ID	WZBD(FM) Berne IN	WQXE(FM) Elizabethtown KY	*WJVH(FM) Belfast ME	KMXK(FM) Cold Spring MN
KTHI(FM) Caldwell ID	WBNL(AM) Boonville IN	WCVQ(FM) Fort Campbell KY	WQSS(FM) Camden ME	KROX(AM) Crookston MN
KLLP(FM) Chubbuck ID	WBPE(FM) Brookston IN	WSTV-FM Frankfort KY	WCXU(FM) Caribou ME	KDLM(AM) Detroit Lakes MN
KXLT-FM Eagle ID	WVBB(FM) Columbia City IN	WUGO(FM) Grayson KY	WCRQ(FM) Dennysville ME	KZLT-FM East Grand Forks MN
KCIX(FM) Garden City ID	WCDQ(FM) Crawfordsville IN	WHLN(AM) Harlan KY	WDME-FM Dover Foxcroft ME	WEVE-FM Eveleth MN
KMVX(FM) Jerome ID	WIKY-FM Evansville IN	WHOP-FM Hopkinsville KY	WKSQ(FM) Ellsworth ME	WLKX-FM Forest Lake MN
KATW(FM) Lewiston ID	WVHI(AM) Evansville IN	WHHT(FM) Horse Cave KY	WHOU-FM Houlton ME	*WTIP(FM) Grand Marais MN
KLER-FM Orofino ID	WAJI(FM) Fort Wayne IN	WZQQ(FM) Hyden KY	*WWLN(FM) Lincoln ME	KMFY(FM) Grand Rapids MN
KWYD(FM) Parma ID	WGL(AM) Fort Wayne IN	WRNZ(FM) Lancaster KY	WCXX(FM) Madawaska ME	WWAX(FM) Hermantown MN
*KSQS(FM) Ririe ID	WMEE(FM) Fort Wayne IN	WKHG(FM) Leitchfield KY	WRMO(FM) Milbridge ME	KLCH(FM) Lake City MN
KSRA(AM) Salmon ID	WSHW(FM) Frankfort IN	WMXL(FM) Lexington KY	WMGX(FM) Portland ME	KFML(FM) Little Falls MN
KSRA-FM Salmon ID	WKAM(AM) Goshen IN	WWEL(FM) London KY	WQHR(FM) Presque Isle ME	KQAD(AM) Luverne MN
KBJX(FM) Shelley ID	WZPL(FM) Greenfield IN	WLUE(FM) Louisville KY	WFMX(FM) Skowhegan ME	KEEZ-FM Mankato MN
WYEC(FM) Cambridge IL	WRZQ-FM Greensburg IN	WVEZ(FM) Louisville KY	WCXV(FM) Van Buren ME	KKCK(FM) Marshall MN
WCXO(FM) Carlyle IL	WKLO(FM) Hardinsburg IN	WXMA(FM) Louisville KY	*WWWA(FM) Winslow ME	KTCZ-FM Minneapolis MN
WUEZ(FM) Carterville IL	WNTR(FM) Indianapolis IN	WYMV(FM) Madisonville KY	XHRM-FM Tijuana MEX	KTLK(FM) Minneapolis MN
WHMS-FM Champaign IL	WITZ(AM) Jasper IN	WFXY(AM) Middlesboro KY	WLEN(FM) Adrian MI	WLTE(FM) Minneapolis MN
WLRW(FM) Champaign IL	WITZ-FM Jasper IN	WMOR-FM Morehead KY	WQBX(FM) Alma MI	KDOG(FM) North Mankato MN
WILV(FM) Chicago IL	WKVI(AM) Knox IN	WCLU-FM Munfordville KY	WHSB(FM) Alpena MI	KYMN(AM) Northfield MN
WLIT-FM Chicago IL	WKVI-FM Knox IN	*WGCF(FM) Paducah KY	WJSZ(FM) Ashley MI	KPRW(FM) Perham MN
WEZC(FM) Clinton IL	WZWZ(FM) Kokomo IN	WKLW-FM Paintsville KY	WLEW-FM Bad Axe MI	KBMX(FM) Proctor MN
KMJM-FM Columbia IL	*WIRE(FM) Lebanon IN	WGKS(FM) Paris KY	WIOG(FM) Bay City MI	KCML(FM) Saint Joseph MN
WDNL(FM) Danville IL	WLME(FM) Lewisport IN	*WWJD(FM) Pippa Passes KY	WYBR(FM) Big Rapids MI	KSTP-FM Saint Paul MN
WITY(AM) Danville IL	WLEG(FM) Ligonier IN	WHVE(FM) Russell Springs KY	WKHM-FM Brooklyn MI	KNUJ-FM Sleepy Eye MN
WDKB(FM) De Kalb IL	WSAL(AM) Logansport IN	WYKY(FM) Science Hill KY	WSMK(FM) Buchanan MI	KNSG(FM) Springfield MN
WDQN(AM) Du Quoin IL	WZVN(FM) Lowell IN	WUHU(FM) Smiths Grove KY	WLXV(FM) Cadillac MI	KSKK(FM) Staples MN
WJEZ(FM) Dwight IL	WORX-FM Madison IN	WLLK-FM Somerset KY	WIDL(FM) Caro MI	KRVY-FM Starbuck MN
WXEF(FM) Effingham IL	WEFM(FM) Michigan City IN	WYSB(FM) Springfield KY	*WPRJ(FM) Coleman MI	KYBA(FM) Stewartville MN
WEBQ-FM Eldorado IL	WPHZ(FM) Mitchell IN	WCDA(FM) Versailles KY	WNIC(FM) Dearborn MI	KQKK(FM) Walker MN
WCFS-FM Elmwood Park IL	WMRS(FM) Monticello IN	KRVE(FM) Brusly LA	WDRQ(FM) Detroit MI	KQIC(FM) Willmar MN
WYST(FM) Fairbury IL	*WWDS(FM) Muncie IN	KQLK(FM) De Ridder LA	WDVD(FM) Detroit MI	KAGE-FM Winona MN
WNOI(FM) Flora IL	WYPW(FM) Nappanee IN	KDDK(FM) Franklin LA	WMGC-FM Detroit MI	KITN(FM) Worthington MN
WISH-FM Galatia IL	WMDH(AM) New Castle IN	WDVW(FM) La Place LA	WFMK(FM) East Lansing MI	KBMV(FM) Birch Tree MO
WDBQ-FM Galena IL	WPGW(AM) Portland IN	KTDY(FM) Lafayette LA	WGLQ(FM) Escanaba MI	KWJK(FM) Boonville MO
WTAO-FM Herrin IL	WFMG(FM) Richmond IN	KBIU(FM) Lake Charles LA	WCRZ(FM) Flint MI	KFMZ(AM) Brookfield MO
WBBE(FM) Heyworth IL	WAXL(FM) Santa Claus IN	KBDV(FM) Leesville LA	WMJZ-FM Gaylord MI	KZBK(FM) Brookfield MO
WVIV-FM Highland Park IL	WZZB(AM) Seymour IN	KZLG(FM) Mansura LA	WSRT(FM) Gaylord MI	KRRY(FM) Canton MO
WLDS(AM) Jacksonville IL	WNSN(FM) South Bend IN	KYMK-FM Maurice LA	WGHN-FM Grand Haven MI	KMXL(FM) Carthage MO
WSSR(FM) Joliet IL	WMYQ(FM) South Whitley IN	WLMG(FM) New Orleans LA	*WCSG(FM) Grand Rapids MI	*KNLH(FM) Cedar Hill MO
WVIX(FM) Joliet IL	WAWC(FM) Syracuse IN	KOGM(FM) Opelousas LA	WFGR(FM) Grand Rapids MI	KREZ(FM) Chaffee MO
WKAY(FM) Knoxville IL	WBOW-FM Terre Haute IN	KVKI(FM) Shreveport LA	WLHT-FM Grand Rapids MI	KPLA(FM) Columbia MO

KLOZ(FM) Eldon MO
KZWV(FM) Eldon MO
KAUL(FM) Ellington MO
*KCFV(FM) Ferguson MO
KCJK(FM) Garden City MO
KGRC(FM) Hannibal MO
KTXY(FM) Jefferson City MO
KCKC(FM) Kansas City MO
KIRK(FM) Macon MO
KLSC(FM) Malden MO
KTRI-FM Mansfield MO
KXEO(AM) Mexico MO
KMCR(FM) Montgomery City MO
KUPH(FM) Mountain View MO
KZMA(FM) Naylor MO
KGBX-FM Nixa MO
KTOZ-FM Pleasant Hope MO
KAHR(FM) Poplar Bluff MO
*KNLP(FM) Potosi MO
KADI-FM Republic MO
KDAA(FM) Rolla MO
KGNM(AM) Saint Joseph MO
KKJO(FM) Saint Joseph MO
KEZK-FM Saint Louis MO
KYKY(FM) Saint Louis MO
KGKS(FM) Scott City MO
KSDL(FM) Sedalia MO
*KWND(FM) Springfield MO
KTTN(AM) Trenton MO
KFNS-FM Troy MO
*KBIY(FM) Van Buren MO
KSLQ-FM Washington MO
KFBD-FM Waynesville MO
KOZQ(AM) Waynesville MO
KJMK(FM) Webb City MO
KULH(FM) Wheeling MO
WKZW(FM) Bay Springs MS
WMJY(FM) Biloxi MS
WMJU(FM) Bude MS
*WOWL(FM) Burnsville MS
*WKVF(FM) Byhalia MS
WMGO(AM) Canton MS
WAID(FM) Clarksdale MS
WFFF-FM Columbia MS
WNMQ(FM) Columbus MS
WLIN-FM Durant MS
WLZA(FM) Eupora MS
WFTA(FM) Fulton MS
WGNL(FM) Greenwood MS
WYMX(FM) Greenwood MS
WUJM(FM) Gulfport MS
WSYE(FM) Houston MS
WNLA-FM Indianola MS
WWJK(FM) Jackson MS
WIQQ(FM) Leland MS
WLSM-FM Louisville MS
WJDQ(FM) Marion MS
WKSO(FM) Natchez MS
WQLJ(FM) Oxford MS
WWSL(FM) Philadelphia MS
WRTM-FM Port Gibson MS
WKZB(FM) Stonewall MS
WUMS(FM) University MS
WJKK(FM) Vicksburg MS
KGLM-FM Anaconda MT
KBBB(FM) Billings MT
KRPM(FM) Billings MT
KOBB(AM) Bozeman MT
KZMY(FM) Bozeman MT
KOPR(FM) Butte MT
KRYK(FM) Chinook MT
KBEV-FM Dillon MT
KVVR(FM) Dutton MT
KLAN(FM) Glasgow MT
KXGN(AM) Glendive MT
KAAK(FM) Great Falls MT
KXDR(FM) Hamilton MT
KHDN(AM) Hardin MT
KOJM(AM) Havre MT
KMTX-FM Helena MT
KALS(FM) Kalispell MT
KATL(AM) Miles City MT
KMSO(FM) Missoula MT
KYJK(FM) Missoula MT
KQRK(FM) Ronan MT
KTHC(FM) Sidney MT

KKVU(FM) Stevensville MT
KENR(FM) Superior MT
KEZQ(FM) West Yellowstone MT
WECR-FM Beech Mountain NC
WSQL(AM) Brevard NC
WKSL(FM) Cary NC
WKQC(FM) Charlotte NC
WLNK(FM) Charlotte NC
WFXC(FM) Durham NC
WKJX(FM) Elizabeth City NC
WIFM-FM Elkin NC
WQNQ(FM) Fletcher NC
WBAV-FM Gastonia NC
WSMW(FM) Greensboro NC
WANG(AM) Havelock NC
WSSM(FM) Havelock NC
WMYI(FM) Hendersonville NC
WLYT(FM) Hickory NC
WMAG(FM) High Point NC
WCXL(FM) Kill Devil Hills NC
WLNC(AM) Laurinburg NC
WTHZ(FM) Lexington NC
WDEX(AM) Monroe NC
WDLZ(FM) Murfreesboro NC
*WAAE(FM) New Bern NC
WNNC(AM) Newton NC
WPNC-FM Plymouth NC
WRAL(FM) Raleigh NC
*WZRU(FM) Roanoke Rapids NC
WLHC(FM) Robbins NC
WAYN(AM) Rockingham NC
WEND(FM) Salisbury NC
WIOZ-FM Southern Pines NC
WRGC(AM) Sylva NC
WFXK(FM) Tarboro NC
WADE(AM) Wadesboro NC
WEQR(FM) Walnut Creek NC
WGNI(FM) Wilmington NC
WILT(FM) Wilmington NC
*WWIL-FM Wilmington NC
*WRCM(FM) Wingate NC
*WSNC(FM) Winston-Salem NC
KYYY(FM) Bismarck ND
KWGO(FM) Burlington ND
KXGT(FM) Carrington ND
KDIX(AM) Dickinson ND
KKXL(AM) Grand Forks ND
KHND(AM) Harvey ND
KNDK-FM Langdon ND
KNDR(FM) Mandan ND
KIZZ(FM) Minot ND
KMXA-FM Minot ND
KQDJ-FM Valley City ND
KYTZ(FM) Walhalla ND
KBRB-FM Ainsworth NE
KRGY(FM) Aurora NE
KWBE(AM) Beatrice NE
KCNB(FM) Chadron NE
KLIR(FM) Columbus NE
*KINI(FM) Crookston NE
KMOR(FM) Gering NE
KRGI(AM) Grand Island NE
KSYZ-FM Grand Island NE
KHAS(AM) Hastings NE
KLIQ(FM) Hastings NE
KMTY(FM) Holdrege NE
KBBK(FM) Lincoln NE
KOOO(FM) Lincoln NE
KICX-FM McCook NE
KSWN(FM) McCook NE
KEXL(FM) Norfolk NE
KELN(FM) North Platte NE
*KJLT-FM North Platte NE
KOMJ(AM) Omaha NE
KQCH(FM) Omaha NE
KSRZ(FM) Omaha NE
KSID-FM Sidney NE
KTMX(FM) York NE
WVMJ(FM) Conway NH
WFTN-FM Franklin NH
WGXL(FM) Hanover NH
*WNEC-FM Henniker NH
WNNH(FM) Henniker NH
WKNE(FM) Keene NH
WLNH-FM Laconia NH
WLTN-FM Lisbon NH

WZID(FM) Manchester NH
WHOM(FM) Mt. Washington NH
WFNQ(FM) Nashua NH
WBYY(FM) Somersworth NH
WSNI(FM) Swanzey NH
WNYN-FM Whitefield NH
WASR(AM) Wolfeboro NH
WLKZ(FM) Wolfeboro NH
WJLK(FM) Asbury Park NJ
WAYV(FM) Atlantic City NJ
WFPG(FM) Atlantic City NJ
WBBO(FM) Bass River Township NJ
WHCY(FM) Blairstown NJ
WNUW(FM) Burlington NJ
WAIV(FM) Cape May NJ
WHTG-FM Eatontown NJ
WSJO(FM) Egg Harbor City NJ
WSUS(FM) Franklin NJ
WWZY(FM) Long Branch NJ
WMGQ(FM) New Brunswick NJ
WPAT-FM Paterson NJ
WOBM-FM Toms River NJ
WBHX(FM) Tuckerton NJ
WCZT(FM) Villas NJ
WAWZ(FM) Zarephath NJ
*KYCM(FM) Alamogordo NM
KIVA(AM) Albuquerque NM
KKOB-FM Albuquerque NM
KMGA(FM) Albuquerque NM
KPEK(FM) Albuquerque NM
KWYK-FM Aztec NM
KAMQ(AM) Carlsbad NM
KCDY(FM) Carlsbad NM
KSMX-FM Clovis NM
KTQM-FM Clovis NM
KSYU(FM) Corrales NM
KDEM(FM) Deming NM
KKOR(FM) Gallup NM
KZOR(FM) Hobbs NM
KLVF(FM) Las Vegas NM
KMVR(FM) Mesilla Park NM
KQNM(AM) Milan NM
KLBU(FM) Pecos NM
KLNN(FM) Questa NM
KRTN(AM) Raton NM
KBIM-FM Roswell NM
KSSR(AM) Santa Rosa NM
KSCQ(FM) Silver City NM
KKIT(FM) Taos NM
KHAC(AM) Tse Bonito NM
KQAY-FM Tucumcari NM
KZMI(FM) Garapan-Saipan NP
KVAL(FM) Cal-Nev-Ari NV
KHIX(FM) Carlin NV
KELK(AM) Elko NV
KLKO(FM) Elko NV
KVLV-FM Fallon NV
KKJJ(FM) Henderson NV
KMXB(FM) Henderson NV
KRNO(FM) Incline Village NV
KKVV(AM) Las Vegas NV
KPLV(FM) Las Vegas NV
KSNE-FM Las Vegas NV
*KSOS(FM) Las Vegas NV
KADD(FM) Logandale NV
KJUL(FM) Moapa Valley NV
KNEV(FM) Reno NV
KJZS(FM) Sparks NV
WYJB(FM) Albany NY
WCSS(AM) Amsterdam NY
*WBXL(FM) Baldwinsville NY
WVIN-FM Bath NY
WBAZ(FM) Bridgehampton NY
WFAS-FM Bronxville NY
WJYE(FM) Buffalo NY
WTSS(FM) Buffalo NY
WVOR(FM) Canandaigua NY
WTOJ(FM) Carthage NY
WCTW(FM) Catskill NY
WLVG(FM) Center Moriches NY
WSDE(AM) Cobleskill NY
WGMM(FM) Corning NY
WNKI(FM) Corning NY
WDNY-FM Dansville NY
WENY-FM Elmira NY
WLVY(FM) Elmira NY

*WHPC(FM) Garden City NY
WENT(AM) Gloversville NY
WHLI(AM) Hempstead NY
WKJY(FM) Hempstead NY
WKPQ(FM) Hornell NY
WNYH(AM) Huntington NY
WCZX(FM) Hyde Park NY
WYXL(FM) Ithaca NY
WWSE(AM) Jamestown NY
WLTB(FM) Johnson City NY
WIZR(AM) Johnstown NY
WKNY(AM) Kingston NY
WSKU(FM) Little Falls NY
WBZZ(FM) Malta NY
WMSA(AM) Massena NY
WSUL(FM) Monticello NY
WFAF(FM) Mount Kisco NY
WBWZ(FM) New Paltz NY
WLTW(FM) New York NY
WPLJ(FM) New York NY
WGNY-FM Newburgh NY
WKXZ(FM) Norwich NY
WVLF(FM) Norwood NY
WMXO(FM) Olean NY
WMCR(AM) Oneida NY
WMCR-FM Oneida NY
WSRK(FM) Oneonta NY
WOLF-FM Oswego NY
WALK-FM Patchogue NY
WDBY(FM) Patterson NY
WHUD(FM) Peekskill NY
WYLF(AM) Penn Yan NY
WZUN(FM) Phoenix NY
WIRY(AM) Plattsburgh NY
WPDM(AM) Potsdam NY
WRNQ(FM) Poughkeepsie NY
WDVI(FM) Rochester NY
WRMM-FM Rochester NY
WNBZ(AM) Saranac Lake NY
WSLP(FM) Saranac Lake NY
WYZY(FM) Saranac Lake NY
WRVE(FM) Schenectady NY
WCDO(AM) Sidney NY
WCDO-FM Sidney NY
WMJC(FM) Smithtown NY
WHFM(FM) Southampton NY
WRCR(AM) Spring Valley NY
WSPQ(AM) Springville NY
WQAR(FM) Stillwater NY
WWLF-FM Sylvan Beach NY
WLTI(FM) Syracuse NY
WYYY(FM) Syracuse NY
WRGR(FM) Tupper Lake NY
WLZW(FM) Utica NY
WMXW(FM) Vestal NY
WNYR-FM Waterloo NY
WAVR(FM) Waverly NY
WQRW(FM) Wellsville NY
WNYV(FM) Whitehall NY
WRIP(FM) Windham NY
WRRQ(FM) Windsor NY
WDJQ(FM) Alliance OH
WREO-FM Ashtabula OH
WJKW(FM) Athens OH
*WOUB-FM Athens OH
WXTQ(FM) Athens OH
WBNV(FM) Barnesville OH
WPKO-FM Bellefontaine OH
WYNT(FM) Caledonia OH
WCMJ(FM) Cambridge OH
WHBC-FM Canton OH
WKDD(FM) Canton OH
WCSM-FM Celina OH
WKKI(FM) Celina OH
WLZT(FM) Chillicothe OH
*WJVS(FM) Cincinnati OH
WKRQ(FM) Cincinnati OH
WNNF(FM) Cincinnati OH
WRRM(FM) Cincinnati OH
WFHM-FM Cleveland OH
WMVX(FM) Cleveland OH
WQAL(FM) Cleveland OH
WNCI(FM) Columbus OH
WSNY(FM) Columbus OH
WTNS(FM) Coshocton OH
WMMX(FM) Dayton OH

WDFM(FM) Defiance OH
WVMX(FM) Delaware OH
WREW(FM) Fairfield OH
WBVI(FM) Fostoria OH
WFRO-FM Fremont OH
*WCVO(FM) Gahanna OH
WXBW(FM) Gallipolis OH
WIMX(FM) Gibsonburg OH
WVNU(FM) Greenfield OH
WNLT(FM) Harrison OH
WKTN(FM) Kenton OH
WLQT(FM) Kettering OH
WAGX(FM) Manchester OH
WVNO-FM Mansfield OH
WYHT(FM) Mansfield OH
WMOA(AM) Marietta OH
WYVK(FM) Middleport OH
WKLM(FM) Millersburg OH
WQIO(FM) Mount Vernon OH
WNDH(FM) Napoleon OH
WWJM(FM) New Lexington OH
WHOF(FM) North Canton OH
WLKR-FM Norwalk OH
WJZE(FM) Oak Harbor OH
WNXT-FM Portsmouth OH
WNTO(FM) Racine OH
WAOL(FM) Ripley OH
WMLX(FM) Saint Mary's OH
WCPZ(FM) Sandusky OH
WMVR-FM Sidney OH
*WCVZ(FM) South Zanesville OH
WWWM-FM Sylvania OH
WTTF(AM) Tiffin OH
WRVF(FM) Toledo OH
WERT(FM) Van Wert OH
WKOV-FM Wellston OH
*WYSO(FM) Yellow Springs OH
WMXY(FM) Youngstown OH
WHIZ-FM Zanesville OH
KYFM(FM) Bartlesville OK
KSEO(AM) Durant OK
KQTZ(FM) Hobart OK
KTLS-FM Holdenville OK
KQIB(FM) Idabel OK
KXLS(FM) Lahoma OK
KBZQ(FM) Lawton OK
KMGZ(FM) Lawton OK
KVRW(FM) Lawton OK
KGLC(FM) Miami OK
KMGL(FM) Oklahoma City OK
KYIS(FM) Oklahoma City OK
*KXTH(FM) Seminole OK
KGFF(AM) Shawnee OK
*KJCM(FM) Snyder OK
KSPI-FM Stillwater OK
KBEZ(FM) Tulsa OK
KRAV(FM) Tulsa OK
KOCD(FM) Wilburton OK
KMZE(FM) Woodward OK
KCMX-FM Ashland OR
KKCW(FM) Beaverton OR
KMGX(FM) Bend OR
KURY-FM Brookings OR
KEHK(FM) Brownsville OR
KCBZ(FM) Cannon Beach OR
KWCQ(FM) Condon OR
KFLY(FM) Corvallis OR
*KLCC(FM) Eugene OR
KMGE(FM) Eugene OR
KCST-FM Florence OR
KGBR(FM) Gold Beach OR
KLDR(FM) Harbeck-Fruitdale OR
KQFM(FM) Hermiston OR
KCGB-FM Hood River OR
KKRB(FM) Klamath Falls OR
KWRL(FM) La Grande OR
KQIK-FM Lakeview OR
KTMT-FM Medford OR
KRSK(FM) Molalla OR
KSND(FM) Monmouth OR
KYTE(FM) Newport OR
*KAVE(FM) Oakridge OR
KSRV-FM Ontario OR
KUMA-FM Pendleton OR
KYCH-FM Portland OR
KLTW-FM Prineville OR

KPPK(FM) Rainier OR
KLRR(FM) Redmond OR
*KLFR(FM) Reedsport OR
*KMPQ(FM) Roseburg OR
KWPK-FM Sisters OR
KMCQ(FM) The Dalles OR
KODL(AM) The Dalles OR
KKMX(FM) Tri City OR
KEUG(FM) Veneta OR
*KWSO(FM) Warm Springs OR
WLEV(FM) Allentown PA
WHJB(AM) Bedford PA
WZWW(FM) Bellefonte PA
WFYY(FM) Bloomsburg PA
WRRK(FM) Braddock PA
WESB(AM) Bradford PA
WXMJ(FM) Cambridge Springs PA
WLNP(FM) Carbondale PA
WIKZ(FM) Chambersburg PA
*WZXQ(FM) Chambersburg PA
WCCR(FM) Clarion PA
WQYX(FM) Clearfield PA
WWCB(AM) Corry PA
WBRX(FM) Cresson PA
WOKW(FM) Curwensville PA
WQKY(FM) Emporium PA
WXBB(FM) Erie PA
WXKC(FM) Erie PA
*WRSD(FM) Folsom PA
WQFN(FM) Forest City PA
WHMJ(FM) Franklin PA
WGET(AM) Gettysburg PA
WRVV(FM) Harrisburg PA
*WBYH(FM) Hawley PA
WMHX(FM) Hershey PA
WRKY-FM Hollidaysburg PA
WCCS(AM) Homer City PA
WDNH-FM Honesdale PA
WLAK(FM) Huntingdon PA
WKYE(FM) Johnstown PA
WLAN-FM Lancaster PA
WROZ(FM) Lancaster PA
WNKZ(FM) Laporte PA
WQTW(AM) Latrobe PA
WQIC(FM) Lebanon PA
*WGRC(FM) Lewisburg PA
WMRF-FM Lewistown PA
WSNU(FM) Lock Haven PA
WNBQ(FM) Mansfield PA
*WRIJ(FM) Masontown PA
WLLF(FM) Mercer PA
*WMSS(FM) Middletown PA
WVRT(FM) Mill Hall PA
WQLV(FM) Millersburg PA
WVLY-FM Milton PA
*WRWJ(FM) Murrysville PA
WQFM(FM) Nanticoke PA
WZPT(FM) New Kensington PA
*WWNW(FM) New Wilmington PA
WNCC(AM) Northern Cambria PA
WPCL(FM) Northern Cambria PA
WKQW-FM Oil City PA
WBEB(FM) Philadelphia PA
WBEN-FM Philadelphia PA
WDAS-FM Philadelphia PA
WISX(FM) Philadelphia PA
*WPTS-FM Pittsburgh PA
WSHH(FM) Pittsburgh PA
WWSH(FM) Pleasant Gap PA
WHKS(FM) Port Allegany PA
WPPA(AM) Pottsville PA
WPXZ-FM Punxsutawney PA
WDSN(FM) Reynoldsville PA
WKMC(AM) Roaring Spring PA
WKBI(AM) Saint Marys PA
WKBI-FM Saint Marys PA
WATS(AM) Sayre PA
WLSW(FM) Scottdale PA
*WBYO(FM) Sellersville PA
WEEO(AM) Shippensburg PA
*WBYX(FM) Stroudsburg PA
WQKX(FM) Sunbury PA
WMGH-FM Tamaqua PA
WTRN(AM) Tyrone PA
WCTL(FM) Union City PA
*WZZD(FM) Warwick PA

*WCYJ-FM Waynesburg PA
WNBT-FM Wellsboro PA
WKSB(FM) Williamsport PA
WLMY(FM) Williamsport PA
WARM-FM York PA
WFDT(FM) Aguada PR
WABA(AM) Aguadilla PR
WTPM(FM) Aguadilla PR
WMIO(FM) Cabo Rojo PR
WNEL(AM) Caguas PR
WVJP(AM) Caguas PR
WVOZ-FM Carolina PR
WCPR(AM) Coamo PR
WXRF(AM) Guayama PR
WOIZ(AM) Guayanilla PR
WIOB(FM) Mayaguez PR
WTIL(AM) Mayaguez PR
WEXS(AM) Patillas PR
WIOC(FM) Ponce PR
*WPUC-FM Ponce PR
WZAR(FM) Ponce PR
WFID(FM) Rio Piedras PR
WIOA(FM) San Juan PR
WLRP(AM) San Sebastian PR
WRSS(AM) San Sebastian PR
WERR(FM) Vega Alta PR
WENA(AM) Yauco PR
WJZS(FM) Block Island RI
WYKZ(FM) Beaufort SC
WCAM(AM) Camden SC
WLTY(FM) Cayce SC
WSSX-FM Charleston SC
WCRE(AM) Cheraw SC
WDAR-FM Darlington SC
WORG(FM) Elloree SC
WZSN(FM) Greenwood SC
WBHC-FM Hampton SC
WAVF(FM) Hanahan SC
WDKD(AM) Kingstree SC
WSIM(FM) Lamar SC
WIHB(FM) Moncks Corner SC
WMYB(FM) Myrtle Beach SC
WKDK(AM) Newberry SC
WTCB(FM) Orangeburg SC
WMGL(FM) Ravenel SC
WSPA-FM Spartanburg SC
KBFO(FM) Aberdeen SD
KDEZ(FM) Brandon SD
KBRK-FM Brookings SD
KFCR(AM) Custer SD
KJBI(FM) Fort Pierre SD
KZKK(FM) Huron SD
KABD(FM) Ipswich SD
KQRN(AM) Mitchell SD
KOLY-FM Mobridge SD
KGFX-FM Pierre SD
KLXS-FM Pierre SD
KKMK(FM) Rapid City SD
KZLK(FM) Rapid City SD
KNBZ(FM) Redfield SD
KELO-FM Sioux Falls SD
KMXC(FM) Sioux Falls SD
KIXX(FM) Watertown SD
KWYR-FM Winner SD
KYNT(AM) Yankton SD
WBGQ(FM) Bulls Gap TN
WCLE-FM Calhoun TN
WRJB(FM) Camden TN
WDEF-FM Chattanooga TN
WKRM(AM) Columbia TN
WGIC(FM) Cookeville TN
WPBX(FM) Crossville TN
WLLJ(FM) Etowah TN
*WVCP(FM) Gallatin TN
WSEV-FM Gatlinburg TN
WKQK(FM) Germantown TN
WRQQ(FM) Goodlettsville TN
WHHM-FM Henderson TN
WKOS(FM) Kingsport TN
WTFM(FM) Kingsport TN
WIFA(AM) Knoxville TN
WJXB-FM Knoxville TN
WDXE-FM Lawrenceburg TN
WZLT(FM) Lexington TN
WYGO(FM) Madisonville TN
WFTZ(FM) Manchester TN

WMC-FM Memphis TN
WRVR(FM) Memphis TN
WYDL(FM) Middleton TN
WKIM(FM) Munford TN
WCJK(FM) Murfreesboro TN
WJXA(FM) Nashville TN
WNRQ(AM) Nashville TN
WJRV(FM) Oliver Springs TN
WBNT-FM Oneida TN
WOCV(AM) Oneida TN
WLZK(FM) Paris TN
WPRT-FM Pegram TN
WSEV(AM) Sevierville TN
WCMT-FM South Fulton TN
WTNE(AM) Trenton TN
WURV(FM) Walden TN
*KACU(FM) Abilene TX
*KGNZ(FM) Abilene TX
KJAV(FM) Alamo TX
KNDA(FM) Alice TX
KMXJ-FM Amarillo TX
KLTY(FM) Arlington TX
KKMJ-FM Austin TX
KNUZ(AM) Bellville TX
KBTS(AM) Big Spring TX
KROO(AM) Breckenridge TX
KLTR(FM) Brenham TX
KBWD(AM) Brownwood TX
KKYS(FM) Bryan TX
KRHC(AM) Burnet TX
KJXJ(FM) Cameron TX
*KETR(FM) Commerce TX
KLTG(FM) Corpus Christi TX
KDMX(FM) Dallas TX
KRNB(FM) Decatur TX
KTDR(FM) Del Rio TX
KAFX-FM Diboll TX
KVLY(FM) Edinburg TX
KINT-FM El Paso TX
KSII(FM) El Paso TX
KTSM-FM El Paso TX
KFST(AM) Fort Stockton TX
KGAF(AM) Gainesville TX
KSOC(FM) Gainesville TX
KFZX(FM) Gardendale TX
KFRO-FM Gilmer TX
KTWL(FM) Hempstead TX
KHMX(FM) Houston TX
KODA(FM) Houston TX
KSYY(FM) Ingram TX
KLJT(FM) Jacksonville TX
KOOI-FM Jacksonville TX
KJAS(FM) Jasper TX
KKBA(FM) Kingsville TX
*KHOY(FM) Laredo TX
KQUR(FM) Laredo TX
KSHN-FM Liberty TX
KONE(AM) Lubbock TX
KYBI(FM) Lufkin TX
KAMX(FM) Luling TX
*KZLV(FM) Lytle TX
KLRK(FM) Marlin TX
KLSR-FM Memphis TX
KHKZ(FM) Mercedes TX
KCHX(FM) Midland TX
KCRS-FM Midland TX
KQRX(FM) Midland TX
KZRB(FM) New Boston TX
KODM(FM) Odessa TX
KKMY(FM) Orange TX
KAZE(FM) Ore City TX
KGRO(AM) Pampa TX
KPLT-FM Paris TX
KPTX(FM) Pecos TX
KDVE(FM) Pittsburg TX
*KPVU(FM) Prairie View TX
KFMK(FM) Round Rock TX
*KNLE-FM Round Rock TX
KELI(FM) San Angelo TX
KIXY-FM San Angelo TX
KMDX(FM) San Angelo TX
KQXT(FM) San Antonio TX
KNVR(AM) San Saba TX
KQDR(FM) Savoy TX
KSMG(FM) Seguin TX
KJIM(AM) Sherman TX

KMMX(FM) Tahoka TX
KLAK(AM) Tom Bean TX
KTYL-FM Tyler TX
KQVT(FM) Victoria TX
KTXN-FM Victoria TX
KVIC(FM) Victoria TX
KQHN(FM) Waskom TX
KZTK(FM) White Oak TX
KBZS(FM) Wichita Falls TX
KALK(FM) Winfield TX
KREC(FM) Brian Head UT
KPLD(FM) Kanab UT
KQMB(FM) Levan UT
KBLQ-FM Logan UT
KMXD(FM) Monroe UT
KUDE(FM) Nephi UT
KBZN(FM) Ogden UT
KTCE(FM) Payson UT
KWSA(FM) Price UT
KSRR(AM) Provo UT
KIFX(FM) Roosevelt UT
KXRQ(FM) Roosevelt UT
*KANN(AM) Roy UT
KUDD(FM) Roy UT
KSNN(FM) Saint George UT
KBEE(FM) Salt Lake City UT
KBEE-FM Salt Lake City UT
KSFI(FM) Salt Lake City UT
KOSY-FM Spanish Fork UT
KYMV(FM) Woodruff UT
WAVA-FM Arlington VA
WWZW(FM) Buena Vista VA
WQMZ(FM) Charlottesville VA
WWTJ(FM) Charlottesville VA
WFNR-FM Christiansburg VA
WNLR(AM) Churchville VA
WXCF(AM) Clifton Forge VA
WXCF-FM Clifton Forge VA
WGCK-FM Coeburn VA
*WPIN-FM Dublin VA
WEVA(AM) Emporia VA
WFLO-FM Farmville VA
WBQB(FM) Fredericksburg VA
WXGM(AM) Gloucester VA
WXGM-FM Gloucester VA
WWDE-FM Hampton VA
WKWI(FM) Kilmarnock VA
WOJL(FM) Louisa VA
WSNZ(FM) Lynchburg VA
WOLD-FM Marion VA
WZVA(FM) Marion VA
WNVA(AM) Norton VA
WESR-FM Onley-Onancock VA
WTVR-FM Richmond VA
WSLQ(FM) Roanoke VA
*WPAR(FM) Salem VA
WSNV(FM) Salem VA
WHLF(FM) South Boston VA
WVBW(FM) Suffolk VA
WRAR-FM Tappahannock VA
WSFF(FM) Vinton VA
WPTE(FM) Virginia Beach VA
WINC-FM Winchester VA
*WIUJ(FM) Charlotte Amalie VI
WVIQ(FM) Christiansted VI
WVVI-FM Christiansted VI
WTSA-FM Brattleboro VT
WEZF(FM) Burlington VT
WMOO(FM) Derby Center VT
WGMT(FM) Lyndon VT
WVNR(AM) Poultney VT
WJJR(FM) Rutland VT
WZRT(FM) Rutland VT
KWLE(AM) Anacortes WA
KQMV(FM) Bellevue WA
KAFE(FM) Bellingham WA
KRWM(FM) Bremerton WA
KOZI(AM) Chelan WA
KOZI-FM Chelan WA
KRAO-FM Colfax WA
KCRK-FM Colville WA
KCMS(FM) Edmonds WA
KLOG(AM) Kelso WA
KLYK(FM) Kelso WA
KONA(AM) Kennewick WA
KONA-FM Kennewick WA

KSWW(FM) Montesano WA
KDRM(FM) Moses Lake WA
KWDB(AM) Oak Harbor WA
KGY(AM) Olympia WA
KXXO(FM) Olympia WA
KEYW(FM) Pasco WA
*KRLF(FM) Pullman WA
KAAP(FM) Rock Island WA
KPLZ(FM) Seattle WA
KUBE(FM) Seattle WA
KWJZ(FM) Seattle WA
*KAGU(FM) Spokane WA
KISC(FM) Spokane WA
KXLY-FM Spokane WA
KZZU-FM Spokane WA
KKSR(FM) Walla Walla WA
KITI-FM Winlock WA
KJOX(FM) Yakima WA
KRSE(FM) Yakima WA
WDKM(FM) Adams WI
WISM-FM Altoona WI
WACD(FM) Antigo WI
*WOVM(FM) Appleton WI
WRPQ(AM) Baraboo WI
WBEV(AM) Beaver Dam WI
WBJZ(FM) Berlin WI
WWIS-FM Black River Falls WI
WCFW(FM) Chippewa Falls WI
WLKN(FM) Cleveland WI
WDRK(FM) Cornell WI
WIAL(FM) Eau Claire WI
WFON(FM) Fond du Lac WI
WSJY(FM) Fort Atkinson WI
WQLH(FM) Green Bay WI
WHSM(AM) Hayward WI
WHSM-FM Hayward WI
WRLS-FM Hayward WI
WLFN(AM) La Crosse WI
WLXR-FM La Crosse WI
WLKG(FM) Lake Geneva WI
*WJTY(FM) Lancaster WI
WFDL-FM Lomira WI
WMGN(FM) Madison WI
WZEE(FM) Madison WI
WOMT(AM) Manitowoc WI
WDLB(AM) Marshfield WI
WRJC-FM Mauston WI
WJMT(AM) Merrill WI
*WGNV(FM) Milladore WI
WLWK-FM Milwaukee WI
WMYX-FM Milwaukee WI
WEKZ-FM Monroe WI
WOFM(FM) Mosinee WI
WNAM(AM) Neenah-Menasha WI
WROE(FM) Neenah-Menasha WI
WPKG(FM) Neillsville WI
WXER(FM) Plymouth WI
WPDR(FM) Portage WI
WBDL(FM) Reedsburg WI
WJMC(AM) Rice Lake WI
WEVR(AM) River Falls WI
WEVR-FM River Falls WI
WIZD(FM) Rudolph WI
WECB(AM) Seymour WI
WOWN(FM) Shawano WI
*WSHS(FM) Sheboygan WI
WKPO(FM) Soldiers Grove WI
WSPT-FM Stevens Point WI
WDOR(AM) Sturgeon Bay WI
WSRG(AM) Sturgeon Bay WI
WGEE(AM) Superior WI
WXYM(FM) Tomah WI
WDUX-FM Waupaca WI
WLJY(FM) Whiting WI
WNNO-FM Wisconsin Dells WI
WHAJ(FM) Bluefield WV
*WPIB(FM) Bluefield WV
WDCI(FM) Bridgeport WV
WBTQ(FM) Buckhannon WV
WVAF(AM) Charleston WV
WOBG(AM) Clarksburg WV
WWLW(FM) Clarksburg WV
WZJO(FM) Dunbar WV
WDNE(AM) Elkins WV
WELK(FM) Elkins WV
WVUS(AM) Grafton WV

WMGA(FM) Kenova WV
WVOW(AM) Logan WV
WVOW-FM Logan WV
WLTF(FM) Martinsburg WV
WYMJ(FM) New Martinsville WV
WXIL(FM) Parkersburg WV
*WQAB(FM) Philippi WV
WDYK(FM) Ridgeley WV
WRRR-FM Saint Marys WV
WMXE(FM) South Charleston WV
WCWV(FM) Summersville WV
WAFD(FM) Webster Springs WV
WELC(AM) Welch WV
WELC-FM Welch WV
WZST(FM) Westover WV
WBTH(AM) Williamson WV
KIGN(FM) Burns WY
KHOC(FM) Casper WY
KJUA(AM) Cheyenne WY
KTAG(FM) Cody WY
KNYN(FM) Fort Bridger WY
KAOX(FM) Kemmerer WY
KIMX(FM) Laramie WY
KZQL(FM) Mills WY
KIQZ(FM) Rawlins WY
KRAL(AM) Rawlins WY
KTRZ(FM) Riverton WY
KTHE(AM) Thermopolis WY
KZEW(FM) Wheatland WY
KKLX(FM) Worland WY

Agriculture

KSIR(AM) Brush CO
KNAB-FM Burlington CO
KSPK(FM) Walsenburg CO
KDSN(AM) Denison IA
WHOW(AM) Clinton IL
WSMI(AM) Litchfield IL
WSMI-FM Litchfield IL
WLBH(AM) Mattoon IL
WMCL(AM) McLeansboro IL
WSLM(AM) Salem IN
WSLM-FM Salem IN
KLOE(AM) Goodland KS
KNDY(AM) Marysville KS
KFRM(AM) Salina KS
KSUM(AM) Fairmont MN
KDHL(AM) Faribault MN
WYRQ(FM) Little Falls MN
KMHL(AM) Marshall MN
KOLV(FM) Olivia MN
KLOH(AM) Pipestone MN
KCUE(AM) Red Wing MN
KKOZ(AM) Ava MO
KKOZ-FM Ava MO
KAOL(AM) Carrollton MO
KMZU(FM) Carrollton MO
KGLE(AM) Glendive MT
KMON(AM) Great Falls MT
WDAY(AM) Fargo ND
KNOX(AM) Grand Forks ND
KZZJ(AM) Rugby ND
KCSR(AM) Chadron NE
KJSK(AM) Columbus NE
KRVN(AM) Lexington NE
KNEB-FM Scottsbluff NE
KTIC(AM) West Point NE
WRFD(AM) Columbus-Worthington OH
KWHW(AM) Altus OK
KBJM(AM) Lemmon SD
KGFX(AM) Pierre SD
KXRB(AM) Sioux Falls SD
KBHB(AM) Sturgis SD
KWAT(AM) Watertown SD
WNAX(AM) Yankton SD
KVWG-FM Dilley TX
KFLP(AM) Floydada TX
KVWC(AM) Vernon TX
KVWC-FM Vernon TX
KBSN(AM) Moses Lake WA
KWNC(AM) Quincy WA
WRDB(AM) Reedsburg WI
WJMC(AM) Rice Lake WI
WCUB(AM) Two Rivers WI
WELD-FM Moorefield WV

Album-Oriented Rock

WTXO(FM) Ashland AL
KKEG(FM) Bentonville AR
KDJE(FM) Jacksonville AR
KERX(FM) Paris AR
KRAB(FM) Green Acres CA
KHDR(FM) Lenwood CA
KHWZ(FM) Ludlow CA
KTYD(FM) Santa Barbara CA
KBPI(FM) Denver CO
WYYX(FM) Bonifay FL
WTKX-FM Pensacola FL
WNDD(FM) Silver Springs FL
WVRK(FM) Columbus GA
WPEZ(FM) Jeffersonville GA
KGUM-FM Dededo GU
KFMW(FM) Waterloo IA
KRVB(FM) Nampa ID
WXRX(FM) Belvidere IL
*WARG(FM) Summit IL
*WMHD-FM Terre Haute IN
KACY(FM) Arkansas City KS
KQRC-FM Leavenworth KS
KDVV(FM) Topeka KS
WZZP(FM) Hopkinsville KY
WMVY(FM) Tisbury MA
WAAF(FM) Westborough MA
WIYY(FM) Baltimore MD
WDLD(FM) Halfway MD
WIMK(FM) Iron Mountain MI
WJXQ(FM) Jackson MI
WUPK(FM) Marquette MI
WRKR(FM) Portage MI
KQDS-FM Duluth MN
KQRA(FM) Brookline MO
KCMQ(FM) Columbia MO
KSHE(FM) Crestwood MO
KMAC(FM) Gainesville MO
KXOQ(FM) Kennett MO
KZRQ-FM Mount Vernon MO
WSMS(FM) Artesia MS
WSFL-FM New Bern NC
KJKJ(FM) Grand Forks ND
WFRD(FM) Hanover NH
WHOM(FM) Mt. Washington NH
*WMNJ(FM) Madison NJ
KZRR(FM) Albuquerque NM
KEND(FM) Roswell NM
*WDWN(FM) Auburn NY
*WGCC-FM Batavia NY
*WBSU(FM) Brockport NY
*WCWP(FM) Brookville NY
*WNYU-FM New York NY
WQBK-FM Rensselaer NY
*WARY(FM) Valhalla NY
WRQK(FM) Canton OH
WEBN(FM) Cincinnati OH
WDOK(FM) Cleveland OH
WTUE(FM) Dayton OH
WBYR(FM) Van Wert OH
KATT-FM Oklahoma City OK
KHBZ-FM Oklahoma City OK
*KRVM-FM Eugene OR
KLRR(FM) Redmond OR
WMMR(FM) Philadelphia PA
*WQSU(FM) Selinsgrove PA
WFXH-FM Hilton Head Island SC
WMFX(FM) Saint Andrews SC
KRRO(FM) Sioux Falls SD
WLQK(FM) Livingston TN
KQQK(FM) Beaumont TX
KFMX-FM Lubbock TX
KISS-FM San Antonio TX
KBZS(FM) Wichita Falls TX
*KWCR-FM Ogden UT
KHTB(FM) Provo UT
WWWV(FM) Charlottesville VA

Alternative

*KRUA(FM) Anchorage AK
*KXLL(FM) Juneau AK
*WEGL(FM) Auburn AL
WZEW(FM) Fairhope AL
*WVUA-FM Tuscaloosa AL
*KCAC(FM) Camden AR
KXNA(FM) Springdale AR
*KZAI(FM) Coolidge AZ
KEDJ(FM) Gilbert AZ
KFMA(FM) Green Valley AZ
KOHT(FM) Marana AZ
KQAZ(FM) Springerville AZ
*KAIC(FM) Tucson AZ
KRDX(FM) Vail AZ
*KSPC(FM) Claremont CA
*KKUP(FM) Cupertino CA
*KFSR(FM) Fresno CA
*KORB(FM) Hopland CA
KSLG-FM Hydesville CA
KROQ-FM Pasadena CA
*KUCR(FM) Riverside CA
KBZT(FM) San Diego CA
*KUSF(FM) San Francisco CA
*KSCU(FM) Santa Clara CA
*KAIB(FM) Shafter CA
KCNL(FM) Sunnyvale CA
*KKZQ(FM) Tehachapi CA
KSRY(FM) Tehachapi CA
KFRR(FM) Woodlake CA
*KLRD(FM) Yucaipa CA
*KMSA(FM) Grand Junction CO
KTCL(FM) Wheat Ridge CO
*WXCI(FM) Danbury CT
*WQAQ(FM) Hamden CT
WJRR(FM) Cocoa Beach FL
*WVUM(FM) Coral Gables FL
WSUN-FM Holiday FL
WPBZ(FM) Indiantown FL
WIIS(FM) Key West FL
WXSR(FM) Quincy FL
*WKPX(FM) Sunrise FL
*WVFS(FM) Tallahassee FL
*WUOG(FM) Athens GA
*WRFG(FM) Atlanta GA
*WGUR(FM) Milledgeville GA
*WVGS(FM) Statesboro GA
*WQAI(FM) Thomson GA
*WPLH(FM) Tifton GA
*WVDA(FM) Valdosta GA
*WVVS(FM) Valdosta GA
KUCD(FM) Pearl City HI
*KHAI(FM) Wahiawa HI
KBVU-FM Alta IA
*KICB(FM) Fort Dodge IA
*KSTM(FM) Indianola IA
*KIGC(FM) Oskaloosa IA
*KPVL(FM) Postville IA
*KMSC(FM) Sioux City IA
*KWDM(FM) West Des Moines IA
KQXR(FM) Payette ID
KEGE(FM) Pocatello ID
KCDA(FM) Post Falls ID
KSKI-FM Sun Valley ID
*WPCD(FM) Champaign IL
WKQX(FM) Chicago IL
WXRT-FM Chicago IL
*WRSE(FM) Elmhurst IL
*WGBK(FM) Glenview IL
*WLCA(FM) Godfrey IL
*WIUS(FM) Macomb IL
*WRRG(FM) River Grove IL
*WARG(FM) Summit IL
*WHJE(FM) Carmel IN
*WJHS(FM) Columbia City IN
*WGRE(FM) Greencastle IN
*WCYT(FM) Lafayette Township IN
*WLAI(FM) Danville KY
*WFPK(FM) Louisville KY
KNXX(FM) Donaldsonville LA
*KSLU(FM) Hammond LA
WNXX(FM) Jackson LA
*KXUL(FM) Monroe LA
*KLPI-FM Ruston LA
*KSCL(FM) Shreveport LA

*KNSU(FM) Thibodaux LA
WBOS(FM) Brookline MA
*WDJM-FM Framingham MA
WFNX(FM) Lynn MA
*WZBC(FM) Newton MA
*WUMD(FM) North Dartmouth MA
*WKKL(FM) West Barnstable MA
*WSKB(FM) Westfield MA
*WCHC(FM) Worcester MA
*WMTB-FM Emmittsburg MD
*WHSN(FM) Bangor ME
WPHX-FM Sanford ME
XETRA-FM Tijuana MEX
*WQAC-FM Alma MI
*WHFR(FM) Dearborn MI
*WDBM(FM) East Lansing MI
WGRD-FM Grand Rapids MI
*WTHS(FM) Holland MI
*WUPX(FM) Marquette MI
*WMHW-FM Mount Pleasant MI
*WOVI(FM) Novi MI
*WPHS(FM) Warren MI
*WYCE(FM) Wyoming MI
*KUMM(FM) Morris MN
*KVSC(FM) Saint Cloud MN
*KSRQ(FM) Thief River Falls MN
KQQX(FM) Hermann MO
*KTRM(FM) Kirksville MO
*KMVC(FM) Marshall MO
KZZK(FM) New London MO
*KGSP(FM) Parkville MO
WHOC(AM) Philadelphia MS
*WMSV(FM) Starkville MS
WUMS(FM) University MS
*KGLT(FM) Bozeman MT
*KMSM-FM Butte MT
KBAZ(FM) Hamilton MT
*KBGA(FM) Missoula MT
*WASU-FM Boone NC
*WZMB(FM) Greenville NC
WSFM(FM) Oak Island NC
WEND(FM) Salisbury NC
*WDCC(FM) Sanford NC
*WZDG(FM) Scotts Hill NC
*KFJM(FM) Grand Forks ND
*KRNU(FM) Lincoln NE
*KDAI(FM) Scottsbluff NE
*KWSC(FM) Wayne NE
WFEX(FM) Peterborough NH
WPNH-FM Plymouth NH
WBBO(FM) Bass River Township NJ
*WDBK(FM) Blackwood NJ
WHTG-FM Eatontown NJ
*WMNJ(FM) Madison NJ
*WLFR(FM) Pomona NJ
*WTSR(FM) Trenton NJ
*WMSC(FM) Upper Montclair NJ
WPSC-FM Wayne NJ
*KQAI(FM) Roswell NM
KTEG(FM) Santa Fe NM
KXTE(FM) Pahrump NV
KRZQ-FM Sparks NV
WHRL(FM) Albany NY
WXPK(FM) Briarcliff Manor NY
WZNE(FM) Brighton NY
*WBSU(FM) Brockport NY
*WBNY(FM) Buffalo NY
*WITC(FM) Cazenovia NY
*WGSU(FM) Geneseo NY
*WDFH(FM) Ossining NY
WBTZ(FM) Plattsburgh NY
WQKE(FM) Plattsburgh NY
*WTSC-FM Potsdam NY
WBER(FM) Rochester NY
WIRQ(FM) Rochester NY
*WSIA(FM) Staten Island NY
WXEG(FM) Beavercreek OH
*WCSB(FM) Cleveland OH
WKRK-FM Cleveland Heights OH
*WHSS(FM) Hamilton OH
WOXY(FM) Oxford OH
*WXUT(FM) Toledo OH
*WOBN(FM) Westerville OH
KPAK(FM) Alva OK
*KRSC-FM Claremore OK
KMYZ-FM Pryor OK

*KSBA(FM) Coos Bay OR
*KBVR(FM) Corvallis OR
KNRQ-FM Eugene OR
*KSLC(FM) McMinnville OR
*KWBX(FM) Salem OR
KVRA(FM) Sisters OR
KRXF(FM) Sunriver OR
*WBUQ(FM) Bloomsburg PA
*WESS(FM) East Stroudsburg PA
*WFSE(FM) Edinboro PA
*WWEC(FM) Elizabethtown PA
*WERG(FM) Erie PA
*WARC(FM) Meadville PA
WXPH(FM) Middletown PA
*WXPN(FM) Philadelphia PA
WJOW(FM) Philipsburg PA
WXDX-FM Pittsburgh PA
WDMT(FM) Pittston PA
*WUSR(FM) Scranton PA
*WVMW-FM Scranton PA
*WSRU(FM) Slippery Rock PA
WCHE(AM) West Chester PA
*WCLH(FM) Wilkes-Barre PA
*WRLC(FM) Williamsport PA
WBRU(FM) Providence RI
*WJMF(FM) Smithfield RI
*KBHU-FM Spearfish SD
*WTTU(FM) Cookeville TN
WTZR(FM) Elizabethton TN
WNFZ(FM) Oak Ridge TN
KEYJ-FM Abilene TX
*KACV-FM Amarillo TX
KTLT(FM) Anson TX
*KVRX(FM) Austin TX
KROX-FM Buda TX
KDGE(FM) Fort Worth-Dallas TX
KHJK(FM) La Porte TX
*KSAU(FM) Nacogdoches TX
*KTSW(FM) San Marcos TX
KJMY(FM) Bountiful UT
*KJQN(FM) Coalville UT
*KOHS(FM) Orem UT
KXRK(FM) Provo UT
*WNRN(FM) Charlottesville VA
*WHRV(FM) Norfolk VA
*WCWM(FM) Williamsburg VA
WZIN(FM) Charlotte Amalie VI
*WJSC-FM Johnson VT
WEQX(FM) Manchester VT
*WVTC(FM) Randolph Center VT
WRJT(FM) Royalton VT
*KASB(FM) Bellevue WA
KFNK(FM) Eatonville WA
*KCWU(FM) Ellensburg WA
KGRG(AM) Enumclaw WA
KTCV(FM) Kennewick WA
*KEXP-FM Seattle WA
KNDD(FM) Seattle WA
KZBD(FM) Spokane WA
*KYVT(FM) Yakima WA
WZNN(FM) Allouez WI
*WBSD(FM) Burlington WI
WMAD(FM) Sauk City WI
*WSUW(FM) Whitewater WI
WQZK(FM) Keyser WV
*WSHC(FM) Shepherdstown WV
*WGLZ(FM) West Liberty WV
KKPL(FM) Cheyenne WY

American Indian

KNDN(AM) Farmington NM
KHAC(AM) Tse Bonito NM
*KWSO(FM) Warm Springs OR
*KILI(FM) Porcupine SD
*KWRR(FM) Ethete WY

Arabic

KXMX(AM) Anaheim CA

Beautiful Music

*KJNP-FM North Pole AK
KBUX(FM) Quartzsite AZ
KWXY-FM Cathedral City CA
*WJMJ(FM) Hartford CT
*WKTZ-FM Jacksonville FL
WVOI(AM) Marco Island FL
*WIVL(FM) Jasper GA
KQWC(AM) Webster City IA
KXLT-FM Eagle ID
WJIL(AM) Jacksonville IL
KVSV-FM Beloit KS
WMST(AM) Mt. Sterling KY
WNBH(AM) New Bedford MA
*WYAR(FM) Yarmouth ME
WMUZ(FM) Detroit MI
KLKS(FM) Breezy Point MN
WBAQ(FM) Greenville MS
WROA(AM) Gulfport MS
*KMTH(FM) Maljamar NM
*KENW-FM Portales NM
*WHPC(FM) Garden City NY
WTLB(AM) Utica NY
WSRW(AM) Hillsboro OH
WSRW(AM) Hillsboro OH
KCFM(AM) Florence OR
*WPGM(AM) Danville PA
*WPGM-FM Danville PA
*WPEL-FM Montrose PA
WNIK-FM Arecibo PR
WVJP(AM) Caguas PR
WVJP-FM Caguas PR
WORO(FM) Corozal PR
WKSA-FM Isabela PR
WIAC-FM San Juan PR
WIOA(FM) San Juan PR
WMUU-FM Greenville SC
KXYL(AM) Brownwood TX
KNNK(FM) Dimmitt TX
*KNCT-FM Killeen TX
KBBT(FM) Schertz TX
*KTXK(FM) Texarkana TX
*WIUJ(FM) Charlotte Amalie VI
WBTN(AM) Bennington VT
WSTJ(AM) Saint Johnsbury VT
*KBCS(FM) Bellevue WA

Big Band

KGOT(FM) Anchorage AK
*KBRW-FM Barrow AK
WAUD(AM) Auburn AL
*KCEA(FM) Atherton CA
KTEA(FM) Cambria CA
KEZW(AM) Aurora CO
WMMB(AM) Melbourne FL
WKII(AM) Solana FL
KCLN(AM) Clinton IA
KQWC(AM) Webster City IA
WAIK(AM) Galesburg IL
WPMB(AM) Vandalia IL
WFRX(AM) West Frankfort IL
*WICN(FM) Worcester MA
*WYAR(FM) Yarmouth ME
WMRX-FM Beaverton MI
WCBY(AM) Cheboygan MI
KLKS(FM) Breezy Point MN
KOMC-FM Kimberling City MO
KRLI(FM) Malta Bend MO
KBFL(AM) Springfield MO
WPAQ(AM) Mount Airy NC
WPNH(AM) Plymouth NH
WOBM(AM) Lakewood NJ
*KNCC(FM) Elko NV
WPTR(FM) Clifton Park NY
WALK(AM) East Patchogue NY
WHUC(AM) Hudson NY
*WKHR(FM) Bainbridge OH
WJAS(AM) Pittsburgh PA
WKDA(AM) Lebanon TN
*KSQX(FM) Springtown TX
*KQXS(FM) Stephenville TX
KPYK(AM) Terrell TX
*WFOS(FM) Chesapeake VA
*WIUJ(FM) Charlotte Amalie VI

WSTJ(AM) Saint Johnsbury VT
KTRW(AM) Opportunity WA
WCCN(AM) Neillsville WI
WBBD(AM) Wheeling WV

Black

WATV(AM) Birmingham AL
WXAL(AM) Demopolis AL
WMGJ(AM) Gadsden AL
WMFC(AM) Monroeville AL
KHKN(AM) Benton AR
*KABF(FM) Little Rock AR
KAKJ(FM) Marianna AR
KTYM(AM) Inglewood CA
*KSRH(FM) San Rafael CA
WZAZ(AM) Jacksonville FL
WWAB(AM) Lakeland FL
WVTJ(AM) Pensacola FL
WYZE(AM) Atlanta GA
WFXA-FM Augusta GA
WWLD(FM) Cairo GA
WOKS(AM) Columbus GA
WBHB(AM) Fitzgerald GA
WJGA-FM Jackson GA
WBBT(AM) Lyons GA
WIBB(AM) Macon GA
*KIGC(FM) Oskaloosa IA
*WIIT(FM) Chicago IL
WVAZ(FM) Oak Park IL
KRUS(AM) Ruston LA
KTKC(FM) Springhill LA
WPRS-FM Waldorf MD
WCHJ(AM) Brookhaven MS
WCLD(AM) Cleveland MS
WTYJ(FM) Fayette MS
WCPC(AM) Houston MS
WXTN(AM) Lexington MS
WMIS(AM) Natchez MS
WFMO(AM) Fairmont NC
WIDU(AM) Fayetteville NC
WFMC(AM) Goldsboro NC
*WNAA(FM) Greensboro NC
WHNC(AM) Henderson NC
WEGG(AM) Rose Hill NC
WWIL(AM) Wilmington NC
*WNEC-FM Henniker NH
*KCEP(FM) Las Vegas NV
WSIV(AM) East Syracuse NY
WTHE(AM) Mineola NY
WBLS(AM) New York NY
*WHCR-FM New York NY
WLIB(AM) New York NY
*WBGU(FM) Bowling Green OH
*WIXQ(FM) Millersville PA
WNAP(AM) Norristown PA
WDAS-FM Philadelphia PA
WDOG(AM) Allendale SC
WDOG-FM Allendale SC
WPJS(AM) Conway SC
WWRK(AM) Darlington SC
WBZF(FM) Hartsville SC
*WLGI(FM) Hemingway SC
WASC(AM) Spartanburg SC
WMRB(AM) Columbia TN
*WVCP(FM) Gallatin TN
WFKX(FM) Henderson TN
WDIA(AM) Memphis TN
*WMTS-FM Murfreesboro TN
KGGR(AM) Dallas TX
KCOH(AM) Houston TX
WKBY(AM) Chatham VA
WILA(AM) Danville VA
WSHV(AM) South Hill VA

Bluegrass

*WPIL(FM) Heflin AL
WRMG(AM) Red Bay AL
KCGS(AM) Marshall AR
*WAMU(FM) Washington DC
WALH(AM) Mountain City GA
WYHG(AM) Young Harris GA
*WAAJ(FM) Benton KY
WSKV(FM) Stanton KY

WTWZ(AM) Clinton MS
WPYB(AM) Benson NC
WKTE(AM) King NC
WKGX(AM) Lenoir NC
WDSL(AM) Mocksville NC
WPAQ(AM) Mount Airy NC
WMPM(AM) Smithfield NC
WADV(AM) Lebanon PA
WAGS(AM) Bishopville SC
WJDJ(AM) Hartsville SC
*WDVX(FM) Clinton TN
WLSB(AM) Copperhill TN
WSDQ(AM) Dunlap TN
*WLMU(FM) Harrogate TN
*WPLN-FM Nashville TN
WUAT(AM) Pikeville TN
WLIJ(AM) Shelbyville TN
*WTML(FM) Tullahoma TN
*KAMU-FM College Station TX
WHAN(AM) Ashland VA
WSVS(AM) Crewe VA
WGFC(AM) Floyd VA
WLRV(AM) Lebanon VA
WNRV(AM) Narrows-Pearisburg VA
WYTI(AM) Rocky Mount VA
WXMY(AM) Saltville VA
*WWED(FM) Spotsylvania VA
KOHO-FM Leavenworth WA

Blues

WREN(AM) Carrollton AL
WQZZ(AM) Eutaw AL
WJLD(AM) Fairfield AL
WZEW(FM) Fairhope AL
WKXN(FM) Greenville AL
WHIY(AM) Huntsville AL
*WJAB(FM) Huntsville AL
WKXK(FM) Pine Hill AL
KAJM(FM) Camp Verde AZ
KOHT(FM) Marana AZ
KRML(AM) Carmel CA
KJLH-FM Compton CA
*KKUP(FM) Cupertino CA
*KSDS(FM) San Diego CA
KQKS(FM) Lakewood CO
WFLM(FM) White City FL
WVKX(FM) Irwinton GA
WLZN(FM) Macon GA
WNUQ(AM) Sylvester GA
KATZ-FM Alton IL
*WSSD(FM) Chicago IL
WFFX(AM) East St. Louis IL
*WDCB(FM) Glen Ellyn IL
*WGLT(FM) Normal IL
WTLC-FM Greenwood IN
WHHH(AM) Indianapolis IN
KBRH(AM) Baton Rouge LA
KJMH(FM) Lake Arthur LA
WATD-FM Marshfield MA
*WESM(FM) Princess Anne MD
*WUCX-FM Bay City MI
WDMK(FM) Detroit MI
WJNZ(AM) Kentwood MI
*WLNZ(FM) Lansing MI
*WNMC-FM Traverse City MI
*WEMU(FM) Ypsilanti MI
*KMVC(FM) Marshall MO
*KCOZ(FM) Point Lookout MO
WJZD(FM) Bay St. Louis MS
WELZ(AM) Belzoni MS
WONG(AM) Canton MS
WROX(AM) Clarksdale MS
WTYJ(FM) Fayette MS
*WURC(FM) Holly Springs MS
*WVSD(FM) Itta Bena MS
*WMPR(FM) Jackson MS
WHJA(AM) Laurel MS
WESY(AM) Leland MS
WNBN(AM) Meridian MS
WMIS(AM) Natchez MS
WABO(AM) Waynesboro MS
WQMG-FM Greensboro NC
WNCT(AM) Greenville NC
WCPS(AM) Tarboro NC
WENC(AM) Whiteville NC

*KCEP(FM) Las Vegas NV
WRKS(FM) New York NY
WJZR(FM) Rochester NY
WDAO(AM) Dayton OH
WRBP(FM) Hubbard OH
WXMG(FM) Upper Arlington OH
*KRVM-FM Eugene OR
*KMHD(FM) Gresham OR
WKSP(FM) Aiken SC
WYNN(AM) Florence SC
WVOL(AM) Berry Hill TN
WBOL(AM) Bolivar TN
*WEVL(FM) Memphis TN
WEUZ(FM) Minor Hill TN
*KAZI-FM Austin TX
KBFB(AM) Dallas TX
*WFOS(FM) Chesapeake VA
WVKL(FM) Norfolk VA
*KPLI(FM) Olympia WA
*KVIX(FM) Port Angeles WA
KRIZ(AM) Renton WA
*KPLU-FM Tacoma WA
WKKV-FM Racine WI

Children

KDIS-FM Little Rock AR
KMIK(AM) Tempe AZ
KMKY(AM) Oakland CA
KDIS(AM) Pasadena CA
KIID(AM) Sacramento CA
KKDD(AM) San Bernardino CA
KDDZ(AM) Arvada CO
WDZK(AM) Bloomfield CT
WAJD(AM) Gainesville FL
WBWL(AM) Jacksonville FL
WMYM(AM) Miami FL
WDYZ(AM) Orlando FL
WDWD(AM) Atlanta GA
WNEX(AM) Macon GA
WPGA(AM) Perry GA
WRDZ(AM) La Grange IL
KQAM(AM) Wichita KS
WDRD(AM) Newburg KY
WBYU(AM) New Orleans LA
KDIZ(AM) Golden Valley MN
KPHN(AM) Kansas City MO
WGFY(AM) Charlotte NC
WCOG(AM) Greensboro NC
WWJZ(AM) Mount Holly NJ
KALY(AM) Los Ranchos de Albuquerque NM
KYDZ(AM) North Las Vegas NV
WWLF(AM) Auburn NY
WQEW(AM) New York NY
WOLF(AM) Syracuse NY
WWMK(AM) Cleveland OH
KOCY(AM) Del City OK
WWCS(AM) Canonsburg PA
*WWCF(FM) McConnellsburg PA
WDDZ(AM) Pawtucket RI
KMIC(AM) Houston TX
KRDY(AM) San Antonio TX
KWDZ(AM) Salt Lake City UT
WDZY(AM) Colonial Heights VA
KKDZ(AM) Seattle WA
*WMLJ(FM) Summersville WV

Chinese

KAZN(AM) Pasadena CA
KAHZ(AM) Pomona CA
KNSN(AM) San Diego CA
KHCM(AM) Honolulu HI
WKDM(AM) New York NY
WZRC(AM) New York NY

Christian

KAFC(FM) Anchorage AK
*KAKL(FM) Anchorage AK
KYKD(FM) Bethel AK
KAGV(AM) Big Lake AK
*KHZK(FM) Kotzebue AK
KAKN(FM) Naknek AK

KIAM(AM) Nenana AK
KICY-FM Nome AK
*KIAM-FM North Nenana AK
*KJLP(FM) Palmer AK
WIZB(FM) Abbeville AL
WAVU(AM) Albertville AL
*WGRW(FM) Anniston AL
WDJC-FM Birmingham AL
*WGIB(FM) Birmingham AL
*WELJ(FM) Brewton AL
*WALN(FM) Carrollton AL
WQUA(AM) Citronelle AL
*WELL-FM Dadeville AL
WKWL(FM) Florala AL
*WTBB(FM) Gadsden AL
*WJIA(FM) Guntersville AL
*WAYH(AM) Harvest AL
WBXR(FM) Hazel Green AL
*WJOU(FM) Huntsville AL
WIXI(AM) Jasper AL
WBHY(AM) Mobile AL
*WBHY-FM Mobile AL
WXVI(AM) Montgomery AL
*WAQG(FM) Ozark AL
WVRV(FM) Pine Level AL
WIJD(AM) Prichard AL
*WAQU(FM) Selma AL
*WAKD(FM) Sheffield AL
WYEA(AM) Sylacauga AL
*WAXU(FM) Troy AL
*WMFT(FM) Tuscaloosa AL
*KJSM-FM Augusta AR
*KOAR(FM) Beebe AR
*KAPG(FM) Bentonville AR
*KBCM(FM) Blytheville AR
*KBHN(FM) Booneville AR
KKSP(FM) Bryant AR
KXRL(FM) Cherry Valley AR
KWXT(AM) Dardanelle AR
*KBPU(FM) De Queen AR
*KAKV(FM) El Dorado AR
*KAYH(FM) Fayetteville AR
*KBNV(FM) Fayetteville AR
KOFC(FM) Fayetteville AR
*KPOS(FM) Fouke AR
*KGSF(FM) Green Forest AR
KZKF-FM Greenwood AR
*KBPW(FM) Hampton AR
*KBPB(FM) Harrison AR
*KBMJ(FM) Heber Springs AR
*KALR(FM) Hot Springs AR
*KLRO(FM) Hot Springs AR
KJLV(FM) Hoxie AR
*KJSB(FM) Jonesboro AR
KJBR(FM) Marked Tree AR
*KLMK(FM) Marvell AR
*KLRM(FM) Melbourne AR
*KNLL(FM) Nashville AR
*KMTC(FM) Russellville AR
*KLRC(FM) Siloam Springs AR
*KKLT(FM) Texarkana AR
KKLV(FM) Turrell AR
*WPLX(AM) Turrell AR
*KLFS(FM) Van Buren AR
KNWJ(FM) Leone AS
KJAL(AM) Tafuna AS
*KWRB(FM) Bisbee AZ
*KLVA(FM) Casa Grande AZ
KCKY(AM) Coolidge AZ
*KZAI(FM) Coolidge AZ
*KRMC(FM) Douglas AZ
*KJTA(FM) Flagstaff AZ
*KLVK(FM) Fountain Hills AZ
*KLKA(FM) Globe AZ
*KVJC(FM) Globe AZ
*KAIH(FM) Lake Havasu City AZ
*KNLB(FM) Lake Havasu City AZ
*KNOG(FM) Nogales AZ
*KFLR-FM Phoenix AZ
KXEG(AM) Phoenix AZ
*KGCB(FM) Prescott AZ
KNXN(AM) Sierra Vista AZ
KTBA(AM) Tuba City AZ
*KFLT(AM) Tucson AZ
*KFLT-FM Tucson AZ
KGMS(AM) Tucson AZ

KWIM(FM) Window Rock AZ
*KCFY(FM) Yuma AZ
*KYRM(FM) Yuma AZ
KFSH-FM Anaheim CA
KERI(AM) Bakersfield CA
*KWTH(FM) Barstow CA
*KWTW(FM) Bishop CA
*KWLU(FM) Chester CA
*KLVS(FM) Citrus Heights CA
*KPSH(FM) Coachella CA
*KDKL(FM) Coalinga CA
*KARQ(FM) East Sonora CA
KIHH(AM) Eureka CA
*KLVY(FM) Fairmead CA
*KYCI(FM) Firebaugh CA
KIRV(AM) Fresno CA
KWRU(AM) Fresno CA
*KLVG(FM) Garberville CA
KKMC(AM) Gonzales CA
KSDT(AM) Hemet CA
*KHRI(FM) Hollister CA
*KORB(FM) Hopland CA
*KZLU(FM) Inyokern CA
*KLVJ(FM) Julian CA
*KWTM(FM) June Lake CA
*KWDS(FM) Kettleman City CA
*KDRH(FM) King City CA
*KTLW(FM) Lancaster CA
*KHKL(FM) Laytonville CA
KKFS(FM) Lincoln CA
*KLVN(FM) Livingston CA
*KRQZ(FM) Lompoc CA
*KFRN(AM) Long Beach CA
KKLA-FM Los Angeles CA
*KLVC(FM) Magalia CA
*KAMB(FM) Merced CA
*KLVR(FM) Middletown CA
KCIV(FM) Mount Bullion CA
*KKLC(FM) Mount Shasta CA
KGDP(AM) Oildale CA
*KLFH(FM) Ojai CA
KDAR(FM) Oxnard CA
*KHCS(FM) Palm Desert CA
*KLVM(FM) Prunedale CA
KNLF(FM) Quincy CA
*KGBM(FM) Randsburg CA
*KLVB(FM) Red Bluff CA
*KKRO(FM) Redding CA
KVIP(AM) Redding CA
KVIP-FM Redding CA
*KWTD(FM) Ridgecrest CA
*KSGN(FM) Riverside CA
KDBV(AM) Salinas CA
KWVE(FM) San Clemente CA
*KLFF-FM San Luis Obispo CA
*KLVH(FM) San Luis Obispo CA
KPRZ(AM) San Marcos-Poway CA
*KSRI(FM) Santa Cruz CA
*KGDP-FM Santa Maria CA
KSBQ(AM) Santa Maria CA
*KQKL(FM) Selma CA
KYIX(FM) South Oroville CA
*KBLV(FM) Tehachapi CA
*KRTM(FM) Temecula CA
*KYKL(FM) Tracy CA
*KULV(FM) Ukiah CA
*KHMS(FM) Victorville CA
*KXRD(FM) Victorville CA
*KARM(FM) Visalia CA
*KSAK(FM) Walnut CA
*KFHL(FM) Wasco CA
KALI(AM) West Covina CA
*KARA(FM) Williams CA
KIQS(AM) Willows CA
*KLRD(FM) Yucaipa CA
KLJH(FM) Bayfield CO
KLVZ(AM) Brighton CO
*KBWA(FM) Brush CO
*KTLC(FM) Canon City CO
*KTMH(FM) Colona CO
*KTLF(FM) Colorado Springs CO
KLTT(AM) Commerce City CO
KDTA(AM) Delta CO
KLZ(AM) Denver CO
*KPOF(AM) Denver CO
*KTCF(FM) Dolores CO

*KTDU(FM) Durango CO
*KGCO(FM) Fort Collins CO
*KLXV(FM) Glenwood Springs CO
KJOL(AM) Grand Junction CO
*KLFV(FM) Grand Junction CO
*KLRY(FM) Gypsum CO
*KTOL(FM) Leadville CO
*KXWA(FM) Loveland CO
KBIQ(FM) Manitou Springs CO
KCBR(AM) Monument CO
*KLDV(FM) Morrison CO
*KTPS(FM) Pagosa Springs CO
*KTEI(FM) Placerville CO
*KFRY(FM) Pueblo CO
KGFT(FM) Pueblo CO
*KTPL(FM) Pueblo CO
*KJWA(FM) Rye CO
*KRWA(FM) Rye CO
*KTPF(FM) Salida CO
*KTML(FM) South Fork CO
*KLBV(FM) Steamboat Springs CO
*KTSG(FM) Steamboat Springs CO
*KDRE(FM) Sterling CO
*KLZV(FM) Sterling CO
*KTAD(FM) Sterling CO
*KTDL(FM) Trinidad CO
*KTAW(FM) Walsenburg CO
*WIHS(FM) Middletown CT
*WSGG(FM) Norfolk CT
WXCT(AM) Southington CT
*WXHL-FM Christiana DE
WHIM(AM) Apopka FL
*WKSG(FM) Cedar Creek FL
*WMYZ(FM) Clermont FL
*WPSF(FM) Clewiston FL
WMCU(AM) Coral Gables FL
WAKU(FM) Crawfordville FL
*WWLC(FM) Cross City FL
*WAQV(FM) Crystal River FL
*WHGN(FM) Crystal River FL
*WREH(FM) Cypress Quarters FL
*WAKJ(FM) De Funiak Springs FL
*WSEB(FM) Englewood FL
*WJLH(FM) Flagler Beach FL
*WMFL(FM) Florida City FL
*WAFG(FM) Fort Lauderdale FL
*WAYJ(FM) Fort Myers FL
WCRM(AM) Fort Myers FL
*WJYO(FM) Fort Myers FL
*WMYE(FM) Fort Myers FL
*WPSM(FM) Fort Walton Beach FL
*WJLF(FM) Gainesville FL
*WYJC(FM) Greenville FL
*WAPN(FM) Holly Hill FL
WEAZ(FM) Holly Hill FL
*WCRJ(FM) Jacksonville FL
WROS(AM) Jacksonville FL
*WGES-FM Key Largo FL
*WMKL(FM) Key Largo FL
*WJIR(FM) Key West FL
*WKWR(FM) Key West FL
*WKZG(FM) Key West FL
*WLAZ(FM) Kissimmee FL
*WBIY(FM) La Belle FL
*WOLR(FM) Lake City FL
*WLMS(FM) Lecanto FL
WAYP(FM) Marianna FL
*WEGS(FM) Milton FL
*WKVH(FM) Monticello FL
*WSOR(FM) Naples FL
*WSRX(FM) Naples FL
WKFP(FM) Navarre FL
*WCIE(FM) New Port Richey FL
*WHIJ(FM) Ocala FL
*WAYR(AM) Orange Park FL
WTLN(AM) Orlando FL
*WHIF(FM) Palatka FL
*WEJF(FM) Palm Bay FL
*WRYZ(FM) Palm Bay FL
*WCNO(FM) Palm City FL
*WFFL(FM) Panama City FL
*WGNK(FM) Pennsuco FL
WVTJ(AM) Pensacola FL
WTBN(AM) Pinellas Park FL
WTWD(AM) Plant City FL
WOKV-FM Ponte Vedra Beach FL

*WAYL(FM) Saint Augustine FL
*WSMR(FM) Sarasota FL
*WTLG(FM) Starke FL
*WFRF(AM) Tallahassee FL
WTAL(AM) Tallahassee FL
*WBVM(FM) Tampa FL
*WPOZ(FM) Union Park FL
*WSCF-FM Vero Beach FL
*WAYF(FM) West Palm Beach FL
*WBJY(FM) Americus GA
*WFFM(FM) Ashburn GA
WFSH-FM Athens GA
*WMSL(FM) Athens GA
WAEC(AM) Atlanta GA
WNIV(AM) Atlanta GA
*WLPE(FM) Augusta GA
WGMI(AM) Bremen GA
*WAYR-FM Brunswick GA
WPMA(FM) Buckhead GA
*WPWB(FM) Byron GA
WCHM(AM) Clarkesville GA
WPBS(AM) Conyers GA
WSRM(AM) Coosa GA
*WAEF(FM) Cordele GA
WWGF(FM) Donalsonville GA
*WAWH(FM) Dublin GA
*WECC-FM Folkston GA
WTHP(AM) Gibson GA
*WMVV(FM) Griffin GA
*WTFH(FM) Helen GA
*WIVL(FM) Jasper GA
*WLPT(FM) Jesup GA
WVFJ-FM Manchester GA
WIGO(AM) Morrow GA
WGTJ(AM) Murrayville GA
*WGCN(FM) Nashville GA
WVKV(FM) Nashville GA
WNEA(AM) Newnan GA
WLPF(FM) Ocilla GA
WTIF-FM Omega GA
*WLFS(FM) Port Wentworth GA
*WLXP(FM) Savannah GA
*WYFS(FM) Savannah GA
WZIQ(FM) Smithville GA
*WHKV(FM) Sylvester GA
*WAYT(FM) Thomasville GA
*WQAI(FM) Thomson GA
*WTXR(FM) Toccoa Falls GA
WBDX(FM) Trenton GA
*WGPH(FM) Vidalia GA
WKTF(AM) Vienna GA
*WASW(FM) Waycross GA
*KSDA-FM Agat GU
*KHMG(FM) Barrigada GU
*KCIF(FM) Hilo HI
KAIM-FM Honolulu HI
KGU(AM) Honolulu HI
*KIHS(FM) Adel IA
KSKB(AM) Brooklyn IA
*KAYP(FM) Burlington IA
*KILV(FM) Castana IA
KCOG(AM) Centerville IA
KLNG(AM) Council Bluffs IA
*KLOX(FM) Creston IA
KPSZ(AM) Des Moines IA
*KIAD(AM) Dubuque IA
*KJYL(FM) Eagle Grove IA
*KXGM-FM Hiawatha IA
*KMDY(FM) Keokuk IA
KNWM(AM) Madrid IA
KCWN(FM) New Sharon IA
*KKLG(FM) Newton IA
*KNWI(FM) Osceola IA
KJCY(FM) Saint Ansgar IA
*KYFR(AM) Shenandoah IA
KSOU(AM) Sioux Center IA
KTFC(FM) Sioux City IA
KTFG(FM) Sioux Rapids IA
*KJIA(FM) Spirit Lake IA
*KTDV(FM) State Center IA
*KAIP(FM) Wapello IA
*KNWS(AM) Waterloo IA
KXGM(AM) Waterloo IA
*KWVI(FM) Waverly IA
KPUL(FM) Winterset IA
KSPD(AM) Boise ID

*KTFY(FM) Buhl ID
KBGN(AM) Caldwell ID
KBXL(AM) Caldwell ID
*KTSY(FM) Caldwell ID
KRTK(AM) Chubbuck ID
KAIO(AM) Idaho Falls ID
*KARJ(FM) Kuna ID
*KAWS(FM) Marsing ID
*KZJB(FM) Pocatello ID
*KLRI(FM) Rigby ID
KSQS(FM) Ririe ID
*KAWZ(FM) Twin Falls ID
*KCIR(FM) Twin Falls ID
*KEFX(FM) Twin Falls ID
*WCLR(FM) Arlington Heights IL
WRMS(AM) Beardstown IL
*WVYN(AM) Bluford IL
*WBEL(FM) Cairo IL
*WIBI(FM) Carlinville IL
*WBVN(FM) Carrier Mills IL
WCBH(FM) Casey IL
WKZI(AM) Casey IL
*WMBI-FM Chicago IL
*WBMF(FM) Crete IL
WYCA(FM) Crete IL
WAIT(AM) Crystal Lake IL
*WARW(FM) Dorsey IL
WDQN-FM Du Quoin IL
*WRYT(AM) Edwardsville IL
*WEFI(FM) Effingham IL
WPIA(FM) Eureka IL
*WAXR(FM) Geneseo IL
WJKL(FM) Glendale Heights IL
WGNU(AM) Granite City IL
WIJR(AM) Highland IL
*WAWF(FM) Kankakee IL
*WONU(FM) Kankakee IL
WLLM(AM) Lincoln IL
*WAWJ(FM) Marion IL
*WJCZ(FM) Milford IL
*WOTW(FM) Monee IL
*WCFL(FM) Morris IL
*WAPO(FM) Mount Vernon IL
*WBMV(FM) Mount Vernon IL
*WPTH(FM) Olney IL
*WWGN(FM) Onarga IL
*WZRS(FM) Pana IL
*WCIC(FM) Pekin IL
*WLWJ(FM) Petersburg IL
*WPJC(FM) Pontiac IL
*WPRC(FM) Princeton IL
*WGCA-FM Quincy IL
*WJLY(FM) Ramsey IL
WLKU(FM) Rock Island IL
*WFEN(FM) Rockford IL
WQFL(FM) Rockford IL
*WGNJ(FM) Saint Joseph IL
*WSLE(FM) Salem IL
WINU(AM) Shelbyville IL
*WLUJ(FM) Springfield IL
*WSCT(FM) Springfield IL
*WSRI(FM) Sugar Grove IL
*WIHM(AM) Taylorville IL
*WETN(FM) Wheaton IL
*WGNR(AM) Anderson IN
*WGNR-FM Anderson IN
WQME(FM) Anderson IN
WHPZ(FM) Bremen IN
*WPFR-FM Clinton IN
WCMR(AM) Elkhart IN
WFRN-FM Elkhart IN
*WBCL(FM) Fort Wayne IN
WFCV(AM) Fort Wayne IN
*WLAB(FM) Fort Wayne IN
WLYV(AM) Fort Wayne IN
*WIKL(FM) Greencastle IN
*WAUZ(FM) Greensburg IN
*WQKO(FM) Howe IN
WBRI(AM) Indianapolis IN
*WQSG(FM) Lafayette IN
*KXJH(FM) Linton IN
*WJCF-FM Morristown IN
WVNI(FM) Nashville IN
WFIA-FM New Albany IN
*WARA(FM) New Washington IN
*WHZN(FM) New Whiteland IN

WGAB(AM) Newburgh IN
*WIKV(FM) Plymouth IN
*WZRP(FM) Richmond IN
*WQKV(FM) Rochester IN
*WJLR(FM) Seymour IN
WHME(FM) South Bend IN
*WHOJ(FM) Terre Haute IN
WPFR(FM) Terre Haute IN
*WJYW(FM) Union City IN
*WTUR(FM) Upland IN
*WATI(FM) Vincennes IN
*WENS(FM) Wadesville IN
WFRR(FM) Walton IN
*WKHL(FM) West Lafayette IN
KDGS(FM) Andover KS
*KAXR(FM) Arkansas City KS
KEOJ(FM) Caney KS
*KHYM(FM) Copeland KS
*KJIL(FM) Copeland KS
KAIG(FM) Dodge City KS
*KTLI(FM) El Dorado KS
*KNGM(FM) Emporia KS
*KBMP(FM) Enterprise KS
KCNW(AM) Fairway KS
*KVCY(FM) Fort Scott KS
*KBDA(FM) Great Bend KS
*KWBI(FM) Great Bend KS
KHYS(FM) Hays KS
*KJRL(FM) Herington KS
*KARF(FM) Independence KS
*KBQC(FM) Independence KS
KCVW(FM) Kingman KS
KKLO(FM) Leavenworth KS
KZQD(FM) Liberal KS
*KGLV(FM) Manhattan KS
*KSNS(FM) Medicine Lodge KS
KJRG(AM) Newton KS
*KRLE(FM) Oberlin KS
KCCV-FM Olathe KS
*KRBW(FM) Ottawa KS
*KTJO-FM Ottawa KS
KCCV(AM) Overland Park KS
KKCV(FM) Rozel KS
*KCVS(FM) Salina KS
KCVT(FM) Silver Lake KS
KHCA(FM) Wamego KS
*KCFN(FM) Wichita KS
*KYFW(FM) Wichita KS
*KYWA(FM) Wichita KS
*KBDD(FM) Winfield KS
*WAYD(FM) Auburn KY
*WTRT(FM) Benton KY
*WCVK(FM) Bowling Green KY
*WAPD(FM) Campbellsville KY
WMTA(AM) Central City KY
*WDFB-FM Danville KY
*WLAI(FM) Danville KY
*WPRZ-FM Fredonia KY
*WRVG(FM) Georgetown KY
*WSGP(FM) Glasgow KY
WKCB(AM) Hindman KY
*WNKJ(FM) Hopkinsville KY
*WHMR(FM) Ledbetter KY
WFIA(AM) Louisville KY
WWLT(FM) Manchester KY
WMIK-FM Middlesboro KY
*WBMK(FM) Morehead KY
*WKVN(FM) Morganfield KY
*WJIE-FM Okolona KY
*WJVK(FM) Owensboro KY
*WGCF(FM) Paducah KY
*WWJD(FM) Pippa Passes KY
*WKVY(FM) Somerset KY
WXKY-FM Stanford KY
WRVI(FM) Valley Station KY
WMTC(AM) Vancleve KY
WMTC-FM Vancleve KY
WZLK(FM) Virgie KY
WVRB(FM) Wilmore KY
WMJR(AM) Winchester KY
*KAPM(FM) Alexandria LA
KJMJ(AM) Alexandria LA
*KLXA-FM Alexandria LA
*KHCL(FM) Arcadia LA
*KAXV(FM) Bastrop LA
*WJFM(FM) Baton Rouge LA

KBCL(AM) Bossier City LA
*WBKL(FM) Clinton LA
*KBAN(FM) De Ridder LA
*KVDP(FM) Dry Prong LA
KBEF(FM) Gibsland LA
KKNO(AM) Gretna LA
KYLA(FM) Homer LA
*KITA(FM) Iota LA
*KTOC-FM Jonesboro LA
*KIKL(FM) Lafayette LA
*KOJO(FM) Lake Charles LA
*KYLC(FM) Lake Charles LA
*KHMD(FM) Mansfield LA
*KMSL(FM) Mansfield LA
*KAVK(FM) Many LA
*KBMQ(FM) Monroe LA
KLIC(AM) Monroe LA
*KYFL(FM) Monroe LA
*KBIO(FM) Natchitoches LA
*WBSN-FM New Orleans LA
WLNO(AM) New Orleans LA
WVOG(FM) New Orleans LA
*WNKV(FM) Norco LA
*KSUL(FM) Port Sulphur LA
KHLL(FM) Richwood LA
*KAPI(FM) Ruston LA
*KSJY(FM) Saint Martinville LA
KSYB(AM) Shreveport LA
*KRLR(FM) Sulphur LA
*WJCI(FM) Baptist Village MA
WROL(AM) Boston MA
WWDJ(AM) Boston MA
WMSX(AM) Brockton MA
*WYCM(FM) Charlton MA
WFGL(AM) Fitchburg MA
WCMX(AM) Leominster MA
*WTKL(FM) North Dartmouth MA
*WRYP(FM) Wellfleet MA
*WKMY(FM) Winchendon MA
WAMD(AM) Aberdeen MD
WRBS(AM) Baltimore MD
WRBS-FM Baltimore MD
WKDI(AM) Denton MD
*WLIC(FM) Frostburg MD
*WAIJ(FM) Grantsville MD
*WZXH(FM) Hagerstown MD
WWGB(AM) Indian Head MD
*WDIH(FM) Salisbury MD
WTHU(AM) Thurmont MD
*WWPN(FM) Westernport MD
*WHCF(FM) Bangor ME
WBCI(FM) Bath ME
*WJVH(FM) Belfast ME
*WRPB(FM) Benedicta ME
*WFST(AM) Caribou ME
*WKVZ(FM) Dexter ME
WMSJ(FM) Freeport ME
*WARX(FM) Lewiston ME
*WHMX(FM) Lincoln ME
*WWLN(FM) Lincoln ME
*WMDR-FM Oakland ME
WJCX(FM) Pittsfield ME
*WHPF(FM) Pittston Farm ME
*WKVV(FM) Searsport ME
*WWWA(FM) Winslow ME
*WUFN(FM) Albion MI
*WVCN(FM) Baraga MI
WBFN(AM) Battle Creek MI
*WLKB(FM) Bay City MI
*WTLI(FM) Bear Creek Township MI
*WSLI(FM) Belding MI
*WCVM(FM) Bronson MI
*WTAC(FM) Burton MI
WLJW(AM) Cadillac MI
*WCWB(FM) Coldwater MI
*WPRJ(FM) Coleman MI
WMUZ(FM) Detroit MI
WHPD(FM) Dowagiac MI
*WJOM(FM) Eagle MI
*WRQC(FM) East Tawas MI
*WLJN(FM) Elmwood Township MI
*WAKL(FM) Flint MI
WSNL(AM) Flint MI
*WTRK(FM) Freeland MI
*WBLW(FM) Gaylord MI
*WJOG(FM) Good Hart MI

*WAYG(FM) Grand Rapids MI
*WCSG(FM) Grand Rapids MI
WCZE(FM) Harbor Beach MI
*WJOJ(FM) Harrisville MI
WLCM(AM) Holt MI
*WWKM(FM) Imlay City MI
*WVCM(FM) Iron Mountain MI
*WLVM(FM) Ironwood MI
*WAYK(FM) Kalamazoo MI
*WLGH(FM) Leroy Township MI
WCAR(AM) Livonia MI
*WKPK(FM) Michigamme MI
*WUGN(FM) Midland MI
*WDTR(FM) Monroe MI
*WMCQ(FM) Muskegon MI
*WPCJ(FM) Pittsford MI
*WJOH(FM) Raco MI
*WSFP(FM) Rust Township MI
*WTHN(FM) Sault Ste. Marie MI
*WJKN-FM Spring Arbor MI
*WSAE(FM) Spring Arbor MI
*WCFG(FM) Springfield MI
*WUFL(AM) Sterling Heights MI
*WLJN-FM Traverse City MI
*WEJC(FM) White Star MI
WDEO(AM) Ypsilanti MI
WJQK(FM) Zeeland MI
*KBHG(FM) Alexandria MN
*KDNW(FM) Duluth MN
*WJRF(FM) Duluth MN
KBGY(FM) Faribault MN
WLKX-FM Forest Lake MN
KKEQ(FM) Fosston MN
*KADU(FM) Hibbing MN
*KBHW(FM) International Falls MN
*KXBR(FM) International Falls MN
WCTS(AM) Maplewood MN
*KTIS(AM) Minneapolis MN
WLOL(AM) Minneapolis MN
*KMKL(FM) North Branch MN
KCGN-FM Ortonville MN
KBHL(FM) Osakis MN
WZFJ(FM) Pequot Lakes MN
KKMS(AM) Richfield MN
*KFSI(FM) Rochester MN
*KKJM(FM) Saint Joseph MN
*KOPJ(FM) Sebeka MN
*KKLW(FM) Willmar MN
*KJWR(FM) Windom MN
KQRB(FM) Windom MN
*KRLP(FM) Windom MN
*KBOJ(FM) Worthington MN
KPVR(FM) Bowling Green MO
*KLFC(FM) Branson MO
KOMC(AM) Branson MO
*KCVY(FM) Cabool MO
*KCVO-FM Camdenton MO
KKLL(AM) Carthage- MO
KMFC(FM) Centralia MO
KSIV(AM) Clayton MO
*KLRQ(FM) Clinton MO
*KJCV(FM) Country Club MO
*KCVZ(FM) Dixon MO
*KTBJ(FM) Festus MO
*KMCV(FM) High Point MO
KBCV(AM) Hollister MO
*KOBC(FM) Joplin MO
*KLJC(FM) Kansas City MO
*KAUF(FM) Kennett MO
KLTE(FM) Kirksville MO
*KCVQ(FM) Knob Noster MO
*KTTK(FM) Lebanon MO
KLRX(FM) Lee's Summit MO
*KNLM(FM) Marshfield MO
*KBKC(FM) Moberly MO
*KCGR(FM) Oran MO
*KCVJ(FM) Osceola MO
*KCVK(FM) Otterville MO
*KBGM(FM) Park Hills MO
*KOKS(FM) Poplar Bluff MO
KHZR(FM) Potosi MO
KADI-FM Republic MO
KAYX(FM) Richmond MO
KGNM(AM) Saint Joseph MO
*KSRD(FM) Saint Joseph MO
KJSL(AM) Saint Louis MO

*KSIV-FM Saint Louis MO
KXEN(AM) Saint Louis MO
*KCVX(FM) Salem MO
*KSCV(FM) Springfield MO
*KWFC(FM) Springfield MO
*KWND(FM) Springfield MO
*KCRL(FM) Sunrise Beach MO
*KRSS(FM) Tarkio MO
KALM(AM) Thayer MO
KULH(FM) Wheeling MO
WCMR-FM Bruce MS
*WKVF(FM) Byhalia MS
WDFX(FM) Cleveland MS
WHJT(FM) Clinton MS
*WLVZ(FM) Collins MS
*WPRG(FM) Columbia MS
*WCSO(FM) Columbus MS
*WMBU(FM) Forest MS
WQST-FM Forest MS
*WQVI(FM) Forest MS
*WSQH(FM) Forest MS
WWUN-FM Friar's Point MS
*WLRK(FM) Greenville MS
*WAOY(FM) Gulfport MS
WCPC(AM) Houston MS
*WYTF(FM) Indianola MS
WSJC(AM) Magee MS
WMER(AM) Meridian MS
*WAVI(FM) Oxford MS
*WPAS(FM) Pascagoula MS
*WLKO(FM) Quitman MS
*WMSB(FM) Senatobia MS
WSAO(AM) Senatobia MS
*WAFR(FM) Tupelo MS
*WAJS(FM) Tupelo MS
WJXN-FM Utica MS
WLRC(AM) Walnut MS
*KJFT(FM) Arlee MT
KCMM(FM) Belgrade MT
*KGCM(FM) Belgrade MT
*KLMT(FM) Billings MT
*KLRV(FM) Billings MT
KMZK(AM) Billings MT
*KLBZ(FM) Bozeman MT
*KFRD(FM) Butte MT
*KFRT(FM) Butte MT
*KAFH(FM) Great Falls MT
*KFRW(FM) Great Falls MT
*KGFA(FM) Great Falls MT
*KMZO(FM) Hamilton MT
*KHLV(FM) Helena MT
KALS(FM) Kalispell MT
*KLKM(FM) Kalispell MT
*KLEU(FM) Lewistown MT
*KYWH(FM) Lockwood MT
*KMZL(FM) Missoula MT
*KBIL(FM) Park City MT
*KQLR(FM) Whitehall MT
*WBKU(FM) Ahoskie NC
*WLFA(FM) Asheville NC
WSKY(AM) Asheville NC
*WZGO(FM) Aurora NC
*WXBE(FM) Beaufort NC
WFGW(AM) Black Mountain NC
WMIT(FM) Black Mountain NC
WVBS(AM) Burgaw NC
WOGR(AM) Charlotte NC
*WYFQ(AM) Charlotte NC
WCSL(AM) Cherryville NC
WHPY(AM) Clayton NC
WCLN-FM Clinton NC
*WYBH(FM) Fayetteville NC
WPFJ(AM) Franklin NC
WSSG(AM) Goldsboro NC
WJSG(FM) Hamlet NC
WLGP(FM) Harkers Island NC
WJCV(AM) Jacksonville NC
*WJKA(FM) Jacksonville NC
WTRU(AM) Kernersville NC
*WGHW(FM) Lockwoods Folly Town NC
WDJS(AM) Mount Olive NC
WECR(AM) Newland NC
*WJIJ(FM) Norlina NC
*WBFY(FM) Pinehurst NC
WGIV(AM) Pineville NC

*WRAE(FM) Raeford NC
WPJL(AM) Raleigh NC
*WPGT(FM) Roanoke Rapids NC
*WRTP(FM) Roanoke Rapids NC
*WZDG(FM) Scotts Hill NC
WKVK(FM) Semora NC
WNCA(AM) Siler City NC
*WAGO(FM) Snow Hill NC
*WZRI(FM) Spring Lake NC
*WKGV(FM) Swansboro NC
WJRM(AM) Troy NC
WJFJ(AM) Tryon NC
WADE(AM) Wadesboro NC
WDRU(AM) Wake Forest NC
*WDVV(FM) Wilmington NC
*WWIL-FM Wilmington NC
WVOT(AM) Wilson NC
*WRCM(FM) Wingate NC
WBFJ(AM) Winston-Salem NC
*WBFJ-FM Winston-Salem NC
WPIP(AM) Winston-Salem NC
*WAJC(FM) Zebulon NC
*KBMK(FM) Bismarck ND
*KNRI(FM) Bismarck ND
*KDVI(FM) Devils Lake ND
*KFBN(FM) Fargo ND
KFNW-FM Fargo ND
*KWTL(AM) Grand Forks ND
KKLQ(FM) Harwood ND
*KLUU(FM) Jamestown ND
*KFNL(FM) Kindred ND
*KGCD(FM) Lincoln ND
KNDR(FM) Mandan ND
KHRT-FM Minot ND
*KNBE(FM) Beatrice NE
*KAMI(AM) Cozad NE
*KCVN(FM) Cozad NE
*KLNB(FM) Grand Island NE
KMMJ(AM) Grand Island NE
*KNFA(FM) Grand Island NE
*KROA(FM) Grand Island NE
*KAYA(FM) Hubbard NE
*KLCV(FM) Lincoln NE
*KJLT(AM) North Platte NE
KCRO(AM) Omaha NE
*KGBI-FM Omaha NE
*KYFG(FM) Omaha NE
*KGRD(FM) Orchard NE
KHZY(FM) Overton NE
*KMLV(FM) Ralston NE
*KDAI(FM) Scottsbluff NE
*KLJV(FM) Scottsbluff NE
KRKR(FM) Valley NE
*KFLV(FM) Wilber NE
*WVNH(FM) Concord NH
*WNHI(FM) Farmington NH
*WVFA(FM) Lebanon NH
*WLMW(FM) Manchester NH
*WANH(FM) Meredith NH
*WVBH(FM) Beach Haven West NJ
*WJPG(FM) Cape May Court House NJ
*WKVP(FM) Cherry Hill NJ
*WXGN(FM) Egg Harbor Township NJ
*WRDR(FM) Freehold Township NJ
*WVBV(FM) Medford Lakes NJ
*WFME(FM) Newark NJ
WNSW(AM) Newark NJ
WIBG(AM) Ocean City NJ
WXMC(AM) Parsippany-Troy Hills NJ
*WKMB(AM) Stirling NJ
WAWZ(FM) Zarephath NJ
KKIM(AM) Albuquerque NM
*KLYT(FM) Albuquerque NM
KSVA(AM) Albuquerque NM
KXKS(AM) Albuquerque NM
*KQGC(FM) Belen NM
*KQRI(FM) Bosque Farms NM
*KKCJ(FM) Cannon AFB NM
KAMQ(AM) Carlsbad NM
*KAQF(FM) Clovis NM
*KELU(FM) Clovis NM
*KZPI(FM) Deming NM
*KNMI(FM) Farmington NM
KPCL(FM) Farmington NM
*KTGW(FM) Fruitland NM

*KGGA(FM) Gallup NM
*KLLU(FM) Gallup NM
*KLGQ(FM) Grants NM
*KLHK(FM) Hobbs NM
*KMBN(FM) Las Cruces NM
KELP-FM Mesquite NM
*KGCN(FM) Roswell NM
*KRLU(FM) Roswell NM
KKIM-FM Santa Fe NM
*KQLV(FM) Santa Fe NM
*KVLK(FM) Socorro NM
*KXFR(FM) Socorro NM
KHAC(AM) Tse Bonito NM
*KVLP(FM) Tucumcari NM
*KNMA(FM) Tularosa NM
*KNIS(FM) Carson City NV
KRNG(AM) Fallon NV
KAVB(FM) Hawthorne NV
*KKVV(AM) Las Vegas NV
*KSOS(FM) Las Vegas NV
*KAIZ(FM) Mesquite NV
KIHM(AM) Reno NV
*KLRH(FM) Sparks NV
WDCD(AM) Albany NY
*WJCA(FM) Albion NY
*WCOF(FM) Arcade NY
*WNGN(FM) Argyle NY
WNYG(AM) Babylon NY
*WCIK(FM) Bath NY
*WIFF(FM) Binghamton NY
WASB(AM) Brockport NY
*WKDL-FM Brockport NY
WDCX-FM Buffalo NY
*WCIY(FM) Canandaigua NY
WRSB(AM) Canandaigua NY
*WMHI(FM) Cape Vincent NY
*WCOV-FM Clyde NY
*WKVJ(FM) Dannemora NY
WSIV(AM) East Syracuse NY
*WCIH(FM) Elmira NY
*WCID(FM) Friendship NY
*WLJH(FM) Glens Falls NY
*WGKR(FM) Grand Gorge NY
WHAZ-FM Hoosick Falls NY
*WHVP(FM) Hudson NY
*WCOT(FM) Jamestown NY
*WFGB(FM) Kingston NY
*WGWR(FM) Liberty NY
*WMHQ(FM) Malone NY
*WLJP(FM) Monroe NY
WRVP(AM) Mount Kisco NY
WMCA(AM) New York NY
*WWRV(AM) New York NY
WZXV(FM) Palmyra NY
*WPGL(FM) Pattersonville NY
*WRPJ(FM) Port Jervis NY
*WGKV(FM) Pulaski NY
*WYKV(FM) Ravena NY
WOKR(FM) Remsen NY
WDCX(FM) Rochester NY
*WSSK(FM) Saratoga Springs NY
WMYY(FM) Schoharie NY
*WYAI(FM) Scotia NY
*WFRS(FM) Smithtown NY
*WCII(FM) Spencer NY
*WMHR(FM) Syracuse NY
WHAZ(AM) Troy NY
*WKVU(FM) Utica NY
WRCK(FM) Utica NY
*WCOU(FM) Warsaw NY
*WKWV(FM) Watertown NY
WLGZ-FM Webster NY
*WMHN(FM) Webster NY
*WBCY(FM) Archbold OH
WJKW(FM) Athens OH
*WCVV(FM) Belpre OH
*WLKP(FM) Belpre OH
*WZCP(FM) Chillicothe OH
WAKW(FM) Cincinnati OH
*WCRF(FM) Cleveland OH
WFHM-FM Cleveland OH
*WHKC(FM) Columbus OH
*WGOJ(FM) Conneaut OH
*WYKL(FM) Crestline OH
*WQRP(FM) Dayton OH
*WORI(FM) Delhi Hills OH

*WTKC(FM) Findlay OH
*WCVO(FM) Gahanna OH
*WWGV(FM) Grove City OH
WPOS-FM Holland OH
*WCVJ(FM) Jefferson OH
*WFCO(FM) Lancaster OH
*WTGN(FM) Lima OH
*WYSM(FM) Lima OH
*WVMC-FM Mansfield OH
WUCO(AM) Marysville OH
*WYSZ(FM) Maumee OH
WFCJ(FM) Miamisburg OH
*WVML(FM) Millersburg OH
*WNZR(FM) Mount Vernon OH
WNPQ(FM) New Philadelphia OH
*WZNP(FM) Newark OH
WRTK(AM) Niles OH
*WHKU(FM) Proctorville OH
WNWT(AM) Rossford OH
*WLRY(FM) Rushville OH
*WVMS(FM) Sandusky OH
*WAUI(FM) Shelby OH
*WOAR(FM) South Vienna OH
*WEKV(FM) South Webster OH
*WBCJ(FM) Spencerville OH
*WEEC(FM) Springfield OH
*WBJV(FM) Steubenville OH
*WOKL(FM) Troy OH
WHKZ(AM) Warren OH
*WNKL(FM) Wauseon OH
*WYSA(FM) Wauseon OH
*WZWP(FM) West Union OH
WKLN(FM) Wilmington OH
*WJIC(FM) Zanesville OH
*KAKO(FM) Ada OK
*KQPD(FM) Ardmore OK
KVSO(AM) Ardmore OK
*KWRI(FM) Bartlesville OK
*KARU(FM) Cache OK
*KJCC(FM) Carnegie OK
KTFR(FM) Chelsea OK
*KAYC(FM) Durant OK
KSEO(AM) Durant OK
*KOKF(FM) Edmond OK
KXOO(FM) Elk City OK
*KWKL(FM) Grandfield OK
*KXRT(FM) Idabel OK
*KJRF(FM) Lawton OK
*KVRS(FM) Lawton OK
KEMX(FM) Locust Grove OK
KTLV(AM) Midwest City OK
*KYLV(FM) Oklahoma City OK
KPGM(AM) Pawhuska OK
*KZTH(FM) Piedmont OK
*KKRI(FM) Pocola OK
*KJTH(FM) Ponca City OK
*KLVV(FM) Ponca City OK
*KARG(FM) Poteau OK
*KXTH(FM) Seminole OK
KQCV-FM Shawnee OK
*KTKL(FM) Stigler OK
KCXR(FM) Taft OK
*KAYM(FM) Weatherford OK
*KJOV(FM) Woodward OK
KHPE(FM) Albany OR
KWIL(AM) Albany OR
*KLOY(FM) Astoria OR
*KWYA(FM) Astoria OR
*KANL(FM) Baker City OR
KNLR(FM) Bend OR
*KVLB(FM) Bend OR
*KMWR(FM) Brookings OR
KYTT-FM Coos Bay OR
*KAPK(FM) Grants Pass OR
*KGCL(FM) Jordan Valley OR
*KPIJ(FM) Junction City OR
*KKLJ(FM) Klamath Falls OR
*KKLP(FM) La Pine OR
*KGRI(FM) Lebanon OR
*KBUG(FM) Malin OR
*KLRF(FM) Milton-Freewater OR
*KYOR(FM) Newport OR
*KEFS(FM) North Powder OR
*KARO(FM) Nyssa OR
*KAPL(AM) Phoenix OR
*KPFR(FM) Pine Grove OR

KKPZ(AM) Portland OR
KPDQ(AM) Portland OR
KPDQ-FM Portland OR
KNLX(FM) Prineville OR
*KKJA(FM) Redmond OR
*KLON(FM) Rockaway Beach OR
KPJC(AM) Salem OR
*KWBX(FM) Salem OR
*KLVP(FM) Sandy OR
KFIS(FM) Scappoose OR
*KJKL(FM) Selma OR
KORE(AM) Springfield-Eugene OR
*KLVU(FM) Sweet Home OR
*KAIK(FM) Tillamook OR
*KZRI(FM) Welches OR
*KLOV(FM) Winchester OR
KGRV(AM) Winston OR
WAVL(AM) Apollo PA
*WTWT(FM) Bradford PA
*WFUZ(FM) Carbondale PA
WHGT(AM) Chambersburg PA
*WZXQ(FM) Chambersburg PA
WPWA(AM) Chester PA
WVCH(AM) Chester PA
*WKEL(FM) Confluence PA
WCOH-FM DuBois PA
*WAWN(FM) Franklin PA
*WCOG-FM Galeton PA
*WVMM(FM) Grantham PA
WEXC(FM) Greenville PA
*WLVU(FM) Halifax PA
WKBO(AM) Harrisburg PA
*WZXM(FM) Harrisburg PA
*WBYH(FM) Hawley PA
*WHHN(FM) Hollidaysburg PA
*WZZH(FM) Honesdale PA
*WFRJ(FM) Johnstown PA
WDAC(FM) Lancaster PA
*WJTL(FM) Lancaster PA
WBYN(AM) Lehighton PA
*WGRC(FM) Lewisburg PA
*WJRC(FM) Lewistown PA
*WRIJ(FM) Masontown PA
*WYFU(FM) Masontown PA
*WQJU(FM) Mifflintown PA
*WRWJ(FM) Murrysville PA
*WPKV(FM) Nanty Glo PA
*WBGM(FM) New Berlin PA
*WVMN(FM) New Castle PA
WPCL(FM) Northern Cambria PA
WWKL(FM) Palmyra PA
WORD-FM Pittsburgh PA
WPIT(AM) Pittsburgh PA
WWNL(AM) Pittsburgh PA
WKVB(FM) Port Matilda PA
WLKJ(FM) Portage PA
WRAW(AM) Reading PA
WREQ(FM) Ridgebury PA
*WBYO(FM) Sellersville PA
*WCIM(FM) Shenandoah PA
WWII(AM) Shiremanstown PA
WLKH(FM) Somerset PA
WBHV-FM State College PA
*WRXV(FM) State College PA
*WTLR(FM) State College PA
*WBYX(FM) Stroudsburg PA
*WLKA(FM) Tafton PA
*WCIT-FM Trout Run PA
WCTL(FM) Union City PA
*WZZD(FM) Warwick PA
WLIH(FM) Whitneyville PA
*WCRG(FM) Williamsport PA
WYYC(AM) York PA
*WTMV(FM) Youngsville PA
WNVM(FM) Cidra PR
WNVE(FM) Culebra PR
WRRH(FM) Hormigueros PR
WNRT(FM) Manati PR
WZNA(AM) Moca PR
WPPC(AM) Penuelas PR
*WNNV(FM) San German PR
WERR(FM) Vega Alta PR
WSTL(AM) Providence RI
*WKIV(FM) Westerly RI
*WAFJ(FM) Belvedere SC
WBAJ(AM) Blythwood SC

WALC(FM) Charleston SC
*WDLL(FM) Dillon SC
WELP(AM) Easley SC
*WLPG(FM) Florence SC
*WYFG(FM) Gaffney SC
WLMC(AM) Georgetown SC
WLFJ(FM) Greenville SC
*WLFJ-FM Greenville SC
*WCKI(AM) Greer SC
WBZT-FM Mauldin SC
*WMBJ(FM) Murrell's Inlet SC
WTBI(AM) Pickens SC
WPAL-FM Ridgeville SC
WSSC(AM) Sumter SC
WBZK(AM) York SC
KLRJ(FM) Aberdeen SD
*KVCF(FM) Freeman SD
*KVCX(FM) Gregory SD
*KWRC(FM) Hermosa SD
*KVFL(FM) Pierre SD
*KASD(FM) Rapid City SD
KTPT(FM) Rapid City SD
*KNWC-FM Sioux Falls SD
*KSFS(FM) Sioux Falls SD
KSLT(FM) Spearfish SD
*KJBB(FM) Watertown SD
*WYLV(FM) Alcoa TN
WATX(AM) Algood TN
WTKB-FM Atwood TN
WBIN(AM) Benton TN
*WHCB(FM) Bristol TN
WJOC(AM) Chattanooga TN
WLMR(AM) Chattanooga TN
*WAYQ(FM) Clarksville TN
*WNRZ(FM) Dickson TN
WCRT(AM) Donelson TN
*WZKV(FM) Dyersburg TN
*WUMC(AM) Elizabethton TN
WLLJ(FM) Etowah TN
WAYB-FM Graysville TN
*WAUO(FM) Hohenwald TN
*WAMP(FM) Jackson TN
*WCQR-FM Kingsport TN
*WKTS(FM) Kingston TN
WFFI(FM) Kingston Springs TN
WIFA(AM) Knoxville TN
WITA(AM) Knoxville TN
WRJZ(AM) Knoxville TN
WBLC(AM) Lenoir City TN
*WIGH(FM) Lexington TN
WFGZ(FM) Lobelville TN
*WDLF(FM) Maynardville TN
*WAJJ(FM) McKenzie TN
WMXK(FM) Morristown TN
WENO(AM) Nashville TN
*WNAZ-FM Nashville TN
*WAYW(FM) New Johnsonville TN
WPRH(FM) Paris TN
*WJBP(FM) Red Bank TN
WDTM(AM) Selmer TN
*WXKV(FM) Selmer TN
*WBIA(FM) Shelbyville TN
WFFH(FM) Smyrna TN
WDBL(AM) Springfield TN
WSBI(AM) Static TN
WJIG(AM) Tullahoma TN
*WTAI(FM) Union City TN
WBOZ(FM) Woodbury TN
*KAGT(FM) Abilene TX
*KAQD(FM) Abilene TX
*KGNZ(FM) Abilene TX
*KAVW(FM) Amarillo TX
*KJJP(FM) Amarillo TX
KTNZ(AM) Amarillo TX
*KXLV(FM) Amarillo TX
*KXRI(AM) Amarillo TX
*KKWV(FM) Aransas Pass TX
*KATG(FM) Athens TX
KPYN(AM) Atlanta TX
*KHIB(FM) Bastrop TX
*KZBJ(FM) Bay City TX
*KLBT(FM) Beaumont TX
*KTXB(FM) Beaumont TX
KIBL(AM) Beeville TX
KPDB(AM) Big Lake TX
*KTAA(FM) Big Sandy TX

*KBCX(FM) Big Spring TX
*KHVT(FM) Bloomington TX
*KUBJ(FM) Brenham TX
KMLU(FM) Brownfield TX
*KPBB(FM) Brownfield TX
*KBUB(FM) Brownwood TX
*KHBW(FM) Brownwood TX
*KPBE(FM) Brownwood TX
KPSM(FM) Brownwood TX
KAGC(AM) Bryan TX
*KLRW(FM) Byrne TX
KAYG(FM) Camp Wood TX
KRDH(AM) Canton TX
KCZO(FM) Carrizo Springs TX
KWDC(FM) Coahoma TX
*KLGS(FM) College Station TX
*KAFR(FM) Conroe TX
*KKLM(FM) Corpus Christi TX
*KCKT(FM) Crockett TX
*KTDA(FM) Dalhart TX
*KCBI(FM) Dallas TX
*KDLI(FM) Del Rio TX
KIXL(AM) Del Valle TX
*KLLR(FM) Dripping Springs TX
*KEPI(FM) Eagle Pass TX
*KEPX(FM) Eagle Pass TX
KELP(AM) El Paso TX
*KKLY(FM) El Paso TX
KLDS(AM) Falfurrias TX
*KZFT(FM) Fannett TX
KIJN(AM) Farwell TX
KIJN-FM Farwell TX
KDFT(AM) Ferris TX
*KPBN(FM) Freer TX
*KYAR(FM) Gatesville TX
*KANJ(FM) Giddings TX
*KMLR(FM) Gonzales TX
*KZAR(FM) Gonzales TX
*KTXG(FM) Greenville TX
*KAZF(FM) Hebronville TX
KEKO(FM) Hebronville TX
*KRLH(FM) Hereford TX
KWRD-FM Highland Village TX
*KHCB-FM Houston TX
*KSBJ(FM) Humble TX
*KHCH(AM) Huntsville TX
*KYLR(FM) Hutto TX
*KBJS(FM) Jacksonville TX
KCOX(AM) Jasper TX
*KHCJ(FM) Jefferson TX
KTXX(FM) Karnes City TX
KERB(AM) Kermit TX
KERB-FM Kermit TX
*KHKV(FM) Kerrville TX
*KKER(FM) Kerrville TX
*KZLO(FM) Kilgore TX
*KYBJ(FM) Lake Jackson TX
*KBKN(FM) Lamesa TX
KLAR(AM) Laredo TX
KBLT(FM) Leakey TX
*KAMY(FM) Lubbock TX
*KKLU(FM) Lubbock TX
*KSWP(FM) Lufkin TX
*KZLV(FM) Lytle TX
*KHML(FM) Madisonville TX
*KBMD(FM) Marble Falls TX
*KSUR(FM) Mart TX
KVMV(FM) McAllen TX
KMXO(AM) Merkel TX
*KMEO(FM) Mertzon TX
KBRZ(AM) Missouri City TX
KBAT(FM) Monahans TX
*KPGA(FM) Morton TX
KLBW(AM) New Boston TX
KTTY(FM) New Boston TX
*KBMM(FM) Odessa TX
*KFLB(AM) Odessa TX
*KLVW(FM) Odessa TX
KAVO(FM) Pampa TX
*KHCP(FM) Paris TX
*KGWP(FM) Pittsburg TX
*KBAH(FM) Plainview TX
*KWLD(FM) Plainview TX
*KHPO(FM) Port O'Connor TX
*KSGR(FM) Portland TX
KCLR(AM) Ralls TX

KLOW(FM) Reno TX
*KTER(FM) Rudolph TX
KCRN-FM San Angelo TX
*KLTP(FM) San Angelo TX
*KNAR(FM) San Angelo TX
KSLR(AM) San Antonio TX
*KYFS(FM) San Antonio TX
KUBR(AM) San Juan TX
KUOL(AM) San Marcos TX
*KVRK(FM) Sanger TX
KMAT(FM) Seadrift TX
KDAE(AM) Sinton TX
*KJAK(FM) Slaton TX
KYTY(AM) Somerset TX
KVRP(AM) Stamford TX
*KBDE(FM) Temple TX
*KVLT(FM) Temple TX
KLGO(FM) Thorndale TX
KTNO(AM) University Park TX
KVOU(AM) Uvalde TX
*KAYK(FM) Victoria TX
*KXBJ(FM) Victoria TX
KBBW(AM) Waco TX
*KVLW(FM) Waco TX
*KHTA(FM) Wake Village TX
KRGE(AM) Weslaco TX
*KFRI(FM) West Odessa TX
KANI(AM) Wharton TX
*KMOC(FM) Wichita Falls TX
*KZKL(FM) Wichita Falls TX
KKHT-FM Winnie TX
KBAW(FM) Zapata TX
*KNKL(FM) North Ogden UT
*KYFO-FM Ogden UT
*KEYY(AM) Provo UT
*KANN(AM) Roy UT
*KAER(FM) Saint George UT
*KUFR(FM) Salt Lake City UT
KUTR(AM) Taylorsville UT
KMRI(AM) West Valley City UT
WAVA(AM) Arlington VA
WAVA-FM Arlington VA
WYFJ(FM) Ashland VA
WLES(AM) Bon Air VA
*WAZP(FM) Cape Charles VA
WYRV(AM) Cedar Bluff VA
*WAUQ(FM) Charles City VA
WJYK(AM) Chase City VA
*WWIP(FM) Cheriton VA
WPMH(AM) Claremont VA
*WARN(FM) Culpeper VA
*WPER(FM) Culpeper VA
*WOKD-FM Danville VA
WPIN-FM Dublin VA
*WJYA(FM) Emporia VA
WKNV(AM) Fairlawn VA
*WJYJ(FM) Fredericksburg VA
*WOKG(FM) Galax VA
*WWMC(FM) Lynchburg VA
*WPIM(FM) Martinsville VA
*WJCN(FM) Nassawadox VA
WLTK(AM) New Market VA
WRJR(AM) Portsmouth VA
WBTK(AM) Richmond VA
*WRIH(FM) Richmond VA
*WRXT(FM) Roanoke VA
WLOY(AM) Rural Retreat VA
*WPAR(FM) Salem VA
WSBV(AM) South Boston VA
*WJLZ(FM) Virginia Beach VA
WVAB(AM) Virginia Beach VA
*WPVA(FM) Waynesboro VA
WEVI(FM) Frederiksted VI
*WCMD-FM Barre VT
*WCMK(FM) Putney VT
WMNV(FM) Rupert VT
*WFTF(FM) Rutland VT
*KJCF(FM) Asotin WA
KGNW(AM) Burien-Seattle WA
*KGTS(FM) College Place WA
*KKRS(FM) Davenport WA
*KLUW(FM) East Wenatchee WA
KCIS(AM) Edmonds WA
KCMS(FM) Edmonds WA
*KYKV(FM) Ellensburg WA
*KTJC(FM) Kelso WA

*KBLD(FM) Kennewick WA
*KJVH(FM) Longview WA
*KWYQ(FM) Longview WA
KWPZ(FM) Lynden WA
KTSL(FM) Medical Lake WA
*KSBC(FM) Nile WA
*KLOP(FM) Ocean Park WA
KGDN(FM) Pasco WA
*KRLF(FM) Pullman WA
*KWFJ(FM) Roy WA
KLFE(AM) Seattle WA
KNTS(AM) Seattle WA
*KEEH(FM) Spokane WA
*KAYB(FM) Sunnyside WA
*KRKL(FM) Walla Walla WA
*KPLW(FM) Wenatchee WA
KJOX(AM) Yakima WA
KYAK(AM) Yakima WA
*KYPL(FM) Yakima WA
*WHEM(FM) Eau Claire WI
*WVCF(FM) Eau Claire WI
*WDKV(FM) Fond du Lac WI
*WVFL(FM) Fond du Lac WI
*WMVM(FM) Goodman WI
*WORQ(FM) Green Bay WI
WWIB(FM) Hallie WI
WJOK(AM) Kaukauna WI
*WSTM(FM) Kiel WI
*WNWC-FM Madison WI
*WGNV(FM) Milladore WI
WJYI(AM) Milwaukee WI
*WMWK(FM) Milwaukee WI
WSSP(AM) Milwaukee WI
*WVCY-FM Milwaukee WI
*WKMZ(FM) Mukwonago WI
*WNLI(FM) Sturgeon Bay WI
*WPFF(FM) Sturgeon Bay WI
*WRVM(FM) Suring WI
*WVCX(FM) Tomah WI
*WEGZ(FM) Washburn WI
*WVRN(FM) Wittenberg WI
*WJJJ(AM) Beckley WV
*WPIB(FM) Bluefield WV
*WCKU(FM) Clarksburg WV
*WKJL(FM) Clarksburg WV
*WBHZ(FM) Elkins WV
*WDKL(FM) Grafton WV
WEMM-FM Huntington WV
WRWB(AM) Huntington WV
WFSP(AM) Kingwood WV
*WKVW(FM) Marmet WV
WZZW(AM) Milton WV
*WLVW(FM) Moundsville WV
WOAY(AM) Oak Hill WV
*WVRR(FM) Point Pleasant WV
*WPWV(FM) Princeton WV
WRLB(FM) Rainelle WV
WRRL(AM) Rainelle WV
*WLKV(FM) Ripley WV
*KCSP-FM Casper WY
*KLWC(FM) Casper WY
*KLWV(FM) Chugwater WY
KUYO(AM) Evansville WY
*KAXG(FM) Gillette WY
*KLOF(FM) Gillette WY
*KLWD(FM) Gillette WY
*KMLT(FM) Jackson WY
*KAIW(FM) Laramie WY
*KTDX(FM) Laramie WY
*KWYC(FM) Orchard Valley WY
*KVLZ(FM) Sheridan WY
*KDNR(FM) South Greeley WY
*KRWT(FM) West Laramie WY

Classic Rock

KBFX(FM) Anchorage AK
KLAM(AM) Cordova AK
KXLR(FM) Fairbanks AK
KSUP(FM) Juneau AK
KSLD(AM) Soldotna AK
*WJSR(FM) Birmingham AL
WZRR(FM) Birmingham AL
WERH-FM Hamilton AL
WTAK-FM Hartselle AL
WRKH(FM) Mobile AL

WXFX(FM) Montgomery AL
WVNA-FM Muscle Shoals AL
WJRL-FM Ozark AL
WMXN-FM Stevenson AL
KDEL-FM Arkadelphia AR
*KSWH(FM) Arkadelphia AR
KFPW-FM Barling AR
KKEG(FM) Bentonville AR
KCJF(FM) Earle AR
KAGL(FM) El Dorado AR
KXJK(AM) Forrest City AR
KCWD(FM) Harrison AR
KEGI(FM) Jonesboro AR
KHBM-FM Monticello AR
KLXQ(FM) Mountain Pine AR
KWLT(FM) North Crossett AR
KYGL(FM) Texarkana AR
KBBQ-FM Van Buren AR
KCUZ(AM) Clifton AZ
KMGN(FM) Flagstaff AZ
KCDX(FM) Florence AZ
KRRK(FM) Lake Havasu City AZ
KZUL-FM Lake Havasu City AZ
KSLX-FM Scottsdale AZ
KFMM(FM) Thatcher AZ
KHYT(FM) Tucson AZ
KLPX(FM) Tucson AZ
KALT-FM Alturas CA
KXGO(FM) Arcata CA
KKBZ(FM) Auberry CA
KHRQ(FM) Baker CA
KVMX(FM) Bakersfield CA
KRHV(FM) Big Pine CA
KOCP(FM) Camarillo CA
KWTY(FM) Cartago CA
KTHU(FM) Corning CA
KDFO(FM) Delano CA
KZRO(FM) Dunsmuir CA
KJFX(FM) Fresno CA
KLBN(FM) Fresno CA
KBAY(FM) Gilroy CA
KHIP(FM) Gonzales CA
KVLI-FM Lake Isabella CA
KHDR(FM) Lenwood CA
KCBS-FM Los Angeles CA
KLOS(FM) Los Angeles CA
KIXA(FM) Lucerne Valley CA
KDJK(FM) Mariposa CA
KHKK(FM) Modesto CA
KVRV(FM) Monte Rio CA
KLUK(FM) Needles CA
KIOO(FM) Porterville CA
KMRJ(FM) Rancho Mirage CA
KLKX(FM) Rosamond CA
KSEG(FM) Sacramento CA
KGB-FM San Diego CA
KUFX(FM) San Jose CA
KZOZ(FM) San Luis Obispo CA
KSAN(FM) San Mateo CA
KXFM(FM) Santa Maria CA
KTMQ(FM) Temecula CA
KHRD(FM) Weaverville CA
KTOR(FM) Westwood CA
KDGL(FM) Yucca Valley CA
KKFM(FM) Colorado Springs CO
KKNN(FM) Delta CO
KQMT(FM) Denver CO
KRFX(FM) Denver CO
KKDC(FM) Dolores CO
KTUN(FM) Eagle CO
KPAW(FM) Fort Collins CO
KRVG(FM) Glenwood Springs CO
KVLE-FM Gunnison CO
KLMR-FM Lamar CO
KSBV(FM) Salida CO
KCRT-FM Trinidad CO
KMAX-FM Wellington CO
WRKI(FM) Brookfield CT
WFOX(FM) Norwalk CT
WMOS(FM) Stonington CT
WJKI(FM) Bethany Beach DE
WGBG(FM) Seaford DE
WRDX(FM) Smyrna DE
WNDT(FM) Alachua FL
WFYV-FM Atlantic Beach FL
WWUS(FM) Big Pine Key FL

WRXK-FM Bonita Springs FL
WCJX(FM) Five Points FL
WBGG-FM Fort Lauderdale FL
WKGR(FM) Fort Pierce FL
WXCV(FM) Homosassa Springs FL
WKYZ(FM) Key Colony Beach FL
WAIL(FM) Key West FL
WAIL(FM) Key West FL
WARO(FM) Naples FL
WRKN(FM) Niceville FL
WHTQ(FM) Orlando FL
WHOG-FM Ormond-by-the-Sea FL
WXGL(FM) Saint Petersburg FL
WHPT(FM) Sarasota FL
WNDD(FM) Silver Springs FL
WRBA(FM) Springfield FL
WGLF(FM) Tallahassee FL
WXOF(FM) Yankeetown FL
WDMG-FM Ambrose GA
WKLS(FM) Atlanta GA
WEKL(FM) Augusta GA
WVRK(FM) Columbus GA
WZTR(FM) Dahlonega GA
WQBZ(FM) Fort Valley GA
WSRV(FM) Gainesville GA
WPCH(FM) Gray GA
WIOL(FM) Greenville GA
WTHG(FM) Hinesville GA
WMGP(FM) Hogansville GA
WYYZ(AM) Jasper GA
WBBT(AM) Lyons GA
WBMZ(FM) Metter GA
WXKT(FM) Royston GA
WIXV(FM) Savannah GA
WZBX(FM) Sylvania GA
*WKEU-FM The Rock GA
WWRQ-FM Valdosta GA
WZCH(FM) Warner Robins GA
WPUP(FM) Watkinsville GA
WDBN(FM) Wrightsville GA
KHWI(FM) Holualoa HI
KPOI-FM Honolulu HI
KRKH(FM) Wailea-Makena HI
KLKK(FM) Clear Lake IA
KCQQ(FM) Davenport IA
KGGO(FM) Des Moines IA
KXGE(FM) Dubuque IA
KKSI(FM) Eddyville IA
KGRR(FM) Epworth IA
KCRR(FM) Grundy Center IA
KKRQ(FM) Iowa City IA
KKGB(FM) Sulphur LA
KGRA(FM) Jefferson IA
KRNQ(FM) Keokuk IA
KKMA(FM) Le Mars IA
KUQQ(FM) Milford IA
KSEZ(FM) Sioux City IA
KJOT(FM) Boise ID
KQEO(FM) Idaho Falls ID
KWYS-FM Island Park ID
KIKX(FM) Ketchum ID
KTPO(FM) Kootenai ID
KKGL(FM) Nampa ID
KMGI(FM) Pocatello ID
KPKY(FM) Pocatello ID
KGTM(FM) Rexburg ID
KOFE(AM) Saint Maries ID
KECH-FM Sun Valley ID
KSNQ(FM) Twin Falls ID
KRVQ(FM) Victor ID
KLZX(FM) Weston ID
WDLJ(FM) Breese IL
WDRV(FM) Chicago IL
WRXQ(FM) Coal City IL
WRHK(FM) Danville IL
WXTT(FM) Danville IL
WMKB(FM) Earlville IL
KUUL(FM) East Moline IL
WYMG(FM) Jacksonville IL
*WMXM(FM) Lake Forest IL
WKGL-FM Loves Park IL
WJEQ(FM) Macomb IL
WGKC(FM) Mahomet IL
WXLP(FM) Moline IL
WZZT(FM) Morrison IL
WIKK(FM) Newton IL
WGLO(FM) Pekin IL

WPBG(FM) Peoria IL
WBZG(FM) Peru IL
WZNX(FM) Sullivan IL
WEBX(FM) Tuscola IL
WHET(FM) West Frankfort IL
WWDV(FM) Zion IL
WMQX(FM) Alexandria IN
WSHP(FM) Attica IN
WJAA(FM) Austin IN
*WHJE(FM) Carmel IN
WSFR(FM) Corydon IN
WXRD(FM) Crown Point IN
WABX(FM) Evansville IN
WFWI(FM) Fort Wayne IN
WXKE(FM) Fort Wayne IN
WZOW(FM) Goshen IN
WMXQ(FM) Hartford City IN
WFBQ(FM) Indianapolis IN
WQMF(FM) Jeffersonville IN
WKHY(FM) Lafayette IN
WRZR(FM) Loogootee IN
WSMM(FM) New Carlisle IN
WMYK(FM) Peru IN
WLCL(FM) Sellersville IN
WWVR(FM) West Terre Haute IN
KNZS(FM) Arlington KS
KFXJ(FM) Augusta KS
KCAR-FM Baxter Springs KS
KKRK(FM) Coffeyville KS
KZRD(FM) Dodge City KS
KOTE(FM) Eureka KS
KSEK-FM Girard KS
KVGB-FM Great Bend KS
KINZ(FM) Humboldt KS
KWKR(FM) Leoti KS
KZUH(FM) Minneapolis KS
KTHR(FM) Wichita KS
WLFX(FM) Berea KY
WDNS(FM) Bowling Green KY
WCBJ(FM) Campton KY
WPTQ(FM) Cave City KY
WTBK(FM) Manchester KY
WQQR(FM) Mayfield KY
WKYM(FM) Monticello KY
WKQQ(FM) Winchester KY
KZMZ(FM) Alexandria LA
KCIJ(FM) Atlanta LA
WDGL(FM) Baton Rouge LA
KLIP(FM) Monroe LA
WKBU(FM) New Orleans LA
KKGB(FM) Sulphur LA
WXRG(FM) Athol MA
WZLX(FM) Boston MA
WROR-FM Framingham MA
*WGAO(FM) Hopedale MA
*WSDH(FM) Sandwich MA
WAQY(FM) Springfield MA
*WYAJ(FM) Sudbury MA
WKGO(FM) Cumberland MD
*WMTB-FM Emmittsburg MD
WDLD(FM) Halfway MD
WTTR(AM) Westminster MD
WZBA(FM) Westminster MD
WKIT-FM Brewer ME
WQDY-FM Calais ME
WWMJ(FM) Ellsworth ME
WCTB(FM) Fairfield ME
WSHK(FM) Kittery ME
WFNK(FM) Lewiston ME
WALZ-FM Machias ME
WHXR(FM) North Windham ME
WBLM(FM) Portland ME
WOZI(FM) Presque Isle ME
WHXQ(FM) Scarborough ME
WNSX(FM) Winter Harbor ME
WZUU(FM) Allegan MI
WFDX(FM) Atlanta MI
WLEW-FM Bad Axe MI
WCSX(FM) Birmingham MI
WCKC(FM) Cadillac MI
WGFM(FM) Cheboygan MI
WMMQ(FM) East Lansing MI
WBFX(FM) Grand Rapids MI
WLAV-FM Grand Rapids MI
WGLI(FM) Hancock MI
WWKR(FM) Hart MI

WKJZ(FM) Hillman MI
WBZV(FM) Hudson MI
WIMK(FM) Iron Mountain MI
WFCX(FM) Leland MI
WUPK(FM) Marquette MI
WKQZ(FM) Midland MI
WRUP(FM) Munising MI
WMRR(FM) Muskegon Heights MI
WIHC(FM) Newberry MI
WAOR(FM) Niles MI
*WOVI(FM) Novi MI
WRSR(FM) Owosso MI
WRKR(FM) Portage MI
WUPF(FM) Powers MI
WILZ(FM) Saginaw MI
WQTX(FM) Saint Johns MI
WYVN(FM) Saugatuck MI
WSUE(FM) Sault Ste. Marie MI
WMXG(FM) Stephenson MI
WQLB(FM) Tawas City MI
WLKM-FM Three Rivers MI
KQPR-FM Albert Lea MN
KXRA-FM Alexandria MN
KKLN(FM) Atwater MN
KLIZ-FM Brainerd MN
KFGI(FM) Crosby MN
KQDS-FM Duluth MN
KXLP(FM) Eagle Lake MN
KLCX(FM) Eyota MN
KFMC(FM) Fairmont MN
KQCL(FM) Faribault MN
KQRS(FM) Golden Valley MN
WXXZ(FM) Grand Marais MN
KRAQ(FM) Jackson MN
KARZ(FM) Marshall MN
KKCK(FM) Marshall MN
KMGM(FM) Montevideo MN
KMFG(FM) Nashwauk MN
KWNG(FM) Red Wing MN
KRCH(FM) Rochester MN
*KRPR(FM) Rochester MN
KRWB(AM) Roseau MN
KRBI-FM Saint Peter MN
KLFN(FM) Sunburg MN
KLZZ(FM) Waite Park MN
KLLZ-FM Walker MN
KHRS(FM) Winthrop MN
KWOA-FM Worthington MN
KWXD(FM) Asbury MO
KKWK(FM) Cameron MO
KGMO(FM) Cape Girardeau MO
KSHE(FM) Crestwood MO
KDFN(AM) Doniphan MO
KKCA(FM) Fulton MO
KCFX(FM) Harrisonville MO
KRXL(FM) Kirksville MO
KPOW-FM La Monte MO
KYRX(FM) Marble Hill MO
KKLH(FM) Marshfield MO
KZZK(FM) New London MO
KMYK(FM) Osage Beach MO
KJEZ(FM) Poplar Bluff MO
KIHT(FM) Saint Louis MO
KIGL(FM) Seligman MO
KXUS(FM) Springfield MO
KXDG(FM) Webb City MO
KSPQ(FM) West Plains MO
WRKG(FM) Drew MS
WMUT(FM) Grenada MS
WXRR(FM) Hattiesburg MS
WZNF(FM) Lumberton MS
WCNA(FM) Potts Camp MS
WSKK(FM) Ripley MS
WSTZ-FM Vicksburg MS
KJJM(FM) Baker MT
KBZM(FM) Big Sky MT
KRKX(FM) Billings MT
KMBR(FM) Butte MT
KTZZ(FM) Conrad MT
KQDI-FM Great Falls MT
KZMT(FM) Helena MT
KBBZ(FM) Kalispell MT
KZMN(FM) Kalispell MT
KLCM(FM) Lewistown MT
KKQX(FM) Manhattan MT
KMTA(AM) Miles City MT

KZOQ-FM Missoula MT
KWMY(FM) Park City MT
KMXE-FM Red Lodge MT
KGCX(FM) Sidney MT
WKRR(FM) Asheboro NC
WBHN(AM) Bryson City NC
WCLN(AM) Clinton NC
WRFX(FM) Kannapolis NC
WSFL-FM New Bern NC
WRVA-FM Rocky Mount NC
WBNE(FM) Shallotte NC
WOBR-FM Wanchese NC
WQNS(FM) Waynesville NC
WNTB(FM) Wrightsville Beach NC
KBYZ(FM) Bismarck ND
KSSS(FM) Bismarck ND
KPFX(FM) Fargo ND
KRWK(FM) Fargo ND
KNOX-FM Grand Forks ND
KTZU(FM) Velva ND
KTGL(FM) Beatrice NE
KBBN-FM Broken Bow NE
KKOT(FM) Columbus NE
KFMT-FM Fremont NE
KMOR(FM) Gering NE
KROR(FM) Hastings NE
KHAQ(FM) Maxwell NE
KQHK(FM) McCook NE
KNEN(FM) Norfolk NE
KQBW(FM) Omaha NE
KBRX(AM) O'Neill NE
WMLL(FM) Bedford NH
WHDQ(FM) Claremont NH
WSAK(FM) Hampton NH
WMTK(FM) Littleton NH
WWHQ(FM) Meredith NH
WMGM(FM) Atlantic City NJ
WCHR-FM Manahawkin NJ
WZXL(FM) Wildwood NJ
KNMZ(FM) Alamogordo NM
KZRM(FM) Chama NM
KYVA-FM Churchrock NM
KEJL(FM) Eunice NM
KDAG(FM) Farmington NM
KXXI(FM) Gallup NM
KMDZ(FM) Las Vegas NM
KIOT(FM) Los Lunas NM
KIDX(FM) Ruidoso NM
KTUM(FM) Tatum NM
KRSI(FM) Garapan-Saipan NP
KKLZ(FM) Las Vegas NV
KOZZ-FM Reno NV
KURK(FM) Reno NV
WPYX(FM) Albany NY
*WGCC-FM Batavia NY
WAAL(FM) Binghamton NY
WTKW(FM) Bridgeport NY
WGRF(FM) Buffalo NY
WKGB-FM Conklin NY
WIII(FM) Cortland NY
*WECW(FM) Elmira NY
WBBI(FM) Endwell NY
WCPV(FM) Essex NY
WLPW(FM) Lake Placid NY
WNGZ(FM) Montour Falls NY
WAXQ(FM) New York NY
WRXP(FM) New York NY
WJJL(AM) Niagara Falls NY
*WRHO(FM) Oneonta NY
WTKV(FM) Oswego NY
WPDH(FM) Poughkeepsie NY
WRCN-FM Riverhead NY
WCMF-FM Rochester NY
WQRS(FM) Salamanca NY
WBPM(FM) Saugerties NY
WLLW(FM) Seneca Falls NY
WRGR(FM) Tupper Lake NY
WLKK(FM) Wethersfield Township NY
WRRQ(FM) Windsor NY
WQEL(FM) Bucyrus OH
*WCWT-FM Centerville OH
WOFX-FM Cincinnati OH
WNCX(FM) Cleveland OH
WLVQ(FM) Columbus OH
WKXA-FM Findlay OH
WFXN-FM Galion OH

*WDUB(FM) Granville OH
WGRR(FM) Hamilton OH
WBWR(FM) Hilliard OH
*WKET(FM) Kettering OH
WEGE(FM) Lima OH
WDLW(AM) Lorain OH
WXXF(FM) Loudonville OH
WAGX(FM) Manchester OH
WYRO(FM) McArthur OH
*WMWX(FM) Miamitown OH
*WLMH(FM) Morrow OH
WNKO(FM) Newark OH
WFXJ-FM North Kingsville OH
WBUK(FM) Ottawa OH
WBIK(FM) Pleasant City OH
WXKR(FM) Port Clinton OH
WZZZ(FM) Portsmouth OH
WODB(FM) Richwood OH
WZLR(FM) Xenia OH
KRKZ(FM) Altus OK
KWCO-FM Chickasha OK
KDDQ(FM) Comanche OK
KCDL(FM) Cordell OK
KTRX(FM) Dickson OK
*KHIM(FM) Mangum OK
KTMC-FM McAlester OK
KRXO(FM) Oklahoma City OK
KLOR-FM Ponca City OK
KKBD(FM) Sallisaw OK
KJSR(FM) Tulsa OK
KTWS(FM) Bend OR
KLOO-FM Corvallis OR
KZEL-FM Eugene OR
KAGO-FM Klamath Falls OR
KFEG(FM) Klamath Falls OR
KUBQ(FM) La Grande OR
KLCR(FM) Lakeview OR
KCRF-FM Lincoln City OR
KBOY-FM Medford OR
KGON(FM) Portland OR
KJMX(FM) Reedsport OR
KCRX-FM Seaside OR
KMSW(FM) The Dalles OR
KPPT-FM Toledo OR
WBVE(FM) Bedford PA
*WBUQ(FM) Bloomsburg PA
WBUS(FM) Boalsburg PA
WMKX(FM) Brookville PA
*WCAL(FM) California PA
WUUZ(FM) Cooperstown PA
WWCB(AM) Corry PA
WODE-FM Easton PA
WQHZ(FM) Erie PA
WQCM(FM) Greencastle PA
*WKVR-FM Huntingdon PA
WJNG(FM) Johnsonburg PA
WCXR(FM) Lewisburg PA
WCHX(FM) Lewistown PA
WBSS(FM) Mount Union PA
WRKT(FM) North East PA
WMGK(FM) Philadelphia PA
WPZX(FM) Pocono Pines PA
WZYY(FM) Renovo PA
WQFX(FM) Russell PA
WUZZ(FM) Saegertown PA
WEZX(FM) Scranton PA
WYFM(FM) Sharon PA
*WSRU(FM) Slippery Rock PA
WXMT(FM) Smethport PA
WZXR(FM) South Williamsport PA
WMTT(FM) Tioga PA
*WRLC(FM) Williamsport PA
*WRIU(FM) Kingston RI
WROQ(FM) Anderson SC
WWNQ(FM) Forest Acres SC
WIOP(FM) Isle of Palms SC
WRFQ(FM) Mt. Pleasant SC
WYAV(FM) Myrtle Beach SC
WQKI(FM) Orangeburg SC
WMXT(FM) Pamplico SC
WMFX(FM) Saint Andrews SC
KSDN-FM Aberdeen SD
KYBB(FM) Canton SD
KDBX(FM) Clear Lake SD
KFXS(FM) Rapid City SD
KJRV(FM) Wessington Springs SD

*WAPX-FM Clarksville TN
WIJV(FM) Harriman TN
*WFHU(FM) Henderson TN
WEKX(FM) Jellico TN
WQUT(FM) Johnson City TN
WIMZ-FM Knoxville TN
WKHT(FM) Knoxville TN
WEGR(FM) Memphis TN
WYNU(FM) Milan TN
WOWC(FM) Morrison TN
WIHG(FM) Rockwood TN
KFGL(FM) Abilene TX
KRXB(FM) Beeville TX
KLUB(FM) Bloomington TX
KNFX-FM Bryan TX
KYYI(FM) Burkburnett TX
KARX(FM) Claude TX
KXIT(FM) Dalhart TX
KZPS(FM) Dallas TX
KWMC(AM) Del Rio TX
KICA-FM Farwell TX
KWKQ(FM) Graham TX
KPUS(FM) Gregory TX
KBRQ(FM) Hillsboro TX
KMFR(FM) Hondo TX
KKRW(FM) Houston TX
*KSHU(FM) Huntsville TX
KJKB(FM) Jacksboro TX
KKVR(FM) Kerrville TX
KDOK(AM) Kilgore TX
KKTX-FM Kilgore TX
KETX-FM Livingston TX
KONE(FM) Lubbock TX
KKHA(FM) Markham TX
KHXS(FM) Merkel TX
KTBQ(FM) Nacogdoches TX
KNRG(FM) New Ulm TX
KIOC(FM) Orange TX
KBUS(FM) Paris TX
KRIA(FM) Plainview TX
KJAZ(FM) Point Comfort TX
KWFR(FM) San Angelo TX
KZEP-FM San Antonio TX
KNRX(FM) Sterling City TX
KLTD(FM) Temple TX
KTAL-FM Texarkana TX
KNAL(AM) Victoria TX
KMAD-FM Whitesboro TX
*KAGJ(FM) Ephraim UT
KCUA(FM) Naples UT
KZHK(FM) Saint George UT
KRSP-FM Salt Lake City UT
WWUZ(FM) Bowling Green VA
WCTG(FM) Chincoteague VA
WKLR(FM) Fort Lee VA
WAFX(FM) Suffolk VA
WIVI(FM) Charlotte Amalie VI
WKVT-FM Brattleboro VT
WOTX(FM) Lunenburg VT
WCVR-FM Randolph VT
*WVTC(FM) Randolph Center VT
WTHK(FM) Wilmington VT
KDUX-FM Aberdeen WA
KISM(FM) Bellingham WA
KWWX(FM) Cashmere WA
KRQT(FM) Castle Rock WA
KCLK-FM Clarkston WA
KVAB(FM) Clarkston WA
*KGHP(FM) Gig Harbor WA
KJR-FM Seattle WA
KZOK-FM Seattle WA
KLSY(FM) South Bend WA
KKZX(FM) Spokane WA
KYNR(AM) Toppenish WA
KFBW(FM) Vancouver WA
KPQ-FM Wenatchee WA
WRLO-FM Antigo WI
WJJH(FM) Ashland WI
WRJO(FM) Eagle River WI
WMEQ-FM Menomonie WI
WKLH(FM) Milwaukee WI
WQBW(FM) Milwaukee WI
WOZZ(FM) New London WI
WTCX(FM) Ripon WI
WGMO(FM) Shell Lake WI
KHQG(FM) Superior WI

WTMB(FM) Tomah WI
WAUH-FM Wautoma WI
WKBH-FM West Salem WI
WGLX-FM Wisconsin Rapids WI
*WVWC(FM) Buckhannon WV
WKQV(FM) Cowen WV
WRZZ(FM) Elizabeth WV
WRLF(FM) Fairmont WV
WQZK-FM Keyser WV
WVKM(FM) Matewan WV
WCLG-FM Morgantown WV
WVJO(FM) Mullens WV
WXCR(FM) New Martinsville WV
WKOY-FM Princeton WV
WVAR(AM) Richwood WV
WOBG-FM Salem WV
WFBY(FM) Weston WV
KASS(FM) Casper WY
KMGW(FM) Casper WY
KGCC(FM) Gillette WY
KZJH(FM) Jackson WY
KARS-FM Laramie WY
KRQU(FM) Laramie WY
KYLZ(FM) Lyman WY
KXXL(FM) Moorcroft WY
KCGL(FM) Powell WY
KSIT(FM) Rock Springs WY
KZWY(FM) Sheridan WY
KRVK(FM) Vista West WY
KDDV-FM Wright WY

Classical

KLEF(FM) Anchorage AK
*KBRW-FM Barrow AK
*KUAC(FM) Fairbanks AK
*WRWA(FM) Dothan AL
*WSGN(FM) Gadsden AL
*WLRH(FM) Huntsville AL
*WLJS-FM Jacksonville AL
*WHIL-FM Mobile AL
*WTSU(FM) Montgomery-Troy AL
*WQPR(FM) Muscle Shoals AL
*WAPR(FM) Selma AL
*WUAL-FM Tuscaloosa AL
*KBSA(FM) El Dorado AR
*KUAF(FM) Fayetteville AR
*KASU Jonesboro AR
*KLRE-FM Little Rock AR
*KNAU(FM) Flagstaff AZ
*KNAG(FM) Grand Canyon AZ
*KBAQ-FM Phoenix AZ
*KNAA(FM) Show Low AZ
*KUAT-FM Tucson AZ
*KAWC-FM Yuma AZ
*KPRX(FM) Bakersfield CA
*KQVO(FM) Calexico CA
*KCHO(FM) Chico CA
*KVPR(FM) Fresno CA
*KXSR(FM) Groveland CA
*KUSC(FM) Los Angeles CA
*KLDD(FM) McCloud CA
*KESC(FM) Morro Bay CA
*KCSN(FM) Northridge CA
*KPSC(FM) Palm Springs CA
*KNHT(FM) Rio Dell CA
*KXPR(FM) Sacramento CA
*KPBS-FM San Diego CA
KDFC-FM San Francisco CA
*KCBX(FM) San Luis Obispo CA
KDB(FM) Santa Barbara CA
*KQSC(FM) Santa Barbara CA
*KSBX(FM) Santa Barbara CA
*KRCB-FM Santa Rosa CA
KBOQ(FM) Seaside CA
*KUOP(FM) Stockton CA
*KKTO(FM) Tahoe City CA
*KDSC(FM) Thousand Oaks CA
KVEN(AM) Ventura CA
*KNYR(FM) Yreka CA
*KAJX(FM) Aspen CO
*KCJX(FM) Carbondale CO
*KVOV(FM) Carbondale CO
*KPRU(FM) Delta CO
*KVOD(FM) Lakewood CO
*KCME(FM) Manitou Springs CO

*KCFP(FM) Pueblo CO
*KPRE(FM) Vail CO
*WSHU(FM) Fairfield CT
*WGRS(FM) Guilford CT
*WJMJ(FM) Hartford CT
*WMNR(FM) Monroe CT
*WSLX(FM) New Canaan CT
*WRXC(FM) Shelton CT
*WGSK(FM) South Kent CT
WCCC(AM) West Hartford CT
*WETA(FM) Washington DC
*WRTX(FM) Dover DE
*WGCU-FM Fort Myers FL
*WQCS(FM) Fort Pierce FL
*WUFT-FM Gainesville FL
*WJUF(FM) Inverness FL
*WJCT-FM Jacksonville FL
*WMKO(FM) Marco FL
*WKCP(FM) Miami FL
WKAT(AM) North Miami FL
*WMFE-FM Orlando FL
*WUWF(FM) Pensacola FL
*WFSQ(FM) Tallahassee FL
*WUSF(FM) Tampa FL
*WXEL-FM West Palm Beach FL
*WPRK(FM) Winter Park FL
*WUNV(FM) Albany GA
*WUGA(FM) Athens GA
*WABE(FM) Atlanta GA
*WACG-FM Augusta GA
*WWIO-FM Brunswick GA
*WUWG(FM) Carrollton GA
*WNGH-FM Chatsworth GA
*WMUM-FM Cochran GA
*WTJB(FM) Columbus GA
*WNGU(FM) Dahlonega GA
*WPPR(FM) Demorest GA
*WJWV(FM) Fort Gaines GA
*WGPB(FM) Rome GA
WWIO(AM) Saint Mary's GA
*WSVH(FM) Savannah GA
*WFSL(FM) Thomasville GA
*WABR(FM) Tifton GA
*WWET(FM) Valdosta GA
*WJSP-FM Warm Springs GA
*WXVS(FM) Waycross GA
*KPRG(FM) Hagatna GU
*KANO(FM) Hilo HI
*KHPR(FM) Honolulu HI
*KKUA(FM) Wailuku HI
*WOI-FM Ames IA
*KWOI(FM) Carroll IA
*KHKE(FM) Cedar Falls IA
*KLCD(FM) Decorah IA
*KHOE(FM) Fairfield IA
*KTPR(FM) Fort Dodge IA
*KSUI(FM) Iowa City IA
*KOWI(FM) Lamoni IA
*KOJI(FM) Okoboji IA
*KUNZ(FM) Ottumwa IA
*KWIT(FM) Sioux City IA
*KBSU-FM Boise ID
*KIBX(FM) Bonners Ferry ID
*KNWO(FM) Cottonwood ID
*KBSM(FM) McCall ID
*KRFA-FM Moscow ID
*KBYI(FM) Rexburg ID
*KWRV(FM) Sun Valley ID
*KBSW(FM) Twin Falls ID
*WSIU(FM) Carbondale IL
WFMT(FM) Chicago IL
*WNIE(FM) Freeport IL
*WNIW(FM) La Salle IL
*WIUM(FM) Macomb IL
*WVSI(FM) Mount Vernon IL
*WUSI(FM) Olney IL
*WCBU(FM) Peoria IL
*WIPA(FM) Pittsfield IL
*WQUB(FM) Quincy IL
*WVIK(FM) Rock Island IL
*WNIU(FM) Rockford IL
*WUIS(FM) Springfield IL
*WNIQ(FM) Sterling IL
*WILL-FM Urbana IL
*WIUW(FM) Warsaw IL
*WETN(FM) Wheaton IL

*WBSB(FM) Anderson IN
*WFIU(FM) Bloomington IN
*WNIN(FM) Evansville IN
*WBSH(FM) Hagerstown IN
*WFYI-FM Indianapolis IN
*WICR(FM) Indianapolis IN
*WBSW(FM) Marion IN
*WBST(FM) Muncie IN
*WSND-FM Notre Dame IN
*WCKZ(FM) Orland IN
*WBSJ(FM) Portland IN
*WECI(FM) Richmond IN
*WBNI-FM Roanoke IN
*WBAA-FM West Lafayette IN
*KANH(FM) Emporia KS
*KANZ(FM) Garden City KS
*KHCT(FM) Great Bend KS
*KZAN(FM) Hays KS
*KZNA(FM) Hill City KS
*KHCC-FM Hutchinson KS
KXTR(AM) Kansas City KS
*KANU(FM) Lawrence KS
*KANV(FM) Olsburg KS
*KRPS(FM) Pittsburg KS
*KHCD(FM) Salina KS
*WKYU-FM Bowling Green KY
*WEKF(FM) Corbin KY
*WKUE(FM) Elizabethtown KY
*WEKH(FM) Hazard KY
*WKPB(FM) Henderson KY
*WUOL(FM) Louisville KY
*WEKU(FM) Richmond KY
*WDCL-FM Somerset KY
WSKV(FM) Stanton KY
*KLSA(FM) Alexandria LA
*WRKF(FM) Baton Rouge LA
*WWNO(FM) New Orleans LA
*KDAQ(FM) Shreveport LA
*KTLN(FM) Thibodaux LA
*WFCR(FM) Amherst MA
*WGBH(FM) Boston MA
WHRB(FM) Cambridge MA
WFCC-FM Chatham MA
WCRB(FM) Lowell MA
*WBJC(FM) Baltimore MD
*WFWM(FM) Frostburg MD
*WGMS(FM) Hagerstown MD
*WSCL(FM) Salisbury MD
*WMEH(FM) Bangor ME
WBQI(FM) Bar Harbor ME
*WMED(FM) Calais ME
*WMEP(FM) Camden ME
*WMEF(FM) Fort Kent ME
WBQQ(FM) Kennebunk ME
WBQW(FM) Kennebunkport ME
*WMEA(FM) Portland ME
*WMEM(FM) Presque Isle ME
WBQX(FM) Thomaston ME
*WMEW(FM) Waterville ME
*WYAR(FM) Yarmouth ME
*WCML-FM Alpena MI
*WAUS(FM) Berrien Springs MI
*WRCJ-FM Detroit MI
*WICV(FM) East Jordan MI
*WKAR-FM East Lansing MI
*WBLU-FM Grand Rapids MI
*WGGL-FM Houghton MI
*WIAA(FM) Interlochen MI
*WMUK(FM) Kalamazoo MI
*WIAB(FM) Mackinaw City MI
*WNMU-FM Marquette MI
*WCMU-FM Mount Pleasant MI
*WCMB-FM Oscoda MI
WKLZ-FM Petoskey MI
*WCMZ-FM Sault Ste. Marie MI
WWCM(FM) Standish MI
*WBLV(FM) Twin Lake MI
*KRSU(FM) Appleton MN
*KCRB-FM Bemidji MN
*KBPR(FM) Brainerd MN
*KSJR-FM Collegeville MN
*KSJR-FM Collegeville MN
*WSCD-FM Duluth MN
*KCMF(FM) Fergus Falls MN
*WMLS(FM) Grand Marais MN
*KSJN(FM) Minneapolis MN

*KCCM(FM) Moorhead MN
*KLSE-FM Rochester MN
*KGAC(FM) Saint Peter MN
*KQMN(FM) Thief River Falls MN
*WIRR(FM) Virginia-Hibbing MN
*KRSW(FM) Worthington MN
*KRCU(FM) Cape Girardeau MO
*KRNW(FM) Chillicothe MO
KFUO-FM Clayton MO
*KBIA(FM) Columbia MO
*KSEF(FM) Farmington MO
*KXMS(FM) Joplin MO
*KKTR(FM) Kirksville MO
*KWJC(FM) Liberty MO
*KXCV(FM) Maryville MO
*KSMS-FM Point Lookout MO
*KMST(FM) Rolla MO
*KSMU(FM) Springfield MO
*KSMW(FM) West Plains MO
*WUSM-FM Hattiesburg MS
*WMPN-FM Jackson MS
*KEMC(FM) Billings MT
*KBMC(FM) Bozeman MT
*KAPC(FM) Butte MT
*KUFN(FM) Hamilton MT
*KNMC(FM) Havre MT
*KUHM(FM) Helena MT
*KUKL(FM) Kalispell MT
KPRK(AM) Livingston MT
*KUFM(FM) Missoula MT
*WCQS(FM) Asheville NC
*WZPE(FM) Bath NC
*WBUX(FM) Buxton NC
*WDAV(FM) Davidson NC
*WFQS(FM) Franklin NC
*WURI(FM) Manteo NC
*WTEB(FM) New Bern NC
*WZRN(FM) Norlina NC
*WCPE(FM) Raleigh NC
*WHQR(FM) Wilmington NC
*WFDD-FM Winston-Salem NC
*KCND(FM) Bismarck ND
*KPPD(FM) Devils Lake ND
*KDPR(FM) Dickinson ND
*KUND-FM Grand Forks ND
*KPRJ(FM) Jamestown ND
*KMPR(FM) Minot ND
*KPPR(FM) Williston ND
*KTNE-FM Alliance NE
*KMNE-FM Bassett NE
*KCNE-FM Chadron NE
*KHNE-FM Hastings NE
*KLNE-FM Lexington NE
*KUCV(FM) Lincoln NE
*KRNE-FM Merriman NE
*KXNE-FM Norfolk NE
*KPNE-FM North Platte NE
*KIOS-FM Omaha NE
*KVNO(FM) Omaha NE
*WWCJ(FM) Cape May NJ
*WWNJ(FM) Dover Township NJ
*WRTQ(FM) Ocean City NJ
WPRB(FM) Princeton NJ
*WWFM(FM) Trenton NJ
*KSJE(FM) Farmington NM
*KRWG(FM) Las Cruces NM
*KMTH(FM) Maljamar NM
*KENW-FM Portales NM
KHFM(FM) Santa Fe NM
*KRNM(FM) Chalan Kanoa-Saipan NP
*KNCC(FM) Elko NV
*KCNV(FM) Las Vegas NV
KXPT(FM) Las Vegas NV
*KUNR(FM) Reno NV
KSVL(FM) Smith NV
*KTPH(FM) Tonopah NV
WEXT(FM) Amsterdam NY
*WSKG-FM Binghamton NY
*WNED-FM Buffalo NY
*WSQE(FM) Corning NY
*WJSL(FM) Houghton NY
*WSQG-FM Ithaca NY
*WNJA(FM) Jamestown NY
*WKCR-FM New York NY
*WNYC-FM New York NY
*WQXR-FM New York NY

*WSQC-FM Oneonta NY
*WRHV(FM) Poughkeepsie NY
*WXXI-FM Rochester NY
*WMHT(FM) Schenectady NY
*WOXR(FM) Schuyler Falls NY
*WCNY-FM Syracuse NY
*WUNY(FM) Utica NY
*WJNY(FM) Watertown NY
*WGBE(FM) Bryan OH
*WGUC(FM) Cincinnati OH
*WOSU-FM Columbus OH
*WOSE(FM) Coshocton OH
*WDPR(FM) Dayton OH
*WGDE(FM) Defiance OH
*WDPG(FM) Greenville OH
*WKSU-FM Kent OH
*WGLE(FM) Lima OH
WCLV(FM) Lorain OH
*WOSV(FM) Mansfield OH
*WMRT(FM) Marietta OH
*WOSB(FM) Marion OH
*WKRJ(FM) New Philadelphia OH
*WNRK(FM) Norwalk OH
*WOSP(FM) Portsmouth OH
*WKSV(FM) Thompson OH
*WGTE-FM Toledo OH
*WKRW(FM) Wooster OH
*WYSU(FM) Youngstown OH
*KOCU(FM) Altus OK
*KLCU(FM) Ardmore OK
*KYCU(FM) Clinton OK
*KCSC(FM) Edmond OK
*KCCU(FM) Lawton OK
*KBCW-FM McAlester OK
*KOSU(FM) Stillwater OK
*KWTU(FM) Tulsa OK
*KSOR(FM) Ashland OR
*KSRG(FM) Ashland OR
*KWAX(FM) Eugene OR
*KWVZ(FM) Florence OR
*KQOC(FM) Gleneden Beach OR
*KQHR(FM) Hood River OR
*KLMF(FM) Klamath Falls OR
*KOOZ(FM) Myrtle Point OR
KCMD(AM) Portland OR
*KQAC(FM) Portland OR
*KWRX(FM) Redmond OR
*KSRS(FM) Roseburg OR
*KQDL(FM) The Dalles OR
*WDIY(FM) Allentown PA
*WMCE(FM) Erie PA
*WQLN-FM Erie PA
*WSAJ-FM Grove City PA
*WITF-FM Harrisburg PA
*WRTY(FM) Jackson Township PA
*WQEJ(FM) Johnstown PA
*WPSX(FM) Kane PA
*WWPJ(FM) Pen Argyl PA
*WRTI(FM) Philadelphia PA
*WQED-FM Pittsburgh PA
*WVIA-FM Scranton PA
*WPSU(FM) State College PA
*WJAZ(FM) Summerdale PA
*WVYA(FM) Williamsport PA
*WIPR-FM San Juan PR
WCRI(FM) Block Island RI
*WSCI(FM) Charleston SC
*WLTR(FM) Columbia SC
*WEPR(FM) Greenville SC
*KESD(FM) Brookings SD
KPSD(FM) Faith SD
*KQSD-FM Lowry SD
*KDSD-FM Pierpont SD
*KBHE-FM Rapid City SD
*KTSD-FM Reliance SD
*KCSD(FM) Sioux Falls SD
*KRSD(FM) Sioux Falls SD
*KUSD(FM) Vermillion SD
*WSMC-FM Collegedale TN
*WHRS(FM) Cookeville TN
*WFHU(FM) Henderson TN
*WKNP(FM) Jackson TN
*WETS(FM) Johnson City TN
*WETS(FM) Johnson City TN
*WUOT(FM) Knoxville TN
*WKNO-FM Memphis TN

*WPLN-FM Nashville TN
*WTML(FM) Tullahoma TN
*KACU(FM) Abilene TX
*KMFA(FM) Austin TX
*KVLU(FM) Beaumont TX
*KAMU-FM College Station TX
*KEDT-FM Corpus Christi TX
WRR(FM) Dallas TX
*KTEP(FM) El Paso TX
*KMBH-FM Harlingen TX
*KUHF(FM) Houston TX
*KSHU(FM) Huntsville TX
*KTXI(FM) Ingram TX
*KNCT-FM Killeen TX
*KOHM(FM) Lubbock TX
*KLDN(FM) Lufkin TX
*KHID(FM) McAllen TX
*KOCV(FM) Odessa TX
*KPAC(FM) San Antonio TX
*KTOT(FM) Spearman TX
*KTXK(FM) Texarkana TX
*KVRT(FM) Victoria TX
*KWBU-FM Waco TX
*KMCU(FM) Wichita Falls TX
*KUSR(FM) Logan UT
*KUSU-FM Logan UT
*KBYU-FM Provo UT
*WVTU(FM) Charlottesville VA
*WVTW(FM) Charlottesville VA
*WMVE(FM) Chase City VA
*WFOS(FM) Chesapeake VA
*WEMC(FM) Harrisonburg VA
*WVTR(FM) Marion VA
*WHRO-FM Norfolk VA
*WCVE(FM) Richmond VA
*WVTF(FM) Roanoke VA
WBQK(FM) West Point VA
*WISE-FM Wise VA
WBTN-FM Bennington VT
*WVPS(FM) Burlington VT
*WNCH(FM) Norwich VT
*WRVT(FM) Rutland VT
*WVPA(FM) Saint Johnsbury VT
WCVT(FM) Stowe VT
*WVTQ(FM) Sunderland VT
*WVPR(FM) Windsor VT
*KZAZ(FM) Bellingham WA
*KNWV(FM) Clarkston WA
*KNWR(FM) Ellensburg WA
KOHO-FM Leavenworth WA
*KQWS(FM) Omak WA
*KNWP(FM) Port Angeles WA
*KWSU(AM) Pullman WA
*KFAE-FM Richland WA
KING-FM Seattle WA
*KPBX-FM Spokane WA
*KNWY(FM) Yakima WA
*WHSA(FM) Brule WI
*WUEC(FM) Eau Claire WI
*WPNE(FM) Green Bay WI
*WGTD(FM) Kenosha WI
*WHLA(FM) La Crosse WI
*WLSU(FM) La Crosse WI
*WERN(FM) Madison WI
*WORT(FM) Madison WI
*WVSS(FM) Menomonie WI
*WSSW(FM) Platteville WI
*WXPR(FM) Rhinelander WI
*WHND(FM) Sister Bay WI
*WHRM(FM) Wausau WI
*WVPB(FM) Beckley WV
*WVPW(FM) Buckhannon WV
*WVPN(FM) Charleston WV
*WVWV(FM) Huntington WV
*WVEP(FM) Martinsburg WV
*WVPM(FM) Morgantown WV
*WVPG(FM) Parkersburg WV
*WAUA(FM) Petersburg WV
*WVNP(FM) Wheeling WV
*KUWA(FM) Afton WY
*KDUW(FM) Douglas WY
*KUWG(FM) Gillette WY
*KUWJ(FM) Jackson WY
*KUWR(FM) Laramie WY
*KUWY(FM) Laramie WY
*KUWN(FM) Newcastle WY

*KUWX(FM) Pinedale WY
*KUWP(FM) Powell WY
*KUWZ(FM) Rock Springs WY
*KPRQ(FM) Sheridan WY
*KSUW(FM) Sundance WY
*KUWD(FM) Sundance WY
KUWT(FM) Thermopolis WY

Comedy

KXDJ(FM) Spearman TX

Contemporary Hit/Top-40

KFAT(FM) Anchorage AK
KGOT(FM) Anchorage AK
KAKQ-FM Fairbanks AK
KWLF(FM) Fairbanks AK
KSLD(AM) Soldotna AK
WZYP(FM) Athens AL
WZBQ(FM) Carrollton AL
WAGF-FM Dothan AL
WKMX(FM) Enterprise AL
WKZJ(FM) Eufaula AL
WABB-FM Mobile AL
WHHY-FM Montgomery AL
WQEN(FM) Trussville AL
*KSWH(FM) Arkadelphia AR
KMRX(FM) El Dorado AR
KHTE-FM England AR
KISR(FM) Fort Smith AR
KIYS(FM) Jonesboro AR
KKPT(FM) Little Rock AR
KMXF(FM) Lowell AR
KMCK(FM) Siloam Springs AR
KFYX(FM) Texarkana AR
KCDQ(FM) Douglas AZ
KOHT(FM) Marana AZ
KZZP(FM) Mesa AZ
KIKO(AM) Miami AZ
KIDR(AM) Phoenix AZ
KVIB(FM) Sun City West AZ
KRQQ(FM) Tucson AZ
KLJZ(FM) Yuma AZ
KEWB(FM) Anderson CA
KISV(FM) Bakersfield CA
KDUC(FM) Barstow CA
KXSB(FM) Big Bear Lake CA
KSIQ(FM) Brawley CA
KBFP-FM Delano CA
KHTS-FM El Cajon CA
KFMI(FM) Eureka CA
KSSD(FM) Fallbrook CA
KWPT(FM) Fortuna CA
*KOHL(FM) Fremont CA
KWYE(FM) Fresno CA
KQCM(FM) Joshua Tree CA
KOKO(FM) Kerman CA
KVPW(FM) Kingsburg CA
KWIN(FM) Lodi CA
KIIS-FM Los Angeles CA
KPWR(FM) Los Angeles CA
KDUQ(FM) Ludlow CA
*KSMC(FM) Moraga CA
*KSFH(FM) Mountain View CA
*KLFH(FM) Ojai CA
KCAQ(FM) Oxnard CA
KPSI-FM Palm Springs CA
KHTN(FM) Planada CA
KNLF(FM) Quincy CA
*KRVH(FM) Rio Vista CA
KGGI(FM) Riverside CA
KVVS(FM) Rosamond CA
KDND(FM) Sacramento CA
KRAY-FM Salinas CA
KYZZ(FM) Salinas CA
KMEL(FM) San Francisco CA
KYLD(FM) San Francisco CA
KWWV(FM) Santa Margarita CA
KLJR(FM) Santa Paula CA
KNNN(FM) Shasta Lake City CA
KBOS-FM Tulare CA
KWNN(FM) Turlock CA
KCDZ(FM) Twentynine Palms CA

KWNE(FM) Ukiah CA
*KDUV(FM) Visalia CA
KSEQ(FM) Visalia CA
*KASF(FM) Alamosa CO
KUUR(FM) Carbondale CO
KMGJ(FM) Grand Junction CO
WQGN-FM Groton CT
WKCI-FM Hamden CT
WKSS(FM) Hartford CT
WWRX(FM) Pawcatuck CT
WILI-FM Willimantic CT
WIHT(FM) Washington DC
*WMPH(FM) Wilmington DE
WFCT(FM) Apalachicola FL
WXKB(FM) Cape Coral FL
WJHM(FM) Daytona Beach FL
WFFY(FM) Destin FL
WRLZ(FM) Eatonville FL
WHYI-FM Fort Lauderdale FL
WLDI(FM) Fort Pierce FL
WZNS(FM) Fort Walton Beach FL
WHTF(FM) Havana FL
WVYB(FM) Holly Hill FL
WIFL(FM) Inglis FL
WAPE-FM Jacksonville FL
WEOW(FM) Key West FL
WLLD(FM) Lakeland FL
WXHT(FM) Madison FL
WAOA-FM Melbourne FL
WEDR(FM) Miami FL
WMYM(AM) Miami FL
WPOW(FM) Miami FL
WBTT(FM) Naples Park FL
WILN(FM) Panama City FL
WPFM-FM Panama City FL
WPRY(AM) Perry FL
WWMI(AM) Saint Petersburg FL
WFLZ-FM Tampa FL
WXXL(FM) Tavares FL
V6AH(AM) Pohnpei FM
*V6AI(AM) Yap FM
WQVE(FM) Albany GA
WCGQ(FM) Columbus GA
WXMK(FM) Dock Junction GA
WBTS(FM) Doraville GA
WKKZ(FM) Dublin GA
WEDB(FM) East Dublin GA
WOAH(FM) Glennville GA
WVFJ-FM Manchester GA
WDRR(FM) Martinez GA
WMGB(FM) Montezuma GA
WAEV(FM) Savannah GA
WZAT(FM) Savannah GA
WSTR(FM) Smyrna GA
WJFL(FM) Tennille GA
KOKU(FM) Hagatna GU
KUAM-FM Hagatna GU
KPMW(FM) Haiimaile HI
KNWB(FM) Hilo HI
KIKI-FM Honolulu HI
KLHI-FM Kahului HI
KPHW(FM) Kaneohe HI
KITH(FM) Kapaa HI
KJMQ(FM) Lihue HI
KNUQ(FM) Paauilo HI
KSRF(FM) Poipu HI
KJMD(FM) Pukalani HI
KDDB(FM) Waipahu HI
KCCQ(FM) Ames IA
KZAT-FM Belle Plaine IA
KZIA(FM) Cedar Rapids IA
KKDM(FM) Des Moines IA
KLYV(FM) Dubuque IA
KRTI(FM) Grinnell IA
KCJJ(AM) Iowa City IA
KXFT(FM) Manson IA
KBEA-FM Muscatine IA
KSMA-FM Osage IA
KOTM-FM Ottumwa IA
KIWA-FM Sheldon IA
KTPZ(FM) Hazelton ID
KFTZ(FM) Idaho Falls ID
KVTY(FM) Lewiston ID
KZFN(FM) Moscow ID
KZMG(FM) New Plymouth ID
KACH(AM) Preston ID

WKIB(FM) Anna IL
WUIL(FM) Arcola IL
WERV-FM Aurora IL
WBNQ(FM) Bloomington IL
WCDD(FM) Canton IL
WCIL-FM Carbondale IL
WLRW(FM) Champaign IL
WBBM-FM Chicago IL
WKSC-FM Chicago IL
WRPW(FM) Colfax IL
WSOY-FM Decatur IL
WYDS(FM) Decatur IL
WISH-FM Galatia IL
WXAJ(FM) Hillsboro IL
WVLI(FM) Kankakee IL
WEAI(FM) Lynnville IL
*WLKL(FM) Mattoon IL
WZPW(FM) Peoria IL
WLCE(FM) Petersburg IL
*WGCA-FM Quincy IL
WQQB(FM) Rantoul IL
WZOK(FM) Rockford IL
WIVQ(FM) Spring Valley IL
WDBR(FM) Springfield IL
WSTQ(FM) Streator IL
WKRV(FM) Vandalia IL
WBWB(FM) Bloomington IN
WNHT(FM) Churubusco IN
WINN(FM) Columbus IN
WIMC(FM) Crawfordsville IN
WXXB(FM) Delphi IN
*WFCI(FM) Franklin IN
*WHWE(FM) Howe IN
*WVSH(FM) Huntington IN
*WBDG(FM) Indianapolis IN
*WEDM(FM) Indianapolis IN
WHHH(FM) Indianapolis IN
WAZY-FM Lafayette IN
*WCYT(FM) Lafayette Township IN
WLHM(FM) Logansport IN
WXXC(FM) Marion IN
*WNAS(FM) New Albany IN
WJFX(FM) New Haven IN
WDKS(FM) Newburgh IN
WUME-FM Paoli IN
WRDZ-FM Plainfield IN
WZKF(FM) Salem IN
WNDV-FM South Bend IN
WNOU(FM) Speedway IN
WMGI(FM) Terre Haute IN
*WVUB(FM) Vincennes IN
*KTCC(FM) Colby KS
KMOQ(FM) Columbus KS
KZCH(FM) Derby KS
KLZR(FM) Lawrence KS
KMXN(FM) Osage City KS
*KTJO-FM Ottawa KS
KACZ(FM) Riley KS
KSAL-FM Salina KS
KSKU(FM) Sterling KS
*KYWA(FM) Wichita KS
WWKF(FM) Fulton KY
WTHX(FM) Hodgenville KY
WZQQ(FM) Hyden KY
WLKT(FM) Lexington-Fayette KY
WDJX(FM) Louisville KY
WFTM-FM Maysville KY
WBTF(FM) Midway KY
WEGI-FM Oak Grove KY
WSTO(FM) Owensboro KY
WDDJ(FM) Paducah KY
*WGCF(FM) Paducah KY
WQHY(FM) Prestonsburg KY
KQID(FM) Alexandria LA
KQIS(FM) Basile LA
WFMF(FM) Baton Rouge LA
KTSR(FM) De Quincy LA
KRKA(FM) Erath LA
WYLK(FM) Lacombe LA
KSMB(FM) Lafayette LA
KNOE-FM Monroe LA
WEZB(FM) New Orleans LA
KRUF(FM) Shreveport LA
WFHN(FM) Fairhaven MA
*WGAO(FM) Franklin MA
WBOQ(FM) Gloucester MA

WXKS-FM Medford MA
*WSDH(FM) Sandwich MA
*WYAJ(FM) Sudbury MA
WOCQ(FM) Berlin MD
WPGC-FM Morningside MD
WMME-FM Augusta ME
*WRBC(FM) Lewiston ME
WBZN(FM) Old Town ME
WJBQ(FM) Portland ME
*WAHS(FM) Auburn Hills MI
WKFR-FM Battle Creek MI
*WBFH(FM) Bloomfield Hills MI
WKHQ-FM Charlevoix MI
WCFX(FM) Clare MI
*WPRJ(FM) Coleman MI
WWCK-FM Flint MI
WRCL(FM) Frankenmuth MI
*WHPR(FM) Highland Park MI
WUPS(FM) Houghton Lake MI
WHMI-FM Howell MI
WHZZ(FM) Lansing MI
WJIM-FM Lansing MI
WTWR-FM Luna Pier MI
WSNX-FM Muskegon MI
WKQS-FM Negaunee MI
*WORW(FM) Port Huron MI
WYSS(FM) Sault Ste. Marie MI
KXRZ(FM) Alexandria MN
*KBSB(FM) Bemidji MN
KCLH(FM) Caledonia MN
KTTB(FM) Glencoe MN
WTBX(FM) Hibbing MN
KDWB-FM Richfield MN
KROC-FM Rochester MN
KCLD-FM Saint Cloud MN
KTNX(FM) Arcadia MO
KSYN(FM) Joplin MO
KMXV(FM) Kansas City MO
*KWJC(FM) Liberty MO
KKBL(FM) Monett MO
KSLZ(FM) Saint Louis MO
KSPW(FM) Sparta MO
WYOY(FM) Gluckstadt MS
WXYK(FM) Gulfport MS
WNSL(FM) Laurel MS
WZYQ(FM) Mound Bayou MS
KISN(FM) Belgrade MT
KBEV-FM Dillon MT
KIKC(AM) Forsyth MT
KOFI(AM) Kalispell MT
KRSQ(FM) Laurel MT
KPLN(FM) Lockwood MT
WNKS(FM) Charlotte NC
WDCG(FM) Durham NC
WQSM(FM) Fayetteville NC
WRHT(FM) Morehead City NC
WKBC-FM North Wilkesboro NC
*WDCC(FM) Sanford NC
WERO(FM) Washington NC
WKZL(FM) Winston-Salem NC
KKCT(FM) Bismarck ND
KKXL-FM Grand Forks ND
*KCNT(FM) Hastings NE
KFRX(FM) Lincoln NE
WJYY(FM) Concord NH
WKNE(FM) Keene NH
WXXS(FM) Lancaster NH
WSNQ(FM) Cape May Court House NJ
*WBZC(FM) Pemberton NJ
WZBZ(FM) Pleasantville NJ
WPST(FM) Trenton NJ
KYEE(FM) Alamogordo NM
KDRF(FM) Albuquerque NM
*KNMI(FM) Farmington NM
KAZX(FM) Kirtland NM
KHQT(FM) Las Cruces NM
KAGM(FM) Los Lunas NM
KBCQ-FM Roswell NM
KKSS(FM) Santa Fe NM
KPXP(FM) Garapan-Saipan NP
KZTQ(FM) Carson City NV
KLUC-FM Las Vegas NV
KQRT(FM) Las Vegas NV
KVEG(FM) Mesquite NV
KWNZ(FM) Sun Valley NV

*WBXL(FM) Baldwinsville NY
WKKF(FM) Ballston Spa NY
*WXBA(FM) Brentwood NY
*WBSU(FM) Brockport NY
*WKRB(FM) Brooklyn NY
WTSS(FM) Buffalo NY
*WCIY(FM) Canandaigua NY
WYUL(FM) Chateaugay NY
WWYL(FM) Chenango Bridge NY
WBDR(FM) Copenhagen NY
WNKI(FM) Corning NY
WDHI(FM) Delhi NY
WLVY(FM) Elmira NY
WMRV-FM Endicott NY
*WCID(FM) Friendship NY
WFNY(FM) Gloversville NY
WKGS(FM) Irondequoit NY
WKZA(FM) Lakewood NY
WSKU(FM) Little Falls NY
WYSX(FM) Morristown NY
WQHT(FM) New York NY
WKSE(FM) Niagara Falls NY
*WOSS(FM) Ossining NY
WBLI(FM) Patchogue NY
WPKF(FM) Poughkeepsie NY
WSPK(FM) Poughkeepsie NY
WPXY-FM Rochester NY
WENU(AM) South Glens Falls NY
*WJPZ-FM Syracuse NY
WNTQ(FM) Syracuse NY
WWHT(FM) Syracuse NY
WFLY(FM) Troy NY
WAJZ(FM) Voorheesville NY
WKBE(FM) Warrensburg NY
WCIZ-FM Watertown NY
WSKS(FM) Whitesboro NY
*WONB(FM) Ada OH
WAKS(FM) Akron OH
*WZIP(FM) Akron OH
WYJK-FM Bellaire OH
WWMK(AM) Cleveland OH
*WUFM(FM) Columbus OH
WLWD(FM) Columbus Grove OH
WXXR(FM) Fredericktown OH
WBKS(FM) Ironton OH
WRVB(FM) Marietta OH
*WYSZ(FM) Maumee OH
WKFS(FM) Milford OH
WXZQ(FM) Piketon OH
WVKF(FM) Shadyside OH
WVKS(FM) Toledo OH
*WYSA(FM) Wauseon OH
*WCWS(FM) Wooster OH
WHOT-FM Youngstown OH
KKWD(FM) Bethany OK
KTBT(FM) Broken Arrow OK
*KSSU(FM) Durant OK
KTIJ(FM) Elk City OK
KHTT(FM) Muskogee OK
KJYO(FM) Oklahoma City OK
KOMA(FM) Oklahoma City OK
KZBB(FM) Poteau OK
KIFS(FM) Ashland OR
KXIX(FM) Bend OR
KYSF(FM) Bonanza OR
KQHC(FM) Burns OR
KDPM(FM) Cottage Grove OR
KDUK-FM Florence OR
KKRB(FM) Klamath Falls OR
*KEOL(FM) La Grande OR
KOOS(FM) North Bend OR
*KMKR(FM) Oakridge OR
KKRZ(FM) Portland OR
KEUG(FM) Veneta OR
WAEB-FM Allentown PA
WHOL(AM) Allentown PA
WWOT(FM) Altoona PA
WASP(AM) Brownsville PA
*WCUC-FM Clarion PA
WRTS(FM) Erie PA
*WZZE(FM) Glen Mills PA
WNNK-FM Harrisburg PA
WJHT(FM) Johnstown PA
WLAN-FM Lancaster PA
*WNTE(FM) Mansfield PA
WVRZ(FM) Mount Carmel PA

WBHT(FM) Mountain Top PA
WBHD(FM) Olyphant PA
WIOQ(FM) Philadelphia PA
WRDW-FM Philadelphia PA
WBZW-FM Pittsburgh PA
WKST-FM Pittsburgh PA
WAVT-FM Pottsville PA
*WYBF(FM) Radnor Township PA
WRFY-FM Reading PA
WAKZ(FM) Sharpsville PA
WRSC-FM State College PA
WKRF(FM) Tobyhanna PA
WNBT-FM Wellsboro PA
WKRZ(FM) Wilkes-Barre PA
WKSB(FM) Williamsport PA
WYCR(FM) York-Hanover PA
WCMN-FM Arecibo PR
WBQN(FM) Barceloneta-Manati PR
WODA(FM) Bayamon PR
WXLX(FM) Lajas PR
WAEL-FM Maricao PR
WPRA(AM) Mayaguez PR
WUKQ-FM Mayaguez PR
WEKO(AM) Morovis PR
WEXS(AM) Patillas PR
WEGM(FM) San German PR
WENA(AM) Yauco PR
*WCVY(FM) Coventry RI
WPRO-FM Providence RI
WWKX(FM) Woonsocket RI
WSEA(FM) Atlantic Beach SC
WSSX-FM Charleston SC
WJMX-FM Cheraw SC
WNOK(FM) Columbia SC
WWXM(FM) Garden City SC
WFBC-FM Greenville SC
WHSC(AM) Hartsville SC
WWKT-FM Kingstree SC
WHZT(FM) Seneca SC
KQRN(FM) Mitchell SD
KQRQ(FM) Rapid City SD
KKLS-FM Sioux Falls SD
KRCS(FM) Sturgis SD
*KAOR(FM) Vermillion SD
KWYR-FM Winner SD
WMSR-FM Collinwood TN
*WUMC(FM) Elizabethton TN
*WVCP(FM) Gallatin TN
WAEZ(FM) Greeneville TN
WTJW(FM) Humboldt TN
WNRX(FM) Jefferson City TN
WRVW(FM) Lebanon TN
*WUTM(FM) Martin TN
WYDL(FM) Middleton TN
WAKQ(FM) Paris TN
WWST(FM) Sevierville TN
WTRZ(FM) Spencer TN
KPRF(FM) Amarillo TX
KQIZ-FM Amarillo TX
KXGL(FM) Amarillo TX
KXSS-FM Amarillo TX
KORQ(FM) Baird TX
KQXY-FM Beaumont TX
*KPFC(FM) Callisburg TX
KDHT(FM) Cedar Park TX
KZFM(FM) Corpus Christi TX
KMMZ(FM) Crane TX
KJKK(FM) Dallas TX
KHKS(FM) Denton TX
KBFM(FM) Edinburg TX
KPRR(FM) El Paso TX
KTFM(FM) Floresville TX
KPMZ(FM) Flower Mound TX
KBXT(FM) Franklin TX
KCDD(FM) Hamlin TX
KPWW(FM) Hooks TX
KKHH(FM) Houston TX
KRBE(FM) Houston TX
KZII-FM Lubbock TX
KZBT(FM) Midland TX
KAZE(FM) Ore City TX
*KWLD(FM) Plainview TX
KKPN(FM) Rockport TX
*KNLE-FM Round Rock TX
KIXY-FM San Angelo TX
KJXK(FM) San Antonio TX

KXXM(FM) San Antonio TX
KSCH(FM) Sulphur Springs TX
KBAR-FM Victoria TX
KVIC(FM) Victoria TX
KWTX-FM Waco TX
KISX(FM) Whitehouse TX
KNIN-FM Wichita Falls TX
KQXC(FM) Wichita Falls TX
KAIQ(FM) Wolfforth TX
KEGH(FM) Brigham City UT
KCIN(FM) Cedar City UT
*KSUU(FM) Cedar City UT
KVFX(FM) Logan UT
*KWCR-FM Ogden UT
KXRQ(FM) Roosevelt UT
KZHT(FM) Salt Lake City UT
KUUU(AM) South Jordan UT
WJJX(FM) Appomattox VA
*WWHS-FM Hampden-Sydney VA
WQPO(FM) Harrisonburg VA
*WHCE(FM) Highland Springs VA
WZVA(FM) Marion VA
WNVZ(FM) Norfolk VA
WNVA-FM Norton VA
WJJS(FM) Roanoke VA
WXLK(FM) Roanoke VA
WHTE-FM Ruckersville VA
WHLF(FM) South Boston VA
WVBX(FM) Spotsylvania VA
WKSI-FM Stephens City VA
WAZR(FM) Woodstock VA
WORK(FM) Barre VT
*WWLR(FM) Lyndonville VT
*WVTC(FM) Randolph Center VT
WXXX(FM) South Burlington VT
KUJ-FM Burbank WA
KBDB-FM Forks WA
KBIS(AM) Forks WA
*KMIH(FM) Mercer Island WA
KZBE(FM) Omak WA
KHTR(FM) Pullman WA
KWWW-FM Quincy WA
*KNHC(FM) Seattle WA
KUBE(FM) Seattle WA
KBKS-FM Tacoma WA
*KVTI(FM) Tacoma WA
KPQ-FM Wenatchee WA
KFFM(FM) Yakima WA
WBIZ-FM Eau Claire WI
WIXX(FM) Green Bay WI
WZEE(FM) Madison WI
WQTC-FM Manitowoc WI
WKEB(FM) Medford WI
WRHN(FM) Rhinelander WI
*WPFF(FM) Sturgeon Bay WI
*WCLQ(FM) Wausau WI
WIFC(FM) Wausau WI
WXSS(FM) Wauwatosa WI
WCIR-FM Beckley WV
WVSR-FM Charleston WV
WQWV(FM) Fisher WV
WKEE-FM Huntington WV
WVAQ(FM) Morgantown WV
WRVZ(FM) Pocatalico WV
KTRS-FM Casper WY
KDLY(FM) Lander WY
KYCS(FM) Rock Springs WY
KZZS(FM) Story WY

Country

KASH-FM Anchorage AK
KBRJ(FM) Anchorage AK
KLAM(AM) Cordova AK
*KDLG(AM) Dillingham AK
KIAK-FM Fairbanks AK
KTKU(FM) Juneau AK
KWHQ-FM Kenai AK
KGTW(FM) Ketchikan AK
KVOK(AM) Kodiak AK
*KJNP(AM) North Pole AK
*KJNP-FM North Pole AK
KRSA(AM) Petersburg AK
KSEW(AM) Seward AK
KSBZ(FM) Sitka AK
KPEN-FM Soldotna AK

KVAK(AM) Valdez AK
KAYO(FM) Wasilla AK
WQAH(FM) Addison AL
WQSB(FM) Albertville AL
WSTH-FM Alexander City AL
WAAO-FM Andalusia AL
WRAB(AM) Arab AL
WCKF(FM) Ashland AL
WKKR(FM) Auburn AL
WZZK-FM Birmingham AL
WAOQ(FM) Brantley AL
WKNU(FM) Brewton AL
WPRN(AM) Butler AL
WEIS(AM) Centre AL
WFXO(FM) Centre AL
WBIB(AM) Centreville AL
WKUL(FM) Cullman AL
WGZZ(FM) Dadeville AL
WDRM(AM) Decatur AL
WTVY-FM Dothan AL
WELB(AM) Elba AL
WVVL(FM) Elba AL
WDJR(FM) Enterprise AL
WPGG(AM) Evergreen AL
WLDX(AM) Fayette AL
WTXT(FM) Fayette AL
WKWL(AM) Florala AL
WXFL(FM) Florence AL
WZOB(AM) Fort Payne AL
WNCB(AM) Gardendale AL
WGEA(AM) Geneva AL
WUSD(FM) Geneva AL
WKGA(FM) Goodwater AL
WQZX(FM) Greenville AL
WBMH(AM) Grove Hill AL
WTWX-FM Guntersville AL
WFMH-FM Hackleburg AL
WJBB-FM Haleyville AL
WERH(AM) Hamilton AL
*WPIL(FM) Heflin AL
WHMA-FM Hobson City AL
WCKA(AM) Jacksonville AL
WDXB(FM) Jasper AL
WINL(FM) Linden AL
WZZX(AM) Lineville AL
WPRN-FM Lisman AL
WNPT-FM Marion AL
WKSJ-FM Mobile AL
WBAM-FM Montgomery AL
WLWI-FM Montgomery AL
WWFF-FM New Market AL
WKLD(FM) Oneonta AL
WAMI(AM) Opp AL
WAMI-FM Opp AL
WOPP(AM) Opp AL
WOAB(FM) Ozark AL
WFHK(AM) Pell City AL
WRMG(AM) Red Bay AL
WELR-FM Roanoke AL
WGOL(AM) Russellville AL
WKEA-FM Scottsboro AL
WWIC(AM) Scottsboro AL
WDXX(FM) Selma AL
WRSM(AM) Sumiton AL
WTDR(FM) Talladega AL
WQRV(FM) Tuscumbia AL
WQSI(FM) Union Springs AL
KPGG(FM) Ashdown AR
KEWI(AM) Benton AR
KTHS(AM) Berryville AR
KTHS-FM Berryville AR
KHLS(FM) Blytheville AR
KLYR(AM) Clarksville AR
KLYR-FM Clarksville AR
KXIO(FM) Clarksville AR
KHPQ(FM) Clinton AR
KMJX(FM) Conway AR
KAGH(AM) Crossett AR
KAGH-FM Crossett AR
KYEL(FM) Danville AR
KCJC(FM) Dardanelle AR
KWXT(AM) Dardanelle AR
KDQN-FM De Queen AR
KDEW-FM De Witt AR
KXSA-FM Dermott AR
KXFE(FM) Dumas AR

KCXY(FM) East Camden AR
KIXB(FM) El Dorado AR
KKIX(FM) Fayetteville AR
KQEW(FM) Fordyce AR
KBFC(FM) Forrest City AR
KMAG(FM) Fort Smith AR
KTCS-FM Fort Smith AR
KAFN(FM) Gould AR
KYXK(FM) Gurdon AR
KWHF(FM) Harrisburg AR
KHOZ-FM Harrison AR
KFFA(AM) Helena AR
KHPA(FM) Hope AR
KKIK(FM) Horseshoe Bend AR
KQUS-FM Hot Springs AR
KFIN(FM) Jonesboro AR
KDXY(FM) Lake City AR
KSSN(AM) Little Rock AR
KBOK(AM) Malvern AR
KAMS(FM) Mammoth Spring AR
KBCN-FM Marshall AR
KENA-FM Mena AR
KVOM-FM Morrilton AR
KPFM(FM) Mountain Home AR
KTLO(AM) Mountain Home AR
KWOZ(FM) Mountain View AR
KMTB(FM) Murfreesboro AR
KOKR(FM) Newport AR
KDYN(AM) Ozark AR
KDYN-FM Ozark AR
KLBL(FM) Pearcy AR
KPBQ-FM Pine Bluff AR
KHOM(FM) Salem AR
KWCK-FM Searcy AR
KZHE(FM) Stamps AR
KOSY(AM) Texarkana AR
KVMZ(FM) Waldo AR
KRLW-FM Walnut Ridge AR
KWRF-FM Warren AR
KWYN(AM) Wynne AR
KWYN-FM Wynne AR
KAVV(FM) Benson AZ
KWCD(FM) Bisbee AZ
KMLE(FM) Chandler AZ
KFXR-FM Chinle AZ
KDDL(FM) Chino Valley AZ
KVRD-FM Cottonwood AZ
KDAP-FM Douglas AZ
KTHQ(FM) Eagar AZ
KAFF(AM) Flagstaff AZ
KAFF-FM Flagstaff AZ
KRDE(FM) Globe AZ
KZUA(FM) Holbrook AZ
KGMN(FM) Kingman AZ
KJJJ(AM) Lake Havasu City AZ
KSAZ(AM) Marana AZ
KQSS(FM) Miami AZ
KPGE(AM) Page AZ
KLPZ(AM) Parker AZ
KMOG(AM) Payson AZ
KNIX-FM Phoenix AZ
KNOT(AM) Prescott AZ
KBUX(FM) Quartzsite AZ
KXKQ(FM) Safford AZ
KSED(FM) Sedona AZ
KIIM-FM Tucson AZ
KSWG(FM) Wickenburg AZ
KHIL(AM) Willcox AZ
KTNN(AM) Window Rock AZ
KWRK(FM) Window Rock AZ
KINO(AM) Winslow AZ
KTTI(FM) Yuma AZ
KCNO(FM) Alturas CA
KBYN(FM) Arnold CA
KIXF(FM) Baker CA
KCWR(FM) Bakersfield CA
KUZZ(AM) Bakersfield CA
KUZZ-FM Bakersfield CA
KFLG-FM Big River CA
KIBS(FM) Bishop CA
KROP(AM) Brawley CA
KUSS(FM) Carlsbad CA
KKHK(FM) Carmel CA
KGRP(FM) Cazadero CA
KKCY(FM) Colusa CA
KPOD-FM Crescent City CA

KWST(AM) El Centro CA
KSOQ-FM Escondido CA
KEKA-FM Eureka CA
KRED-FM Eureka CA
KSKS(FM) Fresno CA
KATJ-FM George CA
KFGY(FM) Healdsburg CA
*KIDE(FM) Hoopa CA
KCNQ(FM) Kernville CA
KRKC(AM) King City CA
KIXW-FM Lenwood CA
KKGO(AM) Los Angeles CA
KRTY(FM) Los Gatos CA
KTOM-FM Marina CA
KUBB(FM) Mariposa CA
KATM(FM) Modesto CA
KTPI-FM Mojave CA
*KSMC(FM) Moraga CA
KPLM(FM) Palm Springs CA
KHSL-FM Paradise CA
KYOE(FM) Point Arena CA
KALF(FM) Red Bluff CA
KNCQ(FM) Redding CA
KEPD(FM) Ridgecrest CA
KZIQ-FM Ridgecrest CA
KNCI(FM) Sacramento CA
KFRG(FM) San Bernardino CA
KTDD(AM) San Bernardino CA
KSON(FM) San Diego CA
KBWF(FM) San Francisco CA
KKJG(FM) San Luis Obispo CA
KSLY-FM San Luis Obispo CA
KSNI-FM Santa Maria CA
KRAZ(FM) Santa Ynez CA
KNTY(FM) Shingle Springs CA
KXFG(FM) Sun City CA
KJDX(FM) Susanville CA
KJUG(AM) Tulare CA
KJUG-FM Tulare CA
KFLS-FM Tulelake CA
KKBN(FM) Twain Harte CA
KXCM(FM) Twentynine Palms CA
KQPM(FM) Ukiah CA
KUKI-FM Ukiah CA
KHAY(FM) Ventura CA
KVFG(FM) Victorville CA
KSYC-FM Yreka CA
KALA-FM Alamosa CO
KWOF(FM) Broomfield CO
KBVC(FM) Buena Vista CO
KNAB-FM Burlington CO
KSTY(FM) Canon City CO
KAVP(AM) Colona CO
KATC-FM Colorado Springs CO
KCSF(AM) Colorado Springs CO
KISZ-FM Cortez CO
KRAI(AM) Craig CO
KYGO-FM Denver CO
KRSJ(FM) Durango CO
KEKB(FM) Fruita CO
KMTS-FM Glenwood Springs CO
KRKY(AM) Granby CO
KMOZ-FM Grand Junction CO
KPKE(AM) Gunnison CO
KQZR(FM) Hayden CO
KJBL(FM) Julesburg CO
KTHN(FM) La Junta CO
KLMR(AM) Lamar CO
KVAY(FM) Lamar CO
KSLV(AM) Monte Vista CO
KYDN(FM) Monte Vista CO
KKXK(FM) Montrose CO
KRYD(FM) Norwood CO
KATR-FM Otis CO
KWGL(FM) Ouray CO
KWUF(AM) Pagosa Springs CO
KCCY(FM) Pueblo CO
KBCR-FM Steamboat Springs CO
KNNG(FM) Sterling CO
KCRT(AM) Trinidad CO
KSKE-FM Vail CO
KSPK(FM) Walsenburg CO
KUAD-FM Windsor CO
WPKX(FM) Enfield CT
WCTY(FM) Norwich CT
WWYZ(FM) Waterbury CT

WMZQ-FM Washington DC
WDSD(FM) Dover DE
WZKT(FM) Lewes DE
WWOJ(FM) Avon Park FL
WQXM(AM) Bartow FL
WPHK(FM) Blountstown FL
WKIS(FM) Boca Raton FL
WAKT-FM Callaway FL
WOCY(FM) Carrabelle FL
WIKX(FM) Charlotte Harbor FL
WAAZ-FM Crestview FL
WJSB(AM) Crestview FL
WZCC(AM) Cross City FL
WDSP(AM) De Funiak Springs FL
WZEP(AM) De Funiak Springs FL
WTRS(FM) Dunnellon FL
WKRO-FM Edgewater FL
WGGR(FM) Fort Myers FL
WDVH(AM) Gainesville FL
WGWD(FM) Gretna FL
WFUS(FM) Gulfport FL
WPLA(FM) Jacksonville FL
WQIK-FM Jacksonville FL
WCNK(FM) Key West FL
WCKT(FM) Lehigh Acres FL
WQHL-FM Live Oak FL
WMAF(AM) Madison FL
WJAQ(FM) Marianna FL
WTYS(AM) Marianna FL
WYZB(FM) Mary Esther FL
WXBM-FM Milton FL
*WBGY(FM) Naples FL
WOGK(FM) Ocala FL
WOKC(FM) Okeechobee FL
WWKA(FM) Orlando FL
WGNE-FM Palatka FL
WIYD(AM) Palatka FL
WPAP-FM Panama City FL
WPCF(AM) Panama City Beach FL
WYCT(FM) Pensacola FL
WNFK(FM) Perry FL
WCTH(FM) Plantation Key FL
WHKR(FM) Rockledge FL
WQYK-FM Saint Petersburg FL
WCTQ(FM) Sarasota FL
WAVW(FM) Stuart FL
WAIB(FM) Tallahassee FL
WTNT-FM Tallahassee FL
WDVH-FM Trenton FL
WQLC(FM) Watertown FL
WIRK-FM West Palm Beach FL
WPCV(FM) Winter Haven FL
WZZS(FM) Zolfo Springs FL
*V6AI(AM) Yap FM
WKAK(FM) Albany GA
WAJQ-FM Alma GA
WISK-FM Americus GA
WUBL(FM) Atlanta GA
WIBL(FM) Augusta GA
WBAF(AM) Barnesville GA
WBYZ(FM) Baxley GA
WKUB(FM) Blackshear/Waycross GA
WPPL(FM) Blue Ridge GA
WTUF(FM) Boston GA
WMOQ(FM) Bostwick GA
WMUV(FM) Brunswick GA
WRJY(FM) Brunswick GA
WJTH(AM) Calhoun GA
WBTR-FM Carrollton GA
WRWH(AM) Cleveland GA
WDCO(AM) Cochran GA
WDXQ-FM Cochran GA
WCON(AM) Cornelia GA
WCON-FM Cornelia GA
WCUG(AM) Cuthbert GA
WZTR(FM) Dahlonega GA
WSEM(AM) Donalsonville GA
WOKA-FM Douglas GA
WQZY(FM) Dublin GA
WXLI(AM) Dublin GA
WUFF(AM) Eastman GA
WSGC-FM Elberton GA
WLJA-FM Ellijay GA
WPGY(AM) Ellijay GA
WYAY(FM) Gainesville GA
WHIE(AM) Griffin GA

WKLY(AM) Hartwell GA	KICD-FM Spencer IA	WBBA-FM Pittsfield IL	KNDY(AM) Marysville KS	WBKR(FM) Owensboro KY
WVOH-FM Hazlehurst GA	KKRF(FM) Stuart IA	WCOY(FM) Quincy IL	KNDY-FM Marysville KS	WKYN(FM) Owingsville KY
WNGA(FM) Helen GA	KNEI-FM Waukon IA	WLFH(AM) Rantoul IL	KFTI-FM Newton KS	WKYQ(FM) Paducah KY
WIFO-FM Jesup GA	KWAY(AM) Waverly IA	WXNU(FM) Saint Anne IL	KFNF(FM) Oberlin KS	WSIP-FM Paintsville KY
WKBX(FM) Kingsland GA	KJJY(FM) West Des Moines IA	WJBD(AM) Salem IL	KOFO(AM) Ottawa KS	WBIO(FM) Philpot KY
WQCH(AM) La Fayette GA	KKYY(FM) Whiting IA	WCCI(FM) Savanna IL	KKOW(AM) Pittsburg KS	WDHR(FM) Pikeville KY
WLHR-FM Lavonia GA	KIZN(FM) Boise ID	WJVO(FM) South Jacksonville IL	KKOW-FM Pittsburg KS	WRIL(FM) Pineville KY
WPEH(AM) Louisville GA	KQFC(FM) Boise ID	WFMB-FM Springfield IL	KQTP(AM) Saint Marys KS	WKCA(FM) Salt Lick KY
WPEH-FM Louisville GA	KICR(FM) Coeur d'Alene ID	WKJT(FM) Teutopolis IL	KSKG(FM) Salina KS	WRLV(AM) Salyersville KY
WKCN(FM) Lumpkin GA	KCHQ(FM) Driggs ID	WSCH(FM) Aurora IN	KYEZ(FM) Salina KS	WRLV-FM Salyersville KY
WLYU(FM) Lyons GA	KORT(AM) Grangeville ID	WXKU-FM Austin IN	KMZA(FM) Seneca KS	WSKV(FM) Stanton KY
WDEN-FM Macon GA	KORT-FM Grangeville ID	WRBI(FM) Batesville IN	KTPK(AM) Topeka KS	WMSK-FM Sturgis KY
WKHX-FM Marietta GA	KYUN(FM) Hailey ID	WUZR(AM) Bicknell IN	WIBW-FM Topeka KS	WKWY(FM) Tompkinsville KY
WKKP(AM) McDonough GA	KID-FM Idaho Falls ID	WSDM-FM Brazil IN	KULY(AM) Ulysses KS	WTKY(AM) Tompkinsville KY
WMCG(FM) Milan GA	KTHK(FM) Idaho Falls ID	WLFW(FM) Chandler IN	KFDI-FM Wichita KS	WTKY-FM Tompkinsville KY
WKZR(FM) Milledgeville GA	KUPI-FM Idaho Falls ID	WKKG(FM) Columbus IN	KFTI(AM) Wichita KS	WKKS(AM) Vanceburg KY
WHKN(FM) Millen GA	KART(AM) Jerome ID	WKZS(FM) Covington IN	KSOK-FM Winfield KS	WKKS-FM Vanceburg KY
WYUM(FM) Mount Vernon GA	KZBG(FM) Lapwai ID	WADM(AM) Decatur IN	KWLS(FM) Winfield KS	WLKS-FM West Liberty KY
WALH(AM) Mountain City GA	KMOK(FM) Lewiston ID	WQHK(FM) Decatur IN	WANY(AM) Albany KY	WTCW(AM) Whitesburg KY
WWLG(FM) Peachtree City GA	KRLC(AM) Lewiston ID	WYGB(FM) Edinburgh IN	WANY-FM Albany KY	WHAY(FM) Whitley City KY
WTSH-FM Rockmart GA	KDZY(FM) McCall ID	WBYT(FM) Elkhart IN	WMDJ-FM Allen KY	WEZJ-FM Williamsburg KY
WSNT-FM Sandersville GA	KVSI(AM) Montpelier ID	WHCC(FM) Ellettsville IN	WDGG(FM) Ashland KY	WNKR(FM) Williamstown KY
WJCL-FM Savannah GA	KMHI(AM) Mountain Home ID	WQKZ(FM) Ferdinand IN	WBVR-FM Auburn KY	KRRV-FM Alexandria LA
WXRS-FM Swainsboro GA	KLER(AM) Orofino ID	WFLQ(FM) French Lick IN	WBRT(AM) Bardstown KY	WABL(AM) Amite LA
WKNG(AM) Tallapoosa GA	KOUU(AM) Pocatello ID	WREB(FM) Greencastle IN	WGGC(FM) Bowling Green KY	WTGE(FM) Baker LA
WTHO-FM Thomson GA	KZBQ(FM) Pocatello ID	WTRE(AM) Greensburg IN	WMMG(AM) Brandenburg KY	KBKK(FM) Ball LA
WOBB(FM) Tifton GA	KKEX(FM) Preston ID	WXCH(FM) Hope IN	WMMG-FM Brandenburg KY	WYNK-FM Baton Rouge LA
WTIF(AM) Tifton GA	KKMV(FM) Rupert ID	WBDC(FM) Huntingburg IN	WKYR-FM Burkesville KY	WYPY(FM) Baton Rouge LA
WNGC(FM) Toccoa GA	KSRA(AM) Salmon ID	WFMS(FM) Indianapolis IN	WSEK(FM) Burnside KY	KQKI(FM) Bayou Vista LA
WAAC(FM) Valdosta GA	KSRA-FM Salmon ID	WBTU(FM) Kendallville IN	WKDZ-FM Cadiz KY	WBOX(AM) Bogalusa LA
WYNR(FM) Waycross GA	KIBR(FM) Sandpoint ID	WIVR(FM) Kentland IN	WCCK(FM) Calvert City KY	KSBH(FM) Coushatta LA
WCJM-FM West Point GA	KBRV(AM) Soda Springs ID	*WKPW(FM) Knightstown IN	WYHY(AM) Cannonsburg KY	KEUN-FM Eunice LA
WKAA(FM) Willacoochee GA	KITT(FM) Soda Springs ID	WWKI(FM) Kokomo IN	WIKI(FM) Carrollton KY	WOMN(AM) Franklinton LA
WFDR-FM Woodbury GA	KEZJ-FM Twin Falls ID	WCOE(FM) La Porte IN	WLLE(FM) Clinton KY	WUUU(FM) Franklinton LA
WYHG(AM) Young Harris GA	KVRG(FM) Victor ID	WKOA(FM) Lafayette IN	WAIN-FM Columbia KY	KLEB(AM) Golden Meadow LA
WEKS(FM) Zebulon GA	KWAL(AM) Wallace ID	WTHD(FM) Lagrange IN	WKDP-FM Corbin KY	WFPR(AM) Hammond LA
KUAI(AM) Eleele HI	WRMJ(FM) Aledo IL	WBTO(AM) Linton IN	WCPM(AM) Cumberland KY	WHMD(FM) Hammond LA
KHCM-FM Honolulu HI	WIBH(AM) Anna IL	WCBK-FM Martinsville IN	WCYN-FM Cynthiana KY	KRLQ(FM) Hodge LA
KDLX(FM) Makawao HI	WLCN(FM) Atlanta IL	WRCY(AM) Mount Vernon IN	WHSX(FM) Edmonton KY	KCIL(FM) Houma LA
KKOA(FM) Volcano HI	WRMS-FM Beardstown IL	WMDH-FM New Castle IN	WFLE(AM) Flemingsburg KY	KJNA-FM Jena LA
KKNE(AM) Waipahu HI	WLMD(FM) Bushnell IL	WARU(AM) Peru IN	WFLE-FM Flemingsburg KY	KMDL(FM) Kaplan LA
KIIC(FM) Albia IA	WRUL(AM) Carmi IL	WPGW-FM Portland IN	WLVK(FM) Fort Knox KY	KNGT(FM) Lake Charles LA
KKSY(FM) Anamosa IA	WIXY(FM) Champaign IL	WRAY-FM Princeton IN	WYGY(FM) Fort Thomas KY	KYKZ(FM) Lake Charles LA
WJOD(FM) Asbury IA	KSGM(AM) Chester IL	*WECI(FM) Richmond IN	WFKY(FM) Frankfort KY	KJAE(FM) Leesville LA
KSOM(FM) Audubon IA	WUSN(FM) Chicago IL	WQLK(FM) Richmond IN	WFKN(AM) Franklin KY	KVVP(FM) Leesville LA
KDMG(FM) Burlington IA	WCCQ(FM) Crest Hill IL	WARU-FM Roann IN	WFUL(AM) Fulton KY	KBON(FM) Mamou LA
KOEL-FM Cedar Falls IA	WDZQ(FM) Decatur IL	WHZR(FM) Royal Center IN	WLYE-FM Glasgow KY	KJVC(FM) Mansfield LA
KHAK(FM) Cedar Rapids IA	WRCV(FM) Dixon IL	WIFE-FM Rushville IN	WGOH(AM) Grayson KY	KWLV(FM) Many LA
KMGO(FM) Centerville IA	WDQN(AM) Du Quoin IL	WSLM(AM) Salem IN	WGRK(AM) Greensburg KY	KAPB-FM Marksville LA
KIAQ(FM) Clarion IA	WCRC(FM) Effingham IL	WMPI(FM) Scottsburg IN	WGRK-FM Greensburg KY	KJLO-FM Monroe LA
KSIB(AM) Creston IA	WFYR(FM) Elmwood IL	WLHK(FM) Shelbyville IN	WLGC-FM Greenup KY	KDBH(FM) Natchitoches LA
KSIB-FM Creston IA	WOKZ(FM) Fairfield IL	WCLS(FM) Spencer IN	WULF(FM) Hardinsburg KY	KXKC(FM) New Iberia LA
WLLR-FM Davenport IA	WFPS(FM) Freeport IL	WNDI(AM) Sullivan IN	WXBC(FM) Hardinsburg KY	WNOE-FM New Orleans LA
KDSN(AM) Denison IA	WXXQ(FM) Freeport IL	WNDI-FM Sullivan IN	WTUK(FM) Harlan KY	KSLO(AM) Opelousas LA
KHKI(FM) Des Moines IA	WAAG(FM) Galesburg IL	WTHI-FM Terre Haute IN	WXLR(FM) Harold KY	KKOO(FM) Rayne LA
KDST(FM) Dyersville IA	WJRE(FM) Galva IL	WLJE(FM) Valparaiso IN	WHBN(AM) Harrodsburg KY	KMYY(FM) Rayville LA
KRKN(FM) Eldon IA	WGEL(FM) Greenville IL	WCJC(FM) Van Buren IN	WKCM(AM) Hawesville KY	KXKZ(FM) Ruston LA
KILR-FM Estherville IA	WEBQ(AM) Harrisburg IL	WKID(FM) Vevay IN	WSGS(FM) Hazard KY	KRMD-FM Shreveport LA
KIOW(FM) Forest City IA	WOOZ-FM Harrisburg IL	WFML(FM) Vincennes IN	WKDQ(FM) Henderson KY	KWKH(AM) Shreveport LA
KWMT(AM) Fort Dodge IA	WDUK(FM) Havana IL	WWBL(FM) Washington IN	WVVR(FM) Hopkinsville KY	KXKS-FM Shreveport LA
KBKB(AM) Fort Madison IA	WRVY-FM Henry IL	KSOK(AM) Arkansas City KS	WCYO(FM) Irvine KY	KLAA-FM Tioga LA
KBKB-FM Fort Madison IA	WXOZ(AM) Highland IL	KVWF(AM) Augusta KS	WJSN-FM Jackson KY	WBOX-FM Varnado LA
KCTN(FM) Garnavillo IA	WHPO(FM) Hoopeston IL	KREP(FM) Belleville KS	WJKY(AM) Jamestown KY	KWTG(FM) Vidalia LA
KXKT(FM) Glenwood IA	WDDD-FM Johnston City IL	KSNP(FM) Burlington KS	WJRS(FM) Jamestown KY	KVPI(AM) Ville Platte LA
KLMJ(FM) Hampton IA	WAKO(AM) Lawrenceville IL	KWGB(FM) Colby KS	WKMO(FM) Lebanon Junction KY	KNCB(AM) Vivian LA
KKIA(FM) Ida Grove IA	WAKO-FM Lawrenceville IL	KXXX(AM) Colby KS	WMTL(AM) Leitchfield KY	KNCB-FM Vivian LA
KNIA(AM) Knoxville IA	WBWN(FM) Le Roy IL	KUSN(FM) Dearing KS	WBUL-FM Lexington KY	KVCL-FM Winnfield LA
KIKD(FM) Lake City IA	WSMI(AM) Litchfield IL	KDNS(FM) Downs KS	WLXX(FM) Lexington KY	KMAR-FM Winnsboro LA
KMCH(FM) Manchester IA	WSMI-FM Litchfield IL	KVOE-FM Emporia KS	WKDO(AM) Liberty KY	WPVQ(FM) Greenfield MA
KMAQ(AM) Maquoketa IA	WLUV(AM) Loves Park IL	KOTE(FM) Eureka KS	WKDO-FM Liberty KY	WCTK(FM) New Bedford MA
KXIA(FM) Marshalltown IA	WZUS(FM) Macon IL	KKJQ(FM) Garden City KS	WFTG(AM) London KY	WKPE-FM South Yarmouth MA
KIAI(FM) Mason City IA	WGGH(AM) Marion IL	KLOE(AM) Goodland KS	WZAQ(FM) Louisa KY	WESO(AM) Southbridge MA
KILJ(AM) Mount Pleasant IA	WMCI(FM) Mattoon IL	KHAZ(FM) Hays KS	WAMZ(FM) Louisville KY	WKLB-FM Waltham MA
KMCS(FM) Muscatine IA	WMCL(AM) McLeansboro IL	KNZA(FM) Hiawatha KS	WRKA(FM) Louisville KY	WGFP(AM) Webster MA
KCZE(FM) New Hampton IA	WGLC-FM Mendota IL	KKQY(FM) Hill City KS	WQNU(FM) Lyndon KY	WPOC(FM) Baltimore MD
KCOB(AM) Newton IA	WMOK(AM) Metropolis IL	KHOK(FM) Hoisington KS	WFMW(AM) Madisonville KY	WTRI(AM) Brunswick MD
KCOB-FM Newton IA	WFXN(AM) Moline IL	KBUF(AM) Holcomb KS	WKLB(AM) Manchester KY	WKIK-FM California MD
KKHQ-FM Oelwein IA	WRAM(AM) Monmouth IL	KAIR-FM Horton KS	WVLC(FM) Mannsville KY	WBEY-FM Crisfield MD
KBOE(AM) Oskaloosa IA	WIBV(AM) Mount Vernon IL	KHUT(FM) Hutchinson KS	WWAG(FM) McKee KY	WROG(AM) Cumberland MD
KBOE-FM Oskaloosa IA	WMIX-FM Mount Vernon IL	KZSN(AM) Hutchinson KS	WMKZ(FM) Monticello KY	WFRE(FM) Frederick MD
KLEE(AM) Ottumwa IA	WALS(FM) Oglesby IL	KERP(AM) Ingalls KS	WMOR(AM) Morehead KY	WFRB-FM Frostburg MD
KZWF(AM) Patterson IA	WSEI(FM) Olney IL	KFKF-FM Kansas City KS	WMSK(AM) Morganfield KY	WKHI(FM) Fruitland MD
KZWU(FM) Pleasantville IA	WMKR(FM) Pana IL	KLDG(AM) Liberal KS	WLBQ(AM) Morgantown KY	WAYZ(FM) Hagerstown MD
KCSI(FM) Red Oak IA	WIBQ(FM) Paris IL	KDJM(FM) Lindsborg KS	WRVK(AM) Mt. Vernon KY	WXCY(FM) Havre de Grace MD
KOAK(AM) Red Oak IA	WXCL(FM) Pekin IL	KXKU(AM) Lyons KS	WLOC(AM) Munfordville KY	WAAI(FM) Hurlock MD
KIHK(FM) Rock Valley IA	WIRL(AM) Peoria IL	KXBZ(FM) Manhattan KS	WFGS(FM) Murray KY	WKIK(AM) La Plata MD

WVMD(FM) Midland MD
WWHC(FM) Oakland MD
WWFG(FM) Ocean City MD
WINX-FM Saint Michaels MD
WKTT(FM) Salisbury MD
WTHT(FM) Auburn ME
WLKE(FM) Bar Harbor ME
WBFB(FM) Belfast ME
WQCB(FM) Brewer ME
WTBM(FM) Mexico ME
WBCQ-FM Monticello ME
WOXO(FM) Norway ME
*WMDR-FM Oakland ME
WPOR(FM) Portland ME
WBPW(FM) Presque Isle ME
WMCM(FM) Rockland ME
WEBB(FM) Waterville ME
WQTE(FM) Adrian MI
WATZ-FM Alpena MI
WWWW-FM Ann Arbor MI
WLEW(AM) Bad Axe MI
WCUZ(FM) Bear Lake MI
WHFB-FM Benton Harbor MI
WBNZ(FM) Beulah MI
WWBR(FM) Big Rapids MI
WBCM(FM) Boyne City MI
WYTZ(FM) Bridgman MI
WKYO(AM) Caro MI
WNWN-FM Coldwater MI
WDTW-FM Detroit MI
WYCD(FM) Detroit MI
WYKX(FM) Escanaba MI
WCXI(AM) Fenton MI
WFBE(FM) Flint MI
WGDN-FM Gladwin MI
WBCT(FM) Grand Rapids MI
WGRY-FM Grayling MI
WCMM(FM) Gulliver MI
*WKKM(FM) Harrison MI
WTWS(FM) Harrison MI
WBCH(AM) Hastings MI
WBCH-FM Hastings MI
WCEN-FM Hemlock MI
WTNR(FM) Holland MI
WHKB(FM) Houghton MI
WJNR-FM Iron Mountain MI
WJMS(AM) Ironwood MI
WJPD(FM) Ishpeming MI
WGLM-FM Lakeview MI
WCUP(FM) L'Anse MI
WITL-FM Lansing MI
WLCO(AM) Lapeer MI
WLJZ(FM) Mackinaw City MI
WBGV(FM) Marlette MI
WFXD(FM) Marquette MI
WAVC(FM) Mio MI
WMUS(FM) Muskegon MI
WLAW(FM) Newaygo MI
WNBY(AM) Newberry MI
WUPY(FM) Ontonagon MI
WARD(AM) Petoskey MI
WSAQ(FM) Port Huron MI
WYZO(FM) Portage MI
WHAK(AM) Rogers City MI
WRGZ(FM) Rogers City MI
WKCQ(FM) Saginaw MI
WMKC(FM) Saint Ignace MI
WMLM(AM) Saint Louis MI
WMIC(AM) Sandusky MI
WKZC(FM) Scottville MI
WKJC(FM) Tawas City MI
WRCI(AM) Three Rivers MI
WLDR-FM Traverse City MI
WTCM-FM Traverse City MI
KRJB(FM) Ada MN
KKIN-FM Aitkin MN
KASM(AM) Albany MN
KAUS-FM Austin MN
KQAQ(AM) Austin MN
KKCQ-FM Bagley MN
KBVB(FM) Barnesville MN
KBHP(FM) Bemidji MN
WBJI(FM) Blackduck MN
KBEW-FM Blue Earth MN
KBMW(AM) Breckenridge MN
KRWC(AM) Buffalo MN

KGPZ(FM) Coleraine MN
KROX(AM) Crookston MN
KARP-FM Dassel MN
KRCQ(FM) Detroit Lakes MN
KKCB(FM) Duluth MN
KTCO(FM) Duluth MN
KLCI(FM) Elk River MN
KJJK-FM Fergus Falls MN
KSDM(FM) International Falls MN
KKOJ(AM) Jackson MN
KKWB(AM) Kelliher MN
KMFX-FM Lake City MN
WYRQ(FM) Little Falls MN
KEYL(AM) Long Prairie MN
KLQL(FM) Luverne MN
KLQP(FM) Madison MN
KYSM-FM Mankato MN
KDMA(AM) Montevideo MN
KVOX-FM Moorhead MN
KKOK-FM Morris MN
KATO-FM New Ulm MN
KNUJ(AM) New Ulm MN
KBLB(FM) Nisswa MN
KOLV(FM) Olivia MN
KDIO(AM) Ortonville MN
KRFO-FM Owatonna MN
KPRM(AM) Park Rapids MN
KXKK(FM) Park Rapids MN
KZPK(FM) Paynesville MN
KBOT(FM) Pelican Rapids MN
WCMP-FM Pine City MN
KLOH(AM) Pipestone MN
KFIL(AM) Preston MN
KFIL-FM Preston MN
WQPM(AM) Princeton MN
KLGR(AM) Redwood Falls MN
KWWK(FM) Rochester MN
KWNO-FM Rushford MN
WWJO(FM) Saint Cloud MN
KRRW(FM) Saint James MN
KEEY-FM Saint Paul MN
KIKV-FM Sauk Centre MN
WVAL(AM) Sauk Rapids MN
KJOE(FM) Slayton MN
KQYB(FM) Spring Grove MN
KNSP(AM) Staples MN
KKAQ(AM) Thief River Falls MN
KKDQ(FM) Thief River Falls MN
KSNR(FM) Thief River Falls MN
KARL(FM) Tracy MN
KVKK(AM) Verndale MN
WUSZ(FM) Virginia MN
KMFX(FM) Wabasha MN
KKWS(FM) Wadena MN
KWAD(AM) Wadena MN
KKWQ(FM) Warroad MN
KDJS-FM Willmar MN
KDOM(AM) Windom MN
KDOM-FM Windom MN
KAGE(AM) Winona MN
KSWF(FM) Aurora MO
KKOZ(AM) Ava MO
KAAN(AM) Bethany MO
KAAN-FM Bethany MO
KYOO(AM) Bolivar MO
KCLR-FM Boonville MO
KWRT(AM) Boonville MO
KRZK(FM) Branson MO
KMAM(AM) Butler MO
KMOE(FM) Butler MO
KATI(FM) California MO
KRLL(AM) California MO
KEZS-FM Cape Girardeau MO
KAOL(AM) Carrollton MO
KMZU(AM) Carrollton MO
KCRV(AM) Caruthersville MO
KRMO(AM) Cassville MO
KWKZ(FM) Charleston MO
KDKD-FM Clinton MO
KESY(FM) Cuba MO
KDEX(AM) Dexter MO
KDEX-FM Dexter MO
KOEA(FM) Doniphan MO
KESM(AM) El Dorado Springs MO
KESM-FM El Dorado Springs MO
KLPW-FM Elsberry MO

KTJJ(FM) Farmington MO
KFAL(AM) Fulton MO
KGOZ(FM) Gallatin MO
KYOO-FM Halfway MO
*WGCQ(FM) Hayti MO
KBTC(AM) Houston MO
KUNQ(FM) Houston MO
KYLS-FM Ironton MO
KZJF(FM) Jefferson City MO
KIXQ(FM) Joplin MO
KBEQ-FM Kansas City MO
KTUF(FM) Kirksville MO
KKKX(FM) Knob Noster MO
KHST(FM) Lamar MO
KCLQ(FM) Lebanon MO
KJEL(FM) Lebanon MO
KLWT(AM) Lebanon MO
KJFM(FM) Louisiana MO
KLTI(AM) Macon MO
KMMO(AM) Marshall MO
KMMO-FM Marshall MO
KMEM-FM Memphis MO
KWWR(FM) Mexico MO
KRES(FM) Moberly MO
KELE-FM Mountain Grove MO
KBTN(AM) Neosho MO
KBTN-FM Neosho MO
KNEM(AM) Nevada MO
KNMO(FM) Nevada MO
KTMO(FM) New Madrid MO
KOMG(FM) Ozark MO
KICK-FM Palmyra MO
KBDZ(FM) Perryville MO
KPWB-FM Piedmont MO
KKLR(FM) Poplar Bluff MO
KPPL(FM) Poplar Bluff MO
KYRO(AM) Potosi MO
KMOZ(AM) Rolla MO
KZNN(FM) Rolla MO
KSD(FM) Saint Louis MO
WIL-FM Saint Louis MO
KKID(FM) Salem MO
KSMO(AM) Salem MO
KSJQ(FM) Savannah MO
KDRO(AM) Sedalia MO
KBXB(FM) Sikeston MO
KRHW(AM) Sikeston MO
KTTS-FM Springfield MO
KRWP(FM) Stockton MO
KTUI-FM Sullivan MO
KSAR(FM) Thayer MO
KTTN-FM Trenton MO
KKAC(FM) Vandalia MO
KTKS(FM) Versailles MO
KFAV(FM) Warrenton MO
KWRE(AM) Warrenton MO
KAYQ(FM) Warsaw MO
KIIK-FM Waynesville MO
KKDY(FM) West Plains MO
KWKJ(FM) Windsor MO
WBLE(FM) Batesville MS
WIZK(AM) Bay Springs MS
WZKX(FM) Bay St. Louis MS
WBYP(FM) Belzoni MS
WBIP(AM) Booneville MS
WBKN(FM) Brookhaven MS
WCKK(FM) Carthage MS
WKJN-FM Centreville MS
WKDJ-FM Clarksdale MS
WMJW(FM) Cleveland MS
WVIM-FM Coldwater MS
WFFF(AM) Columbia MS
WKOR-FM Columbus MS
WADI(FM) Corinth MS
WZKR(FM) Decatur MS
WDMS(FM) Greenville MS
WABG(AM) Greenwood MS
WQXB(FM) Grenada MS
WYKC(AM) Grenada MS
WGCM(AM) Gulfport MS
WHER(FM) Heidelberg MS
WCPC(AM) Houston MS
WKZU(FM) Iuka MS
WMSI(AM) Jackson MS
WAGR-FM Lexington MS
WRBE(AM) Lucedale MS

WRBE-FM Lucedale MS
WUSJ(FM) Madison MS
WAKH(FM) McComb MS
WMSO(FM) Meridian MS
WOKK(FM) Meridian MS
WUCL(FM) Meridian MS
WKXY(FM) Merigold MS
WQNZ(FM) Natchez MS
WWZD-FM New Albany MS
WWMS(FM) Oxford MS
WKNN-FM Pascagoula MS
WRJW(AM) Picayune MS
WJDR(FM) Prentiss MS
WQJB(AM) State College MS
WBBN(FM) Taylorsville MS
WELO(AM) Tupelo MS
WTYL(AM) Tylertown MS
WTYL-FM Tylertown MS
WBBV(FM) Vicksburg MS
WABO(AM) Waynesboro MS
WABO-FM Waynesboro MS
WIGG(AM) Wiggins MS
WONA(AM) Winona MS
WONA-FM Winona MS
KFLN(AM) Baker MT
KCTR-FM Billings MT
KGHL(AM) Billings MT
KGHL-FM Billings MT
KBOZ-FM Bozeman MT
KAAR(FM) Butte MT
*KMSM-FM Butte MT
KIKF(FM) Cascade MT
KHNK(FM) Columbia Falls MT
KQRV(FM) Deer Lodge MT
KDBM(AM) Dillon MT
KHHR-FM East Helena MT
KIKC-FM Forsyth MT
KSCY(FM) Four Corners MT
KLTZ(AM) Glasgow MT
KDZN(FM) Glendive MT
KMON(AM) Great Falls MT
KMON-FM Great Falls MT
KPQX(FM) Havre MT
KBLL-FM Helena MT
KPBR(FM) Joliet MT
KDBR(FM) Kalispell MT
KXLO(AM) Lewistown MT
KLCB(AM) Libby MT
KMMR(FM) Malta MT
KYUS-FM Miles City MT
KGGL(FM) Missoula MT
KYSS-FM Missoula MT
KATQ(AM) Plentywood MT
KATQ-FM Plentywood MT
KERR(AM) Polson MT
KCGM(FM) Scobey MT
KZIN-FM Shelby MT
KVCK-FM Wolf Point MT
WQDK(FM) Ahoskie NC
WKXR(FM) Asheboro NC
WKSF(FM) Asheville NC
WNBB(FM) Bayboro NC
WPYB(AM) Benson NC
WNBR-FM Bethel NC
WKYK(AM) Burnsville NC
WSME(AM) Camp Lejeune NC
WPTL(AM) Canton NC
WSOC-FM Charlotte NC
WRSF(FM) Columbia NC
WAGY(AM) Forest City NC
WNCC-FM Franklin NC
WJSG(FM) Hamlet NC
WCMS-FM Hatteras NC
WIZS(AM) Henderson NC
WMMY(FM) Jefferson NC
WKTE(AM) King NC
WRNS(AM) Kinston NC
WRNS-FM Kinston NC
WKGX(AM) Lenoir NC
WKVS(FM) Lenoir NC
WKXU(FM) Louisburg NC
WKML(FM) Lumberton NC
WBRM(AM) Marion NC
WDSL(AM) Mocksville NC
WIXE(AM) Monroe NC
WMNC(AM) Morganton NC

WMNC-FM Morganton NC
WKRK(AM) Murphy NC
WECR(AM) Newland NC
WKBC(AM) North Wilkesboro NC
WLQB(FM) Ocean Isle Beach NC
WQDR(FM) Raleigh NC
WPTM(FM) Roanoke Rapids NC
WCVP-FM Robbinsville NC
WDWG(FM) Rocky Mount NC
WKRX(FM) Roxboro NC
WRXO(AM) Roxboro NC
WCAB(AM) Rutherfordton NC
WWGP(AM) Sanford NC
WTSB(AM) Selma NC
WADA(AM) Shelby NC
WMPM(AM) Smithfield NC
WCOK(AM) Sparta NC
WKKT(FM) Statesville NC
WTAB(AM) Tabor City NC
WACB(AM) Taylorsville NC
WIST-FM Thomasville NC
WKSK(AM) West Jefferson NC
WRHD(FM) Williamston NC
WWQQ-FM Wilmington NC
WRDU(AM) Wilson NC
WPAW(FM) Winston-Salem NC
WTQR(FM) Winston-Salem NC
KVMI(FM) Arthur ND
*KEYA(FM) Belcourt ND
KBMR(AM) Bismarck ND
KQDY(FM) Bismarck ND
KBTO(FM) Bottineau ND
KPOK(AM) Bowman ND
KDAK(AM) Carrington ND
KAOC(FM) Cavalier ND
KDLR(AM) Devils Lake ND
KZZY(FM) Devils Lake ND
KCAD(FM) Dickinson ND
KLTC(AM) Dickinson ND
KXPO(AM) Grafton ND
KNDC(AM) Hettinger ND
KSJB(AM) Jamestown ND
KYNU(FM) Jamestown ND
KNDK(AM) Langdon ND
KQLX-FM Lisbon ND
KMAV-FM Mayville ND
KCJB(AM) Minot ND
KYYX(FM) Minot ND
KDDR(AM) Oakes ND
KZZJ(AM) Rugby ND
KTGO(AM) Tioga ND
KOVC(AM) Valley City ND
KEYZ(AM) Williston ND
KYYZ(FM) Williston ND
KBRB(AM) Ainsworth NE
KUSO(FM) Albion NE
KAAQ(FM) Alliance NE
KNCY-FM Auburn NE
KTWI(FM) Bennington NE
KBLR-FM Blair NE
KCNI(AM) Broken Bow NE
KZEN(FM) Central City NE
KCSR(AM) Chadron NE
KQSK(FM) Chadron NE
KUTT(FM) Fairbury NE
KSDZ(FM) Gordon NE
KRGI-FM Grand Island NE
KNPQ(FM) Hershey NE
KRNY(FM) Kearney NE
KRVN(AM) Lexington NE
KRVN-FM Lexington NE
KIOD(FM) McCook NE
KFGE(FM) Milford NE
KHYY(FM) Minatare NE
KXNP(FM) North Platte NE
KMCX(FM) Ogallala NE
KBRX-FM O'Neill NE
KNLV-FM Ord NE
KZTL(FM) Paxton NE
KNEB(AM) Scottsbluff NE
KNEB-FM Scottsbluff NE
KZKX(FM) Seward NE
KSID(AM) Sidney NE
KRFS-FM Superior NE
KVSH(AM) Valentine NE
KTCH(AM) Wayne NE

KTIC(AM) West Point NE
KTIC-FM West Point NE
KSUX(FM) Winnebago NE
WNHW(FM) Belmont NH
WOKQ(FM) Dover NH
WYKR-FM Haverhill NH
WYRY(FM) Hinsdale NH
WXXK(FM) Lebanon NH
WSCY(FM) Moultonborough NH
WCNL(AM) Newport NH
WPKQ(FM) North Conway NH
WINQ(FM) Winchester NH
WOF(AM) Andover NJ
WPUR(FM) Atlantic City NJ
*WCVH(FM) Flemington NJ
WKOE(FM) North Cape May NJ
WKMK(FM) Ocean Acres NJ
KZZX(FM) Alamogordo NM
KBQI(FM) Albuquerque NM
KRST(FM) Albuquerque NM
KKTC(FM) Angel Fire NM
KTZA(FM) Artesia NM
KNFT-FM Bayard NM
KARS(AM) Belen NM
KABQ-FM Bosque Farms NM
KATK-FM Carlsbad NM
KLMX(AM) Clayton NM
KNMB(FM) Cloudcroft NM
KCLV-FM Clovis NM
KOTS(AM) Deming NM
KTRA-FM Farmington NM
KGLX(FM) Gallup NM
KYVA(AM) Gallup NM
KMIN(AM) Grants NM
KIXN(FM) Hobbs NM
KPER(FM) Hobbs NM
KRSY-FM La Luz NM
KGRT-FM Las Cruces NM
KBQL(FM) Las Vegas NM
KFUN(AM) Las Vegas NM
KQBA(FM) Los Alamos NM
KWMW(FM) Maljamar NM
KSEL-FM Portales NM
*KTDB(FM) Ramah NM
KBKZ(FM) Raton NM
KCKN(AM) Roswell NM
KMOU(FM) Roswell NM
KWES-FM Ruidoso NM
KSSR(AM) Santa Rosa NM
KMXQ(FM) Socorro NM
KCHS(AM) Truth or Consequences NM
KTNM(AM) Tucumcari NM
KCYE(FM) Boulder City NV
KBUL-FM Carson City NV
KCMY(AM) Carson City NV
KRJC(FM) Elko NV
KDSS(FM) Ely NV
KHWG(AM) Fallon NV
KVLV(AM) Fallon NV
KWNR(FM) Henderson NV
KJUL(FM) Moapa Valley NV
KEBG(FM) Spring Creek NV
KUUB(AM) Sun Valley NV
KBET(AM) Winchester NV
KWNA-FM Winnemucca NV
WGNA-FM Albany NY
WZKZ(FM) Alfred NY
WHWK(FM) Binghamton NY
WBRV(AM) Boonville NY
WBRV-FM Boonville NY
WYRK(FM) Buffalo NY
WNCQ-FM Canton NY
WLYK(FM) Cape Vincent NY
WFFG-FM Corinth NY
WFLR(AM) Dundee NY
WRWC(FM) Ellenville NY
WBUG-FM Fort Plain NY
WBKX(FM) Fredonia NY
WAMF(AM) Fulton NY
WBBS(FM) Fulton NY
WFLK(FM) Geneva NY
WRWD-FM Highland NY
WCKR(FM) Hornell NY
WPGI(FM) Horseheads NY
WQNY(FM) Ithaca NY
WHUG(FM) Jamestown NY

WDNB(FM) Jeffersonville NY
WKXP(FM) Kingston NY
WXRL(AM) Lancaster NY
WVOS(AM) Liberty NY
WLLG(FM) Lowville NY
WVNV(FM) Malone NY
WBGK(FM) Newport Village NY
WBKT(FM) Norwich NY
WPIG(FM) Olean NY
WDOS(AM) Oneonta NY
WTSX(FM) Port Jervis NY
WBYB(FM) Portville NY
WSNN(FM) Potsdam NY
WBEE-FM Rochester NY
WUMX(FM) Rome NY
WSCP(AM) Sandy Creek-Pulaski NY
WUUF(AM) Sodus NY
WROO(FM) South Bristol Township NY
WOKN(FM) Southport NY
WSPQ(AM) Springville NY
WFRG-FM Utica NY
WDLA-FM Walton NY
WCJW(AM) Warsaw NY
WFRY-FM Watertown NY
WRCE(AM) Watkins Glen NY
WLSV(AM) Wellsville NY
WNYV(FM) Whitehall NY
WZAD(FM) Wurtsboro NY
WNCO-FM Ashland OH
WNUS(FM) Belpre OH
WAIS(AM) Buchtel OH
WWKC(FM) Caldwell OH
WKKJ(FM) Chillicothe OH
WUBE-FM Cincinnati OH
WNKK(FM) Circleville OH
WGAR-FM Cleveland OH
WMJK(FM) Clyde OH
WCOL-FM Columbus OH
WTNS(AM) Coshocton OH
WHKO(FM) Dayton OH
WZOM(FM) Defiance OH
WOGF(FM) East Liverpool OH
WEDI(AM) Eaton OH
WKKY(FM) Geneva OH
WDSJ(FM) Greenville OH
WSRW-FM Hillsboro OH
WKFM(FM) Huron OH
WCJO(FM) Jackson OH
WHOK-FM Lancaster OH
WIMT(FM) Lima OH
WKNA(FM) Logan OH
WMRN-FM Marion OH
WQMX(FM) Medina OH
WPFB(AM) Middletown OH
WPFB-FM Middletown OH
WLZZ(FM) Montpelier OH
WSEO(FM) Nelsonville OH
WCLT-FM Newark OH
WOBL(AM) Oberlin OH
WPAY-FM Portsmouth OH
WQXK(FM) Salem OH
*WKTL(FM) Struthers OH
WCKY-FM Tiffin OH
WKKO(FM) Toledo OH
WTOD(AM) Toledo OH
WTUZ(FM) Uhrichsville OH
WTGR(FM) Union City OH
WKSW(FM) Urbana OH
WFGF(FM) Wapakoneta OH
WCHO-FM Washington Court House OH
WXIZ(FM) Waverly OH
WRAC(FM) West Union OH
WKFI(AM) Wilmington OH
WQKT(FM) Wooster OH
WBZI(AM) Xenia OH
KADA-FM Ada OK
KEYB(FM) Altus OK
KWHW(AM) Altus OK
KACO(FM) Apache OK
KKAJ-FM Ardmore OK
KHKC-FM Atoka OK
KREK(FM) Bristow OK
KKBI(FM) Broken Bow OK
KYKC(FM) Byng OK
KWEY(FM) Clinton OK

KKEN(FM) Duncan OK
KLBC(FM) Durant OK
KECO(FM) Elk City OK
KOFM(FM) Enid OK
KTNT(FM) Eufaula OK
KYBE(FM) Frederick OK
KGVE(FM) Grove OK
KGYN(AM) Guymon OK
KICM(FM) Healdton OK
KPRV-FM Heavener OK
KXBL(FM) Henryetta OK
KTJS(AM) Hobart OK
KKRE(FM) Hollis OK
KITX(FM) Hugo OK
KBEL-FM Idabel OK
KLAW(FM) Lawton OK
KBLP(FM) Lindsay OK
KMAD(AM) Madill OK
KFXI(FM) Marlow OK
KNED(AM) McAlester OK
KZLS(AM) Mustang OK
KKNG-FM Newcastle OK
KNID(FM) North Enid OK
KRIG-FM Nowata OK
KTST(FM) Oklahoma City OK
KXXY-FM Oklahoma City OK
KOKL(AM) Okmulgee OK
KPNC(FM) Ponca City OK
KOMS(FM) Poteau OK
KIRC(FM) Seminole OK
KGFY(FM) Stillwater OK
*KLRB(FM) Stuart OK
KIXO(FM) Sulphur OK
KEOK(FM) Tahlequah OK
KTLQ(AM) Tahlequah OK
KVOO-FM Tulsa OK
KWEN(FM) Tulsa OK
KITO-FM Vinita OK
KTFX-FM Warner OK
KWEY(AM) Weatherford OK
KWSH(AM) Wewoka OK
KMCO(FM) Wilburton OK
KWFX(FM) Woodward OK
KWOX(FM) Woodward OK
KRKT-FM Albany OR
KTHH(AM) Albany OR
KCMB(FM) Baker City OR
KBDN(FM) Bandon OR
KMTK(FM) Bend OR
KURY(AM) Brookings OR
KZZR(AM) Burns OR
KJDY-FM Canyon City OR
KMHS(AM) Coos Bay OR
KSHR-FM Coquille OR
KNND(AM) Cottage Grove OR
KWVR-FM Enterprise OR
KCST-FM Florence OR
KSHL(FM) Gleneden Beach OR
KGBR(FM) Gold Beach OR
KRWQ(FM) Gold Hill OR
KOHU(AM) Hermiston OR
KIHR(AM) Hood River OR
KJDY(AM) John Day OR
KLAD-FM Klamath Falls OR
KQIK(AM) Lakeview OR
KNCU(FM) Newport OR
KSRV(AM) Ontario OR
KWHT(FM) Pendleton OR
KAKT(FM) Phoenix OR
KCMD(AM) Portland OR
KUPL-FM Portland OR
KWJJ-FM Portland OR
KRCO(AM) Prineville OR
KSJJ(FM) Redmond OR
KRRM(FM) Rogue River OR
KRSB-FM Roseburg OR
KCYS(FM) Seaside OR
KKNU(FM) Springfield-Eugene OR
KCKX(AM) Stayton OR
WFGY(FM) Altoona PA
WWSM(AM) Annville-Cleona PA
WQBR(FM) Avis PA
WGGI(FM) Benton PA
WLCY(FM) Blairsville PA
WOGH(FM) Burgettstown PA
WVNW(FM) Burnham PA

WBUT(AM) Butler PA
WHGL-FM Canton PA
WCAT-FM Carlisle PA
WIOO(AM) Carlisle PA
WFGI(AM) Charleroi PA
WOGI(FM) Charleroi PA
WKNB(FM) Clarendon PA
WNAE(FM) Clarendon PA
WWCH(AM) Clarion PA
WFRM(AM) Coudersport PA
WDKC(FM) Covington PA
WSJR(FM) Dallas PA
WOWQ(FM) DuBois PA
WCTO(FM) Easton PA
WXTA(FM) Edinboro PA
WYGL-FM Elizabethville PA
WLEM(AM) Emporium PA
WIOV-FM Ephrata PA
WSKE(FM) Everett PA
WTWF(FM) Fairview PA
WLOA(AM) Farrell PA
WGTY(FM) Gettysburg PA
WGRP(AM) Greenville PA
WWGY(FM) Grove City PA
WHVR(AM) Hanover PA
WRBT(FM) Harrisburg PA
WFGI-FM Johnstown PA
WLMI(FM) Kane PA
WADV(AM) Lebanon PA
WGYY(FM) Meadville PA
WPPT(FM) Mercersburg PA
WJUN-FM Mexico PA
WWBE(FM) Mifflinburg PA
WKVE(FM) Mount Pleasant PA
WGYI(FM) Oil City PA
WOGG(FM) Oliver PA
WBXQ(FM) Patton PA
WXTU(FM) Philadelphia PA
WPHB(AM) Philipsburg PA
WDSY-FM Pittsburgh PA
WLGL(FM) Riverside PA
WDDH(AM) Saint Marys PA
WBYL(FM) Salladasburg PA
WGGY(FM) Scranton PA
WYGL(AM) Selinsgrove PA
WBLJ-FM Shamokin PA
*WSRU(FM) Slippery Rock PA
WNTW(AM) Somerset PA
WFGE(FM) Tyrone PA
WKZV(AM) Washington PA
WANB(AM) Waynesburg PA
WILQ(FM) Williamsport PA
WABV(AM) Abbeville SC
WKXC-FM Aiken SC
WDOG(AM) Allendale SC
WDOG-FM Allendale SC
WAGS(AM) Bishopville SC
WGZR(FM) Bluffton SC
WGTR(FM) Bucksport SC
WEZL(FM) Charleston SC
WIWF(FM) Charleston SC
WVSZ(FM) Chesterfield SC
WCOS-FM Columbia SC
WYOR(FM) Cross Hill SC
WEGX(FM) Dillon SC
WNOW-FM Gaffney SC
WZZQ(AM) Gaffney SC
WSSL-FM Gray Court SC
WESC-FM Greenville SC
WJDJ(AM) Hartsville SC
WWNU(FM) Irmo SC
WHYM(AM) Lake City SC
WRHM(FM) Lancaster SC
WHLZ(FM) Marion SC
WYNF(AM) North Augusta SC
WJES(AM) Saluda SC
WSYN(FM) Surfside Beach SC
WBCU(AM) Union SC
WGOG(AM) Walhalla SC
WALI(FM) Walterboro SC
KGIM(AM) Aberdeen SD
KBFS(AM) Belle Fourche SD
KZZI(FM) Belle Fourche SD
KXQL(FM) Flandreau SD
KZMX(AM) Hot Springs SD
KZMX-FM Hot Springs SD

KOKK(AM) Huron SD
KBJM(AM) Lemmon SD
KMLO(FM) Lowry SD
KJAM-FM Madison SD
KXLG(FM) Milbank SD
KMIT(FM) Mitchell SD
KGFX(AM) Pierre SD
KIMM(AM) Rapid City SD
KIQK(FM) Rapid City SD
KOUT(FM) Rapid City SD
KGIM-FM Redfield SD
KPLO-FM Reliance SD
KMOM(FM) Roscoe SD
KIKN-FM Salem SD
KTWB(FM) Sioux Falls SD
KXRB(AM) Sioux Falls SD
KBWS-FM Sisseton SD
KKQQ(FM) Volga SD
KDLO-FM Watertown SD
KSDR-FM Watertown SD
KWYR(AM) Winner SD
KKYA(FM) Yankton SD
WNAX(AM) Yankton SD
WNAX-FM Yankton SD
WJSQ(FM) Athens TN
WLAR(AM) Athens TN
WMOD(FM) Bolivar TN
WXBQ-FM Bristol TN
WTBG(FM) Brownsville TN
WFWL(AM) Camden TN
WUCZ(FM) Carthage TN
WNKX-FM Centerville TN
WUSY(FM) Cleveland TN
WLVS-FM Clifton TN
*WDVX(FM) Clinton TN
WYSH(AM) Clinton TN
WMCP(AM) Columbia TN
WGSQ(FM) Cookeville TN
WHUB(AM) Cookeville TN
WLSB(AM) Copperhill TN
WKBL(AM) Covington TN
WKBQ(FM) Covington TN
WZYX(AM) Cowan TN
WOWF(FM) Crossville TN
WAYA(FM) Decatur TN
WSDQ(AM) Dunlap TN
WTJJ(FM) Dyer TN
WOGT(FM) East Ridge TN
WBEJ(AM) Elizabethton TN
WEMB(AM) Erwin TN
WPFD(AM) Fairview TN
WEKR(AM) Fayetteville TN
WYTM-FM Fayetteville TN
WAKM(AM) Franklin TN
WHIN(AM) Gallatin TN
WGRV(AM) Greeneville TN
WMYL(FM) Halls Crossroads TN
WCXZ(AM) Harrogate TN
*WLMU(FM) Harrogate TN
WTNK(AM) Hartsville TN
WMUF-FM Henry TN
WMLR(AM) Hohenwald TN
WLLI(AM) Humboldt TN
WVHR(AM) Huntingdon TN
WWDX(AM) Huntingdon TN
WOGY(FM) Jackson TN
WDEB(AM) Jamestown TN
WDEB-FM Jamestown TN
WJFC(AM) Jefferson City TN
WCYQ(FM) Karns TN
WIVK-FM Knoxville TN
WTNQ(FM) La Follette TN
WEEN(AM) Lafayette TN
WLCT(FM) Lafayette TN
WDXE(AM) Lawrenceburg TN
WLLX(FM) Lawrenceburg TN
WWLX(AM) Lawrenceburg TN
WANT(FM) Lebanon TN
WKDA(AM) Lebanon TN
WLIL(AM) Lenoir City TN
WAXO(AM) Lewisburg TN
WJJM(AM) Lewisburg TN
WJJM-FM Lewisburg TN
WKSR-FM Loretto TN
WGAP(AM) Maryville TN
WWYN(FM) McKenzie TN

WBMC(AM) McMinnville TN
WGKX(FM) Memphis TN
WMC(AM) Memphis TN
WLIV-FM Monterey TN
WMTN(AM) Morristown TN
WMCT(AM) Mountain City TN
WKDF(FM) Nashville TN
WSIX-FM Nashville TN
WSM(AM) Nashville TN
WSM-FM Nashville TN
WGGQ(AM) Newport TN
WNPC-FM Newport TN
WBNT(AM) Oneida TN
WOCV(AM) Oneida TN
WMUF(AM) Paris TN
WKJQ-FM Parsons TN
WUAT(AM) Pikeville TN
WTRB(AM) Ripley TN
WYHM(AM) Rockwood TN
WJDT(FM) Rogersville TN
WRGS(AM) Rogersville TN
WMXV(FM) Saint Joseph TN
WKWX(FM) Savannah TN
WORM-FM Savannah TN
WXOQ(AM) Selmer TN
WLIJ(AM) Shelbyville TN
WLND(FM) Signal Mountain TN
WJLE(AM) Smithville TN
WJLE-FM Smithville TN
WEPG(AM) South Pittsburg TN
WEYE(FM) Surgoinsville TN
WNTT(AM) Tazewell TN
WTNV(FM) Tiptonville TN
WIKQ(FM) Tusculum TN
WYVY(FM) Union City TN
WECO-FM Wartburg TN
WCDT(AM) Winchester TN
WBRY(AM) Woodbury TN
KEAN-FM Abilene TX
KYYW(AM) Abilene TX
KOPY(AM) Alice TX
KALP(AM) Alpine TX
KATP(FM) Amarillo TX
KDJW(AM) Amarillo TX
KGNC-FM Amarillo TX
KACT-FM Andrews TX
KASE-FM Austin TX
KVET-FM Austin TX
KKCN(FM) Ballinger TX
KRUN(AM) Ballinger TX
KMKS(FM) Bay City TX
KYKR(FM) Beaumont TX
KTKO(FM) Beeville TX
KMKT(FM) Bells TX
KTON(AM) Belton TX
KWTR(FM) Big Lake TX
KBST-FM Big Spring TX
KFYN(AM) Bonham TX
KQTY-FM Borger TX
KNEL-FM Brady TX
KLXK(FM) Breckenridge TX
KTTX(FM) Brenham TX
KWHI(AM) Brenham TX
KKUB(AM) Brownfield TX
KOXE(FM) Brownwood TX
KORA-FM Bryan TX
KCLE(AM) Burleson TX
KBEY(FM) Burnet TX
KMIL(FM) Cameron TX
KTAE(AM) Cameron TX
KGAS-FM Carthage TX
KDET(AM) Center TX
KQBB(FM) Center TX
KCTX-FM Childress TX
KCAR(AM) Clarksville TX
KHFX(AM) Cleburne TX
KTHT(FM) Cleveland TX
KQBZ(FM) Coleman TX
KSTA(AM) Coleman TX
KAUM(FM) Colorado City TX
KVMC(AM) Colorado City TX
KULM-FM Columbus TX
KCOM(AM) Comanche TX
KYOX(FM) Comanche TX
KRYS-FM Corpus Christi TX
KBHT(FM) Crockett TX

KIVY-FM Crockett TX
KSTB(FM) Crystal Beach TX
KNGR(AM) Daingerfield TX
KIXK(AM) Dalhart TX
KDLK-FM Del Rio TX
KRPT(FM) Devine TX
KVWG-FM Dilley TX
KDHN(AM) Dimmitt TX
KSTV-FM Dublin TX
KDDD(AM) Dumas TX
KATX(FM) Eastland TX
KEAS(AM) Eastland TX
KIOX-FM Edna TX
KULP(AM) El Campo TX
KHEY-FM El Paso TX
*KOLI(FM) Electra TX
KNES(AM) Fairfield TX
KPSO-FM Falfurrias TX
KXEZ(FM) Farmersville TX
KFLP-FM Floydada TX
KFST-FM Fort Stockton TX
KPLX(FM) Fort Worth TX
KSCS(FM) Fort Worth TX
KNAF(AM) Fredericksburg TX
KNAF-FM Fredericksburg TX
KHTZ(FM) Ganado TX
KTFW-FM Glen Rose TX
KCTI(AM) Gonzales TX
KSWA(AM) Graham TX
KPIR(AM) Granbury TX
KGVL(AM) Greenville TX
KIKT(FM) Greenville TX
KHLT(AM) Hallettsville TX
KTXM(FM) Hallettsville TX
KCLW(AM) Hamilton TX
KUSJ(FM) Harker Heights TX
KVRP-FM Haskell TX
KPBL(AM) Hemphill TX
KTHP(FM) Hemphill TX
KPAN(AM) Hereford TX
KHBR(AM) Hillsboro TX
KCWM(AM) Hondo TX
KILT-FM Houston TX
KHYI(FM) Howe TX
KSAM-FM Huntsville TX
KRBL(FM) Idalou TX
KEBE(AM) Jacksonville TX
KMBL(AM) Junction TX
KOOK(FM) Junction TX
KHLE(FM) Kempner TX
KAML(AM) Kenedy-Karnes City TX
KRNH(AM) Kerrville TX
KRVL(FM) Kerrville TX
KFTX(FM) Kingsville TX
KBUK(FM) La Grange TX
KVLG(AM) La Grange TX
KPET(AM) Lamesa TX
KCYL(AM) Lampasas TX
KRRG(FM) Laredo TX
KJDL-FM Levelland TX
KLVT(AM) Levelland TX
KSHN-FM Liberty TX
KZZN(AM) Littlefield TX
KETX(AM) Livingston TX
KACQ(FM) Lometa TX
KYKX(FM) Longview TX
KLLL-FM Lubbock TX
KQBR(FM) Lubbock TX
KYKS(FM) Lufkin TX
KAGG(FM) Madisonville TX
KMVL-FM Madisonville TX
KCKL(FM) Malakoff TX
KCUL(AM) Marshall TX
KMHT-FM Marshall TX
KHLB(AM) Mason TX
KLSR-FM Memphis TX
KTEX(FM) Mercedes TX
KRQX(AM) Mexia TX
KRQX-FM Mexia TX
KNFM(FM) Midland TX
KMOO-FM Mineola TX
KFWR(FM) Mineral Wells TX
KMUL(FM) Muleshoe TX
KJCS(FM) Nacogdoches TX
KGNB(AM) New Braunfels TX
KHKX(FM) Odessa TX

KMRK-FM Odessa TX
KOGT(AM) Orange TX
KPXI(FM) Overton TX
KYXX(FM) Ozona TX
KROY(AM) Palacios TX
KNET(AM) Palestine TX
KYYK(FM) Palestine TX
KOMX(FM) Pampa TX
KOYN(FM) Paris TX
KPLT(AM) Paris TX
KZHN(AM) Paris TX
KKBQ(FM) Pasadena TX
KIUN(AM) Pecos TX
KEYE(AM) Perryton TX
KVJY(AM) Pharr TX
KSCN(FM) Pittsburg TX
KKYN-FM Plainview TX
KGCE(FM) Post TX
KOLJ(AM) Quanah TX
KCUB-FM Ranger TX
KRXT(FM) Rockdale TX
KBMI(FM) Roma TX
KDCD(FM) San Angelo TX
KGKL-FM San Angelo TX
KAJA(FM) San Antonio TX
KCYY(FM) San Antonio TX
KKYX(AM) San Antonio TX
KQSI(FM) San Augustine TX
KBAL-FM San Saba TX
KWED(AM) Seguin TX
KIKZ(AM) Seminole TX
KSEM-FM Seminole TX
KAYD-FM Silsbee TX
KOUL(FM) Sinton TX
KSNY(AM) Snyder TX
KSNY-FM Snyder TX
KHOS-FM Sonora TX
KLGD(FM) Stamford TX
KKJW(FM) Stanton TX
*KEQX(FM) Stephenville TX
KSCH(FM) Sulphur Springs TX
KXOX(AM) Sweetwater TX
KXOX-FM Sweetwater TX
KKYR-FM Texarkana TX
KBCY(FM) Tye TX
KKUS(FM) Tyler TX
KNUE(FM) Tyler TX
KBNU(FM) Uvalde TX
KVOU-FM Uvalde TX
KVWC(AM) Vernon TX
KIXS(FM) Victoria TX
KVNN(AM) Victoria TX
WACO-FM Waco TX
KBEC(AM) Waxahachie TX
KLUR(FM) Wichita Falls TX
KWFS-FM Wichita Falls TX
KVST(FM) Willis TX
KGXL(FM) Winters TX
KWUD(AM) Woodville TX
KYKM(FM) Yoakum TX
KCYQ(FM) Elsinore UT
KMTI(AM) Manti UT
KCYN(FM) Moab UT
KEGA(FM) Oakley UT
KENZ(FM) Ogden UT
KKAT-FM Orem UT
KARB(FM) Price UT
KSLL(AM) Price UT
KNEU(AM) Roosevelt UT
KONY(FM) Saint George UT
KKAT(AM) Salt Lake City UT
KSOP-FM Salt Lake City UT
KUBL-FM Salt Lake City UT
KSOP(AM) South Salt Lake UT
KLCY(FM) Vernal UT
WVES(AM) Accomac VA
WKDE-FM Altavista VA
WYYD(FM) Amherst VA
WAXM-FM Big Stone Gap VA
WBBC-FM Blackstone VA
WHKX(FM) Bluefield VA
WHQX(FM) Cedar Bluff VA
WLUS-FM Clarksville VA
WDIC(AM) Clinchco VA
WKHK(FM) Colonial Heights VA
WIQO-FM Covington VA

WSVS(AM) Crewe VA
WJMA-FM Culpeper VA
WAKG(FM) Danville VA
WBNN-FM Dillwyn VA
WLFV(FM) Ettrick VA
WGRX(FM) Falmouth VA
WFLO(AM) Farmville VA
WVHL(FM) Farmville VA
WLQM-FM Franklin VA
WFLS-FM Fredericksburg VA
WFTR(AM) Front Royal VA
WBRF(FM) Galax VA
WMNA(AM) Gretna VA
WMJD(FM) Grundy VA
WKCY-FM Harrisonburg VA
WJNV(FM) Jonesville VA
WLRV(AM) Lebanon VA
WXLZ-FM Lebanon VA
WRAA(AM) Luray VA
WMEV-FM Marion VA
WSIG(FM) Mount Jackson VA
WGH-FM Newport News VA
WNVA-FM Norton VA
WESR(AM) Onley-Onancock VA
WSWV-FM Pennington Gap VA
WUSH(AM) Poquoson VA
WDXC(FM) Pound VA
WPSK-FM Pulaski VA
WSLC-FM Roanoke VA
WYTI(AM) Rocky Mount VA
WXLZ(AM) Saint Paul VA
WXMY(AM) Saltville VA
WKSK-FM South Hill VA
WZBB(AM) Stanleytown VA
WCYK-FM Staunton VA
WKDW(AM) Staunton VA
WKDL(AM) Warrenton VA
WNNT-FM Warsaw VA
WIGO-FM White Stone VA
WUSQ-FM Winchester VA
WYVE(AM) Wytheville VA
WJPK(FM) Barton VT
WZLF(FM) Bellows Falls VT
WWFY(FM) Berlin VT
WTNN(FM) Bristol VT
WOKO(FM) Burlington VT
WJEN(FM) Killington VT
WLVB(FM) Morrisville VT
WIKE(AM) Newport VT
WVNR(AM) Poultney VT
WKXH(FM) Saint Johnsbury VT
WXLF(FM) White River Junction VT
KNBQ(FM) Centralia WA
KMNT(FM) Chehalis WA
KCLX(AM) Colfax WA
KCVL(AM) Colville WA
KYSN(FM) East Wenatchee WA
KXLE-FM Ellensburg WA
KXLE-FM Ellensburg WA
KULE-FM Ephrata WA
KYYT(FM) Goldendale WA
KEYG(AM) Grand Coulee WA
KXXK(FM) Hoquiam-Aberdeen WA
KVAS(AM) Ilwaco WA
KBAM(AM) Longview WA
KUKN(FM) Longview WA
KGY-FM McCleary WA
KWIQ-FM Moses Lake WA
KAPS(AM) Mount Vernon WA
KNCW(FM) Omak WA
KIXZ-FM Opportunity WA
KZZL-FM Pullman WA
KIOK(FM) Richland WA
KORD-FM Richland WA
KKWF(FM) Seattle WA
KMPS-FM Seattle WA
KDRK-FM Spokane WA
KEZE(FM) Spokane WA
KDBL(FM) Toppenish WA
KYNR(AM) Toppenish WA
KKRV(FM) Wenatchee WA
KUTI(AM) Yakima WA
KXDD(FM) Yakima WA
WRLU(FM) Algoma WI
WBSZ(FM) Ashland WI
WLMX-FM Balsam Lake WI

WXRO(FM) Beaver Dam WI
WISS(AM) Berlin WI
WQRB(FM) Bloomer WI
WATQ(FM) Chetek WI
WJMQ(FM) Clintonville WI
WPCK(FM) Denmark WI
WVRE(FM) Dickeyville WI
WDMP(AM) Dodgeville WI
WDMP-FM Dodgeville WI
WDMO(FM) Durand WI
WAXX(FM) Eau Claire WI
WTKM(AM) Hartford WI
WTKM-FM Hartford WI
WJVL(FM) Janesville WI
WQCC(FM) La Crosse WI
WLDY(AM) Ladysmith WI
WGLR(AM) Lancaster WI
WGLR-FM Lancaster WI
WKQH(FM) Marathon WI
WLST(FM) Marinette WI
WYTE(FM) Marshfield WI
WWQM-FM Middleton WI
WOKY(FM) Milwaukee WI
WEKZ(AM) Monroe WI
WWQN(FM) Mount Horeb WI
WNCY-FM Neenah-Menasha WI
WIXK(AM) New Richmond WI
WOCO(AM) Oconto WI
WPKR(FM) Omro WI
WCQM(FM) Park Falls WI
WBKY(FM) Portage WI
WDDC(FM) Portage WI
WQPC(FM) Prairie du Chien WI
WNFM(FM) Reedsburg WI
WHDG(FM) Rhinelander WI
WAQE(FM) Rice Lake WI
WJMC-FM Rice Lake WI
WRCO-FM Richland Center WI
WPLT(FM) Sarona WI
WTCH(AM) Shawano WI
WBFM(FM) Sheboygan WI
WCOW-FM Sparta WI
WCYE(FM) Three Lakes WI
WCUB(AM) Two Rivers WI
WVRQ-FM Viroqua WI
WMIL(FM) Waukesha WI
WDUX(AM) Waupaca WI
WDEZ(FM) Wausau WI
WBKV(AM) West Bend WI
WBWI-FM West Bend WI
WSLD(FM) Whitewater WI
WDLS(FM) Wisconsin Dells WI
WJLS-FM Beckley WV
WDHC(FM) Berkeley Springs WV
WBRB(FM) Buckhannon WV
WKAZ(AM) Charleston WV
WKWS(FM) Charleston WV
WGIE(FM) Clarksburg WV
WPDX(AM) Clarksburg WV
WPDX-FM Clarksburg WV
WZAC-FM Danville WV
WDNE-FM Elkins WV
WKKW(FM) Fairmont WV
WVBD(FM) Fayetteville WV
*WFGH(FM) Fort Gay WV
*WVMR(AM) Frost WV
WTCR-FM Huntington WV
WIHY(AM) Hurricane WV
WKMM(FM) Kingwood WV
WRON-FM Lewisburg WV
WOTR(FM) Lost Creek WV
WGYE(FM) Mannington WV
WELD-FM Moorefield WV
WTNJ(FM) Mount Hope WV
WGGE-FM Parkersburg WV
WHNK(AM) Parkersburg WV
WWYO(AM) Pineville WV
WBYG(FM) Point Pleasant WV
WCEF(FM) Ripley WV
*WVSB(FM) Romney WV
WYKM(AM) Rupert WV
WVRC-FM Spencer WV
WDBS(FM) Sutton WV
WOVK(FM) Wheeling WV
WXCC(FM) Williamson WV
KRSV(AM) Afton WY

KRSV-FM Afton WY
KKAW(FM) Albin WY
KLGT(FM) Buffalo WY
KQLT(FM) Casper WY
KLEN(FM) Cheyenne WY
KOLZ(FM) Cheyenne WY
KXBG(FM) Cheyenne WY
KDWY(FM) Diamondville WY
KKTY(FM) Douglas WY
KEVA(AM) Evanston WY
KRND(AM) Fox Farm WY
KGWY(FM) Gillette WY
KFRZ(FM) Green River WY
KZMQ(AM) Greybull WY
KZMQ-FM Greybull WY
KJAX(FM) Jackson WY
KSGT(AM) Jackson WY
KOVE(AM) Lander WY
KCGY(FM) Laramie WY
KWYW(FM) Lost Cabin WY
KWYY(FM) Midwest WY
KASL(AM) Newcastle WY
KPIN(FM) Pinedale WY
KTAK(FM) Riverton WY
KQSW(FM) Rock Springs WY
KTGA(FM) Saratoga WY
KYTI(FM) Sheridan WY
KYDT(FM) Sundance WY
KDNO(FM) Thermopolis WY
KERM(FM) Torrington WY
KGOS(AM) Torrington WY
KYCN(AM) Wheatland WY

Disco

KIJI(FM) Tumon GU

Diversified

*KUAC(FM) Fairbanks AK
KCAM(AM) Glennallen AK
*KXGA(FM) Glennallen AK
*KRNN(FM) Juneau AK
*KTOO(FM) Juneau AK
*KRBD(FM) Ketchikan AK
KMXT(FM) Kodiak AK
*KXKM(FM) McCarthy AK
KNOM(AM) Nome AK
*KNOM-FM Nome AK
*KSDP(AM) Sand Point AK
*KCAW(FM) Sitka AK
*KTNA(FM) Talkeetna AK
*KCHU(AM) Valdez AK
*KSTK(FM) Wrangell AK
*WLJR(FM) Birmingham AL
*KVMN(FM) Cave City AR
*KABF(FM) Little Rock AR
KVSA(AM) McGehee AR
KBUX(FM) Quartzsite AZ
*KAIC(FM) Tucson AZ
*KNNB(FM) Whiteriver AZ
*KALX(FM) Berkeley CA
*KPFA(FM) Berkeley CA
*KPFB(FM) Berkeley CA
*KZFR(FM) Chico CA
*KSPC(FM) Claremont CA
*KECG(FM) El Cerrito CA
*KMUE(FM) Eureka CA
*KFSR(FM) Fresno CA
*KMUD(FM) Garberville CA
*KCRI(FM) Indio CA
*KUCI(FM) Irvine CA
*KLAI(FM) Laytonville CA
*KPFK(FM) Los Angeles CA
*KKSM(AM) Oceanside CA
*KUCR(FM) Riverside CA
*KBDH(FM) San Ardo CA
*KALW(FM) San Francisco CA
*KPOO(FM) San Francisco CA
*KUSF(FM) San Francisco CA
*KCPR(FM) San Luis Obispo CA
*KUSP(FM) Santa Cruz CA
*KZSC(FM) Santa Cruz CA
*KAIB(FM) Shafter CA
*KCSS(FM) Turlock CA

*KZYZ(FM) Willits CA
*KLRD(FM) Yucaipa CA
KVCU(AM) Boulder CO
*KRCC(FM) Colorado Springs CO
*KBUT(FM) Crested Butte CO
*KGNU(AM) Denver CO
*KDUR(FM) Durango CO
*KUNC(FM) Greeley CO
*KECC(FM) La Junta CO
*KCCS(FM) Starkville CO
*KRNC(FM) Steamboat Springs CO
*WPKN(FM) Bridgeport CT
*WRTC-FM Hartford CT
*WSLX(FM) New Canaan CT
*WHUS(FM) Storrs CT
*WNHU(FM) West Haven CT
*WVUD(FM) Newark DE
*WFCF(FM) Saint Augustine FL
*WMNF(FM) Tampa FL
*WREK(FM) Atlanta GA
*WQAI(FM) Thomson GA
*WVDA(FM) Valdosta GA
*KPRG(FM) Hagatna GU
*KKCR(FM) Hanalei HI
*KAQA(FM) Kilauea HI
*KHAI(FM) Wahiawa HI
*KRUI-FM Iowa City IA
*KWAR(FM) Waverly IA
*KBSQ(FM) McCall ID
*WESN(FM) Bloomington IL
*WDBX(FM) Carbondale IL
*WHPK-FM Chicago IL
*WDGC-FM Downers Grove IL
*WEPS(FM) Elgin IL
*WMXM(FM) Lake Forest IL
*WLRA(FM) Lockport IL
*WHCM(FM) Palatine IL
*WQNA(FM) Springfield IL
*WILL(AM) Urbana IL
*WNTH(FM) Winnetka IL
*WFHB(FM) Bloomington IN
*WPSR(FM) Evansville IN
*WUEV(FM) Evansville IN
*WHWE(FM) Howe IN
*WRFT(FM) Indianapolis IN
WMRS(FM) Monticello IN
*WBKE-FM North Manchester IN
*WVUR-FM Valparaiso IN
*KBTL(FM) El Dorado KS
*KANZ(FM) Garden City KS
*KTJO-FM Ottawa KS
KKAN(AM) Phillipsburg KS
*WOCS(FM) Lerose KY
*KLSP(FM) Angola LA
*WHAB(AM) Acton MA
*WSHL-FM Easton MA
*WUML(FM) Lowell MA
WMLN-FM Milton MA
*WOZQ(FM) Northampton MA
*WNMH(FM) Northfield MA
*WBSL-FM Sheffield MA
*WAIC(FM) Springfield MA
*WSKB(FM) Westfield MA
*WCUW(FM) Worcester MA
*WKHS(FM) Worton MD
*WERU-FM Blue Hill ME
*WBOR(FM) Brunswick ME
*WSHD(FM) Eastport ME
*WMPG(FM) Gorham ME
*WMEB-FM Orono ME
*WUPI(FM) Presque Isle ME
*WMHB(FM) Waterville ME
*WYAR(FM) Yarmouth ME
*WVAC-FM Adrian MI
*WBFH(FM) Bloomfield Hills MI
*WKDS(FM) Kalamazoo MI
*WOCR(FM) Olivet MI
*WNMC-FM Traverse City MI
KDAL(AM) Duluth MN
*KFAI(FM) Minneapolis MN
KOLV(FM) Olivia MN
*KCVO-FM Camdenton MO
*KWUR(FM) Clayton MO
*KOPN(FM) Columbia MO
*KCVQ(FM) Knob Noster MO
*KCVJ(FM) Osceola MO

KLUE(FM) Poplar Bluff MO
*KMST(FM) Rolla MO
*KDHX(FM) Saint Louis MO
*WMUW(FM) Columbus MS
*KGLT(FM) Bozeman MT
*KYPR(FM) Miles City MT
*WXDU(FM) Durham NC
*WSOE(FM) Elon NC
*KMHA-FM Four Bears ND
*KZUM(FM) Lincoln NE
*KDAI(FM) Scottsbluff NE
*WSPS(FM) Concord NH
WAJM(AM) Atlantic City NJ
*WDVR(FM) Delaware Township NJ
*WFMU(FM) East Orange NJ
*WGLS-FM Glassboro NJ
*WNTI(FM) Hackettstown NJ
*KUNM(FM) Albuquerque NM
*KRRT(FM) Arroyo Seco NM
*KCIE(FM) Dulce NM
*KRAR(FM) Espanola NM
KSIL(FM) Hurley NM
*KRRE(FM) Las Vegas NM
*KQAI(FM) Roswell NM
*KBOM(FM) Socorro NM
*KWPR(FM) Lund NV
*WCDB(FM) Albany NY
*WKRB(FM) Brooklyn NY
*WCVF-FM Fredonia NY
*WRCU-FM Hamilton NY
*WPKM(FM) Montauk NY
*WMFU(FM) Mount Hope NY
*WFUV(FM) New York NY
*WONY(FM) Oneonta NY
*WNYO(FM) Oswego NY
*WVKR-FM Poughkeepsie NY
WFTU(AM) Riverhead NY
*WRUR-FM Rochester NY
*WUSB(FM) Stony Brook NY
*WKWZ(FM) Syosset NY
*WPNR-FM Utica NY
*WMCO(FM) New Concord OH
*WOBC-FM Oberlin OH
*WJCU(FM) University Heights OH
*WCWS(FM) Wooster OH
KDOE(FM) Antlers OK
*KPSU(FM) Goodwell OK
*KMUN(FM) Astoria OR
*KWVA(FM) Eugene OR
*KTEC(FM) Klamath Falls OR
*KLCO(FM) Newport OR
*KBOO(FM) Portland OR
*KRRC(FM) Portland OR
KVRA(FM) Sisters OR
*WMUH(FM) Allentown PA
*WDCV-FM Carlisle PA
*WESS(FM) East Stroudsburg PA
*WMCE(FM) Erie PA
*WRSD(FM) Folsom PA
*WHHS(FM) Havertown PA
*WPSX(FM) Kane PA
*WLCH(FM) Lancaster PA
*WIXQ(FM) Millersville PA
*WSFX(FM) Nanticoke PA
*WPEB(FM) Philadelphia PA
WPHE(AM) Phoenixville PA
*WRCT(FM) Pittsburgh PA
*WYBF(FM) Radnor Township PA
*WSRN-FM Swarthmore PA
*WCUR(FM) West Chester PA
*WVYC(FM) York PA
WNIK(AM) Arecibo PR
WQBS(AM) San Juan PR
*WRIU(FM) Kingston RI
*WJHD(FM) Portsmouth RI
*WELH(FM) Providence RI
*KCFS(FM) Sioux Falls SD
*WAPX-FM Clarksville TN
*WAPX-FM Clarksville TN
WSGM(FM) Coalmont TN
*WMTS-FM Murfreesboro TN
*WRVU(FM) Nashville TN
*KTXP(FM) Bushland TX
*KPFT(FM) Houston TX
*KTRU(FM) Houston TX
*KTSU(FM) Houston TX

KOHM(FM) Lubbock TX
KLSR-FM Memphis TX
*KEOM(FM) Mesquite TX
*KWBU-FM Waco TX
*KRCL(FM) Salt Lake City UT
*WUVT-FM Blacksburg VA
*WEHC(FM) Emory VA
*WMLU(FM) Farmville VA
*WWHS-FM Hampden-Sydney VA
*WLUR(FM) Lexington VA
*WVST-FM Petersburg VA
*WDCE(FM) Richmond VA
*WCWM(FM) Williamsburg VA
WSTA(AM) Charlotte Amalie VI
WAXJ(FM) Frederiksted VI
WDHP(AM) Frederiksted VI
WRRA(AM) Frederiksted VI
*WRUV(FM) Burlington VT
*WJSC-FM Johnson VT
*WWLR(FM) Lyndonville VT
*WRMC-FM Middlebury VT
*WGDR(FM) Plainfield VT
WDEV(AM) Waterbury VT
KXPA(AM) Bellevue WA
*KCED(FM) Centralia WA
*KCWU(FM) Ellensburg WA
*KSER(FM) Everett WA
*KAOS(FM) Olympia WA
*KZUU(FM) Pullman WA
*KEXP-FM Seattle WA
KYNR(AM) Toppenish WA
*WRST-FM Oshkosh WI
*WOJB(FM) Reserve WI
*KUWS(FM) Superior WI
*WVBC(FM) Bethany WV
*WVWC(FM) Buckhannon WV
WVMR(AM) Frost WV
*WMUL(FM) Huntington WV
*WWVU-FM Morgantown WV
*WQAB(FM) Philippi WV
*KAIX(FM) Cheyenne WY

Easy Listening

*WVAS(FM) Montgomery AL
KLEZ(FM) Malvern AR
KTLO-FM Mountain Home AR
*KNAI(FM) Phoenix AZ
KAHM(FM) Prescott AZ
*KGUD(FM) Longmont CO
WAVV(FM) Naples Park FL
*WKGC(AM) Panama City Beach FL
WKEZ-FM Tavenier FL
WGPC(AM) Albany GA
*KCMR(FM) Mason City IA
KILJ-FM Mount Pleasant IA
WGCY(FM) Gibson City IL
WLLM(AM) Lincoln IL
KVSV-FM Beloit KS
WJEJ(AM) Hagerstown MD
WEZQ(FM) Bangor ME
WEZR(AM) Lewiston ME
WCZY-FM Mount Pleasant MI
WIOS(AM) Tawas City MI
KTXR(FM) Springfield MO
WBAQ(FM) Greenville MS
WGCM-FM Gulfport MS
WHLC(FM) Highlands NC
KLEA(AM) Lovington NM
KTAT(AM) Frederick OK
WFDT(AM) Aguada PR
WFID(FM) Rio Piedras PR
WDAR-FM Darlington SC
WEZV(FM) North Myrtle Beach SC
WCPH(AM) Etowah TN
*WDNX(FM) Olive Hill TN
KRFE(AM) Lubbock TX
*KLUX(FM) Robstown TX
WJOY(AM) Burlington VT
WLKD(AM) Minocqua WI
WOCO-FM Oconto WI
WEZY(FM) Racine WI
*WJJJ(FM) Beckley WV

Educational

KYKD(FM) Bethel AK
*KBBI(AM) Homer AK
*KXKM(FM) McCarthy AK
*WSTF(FM) Andalusia AL
*WLJR(FM) Birmingham AL
WQEM(FM) Columbiana AL
*WYFD(FM) Decatur AL
*WDYF(FM) Dothan AL
*WVOB(FM) Dothan AL
*WLBF(FM) Montgomery AL
*WTBJ(FM) Oxford AL
*KVMN(FM) Cave City AR
KOFC(AM) Fayetteville AR
KJBN(AM) Little Rock AR
*KCMH(FM) Mountain Home AR
*KWRB(FM) Bisbee AZ
*KRMC(FM) Douglas AZ
*KPUB(FM) Flagstaff AZ
*KNOG(FM) Nogales AZ
*KNNB(FM) Whiteriver AZ
*KALX(FM) Berkeley CA
*KIBC(FM) Burney CA
*KBBF(FM) Calistoga CA
*KHAP(FM) Chico CA
*KECR(AM) El Cajon CA
*KECG(FM) El Cerrito CA
*KMUE(FM) Eureka CA
*KMUD(FM) Garberville CA
*KEFR(FM) Le Grand CA
*KFRN(AM) Long Beach CA
*KAKX(FM) Mendocino CA
*KADV(FM) Modesto CA
*KSMC(FM) Moraga CA
*KSGN(FM) Riverside CA
*KUSF(FM) San Francisco CA
*KZSU(FM) Stanford CA
*KBUT(FM) Crested Butte CO
*KCIC(FM) Grand Junction CO
WADS(AM) Ansonia CT
*WERB(FM) Berlin CT
*WFAR(FM) Danbury CT
*WQTQ(FM) Hartford CT
*WFCS(FM) New Britain CT
*WVUD(FM) Newark DE
*WTJT(FM) Baker FL
*WJED(FM) Dogwood Lakes Estate FL
*WJFP(FM) Fort Pierce FL
WXYB(AM) Indian Rocks Beach FL
*WJIR(FM) Key West FL
*WKES(FM) Lakeland FL
*WYFO(FM) Lakeland FL
*WHIJ(FM) Ocala FL
*WPCS(FM) Pensacola FL
*WVIJ(FM) Port Charlotte FL
*WKZM(FM) Sarasota FL
*WOAK(FM) La Grange GA
*WYFS(FM) Savannah GA
*KKCR(FM) Hanalei HI
*KCIF(FM) Hilo HI
*KAQA(FM) Kilauea HI
*KHJC(FM) Lihue HI
*KHOE(FM) Fairfield IA
*KRUI-FM Iowa City IA
*KBBG(FM) Waterloo IA
*KWAR(FM) Waverly IA
*KCIR(FM) Twin Falls ID
*KEFX(FM) Twin Falls ID
*WBGL(FM) Champaign IL
*WZGL(FM) Charleston IL
*WHPK-FM Chicago IL
*WKKC(FM) Chicago IL
*WMBI-FM Chicago IL
*WZRD(FM) Chicago IL
*WEPS(FM) Elgin IL
*WGNN(FM) Fisher IL
*WGBK(FM) Glenview IL
*WKCC(FM) Kankakee IL
*WLRA(FM) Lockport IL
*WVJC(FM) Mount Carmel IL
*WWGN(FM) Ottawa IL
*WHCM(FM) Palatine IL
*WPSR(FM) Evansville IN
*WGVE(FM) Gary IN
*WHWE(FM) Howe IN

*WQKO(FM) Howe IN
*WRFT(FM) Indianapolis IN
*WWHI(FM) Muncie IN
*WNAS(FM) New Albany IN
*WZRP(FM) Richmond IN
*WJLR(FM) Seymour IN
*WETL(FM) South Bend IN
*WMHD-FM Terre Haute IN
*KONQ(FM) Dodge City KS
*KANZ(FM) Garden City KS
*KZAN(FM) Hays KS
*KZNA(FM) Hill City KS
*KONZ(FM) Riley KS
*WDFB-FM Danville KY
*WSOF-FM Madisonville KY
*WBFI(FM) McDaniels KY
*WTHL(FM) Somerset KY
*KVDP(FM) Dry Prong LA
*KPAE(FM) Erwinville LA
*WRBH(FM) New Orleans LA
WBNW(AM) Concord MA
*WXRB(FM) Dudley MA
*WOZQ(FM) Northampton MA
*WRPS(FM) Rockland MA
*WSDH(FM) Sandwich MA
*WFSI(FM) Annapolis MD
*WOEL-FM Elkton MD
*WGTS(FM) Takoma Park MD
*WERU-FM Blue Hill ME
*WYAR(FM) Yarmouth ME
*WXOU(FM) Auburn Hills MI
*WBFH(FM) Bloomfield Hills MI
*WIDR(FM) Kalamazoo MI
*WKDS(FM) Kalamazoo MI
*WPCJ(FM) Pittsford MI
*KMSK(FM) Austin MN
*KMSU(FM) Mankato MN
*KVSC(FM) Saint Cloud MN
*KRHS(FM) Overland MO
*KMNR(FM) Rolla MO
*WPAE(FM) Centreville MS
*KGLT(FM) Bozeman MT
*KMSM-FM Butte MT
*KDWG(FM) Dillon MT
*KGPR(FM) Great Falls MT
*KBGA(FM) Missoula MT
*WPIR(FM) Hickory NC
*WRSH(FM) Rockingham NC
WBFJ(AM) Winston-Salem NC
*KABU(FM) Fort Totten ND
*KTLX(FM) Columbus NE
*KCNT(FM) Hastings NE
*KIOS-FM Omaha NE
*WVFA(FM) Lebanon NH
*WSCS(FM) New London NH
*WGLS-FM Glassboro NJ
*WFME(FM) Newark NJ
*WVPH(FM) Piscataway NJ
KXNM(FM) Encino NM
*KTDB(FM) Ramah NM
*KSHI(FM) Zuni NM
*KNIS(FM) Carson City NV
*KNCC(FM) Elko NV
*WXBA(FM) Brentwood NY
*WHPC(FM) Garden City NY
*WBAI(FM) New York NY
*WNYE(FM) New York NY
*WONY(FM) Oneonta NY
*WOSS(FM) Ossining NY
*WPSA(FM) Paul Smiths NY
*WPOB-FM Plainview NY
*WFRS(FM) Smithtown NY
*WCII(FM) Spencer NY
*WFRW(FM) Webster NY
*WRDL(FM) Ashland OH
*WZCP(FM) Chillicothe OH
*WHVT(FM) Clyde OH
*WDEQ-FM De Graff OH
*WKET(FM) Kettering OH
*WLMH(FM) Morrow OH
*WMCO(FM) New Concord OH
*WOBC-FM Oberlin OH
*WLHS(FM) West Chester OH
*WZWP(FM) West Union OH
*KKVO(FM) Altus OK
*KOSN(FM) Ketchum OK

*KQCV(AM) Oklahoma City OK
*KOSU(FM) Stillwater OK
KBNP(AM) Portland OR
*KBPS(AM) Portland OR
*WUFR(FM) Bedford PA
*WLCH(FM) Lancaster PA
*WMSS(FM) Middletown PA
*WRCT(FM) Pittsburgh PA
*WREQ(FM) Ridgebury PA
*WXFR(FM) State College PA
*WVYC(FM) York PA
*WIDA-FM Carolina PR
*WJVP(FM) Culebra PR
*WEPC(FM) Belton SC
*WYFV(FM) Cayce SC
*WTBI-FM Greenville SC
WTBI(AM) Pickens SC
*KJBB(FM) Watertown SD
*WHCB(FM) Bristol TN
*WMBW(FM) Chattanooga TN
*WWOG(FM) Cookeville TN
*WMKW(FM) Crossville TN
*WCSK(FM) Kingsport TN
*WCPI(FM) McMinnville TN
*WEVL(FM) Memphis TN
*WQOX(FM) Memphis TN
*WFCM-FM Murfreesboro TN
*WDNX(FM) Olive Hill TN
*WFCM(AM) Smyrna TN
*KJRT(FM) Amarillo TX
KRGN(FM) Amarillo TX
*KASV(FM) Borger TX
*KBNR(FM) Brownsville TX
*KEOS(FM) College Station TX
*KBNJ(FM) Corpus Christi TX
*KVTT(FM) Dallas TX
*KOIR(FM) Edinburg TX
*KVER(FM) El Paso TX
*KTSU(FM) Houston TX
*KAVX(FM) Lufkin TX
KRIO(AM) McAllen TX
*KPHS(FM) Plains TX
*KTER(FM) Rudolph TX
KSLR(AM) San Antonio TX
*KPDR(FM) Wheeler TX
*KRCL(FM) Salt Lake City UT
*WWIP(FM) Cheriton VA
*WFOS(FM) Chesapeake VA
*WOTC(FM) Edinburg VA
*WRVL(FM) Lynchburg VA
WRJR(AM) Portsmouth VA
WGOD-FM Charlotte Amalie VI
*WRUV(FM) Burlington VT
*KKRS(FM) Davenport WA
*KNHC(FM) Seattle WA
*WBCR-FM Beloit WI
*WHHI(FM) Highland WI
*WHLA(FM) La Crosse WI
*WHA(AM) Madison WI
*WSUM(FM) Madison WI
*WHWC(FM) Menomonie WI
*KUWS(FM) Superior WI
*WHRM(FM) Wausau WI
*WVBC(FM) Bethany WV
WQBE-FM Charleston WV
*WWVU-FM Morgantown WV
KVOW(AM) Riverton WY

Ethnic

KAAB(AM) Batesville AR
*KTQX(FM) Bakersfield CA
KIQQ(AM) Barstow CA
*KUBO(FM) Calexico CA
*KHDC(FM) Chualar CA
KQEQ(AM) Fowler CA
*KSJV(FM) Fresno CA
KSRN(FM) Kings Beach CA
*KVUH(FM) Laytonville CA
KBTW(FM) Lenwood CA
KRQK(FM) Lompoc CA
*KMPO(FM) Modesto CA
KLIB(AM) Roseville CA
KTGE(AM) Salinas CA
KRZZ(FM) San Francisco CA
KSQL(FM) Santa Cruz CA

KOBO(AM) Yuba City CA
WLQY(AM) Hollywood FL
WXYB(AM) Indian Rocks Beach FL
WURN(AM) Kendall FL
WMGE(FM) Miami Beach FL
WRUM(AM) Orlando FL
WTIS(AM) Tampa FL
*WREK(FM) Atlanta GA
WATB(AM) Decatur GA
WFSM(AM) Dry Branch GA
WAZX(AM) Smyrna GA
*WWBM(FM) Yates GA
*KKCR(FM) Hanalei HI
KAPA(FM) Hilo HI
KDNN(FM) Honolulu HI
KHUI(FM) Honolulu HI
KINE-FM Honolulu HI
KNDI(AM) Honolulu HI
KORL(AM) Honolulu HI
KPHI(AM) Honolulu HI
KMKK-FM Kaunakakai HI
*KAQA(FM) Kilauea HI
KAGB(FM) Waimea HI
WCEV(AM) Cicero IL
WCGO(AM) Evanston IL
WEEF(AM) Highland Park IL
WPJX(AM) Zion IL
WTUV(AM) Louisville KY
KLCL(AM) Lake Charles LA
KANE(AM) New Iberia LA
WSHO(AM) New Orleans LA
WHTB(AM) Fall River MA
WJDA(AM) Quincy MA
WESX(AM) Salem MA
WRCA(AM) Waltham MA
WAZN(AM) Watertown MA
WNZK(AM) Dearborn Heights MI
KPNP(AM) Watertown MN
WEW(AM) Saint Louis MO
WKRA(AM) Holly Springs MS
WYMY(FM) Goldsboro NC
WWTR(AM) Bridgewater NJ
*WDDM(FM) Hazlet NJ
WSNR(AM) Jersey City NJ
WCAA(AM) Newark NJ
WPAT(AM) Paterson NJ
*KABR(AM) Alamo Community NM
KCNM-FM Garapan-Saipan NP
KWIP(AM) Dallas OR
WNWR(AM) Philadelphia PA
KCHN(AM) Brookshire TX
KRVA(AM) Cockrell Hill TX
KJOJ(AM) Conroe TX
KXTQ-FM Lubbock TX
KTXV(AM) Mabank TX
KREH(AM) Pecan Grove TX
KZMP-FM Pilot Point TX
KEDA(AM) San Antonio TX
KHSE(AM) Wylie TX
WYSK(AM) Fredericksburg VA
WSBV(AM) South Boston VA
KXPA(AM) Bellevue WA
KVRI(AM) Blaine WA
KRPI(AM) Ferndale WA

Farsi

KIRN(AM) Simi Valley CA

Filipino

KTKB-FM Hagatna GU
KNDI(AM) Honolulu HI

Folk

*WDJW(FM) Somers CT
*WGCS(FM) Goshen IN
*WUMB-FM Boston MA
*WFPB-FM Falmouth MA
*WNEF(FM) Newburyport MA
WFPB(AM) Orleans MA
*WBPR(FM) Worcester MA
*WICN(FM) Worcester MA
*WMEH(FM) Bangor ME

*WMED(FM) Calais ME
*WMEP(FM) Camden ME
*WMEF(FM) Fort Kent ME
*WMEA(FM) Portland ME
*WMEM(FM) Presque Isle ME
*WMEW(FM) Waterville ME
*KGPR(FM) Great Falls MT
*KZSD-FM Martin SD
*WETS(FM) Johnson City TN
*KRCL(FM) Salt Lake City UT
*KBCS(FM) Bellevue WA
*WXPR(FM) Rhinelander WI

Foreign/Ethnic

KVTO(AM) Berkeley CA
*KBES(FM) Ceres CA
KSRT(AM) Cloverdale CA
KBIF(AM) Fresno CA
KLOK-FM Greenfield CA
KIGS(AM) Hanford CA
KSQQ(FM) Morgan Hill CA
KLYY(FM) Riverside CA
KEST(AM) San Francisco CA
KEST(AM) San Francisco CA
KSOL(FM) San Francisco CA
KMRB(AM) San Gabriel CA
KSJX(AM) San Jose CA
KALI-FM Santa Ana CA
WDJZ(AM) Bridgeport CT
*WPFW(FM) Washington DC
WUST(AM) Washington DC
WAVS(AM) Davie FL
WSRF(AM) Fort Lauderdale FL
WRTO-FM Goulds FL
WWRF(AM) Lake Worth FL
WAMR-FM Miami FL
WHSR(AM) Pompano Beach FL
KISH(FM) Hagatna GU
KCCN-FM Honolulu HI
*KIPO(FM) Honolulu HI
KZOO(AM) Honolulu HI
KPOA(FM) Lahaina HI
WOJO(FM) Evanston IL
WNWI(AM) Oak Lawn IL
WPNA(AM) Oak Park IL
WUNR(AM) Brookline MA
WLYN(AM) Lynn MA
WJFD-FM New Bedford MA
WBGR(AM) Baltimore MD
WKTX(AM) Cortland OH
WVJP-FM Caguas PR
WMDD(AM) Fajardo PR
WZET(AM) Hormigueros PR
WSOL(AM) San German PR
WPRM-FM San Juan PR
WVOZ(AM) San Juan PR
KHER(FM) Crystal City TX
KFZO(FM) Denton TX
*KEPX(FM) Eagle Pass TX
KGRW(FM) Friona TX
KGOL(AM) Humble TX
KMFM(FM) Premont TX

French

KLEB(AM) Golden Meadow LA

Full Service

WTLS(AM) Tallassee AL
*KHDX(FM) Conway AR
KHTS(AM) Canyon Country CA
WTIC(AM) Hartford CT
WICH(AM) Norwich CT
WILI(AM) Willimantic CT
WDEL(AM) Wilmington DE
WMT(AM) Cedar Rapids IA
KROS(AM) Clinton IA
KDTH(AM) Dubuque IA
WJBC(AM) Bloomington IL
WSPY-FM Plano IL
WZZB(AM) Seymour IN
WZZY(FM) Winchester IN
WCLU(AM) Glasgow KY

WCAP(AM) Lowell MA
WNAW(AM) North Adams MA
WOCN-FM Orleans MA
WBRK(AM) Pittsfield MA
WNAV(AM) Annapolis MD
WTVB(AM) Coldwater MI
WDBC(AM) Escanaba MI
WHTC(AM) Holland MI
WION(AM) Ionia MI
WSJM(AM) Saint Joseph MI
WJJY-FM Brainerd MN
KLFD(AM) Litchfield MN
WJON(AM) Saint Cloud MN
KQRV(FM) Deer Lodge MT
KUSO(FM) Albion NE
KBRL(AM) McCook NE
KELK(AM) Elko NV
WENT(AM) Gloversville NY
WSYR(AM) Syracuse NY
WRIP(FM) Windham NY
WHBC(AM) Canton OH
*WCDR-FM Cedarville OH
WBEX(AM) Chillicothe OH
*WOHC(FM) Chillicothe OH
WHIO(AM) Dayton OH
*WOHP(FM) Portsmouth OH
KBCH(AM) Lincoln City OR
KEX(AM) Portland OR
WBVP(AM) Beaver Falls PA
WCNS(AM) Latrobe PA
WKVA(AM) Lewistown PA
WEEU(AM) Reading PA
WOON(AM) Woonsocket RI
WLSC(AM) Loris SC
KNAF(AM) Fredericksburg TX
KSEY-FM Seymour TX
KSST(AM) Sulphur Springs TX
KTBB(AM) Tyler TX
KMAS(AM) Shelton WA
WOMT(AM) Manitowoc WI
WVRQ(AM) Viroqua WI
WFHR(AM) Wisconsin Rapids WI
WMOV(AM) Ravenswood WV
KFBC(AM) Cheyenne WY

Golden Oldies

KLSZ-FM Fort Smith AR
WYBT(AM) Blountstown FL
WRZN(AM) Hernando FL
WSVU(AM) North Palm Beach FL
WOKA(AM) Douglas GA
WDQX(FM) Morton IL
WQCY(FM) Quincy IL
*WXRB(FM) Dudley MA
WGOP(AM) Pocomoke City MD
WGTO(AM) Cassopolis MI
KOZY(AM) Grand Rapids MN
KBEK(AM) Mora MN
KTNY(FM) Libby MT
WIBT(AM) Shelby NC
WHTG(AM) Eatontown NJ
WCHN(AM) Norwich NY
WIBZ(AM) Wedgefield SC
KSQB(AM) Sioux Falls SD
WRCW(AM) Nekoosa WI
WHTL-FM Whitehall WI
WEIR(AM) Weirton WV

Gospel

*KJHA(FM) Houston AK
KAKN(AM) Naknek AK
KICY(AM) Nome AK
WAVU(AM) Albertville AL
WBNM(AM) Alexander City AL
WHMA(AM) Anniston AL
WRAB(AM) Arab AL
WAGG(AM) Birmingham AL
WAYE(AM) Birmingham AL
*WELJ(FM) Brewton AL
WBYE(AM) Calera AL
WREN(AM) Carrollton AL
WEIS(AM) Centre AL
WLYJ(AM) Centre AL

WBIB(AM) Centreville AL
WQEM(FM) Columbiana AL
WXJC-FM Cordova AL
WMCJ(AM) Cullman AL
WDLK(AM) Dadeville AL
WXAL(AM) Demopolis AL
WAGF(AM) Dothan AL
*WVOB(FM) Dothan AL
WRJL-FM Eva AL
WJLD(AM) Fairfield AL
WXQW(AM) Fairhope AL
WKWL(AM) Florala AL
WGEA(AM) Geneva AL
WJBB(AM) Haleyville AL
WERH(AM) Hamilton AL
WQHC(AM) Hanceville AL
*WKNG-FM Heflin AL
*WPIL(FM) Heflin AL
WDJL(AM) Huntsville AL
WEUP(AM) Huntsville AL
*WJOU(FM) Huntsville AL
WRJX(AM) Jackson AL
WIXI(AM) Jasper AL
WJLX(AM) Jasper AL
WHLW(FM) Luverne AL
WGOK(AM) Mobile AL
WLVV(AM) Mobile AL
WMFC(AM) Monroeville AL
WMGY(AM) Montgomery AL
WURL(AM) Moody AL
WEUV(AM) Moulton AL
*WJIF(FM) Opp AL
WQLS(AM) Ozark AL
WKXK(AM) Pine Hill AL
WLPR(AM) Prichard AL
WVSM(AM) Rainsville AL
WRMG(AM) Red Bay AL
WKAX(AM) Russellville AL
WZCT(AM) Scottsboro AL
WBTG-FM Sheffield AL
WNUZ(AM) Talladega AL
WTSK(AM) Tuscaloosa AL
WWPG(AM) Tuscaloosa AL
WZZA(AM) Tuscumbia AL
WBIL(AM) Tuskegee AL
*WEBT(FM) Valley AL
WJEC(AM) Vernon AL
WAPZ(AM) Wetumpka AL
WYLS(AM) York AL
KNWA(AM) Bellefonte AR
KHKN(FM) Benton AR
KBRI(AM) Brinkley AR
KPZK-FM Cabot AR
KNHD(AM) Camden AR
KWXT(AM) Dardanelle AR
KVDW(AM) England AR
KTCS(AM) Fort Smith AR
KWXI(AM) Glenwood AR
*KBPB(AM) Harrison AR
KJIW-FM Helena AR
KVLO(FM) Humnoke AR
KNEA(AM) Jonesboro AR
KAAY(AM) Little Rock AR
*KABF(FM) Little Rock AR
KJBN(AM) Little Rock AR
KPZK(AM) Little Rock AR
KCGS(AM) Marshall AR
KENA(AM) Mena AR
*KLLN(FM) Newark AR
*KCAT(AM) Pine Bluff AR
KTPA(AM) Prescott AR
KLRG(AM) Sheridan AR
KOSE(AM) Wilson AR
*KYCJ(FM) Camino CA
*KCJH(FM) Livingston CA
KRJY(AM) Sacramento CA
*KYCC(FM) Stockton CA
KDYA(AM) Vallejo CA
KLDC(AM) Denver CO
WDJZ(AM) Bridgeport CT
WYCB(AM) Washington DC
*WDPZ(AM) Dover DE
WFHT(AM) Avon Park FL
WSWN(AM) Belle Glade FL
*WJCB(AM) Clewiston FL
*WJED(FM) Dogwood Lakes Estate FL

*WJBC-FM Fernandina Beach FL
WIRA(AM) Fort Pierce FL
WTMN(AM) Gainesville FL
WRNE(AM) Gulf Breeze FL
WLVF(AM) Haines City FL
*WLVF-FM Haines City FL
WZAZ(AM) Jacksonville FL
WGRO(AM) Lake City FL
WTYS-FM Marianna FL
WMBM(AM) Miami Beach FL
WRMQ(AM) Orlando FL
WBRD(AM) Palmetto FL
WVTJ(AM) Pensacola FL
WPUL(AM) South Daytona FL
WHBT(AM) Tallahassee FL
WEXY(AM) Wilton Manors FL
WOKB(AM) Winter Garden FL
WSIR(AM) Winter Haven FL
WZHR(AM) Zephyrhills FL
WJYZ(AM) Albany GA
WAJQ(AM) Alma GA
WXAG(AM) Athens GA
WAFS(AM) Atlanta GA
WYZE(AM) Atlanta GA
WGUS(AM) Augusta GA
WTHB(AM) Augusta GA
WKUN(AM) Bostwick GA
WGMI(AM) Bremen GA
WULS(FM) Broxton GA
WEAM-FM Buena Vista GA
WQIL(FM) Chauncey GA
WRWH(AM) Cleveland GA
WOKS(AM) Columbus GA
WSHE(AM) Columbus GA
WCON(AM) Cornelia GA
WCUG(AM) Cuthbert GA
WDPC(AM) Dallas GA
WTTI(AM) Dalton GA
WSEM(AM) Donalsonville GA
WMLT(AM) Dublin GA
WTJH(AM) East Point GA
WUFF-FM Eastman GA
WLJA-FM Ellijay GA
WBHB(AM) Fitzgerald GA
WQMJ(FM) Forsyth GA
*WJTG(FM) Fort Valley GA
WXKO(AM) Fort Valley GA
WTHV(AM) Hahira GA
WKLY(AM) Hartwell GA
WVOH(AM) Hazlehurst GA
WGML(AM) Hinesville GA
WVKX(AM) Irwinton GA
*WTLD(FM) Jesup GA
*WMOC(FM) Lumber City GA
WPZE(AM) Mableton GA
WDDO(AM) Macon GA
WFDR(AM) Manchester GA
WHCG(AM) Metter GA
WMNZ(AM) Montezuma GA
WIGO(AM) Morrow GA
WHBS(AM) Moultrie GA
WMTM(AM) Moultrie GA
WALH(AM) Mountain City GA
WRBX(AM) Reidsville GA
WTNL(AM) Reidsville GA
WSSJ(FM) Rincon GA
WZOT(AM) Rockmart GA
WROM(AM) Rome GA
WSOK(AM) Savannah GA
WXRS(AM) Swainsboro GA
WHGH(AM) Thomasville GA
WSTT(AM) Thomasville GA
WLET(AM) Toccoa GA
WJEM(AM) Valdosta GA
WIMO(AM) Winder GA
WTHB-FM Wrens GA
WYHG(AM) Young Harris GA
KTFC(FM) Sioux City IA
KTFG(FM) Sioux Rapids IA
*KBBG(FM) Waterloo IA
WXAN(FM) Ava IL
*WTSG(FM) Carlinville IL
WEIC(AM) Charleston IL
WGRB(AM) Chicago IL
*WSSD(FM) Chicago IL
WFFX(AM) East St. Louis IL

WBGX(AM) Harvey IL
WWHN(AM) Joliet IL
WVEL(AM) Pekin IL
WBCP(AM) Urbana IL
WYGS(FM) Columbus IN
WTLC(AM) Indianapolis IN
WMYJ(AM) Martinsville IN
WRFM(AM) Muncie IN
WFIA(AM) New Albany IN
*WMYJ-FM Oolitic IN
WSLM(AM) Salem IN
WFRI(FM) Winamac IN
WYWY(AM) Barbourville KY
*WAAJ(FM) Benton KY
*WVHM(FM) Benton KY
WCVG(AM) Covington KY
WEKT(AM) Elkton KY
WIOK(FM) Falmouth KY
WFLE(AM) Flemingsburg KY
WEGI(AM) Fort Campbell KY
WFUL(AM) Fulton KY
WOKE(FM) Garrison KY
WLGC(AM) Greenup KY
WFSR(AM) Harlan KY
WHBN(AM) Harrodsburg KY
WEKG(AM) Jackson KY
WKVG(AM) Jenkins KY
*WVCT(FM) Keavy KY
WGWM(AM) London KY
WLLV(AM) Louisville KY
WLOU(AM) Louisville KY
WMIK(AM) Middlesboro KY
WFLW(AM) Monticello KY
WRVK(AM) Mt. Vernon KY
WLOC(AM) Munfordville KY
WCGW(AM) Nicholasville KY
WSIP-FM Paintsville KY
WYGH(AM) Paris KY
WDOC(AM) Prestonsburg KY
WCBR(AM) Richmond KY
WIDS(AM) Russell Springs KY
WBFC(AM) Stanton KY
*WJCR-FM Upton KY
WEKC(AM) Williamsburg KY
KWDF(AM) Ball LA
WXOK(AM) Baton Rouge LA
WIKC(AM) Bogalusa LA
KDLA(AM) De Ridder LA
KGGM(FM) Delhi LA
*KGRM(FM) Grambling LA
KKNO(AM) Gretna LA
KJCB(AM) Lafayette LA
KRJO(AM) Monroe LA
WBOK(AM) New Orleans LA
WODT(AM) New Orleans LA
WYLD(AM) New Orleans LA
KTTP(AM) Pineville LA
WPRF(FM) Reserve LA
KRUS(AM) Ruston LA
KIOU(AM) Shreveport LA
KOKA(AM) Shreveport LA
KSYB(AM) Shreveport LA
KTKC(AM) Springhill LA
KTJZ(FM) Tallulah LA
KNCB(AM) Vivian LA
WCAO(AM) Baltimore MD
WWIN(AM) Baltimore MD
*WLIC(FM) Frostburg MD
*WAIJ(FM) Grantsville MD
WPRS-FM Waldorf MD
*WHCF(FM) Bangor ME
*WRPB(FM) Benedicta ME
*WFST(AM) Caribou ME
*WHPF(FM) Pittston Farm ME
WFLT(AM) Flint MI
*WCTP(FM) Gagetown MI
WDRJ(AM) Inkster MI
*WUNN(AM) Mason MI
WEXL(AM) Royal Oak MI
WWSJ(AM) Saint Johns MI
WCHB(AM) Taylor MI
WWJC(AM) Duluth MN
KNOF(FM) Saint Paul MN
*KGNA-FM Arnold MO
KOMC(AM) Branson MO
*KNLH(FM) Cedar Hill MO

*KYRV(FM) Concordia MO
*KGNN-FM Cuba MO
*KNLQ(FM) Cuba MO
KAUL(FM) Ellington MO
KGGN(AM) Gladstone MO
*KJIR(FM) Hannibal MO
*WGCQ(FM) Hayti MO
KPRT(AM) Kansas City MO
KMHM(AM) Lutesville MO
KMRF(AM) Marshfield MO
*KJAB-FM Mexico MO
*KNLG(FM) New Bloomfield MO
KPWB(AM) Piedmont MO
*KNLP(FM) Potosi MO
KATZ(AM) Saint Louis MO
KSTL(AM) Saint Louis MO
KALM(AM) Thayer MO
*KBIY(FM) Van Buren MO
*KGNV(FM) Washington MO
WFCA(FM) Ackerman MS
WIZK(AM) Bay Springs MS
WBYP(FM) Belzoni MS
WELZ(AM) Belzoni MS
WCHJ(AM) Brookhaven MS
WAJV(FM) Brooksville MS
WMGO(AM) Canton MS
WONG(AM) Canton MS
WCLD(AM) Cleveland MS
WFFF(AM) Columbia MS
WTWG(AM) Columbus MS
*WAUM(FM) Duck Hill MS
WTYJ(FM) Fayette MS
WQST(AM) Forest MS
WJIW(FM) Greenville MS
WGRM(AM) Greenwood MS
WGRM-FM Greenwood MS
WQFX(AM) Gulfport MS
WORV(AM) Hattiesburg MS
WOEG(AM) Hazlehurst MS
WKRA-FM Holly Springs MS
*WURC(FM) Holly Springs MS
WHAL-FM Horn Lake MS
WCPC(AM) Houston MS
WNLA(AM) Indianola MS
*WVSD(FM) Itta Bena MS
WHLH(FM) Jackson MS
*WMPR(FM) Jackson MS
WOAD(AM) Jackson MS
WZRX(AM) Jackson MS
WESY(AM) Leland MS
WXTN(AM) Lexington MS
WAKK(AM) McComb MS
WMER(AM) Meridian MS
WNBN(AM) Meridian MS
WYHL(AM) Meridian MS
WMIS(AM) Natchez MS
WOSM(FM) Ocean Springs MS
WRJW(AM) Picayune MS
WSEL(AM) Pontotoc MS
WSEL-FM Pontotoc MS
WXHB(FM) Richton MS
WSAO(AM) Senatobia MS
WAVN(AM) Southaven MS
*WAQB(FM) Tupelo MS
WFCG(FM) Tylertown MS
WRCS(AM) Ahoskie NC
*WTJY(FM) Asheboro NC
WZOO(AM) Asheboro NC
WSKY(AM) Asheville NC
WPYB(AM) Benson NC
WZGM(AM) Black Mountain NC
WVOE(AM) Chadbourn NC
WRNA(AM) China Grove NC
WYZD(AM) Dobson NC
WCKB(AM) Dunn NC
WCLW(AM) Eden NC
WBXB(AM) Edenton NC
WGQR(AM) Elizabethtown NC
WBOB-FM Enfield NC
WFMO(AM) Fairmont NC
WSTS(FM) Fairmont NC
WIDU(AM) Fayetteville NC
WWOL(AM) Forest City NC
WNNL(AM) Fuquay-Varina NC
WFMC(AM) Goldsboro NC
WYCV(AM) Granite Falls NC

WEAL(AM) Greensboro NC
WKEW(AM) Greensboro NC
*WNAA(FM) Greensboro NC
WPET(AM) Greensboro NC
WKDX(AM) Hamlet NC
WHNC(AM) Henderson NC
*WPIR(FM) Hickory NC
WJCV(AM) Jacksonville NC
WRKB(AM) Kannapolis NC
WKTE(AM) King NC
WELS(AM) Kinston NC
WELS-FM Kinston NC
WEWO(AM) Laurinburg NC
WAGR(AM) Lumberton NC
WHBK(AM) Marshall NC
WDSL(AM) Mocksville NC
WDEX(AM) Monroe NC
WIXE(AM) Monroe NC
WCIS(AM) Morganton NC
WSYD(AM) Mount Airy NC
WWDR(AM) Murfreesboro NC
WCVP(AM) Murphy NC
WAUG(AM) New Hope NC
WCBQ(AM) Oxford NC
WMFA(AM) Raeford NC
WTEL(AM) Red Springs NC
WEGG(AM) Rose Hill NC
*WOGR-FM Salisbury NC
WXKL(AM) Sanford NC
WYAL(AM) Scotland Neck NC
WVCB(AM) Shallotte NC
WMPM(AM) Smithfield NC
*WGAS(AM) South Gastonia NC
WGMA(AM) Spindale NC
WTAB(AM) Tabor City NC
WCPS(AM) Tarboro NC
WTLK(AM) Taylorsville NC
WJRM(AM) Troy NC
WZKB(FM) Wallace NC
WOBX(AM) Wanchese NC
WARR(AM) Warrenton NC
WLGT(FM) Washington NC
WENC(AM) Whiteville NC
WWWC(AM) Wilkesboro NC
WIAM(AM) Williamston NC
WLSG(AM) Wilmington NC
WWIL(AM) Wilmington NC
WGTM(AM) Wilson NC
WLLY(AM) Wilson NC
WBTE(AM) Windsor NC
WGTI(FM) Windsor NC
WPOL(AM) Winston-Salem NC
WSMX(AM) Winston-Salem NC
*WXRI(FM) Winston-Salem NC
WECU(AM) Winterville NC
WYNC(AM) Yanceyville NC
KHRT(AM) Minot ND
KTFJ(AM) Dakota City NE
*KJLT-FM North Platte NE
WIMG(AM) Ewing NJ
*WEHA(FM) Port Republic NJ
WFAI(AM) Salem NJ
WNJC(AM) Washington Township NJ
*KUPR(FM) Alamogordo NM
*KYCM(FM) Alamogordo NM
*KHII(FM) Cloudcroft NM
WUFO(AM) Amherst NY
WBBF(AM) Buffalo NY
WTHE(AM) Mineola NY
WLIB(AM) New York NY
WHLD(AM) Niagara Falls NY
WINW(AM) Canton OH
WDBZ(AM) Cincinnati OH
WJMO(AM) Cleveland OH
*WBIE(FM) Delphos OH
WCNW(AM) Fairfield OH
WJYD(FM) London OH
WRTK(AM) Niles OH
WJTB(AM) North Ridgeville OH
WABQ(AM) Painesville OH
WXIC(AM) Waverly OH
WRAC(FM) West Union OH
WLRD(FM) Willard OH
*KAJT(FM) Ada OK
KZBS(FM) Granite OK
*KVAZ(FM) Henryetta OK

KVIS(AM) Miami OK
KTLV(AM) Midwest City OK
*KLRB(FM) Stuart OK
*KFXT(FM) Sulphur OK
*KTGS(FM) Tishomingo OK
KIMY(FM) Watonga OK
WZUM(AM) Carnegie PA
WPWA(AM) Chester PA
WADV(AM) Lebanon PA
WJSM-FM Martinsburg PA
*WRIJ(FM) Masontown PA
WPGR(AM) Monroeville PA
*WPEL(AM) Montrose PA
*WRWJ(FM) Murrysville PA
WGBN(AM) New Kensington PA
WNAP(AM) Norristown PA
WPCL(FM) Northern Cambria PA
WVGB(AM) Beaufort SC
WBSC(AM) Bennettsville SC
WSPX(FM) Bowman SC
WEAF(AM) Camden SC
WGCV(AM) Cayce SC
WGCD(AM) Chester SC
*WRFE(FM) Chesterfield SC
WWRK(AM) Darlington SC
WDSC(AM) Dillon SC
WYNN(AM) Florence SC
WNOW-FM Gaffney SC
WLMC(AM) Georgetown SC
*WTBI-FM Greenville SC
WCZZ(AM) Greenwood SC
WPJM(AM) Greer SC
WJDJ(AM) Hartsville SC
*WLGI(FM) Hemingway SC
WJBS(AM) Holly Hill SC
WALD(AM) Johnsonville SC
WPDT(FM) Johnsonville SC
WRZE(FM) Kingstree SC
*WKCL(FM) Ladson SC
WAGL(AM) Lancaster SC
WJAY(AM) Mullins SC
WKZK(AM) North Augusta SC
WPJK(AM) Orangeburg SC
*WSSB-FM Orangeburg SC
WPOG(AM) Saint Matthews SC
WTUA(FM) Saint Stephen SC
WCSZ(AM) Sans Souci SC
WAAW(FM) Williston SC
WWGM(FM) Alamo TN
WOJG(AM) Bolivar TN
WIGN(AM) Bristol TN
WJOC(AM) Chattanooga TN
WNOO(AM) Chattanooga TN
WMCH(AM) Church Hill TN
WQZQ(AM) Clarksville TN
WSGM(FM) Coalmont TN
WMRB(AM) Columbia TN
WHUB(AM) Cookeville TN
WENR(AM) Englewood TN
WEMB(AM) Erwin TN
WEKR(AM) Fayetteville TN
WJAK(AM) Jackson TN
WDEB-FM Jamestown TN
WWAM(AM) Jasper TN
WJJT(AM) Jellico TN
WETB(AM) Johnson City TN
WBBX(AM) Kingston TN
WKGN(AM) Knoxville TN
WKXV(AM) Knoxville TN
WQLA(AM) La Follette TN
WEEN(AM) Lafayette TN
WDXL(AM) Lexington TN
WFLI(AM) Lookout Mountain TN
WBMC(AM) McMinnville TN
WBBP(AM) Memphis TN
WLOK(AM) Memphis TN
WXRQ(AM) Mount Pleasant TN
WMCT(AM) Mountain City TN
WMDB(AM) Nashville TN
WNAH(AM) Nashville TN
WUAT(AM) Pikeville TN
WRGS(AM) Rogersville TN
WMXV(FM) Saint Joseph TN
WSIB(FM) Selmer TN
WJBZ-FM Seymour TN
WLIJ(AM) Shelbyville TN

WSMT(AM) Sparta TN
WDEH(AM) Sweetwater TN
WECO(AM) Wartburg TN
WVRY(FM) Waverly TN
WQSE(AM) White Bluff TN
WBOZ(FM) Woodbury TN
KLVQ(AM) Athens TX
KNRB(FM) Atlanta TX
*KAZI-FM Austin TX
KWWJ(AM) Baytown TX
*KGHY(FM) Beaumont TX
KZZB(AM) Beaumont TX
KDET(AM) Center TX
KCOM(AM) Comanche TX
KYOK(AM) Conroe TX
*KDKR(FM) Decatur TX
KNNK(FM) Dimmitt TX
KHVN(AM) Fort Worth TX
KKGM(AM) Fort Worth TX
KTXJ-FM Jasper TX
KJTX(FM) Jefferson TX
KRMY(AM) Killeen TX
KZZN(AM) Littlefield TX
KFIT(AM) Lockhart TX
*KFTG(FM) Pasadena TX
KGCE(FM) Post TX
*KPVU(FM) Prairie View TX
KCHL(AM) San Antonio TX
KFIT EXP STN San Antonio TX
KROI(FM) Seabrook TX
KGLD(AM) Tyler TX
KZEE(AM) Weatherford TX
KWNS(FM) Winnsboro TX
KLLB(AM) West Jordan UT
WWDW(FM) Alberta VA
WAMV(AM) Amherst VA
WTTX-FM Appomattox VA
WBTX(AM) Broadway-Timberville VA
WKBY(AM) Chatham VA
WCPK(AM) Chesapeake VA
WGGM(AM) Chester VA
WFIC(AM) Collinsville VA
WPZZ(FM) Crewe VA
WDVA(AM) Danville VA
WILA(AM) Danville VA
WGFC(FM) Floyd VA
WLQM(AM) Franklin VA
WWWJ(AM) Galax VA
WGAT(AM) Gate City VA
WNRG(AM) Grundy VA
WHHV(AM) Hillsville VA
WHAP(AM) Hopewell VA
WHFD(FM) Lawrenceville VA
WLRV(AM) Lebanon VA
WLLL(AM) Lynchburg VA
WMEV(FM) Marion VA
WTJZ(AM) Newport News VA
WSWV(AM) Pennington Gap VA
WGPL(AM) Portsmouth VA
WPCE(AM) Portsmouth VA
WGTH(AM) Richlands VA
WGTH-FM Richlands VA
WFTH(AM) Richmond VA
WYTI(AM) Rocky Mount VA
WXMY(AM) Saltville VA
*WTRM(FM) Winchester VA
WGOD(AM) Charlotte Amalie VI
KZIZ(AM) Pacific WA
WGLB(AM) Elm Grove WI
WJLS(AM) Beckley WV
*WPJY(FM) Blennerhassett WV
*WKJL(FM) Clarksburg WV
*WFGH(FM) Fort Gay WV
WEMM-FM Huntington WV
WHJC(AM) Matewan WV
WWYO(AM) Pineville WV
WAEY(AM) Princeton WV
WRRL(AM) Rainelle WV
WYKM(AM) Rupert WV
WVRC(AM) Spencer WV
*WMLJ(FM) Summersville WV
*KOFG(FM) Cody WY

Greek

WXYB(AM) Indian Rocks Beach FL
WPSO(AM) New Port Richey FL
WNTN(AM) Newton MA

Inspirational

*KUDU(FM) Tok AK
*WJOU(FM) Huntsville AL
*KFLR-FM Phoenix AZ
*KNAQ(FM) Prescott AZ
*KFLT(AM) Tucson AZ
*KFLT-FM Tucson AZ
*KYCJ(FM) Camino CA
*KAXL(FM) Green Acres CA
*KTLW(FM) Lancaster CA
*KCJH(FM) Livingston CA
*KHCS(FM) Palm Desert CA
*KVIP(AM) Redding CA
*KVIP-FM Redding CA
KRJY(AM) Sacramento CA
*KYCC(FM) Stockton CA
*KARM(FM) Visalia CA
KLLV(AM) Breen CO
*KTPL(FM) Pueblo CO
*KTAD(AM) Sterling CO
*WKZM(FM) Sarasota FL
WTJH(AM) East Point GA
*KSDA-FM Agat GU
*KCMR(FM) Mason City IA
KBGN(AM) Caldwell ID
WRMS(AM) Beardstown IL
*WZRS(FM) Pana IL
*WLWJ(FM) Petersburg IL
*WIHM(AM) Taylorville IL
*WGNR-FM Anderson IN
*KXJH(FM) Linton IN
*WUBS(FM) South Bend IN
*WATI(FM) Vincennes IN
*KFLO-FM Blanchard LA
*KBAN(FM) De Ridder LA
*KYLC(FM) Lake Charles LA
*WHCF(FM) Bangor ME
*WUFN(FM) Albion MI
*WNFA(FM) Port Huron MI
*WNFR(FM) Sandusky MI
*KTGG(AM) Spring Arbor MI
*KDNI(FM) Duluth MN
*KTIS-FM Minneapolis MN
*KBPG(FM) Montevideo MN
*KBHZ(FM) Willmar MN
*KGNA-FM Arnold MO
*KGNN-FM Cuba MO
WBVV(FM) Guntown MS
*KBLW(FM) Billings MT
*KJLF(FM) Butte MT
KMCJ(FM) Colstrip MT
*KGFC(FM) Great Falls MT
*KXEI(FM) Havre MT
*KVCM(FM) Helena MT
WPZS(FM) Albemarle NC
WCLN-FM Clinton NC
*WGPS(FM) Elizabeth City NC
WNNL(FM) Fuquay-Varina NC
*KAYA(FM) Hubbard NE
*KPNO(FM) Norfolk NE
*KJLT-FM North Platte NE
*KGRD(FM) Orchard NE
*KYCM(FM) Alamogordo NM
*KFLQ(FM) Albuquerque NM
*WNGN(FM) Argyle NY
*WCII(FM) Spencer NY
*WCRF(FM) Cleveland OH
WFCO(FM) Lancaster OH
*WVML(FM) Millersburg OH
*WVMS(FM) Sandusky OH
*KSYE(FM) Frederick OK
*KLVV(FM) Ponca City OK
*KMWR(FM) Brookings OR
WCOH-FM DuBois PA
*WAWN(FM) Franklin PA
*WVME(FM) Meadville PA
*WVMN(FM) New Castle PA
WLMC(AM) Georgetown SC
WBZF(FM) Hartsville SC

Italian

WEST(AM) Easton PA

Japanese

KZOO(AM) Honolulu HI

Jazz

WAUD(AM) Auburn AL
*WVSU-FM Birmingham AL
*WJAB(FM) Huntsville AL
*WQPR(FM) Muscle Shoals AL
*WAPR(FM) Selma AL
*WUAL-FM Tuscaloosa AL
*KBSA(FM) El Dorado AR
*KUAF(FM) Fayetteville AR
KASU Jonesboro AR
*KABF(FM) Little Rock AR
*KUAR(FM) Little Rock AR
*KXRJ(FM) Russellville AR
*KJZA(AM) Drake AZ
*KJZZ(FM) Phoenix AZ
KYOT-FM Phoenix AZ
*KUAZ(AM) Tucson AZ
*KUAZ-FM Tucson AZ
*KAWC-FM Yuma AZ
*KNCA(FM) Burney CA
KRML(AM) Carmel CA
*KCHO(FM) Chico CA
*KSPC(FM) Claremont CA
KRVR(FM) Copperopolis CA
*KECG(FM) El Cerrito CA
*KFSR(FM) Fresno CA
KMGQ(FM) Goleta CA
*KKJZ(FM) Long Beach CA
KTWV(FM) Los Angeles CA
*KSBR(FM) Mission Viejo CA
*KNSQ(FM) Mount Shasta CA
*KQNC(FM) Quincy CA
*KXJZ(FM) Sacramento CA
*KSDS(FM) San Diego CA
*KSJS(FM) San Jose CA
*KCBX(FM) San Luis Obispo CA
*KCSM(FM) San Mateo CA
KRUZ(FM) Santa Barbara CA
*KSBX(FM) Santa Barbara CA
*KCRW(FM) Santa Monica CA
*KXJS(FM) Sutter CA
*KRZA(FM) Alamosa CO
*KAJX(FM) Aspen CO
*KCJX(FM) Carbondale CO
*KUVO(FM) Denver CO
*WDJW(FM) Somers CT
*WPFW(FM) Washington DC
*WRTX(FM) Dover DE
*WGCU-FM Fort Myers FL
*WUFT-FM Gainesville FL
*WJUF(FM) Inverness FL
*WMKO(FM) Marco FL
*WDNA(FM) Miami FL

WJNI(FM) Ladson SC
WFMV(FM) South Congaree SC
WLJI(FM) Summerton SC
*KLMP(FM) Rapid City SD
WLRM(AM) Millington TN
KPEZ(FM) Austin TX
*KCBI(FM) Dallas TX
KCRN-FM San Angelo TX
*KHTA(FM) Wake Village TX
*WAUQ(FM) Charles City VA
*WARN(FM) Culpeper VA
WRIS(AM) Roanoke VA
*WCMD-FM Barre VT
*WGLY-FM Bolton VT
*WCKJ(FM) Saint Johnsbury VT
*WGLV(FM) Woodstock VT
KCIS(AM) Edmonds WA
*KCSH(FM) Ellensburg WA
*KAYB(FM) Sunnyside WA
WOTR(FM) Lost Creek WV
WRLB(AM) Rainelle WV
*KOHR(FM) Sheridan WY

*WUCF-FM Orlando FL
*WUSF(FM) Tampa FL
WGYL(FM) Vero Beach FL
WLOQ(FM) Winter Park FL
*WCLK(FM) Atlanta GA
*WSVH(FM) Savannah GA
*KIPO(FM) Honolulu HI
*WOI-FM Ames IA
*KCCK-FM Cedar Rapids IA
*KALA(FM) Davenport IA
*KJMC(FM) Des Moines IA
*KTPR(FM) Fort Dodge IA
*KBBG(FM) Waterloo IA
KBSU(AM) Boise ID
*KIBX(FM) Bonners Ferry ID
*KBSK(FM) McCall ID
KISU-FM Pocatello ID
KYZK(FM) Sun Valley ID
*KEZJ(AM) Twin Falls ID
*WBEZ(FM) Chicago IL
*WHPK-FM Chicago IL
*WNIJ(FM) De Kalb IL
*WSIE(FM) Edwardsville IL
*WNUR-FM Evanston IL
*WDCB(FM) Glen Ellyn IL
*WBEQ(FM) Morris IL
*WGLT(FM) Normal IL
*WCBU(FM) Peoria IL
*WIPA(FM) Pittsfield IL
*WQUB(FM) Quincy IL
*WUIS(FM) Springfield IL
WBCP(AM) Urbana IL
*WFIU(FM) Bloomington IN
*WBEW(FM) Chesterton IN
*WVPE(FM) Elkhart IN
*WUEV(FM) Evansville IN
*WBOI(FM) Fort Wayne IN
*WICR(FM) Indianapolis IN
*WBAA(FM) West Lafayette IN
*KANH(FM) Emporia KS
KKCI(FM) Goodland KS
*KANU(FM) Lawrence KS
*KJHK(FM) Lawrence KS
*KANV(FM) Olsburg KS
*KRPS(FM) Pittsburg KS
*KMUW(FM) Wichita KS
*KLSA(FM) Alexandria LA
*WBRH(FM) Baton Rouge LA
*WWNO(FM) New Orleans LA
*WWOZ(FM) New Orleans LA
*KDAQ(FM) Shreveport LA
*KTLN(FM) Thibodaux LA
*WFCR(FM) Amherst MA
*WGBH(FM) Boston MA
WHRB(FM) Cambridge MA
*WUMD(FM) North Dartmouth MA
*WICN(FM) Worcester MA
*WEAA(FM) Baltimore MD
*WYPR(FM) Baltimore MD
*WFWM(FM) Frostburg MD
*WYPO(FM) Ocean City MD
WQJZ(FM) Ocean Pines MD
*WESM(FM) Princess Anne MD
*WMEH(FM) Bangor ME
*WMED(FM) Calais ME
*WMEP(FM) Camden ME
*WMEF(FM) Fort Kent ME
*WMEA(FM) Portland ME
*WMEM(FM) Presque Isle ME
*WMEW(FM) Waterville ME
*WYAR(FM) Yarmouth ME
*WGVU-FM Allendale MI
*WCML-FM Alpena MI
*WUCX-FM Bay City MI
*WRCJ-FM Detroit MI
*WBLU-FM Grand Rapids MI
*WCMW-FM Harbor Springs MI
*WMUK-FM Kalamazoo MI
*WLNZ(FM) Lansing MI
*WNMU-FM Marquette MI
*WCMU-FM Mount Pleasant MI
*WCMB-FM Oscoda MI
*WSGR-FM Port Huron MI
*WCMZ-FM Sault Ste. Marie MI
WWCM(FM) Standish MI
*WNMC-FM Traverse City MI

*WBLV(FM) Twin Lake MI
WGVS-FM Whitehall MI
*WEMU(FM) Ypsilanti MI
*KBEM-FM Minneapolis MN
*KQAL(FM) Winona MN
*KRCU(FM) Cape Girardeau MO
KRNW(FM) Chillicothe MO
*KWWC-FM Columbia MO
*KJLU(FM) Jefferson City MO
KRLI(FM) Malta Bend MO
*KXCV(FM) Maryville MO
*KCOZ(FM) Point Lookout MO
*WURC(FM) Holly Springs MS
*WVSD(FM) Itta Bena MS
*WJSU(FM) Jackson MS
WMPN-FM Jackson MS
*KEMC(FM) Billings MT
*KBMC(FM) Bozeman MT
*KAPC(FM) Butte MT
*KGPR(FM) Great Falls MT
*KUFN(FM) Hamilton MT
*KNMC(FM) Havre MT
*KUHM(FM) Helena MT
*KUKL(FM) Kalispell MT
*KUFM(FM) Missoula MT
*WCQS(FM) Asheville NC
WVOE(AM) Chadbourn NC
*WNCU(FM) Durham NC
*WFSS(FM) Fayetteville NC
*WFQS(FM) Franklin NC
*WNAA(FM) Greensboro NC
*WSHA(FM) Raleigh NC
*WDCC(FM) Sanford NC
*WSNC(FM) Winston-Salem NC
*KCND(FM) Bismarck ND
*KPPD(FM) Devils Lake ND
*KDPR(FM) Dickinson ND
*KFJM(FM) Grand Forks ND
*KPRJ(FM) Jamestown ND
*KMPR(FM) Minot ND
*KPPR(FM) Williston ND
*KLPR(FM) Kearney NE
*KZUM(FM) Lincoln NE
*KIOS-FM Omaha NE
*WNEC-FM Henniker NH
*WBGO(FM) Newark NJ
*WRTQ(FM) Ocean City NJ
WPRB(FM) Princeton NJ
*KGLP(FM) Gallup NM
*KRWG(FM) Las Cruces NM
KSFR(FM) White Rock NM
*KRNM(FM) Chalan Kanoa-Saipan NP
*KNCC(FM) Elko NV
*KBSJ(FM) Jackpot NV
*KUNV(FM) Las Vegas NV
*KUNR(FM) Reno NV
KJZS(FM) Sparks NV
*WSQX-FM Binghamton NY
*WCWP(FM) Brookville NY
*WBFO(FM) Buffalo NY
*WEOS(FM) Geneva NY
*WGMC(FM) Greece NY
*WRCU-FM Hamilton NY
*WVHC(FM) Herkimer NY
*WSQA(FM) Hornell NY
*WUBJ(FM) Jamestown NY
*WHCR-FM New York NY
*WKCR-FM New York NY
*WOLN(FM) Olean NY
WJZR(FM) Rochester NY
*WLIU(FM) Southampton NY
*WAER(FM) Syracuse NY
*WBGU(FM) Bowling Green OH
*WCPN(FM) Cleveland OH
*WDPS(FM) Dayton OH
*WMRT(FM) Marietta OH
*WMUB(FM) Oxford OH
WJZA(FM) Pickerington OH
*WXTS-FM Toledo OH
*WCSU-FM Wilberforce OH
*KALU(FM) Langston OK
*KGOU(FM) Norman OK
*KROU(FM) Spencer OK
KSMF(FM) Ashland OR
*KSBA(FM) Coos Bay OR

*KBVR(FM) Corvallis OR
*KMHD(FM) Gresham OR
*KSKF(FM) Klamath Falls OR
*KLCO(FM) Newport OR
*WBUQ(FM) Bloomsburg PA
*WRTL(FM) Ephrata PA
*WQLN-FM Erie PA
*WRTY(FM) Jackson Township PA
*WRTI(FM) Philadelphia PA
*WDUQ(FM) Pittsburgh PA
*WXAC(FM) Reading PA
*WUSR(FM) Scranton PA
*WVIA-FM Scranton PA
*WJAZ(FM) Summerdale PA
*WPTC(FM) Williamsport PA
*WVYA(FM) Williamsport PA
WIBS(AM) Guayama PR
WYAS(FM) Vieques PR
*WELH(FM) Providence RI
*WSSB-FM Orangeburg SC
KPSD(FM) Faith SD
*KQSD-FM Lowry SD
*KZSD-FM Martin SD
*KDSD-FM Pierpont SD
*KBHE-FM Rapid City SD
*KTSD-FM Reliance SD
*KUSD-FM Vermillion SD
WBOL(AM) Bolivar TN
*WFHU(FM) Henderson TN
*WUOT(FM) Knoxville TN
*WFMQ(FM) Lebanon TN
*WUMR(FM) Memphis TN
*WMOT(FM) Murfreesboro TN
*WRVU(FM) Nashville TN
*KAZI-FM Austin TX
*KVLU(FM) Beaumont TX
*KAMU-FM College Station TX
*KETR(FM) Commerce TX
*KEDT-FM Corpus Christi TX
*KTEP(FM) El Paso TX
*KTCU-FM Fort Worth TX
*KMBH-FM Harlingen TX
*KTSU(FM) Houston TX
*KSHU(FM) Huntsville TX
*KTXT-FM Lubbock TX
*KLDN(FM) Lufkin TX
*KHID(FM) McAllen TX
*KNTU(FM) McKinney TX
*KSAU(FM) Nacogdoches TX
*KWLD(FM) Plainview TX
*KRTU(FM) San Antonio TX
*KVRT(FM) Victoria TX
*KMCU(FM) Wichita Falls TX
*KUSR(FM) Logan UT
*KUER(FM) Salt Lake City UT
*WVTU(FM) Charlottesville VA
*WVTW(FM) Charlottesville VA
*WVTR(FM) Marion VA
*WHRV(FM) Norfolk VA
*WVST-FM Petersburg VA
*WVRU(FM) Radford VA
*WVTF(FM) Roanoke VA
WISE-FM Wise VA
*WRUV(FM) Burlington VT
*WVPS(FM) Burlington VT
*WNCH(FM) Norwich VT
*WRVT(FM) Rutland VT
*WVPA(FM) Saint Johnsbury VT
*WVPR(FM) Windsor VT
*KBCS(FM) Bellevue WA
*KZAZ(FM) Bellingham WA
*KEWU-FM Cheney WA
KOHO-FM Leavenworth WA
*KPLI(FM) Olympia WA
*KVIX(FM) Port Angeles WA
*KZUU(FM) Pullman WA
*KPBX-FM Spokane WA
*KPLU-FM Tacoma WA
KYNR(AM) Toppenish WA
*WUEC(FM) Eau Claire WI
*WLSU(FM) La Crosse WI
*WWSP(FM) Stevens Point WI
*WVPB(FM) Beckley WV
*WVPW(FM) Buckhannon WV
*WVPN(FM) Charleston WV
*WVWV(FM) Huntington WV

*WVEP(FM) Martinsburg WV
*WVPM(FM) Morgantown WV
*WVPG(FM) Parkersburg WV
*WVNP(FM) Wheeling WV
*KUWL(FM) Laramie WY
*KCWC-FM Riverton WY
*KPRQ(FM) Sheridan WY

Korean

KXMX(AM) Anaheim CA
KMPC(AM) Los Angeles CA
KYPA(AM) Los Angeles CA
KFOX(AM) Torrance CA
KHRA(AM) Honolulu HI
KREA(AM) Honolulu HI
WKTA(AM) Evanston IL
WWRU(AM) Jersey City NJ
WDCT(AM) Fairfax VA
KWYZ(AM) Everett WA
KSUH(AM) Puyallup WA

Light Rock

WPPG(FM) Repton AL
KSMJ(FM) Shafter CA
WLRQ-FM Cocoa FL
WMEZ(FM) Pensacola FL
WEGC(FM) Sasser GA
WTGA(AM) Thomaston GA
WTGA-FM Thomaston GA
KDAT(FM) Cedar Rapids IA
KLLT(FM) Spencer IA
WAVJ(FM) Princeton KY
WVLE(FM) Scottsville KY
KQIS(FM) Basile LA
WCDV(FM) Hammond LA
WVIC(FM) Jackson MI
WSAG(FM) Linwood MI
KBEK(FM) Mora MN
KRVY-FM Starbuck MN
KHME(FM) Winona MN
KYYA-FM Billings MT
KVWE(FM) Frenchtown MT
WOXL-FM Biltmore Forest NC
*WCCE(FM) Buie's Creek NC
WCNG(FM) Murphy NC
KZPR(FM) Minot ND
KOZY-FM Bridgeport NE
KSFT-FM South Sioux City NE
WFPG(FM) Atlantic City NJ
WBTA(AM) Batavia NY
WWFS(FM) New York NY
WDOH(FM) Delphos OH
KDEP(FM) Garibaldi OR
WLTJ(FM) Pittsburgh PA
WSBG(FM) Stroudsburg PA
WWLI(FM) Providence RI
KJAM(AM) Madison SD
KOLY(AM) Mobridge SD
KVIL(FM) Highland Park-Dallas TX
KRSR(FM) Ingleside TX
KLFX(FM) Nolanville TX
KODM(FM) Odessa TX
*KYQX(FM) Weatherford TX
KRPX(FM) Wellington UT
WJDV(FM) Broadway VA
*KTCV(FM) Kennewick WA
WLDB(FM) Milwaukee WI
WSWW-FM Craigsville WV

MOR

KGTL(AM) Homer AK
KIFW(AM) Sitka AK
*WSTF(FM) Andalusia AL
*WDYF(FM) Dothan AL
WHEP(AM) Foley AL
WLVV(AM) Mobile AL
*WLBF(FM) Montgomery AL
WNZZ(AM) Montgomery AL
WTLM(AM) Opelika AL
KFFB(FM) Fairfield Bay AR
KOOU(AM) Hardy AR
KVRE(FM) Hot Springs Village AR

KTLO-FM Mountain Home AR
KYBC(AM) Cottonwood AZ
KGIL(AM) Beverly Hills CA
KWXY-FM Cathedral City CA
KNTI(FM) Lakeport CA
KXBX(AM) Lakeport CA
*KADV(FM) Modesto CA
KESP(AM) Modesto CA
KLXR(AM) Redding CA
KEZW(AM) Aurora CO
*KTSG(FM) Steamboat Springs CO
KRDZ(AM) Wray CO
WQUN(AM) Hamden CT
WWFL(AM) Clermont FL
WROD(AM) Daytona Beach FL
WTOT-FM Graceville FL
WOSN(FM) Indian River Shores FL
WONN(AM) Lakeland FL
*WJTF(FM) Panama City FL
WITS(AM) Sebring FL
WGHC(AM) Clayton GA
WCON(AM) Cornelia GA
WSGC(AM) Elberton GA
WLRR(FM) Milledgeville GA
WMNZ(AM) Montezuma GA
WNEG(AM) Toccoa GA
*WRAF-FM Toccoa Falls GA
WLOV(AM) Washington GA
*WYFW(FM) Winder GA
KUAM(AM) Hagatna GU
KJAN(AM) Atlantic IA
KBUR(AM) Burlington IA
KCHA(AM) Charles City IA
KDEC(AM) Decorah IA
KRNT(AM) Des Moines IA
KMAQ-FM Maquoketa IA
KPTO(AM) Pocatello ID
WFRL(AM) Freeport IL
WAIK(AM) Galesburg IL
WHHL(FM) Jerseyville IL
WLRB(AM) Macomb IL
WLBH(AM) Mattoon IL
WCSJ(AM) Morris IL
WCSJ-FM Morris IL
WNTA(AM) Rockford IL
WBNL(AM) Boonville IN
WGL-FM Huntington IN
WLOI(AM) La Porte IN
KABI(AM) Abilene KS
*KONQ(FM) Dodge City KS
KIND(AM) Independence KS
WCTT(AM) Corbin KY
WSON(AM) Henderson KY
WYMC(AM) Mayfield KY
WEMD(AM) Easton MD
WVAE(AM) Biddeford ME
XETRA(AM) Tijuana MEX
WAAM(AM) Ann Arbor MI
WAKV(AM) Otsego MI
WMJH(AM) Rockford MI
KATE(AM) Albert Lea MN
*KMSK(FM) Austin MN
KROX(AM) Crookston MN
KMRS(AM) Morris MN
WCMP(AM) Pine City MN
WMIN(AM) Sauk Rapids MN
KTRF(AM) Thief River Falls MN
KCXL(AM) Liberty MO
KBFL(AM) Springfield MO
KWKJ(FM) Windsor MO
*KDWG(FM) Dillon MT
KXGF(AM) Great Falls MT
KMMR(FM) Malta MT
WSQL(AM) Brevard NC
WBAG(AM) Burlington-Graham NC
WAZZ(AM) Fayetteville NC
WCVP(AM) Murphy NC
WIOZ(AM) Pinehurst NC
WSAT(AM) Salisbury NC
WAME(AM) Statesville NC
KBRB(AM) Ainsworth NE
WWNH(AM) Madbury NH
WFEA(AM) Manchester NH
WOF(AM) Andover NJ
WCMC(AM) Wildwood NJ
KATK(AM) Carlsbad NM

KKOB Exp Stn Santa Fe NM
WKLI-FM Albany NY
WINR(AM) Binghamton NY
WCGR(AM) Canandaigua NY
*WITR(FM) Henrietta NY
WHUC(AM) Hudson NY
WVIP(AM) New Rochelle NY
WTLA(AM) North Syracuse NY
WOEN(AM) Olean NY
WSGO(AM) Oswego NY
*WPSA(FM) Paul Smiths NY
WTLB(AM) Utica NY
WFAS(AM) White Plains NY
WAKR(AM) Akron OH
WATH(AM) Athens OH
WBNO-FM Bryan OH
WBCO(AM) Bucyrus OH
WILE-FM Byesville OH
WMNI(AM) Columbus OH
WLGN(AM) Logan OH
WIOI(AM) New Boston OH
WCHO(AM) Washington Court House OH
WYPC(AM) Wellston OH
WHIZ(AM) Zanesville OH
*KFXU(FM) Chickasha OK
KAJO(AM) Grants Pass OR
KSHO(AM) Lebanon OR
KBCH(AM) Lincoln City OR
KOOR(AM) Milwaukie OR
KTIL-FM Tillamook OR
WEST(AM) Easton PA
WFRA(AM) Franklin PA
WQMU(FM) Indiana PA
WCRO(AM) Johnstown PA
WEGH(FM) Northumberland PA
WOYL(AM) Oil City PA
WHAT(AM) Philadelphia PA
WJAS(AM) Pittsburgh PA
WNBT(AM) Wellsboro PA
WMSW(AM) Hatillo PR
WISA(AM) Isabela PR
WPPC(AM) Penuelas PR
WBMJ(AM) San Juan PR
WIVV(AM) Vieques PR
WXEW(AM) Yabucoa PR
*WEPC(FM) Belton SC
WCRS(AM) Greenwood SC
*WKCL(FM) Ladson SC
WAVO(AM) Rock Hill SC
WSNW(AM) Seneca SC
KWAT(AM) Watertown SD
WAMB(AM) Nashville TN
WKTI(AM) Powell TN
KAAM(AM) Garland TX
KMVL(AM) Madisonville TX
KLBW(AM) New Boston TX
KAHL(AM) San Antonio TX
KDAE(AM) Sinton TX
KSST(AM) Sulphur Springs TX
KLGN(AM) Logan UT
KOGN(AM) Ogden UT
KENT(AM) Parowan UT
KNFL(AM) Tremonton UT
WPYA(FM) Chesapeake VA
WCVA(AM) Culpeper VA
WMXH-FM Luray VA
WVCV(AM) Orange VA
WMXB(FM) Richmond VA
WRVQ(FM) Richmond VA
WTON-FM Staunton VA
WMBG(AM) Williamsburg VA
KEYF(AM) Dishman WA
KIXI(AM) Mercer Island-Seattle WA
KKAD(AM) Vancouver WA
WATK(AM) Antigo WI
*WLBL(AM) Auburndale WI
*WJTY(FM) Lancaster WI
WOMT(AM) Manitowoc WI
WJMT(AM) Merrill WI
WRIT-FM Milwaukee WI
WJUB(AM) Plymouth WI
WRCO(AM) Richland Center WI
WXCX(FM) Siren WI
WKLP(AM) Keyser WV
*WHFI(FM) Lindside WV

WWYO(AM) Pineville WV
WSLW(AM) White Sulphur Springs WV
KWYO(AM) Sheridan WY

Native American

*KNBA(FM) Anchorage AK
*KUYI(FM) Hotevilla AZ
*KRMH(FM) Red Mesa AZ
*KOHN(FM) Sells AZ
*KGHR(FM) Tuba City AZ
*KSUT(FM) Ignacio CO
WKAM(AM) Goshen IN
*KHEW(FM) Rocky Boy's Reservation MT
*KINI(FM) Crookston NE
KGAK(AM) Gallup NM

New Age

*KFJC(FM) Los Altos CA
KEST(AM) San Francisco CA
*KBSM(FM) McCall ID
*WNUR-FM Evanston IL
*KHCT(FM) Great Bend KS
*KHCC-FM Hutchinson KS
*KHCD(FM) Salina KS
*WYAJ(FM) Sudbury MA
*WMTB-FM Emmittsburg MD
WELY-FM Ely MN
*KCOZ(FM) Point Lookout MO
*KLPR(FM) Kearney NE
*WNEC-FM Henniker NH
WBUZ(FM) La Vergne TN
*KGHP(FM) Gig Harbor WA
*KCWC-FM Riverton WY

News

*KSKA(FM) Anchorage AK
KYKD(FM) Bethel AK
KLAM(AM) Cordova AK
KFBX(AM) Fairbanks AK
*KTOO(FM) Juneau AK
*KDLL(FM) Kenai AK
*KMXT(FM) Kodiak AK
KAKN(FM) Naknek AK
*KCAW(FM) Sitka AK
WNSI-FM Atmore AL
*WBHM(FM) Birmingham AL
WHOS(AM) Decatur AL
*WRWA(FM) Dothan AL
WULA(AM) Eufaula AL
*WSGN(FM) Gadsden AL
WJBB(AM) Haleyville AL
*WLRH(FM) Huntsville AL
WNZZ(AM) Montgomery AL
*WTSU(FM) Montgomery-Troy AL
*WQPR(FM) Muscle Shoals AL
*WAPR(FM) Selma AL
KEWI(AM) Benton AR
*KUCA(FM) Conway AR
*KBSA(FM) El Dorado AR
*KUAF(FM) Fayetteville AR
KXJK(AM) Forrest City AR
*KASU Jonesboro AR
KBOK(AM) Malvern AR
KARN-FM Sheridan AR
KWAK(AM) Stuttgart AR
KFNX(AM) Cave Creek AZ
*KNAU(FM) Flagstaff AZ
*KPUB(FM) Flagstaff AZ
*KNAG(FM) Grand Canyon AZ
*KNAD(FM) Page AZ
*KBAQ-FM Phoenix AZ
KIDR(AM) Phoenix AZ
*KJZZ(FM) Phoenix AZ
*KNAQ(FM) Prescott AZ
*KNAA(FM) Show Low AZ
KCUB(AM) Tucson AZ
KQTH(FM) Tucson AZ
*KUAZ(AM) Tucson AZ
*KAWC-FM Yuma AZ
*KHSU-FM Arcata CA
*KPRX(FM) Bakersfield CA

KSZL(AM) Barstow CA
*KNCA(FM) Burney CA
*KCHO(FM) Chico CA
*KHSR(FM) Crescent City CA
*KVPR(FM) Fresno CA
*KFRN(AM) Long Beach CA
KFWB(AM) Los Angeles CA
KNX(AM) Los Angeles CA
*KLDD(FM) McCloud CA
*KCRY(AM) Mojave CA
*KNSQ(FM) Mount Shasta CA
KTOX(AM) Needles CA
*KCRU(FM) Oxnard CA
*KAZU(FM) Pacific Grove CA
KPSI(AM) Palm Springs CA
KDOW(AM) Palo Alto CA
*KZYX(FM) Philo CA
KAHZ(AM) Pomona CA
*KQNC(FM) Quincy CA
KQMS(AM) Redding CA
*KNHT(FM) Rio Dell CA
*KVCR(FM) San Bernardino CA
KCBS(AM) San Francisco CA
KFRC-FM San Francisco CA
KGO(AM) San Francisco CA
KSFO(AM) San Francisco CA
KLIV(AM) San Jose CA
*KCBX(FM) San Luis Obispo CA
*KCRW(FM) Santa Monica CA
KJPR(AM) Shasta Lake City CA
*KUOP(FM) Stockton CA
*KXJS(FM) Sutter CA
*KKTO(FM) Tahoe City CA
*KCLU-FM Thousand Oaks CA
*KZYZ(FM) Willits CA
*KNYR(FM) Yreka CA
*KRZA(FM) Alamosa CO
KNFO(FM) Basalt CO
KCFC(AM) Boulder CO
*KCJX(FM) Carbondale CO
*KRCC(FM) Colorado Springs CO
*KPYR(FM) Craig CO
*KCFR(AM) Denver CO
*KDNK(FM) Glenwood Springs CO
*KPRN(FM) Grand Junction CO
*KUNC(FM) Greeley CO
KPKE(AM) Gunnison CO
*KECC(FM) La Junta CO
*KPRH(FM) Montrose CO
KVMT(FM) Montrose CO
*KVNF(FM) Paonia CO
*KCFP(FM) Pueblo CO
KKPC(AM) Pueblo CO
*KCCS(FM) Starkville CO
*KRNC(FM) Steamboat Springs CO
*KPRE(FM) Vail CO
WGCH(AM) Greenwich CT
WQUN(AM) Hamden CT
*WFED(AM) Washington DC
WTOP-FM Washington DC
WILM(AM) Wilmington DE
WTAN(AM) Clearwater FL
WMGG(AM) Dunedin FL
*WGCU-FM Fort Myers FL
*WQCS(FM) Fort Pierce FL
*WJUF(FM) Inverness FL
WBXY(FM) La Crosse FL
*WMKO(FM) Marco FL
*WFIT(FM) Melbourne FL
WEBY(AM) Milton FL
WMFE-FM Orlando FL
*WFSW(FM) Panama City FL
*WKGC-FM Panama City FL
WPNN(AM) Pensacola FL
*WUWF(FM) Pensacola FL
*WANM(FM) Tallahassee FL
*WUSF(FM) Tampa FL
*WXEL(FM) West Palm Beach FL
V6AK(AM) Truk FM
*V6AI(AM) Yap FM
*WUNV(FM) Albany GA
*WUGA(FM) Athens GA
*WACG-FM Augusta GA
WBBQ-FM Augusta GA
WNRR(AM) Augusta GA
*WWIO(FM) Brunswick GA

*WUWG(FM) Carrollton GA
WBHF(AM) Cartersville GA
WYXC(AM) Cartersville GA
*WNGH-FM Chatsworth GA
WRBN(FM) Clayton GA
*WMUM-FM Cochran GA
WDAK(AM) Columbus GA
*WTJB(FM) Columbus GA
*WNGU(FM) Dahlonega GA
*WPPR(FM) Demorest GA
WUFF-FM Eastman GA
*WJWV(FM) Fort Gaines GA
WKEU(AM) Griffin GA
WCEH(AM) Hawkinsville GA
WQCH(AM) La Fayette GA
WMVG(AM) Milledgeville GA
WCNN(AM) North Atlanta GA
*WGPB(FM) Rome GA
WWIO(AM) Saint Mary's GA
*WSVH(FM) Savannah GA
WJAT(AM) Swainsboro GA
*WABR(FM) Tifton GA
WNEG(AM) Toccoa GA
*WWET(FM) Valdosta GA
WVOP(AM) Vidalia GA
*WJSP-FM Warm Springs GA
*WXVS(FM) Waycross GA
*KPRG(FM) Hagatna GU
KRTR(AM) Honolulu HI
KJAN(AM) Atlantic IA
*KWOI(FM) Carroll IA
*KUNI(FM) Cedar Falls IA
*KLNI(FM) Decorah IA
KILR-FM Estherville IA
KIOW(FM) Forest City IA
*KTPR(FM) Fort Dodge IA
KVFD(AM) Fort Dodge IA
KXIC(AM) Iowa City IA
KIFG-FM Iowa Falls IA
*KOWI(FM) Lamoni IA
KLEM(AM) Le Mars IA
*KRNI(AM) Mason City IA
*KUNY(FM) Mason City IA
*KDMR(FM) Mitchellville IA
KCOB(AM) Newton IA
KAYL-FM Storm Lake IA
KCII-FM Washington IA
*KBSU-FM Boise ID
*KBSX(FM) Boise ID
*KIBX(FM) Bonners Ferry ID
KVNI(AM) Coeur d'Alene ID
*KNWO(FM) Cottonwood ID
*KBSM(FM) McCall ID
*KBSQ(FM) McCall ID
*KRFA-FM Moscow ID
KIDO(AM) Nampa ID
*KBYI(FM) Rexburg ID
*KBSS(FM) Sun Valley ID
WRMJ(FM) Aledo IL
*WSIU-FM Carbondale IL
WBBM(AM) Chicago IL
*WCRX(FM) Chicago IL
*WNIJ(FM) De Kalb IL
WIXN(AM) Dixon IL
*WNIE(FM) Freeport IL
*WDCB(FM) Glen Ellyn IL
WKIF(FM) Kankakee IL
*WNIW(FM) La Salle IL
WSMI-FM Litchfield IL
*WIUM(FM) Macomb IL
*WVSI(FM) Mount Vernon IL
*WUSI(FM) Olney IL
WPRS(AM) Paris IL
*WIPA(FM) Pittsfield IL
*WQUB(FM) Quincy IL
*WVIK(FM) Rock Island IL
WNTA(AM) Rockford IL
WJBD-FM Salem IL
WCCI(FM) Savanna IL
*WUIS(FM) Springfield IL
WSDR(AM) Sterling IL
*WIUW(FM) Warsaw IL
WFRX(AM) West Frankfort IL
*WBSB(FM) Anderson IN
WBIW(AM) Bedford IN
WZBD(FM) Berne IN

*WFHB(FM) Bloomington IN
*WFIU(FM) Bloomington IN
WREB(FM) Greencastle IN
*WBSH(FM) Hagerstown IN
WXGO(AM) Madison IN
*WBSW(FM) Marion IN
*WBST(FM) Muncie IN
WLBC-FM Muncie IN
*WBSJ(FM) Portland IN
WRAY(AM) Princeton IN
WSLM-FM Salem IN
WZZB(AM) Seymour IN
WAKE(AM) Valparaiso IN
*WBAA-FM West Lafayette IN
KGNO(AM) Dodge City KS
KVOE(AM) Emporia KS
*KHCT(FM) Great Bend KS
KVGB(AM) Great Bend KS
*KHCC-FM Hutchinson KS
KWBW(AM) Hutchinson KS
KKAN(AM) Phillipsburg KS
*KRPS(FM) Pittsburg KS
*KHCD(FM) Salina KS
KMZA(FM) Seneca KS
*KMUW(FM) Wichita KS
*WBRT(AM) Bardstown KY
*WKYU-FM Bowling Green KY
*WEKF(FM) Corbin KY
WCPM(AM) Cumberland KY
*WKUE(FM) Elizabethtown KY
*WEKH(FM) Hazard KY
*WKPB(FM) Henderson KY
*WNKU(FM) Highland Heights KY
WLAP(AM) Lexington KY
*WUKY(FM) Lexington KY
WKJK(AM) Louisville KY
WTTL(AM) Madisonville KY
*WKMS-FM Murray KY
WNBS(AM) Murray KY
*WEKU(FM) Richmond KY
*WDCL-FM Somerset KY
WMSK-FM Sturgis KY
*KLSA(FM) Alexandria LA
WJBO(AM) Baton Rouge LA
KEUN(AM) Eunice LA
WWL-FM Kenner LA
KVOL(AM) Lafayette LA
*WRBH(FM) New Orleans LA
*WWNO(FM) New Orleans LA
KSLO(AM) Opelousas LA
*KDAQ(FM) Shreveport LA
KRMD(AM) Shreveport LA
*WHAB(FM) Acton MA
*WFCR(FM) Amherst MA
*WBUR-FM Boston MA
*WGBH(FM) Boston MA
WHMQ(AM) Greenfield MA
WBIX(AM) Natick MA
WTLP(AM) Braddock Heights MD
WWFD(AM) Frederick MD
*WSCL(FM) Salisbury MD
*WMEH(FM) Bangor ME
*WMED(FM) Calais ME
WCXU(FM) Caribou ME
WCXX(FM) Madawaska ME
WEGP(AM) Presque Isle ME
WCXV(FM) Van Buren ME
*WGVU-FM Allendale MI
*WCML-FM Alpena MI
*WUCX-FM Bay City MI
WNEM(AM) Bridgeport MI
*WNZK(AM) Dearborn Heights MI
*WDET-FM Detroit MI
WJR(AM) Detroit MI
WWJ(AM) Detroit MI
*WICV(FM) East Jordan MI
*WKAR-FM East Lansing MI
WMJZ-FM Gaylord MI
*WBLU(FM) Grand Rapids MI
WGLM(AM) Greenville MI
*WCMW-FM Harbor Springs MI
*WGGL-FM Houghton MI
*WIAA(FM) Interlochen MI
*WMUK(FM) Kalamazoo MI
WJNL(AM) Kingsley MI
WJIM(AM) Lansing MI

*WIAB(FM) Mackinaw City MI
*WNMU-FM Marquette MI
*WCMU-FM Mount Pleasant MI
WKBZ(AM) Muskegon MI
*WCMB-FM Oscoda MI
*WCMZ-FM Sault Ste. Marie MI
WWCM(FM) Standish MI
WMSH(AM) Sturgis MI
*WICA(FM) Traverse City MI
*WBLV(FM) Twin Lake MI
WGVS-FM Whitehall MI
*WEMU(FM) Ypsilanti MI
WPNW(AM) Zeeland MI
KASM(AM) Albany MN
*KNCM(FM) Appleton MN
*KNSE(FM) Austin MN
*KNBJ(FM) Bemidji MN
*KBPN(FM) Brainerd MN
*WIRN(FM) Buhl MN
*WSCN(FM) Cloquet MN
*KNSR(FM) Collegeville MN
KSUM(AM) Fairmont MN
KDHL(AM) Faribault MN
*KNWF(FM) Fergus Falls MN
*WLSN(FM) Grand Marais MN
KDWA(AM) Hastings MN
KDUZ(AM) Hutchinson MN
*KITF(FM) International Falls MN
*KXLC(FM) La Crescent MN
*KMSU(FM) Mankato MN
*KTIS(AM) Minneapolis MN
*KNOW-FM Minneapolis-St. Paul MN
*KCCD(FM) Moorhead MN
WCMP(AM) Pine City MN
WCMP-FM Pine City MN
KLOH(AM) Pipestone MN
*KRFI(FM) Redwood Falls MN
*KZSE(FM) Rochester MN
*KNGA(FM) Saint Peter MN
*KNTN(FM) Thief River Falls MN
KTRF(AM) Thief River Falls MN
KOWZ(AM) Waseca MN
KSGF-FM Ash Grove MO
KAAN(AM) Bethany MO
KAAN-FM Bethany MO
KAPE(AM) Cape Girardeau MO
*KRCU(FM) Cape Girardeau MO
KCHI(AM) Chillicothe MO
KCHI-FM Chillicothe MO
*KRNW(FM) Chillicothe MO
KDKD-FM Clinton MO
*KBIA(FM) Columbia MO
*KSEF(FM) Farmington MO
KYOO-FM Halfway MO
*KCUR-FM Kansas City MO
KMBZ(AM) Kansas City MO
*KKTR(FM) Kirksville MO
KNIM(AM) Maryville MO
*KXCV(FM) Maryville MO
KXEO(AM) Mexico MO
KBDZ(FM) Perryville MO
*KSMS-FM Point Lookout MO
KMIS(AM) Portageville MO
KYRO(AM) Potosi MO
*KMST(FM) Rolla MO
*KWMU(FM) Saint Louis MO
KLFJ(AM) Springfield MO
*KSMU(FM) Springfield MO
KSAR(FM) Thayer MO
KTTN-FM Trenton MO
*KSMW(FM) West Plains MO
WWZQ(AM) Aberdeen MS
*WMAE-FM Booneville MS
WHSY(AM) Hattiesburg MS
*WURC(FM) Holly Springs MS
*WJSU(FM) Jackson MS
*WMPN-FM Jackson MS
*WMAB-FM Mississippi State MS
*WMAV-FM Oxford MS
KBUL(AM) Billings MT
*KEMC(FM) Billings MT
*KBMC(FM) Bozeman MT
*KAPC(FM) Butte MT
*KGPR(FM) Great Falls MT
*KUFN(FM) Hamilton MT
KHDN(AM) Hardin MT

*KUHM(FM) Helena MT
*KUKL(FM) Kalispell MT
KBSR(AM) Laurel MT
*WCQS(FM) Asheville NC
WLOE(AM) Eden NC
*WFSS(FM) Fayetteville NC
*WFQS(FM) Franklin NC
WTRU(AM) Kernersville NC
*WKNS(FM) Kinston NC
WMYN(AM) Mayodan NC
WCVP(AM) Murphy NC
*WTEB(FM) New Bern NC
*WZNB(FM) New Bern NC
*WZRN(FM) Norlina NC
WGCR(AM) Pisgah Forest NC
WAYN(AM) Rockingham NC
*WNCW(FM) Spindale NC
WSIC(AM) Statesville NC
WRGC(AM) Sylva NC
*WHQR(FM) Wilmington NC
*WFDD-FM Winston-Salem NC
*KCND(FM) Bismarck ND
KDAK(AM) Carrington ND
KDLR(AM) Devils Lake ND
*KPPD(FM) Devils Lake ND
*KDPR(FM) Dickinson ND
*KFBN(FM) Fargo ND
KKXL(AM) Grand Forks ND
*KPRJ(FM) Jamestown ND
*KMPR(FM) Minot ND
KDDR(AM) Oakes ND
KOVC(AM) Valley City ND
*KPPR(FM) Williston ND
*KTNE-FM Alliance NE
KNCY-FM Auburn NE
*KMNE-FM Bassett NE
*KCNE-FM Chadron NE
KGMT(AM) Fairbury NE
*KHNE-FM Hastings NE
KRVN(AM) Lexington NE
KRVN-FM Lexington NE
*KUCV(FM) Lincoln NE
*KRNE-FM Merriman NE
*KXNE-FM Norfolk NE
*KPNE-FM North Platte NE
WKBK(AM) Keene NH
WASR(AM) Wolfeboro NH
*WBJB-FM Lincroft NJ
KDEF(AM) Albuquerque NM
*KGLP(FM) Gallup NM
KRSN(AM) Los Alamos NM
KMTH(FM) Maljamar NM
*KTDB(FM) Ramah NM
KRUI(AM) Ruidoso Downs NM
KCHS(AM) Truth or Consequences NM
*KNCC(FM) Elko NV
KRJC(FM) Elko NV
KTSN(AM) Elko NV
*KNPR(FM) Las Vegas NV
KRLV(AM) Las Vegas NV
*KWPR(FM) Lund NV
*KLNR(FM) Panaca NV
*KUNR(FM) Reno NV
*KTPH(FM) Tonopah NV
*WAMC-FM Albany NY
WVTL(AM) Amsterdam NY
WYSL(AM) Avon NY
*WSKG-FM Binghamton NY
*WSQX-FM Binghamton NY
*WCWP(FM) Brookville NY
*WBFO(FM) Buffalo NY
*WSQE(FM) Corning NY
*WGSU(FM) Geneseo NY
*WSQA(FM) Hornell NY
*WSQG-FM Ithaca NY
WJTN(AM) Jamestown NY
*WUBJ(FM) Jamestown NY
WLLG(FM) Lowville NY
*WOSR(FM) Middletown NY
WBBR(AM) New York NY
WCBS(AM) New York NY
WINS(AM) New York NY
*WNYC-FM New York NY
*WOLN(FM) Olean NY
*WSQC-FM Oneonta NY
*WDFH(FM) Ossining NY

WEBO(AM) Owego NY
*WCEL(FM) Plattsburgh NY
WRCR(AM) Spring Valley NY
*WAER(FM) Syracuse NY
*WANC(FM) Ticonderoga NY
WTNY(AM) Watertown NY
WUAM(AM) Watervliet NY
WAKR(AM) Akron OH
*WYBL(FM) Ashtabula OH
*WCVV(FM) Belpre OH
*WGBE(FM) Bryan OH
WAIS(AM) Buchtel OH
WCSM-FM Celina OH
*WCPN(FM) Cleveland OH
*WCBE(FM) Columbus OH
*WGDE(FM) Defiance OH
*WKSU(FM) Kent OH
*WGLE(FM) Lima OH
WLTP(AM) Marietta OH
WMOA(AM) Marietta OH
*WKRJ(FM) New Philadelphia OH
*WNRK(FM) Norwalk OH
*WKSV(FM) Thompson OH
*WGTE-FM Toledo OH
*WKRW(FM) Wooster OH
*WYSO(FM) Yellow Springs OH
*WYSU(FM) Youngstown OH
*KOCU(FM) Altus OK
*KYCU(FM) Clinton OK
KCRC(AM) Enid OK
KIHN(AM) Hugo OK
*KOSN(FM) Ketchum OK
*KCCU(FM) Lawton OK
KOKL(AM) Okmulgee OK
KPGM(AM) Pawhuska OK
*KOSU(FM) Stillwater OK
*KWGS(FM) Tulsa OK
*KSMF(FM) Ashland OR
*KSOR(FM) Ashland OR
*KOAB-FM Bend OR
KZZR(AM) Burns OR
*KSBA(FM) Coos Bay OR
*KLFO(FM) Florence OR
*KAGI(AM) Grants Pass OR
*KLMF(FM) Klamath Falls OR
*KSKF(FM) Klamath Falls OR
*KTVR-FM La Grande OR
*KOAP(FM) Lakeview OR
KGAL(AM) Lebanon OR
*KOOZ(FM) Myrtle Point OR
*KLCO(FM) Newport OR
*KRBM(FM) Pendleton OR
KUMA(AM) Pendleton OR
KCMX(AM) Phoenix OR
KEX(AM) Portland OR
*KOPB-FM Portland OR
*KSRS(FM) Roseburg OR
*KTBR(AM) Roseburg OR
*KSJK(AM) Talent OR
*WDIY(FM) Allentown PA
WBVP(AM) Beaver Falls PA
*WFSE(FM) Edinboro PA
*WQLN-FM Erie PA
WFRA(AM) Franklin PA
WGET(AM) Gettysburg PA
WWBJ(AM) Martinsburg PA
WKQW-FM Oil City PA
KYW(AM) Philadelphia PA
*WHYY-FM Philadelphia PA
KQV(AM) Pittsburgh PA
*WDUQ(FM) Pittsburgh PA
WECZ(AM) Punxsutawney PA
*WVIA-FM Scranton PA
*WPSU(FM) State College PA
WLIH(FM) Whitneyville PA
*WVYA(FM) Williamsport PA
WRXD(FM) Fajardo PR
WORA(AM) Mayaguez PR
WEKO(AM) Morovis PR
WEXS(AM) Patillas PR
WSOL(AM) San German PR
WCNX(AM) Hope Valley RI
WXNI(AM) Westerly RI
*WLJK(AM) Aiken SC
*WJWJ-FM Beaufort SC
*WSCI(FM) Charleston SC

*WLTR(FM) Columbia SC
*WHMC-FM Conway SC
WJMX(AM) Florence SC
*WEPR(FM) Greenville SC
WFXH(AM) Hilton Head Island SC
WRHM(FM) Lancaster SC
*WNSC-FM Rock Hill SC
WSNW(AM) Seneca SC
WBCU(AM) Union SC
KGIM(AM) Aberdeen SD
KBFS(AM) Belle Fourche SD
*KESD(FM) Brookings SD
KDSJ(AM) Deadwood SD
KPSD(FM) Faith SD
*KQSD-FM Lowry SD
KJAM-FM Madison SD
*KZSD-FM Martin SD
*KDSD-FM Pierpont SD
*KBHE-FM Rapid City SD
*KTSD-FM Reliance SD
*KNWC-FM Sioux Falls SD
*KNWC-FM Sioux Falls SD
*KRSD-FM Sioux Falls SD
*KUSD(FM) Vermillion SD
KWAT(AM) Watertown SD
WCTA(AM) Alamo TN
WJZM(AM) Clarksville TN
*WSMC-FM Collegedale TN
*WHRS(FM) Cookeville TN
WDXI(AM) Jackson TN
*WKNP(FM) Jackson TN
*WUOT(FM) Knoxville TN
WLIV(AM) Livingston TN
*WKNO-FM Memphis TN
*WYPL(FM) Memphis TN
*WPLN(FM) Nashville TN
WNTT(AM) Tazewell TN
*WTML(FM) Tullahoma TN
*KACU(FM) Abilene TX
*KUT(FM) Austin TX
KSKY(AM) Balch Springs TX
*KVLU(FM) Beaumont TX
KQTY(AM) Borger TX
KRHC(AM) Burnet TX
*KTXP(FM) Bushland TX
*KAMU-FM College Station TX
*KETR(FM) Commerce TX
*KEDT-FM Corpus Christi TX
KFXR(AM) Dallas TX
KRLD(AM) Dallas TX
*KTEP(FM) El Paso TX
*KMBH-FM Harlingen TX
*KPFT(FM) Houston TX
KTRH(AM) Houston TX
*KUHF(FM) Houston TX
*KSHU(FM) Huntsville TX
*KTXI(FM) Ingram TX
KAML(AM) Kenedy-Karnes City TX
*KLDN(FM) Lufkin TX
KCUL(AM) Marshall TX
*KHID(AM) McAllen TX
KWEL(AM) Midland TX
KGNB(AM) New Braunfels TX
*KOCV(FM) Odessa TX
KOGT(AM) Orange TX
KBUS(FM) Paris TX
KGKL(AM) San Angelo TX
*KUTX(FM) San Angelo TX
*KSTX(FM) San Antonio TX
KJIM(AM) Sherman TX
*KTOT(FM) Spearman TX
*KSQX(FM) Springtown TX
*KQXS(FM) Stephenville TX
*KVRT(FM) Victoria TX
*KMQX(FM) Weatherford TX
*KMCU(FM) Wichita Falls TX
KMTI(AM) Manti UT
KLO(AM) Ogden UT
KOGN(AM) Ogden UT
*KPCW-FM Park City UT
*KUER(FM) Salt Lake City UT
KNFL(AM) Tremonton UT
WKDE(AM) Altavista VA
WOWZ(AM) Appomattox VA
WDIC(AM) Clinchco VA
*WOTC(FM) Edinburg VA

*WEMC(FM) Harrisonburg VA
WLVA(AM) Lynchburg VA
WWWT-FM Manassas VA
WLEE(AM) Richmond VA
*WVTF(FM) Roanoke VA
*WISE-FM Wise VA
WYVE(AM) Wytheville VA
WJOY(AM) Burlington VT
*WVPS(FM) Burlington VT
*WNCH(FM) Norwich VT
*WRVT(FM) Rutland VT
*WVPA(FM) Saint Johnsbury VT
WDEV(AM) Waterbury VT
*WVPR(FM) Windsor VT
*KASB(FM) Bellevue WA
*KZAZ(FM) Bellingham WA
KOZI-FM Chelan WA
*KNWV(FM) Clarkston WA
*KGHP(FM) Gig Harbor WA
KEDO(AM) Longview WA
*KLWS(FM) Moses Lake WA
KOMO-FM Oakville WA
*KPLI(FM) Olympia WA
*KQWS(FM) Omak WA
*KNWP(FM) Port Angeles WA
*KVIX(FM) Port Angeles WA
*KWSU(FM) Pullman WA
KWNC(AM) Quincy WA
KOMO(AM) Seattle WA
KTTH(AM) Seattle WA
*KUOW-FM Seattle WA
KBBO(AM) Selah WA
*KPBX-FM Spokane WA
KSBN(AM) Spokane WA
*KSFC(FM) Spokane WA
*KPLU-FM Tacoma WA
KYNR(AM) Toppenish WA
KUOW(AM) Tumwater WA
*KNWY(FM) Yakima WA
WATW(AM) Ashland WI
*WUEC(FM) Eau Claire WI
*WPNE(FM) Green Bay WI
*WGTD(FM) Kenosha WI
*WLSU(FM) La Crosse WI
*WERN(FM) Madison WI
*WHA(AM) Madison WI
WISN(AM) Milwaukee WI
*WUWM(FM) Milwaukee WI
*WSSW(FM) Platteville WI
WRDB(AM) Reedsburg WI
WRCO-FM Richland Center WI
WEVR-FM River Falls WI
*WHND(FM) Sister Bay WI
WJJQ-FM Tomahawk WI
*WXPW(FM) Wausau WI
*WVPB(FM) Beckley WV
*WVPW(FM) Buckhannon WV
*WVPN(FM) Charleston WV
*WVWV(FM) Huntington WV
*WVEP(FM) Martinsburg WV
*WVPM(FM) Morgantown WV
*WVPG(FM) Parkersburg WV
*WAUA(FM) Petersburg WV
WRON(AM) Ronceverte WV
*WVNP(FM) Wheeling WV
KRSV(AM) Afton WY
*KBUW(FM) Buffalo WY
*KUWC(FM) Casper WY
*KDUW(FM) Douglas WY
*KUWG(FM) Gillette WY
*KUWJ(FM) Jackson WY
*KUWR(FM) Laramie WY
*KUWN(FM) Newcastle WY
*KUWX(FM) Pinedale WY
KPOW(AM) Powell WY
*KUWZ(FM) Rock Springs WY
*KPRQ(FM) Sheridan WY
*KSUW(FM) Sheridan WY
*KUWD(FM) Sundance WY
KYDT(FM) Sundance WY
KUWT(AM) Thermopolis WY

News/talk

KBYR(AM) Anchorage AK
KFQD(AM) Anchorage AK
KAGV(AM) Big Lake AK
*KCDS(FM) Deadhorse AK
KFAR(AM) Fairbanks AK
*KUAC(FM) Fairbanks AK
KTKN(AM) Ketchikan AK
*KXKM(FM) McCarthy AK
KIAM(AM) Nenana AK
*KNOM(AM) Nome AK
*KNOM-FM Nome AK
KIFW(AM) Sitka AK
KSRM(AM) Soldotna AK
*KTNA(FM) Talkeetna AK
WDNG(AM) Anniston AL
WVNN(AM) Athens AL
WAPI(AM) Birmingham AL
WERC(AM) Birmingham AL
WXAL(AM) Demopolis AL
WWNT(AM) Dothan AL
WBCF(AM) Florence AL
WHEP(AM) Foley AL
WAAX(AM) Gadsden AL
WGEA(AM) Geneva AL
WGYV(AM) Greenville AL
WGSV(AM) Guntersville AL
WDBT(FM) Headland AL
WERC-FM Hoover AL
WABB(AM) Mobile AL
WNTM(AM) Mobile AL
WACV(AM) Montgomery AL
WLWI(AM) Montgomery AL
WANI(AM) Opelika AL
WHBB(AM) Selma AL
WFEB(AM) Sylacauga AL
WVNN-FM Trinity AL
WACT(AM) Tuscaloosa AL
WTBC(AM) Tuscaloosa AL
*WUAL-FM Tuscaloosa AL
WVNA(AM) Tuscumbia AL
KVRC(AM) Arkadelphia AR
KAPZ(AM) Bald Knob AR
KLCN(AM) Blytheville AR
KJMT(FM) Calico Rock AR
KCAB(AM) Dardanelle AR
KFAY(AM) Farmington AR
KBJT(AM) Fordyce AR
KFPW(AM) Fort Smith AR
KWHN(AM) Fort Smith AR
KYHN(AM) Fort Smith AR
KURM-FM Gravette AR
KELD-FM Hampton AR
KAWW(AM) Heber Springs AR
KZHS(AM) Hot Springs AR
KZNG(AM) Hot Springs AR
KBTM(AM) Jonesboro AR
*KUAR(FM) Little Rock AR
KNBY(AM) Newport AR
KARV-FM Ola AR
KSMD(FM) Pangburn AR
KCLA(AM) Pine Bluff AR
KOTN(AM) Pine Bluff AR
KARV(AM) Russellville AR
KWYN(AM) Wynne AR
KFNX(AM) Cave Creek AZ
KAPR(AM) Douglas AZ
KVNA(AM) Flagstaff AZ
KTAR-FM Glendale AZ
KJAA(AM) Globe AZ
KDJI(AM) Holbrook AZ
KAAA(AM) Kingman AZ
KNTR(AM) Lake Havasu City AZ
KFNN(AM) Mesa AZ
KLPZ(AM) Parker AZ
KFYI(AM) Phoenix AZ
KKNT(AM) Phoenix AZ
KYCA(AM) Prescott AZ
KQNA(AM) Prescott Valley AZ
KATO(AM) Safford AZ
KAZM(AM) Sedona AZ
KVWM(AM) Show Low AZ
KTAN(AM) Sierra Vista AZ
KJLL(AM) South Tucson AZ
KNST(AM) Tucson AZ

*KUAZ(AM) Tucson AZ	KOA(AM) Denver CO	WDBO(AM) Orlando FL	*KDWI(FM) Ottumwa IA	WIBC(FM) Indianapolis IN
*KUAZ-FM Tucson AZ	KDGO(AM) Durango CO	WELE(AM) Ormond Beach FL	KLEE(AM) Ottumwa IA	WXNT(AM) Indianapolis IN
*KAWC(AM) Yuma AZ	KNRV(AM) Englewood CO	WLTG(AM) Panama City FL	KIWA(AM) Sheldon IA	WIOU(AM) Kokomo IN
KBLU(AM) Yuma AZ	KFTM(AM) Fort Morgan CO	WFLF-FM Parker FL	KMA(AM) Shenandoah IA	WSHY(AM) Lafayette IN
KJOK(AM) Yuma AZ	KNZZ(AM) Grand Junction CO	WCOA(AM) Pensacola FL	KSCJ(AM) Sioux City IA	WSAL(AM) Logansport IN
KATA(AM) Arcata CA	KFKA(AM) Greeley CO	WAMT(AM) Pine Castle-Sky Lake FL	*KWIT(FM) Sioux City IA	*WLPR-FM Lowell IN
KNZR(AM) Bakersfield CA	KHNC(AM) Johnstown CO	WFLF(AM) Pine Hills FL	KXEL(AM) Waterloo IA	WBAT(AM) Marion IN
KMET(AM) Banning CA	KUBC(AM) Montrose CO	WPSL(AM) Port St. Lucie FL	KQWC-FM Webster City IA	WKBV(AM) Richmond IN
KGIL(AM) Beverly Hills CA	KWUF(AM) Pagosa Springs CO	WCCF(AM) Punta Gorda FL	KBOI(AM) Boise ID	WSBT(AM) South Bend IN
*KQVO(FM) Calexico CA	KCSJ(AM) Pueblo CO	WFOY(AM) Saint Augustine FL	*KBSU(AM) Boise ID	WAOV(AM) Vincennes IN
KPAY(AM) Chico CA	KGFT(FM) Pueblo CO	WSDO(AM) Sanford FL	KBFI(AM) Bonners Ferry ID	*WBAA(AM) West Lafayette IN
*KZFR(FM) Chico CA	KVRH(AM) Salida CO	WLSS(AM) Sarasota FL	*KBSY(FM) Burley ID	KGGF(AM) Coffeyville KS
*KPCV(FM) Coachella CA	KRDO-FM Security CO	WSRQ(AM) Sarasota FL	KID(AM) Idaho Falls ID	KQYX(AM) Galena KS
KGOE(AM) Eureka CA	KCOL(AM) Wellington CO	WSTU(AM) Stuart FL	KRLC(AM) Lewiston ID	KIUL(AM) Garden City KS
KINS(AM) Eureka CA	WPRX(AM) Bristol CT	*WFSU-FM Tallahassee FL	*KISU-FM Pocatello ID	KLOE(AM) Goodland KS
KMJ(AM) Fresno CA	WLAD(AM) Danbury CT	WQTL(FM) Tallahassee FL	KSEI(AM) Pocatello ID	*KZAN(FM) Hays KS
KMJ-FM Fresno CA	*WQAQ(FM) Hamden CT	WTAL(AM) Tallahassee FL	KWIK(AM) Pocatello ID	*KZNA(FM) Hill City KS
KYNO(AM) Fresno CA	WDRC(AM) Hartford CT	WFLA(AM) Tampa FL	KSPT(AM) Sandpoint ID	KJCK(AM) Junction City KS
KRLA(AM) Glendale CA	WTIC(AM) Hartford CT	WHNZ(AM) Tampa FL	*KEZJ(FM) Twin Falls ID	KLWN(AM) Lawrence KS
KNCO(AM) Grass Valley CA	WZBG(FM) Litchfield CT	WIXC(AM) Titusville FL	KLIX(AM) Twin Falls ID	KSCB(AM) Liberal KS
KQAB(AM) Lake Isabella CA	WMMW(AM) Meriden CT	WFTL(AM) West Palm Beach FL	KWEI(AM) Weiser ID	KMAN(AM) Manhattan KS
KOSS(AM) Lancaster CA	*WPKT(FM) Meriden CT	WJNO(AM) West Palm Beach FL	WBGZ(AM) Alton IL	KCCV(AM) Overland Park KS
KCAA(AM) Loma Linda CA	WELI(AM) New Haven CT	WPRD(AM) Winter Park FL	WBIG(AM) Aurora IL	KQMA-FM Phillipsburg KS
KSMA(AM) Lompoc CA	WNLK(AM) Norwalk CT	WALG(AM) Albany GA	WBYS(AM) Canton IL	KINA(AM) Salina KS
*KPFK(FM) Los Angeles CA	*WNPR(FM) Norwich CT	WLTA(AM) Alpharetta GA	WCIL(AM) Carbondale IL	KSAL(AM) Salina KS
KTNQ(AM) Los Angeles CA	*WEDW-FM Stamford CT	WGAU(AM) Athens GA	WDWS(AM) Champaign IL	KMAJ(AM) Topeka KS
*KPMO(AM) Mendocino CA	WSTC(AM) Stamford CT	*WABE(FM) Atlanta GA	KSGM(AM) Chester IL	WIBW(AM) Topeka KS
KTIQ(AM) Merced CA	WATR(AM) Waterbury CT	WAOK(AM) Atlanta GA	*WBEZ(FM) Chicago IL	KLEY(AM) Wellington KS
KYOS(AM) Merced CA	WWCO(AM) Waterbury CT	WGKA(AM) Atlanta GA	WGN(AM) Chicago IL	KNSS(AM) Wichita KS
KFIV(AM) Modesto CA	*WSHU(AM) Westport CT	WGST(AM) Atlanta GA	WIND(AM) Chicago IL	WAIA(AM) Beaver Dam KY
KNRY(AM) Monterey CA	WILI(AM) Willimantic CT	WSB(AM) Atlanta GA	WLS(AM) Chicago IL	WKXO(AM) Berea KY
KMJC(AM) Mount Shasta CA	*WAMU(FM) Washington DC	WGAC(AM) Augusta GA	WRTO(AM) Chicago IL	WKCT(AM) Bowling Green KY
KVON(AM) Napa CA	WMAL(AM) Washington DC	WRDW(AM) Augusta GA	WHOW(AM) Clinton IL	WCTT(AM) Corbin KY
*KQEI-FM North Highlands CA	WOL(AM) Washington DC	WGIG(AM) Brunswick GA	WDAN(AM) Danville IL	WKDP(AM) Corbin KY
KNEW(AM) Oakland CA	*WPFW(FM) Washington DC	WMOG(AM) Brunswick GA	WLBK(AM) De Kalb IL	WHIR(AM) Danville KY
KLAA(AM) Orange CA	WDOV(AM) Dover DE	WGRA(AM) Cairo GA	WSOY(AM) Decatur IL	WHOP(AM) Hopkinsville KY
KGAM(AM) Palm Springs CA	WGMD(FM) Rehoboth Beach DE	WJTH(AM) Calhoun GA	WCRA(AM) Effingham IL	WVLK(AM) Lexington KY
KNWQ(AM) Palm Springs CA	WDEL(AM) Wilmington DE	WLBB(AM) Carrollton GA	WRMN(AM) Elgin IL	*WFPL(FM) Louisville KY
KKXX(AM) Paradise CA	WORL(AM) Altamonte Springs FL	WRCG(AM) Columbus GA	WJJG(AM) Elmhurst IL	WGTK(AM) Louisville KY
*KPCC(FM) Pasadena CA	WFLN(AM) Arcadia FL	WBLJ(AM) Dalton GA	WFIW(AM) Fairfield IL	WHAS(AM) Louisville KY
KPRL(AM) Paso Robles CA	WTWB(AM) Auburndale FL	WCFO(AM) East Point GA	*WGNN(FM) Fisher IL	WNGO(AM) Mayfield KY
KWKU(AM) Pomona CA	WWJB(AM) Brooksville FL	WDUN(AM) Gainesville GA	WGIL(AM) Galesburg IL	*WBFI(FM) McDaniels KY
KVTA(AM) Port Hueneme CA	WNZF(AM) Bunnell FL	WHIE(AM) Griffin GA	WGEN(AM) Geneseo IL	WMST(AM) Mt. Sterling KY
KTIP(AM) Porterville CA	WKFL(AM) Bushnell FL	WQXZ(FM) Hawkinsville GA	WKYX-FM Golconda IL	WLRT(AM) Nicholasville KY
KHGQ(FM) Quincy CA	WMMV(AM) Cocoa FL	WVCC(AM) Hogansville GA	WJPF(AM) Herrin IL	WOMI(AM) Owensboro KY
KPCO(AM) Quincy CA	WMEL(AM) Cocoa Beach FL	WVGA(AM) Lakeland GA	WJIL(AM) Jacksonville IL	WKYX(AM) Paducah KY
KWDJ(AM) Ridgecrest CA	WJTK(FM) Columbia City FL	WMAC(AM) Macon GA	WLDS(AM) Jacksonville IL	WKYH(AM) Paintsville KY
KFBK(AM) Sacramento CA	WRHC(AM) Coral Gables FL	WLAQ(AM) Rome GA	WKEI(AM) Kewanee IL	WEKY(AM) Richmond KY
*KXJZ(FM) Sacramento CA	WNDB(AM) Daytona Beach FL	WRGA(AM) Rome GA	WLPO(AM) La Salle IL	KPEL-FM Abbeville LA
KION(AM) Salinas CA	WZEP(AM) De Funiak Springs FL	WBMQ(AM) Savannah GA	WSMI(AM) Litchfield IL	WABL(AM) Amite LA
KTIE(AM) San Bernardino CA	WTJV(AM) De Land FL	WWNS(AM) Statesboro GA	WGGH(AM) Marion IL	*WRKF(FM) Baton Rouge LA
KCBQ(AM) San Diego CA	WYND(AM) De Land FL	WKWN(AM) Trenton GA	WLBH(AM) Mattoon IL	WIKC(AM) Bogalusa LA
KFMB(AM) San Diego CA	WNWF(AM) Destin FL	WNNG(AM) Warner Robins GA	*WBEQ(FM) Morris IL	WASO(AM) Covington LA
KOGO(AM) San Diego CA	WGUL(AM) Dunedin FL	WGAC-FM Warrenton GA	WCSJ(AM) Morris IL	KAOK(AM) Lake Charles LA
*KPBS-FM San Diego CA	WMGG(AM) Dunedin FL	WAYX(AM) Waycross GA	WCSJ-FM Morris IL	KMLB(AM) Monroe LA
KIQI(AM) San Francisco CA	WENG(AM) Englewood FL	WCGA(AM) Woodbine GA	WINI(AM) Murphysboro IL	KNOC(AM) Natchitoches LA
*KQED-FM San Francisco CA	*WAFG(FM) Fort Lauderdale FL	KGUM(AM) Hagatna GU	WCMY(AM) Ottawa IL	WGSO(AM) New Orleans LA
KZSF(AM) San Jose CA	WINK(AM) Fort Myers FL	KHNU(AM) Hilo HI	WMBD(AM) Peoria IL	WRNO-FM New Orleans LA
KVEC(AM) San Luis Obispo CA	WJNX(AM) Fort Pierce FL	KPUA(AM) Hilo HI	WZOE(AM) Princeton IL	WWL(AM) New Orleans LA
KYNS(AM) San Luis Obispo CA	WFTW(AM) Fort Walton Beach FL	KHBZ(AM) Honolulu HI	WGEM-FM Quincy IL	KEEL(AM) Shreveport LA
KCLU(AM) Santa Barbara CA	WRUF(AM) Gainesville FL	KHNR(AM) Honolulu HI	WTAD(AM) Quincy IL	KNCB(AM) Vivian LA
KZSB(AM) Santa Barbara CA	WNRP(AM) Gulf Breeze FL	*KHPR(FM) Honolulu HI	WRHL(AM) Rochelle IL	KVCL(AM) Winnfield LA
KSCO(AM) Santa Cruz CA	WOIR(AM) Homestead FL	KHVH(AM) Honolulu HI	WROK(AM) Rockford IL	WPNI(AM) Amherst MA
KSMX(AM) Santa Maria CA	WXYB(AM) Indian Rocks Beach FL	*KIPO(FM) Honolulu HI	WHCO(AM) Sparta IL	WARL(AM) Attleboro MA
KUHL(AM) Santa Maria CA	WBOB(AM) Jacksonville FL	KWAI(AM) Honolulu HI	WMAY(AM) Springfield IL	WBZ(AM) Boston MA
KKZZ(AM) Santa Paula CA	*WJCT-FM Jacksonville FL	KNUI(AM) Kahului HI	WTAX(AM) Springfield IL	WILD(AM) Boston MA
*KRCB-FM Santa Rosa CA	WOKV(AM) Jacksonville FL	KAOI(AM) Kihei HI	*WNIQ(FM) Sterling IL	WZAI(FM) Brewster MA
KSRO(AM) Santa Rosa CA	WJBW(AM) Jupiter FL	KQNG(AM) Lihue HI	WSPL(AM) Streator IL	WXBR(AM) Brockton MA
KIRN(AM) Simi Valley CA	WLKF(AM) Lakeland FL	*KKUA(FM) Wailuku HI	WTIM-FM Taylorville IL	WBNW(AM) Concord MA
KVML(AM) Sonora CA	WPBR(AM) Lantana FL	KASI(AM) Ames IA	*WILL(AM) Urbana IL	WHNP(AM) East Longmeadow MA
KOWL(AM) South Lake Tahoe CA	WWBA(AM) Largo FL	*WOI(AM) Ames IA	WKRS(AM) Waukegan IL	WSAR(AM) Fall River MA
KSUE(AM) Susanville CA	WFFG(AM) Marathon FL	KWBG(AM) Boone IA	WHBU(AM) Anderson IN	WGAW(AM) Gardner MA
KNWH(AM) Twentynine Palms CA	*WKWM(FM) Marathon FL	KBUR(AM) Burlington IA	WGCL(AM) Bloomington IN	*WAMQ(FM) Great Barrington MA
KERN(AM) Wasco-Greenacres CA	WGUF(AM) Marco FL	WMT(AM) Cedar Rapids IA	*WBEW(FM) Chesterton IN	*WMLN-FM Milton MA
KNTK(FM) Weed CA	WDMC(AM) Melbourne FL	WOC(AM) Davenport IA	WCSI(AM) Columbus IN	*WNAN(FM) Nantucket MA
KUBA(AM) Yuba City CA	WAQI(AM) Miami FL	WHO(AM) Des Moines IA	*WVPE(FM) Elkhart IN	WBSM(AM) New Bedford MA
*KAJX(FM) Aspen CO	WIOD(AM) Miami FL	*KDUB(FM) Dubuque IA	WGBF(AM) Evansville IN	WDIS(AM) Norfolk MA
KRLN(AM) Canon City CO	*WLRN-FM Miami FL	WDBQ(AM) Dubuque IA	*WNIN-FM Evansville IN	WHMP(AM) Northampton MA
KRDO(AM) Colorado Springs CO	WQBA(AM) Miami FL	KILR(AM) Estherville IA	*WBOI(FM) Fort Wayne IN	WBEC(AM) Pittsfield MA
KVOR(AM) Colorado Springs CO	WSUA(AM) Miami FL	KMCD(AM) Fairfield IA	WFCV(AM) Fort Wayne IN	WESO(AM) Southbridge MA
KZNT(AM) Colorado Springs CO	WWFE(AM) Miami FL	*WSUI(AM) Iowa City IA	WOWO(AM) Fort Wayne IN	WHYN(AM) Springfield MA
KVFC(AM) Cortez CO	WSKY-FM Micanopy FL	KOKX(AM) Keokuk IA	WLTH(AM) Gary IN	WGTX(FM) Truro MA
*KBUT(FM) Crested Butte CO	WNOG(AM) Naples FL	KFJB(AM) Marshalltown IA	WTRE(AM) Greensburg IN	*WBUR(AM) West Yarmouth MA
KBNO(AM) Denver CO	WPSO(AM) New Port Richey FL	KOEL(AM) Oelwein IA	*KOJI(FM) Okoboji IA	WXTK(FM) West Yarmouth MA
*KCFR(AM) Denver CO	WKAT(AM) North Miami FL	*KOJI(FM) Okoboji IA	WJOB(AM) Hammond IN	WNNZ(AM) Westfield MA
KNUS(AM) Denver CO	WOCA(AM) Ocala FL	KBIZ(AM) Ottumwa IA	*WFYI-FM Indianapolis IN	*WCAI(FM) Woods Hole MA

WTAG(AM) Worcester MA
WBAL(AM) Baltimore MD
*WEAA(FM) Baltimore MD
WOLB(AM) Baltimore MD
*WYPR(FM) Baltimore MD
WCBC(AM) Cumberland MD
WFMD(AM) Frederick MD
*WYPF(FM) Frederick MD
WHAG(AM) Halfway MD
WJSS(AM) Havre de Grace MD
WPTX(AM) Lexington Park MD
*WSDL(FM) Ocean City MD
*WYPO(FM) Ocean City MD
WICO(AM) Salisbury MD
WJDY(AM) Salisbury MD
WQMR(FM) Snow Hill MD
WVQM(AM) Augusta ME
*WMEP(FM) Camden ME
*WMEF(FM) Fort Kent ME
WVOM(FM) Howland ME
WJCX(FM) Pittsfield ME
WGAN(AM) Portland ME
WLOB(AM) Portland ME
*WMEM(FM) Presque Isle ME
WNZS(AM) Veazie ME
WWNZ(AM) Veazie ME
*WMEW(FM) Waterville ME
WABJ(AM) Adrian MI
WAAM(AM) Ann Arbor MI
*WUOM(FM) Ann Arbor MI
WBCK(AM) Battle Creek MI
WBCK-FM Battle Creek MI
WSJM-FM Benton Harbor MI
WHFB(AM) Benton Harbor-St. Joseph MI
WBRN(AM) Big Rapids MI
WATT(AM) Cadillac MI
WMKT(AM) Charlevoix MI
WDTK(AM) Detroit MI
*WKAR(AM) East Lansing MI
WCHT(AM) Escanaba MI
*WFUM-FM Flint MI
WWCK(AM) Flint MI
WOOD(AM) Grand Rapids MI
*WVGR(FM) Grand Rapids MI
WMPL(AM) Hancock MI
WBCH(AM) Hastings MI
WHTC(AM) Holland MI
WMIQ(AM) Iron Mountain MI
WIAN(AM) Ishpeming MI
WKHM(AM) Jackson MI
WKMI(AM) Kalamazoo MI
WKZO(AM) Kalamazoo MI
WKZO(AM) Kalamazoo MI
*WGVU(AM) Kentwood MI
WILS(AM) Lansing MI
WKLA(AM) Ludington MI
WMTE(AM) Manistee MI
WPIQ(FM) Manistique MI
WDMJ(AM) Marquette MI
WGVS(AM) Muskegon MI
WJML(AM) Petoskey MI
WPHM(AM) Port Huron MI
WSGW(AM) Saginaw MI
WSJM(AM) Saint Joseph MI
WMIC(AM) Sandusky MI
WKNW(AM) Sault Ste. Marie MI
WTCM(AM) Traverse City MI
KATE(AM) Albert Lea MN
KXRA(AM) Alexandria MN
KAUS(AM) Austin MN
WWWI(AM) Baxter MN
KBEW(AM) Blue Earth MN
KRWC(AM) Buffalo MN
KDLM(AM) Detroit Lakes MN
KDAL(AM) Duluth MN
WEBC(AM) Duluth MN
KRBT(AM) Eveleth MN
KBRF(AM) Fergus Falls MN
KLTF(AM) Little Falls MN
WYRQ(FM) Little Falls MN
KTOE(AM) Mankato MN
KMHL(AM) Marshall MN
KTLK-FM Minneapolis MN
WCCO(AM) Minneapolis MN
WWTC(AM) Minneapolis MN

KMRS(AM) Morris MN
WNMT(AM) Nashwauk MN
KCHK(AM) New Prague MN
WWWI-FM Pillager MN
KCUE(AM) Red Wing MN
KROC(AM) Rochester MN
*KRXW(FM) Roseau MN
KNSI(AM) Saint Cloud MN
WJON(AM) Saint Cloud MN
*KNGA(FM) Saint Peter MN
KWLM(AM) Willmar MN
KDOM(AM) Windom MN
KDOM-FM Windom MN
KWNO(AM) Winona MN
KWOA(AM) Worthington MN
*KNSW(FM) Worthington-Marshall MN
*KGNA-FM Arnold MO
KSWM(AM) Aurora MO
KKOZ(AM) Ava MO
KKOZ-FM Ava MO
KBFL-FM Buffalo MO
KMRN(AM) Cameron MO
KZIM(AM) Cape Girardeau MO
KFRU(AM) Columbia MO
*KOPN(FM) Columbia MO
*KGNN-FM Cuba MO
KREI(AM) Farmington MO
KSSZ(FM) Fayette MO
KJFF(AM) Festus MO
KHMO(AM) Hannibal MO
KLIK(AM) Jefferson City MO
KWOS(AM) Jefferson City MO
KZRG(AM) Joplin MO
*KKFI(FM) Kansas City MO
KLWT(AM) Lebanon MO
KMAL(AM) Malden MO
*KNEO(FM) Neosho MO
KRMS(AM) Osage Beach MO
KFMO(AM) Park Hills MO
*KCOZ(FM) Point Lookout MO
KWOC(AM) Poplar Bluff MO
KTTR(AM) Rolla MO
KTTR-FM Saint James MO
KFEQ(AM) Saint Joseph MO
KMOX(AM) Saint Louis MO
KTRS(AM) Saint Louis MO
KSMO(AM) Salem MO
KSIS(AM) Sedalia MO
KSIM(AM) Sikeston MO
KSGF(AM) Springfield MO
KWTO(AM) Springfield MO
KTUI(AM) Sullivan MO
*KGNV(FM) Washington MO
KWPM(AM) West Plains MO
KUKU(AM) Willow Springs MO
WAMY(AM) Amory MS
*WMAH-FM Biloxi MS
WTNI(AM) Biloxi MS
*WMAU-FM Bude MS
WDSK(AM) Cleveland MS
WCJU(AM) Columbia MS
*WMAO-FM Greenwood MS
*WURC(FM) Holly Springs MS
WTCD(FM) Indianola MS
WKOZ(AM) Kosciusko MS
WMXI(FM) Laurel MS
WJZD-FM Long Beach MS
WHNY(AM) McComb MS
*WMAW-FM Meridian MS
WMOX(AM) Meridian MS
WBUV(FM) Moss Point MS
WNAT(AM) Natchez MS
WJNT(AM) Pearl MS
WFMM(FM) Sumrall MS
WVBG(AM) Vicksburg MS
WKBB(AM) West Point MS
KGVW(AM) Belgrade MT
KBLG(AM) Billings MT
KMMS(AM) Bozeman MT
*KGVA(FM) Fort Belknap Agency MT
KQDI(AM) Great Falls MT
KLYQ(AM) Hamilton MT
KBLL(AM) Helena MT
KCAP(AM) Helena MT
KGEZ(AM) Kalispell MT
KOFI(AM) Kalispell MT

KGVO(AM) Missoula MT
KJJR(AM) Whitefish MT
WQNX(AM) Aberdeen NC
WSPC(AM) Albemarle NC
WWNC(AM) Asheville NC
WTKF(AM) Atlantic NC
*WBJD(FM) Atlantic Beach NC
WXIT(AM) Blowing Rock NC
WATA(AM) Boone NC
WCHL(AM) Chapel Hill NC
*WUNC(FM) Chapel Hill NC
WBT(AM) Charlotte NC
*WFAE(FM) Charlotte NC
*WNCU(FM) Durham NC
WGAI(AM) Elizabeth City NC
WFNC(AM) Fayetteville NC
WIDU(AM) Fayetteville NC
WGBR(AM) Goldsboro NC
WSML(AM) Graham NC
*WFHE(FM) Hickory NC
WHKY(AM) Hickory NC
WMFR(AM) High Point NC
WJNC(AM) Jacksonville NC
WAAV(AM) Leland NC
WJRI(AM) Lenoir NC
WLXN(AM) Lexington NC
*WUND-FM Manteo NC
*WYQS(FM) Mars Hill NC
WKRK(AM) Murphy NC
WAUG(AM) New Hope NC
WDOX(AM) Raleigh NC
WPTF(AM) Raleigh NC
*WRQM(FM) Rocky Mount NC
WCAB(AM) Rutherfordton NC
WSTP(AM) Salisbury NC
WLTT(FM) Shallotte NC
WNCA(AM) Siler City NC
WEEB(AM) Southern Pines NC
WTXY(AM) Whiteville NC
WSJS(AM) Winston-Salem NC
KFYR(AM) Bismarck ND
KLXX(AM) Bismarck-Mandan ND
KFGO(AM) Fargo ND
WDAY(AM) Fargo ND
KNOX(AM) Grand Forks ND
KNDK(AM) Langdon ND
KQLX(AM) Lisbon ND
KHRT(AM) Minot ND
KEYZ(AM) Williston ND
KCOW(AM) Alliance NE
KWBE(AM) Beatrice NE
KJSK(AM) Columbus NE
KHUB(AM) Fremont NE
KRGI(AM) Grand Island NE
KGFW(AM) Kearney NE
*KLNE-FM Lexington NE
KFOR(AM) Lincoln NE
KLIN(AM) Lincoln NE
WJAG(AM) Norfolk NE
KODY(AM) North Platte NE
KFAB(AM) Omaha NE
KKAR(AM) Omaha NE
KNEB(AM) Scottsbluff NE
KOLT(AM) Scottsbluff NE
*WEVO(FM) Concord NH
WKXL(AM) Concord NH
WTSN(AM) Dover NH
WXEX(AM) Exeter NH
*WEVC(FM) Gorham NH
*WEVH(FM) Hanover NH
WTSL(AM) Hanover NH
WTPL(FM) Hillsboro NH
WEVJ(FM) Jackson NH
*WEVN(FM) Keene NH
WZBK(AM) Keene NH
WUVR(AM) Lebanon NH
WGIR(AM) Manchester NH
*WEVS(FM) Nashua NH
WSMN(AM) Nashua NH
WNTK-FM New London NH
WGIN(AM) Rochester NH
WQSO(FM) Rochester NH
WCCM(AM) Salem NH
*WNJN-FM Atlantic City NJ
*WNJS-FM Berlin NJ
*WNJB(FM) Bridgeton NJ

*WNJZ(FM) Cape May Court House NJ
WNYM(AM) Hackensack NJ
WRNJ(AM) Hackettstown NJ
WGYM(AM) Hammonton NJ
*WNJM(FM) Manahawkin NJ
*WNJY(FM) Netcong NJ
WVNJ(AM) Oakland NJ
WIBG(AM) Ocean City NJ
WOND(AM) Pleasantville NJ
*WNJP(FM) Sussex NJ
*WNJO(FM) Toms River NJ
*WNJT-FM Trenton NJ
KINN(AM) Alamogordo NM
KKOB(AM) Albuquerque NM
*KUNM(FM) Albuquerque NM
*KRRT(FM) Arroyo Seco NM
*KRAR(FM) Espanola NM
KENN(AM) Farmington NM
KYKK(AM) Hobbs NM
KOBE(AM) Las Cruces NM
KSNM(AM) Las Cruces NM
KNMX(AM) Las Vegas NM
*KRRE(FM) Las Vegas NM
KTBL(AM) Los Ranchos de Albuquerque NM
*KENW-FM Portales NM
KSEL(AM) Portales NM
KBIM(AM) Roswell NM
*KBOM(FM) Socorro NM
KSFR(FM) White Rock NM
*KRNM(FM) Chalan Kanoa-Saipan NP
KKFT(FM) Gardnerville-Minden NV
KDWN(AM) Las Vegas NV
KXNT(AM) North Las Vegas NV
KNUU(AM) Paradise NV
KKOH(AM) Reno NV
KBZZ(AM) Sparks NV
KWNA(AM) Winnemucca NV
*WAMC(AM) Albany NY
WROW(AM) Albany NY
WCSS(AM) Amsterdam NY
WBTA(AM) Batavia NY
WINR(AM) Binghamton NY
WNBF(AM) Binghamton NY
WBEN(AM) Buffalo NY
*WNED(AM) Buffalo NY
*WCAN(FM) Canajoharie NY
WCGR(AM) Canandaigua NY
WENI(AM) Corning NY
WWLE(AM) Cornwall NY
WFLR(AM) Dundee NY
WDOE(AM) Dunkirk NY
WENY(AM) Elmira NY
*WEOS(FM) Geneva NY
WGVA(AM) Geneva NY
WWSC(AM) Glens Falls NY
WLEA(AM) Hornell NY
WWLZ(AM) Horseheads NY
WHCU(AM) Ithaca NY
*WJFF(FM) Jeffersonville NY
*WAMK(FM) Kingston NY
WLVL(AM) Lockport NY
WYBG(AM) Massena NY
WXLM(FM) Montauk NY
WVOX(AM) New Rochelle NY
WADO(AM) New York NY
*WBAI(FM) New York NY
*WNYC(AM) New York NY
WOR(AM) New York NY
WACK(AM) Newark NY
*WSUF(FM) Noyack NY
*WRVO(FM) Oswego NY
WKIP(AM) Poughkeepsie NY
*WRUN-FM Remsen NY
WHAM(AM) Rochester NY
*WXXI(AM) Rochester NY
WGY(AM) Schenectady NY
*WRLI-FM Southampton NY
*WUSB(FM) Stony Brook NY
*WRVD(FM) Syracuse NY
WSYR(AM) Syracuse NY
WIBX(AM) Utica NY
*WRUN(AM) Utica NY
*WRVN(FM) Utica NY
*WRVJ(FM) Watertown NY

WHLO(AM) Akron OH
WATH(AM) Athens OH
*WOUB(AM) Athens OH
WBLL(AM) Bellefontaine OH
*WOUC-FM Cambridge OH
WCER(AM) Canton OH
WBEX(AM) Chillicothe OH
*WOUH-FM Chillicothe OH
WKRC(AM) Cincinnati OH
WLW(AM) Cincinnati OH
*WVXU(FM) Cincinnati OH
*WCSB(FM) Cleveland OH
WTAM(AM) Cleveland OH
WERE(AM) Cleveland Heights OH
*WOSU(AM) Columbus OH
WTVN(AM) Columbus OH
WWOW(AM) Conneaut OH
WHIO(AM) Dayton OH
WONW(AM) Defiance OH
WEOL(AM) Elyria OH
WFIN(AM) Findlay OH
*WOUL-FM Ironton OH
*WFCO(FM) Lancaster OH
WIMA(AM) Lima OH
WMAN(AM) Mansfield OH
*WMRT(FM) Marietta OH
WMRN(AM) Marion OH
WMVO(AM) Mount Vernon OH
WCLT(AM) Newark OH
*WMUB(FM) Oxford OH
WHIO-FM Piqua OH
WULM(AM) Springfield OH
WCWA(AM) Toledo OH
WSPD(AM) Toledo OH
WBTC(AM) Uhrichsville OH
WASN(AM) Youngstown OH
WKBN(AM) Youngstown OH
WHIZ(AM) Zanesville OH
*WOUZ(FM) Zanesville OH
KWHW(AM) Altus OK
KWON(AM) Bartlesville OK
KUSH(AM) Cushing OK
KGWA(AM) Enid OK
KTJS(AM) Hobart OK
*KGOU(FM) Norman OK
KOKC(AM) Oklahoma City OK
KQCV(AM) Oklahoma City OK
KTOK(AM) Oklahoma City OK
KRMG-FM Sand Springs OK
*KROU(FM) Spencer OK
KSPI(AM) Stillwater OK
KRMG(AM) Tulsa OK
KAST(AM) Astoria OR
KBKR(AM) Baker City OR
*KOBK(FM) Baker City OR
KBND(AM) Bend OR
KBNW(AM) Bend OR
KWRO(AM) Coquille OR
KLOO(AM) Corvallis OR
*KOAC(AM) Corvallis OR
KNND(AM) Cottage Grove OR
KWVR(AM) Enterprise OR
*KLCC(FM) Eugene OR
KOPB(AM) Eugene OR
KPNW(AM) Eugene OR
KUGN(AM) Eugene OR
*KOGL(FM) Gleneden Beach OR
KAJO(AM) Grants Pass OR
KUIK(AM) Hillsboro OR
KYKN(AM) Keizer OR
KAGO(AM) Klamath Falls OR
KFLS(AM) Klamath Falls OR
KLBM(AM) La Grande OR
*KDOV(FM) Medford OR
KMED(AM) Medford OR
KNPT(AM) Newport OR
KBBR(AM) North Bend OR
*KAPL(AM) Phoenix OR
KBNP(AM) Portland OR
KPOJ(AM) Portland OR
KXL(AM) Portland OR
KDUN(AM) Reedsport OR
*KLFR(FM) Reedsport OR
*KMPQ(FM) Roseburg OR
KQEN(AM) Roseburg OR
KACI(AM) The Dalles OR

*KOTD(FM) The Dalles OR
KMBD(AM) Tillamook OR
KPAM(AM) Troutdale OR
KWLZ-FM Warm Springs OR
WAEB(AM) Allentown PA
WRTA(AM) Altoona PA
WILK-FM Avoca PA
WBFD(AM) Bedford PA
WBLF(AM) Bellefonte PA
WGPA(AM) Bethlehem PA
*WBUQ(FM) Bloomsburg PA
WISR(AM) Butler PA
WHYL(AM) Carlisle PA
WCHA(AM) Chambersburg PA
WWCH(AM) Clarion PA
WFRM(AM) Coudersport PA
WCED(AM) DuBois PA
WRDD(AM) Ebensburg PA
WJET(AM) Erie PA
WPSE(AM) Erie PA
WZSK(AM) Everett PA
WHP(AM) Harrisburg PA
*WITF-FM Harrisburg PA
WRKK(AM) Hughesville PA
WHUN(AM) Huntingdon PA
WKGE(AM) Johnstown PA
WNTJ(AM) Johnstown PA
WNPV(AM) Lansdale PA
WLBR(AM) Lebanon PA
WIEZ(AM) Lewistown PA
WWGE(AM) Loretto PA
WJSM-FM Martinsburg PA
WMGW(AM) Meadville PA
WPLY(AM) Mount Pocono PA
WKST(AM) New Castle PA
WOYL(AM) Oil City PA
WNTP(AM) Philadelphia PA
WPHB(AM) Philipsburg PA
KDKA(AM) Pittsburgh PA
WDVE(FM) Pittsburgh PA
WPGB(FM) Pittsburgh PA
WPAZ(AM) Pottstown PA
*WYBF(FM) Radnor Township PA
WEEU(AM) Reading PA
WBZU(AM) Scranton PA
WPIC(AM) Sharon PA
WRSC(AM) State College PA
WKOK(AM) Sunbury PA
WTIV(AM) Titusville PA
WGMF(AM) Tunkhannock PA
WKZN(AM) West Hazleton PA
WILK(AM) Wilkes-Barre PA
WRAK(AM) Williamsport PA
*WRLC(FM) Williamsport PA
WWPA(AM) Williamsport PA
WSBA(AM) York PA
WCMN(AM) Arecibo PR
WYAC(AM) Cabo Rojo PR
WNEL(AM) Caguas PR
WLEY(AM) Cayey PR
WOIZ(AM) Guayanilla PR
WMSW(AM) Hatillo PR
WBSG(AM) Lajas PR
WMNT(AM) Manati PR
WKJB(AM) Mayaguez PR
WDEP(AM) Ponce PR
WISO(AM) Ponce PR
WPAB(AM) Ponce PR
WPRP(AM) Ponce PR
WUKQ(AM) Ponce PR
WAPA(AM) San Juan PR
*WIPR(AM) San Juan PR
WKAQ(AM) San Juan PR
WOSO(AM) San Juan PR
WSKN(AM) San Juan PR
WUNO(AM) San Juan PR
WUPR(AM) Utuado PR
WENA(AM) Yauco PR
WKFE(AM) Yauco PR
WRNI-FM Narragansett Pier RI
WADK(AM) Newport RI
WHJJ(AM) Providence RI
WPRO(AM) Providence RI
WRNI(AM) Providence RI
WEAN-FM Wakefield-Peacedale RI
WNRI(AM) Woonsocket RI

WAIM(AM) Anderson SC
WTMA(AM) Charleston SC
WBT-FM Chester SC
WVOC(AM) Columbia SC
WFIS(AM) Fountain Inn SC
WGTN(AM) Georgetown SC
WYRD(AM) Greenville SC
WCRS(AM) Greenwood SC
WHGS(AM) Hampton SC
WRIX-FM Honea Path SC
WRHI(AM) Rock Hill SC
WYRD-FM Simpsonville SC
WOLI(AM) Spartanburg SC
WORD(AM) Spartanburg SC
WSPG(AM) Spartanburg SC
*WRJA-FM Sumter SC
KJAM(AM) Madison SD
KMSD(AM) Milbank SD
KORN(AM) Mitchell SD
KCCR(AM) Pierre SD
KOTA(AM) Rapid City SD
KELO(AM) Sioux Falls SD
KSOO(AM) Sioux Falls SD
WNAX(AM) Yankton SD
WBCR(AM) Alcoa TN
WBIN(AM) Benton TN
WTBG(FM) Brownsville TN
WDEF(AM) Chattanooga TN
WGOW(AM) Chattanooga TN
WBAC(AM) Cleveland TN
WCLE(AM) Cleveland TN
WCRV(AM) Collierville TN
WPTN(AM) Cookeville TN
*WMKW(FM) Crossville TN
WDNT(AM) Dayton TN
WCPH(AM) Etowah TN
WAKM(AM) Franklin TN
WHEW(AM) Franklin TN
WNWS-FM Jackson TN
WTJS(AM) Jackson TN
*WETS(FM) Johnson City TN
WETR(AM) Knoxville TN
WNML(AM) Knoxville TN
WCOR(AM) Lebanon TN
WLOD(AM) Loudon TN
WPLN(AM) Madison TN
WRKQ(AM) Madisonville TN
WWTN(FM) Manchester TN
WCMT(AM) Martin TN
WAKI(AM) McMinnville TN
KWAM(AM) Memphis TN
WREC(AM) Memphis TN
WGNS(AM) Murfreesboro TN
WLAC(AM) Nashville TN
WNOX(FM) Oak Ridge TN
WPLZ(FM) Ooltewah TN
*WFCM(AM) Smyrna TN
WGOW-FM Soddy-Daisy TN
WXQK(AM) Spring City TN
WTNE-FM Trenton TN
KWKC(AM) Abilene TX
KGNC(AM) Amarillo TX
KIXZ(AM) Amarillo TX
KRGN(FM) Amarillo TX
KACT(AM) Andrews TX
KLBJ(AM) Austin TX
KLVI(AM) Beaumont TX
KRCM(AM) Beaumont TX
KBST(AM) Big Spring TX
KBST-FM Big Spring TX
KWHI(AM) Brenham TX
KVNS(AM) Brownsville TX
KXYL-FM Brownwood TX
*KEOS(FM) College Station TX
KTAW(AM) College Station TX
KEYS(AM) Corpus Christi TX
KKTX(AM) Corpus Christi TX
KHER(FM) Crystal City TX
*KERA(AM) Dallas TX
KLIF(AM) Dallas TX
KRLD(AM) Dallas TX
KURV(AM) Edinburg TX
KULP(AM) El Campo TX
KROD(AM) El Paso TX
KTSM(AM) El Paso TX
KFLC(AM) Fort Worth TX

WBAP(AM) Fort Worth TX
KGAF(AM) Gainesville TX
KLAT(AM) Houston TX
KNTH(AM) Houston TX
KPRC(AM) Houston TX
KFRO(AM) Longview TX
KFYO(AM) Lubbock TX
KJDL(AM) Lubbock TX
KJTV(AM) Lubbock TX
KRFE(AM) Lubbock TX
KCRS(AM) Midland TX
KSFA(AM) Nacogdoches TX
KWBC(AM) Navasota TX
KOLE(AM) Port Arthur TX
KKSA(AM) San Angelo TX
KCOR(AM) San Antonio TX
KTSA(AM) San Antonio TX
WOAI(AM) San Antonio TX
*KTSW(FM) San Marcos TX
KWED(AM) Seguin TX
KZSP(FM) South Padre Island TX
KTEM(AM) Temple TX
KLUP(AM) Terrell Hills TX
KTFS(AM) Texarkana TX
KSEV(AM) Tomball TX
KTBB(AM) Tyler TX
KBCT-FM Waco TX
KWTX(AM) Waco TX
KWFS(AM) Wichita Falls TX
KSUB(AM) Cedar City UT
*KUSU-FM Logan UT
KVNU(AM) Logan UT
KSL-FM Midvale UT
KOAL(AM) Price UT
*KBYU-FM Provo UT
KSVC(AM) Richfield UT
KDXU(AM) Saint George UT
KZNU(AM) Saint George UT
*KCPW-FM Salt Lake City UT
KNRS(AM) Salt Lake City UT
KSL(AM) Salt Lake City UT
KHQN(AM) Spanish Fork UT
KVEL(AM) Vernal UT
WFHG-FM Abingdon VA
WBVA(AM) Bayside VA
WFNR(AM) Blacksburg VA
WCHV(AM) Charlottesville VA
WINA(AM) Charlottesville VA
*WMVE(FM) Chase City VA
WPMH(AM) Claremont VA
*WMRY(FM) Crozet VA
WPIN(AM) Dublin VA
WFLO(AM) Farmville VA
WFVA(AM) Fredericksburg VA
*WMRA(FM) Harrisonburg VA
WSVA(AM) Harrisonburg VA
*WCNV(FM) Heathsville VA
*WMRL(FM) Lexington VA
WREL(AM) Lexington VA
WBRG(AM) Lynchburg VA
WLNI(FM) Lynchburg VA
*WHRV(FM) Norfolk VA
WNIS(AM) Norfolk VA
WTPS(AM) Petersburg VA
*WCVE(FM) Richmond VA
WRVA(AM) Richmond VA
WRVA(AM) Richmond VA
WFIR(AM) Roanoke VA
WHEO(AM) Stuart VA
WTZE(AM) Tazewell VA
WKCI(AM) Waynesboro VA
WINC(AM) Winchester VA
WVGN(FM) Charlotte Amalie VI
WVWI(AM) Charlotte Amalie VI
WSNO(AM) Barre VT
WBTN(AM) Bennington VT
WKVT(AM) Brattleboro VT
WVMT(AM) Burlington VT
WTSJ(AM) Randolph VT
WSYB(AM) Rutland VT
WDEV-FM Warren VT
WMXR(AM) Woodstock VT
KBKW(AM) Aberdeen WA
KXRO(AM) Aberdeen WA
KGMI(AM) Bellingham WA
*KUGS(FM) Bellingham WA

KARI(AM) Blaine WA
KELA(AM) Centralia-Chehalis WA
KOZI(AM) Chelan WA
*KNWR(FM) Ellensburg WA
KXLE(AM) Ellensburg WA
KULE(AM) Ephrata WA
KONA(AM) Kennewick WA
KTCR(AM) Kennewick WA
KBSN(AM) Moses Lake WA
*KMWS(FM) Mount Vernon WA
*KSVR(FM) Mount Vernon WA
KONP(AM) Port Angeles WA
KQQQ(AM) Pullman WA
*KFAE-FM Richland WA
KKNW(AM) Seattle WA
KKOL(AM) Seattle WA
KJRB(AM) Spokane WA
KPTQ(AM) Spokane WA
KQNT(AM) Spokane WA
KXLY(AM) Spokane WA
KIRO-FM Tacoma WA
*KXOT(FM) Tacoma WA
KGDC(AM) Walla Walla WA
KUJ(AM) Walla Walla WA
*KWWS(FM) Walla Walla WA
KPQ(AM) Wenatchee WA
*KDNA(FM) Yakima WA
KIT(AM) Yakima WA
WXCE(AM) Amery WI
*WLBL(AM) Auburndale WI
WBEV(AM) Beaver Dam WI
*WHSA(FM) Brule WI
*WHAD(FM) Delafield WI
WAYY(AM) Eau Claire WI
KFIZ(AM) Fond du Lac WI
WFAW(AM) Fort Atkinson WI
WTAQ(AM) Green Bay WI
WOGO(AM) Hallie WI
*WHHI(FM) Highland WI
WCLO(AM) Janesville WI
WHBY(AM) Kimberly WI
WIZM(AM) La Crosse WI
WLDY(AM) Ladysmith WI
WIBA(AM) Madison WI
WTDY(AM) Madison WI
WDLB(AM) Marshfield WI
WMEQ(AM) Menomonie WI
*WVSS(FM) Menomonie WI
WTMJ(AM) Milwaukee WI
WOSH(AM) Oshkosh WI
*WHBM(FM) Park Falls WI
WPDR(AM) Portage WI
WRJN(AM) Racine WI
WJMC(AM) Rice Lake WI
WRPN(AM) Ripon WI
*WRPN-FM Ripon WI
WHBL(AM) Sheboygan WI
WSPT(AM) Stevens Point WI
*KUWS(FM) Superior WI
WFDL(AM) Waupun WI
WSAU(AM) Wausau WI
WFHR(AM) Wisconsin Rapids WI
WWNR(AM) Beckley WV
WCST(AM) Berkeley Springs WV
WHIS(AM) Bluefield WV
WCHS(AM) Charleston WV
WTCS(AM) Fairmont WV
WMTD(AM) Hinton WV
WVHU(AM) Huntington WV
WEPM(AM) Martinsburg WV
WRNR(AM) Martinsburg WV
WAJR(AM) Morgantown WV
WVLY(AM) Moundsville WV
WVNT(AM) Parkersburg WV
WBGS(AM) Point Pleasant WV
WRRL(AM) Rainelle WV
WAJR-FM Salem WV
WWVA(AM) Wheeling WV
*KUWA(FM) Afton WY
KBBS(AM) Buffalo WY
KFBC(AM) Cheyenne WY
KODI(AM) Cody WY
KIML(AM) Gillette WY
KUGR(AM) Green River WY
KOWB(AM) Laramie WY
*KGAB(AM) Orchard Valley WY

KROE(AM) Sheridan WY

Nostalgia

WGMZ(FM) Glencoe AL
WBTG(AM) Sheffield AL
KHBM(AM) Monticello AR
KFTT(FM) Bagdad AZ
KFLG(AM) Bullhead City AZ
KVSL(AM) Show Low AZ
*KCEA(FM) Atherton CA
KXBX(AM) Lakeport CA
KBLF(AM) Red Bluff CA
KTHO(AM) South Lake Tahoe CA
KXDZ(FM) Templeton CA
KEZW(AM) Aurora CO
WFCT(FM) Apalachicola FL
WLQH(AM) Chiefland FL
WROD(AM) Daytona Beach FL
WZFN(AM) Fort Walton Beach FL
WDIZ(AM) Panama City FL
WMOG(AM) Brunswick GA
KWLO(AM) Waterloo IA
WAIK(AM) Galesburg IL
WMIX(AM) Mount Vernon IL
WILO(AM) Frankfort IN
WMRI(AM) Marion IN
WIVY(FM) Morehead KY
WVJS(AM) Owensboro KY
WIZZ(AM) Greenfield MA
WTBO(AM) Cumberland MD
WDEA(AM) Ellsworth ME
WBAE(AM) Portland ME
*WYAR(FM) Yarmouth ME
WCBY(AM) Cheboygan MI
WXLA(AM) Dimondale MI
WDBC(AM) Escanaba MI
WFNT(AM) Flint MI
WGRY(AM) Grayling MI
WCSY(AM) South Haven MI
KKIN(AM) Aitkin MN
KDKK-FM Park Rapids MN
KBFL-FM Buffalo MO
KBFL(AM) Springfield MO
WTZQ(AM) Hendersonville NC
*KFBN(FM) Fargo ND
WMYF(AM) Portsmouth NH
WDNY(AM) Dansville NY
WELG(AM) Ellenville NY
*WRVO(FM) Oswego NY
WBZA(AM) Rochester NY
*WRVD(FM) Syracuse NY
*WRVN(FM) Utica NY
*WRVJ(FM) Watertown NY
WCDK(AM) Cadiz OH
WCHI(AM) Chillicothe OH
WJEH(AM) Gallipolis OH
*WMKV(FM) Reading OH
WSOM(AM) Salem OH
WNIO(AM) Youngstown OH
KTIL-FM Tillamook OR
WJAS(AM) Pittsburgh PA
WCAM(AM) Camden SC
WQMV(AM) Waverly TN
KSLI(AM) Abilene TX
KRHC(AM) Burnet TX
WZEZ(FM) Goochland VA
WRAD(AM) Radford VA
KBRD(AM) Lacey WA
KOMW(AM) Omak WA
KTRW(AM) Opportunity WA
WCCN(AM) Neillsville WI
WETZ(AM) New Martinsville WV
WETZ-FM New Martinsville WV

Oldies

KEAG(AM) Anchorage AK
KHAR(AM) Anchorage AK
*KMJG(FM) Homer AK
KBBO-FM Houston AK
*KWJG(FM) Kasilof AK
KFMJ(AM) Ketchikan AK
KXBA(AM) Nikiski AK
KIFW(AM) Sitka AK

WAFN-FM Arab AL
WKAC(AM) Athens AL
WATV(AM) Birmingham AL
WEBJ(AM) Brewton AL
WTBF-FM Brundidge AL
WACQ(AM) Carrville AL
WZNJ(FM) Demopolis AL
WDGM(FM) Greensboro AL
WGYV(AM) Greenville AL
WBPT(FM) Homewood AL
WLOR(AM) Huntsville AL
WHPH(FM) Jemison AL
WLAY-FM Littleville AL
WMFC-FM Monroeville AL
WQKS-FM Montgomery AL
WOPP(AM) Opp AL
WVOK(AM) Oxford AL
WPID(AM) Piedmont AL
WKZD(AM) Priceville AL
WGAD(AM) Rainbow City AL
WJAM(AM) Selma AL
WJDB(AM) Thomasville AL
WJRD(AM) Tuscaloosa AL
WRLD-FM Valley AL
WKXM-FM Winfield AL
KVLD(FM) Atkins AR
KEWI(AM) Benton AR
KQBK(FM) Booneville AR
KFCM(FM) Cherokee Village AR
KGFL(AM) Clinton AR
KTRQ(FM) Colt AR
KBKG(FM) Corning AR
KFLI(FM) Des Arc AR
KLSZ-FM Fort Smith AR
KBYB(FM) Hope AR
KKIK(FM) Horseshoe Bend AR
KOLL(FM) Lonoke AR
KQOR(FM) Mena AR
KQMJ(FM) Osceola AR
KAMO-FM Rogers AR
KWAK-FM Stuttgart AR
KRLW(AM) Walnut Ridge AR
KWRF(AM) Warren AR
KCTT-FM Yellville AR
KXFF(FM) Colorado City AZ
KKLD(FM) Cottonwood AZ
KGVY(AM) Green Valley AZ
KRCY-FM Lake Havasu City AZ
KIKO(AM) Miami AZ
KGMG(FM) Oracle AZ
KPKR(FM) Parker AZ
KOOL-FM Phoenix AZ
KOY(AM) Phoenix AZ
KAZG(AM) Scottsdale AZ
KZKE(FM) Seligman AZ
KSNX(FM) Show Low AZ
KKYZ(FM) Sierra Vista AZ
KCEE(AM) Tucson AZ
KWFM(AM) Tucson AZ
KJOK(AM) Yuma AZ
KIQO(FM) Atascadero CA
KBRE(FM) Atwater CA
KHYL(FM) Auburn CA
KKBB(FM) Bakersfield CA
KBOV(AM) Bishop CA
KODS(FM) Carnelian Bay CA
KPOD(FM) Crescent City CA
KZRO(FM) Dunsmuir CA
KXO(AM) El Centro CA
KKHB(FM) Eureka CA
*KYAF(FM) Firebaugh CA
KMGV(FM) Fresno CA
KMJ-FM Fresno CA
KAZA(AM) Gilroy CA
KRAK(AM) Hesperia CA
KOKO-FM Kerman CA
KOMY(AM) La Selva Beach CA
KVLI-FM Lake Isabella CA
KBOX(FM) Lompoc CA
KRTH(FM) Los Angeles CA
KCEZ(FM) Los Molinos CA
KABX-FM Merced CA
KNAH(FM) Merced CA
KIDD(AM) Monterey CA
KHOP(FM) Oakdale CA
KOCN(FM) Pacific Grove CA

KDES-FM Palm Springs CA
KNWQ(AM) Palm Springs CA
KCCL(FM) Placerville CA
KLOA(AM) Ridgecrest CA
KOLA(AM) San Bernardino CA
KURS(AM) San Diego CA
KFRC(AM) San Francisco CA
KISQ(FM) San Francisco CA
KKSF(AM) San Francisco CA
KRDG(FM) Shingletown CA
KQOD(FM) Stockton CA
KSTN(AM) Stockton CA
KFSO-FM Visalia CA
KRCV(FM) West Covina CA
KRSX-FM Yermo CA
KUBA(AM) Yuba City CA
KCMN(AM) Colorado Springs CO
KRWZ(AM) Denver CO
KXKL-FM Denver CO
KBKL(FM) Grand Junction CO
KEJJ(FM) Gunnison CO
KZMV(FM) Kremmling CO
KBLJ(AM) La Junta CO
KLIM(AM) Limon CO
KJEB(FM) New Castle CO
KSTC(AM) Sterling CO
WNLC(FM) East Lyme CT
WDRC-FM Hartford CT
WKNL(FM) New London CT
WREF(AM) Ridgefield CT
WQQQ(FM) Sharon CT
WATR(AM) Waterbury CT
WBIG-FM Washington DC
WLBW(FM) Fenwick Island DE
WNCL(FM) Milford DE
*WMHS(FM) Pike Creek DE
WFHT(AM) Avon Park FL
WWBF(AM) Bartow FL
WRGO(FM) Cedar Key FL
WPFL(FM) Century FL
WMMV(AM) Cocoa FL
WSRZ-FM Coral Cove FL
WZEP(AM) De Funiak Springs FL
WBPC(FM) Ebro FL
WNTY(FM) Estero FL
WOLZ(FM) Fort Myers FL
WOLL(FM) Hobe Sound FL
WJGL(FM) Jacksonville FL
WEGT(FM) Lafayette FL
WDSR(AM) Lake City FL
WQHL(AM) Live Oak FL
WEBZ(FM) Mexico Beach FL
WMFQ(FM) Ocala FL
WPLK(AM) Palatka FL
WYCL(FM) Pensacola FL
WMXJ(FM) Pompano Beach FL
WSJF(FM) Saint Augustine Beach FL
WPOI(FM) Saint Petersburg FL
WJCM(AM) Sebring FL
WJQB(FM) Spring Hill FL
WRBQ-FM Tampa FL
WQOL(FM) Vero Beach FL
WTTB(AM) Vero Beach FL
WISK(AM) Americus GA
WMGR(AM) Bainbridge GA
WEBS(AM) Calhoun GA
WBHF(AM) Cartersville GA
WCLA(AM) Claxton GA
WGFS(AM) Covington GA
WCUG(AM) Cuthbert GA
WMRZ(FM) Dawson GA
WXJO(AM) Douglasville GA
WKVQ(AM) Eatonton GA
WDDK(FM) Greensboro GA
WKEU(AM) Griffin GA
WNGM(AM) Hiawassee GA
WTRP(AM) La Grange GA
WPEH(AM) Louisville GA
WAYS(AM) Macon GA
WYTH(AM) Madison GA
WYIS(AM) McRae GA
WYSC(FM) McRae GA
WGCO(FM) Midway GA
WMNZ(AM) Montezuma GA
WMTM-FM Moultrie GA
WSSY(FM) Pinehurst GA

WSFB(AM) Quitman GA
WUUS(AM) Rossville GA
WJFL(FM) Tennille GA
WPAX(AM) Thomasville GA
WATG(FM) Trion GA
WVOP(AM) Vidalia GA
WWUF(AM) Waycross GA
WRLA(AM) West Point GA
KKOL-FM Aiea HI
KQMQ-FM Honolulu HI
KTOH(AM) Kalaheo HI
KBGX(FM) Keaau HI
KONI(AM) Lanai City HI
KIIC(FM) Albia IA
KASI(AM) Ames IA
KOJY(FM) Bloomfield IA
KCIM(AM) Carroll IA
KEDB(FM) Chariton IA
KCHE(AM) Cherokee IA
KCLN(AM) Clinton IA
KJOC(AM) Davenport IA
KIOA(FM) Des Moines IA
*KJMC(FM) Des Moines IA
KGRR(FM) Epworth IA
KIOW(FM) Forest City IA
KVFD(AM) Fort Dodge IA
KLMJ(FM) Hampton IA
KNOD(FM) Harlan IA
KKMA(FM) Le Mars IA
KDAO(AM) Marshalltown IA
KRIB(AM) Mason City IA
KWPC(AM) Muscatine IA
*KIGC(FM) Oskaloosa IA
KIYX(FM) Sageville IA
KWSL(AM) Sioux City IA
KTLB(FM) Twin Lakes IA
KRQN(FM) Vinton IA
KCII(AM) Washington IA
KCII-FM Washington IA
KOKZ(FM) Waterloo IA
KHPP(AM) Waukon IA
KAWO(FM) Boise ID
KGEM(AM) Boise ID
KBAR(AM) Burley ID
KCID(AM) Caldwell ID
KVNI(AM) Coeur d'Alene ID
KDJQ(AM) Meridian ID
KRPL(AM) Moscow ID
KQLZ(FM) Mountain Home ID
KLIX-FM Twin Falls ID
KTFI(AM) Twin Falls ID
WQRL(FM) Benton IL
WROY(AM) Carmi IL
WILY(AM) Centralia IL
WJMK(FM) Chicago IL
WLS-FM Chicago IL
WMQZ(FM) Colchester IL
WPPN(FM) Des Plaines IL
WIXN(AM) Dixon IL
WWYW(FM) Dundee IL
KUUL(FM) East Moline IL
*WRSE(FM) Elmhurst IL
WHPI(FM) Glasford IL
WJBM(AM) Jerseyville IL
WEAI(FM) Lynnville IL
WDKR(FM) Maroa IL
WPWQ(FM) Mount Sterling IL
WHQQ(FM) Neoga IL
WSEY(FM) Oregon IL
WPXN(AM) Paxton IL
WTRX-FM Pontiac IL
WZOE-FM Princeton IL
WTRH(AM) Ramsey IL
WKXQ(FM) Rushville IL
WEJT(FM) Shelbyville IL
WQQL(FM) Springfield IL
WYYS(FM) Streator IL
WCFF(AM) Urbana IL
WYKT(FM) Wilmington IL
WASK-FM Battle Ground IN
WQRK(FM) Bedford IN
WKLU(FM) Brownsburg IN
WIFE(AM) Connersville IN
WOCC(AM) Corydon IN
WCVL(AM) Crawfordsville IN
WIBN(FM) Earl Park IN

WTRC(AM) Elkhart IN
WURK(FM) Elwood IN
WJLT(FM) Evansville IN
WLDE(FM) Fort Wayne IN
WTLC-FM Greenwood IN
WBZQ(AM) Huntington IN
*WJPR(FM) Jasper IN
WAWK(AM) Kendallville IN
*WJEF(FM) Lafayette IN
WQTY(FM) Linton IN
WXGO(AM) Madison IN
WEFM(FM) Michigan City IN
WERK(FM) Muncie IN
WNDA(AM) New Albany IN
WJJK(FM) Noblesville IN
WSEZ(AM) Paoli IN
WTCA(AM) Plymouth IN
WZOC(FM) Plymouth IN
WSJD(FM) Princeton IN
WRIN(AM) Rensselaer IN
WROI(FM) Rochester IN
WAXI(FM) Rockville IN
WZZB(AM) Seymour IN
WTCJ(AM) Tell City IN
WSKL(FM) Veedersburg IN
WJOT(AM) Wabash IN
WJOT-FM Wabash IN
WRSW-FM Warsaw IN
KSAJ-FM Abilene KS
KCAR-FM Baxter Springs KS
KAHE(FM) Dodge City KS
KVOE(AM) Emporia KS
KMDO(AM) Fort Scott KS
KGGF-FM Fredonia KS
KAYS(AM) Hays KS
KWHK(FM) Hutchinson KS
KBGL(FM) Larned KS
KSOB(FM) Larned KS
KBBE(FM) McPherson KS
KLKC-FM Parsons KS
KMMM(AM) Pratt KS
KSKL(FM) Scott City KS
KWIC(FM) Topeka KS
KWME(FM) Wellington KS
KEYN-FM Wichita KS
KFTI(AM) Wichita KS
WMDJ-FM Allen KY
WANV(FM) Annville KY
WCBL-FM Benton KY
WKDZ(AM) Cadiz KY
WBVX(FM) Carlisle KY
WAIN(AM) Columbia KY
WCTT(AM) Corbin KY
WCYN(AM) Cynthiana KY
WEKB(AM) Elkhorn City KY
WKYW(AM) Frankfort KY
WOVO(FM) Glasgow KY
WUGO(FM) Grayson KY
WKYA(FM) Greenville KY
WXMZ(FM) Hartford KY
WKIC(AM) Hazard KY
WQXY(AM) Hazard KY
WHVO(AM) Hopkinsville KY
WIRV(AM) Irvine KY
WLBN(AM) Lebanon KY
WLSK(FM) Lebanon KY
WWXL(AM) Manchester KY
WMJL-FM Marion KY
WFTM(AM) Maysville KY
WMKJ(FM) Mt. Sterling KY
WVJS(AM) Owensboro KY
WSIP(AM) Paintsville KY
WSIP(AM) Paintsville KY
WPKE(AM) Pikeville KY
WANO(AM) Pineville KY
WXKZ-FM Prestonsburg KY
WWKY(AM) Providence KY
WAKY(FM) Radcliff KY
WCND(AM) Shelbyville KY
WKEQ(AM) Somerset KY
WTLO(AM) Somerset KY
WLKS(AM) West Liberty KY
WXKQ(FM) Whitesburg KY
WGKY(FM) Wickliffe KY
WTGG(AM) Amite LA

KSIG(AM) Crowley LA
KFNV-FM Ferriday LA
WTIX-FM Galliano LA
KLEB(AM) Golden Meadow LA
KHLA(AM) Jennings LA
KLLA(AM) Leesville LA
KASO(AM) Minden LA
KLKL(FM) Minden LA
KLIL(FM) Moreauville LA
KMYO-FM Morgan City LA
KZBL(AM) Natchitoches LA
KRDJ(FM) New Iberia LA
WIST(AM) New Orleans LA
KWCL-FM Oak Grove LA
KPCH(FM) Ruston LA
KVPI-FM Ville Platte LA
WODS(FM) Boston MA
*WXRB(FM) Dudley MA
WCIB(FM) Falmouth MA
WATD-FM Marshfield MA
WUPE-FM North Adams MA
WJOE(AM) Orange-Athol MA
WUPE(AM) Pittsfield MA
WARE(AM) Ware MA
WORC-FM Webster MA
WCTR(AM) Chestertown MD
WCMD(AM) Cumberland MD
WTDK(FM) Federalsburg MD
WCTN(AM) Potomac-Cabin John MD
WICL(FM) Williamsport MD
WJZN(AM) Augusta ME
WJTO(AM) Bath ME
WCXU(FM) Caribou ME
WKTJ-FM Farmington ME
WABK-FM Gardiner ME
WLVP(AM) Gorham ME
WBYA(FM) Islesboro ME
WLAM(AM) Lewiston ME
WCXX(FM) Madawaska ME
WCXV(FM) Van Buren ME
WTVL(AM) Waterville ME
WYNZ(FM) Westbrook ME
*WYAR(FM) Yarmouth ME
XHRM-FM Tijuana MEX
WHNN(FM) Bay City MI
WMRX-FM Beaverton MI
WCZW(FM) Charlevoix MI
WTVB(AM) Coldwater MI
WOBE(FM) Crystal Falls MI
WOMC(FM) Detroit MI
WGKL(FM) Gladstone MI
WKAD(FM) Harrietta MI
*WHPR(FM) Highland Park MI
WHTO(FM) Iron Mountain MI
*WJKQ(FM) Jackson MI
WMLQ(FM) Manistee MI
WMTE-FM Manistee MI
WTIQ(AM) Manistique MI
WHLX(AM) Marine City MI
WAGN(AM) Menominee MI
WHYB(FM) Menominee MI
WMPX(AM) Midland MI
WQXO(AM) Munising MI
WNGE(FM) Negaunee MI
WNBY-FM Newberry MI
WLCS(FM) North Muskegon MI
*WAQQ(FM) Onsted MI
WQXC-FM Otsego MI
WLXT(FM) Petoskey MI
WHLS(AM) Port Huron MI
WDEE-FM Reed City MI
WHAK-FM Rogers City MI
WYVN(FM) Saugatuck MI
WCSY-FM South Haven MI
*WSHJ(FM) Southfield MI
WMSH-FM Sturgis MI
WCCW-FM Traverse City MI
WPON(AM) Walled Lake MI
WBMI(FM) West Branch MI
KULO(AM) Alexandria MN
KQQL(FM) Anoka MN
KAUS(AM) Austin MN
KSCR-FM Benson MN
WQXJ(FM) Blackduck MN
KBEW(AM) Blue Earth MN
KUAL-FM Brainerd MN

KRWC(AM) Buffalo MN
WGVY(FM) Cambridge MN
WKLK(AM) Cloquet MN
KLDJ(FM) Duluth MN
WGVZ(FM) Eden Prairie MN
KJJK(AM) Fergus Falls MN
KKCQ(AM) Fosston MN
KKRC(FM) Granite Falls MN
WMFG-FM Hibbing MN
KDUZ(AM) Hutchinson MN
KGHS(AM) International Falls MN
KRAQ(FM) Jackson MN
KQEG(FM) La Crescent MN
WGVX(FM) Lakeville MN
KLQP(FM) Madison MN
KRJM(FM) Mahnomen MN
WMOZ(FM) Moose Lake MN
KRDS-FM New Prague MN
KRFO(AM) Owatonna MN
KISD(FM) Pipestone MN
KWNG(FM) Red Wing MN
KLGR-FM Redwood Falls MN
KNXR(FM) Rochester MN
KXAC(FM) Saint James MN
KZJK(FM) Saint Louis Park MN
KVGO(FM) Spring Valley MN
KLBB(AM) Stillwater MN
KAKK(AM) Walker MN
KRUE(FM) Waseca MN
KDJS(AM) Willmar MN
KWNO(AM) Winona MN
KOZX(FM) Caboool MO
KCRV-FM Caruthersville MO
KCHR(AM) Charleston MO
KCHI(AM) Chillicothe MO
KCHI-FM Chillicothe MO
KDKD(AM) Clinton MO
*KWWC-FM Columbia MO
KDFN(AM) Doniphan MO
KYMO-FM East Prairie MO
KESM(AM) El Dorado Springs MO
KCMO-FM Kansas City MO
KBOA(AM) Kennett MO
KXOQ(FM) Kennett MO
KOMC-FM Kimberling City MO
KIRX(AM) Kirksville MO
KQUL(FM) Lake Ozark MO
KJMO(FM) Linn MO
KRLI(FM) Malta Bend MO
KBHI(AM) Miner MO
KZZT(FM) Moberly MO
KWBZ(FM) Monroe City MO
KXMO-FM Owensville MO
KLID(AM) Poplar Bluff MO
KESJ(AM) Saint Joseph MO
KZQZ(AM) Saint Louis MO
KOKO(AM) Warrensburg MO
KOSP(FM) Willard MO
KUKU-FM Willow Springs MO
WAFM(FM) Amory MS
WIZK(AM) Bay Springs MS
WHKL(FM) Crenshaw MS
WNIX(AM) Greenville MS
WOHT(FM) Grenada MS
WQJQ(AM) Kosciusko MS
WAGR-FM Lexington MS
WAZA(FM) Liberty MS
WNAU(AM) New Albany MS
WOXD(FM) Oxford MS
WMTI(FM) Picayune MS
WCJU-FM Prentiss MS
WVBG-FM Redwood MS
WROB(AM) West Point MS
KANA(AM) Anaconda MT
KKBR(FM) Billings MT
KOBB-FM Bozeman MT
KXTL(AM) Butte MT
KKGR(AM) East Helena MT
KIKC(AM) Forsyth MT
KXGN(AM) Glendive MT
KEIN(AM) Great Falls MT
KLFM(FM) Great Falls MT
KMTX(AM) Helena MT
KOFI(AM) Kalispell MT
KTNY(FM) Libby MT
KBQQ(FM) Pinesdale MT

KSEN(AM) Shelby MT
KWYS(AM) West Yellowstone MT
KWOL-FM Whitefish MT
KVCK(AM) Wolf Point MT
WZKY(AM) Albemarle NC
WPCM(AM) Burlington NC
WCSL(AM) Cherryville NC
WCLN(AM) Clinton NC
WERX-FM Columbia NC
WEGO(AM) Concord NC
WBLA(AM) Elizabethtown NC
WODR(FM) Fair Bluff NC
WWKO(AM) Fair Bluff NC
WFSC(AM) Franklin NC
WTRG(FM) Gaston NC
WGNC(AM) Gastonia NC
WKIX(FM) Goldsboro NC
WNCT(AM) Greenville NC
WNCT-FM Greenville NC
WIZS(AM) Henderson NC
WFMZ(FM) Hertford NC
WAIZ(AM) Hickory NC
WXRC(FM) Hickory NC
WCCG(FM) Hope Mills NC
WTHZ(FM) Lexington NC
WLON(AM) Lincolnton NC
WFVL(FM) Lumberton NC
WHIP(AM) Mooresville NC
WZPR(FM) Nags Head NC
WZAX(FM) Nashville NC
WWMY(FM) Raleigh NC
WLWL(AM) Rockingham NC
WFJA(FM) Sanford NC
WOHS(AM) Shelby NC
WTOE(AM) Spruce Pine NC
WACB(AM) Taylorsville NC
WSVM(AM) Valdese NC
WMXF(AM) Waynesville NC
*KEYA(FM) Belcourt ND
KACL(FM) Bismarck ND
KDVL(FM) Devils Lake ND
KDIX(AM) Dickinson ND
KAUJ(FM) Grafton ND
KKXL(AM) Grand Forks ND
KMJO(FM) Hope ND
KRRZ(AM) Minot ND
KEGK(FM) Wahpeton ND
KCOW(AM) Alliance NE
KGMT(AM) Fairbury NE
KTNC(AM) Falls City NE
KFMT-FM Fremont NE
KSDZ(AM) Gordon NE
KUVR(AM) Holdrege NE
KADL(FM) Imperial NE
KKPR-FM Kearney NE
KYOY(FM) Kimball NE
KLNC(FM) Lincoln NE
KBRL(AM) McCook NE
KOGA(AM) Ogallala NE
KNLV(AM) Ord NE
KRFS(AM) Superior NE
KOAQ(AM) Terrytown NE
KCTY(FM) Wayne NE
KAWL(AM) York NE
WMOU(AM) Berlin NH
WEZS(AM) Laconia NH
WLTN(AM) Littleton NH
WFYX(FM) Walpole NH
WMID(AM) Atlantic City NJ
WIBG-FM Avalon NJ
WRNJ(AM) Hackettstown NJ
WOBM(AM) Lakewood NJ
WJRZ-FM Manahawkin NJ
WMTR(AM) Morristown NJ
WCTC(AM) New Brunswick NJ
WTOC(AM) Newton NJ
WTKU-FM Ocean City NJ
WGHT(AM) Pompton Lakes NJ
WVLT(FM) Vineland NJ
KDEF(AM) Albuquerque NM
KRKE(AM) Albuquerque NM
KKFG(FM) Bloomfield NM
KCCC(AM) Carlsbad NM
KRMQ-FM Clovis NM
KWKA(AM) Clovis NM
KDSK(FM) Grants NM

KVLC(FM) Hatch NM
KHOB(AM) Hobbs NM
*KEDP(FM) Las Vegas NM
KABG(FM) Los Alamos NM
KLEA-FM Lovington NM
KRTN-FM Raton NM
*KRDR(FM) Red River NM
KBCQ(AM) Roswell NM
KCRX(AM) Roswell NM
KBUY(AM) Ruidoso NM
KCHS(AM) Truth or Consequences NM
KNYE(FM) Pahrump NV
WSEN(AM) Baldwinsville NY
WSEN-FM Baldwinsville NY
WABH(AM) Bath NY
WBZO(FM) Bay Shore NY
WENI-FM Big Flats NY
WHTT-FM Buffalo NY
WPTR(FM) Clifton Park NY
WSDE(AM) Cobleskill NY
WIYN(FM) Deposit NY
WDOE(AM) Dunkirk NY
WALK(AM) East Patchogue NY
WFKL(FM) Fairport NY
WGIX-FM Gouverneur NY
WXUR(FM) Herkimer NY
WXHC(FM) Homer NY
WFXF(FM) Honeoye Falls NY
WHHO(AM) Hornell NY
WZCR(FM) Hudson NY
WNYQ(FM) Hudson Falls NY
WHVW(AM) Hyde Park NY
WKSN(AM) Jamestown NY
WCKM-FM Lake George NY
WVOS-FM Liberty NY
WICY(AM) Malone NY
WCBS-FM New York NY
WGNY(AM) Newburgh NY
WPAC(FM) Ogdensburg NY
WHDL(AM) Olean NY
WMCR(AM) Oneida NY
WMCR-FM Oneida NY
WZOZ(FM) Oneonta NY
WKOL(FM) Plattsburgh NY
WVTK(FM) Port Henry NY
WDLC(AM) Port Jervis NY
WCQL(FM) Queensbury NY
WRIV(AM) Riverhead NY
WODZ-FM Rome NY
WTRY-FM Rotterdam NY
WLNG(FM) Sag Harbor NY
WVKZ(AM) Schenectady NY
WCDO-FM Sidney NY
WIPS(AM) Ticonderoga NY
WDLA(AM) Walton NY
WTBQ(AM) Warwick NY
WJQZ(FM) Wellsville NY
WNYV(FM) Whitehall NY
*WRMU(FM) Alliance OH
WOHF(AM) Bellevue OH
WRQN(FM) Bowling Green OH
WQCT(AM) Bryan OH
WYNT(FM) Caledonia OH
WHBC(AM) Canton OH
WCIN(AM) Cincinnati OH
WMJI(FM) Cleveland OH
WBVB(FM) Coal Grove OH
WYBZ(FM) Crooksville OH
WJER(AM) Dover-New Philadelphia OH
WOHI(AM) East Liverpool OH
WGTZ(FM) Eaton OH
WZOO-FM Edgewood OH
WZRX-FM Fort Shawnee OH
WCIT(AM) Lima OH
WDLW(AM) Lorain OH
WAGX(AM) Manchester OH
WMRN(AM) Marion OH
*WLMH(FM) Morrow OH
WBBG(AM) Niles OH
WKSD(FM) Paulding OH
WPTW(AM) Piqua OH
WMLX(FM) Saint Mary's OH
WSWR(FM) Shelby OH
WDIG(AM) Steubenville OH
*WKTL(FM) Struthers OH

WWWM-FM Sylvania OH
WKVX(AM) Wooster OH
KALV(AM) Alva OK
KJMZ(FM) Cache OK
KZLI(AM) Catoosa OK
KRVT(AM) Claremore OK
KTSO(FM) Glenpool OK
KKRX(AM) Lawton OK
KYNZ(FM) Lone Grove OK
KLOR-FM Ponca City OK
WBBZ(AM) Ponca City OK
KVRO(FM) Stillwater OK
KSLE(FM) Wewoka OK
KRAT(FM) Altamont OR
KKBC-FM Baker City OR
KQAK(FM) Bend OR
KURY(AM) Brookings OR
KCNA(FM) Cave Junction OR
KDCQ(FM) Coos Bay OR
KRJT(FM) Elgin OR
KKNX(AM) Eugene OR
KODZ(FM) Eugene OR
KCST-FM Florence OR
KLTH(FM) Lake Oswego OR
KLYC(AM) McMinnville OR
KLDZ(FM) Medford OR
KVAN-FM Pilot Rock OR
KBZY(AM) Salem OR
KSWB(AM) Seaside OR
KACI-FM The Dalles OR
KCUP(AM) Toledo OR
KPPT-FM Toledo OR
WFBG(AM) Altoona PA
WLZS(FM) Beaver Springs PA
WALY(FM) Bellwood PA
WFBS(AM) Berwick PA
WHLM-FM Berwick PA
WKQL(FM) Brookville PA
WCCL(FM) Central City PA
WCPA(AM) Clearfield PA
WKPL(FM) Ellwood City PA
WHPA(FM) Gallitzin PA
WHKF(FM) Harrisburg PA
WTKT(AM) Harrisburg PA
WYCY(FM) Hawley PA
WAZL(AM) Hazleton PA
WDAD(AM) Indiana PA
WTYM(AM) Kittanning PA
WLSH(AM) Lansford PA
WKVA(AM) Lewistown PA
WMVL(FM) Linesville PA
WBPZ(AM) Lock Haven PA
WQZS(FM) Meyersdale PA
WBZD-FM Muncy PA
WJST(AM) New Castle PA
WYNE(AM) North East PA
WNCC(AM) Northern Cambria PA
WKQW(AM) Oil City PA
WOGL(FM) Philadelphia PA
WWSW-FM Pittsburgh PA
WSOX(FM) Red Lion PA
WKBI(AM) Saint Marys PA
WLSW(FM) Scottdale PA
WARM(AM) Scranton PA
WYFM(FM) Sharon PA
WPHD(AM) South Waverly PA
WCDW(FM) Susquehanna PA
WTTC(AM) Towanda PA
WTTC-FM Towanda PA
WPKL(FM) Uniontown PA
WOWY(FM) University Park PA
WRRN(FM) Warren PA
WJPA(AM) Washington PA
WJPA-FM Washington PA
*WRLC(FM) Williamsport PA
WOIZ(AM) Guayanilla PR
WTIL(AM) Mayaguez PR
WYEL(AM) Mayaguez PR
WLEO(AM) Ponce PR
WZAR(FM) Ponce PR
WIDI(FM) Quebradillas PR
WKVM(AM) San Juan PR
WRSS(AM) San Sebastian PR
WWBB(FM) Providence RI
WZLA-FM Abbeville SC
WZLA-FM Abbeville SC

WKSP(FM) Aiken SC
WBSC(AM) Bennettsville SC
WGFG(FM) Branchville SC
WPUB-FM Camden SC
WCRE(AM) Cheraw SC
WAHT(AM) Clemson SC
WLXC(FM) Columbia SC
WYNN(AM) Florence SC
WLFF(FM) Georgetown SC
WPCI(AM) Greenville SC
WOLT(FM) Greer SC
WKSX-FM Johnston SC
WKSC(AM) Kershaw SC
WCOO(FM) Kiawah Island SC
WAGL(AM) Lancaster SC
WOMG(FM) Lexington SC
WYEZ(FM) Murrell's Inlet SC
WGUS-FM New Ellenton SC
WKDK(AM) Newberry SC
WXLY(FM) North Charleston SC
WGZO(FM) Parris Island SC
WLOW(FM) Port Royal SC
*WRBK(FM) Richburg SC
WWJN(FM) Ridgeland SC
WJES(AM) Saluda SC
WSNW(AM) Seneca SC
WWBD(FM) Sumter SC
WJTP(AM) Walhalla SC
*WNBK(FM) Whitmire SC
KAWK(FM) Custer SD
KDSJ(AM) Deadwood SD
KSQB-FM Dell Rapids SD
KBJM(AM) Lemmon SD
KKSD(FM) Milbank SD
KMSD(AM) Milbank SD
KCCR(AM) Pierre SD
KKLS(AM) Rapid City SD
KVHT(FM) Vermillion SD
KUQL(FM) Wessington Springs SD
WVOL(AM) Berry Hill TN
WBOL(AM) Bolivar TN
WOPI(AM) Bristol TN
WDOD(AM) Chattanooga TN
WKOM(FM) Columbia TN
WZYX(AM) Cowan TN
WCDZ(FM) Dresden TN
WTRO(AM) Dyersburg TN
*WVCP(FM) Gallatin TN
WSMG(AM) Greeneville TN
WIRJ(AM) Humboldt TN
WMXX-FM Jackson TN
WKTP(AM) Jonesborough TN
WHGG(AM) Kingsport TN
WKPT(AM) Kingsport TN
*WKCS(FM) Knoxville TN
WKSR-FM Loretto TN
WMSR(AM) Manchester TN
WCMT(AM) Martin TN
WHDM(AM) McKenzie TN
WTPR-FM McKinnon TN
WXMX(FM) Millington TN
WLIK(AM) Newport TN
WATO(AM) Oak Ridge TN
WOKI(FM) Oliver Springs TN
WTPR(AM) Paris TN
WQKR(AM) Portland TN
WKSR(AM) Pulaski TN
WORM(AM) Savannah TN
WSDT(AM) Soddy-Daisy TN
WTZX(AM) Sparta TN
WLOD-FM Sweetwater TN
WNTT(AM) Tazewell TN
WENK(AM) Union City TN
WWON(AM) Waynesboro TN
KULL(FM) Abilene TX
KBYG(AM) Big Spring TX
KNTX(AM) Bowie TX
KNEL(AM) Brady TX
KRVA-FM Campbell TX
KPUR-FM Canyon TX
KCTX(AM) Childress TX
KEFH(FM) Clarendon TX
KGAP(FM) Clarksville TX
KMXR(FM) Corpus Christi TX
KIVY(AM) Crockett TX
KXIT(FM) Dalhart TX

KBFB(FM) Dallas TX
KLUV(FM) Dallas TX
KWMC(AM) Del Rio TX
KDDD-FM Dumas TX
KINL(FM) Eagle Pass TX
KAMA(AM) El Paso TX
KOFX(FM) El Paso TX
KLDE(FM) Eldorado TX
KGBC(AM) Galveston TX
KKDA(AM) Grand Prairie TX
KCOL-FM Groves TX
KONO-FM Helotes TX
KTBZ-FM Houston TX
KHVL(AM) Huntsville TX
KRVF(FM) Kerens TX
KGLK(FM) Lake Jackson TX
KSHN-FM Liberty TX
KITY(FM) Llano TX
KKCL(FM) Lorenzo TX
KDAV(AM) Lubbock TX
KQXX-FM Mission TX
KCKM(AM) Monahans TX
KEWL-FM New Boston TX
KZRB(FM) New Boston TX
KMCM(FM) Odessa TX
KEYE-FM Perryton TX
KREW(AM) Plainview TX
KITE(FM) Port Lavaca TX
KROB(AM) Robstown TX
KTLU(AM) Rusk TX
KWRW(FM) Rusk TX
KONO(AM) San Antonio TX
KBPA(FM) San Marcos TX
KJIM(AM) Sherman TX
*KSQX(FM) Springtown TX
*KQXS(FM) Stephenville TX
KVWC(AM) Vernon TX
KVWC-FM Vernon TX
KNAL(AM) Victoria TX
KBGO(FM) Waco TX
*KMQX(FM) Weatherford TX
KVLL-FM Wells TX
KBDX(FM) Blanding UT
KXBN(FM) Cedar City UT
KLGN(AM) Logan UT
KODJ(FM) Salt Lake City UT
KGNT(FM) Smithfield UT
KDYL(AM) South Salt Lake UT
WABN(AM) Abingdon VA
WODI(AM) Brookneal VA
WBOP(FM) Buffalo Gap VA
*WFOS(FM) Chesapeake VA
WDIC-FM Clinchco VA
WGRQ(FM) Colonial Beach VA
WKEY(AM) Covington VA
WBTM(AM) Danville VA
WILA(AM) Danville VA
WYTT(FM) Emporia VA
WZRV(FM) Front Royal VA
WHAP(AM) Hopewell VA
WLRV(FM) Lebanon VA
WSLK(AM) Moneta VA
WZFM(FM) Narrows VA
WARV-FM Petersburg VA
WBBT-FM Powhatan VA
WRXL(FM) Richmond VA
WXBX(FM) Rural Retreat VA
WSVO(FM) Staunton VA
WKQY(FM) Tazewell VA
WJZW(FM) Woodbridge VA
WSTA(AM) Charlotte Amalie VI
WMNG(FM) Christiansted VI
WUSX(FM) Addison VT
WWOD(FM) Hartford VT
WSKI(AM) Montpelier VT
WVNR(AM) Poultney VT
WCFR(AM) Springfield VT
KOLW(FM) Basin City WA
KRQT(AM) Castle Rock WA
KITI(AM) Chehalis-Centralia WA
KEYF-FM Cheney WA
KLCK(AM) Goldendale WA
KEYG-FM Grand Coulee WA
KARY-FM Grandview WA
KEDO(AM) Longview WA
KBRC(AM) Mount Vernon WA

KRIZ(AM) Renton WA
KMAS(AM) Shelton WA
KBBD(FM) Spokane WA
KYNR(AM) Toppenish WA
KCSY(FM) Twisp WA
KTEL(AM) Walla Walla WA
WBDK(FM) Algoma WI
WATW(AM) Ashland WI
WOLX-FM Baraboo WI
WAQE-FM Barron WI
WGEZ(AM) Beloit WI
WWIS(AM) Black River Falls WI
WOTE(AM) Clintonville WI
WTTN(AM) Columbus WI
WRJO(FM) Eagle River WI
WRKU(FM) Forestville WI
WDGY(AM) Hudson WI
WHRY(AM) Hurley WI
WNXR(FM) Iron River WI
WOGB(FM) Kaukauna WI
WJBL(FM) Ladysmith WI
WHIT(AM) Madison WI
WLTU(FM) Manitowoc WI
WRJC(AM) Mauston WI
WMDC(FM) Mayville WI
WMQA-FM Minocqua WI
WSFQ(FM) Peshtigo WI
WPRE(AM) Prairie du Chien WI
WRDB(AM) Reedsburg WI
WSBW(FM) Sister Bay WI
WBOG(AM) Tomah WI
WJJQ-FM Tomahawk WI
WGBW(AM) Two Rivers WI
WVRQ(AM) Viroqua WI
WKCH(FM) Whitewater WI
WVBO(FM) Winneconne WI
WFGM-FM Barrackville WV
WIWS(AM) Beckley WV
WUKL(FM) Bethlehem WV
WELD(AM) Fisher WV
*WFGH(FM) Fort Gay WV
WVRW(FM) Glenville WV
WMTD(AM) Hinton WV
WMTD-FM Hinton WV
WCBC-FM Keyser WV
WFSP-FM Kingwood WV
WKAZ-FM Miami WV
WCLG(AM) Morgantown WV
WAXS(FM) Oak Hill WV
WADC(AM) Parkersburg WV
WKCJ(FM) Ronceverte WV
WSGB(AM) Sutton WV
WDMX(FM) Vienna WV
WHAW(AM) Weston WV
WBBD(AM) Wheeling WV
WBTH(AM) Williamson WV
KBBS(AM) Buffalo WY
*KKRR(FM) Casper WY
KMLD(FM) Casper WY
KRRR(FM) Cheyenne WY
KMJY(FM) Chugwater WY
KKTY(AM) Douglas WY
KZWB(FM) Green River WY
KANT(FM) Guernsey WY
KMER(AM) Kemmerer WY
KUSZ(FM) Laramie WY
KREO(FM) Pine Bluffs WY
KPIN(FM) Pinedale WY
KVOW(AM) Riverton WY
KRKK(AM) Rock Springs WY
KTHE(AM) Thermopolis WY
KWOR(AM) Worland WY

Other

*KBBI(AM) Homer AK
KRXX(AM) Kodiak AK
WUHT(FM) Birmingham AL
WOZK(AM) Ozark AL
WTBF(AM) Troy AL
KXHT(FM) Marion AR
KFLG(AM) Bullhead City AZ
KLNZ(FM) Glendale AZ
KSZR(FM) Oro Valley AZ
KAZM(AM) Sedona AZ
*KOHN(FM) Sells AZ

KHOV-FM Wickenburg AZ
*KHSU-FM Arcata CA
KDUC(AM) Barstow CA
KSZL(AM) Barstow CA
KXXZ(AM) Barstow CA
KCIK(AM) Blue Lake CA
KOND(FM) Clovis CA
KDAC(AM) Fort Bragg CA
KNCR(AM) Fortuna CA
KXTS(FM) Geyserville CA
KGBA-FM Holtville CA
*KCRY(FM) Mojave CA
*KKSM(AM) Oceanside CA
KMAK(FM) Orange Cove CA
*KCRU(FM) Oxnard CA
KXTZ(FM) Pismo Beach CA
KJAY(AM) Sacramento CA
KLOK(AM) San Jose CA
KWIZ(FM) Santa Ana CA
KYAA(AM) Soquel CA
KGEN(AM) Tulare CA
*KBDG(FM) Turlock CA
KSFM(AM) Woodland CA
KZYR(FM) Avon CO
KLZ(AM) Denver CO
*KDNK(AM) Glenwood Springs CO
KKCH(AM) Glenwood Springs CO
KIDN-FM Hayden CO
*KUTE(FM) Ignacio CO
KQKS(AM) Lakewood CO
KAYW(FM) Meeker CO
*KVMT(FM) Montrose CO
*KPGS(FM) Pagosa Springs CO
*KVNF(FM) Paonia CO
*KTSC-FM Pueblo CO
*KTSC-FM Pueblo CO
KPHT(FM) Rocky Ford CO
KJJD(AM) Windsor CO
WCUM(AM) Bridgeport CT
WZMX(FM) Hartford CT
WFNW(AM) Naugatuck CT
*WMPH(FM) Wilmington DE
WTZB(FM) Englewood FL
WMIB(FM) Fort Lauderdale FL
WMIB(FM) Fort Lauderdale FL
WRNE(AM) Gulf Breeze FL
WAFZ(AM) Immokalee FL
WJAX(AM) Jacksonville FL
WMFM(FM) Key West FL
WWAB(AM) Lakeland FL
WPYO(FM) Maitland FL
WFLC(FM) Miami FL
WFLA-FM Midway FL
WONQ(AM) Oviedo FL
WONQ(AM) Oviedo FL
WMNE(AM) Riviera Beach FL
WSIR(AM) Winter Haven FL
WRBN(FM) Clayton GA
WPLO(AM) Grayson GA
WHLJ(FM) Statenville GA
WHGH(AM) Thomasville GA
WLET(AM) Toccoa GA
WTYB(FM) Tybee Island GA
KUAI(AM) Eleele HI
KSSK(AM) Honolulu HI
KSWI(FM) Atlantic IA
*KJMC(FM) Des Moines IA
KRNA(FM) Iowa City IA
*KSUI(FM) Iowa City IA
KRIB(AM) Mason City IA
*KBBG(FM) Waterloo IA
KRXK(AM) Rexburg ID
KIGO(AM) Saint Anthony ID
WSDZ(AM) Belleville IL
WFUN-FM Bethalto IL
WGCI-FM Chicago IL
WSBC(AM) Chicago IL
WITY(AM) Danville IL
WOJO(AM) Evanston IL
WWHP(FM) Farmer City IL
WSPY(AM) Geneva IL
*WKCC(FM) Kankakee IL
WQLF(FM) Lena IL
*WVJC(FM) Mount Carmel IL
WSQR(AM) Sycamore IL
WBCP(AM) Urbana IL

WEJK(FM) Boonville IN
*WSWI(AM) Evansville IN
WXKE(FM) Fort Wayne IN
WSYW(AM) Indianapolis IN
WLOI(AM) La Porte IN
WNDZ(AM) Portage IN
WLQI(FM) Rensselaer IN
*WZRP(FM) Richmond IN
KNCK(AM) Concordia KS
KOMB(FM) Fort Scott KS
KRSL(AM) Russell KS
KRSL-FM Russell KS
*KMUW(FM) Wichita KS
KSGL(AM) Wichita KS
KQLQ(FM) Columbia LA
*KRVS(FM) Lafayette LA
KLRZ(FM) Larose LA
KMRC(AM) Morgan City LA
KUMX(FM) North Fort Polk LA
KAGY(AM) Port Sulphur LA
WMKI(AM) Boston MA
WVBF(AM) Middleborough Center MA
WNTN(AM) Newton MA
*WUMD(FM) North Dartmouth MA
WORC(AM) Worcester MA
*WFWM(AM) Frostburg MD
*WESM(FM) Princess Anne MD
XHRM-FM Tijuana MEX
WMAX(AM) Bay City MI
*WDET-FM Detroit MI
WFDF(AM) Farmington Hills MI
WBCH-FM Hastings MI
WSRJ(FM) Honor MI
WCCY(AM) Houghton MI
WOLV(FM) Houghton MI
WSAM(AM) Saginaw MI
*WSHJ(FM) Southfield MI
KMGK(FM) Glenwood MN
*KMSU(FM) Mankato MN
*KCCM-FM Moorhead MN
*KRLX(FM) Northfield MN
*KUOM(AM) Saint Louis Park MN
*KGAC(FM) Saint Peter MN
*KSMR(FM) Winona MN
*KSMR(FM) Winona MN
KBXR(FM) Columbia MO
KJXX(AM) Jackson MO
WKCU(AM) Corinth MS
WHTU(FM) Newton MS
KBSR(AM) Laurel MT
WZJS(FM) Banner Elk NC
WKXB(FM) Burgaw NC
WYNA(FM) Calabash NC
*WXYC(FM) Chapel Hill NC
WCRU(AM) Dallas NC
WQNQ(FM) Fletcher NC
WKDX(AM) Hamlet NC
WNOW(AM) Mint Hill NC
WOHS(AM) Shelby NC
WRGC(AM) Sylva NC
*KABU(FM) Fort Totten ND
KSJZ(FM) Jamestown ND
KGOR(FM) Omaha NE
WBNC(AM) Conway NH
WFTN(AM) Franklin NH
WCNL(AM) Newport NH
WTTM(AM) Lindenwald NJ
*WYRS(FM) Manahawkin NJ
*WYRS(FM) Manahawkin NJ
*KUUT(FM) Farmington NM
*KUSW(FM) Flora Vista NM
KRSN(AM) Los Alamos NM
KLEA(AM) Lovington NM
KSFX(AM) Roswell NM
KSHP(AM) North Las Vegas NV
WDDY(AM) Albany NY
WEHH(AM) Elmira Heights-Horseheads NY
WKTU(AM) Lake Success NY
WABY(AM) Mechanicville NY
WBEA(FM) Southold NY
WTOR(AM) Youngstown NY
WCER(AM) Canton OH
*WZCP(FM) Chillicothe OH
*WRUW-FM Cleveland OH
WCKX(FM) Columbus OH

*WZWP(FM) West Union OH
KOJK(FM) Blanchard OK
KTMC(AM) McAlester OK
KMUS(AM) Sperry OK
KWDQ(FM) Woodward OK
*KWYA(FM) Astoria OR
KQFM(FM) Hermiston OR
KDZR(FM) Lake Oswego OR
WAYC(FM) Bedford PA
WBRR(FM) Bradford PA
WLER-FM Butler PA
WYJK(FM) Connellsville PA
WBCB(AM) Levittown-Fairless Hills PA
WPHI-FM Media PA
*WXLV(FM) Schnecksville PA
WWRR(FM) Scranton PA
WVPO(AM) Stroudsburg PA
*WRKC(FM) Wilkes-Barre PA
WGIT(AM) Canovanas PR
WNVE(FM) Culebra PR
WGDL(AM) Lares PR
WZMT(FM) Ponce PR
WIDI(FM) Quebradillas PR
WGTN-FM Andrews SC
WQSC(AM) Charleston SC
WKSX-FM Johnston SC
WVCO(FM) Loris SC
WXBT(FM) West Columbia SC
KBRK(AM) Brookings SD
WMPS(AM) Bartlett TN
WXIS(FM) Erwin TN
WOWW(AM) Germantown TN
*WCSK(FM) Kingsport TN
WQJK(FM) Maryville TN
*KACV-FM Amarillo TX
KBZD(FM) Amarillo TX
KOOC(FM) Belton TX
KQFX(FM) Borger TX
KTAM(AM) Bryan TX
KBSO(FM) Corpus Christi TX
*KTCU-FM Fort Worth TX
KBXX(FM) Houston TX
KHYI(FM) Howe TX
KJBZ(FM) Laredo TX
KQLM(FM) Odessa TX
KIKK(AM) Pasadena TX
*KWMF(FM) Pleasanton TX
KMJR(FM) Portland TX
KROM(FM) San Antonio TX
*KSYM-FM San Antonio TX
*KSYM-FM San Antonio TX
KPYK(AM) Terrell TX
KBTE(FM) Tulia TX
KXOL(AM) Brigham City UT
*KZMU(FM) Moab UT
KMRI(AM) West Valley City UT
WZGN(FM) Crozet VA
WMXH-FM Luray VA
*WHRO-FM Norfolk VA
WJOI(AM) Norfolk VA
WHKT(AM) Portsmouth VA
WBTJ(FM) Richmond VA
*WWPV-FM Colchester VT
WDEV-FM Warren VT
KXAA(FM) Cle Elum WA
KSBN(AM) Spokane WA
*WEMI(FM) Appleton WI
WERL(AM) Eagle River WI
*WEMY(FM) Green Bay WI
*WMSE(FM) Milwaukee WI
WKFX(FM) Rice Lake WI
WKSH(AM) Sussex WI
WMMM-FM Verona WI
*WXPW(FM) Wausau WI
WDZN(FM) Romney WV

Polish

WNWI(AM) Oak Lawn IL
WPNA(AM) Oak Park IL
WNVR(AM) Vernon Hills IL
WRKL(AM) New City NY

Polka

*WOES(FM) Ovid-Elsie MI
KASM(AM) Albany MN
WKTX(AM) Cortland OH
*WKTL(FM) Struthers OH
WTKM(AM) Hartford WI
WTKM-FM Hartford WI

Portugese

KLBS(AM) Los Banos CA
*WFAR(FM) Danbury CT
*WFHL(FM) New Bedford MA

Progressive

*KRUA(FM) Anchorage AK
*KSUA(FM) Fairbanks AK
*KXCI(FM) Tucson AZ
*KSPB(FM) Pebble Beach CA
*KRCB-FM Santa Rosa CA
*KZSU(FM) Stanford CA
*KCSU-FM Fort Collins CO
*WVOF(FM) Fairfield CT
*WDJW(FM) Somers CT
*WVUD(FM) Newark DE
*WKPX(FM) Sunrise FL
*WPRK(FM) Winter Park FL
*WREK(FM) Atlanta GA
*KIWR(FM) Council Bluffs IA
*KALA(FM) Davenport IA
*KWLC(AM) Decorah IA
*KRUI-FM Iowa City IA
*KRNL-FM Mount Vernon IA
*WJMU(FM) Decatur IL
*WNUR-FM Evanston IL
*WLCA(FM) Godfrey IL
*WMXM(FM) Lake Forest IL
*WIUS(FM) Macomb IL
*WMHD-FM Terre Haute IN
*KSDB-FM Manhattan KS
*WWHR(FM) Bowling Green KY
*WTUL(FM) New Orleans LA
*WIQH(FM) Concord MA
*WUML(FM) Lowell MA
*WUMD(FM) North Dartmouth MA
WRNR-FM Grasonville MD
*WUMF-FM Farmington ME
*WMEB-FM Orono ME
*WMEW(FM) Waterville ME
*WYAR(FM) Yarmouth ME
WGRD-FM Grand Rapids MI
*WIDR(FM) Kalamazoo MI
*WSDP(FM) Plymouth MI
*KUOM(AM) Minneapolis MN
*WMCN(FM) Saint Paul MN
*KWUR(FM) Clayton MO
*KCOU(FM) Columbia MO
*WUAG(FM) Greensboro NC
*KDNE(FM) Crete NE
KIBZ(FM) Crete NE
*WUNH(FM) Durham NH
*WNEC-FM Henniker NH
*WKNH(FM) Keene NH
*WPCR-FM Plymouth NH
*WRPR(FM) Mahwah NJ
*WVPH(FM) Piscataway NJ
WPRB(FM) Princeton NJ
*WTSR(FM) Trenton NJ
*WKNJ-FM Union Township NJ
WNJC(AM) Washington Township NJ
WRRB(FM) Arlington NY
*WHCL-FM Clinton NY
WEHN(FM) East Hampton NY
*WCVF-FM Fredonia NY
*WEOS(FM) Geneva NY
*WGFR(FM) Glens Falls NY
*WRCU-FM Hamilton NY
WWRL(AM) New York NY
*WRHO(FM) Oneonta NY
*WFNP(FM) Rosendale NY
*WRUC(FM) Schenectady NY
WEHM(FM) Southampton NY
*WUSB(FM) Stony Brook NY
WCLX(FM) Westport NY

WLKK(FM) Wethersfield Township NY
WDST(FM) Woodstock NY
*WOUB(AM) Athens OH
*WUFM(FM) Columbus OH
*WDUB(FM) Granville OH
*WMCO(FM) New Concord OH
*WUSO(FM) Springfield OH
*WJCU(FM) University Heights OH
*WOBN(FM) Westerville OH
*WYSO(FM) Yellow Springs OH
*KWVA(FM) Eugene OR
*KEOL(FM) La Grande OR
*WWEC(FM) Elizabethtown PA
*WZBT(FM) Gettysburg PA
*WKVR-FM Huntingdon PA
*WMSS(FM) Middletown PA
*WIXQ(FM) Millersville PA
*WKDU(FM) Philadelphia PA
*WPTS-FM Pittsburgh PA
*WXAC(FM) Reading PA
*WSRU(FM) Slippery Rock PA
*WDOM(FM) Providence RI
*WSBF-FM Clemson SC
*KAOR(FM) Vermillion SD
*WNRZ(FM) Dickson TN
*WRVU(FM) Nashville TN
*WUTS(FM) Sewanee TN
*KERA(FM) Dallas TX
*KSAU(FM) Nacogdoches TX
WVAX(AM) Charlottesville VA
*WEHC(FM) Emory VA
*WMLU(FM) Farmville VA
*WWHS-FM Hampden-Sydney VA
*WXJM(FM) Harrisonburg VA
*WDCE(FM) Richmond VA
*WCWM(FM) Williamsburg VA
*WIUV(FM) Castleton VT
*WRMC-FM Middlebury VT
*KUGS(FM) Bellingham WA
*KSVR(FM) Mount Vernon WA
*KEXP-FM Seattle WA
*KUPS(FM) Tacoma WA
*WBSD(FM) Burlington WI
*WWSP(FM) Stevens Point WI
*WVBC(FM) Bethany WV
*WVWC(FM) Buckhannon WV
*WWVU-FM Morgantown WV
*KUWA(FM) Afton WY
*KDUW(FM) Douglas WY
*KUWG(FM) Gillette WY
*KUWJ(FM) Jackson WY
*KUWR(FM) Laramie WY
*KUWN(FM) Newcastle WY
*KUWX(FM) Pinedale WY
*KCWC-FM Riverton WY
*KUWZ(FM) Rock Springs WY
*KSUW(FM) Sheridan WY
*KUWD(FM) Sundance WY
KUWT(FM) Thermopolis WY

Public Affairs

*KYUK(AM) Bethel AK
*KCHU(AM) Valdez AK
KFNN(AM) Mesa AZ
*KNAI(FM) Phoenix AZ
*KPFA(FM) Berkeley CA
*KPFB(FM) Berkeley CA
KLTX(AM) Long Beach CA
*KSJD(FM) Cortez CO
*KAFM(FM) Grand Junction CO
*KVMT(FM) Montrose CO
*KVNF(FM) Paonia CO
WQUN(AM) Hamden CT
*WCSP-FM Washington DC
WTJV(AM) De Land FL
*WUFT-FM Gainesville FL
*WJUF(FM) Inverness FL
WPBR(AM) Lantana FL
*WKFA(FM) Saint Catherine FL
*WPIO(FM) Titusville FL
*WGLT(FM) Normal IL
*WFHB(FM) Bloomington IN
WILO(AM) Frankfort IN
WKCT(AM) Bowling Green KY
*WRPS(FM) Rockland MA

*WDIH(FM) Salisbury MD
*WMEH(FM) Bangor ME
*WMED(FM) Calais ME
*WMEP(FM) Camden ME
*WMEF(FM) Fort Kent ME
*WMEA(FM) Portland ME
*WMEM(FM) Presque Isle ME
KMSK(AM) Austin MN
KMSU(FM) Mankato MN
KAUL(FM) Ellington MO
*KCUR-FM Kansas City MO
*KBIY(FM) Van Buren MO
*WRVS-FM Elizabeth City NC
WSMX(AM) Winston-Salem NC
*KABU(FM) Fort Totten ND
KSWV(AM) Santa Fe NM
*WNYC(AM) New York NY
WOR(AM) New York NY
*WPSA(FM) Paul Smiths NY
*WGBE(FM) Bryan OH
*WOSU(AM) Columbus OH
*WGDE(FM) Defiance OH
*WGLE(FM) Lima OH
*WGTE-FM Toledo OH
KIXR(FM) Ponca City OK
*KTCB(FM) Tillamook OR
*WDIY(FM) Allentown PA
*WDUQ(FM) Pittsburgh PA
WIAC(AM) San Juan PR
*KQSD-FM Lowry SD
*KUSD(FM) Vermillion SD
*WQOX(FM) Memphis TN
*WYPL(FM) Memphis TN
*KUSR(FM) Logan UT
WFHR(AM) Wisconsin Rapids WI

Reggae

WDJA(AM) Delray Beach FL
WJKC(FM) Christiansted VI
WSTX-FM Christiansted VI

Religious

*KATB(FM) Anchorage AK
*KNOM(AM) Nome AK
*KNOM-FM Nome AK
*KJNP(AM) North Pole AK
KRSA(AM) Petersburg AK
*KUDU(FM) Tok AK
*WSTF(FM) Andalusia AL
WRAB(AM) Arab AL
WATV(AM) Birmingham AL
*WBFR(FM) Birmingham AL
*WLJR(FM) Birmingham AL
WBSA(AM) Boaz AL
WGNQ(AM) Bridgeport AL
*WYFD(FM) Decatur AL
*WMBV(FM) Dixons Mills AL
*WDYF(FM) Dothan AL
*WGTF(FM) Dothan AL
*WFIX(FM) Florence AL
*WTBB(FM) Gadsden AL
WGEA(AM) Geneva AL
WBXR(AM) Hazel Green AL
WQOH(AM) Irondale AL
WMOB(AM) Mobile AL
*WLBF(FM) Montgomery AL
*WTBJ(FM) Oxford AL
*WJCK(FM) Piedmont AL
*WRNF(FM) Selma AL
WAPZ(AM) Wetumpka AL
*KVMN(FM) Cave City AR
*KBDO(FM) Des Arc AR
*KARH(FM) Forrest City AR
*KAOW(FM) Fort Smith AR
*KEAF(FM) Fort Smith AR
KFSA(AM) Fort Smith AR
*KLRO(FM) Hot Springs AR
*KAOG(FM) Jonesboro AR
KUUZ(FM) Lake Village AR
KAAY(AM) Little Rock AR
KWLR(FM) Maumelle AR
*KCMH(FM) Mountain Home AR
KSSW(AM) Nashville AR

*KANX(FM) Sheridan AR
KMTL(AM) Sherwood AR
*KLRC(FM) Siloam Springs AR
*KRMB(FM) Bisbee AZ
*KWRB(FM) Bisbee AZ
KPXQ(AM) Glendale AZ
*KNLB(FM) Lake Havasu City AZ
KRIT(FM) Parker AZ
*KWFH(FM) Parker AZ
KASA(AM) Phoenix AZ
*KPHF(FM) Phoenix AZ
*KGCB(FM) Prescott AZ
KXXT(AM) Tolleson AZ
KTBA(AM) Tuba City AZ
KWIM(AM) Window Rock AZ
*KYRM(FM) Yuma AZ
*KNDL(FM) Angwin CA
KLFF(AM) Arroyo Grande CA
KBRT(AM) Avalon CA
*KFRB(FM) Bakersfield CA
KLHC(AM) Bakersfield CA
*KWTH(FM) Barstow CA
*KWTW(FM) Bishop CA
*KIBC(FM) Burney CA
*KMRO(FM) Camarillo CA
KFIA(AM) Carmichael CA
*KHAP(FM) Chico CA
*KFRJ(FM) China Lake CA
*KPSH(FM) Coachella CA
*KFRP(FM) Coalinga CA
KRDU(AM) Dinuba CA
KSAC-FM Dunnigan CA
*KECR(FM) El Cajon CA
*KASK(FM) Fairfield CA
*KJCU(FM) Fort Bragg CA
KJPG(AM) Frazier Park CA
*KEYQ(AM) Fresno CA
*KFNO(FM) Fresno CA
KGED(AM) Fresno CA
*KXBC(FM) Garberville CA
KKMC(AM) Gonzales CA
*KPJP(FM) Greenville CA
KESQ(AM) Indio CA
KTYM(AM) Inglewood CA
*KEFR(FM) Le Grand CA
KJOP(AM) Lemoore CA
*KLWG(FM) Lompoc CA
KLTX(AM) Long Beach CA
KHOT(AM) Madera CA
*KADV(FM) Modesto CA
KKXX(AM) Paradise CA
KCBC(AM) Riverbank CA
KPRO(AM) Riverside CA
*KSGN(FM) Riverside CA
*KEBR(AM) Rocklin CA
*KEAR-FM Sacramento CA
KEZY(AM) San Bernardino CA
KWVE(FM) San Clemente CA
KSDO(AM) San Diego CA
KEAR(AM) San Francisco CA
KFAX(AM) San Francisco CA
KSFB(AM) San Francisco CA
KJDJ(AM) San Luis Obispo CA
*KHFR(FM) Santa Maria CA
*KGZO(FM) Shafter CA
*KFRS(FM) Soledad CA
*KWG(AM) Stockton CA
*KPRA(FM) Ukiah CA
KDIA(AM) Vallejo CA
KRSX(AM) Victorville CA
KSMH(AM) West Sacramento CA
KRKS-FM Boulder CO
KLTT(AM) Commerce City CO
KBJD(AM) Denver CO
KRKS(AM) Denver CO
*KCIC(FM) Grand Junction CO
KPIO(AM) Loveland CO
KFEL(AM) Pueblo CO
KGFT(FM) Pueblo CO
WADS(AM) Ansonia CT
*WFAR(FM) Danbury CT
*WJMJ(FM) Hartford CT
WFIF(AM) Milford CT
*WCTF(AM) Vernon CT
WQOP(AM) Atlantic Beach FL
WSWN(AM) Belle Glade FL

*WYFZ(FM) Belleview FL
WLVJ(AM) Boynton Beach FL
*WRMB(FM) Boynton Beach FL
WNVY(AM) Cantonment FL
WTCL(AM) Chattahoochee FL
*WMIE(FM) Cocoa FL
WWBC(AM) Cocoa FL
WMFJ(AM) Daytona Beach FL
WYND(AM) De Land FL
*WJED(FM) Dogwood Lakes Estate FL
*WKTO(FM) Edgewater FL
*WMFL(FM) Florida City FL
*WAFG(FM) Fort Lauderdale FL
*WJYO(FM) Fort Myers FL
WMYR(AM) Fort Myers FL
*WJFP(FM) Fort Pierce FL
*WYFB(FM) Gainesville FL
WACC(AM) Hialeah FL
WCGL(AM) Jacksonville FL
*WJFR(FM) Jacksonville FL
WZNZ(AM) Jacksonville FL
*WJIR(FM) Key West FL
WKIZ(AM) Key West FL
WOTS(AM) Kissimmee FL
*WKES(FM) Lakeland FL
*WYFO(FM) Lakeland FL
*WAPB(FM) Madison FL
*WGSG(FM) Mayo FL
WCIF(FM) Melbourne FL
*WFRF-FM Monticello FL
*WJLU(FM) New Smyrna Beach FL
WEUS(AM) Orlovista FL
*WJTF(FM) Panama City FL
WDWR(AM) Pensacola FL
*WPCS(FM) Pensacola FL
*WVIJ(FM) Port Charlotte FL
*WFRU(FM) Quincy FL
*WKFA(FM) Saint Catherine FL
*WUJC(AM) Saint Marks FL
*WFTI-FM Saint Petersburg FL
WDEO-FM San Carlos Park FL
*WWFR(FM) Stuart FL
WTAL(AM) Tallahassee FL
WTIS(AM) Tampa FL
*WYFE(FM) Tarpon Springs FL
*WPIO(FM) Titusville FL
*WWVO(FM) Albany GA
WLTA(AM) Alpharetta GA
*WFRP(FM) Americus GA
WAEC(AM) Atlanta GA
WGUN(AM) Atlanta GA
WFAM(AM) Augusta GA
WBAF(AM) Barnesville GA
WUFE(AM) Baxley GA
WGMI(AM) Bremen GA
*WCCV(FM) Cartersville GA
*WFRC(FM) Columbus GA
*WYFK(FM) Columbus GA
WWEV-FM Cumming GA
WDPC(AM) Dallas GA
WDCY(AM) Douglasville GA
*WMVV(FM) Griffin GA
WWWE(AM) Hapeville GA
*WGML(AM) Hinesville GA
*WOAK(FM) La Grange GA
WBML(AM) Macon GA
*WYFS(FM) Savannah GA
*WRAF-FM Toccoa Falls GA
WAFT(FM) Valdosta GA
WGOV(AM) Valdosta GA
WYFA(FM) Waynesboro GA
*WYFW(FM) Winder GA
*KHMG(FM) Barrigada GU
KTWG(AM) Hagatna GU
*KCIF(FM) Hilo HI
KLHT(AM) Honolulu HI
KFFF-FM Boone IA
*KDFR(FM) Des Moines IA
KWKY(AM) Des Moines IA
*KEGR(FM) Fort Dodge IA
*KDCR(FM) Sioux Center IA
KTFC(FM) Sioux City IA
KTFG(FM) Sioux Rapids IA
*KNWS(AM) Waterloo IA
*KNWS-FM Waterloo IA
KNJY(AM) Boise ID

KBXL(FM) Caldwell ID
*KYMS(FM) Rathdrum ID
*KBYR-FM Rexburg ID
*KAWZ(FM) Twin Falls ID
*KEFX(FM) Twin Falls ID
*KTWD(FM) Wallace ID
*WBJW(FM) Albion IL
WXAN(FM) Ava IL
WRMS(AM) Beardstown IL
*WOLG(FM) Carlinville IL
*WTSG(FM) Carlinville IL
*WBGL(FM) Champaign IL
*WZGL(FM) Charleston IL
*WMBI-FM Chicago IL
WNTD(AM) Chicago IL
WYLL(AM) Chicago IL
*WDLM(AM) East Moline IL
*WDLM-FM East Moline IL
*WCBW-FM East St. Louis IL
*WRYT(AM) Edwardsville IL
*WGNN(FM) Fisher IL
*WJCH(FM) Joliet IL
*WGSL(FM) Loves Park IL
*WOTW(FM) Monee IL
*WBNH(FM) Pekin IL
*WCIC(FM) Pekin IL
WVEL(AM) Pekin IL
WPEO(AM) Peoria IL
*WGNJ(FM) Saint Joseph IL
WAUR(AM) Sandwich IL
*WSOG(FM) Spring Valley IL
*WIHM(AM) Taylorville IL
WGLL(AM) Auburn IN
*WSPM(FM) Cloverdale IN
*WFOF(FM) Covington IN
WVHI(AM) Evansville IN
*WBGW(FM) Fort Branch IN
WLYV(AM) Fort Wayne IN
*WHLP(FM) Hanna IN
WBRI(AM) Indianapolis IN
*WIWC(FM) Kokomo IN
*WYTJ(FM) Linton IN
*WBHW(FM) Loogootee IN
*WTMK(FM) Lowell IN
*WMBL(FM) Mitchell IN
WHLY(AM) South Bend IN
*WCRT-FM Terre Haute IN
*WHOJ(FM) Terre Haute IN
*WKRY(FM) Versailles IN
*WATI(FM) Vincennes IN
*WHPL(FM) West Lafayette IN
KAIR(AM) Atchison KS
*KBJQ(FM) Bronson KS
*KHYM(FM) Copeland KS
*KJIL(FM) Copeland KS
KAHS(AM) El Dorado KS
*KPOR(FM) Emporia KS
*KVCY(FM) Fort Scott KS
*KGCR(FM) Goodland KS
*KPRD(FM) Hays KS
KREJ(FM) Medicine Lodge KS
KCCV-FM Olathe KS
KCCV(AM) Overland Park KS
*KAKA(FM) Salina KS
KYUL(AM) Scott City KS
*KBUZ(FM) Topeka KS
*KJTY(FM) Topeka KS
KSGL(AM) Wichita KS
WYWY(AM) Barbourville KY
*WCVK(FM) Bowling Green KY
WKDP(AM) Corbin KY
WCPM(AM) Cumberland KY
WWLK(AM) Eddyville KY
WIOK(FM) Falmouth KY
WJMD(FM) Hazard KY
WKVG(AM) Jenkins KY
WDFB(AM) Junction City KY
WJMM-FM Keene KY
WYGE(AM) London KY
*WSOF-FM Madisonville KY
*WBFI(FM) McDaniels KY
*WEUC(FM) Morganfield KY
WMSK(AM) Morganfield KY
*WAXG(FM) Mt. Sterling KY
WLCR(AM) Mt. Washington KY
WGCK(AM) Neon KY

WNOP(AM) Newport KY
*WPTJ(FM) Paris KY
*WJSO(FM) Pikeville KY
WLCK(AM) Scottsville KY
*WTHL(AM) Somerset KY
WMTC(AM) Vancleve KY
WMTC-FM Vancleve KY
WBCE(AM) Wickliffe KY
WEKC(AM) Williamsburg KY
KJMJ(AM) Alexandria LA
KBZE(FM) Berwick LA
WIKC(AM) Bogalusa LA
*KCKR(FM) Church Point LA
*WWRA(FM) Clinton LA
KAJN-FM Crowley LA
*KVDP(FM) Dry Prong LA
*KPAE(FM) Erwinville LA
*WCKW(AM) Garyville LA
KKNO(AM) Gretna LA
*KAYT(FM) Jena LA
*KOJO(FM) Lake Charles LA
*KBIO(FM) Natchitoches LA
KNIR(AM) New Iberia LA
WLNO(AM) New Orleans LA
WPFC(AM) Port Allen LA
WSRO(AM) Ashland MA
WEZE(AM) Boston MA
WACE(AM) Chicopee MA
*WJWT(FM) Gardner MA
WVNE(AM) Leicester MA
WCMX(AM) Leominster MA
*WSMA(FM) Scituate MA
*WFSI(FM) Annapolis MD
WBGR(AM) Baltimore MD
WBMD(AM) Baltimore MD
*WOEL-FM Elkton MD
*WLIC(FM) Frostburg MD
WOLC(FM) Princess Anne MD
*WGTS(FM) Takoma Park MD
WWPN(AM) Westernport MD
*WCRH(FM) Williamsport MD
*WFST(AM) Caribou ME
*WYFP(FM) Harpswell ME
WJCX(FM) Pittsfield ME
WTME(AM) Rumford ME
*WSEW(FM) Sanford ME
WKTQ(AM) South Paris ME
WLJW(AM) Cadillac MI
*WOLW(FM) Cadillac MI
*WTCK(FM) Charlevoix MI
WLQV(AM) Detroit MI
*WRQC(FM) East Tawas MI
*WLJN(AM) Elmwood Township MI
*WPHN(FM) Gaylord MI
WGDN(AM) Gladwin MI
WFUR(AM) Grand Rapids MI
WFUR-FM Grand Rapids MI
WLCM(AM) Holt MI
WKPR(AM) Kalamazoo MI
*WEUL(AM) Kingsford MI
*WMPC(AM) Lapeer MI
*WHWL(FM) Marquette MI
WRDT(AM) Monroe MI
WMKD(FM) Pickford MI
*WPCJ(FM) Pittsford MI
*WNFA(FM) Port Huron MI
*WMSD(FM) Rose Township MI
WIDG(AM) Saint Ignace MI
*WNFR(FM) Sandusky MI
*WTHN(AM) Sault Ste. Marie MI
*WOFR(FM) Schoolcraft MI
*KTGG(AM) Spring Arbor MI
*WUFL(FM) Sterling Heights MI
*WHST(FM) Tawas City MI
*WLJN-FM Traverse City MI
*WHWG(FM) Trout Lake MI
*WGNB(FM) Zeeland MI
KJLY(FM) Blue Earth MN
WCTS(AM) Maplewood MN
*KTIS(AM) Minneapolis MN
KVXR(AM) Moorhead MN
KCGN-FM Ortonville MN
KTIG(FM) Pequot Lakes MN
KCUE(AM) Red Wing MN
KYES(AM) Rockville MN
*KCFB(FM) Saint Cloud MN

KCWJ(AM) Blue Springs MO
KOMC(AM) Branson MO
*KOZO(FM) Branson MO
KMFC(FM) Centralia MO
*KFUO(AM) Clayton MO
KDJR(FM) De Soto MO
KYMO(AM) East Prairie MO
*KEXS(AM) Excelsior Springs MO
KJXX(AM) Jackson MO
*KHGN(FM) Kirksville MO
KLEX(AM) Lexington MO
KMRF(AM) Marshfield MO
*KCGR(FM) Oran MO
*KLUH(FM) Poplar Bluff MO
*KEXS-FM Ravenwood MO
KSIV-FM Saint Louis MO
KXEN(AM) Saint Louis MO
KRHW(AM) Sikeston MO
*KWFC(FM) Springfield MO
*KNLN(FM) Vienna MO
*WPAE(FM) Centreville MS
WTGY(FM) Charleston MS
WWUN-FM Friar's Point MS
*WAII(FM) Hattiesburg MS
*WATP(FM) Laurel MS
WESY(AM) Leland MS
*WAQL(FM) McComb MS
*WASM(FM) Natchez MS
*WATU(FM) Port Gibson MS
*WJZB(FM) Starkville MS
*WZKM(FM) Waynesboro MS
WJNS-FM Yazoo City MS
KGVW(AM) Belgrade MT
KURL(AM) Billings MT
KGLE(AM) Glendive MT
*KSPL(FM) Kalispell MT
*KPLG(FM) Plains MT
*KPGB(FM) Pryor MT
WCGC(AM) Belmont NC
*WCCE(FM) Buie's Creek NC
WPTL(AM) Canton NC
WMYT(AM) Carolina Beach NC
WHVN(AM) Charlotte NC
WCKB(AM) Dunn NC
WRJD(AM) Durham NC
WLOE(AM) Eden NC
WFMO(AM) Fairmont NC
WWOL(AM) Forest City NC
WFMC(AM) Goldsboro NC
WYCV(AM) Granite Falls NC
WKEW(AM) Greensboro NC
WYFL(AM) Henderson NC
*WHPE-FM High Point NC
WMYN(AM) Mayodan NC
*WOTJ(FM) Morehead City NC
WDJS(AM) Mount Olive NC
WKRK(AM) Murphy NC
*WAAE(FM) New Bern NC
WAUG(AM) New Hope NC
WGCR(AM) Pisgah Forest NC
WCLY(AM) Raleigh NC
WEED(AM) Rocky Mount NC
WEGG(AM) Rose Hill NC
WVCB(AM) Shallotte NC
*WAGO(FM) Snow Hill NC
WCOK(AM) Sparta NC
WGMA(AM) Spindale NC
*WYFQ-FM Wadesboro NC
WOBX(AM) Wanchese NC
WSMY(AM) Weldon NC
WIAM(AM) Williamston NC
WLSG(AM) Wilmington NC
WBTE(AM) Windsor NC
WPOL(AM) Winston-Salem NC
*WSNC(FM) Winston-Salem NC
*KBFR(FM) Bismarck ND
KHRT(AM) Minot ND
KCVD(AM) New England ND
*KFNW(AM) West Fargo ND
KPNY(FM) Alliance NE
*KNBE(FM) Beatrice NE
*KTLX(FM) Columbus NE
*KNFA(FM) Grand Island NE
*KAYA(FM) Hubbard NE
KVSS(FM) Lincoln NE
*KNGN(AM) McCook NE

*KPNO(FM) Norfolk NE
KOTK(AM) Omaha NE
*KYFG(FM) Omaha NE
*KFHC(FM) Ponca NE
KHZZ(FM) Sargent NE
KCMI(FM) Terrytown NE
WDER(AM) Derry NH
*WVFA(AM) Lebanon NH
*WYGG(FM) Asbury Park NJ
*WKDN-FM Camden NJ
WTMR(AM) Camden NJ
WIFI(AM) Florence NJ
WXMC(AM) Parsippany-Troy Hills NJ
WCHR(AM) Trenton NJ
WFJS(AM) Trenton NJ
*WJPH(FM) Woodbine NJ
*KFLQ(FM) Albuquerque NM
KNKT(FM) Armijo, Albuquerque NM
*KZPI(FM) Deming NM
*KRUC(FM) Las Cruces NM
*KXXQ(FM) Milan NM
KCKN(AM) Roswell NM
*KWFL(FM) Roswell NM
KHAC(AM) Tse Bonito NM
KCNM(AM) Garapan-Saipan NP
KKVV(AM) Las Vegas NV
*KIHM(FM) Reno NV
KXTO(AM) Reno NV
WLOF(AM) Attica NY
WDCX-FM Buffalo NY
*WFBF(FM) Buffalo NY
*WMHI(FM) Cape Vincent NY
WCHP(AM) Champlain NY
WJIV(FM) Cherry Valley NY
WYBY(FM) Cortland NY
WVOA-FM DeRuyter NY
WSIV(AM) East Syracuse NY
WLNL(AM) Horseheads NY
*WFRH(FM) Kingston NY
WBAR-FM Lake Luzerne NY
WVOU(AM) Mexico NY
WTHE(AM) Mineola NY
WJUX(FM) Monticello NY
*WWRV(AM) New York NY
*WFSO(FM) Olivebridge NY
WZXV(FM) Palmyra NY
WHIC(AM) Rochester NY
WYFY(FM) Rome NY
*WFRS(FM) Smithtown NY
*WFRW(FM) Webster NY
*WHJM(FM) Anna OH
*WOFN(FM) Beach City OH
WJYM(AM) Bowling Green OH
WILB(AM) Canton OH
WGGN(FM) Castalia OH
*WCDR-FM Cedarville OH
*WOHC(FM) Chillicothe OH
WCVX(AM) Cincinnati OH
*WCRF(FM) Cleveland OH
*WHVT(FM) Clyde OH
WVKO(AM) Columbus OH
WRFD(AM) Columbus-Worthington OH
*WCUE(AM) Cuyahoga Falls OH
*WJJE(FM) Delaware OH
WGNZ(AM) Fairborn OH
WNLT(AM) Harrison OH
*WFOT(FM) Lexington OH
*WVML(FM) Millersburg OH
WCCD(AM) Parma OH
*WOHP(FM) Portsmouth OH
*WLRY(FM) Rushville OH
*WVMS(FM) Sandusky OH
*WEEC(FM) Springfield OH
*WOTL(FM) Toledo OH
*WXML(FM) Upper Sandusky OH
*WYTN(FM) Youngstown OH
*WJIC(FM) Zanesville OH
*KKVO(AM) Altus OK
*KNYD(FM) Broken Arrow OK
*KDIM(FM) Coweta OK
*KKRD(FM) Enid OK
KMFS(AM) Guthrie OK
KBIJ(FM) Guymon OK
*KALU(FM) Langston OK
*KMSI(FM) Moore OK
KQCV(AM) Oklahoma City OK

KXOJ-FM Sapulpa OK
KCFO(AM) Tulsa OK
*KGIO(FM) Astoria OR
*KDJC(FM) Baker City OR
*KJCH(FM) Coos Bay OR
KDOV(FM) Medford OR
*KLRF(FM) Milton-Freewater OR
KBVM(FM) Portland OR
*KAJC(FM) Salem OR
*KQFE(FM) Springfield OR
KGRV(AM) Winston OR
*WITX(FM) Beaver Falls PA
WHJB(AM) Bedford PA
*WUFR(FM) Bedford PA
*WFKJ(FM) Cashtown PA
*WZXQ(FM) Chambersburg PA
WPWA(AM) Chester PA
WVCH(AM) Chester PA
WCOJ(AM) Coatesville PA
WCIG(AM) Dallas PA
*WPGM(AM) Danville PA
*WPGM-FM Danville PA
WISP(AM) Doylestown PA
*WEFR(FM) Erie PA
*WBYH(FM) Hawley PA
*WHHN(FM) Hollidaysburg PA
WPPZ-FM Jenkintown PA
WJSA(FM) Jersey Shore PA
WJSA-FM Jersey Shore PA
WJSM-FM Martinsburg PA
WWBJ(FM) Martinsburg PA
*WRIJ(FM) Masontown PA
*WPEL-FM Montrose PA
*WRWJ(FM) Murrysville PA
*WBGM(FM) New Berlin PA
*WVMN(FM) New Castle PA
WPCL(FM) Northern Cambria PA
WQOR(AM) Olyphant PA
WFIL(AM) Philadelphia PA
WPHE(AM) Phoenixville PA
WITK(AM) Pittston PA
*WBYO(FM) Sellersville PA
*WXFR(FM) State College PA
*WBYX(FM) Stroudsburg PA
*WRGN(FM) Sweet Valley PA
*WBMR(FM) Telford PA
*WZZD(FM) Warwick PA
WLIH(FM) Whitneyville PA
*WYTL(FM) Wyomissing PA
WFAB(AM) Ceiba PR
*WJVP(FM) Culebra PR
*WCRP(FM) Guayama PR
WCGB(AM) Juana Diaz PR
WRRE(AM) Juncos PR
*WPLI(FM) Levittown PR
WZOL(FM) Luquillo PR
WCHQ(AM) Quebradillas PR
WBMJ(AM) San Juan PR
WKVM(AM) San Juan PR
WIVV(AM) Vieques PR
WARV(AM) Warwick RI
WMIR(AM) Atlantic Beach SC
WVCD(AM) Bamberg-Denmark SC
*WAGP(AM) Beaufort SC
WVGB(AM) Beaufort SC
*WEPC(FM) Belton SC
*WYFV(FM) Cayce SC
*WFCH(FM) Charleston SC
*WMHK(FM) Columbia SC
WQXL(AM) Columbia SC
WFGN(AM) Gaffney SC
*WYFG(FM) Gaffney SC
WPJF(AM) Greenville SC
*WTBI-FM Greenville SC
WRIX(AM) Homeland Park SC
WKZK(AM) North Augusta SC
*WYFH(FM) North Charleston SC
*WKVC(FM) North Myrtle Beach SC
WNMB(AM) North Myrtle Beach SC
WPJK(AM) Orangeburg SC
WQIZ(AM) Saint George SC
WDRF(AM) Woodruff SC
*KKAA(AM) Aberdeen SD
*KVCF(FM) Freeman SD
*KVCX(FM) Gregory SD
*KVFL(FM) Pierre SD

*KQFR(FM) Rapid City SD
*KQKD(AM) Redfield SD
*KNWC(AM) Sioux Falls SD
*KJBB(AM) Watertown SD
WWGM(FM) Alamo TN
WBIN(AM) Benton TN
*WDYN-FM Chattanooga TN
WLMR(AM) Chattanooga TN
*WMBW(FM) Chattanooga TN
WMCH(AM) Church Hill TN
*WYFC(FM) Clinton TN
WSGM(FM) Coalmont TN
WCRV(AM) Collierville TN
*WAYM(FM) Columbia TN
WMRB(AM) Columbia TN
*WWOG(FM) Cookeville TN
*WMKW(FM) Crossville TN
WYXE(AM) Gallatin TN
WCLC(AM) Jamestown TN
WCLC-FM Jamestown TN
WDEB(AM) Jamestown TN
WKXV(AM) Knoxville TN
WLAF(AM) La Follette TN
WMQM(AM) Lakeland TN
*WAWI(FM) Lawrenceburg TN
WBLC(AM) Lenoir City TN
WFLI(AM) Lookout Mountain TN
WBBP(AM) Memphis TN
*WFCM-FM Murfreesboro TN
WENO(AM) Nashville TN
WLAC(AM) Nashville TN
WNQM(AM) Nashville TN
WYFN(AM) Nashville TN
*WDNX(FM) Olive Hill TN
WKJQ(AM) Parsons TN
*WAUV(FM) Ripley TN
*WAZD(FM) Savannah TN
*WFCM(AM) Smyrna TN
*WZYZ(FM) Spencer TN
*WAUT-FM Tullahoma TN
KDRY(AM) Alamo Heights TX
*KJRT(FM) Amarillo TX
KRGN(FM) Amarillo TX
*KEDR(FM) Bay City TX
KPDB(FM) Big Lake TX
KMZZ(FM) Bishop TX
*KASV(FM) Borger TX
*KBNR(FM) Brownsville TX
KBEN(AM) Carrizo Springs TX
KJON(AM) Carrollton TX
KUZN(FM) Centerville TX
*KBNJ(FM) Corpus Christi TX
KCTA(AM) Corpus Christi TX
KGGR(AM) Dallas TX
*KDKR(FM) Decatur TX
KVOZ(AM) Del Mar Hills TX
*KYFB(FM) Denison TX
KDHN(AM) Dimmitt TX
*KOIR(FM) Edinburg TX
*KVER(FM) El Paso TX
KVIV(AM) El Paso TX
KPAS(FM) Fabens TX
KIJN(AM) Farwell TX
KIJN-FM Farwell TX
*KJMA(FM) Floresville TX
KFST(AM) Fort Stockton TX
*KHCB(AM) Galveston TX
*KBJS(FM) Jacksonville TX
*KJCR(FM) Keene TX
KRMY(AM) Killeen TX
KINE(AM) Kingsville TX
*KBNL(FM) Laredo TX
*KAMY(FM) Lubbock TX
KRIO(AM) McAllen TX
*KCAS(FM) McCook TX
KLPF(AM) Midland TX
*KFLB(AM) Odessa TX
*KYFP(FM) Palestine TX
*KPMB(FM) Plainview TX
*KDEI(AM) Port Arthur TX
KBPO(AM) Port Neches TX
KMFM(FM) Premont TX
KBIC(FM) Raymondville TX
KRTX(AM) Rosenberg-Richmond TX
KCRN-FM San Angelo TX

*KFLB-FM Stanton TX
KTUE(AM) Tulia TX
*KGLY(FM) Tyler TX
*KVNE(FM) Tyler TX
*KXBJ(FM) Victoria TX
KANI(AM) Wharton TX
*KPDR(FM) Wheeler TX
KNAK(AM) Delta UT
KIHU(AM) Tooele UT
WYFJ(FM) Ashland VA
WLSD(AM) Big Stone Gap VA
WZAP(AM) Bristol VA
WNLR(AM) Churchville VA
*WOTC(FM) Edinburg VA
WKNV(AM) Fairlawn VA
WFAX(AM) Falls Church VA
WPAK(AM) Farmville VA
WYFT(FM) Luray VA
WKPA(AM) Lynchburg VA
*WRVL(FM) Lynchburg VA
WYFI(FM) Norfolk VA
WYRM(AM) Norfolk VA
WGTH-FM Richlands VA
WREJ(AM) Richmond VA
WRIS(AM) Roanoke VA
WXLZ(AM) Saint Paul VA
WKGM(AM) Smithfield VA
WKBA(AM) Vinton VA
*WYCS(FM) Yorktown VA
WGOD-FM Charlotte Amalie VI
*WIVH(FM) Christiansted VI
WTWN(AM) Wells River VT
KARI(AM) Blaine WA
*KACS(FM) Chehalis WA
KSPO(FM) Dishman WA
*KCSH(FM) Ellensburg WA
KTAC(FM) Ephrata WA
KTBI(AM) Ephrata WA
*KARR(AM) Kirkland WA
KWPZ(FM) Lynden WA
*KMLW(FM) Moses Lake WA
*KOLU(FM) Pasco WA
*KBLE(AM) Seattle WA
*KMBI(AM) Spokane WA
*KMBI-FM Spokane WA
KTTO(AM) Spokane WA
KHSS(FM) Walla Walla WA
*KSOH(FM) Wapato WA
*KPLW(FM) Wenatchee WA
*KBNO-FM White Salmon WA
WYNW(FM) Birnamwood WI
*WDVM(AM) Eau Claire WI
*WVCF(FM) Eau Claire WI
*WVFL(FM) Fond du Lac WI
*WJTY(FM) Lancaster WI
*WJWD(FM) Marshall WI
*WVCY-FM Milwaukee WI
WMMA(FM) Nekoosa WI
*WVCY(FM) Oshkosh WI
WHFA(AM) Poynette WI
*WNWC(AM) Sun Prairie WI
*WVCX(FM) Tomah WI
*WEGZ(FM) Washburn WI
*WVRN(FM) Wittenberg WI
WJLS(AM) Beckley WV
WRWB(AM) Huntington WV
WFSP(AM) Kingwood WV
WMON(AM) Montgomery WV
WELD-FM Moorefield WV
WJYP(AM) Saint Albans WV
WMXE(FM) South Charleston WV
WSCW(AM) South Charleston WV
KUYO(AM) Evansville WY
*KWCF(FM) Sheridan WY

Rock/AOR

KWHL(FM) Anchorage AK
*KDLG(AM) Dillingham AK
KKED(FM) Fairbanks AK
KKED(AM) Fairbanks AK
KXLW(AM) Houston AK
KZND-FM Houston AK
KSUP(FM) Juneau AK
KFSE(FM) Kasilof AK
WESP(AM) Dothan AL

WRTT-FM Huntsville AL
WQNR(FM) Tallassee AL
*WVUA-FM Tuscaloosa AL
WTGZ(FM) Tuskegee AL
KCCB(AM) Corning AR
KTRN(FM) White Hall AR
KDKB(FM) Mesa AZ
KUPD-FM Tempe AZ
KMXZ-FM Tucson AZ
KWCX-FM Willcox AZ
KWMX(FM) Williams AZ
KBRE(FM) Atwater CA
KRRX(FM) Burney CA
KWTY(FM) Cartago CA
KFMF(FM) Chico CA
KSSI(FM) China Lake CA
KCLB-FM Coachella CA
*KVHS(FM) Concord CA
*KDVS(FM) Davis CA
KSOF(FM) Dinuba CA
KGBB(FM) Edwards CA
KRAB(FM) Green Acres CA
KURQ(FM) Grover Beach CA
KRZR(FM) Hanford CA
KCXX(FM) Lake Arrowhead CA
*KRQZ(FM) Lompoc CA
KFFG(FM) Los Altos CA
*KXLU(FM) Los Angeles CA
KMRQ(FM) Manteca CA
KRCK-FM Mecca CA
*KAKX(FM) Mendocino CA
KMFB(FM) Mendocino CA
KHKK(FM) Modesto CA
KJEE(FM) Montecito CA
*KSFH(FM) Mountain View CA
KRQR(FM) Orland CA
KCAL-FM Redlands CA
KRXQ(FM) Sacramento CA
KIOZ(FM) San Diego CA
KYXY(FM) San Diego CA
KFOG(FM) San Francisco CA
KITS(FM) San Francisco CA
*KSJS(FM) San Jose CA
KZOZ(FM) San Luis Obispo CA
*KSCU(FM) Santa Clara CA
KXFX(FM) Santa Rosa CA
KWSX(AM) Stockton CA
KMKX(FM) Willits CA
KILO(FM) Colorado Springs CO
KRKV-FM Las Animas CO
KSTR-FM Montrose CO
KENG(FM) Parachute CO
KDZA-FM Pueblo CO
KRXP(FM) Pueblo West CO
*KDRE(FM) Sterling CO
*WERB(FM) Berlin CT
*WQAQ(FM) Hamden CT
WCCC-FM Hartford CT
WHCN(FM) Hartford CT
WPLR(FM) New Haven CT
WMRQ-FM Waterbury CT
*WECS(FM) Willimantic CT
WWDC-FM Washington DC
WOSC(FM) Bethany Beach DE
WZBH(FM) Georgetown DE
WYYX(FM) Bonifay FL
WNDN(FM) Chiefland FL
WXTB(FM) Clearwater FL
WJRR(FM) Cocoa Beach FL
WJBX(FM) Fort Myers Beach FL
WJBX(AM) Fort Myers Beach FL
WKSM(FM) Fort Walton Beach FL
WRUF-FM Gainesville FL
WXXJ(FM) Jacksonville FL
WHDR(FM) Miami FL
WHHZ(FM) Newberry FL
WMMO(FM) Orlando FL
WHOG-FM Ormond-by-the-Sea FL
WFKZ(FM) Plantation Key FL
WXSR(FM) Quincy FL
WSJZ-FM Sebastian FL
WGLF(FM) Tallahassee FL
WLTQ-FM Venice FL
*WRAS(FM) Atlanta GA
WHFX(FM) Darien GA
WCHZ(FM) Harlem GA

WJAD(FM) Leesburg GA
WRHQ(FM) Richmond Hill GA
WRXR-FM Rossville GA
WWRQ-FM Valdosta GA
WACF(FM) Young Harris GA
KUMU-FM Honolulu HI
KQCS(FM) Bettendorf IA
KBOB-FM De Witt IA
KUEL(FM) Fort Dodge IA
KYTC(FM) Northwood IA
KAZR(FM) Pella IA
KSEZ(FM) Sioux City IA
KCVI(FM) Blackfoot ID
KZDX(FM) Burley ID
KHTQ(FM) Hayden ID
KOZE-FM Lewiston ID
KQXR(FM) Payette ID
KSNA(FM) Rexburg ID
KIRQ(FM) Twin Falls ID
WWCT(FM) Bartonville IL
WXRX(FM) Belvidere IL
WQKQ(FM) Carthage IL
WRXX(FM) Centralia IL
WWGO(FM) Charleston IL
WKQX(FM) Chicago IL
WLUP-FM Chicago IL
WXRT-FM Chicago IL
*WRSE(FM) Elmhurst IL
WKTA(AM) Evanston IL
*WHFH(FM) Flossmoor IL
WLSR(FM) Galesburg IL
*WLCA(FM) Godfrey IL
*WCSF(FM) Joliet IL
*WLTL(FM) La Grange IL
WDQZ(FM) Lexington IL
*WLNX(FM) Lincoln IL
WNLF(FM) Macomb IL
*WLKL(FM) Mattoon IL
WVZA(FM) Murphysboro IL
*WONC(FM) Naperville IL
WIHN(FM) Normal IL
WIXO(FM) Peoria IL
WQLZ(FM) Taylorville IL
WPGU(FM) Urbana IL
WCVS-FM Virden IL
WDML(FM) Woodlawn IL
WSDM-FM Brazil IN
*WDSO(FM) Chesterton IN
WTFX-FM Clarksville IN
*WRGF(FM) Greenfield IN
*WBDG(FM) Indianapolis IN
WRZX(FM) Indianapolis IN
WYXB(FM) Indianapolis IN
WKHY(FM) Lafayette IN
*WCYT(FM) Lafayette Township IN
WWWY(FM) North Vernon IN
WBTO-FM Petersburg IN
*WPUM(FM) Rensselaer IN
WWSY(FM) Seelyville IN
WRBR-FM South Bend IN
*WISU(FM) Terre Haute IN
KBZI(FM) Columbus KS
KMDO(AM) Fort Scott KS
*KJHK(FM) Lawrence KS
KQRC-FM Leavenworth KS
KMKF(FM) Manhattan KS
*KSDB-FM Manhattan KS
KFIX(FM) Plainville KS
KICT-FM Wichita KS
*KSWC(FM) Winfield KS
WCMI-FM Catlettsburg KY
WPKE-FM Coal Run KY
WXZZ(FM) Georgetown KY
WGBF-FM Henderson KY
WKCB-FM Hindman KY
WIFX-FM Jenkins KY
WKTG(FM) Madisonville KY
WZZL(FM) Reidland KY
WRZI(FM) Vine Grove KY
WXCM(FM) Whitesville KY
KFTE(FM) Breaux Bridge LA
KEZP(FM) Bunkie LA
KNXX(FM) Donaldsonville LA
KYRK(FM) Houma LA
KXRR(FM) Monroe LA
*KXUL(FM) Monroe LA

KXOR-FM Thibodaux LA
WMJX(FM) Boston MA
*WBMT(FM) Boxford MA
WKAF(FM) Brockton MA
WHRB(FM) Cambridge MA
*WIQH(FM) Concord MA
WPXC(FM) Hyannis MA
WLZX(FM) Northampton MA
WOCN-FM Orleans MA
*WMHC(FM) South Hadley MA
WWFX(FM) Southbridge MA
WCHH(FM) Baltimore MD
WMDM(FM) Lexington Park MD
WCYY(FM) Biddeford ME
WTQX(FM) Boothbay Harbor ME
*WUMF(FM) Farmington ME
*WMEB-FM Orono ME
WTOS-FM Skowhegan ME
*WCHW-FM Bay City MI
WRIF(FM) Detroit MI
WOUF(FM) Frankfort MI
WGFN(FM) Glen Arbor MI
WJZJ(FM) Glen Arbor MI
WKLT(FM) Kalkaska MI
WQUS(FM) Lapeer MI
WKQZ(FM) Midland MI
*WBLD(FM) Orchard Lake MI
WKLZ-FM Petoskey MI
WRKR(FM) Portage MI
WIRX(FM) Saint Joseph MI
*WNMC-FM Traverse City MI
WWBN(FM) Tuscola MI
KAOD(FM) Babbitt MN
KQHT(FM) Crookston MN
KBAJ(FM) Deer River MN
KZCR(FM) Fergus Falls MN
KQYK(FM) Lake Crystal MN
KXXR(FM) Minneapolis MN
KQWB-FM Moorhead MN
KPHR(FM) Ortonville MN
KDZZ(FM) Saint Charles MN
*KDXL(FM) Saint Louis Park MN
KZRV(FM) Sartell MN
WHMH-FM Sauk Rapids MN
KZIO(FM) Two Harbors MN
*KQAL(FM) Winona MN
*KSMR(FM) Winona MN
KDBB(FM) Bonne Terre MO
KFEB(FM) Campbell MO
*KCOU(FM) Columbia MO
KCGQ-FM Gordonville MO
KBBM(FM) Jefferson City MO
KRBZ(FM) Kansas City MO
*KWJC(FM) Liberty MO
KNIM-FM Maryville MO
KMYK(FM) Osage Beach MO
KJEZ(FM) Poplar Bluff MO
KFLW(FM) Saint Robert MO
KPNT(FM) Sainte Genevieve MO
WCPR-FM D'Iberville MS
WUSW(FM) Hattiesburg MS
WRXW(FM) Pearl MS
WZLQ(FM) Tupelo MS
KRZN(FM) Billings MT
*KDWG(FM) Dillon MT
KQDI-FM Great Falls MT
KMHK(FM) Hardin MT
KBBZ(FM) Kalispell MT
KOZB(FM) Livingston MT
*KBGA(FM) Missoula MT
WRCQ(FM) Dunn NC
WTPT(FM) Forest City NC
WXNR(FM) Grifton NC
WVBZ(FM) High Point NC
WXQR(FM) Jacksonville NC
WRFX(FM) Kannapolis NC
WOBX-FM Manteo NC
WMGV(FM) Newport NC
WBBB(AM) Raleigh NC
*WKNC-FM Raleigh NC
WEND(FM) Salisbury NC
WAZO(FM) Southport NC
WTMT(FM) Weaverville NC
*KEYA(FM) Belcourt ND
KQZZ(FM) Devils Lake ND
KZRX(FM) Dickinson ND

KDSR(FM) Williston ND
KRVX(FM) Wimbledon ND
KTWI(FM) Bennington NE
*KINI(FM) Crookston NE
KLZA(FM) Falls City NE
*KLPR(FM) Kearney NE
KZMC(FM) McCook NE
KETT(FM) Mitchell NE
KOGA-FM Ogallala NE
KEZO-FM Omaha NE
KKCD(FM) Omaha NE
KKJK(FM) Ravenna NE
KRNP(FM) Sutherland NE
*KWSC(FM) Wayne NE
WWHK(FM) Concord NH
WDCR(AM) Hanover NH
WFRD(FM) Hanover NH
WGIR-FM Manchester NH
*WPCR-FM Plymouth NH
WHEB(FM) Portsmouth NH
WWYY(FM) Belvidere NJ
WDHA-FM Dover NJ
*WNTI(FM) Hackettstown NJ
*WJSV(FM) Morristown NJ
WNNJ(FM) Newton NJ
WJSE(FM) Petersburg NJ
WRAT(FM) Point Pleasant NJ
*WSOU(FM) South Orange NJ
*WMCX(FM) West Long Branch NJ
KRWN(FM) Farmington NM
KFMQ(FM) Gallup NM
KXPZ(FM) Las Cruces NM
*KEDP(FM) Las Vegas NM
KPSA-FM Lordsburg NM
KQBA(FM) Los Alamos NM
*KRDR(FM) Red River NM
KSFX(FM) Roswell NM
KRSI(FM) Garapan-Saipan NP
KOYT(FM) Elko NV
KRNO(FM) Incline Village NV
KMZQ(AM) Las Vegas NV
KOMP(FM) Las Vegas NV
KDOT(FM) Reno NV
KRZQ-FM Sparks NV
*WCDB(FM) Albany NY
*WETD(FM) Alfred NY
WZMR(FM) Altamont NY
WRRB(FM) Arlington NY
WBAB(FM) Babylon NY
*WGCC-FM Batavia NY
WEDG(FM) Buffalo NY
WOTT(FM) Calcium NY
WRCD(FM) Canton NY
*WHCL-FM Clinton NY
WQBJ(FM) Cobleskill NY
WKGB-FM Conklin NY
*WSUC-FM Cortland NY
WEHN(FM) East Hampton NY
WKLL(FM) Frankfort NY
*WGFR(FM) Glens Falls NY
WEFX(FM) Henderson NY
*WICB(FM) Ithaca NY
WVBR-FM Ithaca NY
WPDA(FM) Jeffersonville NY
WAQX-FM Manlius NY
WRRV(FM) Middletown NY
WKRH(FM) Minetto NY
WKRL-FM North Syracuse NY
*WRHO(FM) Oneonta NY
*WNYO(FM) Oswego NY
*WPOB-FM Plainview NY
WRCN-FM Riverhead NY
*WSBU(FM) Saint Bonaventure NY
WEHM(FM) Southampton NY
WHFM(FM) Southampton NY
WOUR(FM) Utica NY
*WPNR-FM Utica NY
WDST(FM) Woodstock NY
WONE-FM Akron OH
*WZIP(FM) Akron OH
*WRMU(FM) Alliance OH
*WRDL(FM) Ashland OH
*WBWC(FM) Berea OH
WMMS(FM) Cleveland OH
WRKZ(FM) Columbus OH
*WUFM(FM) Columbus OH

WTUE(FM) Dayton OH
WRXS(FM) Dublin OH
*WLFC(FM) Findlay OH
WZRX-FM Fort Shawnee OH
WWCD(FM) Grove City OH
*WHSS(FM) Hamilton OH
*WKET(FM) Kettering OH
WFTK(FM) Lebanon OH
*WCMO(FM) Marietta OH
*WYSZ(FM) Maumee OH
*WUSO(FM) Springfield OH
*WSTB(FM) Streetsboro OH
WIOT(FM) Toledo OH
*WYSA(FM) Wauseon OH
*WLHS(FM) West Chester OH
*WOBN(FM) Westerville OH
*WCWS(FM) Wooster OH
WNCD(FM) Youngstown OH
KKBS(FM) Guymon OK
KZCD(FM) Lawton OK
KMYZ-FM Pryor OK
KMMY(FM) Soper OK
KMOD-FM Tulsa OK
KZZE(FM) Eagle Point OR
KROG(FM) Grants Pass OR
KUFO-FM Portland OR
KORC(AM) Waldport OR
WZZO(FM) Bethlehem PA
*WBUQ(FM) Bloomsburg PA
WRKW(FM) Ebensburg PA
*WFSE(FM) Edinboro PA
*WERG(FM) Erie PA
*WVMM(FM) Grantham PA
WEXC(FM) Greenville PA
WRVV(FM) Harrisburg PA
WBSX(FM) Hazleton PA
WRKY-FM Hollidaysburg PA
WRKK(AM) Hughesville PA
*WKVR-FM Huntingdon PA
*WVBU-FM Lewisburg PA
*WNTE(FM) Mansfield PA
WEEO-FM McConnellsburg PA
WTPA(FM) Mechanicsburg PA
WWIZ(FM) Mercer PA
*WKDU(FM) Philadelphia PA
WRFF(FM) Philadelphia PA
WYSP(FM) Philadelphia PA
WJOW(FM) Philipsburg PA
WDVE(FM) Pittsburgh PA
WPAM(AM) Pottsville PA
*WXAC(FM) Reading PA
*WUSR(FM) Scranton PA
WZXR(FM) South Williamsport PA
WMTT(FM) Tioga PA
WBHB-FM Waynesboro PA
*WRKC(FM) Wilkes-Barre PA
*WRKC(FM) Wilkes-Barre PA
*WPTC(FM) Williamsport PA
WQXA-FM York PA
WMEG(FM) Guayama PR
WCAD(FM) San Juan PR
WIAC-FM San Juan PR
*WQRI(FM) Bristol RI
WHJY(FM) Providence RI
WRXZ(FM) Briarcliff Acres SC
WARQ(FM) Columbia SC
WYBB(FM) Folly Beach SC
WKZQ-FM Forestbrook SC
KVAR(FM) Pine Ridge SD
KDDX(FM) Spearfish SD
*KAOR(FM) Vermillion SD
WBXE(FM) Baxter TN
WSKZ(FM) Chattanooga TN
WRZK(FM) Colonial Heights TN
WASL(FM) Dyersburg TN
WZDQ(FM) Humboldt TN
*WUTK-FM Knoxville TN
WKXD-FM Monterey TN
*KACC(FM) Alvin TX
KLBJ-FM Austin TX
KROX-FM Buda TX
*KWTS(FM) Canyon TX
KZRK-FM Canyon TX
KTUX(FM) Carthage TX
KLAQ(FM) El Paso TX
KEGL(FM) Fort Worth TX

*KTCU-FM Fort Worth TX
KHFI-FM Georgetown TX
KDBN(FM) Haltom City TX
KFRQ(FM) Harlingen TX
KZXL(FM) Hudson TX
*KTAI(FM) Kingsville TX
KFMX-FM Lubbock TX
KLTO-FM McQueeney TX
KMJR(FM) Portland TX
KISS-FM San Antonio TX
*KVRK(FM) Sanger TX
KNCN(FM) Sinton TX
KLYD(FM) Snyder TX
KZZQ(FM) Coalville UT
KAUU(FM) Manti UT
KBER(FM) Ogden UT
WLEQ(FM) Bedford VA
WWRE(FM) Berryville VA
WBRW(FM) Blacksburg VA
WWTJ(FM) Charlottesville VA
WDYL(FM) Chester VA
WACL(FM) Elkton VA
WROX-FM Exmore VA
WFQX(FM) Front Royal VA
WZZU(FM) Lynchburg VA
WROV-FM Martinsville VA
WNOR(FM) Norfolk VA
WRXL(FM) Richmond VA
WWRT(FM) Strasburg VA
*WNRS-FM Sweet Briar VA
WZZI(FM) Vinton VA
WEXP(FM) Brandon VT
*WWLR(FM) Lyndonville VT
*WNUB-FM Northfield VT
*WVTC(FM) Randolph Center VT
WDVT(FM) Rutland VT
WLFE-FM Saint Albans VT
WIZN(FM) Vergennes VT
WKKN(FM) Westminster VT
*KGRG-FM Auburn WA
KNRK(FM) Camas WA
*KCWU(FM) Ellensburg WA
KBIS(FM) Forks WA
*KZUU(FM) Pullman WA
KEGX(FM) Richland WA
KISW(FM) Seattle WA
KXRX(FM) Walla Walla WA
KATS(FM) Yakima WA
WAPL(FM) Appleton WI
WLGE(FM) Bailey's Harbor WI
WWHG(FM) Evansville WI
WIIL(FM) Kenosha WI
WRQT(FM) La Crosse WI
WIBA-FM Madison WI
WMZK(FM) Merrill WI
WHQG(FM) Milwaukee WI
WLUM-FM Milwaukee WI
WZOR(FM) Mishicot WI
WCCN-FM Neillsville WI
WWWX(FM) Oshkosh WI
*WSUP(FM) Platteville WI
*WSHS(FM) Sheboygan WI
WHBZ(FM) Sheboygan Falls WI
*WNLI(FM) Sturgeon Bay WI
WRQE(FM) Sturgeon Bay WI
WJJO(FM) Watertown WI
WBCV(FM) Wausau WI
WAMX(FM) Milton WV
WHBR-FM Parkersburg WV
WKLC-FM Saint Albans WV
WEGW(FM) Wheeling WV
KAZY(FM) Cheyenne WY
KDAD(FM) Douglas WY
KMTN(FM) Jackson WY

Russian

KICY(AM) Nome AK
WKTA(AM) Evanston IL
WAZN(AM) Watertown MA

Smooth Jazz

KNIK-FM Anchorage AK
*WVAS(FM) Montgomery AL
*KUAP(FM) Pine Bluff AR
KOAS(FM) Dolan Springs AZ
KSSJ(FM) Fair Oaks CA
KJJZ(FM) Indio CA
KIFM(FM) San Diego CA
KJZY(FM) Sebastopol CA
KKXS(FM) Shingletown CA
KMYT(FM) Temecula CA
KKHI(FM) Centennial CO
WXJZ(FM) Gainesville FL
WSJT(FM) Holmes Beach FL
WSBZ(FM) Miramar Beach FL
WJZT(FM) Woodville FL
WAEG(FM) Evans GA
KORL-FM Waianae HI
KQZB(FM) Troy ID
WARH(FM) Granite City IL
WKYL(FM) Lawrenceburg KY
WJSH(FM) Folsom LA
WEIB(FM) Northampton MA
WJZQ(FM) Cadillac MI
WJZL(FM) Charlotte MI
WVMV(FM) Detroit MI
WMFN(FM) Zeeland MI
KTLK-FM Minneapolis MN
KZWV(FM) Eldon MO
WDAF-FM Liberty MO
KQJZ(AM) Evergreen MT
*WCCE(FM) Buie's Creek NC
*WRMU(FM) Alliance OH
WNWV(FM) Elyria OH
KYSJ(FM) Coos Bay OR
KUJJ(FM) Weston OR
WSJW(FM) Starview PA
*WFSK-FM Nashville TN
KERV(AM) Kerrville TX
*KPVU(FM) Prairie View TX
WWTJ(FM) Charlottesville VA
WJCD(FM) Windsor VA
KZAL(FM) Manson WA
KWJZ(FM) Seattle WA
WJZX(FM) Brookfield WI
WAUN(FM) Kewaunee WI

Soul

WZZA(AM) Tuscumbia AL
KOKY(FM) Sherwood AR
WTYB(FM) Tybee Island GA
WFUN-FM Bethalto IL
WYRB(FM) Genoa IL
WSRB(FM) Lansing IL
KXZZ(AM) Lake Charles LA
WRBO(FM) Como MS
WQMG-FM Greensboro NC
WRKS(FM) New York NY
WAMO(AM) Millvale PA

Spanish

WQCR(AM) Alabaster AL
WWGC(AM) Albertville AL
WZGX(AM) Bessemer AL
WENN(AM) Birmingham AL
WYAM(AM) Hartselle AL
WJHX(AM) Lexington AL
WCRL(AM) Oneonta AL
WKAX(AM) Russellville AL
WQRX(AM) Valley Head AL
KSEC(FM) Bentonville AR
KZTD(AM) Cabot AR
KLTK(AM) Centerton AR
KDQN(AM) De Queen AR
KAKS(FM) Huntsville AR
KTUV(AM) Little Rock AR
KBHC(AM) Nashville AR
KYNG(AM) Springdale AR
KOAI(AM) Van Buren AR
KVVA-FM Apache Junction AZ
KKMR(FM) Arizona City AZ
*KRMB(FM) Bisbee AZ
KMIA(AM) Black Canyon City AZ

KCKY(AM) Coolidge AZ
KDAP(AM) Douglas AZ
*KRMC(FM) Douglas AZ
KLNZ(FM) Glendale AZ
KQMR(FM) Globe AZ
KTZR-FM Green Valley AZ
KZLZ(FM) Kearny AZ
KRRN(FM) Kingman AZ
*KNOG(FM) Nogales AZ
KOFH(FM) Nogales AZ
KCMT(FM) Oro Valley AZ
KHOT-FM Paradise Valley AZ
KRIT(FM) Parker AZ
KIDR(AM) Phoenix AZ
*KNAI(FM) Phoenix AZ
KSUN(AM) Phoenix AZ
KEVT(AM) Sahuarita AZ
KOMR(FM) Sun City AZ
KVIB(FM) Sun City West AZ
KTKT(AM) Tucson AZ
KCEC-FM Wellton AZ
*KYRM(FM) Yuma AZ
KWRN(AM) Apple Valley CA
KSSE(FM) Arcadia CA
KBYN(FM) Arnold CA
*KCFA(FM) Arnold CA
KMYX-FM Arvin CA
KAFY(AM) Bakersfield CA
KLHC(FM) Bakersfield CA
KPSL-FM Bakersfield CA
*KTQX(FM) Bakersfield CA
KWAC(AM) Bakersfield CA
KIQQ(AM) Barstow CA
*KODV(FM) Barstow CA
KAEH(FM) Beaumont CA
KXSB(FM) Big Bear Lake CA
KSEH(FM) Brawley CA
KGBA(AM) Calexico CA
*KUBO(FM) Calexico CA
KMVE(FM) California City CA
KSSB(FM) Calipatria CA
*KBBF(FM) Calistoga CA
*KMRO(FM) Camarillo CA
KNTO(FM) Chowchilla CA
*KHDC(FM) Chualar CA
KCVR-FM Columbia CA
KBLO(FM) Corcoran CA
KFVR(AM) Crescent City CA
KXSE(FM) Davis CA
KCHJ(AM) Delano CA
KCHJ(FM) Delano CA
KSAC-FM Dunnigan CA
KLAX-FM East Los Angeles CA
KMQA(FM) East Porterville CA
KMLA(FM) El Rio CA
KSPE-FM Ellwood CA
KLMG(FM) Esparto CA
KSSD(FM) Fallbrook CA
KXZM(FM) Felton CA
*KEYQ(AM) Fresno CA
KGED(AM) Fresno CA
KGST(AM) Fresno CA
KIRV(AM) Fresno CA
*KSJV(FM) Fresno CA
KWRU(FM) Fresno CA
KXEX(AM) Fresno CA
KEBN(FM) Garden Grove CA
KAZA(AM) Gilroy CA
KSCA(FM) Glendale CA
KBAA(FM) Grass Valley CA
KLOK-FM Greenfield CA
KSEA(FM) Greenfield CA
KHHZ(FM) Gridley CA
KRTO(FM) Guadalupe CA
KGEN-FM Hanford CA
KRDA(FM) Hanford CA
KXRS(FM) Hemet CA
KMPG(AM) Hollister CA
KXSM(FM) Hollister CA
KMXX(FM) Imperial CA
KESQ(AM) Indio CA
KRCD(FM) Inglewood CA
KTTA(FM) Jackson CA
KBHH(FM) Kerman CA
KSRN(FM) Kings Beach CA
KUNA-FM La Quinta CA

*KVUH(FM) Laytonville CA
KBTW(FM) Lenwood CA
KSKD(FM) Livingston CA
KCVR(AM) Lodi CA
KIDI-FM Lompoc CA
KRQK(FM) Lompoc CA
KSMY(FM) Lompoc CA
KBUE(FM) Long Beach CA
KLTX(FM) Long Beach CA
KHJ(AM) Los Angeles CA
KLVE(FM) Los Angeles CA
KTNQ(AM) Los Angeles CA
KXOL-FM Los Angeles CA
KXOS(FM) Los Angeles CA
KQLB(AM) Los Banos CA
KEBT(FM) Lost Hills CA
KHIT-FM Madera CA
KRCX-FM Marysville CA
KIWI(FM) McFarland CA
KMEN(FM) Mendota CA
KTIQ(AM) Merced CA
KBBU(FM) Modesto CA
KHPY(AM) Moreno Valley CA
KLMM(FM) Morro Bay CA
KIQQ-FM Newberry Springs CA
KDLE(FM) Newport Beach CA
KLLE(FM) North Fork CA
KAAT(FM) Oakhurst CA
KEWE(AM) Oroville CA
KOXR(AM) Oxnard CA
KXLM(FM) Oxnard CA
KUTY(AM) Palmdale CA
KLUN(FM) Paso Robles CA
KTSE-FM Patterson CA
KTOB(AM) Petaluma CA
KATD(AM) Pittsburg CA
KWKU(AM) Pomona CA
KCAL(AM) Redlands CA
KDIF(AM) Riverside CA
KFSG(FM) Roseville CA
KDBV(AM) Salinas CA
KPRC-FM Salinas CA
KRAY-FM Salinas CA
KTGE(AM) Salinas CA
KEZY(AM) San Bernardino CA
KLNV(FM) San Diego CA
KLQV(FM) San Diego CA
KSDO(AM) San Diego CA
KBUA(FM) San Fernando CA
KIQI(AM) San Francisco CA
KSOL(FM) San Francisco CA
KRQB(FM) San Jacinto CA
KBRG(FM) San Jose CA
KSJO(AM) San Jose CA
KZSF(AM) San Jose CA
KVVZ(FM) San Rafael CA
KWIZ(FM) Santa Ana CA
KIST(AM) Santa Barbara CA
KIST-FM Santa Barbara CA
KZER(AM) Santa Barbara CA
KVVF(FM) Santa Clara CA
KSQL(FM) Santa Cruz CA
KSBQ(AM) Santa Maria CA
KTAP(AM) Santa Maria CA
KBLA(AM) Santa Monica CA
KDLD(FM) Santa Monica CA
KLJR-FM Santa Paula CA
KRRS(AM) Santa Rosa CA
KSES-FM Seaside CA
*KGZO(FM) Shafter CA
KMBX(AM) Soledad CA
KMJV(FM) Soledad CA
KSTN-FM Stockton CA
KMIX(FM) Tracy CA
KGEN(AM) Tulare CA
KLOC(AM) Turlock CA
KUKI(AM) Ukiah CA
KSSC(FM) Ventura CA
KUNX(AM) Ventura CA
KRSX(AM) Victorville CA
KWCA(FM) Weaverville CA
KALI(AM) West Covina CA
KLLK(AM) Willits CA
KJOR(FM) Windsor CA
KLOQ-FM Winton CA
KOBO(AM) Yuba City CA

KPVW(FM) Aspen CO
KMXA(AM) Aurora CO
KLVZ(AM) Brighton CO
KJMN(FM) Castle Rock CO
KBJD(AM) Denver CO
KBNO(AM) Denver CO
KNRV(AM) Englewood CO
KXPK(FM) Evergreen CO
KFTM(AM) Fort Morgan CO
KGRE(AM) Greeley CO
KQSE(FM) Gypsum CO
KFVR-FM La Junta CO
KXRE(AM) Manitou Springs CO
KAVA(AM) Pueblo CO
KIQN(FM) Pueblo CO
KWRP(AM) Pueblo CO
KRYE(FM) Rye CO
KXCL(FM) Westcliffe CO
KJJD(AM) Windsor CO
WADS(AM) Ansonia CT
WCUM(AM) Bridgeport CT
WPRX(AM) Bristol CT
WSUB(AM) Groton CT
WNEZ(AM) Manchester CT
WFNW(AM) Naugatuck CT
WLAT(AM) New Britain CT
WRYM(AM) New Britain CT
WXCT(AM) Southington CT
WJWL(AM) Georgetown DE
WYUS(AM) Milford DE
WNWK(AM) Newark DE
WNTF(AM) Bithlo FL
WLCC(AM) Brandon FL
WEWC(AM) Callahan FL
WAFC(AM) Clewiston FL
WAFC-FM Clewiston FL
WRHC(AM) Coral Gables FL
WDCF(AM) Dade City FL
WRLZ(AM) Eatonville FL
WVOJ(AM) Fernandina Beach FL
WRMA(FM) Fort Lauderdale FL
WCRM(AM) Fort Myers FL
WJNX(AM) Fort Pierce FL
WRTO-FM Goulds FL
WACC(AM) Hialeah FL
WCMQ-FM Hialeah FL
WOIR(AM) Homestead FL
WAFZ-FM Immokalee FL
WWWK(FM) Islamorada FL
*WGES-FM Key Largo FL
WKIZ(AM) Key West FL
*WLAZ(FM) Kissimmee FL
WOTS(AM) Kissimmee FL
*WBIY(FM) La Belle FL
WIPC(AM) Lake Wales FL
WWRF(AM) Lake Worth FL
WQBQ(AM) Leesburg FL
WRAZ-FM Leisure City FL
WAMR-FM Miami FL
WAQI(AM) Miami FL
*WDNA(FM) Miami FL
WOCN(AM) Miami FL
WQBA(AM) Miami FL
WSUA(AM) Miami FL
WWFE(AM) Miami FL
WNMA(AM) Miami Springs FL
WECM(AM) Milton FL
WZSP(FM) Nocatee FL
WXDJ(AM) North Miami Beach FL
WUNA(AM) Ocoee FL
WRUM(FM) Orlando FL
*WGNK(FM) Pennsuco FL
WTLQ-FM Punta Rassa FL
WPSP(AM) Royal Palm Beach FL
WYUU(FM) Safety Harbor FL
WIWA(AM) Saint Cloud FL
WGES(AM) Saint Petersburg FL
WSDO(AM) Sanford FL
WPIK(FM) Summerland Key FL
WAMA(AM) Tampa FL
WQBN(AM) Temple Terrace FL
WNUE-FM Titusville FL
WAUC(AM) Wauchula FL
WRLX(FM) West Palm Beach FL
WLAA(AM) Winter Garden FL
WPRD(AM) Winter Park FL

WAOS(AM) Austell GA
WBZY(FM) Bowdon GA
WLKQ-FM Buford GA
WXEM(AM) Buford GA
WWVA-FM Canton GA
WPBS(AM) Conyers GA
WDAL(AM) Dalton GA
WLBA(AM) Gainesville GA
WPLO(AM) Grayson GA
WWWE(AM) Hapeville GA
*WTMQ(FM) Lumpkin GA
WFTD(AM) Marietta GA
WSBX(AM) Ochlocknee GA
WOCE(AM) Ringgold GA
WKTM(AM) Soperton GA
*WJDS(FM) Sparta GA
WNSY(FM) Talking Rock GA
KDNZ(AM) Cedar Falls IA
*KOJI(FM) Okoboji IA
KDLS-FM Perry IA
*KWIT(FM) Sioux City IA
KAYL(AM) Storm Lake IA
KSPZ(AM) Ammon ID
KDBI(FM) Emmett ID
KWEI-FM Fruitland ID
KPDA(FM) Gooding ID
KRXR(AM) Gooding ID
KQTA(FM) Homedale ID
KFTA(AM) Rupert ID
KWEI(AM) Weiser ID
WLEY-FM Aurora IL
WNUA(FM) Chicago IL
WRTO(AM) Chicago IL
WRLL(AM) Cicero IL
WAIT(AM) Crystal Lake IL
WPPN(FM) Des Plaines IL
WCGO(AM) Evanston IL
WVIV-FM Highland Park IL
WKBF(AM) Rock Island IL
WGBJ(FM) Auburn IN
WNTS(AM) Beech Grove IN
WEDJ(FM) Danville IN
KYQQ(FM) Arkansas City KS
KANR(FM) Belle Plaine KS
KMML(FM) Cimarron KS
KFXX-FM Hugoton KS
KSSA(FM) Ingalls KS
KDTD(AM) Kansas City KS
KYYS(AM) Kansas City KS
KSMM(AM) Liberal KS
KSMM-FM Liberal KS
KCZZ(AM) Mission KS
WNTC(FM) Drakesboro KY
WTSZ(AM) Eminence KY
WTUV-FM Eminence KY
KSYR(FM) Benton LA
*WWRA(FM) Clinton LA
KGLA(AM) Gretna LA
WFNO(AM) Norco LA
WWDJ(AM) Boston MA
WUNR(AM) Brookline MA
WXKS(AM) Everett MA
WKOX(AM) Framingham MA
WCEC(AM) Haverhill MA
WNNW(AM) Lawrence MA
*WFHL(FM) New Bedford MA
WSPR(AM) Springfield MA
WRCA(AM) Waltham MA
WACM(AM) West Springfield MA
WNEB(AM) Worcester MA
WLZL(FM) Annapolis MD
WYRE(AM) Annapolis MD
WWGB(AM) Indian Head MD
WILC(AM) Laurel MD
WLXE(AM) Rockville MD
WACA(AM) Wheaton MD
WNWZ(AM) Grand Rapids MI
WSDS(AM) Salem Township MI
WYGR(AM) Wyoming MI
KMNQ(AM) Brooklyn Park MN
KMNV(AM) Saint Paul MN
KQMO(FM) Shell Knob MO
WIVG(FM) Tunica MS
WLLQ(AM) Chapel Hill NC
WGSP(AM) Charlotte NC
WCXN(AM) Claremont NC

WRRZ(AM) Clinton NC
WTIK(AM) Durham NC
WGBT(FM) Eden NC
WZBO(AM) Edenton NC
WCNC(AM) Elizabeth City NC
WRTG(AM) Garner NC
WYMY(FM) Goldsboro NC
WWBG(AM) Greensboro NC
WGOS(AM) High Point NC
WLGD(FM) Jacksonville NC
WZUP(FM) La Grange NC
WSGH(AM) Lewisville NC
*WLLN(AM) Lillington NC
WXNC(AM) Monroe NC
WREV(AM) Reidsville NC
WNCA(AM) Siler City NC
WOLS(FM) Waxhaw NC
WETC(AM) Wendell-Zebulon NC
WTOB(AM) Winston-Salem NC
KOIL(AM) Bellevue NE
KBBX-FM Nebraska City NE
KOTK(AM) Omaha NE
KMMQ(AM) Plattsmouth NE
WENJ(AM) Atlantic City NJ
WEMG(AM) Camden NJ
WJDM(AM) Elizabeth NJ
WCAA(FM) Newark NJ
WNSW(AM) Newark NJ
WXMC(AM) Parsippany-Troy Hills NJ
WPAT(AM) Paterson NJ
WPAT-FM Paterson NJ
WTAA(AM) Pleasantville NJ
WMIZ(AM) Vineland NJ
*KANW(FM) Albuquerque NM
KBZU(FM) Albuquerque NM
KKRG(FM) Albuquerque NM
KRZY(AM) Albuquerque NM
KDLW(FM) Belen NM
KPZE-FM Carlsbad NM
KKNS(AM) Corrales NM
*KZPI(FM) Deming NM
KDCE(AM) Espanola NM
KYBR(FM) Espanola NM
KRZE(AM) Farmington NM
KLMA(FM) Hobbs NM
KPZA-FM Jal NM
*KRUC(FM) Las Cruces NM
*KRWG(FM) Las Cruces NM
KFUN(AM) Las Vegas NM
KNMX(AM) Las Vegas NM
KLVO(FM) Los Alamos NM
KRDD(AM) Roswell NM
KNUW(FM) Santa Clara NM
KJFA(FM) Santa Fe NM
KRZY-FM Santa Fe NM
KSWV(AM) Santa Fe NM
*KNLK(FM) Santa Rosa NM
KSSR(AM) Santa Rosa NM
KXMT(FM) Taos NM
KKVS(FM) Truth or Consequences NM
KAVB(FM) Hawthorne NV
KDOX(AM) Henderson NV
KRGT(FM) Indian Springs NV
KENO(AM) Las Vegas NV
KISF(FM) Las Vegas NV
KKVV(AM) Las Vegas NV
KQRT(FM) Las Vegas NV
KRLV(AM) Las Vegas NV
KWID(FM) Las Vegas NV
KRNV-FM Reno NV
KXEQ(AM) Reno NV
KXTO(AM) Reno NV
KBDB(AM) Sparks NV
KQLO(AM) Sun Valley NV
KLSQ(AM) Whitney NV
WQBU-FM Garden City NY
WADO(AM) New York NY
*WHCR-FM New York NY
WKDM(AM) New York NY
WSKQ-FM New York NY
*WWRV(AM) New York NY
WLIM(AM) Patchogue NY
WEOK(AM) Poughkeepsie NY
WBON(FM) Westhampton NY
WDLR(AM) Delaware OH
WVKO-FM Johnstown OH

*WNZN(FM) Lorain OH
KCLI(AM) Clinton OK
KIZS(AM) Collinsville OK
KZUE(AM) El Reno OK
KINB(FM) Kingfisher OK
KTUZ-FM Okarche OK
KREU(FM) Roland OK
KXTD(AM) Wagoner OK
KGAY(AM) Ashland OR
*KGIO(FM) Astoria OR
KRYP(FM) Gladstone OR
KSZN(AM) Gresham OR
KUIK(AM) Hillsboro OR
KXOR(AM) Junction City OR
KRTA(AM) Medford OR
KZTB(FM) Milton-Freewater OR
KGDD(AM) Oregon City OR
KLPM(AM) Portland OR
KRDM(AM) Redmond OR
KWOD(AM) Salem OR
*KXPD(AM) Tigard OR
KWBY(AM) Woodburn OR
WHOL(AM) Allentown PA
WCDL(AM) Carbondale PA
*WLCH(FM) Lancaster PA
WNAK(AM) Nanticoke PA
WUBA(AM) Philadelphia PA
WPHE(AM) Phoenixville PA
*WXAC(FM) Reading PA
WOQI(AM) Adjuntas PR
WIVA-FM Aguadilla PR
WTPM(FM) Aguadilla PR
WWNA(AM) Aguadilla PR
WCMN(AM) Arecibo PR
WCMN-FM Arecibo PR
WMIA(AM) Arecibo PR
WNIK(AM) Arecibo PR
WBQN(AM) Barceloneta-Manati PR
WOLA(AM) Barranquitas PR
WODA(FM) Bayamon PR
WRSJ(AM) Bayamon PR
WYAC(AM) Cabo Rojo PR
WNEL(AM) Caguas PR
WVJP(AM) Caguas PR
WVJP-FM Caguas PR
WDIN(AM) Camuy PR
WGIT(AM) Canovanas PR
WIDA(AM) Carolina PR
WNVM(FM) Cidra PR
WNVE(FM) Culebra PR
WRXD(FM) Fajardo PR
*WCRP(FM) Guayama PR
WIBS(AM) Guayama PR
WZET(AM) Hormigueros PR
WALO(AM) Humacao PR
WCGB(AM) Juana Diaz PR
WBSG(AM) Lajas PR
WGDL(AM) Lares PR
WMNT(AM) Manati PR
WAEL-FM Maricao PR
WIOB(AM) Mayaguez PR
WPRA(AM) Mayaguez PR
*WRUO(FM) Mayaguez PR
WTIL(AM) Mayaguez PR
WEKO(AM) Morovis PR
WYQE(FM) Naguabo PR
WPPC(AM) Penuelas PR
WDEP(AM) Ponce PR
WPAB(AM) Ponce PR
WPRP(AM) Ponce PR
WRIO(FM) Ponce PR
WZAR(FM) Ponce PR
WZMT(FM) Ponce PR
WCHQ(AM) Quebradillas PR
WIDI(FM) Quebradillas PR
WHOY(AM) Salinas PR
WSOL(AM) San German PR
WAPA(AM) San Juan PR
WIAC(AM) San Juan PR
WIOA(AM) San Juan PR
WQBS(AM) San Juan PR
*WRTU(FM) San Juan PR
WSKN(AM) San Juan PR
WZNT(AM) San Juan PR
WRSS(AM) San Sebastian PR
WRSS(AM) San Sebastian PR

WUPR(AM) Utuado PR
WERR(FM) Vega Alta PR
WIVV(AM) Vieques PR
WIVV(AM) Vieques PR
WIVV(AM) Vieques PR
WXEW(AM) Yabucoa PR
WKFE(AM) Yauco PR
WALE(AM) Greenville RI
WKKB(FM) Middletown RI
*WELH(FM) Providence RI
WPMZ(AM) Providence RI
WBLR(AM) Batesburg SC
WCEO(AM) Columbia SC
WOLI-FM Easley SC
WGVL(AM) Greenville SC
WPJF(AM) Greenville SC
WQVA(AM) Lexington SC
WWIK(FM) McClellanville SC
WKMG(AM) Newberry SC
WGSP-FM Pageland SC
WNFO(AM) Ridgeland SC
WAZS(AM) Summerville SC
WBZK(AM) York SC
WSAA(FM) Benton TN
WNWS(AM) Brownsville TN
WHEW(AM) Franklin TN
WYXE(AM) Gallatin TN
WKZX-FM Lenoir City TN
WKCE(AM) Maryville TN
WGSF(AM) Memphis TN
WMGC(AM) Murfreesboro TN
*WMTS-FM Murfreesboro TN
WNQM(AM) Nashville TN
WNVL(AM) Nashville TN
WSBI(AM) Static TN
KKHR(FM) Abilene TX
KTCY(FM) Azle TX
KXGJ(FM) Bay City TX
KQQK(FM) Beaumont TX
KIBL(AM) Beeville TX
KDXX(FM) Benbrook TX
KPDB(AM) Big Lake TX
KBYG(AM) Big Spring TX
KBRN(AM) Boerne TX
KBOC(FM) Bridgeport TX
KKUB(AM) Brownfield TX
*KPBB(FM) Brownfield TX
*KBNR(FM) Brownsville TX
KKPS(FM) Brownsville TX
*KPBE(FM) Brownwood TX
KXYL(AM) Brownwood TX
KTAE(AM) Cameron TX
KAYG(FM) Camp Wood TX
KBEN(AM) Carrizo Springs TX
KCZO(FM) Carrizo Springs TX
KJON(AM) Carrollton TX
KDET(AM) Center TX
KUZN(FM) Centerville TX
*KFCH(FM) Childress TX
KWOW(FM) Clifton TX
KGSX(FM) Comfort TX
KUNO(AM) Corpus Christi TX
KMMZ(FM) Crane TX
KXOI(AM) Crane TX
KHER(FM) Crystal City TX
KNIT(AM) Dallas TX
KFZO(FM) Denton TX
KSML(AM) Diboll TX
KLMO-FM Dilley TX
KDHN(AM) Dimmitt TX
KXBT(FM) Dripping Springs TX
KEPS(AM) Eagle Pass TX
*KEPX(FM) Eagle Pass TX
*KOIR(FM) Edinburg TX
KVLY(FM) Edinburg TX
KAMA(AM) El Paso TX
KBNA-FM El Paso TX
KINT-FM El Paso TX
KSVE(AM) El Paso TX
*KVER(FM) El Paso TX
KVIV(AM) El Paso TX
KXPL(AM) El Paso TX
KYSE(FM) El Paso TX
KXXS(FM) Elgin TX
KDFM(AM) Falfurrias TX
KLDS(AM) Falfurrias TX

KPSO-FM Falfurrias TX
KIJN(AM) Farwell TX
KMUL(AM) Farwell TX
KDFT(AM) Ferris TX
KFST-FM Fort Stockton TX
KFJZ(AM) Fort Worth TX
KFLC(AM) Fort Worth TX
KLNO(FM) Fort Worth TX
KMVK(FM) Fort Worth TX
KOYE(FM) Frankston TX
KJOJ-FM Freeport TX
*KPBN(FM) Freer TX
KGRW(FM) Friona TX
KATH(AM) Frisco TX
*KHCB(AM) Galveston TX
KOVE-FM Galveston TX
KHZS(FM) Georgetown TX
KHMC(FM) Goliad TX
KGBT(AM) Harlingen TX
KVJM(FM) Hearne TX
KEKO(FM) Hebronville TX
KJNZ(FM) Hereford TX
KEYH(AM) Houston TX
KLAT(AM) Houston TX
KLOL(FM) Houston TX
KLTN(FM) Houston TX
KQUE(AM) Houston TX
KXYZ(AM) Houston TX
KSML-FM Huntington TX
*KHCH(AM) Huntsville TX
KLEY-FM Jourdanton TX
KTXX(FM) Karnes City TX
KERB(AM) Kermit TX
KERB-FM Kermit TX
*KHKV(FM) Kerrville TX
KINE(AM) Kingsville TX
KNOR(FM) Krum TX
KTXC(FM) Lamesa TX
*KBNL(FM) Laredo TX
*KHOY(FM) Laredo TX
KLAR(AM) Laredo TX
KLNT(AM) Laredo TX
KNEX(AM) Laredo TX
KHHL(FM) Leander TX
KESS-FM Lewisville TX
KBZO(AM) Lubbock TX
KXTQ-FM Lubbock TX
KELG(AM) Manor TX
*KBIB(AM) Marion TX
KCUL-FM Marshall TX
KGBT-FM McAllen TX
KRIO(AM) McAllen TX
KJSA(AM) Mineral Wells TX
KBDR(FM) Mirando City TX
KIRT(AM) Mission TX
KAMA-FM Missouri City TX
KBRZ(AM) Missouri City TX
KIMP(AM) Mount Pleasant TX
KZZA(FM) Muenster TX
KLHB(FM) Odem TX
KLVL(AM) Pasadena TX
KRIO-FM Pearsall TX
KOKE(FM) Pflugerville TX
KDVE(FM) Pittsburg TX
*KGWP(FM) Pittsburg TX
*KPMB(FM) Plainview TX
KREW(AM) Plainview TX
*KWMF(FM) Pleasanton TX
KQBU-FM Port Arthur TX
KTJM(FM) Port Arthur TX
KNVO-FM Port Isabel TX
KBPO(AM) Port Neches TX
KMFM(FM) Premont TX
KCLR(FM) Ralls TX
KBIC(FM) Raymondville TX
KBUC(FM) Raymondville TX
KQBO(FM) Rio Grande City TX
KHCK-FM Robinson TX
KROB(AM) Robstown TX
KSAB(AM) Robstown TX
KRTX(AM) Rosenberg-Richmond TX
*KTER(FM) Rudolph TX
KSJT-FM San Angelo TX
KCOR(AM) San Antonio TX
KROM(FM) San Antonio TX

KXTN-FM San Antonio TX
KQSI(FM) San Augustine TX
KUKA(FM) San Diego TX
KUBR(AM) San Juan TX
KUOL(AM) San Marcos TX
KMAT(FM) Seadrift TX
KDAE(AM) Sinton TX
KESO(FM) South Padre Island TX
KSTV(AM) Stephenville TX
KAMZ(FM) Tahoka TX
KXAL-FM Tatum TX
KLQB(FM) Taylor TX
KWNX(AM) Taylor TX
KYST(AM) Texas City TX
KTUE(AM) Tulia TX
KSAH(AM) Universal City TX
KTNO(AM) University Park TX
KZMP(AM) University Park TX
KUVA(FM) Uvalde TX
KRGE(AM) Weslaco TX
KAIQ(FM) Wolfforth TX
KBAW(FM) Zapata TX
KTUB(AM) Centerville UT
KSVN(AM) Ogden UT
KDUT(FM) Randolph UT
KBJA(AM) Sandy UT
WXTR(AM) Alexandria VA
WZHF(AM) Arlington VA
WTGD(FM) Bridgewater VA
WPWC(AM) Dumfries-Triangle VA
WTOX(AM) Glen Allen VA
WKDV(AM) Manassas VA
WVXX(AM) Norfolk VA
WBTK(AM) Richmond VA
WVNZ(AM) Richmond VA
WKCW(AM) Warrenton VA
WAMM(AM) Woodstock VA
WAXJ(FM) Frederiksted VI
WMYP(FM) Frederiksted VI
KBKW(AM) Aberdeen WA
KTBK(AM) Auburn-Federal Way WA
KXPA(AM) Bellevue WA
KMMG(FM) Benton City WA
KBRO(AM) Bremerton WA
*KCED(FM) Centralia WA
KZHR(FM) Dayton WA
KDDS-FM Elma WA
KLDY(AM) Lacey WA
KNTB(AM) Lakewood WA
KMNA(FM) Mabton WA
*KSVR(FM) Mount Vernon WA
KZTA(FM) Naches WA
KLES(FM) Prosser WA
KZML(FM) Quincy WA
KRCW(FM) Royal City WA
KNTS(AM) Seattle WA
KDYM(AM) Sunnyside WA
KKMO(FM) Tacoma WA
KDYK(AM) Union Gap WA
KTRO(AM) Vancouver WA
KZNW(AM) Wenatchee WA
*KBNO-FM White Salmon WA
KWLN(AM) Wilson Creek WA
*KDNA(FM) Yakima WA
WREY(AM) Hudson WI
WLMV(AM) Madison WI
WJTI(AM) Racine WI
WDDW(FM) Sturtevant WI
WRRD(AM) Waukesha WI
KBMG(FM) Evanston WY
KLMI(FM) Rock River WY
KMRZ-FM Superior WY
KOLT-FM Warren AFB WY

Sports

KTZN(AM) Anchorage AK
KCBF(AM) Fairbanks AK
WBNM(AM) Alexander City AL
WNSI-FM Atmore AL
WAUD(AM) Auburn AL
WNSP(FM) Bay Minette AL
WJOX(FM) Birmingham AL
WSPZ(AM) Birmingham AL
WFMH(AM) Cullman AL
WKUL(AM) Cullman AL

WWTM(AM) Decatur AL
WZNJ(FM) Demopolis AL
WOOF(AM) Dothan AL
WSBM(AM) Florence AL
WHEP(AM) Foley AL
WJBY(AM) Gadsden AL
WUMP(AM) Madison AL
WMSP(AM) Montgomery AL
WNTM(AM) Mobile AL
WLAY(AM) Muscle Shoals AL
WHAL(AM) Phenix City AL
WIQR(AM) Prattville AL
WELR(AM) Roanoke AL
WNSI(AM) Robertsdale AL
WYTK(FM) Rogersville AL
WWIC(AM) Scottsboro AL
WFEB(AM) Sylacauga AL
WTLS(AM) Tallassee AL
WTBC(AM) Tuscaloosa AL
WVNA(AM) Tuscumbia AL
WVSA(AM) Vernon AL
WKXM(AM) Winfield AL
WSLY(FM) York AL
KBTA(AM) Batesville AR
KEWI(AM) Benton AR
KREB(AM) Bentonville-Bella Vista AR
KASR(FM) Conway AR
KXXA(AM) Conway AR
KELD(AM) El Dorado AR
KQSM-FM Fayetteville AR
KFFA-FM Helena AR
KZHS(AM) Hot Springs AR
KARN(AM) Little Rock AR
KTTG(FM) Mena AR
KVOM(AM) Morrilton AR
KDXE(AM) North Little Rock AR
KDRS(AM) Paragould AR
KOTN(AM) Pine Bluff AR
KFFK(AM) Rogers AR
KARV(AM) Russellville AR
KUOA(AM) Siloam Springs AR
KWAK(AM) Stuttgart AR
KHGG(AM) Van Buren AR
KHGG-FM Waldron AR
KQPN(AM) West Memphis AR
KMIA(AM) Black Canyon City AZ
KVNA(FM) Flagstaff AZ
KIKO(AM) Miami AZ
KGME(AM) Phoenix AZ
KIDR(AM) Phoenix AZ
KMVP(AM) Phoenix AZ
KTAR(AM) Phoenix AZ
KQNA(AM) Prescott Valley AZ
KATO(AM) Safford AZ
KAZM(AM) Sedona AZ
KTAN(AM) Sierra Vista AZ
KDUS(AM) Tempe AZ
KCUB(AM) Tucson AZ
KFFN(AM) Tucson AZ
KTKT(AM) Tucson AZ
KJOK(AM) Yuma AZ
KATA(AM) Arcata CA
KXTK(AM) Arroyo Grande CA
KBFP(AM) Bakersfield CA
KGEO(AM) Bakersfield CA
KHTY(AM) Bakersfield CA
KMET(AM) Banning CA
KFPT(AM) Clovis CA
KWRM(AM) Corona CA
KCBL(AM) Fresno CA
KFIG(AM) Fresno CA
KGST(AM) Fresno CA
KRER(FM) Hamilton City CA
KAVL(AM) Lancaster CA
KLAC(AM) Los Angeles CA
KSPN(AM) Los Angeles CA
KWKW(AM) Los Angeles CA
KMFB(FM) Mendocino CA
KESP(AM) Modesto CA
KLAA(AM) Orange CA
KDOW(AM) Palo Alto CA
KPRL(AM) Paso Robles CA
KWKU(AM) Pomona CA
KNLF(FM) Quincy CA
KWDJ(AM) Ridgecrest CA
KHTK(AM) Sacramento CA

KLSD(AM) San Diego CA
KNBR(AM) San Francisco CA
KKJL(AM) San Luis Obispo CA
KTCT(AM) San Mateo CA
KCNR(AM) Shasta CA
KIRN(AM) Simi Valley CA
KOWL(AM) South Lake Tahoe CA
KSUE(AM) Susanville CA
KXPS(AM) Thousand Palms CA
KEZL(AM) Visalia CA
KSLK(FM) Visalia CA
KCTC(AM) West Sacramento CA
KNFO(AM) Basalt CO
KSIR(AM) Brush CO
KVOR(AM) Colorado Springs CO
KBNO(AM) Denver CO
KOA(AM) Denver CO
KIUP(AM) Durango CO
KIIX(AM) Fort Collins CO
KTMM(AM) Grand Junction CO
KEPN(AM) Lakewood CO
KCKK(AM) Littleton CO
KKFN(FM) Longmont CO
KWUF(AM) Pagosa Springs CO
KJMP(AM) Pierce CO
KDZA(AM) Pueblo CO
KRGS(AM) Rifle CO
KBCR(AM) Steamboat Springs CO
KSPK(FM) Walsenburg CO
WINE(AM) Brookfield CT
WPOP(AM) Hartford CT
WMMW(AM) Meriden CT
WAVZ(AM) New Haven CT
WTEM(AM) Washington DC
WDOV(AM) Dover DE
WWTX(AM) Wilmington DE
WBGF(FM) Belle Glade FL
WWJB(AM) Brooksville FL
WKFL(AM) Bushnell FL
WMEL(AM) Cocoa Beach FL
WRHC(AM) Coral Gables FL
WNDB(AM) Daytona Beach FL
WTJV(AM) De Land FL
WFLL(AM) Fort Lauderdale FL
WGGG(AM) Gainesville FL
WRUF(AM) Gainesville FL
WNPL(AM) Golden Gate FL
WYGC(FM) High Springs FL
WTKE-FM Holt FL
WFXJ(AM) Jacksonville FL
WNNR(AM) Jacksonville FL
WJXL(AM) Jacksonville Beach FL
WKWF(AM) Key West FL
WHOO(AM) Kissimmee FL
WBXY(FM) La Crosse FL
WFFG(AM) Marathon FL
WDMC(AM) Melbourne FL
WINT(AM) Melbourne FL
WINZ(AM) Miami FL
WOCN(AM) Miami FL
WQAM(AM) Miami FL
WNMA(AM) Miami Springs FL
WWCN(AM) North Fort Myers FL
WMOP(AM) Ocala FL
WYGM(AM) Orlando FL
WELE(AM) Ormond Beach FL
WLTG(AM) Panama City FL
WASJ(FM) Panama City Beach FL
WPTK(AM) Pine Island Center FL
WHBO(AM) Pinellas Park FL
WPSL(AM) Port St. Lucie FL
WMEN(AM) Royal Palm Beach FL
WAOC(AM) Saint Augustine FL
WFOY(AM) Saint Augustine FL
WDAE(AM) Saint Petersburg FL
WSRQ(AM) Sarasota FL
WQYK(AM) Seffner FL
WAXY(AM) South Miami FL
WSTU(AM) Stuart FL
*WANM(FM) Tallahassee FL
WNLS(AM) Tallahassee FL
WHNZ(AM) Tampa FL
WEFL(AM) Tequesta FL
WJNO(AM) West Palm Beach FL
WGPC(AM) Albany GA
WSRA(AM) Albany GA

WRFC(AM) Athens GA
WALR(AM) Atlanta GA
WQXI(AM) Atlanta GA
WGAC(AM) Augusta GA
WNRR(AM) Augusta GA
WRDW(AM) Augusta GA
WSGF(AM) Augusta GA
WFNS(AM) Blackshear GA
WPPL(FM) Blue Ridge GA
WMOG(AM) Brunswick GA
WSFN(AM) Brunswick GA
WBHF(AM) Cartersville GA
WYXC(AM) Cartersville GA
WEAM(AM) Columbus GA
WRCG(AM) Columbus GA
WSHE(AM) Columbus GA
WSHE(AM) Columbus GA
WDMG(AM) Douglas GA
WGGA(AM) Gainesville GA
WHIE(AM) Griffin GA
WCEH(AM) Hawkinsville GA
WLOP(AM) Jesup GA
WLAG(AM) La Grange GA
WIFN(FM) Macon GA
WFOM(AM) Marietta GA
WMVG(AM) Milledgeville GA
WCOH(AM) Newnan GA
WCNN(AM) North Atlanta GA
WLAQ(AM) Rome GA
WSNT(AM) Sandersville GA
WJLG(AM) Savannah GA
WTKS(AM) Savannah GA
WPTB(AM) Statesboro GA
WWNS(AM) Statesboro GA
WJAT(AM) Swainsboro GA
WVLD(AM) Valdosta GA
WVOP(AM) Vidalia GA
WNNG(AM) Warner Robins GA
KHLO(AM) Hilo HI
KPUA(AM) Hilo HI
KKEA(AM) Honolulu HI
KKON(AM) Kealakekua HI
KAOI(AM) Kihei HI
KQNG(AM) Lihue HI
KUPA(AM) Pearl City HI
KMVI(AM) Wailuku HI
KCNZ(AM) Cedar Falls IA
KGYM(AM) Cedar Rapids IA
KMJM(AM) Cedar Rapids IA
KBGG(AM) Des Moines IA
KWKY(AM) Des Moines IA
KXNO(AM) Des Moines IA
WDBQ(AM) Dubuque IA
KILR-FM Estherville IA
KVFD(AM) Fort Dodge IA
KIFG-FM Iowa Falls IA
KOKX(AM) Keokuk IA
KLEM(AM) Le Mars IA
KOEL(AM) Oelwein IA
KMNS(AM) Sioux City IA
KSCJ(AM) Sioux City IA
KAYL-FM Storm Lake IA
KBFI(AM) Bonners Ferry ID
KRLC(AM) Lewiston ID
KTIK(AM) Nampa ID
KIOV(AM) Payette ID
KWIK(AM) Pocatello ID
KSPT(AM) Sandpoint ID
WBIG(AM) Aurora IL
WBYS(AM) Canton IL
WCIL(AM) Carbondale IL
WDWS(AM) Champaign IL
*WCRX(FM) Chicago IL
WGN(AM) Chicago IL
WMVP(AM) Chicago IL
WSCR(AM) Chicago IL
WXLT(FM) Christopher IL
WDAN(AM) Danville IL
WDZ(AM) Decatur IL
WSOY(AM) Decatur IL
WXOS(FM) East St. Louis IL
WZPN(FM) Farmington IL
WGIL(AM) Galesburg IL
*WGBK(FM) Glenview IL
WJPF(AM) Herrin IL
WDDD(AM) Johnston City IL

WLPO(AM) La Salle IL
WSMI-FM Litchfield IL
WLUV(AM) Loves Park IL
WZZT(FM) Morrison IL
WVMC(AM) Mount Carmel IL
WVLN(AM) Olney IL
WPRS(AM) Paris IL
WZOE(AM) Princeton IL
WGEM(AM) Quincy IL
WKJR(AM) Rantoul IL
WTJK(AM) South Beloit IL
WHCO(AM) Sparta IL
WFMB(AM) Springfield IL
WTAX(AM) Springfield IL
WSDR(AM) Sterling IL
WSPL(AM) Streator IL
WVIL(FM) Virginia IL
KFNS(AM) Wood River IL
WHBU(AM) Anderson IN
WBIW(AM) Bedford IN
WNUY(FM) Bluffton IN
WSDX(AM) Brazil IN
WCSI(AM) Columbus IN
WKJG(AM) Fort Wayne IN
WOWO(AM) Fort Wayne IN
WLTH(AM) Gary IN
WREB(FM) Greencastle IN
WFNI(AM) Indianapolis IN
WNDE(AM) Indianapolis IN
WXLW(AM) Indianapolis IN
WQKC(AM) Jeffersonville IN
WIOU(AM) Kokomo IN
WASK(AM) Lafayette IN
WBAT(AM) Marion IN
WYFX(FM) Mount Vernon IN
WLBC-FM Muncie IN
WXFN(AM) Muncie IN
WJCP(AM) North Vernon IN
WZZB(AM) Seymour IN
WDND(AM) South Bend IN
WSBT(AM) South Bend IN
WBOW(AM) Terre Haute IN
WAOV(AM) Vincennes IN
WRSW(AM) Warsaw IN
KKOY(AM) Chanute KS
KFH-FM Clearwater KS
KGGF(AM) Coffeyville KS
KDCC(AM) Dodge City KS
KGNO(AM) Dodge City KS
KIUL(AM) Garden City KS
KKCI(FM) Goodland KS
KVGB(AM) Great Bend KS
KNNS(AM) Larned KS
KLWN(AM) Lawrence KS
KMAN(AM) Manhattan KS
KLKC(AM) Parsons KS
KSEK(AM) Pittsburg KS
KINA(AM) Salina KS
KMAJ(AM) Topeka KS
KTOP(AM) Topeka KS
WIBW(AM) Topeka KS
KFH(AM) Wichita KS
KGSO(AM) Wichita KS
KKLE(AM) Winfield KS
WAIA(AM) Beaver Dam KY
WCBL(AM) Benton KY
WBGN(AM) Bowling Green KY
WXAM(AM) Buffalo KY
WTCO(AM) Campbellsville KY
WNES(AM) Central City KY
WIEL(AM) Elizabethtown KY
WCDS(AM) Glasgow KY
WWKU(AM) Glasgow KY
WLGC(AM) Greenup KY
WLXG(AM) Lexington KY
WVLK(AM) Lexington KY
WKRD(AM) Louisville KY
WTTL(AM) Madisonville KY
WNBS(AM) Murray KY
WOFC(AM) Murray KY
WPAD(AM) Paducah KY
WKYH(AM) Paintsville KY
WPKY(AM) Princeton KY
WVLK-FM Richmond KY
WKRD-FM Shelbyville KY
WMSK-FM Sturgis KY

KDBS(AM) Alexandria LA
WIBR(AM) Baton Rouge LA
WJBO(AM) Baton Rouge LA
KBZE(FM) Berwick LA
KRRP(AM) Coushatta LA
WSKR(AM) Denham Springs LA
KNBB(FM) Dubach LA
KBYO-FM Farmerville LA
KRLQ(FM) Hodge LA
KJIN(AM) Houma LA
KFXZ(AM) Lafayette LA
KPEL(AM) Lafayette LA
WWL(AM) New Orleans LA
WWWL(AM) New Orleans LA
KRMD(AM) Shreveport LA
WSLA(AM) Slidell LA
KEZM(AM) Sulphur LA
KMBS(AM) West Monroe LA
WARL(AM) Attleboro MA
WBZ-FM Boston MA
WEEI(AM) Boston MA
WWZN(AM) Boston MA
WXBR(AM) Brockton MA
WAMG(AM) Dedham MA
WEII(FM) Dennis MA
WVEI-FM Easthampton MA
WSAR(AM) Fall River MA
WPKZ(AM) Fitchburg MA
WLLH(AM) Lowell MA
WBSM(AM) New Bedford MA
WBEC(AM) Pittsfield MA
WESO(AM) Southbridge MA
WHLL(AM) Springfield MA
WXTK(FM) West Yarmouth MA
WVEI(AM) Worcester MA
WBAL(AM) Baltimore MD
WJZ(AM) Baltimore MD
WCEM(AM) Cambridge MD
WJZ-FM Catonsville MD
WSRY(AM) Elkton MD
WFMD(AM) Frederick MD
WVIE(AM) Pikesville MD
WWXT(FM) Prince Frederick MD
WICO(AM) Salisbury MD
WTGM(AM) Salisbury MD
WQMR(FM) Snow Hill MD
WNST(AM) Towson MD
WAEI(AM) Bangor ME
WAEI-FM Bangor ME
WZON(AM) Bangor ME
WCME(AM) Brunswick ME
WFAU(AM) Gardiner ME
WJJB-FM Gary ME
WIGY(FM) Madison ME
WTBM(FM) Mexico ME
WSYY(AM) Millinocket ME
WOXO-FM Norway ME
WRKD(AM) Rockland ME
WPEI(FM) Saco ME
WPHX(AM) Sanford ME
WSKW(AM) Skowhegan ME
WRED(AM) Westbrook ME
WFYC(AM) Alma MI
WTKA(AM) Ann Arbor MI
WBRN(AM) Big Rapids MI
WDFN(AM) Detroit MI
WXYT(AM) Detroit MI
WXYT-FM Detroit MI
WDOW(AM) Dowagiac MI
WVFN(AM) East Lansing MI
WTRX(AM) Flint MI
WSHN(AM) Fremont MI
WMJZ-FM Gaylord MI
WGHN(AM) Grand Haven MI
WBBL-FM Greenville MI
WGLM(AM) Greenville MI
WKMJ-FM Hancock MI
WMPL(AM) Hancock MI
WMAX-FM Holland MI
WCCY(AM) Houghton MI
WMIQ(AM) Iron Mountain MI
WZAM(AM) Ishpeming MI
WIBM(AM) Jackson MI
WQLR(AM) Kalamazoo MI
WJNL(AM) Kingsley MI
WLUN(FM) Pinconning MI

WSJM(AM) Saint Joseph MI
WKNW(AM) Sault Ste. Marie MI
WCCW(AM) Traverse City MI
WEFG-FM Whitehall MI
KBUN(AM) Bemidji MN
KLIZ(AM) Brainerd MN
KVBR(AM) Brainerd MN
KDLM(AM) Detroit Lakes MN
KQDS(AM) Duluth MN
WEBC(AM) Duluth MN
KCNN(AM) East Grand Forks MN
KSUM(AM) Fairmont MN
KDHL(AM) Faribault MN
KDWA(AM) Hastings MN
WMFG(AM) Hibbing MN
KDUZ(AM) Hutchinson MN
KYSM(AM) Mankato MN
KFAN(AM) Minneapolis MN
KFXN(AM) Minneapolis MN
WCMP-FM Pine City MN
KOLM(AM) Rochester MN
KWEB(AM) Rochester MN
WBHR(AM) Sauk Rapids MN
KXSS(AM) Waite Park MN
KDOM(AM) Windom MN
KDOM-FM Windom MN
KWNO(AM) Winona MN
KBFL-FM Buffalo MO
KAPE(AM) Cape Girardeau MO
KGIR(AM) Cape Girardeau MO
KDKD-FM Clinton MO
KTGR(AM) Columbia MO
KRFT(AM) De Soto MO
KYLS(AM) Fredericktown MO
KHMO(AM) Hannibal MO
KCTE(AM) Independence MO
KCSP(AM) Kansas City MO
KLWT(AM) Lebanon MO
KNIM(AM) Maryville MO
KXEO(AM) Mexico MO
KFMO(AM) Park Hills MO
KLID(AM) Poplar Bluff MO
KMIS(AM) Portageville MO
KTTR(AM) Rolla MO
KFEQ(AM) Saint Joseph MO
KMOX(AM) Saint Louis MO
KSLG(AM) Saint Louis MO
KTRS(AM) Saint Louis MO
KSMO(AM) Salem MO
KGMY(AM) Springfield MO
KWTO(AM) Springfield MO
KWTO-FM Springfield MO
KTUI-FM Sullivan MO
KTTN-FM Trenton MO
KOKO(AM) Warrensburg MO
WWZQ(AM) Aberdeen MS
WAMY(AM) Amory MS
WXBD(AM) Biloxi MS
WJFN(AM) Brandon MS
WDTL-FM Cleveland MS
WCJU(AM) Columbia MS
WJWF(AM) Columbus MS
WPBQ(AM) Flowood MS
WFOR(AM) Hattiesburg MS
WHSY(AM) Hattiesburg MS
WDXO(FM) Hazlehurst MS
WJDX(AM) Jackson MS
WSFZ(AM) Jackson MS
WAML(AM) Laurel MS
WXWX(FM) Marietta MS
WAPF(AM) McComb MS
WHNY(AM) McComb MS
WMOX(AM) Meridian MS
WMLC(AM) Monticello MS
WNAT(AM) Natchez MS
WZNO(FM) Pickens MS
WQMS(AM) Quitman MS
WKOR(AM) Starkville MS
WSSO(AM) Starkville MS
WTUP(AM) Tupelo MS
WQBC(AM) Vicksburg MS
KBLG(AM) Billings MT
KQBL(FM) Billings MT
KMMS(AM) Bozeman MT
KBOW(AM) Butte MT

KGEZ(AM) Kalispell MT
KGRZ(AM) Missoula MT
KYLT(AM) Missoula MT
WISE(AM) Asheville NC
WTKF(FM) Atlantic NC
WATA(AM) Boone NC
WYSE(AM) Canton NC
WBCN(AM) Charlotte NC
WFNZ(AM) Charlotte NC
WCMC-FM Creedmoor NC
*WWCU(FM) Cullowhee NC
WDNC(AM) Durham NC
WDUR(AM) Durham NC
WGAI(AM) Elizabeth City NC
WGHB(AM) Farmville NC
WFAY(AM) Fayetteville NC
WGNC(AM) Gastonia NC
WYND-FM Hatteras NC
WYSR(AM) High Point NC
WJNC(AM) Jacksonville NC
WLXN(AM) Lexington NC
WLON(AM) Lincolnton NC
WNOS(AM) New Bern NC
WWNB(AM) New Bern NC
WRBZ(AM) Raleigh NC
WCBT(AM) Roanoke Rapids NC
WRMT(AM) Rocky Mount NC
WCAB(AM) Rutherfordton NC
WOHS(AM) Shelby NC
WNCA(AM) Siler City NC
WFBX(AM) Spring Lake NC
WSIC(AM) Statesville NC
WBLO(AM) Thomasville NC
WMFD(AM) Wilmington NC
WVOT(AM) Wilson NC
WTIX(AM) Winston-Salem NC
KDKT(AM) Beulah ND
KXMR(AM) Bismarck ND
KLXX(AM) Bismarck-Mandan ND
KVOX(AM) Fargo ND
WDAY(AM) Fargo ND
KQDJ(AM) Jamestown ND
KMSR(AM) Mayville ND
KOVC(AM) Valley City ND
KOZN(AM) Bellevue NE
KJSK(AM) Columbus NE
KICS(AM) Hastings NE
KXPN(AM) Kearney NE
KLMS(AM) Lincoln NE
KSWN(FM) McCook NE
WJAG(AM) Norfolk NE
KOOQ(AM) North Platte NE
KXSP(AM) Omaha NE
KOLT(AM) Scottsbluff NE
WTSV(AM) Claremont NH
WTSN(AM) Dover NH
WXEX(AM) Exeter NH
WTSL(AM) Hanover NH
WTPL(FM) Hillsboro NH
WLTN(AM) Littleton NH
WGAM(AM) Manchester NH
WGIR(AM) Manchester NH
WGHM(AM) Nashua NH
WSMN(AM) Nashua NH
WGIN(AM) Rochester NH
WADB(AM) Asbury Park NJ
WENJ(AM) Atlantic City NJ
WNJE(AM) Flemington NJ
WSNR(AM) Jersey City NJ
WENJ-FM Millville NJ
WPAT(AM) Paterson NJ
KRSY(AM) Alamogordo NM
KBZU(FM) Albuquerque NM
KDEF(AM) Albuquerque NM
KNML(AM) Albuquerque NM
KCQL(AM) Aztec NM
KNFT(AM) Bayard NM
KCLV(AM) Clovis NM
KENN(AM) Farmington NM
KYKK(AM) Hobbs NM
KOBE(AM) Las Cruces NM
KSNM(AM) Las Cruces NM
KRSN(AM) Los Alamos NM
KQTM(FM) Rio Rancho NM
KWES(AM) Ruidoso NM
KRUI(AM) Ruidoso Downs NM

KVSF(AM) Santa Fe NM
KTSN(AM) Elko NV
KBAD(AM) Las Vegas NV
KENO(AM) Las Vegas NV
KLAV(AM) Las Vegas NV
KRLV(AM) Las Vegas NV
KWWN(AM) Las Vegas NV
KSHP(AM) North Las Vegas NV
KHIT(AM) Reno NV
KPLY(AM) Reno NV
KBZZ(AM) Sparks NV
WCSS(AM) Amsterdam NY
WVTL(AM) Amsterdam NY
WYSL(AM) Avon NY
WBNR(AM) Beacon NY
WYOS(AM) Binghamton NY
WPUT(AM) Brewster NY
WBEN(AM) Buffalo NY
WGR(AM) Buffalo NY
WSDE(AM) Cobleskill NY
WCBA(AM) Corning NY
WELM(AM) Elmira NY
WENE(AM) Endicott NY
WMML(AM) Glens Falls NY
WWSC(AM) Glens Falls NY
WLIR-FM Hampton Bays NY
WNRS(AM) Herkimer NY
WHCU(AM) Ithaca NY
WJTN(AM) Jamestown NY
WGHQ(AM) Kingston NY
WIRD(AM) Lake Placid NY
WIXT(AM) Little Falls NY
WLVL(AM) Lockport NY
WTMM-FM Mechanicville NY
WADO(AM) New York NY
WEPN(AM) New York NY
WFAN(AM) New York NY
WACK(AM) Newark NY
WSLB(AM) Ogdensburg NY
WLNA(AM) Peekskill NY
WEAV(AM) Plattsburgh NY
WADR(AM) Remsen NY
WROC(AM) Rochester NY
WRNY(AM) Rome NY
WGGO(AM) Salamanca NY
WSPQ(AM) Springville NY
*WAER(FM) Syracuse NY
WHEN(AM) Syracuse NY
WNSS(AM) Syracuse NY
WOFX(AM) Troy NY
WPIE(AM) Trumansburg NY
WIBX(AM) Utica NY
WUTQ(AM) Utica NY
WNER(AM) Watertown NY
WARF(AM) Akron OH
WFUN(AM) Ashtabula OH
WATH(AM) Athens OH
WOMP(AM) Bellaire OH
WBLL(AM) Bellefontaine OH
WQEL(FM) Bucyrus OH
WILE(AM) Cambridge OH
WCER(AM) Canton OH
WCSM-FM Celina OH
WKKI(FM) Celina OH
WCKY(AM) Cincinnati OH
WSAI(AM) Cincinnati OH
WKNR(AM) Cleveland OH
WTAM(AM) Cleveland OH
WWGK(AM) Cleveland OH
WBNS(AM) Columbus OH
WBNS-FM Columbus OH
WYTS(AM) Columbus OH
WING(AM) Dayton OH
WONE(AM) Dayton OH
WONW(AM) Defiance OH
WLQR(AM) Delta OH
WEOL(AM) Elyria OH
WFOB(AM) Fostoria OH
WMOH(AM) Hamilton OH
WIRO(AM) Ironton OH
WIMA(AM) Lima OH
WWSR(AM) Lima OH
WMOA(AM) Marietta OH
WTIG(AM) Massillon OH
WJAW-FM McConnelsville OH
WMPO(AM) Middleport-Pomeroy OH

WLKR(AM) Norwalk OH
WLKR-FM Norwalk OH
WRGM(AM) Ontario OH
WKSD(FM) Paulding OH
WNXT(AM) Portsmouth OH
WLEC(AM) Sandusky OH
WIZE(AM) Springfield OH
WSTV(AM) Steubenville OH
WLQR(AM) Toledo OH
WBTC(AM) Uhrichsville OH
WANR(AM) Warren OH
WELW(AM) Willoughby-Eastlake OH
WQKT(AM) Wooster OH
WBBW(AM) Youngstown OH
WKBN(AM) Youngstown OH
KADA(AM) Ada OK
KOKB(AM) Blackwell OK
KUSH(AM) Cushing OK
KPNS(AM) Duncan OK
WWLS-FM Edmond OK
KADS(AM) Elk City OK
KFXY(AM) Enid OK
KXCA(AM) Lawton OK
KEBC(AM) Midwest City OK
WWLS(AM) Moore OK
KBIX(AM) Muskogee OK
KYAL-FM Muskogee OK
KREF(AM) Norman OK
KOKC(AM) Oklahoma City OK
WKY(AM) Oklahoma City OK
KOKL(AM) Okmulgee OK
KOKP(AM) Perry OK
KOSB(FM) Perry OK
KYAL(AM) Sapulpa OK
KSPI(AM) Stillwater OK
KTLQ(AM) Tahlequah OK
KAKC(AM) Tulsa OK
KCFO(AM) Tulsa OK
KTBZ(AM) Tulsa OK
KGND(AM) Vinita OK
KSIW(AM) Woodward OK
KAST(AM) Astoria OR
KBND(AM) Bend OR
KICE(AM) Bend OR
KHSN(AM) Coos Bay OR
KLOO(AM) Corvallis OR
KUJZ(FM) Creswell OR
KSCR(AM) Eugene OR
KUIK(AM) Hillsboro OR
KFLS(AM) Klamath Falls OR
KLAD(AM) Klamath Falls OR
KGAL(AM) Lebanon OR
*KEZX(AM) Medford OR
KNPT(AM) Newport OR
KTIX(AM) Pendleton OR
KFXX(AM) Portland OR
KXTG(FM) Portland OR
KQEN(AM) Roseburg OR
KSKR(AM) Roseburg OR
KOHI(AM) Saint Helens OR
KWOD(AM) Salem OR
KSKR-FM Sutherlin OR
KMBD(AM) Tillamook OR
WSAN(AM) Allentown PA
WTKZ(AM) Allentown PA
WVAM(AM) Altoona PA
WMBA(AM) Ambridge PA
WBVP(AM) Beaver Falls PA
*WBUQ(FM) Bloomsburg PA
WISR(AM) Butler PA
WWCB(AM) Corry PA
*WESS(FM) East Stroudsburg PA
WEEX(AM) Easton PA
WPDC(AM) Elizabethtown PA
WFNN(AM) Erie PA
WPSE(AM) Erie PA
WRIE(AM) Erie PA
WFRA(AM) Franklin PA
WGET(AM) Gettysburg PA
WHGB(AM) Harrisburg PA
WTKT(AM) Harrisburg PA
WPSN(AM) Honesdale PA
WKGE(AM) Johnstown PA
WTYM(AM) Kittanning PA
WLPA(AM) Lancaster PA
WNPV(AM) Lansdale PA

WWGE(AM) Loretto PA
WMGW(AM) Meadville PA
WJUN(AM) Mexico PA
WKST(AM) New Castle PA
WIP(AM) Philadelphia PA
WPEN(AM) Philadelphia PA
WPHB(AM) Philipsburg PA
WBGG(AM) Pittsburgh PA
WEAE(AM) Pittsburgh PA
WPGB(FM) Pittsburgh PA
WYCK(AM) Plains PA
WEEU(AM) Reading PA
WIOV(AM) Reading PA
WGLD(AM) Red Lion PA
WKBI(AM) Saint Marys PA
WEJL(AM) Scranton PA
WICK(AM) Scranton PA
WBHV(AM) Somerset PA
WQWK(AM) State College PA
WKOK(AM) Sunbury PA
WTZN(AM) Troy PA
WCBG(AM) Waynesboro PA
WBAX(AM) Wilkes-Barre PA
WLYC(AM) Williamsport PA
WRAK(AM) Williamsport PA
WOYK(AM) York PA
WGIT(AM) Canovanas PR
WXRF(AM) Guayama PR
WMNT(AM) Manati PR
WYEL(AM) Mayaguez PR
WVOZ(AM) San Juan PR
WADK(AM) Newport RI
WPRO(AM) Providence RI
WLKW(AM) West Warwick RI
WEEI-FM Westerly RI
WANS(AM) Anderson SC
WZMJ(FM) Batesburg SC
WQNT(AM) Charleston SC
WSPO(AM) Charleston SC
WCCP-FM Clemson SC
WPCC(AM) Clinton SC
WCOS(AM) Columbia SC
WVOC(AM) Columbia SC
WIQB(AM) Conway SC
WJXY-FM Conway SC
WTMZ(AM) Dorchester
   Terrace-Brentwood SC
WNKT(FM) Eastover SC
WOLH(AM) Florence SC
WFIS(AM) Fountain Inn SC
WXJY(FM) Georgetown SC
WFXH(AM) Hilton Head Island SC
WWFN-FM Lake City SC
WRHM(FM) Lancaster SC
WJKB(AM) Moncks Corner SC
WRNN(AM) Myrtle Beach SC
WRHI(AM) Rock Hill SC
WOLI(AM) Spartanburg SC
WSPG(AM) Spartanburg SC
WALI(FM) Walterboro SC
KGIM(AM) Aberdeen SD
KBFS(AM) Belle Fourche SD
KIJV(AM) Huron SD
KSOO-FM Lennox SD
KORN(AM) Mitchell SD
KSOO(AM) Sioux Falls SD
KWSN(AM) Sioux Falls SD
KVTK(AM) Vermillion SD
KJJQ(AM) Volga SD
WMFS-FM Bartlett TN
WXSM(AM) Blountville TN
WNSR(AM) Brentwood TN
WRKM(AM) Carthage TN
WVFB(FM) Celina TN
WDEF(AM) Chattanooga TN
WJZM(AM) Clarksville TN
WKFN(AM) Clarksville TN
WCSV(AM) Crossville TN
WEMB(AM) Erwin TN
WCPH(AM) Etowah TN
WEKR(AM) Fayetteville TN
WHEW(AM) Franklin TN
WGFX(FM) Gallatin TN
WMLR(AM) Hohenwald TN
WGOC(AM) Kingsport TN
WNML(AM) Knoxville TN

WVLZ(AM) Knoxville TN
WTNQ(FM) La Follette TN
WALV-FM Lakesite TN
WCOR(AM) Lebanon TN
WLIV(AM) Livingston TN
WNML-FM Loudon TN
WMSR(AM) Manchester TN
WWTN(FM) Manchester TN
WKCE(AM) Maryville TN
WHBQ(AM) Memphis TN
WMFS(AM) Memphis TN
WREC(AM) Memphis TN
*WUMR(FM) Memphis TN
WLIV-FM Monterey TN
WGNS(AM) Murfreesboro TN
WBFG(FM) Parker's Crossroads TN
WTNE-FM Trenton TN
KZQQ(AM) Abilene TX
KESN(FM) Allen TX
KPUR(AM) Amarillo TX
KACT(AM) Andrews TX
KVET(AM) Austin TX
KRUN(AM) Ballinger TX
KFNC(FM) Beaumont TX
KIKR(AM) Beaumont TX
KGOW(AM) Bellaire TX
KBST(AM) Big Spring TX
KQTY(AM) Borger TX
KTTU-FM Brownfield TX
KZRK(AM) Canyon TX
KGAS(AM) Carthage TX
KZNE(AM) College Station TX
KEYS(AM) Corpus Christi TX
KSIX(AM) Corpus Christi TX
KZNX(AM) Creedmoor TX
KNIT(AM) Dallas TX
KRLD(AM) Dallas TX
KRLD-FM Dallas TX
KTCK(AM) Dallas TX
KURV(AM) Edinburg TX
KULP(AM) El Campo TX
KHEY(AM) El Paso TX
KROD(AM) El Paso TX
KFLC(AM) Fort Worth TX
KKGM(AM) Fort Worth TX
KATH(AM) Frisco TX
KWRD(AM) Henderson TX
KBME(AM) Houston TX
KILT(AM) Houston TX
KTRH(AM) Houston TX
*KSHU(FM) Huntsville TX
KAML(AM) Kenedy-Karnes City TX
KFRO(AM) Longview TX
KKAM(AM) Lubbock TX
KMHT(AM) Marshall TX
KMND(AM) Midland TX
KBED(AM) Nederland TX
KRIL(AM) Odessa TX
KOGT(AM) Orange TX
KLVL(AM) Pasadena TX
KVOP(AM) Plainview TX
KSOX(AM) Raymondville TX
KKLF(AM) Richardson TX
KGKL(AM) San Angelo TX
KKSA(AM) San Angelo TX
KTKR(AM) San Antonio TX
KZDC(AM) San Antonio TX
*KTSW(FM) San Marcos TX
KTDK(FM) Sanger TX
KJIM(AM) Sherman TX
KSET(AM) Silsbee TX
*KSQX(FM) Springtown TX
KWNX(AM) Taylor TX
KTEM(AM) Temple TX
KCMC(AM) Texarkana TX
KTBB(AM) Tyler TX
KYZS(AM) Tyler TX
KZMP(AM) University Park TX
KRZI(AM) Waco TX
*KMQX(FM) Weatherford TX
KSL-FM Midvale UT
KJQS(AM) Murray UT
KALL(AM) North Salt Lake City UT
KLO(AM) Ogden UT
KOAL(AM) Price UT
KOVO(AM) Provo UT

KSVC(AM) Richfield UT
KFNZ(AM) Salt Lake City UT
KSL(AM) Salt Lake City UT
KZNS(AM) Salt Lake City UT
KHQN(AM) Spanish Fork UT
KVEL(AM) Vernal UT
KUNF(AM) Washington UT
WXTR(AM) Alexandria VA
WCBX(AM) Bassett VA
WBLT(AM) Bedford VA
WKEX(AM) Blacksburg VA
WKLV(AM) Blackstone VA
WFHG(AM) Bristol VA
WINA(AM) Charlottesville VA
WKAV(AM) Charlottesville VA
WDIC-FM Clinchco VA
WKTR(AM) Earlysville VA
WODY(AM) Fieldale VA
WGAT(AM) Gate City VA
WXTG(AM) Hampton VA
WHBG(AM) Harrisonburg VA
WREL(AM) Lexington VA
WBRG(AM) Lynchburg VA
WVGM(AM) Lynchburg VA
*WWMC(FM) Lynchburg VA
WJFK-FM Manassas VA
WCMS(AM) Newport News VA
WTAR(AM) Norfolk VA
WRAD(AM) Radford VA
WRNL(AM) Richmond VA
WXGI(AM) Richmond VA
WGMN(AM) Roanoke VA
WTON(AM) Staunton VA
WXTG-FM Virginia Beach VA
WWXX(FM) Warrenton VA
WINC(AM) Winchester VA
WYVE(AM) Wytheville VA
WVWI(AM) Charlotte Amalie VI
WSNO(AM) Barre VT
WTSA(AM) Brattleboro VT
WCAT(AM) Burlington VT
WVMT(AM) Burlington VT
WFAD(AM) Middlebury VT
WEEY(FM) Springfield VT
WDEV-FM Warren VT
WDEV(AM) Waterbury VT
WNHV(AM) White River Junction VT
WMXR(FM) Woodstock VT
KXLX(AM) Airway Heights WA
KCLK(AM) Asotin WA
KPUG(AM) Bellingham WA
KELA(AM) Centralia-Chehalis WA
KXLE(AM) Ellensburg WA
KULE(AM) Ephrata WA
KRKO(AM) Everett WA
KWOK(AM) Hoquiam WA
KJOX-FM Long Beach WA
KBSN(AM) Moses Lake WA
KWIQ(AM) Moses Lake North WA
KFLD(AM) Pasco WA
KALE(AM) Richland WA
KIRO(AM) Seattle WA
KJR(AM) Seattle WA
KBBO(AM) Selah WA
KGA(AM) Spokane WA
KHHO(AM) Tacoma WA
KIRO-FM Tacoma WA
KYNR(AM) Toppenish WA
KTRO(AM) Vancouver WA
KUJ(AM) Walla Walla WA
KKRT(AM) Wenatchee WA
WSCO(AM) Appleton WI
WDUZ-FM Brillion WI
WMBE(AM) Chilton WI
WEAQ(AM) Chippewa Falls WI
WTLX(FM) Columbus WI
WBIZ(AM) Eau Claire WI
KFIZ(AM) Fond du Lac WI
WFAW(AM) Fort Atkinson WI
WDUZ(AM) Green Bay WI
WNFL(AM) Green Bay WI
WAUK(AM) Jackson WI
WKTY(AM) La Crosse WI
WTSO(AM) Madison WI
WMAM(AM) Marinette WI
WDLB(AM) Marshfield WI

WIGM(AM) Medford WI
WMEQ(AM) Menomonie WI
WTMJ(AM) Milwaukee WI
WOSH(AM) Oshkosh WI
WNBI(AM) Park Falls WI
WPVL(AM) Platteville WI
WOBT(AM) Rhinelander WI
WRCO-FM Richland Center WI
WEVR(AM) River Falls WI
WEVR-FM River Falls WI
WRIG(AM) Schofield WI
WCLB(AM) Sheboygan WI
WKLJ(AM) Sparta WI
WOSQ(FM) Spencer WI
WDOR-FM Sturgeon Bay WI
WJJQ(AM) Tomahawk WI
WJJQ-FM Tomahawk WI
WFBZ(FM) Trempealeau WI
WRRD(AM) Waukesha WI
WXCO(AM) Wausau WI
WKEZ(AM) Bluefield WV
WMRE(AM) Charles Town WV
WCHS(AM) Charleston WV
WSWW(AM) Charleston WV
WKKX(AM) Clarksburg WV
WBES(AM) Dunbar WV
WMMN(AM) Fairmont WV
WAMN(AM) Green Valley WV
WRVC(AM) Huntington WV
WTCR(AM) Kenova WV
WEPM(AM) Martinsburg WV
WRNR(AM) Martinsburg WV
WVLY(AM) Moundsville WV
WJAW(AM) Saint Marys WV
WKKX(AM) Wheeling WV
KRSV(AM) Afton WY
KBBS(AM) Buffalo WY
KKTL(AM) Casper WY
KVOC(AM) Casper WY
KFBC(AM) Cheyenne WY
KRAE(AM) Cheyenne WY
KODI(AM) Cody WY
KIML(AM) Gillette WY
KHAT(AM) Laramie WY
KOWB(AM) Laramie WY
KRKI(FM) Newcastle WY
KYDT(FM) Sundance WY

Talk

KENI(AM) Anchorage AK
KUDO(AM) Anchorage AK
*KYUK(AM) Bethel AK
KRUP(FM) Dillingham AK
KOAN(AM) Eagle River AK
KFBX(AM) Fairbanks AK
KJNO(AM) Juneau AK
KXLJ(AM) Juneau AK
KVOK(AM) Kodiak AK
*KUDU(FM) Tok AK
KVAK(AM) Valdez AK
WXJC(AM) Birmingham AL
WGNQ(AM) Bridgeport AL
WRTR(FM) Brookwood AL
WKUL(FM) Cullman AL
WAVH(FM) Daphne AL
WOOF(AM) Dothan AL
WULA(AM) Eufaula AL
WJLD(AM) Fairfield AL
WBHP(AM) Huntsville AL
WIJD(AM) Prichard AL
WNSI(AM) Robertsdale AL
WMRK-FM Shorter AL
WTLS(AM) Tallassee AL
WTBF(AM) Troy AL
WAPZ(AM) Wetumpka AL
KEWI(AM) Benton AR
KREB(AM) Bentonville-Bella Vista AR
KVDW(AM) England AR
*KAYH(FM) Fayetteville AR
KXJK(AM) Forrest City AR
KHOZ(AM) Harrison AR
KXAR(AM) Hope AR
KABZ(FM) Little Rock AR
KVMA(AM) Magnolia AR
KTTG(FM) Mena AR

KWCK(AM) Searcy AR
KARN-FM Sheridan AR
KZZZ(AM) Bullhead City AZ
KFNX(AM) Cave Creek AZ
KVOI(AM) Cortaro AZ
KGME(AM) Phoenix AZ
KIDR(AM) Phoenix AZ
KPHX(AM) Phoenix AZ
KZON(FM) Phoenix AZ
KNXN(AM) Sierra Vista AZ
KRVZ(AM) Springerville AZ
KXMX(AM) Anaheim CA
KIXW(AM) Apple Valley CA
KBRT(AM) Avalon CA
KAFY(AM) Bakersfield CA
KSZL(AM) Barstow CA
KRXA(AM) Carmel Valley CA
KPTR(AM) Cathedral City CA
KNWZ(AM) Coachella CA
*KMUE(FM) Eureka CA
KWSW(AM) Eureka CA
KIRV(AM) Fresno CA
*KMUD(FM) Garberville CA
KGBA-FM Holtville CA
KABC(AM) Los Angeles CA
KFI(AM) Los Angeles CA
KTLK(AM) Los Angeles CA
KMYC(AM) Marysville CA
KMPH(AM) Modesto CA
KTOX(AM) Needles CA
KKGN(AM) Oakland CA
KGDP(AM) Oildale CA
KDAR(FM) Oxnard CA
KGAM(AM) Palm Springs CA
KPSI(AM) Palm Springs CA
KDOW(AM) Palo Alto CA
*KZYX(FM) Philo CA
KAHZ(AM) Pomona CA
KNLF(FM) Quincy CA
KSTE(AM) Rancho Cordova CA
KQMS(AM) Redding CA
*KVIP(FM) Redding CA
KTKZ(AM) Sacramento CA
*KVCR(FM) San Bernardino CA
KEST(AM) San Francisco CA
KFAX(AM) San Francisco CA
KGO(AM) San Francisco CA
KSFO(AM) San Francisco CA
KTRB(AM) San Francisco CA
KJZN(FM) San Joaquin CA
KPRZ(AM) San Marcos-Poway CA
KTMS(AM) Santa Barbara CA
KCNR(AM) Shasta CA
KFUT(AM) Thousand Palms CA
KXPS(AM) Thousand Palms CA
KCEO(AM) Vista CA
*KZYZ(FM) Willits CA
KNFO(FM) Basalt CO
KSIR(AM) Brush CO
KSKE(AM) Buena Vista CO
KKKK(AM) Colorado Springs CO
KLTT(AM) Commerce City CO
KBJD(AM) Denver CO
KHOW(AM) Denver CO
KEPL(AM) Estes Park CO
KGLN(AM) Glenwood Springs CO
KEXO(AM) Grand Junction CO
KJOL(AM) Grand Junction CO
KRCN(AM) Longmont CO
KTNI-FM Strasburg CO
KKZN(AM) Thornton CO
KVLE(AM) Vail CO
WICC(AM) Bridgeport CT
WGCH(AM) Greenwich CT
WMMW(AM) Meriden CT
WMRD(AM) Middletown CT
WLIS(AM) Old Saybrook CT
WHDD(AM) Sharon CT
WSNG(AM) Torrington CT
WKND(AM) Windsor CT
WTEM(AM) Washington DC
WWRC(AM) Washington DC
WILM(AM) Wilmington DE
WTMC(AM) Wilmington DE
WHIM(AM) Apopka FL
WQOP(AM) Atlantic Beach FL

WHJX(FM) Baldwin FL
WSBR(AM) Boca Raton FL
WWPR(AM) Bradenton FL
WTAN(AM) Clearwater FL
WWBC(AM) Cocoa FL
WTKS-FM Cocoa Beach FL
WACC(AM) Hialeah FL
WTKE-FM Holt FL
WYMM(AM) Jacksonville FL
WBXY(FM) La Crosse FL
WWTK(AM) Lake Placid FL
WWAB(AM) Lakeland FL
WLBE(AM) Leesburg FL
WJXR(FM) Macclenny FL
*WCNZ(AM) Marco Island FL
WMBM(AM) Miami Beach FL
WNMA(AM) Miami Springs FL
WFLA-FM Midway FL
WEBY(AM) Milton FL
*WEGS(FM) Milton FL
WPGS(AM) Mims FL
*WSOR(FM) Naples FL
WWCN(AM) North Fort Myers FL
WMOP(AM) Ocala FL
WTLN(AM) Orlando FL
WYOO(FM) Springfield FL
WZAB(AM) Sweetwater FL
WCZR(FM) Vero Beach FL
WTTB(AM) Vero Beach FL
WZTA(AM) Vero Beach FL
WBZT(AM) West Palm Beach FL
WZHR(AM) Zephyrhills FL
WDDQ(FM) Adel GA
WRFC(AM) Athens GA
WGUN(AM) Atlanta GA
WNIV(AM) Atlanta GA
WQXI(AM) Atlanta GA
WNRR(AM) Augusta GA
WBBK(AM) Blakely GA
WYXC(AM) Cartersville GA
WGHC(AM) Clayton GA
WJJC(AM) Commerce GA
WSEM(AM) Donalsonville GA
WSGC(AM) Elberton GA
WFJO(FM) Folkston GA
WDDK(FM) Greensboro GA
WKLY(AM) Hartwell GA
WIBB(AM) Macon GA
WXFO(AM) Royston GA
WJAT(AM) Swainsboro GA
WZQZ(AM) Trion GA
*WJSP-FM Warm Springs GA
WPLV(AM) West Point GA
WIMO(AM) Winder GA
KKEA(AM) Honolulu HI
KRTR(AM) Honolulu HI
KUMU(AM) Honolulu HI
KFFF(AM) Boone IA
KWQW(FM) Boone IA
KCPS(AM) Burlington IA
KCNZ(AM) Cedar Falls IA
*KUNI(FM) Cedar Falls IA
KWKY(AM) Des Moines IA
KCJJ(AM) Iowa City IA
KGLO(AM) Mason City IA
*KDMR(FM) Mitchellville IA
KICD(AM) Spencer IA
*KNWS(AM) Waterloo IA
KBLI(AM) Blackfoot ID
KFXD(AM) Boise ID
KSPD(AM) Boise ID
KBAR(AM) Burley ID
KBGN(AM) Caldwell ID
KBLY(AM) Idaho Falls ID
KOZE(AM) Lewiston ID
KIDO(AM) Nampa ID
KTIK(AM) Nampa ID
*KBSW(FM) Twin Falls ID

WCPT-FM Arlington Heights IL
WVON(AM) Berwyn IL
WTHQ(AM) Brookport IL
WCAZ(AM) Carthage IL
WMVP(AM) Chicago IL
*WSSD(FM) Chicago IL
WYLL(AM) Chicago IL
WCPY(FM) De Kalb IL
WDDD(AM) Johnston City IL
WJOL(AM) Joliet IL
WKAN(AM) Kankakee IL
WLLM(AM) Lincoln IL
WFXN(AM) Moline IL
WMIX(AM) Mount Vernon IL
*WPTH(FM) Olney IL
WPRS(AM) Paris IL
WCPQ(FM) Park Forest IL
WPEO(AM) Peoria IL
WTRH(AM) Ramsey IL
WNTA(AM) Rockford IL
*WGNJ(FM) Saint Joseph IL
WAUR(AM) Sandwich IL
WFMB(AM) Springfield IL
WSDR(AM) Sterling IL
WGFA(AM) Watseka IL
WCPT(AM) Willow Springs IL
*WGNR(AM) Anderson IN
WBIW(AM) Bedford IN
WNUY(FM) Bluffton IN
WCMR(AM) Elkhart IN
WFDM(AM) Franklin IN
*WGVE(FM) Gary IN
WWCA(AM) Gary IN
WNDE(AM) Indianapolis IN
WTLC(AM) Indianapolis IN
WIMS(AM) Michigan City IN
WMRS(FM) Monticello IN
WYFX(FM) Mount Vernon IN
WFIA-FM New Albany IN
WRAY(AM) Princeton IN
*WZRP(FM) Richmond IN
WSLM-FM Salem IN
*WHOJ(FM) Terre Haute IN
KFH-FM Clearwater KS
KGNO(AM) Dodge City KS
KCNW(AM) Fairway KS
KVGB(AM) Great Bend KS
KRMR(FM) Hays KS
KBUF(AM) Holcomb KS
KWBW(AM) Hutchinson KS
KIOL(AM) Iola KS
KCVW(FM) Kingman KS
KNGL(AM) McPherson KS
KCCV-FM Olathe KS
KLKC(AM) Parsons KS
KFRM(AM) Salina KS
KCVT(FM) Silver Lake KS
KFH(AM) Wichita KS
WCMI(AM) Ashland KY
WCBL(AM) Benton KY
WSFE(AM) Burnside KY
WNES(AM) Central City KY
WKFO(AM) Corbin KY
WQRT(AM) Florence KY
WLGC(AM) Greenup KY
WFIA(AM) Louisville KY
WKJK(AM) Louisville KY
WTTL(AM) Madisonville KY
WNBS(AM) Murray KY
WLSI(AM) Pikeville KY
WPRT(AM) Prestonsburg KY
WLRS(FM) Shepherdsville KY
WSFC(AM) Somerset KY
WLXO(FM) Stamping Ground KY
KJMJ(AM) Alexandria LA
KSYL(AM) Alexandria LA
WJBO(AM) Baton Rouge LA
WPYR(AM) Baton Rouge LA
KBCL(AM) Bossier City LA
KEUN(AM) Eunice LA
KBYO-FM Farmerville LA
KRLQ(FM) Hodge LA
WWL-FM Kenner LA
KFXZ(AM) Lafayette LA
KVOL(AM) Lafayette LA
*KOJO(FM) Lake Charles LA

KLIC(AM) Monroe LA
*KBIO(FM) Natchitoches LA
WIST(AM) New Orleans LA
WSHO(AM) New Orleans LA
KRMD(AM) Shreveport LA
WSRO(AM) Ashland MA
WNSH(AM) Beverly MA
*WBUR-FM Boston MA
WEZE(AM) Boston MA
WRKO(AM) Boston MA
WTKK(FM) Boston MA
WACE(AM) Chicopee MA
WHTB(AM) Fall River MA
WPKZ(AM) Fitchburg MA
*WCCT-FM Harwich MA
WCAP(AM) Lowell MA
WBIX(AM) Natick MA
WPLM(AM) Plymouth MA
WESO(AM) Southbridge MA
*WSKB(FM) Westfield MA
WCRN(AM) Worcester MA
WBIS(AM) Annapolis MD
WCBM(AM) Baltimore MD
WJZ(AM) Baltimore MD
WTNT(AM) Bethesda MD
WKDI(AM) Denton MD
WFRB(AM) Frostburg MD
WARK(AM) Hagerstown MD
WHFS(AM) Morningside MD
WICO-FM Pocomoke City MD
WZAA(AM) Silver Spring MD
*WMDR(AM) Augusta ME
WZON(AM) Bangor ME
WBCI(FM) Bath ME
WCME(AM) Brunswick ME
WXME(AM) Monticello ME
WZAN(AM) Portland ME
WEGP(AM) Presque Isle ME
WTME(AM) Rumford ME
WKTQ(AM) South Paris ME
WLOB-FM Topsham ME
WPRR(AM) Ada MI
WATZ(AM) Alpena MI
WMAX(AM) Bay City MI
WSGW-FM Carrollton MI
WDTW(AM) Dearborn MI
WNZK(AM) Dearborn Heights MI
WDFN(AM) Detroit MI
WVFN(AM) East Lansing MI
*WLJN(AM) Elmwood Township MI
WSNL(AM) Flint MI
WTRX(AM) Flint MI
WSHN(AM) Fremont MI
WJRW(AM) Grand Rapids MI
WTKG(AM) Grand Rapids MI
WGLM(AM) Greenville MI
*WHPR(FM) Highland Park MI
WJMS(AM) Ironwood MI
WJNL(AM) Kingsley MI
WJIM(AM) Lansing MI
WKBZ(AM) Muskegon MI
WNIL(AM) Niles MI
WLBY(AM) Saline MI
WMMI(AM) Shepherd MI
WIOS(AM) Tawas City MI
*WICA(FM) Traverse City MI
*WLJN-FM Traverse City MI
WPON(AM) Walled Lake MI
WKLQ(AM) Whitehall MI
WDEO(AM) Ypsilanti MI
WPNW(AM) Zeeland MI
KKBJ(AM) Bemidji MN
WFMP(AM) Coon Rapids MN
KROX(AM) Crookston MN
WZFG(AM) Dilworth MN
*KDNI(FM) Duluth MN
WWJC(AM) Duluth MN
KKCQ(AM) Fosston MN
KYCR(AM) Golden Valley MN
KDWA(AM) Hastings MN
WMFG(AM) Hibbing MN
KFAN(AM) Minneapolis MN
KFXN(AM) Minneapolis MN
KLOH(AM) Pipestone MN
KKMS(AM) Richfield MN
KWEB(AM) Rochester MN

KTNF(AM) Saint Louis Park MN
KSTP(AM) Saint Paul MN
KOWZ(AM) Waseca MN
KSGF-FM Ash Grove MO
KAPE(AM) Cape Girardeau MO
*KNLH(FM) Cedar Hill MO
KCHR(AM) Charleston MO
*KFUO(AM) Clayton MO
KCTO(AM) Cleveland MO
*KJCV(FM) Country Club MO
KFTK(FM) Florissant MO
KBCV(AM) Hollister MO
KCTE(AM) Independence MO
KZYM(AM) Joplin MO
KCMO(AM) Kansas City MO
KOTC(AM) Kennett MO
*KKTR(FM) Kirksville MO
KBNN(AM) Lebanon MO
KCXL(AM) Liberty MO
KWIX(AM) Moberly MO
KLID(AM) Poplar Bluff MO
*KNLP(FM) Potosi MO
KJSL(AM) Saint Louis MO
KADI(AM) Springfield MO
KLFJ(AM) Springfield MO
*KSCV(FM) Springfield MO
KWTO-FM Springfield MO
KSAR(FM) Thayer MO
KLPW(AM) Union MO
KWMO(AM) Washington MO
KJPW(AM) Waynesville MO
WWZQ(AM) Aberdeen MS
WJZD(AM) Bay St. Louis MS
WXRZ(FM) Corinth MS
WFMN(FM) Flora MS
WYAB(FM) Flora MS
WABG(AM) Greenwood MS
WHSY(AM) Hattiesburg MS
WJDX(AM) Jackson MS
WJQS(AM) Jackson MS
WALT(AM) Meridian MS
WRQO(FM) Monticello MS
WPMP(AM) Pascagoula-Moss Point MS
WHOC(AM) Philadelphia MS
WWMR(FM) Saltillo MS
WKMQ(AM) Tupelo MS
WTNM(AM) Water Valley MS
KURL(AM) Billings MT
KBOZ(AM) Bozeman MT
KMPT(AM) East Missoula MT
KBSR(AM) Laurel MT
KGRZ(AM) Missoula MT
*KUFM(FM) Missoula MT
WCGC(AM) Belmont NC
WFGW(AM) Black Mountain NC
WATA(AM) Boone NC
WSQL(AM) Brevard NC
WZTK(FM) Burlington NC
WBAG(AM) Burlington-Graham NC
WMYT(AM) Carolina Beach NC
WOGR(AM) Charlotte NC
WCRU(AM) Dallas NC
WLOE(AM) Eden NC
WPEK(AM) Fairview NC
WGHB(AM) Farmville NC
WTIB(FM) Farmville NC
WQNC(FM) Harrisburg NC
WIZS(AM) Henderson NC
WGOS(AM) High Point NC
WYSR(AM) High Point NC
WKXU(FM) Louisburg NC
WYRN(AM) Louisburg NC
WIXE(AM) Monroe NC
*WAAE(FM) New Bern NC
WNOS(AM) New Bern NC
*WZRN(FM) Norlina NC
WNBU(AM) Oriental NC
WFMI(FM) Southern Shores NC
WBLO(AM) Thomasville NC
WDLX(AM) Washington NC
WBFJ(AM) Winston-Salem NC
WTIX(AM) Winston-Salem NC
KQWB(AM) West Fargo ND
KTTT(AM) Columbus NE
KAWL(AM) York NE

WDER(AM) Derry NH
WKBK(AM) Keene NH
WEMJ(AM) Laconia NH
WTMR(AM) Camden NJ
WOBM(AM) Lakewood NJ
*WVPH(FM) Piscataway NJ
WGHT(AM) Pompton Lakes NJ
WKMB(AM) Stirling NJ
WKXW(FM) Trenton NJ
WNJC(AM) Washington Township NJ
KRSY(AM) Alamogordo NM
KABQ(AM) Albuquerque NM
KKIM(AM) Albuquerque NM
KSVP(AM) Artesia NM
KNFT(AM) Bayard NM
KICA(AM) Clovis NM
*KNMI(FM) Farmington NM
KZXQ(FM) Reserve NM
KRUI(AM) Ruidoso Downs NM
KTRC(AM) Santa Fe NM
KVOT(AM) Taos NM
*KNIS(FM) Carson City NV
KTSN(AM) Elko NV
KCLS(FM) Ely NV
KELY(AM) Ely NV
KKVV(AM) Las Vegas NV
KLAV(AM) Las Vegas NV
KXTE(FM) Pahrump NV
KJFK(AM) Reno NV
KRZQ-FM Sparks NV
*WAMC-FM Albany NY
WVTL(AM) Amsterdam NY
WAUB(AM) Auburn NY
WBNR(AM) Beacon NY
WBUF(FM) Buffalo NY
WWKB(AM) Buffalo NY
WCKL(AM) Catskill NY
WCHP(AM) Champlain NY
WECK(AM) Cheektowaga NY
WJIV(FM) Cherry Valley NY
WNMR(FM) Dannemora NY
WENE(AM) Endicott NY
WLIE(AM) Islip NY
WNYY(AM) Ithaca NY
WJTN(AM) Jamestown NY
WGHQ(AM) Kingston NY
*WOSR(FM) Middletown NY
WABC(AM) New York NY
WEPN(AM) New York NY
WFAN(AM) New York NY
WMCA(AM) New York NY
WWRL(AM) New York NY
WQTK(FM) Ogdensburg NY
WEBO(AM) Owego NY
WLNA(AM) Peekskill NY
*WCEL(AM) Plattsburgh NY
WEAV(AM) Plattsburgh NY
WTWK(AM) Plattsburgh NY
*WAIH(FM) Potsdam NY
WGDJ(AM) Rensselaer NY
WHTK(AM) Rochester NY
WSFW(AM) Seneca Falls NY
WFBL(AM) Syracuse NY
WNSS(AM) Syracuse NY
*WANC(FM) Ticonderoga NY
WTBQ(AM) Warwick NY
WATN(AM) Watertown NY
WLGZ-FM Webster NY
WXZO(AM) Willsboro NY
WNCO(AM) Ashland OH
WAIS(AM) Buchtel OH
WGFT(AM) Campbell OH
*WZCP(FM) Chillicothe OH
WCVX(AM) Cincinnati OH
*WCPN(FM) Cleveland OH
WHK(AM) Cleveland OH
WHKW(AM) Cleveland OH
*WHKC(FM) Columbus OH
WHTH(AM) Heath OH
WJMP(AM) Kent OH
WNIR(AM) Kent OH
WLOH(AM) Lancaster OH
WLTP(AM) Marietta OH
WUCO(AM) Marysville OH
WCCD(AM) Parma OH
WNXT(AM) Portsmouth OH

WPAY(AM) Portsmouth OH
*WEEC(FM) Springfield OH
*WZWP(FM) West Union OH
WTDA(FM) Westerville OH
WELW(AM) Willoughby-Eastlake OH
KOKB(AM) Blackwell OK
KPNS(AM) Duncan OK
WWLS-FM Edmond OK
*KWXC(FM) Grove OK
KXCA(AM) Lawton OK
WWLS(AM) Moore OK
KTLR(AM) Oklahoma City OK
KOKL(AM) Okmulgee OK
KCFO(AM) Tulsa OK
KFAQ(AM) Tulsa OK
KSIW(AM) Woodward OK
KKEE(AM) Astoria OR
KICE(AM) Bend OR
KZZR(AM) Burns OR
KEJO(AM) Corvallis OR
KLZS(AM) Eugene OR
*KRVM(AM) Eugene OR
KGAL(AM) Lebanon OR
KUMA(AM) Pendleton OR
KCMX(AM) Phoenix OR
KEX(AM) Portland OR
KKPZ(AM) Portland OR
KPDQ(AM) Portland OR
KPDQ-FM Portland OR
KOHI(AM) Saint Helens OR
KFIR(AM) Sweet Home OR
WMBA(AM) Ambridge PA
WBVP(AM) Beaver Falls PA
*WBUQ(FM) Bloomsburg PA
WLFP(AM) Braddock PA
*WHHN(FM) Hollidaysburg PA
WFYL(AM) King of Prussia PA
WDAC(FM) Lancaster PA
WWBJ(AM) Martinsburg PA
WEDO(AM) McKeesport PA
WMNY(AM) McKeesport PA
WMLP(AM) Milton PA
WFIL(AM) Philadelphia PA
*WHYY-FM Philadelphia PA
WPHT(AM) Philadelphia PA
WURD(AM) Philadelphia PA
WWDB(AM) Philadelphia PA
WEAE(AM) Pittsburgh PA
WWNL(AM) Pittsburgh PA
WECZ(AM) Punxsutawney PA
WNAE(AM) Warren PA
WCHE(AM) West Chester PA
WPYT(AM) Wilkinsburg PA
WYYC(AM) York PA
WABA(AM) Aguadilla PR
WPRA(AM) Mayaguez PR
WTIL(AM) Mayaguez PR
WBMJ(AM) San Juan PR
WQII(AM) San Juan PR
WRSS(AM) San Sebastian PR
WIVV(AM) Vieques PR
WXEW(AM) Yabucoa PR
WPRV(AM) Providence RI
WEEI-FM Westerly RI
WXNI(AM) Westerly RI
WISW(AM) Columbia SC
WOIC(AM) Columbia SC
WELP(AM) Easley SC
WJMX(AM) Florence SC
WOLH(AM) Florence SC
WSCC-FM Goose Creek SC
WLFJ(AM) Greenville SC
WCKI(AM) Greer SC
WZJY(AM) Mt. Pleasant SC
WSNW(AM) Seneca SC
WRNN-FM Socastee SC
WDXY(AM) Sumter SC
WJTP(AM) Walhalla SC
KSDN(AM) Aberdeen SD
KBFS(AM) Belle Fourche SD
KIJV(AM) Huron SD
KORN(AM) Mitchell SD
KTOQ(AM) Rapid City SD
KJJQ(AM) Volga SD
KSDR(AM) Watertown SD
WCTA(AM) Alamo TN

WYXI(AM) Athens TN
*WHCB(FM) Bristol TN
WNWS(AM) Brownsville TN
WNOO(AM) Chattanooga TN
WJZM(AM) Clarksville TN
WKFN(AM) Clarksville TN
WQZQ(AM) Clarksville TN
WPWT(AM) Colonial Heights TN
WZYX(AM) Cowan TN
WAEW(AM) Crossville TN
WMTY(AM) Farragut TN
WIRJ(AM) Humboldt TN
WJCW(AM) Johnson City TN
WIFA(AM) Knoxville TN
WKVL(AM) Knoxville TN
WRJZ(AM) Knoxville TN
WNML-FM Loudon TN
WMSR(AM) Manchester TN
WLOK(AM) Memphis TN
*WFSK-FM Nashville TN
WZNG(AM) Shelbyville TN
KZQQ(AM) Abilene TX
KTEK(AM) Alvin TX
KPUR(AM) Amarillo TX
KZIP(AM) Amarillo TX
KVET(AM) Austin TX
KSKY(AM) Balch Springs TX
KBYG(AM) Big Spring TX
KQTY(AM) Borger TX
KTMR(AM) Converse TX
KCCT(AM) Corpus Christi TX
KAND(AM) Corsicana TX
KZNX(AM) Creedmoor TX
KGGR(AM) Dallas TX
KTCK(AM) Dallas TX
KIXL(AM) Del Valle TX
KATX(FM) Eastland TX
KEAS(AM) Eastland TX
KHRO(AM) El Paso TX
KQBU(AM) El Paso TX
KFCD(AM) Farmersville TX
KNAF(AM) Fredericksburg TX
KEES(AM) Gladewater TX
KVCE(AM) Highland Park TX
KCOH(AM) Houston TX
KILT(AM) Houston TX
KXYZ(AM) Houston TX
KMNY(AM) Hurst TX
KERV(AM) Kerrville TX
*KAVX(FM) Lufkin TX
KWEL(AM) Midland TX
KVOP(AM) Plainview TX
KJCE(AM) Rollingwood TX
KGKL(AM) San Angelo TX
KSLR(AM) San Antonio TX
*KSQX(FM) Springtown TX
KPWT(FM) Terrell Hills TX
KKTK(AM) Texarkana TX
KLGO(FM) Thorndale TX
KTBB-FM Tyler TX
KTNO(AM) University Park TX
KNRS-FM Centerville UT
KALL(AM) North Salt Lake City UT
KLO(AM) Ogden UT
KTKK(AM) Sandy UT
KCPX(AM) Spanish Valley UT
KUNF(AM) Washington UT
WAVA-FM Arlington VA
WHAN(AM) Ashland VA
WLES(AM) Bon Air VA
*WWVT(AM) Christiansburg VA
WEVA(AM) Emporia VA
*WFFC(FM) Ferrum VA
WODY(AM) Fieldale VA
WMNA-FM Gretna VA
WKCY(AM) Harrisonburg VA
WHEE(AM) Martinsville VA
WMVA(AM) Martinsville VA
WSVG(AM) Mount Jackson VA
WCMS(AM) Newport News VA
WESR(AM) Onley-Onancock VA
WWBU(FM) Radford VA
WLEE(AM) Richmond VA
WWWR(AM) Roanoke VA
*WRAR(AM) Tappahannock VA
WXTG-FM Virginia Beach VA

WDHP(AM) Frederiksted VI
WRSA(AM) Saint Albans VT
KCLK(AM) Asotin WA
KBAI(AM) Bellingham WA
KPUG(AM) Bellingham WA
KGNW(AM) Burien-Seattle WA
KOZI-FM Chelan WA
KMAX(AM) Colfax WA
KSPO(FM) Dishman WA
KTAC(FM) Ephrata WA
KTBI(AM) Ephrata WA
KRKO(AM) Everett WA
KLAY(AM) Lakewood WA
KGTK(AM) Olympia WA
KOMW(AM) Omak WA
KTRW(AM) Opportunity WA
KPTK(AM) Seattle WA
*KUOW-FM Seattle WA
KVI(AM) Seattle WA
KBBO(AM) Selah WA
KITZ(AM) Silverdale WA
KSBN(AM) Spokane WA
KUOW(AM) Tumwater WA
KBMS(AM) Vancouver WA
WEAQ(AM) Chippewa Falls WI
*WDVM(AM) Eau Claire WI
*WHID(FM) Green Bay WI
WMCS(AM) Greenfield WI
WTKM(AM) Hartford WI
WTKM-FM Hartford WI
WKBH(AM) Holmen WI
*WHLA(FM) La Crosse WI
WKTY(AM) La Crosse WI
WMAM(AM) Marinette WI
*WHWC(FM) Menomonie WI
WJMT(AM) Merrill WI
WISN(AM) Milwaukee WI
WCSW(AM) Shell Lake WI
*WHDI(FM) Sister Bay WI
*WNWC(AM) Sun Prairie WI
WXXM(FM) Sun Prairie WI
WDSM(AM) Superior WI
*WVCX(FM) Tomah WI
WJJQ(AM) Tomahawk WI
*WEGZ(FM) Washburn WI
*WLBL-FM Wausau WI
WBUC(AM) Buckhannon WV
WVTS(AM) Charleston WV
WSWW-FM Craigsville WV
WBES(AM) Dunbar WV
WOAY(AM) Oak Hill WV
WRON(AM) Ronceverte WV
WEIR(AM) Weirton WV
KTWO(AM) Casper WY
KUYO(AM) Evansville WY
KYOD(FM) Glendo WY
KPOW(AM) Powell WY

Tejano

KXEW(AM) South Tucson AZ
KOPY-FM Alice TX
KFON(AM) Austin TX
KKPS(FM) Brownsville TX
KTJK(AM) Del Rio TX
KFZO(FM) Denton TX
KNTE-FM El Campo TX
KXXS(FM) Elgin TX
KPSO-FM Falfurrias TX
KGRW(FM) Friona TX
KHMC(FM) Goliad TX
KBTQ(FM) Harlingen TX
KEJS(FM) Lubbock TX
KHCK-FM Robinson TX
KMIQ(FM) Robstown TX
KSAB(FM) Robstown TX
KCLL(FM) San Angelo TX
KXTN-FM San Antonio TX
KUVA(AM) Uvalde TX
KTXZ(AM) West Lake Hills TX
KZXR(AM) Prosser WA

Top-40

WJDB-FM Thomasville AL
KLBQ(FM) El Dorado AR
KOFH(FM) Nogales AZ
KXAZ(FM) Page AZ
KQST(FM) Sedona AZ
KWRN(AM) Apple Valley CA
KRVC(FM) Hornbrook CA
KAMP-FM Los Angeles CA
KNKK(FM) Needles CA
KKXX-FM Shafter CA
KSME(FM) Greeley CO
KKMG(FM) Pueblo CO
WKCI-FM Hamden CT
WYKS(FM) Gainesville FL
WBVD(FM) Melbourne FL
WFKS(FM) Neptune Beach FL
WWWQ(FM) Atlanta GA
WNNX(FM) College Park GA
WBTY(FM) Homerville GA
KSHK(FM) Kekaha HI
KHDK(FM) New London IA
KSAS-FM Caldwell ID
WAZY-FM Lafayette IN
WRWM(FM) Lawrence IN
WSVX(AM) Shelbyville IN
KJCK-FM Junction City KS
KLZR(FM) Lawrence KS
KCHZ(FM) Ottawa KS
WLTO(FM) Nicholasville KY
WKKS-FM Vanceburg KY
KSMB(FM) Lafayette LA
WJMN(FM) Boston MA
WKHZ(AM) Ocean City MD
WDKZ(FM) Salisbury MD
WSKX(FM) York Center ME
WHTS(FM) Coopersville MI
WKQI(FM) Detroit MI
WMXG(FM) Stephenson MI
KCAJ-FM Roseau MN
KOQL(FM) Ashland MO
WHGO(FM) Pascagoula MS
KBUD(FM) Sardis MS
WFLB(FM) Laurinburg NC
WDAY-FM Fargo ND
KQKY(FM) Kearney NE
WERZ(FM) Exeter NH
WHTZ(FM) Newark NJ
KKYC(FM) Clovis NM
KFRH(FM) North Las Vegas NV
WDRE(FM) Calverton-Roanoke NY
*WECW(FM) Elmira NY
WXRK(FM) New York NY
WFIZ(FM) Odessa NY
WMCR(AM) Oneida NY
WMCR-FM Oneida NY
WLNG(FM) Sag Harbor NY
WMTR-FM Archbold OH
WDKF(FM) Englewood OH
KXFC(FM) Coalgate OK
KQLL-FM Owasso OK
KOSG(FM) Pawhuska OK
*KAYE-FM Tonkawa OK
*KMHS-FM Coos Bay OR
KKKJ(FM) Merrill OR
KLKY(FM) Stanfield OR
WBYN-FM Boyertown PA
WXYX(FM) Bayamon PR
WNOD(FM) Mayaguez PR
WKAQ-FM San Juan PR
WSSX-FM Charleston SC
WHHD(FM) Clearwater SC
WYMB(AM) Manning SC
KDSJ(AM) Deadwood SD
WDOD-FM Chattanooga TN
WHBQ-FM Germantown TN
WBMC(AM) McMinnville TN
WYDL(FM) Middleton TN
WNFN(FM) Millersville TN
WCRK(AM) Morristown TN
WUUQ(FM) South Pittsburg TN
KNDE(FM) College Station TX
KYSE(FM) El Paso TX
KMKI(AM) Plano TX
WVHT(FM) Norfolk VA

WRIC-FM Richlands VA
KJET(FM) Raymond WA
KRXY(FM) Shelton WA
WKSZ(FM) De Pere WI
WIZM-FM La Crosse WI
WPVL-FM Platteville WI
WELK(FM) Elkins WV
*WQAB(FM) Philippi WV
WSTG(FM) Princeton WV
*WPHP(FM) Wheeling WV
KLQQ(FM) Clearmont WY
KAML-FM Gillette WY

Triple A

*KXLL(FM) Juneau AK
WWMM(FM) Northport AL
KWBF-FM North Little Rock AR
KZGL(FM) Flagstaff AZ
*KGHR(FM) Tuba City AZ
KWMT-FM Tucson AZ
KBHR(FM) Big Bear City CA
*KNCA(FM) Burney CA
KPYG(FM) Cayucos CA
KPRI(FM) Encinitas CA
KOZT(FM) Fort Bragg CA
KPIG-FM Freedom CA
KHUM(FM) Garberville CA
KRSH(FM) Healdsburg CA
KSWD(FM) Los Angeles CA
*KNSQ(FM) Mount Shasta CA
KZAP(FM) Paradise CA
KPIG(AM) Piedmont CA
KNRO(AM) Redding CA
KTKE(FM) Truckee CA
KSPN-FM Aspen CO
KBCO(FM) Boulder CO
KSMT(FM) Breckenridge CO
KRKY-FM Estes Park CO
KYSL(FM) Frisco CO
*KUTE(FM) Ignacio CO
KFMU-FM Oak Creek CO
*KPGS(FM) Pagosa Springs CO
KSNO-FM Snowmass Village CO
WKZE-FM Salisbury CT
WOCM(FM) Selbyville DE
*WFIT(FM) Melbourne FL
*WUWF(FM) Pensacola FL
WZGC(FM) Atlanta GA
KPTL(FM) Ankeny IA
KUNI(FM) Cedar Falls IA
KDEC-FM Decorah IA
*KRNI(AM) Mason City IA
*KUNY(FM) Mason City IA
*KDMR(FM) Mitchellville IA
*KDWI(FM) Ottumwa IA
*KISU-FM Pocatello ID
KPND(FM) Sandpoint ID
WTTS(FM) Bloomington IN
*WEEM-FM Pendleton IN
KACY(FM) Arkansas City KS
*WNKU(FM) Highland Heights KY
*WUKY(FM) Lexington KY
*WKWC(FM) Owensboro KY
KROK(FM) South Fort Polk LA
WRNX(FM) Amherst MA
WXRV(FM) Andover MA
WRSI(FM) Turners Falls MA
*WTMD(FM) Towson MD
WCLZ(FM) Brunswick ME
WQKL(FM) Ann Arbor MI
*WLNZ(FM) Lansing MI
KDAL-FM Duluth MN
*KUMD-FM Duluth MN
*WTIP(FM) Grand Marais MN
*KCMP(FM) Northfield MN
*KMSE(FM) Rochester MN
*KSRQ(FM) Thief River Falls MN
KKSN(FM) Kansas City MO
*KCLC(FM) Saint Charles MO
*KTBG(FM) Warrensburg MO
*WUSM(FM) Hattiesburg MS
KMMS-FM Bozeman MT
KDTR(FM) Florence MT
*WGWG(FM) Boiling Springs NC
WUIN(FM) Carolina Beach NC

*WSGE(FM) Dallas NC
WVOD(FM) Manteo NC
*WNCW(FM) Spindale NC
WLKC(FM) Campton NH
WMWV(FM) Conway NH
*WBJB-FM Lincroft NJ
*KUUT(FM) Farmington NM
*KUSW(FM) Flora Vista NM
KTAO(FM) Taos NM
WGFR(FM) Glens Falls NY
*WFUV(FM) New York NY
*WAPS(FM) Akron OH
*WDPS(FM) Dayton OH
*WYSO(FM) Yellow Springs OH
*KSMF(FM) Ashland OR
*KRVM-FM Eugene OR
*KSKF(FM) Klamath Falls OR
KTEE(FM) North Bend OR
KINK(FM) Portland OR
KLRR(FM) Redmond OR
*KSYD(FM) Reedsport OR
*WVMM(FM) Grantham PA
*WYEP-FM Pittsburgh PA
*KSDJ(FM) Brookings SD
KSQY(FM) Deadwood SD
*WUTC(FM) Chattanooga TN
WRLT(FM) Franklin TN
WFIV-FM Loudon TN
KEEP(FM) Bandera TX
KGSR(FM) Bastrop TX
*KTCU-FM Fort Worth TX
KFAN-FM Johnson City TX
*KSYM-FM San Antonio TX
*KPCW-FM Park City UT
*WNRN(FM) Charlottesville VA
WTYD(FM) Deltaville VA
WCNR(FM) Keswick VA
*WVRU(FM) Radford VA
WIVI(FM) Charlotte Amalie VI
WDOT(FM) Danville VT
WRSY(FM) Marlboro VT
WNCS(FM) Montpelier VT
*WNUB-FM Northfield VT
*KGHP(FM) Gig Harbor WA
KMTT(FM) Tacoma WA
*WUWM(FM) Milwaukee WI
*WYMS(FM) Milwaukee WI
*KBUW(FM) Buffalo WY
*KUWC(FM) Casper WY

Urban Contemporary

WDLT-FM Chickasaw AL
WJJN(FM) Columbia AL
WQZZ(FM) Eutaw AL
WBFA(FM) Fort Mitchell AL
WMGJ(AM) Gadsden AL
WKXN(FM) Greenville AL
WHRP(FM) Gurley AL
WHOG(AM) Hobson City AL
WJUS(AM) Marion AL
WBHJ(FM) Midfield AL
WBLX-FM Mobile AL
WEUP-FM Moulton AL
WTUG-FM Northport AL
WZMG(AM) Pepperell AL
WKXK(FM) Pine Hill AL
WBFZ(FM) Selma AL
WAGH(FM) Smiths AL
WZHT(FM) Troy AL
WBHK(FM) Warrior AL
WJWZ(FM) Wetumpka AL
*KSWH(FM) Arkadelphia AR
KMGC(FM) Camden AR
KAPW(FM) Cotton Plant AR
KMLK(FM) El Dorado AR
KAMJ-FM Gosnell AR
KZYQ(FM) Lake Village AR
KAKJ(FM) Marianna AR
KIPR(FM) Pine Bluff AR
KZYP(FM) Pine Bluff AR
KTOY(FM) Texarkana AR
KCLT(FM) West Helena AR
KKFR(FM) Mayer AZ
KNRJ(FM) Payson AZ
KTUC(AM) Tucson AZ

KNGY(FM) Alameda CA
KVIN(AM) Ceres CA
KJLH(FM) Compton CA
*KCRH(FM) Hayward CA
KKUU(FM) Indio CA
KRAJ(FM) Johannesburg CA
KHHT(FM) Los Angeles CA
*KSFH(FM) Mountain View CA
KWIE(FM) Ontario CA
KPAT(FM) Orcutt CA
KDAY(FM) Redondo Beach CA
KBMB(FM) Sacramento CA
KDON-FM Salinas CA
KYLD(FM) San Francisco CA
*KSJS(FM) San Jose CA
KKJL(AM) San Luis Obispo CA
KVYB(FM) Santa Barbara CA
KWYL(FM) South Lake Tahoe CA
*KSAK(FM) Walnut CA
KNAB(FM) Burlington CO
KIBT(FM) Fountain CO
*WQTQ(FM) Hartford CT
WYBC-FM New Haven CT
*WECS(FM) Willimantic CT
WKND(AM) Windsor CT
WHUR-FM Washington DC
WKYS(FM) Washington DC
WJBT(FM) Callahan FL
WBTP(FM) Clearwater FL
*WJCB(FM) Clewiston FL
WHQT(FM) Coral Gables FL
WHNR(AM) Cypress Gardens FL
WTMP-FM Dade City FL
WCFB(FM) Daytona Beach FL
WTMP(AM) Egypt Lake FL
WKIQ(AM) Eustis FL
*WJFP(FM) Fort Pierce FL
WRNE(AM) Gulf Breeze FL
WRRX(FM) Gulf Breeze FL
WNEW(FM) Jupiter FL
WSBB(AM) New Smyrna Beach FL
WPBH(FM) Port St. Joe FL
WRXB(FM) Saint Petersburg Beach FL
WHBX(FM) Tallahassee FL
WTMG(FM) Williston FL
*WPRK(FM) Winter Park FL
WJIZ-FM Albany GA
WVEE(FM) Atlanta GA
WFXA-FM Augusta GA
WBBK-FM Blakely GA
WSOL-FM Brunswick GA
WWLD(FM) Cairo GA
WZBN(FM) Camilla GA
WFXE(FM) Columbus GA
WMRZ(AM) Dawson GA
WUMJ(FM) Fayetteville GA
WQMJ(FM) Forsyth GA
WIBB-FM Fort Valley GA
WFXM(FM) Gordon GA
WHTA(FM) Hampton GA
WVKX(FM) Irwinton GA
WALR-FM La Grange GA
WLZN(FM) Macon GA
WPRW-FM Martinez GA
WHBS(FM) Moultrie GA
WMPZ(FM) Ringgold GA
WAMJ(FM) Roswell GA
WBGA(FM) Saint Simons Island GA
WQBT(FM) Savannah GA
WEAS-FM Springfield GA
WHLJ(FM) Statenville GA
WNUQ(FM) Sylvester GA
WGOV(FM) Valdosta GA
WLYX(FM) Valdosta GA
*WVVS(FM) Valdosta GA
WRBV(FM) Warner Robins GA
WAKB(FM) Waynesboro GA
KZGZ(FM) Hagatna GU
*KALA(FM) Davenport IA
KJMC(FM) Des Moines IA
KATZ-FM Alton IL
WKRO(AM) Cairo IL
*WPCD(FM) Champaign IL
*WKKC(FM) Chicago IL
*WMBI(AM) Chicago IL
*WIUS(FM) Macomb IL

WCZQ(FM) Monticello IL
WMOJ-FM Connersville IN
WEOA(AM) Evansville IN
WPWX(FM) Hammond IN
*WBDG(FM) Indianapolis IN
WHHH(FM) Indianapolis IN
WGZB-FM Lanesville IN
WUBU(FM) South Bend IN
*WISU(FM) Terre Haute IN
*KSDB-FM Manhattan KS
WIZF(FM) Erlanger KY
WGVN(AM) Georgetown KY
WMJM(FM) Jeffersontown KY
WBTF(FM) Midway KY
WDXR(AM) Paducah KY
WUBT(FM) Russellville KY
KEDG(FM) Alexandria LA
KMXH(FM) Alexandria LA
KJMG(FM) Bastrop LA
KRVV(FM) Bastrop LA
KKND(FM) Belle Chasse LA
KBZE(FM) Berwick LA
KDKS-FM Blanchard LA
KBCE(FM) Boyce LA
KNOU(FM) Empire LA
*KGRM(FM) Grambling LA
KBTT(FM) Haughton LA
KTGV(FM) Jonesville LA
WEMX(FM) Kentwood LA
KJCB(AM) Lafayette LA
KRRQ(FM) Lafayette LA
KJMH(FM) Lake Arthur LA
KZWA(FM) Moss Bluff LA
WQUE-FM New Orleans LA
*WWOZ(FM) New Orleans LA
WYLD-FM New Orleans LA
KCLF(FM) New Roads LA
KQXL-FM New Roads LA
KKST(FM) Oakdale LA
KFXZ-FM Opelousas LA
KMEZ(FM) Port Sulphur LA
KMJJ-FM Shreveport LA
KVMA-FM Shreveport LA
KTJZ(FM) Tallulah LA
KNEK(AM) Washington LA
*WOZQ(FM) Northampton MA
*WMHC(FM) South Hadley MA
WERQ-FM Baltimore MD
WTBO(AM) Cumberland MD
WWIN-FM Glen Burnie MD
WSBY-FM Salisbury MD
WDMK(FM) Detroit MI
WGPR(FM) Detroit MI
WJLB(FM) Detroit MI
WMXD(FM) Detroit MI
WQHH(FM) Dewitt MI
WDZZ-FM Flint MI
WVIB(FM) Holton MI
WIKB(AM) Iron River MI
WJNZ(AM) Kentwood MI
WHTD(FM) Mount Clemens MI
WSNX-FM Muskegon MI
WNWN(AM) Portage MI
WTLZ(FM) Saginaw MI
WOWE(FM) Vassar MI
WMFN(AM) Zeeland MI
*KMOJ(FM) Minneapolis MN
KDMO(AM) Carthage MO
WMBH(AM) Joplin MO
KPRS(FM) Kansas City MO
KMJK(FM) Lexington MO
WESE(FM) Baldwyn MS
WJBI(AM) Batesville MS
WRBJ-FM Brandon MS
WAJV(FM) Brooksville MS
WMGO(AM) Canton MS
WCLD-FM Cleveland MS
WWKZ(FM) Columbus MS
WACR-FM Columbus AFB MS
WJXM(FM) De Kalb MS
WJKX(FM) Ellisville MS
WJMG(FM) Hattiesburg MS
WKRA-FM Holly Springs MS
WJMI(FM) Jackson MS
*WMPR(FM) Jackson MS
WBAD(FM) Leland MS

WJZD-FM Long Beach MS
WKXI-FM Magee MS
WQYZ(FM) Ocean Springs MS
KJMS(FM) Olive Branch MS
WZLD(FM) Petal MS
WMSU(FM) Starkville MS
WMXU(FM) Starkville MS
WGNG(FM) Tchula MS
WZKS(FM) Union MS
KLSK(FM) Great Falls MT
WQZL(FM) Belhaven NC
WVOE(AM) Chadbourn NC
WMKS(FM) Clemmons NC
WPEG(FM) Concord NC
WFXC(FM) Durham NC
*WRVS-FM Elizabeth City NC
WBAV-FM Gastonia NC
WQNC(FM) Harrisburg NC
WCCG(FM) Hope Mills NC
WQSL(FM) Jacksonville NC
WKXS-FM Leland NC
WCDG(FM) Moyock NC
WIKS(FM) New Bern NC
WPWZ(FM) Pinetops NC
*WKNC-FM Raleigh NC
WJMH(FM) Reidsville NC
WRSV(FM) Rocky Mount NC
WUKS(FM) Saint Pauls NC
WMGU(FM) Southern Pines NC
WFXK(FM) Tarboro NC
WSMY(AM) Weldon NC
WENC(AM) Whiteville NC
WZFX(FM) Whiteville NC
WMNX(FM) Wilmington NC
*KZUM(FM) Lincoln NE
KOPW(FM) Plattsmouth NE
*WSPS(FM) Concord NH
*WNEC-FM Henniker NH
WJKS(FM) Canton NJ
WIMG(AM) Ewing NJ
WTTH(FM) Margate City NJ
WRNB(FM) Pennsauken NJ
WEZW(FM) Wildwood Crest NJ
*KCEP(FM) Las Vegas NV
KVGS(FM) Laughlin NV
*WCDB(FM) Albany NY
WPHR-FM Auburn NY
*WCWP(FM) Brookville NY
WWWS(AM) Buffalo NY
WBLK(FM) Depew NY
*WRCU-FM Hamilton NY
WVHC(FM) Herkimer NY
*WICB(FM) Ithaca NY
WBLS(FM) New York NY
WWPR-FM New York NY
*WOSS(FM) Ossining NY
*WNYO(FM) Oswego NY
WDKX(FM) Rochester NY
*WFNP(FM) Rosendale NY
*WPNR-FM Utica NY
WENZ(FM) Cleveland OH
WZAK(FM) Cleveland OH
WIMX(FM) Gibsonburg OH
WRBP(FM) Hubbard OH
WJTB(AM) North Ridgeville OH
WDHT(FM) Springfield OH
WDIG(AM) Steubenville OH
WJUC(FM) Swanton OH
WROU-FM West Carrollton OH
*WCSU-FM Wilberforce OH
KJMM(FM) Bixby OK
*KALU(FM) Langston OK
KRMP(AM) Oklahoma City OK
KVSP(FM) Oklahoma City OK
KJMU(AM) Sand Springs OK
KGTO(AM) Tulsa OK
KXJM(FM) Banks OR
*KBVR(FM) Corvallis OR
*KWVA(FM) Eugene OR
WAMO-FM Beaver Falls PA
*WERG(FM) Erie PA
WLAN(AM) Lancaster PA
*WWLU(FM) Lincoln University PA
WUSL(FM) Philadelphia PA
*WCLH(FM) Wilkes-Barre PA
*WRLC(FM) Williamsport PA

WBRU(FM) Providence RI
*WJMF(FM) Smithfield RI
WJMZ-FM Anderson SC
WIIZ(FM) Blackville SC
WYNN-FM Florence SC
WLVH(FM) Hardeeville SC
*WLGI(FM) Hemingway SC
WXST(FM) Hollywood SC
WJNI(FM) Ladson SC
WCMG(FM) Latta SC
WHXT(FM) Orangeburg SC
WPJK(AM) Orangeburg SC
*WSSB-FM Orangeburg SC
WDAI(FM) Pawley's Island SC
WZTF(FM) Scranton SC
WASC(AM) Spartanburg SC
WWWZ(FM) Summerville SC
WWDM(FM) Sumter SC
WXBT(FM) West Columbia SC
WFKX(FM) Henderson TN
WQQK(FM) Hendersonville TN
WKGN(AM) Knoxville TN
WDIA(AM) Memphis TN
WHRK(FM) Memphis TN
*WQOX(FM) Memphis TN
WEUZ(FM) Minor Hill TN
WJTT(FM) Red Bank TN
*KAZI-FM Austin TX
KTCX(FM) Beaumont TX
KHPT(FM) Conroe TX
KSSM(FM) Copperas Cove TX
KBFB(FM) Dallas TX
KKDA-FM Dallas TX
KEPS(AM) Eagle Pass TX
KSOC(FM) Gainesville TX
KCOH(AM) Houston TX
KMJQ(FM) Houston TX
KIIZ-FM Killeen TX
KAJZ(FM) Llano TX
KDAV(AM) Lubbock TX
*KBWC(FM) Marshall TX
KZRB(FM) New Boston TX
KGEE(FM) Pecos TX
KZEY(AM) Tyler TX
KBLZ(FM) Winona TX
*WNRN(FM) Charlottesville VA
WUVA(FM) Charlottesville VA
WVBE-FM Lynchburg VA
WCDX(FM) Mechanicsville VA
WKUS(FM) Norfolk VA
*WNSB(FM) Norfolk VA
WOWI(FM) Norfolk VA
WKJM(FM) Petersburg VA
WBTJ(FM) Richmond VA
WKJS(FM) Richmond VA
WVBE(AM) Roanoke VA
WTOY(AM) Salem VA
WQOK(FM) South Boston VA
WXEZ(FM) Yorktown VA
WSTA(AM) Charlotte Amalie VI
WVJZ(FM) Charlotte Amalie VI
WJKC(FM) Christiansted VI
WWKS(FM) Cruz Bay VI
*WVTC(FM) Randolph Center VT
KYIZ(AM) Renton WA
KYNR(AM) Toppenish WA
KBMS(AM) Vancouver WA
KHHK(FM) Yakima WA
WJQM(FM) De Forest WI
WJMR-FM Menomonee Falls WI
WNOV(AM) Milwaukee WI
*WSUW(FM) Whitewater WI

Variety/Diverse

*KBRW(AM) Barrow AK
*KYUK(AM) Bethel AK
*KCUK(FM) Chevak AK
*KZPA(AM) Fort Yukon AK
*KIYU(AM) Galena AK
*KIYU-FM Galena AK
*KEUL(FM) Girdwood AK
*KHNS(FM) Haines AK
*KMJG(FM) Homer AK
*KWJG(FM) Kasilof AK
*KDLL(FM) Kenai AK

*KOTZ(AM) Kotzebue AK
*KFSK(FM) Petersburg AK
*KUHB(FM) Saint Paul AK
*KCAW(FM) Sitka AK
KNSA(AM) Unalakleet AK
*KUCB(FM) Unalaska AK
WRVX(FM) Eufaula AL
*WLRH(FM) Huntsville AL
*WLJS-FM Jacksonville AL
KBVA(FM) Bella Vista AR
KAVH(FM) Eudora AR
*KXUA(FM) Fayetteville AR
KURM(AM) Rogers AR
KXRJ(FM) Russellville AR
*KRMH(FM) Red Mesa AZ
KSED(FM) Sedona AZ
*KXCI(FM) Tucson AZ
KBSZ(AM) Wickenburg AZ
*KHSU-FM Arcata CA
KAHI(AM) Auburn CA
*KISL(FM) Avalon CA
KWRM(AM) Corona CA
*KHSR(FM) Crescent City CA
*KKUP(FM) Cupertino CA
*KDVS(FM) Davis CA
KFCF(FM) Fresno CA
KTDE(FM) Gualala CA
*KCRH(FM) Hayward CA
KTYM(AM) Inglewood CA
*KFJC(FM) Los Altos CA
*KAKX(FM) Mendocino CA
KVMR(FM) Nevada City CA
*KCSN(FM) Northridge CA
KZYX(FM) Philo CA
*KWMR(FM) Point Reyes Station CA
*KFPR(FM) Redding CA
*KYDS(FM) Sacramento CA
*KSRH(FM) San Rafael CA
*KCSB-FM Santa Barbara CA
*KFER(FM) Santa Cruz CA
KSVY(FM) Sonoma CA
*KRZA(FM) Alamosa CO
KONN-FM Bennett CO
*KGNU-FM Boulder CO
*KEPC(FM) Colorado Springs CO
*KRFC(FM) Fort Collins CO
*KMPB(FM) Frisco CO
KCUV(FM) Greenwood Village CO
*KWSB-FM Gunnison CO
*KOTO(FM) Telluride CO
KJAC(FM) Timnath CO
*WVOF(FM) Fairfield CT
*WESU(FM) Middletown CT
*WCNI(FM) New London CT
*WBVC(FM) Pomfret CT
*WAPJ(FM) Torrington CT
*WWEB(FM) Wallingford CT
*WWUH(FM) West Hartford CT
*WWPT(FM) Westport CT
WJWK(AM) Seaford DE
WBGC(AM) Chipley FL
*WRGP(FM) Homestead FL
WWFE(AM) Miami FL
*WEJF(FM) Palm Bay FL
WPIK(FM) Summerland Key FL
WVLG(AM) Wildwood FL
*WRFG(FM) Atlanta GA
WMLB(AM) Avondale Estates GA
WMJE(FM) Clarkesville GA
*WBCX(FM) Gainesville GA
*WHCJ(FM) Savannah GA
WZAT(FM) Savannah GA
*KURE(FM) Ames IA
*KWLC(AM) Decorah IA
*KHOE(FM) Fairfield IA
KOKX-FM Keokuk IA
*KRNL-FM Mount Vernon IA
KZSR(AM) Onawa IA
KDLS(AM) Perry IA
*KLCZ(FM) Lewiston ID
*KUOI-FM Moscow ID
*WEFT(FM) Champaign IL
*WEIU(FM) Charleston IL
*WIIT(FM) Chicago IL
*WKKC(FM) Chicago IL
*WLUW(FM) Chicago IL

*WRTE(FM) Chicago IL
*WZRD(FM) Chicago IL
WCFJ(AM) Chicago Heights IL
WFIW-FM Fairfield IL
*WVKC(FM) Galesburg IL
WDUK(FM) Havana IL
*WHSD(FM) Hinsdale IL
*WLTL(FM) La Grange IL
*WAES(FM) Lincolnshire IL
WKOT(FM) Marseilles IL
*WMTH(FM) Park Ridge IL
*WILL-FM Urbana IL
*WFWR(FM) Attica IN
*WNDY(FM) Crawfordsville IN
*WPSR(FM) Evansville IN
WTRE(AM) Greensburg IN
*WHCI(FM) Hartford City IN
*WJEL(FM) Indianapolis IN
WAWK(AM) Kendallville IN
*WLPR-FM Lowell IN
*WBRO(FM) Marengo IN
*WECI(FM) Richmond IN
*WITT(FM) Zionsville IN
*KVCO(FM) Concordia KS
*KONQ(FM) Dodge City KS
*KBCU(FM) North Newton KS
KQMA-FM Phillipsburg KS
*WRFL(FM) Lexington KY
*WMKY(FM) Morehead KY
*WKMS-FM Murray KY
WKFC(FM) North Corbin KY
WRUS(AM) Russellville KY
*WMMT(FM) Whitesburg KY
*KLSU(FM) Baton Rouge LA
*KRVS(FM) Lafayette LA
*KEDM(FM) Monroe LA
*KNWD(FM) Natchitoches LA
KKAY(AM) White Castle LA
*WAMH(FM) Amherst MA
*WMUA(FM) Amherst MA
*WERS(FM) Boston MA
*WRBB(FM) Boston MA
*WBIM-FM Bridgewater MA
*WMBR(FM) Cambridge MA
*WGAJ(FM) Deerfield MA
*WXPL(FM) Fitchburg MA
*WHHB(FM) Holliston MA
*WCCH(FM) Holyoke MA
WMKK(FM) Lawrence MA
*WWTA(FM) Marion MA
*WAVM(FM) Maynard MA
*WMFO(FM) Medford MA
WMRC(AM) Milford MA
*WNCK(FM) Nantucket MA
WNBP(AM) Newburyport MA
WNTN(AM) Newton MA
*WOMR(FM) Provincetown MA
*WMWM(FM) Salem MA
*WMHC(FM) South Hadley MA
*WNEK-FM Springfield MA
*WSCB(FM) Springfield MA
*WTCC(FM) Springfield MA
*WZLY(FM) Wellesley MA
WQSR(FM) Baltimore MD
*WHFC(FM) Bel Air MD
*WMUC-FM College Park MD
WMET(AM) Gaithersburg MD
*WUMF-FM Farmington ME
*WUMM(FM) Machias ME
WSYY-FM Millinocket ME
*WCBN-FM Ann Arbor MI
*WHFR(FM) Dearborn MI
WMJO(FM) Essexville MI
*WMTU-FM Houghton MI
*WIDR(FM) Kalamazoo MI
*WYDM(FM) Monroe MI
*WOAS(FM) Ontonagon MI
*WBLD(FM) Orchard Lake MI
*WLSO(FM) Sault Ste. Marie MI
*WYCE(FM) Wyoming MI
WELY(AM) Ely MN
WELY-FM Ely MN
*WTIP(FM) Grand Marais MN
*KAXE(FM) Grand Rapids MN
*KSMR(FM) Winona MN
*KZGM(FM) Cabool MO

KCXL(AM) Liberty MO
*KGSP(FM) Parkville MO
*KMNR(FM) Rolla MO
*WUSM-FM Hattiesburg MS
*WPRL(FM) Lorman MS
*KGVA(FM) Fort Belknap Agency MT
*KGPR(FM) Great Falls MT
KINX(FM) Great Falls MT
*WSGE(FM) Dallas NC
WRVS-FM Elizabeth City NC
*WUAW(FM) Erwin NC
WQFS(FM) Greensboro NC
*WZMB(FM) Greenville NC
WHKP(AM) Hendersonville NC
*WHYC(FM) Swanquarter NC
*KDSU(FM) Fargo ND
*KDCV-FM Blair NE
KNCY(AM) Nebraska City NE
*WPEA(FM) Exeter NH
WSNJ(AM) Bridgeton NJ
*WRRC(FM) Lawrenceville NJ
WMVB(AM) Millville NJ
*WRSU-FM New Brunswick NJ
*WLFR(FM) Pomona NJ
*WWPH(FM) Princeton Junction NJ
*WFDU(FM) Teaneck NJ
KDAZ(AM) Albuquerque NM
*KRUX(FM) Las Cruces NM
KVSF-FM Pecos NM
KRSI(FM) Garapan-Saipan NP
*WALF(FM) Alfred NY
*WHRW(FM) Binghamton NY
*WXLH(FM) Blue Mountain Lake NY
*WXLB(FM) Boonville NY
*WSLU(FM) Canton NY
*WHCL-FM Clinton NY
*WSUC-FM Cortland NY
*WXXE(FM) Fenner NY
WGBB(AM) Freeport NY
*WHPC(FM) Garden City NY
*WRHU(FM) Hempstead NY
*WJFF(FM) Jeffersonville NY
*WSHR(FM) Lake Ronkonkoma NY
*WVCR-FM Loudonville NY
*WSLO(FM) Malone NY
*WBAI(FM) New York NY
*WKCR-FM New York NY
*WXLG(FM) North Creek NY
*WXLU(FM) Peru NY
*WAIH(FM) Potsdam NY
*WSLL(FM) Saranac Lake NY
*WSPN(FM) Saratoga Springs NY
WSPQ(AM) Springville NY
*WRPI(FM) Troy NY
*WSLJ(FM) Watertown NY
*WAPS(FM) Akron OH
*WOBO(FM) Batavia OH
*WBGU(FM) Bowling Green OH
*WRUW-FM Cleveland OH
*WCBE(FM) Columbus OH
WKTX(AM) Cortland OH
*WUDR(FM) Dayton OH
*WWSU(FM) Dayton OH
*WSLN(FM) Delaware OH
*WKCO(FM) Gambier OH
*WDUB(FM) Granville OH
*WFGA(FM) Hicksville OH
WMVO(AM) Mount Vernon OH
*WYNS(FM) Waynesville OH
KQOB(FM) Enid OK
KIHN(FM) Hugo OK
*KSRG(FM) Ashland OR
*KLFO(FM) Florence OR
*KEOL(FM) La Grande OR
*WJCS(FM) Allentown PA
WGPA(AM) Bethlehem PA
*WLVR(FM) Bethlehem PA
WHLM(AM) Bloomsburg PA
*WLBS(FM) Bristol PA
WMAJ-FM Centre Hall PA
*WDNR(FM) Chester PA
*WJRH(FM) Easton PA
WGSM(FM) Greensburg PA
*WIUP-FM Indiana PA
WKHB(AM) Irwin PA
WKFB(AM) Jeannette PA

*WFNM(FM) Lancaster PA
WEDO(AM) McKeesport PA
*WKDU(FM) Philadelphia PA
WNWR(AM) Philadelphia PA
*WSYC-FM Shippensburg PA
*WKPS(FM) State College PA
*WPSU(FM) State College PA
WMBS(AM) Uniontown PA
*WXVU(FM) Villanova PA
*WRDV(FM) Warminster PA
*WNJR(FM) Washington PA
*WVYC(FM) York PA
WOQI(AM) Adjuntas PR
WCGB(AM) Juana Diaz PR
WDEP(AM) Ponce PR
WJIT(AM) Sabana PR
WEGA(AM) Vega Baja PR
WJZS(FM) Block Island RI

*WUSC-FM Columbia SC
WLBG(AM) Laurens SC
*KLND(FM) Little Eagle SD
*KILI(FM) Porcupine SD
WQSV(AM) Ashland City TN
*WAPX-FM Clarksville TN
WHHM-FM Henderson TN
WYGO(FM) Madisonville TN
*WEVL(FM) Memphis TN
*WUTS(FM) Sewanee TN
WSGI(AM) Springfield TN
WQAK(FM) Union City TN
KVLF(AM) Alpine TX
*KNON(FM) Dallas TX
*KOOP(FM) Hornsby TX
KRBA(AM) Lufkin TX
*KEOM(FM) Mesquite TX
KNBT(FM) New Braunfels TX

KLVL(AM) Pasadena TX
KWFB(FM) Quanah TX
*KGWB(FM) Snyder TX
*KZMU(FM) Moab UT
*KPGR(FM) Pleasant Grove UT
KLGL(FM) Richfield UT
*WTJU(FM) Charlottesville VA
*WVTW(FM) Charlottesville VA
*WMRY(FM) Crozet VA
*WHOV(FM) Hampton VA
*WEMC(FM) Harrisonburg VA
*WMRA(FM) Harrisonburg VA
WCLM(AM) Highland Springs VA
WHAP(AM) Hopewell VA
*WCHG(FM) Hot Springs VA
*WMRL(FM) Lexington VA
*WWMC(FM) Lynchburg VA
WWLB(FM) Midlothian VA

*WVLS(FM) Monterey VA
WSTX(AM) Christiansted VI
*WXLQ(FM) Bristol VT
*WIUV(FM) Castleton VT
WWMP(FM) Waterbury VT
*KUBS(FM) Newport WA
KSUH(AM) Puyallup WA
*KWCW(FM) Walla Walla WA
KTRT(FM) Winthrop WA
*WBCR-FM Beloit WI
*WORT(FM) Madison WI
WOCO(AM) Oconto WI
*WXPR(FM) Rhinelander WI
*WRFW(FM) River Falls WI
*WCCX(FM) Waukesha WI
WQWV(FM) Fisher WV
*WRSG(FM) Middlebourne WV
WKWK-FM Wheeling WV

WVVV(FM) Williamstown WV
*KWRR(FM) Ethete WY
KYOD(FM) Glendo WY
*KHOL(FM) Jackson WY

Vietnamese

KZSJ(AM) San Martin CA
KVNR(AM) Santa Ana CA
KVVN(AM) Santa Clara CA
KJOJ(AM) Conroe TX
KYND(AM) Cypress TX
KREH(AM) Pecan Grove TX

Women

WNSH(AM) Beverly MA

Programming on Radio Stations in Canada

Adult Contemp

CFIT-FM Airdrie AB
CKBA-FM Athabasca AB
CIXF-FM Brooks AB
CHFM-FM Calgary AB
CKCE-FM Calgary AB
CKMX(AM) Calgary AB
CHMN-FM Canmore AB
CHOO-FM Drumheller AB
CFXE-FM Edson AB
*CKRP-FM Falher AB
CFVR-FM Fort McMurray AB
CKOS-FM Fort McMurray AB
CJUV-FM Lacombe AB
CFRV-FM Lethbridge AB
CJOC-FM Lethbridge AB
CFMY-FM Medicine Hat AB
CJCY-FM Medicine Hat AB
CKKX-FM Peace River AB
CHUB-FM Red Deer AB
CIZZ-FM Red Deer AB
CFMG-FM Saint Albert AB
CHSL-FM Slave Lake AB
CJBZ-FM Taber AB
CKWY-FM Wainwright AB
CKGO-FM-1 Boston Bar BC
CFLD(AM) Burns Lake BC
CIQC-FM Campbell River BC
CFKC(AM) Creston BC
CJSU-FM Duncan BC
CIEG-FM Egmont BC
CISC-FM Gibsons BC
CFSR-FM Hope BC
CKBZ-FM Kamloops BC
CHSU-FM Kelowna BC
CILK-FM Kelowna BC
CJNL(AM) Merritt BC
CKWV-FM Nanaimo BC
CKKC-FM Nelson BC
CKZX-FM New Denver BC
CJOR(AM) Osoyoos BC
CIBH-FM Parksville BC
CISP-FM Pemberton BC
CIPN-FM Pender Harbour BC
CIGV-FM Penticton BC
CJAV-FM Port Alberni BC
CFNI(AM) Port Hardy BC
CFPW-FM Powell River BC
CKKN-FM Prince George BC
CIOR(AM) Princeton BC
CKXR-FM Salmon Arm BC
CKAY-FM Sechelt BC
CFBV(AM) Smithers BC
CISQ-FM Squamish BC
CJAT-FM Trail BC
CHQM-FM Vancouver BC
CKLG-FM Vancouver BC
CKZZ-FM Vancouver BC
CICF-FM Vernon BC
CHBE-FM Victoria BC
CIOC-FM Victoria BC
CISW-FM Whistler BC
CKLF-FM Brandon MB
CKDM(AM) Dauphin MB
CFAR(AM) Flin Flon MB
CILT-FM Steinbach MB
CJAR(AM) The Pas MB
CHTM(AM) Thompson MB
CJEL-FM Winkler MB
CFWM-FM Winnipeg MB
CKY-FM Winnipeg MB
CKBC-FM Bathurst NB
CKNB(AM) Campbellton NB
CJVA(AM) Caraquet NB
CJEM-FM Edmundston NB
*CJPN-FM Fredericton NB
CIKX-FM Grand Falls NB
CKMV-FM Grand Falls NB
CFAN-FM Miramichi City NB
CFBO-FM Moncton NB

CFQM-FM Moncton NB
CIOK-FM Saint John NB
CJCW(AM) Sussex NB
CJCJ-FM Woodstock NB
CFOZ-FM Argentia NF
CJOZ-FM Bonavista Bay NF
CFLC-FM Churchill Falls NF
CJKK-FM Clarenville NF
CKOZ-FM Corner Brook NF
CFLN(AM) Goose Bay NF
CIFX-FM Lewisporte NF
CIOZ-FM Marystown NF
CHOS-FM Rattling Brook NF
CKSS-FM Red Rocks NF
CHOZ-FM Saint John's NF
CKSJ-FM Saint John's NF
VOCM(AM) Saint John's NF
CIOS-FM Stephenville NF
CJLS-FM-1 Barrington NS
CKBW-FM Bridgewater NS
CIOO-FM Halifax NS
CKWM-FM Kentville NS
CKBW-1 Liverpool NS
CKEC-FM New Glasgow NS
CJLS-FM-2 New Tusket NS
CIGO-FM Port Hawkesbury NS
CKBW-FM-2 Shelburne NS
CBI-FM Sydney NS
CKTO-FM Truro NS
CJLS-FM Yarmouth NS
CJCD-FM-1 Hay River NT
CJCD-FM Yellowknife NT
CBQR-FM Rankin Inlet NU
CFAO-FM Alliston ON
CHAY-FM Barrie ON
CIQB-FM Barrie ON
CIGL-FM Belleville ON
CJOJ-FM Belleville ON
CJFB-FM Bolton ON
CFBG-FM Bracebridge ON
CKPC-FM Brantford ON
CFJR-FM Brockville ON
CJPT-FM Brockville ON
CKSY-FM Chatham ON
CHUC-FM Cobourg ON
CKSG-FM Cobourg ON
CHPB-FM Cochrane ON
CKCB-FM Collingwood ON
CFLG-FM Cornwall ON
CJUL(AM) Cornwall ON
CKDR-FM Dryden ON
CJBB-FM Englehart ON
CFOB-FM Fort Frances ON
CHWC-FM Goderich ON
CIMJ-FM Guelph ON
CKLH-FM Hamilton ON
CKHK-FM Hawkesbury ON
CHYK-FM-3 Hearst ON
*CINN-FM Hearst ON
CFBK-FM Huntsville ON
CJRL-FM Kenora ON
CIYN-FM Kincardine ON
CFLY-FM Kingston ON
CJKL-FM Kirkland Lake ON
CKWR-FM Kitchener ON
CHYR-FM Leamington ON
CKLY-FM Lindsay (city of Kawartha Lakes) ON
CFPL(AM) London ON
CFPL-FM London ON
CIQM-FM London ON
CFNO-FM Marathon ON
CKDX-FM Newmarket ON
CFLZ-FM Niagara Falls ON
CHUR-FM North Bay ON
CISS-FM Ottawa ON
CJMJ-FM Ottawa ON
CJWL-FM Ottawa ON
CIXK-FM Owen Sound ON
CKLP-FM Parry Sound ON
CIMY-FM Pembroke ON

*CFRH-FM Penetanguishene ON
CHLK-FM Perth ON
CKPT-FM Peterborough ON
CFPS-FM Port Elgin ON
CHMY-FM Renfrew ON
CHSC(AM) Saint Catharines ON
CFGX-FM Sarnia ON
CHAS-FM Sault Ste. Marie ON
CHCD-FM Simcoe ON
CHGK-FM Stratford ON
CJMI-FM Strathroy ON
CFSF-FM Sturgeon Falls ON
CHYC-FM Sudbury ON
CJMX-FM Sudbury ON
CJUK-FM Thunder Bay ON
CJUK-FM Thunder Bay ON
CKPR-FM Thunder Bay ON
CHYK-FM Timmins ON
CHFI-FM Toronto ON
CHUM-FM Toronto ON
CJEZ-FM Toronto ON
CKFM-FM Toronto ON
CKQV-FM Vermillion Bay ON
CHGB-FM Wasaga Beach ON
CJWA-FM Wawa ON
CIDR-FM Windsor ON
CKWW(AM) Windsor ON
CKNX-FM Wingham ON
CIHR-FM Woodstock ON
CHLQ-FM Charlottetown PE
CFVM-FM Amqui PQ
CJAN-FM Asbestos PQ
CHLC-FM Baie Comeau PQ
CIEU-FM Carleton PQ
CHAI-FM Chateauguay PQ
CBJ-FM Chicoutimi PQ
CFVD-FM Degelis PQ
CHRD-FM Drummondville PQ
CJDM-FM Drummondville PQ
CFRP(AM) Forestville PQ
CFXM-FM Granby PQ
*CFTH-FM-1 Harrington Harbour PQ
*CKRK-FM Kahnawake PQ
CHOX-FM La Pocatiere PQ
CFLM(AM) La Tuque PQ
CJLA-FM Lachute PQ
CFGL-FM Laval PQ
CFOM-FM Levis PQ
CHAA-FM Longueuil PQ
CHGA-FM Maniwaki PQ
CFLO-FM Mont-Laurier PQ
CFEL-FM Montmagny PQ
CFQR-FM Montreal PQ
CITE-FM Montreal PQ
CJFM-FM Montreal PQ
CHIK-FM Quebec PQ
*CION-FM Quebec PQ
CITF-FM Quebec PQ
CJEC-FM Quebec PQ
*CKRL-FM Quebec PQ
CJBR-FM Rimouski PQ
CKMN-FM Rimouski-Mont Joli PQ
CIEL-FM Riviere du Loup PQ
CHOA-FM Rouyn-Noranda PQ
CJAB-FM Saguenay PQ
CJAS-FM Saint Augustin PQ
CKRB-FM Saint Georges-de-Beauce PQ
CIME-FM Saint Jerome PQ
CHEQ-FM Sainte-Marie-de-Beauce PQ
CKCN-FM Sept-Iles PQ
CKSM(AM) Shawinigan PQ
CFGE-FM Sherbrooke PQ
CITE-FM-1 Sherbrooke PQ
CKLD-FM Thetford Mines PQ
CJEB-FM Trois Rivieres PQ
CKOD-FM Valleyfield PQ
CFDA-FM Victoriaville PQ
CKVM-FM Ville-Marie PQ
CFYM(AM) Kindersley SK
CJAW-FM Moose Jaw SK

CFNK-FM Pinehouse Lake SK
CKBI(AM) Prince Albert SK
CHMX-FM Regina SK
CIZL-FM Regina SK
CFMC-FM Saskatoon SK
CJMK-FM Saskatoon SK
CKFI-FM Swift Current SK
CFGW-FM Yorkton SK
CIAY-FM Whitehorse YT

Agriculture

CFAM(AM) Altona MB
CJRB(AM) Boissevain MB
CKRM(AM) Regina SK

Album-Oriented Rock

CKLZ-FM Kelowna BC
CJAR(AM) The Pas MB
CHRE-FM Saint Catharines ON
CJMX-FM Sudbury ON
CJQQ-FM Timmins ON
CIZL-FM Regina SK

Alternative

CFEX-FM Calgary AB
*CJSW-FM Calgary AB
*CJSR-FM Edmonton AB
CHIQ-FM Winnipeg MB
CKIC-FM Winnipeg MB
*CHMR-FM Saint John's NF
*CIOI-FM Hamilton ON
CKLC-FM Kingston ON
*CHRW-FM London ON
CILV-FM Ottawa ON
*CKDJ-FM Ottawa ON
CHRY-FM Toronto ON
*CKLN-FM Toronto ON
CIMI-FM Charlesbourg PQ
*CISM-FM Montreal PQ
CHOI-FM Quebec PQ

American Indian

CHDH-FM Siksika AB
CHFN-FM Cape Croker (Neyaashiinigmiing) ON
CFNK-FM Pinehouse Lake SK

Arabic

CHOU(AM) Montreal PQ

Beautiful Music

CBX-FM Edmonton AB
*CION-FM Quebec PQ

Big Band

*CFEP-FM Eastern Passage NS

Black

CHRY-FM Toronto ON

Blues

*CBR-FM Calgary AB
CHMC-FM Edmonton AB
*CHRW-FM London ON
*CKRZ-FM Ohsweken ON
CKLX-FM Montreal PQ

Chinese

CKER-FM Edmonton AB
CJVB(AM) Richmond BC
CHMB(AM) Vancouver BC
CHKT(AM) Toronto ON

Christian

CJSI-FM Calgary AB
CJCA(AM) Edmonton AB
CJGY-FM Grande Prairie AB
CKVN-FM Lethbridge AB
CJLT-FM Medicine Hat AB
CIAJ-FM Prince Rupert BC
CFEQ-FM Winnipeg MB
CHVN-FM Winnipeg MB
CKJS(AM) Winnipeg MB
CJFY-FM Blackville NB
CIXN-FM Fredericton NB
CJRI-FM Fredericton NB
CITA-FM Moncton NB
CKOE-FM Moncton NB
CINB-FM Saint John NB
CJLU-FM Halifax NS
CINU-FM Truro NS
CFSH-FM Apsley ON
CJLF-FM Barrie ON
CKJJ-FM Belleville ON
CFWC-FM Brantford ON
CKGW-FM Chatham ON
*CJIV-FM Dryden ON
CJTW-FM Kitchener-Waterloo ON
CHJX-FM London ON
CJYE(AM) Oakville ON
CHRI-FM Ottawa ON
CJTL-FM Pickle Lake ON
CJTK-FM Sudbury ON
CKSO-FM Sudbury ON
*CJOA-FM Thunder Bay ON
*CHIM-FM Timmins ON
CJFH-FM Woodstock ON
CHIC-FM Rouyn-Noranda PQ
CFAQ-FM Blucher SK
CIOT-FM Nipawin SK
CJJC-FM Yorkton SK
CIAY-FM Whitehorse YT

Classic Rock

CFGQ-FM Calgary AB
CJAQ-FM Calgary AB
CJXK-FM Cold Lake AB
CFBR-FM Edmonton AB
CIRK-FM Edmonton AB
CJRY-FM Edmonton AB
CHFT-FM Fort McMurray AB
CKYX-FM Fort McMurray AB
CFRI-FM Grande Prairie AB
CFRV-FM Lethbridge AB
CKJX-FM Olds AB
CFDV-FM Red Deer AB
CFXW-FM Whitecourt AB
CKQR-FM Castlegar BC
CKNL-FM Fort St. John BC
CKGF-FM-2 Greenwood BC
CJUI-FM Kelowna BC
CKKO-FM Kelowna BC
CFMI-FM New Westminster BC
CKDV-FM Prince George BC
CFNR-FM Terrace BC
CKKQ-FM Victoria BC
CKX-FM Brandon MB
CHTM(AM) Thompson MB
CITI-FM Winnipeg MB
CFAI-FM Edmundston NB
CIBX-FM Fredericton NB
CJMO-FM Moncton NB
CJYC-FM Saint John NB
CFOZ-FM Argentia NF

CJOZ-FM Bonavista Bay NF
CJKK-FM Clarenville NF
CKOZ-FM Corner Brook NF
CKXD-FM Gander NF
CKXG-FM Grand Falls-Windsor NF
CIOZ-FM Marystown NF
CHOS-FM Rattling Brook NF
CKSS-FM Red Rocks NF
CHOZ-FM Saint John's NF
VOCM-FM Saint John's NF
CIOS-FM Stephenville NF
CFRQ-FM Dartmouth NS
CHNS-FM Halifax NS
CHER-FM Sydney NS
CJIJ-FM Sydney NS
CKIQ-FM Iqaluit NU
CFJB-FM Barrie ON
CJXY-FM Burlington ON
CJJM-FM Espanola ON
CFZN-FM Haliburton ON
CKTI-FM Kettle Point ON
CFMK-FM Kingston ON
CFCA-FM Kitchener ON
CICZ-FM Midland ON
CILQ-FM North York ON
*CKRZ-FM Ohsweken ON
CKDO(AM) Oshawa ON
CKGE-FM Oshawa ON
CHEZ-FM Ottawa ON
CKQB-FM Ottawa ON
CJTN-FM Quinte West ON
CHNO-FM Sudbury ON
CKTG-FM Thunder Bay ON
CIXL-FM Welland ON
CKDK-FM Woodstock ON
CKQK-FM Charlottetown PE
CJRW-FM Summerside PE
CFVM-FM Amqui PQ
CFOM-FM Levis PQ
CHOM-FM Montreal PQ
CHNC-FM New Carlisle PQ
CJMF-FM Quebec PQ
CKIA-FM Quebec PQ
CFYX-FM Rimouski PQ
CFJO-FM Thetford Mines PQ
CHGO-FM Val d'Or PQ
CJNE-FM Nipawin SK
CFMM-FM Prince Albert SK
CFWF-FM Regina SK
CIZL-FM Regina SK
CKCK-FM Regina SK
CFET-FM Tagish YT
CHON-FM Whitehorse YT

Classical

*CBR-FM Calgary AB
CBX-FM Edmonton AB
CKUA(AM) Edmonton AB
*CKUA-FM Edmonton AB
*CBZ-FM Fredericton NB
CBA-FM Moncton NB
*CBN-FM Saint John's NF
*VOWR(AM) Saint John's NF
*CBH-FM Halifax NS
CFMX-FM Cobourg ON
*CBOQ-FM Ottawa ON
*CBOX-FM Ottawa ON
CBL-FM Toronto ON
CFMZ-FM Toronto ON
CJBC-FM Toronto ON
*CBE-FM Windsor ON
*CBJX-FM Chicoutimi PQ
CHLX-FM Gatineau PQ
CBF-FM Montreal PQ
CBM-FM Montreal PQ
CJPX-FM Montreal PQ
*CBVX-FM Quebec PQ
CJSQ-FM Quebec PQ
*CKRL-FM Quebec PQ
*CBRX-FM Rimouski PQ
CBF-FM-1 Trois Rivieres PQ
*CBK-FM Regina SK
*CBKS-FM Saskatoon SK

Comedy

CJRP-FM Saint John NB

Contemporary Hit/Top-40

CJEG-FM Bonnyville AB
CIBQ(AM) Brooks AB
CIBK-FM Calgary AB
CHBN-FM Edmonton AB
CKNG-FM Edmonton AB
CFXE-FM Edson AB
CKOS-FM Fort McMurray AB
CFGP-FM Grande Prairie AB
CFRV-FM Lethbridge AB
CIZZ-FM Red Deer AB
CKIK-FM Red Deer AB
CJBZ-FM Taber AB
CFCP-FM Courtenay BC
CKRX-FM Fort Nelson BC
CKRV-FM Kamloops BC
CKTK-FM Kitimat BC
CHTK(AM) Prince Rupert BC
CKDM(AM) Dauphin MB
CJPG-FM Portage la Prairie MB
CICY-FM Selkirk MB
CKMM-FM Winnipeg MB
CKLE-FM Bathurst NB
CKNB(AM) Campbellton NB
CJEM-FM Edmundston NB
CKTP-FM Fredericton Centre NB
CKMV-FM Grand Falls NB
CHWV-FM Saint John NB
CFOZ-FM Argentia NF
CJOZ-FM Bonavista Bay NF
CJKK-FM Clarenville NF
CKOZ-FM Corner Brook NF
CIFX-FM Lewisporte NF
CIOZ-FM Marystown NF
CHOS-FM Rattling Brook NF
CKSS-FM Red Rocks NF
CHOZ-FM Saint John's NF
CKIX-FM Saint John's NF
CIOS-FM Stephenville NF
CJFX-FM Antigonish NS
CJIJ-FM Sydney NS
CKPE-FM Sydney NS
CKMB-FM Barrie ON
CJOJ-FM Belleville ON
CKPC(AM) Brantford ON
CKEY-FM Fort Erie ON
CKAP-FM Kapuskasing ON
CKBT-FM Kitchener-Waterloo ON
CHST-FM London ON
CIDC-FM Orangeville ON
CHRI-FM Ottawa ON
CIHT-FM Ottawa ON
CKDR-FM-5 Red Lake ON
CKDR-FM-2 Sioux Lookout ON
CFHK-FM St. Thomas ON
CHYC-FM Sudbury ON
CKIS-FM Toronto ON
CKYK-FM Alma PQ
CFVM-FM Amqui PQ
CIEU-FM Carleton PQ
CHAI-FM Chateauguay PQ
CKXO-FM Chibougamau PQ
CFVD-FM Degelis PQ
CFTX-FM Gatineau PQ
*CKRK-FM Kahnawake PQ
CHOX-FM La Pocatiere PQ
CFLM(AM) La Tuque PQ
CBGA-FM Matane PQ
CKMF-FM Montreal PQ
CFVD-FM-2 Pohenegamook PQ
CIPC-FM Port-Cartier PQ
CKMN-FM Rimouski-Mont Joli PQ
CJMM-FM Rouyn-Noranda PQ
CIGB-FM Trois Rivieres PQ
CKOI-FM Verdun PQ
CKJH(AM) Melfort SK
CFMM-FM Prince Albert SK
CKRW(AM) Whitehorse YT

Country

CJPR-FM Blairmore AB
CIBQ(AM) Brooks AB
CKRY-FM Calgary AB
CFCW(AM) Camrose AB
CIBW-FM Drayton Valley AB
CKDQ(AM) Drumheller AB
CFWE-FM-4 Edmonton AB
CISN-FM Edmonton AB
CJOK-FM Fort McMurray AB
CFRI-FM Grande Prairie AB
CJXX-FM Grande Prairie AB
CKHL-FM High Level AB
CKVH(AM) High Prairie AB
CHRB(AM) High River AB
CFXO-FM High River-Okotoks AB
CHLB-FM Lethbridge AB
CKSA-FM Lloydminster AB
CHAT-FM Medicine Hat AB
CKLJ-FM Olds AB
CKYL(AM) Peace River AB
CKGY-FM Red Deer AB
CHBW-FM Rocky Mountain House AB
CHLW-FM Saint Paul AB
CKSQ-FM Stettler AB
CKKY-FM Wainwright AB
CFOK(AM) Westlock AB
CIHS-FM Wetaskiwin AB
CKJR(AM) Wetaskiwin AB
CIXM-FM Whitecourt AB
CKBX(AM) 100 Mile House BC
CKQC-FM Abbotsford BC
CHBZ-FM Cranbrook BC
CJDC(AM) Dawson Creek BC
CKFU-FM Fort St. John BC
CJKC-FM Kamloops BC
CKOV-FM Kelowna BC
CIGV-FM Penticton BC
CJCI-FM Prince George BC
CKCQ-FM Quesnel BC
CJFW-FM Terrace BC
CHMZ-FM Tofino BC
CJJR-FM Vancouver BC
CIVH(AM) Vanderhoof BC
CKWL(AM) Williams Lake BC
CKLQ(AM) Brandon MB
CKXA-FM Brandon MB
CKDM(AM) Dauphin MB
CFRY(AM) Portage la Prairie MB
CFRY-FM Portage la Prairie MB
CFPX-FM Pukatawagan MB
CFQX-FM Selkirk MB
CICY-FM Selkirk MB
CJAR(AM) The Pas MB
CHTM(AM) Thompson MB
CKMW(AM) Winkler-Morden MB
CHNK-FM Winnipeg MB
CKNB(AM) Campbellton NB
CFXY-FM Fredericton NB
CKHJ(AM) Fredericton NB
CJXL-FM Moncton NB
CHSJ-FM Saint John NB
CHTD-FM Saint Stephen NB
CJSE-FM Shediac NB
CKIM(AM) Baie Verte NF
CHVO-FM Carbonear NF
CFLC-FM Churchill Falls NF
CKVO(AM) Clarenville NF
CFCB(AM) Corner Brook NF
CKGA(AM) Gander NF
CKCM(AM) Grand Falls NF
CHCM(AM) Marystown NF
CFNW(AM) Port au Choix NF
CFCV-FM Saint Andrews NF
CJYQ(AM) Saint John's NF
VOCM(AM) Saint John's NF
*VOWR(AM) Saint John's NF
CFSX(AM) Stephenville NF
CFLW(AM) Wabush NF
*CKJM-FM Cheticamp NS
CKDY(AM) Digby NS
CHFX-FM Halifax NS
CKEN-FM Kentville NS
CKAD(AM) Middleton NS
CJCB(AM) Sydney NS

CKCH-FM Sydney NS
CKTY-FM Truro NS
CFAB(AM) Windsor NS
CKLB-FM Yellowknife NT
CJKX-FM Ajax ON
CHCQ-FM Belleville ON
CJBQ(AM) Belleville ON
CFCO(AM) Chatham ON
CING-FM Hamilton ON
CFQK-FM Kaministiquia ON
CKTI-FM Kettle Point ON
CKXC-FM Kingston ON
CIKZ-FM Kitchener-Waterloo ON
CJSP-FM Leamington ON
CFRM-FM Little Current ON
CJBX-FM London ON
*CHMO(AM) Moosonee ON
CKAT-FM North Bay ON
*CKRZ-FM Ohsweken ON
CICX-FM Orillia ON
CKYC-FM Owen Sound ON
CHVR-FM Pembroke ON
CKQM-FM Peterborough ON
CJHR-FM Renfrew ON
CHOK(AM) Sarnia ON
CJQM-FM Sault Ste. Marie ON
CKBY-FM Smiths Falls ON
CICS-FM Sudbury ON
CJDL-FM Tillsonburg ON
CKOT(AM) Tillsonburg ON
CKNX(AM) Wingham ON
CFCY-FM Charlottetown PE
CFGT(AM) Alma PQ
CFVD-FM Degelis PQ
CHIP-FM Fort Coulonge PQ
*CFTH-FM-1 Harrington Harbour PQ
CKAJ-FM Jonquiere PQ
*CKRK-FM Kahnawake PQ
*CFIN-FM Lac-Etchemin PQ
CFIC-FM Listuguj PQ
CHRG-FM Maria (Reserve) PQ
CHNC-FM New Carlisle PQ
CKIA-FM Quebec PQ
CKMN-FM Rimouski-Mont Joli PQ
CJMS(AM) Saint Constant PQ
CJSL(AM) Estevan SK
CFMQ-FM Hudson Bay SK
CKVX-FM Kindersley SK
CJLR-FM La Ronge SK
CFDM-FM Meadow Lake SK
CJNS-FM Meadow Lake SK
CJNS-FM Meadow Lake SK
CJVR-FM Melfort SK
CILG-FM Moose Jaw SK
CJNB(AM) North Battleford SK
CHBD-FM Regina SK
CKRM(AM) Regina SK
CJWW(AM) Saskatoon SK
CJSN(AM) Shaunavon SK
CKSW(AM) Swift Current SK
CFSL(AM) Weyburn SK
CJGX(AM) Yorkton SK
CHON-FM Whitehorse YT

Diversified

*CBR(AM) Calgary AB
*CHFA(AM) Edmonton AB
CKUA(AM) Edmonton AB
*CKUA-FM Edmonton AB
*CJSF-FM Burnaby BC
CHET-FM Chetwynd BC
CHAD-FM Dawson Creek BC
CFBX-FM Kamloops BC
CHLY-FM Nanaimo BC
*CJLY-FM Nelson BC
*CFUR-FM Prince George BC
CBUF-FM Vancouver BC
*CITR-FM Vancouver BC
*CFUV-FM Victoria BC
*CKSB(AM) Saint Boniface MB
CKXL-FM Saint Boniface MB
CICY-FM Selkirk MB
*CBWK-FM Thompson MB
CBW(AM) Winnipeg MB
CBW-FM Winnipeg MB

*CKUW-FM Winnipeg MB
CJVA(AM) Caraquet NB
CBZF-FM Fredericton NB
CHSR-FM Fredericton NB
*CFJU-FM Kedgwick NB
*CHMA-FM Sackville NB
CJRM-FM Labrador City NF
*CBN(AM) Saint John's NF
*CHMR-FM Saint John's NF
*VOWR(AM) Saint John's NF
*CIFA-FM Comeauville NS
CBHA-FM Halifax NS
*CBH-FM Halifax NS
*CKDU-FM Halifax NS
CFCT(AM) Tuktoyaktuk NT
*CFYK(AM) Yellowknife NT
CKON-FM Akwesasne ON
CKOL-FM Campbellford ON
CKUN-FM Christian Island ON
CFDY-FM Cochrane ON
*CFRU-FM Guelph ON
*CFMU-FM Hamilton ON
CFBW-FM Hanover ON
CHCR-FM Killaloe ON
CBBK-FM Kingston ON
*CFRC-FM Kingston ON
*CKVI-FM Kingston ON
CKWR-FM Kitchener ON
CJIQ-FM Kitchener/Paris ON
CBBL-FM London ON
CJBC-FM-4 London ON
*CHMO(AM) Moosonee ON
*CKRZ-FM Ohsweken ON
*CBOQ-FM Ottawa ON
*CBOX-FM Ottawa ON
CKAV-FM-9 Ottawa ON
CKCU-FM Ottawa ON
CKQB-FM Ottawa ON
CFFF-FM Peterborough ON
CHRY-FM Toronto ON
*CKMS-FM Waterloo ON
*CBE(AM) Windsor ON
*CBEF-FM Windsor ON
*CBE-FM Windsor ON
CFMF-FM Fermont PQ
CFIM-FM Iles-de-la-Madeleine PQ
CKAJ-FM Jonquiere PQ
CBOF-1(AM) Maniwaki PQ
CBGA-FM Matane PQ
CIRA-FM Montreal PQ
*CKUT-FM Montreal PQ
CKVL-FM Montreal (zone LaSalle) PQ
CKAG-FM Pikogan PQ
CFVD-FM-2 Pohenegamook PQ
CBVE-FM Quebec PQ
CKIA-FM Quebec PQ
CHRL-FM Roberval PQ
*CBSI-FM Sept-Iles PQ
CFLX-FM Sherbrooke PQ
CFOU-FM Trois Rivieres PQ
CIAX-FM Windsor PQ
*CBKF-1(AM) Gravelbourg SK
CFMQ-FM Hudson Bay SK
CJLR-FM La Ronge SK
*CBK(AM) Regina SK
CBKF-FM Regina SK
*CJTR-FM Regina SK
CBKF-2(AM) Saskatoon SK
*CBKS-FM Saskatoon SK
CIDD-FM White Bear Lake Resort SK

Drama/Literature

CBF-FM-1 Trois Rivieres PQ

Easy Listening

CKOR(AM) Penticton BC
CHOR(AM) Summerland BC
CJRB(AM) Boissevain MB
*CFEP-FM Eastern Passage NS
CHPR-FM Hawkesbury ON
CKHK-FM Hawkesbury ON
CFFX-FM Kingston ON
CJHR-FM Renfrew ON

CKOT-FM Tillsonburg ON
CFMQ-FM Hudson Bay SK

Educational

CHDH-FM Siksika AB
*CBG(AM) Gander NF
CBT(AM) Grand Falls-Windsor NF
*CFGB-FM Happy Valley NF
*CBCS-FM Sudbury ON
CJBC(AM) Toronto ON
*CHYZ-FM Sainte Foy PQ
*CBSI-FM Sept-Iles PQ

Eskimo

CKQN-FM Baker Lake NU

Ethnic

CHKF-FM Calgary AB
CFWE-FM-4 Edmonton AB
CKER-FM Edmonton AB
CJVB(AM) Richmond BC
CHKG-FM Vancouver BC
CJRJ(AM) Vancouver BC
CKYE-FM Vancouver BC
CKJS(AM) Winnipeg MB
*CFRU-FM Guelph ON
*CFMU-FM Hamilton ON
CINA(AM) Mississauga ON
CJMR(AM) Oakville ON
CJLL-FM Ottawa ON
CHHA(AM) Toronto ON
CHKT(AM) Toronto ON
CHTO(AM) Toronto ON
CJSA-FM Toronto ON
CKHC-FM Toronto ON
*CJAM-FM Windsor ON
CHUK-FM Mashteuiatsh (Pointe-Bleue) PQ
CFMB(AM) Montreal PQ
CHOU(AM) Montreal PQ
CJWI(AM) Montreal PQ
CKDG-FM Montreal PQ
CJLR-FM La Ronge SK

Filipino

CJSA-FM Toronto ON

Folk

*VOWR(AM) Saint John's NF
*CKJM-FM Cheticamp NS

Foreign/Ethnic

CHMB(AM) Vancouver BC
CKQN-FM Baker Lake NU
CIAO(AM) Brampton ON
CHIN(AM) Toronto ON
CHIN-FM Toronto ON
CIRV-FM Toronto ON
CINQ-FM Montreal PQ
CJCF-FM Cumberland House SK

French

CBCX-FM Calgary AB
CBRF-FM Calgary AB
*CKRP-FM Falher AB
CKXU-FM Lethbridge AB
CBUX-FM Vancouver BC
CILS-FM Victoria BC
*CKSB(AM) Saint Boniface MB
CKXL-FM Saint Boniface MB
*CFJU-FM Kedgwick NB
CKMA-FM Miramichi NB
*CBAF-FM Moncton NB
CFBO-FM Moncton NB
CHOY-FM Moncton NB
CKUM-FM Moncton NB
CKRO-FM Pokemouche NB

CHQC-FM Saint John NB
CJRM-FM Labrador City NF
CKRH-FM Halifax NS
CIVR-FM Yellowknife NT
CFRT-FM Iqaluit NU
CHOD-FM Cornwall ON
CHYK-FM-3 Hearst ON
CKGN-FM Kapuskasing ON
CJBC-FM-4 London ON
*CHUO-FM Ottawa ON
*CFRH-FM Penetanguishene ON
CFSF-FM Sturgeon Falls ON
CHYK-FM Timmins ON
CHOQ-FM Toronto ON
CFID-FM Acton Vale PQ
CHOW-FM Amos PQ
CFMV-FM Chandler PQ
CKII-FM Dolbeau-Mistassini PQ
CJDM-FM Drummondville PQ
CFMF-FM Fermont PQ
CHIP-FM Fort Coulonge PQ
CFTX-FM Gatineau PQ
CHLX-FM Gatineau PQ
CJRC-FM Gatineau PQ
CHME-FM Les Escoumins PQ
CHHO-FM Louiseville PQ
CHUK-FM Mashteuiatsh (Pointe-Bleue) PQ
CHEF-FM Matagami PQ
CFLO-FM Mont-Laurier PQ
CINQ-FM Montreal PQ
CHOI-FM Quebec PQ
CHIC-FM Rouyn-Noranda PQ
*CHYZ-FM Sainte Foy PQ
CFUT-FM Shawinigan PQ
CFAK-FM Sherbrooke PQ
CFLX-FM Sherbrooke PQ
CKOY-FM Sherbrooke PQ
CJTB-FM Tete-a-la-Baleine PQ
CJEB-FM Trois Rivieres PQ
CJVD-FM Vaudreuil-Dorion PQ
CFRG-FM Gravelbourg SK

Full Service

CHMS-FM Bancroft ON

German

CHPD-FM Aylmer ON

Golden Oldies

CHAB(AM) Moose Jaw SK
CJNE-FM Nipawin SK

Gospel

CIHS-FM Wetaskiwin AB
CJRI-FM Fredericton NB
*VOAR(AM) Mount Pearl NF

Greek

CHTO(AM) Toronto ON

Hindi

CJSA-FM Toronto ON

Inspirational

CJRB(AM) Boissevain MB

Jazz

*CJSW-FM Calgary AB
CKUA(AM) Edmonton AB
*CKUA-FM Edmonton AB
CBAX-FM Halifax NS
CBHA-FM Halifax NS
CBBL-FM London ON
*CHRW-FM London ON
CBBS-FM Sudbury ON

*CKLU-FM Sudbury ON
*CJRT-FM Toronto ON
*CBJX-FM Chicoutimi PQ
CHLX-FM Gatineau PQ
CKLX-FM Montreal PQ
*CKRL-FM Quebec PQ
*CBRX-FM Rimouski PQ
*CBK-FM Regina SK
*CBKS-FM Saskatoon SK

Jewish

CJRS(AM) Montreal PQ

Light Rock

CHMC-FM Edmonton AB
CIOC-FM Victoria BC
CKXL-FM Saint Boniface MB
CKDH(AM) Amherst NS
CFLT-FM Dartmouth NS
CKNR-FM Elliot Lake ON
CFFX-FM Kingston ON
CKGB-FM Timmins ON
CIMF-FM Gatineau PQ
CHOE-FM Matane PQ
CHEY-FM Trois Rivieres PQ
CHSN-FM Estevan SK

MOR

*CHFA(AM) Edmonton AB
CHET-FM Chetwynd BC
CHAD-FM Dawson Creek BC
CISL(AM) Richmond BC
CFTK(AM) Terrace BC
CFAM(AM) Altona MB
CHSM(AM) Steinbach MB
CJVA(AM) Caraquet NB
CKRO-FM Pokemouche NB
CKHR-FM Hay River NT
CHOD-FM Cornwall ON
CJMI-FM Strathroy ON
CFZM(AM) Toronto ON
CJAN-FM Asbestos PQ
CHLC-FM Baie Comeau PQ
CFIX-FM Chicoutimi PQ
CHVD-FM Dolbeau-Mistassini PQ
CHRD-FM Drummondville PQ
CFRP(AM) Forestville PQ
CJRG-FM Gaspe PQ
CILE-FM Havre-Saint-Pierre PQ
CJLM-FM Joliette PQ
CJIT-FM Lac Megantic PQ
*CFIN-FM Lac-Etchemin PQ
CHEF-FM Matagami PQ
CHRM-FM Matane PQ
CKNA-FM Natashquan PQ
CKYQ-FM Plessisville PQ
CJBR-FM Rimouski PQ
CJRE-FM Riviere au Renard PQ
CFNJ-FM Saint Gabriel-de-Brandon PQ
CIHO-FM Saint Hilarion PQ
CJDS-FM Saint Pamphile PQ
CJMC-FM Sainte Anne des Monts PQ
CHEQ-FM Sainte-Marie-de-Beauce PQ
CKBI(AM) Prince Albert SK
CJSN(AM) Shaunavon SK
CIMG-FM Swift Current SK

Native American

CKAV-FM-2 Vancouver BC
CICU-FM Eskasoni Indian Reserve NS
CKAV-FM Toronto ON
CKUJ-FM Kuujjuaq PQ

News

CFFR(AM) Calgary AB
*CJSW-FM Calgary AB
CBX-FM Edmonton AB
CHQT(AM) Edmonton AB
CFML-FM Burnaby BC

CBTE-FM Crawford Bay BC
CHNL(AM) Kamloops BC
*CBTK-FM Kelowna BC
CJNL(AM) Merritt BC
*CFPR-FM Prince Rupert BC
CKWX(AM) Vancouver BC
CKIZ-FM Vernon BC
*CBAF-FM Moncton NB
CBAM-FM Moncton NB
CBD-FM Saint John NB
CBGY(AM) Bonavista Bay NF
*CIFA-FM Comeauville NS
CBHA-FM Halifax NS
CBQX-FM Kenora ON
CHSC(AM) Saint Catharines ON
CBEG-FM Sarnia ON
*CBQT-FM Thunder Bay ON
CFTR(AM) Toronto ON
CHUM(AM) Toronto ON
CBMI-FM Baie Comeau PQ
CHRD-FM Drummondville PQ
*CBV-FM-6 La Malbaie PQ
CFBS-FM Lourdes-de-Blanc-Sablon PQ
CKWE-FM Maniwaki (Kitigan Zibi Anishinabeg Reserve) PQ
CBME-FM Montreal PQ
CFEI-FM Saint Hyacinthe PQ
CINF(AM) Verdun PQ
CFMM-FM Prince Albert SK
*CBK(AM) Regina SK

News/talk

*CBR(AM) Calgary AB
CHQR(AM) Calgary AB
CBX(AM) Edmonton AB
*CHFA(AM) Edmonton AB
CHDH-FM Siksika AB
CKFR(AM) Kelowna BC
CKNW(AM) New Westminster BC
*CBU(AM) Vancouver BC
*CFRO-FM Vancouver BC
CFAX(AM) Victoria BC
CJOB(AM) Winnipeg MB
*CKUW-FM Winnipeg MB
*CBZ-FM Fredericton NB
CKNI-FM Moncton NB
CHNI-FM Saint John NB
CKIM(AM) Baie Verte NF
*CBY(AM) Corner Brook NF
*CBG(AM) Gander NF
CKGA-FM Gander NF
*CBN-FM Saint John's NF
VOCM(AM) Saint John's NF
CJNI-FM Halifax NS
*CHAK(AM) Inuvik NT
*CFYK-FM Yellowknife NT
CFFB(AM) Iqaluit NU
CJUL(AM) Cornwall ON
CHML(AM) Hamilton ON
CKGL-FM Kitchener ON
CFPL(AM) London ON
CJBK(AM) London ON
CFRA(AM) Ottawa ON
CFOS(AM) Owen Sound ON
CKTB(AM) Saint Catharines ON
*CBCS-FM Sudbury ON
*CKLU-FM Sudbury ON
*CBQ-FM Thunder Bay ON
CFMJ(AM) Toronto ON
CFRB(AM) Toronto ON
*CBE(AM) Windsor ON
CKLW(AM) Windsor ON
CBJ-FM Chicoutimi PQ
CHXX-FM Donnacona PQ
CFIM-FM Iles-de-la-Madeleine PQ
CBGA-FM Matane PQ
CJAD(AM) Montreal PQ
CBVE-FM Quebec PQ
*CBV-FM Quebec PQ
CJBR-FM Rimouski PQ
CBGN(AM) Sainte Anne des Monts PQ
CKCN-FM Sept-Iles PQ
CKSM(AM) Shawinigan PQ
CFLX-FM Sherbrooke PQ

CJME(AM) Regina SK
CJWW(AM) Saskatoon SK
CKOM(AM) Saskatoon SK

Nostalgia

CJNU-FM Winnipeg MB
*CFIN-FM Lac-Etchemin PQ
CFAV(AM) Laval PQ

Oldies

CFXL-FM Calgary AB
CFXH-FM Hinton AB
CKCL-FM Chilliwack BC
CKLR-FM Courtenay BC
CHAD-FM Dawson Creek BC
CJNL(AM) Merritt BC
CIBH-FM Parksville BC
CFIS-FM Prince George BC
CKKS-FM Sechelt BC
CFRW(AM) Winnipeg MB
CFRK-FM Fredericton NB
CFBC(AM) Saint John NB
CFCV-FM Saint Andrews NF
*VOWR(AM) Saint John's NF
CBI-FM Sydney NS
CKPC(AM) Brantford ON
CJOY(AM) Guelph ON
CKOC(AM) Hamilton ON
CKKW-FM Kitchener ON
CKSL(AM) London ON
CIWW(AM) Ottawa ON
CJMJ-FM Ottawa ON
CKKL-FM Ottawa ON
CFOS(AM) Owen Sound ON
CKRU(AM) Peterborough ON
CKDR-FM-2 Sioux Lookout ON
CJCS(AM) Stratford ON
CHTN-FM Charlottetown PE
*CFTH-FM-1 Harrington Harbour PQ
CFOM-FM Levis PQ
CHRG-FM Maria (Reserve) PQ
CINW(AM) Montreal PQ
CFEI-FM Saint Hyacinthe PQ
CFZZ-FM Saint Jean-Iberville PQ
CJVD-FM Vaudreuil-Dorion PQ
CFYM(AM) Kindersley SK
CFNK-FM Pinehouse Lake SK
CKBI(AM) Prince Albert SK
CJYM(AM) Rosetown SK

Other

*CBR(AM) Calgary AB
CFCW-FM Camrose AB
CKRA-FM Edmonton AB
CHET-FM Chetwynd BC
*CFPR(AM) Prince Rupert BC
CKIZ-FM Vernon BC
*CBCV-FM Victoria BC
CHTT-FM Victoria BC
*CBAF-FM Moncton NB
*CBAL-FM Moncton NB
CKCW-FM Moncton NB
CKUL-FM Halifax NS
CFFB(AM) Iqaluit NU
CJDV-FM Cambridge ON
CKGN-FM Kapuskasing ON
CJTT-FM New Liskeard ON
CFXN-FM North Bay ON
CBQS-FM Sioux Narrows ON
CJET-FM Smiths Falls ON
CHIP-FM Fort Coulonge PQ
CKAJ-FM Jonquiere PQ
*CBV-FM-6 La Malbaie PQ
CHUT-FM Lac-Simon (Louvicourt) PQ
CINQ-FM Montreal PQ
CKIA-FM Quebec PQ
CFRG-FM Gravelbourg SK

Progressive

CKCU-FM Ottawa ON
CFNY-FM Toronto ON
*CJAM-FM Windsor ON

Public Affairs

*CKRP-FM Falher AB
CBTE-FM Crawford Bay BC
*CBTK-FM Kelowna BC
CBYG-FM Prince George BC
*CFRO-FM Vancouver BC
CFNC(AM) Cross Lake MB
CBAM-FM Moncton NB
CBGY(AM) Bonavista Bay NF
CBI(AM) Sydney NS
CJLX-FM Belleville ON
*CFMU-FM Hamilton ON
CBQX-FM Kenora ON
CKCU-FM Ottawa ON
CBQL-FM Savant Lake ON
*CBQ-FM Thunder Bay ON
CBLA-FM Toronto ON
CBL-FM Toronto ON
*CKMS-FM Waterloo ON
CBMI-FM Baie Comeau PQ
*CHOC-FM Saint Remi PQ
*CBKA-FM La Ronge SK

Religious

CHRB(AM) High River AB
*VOAR(AM) Mount Pearl NF
CHSB-FM Bedford NS
CKKK-FM Peterborough ON
CJTK-FM Sudbury ON
CIRA-FM Montreal PQ
CJRS(AM) Montreal PQ
*CION-FM Quebec PQ
CKSW(AM) Swift Current SK

Rock/AOR

CFNA-FM Bonnyville AB
CJAY-FM Calgary AB
CFBR-FM Edmonton AB
CHDI-FM Edmonton AB
CJRX-FM Lethbridge AB
CKLM-FM Lloydminster AB
CKMH-FM Medicine Hat AB
CKBX(AM) 100 Mile House BC
CHWK-FM Chilliwack BC
CKSR-FM Chilliwack BC
CHDR-FM Cranbrook BC
CJDR-FM Fernie BC
CHRX-FM Fort St. John BC
CKGR(AM) Golden BC
CKIR(AM) Invermere BC
CIFM-FM Kamloops BC

CHWF-FM Nanaimo BC
CHNV-FM Nelson BC
CJMG-FM Penticton BC
CFNI(AM) Port Hardy BC
CIRX-FM Prince George BC
CJCI-FM Prince George BC
CKCQ-FM Quesnel BC
CKCR(AM) Revelstoke BC
CHMZ-FM Tofino BC
CFOX-FM Vancouver BC
CIVH(AM) Vanderhoof BC
CJZN-FM Victoria BC
CFFM-FM Williams Lake BC
CKWL(AM) Williams Lake BC
CFPX-FM Pukatawagan MB
CFEQ-FM Winnipeg MB
CJKR-FM Winnipeg MB
*CKUW-FM Winnipeg MB
CFXY-FM Fredericton NB
CJRP-FM Saint John NB
CKXX-FM Corner Brook NF
CIJK-FM Kentville NS
CKTO-FM Truro NS
CFJB-FM Barrie ON
CJLX-FM Belleville ON
CKUE-FM Chatham ON
CJSS-FM Cornwall ON
CJBB-FM Englehart ON
CKJN-FM Haldimand County ON
CIKR-FM Kingston ON
CHYM-FM Kitchener ON
CKFX-FM North Bay ON
CKGE-FM Oshawa ON
CKQB-FM Ottawa ON
CKWF-FM Peterborough ON
CHTZ-FM Saint Catharines ON
CHKS-FM Sarnia ON
CJRQ-FM Sudbury ON
CJSD-FM Thunder Bay ON
CFNY-FM Toronto ON
CIMX-FM Windsor ON
CIBU-FM Wingham ON
CFMV-FM Chandler PQ
CKTF-FM Gatineau PQ
CFOR-FM Maniwaki PQ
*CKRL-FM Quebec PQ
CIKI-FM Rimouski PQ
CIBM-FM Riviere du Loup PQ
CHUN-FM Rouyn-Noranda PQ
CKGS-FM Saguenay (zone La Baie) PQ
CHJM-FM Saint Georges PQ
CKOY-FM Sherbrooke PQ
CJSO-FM Sorel PQ
CFJO-FM Thetford Mines PQ
CJCQ-FM North Battleford SK
CJHD-FM North Battleford SK
CHQX-FM Prince Albert SK
CJDJ-FM Saskatoon SK
CKRC-FM Weyburn SK

Smooth Jazz

CHMC-FM Edmonton AB
CJGV-FM Winnipeg MB
CIWV-FM Hamilton ON

Spanish

CHHA(AM) Toronto ON

Sports

CFAC(AM) Calgary AB
CHQR(AM) Calgary AB
CFRN(AM) Edmonton AB
CHED(AM) Edmonton AB
CHNL(AM) Kamloops BC
CKFR(AM) Kelowna BC
CKNW(AM) New Westminster BC
CKST(AM) Vancouver BC
CHML(AM) Hamilton ON
CKGL(AM) Kitchener ON
CFPL(AM) London ON
CFGO(AM) Ottawa ON
CJCL(AM) Toronto ON
CKAC(AM) Montreal PQ
CKGM(AM) Montreal PQ
CHRC(AM) Quebec PQ
CKSM(AM) Shawinigan PQ

Talk

CHED(AM) Edmonton AB
CHNL(AM) Kamloops BC
CFUN(AM) Vancouver BC
CHMJ(AM) Vancouver BC
*CBWK-FM Thompson MB
CBD-FM Saint John NB
CBDQ-FM Labrador City NF
CIFX-FM Lewisporte NF
CBQR-FM Rankin Inlet NU
CJBQ(AM) Belleville ON
CHAM(AM) Hamilton ON
CFGO(AM) Ottawa ON
CBLA-FM Toronto ON
CIRR-FM Toronto ON
CJCL(AM) Toronto ON
*CJAM-FM Windsor ON
*CBCT-FM Charlottetown PE
CFGT(AM) Alma PQ
CBJE-FM Chicoutimi PQ
CIDI-FM Lac-Brome PQ
CHMP-FM Longueuil PQ
CKWE-FM Maniwaki (Kitigan Zibi Anishinabeg Reserve) PQ
*CIBL-FM Montreal PQ
CJMF-FM Quebec PQ
*CBRX-FM Rimouski PQ
CKRS-FM Saguenay PQ
CFND-FM Saint Jerome PQ

*CBSI-FM Sept-Iles PQ
CHLT-FM Sherbrooke PQ
CHLN-FM Trois Rivieres PQ
*CBK(AM) Regina SK
*CFWH(AM) Whitehorse YT

Top-40

CFUL-FM Calgary AB
CFBT-FM Vancouver BC
CJCH-FM Halifax NS
CKHZ-FM Halifax NS
CHRK-FM Sydney NS
CFIF-FM Iroquois Falls ON
CIDC-FM Orangeville ON
CISS-FM Ottawa ON
CFSF-FM Sturgeon Falls ON
CHMT-FM Timmins ON
CIRR-FM Toronto ON
CFMF-FM Fermont PQ
CKTF-FM Gatineau PQ
CJIT-FM Lac Megantic PQ
CIMO-FM Magog PQ
CJMV-FM Val d'Or PQ
CFDM-FM Meadow Lake SK
CFWD-FM Saskatoon SK

Triple A

CFML-FM Burnaby BC
CHHR-FM Vancouver BC
CKPK-FM Vancouver BC

Urban Contemporary

CHPQ-FM Parksville BC
*CKUW-FM Winnipeg MB
CJRP-FM Saint John NB
*CIXX-FM London ON
CFXJ-FM Toronto ON

Variety/Diverse

CIGY-FM Calgary AB
CIAM-FM Fort Vermilion AB
CIKT-FM Grande Prairie AB
CKXU-FM Lethbridge AB
CIVL-FM Abbotsford BC
CFCH-FM Chase BC
CIDO-FM Creston BC
*CBTK-FM Kelowna BC
CHLS-FM Lillooet BC
CHMM-FM MacKenzie BC
CJMP-FM Powell River BC
CIMM-FM Ucluelet BC
*CBU(AM) Vancouver BC
CBUX-FM Vancouver BC
CJJJ-FM Brandon MB
CJSB-FM Swan River MB

CINC-FM Thompson MB
CJUM-FM Winnipeg MB
CIMS-FM Balmoral NB
CKUM-FM Moncton NB
CFMH-FM Saint John NB
*CBY(AM) Corner Brook NF
CFXU-FM Antigonish NS
*CKJM-FM Cheticamp NS
CKOA-FM Glace Bay NS
CBAX-FM Halifax NS
CKHR-FM Hay River NT
CBQR-FM Rankin Inlet NU
CHES-FM Erin ON
CFGI-FM Georgina Island ON
CKHA-FM Haliburton ON
CKGN-FM Kapuskasing ON
CKYM-FM Napanee ON
*CHOP-FM Newmarket ON
*CBOF-FM Ottawa ON
*CBO-FM Ottawa ON
CFBU-FM Saint Catharines ON
CJAI-FM Stella ON
CBBX-FM Sudbury ON
*CBON-FM Sudbury ON
*CKLU-FM Sudbury ON
CILU-FM Thunder Bay ON
CHOQ-FM Toronto ON
*CIUT-FM Toronto ON
CJBC(AM) Toronto ON
CFWP-FM Wahta Mohawk Territory near Bala ON
CIWS-FM Whitchurch-Stouffville ON
CFID-FM Acton Vale PQ
CHOW-FM Amos PQ
CJRD-FM Drummondville PQ
CFTH-FM-2 La Tabatiere PQ
CFLM(AM) La Tuque PQ
CIDI-FM Lac-Brome PQ
CHHO-FM Louiseville PQ
CKAU-FM Maliotenam PQ
CHGA-FM Maniwaki PQ
CKWE-FM Maniwaki (Kitigan Zibi Anishinabeg Reserve) PQ
CHRG-FM Maria (Reserve) PQ
CBFX-FM Montreal PQ
CJLO(AM) Montreal PQ
CJBE-FM Port-Menier PQ
*CBV-FM Quebec PQ
CIAU-FM Radisson PQ
*CHYZ-FM Sainte Foy PQ
CIBO-FM Senneterre PQ
CJMQ-FM Sherbrooke PQ
CHXL-FM Okanese Indian Reserve SK
*CBK-FM Regina SK
CFCR-FM Saskatoon SK
CKZP-FM Zenon Park SK
CFYT-FM Dawson City YT
CFET-FM Tagish YT

Special Programming on Radio Stations in the U.S.

Adult Contemp
KNTI(FM) Lakeport CA 3 hrs
KOLV(FM) Olivia MN
WKBO(AM) Harrisburg PA
WRDW-FM Philadelphia PA 11 hrs

Agriculture
WKAC(AM) Athens AL 5 hrs
WNSI-FM Atmore AL 5 hrs
WACQ(AM) Carrville AL 1 hr
WLYJ(AM) Centre AL 1 hr
WKUL(AM) Cullman AL 15 hrs
WTVY-FM Dothan AL 5 hrs
WULA(AM) Eufaula AL 2 hrs
WABF(AM) Fairhope AL 1 hr
WKWL(AM) Florala AL 1 hr
WHEP(AM) Foley AL 2 hrs
WZOB(AM) Fort Payne AL 2 hrs
WJBB(AM) Haleyville AL 3 hrs
WERH(AM) Hamilton AL
WINL(FM) Linden AL 10 hrs
WACV(AM) Montgomery AL 5 hrs
WOPP(AM) Opp AL 2 hrs
WKEA-FM Scottsboro AL 1 hr
WHBB(AM) Selma AL 10 hrs
WBTG-FM Sheffield AL 1 hr
WTLS(AM) Tallassee AL 6 hrs
WTBF(AM) Troy AL 17 hrs
KAPZ(AM) Bald Knob AR 3 hrs
KAAB(AM) Batesville AR 5 hrs
KEWI(AM) Benton AR 4 hrs
KTHS(AM) Berryville AR 15 hrs
KTHS-FM Berryville AR 15 hrs
KXXA(AM) Conway AR 6 hrs
KHTE-FM England AR 5 hrs
KVDW(AM) England AR 5 hrs
KXJK(AM) Forrest City AR 16 hrs
KFFA(AM) Helena AR 16 hrs
KFIN(FM) Jonesboro AR 13 hrs
KNEA(AM) Jonesboro AR 6 hrs
KVMA(AM) Magnolia AR 2 hrs
KVSA(AM) McGehee AR 5 hrs
KBOA-FM Piggott AR 5 hrs
KPBQ-FM Pine Bluff AR 2 hrs
KPOC(AM) Pocahontas AR 10 hrs
KPOC-FM Pocahontas AR 10 hrs
KURM(AM) Rogers AR 10 hrs
KARV(AM) Russellville AR 5 hrs
KWCK(AM) Searcy AR 10 hrs
KWCK-FM Searcy AR 3 hrs
KWAK(AM) Stuttgart AR 6 hrs
KOSE(AM) Wilson AR 5 hrs
KWYN(AM) Wynne AR 6 hrs
KDJI(AM) Holbrook AZ 8 hrs
KLPZ(AM) Parker AZ 1 hr
KVSL(AM) Show Low AZ 2 hrs
KCFJ(AM) Alturas CA 1 hr
KISV(AM) Bakersfield CA 1 hr
KJMB(FM) Blythe CA 5 hrs
KXO(AM) El Centro CA 7 hrs
KRKC(AM) King City CA 10 hrs
KUBB(FM) Mariposa CA 2 hrs
KYOS(AM) Merced CA 5 hrs
KESP(AM) Modesto CA 3 hrs
KBLF(AM) Red Bluff CA 5 hrs
KSTN(AM) Stockton CA 3 hrs
KJUG(AM) Tulare CA 5 hrs
KJUG-FM Tulare CA 5 hrs
KWNE(FM) Ukiah CA 1 hr
KUBA(AM) Yuba City CA 4 hrs
KGIW(AM) Alamosa CO 6 hrs
KRAI(AM) Craig CO 1 hr
KFTM(AM) Fort Morgan CO 6 hrs
KRKY(AM) Granby CO 1 hr
KFKA(AM) Greeley CO 15 hrs
KSLV(AM) Monte Vista CO 1 hr
KSTC(AM) Sterling CO 15 hrs
KCRT(AM) Trinidad CO 1 hr
KCOL(AM) Wellington CO 2 hrs

KRDZ(AM) Wray CO 10 hrs
WGMD(FM) Rehoboth Beach DE 2 hrs
WGBG(FM) Seaford DE 1 hr
WBGF(FM) Belle Glade FL 5 hrs
WLBE(AM) Leesburg FL 3 hrs
WTYS(AM) Marianna FL 1 hr
WDVH-FM Trenton FL 2 hrs
WZZS(FM) Zolfo Springs FL 1 hr
V6AH(AM) Pohnpei FM 20 hrs
WAJQ(AM) Alma GA 2 hrs
WAJQ-FM Alma GA 2 hrs
WDEC-FM Americus GA 1 hr
WGAC(AM) Augusta GA 4 hrs
WMGR(AM) Bainbridge GA 3 hrs
WJTH(AM) Calhoun GA 1 hr
WCLA(AM) Claxton GA 1.5 hrs
WDCO(AM) Cochran GA 3 hrs
WDXQ-FM Cochran GA 3 hrs
WRCG(AM) Columbus GA 3 hrs
WCUG(AM) Cuthbert GA 8 hrs
WDMG(AM) Douglas GA 4 hrs
WVOH(AM) Hazlehurst GA 2 hrs
WIFO-FM Jesup GA 5 hrs
WQCH(AM) La Fayette GA 2 hrs
WMCG(FM) Milan GA 1 hr
WHKN(FM) Millen GA 10 hrs
WMTM(AM) Moultrie GA 16 hrs
WALH(AM) Mountain City GA 2 hrs
WSTI-FM Quitman GA 5 hrs
WWNS(AM) Statesboro GA 12 hrs
WJAT(AM) Swainsboro GA 5 hrs
WTHO-FM Thomson GA 3 hrs
WTIF(AM) Tifton GA 5 hrs
KLGA(AM) Algona IA
KLGA-FM Algona IA
KJAN(AM) Atlantic IA 12 hrs
KWBG(AM) Boone IA 15 hrs
KBUR(AM) Burlington IA 19 hrs
KCPS(AM) Burlington IA 10 hrs
WMT(AM) Cedar Rapids IA 19 hrs
KCHA-FM Charles City IA 12 hrs
KCHE(AM) Cherokee IA 12 hrs
KCLN(AM) Clinton IA 10 hrs
KROS(AM) Clinton IA 5 hrs
KCZQ(AM) Cresco IA 12 hrs
WOC(AM) Davenport IA 10 hrs
KDSN(AM) Denison IA 12 hrs
KDSN-FM Denison IA 7 hrs
WHO(AM) Des Moines IA 15 hrs
KDTH(AM) Dubuque IA 17 hrs
KDST(FM) Dyersville IA
KILR(AM) Estherville IA 9 hrs
KILR-FM Estherville IA 4 hrs
KIOW(FM) Forest City IA 15 hrs
KWMT(AM) Fort Dodge IA
KGRN(AM) Grinnell IA 12 hrs
KLMJ(FM) Hampton IA 8 hrs
KNOD(FM) Harlan IA 3 hrs
KHBT(FM) Humboldt IA 10 hrs
KKIA(FM) Ida Grove IA 10 hrs
KIFG(AM) Iowa Falls IA 5 hrs
KOKX(AM) Keokuk IA 6 hrs
KOKX-FM Keokuk IA 3 hrs
KLEM(AM) Le Mars IA 18 hrs
KMCH(FM) Manchester IA 7 hrs
KMAQ(AM) Maquoketa IA 10 hrs
KGLO(AM) Mason City IA 15 hrs
KCZE(FM) New Hampton IA 12 hrs
KCOB(AM) Newton IA 2 hrs
KOEL(AM) Oelwein IA 16 hrs
KMA(AM) Shenandoah IA
*KDCR(FM) Sioux Center IA 2 hrs
KSCJ(AM) Sioux City IA 5 hrs
KTFC(FM) Sioux City IA 1 hr
KKRF(AM) Stuart IA 5 hrs
KTLB(FM) Twin Lakes IA 15 hrs
KCII-FM Washington IA
KQWC(AM) Webster City IA 8 hrs
KNJY(AM) Boise ID 5 hrs
KORT(AM) Grangeville ID 2 hrs

KID(AM) Idaho Falls ID 18 hrs
KOZE(AM) Lewiston ID 2 hrs
KRLC(AM) Lewiston ID 5 hrs
KVSI(AM) Montpelier ID 2 hrs
KRPL(AM) Moscow ID 4 hrs
KWIK(AM) Pocatello ID 3 hrs
KACH(AM) Preston ID 3 hrs
KSRA(AM) Salmon ID 4 hrs
KSRA-FM Salmon ID 4 hrs
KLIX(AM) Twin Falls ID 2 hrs
KTFI(AM) Twin Falls ID 3 hrs
WQRL(FM) Benton IL 3 hrs
WBNQ(FM) Bloomington IL 1 hr
WJBC(AM) Bloomington IL 13 hrs
WLMD(FM) Bushnell IL 3 hrs
WKRO(AM) Cairo IL 12 hrs
WBYS(AM) Canton IL 10 hrs
WCIL(AM) Carbondale IL 1 hr
WROY(AM) Carmi IL 6 hrs
WDWS(AM) Champaign IL 10 hrs
WEIC(AM) Charleston IL 8 hrs
KSGM(AM) Chester IL 2 hrs
WDAN(AM) Danville IL 20 hrs
WITY(AM) Danville IL 12 hrs
WLBK(AM) De Kalb IL 12 hrs
WSOY(AM) Decatur IL 10 hrs
WIXN(AM) Dixon IL 11 hrs
WDQN(AM) Du Quoin IL 3 hrs
KUUL(FM) East Moline IL 1 hr
WFIW(AM) Fairfield IL 16 hrs
WFIW-FM Fairfield IL 12 hrs
WFRL(AM) Freeport IL 15 hrs
WAAG(FM) Galesburg IL 5 hrs
WGIL(AM) Galesburg IL 10 hrs
WGEL(FM) Greenville IL 19 hrs
WEBQ(AM) Harrisburg IL 6 hrs
WDUK(FM) Havana IL 8 hrs
WRVY-FM Henry IL 4 hrs
WJRJ(AM) Highland IL 5 hrs
WJIL(AM) Jacksonville IL 8 hrs
WLDS(AM) Jacksonville IL 20 hrs
WJBM(AM) Jerseyville IL 18 hrs
WJOL(AM) Joliet IL 3 hrs
WKAN(AM) Kankakee IL 10 hrs
WKEI(AM) Kewanee IL 20 hrs
WSMI(AM) Litchfield IL 18 hrs
WSMI-FM Litchfield IL 18 hrs
WLUV(AM) Loves Park IL 6 hrs
WJEQ(FM) Macomb IL 1 hr
WLRB(AM) Macomb IL 1.25 hrs
WZUS(AM) Macon IL 5 hrs
WLBH-FM Mattoon IL 9 hrs
WMCI(FM) Mattoon IL 5 hrs
WFXN(AM) Moline IL 1 hr
WRAM(AM) Monmouth IL 18 hrs
WCZQ(FM) Monticello IL 11 hrs
WCSJ-FM Morris IL 10 hrs
WVMC(AM) Mount Carmel IL 5 hrs
WMIX(AM) Mount Vernon IL 18 hrs
WMIX-FM Mount Vernon IL 12 hrs
WHQQ(FM) Neoga IL 7 hrs
WCMY(AM) Ottawa IL 9 hrs
WPXN(AM) Paxton IL 10 hrs
WMBD(AM) Peoria IL 15 hrs
WBBA-FM Pittsfield IL 10 hrs
WSPY-FM Plano IL 18 hrs
WZOE(AM) Princeton IL 15 hrs
WTAY(AM) Robinson IL 3 hrs
WTYE(FM) Robinson IL 6 hrs
WKXQ(FM) Rushville IL 6 hrs
WJBD(AM) Salem IL 4 hrs
WJBD-FM Salem IL 4 hrs
WAUR(AM) Sandwich IL 15 hrs
WHCO(AM) Sparta IL 20 hrs
WTAX(AM) Springfield IL 16 hrs
WSDR(AM) Sterling IL 16 hrs
WSQR(AM) Sycamore IL 6 hrs
WTIM-FM Taylorville IL 20 hrs
WRAN(FM) Tower Hill IL 6 hrs
*WILL(AM) Urbana IL 7 hrs

WPMB(AM) Vandalia IL 4 hrs
WGFA-FM Watseka IL 18 hrs
WRBI(FM) Batesville IN 5 hrs
WBIW(AM) Bedford IN 3 hrs
WADM(AM) Decatur IN 2 hrs
WIKY-FM Evansville IN 17 hrs
WILO(AM) Frankfort IN 12 hrs
WSHW(FM) Frankfort IN 8 hrs
WFLQ(FM) French Lick IN 3 hrs
WREB(AM) Greencastle IN 5 hrs
WTRE(AM) Greensburg IN 10 hrs
WBDC(FM) Huntingburg IN 5 hrs
WAWK(AM) Kendallville IN 1 hr
WLOI(AM) La Porte IN 8 hrs
WASK(AM) Lafayette IN 2 hrs
WKOA(AM) Lafayette IN 3 hrs
WSAL(AM) Logansport IN 10 hrs
WRZR(FM) Loogootee IN 2 hrs
WORX-FM Madison IN 3 hrs
WXGO(AM) Madison IN 3 hrs
WCBK-FM Martinsville IN 1 hr
WMYJ(AM) Martinsville IN 1 hr
WEFM(FM) Michigan City IN
WRCY(AM) Mount Vernon IN 5 hrs
WMDH(AM) New Castle IN 2 hrs
WMDH-FM New Castle IN 1 hr
WSEZ(AM) Paoli IN 7 hrs
WTCA(AM) Plymouth IN 3 hrs
WLQI(FM) Rensselaer IN 15 hrs
WRIN(AM) Rensselaer IN 12 hrs
WKBV(AM) Richmond IN 4 hrs
WROI(FM) Rochester IN 10 hrs
WIFE-FM Rushville IN 18 hrs
WAXL(AM) Santa Claus IN 3 hrs
WZZB(AM) Seymour IN 2 hrs
WNDI(AM) Sullivan IN 6 hrs
WKUZ(AM) Wabash IN 5 hrs
WWBL(FM) Washington IN 15 hrs
KAIR(AM) Atchison KS 7 hrs
KVSV(AM) Beloit KS 9 hrs
KSNP(FM) Burlington KS 8 hrs
KGNO(AM) Dodge City KS 15 hrs
KDNS(FM) Downs KS 5 hrs
KIUL(AM) Garden City KS 5 hrs
*KGCR(FM) Goodland KS 2 hrs
KVGB(AM) Great Bend KS 7 hrs
KHAZ(FM) Hays KS 10 hrs
KNZA(FM) Hiawatha KS 14 hrs
KBUF(AM) Holcomb KS 15 hrs
KNNS(AM) Larned KS 10 hrs
KSCB(AM) Liberal KS 6 hrs
KSMM-FM Liberal KS 12 hrs
KOFO(AM) Ottawa KS 2 hrs
KLKC(AM) Parsons KS 2 hrs
KKAN(AM) Phillipsburg KS 10 hrs
KRSL(AM) Russell KS 2 hrs
KSAL(AM) Salina KS 3 hrs
KYUL(AM) Scott City KS 5 hrs
KMZA(FM) Seneca KS 7 hrs
KULY(AM) Ulysses KS 12 hrs
KLEY(AM) Wellington KS 10 hrs
WANY(AM) Albany KY 2 hrs
WBRT(AM) Bardstown KY 10 hrs
WKDZ(AM) Cadiz KY 2 hrs
WNES(AM) Central City KY 7 hrs
WAIN(AM) Columbia KY 2 hrs
WCPM(AM) Cumberland KY 1 hr
WHSX(FM) Edmonton KY 15 hrs
WFKN(AM) Franklin KY 6 hrs
WKCM(AM) Hawesville KY 3 hrs
WSON(AM) Henderson KY 2 hrs
WTHX(FM) Hodgenville KY 2 hrs
WHOP-FM Hopkinsville KY 15 hrs
WMJL-FM Marion KY 3 hrs
WQQR(FM) Mayfield KY 4 hrs
WFTM(AM) Maysville KY 6 hrs
WFTM-FM Maysville KY 6 hrs
WMIK(AM) Middlesboro KY 1 hr
WFLW(AM) Monticello KY 5 hrs
WMST(AM) Mt. Sterling KY 2 hrs

WBKR(FM) Owensboro KY 2 hrs
WVJS(AM) Owensboro KY 1 hr
WBIO(FM) Philpot KY 5 hrs
WKCA(FM) Salt Lick KY 10 hrs
WVLE(AM) Scottsville KY 3 hrs
WKEQ(FM) Somerset KY 1 hr
WTLO(AM) Somerset KY 1 hr
WYSB(FM) Springfield KY 10 hrs
WMTC(AM) Vancleve KY 1 hr
WMTC-FM Vancleve KY 2 hrs
WLKS(AM) West Liberty KY 5 hrs
KQLQ(FM) Columbia LA 3 hrs
KSIG(AM) Crowley LA 5 hrs
WFPR(AM) Hammond LA 1 hr
WSRY(AM) Elkton MD 1 hr
WICO(AM) Salisbury MD 1 hr
WTTR(AM) Westminster MD 4 hrs
WABJ(AM) Adrian MI 7 hrs
WFYC(AM) Alma MI 4 hrs
WQBX(FM) Alma MI 4 hrs
WATZ(AM) Alpena MI 3 hrs
WLEW(AM) Bad Axe MI 4 hrs
WBCM(FM) Boyne City MI 1 hr
WKYO(AM) Caro MI 18 hrs
WTVB(AM) Coldwater MI 6 hrs
WDOW(AM) Dowagiac MI 7 hrs
WCHT(AM) Escanaba MI 1 hr
WGHN-FM Grand Haven MI 5 hrs
WCSR(AM) Hillsdale MI 3 hrs
WKZO(AM) Kalamazoo MI 10 hrs
WSGW(AM) Saginaw MI 10 hrs
WMLM(AM) Saint Louis MI 5 hrs
WMIC(AM) Sandusky MI 12 hrs
WCSY(AM) South Haven MI 3 hrs
WTCM(AM) Traverse City MI 5 hrs
WPNW(AM) Zeeland MI 1 hr
KASM(AM) Albany MN 6 hrs
KATE(AM) Albert Lea MN 18 hrs
KXRA(AM) Alexandria MN 5 hrs
KKCQ-FM Bagley MN 5 hrs
KBMO(AM) Benson MN 10 hrs
KSCR-FM Benson MN 10 hrs
KBEW(AM) Blue Earth MN 15 hrs
KJLY(FM) Blue Earth MN 5 hrs
WGVY(FM) Cambridge MN 8 hrs
WFMP(FM) Coon Rapids MN
KROX(AM) Crookston MN 10 hrs
KDLM(AM) Detroit Lakes MN 1 hr
KCNN(AM) East Grand Forks MN 6 hrs
KFMC(FM) Fairmont MN 6 hrs
KBRF(AM) Fergus Falls MN 15 hrs
KKCQ(AM) Fosston MN 5 hrs
KDUZ(AM) Hutchinson MN 18 hrs
KKOJ(AM) Jackson MN 15 hrs
KLFD(AM) Litchfield MN 20 hrs
KLTF(AM) Little Falls MN 8 hrs
KEYL(AM) Long Prairie MN 5 hrs
KLQL(FM) Luverne MN 5 hrs
KLQP(FM) Madison MN 5 hrs
KDMA(AM) Montevideo MN 7 hrs
KYMN(AM) Northfield MN 6 hrs
KDIO(AM) Ortonville MN 18 hrs
WCMP(AM) Pine City MN 6 hrs
WQPM(AM) Princeton MN 2 hrs
KROC(AM) Rochester MN 12 hrs
KIKV-FM Sauk Centre MN 20 hrs
KNSG(FM) Springfield MN 15 hrs
KNSP(AM) Staples MN 10 hrs
KSNR(FM) Thief River Falls MN 1 hr
KTRF(AM) Thief River Falls MN 12 hrs
KARL(FM) Tracy MN 15 hrs
KWAD(AM) Wadena MN 10 hrs
KDJS(AM) Willmar MN 5 hrs
KDJS-FM Willmar MN
KWLM(AM) Willmar MN 8 hrs
KAGE(AM) Winona MN
KWOA(AM) Worthington MN
KAAN(AM) Bethany MO 10 hrs
KWRT(AM) Boonville MO 5 hrs
KMAM(AM) Butler MO

KMOE(FM) Butler MO 15 hrs
KOZX(FM) Cabool MO 2 hrs
KATI(FM) California MO 5 hrs
KRLL(AM) California MO 5 hrs
KMRN(AM) Cameron MO 12 hrs
KDFN(AM) Doniphan MO 5 hrs
KTJJ(FM) Farmington MO 6 hrs
KUNQ(FM) Houston MO 2 hrs
KWOS(AM) Jefferson City MO 12 hrs
KBOA(AM) Kennett MO 5 hrs
KIRX(AM) Kirksville MO 10 hrs
KBNN(AM) Lebanon MO 8 hrs
KNIM(AM) Maryville MO 5 hrs
KMEM-FM Memphis MO 8 hrs
KWWR(FM) Mexico MO
KMCR(FM) Montgomery City MO 2 hrs
KBTN(AM) Neosho MO 6 hrs
KNEM(AM) Nevada MO 1 hr
KNMO(FM) Nevada MO 1 hr
KBDZ(FM) Perryville MO 2 hrs
KZNN(FM) Rolla MO 3 hrs
KFEQ(AM) Saint Joseph MO 20 hrs
KSMO(AM) Salem MO 18 hrs
KDRO(AM) Sedalia MO 6 hrs
KBXB(AM) Sikeston MO 3 hrs
KRHW(AM) Sikeston MO 6 hrs
KSIM(AM) Sikeston MO 12 hrs
KTTS-FM Springfield MO 5 hrs
KWTO(AM) Springfield MO 20 hrs
KRWP(FM) Stockton MO 8 hrs
KSAR(FM) Thayer MO 4 hrs
KTKS(FM) Versailles MO 2 hrs
KWRE(AM) Warrenton MO 1 hr
KUKU-FM Willow Springs MO 6 hrs
WCKK(FM) Carthage MS
WBAQ(FM) Greenville MS 1 hr
WROA(AM) Gulfport MS 1 hr
WTCD(AM) Indianola MS 5 hrs
WJDX(AM) Jackson MS 2 hrs
WMSI(FM) Jackson MS 1 hr
WIQQ(FM) Leland MS 6 hrs
WRQO(FM) Monticello MS 1 hr
WWMS(FM) Oxford MS 2 hrs
WHOC(AM) Philadelphia MS 2 hrs
WRJW(AM) Picayune MS 6 hrs
WTYL(AM) Tylertown MS 6 hrs
WJNS-FM Yazoo City MS 16 hrs
KFLN(AM) Baker MT 10 hrs
KBOW(AM) Butte MT 5 hrs
KXGN(AM) Glendive MT 2 hrs
KXGF(AM) Great Falls MT 2 hrs
KOJM(AM) Havre MT 4 hrs
KPQX(FM) Havre MT 10 hrs
*KXEI(FM) Havre MT 1 hr
KXLO(AM) Lewistown MT
KYUS-FM Miles City MT 1 hr
KATQ(AM) Plentywood MT 5 hrs
KATQ-FM Plentywood MT 5 hrs
KCGM(FM) Scobey MT 6 hrs
KSEN(AM) Shelby MT 8 hrs
KZIN-FM Shelby MT 4 hrs
KVCK(AM) Wolf Point MT 6 hrs
KVCK-FM Wolf Point MT 6 hrs
WQDK(FM) Ahoskie NC 7 hrs
WKXR(AM) Asheboro NC 1 hr
WWNC(AM) Asheville NC 1 hr
WGAI(AM) Elizabeth City NC 3 hrs
WFMO(AM) Fairmont NC 5 hrs
WCXL(FM) Kill Devil Hills NC 2 hrs
WKTE(AM) King NC 2 hrs
WHBK(AM) Marshall NC 3 hrs
WPAQ(AM) Mount Airy NC 1 hr
WWDR(AM) Murfreesboro NC 10 hrs
WCVP(AM) Murphy NC 3 hrs
WCBQ(AM) Oxford NC
WPTF(AM) Raleigh NC 10 hrs
WTEL(AM) Red Springs NC 5 hrs
WPTM(FM) Roanoke Rapids NC 15 hrs
WEGG(AM) Rose Hill NC 9 hrs
WKRX(FM) Roxboro NC 5 hrs
WRXO(AM) Roxboro NC 5 hrs
WWGP(AM) Sanford NC 7 hrs
WYAL(AM) Scotland Neck NC 2 hrs
WMPM(AM) Smithfield NC 2 hrs
WTAB(AM) Tabor City NC 12 hrs

WADE(AM) Wadesboro NC 1 hr
WKSK(AM) West Jefferson NC 3 hrs
WENC(AM) Whiteville NC 5 hrs
WTXY(AM) Whiteville NC 2 hrs
KBMR(AM) Bismarck ND 4 hrs
KPOK(AM) Bowman ND 2 hrs
*KMHA(FM) Four Bears ND 1 hr
KAUJ(FM) Grafton ND 18 hrs
KXPO(AM) Grafton ND 18 hrs
KNDC(AM) Hettinger ND
KSJB(AM) Jamestown ND 12 hrs
KNDK(AM) Langdon ND 12 hrs
KQLX(AM) Lisbon ND 14 hrs
KCJB(AM) Minot ND 4 hrs
KHRT(AM) Minot ND 1 hr
KZPR(FM) Minot ND 4 hrs
KUSO(FM) Albion NE 10 hrs
KAAQ(FM) Alliance NE 4 hrs
KCOW(AM) Alliance NE 18 hrs
KWBE(AM) Beatrice NE 14 hrs
KZEN(FM) Central City NE 20 hrs
KCSR(AM) Chadron NE 5 hrs
KQSK(FM) Chadron NE 4 hrs
KKOT(FM) Columbus NE 8 hrs
KTTT(AM) Columbus NE 5 hrs
KGMT(AM) Fairbury NE 18 hrs
KHUB(AM) Fremont NE 6 hrs
KHAS(AM) Hastings NE 2 hrs
KMTY(FM) Holdrege NE 5 hrs
KUVR(AM) Holdrege NE 5 hrs
KGFW(AM) Kearney NE 8 hrs
KRVN-FM Lexington NE 10 hrs
KICX(FM) McCook NE 6 hrs
KIOD(FM) McCook NE 6 hrs
KNCY(AM) Nebraska City NE 3 hrs
KNEN(FM) Norfolk NE 10 hrs
KMCX(FM) Ogallala NE 2 hrs
KOGA(AM) Ogallala NE 10 hrs
KFAB(AM) Omaha NE 5 hrs
KBRX(AM) O'Neill NE 12 hrs
KNLV(AM) Ord NE 8 hrs
KNLV-FM Ord NE 8 hrs
KNEB(AM) Scottsbluff NE 18 hrs
KNEB-FM Scottsbluff NE 18 hrs
KSID(AM) Sidney NE 5 hrs
KRFS(AM) Superior NE 5 hrs
KRFS-FM Superior NE
KTCH(AM) Wayne NE 20 hrs
KTIC-FM West Point NE 10 hrs
KAWL(AM) York NE 7 hrs
*WNEC-FM Henniker NH 4 hrs
WSNJ(AM) Bridgeton NJ 10 hrs
WFAI(AM) Salem NJ 8 hrs
KRSY(AM) Alamogordo NM 1 hr
KICA(AM) Clovis NM 5 hrs
KOTS(AM) Deming NM 5 hrs
KSEL-FM Portales NM 4 hrs
KMXQ(FM) Socorro NM 2 hrs
KWNA(AM) Winnemucca NV 2 hrs
WABH(AM) Bath NY 5 hrs
WVIN-FM Bath NY 1 hr
WBRV-FM Boonville NY 3 hrs
WKGB-FM Conklin NY 1 hr
WWLE(AM) Cornwall NY 1 hr
WRWD-FM Highland NY 1 hr
WJTN(AM) Jamestown NY 1 hr
WIXT(AM) Little Falls NY 1 hr
WLVL(AM) Lockport NY 6 hrs
WLLG(FM) Lowville NY 3 hrs
WICY(AM) Malone NY 1 hr
WYBG(AM) Massena NY
WACK(AM) Newark NY 5 hrs
WEOK(AM) Poughkeepsie NY 2 hrs
WRIV(AM) Riverhead NY 8 hrs
WSPQ(AM) Springville NY 5 hrs
WIPS(AM) Ticonderoga NY 6 hrs
WIBX(AM) Utica NY 14 hrs
WDLA(AM) Walton NY 2 hrs
WCJW(AM) Warsaw NY 11 hrs
WTNY(AM) Watertown NY 3 hrs
WNCO(AM) Ashland OH 3 hrs
WAIS(AM) Buchtel OH 5 hrs
WBCO(AM) Bucyrus OH 4 hrs
WYNT(FM) Caledonia OH 3 hrs
WCER(AM) Canton OH 6 hrs
WHBC(AM) Canton OH 1 hr

WDOH(FM) Delphos OH 8 hrs
WEDI(AM) Eaton OH 2 hrs
WFIN(AM) Findlay OH 7 hrs
WKTN(FM) Kenton OH 2 hrs
WLOH(AM) Lancaster OH 1 hr
WIMA(AM) Lima OH 5 hrs
WIMT(FM) Lima OH 5 hrs
WMOA(AM) Marietta OH 1 hr
WMRN(AM) Marion OH 5 hrs
WMPO(AM) Middleport-Pomeroy OH 1 hr
WSEO(FM) Nelsonville OH
WHOF(AM) North Canton OH 2 hrs
WLKR-FM Norwalk OH 3 hrs
WBUK(AM) Ottawa OH 5 hrs
WPTW(AM) Piqua OH 2 hrs
WNTO(AM) Racine OH 1 hr
WSOM(AM) Salem OH 2 hrs
WTUZ(AM) Uhrichsville OH 2 hrs
WCHO(AM) Washington Court House OH 5 hrs
WRAC(FM) West Union OH 10 hrs
WKFI(AM) Wilmington OH 2 hrs
WQKT(FM) Wooster OH 2 hrs
WBZI(AM) Xenia OH 2 hrs
WHIZ(AM) Zanesville OH 2 hrs
KEYB(FM) Altus OK 2 hrs
KKBI(FM) Broken Bow OK 5 hrs
KGWA(AM) Enid OK 3 hrs
KIHN(AM) Hugo OK 1 hr
KMAD(AM) Madill OK 2 hrs
KYAL-FM Muskogee OK 5 hrs
KPNC(FM) Ponca City OK 5 hrs
KFAQ(AM) Tulsa OK 5 hrs
KBKR(AM) Baker City OR 2 hrs
KZZR(AM) Burns OR 6 hrs
KWVR(AM) Enterprise OR 4 hrs
KWVR-FM Enterprise OR 4 hrs
KAGO(AM) Klamath Falls OR 3 hrs
KLBM(AM) La Grande OR 2 hrs
KSRV(AM) Ontario OR 15 hrs
KUMA(AM) Pendleton OR 10 hrs
KCKX(AM) Stayton OR 15 hrs
KACI(AM) The Dalles OR 1 hr
KODL(AM) The Dalles OR 4 hrs
WHLM(AM) Bloomsburg PA 1 hr
WFRM(AM) Coudersport PA 2 hrs
WDAC(AM) Lancaster PA 4 hrs
WWBJ(AM) Martinsburg PA 1 hr
*WPEL(AM) Montrose PA 1 hr
WATS(AM) Sayre PA 1 hr
WSBA(AM) York PA 4 hrs
WSOL(AM) San German PR 2 hrs
WVCD(AM) Bamberg-Denmark SC 1 hr
WOLH(AM) Florence SC 1 hr
WHSC(AM) Hartsville SC 3 hrs
WJBS(AM) Holly Hill SC 2 hrs
WJAY(AM) Mullins SC 10 hrs
KGIM(AM) Aberdeen SD 12 hrs
KSDN(AM) Aberdeen SD 15 hrs
KBFS(AM) Belle Fourche SD 20 hrs
KBRK(AM) Brookings SD 9 hrs
KZMX(AM) Hot Springs SD 6 hrs
KJAM(AM) Madison SD 11 hrs
KMSD(AM) Milbank SD 6 hrs
KMIT(FM) Mitchell SD 18 hrs
KORN(AM) Mitchell SD 10 hrs
KOLY(AM) Mobridge SD
KIMM(AM) Rapid City SD 1 hr
KTOQ(AM) Rapid City SD 2 hrs
KPLO-FM Reliance SD 5 hrs
KSDR-FM Watertown SD 8 hrs
KKYA(FM) Yankton SD 5 hrs
KYNT(AM) Yankton SD 5 hrs
WNAX(AM) Yankton SD 35 hrs
WLAR(AM) Athens TN 2 hrs
*WHCB(FM) Bristol TN 1 hr
WNKX-FM Centerville TN
WMCP(AM) Columbia TN 4 hrs
WZYX(AM) Cowan TN 2 hrs
WEKR(AM) Fayetteville TN 1 hr
WHIN(AM) Gallatin TN 5 hrs
WMYL(FM) Halls Crossroads TN 2 hrs

WDXI(AM) Jackson TN 12 hrs
WCLC(AM) Jamestown TN 2 hrs
WDEB(AM) Jamestown TN 3 hrs
WJFC(AM) Jefferson City TN 1 hr
WBUZ(FM) La Vergne TN 1 hr
WEEN(AM) Lafayette TN 5 hrs
WLIL(AM) Lenoir City TN 4 hrs
WLIV(AM) Livingston TN 2 hrs
WMSR(AM) Manchester TN
WAKI(AM) McMinnville TN 2 hrs
WBMC(AM) McMinnville TN 5 hrs
WREC(AM) Memphis TN 3 hrs
WGNS(AM) Murfreesboro TN 3 hrs
WSM(AM) Nashville TN 6 hrs
*WDNX(FM) Olive Hill TN 1 hr
WMUF(AM) Paris TN 2 hrs
WUAT(AM) Pikeville TN 5 hrs
WLIJ(AM) Shelbyville TN 5 hrs
WDBL(AM) Springfield TN 10 hrs
WCDT(AM) Winchester TN 15 hrs
KFYN(AM) Bonham TX 6 hrs
KLXK(FM) Breckenridge TX 5 hrs wkly hrs
KWHI(AM) Brenham TX 3 hrs
KCAR(AM) Clarksville TX 2 hrs
KQBZ(FM) Coleman TX 14 hrs
KSTA(AM) Coleman TX 14 hrs
KZNE(AM) College Station TX 10 hrs
KIXK(AM) Dalhart TX 7 hrs
KDDD-FM Dumas TX 5 hrs
KNES(AM) Fairfield TX 3 hrs
KMUL(AM) Farwell TX 3 hrs
WBAP(AM) Fort Worth TX 6 hrs
KNAF(AM) Fredericksburg TX 5 hrs
KGAF(AM) Gainesville TX 3 hrs
KPIR(AM) Granbury TX 1 hr
KGVL(AM) Greenville TX 5 hrs
KHLT(AM) Hallettsville TX 5 hrs
KVRP-FM Haskell TX 5 hrs
KPAN(AM) Hereford TX 12 hrs
KEBE(AM) Jacksonville TX 9 hrs
KOOI-FM Jacksonville TX 9 hrs
KMBL(AM) Junction TX 6 hrs
KVLG(AM) La Grange TX 4 hrs
KCYL(AM) Lampasas TX 5 hrs
KZZN(AM) Littlefield TX 7 hrs
KCUL(AM) Marshall TX 3 hrs
KRQX(AM) Mexia TX 12 hrs
KSFA(AM) Nacogdoches TX 7 hrs
KNET(AM) Palestine TX 6 hrs
KOMX(FM) Pampa TX 10 hrs
KBUS(FM) Paris TX 6 hrs
KEYE(AM) Perryton TX 2 hrs
KEYE-FM Perryton TX 2 hrs
KKYN-FM Plainview TX 12 hrs
KVOP(AM) Plainview TX 12 hrs
KITE(FM) Port Lavaca TX 1 hr
KWFB(AM) Quanah TX 3 hrs
KGKL(AM) San Angelo TX 6 hrs
KWED(AM) Seguin TX 6 hrs
KDAE(AM) Sinton TX 6 hrs
KSTV(AM) Stephenville TX 5 hrs
KXOX(AM) Sweetwater TX 5 hrs
KVOU(AM) Uvalde TX 12 hrs
KBEC(AM) Waxahachie TX 5 hrs
KWUD(AM) Woodville TX 02 hrs
KSUB(AM) Cedar City UT 6 hrs
KNAK(AM) Delta UT 5 hrs
KVNU(AM) Logan UT 2 hrs
KMTI(AM) Manti UT 5 hrs
KOAL(AM) Price UT 5 hrs
KSVC(AM) Richfield UT 1 hr
KVEL(AM) Vernal UT 2 hrs
WBTX(AM) Broadway-Timberville VA 1 hr
WPZZ(FM) Crewe VA 10 hrs
WPAK(AM) Farmville VA 1 hr
WWWJ(AM) Galax VA 1 hr
WXGM(AM) Gloucester VA 2 hrs
WXGM-FM Gloucester VA 2 hrs
WMNA(AM) Gretna VA 8 hrs
WNRG(AM) Grundy VA 5 hrs
WSVA(AM) Harrisonburg VA 8 hrs
WHHV(AM) Hillsville VA 1 hr
WKWI(AM) Kilmarnock VA 2 hrs
WRVA(AM) Richmond VA 3 hrs

WXLZ(AM) Saint Paul VA 2 hrs
WKGM(AM) Smithfield VA 02 hrs
WSBV(AM) South Boston VA 1 hr
WKDW(AM) Staunton VA 1 hr
WHEO(AM) Stuart VA 4 hrs
WKCW(AM) Warrenton VA 1 hr
WKCI(AM) Waynesboro VA 2 hrs
WZLF(FM) Bellows Falls VT 1 hr
KNBQ(FM) Centralia WA 1 hr
KOZI(AM) Chelan WA 3 hrs
KCLX(AM) Colfax WA 5 hrs
KYSN(FM) East Wenatchee WA 1 hr
KTBI(AM) Ephrata WA 15 hrs
KULE(AM) Ephrata WA 1 hr
KULE-FM Ephrata WA 5 hrs
KONA(AM) Kennewick WA 3 hrs
KBRC(AM) Mount Vernon WA 5 hrs
KNCW(FM) Omak WA 1 hr
KOMW(AM) Omak WA 2 hrs
KQQQ(AM) Pullman WA 3 hrs
KWNC(AM) Quincy WA 5 hrs
KGA(AM) Spokane WA 1 hr
KTEL(AM) Walla Walla WA 5 hrs
KPQ(AM) Wenatchee WA 3 hrs
KIT(AM) Yakima WA 6 hrs
WBEV(AM) Beaver Dam WI 8 hrs
WXRO(FM) Beaver Dam WI 6 hrs
WOTE(AM) Clintonville WI 8 hrs
WAXX(FM) Eau Claire WI 15 hrs
WAYY(AM) Eau Claire WI 5 hrs
KFIZ(AM) Fond du Lac WI 10 hrs
WTAQ(AM) Green Bay WI 5 hrs
WAUN(FM) Kewaunee WI 10 hrs
WKTY(AM) La Crosse WI 5 hrs
WGLR(AM) Lancaster WI 10 hrs
WGLR-FM Lancaster WI
WTSO(AM) Madison WI 20 hrs
WMAM(AM) Marinette WI 3 hrs
WJMT(AM) Merrill WI 7 hrs
WCCN(AM) Neillsville WI 19 hrs
WPKR(AM) Omro WI 1 hr
WPVL(AM) Platteville WI 12 hrs
WJUB(AM) Plymouth WI 5 hrs
WPDR(AM) Portage WI 6 hrs
WNFM(FM) Reedsburg WI 18 hrs
WRCO(AM) Richland Center WI 2 hrs
WRCO-FM Richland Center WI 18 hrs
WEVR(AM) River Falls WI 18 hrs
*WRFW(FM) River Falls WI 10 hrs
WTCH(AM) Shawano WI 21 hrs
WHBL(AM) Sheboygan WI 10 hrs
WCSW(AM) Shell Lake WI 3 hrs
WDOR-FM Sturgeon Bay WI 5 hrs
WVRQ(AM) Viroqua WI 1 hr
WVRQ-FM Viroqua WI 1 hr
WDUX(AM) Waupaca WI 6 hrs
WFDL(AM) Waupun WI 5 hrs
WDEZ(AM) Wausau WI 4 hrs
WSAU(AM) Wausau WI 5 hrs
WELD(AM) Fisher WV 3 hrs
*WVMR(AM) Frost WV 5 hrs
WRON-FM Lewisburg WV 3 hrs
WGGE(FM) Parkersburg WV 2 hrs
WWVA(AM) Wheeling WV 2 hrs
KFBC(AM) Cheyenne WY 1 hr
KMER(AM) Kemmerer WY 3 hrs
KCGY(FM) Laramie WY 1 hr
KHAT(AM) Laramie WY 1 hr
KASL(AM) Newcastle WY 5 hrs
KPOW(AM) Powell WY 19 hrs
KTAK(FM) Riverton WY 5 hrs
KVOW(AM) Riverton WY 5 hrs
KYCN(AM) Wheatland WY 3 hrs

Alternative

KWKM(FM) Saint Johns AZ 3 hrs
*KALW(FM) San Francisco CA 4 hrs
KFMU-FM Oak Creek CO 4 hrs
WRUF-FM Gainesville FL 6 hrs
WXXL(FM) Tavares FL 6 hrs
KECH-FM Sun Valley ID 5 hrs
*WQUB(FM) Quincy IL 12 hrs
*WEEM-FM Pendleton IN 2 hrs
KIND-FM Independence KS 4 hrs
WFRD(FM) Hanover NH 1 hr

KAGM(FM) Los Lunas NM 18 hrs
KSPI-FM Stillwater OK
WFBC-FM Greenville SC 2 hrs
WRLT(FM) Franklin TN 1 hr
KWKQ(FM) Graham TX 10 hrs
*KRLF(FM) Pullman WA 1 hr
*KYVT(FM) Yakima WA 3 hrs
*KUWS(FM) Superior WI 16 hrs

American Indian

*KDLG(AM) Dillingham AK 1 hr
*KIYU(AM) Galena AK 2 hrs
KCAM(AM) Glennallen AK 1 hr
*KTOO(FM) Juneau AK 1 hr
*KDLL(FM) Kenai AK 10 hrs
KIAM(AM) Nenana AK 3 hrs
*KJNP(AM) North Pole AK 2 hrs
WNSI-FM Atmore AL 1 hr
*KABF(FM) Little Rock AR 2 hrs
*KXCI(FM) Tucson AZ 2 hrs
*KNNB(FM) Whiteriver AZ 8 hrs
*KZFR(FM) Chico CA 2 hrs
*KFCF(FM) Fresno CA 2 hrs
*KMUD(FM) Garberville CA 1 hr
*KIDE(FM) Hoopa CA 20 hrs
*KCSB-FM Santa Barbara CA 3 hrs
KRTZ(FM) Cortez CO 1 hr
*KSUT(FM) Ignacio CO 7 hrs
WZTR(FM) Dahlonega GA 1 hr
*WBCX(FM) Gainesville GA 4 hrs
KWIK(AM) Pocatello ID 1 hr
*WUEV(FM) Evansville IN 1 hr
*WHFC(FM) Bel Air MD 3 hrs
WCUP(FM) L'Anse MI 2 hrs
*WLNZ(FM) Lansing MI 3. hrs
*WNMC-FM Traverse City MI 1 hr
*KBSB(FM) Bemidji MN 3 hrs
*KKFI(FM) Kansas City MO 2 hrs
*WWCU(FM) Cullowhee NC 5. hrs
*KEYA(FM) Belcourt ND 9 hrs
*KCND(FM) Bismarck ND 2 hrs
*KDPR(FM) Dickinson ND 2 hrs
*KABU(FM) Fort Totten ND 19 hrs
*KMHA(FM) Four Bears ND 4 hrs
*KPRJ(FM) Jamestown ND 2 hrs
*KMPR(FM) Minot ND 2 hrs
*KPPR(FM) Williston ND 2 hrs
*KINI(FM) Crookston NE 15 hrs
*WNEC-FM Henniker NH 18 hrs
*KABR(AM) Alamo Community NM 10 hrs
KYVA-FM Churchrock NM 10 hrs
KPCL(FM) Farmington NM 7 hrs
KGLX(FM) Gallup NM 3 hrs
*KTDB(FM) Ramah NM 8 hrs
KSFR(FM) White Rock NM 4 hrs
*KSHI(FM) Zuni NM 20 hrs
WYBG(AM) Massena NY
*WBAI(FM) New York NY 1 hr
WNTO(FM) Racine OH 1 hr
*KOSN(FM) Ketchum OK 1 hr
KVSP(FM) Oklahoma City OK 1 hr
KIRC(FM) Seminole OK 1 hr
*KOSU(FM) Stillwater OK 1 hr
KWSH(AM) Wewoka OK 1 hr
*KMUN(FM) Astoria OR 2 hrs
*KTEC(FM) Klamath Falls OR 1 hr
KOLY(AM) Mobridge SD
KOLY-FM Mobridge SD 1 hr
*KBHE-FM Rapid City SD 1 hr
*KTSD-FM Reliance SD 1 hr
KBHB(AM) Sturgis SD 1 hr
*KAOR(FM) Vermillion SD 2 hrs
*KUSD(FM) Vermillion SD 1 hr
WLIL(AM) Lenoir City TN 1 hr
*WRVU(FM) Nashville TN 2 hrs
*KOOP(FM) Hornsby TX 1 hr
*KZMU(FM) Moab UT 5 hrs
*KRCL(FM) Salt Lake City UT 4 hrs
*WUVT-FM Blacksburg VA 2 hrs
*KSER(FM) Everett WA 2 hrs
*KAOS(FM) Olympia WA 3 hrs
*KSFC(FM) Spokane WA 5 hrs
KYNR(AM) Toppenish WA 20 hrs
*WOJB(FM) Reserve WI 15 hrs

Arabic

WPNA(AM) Oak Park IL 2 hrs
KLAV(AM) Las Vegas NV 7 hrs
*WDIY(FM) Allentown PA 1 hr
*WMUH(FM) Allentown PA 2 hrs
KARI(AM) Blaine WA 1 hr

Armenian

*KUSF(FM) San Francisco CA 1 hr

Beautiful Music

*KNOG(FM) Nogales AZ 5 hrs
WMRX-FM Beaverton MI 2 hrs
WALK-FM Patchogue NY
WORG(FM) Elloree SC
KNNK(FM) Dimmitt TX 20 hrs
*KZAZ(FM) Bellingham WA 7 hrs

Big Band

*KASU Jonesboro AR 2 hrs
*WGRS(FM) Guilford CT 8 hrs
WQUN(AM) Hamden CT 4 hrs
*WMNR(FM) Monroe CT 8 hrs
*WRXC(FM) Shelton CT 8 hrs
*WGSK(FM) South Kent CT 8 hrs
WTAN(AM) Clearwater FL 40 hrs
KROS(AM) Clinton IA 3 hrs
*WSIU(FM) Carbondale IL 4 hrs
WHPO(FM) Hoopeston IL 2 hrs
WTAY(AM) Robinson IL 10 hrs
WTYE(FM) Robinson IL 10 hrs
WMAY(AM) Springfield IL 5 hrs
WXNT(AM) Indianapolis IN 2 hrs
WAWK(AM) Kendallville IN 2 hrs
KIND(AM) Independence KS 2 hrs
KLKC(AM) Parsons KS 3 hrs
*WESM(FM) Princess Anne MD 10 hrs
*WKHS(FM) Worton MD 2 hrs
*WHFR(FM) Dearborn MI 6 hrs
WOUF(FM) Frankfort MI 2 hrs
*WLNZ(FM) Lansing MI 3 hrs
WIOS(AM) Tawas City MI 6 hrs
KYMN(AM) Northfield MN 3 hrs
KOLV(FM) Olivia MN
*KXMS(FM) Joplin MO 2 hrs
KPRK(AM) Livingston MT 4 hrs
WXIT(AM) Blowing Rock NC 4 hrs
*WCCE(FM) Buie's Creek NC 4 hrs
*WZRU(FM) Roanoke Rapids NC 4 hrs
KMTY(FM) Holdrege NE 5 hrs
KUVR(AM) Holdrege NE 5 hrs
WSNJ(AM) Bridgeton NJ
*WNTI(FM) Hackettstown NJ 4 hrs
KRSY(AM) Alamogordo NM 6 hrs
KRSN(AM) Los Alamos NM 8 hrs
WDNY(AM) Dansville NY 3 hrs
WDNY-FM Dansville NY 3 hrs
*WNYC(FM) New York NY 2 hrs
WDOS(AM) Oneonta NY 7 hrs
WRGR(FM) Tupper Lake NY 2 hrs
WNYV(FM) Whitehall NY 3 hrs
WATH(AM) Athens OH 15 hrs
WBBZ(AM) Ponca City OK 3 hrs
WNPV(AM) Lansdale PA 3 hrs
WLSH(AM) Lansford PA 4 hrs
WPHB(AM) Philipsburg PA 5 hrs
WCRI(FM) Block Island RI 4 hrs
WJMX(AM) Florence SC 3 hrs
WHSC(AM) Hartsville SC 3 hrs
WMYB(FM) Myrtle Beach SC
*KNCT-FM Killeen TX 6 hrs
WVNR(AM) Poultney VT 3 hrs
KEYG(AM) Grand Coulee WA 4 hrs
*WVMR(AM) Frost WV 3 hrs
*WWVU-FM Morgantown WV 2 hrs

Black

*KSUA(FM) Fairbanks AK 8 hrs
WNSI-FM Atmore AL 1 hr
WULA(AM) Eufaula AL 3 hrs
WGYV(AM) Greenville AL 6 hrs
WHMA-FM Hobson City AL 6 hrs
*WJAB(AM) Huntsville AL 3 hrs
WMGY(AM) Montgomery AL 15 hrs
WOPP(AM) Opp AL 4 hrs
WKAX(AM) Russellville AL 4 hrs
WHBB(AM) Selma AL 18 hrs
KAMD-FM Camden AR 5 hrs
*KUAF(FM) Fayetteville AR 5 hrs
KFFA(AM) Helena AR 10 hrs
KOSE(AM) Wilson AR 6 hrs
KDVA(AM) Buckeye AZ 6 hrs
KTKT(AM) Tucson AZ 1 hr
*KXCI(FM) Tucson AZ 4 hrs
*KPFA(FM) Berkeley CA 18 hrs
*KMUD(FM) Garberville CA 3 hrs
*KXLU(FM) Los Angeles CA 10 hrs
*KMPO(FM) Modesto CA 3 hrs
KVMR(FM) Nevada City CA 4 hrs
*KSPB(FM) Pebble Beach CA 18 hrs
*KZYX(FM) Philo CA 6 hrs
*KUCR(FM) Riverside CA 18 hrs
*KYCC(FM) Stockton CA 6 hrs
KDIA(AM) Vallejo CA 2 hrs
KDYA(AM) Vallejo CA 2 hrs
*KGNU-FM Boulder CO 7 hrs
KLDC(AM) Denver CO 2 hrs
*KCSU-FM Fort Collins CO 3 hrs
*KMSA(FM) Grand Junction CO 6 hrs
*WPKN(FM) Bridgeport CT 4 hrs
WFIF(AM) Milford CT 6 hrs
*WCNI(FM) New London CT 3 hrs
*WVUD(FM) Newark DE 10 hrs
WPHK(FM) Blountstown FL 12 hrs
*WVUM(FM) Coral Gables FL 7 hrs
WAVS(AM) Davie FL
WRUF(AM) Gainesville FL 4 hrs
*WUFT-FM Gainesville FL 4 hrs
WGWD(FM) Gretna FL 20 hrs
WDSR(AM) Lake City FL 1 hr
WLBE(AM) Leesburg FL 3 hrs
WOCA(AM) Ocala FL 2 hrs
*WKGC-FM Panama City FL 6 hrs
WPRY(AM) Perry FL 2 hrs
*WKPX(FM) Sunrise FL 3 hrs
*WVFS(FM) Tallahassee FL 8 hrs
*WBVM(FM) Tampa FL 4 hrs
WDEC(AM) Americus GA 5 hrs
WRFC(AM) Athens GA 15 hrs
WMOG(AM) Brunswick GA 8 hrs
WGRA(AM) Cairo GA 6 hrs
WEBS(AM) Calhoun GA 2 hrs
WBTR-FM Carrollton GA 5 hrs
WDCO(AM) Cochran GA 6 hrs
WDXQ-FM Cochran GA 6 hrs
WCUG(AM) Cuthbert GA 4 hrs
WUFF(AM) Eastman GA 5 hrs
*WBCX(FM) Gainesville GA 12 hrs
WFDR(AM) Manchester GA 13 hrs
WYIS(AM) McRae GA 4 hrs
WMVG(AM) Milledgeville GA 4 hrs
WTGA(AM) Thomaston GA 4 hrs
WLET(AM) Toccoa GA
KLNG(AM) Council Bluffs IA 6 hrs
*KUOI-FM Moscow ID 3 hrs
KATZ-FM Alton IL
*WESN(FM) Bloomington IL 18 hrs
*WEFT(FM) Champaign IL 8 hrs
*WVKC(FM) Galesburg IL 6 hrs
*WCSF(FM) Joliet IL 2 hrs
WJOL(AM) Joliet IL 1 hr
*WMXM(FM) Lake Forest IL 6 hrs
*WLRA(FM) Lockport IL 15 hrs
*WQNA(FM) Springfield IL 9 hrs
*WFYI-FM Indianapolis IN 5 hrs
WXFN(AM) Muncie IN 3 hrs
WWVR(FM) West Terre Haute IN 6 hrs
*KONQ(FM) Dodge City KS 10 hrs
KWBW(AM) Hutchinson KS 2 hrs
*KSDB-FM Manhattan KS 4 hrs
WCPM(AM) Cumberland KY 3 hrs
*WNKJ(FM) Hopkinsville KY 4.5 hrs
WFXY(AM) Middlesboro KY 2 hrs
WEKY(AM) Richmond KY 12 hrs
*KLSP(FM) Angola LA 10 hrs
KAJN-FM Crowley LA 2 hrs
KVPI-FM Ville Platte LA 10 hrs
*WOMR(FM) Provincetown MA 6 hrs
*WBSL-FM Sheffield MA 2 hrs
WHLL(AM) Springfield MA 1 hr
*WYAJ(FM) Sudbury MA 6 hrs
*WCHC(FM) Worcester MA 8 hrs
WKHI(FM) Fruitland MD 5 hrs
*WUPX(FM) Marquette MI 6 hrs
WHLS(AM) Port Huron MI 1 hr
WSJM(AM) Saint Joseph MI 5 hrs
*WNMC-FM Traverse City MI 20 hrs
WMFN(AM) Zeeland MI 2hrs
*KFAI(FM) Minneapolis MN 10 hrs
KNOF(FM) Saint Paul MN 5 hrs
KMFC(FM) Centralia MO 3 hrs
*KOPN(FM) Columbia MO 10 hrs
*KCFV(FM) Ferguson MO 4 hrs
KLSC(FM) Malden MO 6 hrs
*KMVC(FM) Marshall MO 10 hrs
KLID(AM) Poplar Bluff MO 2 hrs
KDRO(AM) Sedalia MO 1 hr
WCJU(AM) Columbia MS 112 hrs
WKCU(AM) Corinth MS 2 hrs
WABG(AM) Greenwood MS 4 hrs
WGRM(AM) Greenwood MS 2 hrs
WNBN(AM) Meridian MS
WRJW(AM) Picayune MS 8 hrs
WJDR(FM) Prentiss MS 5 hrs
WSSO(AM) Starkville MS 12 hrs
*KGLT(FM) Bozeman MT 3 hrs
WFGW(AM) Black Mountain NC 1 hr
WRRZ(AM) Clinton NC 5 hrs
WGAI(AM) Elizabeth City NC 4 hrs
WSML(AM) Graham NC 18 hrs
WYRN(AM) Louisburg NC
WHIP(AM) Mooresville NC 6 hrs
WDJS(AM) Mount Olive NC 5 hrs
WNNC(AM) Newton NC 2 hrs
WRXO(AM) Roxboro NC 4 hrs
*KZUM(FM) Lincoln NE 13 hrs
*KWSC(FM) Wayne NE 4 hrs
*WUNH(FM) Durham NH 4 hrs
*WGLS-FM Glassboro NJ 10 hrs
*WRRC(FM) Lawrenceville NJ 10 hrs
*WKNJ-FM Union Township NJ 2 hrs
*WMSC(FM) Upper Montclair NJ 4 hrs
KKIM(AM) Albuquerque NM 2 hrs
*WXBA(FM) Brentwood NY 5 hrs
*WBSU(FM) Brockport NY 1 hr
*WBNY(FM) Buffalo NY 12 hrs
*WSLU(FM) Canton NY
WSIV(AM) East Syracuse NY 20 hrs
*WRCU-FM Hamilton NY 10 hrs
WHLI(AM) Hempstead NY 1 hr
WKJY(FM) Hempstead NY 1 hr
WLNL(AM) Horseheads NY 1 hr
WVOX(AM) New Rochelle NY 1 hr
*WBAI(FM) New York NY 10 hrs
*WKCR-FM New York NY 12 hrs
*WNYU-FM New York NY 5 hrs
WJJL(AM) Niagara Falls NY 2 hrs
*WQKE(FM) Plattsburgh NY 9 hrs
WRNY(AM) Rome NY 3 hrs
*WFNP(FM) Rosendale NY 14 hrs
*WUSB(FM) Stony Brook NY 12 hrs
*WJPZ-FM Syracuse NY 12 hrs
*WOUB(AM) Athens OH 8 hrs
*WCDR-FM Cedarville OH 2 hrs
*WOHC(FM) Chillicothe OH 2 hrs
*WOSU(AM) Columbus OH 1 hr
*WWSU(FM) Dayton OH 12 hrs
*WDUB(FM) Granville OH 9 hrs
WRBP(FM) Hubbard OH
WFCJ(FM) Miamisburg OH 3 hrs
WNPQ(FM) New Philadelphia OH 4 hrs
WCCD(AM) Parma OH 3 hrs
*WOHP(AM) Portsmouth OH 2 hrs
WNTO(FM) Racine OH 1 hr
*WEEC(FM) Springfield OH 1 hr
*WXUT(FM) Toledo OH 8 hrs
*WOBN(FM) Westerville OH 2 hrs
KZBB(FM) Poteau OK 2 hrs
*KMUN(FM) Astoria OR 2 hrs
KKNX(FM) Eugene OR 3 hrs
*KLCC(FM) Eugene OR 2 hrs
*KRVM-FM Eugene OR 2 hrs
*KWVA(FM) Eugene OR 4 hrs
*KTEC(FM) Klamath Falls OR 3 hrs
*KEOL(FM) La Grande OR 12 hrs
*KSLC(FM) McMinnville OR 2 hrs
KLCO(FM) Newport OR 3 hrs
KLPM(AM) Portland OR 1 hr
*KRRC(FM) Portland OR 10 hrs
*WLVR(FM) Bethlehem PA 12 hrs
*WCAL(FM) California PA 4 hrs
*WFSE(FM) Edinboro PA 15 hrs
*WKVR-FM Huntingdon PA 10 hrs
WIUP-FM Indiana PA 14 hrs
*WFNM(FM) Lancaster PA 6 hrs
*WNTE(FM) Mansfield PA 5 hrs
*WARC(FM) Meadville PA 8 hrs
WJST(FM) New Castle PA 1 hr
*WKDU(FM) Philadelphia PA 8 hrs
*WRCT(FM) Pittsburgh PA 12 hrs
WVMW-FM Scranton PA 2 hrs
*WSYC-FM Shippensburg PA 9 hrs
*WXVU(FM) Villanova PA 10 hrs
WSBA(AM) York PA 3 hrs
WBRU(FM) Providence RI 20 hrs
WARV(AM) Warwick RI 2 hrs
WOON(AM) Woonsocket RI 1 hr
WBSC(AM) Bennettsville SC 15 hrs
WCRE(AM) Cheraw SC 5 hrs
WFIS(AM) Fountain Inn SC 4 hrs
WJBS(AM) Holly Hill SC 17 hrs
WRIX(AM) Homeland Park SC 7 hrs
*KSDJ(FM) Brookings SD 8 hrs
*WYXI(AM) Athens TN 1 hr
*WHCB(FM) Bristol TN 1 hr
*WMBW(FM) Chattanooga TN 1 hr
*WAPX-FM Clarksville TN 6 hrs
WKBL(AM) Covington TN 4 hrs
WHIN(AM) Gallatin TN 2 hrs
*WVCP(FM) Gallatin TN 8 hrs
WITA(AM) Knoxville TN 8 hrs
WLIL(AM) Lenoir City TN 1 hr
WDXL(AM) Lexington TN 4 hrs
*WEVL(FM) Memphis TN 10 hrs
WXRQ(AM) Mount Pleasant TN 4 hrs
WGNS(AM) Murfreesboro TN 7 hrs
WLAC(AM) Nashville TN 20 hrs
*WRVU(FM) Nashville TN 3 hrs
*WUTS(FM) Sewanee TN 2 hrs
WLIJ(AM) Shelbyville TN 1 hr
*KGNZ(AM) Abilene TX 2 hrs
KLVQ(AM) Athens TX 1 hr
KAGC(AM) Bryan TX 2 hrs
*KWTS(FM) Canyon TX 3 hrs
KNES(FM) Fairfield TX 3 hrs
KGVL(AM) Greenville TX 1 hr
*KOOP(FM) Hornsby TX 2 hrs
*KPFT(FM) Houston TX 15 hrs
KHVL(AM) Huntsville TX 5 hrs
*KBJS(FM) Jacksonville TX 1 hr
*KTAI(FM) Kingsville TX 8 hrs
KVLG(AM) La Grange TX 1 hr
KSHN-FM Liberty TX 3 hrs
KFRO(AM) Longview TX 3 hrs
KHKZ(FM) Mercedes TX 3 hrs
KLVL(AM) Pasadena TX 4 hrs
KLGO(FM) Thorndale TX 6 hrs
*KZMU(FM) Moab UT 3 hrs
*KRCL(FM) Salt Lake City UT 20 hrs
*WTJU(FM) Charlottesville VA 8 hrs
WKEY(AM) Covington VA 1 hr
WFAX(AM) Falls Church VA 15 hrs
WMNA(AM) Gretna VA 2 hrs
WKWI(FM) Kilmarnock VA 6 hrs
*WVRU(FM) Radford VA 6 hrs
WKBA(AM) Vinton VA 10 hrs
WKCI(AM) Waynesboro VA 3 hrs
*KUGS(FM) Bellingham WA 10 hrs
*KZUU(FM) Pullman WA 12 hrs
*KNHC(FM) Seattle WA
*KSFC(FM) Spokane WA 2 hrs
*KUPS(FM) Tacoma WA 18 hrs

KJOX(AM) Yakima WA 2 hrs
*WORT(FM) Madison WI 3 hrs
*WMSE(FM) Milwaukee WI 13 hrs
*KUWS(FM) Superior WI 4 hrs
*WCCX(FM) Waukesha WI 3 hrs
*WVWC(FM) Buckhannon WV 4 hrs
*WWVU-FM Morgantown WV 9 hrs
*WQAB(FM) Philippi WV 2 hrs
*WPHP(FM) Wheeling WV 4 hrs

Bluegrass

*WQPR(FM) Muscle Shoals AL
WNUZ(AM) Talladega AL 6 hrs
*KABF(FM) Little Rock AR 6 hrs
*KFJC(FM) Los Altos CA 8 hrs
*KCSN(FM) Northridge CA 5 hrs
*KAJX(FM) Aspen CO 2 hrs
*KDUR(FM) Durango CO 6 hrs
WWOJ(FM) Avon Park FL 2 hrs
WTUF(FM) Boston GA 5 hrs
*WUWG(FM) Carrollton GA 2 hrs
*WQNA(FM) Springfield IL 6 hrs
*WUIS(FM) Springfield IL 2 hrs
WAWK(AM) Kendallville IN 2 hrs
WMRS(FM) Monticello IN 2 hrs
*WPUM(FM) Rensselaer IN 3 hrs
*WECI(FM) Richmond IN 19 hrs
*WMHD-FM Terre Haute IN 1 hr
*KANU(FM) Lawrence KS 4 hrs
WGOH(AM) Grayson KY
WWAG(FM) McKee KY 9 hrs
*WKMS-FM Murray KY 3 hrs
WTKY-FM Tompkinsville KY 6 hrs
*WDET-FM Detroit MI 2 hrs
*WMUK(FM) Kalamazoo MI 4 hrs
*KBEM-FM Minneapolis MN 4 hrs
*KOPN(FM) Columbia MO 6 hrs
KTJJ(FM) Farmington MO 2 hrs
*KMST(FM) Rolla MO 5 hrs
WSKK(FM) Ripley MS 2 hrs
*WCCE(FM) Buie's Creek NC 3 hrs
*WUAG(FM) Greensboro NC 2 hrs
WECR(AM) Newland NC 2 hrs
WQDR(FM) Raleigh NC
WLHC(FM) Robbins NC 5 hrs
WEGG(AM) Rose Hill NC 10 hrs
WTQR(FM) Winston-Salem NC 2 hrs
*WDVR(FM) Delaware Township NJ 6 hrs
*WBJB-FM Lincroft NJ 3 hrs
*WBZC(FM) Pemberton NJ 4 hrs
*KRWG(FM) Las Cruces NM 8 hrs
*WBFO(FM) Buffalo NY 3 hrs
*WSQG-FM Ithaca NY 5 hrs
*WUBJ(FM) Jamestown NY 3 hrs
*WOLN(FM) Olean NY 3 hrs
*WCNY-FM Syracuse NY 3 hrs
WUNY(FM) Utica NY 3 hrs
*WJNY(FM) Watertown NY 3 hrs
*WOSU(FM) Columbus OH 12 hrs
*WYSO(FM) Yellow Springs OH 6 hrs
KVSP(AM) Oklahoma City OK 2 hrs
WWSM(AM) Annville-Cleona PA 3 hrs
WSKE(FM) Everett PA 3 hrs
*WVMM(FM) Grantham PA 1 hr
WJSA(AM) Jersey Shore PA 1 hr
WJSA-FM Jersey Shore PA 1 hr
WLMI(FM) Kane PA 1 hr
WPHB(AM) Philipsburg PA 4 hrs
*WYEP-FM Pittsburgh PA 4 hrs
*WXLV(FM) Schnecksville PA
*WQSU(FM) Selinsgrove PA 7 hrs
*WBYO(FM) Sellersville PA 2 hrs
*WBYX(FM) Stroudsburg PA 3. hrs
*WZZD(FM) Warwick PA 3 hrs
WCRI(FM) Block Island RI 4 hrs
WVFB(FM) Celina TN 6 hrs
*WHRS(FM) Cookeville TN 1 hr
WEMB(AM) Erwin TN 2 hrs
*WVCP(FM) Gallatin TN 2 hrs
WCLC(AM) Jamestown TN 3 hrs
WWAM(AM) Jasper TN 1 hr
WLAF(AM) La Follette TN 7 hrs
*WRVU(FM) Nashville TN 3 hrs
*KETR(FM) Commerce TX 3 hrs

KSWA(AM) Graham TX 2 hrs
KSHN-FM Liberty TX 2 hrs
*KOCV(AM) Odessa TX 2 hrs
KZHN(AM) Paris TX
WKDE-FM Altavista VA 10 hrs
WMNA(AM) Gretna VA 20 hrs
WSIG(FM) Mount Jackson VA 6 hrs
*WKDW(AM) Staunton VA 1 hr
WKCW(AM) Warrenton VA
*KBCS(FM) Bellevue WA
*WOJB(FM) Reserve WI 2 hrs
WVRQ-FM Viroqua WI 2 hrs
*WVMR(AM) Frost WV 5 hrs
*WWVU-FM Morgantown WV 1 hr
WMOV(AM) Ravenswood WV 10 hrs
WHAW(AM) Weston WV 8 hrs
KKTY-FM Douglas WY 1 hr

Blues

*KUAC(FM) Fairbanks AK 4 hrs
*KTNA(FM) Talkeetna AK 5 hrs
WDLT-FM Chickasaw AL 18 hrs
*WVAS(FM) Montgomery AL 9 hrs
*WQPR(FM) Muscle Shoals AL
*WVUA-FM Tuscaloosa AL 3 hrs
KFFA(AM) Helena AR 8 hrs
*KASU Jonesboro AR
KERX(FM) Paris AR 3 hrs
KWKM(FM) Saint Johns AZ 1 hr
*KNCA(FM) Burney CA 6 hrs
*KSPC(FM) Claremont CA 4 hrs
*KFSR(FM) Fresno CA 6 hrs
*KKJZ(FM) Long Beach CA 15 hrs
*KSBR(FM) Mission Viejo CA 3 hrs
*KNSQ(FM) Mount Shasta CA 6 hrs
*KVMR(FM) Nevada City CA 7 hrs
KHOP(FM) Oakdale CA 2 hrs
*KZYX(FM) Philo CA 3 hrs
KRXQ(FM) Sacramento CA 1 hr
*KXJZ(FM) Sacramento CA 7 hrs
*KCPR(FM) San Luis Obispo CA 3 hrs
*KCSM(FM) San Mateo CA 5 hrs
*KSCU(FM) Santa Clara CA 3 hrs
*KRCC(FM) Colorado Springs CO 5 hrs
*KDUR(FM) Durango CO 6 hrs
KIBT(FM) Fountain CO 3 hrs
*KWSB-FM Gunnison CO 3 hrs
KWUF-FM Pagosa Springs CO 10 hrs
*KVNF(FM) Paonia CO 3 hrs
*KOTO(FM) Telluride CO 7 hrs
*WESU(FM) Middletown CT 10 hrs
*WFCS(FM) New Britain CT 12 hrs
*WUCF-FM Orlando FL 4 hrs
*WFCF(FM) Saint Augustine FL 4 hrs
*WKPX(FM) Sunrise FL 3 hrs
*WCLK(FM) Atlanta GA 3 hrs
WZBN(FM) Camilla GA 5 hrs
*KUNI(FM) Cedar Falls IA 2 hrs
*KCCK-FM Cedar Rapids IA 12 hrs
KROS(AM) Clinton IA 1 hr
*KDUB(FM) Dubuque IA 5 hrs
*KRNI(AM) Mason City IA 5 hrs
*KUNY(FM) Mason City IA 5 hrs
*KDMR(FM) Mitchellville IA 5 hrs
*KOJI(FM) Okoboji IA 4 hrs
*KWIT(FM) Sioux City IA 2 hrs
KECH-FM Sun Valley ID 8. hrs
*WEFT(FM) Champaign IL 10 hrs
WMKB(FM) Earlville IL 5 hrs
*WIUM(FM) Macomb IL 7 hrs
*WIUS(FM) Macomb IL 4 hrs
*WQUB(FM) Quincy IL 2 hrs
*WNIU(FM) Rockford IL 4 hrs
*WDML(FM) Woodlawn IL 1 hr
WTTS(FM) Bloomington IN 2 hrs
*WVPE(FM) Elkhart IN 15 hrs
*WFYI-FM Indianapolis IN 4 hrs
*WCYT(FM) Lafayette Township IN 2 hrs
*WSND-FM Notre Dame IN
*KTCC(FM) Colby KS 3 hrs
*KANU(FM) Lawrence KS 4 hrs
*KJHK(FM) Lawrence KS 2 hrs

WTKY(AM) Tompkinsville KY
KJMG(FM) Bastrop LA 12 hrs
*WGBH(FM) Boston MA 8 hrs
*WESM(FM) Princess Anne MD 5 hrs
WBQI(FM) Bar Harbor ME 15 hrs
*WMHB(FM) Waterville ME
WGTO(AM) Cassopolis MI 4 hrs
*WHFR(FM) Dearborn MI 12 hrs
*WDET-FM Detroit MI 3 hrs
*WDBM(FM) East Lansing MI 4 hrs
WKLT(FM) Kalkaska MI 2 hrs
WNWN(AM) Portage MI 3 hrs
WKRR(FM) Portage MI 4 hrs
*WPHS(FM) Warren MI 3 hrs
*WTIP(FM) Grand Marais MN 15 hrs
*KOPN(FM) Columbia MO 13 hrs
*KKFI(FM) Kansas City MO 9 hrs
KPOW-FM La Monte MO 6 hrs
*KGSP(FM) Parkville MO 12 hrs
KBFL(AM) Springfield MO 4 hrs
WESE(FM) Baldwyn MS 6 hrs
WJZD-FM Long Beach MS
*WASU-FM Boone NC 2 hrs
*WNAA(FM) Greensboro NC 3 hrs
*WUAG(FM) Greensboro NC 4 hrs
WVOD(FM) Manteo NC 2 hrs
*WSHA(FM) Raleigh NC 8 hrs
*WNCW(FM) Spindale NC 4 hrs
*KCND(FM) Bismarck ND 2 hrs
*KFJM(FM) Grand Forks ND 3 hrs
*KZUM(FM) Lincoln NE 13 hrs
*KKCD(FM) Omaha NE 1 hr
*KWSC(FM) Wayne NE 2 hrs
WHDQ(AM) Claremont NH 3 hrs
*WUNH(FM) Durham NH 3 hrs
WFRD(FM) Hanover NH 1 hr
*WNEC-FM Henniker NH 4 hrs
*WKNH(FM) Keene NH 3 hrs
*WPCR-FM Plymouth NH 3 hrs
*WNTI(FM) Hackettstown NJ 11 hrs
*WBJB-FM Lincroft NJ 4 hrs
KRSI(FM) Garapan-Saipan NP 6 hrs
*WBFO(FM) Buffalo NY 8 hrs
*WGMC(FM) Greece NY 3 hrs
*WICB(FM) Ithaca NY 2 hrs
WVBR-FM Ithaca NY 5 hrs
*WUBJ(FM) Jamestown NY 8 hrs
*WOLN(FM) Olean NY 8 hrs
WZOZ(FM) Oneonta NY 2 hrs
WTKV(FM) Oswego NY 1 hr
WPDH(FM) Poughkeepsie NY
*WSPN(FM) Saratoga Springs NY 9 hrs
*WUSB(FM) Stony Brook NY 10 hrs
*WAER(FM) Syracuse NY 3 hrs
*WCBE(FM) Columbus OH 3 hrs
WJZE(FM) Oak Harbor OH
*WUSO(FM) Springfield OH 3 hrs
WJUC(FM) Swanton OH 5 hrs wkly
*WXTS-FM Toledo OH 5 hrs
*WXUT(FM) Toledo OH 2 hrs
*WYSO(FM) Yellow Springs OH 4 hrs
*KGOU(FM) Norman OK 8 hrs
KROU(FM) Spencer OK 8 hrs
*KSMF(FM) Ashland OR 6 hrs
*KSBA(FM) Coos Bay OR 6 hrs
*KLCC(FM) Eugene OR 3 hrs
*KMHD(FM) Gresham OR 15 hrs
*KSKF(FM) Klamath Falls OR 6 hrs
*KLCO(FM) Newport OR 4 hrs
KYTE(FM) Newport OR 2 hrs
KMCQ(FM) The Dalles OR 4 hrs
*WDCV-FM Carlisle PA 6 hrs
*WDNR(FM) Chester PA 2 hrs
WPSX(FM) Kane PA 3 hrs
*WKDU(FM) Philadelphia PA 3 hrs
*WYEP-FM Pittsburgh PA 7 hrs
WSYC-FM Shippensburg PA 2 hrs
WWII(AM) Shiremanstown PA 4 hrs
WPSU(FM) State College PA 3 hrs
*WRDV(FM) Warminster PA 3 hrs
WRLC(FM) Williamsport PA 3 hrs
*WRIU(FM) Kingston RI 3 hrs
*WSSB-FM Orangeburg SC 2 hrs
WRLT(FM) Franklin TN 2 hrs

*WETS(FM) Johnson City TN 12 hrs
*WRVU(FM) Nashville TN 3 hrs
*KAZI-FM Austin TX 6 hrs
*KUT(FM) Austin TX 6 hrs
*KLUB(FM) Bloomington TX 1 hr
*KOCV(FM) Odessa TX 4 hrs
*KUTX(FM) San Angelo TX 6 hrs
*KSTX(FM) San Antonio TX 6 hrs
KNCN(FM) Sinton TX 2 hrs
*KSUU(FM) Cedar City UT 4 hrs
*KZMU(FM) Moab UT 19 hrs
*WMRY(FM) Crozet VA 5 hrs
*WWHS-FM Hampden-Sydney VA 2 hrs
*WHOV(FM) Hampton VA 3 hrs
*WMRA(FM) Harrisonburg VA 5 hrs
*WMRL(FM) Lexington VA 5 hrs
*WVRU(FM) Radford VA 2 hrs
*WCVE(FM) Richmond VA 3 hrs
*WCWM(FM) Williamsburg VA 3 hrs
*WRMC-FM Middlebury VT 10 hrs
WIZN(FM) Vergennes VT 3 hrs
*KSER(FM) Everett WA 3 hrs
KKZX(FM) Spokane WA 2 hrs
*KUPS(FM) Tacoma WA 6 hrs
*WBSD(FM) Burlington WI 3 hrs
*WUEC(FM) Eau Claire WI 3 hrs
*WPNE(FM) Green Bay WI 2 hrs
WMCS(AM) Greenfield WI 6 hrs
*WHND(FM) Sister Bay WI 3 hrs
*WWSP(FM) Stevens Point WI 4 hrs
*WVWC(FM) Buckhannon WV 2 hrs

Children

KLEF(FM) Anchorage AK 1 hr
*KTOO(FM) Juneau AK 1 hr
KRSA(AM) Petersburg AK 10 hrs
*WMBV(FM) Dixons Mills AL 3 hrs
*WRWA(FM) Dothan AL 1 hr
*WTSU(FM) Montgomery-Troy AL 1 hr
KFMM(FM) Thatcher AZ 2 hrs
*KCFY(FM) Yuma AZ 7 hrs wkly
*KYRM(FM) Yuma AZ 6 hrs
KZRO(FM) Dunsmuir CA 2 hrs
KGBA-FM Holtville CA 4 hrs
*KPFK(FM) Los Angeles CA 1 hr
KSPN(FM) Los Angeles CA 24 hrs
*KXLU(FM) Los Angeles CA 1 hr
KWVE(FM) San Clemente CA 3 hrs
KFAX(AM) San Francisco CA 1 hr
*WIHS(FM) Middletown CT 9 hrs
*WAFG(FM) Fort Lauderdale FL 4 hrs
*WJYO(FM) Fort Myers FL 5 hrs
*WJLF(FM) Gainesville FL 1 hr
*WGNK(FM) Pennsuco FL 6 hrs
*WBVM(FM) Tampa FL 4 hrs
*WTJB(FM) Columbus GA 1 hr
*KHMG(FM) Barrigada GU 2 hrs
*KHOE(FM) Fairfield IA 3 hrs
KTFC(FM) Sioux City IA 5 hrs
KTFG(FM) Sioux Rapids IA 5 hrs
*KCIR(FM) Twin Falls ID 2 hrs
*WUEV(FM) Evansville IN 5 hrs
*KJTY(FM) Topeka KS 5 hrs
*WKHS(FM) Worton MD 5 hrs
WMDR(AM) Augusta ME
WHCF(FM) Bangor ME 5 1/2 hrs
WBQX(FM) Thomaston ME 1 hr
WDBC(AM) Escanaba MI 1 hr
*WLNZ(FM) Lansing MI 1 hr
*KJLY(FM) Blue Earth MN 4 hrs
*WTIP(FM) Grand Marais MN
*KGNN-FM Cuba MO 7 hrs
KKBL(FM) Monett MO 2 hrs
*KGNV(FM) Washington MO 6 hrs
*WPAE(FM) Centreville MS 5 hrs
*WMBU(FM) Forest MS 5 hrs
*KABU(FM) Fort Totten ND 12 hrs
WMVB(AM) Millville NJ 3 hrs
*WMHI(FM) Cape Vincent NY 11 hrs
WYBG(AM) Massena NY
*WRHO(FM) Oneonta NY 2 hrs
*WMHR(FM) Syracuse NY 11 hrs
*WMHN(FM) Webster NY 11 hrs
WFCJ(FM) Miamisburg OH 2 hrs

*KIHN(AM) Hugo OK 1 hr
*KMUN(FM) Astoria OR 6 hrs
*KWVA(FM) Eugene OR 4 hrs
*WFKJ(FM) Cashtown PA 12 hrs
*WDNR(FM) Chester PA 2 hrs
WCOH-FM DuBois PA 2 hrs
*WXPN(FM) Philadelphia PA 5 hrs
WCTL(FM) Union City PA 1 hr
*WTMV(FM) Youngsville PA 10 hrs
*KLND(FM) Little Eagle SD 4 hrs
*WHCB(FM) Bristol TN 10 hrs
KBYG(AM) Big Spring TX 1 hr
KPSM(FM) Brownwood TX 3 hrs
WRR(FM) Dallas TX 2 hrs
*KNLE-FM Round Rock TX 4 hrs
*KTER(FM) Rudolph TX 4 hrs
*KVNE(FM) Tyler TX 4 hrs
*WTJU(FM) Charlottesville VA 2 hrs
*WVPS(FM) Burlington VT .5 hrs
WWOD(FM) Hartford VT 3 hrs
WCVT(FM) Stowe VT 1 hr
*WWMP(FM) Waterbury VT 3 hrs
WTWN(AM) Wells River VT
*KRLF(FM) Pullman WA 5 hrs
*KDNA(FM) Yakima WA 5. hrs
*WGNV(FM) Milladore WI 4 hrs
*WVPG(FM) Parkersburg WV 1 hr
*WQAB(FM) Philippi WV 2 hrs

Chinese

KGBA-FM Holtville CA 14 hrs
KKLA-FM Los Angeles CA 2 hrs
KEST(AM) San Francisco CA
*KUSF(FM) San Francisco CA 7.5 hrs
KSJX(AM) San Jose CA 10 hrs
WJDA(AM) Quincy MA 3 hrs
*WDBM(FM) East Lansing MI 4 hrs
*KRNM(FM) Chalan Kanoa-Saipan NP 1 hr
*WUSB(FM) Stony Brook NY 1 hr
*WJCU(FM) University Heights OH 1 hr
WBZK(AM) York SC 10 hrs
*KHCB(AM) Galveston TX 13 hrs
*KHCB-FM Houston TX 1 hr
*KKER(FM) Kerrville TX 1 hr
*WUVT-FM Blacksburg VA 2 hrs

Christian

KYKD(FM) Bethel AK
KCAM(AM) Glennallen AK 8 hrs
KJLH-FM Compton CA 6 hrs
KNCO(FM) Grass Valley CA 4 hrs
KFTM(AM) Fort Morgan CO 6 hrs
WEBY(AM) Milton FL 7 hrs
WMGF(FM) Mount Dora FL 20 hrs
WROM(AM) Rome GA
WDML(FM) Woodlawn IL 3 hrs
*WMHD-FM Terre Haute IN 2 hrs
KIND-FM Independence KS 2 hrs
*WCVK(FM) Bowling Green KY 10 hrs
*WHFC(FM) Bel Air MD 6 hrs
*WPHS(FM) Warren MI 4 hrs
*KWJC(FM) Liberty MO 10 hrs
KNEM(AM) Nevada MO 5 hrs
KNMO(FM) Nevada MO 5 hrs
KAYX(FM) Richmond MO
*KKDY(FM) West Plains MO 3 hrs
*WASU-FM Boone NC 3 hrs
WLHC(FM) Robbins NC 5 hrs
KTNC(AM) Falls City NE 1 hr
*WKNH(FM) Keene NH 3 hrs
*WITR(FM) Henrietta NY 10 hrs
WRIP(FM) Windham NY 2 hrs
*WRDL(FM) Ashland OH 7 hrs
KGFY(FM) Stillwater OK 4 hrs
*WCYJ-FM Waynesburg PA 3 hrs
WFIS(AM) Fountain Inn SC 3 hrs
*WKTS(FM) Kingston TN 2 hrs wkly
WNRQ(FM) Nashville TN 6 hrs
KRUN(AM) Ballinger TX 4 hrs
KQTY-FM Borger TX 5 hrs
*KVTT(FM) Dallas TX 6 hrs

*KRTU(FM) San Antonio TX 2 hrs
WELD-FM Moorefield WV

Classic Rock

KMMT(FM) Mammoth Lakes CA 4 hrs
KVAY(FM) Lamar CO 4 hrs
*WXCI(FM) Danbury CT 3 hrs
WSGL(FM) Naples FL 5 hrs
*WCSF(FM) Joliet IL 4 hrs
*WRRG(FM) River Grove IL 2 hrs
*WBKE-FM North Manchester IN 6 hrs
*WECI(FM) Richmond IN 16 hrs
*WVUR-FM Valparaiso IN 3 hrs
*KTCC(FM) Colby KS 3 hrs
*KMVC(FM) Marshall MO 4 hrs
WERX-FM Columbia NC
KHND(FM) Harvey ND
*WPSC-FM Wayne NJ 12 hrs
*WCWP(FM) Brookville NY 2 hrs
*WQKE(FM) Plattsburgh NY 12 hrs
WRIP(FM) Windham NY 4 hrs
WMKX(FM) Brookville PA 6 hrs
*WJRH(FM) Easton PA 4 hrs
*WCYJ-FM Waynesburg PA 3 hrs
*WDOM(FM) Providence RI 3 hrs
KNCN(FM) Sinton TX 2 hrs
*WVBC(FM) Bethany WV 8 hrs
KKTY-FM Douglas WY 3 hrs

Classical

*KBRW(AM) Barrow AK 2 hrs
*KYUK(AM) Bethel AK 4 hrs
KCAM(AM) Glennallen AK 10 hrs
*KRBD(FM) Ketchikan AK 11 hrs
KIAM(AM) Nenana AK 1 hr
KICY-FM Nome AK 2 hrs
*KNOM(AM) Nome AK 5 hrs
*KNOM-FM Nome AK 5 hrs
KRSA(AM) Petersburg AK 5 hrs
*KCAW(FM) Sitka AK 15 hrs
*KSTK(FM) Wrangell AK 4 hrs
KKEG(FM) Bentonville AR 2 hrs
KESA(FM) Eureka Springs AR 5 hrs
*KSMC(FM) Moraga CA 4 hrs
*KAZU(FM) Pacific Grove CA 3 hrs
*KZYX(FM) Philo CA 14 hrs
*KUCR(FM) Riverside CA 14 hrs
KJDX(FM) Susanville CA 5 hrs
*KCSS(FM) Turlock CA 9 hrs
*KGNU-FM Boulder CO 13 hrs
*KDUR(FM) Durango CO 6 hrs
*KCIC(FM) Grand Junction CO 14 hrs
*KSUT(FM) Ignacio CO 8 hrs
*KVNF(FM) Paonia CO 15 hrs
*KOTO(FM) Telluride CO 6 hrs
*WPKN(FM) Bridgeport CT 2 hrs
*WRTC-FM Hartford CT 4 hrs
*WCNI(FM) New London CT 6 hrs
*WGSK(FM) South Kent CT 1 hr
*WWEB(FM) Wallingford CT 2 hrs
*WNHU(FM) West Haven CT 9 hrs
*WVUD(FM) Newark DE 10 hrs
WKEY-FM Key West FL 4 hrs
*WRAS(FM) Atlanta GA 3 hrs
*WREK(FM) Atlanta GA 15 hrs
WMOG(AM) Brunswick GA 1 hr
*WBCX(FM) Gainesville GA 20 hrs
*KDFR(FM) Des Moines IA 2 hrs
*KCMR(FM) Mason City IA 5 hrs
KSAS-FM Caldwell ID 2 hrs
KSRA(AM) Salmon ID 1 hr
KSRA-FM Salmon ID 1 hr
*WESN(FM) Bloomington IL 6 hrs
*WHPK-FM Chicago IL 10 hrs
*WEPS(FM) Elgin IL 4 hrs
*WVKC(FM) Galesburg IL 18 hrs
*WJCH(FM) Joliet IL 2 hrs
*WMXM(FM) Lake Forest IL 3 hrs
*WLRA(FM) Lockport IL 6 hrs
*WDSO(FM) Chesterton IN 1 hr
*WBKE-FM North Manchester IN 10 hrs
*WPUM(FM) Rensselaer IN 3 hrs
*WMHD-FM Terre Haute IN 4 hrs

*WVUR-FM Valparaiso IN 3 hrs
*WVUB(FM) Vincennes IN 6 hrs
KIND(AM) Independence KS 3 hrs
*WKMS-FM Murray KY 15 hrs
*WOMR(FM) Provincetown MA 16 hrs
*WYAJ(FM) Sudbury MA 3 hrs
WMVY(FM) Tisbury MA 4 hrs
*WCHC(FM) Worcester MA 6 hrs
*WHFC(FM) Bel Air MD 18 hrs
WRSR(FM) Owosso MI 1 hr
KNXR(FM) Rochester MN 4 hrs
*WMCN(FM) Saint Paul MN 4 hrs
*KQAL(FM) Winona MN 14 hrs
KIXQ(FM) Joplin MO 3 hrs
*KWJC(FM) Liberty MO 10 hrs
*KGNV(FM) Washington MO 5 hrs
*KGLT(FM) Bozeman MT 11 hrs
*KMSM-FM Butte MT 2 hrs
*KNMC(FM) Havre MT 10 hrs
KALS(FM) Kalispell MT 1 hr
*WFSS(FM) Fayetteville NC 5 hrs
WVOD(FM) Manteo NC 6 hrs
WCVP(AM) Murphy NC 20 hrs
KHAS(AM) Hastings NE 2 hrs
*KLPR(FM) Kearney NE 18 hrs
KCMI(FM) Terrytown NE 4 hrs
*WKNH(FM) Keene NH 4 hrs
*WPCR-FM Plymouth NH 3 hrs
*WKDN-FM Camden NJ 2 hrs
WKOE(FM) North Cape May NJ 3 hrs
*WLFR(FM) Pomona NJ 4 hrs
*KUNM(FM) Albuquerque NM 12 hrs
KPCL(FM) Farmington NM 1 hr
*WXLH(FM) Blue Mountain Lake NY
*WBFO(FM) Buffalo NY 1 hr
*WSLU(FM) Canton NY
*WHCL-FM Clinton NY 9 hrs
*WRCU-FM Hamilton NY 4 hrs
*WJSL(FM) Houghton NY 5 hrs
WHVW(FM) Hyde Park NY 16 hrs
*WBAI(FM) New York NY 5 hrs
WSRK(FM) Oneonta NY 1 hr
WLIM(AM) Patchogue NY 7 hrs
*WPNR-FM Utica NY 10 hrs
*WFRW(FM) Webster NY 2 hrs
*WBGU(FM) Bowling Green OH 3 hrs
*WCUE(FM) Cuyahoga Falls OH 2 hrs
*WLFC(FM) Findlay OH 3 hrs
*WMCO(FM) New Concord OH 4 hrs
*WUSO(FM) Springfield OH 3 hrs
*WYTN(FM) Youngstown OH 2 hrs
WBBZ(AM) Ponca City OK 5 hrs
*KBVR(FM) Corvallis OR 4 hrs
*KEOL(FM) La Grande OR 4 hrs
*KRRC(FM) Portland OR 4 hrs
*WLVR(FM) Bethlehem PA 8 hrs
*WESS(FM) East Stroudsburg PA 4 hrs
*WZBT(FM) Gettysburg PA 3 hrs
*WIUP-FM Indiana PA 15 hrs
WJSA(AM) Jersey Shore PA 1 hr
WJSA-FM Jersey Shore PA 1 hr
*WFNM(FM) Lancaster PA 2 hrs
*WARC(FM) Meadville PA 10 hrs
*WPEL(FM) Montrose PA 1 hr
WJST(AM) New Castle PA 1 hr
*WHYY-FM Philadelphia PA 4 hrs
*WRCT(FM) Pittsburgh PA 3 hrs
*WUSR(FM) Scranton PA 5 hrs
*WVMW-FM Scranton PA 7 hrs
*WSYC-FM Shippensburg PA 2 hrs
*WRLC(FM) Williamsport PA 1 hr
*WVYC(FM) York PA 8 hrs
*WTMV(FM) Youngsville PA 2.5 hrs
WTPM(FM) Aguadilla PR 7 hrs
WMUU-FM Greenville SC 14 hrs
WMYB(FM) Myrtle Beach SC
*WHCB(FM) Bristol TN 1 hr
*WFHU(FM) Henderson TN 7 hrs
*WFMQ(FM) Lebanon TN 6 hrs
*WRVU(FM) Nashville TN 6 hrs
*WDNX(FM) Olive Hill TN 5 hrs
*WUTS(FM) Sewanee TN 4 hrs
*KWTS(FM) Canyon TX 4 hrs

*KTRU(FM) Houston TX 3 hrs
*KNTU(FM) McKinney TX 6 hrs
*KSUU(FM) Cedar City UT 3 hrs
*KPCW(FM) Park City UT 17 hrs
*WWHS-FM Hampden-Sydney VA 2 hrs
*WVRU(FM) Radford VA 15 hrs
*WDCE(FM) Richmond VA 3 hrs
*WCWM(FM) Williamsburg VA 11 hrs
*WIUJ(FM) Charlotte Amalie VI 5 hrs
*WIUV(FM) Castleton VT 3 hrs
*WJSC-FM Johnson VT 3 hrs
*WWLR(FM) Lyndonville VT 2 hrs
*WRMC-FM Middlebury VT 15 hrs
WDEV(AM) Waterbury VT 1 hr
KULE-FM Ephrata WA 5 hrs
KEYG(AM) Grand Coulee WA 4 hrs
*KMLW(FM) Moses Lake WA 1 hr
*KAGU(FM) Spokane WA 2 hrs
*WMSE(FM) Milwaukee WI 3 hrs
*WSUP(FM) Platteville WI 4 hrs
WRJN(AM) Racine WI 2 hrs
*WVBC(FM) Bethany WV 2 hrs
*WVWC(FM) Buckhannon WV 2 hrs
WZJO(FM) Dunbar WV 2 hrs
*WWVU-FM Morgantown WV 4 hrs
KMTN(FM) Jackson WY

Comedy

KTCL(FM) Wheat Ridge CO 1 hr
WWHP(FM) Farmer City IL 1 hr
KEYN-FM Wichita KS 2 hrs
*WVSD(FM) Itta Bena MS 2 hrs
*WPCR-FM Plymouth NH 3 hrs

Contemporary Hit/Top-40

*KNOM(AM) Nome AK 12 hrs
*KNOM-FM Nome AK 12 hrs
*KCSS(FM) Turlock CA 10 hrs
*WXCI(FM) Danbury CT 3 hrs
WZHR(AM) Zephyrhills FL 10 hrs
KIOW(FM) Forest City IA 19 hrs
*WBKE-FM North Manchester IN 10 hrs
WTNM(FM) Water Valley MS 4 hrs
KATQ-FM Plentywood MT
*WIRQ(FM) Rochester NY 3 hrs
WQIO(FM) Mount Vernon OH 4 hrs
*WKVR-FM Huntingdon PA 15 hrs
WVOZ(AM) San Juan PR 15 hrs
*KRLF(FM) Pullman WA 1 hr
*KVTI(FM) Tacoma WA 3 hrs

Country

*KBRW(AM) Barrow AK 7 hrs
*KYUK(AM) Bethel AK 4 hrs
*KRBD(FM) Ketchikan AK 14 hrs
*KSTK(FM) Wrangell AK 16 hrs
*KPFA(FM) Berkeley CA 18 hrs
*KFJC(FM) Los Altos CA 8 hrs
*KVMR(FM) Nevada City CA 7 hrs
*KAZU(FM) Pacific Grove CA 6 hrs
*KVNF(FM) Paonia CO 5 hrs
*KOTO(FM) Telluride CO 12 hrs
*WWEB(FM) Wallingford CT 2 hrs
*WAMU(FM) Washington DC 4 hrs
KSTO(FM) Hagatna GU 14 hrs
KROS(AM) Clinton IA 6 hrs
KGRN(AM) Grinnell IA 12 hrs
WTAY(AM) Robinson IL 12 hrs
WTYE(FM) Robinson IL 12 hrs
*WPUM(FM) Rensselaer IN 3 hrs
WLVK(FM) Fort Knox KY
*KLSP(FM) Angola LA 6 hrs
*WKHS(FM) Worton MD 2 hrs
WBPW(FM) Presque Isle ME
*WDBM(FM) East Lansing MI 4 hrs
*WPHS(FM) Warren MI 4 hrs
*WMCN(FM) Saint Paul MN 2 hrs
*KXEI(FM) Havre MT 1 hr
*WASU-FM Boone NC 8 hrs

WCVP(AM) Murphy NC 12 hrs
*KMHA(FM) Four Bears ND 8 hrs
*WNEC-FM Henniker NH 3 hrs
*WDVR(FM) Delaware Township NJ 12 hrs
WLNL(AM) Horseheads NY 1 hr
WVBR-FM Ithaca NY 4 hrs
*WKCR-FM New York NY 6 hrs
*WGGO(AM) Salamanca NY 5 hrs
*WKWZ(FM) Syosset NY 6 hrs
*WBGU(FM) Bowling Green OH 4 hrs
*KRSC-FM Claremore OK 5 hrs
*KRVM-FM Eugene OR 1 hr
*KWVA(FM) Eugene OR 3 hrs
*KRRC(FM) Portland OR 2 hrs
*WFKJ(AM) Cashtown PA 4 hrs
*WCUC-FM Clarion PA 6 hrs
WSKE(FM) Everett PA 2 hrs
*WRCT(FM) Pittsburgh PA 3 hrs
*WXLV(FM) Schnecksville PA
*WQSU(FM) Selinsgrove PA 6 hrs
*WRDV(FM) Warminster PA 4 hrs
*WCYJ-FM Waynesburg PA 3 hrs
WCHE(AM) West Chester PA 2 hrs
*WDOM(FM) Providence RI 2 hrs
WWLX(AM) Lawrenceburg TN 8 hrs
*WEVL(FM) Memphis TN 15 hrs
WSM(AM) Nashville TN 12 hrs
*WUTS(FM) Sewanee TN 2 hrs
*KPCW(FM) Park City UT 18 hrs
WCLM(AM) Highland Springs VA
*WJSC-FM Johnson VT 3 hrs
*WBSD(FM) Burlington WI 4 hrs
*WOJB(FM) Reserve WI 15 hrs

Croation

WELW(AM) Willoughby-Eastlake OH 3 hrs
WKBN(AM) Youngstown OH 2 hrs
WFGI(AM) Charleroi PA 1 hr
WOGI(FM) Charleroi PA 1 hr
WEDO(AM) McKeesport PA 1 hr
WKZV(AM) Washington PA 1 hr

Czech

KMRY(AM) Cedar Rapids IA 3 hrs
WAAL(FM) Binghamton NY 1 hr
WOMP(AM) Bellaire OH 2 hrs
KAGC(AM) Bryan TX 2 hrs
KTAE(AM) Cameron TX 8 hrs
KULP(AM) El Campo TX 5 hrs
KHLT(AM) Hallettsville TX 5 hrs
KHBR(AM) Hillsboro TX 2 hrs
KVLG(AM) La Grange TX 6 hrs
KTEM(AM) Temple TX 3 hrs
WAUN(FM) Kewaunee WI 1 hr

Disco

*WVBU-FM Lewisburg PA 6 hrs

Discussion

WNDN(FM) Chiefland FL

Diversified

*KALW(FM) San Francisco CA 1 1/2 hrs
WUMS(FM) University MS 2 hrs
*WNAA(FM) Greensboro NC 7 hrs

Drama/Literature

*KUAR(FM) Little Rock AR 2 hrs
*KZYX(FM) Philo CA 3 hrs
*KOTO(FM) Telluride CO 3 hrs
*WGLT(FM) Normal IL 2 hrs
*KMSK(FM) Austin MN 3 hrs
*KMSU(FM) Mankato MN 3 hrs
WNCW(FM) Spindale NC 3 hrs
*WNYC-FM New York NY 5 hrs
*KAGU(FM) Spokane WA 2 hrs

*WQAB(FM) Philippi WV 2 hrs

Easy Listening

KRBB(FM) Wichita KS 18 hrs
KCHR(AM) Charleston MO

Educational

*KXRJ(FM) Russellville AR
*KCRH(FM) Hayward CA 1 hr
KVEC(AM) San Luis Obispo CA
*KYCC(FM) Stockton CA 1 hr
WGCH(AM) Greenwich CT 2 hrs
*WJMJ(FM) Hartford CT
*WHIF(FM) Palatka FL 10 hrs
*WKGC(FM) Panama City Beach FL 8 hrs
KGUM(AM) Hagatna GU 1 hr
*WEPS(FM) Elgin IL 1 hr
*WDCB(FM) Glen Ellyn IL 12 hrs
*WEEM-FM Pendleton IN 4 hrs
*WOMR(FM) Provincetown MA 10 hrs
*WFWM(FM) Frostburg MD 5 hrs
*WNMU-FM Marquette MI
*WBAI(FM) New York NY
*WCWS(FM) Wooster OH 8 hrs
KBNP(AM) Portland OR
*WESS(FM) East Stroudsburg PA 7 hrs
WPWT(AM) Colonial Heights TN 1 hr
*KMFA(FM) Austin TX 2 hrs
WRVA(AM) Richmond VA 2 hrs
WWYO(AM) Pineville WV 2 hrs

Eskimo

KAGV(AM) Big Lake AK 3 hrs
*KNOM(AM) Nome AK 6 hrs
*KNOM-FM Nome AK 6 hrs

Ethnic

*KRBD(FM) Ketchikan AK 5 hrs
*KALW(FM) San Francisco CA 1 hr
*KALW(FM) San Francisco CA 4 hrs
*WJFP(FM) Fort Pierce FL 8 hrs
WPSO(AM) New Port Richey FL
WCLA(AM) Claxton GA 6 hrs
*WUIS(FM) Springfield IL 1 hr
KVPI(AM) Ville Platte LA 12 hrs
WCAR(AM) Livonia MI
*KGVA(FM) Fort Belknap Agency MT 15 hrs
*WSOU(FM) South Orange NJ 10 hrs
*KRNM(FM) Chalan Kanoa-Saipan NP 2 hrs
KRSI(AM) Garapan-Saipan NP 6 hrs
WVBR-FM Ithaca NY 5 hrs
WLIM(AM) Patchogue NY 1 hr
*KWVA(FM) Eugene OR 4 hrs
*WDIY(FM) Allentown PA 1 hr
WVWI(AM) Charlotte Amalie VI 2 hrs
WWKS(FM) Cruz Bay VI 25 hrs
WIZM(AM) La Crosse WI 2 hrs

Farsi

WUST(AM) Washington DC 5 hrs

Filipino

*KBRW(AM) Barrow AK 2 hrs
KCHJ(AM) Delano CA 3 hrs
*KECG(FM) El Cerrito CA 2 hrs
KKLA-FM Los Angeles CA 1
*KMPO(FM) Modesto CA 1 hr
KSJX(AM) San Jose CA 2 hrs
WPSO(AM) New Port Richey FL 1 hr
*V6AI(AM) Yap FM 5 hrs
KWAI(AM) Honolulu HI 7 hrs
KLAV(AM) Las Vegas NV 5 hrs

Finnish

*KUSF(FM) San Francisco CA 1 hr
*WFHB(FM) Bloomington IN 3 hrs
KRBT(AM) Eveleth MN 1 hr
*WBXL(FM) Baldwinsville NY 2 hrs

Folk

*KUAC(FM) Fairbanks AK 10 hrs
*KRBD(FM) Ketchikan AK 10 hrs
*WSGN(FM) Gadsden AL 2 hrs
*WQPR(FM) Muscle Shoals AL 5 hrs
*WUAL-FM Tuscaloosa AL 5 hrs
*KUAF(FM) Fayetteville AR 5 hrs
*KASU Jonesboro AR 4 hrs
*KABF(FM) Little Rock AR 10 hrs
*KUAR(FM) Little Rock AR 3 hrs
KCTT-FM Yellville AR 10 hrs
KVNA(AM) Flagstaff AZ 4hrs
*KXCI(FM) Tucson AZ 2 hrs
*KPFA(FM) Berkeley CA 10 hrs
*KNCA(FM) Burney CA 3 hrs
*KFSR(FM) Fresno CA 3 hrs
*KXLU(FM) Los Angeles CA 1 hr
*KSBR(FM) Mission Viejo CA 2 hrs
*KMPO(FM) Modesto CA 4 hrs
*KNSQ(FM) Mount Shasta CA 3 hrs
*KVMR(FM) Nevada City CA 13 hrs
*KAZU(FM) Pacific Grove CA 6 hrs
*KZYX(FM) Philo CA 8 hrs
KVYN(FM) Saint Helena CA 2 hrs
*KCBX(FM) San Luis Obispo CA 15 hrs
*KRCB-FM Santa Rosa CA 6 hrs
*KGNU-FM Boulder CO 20 hrs
*KMSA(FM) Grand Junction CO 2 hrs
*WSHU(FM) Fairfield CT 5 hrs
*WGRS(FM) Guilford CT 2 hrs
*WMNR(FM) Monroe CT 2 hrs
WYBC-FM New Haven CT 4 hrs
*WCNI(FM) New London CT 9 hrs
*WRXC(FM) Shelton CT 2 hrs
*WGSK(FM) South Kent CT 2 hrs
*WNHU(FM) West Haven CT 6 hrs
*WVUD(FM) Newark DE 15 hrs
*WUFT-FM Gainesville FL 1 hr
*WKGC(FM) Panama City Beach FL 2 hrs
*WFCF(FM) Saint Augustine FL 3 hrs
*WVFS(FM) Tallahassee FL 3 hrs
V6AH(AM) Pohnpei FM 20 hrs
*WUGA(FM) Athens GA 4 hrs
*WUWG(FM) Carrollton GA 2 hrs
*KUNI(FM) Cedar Falls IA 4 hrs
KROS(AM) Clinton IA 2 hrs
*KIWR(FM) Council Bluffs IA 2 hrs
*KDUB(FM) Dubuque IA 4 hrs
*KHOE(FM) Fairfield IA 6 hrs
*KRNI(AM) Mason City IA 4 hrs
*KUNY(FM) Mason City IA 4 hrs
*KDMR(FM) Mitchellville IA 2 hrs
*KRNL-FM Mount Vernon IA 2 hrs
*KBSU(AM) Boise ID
*KRFA-FM Moscow ID
*KUOI-FM Moscow ID 3 hrs
*WSIU(FM) Carbondale IL 3 hrs
*WEFT(FM) Champaign IL 10 hrs
WFMT(FM) Chicago IL 4 hrs
*WNIJ(FM) De Kalb IL 4 hrs
*WNUR-FM Evanston IL 3 hrs
*WDCB(FM) Glen Ellyn IL 12 hrs
*WIUM(FM) Macomb IL 7 hrs
*WGLT(FM) Normal IL 4 hrs
*WQUB(FM) Quincy IL 2 hrs
*WQNA(FM) Springfield IL 8 hrs
*WFHB(FM) Bloomington IN 10 hrs
*WVPE(FM) Elkhart IN 9 hrs
*WICR(FM) Indianapolis IN 1 hr
*KANZ(FM) Garden City KS 6 hrs
*KZNA(FM) Hill City KS 6 hrs
*KRPS(FM) Pittsburg KS 3 hrs
*KMUW(FM) Wichita KS 6 hrs
*WKUE(FM) Elizabethtown KY 5 hrs
*WKMS-FM Murray KY 3 hrs

*WDCL-FM Somerset KY 5 hrs
*WGBH(FM) Boston MA 10 hrs
*WAMQ(FM) Great Barrington MA 7 hrs
*WOMR(FM) Provincetown MA 19 hrs
*WBSL-FM Sheffield MA 2 hrs
*WMTB-FM Emmitsburg MD 1 hr
*WMHB(FM) Waterville ME
*WDET-FM Detroit MI 3 hrs
WOUF(FM) Frankfort MI 2 hrs
*WBLU-FM Grand Rapids MI 5 hrs
*WCMW(FM) Harbor Springs MI 3 hrs
*WLNZ(FM) Lansing MI 4 hrs
*WNMC-FM Traverse City MI 11 hrs
*WBLV(FM) Twin Lake MI 5 hrs
*WYCE(FM) Wyoming MI 1 hr
*KMSK(FM) Austin MN 5 hrs
*KBSB(FM) Bemidji MN 3 hrs
WMFG(FM) Hibbing MN
*KMSU(FM) Mankato MN 5 hrs
*KFAI(FM) Minneapolis MN 6 hrs
KVSC(FM) Saint Cloud MN
*WMCN(FM) Saint Paul MN 2 hrs
*KGAC(FM) Saint Peter MN 9 hrs
*KOPN(FM) Columbia MO 2 hrs
*KKFI(FM) Kansas City MO 4 hrs
*KCOZ(FM) Point Lookout MO 10 hrs
*KMST(FM) Rolla MO 5 hrs
*KEMC(FM) Billings MT 5 hrs
*KGLT(FM) Bozeman MT 12 hrs
*WCQS(FM) Asheville NC 9 hrs
*WBUX(FM) Buxton NC 20 hrs
*WUNC(FM) Chapel Hill NC 20 hrs
*WWCU(FM) Cullowhee NC 4. hrs
*WFSS(FM) Fayetteville NC 3 hrs
*WFQS(FM) Franklin NC 9 hrs
*WUND-FM Manteo NC 20 hrs
*WURI(FM) Manteo NC 20 hrs
*WZRU(FM) Roanoke Rapids NC 5 hrs
*WNCW(FM) Spindale NC 12 hrs
*KEYA(FM) Belcourt ND 4 hrs
*KCND(FM) Bismarck ND 6 hrs
*KDPR(FM) Dickinson ND 6 hrs
*KPRJ(FM) Jamestown ND 6 hrs
*KMPR(FM) Minot ND 6 hrs
*KPPR(FM) Williston ND 6 hrs
*KZUM(FM) Lincoln NE 8 hrs
*WEVO(FM) Concord NH 3 hrs
*WUNH(FM) Durham NH 4 hrs
*WEVC(FM) Gorham NH 4 hrs
*WEVH(FM) Hanover NH 3 hrs
*WNEC-FM Henniker NH 18 hrs
WEVJ(FM) Jackson NH 3 hrs wklly hrs
*WEVN(FM) Keene NH 3 hrs
*WKNH(FM) Keene NH 6 hrs
*WDVR(FM) Delaware Township NJ 6 hrs
*WBZC(FM) Pemberton NJ 4 hrs
*WLFR(FM) Pomona NJ 3 hrs
*WTSR(FM) Trenton NJ 4 hrs
*KSJE(FM) Farmington NM 15 hrs
*KRWG(FM) Las Cruces NM 8 hrs
*KUNR(FM) Reno NV 2 hrs
*WAMC-FM Albany NY 7 hrs
*WSKG-FM Binghamton NY 5 hrs
*WXLH(FM) Blue Mountain Lake NY
*WBNY(FM) Buffalo NY 3 hrs
*WCAN(FM) Canajoharie NY 7 hrs
*WSLU(FM) Canton NY
*WSQE(FM) Corning NY 5 hrs
*WCVF-FM Fredonia NY 4 hrs
*WICB(FM) Ithaca NY 2 hrs
*WSQG-FM Ithaca NY 5 hrs
WVBR-FM Ithaca NY 8 hrs
*WAMK(FM) Kingston NY 7 hrs
WYBG(AM) Massena NY
*WOSR(FM) Middletown NY 7 hrs
*WBAI(FM) New York NY 2 hrs
*WSUF(FM) Noyack NY 5 hrs
*WRHO(FM) Oneonta NY 5 hrs
*WSQC-FM Oneonta NY 5 hrs
WTKV(FM) Oswego NY 3 hrs
*WCEL(FM) Plattsburgh NY 7 hrs
*WSPN(FM) Saratoga Springs NY 6 hrs

*WUSB(FM) Stony Brook NY 15 hrs
*WANC(FM) Ticonderoga NY 6 hrs
*WBGU(FM) Bowling Green OH 4 hrs
*WLFC(FM) Findlay OH 3 hrs
*WKSU-FM Kent OH 12 hrs
*WOBC-FM Oberlin OH 12 hrs
WNTO(FM) Racine OH 2 hrs
*WKRW(FM) Wooster OH 12 hrs
*WYSO(FM) Yellow Springs OH 2 hrs
*WYSU(FM) Youngstown OH 3 hrs
*KRSC-FM Claremore OK 5 hrs
*KSMF(FM) Ashland OR 3 hrs
*KMUN(FM) Astoria OR 18 hrs
*KSBA(FM) Coos Bay OR 3 hrs
*KBVR(FM) Corvallis OR 4 hrs
*KLCC(FM) Eugene OR 12 hrs
*KRVM-FM Eugene OR 3 hrs
*KSKF(FM) Klamath Falls OR 3 hrs
*KTEC(FM) Klamath Falls OR 3 hrs
*KLCO(FM) Newport OR 12 hrs
*WDIY(FM) Allentown PA 12 hrs
WWCS(AM) Canonsburg PA 2 hrs
*WZBT(FM) Gettysburg PA 6 hrs
*WIUP-FM Indiana PA 4 hrs
*WPSX(FM) Kane PA 10 hrs
*WHYY-FM Philadelphia PA 4 hrs
*WXPN(FM) Philadelphia PA 5 hrs
*WRCT(FM) Pittsburgh PA 3 hrs
*WYEP-FM Pittsburgh PA 9 hrs
WEEU(AM) Reading PA 3 hrs
*WPSU(FM) State College PA 12 hrs
*WRDV(FM) Warminster PA 4 hrs
*WRIU(FM) Kingston RI 15 hrs
*WJMF(FM) Smithfield RI 4 hrs
*KCSD(FM) Sioux Falls SD 5 hrs
*WHCB(FM) Bristol TN 1 hr
*WTTU(FM) Cookeville TN
*WRVU(FM) Nashville TN 3 hrs
*KUT(FM) Austin TX 4 hrs
*KAMU-FM College Station TX 3 hrs
*KEOS(FM) College Station TX 10 hrs
*KTEP(FM) El Paso TX 3 hrs
*KOOP(FM) Hornsby TX 7 hrs
*KTRU(FM) Houston TX 3 hrs
*KOCV(FM) Odessa TX 4 hrs
*KUTX(FM) San Angelo TX 4 hrs
*KSTX(FM) San Antonio TX 5 hrs
*KZMU(FM) Moab UT 6 hrs
*WNRN(FM) Charlottesville VA 19 hrs
*WTJU(FM) Charlottesville VA 20 hrs
*WMRY(FM) Crozet VA 8 hrs
*WMRA(FM) Harrisonburg VA 8 hrs
*WMRL(FM) Lexington VA 8 hrs
*WHRV(FM) Norfolk VA 7 hrs
*WVRU(FM) Radford VA 1 hr
*WCVE(FM) Richmond VA 6 hrs
*WVPS(FM) Burlington VT 4 hrs
*WIUV(FM) Castleton VT 4 hrs
*WRMC-FM Middlebury VT 15 hrs
WNCS(FM) Montpelier VT 4 hrs
*WRVT(FM) Rutland VT 4 hrs
*WVPR(FM) Windsor VT 6 hrs
*KUGS(FM) Bellingham WA 6 hrs wkly hrs
*KZAZ(FM) Bellingham WA 8 hrs
*KNWR(FM) Ellensburg WA
*KSER(FM) Everett WA 2 hrs
*KAOS(FM) Olympia WA 16 hrs
*KZUU(FM) Pullman WA 4 hrs
KFAE-FM Richland WA
*KAGU(FM) Spokane WA 2 hrs
*KPBX-FM Spokane WA
*WHSA(FM) Brule WI 3 hrs
*WBSD(FM) Burlington WI 5 hrs
*WUEC(FM) Eau Claire WI 3 hrs
*WPNE(FM) Green Bay WI 3 hrs
*WVSS(FM) Menomonie WI 6 hrs
*WHND(FM) Sister Bay WI 3 hrs
*WLBL-FM Wausau WI 3 hrs
*WVBC(FM) Bethany WV 2 hrs
WWYO(AM) Pineville WV 1 hr
WMOV(AM) Ravenswood WV 2 hrs
WHAW(AM) Weston WV 4 hrs
*KUWA(FM) Afton WY 5 hrs
*KUWJ(FM) Jackson WY 10 hrs
*KUWR(FM) Laramie WY 10 hrs

*KUWZ(FM) Rock Springs WY 10 hrs

Foreign/Ethnic

*KJHA(FM) Houston AK 3 hrs
*KJNP(AM) North Pole AK 1 hr
*KCAW(FM) Sitka AK 3 hrs
KSAZ(AM) Marana AZ 2 hrs
*KKUP(FM) Cupertino CA 19 hrs
KBIF(AM) Fresno CA 56 hrs
*KFCF(FM) Fresno CA 1 hr
*KMUD(FM) Garberville CA 1 hr
KMYC(AM) Marysville CA 2 hrs
*KVMR(FM) Nevada City CA 20 hrs
*KAZU(FM) Pacific Grove CA 6 hrs
*KXJZ(FM) Sacramento CA 2 hrs
KEST(AM) San Francisco CA
*KUSF(FM) San Francisco CA 2 hrs
KMRB(AM) San Gabriel CA 4 hrs
*KCSB-FM Santa Barbara CA 2 hrs
KOBO(AM) Yuba City CA 3 hrs
*KRZA(FM) Alamosa CO 3 hrs
*WJMJ(FM) Hartford CT 1 hr
*WWUH(FM) West Hartford CT 14 hrs
WHUR-FM Washington DC 6 hrs
WYUS(AM) Milford DE 3 hrs
WXYB(AM) Indian Rocks Beach FL 5 hrs
*WDNA(FM) Miami FL 10 hrs
*WLRN-FM Miami FL 3 hrs
WTMY(AM) Sarasota FL 4 hrs
*WRFG(FM) Atlanta GA 9 hrs
WWWE(AM) Hapeville GA 6 hrs
KUAI(AM) Eleele HI 5 hrs
KWAI(AM) Honolulu HI 2 hrs
KKON(AM) Kealakekua HI
*KDCR(FM) Sioux Center IA 1 hr
*WHPK-FM Chicago IL 4 hrs
WCGO(AM) Evanston IL 28 hrs
*WQNA(FM) Springfield IL 3 hrs
*WFHB(FM) Bloomington IN 3 hrs
*WCUW(FM) Worcester MA 10 hrs
*WEAA(FM) Baltimore MD 7 hrs
*WMHB(FM) Waterville ME
*WHFR(FM) Dearborn MI 2 hrs
KNOF(AM) Saint Paul MN 1 hr
*WMCN(FM) Saint Paul MN 16 hrs
*WSHA(FM) Raleigh NC 6 hrs
KMTY(FM) Holdrege NE 1 hr
KNLV(AM) Ord NE 4 hrs
*WFMU(FM) East Orange NJ 15 hrs
*WBJB-FM Lincroft NJ 3 hrs
WPRB(FM) Princeton NJ 6 hrs
*KUNM(FM) Albuquerque NM 9 hrs
KTAO(FM) Taos NM 5 hrs
*KUNR(FM) Reno NV 9 hrs
*WGMC(FM) Greece NY 1 hr
*WICB(FM) Ithaca NY 2 hrs
WJTN(AM) Jamestown NY 1 hr
WKSN(AM) Jamestown NY 1 hr
*WRHO(FM) Oneonta NY 2 hrs
*WRHV(FM) Poughkeepsie NY 1 hr
*WSPN(FM) Saratoga Springs NY 3 hrs
*WAER(FM) Syracuse NY 4 hrs
*WAPS(FM) Akron OH 3 hrs
*WDUB(FM) Granville OH 2 hrs
*KLCO(FM) Newport OR 3 hrs
*KBOO(FM) Portland OR 4 hrs
KLPM(AM) Portland OR 1 hr
WWCS(AM) Canonsburg PA 2 hrs
*WKDU(FM) Philadelphia PA 12 hrs
WTPM(FM) Aguadilla PR 1 hr
KEDA(AM) San Antonio TX 4 hrs
*KZMU(FM) Moab UT 1 hr
*KRCL(FM) Salt Lake City UT 5 hrs
*WUVT-FM Blacksburg VA 8 hrs
*KAOS(FM) Olympia WA 3 hrs
*KPBX-FM Spokane WA
WEKZ(AM) Monroe WI 3 hrs
KBBS(AM) Buffalo WY 1 hr

French

*KTOO(FM) Juneau AK 2 hrs
*KUSF(FM) San Francisco CA 1 hr
*KSRH(FM) San Rafael CA 1 hr
*WPKN(FM) Bridgeport CT 2 hrs
WUST(AM) Washington DC 15 hrs
KSIG(AM) Crowley LA 18 hrs
KVPI-FM Ville Platte LA 18 hrs
WJIB(AM) Cambridge MA 10 hrs
WHTB(AM) Fall River MA 1 hr
*WCUW(FM) Worcester MA 2 hrs
*KFAI(FM) Minneapolis MN 2 hrs
WMOU(AM) Berlin NH 3 hrs
WFEA(AM) Manchester NH 3 hrs
WCHP(AM) Champlain NY
*WOBC-FM Oberlin OH 1 hr
*KRRC(FM) Portland OR 2 hrs
WWCS(AM) Canonsburg PA 2 hrs
WNRI(AM) Woonsocket RI 4 hrs
WOON(AM) Woonsocket RI 1 hr
*WEVL(FM) Memphis TN 1 hr
*WRVU(FM) Nashville TN 1 hr
*WUTS(FM) Sewanee TN 2 hrs
*WIUJ(FM) Charlotte Amalie VI 4 hrs

Full Service

WTMY(AM) Sarasota FL 2 hrs

German

*KCSN(FM) Northridge CA 3 hrs
*KUSF(FM) San Francisco CA 1.5 hr
KFKA(AM) Greeley CO 1 hr
WUST(AM) Washington DC 7 hrs
*WKTO(FM) Edgewater FL 1.5 hr
KSKB(FM) Brooklyn IA 1 hr
*KRNL-FM Mount Vernon IA 2 hrs
*WIIT(FM) Chicago IL 3 hrs
WKTA(FM) Evanston IL 5 hrs
WIJR(AM) Highland IL 1 hr
*WICR(FM) Indianapolis IN 1 hr
*WCUW(FM) Worcester MA 2 hrs
WBMD(AM) Baltimore MD 1 hr
WATZ(AM) Alpena MI 2 hrs
WKCQ(FM) Saginaw MI 3 hrs
KASM(AM) Albany MN 2 hrs
WEW(AM) Saint Louis MO 3 hrs
KTTT(AM) Columbus NE 5 hrs
KBRX(AM) O'Neill NE 6 hrs
*KUNV(FM) Las Vegas NV 1 hr
*WBXL(FM) Baldwinsville NY 3 hrs
WHVW(AM) Hyde Park NY 1 hr
WKNY(AM) Kingston NY 1 hr
WXRL(AM) Lancaster NY 1 hr
WVOU(FM) Mexico NY 2 hrs
WTLA(AM) North Syracuse NY 2 hrs
WSGO(AM) Oswego NY 2 hrs
*WAPS(FM) Akron OH 2 hrs
*WOBO(FM) Batavia OH 5 hrs
*WCPN(FM) Cleveland OH 1 hr
WKTX(AM) Cortland OH 5 hrs
WONW(AM) Defiance OH 4 hrs
WCWA(AM) Toledo OH 1 hr
WELW(AM) Willoughby-Eastlake OH 1 hr
KKRX(AM) Lawton OK 1 hr
*WMUH(FM) Allentown PA 2 hrs
WGPA(AM) Bethlehem PA 2 hrs
WWCS(AM) Canonsburg PA 2 hrs
*WDCV-FM Carlisle PA 1 hr
*WMCE(FM) Erie PA 4 hrs
WKST(AM) New Castle PA 1 hr
WEEU(AM) Reading PA 2 hrs
*WCLH(FM) Wilkes-Barre PA 3 hrs
*WRVU(FM) Nashville TN 1 hr
KHLT(AM) Hallettsville TX 5 hrs
*KOOP(FM) Hornsby TX .5 hr
KVLG(AM) La Grange TX 1 hr
*WKGM(AM) Smithfield VA 1 hr
KARI(AM) Blaine WA 2 hrs
*WGTD(FM) Kenosha WI 1 hr
WSSP(FM) Milwaukee WI 8 hrs
WEKZ(AM) Monroe WI 3 hrs
WXER(FM) Plymouth WI 3 hrs

Golden Oldies

KGFT(FM) Pueblo CO 11 hrs
WSYY-FM Millinocket ME

Gospel

KFAR(AM) Fairbanks AK 2 hrs
*KSDP(AM) Sand Point AK 3 hrs
WNSI-FM Atmore AL 12 hrs
WSPZ(AM) Birmingham AL 5 hrs
WBSA(AM) Boaz AL
WAOQ(FM) Brantley AL 14. hrs
WKNU(FM) Brewton AL 2 hrs
WACQ(AM) Carrville AL 5 hrs
WGZZ(FM) Dadeville AL 3 hrs
WOOF(AM) Dothan AL 17 hrs
WTVY-FM Dothan AL 4 hrs
WELB(AM) Elba AL 12 hrs
*WFIX(FM) Florence AL 6 hrs
WZOB(AM) Fort Payne AL 5 hrs
WDJL(AM) Huntsville AL 6 hrs
*WJAB(FM) Huntsville AL 14 hrs
WCKA(AM) Jacksonville AL 2 hrs
WIXI(AM) Jasper AL 6 hrs
WINL(FM) Linden AL 5 hrs
WLWI-FM Montgomery AL 4 hrs
*WVAS(FM) Montgomery AL 5 hrs
WAMI(AM) Opp AL 15 hrs
WAMI-FM Opp AL 15 hrs
WOPP(AM) Opp AL 19 hrs
WJRL-FM Ozark AL 8 hrs
WGOL(AM) Russellville AL 4 hrs
WFEB(AM) Sylacauga AL 6 hrs
WNUZ(AM) Talladega AL 7 hrs
*WEBT(AM) Valley AL
KEWI(AM) Benton AR 10 hrs
KAMD-FM Camden AR 19 hrs
KBJT(AM) Fordyce AR 11 hrs
KHOZ(AM) Harrison AR 10 hrs
KFFA(AM) Helena AR 4 hrs
KBOK(AM) Malvern AR 8 hrs
KZHE(AM) Stamps AR 8 hrs
KWRF(AM) Warren AR 8 hrs
KWRF-FM Warren AR 8 hrs
KCLT(FM) West Helena AR 15 hrs
KDVA(FM) Buckeye AZ 7 hrs
*KXCI(FM) Tucson AZ 2 hrs
KXMX(AM) Anaheim CA
KMVE(FM) California City CA 3 hrs
KRML(AM) Carmel CA 6 hrs
KJLH-FM Compton CA 6 hrs
*KECG(FM) El Cerrito CA 5 hrs
KTDE(FM) Gualala CA 1 hr
KGBA-FM Holtville CA 7 hrs
KSRN(FM) Kings Beach CA 1 hr
*KPFK(FM) Los Angeles CA 2 hrs
KYOS(AM) Merced CA 1 hr
*KAZU(FM) Pacific Grove CA 4 hrs
*KZYX(FM) Philo CA 2 hrs
KEST(AM) San Francisco CA
KISQ(FM) San Francisco CA 3 hrs
KDIA(AM) Vallejo CA 7 hrs
KDYA(AM) Vallejo CA 7 hrs
KUBA(AM) Yuba City CA 2 hrs
*KASF(FM) Alamosa CO 4 hrs
KRTZ(FM) Cortez CO 1 hr
KVAY(FM) Lamar CO 4 hrs
KSLV(AM) Monte Vista CO 4 hrs
*KVNF(FM) Paonia CO 3 hrs
KGFT(FM) Pueblo CO 3 3 hrs
*WQTQ(FM) Hartford CT 12 hrs
*WRTC-FM Hartford CT 6 hrs
*WESU(FM) Middletown CT 6 hrs
WYBC-FM New Haven CT 8 hrs
*WCNI(FM) New London CT 3 hrs
*WNHU(FM) West Haven CT 4 hrs
WKND(AM) Windsor CT 5 hrs
WHUR-FM Washington DC 14 hrs
WAFL(FM) Milford DE 2 hrs
WYBT(AM) Blountstown FL 15 hrs
WWPR(AM) Bradenton FL 6 hrs
WZEP(AM) De Funiak Springs FL 10 hrs
WRNE(AM) Gulf Breeze FL
WWAB(AM) Lakeland FL 12 hrs

WLBE(AM) Leesburg FL 4 hrs
WQHL(AM) Live Oak FL 7 hrs
WMAF(AM) Madison FL
WTYS(AM) Marianna FL 11 hrs
WLTG(AM) Panama City FL 7 hrs
WTMY(AM) Sarasota FL 5 hrs
WPUL(AM) South Daytona FL
*WANM(AM) Tallahassee FL 18 hrs
WQLC(FM) Watertown FL 4 hrs
WFLM(FM) White City FL 20 hrs
WZZS(FM) Zolfo Springs FL 2 hrs
V6AH(AM) Pohnpei FM 2 hrs
WFSH-FM Athens GA 2 hrs
*WCLK(FM) Atlanta GA 17 hrs
WTUF(AM) Boston GA 7 hrs
WJTH(AM) Calhoun GA 2 hrs
WZBN(FM) Camilla GA 16 hrs
WDCO(AM) Cochran GA 6 hrs
WDXQ-FM Cochran GA 6 hrs
WCON-FM Cornelia GA 10 hrs
WOKA-FM Douglas GA 4 hrs
WQZY(FM) Dublin GA 3 hrs
WRDO(AM) Fitzgerald GA 6 hrs
*WBCX(FM) Gainesville GA 6 hrs
WJGA-FM Jackson GA 15 hrs
WNEA(AM) Newnan GA 15 hrs
WPTB(AM) Statesboro GA 6 hrs
WTHO-FM Thomson GA 1 hr
WLET(AM) Toccoa GA
WGOV(AM) Valdosta GA 14 hrs
WVLD(AM) Valdosta GA 2 hrs
KSTO(FM) Hagatna GU 6 hrs
*KEDB(FM) Chariton IA 5 hrs
KROS(AM) Clinton IA 5 hrs
*KALA(FM) Davenport IA 13 hrs
*KHOE(FM) Fairfield IA 3 hrs
KYTC(FM) Northwood IA 1 hr
KBOE(AM) Oskaloosa IA 9 hrs
*KIGC(FM) Oskaloosa IA 12 hrs
KLEE(AM) Ottumwa IA 6 hrs
KIHK(FM) Rock Valley IA 3 hrs
KTLB(FM) Twin Lakes IA 2 hrs
KWIK(AM) Pocatello ID 2 hrs
WBGZ(AM) Alton IL 4 hrs
WKRO(AM) Cairo IL 12 hrs
*WSSD(FM) Chicago IL
WWHP(AM) Farmer City IL 3 hrs
WJRE(AM) Galva IL 1 hr
*WDCB(FM) Glen Ellyn IL 2 hrs
WHPO(FM) Hoopeston IL 7 hrs
WJOL(AM) Joliet IL 1 hr
*WMXM(FM) Lake Forest IL 3 hrs
WPNA(AM) Oak Park IL 2 hrs
WVAZ(FM) Oak Park IL 4 hrs
WBBA-FM Pittsfield IL 3 hrs
WNTA(AM) Rockford IL 20 hrs
WPMB(AM) Vandalia IL 3 hrs
WYKT(FM) Wilmington IL 4 hrs
WBNL(AM) Boonville IN 5 hrs
WURK(FM) Elwood IN 4 hrs
WFLQ(FM) French Lick IN 4 hrs
WKAM(AM) Goshen IN 6 hrs
WXLW(AM) Indianapolis IN 5 hrs
WYXB(FM) Indianapolis IN 10 hrs
*WKPW(FM) Knightstown IN
WMRS(FM) Monticello IN 5 hrs
WRIN(AM) Rensselaer IN 2 hrs
WAXI(FM) Rockville IN 2 hrs
WTCJ(AM) Tell City IN 6 hrs
WWVR(FM) West Terre Haute IN
KDNS(FM) Downs KS 5 hrs
KHAZ(FM) Hays KS 3 hrs
KINZ(FM) Humboldt KS 3 hrs
KHUT(FM) Hutchinson KS 5 hrs
KWBW(AM) Hutchinson KS 11 hrs
KNNS(AM) Larned KS 6 hrs
*KSDB-FM Manhattan KS 3 hrs
KFNF(FM) Oberlin KS 3 hrs
KKAN(AM) Phillipsburg KS 12 hrs
KFRM(AM) Salina KS 3 hrs
KSKG(FM) Salina KS 3 hrs
*KMUW(FM) Wichita KS 3 hrs
WANY(AM) Albany KY 6 hrs
WLFX(FM) Berea KY 12 hrs
WAIN-FM Columbia KY 15 hrs
WHVO(AM) Hopkinsville KY 3 hrs

WLBN(AM) Lebanon KY 5 hrs
WFTM(AM) Maysville KY 5 hrs
WFTM-FM Maysville KY 5 hrs
WFXY(AM) Middlesboro KY 3 hrs
WMIK(AM) Middlesboro KY 2 hrs
WKYQ(FM) Paducah KY 2 hrs
WRLV-FM Salyersville KY 4 hrs
WTKY(AM) Tompkinsville KY
WTKY-FM Tompkinsville KY 8 hrs
KRVV(AM) Bastrop LA 4 hrs
WFPR(AM) Hammond LA 12 hrs
WHMD(AM) Hammond LA 4 hrs
KJLO-FM Monroe LA 4 hrs
WJIB(AM) Cambridge MA 4 hrs
*WAIC(FM) Springfield MA
*WEAA(FM) Baltimore MD 13 hrs
*WMTB-FM Emmitsburg MD 1 hr
WKHI(AM) Fruitland MD 5 hrs
WAAI(FM) Hurlock MD 3 hrs
*WESM(FM) Princess Anne MD 20 hrs
WQTE(FM) Adrian MI 2 hrs
WGTO(AM) Cassopolis MI 10 hrs
*WDET-FM Detroit MI 2 hrs
WDZZ-FM Flint MI 8 hrs
WLCM(AM) Holt MI 3 hrs
WJNZ(AM) Kentwood MI 4 hrs
WTLZ(FM) Saginaw MI 6 hrs
WMLM(AM) Saint Louis MI 2 hrs
KDUZ(AM) Hutchinson MN 3 hrs
KLQL(FM) Luverne MN 4 hrs
KYOO(AM) Bolivar MO 2 hrs
KBFL-FM Buffalo MO 3 hrs
KATI(FM) California MO 3 hrs
KRLL(AM) California MO 3 hrs
KMFC(FM) Centralia MO 2 hrs
KCHR(AM) Charleston MO 10 hrs
*KOPN(FM) Columbia MO 3 hrs
KUNQ(FM) Houston MO 10 hrs
*KTTK(FM) Lebanon MO 7 hrs
*KJAB-FM Mexico MO 20 hrs
*KGSP(FM) Parkville MO 3 hrs
KDRO(AM) Sedalia MO 6 hrs
*KWND(FM) Springfield MO 3 hrs
KTTN-FM Trenton MO 6 hrs
WWZQ(AM) Aberdeen MS 8 hrs
WAMY(AM) Amory MS 6 hrs
WESE(FM) Baldwyn MS 6 hrs
WJZD(FM) Bay St. Louis MS 13 hrs
WBKN(AM) Brookhaven MS 3 hrs
*WPAE(FM) Centreville MS 15 hrs
WKRA(AM) Holly Springs MS 12 hrs
WNAT(AM) Natchez MS 18 hrs
WNAU(AM) New Albany MS
WWZD-FM New Albany MS 4 hrs
WOXD(AM) Oxford MS 12 hrs
WSKK(AM) Ripley MS 6 hrs
WAVN(AM) Southaven MS 19 hrs
WIGG(AM) Wiggins MS
WKXR(AM) Asheboro NC 10 hrs
WWNC(AM) Asheville NC 3 hrs
*WGWG(FM) Boiling Springs NC 15 hrs
WATA(AM) Boone NC 5 hrs
WSQL(AM) Brevard NC 8 hrs
*WCCE(FM) Buie's Creek NC 11 hrs
WKYK(AM) Burnsville NC 12 hrs
WCLN(AM) Clinton NC 7.5 hrs
WPEG(FM) Concord NC 6 hrs
WFXC(FM) Durham NC 4 hrs
*WRVS-FM Elizabeth City NC 20 hrs
WBLA(AM) Elizabethtown NC 8 hrs
*WFSS(FM) Fayetteville NC 2 hrs
*WNAA(FM) Greensboro NC 3 hrs
WLNC(AM) Laurinburg NC 4 hrs
WLON(AM) Lincolnton NC 5 hrs
WBRM(AM) Marion NC 5 hrs
WDJS(AM) Mount Olive NC 5 hrs
WIKS(AM) New Bern NC 4 hrs
WECR(AM) Newland NC 10 hrs
WGCR(AM) Pisgah Forest NC
WPJL(AM) Raleigh NC
*WSHA(FM) Raleigh NC 6 hrs
*WZRU(FM) Roanoke Rapids NC 6 hrs
WRSV(FM) Rocky Mount NC 20 hrs
WKRX(FM) Roxboro NC 4 hrs

WKRX(FM) Roxboro NC 5 hrs
WRXO(AM) Roxboro NC 5 hrs
WNCA(AM) Siler City NC 10 hrs
WEEB(AM) Southern Pines NC 6 hrs
*WNCW(FM) Spindale NC 2 hrs
WAME(AM) Statesville NC 5 hrs
WFXK(FM) Tarboro NC 3 hrs
WACB(AM) Taylorsville NC 12 hrs
WSVM(AM) Valdese NC 4 hrs
WKSK(AM) West Jefferson NC 5 hrs
WYNC(AM) Yanceyville NC
*KABU(FM) Fort Totten ND 7 hrs
KAUJ(AM) Grafton ND 4 hrs
KXPO(AM) Grafton ND 5 hrs
KQLX(AM) Lisbon ND 6 hrs
KTGO(AM) Tioga ND 11 hrs
*KINI(FM) Crookston NE 6 hrs
KMTY(FM) Holdrege NE 5 hrs
KUVR(AM) Holdrege NE 5 hrs
*KRNU(FM) Lincoln NE 2 hrs
KRFS(AM) Superior NE 3 hrs
WTMR(AM) Camden NJ 20 hrs
*WJPG(FM) Cape May Court House NJ 1 hr
WTTH(FM) Margate City NJ 5 hrs
WMVB(AM) Millville NJ 8 hrs
*WTSR(FM) Trenton NJ 6 hrs
*WMSC(FM) Upper Montclair NJ 2 hrs
*WMCX(FM) West Long Branch NJ 6 hrs
*WJPH(FM) Woodbine NJ 1 hr
KRSY(AM) Alamogordo NM 8 hrs
KATK(AM) Carlsbad NM 2 hrs
*KCEP(FM) Las Vegas NV 14 hrs
*WCDB(FM) Albany NY 3 hrs
WROW(AM) Albany NY 3 hrs
*WXLH(FM) Blue Mountain Lake NY
*WSLU(FM) Canton NY
WSIV(AM) East Syracuse NY 1 hr
*WEOS(FM) Geneva NY 3 hrs
*WITR(FM) Henrietta NY 8 hrs
WHVW(AM) Hyde Park NY 1.5 hr
*WVCR-FM Loudonville NY 3 hrs
WVOX(AM) New Rochelle NY 1 hr
WJJL(AM) Niagara Falls NY 1 hr
WLIM(AM) Patchogue NY 2 hrs
WDKX(FM) Rochester NY 7 hrs
WMYY(FM) Schoharie NY
*WAER(FM) Syracuse NY 3 hrs
*WONB(AM) Ada OH 3 hrs
*WRMU(FM) Alliance OH 2 hrs
WAIS(AM) Buchtel OH 3 hrs
WCER(AM) Canton OH 11 hrs
WCVX(AM) Cincinnati OH 15 hrs
*WWSU(FM) Dayton OH 3 hrs
WEDI(AM) Eaton OH 5 hrs
*WCVO(FM) Gahanna OH 6 hrs
WPOS-FM Holland OH 20 hrs
WJYD(FM) London OH 10 hrs
WTIG(AM) Massillon OH 6 hrs
WMPO(AM) Middleport-Pomeroy OH 18 hrs
WQIO(FM) Mount Vernon OH 2 hrs
WNPQ(FM) New Philadelphia OH 4 hrs
WPAY(AM) Portsmouth OH 6 hrs
WNTO(FM) Racine OH 7 hrs
WDIG(AM) Steubenville OH
WJUC(FM) Swanton OH 12 hrs wkly hrs
WERT(AM) Van Wert OH 3 hrs
WKFI(AM) Wilmington OH 5 hrs
WBZI(AM) Xenia OH 5 hrs
KADA(AM) Ada OK 5 hrs
KADA-FM Ada OK 5 hrs
KYFM(FM) Bartlesville OK 4 hrs
KKBI(FM) Broken Bow OK 4 hrs
KDDQ(FM) Comanche OK 2 hrs
KTNT(AM) Eufaula OK 3 hrs
KIHN(AM) Hugo OK 5 hrs
KFXI(FM) Marlow OK 8 hrs
KTMC(AM) McAlester OK 5 hrs
KTMC-FM McAlester OK 2 hrs
KKNG-FM Newcastle OK 8 hrs
KRIG-FM Nowata OK 4 hrs
KFAQ(AM) Tulsa OK 2 hrs

KAJO(AM) Grants Pass OR 1 hr
KYKN(AM) Keizer OR 6 hrs
KWBY(AM) Woodburn OR 3 hrs
WWSM(AM) Annville-Cleona PA 3 hrs
WBVP(AM) Beaver Falls PA 2 hrs
WCHA(AM) Chambersburg PA 2 hrs
WSKE(FM) Everett PA 1 hr
*WZBT(FM) Gettysburg PA 1 hr
*WVMM(FM) Grantham PA 5 hrs
WTKT(AM) Harrisburg PA 2 hrs
*WIUP-FM Indiana PA 1 hr
WJSA(AM) Jersey Shore PA 4 hrs
WJSA-FM Jersey Shore PA 3 hrs
WQZS(FM) Meyersdale PA 5 hrs
WWBE(FM) Mifflinburg PA 2 hrs
*WKDU(FM) Philadelphia PA 4 hrs
WURD(AM) Philadelphia PA 9 hrs
WUSL(FM) Philadelphia PA 4 hrs
WPHB(AM) Philipsburg PA 6 hrs
WPAM(AM) Pottsville PA
*WBYO(FM) Sellersville PA 2 hrs
WWII(AM) Shiremanstown PA 2 hrs
*WZZD(FM) Warwick PA 3 hrs
WKZV(AM) Washington PA 1 hr
*WRLC(FM) Williamsport PA 6 hrs
*WTMV(FM) Youngsville PA 2 hrs
*WJMF(FM) Smithfield RI 2 hrs
WOON(AM) Woonsocket RI 1 hr
WZLA-FM Abbeville SC 8 hrs
WBT-FM Chester SC 6 hrs
WOLH(AM) Florence SC 4 hrs
WFIS(AM) Fountain Inn SC 4 hrs
WHSC(AM) Hartsville SC 3 hrs
WKMG(AM) Newberry SC 3 hrs
WALI(AM) Walterboro SC 5 hrs
*KLND(FM) Little Eagle SD 3 hrs
KBHB(AM) Sturgis SD 3 hrs
WATX(AM) Algood TN
WVOL(AM) Berry Hill TN 6 hrs
*WHCB(FM) Bristol TN 15 hrs
WFWL(AM) Camden TN 8 hrs
WRJB(FM) Camden TN 4 hrs
WVFB(AM) Celina TN 7 hrs
WNKX-FM Centerville TN
WMSR-FM Collinwood TN
WHUB(AM) Cookeville TN 11 hrs
WZYX(AM) Cowan TN 10 hrs
WSDQ(AM) Dunlap TN 7 hrs
WEMB(AM) Erwin TN 10 hrs
*WVCP(AM) Gallatin TN 6 hrs
WMYL(FM) Halls Crossroads TN 2 hrs
WTNK(AM) Hartsville TN 4 hrs
*WFHU(FM) Henderson TN 9 hrs
WFKX(FM) Henderson TN 3 hrs
WHHM-FM Henderson TN 10 hrs
WQQK(FM) Hendersonville TN 6 hrs
WMLR(AM) Hohenwald TN 4 hrs
WDXI(AM) Jackson TN 16 hrs
WNRX(FM) Jefferson City TN 4 hrs
WLIL(AM) Lenoir City TN 18 hrs
WAXO(AM) Lewisburg TN 12 hrs
WDXL(AM) Lexington TN 10 hrs
WLIV(AM) Livingston TN 18 hrs
WDIA(AM) Memphis TN
WTRB(AM) Ripley TN 6 hrs
WJLE(AM) Smithville TN 15 hrs
WJLE-FM Smithville TN 15 hrs
WEPG(AM) South Pittsburg TN 10 hrs
WDBL(AM) Springfield TN 10 hrs
*KGNZ(FM) Abilene TX 2 hrs
KIXZ(AM) Amarillo TX 6 hrs
*KAZI-FM Austin TX 18 hrs
KORQ(AM) Baird TX 3 hrs
KBYG(AM) Big Spring TX 6 hrs
KQTY-FM Borger TX 4 hrs
KNTX(AM) Bowie TX 4 hrs
KLTR(FM) Brenham TX 10 hrs
KPSM(FM) Brownwood TX 2 hrs
KTAE(AM) Cameron TX 6 hrs
KCAR(AM) Clarksville TX 9 hrs
KQBZ(FM) Coleman TX 7 hrs
KSTA(AM) Coleman TX 7 hrs
*KEOS(FM) College Station TX 3 hrs
KCOM(AM) Comanche TX 5 hrs
KSSM(FM) Copperas Cove TX
KBHT(AM) Crockett TX 6 hrs

KDDD-FM Dumas TX 5 hrs
KATX(FM) Eastland TX 5 hrs
KEAS(AM) Eastland TX 5 hrs
*KTEP(FM) El Paso TX 4 hrs
KNES(FM) Fairfield TX 3 hrs
KSWA(AM) Graham TX 2 hrs
KHBR(AM) Hillsboro TX 6 hrs
KOOK(FM) Junction TX 2 hrs
KRVL(FM) Kerrville TX 1 hr
*KTAI(FM) Kingsville TX 6 hrs
KHKZ(FM) Mercedes TX 2 hrs
KRQX(AM) Mexia TX 3 hrs
KCKM(AM) Monahans TX 3 hrs
KJCS(FM) Nacogdoches TX 3 hrs
KPLT(AM) Paris TX 4 hrs
KZHN(AM) Paris TX
KXOX(AM) Sweetwater TX 4 hrs
KTBB(AM) Tyler TX 5 hrs
*KVNE(FM) Tyler TX 4 hrs
KVWC(AM) Vernon TX 16 hrs
KALK(AM) Winfield TX 1 hr
KWUD(AM) Woodville TX 6 hrs
KBLQ-FM Logan UT 8 hrs
*KWCR-FM Ogden UT 3 hrs
WKDE(AM) Altavista VA 5 hrs
WKDE-FM Altavista VA 5 hrs
*WTJU(FM) Charlottesville VA 1 hr
WKEY(AM) Covington VA 2 hrs
WEVA(AM) Emporia VA 3 hrs
WPAK(AM) Farmville VA 12 hrs
WGAT(AM) Gate City VA 20 hrs
WMNA(AM) Gretna VA 15 hrs
WCLM(AM) Highland Springs VA 5 wkly hrs
WKWI(FM) Kilmarnock VA 5 hrs
WMEV(AM) Marion VA 2 hrs
WSIG(AM) Mount Jackson VA 4 hrs
WNVA(AM) Norton VA 15 hrs
WVCV(AM) Orange VA 2 hrs
*WVST-FM Petersburg VA 13 hrs
WXLZ(AM) Saint Paul VA 15 hrs
WKGM(AM) Smithfield VA 5 hrs
WQOK(FM) South Boston VA 9 hrs
WTZE(AM) Tazewell VA 5 hrs
WKCW(AM) Warrenton VA 6 hrs
WMBG(AM) Williamsburg VA 5 hrs
WYVE(AM) Wytheville VA 4 hrs
WRRA(AM) Frederiksted VI 12 hrs
WWOD(FM) Hartford VT 2 hrs
WMNV(FM) Rupert VT
WTWN(AM) Wells River VT
KBDB-FM Forks WA 4 hrs
KBIS(AM) Forks WA 6.5 hrs
*KNHC(FM) Seattle WA 6 hrs
KITZ(AM) Silverdale WA 2 hrs
KJOX(AM) Yakima WA 2 hrs
WATK(AM) Antigo WI 1 hr
WMCS(AM) Greenfield WI 5 hrs
WKKV-FM Racine WI 6 hrs
WRCO-FM Richland Center WI 6 hrs
WRON-FM Lewisburg WV 6 hrs
WELD-FM Moorefield WV 3 hrs
WVNT(AM) Parkersburg WV 4 hrs
WCWV(FM) Summersville WV 15 hrs
WHAW(AM) Weston WV 18 hrs
WXCC(FM) Williamson WV 8 hrs
KJUA(AM) Cheyenne WY 1 hr
KKTY-FM Douglas WY 1 hr

Greek

WCGO(AM) Evanston IL 2 hrs
WJOB(AM) Hammond IN 1 hr
WLYN(AM) Lynn MA 2 hrs
WBMD(AM) Baltimore MD 2 hrs
WAAL(FM) Binghamton NY 1 hr
WKTX(AM) Cortland OH 2 hrs
WCCD(AM) Parma OH 2 hrs
WEDO(AM) McKeesport PA 1 hr
WKST(AM) New Castle PA 1 hr
WBZK(AM) York SC 10 hrs
*WUVT-FM Blacksburg VA 2 hrs
WEIR(AM) Weirton WV 1 hr

Hardcore

*WITR(FM) Henrietta NY 2 hrs
*WNRN(FM) Charlottesville VA 4 hrs
*WWHS-FM Hampden-Sydney VA 4 hrs

Hebrew

*WHPK-FM Chicago IL 1 hr
KLAV(AM) Las Vegas NV 1 hr
*WKDU(FM) Philadelphia PA 3 hrs

Hindi

*WAPS(FM) Akron OH 1 hr
*WCPN(FM) Cleveland OH 1 hr
WKTX(AM) Cortland OH 7 hrs
*WJCU(FM) University Heights OH 3 hrs

Inspirational

WNBN(AM) Meridian MS

Irish

*KUSF(FM) San Francisco CA 1 hr
*KRCC(FM) Colorado Springs CO 5 hrs
WQUN(AM) Hamden CT 2 hrs
WMRD(AM) Middletown CT 1 hr
*WNHU(FM) West Haven CT 5 hrs
*WHPK-FM Chicago IL 1 hr
WPNA(AM) Oak Park IL 7 hrs
*KANU(AM) Lawrence KS 2 hrs
*WGBH(FM) Boston MA 2 hrs
WROL(AM) Boston MA
WACE(AM) Chicopee MA 2 hrs
WNBP(AM) Newburyport MA 4 hrs
WNTN(AM) Newton MA 6 hrs
WBRK(AM) Pittsfield MA 1 hr
*WUNH(FM) Durham NH 2 hrs
WHVW(AM) Hyde Park NY 1 hr
WKNY(AM) Kingston NY 1 hr
*WVCR-FM Loudonville NY 3 hrs
WVOX(AM) New Rochelle NY 1 hr
*WFUV(FM) New York NY 10 hrs
WLIM(AM) Patchogue NY 1 hr
WLLW(FM) Seneca Falls NY 2 hrs
WSFW(AM) Seneca Falls NY 2 hrs
WTBQ(AM) Warwick NY 1 hr
WTBQ(AM) Warwick NY 2 hrs
*WCBE(FM) Columbus OH 4 hrs
WGBN(AM) New Kensington PA 2 hrs
*WYEP-FM Pittsburgh PA 2 hrs
WADK(AM) Newport RI 2 hrs
*WEVL(FM) Memphis TN 4 hrs

Italian

*KUSF(FM) San Francisco CA 1 hr
WICC(AM) Bridgeport CT 5 hrs
WGCH(AM) Greenwich CT 1 hr
WMRD(AM) Middletown CT 2 hrs
WRYM(AM) New Britain CT 1 hr
WATR(AM) Waterbury CT 3 hrs
*WWUH(FM) West Hartford CT 3 hrs
WXYB(AM) Indian Rocks Beach FL 2 hrs
WDUV(FM) New Port Richey FL 1 hr
WPSO(AM) New Port Richey FL 2 hrs
WNTN(AM) Newton MA 2 hrs
*WHRW(FM) Binghamton NY 3 hrs
WAMF(AM) Fulton NY 2 hrs
WHVW(AM) Hyde Park NY 1 hr
WJTN(AM) Jamestown NY 1 hr
WIZR(AM) Johnstown NY 1 hr
WLVL(AM) Lockport NY 2 hrs
WVOU(AM) Mexico NY 2 hrs
WVIP(FM) New Rochelle NY 6 hrs
WJJL(AM) Niagara Falls NY 4 hrs
WLIM(AM) Patchogue NY 4 hrs
*WRUC(FM) Schenectady NY 1 hr

WLLW(FM) Seneca Falls NY 2 hrs
WSFW(AM) Seneca Falls NY 2 hrs
WUTQ(AM) Utica NY 2 hrs
*WAPS(FM) Akron OH 2 hrs
WRTK(AM) Niles OH 1 hr
*WJCU(FM) University Heights OH 2 hrs
WELW(AM) Willoughby-Eastlake OH 1 hr
WNIO(AM) Youngstown OH 3 hrs
KLPM(AM) Portland OR 1 hr
*WMUH(FM) Allentown PA 2 hrs
WWCS(AM) Canonsburg PA 2 hrs
WEDO(AM) McKeesport PA 1 hr
WGBN(AM) New Kensington PA 2 hrs
WURD(AM) Philadelphia PA 3 hrs
WPIC(AM) Sharon PA 2 hrs
WFAX(AM) Falls Church VA 1 hr
*WMSE(FM) Milwaukee WI 3 hrs
WRJN(AM) Racine WI 2.5 hrs
WRLF(FM) Fairmont WV 3 hrs
WTCS(AM) Fairmont WV 3 hrs
WEIR(AM) Weirton WV 3 hrs

Japanese

KTYM(AM) Inglewood CA 1 hr
KEST(AM) San Francisco CA
*KCSB-FM Santa Barbara CA 1 hr
*V6AI(AM) Yap FM 5 hrs
KPUA(AM) Hilo HI 6 hrs
*WBXL(FM) Baldwinsville NY 1 hr
*KWVA(FM) Eugene OR 2 hrs
*WRVU(FM) Nashville TN 2 hrs

Jazz

*KBRW(AM) Barrow AK 6 hrs
*KUAC(FM) Fairbanks AK 15 hrs
*KIYU(AM) Galena AK 4 hrs
*KBBI(AM) Homer AK
*KTOO(FM) Juneau AK 14 hrs
*KRBD(FM) Ketchikan AK 10 hrs
*KSTK(FM) Wrangell AK 8 hrs
WDLT-FM Chickasaw AL 5 hrs
WZEW(FM) Fairhope AL 6 hrs
*WFIX(FM) Florence AL 6 hrs
WJRL-FM Ozark AL 4 hrs
WWPG(AM) Tuscaloosa AL 2 hrs
KEZA(FM) Fayetteville AR
*KXRJ(FM) Russellville AR 15 hrs
KNOT(AM) Prescott AZ 2 hrs
*KXCI(FM) Tucson AZ 2 hrs
*KHSU-FM Arcata CA 10 hrs
*KPFA(FM) Berkeley CA 15 hrs
KRML(AM) Carmel CA 140 hrs
*KHSR(FM) Crescent City CA 10 hrs
*KMUD(FM) Garberville CA 6 hrs
KFGY(FM) Healdsburg CA 5 hrs
*KFJC(FM) Los Altos CA 7 hrs
*KPFK(FM) Los Angeles CA 5 hrs
KMMT(FM) Mammoth Lakes CA 2 hrs
*KSMC(FM) Moraga CA 5 hrs
KHOP(FM) Oakdale CA 4 hrs
*KZYX(FM) Philo CA 11 hrs
*KUCR(FM) Riverside CA 6 hrs
KFRC(AM) San Francisco CA
*KRCB-FM Santa Rosa CA 6 hrs
KNNN(FM) Shasta Lake City CA 3 hrs
KZSQ-FM Sonora CA 3 hrs
KTHO(AM) South Lake Tahoe CA
*KCSS(FM) Turlock CA 4 hrs
*KASF(FM) Alamosa CO 6 hrs
*KGNU-FM Boulder CO 15 hrs
KVCU(AM) Boulder CO 3 hrs
*KRCC(FM) Colorado Springs CO 15 hrs
*KDUR(FM) Durango CO 9 hrs
KIQX(FM) Durango CO 7 hrs
KCSU-FM Fort Collins CO 3 hrs
*KMSA(FM) Grand Junction CO 12 hrs
*KWSB-FM Gunnison CO 3 hrs
*KSUT(FM) Ignacio CO 15 hrs
KFMU-FM Oak Creek CO 4 hrs
KWUF(AM) Pagosa Springs CO 10 hrs
*KVNF(FM) Paonia CO 17 hrs

*KOTO(FM) Telluride CO 9 hrs
*WPKN(FM) Bridgeport CT 16 hrs
*WXCI(FM) Danbury CT 3 hrs
*WQTQ(FM) Hartford CT 12 hrs
WZBG(FM) Litchfield CT 2 hrs
WMRD(AM) Middletown CT 4 hrs. weekly hrs
WYBC-FM New Haven CT 8 hrs
*WCNI(FM) New London CT 9 hrs
WLIS(AM) Old Saybrook CT 4 hrs
*WNHU(FM) West Haven CT 12 hrs
*WECS(FM) Willimantic CT 16 hrs
WKND(AM) Windsor CT 3 hrs
*WAMU(AM) Washington DC 3 hrs
*WVUD(FM) Newark DE 15 hrs
WGMD(FM) Rehoboth Beach DE 2 hrs
*WKTO(FM) Edgewater FL 4 hrs
*WJLF(FM) Gainesville FL 2 hrs
WXCV(FM) Homosassa Springs FL 7 hrs
WAVV(FM) Naples Park FL 3 hrs
WRXB(AM) Saint Petersburg Beach FL 15 hrs
*WANM(FM) Tallahassee FL 15 hrs
*WFSU-FM Tallahassee FL 8 hrs
WFLM(FM) White City FL 4 hrs
*WPRK(FM) Winter Park FL 3 hrs
*WUGA(FM) Athens GA 4 hrs
*WABE(FM) Atlanta GA 7 hrs
*WREK(FM) Atlanta GA 15 hrs
*WACG-FM Augusta GA 18 hrs
*WNGH-FM Chatsworth GA 16 hrs
*WMUM-FM Cochran GA 18 hrs
*WNGU(FM) Dahlonega GA 16 hrs
*WPPR(FM) Demorest GA 16 hrs
*WJWV(FM) Fort Gaines GA 16 hrs
WFXM(FM) Gordon GA 3 hrs
*WGPB(FM) Rome GA
*WSVH(FM) Savannah GA 4 hrs
*WABR(FM) Tifton GA 4 hrs
*WWET(FM) Valdosta GA 16 hrs
*WJSP-FM Warm Springs GA 18 hrs
WWSN(FM) Waycross GA 5 hrs
*WXVS(FM) Waycross GA 16 hrs
KUAI(AM) Eleele HI 4 hrs
KMXG(FM) Clinton IA 3 hrs
KROS(AM) Clinton IA 1 hr
*KHOE(FM) Fairfield IA 2 hrs
*KRNL-FM Mount Vernon IA 2 hrs
*KOJI(FM) Okoboji IA 4 hrs
*KIGC(FM) Oskaloosa IA 12 hrs
*KWIT(FM) Sioux City IA 17 hrs
KSAS-FM Caldwell ID 4 hrs
*KBSM(FM) McCall ID
*KRFA-FM Moscow ID
*KUOI(FM) Moscow ID 4 hrs
KECH-FM Sun Valley ID 6. hrs
*WESN(FM) Bloomington IL 6 hrs
*WEIU(FM) Charleston IL 4 hrs
WFMT(FM) Chicago IL 5 hrs
*WIIT(FM) Chicago IL 9 hrs
*WSSD(FM) Chicago IL
*WEPS(FM) Elgin IL 6 hrs
*WVKC(FM) Galesburg IL 15 hrs
WYMG(FM) Jacksonville IL 2 hrs
*WCSF(FM) Joliet IL 2 hrs
*WMXM(FM) Lake Forest IL 6 hrs
*WLRA(FM) Lockport IL 15 hrs
*WIUM(FM) Macomb IL 5 hrs
*WIUS(FM) Macomb IL 2 hrs
WPNA(AM) Oak Park IL 4 hrs
*WRRG(FM) River Grove IL 5 hrs
*WVIK(FM) Rock Island IL 9 hrs
WNNS(FM) Springfield IL 6 hrs
*WGRE(FM) Greencastle IN 3 hrs
WNTR(FM) Indianapolis IN 6 hrs
*WSND-FM Notre Dame IN
*WMHD(FM) Terre Haute IN 2 hrs
*WVUR-FM Valparaiso IN 3 hrs
*KANZ(FM) Garden City KS 15 hrs
*KZNA(FM) Hill City KS 15 hrs
*KSDB-FM Manhattan KS 3 hrs
KRBB(FM) Wichita KS 2 hrs
*WKUE(FM) Elizabethtown KY 15 hrs
WRNZ(FM) Lancaster KY 2 hrs
*WDCL-FM Somerset KY 15 hrs

*KLSP(FM) Angola LA 7 hrs
*WAMQ(FM) Great Barrington MA 13 hrs
WFNX(FM) Lynn MA 8 hrs
*WBSL-FM Sheffield MA 8 hrs
*WYAJ(FM) Sudbury MA 5 hrs
WMVY(FM) Tisbury MA 4 hrs
*WCHC(FM) Worcester MA 6 hrs
WLIF(FM) Baltimore MD 8 hrs
*WHFC(FM) Bel Air MD 18 hrs
*WKHS(FM) Worton MD 2 hrs
*WUMF-FM Farmington ME 15 hrs
WBQW(FM) Kennebunkport ME 5 hrs
WPHX-FM Sanford ME 6 hrs
WBQX(FM) Thomaston ME 2 hrs
*WMHB(FM) Waterville ME
*WHFR(FM) Dearborn MI 10 hrs
*WDET-FM Detroit MI 15 hrs
*WDBM(FM) East Lansing MI 5 hrs
*WKAR-FM East Lansing MI 7 hrs
*WTHS(FM) Holland MI 6 hrs
WJNZ(AM) Kentwood MI 6 hrs
*WUPX(FM) Marquette MI 2 hrs
WRKR(FM) Portage MI
*KFAI(FM) Minneapolis MN 12 hrs
*KVSC(FM) Saint Cloud MN
*WMCN(FM) Saint Paul MN 4 hrs
*KOPN(FM) Columbia MO 4 hrs
*KCFV(FM) Ferguson MO 4 hrs
*KKFI(FM) Kansas City MO 10 hrs
*KGSP(FM) Parkville MO 14 hrs
*KMST(FM) Rolla MO 3 hrs
KMOX(AM) Saint Louis MO 4 hrs
KBFL(AM) Springfield MO 12 hrs
*KSMU(FM) Springfield MO 10 hrs
WGNL(FM) Greenwood MS 6 hrs
*KMSM-FM Butte MT 5 hrs
WSQL(AM) Brevard NC 5 hrs
*WXDU(FM) Durham NC 18 hrs
*WRVS-FM Elizabeth City NC 6 hrs
*WKNS(FM) Kinston NC 6 hrs
WIKS(FM) New Bern NC 2 hrs
WNOS(AM) New Bern NC 12 hrs
*WTEB(FM) New Bern NC 4 hrs
WNNC(AM) Newton NC 3 hrs
*WZRU(FM) Roanoke Rapids NC 6 hrs
WLHC(FM) Robbins NC 2 hrs
*WNCW(FM) Spindale NC 5 hrs
WFXK(FM) Tarboro NC 4 hrs
*WFDD-FM Winston-Salem NC 16 hrs
*KRNU(FM) Lincoln NE 2 hrs
KEZO-FM Omaha NE 3 hrs
*KIOS-FM Omaha NE 15 hrs
*KKCD(FM) Omaha NE 4 hrs
*KWSC(FM) Wayne NE 2 hrs
*WUNH(FM) Durham NH 5 hrs
*WKNH(FM) Keene NH 3 hrs
WFEX(FM) Peterborough NH 6 hrs
*WPCR-FM Plymouth NH 3 hrs
*WDVR(FM) Delaware Township NJ 11 hrs
*WNTI(FM) Hackettstown NJ 9 hrs
*WBZC(FM) Pemberton NJ 4 hrs
*WLFR(FM) Pomona NJ 10 hrs
*WTSR(FM) Trenton NJ 4 hrs
*WKNJ-FM Union Township NJ 8 hrs
*WMSC(FM) Upper Montclair NJ 2 hrs
*WPSC-FM Wayne NJ 12 hrs
*WMCX(FM) West Long Branch NJ 3 hrs
KKTC(FM) Angel Fire NM 4 hrs
*KSJE(FM) Farmington NM 15 hrs
KRSN(AM) Los Alamos NM 5 hrs
KTAO(FM) Taos NM 5 hrs
KRSI(FM) Garapan-Saipan NP 1 hr
*KCEP(FM) Las Vegas NV 12 hrs
KNEV(FM) Reno NV 2 hrs
*WAMC-FM Albany NY 18 hrs
*WCDB(FM) Albany NY 10 hrs
WVIN-FM Bath NY 2 hrs
*WHRW(FM) Binghamton NY 9 hrs
*WSKG-FM Binghamton NY
*WXLH(FM) Blue Mountain Lake NY
*WBNY(FM) Buffalo NY 3 hrs
*WCAN(FM) Canajoharie NY 17 hrs

*WSLU(FM) Canton NY
*WHCL-FM Clinton NY 9 hrs
WKGB-FM Conklin NY 2 hrs
*WSQE(FM) Corning NY
*WRCU-FM Hamilton NY 12 hrs
*WITR(FM) Henrietta NY 8 hrs
*WICB(FM) Ithaca NY 13 hrs
*WSQG-FM Ithaca NY 7 hrs
*WAMK(FM) Kingston NY 13 hrs
*WOSR(FM) Middletown NY 13 hrs
*WBAI(FM) New York NY 5 hrs
*WNYC-FM New York NY 4 hrs
WQXR-FM New York NY 2 hrs
*WRHO(FM) Oneonta NY 4 hrs
*WSQC-FM Oneonta NY
WZOZ(FM) Oneonta NY 2 hrs
WLIM(AM) Patchogue NY 4 hrs
*WCEL(FM) Plattsburgh NY 13 hrs
*WRHV(FM) Poughkeepsie NY 2 hrs
WDKX(FM) Rochester NY 4 hrs
*WFNP(FM) Rosendale NY 4 hrs
*WMHT-FM Schenectady NY 1 hr
*WRUC(FM) Schenectady NY 15 hrs
WLLW(FM) Seneca Falls NY 1 hr
WSFW(AM) Seneca Falls NY 1 hr
*WKWZ(FM) Syosset NY 12 hrs
*WCNY-FM Syracuse NY 7 hrs
*WANC(FM) Ticonderoga NY 17 hrs
*WPNR-FM Utica NY 14 hrs
*WUNY(FM) Utica NY 7 hrs
*WJNY(FM) Watertown NY 5 hrs
WRIP(FM) Windham NY 2 hrs
*WRDL(FM) Ashland OH 5 hrs
*WGBE(FM) Bryan OH
*WCBE(FM) Columbus OH 4 hrs
*WWSU(FM) Dayton OH 3 hrs
*WGDE(FM) Defiance OH 16 hrs
WBVI(FM) Fostoria OH 3 hrs
WWCD(FM) Grove City OH 3 hrs
WRBP(FM) Hubbard OH 12 hrs
WVKO-FM Johnstown OH 10 hrs
WCIT(AM) Lima OH 2 hrs
*WGLE(FM) Lima OH 16 hrs
WCLV(FM) Lorain OH 5 hrs
*WMCO(FM) New Concord OH 10 hrs
*WOBC-FM Oberlin OH 15 hrs
*WUSO(FM) Springfield OH 6 hrs
*WGTE-FM Toledo OH 16 hrs
WRVF(FM) Toledo OH 6 hrs
*WOBN(FM) Westerville OH 1 hr
*WYSO(FM) Yellow Springs OH 12 hrs
*KRSC-FM Claremore OK 5 hrs
KBZQ(FM) Lawton OK 4 hrs
*KCCU(FM) Lawton OK
KZBB(FM) Poteau OK 2 hrs
*KOAC(FM) Corvallis OR 12 hrs
*KWVA(FM) Eugene OR 6 hrs
*KEOL(FM) La Grande OR 6 hrs
KYTE(FM) Newport OR 4 hrs
*KRRC(FM) Portland OR 10 hrs
KLRR(FM) Redmond OR 5 hrs
*WDIY(FM) Allentown PA 10 hrs
*WLVR(FM) Bethlehem PA 12 hrs
WMKX(FM) Brookville PA 3 hrs
*WDCV-FM Carlisle PA 6 hrs
*WDNR(FM) Chester PA 2 hrs
*WCUC-FM Clarion PA 3 hrs
*WESS(FM) East Stroudsburg PA 6 hrs
*WJRH(FM) Easton PA 9 hrs
*WMCE(FM) Erie PA 4 hrs
*WZBT(FM) Gettysburg PA 4 hrs
*WKVR-FM Huntingdon PA 3 hrs
*WIUP-FM Indiana PA 15 hrs
*WPSX(FM) Kane PA 3 hrs
*WFNM(FM) Lancaster PA 8 hrs
*WVBU-FM Lewisburg PA 3 hrs
*WNTE(FM) Mansfield PA 2 hrs
*WARC(FM) Meadville PA 4 hrs
*WIXQ(FM) Millersville PA 2 hrs
*WHYY-FM Philadelphia PA 4 hrs
*WRCT(FM) Pittsburgh PA 18 hrs
*WVMW-FM Scranton PA 10 hrs
WSYC-FM Shippensburg PA 3 hrs
*WPSU(FM) State College PA 4 hrs
*WRDV(FM) Warminster PA 3 hrs

*WNJR(FM) Washington PA 3 hrs
*WRLC(FM) Williamsport PA 8 hrs
*WVYC(FM) York PA 8 hrs
WWNA(AM) Aguadilla PR 3 hrs
WOLA(AM) Barranquitas PR 5 hrs
WUKQ-FM Mayaguez PR 6 hrs
WADK(AM) Newport RI 7 hrs
WBRU(FM) Providence RI 18 hrs
WEGX(FM) Dillon SC 1 hr
WOLH(AM) Florence SC 4 hrs
WYNN(AM) Florence SC
*WLGI(FM) Hemingway SC 18 hrs
*WSSB-FM Orangeburg SC 10 hrs
WSPA-FM Spartanburg SC 4 hrs
*KSDJ(FM) Brookings SD 2 hrs
*KCSD(FM) Sioux Falls SD 10 hrs
*WAPX-FM Clarksville TN 6 hrs
*WTTU(FM) Cookeville TN
*WFHU(FM) Henderson TN 45 hrs
*WEVL(FM) Memphis TN 15 hrs
*WMTS-FM Murfreesboro TN 4 hrs
*WRVU(FM) Nashville TN 18 hrs
*WUTS(FM) Sewanee TN 4 hrs
*KACU(FM) Abilene TX 3 hrs
*KACV-FM Amarillo TX 12 hrs
KGSR(FM) Bastrop TX 6 hrs
*KWTS(FM) Canyon TX 3 hrs
*KEOS(FM) College Station TX 3 hrs
KODA(FM) Houston TX 4 hrs
*KTRU(FM) Houston TX 10 hrs
KFAN-FM Johnson City TX
*KNCT-FM Killeen TX 15 hrs
KMND(AM) Midland TX 1 hr
*KOCV(FM) Odessa TX 4 hrs
KQXT(FM) San Antonio TX 4 hrs
*KSTX(FM) San Antonio TX 6 hrs
*KTXK(FM) Texarkana TX 15 hrs
*KWBU-FM Waco TX 10 hrs
KBLQ-FM Logan UT 4 hrs
*KPCW-FM Park City UT 12 hrs
*WWHS-FM Hampden-Sydney VA 6 hrs
*WXJM(FM) Harrisonburg VA 14 hrs
*WVRU(FM) Radford VA 19 hrs
*WCVE-FM Richmond VA 18 hrs
*WDCE(FM) Richmond VA 9 hrs
*WCWM(FM) Williamsburg VA 13 hrs
*WISE-FM Wise VA 9 hrs
*WIUJ(FM) Charlotte Amalie VI 6 hrs
WRRA(AM) Frederiksted VI 6 hrs
*WIUV(FM) Castleton VT 10 hrs
*WWLR(FM) Lyndonville VT 3 hrs
WEQX(FM) Manchester VT 4 hrs
*WRMC-FM Middlebury VT 10 hrs
WNCS(FM) Montpelier VT 5 hrs
*KUGS(FM) Bellingham WA 10 hrs wkly hrs
*KNWR(FM) Ellensburg WA
*KSER(FM) Everett WA 3 hrs
KBRD(AM) Lacey WA 1 hr
*KWSU(AM) Pullman WA 14 hrs
*KZUU(FM) Pullman WA 12 hrs
*KFAE-FM Richland WA 15 hrs
*KUOW-FM Seattle WA 5 hrs
*KAGU(FM) Spokane WA 2 hrs
*KPBX-FM Spokane WA
*KUPS(FM) Tacoma WA 12 hrs
*WHSA(FM) Brule WI 6 hrs
*WBSD(FM) Burlington WI 4 hrs
*WPNE(FM) Green Bay WI 10 hrs
*WORT(FM) Madison WI 5 hrs
*WHWC(FM) Menomonie WI 3 hrs
*WVSS(FM) Menomonie WI 5 hrs
*WMSE(FM) Milwaukee WI 15 hrs
*WSUP(FM) Platteville WI 3 hrs
*WOJB(FM) Reserve WI 10 hrs
*WXPR(FM) Rhinelander WI 8 hrs
*WHND(FM) Sister Bay WI 10 hrs
*KUWS(FM) Superior WI 15 hrs
*WSUW(FM) Whitewater WI 6 hrs
*WVWC(FM) Buckhannon WV 8 hrs
WQZK-FM Keyser WV 2 hrs
*WWVU-FM Morgantown WV 9 hrs
*WQAB(FM) Philippi WV 4 hrs
WMOV(AM) Ravenswood WV 2 hrs
*WPHP(FM) Wheeling WV 1 hr

*KUWA(FM) Afton WY 5 hrs
KMTN(AM) Jackson WY
*KUWJ(FM) Jackson WY 6 hrs
*KUWR(FM) Laramie WY 6 hrs
*KUWZ(FM) Rock Springs WY 6 hrs

Jewish

*KCSN(FM) Northridge CA 3 hrs
WMRD(AM) Middletown CT 1 hr
WPBR(AM) Lantana FL 3 hrs
WVIP(FM) New Rochelle NY 1 hr
WVOX(AM) New Rochelle NY 2 hrs
WMCA(AM) New York NY 9 hrs
*WDIY(FM) Allentown PA 1 hr
*WHCB(FM) Bristol TN 1 hr
*KEOS(FM) College Station TX 2 hrs

Korean

WCGO(AM) Evanston IL 20 hrs
*WNKJ(FM) Hopkinsville KY 1/2 hrs
*KRNM(FM) Chalan Kanoa-Saipan NP 1 hr
*WUSB(FM) Stony Brook NY 1 hr

Light Rock

*KTNA(FM) Talkeetna AK 5 hrs

Lithuanian

WCGO(AM) Evanston IL 1 hr
WBMD(AM) Baltimore MD 1 hr
*WGMC(FM) Greece NY 1 hr
*WCPN(FM) Cleveland OH 1 hr
*WJCU(FM) University Heights OH 2 hrs

MOR

WSNJ(AM) Bridgeton NJ
WBUK(FM) Ottawa OH 4 hrs

Native American

KTNN(AM) Window Rock AZ
*KDUR(FM) Durango CO 3 hrs
KIXR(FM) Ponca City OK 3 hrs
*KRVM-FM Eugene OR 2 hrs
*WPNE(FM) Green Bay WI 2. hrs
*WHND(FM) Sister Bay WI 2 hrs

New Age

*KUAC(FM) Fairbanks AK 3 hrs
*WBHM(FM) Birmingham AL 6 hrs
*WSGN(FM) Gadsden AL 10 hrs
*WQPR(FM) Muscle Shoals AL 20 hrs
*WUAL-FM Tuscaloosa AL 20 hrs
*KASU Jonesboro AR
KEST(AM) San Francisco CA
*KVNF(FM) Paonia CO 6 hrs
*WXCI(FM) Danbury CT 3 hrs
*WSHU(FM) Fairfield CT 6 hrs
*WGRS(FM) Guilford CT 1 hr
*WMNR(FM) Monroe CT 1 hr
*WRXC(FM) Shelton CT 1 hr
*WGSK(FM) South Kent CT 1 hr
*WMFE-FM Orlando FL 4 hrs
*WFCF(FM) Saint Augustine FL 4 hrs
*WRAS(FM) Atlanta GA 3 hrs
*WUWG(FM) Carrollton GA 3 hrs
*KCCK-FM Cedar Rapids IA 7 hrs
*WSIU(FM) Carbondale IL 4 hrs
*WSIE(FM) Edwardsville IL 10 hrs
*WNIU(FM) Rockford IL 2 hrs
*KMSK(FM) Austin MN 5 hrs
*KMSU(FM) Mankato MN 5 hrs
*KCOZ(FM) Point Lookout MO 10 hrs
*WZRU(FM) Roanoke Rapids NC 10 hrs
*KUND-FM Grand Forks ND 4 hrs
*KZUM(FM) Lincoln NE 8 hrs

*WKNH(FM) Keene NH 4 hrs
*WKNJ-FM Union Township NJ 8 hrs
*WCVF-FM Fredonia NY 4 hrs
*WSUF(FM) Noyack NY 6 hrs
*WAER(FM) Syracuse NY 3 hrs
*WGDE(FM) Defiance OH 4 hrs
*WGLE(FM) Lima OH
*WGTE-FM Toledo OH 4 hrs
*WYSO(FM) Yellow Springs OH 4 hrs
*WQLN-FM Erie PA 2 hrs
*WIUP-FM Indiana PA 4 hrs
*WVBU(FM) Lewisburg PA 1 hr
*WKDU(FM) Philadelphia PA 2 hrs
*WRDV(FM) Warminster PA 3 hrs
WCRI(FM) Block Island RI 4 hrs
*KAMU-FM College Station TX 5 hrs
*KTRU(FM) Houston TX 1 hr
*KNTU(FM) McKinney TX 3 hrs
*WVRU(FM) Radford VA 3 hrs
*KPBX-FM Spokane WA
*WWVU-FM Morgantown WV 6 hrs
KMTN(AM) Jackson WY

New Wave

*WVUA-FM Tuscaloosa AL 4 hrs

News

WBCF(AM) Florence AL 10 hrs
KWBF-FM North Little Rock AR 15 hrs
KBHR(FM) Big Bear City CA 8 hrs
KWXY-FM Cathedral City CA 2 hrs
*KRZA(FM) Alamosa CO 4 hrs
WILI-FM Willimantic CT 1 hr
WRZN(AM) Hernando FL 4 hrs
*WRGP(FM) Homestead FL 3 hrs
WCNK(FM) Key West FL 1 hr
KLGA(AM) Algona IA
KLGA-FM Algona IA
KTFC(FM) Sioux City IA 10 hrs
*WPCD(FM) Champaign IL 8 hrs
*WGCS(FM) Goshen IN 8 hrs
WMJL-FM Marion KY
WKIK(FM) La Plata MD
WSMD-FM Mechanicsville MD
*WPHS(FM) Warren MI 5 hrs
KMAM(AM) Butler MO
KBNN(AM) Lebanon MO
KCXL(AM) Liberty MO 4 hrs
KWWR(FM) Mexico MO
KSIM(AM) Sikeston MO
KRWP(FM) Stockton MO
WKXU(FM) Louisburg NC
KHND(AM) Harvey ND
*KZUM(FM) Lincoln NE 11 hrs
WBAZ(FM) Bridgehampton NY
*WKCR-FM New York NY 3 hrs
WJZR(FM) Rochester NY 1 hr
WBEA(FM) Southold NY
*WCII(FM) Spencer NY 14 hrs
WCLV(FM) Lorain OH 1 hr
KSPI(AM) Stillwater OK
*KMHD(FM) Gresham OR 5 hrs
KSZN(AM) Gresham OR 3 hrs
WIVV(AM) Vieques PR 7 hrs
WHYM(AM) Lake City SC
KORA-FM Bryan TX
KTAM(AM) Bryan TX
KCYL(AM) Lampasas TX 14 hrs
*KSUU(FM) Cedar City UT
WEVA(AM) Emporia VA 14 hrs
WVCV(AM) Orange VA 18 hrs
WHEO(AM) Stuart VA 10 hrs
*KASB(FM) Bellevue WA 3 hrs
KQQQ(AM) Pullman WA 10 hrs
WGLR-FM Lancaster WI
WOMT(AM) Manitowoc WI 18 hrs
*KUWJ(FM) Jackson WY 3 hrs
*KUWR(FM) Laramie WY 3 hrs

News/talk

*WVAS(FM) Montgomery AL 7 hrs
KWKM(FM) Saint Johns AZ 2 hrs
WCCC-FM Hartford CT 10 hrs
WILM(AM) Wilmington DE
WWWE(AM) Hapeville GA 14 hrs
*WHFH(FM) Flossmoor IL 1 hr
*WHHL(FM) Jerseyville IL 3 hrs
*WLTL(FM) La Grange IL 10 hrs
WITZ-FM Jasper IN 3 hrs
WWVR(FM) West Terre Haute IN
*KCFN(FM) Wichita KS
WFLW(AM) Monticello KY 10 hrs
WCBR(AM) Richmond KY
KJXX(AM) Jackson MO
WQNQ(FM) Fletcher NC 5 hrs
WCBQ(AM) Oxford NC
WMPM(AM) Smithfield NC 12 hrs
KLIQ(FM) Hastings NE
WSNJ(AM) Bridgeton NJ
*WJSV(FM) Morristown NJ 3 hrs
KSNE-FM Las Vegas NV 1 hr
*WCDB(FM) Albany NY 1 hr
*WITC(FM) Cazenovia NY 3 hrs
WCKM-FM Lake George NY
WJJL(AM) Niagara Falls NY 5 hrs
*WNYO(FM) Oswego NY 4 hrs
*WFNP(FM) Rosendale NY 5 hrs
*WRMU(FM) Alliance OH 5 hrs
WRBP(FM) Hubbard OH
*WESS(FM) East Stroudsburg PA 6 hrs
*WFSE(FM) Edinboro PA 3 hrs
*WQLN-FM Erie PA 3 hrs
WXTU(FM) Philadelphia PA 1/2 hr
WBCU(AM) Union SC 10 hrs
*KLND(FM) Little Eagle SD 5 hrs
KRFE(AM) Lubbock TX 15 hrs
KMER(AM) Kemmerer WY 7 hrs
*KUWZ(FM) Rock Springs WY 3 hrs

Nostalgia

KNTK(FM) Weed CA 2 hrs
*WAMU(FM) Washington DC 4 hrs
*KCMR(FM) Mason City IA 10 hrs
WAAM(AM) Ann Arbor MI 6 hrs
KRDS-FM New Prague MN 18 hrs
WDOS(AM) Oneonta NY 2 hrs
WDJQ(FM) Alliance OH
*WFSE(FM) Edinboro PA 2 hrs
KLSR-FM Memphis TX 10 hrs
KEYG(AM) Grand Coulee WA 4 hrs
KARS-FM Laramie WY 6 hrs

Oldies

KRSA(AM) Petersburg AK 5 hrs
WJAB(FM) Huntsville AL 8 hrs
WJRL-FM Ozark AL 6 hrs
KESA(AM) Eureka Springs AR 2 hrs
KEZA(FM) Fayetteville AR
*KAZU(FM) Pacific Grove CA 5 hrs
*KSPB(FM) Pebble Beach CA 4 hrs
*KWSB-FM Gunnison CO 3 hrs
*WPFW(FM) Washington DC 3 hrs
*WVUM(FM) Coral Gables FL 5 hrs
WXCV(FM) Homosassa Springs FL 6 hrs
WMAF(AM) Madison FL
WGOV(AM) Valdosta GA 10 hrs
*WQUB(FM) Quincy IL 2 hrs
*WRRG(FM) River Grove IL 11 hrs
WJVO(FM) South Jacksonville IL 5 hrs
WBIW(AM) Bedford IN
*WCYT(FM) Lafayette Township IN 2 hrs
WXLO(FM) Fitchburg MA 5 hrs
WHAI(FM) Greenfield MA 13 hrs
*WOMR(FM) Provincetown MA 9 hrs
*WEAA(FM) Baltimore MD 5 hrs
*WKHS(FM) Worton MD 6 hrs
WMPX(AM) Midland MI 2 hrs
KASM(AM) Albany MN
KXLP(FM) Eagle Lake MN 15 hrs

KEYL(AM) Long Prairie MN 3 hrs
KNUJ(AM) New Ulm MN 8 hrs
KOLV(FM) Olivia MN
KKAQ(AM) Thief River Falls MN 6 hrs
KKDQ(FM) Thief River Falls MN 6 hrs
KBFL(AM) Springfield MO 4 hrs
*WVSD(AM) Itta Bena MS 10 hrs
WUMS(FM) University MS 2 hrs
KBAZ(FM) Hamilton MT 3 hrs
KPRK(AM) Livingston MT 5 hrs
WIXE(AM) Monroe NC 5 hrs
*WZRU(FM) Roanoke Rapids NC 4 hrs
WLTT(FM) Shallotte NC 6 hrs
KAUJ(AM) Grafton ND 4 hrs
KLIR(FM) Columbus NE 12 hrs
*WDVR(FM) Delaware Township NJ 13 hrs
*WNTI(FM) Hackettstown NJ 3 hrs
*WTSR(FM) Trenton NJ 6 hrs
WVBR-FM Ithaca NY 5 hrs
*WNYU-FM New York NY 3 hrs
WZOZ(FM) Oneonta NY 2 hrs
WPDH(FM) Poughkeepsie NY 4 hrs
WSFW(AM) Seneca Falls NY 3 hrs
*WRDL(FM) Ashland OH 4 hrs
KBZQ(FM) Lawton OK 6 hrs
WMBA(AM) Ambridge PA 3 hrs
WMKX(FM) Brookville PA 8 hrs
WWCS(AM) Canonsburg PA 4 hrs
*WDNR(FM) Chester PA 2 hrs
WOKW(FM) Curwensville PA 2 hrs
*WESS(FM) East Stroudsburg PA 8 hrs
WCCS(AM) Homer City PA 9 hrs
WLSH(AM) Lansford PA 18 hrs
WMNY(AM) McKeesport PA 9 hrs
WMGH-FM Tamaqua PA 7 hrs
*WNJR(FM) Washington PA 3 hrs
*WCYJ-FM Waynesburg PA 3 hrs
WYKZ(FM) Beaufort SC 5 hrs
WHSC(AM) Hartsville SC 6 hrs
WSPA-FM Spartanburg SC 10 hrs
WMXX-FM Jackson TN 15 hrs
WWLX(AM) Lawrenceburg TN 8 hrs
KFGL(FM) Abilene TX 2 hrs
KFYN(AM) Bonham TX 6 hrs
*KTRU(FM) Houston TX 3 hrs
KJAS(FM) Jasper TX 3 hrs
WPCE(AM) Portsmouth VA
*WVRU(FM) Radford VA 5 hrs
WTSA-FM Brattleboro VT 16 hrs
WIZN(FM) Vergennes VT 3 hrs
WLKG(FM) Lake Geneva WI 10 hrs
*WFGH(FM) Fort Gay WV 19 hrs
*WWVU-FM Morgantown WV 8 hrs

Other

*KSUA(FM) Fairbanks AK 19 hrs
*KTOO(FM) Juneau AK 1 hr
*KNOM(AM) Nome AK 14 hrs
*KNOM-FM Nome AK 14 hrs
KIFW(AM) Sitka AK 3 hrs
*WMBV(AM) Dixons Mills AL 3 hrs
WABF(AM) Fairhope AL 6 hrs
*WVUA-FM Tuscaloosa AL 3 hrs
WAPZ(AM) Wetumpka AL
*KUAR(FM) Little Rock AR 4 hrs
*KHSU-FM Arcata CA 14 hrs
KAHI(AM) Auburn CA
KIXF(FM) Baker CA
*KSPC(FM) Claremont CA 6 hrs
*KHSR(FM) Crescent City CA 14 hrs
*KFSR(FM) Fresno CA 1 hr
*KFSR(FM) Fresno CA 9 hrs
KCAA(AM) Loma Linda CA
*KSBR(FM) Mission Viejo CA 9 hrs
*KZYX(FM) Philo CA 8 hrs
KTIP(AM) Porterville CA
KTIP(AM) Porterville CA 1 hr
*KUSF(FM) San Francisco CA
*KUSF(FM) San Francisco CA 1 hr
KVEC(AM) San Luis Obispo CA
*KSCU(FM) Santa Clara CA 1 hr
*KSCU(FM) Santa Clara CA 6 hrs

KLCA(FM) Tahoe City CA 2 hrs
KTCL(FM) Wheat Ridge CO 1 hr
KRDZ(AM) Wray CO 3 hrs
*WGRS(FM) Guilford CT 1 hr
WQUN(AM) Hamden CT 2 hrs
WCCC-FM Hartford CT 10 hrs
*WQTQ(FM) Hartford CT 18 hrs
*WRTC-FM Hartford CT 6 hrs
*WESU(FM) Middletown CT
*WESU(FM) Middletown CT 5 hrs
*WMNR(FM) Monroe CT 1 hr
*WRXC(FM) Shelton CT 1 hr
*WPFW(FM) Washington DC 1 hr
WWUS(FM) Big Pine Key FL 4 hrs
WZFN(AM) Fort Walton Beach FL 1 hr
*WJLF(FM) Gainesville FL 5 hrs
WIIS(FM) Key West FL 4 hrs
WPBR(AM) Lantana FL 17 hrs
*WKWM(FM) Marathon FL 3 hrs
WPSO(AM) New Port Richey FL
*WUCF-FM Orlando FL
WCTH(FM) Plantation Key FL 3 hrs
WHKR(FM) Rockledge FL 1 hr
*WFCF(FM) Saint Augustine FL 4 hrs
*WCLK(FM) Atlanta GA 12 hrs
*WRAS(FM) Atlanta GA 3 hrs
*WRAS(FM) Atlanta GA 6 hrs
*WREK(FM) Atlanta GA 18 hrs
WGAC(AM) Augusta GA 3 hrs
WJJC(AM) Commerce GA
*WBCX(FM) Gainesville GA 6 hrs
KGUM(AM) Hagatna GU 7 hrs
KWXX-FM Hilo HI 20 hrs
KWAI(AM) Honolulu HI 14 hrs
KWAI(AM) Honolulu HI 2 hrs
*KKUA(FM) Wailuku HI 3 hrs
KLGA(AM) Algona IA
KLGA-FM Algona IA
*KIWR(FM) Council Bluffs IA 4 hrs
*KMSC(FM) Sioux City IA 4 hrs
KRLC(AM) Lewiston ID 2 hrs
WILY(AM) Centralia IL
*WRSE(FM) Elmhurst IL 3 hrs
*WRSE(FM) Elmhurst IL 6 hrs
WWHP(FM) Farmer City IL 2 hrs
WYMG(FM) Jacksonville IL 1 hr
*WLRA(FM) Lockport IL 15 hrs
*WUIS(FM) Springfield IL 19 hrs
WGFA-FM Watseka IL 2 hrs
WETN(FM) Wheaton IL 2 hrs
*WGRE(FM) Greencastle IN 2 hrs
*WSND-FM Notre Dame IN
*WWHR(FM) Bowling Green KY 2 hrs
WVLC(FM) Mannsville KY 5 hrs
WRLV-FM Salyersville KY 6 1/2 hrs
WTKY-FM Tompkinsville KY 1 hr
*KLSP(FM) Angola LA 4 hrs
KEUN(AM) Eunice LA 1 hr
KEUN-FM Eunice LA 2 hrs
KUMX(FM) North Fort Polk LA
*WGBH(FM) Boston MA 3 hrs
WROL(AM) Boston MA
WHTB(AM) Fall River MA 11 hrs
WFNX(FM) Lynn MA 2 hrs
WNTN(AM) Newton MA 2 hrs
WESX(AM) Salem MA 8 hrs
*WHFC(FM) Bel Air MD 15 hrs
*WUMF-FM Farmington ME 15 hrs
*WMPG(FM) Gorham ME 14 hrs
*WMHB(FM) Waterville ME
*WDBM(AM) East Lansing MI 4 hrs
WCHT(AM) Escanaba MI 1 hr
WSRT(FM) Gaylord MI 5. hrs
WSDS(AM) Salem Township MI
WMFN(AM) Zeeland MI 1 hr
WLKX-FM Forest Lake MN 9 hrs
KLTF(AM) Little Falls MN 5 hrs
KCHK(AM) New Prague MN 40 hrs
*KVSC(FM) Saint Cloud MN
*WMCN(FM) Saint Paul MN 4 hrs
KYOO(AM) Bolivar MO 3 hrs
KKWK(FM) Cameron MO
*KCFV(FM) Ferguson MO 4 hrs
*KCFV(FM) Ferguson MO 8 hrs
KFAL(AM) Fulton MO 6 hrs
KCXL(AM) Liberty MO 17 hrs

KRWP(FM) Stockton MO
*KGNV(FM) Washington MO 5 hrs
WJNS-FM Yazoo City MS 16 hrs
KXGN(AM) Glendive MT 5 hrs
WERX-FM Columbia NC
*WWCU(FM) Cullowhee NC 5. hrs
WCKB(AM) Dunn NC 9 hrs
*WFSS(FM) Fayetteville NC 2 hrs
WBAV-FM Gastonia NC 8 hrs
*WUAG(FM) Greensboro NC 2 hrs
WKGX(AM) Lenoir NC 16 hrs
WPAQ(AM) Mount Airy NC 15 hrs
WTAB(AM) Tabor City NC
KBTO(FM) Bottineau ND 5 hrs wkly hrs
KHND(AM) Harvey ND
WMOU(AM) Berlin NH 3 hrs
WFRD(FM) Hanover NH 2 hrs
*WKNH(FM) Keene NH 7 hrs
WWNH(AM) Madbury NH 24 hrs
WFEX(FM) Peterborough NH 2 hrs
WPNH(AM) Plymouth NH 6 hrs
*WPSC-FM Wayne NJ 18 hrs
*WPSC-FM Wayne NJ 3 hrs
KRSY-FM La Luz NM
KLAV(AM) Las Vegas NV 4 hrs
*KUNV(FM) Las Vegas NV 2 hrs
*WCDB(FM) Albany NY 10 hrs
*WCDB(FM) Albany NY 3 hrs
WCSS(AM) Amsterdam NY 12 hrs
*WBNY(FM) Buffalo NY 3 hrs
WDNY(FM) Dansville NY 4 hrs
WCVF-FM Fredonia NY 4 hrs
*WEOS(FM) Geneva NY 10 hrs
WVBR-FM Ithaca NY 6 hrs
*WKCR-FM New York NY 6 hrs
*WKCR-FM New York NY 8 hrs
*WNYU-FM New York NY 13 hrs
WEOK(AM) Poughkeepsie NY 2 hrs
WBEA(FM) Southold NY
*WOBO(FM) Batavia OH 3 hrs
WXXR(FM) Fredericktown OH 2hrs
WFXN-FM Galion OH 2hrs
WWCD(FM) Grove City OH 4 hrs
WXXF(FM) Loudonville OH 2hrs
WPFB(AM) Middletown OH 1 hr
*WOBC(FM) Oberlin OH 20 hrs
*WOBC-FM Oberlin OH 8 hrs
WSTV(AM) Steubenville OH 2 hrs
*WOBN(FM) Westerville OH 2 hrs
*WYSO(FM) Yellow Springs OH 3 hrs
KKBS(FM) Guymon OK 5 hrs
KSPI(AM) Stillwater OK
*KLCC(FM) Eugene OR 9 hrs
*KTEC(FM) Klamath Falls OR 15 hrs
KLCO(FM) Newport OR 6 hrs
KACI(AM) The Dalles OR 3 hrs
KMCQ(FM) The Dalles OR 3 hrs
WBVP(AM) Beaver Falls PA
*WBUQ(FM) Bloomsburg PA 10 hrs
*WDCV-FM Carlisle PA 1 hr
WCCR(FM) Clarion PA
*WCUC-FM Clarion PA 12 hrs
*WVMM(FM) Grantham PA 7 hrs
*WVBU-FM Lewisburg PA 2 hrs
WRKT(FM) North East PA 1 hr
*WKDU(FM) Philadelphia PA 4 hrs
KQV(AM) Pittsburgh PA
WJAS(AM) Pittsburgh PA 2 hrs
*WRCT(FM) Pittsburgh PA 12 hrs
WARM(AM) Scranton PA 2 hrs
*WUSR(FM) Scranton PA 10 hrs
WPIC(AM) Sharon PA 12 hrs
WMBS(AM) Uniontown PA 3 hrs
*WCYJ-FM Waynesburg PA 3 hrs
*WPTC(FM) Williamsport PA 1 hr
WMNT(AM) Manati PR
*WRIU(FM) Kingston RI 6 hrs
WADK(AM) Newport RI 1 hr
WADK(AM) Newport RI 2 hrs
WVGB(AM) Beaufort SC
WHHD(AM) Clearwater SC
WJDJ(AM) Hartsville SC 2 hrs
WJBS(AM) Holly Hill SC 2 hrs
WMXT(FM) Pamplico SC 5 hrs
KGIM(AM) Aberdeen SD

*KLND(FM) Little Eagle SD 2 hrs
WNAX(AM) Yankton SD 15 hrs
*WHCB(FM) Bristol TN 2 hrs
*WHRS(FM) Cookeville TN 1 hr
*WTTU(FM) Cookeville TN
WKBQ(FM) Covington TN
WWAM(AM) Jasper TN 1 hr
WKGN(AM) Knoxville TN 1 hr
WEGR(FM) Memphis TN
*WMTS-FM Murfreesboro TN 2 hrs
*WRVU(FM) Nashville TN 11 hrs
*KACV-FM Amarillo TX 6 hrs
KBYG(AM) Big Spring TX 12 hrs
KPSM(AM) Brownwood TX 5 hrs
*KWTS(FM) Canyon TX 11 hrs
*KAMU-FM College Station TX 5 hrs
KTSM(AM) El Paso TX 1 hr
*KTCU-FM Fort Worth TX
KSWA(AM) Graham TX 2 hrs
KPRC(AM) Houston TX 16 hrs
*KTRU(FM) Houston TX 3 hrs
KRVL(FM) Kerrville TX 1 hr
KHKZ(FM) Mercedes TX 3 hrs
*KOCV(FM) Odessa TX 4 hrs
KNCN(FM) Sinton TX 1 hr
*WNRN(FM) Charlottesville VA 6 hrs
WDIC(AM) Clinchco VA
WEVA(AM) Emporia VA 3 hrs
WRVA(AM) Richmond VA 2 hrs
WVBW(FM) Suffolk VA 1 hr
*WISE-FM Wise VA 2 hrs
*WVPS(FM) Burlington VT 8 hrs
WEQX(FM) Manchester VT 5 hrs
WIKE(AM) Newport VT 5 hrs
WVNR(AM) Poultney VT 3 hrs
*WRVT(FM) Rutland VT 3 hrs
*WVPR(FM) Windsor VT 3 hrs
*KGRG-FM Auburn WA 3 hrs
*KUGS(FM) Bellingham WA 17 hrs wkly hrs
*KUGS(FM) Bellingham WA 2 hrs wkly hrs
KGNW(AM) Burien-Seattle WA
KELA(AM) Centralia-Chehalis WA
*KZUU(FM) Pullman WA 2 hrs
*KNHC(FM) Seattle WA 6 hrs
KPLZ(FM) Seattle WA
*KPBX-FM Spokane WA
*KUPS(FM) Tacoma WA 4 hrs
*WBSD(FM) Burlington WI 5 hrs
*WHID(FM) Green Bay WI 2 hrs
*WPNE(FM) Green Bay WI 2 hrs
WMEQ-FM Menomonie WI
*WHND(FM) Sister Bay WI 2 hrs
*WWSP(FM) Stevens Point WI 1 hr
*WCCX(FM) Waukesha WI 3 hrs
WDLS(AM) Wisconsin Dells WI 5 hrs
WGGE(AM) Parkersburg WV 5 hrs
*WVPG(FM) Parkersburg WV 2 hrs

Polish

KXMX(AM) Anaheim CA
*KSPC(FM) Claremont CA 3 hrs
KTYM(AM) Inglewood CA 2 hrs
*KUSF(FM) San Francisco CA 1 hr
WPRX(AM) Bristol CT 2 hrs
WGCH(AM) Greenwich CT 1 hr
*WRTC-FM Hartford CT 3 hrs
WMMW(AM) Meriden CT 1 hr
WMRD(AM) Middletown CT 2 hrs
WRYM(AM) New Britain CT 5 hrs
*WCNI(FM) New London CT 3 hrs
WICH(AM) Norwich CT 2 hrs
WATR(AM) Waterbury CT 2 hrs
*WWUH(FM) West Hartford CT 3 hrs
*WKTO(FM) Edgewater FL 1.5 hrs
WXYB(AM) Indian Rocks Beach FL 2 hrs
WLBE(AM) Leesburg FL 2 hrs
WPSO(AM) New Port Richey FL 1 hr
WTMY(AM) Sarasota FL 1 hr
KSKB(FM) Brooklyn IA 1 hr
WJOL(AM) Joliet IL 1 hr
WHCO(AM) Sparta IL 2 hrs
WJOB(AM) Hammond IN 2 hrs

WIMS(AM) Michigan City IN 3 hrs
WACE(AM) Chicopee MA 1 hr
WHTB(AM) Fall River MA 1 hr
WNBH(AM) New Bedford MA 2 hrs
WHMP(AM) Northampton MA 3 hrs
WBRK(AM) Pittsfield MA 1 hr
WESX(AM) Salem MA 2 hrs
*WBSL-FM Sheffield MA 1 hr
WESO(AM) Southbridge MA 3 hrs
WARE(AM) Ware MA 4 hrs
*WCUW(FM) Worcester MA 6 hrs
WORC(AM) Worcester MA 4 hrs
WBMD(AM) Baltimore MD 2 hrs
WATZ(AM) Alpena MI 2 hrs
WATZ-FM Alpena MI 2 hrs
WLEW(AM) Bad Axe MI 2 hrs
WIBM(AM) Jackson MI 1.5 hrs
WMTE-FM Manistee MI 6 hrs
WMIC(AM) Sandusky MI 5 hrs
*WPHS(FM) Warren MI 2 hrs
WBMI(AM) West Branch MI 6 hrs
WNMT(AM) Nashwauk MN 2 hrs
KRDS-FM New Prague MN 18 hrs
WEW(AM) Saint Louis MO 2 hrs
KJSK(AM) Columbus NE 4 hrs
KTTT(AM) Columbus NE 5 hrs
*WUNH(FM) Durham NH 2 hrs
*WSOU(FM) South Orange NJ 2 hrs
WAAL(FM) Binghamton NY 3 hrs
*WHRW(FM) Binghamton NY 3 hrs
*WBFO(FM) Buffalo NY 3 hrs
WECK(AM) Cheektowaga NY 2 hrs
WDOE(AM) Dunkirk NY 6 hrs
WAMF(AM) Fulton NY 5 hrs
*WGMC(FM) Greece NY 2 hrs
*WUBJ(FM) Jamestown NY 3 hrs
WIZR(FM) Johnstown NY 1 hr
WKNY(AM) Kingston NY 1 hr
WXRL(AM) Lancaster NY 19 hrs
WLVL(AM) Lockport NY 1 hr
*WVCR-FM Loudonville NY 3 hrs
WVOU(AM) Mexico NY 4 hrs
*WJJL(AM) Niagara Falls NY 2 hrs
WTLA(AM) North Syracuse NY 2 hrs
*WOLN(FM) Olean NY 3 hrs
WSGO(AM) Oswego NY 2 hrs
WEOK(AM) Poughkeepsie NY 1 hr
WRIV(AM) Riverhead NY 4 hrs
WGGO(AM) Salamanca NY 1 hr
*WSPN(FM) Saratoga Springs NY 3 hrs
WLLW(FM) Seneca Falls NY 2 hrs
WSFW(AM) Seneca Falls NY 2 hrs
*WUSB(FM) Stony Brook NY 1 hr
WIBX(AM) Utica NY 3 hrs
WUTQ(AM) Utica NY 4 hrs
WNYV(FM) Whitehall NY 1 hr
*WOBO(FM) Batavia OH 3 hrs
WOMP(AM) Bellaire OH 2 hrs
*WCPN(FM) Cleveland OH 1 hr
WKTX(AM) Cortland OH 1 hr
WRTK(AM) Niles OH 1 hr
WSTV(AM) Steubenville OH 2 hrs
WCWA(AM) Toledo OH 1 hr
WTOD(AM) Toledo OH 4 hrs
*WJCU(FM) University Heights OH 2 hrs
WELW(AM) Willoughby-Eastlake OH 1 hr
*WMUH(FM) Allentown PA 2 hrs
WVAM(AM) Altoona PA 1 hr
WMBA(AM) Ambridge PA 2 hrs
WWSM(AM) Annville-Cleona PA 2 hrs
WWCS(AM) Canonsburg PA 2 hrs
WFGI(AM) Charleroi PA 2 hrs
WOGI(FM) Charleroi PA 2 hrs
*WMCE(FM) Erie PA 3 hrs
WCCS(AM) Homer City PA 3 hrs
WQFM(AM) Nanticoke PA 3 hrs
WKST(AM) New Castle PA 1 hr
WGBN(AM) New Kensington PA 3 hrs
WYCK(AM) Plains PA 3 hrs
WPAZ(AM) Pottstown PA 1 hr
WECZ(AM) Punxsutawney PA 3 hrs
WICK(AM) Scranton PA 2 hrs
WPIC(AM) Sharon PA 3 hrs

WCDW(FM) Susquehanna PA 5 hrs
WKZV(FM) Washington PA 3 hrs
WLKW(AM) West Warwick RI 2 hrs
WNRI(AM) Woonsocket RI 2 hrs
WOON(AM) Woonsocket RI 3 hrs
KYNT(AM) Yankton SD 1 hr
*KOOP(FM) Hornsby TX .5 hrs
KVLG(AM) La Grange TX 6 hrs
KANI(AM) Wharton TX 6 hrs
WVNR(AM) Poultney VT 1 hr
WJMT(AM) Merrill WI 3 hrs
*WRPN-FM Ripon WI 1 hr
WSPT(AM) Stevens Point WI 1 hr
WSAU(AM) Wausau WI 3 hrs
WMOV(AM) Ravenswood WV 1 hr
WBBD(AM) Wheeling WV 2 hrs

Polka

KCAA(AM) Loma Linda CA
KZAT-FM Belle Plaine IA 2 hrs
KDSN(AM) Denison IA 4 hrs
KMAQ(AM) Maquoketa IA 3 hrs
KLEE(AM) Ottumwa IA 1 hr
WLUV(AM) Loves Park IL 6 hrs
WPNA(AM) Oak Park IL 15 hrs
WTAY(AM) Robinson IL 3 hrs
KRSL(AM) Russell KS 4 hrs
KRSL-FM Russell KS
WCUP(FM) L'Anse MI 2 hrs
WNBY(AM) Newberry MI 2 hrs
WUPY(FM) Ontonagon MI 1 hr
WYGR(AM) Wyoming MI 3 hrs
KRBT(AM) Eveleth MN 3 hrs
WMFG(AM) Hibbing MN 4 hrs
KDUZ(AM) Hutchinson MN 8 hrs
KLTF(AM) Little Falls MN 2 hrs
KWNO(AM) Winona MN 5 hrs
KHND(AM) Harvey ND 3 hrs
KTTT(AM) Columbus NE
WGHT(AM) Pompton Lakes NJ 1 hr
WAAL(FM) Binghamton NY 4 hrs
*WZIP(FM) Akron OH 4 hrs
WNDH(FM) Napoleon OH 2 hrs
WELW(AM) Willoughby-Eastlake OH 15 hrs
WKBN(AM) Youngstown OH 2 hrs
WMBA(AM) Ambridge PA 2 hrs
WGPA(AM) Bethlehem PA 12 hrs
WHYL(AM) Carlisle PA 2 hrs
*WERG(FM) Erie PA 4 hrs
WLMI(FM) Kane PA 1 hr
WMNY(AM) McKeesport PA 2 hrs
WPHB(AM) Philipsburg PA 6 hrs
WWII(AM) Shiremanstown PA 7 hrs
WMGH-FM Tamaqua PA 3 hrs
WKZV(AM) Washington PA 2 hrs
KYNT(AM) Yankton SD 1 hr
*WMTS-FM Murfreesboro TN 2 hrs
KWHI(AM) Brenham TX 2 hrs
KULM-FM Columbus TX 12 hrs
KNAF(AM) Fredericksburg TX 4.5 hrs
KYKM(FM) Yoakum TX 9 hrs
WDKM(AM) Adams WI 14 hrs
WLDY(AM) Ladysmith WI 3 hrs
WCCN(AM) Neillsville WI 2 hrs
WVRQ(AM) Viroqua WI 6 hrs

Portugese

KSTN-FM Stockton CA 4 hrs
*WRTC-FM Hartford CT 8 hrs
*WWUH(FM) West Hartford CT 3 hrs
WACE(AM) Chicopee MA 1 hr
WSAR(AM) Fall River MA 3 hrs
WPHE(AM) Phoenixville PA 3 hrs
WNRI(AM) Woonsocket RI 2 hrs
*WRVU(FM) Nashville TN 2 hrs

Progressive

*KFJC(FM) Los Altos CA 4 hrs
*WONC(FM) Naperville IL 14 hrs
WTTS(FM) Bloomington IN 4 hrs
*WDSO(FM) Chesterton IN 8 hrs
*WBKE-FM North Manchester IN 7 hrs
*WECI(FM) Richmond IN 18 hrs
*KMVC(FM) Marshall MO 10 hrs
*KZUM(FM) Lincoln NE 15 hrs
WRRV(FM) Middletown NY 2 hrs
*WIRQ(FM) Rochester NY 3 hrs
WIOT(FM) Toledo OH 2 hrs
*KRSC-FM Claremore OK 12 hrs
*WCAL(FM) California PA 6 hrs
*WHRV(FM) Norfolk VA 14 hrs
WIZN(AM) Vergennes VT 1 hr
*KZUU(FM) Pullman WA 10 hrs
*WSUP(FM) Platteville WI 6 hrs

Public Affairs

WDLT-FM Chickasaw AL 4 hrs
KMLE(FM) Chandler AZ 1 hr
*KGHR(FM) Tuba City AZ 5 hrs
*KPFA(FM) Berkeley CA 18 hrs
*KNCA(FM) Burney CA 7 hrs
*KSPC(FM) Claremont CA 3 hrs
*KCRH(FM) Hayward CA 5 hrs
KYSR(FM) Los Angeles CA 2 hrs
*KNSQ(FM) Mount Shasta CA 7 hrs
KTYD(FM) Santa Barbara CA 1 hr
KIMN(FM) Denver CO 2 hrs
KJJD(AM) Windsor CO
WSTW(FM) Wilmington DE 1 hr
WXTB(FM) Clearwater FL 4 hrs
WIRA(AM) Fort Pierce FL 1 hr
WVOP(AM) Vidalia GA 1 hr
*WEFT(FM) Champaign IL 5 hrs
*WDGC-FM Downers Grove IL 6 hrs
KUUL(FM) East Moline IL 6 hrs
*WEPS(FM) Elgin IL 3 hrs
WFXN(AM) Moline IL 4 hrs
WPNA(AM) Oak Park IL 5 hrs
WVAZ(FM) Oak Park IL 2 hrs
WYKT(FM) Wilmington IL 4 hrs
KNCK(AM) Concordia KS 2 hrs
WMJL-FM Marion KY 1 hr
WSNE-FM Taunton MA 4 hrs
WDMK(FM) Detroit MI 2 hrs
WCCY(AM) Houghton MI 1 hr
*KQAL(FM) Winona MN 10 hrs
KCMO(AM) Kansas City MO 1 1/2 hrs
KCMO-FM Kansas City MO 1 1/2 hrs
WCLN(AM) Clinton NC
WPAQ(AM) Mount Airy NC 1 hr
WKRK(AM) Murphy NC 3 hrs
*KABU(FM) Fort Totten ND 5 hrs
KLIQ(AM) Hastings NE
*KZUM(FM) Lincoln NE 11 hrs
*WBJB-FM Lincroft NJ 5 hrs
*WRPR(FM) Mahwah NJ 12 hrs
WMTR(AM) Morristown NJ 5 hrs
WTOC(AM) Newton NJ 1 hr
*WSOU(FM) South Orange NJ 5 hrs
*WTSR(FM) Trenton NJ 8 hrs
*KUNV(FM) Las Vegas NV 4 hrs
*WXLH(FM) Blue Mountain Lake NY
*WBSU(FM) Brockport NY 8 hrs
*WCWP(FM) Brookville NY 5 hrs
WJYE(FM) Buffalo NY 2 hrs
*WNED(FM) Buffalo NY
*WSLU(FM) Canton NY
WAQX-FM Manlius NY 1 hr
*WDFH(FM) Ossining NY 20 hrs
WUMX(FM) Rome NY 1 hr
WQAR(FM) Stillwater NY
*WJPZ-FM Syracuse NY 13 hrs
*WARY(FM) Valhalla NY 10 hrs
WNYV(FM) Whitehall NY 5 hrs
*WZIP(FM) Akron OH 11 hrs
WRQN(FM) Bowling Green OH 1 hr
WKKY(FM) Geneva OH 2 hrs
KJSR(FM) Tulsa OK 2 hrs
*KSMF(FM) Ashland OR 7 hrs
*KSOR(FM) Ashland OR 7 hrs

*KSBA(FM) Coos Bay OR 7 hrs
*KSKF(FM) Klamath Falls OR 7 hrs
KBNP(AM) Portland OR
KACI(AM) The Dalles OR 1 hr
WWCH(AM) Clarion PA
WSJR(FM) Dallas PA 1 hr
*WQLN-FM Erie PA 5 hrs
WRTS(FM) Erie PA 1 hr
WTKT(AM) Harrisburg PA 2 hrs
WIOQ(FM) Philadelphia PA
WSHH(FM) Pittsburgh PA 1 hr
*WSRU(FM) Slippery Rock PA 1 hr
*WRLC(FM) Williamsport PA 2 hrs
WAGS(AM) Bishopville SC 2 hrs
WSAA(AM) Benton TN 2 hrs
WKHT(AM) Knoxville TN 2 hrs
WKTI(AM) Powell TN 2 hrs
KDHT(AM) Cedar Park TX 2 hrs
KBFM(AM) Edinburg TX
KTSM(AM) El Paso TX 1 hr
KTBZ-FM Houston TX 1 hr
*KSWP(FM) Lufkin TX 2 hrs
KAMX(AM) Luling TX 2 hrs
*KNTU(FM) McKinney TX 2 hrs
KCYY(AM) San Antonio TX 2 hrs
KKYX(AM) San Antonio TX 2 hrs
KQXT(FM) San Antonio TX 1 hr
KNCN(AM) Sinton TX 1 hr
KVEL(AM) Vernal UT 1 hr
*WVRU(AM) Radford VA 6 hrs
WMOO(FM) Derby Center VT 8 hrs
WJJR(AM) Rutland VT 1 hr
KEDO(AM) Longview WA 2 hrs
WNBI(AM) Park Falls WI 5 hrs
*WWSP(FM) Stevens Point WI 5 hrs
WWYO(AM) Pineville WV 8 hrs

Reggae

*WJAB(FM) Huntsville AL 4 hrs
*WVUA-FM Tuscaloosa AL 3 hrs
*KABF(FM) Little Rock AR 4 hrs
*KSPC(FM) Claremont CA 8 hrs
*KFSR(FM) Fresno CA 6 hrs
*KSBR(FM) Mission Viejo CA 3 hrs
*KSPB(FM) Pebble Beach CA 2 hrs
*KZYX(FM) Philo CA 4 hrs
*KCSB-FM Santa Barbara CA 6 hrs
*KCSS(FM) Turlock CA
*KASF(FM) Alamosa CO 5 hrs
KSMT(FM) Breckenridge CO 2 hrs
*KRCC(FM) Colorado Springs CO 6 hrs
*KWSB-FM Gunnison CO 6 hrs
KTCL(FM) Wheat Ridge CO 2 hrs
*WXCI(FM) Danbury CT 2 hrs
*WQTQ(FM) Hartford CT 4 hrs
*WESU(FM) Middletown CT 10 hrs
WMRD(AM) Middletown CT 1 hr
*WRGP(FM) Homestead FL 3 hrs
WIIS(FM) Key West FL 4 hrs
*WFCF(FM) Saint Augustine FL 4 hrs
*WANM(FM) Tallahassee FL 3 hrs
WFLM(FM) White City FL 4 hrs
*WCLK(FM) Atlanta GA 3 hrs
*WRAS(FM) Atlanta GA 4 hrs
KWXX-FM Hilo HI 20 hrs
KAOY(FM) Kealakekua HI 4 hrs
*WNUR-FM Evanston IL 4 hrs
*WSND-FM Notre Dame IN
*KJHK(FM) Lawrence KS 3 hrs
*WESM(FM) Princess Anne MD 2 hrs
*WDET-FM Detroit MI 2 hrs
*WLNZ(FM) Lansing MI 4 hrs
*WVSD(FM) Itta Bena MS 3 hrs
WNAA(FM) Greensboro NC 7 hrs
WVOD(FM) Manteo NC 2 hrs
WKKCD(FM) Omaha NE 1 hr
*WKNH(FM) Keene NH 3 hrs
*WPCR-FM Plymouth NH 3 hrs
*WNTI(FM) Hackettstown NJ 3 hrs
*WBZC(FM) Pemberton NJ 4 hrs
KRSI(AM) Garapan-Saipan NP 22 hrs
*WBNY(FM) Buffalo NY 3 hrs
*WHCL-FM Clinton NY 2 hrs
*WCVF-FM Fredonia NY 4 hrs

*WEOS(FM) Geneva NY 3 hrs
*WITR(FM) Henrietta NY 5 hrs
*WICB(FM) Ithaca NY 2 hrs
*WNYU-FM New York NY 2 hrs
*WPNR-FM Utica NY 5 hrs
*WDUB(FM) Granville OH 2 hrs
WVKO-FM Johnstown OH 5 hrs
*KEOL(FM) La Grande OR 7 hrs
*KBOO(FM) Portland OR 10 hrs
*WLVR(FM) Bethlehem PA 6 hrs
WWCS(AM) Canonsburg PA 2 hrs
*WJRH(FM) Easton PA 6 hrs
*WKVR-FM Huntingdon PA 3 hrs
*WRIU(FM) Kingston RI 7 hrs
*WSSB-FM Orangeburg SC 4 hrs
*WRVU(FM) Nashville TN 3 hrs
*KAZI-FM Austin TX 6 hrs
*KTRU(FM) Houston TX 6 hrs
*KTSU(FM) Houston TX 8 hrs
*WWHS-FM Hampden-Sydney VA 4 hrs
*WHOV(FM) Hampton VA 4 hrs
*WCWM(FM) Williamsburg VA 6 hrs
WIZN(AM) Vergennes VT 1 hr
*KGRG-FM Auburn WA 3 hrs
*KSER(FM) Everett WA 2 hrs
*KUPS(FM) Tacoma WA 6 hrs
*WBSD(FM) Burlington WI 3 hrs
*WWVU-FM Morgantown WV 4 hrs

Religious

KYMG(FM) Anchorage AK 1 hr
*KBRW(AM) Barrow AK 1 hr
*KNOM(AM) Nome AK 20 hrs
*KNOM-FM Nome AK 20 hrs
WKNU(FM) Brewton AL 2 hrs
WABF(AM) Fairhope AL 6 hrs
WKWL(AM) Florala AL 12 hrs
WBFA(FM) Fort Mitchell AL 6 hrs
WZOB(AM) Fort Payne AL 5 hrs
*WLJS-FM Jacksonville AL 3 hrs
WEUP-FM Moulton AL 1 hr
WNSI(AM) Robertsdale AL 6 hrs
WGOL(AM) Russellville AL 10 hrs
WKEA-FM Scottsboro AL 4 hrs
WTBC(AM) Tuscaloosa AL 3 hrs
*WVUA-FM Tuscaloosa AL 3 hrs
KMJI(AM) Ashdown AR 4 hrs
KEWI(AM) Benton AR 5 hrs
KLYR(AM) Clarksville AR 8 hrs
KAVV(AM) Benson AZ 3 hrs
KCUZ(AM) Clifton AZ 2 hrs
KFYI(AM) Phoenix AZ 2 hrs
KTKT(AM) Tucson AZ 2 hrs
KXMX(AM) Anaheim CA
KISV(FM) Bakersfield CA 1 hr
KSSB(AM) Calipatria CA 6 hrs
KJLH-FM Compton CA 7 hrs
KCNQ(FM) Kernville CA 1 hr
KLBS(AM) Los Banos CA 8 hrs
KDUQ(AM) Ludlow CA 1 hr
*KSMC(FM) Moraga CA 2 hrs
KAAT(AM) Oakhurst CA 2 hrs
KWKU(AM) Pomona CA 15 hrs
KVML(AM) Sonora CA 3 hrs
KSTN(AM) Stockton CA 5 hrs
KSUE(AM) Susanville CA 3 hrs
KXPS(AM) Thousand Palms CA 17 hrs
KDIA(AM) Vallejo CA 5 hrs
KDYA(AM) Vallejo CA 5 hrs
KUBA(AM) Yuba City CA 2 hrs
KCMN(AM) Colorado Springs CO 3 hrs
*KSJD(AM) Cortez CO 1 hr
KFKA(AM) Greeley CO 4 hrs
KUBC(AM) Montrose CO 3 hrs
KCRT(AM) Trinidad CO 5 hrs
KSPK(FM) Walsenburg CO 2 hrs
KCOL(AM) Wellington CO 1 hr
WGCH(AM) Greenwich CT 3 hrs
WMMW(AM) Meriden CT 4 hrs
*WECS(FM) Willimantic CT 3 hrs
WILI(AM) Willimantic CT 2 hrs
WJWL(AM) Georgetown DE 6 hrs

WYUS(AM) Milford DE 10 hrs
WGMD(FM) Rehoboth Beach DE 2 hrs
WSTW(FM) Wilmington DE 1 hr
WYBT(AM) Blountstown FL
WWPR(AM) Bradenton FL 5 hrs
WLQH(AM) Chiefland FL 9 hrs
*WVUM(FM) Coral Gables FL 6 hrs
WHNR(AM) Cypress Gardens FL 10 hrs
WNDB(AM) Daytona Beach FL 5 hrs
WMGG(AM) Dunedin FL 2 hrs
WENG(AM) Englewood FL 2 hrs
WIRA(AM) Fort Pierce FL 1 hr
WXYB(AM) Indian Rocks Beach FL 8 hrs
WPLA(AM) Jacksonville FL 2 hrs
WWRF(AM) Lake Worth FL 4 hrs
WONN(AM) Lakeland FL 2 hrs
WQHL(AM) Live Oak FL 6 hrs
WARO(AM) Naples FL 2 hrs
WPSO(AM) New Port Richey FL 8 hrs
*WHIF(FM) Palatka FL 10 hrs
WIYD(AM) Palatka FL 5 hrs
WFLF-FM Parker FL 5 hrs
WCOA(AM) Pensacola FL
WPSL(AM) Port St. Lucie FL 6 hrs
WSDO(AM) Sanford FL 3 hrs
WKII(AM) Solana FL 4 hrs
WSIR(AM) Winter Haven FL 14 hrs
V6AH(AM) Pohnpei FM 2 hrs
*V6AI(AM) Yap FM 4 hrs
WMGR(AM) Bainbridge GA 12 hrs
WJTH(AM) Calhoun GA 16 hrs
WCLA(AM) Claxton GA 4 hrs
WBLJ(AM) Dalton GA
WDMG(AM) Douglas GA 6 hrs
WWWE(AM) Hapeville GA 12 hrs
WMAC(AM) Macon GA 4 hrs
WHKN(FM) Millen GA 2 hrs
WROM(AM) Rome GA
WTHO-FM Thomson GA 6 hrs
WLET(AM) Toccoa GA
WVOP(AM) Vidalia GA 8 hrs
KROS(AM) Clinton IA 4 hrs
KCQQ(FM) Davenport IA 1 hr
KILR(AM) Estherville IA 11 hrs
KILR-FM Estherville IA 11 hrs
KNOD(AM) Harlan IA 2 hrs
KNIA(AM) Knoxville IA 18 hrs
KMCH(FM) Manchester IA 4 hrs
KRIB(AM) Mason City IA 5 hrs
KYTC(FM) Northwood IA 2 hrs
KLLT(FM) Spencer IA 2 hrs
KTLB(FM) Twin Lakes IA 2 hrs
KXEL(AM) Waterloo IA 20 hrs
KVNI(AM) Coeur d'Alene ID 3 hrs
KVSI(AM) Montpelier ID 2 hrs
KRPL(AM) Moscow ID 2 hrs
KWYD(AM) Parma ID 1 hr
KWIK(AM) Pocatello ID 1 hr
KSPT(AM) Sandpoint ID 2 hrs
KTFI(AM) Twin Falls ID 5 hrs
WRMJ(AM) Aledo IL 3 hrs
KATZ-FM Alton IL 2 hrs
WBGZ(AM) Alton IL 3 hrs
WBIG(AM) Aurora IL 6 hrs
WDWS(AM) Champaign IL 4 hrs
KSGM(AM) Chester IL 6 hrs
*WIIT(FM) Chicago IL 2 hrs
WITY(AM) Danville IL 6 hrs
WDKB(FM) De Kalb IL 1 hr
WDQN(AM) Du Quoin IL 5 hrs
WAIK(AM) Galesburg IL 6 hrs
WGIL(AM) Galesburg IL 4 hrs
WLSR(FM) Galesburg IL 6 hrs
WKYX-FM Golconda IL 1 hr
WJBM(AM) Jerseyville IL 3 hrs
WKEI(AM) Kewanee IL 6 hrs
WLBH(AM) Mattoon IL 5 hrs
WMOK(AM) Metropolis IL 5 hrs
WRAM(AM) Monmouth IL 3 hrs
WDQX(AM) Morton IL 1 hr
WINI(AM) Murphysboro IL 6 hrs
*WONC(FM) Naperville IL 4 hrs
WPNA(AM) Oak Park IL 4 hrs
WLCE(FM) Petersburg IL 5 hrs

WBBA-FM Pittsfield IL 3 hrs
WKKQ(FM) Rushville IL 6 hrs
WJBD(AM) Salem IL 6 hrs
WHCO(AM) Sparta IL 10 hrs
WTIM-FM Taylorville IL 4 hrs
WRAN(FM) Tower Hill IL 3 hrs
*WETN(FM) Wheaton IL 3 hrs
WZSR(FM) Woodstock IL 1 hr
WQME(FM) Anderson IN 9 hrs
WNUY(FM) Bluffton IN 4 hrs
WIFE(AM) Connersville IN 12 hrs
WBYT(FM) Elkhart IN 2 hrs
WFLQ(FM) French Lick IN 6 hrs
*WGRE(FM) Greencastle IN 2 hrs
WTRE(AM) Greensburg IN 3 hrs
WJOB(AM) Hammond IN 2 hrs
WBDC(FM) Huntingburg IN 4 hrs
WRWM(FM) Lawrence IN 3 hrs
WXGO(AM) Madison IN 6 hrs
WEFM(FM) Michigan City IN 4 hrs
WMDH(AM) New Castle IN 2 hrs
WTCA(AM) Plymouth IN 4 hrs
WRIN(AM) Rensselaer IN 10 hrs
WROI(FM) Rochester IN 6 hrs
WZZB(AM) Seymour IN 6 hrs
WSBT(AM) South Bend IN 2 hrs
WCLS(FM) Spencer IN 6 hrs
WAWC(FM) Syracuse IN 4 hrs
WCJC(FM) Van Buren IN 3 hrs
KABI(AM) Abilene KS 4 hrs
KSNP(FM) Burlington KS 3 hrs
KVGB(AM) Great Bend KS 2 hrs
KFBZ(FM) Haysville KS 2 hrs
KHOK(FM) Hoisington KS 2 hrs
KNNS(AM) Larned KS 5 hrs
KLWN(AM) Lawrence KS 4 hrs
KNGL(AM) McPherson KS 5 hrs
KLKC(AM) Parsons KS 2 hrs
KLEY(AM) Wellington KS 4 hrs
*KCFN(FM) Wichita KS
WMMG(AM) Brandenburg KY 8 hrs
WKDP-FM Corbin KY 5 hrs
WFKN(AM) Franklin KY
WHVO(AM) Hopkinsville KY 6 hrs
WRNZ(FM) Lancaster KY 4 hrs
WKYL(FM) Lawrenceburg KY 2 hrs
WQQR(FM) Mayfield KY 10 hrs
WFTM(AM) Maysville KY 5 hrs
WFXY(AM) Middlesboro KY 3 hrs
WCBR(AM) Richmond KY 35 hrs
WEKY(AM) Richmond KY 6 hrs
WTLO(AM) Somerset KY 4 hrs
*WJCR-FM Upton KY
KVVP(FM) Leesville LA 9 hrs
*WGAO(FM) Franklin MA 8 hrs
WBEC(AM) Pittsfield MA 3 hrs
WBRK(AM) Pittsfield MA 2 hrs
WHLL(AM) Springfield MA 2 hrs
WOLB(AM) Baltimore MD 2 hrs
WCEM(AM) Cambridge MD 5 hrs
WSRY(AM) Elkton MD 3 hrs
*WMTB-FM Emmitsburg MD 4 hrs
WAYZ(FM) Hagerstown MD 3 hrs
WXCY(FM) Havre de Grace MD 2 hrs
WVAE(AM) Biddeford ME 2 hrs
WABJ(AM) Adrian MI 3 hrs
WATZ(AM) Alpena MI 2 hrs
WATZ-FM Alpena MI 1 hr
WAAM(AM) Ann Arbor MI 4 hrs
*WAUS(FM) Berrien Springs MI 10 hrs
WYBR(FM) Big Rapids MI 1 hr
WDBC(AM) Escanaba MI 4 hrs
WDZZ-FM Flint MI 1 hr
WWKR(FM) Hart MI 3 hrs
WCSR(AM) Hillsdale MI 10 hrs
*WTHS(FM) Holland MI 14 hrs
WCCY(AM) Houghton MI 1 hr
WKHM(AM) Jackson MI 4 hrs
WKZO(AM) Kalamazoo MI 5 hrs
WFCX(FM) Leland MI 1 hr
WTWR-FM Luna Pier MI 3 hrs
WMTE-FM Manistee MI 2 hrs
WMPX(AM) Midland MI 3 hrs
WNIL(AM) Niles MI 6 hrs
WUPY(FM) Ontonagon MI 3 hrs
WRSR(FM) Owosso MI 1 hr

WJML(AM) Petoskey MI 4 hrs
KXRA(AM) Alexandria MN 2 hrs
KXRZ(FM) Alexandria MN 3 hrs
KKCQ-FM Bagley MN 9 hrs
KDLM(AM) Detroit Lakes MN 8 hrs
KBRF(AM) Fergus Falls MN 7 hrs
KJJK(AM) Fergus Falls MN 3 hrs
WLKX-FM Forest Lake MN 6 hrs
KKCQ(AM) Fosston MN 4 hrs
WMFG(AM) Hibbing MN 4 hrs
KLFD(AM) Litchfield MN 3 hrs
KFML(FM) Little Falls MN 6 hrs
KLTF(AM) Little Falls MN 4 hrs
KEYL(AM) Long Prairie MN 4 hrs
KQAD(AM) Luverne MN 5 hrs
KMHL(AM) Marshall MN 7 hrs
KYMN(AM) Northfield MN 2 hrs
KDIO(AM) Ortonville MN 5 hrs
KLOH(AM) Pipestone MN 5 hrs
KQIC(FM) Willmar MN 2 hrs
KAGE(AM) Winona MN
KAAN(AM) Bethany MO 1 hr
KMRN(AM) Cameron MO 4 hrs
KCRV(AM) Caruthersville MO 20 hrs
KCXL(AM) Liberty MO 3 hrs
*KMVC(FM) Marshall MO 16 hrs
KMEM-FM Memphis MO 4 hrs
*KJAB(AM) Mexico MO 20 hrs
KMCR(FM) Montgomery City MO 2 hrs
KELE-FM Mountain Grove MO 3 hrs
KBDZ(FM) Perryville MO 5 hrs
KLID(AM) Poplar Bluff MO 2 hrs
KMIS(AM) Portageville MO 5 hrs
KMOX(AM) Saint Louis MO 1 hr
KDRO(AM) Sedalia MO 3 hrs
KWTO(AM) Springfield MO 1 hr
KLPW(AM) Union MO 6 hrs
KTKS(AM) Versailles MO 3 hrs
KJPW(AM) Waynesville MO 3 hrs
WAFM(FM) Amory MS 2 hrs
WAMY(AM) Amory MS 6 hrs
WHJT(FM) Clinton MS 6 hrs
WBAQ(FM) Greenville MS 4 hrs
WDMS(FM) Greenville MS 1 hr
WTCD(FM) Indianola MS 11 hrs
WIQQ(FM) Leland MS 6 hrs
WMOX(AM) Meridian MS 8 hrs
WRQO(FM) Monticello MS 10 hrs
WRJW(AM) Picayune MS 16 hrs
WSKK(FM) Ripley MS 2 hrs
KBOW(AM) Butte MT 2 hrs
*KMSM-FM Butte MT 3 hrs
KXTL(AM) Butte MT 1 hr
KMSO(FM) Missoula MT 1 hr
KATQ(AM) Plentywood MT 6 hrs
KATQ-FM Plentywood MT 6 hrs
WWNC(AM) Asheville NC 3 hrs
WXIT(AM) Blowing Rock NC 8 hrs
WSQL(AM) Brevard NC 4 hrs
WBAG(AM) Burlington-Graham NC 5 hrs
WRRZ(AM) Clinton NC 6 hrs
WGAI(AM) Elizabeth City NC 4 hrs
WQNQ(FM) Fletcher NC 2 hrs
WBRM(AM) Marion NC 7 hrs
WHIP(AM) Mooresville NC 6 hrs
WECR(AM) Newland NC 5 hrs
WPTM(FM) Roanoke Rapids NC 3 hrs
WNCA(AM) Siler City NC 15 hrs
WMPM(AM) Smithfield NC 8 hrs
WTOE(AM) Spruce Pine NC 8 hrs
WMXF(AM) Waynesville NC 3 hrs
WENC(AM) Whiteville NC 4 hrs
WTXY(AM) Whiteville NC 10 hrs
*KEYA(FM) Belcourt ND 10 hrs
KAUJ(FM) Grafton ND 3 hrs
KXPO(AM) Grafton ND 3 hrs
KNDK(AM) Langdon ND 4 hrs
KEYZ(AM) Williston ND 5 hrs
KZEN(FM) Central City NE 5 hrs
KJSK(AM) Columbus NE 20 hrs
KLIR(FM) Columbus NE 4 hrs
*KINI(FM) Crookston NE 6 hrs
KRVN(AM) Lexington NE 12 hrs
KRFS(AM) Superior NE 3 hrs
WHCY(FM) Blairstown NJ 1 hr

*WDVR(FM) Delaware Township NJ 6 hrs
WSJO(FM) Egg Harbor City NJ 4 hrs
*WRDR(FM) Freehold Township NJ 6 hrs
*WNTI(FM) Hackettstown NJ 4 hrs
WTTH(FM) Margate City NJ 1 hr
WTOC(AM) Newton NJ 1 hr
WGHT(AM) Pompton Lakes NJ 2 hrs
*WSOU(FM) South Orange NJ 5 hrs
WNJC(AM) Washington Township NJ 6 hrs
KRSY(AM) Alamogordo NM 4 hrs
KKTC(AM) Angel Fire NM 8 hrs
KARS(AM) Belen NM
KLEA(AM) Lovington NM 3 hrs
KLAV(AM) Las Vegas NV 3 hrs
KSNE-FM Las Vegas NV 1 hr
KNEV(FM) Reno NV 1 hr
WYSL(AM) Avon NY 4 hrs
WAAL(AM) Binghamton NY 3 hrs
*WHRW(FM) Binghamton NY 6 hrs
WBRV-FM Boonville NY 3 hrs
*WCWP(FM) Brookville NY 4 hrs
*WHCL-FM Clinton NY 2 hrs
WDNY(AM) Dansville NY 1 hr
WDNY-FM Dansville NY 1 hr
WFLR(AM) Dundee NY 5 hrs
WELM(AM) Elmira NY 1 hr
WGBB(AM) Freeport NY 6 hrs
WMML(AM) Glens Falls NY 3 hrs
WLIE(AM) Islip NY 3 hrs
WKSN(AM) Jamestown NY 2 hrs
WIXT(AM) Little Falls NY 1 hr
WLVL(AM) Lockport NY 3 hrs
WLLG(FM) Lowville NY 2 hrs
WVOX(AM) New Rochelle NY 3 hrs
WOR(AM) New York NY 4 hrs
WGNY(AM) Newburgh NY 4 hrs
WTLA(AM) North Syracuse NY 2 hrs
WDOS(AM) Oneonta NY 7 hrs
WEBO(AM) Owego NY 6 hrs
*WQKE(FM) Plattsburgh NY 3 hrs
WEOK(AM) Poughkeepsie NY 2 hrs
WMYY(FM) Schoharie NY
WSPQ(AM) Springville NY 2 hrs
WRGR(FM) Tupper Lake NY 1 hr
WAJZ(FM) Voorheesville NY 1 hr
WNYV(FM) Whitehall NY 2 hrs
*WONB(FM) Ada OH 1 hr
WBLL(AM) Bellefontaine OH 6 hrs
WBCO(AM) Bucyrus OH 4 hrs
WQEL(FM) Bucyrus OH 5 hrs
WCER(AM) Canton OH 5 hrs
WKKI(FM) Celina OH 2 hrs
WMNI(AM) Columbus OH 4 hrs
WHIO(AM) Dayton OH 2 hrs
*WWSU(FM) Dayton OH 11 hrs
WDFM(AM) Defiance OH 3 hrs
WZOM(FM) Defiance OH 6 hrs
*WLFC(FM) Findlay OH 3 hrs
WRBP(AM) Hubbard OH 6 hrs
WBKS(FM) Ironton OH 2 hrs
WVKO-FM Johnstown OH 13 hrs
WCIT(AM) Lima OH 11 hrs
WMOA(AM) Marietta OH 1 hr
WMPO(AM) Middleport-Pomeroy OH 6 hrs
WMVO(AM) Mount Vernon OH 7 hrs
*WMCO(FM) New Concord OH 2 hrs
WNTO(AM) Racine OH 1 hr
WCWA(AM) Toledo OH 3 hrs
WSPD(AM) Toledo OH 5 hrs
WBTC(AM) Uhrichsville OH 2 hrs
WTUZ(FM) Uhrichsville OH 1 hr
*WOBN(FM) Westerville OH 4 hrs
WHIZ-FM Zanesville OH 1 hr
KWON(AM) Bartlesville OK 5 hrs
KGYN(AM) Guymon OK 8 hrs
KICM(FM) Healdton OK 5 hrs
KTJS(AM) Hobart OK 12 hrs
KTMC-FM McAlester OK 5 hrs
KVSP(FM) Oklahoma City OK 5 hrs
WBBZ(AM) Ponca City OK 5 hrs
KZBB(FM) Poteau OK 1 hr
KGFF(AM) Shawnee OK 4 hrs

KWIL(AM) Albany OR 168 hrs
KNND(AM) Cottage Grove OR 3 hrs
KAJO(AM) Grants Pass OR 8 hrs
KSZN(AM) Gresham OR 1 hr
KUIK(AM) Hillsboro OR 2 hrs
KQIK(AM) Lakeview OR 2 hrs
KQIK-FM Lakeview OR 2 hrs
*KSLC(FM) McMinnville OR 2 hrs
KNPT(AM) Newport OR 3 hrs
KOHI(AM) Saint Helens OR
KWBY(AM) Woodburn OR 5 hrs
WBVP(AM) Beaver Falls PA 3 hrs
WHLM(AM) Bloomsburg PA 2 hrs
WISR(AM) Butler PA 6 hrs
*WCAL(FM) California PA 6 hrs
WWCS(AM) Canonsburg PA 2 hrs
WIOO(AM) Carlisle PA 5 hrs
WCCL(FM) Central City PA 4 hrs
WCHA(AM) Chambersburg PA 8 hrs
WHGT(AM) Chambersburg PA 1 hr
WCCR(FM) Clarion PA 4 hrs
WWCH(AM) Clarion PA 8 hrs
*WFSE(FM) Edinboro PA 4 hrs
*WWEC(FM) Elizabethtown PA 4 hrs
WHUN(AM) Huntingdon PA 2 hrs
*WKVR-FM Huntingdon PA 3 hrs
WDAD(AM) Indiana PA 2 hrs
WTYM(AM) Kittanning PA 4 hrs
WNPV(AM) Lansdale PA 5 hrs
WCNS(AM) Latrobe PA 5 hrs
WJUN(AM) Mexico PA 2 hrs
*WMSS(FM) Middletown PA 8 hrs
WPGR(AM) Monroeville PA 6 hrs
WGBN(AM) New Kensington PA 2 hrs
*WWNW(FM) New Wilmington PA 3 hrs
WWKL(FM) Palmyra PA 6 hrs
WHKS(FM) Port Allegany PA 1 hr
WPAZ(AM) Pottstown PA 12 hrs
WKBI-FM Saint Marys PA 2 hrs
WBZU(AM) Scranton PA 1 hr
WICK(AM) Scranton PA 3 hrs
*WUSR(FM) Scranton PA 4 hrs
WPIC(AM) Sharon PA 2 hrs
*WSRU(FM) Slippery Rock PA 1 hr
WTRN(AM) Tyrone PA 4 hrs
*WXVU(FM) Villanova PA 2 hrs
WKZV(AM) Washington PA 1 hr
WCHE(AM) West Chester PA 8 hrs
WKZN(AM) West Hazleton PA 1 hr
WILK(AM) Wilkes-Barre PA 1 hr
*WRLC(FM) Williamsport PA 3 hrs
WALO(AM) Humacao PR 2 hrs
WEXS(AM) Patillas PR 2 hrs
WKVM(AM) San Juan PR 40 hrs wkly hrs
WCRI(FM) Block Island RI 2 hrs
*WJMF(FM) Smithfield RI 2 hrs
WAGS(AM) Bishopville SC 7 hrs
WQNT(AM) Charleston SC 1 hr
WMUU-FM Greenville SC 20 hrs
WBHC-FM Hampton SC 11 hrs
WHSC(AM) Hartsville SC 6 hrs
WJDJ(AM) Hartsville SC 7 hrs
WKMG(AM) Newberry SC 2 hrs
WQKI-FM Orangeburg SC 6 hrs
WOLI(AM) Spartanburg SC 5 hrs
WSPA-FM Spartanburg SC 3 hrs
KBFS(AM) Belle Fourche SD 2 hrs
WNAX(AM) Yankton SD 16 hrs
WCTA(AM) Alamo TN 9 hrs
WYXI(AM) Athens TN 8 hrs
WMPS(AM) Bartlett TN 7 hrs
WJZM(AM) Clarksville TN
WYSH(AM) Clinton TN 15 hrs
WKRM(AM) Columbia TN 4 hrs
WZYX(AM) Cowan TN 12 hrs
WAKM(AM) Franklin TN 6 hrs
WMYL(FM) Halls Crossroads TN 2 hrs
WJFC(AM) Jefferson City TN 4 hrs
WNRX(AM) Jefferson City TN 2 hrs
WJCW(AM) Johnson City TN 4 hrs
WKGN(AM) Knoxville TN 5 hrs
WLIV(AM) Livingston TN 15 hrs
WREC(AM) Memphis TN 4 hrs

WGNS(AM) Murfreesboro TN 6 hrs
WMGC(AM) Murfreesboro TN 4 hrs
WLIK(AM) Newport TN 18 hrs
WUAT(AM) Pikeville TN 15 hrs
WJTT(FM) Red Bank TN 4 hrs
WLIJ(AM) Shelbyville TN 11 hrs
WZNG(AM) Shelbyville TN 5 hrs
WSMT(AM) Sparta TN 10 hrs
WCDT(AM) Winchester TN 6 hrs
KQIZ-FM Amarillo TX 2 hrs
KLVQ(AM) Athens TX 8 hrs
KFYN(AM) Bonham TX 6 hrs
KQTY-FM Borger TX 1 hr
KWHI(AM) Brenham TX 3 hrs
*KWTS(FM) Canyon TX 3 hrs
KCTX-FM Childress TX 5 hrs
KHER(AM) Crystal City TX 2 hrs
KTDR(FM) Del Rio TX 3 hrs
KWMC(AM) Del Rio TX 5 hrs
KTSM(AM) El Paso TX 3 hrs
KGVL(AM) Greenville TX 6 hrs
KIKT(FM) Greenville TX 5 hrs
KCLW(AM) Hamilton TX 6 hrs
KVRP-FM Haskell TX 6 hrs
KTBZ-FM Houston TX 1 hr
KVLG(AM) La Grange TX 5 hrs
KCYL(AM) Lampasas TX 10 hrs
KSHN-FM Liberty TX 5 hrs
KZZN(AM) Littlefield TX 5 hrs
*KAVX(FM) Lufkin TX
KCKL(FM) Malakoff TX 7 hrs
KLSR-FM Memphis TX 5 hrs
KBED(AM) Nederland TX 4 hrs
KNBT(FM) New Braunfels TX 3 hrs
KNET(AM) Palestine TX 7 hrs
KZHN(AM) Paris TX
KEYE(AM) Perryton TX 3 hrs
KEYE-FM Perryton TX 3 hrs
KWFB(AM) Quanah TX 2 hrs
KMIQ(FM) Robstown TX 6 hrs
KDCD(FM) San Angelo TX 2 hrs
KELI(FM) San Angelo TX 6 hrs
KQXT(FM) San Antonio TX 2 hrs
KSTV(AM) Stephenville TX 6 hrs
KBCY(FM) Tye TX 5 hrs
KTXZ(AM) West Lake Hills TX 6 hrs
KWUD(AM) Woodville TX 03 hrs
KSUB(AM) Cedar City UT
KVNU(AM) Logan UT 2 hrs
*KWCR-FM Ogden UT 3 hrs
*KBYU-FM Provo UT 2 hrs
KXRQ(FM) Roosevelt UT 8 hrs
KDXU(AM) Saint George UT 4 hrs
KVEL(AM) Vernal UT
WBNN-FM Dillwyn VA
WFLO(AM) Farmville VA 10 hrs
WFLO-FM Farmville VA 1 hr
WXGM(AM) Gloucester VA 2 hrs
WXGM-FM Gloucester VA 2 hrs
WKCY(AM) Harrisonburg VA 2 hrs
WMXH-FM Luray VA 5 hrs
WRAA(AM) Luray VA 7 hrs
WZZU(FM) Lynchburg VA 1 hr
WMEV(AM) Marion VA 8 hrs
WNVA(AM) Norton VA 2 hrs
WVCV(AM) Orange VA 1 hr
*WDCE(FM) Richmond VA 3 hrs
WRVA(AM) Richmond VA 10 hrs
WYTI(AM) Rocky Mount VA 10 hrs
WHEO(AM) Stuart VA 10 hrs
WVBW(FM) Suffolk VA 2 hrs
WKCW(AM) Warrenton VA 6 hrs
WVVI(AM) Charlotte Amalie VI 6 hrs
WVVI-FM Christiansted VI 3 hrs
WRRA(AM) Frederiksted VI 10 hrs
*WRMC-FM Middlebury VT 1 hr
WVNR(AM) Poultney VT 2 hrs
WMNV(FM) Rupert VT
KWLE(AM) Anacortes WA 1 hr
KYSN(FM) East Wenatchee WA 1 hr
KARY-FM Grandview WA 8 hrs
KZIZ(AM) Pacific WA 18 hrs
KRIZ(AM) Renton WA 18 hrs
KMAS(AM) Shelton WA 4 hrs
KHSS(FM) Walla Walla WA 3 hrs
*KDNA(FM) Yakima WA 4. hrs

WATW(AM) Ashland WI 5 hrs
WRPQ(AM) Baraboo WI 4 hrs
WCFW(FM) Chippewa Falls WI 2 hrs
WTTN(AM) Columbus WI 4 hrs
WMCS(AM) Greenfield WI 3.25 hrs
WJOK(AM) Kaukauna WI 2 hrs
WAUN(AM) Kewaunee WI 3 hrs
WJMT(AM) Merrill WI 3 hrs
WMYX(FM) Milwaukee WI 1 hr
WSSP(AM) Milwaukee WI 3 hrs
WTMJ(AM) Milwaukee WI 2 hrs
WNBI(AM) Park Falls WI 1 hr
WVRQ(AM) Viroqua WI 6 hrs
WSAU(AM) Wausau WI 3 hrs
*WVBC(FM) Bethany WV 4 hrs
WKEZ(AM) Bluefield WV 5 hrs
WBUC(AM) Buckhannon WV 7 hrs
*WVWC(FM) Buckhannon WV 4 hrs
WELD(AM) Fisher WV 10 hrs
*WVMR(FM) Frost WV 10 hrs
WRVC(AM) Huntington WV 3 hrs
WRON-FM Lewisburg WV 4 hrs
WEPM(AM) Martinsburg WV 6 hrs
WADC(AM) Parkersburg WV 3 hrs
WRON(AM) Ronceverte WV 2 hrs
WCWV(FM) Summersville WV 18 hrs
WELC(AM) Welch WV 15 hrs
WZST(FM) Westover WV 2 hrs
KLGT(FM) Buffalo WY 1 hr
KYOD(FM) Glendo WY 2 hrs wkly hrs
KASL(AM) Newcastle WY 2 hrs

Rock/AOR

*KBBI(AM) Homer AK
*KSPB(FM) Pebble Beach CA 2 hrs
*KZYX(FM) Philo CA 6 hrs
*WXCI(FM) Danbury CT 3 hrs
*WNHU(FM) West Haven CT 9 hrs
*KMSC(FM) Sioux City IA 4 hrs
*WBKE-FM North Manchester IN 6 hrs
*WVUR-FM Valparaiso IN 3 hrs
*KTCC(FM) Colby KS 7 hrs
*WYAJ(FM) Sudbury MA 3 hrs
*WCHC(FM) Worcester MA 9 hrs
*WYFP(FM) Harpswell ME 4 hrs
*WMHB(FM) Waterville ME
*WSGR-FM Port Huron MI 12 hrs
*WTIP(FM) Grand Marais MN 15 hrs
*KOPN(FM) Columbia MO 6 hrs
*KWSC(FM) Wayne NE 2 hrs
*WNTI(FM) Hackettstown NJ 6 hrs
*WRRC(FM) Lawrenceville NJ 10 hrs
*WEOS(FM) Geneva NY 6 hrs
*WQKE(FM) Plattsburgh NY 10 hrs
*WFNP(FM) Rosendale NY 7 hrs
WIOT(FM) Toledo OH 2 hrs
*WXUT(FM) Toledo OH 4 hrs
*KSLC(FM) McMinnville OR 7 hrs
*WCAL(FM) California PA 5 hrs
*WJRH(FM) Easton PA 6 hrs
*WXLV(FM) Schnecksville PA
*WUSR(FM) Scranton PA 8 hrs
WSBG(FM) Stroudsburg PA 3 hrs
*WNJR(FM) Washington PA 10 hrs
*WDOM(FM) Providence RI 6 hrs
WRLT(FM) Franklin TN 4 hrs
*WVCP(FM) Gallatin TN 15 hrs
WHHM-FM Henderson TN 6 hrs
*KRTU(FM) San Antonio TX 2 hrs
KNCN(FM) Sinton TX 2 hrs
*KSUU(FM) Cedar City UT 4 hrs
*KGRG-FM Auburn WA 6 hrs
*KRLF(FM) Pullman WA 1 hr
*KUPS(FM) Tacoma WA 8 hrs
*WSUP(FM) Platteville WI 6 hrs
*WSUW(FM) Whitewater WI 14 hrs
*WWVU-FM Morgantown WV 3 hrs
KYOD(FM) Glendo WY 2 hrs

Russian

*KJNP(AM) North Pole AK 11 hrs
KTYM(AM) Inglewood CA 2 hrs
WUST(AM) Washington DC 5 hrs
*WDCV-FM Carlisle PA 1 hr
*WRVU(FM) Nashville TN 1 hr
*KUGS(FM) Bellingham WA 2 hrs wkly hrs
KKNW(AM) Seattle WA 5 hrs
KLFE(AM) Seattle WA 12 hrs

Sacred

WHOU-FM Houlton ME 1 hr

Scottish

*WOBO(FM) Batavia OH 1 hr
*KBCS(FM) Bellevue WA 5 hrs

Serbian

WRJN(AM) Racine WI 2 hrs

Slovak

*WWPT(FM) Westport CT 3 hrs
WPNA(AM) Oak Park IL
*WCPN(FM) Cleveland OH 1 hr
WEDO(AM) McKeesport PA 1 hr

Slovenian

*WAPS(FM) Akron OH 2 hrs
WKTX(AM) Cortland OH 2 hrs
WEDO(AM) McKeesport PA 1 hr

Smooth Jazz

*WONB(FM) Ada OH 10 hrs
WVLY-FM Milton PA 6 hrs

Soul

*WWHR(FM) Bowling Green KY 2 hrs
*WYEP-FM Pittsburgh PA 3 hrs

Spanish

*KSUA(FM) Fairbanks AK 3 hrs
*KTOO(FM) Juneau AK 2 hrs
*WTBB(FM) Gadsden AL 1 hr
*WTBJ(FM) Oxford AL 1 hr
KFPW(AM) Fort Smith AR 6 hrs
KLSZ-FM Fort Smith AR 6 hrs
KAAY(AM) Little Rock AR 2 hrs
*KABF(FM) Little Rock AR 10 hrs
KVNA(AM) Flagstaff AZ 3 hrs
KXEG(AM) Phoenix AZ 5 hrs
*KXCI(FM) Tucson AZ 4 hrs
KINO(AM) Winslow AZ 3 hrs
*KAWC(AM) Yuma AZ 15 hrs
KXMX(AM) Anaheim CA
*KZFR(FM) Chico CA 6 hrs
KKCY(AM) Colusa CA 1 hr
KTHU(AM) Corning CA 1 hr
*KKUP(FM) Cupertino CA 3 hrs
*KECG(FM) El Cerrito CA 3 hrs
KBIF(AM) Fresno CA 6 hrs
*KFCF(FM) Fresno CA 5 hrs
*KMUD(FM) Garberville CA 2 hrs
KAZA(AM) Gilroy CA 133 hrs
KKMC(AM) Gonzales CA 3 hrs
KNTI(FM) Lakeport CA 3 hrs
KXBX(AM) Lakeport CA 3 hrs
*KPFK(FM) Los Angeles CA 15 hrs
*KADV(AM) Modesto CA 1 hr
*KSMC(FM) Moraga CA 1 hr
KVON(AM) Napa CA 5 hrs
KBLF(AM) Red Bluff CA 4 hrs
*KFPR(FM) Redding CA 4 hrs
KDIF(AM) Riverside CA 168 hrs
*KCPR(FM) San Luis Obispo CA 3 hrs

KPRZ(AM) San Marcos-Poway CA 22 hrs
*KCSB-FM Santa Barbara CA 12 hrs
KSTN-FM Stockton CA
KWNE(AM) Ukiah CA 4 hrs
KGIW(AM) Alamosa CO 6 hrs
*KRZA(FM) Alamosa CO 14 hrs
*KGNU-FM Boulder CO 3 hrs
KSMT(FM) Breckenridge CO 2 hrs
*KUVO(FM) Denver CO 15 hrs
KRKY(AM) Granby CO 1 hr
*KLFV(FM) Grand Junction CO 2 hrs
*KWSB-FM Gunnison CO 1 hr
KSLV(AM) Monte Vista CO 10 hrs
*KVNF(FM) Paonia CO 2 hrs
*WPKN(FM) Bridgeport CT 4 hrs
*WFAR(FM) Danbury CT 2 hrs
*WRTC-FM Hartford CT 6 hrs
*WFCS(FM) New Britain CT 2 hrs
*WCNI(FM) New London CT 3 hrs
*WHUS(FM) Storrs CT 3 hrs
*WWUH(FM) West Hartford CT 3 hrs
*WECS(FM) Willimantic CT 9 hrs
WILI(AM) Willimantic CT 1 hr
WUST(AM) Washington DC 15 hrs
*WVUD(FM) Newark DE 1 hr
WDEL(AM) Wilmington DE 2 hrs
WWPR(AM) Bradenton FL 40 hrs
*WVUM(FM) Coral Gables FL 2 hrs
*WKTO(FM) Edgewater FL 2 hrs
*WJFP(FM) Fort Pierce FL 2 hrs
*WAPN(FM) Holly Hill FL 4 hrs
*WRGP(FM) Homestead FL 3 hrs
WXYB(AM) Indian Rocks Beach FL 2 hrs
WKEY-FM Key West FL 3 hrs
WMNE(AM) Riviera Beach FL
*WFCF(FM) Saint Augustine FL 4 hrs
*WVFS(FM) Tallahassee FL 2 hrs
*WBVM(FM) Tampa FL 4 hrs
WTIS(AM) Tampa FL 1 hr
WSIR(AM) Winter Haven FL 10 hrs
*WRFG(FM) Atlanta GA 5 hrs
WTHV(AM) Hahira GA 5 hrs
WGML(AM) Hinesville GA 1 hr
KWAI(AM) Honolulu HI 3 hrs
KCHE(AM) Cherokee IA 1 hr
KLNG(AM) Council Bluffs IA 10 hrs
*KALA(FM) Davenport IA 15 hrs
KDSN(AM) Denison IA 4 hrs
*KHOE(FM) Fairfield IA 2 hrs
*KRNL-FM Mount Vernon IA 1 hr
KBGN(AM) Caldwell ID 5 hrs
KLLP(AM) Chubbuck ID 4 hrs
KART(AM) Jerome ID 9 hrs
KMHI(AM) Mountain Home ID 7 hrs
*WEFT(FM) Champaign IL 3 hrs
*WPCD(FM) Champaign IL 4 hrs
*WIIT(FM) Chicago IL 5 hrs
*WMBI(FM) Chicago IL 12 hrs
WRMN(AM) Elgin IL 10 hrs
WWHN(AM) Joliet IL 1 hr
*WIUS(FM) Macomb IL 3 hrs
*WFEN(FM) Rockford IL 1 hr
WSDR(AM) Sterling IL 4 hrs
WLYV(AM) Fort Wayne IN 1 hr
*WGCS(FM) Goshen IN 8 hrs
WBDC(FM) Huntingburg IN .5 hrs
*WBKE-FM North Manchester IN 1 hr
KFFX(AM) Emporia KS 2 hrs
KVOE(AM) Emporia KS 4 hrs
*KANZ(FM) Garden City KS 6 hrs
KKCI(FM) Goodland KS 1 hr
*KZNA(FM) Hill City KS 6 hrs
KWKR(FM) Leoti KS 3 hrs
KSMM-FM Liberal KS 5 hrs
*KBCU(FM) North Newton KS 2 hrs
KULY(AM) Ulysses KS 3 hrs
*KMUW(FM) Wichita KS 2 hrs
KRBB(FM) Wichita KS 3 hrs
*WNKJ(FM) Hopkinsville KY 3/4 hrs
WYGH(AM) Paris KY
*WFCR(FM) Amherst MA 2 hrs
*WBSL-FM Sheffield MA 2 hrs
WORC(AM) Webster MA 1 hr
*WBUR(AM) West Yarmouth MA 5 hrs

*WCUW(FM) Worcester MA 19 hrs
WOLB(AM) Baltimore MD 2 hrs
*WMPG(FM) Gorham ME 4 hrs
WLEN(AM) Adrian MI 4 hrs
WQTE(AM) Adrian MI 3 hrs
*WKAR(AM) East Lansing MI 3 hrs
WHTC(AM) Holland MI 3 hrs
*WTHS(FM) Holland MI 8 hrs
WIBM(AM) Jackson MI 1 hr
*WLNZ(FM) Lansing MI 4 hrs
WHLS(AM) Port Huron MI 1 hr
*WNMC-FM Traverse City MI 2 hrs
*WYCE(FM) Wyoming MI 10 hrs
WPNW(AM) Zeeland MI 2 hrs
KATE(AM) Albert Lea MN 2 hrs
KYCR(AM) Golden Valley MN 14 hrs
KDUZ(AM) Hutchinson MN 1 hr
KYSM-FM Mankato MN 1 hr
*KBEM-FM Minneapolis MN 4 hrs
*KFAI(FM) Minneapolis MN 8 hrs
KCHK(AM) New Prague MN 6 hrs
KYMN(AM) Northfield MN 2 hrs
KRFO(AM) Owatonna MN 2 hrs
KLOH(AM) Pipestone MN 2 hrs
KRRW(AM) Saint James MN 1 hr
KNOF(FM) Saint Paul MN 1 hr
*KSRQ(FM) Thief River Falls MN 1 hr
KAOL(AM) Carrollton MO 3 hrs
KMZU(AM) Carrollton MO 3 hrs
KDMO(AM) Carthage MO 1 hr
KMFC(FM) Centralia MO 1 hr
*KCUR-FM Kansas City MO 2 hrs
*KKFI(FM) Kansas City MO 16 hrs
WHB(AM) Kansas City MO 2 hrs
KCXL(AM) Liberty MO 5 hrs
WEW(AM) Saint Louis MO 10 hrs
WRRZ(AM) Clinton NC 5 hrs
WCLW(AM) Eden NC 6 hrs
WDJS(AM) Mount Olive NC 5 hrs
WMFA(AM) Raeford NC 6 hrs
*WSHA(FM) Raleigh NC 3 hrs
WNCA(AM) Siler City NC 25 hrs
WKSK(AM) West Jefferson NC 1 hr
KAUJ(FM) Grafton ND 2 hrs
KJSK(AM) Columbus NE 6 hrs
*KZUM(FM) Lincoln NE 4 hrs
*KJLT(AM) North Platte NE 1 hr
KNEB(AM) Scottsbluff NE 5 hrs
WFEA(AM) Manchester NH 2 hrs
WOF(AM) Andover NJ 3 hrs
*WBJB-FM Lincroft NJ 4 hrs
WMVB(AM) Millville NJ 2 hrs
*WFDU(FM) Teaneck NJ 3 hrs
*WMSC(FM) Upper Montclair NJ 2 hrs
KSVA(AM) Albuquerque NM 4 hrs
*KUNM(FM) Albuquerque NM 9 hrs
KCQL(AM) Aztec NM 6 hrs
KYVA-FM Churchrock NM 4 hrs
KLMX(AM) Clayton NM 3 hrs
KOTS(AM) Deming NM 8 hrs
KVLC(FM) Hatch NM 6 hrs
*KRWG(FM) Las Cruces NM 10 hrs
KBUY(AM) Ruidoso NM 4 hrs
KTNM(AM) Tucumcari NM 18 hrs
KSFR(FM) White Rock NM 4 hrs
KKVV(AM) Las Vegas NV 20 hrs
*KUNV(FM) Las Vegas NV 5 hrs
KKOH(AM) Reno NV 2 hrs
*WCDB(FM) Albany NY 3 hrs
*WHRW(FM) Binghamton NY 9 hrs
*WCWP(FM) Brookville NY 1 hr
WCHP(AM) Champlain NY
WDOE(AM) Dunkirk NY 2 hrs
*WCVF-FM Fredonia NY 4 hrs
WGBB(AM) Freeport NY 2 hrs
*WGMC(FM) Greece NY 10 hrs
WJTN(AM) Jamestown NY 1 hr
WIZR(AM) Johnstown NY 1 hr
*WVCR-FM Loudonville NY 3 hrs
WVOU(FM) Mexico NY 15 hrs
*WBAI(FM) New York NY 3 hrs
*WKCR(FM) New York NY 10 hrs
*WNYU-FM New York NY 2 hrs
WGNY(AM) Newburgh NY 1 hr
*WRHO(FM) Oneonta NY 2 hrs
*WNYO(FM) Oswego NY 6 hrs

*WFNP(FM) Rosendale NY 3 hrs
*WSPN(FM) Saratoga Springs NY 3 hrs
*WRUC(FM) Schenectady NY 3 hrs
*WUSB(FM) Stony Brook NY 3 hrs
*WBGU(FM) Bowling Green OH 4 hrs
WCVX(AM) Cincinnati OH 3 hrs
*WWSU(FM) Dayton OH 3 hrs
WEOL(AM) Elyria OH 2 hrs
*WLFC(FM) Findlay OH 3 hrs
WFOB(AM) Fostoria OH 3 hrs
*WDUB(FM) Granville OH 2 hrs
WRBP(FM) Hubbard OH 3 hrs
WXKR(FM) Port Clinton OH 1 hr
*WJCU(FM) University Heights OH 4 hrs
WERT(AM) Van Wert OH 1 hr
WELW(AM) Willoughby-Eastlake OH 1 hr
KWHW(AM) Altus OK 16 hrs
KGYN(AM) Guymon OK 8 hrs
KBZQ(FM) Lawton OK 4 hrs
KTLR(AM) Oklahoma City OK 3 hrs
*KMUN(FM) Astoria OR 3 hrs
*KBVR(FM) Corvallis OR 4 hrs
*KLCC(FM) Eugene OR 5 hrs
*KWVA(FM) Eugene OR 6 hrs
*KAGI(FM) Grants Pass OR 6 hrs
KOHU(AM) Hermiston OR 6 hrs
KUIK(AM) Hillsboro OR 21 hrs
KCGB-FM Hood River OR 4 hrs
KIHR(AM) Hood River OR 14 hrs
KAGO(AM) Klamath Falls OR 5 hrs
*KTEC(FM) Klamath Falls OR 3 hrs
*KLCO(FM) Newport OR 5 hrs
*KBOO(FM) Portland OR 10 hrs
*KBPS(AM) Portland OR 1 hr
*KBVM(FM) Portland OR 14 hrs
KKPZ(AM) Portland OR 20 hrs
*KRRC(FM) Portland OR 2 hrs
KACI-FM The Dalles OR 1 hr
KODL(AM) The Dalles OR 2 hrs
*WDIY(FM) Allentown PA 3 hrs
*WMUH(FM) Allentown PA 4 hrs
WGPA(AM) Bethlehem PA 2-4 hrs
WWCS(AM) Canonsburg PA 2 hrs
*WDCV-FM Carlisle PA 1 hr
*WJRH(FM) Easton PA 6 hrs
*WERG(FM) Erie PA 3 hrs
*WMCE(FM) Erie PA 3 hrs
*WQLN-FM Erie PA 1 hr
*WZBT(FM) Gettysburg PA 4 hrs
WWKL(FM) Palmyra PA 14 hrs
WNTP(AM) Philadelphia PA 2 hrs
*WCLH(FM) Wilkes-Barre PA 3 hrs
*WVYC(FM) York PA 1 hr
WKJB(AM) Mayaguez PR 1 hr
*WRIU(FM) Kingston RI 3 hrs
WKMG(AM) Newberry SC 10 hrs
*KLND(FM) Little Eagle SD 1 hr
WHCB(FM) Bristol TN 1 hr
*WETS(FM) Johnson City TN 1 hr
*WYPL(FM) Memphis TN 1 hr
WNQM(AM) Nashville TN
*WRVU(FM) Nashville TN 2 hrs
KVLF(AM) Alpine TX 10 hrs
KKCN(FM) Ballinger TX 4 hrs
*KVLU(FM) Beaumont TX 5 hrs
KHVT(FM) Bloomington TX 6 hrs
KXYL(AM) Brownwood TX 36 hrs
*KWTS(FM) Canyon TX 3 hrs
KDHT(FM) Cedar Park TX 2 hrs
KQBZ(FM) Coleman TX 5 hrs
KSTA(AM) Coleman TX 5 hrs
KCTA(AM) Corpus Christi TX 6 hrs
*KEDT-FM Corpus Christi TX 4 hrs
KDHN(AM) Dimmitt TX 17 hrs
KULP(AM) El Campo TX 14 hrs
KELP(AM) El Paso TX 12 hrs
KCLW(AM) Hamilton TX 12 hrs
KMBH-FM Harlingen TX 5 hrs
*KOOP(FM) Hornsby TX 10 hrs
KHCB-FM Houston TX 10 hrs
*KSHU(FM) Huntsville TX 4 hrs
*KBJS(FM) Jacksonville TX 1 hr
*KKER(FM) Kerrville TX 6 hrs

*KTAI(FM) Kingsville TX 3 hrs
*KHML(FM) Madisonville TX 6 hrs
*KNTU(FM) McKinney TX 6 hrs
KLSR-FM Memphis TX 6 hrs
*KLUX(FM) Robstown TX 3 hrs
KTLU(AM) Rusk TX 10 hrs
KWRW(FM) Rusk TX 10 hrs
KSLR(AM) San Antonio TX 18 hrs
KXOX(AM) Sweetwater TX 8 hrs
*KVNE(FM) Tyler TX 2 hrs
KANI(AM) Wharton TX 3 hrs
*KPDR(FM) Wheeler TX 5 hrs
KWFS(AM) Wichita Falls TX 4 hrs
*KWCR-FM Ogden UT 16 hrs
*KEYY(AM) Provo UT 5 hrs
*KRCL(FM) Salt Lake City UT 9 hrs
KVEL(AM) Vernal UT
*WTJU(FM) Charlottesville VA 2 hrs
WWWJ(AM) Galax VA 20 hrs
*WHOV(FM) Hampton VA 12 hrs
*WXJM(FM) Harrisonburg VA 2 hrs
WKGM(AM) Smithfield VA 01 hrs
*WIUJ(FM) Charlotte Amalie VI 4 hrs
*WIUV(FM) Castleton VT 1 hr
*WRMC-FM Middlebury VT 1 hr
KWLE(AM) Anacortes WA 6 hrs
KOZI(AM) Chelan WA 5 hrs
KBSN(AM) Moses Lake WA 9 hrs
KBRC(AM) Mount Vernon WA 3 hrs
*KAOS(FM) Olympia WA 6 hrs
KOMW(AM) Omak WA 2 hrs
*KZUU(FM) Pullman WA 3 hrs
*KUOW-FM Seattle WA 2 hrs
*KDNA(FM) Yakima WA 106 hrs
WMCS(AM) Greenfield WI 5 hrs
*WMSE(FM) Milwaukee WI 3 hrs
WSSP(AM) Milwaukee WI 3 hrs
*WSHS(AM) Sheboygan WI 3. hrs
*WCCX(FM) Waukesha WI 8 hrs
*WMLJ(FM) Summersville WV 1 hr
KRAE(AM) Cheyenne WY 2 hrs
KUGR(AM) Green River WY 5 hrs

Sports

*KRUA(FM) Anchorage AK 1 hr
*WMBV(FM) Dixons Mills AL 1 hr
*WFIX(FM) Florence AL 6 hrs
WUMP(AM) Madison AL
WMGY(AM) Montgomery AL 6 hrs
WKLD(FM) Oneonta AL
WZCT(AM) Scottsboro AL 19 hrs
WKXM-FM Winfield AL 10 hrs
KYEL(FM) Danville AR
KFFA(AM) Helena AR 15 hrs
*KLVA(FM) Casa Grande AZ 7 hrs
KDJI(AM) Holbrook AZ 10 hrs
KAAA(AM) Kingman AZ
KNOT(AM) Prescott AZ 8 hrs
KRKC(AM) King City CA 9 hrs
KCAA(AM) Loma Linda CA
KLAA(AM) Orange CA
KTIP(AM) Porterville CA 6 hrs
KLIV(AM) San Jose CA
KKJL(AM) San Luis Obispo CA
KVEC(AM) San Luis Obispo CA
KVML(AM) Sonora CA 15 hrs
KFTM(AM) Fort Morgan CO 10 hrs
KUBC(AM) Montrose CO 5 hrs
KCOL(AM) Wellington CO 7 hrs
WGCH(AM) Greenwich CT 6 hrs
WZKT(FM) Lewes DE
WWBF(AM) Bartow FL
WSWN(AM) Belle Glade FL
*WVUM(FM) Coral Gables FL 5 hrs
WAAZ-FM Crestview FL
WNDB(AM) Daytona Beach FL
WDSP(AM) De Funiak Springs FL
WQHL-FM Live Oak FL
WFLF(AM) Pine Hills FL
WTBN(AM) Pinellas Park FL varies hrs
WAOC(AM) Saint Augustine FL
WKII(AM) Solana FL
WMGR(AM) Bainbridge GA 15 hrs
WFNS(AM) Blackshear GA 10 hrs
WGMI(AM) Bremen GA

WCLA(AM) Claxton GA
WRBN(AM) Clayton GA
WFOM(AM) Marietta GA fall hrs
WJAT(AM) Swainsboro GA
KPUA(AM) Hilo HI
KCPS(AM) Burlington IA 10 hrs
KLMJ(FM) Hampton IA
KIKD(FM) Lake City IA
KMCH(FM) Manchester IA 7 hrs
*KWDM(FM) West Des Moines IA 3
  hrs
KWYD(FM) Parma ID 1 hr
KTFI(AM) Twin Falls ID 3 hrs
WCDD(FM) Canton IL
WRXX(FM) Centralia IL
WGN(AM) Chicago IL
WXEF(FM) Effingham IL
*WHFH(FM) Flossmoor IL 4 hrs
WAIK(AM) Galesburg IL 10 hrs
WGIL(AM) Galesburg IL 15 hrs
*WGBK(FM) Glenview IL 9 hrs
WJBM(AM) Jerseyville IL 13 hrs
*WLTL(FM) La Grange IL 5 hrs
WFXN(AM) Moline IL 8 hrs
WBBA-FM Pittsfield IL 6 hrs
WGFA-FM Watseka IL 18 hrs
*WETN(FM) Wheaton IL 5 hrs
WYKT(FM) Wilmington IL 12 hrs
WBIW(AM) Bedford IN
WUZR(FM) Bicknell IN
*WGCS(FM) Goshen IN 10 hrs
WJOB(AM) Hammond IN
WBDC(FM) Huntingburg IN 6 hrs
WLME(FM) Lewisport IN 6 hrs
*WEEM-FM Pendleton IN 10 hrs
WFMG(FM) Richmond IN 8 hrs
*KTCC(FM) Colby KS 3 hrs
*KONQ(FM) Dodge City KS 5 hrs
KAYS(AM) Hays KS
KSEK(AM) Pittsburg KS
WKCM(AM) Hawesville KY 6 hrs
WCBR(AM) Richmond KY
WYSB(FM) Springfield KY 12 hrs
WEZJ-FM Williamsburg KY
WTGE(FM) Baker LA
WDGL(FM) Baton Rouge LA
*WXRB(FM) Dudley MA
WGFP(AM) Webster MA
WORC(AM) Worcester MA 6 hrs
WTAG(AM) Worcester MA
WNAV(AM) Annapolis MD
WXCY(FM) Havre de Grace MD 6 hrs
WKIK(AM) La Plata MD
WBPW(FM) Presque Isle ME
WMCM(FM) Rockland ME
*WBFH(FM) Bloomfield Hills MI 6 hrs
WDMK(FM) Detroit MI 2 hrs
WKMI(AM) Kalamazoo MI
WRSR(FM) Owosso MI 4 hrs
WJML(AM) Petoskey MI
WBJI(FM) Blackduck MN 4 hrs
KXDL(FM) Browerville MN 2 hrs
*WTIP(FM) Grand Marais MN 2 hrs
KEYL(AM) Long Prairie MN 10 hrs
KWWR(FM) Mexico MO
KBDZ(FM) Perryville MO 5 hrs
KSIM(AM) Sikeston MO
KTXR(FM) Springfield MO
WZLD(FM) Petal MS 3 hrs
WRJW(AM) Picayune MS 4 hrs
WIGG(AM) Wiggins MS
KMON(AM) Great Falls MT 5 hrs
WCSL(AM) Cherryville NC 3 hrs
WAZZ(AM) Fayetteville NC
WIZS(AM) Henderson NC
WGOS(AM) High Point NC 10 hrs
WELS-FM Kinston NC
WRNS-FM Kinston NC 6 hrs
WFLB(FM) Laurinburg NC
WKXU(AM) Louisburg NC
WECR(AM) Newland NC
WCBQ(AM) Oxford NC
WQDR(FM) Raleigh NC
WNCA(AM) Siler City NC 6 hrs
WEEB(AM) Southern Pines NC
WRGC(AM) Sylva NC

WSVM(AM) Valdese NC 15 hrs
WTQR(FM) Winston-Salem NC
KLXX(AM) Bismarck-Mandan ND 6 hrs
KDLR(AM) Devils Lake ND
KDIX(AM) Dickinson ND
KRRZ(AM) Minot ND
KGFW(AM) Kearney NE 10 hrs
*KRNU(FM) Lincoln NE 4 hrs
KIOD(FM) McCook NE 10 hrs
KNCY(AM) Nebraska City NE 6 hrs
WHTG(AM) Eatontown NJ 29 hrs
*WJSV(FM) Morristown NJ 3 hrs
WCTC(AM) New Brunswick NJ
WGHT(AM) Pompton Lakes NJ 2 hrs
*WMSC(FM) Upper Montclair NJ 3 hrs
*WMCX(FM) West Long Branch NJ 11
  hrs
KICA(AM) Clovis NM 4 hrs
KBIM-FM Roswell NM
KELY(AM) Ely NV
KKOH(AM) Reno NV
WBTA(AM) Batavia NY 9 hrs
WBAZ(FM) Bridgehampton NY
*WCWP(FM) Brookville NY 3 hrs
WBEN(AM) Buffalo NY
*WHCL-FM Clinton NY 6 hrs
WDNY-FM Dansville NY 4 hrs
*WKCR-FM New York NY 3 hrs
WEBO(AM) Owego NY 16 hrs
WODZ-FM Rome NY
*WRUC(FM) Schenectady NY 4 hrs
WUUF(AM) Sodus NY 5 hrs
WFAS(AM) White Plains NY 8 hrs
*WZIP(FM) Akron OH 3 hrs
WXTQ(AM) Athens OH
WBNO-FM Bryan OH
WCDK(FM) Cadiz OH
WBVB(FM) Coal Grove OH
WEOL(AM) Elyria OH
WFIN(AM) Findlay OH 12 hrs
WWSR(FM) Lima OH
WMOA(AM) Marietta OH 15 hrs
WKLM(FM) Millersburg OH
WBUK(FM) Ottawa OH 2 hrs
WPTW(AM) Piqua OH 30 hrs
WCWA(AM) Toledo OH 15 hrs
WHIZ-FM Zanesville OH 3 hrs
KADA-FM Ada OK 3 hrs
KRVT(AM) Claremore OK 4 hrs
KOCY(AM) Del City OK
KXXY-FM Oklahoma City OK
KOKL(AM) Okmulgee OK 10 hrs
KSPI(AM) Stillwater OK
KURY-FM Brookings OR
KPNW(AM) Eugene OR
KYKN(AM) Keizer OR
KBBR(AM) North Bend OR
KEX(AM) Portland OR
KQEN(AM) Roseburg OR
KOHI(AM) Saint Helens OR
KCKX(AM) Stayton OR
WRTA(AM) Altoona PA
WBVE(AM) Bedford PA
WZWW(FM) Bellefonte PA 3 hrs
*WFSE(FM) Edinboro PA
*WFNM(FM) Lancaster PA 2 hrs
WNPV(AM) Lansdale PA 6 hrs
WBPZ(AM) Lock Haven PA
*WMSS(FM) Middletown PA 5 hrs
WQLV(FM) Millersburg PA 6 hrs
WWKL(FM) Palmyra PA
WNTP(AM) Philadelphia PA 5 hrs
KQV(AM) Pittsburgh PA
WEAE(AM) Pittsburgh PA
WDMT(FM) Pittston PA
*WQSU(FM) Selinsgrove PA 4 hrs
*WSRU(FM) Slippery Rock PA 1 hr
WMBS(AM) Uniontown PA
WKZV(AM) Washington PA 1 hr
WBAX(AM) Wilkes-Barre PA
WEXS(AM) Patillas PR 6 hrs
WLEO(AM) Ponce PR
*WDOM(FM) Providence RI 2 hrs
WVGB(AM) Beaufort SC
WGTR(FM) Bucksport SC 8 hrs
WPCC(AM) Clinton SC

WISW(AM) Columbia SC
WNOW-FM Gaffney SC
WAVO(AM) Rock Hill SC
WSNW(AM) Seneca SC
WOLI(AM) Spartanburg SC 12 hrs
WBCU(AM) Union SC 10 hrs
KZKK(AM) Huron SD
KKSD(FM) Milbank SD 5 hrs
KIMM(AM) Rapid City SD
KSDR(AM) Watertown SD 8 hrs
WNAX(AM) Yankton SD 10 hrs
WSAA(FM) Benton TN
WHUB(AM) Cookeville TN 10 hrs
WAKM(AM) Franklin TN 6 hrs
WAEZ(AM) Greeneville TN
WDXI(AM) Jackson TN 16 hrs
WMSR(AM) Manchester TN
WTNE(AM) Trenton TN 20 hrs
WBOZ(AM) Woodbury TN 5 hrs
KSKY(AM) Balch Springs TX
KTAM(AM) Bryan TX
KCAR(AM) Clarksville TX 10 hrs
KRLD(AM) Dallas TX
WBAP(AM) Fort Worth TX
KGAF(AM) Gainesville TX 3 hrs
KCOH(AM) Houston TX
KCYL(AM) Lampasas TX 8 hrs
KSFA(AM) Nacogdoches TX
KJAK(FM) Slaton TX 5 hrs
KGLD(AM) Tyler TX
KVOU-FM Uvalde TX
*KPGR(FM) Pleasant Grove UT 4 hrs
WKEX(AM) Blacksburg VA
WMNA(AM) Gretna VA 10 hrs
*WRVL(FM) Lynchburg VA
WMEV-FM Marion VA
WYTI(AM) Rocky Mount VA
WTON(AM) Staunton VA
WKVT-FM Brattleboro VT 6 hrs
WVNR(AM) Poultney VT 10 hrs
*KASB(AM) Bellevue WA 6 hrs
*KCED(AM) Centralia WA 4 hrs
KMNT(AM) Chehalis WA
KCLX(AM) Colfax WA 7 hrs
KBDB-FM Forks WA 20 hrs
KBIS(AM) Forks WA 20 hrs
KONA(AM) Kennewick WA 8 hrs
KKNW(AM) Seattle WA 15 hrs
KXLY(AM) Spokane WA 20 hrs
KKAD(AM) Vancouver WA 18 hrs
WBEV(AM) Beaver Dam WI 18 hrs
WLKG(FM) Lake Geneva WI 2 hrs
WGLR-FM Lancaster WI
WMAM(AM) Marinette WI
WPVL(AM) Platteville WI 15 hrs
*WRPN-FM Ripon WI 15 hrs
WCOW-FM Sparta WI
*WWSP(FM) Stevens Point WI 3 hrs
*KUWS(FM) Superior WI 6 hrs
WDUX-FM Waupaca WI 15 hrs
WJLS(AM) Beckley WV 3 hrs
WXKX(AM) Clarksburg WV
WTNJ(FM) Mount Hope WV
WWYO(AM) Pineville WV 18 hrs

Talk

WBCF(AM) Florence AL 24 hrs
WNUZ(AM) Talladega AL 5 hrs
KHTE-FM England AR 10 hrs
KVDW(AM) England AR 10 hrs
KBOK(AM) Malvern AR 6 hrs
KCGS(AM) Marshall AR 7 hrs
KCUZ(AM) Clifton AZ 8 hrs
KJLH-FM Compton CA 8.5 hrs
KXBX(AM) Lakeport CA 5 hrs
KTOX(AM) Needles CA 22 hrs
KXTZ(FM) Pismo Beach CA 1 hr
*KASF(AM) Alamosa CO 6 hrs
KFTM(AM) Fort Morgan CO 5 hrs
KGRE(AM) Greeley CO 1 hr
WICH(AM) Norwich CT 15 hrs
WINY(AM) Putnam CT 11 hrs
WEBE(FM) Westport CT 1 hr
WWPR(AM) Bradenton FL 15 hrs
WRNE(AM) Gulf Breeze FL

WOTS(AM) Kissimmee FL 20 hrs
WFOY(AM) Saint Augustine FL
*WWFR(FM) Stuart FL 1 hr
WBAF(AM) Barnesville GA 5 hrs
*WFRC(FM) Columbus GA 8 hrs
WSDZ(AM) Belleville IL 1/2 hrs
*WSSD(FM) Chicago IL 6 hrs
*WHFH(FM) Flossmoor IL 1 hr
WAIK(AM) Galesburg IL 10 hrs
*WCSF(FM) Joliet IL 4 hrs
*WLRA(FM) Lockport IL 15 hrs
WKLU(AM) Brownsburg IN
WRWM(FM) Lawrence IN 1 hr
*WPUM(FM) Rensselaer IN 1 hr
WLBN(AM) Lebanon KY 5 hrs
WTBK(FM) Manchester KY 8 hrs
WPHX-FM Sanford ME 2 hrs
WDZZ-FM Flint MI 1 hr
WGLI(AM) Hancock MI 5 hrs
KNXR(FM) Rochester MN 2 hrs
KAYX(FM) Richmond MO
KSIM(AM) Sikeston MO
WTCD(FM) Indianola MS 10 hrs
WATA(AM) Boone NC 20 hrs
WIZS(AM) Henderson NC
WRFX(FM) Kannapolis NC 3 hrs
WENC(AM) Whiteville NC 5 hrs
KHND(AM) Harvey ND 8 hrs
WMOU(AM) Berlin NH 2 hrs
WRNJ(AM) Hackettstown NJ 10 hrs
WOBM(AM) Lakewood NJ 12 hrs
KWKA(AM) Clovis NM
KBCQ(AM) Roswell NM 15 hrs
KMXQ(FM) Socorro NM 1 hr
WUFO(AM) Amherst NY 8 hrs
*WSQX-FM Binghamton NY 10 hrs
WENT(AM) Gloversville NY 1 hr
*WNYC(AM) New York NY 3 hrs
WEOK(AM) Poughkeepsie NY 5 hrs
WBEA(FM) Southold NY
WONW(AM) Defiance OH 3 hrs
WEGE(FM) Lima OH 5 hrs
*WLRY(FM) Rushville OH 16 hrs
KGFF(AM) Shawnee OK
KWIP(AM) Dallas OR 5 hrs
KWVR-FM Enterprise OR 15 hrs
KGAL(AM) Lebanon OR 5 hrs
KQEN(AM) Roseburg OR
*KSJK(AM) Talent OR 6 hrs
KACI(AM) The Dalles OR 10 hrs
*WBUQ(FM) Bloomsburg PA 10 hrs
WBHD(FM) Olyphant PA
WPAM(AM) Pottsville PA
WMBS(AM) Uniontown PA
WZAR(FM) Ponce PR 15 hrs
WOLH(AM) Florence SC 16 hrs
WNOW-FM Gaffney SC 10 hrs
WLMC(AM) Georgetown SC 4 hrs
WRIX-FM Honea Path SC 20 hrs
WSAA(FM) Benton TN
WZYX(AM) Cowan TN
KIXZ(AM) Amarillo TX 2 hrs
*KAZI-FM Austin TX 10 hrs
KNES(FM) Fairfield TX 15 hrs
KMJQ(FM) Houston TX 3 hrs
KTBZ-FM Houston TX 2 hrs
KKCL(FM) Lorenzo TX 17 hrs
*KSTX(FM) San Antonio TX 6 hrs
KSUB(AM) Cedar City UT
WRVA(AM) Richmond VA 1 hr
KBKW(AM) Aberdeen WA
KGNW(AM) Burien-Seattle WA
KXLY(AM) Spokane WA 5 hrs
KXLY(AM) Spokane WA 5 hrs
*KVTI(FM) Tacoma WA 4 hrs
WELD-FM Moorefield WV 6 hrs
WMOV(AM) Ravenswood WV 2 hrs
KOVE(AM) Lander WY 15 hrs

Tejano

KPAN(AM) Hereford TX 15 hrs

Top-40

WKPE-FM South Yarmouth MA
KOLV(FM) Olivia MN
KATQ(AM) Plentywood MT
WCLM(AM) Highland Springs VA
KMPS-FM Seattle WA

Triple A

*KBBI(AM) Homer AK
*KOJI(FM) Okoboji IA 18 hrs
*KWIT(FM) Sioux City IA 12 hrs
*KMUW(FM) Wichita KS 14 hrs
*WKMS-FM Murray KY 3 hrs
*KOPN(FM) Columbia MO 10 hrs
*WEOS(FM) Geneva NY 12 hrs
WRIP(FM) Windham NY 5 hrs
WEQX(FM) Manchester VT 4 hrs

Ukranian

WILI(AM) Willimantic CT 1 hr
WPNA(AM) Oak Park IL
WCCD(AM) Parma OH 1 hr
KARI(AM) Blaine WA 1 hr

Underground

*WMTS-FM Murfreesboro TN 10 hrs

Urban Contemporary

*KSCU(FM) Santa Clara CA 15 hrs
*KCSU-FM Fort Collins CO 3 hrs
*WQTQ(FM) Hartford CT 19 hrs
*WRGP(FM) Homestead FL 12 hrs
*KICB(FM) Fort Dodge IA 2 hrs
*KMSC(FM) Sioux City IA 4 hrs
*WQUB(FM) Quincy IL 2 hrs
*WVUR-FM Valparaiso IN 3 hrs
*KTCC(FM) Colby KS 4 hrs
*WKMS-FM Murray KY 3 hrs

*WEAA(FM) Baltimore MD 5 hrs
*WKHS(FM) Worton MD 2 hrs
*WSGR-FM Port Huron MI 6 hrs
*KSRQ(FM) Thief River Falls MN 5 hrs
*KMVC(FM) Marshall MO 20 hrs
*WASU-FM Boone NC 6 hrs
*WXDU(FM) Durham NC 12 hrs
*WUAG(FM) Greensboro NC 6 hrs
*WKNH(FM) Keene NH 4 hrs
*WPSC-FM Wayne NJ 18 hrs
*WIRQ(FM) Rochester NY 3 hrs
*WUSO(FM) Springfield OH 9 hrs
*WBUQ(FM) Bloomsburg PA 10 hrs
*WCAL(FM) California PA 12 hrs
*WDCV-FM Carlisle PA 15 hrs
*WCUC-FM Clarion PA 6 hrs
*WUSR(FM) Scranton PA 6 hrs
WBRU(FM) Providence RI 20 hrs
*WDOM(FM) Providence RI 16 hrs
*KCFS(FM) Sioux Falls SD 6 hrs
*WTTU(FM) Cookeville TN
*WNRN(FM) Charlottesville VA 16 hrs
*WIUV(FM) Castleton VT 5 hrs

*WRMC-FM Middlebury VT 12 hrs
*KGRG-FM Auburn WA 3 hrs
*WSUP(FM) Platteville WI 4 hrs
*WSUW(FM) Whitewater WI 14 hrs

Variety/Diverse

*KRUA(FM) Anchorage AK 20 hrs
*WEGL(FM) Auburn AL
KBHR(FM) Big Bear City CA 2 hrs
*KIWR(FM) Council Bluffs IA 16 hrs
*WNUR-FM Evanston IL 12 hrs
*WDCB(FM) Glen Ellyn IL 7 hrs
WVEZ(FM) Louisville KY 5 hrs
*KGAC(FM) Saint Peter MN 8 hrs
WPEG(FM) Concord NC 8 hrs
WHKP(AM) Hendersonville NC 18 hrs
*WITC(FM) Cazenovia NY 10 hrs
*WBAI(FM) New York NY
WJZA(FM) Pickerington OH 15 hrs
WODB(FM) Richwood OH 15v hrs
WEZY(FM) Racine WI

Vietnamese

KXMX(AM) Anaheim CA 2 hrs
*KHCB(AM) Galveston TX 4 hrs
*WSHS(FM) Sheboygan WI 3 hrs

Women

*KPFA(FM) Berkeley CA 10 hrs
*KAZU(FM) Pacific Grove CA 6 hrs
*WCNI(FM) New London CT 3 hrs
*WPFW(FM) Washington DC 3 hrs
KROS(AM) Clinton IA 5 hrs
*KMSC(FM) Sioux City IA 5 hrs
KNSG(FM) Springfield MN 3 hrs
WNBN(AM) Meridian MS
WUMS(FM) University MS 1 hr
KAWL(AM) York NE 3 hrs
*WXUT(FM) Toledo OH 2 hrs
KGNW(AM) Burien-Seattle WA

Special Programming on Radio Stations in Canada

Agriculture

CFAC(AM) Calgary AB 10 hrs
CFCW(AM) Camrose AB 5 hrs
CKDQ(AM) Drumheller AB 8 hrs
CFXE-FM Edson AB 2 hrs
CHRB(AM) High River AB 5 hrs
CHLW(AM) Saint Paul AB 5 hrs
CKKY(AM) Wainwright AB 10 hrs
CFOK(AM) Westlock AB 5 hrs
CIGV-FM Penticton BC 1 hr hrs
CKLQ(AM) Brandon MB 18 hrs
CFRY(AM) Portage la Prairie MB 4 hrs
CBW(AM) Winnipeg MB 6 hrs
CKDH(AM) Amherst NS 2 hrs
CKDY(AM) Digby NS 7 hrs
CKEN-FM Kentville NS 5 hrs
CKAD(AM) Middleton NS 3 hrs
CJBQ(AM) Belleville ON 3 hrs
CFCO(AM) Chatham ON 3 hrs
CHCD-FM Simcoe ON 5 hrs
CFRB(AM) Toronto ON 2 hrs
CJSL(AM) Estevan SK 4 hrs
CJNB(AM) North Battleford SK 7 hrs
CKBI(AM) Prince Albert SK 2 hrs
*CBK(AM) Regina SK 5 hrs
CKSW(AM) Swift Current SK 5 hrs
CFSL(AM) Weyburn SK 3 hrs

American Indian

*CJSR-FM Edmonton AB 2 hrs
CFNR-FM Terrace BC 9 hrs
CHMB(AM) Vancouver BC 1 hr hrs
*CFUV-FM Victoria BC 1 hr hrs
CHTM(AM) Thompson MB 10 hrs
CHSR-FM Fredericton NB 1 hr hrs
CKON-FM Akwesasne ON
*CHMO(AM) Moosonee ON 5 hrs
CKCU-FM Ottawa ON 2 hrs
CKLP-FM Parry Sound ON 1 hr hrs
CFBU-FM Saint Catharines ON 1 hr hrs
CBQS-FM Sioux Narrows ON 1 hr hrs
*CKRK-FM Kahnawake PQ 10 hrs
*CBKA-FM La Ronge SK 20 hrs
*CJTR-FM Regina SK 4 hrs

Arabic

*CKRL-FM Quebec PQ 3 hrs

Big Band

CJLX-FM Belleville ON 2 hrs
CFBG-FM Bracebridge ON 1 hr hrs

Black

*CJSR-FM Edmonton AB 7 hrs
*CFRO-FM Vancouver BC 14 hrs
CHSR-FM Fredericton NB 3 hrs
CKLB-FM Yellowknife NT 1 hr hrs
*CFMU-FM Hamilton ON 4 hrs
CKCU-FM Ottawa ON 12 hrs
CHRY-FM Toronto ON
*CJAM-FM Windsor ON 10 hrs
*CIBL-FM Montreal PQ 13 hrs
*CKUT-FM Montreal PQ 20 hrs
*CKRL-FM Quebec PQ 6 hrs
CFNJ-FM Saint Gabriel-de-Brandon PQ 1 hr hrs
*CJTR-FM Regina SK 2 hrs

Bluegrass

CKOL-FM Campbellford ON 3 hrs
CHCR-FM Killaloe ON 6 hrs

Blues

CKXL-FM Saint Boniface MB 2 hrs
*CHMR-FM Saint John's NF 6 hrs
CJLX-FM Belleville ON 1 hr hrs
*CFMU-FM Hamilton ON 5 hrs
CFBW-FM Hanover ON 2 hrs
CFBU-FM Saint Catharines ON 2 hrs
CIEU-FM Carleton PQ 5 hrs

Children

CHVN-FM Winnipeg MB 1 hr hrs
*CKUW-FM Winnipeg MB 2 hrs
CHRI-FM Ottawa ON 4 hrs

Chinese

*CFRO-FM Vancouver BC 2 hrs
CHSR-FM Fredericton NB 3 hrs
*CHUO-FM Ottawa ON 2 hrs
CFBU-FM Saint Catharines ON 2 hrs
CHRY-FM Toronto ON
CINQ-FM Montreal PQ 5 hrs
*CJTR-FM Regina SK 1 hr hrs

Christian

*CIXX-FM London ON 3 hrs

Classical

*CJSR-FM Edmonton AB 2 hrs
CKBX(AM) 100 Mile House BC 1 hr
CIGV-FM Penticton BC 2 hrs
CHOR(AM) Summerland BC 3 hrs
CFAM(AM) Altona MB 15 hrs
CBW(AM) Winnipeg MB 8 hrs
*CKUW-FM Winnipeg MB 4 hrs
CHSR-FM Fredericton NB 6 hrs
*CHMR-FM Saint John's NF 10 hrs
CJLX-FM Belleville ON 2 hrs
CHOD-FM Cornwall ON 4 hrs
*CFMU-FM Hamilton ON 5 hrs
CFBU-FM Saint Catharines ON 1 hr hrs
CHAS-FM Sault Ste. Marie ON 5 hrs
CFRB(AM) Toronto ON 7 hrs
*CBE(AM) Windsor ON 4 hrs
*CJAM-FM Windsor ON 4 hrs
CIEU-FM Carleton PQ 3 hrs
CHIP-FM Fort Coulonge PQ 2 hrs
CJRG-FM Gaspe PQ 2 hrs
*CFIN-FM Lac-Etchemin PQ 4 hrs
CHGA-FM Maniwaki PQ 1 hr hrs
*CIBL-FM Montreal PQ 4 hrs
CKIA-FM Quebec PQ 3 hrs
CKMN-FM Rimouski-Mont Joli PQ 3 hrs
CFNJ-FM Saint Gabriel-de-Brandon PQ 2 hrs
CIHO-FM Saint Hilarion PQ 2 hrs
CJMC-FM Sainte Anne des Monts PQ 2 hrs
CFLX-FM Sherbrooke PQ 7 hrs
CJSO-FM Sorel PQ 2 hrs
CFMC-FM Saskatoon SK 2 hrs

Country

CBW(AM) Winnipeg MB 1 hr hrs
CJVA(AM) Caraquet NB 15 hrs
*CFJU-FM Kedgwick NB 12 hrs
CKDH(AM) Amherst NS 11 hrs
CFNO-FM Marathon ON 12 hrs
CFMF-FM Fermont PQ 4 hrs
*CFIN-FM Lac-Etchemin PQ 6 hrs
CHGA-FM Maniwaki PQ 8 hrs

Disco

CKMF-FM Montreal PQ

Educational

CKUA(AM) Edmonton AB
CBW-FM Winnipeg MB 5 hrs
CJLX-FM Belleville ON 4 hrs
*CIXX-FM London ON 4 hrs
CHRY-FM Toronto ON

Ethnic

CKER-FM Edmonton AB 10 hrs
*CHUO-FM Ottawa ON 6 hrs

Filipino

CKJS(AM) Winnipeg MB 20 hrs

Finnish

CKTG-FM Thunder Bay ON 1 hr hrs

Folk

*CJSR-FM Edmonton AB 16 hrs
CKXL-FM Saint Boniface MB 2 hrs
*CKUW-FM Winnipeg MB 2 hrs
CFAN-FM Miramichi City NB 2 hrs
*CHMR-FM Saint John's NF 6 hrs
*VOWR(AM) Saint John's NF 15 hrs
CJLX-FM Belleville ON 1 hr hrs
CKCU-FM Ottawa ON 12 hrs
*CJAM-FM Windsor ON 4 hrs
CIEU-FM Carleton PQ 3 hrs
CHGA-FM Maniwaki PQ 5 hrs
*CKUT-FM Montreal PQ 3 hrs

Foreign/Ethnic

*CJSF-FM Burnaby BC 2 hrs
*CFRO-FM Vancouver BC 8 hrs
CHSR-FM Fredericton NB 5 hrs
*CKJM-FM Cheticamp NS 1 hr hrs
*CHAK(AM) Inuvik NT 18 hrs
CFCT(AM) Tuktoyaktuk NT 5 hrs
*CFYK(AM) Yellowknife NT 16 hrs
CBQR-FM Rankin Inlet NU 10 hrs
CKWR-FM Kitchener ON 4 hrs
*CBQT-FM Thunder Bay ON 1 hr hrs
CJDL-FM Tillsonburg ON 2 hrs
CKOT(AM) Tillsonburg ON 2 hrs
CHRY-FM Toronto ON
CINQ-FM Montreal PQ 18 hrs
CKIA-FM Quebec PQ 3 hrs
CHON-FM Whitehorse YT 15 hrs

French

*CJSW-FM Calgary AB 1 hr hrs
*CJSR-FM Edmonton AB 1 hr hrs
*CFUV-FM Victoria BC 2 hrs
CKBC-FM Bathurst NB 9 hrs
CKNB(AM) Campbellton NB 18 hrs
CHSR-FM Fredericton NB 2 hrs
CKHJ(AM) Fredericton NB 1 hr hrs
*CHMR-FM Saint John's NF 2 hrs
CFDY-FM Cochrane ON 5 hrs
*CFMU-FM Hamilton ON 1 hr hrs

CFNJ-FM Saint Gabriel-de-Brandon PQ 4 hrs
CJMC-FM Sainte Anne des Monts PQ 2 hrs
CKCN-FM Sept-Iles PQ 8 hrs
CFDA-FM Victoriaville PQ 3 hrs

German

*CJSW-FM Calgary AB 2 hrs
CKJS(AM) Winnipeg MB 6 hrs
CKWR-FM Kitchener ON 3 hrs
*CHUO-FM Ottawa ON 2 hrs
*CKLU-FM Sudbury ON 1 hr hrs
CJDL-FM Tillsonburg ON 1 hr hrs
CKOT(AM) Tillsonburg ON 1 hr hrs
CFCR-FM Saskatoon SK 2 hrs
CKSW(AM) Swift Current SK 1 hr hrs

Gospel

*CJSR-FM Edmonton AB 2 hrs
CILK-FM Kelowna BC 3 hrs
CHVN-FM Winnipeg MB 4 hrs
CKOL-FM Campbellford ON 3 hrs
CFCO(AM) Chatham ON 2 hrs
CKSY-FM Chatham ON 2 hrs
CFBW-FM Hanover ON 6 hrs
CKOT-FM Tillsonburg ON 1 hr hrs
CHRY-FM Toronto ON
CHIP-FM Fort Coulonge PQ 7 hrs
*CKUT-FM Montreal PQ 2 hrs
CJWW(AM) Saskatoon SK 3 hrs

Greek

CKJR(AM) Wetaskiwin AB 2 hrs
*CFRO-FM Vancouver BC 1 hr hrs
CHMB(AM) Vancouver BC 1/2 hrs
CKJS(AM) Winnipeg MB 1 hr hrs
CJLX-FM Belleville ON 1 hr hrs
CKWR-FM Kitchener ON 2 hrs
CHAA-FM Longueuil PQ 5 hrs
CINQ-FM Montreal PQ 13 hrs

Hebrew

CHRY-FM Toronto ON

Hindi

CJDL-FM Tillsonburg ON 1 hr hrs
CKOT(AM) Tillsonburg ON 1 hr hrs

Irish

CKXD-FM Gander NF 12 hrs
CIGO-FM Port Hawkesbury NS 1 hr hrs
CFZM(AM) Toronto ON 1 hr hrs

Italian

*CJSW-FM Calgary AB 1 hr hrs
CKER-FM Edmonton AB 3 hrs
CHMB(AM) Vancouver BC 1 hr hrs
*CFUV-FM Victoria BC 2 hrs
CKJS(AM) Winnipeg MB 5 hrs
*CFRU-FM Guelph ON 1 hr hrs
*CFMU-FM Hamilton ON 1 hr hrs
CKCU-FM Ottawa ON 1 hr hrs
CHAS-FM Sault Ste. Marie ON 2 hrs
CJQM-FM Sault Ste. Marie ON 4 hrs
*CKLU-FM Sudbury ON 1 hr hrs
CKTG-FM Thunder Bay ON

(column 4 continued)

CHCR-FM Killaloe ON 8 hrs
CKCU-FM Ottawa ON 2 hrs
*CKLU-FM Sudbury ON 19 hrs
CHRY-FM Toronto ON
*CIUT-FM Toronto ON 2 hrs
CHAA-FM Longueuil PQ 18 hrs
*CKUT-FM Montreal PQ 9 hrs
CJBR-FM Rimouski PQ
CFCR-FM Saskatoon SK 1 hr hrs
*CFWH(AM) Whitehorse YT 1 hr hrs

Japanese

CHMB(AM) Vancouver BC 1 hr hrs

Jazz

CKMX(AM) Calgary AB 5 hrs
CFOX-FM Vancouver BC 2 hrs
*CFRO-FM Vancouver BC 16 hrs
CKXL-FM Saint Boniface MB 4 hrs
CBW-FM Winnipeg MB 3 hrs
*CKUW-FM Winnipeg MB 8 hrs
CKLE-FM Bathurst NB 2 hrs
CHSR-FM Fredericton NB 6 hrs
CJMO-FM Moncton NB 2 hrs
CKUM-FM Moncton NB 4 hrs
*CHMR-FM Saint John's NF 6 hrs
*CKJM-FM Cheticamp NS 3 hrs
CFRQ-FM Dartmouth NS 3 hrs
CIVR-FM Yellowknife NT 4 hrs
CJLX-FM Belleville ON 3 hrs
CFBG-FM Bracebridge ON 2 hrs
CHOD-FM Cornwall ON 4 hrs
*CFMU-FM Hamilton ON 10 hrs
*CHUO-FM Ottawa ON 5 hrs
CKCU-FM Ottawa ON 15 hrs
CKWF-FM Peterborough ON 12 hrs
CFBU-FM Saint Catharines ON 4 hrs
CHAS-FM Sault Ste. Marie ON 2 hrs
CHRY-FM Toronto ON
*CBE(AM) Windsor ON 2 hrs
*CJAM-FM Windsor ON 6 hrs
CIEU-FM Carleton PQ 3 hrs
CFMF-FM Fermont PQ 1 hr hrs
CJRG-FM Gaspe PQ 2 hrs
*CFIN-FM Lac-Etchemin PQ 6 hrs
CHGA-FM Maniwaki PQ 3 hrs
*CIBL-FM Montreal PQ 14 hrs
*CBVX-FM Quebec PQ 16 hrs
CKIA-FM Quebec PQ 4 hrs
CFNJ-FM Saint Gabriel-de-Brandon PQ 2 hrs
CIHO-FM Saint Hilarion PQ 2 hrs
CFLX-FM Sherbrooke PQ 8 hrs
CFMC-FM Saskatoon SK 2 hrs

New Age

CFGX-FM Sarnia ON 7 hrs

News

*CFPR(AM) Prince Rupert BC
*CBVX-FM Quebec PQ 7 hrs

News/talk

CKPR-FM Thunder Bay ON 10 hrs

Oldies

CJSU-FM Duncan BC 12 hrs
CKXX-FM Corner Brook NF 3 hrs
CHIP-FM Fort Coulonge PQ
CJLM-FM Joliette PQ 6 hrs
CHAA-FM Longueuil PQ 9 hrs
CKMN-FM Rimouski-Mont Joli PQ 3 hrs
CFDA-FM Victoriaville PQ 3 hrs

Other

*CJSR-FM Edmonton AB 4 hrs hrs
CKUA(AM) Edmonton AB
CISC-FM Gibsons BC 3 hrs
CKFR(AM) Kelowna BC 2 hrs
CKFR(AM) Kelowna BC 4 hrs
CHLS-FM Lillooet BC 16 hrs
CKKS-FM Sechelt BC 3 hrs
CHMB(AM) Vancouver BC 1 hr hrs
CHMB(AM) Vancouver BC 1/2 hrs
CJAR(AM) The Pas MB 5 hrs
CHVN-FM Winnipeg MB 6 hrs
CIOK-FM Saint John NB 4 hrs
*CBN(AM) Saint John's NF 3 hrs
CIGO-FM Port Hawkesbury NS 3 hrs
CIVR-FM Yellowknife NT 3 hrs
CFBG-FM Bracebridge ON 1 hr hrs
CFMJ(AM) Toronto ON
CFZM(AM) Toronto ON 1 hr hrs
*CIUT-FM Toronto ON 5 hrs
*CIBL-FM Montreal PQ 8 hrs
CINQ-FM Montreal PQ 16 hrs

Polish

*CJSR-FM Edmonton AB 2 hrs
CKER-FM Edmonton AB 6 hrs
*CFRO-FM Vancouver BC 5 hrs
*CFUV-FM Victoria BC 1 hr
CKJS(AM) Winnipeg MB 7 hrs
CHCR-FM Killaloe ON 1 hr hrs

CKWR-FM Kitchener ON 4 hrs
CKCU-FM Ottawa ON 1 hr hrs
*CKLU-FM Sudbury ON 1 hr hrs
*CJAM-FM Windsor ON 1 hr hrs
CFCR-FM Saskatoon SK 1 hr hrs

Portugese

CKER-FM Edmonton AB 2 hrs
CFOK(AM) Westlock AB 5 hrs
*CJSF-FM Burnaby BC 2 hrs
CJOR(AM) Osoyoos BC 3 hrs
CHMB(AM) Vancouver BC 1 hr hrs
CKJS(AM) Winnipeg MB 8 hrs
CJDV-FM Cambridge ON 2 hrs
CKWR-FM Kitchener ON 5 hrs
CFBU-FM Saint Catharines ON 2 hrs
CINQ-FM Montreal PQ 12 hrs
*CJTR-FM Regina SK 1 hr

Public Affairs

*CFPR(AM) Prince Rupert BC

Reggae

CKXL-FM Saint Boniface MB 2 hrs
*CHMR-FM Saint John's NF 2 hrs
CJLX-FM Belleville ON 1 hr
*CFMU-FM Hamilton ON 4 hrs
*CIBL-FM Montreal PQ 4 hrs

Religious

CKDQ(AM) Drumheller AB 2 hrs
CHLW(AM) Saint Paul AB 5 hrs
CFOK(AM) Westlock AB 6 hrs
CIVH(AM) Vanderhoof BC 5 hrs
CHTM(AM) Thompson MB 12 hrs
CFAN-FM Miramichi City NB 4 hrs
CJCW(AM) Sussex NB 4 hrs
*CHMR-FM Saint John's NF 4 hrs
*VOWR(AM) Saint John's NF 10 hrs
CFSX(AM) Stephenville NF 1 hr hrs
CJSS-FM Cornwall ON 1 hr hrs
*CFRU-FM Guelph ON 1 hr hrs
CKDO(AM) Oshawa ON 1 hr hrs
*CHUO-FM Ottawa ON 2 hrs
CKCU-FM Ottawa ON 3 hrs
CKTG-FM Thunder Bay ON
CKNX(AM) Wingham ON 6 hrs
CHRD-FM Drummondville PQ 1 hr hrs
*CFIN-FM Lac-Etchemin PQ 1 hr hrs
CJSL(AM) Estevan SK 10 hrs
CKJH(AM) Melfort SK 9 hrs
CJNB(AM) North Battleford SK 10 hrs
CJDJ-FM Saskatoon SK 6 hrs
CFSL(AM) Weyburn SK 9 hrs

Rock/AOR

CHIP-FM Fort Coulonge PQ

Scottish

CKEC-FM New Glasgow NS
CIGO-FM Port Hawkesbury NS 1 hr hrs
CFBW-FM Hanover ON 2 hrs
CFZM(AM) Toronto ON 2 hrs hrs

Spanish

*CJSW-FM Calgary AB 1 hr hrs
*CJSR-FM Edmonton AB 2 hrs
CKER-FM Edmonton AB 8 hrs
*CJSF-FM Burnaby BC 4 hrs
*CFUV-FM Victoria BC 2 hrs
CKXL-FM Saint Boniface MB 2 hrs
CKJS(AM) Winnipeg MB 3 hrs
*CFRU-FM Guelph ON
*CFMU-FM Hamilton ON 1 hr hrs
CKWR-FM Kitchener ON 4 hrs
*CHUO-FM Ottawa ON 3 hrs
CFBU-FM Saint Catharines ON 4 hrs
*CKLU-FM Sudbury ON 1 hr hrs
CHRY-FM Toronto ON
*CIUT-FM Toronto ON 4 hrs
*CJAM-FM Windsor ON 1 hr hrs
CHAA-FM Longueuil PQ 3 hrs
CINQ-FM Montreal PQ 16 hrs
*CKUT-FM Montreal PQ 6 hrs
CKIA-FM Quebec PQ 4 hrs
*CKRL-FM Quebec PQ 2 hrs
CFLX-FM Sherbrooke PQ 3 hrs

CFCR-FM Saskatoon SK 2 hrs

Sports

CFFR(AM) Calgary AB 15 hrs
CJBX-FM London ON
CHOK(AM) Sarnia ON
CFMJ(AM) Toronto ON

Talk

CISQ-FM Squamish BC 5 hrs

Ukranian

CKER-FM Edmonton AB 10 hrs
CHMB(AM) Vancouver BC 1 hr hrs

Urban Contemporary

*CHYZ-FM Sainte Foy PQ 15 hrs

Vietnamese

CHMB(AM) Vancouver BC 1 hr hrs
CKCU-FM Ottawa ON 1 hr hrs
CHAA-FM Longueuil PQ 5 hrs

U.S. Radio Markets: Arbitron Metro Survey Area Ranking

This chart ranks the 300 radio markets by Metro Survey Area population. Figures include all persons aged 12 or older and are based on 2000 U.S. Bureau of Census estimates updated and projected to January 1, 2009. Data reflects the Spring 2009 Arbitron market definitions. See U.S. Radio Markets beginning on pg. D-810 for details.

1. New York	15,393,700	71. Knoxville 669,900
2. Los Angeles	10,877,600	72. Omaha-Council Bluffs ... 627,500
3. Chicago	7,813,900	73. Sarasota-Bradenton ... 626,700
4. San Francisco	6,013,700	74. Bakersfield ... 596,900
5. Dallas-Ft. Worth	5,120,100	75. Akron ... 596,500
6. Houston-Galveston	4,759,600	76. El Paso ... 594,700
7. Atlanta	4,378,000	77. Wilmington, DE ... 592,000
8. Philadelphia	4,352,800	78. Baton Rouge ... 570,300
9. Washington, DC	4,238,100	79. Harrisburg-Lebanon-Carlisle ... 569,800
10. Boston	3,912,000	80. Stockton ... 561,100
11. Detroit	3,866,900	81. Gainesville-Ocala ... 560,700
12. Miami-Ft. Lauderdale-Hollywood	3,559,700	82. Monterey-Salinas-Santa Cruz ... 556,200
13. Seattle-Tacoma	3,353,200	83. Syracuse ... 550,800
14. Puerto Rico	3,327,100	84. Charleston, SC ... 542,700
15. Phoenix	3,249,200	85. Little Rock ... 542,000
16. Minneapolis-St. Paul	2,697,500	86. Daytona Beach ... 538,900
17. San Diego	2,536,000	87. Greenville-New Bern-Jacksonville ... 528,900
18. Tampa-St. Petersburg-Clearwater	2,387,300	88. Springfield, MA ... 525,800
19. Nassau-Suffolk (Long Island)	2,325,200	89. Columbia, SC ... 519,500
20. St. Louis	2,299,000	90. Des Moines ... 516,400
21. Denver-Boulder	2,298,100	91. Toledo ... 511,400
22. Baltimore	2,271,500	92. Spokane ... 510,000
23. Portland, OR	2,078,300	93. Lakeland-Winter Haven ... 501,400
24. Pittsburgh, PA	1,975,700	94. Colorado Springs ... 498,800
25. Charlotte-Gastonia-Rock Hill	1,962,300	95. Ft. Pierce-Stuart-Vero Beach ... 491,500
26. Riverside-San Bernardino	1,854,600	96. Mobile ... 489,300
27. Sacramento	1,824,400	97. Melbourne-Titusville-Cocoa ... 485,600
28. Cincinnati	1,773,000	98. Madison ... 477,300
29. Cleveland	1,764,400	99. Wichita ... 475,100
30. Salt Lake City-Ogden-Provo	1,676,000	100. Boise ... 472,700
31. San Antonio	1,675,200	101. Visalia-Tulare-Hanford ... 468,200
32. Kansas City	1,599,600	102. Johnson City-Kingsport-Bristol ... 462,500
33. Las Vegas	1,586,300	103. York ... 456,600
34. Orlando	1,519,700	104. Lexington-Fayette ... 454,800
35. San Jose	1,482,100	105. Lafayette, LA ... 452,600
36. Columbus, OH	1,448,200	106. Chattanooga ... 444,900
37. Milwaukee-Racine	1,447,700	107. Ft. Wayne ... 435,100
38. Middlesex-Somerset-Union	1,381,900	108. Huntsville ... 435,000
39. Austin	1,381,800	109. Modesto ... 428,400
40. Indianapolis	1,379,600	110. Augusta, GA ... 428,100
41. Providence-Warwick-Pawtucket	1,368,300	111. Roanoke-Lynchburg ... 422,700
42. Norfolk-Virginia Beach-Newport News	1,334,800	112. Lancaster ... 421,100
43. Raleigh-Durham	1,286,600	113. New Haven ... 418,800
44. Nashville	1,237,500	114. Worcester ... 416,600
45. Greensboro-Winston-Salem-High Point	1,179,100	115. Morristown, NJ ... 415,300
46. Jacksonville	1,140,100	116. Portsmouth-Dover-Rochester ... 414,500
47. West Palm Beach-Boca Raton	1,117,800	117. Victor Valley ... 412,900
48. Oklahoma City	1,099,900	118. Oxnard-Ventura ... 405,900
49. Memphis	1,069,400	119. Santa Rosa ... 403,900
50. Hartford-New Britain-Middletown	1,051,800	120. Ft. Collins-Greeley, CO ... 403,600
51. Monmouth-Ocean	1,033,700	121. Jackson, MS ... 397,600
52. Buffalo-Niagara Falls	966,000	122. Reno ... 393,800
53. Louisville	953,500	123. Bridgeport ... 393,400
54. Richmond	941,600	124. Pensacola ... 389,900
55. New Orleans	936,700	125. Lansing-East Lansing ... 389,200
56. Rochester, NY	932,800	126. Youngstown-Warren ... 387,500
57. Birmingham	886,400	127. Flint ... 360,300
58. McAllen-Brownsville-Harlingen	868,900	128. Fayetteville, NC ... 354,300
59. Greenville-Spartanburg	863,400	129. Canton ... 347,800
60. Tucson	839,600	130. Reading, PA ... 346,800
61. Ft. Myers-Naples-Marco Island	836,700	131. Palm Springs ... 346,400
62. Dayton	824,200	132. Fayetteville (North West Arkansas) ... 340,600
63. Albany-Schenectady-Troy	784,400	133. Shreveport ... 338,000
64. Honolulu	766,100	134. Saginaw-Bay City-Midland ... 331,100
65. Tulsa	747,400	135. Appleton-Oshkosh ... 326,800
66. Fresno	741,800	136. Springfield, MO ... 325,400
67. Grand Rapids	717,900	137. Corpus Christi ... 319,600
68. Albuquerque	701,300	138. Burlington-Plattsburgh ... 318,300
69. Allentown-Bethlehem	700,600	139. Newburgh-Middletown, NY (Mid-Hudson Valley) ... 318,100
70. Wilkes Barre-Scranton	682,900	140. Beaumont-Port Arthur, TX ... 316,600

141. Atlantic City-Cape May	315,200	221. Winchester, VA ... 165,700
142. Trenton	312,700	222. Las Cruces, NM ... 165,400
143. Salisbury-Ocean City	311,300	223. Bangor ... 164,100
144. Tyler-Longview	306,500	224. Olean, NY ... 163,000
145. Flagstaff-Prescott, AZ	306,200	224. Laurel-Hattiesburg, MS ... 162,300
146. Quad Cities (Davenport-Rock Island-Moline)	303,800	226. Alexandria, LA ... 161,700
147. Eugene-Springfield	303,100	227. Ft. Walton Beach, FL ... 159,400
148. Ann Arbor	303,000	228. Elmira-Corning, NY ... 158,400
149. Rockford	301,500	229. La Crosse, WI ... 157,600
150. Stamford-Norwalk, CT	300,600	230. Redding, CA ... 157,200
151. Fredericksburg	299,500	231. Charlottesville, VA ... 156,500
152. Peoria	299,000	232. Lake Charles, LA ... 154,200
153. Montgomery	298,400	233. Tuscaloosa, AL ... 153,700
154. Killeen-Temple, TX	292,200	234. Rochester, MN ... 152,900
155. Biloxi-Gulfport-Pascagoula	291,800	235. Bryan-College Station, TX ... 147,000
156. Macon	284,300	236. Muskegon, MI ... 146,800
157. Savannah	280,300	237. Joplin, MO ... 144,700
158. Myrtle Beach, SC	278,600	238. Twin Falls (Sun Valley), ID ... 144,600
159. Asheville	267,200	239. Panama City, FL ... 142,500
160. Huntington-Ashland	267,000	240. Lafayette, IN ... 142,100
161. Wilmington, NC	259,900	241. Bloomington ... 141,600
162. Tallahassee	259,100	242. Marion-Carbondale (Southern IL) ... 141,400
163. Evansville	258,300	243. Dubuque, IA ... 141,300
164. Utica-Rome	254,900	244. Eau Claire, WI ... 137,800
165. Poughkeepsie, NY	253,600	245. Pittsburg, KS (Southeast Kansas) ... 134,200
166. Hagerstown-Chambersburg-Waynesboro, MD-PA	250,000	246. Abilene, TX ... 133,600
167. Portland, ME	239,300	247. Pueblo ... 133,200
168. Wausau-Stevens Point, WI (Central WI)	237,700	248. Columbia, MO ... 132,700
169. Erie	237,400	249. LaSalle-Peru, IL ... 131,600
170. Concord (Lakes Region)	237,300	250. Sussex, NJ ... 130,800
171. Anchorage	236,900	251. State College, PA ... 130,500
172. Lincoln	234,300	252. Waterloo-Cedar Falls ... 129,000
173. San Luis Obispo, CA	233,600	253. Lufkin-Nacogdoches, TX ... 128,800
174. New London, CT	229,700	254. Lima, OH ... 126,600
175. Ft. Smith, AR	228,000	255. Parkersburg-Marietta, WV-OH ... 126,600
176. Wenatchee, WA	227,900	256. Wheeling ... 126,000
177. Morgantown-Clarksburg-Fairmont, WV	226,700	257. Florence-Muscle Shoals, AL ... 124,100
178. South Bend	221,600	258. Monroe, LA ... 124,100
179. New Bedford-Fall River, MA	221,400	259. Grand Junction, CO ... 123,000
180. Merced, CA	218,900	260. Billings, MT ... 119,900
181. Lubbock	216,400	261. Kalispell-Flathead Valley, MT ... 117,400
182. Binghamton	213,800	262. Hamptons-Riverhead ... 116,400
183. Lebanon-Rutland-White River Junction	212,300	263. Texarkana, TX-AR ... 115,200
184. Odessa-Midland, TX	211,700	264. Battle Creek, MI ... 114,400
185. Charleston, WV	210,200	265. Wichita Falls, TX ... 114,300
186. Kalamazoo	208,800	266. Grand Island-Kearney, NE ... 112,200
187. Green Bay	206,300	267. Valdosta, GA ... 109,600
188. Columbus, GA	204,900	268. Altoona ... 107,800
189. Tupelo, MS	200,600	269. Montpelier-Barre-St. Johnsbury ... 107,800
190. Dothan, AL	199,400	270. Albany, GA ... 107,600
191. Manchester	198,200	271. Augusta-Waterville, ME ... 105,800
192. Traverse City-Petoskey, MI	197,100	272. Harrisonburg, VA ... 104,200
193. Cape Cod, MA	196,800	273. Columbus-Starkville-West Point, MS ... 103,300
194. Amarillo, TX	195,300	274. Mankato-New Ulm-St. Peter, MN ... 101,900
195. Clarksville-Hopkinsville, TN-KY	193,500	275. Rapid City, SD ... 100,800
196. Tri-Cities, WA (Richland-Kennewick-Pasco)	193,100	276. Williamsport, PA ... 100,700
197. Topeka	193,000	277. Elkins-Buckhannon-Weston, WV ... 100,000
198. Frederick, MD	192,000	277. Sioux City, IA ... 99,300
199. Waco, TX	191,000	279. Watertown, NY ... 99,100
200. Chico, CA	190,800	280. Sheboygan, WI ... 98,900
201. Danbury, CT	190,000	281. Lawton, OK ... 91,900
202. Rocky Mount-Wilson, NC	188,300	282. Decatur, IL ... 91,800
203. Salina-Manhattan, KS	188,200	283. Ithaca, NY ... 91,600
204. Yakima, WA	187,600	284. Lewiston-Auburn, ME ... 91,600
205. Bend, OR	182,300	285. Bismarck, ND ... 90,600
206. Laredo, TX	179,200	286. Bluefield, WV ... 90,300
207. Bowling Green, KY	177,000	287. Sebring, FL ... 88,800
208. Medford-Ashland, OR	176,900	288. Cookeville, TN ... 88,500
209. Terre Haute	175,100	289. San Angelo, TX ... 87,600
210. Cedar Rapids	174,900	290. Hot Springs, AR ... 84,600
211. Duluth-Superior	174,500	291. Grand Forks, ND-MN ... 83,800
212. Santa Maria-Lompoc, CA	174,400	292. Jackson, TN ... 81,400
213. Hilton Head, SC	172,100	293. Jonesboro, AR ... 78,200
214. Santa Barbara	172,100	294. Cheyenne, WY ... 72,900
215. Muncie-Marion, IN	168,800	295. Beckley, WV ... 68,900
216. St. Cloud, MN	167,900	296. Mason City, IA ... 67,600
217. Florence, SC	167,200	297. Clovis, NM ... 65,500
218. Fargo-Moorhead	167,000	298. Brunswick, GA ... 64,400
219. Sunbury-Selinsgrove-Lewisburg, PA	166,300	299. Meridian, MS ... 63,200
220. Champaign, IL	166,000	300. Casper, WY ... 61,600

U.S. Radio Markets

Abilene, TX: Rank 246
American Family Radio KAQD(FM)
Cumulus Media Inc. KBCY(FM), KCDD(FM), KHXS-FM, KTLT(FM)
Graham Newspapers Inc. KLXK(FM), KROO(AM)
EMF Broadcasting KAGT(FM)
Weston Entertainment L.P. KVRP, KVRP-FM
Canfin Enterprises Inc. KKHR-FM, KWKC(AM), KZQQ(AM)
GAP Broadcasting LLC KEAN-FM, KEYJ-FM, KFGL(FM), KSLI(AM), KULL-FM, KYYW(AM)

Akron, OH: Rank 75
Clear Channel Communications Inc. WARF(AM), WHLO
Family Stations Inc. WCUE
Rubber City Radio Group Inc. WAKR, WQMX-FM WAKS(FM), WJMP, WNIR-FM, WONE-FM

Albany, GA: Rank 270
Clear Channel Communications Inc. WJIZ-FM, WJYZ, WOBB-FM, WRAK-FM
Cumulus Media Inc. WALG, WEGC-FM, WGPC, WJAD-FM, WQVE(FM)
Good News Network WZIQ-FM
EMF Broadcasting WHKV(FM) WKAK-FM, WMTM-FM, WZBN(FM)

Albany-Schenectady-Troy, NY: Rank 63
ABC Inc. WDDY(AM)
Vox Communications WUPE(AM)
Clear Channel Communications Inc. WGY, WHRL-FM, WKKF(FM), WOFX(AM), WPYX-FM, WRVE-FM, WTRY-FM
Crawford Broadcasting Co. WDCD(AM), WPTR(FM)
Regent Communications Inc. WBZZ(FM), WGNA-FM, WQBJ-FM, WQBK-FM, WTMM-FM
WAMC/Northeast Public Radio WAMC(AM), WAMC-FM, WCAN-FM
Pamal Broadcasting Ltd. WAJZ(FM), WENU(AM), WFLY-FM, WIZR, WKLI-FM, WROW(AM), WYJB(FM), WZMR-FM
Capital Media Corp. WHAZ, WHAZ-FM, WMYY-FM
Anastos Media Group Inc. WABY(AM), WQAR-FM, WUAM(AM), WVKZ
EMF Broadcasting WYAI(FM), WYKV(FM) WGDJ(AM)
Roser Communications Network Inc. WBUG-FM, WVTL(AM)
Regional Radio Group LLC WCKM-FM

Albuquerque, NM: Rank 68
Wilkins Communications Network Inc. KXKS(AM)
ABC Inc. KALY
Citadel Broadcasting Corp. KDRF(FM), KKOB(AM), KKOB-FM, KNML(AM), KRST-FM, KTBL(AM)
Clear Channel Communications Inc. KABQ, KBQI(FM), KPEK-FM, KTEG(FM), KZRR-FM
Family Life Communications Inc. KFLQ(FM)
Univision Radio KJFA(FM), KKRG(FM), KKSS-FM
American General Media KABG(FM), KAGM(FM), KARS, KDLW(FM), KHFM(AM), KKIM
Entravision Communications Corp. KRZY, KRZY-FM
Four Corners Broadcasting L.L.C. KIQX(FM)
EMF Broadcasting KQRI(FM) KABQ-FM, KBZU(FM), KIOT-FM, KKNS(AM), KQTM(FM)

Alexandria, LA: Rank 226
Wilkins Communications Network Inc. KWDF
American Family Radio KAPM(FM)
The Radio Group KAPB-FM
Opus Media Holdings LLC KBKK(FM), KEZP-FM, KLAA-FM
EMF Broadcasting KLXA-FM
Radio Maria Inc. KJMJ(AM)
Cenla Broadcasting Co. Inc. KDBS, KKST-FM, KQID-FM, KRRV-FM, KSYL, KZMZ-FM

Allentown-Bethlehem, PA: Rank 69
Citadel Broadcasting Corp. WCTO-FM, WLEV-FM
Clear Channel Communications Inc. WAEB, WSAN(AM), WZZO-FM
J-Systems Franchising Corp. WLSH
Nassau Broadcasting Partners L.P. WBYN(AM), WEEX, WODE-FM, WTKZ, WWYY-FM WAEB-FM

Altoona, PA: Rank 268
Allegheny Mountain Network Stations WTRN
Forever Broadcasting WALY-FM, WFBG, WRKY-FM, WVAM, WWOT(FM)
Vernal Enterprises Inc. WHPA(FM) WFGY-FM, WJSM-FM, WKMC, WWBJ(AM)

Amarillo, TX: Rank 194
American Family Radio KAVW(FM)
Family Life Communications Inc. KRGN-FM
Morris Radio LLC KGNC, KGNC-FM
Cumulus Media Inc. KARX(FM), KPUR, KPUR-FM, KQIZ-FM, KZRK(AM), KZRK-FM
Tejas Broadcasting Ltd. LLP KBZD(FM), KQFX-FM, KTNZ

EMF Broadcasting KXLV(FM), KXRI(FM)
GAP Broadcasting LLC KATP(FM), KIXZ, KMXJ-FM, KPRF(FM), KXSS-FM

Anchorage, AK: Rank 171
New Northwest Broadcasters LLC KBBO-FM, KDBZ(FM), KFAT(FM)
Clear Channel Communications Inc. KASH-FM, KBFX(FM), KENI, KGOT-FM, KTZN, KYMG-FM
Morris Radio LLC KAYO(FM), KBRJ(FM), KEAG-FM, KFQD, KHAR, KMXS-FM, KWHL-FM
EMF Broadcasting KAKL(FM) KLEF-FM, KOAN(AM), KUDO(AM), KZND-FM
World Radio Link Inc. KMVV(FM)

Ann Arbor, MI: Rank 148
Birach Broadcasting Corp. WSDS(AM)
Clear Channel Communications Inc. WLBY(AM), WTKA, WWWW-FM WAAM, WDEO(AM), WQKL(FM)

Appleton-Oshkosh, WI: Rank 135
Clear Channel Communications Inc. WOGB-FM
Evangel Ministries Inc. WEMI(FM)
Midwest Communications Inc. WNCY-FM, WOZZ-FM, WROE-FM
VCY America Inc. WVCY
Woodward Communications Inc. WAPL(FM), WHBY(AM), WSCO(AM)
Cumulus Media Inc. WNAM, WOSH, WPKR-FM
Relevant Radio WJOK, WOVM(FM)
Mountain Dog Media WFON(FM)
Results Broadcasting WJMQ(FM), WOTE(AM) WVBO-FM, WWWX-FM

Asheville, NC: Rank 159
Wilkins Communications Network Inc. WSKY(AM)
Clear Channel Communications Inc. WPEK(AM), WQNQ(FM), WQNS-FM, WWNC
Saga Communications Inc. WTMT(FM), WYSE(AM) WFGW, WKSF-FM, WMIT-FM
HRN Broadcasting Inc. WZGM(AM)

Atlanta, GA: Rank 7
Beasley Broadcast Group Inc. WAEC, WWWE(AM)
ABC Inc. WDWD
Citadel Broadcasting Corp. WKHX-FM, WYAY-FM
Clear Channel Communications Inc. WBZY(FM), WCOH, WGST, WKLS(FM), WUBL(FM), WWLG(FM), WWVA-FM
Cox Radio Inc. WALR-FM, WBTS-FM, WSB, WSB-FM, WSRV(FM)
Davis Broadcasting Inc. WCHK, WLKQ-FM
GHB Radio Group WYZE
CBS Radio WAOK, WZGC(FM)
Lincoln Financial Media WQXI, WSTR-FM
Salem Communications Corp. WAFS(AM), WFSH-FM, WGKA(AM), WLTA, WNIV
Cumulus Media Partners LLC WNNX(FM), WWWQ(FM)
Jacobs Media Corp. WGGA(AM)
Willis Broadcasting Corp. WTJH
Multicultural Radio Broadcasting Inc. WGFS
Radio One Inc. WAMJ(FM), WHTA(FM), WPZE(FM), WUMJ(FM)
Sheridan Broadcasting Corp. WIGO(AM)
Dickey Broadcasting Co. WALR, WCNN, WFOM WVEE-FM, WVFJ-FM, WXJO(AM)
Prieto Broadcasting Inc. WFTD

Atlantic City-Cape May, NJ: Rank 141
Equity Communications LP WAIV(FM), WAYV(FM), WCMC(AM), WEZW(FM), WMID(AM), WSNQ(FM), WTTH(FM), WZBZ(FM), WZXL(FM)
Access.1 Communications Corp. WGYM(AM)
Millennium Radio Group LLC WENJ(AM), WENJ-FM, WFPG(FM), WPUR-FM, WSJO(FM)
Press Communications L.L.C. WBBO(FM) WCZT(FM), WIBG-FM, WKOE(FM)
Atlantic Broadcasting WJSE-FM, WMGM(FM), WOND(AM), WTAA(AM), WTKU-FM

Augusta, GA: Rank 110
Wilkins Communications Network Inc. WFAM(AM)
Beasley Broadcast Group Inc. WCHZ-FM, WDRR(FM), WGAC, WGAC-FM, WGUS(AM), WGUS-FM, WHHD(FM), WKXC-FM, WRDW(AM)
Bible Broadcasting Network WYFA-FM
Clear Channel Communications Inc. WBBQ-FM, WEKL(FM), WKSP(FM), WPRW-FM, WSGF(AM), WYNF(AM)
Perry Publishing & Broadcasting Co. WAEG-FM, WAKB(FM), WFXA-FM, WTHB, WTHB-FM WIBL(FM), WKSX-FM, WLPE(FM), WNRR(AM), WTHO-FM, WTWA

Augusta-Waterville, ME: Rank 271

Citadel Broadcasting Corp. WEBB-FM, WJZN(AM), WMME-FM, WTVL(AM)
Mountain Wireless Inc. WCTB-FM, WFMX(FM), WSKW
Blueberry Broadcasting LLC WABK-FM, WFAU, WTOS-FM, WVQM(FM)

Austin, TX: Rank 39
Clear Channel Communications Inc. KASE-FM, KHFI-FM, KPEZ-FM, KVET, KVET-FM
Emmis Communications Corp. KBPA(FM), KDHT(FM), KGSR-FM, KLBJ, KLBJ-FM, KROX-FM
Entercom Communications Corp. KAMX(FM), KJCE, KKMJ-FM, KLQB(FM)
Univision Radio KHZS(FM)
Houston Christian Broadcasters Inc. KHIB(FM)
Simmons Media Group KWNX(AM), KZNX(AM)
Relevant Radio KIXL(AM)
EMF Broadcasting KYLR(FM)
Border Media Partners LLC KFON, KHHL(FM), KXBT(FM), KXXS(FM) KFMK-FM
Encino Broadcasting LLC KELG(AM), KTXZ

Bakersfield, CA: Rank 74
Buckley Broadcasting Corp. KKBB-FM, KLLY-FM, KNZR, KSMJ(FM)
Clear Channel Communications Inc. KBFP(AM), KBFP-FM, KDFO(FM), KHTY(AM), KRAB-FM
Family Stations Inc. KFRB-FM
Lotus Communications Corp. KCHJ, KIWI(FM), KPSL-FM, KVMX(FM), KWAC
Buck Owens Productions Inc. KCWR(FM), KUZZ, KUZZ-FM
American General Media KEBT(FM), KERI(AM), KERN(AM), KGEO, KGFM-FM, KISV(FM), KKXX-FM
Gore-Overgaard Broadcasting Inc. KLHC(AM)
Lazer Broadcasting Corp. KEAL(AM), KXTT(FM)
IHR Educational Broadcasting KJPG(AM) KQAB, KVLI-FM

Baltimore, MD: Rank 22
Clear Channel Communications Inc. WCAO, WCHH(FM), WPOC-FM, WQSR(FM)
Family Stations Inc. WBGR, WBMD
CBS Radio WJZ(AM), WJZ-FM, WLIF-FM, WWMX-FM
Salem Communications Corp. WAMD
Shamrock Communications Inc. WZBA(FM)
Radio One Inc. WERQ-FM, WOLB(AM), WWIN, WWIN-FM WBAL, WFBR(AM), WIYY-FM, WRBS(AM), WTTR(AM)

Bangor, ME: Rank 223
The Zone Corp. WKIT-FM, WZON
Cumulus Media Inc. WBZN-FM, WEZQ-FM, WQCB-FM
EMF Broadcasting WKVZ(FM) WFGO(AM), WNSX(FM), WNZS(AM), WSYY(AM), WSYY-FM, WWMJ-FM, WWNZ(AM)
Charles A. Hecht and Alfredo Alonso Stns WRME(AM)
Blueberry Broadcasting LLC WAEI(AM), WAEI-FM, WBFB-FM, WKSQ-FM, WVOM-FM

Baton Rouge, LA: Rank 78
Citadel Broadcasting Corp. KQXL-FM, KRDJ(FM), WCDV-FM, WEMX-FM, WIBR, WXOK
Clear Channel Communications Inc. KRVE-FM, WFMF(FM), WJBO, WSKR, WYNK-FM
Communications Capital Managers LLC WUBR(AM)
Family Worship Center Church Inc. WJFM-FM
EMF Broadcasting WBKL(FM)
Guaranty Broadcasting Co. of Baton Rouge, LLC KNXX(FM), WDGL(FM), WNXX(FM), WTGE(FM), WYPY(FM)
Davidson Media Group LLC WPYR(AM) KBRH, WBRH-FM

Battle Creek, MI: Rank 264
Clear Channel Communications Inc. WBCK-FM, WBXX(FM)
Family Life Communications Inc. WUFN(FM) WBCK, WBFN(AM)

Beaumont-Port Arthur, TX: Rank 140
Birach Broadcasting Corp. KOLE
Clear Channel Communications Inc. KCOL-FM, KIOC-FM, KKMY-FM, KLVI, KYKR-FM
Family Stations Inc. KTXB-FM
Martin Broadcasting Inc. KZZB
Univision Radio KPTY(FM)
Cumulus Media Inc. KAYD-FM, KBED(AM), KIKR, KQXY-FM, KTCX-FM
Radio Maria Inc. KDEI(AM)

Beckley, WV: Rank 295
Southern Communications Corp. WAXS-FM, WCIR-FM, WIWS, WMTD, WMTD-FM, WTNJ-FM, WWNR
First Media Radio LLC WJLS, WJLS-FM

Bend, OR: Rank 205
Horizon Broadcasting Group LLC KLTW-FM, KQAK(FM), KRCO(AM), KWLZ-FM, KWPK-FM

Billings, MT: Rank 260
New Northwest Broadcasters LLC KGHL, KGHL-FM, KQBL(FM), KRPM(FM), KRSQ-FM
Chaparral Communications KWMY(FM)
EMF Broadcasting KBIL(FM), KLRV(FM)
Cherry Creek Radio LLC KBLG, KRKX(FM), KRZN(FM), KYYA-FM
Connoisseur Media LLC KPBR(FM), KPLN(FM)
Sun Mountain Inc. KBSR
GAPWEST Broadcasting KBBB(FM), KBUL, KCTR-FM, KKBR-FM, KMHK-FM

Biloxi-Gulfport-Pascagoula, MS: Rank 155
American Family Radio WAOY-FM
Clear Channel Communications Inc. WBUV(FM), WKNN-FM, WMJY-FM, WQYZ-FM
Triad Broadcasting Co. L.L.C. WCPR-FM, WHGO(FM), WTNI(AM), WUJM(FM), WXBD, WXYK-FM WGCM, WGCM-FM, WZKX(FM)
Walking by Faith Ministries Inc. WQFX

Binghamton, NY: Rank 182
Citadel Broadcasting Corp. WHWK-FM, WNBF, WWYL(FM), WYOS(AM)
Clear Channel Communications Inc. WBBI(FM), WENE(AM), WINR, WKGB-FM, WMRV-FM, WMXW-FM
CSN International WIFF(FM)
Double O Radio L.L.C. WIYN-FM WAAL-FM

Birmingham, AL: Rank 57
Citadel Broadcasting Corp. WAPI, WFFN-FM, WJOX(FM), WSPZ(AM), WUHT(FM), WZRR-FM
Clear Channel Communications Inc. WDXB(FM), WERC, WERC-FM, WMJJ-FM, WQEN(FM)
Cox Radio Inc. WAGG(AM), WBHJ(FM), WBHK-FM, WBPT(FM), WENN(AM), WNCB(FM), WZZK-FM
Crawford Broadcasting Co. WDJC-FM, WXJC(AM), WXJC-FM, WYDE(AM), WYDE-FM
Family Stations Inc. WBFR-FM
Sheridan Broadcasting Corp. WATV(AM)
Davidson Media Group LLC WAYE WCRL, WJLX(AM), WKLD-FM, WQOH(AM)

Bismarck, ND: Rank 285
Clear Channel Communications Inc. KBMR, KFYR, KQDY(FM), KSSS-FM, KXMR, KYYY-FM
Family Stations Inc. KBFR(FM)
Cumulus Media Inc. KACL(FM), KBYZ(FM), KKCT-FM, KLXX, KUSB(FM)
EMF Broadcasting KNRI(FM)
Connoisseur Media LLC KKBO(FM)
World Radio Link Inc. KXRV(FM)

Bloomington, IL: Rank 241
Regent Communications Inc. WBNQ-FM, WBWN-FM, WJBC
Connoisseur Media LLC WIHN-FM
Great Plains Media Inc. WYST(FM)

Bluefield, WV: Rank 286
Baker Family Stations WAMN
Triad Broadcasting Co. L.L.C. WBDY, WHAJ-FM, WHIS, WHQX-FM, WKEZ, WKOY-FM, WTZE WAEY, WGTH, WGTH-FM, WHKX-FM, WKQY-FM, WSTG-FM

Boise, ID: Rank 100
Citadel Broadcasting Corp. KBOI, KIZN-FM, KKGL-FM, KQFC-FM, KTIK, KZMG(FM)
Journal Communications Inc. KCID(AM), KGEM(AM), KJOT(FM), KQXR-FM, KRVB(FM), KTHI(FM)
KSPD Inc. KBXL(FM), KSPD KWEI(AM), KWEI-FM
FM Idaho Co. LLC KPDA(FM), KQLZ(FM), KSRV-FM, KWYD(FM)
Peak Broadcasting LLC KAWO(FM), KCIX(FM), KFXD(AM), KIDO(AM), KSAS-FM, KXLT-FM

Boston: Rank 10
Beasley Broadcast Group Inc. WRCA
ABC Inc. WMKI(AM)
Clear Channel Communications Inc. WJMN-FM, WKOX, WXKS, WXKS-FM
Entercom Communications Corp. WAAF(FM), WEEI, WKAF(FM), WMKK(FM), WRKO
Greater Media Inc. WBOS-FM, WKLB-FM, WMJX-FM, WROR-FM, WTKK(FM)
CBS Radio WBMX(FM), WBZ, WBZ-FM, WODS-FM, WZLX-FM
Northeast Broadcasting Company Inc. WXRV(FM)
Salem Communications Corp. WEZE, WROL, WWDJ(AM)
Nassau Broadcasting Partners L.P. WCRB(FM)
Langer Broadcasting Group L.L.C. WBIX(AM), WSRO(AM)
Multicultural Radio Broadcasting Inc. WAZN(AM), WLYN
Costa-Eagle Radio Ventures L.P. WCEC(AM), WNNW(AM)
Radio One Inc. WILD
Rose City Radio Corp. WWZN(AM)
Phoenix Media Communications Group WFEX(FM), WFNX(FM) WAMG(AM), WJIB, WLLH, WPLM, WPLM-FM
BusinessTalkRadio.Net Inc. WXBR(AM)

Bowling Green, KY: Rank 207
Commonwealth Broadcasting Corp. WHHT(FM), WOVO(FM), WPTQ(FM), WWKU(AM)
Forever Communications Inc. WBGN(AM), WBVR-FM, WLYE-FM, WUHU(AM) WDNS(FM), WKCT(AM), WLCK(AM), WVLE(FM)

Bridgeport, CT: Rank 123
Blount Communications Group WFIF
Cox Radio Inc. WEZN-FM
Cumulus Media Inc. WICC

Brunswick, GA: Rank 298
Qantum Communications Corp. WBGA(FM), WGIG(AM), WHFX(FM), WMOG, WWSN-FM, WYNR(FM)
MarMac Communications LLC WSFN

Bryan-College Station, TX: Rank 235
American Family Radio KLGS(FM)
Clear Channel Communications Inc. KAGG(FM), KKYS-FM, KNFX-FM
Brazos Valley Communications Ltd. KBXT(FM), KJXJ(FM), KORA-FM, KTAM(AM)
Bryan Broadcasting Corp. KNDE(FM), KZNE(AM), WTAW(AM) KTTX-FM, KWUP(FM)

Buffalo-Niagara Falls, NY: Rank 52
Citadel Broadcasting Corp. WBBF(AM), WEDG-FM, WGRF-FM, WHLD, WHTT-FM
Crawford Broadcasting Co. WDCX-FM
Entercom Communications Corp. WBEN, WGR, WKSE-FM, WLKK(FM), WWKB, WWWS
Family Stations Inc. WFBF-FM
Regent Communications Inc. WBLK-FM, WBUF(FM), WJYE-FM, WYRK-FM
Corus Entertainment Inc. CFNY-FM
Sheridan Broadcasting Corp. WUFO WECK, WNED, WNED-FM, WTSS(FM)

Burlington-Plattsburgh, VT-NY: Rank 138
Hall Communications Inc. WBTZ-FM, WIZN-FM, WJOY(AM), WKOL-FM, WOKO-FM
Northeast Broadcasting Company Inc. WCAT(AM), WTWK(AM), WWMP(FM)
Radio Vermont Group Inc. WCVT-FM, WDEV-FM WLFE-FM
Radioactive LLC WNMR(FM), WYME(FM)
Charles A. Hecht and Alfredo Alonso Stns WVVT(AM)
Vox AM/FM LLC WCPV-FM, WEAV, WEZF-FM, WVTK(FM), WXZO(FM)

Canton, OH: Rank 129
Clear Channel Communications Inc. WHOF(FM), WKDD(FM), WRQK-FM
NextMedia Group Inc. WHBC, WHBC-FM WDJQ(FM), WDPN

Cape Cod, MA: Rank 193
Nassau Broadcasting Partners L.P. WFQR(FM), WFRQ(FM), WPXC-FM
Sandab Communications L.P. II WFCC-FM, WKPE-FM, WOCN-FM, WQRC(FM)
Qantum Communications Corp. WCIB(FM), WCOD(FM), WEII(FM), WXTK-FM

Casper, WY: Rank 300
Northeast Broadcasting Company Inc. KTED(FM), KZQL(FM)
Mt. Rushmore Broadcasting Inc. KASS(FM), KHOC-FM, KMLD(FM), KQLT-FM, KVOC
Cochise Broadcasting LLC KWYX(FM)
GAPWEST Broadcasting KKTL, KMGW(FM), KRVK(FM), KTRS-FM, KTWO, KWYY(FM)

Cedar Rapids, IA: Rank 210
Clear Channel Communications Inc. KKRQ-FM, KKSY(FM), KMJM(AM), KXIC, WMT, WMT-FM
Cumulus Media Inc. KDAT(FM), KHAK(FM), KRNA(FM) KGYM(AM)

Champaign, IL: Rank 220
Illinois Bible Institute Inc. WBGL-FM
Saga Communications Inc. WCFF(FM), WIXY-FM, WLRW-FM, WXTT(FM) WDWS(AM), WHMS-FM, WILL(AM), WILL-FM
RadioStar Inc. WEBX-FM, WGKC-FM, WLFH(FM), WQQB(FM)

Charleston, SC: Rank 84
Bible Broadcasting Network WYFH-FM
Citadel Broadcasting Corp. WIWF(FM), WSSX-FM, WTMA, WWWZ-FM
Clear Channel Communications Inc. WEZL-FM, WRFQ(FM), WSCC-FM, WXLY-FM
Family Stations Inc. WFCH-FM
L M Communications Inc. WCOO(FM), WYBB-FM
Apex Broadcasting Inc. WAVF(FM), WIHB(FM), WIOP(FM), WSPO(AM), WXST(FM)
Glory Communications Inc. WTUA-FM
Kirkman Broadcasting Inc. WJKB(AM), WQNT(AM), WQSC, WTMZ
Jabar Communications Inc. WAZS(AM), WWIK(FM) WALC-FM, WLTQ(AM), WMGL(FM)

Charleston, WV: Rank 185
Baker Family Stations WIHY(AM)
L M Communications Inc. WJYP(AM), WKLC-FM, WMXE(FM), WSCW
Bristol Broadcasting Co. Inc. WBES(AM), WVTS(AM), WZJO(FM)
West Virginia Radio Corp. WCHS, WKAZ, WKAZ-FM, WKWS-FM, WRVZ-FM, WSWW, WVAF-FM WQBE-FM, WVSR-FM

Charlotte-Gastonia-Rock Hill, NC-SC: Rank 25
Bible Broadcasting Network WYFQ(AM)
ABC Inc. WGFY
Clear Channel Communications Inc. WEND-FM, WIBT(FM), WKKT-FM, WLYT-FM, WRFX(FM)
GHB Radio Group WAVO, WCGC, WEGO, WHVN, WOLS(FM)
Greater Media Inc. WBT, WBT-FM, WLNK(FM)
CBS Radio WBAV-FM, WBCN(AM), WFNZ, WKQC(FM), WNKS-FM, WPEG-FM, WSOC-FM
Our Three Sons Broadcasting L.L.P. WRHI(AM)
Radio One Inc. WQNC(FM)
Truth Broadcasting Corp. WCRU(AM)
Wisdom LLC WGIV(AM)
Davidson Media Group LLC WNOW WBZK, WRKB, WRNA, WTCG(AM)
Norsan Consulting and Management Inc. WGSP, WXNC(AM)
HRN Broadcasting Inc. WCSL, WGNC, WLON, WOHS

Charlottesville, VA: Rank 231
Baker Family Stations WKTR
Saga Communications Inc. WCNR(FM), WINA, WQMZ(FM), WVAX(AM), WWWV-FM
Piedmont Communications Inc. WOJL(FM)
Monticello Media LLC WCHV, WCYK-FM, WHTE-FM, WKAV, WWTJ(FM), WZGN(FM)

Chattanooga, TN: Rank 106
Wilkins Communications Network Inc. WLMR(FM)
Bahakel Communications WDEF, WDEF-FM, WDOD
Brewer Broadcasting Corp. WALV-FM, WJTT-FM, WMPZ-FM, WPLZ(FM)
Citadel Broadcasting Corp. WGOW, WGOW-FM, WOGT-FM
Clear Channel Communications Inc. WLND(FM), WRXR-FM, WURV(FM), WUSY-FM
Family Life Communications Inc. WJBP(FM)
The Moody Bible Institute of Chicago WMBW-FM WDOD-FM, WNOO(AM), WSDT, WSKZ-FM
3 Daughters Media Inc. WUUQ(FM), WUUS(AM)
North Georgia Radio Group L.P. WOCE(FM)

Cheyenne, WY: Rank 294
Clear Channel Communications Inc. KOLZ-FM, KXBG(FM)
Northeast Broadcasting Company Inc. KAZY(FM), KHAT(AM), KRAE, KRAN(FM)
Regent Communications Inc. KARS-FM, KKPL(FM)
EMF Broadcasting KAIX(FM) KOLT-FM, KRRR(FM)
GAPWEST Broadcasting KCGY(FM), KGAB, KIGN(FM), KLEN-FM
Cedar Cove Broadcasting Inc. KDNR(FM)

Chicago: Rank 3
Birach Broadcasting Corp. WNWI
Bonneville International Corporation WDRV(FM), WILV(FM), WTMX-FM, WWDV(FM)
ABC Inc. WMVP, WRDZ
Citadel Broadcasting Corp. WLS, WLS-FM
Clear Channel Communications Inc. WGCI-FM, WGRB(AM), WKSC-FM, WLIT-FM, WNUA-FM, WVAZ-FM, WVON(AM)
Crawford Broadcasting Co. WPWX(FM), WSRB(FM), WYCA(FM)
Emmis Communications Corp. WKQX-FM, WLUP-FM
Family Stations Inc. WJCH-FM
CBS Radio WBBM(AM), WBBM-FM, WCFS-FM, WJMK-FM, WSCR(AM), WUSN-FM, WXRT-FM
McNaughton-Jakle Stations WBIG, WRMN
The Moody Bible Institute of Chicago WMBI(AM), WMBI-FM
Newsweb Corp. WAIT(AM), WCFJ, WCPQ(FM), WCPT(AM), WCPT-FM, WNDZ, WSBC(AM)
NextMedia Group Inc. WCCQ-FM, WERV-FM, WJOL, WKRS, WLIP, WRXQ(FM), WSSR(FM), WWYW(FM), WXLC-FM, WZSR-FM
STARadio Corp. WYKT-FM
Salem Communications Corp. WIND, WYLL(AM)
Spanish Broadcasting System Inc. WLEY-FM
Univision Radio WOJO-FM, WPPN(FM), WRTO(AM), WVIV-FM, WVIX(FM)
Tribune Broadcasting Co. WGN(AM)
Polnet Communications Ltd. WEEF, WKTA, WNVR, WPJX(AM)
Relevant Radio WAUR, WNTD, WWCA
EMF Broadcasting WCLR(FM), WJKL(FM), WSRI(FM)
Porter County Broadcasting Corp. WAKE, WLJE-FM, WXRD-FM, WZVN-FM WIIL-FM

Chico, CA: Rank 200
Family Stations Inc. KHAP(FM)
Fritz Communications Inc. KBQB(FM), KCEZ(FM), KKCY-FM, KMJE-FM, KRQR-FM, KTHU(FM)
Mapleton Communications LLC KALF(FM), KFMF-FM, KQPT(FM), KZAP-FM
Deer Creek Broadcasting LLC KEWE(AM), KHHZ(FM), KHSL-FM, KMXI-FM, KPAY

Cincinnati, OH: Rank 28
Vernon R Baldwin Inc. WCNW, WMOH, WNLT-FM
Bonneville International Corporation WKRQ-FM, WREW(FM), WUBE-FM, WYGY(FM)
Clear Channel Communications Inc. WCKY(AM), WEBN(FM), WKFS-FM, WKRC, WLW, WSAI(AM)
Pillar of Fire Inc. WAKW-FM
Cumulus Media Partners LLC WFTK(FM), WGRR-FM, WRRM-FM
Cumulus Media Inc. WNNF(FM), WOFX-FM
Christian Broadcasting System Ltd. WCVX(AM), WQRT(AM)
Radio One Inc. WDBZ(AM), WIZF-FM
First Broadcast Operating Inc. WAOL-FM, WOXY-FM
EMF Broadcasting WORI(FM)
Davidson Media Group LLC WCVG
Wagon Wheel Broadcasting LLC WSCH-FM

Clarksville-Hopkinsville, TN-KY: Rank 195
Key Broadcasting Inc. WHOP(AM), WHOP-FM
Saga Communications Inc. WEGI-FM, WVVR(FM)

Cleveland, OH: Rank 29
ABC Inc. WWMK
Clear Channel Communications Inc. WGAR-FM, WMJI-FM, WMMS-FM, WMVX-FM, WTAM
CBS Radio WDOK-FM, WKRK-FM, WNCX(FM), WQAL-FM
The Moody Bible Institute of Chicago WCRF-FM
Salem Communications Corp. WFHM-FM, WHK(AM), WHKW(AM)
Elyria-Lorain Broadcasting Co. WEOL, WNWV-FM
Good Karma Broadcasting L.L.C. WKNR(AM), WWGK(AM)
Radio One Inc. WENZ-FM, WERE(AM), WJMO(AM), WZAK-FM WCCD(AM)

Clovis, NM: Rank 297

Colorado Springs, CO: Rank 94
Bahakel Communications KILO-FM
Citadel Broadcasting Corp. KATC-FM, KCSF(AM), KKFM-FM, KKMG-FM, KKPK(FM), KVOR
Clear Channel Communications Inc. KIBT(FM), KKLI-FM, KVUU-FM
Crawford Broadcasting Co. KCBR, KCMN
Salem Communications Corp. KBIQ(FM), KGFT-FM, KZNT(AM)
News-Press & Gazette Co. KRDO(AM)
Pilgrim Communications Inc. KKKK(AM)
Latino Communications LLC KXRE(AM)

Columbia, MO: Rank 248
The Curators of the University of Missouri KBIA(FM)
Cumulus Media Inc. KBXR(FM), KFRU, KOQL-FM, KPLA(FM)
Best Broadcast Group KZZT-FM KATI(FM), KCMQ(FM), KFAL, KTGR, KTXY-FM, KWRT(AM), KWWR-FM

Columbia, SC: Rank 89
Bible Broadcasting Network WYFV-FM
Citadel Broadcasting Corp. WISW, WLXC(FM), WNKT(FM), WOMG(FM), WTCB-FM
Clear Channel Communications Inc. WCOS, WLTY-FM, WNOK(FM), WVOC, WXBT(FM)
Inner City Broadcasting WARQ(FM), WHXT-FM, WMFX(FM), WOIC(AM), WWDM(FM), WZMJ-FM
Miller Communications Inc. WIGL(FM)
Glory Communications Inc. WFMV(FM), WGCV(AM), WQXL
Double O Radio L.L.C. WWNQ(FM), WWNU(FM) WBLR, WCOS-FM, WPOG(AM)
Norsan Consulting and Management Inc. WCEO(AM)

Columbus, GA: Rank 188
Bible Broadcasting Network WYFK-FM
Clear Channel Communications Inc. WBFA(FM), WDAK, WGSY-FM, WHAL(AM), WSHE(AM), WSTH-FM, WVRK-FM
Davis Broadcasting Inc. WEAM, WEAM-FM, WIOL(FM), WKZJ(FM), WOKS
Family Stations Inc. WFRC-FM WFXE-FM
PMB Broadcasting LLC WCGQ-FM, WKCN-FM, WRCG, WRLD-FM

Columbus, OH: Rank 36
American Family Radio WWGV(FM)
Clear Channel Communications Inc. WBWR(FM), WCOL-FM, WKKJ(FM), WLZT(FM), WNCI-FM, WRXS(FM), WTVN(AM), WYTS(AM)
Dispatch Broadcast Group WBNS, WBNS-FM
Saga Communications Inc. WJZA(FM), WODB(FM), WSNY(FM), WVMX(FM)
Radio One Inc. WCKX-FM, WJYD(FM), WXMG-FM
North American Broadcasting Co. Inc. WMNI, WRKZ(FM), WTDA(FM) WCLT(AM), WCLT-FM, WOSU, WOSU-FM
Wilks Broadcast Group LLC WHOK-FM, WLVQ(FM), WNKK(FM)
Christian Voice of Central Ohio Inc. WRFD(AM)
Bernard Radio LLC WVKO, WVKO-FM
BAS Broadcasting Inc. WQIO-FM

Columbus-Starkville-West Point, MS: Rank 273
Air South Radio Inc. WLZA(FM)
American Family Radio WCSO(FM), WJZB(FM)

Cumulus Media Inc. WJWF(AM), WKOR(AM), WKOR-FM, WNMQ(FM), WSMS(FM), WSSO(AM)
TeleSouth Communications Inc. WROB(AM) WKBB(FM), WTWG(AM)
Urban Radio Licenses LLC WACR-FM, WMSU(FM)

Concord (Lake Regions), NH: Rank 170
Citadel Broadcasting Corp. WPKQ(FM)

Cookeville, TN: Rank 288
JWC Broadcasting WKXD-FM
Great Plains Media Inc. WGIC-FM, WGSQ-FM, WHUB, WPTN

Corpus Christi, TX: Rank 137
Clear Channel Communications Inc. KKTX(AM), KMXR-FM, KNCN-FM, KRYS-FM, KSAB-FM, KUNO
Malkan Broadcast Associates KEYS(AM), KKBA(FM), KZFM(FM)
World Radio Network Inc. KBNJ(FM)
Tejas Broadcasting Ltd. LLP KLHB(FM), KLTG-FM, KMJR(FM), KOUL-FM
EMF Broadcasting KKLM(FM), KKWV(FM)
Convergent Broadcasting LLC KKPN(FM), KPUS(FM), KRSR(FM)
Claro Communications Ltd. KMZZ(FM), KROB(AM)

Dallas-Fort Worth: Rank 5
ABC Inc. KESN(FM), KMKI
Citadel Broadcasting Corp. KPMZ(FM), KSCS-FM, WBAP
Clear Channel Communications Inc. KDGE(FM), KDMX(FM), KEGL-FM, KFXR(AM), KHKS-FM, KZPS-FM
Crawford Broadcasting Co. KAAM(AM)
Criswell Communications KCBI(FM)
CBS Radio KJKK(FM), KLUV(FM), KMVK(FM), KRLD, KRLD-FM, KVIL(FM)
Mortenson Broadcasting Co. KGGR, KHVN, KKGM(AM), KRVA, KTNO(AM)
NextMedia Group Inc. KLAK(FM)
Salem Communications Corp. KLTY(FM), KSKY(AM)
Cumulus Media Partners LLC KDBN(FM), KKLF(AM), KLIF(AM), KPLX(FM), KTCK, KTDK(FM)
Univision Radio KDXX(FM), KFLC(AM), KFZO(FM), KLNO(FM)
CSN International KDKR(FM)
Service Broadcasting Group LLC KKDA, KKDA-FM, KRNB-FM
Liberman Broadcasting Inc. KBOC(FM), KNOR(FM), KTCY(FM), KZMP(AM), KZMP-FM, KZZA(FM)
Multicultural Radio Broadcasting Inc. KDFT, KMNY(AM)
James Crystal Inc. KNIT(AM)
Radio One Inc. KBFB(FM), KSOC(FM)
LKCM Radio Group L.P. KFWR(FM), KRVA-FM, KRVF(FM), KTFW-FM
SIGA Broadcasting Corp. KFJZ, KHFX(AM) KATH(AM), KCLE(AM), KHYI-FM, KJON(AM), KJSA, KVCE(AM)
Bernard Radio LLC KHSE(AM)

Danbury, CT: Rank 201
Berkshire Broadcasting Corp. WDAQ(FM), WLAD, WREF(AM)
Cumulus Media Inc. WDBY(FM), WINE, WRKI-FM

Dayton, OH: Rank 62
Brewer Broadcasting Corp. WQLK-FM
Clear Channel Communications Inc. WIZE, WLQT-FM, WMMX-FM, WONE, WTUE-FM, WXEG-FM
Cox Radio Inc. WHIO, WHIO-FM, WHKO-FM, WZLR-FM
Radio Stations WPAY/WPFB Inc. WPFB, WPFB-FM
EMF Broadcasting WOKL(FM), WQRP-FM
Radio Maria Inc. WULM(AM), WDKF(FM)
Main Line Broadcasting LLC WDHT(FM), WGTZ-FM, WING, WKSW-FM, WROU-FM
Town and Country Broadcasting Inc. WBZI, WEDI(AM)

Daytona Beach, FL: Rank 86
Renda Broadcasting Corp. WGNE-FM
J&V Communications Inc. WTJV(AM)
Entravision Communications Corp. WNUE-FM
Gore-Overgaard Broadcasting Inc. WROD, WSBB
Black Crow Media Group LLC WHOG-FM, WKRO-FM, WNDB, WVYB-FM
Buddy Tucker Association Inc. WYND

Decatur, IL: Rank 282
The Cromwell Group Inc. WZNX(FM), WZUS(FM)
Neuhoff Family L.P. WDZ(AM), WSOY(AM), WSOY-FM

Denver-Boulder, CO: Rank 21
Clear Channel Communications Inc. KBCO(FM), KBPI(FM), KHOW, KKZN(AM), KOA, KPTT(FM), KRFX-FM, KTCL(FM)
Crawford Broadcasting Co. KLDC(AM), KLTT, KLVZ(AM), KLZ
Entercom Communications Corp. KALC(FM), KEZW, KOSI-FM, KQMT(FM)
Lincoln Financial Media KEPN(AM), KKFN(FM), KQKS-FM, KRWZ(AM), KYGO-FM
Pillar of Fire Inc. KPOF
Salem Communications Corp. KBJD, KNUS, KRKS(AM), KRKS-FM
Entravision Communications Corp. KJMN-FM, KMXA, KXPK-FM
Pilgrim Communications Inc. KRCN(AM)
Latino Communications LLC KBNO(AM)

EMF Broadcasting KLDV(FM)
Bustos Media LLC KKHI(FM)
NRC Broadcasting Inc. KCKK(AM), KCUV(FM) KNRV(AM), KTNI-FM, KVOD(FM)
Wilks Broadcast Group LLC KIMN-FM, KWOF(FM), KXKL-FM

Des Moines, IA: Rank 90
Citadel Broadcasting Corp. KGGO-FM, KHKI-FM, KJJY(FM), KWQW(FM)
Clear Channel Communications Inc. KASI, KCCQ(FM), KDRB(FM), KKDM-FM, KPTL(FM), KXNO(AM), WHO(AM)
Family Stations Inc. KDFR(FM)
Northwestern College & Radio KNWI(FM), KNWM(FM)
Saga Communications Inc. KAZR(FM), KIOA(AM), KLTI-FM, KPSZ(AM), KRNT, KSTZ(FM) KDLS-FM
Birch Broadcasting Corp. KXLQ
Connoisseur Media LLC KZWF(FM)
Coon Valley Communications Inc. KDLS

Detroit: Rank 11
Birach Broadcasting Corp. WNZK, WPON
CTVglobemedia CIDR-FM, CIMX-FM, CKLW, CKWW
ABC Inc. WFDF(AM)
Citadel Broadcasting Corp. WDRQ(FM), WDVD(FM), WJR
Clear Channel Communications Inc. WDFN, WDTW(AM), WDTW-FM, WJLB-FM, WKQI-FM, WMXD-FM, WNIC-FM
Crawford Broadcasting Co. WEXL, WMUZ-FM, WRDT(AM)
Family Life Communications Inc. WUFL
Greater Media Inc. WCSX-FM, WMGC-FM, WRIF(FM)
CBS Radio WOMC-FM, WVMV-FM, WWJ, WXYT, WXYT-FM, WYCD-FM
Salem Communications Corp. WDTK(AM), WLQV
Liggett Communications L.L.C. WHLX(AM), WPHM
Radio One Inc. WCHB, WDMK(FM), WHTD(FM)
Davidson Media Group LLC WDRJ(AM) WHLS, WSAQ-FM

Dothan, AL: Rank 190
Wilson Broadcasting Inc. WAGF, WAGF-FM, WJJN-FM
Magic Broadcasting LLC WJRL-FM, WKMX-FM, WLDA(FM), WTVY-FM WELB, WOAB-FM, WOOF, WOOF-FM, WOZK, WQLS, WVVL(FM)

Dubuque, IA: Rank 243
American Family Radio KIAD(FM)
Family Life Communications Inc. WJTY-FM
Morgan Murphy Media WGLR, WGLR-FM, WPVL, WPVL-FM
Cumulus Media Inc. KLYV-FM, KXGE-FM, WDBQ, WDBQ-FM, WJOD-FM
Radio Dubuque Inc. KATF(FM), KDTH, KGRR-FM

Duluth-Superior, MN-WI: Rank 211
Midwest Communications Inc. KDAL, KDAL-FM, KHQG(FM), KTCO-FM, WDSM, WGEE(AM), WUSZ-FM
Northwestern College & Radio KDNI(FM), KDNW(FM)
Red Rock Radio Corp. KQDS, KQDS-FM, KZIO-FM, WWAX-FM
Heartland Communications Group LLC WNXR(FM) KMFY-FM
GAPWEST Broadcasting KBMX(FM), KKCB-FM, KLDJ-FM, WEBC

Eau Claire, WI: Rank 244
Clear Channel Communications Inc. WATQ(FM), WBIZ, WBIZ-FM, WMEQ(AM), WMEQ-FM, WQRB(FM)
VCY America Inc. WVCF-FM
Maverick Media LLC WAXX-FM, WAYY(AM), WDRK(FM), WEAQ, WECL-FM, WIAL-FM
Zoe Communications Inc. WQOQ(AM)
Relevant Radio WDVM(AM) WISM-FM, WOGO, WWIB-FM

El Paso, TX: Rank 76
Clear Channel Communications Inc. KHEY(AM), KPRR-FM, KTSM(AM), KTSM-FM
Regent Communications Inc. KROD, KSII-FM
Univision Radio KAMA, KBNA-FM, KQBU(AM)
World Radio Network Inc. KVER-FM
Entravision Communications Corp. KHRO(AM), KINT-FM, KOFX-FM, KSVE(AM), KYSE(AM)
EMF Broadcasting KKLY(FM) KHEY-FM, KLAQ-FM
Bravo Mic Communications LLC KXPZ(FM)

Elkins-Buckhannon-Weston, WV: Rank 277

Elmira-Corning, NY: Rank 228
Pembrook Pines Media Group WABH, WEHH, WELM, WOKN-FM
CSN International WREQ-FM
Backyard Broadcasting LLC WNKI-FM, WPGI-FM, WWLZ
Family Life Network WCIH-FM, WCIK-FM
WS2K Radio LLC dba WS Media WCBA, WENI(AM), WENI-FM, WENY, WENY-FM, WGMM(FM) WCKR-FM, WHHO, WKPQ-FM, WLEA, WLVY-FM, WVIN-FM

Erie, PA: Rank 169
Forever Broadcasting WGYY(FM)
Citadel Broadcasting Corp. WQHZ(FM), WRIE, WXTA-FM
Family Stations Inc. WEFR-FM WXKC-FM
Connoisseur Media LLC WFNN(AM), WJET(AM), WRKT-FM, WRTS-FM, WXBB(FM)

Eugene-Springfield, OR: Rank 147
Family Stations Inc. KQFE-FM
Cumulus Media Inc. KEHK-FM, KSCR(AM), KUGN, KUJZ(FM), KZEL-FM
Bicoastal Media L.L.C. KDUK-FM, KODZ-FM, KOOS(FM), KPNW
McKenzie River Broadcasting Company, Inc. KEUG(FM), KKNU(FM), KMGE-FM KCFM(AM), KCST-FM, KNRQ-FM, KOPB(AM), KRVM(AM), KRVM-FM
Churchill Communications LLC KLZS(AM), KXOR(AM)

Evansville, IN: Rank 163
Regent Communications Inc. WDKS-FM, WGBF, WGBF-FM, WJLT(FM), WKDQ-FM
South Central Communications Corp. WABX-FM, WEJK(FM), WEOA, WIKY-FM, WLFW(FM), WSTO-FM
The Original Company Inc. WRCY(AM), WYFX(FM)
Withers Broadcasting Co. WYNG(FM)
Word Broadcasting Network Inc. WVHI
EMF Broadcasting WKVN(FM)

Fargo-Moorhead, ND-MN: Rank 218
Forum Communications Co. WDAY
Leighton Enterprises Inc. KBOQ(FM)
Northwestern College & Radio KFNL(FM), KFNW(AM)
Triad Broadcasting Co. L.L.C. KLTA(FM), KPFX(FM), KQWB-FM, KVOX-FM KQLX-FM, KVXR(AM), WZFG(AM)
Radio Fargo-Moorhead Inc. KBVB(FM), KFGO, KRWK(FM), KVOX(AM), WDAY-FM

Fayetteville (Northwest Arkansas), AR: Rank 132
American Family Radio KBNV(FM)
Bott Radio Network KAYH(FM), KOFC
Clear Channel Communications Inc. KEZA-FM, KIGL(FM), KKIX-FM, KMXF(FM)
Cumulus Media Inc. KAMO-FM, KFAY, KKEG(FM), KMCK-FM, KQSM-FM, KYNF(FM), KYNG(AM)
KERM Inc. KURM
Davidson Media Group LLC KAKS(FM)

Fayetteville, NC: Rank 132
Beasley Broadcast Group Inc. WAZZ(AM), WFLB-FM, WKML-FM, WTEL(AM), WUKS(FM), WZFX-FM
Bible Broadcasting Network WYBH(FM)
Cumulus Media Inc. WFNC, WFVL(FM), WMGU(FM), WRCQ-FM
Davidson Media Group LLC WSTS-FM WFMO, WGQR-FM, WQSM-FM
Norsan Consulting and Management Inc. WFAY(AM)

Flagstaff-Prescott, AZ: Rank 145
Yavapai Broadcasting Corp. KKLD(FM), KVNA(AM), KVNA-FM, KVRD-FM, KYBC(AM)
LKCM Radio Group L.P. KFSZ(FM) KAHM(FM), KYCA(AM), KZGL(FM)
Cochise Broadcasting LLC KZXK(FM)
Prescott Valley Broadcasting Co. Inc. KPPV(FM), KQNA(AM)

Flint, MI: Rank 127
Birach Broadcasting Corp. WCXI(AM)
Citadel Broadcasting Corp. WFBE-FM, WTRX
Regent Communications Inc. WFNT, WLCO(AM), WQUS(FM), WWBN-FM
Cumulus Media Inc. WDZZ-FM, WRSR-FM, WWCK
Christian Broadcasting System Ltd. WSNL(AM)
EMF Broadcasting WAKL(FM), WCRZ-FM, WWCK-FM
Superior Communications WTAC(AM)

Florence, SC: Rank 217
American Family Radio WDLL(FM)
Miller Communications Inc. WHYM(AM), WOLH(AM), WSIM(FM)
Cumulus Media Inc. WBZF-FM, WCMG-FM, WHLZ(FM), WHSC, WMXT-FM, WWFN-FM, WYNN
Glory Communications Inc. WPDT-FM
Qantum Communications Corp. WDAR-FM, WEGX-FM, WJMX, WJMX-FM, WWRK(AM), WZTF(FM) WLPG-FM, WYNN-FM

Florence-Muscle Shoals, AL: Rank 257
Big River Broadcasting Corp. WQLT-FM, WSBM(AM), WXFL(FM) WMSR-FM
Urban Radio Licenses LLC WLAY-FM, WMXV(FM)

Fort Collins-Greeley, CO: Rank 120
Clear Channel Communications Inc. KIIX(AM), KPAW-FM, KSME(FM)
WAY-FM Media Group Inc. KXWA(FM)
EMF Broadcasting KGCO(FM)
NRC Broadcasting Inc. KJAC(FM), KRKY-FM
College Creek Media LLC KYEN(FM)
Greeley Broadcasting Corp. KGRE

Fort Myers-Naples-Marco Island, FL: Rank 61
Beasley Broadcast Group Inc. WJBX-FM, WJPT(FM), WRXK-FM, WWCN, WXKB-FM
Clear Channel Communications Inc. WBTT(FM), WCKT(FM), WOLZ-FM, WZJZ(FM)
Renda Broadcasting Corp. WGUF-FM, WJGO(FM), WSGL-FM, WWGR-FM

Fort Myers Broadcasting Co. WINK-FM, WPTK(AM), WTLQ-FM
Meridian Broadcasting Inc. WARO-FM, WINK(AM), WNOG, WNTY(FM), WTLT-FM
WAY-FM Media Group Inc. WAYJ-FM WCNZ(AM), WMYR, WVOI(AM)

Fort Pierce-Stuart-Vero Beach, FL: Rank 95
Clear Channel Communications Inc. WAVW(FM), WQOL-FM, WZTA(AM)
Vero Beach Broadcasters LLC WGYL-FM, WJKD(FM), WOSN-FM, WTTB
Black Media Works Inc. WJFP-FM, WCZR(FM), WSYR-FM

Fort Smith, AR: Rank 175
American Family Radio KAOW(FM)
Clear Channel Communications Inc. KKBD-FM, KMAG-FM, KWHN(AM), KYHN(AM), KZBB-FM
Family Stations Inc. KEAF(FM)
Pearson Broadcasting KERX(FM), KTTG-FM
Cumulus Media Inc. KBBQ-FM, KLSZ-FM, KOAI(AM), KOMS-FM
Pharis Broadcasting KFPW, KFPW-FM, KHGG(AM), KQBK(FM) KFSA, KISR-FM, KTCS, KTCS-FM

Fort Walton Beach, FL: Rank 227
Cumulus Media Inc. WFTW, WNCV(FM), WYZB-FM, WZNS-FM
Qantum Communications Corp. WFFY(FM), WMXZ(FM), WWAV-FM WAAZ-FM, WJSB, WKSM-FM
Star Broadcasting Inc. WRKN(FM), WTKE-FM, WZFN(AM)

Fort Wayne, IN: Rank 107
Bott Radio Network WFCV
Federated Media WBYR-FM, WFWI-FM, WKJG(AM), WMEE-FM, WOWO, WQHK-FM
Sarkes Tarzian Inc. WAJI(FM), WLDE-FM
Summit City Radio Group WGL, WGL-FM, WNHT(FM), WXKE(FM) WBNI-FM, WGBJ(FM), WLYV, WNBR-FM
Independence Media Holdings LLC WNUY(FM)

Frederick, MD: Rank 198
WFMD(AM), WFRE(FM)

Fredericksburg, VA: Rank 151

Fresno, CA: Rank 66
Clear Channel Communications Inc. KALZ(FM), KBOS-FM, KCBL, KFSO-FM, KHGE(FM), KRDU, KRZR-FM
Family Stations Inc. KFNO-FM
Lotus Communications Corp. KGST, KHIT-FM, KKBZ(FM), KLBN(FM)
Univision Radio KLLE(FM), KOND(FM), KRDA(FM)
Gore-Overgaard Broadcasting Inc. KBIF, KIRV
Multicultural Radio Broadcasting Inc. KWRU(AM)
Moon Broadcasting KAAT(FM) KSOF-FM, KVPW(FM)
Wilks Broadcast Group LLC KFRR-FM, KJFX-FM, KJZN(FM)
Peak Broadcasting LLC KFPT(AM), KMGV-FM, KMJ, KMJ-FM, KSKS-FM, KWYE(FM)

Gainesville-Ocala, FL: Rank 81
Asterisk Inc. WMFQ-FM, WXJZ(FM), WYGC(FM)
Bible Broadcasting Network WYFB-FM, WYFZ(FM)
Wooster Republican Printing Co. WNDD-FM, WNDT(FM), WOGK(FM)
Entercom Communications Corp. WKTK-FM, WSKY-FM
Pamal Broadcasting Ltd. WDVH(AM), WDVH-FM, WHHZ(FM), WKZY(FM), WTMG-FM, WTMN(AM) WAJD, WRUF, WRUF-FM, WYKS-FM

Grand Forks, ND-MN: Rank 291
Clear Channel Communications Inc. KJKJ-FM, KKXL, KQHT-FM, KSNR-FM
Leighton Enterprises Inc. KCNN, KNOX, KNOX-FM, KYCK-FM, KZLT-FM KKCQ, KKEQ-FM, KKXL-FM

Grand Island-Kearney, NE: Rank 256

Grand Junction, CO: Rank 259
Cumulus Media Inc. KBKL(FM), KEKB-FM, KEXO, KKNN-FM, KMXY-FM
MBC Grand Broadcasting Inc. KJYE-FM, KMGJ-FM, KMOZ-FM, KNZZ(AM), KSTR-FM, KTMM(AM)
EMF Broadcasting KLFV(FM)
Cherry Creek Radio LLC KKXK-FM, KUBC(AM)
United Ministries KJOL(AM)

Grand Rapids, MI: Rank 67
Birach Broadcasting Corp. WMFN, WMJH
Citadel Broadcasting Corp. WBBL-FM, WHTS(FM), WJRW(AM), WLAV-FM, WTNR(FM)
Clear Channel Communications Inc. WBCT-FM, WBFX(FM), WMAX-FM, WMRR-FM, WOOD, WOOD-FM, WSNX-FM, WTKG
Kuiper Stns WFUR
Midwest Communications Inc. WHTC(AM)
The Moody Bible Institute of Chicago WGNB(FM)
Regent Communications Inc. WFGR-FM, WGRD-FM, WNWZ, WTRV-FM WFUR-FM, WGHN, WGHN-FM, WLHT-FM

Green Bay, WI: Rank 187
Clear Channel Communications Inc. WDUZ(AM), WDUZ-FM, WPCK(FM), WQLH-FM
Evangel Ministries Inc. WEMY-FM
Midwest Communications Inc. WIXX-FM, WNFL, WRQE(FM), WTAQ(AM), WTAQ-FM
Woodward Communications Inc. WECB(FM), WKSZ(FM), WZOR(FM)
Results Broadcasting WOWN-FM, WTCH WZNN(FM)

Greensboro-Winston Salem-High Point, NC: Rank 45
ABC Inc. WCOG
Clear Channel Communications Inc. WGBT(FM), WMAG(FM), WMKS(FM), WTQR-FM, WVBZ(FM)
Curtis Media Group WMFR, WPCM, WSJS, WSML, WZTK(FM)
Entercom Communications Corp. WEAL, WJMH-FM, WPAW(FM), WPET, WQMG-FM, WSMW(FM)
GHB Radio Group WBLO(AM), WIST-FM, WTIX(AM)
Truth Broadcasting Corp. WKEW, WPOL, WTRU(AM)
Davidson Media Group LLC WSGH(AM), WTOB, WWBG WLXN, WTHZ(FM), WYSR(AM)
Blue Ridge Radio Inc. WBRF(FM)
Positive Alternative Radio Inc. WXRI-FM

Greenville-New Bern-Jacksonville, NC: Rank 87
American Family Radio WAAE-FM, WJKA(FM)
Beasley Broadcast Group Inc. WIKS-FM, WMGV-FM, WNCT, WNCT-FM, WSFL-FM, WXNR-FM
Capitol Broadcasting Co. Inc. WLGD(FM)
NextMedia Group Inc. WANG, WERO(FM), WQSL-FM, WQZL(FM), WRNS, WRNS-FM, WSSM(FM), WXQR-FM
CTC Media Group Inc. WECU(AM), WNOS, WSME(AM), WWNB
Radio La Grande WLNR, WSRP(AM) WDLX, WELS, WELS-FM, WLGT(FM), WNBR-FM
Inner Banks Media LLC WNBU(FM), WRHD(FM), WRHT-FM, WTIB(FM)
Conner Media Corp. WAVQ(AM), WJNC

Greenville-Spartanburg, SC: Rank 59
Wilkins Communications Network Inc. WELP(AM)
Clear Channel Communications Inc. WESC-FM, WGVL, WLFJ(AM), WMYI(FM), WSSL-FM
Cox Radio Inc. WHZT(FM), WJMZ-FM
Entercom Communications Corp. WORD(AM), WROQ-FM, WSPA-FM, WTPT-FM, WYRD, WYRD-FM
Davidson Media Group LLC WNOW-FM, WOLI(AM), WOLI-FM, WOLT-FM WAHT, WCCP-FM, WFBC-FM, WMUU-FM, WPJF(AM)

Hagerstown-Chambersburg-Waynesboro, MD-PA: Rank 166
Allegheny Mountain Network Stations WEEO-FM
VerStandig Broadcasting WAYZ(FM), WBHB-FM, WCBG(AM), WPPT(FM)
Nassau Broadcasting Partners L.P. WARK, WWEG(FM)
Prettyman Broadcasting Co. WICL(FM), WLTF(FM)
Main Line Broadcasting LLC WCHA, WDLD(FM), WHAG, WIKZ-FM, WQCM(FM)

Hamptons-Riverhead, NY: Rank 262

Harrisburg-Lebanon-Carlisle, PA: Rank 79
Citadel Broadcasting Corp. WCAT-FM, WMHX(FM)
Clear Channel Communications Inc. WHP, WKBO, WRBT-FM, WRVV-FM, WTKT(AM)
MAX Media L.L.C. WYGL-FM
Cumulus Media Inc. WHGB(AM), WTPA-FM, WWKL(FM)
WS2K Radio LLC dba WS Media WHYL WHKF(FM), WLBR, WNNK-FM, WQIC-FM

Harrisonburg, VA: Rank 272
Clear Channel Communications Inc. WACL-FM, WKCY, WKCY-FM
VerStandig Broadcasting WHBG, WJDV(FM), WQPO-FM, WSVA, WTGD(FM) WBTX, WLTK(FM), WTON-FM

Hartford-New Britain-Middletown, CT: Rank 50
Buckley Broadcasting Corp. WDRC(AM), WDRC-FM
ABC Inc. WDZK
Clear Channel Communications Inc. WHCN-FM, WKSS-FM, WPOP, WWYZ-FM
Family Stations Inc. WCTF
CBS Radio WRCH-FM, WTIC, WZMX-FM
Davidson Media Group LLC WXCT(AM) WCCC(AM), WCCC-FM, WMRQ-FM, WTIC-FM
Freedom Communications of Connecticut Inc. WKND(AM), WLAT(AM), WNEZ(AM)

Hilton Head, SC: Rank 213

Honolulu, HI: Rank 64
Clear Channel Communications Inc. KDNN(FM), KHBZ(AM), KHVH, KIKI-FM, KSSK(AM), KSSK-FM, KUCD(FM)
Cox Radio Inc. KCCN-FM, KINE-FM, KKNE(AM), KPHW(FM), KRTR(AM), KRTR-FM
Salem Communications Corp. KAIM-FM, KGU, KHCM(AM), KHCM-FM, KHUI(FM), KKOL-FM

Visionary Related Entertainment L.L.C. KDDB(FM), KPOI-FM, KQMQ-FM, KUMU, KUMU-FM
KM Communications Inc. KEWA(AM) KORL(AM)

Hot Springs, AR: Rank 290
US Stations LLC KLBL(FM)

Houston-Galveston: Rank 6
ABC Inc. KMIC(AM)
Clear Channel Communications Inc. KBME, KKRW-FM, KODA-FM, KPRC, KTBZ-FM, KTRH
Cox Radio Inc. KGLK(FM), KHPT(FM), KKBQ-FM, KTHT(FM)
CBS Radio KHMX-FM, KIKK, KILT, KILT-FM, KKHH(FM), KLOL-FM
Martin Broadcasting Inc. KYOK(AM)
Pacifica Foundation Inc. KPFT-FM
Salem Communications Corp. KKHT-FM, KNTH(AM)
Cumulus Media Partners LLC KFNC(FM), KHJK(FM), KRBE(FM)
Univision Radio KAMA-FM, KLAT, KLTN(FM), KOVE-FM, KQBU-FM
Entravision Communications Corp. KGOL
Liberman Broadcasting Inc. KEYH, KJOJ, KJOJ-FM, KQQK(FM), KQUE, KSEV(AM), KTJM-FM
Cumulus Media Inc. KSTB-FM
Houston Christian Broadcasters Inc. KHCB, KHCB-FM
Multicultural Radio Broadcasting Inc. KXYZ
Radio One Inc. KBXX(FM), KMJQ-FM, KROI(FM)
SIGA Broadcasting Corp. KGBC, KLVL KGOW(AM), KTEK
Aleluya Christian Broadcasting Inc. KBRZ(AM), KFTG-FM, KRTX

Huntington-Ashland, WV-KY: Rank 160
Baker Family Stations WYHY(AM)
Clear Channel Communications Inc. WAMX-FM, WBVB-FM, WKEE-FM, WTCR, WTCR-FM, WVHU(AM)
Mortenson Broadcasting Co. WEMM-FM, WRWB(AM)
Kindred Communications Inc. WCMI, WCMI-FM, WDGG-FM, WRVC WBKS(FM), WGOH, WIRO, WLGC, WLGC-FM, WUGO-FM, WZZW
Connoisseur Media LLC WMGA(FM), WXBW(FM)
Positive Alternative Radio Inc. WKAO(FM)

Huntsville, AL: Rank 108
Wilkins Communications Network Inc. WBXR(AM)
Clear Channel Communications Inc. WBHP, WDRM-FM, WHOS, WTAK-FM
Cumulus Media Inc. WHRP(FM), WUMP, WVNN, WVNN-FM, WWFF-FM, WZYP-FM
Black Crow Media Group LLC WAHR-FM, WLOR, WRTT-FM
Christian Voice of Central Ohio Inc. WDPT(AM), WTKI(AM)

Indianapolis, IN: Rank 40
Wilkins Communications Network Inc. WBRI(AM)
ABC Inc. WRDZ-FM
Clear Channel Communications Inc. WFBQ-FM, WNDE, WRZX-FM
Emmis Communications Corp. WFNI(AM), WIBC(FM), WLHK(FM), WYXB(FM)
Entercom Communications Corp. WNTR(FM), WXNT(AM), WZPL-FM
Mid-America Radio Group Inc. WCBK-FM, WMYJ(FM)
The Moody Bible Institute of Chicago WGNR-FM
Rodgers Broadcasting Corp. WIFE(AM)
Cumulus Media Partners LLC WFMS-FM, WJJK(FM), WRWM(FM)
Sarkes Tarzian Inc. WTTS-FM
Radio One Inc. WHHH-FM, WNOU(FM), WTLC, WTLC-FM
Pilgrim Communications Inc. WFDM(FM)
EMF Broadcasting WIKL(FM)
Davidson Media Group LLC WNTS WHZN(FM), WQRK(FM)

Ithaca, NY: Rank 283
Bible Broadcasting Network WYBY(AM)
Pembrook Pines Media Group WPIE
Saga Communications Inc. WHCU, WIII(FM), WNYY(AM), WQNY-FM, WYXL-FM
Finger Lakes Radio Group WFIZ(FM)

Jackson, MS: Rank 121
Clear Channel Communications Inc. WHLH(FM), WJDX, WMSI-FM, WQJQ-FM, WSTZ-FM, WZRX
Inner City Broadcasting WJMI-FM, WJNT, WJQS(AM), WKXI-FM, WOAD, WZNO(FM)
New South Communications Inc. WIIN, WJKK-FM, WUSJ(FM), WYOY-FM
Backyard Broadcasting LLC WRXW(FM), WWJK(FM)
TeleSouth Communications Inc. WFMN-FM
Marion R. Williams Stns WONG WRBJ-FM

Jackson, TN: Rank 292
Forever Communications Inc. WTJS, WTJW(FM), WYNU-FM
Black Crow Media Group LLC WFKX(FM), WHHM-FM, WWYN(FM), WZDQ(FM)
Grace Broadcasting Services Inc. WWGM(FM)

Jacksonville, FL: Rank 46
ABC Inc. WBWL
Clear Channel Communications Inc. WFKS(FM), WFXJ(AM), WJBT(FM), WPLA(FM), WQIK-FM, WSOL-FM

Cox Radio Inc. WAPE-FM, WFYV-FM, WJGL(FM), WOKV, WOKV-FM, WXXJ(FM)
Renda Broadcasting Corp. WEJZ-FM, WMUV(FM), WSOS-FM
Salem Communications Corp. WZAZ
Word Broadcasting Network Inc. WYMM(AM) WFOY(AM), WHJX(FM), WJAX, WJSJ(FM), WKTZ-FM, WSJF(FM), WZNZ
Norsan Consulting and Management Inc. WEWC(AM), WNNR(AM), WSOS(AM), WVOJ(AM)
Chesapeake-Portsmouth Broadcasting Corp. WBOB(AM)

Johnson City-Kingsport-Bristol, TN-VA: Rank 102
Citadel Broadcasting Corp. WGOC(AM), WJCW, WKOS-FM, WQUT-FM, WXSM(AM)
Glenwood Communications Corp. WKPT, WKTP, WMEV, WMEV-FM, WOPI, WRZK-FM, WTFM-FM, WVEK-FM
Bristol Broadcasting Co. Inc. WAEZ(FM), WFHG(AM), WFHG-FM, WTZR(FM), WXBQ-FM WEMB
Information Communications Corp. WABN, WHGG(AM), WPWT(AM)
Positive Alternative Radio Inc. WCQR-FM

Jonesboro, AR: Rank 293
American Family Radio KAOG(FM), KJSB(FM)
Clear Channel Communications Inc. KBTM(AM), KFIN(FM), KIYS(FM), KNEA(AM)
Saga Communications Inc. KEGI(FM), KJBX(FM)
EMF Broadcasting KJLV(FM)

Joplin, MO: Rank 237
Zimmer Radio Inc. KIXQ(FM), KJMK-FM, KSYN-FM, KXDG-FM, KZRG(AM), KZYM(AM)
My Town Media Inc. KHST(FM), KWXD-FM
EMF Broadcasting KOBC-FM KDMO, KMXL-FM, WMBH(AM)
American Media Investments Inc. KBTN(AM), KBZI(FM), KCAR-FM, KMOQ(FM), KQYX(AM)

Kalamazoo, MI: Rank 186
Forum Communications Co. WZUU-FM
Kuiper Stns WKPR
Midwest Communications Inc. WKZO(AM), WNWN, WNWN-FM, WQLR(AM), WVFM(FM), WYZO(FM)
Cumulus Media Inc. WKFR-FM, WKMI, WRKR-FM

Kalispell-Flathead Valley, MT: Rank 261

Kansas City, MO-KS: Rank 32
Wilkins Communications Network Inc. KCNW(AM)
Bick Broadcasting Co. KSIS(AM)
Bott Radio Network KAYX(AM), KCCV, KCCV-FM, KLEX
ABC Inc. KPHN
The Curators of the University of Missouri KCUR-FM
Entercom Communications Corp. KCSP(AM), KKSN(FM), KMBZ, KQRC-FM, KRBZ(FM), KUDL-FM, KXTR(AM), KYYS(AM), WDAF-FM
Cumulus Media Partners LLC KCFX(FM), KCHZ(FM), KCJK(FM), KCMO, KCMO-FM, KMJK(FM)
Carter Broadcast Group Inc. KPRS-FM, KPRT
Davidson Media Group LLC KCZZ(AM), KDTD(AM)
Wilks Broadcast Group LLC KBEQ-FM, KCKC(FM), KFKF-FM, KMXV-FM
Catholic Radio Network Inc. KEXS(AM)

Killeen-Temple, TX: Rank 154
Clear Channel Communications Inc. KIIZ-FM, KLFX-FM
Martin Broadcasting Inc. KRMY
Cumulus Media Inc. KLTD-FM, KOOC(FM), KSSM(FM), KTEM, KUSJ(FM)
EMF Broadcasting KYAR(FM)
Munbilla Broadcasting Properties Ltd. KHLE(FM)
The RAFTT Corp. KTON

Knoxville, TN: Rank 71
Citadel Broadcasting Corp. WIVK-FM, WNML(AM), WNML-FM, WOKI(FM)
South Central Communications Corp. WIMZ-FM, WJXB-FM, WQJK(FM)
Journal Communications Inc. WCYQ(FM), WKHT(FM), WKTI(AM), WWST(FM)
Horne Radio Group WATO, WFIV-FM, WGAP, WKVL(AM), WLOD, WMTY(AM)
Peg Broadcasting Crossville LLC WPBX(FM) WIFA(AM), WIHG(FM), WIJV(FM), WITA, WKZX-FM, WLIL(AM), WSEV
Norsan Consulting and Management Inc. WKGN
East Tennessee Radio Group L.P. WSEV-FM

La Crosse, WI: Rank 229

La Salle-Peru, IL: Rank 249
Studstill Broadcasting WALS(FM), WBZG(FM), WGLC-FM, WIVQ(FM), WSPL(AM), WSTQ(FM), WYYS(FM)

Lafayette, IN: Rank 240
RadioWorks Inc. WKHY(FM)
American Family Radio WQSG(FM)
The Moody Bible Institute of Chicago WHPL-FM
Schurz Communications Inc. WASK, WASK-FM, WKOA-FM, WXXB(FM)

Artistic Media Partners Inc. WAZY-FM, WBPE(FM), WSHP(FM), WSHY(AM)
Kaspar Broadcasting Group WSHW-FM
EMF Broadcasting WKHL(FM) WBAA(AM), WBAA-FM

Lafayette, LA: Rank 105
Citadel Broadcasting Corp. KNEK, KRRQ-FM, KSMB-FM, KXKC(FM)
Regent Communications Inc. KFTE-FM, KMDL-FM, KPEL, KPEL-FM, KRKA(FM), KROF, KTDY-FM
Family Worship Center Church Inc. KCKR(FM)
EMF Broadcasting KIKL(FM)
Pittman Broadcasting Services LLC KFXZ(AM), KFXZ-FM, KVOL, KYMK-FM
Radio Maria Inc. KNIR KEUN, KEUN-FM, KNEK-FM, KOGM-FM, KSLO(AM)

Lake Charles, LA: Rank 232
American Family Radio KYLC(FM)
Cumulus Media Inc. KAOK, KBIU(FM), KKGB-FM, KQLK(FM), KXZZ, KYKZ-FM
EMF Broadcasting KRLR(FM)
Radio Maria Inc. KOJO-FM
GAP Broadcasting LLC KLCL, KNGT(FM), KTSR(FM)

Lakeland-Winter Haven, FL: Rank 93
Bible Broadcasting Network WYFO-FM
Hall Communications Inc. WLKF(AM), WONN(AM), WPCV(FM), WWRZ-FM
The Moody Bible Institute of Chicago WKES-FM WLVF

Lancaster, PA: Rank 112
Citadel Broadcasting Corp. WIOV-FM
Clear Channel Communications Inc. WLAN, WLAN-FM
Hall Communications Inc. WLPA, WROZ-FM

Lansing-East Lansing, MI: Rank 125
Citadel Broadcasting Corp. WFMK(FM), WITL-FM, WJIM(AM), WJIM-FM, WVFN(AM)
Family Life Communications Inc. WUNN(AM)
MacDonald Broadcasting Co. WHZZ-FM, WILS, WQHH-FM, WXLA
Rubber City Radio Group Inc. WJXQ-FM, WJZL(FM), WQTX(FM), WVIC(FM)
Christian Broadcasting System Ltd. WLCM(AM) WKAR, WKAR-FM, WMMQ(FM)

Laredo, TX: Rank 206
World Radio Network Inc. KBNL(FM)
Border Media Partners LLC KBDR(FM), KLNT, KNEX-FM

Las Cruces, NM: Rank 222
Bravo Mic Communications LLC KVLC(FM)

Las Vegas, NV: Rank 33
Beasley Broadcast Group Inc. KCYE(FM), KDWN, KFRH(FM), KKLZ-FM
Clear Channel Communications Inc. KPLV(FM), KSNE-FM, KWNR-FM
CBS Radio KKJJ(FM), KLUC-FM, KMXB(FM), KXNT, KXTE-FM, KYDZ(AM)
Lotus Communications Corp. KBAD, KENO, KOMP-FM, KWID(FM), KWWN(AM), KXPT-FM
McNaughton-Jakle Stations KSHP
Univision Radio KISF-FM, KLSQ(AM)
Entravision Communications Corp. KQRT(FM) KADD(FM)
Riviera Broadcast Group LLC KOAS(FM), KVGS(FM)
College Creek Media LLC KHIJ(FM)
Faith Communications Corp. KSOS(FM)
Kemp Communications Inc. KMZQ(FM), KONV(FM), KVEG(FM)
BusinessTalkRadio.Net LLC KNUU(AM)

Laurel-Hattiesburg, MS: Rank 225
American Family Radio WAII-FM, WATP-FM
Clear Channel Communications Inc. WFOR, WHER-FM, WHJA(AM), WJKX-FM, WNSL-FM, WUSW-FM, WZLD(FM)
Blakeney Communications Inc. WBBN(FM), WKZW-FM, WXHB(FM), WXRR-FM
EMF Broadcasting WLVZ(FM) WJMG(FM), WORV
Walking by Faith Ministries Inc. WAML

Lawton, OK: Rank 281
American Family Radio KVRS-FM
Perry Publishing & Broadcasting Co. KJMZ(FM), KKRX, KVSP(FM), KXCA(AM)
Monarch Broadcasting Inc. KQTZ-FM
GAP Broadcasting LLC KLAW(FM), KVRW-FM, KZCD(FM)

Lebanon-Rutland-White River Junction, NH-VT: Rank 183

Lewiston-Auburn, ME: Rank 283
Gleason Radio Group WEZR(AM)
Nassau Broadcasting Partners L.P. WLAM(AM)

Lexington-Fayette, KY: Rank 104
Vernon R Baldwin Inc. WVRB-FM
Clear Channel Communications Inc. WBUL-FM, WGVN(AM), WKQQ-FM, WLAP, WLKT-FM, WMXL-FM
L M Communications Inc. WBTF-FM, WBVX(FM), WCDA-FM, WGKS-FM, WLXG
Cumulus Media Inc. WLTO-FM, WVLK, WVLK-FM, WXZZ-FM
Christian Broadcasting System Ltd. WCGW, WLRT(AM)
Wallingford Broadcasting Co. WEKY, WKXO, WLFX(FM)
EMF Broadcasting WRVG(FM) WLXX(FM)

Lima, OH: Rank 254
Clear Channel Communications Inc. WIMA, WIMT(FM), WZRX-FM
Maverick Media LLC WCIT(AM), WDOH-FM, WEGE(FM), WFGF(FM), WWSR(FM) WCSM, WCSM-FM

Lincoln, NE: Rank 172
Bott Radio Network KLCV-FM
Three Eagles Communications KFOR(AM), KFRX(FM), KIBZ(FM), KLMS(AM), KTGL-FM, KZKX-FM
Family Worship Center Church Inc. KNBE(FM)
NRG Media LLC KBBK(FM), KLIN, KLNC(FM) KVSS(FM)

Little Rock, AR: Rank 85
Birach Broadcasting Corp. KTUV(AM)
ABC Inc. KDIS-FM
Citadel Broadcasting Corp. KAAY, KARN, KIPR-FM, KLAL-FM, KOKY-FM, KPZK(AM), KURB-FM
Clear Channel Communications Inc. KDJE(FM), KHKN(FM), KHLR(FM), KMJX-FM, KSSN-FM
Noalmark Broadcasting Corp. KBOK(AM)
Simmons Media Group KDXE(AM)
Wagenvoord Advertising Group Inc. KLRG(AM)
US Stations LLC KQUS-FM
Crain Media Group LLC KHTE-FM, KKSP(FM), KOLL(FM) KARN-FM, KASR(FM), KPZK-FM, KXXA(AM), KZTD(AM)

Los Angeles: Rank 2
Bonneville International Corporation KSWD(FM)
ABC Inc. KDIS(AM), KSPN(AM)
Citadel Broadcasting Corp. KABC, KLOS-FM
Clear Channel Communications Inc. KBIG-FM, KFI, KHHT(FM), KIIS-FM, KLAC, KOST-FM, KSRY(FM), KTLK(AM), KVVS(FM), KYSR-FM
Crawford Broadcasting Co. KBRT
Emmis Communications Corp. KPWR-FM, KXOS(FM)
Family Stations Inc. KFRN
CBS Radio KAMP-FM, KFWB, KNX, KROQ-FM, KRTH-FM, KTWV-FM
Lotus Broadcasting KIRN(AM), KWKU(AM), KWKW
Pacifica Foundation Inc. KPFK-FM
Salem Communications Corp. KFSH-FM, KKLA-FM, KRLA(AM), KXMX(AM)
Spanish Broadcasting System Inc. KLAX-FM, KXOL-FM
Univision Radio KLVE-FM, KRCD(FM), KRCV-FM, KSCA-FM, KTNQ
Entravision Communications Corp. KDLD(FM), KDLE(FM), KLYY(FM), KSSE(FM)
Liberman Broadcasting Inc. KBUA(FM), KBUE(FM), KEBN(FM), KHJ(AM), KVNR, KWIZ-FM
Multicultural Radio Broadcasting Inc. KAHZ(AM), KALI, KAZN, KBLA, KYPA
High Desert Broadcasting LLC KGMX-FM, KOSS(AM), KUTY
Magic Broadcasting LLC KDAY(FM)
Hi-Favor Broadcasting LLC KLTX KAVL, KCBS-FM, KMPC(AM)

Louisville, KY: Rank 53
Birach Broadcasting Corp. WCND
ABC Inc. WDRD(AM)
Clear Channel Communications Inc. WAMZ(FM), WHAS, WKJK(AM), WKRD(AM), WKRD-FM, WLUE(FM), WQMF-FM, WTFX-FM, WZKF(FM)
Cox Radio Inc. WQNU(FM), WRKA(FM), WSFR(FM), WVEZ(FM)
Salem Communications Corp. WFIA, WFIA-FM, WGTK(AM)
Cumulus Media Partners WLCL(FM), WQKC(AM)
Commonwealth Broadcasting Corp. WTSZ(AM)
WAY-FM Media Group Inc. WAYI(FM), WRVI-FM
EMF Broadcasting WARA(FM)
Davidson Media Group LLC WLLV, WLOU, WTUV(AM), WTUV-FM WNDA(AM)
Main Line Broadcasting LLC WDJX-FM, WGZB-FM, WLRS(FM), WMJM-FM, WXMA(FM)

Lubbock, TX: Rank 181
Family Life Communications Inc. KAMY(FM)
Ramar Communications II Ltd. KJTV(AM), KLZK(FM), KTTU-FM, KXTQ-FM
Entravision Communications Corp. KAIQ(FM), KBZO
EMF Broadcasting KKLU(FM), KPGA(FM) KTXT-FM
Wilks Broadcast Group LLC KLLL-FM, KMMX(FM), KONE(FM)
GAP Broadcasting LLC KFMX-FM, KFYO, KKAM, KKCL-FM, KQBR(FM), KZII-FM

Lufkin-Nacogdoches, TX: Rank 253
KRBA(AM), KYBI(FM)
GAP Broadcasting LLC KAFX-FM, KSFA(AM), KTBQ(FM), KYKS(FM)

Macon, GA: Rank 156
American Family Radio WBKG-FM
Clear Channel Communications Inc. WFSM(AM), WIBB(AM), WIBB-FM, WPCH(FM), WQBZ-FM, WRBV-FM
Family Life Communications Inc. WJTG(FM)
Rodgers Broadcasting Corp. WBML
Cumulus Media Inc. WAYS(AM), WDDO, WDEN-FM, WIFN(FM), WLZN(FM), WMAC, WMGB(FM), WPEZ(FM)
Georgia Eagle Broadcasting Inc. WNNG(AM) WFXM(FM), WPGA, WPGA-FM, WQMJ(FM), WXKO, WZCH(FM)

Madison, WI: Rank 98
Clear Channel Communications Inc. WIBA, WIBA-FM, WMAD(FM), WTSO, WXXM(FM)
Entercom Communications Corp. WCHY(FM), WMMM-FM, WOLX-FM
The Mid-West Family Broadcast Group WHIT(AM), WJJO-FM, WLMV(AM), WMGN-FM, WTDY, WWQM-FM, WWQN(FM)
Northwestern College & Radio WNWC(AM), WNWC-FM
Good Karma Broadcasting L.L.C. WTLX(FM)
Relevant Radio WHFA(AM)
NRG Media LLC WSJY-FM WDMP(AM), WZEE-FM
Magnum Communications Inc. WBKY(FM)

Manchester, NH: Rank 191
Blount Communications Group WDER(AM)
Saga Communications Inc. WFEA, WMLL(FM), WZID(FM)
Absolute Broadcasting LLC WGAM(AM)
Great Eastern Radio LLC WTPL(FM)

Mankato-New Ulm-St. Peter, MN: Rank 274
Linder Broadcasting Group KATO-FM, KDOG(FM), KTOE(AM)
Three Eagles Communications KEEZ-FM, KRBI-FM
Ingstad Brothers Broadcasting LLC KNUJ(AM) KGLB(AM)
Radioactive LLC KXLP(FM)

Marion-Carbondale (Southern Illinois): Rank 242
American Family Radio WAWJ(FM)
Clear Channel Communications Inc. WDDD
MAX Media L.L.C. WCIL, WJPF, WOOZ-FM, WUEZ(FM), WXLT(FM)
Withers Broadcasting Inc. WDDD-FM, WFRX, WHET(FM), WTAO-FM, WVZA(FM) WCIL-FM

Mason City, IA: Rank 296
American Family Radio KBDC(FM)
Three Eagles Communications KGLO(AM), KIAI(FM), KLSS-FM, KRIB(AM) KRNI(AM), KSMA-FM, KUNY(FM)
Coloff Media LLC KLKK(FM)

McAllen-Brownsville-Harlingen, TX: Rank 58
Clear Channel Communications Inc. KBFM(FM), KHKZ(FM), KQXX-FM, KTEX(FM), KVNS(AM)
Univision Radio KBTQ(FM), KGBT, KGBT-FM
World Radio Network Inc. KBNR(FM), KVMV-FM
Entravision Communications Corp. KFRQ(FM), KKPS-FM, KNVO-FM, KVLY-FM
Border Media Partners LLC KBUC(FM), KESO-FM, KJAV-FM, KSOX, KURV, KVJY, KZSP-FM

Medford-Ashland, OR: Rank 208
Bicoastal Media L.L.C. KIFS(FM), KLDZ(FM), KMED, KRWQ-FM, KZZE-FM
Mapleton Communications LLC KAKT(FM), KBOY-FM, KCMX, KCMX-FM, KGAY(AM), KTMT-FM
Opus Broadcasting Systems Inc. KCNA(FM), KEZX(AM), KROG-FM, KRTA, KRVC(FM)

Melbourne-Titusville-Cocoa, FL: Rank 97
Clear Channel Communications Inc. WBVD-FM, WMMB, WMMV
Genesis Communications Inc. WIXC(FM)
Cumulus Media Inc. WAOA-FM, WHKR-FM, WINT(AM), WSJZ-FM
Rama Communications Inc. WMEL(AM)

Memphis, TN: Rank 49
Bott Radio Network WCRV
Citadel Broadcasting Corp. WGKX-FM, WRBO(FM), WXMX(FM)
Clear Channel Communications Inc. KJMS(FM), WDIA, WEGR(FM), WHAL-FM, WHRK-FM, WREC(AM)
Entercom Communications Corp. WMQK(FM), WMC(AM), WMC-FM, WMFS(AM), WMFS-FM, WRVR(FM)
F W Robbert Broadcasting Co. Inc. WMQM(AM)
Sudbury Services Inc. KHLS-FM, WLCN, KOSE, KQMJ(AM)
Simmons Media Group KQPN(AM)
EMF Broadcasting KKLV(FM), WPLX(AM) WKBL(AM), WKBQ(FM), WKRA, WKRA-FM, WVIM-FM

Merced, CA: Rank 180
Bott Radio Network KCIV(FM)
Buckley Broadcasting Corp. KHTN(FM), KUBB-FM
Citadel Broadcasting Corp. KDJK(FM)
Mapleton Communications LLC KABX-FM, KLOQ-FM, KNAH(FM), KTIQ(AM), KYOS
EMF Broadcasting KLVN(FM)

Meridian, MS: Rank 299
Clear Channel Communications Inc. WJDQ(FM), WMSO(FM), WYHL(AM)
New South Communications Inc. WALT
Mississippi Broadcasters L.L.C. WJXM(AM), WKZB(FM), WUCL(FM) WOKK-FM

Miami-Fort Lauderdale-Hollywood, FL: Rank 12
Beasley Broadcast Group Inc. WHSR, WKIS-FM, WPOW-FM, WQAM, WWNN
ABC Inc. WMYM(AM)
Clear Channel Communications Inc. WBGG-FM, WHYI-FM, WINZ(AM), WIOD, WMGE(FM), WMIA-FM, WMIB(FM)
Cox Radio Inc. WEDR-FM, WFLC-FM, WHDR(FM), WHQT-FM
Lincoln Financial Media WAXY, WLYF(FM), WMXJ-FM
Salem Communications Corp. WKAT, WMCU(AM)
Spanish Broadcasting System Inc. WCMQ-FM, WRMA-FM, WXDJ-FM
Univision Radio WAMR-FM, WAQI, WQBA, WRTO-FM
Entravision Communications Corp. WLQY
Multicultural Radio Broadcasting Inc. WEXY, WNMA
James Crystal Inc. WFLL(AM) WSRF
Independence Media Holdings LLC WOCN

Middlesex-Somerset-Union, NJ: Rank 38

Milwaukee-Racine, WI: Rank 37
ABC Inc. WKSH(AM)
Clear Channel Communications Inc. WISN, WKKV-FM, WMIL-FM, WOKY, WQBW(FM), WRIT-FM
Entercom Communications Corp. WMYX-FM, WSSP(AM), WXSS-FM
Family Stations Inc. WMWK-FM
Bliss Communications Inc. WBKV(AM), WBWI-FM, WRJN
Saga Communications Inc. WHQG(FM), WJMR-FM, WJYI, WJZX(FM), WKLH-FM
Journal Communications Inc. WLWK-FM, WTMJ
VCY America Inc. WVCY-FM
Milwaukee Radio Alliance L.L.C. WLDB(FM), WLUM-FM, WMCS
Good Karma Broadcasting L.L.C. WAUK(AM), WRRD(AM)
Relevant Radio WPJP(FM)
EMF Broadcasting WKMZ(FM)
Bustos Media LLC WDDW(FM) WEZY-FM, WTKM(AM), WTKM-FM, WZRK(AM)

Minneapolis-St. Paul, MN: Rank 16
ABC Inc. KDIZ
Citadel Broadcasting Corp. KQRS-FM, KXXR(FM), WGVY(FM), WGVZ(FM)
Clear Channel Communications Inc. KDWB-FM, KEEY-FM, KFAN, KFXN, KQQL-FM, KTCZ-FM, KTLK-FM
Hubbard Broadcasting Inc. KSTP(AM), KSTP-FM, WFMP(FM), WIXK(AM)
CBS Radio KZJK(FM), WCCO
Northwestern College & Radio KTIS, KTIS-FM
Salem Communications Corp. KKMS, KYCR, WWTC
Relevant Radio WLOL(AM)
Davidson Media Group LLC KMNQ(AM), KMNV(AM)
Ingstad Brothers Broadcasting LLC KCHK, KRDS-FM KLCI(FM), KQSP(AM), KTNF(AM), WEVR, WEVR-FM, WLTE-FM

Mobile, AL: Rank 96
Wilkins Communications Network Inc. WIJD(AM)
Clear Channel Communications Inc. WKSJ-FM, WMXC-FM, WNTM(AM), WRKH-FM
Martin Broadcasting Inc. WLVV
Goforth Media Inc. WBHY, WBHY-FM
Cumulus Media Inc. WBLX-FM, WDLT-FM, WGOK, WXQW(AM), WYOK-FM
Family Worship Center Church Inc. WQUA-FM WABB, WABB-FM, WABF(AM), WCSN-FM, WHOA(AM)
Buddy Tucker Association Inc. WMOB, WTOF(AM)

Modesto, CA: Rank 109
Citadel Broadcasting Corp. KATM(FM), KESP(AM), KHKK-FM, KHOP-FM, KWNN-FM
Clear Channel Communications Inc. KFIV, KJSN-FM, KMRQ(FM), KOSO-FM
Pappas Telecasting Companies KMPH(FM)
Entravision Communications Corp. KTSE-FM
Bustos Media LLC KBBU(FM)

Monmouth-Ocean, NJ: Rank 51

Monroe, LA: Rank 257
Bible Broadcasting Network KYFL-FM
Communications Capital Managers LLC KNBB(FM), KXKZ-FM
Opus Media Holdings LLC KMYY(FM), KXRR(FM), KZRZ(FM)
Holladay Broadcasting of Louisiana LLC KJLO-FM, KJMG-FM, KLIP-FM, KMLB(AM), KRJO(AM), KRVV-FM KNOE-FM

Monterey-Salinas-Santa Cruz, CA: Rank 82
Buckley Broadcasting Corp. KIDD, KWAV-FM, KYZZ(FM)
Clear Channel Communications Inc. KDON-FM, KION(AM), KOCN-FM, KPRC-FM, KTOM-FM
Univision Radio KSQL(FM)
Entravision Communications Corp. KMBX(AM), KSES-FM

Lazer Broadcasting Corp. KXSM(FM)
Mapleton Communications LLC KBOQ(FM), KCDU(FM), KHIP(FM), KKHK(FM), KPIG-FM
Bustos Media LLC KZSJ(AM) KNRY, KRXA(AM), KYAA(AM)
Wolfhouse Radio Group Inc. KEXA(FM), KMJV(FM), KRAY-FM, KTGE

Montgomery, AL: Rank 153
Clear Channel Communications Inc. WHLW(FM), WWMG(FM), WZHT-FM
GHB Radio Group WMGY
Cumulus Media Partners LLC WMXS-FM
Cumulus Media Inc. WHHY-FM, WLWI(AM), WLWI-FM, WMSP, WNZZ, WXFX(FM)
Scott Communications Inc. WMRK-FM
Tiger Communications Inc. WQSI(FM), WTGZ(FM)

Montpelier-Barre-St. Johnsbury, VT: Rank 268

Morgantown-Clarksburg-Fairmont, WV: Rank 177
Burbach Broadcasting Group WGIE(FM), WGYE(FM), WOBG, WOBG-FM, WXKX(AM)
West Virginia Radio Corp. WAJR, WAJR-FM, WBRB(FM), WVAQ-FM, WWLW(FM)
EMF Broadcasting WCKU(FM) WCLG, WCLG-FM, WFGM-FM, WPDX(AM), WPDX-FM
Fantasia Broadcasting Inc. WMMN, WRLF-FM, WTCS, WZST-FM

Morristown, NJ: Rank 115
Greater Media Inc. WMTR(AM)

Muncie-Marion, IN: Rank 215
Citadel Broadcasting Corp. WMDH-FM

Muskegon, MI: Rank 236
American Family Radio WMCQ(FM)
Citadel Broadcasting Corp. WVIB(FM)
Clear Channel Communications Inc. WKBZ(AM), WMUS(FM), WSHZ(FM) WGVS(AM), WGVS-FM

Myrtle Beach, SC: Rank 158
NextMedia Group Inc. WKZQ-FM, WMYB(FM), WRNN(AM), WRNN-FM, WYAV(FM)
Cumulus Media Inc. WDAI-FM, WIQB(AM), WJXY-FM, WLFF(FM), WSEA(FM), WSYN(FM), WXJY-FM
Qantum Communications Corp. WGTR-FM, WRXZ(FM), WWXM(FM), WYNA-FM

Nashville, TN: Rank 44
Bible Broadcasting Network WYFN
Bott Radio Network WCRT(AM)
Citadel Broadcasting Corp. WGFX-FM, WKDF-FM
Clear Channel Communications Inc. WLAC, WRVW-FM, WSIX-FM, WUBT(FM)
The Cromwell Group Inc. WBUZ(FM), WPRT-FM
F W Robbert Broadcasting Co. Inc. WNQM
Salem Communications Corp. WBOZ(FM), WFFH(FM), WFFI(FM), WVRY-FM
South Central Communications Corp. WCJK(FM), WJXA-FM
Cumulus Media Inc. WNFN(FM), WQQK-FM, WRQQ(FM), WSM-FM, WWTN-FM
Southern Wabash Communications Corp. WMGC, WNSR
WAY-FM Media Group Inc. WAYM(FM)
Davidson Media Group LLC WMDB(AM), WNVL(AM) WENO, WNAZ-FM, WNKX-FM, WNRQ-FM
Grace Broadcasting Services Inc. WFGZ-FM, WNKX

Nassau-Suffolk, NY (Long Island): Rank 18

New Bedford-Fall River, MA: Rank 179

New Haven, CT: Rank 113
Buckley Broadcasting Corp. WMMW
Clear Channel Communications Inc. WAVZ, WELI, WKCI-FM
Cox Radio Inc. WPLR-FM WQAQ-FM, WQUN(AM), WYBC, WYBC-FM

New London, CT: Rank 174
Citadel Broadcasting Corp. WMOS(FM), WSUB
Hall Communications Inc. WCTY(FM), WICH(AM), WILI-FM, WKNL(FM), WNLC-FM WQGN-FM

New Orleans, LA: Rank 55
ABC Inc. WBYU
Citadel Broadcasting Corp. KKND(FM), KMEZ(FM), WDVW(FM), WMTI(FM)
Clear Channel Communications Inc. KYRK(FM), WNOE-FM, WODT, WQUE-FM, WRNO-FM, WYLD, WYLD-FM
Entercom Communications Corp. WEZB-FM, WKBU(FM), WLMG(FM), WWL, WWL-FM, WWWL(AM)
GHB Radio Group WIST(AM)
F W Robbert Broadcasting Co. Inc. WVOG

Southwest Broadcasting Inc. WJSH(FM)
Spotlight Broadcasting LLC KAGY
Davidson Media Group LLC WFNO KLRZ-FM, WBOK, WPRF(FM), WYLK(FM)
Sunburst Media-Louisiana LLC KCIL(FM)
Covenant Network WCKW(AM)

New York: Rank 1
Barnstable Corporation WBZO-FM, WHLI, WKJY-FM, WMJC(FM), WRCN-FM
Buckley Broadcasting Corp. WOR
ABC Inc. WEPN(AM), WQEW
Citadel Broadcasting Corp. WABC(AM), WPLJ(FM), WXLM(FM)
Clear Channel Communications Inc. WALK(AM), WAXQ-FM, WHTZ-FM, WKTU(FM), WLTW-FM, WWPR-FM
Cox Radio Inc. WBAB(FM), WBLI-FM, WCTZ(FM), WFOX(FM), WGBB, WHFM-FM, WNLK(AM), WSTC(AM)
Emmis Communications Corp. WQHT-FM, WRKS(FM), WRXP(FM)
Family Stations Inc. WFME-FM
Greater Media Inc. WCTC(AM), WDHA-FM, WMGQ(FM), WWTR(AM)
CBS Radio WCBS, WCBS-FM, WFAN, WINS, WWFS(FM), WXRK(FM)
Inner City Broadcasting WBLS-FM, WLIB
Pacifica Foundation Inc. WBAI-FM
Pillar of Fire Inc. WAWZ(FM)
Salem Communications Corp. WMCA, WNYM(AM)
Spanish Broadcasting System Inc. WPAT-FM, WSKQ-FM
Univision Radio WADO, WCAA-FM, WQBU-FM
Universal Broadcasting of New York Inc. WTHE(AM), WVNJ(AM)
Pamal Broadcasting Ltd. WHUD-FM, WLNA(AM), WXPK(FM)
Back Bay Broadcasters LLC WBAZ(FM), WBEA(FM), WEHN(FM)
Cumulus Media Inc. WEBE-FM, WFAS-FM, WPUT(AM)
Multicultural Radio Broadcasting Inc. WJDM, WKDM(AM), WNSW, WNYG, WPAT, WZRC
Access.1 Communications Corp. WWRL(AM)
Millennium Radio Group LLC WADB(AM), WJLK(FM)
Polnet Communications Ltd. WLIM, WRKL
Rose City Radio Corp. WSNR(AM)
Press Communications L.L.C. WHTG, WHTG-FM, WWZY-FM
The Morey Organization Inc. WBON(FM), WDRE(FM), WLIR-FM WALK-FM, WNYC, WNYC-FM, WQXR-FM, WVIP(FM), WVOX
BusinessTalkRadio.Net Inc. WGCH(AM)

Newburgh-Middletown, NY (Mid-Hudson Valley): Rank 139
Clear Channel Communications Inc. WRWC(FM)
Sunrise Broadcasting Corp. WGNY, WGNY-FM
WAMC/Northeast Public Radio WOSR-FM
Cumulus Media Inc. WALL, WZAD-FM WDLC, WRRV-FM, WTSX-FM
Digital Radio Broadcasting Inc. WYNY(AM)

Norfolk-Virginia Beach-Newport News, VA: Rank 42
Baker Family Stations WKGM
Bible Broadcasting Network WYFI-FM
ABC Inc. WHKT, WRJR(AM)
Clear Channel Communications Inc. WCDG(FM), WJCD(FM), WKUS(FM), WOWI-FM
MAX Media L.L.C. WCMS(AM), WGH-FM, WVBW(FM), WVHT(FM), WXEZ-FM
Entercom Communications Corp. WNVZ-FM, WPTE-FM, WVKL-FM, WWDE-FM
Saga Communications Inc. WAFX-FM, WJOI, WNOR(FM)
Sinclair Communications Inc. WNIS, WPYA(FM), WROX-FM, WTAR(AM), WUSH(FM)
Willis Broadcasting Corp. WCPK, WGPL, WPCE
Word Broadcasting Network Inc. WYRM(AM)
Davidson Media Group LLC WVXX(AM) WXGM, WXGM-FM
Red Zebra Holdings LLC WXTG(AM), WXTG-FM
Chesapeake-Portsmouth Broadcasting Corp. WTJZ

Odessa-Midland, TX: Rank 184
American Family Radio KBMM(FM)
Family Life Communications Inc. KFLB(AM)
Cumulus Media Inc. KBAT(FM), KMND, KODM-FM, KRIL, KZBT(FM)
EMF Broadcasting KFRI(FM), KLVW(FM)
Double O Radio L.L.C. KHKX(FM), KMCM-FM, KQRX-FM KERB, KERB-FM, KNFM-FM
La Promesa Foundation KLPF(AM), KVDG(FM)
GAP Broadcasting LLC KCHX(FM), KCRS(AM), KCRS-FM, KFZX(FM), KMRK-FM

Oklahoma City, OK: Rank 48
Bott Radio Network KQCV, KQCV-FM
Citadel Broadcasting Corp. KATT-FM, KYIS(FM), WKY, WWLS(AM), WWLS-FM
Clear Channel Communications Inc. KHBZ-FM, KTOK(AM), KTST-FM, KXXY-FM
Renda Broadcasting Corp. KMGL-FM, KOKC(AM), KOMA(FM), KRXO-FM
Tyler Media Broadcasting Corp. KOCY(AM), KOJK(FM), KTLR(AM), KTUZ-FM
Perry Publishing & Broadcasting Co. KRMP(AM)
One Ten Broadcast Group Inc. KIRC-FM
Family Worship Center Church Inc. KMFS(AM)
EMF Broadcasting KOKF-FM, KYLV-FM KINB(FM), KJYO-FM, KKWD(FM)

Olean, NY: Rank 224
WBRR(FM), WESB(AM)

Colonial Radio Group Inc. WBYB(FM)

Omaha-Council Bluffs, NE-IA: Rank 72
Wilkins Communications Network Inc. KLNG(AM)
Bible Broadcasting Network KYFG(FM)
Clear Channel Communications Inc. KFAB, KGOR-FM, KQBW(FM), KTWI(FM), KXKT(FM)
Nebraska Rural Radio Association KTIC-FM
Salem Communications Corp. KCRO, KGBI-FM, KOTK(AM)
Journal Communications Inc. KEZO-FM, KKCD-FM, KQCH(FM), KSRZ-FM, KXSP(AM)
Waitt Omaha LLC KKAR, KMMQ(AM), KOIL(AM), KOOO(FM), KOPW(FM), KOZN(AM), KQKQ-FM
EMF Broadcasting KMLV(FM) KRKR(FM)
Connoisseur Media LLC KGGG(FM)
Cochise Broadcasting LLC KOMJ(AM)

Orlando, FL: Rank 34
ABC Inc. WDYZ(AM)
Clear Channel Communications Inc. WFLF(AM), WJRR-FM, WMGF(FM), WRUM(FM), WTKS-FM, WXXL-FM, WYGM(AM)
Cox Radio Inc. WCFB-FM, WDBO, WHTQ-FM, WMMO-FM, WPYO(FM)
Genesis Communications Inc. WAMT(AM), WHOO(AM)
CBS Radio WJHM-FM, WOCL-FM, WOMX-FM
Salem Communications Corp. WHIM, WORL(AM), WTLN(AM)
J&V Communications Inc. WOTS, WPRD, WSDO(AM)
Rama Communications Inc. WLAA(AM), WNTF, WOKB(AM) WWKA(AM)

Oxnard-Ventura, CA: Rank 118
Salem Communications Corp. KDAR(FM)
Entravision Communications Corp. KSSC(FM)
Gold Coast Broadcasting LLC KCAQ(FM), KFYV(FM), KKZZ(AM), KOCP-FM, KUNX(AM), KVTA
Cumulus Media Inc. KBBY-FM, KHAY-FM, KVEN
Lazer Broadcasting Corp. KLJR-FM, KOXR

Palm Springs, CA: Rank 131
CBS Radio KEZN-FM
Morris Radio LLC KDGL(FM), KFUT(AM), KKUU(FM), KNWQ(AM), KNWZ(AM), KXPS(AM)
News-Press & Gazette Co. KESQ, KUNA-FM
Entravision Communications Corp. KLOB-FM
RR Broadcasting KDES-FM, KGAM, KPSI, KPSI-FM, KPTR(AM) KCLB-FM, KWXY-FM

Panama City, FL: Rank 239
Clear Channel Communications Inc. WDIZ, WFLF-FM, WFSY-FM, WPAP-FM, WPBH(FM)
Family Life Communications Inc. WJTF-FM
WAY-FM Media Group Inc. WAYP(FM)
Family Worship Center Church Inc. WFFL(FM)
Magic Broadcasting LLC WILN-FM, WPCF(AM), WVVE(FM), WYOO-FM, WYYX-FM
Williams Communications Inc. WLTG
Double O Radio L.L.C. WAKT-FM, WASJ(FM), WPFM-FM, WRBA(FM)

Parkersburg-Marietta, WV-OH: Rank 254
Burbach Broadcasting Group WADC, WGGE(FM), WHBR-FM, WRZZ-FM, WVNT(AM), WXIL-FM
Clear Channel Communications Inc. WDMX-FM, WHNK(AM), WLTP(AM), WNUS-FM, WRVB-FM
Positive Alternative Radio Inc. WPJY(FM)

Pensacola, FL: Rank 124
Wilkins Communications Network Inc. WNVY, WVTJ(AM)
Clear Channel Communications Inc. WTKX-FM, WYCL-FM
Pamal Broadcasting Ltd. WMEZ-FM, WXBM-FM
Cumulus Media Inc. WCOA WJLQ(FM)

Peoria, IL: Rank 152
Illinois Bible Institute Inc. WCIC-FM
Regent Communications Inc. WFYR-FM, WGLO-FM, WIXO(FM), WVEL, WZPW(FM)
Triad Broadcasting Co. L.L.C. WDQX(FM), WIRL(AM), WMBD, WPBG-FM, WSWT-FM, WXCL(FM)
Prairie Radio Communications WCDD(FM)
Independence Media Holdings LLC WHPI(FM), WPIA(FM), WWCT(FM)

Philadelphia: Rank 8
Beasley Broadcast Group Inc. WRDW-FM, WTMR, WWDB(AM), WXTU-FM
ABC Inc. WWJZ
Clear Channel Communications Inc. WDAS-FM, WIOQ-FM, WISX(FM), WRFF(FM), WUBA(AM), WUSL-FM
Family Stations Inc. WKDN-FM
GHB Radio Group WNAP
Great Scott Broadcasting WPAZ
Greater Media Inc. WBEN-FM, WMMR-FM, WNUW(FM), WPEN
CBS Radio KYW, WIP, WOGL(FM), WPHT, WYSP-FM
Salem Communications Corp. WFIL(AM), WNTP(AM)
Langer Broadcasting Group L.L.C. WFYL(AM)
Multicultural Radio Broadcasting Inc. WTTM(AM)

Radio One Inc. WPHI-FM, WPPZ-FM, WRNB(FM)
EMF Broadcasting WKVP(FM)
Davidson Media Group LLC WEMG(AM) WCOJ(AM), WHAT, WMGK-FM, WURD(AM)
Mountain Broadcasting Corp. WPWA

Phoenix, AZ: Rank 15
Bonneville International Corporation KMVP, KPKX(FM), KTAR(AM), KTAR-FM
ABC Inc. KMIK
Clear Channel Communications Inc. KESZ-FM, KFYI(AM), KGME(AM), KMXP-FM, KNIX-FM, KOY, KYOT-FM, KZZP-FM
Family Life Communications Inc. KFLR-FM
Family Stations Inc. KPHF-FM
CBS Radio KMLE-FM, KOOL-FM, KZON(FM)
Salem Communications Corp. KKNT(AM), KPXQ(AM)
Sandusky Radio KAZG(AM), KDKB(FM), KDUS, KSLX-FM, KUPD-FM
Univision Radio KHOT-FM, KHOV-FM, KOMR(FM), KQMR(FM)
Entravision Communications Corp. KDVA(FM), KLNZ-FM, KMIA(AM), KVVA-FM
EMF Broadcasting KLVK(FM) KASA, KIDR, KMVA(FM)
Riviera Broadcast Group LLC KEDJ(FM), KKFR(FM)
Communicom Broadcasting LLC KXEG(AM), KXXT(AM)
1TV.Com Inc. KBSZ

Pittsburg, KS (Southeast Kansas): Rank 245

Pittsburgh, PA: Rank 24
Wilkins Communications Network Inc. WWNL(AM)
Birach Broadcasting Corp. WWCS
ABC Inc. WEAE
Clear Channel Communications Inc. WBGG(AM), WDVE-FM, WKST-FM, WPGB(FM), WWSW-FM, WXDX-FM
CBS Radio KDKA, WBZW-FM, WDSY-FM, WZPT-FM
Renda Broadcasting Corp. WGSM(FM), WJAS, WSHH-FM
Salem Communications Corp. WORD-FM, WPIT
Langer Broadcasting Group L.L.C. WPYT(AM)
Butler County Radio Network Inc. WBUT, WISR, WLER-FM
Sheridan Broadcasting Corp. WAMO(AM), WAMO-FM, WPGR(AM)
Keymarket Communications LLC WASP, WFGI(AM), WOGF(FM), WOGG(FM), WPKL(FM), WYJK(AM)
Broadcast Communications Inc. WKFB(AM), WKHB(AM), WKVE(FM), WJPA, WJPA-FM, WOGI(FM)
BusinessTalkRadio.Net Inc. WLFP(AM)
Iorio Broadcasting Inc. WBVP(AM), WMBA

Portland, ME: Rank 167
Blount Communications Group WBCI-FM
Citadel Broadcasting Corp. WBLM-FM, WCYY-FM, WHOM-FM, WJBQ-FM
Gleason Radio Group WOXO-FM, WTBM(FM)
Saga Communications Inc. WBAE, WCLZ(FM), WGAN(AM), WMGX(FM), WPOR(FM), WYNZ-FM, WZAN
Nassau Broadcasting Partners L.P. WFNK(FM), WHXQ(FM), WHXR(FM), WLVP(AM), WTHT(FM)
Atlantic Coast Radio L.L.C. WJJB-FM, WLOB, WPEI(FM), WRED(AM)
EMF Broadcasting WARX(FM) WCME(AM), WJTO

Portland, OR: Rank 23
ABC Inc. KDZR(AM)
Clear Channel Communications Inc. KEX, KFBW(FM), KKCW-FM, KKRZ-FM, KLTH(FM), KPOJ(AM), KXJM(FM)
Crawford Broadcasting Co. KKPZ(AM)
Entercom Communications Corp. KFXX(AM), KGON-FM, KNRK-FM, KRSK(FM), KTRO(AM), KWJJ-FM, KWOD(AM), KYCH-FM
CBS Radio KCMD(AM), KINK(FM), KUFO-FM, KUPL-FM
Salem Communications Corp. KPDQ, KPDQ-FM, KRYP(FM)
Pamplin Broadcasting KKAD(AM), KPAM
Rose City Radio Corp. KXL, KXTG(FM)
EMF Broadcasting KLVP(FM), KZRI(FM)
Bustos Media LLC KGDD(AM), KLPM(AM), KOOR(AM), KSZN(AM)
Churchill Communications LLC KXPD(AM)

Portsmouth-Dover-Rochester, NH: Rank 116
Citadel Broadcasting Corp. WOKQ-FM, WSAK(FM), WSHK(FM)
Clear Channel Communications Inc. WERZ-FM, WGIN, WHEB-FM, WMYF, WQSO-FM, WSKX(FM)
Costa-Eagle Radio Ventures L.P. WCCM(AM)
Phoenix Media Communications Group WPHX-FM
EMF Broadcasting WNHI(FM) WXEX(AM)

Poughkeepsie, NY: Rank 165
Clear Channel Communications Inc. WBWZ-FM, WKIP, WPKF(FM), WRNQ-FM, WRWD-FM
Pamal Broadcasting Ltd. WBNR, WBPM(FM), WSPK-FM
Cumulus Media Inc. WCZX-FM, WEOK, WRRB(FM) WPDH-FM

Providence-Warwick-Pawtucket, RI: Rank 41
Blount Communications Group WARV
ABC Inc. WDDZ(AM)
Citadel Broadcasting Corp. WBSM, WEAN-FM, WFHN-FM, WPRO, WPRV(AM), WWKX-FM, WWLI-FM
Clear Channel Communications Inc. WHJJ, WHJY-FM, WSNE-FM, WWBB-FM

Entercom Communications Corp. WEEI-FM
Hall Communications Inc. WCTK(FM), WLKW(AM), WNBH
Davidson Media Group LLC WKKB(FM) WNRI, WPRO-FM, WRNI-FM
Astro Tele-Communications Corp. Rhode Island WADK, WJZS(FM), WKFD(AM)

Pueblo, CO: Rank 247
Bahakel Communications KRXP(FM)
Clear Channel Communications Inc. KCCY(FM), KCSJ, KDZA(AM), KDZA-FM
Family Stations Inc. KFRY(FM)
WAY-FM Media Group Inc. KRWA(FM)
Latino Communications LLC KAVA KIQN(FM), KRLN(AM), KSTY(FM), KWRP(AM)
Catholic Radio Network Inc. KFEL

Puerto Rico: Rank 14
Uno Radio Group WCMN, WCMN-FM, WFDT(FM), WFID-FM, WIVA-FM, WLEO(AM), WMIO(FM), WNEL, WORA, WPRM-FM, WPRP, WRIO-FM, WUNO(AM)
Spanish Broadcasting System Inc. WEGM(FM), WIOA(FM), WIOB-FM, WIOC(FM), WMEG-FM, WNOD(FM), WODA(FM), WRXD(FM), WZET(FM), WZMT-FM, WZNT-FM
Univision Radio WKAQ, WUKQ(AM), WUKQ-FM, WYEL(AM)
International Broadcasting Corp. WCHQ(AM), WEKO(AM), WIBS, WRSJ(AM), WTIL, WVOZ-FM, WXRF
Media Power Group Inc. WDEP(AM), WKFE, WLEY, WSKN(AM) WIAC, WIAC-FM, WIDA, WIDA-FM, WIPR(AM), WIPR-FM, WISA, WKAQ-FM, WKSA-FM, WNIK, WNIK-FM, WQBS, WVJP, WVJP-FM, WYAC(AM), WZAR-FM
Calvary Evangelistic Mission Inc. WBMJ, WCGB, WIVV

Quad Cities, IA-IL (Davenport-Rock Island-Moline): Rank 146
Clear Channel Communications Inc. KCQQ(FM), KMXG(FM), KUUL(FM), WFXN(AM), WLLR-FM, WOC
Miller Media Group WKEI(AM), WYEC(FM)
Cumulus Media Inc. KBEA-FM, KBOB-FM, KJOC, KQCS(FM), WXLP-FM
EMF Broadcasting WLKU(FM) WGEN, WKBF

Raleigh-Durham, NC: Rank 43
Capitol Broadcasting Co. Inc. WCMC-FM, WRAL(FM)
Clear Channel Communications Inc. WDCG-FM, WKSL(FM), WRDU-FM, WRVA-FM
Curtis Media Group WBBB-FM, WCLY, WDNC(AM), WDOX(AM), WFMC(AM), WKXU(FM), WPTF, WQDR-FM, WWMY(FM), WYMY(FM), WYRN(AM)
Radio One Inc. WFXC-FM, WFXK-FM, WNNL-FM, WQOK-FM
Truth Broadcasting Corp. WDRU(AM)
Davidson Media Group LLC WRJD(AM), WTIK
Radio La Grande WGSB, WLLQ(AM), WRTG WRXO(AM)
Prieto Broadcasting Inc. WDUR, WETC

Rapid City, SD: Rank 275
American Family Radio KASD(FM)
Duhamel Broadcasting Enterprises KDDX(AM), KOTA
Family Stations Inc. KQFR(FM)
Schurz Communications Inc. KBHB, KFXS-FM, KKLS, KKMK-FM, KOUT-FM, KRCS-FM
Bethesda Christian Broadcasting KLMP(FM), KSLT-FM, KTPT(FM)
Haugo Broadcasting Inc. KSQY-FM, KTOQ KIQK-FM
Michael Radio Group KRKI(FM)
Connoisseur Media LLC KXMZ(FM)
JER Licenses LLC KXZS(FM)

Reading, PA: Rank 130
Citadel Broadcasting Corp. WIOV
Clear Channel Communications Inc. WRAW(AM), WRFY-FM

Redding, CA: Rank 230
Fritz Communications Inc. KESR(FM), KEWB-FM, KHRD(FM), KNCQ-FM
Mapleton Communications LLC KNNN(FM), KNRO(AM), KQMS, KRRX-FM, KSHA-FM
EMF Broadcasting KKRO(FM), KLVB(FM)
Pacific Cascade Communications Corp. KVIP, KVIP-FM

Reno, NV: Rank 122
Americom KBZZ(AM), KJFK(AM), KLCA-FM, KRNO(FM), KZTQ(FM)
Citadel Broadcasting Corp. KBUL-FM, KKOH, KNEV-FM
Lotus Communications Corp. KDOT-FM, KHIT, KOZZ-FM, KPLY(AM), KUUB(FM)
Entravision Communications Corp. KRNV-FM
Azteca Broadcasting Corp. KXEQ
IHR Educational Broadcasting KIHM(AM)
Wilks Broadcast Group LLC KJZS(FM), KRZQ-FM, KTHX-FM, KURK(FM)

Richmond, VA: Rank 54
American Family Radio WRIH(FM)
ABC Inc. WDZY
Clear Channel Communications Inc. WBTJ(FM), WRNL, WRVA, WRVQ-FM, WRXL-FM, WTVR-FM
Cox Radio Inc. WDYL-FM, WKHK-FM, WKLR-FM, WMXB-FM
Radio One Inc. WCDX-FM, WKJM(FM), WKJS(FM), WPZZ(FM), WTPS(AM)

Davidson Media Group LLC WLEE(AM), WREJ(AM), WVNZ(AM) WHAP
Main Line Broadcasting LLC WARV-FM, WBBT-FM, WLFV(FM)
Red Zebra Holdings LLC WXGI
Mountain Broadcasting Corp. WBTK(AM)
Chesapeake-Portsmouth Broadcasting Corp. WLES(AM)

Riverside-San Bernardino, CA: Rank 26
Anaheim Broadcasting Corp. KCAL-FM, KOLA(FM)
Clear Channel Communications Inc. KDIF, KGGI-FM, KKDD, KTDD(AM)
CBS Radio KFRG-FM
Salem Communications Corp. KTIE(AM)
Liberman Broadcasting Inc. KRQB(FM)
Lazer Broadcasting Corp. KCAL, KXRS-FM, KXSB-FM
Hi-Favor Broadcasting LLC KEZY(AM) KVCR-FM

Roanoke-Lynchburg, VA: Rank 111
Clear Channel Communications Inc. WJJS(FM), WJJX(FM), WROV-FM, WYYD-FM
Mel Wheeler Inc. WFIR(AM), WSLC-FM, WSLQ-FM, WVBE(AM), WVBE-FM, WXLK-FM WKDE, WKDE-FM, WSFF(FM), WSLK(AM), WSNV(FM), WSNZ(FM), WWWR
Centennial Broadcasting LLC WLEQ(FM), WLNI-FM, WZZI-FM, WZZU(FM)
3 Daughters Media Inc. WGMN, WVGM
Chesapeake-Portsmouth Broadcasting Corp. WLVA
Positive Alternative Radio Inc. WPAR-FM, WRXT-FM, WTTX-FM

Rochester, MN: Rank 234
Clear Channel Communications Inc. KRCH(FM), KWEB(AM)
Cumulus Media Inc. KLCX(FM), KOLM(AM), KROC(AM), KROC-FM, KWWK(FM)

Rochester, NY: Rank 56
Clear Channel Communications Inc. WDVI(FM), WFXF(FM), WHAM, WHTK, WKGS-FM, WVOR(FM)
Crawford Broadcasting Co. WDCX(AM), WLGZ-FM
Entercom Communications Corp. WBEE-FM, WBZA(FM), WCMF-FM, WPXY-FM, WROC(AM)
M.B. Communications WFLK-FM, WYLF(FM)
Finger Lakes Radio Group WCGR
Holy Family Communications WHIC(AM) WACK(AM), WASB, WDNY(AM), WXXI(AM), WXXI-FM
Stephens Family L.P. WFKL(FM), WRMM-FM

Rockford, IL: Rank 149
Cumulus Media Inc. WKGL-FM, WROK, WXXQ-FM, WZOK-FM
Good Karma Broadcasting L.L.C. WTJK
Maverick Media LLC WGFB(FM), WNTA, WRTB(FM), WXRX-FM
EMF Broadcasting WGSL-FM, WQFL-FM

Rocky Mount-Wilson, NC: Rank 202
Capitol Broadcasting Co. Inc. WNCM(FM)
First Media Radio LLC WDWG(FM), WPWZ(FM), WRMT(AM), WZAX(FM), WRSV(FM)

Sacramento, CA: Rank 27
ABC Inc. KIID(AM)
Citadel Broadcasting Corp. KWYL(FM)
Clear Channel Communications Inc. KFBK, KGBY-FM, KHLX(FM), KHYL-FM, KQJK(FM), KSTE
Entercom Communications Corp. KBZC(FM), KCTC(AM), KDND(FM), KRXQ-FM, KSEG-FM, KSSJ-FM
Family Stations Inc. KEAR-FM
CBS Radio KHTK, KNCI-FM, KSFM-FM, KYMX-FM, KZZO-FM
Salem Communications Corp. KFIA, KTKZ
Entravision Communications Corp. KBMB(FM), KNTY(FM), KRCX-FM, KXSE(FM)
Fritz Communications Inc. KCCL(FM)
Lazer Broadcasting Corp. KSRN(FM)
EMF Broadcasting KLRS(FM), KLVS(FM)
Bustos Media LLC KLMG(FM)
Cherry Creek Radio LLC KRLT-FM
IHR Educational Broadcasting KAHI, KSMH(AM)
Nevada County Broadcasters Inc. KNCO(AM) KRJY(AM)

Saginaw-Bay City-Midland, MI: Rank 134
Citadel Broadcasting Corp. WHNN-FM, WILZ-FM, WIOG(FM), WKQZ-FM
MacDonald Broadcasting Co. WKCQ-FM, WMJO(FM), WSAG(FM), WSAM
Meredith Broadcasting Group, Meredith Corp. WNEM(AM)
NextMedia Group Inc. WCEN-FM, WSGW, WSGW-FM, WTLZ-FM
EMF Broadcasting WLKB(FM) WGER(FM), WLUN(FM)

Salina-Manhattan, KS: Rank 203

Salisbury-Ocean City, MD: Rank 143
Birach Broadcasting Corp. WGOP(AM)
Clear Channel Communications Inc. WJDY(AM), WOSC-FM, WSBY-FM, WTGM, WWFG-FM
Great Scott Broadcasting WGBG-FM, WJWK, WJWL, WKDB(FM), WKHI(FM), WOCQ-FM, WXSH(FM), WZBH-FM, WZEB(FM)

Delmarva Broadcasting Co. WAFL-FM, WICO(AM), WICO-FM, WKTT(FM), WNCL(FM), WQJZ-FM, WYUS, WZKT(FM) WDKZ(FM), WLBW-FM, WQHQ-FM

Salt Lake City-Ogden-Provo, UT: Rank 30
Bible Broadcasting Network KYFO-FM
Bonneville International Corporation KRSP-FM, KSFI-FM, KSL, KSL-FM
ABC Inc. KWDZ(AM)
Citadel Broadcasting Corp. KBEE(FM), KBER(FM), KENZ(FM), KFNZ, KHTB(FM), KJQS(AM), KKAT(AM), KKAT-FM
Clear Channel Communications Inc. KJMY(FM), KNRS, KNRS-FM, KODJ-FM, KOSY-FM, KZHT(FM)
Family Stations Inc. KUFR-FM
Legacy Media Corporation KOGN(AM)
Azteca Broadcasting Corp. KSVN
Simmons Media Group KEGH(FM), KOVO, KXOL, KXRK-FM, KYMV(FM), KZNS(AM)
Millcreek Broadcasting L.L.C. KUDD(FM), KUUU(FM)
Bustos Media LLC KDUT(FM), KTUB(AM)
IHR Educational Broadcasting KIHU(AM)
Carlson Communications International KDYL(AM) KALL(AM), KSOP, KSOP-FM, KUBL-FM, KUTR(AM)
3 Point Media KYLZ(FM), KZZQ(FM)
Faith Communications Corp. KANN

San Angelo, TX: Rank 289
Criswell Communications KCRN, KCRN-FM
EMF Broadcasting KLRW(FM), KNAR(FM)
Double O Radio L.L.C. KELI-FM, KGKL, KGKL-FM, KKCN(FM), KNRX(FM)
Foster Communications Co. Inc. KCLL(FM), KIXY-FM, KKSA, KWFR-FM KLTP(FM)

San Antonio, TX: Rank 31
Bible Broadcasting Network KYFS-FM
ABC Inc. KRDY(AM)
Clear Channel Communications Inc. KAJA(FM), KQXT-FM, KTKR, KXXM-FM, KZEP-FM, WOAI
Cox Radio Inc. KCYY(FM), KISS-FM, KKYX, KONO, KONO-FM, KPWT(FM), KSMG(FM)
Martin Broadcasting Inc. KCHL
Salem Communications Corp. KLUP(AM), KSLR
Univision Radio KBBT(FM), KCOR(AM), KGSX(FM), KLTO-FM, KROM(FM), KXTN-FM
Victoria RadioWorks Ltd. KBAR-FM, KNAL(AM)
Border Media Partners LLC KJXK(FM), KSAH(AM), KTFM(FM), KTSA, KZDC
SIGA Broadcasting Corp. KTMR(AM) KAHL(AM), KGNB, KNBT-FM, KYTY(AM)
La Promesa Foundation KJMA(FM), KWMF(AM)
GAP Broadcasting LLC KIXS-FM

San Diego, CA: Rank 17
Clear Channel Communications Inc. KGB-FM, KHTS-FM, KIOZ-FM, KLSD(AM), KMYI(FM), KOGO(AM), KUSS(FM)
CBS Radio KSCF(FM), KYXY-FM
Lincoln Financial Media KBZT(FM), KIFM-FM, KNSN(AM), KSON(FM), KSOQ-FM
Salem Communications Corp. KCBQ, KPRZ
Univision Radio KLNV-FM, KLQV-FM
Entravision Communications Corp. KSSD(FM)
Astor Broadcast Group KCEO, KFSD(AM)
EMF Broadcasting KLVJ-FM
Hi-Favor Broadcasting LLC KSDO KFMB, KFMB-FM, XETRA, XETRA-FM

San Francisco: Rank 4
ABC Inc. KMKY
Citadel Broadcasting Corp. KGO, KSFO
Clear Channel Communications Inc. KCNL(FM), KIOI-FM, KISQ-FM, KKGN(AM), KKSF-FM, KMEL-FM, KNEW, KYLD-FM
Entercom Communications Corp. KBWF(FM), KDFC-FM, KOIT-FM
Family Stations Inc. KEAR(AM)
CBS Radio KCBS, KFRC(AM), KFRC-FM, KITS-FM, KLLC-FM, KMVQ-FM
Inner City Broadcasting KBLX-FM, KVTO, KVVN
Pacifica Foundation Inc. KPFA-FM, KPFB-FM
Pappas Telecasting Companies KTRB(AM)
NextMedia Group Inc. KBAY(FM), KEZR(FM)
Salem Communications Corp. KDOW(FM), KFAX
Sinclair Communications Inc. KXTS(FM)
Spanish Broadcasting System Inc. KRZZ(FM)
Cumulus Media Partners LLC KFFG-FM, KFOG-FM, KNBR, KSAN-FM, KTCT
Univision Radio KBRG(FM), KLOK, KSOL(FM), KVVF(FM), KVVZ(FM)
Multicultural Radio Broadcasting Inc. KATD, KEST, KIQI
Bicoastal Media L.L.C. KLLK
Maverick Media LLC KMHX(FM), KSRO, KVRV-FM, KXFX-FM
Mapleton Communications LLC KPIG(AM)
Moon Broadcasting KRRS, KTOB(AM)
EMF Broadcasting KLVR(FM)
IHR Educational Broadcasting KSFB(AM) KFGY-FM, KSJO-FM
Coast Radio Company Inc. KKDV(FM), KKIQ-FM, KUIC-FM
Redwood Empire Stereocasters KZST-FM

San Jose, CA: Rank 35

Multicultural Radio Broadcasting Inc. KSJX(AM)

San Luis Obispo, CA: Rank 173
American General Media KIQO-FM, KKAL(FM), KKJG-FM, KZOZ-FM
Lazer Broadcasting Corp. KLMM(FM)
Mapleton Communications LLC KPYG(FM), KWWV(FM), KXTZ-FM, KYNS(AM)
EMF Broadcasting KLVH(FM) KESC(FM)
Frontier Radio Management Inc. KSLY-FM, KSTT-FM, KURQ(FM), KVEC

Santa Barbara, CA: Rank 213
Cumulus Media Inc. KMGQ(FM), KRUZ(FM), KVYB(FM)
Point Broadcasting Company KIST(AM), KIST-FM, KSBL-FM, KSPE-FM, KTMS, KTYD-FM
Lazer Broadcasting Corp. KZER(AM) KCLU(AM)

Santa Maria-Lompoc, CA: Rank 212
Family Stations Inc. KHFR(FM)
American General Media KBOX(FM), KPAT-FM, KRQK-FM
Lazer Broadcasting Corp. KSBQ
Knight Broadcasting Inc. KSMA(FM), KSYV-FM, KUHL(AM)
Emerald Wave Media KIDI-FM, KRTO(FM), KTAP
Frontier Radio Management Inc. KSMX(FM), KSMY(FM), KSNI-FM, KXFM-FM

Santa Rosa, CA: Rank 119
Redwood Empire Stereocasters KGRP(FM)

Sarasota-Bradenton, FL: Rank 73
Clear Channel Communications Inc. WCTQ(FM), WDDV(AM), WLTQ-FM, WSDV(AM), WSRZ-FM, WTZB(FM)
Cox Radio Inc. WHPT(FM)
CBS Radio WSJT(FM)
The Moody Bible Institute of Chicago WKZM-FM
Northwestern College & Radio WSMR-FM
Salem Communications Corp. WLSS(AM)
Metropolitan Radio Group Inc. WBRD, WTMY
Viper Communications Broadcast Group WENG

Savannah, GA: Rank 157
Bible Broadcasting Network WYFS-FM
Clear Channel Communications Inc. WAEV-FM, WLVH-FM, WSOK, WTKS(AM), WYKZ(FM)
Triad Broadcasting Co. L.L.C. WFXH(FM), WGCO(FM), WGZR(FM), WLOW(FM)
Cumulus Media Inc. WBMQ, WEAS-FM, WIXV-FM, WJCL-FM, WJLG, WTYB(FM), WZAT-FM
Tama Broadcasting Inc. WSSJ(FM), WTHG(FM) WFXH-FM, WQBT(FM), WRHQ-FM, WWJN(FM)
MarMac Communications LLC WSEG(AM)

Seattle-Tacoma, WA: Rank 13
CRISTA Broadcasting KCIS(AM), KCMS(FM)
Bonneville International Corporation KIRO, KIRO-FM, KTTH(AM)
ABC Inc. KKDZ
Clear Channel Communications Inc. KBKS-FM, KFNK(FM), KHHO, KJR, KJR-FM, KUBE-FM
Entercom Communications Corp. KISW-FM, KKWF(FM), KMTT-FM, KNDD-FM
Family Stations Inc. KARR
Fisher Communications Inc. KOMO(AM), KPLZ(FM), KVI(AM)
CBS Radio KJAQ(FM), KMPS-FM, KPTK(AM), KZOK-FM
Premier Broadcasters KRXY-FM
Salem Communications Corp. KGNW, KKMO, KKOL, KLFE, KNTS(AM)
Sandusky Radio KIXI, KKNW(AM), KQMV(FM), KRWM-FM, KWJZ(FM)
Multicultural Radio Broadcasting Inc. KXPA
Bustos Media LLC KTBK(AM)
Seattle Streaming Radio LLC KBRO, KLDY, KNTB

Sebring, FL: Rank 287
Cohan Radio Group Inc. WITS(AM), WJCM(AM), WWLL(FM), WWOJ(FM), WWTK(AM)

Sheboygan, WI : Rank 280
Midwest Communications Inc. WBFM(FM), WHBL(AM), WHBZ(FM), WXER(FM)
Mountain Dog Media WCLB(AM)

Shreveport, LA: Rank 133
Wilkins Communications Network Inc. KIOU
Noalmark Broadcasting Corp. KVMA(FM)
Metropolitan Radio Group Inc. KTKC-FM
Cumulus Media Inc. KMJJ-FM, KQHN(FM), KRMD, KRMD-FM, KVMA-FM
Houston Christian Broadcasters Inc. KHMD(FM)
Access.1 Communications Corp. KBTT(FM), KLKL(FM), KOKA, KSYR(FM), KTAL-FM KNCB, KNCB-FM
Amistad Communications Inc. KASO, KSYB(AM)
GAP Broadcasting LLC KEEL(AM), KRUF(FM), KTUX-FM, KVKI-FM, KWKH(AM), KXKS-FM
The RAFTT Corp. KBSF

Sioux City, IA: Rank 278
Bott Radio Network KTFC-FM
Clear Channel Communications Inc. KGLI-FM, KMNS, KSEZ-FM, KSFT-FM, KWSL WNAX(AM), WNAX-FM
Powell Broadcasting Co. Inc. KKMA(FM), KKYY(FM), KSCJ, KSUX(FM)

South Bend, IN: Rank 178
Federated Media WAOR-FM, WBYT-FM
Le Sea Broadcasting WHME-FM
Schurz Communications Inc. WNSN-FM, WSBT
Artistic Media Partners Inc. WDND(AM), WNDV-FM, WPNT(AM), WSMM(FM)
Marion R. Williams Stns WSMK-FM
Progressive Broadcasting System Inc. WFRN-FM
Talking Stick Communications LLC WRBR-FM WHLY(AM)

Spokane, WA: Rank 92
Clear Channel Communications Inc. KCDA(FM), KIXZ-FM, KKZX-FM, KPTQ(AM), KQNT(AM)
The Moody Bible Institute of Chicago KMBI, KMBI-FM
Morgan Murphy Media KEZE-FM, KXLY, KZZU-FM
Morris Radio LLC KWIQ(AM)
Mapleton Communications LLC KBBD(FM), KDRK-FM, KEYF(AM), KEYF-FM, KGA, KJRB, KZBD(FM)
EMF Broadcasting KTSL-FM KAZZ(FM), KHTQ-FM, KISC-FM, KTRW(AM), KVNI, KXLY-FM

Springfield, MA: Rank 88
Citadel Broadcasting Corp. WHLL(AM), WMAS-FM
Clear Channel Communications Inc. WHYN, WHYN-FM, WNNZ, WPKX-FM, WRNX-FM
Entercom Communications Corp. WVEI-FM
Saga Communications Inc. WAQY-FM, WHMP, WHNP(AM), WLZX(FM), WRSI(FM)
Pamal Broadcasting Ltd. WPNI(AM)
Davidson Media Group LLC WACM, WSPR

Springfield, MO: Rank 136
Bott Radio Network KSCV(FM)
Clear Channel Communications Inc. KGBX-FM, KGMY, KSWF(FM), KTOZ-FM, KXUS-FM
Meyer Communications Inc. KBFL(AM), KTXR-FM, KWTO, KWTO-FM
The Mid-West Family Broadcast Group KKLH(FM), KOMG(FM), KOSP(FM), KQRA(FM)
Journal Communications Inc. KSGF(AM), KSGF-FM, KSPW(FM), KTTS-FM KMRF

St. Cloud, MN: Rank 216
Leighton Enterprises Inc. KCLD-FM, KCML(FM), KNSI, KZPK-FM
Regent Communications Inc. KLZZ-FM, KMXK-FM, KXSS(AM), KZRV(FM), WJON, WWJO-FM KASM, KDDG(AM)
Tri-County Broadcasting Inc. WBHR, WHMH-FM

St. Louis, MO: Rank 20
Birach Broadcasting Corp. WEW, WIJR(AM)
Bonneville International Corporation WARH(FM), WIL-FM, WXOS(FM)
Bott Radio Network KSIV(AM), KSIV-FM
ABC Inc. WSDZ
Clear Channel Communications Inc. KATZ(AM), KATZ-FM, KLOU(FM), KMJM-FM, KSD(FM), KSLZ(FM)
Crawford Broadcasting Co. KJSL, KSTL
The Curators of the University of Missouri KWMU-FM
Emmis Communications Corp. KFTK(FM), KIHT-FM, KPNT(AM), KSHE(FM)
CBS Radio KEZK-FM, KMOX, KYKY-FM
Radio One Inc. WFUN-FM, WHHL(FM)
Simmons Media Group KSLG(AM), WFFX(AM)
Family Worship Center Church Inc. KDJR(FM)
Kaspar Broadcasting Group KFAV-FM, KWRE(AM)
Big League Broadcasting LLC KFNS(AM), KFNS-FM, KRFT(AM) KFUO(AM), KFUO-FM, KSLQ-FM, KTUI, KTUI-FM, KWMO, KZQZ(AM)
Missouri River Christian Broadcasting Inc. KGNA-FM
Covenant Network KHOJ(AM), WRYT(AM)
GoodRadio.TV KJFF(AM)

Stamford-Norwalk, CT: Rank 150

State College, PA: Rank 251
Forever Broadcasting WBUS(FM), WFGE(FM), WMAJ-FM, WQWK(FM), WRSC, WRSC-FM
Family Stations Inc. WXFR(FM)
First Media Radio LLC WZWW-FM
2510 Licenses LLC WBHV-FM, WOWY(FM), WWSH(FM)
Magnum Broadcasting Inc. WBLF, WJOW(FM), WPHB

Stockton, CA: Rank 90
Citadel Broadcasting Corp. KJOY-FM, KWIN-FM
Clear Channel Communications Inc. KQOD-FM, KWSX(AM)
Entravision Communications Corp. KCVR, KMIX-FM
IHR Educational Broadcasting KWG(AM) KSTN, KSTN-FM

Sunbury-Selinsgrove-Lewisburg, PA: Rank 219

Backyard Broadcasting LLC WCXR(FM)
Sunbury Broadcasting Corp. WMLP(AM), WVLY-FM

Sussex, NJ: Rank 250
Clear Channel Communications Inc. WNNJ(FM), WSUS-FM, WTOC(AM)

Syracuse, NY: Rank 83
Buckley Broadcasting Corp. WFBL(AM), WSEN(AM)
Citadel Broadcasting Corp. WAQX-FM, WLTI(FM), WNSS(AM), WNTQ(FM)
Clear Channel Communications Inc. WBBS-FM, WHEN, WPHR-FM, WSYR, WWHT-FM, WYYY-FM
Mars Hill Network WMHR-FM
Galaxy Communications L.P. WKRH-FM, WKRL-FM, WSCP, WSGO, WTKV-FM, WTKW-FM, WTLA, WZUN(FM)
WOLF Radio Inc. WOLF, WOLF-FM WMCR, WMCR-FM, WSEN-FM, WVOA-FM
Cram Communications LLC WAMF(AM), WSIV

Tallahassee, FL: Rank 162
Clear Channel Communications Inc. WFLA-FM, WNLS, WTLY(FM), WTNT-FM, WXSR-FM
Cumulus Media Inc. WBZE(FM), WGLF(FM), WHBT(FM), WHBX(FM), WWLD(FM)
Marion R. Williams Stns WSTT
Opus Media Holdings LLC WAIB-FM, WEGT(FM), WHTF-FM, WQTL(FM)

Tampa-St. Petersburg-Clearwater, FL: Rank 18
Bible Broadcasting Network WYFE-FM
ABC Inc. WWMI
Clear Channel Communications Inc. WBTP(FM), WFLA(AM), WFUS(FM), WHNZ(AM), WMTX(FM), WXTB-FM
Cox Radio Inc. WDUV-FM, WPOI(FM), WSUN-FM, WWRM(FM), WXGL(FM)
Family Stations Inc. WFTI-FM
Genesis Communications Inc. WHBO(AM), WMGG(AM), WWBA(AM)
CBS Radio WLLD(FM), WQYK(AM), WQYK-FM, WRBQ-FM, WYUU(FM)
Salem Communications Corp. WGUL(AM), WTBN(AM), WTWD(AM)
Metropolitan Radio Group Inc. WRXB
Wagenvoord Advertising Group Inc. WDCF, WTAN(AM), WZHR(AM)
Tama Broadcasting Inc. WTMP, WTMP-FM WFLZ-FM, WLCC

Terre Haute, IN: Rank 209
The Cromwell Group Inc. WCBH-FM
Emmis Communications Corp. WTHI-FM, WWVR-FM
Illinois Bible Institute Inc. WCRT-FM
Midwest Communications Inc. WIBQ(FM), WMGI-FM, WPRS
The Original Company Inc. WQTY-FM
Crossroads Communications Inc. WAXI-FM, WBOW(AM), WBOW-FM, WSDM-FM, WSDX(AM) WKZI, WNDI, WNDI-FM
Covenant Network WHOJ(FM)

Texarkana, TX-AR: Rank 263
American Family Radio KNLL(FM)
Arklatex LLC KBYB(FM), KCMC, KFYX(FM), KTFS(AM), KTOY(FM)
Family Worship Center Church Inc. KNRB(FM)
EMF Broadcasting KKLT(FM)
Tower Investment Trust Inc. KTTY(FM)
GAP Broadcasting LLC KKYR-FM, KOSY(AM), KPWW-FM, KYGL-FM
American Media Investments Inc. KEWL-FM, KKTK(AM), KPGG(AM)

Toledo, OH: Rank 91
Clear Channel Communications Inc. WCWA, WIOT(FM), WRVF(FM), WSPD, WVKS-FM
Family Stations Inc. WOTL-FM
Cumulus Media Inc. WLQR, WLQR-FM, WRQN-FM, WTOD, WTWR-FM, WWWM-FM, WXKR-FM
Lake Cities Broadcasting Corp. WLZZ(FM)
Family Worship Center Church Inc. WJYM
EMF Broadcasting WNWT(AM) WKKO-FM
Urban Radio Licenses LLC WIMX-FM, WJZE-FM
BAS Broadcasting Inc. WPFX-FM

Topeka, KS: Rank 197
American Family Radio KBUZ(FM)
Bott Radio Network KCVT(FM)
Family Life Communications Inc. KJTY-FM
Morris Radio LLC WIBW, WIBW-FM
Cumulus Media Inc. KDVV-FM, KMAJ, KTOP, KWIC-FM
EMF Broadcasting KGLV(FM) KMAJ-FM, KMKF-FM
Great Plains Media Inc. KLZR(FM), KMXN(FM)

Traverse City-Petoskey, MI: Rank 192
Midwestern Broadcasting Co. WBCM(FM), WCCW(AM), WJZQ(FM), WTCM(FM)
Northern Star Broadcasting L.L.C. WGFM(FM), WGFN(FM), WJZJ(FM), WLJZ(FM), WMKC(FM)
MacDonald Garber Broadcasting Co. WKHQ-FM, WLXT(FM), WLXV(FM), WMBN(AM), WMKT(AM)
Fort Bend Broadcasting Co. WARD(AM), WLDR-FM
Good News Media Inc. WLJN-FM WCCW-FM, WOUF(FM), WTCM-FM

Trenton, NJ: Rank 142
Nassau Broadcasting Partners L.P. WCHR(AM), WPST(FM)
Multicultural Radio Broadcasting Inc. WHWH
Millennium Radio Group LLC WKXW(FM) WFJS(AM)

Tri-Cities, WA (Richland-Kennewick-Pasco): Rank 196
New Northwest Broadcasters LLC KALE, KEGX(FM), KIOK-FM, KKSR(FM), KTCR, KUJ-FM
CSN International KBLD(FM)
Moon Broadcasting KLES(FM), KZXR
EMF Broadcasting KRKL(FM)
Bustos Media LLC KMMG(FM), KZTB(FM)
Cherry Creek Radio LLC KONA, KONA-FM KVAN(AM)
GAPWEST Broadcasting KEYW-FM, KFLD, KOLW(FM), KORD-FM

Tucson, AZ: Rank 60
Citadel Broadcasting Corp. KCUB, KHYT-FM, KIIM-FM, KSZR(FM), KTUC
Clear Channel Communications Inc. KNST, KOHT-FM, KRQQ-FM, KTZR-FM, KWFM(AM), KWMT-FM, KXEW
Family Life Communications Inc. KFLT, KFLT-FM
Lotus Communications Corp. KFMA-FM, KLPX-FM, KTKT
Journal Communications Inc. KFFN, KGMG-FM, KMXZ-FM, KQTH(FM)
Good News Communications Inc. KCEE(AM), KGMS(AM), KVOI(AM)
EMF Broadcasting KAIC(FM) KEVT(AM), KUAT-FM, KUAZ(AM), KUAZ-FM

Tulsa, OK: Rank 65
Birach Broadcasting Corp. KJMU(AM)
Clear Channel Communications Inc. KAKC(AM), KIZS(FM), KMOD-FM, KQLL-FM, KTBT(FM), KTBZ(AM)
Cox Radio Inc. KJSR-FM, KRAV-FM, KRMG, KRMG-FM, KWEN-FM
Adonai Radio Group KCXR(FM), KEMX-FM, KXOJ-FM, KYAL(AM), KYAL-FM
Renda Broadcasting Corp. KBEZ(FM), KHTT-FM
Shamrock Communications Inc. KMYZ-FM, KTSO(FM)
Journal Communications Inc. KFAQ(AM), KVOO-FM, KXBL(FM)
Perry Publishing & Broadcasting Co. KGTO, KJMM-FM
KCD Enterprises Inc. KPGM(AM)
K95.5 Inc. KTFX-FM KEOR(AM), KMUS(AM), KRVT(AM), KZLI(AM)

Tupelo, MS: Rank 189
Wilkins Communications Network Inc. WCPC
Air South Radio Inc. WFTA-FM
American Family Radio WAFR-FM, WAQB-FM
Clear Channel Communications Inc. WBVV(FM), WESE-FM, WKMQ(AM), WTUP, WWKZ(FM), WWZD-FM
Stanford Communications Inc. WAFM-FM, WAMY, WWZQ WELO, WSEL, WSEL-FM, WZLQ-FM

Tuscaloosa, AL: Rank 233
Citadel Broadcasting Corp. WBEI(FM), WTSK(AM), WTUG-FM, WWMM(FM)
Clear Channel Communications Inc. WACT(AM), WRTR(FM), WTXT-FM, WZBQ-FM
The Moody Bible Institute of Chicago WMFT(FM) WJRD(AM)

Twin Falls (Sun Valley), ID: Rank 238

Tyler-Longview, TX: Rank 144
American Family Radio KATG(FM)
Bible Broadcasting Network KYFP(FM)
Bott Radio Network KTAA(FM)
Salem Communications Corp. KPXI-FM
Gleiser Communications LLC KEES, KTBB, KTBB-FM, KYZS
Reynolds Radio LLC KZTK(FM)
Access.1 Communications Corp. KFRO, KKUS(FM), KOOI-FM, KOYE(FM), KYKX-FM
Waller Broadcasting KEBE, KFRO-FM, KLJT-FM, KXAL-FM
EMF Broadcasting KZLO(FM) KTLU, KWRW-FM
GAP Broadcasting LLC KDOK(AM), KISX-FM, KKTX-FM, KNUE(FM), KTYL-FM

Utica-Rome, NY: Rank 164
Bible Broadcasting Network WYFY
Clear Channel Communications Inc. WUMX(FM)
Regent Communications Inc. WFRG-FM, WIBX, WLZW-FM, WODZ-FM
WAMC/Northeast Public Radio WRUN(AM), WRUN-FM
Galaxy Communications L.P. WIXT(AM), WKLL-FM, WOUR-FM, WRNY, WTLB
EMF Broadcasting WKVU(FM), WOKR(FM), WRCK-FM WBRV, WBRV-FM, WXUR-FM
Roser Communications Network Inc. WADR, WBGK(FM), WSKS(FM), WSKU(FM), WUTQ

Valdosta, GA: Rank 267
Rama Communications Inc. WRFV(AM)
Black Crow Media Group LLC WQPW(FM), WSTI-FM, WVGA(AM), WVLD(AM), WWRQ-FM, WXHT(FM)
EMF Broadcasting WVDA(FM), WVKV(FM)
Dee Rivers Radio Group WAAC(FM), WGOV(AM), WLYX(FM)

Victor Valley, CA: Rank 117

Visalia-Tulare-Hanford, CA: Rank 101
Buckley Broadcasting Corp. KIOO-FM, KSEQ-FM
Clear Channel Communications Inc. KEZL(AM)
Azteca Broadcasting Corp. KGEN, KGEN-FM
Moon Broadcasting KMQA-FM
IHR Educational Broadcasting KJOP KJUG, KJUG-FM

Waco, TX: Rank 199
American Family Radio KBDE(FM), KSUR(FM)
Clear Channel Communications Inc. KBGO(FM), KWTX, KWTX-FM, WACO-FM
Univision Radio KHCK-FM
Simmons Media Group KLRK(FM), KRZI(AM)
Border Media Partners LLC KWOW-FM KBRQ(FM)
William W. McCutchen III Stns KDRW(FM)

Washington, DC: Rank 9
Bonneville International Corporation WFED(AM), WTLP(FM), WTOP-FM, WWFD(AM), WWWT-FM, WZAA(AM)
Citadel Broadcasting Corp. WJZW-FM, WMAL, WRQX-FM
Clear Channel Communications Inc. WASH-FM, WBIG-FM, WIHT(FM), WMZQ-FM, WWDC-FM
CBS Radio WHFS(AM), WJFK-FM, WLZL(FM), WPGC-FM, WTGB-FM
Pacifica Foundation Inc. WPFW-FM
Salem Communications Corp. WAVA(AM), WAVA-FM
Nassau Broadcasting Partners L.P. WAFY-FM
Entravision Communications Corp. WACA
Multicultural Broadcasting Inc. WLXE(AM), WZHF
Radio One Inc. WKYS-FM, WMMJ-FM, WOL, WPRS-FM, WYCB
Somar Communications Inc. WKIK, WMDM(FM)
Red Zebra Holdings LLC WTEM, WTNT(AM), WWRC(AM), WWXT(FM), WWXX(FM), WXTR(AM)
Mountain Broadcasting Group WWGB
Metro Radio Inc. WKDV

Waterloo-Cedar Falls, IA: Rank 252
Bahakel Communications KFMW-FM, KOKZ-FM, KWLO(AM), KXEL
Northwestern College & Radio KNWS
KM Communications Inc. KQMG, KQMG-FM
Cumulus Media Inc. KCRR(FM), KKHQ-FM, KOEL-FM KNWS-FM, KWAY, KWAY-FM
Ace Radio Corp. KCOO(FM)

Watertown, NY: Rank 279
Clancy-Mance Communications WLYK(FM)
Mars Hill Network WMHI-FM
EMF Broadcasting WKWV(FM)
Radioactive LLC WBLH(FM)
Community Broadcasters LLC WATN, WBDR(FM), WEFX(FM), WOTT(FM), WTOJ(FM)
Stephens Family L.P. WCIZ-FM, WFRY-FM, WNER(AM), WTNY

Wausau-Stevens Point, WI (Central Wisconsin): Rank 168
Muzzy Broadcasting L.L.C. WKQH(FM), WSPT, WSPT-FM
Evangel Ministries Inc. WGNV(FM)
Midwest Communications Inc. WDEZ-FM, WIZD-FM, WOFM-FM, WRIG, WSAU
NRG Media LLC WBCV(FM), WGLX-FM, WLJY(FM), WYTE(FM) WDUX(AM), WIFC-FM, WMZK-FM
Seehafer Broadcasting Corp. WDLB, WFHR, WOSQ-FM, WXCO
JER Licenses LLC WDTX(FM)

Wenatchee, WA: Rank 176

West Palm Beach-Boca Raton, FL: Rank 47
Beasley Broadcast Group Inc. WSBR
ABC Inc. WMNE(AM)
Clear Channel Communications Inc. WBZT(AM), WJNO(AM), WKGR-FM, WLDI-FM, WRLX-FM, WZZR(FM)
CBS Radio WEAT-FM, WIRK-FM, WMBX-FM, WNEW(FM), WPBZ-FM
James Crystal Inc. WFTL(AM), WMEN(AM)
WAY-FM Media Group Inc. WAYF(FM) WAFC, WAFC-FM, WDJA(AM), WJBW(AM), WOLL-FM
Communicom Broadcasting LLC WLVJ(AM)

Wheeling, WV: Rank 256
Clear Channel Communications Inc. WBBD, WEGW-FM, WKWK-FM, WVKF(FM), WWVA(AM)
Keymarket Communications LLC WOMP, WUKL(FM), WYJK-FM
EMF Broadcasting WLVW(FM)
Priority Radio Inc. WXHZ(FM) WOVK-FM

Wichita Falls, TX: Rank 265
Cumulus Media Inc. KLUR-FM, KOLI-FM, KQXC-FM, KYYI-FM
Graham Newspapers Inc. KSWA(AM)
EMF Broadcasting KZKL(FM)
Tower Investment Trust Inc. KXXN(FM)
GAP Broadcasting LLC KBZS(FM), KNIN-FM, KWFS, KWFS-FM
South Texas FM Investments LLC KZAM(FM)

Wichita, KS: Rank 99
American Family Radio KCFN(FM)
Bible Broadcasting Network KYFW-FM
Bott Radio Network KJRG
ABC Inc. KQAM
Clear Channel Communications Inc. KRBB-FM, KTHR(FM), KZCH(FM), KZSN(FM)
Entercom Communications Corp. KDGS(FM), KEYN-FM, KFBZ(FM), KFH(AM), KFH-FM, KNSS(AM)
Robert Ingstad Broadcast Properties KBUF(AM)
Journal Communications Inc. KFDI-FM, KFTI(AM), KFTI-FM, KFXJ(FM), KICT-FM, KYQQ(FM)
WAY-FM Media Group Inc. KYWA(FM)
EMF Broadcasting KTLI(FM)
Connoisseur Media LLC KIBB(FM), KVWF(FM)
Steckline Communications Inc. KGSO(AM)
Catholic Radio Network Inc. KAHS(AM)

Wilkes Barre-Scranton, PA: Rank 70
Wilkins Communications Network Inc. WITK(AM)
Citadel Broadcasting Corp. WARM, WBHD(FM), WBHT-FM, WBSX(FM), WMGS-FM, WSJR(FM)
Clear Channel Communications Inc. WHCY-FM
MAX Media L.L.C. WFYY(FM)
Entercom Communications Corp. WBZU(AM), WDMT(FM), WGGI-FM, WGGY-FM, WILK, WILK-FM, WKRF(FM), WKRZ-FM, WKZN(AM)
Shamrock Communications Inc. WBAX, WEJL, WEZX-FM, WQFM-FM, WQFN(FM)
Nassau Broadcasting Partners L.P. WVPO
Family Life Network WCIG(FM)
Bold Gold Media Group LP WFBS(AM), WICK, WWRR(FM), WYCK
Holy Family Communications WQOR(AM)
WS2K Radio LLC dba WS Media WAZL, WCDL(AM), WLNP(FM), WNAK WSBG-FM

Geos Communications WGMF(AM)

Williamsport, PA: Rank 276
Clear Channel Communications Inc. WBYL(FM), WRAK, WRKK, WVRT(FM)
Backyard Broadcasting LLC WBZD-FM, WILQ-FM, WLMY(FM), WWPA WJSA, WJSA-FM, WKSB-FM, WSNU-FM
Geos Communications WNKZ(FM)

Wilmington, DE: Rank 77
Clear Channel Communications Inc. WDSD(FM), WILM, WRDX(FM), WWTX(AM)
NextMedia Group Inc. WJBR-FM
Delmarva Broadcasting Co. WDEL, WSTW-FM, WXCY(FM)
Priority Radio Inc. WSRY(AM)

Wilmington, NC: Rank 161
Capitol Broadcasting Co. Inc. WAZO(FM), WILT(FM), WKXB-FM, WMFD
Cumulus Media Inc. WAAV, WGNI-FM, WMNX-FM, WWQQ-FM
Sea-Comm Inc. WBNE(FM), WLTT(FM), WNTB(FM)
Carolina Christian Radio WDVV-FM, WLSG(AM), WMYT, WWIL, WWIL-FM, WZDG(FM) WKXS-FM
Charles A. Hecht and Alfredo Alonso Stns WVNC(AM)

Winchester, VA: Rank 221
Vox Communications WSIG(FM)
Clear Channel Communications Inc. WAZR-FM, WFQX-FM, WLVE(AM)
Mid Atlantic Network WINC, WINC-FM, WWRE(FM), WWRT(FM) WFTR, WSVG(AM), WUSQ-FM, WZRV(FM)

Worcester, MA: Rank 114
Blount Communications Group WNEB, WVNE(AM)
Citadel Broadcasting Corp. WORC-FM, WWFX(FM), WXLO-FM
Clear Channel Communications Inc. WSRS-FM, WTAG
Entercom Communications Corp. WVEI(AM)
Northeast Broadcasting Company Inc. WJOE(AM), WXRG(FM) WORC

Yakima, WA: Rank 204
New Northwest Broadcasters LLC KARY-FM, KBBO(AM), KHHK-FM, KJOX(AM), KRSE-FM, KXDD-FM
Bustos Media LLC KDYK(AM), KDYM(AM), KZTA-FM
GAPWEST Broadcasting KATS(FM), KDBL(FM), KFFM-FM, KIT, KUTI(AM)

York, PA: Rank 103
Wilkins Communications Network Inc. WYYC(AM)
Citadel Broadcasting Corp. WQXA-FM
Hall Communications Inc. WSJW(FM)
Cumulus Media Partners LLC WARM, WGLD(AM), WSBA, WSOX-FM WGET, WGTY-FM, WHVR, WYCR-FM

Youngstown-Warren, OH: Rank 126
Forever Broadcasting WWGY(FM)
Clear Channel Communications Inc. WAKZ(FM), WBBG(FM), WKBN, WMXY(FM), WNCD(FM), WNIO(AM)
Family Stations Inc. WYTN-FM
Cumulus Media Inc. WBBW, WLLF-FM, WPIC, WSOM, WWIZ-FM WHKZ(AM), WHOT-FM, WQXK-FM, WYFM-FM
Beacon Broadcasting Inc. WANR, WLOA(AM), WRTK(AM)
Bernard Radio LLC WASN(AM), WGFT(AM), WRBP(FM)

Section E
Programming

Major Broadcast TV Networks

ABC

77 W. 66th St., New York, NY 10023. Phone: 212-456-7777.

ABC Inc., 500 S. Buena Vista St., Burbank, CA 91521. Phone: 818-460-7477; Web site: abc.go.com.

ABC Daytime 2300 Riverside Dr., Burbank, CA 91506. Phone: 818-249-9999. Brain Frons, pres ABC Daytime.

Walter Liss, pres, ABC Owned Television; Anne Sweeney, co-chmn/Disney Media Networks, pres, Disney-ABC Television Group; Felicia Minei Behr, sr VP, Daytime progmg Capital Cities; Angela Shapiro, pres, Daytime progmg Capital Cities; George Bodenheimer, co-chmn/Disney Media Neworks, pres, ABC Sports/ESPN Inc.

Andy Bird, chmn/Walt Disney International; Robert A. Iger, pres/CEO; Thomas O. Staggs, sr exec VP/CFO; Christine M. McCarthy, exec VP/corporate finance; Alan Braveman, sr exec VP/gen counsel and sec; Zenia Mucha, exec VP corporate communication; Preston Padden, exec VP/govt rel; Brent Woodford, sr VP pres, planning and control.

Ownership The Walt Disney Co., 500 S. Buena Vista St., Burbank, CA 91521-9722. Phone: (818) 560-1000; Web site: www.disney.com.

Primetime & Late Night: According to Jim, Brothers & Sister, Boston Legal, Eli Stone, Cavemen, Carpoolers, Dancing With The Stars, Desperate Housewives, Extreme Makeover: Home Edition, Grey's Anatomy, Men In Trees, Lost, Pushing Daisies, Samantha Who?, Supernanny, Ugly Betty, Wife Swap, Women's Murder Club, Cashmere Mafia, October Road and Late Night: Jimmy Kimmel Live.

CBS

CBS Television Network, 51 W. 52nd St., New York, NY 10019. Phone: 212-975-4321; Web site: www.cbs.com.

7800 Beverly Blvd., Los Angeles, CA 90036. Phone: 323-575-2200.

Leslie Moonves, pres/CEO; Louis J. Briskman, exec VP/gen counsel; Gil Schwartz, exec VP, corporate communications; Martin Shea, exec VP pres, investor rel; Frederic Reynolds, exec VP/CFO; Martin D. Franks, exec VP pres, policy, planning and govt rel; Susan C. Gordon, sr VP pres, corporate controller and chief accounting officer; David F. Poltrack; chief rsch officer; Angeline Straka, sr VP, deputy gen counsel and sec; Joseph Ianniello, sr VP pres, chief dev officer and treas; Kelly Kahl, sr exec VP of progmg.

Ownership: CBS Corporation (formerly known as Viacom Inc.), 1515 Broadway, New York, NY 10036. Phone: 212-258-6000; Web site: www.viacom.com.

Sumner Redstone, chmn and founder; Martin She, exec VP pres/investor rel.

Primetime: The Amazing Race, Big Brother, Cold Case, Criminal Minds, CSI: Crime Scene Investigation, CSI: Miami, CSI: NY, Dexter, Ghost Whisper, How I Met Your Mother, Moonlight, NCIS, New Advs. Of Old Christine, Rules of Engagement, Numb3rs, Shark, Survivors, Two and a Half Men, The Unit, Without A Trace. Daytime: Guiding Light, The Price is Right, The Bold and the Beautiful, The Young and the Restless, As the World Turns. Late Night: Late Show with David Letterman, The Late Show with Craig Ferguson.

The CW Television Network

Headquarters: 4000 Warner Blvd., Burbank, CA 91522. Phone: 818-977-2500; Fax: 818-954-7667. Web site: www.cwtv.com.
3300 W Olive Ave., Burbank, CA 91502. Phone: 818-977-2500.

The CW is a joint venture between CBS Corporation and Warner Bros. Entertainment, a subsidiary of Time Warner.

Dawn Ostroff, pres, entertainment; John Maatta, COO; Michael Roberts, exec VP of current progmg; Harold Protter, sr VP technology; Betsy McGowen sr VP/gen mgr of children's progmg; Rick Mater, sr VP, bcst standards; Eric Cardinal, sr VP, rsch; Kim Fleary, exec VP comedy dev.

Ownership: CBS Corporation; Warner Bros. Entertainment Inc. (Time Warner).

Features: Gossip Girls, One Tree Hill, Beauty and the Geek, America's Next Top Model, Everybody Hates Chris, Smallville, Reaper, Supernatural. CW Kids: Pokemon, YuGi, Xiaolin, The Bateman, Jackie Chan Adventure, Mucha Lucha! Gigante.

FOX

Twentieth Century Fox Television, 10201 W. Pico Blvd., Los Angeles, CA 90035. Phone: 310-369-1000; Web site: www.fox.com.

Peter Liguori, pres; Marcy Ross, sr VP, Fox Broadcasting Co; Preston Beckman, exec VP, strategic program planning; David Hill, chmn/CEO, Fox Sports Television Group; Roger Ailes, chmn/pres Fox News channel; Leslie Oren, sr VP/publicity and corporate communications, Fox Television studios; Scott Grogin (press contact), sr VP corporate communications, Fox Film Corp.

Ownership: News Corp., 1211 Ave. of the Americas, New York, NY 10036. Phone: 212-852-7000; Web site: wwww.newscorp.com.

K. Rupert Murdoch, chmn/CEO; Peter Chernin, pres/COO; David F. DeVoe, CFO; Natalie Bancroft, dir; James Murdoch, chmn/chief exec, Europe and Asia; Leon Hertz, exec VP; John Nallen, exec VP/deputy CFO.

Shows: 24, American Dad, American Idol, America's Most Waneted, Are You Smarter Than A 5th Grader, Back To You, Bones, Cops, Don't Forget The Lyrics, Family Guy, Hell Kitchen, House, King Of The Of The Hill, K-Ville, MADtv, Nashville, New Amsterdam, Prison Break, The Simpsons, So You Think You Can Dance, Till Death.

ION Media Networks Inc

601 Clearwater Park Rd., West Palm Beach, FL 33401. Phone: 561-682-4100; Web site: www.ionmedianetworks.com.

Brandon Burgess, chmn/CEO; Richard Garcia, sr VP/CFO; Adam K. Weinstein, sr VP, sec/chief legal officer; Steven J. Friedman, pres cable; Stephen Appel, pres, sls/mktg; David A. Glenn, pres engrg.

Ownership: Paxson Communications Corp. (dba ION Media Networks), 601 Clearwater Park Rd., West Palm Beach, FL 33401. Phone: 888-467-2988.

Lowell Paxson, chmn Emeritus; Directors: W. Lawrence Patrick, chmn; Henry Brandon; Brandon Burges; Raymond S. Rajewski; William A. Roskin; Lucille S. Salhany.

NBC

30 Rockefeller Plaza, #2., New York, NY 10112. Phone: 212-664-4444; Web site: www.nbc.com.

3000 W. Alameda Ave., Los Angeles, CA 91505.

Jeff Zucker, pres/CEO, NBC Universal; Lynn Calpeter, exec VP/CFO; John Eck, pres Media Works/CIO/NBC Universal; Jay Ireland, pres, NBC Universal; Vivi Zigler, exec VP/digital entertainment and New Media; Hohn Damiano, exec rel; John Miller, chief mktg officer/NBC agency.

Ownership: NBC Universal, a subsidiary of General Electric; NBC Universal, 30 Rockefeller Plaza, New York, NY 10112. Phone: 212-664-4444; Web site: www.nbcuni.com.

General Electric, 3135 Eastern Tpke., Fairfield, CT 06828. Phone: 203-373-2211; Web site: www.ge.com.

Jeffrey Immelt, chmn/CEO; Richard Cotton, exec VP/gen counsel; Lynn Calpeter, exec VP/CFO; James Damiano, exec VP affil rel; Brackett Denniston III, sr VP/gen counsel; Pamela Daley, sr VP/divisional; John Lynch, sr VP/divisional; Dan Henson, chief mktg officer; Kathryn A. Cassidy, VP/treas.

Primetime: Daytime and Late Night Deal or No Deal, Medium, Law & Order:SVU, Law & Order:Criminal Intent, Scrubs, The Office, 30 Rock, ER, My Name Is Earl, The Biggest Loser, Tonight Show with Jay Leno, Late Night with Conan O'Brien, Last Call with Carson Daly, Las Vegas, Monk, Psych, Most Outrageous, Lipstick Jungle, Last Comic Standing, Chuck, Heroes, Celebrity Apprentice.

Major TV Program Syndicators/Distributors

Disney-ABC Domestic Television (Formerly known as Buena Vista Television).

Head Office: 500 S. Buena Vista St., Burbank, CA 91521; Tel: 818-560-1000.

Officers: Janice Marinelli, pres; Tom Malanga, sr VP finance; Sal Sardo, exec VP/mktg.

New York Office: Advertising/Media Sales, 7 W. 66th St., New York, NY 10023; Tel: 212-456-1740; Fax: 212-456-0395.

Management: Howard Levy, exec VP; Norman Lesser, sr VP; Irv Schulman, VP; Deb Kerins, account exec/east.

Major first-run programming: Who Wants To Be A Millionaire, Live with Regis and Kelly, Ebert & Roeper.

Major off-net comedies: According to Jim, Scrubs, My Wife and Kids.

King World Productions

Head Office: 2401 Colorado Ave., Suite 110, Santa Monica, CA 90404; Tel: 310-264-3300; Fax: 310-264-3301.

Management: John Nogawski, pres/CBS Television Distribution; Steven A. LoCascio, exec VP/CFO; Robert Madden, sr VP, CBS Television; Delilah Loud, sr VP, adv/promotion.

New York Office: 1700 Broadway, 32nd & 33rd Fl., New York, NY 10019; Tel: 212-315-4000; Fax: 212-582-9255.

Management: Joe DiSalvo, pres/sls CBS Television Distribution; Steve Hirsch, pres; Michael Auerbach, sr VP, King World media sls.

Major first-run programming: The Oprah Winfrey Show, Dr. Phil, Wheel of Fortune, Jeopardy!, Inside Edition, Mr. Food, CBS MarketWatch and Bob Vila's Home Again.

Major off-net programming: Everybody Loves Raymond, CSI: Crime Scene Investigation, CSI:NY and CSI: Miami.

NBC Universal Television Distribution (NUTD)

Head Office: 3400 W. Olive Ave., 6th Fl., Burbank, CA 91505; Tel: 818-526-6900.

Management: NBC Universal, Jeff Zucker, pres/CEO; Lynn Calpeter, exec VP/CEO; John Eck, chief info officer; Richard Cotton, exec VP/gen counsel.

Domestic syndication programming: Martha Stewart, Access Hollywood, Blind Date, Jerry Springer Show and Maury.

First-run weekly syndicated programming: The Chris Matthews Show, The Wall Street Journal Report with Maria Bartiromo and Your Total Health.

Off-Network Distribution: Crossing Jordan, Fear Factor and the Law & Order franchise.

International Television Distribution Featured Shows: Bionic Women, Life and Lipstick Jungle.

Paramount Worldwide Television Distribution

Head Office: 5555 Melrose Ave., Hollywood, CA 90038-3197; Tel: 323-956-5000.

Management: Joel Berman, pres.

New York Office: 1515 Broadway, 33rd Fl., New York, NY 10036; Tel: (212) 258-6000.

Scott Koondel, SVP, natl sls mgr.

CBS Paramount International Television: Armando Nunez, pres.

CBS Paramount Domestic Television: John Nogawski, pres.

First-run syndication: Dr. Phil, Entertainment Tonight, The Insider, Judge Joe Brown, Judge Judy, The Montel Williams Show.

Off-network syndicated: I Love Lucy, Hawaii Five-O, Cheers, Frasier, The Andy Griffith Show, The Parkers.

Sony Pictures Television

Head Office: 9336 Washington Blvd., Culver City, CA 90232; Tel: 310-202-1234.

Sony Pictures Entertainment: 10202 W. Washington Blvd., Culver City, CA 90232; Tel: 310-244-4000.

Senior Management: Michael Lynton, chmn/CEO; Amy Pascal, co-chm; Jeff Blake, vice-chmn; Yair Landua, vice-chmn.

New York Office: 550 Madison Ave., New York, NY 10022; Tel: 212-833-8500.

Daytime Dramas: The Young and the Restless and Days of our Lives.

Dramas: Breaking Bad, Caterbury's Law, Damages, Cashmere Mafia, Rescue Me, The Shield, Strong Medicine and Walker, Texas Ranger.

Comedies: The Nanny, Rules of Engagement, Seinfeld, The King of Queens, Mad About You and Married with Children.

Twentieth Television

Head Office: 2121 Avenues of the Stars, 21st Fl., Los Angeles, CA 90067. Tel: 310-369-1000; Fax: 310-369-3899. Web site: www.fox.com.

Primary Contact: Brian Lewis, exec VP corporate communications.

First-run programs Court Show: Cristina's Court, Divorce Court and Judge Alex.

Major off-network programming: The Simpsons, Malcolm in the Middle, Yes, Dear, "24", Reba, The Bernie Mac Show, Dharma & Greg and King of the Hill.

Warner Bros. Domestic Cable Distribution

Head Office: 3400 Riverside Dr. Burbank, CA 91522; Tel: 818-977-4340; Fax: 818-977-7066.

Management: Eric Frankel, pres; Gus Lucas, sr VP; Linda Abrams, sr VP, mktg; Maury Litner, VP mktg; Mike Russo, VP, sls/mktg.

Major Cable Network: ER, The West Wing, The Gilmore Girls, Smallville, Cold Case, Without a Trace, Nip/Tuck and Two and a Half Men.

Warner Bros. Domestic Television Distribution

Head Office: 4000 Warner Blvd., Burbank, CA 91522; Tel: 818-954-6000; Fax: 212-954-7667.

Management: Kenneth Werner, pres; Andy Lewis, exec VP/gen mgr.

New York Office: 1325 Ave. of the Americas, 31st Fl., New York, NY 10019; Tel: 212-636-5300.

Management: Michael Teicher, exec VP/media sls; Roseann Cacciola, sr VP, gen sls mgr/media sls.

First-run primetime series: Smallville and ER.

Syndicated shows: The Ellen DeGeneres Show and Extra.

Syndicated off-net programming: Friends and Will & Grace.

Regional Broadcast TV Networks

ALIN-TV, 149 Madison Ave., Suite 602, New York, NY, 10016. Phone: (212) 889-1327. Web Site:http://www.alintv.com

Alan Cohen, pres.

ALIN-TV offers locally originated progmg on a line-up of leading ind stns providing natl participation on a daily basis. Specific networks are provided to zero in on target audience progmg: prime, prime access, teen/young adult, late night entertainment, daytime, weekend entertainment, news & kids.

American Public Television, 55 Summer St. 4th Fl., Boston, MA, 02110. Phone: (617) 338-4455. Fax: (617) 338-5369.E-mail: info@aptonline.org Web Site:www.aptonline.org

Cynthia Fennerman, pres; Chris Funkhauser, VP/exch & distr svs.

Comprises WETA-TV, WHMM, both Washington, DC; WEDW(TV) Bridgeport, WEDY(TV) New Haven, WEDH(TV) Hartford, WEDN(TV) Norwich, all Connecticut; WCBB(TV) Augusta, WMED-TV Calais, WMEB-TV Orono, WMEM-TV Presque Isle, all Maine; WGBH-TV Boston, WGBX-TV Boston, WGBY-TV Springfield, all Massachusetts; WENH-TV Durham, WEKW-TV Keene, WLED-TV Littleton, all New Hampshire; WNJT-TV Trenton, New Jersey; WSKG(TV) Binghamton, WNED-TV Buffalo, WNET(TV) New York, WLIW-TV Plainview, WXXI(TV) Rochester, WMHT(TV) Schenectady, WCNY-TV Syracuse, WNPE-TV Watertown, all New York; WCET-TV Cincinnati, WVIZ-TV Cleveland, WPTD-TV Dayton, all Ohio; WLVT-TV Bethlehem-Allentown, WPSX-TV Clearfield, WITF-TV Harrisburg, WHYY-TV Philadelphia, WQED(TV) Pittsburgh, WVIA(TV) Scranton-Wilkes Barre, WQLN Erie, all Pennsylvania; WSBE-TV Providence, Rhode Island; WMPT-TV Annapolis, WMPB(TV) Baltimore, WWPB(TV) Hagerstown, WCPB-TV Salisbury, all Maryland. Service virtually all Public Television stations in the U.S.

California Farm Network, 2300 River Plaza Dr., Sacramento, CA, 95833. Phone: (916) 561-5550. Fax: (916) 561-5695.E-mail: cfbf@cfbf.com Web Site:www.cfbf.com

Bob Krauter, exec dir; Ron Miller, opns mgr; Doug Mosebar, pres.

Comprises KUVI-TV Bakersfield, KAEF-TV Eureka, KSEE-TV Fresno, KIXE-TV Redding, KRCR-TV Redding, KSBW-TV Salinas, KSBY-TV San Luis Obispo, K26AY Lakeport, KXTV-TV Sacramento, KPXN-TV Los Angeles, KFTY-TV Santa Rosa, KBHAA-TV San Francisco, all California; KYMA(TV) Yuma, Arizona; RFD-TV dish net direct TV.

California-Oregon Broadcasting Inc., Box 1489, Medford, OR, 97501. Phone: (541) 779-5555. Fax: (541) 779-1151.E-mail: kobi@kobi5.com Web Site:www.localnewscomesfirst.com

Patricia C. Smullin, pres.

EugeneOR . KEVU-KISR-TV, 2940 Chad Dr. Phone: MedfordOR . KOBI-TV, 125 S.Fir St. Phone:

Comprises KLSR-TV & KEVU-TV Eugene, KOTI(TV) Klamath Falls, KOBI(TV) Medford, all Oregon. Represented by John Blair & Co., Northwest.

4X Network, Box 1686, 3425 S. Broadway, Minot, ND, 58701. Phone: (701) 852-2104. Fax: (701) 838-9360.E-mail: webmaster@kxmcnews.com Web Site:www.kxmc.com

David Reiten, gen mgr .

Comprises KXMB-TV Bismarck, KXMA-TV Dickinson, KXMC-TV Minot, KXMD-TV Williston, all North Dakota. Represented by Katz Continental.

KMWB, (Sinclair Communication Inc.). 1640 Como Ave., St. Paul, MN, 55108. Phone: (651) 646-2300. Fax: (651) 646-1220.E-mail: sales@kmwb23.com Web Site:www.kmwb23.com

Art Lanham, pres, gen mgr; Miles Kennedy, VP &

controller; Bob Weinstein, natl sls mgr; Jeff Ongstad, creative svcs dir.

Minnesota, Wisconsin. Represented by Millenium.

KSN Television Group, Box 333, 833 N. Main St., Wichita, KS, 67201. Phone: (316) 265-3333. Fax: (316) 292-1197. Web Site:www.ksn.com

Comprises KSNG Garden City, KSNC Great Bend, KSNT Topeka, KSNW Wichita, KSNK Oberlin, all Kansas. Represented by TeleRep. Above TV stns affiliated with NBC Television Network. Owned by SJL of KS.

KWCH-TV, Sunflower Broadcasting Inc., (formerly KWCH-TV Schurz Communications Inc.). 2815 E. 37th St., N., Wichita, KS, 67219. Phone: (316) 838-1212. Fax: (316) 831-6198. Web Site:www.kwch.com

Joan M. Barrett, pres & gen mgr .

Comprises KBSD-TV Ensign-Dodge City, KBSL-TV Goodland, KBSH-TV Hays, KWCH-TV Wichita-Hutchinson, all Kansas. Represented by HRP.

Kansas Television Network, 1500 N. West St., Wichita, KS, 67203. Phone: (316) 943-4221. Fax: (316) 943-5493. Web Site:www.kake.com

Terry Cole, gen mgr .

Comprises KLBY-TV Colby, KUPK-TV Garden City, KAKE-TV Wichita, all Kansas. Represented by Katz.

Keloland TV Young Broadcasting of Sioux Falls Inc., KELO TV Bldg., 501 S. Phillips Ave., Sioux Falls, SD, 57104. Phone: (605) 336-1100. Fax: (605) 334-3447. Fax: (605) 336-0202. Web Site:www.keloland.com

Vincent Young, chmn; Mark Millage, news dir.

Comprises KDLO-TV Florence, KPLO-TV Reliance, KELO-TV Sioux Falls, KCLO-TV Rapid City, all South Dakota. Represented by Adam Young Inc.

National Educational Telecommunications Association, Box 50008, Columbia, SC, 29250. Phone: (803) 799-5517. Fax: (803) 771-4831.E-mail: skip@netaonline.org Web Site:www.netaonline.org

Skip Hinton, pres.

Comprises Alabama PTV Birmingham, Alabama; KUAC Fairbanks, KYUK Bethel, Alaska; KUAT Tucson, Arizona; Arkansas ETV Conway, Arkansas; KOCE Huntington Beach, KLCS Los Angeles, both California; WBCC Cocoa, WCEU Daytona Beach, WFSU Tallahassee, WGCU Fort Myers, WLRN Miami, WSRE Pensacola, WUFT Gainesville, WUSF Tampa, WXEL West Palm Beach, all Florida; Georgia Public Broadcasting Atlanta, WPBA Atlanta, both Georgia; Idaho PTV Boise, Idaho; WNIT, Elkhart, WYIN Merrillville, both Indiana; Iowa PTV Johnston, Iowa; KOOD Bunker Hill, Kansas; Kentucky ETV Lexington, WKYU Bowling Green, both Kentucky; LA Public Broadcasting Baton Rouge, WLAE New Orleans, both Louisiana; Maryland Public Broadcasting Owings Mills, Maryland; WKAR, E. Lansing, WGVU Grand Rapids, Michigan; Minnesota, Twin Cities PTV St. Paul, Minnesota; Mississippi EB Jackson, Mississippi; KCPT Kansas City, KETC St. Louis, KMOS Warrensburg, KOZK Ozarks Public TV Springfield, all Missouri; Montana PTV Bozeman, Montana; Nebraska ETV Lincoln, Nebraska; KLVX Las Vegas, Nevada; New Hampshire PTV Durham, New Hampshire; NJN Trenton, New Jersey; KENW Portales, KNME Albuquerque, KRWG Las Cruces, all New Mexico; WLIW Long Island, WMHT Schenectady, WNET New York, WPBS Watertown, all New York; UNC-TV Research Triangle Park, North Carolina; Prairie Public Television Fargo, North Dakota; WOUB Athens, WOSU, Columbus, WPTD Dayton, WNEO, Kent, all Ohio; KRSC Claremore, Oklahoma ETV Oklahoma City, both Oklahoma; Oregon Public Broadcasting Portland, Oregon; WLVT Allentown, WPSU, University Park, WYBE Philadelphia, all Pennsylvania; WSBE Providence, Rhode Island; South Carolina ETV Columbia, South Carolina; South Dakota Public Television Vermillion, South Dakota,

WCTE Cookeville, WNPT Nashville, WKNO Memphis, WLJT Martin, WSJK Knoxville, WTCI Chattanooga, all Tennessee; KAMU College Station, KWBU Waco, KEDT Corpus Christi, KERA Dallas, KLRU Austin, KMBH Harlingen, KNCT Killeen, KOCV Odessa, KTXT Lubbock, all Texas; KBYU Provo, KUED Salt Lake City, Utah; Vermont PTV Colchester, Vermont; WTJX St. Thomas, Virgin Islands; WBRA Roanoke, WCVE Richmond, WHRO Norfolk, WVPT Harrisonburg, all Virginia; KSPS Spokane, Washington; West Virginia Public Broadcasting Charleston, West Virginia; Wisconsin PTV Milwaukee , ETV Madison, both Wisconsin; Wyoming PTV Riverton, Wyoming.

Nebraska Television Network (NTV), Box 220, Kearney, NE, 68848. Phone: (308) 743-2494. Fax: (308) 743-2644.E-mail: news@nebraskatv.net Web Site:www.nebraska.tv

Janet Noll, gen mgr .

Comprises KTVG(TV) Grand Island; KHGI-TV13, Kearney, Hastings, Grand Island; KWNB-TV North Platte & KSNB-TV Superior and the translators of K02HB, K17CI, K11KV, K12KW, K13OM, K13NP, K13VO, K06EY. Represented by Petry.

North Dakota Television, 200 N. 4th St., Bismarck, ND, 58501. Phone: (701) 255-5757. Fax: (701) 255-8220. Web Site:www.kfyrtv.com E-mail: kfyrtv@kfyrtv.com

Julie Jensen, natl sls mgr; Barry Shumaier, rgnl sls mgr; Dick Heidt, gen mgr .

Comprises KFYR-TV Bismarck, KQCD-TV Dickinson, KMOT-TV Minot, KUMV-TV Williston, all North Dakota; KVLY-TV, serving North Dakota, South Dakota & Montana. Represented by Blair.

Ohio Educational Telecommunications Network Commission, 2470 North Star Rd., Columbus, OH, 43221. Phone: (614) 644-1714. Fax: (614) 644-3112.E-mail: christofi@oet.state.oh.us Web Site:www.oet.edu

Denos Christofi, exec dir.

Comprises WEAO Akron, WNEO-TV Alliance, WOUB-TV Athens, WBGU-TV Bowling Green, WOUC-TV Cambridge, WCET Cincinnati, WVIZ-TV Cleveland, WOSU-TV Columbus, WPTD Dayton, WPTO Oxford, WPBO-TV Portsmouth, WGTE-TV Toledo, all Ohio.

Pennsylvania Public Television Network, 24 Northeast Dr., Hershey, PA, 17033. Phone: (717) 533-6011. Fax: (717) 533-4236.E-mail: sstrobel@state.pa.us Web Site:www.pptn.pa.us

Sylvia L. Strobel, pres.

PPTN provides leadership & acountablity in guiding, supporting & advocating public telecommunications to educate, enlighten, inspire & connect the citizens of PA. Public stns operating across PA: WQLN-TV Erie; WITF-TV Harrisburg; WHYY-TV & WYBE-TV Philadelphia; WQED-TV Pittsburgh; WVIA-TV Scranton; WPSU-TV University Park.

SJL Broadcast Management Corp., (formerly Montecito Broadcast Group LLC). 1482 E. Valley Rd., Suite 712, Montecito, CA, 93108. Phone: (805) 969-9278. Fax: (805) 969-2399.

George Lilly, chmn/CEO.

San Luis ObispoCA , 3889 Long St., Suite 200.

Comprise WICU-TV, Erie, PA.

Wisconsin Educational Communications Board, 3319 W. Beltline Hwy., Madison, WI, 53713-4296. Phone: (608) 264-9600. Fax: (608) 264-9664. Web Site:www.ecb.org

Comprises WPNE(TV) Green Bay, WHLA-TV La Crosse, WHWC-TV Menomonie/Eau Claire, WLEF-TV Park Falls, WHRM-TV Wausau, all Wisconsin. Affils: Wisconsin: WMVS(TV) Milwaukee; WDSE-TV Duluth, Minnesota.

National Cable Networks

A&E Network, 235 E. 45th St., New York, NY, 10017. Phone: (212) 210-1400. Fax: (212) 210-9755. Web Site:www.aetv.com

Abbe Raven, pres; David Zagin, sr VP; Mel Berning, exec VP.

A&E Network offers discerning viewers a unique blend of original progmg featuring its signature series BIOGRAPHY, original movies, dramas, series & documentaries. On 10,000 cable systems. Satellite: Galaxy V, transponder 23.

ABC Family Channel, 500 S. Buena Vista St., Burbank, CA, 91521. Phone: (818) 560-1000. Fax: (818) 560-1930. Web Site:www.abcfamily.com

Ben Pyne, sr VP; Laura Nathanson, exec VP; Nicole Nochols, VP; Anne Sweeney, chmn.

Newport BeachCA , 660 Newport Center Dr, Suite 770. Phone:

EnglewoodCO , 5445 DCT Pkwy, Suite 525. Phone:

AtlantaGA , Box 492347. Phone:

OakbrookIL , 1301 W. 22nd St, Suite 902. Phone:

New YorkNY , 1133 Ave. of the Americas, 36th Fl. Phone:

LewisvilleTX , 1422 W. Main St, Suite 201. Phone:

Virginia BeachVA , Box 2050, 2877 Guardian Ln. Phone: Basic cable network available in over 87 million homes nationwide 24 hours; delivers a dynamic mix of quality entertainment with original series & movies, classics from Disney. Satellite: Galaxy V, transponder 11.

ABS-CBN (The Flilipino Channel), 859 Cowan Rd., Burlingame, CA, 94010. Phone: (650) 697-3700. Fax: (650) 697-3500. Web Site:www.abs-bn.com

Rafael Lopez, mgng dir; Eugenio Lopezill, chmn; Augusto Almeda-Lopez, vice chmn.

A 24-hour all Filipino premium svc ch delivered via satellite from the Philippines. Serving 35,000 subs on 11 systems. Satellite: Galaxy 11, transponder 24.

ANA Television Network, 1510 H St. N.W., Suite 400, Washington, DC, 20005. Phone: (202) 898-8222.

Angelyn Adams, CFO.

Arabic-language TV net bcstg to the Arab-American community 24 hours via cable, wireless cable. Satellite: DIRECTV Plus. Satellite: Galaxy V, transponder 11.

ART (Arab Radio & Television), 315 Arden Ave., Suite 26, Glendale, 91203. Phone: (818) 243-0278. Fax: (818) 243-9278. Web Site:www.art.tv.net

Michael Scott, VP.

ART's foundation is based on the largest gen entertainment library in the Middle East. Available 24 hours a day in North America, has progmg targeted to second generation Arab Americans. Satellite: Galaxy 11, transponder 24.

AYM Sports, Avenida Chapultepac 405, Colonia Juarez, Delegacion Cuauhtemoc, Mexico, 06600. Web Site:www.aymsports.tv

Benjamin Hinojosa, pres; Carlos Carrillo, progmg VP.

Available 24 hours a day, 100% Mexican network consisting of soccer, basketball, rodeo charreadas, horse racing, boxing, kick boxing, jujitsu, karate, tae kwon do, swimming, driving, truck series, rallies and much more. Satellite: Telestar 7, transponder 12.

ABS-CBN International, (formerly 14BS-CBN International). 150 Shoreline Dr., Redwood City, CA, 94065-1400. Phone: (650) 508-6000. Fax: (650) 551-1062.E-mail: tfc@abs-cbni.com Web Site:www.abs-cbni.com

Rafael Lopez, COO & sr VP; Jun del Rosario, production mgr.

A 24-hour svc for Filipinos worldwide. Progmg originates at ABS-CBN, the Philippines top-rated net. Time-shifted for North America.

Satellite: Galaxy 11, PAS-2 for Pacific delivery, Telstar 5 (ku) transponder 22 for North America. On 144 cable systems. 100,000 subs.

Access Television Network Inc., 2600 Michelson Dr., Suite 1650, Irvine, CA, 92612. Phone: (949) 263-9900. Fax: (949) 622-6295. Web Site:www.accesstv.com E-mail: info@accesstv.com

George Henry, CEO; Robert T. Tyler, CFO; Mark R. Russo, sr VP opns.

DenverCO , 1020 15th St, Unit 30.

Organized natl marketplace for paid progmg on loc cable systems. Galaxy 11. On 650 cable systems. 40 million subs. transponder 9.

African Independent Television (AIT), One AIT Rd., PMB 1309, Apapa, Alagbado-Lagos Nigeria. Phone: (212) 213-2070. Web Site:www.aittv.com

Ladi Lawal, COO.

AIT is a Pan-African gen entertainment ch offering news, talk show, soap opera, sports, Afician culture & music 24 hours a day. Areas: United States & Afica. Satellite: Telstar 5, transponder 5.

AMC, (Rainbow Programming Service Holdings Inc.). 200 Jericho Quadrangle, Jericho, NY, 11753. Phone: (516) 803-2300. Web Site:www.amctv.com

David Sehring, sr VP; Charlie Collier, pres.

AMC is a 24 hour, movie-based mix or original series, documentaries & specials. 85 million subs. Satellite: Satcom C-4, transponder 1.

AmericanLife TV Network, (formerly GoodLife TV Network). 650 Massachusetts Ave. N.W., Suite 202, Washington, DC, 20001. Phone: (202) 289-6633. Fax: (202) 289-6632. Web Site:www.americanlifetv.com

Mark Ringwald, VP progmg; Shera Higgs Thompson, mktg mgr.

Speaks to the interests & values of the unstopable Baby Boomer delivering enteraining classic programs & awarding-winning originals. Satellite: Galaxy IR, transponder 22.

America's Collectibles Network (ACNTV), 10001 Kingston Park, Suite 57, Knoxville, 37922. Phone: (865) 693-8471. Fax: (865) 560-3298. Web Site:www.acntv.com

F. Robert Hall, pres; Harris Bagley, VP.

ACNT offers a wide var of jewelry & gemstones at reduced prices, 24 hours a day home shopping, in the United States & Canada. Serving more than 63 million subs. Satellite: Telstar7, Transponder 21, Galaxy 11, Transponder 19.

Animal Planet, One Discovery Pl., Silver Spring , MD, 20910. Phone: (240) 662-2000. Fax: (240) 662-1854.E-mail: first_last@discovery.com Web Site:www.animalplanet.com

Marjorie Kaplan, gen mgr & pres.

Available in more than 94 million homes in the U.S., online assets, the ultimate online destination for all things animal, 24/7 broadband ch, Animal Planet Beyond, Petfinder.com, pet adoption, PetsIncredible, a major producer & distributor of pet-training videos & web svc & other media platforms, a robust VOD svc, mobile content & merchandising extensions.

Anime Network, 10114 West Sam Houston Pkwy. S., Suite 200, Houston, 77099. Phone: (713) 341-7200. Fax: (713) 341-7199. Web Site:www.theanimenetwork.com

John Ledford, chmn/CEO; Kevin Corcoran, pres.

Anime is an exploration of Western pop culture. Anime reaches males 18-35 demographic with four different genres, including martial arts, comedy, science fiction & drama 24 hours a day, basic ad-supported. Serving more than 84 million subs.

Automotive Networks Corp., WheelsTV. 289 Great Rd., Acton, MA, 01720. Phone: (978) 264-4333. Fax: (978) 264-9547.E-mail: jimbar@wheelstv.net Web Site:www.wheelstv.net

Automotive entertainment & info via video on demand, worldwide web & dir mktg.

Serving 9.1 million subs.

BBC America, 747 3rd Ave., Fl. 6, New York, NY, 10017-2871. Phone: (301) 347-2222. Phone: (212) 705-9387. Web Site:www.bbcamerica.com

Bill Hilary, pres/CEO; Kathryn Mitchell, gen mgr .

BBC America is a 24 hour award-winning TV featuring razor-sharp comedies, provocative dramas & life changing makeovers. Digital, Analog & DBS. Satellite: Satcom C3. 37 million. Satellite: Galaxy VII, transponder 22.

BET (Black Entertainment Television), 1235 W St. N.E., Washington, DC, 20018. Phone: (202) 608-2000. Fax: (202) 608-2631.E-mail: bet-tv_bizdev@bet.com Web Site:www.bet.com

Scott Mills, pres/COO.

BurbankCA . BET/Los Angeles - Production, 2801 W. Olive Ave. Phone:

WashingtonDC . Network Operations, 1899 Ninth St. N.E. Phone:

WashingtonDC . BET Film Production Facility, 2000 West Pl. N.E. Phone:

ChicagoIL . BET/Chicago, 180 N. Stetson Ct, Suite 4350. Phone:

New YorkNY . BET/New York, 380 Madison Ave, 20th Fl. Phone:

BET is the nation's leading TV network providing 24 hour for African-American audience in the United States, Canada & the Caribbean. BET Digital Networks-BET jazz, BET Gospel & BET Hip-Hop. 78 million subs. Satellite: Galaxy V, transponder 20.

BET Jazz: The Jazz Channel, 1235 W St. N. E., Washington, DC, 20018. Phone: (202) 608-2000. Fax: (202) 608-2631. Web Site:www.bet.com

Robert L. Johnson, chmn/CEO; Debra L. Lee, pres/COO.

The Jazz Channel is a 24-hour TV progmg svc dedicated exclusively to jazz through in-studio performances, documentaries,concert coverage & celebrity interviews. 9 million subs. Satellite: Galaxy VII, transponder 21.

BabyFirstTV, Box 25639, Los Angeles, CA, 90025. Phone: (888) 251-2229. Web Site:www.babyfirsttv.com

Guy Oranim, CEO; Sharon Rechter, exec VP; Arik Kerman, sr VP.

Bandamax, 5999 Center Dr., Los Angeles, 90045. Phone: (301) 348-3371. Web Site:www.tutv.tv

Mark Feldman, pres/CEO; Carlos Madrazo, CFO; Chris Fager, exec VP; Ariela Nerobay, VP sls.

Bandamax features a 24-hour a day country music video, including best artists in Tex-Mex, Norteno, Banda & Manachi genres. De Pelicula Sp-language films, De Pelicula Clasico films of Mexico's golden era.

BLACK BELT TV/The Martial Arts Network, 880 Calle Primavera, San Dimas, CA, 91773. Phone: (909) 971-9300. Fax: (909) 854-9329.E-mail: info@blackbelttv.com Web Site:www.blackbelttv.com

Erik D. Jones, pres.

A 24/7 cable TV net that targets demographics highly desired by advertisers. Our appeal focuses on all income level individuals & families. Provides progmg for advertisers seeking to attract martial arts practitioners/enthusiasts, health/fitness-minded individuals, as well as sports suppliers of exercise equipment, & other companies & product manufacturers that can directly reach their target audience. Our progmg includes martial arts movies, martial arts training/self-defense, self-improvement programs, sports, women, & children-oriented programs, martial arts news, & much more.

Bloomberg Television, 499 Park Ave., New York, NY, 10022. Phone: (212) 893-3331. Fax: (202) 522-2400. Web Site:www.bloomberg.com/media/tv

Kenneth Kohn, editor; Betsy Alekman, mktg.

A sophisticated 24-hour business & financial news ch. Serving over 200 million subs worldwide, United States, Canada, Central & South America, Europe,& Asia/Pacific. Satellite: Galaxy 11, HITS, C3.

BlueHighways TV, 111 Shivel Dr., Hendersonville, TN, 37075. Phone: (615) 264-3292. Fax: (615) 264-3308.E-mail: feedback@bluehighwaystv.com Web Site:www.bluehighwaystv.com

Alan McLaughlin, COO; Stan Hitchcock, chmn/CEO; Lee Clayton Roper, pres.

BlueHighways TV is a multi-platform progmg svc featuring roots music, American culture & back roads exploration. Satelite: AMC-10. Transponder 15.

The Boating Channel (TBC), Box 1148, Sag Harbor, NY, 11963. Phone: (631) 725-4440. Fax: (631) 725-0748. Web Site:www.boatingchannel.com E-mail: service@baotingchannel.com

Barbara London, pres; Daniel E. London, COO; Gregory Hahn, exec producer.

Marine news & weather, entertainment, info & educ for the recreational, professional boater & cruise vacationer.

Boston Kids & Family TV, 43 Hawkins St., Suite 1B, Boston, 02114. Phone: (617) 635-3112. Fax: (617) 635-4475.E-mail: cable@ci.boston.ma.us Web Site:www.cityofboston.gov/cable

Michael Lynch, dir; David Burt, stn mgr.

A partnership between the City of Boston & WGBH. Available 24 hour a day , edu TV progmg. PBS Kids from WGBH in Boston.

Bravo, (NBC Cable Network). 30 Rockefeller Plaza, 14th Fl. E., New York, NY, 10112. Phone: (212) 664-4444. E-mail: support@bravotv.com Web Site:www.bravotv.com

Lauren Zalaznick, pres.

Bravo offers innovative arts & entertainment progmg with a unique point of view featuring original series, theater, dance, music & documentaries 24 hours.

Buzztime Entertainment, Inc., 5966 La Place Ct., Suite 100, Carlsbad, 92008. Phone: (760) 476-1976. Fax: (760) 438-3505. Web Site:www.buzztime.com

Stanley Kinsey, chmn/CEO; Tyrone Lam, pres/COO; Dan Sweeney, sr VP; Pat Ruble, VP.

Buzztime is the only 24-hour interactive entertainment bcst created exclusively for TV audiences. Featuring play-along trivia games for players of all interests & ability levels.

CBS College Sports Network, 85 10th Ave., 3rd Fl., New York, NY, 10011. Phone: (212) 342-8700. Fax: (212) 342-8899. Web Site:www.cstv.com

The network televises regular season & championship events coverage from every major collegiate athletic conference & televises nine NCAA Championships available 24-hour, ad-supported. 15 million subs. Satellite: Galaxy IR, transponder 22.

CCTV 4, 11 Fuxing Rd., Beijing, 100859. China. Phone: (310) 414-2110. Phone: 011-86-10-6-850-6517. Fax: (310) 141-2101. Fax: 011-86-10-6-851-4993. Web Site:www.cctv-4.com

Michael Scott, VP.

China Central TV (CCTV) China's only national bcstg network. Provide Info about China's politics, economy, society, culture, science, edu & history, also Chinese viewers, living outside of China, 24 hours a day. Serving more than 100 million subs. Satellite: Galaxy 11, transponder 24.

CMT: Country Music Television, 330 Commerce St., Nashville, TN, 37201. Phone: (615) 335-8400. Fax: (615) 335-8615. Web Site:www.cmt.com

CMT, America's # one country music network, 24 hours a day. CMT, owned & operated by MTV networks. Serving 80 million subs. Satellite: Satcom C-4, transponder 24, Satcom C3, transponder 18 west coast.

CNBC, 900 Sylvan Ave., Englewood Cliffs, NJ, 07632. Phone: (201) 735-2622. Web Site:www.cnbc.com

Mark Hoffman, pres.

CNBC set the standard for up-to-the-minute business news & incisive analysis of global financial markets. During primetime, the network presents broad-base news, talk, interview & entertainment progmg.

Serving 86 million subs. Satellite: Galaxy 5, transponder 13.

CNN-Cable News Network, 1 CNN Ctr., Atlanta, GA, 30303. Phone: (404) 827-2300. Web Site:www.cnn.com

David Payne, sr VP & gen mgr; Mich Gelman, sr VP & exec producer; Susan Grant, sr. VP news svcs.

CNN provides coverage of major breaking stories, business, weather, sports & special reports, worldwide audience, 24 hours.

CNN en Espanol, One CNN Ctr., Atlanta, GA, 30303. Phone: (404) 878-1555. Fax: (404) 878-0050.E-mail: espanol.mesa@turner.com

Christopher Crommett, sr VP.

A 24-hour Sp-language news network in the United States & Latin America. The network keeps its loyal viewers connected with the events, issues trends that matter most to them & their families.

Serving more than 24 million subs.

CNN Headline News, One CNN Ctr., Atlanta, GA, 30348-5366. Phone: (404) 827-1500. Fax: (404) 827-1995. Web Site:www.cnn.com/hln

Roland Santo, exec VP & gen mgr.

Provides viewers with a 30-minute news, 24-hours. Each half-hour covers major news stories as well as business, sports, medicine, entertainment, weather & human interest topics. Areas: United States, Canada, Mexico & Caribbean.

CNNI (CNN International), One CNN Ctr., 3rd Flr., Atlanta, GA, 30348. Phone: (404) 827-1500. Fax: (404) 827-1995. Web Site:www.cnn.com/cnni

Rena Golden, sr VP; Eric Ludgood, VP; Chris Cramer, mgng dir; Debra Kocker, VP.

A 24-hour global news & info, with live, breaking world news, sports, features & weather. Serving 170 million worldwide.

c/net: the computer network, 235 Second St., San Francisco, CA, 94105. Phone: (415) 344-2000. Web Site:www.cnet.com

Shelby Bonnie, CEO.

CNET news.com, airs weekly on CNBC & CNET tv.com airs on syndication.

C-SPAN (Cable Satellite Public Affairs Network), 400 N. Capitol St. N.W., Suite 650, Washington, DC, 20001. Phone: (202) 737-3220. Fax: (202) 737-3323. Web Site:www.c-span.org

Brian P. Lamb, chmn/CEO; Rob Kennedy, exec VP & COO; Susan Swain, exec VP & COO; Bruce Collins, exec VP & corporate counsel.

C-SPAN progmg includes live coverage of the House of Representatives, National Pres Club speeches & congressional hearings. C-SPAN 2 live coverage of the U.S. Senate & C-SPAN 3 pub affrs TV. 87 million subs. Satellite: Satcom C-3, transponder 7.

CTI Zhong Tian Channel, 1255 Corporate Center Dr., Suite 212, Monterey Park, 91754. Phone: (323) 415-0068.

Andy Chung, gen mgr .

A 24-hour Mandarin-Chinese ch, consists of progmg derived from Chinese TV Int'l reputable Zhong Tian news. Satelite: Galaxy 11, transponder 24.

The California Channel, 1121 L St., Suite 110, Sacramento, CA, 95814. Phone: (916) 444-9792. Fax: (916) 444-9812.E-mail: contactus@calchannel.com Web Site:www.calchannel.com

John Hancock, pres.

Televised coverage of California state legislature & govt agency proceedings. M-F, 9 AM-3:30 PM. Satellite: Galaxy 15. On 114 cable systems. 5.8 million subs. transponder 3 C.

Canal 24 Horas, 1100 Ponce de Leon Blvd., Coral Gables, 33134. Phone: (305) 444-4402. Fax: (305) 444-6301.E-mail: aragon@tveamerica.com Web Site:www.rtve.es

Mariano Aragon, mgr.

A 24 hour news network from TVE which offers a Headline News fromat with 30 minute blocks. The network also produces 17 different 30 minutes daily & wkly news magazines. Areas: United States, Mexico, Caribbean, Central & South America & Europe. 250,000 subs. Satellite: Telstar 5, transponder 1.

Cartoon Network, 1050 Techwood Dr. N.W., Altanta, GA, 30318. Phone: (404) 827-4700. Phone: (404) 827-1700. Web Site:www.cartoonnetwork.com

Dennis Adamovich, mktg VP; Gary Albright, sr VP; Bob Higgins, progmg VP.

A Turner Broadcasting System. Inc.'s 24-hour Cartoon Network offers the best in animated entertainment. Drawing from the world's largest cartoon library, also showcases unique original ventures such as "Johnny Bravo," "Cow and Chicken," "Dexter's Laboratory," "Ed, Edd n Eddy," and "Cartoon Cartoon." Serving 86 million subs around the world. Satellite: Galaxy 1, transponder 15 (West). Satellite: Galaxy IR, transponder 8 (East).

Cartoon Network Latin America, 1050 Techwood Dr., N.W., Altanta, GA, 30318. Phone: (404) 885-4398. Phone: (404) 827-1700. Fax: (404) 885-2157.E-mail: larissa.pissarra@turner.com Web Site:www.cartoonnetworkla.com

The first global 24-hour cable ch programmed entirely with cartoons. Available in Sp, Portuguese or English.

Serving more than 10.9 million subs. Satellite: PanAmSat 3R.

Channel One Russia Worldwide Network, 20 Frunzenskaya Daberezhmaya, Suite D, Moscow, 119146. Phone: (310) 414-2110. Fax: (310) 414-2101. Web Site:www.firstchannel.tv

David Quinn, dir.

A 24-hour Russian language ch for Russian communities throughout the United States. The ch consists of dramas, movies, news, children progmg, sports, talk show and more. Satellite: Galaxy 11, transponder 24.

Chronicle DTV, 53 W. 36th St., Suite 203, New York, 10018. Phone: (212) 337-9700 ext.105. Fax: (212) 352-1190. Web Site:www.chronicledtv.com

David Peipers, chmn; Richard Blume, pres/CEO.

A 24-hour digital TV progmg network offering diverse selection of feature length non-fiction & documentary programs. Chronicle is seen in 35 cities in the United States, Los Angeles, Miami, West Palm Beach & Orlando. one million subs. Satellite: Telstar 5, transponder 22.

Cinemax, (Home Box Office). 1100 Ave. of the Americas, New York, NY, 10036. Phone: (212) 512-1000. Fax: (212) 512-5637. Web Site:www.cinemax.com

Cinemax is a 24-hour digital pay-TV svc designed to provide viewers with the most movies & fewest repeats. Multiplex chs: Cinemax, MoreMAX, ActionMAX, ThrillerMAX, WMAX, @MAX, 5StarMAX, OuterMAX. Cinemax is seen in the U.S. & Puerto Rico. 39 million subs. Satellite: Galaxy IR, transponder 23.

Classic Arts Showcase, Box 828, Burbank, CA, 91503. Phone: (323) 878-0283. Fax: (323) 878-0329.E-mail: casmail@sbcglobal.net Web Site:www.classicartsshowcase.org

James Rigler, pres & dir progmg; Charlie Mount, gen mgr .

CAS is a non-profit arts progmg svc that include 16 art disciplines. The svc also features classic video from independent producers with the right to show clips. We require copies from masters on BetaCam-SP Tap. Available 24 hour.

Serving 60 million subs. Satellite: Galaxy 1R, transponder 5.

College Entertainment Network, 6255 Sunset Blvd., Suite 611, Hollywood, 90028. Phone: (323) 465-9880. Fax: (323) 465-9881. Web Site:www.collegeentertainment.com

Robert Artura, pres/CEO; Georgina Montalvan, VP mktg.

College Entertainment Network is a world of college TV stn on one network, it features block of programs, from extreme sports to entertainment. 10 million subs.

Comedy Central, 345 Hudson St, New York, NY, 10014. Phone: (212) 767-8600. Fax: (212) 767-8592. Web Site:www.comedycentral.com

Michele Ganeless, pres.

Los AngelesCA , 2049 Century Park E, Suite 4250. Phone:

A 24-hour all comedy TV network that covers stand-up, sketch comedy, movies, talk shows, sitcoms, specials & classics TV shows. Serving 84.8 million subs. Satellites: Satcom C-3, transponder 21 (east), Galaxy 1R, transponder 1 (west).

The Crime Channel, 78206 Varner Rd., Suite D131, Palm Desert, CA, 92211. Phone: (760) 360-6151. Fax: (760) 360-3258.E-mail: crimechannel@dcrr.com

Arnie Frank, pres.

The Crime Channel offers series, movies, documentaries, original productions, on the spot crime news & foreign programs. Satellite: Satcom C-1, transponder 11.

Daystar Television Network, 4201 Pool Rd., Colleyville, 76034. Phone: (817) 571-1229. Fax: (817) 571-7458.E-mail: comments@daystar.com Web Site:www.daystar.com

Janice Smith, VP progmg; David Troxel, VP.

Our progmg is multi-ch & interdenominational. Christian TV net, is available from DirectTV, Dish Network 24-hours a day.

De Pelicula, 5999 Center Dr., Los Angeles, 90045. Phone: (301) 348-3371. Web Site:www.tutv.tv

Mark Feldman, pres/CEO; Carlos Madrazo, CFO.

A 24-hour contemporary & classic movie ch featuring the best Sp language films.

Multiplex ch: De Pelicula Clasico is a 24-hour movie ch featuring the best films of Mexico's golden era.

TeleHit is a young, hip & cutting-edge, trend setting lite-style & music ch. 750,000 subs.

Deep Dish TV, 339 Lafayette St., New York, NY, 10012. Phone: (212) 473-8933. Fax: (212) 420-8223.E-mail: deepdish@igc.org Web Site:www.deepdishtv.org

Ron Davis, chmn; Tom Pool, exec dir; Victoria Macdonado, VP.

Educational progmg (one hour a wk) distributed to PBS & pub access chs. Satellite: Galaxy IR, transponder 15.

Discovery Channel, One Discovery Pl., Silver Springs, MD, 20910. Phone: (240) 662-2000. Fax: (240) 662-1854.E-mail: first_last@discovery.com Web Site:www.discovery.com

John Ford, pres; Joe Abruzzese, pres, adv sls; Billy Goodwyn, pres, affil sls & mktg.

The United States largest cable TV net, the nation's premier provider of real-world entertainment, offering a signature mix of compelling, high-end production values & vivid cinematography that consistently represents qulity for viewers. Primetime progmg features science & technology, exploration, adventure, history and in-depth, behind-the scenes glimpses at the people, places, organizations that shape, share our world & is dedicated to creating the highest quality TV & media to inspire audiences by delivering knowledge about the world in an energizing way; evolving a timeless brand for a changing world. 74.9 million subs. Satellite: Satcom C-4, Transponder 13.

Discovery en Espanol, One Discovery Place, Silver Spring, MD, 20910. Phone: (240) 662-2000. Fax: (240) 662-1854.E-mail: first_last@discovery.com Web Site:www.discovery.com

Billy Campbell, pres; Joe Abruzzese, pres, adv sls; Bill Goodwyn, pres, affil sls & mktg; Luis Silberwasser, exec VP & gen mgr.

Provider of high quality nonfiction entertainment for Sp-speaking audiences in the United States. Offering original progmg, some of the best Discovery content from around the world, the portfolio includes Discovery en Espanol & Discovery Familia.

Discovery HD Theater, One Discovery Pl., Silver Spring, MD, 20910. Phone: (240) 662-2000. Fax: (240) 662-1854.E-mail: first_last@discovery.com Web Site:www.dhd.discovery.com

Billy Campbell, pres; Joe Abruzzese, pres, adv sls; Patrick Younge, exec VP & gen mgr; Bill Goodwyn, pres, affil sls & mktg.

Provide viewers with the hightest-quality TV experience available with spectacular images, dynamic sound & compelling stories from across the globe. A broad array of rich, original HD content across several progmg categories such as world cultures, wildlife, high-end auto & adventure.

Discovery Kids Channel, (Discovery Communications). One Discovery Pl., Silver Spring, MD, 20910. Phone: (240) 662-2000. Fax: (240) 662-1854.E-mail: first_last @discovery.com Web Site:www.discoverykids.com

Billy Campbell, pres; Joe Abruzzese, pres, adv sls; Bill Goodwyn, pres, affil sls & mktg; Marjorie Kaplan, exec VP & gen mgr.

Provides entertaining, engaging & high-quality real-world progmg that kids enjoy & parent trust. Kids can learn about science, adventure, exploration & natural history through documentaries, reality shows, scripted dramas & animated stories.

Discovery Kids en Espanol, One Discovery Pl., Silver Spring, MD, 20910. Phone: (240) 662-2000. Fax: (240) 662-1854.E-mail: first_last@discovery.com Web Site:www.discovery.com

Billy Campbell, pres; Joe Abruzzese, pres, adv sls ; Bill Goodwyn, pres, affil sls & mktg; Luis Silberwasser, exec VP & gen mgr.

Offering original progmg develop for Sp-speaking audiences, in addition to some of the best Discovery content from around the world, the portfolio includes Discovery en Espanol & Discovery Familia.

Disney Channel, 3800 W. Alameda Ave., Burbank, CA, 91505. Phone: (818) 569-7500. Fax: (818) 566-1358. Web Site:www.disneychannel.com

Rich Ross, pres.

A 24-hour gen entertainment network for kids & families through original series, movies & contemporay acquired progmg. Serving over 87 million subs. Satellite: Galaxy 5, transponder 1 east, Galaxy 1-R, transponder 7 west.

The Dream Network, 9300 Georgia Ave., Suite 206, Silver Springs, 20910. Phone: (301) 587-0000. Fax: (301) 587-7464. Web Site:www.thedreamnetwork.com

Alvin Augustus Jones, pres/CEO.

The Dream Network is the urban family choice for news, talk, sports & gospel music. Seen in the United States, Canada, Caribbean, Europe, Africa & Asia. Serving 25 million subs on 10 million cable systems. Satellite: DirecTV.

E! Entertainment Television, 5750 Wilshire Blvd., Los Angeles, CA, 90036-3709. Phone: (323) 954-2400. Fax: (323) 954-2500. Web Site:www.eonline.com

Neil Baker, sr VP, adv sls; Ted Harbert, pres/CEO; Ken Bettsteller, CEO.

New YorkNY , 11 W. 42nd St. Phone:

A 24-hours progmg net covering celebrities, entertainment news, gossip & pop-culture, feature behind the scenes with today's biggest stars. 84 million subs. Satellite: Satcom C-3, transponder 23.

ESPN, ESPN Plaza, Bristol, CT, 06010-9454. Phone: (860) 766-2000. Fax: (860) 766-2400. Web Site:www.espn.com

Edward Erhardt, pres; Ed Durso, exec VP, admin; Lee Ann Daly, exec VP mktg; Chris Driessen, exec VP & CFO.

New YorkNY , 605 3rd Ave. Phone:

A 24-hour svc covering sports events, news, info, & lifestyle progmg.

ESPN CLASSIC is a 24-hour, all sports network devoted to telecasting the greatest games, stories, heroes & memories in the history of sports. ESPN DEPORTE offers a wide var of domestic & intl sports progmg 24-hours. ESPN HD offers a 24-hours high definition TV svc from ESPN, features high profile telecast. ESPNEWS, the nation's only 24-hours TV sports news svc, provides an expanded window for news & highlights,as well as live coverage of

beaking news. 88 million subs. Satellite: Galaxy V, transponder 9.

ESPN2, ESPN Plaza, Bristol, CT, 06010-9454. Phone: (860) 766-2000. Fax: (860) 766-2400. Web Site:www.espn.com

George Bodenheimer, pres; Sean Bratches, exec VP/sls mktg.

A 24-hour sports net features a progmg line-up on par with ESPN. 86 million subs. Satellite: Galaxy V, transponder 14.

ESPNU, c/o ESPN Regional Television, 11001 Rushmore Dr., Charlotte, NC, 28277. Phone: (704) 973-5000. Fax: (704) 973-5090. Web Site:www.espn.com

Rosalyn Durant, VP/gen mgr.

ESPNU is a TV ch that specializes in college sports & is produced by affil with & owned by parent Network ESPN.

EWTN, The Global Catholic Network. 5817 Old Leeds Rd., Irondale, AL, 35210. Phone: (205) 271-2900. Fax: (205) 271-2925. Web Site:www.ewtn.com

R. William Steltemeier, chmn/CEO; Michael P. Warsaw, pres; Chris Wegemer, VP mktg; Scott Hults, dir; Doug Keck, VP.

America's largest relg cable network offers coml-free family-oriented progmg in English & Sp. EWTN features documentaries, music, drama, live talk shows, animated children shows & special church events from around the world. 53 million subs. Satellite: Galaxy IR, transponder 11.

Ecology Communications , 9171 Victoria Dr., Ellicott City, 21042. Phone: (410) 465-0480. Fax: (410) 461-5152. Web Site:www.ecology.com

Shelley Duvall, chmn/CEO; Eric McLamb, pres.

Ecology Communications focuse on ecology & enviroment in a var of entertainment-driven formats wkly. 10 million subs.

eSignal, 3955 Point Eden Way, Hayward, CA, 94545. Phone: (510) 266-6000. Fax: (510) 266-6100. Web Site:www.esignal.com

Chuck Thompson, pres; Grant Mader, VP net ops & telecommunications.

Real-time stock, option, commodity quotation service & sports service delivered via cable TV, FM frequency & bcst VBI to end user PC.

Serving more than 20,000 subs on more than 850 systems. Satellites: Satcom F3, transponder 11; Galaxy 3, transponder 24.

EUROCINEMA, European Movies on TV. 387 Park Ave., 3rd Fl., New York, NY, 10016. Phone: (212) 763-5533.E-mail: eurocinema@envrocinema.com Web Site:www.eurocinema.com

Sebastiaen Perioche, chmn/CEO; Steve Matela, VP affil rel.

Non-Hollywood movies service for Broadband & Digital TV

FX Networks Inc., (A subsidiary of Fox, Inc.). 1440 S. Sepulveda Blvd., Los Angeles, CA, 90025. Phone: (310) 444-8777. Fax: (310) 444-8266. Web Site:www.fxnetworks.com

John Landgraf, pres; Chuck Saftler, VP progmg; Christy Dees, dev dir; Michael Sakin, sr VP; Mark DeVitre, sr VP; Chris Carlisle, VP mgr; Lindsay Gardner, exec VP; Steve LeBlang, rsch dir; John Solberg, VP; Steve Webster, VP; Eric Shiu, VP.

An entertainment basic cable net from Fox Television involving hit series, daily films, original programs & sports.

Serving more than 53 million subs on 3,293 cable systems. Satellite: Hughes Communications Galaxy 7, transponder 4 & 5.

FamilyNet Television & Radio, 6350 West Fwy., Fort Worth, TX, 76116. Phone: (800) 832-6638. Phone: (817) 570-1423. Fax: (817) 737-7853.E-mail: info@familynet.com Web Site:www.familynet.com

Martin Coleman, COO; R. Chip Turner, VP mktg; Randy Singer, pres/CEO; Ray Raley, engrg VP.

FamilyNet TV is a full-time cable network, including original values-based programs & operates Christian talk ch 161 on sirius stattelite radio. Reliable, safe TV for today's family.

FitTV, One Discovery Pl., Silver Spring, MD, 20910. Phone: (240) 662-2000. Fax: (240) 662-1854.E-mail: first_last @discovery.com Web Site:www.fittv.com

Billy Campbell, pres; Joe Abruzzese, pres & adv sls; Bill Goodwyn, pres, affil sls & mktg; Eileen O'Neill, exec VP & gen mgr.

FitTV is the premier, interactive fitness brand that inspires consumers to improve their fitness & well-being-on their terms. FitTV features approachable experts & entertaining

shows that help real people learn how to incorporate fitness in to their busy lives.

Food Network, 1180 6th Ave., 12th Fl., New York, NY, 10036. Phone: (212) 398-8836. Fax: (212) 736-7716. Web Site:www.foodnetwork.com

Brooke Johnson, pres; Adam Rockmore, VP mktg.

A 24-hour net dedicated to exploring new, different & interesting ways to approach food. 82 million subs. Satellite: Galaxy IR, transponder 4.

Fox Business Network, 1211 Avenue of the Americas, New York, NY, 10036. Phone: (888) 369-4762. Phone: (212) 601-7000. Fax: (212) 601-7990. Web Site:www.foxbusiness.com

Roger Ailes, chmn/CEO; Neil Cavuto, sr VP/mgng editor business news.

Fox Movie Channel, (FX Networks Inc.). 10201 W. Pico Blvd., Bldg. 103, 4th Fl., Los Angeles, CA, 90035. Phone: (310) 369-0586. Fax: (310) 969-4687. Web Site:www.foxmoviechannel.com

Chuck Saftler, gen mgr .

The network is dedicated to preserving Hollywood history through original series & specials.

Fox Net, 10201 W. Pico Blvd., Bldg. 100, Los Angeles, CA, 90064. Phone: (310) 369-1000. Web Site:www.fox.com

Susan Kiel, VP; Dwayne Bright, progmg dir; Wendy Chambers, dir; Betty Wang, dir mktg; Keith Goldberg, dir; Mark Handwerger, natl sls mgr; Julie Allen, natl sls mgr; Steve Nazar, opns mgr.

Los AngelesCA . FOX Broadcasting Co, 10201 W. Pico Blvd. Phone:

A 24-hours basic cable affil to Fox Broadcasting Co.

Fox News Channel

See isting in Major National TV News Organizations, this section.

Free Speech TV, Box 44099, Denver, CO, 80201. Phone: (303) 442-8445. Fax: (303) 442-6472.E-mail: jon@freespeech.org Web Site:www.freespeech.org

Jon Stout, gen mgr .

FSTV airs primarily social, political, cultural & environmental documentaries & news programs, 24-hours a day. Serving 30 million subs, on 180 cable systems & DISH Network.

Fuel, 1440 S. Sepulveda Blvd., Suite 1900, Los Angeles, 90025. Fax: (310) 444-8559.E-mail: hookup@fuel.tv Web Site:www.fuel.tv

Cj Olivares, VP progmg; David Sternberg, gen mgr; Kelsey Martinez, dir.

A 24-hour sports network featuring snowboarding, wakeboarding, surfing, BMX, motorcross & skateboading. Serving 5 million subs. Satellite: Galaxy II, transponder 5.

Fuse, 11 Penn Plaza, 15th Fl., New York, NY, 10001. Phone: (212) 324-8500. Fax: (212) 324-3445. Web Site:www.fuse.tv

Eric Sherman, pres; Norman Schoenfeld, VP progmg; Michael Goldstein, VP; Kim Martin, exec VP; Theano Apostolou, VP.

Santa MonicaCA . The Water Garden, 2425 W. Olympic Blvd, Suite 5050. Phone:

ChicagoIL . Chicago Office, 205 N. Michigan, Suite 803A. Phone:

Fuse is the only all-music, viewer-influenced TV network, featuring music videos, exclusive artist interviews, live concerts & specials. Serving 35 million subs. Satellite: Loral Skynet Telstar 7, transponder 14.

Galavision, 605 3rd Ave., 12th Fl., New York, NY, 10158. Phone: (212) 455-5200. Fax: (212) 867-6710. Web Site:www.univision.com

Tim Krass, exec VP affil affrs; Timothy Spillane, VP.

Los AngelesCA , 6701 Center Dr. W, Suite 650. Phone:

ChicagoIL , 541 N. Fairbanks Ct, Suite 1240. Phone:

DallasTX , 2323 Bryan St, Suite 1900. Phone:

A 24-hr Sp language cable network for United States Hispanics in distribution & viewership. 37 million subs. Satellite: Satcom C-4, transponder 4.

Game Show Network, 2150 Colorado Ave., Santa Monica, CA, 90404. Phone: (310) 255-6800. Fax: (310) 255-6810. Web Site:www.gsn.com E-mail: distribution@gsn.com

ChicagoIL , 515 N. State St. Suite 2120. Phone:

New YorkNY , 680 Fifth Ave. 11th Fl. Phone:

DallasTX , The Republic Center, 325 N. St. Paul St. Suite 1500. Phone:

Game Show Network (GSN) is the only U.S. television network dedicated to game progmg & interactive game playing, featuring over 65 hours per week of original

progmg & enhanced classics.

Reaching 50 million subs.

The Golf Channel, 7580 Commerce Center Dr., Orlando, FL, 32819. Phone: (407) 355-4653. Fax: (407) 363-7976. Web Site:www.thegolfchannel.com

Page H. Thompson, pres.

A 24-hour ch offering a blend of tournament coverage from the PGA, LPGA, Sr Tour, Nike, EPGA Tours, as well as instruction, interactive talk, news, profiles, classics, travel & more.

Serving 30 million subs on 2,200 cable systems. Satellite: Galaxy VI, Transponder 7.

Great American Country, 49 Music Sq. W., Suite 301, Nashville, TN, 37203. Phone: (615) 327-7525. Fax: (615) 329-8770. Web Site:www.gactv.com

Ed Hardy, pres.

GAC is a country music video net, features natl & loc adv, also featuring a broad var of videos programs. 24 million subs. Satellite: Satcom C-3, transponder 20.

Guthy-Renker Television, 41-550 Eclectic St., Suite 200, Palm Desert, CA, 92260. Phone: (760) 773-9022. Fax: (760) 773-9016. Web Site:www.guthy-renker.com

Direct-response TV.

HBO (Home Box Office), 1100 Ave. of the Americas, New York, NY, 10036. Phone: (212) 512-1000. Web Site:www.hbo.com E-mail: info@hob.com

Bill Nelson, chmn/CEO.

Features 24-hour var progmg including theatrical films, original movies, specials, documentaries, sports, & series. Multiplex chs. HBO, HBO 2, HBO Latino, HBO Signature, HBO Family, HBO Comedy, HBO Zone - known collectively as HBO The Works. MoreMAX.

HDNET, 2400 N. Ulster St., Denver, 80238. Phone: (303) 388-8500. Fax: (303) 388-9600.E-mail: info@hd.net Web Site:www.hd.net

Mark Cuban, chmn/pres; Philip Garvin, gen mgr .

HDNET, the leader in high-indefinition bcstg, produces & televises 24-hour a day. Satellite: Galaxy 9, transponder 19C.

HDNET Movies is a 24-hour coml-free schedule of full-length feature films. Satellite: Galaxy 9, transponder 19C.

HSN, The Home Shopping Network, One HSN Dr., St. Petersburg, FL, 33729. Phone: (727) 872-1000. Fax: (727) 872-7356. Web Site:www.hsn.com

Bob Rosenblatt, pres; Peter Ruben, exec VP; Tom McInerney, CEO.

HSN offers live, 24-hour video retailing. 81 million subs. Satellite: Satcom C-4, transponder 10.

Hallmark Channel, 12700 Ventura Blvd., Suite 200, Studio City, CA, 91604-2463. Phone: (818) 755-2400. Fax: (818) 755-2564. Web Site:www.hallmarkchannel.com

David Kenin, VP progmg.

A 24-hour basic cable ch that provides high quality entertainment progmg to a national audience. 56 million subs. Satellite: Satcom C-3, transponder 5.

Home & Garden Television Network (HGTV), 9721 Sherrill Blvd., Knoxville, TN, 37932. Phone: (865) 694-2700. Fax: (865) 531-1588. Web Site:www.hgtv.com

Mike Boyd, VP mktg; Jim Samples, pres.

HGTV is a 24-hour network that provides practical info & creative ideas to help the viewers to make the most of their lives at home & is designed to appeal to all ages & lifestyles. Satellite: Galaxy IR, transponder 4.

Home Improvement Television Network, 3441 Baker St., San Diego, CA, 92117. Phone: (858) 273-0572. Fax: (858) 273-8410.E-mail: homefix@hometvnet.com Web Site:www.hometvnet.com

Bruce Lamb, pres.

Providers of home improvement progmg & 90-second video vignettes.

IFC, 11 Penn Plaza, New York, NY, 10001. Phone: (917) 542-6320. Fax: (917) 542-6395. Web Site:www.ifc.com E-mail: help@ifcentetainment.com

Jonathan Sehring, pres. Satellite: Galaxy VII.

I.M.A.G.E. LLC, (Interactive Meet and Greet Entertainment). Box 702, 67 River St., Hudson, MA, 01749-0702. Phone: (508) 788-5474.E-mail: wexrex@aol.com Web Site:www.allcollectors.com

Gary Sohmers, chmn/pres; Chip Sohmers, CEO.

Basic svc, 24-hour progmg targeted to collectors of various merchandise & memorabilia, educ & entertaining

progmg with a shopping element, with patent pending interactive applications.

iN DEAMAND, (formerly Viewers Choice). 345 Hudson St., 17tt Fl., New York, NY, 10014. Phone: (646) 638-8200. Web Site:www.indemand.com

Rob Jacobson, pres/CEO.

Los AngelesCA , 1888 Century Park E. Phone: AtlantaGA , 1117 Perimeter Ctr. W, Suite 500 E. Phone: SouthfieldMI , 26677 W. Twelve Mile Rd. Phone: Pay-Per-View (PPV), Video-On-Demand (VOD) & high-definition (HD) progmg 24-hrs. National Cable Program Services. Programming genres: gen entertainment.

The Independent Film Channel (IFC), (A division of Rainbow Media Programming Holdings). 11 Penn Plaza, 18th Fl., New York, NY, 10001. Phone: (917) 542-6200. Fax: (917) 542-6395. Web Site:www.ifc.com E-mail: webmaster@ifctv.com

A 24-hour uncut coml-free ch, capturing the true spirit of ind film, original series, live events & enchanced new media progmg.

The Inspiration Network INSP, Box 7750, Charlotte, NC, 28241. Phone: (803) 578-1000. Web Site:www.insp.com

David Cerullo, pres/CEO; Rod Tapp, exec VP; Tom Hohman, sr VP; Larry Simms, VP sls; Ron Shuping, VP progmg.

INSP blends ministry programs with family-oriented movies, dramas, music & children's programs along with concerts & specials. 21 million subs. Satellite: Galaxy IR, transponder 17.

Inspirational Life Television, (I-Lifetv). 7910 Crescent Executive Dr., 5th Fl., Charlotte, NC, 28217. Phone: (704) 525-9800. Fax: (704) 525-9899.

David Cerullo, pres/CEO; Tom Hohman, sr VP; Larry Sims, VP sls.

TV net which distributes life-enriching, edu entertainment progmg & digital, 24-hours. 6 million subs. Satellite: Galaxy IR, transponder 7.

International Networks, 4100 E. Dry Creek Rd., Centennial, CO, 80122. Phone: (303) 712-5400. Fax: (303) 712-5401. Web Site:internationalnetworks.com

Rod Shanks, mgng dir; Scott Wheeler, sr VP net dev; Michael Scott, VP distribution; Victor Perez, VP technology.

New YorkNY , 1114 Ave. of the Americas, 22nd Fl. Phone:

Los AngelesCA , 12100 W. Olympic Blvd, Suite 200. Phone:

Offer in-language progmg from a var of international sources: Arabic Radio & Television, ATV (Cantonese), China Central Television-4 (Mandarin), Channel One Russia, CTI-Zhong Tian Channel (Mandarin), Deutsche Welle (German), MYX (Asian American), Phoenix North America Chinese Channel (Mandarin), Phoenix InfoNews (Mandarin), ProSiebenSat.1 Welt (German), RAITALIA (Italian), Russian Television Network (Russian), Saigon Broadcasting Television Network (Vietnamese), STAR India GOLD, STAR India NEWS, STAR India ONE & STAR India PLUS (all Hindi), The Filipino Channel, TV Asia (South Asian), TV JAPAN, tvK (Korean), TV5MONDE (French), TV Polonia (Polish) & VIJAY (Tamil). 14 Million. 24.

Investigation Discovery, One Discovery Pl., Silver Spring , MD, 20910. Phone: (240) 662-2000. Fax: (240) 662-1854.E-mail: first_last@discovery.com Web Site:www.investigationdiscovery.com

Henry Schleiff, pres; Joe Abruzzese, pres, adv sls; Bill Goodwyn, pres, affil sls & mktg; Vivian Schiller, exec VP & gen mgr.

Provides the highest quality investigative progmg focused on dynamic stories of human nature from the past to the present.

The Irish Channel (CelticVision), 179 Amory St., Brookline, MA, 02445. Phone: (617) 731-8566.E-mail: celtictv@aol.com

Serving 140,000 subs on 2 cable systems.

Jewelry Television By ACN, 10001 Kingston Pike, Knoxville, TN, 37922. Phone: (865) 692-6000. Fax: (865) 692-6050. Web Site:www.jtv.com

Harry Bagley, sr VP.

Jewerly TV the only network that focuses exclusively on the sls of fine jewelry & gemstones, 24-hours a day. Satellite: Telstar 5. Serving 32 milion subs, on 11 million cable systems, transponder 19. s.

Jewish Television Network, 13743 Ventura Blvd., Suite 200, Sherman Oaks, CA, 91423. Phone: (818) 789-5891.E-mail: jewishtv@earthlink.net Web Site:www.jewishtvnetwork.com

Jay Sanderson, CEO.

Production & cablecasting of net quality Jewish progmg

in news, pub affrs, educ, arts, PBS & entertainment.

The Jones Companies, 9697 E. Mineral Ave., Centennial, CO, 80112. Phone: (303) 792-3111. Fax: (303) 784-8454.E-mail: publicrelations@jones.com Web Site:www.jones.com

Glenn R. Jones, pres/CEO; Timothy J. Burke, VP.

A 24-hour revenue providing svc that features full-length product demonstrations & introduction of new products in a hands-on demonstration format.

KTLA, United Video (a company of the United Video Satellite Group). 5800 Sunset Blvd., Los Angeles, CA, 90028. Phone: (323) 460-5500. Fax: (323) 460-5333.E-mail: ktla-am-news@tribune.com Web Site:www.ktla.com

John Reardon, VP/gen mgr.

Los Angeles CW stn offers movies, news, specials & live sporting events, featuring the Los Angeles Clippers basketball. Services offered: Ind satellite carrier serving CATV, SMATV & MMDS distributing WGN, WPIX, KTLA & WFMT (FM) Network svcs. Satellite: Spacenet 6E. On 220 cable systems. 1 million subs. transponder 15.

The Learning Channel (TLC), (Discovery Communications). One Discovery Pl., Silver Spring, MD, 20910. Phone: (240) 662-2000. Fax: (240) 662-1854.E-mail: first_last @discovery.com Web Site:www.tlc.com

Eileen O'Neill, pres; Joe Abruzzese, pres & adv sls; Bill Goodwyn, pres, affil sls & mktg; David Abraham, exec VP & gen mgr.

TLC's themed nights that focus on real families , relationship, careers & entertaining consist of perennial fashion favorite, makeover sensation, humorous & fun workplace competion. Real-life progmg portrays relatable people with compelling stories in the blockbuster hits Jon & Kate Plus 8, Little People, Big World & LA Ink.

Lifetime, (A&E Television Networks). 309 West 49th St., 17th Fl., New York, NY, 10019. Phone: (212) 424-7000. Fax: (212) 957-4264.E-mail: morgenstein@lifetimetv.com Web Site:www.mylifetime.com

Nickolas Davatzes, pres/CEO; Dan Davids, VP/gen mgr; Charles Maday, sr VP.

Offering the highest quality entertainment, info progmg & advocating a wide range of issues affecting women & their families. 86 million subs. Satellite: Satcom C-3, transponder 12.

Lifetime Movie Network, 309 W. 49th St., New York, NY, 10019. Phone: (212) 424-7000. Fax: (212) 957-4264. Web Site:www.lifemetv.com

Andrea Wong, pres/CEO; James Wesley, CFO; Rick Haskins, VP/gen mgr.

Offering the highest quality entertainment & info progmg 24-hours.

LIFETIME Television, 309 W. 49th St., New York, NY, 10019. Phone: (212) 424-7000. Fax: (212) 957-4264. Web Site:www.lifetimetv.com

Andrea Wong, pres/CEO; Barbara Fisher, exec VP; James Wesley, CFO; Lynn Picard, exec VP; Louise Henry Bryson, exec VP; Patricia Langer, VP business affrs; Meredith Wagner, exec VP; Tim Brooks, VP rsch; Richard Basso, sr VP; Gwynne McConkey, opns VP.

Offering the highest quality entertainment, info progmg & advocating a wide range of issues affecting women & their families, 24 hours nationwide . Satellite: Galaxy V, transponder 21.

The Locomotion Channel, 420 Lincoln Rd., Suite 235, Miami Beach, FL, 33139. Phone: (786) 276-1140. Fax: (786) 276-1141.

Rodrigo Piza, gen mgr .

The Locomotion features the best intl productions created specifically for viewers ages 18-35, combining electronic music & digital culture 24-hrs a day.

MLB Network, 40 Hartz Way, Suite 10, Secaucus, NJ, 07094. Phone: (201) 520-6400. Web Site:mlb.mlb.com/network/

Tony Petitti, pres/CEO; Bill Morningstar, exec VP.

MSNBC, One MSNBC Plaza, Secaucus, NJ, 07094. Phone: (201) 583-5000. Fax: (201) 583-5179. Web Site:www.msnbc.com

Val Nicholas, VP mktg; Dan Abrams, gen mgr .

MSNBC is an all news net 24-hours. 82 million subs. Satellite: Galaxy IR, transponder 10.

MTV: Music Television, MTV Networks Inc. 1515 Broadway, New York, NY, 10036. Phone: (212) 258-8000. Fax: (212) 258-8100. Web Site:www.mtv.com

Judy McGrath, chmn/CEO.

A 24-hrs music video ch in stereo, with 22 worldwide music on the web, original, innovative online music &

entertainment progmg to each net. Also includes 14 international destinations throughout Europe, Asia, & Latin America.

MTV Networks, 1515 Broadway, New York, NY, 10036. Phone: (212) 258-8000. Fax: (212) 258-8100. Web Site:www.mtvn.com

MTV2 is the premier destination to find the hottest mix of music videos, long form music programs, exclusive access to their favorite bands, and ground-breaking music before it hits mainstream.

MTV Networks Latin America, (formerly MTV Latino). 1111 Lincoln Rd., 6th Fl., Miami Beach, FL, 33139. Phone: (305) 535-3700. Fax: (305) 535-8388. Web Site:www.mtvla.com

MTV's sixth global network, 24-hour progmg, advertiser supported & available in Latin America & the United States. Serving over 8.5 million subs. Satellite: Satcom C3, transponder 19 (USA); PanAm Sat 3, transponder 5C & 6C (Latin America).

Military Channel, One Discovery Pl., Silver Spring, MD, 20910. Phone: (240) 662-2000. Fax: (240) 662-1854.E-mail: first_last@discovery.com Web Site:www.military.discovery.com

Billy Campbell, pres; Joe Abruzzese, pres & adv sls; Bill Goodwyn, pres, affil sls & mktg; Deborah Adler Myers, exec VP.

Real-world stories of heroism, military strategy, technological breakthroughs & turning points in history. Takes viewers "behind the lines" to hear the personal stories of servicemen & women & offers in-depth explorations of military technology, battlefield strategy, aviation & history. It also provides unique access to this world, allowing viewers to experience & understand a world full of human drama, courage, innovation & long-held military traditions.

The Movie Channel (TMC), (Showtime Networks Inc.). 1633 Broadway, New York, NY, 10019. Phone: (212) 708-1600. Fax: (212) 708-1212. Web Site:www.sho.com

TMC features daily movie marathons, overnight & double vision weekends & Movie Channel Xtra, offers more of viewers favorite movies, 24-hours a day. Serving 34.8 million subs. Satellites: Satcom C-3, transponder 19 east; Satcom G-9, transponder 5 west.

NFL Network, 10950 Washington Blvd., Culver City, CA, 90232. Phone: (310) 840-4635. Fax: (310) 280-1132.E-mail: krista.ostensen@la.nfl.net Web Site:www.nfl.com/nflnetwork/home

Steve Bornstein, pres/CEO; Adam Shaw, sr VP.

A national cable & satellite ch telecasting NFL content 24 hrs a day. Satellites: Galaxy 11, Transponder 9. Serving 30 million subs. On more than 60 cable systems.

National Geographic Channel, 1145 17th St. N.W., Washington, DC, 20036-4688. Phone: (202) 912-6500. Fax: (202) 912-6603.E-mail: comments@natgeochannel.com Web Site:www.natgeotv.com

John Ford, exec VP progmg; Kiera Hynninen, sr VP mktg; David Haslingden, CEO.

NGC provides the spectacular imagery that the National Geographic is know for in stunning high-definition. 47 million subs. Satellite: Satcom C-3, Transponder one.

National Jewish Television Network, Box 480, Wilton, CT, 06897. Phone: (203) 834-3799.E-mail: nj@jewishmail.com

Joel A. Levitch, pres/CEO.

NJT offers documentaries, children's programs, news magazines, Info, cultural & relg progmg for the Jewish community, presented 3-hours every Sunday.

Nationality Broadcasting Network, (Radio-WKTX 830 AM/NBN TV). 11906 Madison Ave., Lakewood, OH, 44107. Phone: (216) 221-0330. Fax: (216) 221-3638.

Jim Georgiades, opns mgr.

Provides internationally & locally-produced nationality TV & radio progmg, special programs & comls; also full-svc production house. Serving one cable system. On SCOLA TV network.

Newsworld International, (North American Television Inc.). 1230 Ave. of the America, New York, NY, 10020. Phone: (212) 413-5000. Web Site:www.nwitv.com E-mail: nwifeedback@indtvholdings.com

Lou Cooper, VP progmg; John Bernbach, chmn; Patrick Vien, pres/CEO; Doug Halloway, pres network distribution.

Intl progmg covering top stories from around the world plus current affrs, documentaries, the latest business, financial & sports news, 24-hours.

NICK at NITE

See ickelodeon.

Nickelodeon, (MTV Networks Inc.). 1515 Broadway, New York, NY, 10036. Phone: (212) 258-8000. Fax: (212) 258-6284. Web Site:www.nickelodeon.com

Tom Freston, chmn/CEO; Cyma Zarghami, VP/gen mgr; Jeff Dunn, CEO.

Nickelodeon cable net targets kids. NICK at NITE provides entertainment svc for the TV generation. NICKTOONS is the 24-hours digital destination for the next generation of animation. NICK2 gives viewers the convenience of watching their favorite Nickelodeon & NICK at NITE shows at different times of the day.

Noah's World International, 11448 Kanapali Ln., Boynton Beach, 33437. Phone: (561) 732-2108. Fax: (516) 732-5108. Web Site:www.noahsworldtv.com

Ken Klein, pres; Ilan Klein, exec VP.

Noah's World Internation profiles & present enlightened countries around the globe, 24-hours a day.

Noggin/The N, 1633 Broadway, 7th Fl., New York, NY, 10019. Phone: (212) 654-7707. Fax: (212) 654-4867. Web Site:www.noggin.com

Tom Ascheim, VP/gen mgr; Kenny Miller, VP progmg.

The N, the nighttime net for teens, 24-hours. Satellite: Satcom C-3, transponder 15.

OWN: The Oprah Winfrey Network, 9150 Wilshire Blvd., Suite 240, Beverly Hills, CA, 90212. Phone: (424) 204-1800.

Robin Schwartz, pres; Christina Norman, CEO.

OASIS TV, 1875 Century Park E., Suite 600, Los Angeles, CA, 90067-2507. Phone: (310) 553-4300. Fax: (310) 553-4300.E-mail: service@oasistv.com Web Site:www.oasistv.com

Robert Schnitzer, CEO; Azim Khamisa, chmn.

Independent content provider of branded Body-Mind-Spirit video progmg. Range of topics: Health, Healing, Metaphysics, Spirituality, Earth, Environment, World Peace, Visionary Arts & Personal Growth. On 16 cable systems. 1.8 million subs.

Open TV, 350 5th Ave., Fl. 59, New York, NY, 10118-5999. Phone: (212) 601-2719.

David Reese, pres/CEO.

BranchburgNJ , 3040 Rte 22 W., Suite 210. Phone:

Individualized TV progmg for educ & entertainment.

The Outdoor Channel, 43445 Business Park Dr., Suite 103, Temecula, CA, 92590. Phone: (800) 770-5750. Web Site:www.outdoorchannel.com

Roger Werner, pres/CEO.

Outdoor Channel offers progmg such as fishing, hunting, hiking, competitive shooting & motor sports, 24-hours.

OVATION-The Arts Network, 5801 Duke St., Suite D-112, Alexandria, VA, 22304. Phone: (703) 813-6310. Fax: (703) 813-6340.E-mail: info@ovationtv.com Web Site:www.ovationtv.com

Edward J. Mathias, chmn; Harold E. Morse, pres/CEO; Susan Wittenberg, VP progmg; Lee J. Lindbloom, VP network opns.

The net covers arts news from around the world & children's arts programs, 20 hours a day. 6.6 million subs. Satellite: Galaxy VII, transponder 13.

Oxygen Media Inc., 75 9th Ave., 7th Fl., New York, NY, 10011. Phone: (212) 651-2070. Fax: (212) 651-2099.E-mail: feedback@oxygen.com Web Site:www.oxygen.com

Lisa Gersh, pres/COO; Mary G. Murano, exec VP; Daniel H. Taitz, gen counsel.

Oxygen Media is a 24-hour cable network for women.

Pennsylvania Cable Network (PCN), 401 Fallowfield Rd, Camp Hill, PA, 17011. Phone: (717) 730-6000. Fax: (717) 730-6005. Fax: (717) 441-4540.E-mail: pcntv@pcntv.com Web Site:www.pcntv.com

Brian Lockman, pres/CEO; William J. Bova, VP progmg; Debra Kohr Sheppard, opns VP; Rick Cochran, VP mktg; Michelle Harter, VP.

PhiladelphiaPA , 400 N. Broad St. Phone:

PittsburghPA , Pittsburgh Post Gazette Bldg, 34 Blvd. Phone:

The nation's preeminent state pub affrs net, with live & same-day coverage of the Pennsylvania General Assembly. PCN also covers significant state events, such as high school sports finals. Serving 3.3 million subs on 150 cable systems, transponder 13C. Satellite: AMC-6.

Pentagon Channel, 601 North Fairfax St., Alexandria, 22314. Phone: (703) 428-0265. Fax: (703) 428-0466.E-mail: pentagonchannel@hq.afis.osd.mil

Gene Brink, gen mgr .

Pentagon Channel is a gov owned TV of the Department of Defense, providing internal communications to svc

members, families, the National Guard, the Reserve & military retirees, available 24-hours. 5.3 million subs.

Planet Green, (formerly Discovery Home Channel). One Discovery Pl., Silver Spring, MD, 20910. Phone: (240) 662-2000. Fax: (240) 662-1854.E-mail: first_last @discovery.com Web Site:www.planetgreen.com

Laura Michalchyshyn, pres.

Planet Green will provide entertaining, authentic & quality info for such categories as eco-design, organic food & green architecture, progmg for a green lifestyle.

Plato Learning Inc., 10801 Nesbitt Ave. S., Bloomington, MN, 55437. Phone: (800) 447-5286. Web Site:www.plato.com E-mail: info@plato.com

Terri Reden, dir communications.

Interactive TV progmg for children.

Playboy TV, (Playboy Entertainment Group). 2706 Media Center Dr., Los Angeles, CA, 90065. Phone: (323) 276-4000. Fax: (323) 276-4500. Web Site:www.playboytv.com

James English, pres; Sol Weisel, exec VP; Jeff Jenest, exec VP; Craig Simon, sr VP.

Entertainment targeted to adults. Schedule consists of nearly 100% original Playboy programs with the balance comprised of acquired programs & feature films. Serving 4.5 under PPV svc. Satellite: Galaxy 5, transponder 2.

Hot Zone is a 24-hour Pay-Per-View ch for adults. Satellite: Telstar 7, transponder 5.

Hot Networks is a 24-hour Pay-Per-View ch for adults. Satellite: Telstar 7, transponder 5.

Praise Television, 28059 US Hwy. 19 N., Suite 300, Clearwater, 33761. Phone: (800) 921-9692. Fax: (727) 530-0671.

Dustin Rubeck, pres.

A 24-hours, Christian music for family entertainment. Satellite: GE-1, transponder 7.

Product Information Network (PIN), 9697 East Mineral Ave., Englewood, 80155-3309. Phone: (303) 784-8321. Fax: (303) 784-8549.

Jon Shaver, COO; Richard Steele, VP sls; Tom Cahill, VP mktg.

A 24-hours info net, ad-supported. 35 million subs. Satellite: Satcom C-3, transponder 20.

Puma TV, 2029 S.W. 105th Ct., Miami, 33165-7937. Phone: (305) 554-1876. Fax: (305) 554-6776.

Jose Luis Rodriguez, pres; Osvaldo Rodriguez, VP.

Puma TV offers a wide var of info programs on fashion, modeling & entertainment, music ch by Hispanic for Hispanic, 24-hours. 2.7 million subs. Satellite: Telstar 5.

QVC, Studio Park, West Chester, PA, 19380. Phone: (484) 701-1000.E-mail: webmaster@qvc.com Web Site:www.qvc.com

Douglas S. Briggs, pres; Tim Megaw, sr VP.

Preeminent electronic retailer mktg a wide var of brand name products, categories as home furnishings, licensed products, fashions, beauty, electronics & fine jewelry. 85.4 million subs. Satellite: Satcom C-4, transponder 9.

The Real Estate Network-TREN, 325 Sharon Park Dr., Suite 512, Menlo Park, CA, 94025. Phone: (650) 361-1000. Fax: (650) 332-1605.E-mail: kevintren@yahoo.com

Kevin L. Keithley, CEO; Ronald D. Keithley, COO.

Niche advertiser-supported entertainment progmg & interactive svc focusing on mdse real estate listings & related products & svcs throughout America.

Recovery Network, 1411 5th St., Suite 250, Santa Monica, CA, 90401. Phone: (310) 393-3979.E-mail: info@recoverynetwork.com Web Site:www.recoverynetwork.org

Progmg addresses behavioral & alternative health care issues & treatments for eating disorders, addictions, depression, sexual addictions, substance abuse, etc.

Serving 5 million subs on 36 systems. Satellite: Galaxy 7. Launched Spring 1996.

SCOLA, 21557 270th St., McClelland, IA, 51548-0619. Phone: (712) 566-2202. Fax: (712) 566-2502.E-mail: scola@scola.org Web Site:www.scola.org

Francis Lajba, pres; John Millar, VP.

Foreign language news & educ progmg, 24-hours a day. Satellite: Telstar 5.

STARNET, 1332 Enterprise Dr., Suite 200, West Chester, PA, 19380. Phone: (610) 427-4163.

Jerry Lenfest, pres/CEO; Joy Tartar, CFO.

Automatic cross-ch tune-in promotion svc for basic, PPV delivered via satellite. Nu-Star - automatic cross ch tune-in promotion svc for basic PPV delivered via satellite. The

Promoter-individualized tune-in promotion for PPV delivered via satellite.

The Science Channel, One Discovery Pl., Silver Spring, MD, 20910. Phone: (240) 662-2000. Fax: (240) 662-1854. E-mail: first_last@discovery.com Web Site:www.sciencechannel.com

Billy Campbell, pres; Joe Abruzzese, pres & adv sls; Bill Goodwyn, pres, affil sls & mktg; Deborah Adler Myers, exec VP & gen mgr.

Scientific topics ranging form string theory & futuristic cities to accidental discoveries & outrageous inventions. Reaching more than 50 million homes nationwide.

Sci-Fi Channel, (USA Networks). 30 Rockefeller Plaza, New York, NY, 10112. Phone: (212) 644-4444. Fax: (212) 703-8533. Web Site:www.scifi.com

David Howe, VP/gen mgr.

Dedicated to a broad range of science fiction & fact, fantasy, & horror programs, 24-hours.

Scripps Networks, 9721 Sherrill Blvd., Knoxville, TN, 37932. Phone: (865) 694-2700. Fax: (865) 690-9281. Web Site:www.scrippsnetworks.com

Bob Baskerville, pres; Robyn Ulrich, VP mktg; Jeff Sears, VP.

DIY cable TV net operated by Scripps Networks, providing in depth demonstrations & tips for categories such as home improvement, home bldg, tools, products, gardening, landscaping, automotive, boating, decorating, design, arts, crafts, cooking, hobby & recreations, 24-hours. 25 million subs. Satellite: Galaxy IR, transponder 4.

ShopNBC, ValueVision Media Inc., 6740 Shady Oak Rd., Eden Prairie, MN, 55344. Phone: (952) 943-6000. Fax: (952) 943-6011. Web Site:www.shopnbc.com

Will Lansing, CEO; Frank Elsenbast, CFO.

ValueVision Media (Nasdaq: VVTV) operates in the rapidly growing converged world of TV, the Internet & e-commerce. The company flagship media property, ShopNBC, the nation's fastest growing shoppng network, is bcst into 70 million homes 24 hrs a day. GE Equity & NBC own approximately 27% of ValueVision Media. Satellite used and transponder: Galaxy 15, transponder 12. 1,900.

Short TV, 580 Broadway, Suite 1104, New York, 10012. Phone: (212) 226-6258. Fax: (212) 925-5802. E-mail: info@shorttv.com Web Site:www.shorttv.com

Roland Dib, pres.

Short films, available 24-hours, ad-supported. 2.5 million subs.

Showtime Networks Inc., 1633 Broadway, New York, NY, 10019. Phone: (212) 708-1600. Fax: (212) 708-1212. Web Site:www.sho.com

Matthew C. Blank, chmn/CEO.

THE MOVIE CHANNEL & FLIX. SNI also operates & manages the premium TV net SUNDANCE CHANNEL, SHOWTIME on Espanol, a separate audio feed of SHOWTIME, available for the Sp-speaking audience. SNI also markets & distributes sports & entertainment events for exhibition to subscribers on a pay-per-view basis. Multiplex chs: SHOWTIME BEYOND, SHOWTIME PAY-PER-VIEW. SHOWTIME EXTREME, SHOWTIME FAMILY ZONE, SHOWTIME NEXT, targeting gen young adults 18-24, SHOWTIME SHOWCASE, SHOWTIME TOO, SHOWTIME WOMEN. 34.8 million subs. Satellite: Satcom C-3, transponder 19 (east).

Si TV, 3030 Andrita St., Bldg. A, Los Angeles, 90065. Phone: (323) 256-8900. Fax: (323) 256-9888. Web Site:www.sitv.com

Jeff Valdez, chmn/CEO; Leo Perez, COO; Rita Morales, VP progmg.

SiTV is a Latino-themed network in English that features original progmg, comedy, drama, var shows, talk-format strips, music & style shows, available 24-hours.

The Ski Channel, 881 Alma Real Dr., Terrace 8, Pacific Palisades, CA, 90272. Phone: (310) 230-2050. E-mail: info@theskichannel.com

Steve Bellamy, chmn/CEO.

Skyview World Media, Two Executive Dr., Suite 6000, Fort Lee, 07024. Phone: (201) 242-3000. Fax: (201) 944-5961. E-mail: info@kskyviewmedia.com Web Site:www.skyviewmedia.com

John Lunsford, pres/CEO; James Helfott, sr VP.

Skyview World Media is North America's leading provider of foreign ethnic progmg. 100,000 subs.

Sleuth, NBC Universal Cable, 900 Sylvan Ave., 1 CNBC Plaza, Englewood Cliffs, NJ, 07632. Phone: (201) 735-3604. Web Site:www.sleuthchannel.com

Soapnet, 3800 West Alameda Ave., Burbank, 91505. Phone: (818) 569-7500. Fax: (818) 566-1358. Web Site:www.soapnet.com

Deborah Blackwell, sr VP; Mary Ellen DiPrisco, VP progmg; Sherri York, VP mktg.

Soapnet features today's soaps tonight, classic soaps, news & info from the world of soaps, 24-hours. Serving 35.7 million subs. Satellite: Galaxy 10 R.

Sorpresa, 6125 Airport Fwy., Suite 200, Fort Worth, 76117. Phone: (817) 222-1234. Fax: (817) 222-9809. Web Site:www.sorpresatv.net

Leonard Firestone, chmn/CEO; Michael Fletcher, pres.

The nation's first network dedicated to America's Hispanic children, available 24-hours, ad-supported, Digital Premium. Satellite: Telstar 5, transponder 24.

SourceSuite, LLC, 5601 MacArthur Blvd., Suite 201, Irving, 75038. Phone: (469) 524-0116. Fax: (469) 417-0314. Web Site:www.intchan.com

Charlie Barnes, gen mgr .

SourceSuite is a leading provider of interactive TV products, available 24-hours. 400,000 subs.

SPEED, 9711 Southern Pines Blvd., Charlotte, NC, 28273. Phone: (704) 731-2222. Phone: (704) 731-2285. Fax: (704) 731-2197. Web Site:www.speedtv.com

Rick Miner, sr VP & exec producer; Bill Osborn, sr VP mktg; Bob Ecker, progmg VP; Kevin Annison, VP opns & business dev; Kevin Wilson, VP business & legal; Chris Long, VP/exec producer; Francois McGillicuddy, VP finance & admin; Hunter Nickell, exec VP & gen mgr.

Providing insight & action, number one authority for anything motorsports. 57.1 million subs. Satellite: Satcom C-4, transponder 11.

Spice 1, 2706 Media Center Dr., Los Angeles, 90065. Phone: (323) 276-4000. Fax: (323) 276-4500. Web Site:www.spicetv.com

James English, pres.

An erotic adult-theme movie net, Premium, Pay-Per-View, available 24-hours. Multiplex ch: Spice 2. 11,000 subs. Satellite: Telstar 5.

Spike TV, (division of MTV Networks). 1775 Broadway, 37th Fl., New York, NY, 10019. Phone: (212) 846-8705. Phone: (212) 767-4275. Web Site:www.spiketv.com

Kevin Kay, pres.

NashvilleTN , 2806 Opryland Dr. Phone:

Network for men. 87.2 million subs. Satellite: Satcom C-3, transponder 18.

The Sportsman Channel, 2855 S. James Dr., Suite 101, New Berlin, WI, 53151. Phone: (262) 432-9100. Fax: (262) 432-9101. Web Site:www.thesportsmanchannel.com

C. Michael Cooley, pres/CEO; Todd D. Hansen, sr VP; Jim Seley, progmg dir; Darrell Lake, VP sls.

The Sportsman Channel provides continuous hunting & fishing progmg 24-hours a day. 10.7 million subs. Satellite: Telstar 5, Transponder 1.

Starz!, See Encore Media Corp.

Starz Entertainment LLC, (formerly Encore Media Corp.). 8900 Liberty Cir., Englewood, CO, 80112. Phone: (720) 852-7700. Fax: (720) 852-7710. Web Site:www.starz.com

Bill Myers, exec VP, CFO; Jerry Maglio, exec VP, mktg; Robert B. Clasen, pres/CEO.

Los AngelesCA . International Channel, 11766 Wilshire Blvd, Suite 710. Phone:

EnglewoodCO . Founders, 5445 DTC Pkwy, Suite 600. Phone:

EnglewoodCO . New Media, 5445 DTC Pkwy, Suite 600. Phone:

AtlantaGA . southeast region, 5775 Peachtree Dunwoody Rd, Suite D-620. Phone:

ChicagoIL . central region, 111 E. Wacker Dr, Suite 1300. Phone:

HobokenNJ . eastern region, 70 Hudson St. Phone:

CarrolltonTX . Time Warner & Central region office, 2340 E. Trinity Mills Rd, Suite 300. Phone:

Offers 16 movie channels including the flagship Starz & Encore brands with approximately 16.8 million & 31.4 million subs. Advanced svcs including Starz HD, Encore HD, Starz On Demand, Encore On Demand, MoviePlex On Demand, Starz HD On Demand, Encore On HD Demand, MoviePlex HD On Demand, Starz Play & Vongo.

The Style Network, 5750 Wilshire Blvd., Los Angeles, CA, 90036-3709. Phone: (323) 954-2400. Fax: (323) 954-2500. Web Site:www.eonline.com

Style Network covers the gamut of the lifestyle genre. 34 million subs.

Sun TV, 2245 Godby Rd., Atlanta, 30349. Phone: (404) 766-9197. Fax: (404) 767-5264.

David C. Simon, pres/CEO; Virgil Scott, VP.

Sun TV network features news, sports, entertainment, sitcoms, soaps, talk shows from 6:30 AM-midnight Saturday-Sunday (EST). Original progmg from the Caribbean, Central & South America. Serving 700,000 subs. Satellite: Galaxy 4-13.

Sundance Channel, 1633 Broadway, 8th Fl., New York, NY, 10019. Phone: (212) 654-1500. Phone: (212) 708-8025. Web Site:www.sundancechannel.com

Larry Aidem, pres/CEO; Kim Gabelmann, VP.

Sundance Channel is a 24-hours a day ch, featuring uncut coml-free programs, providing TV viewers daring & engaging feature films, short, documentaries, world cinema & animation. 17 million subs. Satellite: Satcom C-4, transponder 20.

TBN-Trinity Broadcasting Network, (TBN Cable Network). 2823 W. Irving Blvd., Irving, TX, 75061. Phone: (972) 313-9500. Phone: (800) 735-5542. Fax: (972) 313-1010. E-mail: comments@tbn.org Web Site:www.tbn.org

Paul Crouch, pres; Robert Higley, VP mktg.

TBN is America's most watched relg network, offering 24-hours of coml-free inspiritional original programs, that appeal to viewers in many denominations. Progmg includes Nashville gospel concerts, health & fitness, talk shows & svcs from America's largest Churches. Multiplex ch: TBN Enlace USA is a 24-hour multi-faith Hispanic ch from Trinity Broadcasting Network. The Church Channel is a new digital network from TBN features church svc program from Protestant, Catholic & Jewish faith groups, 24-hours. On 43.4 million cable systems. 49 million subs. Satellite: Galaxy V, transponder 3.

TBS, 1050 Techwood Dr. N.W., Atlanta, GA, 30318. Phone: (404) 885-4339. Fax: (404) 885-4319. Web Site:tbs.com

Ken Schwab, sr VP progmg/TBS; Steve Koonin, exec VP/COO.

TBS is TV top-rated comedy network. It serves as home to such original comedy series (just name a few) as MY Boys, The Bill Engvall Show, Tyler Perry's House of Payne, Tyler Perry's Meet The Browns & George Lopez's Lopez Tonight, blockbuster movies; & hosted movie showcases. 90.9 million subs. Satellite: Galaxy V, transponder 6.

TEN-The Erotic Network, 7007 Winchester Cir., Suite 200, Boulder, 80301. Phone: (303) 786-8700. Fax: (303) 938-8388. Web Site:www.noof.com

Ken Boenish, pres; Michael Weiner, CEO; William Mossa, VP mktg.

TEN is a network that uses the "un-inhibited" editing standard, 24-hours a day. Multiplex chs: TEN On Demand, TENBlox, TENBlue, TENClips & TENXtsy, PLEASURE. Serving 13.7 million subs. Satellite: Telstar 7-24, TUN, G10R-7.

TNT Latin America, 1050 Techwood Dr. N.W., Atlanta, GA, 30318. Phone: (404) 827-1700. Fax: (404) 575-5341. E-mail: patricia.brito@turner.com Web Site:www.tntla.com

Rick Perez, VP/gen mgr.

Cable network bcst in Sp, Portuguese, English featuring contemp, original movies, NBA coverage & exclusive premieres, 24-hours a day. Serving more than 8.5 million subs in 39 countries in the rgn. Satellite: PanAmSat 1, transponder 3.

TNT (Turner Network Television), 1050 Techwood Dr. N.W., Atlanta, GA, 30318. Phone: (404) 885-4339. Fax: (404) 885-4319. Web Site:www.tnt.tv

Mark Lazarus, pres; Steve Koonin, exec VP.

Top-rated networks, offers original series, also home to powerful one-hr dramas, bcst premiere movies, compelling prime-time specials & championship sports coverage. Available in high definition. 90.3 million subs. Satellite: Galaxy V, transponder 17.

TR!O, 1230 Ave. of the Americas, New York, 10020. Phone: (212) 413-5000. Fax: (212) 413-6552. Web Site:www.triotv.com

Lauren Zalaznick, pres.

TR!O is an entertainment cable TV ch reflecting pop culture, 24-hours a day. Serving 20 million subs. Satellite: Galaxy 1R, transponder 24, Satcom C3, transponder 8.

TV Asia, (Asian Star Broadcasting Network Inc.). 76 National Rd., Edison, NJ, 08817. Phone: (732) 650-1100. Fax: (732) 650-1112. E-mail: info@tvasiausa.com Web Site:www.tvasiausa.com

TV Asia provides a wide range of prgmg produced for South Asian Americans, 24-hrs.

TV Games (TVG) Network, 6701 Center Dr. W., Los Angeles, 90045. Phone: (310) 242-9500. Web Site:www.tvgnetwork.com

Ryan O'Hara, COO. 12 million subs. Satellite: GE-1, transponder 23.

TV Guide Channel, 6922 Hollywood Blvd., Los Angeles, CA, 90028. Phone: (323) 817-4600. Fax: (323) 762-8815. Web Site:www.tvguide.com

Ray Hopkins, exec VP.

New YorkNY , 708 Third Ave., 21st Fl. Phone:

The network combines original etertaining long-form progmg with comprehensive listing info 24-hours a day. 70 million subs. Satellite: Satcom C-4.

TV Japan, (Japan Network Group Inc.). 100 Broadway, 15th Fl., New York, NY, 10005. Phone: (212) 262-3377. Fax: (212) 262-5577.E-mail: takeuchi@tvjapan.net Web Site:www.tvjapan.net

Mitsuo Sekino, pres/CEO; Masao Watari, exec VP; Koki Matsumoto, exec VP.

TV Japan is a Japanese language ch, available 24-hours a day. Satellite: Galaxy II, transponder 24.

TV Land, 1515 Broadway, New York, 10036. Phone: (212) 258-8000. Fax: (212) 846-1775.

Larry W. Jones, VP/gen mgr.

TV Land is the only network dedicated to the best of everything TV from the past 50 years, available 24-hours. 82.1 million subs. Satellite: Satcom C-3, transponder 18.

Talk Internetwork, Inc., 9662 E. Volture Dr., Scottsdale, AZ, 85260. Phone: (480) 551-9774.E-mail: info@talkinternet@aol.com Web Site:www.talkinternet.com

Edwin Cooperstein, pres/CEO; Pat McMahon, progmg dir.

A 24-hour, live, all-talk progmg internet site.

Talkline Communications Television Network, Box 20108, Park West Stn., New York, NY, 10025-1510. Phone: (212) 769-1925. Fax: (212) 799-4195.E-mail: info@talklinecommunications.com Web Site:www.talklinecommunications.com

Zev Brenner, pres/CEO.

Jewish programs with newsmaker guests, celebrity interviews as well as informational progmg. Presented Sundays 11 AM-6 PM, nationally & Sundays 2-5 PM, 9-11 PM & Fridays, 8 AM-noon all EST in the New York area. Serving more than 18 million subs on 825 cable systems.

TechTV, 650 Townsend St., 3rd Fl., San Francisco, 94103. Phone: (415) 355-4000. Fax: (415) 355-4670.E-mail: techtvinfo@techtv.com

Joseph Gillespie, exec VP; Greg Brannan, sr VP; Peter Gochis, VP sls.

TechTV intrigues viewers with everything from help & info to cutting-edge factual progmg to outrageous late-night fun. 43 milion subs. Satellite: Satcom C-4, transponder 12.

Telemundo, 2290 W. 8th Ave., Hialeah, 10019. Phone: (305) 889-7200. Fax: (305) 889-7205.

Jim McNamara, pres/CEO; Don Brown, CFO; Ramon Escobar, exec VP.

Telemundo, a United States Sp-language TV network, available 24-hours. Multiplex ch: Telemundo Internacional. Serving 32 million subs. Satellite: Satcom, transponder 20 east, AMC-4, transponder 8 west.

The Tennis Channel, 2850 Ocean Park Blvd., Santa Monica, 90405. Phone: (310) 314-9400. Fax: (310) 314-9433. Web Site:www.thetennischannel.com

Steve Bellamy, pres; Ken Solomon, chmn/CEO; John Brady, CFO; Keith Manasco, VP opns.

The Tennis Channel is the 24-hour cable TV network devoted to tennis & other racquet sports, ad-supported. 3 million subs. Satellite: Telstar 5, transponder 15.

The Theatre Channel, Box 2676, Venice, CA, 90294. Phone: (310) 823-6508.E-mail: info@theatrechannel.com Web Site:www.theatrechannel.com

Cheryl Beach, CEO.

Traditional & alternative live theatre dance, opera, children's theatre in a videotape format.

Time Warner Cable, One Time Warner Ctr., New York, NY, 10019. Phone: (212) 598-7200. Web Site:www.timewarner.com

Jeffrey L. Bewkes, pres/CEO.

FlushingNY , 41-61 Kissena Blvd.

Cable svc. Serving over 1.3 million subs.

Toon Disney, 3800 W. Alameda Ave., Burbank, CA, 91505. Phone: (818) 569-7500. Fax: (818) 566-1358. Web Site:www.toondisney.com

Ann Sweeney, pres.

Toon Disney is a var of acquired animated programs, 24-hours a day. Serving more than 43 million subs. Satellite: Galaxy 10R.

Travel Channel, 5425 Wisconsin Ave., Suite 500, Chevy Chase, MD, 20815. Phone: (301) 244-7500. Fax: (301) 244-7507. Web Site:www.travelchannel.com

Billy Campbell, pres; Joe Abruzzese, pres, adv sls; Bill Goodwyn, pres, affil sls & mktg; Patrick Younge, pres/gen mgr.

Bringing knowledge, insight & info to a community of people who want to experience their world & satisfy their curiosity. Serving more than 90 million U.S. cable homes.

truTV, 600 3rd Ave., 2nd Fl., New York, NY, 10016. Phone: (212) 973-2800. Fax: (212) 973-3210. Web Site:www.courttv.com

Marc Juris, gen mgr; Ira Fields, exec VP & CFO; Art Bell, pres/COO.

Court TV telecast trails day by day & high profile original programs 24-hours. Serving 80 million subs.

Turner Classic Movies (TCM), 1050 Techwood Dr. N.W., Atlanta, GA, 30318. Phone: (404) 885-5535. Web Site:www.turnerclassicmovies.com

Tom Karsch, VP/gen mgr; Mark Lazarus, pres.

Features Hollywood's greatest movies of all time, presented 24-hours, coml-free. 63.9 million subs.

USA Network, 30 Rockefeller Plaza, c/o NBC, New York, NY, 10112. Phone: (212) 664-4444. Fax: (212) 413-6509. Web Site:www.wnbc.com

Bonnie Hammer, pres; Jeff Wachtel, exec VP/original progmg.

Nework featuring movies, original series, sports specials, teen & children's progmg, 24-hours.

Univision Television Group, 605 3rd Ave., 12th Fl., New York, NY, 10158. Phone: (212) 455-5200. Fax: (212) 867-6710. Web Site:www.univision.com

New YorkNY . East, 605 Third Ave, 26 Fl. Phone:

DallasTX . Central, 2323 Bryan St, Suite 1900. Phone:

Univision Network, the most-watched Spanish-language broadcast television network in the U.S. reaching 97% of U.S. Hispanic households.

Serving 34.5 million subs. Satellite: Galaxy 1R.

TeleFutura Network, a general-interest Spanish-language broadcast television network, which was launched in 2002 and now reaches 85% of U.S. Hispanic households. Serves 7.2 million subs. Satellite: Galaxy 1. Satellite: Galaxy IR.

Urban Television Network Corp., 300 Radio Shack Cir., Suite T3-381, Fort Worth, TX, 76102. Phone: (817) 415-4816.E-mail: info@uatvn.com Web Site:www.uatvn.com

Jacob R. Miles III, CEO; Randy Moseley, exec VP/CFO & dir.

VH1 (Music First), (MTV Networks Inc.). 1515 Broadway, New York, NY, 10036. Phone: (212) 846-7840. Web Site:www.vh1.com

VH1 is a 24-hours ch that features new, current & classic music video, for viewers ages 18-49 who grew up with music videos. Multiplex chs: VH1 Classic, VH1 Country, VH1 Megahits, VH1 Soul & VH Uno. 86.3 million subs. Satellite: Satcom C-4, transponder 23.

Versus, One Comcast Ctr., 27th Fl., Philadelphia, PA, 19103. Phone: (215) 665-1700. Web Site:www.versus.com

Los AngelesCA , 11835 W. Olympic Blvd, Suite 980. Phone:

New YorkNY , 90 Park Ave., 2nd Fl. Phone:

Offers collegiate sports featuring nationally-ranked teams from top conference, features the best field sports progmg on TV & is a destination for sports fans, athletes & sportsmen to find exclusive, competitive events that audiences can't find elsewhere. On 4,893 cable systems.

WGN America, 2501 W. Bradley Pl., Chicago, IL, 60618-4718. Phone: (773) 528-2311. Phone: (773) 883-3241, (212) 210-5900. Fax: (773) 883-6299. Web Site:www.WGNAmerica.com

Bill Shaw; Sean Compton, sr VP of progmg & dev; Chris Manning, VP/gen sls mgr.

Broad scope entertainment network offering blockbuster movies & series, including MLB baseball & NBA basketball in HD. Total subscribers: 72 million. Satellite used and transponder: Galaxy 14. transponder 13C.

WSBK-TV, (Boscom). 1170 Soldiers Field Rd., Boston, MA, 02134. Phone: (617) 787-7000. Fax: (617) 254-6383. Web Site:www.boston.cbs.com

Ed Piette, pres/gen mgr.

WSBK-TV is a 24-hours ind ch from Boston featuring sports, movies, news & specials. Satellite: GE-3, Transponder 3.

The Weather Channel, 300 Interstate North Pkwy., Atlanta, GA, 30339. Phone: (770) 226-0000. Fax: (770) 226-2950. Web Site:www.weather.com

Terry Connelly, sr VP/gen mgr.

New YorkNY , 845 Third Ave, 11th Floor. Phone:

All-weather progmg 24-hours a day; natl, international, rgnl & loc weather forecasts & features. Multiplex ch: WeatherScan.

Serving 87.5 million subs. Satellite: GE Satcom C-3, transponder 13.

WE-Women's Entertainment, 11 Penn Plaza, 19th Fl., New York, NY, 10001. Phone: (516) 803-4400. Web Site:www.wetv.com

Kim Martin, gen mgr .

A 24-hours cable net featuring classic movies & TV progmg devoted entirely to romance.

Worship Network, Box 428, Safe Harbor, FL, 34695-0365. Phone: (727) 536-0036. Web Site:www.worship.net

Bruce Kobish, pres/CEO.

Worship Network features, scenery from around the world with words of wisdom from scriptures & inspirational music. Available 24 hours a day. 66 million subs. transponder 7.

Regional Cable News Networks

Allbritton Communications, 1000 Wilson Blvd., Suite 2700, Arlington, VA, 22209. Phone: (703) 647-8745. Fax: (703) 647-8746.E-mail: jkillen@allbrittontv.com Web Site:www.newschannel8.net

James Killen, sls VP.

There are 8 stns: WJLA. Newschannel 8. WHTM, WSET, WCIU, WBMA, KATV, KTUL.

The Arizona News Channel, 5555 N 7th Ave., Phoenix, AZ, 85013. Phone: (602) 207-3762. Fax: (602) 379-2459.E-mail: advertising@azfamily.com Web Site:www.azfamily.com

Arizona's first & only 24-hour loc news svc built on a unique partnership; live loc breaking coverage gives viewers the latest news from around the Valley; NewsChannel 3's "Good Morning Arizona," "Good Day Arizona," "Good Evening Arizona" & "The News Show" replay throughout the day on the AZ News Channel, Cox Cable Channel 14; progmg also includes loc productions exclusive to cable, such as "Project Parenting."

Bay News 9, 700 Carillon Pkwy., Ste. 9, St. Petersburg, FL, 33716. Phone: (727) 329-2300. Fax: (727) 329-2434.E-mail: viewer@baynews9.com Web Site:www.baynews9.com

Elliott Wiser, VP/gen mgr; Mike Gautreau, news dir.

Bay News 9 is a 24-hour ch owned & operated by Bright House Network. The ch serves over 1 million cable customers in Tampa Bay. Also programs a 24-hour Sp & sports ch.

Bay TV, (KRON 4). 1001 Van Ness Ave., San Francisco, CA, 94109. Phone: (415) 441-4444.E-mail: 4listens@kron4.com Web Site:www.baytv.com

A 24-hour loc news, sports & info cable ch.

CLTV News (ChicagoLand Television News), 2000 York Rd., Suite 114 , Oak Brook, IL, 60523. Phone: (630) 368-4000. Fax: (630) 571-0489. Web Site:www.cltv.com

Steve Farber, gen mgr .

Covers Chicago loc & rgnl news, sports, news, weather & traf info, serving 1.9 million subs.

CN8 - The Comcast Network, 1500 Market St., 28th Fl., W. Tower, Philadelphia, PA, 19102. Phone: (215) 981-7750. Fax: (215) 981-8420. Web Site:www.cn8.com

Michael A. Doyle, pres; Melissa Kennedy, dir mktg.

CN8, The Comcast Network, is an award-winning, 24-hours news, talk, sports & entertainment cable net created by Comcast Cable Communications, that has steadily won viewers, awards & accolades since its inception in 1996. CN8 provides quality locally-produced progmg in four main areas-live, interactive television; rgnl news; entertainment; coverage of high school, college & professional sports. CN8 continues to expand its compelling mix of news, talk, sports & entertainment progmg throughout the eastern seaboard, from Washington DC, to the new England area, broadcasting to 6.2 million viewers everyday.

CablePulse (CP 24), 299 Queen St. W., Toronto, ON, M5V 2Z5. Canada. Phone: (416) 591-5757. Fax: (416) 593-6397.E-mail: info@cp24.com Web Site:www.pulse24.com

Stephen Hurlbut, VP/gen mgr; Dan Hamilton, VP sls; Tina Cortese, dir of news progmg; Keith Wilson, opns dir; Karen Reid, news dir; David Kirkwood, VP; Jenny Norush, adv dir; Bev Nenson, dir of publicity; Allan Schwebel, VP mktg, VP sls.

Rgnl 24-hour a day English language news & information channel.

The California Channel, 1121 L St, Suite 110, Sacramento, CA, 95814. Phone: (916) 444-9792. Fax: (916) 444-9812. Web Site:www.calchannel.com

John Hancock, pres.

The California Channel is an independent, nonprofit, public affairs cable television network. Programming includes coverage of California Assembly and Senate floor sessions and committee meetings, capitol press conferences, and proceedings of regulatory boards and state commissions. 33.5 hours/week, serving 5,800,000 subs.

CBS News 4, 8900 N.W. 18th Terr., Doral, FL, 33172. Phone: (305) 591-4444. Web Site:www.cbs4news.com

Central Florida News 13, 20 N. Orange Ave., Suite 13, Orlando, FL, 32801. Phone: (407) 513-1300. Fax: (407) 513-1310.E-mail: newsdesk@cfnews13.com Web Site:www.cfnews13.com

Robin A. Smythe, VP/gen mgr.

Central Florida News 13 is Orlando & the Central Florida Region's only 24-hour loc cable news ch seen only on Bright House Networks.

Country Television Network San Diego, 1600 Pacific Hwy., Rm. 208, San Diego, CA, 92101-2422. Phone: (619) 595-4600. Fax: (619)557-4027.E-mail: ctn@sdcountry.ca.gov Web Site:www.ctn.org

Michael Workman, dir; Janice McGee, owner; Barry Fraser, cable franchise admin.

Country Television Network San Diego makes country govt more accessible & understandable to the citizens of San Diego County through informational progmg focusing on the svcs, programs & current issues of county gov, 24 hr a day, serving 708,700 subs.

Las Vegas One, 3228 Channel 8 Dr., Las Vegas, NV, 89109. Phone: (702) 792-8888. Fax: (702) 792-2977. Web Site:www.klas-tv.com

Robert Stoldal, VP opns; Emily Neilson, pres.

Las Vegas One is a 24-hours loc news ch serving the Las Vegas area.

Michigan Government Television, 111 S. Capitol Ave., 4th Fl., Romney Bldg., Lansing, MI, 48909. Phone: (517) 373-4250. Fax: (517) 335-7342.E-mail: mgtv@mgtv.org Web Site:www.mgtv.org

Bill Trevarthen, exec dir.

Cable network covering all branches of Michigan's state government.

Neighborhood News 12, 111 New South Rd., Hicksville, NY, 11801. Phone: (516) 393-3378. Web Site:www.news12.com

Barry J. Romanski, gen mgr .

Neighborhood News 12 is a 24-hrs news ch for individual communities.

New England Cable News, 160 Wells Ave., Newton, MA, 02459. Phone: (617) 630-5000. Fax: (617) 630-5057. Fax: (617) 630-5055. Web Site:www.necn.com

Charles J. Kravetz, pres, gen mgr; Tom Melville, news dir.

A 24-hour rgnl news net.

New York 1 News, 75 9th Ave., 6th Fl., New York, NY, 10011. Phone: (212) 691-6397. Fax: (212) 563-7154.E-mail: ny/news@ny1.com Web Site:www.ny1.com

Steve Paulus, sr VP; Brad Shapiro, dir; Marc Nathanson, exec producer; Bernie Han, news dir; Kevin Dugan, producer.

A 24-hour, all-news cable ch devoted primarily to coverage of New York City & its neighborhoods.

News 12 Bronx, 930 Soundview Ave., Bronx, NY, 10473. Phone: (718) 861-6800.E-mail: customerservice@news12.com Web Site:www.news12.com

News 12 Bronx is a 24-hours rgnl news progmg svc (a News 12 Regional Network).

News 14 Carolina, 316 East Morehead St., Suite 100, Charlotte, NC, 28202. Phone: (704) 973-5800. Fax: (704) 731-2760.E-mail: feedback@news14.com Web Site:www.news14.com

New 14 Carolina offers 24-hours loc news & weather every ten minutes on the Ones.

News Channel 8, 1100 Wilson Blvd., 6th Fl., Arlington, VA, 22209. Phone: (703) 236-9555. Fax: (703) 236-2331. Web Site:www.news8.net

A 24-hour news svc offered in the Washington, DC metropolitan area over all cable svcs. It is available to cable subs in Alexandria, Arlington County, Fairfax City, Fairfax County & Loudoun County in Virginia, Montgomery & Prince George's Counties in Maryland & Washington, DC.

News Now 53, 777 Northwest Grand Blvd., Suite 600, Oklahoma City, OK, 73118. Phone: (405) 600-6600. Fax: (405) 600-0670. Web Site:www.kotv.com

News On One, 3501 Farnam St., Omaha, NE, 68131. Phone: (402) 346-6666. Fax: (402) 233-7888.E-mail: sixonlin@wowt.com Web Site:www.wowt.com

Dir of prom & production & tech opns.

News 10 Now, 815 Erie Blvd. E., Syracuse, NY, 13210. Phone: (315) 234-1000. Fax: (315) 234-0635.E-mail: info@news10now.com Web Site:www.news10now.com

Ron Lombard, gen mgr & news dir.

A 24-hour loc/rgnl news ch serving 560,000 Time Warner cable subscribers throughout central/upstate New York.

News 12 Connecticut, 28 Cross St., Norwalk, CT, 06851. Phone: (203) 849-1321. Fax: (203) 849-1327.E-mail: news12.ct@news12.com Web Site:www.news12.com

Tom Appleby, news dir; Carmela Williams, news coord.

24 hour, 7 day week reg news ch featuring hyper-loc news coverage including sports & weather.

News 12 Long Island, One Media Crossways, Woodbury, NY, 11797. Phone: (516) 393-1200. Fax: (516) 393-1456. Web Site:www.news12.com E-mail: new12li@news12.com

Patrick Dolan, news dir.

A 24-hours rgnl news svc.

News 12 New Jersey, 450 Raritan Ctr. Pkwy., Edison, NJ, 08837-3994. Phone: (732) 346-3200. Fax: (732) 417-5155.E-mail: news12nj@news12.com Web Site:www.news12.com

Larry Meyrowitz, dir opns, engrg dir; Laura Johnson, sls dir; Randal W. Stanley, news dir & gen mgr; Patrick O. Young, dir mktg, prom dir.

Provides 24-hour coverage of breaking news & events throughout New Jersey, in addition to pub affrs, info & lifestyle progmg of loc interest. Serving 1.8 million households in 14 northern & central counties in New Jersey .

News 12 Westchester, 6 Executive Plaza, Yonkers, NY, 10701. Phone: (914) 378-8916. Fax: (914) 378-8938.E-mail: news12wc@news12.com Web Site:www.news12.com

Marguerite Tolliver, mgr.

24-hour news organization covering Westchester County.

NewsChannel 5+, 474 James Robertson Pkwy., Nashville, TN, 37219. Phone: (615) 248-5371. Fax: (615) 248-5394.E-mail: mbonnett@newschannel5.com Web Site:www.newschannel5.com

Michelle Bonnett, exec dir.

NewsChannel 5+ is a loc news & info stn, serving 550,000 homes in Middle Tennessee & Southern Kentucky.

Ohio News Network, 770 Twin Rivers Dr., Columbus, OH, 43215. Phone: (614) 280-3700. Fax: (614) 280-6305. Web Site:www.ohionewsnow.com

Tom Griesdorn, VP/gen mgr; Frank Willson, mktg dir; Barb Geller, affil rel mgr; Greg Fisher, news dir; Jason Pheister, progmg dir; Vince Jones, opns mgr; Chuck DeVendra, sls dir.

A 24-hour cable news ch featuring loc news, weather & sports for the people of Ohio. Currently seen in over 1.5 million homes.

Orange County Newschannel, 625 North Grand Avenue, Santa Ana, CA, 92701. Phone: (714) 565-3850. Web Site:www.rtnda.org

Mike Sweeney, gen mgr; Don Engelhardt, chief engr; Mya Bulwa, exec producer; Susanne Lysak, news dir.

Orange County Newschannel features exclusive coverage of loc news, sports, weather & traf in southern California's Orange County, 24 hours serving over 575,000 subs.

Pennsylvania Cable Network (PCN), 401 Fallowfield Rd., Camp Hill, PA, 17011. Phone: (717) 730-6000. Fax: (717) 730-6005.E-mail: pcntv@pcntv.com Web Site:www.pcntv.com

Brian Lockman, pres/CEO; William Bova, VP progmg; Debra Kohr Sheppard, VP opns; Richard Cochran, VP mktg; Michelle Harter, VP.

PCN is the nation's pre-eminent state pub affrs network, with live & same day coverage of the Pennsylvania Senate/House & other govt activities. PCN televises significant state events (such as high school sports championships), tours museums & mfg facilities in the state & distributes educ progmg.

Pittsburgh Cable News Channel (PCNC), 4145 Evergreen Rd., Pittsburgh, PA, 15214. Phone: (412) 237-1190. Fax: (412) 237-1286. Web Site:www.wpxi.com E-mail: mbarash@wpxi.com

Paul Curran, gen sls mgr; Mark W. Barash, stn mgr; Brian Abzanka, opns mgr.

Loc & rgnl news, talk & info.

R News/Time Warner Communications, 71 Mt. Hope Ave., Rochester, NY, 14620. Phone: (585) 756-2424. Fax: (585) 756-1673. Web Site:www.rnews.com E-mail: assignment@rnews.com

Ed Buttaccio, news dir.

Loc news 24-hours 7 days per week. Interactive daily call-in show. Nightly loc Sp newscast.

Regional News Network (RNN), 721 Broadway, Kingston, NY, 12401. Phone: (914) 417-2700.

Richard French, gen mgr .

RNN is a 24 hour provider of news & pub info targeted to suburban New York, Connecticut & and New Jersey serving over 250,000 subs.

Rhode Island News Channel, 10 Orms St., Providence, RI, 02904. Phone: (401) 453-8000. Fax: (401) 331-4431.E-mail: radeszkoza@abc6.com Web Site:www.abc6.com

Ronald Adeszko, gen mgr .

Rhode Island News Channel is a simulcast & rebroadcast of WLNE newscasts for Rhode Island.

SNN News 6, 1741 Main St., Sarasota, FL, 34236. Phone: (941) 361-4600. Fax: (941) 361-4699. Web Site:www.snn6.com

Linda DesMarais, gen mgr .

A 24-hour cable news ch with focus on loc news & info. The Sarasota Herald -Tribune newspaper owned by the New York Times Co.

San Diego's Newchannel 15, Box 85347, San Diego, CA, 92186. Phone: (619) 237-1010. Fax: (619) 527-0369. Web Site:www.10news.com

San Diego's Newchannel 15 provides original newscasts, repeats of KGTV-10 newscasts & live break-ins 24 hours.

Texas Cable News, 570 Young St., Dallas, TX, 75202. Phone: (214) 977-4500. Web Site:www.txcn.com

James T. Aitken, gen mgr .

News ch covering the state of Texas, 24-hours loc & rgnl.

Tri-State Media News (TSM news), 2215 DuPont Pkwy., New Castle, DE, 19770. Phone: (877) TSM-NEWS. Web Site:www.tsmnews.com

Stanley H. Green, pres/CEO.

WJLA-TV/Newschannel 8, 1100 Wilson Blvd., 6th Fl., Arlington, VA, 22209. Phone: (703) 647-8745. Fax: (703) 647-8746. Web Site:www.newschannel8.net E-mail: jkillen@allbrittontv.com

James Killen, sls VP.

A 24-hours rgnl news svc for Washington, DC, suburban Maryland & northern Virginia. On 15 cable systems serving 1,125,000 subs.

Regional Cable Sports Networks

Big Ten Network, 444 N. Michigan Ave., Suite 1200, Chicago, IL, 60611. Phone: (312) 665-0700. Fax: (312) 665-0740. Web Site:www.bigten.org

Mark Silverman, pres.

CBS College Sports Network, Chelsea Piers, Pier 62, Suite 316, New York, NY, 10011. Phone: (212) 342-8700. Fax: (212) 342-8899.E-mail: customerservice @website.cstv.com Web Site:www.cstv.com

Eric Krasnoo, VP.

Channel 4 San Diego, 350 10th Ave., Suite 500, San Diego, CA, 92101. Phone: (619) 683-1900. Fax: (619) 876-4993. Web Site:4sd.com

Craig Nichols, VP/gen mgr.

San Diego Padres baseball, etc.

Comcast SportsNet, 3601 South Broad St., Philadelphia, PA, 19148. Phone: (215) 336-3500. Fax: (215) 952-5996.E-mail: askcsn@comcastsportsnetwork.com Web Site:www.comcastsportsnet.com

Jack Williams, pres.

Rgnl TV progmg svcs includes live coverage of Philadelphia Flyers ice hockey, Philadelphia '76ers basketball, Philadelphia Phillies baseball, pro boxing, college basketball, football, indoor lacrosse, ABL, loc sports news & sports talk programs.

Serving 3 million subs on MSOS(16).

Comcast SportsNet Mid-Atlantic, 7700 Wisconsin Ave., Suite 200, Bethesda, MD, 20814. Phone: (301) 718-3200. Fax:(301) 718-3300.E-mail: viewmail@comcastsportsnet.com Web Site:midatlantic.comcastsportsnet.com

Rgnl sports net serving mid-Atlantic. Progmg includes Orioles baseball, Capitals, hockey, Wizards, basketball, ACC & CAA.

Serving 4.4 million subs on over 200 cable systems.

Satellite: Spacenet III, transponder 12-H, ch 23 (scrambled).

Connecticut Sports Network, 1049 Asylum Ave., Hartford, CT, 06105. Phone: (860) 278-5310.

Anthony Meliso, gen mgr .

Cox Sports AZ, 20401 N. 29th Ave., Phoenix, AZ, 85027. Phone: (623) 322-8001. Fax: (623) 322-7424. Web Site:phoenix.cox.net

Phoenix Suns basketball, sports specials, high school sports & high school championships, etc. Phoenix metropolitan area serving over 500,000 subs. Loc microwave/fiber distributed regionally to additional operators.

Cox Sports Television, 2121 Airline Dr., Metairie, LA, 70001. Phone: 504-304-2740. Fax: 504-304-2243.E-mail: coxsportstv@cox.com Web Site:www.coxsportstv.com

Rod Mickler, VP.

Cox Sports TV is an innovated, 24 hours net providing compelling & rgnl sports progmg. Satellite: Galaxy 23. Serving 1.3 million sub, on 79 cable systems, transponder one.

CSS - Comcast/Charter Sports Southeast, 2995 Courtyards Dr., Norcross, GA, 30071. Phone: (770) 559-7800. Phone: (770) 559-2742 (Jeff Miller). Fax: (770) 559-2329.E-mail: css@csssports.com Web Site:www.csssports.com

ESPN Inc., ESPN Plaza, 545 Middle St., Bristol, CT, 06010. Phone: (860) 766-2000. Fax: (860) 766-2400. Web Site:www.espn.com

ESPN offers a var of professional & amateur sports, including NFL, college basketball, NHL major league baseball, the woman's NCAA tournament.

On 28,000 affiliating cable systems serving over 77 million subs.

ESPNews, ESPN Plaza, 545 Middle St., Bristol, CT, 06010-9454. Phone: (860) 585-2000. Fax: (860) 766-2400. Web Site:www.espn.com

ESPN Classic, ESPN Plaza, 545 Middle St., Bristol, CT, 06010. Phone: (860) 766-2000. Fax: (860) 766-2400. Web Site:www.espn.com

Classic sporting events, sports series, documentaries & movies; home shopping for sports merchandise & interactive sports games.

Serving 20 million subs on 400 plus cable systems.

Satellite: Galaxy 7, transponder 13 (compressed).

FSN Arizona, 2 North Central Ave., Suite 1700, One Renaissance Sq., Phoenix, AZ, 85004. Phone: (602) 257-9500. Fax: (602) 257-0848. Web Site:www.foxsports.com/arizona

Mike Connelly, VP/gen mgr; Amy Serafin, progmg mgr; Brett Hansen, dir mktg; Jen Baker, account exec; Michael Bardess, producer.

Provides rgnl coverage of loc interest sports progmg. Serving 2.3 million subs in Arizona & Mexico. Satellite: C-1/16.

FSN Florida, 1550 Sawgrass Corporate Pkwy., Suite 350, Sunrise, FL, 33323. Phone: (954) 845-9994. Web Site:www.fsnflorida.com

Jeff Genthner, VP/gen mgr.

FSN Florida progmg includes Major League Baseball's Marlins, Tampa Bay Devil Rays & National Hockey League's Florida Panthers.

FSN Pittsburgh, 323 North Shore Dr., Suite 200, Pittsburgh, PA, 15212. Phone: (412) 316-3800. Fax: (412) 316-3892. Web Site:www.fsninsider.com

Ted Black, VP/gen mgr.

FSN Pittsburgh telecasts more than 2,000 hours loc progmg each year including the Pittsburgh Pirates, Penguins & Steelers. Also carries athletic contsts & progmg from the University of Pittsburgh, West Virginia & the WPIAL, among others. Satellite: Galaxy 17. On 60 cable systems. 2.3 million subs.

FSN South, 1175 Peachtree St. N.E., Bldg. 100, Suite 200, Atlanta, GA, 30361. Phone: (404) 230-7300. Fax: (404) 230-7399. Web Site:www.foxsports.com

Chris Killebrew, VP sls; Bill Irish, VP progmg, VP progmg; Cheryl Raiford, controller; Jamie Kimbrough, dir; Brian Hogan, gen sls mgr; Steve Craddock, exec producer & VP; Jeff Genthner, VP/gen mgr.

NCAA sports, Atlanta Hawks, Memphis Grizzlies basketball, Atlanta Braves, Baltimore Orioles, Cincinnati Reds, St. Louis Cardinals baseball, Carolina Hurricanes, Nashville Predators hockey, NASCAR, golf, tennis & much more.

Serving 11.3 million subs on more than 1,100 cable systems.

Satellite: Galaxy 11, transponder 4, ch 2.

FSN West, 1100 S. Flower St. #2200, Los Angeles, CA, 90015. Phone: (213) 743-7800. Fax: (213) 743-7841. Web Site:msn.foxsports.com/regional/west

Steve Simpson, VP/gen mgr.

Los Angeles Lakers basketball, Kings hockey, Lazers indoor soccer, Strings tennis, San Diego Soccers soccer & collegiate sports, etc.

FSN West 2, 1100 S. Flower St., #2200, Los Angeles, CA, 90015. Phone: (213) 743-7800. Fax: (213) 743-7841. Web Site:msn.foxsports.com/regional/west

LaVada Heath, sls VP; Lisa Laky, VP sls; Alex Tevllin, progmg mgr; Greg Dowling, news dir; Steve Simpson, VP/gen mgr; Amy Wilson, dir mktg.

Rgnl sports net featuring the Los Angeles Dodgers, Los Angeles Clippers, Los Angeles Galaxy, Mighty Ducks of Anaheim, USC & UCLA athletic events & other sports.

Serving 3 million subs.

Satellite: G1, transponder 21. 4,800,000.

Fox Soccer Channel, 1440 S. Sepulveda Blvd., 2nd Fl., Los Angeles, CA, 90025. Phone: (310) 444-8642. Fax: (310) 444-8445. Web Site:www.foxsoccer.com E-mail: ben.alkaly@fox.com

Frank Uddo, VP progmg; Dermot McQuarrie, sr VP; Sean Riley, sr VP; David Sternberg, exec VP; Raul de Quesada, sr VP; David Stenberg, gen mgr; Ed Derse, VP, interactive media; Raul Palma, VP, production; Fausto Ceballos, VP, on-air promotions; Mike Petruzzi, natl adv sls mgr; Veronica Alvarez, dir of mktg & promotions.

Fox Soccer Channel is the nation's leading TV destination for young, passionate & affluent soccer fans. The best in exclusive coverage of professional, college & youth soccer. Satellite: Galaxy 11, transponder 8. 550+. over 30 million.

Fox Sports en Espanol, 1440 S. Sepulveda Blvd., Los Angeles, CA, 90025. Phone: (310) 444-8658. Fax: (310) 444-8445.E-mail: patrick.ilabaca@fox.com Web Site:www.fse.tv

New YorkNY , 1211 Ave. of the Americas. Phone:

Live, exclusive coverage in Sp of the Copa Toyota Libertadores & Major League Baseball's All-Star game & World Series postseason, boxing & nightly sports news. Serving 7.9 million subs on 1,321 cable systems. Satellite: Satcom C1, Transponder 1, ch 8 (SA Power VU IRD D9225).

Fox Sports Net, 10201 W. Pico Blvd., FNC/Bldg. 101, 5th Fl., Los Angeles, CA, 90035. Phone: (310) 369-6000. Fax: (310) 969-6700. Web Site:www.foxsports.com

Tracy Dolgin, exec VP; Arthur Smith, VP progmg; Jim Martin, exec VP; Jeff Shell, CFO; Randy Freer, pres.

A natl, rgnl & loc supplier of sports progmg.

Serves 68 million subs through 22 rgnl sports nets.

Fox Sports Net Bay Area, 77 Geary St., 5th Fl., San Francisco, CA, 94108. Phone: (415) 296-8900. Fax: (415) 296-9198.E-mail: fsnbayinfo@fsnbayarea.com Web Site:www.fsnbayarea.com

Jeff Krolik, VP/gen mgr; Chris Geer, VP sls; Ted Griggs, VP progmg; Michael McCright, gen sls mgr.

Programing: San Francisco Giants, Oakland Athletics, Golden State Warriors, San Jose Sharks, San Jose Saber Cats & San Jose Stealth.

Serving more than 4 million households in Northern California & Northern Nevada.

Satellite: Compressed, AMC 1, T 18 Channel 110.

Fox Sports Net Detroit, 26555 Evergreen Rd., Suite 90, Southfield, MI, 480276. Phone: (248) 226-9700. Fax: (248) 226-9725. Web Site:www.foxsports.com/detroit E-mail: detroit@foxsports.net

Lisa Giles, progmg dir; Greg Hammaren, VP/gen mgr; John Tuohey, exec producer.

Cable sports net featuring Detroit Pistons, Red Wings, Tigers, Fury, Shock, CCHA hockey & Michigan High School Association championship contests.

Serving 3.2 million subs on more than 70 cable systems.

Fox Sports Net Midwest, 700 St. Louis Union Station, Suite 300, St. Louis, MO Phone: (314) 206-7020. Fax: (314) 206-7070.E-mail: midwest@foxsports.net Web Site:www.foxsports.com

Jack Donovan, VP/gen mgr.

IndianapolisIN . FSN Indiana, 135 N. Pennsylvania St., Suite 720.

Fox Sports Net Midwest reaches more than 5.4 million cable & satellite TV homes in six Midwest states. It telecasts more than 2,000 hours of loc progmg each year, including coverage of St. Louis Cardinals baseball, St. Louis Blues hockey, Indiana Pacers basketball, Indiana Fever basketball, Kansas City Royals baseball, Cincinnati Reds baseball, Big 12: football, women's basketball & showcase, Univ. of Missouri athletics, Kansas State Univ. athletics, Univ. of Nebraska Basketball, Missouri Valley Conference basketball, championship events, Gateway Conference football, & loc high school sports programs, collegiate coaches shows.

Fox Sports Net New England, 42 3rd Ave., Burlington, MA, 01803-4414. Phone: (781) 270-7200. Web Site:www.foxsportsnewengland.com

Boston Celtics basketball, New York Mets (Connecticut only), college basketball, golf, football, hockey, professional tennis, soccer & auto racing.

On 215 cable systems serving 2.9 million subs.

Satellite: GE1, transponder 14.

Fox Sports Net New York, Two Penn Plaza, 4th Fl., New York, NY, 10001. Phone: (212) 465-6000. Fax: (212) 465-6024. Web Site:msn.foxsports.com

A two-ch rgnl sports network that delivers approximately 300 live games of the New York Islanders, Mets, New Jersey Nets & Devils, in addition to horse racing, college football, basketball & variety of sports specials.

On 128 affil cable systems serving more than 2.7 million subs.

Satellite: GE SpaceNet 2, transponders 1.

Fox Sports Net North, 1 Main St. S.E., #600, Minneapolis, MN, 55414-1036. Phone: (612) 330-2468. Phone: (612) 486-9500. Web Site:www.foxcable.com

Rgnl Sports Network: Minnesota, Iowa, Wisconsin, South Dakota & North Dakota. MLB & Brewers, NBA Timberwolves & Bucks, University of Minnesota hockey, & women's athletics, University of Wisconsin men's & women's athletics, Marquette University athletics.

Serving 3 million subs.

Satellite: GE 3, transponder 6.

Fox Sports Net Northwest, 3626 156th Ave. S.E., Bellevue, WA, 98006. Phone: (425) 641-0104. Fax: (425) 641-9811. Web Site:www.foxsports.com/northwest

Mark Shuken, VP/gen mgr; Amy Affeld, progmg dir; Mike Smith, controller; Liz Serrette, opns mgr; Julie McCormack, mgr; Brett Bibby, gen sls mgr.

Coverage of PAC-10, Big Sky, other collegiate conference athletic events; Mariners, SuperSonics & other professional & high school events in the Pacific Northwest rgn.

Serving 2.4 million subs on 100 cable systems.

Satellite: G7, transponder 4.

Fox Sports Net Ohio, 9200 S. Hills Blvd., Suite 200, Broadview Heights, OH, 44147. Phone: (440) 746-8000. Fax: (440) 746-9480. Web Site:www.foxsports.com

Steve Pawlowski, communications dir.

CincinnatiOH , 11311 Cornell Park Dr, Suite 406. Phone: Live sports progmg: Cleveland Indians, Cleveland Cavaliers, Cincinnati Reds, Columbus Blue Jackets, college football, basketball & sports news.

Serving 4.5 million subs on 206 cable systems.

Satellite: Satcom GE1, transponder T4. Alternate: GE1 T17.

Fox Sports Net Rocky Mountain, 2300 15th St., Suite 300, Denver, CO, 80202. Phone: (720) 898-2700. Fax: (720) 898-2735. Web Site:www.foxsports.com

Steven Gravlin, dir; Tim Griggs, gen mgr; Amy Turner, dir.

Rgnl sports net serving 8 states. Progmg includes Denver Nuggets, Utah Jazz, Colorado Avalanche, Colorado Rockies, Univ of Denver & Big 12 conference. Serving 2.2 million subs on 300 cable systems.

Satellites: G7.

Fox Sports Net Southwest, 100 E. Royal Ln., Suite 200, Irving, TX, 75039. Phone: (972) 868-1800. Fax: (972) 868-1678. Web Site:www.foxsports.com

Jon Heidtke, VP/gen mgr; Mike Anastassiou, exec producer; Mike Ibanez, affil sls dir.

Rgnl sports net serving Texas, Oklahoma, Arkansas, Louisiana & parts of New Mexico. Serving 9 million subs on 1,300 cable and satellite systems. Satellite: Galaxy 11, transponder 4 (digitally compressed).

Madison Square Garden Network, Two Penn Plaza, 4th Fl., New York, NY, 10001. Phone: (212) 465-6000. Fax: (212) 465-6024. Web Site:www.msgnetwork.com E-mail: mscnetpr@msgnetwork.com

New York Knicks, Rangers & Yankees; college football & basketball games; boxing. Exclusive Garden events as well as original series progmg.

Serving more than 6.1 million subs on more than 250 cable systems.

Satellite: Satcom 4, transponder 6.

Mid-Atlantic Sports Network, 333 W. Camden St., Baltimore, MD, 21201. Phone: (410) 625-7100. Web Site:www.masnsports.com

New England Sports Network (NESN), 480 Arsenal St. #1, Watertown, MA, 02472-2805. Phone: (617) 536-9233. Fax: (617) 536-7814. Web Site:www.boston.com/sports.nesn

NESN is a cable sports svc that delivers Boston Bruins, Red Sox, New England college sports as well as boxing, tennis, fishing, bowling & wrestling.

Serving 3.5 million subs on 28 cable systems.

Satellites: Satcom F-4, transponder 13; GE C-3, transponder 14.

The Sports Network, 2200 Byberry Rd., Hatboro, PA, 19040. Phone: (215) 441-8444. Fax: (215) 441-5767.E-mail: kzajac@sportsnetwork.com Web Site:www.sportsnetwork.com

International real-time sports wire svc providing content, branded web pages, satellite and/or computer feeds directly to broadcasters (radio & TV), print, Internet sites, wireless with state of the art technology.

SportsNet New York, 75 Rockefeller Plaza, 29th Fl., New York, NY, 10019. Phone: (212) 485-4800. Fax: (212) 485-4802. Web Site:www.sny.tv

Jon Litner, pres.

Sun Sports, 1000 Legion Place, Suite1600, Orlando, FL, 32801-1060. Phone: (407) 648-1150. Fax: (407) 245-2571.E-mail: askus@foxsports.net Web Site:www.sunsportstv.com

Cathy Weeden, VP/gen mgr.

SunriseFL , 1550 Sawgrass Corp. Pkwy, Suite 350.

Rgnl sports cable net. Progmg includes Orlando Magic & Miami Heat NBA basketball, Tampa Bay Lightning NHL hockey, Florida State, Univ. of Florida, SEC, & FHSAA, athletics, as well as a wide var of loc & rgnl sports events plus Chevy Tailgate Saturday, In My Own Words, Chevy FL Fishing Report. Serving 6.3 million subs.

Satellites: Galaxy II, transponder 4.

Victory Sports One, 60 S. 6th St., Suite 3700, Minneapolis, MN, 55403. Phone: (612) 661-3778.E-mail: info@victorysports.com Web Site:www.victorysports.com

VideoSeat Pay-Per-View, (A division of Host Communications Inc.). 546 E. Main St., Lexington, KY, 40508. Phone: (859) 226-4678. Fax: (859) 226-4391.E-mail: dossd@hcionline.com Web Site:www.hostcommunications.com

Lawthon Logan, sr exec VP sls.

VideoSeat handles turnkey pay-per-view syndication of several top schools in college football, including: Kentucky, Mississippi State, South Carolina, & Tennessee. Systems in Kentucky, Georgia, Mississippi, South Carolina & Tennessee.

Yankees Entertainment and Sports Network LLC, The Chrysler Bldg., 405 Lexington Ave., 36th Fl., New York, NY, 10174-3699. Phone: (646) 487-3600. Fax: (646) 487-3612.E-mail: info@yesnetwork.com Web Site:www.yesnetwork.com

Michael Wach, exec VP.

Cable Audio Services

CRN Digital Talk Radio, 10487 Sunland Blvd., Sunland, CA, 91040. Phone: (818) 352-7152. Fax: (818) 352-3229. E-mail: info@crni.net Web Site:www.crntalk.com

Michael Horn, pres/CEO; Jennifer Horn, VP sls, mktg VP.

Premier provider for radio syndication. CRN develops the hottest new, unique talk talent & distributes it worldwide via cable TV audio, radio, satellite audio & the internet. ON 125 cable systems nationwide serving 26 million subs. Satellite: IA 13, transponder 15, virtual ch 521-526. CRN 1-8 with 8 talk networks, featuring Sp & world talk radio.

The Classical Station, WCPE, Box 897, Wake Forest, NC, 27588. Phone: (919) 556-5178. Fax: (919) 556-9273. E-mail: wcpe@wcpe.org Web Site:theclassicalstation.org

Deborah S. Proctor, gen mgr .

Free 24-hour classical music progmg with live announcers for radio, cable, other distributors. Weekly request programs, opera and features. Satellite: AMC 1, Transponder 12 k, Vert, 1,1942 MHz.

DMX, Inc., 600 Congress Ave., Fl. 14, Austin, TX, 78701. Phone: (512) 380-8500. Fax: (512) 380-8501. Web Site:www.dmx.com

Steve Hicks, chmn; John Cullins, pres; Paul Stove, COO; Kim Shipman, CFO.

Offers uninterrupted premium digital audio music progmg via satellite & cable to residential & coml subs.

Moody Radio, (Formerly Moody Broadcasting Network). 820 N. LaSalle Blvd., Chicago, IL, 60610. Phone: (800) 621-7031. Phone: (312) 329-4433. Fax: (312) 329-4339. E-mail: moodyradio@moody.edu Web Site:www.whereyouturn.org

Scott Krus, pres; Wayne Pederson, VP.

Provides 24-hours format of relg & educ progmg; music, drama, talk, news & pub affrs.

On 461 radio stns nationwide.

Satellites: AMC-3, transponder 17H (DVB-stereo digital) on AMC-8 (SCPC, digital stereo).

Music Choice, 110 Gibraltar Rd., Suite 200, Horsham, PA, 19044. Phone: (215) 784-5840. Fax: (215) 784-5869. Web Site:www.musicchoice.com

David J. Del Beccaro, pres/CEO; Damon Williams, sr VP.

Music Choice is the premier music television network, reaching U.S .households through digital cable and satellite television. Music Choice programs interruption-free music for homes and businesses and distributes televised concerts and music shows. The Music Choice music channels reach 33 million households and the Music Choice Concert Series airs in 44 million homes nationally. Music Choice is a partnership among subsidiaries of Microsoft Corporation, Motorola, Inc., Sony Corporation of America, Warner Music Group, Inc., EMI Music and several leading U.S. cable providers:Adelphia Cable Communications, Comcast Cable Communications, Cox Communications, and Time Warner Cable.

WFMT Radio Network, 5400 N. St. Louis Ave., Chicago, IL, 60625. Phone: (773) 279-2112. Phone: (773) 279-2114. Fax: (773) 279-2199. E-mail: cmartinez@wfmt.com Web Site:www.wfmt.com

Steve Robinson, gen mgr & sr VP.

Classical music, spoken arts & fine arts program series & specials. Satellite- & tape-delivered. Major symphony orchestras, opera, jazz, exclusive BBC & Radio Deutsche Welle progmg, WFMT-produced archival & spoken-word progmg, live studio performances, folk music. Since 1976.

Serving more than 900 radio outlets worldwide.

Satellite: Galaxy 4, digital frequeney B72.0.

"The Weather Center", (a broadcast service of Aviation Weather Inc.). 701 Gervais St., Suite 224, Columbia, SC, 29201. Phone: (803) 422-4823. E-mail: wxcenter@aviationweatherinc.com Web Site:www.aviationweatherinc.com

Liam Richard Ferguson, pres.

"Regional Radio Broadcast/Weathercast Network" across the Carolinas & Georgia in over 20 bcst markets. Weather forecasting, site-specific bcst svc for stns all across America. 100% barter.

Yesterday U.S.A., 2001 Plymouth Rock, Richardson, TX, 75081. Phone: (972) 889-8255. Fax: (972) 889-4415. E-mail: yesterdayusa@mail.com Web Site:www.yesterdayusa.com

William J. Bragg, founder.

A 24-hour natl radio voice of the National Museum of Communication of Irving, TX. Presenting public domain old-time radio shows & vintage music free of charge & without comls.

Satellites: Galaxy 11, transponder 18, Ku verticel, frequency 12060, audio PID 1620 left ch .

Major National TV News Organizations

ABC News

7 W. 66th St., York, NY 10023; Tel: 212-456-2700; Fax: 212-456-2795.

Ownership: Walt Disney Company

147 Columbus Ave., New York, NY 10023; Tel: 212-456-1000.

Executives: David Westin, pres; Paul Mason, sr VP; Paul Slavin, sr VP producer; Phyllis McGrady, exec producer/special progmg; Bob Murphy, sr VP/multimedia; Chris Isham, sr producer; Amy Entelis, sr VP, talent recruitment/business affrs; Kerry Marash, VP/editorial quality; Dawn Porter, dir/news practices; Barbara Fedida, dir/news practices; Andrea Cohen, VP/business affrs; Jeffrey Schneider, VP/news media; Derek Medina, sr VP/business dev; Dick Wald, sr VP/consultant; Jacqueline Shire, news consultant; Roger Goodman, VP/special projects.

Domestic Bureau

Atlanta: 2580 Cumberland Pkwy. S.E., Suite 160, Atlanta, GA 30339; Tel: 770-431-2380; Fax: 770-431-7800.

Chicago: 190 N. State St., Chicago, IL 60601; Tel: 312-899-4015; Fax: 312-899-4050.

Ron Schofield, Midwest bureau chief.

Los Angeles: 4151 Prospect Ave., Los Angeles, CA 90027; Tel: 323-671-5261; Fax: 323-671-5210.

David Eaton; Charlie Herman, deputy bureau chief; Michael Ray Gammon; Derick Yanehiro and Marilyn Heck, assignment editors; Roger Scott; Chris Cahan, field producer.

New York: 47 W. 66th St., 3rd Fl., New York, NY 10023; Tel: 212-456-2700, 212-456-7777; Fax: 212-456-2214.

Kris Sebastian, VP, Northeast bureau chief; Chuck Lustig, dir of foreign news; Barbara Chen, network producer; Assignment editors: Justin Anderson; Ed Bailey; Wendy Fisher; Michael Kreisel; Barbara Garci; Eva Price; Ursula Fahy, International domestic/assignment editor.

Washington: 1717 DeSales St., N.W., Washington, DC 20036; Tel: 202-222-7300; Fax: 202-222-7684.

Robin Sproul, bureau chief; Assignment editors: Dianne Boozer; Dee Carden; Theresa Cook; George Sanchez; Zack Wolf and Julianne Donofrio.

Dallas: 606 Young St., Dallas, TX 75202; Tel: 214-749-7013.

Denver: 123 Speer Blvd., Denver, CO 80203; Tel: 303-832-7777.

Miami: 1320 South Dixie Hwy., Coral Gables, FL 33146; Tel: 305-662-2116.

International Bureaus

Beijing: 4-1-71 Jian Guo Men Wai Diplomatic Compound, Beijing, China; Tel: 861 06532 2671; Fax: 861 06532 2668.

Josh Gerstein; Chito Romana.

Jerusalem: 206 Jaffa Rd., Jerusalem, Israel; Tel: 9722 500 5911; Fax: 9722 500 2051.

Tim Heritage Gerald Holmes; Bruno Nota.

Kenya: Tel: 2542 522 624.

Martin Seemungal.

London: 3 Queen Caroline St., London W6 9PE, UK; Tel: 44 208 222 5500.

Marcus Wilford; Robin Wiener.

Primetime Shows Executive Producers: 20/20: David Sloan; Good Morning America: Shelley Ross; Nightline: Leroy Sievers; Primetime Thursday: David Doss; This Week with George Stephanopoulos: Tom Bettag; World News Tonight with Charles Gibson: Julia Bain; World News Tonight Saturday/Sunday: Craig Bengtson.

Affiliate News Service: ABSAT, 47 W. 66th St., New York, NY 10023; Tel: 212-456-3680; Mike Huitt, dir; Chris Myers, opns mgr.

CBS News

555 W. 57th St., New York, NY 10019; 212-975-4114. Web site: www.cbs.com.

Executives: Marcy McGinnis, sr VP/news coverage; John Frazee, sr VP/news svcs; Sandra Genelius, spokeswoman CBS; Frank Governale, VP/news opns; Linda Mason, sr VP, standards/special projects; James McKenna, VP, finance/admin; Christopher Isham, VP/Washington, DC bureau chief; John Paxson, VP, Europe/London bureau chief.

Domestic Bureaus

Atlanta: 260 14th St. NE, Atlanta, GA 30309; Tel: 404-685-2400.

Dallas: 10111 N. Central Expwy, Dallas, TX 75231; Tel: 817-451-1111; Fax: 214-696-9011.

Los Angeles: 7800 Beverly Blvd., Los Angeles, CA 90036; Tel: 323-575-2345

Jennifer Siebens, bureau chief.

Miami: 4770 Biscayne Blvd., Miami, FL 33101; Tel: 305-571-4400.

San Francisco: 825 Battery St., San Francisco, CA 94111; Tel: 415-362-8177

Washington: 2000 M St., N.W., Washington, DC 20036; Tel: 202-457-44444.

International Bureaus

Amman, Jordan; Baghdad, Iraq; Beijing, China; Bonn, Germany; Hong Kong; Johannesburg, South Africa; London, England; Moscow, Russia; Paris, France; Rome, Italy; Tel Aviv, Israel; Tokyo, Japan.

CBS News: The Early Show, Evening News, Up to the Minute, Morning News, 60 Minutes (Sunday Edition), 48 Hours Mystery, Sunday Morning, The Saturday Early Show, Face the Nation.

CNBC

CNBC, Inc., 900 Sylvan Ave., Englewood Cliffs, NJ 07632; Tel: 201-735-2622; Fax: 201-735-3200. Web site: www.cnbc.com.

Executives: Mark Hoffman, pres; Lilach Asofsky, sr VP, mktg/rsch; Judith H. Dobrzynski, exec editor; Lauren Donovan, sr VP; Robert Foothorap, sr VP/adv sls; Scott Drake, VP; Nikki Gonzalez, VP, human resources; Bob Meyers, sr VP/primetime progmg; Kevin Egan, VP/CFO; Steve Fastook, VP, tech/coml opns; Amy Zelvin, VP, PR.
Anchors & Reporters David Faber and Melissa Francis, anchor/reporters; Erin Burnett and Maria Bartiromo, anchors; Margaret Brennan and Bertha Coomb, reporters; Michelle Caruso-Cabrera, gen assignment reporter; Julia Boorstin, media entertainment reporter; Scott Cohn, sr correspondent reporter; Sharon Epperson, personal finance reporter.

Domestic Bureaus

Washington: 1025 Connecticut Ave., N.W., Suite 800, Washington, DC 20036; Tel: 202-467-5400; Fax: 202-737-4985.

Alan Murray, bureau chief/anchor.

Los Angeles: 3000 W. Alameda Ave., Burbank, CA 91523; Tel: 818-840-3214; Fax: 818-840-3537.

Heather Allen, bureau chief.

International Bureaus: London; Singapore.

Programs: Worldwide Exchange, Squawk Box, Squawk on the Street, The Call, Power Lunch, Street Signs, Closing Bell, Fast Money, Mad Money, Kudlow & Company, Big Idea wit Donny Deutsch. Weekend: High Net Worth, The Suze Orman Show, The Wall Street Journal Report.

CNN

One CNN Center, Atlanta, GA 30303; Tel: 404-827-1700.

Executives: Jim Walton, pres; Greg D'Alba, exec sr VP, news COO, adv sls/mktg; Brad Ferrer, exec VP finance/admin; Nancy Lance, sr VP editorial.

Domestic Bureaus

New York: One Time Warner Center, New York, NY 10019; Tel: 212-275-7800; 212-484-8000.

Karen Curry, bureau chief.

Boston: 637 Washington St., Suite 208, Brookline, MA 02446; Tel: 617-264-9905

Dan Lothian, bureau chief.

Chicago: 435 N. Michigan Ave., Chicago, IL 60611; Tel: 312-645-8555

Ron Hess, deputy bureau chief.

Los Angeles: 6430 W. Sunset Blvd., Los Angeles, CA 90028; Tel: 323-993-5000

Miami: 12000 Biscayne Blvd. N., Miami, FL 33181; Tel: (America) 305-892-5100.

John Zarrella, bureau chief.

Washington: 820 First St. N.E., Washington, DC 20022; Tel: 202-898-7900

David Bohrman, bureau chief.

International Bureaus

Hong Kong: 30/F Oxford House, Taikoo Pl., 979 Kings Rd., Quarry Bay, Hong Kong SAR.

CNN TV Programs: Morning: Anderson Cooper 360, American Morning, Issue#1, CNN Newsroom, The Situation Room. Evening: The Situation Room, Lou Dobbs Tonight, CNN Election Center, Larry King Live, Anderson Cooper 360. CNN Overnight: Larry King Live, Anderson Cooper 360.

Fox News Channel

Ownership: News Corp.

1211 Ave. of the Americas, New York, NY 10036; Tel: 212 301-3000. Web site: www.foxnews.com.

Executives: Roger Ailes, chmn/CEO; Kevin Magee, sr VP/radio; Mark Kranz, CFO; John Moody, exec VP, news/editorial; Paul Rittenberg, sr VP/adv sls; Bill Shine, VP/progmg; News Corp.; Rupert Murdoch, chmn/CEO, News Corp.; Peter Chernin, pres/COO, News Corp.; Martin Pompadur, exec VP, News Corp.; David DeVoe, CFO; Brian Lewis, exec VP/corporate communcations.

Domestic Bureaus

Atlanta: 260 14th St., N.W., Atlanta, GA 30318; Tel: 404-685-2280.

John Boswell, bureau chief.

Denver: 999 18th St., Suite 1665, Denver, CO 80202; Tel: 303-383-1170.

Denis King, bureau chief.

Dallas: 301 N. Market St., Suite 450, Dallas, TX 75202; Tel: 214-742-5005; Fax: 214-742-1067.

Russell Cosby, bureau chief.

Los Angeles: 2044 Armocast Ave., Los Angeles, CA 90025; Tel: 310-571-2000/5/7; Fax: 310-571-2009

John Brady, bureau chief.

Miami: 1440 79th St. Causeway, Suite 208, North Bay Village, FL 33141; Tel: 305-866-8007.

Nancy Harmeyer, bureau chief.

San Francisco: 901 Battery St., Suite 210, San Francisco, CA 94111; Tel: 415-951-8550

Washington: 2201 C St., N.W., Washington, DC 20520; Tel: 202-496-0109; Fax: 202-824-6426

Brian Wilson, bureau chief

Primetime Shows: Special Report with Brit Hume; The O'Reilly Factor; Hannity and Colmes; On the Record with Greta Van Susteren; Your World with Neil Cavuto; The Big Story with John Gibson.

MSNBC

1 MSNBC Plaza, Seacaucus, NJ 07094; Tel: 201-583-5000; Fax: 201-583-5453. Web site: msnbc.com.

Executives: Rick Kaplan, pres/gen mgr; Phil Griffin, exec in charge; Mark Effron, VP, news/daytime progmg; Robin Garfield, VP, strategic opns; Val Nicholas, MSNBC/Microsoft-NBC, adv sls VP; Jeremy Gaines, VP, communications.

MSNBC Featuring: Today Show, Nightly News, Dateline, Meet the Press, MSNBC TV.

NBC News

Ownership: NBC Universal

30 Rockefeller Plaza, New York, NY 10112; Tel: 212-664-4444.

Executives: Steve Capus, pres, NBC News; Jeff Zucker, pres/CEO, NBC Universal.

Domestic Bureaus

Midwest Bureau: 454 N. Columbus Dr., 1st Fl., Chicago, IL 60611

Tom Lea, bureau chief.

News: Nightly News, TODAY, Dateline NBC, Meet the Press, Weekend Today, Weekend Nightly News, NBC sports.

TV News Services

ABC News

See BC listing in Major National TV News Organizations, this section.

APTN Productions, The Interchange, Oval Rd., Camden Lock, London, NW1 7DZ. United Kingdom. Phone: (0) 20 7482 7400. Fax: (0) 20 7413 8312. Web Site:www.aptn.com

Eric Braun, mgng dir; Nigel Baker, exec dir.

New YorkNY , 1995 Broadway. Phone:

International TV svcs company, daily satellite news feeds to bcstrs worldwide, tech facilities, camera crew hire worldwide.

Serves TV.

AccuWeather Inc., 385 Science Park Rd., State College, PA, 16803. Phone: (814) 235-8600. Phone: (800) 566-6606. Fax: (814) 235-8609.E-mail: sales@accuweather.com Web Site:www.accuweather.com

Dr. Joel N. Myers, pres; Evan Myers, sr VP/dir opns.

TV, radio, weather progmg & systems, plus turnkey solutions to take your loc news to the mobile web.

Agence France-Presse, 1500 K St. N.W., Suite 600, Washington, DC, 20005. Phone: (202) 289-0700. Fax: (202) 414-0632. Web Site:www.afp.com E-mail: afp-usa@afp.com

Peter Mackler, editor-in-chief English; Philipe Raater, editor-in-chief & Fr edition.

Produces a variety of international news svcs for radio & TV, including text wires in six languages, photo wires, graphics & financial wires plus video svcs.

All Africa Global Media, 920 M Street S.E., Washington, DC, 20003. Phone: (202) 546-0777. Fax: (202) 546-0676. Web Site:www.allafrica.com E-mail: newsdesk@allafrica.com

Reed Kramer, CEO; Amadou Mahtar Ba, pres.

A news & info svc on African affrs for TV, radio & print news svcs.

American Academy of Dermatology, Communications Dept., American Academy of Dermatology. Box 4014, Schaumburg, IL, 60168-4014. Phone: (847) 330-0230. Fax: (847) 330-8907. Web Site:www.aad.org E-mail: mediarelations@aad.org

WashingtonDC , 1350 I Street NW, Suite 870. Phone:

Expert physicians available for TV & radio interviews, audio & video tapes on skin cancer pevention & detection, as well as info on skin, hair & nail conditions.

American Heart Association National Center, 7272 Greenville Ave., Dallas, TX, 75231. Phone: (214) 706-1330. Phone: (800) 242-8721 (aha-usa1). Fax: (214) 706-5243. Web Site:www.americanheart.org

Julie Del Barto, bcst mgr.

Periodic satellite news feeds of medical rsch stories.

The Associated Press, AP Broadcast News Center, 1100 13th St., Suite 700, Washington, DC, 20005. Phone: (202) 736-1100. Phone: (800) 821-4747. Fax: (202) 736-1124. Web Site:www.apbroadcast.com

James R. Williams III, VP.

AP Services for TV: Video: APTN Video News. Wires: APTV Wire, AP News Tickers, AP NewsPower, AP Data Stream. AP Alert Graphics: AP GraphicsBank. Software: AP NewsCenter; AP NewsDesk; AP NewsDesk (LAN), ENPS, SNAPfeed Satellite Delivery: AP Express. Elections: ENPS Stats, AP Politics, AP Election Wire. Online content: CustomNews, AP Online, Online Video Network, AP Spanish Online. Photos: Photo Archive, Photo Stream.

Audio-Video News, 3622 Stanford Cir., Falls Church, VA, 22041. Phone: (703) 354-6795.E-mail: connielawn@aol.com Web Site:dcski.com

Covers major natl, international & specialty stories for radio & TV stns in the U.S. & around the world. Also do live talk-back features. Serves radio, TV & write ski reports.

Bloomberg Financial L.P., (formerly Bloomberg L.P. 731 Lexington Ave., New York, NY, 10022. Phone: (212) 318-2200, EXT. 2201. Fax: (917) 369-5000. Web Site:www.bloomberg.com

John Meehan, chief of bcstg.

Offers business & news reports for radio & TV stns. 24-hours a day. Full news svc.

British Information Services, 845 3rd Ave., New York, NY, 10022. Phone: (212) 745-0277. Fax: (212) 745-0359. Web Site:www.britianusa.com

Mark Hopkinson, Head Radio/TV div; Sarah Kendall, mktg.

Assists radio & TV crews visiting the United Kingdom. Serves radio & TV.

Broadcast Interview Source, 2233 Wisconsin Ave. N.W., Washington, DC. Phone: (202) 333-5000. Fax: (202) 342-5411.E-mail: expertclick@gmail.com Web Site:www.expertclick.com

Mitchell P. Davis, editor.

Free source of interview contacts

CBS News

See BS listing in Major National TV News Organizations, this section.

CNN and CNN Headline News

See isting in Major National TV News Organizations, this section.

CW11.com WPIX-TV New York, 220 E. 42nd St., 10th Fl., New York, NY, 10017. Phone: (212) 949-1100. Fax: (212) 210-2591. Web Site:www.cw11.com E-mail: jziegler@tribune.com

Betty Ellen Berlamino, gen mgr; John Ziegler, mktg dir.

Camera Planet, 253 Fifth Ave., New York, NY, 10016. Phone: (212) 779-0500.E-mail: archive@cameraplanet.com Web Site:www.cameraplanet.com

Steve Carlis, pres/COO; Steve Rosenbaum, pres/CEO.

Canada NewsWire Ltd., 1500, 20 Bay St., WaterPark Pl., Toronto, ON, M5J 2N8. Canada. Phone: (416) 863-9350. Phone: (866) 805-9530. Fax: (416) 863-9429.E-mail: cnwtor@newswire.ca Web Site:www.newswire.ca

Sylvia Kavanagh, mgr; Tim Griffin, bcst mgr; Carolyn McGill, dir mktg.

CalgaryAB Canada, Gulf Canada Sq, 401 Ninth Ave. S.W., Suite 835. Phone:Michle.dauphine@newswire.ca Krista Wightman, mgr.

VancouverBC Canada, 650 West Georgia St, Suite 1103. Phone:

HalifaxNS Canada, Sun Tower, 1550 Bedford Hwy., Suite 410. Phone:jgallant@newswire.ca Robert Moffatt, mgr Atlantic Canada.

OttawaON Canada, 255 Albert St, Suite 460. Phone:

MontrealPQ Canada, 1155 Rene Levesque Blvd. W, Suite 3310. Phone:scmtl@newswire.ca Elaire Carr, VP Quebec.

Offers a range of industry leading communication products & svcs for companies looking to maximize the strength of their news. Whether you are an investor rel off, or a specialist in PR, CNW offers the right tools for your communications.

The Canadian Press, 36 King St. E., Toronto, ON, M5C 2L9. Canada. Phone: (416) 364-3172. Fax: (416) 364-1325.E-mail: broadcast@thecanadianpress.com Web Site:www.thecanadianpress.com

Wayne Waldroff, gen mgr; David Ross, CFO/dir opns; Terry Scott, news dir.

Full wire & audio svcs (news agency), satellite delivery for radio program syndicators.

Serves radio & TV.

Capital Television News Service (CTNS), 1629 S. St., Sacramento, CA, 95811. Phone: (916) 446-7890. Fax: (916) 446-7893.E-mail: pacsat@pacsat.com Web Site:www.pacsat.com

Video wire svc providing daily news coverage, via satellite, of California's capitol for subscribing TV stns throughout the state.

Compu-Weather Inc., 2566 Rt. 52, Hopewell Junction, NY, 12533. Phone: (800) 284-7246. Fax: (845) 226-1918.E-mail: sales@compuweather.com Web Site:www.compuweather.com

Jeff Wimmer, pres.

TV & radio svc providing weather forecasts, features, info & actualities.

Congressional Quarterly Inc., 1255 22nd St. NW, Washington, DC, 20037. Phone: (202) 419-8500. Phone: (800) 432-2250. Fax: (202) 419-8760.E-mail: marketing@cq.com Web Site:www.cq.com

David Rapp, editor-in-chief.

Congressional Quarterly Weekly Report & News Service, editorial rsch reports, newsletters, seminars, rsch, reference volumes, paperbacks; daily & wkly congressional info publications.

Connecticut Weather Center Inc., 18 Woodside Ave., Danbury, CT, 06810-7123. Phone: (203) 730-2899. Fax: (203) 730-2839.E-mail: weatherlab@ctweather.com Web Site:www.ctweather.com

William Jacquemin, pres.

Weather forecasts for all media. Custom intros/outros/lives. Accurate forecasts. Barter or cash arrangement available.

Feature Story News, 1730 Rhode Island Ave. N.W., Suite 405, Washington, DC, 20036. Phone: (202) 296-9012. Fax: (202) 296-9205.E-mail: markss@featurestory.com Web Site:www.featurestorynews.com

Simon Marks, pres.

OrlandoFL , 1103 Palmer St. Phone:

New YorkNY , 1133 Broadway, Suite 1420. Phone:

Ind supplier of radio & TV news to English-language bcstrs worldwide. Bureaus in Washington, Moscow, London, New York, Orlando & San Francisco.

Fox News Channel

See isting in Major National TV News Organizations, this section.

Golden Lamb Productions, Box 47, Schoolhouse Rd., Nassau, NY, 12123. Phone: (866) 457-2739. Web Site:www.glpvideoproduction.com

Dow Haynor, pres.

ENG, EFP crews, HD & SD, SNG available. Serves the Northeast, 24-hour call, packages, live remotes, camera crane news & sports.

Hollywood News Service, 13636 Ventura Blvd., Suite 303, Sherman Oaks, CA, 91423. Phone: (818) 986-8168. Phone: (818) 990-5945. Fax: (818) 789-8047.E-mail: editor@newscalender.com Web Site:www.newscalender.com

A wire svc to the entertainment media. Publisher of Hollywood News Calendar in Los Angeles; Entertainment News Calendar in New York.

Independent Television News of London Ltd., 400 N. Capital St., Suite 850, Washington, DC, 20001. Phone: (202) 429-9080. Fax: (202) 429-8948.E-mail: michael.herrod@itn.co.uk Web Site:www.itn.co.uk

London, ITN House, 200 Grays Inn Rd. Phone:

Other branches: South Africa, Moscow, London. Hong Kong. British TV news, Washington bureau.

Israel Broadcasting Service, 800 2nd Ave., New York, NY, 10017. Phone: (212) 499-5402. Fax: (212) 499-5425.E-mail: yonih@newyork.mfa.gov.il Web Site:www.israel.org

Yoni Heilman, dir community & interrelg affrs.

Free radio & TV programs & footage about Israel.

Kyodo News New York Bureau, 747 Third Ave., Suite 1801, New York, NY, 10017. Phone: (212) 508-5460. Fax: (212) 508-5461. Web Site:www.kyodo.co.jp

Japan's leading newsgathering organization serving virtually all media in all parts of the world. The combined circulation of nwspr subscribers is about 50 million.

Medialink, 708 Third Ave., New York, NY, 10017. Phone: (212) 682-8300. Phone: (800) 843-0677. Fax: (212) 682-5260. Web Site:www.medialink.com E-mail: info@medialink.com

Michele Wallace, sr VP; Larry Thomas, COO.

London, 7 Fitzroy Sq. Phone:

Los AngelesCA , 6430 Sunset Blvd, Suite 1100. Phone:

San FranciscoCA , One Maritime Plaza, Suite 1670. Phone:

WashingtonDC , Natl. Press Bldg., 529 14th St. N.W., Suite 1230-A. Phone:

ChicagoIL , The Time & Life Bldg, 541 N. Fairbanks Ct, Suite 1910. Phone:

DallasTX , 5000 Quorum, Suite 450. Phone:

International video & audio PR, satellite feed & news advisory service. Accessible by computer/newswire in

U.S. & European newsrooms.
Serves radio & TV.

MediaOne Services, 901 Battery St., Suite 220, San Francisco, CA, 94111. Phone: (415) 693-5000. Fax: (415) 693-5005.E-mail: info@mediaoneservices.com Web Site:www.mediaoneservices.com

Benjamin Schick, pres/COO; Nelson Ferreira, opns mgr.

Satellite uplinking & fiber-optic transmission capabilities. 20'x 40'& 30' x 30' studios for production of cable progmg, teleconferences, live interviews, satellite press tours. Serves radio & TV.

Metro Weather Service Inc., 788 Franklin Ave., Valley Stream, NY, 11580. Phone: (516) 568-8853.E-mail: metrowx@aol.com Web Site:www.metrowx.com

Pat Pagano, pres.

Tailored weather forecasts for TV & briefings to weathercasters. Serves radio & TV.

Miami News Net, 2641 S.W. 27th St., Miami, FL, 33133. Phone: (305) 285-0044. Fax: (305) 285-0074.E-mail: mnn@bellsouth.net Web Site:www.miaminewsnet.com

Catherine A. Scull, pres.

A 24-hour TV news, sports & entertainment svc that provides crews, video archive, avid, beta edit & feed facilities. Live talkback studio facilities, dual path digital KU uplink trunk.

Mountain News Corporation, 50 Vashell Way, Suite 400, Orinda, CA, 94563. Phone: (925) 254-4456. Fax: (925) 254-7923.E-mail: info@mountainnews.com Web Site:www.mountainnews.com

Rob Brown, producer.

Mountain News Corporation, formally AMI News, is the largest & oldest producer of winter & summer progmg for media. We deliver the most accurate & timely news & info covering mountain activities.

NBC News

See BC listing in Major National TV News Organizations, this section.

NOAA/National Weather Service Headquarters, 1325 East-West Hwy., Silver Spring, MD, 20910. Phone: (301) 713-0700. Fax: (301) 713-1598. Web Site:www.nws.noaa.gov

AnchorageAK , 222 W. Seventh Ave, 23, Rm. 517. Phone:

HonoluluHI , Grosvenor Ctr. Mauka Tower, 737 Bishop St., Suite 2200. Phone:

Kansas CityMO , 7220 N.W. 101 Terr. Phone:

BohemiaNY , 630 Johnson Ave. Phone:

Fort WorthTX , 819 Taylor St, Rm. 10A06. Phone:

Salt Lake CityUT , Federal Bldg., 125 S. State St., Rm. 1311. Phone:

Weather & flood warnings, forecasts & related info for the media & gen public.

The Nasdaq Stock Market, 1 Liberty Plaza, New York, NY, 10006. Phone: (212) 858-5211. Phone: (212) 401-8700. Fax: (646) 625-6548.E-mail: petersos@nasdaq.com Web Site:www.nasdaq.com

Robert Greifeld, pres/CEO.

Customized loc data for the stock market.

Serves radio & TV.

Nielsen Entertainment News Wire, 101 Federal St., Suite 600, Boston, MA, 02110. Phone: (617) 478-5500. Fax: (617) 478-5501.E-mail: donald.gallagher@nielsen.com Web Site:www.nielsenenw.com

Donald Gallagher, mngng editor.

Advance news from Nielsen-owned publications serving radio, TV, nwsprs & online.

Nippon TV Network Corp., 645 5th Ave., Suite 303, New York, NY, 10022. Phone: (212) 660-6900. Fax: (212) 660-6998. Fax: (212) 265-8495.E-mail: motoko@ntvic.com Web Site:www.ntv.co.jp

Motoko Hasegawa, editor-in-chief; Jusaburo Hayashi, pres.

International media svcs.

NorthStar Studios Inc., 3201 Dickerson Pike, Nashville, TN, 37207. Phone: (615) 650-6000 ext. 6031 (Grant Barbre). Phone: (615) 650-6000. Fax: (615) 650-6300.E-mail: grant.barbre@northstarstudios.tv Web Site:www.northstarstudios.tv

Grant Barbre, pres.

Complete TV production svcs: 7 stages, mobile production/uplink trucks, network origination, transmissions, digital archiving, Avid/DS, linear editing, graphics/animations & ENG crews.

Potomac Television - News & Video Service, 1510 H. St. N.W., Suite 202B, Washington, DC, 20005. Phone: (202) 783-6464. Fax: (202) 783-1132.E-mail: jnorins@potomactv.com Web Site:www.ptpngroup.com

Jamie Norins, news bureau chief.

Washington, DC, news coverage, studios, editing facilities, live shots, crews, satellite capability & duplications.

Presson Perspectives, 600 Druid Rd. E., Clearwater, FL, 33756. Phone: (800) 249-4521. Fax: (727) 443-1984.E-mail: gpresson@tampabayrr.com

Gina Presson, producer & pres.

Specializing in TV news & documentary production & electronic publishing. Svcs include rsch, field production, videography, postproduction, & satellite feeds for radio & TV.

Serves radio & TV.

Reuters America, 3 Times Sq., New York, NY, 10036. Phone: (646) 223-4000. Web Site:www.reuters.com E-mail: boblagrassa@reuters.com

Bob Lagrassa, dir tv opns.

Worldwide TV news production & transmission svcs for loc TV stns/producers. Camera crews, production facilities, news bureaus, satellite svcs, video/slide archives.

The Seattle Video Bureau, Box 99218, Seattle, WA, 98199. Phone: (206) 448-2500. Fax: (206) 378-1700.E-mail: dave@seattlevideo.com Web Site:www.seattlevideo.com

David Oglevie, pres.

ENG/EFP crews with BETACAM SP kits. Net experienced.

Skywatch Weather Center, 347 Prestley Rd., Bridgeville, PA, 15017. Phone: (412) 221-6000. Phone: (800) 759-9282. Fax: (412) 221-3160.E-mail: airsci@skywatchweather.com Web Site:www.skywatchweather.com

Dr.Stanley J. Penkala, pres; Daniel Krzywiecki, VP; Stanley Bostjancic, treas; Harry Green, sec.

Weather forecasts targeted to the viewing area, & comprehensive briefings for on-air talent. Serves radio & TV.

Skyways Communications, L.L.C., 89 Access Rd., Suite 20, Norwood, MA, 02062. Phone: (781) 551-9960. Fax: (781) 551-5956.E-mail: scott@skyways.net Web Site:www.skyways.net

LuAnn Reeb, pres; Kate Kenney, producer.

Custom TV news gathering, producing & mobile satellite uplinking svcs. Provides bcst-experienced crews, producers, reporters & technicians for breaking news, live-event coverage & webcasting.

The Sports Network, 2200 Byberry Rd., Suite 200, Hatboro, PA, 19040. Phone: (215) 441-8444. Fax: (215) 441-5767.E-mail: kzajac@sportsnetwork.com Web Site:www.sportsnetwork.com

Mickey Charles, pres/CEO; Ken Zajac, sls dir.

International real-time sports wire svc providing content, branded web pages, satellite and/or computer feeds directly to broadcasters (radio & TV), print, Internet sites, wireless with state of the art technology.

Tankersley Productions, Inc., St. Louis, 858 Hanley Industrial Ct., St. Louis, MO, 63144. Phone: (314) 725-0116.E-mail: randy@tankersleyproductions.com Web Site:www.tankersleyproductions.com

Randy Tankersley, pres.

Full-bcst svcs. ENG/EFP Beta SP crews with/without producers, avid nonlinear editing.

U.S. Conference of Catholic Bishops, Department of Communication, Film/TV Review Svcs. Office for Film & Broadcasting, 1011 First Ave., New York, NY, 10022. Phone: (212) 644-1880. Fax: (212) 644-1886.E-mail: ofb@msn.com Web Site:www.usccb.org

Harry Forbes, dir.

Publishes wkly reviews of movies, TV with artistic & moral observations.

WSI (Weather Services International), 400 Minuteman Rd., Andover, MA, 01810. Phone: (978) 983-6300. Fax: (978) 983-6400. Web Site:www.wsi.com

Mark Gildersleeve, pres; Linda Maynard, VP mktg.

WSI is the leading source of professional on-air weather systems, solutions & forecasting svc for TV, including TrueView, the most innovative weather storytelling tool available.

The Washington Bureau, 400 N. Capitol St. N.W., Suite 775, Washington, DC, 20001. Phone: (202) 347-6396. Fax: (202) 628-6295.E-mail: rtillery@twbnews.com Web Site:www.twbnews.com

Richard Tillery, bureau chief; Julia Rockler, CEO.

Custom TV news coverage: ENG crews, producers & talent. Prod svcs: editing, studio, remote & satellite capabilities. Two live studios. Teleconference capability. Fiber Optic connectivity with Capital, White House & other locations.

"The Weather Center", (a broadcast service of Aviation Weather Inc.). 701 Gervais St., Suite 224, Columbia, SC, 29201. Phone: (803) 422-4823.E-mail: wxcenter@aviationweatherinc.com Web Site:www.aviationweatherinc.com

Liam Richard Ferguson, pres.

"Regional Radio Broadcast/Weathercast Network" across the Carolinas & Georgia in over 20 bcst markets. Weather forecasting, site-specific bcst svc for stns all across America. 100% barter.

WeatherData Inc., 245 N. Waco St., Suite 310, Wichita, KS, 67202. Phone: (316) 265-9127. Fax: (316) 265-1949. Web Site:www.weatherdata.com E-mail: ceo@weatherdata.com

Mike Smith, CEO.

Forecasts for radio & TV, meteorology training, slides & videotape of weather & related phenomena. Nexrad radar interpretation seminar; distributor of Nexrad weather display systems. Meteorologist 24/7, storm monitoring & customer svc.

WeatherVision Inc., 916 Foley St., Jackson, MS, 39202-3406. Phone: (601) 948-7018. Phone: (800) 353-9177. Fax: (601) 948-6052.E-mail: edward@weathervision.com Web Site:www.weathervision.com

Edward Saint-Pe', pres; Jason McCleaver, VP.

Customized, localized TV weathercasts with or without meteorologists. Barter/cash via Ku-band satellite. Complete studio teleport for use by news media on site. Avid editing available on site. Serves radio, TV & 3-D branding animation svcs.

National Radio Programming Services

ABC Radio Networks

Headquarters: 444 Madison Ave., New York, NY 10022. (212) 735-1700. Web site: www.abcradionetworks.com.

Executives: John Hare, pres; David Westin, pres, ABC News; Larry Hyams, chief rsch; John E. McConnell, sr VP; Anne Gatoff, VP/dir finance; Kevin Miller, sr VP/chief mktg; Chip Gedney, VP sls.

ABC 24-Hour Formats: ABC AC, Classic R&B (Urban Oldies),Today's Hits & Yesterday's Favorites (Best of the 70s through today), Classic Rock (Classic AOR), Country Coast-to-Coast (Contemporary Country), Hot AC (Young AC), Memories (Adult Soft Oldies), Oldies Radio, Real Country, Rejoice! (Gospel), Stardust (MOR), The Touch (Urban AC).

Music: *American Country Countdown, American Gold, Rock & Roll's Greatest Hits, The Dick Bartley, The Ride with Doug and DeDe, The Michael Baisden Show, GAC Nights, Oldies Radio, Touch, Timeless, Classic Rock, Today's Best Country.*

Urban Programming: *The Travis Smiley Report, The Tom Joyner Morning Show.*

News: *ABC News, ABC Sports.*

Talk Programming: *America's Most Wanted, Focus on the Family, MoneyTalk with Bob Brinker, Imus in the Morning, Ric Edelman, The Mark Levin Show, Sean Hannity.*

East Region

ABC, Inc., 77 W. 66th St., New York, NY 10023. (212) 456-7777.

Departments: Advertising Sales, Affiliate Marketing East, Finance, Research, MIS.

Executive: Geoff Rich, exec VP/progmg, ABC Radio Today Entertainment.

125 West End Ave., New York 10023. (212) 735-1700.

Departments: ABC News Radio, Engineering, Network Programming, International.

Executive: Chris Berry, VP News radio.

West Region

13725 Montfort Dr., Dallas, TX 75240. (972) 991-9200.

Departments: Affiliate Marketing West; Entertainment Programming; Marketing & Promotion; ABC 24-Hour Formats; Advertising Sales (Southwest); Engineering; Finance; MIS; Research; Clearance; International.

Executives: James Robinson, pres, ABC Radio Division; Michael Connolly, sr VP/ad sls; Kevin Miller, sr VP/business dev.

American Urban Radio Networks

Executive Headquarters: 432 Park Ave., 14th Fl., New York, NY 10016. (212) 883-2100. Fax: (212) 297-2571. Web site: www.aurn.com.

Officers: Howard Eisen, exec VP/sls; Basil Murrain, VP/promotion; Barry Feldman, exec dir/mktg.

Programming and Operations Headquarters: 960 Penn Ave., Suite 200, Pittsburgh, PA 15222-3811. (412) 456-4000. Fax: (412) 456-4040.

Officers: Jerry Lopes, pres, program opns/ affiliations; Glenn Bryant, sr VP/opns; Kathy Gersna, VP human resources/corporate opns; Adele Lawhead, VP/controller; Tene Croom, dir news; Dian Sirko, dir/corporate traf; Bob Sharkey, chief engr; Ty Miller, dir sports; Jay

Silvers, production dir; Laurene Gaines, exec producer, The Bev Smith Show.

Chicago Office: 30 N. Michigan Ave., Suite 1218, Chicago, IL. (312) 558-9090. Fax: (312) 558-9280. Contact: Jon Krongard, VP/sls Western Region.

Detroit Office: 1133 Whittier Rd., Grosse Pointe, MI 48230. (313) 885-4243. Fax: (313) 885-2192. Contact: J.D. MacKay, exec sls dir.

AP Radio Networks

AP All News Radio (ANR) and AP Network News (APNN), both administered by the Radio Division of the AP Broadcast organization. ANR is a live news network that taps AP's worldwide resources to deliver the latest audio news from around the globe 24 hours a day. APNN provides newscasts, sportscasts, business reports, entertainment reports and features plus actuality feeds. APNN provides regularly scheduled progmg on the Main Channel and live, long-form coverage of special events and major breaking news on the Hotline ch.

AP (Associated Press)

AP is a not-for-profit cooperative with more than 4,000 employees working in more than 240 worldwide bureau owned by its U.S. daily nwspr members. Any nwspr, radio or TV stn can become a member.

International Headquarters: 450 W. 33rd St., New York, NY 10001. (212) 621-1500. General/National Desk: (212) 621-1600. International Desk: (212) 621-1750. Fax: (212) 621-5469, arts and entertainment; (212) 621-1587 business news. Web site: www.ap.org. E-mail: info@p.org (no attachments).

AP Broadcast

AP Broadcast News Center: Mailing, 1100 13th St., Suite 700, Washington, DC 20005. Web site: www.apbroadcast.com.

AP Radio Contacts: General information, (800) 527-7234. E-mail: apradio@a]p.org. Thom Callahan, gen mgr/radio division and radio division I mgr (202)641-9051, tcallahan@a]p.org; Susan Spaulding, dir Radio Group/Internet sls (202) 641-9053, sspaulding@a]p.org; Dave Herring, dir radio network sls (202) 641-9054. E-mail: dherring@a]p.org; Carol Robinson, dir/group sls (202) 641-9055. crobinson@a]p.org.

Advisory Board for Radio: Ken Beck, VP news, talk, sports progmg and technical opons, Entercom, Inc. Seatle, WA; Don Benson, pres/radio Division Lincoln Financial Media, Atlanta, GA; Rick Feinblatt, sr VP pres/Radio Greater Media, Bala Cynwyd, PA; Carl Gardner, exec VP Television and radio opns Milwaukee, WI; Dan Lawrie, VP/mkt mgr Tulsa, OK; Mark Mason, VP/news progmg CBS Radio New York, NY; W. Russell Withers Jr., owner/pres Withers Broadcasting Group Mt Vernon, IL.

Senior Management: James R. Williams III, VP/dir Global Broadcast; Greg Groce, dir business opns/dev; Brad Kalbfeld, deputy dir/mgr editor; Roger Lockhart, dir mktg communications; Lee Perryman, deputy dir bcst svcs/dir bcst tech; John Phillips, dir financial planning; Montrese Garner-Sampson, dir human resources.

Sales Management: Bill Burke, product mgr/bcst tech; Carol Robinson, dir group sls; Susan Spaulding, dir radio groups/internet sls.

Newsroom Management: Denise Vance, international mgr/Americas for APTN; Wally Hindes, asst mgng editor/radio; Ed Tobias, asst mgng editor bcst news; Barbara Worth, asst mgng editor news wire; Brad Kalbfeld, deputy dir/mgng editor.

AP Radio News Anchors: Jon Belmont; Ross Simpson;

Rita Foley; Tim Maguire; Ed Donahue; Sandy Kozel; Camille Bohannon.

AP Radio Sports Anchors: Dave Lubeski, dir; Jack Briggs, asst dir; Mike Gracia; Mark Hamrick, business anchor.

CBS Radio

Headquarters: 1515 Broadway, New York, NY 10036; (212) 846-3939.

Executive Management: Dan Mason, pres/CEO; Anton Guitano, sr exec VP finance/opns and CFO; David Goodman, pres/digital media and integrated mktg; Scott Herman, exec VP opns; Rich Lobel, exec VP/CBS Altitude Group; Sue McNamara, sr VP sls; Karen Mateo, VP communications; Chris Oliviero, VP progmg; Oli Stephensen, VP/chief tech officer; Greg Strassell, sr VP progmg; Glynn Walden, sr VP engrg; Michael Weiss, pres/sls; Mark Zulli, sr VP human resources.

CNN Radio Networks

Headquarters: Turner Broadcasting 1 CNN Ctr. N.W., Atlanta, GA 30303-2762. (301) 628-2510 (USA Jim Jones). Web Site: www.cnnradionet.com.

CNN Radio: Natl & International radio news network. CNN Radio is a full svc network.

Principal Executives: Robert Garcia, VP; Harley Hotchkiss, dir opns; Richard Benson, exec producer.

Bureaus: Atlanta, Boston, Chicago, Dallas, Denver, Los Angeles, Miami, New York, San Francisco, Seattle, Washington, DC, Baghdad, Bangkok, Beijing, Beirut, Berlin, Buenos Aires, Cairo, Dubai, Frankfurt, Havana, Hong Kong, Islamabad, Istanbul, Jakarta, Jerusalem, Johannesburg, Lagos, London; Madrid, Mexico City,, Moscow, Nairobi, New Delhi, Paris, Rome, Tokyo, Seoul, Sidney.

Eastern Region Public Media (Eastern Public Radio)

Mailing: Georgette Bronfman, PO Box 615, Kensington, MD 20895. Phone: (301) 943-2930. Web Site: http://www.easternpublicradio.org.

Executive Committee: Georgette Bronfman, exec dir; Lee Ferraro (co-chmn) gen mgr, WYEP Pittsburgh, PA; Jeanne Fisher (vice-chair) VP of radio WXXI-FM Rochester, NY; Michael Black (sec) gen mgr, WEOS Geneva, NY; Glenn Gleixner (treas) gen mgr, WVTF Roanoke, VA; Quyen Shanahan (at-large) assoc gen mgr, WXPN Philadelphia, PA; Rob Gordon (at-large) gen mgr, WPLN Nashville, TN; Maxie Jackson (at-large) sr dir prgram dev, WNYC New York, NY; Dave Spizale (co-chmn) gen mgr, KRVS Lafayette, LA; Kate Lochte (at-large) gen mgr, WKMS Murray, KY; Earl Johnson (co-vice-chair) gen mgr, WABE Atlanta, GA.

Family Stations Inc.

Headquarters: 290 Hegenberger Rd., Oakland, CA 94621. (510) 568-6200. E-Mail: info@fa]milyradio.com; Web site: www.familyradio.org.

Executives: Harold Camping, pres/gen mgr; David Hoff, progmg mgr; Dan Elyea, engrg mgr.

Family Radio is a nondenominational, noncommercial, nonprofit, listener-supported, 24-hour, Christian ministry. Conservative Christian music & progmg. Some talk, limited news six days per week. Aired its first bcst February 1959.

Jones Radio Networks

Headquarters: 8200 S. Akron St., Suite 103, Centennial, CO 80112. (800) 609-5663 (CO); (800) 426-9082 (Seattle); (800) 611-5663 (Washington, DC). Fax: (303) 784-8615. Web site: www.jonesradio.com.

Executives: Glenn R. Jones, chmn; Phil Barry, VP/gen mgr (Denver); Frank De Santis, VP, gen mgr news/talk; James LaMarca, exec VP/COO; Amy Bolton, VP, gen mgr news/talk (DC); Susan Stephens, VP/gen mgr (Seattle).

Sales & Marketing: Patrick Crocker, sls dir; Kim Ketchel, ad sls/mktg.

Formats: Country, CD Country, Classic Hit Country, Adult Contemporary, Adult Hit Radio, Rock Classics, Good Time Oldies, Music of Your Life, Smooth Jazz, Branding Power.

News & Talk Programming: Long Form: Neal Boortz, Stephanie Miller, Ed Schultz, Bill Press & Midnight Radio. Short Form: Fight Back with David Horowitz, The Clark Howard Minute, Wall Street Wake-Up with Chris Byron, Something You Should Know. Weekends: Newsweek On-Air, Best of Stephanie Miller, Best of Neal Boortz. Newsweek on Air, The Ed Schultz Show.

Prep & Short Features: American Comedy Network, Jimmy Carter Entertainment Report, Gossip To Go With Flo, Jones Research Network, Jones Prep Country, AC, CHR, Rock and Oldies stns.

Moody Broadcasting Network

Mailing Address: 820 N. LaSalle Blvd., Chicago, IL 60610. (800) 621-7031; (312) 329-4271. Fax: (312) 329-4368. Web Site: http://www.mbn.org; E-mail: mbnmoody.edu.

Leadership: Michael Easley, pres/Moody Bible Institute; Wayne Pederson, VP; Doug Hastings, division mgr; Denny Nugent, national program dir; Mark Williames, dir tech svcs; Mike Bingham, group division mgr.

Moody Network Team provides progmg including: Midday Connection, Primetime America, Open Line, Music Thru the Night and Proclaim. Relg & educ stereo audio progmg, music, talk, news and pub affrs 24 hours a day. Services 370 radio affils in 50 states, Washington, DC, Puerto Rico and the Virgin Islands.

National Public Radio (NPR)

Headquarters: 635 Massachusetts Ave. N.W., Washington, DC 20001. (202) 513-2000. Fax: (202) 513-3329. Web Site: http://www.npr.org.

Corporate Officers: Kevin Klose, pres/CEO; Mitch Praver, exec VP pres/COO; Dennis L. Haarasger, Interim CEO; Ellen Weiss, VP news; Audi Sporkin, VP communications; Jim Elder, CFO/treas, VP

finance and admin; Kathleen Jackson, VP/human resources; Peter Lowenstein, VP/distribution; Jackie Nixon, dir, audience/corporate rsch; Dana Davis Rehm, sr VP, strategy and partnership; Margaret Low Smith, VP/progmg; Mike Starling, chief technology officer/exec dir, NPR Labs; Maria C. Thomas, sr VP, NPR Digital Media; Walt Swanston, dir diversity mgmt; Bob Holstein, VP/info tech and chief info officer; Annie Callaway Davis, VP/dev and exec dir, NPR Foundation; Carlos Barrionuevo, dir business dev.

Members Board: John A. Herrmann Jr., vice-chmn NPR Foundation; Carol Cartwright, pres emeritus, Kent State University; Howard H. Stevenson, vice-chair and acting chair; Lyle Logan, exec VP/Northern Trust Global; Eduardo A. Hauser, CEO/DailyMe Inc.

This noncommercial, satellite-delivered radio system serves a growing audience of more than 15 million Americans each week via 620 public radio stns and the Internet. NPR also serves: Europe, Asia, Australia and Africa via NPR Worldwide; military installations overseas via American Forces Network; and Japan via cable.

NPR provides member stns with progmg, professional dev, promotional support, program distribution/representation in Washington on issues affecting bcstg. News Talk Programs include: All Things Considered, The Bryant Park Project, Morning Edition, News & Notes, Weekend Edition Saturday, Weekend Edition Sunday and Talk of the Nation, Fresh Air, Day To Day, Tell Me More. Music Programs include: World Cafe From the Top, JazzSet, Marian McPartland's Piano Jazz and World of Opera.

Public Radio International

Mailing Address: 100 N. 6th St., Suite 900A, Minneapolis, MN 55403. (612) 338-5000. Web Site: http://www.pri.org.

Management Staff: Alisa Miller, pres/CEO; Timothy J. Engel, sr VP/CFO; Melinda Ward, sr VP; Eleanor Harris, sr VP, head mktg/distribution; Elinor Gould Zimmerman, VP/resource dev; Dan Jensen, dir.

Background Information: PRI is a Minneapolis-based pub radio network and audio publisher that provides over 400 hours each week of original progmg bcst by over 715 pub radio stn affils. Its progmg also is available on locally branded pub radio stn Web sites, internationally through the World Radio Network, and nationwide via Sirius Satellite Radio. PRI was founded in 1983 as American Public Radio by five leading public radio stns to dev distinctive radio programs and to div the pub radio offerings available to American listeners. Programs includes: BBC World Service, Living on Earth, Open Source, PRI's The World, Bob Edwards Weekends, Fair Game, This America Life, The Travis Smiley Show, Studio 360 and Michael Feldmam's What d'Ya Know?. Classical Music Progams includes: Classical 24, Schickel Mix Major symphony orchestras.

Superadio Network

Headquarters MA: 1661 Worcester Rd., Suite 205, Framingham, MA 01701. (508) 620-0006. Fax: (508) 628-1590. Web Site: http://www.superadio.com; E-mail: mixessuperadio.com.

Executives: Rich O'Brien, sr VP progmg/affil rels; Joan Brooks, business mgr; Alexis Coble, distribution mgr; Sheila Pellegrini, network affil coord.

Headquarters NY: 11 Penn Plaza, 16th Fl., New York, New York. (212) 714-1000. Fax: (212) 714-1563.

Executives: Jack Bryant, COO; Eric Faison, VP affil rel; John Campanario, VP/dir urban progmg; Robert Massey, dir affil rels.

Urban/Rhythmic Programs: Black Spin (with Spinderella), Classic Jam (80s & 90s Hip-Hop and R&B), Classic Jam Mini-Mixx, Kool Jam (The Original Old School R&B Show), Lost in the 80s(Derick Jonzun), New School Mini-Mix, Old Skool Mini Mix, Oldies Jam, Slam Jam (Today's Hip-Hop and R&B), Smooth Jam, Sunday Nite Show Jams (with R Dub!) Old Skool Show (with MC Serch), Supermixx Rhythm and Sol Kafe.

CHR Programs: Open House Party (with John Garabedian), Open House Party Sunday (with Kannon), Romeo's Playhouse, Supermixx Mainstream, Supermixx Rhythm

Gospel: BeBe Winans Radio Show, Holy Hip Hop Radio, Inspiration Jam.

Country: Retro Country USA (with Ken Cooper).

United Press International

Headquarters: 1133 19th St. N.W., Washington, DC 20036. (202) 898-8000. Fax: (202) 898-8048. E-mail: tipsupi.com (news); salesupi.com (general); supportupi.com (customer svc). Web site: www.upi.com.

Leadership Team: Nicholas Chiaia, pres; Michael Marshall (editor in chief); Dr. Chung Hwan Kwak, (chmn); Christopher Ching, VP of finance; Marc Oram, gen counsel.

Broadcast History: UPI is a global opn hqtr in Washington, DC with offices in Seoul, Korea, United Kingdom, Beirut Lebanon, Tokyo, Japan, Santiago, Chile and Hong Kong, China. UPI was founded in 1907 by E.W. Scripps as the United Press (UP). It became known as UPI when the UP merged with the International News Service in 1958, which was founded in 1909 by William Randolph Hearst. UPI is owned by News World Communications, a global multi-media company. In 1935, UPI became the first news svc to supply news to bcstrs. Ten years later, UPI started the first sports wire. In 1958, UPI began the first wire svc radio network, providing radio stns with voice reports from correspondents all over the globe.

USA Radio Networks, Inc.

Headquarters: 2290 Springlake Rd., Suite 107, Dallas, TX 75234. (972) 484-3900; (800) 829-8111. Web site: www.usaradio.com

Executives: Mark Maddoux, pres; Tim Maddoux, VP/progmg and program dev; David Maddoux, IS technology; Tim King, engrg; Andrew Hydock, opns.

Affiliate Sales Director: Robert Jimenez.

Advertising Sales: Buddy Vaughn; Tiffany Forney.

Foreign Correspondents: Andrew Adams, Tokyo; Anya Ardayeva and Guy Chazan, Moscow; Susan Lackey, London; Ellen Ratner, DC; Laurence Frost, Paris; Nathan Morley, Cyprus; Ronnie Nathaniels, Manila; David Bendo, Jerusalem.

News: Bob Morrison, dir; Judy Hydock, asst news dir; Charlie Butts, relg editor; Ray Canevari, sports (leave

massage); Anchors: John Scott, Allen Stone and Jason Walker; Jack Dereat Cynthia King, anchors weekend; Connie Lawn, White House correspondent.

Dallas News Desk, Editors/Producers: Curt Lewis and Richard Curtis (weekday); Lindsay Hooker (weekend).

Service available via Satcom C-5 & through other nets & outlets. The USA Radio Network includes over 1,500 affiliated radio stns.

Weekday Programs: DayBreak USA, Point of View, The Roth Show; The Jim Sumpter Show; Politics & Religion; Marriage Builders, Golden Age of Radio Theater.

Weekend Programs: Outdoors this week, Cruise Control, Ask Andrea, The Radio Show, The Jim Sumpter Show, Smart Money, Phyllis Schlafly Live, Ed McMahon's Lifestyles Live, The Ron Seggi Show Live from Universal Studio Florida, ick Williams Cyber Line, America's Greatest Heroes, Bible Greatest Heroes, MidEast Week.

News:

USA News: Top of the Hour, Non-Commercial, NewsBreaks Sports.

The Wall Street Journal Radio Network

Mailing Address: 1155 Avenue of the Americas, 8th Fl., New York, NY 10036. (212) 659-1208. Fax: (212) 659-1908. E-Mail: wsjradio@]owjones.com. Web site: www.wsjradio.com.

Radio Staff: Nancy Abramson, exec dir; Ken Martin, affil mktg; Jeff Bellinger, morning news editor/news inquiries; Janie Edwards, traf dir; Patrice Sikora, mngg editor; Amy Francis, New Media project mgr; Paul von Zech, afternoon newsroom editor/news inquiries.

Programs: *The Wall Street Journal Report; The Dow Jones Money Report; The Wall Street Journal This Morning; The Wall Street Journal This Weekend; Barron's on Investment.*

Westwood One

Headquarters: 40 W. 57th St. 5th Fl., New York, NY 10019. (212) 641-2000. Fax: (212) 641-2185. Web site: www.westwoodone.com.

Corporate: Tom Beusse, pres/CEO; Gary Yusko, CFO; Roby Wiener, chief/ mktg officer; Paul Gregrey, exec VP/dir sls; Dennis Green, sr VP/affil sls; James Starace, VP, affil info/compliance; David Hillman, chief admin officer/exec VP/gen counsel; Carolyn Jones, VP/human resources; Paul Bronstein, VP rsch; Luis Rodriguez, chief info officer; Conrad Trautman, sr VP, opn/engrg; Max Krasny, sr VP/entertainment; Patrick

Parnham, VP/technical svcs: Nicole Horsford, VP/interactive sls and mktg; David Halberstam, exec VP/gen mgr sports.

Westwood One Programming

News Networks: *CBS Radio News, CNBC Business Radio, CNN Radio News, Marketwatch.com, NBC News Radio, Westwood One News.*

Features Programs: *ET Radio Minute, CBS Healthwatch, Dave Ross, Meet The Press, In the Marketplace, Late Night on Jimmy Kimmel Live, Osgood File, Raising our Kids, What's in the News, World News Roundup, Harry Smith Reporting.*

Talk Programs: *America in the Morning, America this Week, The Jim Bonhannon Show, The Don & Mike Show, First Light, The Adam Carolla Show, Phil Valentine Show, Dennis Miller, The Lars Larson Show, Larry King Live, Loveline, The Tom Leykis Show, On the Garden Line with Jerry Baker, The Radio Factor with Bill O'Reilly, Troubleshooter Tom Martino, The Week in Review.*

Sports

Football: *Monday Night Football, Sunday Night Football, NFL Playoffs, NFL Championships, NFL Super Bowl, NFL Pro Bowl, NFL Sunday Doubleheaders, NCAA Football, NFL Insider, NFL Preview, The NFL Today.*

Basketball: *NCAA Basketball, March To Madness, National Invitational Tournament.*

Golf: *British Open Championship, Masters, PGA Championship, US Open.*

Other Sports: *Focus on Racing Radio, Wimbledon, HBO Boxing.*

Sports Features: *John Madden Sports Quiz, The Madden Minute, Scoreboard, Sports Central USA, Sports Time, Sports World Roundup, Sports Feed, Today in Auto Racing, Today in Golf, Today in Sports, Westwood One Sports Report, 3rd & Long with Howie Long.*

Entertainment

Features: *Daily Show with John Stewart, ET Radio Minute, Late Show with David Letterman, Late Late Show with Craig Kilborn, Randy Jackson Hit List.*

Music

Alt/Modern Rock: *Absolutely Live, The Fax Prep Service, Loveline, MTV Radio Network, Out of Order.*

Contemporary/CHR: *The E! Radio Network Prep Service, MTV Radio Network, MTV's Total Request Live Weekend Countdown, Night Flight, Saturday Night All Request 80s, VH1 Behind the Music, Storytellers and Concerts, VH1 Radio Network.*

Classic Rock: *The Beatle Brunch, The Beatle Years, Off the Record, Superstar Concert Series, VH1 Behind the Music, Storytellers and Concerts, VH1 Radio Network.*

Country: *CMT Radio Network, Country's Cutting Edge, Country Gold, Country's Inside Trak, Country Six Pack, CMT's Country Countdown USA with Lon Helton, Grand Ole Opry, Stars of Country, The Weekly Country Music Countdown, Young and Verna.*

Oldies: *The Beatle Brunch, The Beatle Years, Doo Wop Heaven, The Motown Show, Oldies Six Pack.*

Urban/Hip Hop: *BET Radio Network, MTV Radio Network, MTV's TRL Weekend Countdown (Rhythmic).*

Urban/Hip Hop: *The Academy Of Country Music Awards, The BET Awards, Country Artist Album Premieres and Specials, The GRAMMY Awards, MTV Concerts and Specials, Music Events and Concerts, NFL Kickoff, VH1 Concerts and Specials.*

Prep Services

BET Radio Network, The CBS Morning Resource, The E! Radio Network, CMT Radio Morning Facts, MTV Radio Prep, VH1 Morning Prep, Westwood One Prep, BET Prep, Entertainment Newsfeed, Westwood One Celebrity Satellite Tours.

24-Hour Formats

Adult Rock & Roll, Adult Standards, Bright AC, CNN Headline News, Hot Country, Mainstream Country, The Oldies Channel, Soft AC.

WFMT Radio Network

Headquarters: 5400 N. St. Louis Ave., Chicago, IL 60625. (773) 279-2000. Fax: (773) 279-2199. Web Site: http://www.wfmt.com

Management: Daniel J. Schmidt, pres/CEO; Steve Robinson, sr VP radio; Reese P. Marcusson, exec VP/CFO; Farrell Frentress, exec VP/dev; V.J. McAleer, sr VP/production; Joanie Bayhack, sr VP, corporate communication/direct mktg; Donna L. Davies, sr VP/dev.

Trustees Board: Sandra P. Guthman, chmn; Daniel Schmidt, pres; John J. Brennan, (treas); Renee Crown (vice-chmn); Roger Plummer (vice-chmn); Deborah L. DeHaas, (vice-chmn); Robert S. Silver, sec.

Satellite-delivered performing arts, jazz & spoken word progmg to over 1500 coml & pub radio stns domestically & 40 countries abroad. Among the feature programs are concerts by major symphony orchestras, productions by opera companies, concerts from Europe, concerts & spoken word from the BBC, music & verbal documentaries, folk music. Beethoven Satellite Network is the all classical 12 hr svc, hosted by Peter Van Graaff. Jazz Satellite Network the leader in mainstream nightly satellite, 12 hr nightly, hosted by legendary jazz expert Bob Parlocha.

Regional Radio Programming Services

Alaska Public Radio Network, 3877 University Dr., Anchorage, AK, 99508. Phone: (907) 550-8400. Fax: (907) 550-8401.E-mail: aprn@alaska.net Web Site:www.aprn.org

Bede Trantina, stn mgr; Duncan Moon, news dir.

JuneauAK . Juneau Alaska News Bureau, 530 Park St. Phone:

WashingtonDC . Washington, DC News Bureau, 2801 Quebec St. N.W, Suite 505. Phone:

Satellite-delivered news/info programs to 26 member stn across Alaska from state-of-the-art studios, hqtr in Anchorage.

Allegheny Mountain Network, Box 247, Tyrone, PA, 16686. Phone: (814) 684-3200. Fax: (814) 684-1220.E-mail: amnnet@aol.com

Cary Simpson, pres; Alfred Haper, VP.

WellsboroPA , Box 98. Phone:

Comprises 9 stns in Pennsylvania. Represented by Dome & Associates.

American Ag Network, 214 W. Pleasant Dr., Pierre, SD, 57501-2472. Phone: (605) 224-9911. Fax: (605) 224-8984.E-mail: markswendsen@amfmradio.biz Web Site:americanagnetwork.com

Mark Swendsen, pres.

FargoND , 2501 13th Ave., Suite 201. Phone:

Grand ForksND , Box 13919. Phone:

Comprises 40 stns: 16 in South Dakota, 22 in North Dakota & 2 in Montana.

Arkansas Radio Network, 700 Wellington Hills Rd., Little Rock, AR, 72211. Phone: (501) 401-0228. Phone: (800) 839.4610. Fax: (501) 401-0367.E-mail: gordon.stephan@citcomm.com Web Site:www.arkansasradionetwork.com

Ross McKenney, producer.

Comprises 55 interconnected stns, all in Arkansas, Texas & Mississippi. Represented by StateNets & McGauren Guild.

Beasley Broadcast Group, 3033 Riviera Dr., Suite 200, Naples, FL, 34103. Phone: (239) 263-5000. Fax: (239) 263-8191.E-mail: email@bbgi.com Web Site:www.bbgi.com

George G. Beasley, chmn/CEO.

Radio stns 44: 27 FMs & 17 AMs in 11 large, mid-sized markets.

Brownfield Network, (A division of Learfield Communications Inc.). 505 Hobbs Rd., Jefferson City, MO, 65109-6829. Phone: (573) 893-5700. Fax: (573) 893-8094.E-mail: jsteinman@learfield.com Web Site:www.brownfieldnetwork.com

Bruce Beasley, pres; Joyce Steinman, adv.

Comprises 280 stns in Illinois, Iowa, Missouri, Nebraska, Indiana, South Dakota & Wisconsin. Represented by In-House.

CRN International, Inc., One Circular Ave., Hamden, CT, 06514. Phone: (203) 288-2002. Fax: (203) 281-3291.E-mail: info@crnradio.com Web Site:www.crnradio.com

Barry Berman, pres; S. Richard Kalt, exec VP; Patrick Kane, sr VP; Steve Wakeen, VP.

Stragtegy & execution, retail mktg, lifestyle progmg, promotions, digital media & other non-traditional communication tactics, small business, collaborative mktg, weather-triggered media placement, Ethnic, Just -In-Time Marketing. Branch Office: Minneapolis, MN.

California News Radio, 14605 N. Airport Dr., Suite 370, Scottsdale, AZ, 85260. Phone: (480) 503-8700. Fax: (480) 998-5751. Web Site:www.skyviewsatellite.com

Jeanne-Marie Condo, gen mgr; Ken Thiele, pres.

Comprises 26 stns in California.

Compu-Weather Inc., 2566 Rt. 52, Hopewell Junction, NY, 12533. Phone: (800) 284-7246. Fax: (845) 226-1918.E-mail: sales@compuweather.com Web Site:www.compuweather.com

Jeff Wimmer, pres.

Florida Public Radio Network, 1600 Red Barber Plaza, Tallahassee, FL, 32310. Phone: (850) 487-3194. Fax: (850) 487-3293.E-mail: fpr@wfsu.org Web Site:www.wfsu.org

Carolina Austin, opns mgr; Tom Flanigan, news dir.

Serves 13 FM public radio stns in Florida.

Florida News Network, 2500 Maitland Ctr. Pkwy., Suite 407, Maitland, FL, 32751. Phone: (407) 916-7810. Phone: (407) 916-7800. Fax: (407) 916-7425.E-mail: jimpoling@fnnonline.net Web Site:www.fnnonline.net

Jim Poling, opns mgr; Rick Green, gen mgr; Jim Underwood, sls dir.

Comprises 58 stns in Florida. Represented by StateNets Inc.

Georgia News Network, 1819 Peachtree Rd., Suite 700, Atlanta, GA, 30309. Phone: (404) 607-9045. Phone: (800) 776-4638. Fax: (404) 367-6404.E-mail: robmaynard @clearchannel.com Web Site:www.georgianewsnetwork.com

Linda Kent, sls; Rob Maynard, progmg.

Comprises 108 stns in Georgia. Represented by StateNts.

Hawkeye Network, 505 Hobbs Rd., Jefferson City, MO, 65109. Phone: (573) 893-7200. Fax: (573) 893-8076. Web Site:www.learfield.com

Clyde G. Lear, pres; Greg Brown, VP; Keith Sampson, exec producer; Bob Agramonte, gen mgr .

Comprises 50 stns in Iowa. Sports Network.

Hispanic Communications Network, 1126 16th St. N.W., Suite 350, Washington, DC, 20036. Phone: (202) 637-8800. Fax: (202) 637-8801.E-mail: info@hcnmedia.com Web Site:www.hcnmedia.com

Carlos Alcazar, pres/CEO.

National-All 50 states & Puerto Rico: 200 radio stns.

Hometown Radio Network, 1100 Chester Ave., Suite 100, Cleveland, OH, 44115. Phone: (216) 781-0035. Fax: (216) 781-7508.E-mail: sjsharpe@regionalreps.com Web Site:www.regionalreps.com

Stuart J. Sharpe, pres.

Comprises over 1000 affils in Delaware, Florida, Georgia, Iowa, Illinois, Indiana, Kansas, Kentucky, Maryland, Nebraska, North Carolina, Ohio, Oklahoma, Pennsylvania, South Carolina, Virginia, & West Virginia. Represented by: Rgnl Reps Corp.

ION Radio Network, Box 1223, Airport Rd., Morristown, NJ, 07960. Phone: (973) 983-8222. Fax: (973) 983-1390.E-mail: steve@ionweather.com Web Site:www.ionweather.com

Stephen Pellettiere, pres.

Comprises 10 stns, four in New Jersey, four in New York, one in Pennsylvania & one in Connecticut.

Illinois Radio Network, 430 W. Erie, Suite 505, Chicago, IL, 60610. Phone: (312) 943-6363. Fax: (312) 943-5109. Web Site:www.illinoisradionetwork.com

Dennis Mellott, gen mgr & pres.

A statewide satellite-delivered net providing news, sports, business & special progmg. IRN 67 affils. Representative: StateNets.

KEDA Radio, 510 S. Flores, San Antonio, TX, 78204. Phone: (210) 226-5254.E-mail: kedakid@aol.com Web Site:www.kedaradio.com

Comprises three stns in Texas, three affiliates. Represented by Caballero Spanish Media.

Kansas Agriculture Network, Box 1818, Topeka, KS, 66601-1818. Phone: (785) 272-3456. Fax: (785) 272-7282. Web Site:www.radionetworks.com E-mail: dan.johnson@morris.com

Comprises 30 stns in Kansas. Represented by Learfield Radio.

Kansas Information Network, Box 1818, Topeka, KS, 66601-1818. Phone: (785) 272-3456. Fax: (785) 228-7282. Web Site:www.radionetworks.com E-mail: dan.johnson@morris.com

Comprises 32 stns in Kansas. Represented by StateNets.

Kansas State Sports Network, 1632 S. Maze Rd., Wichita, 67209. Phone: (316) 721-8484.

Kentucky News Network, (A subsidiary of Clear Channel Radio Inc.). 4000 # 1 Radio Dr., Louisville, KY, 40218. Phone: (502) 479-2248. Fax: (502) 479-2231.E-mail: nathanbutler@clearchannel.com Web Site:www.kentuckynewsnetwork.com

Comprises 87 stns in Kentucky. Represented by StatesNets. Live via satellite.

Linder Farm Network, 255 Cedardale Dr., Owatonna, MN, 55060. Phone: (507) 444-9224. Fax: (507) 444-9080.E-mail: farm@linderradio.com Web Site:www.linderfarmnetwork.com

Jeff Stewart, sls mgr; Lynn Ketelsen, gen mgr .

Comprises 22 stns in Minnesota. Represented by Katz Radio.

Louisiana Agri-News Network, 10500 Coursey Blvd., Ste. 104, Baton Rouge, LA, 70816. Phone: (225) 291-2727. Fax: (225) 297-7539.E-mail: jim@la-net.net Web Site:www.la-net.net

Bill Rigell, pres/CEO; Jim Engster, gen mgr .

Comprises 46 stns in Louisiana & Mississippi. Represented by McGavren Guild.

Louisiana Network Inc., 10500 Coursey Blvd., Suite 104, Baton Rouge, LA, 70816. Phone: (225) 291-2727. Fax: (225) 297-7539.E-mail: jim@la-net.net Web Site:www.la-net.net

Comprises 84 stns in Louisiana. Represented by news net: State Nets, Agri-News Network: McGavren Guild.

Michigan Farm Radio Network, 325 South Walnut, Lansing, MI, 48933. Phone: (517) 484-4888. Fax: (517) 484-5015.E-mail: rhermes@irnradionet.com Web Site:www.mfrn.com

Dennis Mellott, gen mgr , pres; Kirsten Buys, dir; Janelle Brose, dir.

Comprises 21 Michigan, affils. Represented by J.L. Farmakis.

Michigan Radio Network, 325 S. Walnut, Lansing, MI, 48933. Phone: (517) 484-4888. Fax: (517) 484-9404.E-mail: news@mrnradionet.com Web Site:www.michiganradionetwork.com

Dennis Mellott, pres; Rob Baykian, news dir; Kirsten Buys, dir.

A statewide satellite-delivered net providing news, sports, business & special progmg. MRN 55 affils. Representative: StateNets.

Mid-America Ag Network, 1632 S. Maize Rd., Wichita, KS, 67209. Phone: (316) 721-8484. Fax: (316) 721-8276. Web Site:www.maanradio.com

Rick Betzen, gen mgr; Greg Steckline, pres.

Comprises 33 stns in Colorado, Kansas & Nebraska. Represented by Torbet Radio.

Midwestern Broadcsting Company, (Formerly Paul Bunyan Network). Paul Bunyan Bldg., 314 E. Front, Traverse City, MI, 49684. Phone: (231) 947-7675. Fax: (231) 929-3988.E-mail: chrisw@wtcmradio.com Web Site:www.wtcmradio.com

Ross Biederman, pres/CEO; Chris Warren, gen mgr .

Comprises 10 stns in Michigan. Represented by Katz Radio.

Mississippi Agri Network, 6311 Ridgewood Rd., Jackson, MS, 39211. Phone: (601) 957-1700. Fax: (601) 956-5228.E-mail: lsheldon@telesouth.com Web Site:www.supertalk.com

Stacy Long, gen sls mgr.

Comprises 35 affils in Mississippi. Represented by McGavren/Guild.

Mississippi News Network, 6311 Ridgewood Rd., Jackson, MS, 39211. Phone: (601) 957-1700. Fax: (601) 956-5228.E-mail: lsheldon@telesouth.com Web Site:www.supertalkms.com

Stacy Long, gen sls mgr.

Comprises 82 affils in Mississippi. Represented by StateNets.

Mississippi State Basketball Network, 6311 Ridgewood Rd., Jackson, MS, 39211. Phone: (601) 957-1700. Fax: (601) 956-5228.E-mail: kdillon@telesouth.com Web Site:www.supertalkms.com

Kim Dillon, mktg dir.

Comprises 28 affils in Mississippi & one in Tennessee.

Mississippi State Football Network, 6311 Ridgewood Rd., Jackson, MS, 39211. Phone: (601) 957-1700. Fax: (601) 956-5228.E-mail: kdillon@telesouth.com Web Site:www.supertalkms.com

Steve Davenport, pres/CEO.

Comprises 30 affils in Mississippi & one in Alabama. Represented by Kim Dillon.

Missourinet, (A division of Learfield Communications Inc.). 505 Hobbs Rd., Jefferson City, MO, 65109. Phone: (573) 893-2829. Fax: (573) 893-8094.E-mail: info@missourinet.com Web Site:www.missourinet.com

Serves Missouri, 50-60 affils.

Mountain News Network, 50 Vashell Way, Suite 200, Orinda, CA, 94563. Phone: (925) 254-4456. Phone: (800) 736-0370 Eastern Bureau. Fax: (925) 254-6135.E-mail: news@mnn.net Web Site:www.mnn.net

Comprises 1,537 stns nationwide.

NRG Media, LLC, Box 94, Fort Atkinson, WI, 53538. Phone: (920) 563-2667. Fax: (920) 563-0315.E-mail: jvriezen@nrgmedia.com Web Site:www.lite1073.com

Jim Vriezen, gen mgr .

Comprises 55 radio stns in Illinois, Iowa, Nebraska & Wisconsin.

National Educational Telecommunications Association, Box 50008, Columbia, SC, 29250. Phone: (803) 799-5517. Fax: (803) 771-4831.E-mail: skip@netaonline.org Web Site:www.netaonline.org

Skip Hinton, pres.

Ninety-five members in 45 states & the U.S. Virgin Islands.

New South Communications Inc., Box 5797, Meridian, MS, 39302. Phone: (601) 693-2661. Fax: (601) 483-0826.

Ed Holladau, pres.

Comprises 18 stns: five in Louisiana, ten in Mississippi & three in Alabama. Represented by McGavren Guild.

North Carolina News Network, 711 Hillsborough St., Raleigh, NC, 27603. Phone: (919) 890-6128. Fax: (919) 890-6146.E-mail: rhankin@ncnn.com Web Site:www.ncnn.com

Ardie Gregory, VP/gen mgr.

Comprises 75 stns in North Carolina. Represented by StateNets.

North Dakota News Network, Box 1197, Pierre, SD, 57501. Phone: (605) 224-9911. Fax: (605) 224-8984.E-mail: markswendsen@amfmradio.biz

Mark Swendsen, pres.

Comprises 24 stns in North Dakota. Represented by StateNets.

Ohio Educational Telecommunications Network Commission, 2470 North Star Rd., Columbus, OH, 43221. Phone: (614) 228-4526. Fax: (614) 644-3112.

Oklahoma News Network, (Oklahoma Agrinet). Box 1000, Oklahoma City, OK, 73101. Phone: (405) 840-5271 Ext. 278. Fax: (405) 840-5808.

Jerry Bohnen, news dir.

Comprises 55 stns in Oklahoma.

Pittsburgh Country Network, 1439 Denniston St., Pittsburgh, PA, 15217. Phone: (412) 421-2600. Fax: (412) 421-6001.E-mail: rafson@cmsradio.com Web Site:www.cmsradio.com

Roger Rafson, pres.

Comprises three stns in Pennsylvania. Represented by Commercial Media Sales.

Radio Iowa, (A division of Learfield Communications Inc.). 2700 Grand Ave., Suite 103, Des Moines, IA, 50312. Phone: (515) 282-1984. Fax: (515) 282-1879.E-mail: radioiowa@learfield.com Web Site:www.radioiowa.com

Clyde G. Lear, pres/CEO; Jennifer Shaefer, adv; O. Kay Henderson, news dir.

Comprises 66 affils in Iowa.

Radio Pennsylvania Network, (A Division of WITF Inc.). 4801 Lindle Rd., Harrisburg, PA, 17111. Phone: (717) 704-3000. Fax: (717) 704-3659.E-mail: craig_rhodes@radiopa.com Web Site:www.radiopa.com

Craig Rhodes, opns mgr; Brad Christman, editor.

Bcsts state news, sports & features to affils in Pennsylvania. Comprises 80 stns. Represented by NASRN.

Saga Communications, Inc,, 73 Kercheval Ave., Suite 201, Grosse Pointe Farms, MI, 48236. Phone: (313) 886-7070. Fax: (313) 886-7150.

Warren Lada, sr VP/opns; Edward hrstian, pres/CEO.

South Carolina News Network, (A division of Learfield Communications). 3710 Landmark Dr., Suite 100, Columbia, SC, 29204. Phone: (803) 790-4300. Fax: (803) 790-4309.

Scott Brandon, .

Comprises 45 affils in South Carolina.

South Dakota News Network, Box 1197, Pierre, SD, 57501. Phone: (605) 224-9911. Fax: (605) 224-8984.E-mail: markswendsen@amfmradio.biz

Mark Swendsen, pres.

Comprises 20 stns in South Dakota. Represented by StateNets.

Southeast AgNet, 5053 N.W. Hwy. 225 A, Ocala, FL, 34482. Phone: (352) 671-1909. Fax: (352) 671-1364.E-mail: gary@southeastagnet.com Web Site:www.southeastagnet.com

Gary Cooper, pres; Robin Loftin, VP.

Stns interconnected via Internet. Comprises 65 affils in Florida, Georgia & the Alabama rgn.

Southern Farm Network, 3012 Highwoods Blvd., Suite 200, Raleigh, NC, 27604. Phone: (919) 876-0674. Fax: (919) 790-8369.E-mail: bprice@southernfarmnetwork.com Web Site:www.southernfarmnetwork.com

Barbara G. Price, opns mgr & sls.

Comprises 20 affils in North Carolina & South Carolina.

Tennessee Agri-Net, (Subsidiary of Clear Channel Communications Inc.). 55 Music Square West, Nashville, TN, 37203. Phone: (615) 664-2400. Fax: (615) 687-9797.E-mail: craighahn@clearchannel.com Web Site:www.tennesseeradionetwork.com

Tom English, .

Comprises 48 stns in Tennessee.

Tennessee Radio Network, (A subsidiary of Clear Channel Broadcasting Inc.). 55 Music Sq. W., Nashville, TN, 37203. Phone: (615) 664-2400. Fax: (615) 687-9797.E-mail: craighahn@clearchannel.com Web Site:www.tennesseeradionetwork.com

Tom English, mktg mgr/VP.

Comprises 74 stns in Tennessee. Representative Nathan Butler (Loisville, KY location) affil rel dir.

Texas State Network, 4131 N. Central Expwy., Suite 500, Dallas, TX, 75204. Phone: (214) 525-7400. Fax: (214) 525-7371.E-mail: dbell@cbs.com Web Site:www.tsnradio.com

Jerry Bobo, VP, gen mgr; Dan Bell, gen sls mgr; Julis Graw, dir news & opns; Brian Purdy, VP/mktg mgr.

AustinTX , 502 E. 11th St, Suite 320. Phone:

Provides newscasts, sportscasts, agriculture reports, longform programs to 165 stns in Texas & the Texas Rangers Radio Network. The oldest & largest state radio net owned by CBS Radio. Represented by StateNets.

Tiger Network, (A division of Learfield Communications Inc.). 505 Hobbs Rd., Jefferson City, MO, 65109. Phone: (573) 893-7200. Fax: (573) 893-2321. Web Site:www.learfield.com

Clyde G. Lear, pres; Greg Brown, VP; Keith Sampson, exec producer; Bob Agramonte, gen mgr; Aaron Worsham, VP opns.

Comprises 55 stns in Missouri.

Tribune Radio Networks, 435 N. Michigan Ave., Chicago, IL, 60611. Phone: (312) 222-3342.E-mail: bpabst@tribune.com Web Site:www.tribuneradio.com

Barbra Pabst, opns; Kurt Vanderan, opns mgr.

Network comprised of: Chicago Cubs Network (50 stns), National Farm Report (260 stns), Farming America (200 stns), Agri-Voice Network (95 stns), Samuelson's Soapbox (150 stns). Represented by Eastman.

University of Mississippi Baseball Network, 6311 Ridgewood Rd., Jackson, MS, 39211. Phone: (601) 957-1700. Fax: (601) 956-5228.E-mail: kdillon@telesouth.com Web Site: www.supertalkms.com

Comprises 30 affils in Mississippi & one in Tennessee. Represented by Kim Dillon.

University of Mississippi Basketball Network, 6311 Ridgewood Rd., Jackson, MS, 39211. Phone: (601) 957-1700. Fax: (601) 956-5228. Web Site:www.telesouth.com

Steve Davenport, pres; Stacy Long, gen sls mgr.

Comprises 30 affils in Mississippi & one in Tennessee. Represented by Kim Dillon.

University of Mississippi Football Network, 6311 Ridgewood Rd., Jackson, MS, 39211. Phone: (601) 957-1700. Fax: (601) 956-5228.E-mail: kdillon@telesouth.com Web Site:www.supertalkms.com

Steve Davenport, pres.

Comprises 30 affils in Mississippi & one in Tennessee. Represented by Tim Fritts.

Univision Radio, 3102 Oak Lawn Ave., Suite 215, Dallas, TX, 75219. Phone: (214) 525-7700. Fax: (214) 525-7750. Web Site:www.univision.com

Alan F. Horn, pres/COO.

Comprises 72 stns, 18 in California, four in Florida, five in Illinois, three in Nevada, three in New York, 26 in Texas & five in Arizona, four in New Mexico, four in Puerto Rico.

Vox Communications, (formerly Berkshire Broadcasting Co. Inc.). 211 Jason St., Pittsfield, MA, 01201. Phone: (413) 499-3333. Fax: (413) 442-1590.E-mail: wnaw@wnaw.com Web Site:www.wnaw.com

Comprises 6 stns in Berkshire County, MA.

WRTI-FM, 1509 Cecil B. Moore, 3rd Fl., Philadelphia, PA, 19121-3410. Phone: (215) 204-8405. Fax: (215) 204-7027. Web Site:www.wrti.org

David S. Conant, exec dir; Patty Prevost, dev dir; Tobias Poole, opns.

Comprises four stns in Pennsylvania, one in New Jersey & one in Delaware.

WV Radio Corp. and Metronews Radio Network, Greer Bldg., 1251 Earl L. Core Rd., Morgantown, WV, 26505. Phone: (304) 296-0029. Fax: (304) 296-3876. Web Site:www.wvmetronews.com E-mail: dmiller@wvradio.com

Dale B. Miller, pres; Hoppy Kercheval, VP opns. CharlestonWV , 1111 Virginia St. E. Phone:

Comprises West Virginia News, 58 stns in West Virginia & Mountaineer Sports Network, 72 stns in West Virginia.

"The Weather Center", (A broadcast service of Aviation Weather Inc.). 701 Gervais St., Suite 224, Columbia, SC, 29201. Phone: (803) 422-4823.E-mail: wxcenter@aviationweatherinc.com Web Site:www.aviationweatherinc.com

"Regional Radio Broadcast/Weathercast Network" across the Carolinas & Georgia in over 20 bcst markets. Weather forecasting, site-specific bcst svc for stns all across America.

Western Agri-Radio Networks Inc., (dba California Agri-Radio Network & Southwest Agri-Radio Network). 1700 S. 1st Ave., Suite 214, Yuma, AZ, 85364. Phone: (928) 782-1440. Fax: (928) 782-1474.E-mail: ggatley@sprynet.com Web Site:www.farmnewswest.com

George G. Gatley, pres.

YumaAZ . Southwest Agri-Radio Network , 1700 S. 1st Ave, Suite 214. Phone:ggatley@sprynet.com Web Site: www.home.com/sprynet/ggatley.

YumaAZ . California Agri-Radio Network, 1700 S. 1st Ave, Suite 214. Phone:ggatley@sprynet.com Web Site: www.home.com/sprynet/ggatley.

Fifteen radio stns in California, two in Arizona & one in Texas. Represented by J.L. Famakis.

Wisconsin Radio Network, 222 State St., Suite 401, Madison, WI, 53703. Phone: (608) 251-3900. Fax: (608) 251-7233.E-mail: info@wrn.com Web Site:www.wrn.com

Joyce Steinman, adv; Bob Hague, news dir.

Statewide satellite-delivered net providing Wisconsin news & sports.

Yancey AG Network, Box 1000, Oklahoma City, OK, 73101. Phone: (405) 858-10297. Web Site:www.oklahomaagrinet.net E-mail: ashliacker@clearchannel.com

Ron Hays, progmg dir; Ben Buckland, network mgr.

A satellite delivered Agsource providing affil radio stns with agricultural markets, news & weather. Represents 17 stns.

Radio News Services

ABC News Radio, 125 West End Ave., New York, NY, 10023. Phone: (212) 456-5100. Fax: (212) 456-5150. E-mail: customerservice@abc.com Web Site:www.abcradionetworks.com

Steve Jones, VP; Andrew Kalb, exec dir, news progmg; Michael Rizzo, exec dir, news & sports coverage; Robert Garcia, exec dir, Washington bureau chief.

Serves 2,500 affiliates & 92.5 million wkly listeners nationwide, with bcst facilities in New York City & Washington, DC.

AMI News, 50 Vashell Way, Suite 200, Orinda, CA, 94563. Phone: (925) 254-4456. Web Site:www.theamigroup.com

Chad Dyer, VP/internet news svcs., Eastern Bureau. Phone:

MP3 Wave phone- & tape-supplied features focusing on skiing, fishing, camping, travel & beach conditions with related news & information. Offered seasonally. Available on the Internet.

AccuWeather Inc., 385 Science Park Rd., State College, PA, 16803. Phone: (814) 235-8600. Fax: (814) 235-8609. E-mail: info@accuweather.com Web Site:www.accuweather.com

Gary Kemp, sls VP; Dr. Joel N. Myers, pres/CEO.

World's most accurate svc provides products & svcs for TV, radio, internet, mobile web & all new media platforms.

Agence France-Presse, 1500 K St. N.W., Suite 600, Washington, DC, 20005. Phone: (202) 289-0700. Fax: (202) 414-0632. E-mail: afp-usa@afp.com Web Site:www.afp.com

Pierre Louette, chief exec; Denis Hiault, dir; Jean-Pierre Vignolle, dir.

Produces a var of international news svcs, including text wires in six languages, photo wires, graphics & financial wires.

Alaska Public Radio Network, 3877 University Dr., Anchorage, AK, 99508. Phone: (907) 550-8400. Fax: (907) 550-8401. E-mail: aprn@alaska.net Web Site:www.aprn.org

Bede Trantina, stn mgr; Duncan Moon, news dir.

JuneauAK . Juneau Alaska News Bureau, 530 Park St. Phone:

WashingtonDC . Washington, DC News Bureau, 2801 Quebec St. N.W, Suite 505. Phone:

Satellite-delivered news/info programs to 26 member stn across Alaska from state-of-the-art studios, hqtr in Anchorage.

American Academy of Dermatology, Communications Dept., American Academy of Dermatology. Box 4014, Schaumburg, IL, 60168-4014. Phone: (847) 330-0230. Fax: (847) 330-8907. Web Site:www.aad.org E-mail: mediarelations@aad.org

WashingtonDC , 1350 I Street NW, Suite 870. Phone:

Expert physicians available for TV & radio interviews, audio & video tapes on skin cancer pevention & detection, as well as info on skin, hair & nail conditions.

American Heart Association, 7272 Greenville Ave., Dallas, TX, 75231-4596. Phone: (214) 706-1330. Phone: (800) 242-8721 (aha-usa1). Fax: (214) 706-5243. Web Site:www.americanheart.org

M. Cass Wheeler, CEO.

Rsch & lifestyle reports, distributed via podcast.

American Urban Radio Networks, 960 Penn Ave., Suite 200, Pittsburgh, PA, 15222. Phone: (412) 456-4000. Fax: (412) 456-4040. E-mail: jlopes@aurn.com Web Site:www.aurn.com

Jerry Lopes, opns.

New YorkNY , 432 Park Ave. S., 14th Fl. Phone:jay@aurn.com E.J. "Jay" Williams, pres.

Info, news, sports & entertainment of special interest to Blacks & other minorities.

Associated Press Broadcast Services, 1825 K St. N.W., Suite 800, Washington, DC, 20006-1202. Phone: (202) 641-9281. Web Site:www.apbroadcast.com

Audio: PrimeCuts, Sound Bank. On Air: Radio News. On Line: News Tickers, Online Video Network; Custom News, Sp Online. Prep: Power Prep. Software: News Desk, APENPS. Sound Desk, News Center. Text Headlines, Sp, Sports Power, News Power, Images & Multimedia: asap, all AP.

Associated Press Network News

See ssociated Press listing in Major National Radio Networks, this section.

Audio-Video News, 3622 Stanford Cir., Falls Church, VA, 22041. Phone: (703) 354-6795. E-mail: connielawn@aol.com Web Site:www.dcski.com

Connie Lawn, pres.

Covers major natl, international & ski stories for radio & TV stns in the United States & around the world. Also live "inserts" into radio & TV shows.

The Berns Bureau, Box 2939, Washington, DC, 20013-2939. Phone: (202) 314-5165.

Matt Kaye, .

Complete "localized" coverage of Washington, DC. Satellite ISDN & telephone transmission. Audio news releases. Govt, politics, farm, relg & other progmg for radio. Audio svc for TV.

Black Radio Network Inc. (BRN), 166 Madison Ave., New York, NY, 10016. Phone: (212) 686-6850. Fax: (212) 686-7308. E-mail: news@blackradionetwork.com

Roy Thompson, VP.

Provides a daily actuality news service emphasizing minority-oriented items.

British Information Services, 845 Third Ave., New York, NY, 10022. Phone: (212) 745-0395. Fax: (212) 745-0463. Web Site:www.britainusa.com

Provides daily audio news feed svc filed by digital line from London at no cost to stns. Assists radio & TV crews visiting the United Kingdom.

CBS News

See BS listing in National Radio Programming Services, this section.

CNN Radio News, One CNN Ctr., 4 S.W., Atlanta, GA, 30303. Phone: (404) 827-2751. Fax: (404) 827-5363. Web Site:www.westwoodone.com

Fred Bennett, sr VP.

Top- & bottom-of-the-hour radio newscasts 24-hours a day plus business, sports & lifestyle updates.

Canada NewsWire Ltd., 1500, 20 Bay St., WaterPark Pl., Toronto, ON, M5J 2N8. Canada. Phone: (416) 863-9350. Phone: (866) 805-9530. Fax: (416) 863-9429. E-mail: cnwtor@newswire.ca Web Site:www.newswire.ca

Sylvia Kavanagh, mgr; Tim Griffin, bcst mgr; Carolyn McGill, dir mktg.

CalgaryAB Canada, Gulf Canada Sq, 401 Ninth Ave. S.W., Suite 835. Phone:Michle.dauphine@newswire.ca Krista Wightman, mgr.

VancouverBC Canada, 650 West Georgia St, Suite 1103. Phone:

HalifaxNS Canada, Sun Tower, 1550 Bedford Hwy., Suite 410. Phone:jgallant@newswire.ca Robert Moffatt, mgr Atlantic Canada.

OttawaON Canada, 255 Albert St, Suite 460. Phone: MontrealPQ Canada, 1155 Rene Levesque Blvd. W, Suite 3310. Phone:scmtl@newswire.ca Elaire Carr, VP Quebec.

Offers a range of industry leading communication products & svcs for companies looking to maximize the strength of their news. Whether you are an investor rel off, or a specialist in PR, CNW offers the right tools for your communications.

The Canadian Press, 36 King St. E., Toronto, ON, M5C 2L9. Canada. Phone: (416) 364-3172. Fax: (416) 364-8896. Web Site:www.thecanadianpress.com E-mail: broadcast@thecanadianpress.com

Full wire & audio svcs (news agency), satellite delivery for radio program syndicators.

The Church of Jesus Christ of Latter-day Saints (Mormons), 50 East North Temple, Salt Lake City, UT, 84150. Phone: (801) 240-1000. E-mail: russelldg@chq.byu.edu Web Site:www.lds.org

Gordon Hinckley, pres; Donald G. Russell, media rel.

Offers free pub affrs, news & feature progmg for TV & radio; also guests for talk shows. Pub affrs progmg is not church-oriented.

Compu-Weather Inc., 2566 Rt. 52, Hopewell Junction, NY, 12533. Phone: (800) 284-7246. Fax: (845) 226-1918. E-mail: sales@compuweather.com Web Site:www.compuweather.com

Jeff Wimmer, pres.

Weather forecasts, features, info & actualities for TV & radio.

Congressional Quarterly Inc., 1255 22nd St. N.W., Washington, DC, 20037. Phone: (202) 419-8500. Fax: (202) 419-8760. E-mail: customerservice@cq.com Web Site:www.cq.com

Keith A. White, VP/gen mgr; David Rapp, editor.

Print & Web-based info products & svcs on govt, politics & current interest topics. Daily & wkly publications, reference books & newsletters.

Connecticut Weather Center Inc., 18 Woodside Ave., Danbury, CT, 06810-7123. Phone: (203) 730-2899. Fax: (203) 730-2839. E-mail: weatherlab@ctweather.com Web Site:www.ctweather.com

William Jacquemin, pres.

Weather forecasts for all media. Custom intros/outros/lives. Accurate forecasts. Barter or cash arrangement available.

Corus Radio Network, 700 W. Georgia St., Suite 2000, Vancouver, BC, V7Y 1K9. Canada. Phone: (604) 331-2830. Fax: (604) 331-2722. E-mail: akrueger@cknw.com Web Site:www.corusent.com

Allan Krueger, opns mgr; John P. Hayes, pres.

Live & pre-recorded info & entertainment program production & satellite delivery to rgnl & natl Canadian radio stns.

Dairyline Radio, 1843 Front St., Suite A, Lynden, WA, 98264. Phone: (360) 354-5596, EXT. 101. Fax: (360) 354-7517. E-mail: bbaker@dairyline.com Web Site:www.dairyline.com

Lee Mielke, pres; Bill Baker, mktg dir.

WilmingtonNC . DairyBusiness Communications, 7225 Wrightsville Ave, 204.

LyndenWA

Five minute & 9 1/2 minute Dairy Report- weekdays. Daily updates of news affecting the dairy industry.

Entertainment News Calendar, 13636 Ventura, Suite 303, Sherman Oaks, CA, 91423. Phone: (818) 990-5945. Fax: (818) 789-8047. Fax: (212) 563-3488. E-mail: editor@newscalendar.com Web Site:www.newscalendar.com

Evelyn Heyward, editor.

Sherman OaksCA . Hollywood News Calender, 15030 Ventura Blvd., Ste 742. Phone:

Daily entertainment news svc.

Fairchild Broadcast News, Box 535, Hewlett, NY, 11557. Phone: (212) 686-6850. Fax: (212) 686-7308. Web Site:www.fairchildgroup.com/news

Gathers & disseminates news around the world.

Feature Story News, 1730 Rhode Island Ave. N.W., Suite 405, Washington, DC, 20036. Phone: (202) 296-9012. Fax: (202) 296-9205. E-mail: markss@featurestory.com Web Site:www.featurestorynews.com

Simon Marks, pres.

OrlandoFL , 1103 Palmer St. Phone:

New YorkNY , 1133 Broadway, Suite 1420. Phone:

Ind supplier of radio & TV news to English-language bcstrs worldwide. Bureaus in Washington, Moscow, London, New York, Orlando & San Francisco.

Hollywood News Calendar, 13636 Ventura Blvd., #303, Sherman Oaks, CA, 91423. Phone: (818) 990-5945. Phone: (818) 986-8186. Fax: (818) 789-8047. E-mail: editor@newscalendar.com Web Site:www.newscalendar.com

Carolyn Fox, publisher.

New YorkNY . Entertainment News Calender, 250 W. 57th St, #1431. Phone:

Daily entertainment news svc. Publisher of Hollywood News Calendar in Los Angeles & Entertainment News Calendar in New York.

Israel Broadcasting Service, 800 Second Ave., New York, NY, 10017. Phone: (212) 499-5402.

Free radio & TV programs, features from & about Israel.

Medialink, 708 3rd Ave., 9th Fl., New York, NY, 10017. Phone: (212) 682-8300. Fax: (212) 682-5260. Web Site:www.medialink.com

Mary C. Buhhay, sr VP; Laurence Moskowitz, pres; Larry Thomas, COO.

London, 37/38 Golden Sq. Phone:

Los AngelesCA , 6430 Sunset Blvd, Suite 1100. Phone:

San FranciscoCA , One Maritime Plaza. Phone:

WashingtonDC , 1401 New York Ave. N.W, Suite 520. Phone:

AtlantaGA , 3340 Peachtree Rd. N.E, Suite 1520. Phone:

ChicagoIL , The Time & Life Bldg., 541 N. Fairbanks Ct., Suite 1910. Phone:

DallasTX , 4851 LBJ Fwy, Suite 605. Phone:

International video & audio PR, satellite feed & news advisory svc. Advisories accessible by computer/newswire in United States & Europe.

Metro Networks/Shadow Broadcast Services, a Westwood One Co., 2800 Post Oak, Suite 4000, Houston, TX, 77056. Phone: (713) 407-6000. Phone: (713) 407-6911. Fax: (713) 407-6849. Web Site:www.westwoodone.com

Chuck Bortnick, pres; Peter Kosann, pres/CEO.

Provider of traf reporting svcs & leading supplier of loc news, sports, weather & video news svcs to the TV & radio bcst industries.

Metro Weather Service Inc., 788 Franklin Ave., Valley Stream, NY, 11580. Phone: (516) 568-8844. Fax: (516) 568-8853.E-mail: metrowx@aol.com Web Site:www.metroweather.com

Pat Pagano, pres; Brettt Zueiback, mgr.

Tailored weather forecasts for radio & TV. Feature reports farming, marine, ski, long-range forecasts via phone, computer, fax, ISDN, MP3 & Skype.

NOAA/National Weather Service, 1325 East-West Hwy., Silver Spring, MD, 20910. Phone: (301) 713-0622. Fax: (301) 713-1292. Web Site:www.nws.noaa.gov

Jack F. Kelly, dir; Curtis Carey, pub affrs dir; George Hernandez, editor.

Weather & flood warnings, forecasts & related info for the media & general pub.

News Broadcast Network, 75 Broad St., 15th Fl., New York, NY, 10004. Phone: (212) 684-8910. Phone: (800) 920-6397. Fax: (212) 684-9650.E-mail: info@newbroadcastnetwork.com Web Site:www.newsbroadcastnetwork.com

Robert Hill, exec producer; Michael J. Hill, pres.

Washington Phone:

Los AngelesCA Phone:

ChicagoIL Phone:

SeattleWA Phone:

MilwaukeeWI Phone:

Production & distribution of electronic news releases, actualities & pub affrs programs distributed by satellite, telephone & tape.

Nielsen Entertainment News Wire, (formerly VNU Entertainment News Wire). 101 Federal St., Suite 600, Boston, MA, 02110. Phone: (617) 478-5500. Fax: (617) 478-5501. Web Site:www.vnuenw.com

Advance news from Nielsen owned publications.

North American Network, 5335 Wisconsin Ave. N.W., Washington, DC, 20015. Phone: (301) 654-9810. Fax: (301) 654-9828. Web Site:www.radiospace.com

Tom Sweeney, pres.

Audio news releases & talk show interviews. On-site coverage for corps, govt agencies & assns.

PA-SportsTicker, 989 6th Ave., 2nd Fl., New York, NY, 10018. Phone: (212) 738-5611. Fax: (212) 695-8560.E-mail: newsroom@sportsticker.com Web Site:www.pa-sportsticker.com

Jim Morganthaler, gen mgr; Jay Imus, sls dir.

BostonMA , Boston Fish Pier, West Bldg. #1, Suite 302. Phone:

New YorkNY , 19 E 34th St. Phone:

Provides 24-hr sports news, info, instant scores & complete sports news coverage on all professional & major college events.

Radio America, 1100 N. Glebe Rd., Suite 900, Arlington, VA, 22201. Phone: (703) 302-1000. Phone: (800) 807-4703. Fax: (571) 480-4140.E-mail: radio@radioamerica.org Web Site:www.radioamerica.org

Michael Paradiso, COO; Rich McFadden, news dir.

Short & long-form programs, special series, documentaries, daily one hr news show & conservative talk radio.

Radio Press News Services, 8633 Arbor Dr., El Cerrito, CA, 94530-2728. Phone: (510) 524-9559.E-mail: jag4jl@aol.com

Robert Miles Master, editor-in-chief.

Natl coverage, with special unit for northern California, Bay Area of California & adjacent states, photographer on staff. Multimedia news, Travellands & Vacationland. Special features, articles, transcriptions & video features. TV assignment accepted.

Radio Pulsebeat News, Box 418, Hewlett, NY, 11557. Phone: (212) 686-6850. Fax: (212) 686-7308.

Jay R. Levy, pres.

Gen actuality news svc.

RadioTour.com, 2233 Wisconsin Ave. N.W., Washington, DC, 20007. Phone: (202) 333-4904. Fax: (202) 342-5411.E-mail: expertclick@gmail.com Web Site:www.expertclick.com

Publisher of free Yearbook of Experts, Authorities & Spokespersons.

Reuters America Inc., 1333 H St. N.W., #500, Washington, DC, 20005. Phone: (202) 898-8300. Fax: (202) 898-8383. Web Site:www.reuters.com

Mitch Koppelman, VP.

The Reuter Broadcast Report & Reuter Broadcast PLUS, features natl & international news, sports, business news, entertainment & weather.

Skywatch Weather Center, 347 Prestley Rd., Bridgeville, PA, 15017. Phone: (800) SKY-WATCH. Fax: (412) 221-3160.E-mail: airsci@skywatchweather.com Web Site:www.skywatchweather.com

Dr.Stanley Penkala, pres.

Taped, live & MP3 weathercasts targeted to the listening area, in stn-specified formats. Featuring accuracy, clarity & mature voices.

The Sports Network, 2200 Byberry Rd., Hatboro, PA, 19040. Phone: (215) 441-8444. Fax: (215) 441-5767. Web Site:www.sportsnetwork.com E-mail: kzajac@sportshetwork.com

Mickey Charles, CEO; Ken Zajac, sls dir.

International real-time sports wire svc providing content, branded web pages, XML feeds directly to bcstrs (radio & TV), print, Internet sites, wireless with state of the art technology.

Studio M Productions, 4032 Wilshire Blvd., Ste 403, Los Angeles, CA, 90010. Phone: (213) 389-7372.E-mail: senator@sound4film-tv.com Web Site:www.sound4film-tv.com

Mike Michaels, owner.

HonoluluHI , 8715 Waikiki Stn. Phone:senator@sound4film -tv.com Web Site: www.sound4film-tv.com.

Stringers, crew news, sports, features, remote bcsts, engrs, announcers, reporters, equipment for radio, TV, film & video.

Texas State Networks, 4131 N. Central Expwy., Suite 500, Dallas, TX, 75204-2175. Phone: (214) 525-7400. Fax: (214) 525-7372.E-mail: tsnnews@cbs.com Web Site:www.tsnradio.com

Dan Bell, gen sls mgr; Brian Purdy, gen mgr .

AustinTX . Austin News Bureau, 502 E. 11th, Suite 320. Phone:

News svc of the Texas State Networks. Provides Texas news, sports, agriculture, business & weather, Texas Rangers Radio Network & special features & long form programs.

Trans World Communications Inc., Box 418, Hewlett, NY, 11557. Phone: (212) 686-6850. Fax: (212) 686-7308.

Jay Levy, VP.

Produces audio news svcs for radio & TV bcstg.

United Press International Inc., 1510 H St. N.W., Washington, DC, 20005. Phone: (202) 898-8000. Fax: (202) 898-8048.E-mail: editorforms@upi.com Web Site:www.upi.com

Nicholas Chiaia, COO; Christopher Ching, VP finance.

Full global text, audio, photo news , info svcs, morning drive progmg, world, natl news, sports, weather, features & financial reports 24 hours.

WINGS: Women's International News Gathering Service, Box 95090, Vancouver, BC, BC V5T 4T8. Canada. Phone: (604) 876-6994. Web Site:www.wings.org E-mail: wings@wings.org

Frieda Werden, producer.

AustinTX , Box 33220. Stacy Pettigrew, bureau mgr.

Syndicate audio news & current affrs program, both produced in-house & acquired, focus on women & hard news. Distribution CD, satellite, & FTP.

The Wall Street Journal Radio Network, 1155 Avenue of Americas, 8th Fl., New York, NY, 10017. Phone: (800) 828-6397. Phone: (212) 659-1208. Fax: (212) 659-1908.E-mail: wsjradio@dowjones.com Web Site:www.wsjradio.com

Nancy Abramson, exec dir.

Hourly business & financial news reports transmitted live via satellite 18 times daily from the Journal's New York newsroom. Dow Jones Money Report also transmitted 18 times daily.

"The Weather Center", (a broadcast service of Aviation Weather Inc.). 701 Gervais St., Suite 224, Columbia, SC, 29201. Phone: (803) 422-4823.E-mail: wxcenter@aviationweatherinc.com Web Site:www.aviationweatherinc.com

Liam Richard Ferguson, pres.

"Regional Radio Broadcast/Weathercast Network" across the Carolinas & Georgia in over 20 bcst markets. Weather forecasting, site-specific bcst svc for stns all across America. 100% barter.

Weather-One, (A wholly-owned division of Liberty Hill Broadcasting). 5829 West Maple Rd., Suite 115, West Bloomfield, MI, 48322. Phone: (248) 737-3000. Fax: (248) 737-3555.E-mail: bzate@imageteleproducts.com

Barry Zate, sr VP.

Provides weather forecasting svcs, advanced storm warnings, agricultural & ski info to radio stns.

WeatherData Inc., 245 N. Waco, Suite 310, Wichita, KS, 67202. Phone: (316) 265-9127. Fax: (316) 265-1949. Web Site:www.weatherdata.com E-mail: ceo@weatherdata.com

Mike Smith, CEO.

Weather radar, graphic & info display systems, training, on air forecast & storm warning svcs. Select Warn, Storm Hawk, 24/7 storm monitoring, & customer svc. Complete system integration & training.

Evan Weiner Productions, Box 1656, Mount Vernon, NY, 10552. Phone: (914) 667-9070. Phone: (203) 288-2597 (producer).E-mail: evan4256@aol.com Web Site:www.bickley.com/evan_weiner.html

Evan Weiner, exec producer.

Sports commentaries & reporting. Current program: The Business of Sports, commentaries on Metro Source.

Westwood One, Radio New Services. 40 W. 57th St., 5th Fl., New York, NY, 10019. Phone: (212) 641-2000. Fax: (212) 641-2185. Web Site:www.westwoodone.com

Rod Sherwood; Steven Kalin, COO Metro; Gary Schonfeld, pres net division.

Producer & distributor of radio progmg including CNN, NBC, Mutual, CNBC Business Radio, 24-hours music formats, long-short-form talk, music & news programs.

World Radio Network, Box 1212, London, SW8 2ZF. United Kingdom. Phone: 44-20-7896-9000. Fax: 44-20-7896-9007.E-mail: contactus@wrn.org Web Site:www.wrn.org

Karl Miosga, chmn; Jeff Cohen, dev dir; Tim Ashburner, tech dir.

World Radio Network (via Galaxy 25) news & features ch, comprising live progmg segments in English & languages from more than 20 international bcstrs. WRN can also supply many customized progmg feeds to radio stns as well as progmg distribution, satellite uplink & internet streaming.

TV-CATV-Radio.

Radio Format Providers

ABC Radio Networks, 13725 Montfort Dr., Dallas, TX, 75240. Phone: (972) 991-9200. Fax: (972) 448-3378. Web Site:www.abcradionetwork.com

James Robinson, pres; Julie Atherton, dir mktg.

Bcsts five full-service line nets, Paul Harvey News & Comment, ESPN Radio, long-form progmg, 24-hour formats, ABC News, ABC Sports, & d/wkly features.

Alternative Programming, 4215 Brendenwood Rd., Rockford, IL, 61107. Phone: (815) 229-3995. Fax: (815) 229-5043.E-mail: altprog@sbcglobal.net   Web Site:www.alternative-programming.com

Gary A. Knoll, owner.

Complete music formats for radio - current music for various formats - custom CD svc.

American Blues Network, Box 6216, Gulfport, MS, 39506. Phone: (800) 896-5307. Fax: (228) 896-5703.E-mail: info@americianbluesnetwork.com   Web Site:www.americanbluesnetwork.com

Stan Daniels, CEO.

The only 24-hour blues syndication.

American Comedy Network & Onion Radio News, 91 River St., Milford, CT, 06460. Phone: (203) 877-8210. Fax: (203) 877-8242.E-mail: acn@americancomedynetwork.com Web Site:www.americancomedynetwork.com

Adrienne Munos, sls; Kurt Luchs, gen mgr; Ben Churchill, producer.

Comedy svc providing daily topical audio sound bites, song parodies, fake comls. Comedy CD, e-mail prep & gold library. Onion Radio News 10 features every week via web and more.

Toby Arnold & Associates, 3234 Commander Dr., Carrollton, TX, 75006. Phone: (972) 661-8201. Phone: (800) 527-5335. Fax: (972) 250-6014.E-mail: toby@taamusic.com Web Site:www.taamusic.com

Toby Arnold, pres/CEO; Dolly Arnold, VP, COO; Lawrence Mangiameli, VP, dir.

Audio Production libraries for radio. Station Imaging, Morning show promo sweeper, stager packages for all formats. Cash or Barter.

Beethoven Satellite Network, (BSN Around the Clock). 5400 N. St. Louis Ave., Chicago, IL, 60625. Phone: (773) 279-2112. Fax: (773) 279-2199.E-mail: cmartinez@wfmt.com Web Site:www.wfmt.com

Steve Robinson, VP; Terry Medina, dir syndication.

Satellite-delivered classical music format svc 12-hours overnight serving over 300 outlets nationwide. Produced by WFMT-FM Chicago. Since 1986.

Satellite: Galaxy 6, Digital frequency B72.4.

CBS Radio Networks, 524 West 57th St., New York, NY, 10019. Phone: (212) 975-2044. Fax: (212) 974-0615.E-mail: barobinson@cbs.com Web Site:www.westwoodone.com

Beth Robinson, VP progmg; Peter Kosann, pres/CEO; Andrew Zaref, CFO.

This division currently offers NFL Football, NCAA Basketball & College Football. Also syndicates *David Letterman's Top Ten List*.

CRN International Inc., One Circular Ave., Hamden, CT, 06514. Phone: (203) 288-2002. Fax: (203) 281-3291.E-mail: info@crnradio.com Web Site:www.crnradio.com

Barry Berman, pres; S. Richard Kalt, exec VP; Patrick Kane, sr VP; Doug Harris, dir.

Features include *Ski Watch®*, a 60-second, daily ski conditions update. Summer-oriented progmg includes *Beach Watch® & Summer Watch.®* Small business programs include the *Small Business Report & Small Business Profile*. All programs available on a barter basis.

The Classical Station, WCPE, Box 897, Wake Forest, NC, 27588. Phone: (919) 556-5178. Fax: (919) 556-9273.E-mail: wcpe@wcpe.org   Web Site:theclassicalstation.org

Deborah Proctor, gen mgr; Dick Storck, progmg dir; Rae Weaver, dev dir; Curtis Brothers, outreach dir; Peter Blume, business dev dir.

Free 24-hour classical music progmg with live announcers for radio, cable, other distributors. Wkly request programs, opera & features.

Creative Radio Network, Box 7749, Thousand Oaks, CA, 91359. Phone: (818) 991-3892. Fax: (818) 991-3894.

Darwin Lamm, pres/CEO.

Radio music program for A/C—country & modern. Elvis international forum magazine.

Dialogue, One Woodrow Wilson Plaza, 1300 Pennsylvania Ave., N.W., Washington, DC, 20004-3027. Phone: (202) 691-4146. Fax: (202) 691-4141.E-mail: dialogue@wwic.si.edu Web Site:www.wilsoncenter.org/dialogue

George Liston Seay, exec producer.

Wkly half-hour program of conversations on natl, internatl affrs, history & culture. Available to pub & coml stns free of charge on CD. Progmg produced by the Woodrow Wilson International Center for Scholars.

Eagle Media Productions Ltd., Box 580, Northford, CT, 06472. Phone: (203) 294-1190. Fax: (203) 294-9512.E-mail: lou.adler@sbcglobal.net Web Site:www.louadler.com

Louis Adler, pres; Thalia Adler, VP.

Offers *Medical Journal*, 90-second feature-barter; CD delivery.

Excelsior Radio Networks, 220 W. 42nd St., New York, NY, 10036-7202. Phone: (212) 419-2929. Fax: (212) 681-1952.E-mail: robscolaro@aol.com Web Site:www.exradio.com

Michael R. Ewing, pres/COO; Jonathan Goldman, exec VP.

Las VegasNV , 1445 E. Tropicana Ave. Phil Hall, gen mgr.

Sports talk 24-hours a day. Sports analysis & commentary on AOL & the internet.

Executive Broadcast Services, 30 Mobray Ct., Colorado Springs, CO, 80906. Phone: (719) 579-6676. Fax: (719) 579-6664.E-mail: skip@executivebroadcast.com

Skip Joeckel, pres.

Markets & sells a select line of programs, products & svcs to U.S. radio stns.

Fischer Broadcast Services, 10841 Bittersweet Lane, Fishers, IN, 46038-2203. Phone: (317) 514-5757. Fax: (317) 578-3884.E-mail: superfisch@midspring.com Web Site:www.superfisch.com

Scott Fischer, pres.

SUPERFISCH—VOICE IMAGING & BRANDING. Scott Fischer voice artist for radio & TV loc, cable, Netw. Promax & Emmy award voice. A versitile-VO-value! Yes you CAN afford me-can you afford not to check me out?

Ghostwriters/Radio Mall, 2412 Unity Ave. N., Dept BCY, Minneapolis, MN, 55422-3450. Phone: (800) 759-4561. Fax: (763) 522-6256.E-mail: info@radio-mall.com Web Site:www.radiomall.com

David Dworkin, owner.

Over 23 years experience with products sold to more than 7,300 radio stns worldwide as well as TV stns, audio-video producers & cable operators. If you have a product that you'd like to mkt to radio or TV stns, contact us.

Hispanic Communications Network, 1126 16th St., N.W., Suite 350, Washington, DC, 20036. Phone: (202) 637-8800. Fax: (202) 637-8801.E-mail: info@hcnmedia.com Web Site:www.hcnmedia.org

Jeff Kline, chmn/CEO.

Produces six daily Spanish radio programs & distributes them to Hispanic Radio net affiliates.

J.N. Productions, 902-1790 Bayshore Dr., Vancouver, BC, V6G 3G5. Canada. Phone: 604-331-0690.E-mail: jnproductions@telus.net Web Site:www.jnproductions.bc.ca

Jakob Nortman, pres.

For all your voice-over needs, including narration, corporate videos, on-hold telephone messages & announcements for GPS systems. Radio production facilities available.

Jameson Broadcast Inc., 1644 Hawthorne St., Sarasota, FL, 34239. Phone: (941) 906-8800.E-mail: jamie@jamesonbcast.com   Web Site:www.jamesonbroadcast.com/radio

Specializes in short-form entertainment, info programs & promotions.

Launch Radio Networks, (a division of United Stations Radio Network). 1065 Ave. of the Americas, 3rd Fl., New York, NY, 10018. Phone: (212) 536-3600. Fax: (212) 536-3601. Web Site:www.launchradionetworks.com E-mail: ccolombo@launchradionetworks.com

Dave Ankers, VP/gen mgr; Judy Rosen, dir opns.

Launch Radio Networks produces, distributes music, entertainment news & svcs for radio stns as well as other media worldwide.

MRN Radio (Motor Racing Network), 555 MRN Dr., Concord, NC, 28027. Phone: (704) 262-6700. Fax: (704) 262-6811. Web Site:www.mrnradio.com

David Hyatt, pres; Cheryl Knight, dir.

Live bcsts of NASCAR stock car racing & related programs via satellite.

J J McKay Productions Inc., 800 Pennsylvania St., Suite 305, Denver, CO, 80203. Phone: (303) 880-6926. Web Site:www.jjmckay.com

J.J. McKay, pres.

Maximum-impact production & versatile voice-over talent. All formats. Choose the voice for today AND tomorrow! Delivered via analog tape, DAT, ISDN/Zephyr, MP3, DCI.

Miller Broadcast Management, 616 W. Fulton St., Suite 516, Chicago, IL, 60661. Phone: (312) 454-1111. Fax: (312) 454-0044. Web Site:info@millerbroadcast.com

Lisa Miller, pres; Matt Miller, VP.

Musical Starstreams, Box 12685, LaJolla, CA, 92039-2685. Phone: (619) 276-8989.E-mail: info@starstreams.com Web Site:www.starstreams.com

Musical Starstreams is a wkly two-hour program of "exotic electronica" targeted to adults age 25-54.

Orange Productions, 523 Righters Ferry Rd., 1st Fl., Bala Cynwyd, PA, 19004. Phone: (610) 667-8620. Fax: (610) 667-8939.E-mail: orange@snip.net Web Site:www.soundsofsinatra.com

Sid Mark, pres; Jon Harmelin, VP/gen mgr.

Production & distribution of a wkly two-hour program *Sounds of Sinatra*.

Premiere Radio Networks Inc., 15260 Ventura Blvd., 4th Fl., Sherman Oaks, CA, 91403-5339. Phone: (818) 377-5300. Fax: (818) 377-5333.E-mail: webmaster@premradio.com Web Site:www.premrad.com

Kraig T. Kitchin, pres/COO.

Sherman OaksCA , 15260 Ventura Blvd., 5th Fl. Phone: AtlantaGA , 3405 Piedmont Rd, Suite 500. Phone: ChicagoIL , 875 N. Michigan Ave, Suite 1450. Phone: Royal OakMI , 306 S. Washington Ave, Suite 214. New YorkNY , 1270 Ave. of the Americas. Phone: DallasTX , 14001 N. Dallas Pkwy, Suite 500. Phone: Premiere Radio features the following personalities: Rush Limbaugh, Delilah Ryan Seacrest, Steve Harvey, Jim Rome, Glenn Beck, Ty Pennington, Blair Garner, Whoopi Goldberg, Dr. Laura Schlessinger, Maria Bartiromo, George Noory, Casey Kasem, Ben & Brian, Bill Handel, Bob (Kevoian) & Tom (Griswold), Jeff Foxworthy, Jay Leno, Hohn Boy & Billy, T.D. Jakes, Matt Drudge, Big Tigger, Art Bell, Big D & Bubba, & Dr. Dean Edell.

RPM Radio Programming and Management Inc., 1133 West Long Lake Rd., Bloomfield Hills, MI, 48302. Phone: (800) 521-2537. Phone: (248) 647-1068. Fax: (248) 647-3936. Fax: (888) 776-0006.E-mail: info@tophitsusa.com Web Site:www.tophitsusa.com

Thomas M. Krikorian, pres.

Top Hits USA wkly CD svc & CD libraries including Solid Gold, Spectrum A/C & Country One. Classic rock, CD Christmas library.

Radio Center for People with Disabilities (RCPD), 230 E. Ohio St., Suite 101, Chicago, IL, 60611. Phone: (312) 640-5000. Fax: (312) 640-5010.E-mail: rc4pd@aol.com Web Site:www.rcpd.org

Brad Saul, CEO.

PCPD is a non-profit agency founded to recruit, train & place people with disabilities in paying, off-air jobs in the radio business.

Radio Express Inc., 1415 W. Magnolia Blvd., Suite 201, Burbank, CA, 91506. Phone: (818) 295-5800. Fax: (818) 295-5801.E-mail: radioinfo@radioexpress.com Web Site:www.radioexpress.com

Tom Rounds, CEO; John Fleck, pres.

Distributors outside the United States: *The World Chart Show, Rick Dees Weekly Top 40, Country Countdown, Hot Mix, Hitdisc, Golddisc, Supercharger Production tool kit & Production libraries by firstcom music*. Programs available by cash or barter, libraries & products cash only.

Radio Spirits, Box 3107, Wallingford, CT, 06492. Phone: (203) 265-8044. Web Site:www.radiospirits.com

Hakan Lindskog, pres.

Radio producers of the nationally-syndicated old time radio program *When Radio Was*. Complete digital recording studio features Sonic Solutions Digital Work Station with No-Noise.

SFX Radio Network, Clear Channel Entertainment, 220 W. 42nd St., New York, NY, 10036. Phone: (917) 421-4000. Web Site:www.sfxnet.com

Offers both wkly & mthy shows featuring classic rock, country, urban contemp & live concerts in addition to stn prep svcs.

Salem Music Network Inc., (A division of Salem Music Networks/Salem Radio Network). 402 BNA Dr., Suite 400, Nashville, TN, 37217. Phone: (615) 367-2210. Fax: (615) 367-0758.E-mail: info@salemmusicnetwork.com Web Site:www.salemmusicnetwork.com

Michael S. Miller, gen mgr .

Provider of three different 24-hour Christian music formats via digital satellite to 230 plus radio stns throughout the US, Canada & operator of two greater Nashville (TN) radio stns.

Sheridan Broadcasting Corp., 960 Penn Ave., Suite 200, Pittsburgh, PA, 15222. Phone: (412) 456-4008. Phone: (800) 456-4211. Fax: (412) 456-4040 (progmg). Fax: (412) 457-4077 (admin).

Ronald Davenport, chmn..

Provides hourly news & sports, longform talk & mus progmg as well as *USA Music Magazine*. Other alternative progmg includes *Coming Soon* movie review, *Straight Up* with Bev Smith & *White House Report* with White House correspondent April Ryan.

Sirius Satellite Radio, 1221 Ave. of the Americas, 36th Fl., New York, NY, 10020. Phone: (212) 584-5100. Fax: (212) 584-5200.E-mail: rshnall@siriusradio.com Web Site:www.sirius.com

Rebecca Schnall, media rel.

Southcott Productions, Box 33185, Granada Hills, CA, 91394. Phone: (818) 368-4938. Fax: (818) 368-4938.E-mail: chucksongs@aol.com Web Site:www.chucksouthcott.com

Chuck Southcott, owner.

North HollywoodCA , 4605 Lankershim Blvd, Suite 702. Phone:

Adult pop standards format-This Is Music & Holiday Magic to cover all American holidays.

TM Century Inc., 2002 Academy, Dallas, TX, 75234. Phone: (972) 406-6800. Fax: (972) 406-6890.E-mail: tmci@tmcentury.com Web Site:www.tmcentury.com

David Graupner, pres/CEO; Eve Mayer Orsburn, VP Sales & Marketing; Erik Hastings, exec producer.

GoldDisc music libraries, HitDisc wkly mus svc, music on hard drive, jingles, mus libraries production, special programs, CD-ROM.

Talkline Communications Network, Box 20108, Park West Station, New York, NY, 10025-1510. Phone: (212) 769-1925. Fax: (212) 799-4195.E-mail: tcntalk@aol.com Web Site:www.talkline communication.com

Zev J. Brenner, pres.

National Jewish radio net featuring news, interviews with newsmaker guests & celebrities; live call-in format; live segments from Israel; satellite delivered. Available on barter.

United Press International, 1510 H St. N.W., Washington, DC, 20005. Phone: (202) 898-8111. Phone: (202) 898-8100. Fax: (202) 898-8057.E-mail: editorforms@upi.com Web Site:www.upi.com

Tobin C. Beck, news dir; Michael Marshall, editor.

Full-svc company offers a number of short-form info features to its affil radio stns.

Virtual Radio, 4521 Campus Dr., Suite 579, Irvine, CA, 92612. Phone: (800) 601-6923.E-mail: joel@virtualradio.com Web Site:www.vradio.com

Joel Easton, mgng dir.

Virtual Radio is the oldest music website providing a new radio format, content & internet expertise to bcstrs world wide.

WFMT Fine Arts Radio, 5400 N. St. Louis Ave., Chicago, IL, 60625. Phone: (773) 279-2000. Fax: (773) 279-2199.E-mail: guide@networkchicago.com Web Site:www.wfmt.com

Daniel Schmidt, pres/CEO; Peter Whorf, progmg dir.

Classical, opera & folk mus, news & fine art progmg 24-hours per day through United Video Inc. Serving 200 cable systems in 30 states with 850,000 subs.

"The Weather Center", (a broadcast service of Aviation Weather Inc.). 701 Gervais St., Suite 224, Columbia, SC, 29201. Phone: (803) 422-4823.E-mail: wxcenter@aviationweatherinc.com Web Site:www.aviationweatherinc.com

Liam Richard Ferguson, pres.

"Regional Radio Broadcast/Weathercast Network" across the Carolinas & Georgia in over 20 bcst markets. Weather forecasting, site-specific bcst svc for stns all across America. 100% barter.

Westwood One, Radio New Services. 40 W. 57th St., 5th Fl., New York, NY, 10019. Phone: (212) 641-2000. Fax: (212) 641-2185. Web Site:www.westwoodone.com

Rod Sherwood; Steven Kalin, COO Metro; Gary Schonfeld, pres net division.

Producer & distributor of radio progmg including CNN, NBC, Mutual, CNBC Business Radio, 24-hours music formats, long-short-form talk, music & news programs.

World Radio Network, Box 1212, London, SW8 2ZF. United Kingdom. Phone: 44-20-7896-9000. Fax: 44-20-7896-9007.E-mail: contactus@wrn.org Web Site:www.wrn.org

Karl Miosga, chmn; Jeff Cohen, dev dir; Tim Ashburner, tech dir.

World Radio Network (via Galaxy 25) news & features ch, comprising live progmg segments in English & languages from more than 20 international bcstrs. WRN can also supply many customized progmg feeds to radio stns as well as progmg distribution, satellite uplink & internet streaming.

Music Licensing

APM Music, 6255 Sunset Blvd., Suite 820, Hollywood, CA, 90028. Phone: (323) 461-3211. Fax: (323) 461-9102. E-mail: accountservices@apmmusic.com Web Site:www.apmmusic.com

Sharon Jennings, dir mktg; Adam Taylor, pres; George Mecias, VP sls.

New YorkNY , 381 Park Ave. S., Suite 1101. Phone:

Sixteen libraries: KPM, Bruton, Sonoton, Carlin, Castle, NFL. Over 3,000 CDs, personalized packages, music search, 15-20 new CD releases mthy.

American Society of Composers, Authors & Publishers (ASCAP), One Lincoln Plaza, New York, NY, 10023. Phone: (212) 621-6000. Fax: (212) 724-9064. E-mail: info@ascap.com Web Site:www.ascap.com

Marilyn Bergman, chmn/pres; Lauren Lossa, VP mktg.

London. ASCAP - London, 8 Cork St. Phone:

Los AngelesCA . ASCAP - Los Angeles, 7920 W. Sunset Blvd., 3rd Fl. Phone:

Miami BeachFL . ASCAP - Miami, 420 Lincoln Rd, Suite 385. Phone:

AtlantaGA . ASCAP - Atlanta, PMB 400, 541 Tenth St. N.W. Phone:

ChicagoIL . ASCAP - Midwest, 1608 N. Milwaukee Ave, Suite 1007. Phone:

NashvilleTN . ASCAP - Nashville, 2 Music Sq. W. Phone:

A membership assn of more than 275,000 composers, lyricists, & music publishers, ASCAP licenses the pub performances of its members' works. ASCAP has reciprocal agreements with foreign societies representing virtually every country that has laws protecting copyright.

BMI-Broadcast Music Inc., 320 W. 57th St., New York, NY, 10019. Phone: (212) 586-2000. Fax: (212) 582-5972. Web Site:www.bmi.com

Del Bryant, pres/CEO; John E. Cody, COO.

MiamiFL , 1691 Michigan Ave., Suite 350. Phone:

AtlantaGA , Tower Pl. 100, 3340 Peachtree Rd. N.E., Suite 570. Phone:

Hato ReyPR , Bank Trust Plaza, 255 Ponce de leon Ave, East Wing, Suite A-262. Phone:

LondonNO United Kingdom, 84 Harley House, Marlebone Rd. Phone:

Los AngelesCA , 8730 Sunset Blvd. Phone:

NashvilleTN , 10 Music Sq. E. Phone:

Licenses the pub performance rights of musical compositions for more than 300,000 songwriters, composers & music publishers; maintains reciprocal arrangements with more than 40 licensing organizations worldwide.

European American Music Distributors L.L.C., 254 W. 31st St., 15th Fl., New York, NY, 10000. Phone: (212) 461-6940. Fax: (212) 810-4565. E-mail: info@eamdllc.com Web Site:www.eamdllc.com

Jim Kendrick, pres.

Music publisher & distributor.

The Harry Fox Agency Inc., 601 W. 26th St., Suite 500, New York, NY, 10001. Phone: (212) 834-0186. Phone: (212) 834-0100. Fax: (646) 487-6779. Web Site:www.harryfox.com E-mail: press@harryfox.com

Music licensing.

SESAC Inc., 55 Music Sq. E., Nashville, TN, 37203. Phone: (615) 320-0055. Fax: (615) 329-9627. E-mail: dhoughton@sesac.com Web Site:www.sesac.com

Santa MonicaCA , 501 Santa Monica Blvd., Suite 450.

Phone:

MiamiFL , 420 Lincoln Rd., Suite 502. Phone:

AtlantaGA , 981 Joseph E. Lowery Blvd. N.W., Suite 11. Phone:

London United Kingdom, 67 Upper Berkeley St.

New YorkNY , 152 W. 57th St., 57th Fl. Phone:

Performing rights organization representing a diversity of copyrighted music.

Society of Composers, Authors & Music Publishers of Canada (SOCAN), Societe Canadienne des auteurs, compositeurs et editeurs de musique. 41 Valleybrook Dr., Toronto, ON, M3B 2S6. Canada. Phone: (416) 445-8700. Phone: (866) 307-6226. Fax: (416) 445-7108. E-mail: socan@socan.ca Web Site:www.socan.ca

Dartmouth, Queen Sq., 45 Alderney Dr., Suite 802. Phone:

Edmonton, 1145 Weber Centre, 5555 Calgary Tr. Phone:

Montreal, 600, boul. de Maisonneuve Ouest, Bureau 500. Phone:

Vancouver, 1201 W. Pender St, Suite 400. Phone:

SOCAN licenses the public performance of music in Canada & distributes performance royalties to copyright holders worldwide.

Warner Bros. Publications, 15800 N.W. 48th Ave., Miami, FL, 33014. Phone: (305) 620-1500. Web Site:www.warnerbros.com

Full-line music publishers of popular, standard & educ music as well as instructional videos from influential musicians. International market.

Canadian Broadcast Networks

Astral Television Networks Inc.

Head Office: Brookfield Place 181 Bay St., PO Box 787, Suite 100, Toronto, ON M5J 2T3. (English) (416) 956-2010. Fax: (416) 956-2018. Web site: www.astralmedia.com.

Television Division (French): 2100 rue Sainte-Catherine Ouest, Bureau 900, Montreal, PQ H3H 2T3. (514) 939-5090. Fax: (514) 939-5098.

Management: John Riley, pres; Domenic Vivolo, sr VP sls/mktg; Kevin Wright, sr VP progmg; Deborah Wilson, VP communications; Roopa Shah, communications mgr; Chris Bell, VP technology; John Pow, VP finance admin; Kim Crter, VP human resources; Megan O'Neal, dir business/legal affrs; Alicia Barin, VP strategic planning; Mark Waschulzik, dir affil mktg.

Television: Pay Television: The Movie Network, Super Ecran, Mpix, cinepop, Viewer's Choice; Speciality Television: Family, Playhouse Disney, Canal Vie, VRAK.TV, Ztele, Canal D, Historia, Series, Musique Plus, TELETOON, TELETOON Retro.

CTV Inc.

CTV Head Office: Box 9, Station, Scarborough, ON, Canada M4A 2M9. (416) 332-5000. Fax: (416) 332-5022. Web site: www.ctv.ca.

CTV Executives: Ivan Fecan, CEO; Rick Brace, pres/revenue, business planning and sports; Susanne Boyce, pres/creative, content and ch. **Ownership:** CTVglobemedia Inc., 9 Channel Nine Court, Scarborough, Ontario, Canada M1S 4B5. (416) 332-5000. Fax: (416) 332-4346. Web site: www.ctvglobemedia.com.

CTVglobemedia Sales Centre

Ontario, CTV Inc., 9 Channel Nine Court, Scarborough, Ontario, Canada M1S 4B5. (416) 323-4311. Fax: (416) 332-4533.

CTVglobemedia Management: Rita Fabian, exec VP/sls and mktg, (contact); Ivan Fecan, pres/CEO; Robin Fillingham, CFO; Joe Carter, sr VP, CTV Specialty Television Sales; Andre Serero, exec VP business, legal affrs/corporate sec; Dawn Fell, exec VP human resources/ opns; Paul Sparkes, exec VP/corporate affrs.

Canadian Broadcasting Corp.

The Canadian Broadcasting Corp. (CBC) is a publicly owned corporation established by the Broadcasting Act (1936) of the Canadian Parliament to provide the natl bcstg svc in Canada in the two official languages English and French. Under this legislation, the CBC is subject to regulations of the Canadian Radio-Television & Telecommunications Commission (CRTC).

Program Services: The progmg on CBC networks is nearly all Canadian and virtually free of coml adv. Newsworld is a 24-hour natl satellite to cable English-language news & info svc. Le Réseau de l'information (RDI) is a 24-hour natl satellite-to-cable French-language news & info svc. The heart of CBC's natl distribution system is Canada's Anik E2 satellite, carrying progmg through six different time zones.

Head Office: 181 Queen Street, Box 3220, Station C, Ottawa, ON K1P 1K9. (613) 288-6000. TDD: (613) 288-6455. E-mail: liaison@cbl.ca.

CBC Management: Hubert T. Lacroix, pres/CEO; Alex Allard, co-pres, CBC Television; Timothy Casgrain, C.M.-chmn/bd of dir/Toronto, Ontario; Bernd Christmas, CEO/Membertou Band, Membertou, Nova Scotia; Richard Stursberg, exec VP, CBC Television; Johanne Charbonneau, VP/CFO; Raymond Carnovale, VP/chief technology officer; Michel Tremblay, VP, strategy/business dev; William Chambers, VP/communications; Michel Saint-Cyr, pres/real estate division; Pierre Nollet, VP, gen counsel/corporate sec; George Smith, sr VP, human resources/organization.

CBC Ombudsman: Julie Miville-Dechene, French svcs; Vince Carlin and William Morgan, English svcs.

CBC Ombudsman: English svcs, Canadian Broadcasting Corporation, Box 500, Station A, Toronto, ON M5W 1E6; E-mail: ombudsman@ca. Web Site: www.cbc.ca/obudsman. Renaud Gilbert, French svcs, 1400 Rene-Levesque Boulevard East, Box 6000, Montreal, PQ H3C 3A8; E-mail: ombudsmanradio-canada.ca. Web Site: www.radio-canada-ca/obudsman.

English Services: 250 Front Street West, Box 500, Station A, Toronto, ON M5W 1E6. (416) 205-3311. TDD: (416) 205-6688; E-mail: cbcinput@cbl.ca.

French Services: 1400 Rene-Levesque Boulevard East, Box 6000, Montreal, PQ H3C 3A8. (514) 597-6000. TDD: (514) 597-6013; E-mail: auditoireradio-canada.ca.

Newfoundland Region (English svcs): Radio bldg.: 25 Henry Street, Television bldg.: 95 University Ave., Box 12010, Station A, St. John's, NF A1B 3T8. (709) 576-5000.

Maritime Region (English svcs): Radio bldg.: 5600 Sackville Street, Television bldg.: 1840 Bell Street, Box 3000, Halifax, NS B3J 3E9. (902) 420-8311.

Atlantic Provinces (French svcs): 250 Universite Ave., Box 950, Moncton, NB E1C 8N8. (506) 853-6666.

Quebec Region (English svcs): 1400 Rene-Levesque Boulevard East, Box 6000, Montreal, PQ H3C 3A8. (514) 597-6000.

Quebec City & Eastern Quebec Region (French svcs): 888 St-Jean Street, Box 18800, QC City, QC G1K 9L4. (418) 654-1341.

Ontario Region (English svcs): 250 Front Street West, Box 500, Station A, Toronto, ON M5W 1E6. (416) 205-3311. TDD: (866) 220-6045.

Ontario Region (French svcs): 181 Queen Street, Box 3220, Station C, Ottawa, ON K1P 1K9. (613) 724-1200. TDD: (613) 288-6455.

Manitoba Region (English & French svcs): 541 Portage Ave., Box 160, Winnipeg, MB R3C 2H1. (204) 788-3222.

Saskatchewan Region (English & French svcs): 2440 Broad Street, Box 540, Regina, SK S4P 4A1. (306) 347-9540.

Alberta Region (English & French svcs): 10062-102nd Ave., Room 123, Edmonton City Centre, Box 555, Edmonton, AB T5J 2P4. (780) 468-7500.

British Columbia Region (English & French svcs): Box 4600, Vancouver, BC V6B 4A2. (604) 662-6000.

CBC North: 5129 49th Street, Box 160, Yellowknife, NT X1A 1P8. (867) 920-5400.

Global Television Network

Head Office: 81 Barber Greene Rd., Toronto, ON M3C 2A2. (416) 446-5311. Fax: (416) 446-5449. Web site: www.canada.com/globaltv.com.

CanWest Global Executive Management: Leonard Asper, CEO; Kathleen Dore, pres; CanWest Broadcasting; Steve Wyatt, sr VP/news and info; Barbara Williams, exec VP/content; Walter Levitt, chief mktg officer.

TVA

Head Office: Groupe TVA Inc., 1600 de Maisonneuve Boulevard. E., Montreal, PQ H2L 4P2. (514) 526-2951; Fax: (514) 598-6086. Web site: www.tva.ca.

Executive: Pierre Dion, pres/CEO.

TVA Owned: CFTM-Montreal; CFCM-Quebec City; CHLT-Sherbrooke; CHEM-Trois-Rivieres; CFER-Rimouski; CJPM-Saguenay.

Regional Affiliates: CHAU-Carleton; CIMT-Riviere-du-Loup; CFEM-Rouyn; CHOT-Gatineau.

Television Quatre Saisons

Head Office: Corp Owner: TQS Inc., 612 rue Saint-Jacques, Montreal, PQ H3C 5R1. (514) 390-6035. Web site: www.tqs.ca.

Board of Directors: Louis V. Audet, chmn of bd; Andre Brousseau, chmn/audit committee; Alain Gourd (presiding) the human resources strategic. **Principal Officers:** Jean Rodrigue, (acting) gen mgr; Michel Cloutier, dir/gen, Sherbrooke /Trois-Rivieres; Claude Deraiche, dir/gen communications; Renaud Francoeur, dir/gen, Quebec; Martin Gagnon, dir/gen, Saguenay; Bernard Guerin, dirgen/legal affrs; Robert Montour, dir/gen progmg; Luica Quenneville, dir gen/dev and acquistitions.

Affiliates Television Stations: CFJP Montreal, PQ; CFAP Quebec City, PQ; CFRS Saguenay, PQ; CFKS Sherbrooke, PQ; CFKM Trois Rivieres.

Canadian Cable Networks

ARTV, 1400 boul. Rene-Levesque Est, Bureau A-53-1, Montreal, PQ, H2L 2M2. Canada. Phone: (514) 597-3636. Fax: (514) 597-3633. Web Site:www.artv.ca Marie Cote, gen mgr; Jacinthe Brisebois, production mgr; Catherine Dupont, opns mgr; Luc Leblanc, artistic dir; Gilbert Morin, comptroller; Gilles Desjardins, head, distribution; Marc Pichette, head, communications.

ARTV is a French-language channel dedicated entirely to arts and culture. Twenty-four hours a day of great performances, films, documentaries, dramas & design. The pleasure of capturing the art and culture of Quebec, Canada & the whole world.

Aboriginal Peoples Television Network, 339 Portage Ave., Winnipeg, MB, R3B 2C3. Canada. Phone: (204) 947-9331. Fax: (204) 947-9307.E-mail: info@aptn.ca Web Site:www.aptn.ca Jean LaRose, CEO.

Alliance Broadcasting, (dba Showcase TV & History TV). 121 Bloor St. E., Toronto, ON, M4W 3M5. Canada. Phone: (416) 967-1174. Fax: (416) 960-0971. Web Site:www.allianceatlantis.com Phyllis Yaffe, pres/CEO.

Best of Canadian & international TV series & movies. Serving 5 million subs on 100 cable systems. Satellite: ANIK-E2.

Atlantic Satellite Network (ASN), 2885 Robie St., Halifax, NS, B3K 5Z4. Canada. Phone: (902) 453-4000. Fax: (902) 454-3302.E-mail: bt@ctv.ca Web Site:www.ctv.ca Rich Marchand, gen sls mgr; L. Wartman, opns dir.

Movies & news, educ programs weekend mornings. Serves 51 cable systems. Satellite: Anik C-1.

BookTelevision: The Channel, 299 Queen St. W., Toronto, ON, M5V 2Z5. Canada. Phone: (416) 591-5757.E-mail: info@booktelevision.com Web Site:www.booktelevision.com

BookTelevision: The Channel spotlights all the writing that informs & entertains us in our daily lives.

Bravo!, 299 Queen St. W., Toronto, ON, M5V 2Z5. Canada. Phone: (416) 591-5757. Fax: (416) 591-8497.E-mail: bravomail@bravo.ca Web Site:www.bravo.ca

Bravo! NewStyle Arts Channel is dedicated to entertaining, stimulating & enlightening veiwers who have a taste for more complex TV. Bravo! delivers a wide array of fine arts progmg, balancing longer-form structured shows & shorter pieces that appear in a more random way as "flow" to create a fluid mix of distinctive music, dance, opera, drama, literature, cinema, visual art, the art of TV & the art of talk. Serving 5.8 million subs on 700 cable systems.

CBC Newsworld, Box 500, Station A, Toronto, ON, M5W 1E6. Canada. Phone: (416) 205-2409. Fax: (416) 205-8684. Web Site:www.newsworld.com E-mail: maria_mirowicz@cbc.ca Maria Mirowicz, program dir.

Live 24-hours news & info net on basic cable, satellite & wireless in Canada.

On 1500 cable systems serving 8 million subs. Satellite: Anik E2 (Ku-band).

CPAC-Cable Public Affairs Channel, (A subsidiary of Consortium of Canadian Cable Companies). 1750-45 O'Connor St., Ottawa, ON, K1P 1A4. Canada. Phone: (613) 567-2722. Fax: (613) 567-2741.E-mail: comments@cpac.ca Web Site:www.cpac.ca

Uncut, unfiltered coverage of Canadian pub affrs issues including LIVE bcsts of the House of Commons & its Standing Committees. Serving 7.2 million subs.

CTV News Channel, Box 9, Station "O", Toronto, ON, M4A 2M9. Canada. Phone: (416) 332-5000. Fax: (416) 291-5337.E-mail: news@ctv.ca Web Site:www.ctv.ca Jana Juginovic, progmg dir & news dir.

Continually updated headline news, business, sports, weather & entertainment, every 15 minutes.

Canadian Satellite Communications Inc. (CANCOM), 2055 Flavelle Blvd., Mississauga, ON, L5K 1Z8. Canada. Phone: (905) 403-2020. Fax: (905) 403-2022. Web Site:www.cancom.ca Don Fletcher, VP.

Expert in evaluating, selecting, integrating & implementing satellite-based solutions for business. Cancom operates in four main lines of business: broadcast solutions, tracking solutions, learning solutions & data solutions.

Le Canal Nouvelles, 1600 boul. de Maisonneuve est, Montreal, PQ, H2L 4P2. Canada. Phone: (514) 598-2869. Fax: (514) 598-6037. Web Site:www.tva.canoe.ca Martin Cloutier, gen mgr .

Les Chaines Tele Astral, Les Chaines Tele Astral, Une division d'Astra Media, 2100, Ste-Catherine St. W., Rm. 700, Montreal, PQ, H3H 2T3. Canada. Phone: (514) 939-3150. Fax: (514) 939-3151. Web Site:www.astral.com Pierre Roy, pres; Johanne Saint-Laurent, VP.

Progmg includes Super cran, the Fr pay-TV stn; Canal Famille, children's progmg stn devoted to children from ages 3 to 14; Canal D, a specialty ch featuring mainly documentaries.

Serving 245,000 subs (Super Ecran); 2,110,000 subs (Canal Famille), &1,705,000 subs (Canal D).

Serving 370 cable systems.

Satellite: Anik E-2, transponder 11-A.

The Comedy Network, Box 1000, Station "O", Toronto, ON, M4A 2W3. Canada. Phone: (416) 332-5300. Fax: (416) 332-5283. Rick Brace, pres; Brent Haynes, program dir.

A 24-hour service featuring Canadian & international programs devoted exclusively to comedy sketches, standup comedy, & ongoing comedy series. Coverage area: national.

Country Music Television (Canada), 64 Jefferson Ave., Unit 18, Toronto, ON, M6K 3H4. Canada. Phone: (416) 534-1191. Fax: (416) 530-2215.E-mail: info@cmt.ca Web Site:www.cmtcanada.ca Michael Harris, CEO.

A 24-hour mus & entertainment net that combines mus videos with programs and features that focus on the artists and their mus.

Serving 7 million subs on 1,487 cable systems in Canada.

Satellite: Anik E2 (Ku-Band), transponder T4.

Court TV Canada, 10212 Jasper Ave., Edmonton, AB, T5J 5A3. Canada. Phone: (780) 440-7777. Fax: (780) 440-8899.E-mail: info@courttvcanada.ca Web Site:www.courttvcanada.ca Jill Bonenfant, news dir & progmg dir.

Court TV Canada, in partnership with the U.S. based Court TV, combines Court TV's compelling daytime live trial coverage, legal analysis from inside U.S. courts with legal & police dramas, movies, documentaries & series from Canada & abroad.

DMX Music-Canada, 7260 12th St. S.E., Suite 120, Calgary, AB, T2H 2S5. Canada. Phone: (403) 640-8527. Fax: (403) 253-2788.E-mail: brad.trumble@dmxmusic.com Web Site:www.dmx.ca Brad Trumble, VP.

Formerly a residential svc, now a coml svc exculsively. Considering a return to the Canadian market. DMX commercial audio svc; 102 formats digital audio.

Serving 8000 subs. Satellites: C3 Bank, TBA (Ku-band) delivered by satellite ant.

Discovery Channel, #9 Channel 9 Ct., Toronto, ON, M1S 4B5. Canada. Phone: (416) 332-5000. Web Site:www.ctv.ca Ivan Fecan, pres/CEO; Corrie Coe, program dir.

Non-fiction documentary TV progmg focusing on the themes of nature, science & technology, adventure.

On 385 cable systems serving 5.6 million subs.

Satellite: Anik E2, Channel 210.

Drive-In Classics, 299 Queen St. W., Toronto, ON, M5V 2Z5. Canada. Phone: (416) 591-5757.E-mail: driveinclassics @driveinclassics.ca Web Site:www.driveinclassics.ca

Drive-In classics is a movie ch that celebrates the funny, entertaining & sometimes thought-provoking drive-in movies of the 50s, 60s & 70s.

Fairchild Television Ltd., #3300-415, Hazelbridge Way, Aberdeen Centre, Richmond, BC, V6X 4J7. Canada. Phone: (604) 295-1313. Fax: (604) 295-1300.E-mail: info@fairchildtv.com Web Site:www.fairchildtv.com Joseph Chan, pres.

The only Chinese language specialty TV across Canada. Serving 360,000 subs on 8 cable systems & DTH.

The Family Channel Inc., Box 787, BCE Place, 181 Bay St., Toronto, ON, M5J 2T3. Canada. Phone: (416) 956-2030. Fax: (416) 956-2035.E-mail: info@family.ca Web Site:www.family.ca Kevin Wright, VP progmg; Barbara Bailie, dir.

Premium TV net offering family entertainment based on 60% from the Disney Channel, 25% Canadian & 15% international progmg.

Serving 5.4 million subs, on 300 cable systems, transponder T20.

FashionTelevisionChannel, 299 Queen St. W., Toronto, ON, M5V 2Z5. Canada. Phone: (416) 591-5757.E-mail: infoft@ftchannel.com Web Site:www.ftchannel.com Marcia Martin, VP/gen mgr; David Kirkwood, VP sls; Ellen Baine, VP progmg; Scott Greig, creative dir; Jay Levine, production supvr; Bev Nenson, dir publicity; Allan Schwebel, VP-affil sls & mktg.

Canada's first & only 24-hour English language fashion channel dedicated to the world of art, architecture, photgrafy & designb with a celebration of style. Designer TV 24-hours a day.

Food Network Canada, 121 Bloor St. E., Toronto, ON, M4W 3M5. Canada. Phone: (416) 967-1174.E-mail: info@allianceatlantis.com Web Site:www.foodtv.ca Bill Kossman, program dir.

HGTV Canada, 121 Bloor St. E., Suite 200, Toronto, ON, M4W 3M5. Canada. Phone: (866) 967-4488 (viewer relations). Phone: (416) 967-0022 (main reception). Fax: (416) 960-0971.E-mail: feedback@hgtv.ca Web Site:www.hgtv.ca Norm Bolen, exec VP.

A 24-hour Canadian home & garden progmg resource.

Serving 5.2 million subs.

Satellite: F1, transponder T19.

History Television, 121 Bloor St. E., Suite B1, Toronto, ON, M4W 3M5. Canada. Phone: (416) 967-1174. Fax: (416) 960-0971. Web Site:www.allianceatlantis.com Marc Etkind, progmg dir.

A 24-hour program svc featuring current & world history told in documentaries, mini-series & feature films.

Satellite: Launching September 1997. On 350 cable systems serving 4 million subs.

Satellite: Anik e-2, transponder 19.

Life Network, 121 Bloor St. E., Suite 200, Toronto, ON, M4W 3M5. Canada. Phone: (416) 967-1174. Fax: (416) 960-0971.E-mail: info@lifenetwork.ca Web Site:www.lifenetwork.ca Kirstine Layfield, exec dir.

Offers lifestyle entertainment progmg about the people, places & experiences that make the journey of life worthwhile & interesting.

Serving 26 million English & Fr subs on 100 cable systems.

Satellite: Anik E2 (Ku-band), transponder T19 (horizontal).

La Magnetotheque, 1055 Rene Levesque E., Suite 501, Montreal, PQ, H2L 4S5. Canada. Phone: (514) 282-1999. Fax: (514) 282-1676. Web Site:www.lamagnetotheque.qc.ca E-mail: info@lamagnetotheque.qc.ca Majorie Theodore, gen mgr .

French-language reading svc for persons who are blind, visually impaired, or print-handicapped.

Movie Central, 5324 Calgary Tr., Suite 200, Edmonton, AB, T6H 4J8. Canada. Phone: (780) 430-2800. Fax: (780) 437-3188. Web Site:www.moviecentral.com Sandy Perkins, progmg dir; Andrew Eddy, VP/gen mgr.

Coml-free premium pay TV svc including movies, mus & comedy specials, major sports events & boxing (Superchannel, Movie Max!, Viewers Choice, Pay-Per-View).

Serving 300,000 subs on 170 cable systems.

Satellite: Anik E2.

MuchLOUD, 299 Queen St. W., Toronto, ON, M5V 2Z5. Canada. Phone: (416) 591-5757.E-mail: muchloud@muchmusic.com Web Site:www.muchloud.com

For fans of hard music everywhere - MuchLOUD delivers. Alternative, metal and punk music videos, featured alongside exclusive artist interviews, specials, classic archival material and up-to-the-minute concert info.

MuchMoreMusic, 299 Queen St. W., Toronto, ON, M5V 2Z5. Canada. Phone: (416) 591-5757. Fax: (416) 926-4026.E-mail: muchmoremail@muchmoremusic.com Web Site:www.muchmoremusic.com David Kines, VP/gen mgr.

Brings music fans Hot AC MusicVideo, top international specials, documentaries, movies and a growing roster of exclusive, original programming they can't find anywhere else.

MuchMoreRetro, 299 Queen St. W., Toronto, ON, M5V 2Z5. Canada. Phone: (416) 591-5757. Fax: (416) 926-4026.E-mail: request@muchmoreretro.com Web Site:www.muchmoreretro.com David Kines, VP/gen mgr.

Source for 24/7 classic videoflow from artists including The Police, Madonna, Bon Jovi, Corey Hart, Prince, Aerosmith,

Duran Duran, Janet Jackson, Rush, Nirvana and Alanis Morissette and more.

MuchMusic, 299 Queen St. W., Toronto, ON, M5V 2Z5. Canada. Phone: (416) 591-5757. E-mail: muchmail@muchmusic.com Web Site:www.muchmusic.com

Live to air approximately 8 hours daily from streetfront headquarters in downtown Toronto, with videoflow showcasing live performance & interviews from musical artists & celebrity guests.

Serving 7,063,468 subs.

Satellite: Anik F1, transponder 17, L-Band Frequency 977.75 mhz.

MuchVibe, 299 Queen St. W., Toronto, ON, M5V 2Z5. Canada. Phone: (416) 591-5757. E-mail: muchvibe@muchmusic.com Web Site:www.muchvibe.ca

The source for top music videos, interviews, concert specials, concert listings and classic clips from the CHUM music video archive. Hip Hop, Rap, R&B, Old School, Reggae and more.

MusiMax & MusiquePlus, 355 rue Ste- Catherine O., Montreal, PQ, H3B 1A5. Canada. Phone: (514) 284-7587. Fax: (514) 284-1889. Web Site:www.musiqueplus.com Pierre Marchand, VP/gen mgr.

Musimax is a French-language speciality svc owned equally by Astral Media Inc. of Montreal and CHUM Ltd. of Toronto. MusiquePlus is MuchMusic's French-language counterpart in Quebec. Serving 2.078 million subs on approximately 120 cable systems . Satellite: Anik F1, transponder 9B.

OLN, Outdoor Life Network. 9 Channel Nine Crt., Scarborough, ON, M1S 4B5. Canada. Phone: (416) 332-5000. Fax: (416) 332-5861. Web Site:www.tsn.ca/oln Anna Stamboic, dir.

Canada's destination for adventurous entertainment. Going beyond the comforts of home, OLN's progmg reveals the onsatible human drive for adventure.

Prime TV, 2100 One Lombard Pl., Winnipeg, MB, R3B-OX3. Canada. Phone: (204) 926-4800. Web Site:www.globaltv.com Tim Schellenberg, gen mgr .

The best of TV. Classy & classic entertainment & informational progmg for those moving on from youth-skewed traditional TV fare. 5 million subs.

RDI-Le Reseau de l'information, (Formerly RDI-Le Reseau de l'information de Radio - Canada). 1400 Blvd. Rene-Levesque E., Montreal, PQ, H2L 2M2. Canada. Phone: (514) 597-7224. Fax: (514) 597-5226. E-mail: gilles.desjardins@radio-canada.ca Web Site:www.radio-canada.ca/rdi

RDI-Le Reseau de l'information is Canada's French-language news network. RDI provide live of coverage major events, newscasts every 15 minutes, sports, financial news, as well as info programs on a wide range of topics. 9.2 million subs.

Report on Business Television, 720 King St. W., 10th Fl., Toronto, ON, M5V 2T3. Canada. Phone: (416) 957-8100. Fax: (416) 957-8180. Web Site:www.robtv.com Jack Fleischmann, gen mgr .

Le Reseau des sports (RDS), 1755 Blvd. Rene-Levesque Est, Suite 300, Montreal, PQ, H2K 4P6. Canada. Phone: (514) 599-2244. Fax: (514) 599-2299. E-mail: webmaster@rds.ca Web Site:www.rds.ca Jerry Frappier, gen mgr .

Provides 24-hour sports TV in Fr.

Satellite: ANIK E-2, transponder T-18.

The Score Television Network, 370 King St. W., Suite 304, Toronto, ON, M5V 1J9. Canada. Phone: (416) 977-6787. Fax: (416) 977-0238. E-mail: info@thescore.ca Web Site:www.thescore.ca John Levy, CEO; David Errington, VP/gen mgr.

Delivers the most comprehensive svc of professional & amateur sports news & info from Canada & around the world & is in every major Canadian cable market. Available in more than 5 million cable homes.

Serving 5.4 million subs on 370 cable systems.

Satellite: Anik F1, transponder 19.

Sex TV: The Channel, 299 Queen St. W., Toronto, ON, M5V 2Z5. Canada. Phone: (416) 591-5757.E-mail: sextvchannel@cum.com Web Site:www.sextvthechannel.com

The Shopping Channel, 59 Ambassador Dr., Mississauga, ON, L5T 2P9. Canada. Phone: (905) 565-3500. Phone: (905) 565-2600 (voicemail attendant) . Fax: (905) 565-2641. Web Site:www.theshoppingchannel.ca Ted Starkman, VP/gen mgr.

Live, shop-at-home televised retail svc, offering a var of consumer products.

Serving 5.7 million subs across Canada via cable & satellite.

Satellite: Anik E2, transponder 5.

SPACE: The Imagination Station, 299 Queen St. W., Toronto, ON, M5V 2Z5. Canada. Phone: (416) 591-5757.E-mail: space@spacecast.com Web Site:www.spacecast.com

Cable-delivered, national, 24 hour, English-language Science Fiction, Science Fact, Speculation and Fantasy channel. The program mix includes memorable sci-fi classics and current popular series, plus feature films, documentaries, specials and daily original productions with a tilt to information and new age speculation.

Star! The Entertainment Information Station, 299 Queen St. W., Toronto, ON, M5V 2Z5. Canada. Phone: (416) 591-7400.E-mail: info@star-tv.com Web Site:www.star-tv.com

Canada's only 24-hour national specialty service dedicated to the world of showbiz news and information. Programming includes in-depth specials and events, detailed behind-the scene features on major movies, exclusive interviews with the world's biggest celebrities and extensive live coverage of award shows, premieres and galas.

TMN—The Movie Network/MOVIEPIX, Box 787 , BCE Place, Suite 100 , 181 Bay St., Toronto, ON, M5J 2T3. Canada. Phone: (416) 956-2010. Fax: (416) 956-2018.E-mail: kwright@tv.astral.com Web Site:www.movienetwork.ca Kevin Wright, VP progmg.

Two English-language, gen interest, pay TV nets featuring recent movie titles on the multi-channeled TMN, & new classics on MOVIEPIX.

Serving 350,000 subs on 200 cable systems.

Satellite: Anik E1 (Ku-band), transponder T31 (TMN); Anik E2 (Ku-band), transponder T27 (MOVIEPIX).

TSN—The Sports Network, 9 Channel Nine Crt., Toronto, ON, M1S 4B5. Canada. Phone: (416) 332-5000. Fax: (416) 332-7656. Web Site:www.tsn.ca Adam Ashton, VP mktg; Rick Chisholm, sr VP; Andrea Goldstein, dir; Phil King, pres; Kim McKenney, dir; Judy Needham, dir; Nikki Moffat, dir.

TSN's flagship news program, SportsCentre, NHL & first three rounds of the Stanley Cups Playoffs, Toronto Maple Leafs hockey, International Hockey including the IIHF World Junior Championship, the Olympic Games through 2012. CFL, NFL, PGA Tour & all four golf Majors, Season of Champions Curling, NASCAR. A 24-hour sports ch distributed on cable in Canada. Covers all major professional & amateur sports.

Serving 8.8 million subs on more than 2,000 cable systems.

Satellite: Anik E1, transponder 18 KU-H.

TVOntario, 2180 Yonge St., Toronto, ON, M4T 2T1. Canada. Phone: (416) 484-2600. Fax: (416) 484-6285.E-mail: jjavet@tvontario.org Web Site:www.tvontario.org Lee Robock, gen mgr; Ray Newell, dir opns.

Provides educ progmg in English & Fr off air & via cable systems throughout Ontario.

TVO network (English) serves 98% of Ontario households. (Fr) serves 75% of Ontario households & 300,000 households in Quebec. Together the nets are on 327 cable systems.

Satellites: Anik F1, transponder 21.

Talk TV, Box 9, Station "O", Toronto, ON, M4A 2M9. Canada. Phone: (416) 332-5030. Fax: (416) 332-5283. Web Site:www.talktv.ca Ed Robinson, gen mgr; Patrick Patterson, sls dir.

TELETOON, Box 787, 181 Bay St., Toronto, ON, M5J 2T3. Canada. Phone: (416) 956-2060. Fax: (416) 956-2070.E-mail: info@teleton.com Web Site:www.teleton.com Darrell Atherley, mktg VP, sls VP; Leslie Kruger, dir mktg & prom dir.

This specialty net shows the best in animation from Canada & around the planet.

Serving 6 million subs on 1,000 cable systems.

Satellite: Anik E2, transponder 20. 1000. 6 Million.

Treehouse TV, 64 Jefferson Ave., Unit 18, Toronto, ON, M6K-3H4. Canada. Phone: (416) 534-1191. Web Site:www.treehousetv.ca Phil Piazza, VP progmg; Susan Ross, VP/gen mgr.

Treehouse TV is a specialty net dedicated to providing a variety of imaginative, stimulating and coml-free progmg for preschoolers from morning until bedtime.

Serving 4 million subs on 180 cable systems.

Satellite: Anik E-2, transponder 5.

VIVA, Corus Specialty Television, 64 Jefferson Ave., Unit 18, Toronto, ON, M6K 3H4. Canada. Phone: (416) 534-1191. Fax: (416) 588-9341. Web Site:www.myviva.ca

Viewer's Choice Canada, Box 787, BCE Place, Suite 100 , 181 Bay St., Toronto, ON, M5J 2T3. Canada. Phone: (416) 956-2010. Fax: (416) 956-2055. Web Site:www.viewerschoice.com John Riley, pres/CEO.

Eastern Canada's pay-per-view network.

On 50 cable systems serving 600,000 addressable subs.

Satellites: Anik E1; Anik E2.

Vision TV: (Canada's Multi Faith Network), 80 Bond St., Toronto, ON, M5B 1X2. Canada. Phone: (416) 368-3194. Fax: (416) 368-9774. Web Site:www.visiontv.ca E-mail: estella@visiontv.ca Bill Roberts, pres/CEO; Mark Prasuhn, COO.

Programs presented by 30 plus faith groups, British comedies, movies dramas, documentaries, pub affrs, music & performance.

Serving 7.8 million subs on 12 cable systems. Satellite: Anik F1, transponder 5.

VoicePrint(TM), (A division of The National Broadcast Reading Service Inc.). 1090 Don Mills Rd., Suite 303, Toronto, ON, M3C 3R6. Canada. Phone: (416) 422-4222. Fax: (416) 422-1633.E-mail: nbrs@nbrscanada.com Web Site:www.voiceprintcanada.com Robert S. Trimbee, pres; Mike Hanson, mgng dir.

Read published news in audio format for blind, vision-restricted & sr Canadians.

W Network, 64 Jefferson Ave., Unit 18, Toronto, ON, M6K 3H4. Canada. Phone: (416) 534-1191. Web Site:www.wnetwork.com

The Weather Network/MeteoMedia Inc., (A division of Pelmorex Communications Inc.). 1755 Rene-Levesque Blvd. E., Suite 251, Montreal, PQ, H2K 4P6. Canada. Phone: (514) 597-1700. Fax: (514) 597-2981. Web Site:www.theweathernetwork.com Pierre L. Morrissette, pres/CEO; Luc Perreault, VP.

Natl satellite-to-cable TV network bcstg in Fr (MétéoMédia) & English (The Weather Network) offering weather & environmental info 24-hours a day, 7 days a week.

Serving 8.2 million subs on 752 headends.

Satellite: Anik E2, transponder 1A.

YTV Canada Inc., 64 Jefferson Ave., Unit 18, Toronto, ON, M6K 3H4. Canada. Phone: (416) 534-1191. Fax: (416) 533-0346.E-mail: info@ytv.ca Web Site:www.ytv.ca Susan Schaefer, mktg VP; Phil Piazza, VP progmg.

English language basic cable specialty svc dedicated to children, teens & their families.

On approximately 1,200 cable systems serving an estimated 8.1 million subs.

Satellite: ANIK E1 East/West-DVC, transponder 7 (nationwide), 111 degrees (Ku-band), vert polarization, 11900 MHZ.

Canadian Radio Networks and Services

Astral Radio and Énergie

Head Office: Astral Media Inc., 2100, rue Sainte-Catherine, Bureau 1000, Montreal, PQ H3H 2T3. (514) 939-5000. Web site: www.astralmedia.com.

Radio Division: 1717 boul. Rene-Levesque E. St., Bureau 200, Montreal, PQ H2L 4T9. (514) 529-3229. FAX: (514) 529-9308. Web site: www.radioenergie.com.

Principal Officers: Ian Greenberg, pres/CEO, Astral Media Inc.; Jacques Parisien, pres, Astral Radio; Charles Benoit, VP, Radio Energie/VP New Media Astral Media; Luc Sabbatini, exec VP, Astral Radio; Andre Bureau, chmn of bd; Sidney Greenberg, VP Astral Media Inc.; Louis Ryan, VP strategic planning; Alain Bergaron, VP Brand mgmt/corporate communications; Sophie Emond, VP reg/govt affrs; Claude Laflamme, VP corporate affrs; Andra Gagnon, VP/opns Astral Radio; Denis Rozon, VP finance, Astral Radio; Brigitte Catellier, VP legal affrs Astral Media Inc.; Michael Arpin, sr advisor reg/govt affrs; Claude Gagnon, sr VP/CFO; Danielle Chagnon, VP/product, Astral Radio; Anne McNamara, VP human resource, Astral Radio.

Radio Energie FM Stations CKMF 94.3 (Montreal); CHIK 98.9 (Quebec); CKTF 104.1 (Gatineau/Hull); CIGB 102.3 (Trois-Rivieres); CJMV 102.7 (Val d'Or); CIMO 106.1 (Sherbrooke/Magog); CJMM 99.1 (Rouyn-Noranda); CJAB 94.5 (Chicoutimi/Jonquiere). **Astral Radio AM Stations** CJRC 1150 (Ottawa/Hull); CKRS 590 (Chicoutimi/Jonquiere); CKSM 1220 (Shawinigan).

Canadian Broadcasting Corp.

The **Canadian Broadcasting Corp.** (CBC) is a publ owned corporation established by the Broadcasting Act (1936) of the Canadian Parliament to provide the natl bcstg svc in Canada in the two official languages, English & French. CBC/Radio is Canada's natl public bcstr and one of its largest cultural institutions.

Program Services: The CBC operates English and French AM & FM stereo networks. The progmg on these networks is nearly all Canadian and virtually free of coml adv. CBC North bcsts radio programs to Canada's north in English, French and eight native languages, serving the special needs of native and non-native groups in the Yukon, the Northwest Territories and northern Quebec. With 29 svcs offered on Radio, Television, the internet, satellite radio, digital audio,distribution svcs, wireless WAP and SMS mgng svcs. Under this legislation CBC is governed by the 1991 Broadcasting Act and subject to regulations of the Canadian Radio-Television and Telecommunications Commission (CRTC).

Office: Box 500 Stn. A, Toronto, ON M5W 1E6. (416) 205-7264. Fax: (416) 205-2400. Web site: www.cbc.ca.

CBC Board of Directors: Timothy W. Casgrain, chair, Toronto; Helene F. Fortin, ptnr.

Senior Executive Team: Hubert T. Lacriox, pres/CEO; Jane Chalmers, VP CBC Radio; Sylvain Lafrance, exec VP French Services; Richard Stursberg, exec VP English Services; Pierre Nollet, VP/gen counsel/corporate sec; George C.B. Smith, sr VP human resources and organization; Johanne Charbonneau, VP/CFO; Raymond Carnovale, VP/chief technology officer; Michel Tremblay, VP strategy/business dev; William B. Chambers, VP communications; Michel Saint-Cyr, pres Real Estate div.

CBC Ombudsman: Vince Carlin and William Morgan, English svcs, Box 500, Station A, Toronto, ON M5W 1E6; E-mail: ombudsman@cb].ca. Web site: www.cbc.ca/ombudsman. Julie Miville-Dechene, French svcs, 1400 Rene-Levesque Blvd. East. Box 6000, Montreal, PQ H3C 3A8; E-mail ombudsmanradio-canada.ca. Web Site: www.radio-canda-ca/ombudsman.

Ombudsman English Services: Canadian Broadcasting Corporation, Box 500, Station A, Toronto, ON M5W 1E6. E-mail: ombudsman@cb].ca. Web site: www.cbc.ca/ombudsman.

Ombudsman French Services: Box 6000, Montreal, PQ H3C 3A8. E-mail: ombudsmanradio-canada.ca. Web site: www.radio-canada.ca/ombudsman.

Communications-English Networks: 250 Front Street West, Box 500, Station A, Toronto, ON M5W 1E6. (866) 306-4636. TDD: (416) 205-6688; E-mail: cbcinput@cb].ca.

Communications-French Services: Box 6000, Montreal, PQ H3C 3A8. (514) 597-6000. TDD: (514) 597-6013; E-mail: auditoireradio-canada.ca.

Newfoundland Region (English): 95 University Ave., Box 12010, Station A, St. John's, NF A1B 3T8. (709) 576-5000.

Maritimes Region (English): 5600 Sackville Street, Box 3000, Halifax, NS B3J 3E9. (902) 420-8311.

Atlantic Provinces (French): 250 Archibald Street, Box 950, Moncton, NB E1C 8N8. (506) 853-6666.

Quebec Region (English): 1400 Rene-Levesque Boulevard East, Box 6000, Montreal, PQ H3C 3A8. (514) 597-6000.

Quebec City & Eastern Quebec Region (French): 2505 Laurier Boulevard, Box 18800, Ste-Foy, PQ G1V 9L4. (418) 654-1341.

Ontario Region (English): 205 Wellington Street, Box 500, Station A, Toronto, ON M5W 1E6. (416) 205-3311.

Ontario Region (French): 250 Lanark Avenue, Box 3220, Station C, Ottawa, ON K1Y 1E4. (613) 724-1200.

Manitoba Region (English & French): 541 Portage Ave., Box 160, Winnipeg, MB R3C 2H1. (204) 788-3222.

Saskatchewan Region (English & French): 2440 Broad St., Box 540, Regina, SK S4P 4A1. (306) 347-9540.

Alberta Region (English & French): 10062-102nd Ave., Room 123, Edmonton City Centre, Box 555, Edmonton, AB T5J 2P4. (780) 468-7500.

British Columbia Region (English & French): 700 Hamilton Road, Box 4600, Vancouver, BC V6B 4A2. (604) 662-6000.

CBC North: 5129 49th Street, Box 160, Yellowknife, NT X1A 1P8. (867) 920-5400.

Producers, Distributors, and Production Services Alphabetical Index

A

ABC Family, 3800 W. Alameda Ave., Burbank, CA, 91521. Phone: (818) 560-1000. Fax: (818) 840-1922. Web Site:www.abcfamily.com

TV-CATV only.

ABC Family features quality, contemp entertainment for all members of the family including original series, movies & specials. Available in over 87 million homes via basic cable.

ACC Entertainment, Bavariafilmplatz 7, 82031 Grünwald, Munich Phone: 49-89 64981-332. Phone: 49-89 64981-232.E-mail: accficm@acc.com

TV-CATV only.

Film & TV producers, distributors.

ACTV Inc., 233 Park Ave., 10th Floor, New York, NY, 10020. Phone: (212) 497-7000. Fax: (212) 459-9548.E-mail: info@actv.com Christopher Cline, CFO; David Reese, chmn/CEO.

TV-CATV only.

Interactive TV progmg for educ & entertainment.

ADM—International Film & TV Distribution, Drienerwolde House, Drienerwoldeweg, Hengelo, IL, 7552 PC. Netherlands. Phone: 31 74 250 6843. Fax: 31 74 250 1874. Carole K. Hodson, mngd dir; Herman Melzer, chmn acquisitions; Sarah J. Mydlak, dir sales & mktg.

TV-CATV only.

International distributor of film & TV programs including features, classics, documentaries, children's, plus much more.

ALIN TV, 149 Madison Ave., Suite 602, New York, NY, 10016. Phone: (212) 889-1327. Fax: (212) 213-6968. Web Site:www.alintv.com Alan Cohen, pres.

TV-CATV only.

Unwired TV natl network, syndication, digital media sls & mktg.

ANA Television Network, 1510 H St. N.W., Suite 400, Washington, DC, 20005. Phone: (202) 898-8222. Angelyn Adams, CFO.

TV-CATV only.

Arabic-language TV net bcstg to the Arab-American community 24 hours via cable, wireless cable. Satellite: DIRECTV Plus.

APA International Film Distributors Inc., 7152 S.W. 47th St., Miami, FL, 33155. Phone: (305) 666-0020. Fax: (305) 666-1725.E-mail: apafilm@bellsouth.net Rafael Fusaro, pres.

TV-CATV only.

TV program production & distribution.

APM/Associated Production Music LLC, 6255 Sunset Blvd., Suite 820, Hollywood, CA, 90028. Phone: (323) 461-3211. Phone: (800) 543-4276. Fax: (323) 461-9102.E-mail: sales@apmmusic.com Web Site:www.apmmusic.com

New YorkNY , 342 Madison Ave, Suite 1200. Phone:

TV-CATV only.

Sixteen Libraries: KPM, Bruton, Sonoton, Carlin, Castle, NFL. Over 5,000 CDs, personalized packages, music search, 15-20 New CD releases mthy.

ATA Trading Corp., Box 307, Massapequa Park, NY, 11762. Phone: (516) 541-5336. Fax: (516) 541-5336.E-mail: atat@verizon.net Harold G. Lewis, pres; Susan Lewis, VP.

TV-CATV only.

Worldwide distributors for ind producers in all areas of feature films, made-for-TV productions, series, documentaries & children's programs.

Academy Entertainment, 611 Cedar Ln., Teaneck, NJ, 07666. Phone: (201) 394-1849. Fax: (201) 357-8482.E-mail: mlrfilms@aol.com Alan Miller, pres; Al Leifer, co-pres.

TV-CATV only.

Distribution of film, TV & video progmg worldwide.

Accuracy in Media Inc., 4455 Connecticut Ave. N.W., Suite 330, Washington, DC, 20008. Phone: (202) 364-4401. Fax: (202) 364-4098.E-mail: info@aim.org Web Site:www.aim.org Don Irvine, chmn; Cliff Kincaid, editor; Roger Aronoff, media analyst.

TV-CATV-Radio.

Nationwide media monitoring organization produces documentary TV films, radio & podcast commentaries, bi-monthly printed publications, daily website updates & programs that critique media coverage.

Acme, 9976 W. Wanda Dr., Beverly Hills, CA, 90210. Phone: (310) 276-5509. Fax: (310) 276-1183.E-mail: acmetoy@yahoo.com Bradley Friedman, pres; David Temianka, dir; Fred Wietzchz, CEO.

TV-CATV only.

Feature film & TV production, music videos, childrens progmg, commercials, robotics, scripting, tin toy props, rock music stock footage, space stock footage.

Advanced Digital Services, Inc., 948 N. Cahuenga Blvd., Hollywood, CA, 90038. Phone: (323) 468-2200. Fax: (323) 468-2211. Web Site:www.adshollywood.com Andrew McIntyre, chmn/CEO; Kevin Yates, COO; Jack Fleming, pres.

TV-CATV only.

Video duplication, standard conversion & digital postproduction.

Adventist Media Center, 101 W. Cochran, Simi Valley, CA, 93065. Phone: (805) 955-7777. Fax: (805) 522-1082.E-mail: info@faithfortoday.tv Marshall Chase, gen mgr .

TV-CATV-Radio.

TV program production & distribution.

Aegis People Support Transcription and Captioning, (Formerly The Transcription Company). 111 North First St., Suite 201, Burbank, CA, 91502. Phone: (818) 848-6500. Fax: (818) 556-4150. Web Site:www.aegisbpo.com E-mail: customerservice@transcripts.tv Glory Johnson, dir VP media svcs; Stephanie Gray, dir transcript.

Newport BeachCA . Rapidtext Inc., 1801 Dove St, Suite 101. Phone:

TV-CATV only.

Transcribe all media: TV shows, films, news, sports, documentaries, meetings interviews. Provide closed captioning. Provide translations.

African Family Film Foundation, Box 630, Santa Cruz, CA, 95061-0630. Phone: (831) 426-3133.E-mail: taale@africanfamily.org Web Site:www.africanfamily.org Taale Laafi Rosellini, dir.

TV-CATV only.

Production & distribution of films & videotapes promoting African family life & culture.

Agency for Instructional Technology (AIT), Box A, Bloomington, IN, 47402-0120. Phone: (800) 457-4509. Phone: (812) 339-2203. Fax: (812) 333-4218.E-mail: info@ait.net Web Site:www.ait.net Chuck Wilson, dir.

BloomingtonIN , 1800 N. Stonelake Dr. (Shipping address). TV-CATV-Radio.

Produces, acquires & distributes technology-based learning resources including video, videodisc, software & print—for all K-12 curricular areas, vocational educ/tech prep, early childhood, & professional dev.

Agora TV, 195 Hicks Dr. S.E., Marietta, GA, 30060. Phone: (404) 226-4503. Fax: (678) 581-3750.E-mail: joe@agoratv.tv Web Site:www.agoratv.tv Joseph Gora, pres.

TV-CATV only.

TV production & equipment rental, Fly packages.

Agrinet News Network, 176 Radio Rd., Powells Point, NC, 27966. Phone: (252) 491-2414. Fax: (252) 491-2959. Web Site:www.agrinetradio.com Bill Ray, host; Bob Yanacek, office mgr; Lisa Ray, stn affiliates mgr.

TV-CATV-Radio.

290 radio partners coast-to-coast. Program available via internet. Contract required for distribution.

Airwaves Audio Inc., 150 Mutual St., Toronto, ON, M5B 2M1. Canada. Phone: (416) 977-1098. Fax: (416) 997-5701.

TV-CATV only.

Audiovisual & industrial postproduction. Audio recording & mixing for radio & TV.

Alden Films, Box 449, Clarksburg, NJ, 08510. Phone: (732) 462-3522. Fax: (732) 294-0330.E-mail: info@aldenfilms.com Web Site:www.aldenfilms.com Paul Weinberg, pres; Fran Fried, admin asst.

TV-CATV only.

Distributes nearly 200 DVD's, CD's on Israel & Judaica. Official distributor for state of Israel.

All Media Productions Inc., 12261 Cleveland Ave. Ste F, Nunica, MI, 49448-9309. Phone: (616) 837-0899. Fax: (616) 837-0897. Web Site:www.allmediaproductions.com E-mail: linda@allmediaproductions.com Linda Langs, pres.

TV-CATV only.

Web dev, internet mktg & film distribution.

All My Features Inc., 9190 Clearstream Terr., Mechanicsville, VA, 23111. Phone: (804) 730-1534. Fax: (804) 559-4809.

TV-CATV only.

Provides daily entertainment news, entertainment-related features via audio & computer feeds.

All Productions, 7025 Regner Rd., Suite 5, San Diego, CA, 92119. Phone: (619) 284-2566. Phone: (619) 460-4837. Fax: (619) 460-6160.E-mail: mikeall@eudoramail.com Web Site:www.allproductions.com Michael J. All, CEO; Stephen A. All, CFO; Jean M. All, pres; George Kay, script editor; Tony Stevens, producer & dir.

San DiegoCA , 7025 Regner Rd. Phone:

TV-CATV-Radio.

TV & radio program production, distribution; cable-ready TV progmg; promotion film production, production svcs; TV, radio spots, coml announcers & printed books.

Allegro Productions Inc., 1000 Clint Moore Rd., Suite 108, Boca Raton, FL, 33487. Phone: (800) 275-4636. Fax: (888) 329-3737. Fax: (561) 241-0707.E-mail: allegro@ssrvideo.com Web Site:www.ssrvideo.com Scott Forman, pres.

TV-CATV only.

Educational & corporate progmg, including documentary/bcst. From concept to completion, offering full service video post production, CD-ROM/DVD authoring, multi-format duplication, 3D animation & effects.

Alliance for Christian Media/Day1, (Formerly Protestant Hour Inc.). 644 W. Peachtree St., Suite 300, Atlanta, GA, 30309-1925. Phone: (404) 815-9110. Fax: (404) 815-0495.E-mail: info@day1.org Web Site:www.day1.org Peter Wallace, VP & exec producer; Louis Schueddig, pres.

Radio Only.

Radio program production & distribution; relg ecumenical media.

Allied Production and Distribution Services, 135 W. Hancock St., Decatur, GA, 30030. Phone: (404) 373-1227. Fax: (404) 373-1227. Edwin Clark, pres.

TV-CATV only.

TV program production & distribution.

Allumination FilmWorks, LLC, (Formerly Ardustry Home Entertainment LLC). 21250 Califa St., Suite 102, Woodland Hills, CA, 91367. Phone: (818) 712-9000. Fax: (818) 712-9074.E-mail: info@alluminationfilmworks.com Web Site:www.alluminationfilmworks.com Cheryl Freeman, CEO.

TV-CATV only.

Distribution, dev, production documentaries, TV series, kids, specials.

Aloha Productions, Box 33648, San Diego, CA, 92163. Phone: (619) 275-7357. Phone: (800) 223-2564. Fax: (619) 296-5909.E-mail: jhal@alohajingles.com Hal Hodgson, exec producer.

TV-CATV-Radio.

Original coml music production, scoring, jingles, long-form; movie & TV scores.

Alternative Programming, 4215 Brendenwood Rd., Rockford, IL, 61107. Phone: (815) 229-3995. Fax: (815) 229-5043.E-mail: altprog@sbcglobal.net Web Site:www.alternative-programming.com Gary A. Knoll, owner.

Radio Only.

Complete music formats for radio - current music for various formats - custom CD svc.

Altman Productions, 3401 Macomb St. N.W., Washington, DC, 20016. Phone: (202) 362-3088.E-mail: itsacademicquiz@aol.com Susan Altman, producer; Susan Lechner, editor.

TV-CATV only.

TV & radio program production. Producers of It's Academic,

the high school quiz program, longest running TV quiz program in the world.

Altruist Media, 2601A Wilson Blvd., Arlington, VA, 22201. Phone: (703) 812-8813. Fax: (703) 812-9710.E-mail: info@altruistmedia.com Web Site:www.altruistmedia.com Jan Dearth, pres.

TV-CATV only.

A full-svc visual communications firm. Staff producers, writers & dirs provide full creative direction & project mgmt from concept dev, treatment, scripting & graphics design to production & delivery. Offers videotape, live event production, consulting svcs for organizational communications. Provides comprehensive production svcs for videotape, special event & live business TV-video conference progmg. Also offers media training, VNR production, video press tours, consulting for private networks, new media svcs including distributed multimedia, WWW design & CD-ROM dev.

Americ Disc, 2525 Canadian, Drummondville, PQ, J2C 7W2. Canada. Phone: (819) 474-2655. Phone: (800) 263-0419. Fax: (819) 478-4575.E-mail: info@americdisc.com Web Site:www.americdisc.com

TV-CATV only.

CD & DVD replication & fulfillment.

America On The Road Inc., 1767 Lakewood Ranch Blvd., Suite 183, Bradenton, FL, 34211. Phone: (941) 750-6590. Fax: (941) 708-6523.E-mail: info@americaontheroad.com Web Site:www.americaontheroad.com Jack Nerad, producer; Al Herskovitz, business mgr; Mike Anson, co-host.

TV-CATV-Radio.

One hour wkly, 2.5-minute daily automotive consumer show.

America One Television Network, 6125 Airport Freeway, Suite 100, Ft. Worth, TX, 76117. Phone: (817) 546-1400. Fax: (682) 647-0756. Web Site:www.americaone.com Matt Reiff, pres; Preston Bornman, sr VP.

TV-CATV only.

24 hour gen entertainment bcst network.

American Blues Network, Box 6216, Gulfport, MS, 39506. Phone: (800) 896-5307. Fax: (228) 896-5703.E-mail: info@americianbluesnetwork.com Web Site:www.americianbluesnetwork.com Stan Daniels, CEO.

Radio Only.

The only 24-hour blues syndication.

American Chiropractic Association Inc., 1701 Clarendon Blvd., Arlington, VA, 22209. Phone: (703) 276-8800. Fax: (703) 243-2593.E-mail: memberinfo@acatoday.org Web Site:www.acatoday.org

TV-CATV-Radio.

Professional membership organization.

American Farm Bureau Inc., 600 Maryland Ave. S.W., Suite 100W, Washington, DC, 20024. Phone: (202) 406-3600. Fax: (202) 406-3602. Web Site:www.fb.org Don Lipton, dir & pub rel.

TV-CATV only.

AGFeed, mthy video feed of news stories about food & agriculture, *Newsline* radio svc, *Focus on Agriculture* commentary, stock footage.

American Foundation for the Blind, 11 Penn Plaza, Suite 300, New York, NY, 10001. Phone: (212) 502-7600. Phone: (800) 232-5463. Fax: (212) 502-7777.E-mail: afbinfo@afb.net Web Site:www.afb.org Carl Augusto, pres; Liz Greco-Rocks, dir.

TV-CATV only.

Provides consultation & referrals, social & technological rsch, publications, info svcs, public educ, govt rel & talking books.

American Heart Association, 7272 Greenville Ave., Dallas, TX, 75231-4596. Phone: (214) 706-1330. Fax: (214) 706-5243. Web Site:americanheart.org Julie Del Barto, communications mgr & natl bcst.

TV-CATV-Radio.

Video news releases, podcasts, stock footage, limited animation related to heart & disease for news programs.

American Public Television, 55 Summer St., Boston, MA, 02110. Phone: (617) 338-4455. Fax: (617) 338-5369.E-mail: info@aptonline.org Web Site:www.aptonline.org Cynthia Fenneman, pres/CEO.

TV-CATV only.

Major distributor of high quality TV programs to all U.S. public TV stns. Also distributor of programs to international media.

American Stock Exchange, 86 Trinity Pl., New York, NY, 10006. Phone: (212) 306-1229. Fax: (212) 306-5489.E-mail: kenneth.meyer@amex.com Web Site:www.amex.com Kimberly Zapien, dir.

TV-CATV only.

TV studio location on a trading floor, teleprompters, access to industry analysts, production and postproduction svcs.

American TelNet, 855 SW 78th Ave., Plantation, FL, 33324. Phone: (954) 453-7000. Fax: (954) 453-7809.E-mail: success@americantelnet.com

An 800/900 Interactive svc bureau offering a wide var of turnkey pay-per-call entertainment & business programs.

AmericaNurse TV Productions, Box 7717, Romeoville, IL, 60446. Phone: (815) 773-4497.E-mail: asktvnurse@yahoo.com Web Site:www.americanurse.com Karon Gibson, R.N., producer.

TV-CATV only.

Consumer educ shows on health, safety & other self-help titles. Entertaining introduction to optional alternative & mainstream medicine & Rx. Travel, entainment, legal & reality TV. Also internet progmg on ustream.tv, "Outspocken" with Karen.

America's Most Wanted, 2 Bethesda Metro Ctr., Suite 800, Bethesda, MD, 20814. Phone: (240) 482-1100. Fax: (240) 482-1181.E-mail: feedback@amw.com Web Site:www.amw.com Marc Kaplan, .

TV-CATV only.

Wkly reality-based program for Fox TV.

Anderson Productions Ltd. (APL), 55 W. 39th St., Suite 800, New York, NY, 10018. Phone: (212) 414-9220. Fax: (212) 206-0279.E-mail: steveanderson@apltv.com Web Site:www.apltv.com Steven C. F. Anderson, exec producer & pres.

TV-CATV only.

TV program production for bcst, cable TV & nonprofit orgs.

Angel Films Co., 967 Hwy. 40, New Franklin, MO, 65274-9778. Phone: (573) 698-3900. Fax: (573) 698-3900.E-mail: phoeenix@phoeenix.org William H. Hoehne Jr., chmn; Joyce L. Chow, CEO; Arlene Hulse, pres; Leana Le Gee, VP mktg, adv VP; Matthew P. Eastman, VP production.

TV-CATV only.

Production, distribution, syndication of progmg for adults & children.

Animated Production Services, 321 W. 44th St., New York, NY, 10036. Phone: (212) 265-2942. Fax: (212) 265-2944.E-mail: info@digitaltofilm.com Web Site:www.digitaltofilm.com

TV-CATV only.

TV program, coml, promotional film production, distribution & production svcs, digital film.

Antenne 2 - French TV 2, 1290 Ave. of the Americas, Suite 3410, New York, NY, 10104. Phone: (212) 581-1771. Fax: (212) 541-4309. Web Site:www.france2.fr

TV-CATV only.

TV program production.

The Arabic Channel, 366 86 St., 1st Fl., Brooklyn, NY, 11209-5002. Phone: (718) 238-2450. Fax: (718) 238-2465. Gamil M. Tawfik, pres/CEO; Marguerite M. Moore, VP.

TV-CATV only.

Arabic language progmg bcst Time Warner Cable.

Archive Films/Archive Photos, 75 Varick St., 5th Floor, New York, NY, 10013. Phone: (646) 613-4000. Phone: (800) 462-4379. Fax: (646) 613-4140.E-mail: sales@gettyimages.com Web Site:www.gettyimages.com

111 45 Stockholm. Archive Films/Archive Photos Scandinavia, Birger Jarlsgatan 55. Phone:

Cologne. Archive Films GMBH, Bremstrasse 12. Phone:

London. Archive Films/Archive Photos, 17 Conway St. Phone:

Milan. Archive Films/Archive Photos Italy, Via Terraggio 17. Phone:

Paris Ducaud. Archive Films/Archive Photos, 4 Boulevard Poissonniere. Phone:

TV-CATV only.

Stock footage/photo library providing all types of historical footage & photos for use in products for TV/CATV.

Arkadia Entertainment Corp., 34 E. 23rd St., 3rd Fl., New York, 10010. Phone: (212) 533-0007. Fax: (212) 979-0266.E-mail: arkadian@aol.com Web Site:www.arkadiarecords.com Bob Karcy, CEO.

Radio Only.

CD, DVD, video production & distribution worldwide. A broad range of exclusive progmg.

Armedia Communications, 307-3219 Yonge St., Toronto, ON, M4N 2L3. Canada. Phone: (905) 889-0076. Fax: (905) 889-0078.E-mail: armedia@msn.com Web Site:www.david-mazmanian.vpweb.com David Mazmanian, principal.

TV-CATV-Radio.

Audio, video, music production & bcst svcs.

J. Arnold Productions, 363 Massachusetts Ave., Lexington, MA, 02420. Phone: (781) 674-2277. Fax: (781) 674-0272.E-mail: jarpro@aol.com James Arnold, pres; Lori Arnold, production mgr; Eric Fisher, production mgr.

CharlotteNC , 147 Cove Creek Rd. Phone:

TV-CATV only.

Full-svc on location video production. ENG-EFP crews & Betacam equipment packages.

The Kay Arnold Group, 34 Kramer Dr., Paramus, NJ, 07652. Phone: (201) 652-6037. Fax: (201) 612-8578. Kay Arnold, pres.

TV-CATV only.

Production & distribution of film & tape programs for TV, satellite, cable, home video & non-theatrical.

Toby Arnold and Associates Inc., 3234 Commander Dr., Carrollton, TX, 75006. Phone: (800) 527-5335. Phone: (972) 661-8200. Fax: (972) 250-6014.E-mail: toby@taamusic.com Web Site:www.taamusic.com Grady Sanders, pres; Susan Bedwell, VP & COO; Lawrence Mangiameli, VP, creative dir.

TV-CATV-Radio.

Audio production libraries for TV & radio, stn imaging, morning show promo sweeper & stager packages for all formats.

Artisan PictureWorks Ltd., 800 Forrest St. N.W., Atlanta, GA, 30318. Phone: (404) 355-3398. Fax: (404) 350-0302.E-mail: info@artisanpicture.com Web Site:www.artisanpictureworks.com Bryan Gartman, pres; Amy Thompson, production mgr; Ben Smart, studio mgr.

TV-CATV only.

Studio facilities feature Ultimatte, fiber optics to satellite uplink. Live multicam specialists. Remote & in-house production facilities.

Artist View Entertainment Inc., 4425 Irvine Ave., Studio City, CA, 91502-1919. Phone: (818) 752-2480. Fax: (818) 752-9339.E-mail: info@artistviewent.com Web Site:www.artistviewent.com Scott J. Jones, pres; Jay E. Joyce, VP.

TV-CATV only.

Worldwide distribution in all media specializing in feature films.

Ascent Media Group, (Formerly Ascent Entertainment Group Inc.). 520 Broadway, 5th Fl., Santa Monica, CA, 91401. Phone: (310) 434-7000. Web Site:www.ascentmedia.com

TV-CATV-Radio.

Network svcs, syndication, advertising solutions, satellite bcst distribution, & net construction & maintenance.

Ascent Media Management East, 235 Pegasus Ave., Northvale, NJ, 07647. Phone: (201) 767-3800. Fax: (201) 784-2769.E-mail: agavin@apvi.com Web Site:www.apvi.com Don Buck, pres; Al Gavin, sls VP; Tony Beswick, VP/gen mgr.

BurbankCA . Audio Plus Video - West, 200 S. Flower St. Phone:

TV-CATV only.

Standards & aspect ratio conversion, international duplication, PAL/NTSC editing, film-to-tape transfers, 16 X 9 audio layback, restoration & satellite svcs, dud authoring, compression, streaming.

Ascent Media Network, (formerly Ascent Media Network Services). 250 Harbor Dr., Stamford, CT, 06902. Phone: (203) 965-6000. Fax: (203) 965-6405. Web Site:www.ascentmedia.com Peter Brickman, mgng dir.

Singapore. Asia Bcst Centre Phone:vhendra@abc.gwns.com Vincent Helseth.

MinneapolisMN . GWNS Minneapolis, 6845 20th Ave. Phone:

TV-CATV only.

Video transmission, origination; tech consulting, new

media products; private networks, post production, studio, graphics; bcst event svcs & satellite svcs.

Ascent Media Network Services, 2901 W. Alameda Ave., Burbank, CA, 91505. Phone: (818) 840-7174. Fax: (818) 567-1131. Web Site:www.ascentmedia.com Sharon Pyne, opns dir; Lennis Schwartz, VP opns; Jodynne Wood, sls dir.

London NO United Kingdom, 48 Charlotte St.

TV-CATV only.

AM NS powers the bcst-cable nets around the world. We distribute progmg content over our integrated fiber & satellite net.

Asia Pacific Productions USA, Ltd., 19698 S.E. Cottonwood St., Portland, OR, 97267. Phone: (503) 723-6456.E-mail: info@approd.com Web Site:approd.com Thomas F. Hopkins, pres; Miyuki Shigeji, VP.

Kobe Japan. Asia Pacific Productions Japan, 3-17 Higashi Maruyama Cho. Phone:

TV-CATV only.

Provides news, documentary & program production; coml production; business/promotional film & video production; production svcs for TV/CATV.

Associated Press Television News, 1825 K St., N.W., Suite 800, Washington, DC, 20036. Phone: (202) 736-9595. Fax: (202) 736-9619. Web Site:www.ap.org

TV-CATV only.

TV news production, news library, video editing & ENG production.

Associated Television International, 4401 Wilshire Blvd., Los Angeles, CA, 90010. Phone: (323) 556-5600. Fax: (323) 556-5610. Fax: www.associatedtelevision.com E-mail: atiwest@aol.com David McKenzie, pres; Jim Romanovich, pres/World Media; Justin Pierce, sr VP dev.

TV-CATV-Radio.

Full-svc production, distribution & syndication company in business for over 20 years.

Association of Islamic Charitable Projects, 4431 Walnut St., Philadelphia, PA, 19104. Phone: (215) 387-8888. Fax: (215) 387-3815. Web Site:www.aicp.org

TV-CATV only.

Islamic progmg. Educational micro-bcst net svc for metro Philadelphia.

At a Glance, 6350 W. Freeway, Fort Worth, TX, 76116. Phone: (817) 570-1400. Phone: (800) 266-1837. Fax: (817) 737-9436.E-mail: info@familynet.com Web Site:www.familynetradio.com Lisa Bratton, radio mktg & distribution; Donna Senn, radio Distribution; Chuck Ries, producer.

Radio Only.

Variety of topics: health, fitness, character, parenting, etc. 60 second spots, 10 per month, on CD.

Atlantic Video Inc., 650 Massachusetts Ave. N.W., Washington, DC, 20001. Phone: (202) 408-0900. Fax: (202) 408-8496. Web Site:www.atlanticvideo.com Doug Moon Joo, pres; John Sommers, VP/gen mgr; Amy Schwab, mktg dir.

Alexandria VA , 150 S. Gordon St. Phone:

TV-CATV only.

Soundstages, postproduction, graphics, duplication, remote, satellite uplink, videoconferencing, film-to-tape, D-2, digital 110 pathways & audio sweetening.

Auburn Television Satellite Uplink, (Formerly Auburn Television). Auburn University, Admin. Bldg., Corner of Samford & Donahue, Auburn, AL, 36849-5423. Phone: (334) 844-5707. Fax: (334) 844-5708.E-mail: taylody@auburn.edu Web Site:www.auburn.edu Bliss Bailey, exec dir; John Gober, engr; Deborah Howard, opns mgr.

Montgomery AL . Broadview Media, 401 Adams St., Suite 740. Phone:

TV-CATV-Radio.

Tape/CD/DVD duplication, satellite uplink/downlink facilities & CATV. Affiliate studio production facilities (Broadview Media) are available in Montgomery, AL via microwave link to the uplink.l

The Audio Department Inc., 119 W. 57th St., 4th Fl., New York, NY, 10019. Phone: (212) 586-3503. Fax: (212) 245-1675. Web Site:www.theaudiodepartment.com Aimee Mitchaud, mgr; Lola Norarevian, mgr.

TV-CATV only.

Audio & audio for video, adv & media promotion.

Audio Production Services, University of Colorado, Campus Box 379, 312 Stadium Bldg., Boulder, CO, 80309. Phone: (303) 492-2675. Fax: (303) 492-7017.

Radio Only.

Radio program production.

Auritt Communications Group, 555 8th Ave., Suite 709, New York, NY, 10018. Phone: (212) 302-6230. Fax: (212) 302-2969. Web Site:www.auritt.com E-mail: info@auritt.com Joan Auritt, pres.

TV-CATV-Radio.

Satellite media tours, event coverage, video news releases, B-roll packages, radio tours, audio news releases, sls/corporate videos, web casting & print tours.

Australian Tourist Commission, 2049 Century Park E., Fl. 19, Los Angeles, CA, 90067-3121. Phone: (310) 229-4871. Fax: (310) 552-1215.E-mail: rmonfrini@atc.australia.com Web Site:www.australia.com Robert Monfrini, dir.

TV-CATV only.

TV program distribution.

Avid Technology Inc., Avid Technology Park, One Park W., Tewksbury, MA, 01876. Phone: (800) 949-2843. Phone: (978) 640-6789. Fax: (978) 640-1366.E-mail: info@avid.com Web Site:www.avid.com

TV-CATV only.

Avid Technology is a leading supplier of newsroom computer, editing, playback & effects systems. Implemented as stand-alone or networked systems, Avid solutions provide speed, creativity & operating efficiencies throughout the newsroom.

Axcess Broadcast Services Inc., 4801 Spring Valley, Suite 105-B, Dallas, TX, 75244. Phone: (972) 386-6847. Fax: (972) 386-5207.

TV-CATV only.

Sls consulting for new businesses in the top 100 markets. CD production library, radio, TV promotions & IDs.

B

BBC Worldwide Americas Inc., 747 3rd Ave., 7th Fl., New York, NY, 10017. Phone: (212) 705-9300. Fax: (212) 888-0576.

TV-CATV only.

TV program production & distribution, home video, library sls, licensing.

BBC Worldwide Television Ltd., 80 Woodlands, London, W12 0TT. Fax: (181) 749-0538. Fax: (181) 576-2000.E-mail: webguide@bbc.co.uk Web Site:www.bbc.co.uk

TV-CATV-Radio.

Program licensing to international bcstrs & generation of co-production business. Dev of BBC branded satellite & cable channels worldwide.

S. Banks Group Inc., 174 Johnston Ave., Toronto, ON, M2N 1H3. Canada. Phone: (416) 224-0296. Fax: (416) 224-8542. Sydney Banks, pres.

TV-CATV only.

Feature film and TV program production.

Bardel Entertainment Inc., 548 Beatty St., Vancouver, BC, V6B 2L3. Canada. Phone: (604) 669-5589. Fax: (604) 669-9079.E-mail: info@bardel.ca Web Site:www.bardelentertainment.com Barry Ward, pres; Delna Bhesania, co-CEO; Michael Remedios, co-CEO.

TV-CATV only.

High quality 3D, Maya, Flash, Harmony & hybrids of digital & traditional animation for feature film, TV, interactive media, internet & commercials. Specializing in virtual worlds & online casual games.

Bavaria Film GmbH, Bavariafilmplatz 7, 82031 Geiselgasteig/Munich Phone: 49 89 6499 0. Fax: 49 89 6492 507.E-mail: presse@bavaria-film.de Web Site:www.bavaria-film.de Dieter Frank, pres; Thilo Kleine, pres; Peter Kussius, sls mgr.

TV-CATV only.

Dubbing, film laboratories, film & tape transfers, film & TV production, production svcs, multimedia svcs.

Bayliss, (Formerly Gene Bayliss). 208 Good Hill Rd., Weston, CT, 06883-2326. Phone: (203) 227-7521. Fax: (203) 454-1032. Web Site:www.genebayliss.com Gene Bayliss, producer & consultant.

Produces, directs video conferences, videotapes for corporations & industries, meetings & special events.

Beckmann International, Meadow Ct., West St., Ramsey, Isle of Man, IM8 1AE. Phone: 44 01624 816585. Fax: 44 01624 816589.E-mail: beckmann@enterprise.net Web Site:www.beckmanngroup.co.uk

TV-CATV only.

International sls distributor specializing in non-fiction progmg.

Beethoven Satellite Network, (Classical Music Format Service). c/o WFMT Fine Arts Radio, 5400 N. St. Louis Ave., Chicago, IL, 60625. Phone: (773) 279-2000. Phone: (800) USA-WFMT. Fax: (773) 279-2199. Web Site:www.wfmt.com Steve Robinson, sr VP; Peter Vandegraaff, progmg dir; Carol Martinez, stn rel mgr; Terry Medina, mktg dir.

Radio Only.

Program production & distribution; 84 hour-a-week classical music format with program hosts in one-hour modules, loc sound included.

Dave Bell Associates Inc., 3211 Cahuenga Blvd. W., Hollywood, CA, 90068. Phone: (323) 851-7801. Fax: (323) 851-9349.E-mail: dbmovies@aol.com Dave Bell, pres; Ted Weiant, VP; Fred Putman, VP; Kitty Stallings, Associate.

TV-CATV only.

Dev & production of TV movies, reality series, feature films, documentaries & game shows.

Bell Foto Art Productions, 2577 S. Pennsylvania St., Denver, CO, 80210-5722. Phone: (303) 377-4606. Fax: (303) 322-2443.E-mail: bellfoto@att.net Web Site:www.bellfoto.tv Chris Bell, owner.

TV-CATV only.

Award winning High Definition video production: VNR, corporate, news sports, medical, training & legal. Story tellers with AJ-HDX 900, HVX-200, Sony Z1-U, Sony EX-3 and now the Sony XD-HD

Bellon Entertainment, 250 W. 57th St., Suite 1414, New York, NY, 10107. Phone: (212) 265-1222. Fax: (212) 265-7318.E-mail: bellonent@aol.com Gregory P. Bellon, pres.

TV-CATV only.

Represent and develop TV formats for worldwide distribution.

Best Film & Video Corp., 157 Fairview Ave., East Meadow, NY, 11554. Phone: (516) 931-6969. Fax: (516) 931-5959. Roy B. Winnick, pres; Dana Miller, dir mktg.

Beverly Hills CA , 242 N. Canon Dr. Phone:

TV program production & distribution of home video.

Black Audio Devices, Box 106, Ventura, CA, 93002-0106. Phone: (805) 653-5557. Fax: (805) 653-5557. Web Site:www.blackaudio.com

TV-CATV only.

Blackbird Productions, 6 Molasses Row, London, SWI1 3UX. United Kingdom. Phone: +44 20 792 46440.

TV-CATV only.

Program production & distribution.

Blackstone Stock Footage, 509 Upsall Drive, Antioch, TN, 37013. Phone: (615) 731-5310. Fax: (615) 731-5232.E-mail: g.clifford@worldnet.att.net Web Site:www.blackstonestockfootage.com Glenda Clifford, pres.

TV-CATV only.

We offer: Archival newsreel footage, medical, extreme sports, landmarks from around the world, food, people, animals, underwater, timelapse cities & nature.

Blanc Communications Corp., 171 Pier Ave., Suite 517, Santa Monica, CA, 90405. Phone: (310) 278-2600. Fax: (310) 396-8434.

TV program production; TV & radio coml production & distribution.

The Chuck Blore Co., 17428 Tarzana St., Encino, CA, 91316. Phone: (818) 784-5104. Fax: (818) 986-1196.E-mail: bloregroup@aol.com Web Site:www.chuckblore.com Chuck Blore, CEO.

TV-CATV-Radio.

TV programs & coml production svcs. Radio coml production svcs. TV programs consultation.

Blue Canyon Productions, Box 6622, Santa Fe, NM, 87502. Phone: (505) 989-9298. Web Site:www.bluecanyonproductions.com Jim Terr, pres.

TV-CATV-Radio.

Award-winning, nationally-bcst jingle, PSA & radio spot production, voice-overs, video production, as well as music production, scoring & scripting.

Blue Heaven Productions, 11 Glenwood Rd., Toms River, NJ, 08753-4117. Phone: (732) 349-8569.E-mail: raynorman3@juno.com Ray Norman, pres.

Radio Only.

Nostalgia music production library, CD masters made

Blue Sky Studios, 44 S. Broadway, White Plains, NY, 10601. Phone: (914) 259-6500. Fax: (914) 259-6499.E-mail: query@blueskystudios.com Web Site:www.blueskystudios.com Brian Keane, gen mgr .

TV-CATV only.

Dev & production of CG animated films.

Blue Star Media, Dallas Cowboys Broadcasting. Dallas Cowboys Football Club, One Cowboys Pkwy., Irving, TX, 75063. Phone: (972) 556-9345. Fax: (972) 556-9339. Web Site:dallascowboys.com Scott Purcel, dir bcstg.

TV-CATV-Radio.

Radio play by play, wkly sports TV for NFL Dallas Cowboys & show for Dallas Cowboys.

Robert L. Bocchino, 264 Montgomery Ave., Haverford, PA, 19041-1531. Phone: (610) 649-0993. Fax: (610) 649-0895. Robert L. Bocchino, owner.

TV-CATV only.

Voice over artist, coml spokesperson.

Bonneville Communications, 5 Triad Ctr., Suite 700, Salt Lake City, UT, 84180-1121. Phone: (801) 237-2600. Fax: (801) 237-2614.E-mail: bonneville@bonneville.com Web Site:www.bonneville.com Gregg D. Garber, gen mgr; Marc Lee, dir; Paul Yates, controller & VP.

TV-CATV only.

A values-driven adv agency engaged in communications for quality life.

Boston Symphony Orchestra, Symphony Hall, 301 Massachusetts Ave., Boston, MA, 02115. Phone: (617) 266-1492. Fax: (617) 638-9367. Web Site:www.bso.org Mark Volpe, mng dir.

TV-CATV only.

Evening at Pops TV series & other special TV productions. Originates regular radio bcst of BSO concerts.

Dick Brescia Associates, 164 Garfield St., Haworth, NJ, 07641. Phone: (201) 385-6566. Fax: (201) 385-6449.E-mail: dbasyndicators@prodigy.net Web Site:www.ictx.com/dba

Radio Only.

Radio shows: *When Radio Was, Stan Freberg Here.* Radio movie classics, radio super heroes.

Brillig Productions Inc., 770 Amalfi Dr., Pacific Palisades, CA, 90272. Phone: (310) 459-4450. Fax: (310) 459-4456.E-mail: brilligprod@cooliwk.net Barry Brown, pres; Joy Brown, VP.

TV-CATV only.

Feature films, TV features, TV comls, documentaries.

British Broadcasting Corp., (Fine Arts Programs.). c/o WFMT Radio Network, 5400 N. St. Louis Ave., Chicago, IL, 60625. Phone: (773) 279-2112. Phone: (773) 279-2114. Fax: (773) 279-2199.E-mail: finearts@wfmt.com Web Site:www.wfmt.com Carol Martinez, stn rel mgr; Steve Robinson, sr VP.

Radio Only.

Distribute wkly series *My Music*, & *My Word* for coml & public stns in the United States by WFMT Fine Arts Network.

Broadcast News Service, Box 919, Norwood, MA, 02062-0919. Phone: (781) 344-6988. Fax: (781) 344-8928. P. J. Romano, dir.

TV-CATV only.

Radio, TV features & productions, audio news & features.

Broadcast Programming, 2211 5th Ave., Seattle, WA, 98121. Phone: (206) 728-2741. Phone: (800) 426-9082. Fax: (206) 441-6582.E-mail: experts@jmseattle.com Web Site:www.jonesradio.com

Radio Only.

Daypart personality progmg, music log & consulting services.

Broadcast Studio Inc., (Formerly KJD Teleproductions). 30 Whyte Dr., Voorhees, NJ, 08043. Phone: (856) 751-3500. Fax: (856) 751-7729.E-mail: mactoday@earthlink.net Web Site:www.kjdteleproductions.com Larry Scott, pres/CEO.

TV-CATV-Radio.

TV, radio program, coml, promotion film production & distribution; production svcs; TV processing lab.

Broadview Media, 4455 W. 77th St., Minneapolis, MN, 55435. Phone: (952) 835-4455. Fax: (952) 835-0971.E-mail: michaels@broadviewmedia.com Michael Smith, VP progmg.

TV-CATV only.

Full-svc production, postproduction & creative svcs for the production of TV programs.

Bruder Releasing Inc. (BRI), 2020 Broadway, Santa Monica, CA, 90404. Phone: (310) 829-2222. Fax: (310) 829-0202.E-mail: bruder@brivideo.net Web Site:www.46ri.net Marc Bruder, pres.

TV-CATV only.

Supplies ind films to pay-per-view, cable, bcst & video markets worldwide.

Bulbeck & Mas SL, Quinones, 2, 28015 Madrid Phone: 34 91 594 2709. Fax: 34 91 445 7212.E-mail: bymfilms@bulbeckymas.com

TV-CATV only.

Specialists in libraries of Spanish features.

Burrud Productions Inc., 16351 Gothard St., Unit D, Huntington Beach, CA, 92647. Phone: (714) 842-8422. Fax: (714) 842-0433.E-mail: burrudprod@aol.com Web Site:www.burrud.com John Burrund, pres/CEO; Linda Karabin, VP; Drew Horton, VP; Valerie Chow, VP; Shannon Mead, exec dir, CEO.

TV-CATV only.

Feature film & TV production of reality, wildlife, oceanic, human adventure, documentary & world exploration progmg.

Buzzco Associates Inc., 33 Bleecker St., Suite 5A, New York, NY, 10012. Phone: (212) 473-8800. Fax: (212) 473-8891.E-mail: info@buzzzco.com Web Site:www.buzzzco.com Candy Kugel, dir; Vincent Cafarelli, dir.

TV-CATV only.

A full range of animation from traditional to innovative computer 2-D.

C

CABLEready Corp., 98 East Ave., Norwalk, CT, 06851-5029. Phone: (203) 855-7979. Fax: (203) 855-8370.E-mail: info@cableready.net Web Site:www.cableready.net Gary Lico, pres; Lou Occhicone, sr VP opns; Sabrina Toledo, VP sls; Liz Levenson, dir devt.

TV-CATV only.

Dev & sls of programs to U.S. cable TV networks & systems & all international telecasters.

CA Media Development, 1144 Hooper Ave., Suite 208, Toms River, NJ, 08753. Phone: (732) 797-1965. Fax: (732) 797-1260.E-mail: ca.media@comcast.net Gregory Koziar, pres.

TV-CATV-Radio.

Full svc adv agency, as well as coml production, for radio & cable TV.

CBC International Sales, Box 500, Stn. A, Toronto, ON, M5W 1E6. Canada. Phone: (416) 205-3500. Fax: (416) 205-3482.E-mail: cbcis@toronto.cbc.ca Christina Criss Hajek; Susan Hewitt, head international sls (London) & new business dev; Sandra Sarciada-Naughton, .

London, 43/51 Great Titchfield St.

Los AngelesCA , 1950 Sawtelle Blvd, Suite 333.

TV-CATV only.

CBC is Canada's natl bcstr. Produces & distributes TV progmg in both English & French.

CBS Studio International, (Formerly CBS Paramount International Television). 7800 Beverly Blvd., Los Angeles, CA, 90036. Phone: (323) 575-5460. Fax: (323) 575-5469.E-mail: firstname.lastname@cbs.com Web Site:www.cbscorporation.com Armando Nunez, pres; Joe Lucas, exec VP & sls & mktg; Barry Chamberlain, sr VP sls.

TV-CATV only.

International TV distribution, co-production, loc production formats, & channel mgmt.

CBS Television Distribution, 2401 Colorado Ave., Suite 110, Santa Monica, CA, 90404. Phone: (310) 264-3300. Fax: (310) 264-3301. Web Site:www.cbscorporation.com Robert Madden, sr exec VP; John Nogawski, pres; Terry Wood, pres & creative affrs & dev.

TV-CATV only.

TV program production, distribution, mktg to domestic syndication & other TV venues.

CBS Worldwide Distribution, (Formerly Viacom Video Services). 524 W. 57th St., New York, NY, 10019-2924. Phone: (212) 975-8139. Fax: (212) 975-7272.E-mail: mjeffers@cbs.com Web Site:www.cbs.com Jaime Rockman, VP distribution & opns.

Los AngelesCA , 10877 Wilshire Blvd. Phone:

TV-CATV only.

Duplicate & distribute syndicated TV progmg via tape & satellite, coml integration, international standards conversion, uplink/downlink, tape duplication, space segment & HD.

CCI Entertainment Ltd., 18 Dupont St., Toronto, ON, MSR 1V2. Canada. Phone: (416) 964-8750. Fax: (416) 964-1980. Arnie Zipursky, pres/CEO; Annette Frymer, COO.

TV-CATV only.

Distributor & co-producer, producer

CCM Media Services, 750 old Hickory Blvd, Ste 150-1, Brentwood, TN, 37027. Phone: (615) 312-4244. Fax: (615) 312-4266.E-mail: jcharles@salempublishing.com Web Site:www.salempublishing.com

Publisher of Homecoming, Preaching, YouthWorker Journal, Singing News and Townhall magazines

CDC United Network, 40 Rue Souveraine, 1050 Brussels Phone: (322) 502-6640. Fax: (322) 502-6656.E-mail: alexandre@cdc.skynet.be MOBILE: 3275713057

TV-CATV only.

TV distribution & merchandising in Latin America.

CDR Communications Inc., 9310-B Old Keene Mill Rd., Burke, VA, 22015. Phone: (703) 569-3400. Fax: (703) 569-3448.E-mail: chris@cdrcommunications.com Web Site:www.cdrcommunications.com Christopher D. Rogers, pres; Nancy B. Rogers, VP.

BurkeVA , 9302 C Old Keene Mill Rd.

TV-CATV-Radio.

Film, TV, video & radio production: teleconferences, documentaries, adv campaigns, PSAs; graphics, animation, syndication, promotion, publishing, distribution, postproduction & mktg.

CFP Video Productions, Box 86, Caldwell, NJ, 07006-0086. Phone: (973) 226-2481. Fax: (973) 226-2480.E-mail: don.spitzmiller@verizon.net Web Site:www.cfpvideo.com Donald Spitzmiller, pres.

TV-CATV-Radio.

Full video, audio svcs for TV & industrial productions. Avid edit svc/post production.

CIFEX International Inc., One Peconic Hills Ct., Southampton, NY, 11968-1618. Phone: (631) 283-9454. Fax: (631) 283-4210.E-mail: cifex@prodigy.net Gerald J. Rappoport, pres; Beulah Rappoport, VP business affrs; Shirley Clarke, VP mktg.

TV-CATV only.

Distributor of foreign-language feature films, animated & live-action short films & documentaries.

CMT, 330 Commerce St., Nashville, TN, 37201. Phone: (615) 335-8400. Fax: (615) 335-8615. Web Site:www.cmt.com Brian Philips, exec VP/gen mgr; Neil Holt, sr VP/ad sls; Jay Frank, sr VP/music strategy; Martin Clayton, VP digital media; Mary Beth Cunin, VP progmg strategy; John Hamlin, sr VP/production & dev; Bob Kusbit, head dev; Suzanne Norman, sr VP/strategy & opns.

TV-CATV only.

America's #1 country music net, provides original progmg, live concerts, events, music videos by established & cutting edge artists, news & info.

CNBC Syndication, 900 Sylvan Ave., Englewood Cliffs, NJ, 07632. Phone: (201) 735-2622. Fax: (201) 585-3365. Howard Homonoff, VP/gen mgr; Steve Blechman, mgr; Margaret Agsteribbe, mgr; Pamela Thomas Graham, CEO.

TV-CATV only.

Syndicated TV program, *Wall Street Journal Report*, business events.

CN8, The Comcast Network, Penns Landing Studio, 1351 S. Columbus Blvd., Philadelphia, PA, 19147. Phone: (215) 468-2222. Fax: (215) 468-3812. Web Site:www.cn8.tv Jonathan Gorchow; David Shane, dir of progmg, CN8; Cheryl Flamini, VP of business dev, Eastern division; Peggy Giordano, mgr, CN8 progmg; Denise Pettyford, dir of network adv sls, CN8; Larry Watzman, creative svcs dir, CN8; Alex Soumbenioits, mktg & PR mgr, CN8; Brian McLendon, dir of network productions, CN8; Scott Clark, dir of engrg, CN8; Stephanie Millagranna, admin coord; Mark Dudzinski, stn mgr; Rich Frantz, mgr engr; Jon Gurevitch, VP sports; Buck Dopp, VP.

New CastleDE . New Castle Studio, 2215 N. Dupont Hwy. Phone:

TV-CATV only.

CN8, The Comcast Network, is a rgnl cable net offering news, sports, & entertainment progmg to 3.9 million cable homes.

CNN Newsource Sales Inc., One CNN Center, 12 North, Atlanta, GA, 30303. Phone: (404) 827-5475. Fax: (404) 827-4466.E-mail: cnn.newsource@turner.com Web Site:http://newsource.cnn.com Taylor Fuller, VP/gen sls mgr; Ed Stephen, sr VP.

TV-CATV only.

Provider of news & info content to the loc bcst news industry.

C N R Radio, Box 27532, Minneapolis, MN, 55427-0532. Phone: (763) 537-5868.E-mail: CNRadio@comcast.net Web Site:www.cnradio.notlong.com George Carden, pres & producer.

Radio Only.

News interviews, soundbites & features with newsmakers for primarily Christian radio stns & nets.

CONUS Archive, 3415 University Ave., St. Paul, MN, 55114. Phone: (651) 642-4576. Fax: (651) 642-4669. Web Site:www.conus.com Chris Bridson, sr sls exec; Jim Richter, VP/gen mgr.

TV-CATV only.

Video archive svcs to natl & international program producers.

CRM Learning, 2215 Faraday Ave., Carlsbad, CA, 92008-7295. Phone: (800) 421-0833. Fax: (760) 931-5792. Web Site:www.crmlearning.com Peter J. Jordan, pres/CEO.

TV-CATV only.

Production & distribution of business training films.

CRN International, One Circular Ave., Hamden, CT, 06514. Phone: (203) 288-2002. Fax: (203) 281-3291. Web Site:www.crnradio.com Barry Berman, pres; S. Richard Kalt, exec VP.

Radio Only.

Short-form customized radio progms & promotions; *SkiWatch® BeachWatch* & small business reports.

CS Associates, 200 Dexter Ave, Watertown, MA, 02472-4236. Phone: (617) 923-0077. Fax: (617) 923-0025.E-mail: programs@csassociates.com Charles Schuerhoff, pres; Brian Gilbert, aquisitions; Lisa Carey, VP intl sales; Jason Redmond, Mgr of Acquisitions.

TV-CATV only.

Program distribution, specializing in documentaries, foreign & domestic TV & cable; broker co-productions.

CTVC Hillside Studios, Merry Hill Rd., Bushey, Watford, Herts, WD23 1DR. Phone: 020 8950 4426. Fax: 020 8950 1437.E-mail: barrie.allcott@ctvc.co.uk Web Site:www.ctvc.co.uk Barrie Allcott, mng dir; Ray Bruce, producer.

TV-CATV only.

Producers of programs with humanitarian values, especially relg. Also full bcst facilities available for hire.

CTV Television Inc., Box 9, Stn. O, Toronto, ON, M4A 2M9. Canada. Phone: (416) 332-5000. Fax: (416) 332-5065. Web Site:www.ctv.ca Susanne Boyce, pres CTV progmg.

TV-CATV only.

TV bcstg, program production & distribution.

C 2 Productions Inc., 15430 Catalpa Cove Ln., Fort Myers, FL, 33908. Phone: (239) 437-4222. Fax: (239) 437-2042.E-mail: chris@chriscorley.com Web Site:chriscorley.com Chris Corley, pres.

TV-CATV-Radio.

Voice-overs delivered digitally or in person.

Cable Films & Video, Box 7171, Country Club Station, Kansas City, MO, 64113. Phone: (913) 362-2804. Phone: (800) 514-2804. Fax: (913) 362-2804.E-mail: cablesfilms @kc.rr.com Web Site:www.onlineworld.com/movies Herbert Miller, CEO.

TV-CATV only.

Classic films, all formats: one inch BETA SP, CD-ROM, U-Matic, PAL, NTSC, SECAM, DVD. Over 300 motion pictures & classic cartoons, clips available.

Call For Action Inc., 5272 River Rd., Suite 300, Bethesda, MD, 20816. Phone: (301) 657-8260. Fax: (301) 657-2914. Web Site:www.callforaction.org Shirley L. Rooker, pres.

TV-CATV only.

International hotline svc, affiliated with the bcst media, that provides info, assistance to individuals & small businesses with consumer problems.

Camera Group, 3920 N. 29th Ave., Hollywood, FL, 33022. Phone: (305) 945-2020. Fax: (305) 945-1117.E-mail: cameragrp@aol.com Web Site:www.cameragroup.com Eileen Garcia-Di Rosa, pres.

TV-CATV only.

Rental, sls, svc & maintenance of motion picture, TV & video production equipment.

CamMate Studios, 425 E. Comstock, Chandler, AZ, 85225. Phone: (480) 813-9500. Fax: (480) 813-9292.E-mail: cammate@cammate.com Web Site:www.cammate.com Linda Mitchell, pres/CEO; James Mitchell, mktg dir.

TV-CATV only.

Camera cranes, telescopic cranes & mini cranes.

Campbell-Ewald Advertising, 30400 Van Dyke, Warren, MI, 48093. Phone: (586) 574-3400. Fax: (586) 558-5891. Web Site:www.campbell-ewald.com Anthony J. Hopp, CEO/chmn/pres; S.H. Gilbert, exec VP/CFO; D.A. Kamowsky, VP; W.J. Ludwig, VP; L.M. Schultz, VP; J.T. Seregny, VP.

Los AngelesCA , 11100 Santa Monica Blvd, 6th Fl. Phone:

ChicagoIL , One Magnificent Mile, 930 N. Michigan Ave, Suite 1060. Phone:

New YorkNY , One Dag Hammarskjold Plaza. Phone:

TV-CATV only.

TV programs, TV radio coml, promotion film production.

Canamedia Inc., (formerly Canamedia Productions Ltd.). 381 Richmond St. E., Suite 200, Toronto, ON, M5A 1P6. Canada. Phone: (416) 483-7446. Fax: (416) 483-7529.E-mail: canamed@canamedia.com Web Site:www.canamedia.com Les Harris, pres; Andrea Stokes, intl sls & acquisitions mgr.

TV-CATV only.

Canamedia offers production & international distribution svcs. It also exclusively represents in Canada the ITN source Archive & Natural History New Zealand Archives as well as the PUMP audio music archive.

CanLib Inc., 4819 Galendo St., Woodland Hills, CA, 91364-4326. Phone: (818) 888-6005. Fax: (818) 888-2505.E-mail: canlibinc@adelphia.net Gene Accas, pres; Carol Stevens, exec VP, sec/treas.

TV-CATV only.

Bcstg & media consulting: rsch for producers, distributors, advertisers, agencies & law firms (legal expert witness).

Cannell Studios, 7083 Hollywood Blvd., Suite 600, Hollywood, CA, 90028. Phone: (323) 465-5800. Fax: (323) 856-7390. Web Site:www.cannell.com Stephen J. Cannell, chmn/CEO.

TV-CATV only.

Capital Communications, 2357-3 South Tamiami Trl., Venice, FL, 34293. Phone: (941) 492-4688. Fax: (941) 492-4923.E-mail: cap5678@isp.com Web Site:www.isp.com James Springer, pres/CEO.

TV-CATV only.

International distributor of pre-packaged TV programs.

Carden & Cherry Syndication Inc., 1220 McGavock St., Nashville, TN, 37203. Phone: (615) 255-6694. Fax: (615) 255-8345.

TV-CATV only.

TV & radio coml production & distribution; production svcs.

Careco Television Productions, 5717 N.W. Pkwy., Suite 104, San Antonio, TX, 78249. Phone: (800) 668-8081. Fax: (210) 697-0150. Web Site:www.outdooraction.com Charles Goodloe, pres; Lavonne Kacalek, VP.

TV-CATV only.

Producer of *American Outdoors* & *Fishing Texas*, weekly half hour series.

Caridi Entertainment, 250 W. 57th St., Suite 1326, New York, NY, 10107. Phone: (212) 581-2277. Fax: (212) 581-2278.E-mail: c.caridi@att.net

TV-CATV only.

Full-svc international distributor & production company.

Carleton Productions International Inc., 1500 Merivale Rd., 5th Fl., Nepean, ON, K2E 6Z5. Canada. Phone: (613) 224-9666. Fax: (613) 224-9074.E-mail: cpi@magi.com Web Site:www.carletonproductions.com Mark Ross, pres.

TV & radio programs, coml production & distribution & production svcs.

George Carlson & Associates, 323 First Ave. W., Seattle, WA, 98119. Phone: (206) 213-0562. Fax: (206) 213-0562. George Carlson, producer.

TV-CATV only.

Producers/distributors of 1/2-hour color, true life, travel adventure series to all parts of the world called *The Traveler & Northwest Traveler.*

Carlton International Media Inc., 11145 N.W. 1st Pl., Coral Springs, FL, 33071. Phone: (954) 345-1620. Fax: (954) 345-1490.E-mail: clarea@msn.com Web Site:www.carltonint.co.uk Claire Alter, VP; Rupert Dillnot-Cooper, CEO; Louise Pedersen, mgr.

Studio CityCA Phone:

TV-CATV only.

British TV distributor, licenses a wide range of programs worldwide.

Carpel Video Inc., 429 E. Patrick St., Frederick, MD, 21701. Phone: (800) 238-4300. Phone: (301) 694-3500. Fax: (301) 694-9510. Web Site:www.carpelvideo.com Andy Carpel, pres.

TV-CATV only.

Videotape recyclers; production svcs, video tape to DVD duplication.

Carriage House Studios, 119 Westhill Rd., Stamford, CT, 06902. Phone: (203) 358-0065. Fax: (203) 964-4988.E-mail: chstudios@aol.com John Montagnese, pres & Studio mgr.

TV-CATV only.

Recording studio.

Carsey-Werner Distribution, 12001 Ventura Pl., Suite 600, Studio City, CA, 91604. Phone: (818) 299-9600. Fax: (818) 299-9650. Web Site:www.carseywerner.com Bob Dubelko, pres/COO; Herbert Lazarus, pres; James Kraus, pres.

TV-CATV only.

TV program distribution.

Sandra Carter Global, Inc., 230 W. 79th St., Suite 102, New York, NY, 10024. Phone: (212) 875-1811. Fax: (212) 875-0088.E-mail: sales@sandra-carter.com Web Site:www.sandra-carter.com Sandra Carter, pres.

TV-CATV only.

Distribution to all media, co-production deals, production, principle product in factual series.

Castle Hill Productions Inc., 36 W. 25th St., 2nd Fl., New York, NY, 10010. Phone: (212) 242-1500. Fax: (212) 414-5737.E-mail: mm@castlehillproductions.com Web Site:www.castlehillproductions.com Julian Schlossberg, chmn; Mel Maron, pres; Barbara Karmel, VP TV sls.

Boca RatonFL , 2385 Executive Center Dr, Suite 100.

TV-CATV only.

Movie distribution for theater, TV, cable, and video.

Catholic Communications Corp., 65 Elliot St., Springfield, MA, 01101. Phone: (413) 452-0648. Fax: (413) 747-0273.E-mail: m.graziano@diospringfield.org Mark Duport, CEO.

TV-CATV-Radio.

TV & radio production svcs.

Catholic Television Network, Box 430, 9531 Akron-Canfield Rd., Canfield, OH, 44406-0430. Phone: (330) 533-2243. Fax: (330) 533-1907.E-mail: judyctny@aol.com Web Site:www.doy.org Bob Gavalier, gen mgr .

TV-CATV only.

24-hour ecumenical TV ch.

Celebrities Productions, 230 S. Bemiston Ave., Suite 1400, St. Louis, MO, 63105. Phone: (314) 862-7800. Fax: (314) 721-5171. I.J. Davis, pres; David Dovich, VP; Walt Williams, VP.

TV-CATV-Radio.

Creation, production of radio, TV spots, programs, audio visuals; arrangement for celebrity talent, music, syndication & video conference production.

CelebrityFootage, 320 South Almont Dr., Beverly Hills, CA, 90211. Phone: (310) 360-9600. Fax: (310) 360-9696.E-mail: michael@celebrityfootage.com Web Site:www.celebrityfootage.com Michael Goldberg, pres.

TV-CATV only.

Provides media outlets with celebrity entertainment news from the Los Angeles area, including movie premieres, award shows & charity benefits.

Celluloid Dreams, 24 rue Lamartine 75009, Paris Phone: (33) 1 49 70 83 20. Fax: (33) 1 49 70 03 71. Web Site:www.celluloid-dreams.com

TV-CATV only.

International distribution of ind features, documentaries & animation films.

Center City Film & Video, 1503-05 Walnut St., Philadelphia, PA, 19102. Phone: (215) 568-4134. Fax: (215) 568-6011.E-mail: centercity@ccfv.com Web Site:www.ccfv.com Jordan M. Schwartz, chmn/pres; Brian Isely, VP/gen mgr; John Gillespie, exec producer.

TV-CATV only.

Award winning production staff, video; film production, studio; remote camera packages including ultimatte, digital audio suite, flint, complete post production.

Central City Productions, Inc., 212 East Ohio St. #3, Chicago, IL, 60611. Phone: (312) 654-1100. Fax: (312) 321-9921. Web Site:www.ccptv.com Don Jackson, chmn/CEO; Rosemary Jackson, VP; Erma Gray Davis, pres/COO; Jennifer J. Jackson, gen mgr; Heather Davis, sls VP.

TV-CATV only.

Production & mktg of bcst & cable TV progmg targeted towards minority viewers.

Central Park Media Corp., (formerly Central Park Media). 331 W. 57th St., Suite 554, New York, NY, 10019. Phone: (646) 957-8301 (X-8303). Fax: (646) 957-8316.E-mail: jod@teamcpm.com Web Site:www.centralparkmedia.com John O'Donnell, mgng dir.

TV-CATV only.

Over 200 Japanese Anime titles available for TV & cable.

Century III at Universal Studios Florida, 2000 Universal Studios Plaza, Orlando, FL, 32819-7606. Phone: (407) 354-1000. Fax: (407) 352-8662.E-mail: rcibella@century3.com Web Site:www.century3.com

TV-CATV-Radio.

Full-svc production & postproduction facility, audio department, custom graphics, digital editing capabilities, film transfers, interactive department, satellite uplink svcs.

Channel Four Television, 124 Horseferry Rd., London, SW1 2TX. Phone: 44 20 7396 4444.E-mail: righttoreply@channel.4.com Web Site:www.channel4.com

TV-CATV only.

UK bcstr.

Chicago Radio Syndicate Inc., 15003 Lemay St., Van Nuys, CA, 91405. Phone: (800) 621-6949. Fax: (818) 376-8529. Web Site:www.sandyorkin-crs.com E-mail: sandyo@earthlink.net Sandy Orkin, pres.

Radio Only.

Syndication of Dick Orkin comedy features—*Chickenman*, *Tooth Fairy & Mini-People* & commercial camgaigns.

Children's Media Productions, Box 40400, Pasadena, CA, 91114-7400. Phone: (626) 797-5462.E-mail: childrensmedia@yahoo.com Web Site:www.childrensmedia.com C. Ray Carlson, pres; Joy Carlson, PR.

TV-CATV only.

Producer & distributor of children's progmg, videos & feature films, worldwide.

Chinamerica Hit Radio, (Formerly The Radio-Studio Network). Box 683, New York, 10108. Phone: (800) 827-1722. Fax: (212) 868-5663.E-mail: programming @chinamericahitradio.com Web Site:www.chinamericahitradio.com Steve Warren, exec producer.

Chinese hit music, 24 hour pop contemp, hosted in English

Christian Children's Associates Inc., Box 446, Toms River, NJ, 08754. Phone: (732) 240-3003. Fax: (732) 286-4244.E-mail: adventurepals@juno.com Web Site:www.adventurepals.com Jean Donaldson, pres; Frank Troilo, VP; ReverendWilliam Cook, dir.

TV-CATV-Radio.

Production, distribution of radio & TV progmg for children.

Christian Media Network, Box 448, Jacksonville, OR, 97530. Phone: (541) 899-8888. Web Site:www.christianmedianetwork.com

TV-CATV-Radio.

Christian Science Sentinel - Radio Edition, One Norway St., C4-20, Boston, MA, 02115-3122. Phone: (617) 450-2000. Fax: (617) 450-3997.E-mail: sentinelradio@csps.com Web Site:www.sentinelradio.com Susan Kerr, producer.

Radio Only.

Religious radio programs.

Christian TV Services of Ellicottville Inc., P. O. Box 209, Ellicottville, NY, 14731-0209. Phone: (716) 699-2549. Fax: (716) 699-2590.E-mail: geothayer@yahoo.com Web Site:www.christiantvservices.com Rev. George A. Thayer, pres/CEO.

TV-CATV only.

Christian media consultants "Ministering to ministries around the world"; locally linked area worship places, internet listing places; svcs , inc. 1974 internet.

The Christophers Inc., 12 E. 48th St., New York, NY, 10017. Phone: (212) 759-4050. Fax: (212) 838-5073.E-mail: mail@christophers.org Web Site:www.christophers.org Tony Rossi, producer.

TV-CATV-Radio.

We produce & distribute only our own media (radio, print).

Chrysalis Distribution, 13 Bramley Rd., London, W10 6SP. Phone: (44) 207 4674. Fax: (44) 207 221 6286.E-mail: distribution@chrysalis.co.uk Christina Willoughby, mgng dir.

TV-CATV only.

International sale of TV programs to all media worldwide.

Cimarron Group, 6855 Santa Monica Blvd., Hollywood, CA, 90038. Phone: (323) 337-0300. Fax: (323) 337-0333. Web Site:www.cimarrongroup.com Cheryl Savala, sr art dir; Bob Farina, owner.

TV-CATV only.

TV promotions, spec shoots, graphics, sls presentations, trade & consumer print design, title treatment & image campaigns.

Cinecraft Productions Inc., 2515 Franklin Blvd., Cleveland, OH, 44113. Phone: (216) 781-2300. Fax: (216) 781-1067.E-mail: info@cinecraft.com Web Site:www.cinecraft.com Neil G. McCormick, chmn; Neil G. MCCormick, mgr; Maria E. Keckan, pres.

TV-CATV only.

Betacam field production; 60' x 70' sound stage with hard cyc; AVID MC1000NT; Animation with Soft Image; interactive DVD & CD-R dev.

CineFilm/CineTransfer, 2156 Faulkner Rd. N.E., Atlanta, GA, 30324. Phone: (404) 633-1448. Phone: (800) 633-1448. Fax: (404) 633-3867.E-mail: csr@cinefilmlab.com Web Site:www.cinefilmlab.com William G. Thorton, pres; Jim Ogburn, gen mgr .

TV-CATV only.

16mm, super 16mm, 35mm color negative processing & printing. Dailies thru release prints. State-of-the-art video dailies & scene-to-scene transfers. Spirit Data Cini, all HD Formats

CineGroupe Corporation, (Formerly CineGroupe). 1151 Alexandre-DeSeve St., Montreal, PQ, H2L 2T7. Canada. Phone: (514) 524-7567. Fax: (514) 849-5001.E-mail: distribution@cinegroupe.ca Web Site:www.cinegroupe.com Michael Lemire, exec VP; Jacques Pettigrew, pres/CEO; Linda Caron, exec VP/finance & admin; Elaine Bigras, sls & client svcs coord.

TV-CATV only.

Animation, TV production, postproduction, paint & trace studio, distribution of animation TV series for children.

Cinema Concepts Animation Studio, 2030 Powers Ferry Rd., #214, Atlanta, GA, 30339. Phone: (770) 956-7460. Fax: (770) 956-8358.E-mail: info@cinemaconcepts.com Web Site:www.cinemaconcepts.com Stewart D. Harnell, CEO; Sharron A. Harnell, VP; John Price, studio dir; Theresa Dickey, gen mgr .

TV-CATV-Radio.

Animated corporate IDs, presentation/policy trailers for TV, cable & motion picture theatres, theatrical trailer fulfillment.

The Cinema Guild Inc., 115 W. 30th St., Suite 800, New York, NY, 10001. Phone: (212) 685-6242. Fax: (212) 685-4717.E-mail: info@cinemaguild.com Web Site:www.cinemaguild.com Ryan Krivoshey, dir distribution; Philip Hobel, chmn/CEO; Mary Ann Hobel, co-chmn.

TV-CATV only.

Film & video distribution to theatrical, non-theatrical, TV & home video mkts, worldwide.

Circle Oak Productions Inc., 33 N. Birch Hill Rd., Patterson, NY, 12563. Phone: (845) 878-9017. Fax: (845) 878-9018.

Educ film production.

Tim Cissell Music, 1120 Grassmere Dr., Richardson, TX, 75080-2909. Phone: (972) 680-0817. Fax: (972) 680-0866.E-mail: tcissell@wt.net Web Site:www.web.wt.net/~tcissell Tim Cissell, owner.

TV-CATV-Radio.

Offers music composition & production for all media (TV/CATV & radio)—jingles, IDs, film & video.

Citadel Media, (Formerly ABC Radio Networks). 261 Madison Ave., 3rd Fl., New York, NY, 100162. Phone: (212) 735-1700. Fax: (212) 735-1799. Web Site:www.citadelmedianetworks.com Tom Powell, VP; Dan Formento, VP.

Radio Only.

Producers of natl & international radio features, such as *Flashback, Flashback Pop Quiz & Rock Slides*.

Citadel Media, (Formerly ABC Radio Networks). 13725 Montfort Dr., Dallas, TX, 75240. Phone: (972) 991-9200. Fax: (972) 991-9890. Web Site:www.citadelmedianetworks.com Jim Robinson, pres; Darryl Brown, exec VP; Carl Anderson, progmg VP; Omar Thompson, mktg VP; Michael Knize, sls VP.

Radio Only.

Live 24-hour premium progmg available featuring 9 radio formats. Include advanced digital media platforms with online interactive advertising, streaming audio & podcasts, syndicated music & talk programs including Flashback, format-specific e-PREP, production libraries

The Dick Clark Productions, 2900 Olympic Blvd., Santa Monica, CA, 90404. Phone: (310) 255-4600. Web Site:www.dickclarkproductions.com Dick Clark, chmn; Orly Adelson, pres.

TV-CATV only.

TV production for networks, cable & syndication. Produces series, specials & movies for TV.

Classic Media, 860 Broadway, 6th Fl., New York, NY, 10003. Phone: (212) 659-3011. Fax: (212) 659-1958. Douglas Schwalbe, head of international; Bob Higgins, head of creative affrs & production.

Beverly HillsCA , 8640 Wilshire Blvd. Phone:

TV-CATV only.

Classic Media is a New York-based entertainment company that manages some of the most recognizable family oriented properties across all media including feature film, television, home video & consumer products.

The Classical Station, WCPE, Box 897, Wake Forest, NC, 27588. Phone: (919) 556-5178. Fax: (919) 556-9273.E-mail: wcpe@wcpe.org Web Site:theclassicalstation.org Deborah Proctor, gen mgr; Dick Storck, progmg dir; Rae Weaver, dev dir; Curtis Brothers, outreach dir; Peter Blume, business dev dir.

TV-CATV-Radio.

Free 24-hour classical music progmg with live announcers for radio, cable, other distributors. Wkly request programs, opera & features.

Clayton-Davis & Associates Inc., 230 S. Bemiston Ave., Suite 1400, St. Louis, MO, 63105. Phone: (314) 862-7800. Fax: (314) 721-5171. Web Site:www.claytondavis.com Jennifer Jermak, pres; Steve Pezold, VP.

TV-CATV-Radio.

Program production, syndication & barter.

Clear Channel Broadcasting Inc., 55 Music Sq. West, Nashville, TN, 37203. Phone: (615) 664-2400. Fax: (615) 664-2457.E-mail: davealpert@clearchannel.com Dave Alpert, pres; Kevin Moore, VP sls; Tom Stevens, opns dir.

TV-CATV-Radio.

State radio networking, collegiate radio & TV networking.

Clear Channel Entertainment Television, 220 W. 42nd St., 9th Fl., New York, NY, 10036. Phone: (917) 421-5206. Fax: (917) 421-5239. Web Site:www.clearchannelentertainment.com Steve Stern, exec producer; Joe Townley, pres; Marc Forest, progmg VP; Dawn Olejar, opns VP.

TV-CATV only.

Produces TV programs & promotion films, documentary film production, sports event TV production.

Clever Cleaver Productions, 4718 N. Placita Ventana Del Rio, Tucson, AZ, 85750. Phone: (520) 615-1582. Fax: (520) 615-1586.E-mail: clevercook@comcast.net Web Site:www.clevercleaver.com Lee N. Gerovitz, pres; Steve Cassarino, VP.

TV-CATV only.

Offers 260, 3-minute entertaining cooking vignettes & 27, 30-minute cooking shows, 90-second HD cooking vignettes (cash or barter) & 2-minute tailgate cooking vignettes (free licensing).

Coe Film Associates Inc., 70 E. 96th St., New York, NY, 10128. Phone: (212) 831-5355. Fax: (212) 996-6728.E-mail: cfainc@juno.com

TV-CATV only.

TV program distribution.

Colon & Associates Inc., 7100 Blvd. East, Guttenberg, NJ, 07093. Phone: (201) 869-4615. Fax: (201) 869-6217.E-mail: rei616@aol.com Web Site:www.saptv.com Reinaldo Colon, pres & CEO.

TV-CATV-Radio.

Program distribution, production, Sp language dubbing.

ComBridges, 70 Irwin St., San Rafael, CA, 94901. Phone: (415) 454-5505. Fax: (415) 454-1941. Web Site:www.combridges.com E-mail: info@combridges.com Jon Leland, pres & creative dir; Donna Nieddu, mgr; John Kraus, exec producer.

TV-CATV only.

Source of videos, seminars & interactive media. Producer, websites.

Combs Music, 421 Cedar Trail, Winston-Salem, NC, 27104. Phone: (336) 760-3905. Fax: (336) 760-3855.E-mail: dave@combsmusic.com Web Site:www.combsmusic.com

TV-CATV only.

Composes, produces, publishes & distributes easy lstng instrumental music, e.g., *Rachel's Song*.

Comcast Media Center, 4100 E. Dry Creek Rd., Littleton, CO, 80122. Phone: (303) 486-3800. Fax: (303) 486-3891. Web Site:www.comcast.com

TV-CATV only.

Network origination, production, postproduction, uplinking, compression, remote production, audio production.

Command Productions, Box 3000, Sausalito, CA, 94966-3000. Phone: (415) 332-3161. Fax: (415) 332-1901.E-mail: audio@commandproductions.com Web Site:www.commandproductions.com Warren Weagant, pres; Kitt Weagant, VP.

TV-CATV-Radio.

Radio-TV, CATV audio voice identification & promotion production.

Communications III Inc., 921 Eastwind Dr., Suite 104, Westerville, OH, 43081. Phone: (614) 901-7720. Fax: (614) 901-7721.E-mail: shalliday@comiii.com Web Site:www.comIII.com Scott Halliday, pres.

TV-CATV only.

Central Ohio C-band satellite & Teleport svc, with access to studio, edit suites, at Ohio State University & various downtown locations.

CompuWeather Inc., 2566 Rt. 52, Hopewell Junction, NY, 12533. Phone: (800) 825-4445. Fax: (800) 825-4441.E-mail: forecasts@compuweather.com Web Site:www.compuweather.com Jeff Wimmer, principal; Todd Gross, principal.

TV-CATV-Radio.

Weather, environmental features, actualities, forecasts, info, worldwide weather consulting svc, forecast, outcodes, studies, advice, site specific, 24/7 & 31 years experience.

Concept Videos, 5371 Punta Alta, Apt.1E, Laguna Hills, CA, 92653. Phone: (800) 333-8252. Fax: (877) 523-5592.E-mail: wjconnell@preschoolpower.com Web Site:www.preschoolpower.com William Connell, pres.

TV-CATV only.

Gold medal winning children's series, *Pre-School Power*, (13 x 30) recently telecast on 190 public TV stns.

Consolidated Film Industries (CFI), 959 N. Seward St., Hollywood, CA, 90038. Phone: (323) 960-7444. Fax: (323) 960-7573. Web Site:www.technicolor.com

TV-CATV only.

Film processing; titles & opticals; videotape transfers; office rentals.

Continental Recordings Inc., 23 Mirimichi Street, Plainville, MA, 02762-1710. Phone: (508) 699- 0003. Fax: (617) 699-0005.E-mail: danf31@earthlink.net L. Daniel Flynn, pres.

TV-CATV-Radio.

Coml jingles, stn IDs, original music creation & production, cassette duplication & bcstg adv consultation, CD & DVD duplicator.

William F. Cooke Television Programs, 307-23 Lesmill Rd., Toronto, ON, M3B 3P6. Canada. Phone: (416) 967-6141. Fax: (416) 967-5133.E-mail: info@cooketv.com William F. Cooke, pres/CEO; Alex McWilliams, pres distribution.

TV-CATV only.

TV program production & distribution.

Cookie Jar Group, 266 King St. W., 2nd Fl., Toronto, ON, M5V 1H8. Canada. Phone: (416) 977-3238. Fax: (416) 977-4526. Web Site:www.cookiejarentertainment.com Michael Hirsh, CEO; Scott McCaw, CFO; Toper Taylor, pres/COO; Kirk Bloomgarden, exec VP, worldwide consumer products, mktg.

BurbankCA . Cookie Jar Entertainment, 4100 W. Alameda Ave. Phone:

ParisBC France. Cookie Jar Entertainment, 11 Rue Torricelli. Phone:

London United Kingdom. CPLG, 3 Shortlands. Phone:

TV-CATV only.

International dev, production, postproduction & distributer of live action, animated & educ progmg. Worldwide consumer products & licensing division including ownership of CPLG.

Coote Communications, 568 Carver Hill, Milton, ON, LQT 5K5. Canada. Phone: (905) 203-0065.E-mail: amcoote@hotmail.com Morgan Coote, pres; Donald Coote, VP.

TV-CATV only.

Complete film & videotape production from script to screen.

Cornell University Educational Television Center, 126 CCCGarden Ave., Ithaca, NY, 14853-6601. Phone: (607) 255-8162. Fax: (607) 255-1563.E-mail: grp2@cornell.edu Web Site:www.DLS.cornell.edu Glen Palmer, mgr business/production svcs.

TV-CATV only.

Satellite uplinks, Betacam DvcPro video production & postproduction, audio production

Country Crossroads, 6350 W. Freeway, Fort Worth, TX, 76116. Phone: (817) 570-1491. Phone: (800) 292-2287. Fax: (817) 737-9436.E-mail: cries@familynetradio.com Web Site:www.countrycrossroadsradio.com Chuck Ries, producer; Kirk Teegarden, producer.

Radio Only.

Country music with interviews. Program hosted by Brother Jon Rivers, 30 minute wkly on CD or download.

Cramer, (formerly Cramer Productions Center). 425 University Ave., Norwood, MA, 02062. Phone: (781) 278-2300. Fax: (781) 255-0721.E-mail: info@cameronline.com Web Site:www.crameronline.com Tom Martin, CEO; Rich Sturchio, exec VP; T.J. Martin, exec VP.

TV-CATV-Radio.

Film & video production svcs from design to presentation; staging svcs; video duplications. Web-casting, interactive media.

Thomas Craven Film Corp., 5 W. 19th St., New York, NY, 10011-4216. Phone: (212) 463-7190. Fax: (212) 627-4761.E-mail: michael@cravenfilms.com Web Site:www.cravenfilms.com Michael Craven, pres; Ernest Barbieri, VP.

TV-CATV-Radio.

Complete film & video production svcs from scripting through shooting & editing to distribution.

Crawford Communications, 3845 Pleasantdale Rd., Atlanta, GA, 30340. Phone: (404) 876-7149. Fax: (678) 421-6717. Web Site:www.crawford.com Jesse C. Crawford, owner; Paul Hansel, pres; Bill Thompson, sls dir; Jessica Moore, mktg dir.

TV-CATV-Radio.

Computer graphics, animation, production & postproduction svcs domestic & international teleport.

Creative International Activities Ltd., 372 Central Park W., New York, NY, 10025. Phone: (212) 663-8944. Fax: (212) 865-8486.E-mail: ciaklaus@aol.com Klaud J. Lehmann, pres.

International TV program syndication & consultation.

Creative Marketing & Communications Corp., 7633 Athenia Dr., Cincinnati, OH, 45244. Phone: (513) 624-8301. Phone: (800) 845-8477. Fax: (513) 624-8302. Web Site:www.cmcideas.com Terry Dean, pres; Susan Dean, VP.

Radio Only.

Syndicated 30-60-second coml wraparounds.

Creative Radio Network, Box 7749, Thousand Oaks, CA, 91359. Phone: (818) 991-3892. Fax: (818) 991-3894. Darwin Lamm, pres.

Radio Only.

Radio program production & syndication—all formats; holiday & artist specials.

Crest National Digital Media Complex, 1000 N. Highland Ave., Hollywood, CA, 90038. Phone: (323) 466-0624. Fax: (323) 461-8901. Web Site:www.crestnational.com E-mail: info@crestnational.com Ron Stein, pres; John Walker, exec sls mgr.

TV-CATV only.

Full videotape postproduction including film transfer, processing, sweetening & duplication.

The Crime Channel, 78206 Varner Rd. (D131), Palm Desert, CA, 92211. Phone: (760) 360-6151, Ext. 3. Fax: (760) 360-3258.E-mail: crimechannel@dc.rr.com Web Site:www.crimechannel.com Arnie Frank, pres.

TV-CATV-Radio.

TV program distribution & bcstg.

Critical Mass Releasing Inc., 77 Mowat Ave., Suite 110, Toronto, ON, M6K 3E3. Canada. Phone: (416) 538-2535. Fax: (416) 538-3367.E-mail: cmass@netcom.ca William Alexander, pres; Lisa-Marie Doorey, Dir of International sls.

TV-CATV only.

International TV & domestic distribution, TV & film, film & series production, theatrical & video releasing.

Ben Cromer Communications, Box 526, Round Hill, VA, 20142. Phone: (540) 338-5486. Fax: (540) 338-5486.E-mail: info@bencromer.com Ben Cromer, pres.

TV-CATV-Radio.

Feature writing & script preparation for print & bcst media; specializing in the music & entertainment industry; telecommunications; business/economics & travel/history.

Crossroads Christian Communications Inc., Box 5100, Burlington, ON, L7R 4M2. Canada. Phone: (905) 335-7100. Web Site:www.crossroads.ca Ron Mainse, pres; Doug McKenzie, CEO.

TV-CATV only.

Produces 100 Huntley Street program.

Crown International Pictures Inc., 8701 Wilshire Blvd., Beverly Hills, CA, 90211. Phone: (310) 657-6700. Fax: (310) 657-4489.E-mail: crown@crownintlpictures.com Web Site:www.crownintlpictures.com Scott E. Schwimer, sr VP; Mark Tenser, pres/CEO; Lisa Agay, dir publ & adv.

TV-CATV only.

Film production & distribution.

Crystal Pictures Inc., 200 Riverside Dr., Bldg. 22 1st Fl., Asheville, NC, 28804. Phone: (828) 285-9995. Fax: (828) 285-9997.E-mail: cryspic@aol.com Joshua Tager, pres; Jane Anne Rolston, gen sls mgr.

TV-CATV only.

Distribution of feature film & svcs to all TV outlets in United States & abroad.

Cube International, Box 307, Lehi, UT, 84043-0307. Phone: (801) 722-1000. Fax: (801) 722-1000.E-mail: phillcatheral@earthlink.net Web Site:www.cubeinternational.com Olivier de Courson, mgng dir; Phillip G. Catherall, mgng dir.

TV-CATV only.

Film & TV distribution to all worldwide markets & media.

Curb Entertainment International Corp., 3907 W. Alameda Ave., Burbank, CA, 91505. Phone: (818) 843-8580. Fax: (818) 566-1719.E-mail: info@curbentertainment.com Web Site:www.curbentertainment.com Carole Curb, pres; Mike Curb, chmn; Ilda Toth, exec dir.

TV-CATV only.

International production & distribution co.

Custom Productions Inc., 1334 3rd St. Promenade, Suite 300, Santa Monica, CA, 90401. Phone: (310) 393-4144. Fax: (310) 393-1143. Web Site:www.customproductions.TV Steve Stockman, pres.

TV-CATV only.

Creation & production of custom TV campaigns for radio stns and TV news stns in the top 25 markets.

D

DC Audio, (Dryden Clarke Audio & Daily Feed). 1783 Lanier Pl. N.W., Suite B, Washington, DC, 20009. Phone: (202) 667-1234. Fax: (202) 667-5578. E-mail: dfeed@dailyfeed.com Web Site:www.dailyfeed.com John Dryden, pres.

Radio Only.

Produces The Daily Feed, a 90-second political, social satire radio commentary. Markets cash and bartered radio inventory to 18 + demos.

DG Systems, 750 W. John Carpenter Fwy., Irving, TX, 75039. Phone: (972) 581-2000. Fax: (972) 581-2001. Web Site:www.dgsystems.com Marty Melody, VP sls.

TV-CATV-Radio.

Duplication & distribution of corporate training & educ, TV & radio programs. Distribution of syndicated TV programs via satellite & videotape.

DIC Entertainment, 4100 W. Alameda Ave., Burbank, CA, 91505. Phone: (818) 955-5400. Fax: (818) 955-5696. Web Site:www.dicentertainment.com Andy Heyward, chmn/CEO; Brad Brooks, pres; Jedd Gold, mktg VP.

TV-CATV only.

DIC Entertainment, a leading children's entertainment company, is a full-service studio dedicated to creating, developing, producing, distributing, mktg & mdsg children's & family-based intellectual properties.

DLT Entertainment Ltd., 124 E. 55th St., New York, NY, 10022-4501. Phone: (212) 245-4680. Fax: (212) 315-1132. Web Site:www.dltentertainment.com Donald L. Taffner, owner; John Fitzgerald, CEO; Donald Taffner Jr., VP; Jeff Cotugno, VP.

TV-CATV only.

TV program production & distribution.

DMX Music, 900 E. Pine St., Seattle, WA, 98122. Phone: (800) 831-8001. Fax: (206) 329-9952. Web Site:www.dmxmusic.com Liberty Media, owner.

TV-CATV-Radio.

Programmer & supplier of satellite-delivered music svcs for business & cable TV. Available satellite direct or through FM subcarrier.

D-Squared Media, 210 E. 38th St., Suite 5H, New York, NY, 10016. Phone: (212) 254-3489. Fax: (212) 254-3489. E-mail: solutions@dsquaredmedia.com Web Site:www.dsquaredmedia.com Adriana E. Davis, producer & editor/writer.

TV-CATV-Radio.

Film, video, & radio production svcs from script to screen.

D-V-X International, (A division of Demo-Vox Sound Studio Inc.). 1038 Bay Ridge Ave., Brooklyn, NY, 11219. Phone: (718) 680-7234. Fax: (718) 680-7234.

TV-CATV only.

Video recording, creative production & postproduction svcs.

DWJ Television, One Robinson Ln., Ridgewood, NJ, 07450. Phone: (201) 445-1711. Fax: (201) 445-8352. E-mail: dwjinfo@dwjtv.com Web Site:www.dwjtv.com Daniel G. Johnson, pres; Michael L. Friedman, exec VP; Cynthia Boseski, sr VP.

TV-CATV-Radio.

Provides TV, radio progmg, production; promotional video production & production svcs.

Daley Video, 4095 Hitchcock Rd., Concord, CA, 94518. Phone: (925) 676-7260. Fax: (413) 541-8354. E-mail: gadaley@aol.com Greg Daley, owner/CEO.

TV-CATV only.

Betacam SP, D1 digital betacom editing & 3/4-inch postproduction; TV production.

Dargaud-Marina, 15-27 rue Moussorgski, Paris, 75018. France. Phone: 331-5326-3100. Fax: 331-5326-3113. E-mail: sales@dargaudmarina.fr Gaspard De Chavagnac, mngg dir; Claude De Saint Vincent, pres; Patrick Desiev, VP finance; G. Guillot, sls.

TV-CATV only.

Distribution & production company specialized in children's progmg, mainly animation.

Darino Films/Library of Special Effects, 222 Park Ave. S., New York, NY, 10003. Phone: (212) 228-4024. E-mail: edarino@hotmail.com Ed Darino, owner.

TV-CATV only.

Distributors of TV programs, video, CD, animation, educationals, effects libraries, stock footage libraries, production CD & DVD.

Daro Film Distribution, Le Victoria, 13 Blvd. Princess Charlotte, MC, 98000. Phone: (377) 979-1600. Fax: (377) 979-1590. E-mail: daro@meditnet.com

TV-CATV only.

International distribution, co-production, co-financing of TV programs & films.

Jeff Davis Productions Inc., 6166 Mulholland Hwy., Los Angeles, CA, 90068. Phone: (323) 464-3500. Fax: (323) 464-1414. E-mail: jeffdavies@jeffdavies.com Web Site:www.jeffdavis.com Jeff Davies, CEO.

TV-CATV-Radio.

Voiceover, production, TV & radio.

DaviSound, Box 521, 1504 Sunset, Newberry, SC, 29108. Phone: (803) 276-0639. E-mail: davisound@hotmail.com Web Site:www.davisound.com Hayne Davis; Annette Davis, opns mgr.

TV-CATV only.

Coml & promotional writing & producing for radio, jingles & program production & distribution. Also provides DaviSound "Tool Boxes," custom fabricated pro audio equipment.

De Wolfe Music Library Inc., 25 W. 45th St., New York, NY, 10036. Phone: (212) 382-0220. Fax: (212) 382-0278. E-mail: info@dewolfmusic.com Web Site:www.dewolfemusic.com Andrew M. Jacobs, pres; Jamie Gillespie, Mgr Music Sls.

TV-CATV-Radio.

The largest independant production music library in the world!

DeLuxe Laboratories, 1377 N. Serrano Ave., Hollywood, CA, 90027. Phone: (323) 462-6171. Fax: (323) 461-0608. Web Site:www.bydeluxe.com Cyril Drabinsky, pres; Steve Van Anda, sls VP.

TV-CATV only.

Full svc motion picture processing lab with labs in Toronto, London, Rome.

Design Partners Inc., 2919 W. Burbank Blvd., Suite B, Burbank, CA, 91505. Phone: (818) 845-9191. Fax: (818) 845-9258. E-mail: designpartners@dpi-ld.com Web Site:www.dpi-ld.com Greg Brunton, pres.

TV-CATV only.

TV, lighting design, industrial production & TV production & tech supervision svcs.

Devillier Donegan Enterprises L.P., 4401 Connecticut Ave. N.W., 6th Floor, Washington, DC, 20008. Phone: (202) 686-3980. Fax: (202) 686-3999. Web Site:www.ddegroup.com Ronald J. Devillier, pres/CEO; Brian Donegan, exec VP; Joan Lanigan, VP business legal affrs; Linda Ekizian, VP mktg; Gregory Diefenbach, production & dev; John Esteban, VP finance/admin.

TV-CATV only.

Worldwide distribution of progmg: international & ind documentaries, Hollywood profiles, science series, drama, natural history progmg & the performing arts.

Devlin Design Group Inc., 12526 High Bluff, # 300, San Diego, CA, 92130. Phone: (760) 634-6515. Fax: (760) 634-6929. E-mail: creative@ddgtv.com Web Site:www.ddgtv.com Dan Devlin, .

TV-CATV only.

Designs, builds & installs news sets & newsrooms. Facility planning, broadcast consulting, tech & lighting direction. Virtual Reality Rsch & Dev Ctr. Virtual sets, soft sets.

Digital Brewery L.L.C., 3820 Packard, Suite 150, Ann Arbor, MI, 48108. Phone: (800) 572-0098. Phone: (734) 975-8880. Fax: (734) 975-8915. Web Site:www.digitalbrewery.com Terry Dollhoff, co-pres; Sal Calabrese, co-pres.

TV-CATV only.

Packaged animations include backgrounds, holidays, corporate, adv & globes, maps & flags.

Digital Force, 149 Madison Ave., 12th Fl., New York, NY, 10016. Phone: (212) 252-9300. Fax: (212) 252-7377. E-mail: info@digitalforce.com Web Site:www.digitalforce.com Jerome Bunke, pres; Vanessa Towle-Mullin, production mgr; Arthur Crumlish, sr VP.

TV-CATV only.

Compact disc, CD-ROM & DVD production service to meet the needs of bcstrs, cable networks, & small labels/ind artists. Clients include the National Football League (NFL) & National Hockey League (NHL) on Fox TV as well as PSAs & promotional discs from bcstrs nationwide, ABC-TV & NBC, Westwood One & CBS.

Dimension 3 Corp, 5240 Medina Rd., Woodland Hills, CA, 91364-1913. Phone: (818) 592-0999. Fax: (818) 592-0987. E-mail: info@d3.com Web Site:www.d3.com Daniel L. Symmes, pres.

TV-CATV only.

Supplies 3-D bcst TV process & 3-D film; equipment, consultation & 3-D glasses.

Disney Channel, 3800 W. Alameda Ave., Burbank, CA, 91505. Phone: (818) 569-7700. Fax: (818) 845-8249. Web Site:www.disneychannel.com Anne M. Sweeney, pres.

TV-CATV only.

Original TV program production & distribution.

Walt Disney Company, 500 S. Buena Vista St., Burbank, CA, 91521-0990. Phone: (818) 560-1000. Fax: (818) 560-1930. Zenia Mucha, exec VP corporate communications.

TV-CATV only.

The Walt Disney Company subsidiary; devs & syndicates first-run adult & children's progmg, off-net progmg & feature film packages.

The Walt Disney Company, 500 S. Buena Vista St., Burbank, CA, 91521. Phone: (818) 560-1000. Fax: (818) 560-1930. Web Site:www.disney.com Michael Eisner, chmn/CEO.

TV-CATV only.

Diversified Communications Inc., 2000 M St. N.W., Suite 340, Washington, DC, 20036. Phone: (202) 775-4300. Fax: (202) 775-4363. Web Site:www.dciteleport.com Al Levin, pres; Nelson Crumling, VP.

TV-CATV only.

Complete mobile facilities, Ku-band uplink trucks, extensive loc & global connectivity; internationally compliant, fully redundant Ku-band air transportable uplink.

D'Ocon Films Productions, C/Calaf.3 Bajos, Barcelona, 08021. Spain. Phone: 34-93-240-41-22 . Fax: 34-93-240-41-24. E-mail: docon@docon.es

TV-CATV only.

Principally an animation company offering full range of pre-production, production & postproduction svcs either developing our own concepts or co-producing.

The Dolmatch Group Ltd., Box 3298, 19697 Glen Brae Dr., Saratoga, CA, 95070. Phone: (408) 741-8620. Fax: (408) 741-8620. E-mail: tdgdolmatch@yahoo.com Murray Dolmatch, pres; Sandra Dolmatch, VP.

TV-CATV only.

Represents producers in the United States, United Kingdom, Germany, France & Italy; distributes feature films, documentaries & animation; active in co-production & co-financing.

Dome Productions, 1 Blue Jays Way, Suite #3400, Toronto, ON, M5V1J3. Canada. Phone: (416) 341-2001. Phone: (514) 731-3663. Fax: (416) 341-2020. Fax: (514) 731-4646. E-mail: mcarlyle@domeprod.com Web Site:www.domeproductions.com Mary Ellen Carlyle, VP/gen mgr.

Mont-RoyalPQ Canada, 5647 Ferrier.

TV-CATV only.

Mobile production trucks/airpacks (High Definition, Digital, Analog), telecommunications (Fibre/Satellite transmission, satellite media tours, playouts), Host bcst (Design, production, engrg, opons).

Donnelly & Associates, 7507 Sunset Blvd., Suite 205, Los Angeles, CA, 90046. Phone: (323) 850-5861. Fax: (323) 850-5866. E-mail: wpdonnelly@earthlink.net W.P. Donnelly, pres.

TV-CATV only.

Mktg & licensing films to pay-TV, network & syndication packages.

Dorling Kindersley Vision, 80 Strand, London, WC2R 0RL. Phone: 0044 207 010 3000. Fax: 0044 207 010 6636. E-mail: dkvision@dk-uk.com Web Site:www.dk-uk.com

TV-CATV only.

Produces programs for the international TV & video markets, incorporating visual design with universally appealing subjects.

John Driscoll/VoiceOver America, Box 1996, Studio City, CA, 91614. Phone: (888) 766-2049. Phone: (818) 373-9849. E-mail: johndriscoll@voiceoveramerica.com Web Site:www.johndriscoll.com John Moore, pres/CEO.

TV-CATV-Radio.

Voice Over America heard on TNT, VH-1, NBC-TV, FOX-TV, Spike TV, NBA, NFL, MLB & affil. Comcast, HBO/Cinemax, Global, Corus, Rogers, RTE, CBC, CTV & Direct TV.

Mark Druck Productions Inc., 300 E. 40th St., New York, NY, 10016. Phone: (212) 682-5980. Fax: (212) 682-5981.E-mail: markdruck@aol.com Mark Druck, pres; Lisa Dodenhoff, producer.

TV-CATV only.

TV & video tape industrial progmg, prom film production & distribution.

Duke International, Box 46, Douglas, Isle of Man, IM99 1DD. Phone: (+44) 1624 640020. Fax: (+44) 1624 640001.E-mail: info@dukesales.com Web Site:www.dukesales.com Jon Quayle, sls dir.

TV-CATV only.

A wide range of powersport progmg, documentaries, clips; also production & editing facilities.

The D.L. Dykes Jr. Foundation, 111 E. Capitol St., Jackson, MS, 39201. Phone: (601) 354-0767. Joe Todaro, production mgr; David R. Dyker, CEO.

TV-CATV only.

Educ progmg.

E

E! Entertainment Television, 5750 Wilshire Blvd., Los Angeles, CA, 90036-3709. Phone: (323) 954-2400. Fax: (323) 954-2500. Web Site:www.eonline.com Neil Baker, sr VP, adv sls; Ted Harbert, pres/CEO; Ken Bettsteller, CEO.

New YorkNY , 11 W. 42nd St. Phone:

TV-CATV only.

A 24-hours progmg net covering celebrities, entertainment news, gossip & pop-culture, feature behind the scenes with today's biggest stars.

E1 Entertainment, 70 Driver Rd., Unit 1, Brampton, ON, L6T 5V2. Canada. Phone: (905) 624-7337. Fax: (905) 624-7310. Web Site:www.entertainmentonegroup.com Darren Throop, pres/CEO; Noreen Halpern, pres & dramatic progmg.

E1 Entertainment is involved in production and distribution of multimedia content for film, TV, video & on-line communication marketplace.

ESPI Video, 4801 Spring Valley Rd., Suite 116, Dallas, TX, 75244. Phone: (214) 522-6699. Fax: (214) 522-7699.E-mail: gsleeper@espivideo.com Web Site:www.espivideo.com Gary Sleeper, pres.

TV-CATV only.

Full-svc production company specializing in corporate video production. Postproduction facilities & on-location svcs also available.

ESPN Radio Network, ESPN Plaza, Bristol, CT, 06010. Phone: (860) 766-2661. Fax: (860) 860-5523. Web Site:www.espnradio.com John A. Walsh, exec editor; Len Weiner, progmg dir; John Martin, exec producer.

Radio Only.

NBA On ESPN Radio; College Game Day (Sat); ESPN Radio weekends; Brent Musburger afternoon drive sportscasts; AM & PM drive commentaries; NFL Gameday (Sun)

ESPN Regional Television, 11001 Rushmore Dr., Charlotte, NC, 28277. Phone: (704) 973-5000. Fax: (704) 973-5090. Web Site:www.espn.com Chuck Gerber, exec VP/gen mgr.

TV-CATV only.

Producer & distributor of TV sports events including college & professional basketball, boxing & auto racing for over-the-air & cable.

EUE Screen Gems Studios, 222 E. 44th St., New York, NY, 10017. Phone: (212) 450-1600. Fax: (212) 450-1610. Mitchell Brill, exec VP; Ed Brancaccio, chief technology officer.

WilmingtonNC , 1223 N. 23rd St. Phone:

TV program, coml production & distribution.

Eagle Eye Film Company, 824 N. Victory Blvd., Burbank, CA, 91502. Phone: (818) 506-6100. Fax: (818) 506-4313. Web Site:www.eagleyepost.com Chuck Spatariu, pres; Joel Minnich, opns coord.

TV-CATV only.

Editing facility, editing rentals & RAID storage solutions.

Eagle Media Productions Ltd., Box 580, Northford, CT, 06472. Phone: (203) 294-1190. Fax: (203) 294-9512.E-mail: louadler@sbcglobal.net Louis C. Adler, pres; Thalia Adler, VP.

TV-CATV only.

Radio program syndication, program & news consultant. Producers of *Medical Journal.*

Eaton Films Ltd., 10 Holbein Mews, London, SW1W 8NN. Phone: (44) 207-823-6173. Fax: (44) 207-823-6017.E-mail: eaton.films@talk21.com Judith Bland, dir; Liz Cook, dir internatonal sls.

TV & video distribution.

Echo Radio Productions Inc., 44895 Hwy. 82, Aspen, CO, 81611. Phone: (800) 385-4612. Fax: (970) 925-2640. Fax: (970) 925-9369.E-mail: kayla@echoradio.com Web Site:www.echoradio.com Kayla Hoffman-Cook, VP; Rodney H. Jacobs, CEO.

Radio Only.

Syndicator & producer of radio vignette progmg.

Ecumedia News Service, Box 358, Ridgefield, CT, 06877. Phone: (203) 431-6092. Fax: (212) 870-2030.E-mail: roy.lloyd@ecunet.org Roy T. Lloyd, dir.

Radio Only.

News stories, features & actualities about ethics & relg produced for radio.

Ecumenical Communications, 48 Eastview Rd., Terryville, CT, 06786. Phone: (860) 585-5090.E-mail: info@ecucomm.ro Web Site:www.ecucomm.ro Robert J. Geckler, owner.

Radio Only.

Radio, podcast program production, distribution; production, restoration svcs, internet, website & podcast svcs.

Educational Technologies Network (ETN), (formerly ETN—Educational Telecommunications Network). 9300 Imperial Hwy., Rm. 126, Los Angeles County Office of Education, Downey, CA, 90242-2890. Phone: (562) 922-6641. Fax: (562) 922-8841.E-mail: ENT_Productions@lacoe.edu Web Site:www.lacoe.edu Richard Quinones PhD., division dir; Rodney Conner PhD., media coord.

TV-CATV only.

ETN provides multimeda production svcs to LACOE division & school districts throughout Los Angeles county. Include: studio & remote video production, distance learning & vitual meetings, video streaming, videoconferencing, interactive CD-ROM & DVD authoring & live event video coverage,

Ellis Entertainment, 1300 Yonge St., Suite 300, Toronto, ON, M4T 1X3. Canada. Phone: (416) 924-2186. Fax: (416) 924-6115.E-mail: sales@ellisent.com Web Site:www.ellisent.com Grace Lo, mgr; Stephen Ellis, pres & CEO.

TV-CATV only.

Producers and distributors of 1000+ hrs of non-fiction and family entertainment for TV and video for four decades.

Empire Burbank Studio, 1845 Empire Ave., Burbank, CA, 91504. Phone: (818) 840-1400. Fax: (818) 567-1062.

TV-CATV only.

Sound stage studio rental, audience rated TV studios, full-svc production facilities & equipment, ultimate stage.

Encore Video Productions Inc., 811 Main St., Myrtle Beach, SC, 29577. Phone: (843) 448-9900. Fax: (843) 448-9235.E-mail: frank@encorevideo.biz Web Site:www.encorevideo.biz Rik Dickinson, pres; Frank Payne, VP.

TV-CATV only.

Location & studio production, specializing in EFP/ENG 1-Camera productions, full script to screen svc, VNR, EPK satellite media tours, teleconferences, & magazine TV production. Betagami SP, non-linear editing.

Enoki Films U.S.A. Inc., 16430 Ventura Blvd., Suite 308, Encino, CA, 91436. Phone: (818) 907-6503. Fax: (818) 907-6506.E-mail: info@enokifilmsusa.com Web Site:www.enokifilmsusa.com Yoshi Enoki, pres; Ricki Ames, VP worldwide distribution; Madoka Koike, distribution coord.

TV-CATV only.

Producer & distributor of children's animation for TV & video.

Envoy Productions, 660 Mason Ridge Ctr. Dr., St. Louis, MO, 63141-8557. Phone: (314) 317-4216. Fax: (314) 317-4299.E-mail: sandi.clement@lhm.org Web Site:www.envoyproductions.com Sandi Clement, Manager; Kurt R. Klaus, pres.

TV-CATV only.

TV, radio production, distribution (English & Sp). Syndicates 30-minute wkly radio shows, The Lutheran Hour & TV holiday specials.

Episcopal Church Center, 815 2nd Ave., New York, NY, 10017. Phone: (212) 716-6102. Fax: (212) 949-8059. Web Site:www.episcopalchurch.org

Spokespersons for church & society issues.

Essence Television Productions Inc., 135 W. 50th St., Frnt 4, New York, NY, 10020-1201. Phone: (212) 642-0600. Fax: (212) 921-5173. Web Site:www.essence.com Edward Lewis, chmn/CEO.

TV-CATV only.

TV program production.

Ethnic-American Broadcasting Co., Two Executive Drive, Fort Lee, NJ, 07024. Phone: (201) 242-3000. Fax: (201) 944-5961.E-mail: info@skyview

Fort LeeNJ , 2 Executive Dr, Suite 600. Phone:

TV-CATV-Radio.

Provides ethnic radio & TV language svcs via DBS & through cable systems throughout North America.

Eurocine, 33 Ave. Des Champs Elysees, Paris, 75008. France. Phone: 33.1.42.25.6492. Fax: 33.1.42.25.7338.E-mail: eurocine@club-internet.fr Web Site:www.eurocine.net Kunesova Ilona, .

TV-CATV only.

Production & distribution in all media.

Europe Images International, 1 Rond-Point Victor Hugo, F-92130, Issy-Les-Moulineaux France. Phone: (33) 1 55 95 58 00. Fax: (33) 1 55 95 58 10.E-mail: Europe-Images @europeimages.com Web Site:www.europeimages.com John Rouilly, CEO.

TV-CATV only.

Acquires, distributes & invests in international TV progmg. Catalog close to 5 hours broken into three categories, drama, children's documentaries.

Evangelical Lutheran Church in America, 8765 W. Higgins Rd., Chicago, IL, 60631. Phone: (773) 380-2941. Fax: (773) 380-2406.E-mail: ava.martin@elca.org Web Site:www.elca.org Ava Martin, dir.

TV-CATV-Radio.

TV & radio progmg, promotional film production, distribution, production svcs & news.

Evergreen Entertainment Group, 1825 Ponce De Leon Blvd., Suite 450, Coral Gables, FL, 33134-3626. Phone: (305) 460-4448.E-mail: evergreenenter@juno.com Migdalia Inocencio, pres.

TV-CATV only.

Worldwide programs distribution; international co-production liaison; mktg & progmg cable/satellite.

Expand Images, 7 Rue Taylor, Paris, 75010. Phone: (33) 0148-0305-44. Fax: (33) 0148-0345-04.E-mail: communication@expand.fr Web Site:www.expand.fr

TV-CATV only.

Production & distribution company.

Eye in the Woods, Box 89, Brewton, AL, 36427. Phone: (251) 809-1909. Fax: (251) 809-0729. Web Site:www.eyeinthewoods.com Dale Faust, pres/exec producer.

TV-CATV only.

Produce a weekly show viewed on The Outdoor Channel.

Eyewitness Kids News, LLC, 182 Sound Beach Ave., Old Greenwich, CT, 06870-0116. Phone: (203) 637-0044. Fax: (203) 698-0812.E-mail: primonews@aol.com Web Site:www.educationtelevisionfund.org Albert T. Primo, pres.

New YorkNY , 355 W. 52nd St., , 3rd Fl.

TV-CATV only.

Coaching of TV news, program talent, strategic planning & production svcs.

F

FTC/Orlando, 324 DeSota Cir., Orlando, FL, 32804. Phone: (407) 422-8246. Fax: (407) 843-0738.E-mail: ftcorlando@aol.com Web Site:www.ftcorlando.com A.J. Foresta, pres.

TV-CATV only.

Full-svc film & TV production company, specializing in coml & feature production. Area specialty: steadicam.

Faith for Today, 101 W. Cochran St., Simi Valley, CA, 93065. Phone: (888) 940-0062. Fax: (805) 522-2114.E-mail: info@faithfortoday.tv Web Site:www.faithfortoday.tv Michael Tucker, Speaker/Director.

TV-CATV only.

Producer & distributor of *Lifestyle Magazine, McDougall M.D. & The Evidence.*

Family Stations Inc., 290 Hegenberger Rd., Oakland, CA, 94621. Phone: (510) 568-6200. Phone: (800) 543-1495. Fax: (510) 633-7983. E-mail: famradio@familyradio.com Web Site:www.familyradio.com Harold E. Camping, pres/gen mgr; Rick Prime, tech dir; W. Craig Hulsebos, progmg mgr; William Thornton, VP.

Radio Only.

Radio program production & distribution.

FamilyNet, 6350 W. Freeway, Fort Worth, TX, 76116. Phone: (817) 737-4011. Fax: (817) 377-4372.E-mail: ddavis@familynet.com Web Site:www.familynet.com David Clark, pres; Glenn McEowen, VP tech opns; Martin Coleman, VP production team; Chip Turner, VP mktg; Darin Davis, VP sls & traffic.

TV-CATV only.

FamilyNet is a 24/7 cable net. In addition, FamilyNet produces 5 syndicated radio progms. Values based, family oriented progmg.

FamilyNet Radio, 6350 W. Freeway, Fort Worth, TX, 76116-4511. Phone: (817) 570-1416. Phone: (800) 266-1837. Fax: (817) 735-1790.E-mail: smiller@familynet.com Web Site:www.familynetradio.com Scott Miller, dir progmg; Dale Weller, COO.

Radio Only.

FamilyNet Radio is SIRIUS 161, Christian talk. We produce "Mornings" which airs only on SIRIUS .

Faraone Communications Inc., 75 West End Ave., R-9A, New York, NY, 10023. Phone: (212) 489-1313. Fax: (212) 489-8978.E-mail: ted.faraone@verizon.net Web Site:www.worldwidepublicrelations.com Ted Faraone, principal; Randolph Nader, VP.

Valley VillageCA . Valley Village, 4804 Laurel Canyon Blvd., Ste 516.

TV-CATV-Radio.

Media rel svcs to producers, distributors of radio, TV programs, talent & home video.

Federal Citizen Information Center, 1800 F St. N.W., Rm. G-142, Washington, DC, 20405. Phone: (202) 501-1794. Fax: (202) 501-4281.E-mail: nancy.tyler@gsa.gov Web Site:www.pueblo.gsa.gov Teresa Nasif, dir; Nancy Tyler, pub svc mgr.

TV-CATV-Radio.

TV & radio PSAs promoting USA.gov, the official web portal of the federal government.

Festival de Television de Monte-Carlo, 4, Boulevard du Jardin Exotique, Monte Carlo, 98000. Phone: 377 93 10 40 60. Fax: 377 93 50 70 14.E-mail: info@tvfestival.com Web Site:www.tvfestival.com

TV-CATV only.

Competition of TV films & miniseries; news programs; producers. Conferences, panels & other market-related activities.

Film House Inc., 810 Dominican Dr., Nashville, TN, 37228. Phone: (615) 255-4000. Fax: (615) 255-4111.E-mail: results@filmhouse.com Curt Hahn, CEO; Ron Routson, pres/COO; Wayne Campbell, VP mktg; Andy Cohen, CFO.

TV-CATV only.

Creates & produces TV mktg campaigns for radio & TV stns worldwide.

Film Roman Inc., 12020 Chandler Blvd., Suite 200, North Hollywood, CA, 91607. Phone: (818) 761-2544. Fax: (818) 985-2973. Web Site:www.filmroman.com John Hyde, pres/CEO.

TV-CATV only.

Animation production studio.

Filmoption International Inc., 3401 St. Antoine St., Westmount, PQ, H3Z 1X1. Canada. Phone: (416) 598-1557. Fax: (416) 593-0013.E-mail: mrosilo@filmoption.com Web Site:www.filmoption.com Maryse Rouillard, pres; Lizanne Rouillard, VP; Muriel Rosilio, sr exec sls & co-productions; Evangelia Ozek, sls exec.

TorontoON Canada, 144 Front St. West, Suite 760. Phone:mrosilio@filmoption.com Muriel rosilio, sr exec sls co-productions.

WestmountPQ Canada, 3401 St-Antoine. Phone:mrouilla @filmoption.com Maryse Rouillard, pres.

TV-CATV only.

International distribution of TV programs.

Films Media Group, Box 2053, Princeton, NJ, 08543-2053. Phone: (609) 671-0266. Phone: (800) 257-5126. Fax: (609) 671-5772.E-mail: custserv@films.com Web Site:www.films.com Amy Bevilacqua, exec VP/ gen mgr; Diane Bilello, VP sls.

TV-CATV only.

Distributes programs for bcst & cable industries to non-theatrical, educ, institutional, home video & business markets.

Films of the Nations, Box 449, Clarksburg, NJ, 08510. Phone: (732) 462-3522. Fax: (732) 294-0330.E-mail: aldfilms@bellatlantic.net Web Site:www.aldenfilms.com Paul Weinberg, pres.

TV-CATV only.

TV program, promotion & educ film distribution.

Financial Media Services, Inc., Box 870928, Stone Mountain, GA, 30087. Phone: (770) 413-2258. Fax: (770) 465-0180.E-mail: charles@charlesross.com

TV-CATV-Radio.

Produces & syndicates nationally syndicated radio show *Your Personal Finance.*

David Finch Distribution Ltd., Box 264, Walton-on-Thames, KT12 3YR. United Kingdom. Phone: 44-1932-882733. Fax: 44-1932-882108.E-mail: sales@david-finch.com David Finch, chief exec.

TV-CATV only.

Supply of programs for home video & TV worldwide. Acquisition for United Kingdom home video.

Finger Lakes Productions International, 119 S. Cayuga St., Ithaca, NY, 14850. Phone: (607) 275-9400. Fax: (607) 277-0961.E-mail: info@flpradio.com Web Site:www.flpradio.com Paul Bartishevich, pres/CEO.

Radio Only.

Full-service radio mktg, production & syndication of short-form radio features. International mktg, sls & consulting.

First Marketing, 3300 Gateway Dr., Pompano Beach, FL, 33069. Phone: (954) 979-0700. Phone: (800) 641-9251. Fax: (954) 971-4707. Web Site:www.first-marketing.com Ronald Drenning, pres; Neil Rosenblum, VP/business dev.

TV-CATV only.

First Marketing offers 30 yrs of experience partnering with marketing professionals to dev custom communications programs designed to enhance custom relationships & profitability.

1st Miracle Productions, 3439 W. Cahuenga Blvd., Hollywood, CA, 90068. Phone: (323) 874-6000. Fax: (323) 874-4252.E-mail: sales@1stmiracleproductions.com Web Site:www.1stmiracleproductions.com Moshe Bibiyan, CEO; Simon Bibiyan, pres.

TV-CATV only.

International distribution, co-production, postproduction finance.

First Run/Icarus Films, 32 Court St., 21st Fl., Brooklyn, NY, 10201. Phone: (718) 488-8900. Fax: (718) 488-8642.E-mail: info@frif.com Web Site:www.frif.com Jonathan Miller, pres.

TV-CATV only.

International TV program distribution: documentaries, current affrs, music, arts, cultural programs.

FirstCom Music, 1325 Capital Pkwy., Suite 109, Carrollton, TX, 75006. Phone: (800) 858-8880. Fax: (972) 242-6526.E-mail: info@firstcom.com Web Site:www.firstcom.com Carol Riffert, VP/gen mgr; Ken Nelson, exec producer & sr VP.

Beverly HillsCA , 8750 Wilshire Blvd., 2nd Fl.

TV-CATV-Radio.

FirstCom's 18 spectacular libraries deliver the combined power of 186,000 compositions & growing by 6,000 new tracks a year. Delivery options include DVD, CD, Hard-drive & online. Guaranteed to add creativity to your production!

Fischer Broadcast Services, 10841 Bittersweet Lane, Fishers, IN, 46038-2203. Phone: (317) 514-5757. Fax: (317) 578-3884.E-mail: superfisch@midspring.com Web Site:www.superfisch.com Scott Fischer, pres.

TV-CATV-Radio.

SUPERFISCH—VOICE IMAGING & BRANDING. Scott Fischer voice artist for radio & TV loc, cable, Netw. Promax & Emmy award voice. A versitile-VO-value! Yes you CAN afford me-can you afford not to check me out?

Forde Motion Picture Labs, 1001 Lenora St., Seattle, WA, 98121-2706. Phone: (206) 682-2510. Phone: (800) 682-2510. Fax: (206) 682-2560. Web Site:www.fordelabs.com Richard E. Vedvick, pres.

TV-CATV only.

Overnight processing of 35mm/16mm Eastman color negative dailies; release printing.

4 Kids Entertainment (Sub 4 Kids Entertainment), (Formerly The Summit Media Group Inc. (Sub 4 Kids Entertainment). 1414 Ave. of the Americas, New York, NY, 10019. Phone: (212) 754-4900. Fax: (212) 754-5480.E-mail: shirsch@4kidsent.com Alfred Kahn, chmn/CEO.

Distribution of programs in the United States with emphasis on programs for children.

Fox Digital, Fox Network Ctr., 10201 W. Pico Blvd., Los Angeles, CA, 90035. Phone: (310) 369-6622. Fax: (310) 969-6125. Web Site:www.fox.com

TV-CATV only.

Videotape production facilities, stages & equipment.

Fox 17 Studio Productions, 631 Mainstream Dr., Nashville, TN, 37228. Phone: (615) 244-1717. Fax: (615) 259-3962. Web Site:www.wztv.com E-mail: production@fox17.com Bill Zuckerman, prom dir.

TV-CATV only.

Full range video & film production facility; 25 x 40 studio & 60 x 60 studio soundstage; betacams & a var of tape formats for TV/CATV.

Fox Sports West, 1100 S. Flower St., Los Angeles, CA, 90015. Phone: (213) 743-7800. Fax: (213) 743-7835. Web Site:www.foxsports.com Steve Simpson, gen mgr; Dennis Johnson, public relations dir.

TV-CATV only.

TV program production & distribution.

Fox 29 WUTV Sinclair, 951 Whitehaven Rd., Grand Island, NY, 14072. Phone: (716) 773-7531. Fax: (716) 773-5753. Web Site:www.wutv.com Don Moran, gen mgr; Jon May, progmg coord.

TV-CATV only.

TV coml production; U.S. rep, Katz; Canadian rep, Airtime.

Sandy Frank Entertainment Inc., 954 Lexington Ave., Suite 255, New York, NY, 10021. Phone: (212) 772-1889. Fax: (212) 772-2297.E-mail: sfe@aol.com Web Site:www.sandyfrankent.com Sandy Frank, chmn/CEO; Nora Maria Diaz, sls dir; Rosalie Perrone, controller; Sandi Spidell, VP opns; Maury Shields, VP business affrs; Barbara Kalicinska, sls; Sophia Evans, sls; Susan Piscitello, sls.

TV-CATV only.

TV production & syndication.

Free Speech TV (FSTV), Box 44099, Denver, CO, 80201. Phone: (303) 442-8445. Fax: (303) 442-6472. Web Site:www.freespeech.org E-mail: viewercomments@fstv.org John Schwartz, bd pres; Jon Stout, gen mgr; Nathaniel Reeder, opns dir; Eric Galatas, progmg dir; Jason McKain, dir outreach/member svcs.

TV-CATV only.

Acquires works from activists, independent film/video artists & community based media; providing exposure to progressive ideas.

Freewheelin' Films Ltd., 44895 Hwy. 82, Aspen, CO, 81611. Phone: (970) 925-2640. Fax: (970) 925-9369. Web Site:www.fwf.com E-mail: kalyla@fwf.com Rodney H. Jacobs, CEO; Kayla Hoffman-Cook, VP.

TV-CATV only.

25-yr old production company specializing in entertainment, sports & lifestyle specials.

The Fremantle Corp., 25 Lesmill Road, #5, Toronto, ON, M3B 2T3. Canada. Phone: (416) 443-9204. Fax: (416) 443-8685. Web Site:www.fremantlecorp.com Randy Zalken, pres; Marshall Kesten, CEO; Lisa Dunn, VP sls; Irv Holender, principal; Diane Tripp, sls dir.

TV-CATV only.

International TV program distribution & co-production.

Fremantle Media Ltd., 1 Stephen St., London, W1T 1AL. United Kingdom. Phone: 44 (0)20 7691-6000. Fax: 44 (0)20 7691-6100.E-mail: feedback@freemantlemedia.com Web Site:www.pearsontv.com Greg Dyke, CEO; Tony Cohen, mgng dir; James Bennet, CEO.

TV production & distribution.

FremantleMedia North America Inc., 2700 Colorado Ave., Suite 450, Santa Monica, CA, 90404. Phone: (310) 255-4700. Fax: (310) 255-4800. Web Site:www.fremantlemedia.com David Lyle, pres; Cecile Frot Coutaz, COO.

New YorkNY , 1540 Broadway. Catherine V, MacKay, Deputy CEO.

TV-CATV only.

TV production.

Chuck Fries Productions Inc., 6922 Hollywood Blvd., 12th Fl., Hollywood, CA, 90028. Phone: (310) 203-9520. Fax: (323) 466-2266.E-mail: chuckfries@aol.com

TV-CATV only.

Domestic & international TV, home video, & feature film production & distribution.

G

GLL TV Enterprises Inc., 8009 Via Fiore, Sarasota, FL, 34238. Phone: (941) 925-4339. Fax: (941) 925-3976.E-mail: glltv@pobox.com Gunther L. Less, pres; Ellen G. Less, sec/treas.

TV-CATV only.

TV program, coml, promotional film production & distribution. Journey to Adventure, the longest-running syndicated travel show on TV.

GMI Media L.L.C., 325 Washington Ave. S., #399, Kent, WA, 98032. Phone: (206) 374-8889. Web Site:www.gmimedia.com/contact.htm Ron Erak, pres; Richard Germaine, VP/gen mgr.

TV-CATV-Radio.

Custom ID jingle packages for all radio & TV formats as well as coml jingle for loc ad sls. CD production libraries, Voice overs & production for promotions & spots.

GPN Inc & Destination Education Inc., (formerly Great Plains National (GPN). Box 6124, Lincoln, NE, 68506. Phone: (402) 435-0110. Fax: (402) 435-0119.E-mail: serevice@shopdei.com Web Site:www.shopdei.com Stephen C. Lenzen, pres.

TV-CATV only.

Acquires, produces, promotes & distributes videotaped instructional videos for bcst, cablecast & audiovisual use.

GRB Entertainment, 13400 Riverside Dr., 3rd Fl., Studio City, CA, 91423. Phone: (818) 728-7697. Fax: (818) 728-7601.E-mail: gbenz@grbtv.com Web Site:www.grbtv.com Gary R. Benz, pres/CEO.

TV-CATV only.

Production & distribution (TV).

GTN, 13320 Northend Ave., Oak Park, MI, 48237. Phone: (248) 548-2500. Fax: (248) 548-1916. Web Site:www.gtninc.com Doug Cheek, pres.

TV-CATV only.

Studios, remote equipment, multi-format editing, film transfer, audio & duplication svcs, on-site satellite svcs & graphics.

GVI, 1775 K St. N.W., Suite 220, Washington, DC, 20006. Phone: (202) 293-4488. Fax: (202) 293-3293. Web Site:www.g-v-i.com Andy Hemmindinger, pres; Bob Burnett, VP.

TV-CATV only.

Full creative script-to-screen production, camera crews, Avid editing, DVD authoring & equipment rental.

Galavision, 605 Third Ave., 12th Fl., New York, NY, 10158-0180. Phone: (212) 455-5300. Fax: (212) 953-0198. Web Site:www.univision.com Ray Rodriguez, pres/COO; Joanne Lynch, gen mgr; Cesar Conde, opns mgr.

MiamiFL , 9405 N.W. 41st St. Phone:

ChicagoIL , 541 N. Fairbanks Ct., 12th Fl., Suite 1240. Phone:

Los AngelesCA , 5999 Center Dr. Phone:

DallasTX , 2323 Bryan St, Suite 1900. Phone:

TV-CATV only.

Spanish TV program distribution, cable.

Gedeon Programmes, 44-50 av du Capitaine Glarner, Saint-Quen, 93585. Fax: 33 01 49 48 65 03. Phone: 33 01 49 48 65 00. Web Site:www.gedeonprogrammes.com

TV-CATV only.

Films, TV movies, TV series, interactive fiction.

General Broadcasting Co. Inc., 8 N. Bothwell St., Suite 103, Palatine, IL, 60067. Phone: (847) 202-8804. Fax: (847) 202-8834. Robert E. Potter, pres; Charles E. Maples, VP; Dean Mulchaey, production mgr; Eric Edgerton, gen mgr .

Background music, environmental music progmg.

Georgia Film, Video & Music Office, Georgia Department of Economic Dev, 75 Fifth St. N.W., Atlanta, GA, 30308. Phone: (404) 962-4052. Fax: (404) 962-4053.E-mail: film@georgia.org Web Site:www.georgia.org Bill Thompson, dir.

TV-CATV only.

Location scouting & preproduction svcs provided to feature film, TV movie, coml & multimedia production companies.

Getty Images, 601 N. 34th St., Seattle, WA, 98103. Phone: (206) 925-5000. Fax: (206) 925-5001.E-mail: sales@gettyimages.com Web Site:www.gettyimages.com

TV-CATV only.

Getty Images is an imagery company creating and providing still and moving images to communications professionals around the globe.

Ghostwriters/Radio Mall, 2412 Unity Ave. N., Dept BCY, Minneapolis, MN, 55422-3450. Phone: (800) 759-4561. Fax: (763) 522-6256.E-mail: info@radio-mall.com Web Site:www.radiomall.com David Dworkin, owner.

TV-CATV-Radio.

Over 23 years experience with products sold to more than 7,300 radio stns worldwide as well as TV stns, audio-video producers & cable operators. If you have a product that you'd like to mkt to radio or TV stns, contact us.

Lon Gibby Productions, Inc./ Gibby Media Group, 1213 S Pines Rd., Ste C, Spokane Valley, WA, 99206-5485. Phone: (509) 467-1113. Phone: (800) 200-1113. Fax: (509) 467-4763.E-mail: lon@longibby.com Web Site:www.longibby.com Lon Gibby, pres/CEO.

Multimedia productions, video, CD-Rom, CD-I, producers of bcst TV programs, comls, infomercials, corporate videos & webcasting

Gladney Communications Ltd., 101 Reni Rd., Manhasset, NY, 11030. Phone: (516) 627-3016. Fax: (516) 767-1957. Norman Gladney, pres; Marion Gladney, exec VP.

TV-CATV only.

TV & radio production & distribution.

Glenray Productions Inc., Box 40400, Pasadena, CA, 91114-7400. Phone: (626) 797-5462.E-mail: glenray@pacbell.net Web Site:www.familymedia.net C. Ray Carlson, pres.

TV-CATV only.

Films, TV series, video distribution & production, primarily for family & children.

Global Entertainment Media, 1200 N.W. 78th Ave., Suite 104, Miami, FL, 33126. Phone: (786) 206-4873. Fax: (786) 206-4889.E-mail: sales@gem-media.com Web Site:www.gem-media.com Alexander A. Fiore, CEO; Mercedes M. Fiore, pres.

TV-CATV only.

Production & distribution company.

Global Telemedia Inc., 1698 Post Rd. E., Suite 1B, Westport, CT, 06880. Phone: (203) 259-9985. Fax: (203) 259-9986.E-mail: anne@globaltelemedia.com Web Site:www.globaltelemedia.com Greg Kimmelman, pres/CEO; Anne Corsak, VP sls, mktg.

TV-CATV only.

Production & distribution of bcst TV & DVD progmg worldwide.

GlobeCast, 1270 Avenue of the Americas, Ste 2800, New York, NY, 10020. Phone: (212) 373-5140. Fax: (212) 399-1949.E-mail: info@globecastna.com Web Site:www.globecast.com David Sprechman, pres/CEO; Mary Frost, Sr sls VP; Jonathan Feldman, VP business affrs; Keven Cahoon, VP mktg.

Culver CityCA . GlobeCast Los Angeles/California, 10525 W. Washington Blvd. Phone:

WashingtonDC . GlobeCast Washington/DC, 1120 G Street, NW - 2nd Floor. Phone:

MiamiFL . GlobeCast Miami Headquarters America/Florida, 7291 NW 74th St. Phone:

Salt Lake CityUT . GlobeCast Salt Lake City/Utah, 1193 West 2400 South, Suite A. Phone:

TV-CATV only.

GlobeCast Audio division supports a comprehensive package of audio transmission svcs:

ABC/Keystone Ventures provides Satcom C5 DATS/SEDAT distribution svcs to 7,000 radio stns.

3D2, a high-quality digital net designed to svc the entertainment industry, connections post-production facilities, recording studios & voice-over talent worldwide.

A/FX Network utilizing Telos Zephyr code located at venues for sports backhauls & special events.

"Hybrid" bridging svcs to simplify a digital world full of different flavored audio codecs.

Remote Production Packages for single or multi-stn remote bcsts.

GlobeCast North America, 10525 W. Washington Blvd., Culver City, CA, 90230. Phone: (310) 845-3900. Fax: (310) 845-3904. Web Site:www.globecast.com Ken Drake, dir opns.

TV-CATV only.

In the center of Hollywood, GlobeCast North America's Sunset facility provides studio production second audio progmg (SAP), & related client facility svcs on an as-scheduled or contractual basis. GlobeCast's studio is completely integrated w/GlobeCast's network of global, end-to-end connectivity via satellite, fiber optics & microwave.

GlobeCast North America, provides the bcstg industry with a unique combination of both recognized expertise & extensive inter-continental svcs. Through GlobeCast's vast global infrastructure of over 100 transponders, 30 teleports & interconnect facilities, the company provides instant access to the world's major media markets. GlobeCast North America is part of France Telecom, one of the worlds largest telecommunications companies.

Jeff Gold Productions Inc., 13900 Panay Way, Marina del Rey, CA, 90292. Phone: (310) 827-9165. Jeff Gold, dir.

Golden Gate Studios, (KTLN TV 68). 400 Tamal Plaza, Suite 428, Corte Madera, CA, 94925. Phone: (415) 945-7500. Fax: (415) 924-0264. Web Site:www.goldengatestudios.com

TV-CATV only.

2 Studios, Green Screen Options, Full Production Packages

The Samuel Goldwyn Films, 9570 W. Pico Blvd., Suite 400, Los Angeles, CA, 90035-6405. Phone: (310) 860-3100. Fax: (310) 860-3195. Samuel Goldwyn Jr., chmn/CEO; Meyer Gottlieb, pres/COO.

Movie acquisition & distribution.

Good Life Associates, Box 82808, Lincoln, NE, 68501-2808. Phone: (402) 464-6440. Fax: (402) 464-6880.E-mail: martinj@backtothebible.org Web Site:www.goodlifeassociates.org Thomas C. Schindler, pres; Martin Jones, dir.

Radio Only.

Radio program, coml production & distribution svcs.

Good News Broadcasting Association Inc., 6400 Comhusker Hwy., Lincoln, NE, 68501. Phone: (402) 464-7200. Fax: (402) 464-7474.E-mail: info@backtothebible /backtothebible.com Web Site:www.backtothebible.org Woodrow Kroll, pres.

TV-CATV only.

Radio & TV program production & distribution.

Gordon Productions, 1557 Pine St., San Francisco, CA, 94109. Phone: (415) 776-7484. Fax: (415) 776-7822.E-mail: john@gpvideo.com Web Site:www.gpvideo.com John Gordon, pres; Les Lieurance, VP; Jerry Gordon, CEO.

TV-CATV-Radio.

Broadcast pub rels svcs include: B-roll & VNR production & distribution, TV, radio PSA's & audio news releases. Corporate video production include: trade shows, patient educ, training & employee presentations.

Billy Graham Evangelistic Association, Radio Department, Box 1270, Charlotte, NC, 28201. Phone: (704) 401-2432. Fax: (704) 401-3028.E-mail: had@bgea.org Franklin Graham, pres; Roger Flessing, dir.

Radio Only.

Granada America, 15303 Ventura Blvd., Suite C-800, Sherman Oaks, CA, 91403. Phone: (818) 455-4600. Fax: (818) 455-4700. Web Site:www.granadaamerica.com Paul Buccieri, CEO; Sam Zoda, exec VP; Emily Brecher, CFO.

GranadaNY , 609 Greenwich St., 9th Fl.

TV-CATV only.

Worldwide distribution, production of TV series & made-for-TV movies.

Great Chefs Television/Publishing, (A division of G.C.I., Inc.). 747 Magazine St., New Orleans, LA, 70156. Phone: (504) 581-5000. Fax: (504) 581-1188.E-mail: info@greatchefs.com Web Site:www.greatchefs.com John Shoup, pres/CEO.

TV-CATV only.

Production, distribution of cooking, jazz TV programs, videos, CDs, CD-ROMs & books.

Great North Productions, 3720-76 Ave., Edmonton, AB, T6B 2N9. Canada. Phone: (780) 440-2022. Fax: (403) 440-3400. Web Site:www.greatnorth.ab.ca Penny Ritco, VP.
TV-CATV only.
A full-svc international production & distribution company, providing worldwide distribution for bcst home video, non-theatrical markets & co-production opportunities.

The Griffin Group, 130 S. El Camino Dr., Beverly Hills, CA, 90212. Phone: (310) 385-2700. Fax: (310) 358-2701. Web Site:www.merv.com Rob Pritchard, pres; Ronnie Ward, vice chmn.
TV-CATV only.
Full-service dev & production company, slate includes series, specials & films, also real estate & hotel ownership.

Grinberg Film Libraries Inc., 21011 Itasca St., Unit D, Chatworth, CA, 91311. Phone: (818) 709-2450. Fax: (818) 709-8540. Web Site:www.grinberg.com W. "Bill" Brewington, CEO.
TV-CATV only.
Stock footage & news library.

Groove Addicts, 12211 West Washington Blvd., Los Angeles, CA, 90066. Phone: (310) 572-4646. Fax: (310) 572-4647.E-mail: info@grooveaddicts.com Web Site:www.grooveaddicts.com Dain Eric Blair, CEO; Bill Stolier, VP/gen mgr.
ChicagoIL . Groove Addicts - Chicago, 108 W. Hubbard St. Phone:
TV-CATV-Radio.
Adward winning custom scoring & syndicated branding & ID packages for bcsts & entertainment projects worldwide.

Groove Addicts Production Music Catalog, 12211 West Washington Blvd., Los Angeles, CA, 90066. Phone: (310) 572-4644. Fax: (310) 572-4647.E-mail: info@grooveaddicts.com Web Site:www.grooveaddicts.com Bill Stolier, VP/gen mgr.
TV-CATV-Radio.
Continuously updated, sound design & SFX. Annual blanket license & custom music packages. 17 library collection with over 750 releases.

Grove Television Enterprises Inc., 46216 Dry Creek Dr., Badger, CA, 93603. Phone: (323) 645-6444. Fax: (323) 645-6445.E-mail: brett@rehabent.com John W. Hyde, pres/CEO.
TV-CATV only.
TV production & distribution international & domestic.

H

HAVE Inc., 350 Power Ave., Hudson, NY, 12534-2448. Phone: (518) 828-2000. Phone: (800) 999-4283. Fax: (518) 828-2008.E-mail: have@haveinc.com Web Site:www.haveinc.com Nancy Gordon, pres; Paul Swedenburg, VP.
TV-CATV only.
Distribution of cable connected products, equipment, accessories & supplies, featuring BELDEN, CANARE, MOGAMI & GEPCO cable. Duplication, video/audio postproduction svcs & CD-Audio & CD-ROM, DVD & Blu-ray replication & duplication, DVD & Blu-ray authoring. Digital Archiving & file delivery & order fulfillment svcs.

HEA Productions, 313 Gahbauer Rd., Hudson, NY, 12534. Phone: (518) 822-1717. Fax: (518) 822-1042.E-mail: susan@susanhamilton.com Susan Hamilton, pres.
TV-CATV only.
Radio & TV music production.

HIT Entertainment P.L.C., Maple House, 149-150 Tottenham Ct. Rd., 5th Fl., London, W1T 7NF. United Kingdom. Phone: 20-7554-2500. Fax: 20-7388-9321.E-mail: contactus@hitentertainment.com Web Site:www.hitentertainment.com Rob Lawes, CEO; Peter Orton, chmn; Charles Caminada, sls dir; Steve Ruffini, CFO.
Beverly HillsCA , 9300 Wilshire Blvd., 2nd Fl. Phone:
AllenTX , 830 Greenville Ave. Phone:
TV-CATV only.
Distributor, co-producer & financier of quality animiation, children's & natural history progmg.

Alfred Haber Distribution Inc., 111 Grand Ave., Suite 203, Palisades Park, NJ, 07650. Phone: (201) 224-8000. Fax: (201) 947-4500.E-mail: info@haberinc.com Web Site:www.alfredhaber.com George Scanlon, COO; Alfred Haber, pres.
TV-CATV only.
TV program distribution.

Halland Broadcast Services, 2412 Unity Ave. N., Dept. BCY, Minneapolis, MN, 55422. Phone: (763) 522-6256. Fax: (763) 522-6256.E-mail: info@radio-mall.com Web Site:www.h-b-s.com Dave Dworkin, mgr.
Radio Only.
Rock 'n' Roll Graffiti oldies library on compact disc, *The Eighties Plus* AC/CHR library on compact disc & *The Seventies* AC/CHR gold library on compact disc. Country music libraries on compact disc. Also available on hard drive.

Hamilton Productions Inc., 7732 Georgetown Pike, McLean, VA, 22102. Phone: (703) 734-5444. Fax: (703) 734-5449.E-mail: jah@dgsys.net John Hamilton, pres; Jay Hamilton, VP; Anne H. Deger, VP.
TV-CATV only.
Ind TV production firm.

Hanna-Barbera Productions Inc., 15303 Ventura Blvd., Suite 1400, Sherman Oaks, CA, 91403. Phone: (818) 977-7500. Fax: (818) 977-7510. Web Site:www.hanna-barbera.com William Hanna, co-chmn; Joseph Barbera, co-chmn.
TV program production.

Happi Associates, Box 110892, Nashville, TN, 37222. Phone: (615) 220-6050. Phone: (615) 604-1981.E-mail: doddrace@aol.com Skeeter Dodd, gen mgr .
Radio Only.
Radio program & mgmt; country formats; motivational speaking, jingles ID & coml, production music, features, customized productions.

Larry Harmon Pictures Corp., 7080 Hollywood Blvd., Suite 202, Hollywood, CA, 90028. Phone: (323) 463-2331. Fax: (818) 377-3342.E-mail: tellbozo@aol.com Web Site:www.bozo.com Larry Harmon, pres; Susan Harmon, exec VP; Marci Breth, VP corporate affrs.
TV-CATV only.
Owner & distributor of *Bozo* cartoons & live show franchise, & *Laurel & Hardy* cartoons.

Harmony Gold U.S.A. Inc., 7655 Sunset Blvd., Los Angeles, CA, 90046. Phone: (323) 851-4900. Fax: (323) 851-5599.E-mail: sales@harmonygold.com Web Site:www.harmonygold.com Frank Agrama, chmn/CEO; Melissa Wohl, VP sls & acquisition.
TV-CATV only.
TV production, international TV distribution.

Harpo Productions, 110 N. Carpenter St., Chicago, IL, 60607. Phone: (312) 633-1000. Web Site:www.oprah.com
Produces "The Oprah Winfrey Show."

Health Net Productions & Pet Talk, 185 N. New Ballas Rd., St. Louis, MO, 63141. Phone: (314) 997-5422. Fax: (314) 997-5422.E-mail: judyleven@aol.com Judy Leventhal, pres; Chuck LeRoi, VP.
TV-CATV only.
Distributes 90-second pharmacy vignettes, 45 to 60-second pet care vignettes & 90-second sports medicine vignettes.

Hearst Entertainment, Inc., 300 W. 57th St., 15th Fl., New York, NY, 10019. Phone: (212) 969-7553. Fax: (646) 280-1553. Web Site:www.hearstent.com Bruce L. Paisner, pres; Stacey Valenza, VP sls.
Woodland HillsCA . Hearst Entertainment Productions, 20335 Ventura Blvd., Suite 300. Phone:
TV-CATV only.
Leading producer & distributor of made-for-television movies, first-run entertainment, animated series, reality & documentary progmg for the global marketplace.

Hearts of Space Inc., 454 Las Gallinas #333, San Rafael, CA, 94903. Phone: (415) 499-9901. Fax: (415) 499-9903.E-mail: help@hos.com Web Site:www.hos.com Stephen M. Hill, pres & producer; Leyla Rael Hill, VP/gen mgr.
Radio Only.
Slow Music for Fast Times. Syndicated one-hour progmg of ambient, electronic, multi-cultural & contemplative spacemusic via NPR satellite transmission & by direct subscription online at www.hos.com.

Heil Enterprises, Box 1372, Lancaster, PA, 17608-1372. Phone: (717) 898-9100. Fax: (717) 898-6600.E-mail: radio@thegospelgreats.com Web Site:www.thegospelgreats.com Paul Heil, owner; Shelia Heil, co-owner/office mgr.
Radio Only.
Radio program

Arthur Henley Productions, 101 W. 23rd St., #2462, New York, NY, 10011. Phone: (718) 263-0136.E-mail: ah55@webtv.net Arthur Henley, pres.
TV-CATV only.
TV & radio program production; radio program distribution.

Henninger Media Services, Inc., 2601-A Wilson Blvd., Arlington, VA, 22201. Phone: (703) 243-3444. Phone: (888) 243-3444. Fax: (703) 243-5697. Fax: (703) 243-4023. Web Site:www.henninger.com Rob Henninger, CEO.
WashingtonDC . Henninger Capitol, 2121 Wisconsin Ave. N.W. Phone:
WashingtonDC . Henninger Media Services, 1150 17th St, Suite 401. Phone:
NashvilleTN . Henninger Elite, Metro Center, 50 Vantage Way, Suite 100. Phone:
RichmondVA . Henninger Richmond, 1901 E. Franklin St, Suite 103. Phone:
RichmondVA . Commonwealth Film Labs, 1500 Brook Rd. Phone:
TV-CATV-Radio.
TV postproduction, film & video, film processing, 2-D & 3-D graphics, TV progmg dev, distribution; multi-media & DVDs.

Heritage/Baruch Television Distribution, 1025 Connecticut Ave. N.W., Suite 1012, Washington, DC, 20036-5417. Phone: (202) 833-1777. Fax: (202) 496-0162. Ed Baruch, pres; Steve Smallwood, VP; Valerie Cooley-Elliott, dir mktg.
TV-CATV only.
Mktg, syndication & production/distribution of progmg to network syndication international.

Highland Laboratories, Administration Bldg., Pier 96, San Francisco, CA, 94124. Phone: (415) 981-5010. Fax: (415) 981-5019. Web Site:www.highlandlab.com B.J. Brose, pres.
TV-CATV only.
Video, audio, film duplication, film transfers: D-2, Betacam, 2 inches, 1 inch, 3/4 inch, 1/2 inch.

Jack Hilton Inc., 230 Park Ave., Suite 1530, New York, NY, 10169. Phone: (212) 687-2002. Fax: (212) 697-9008.
TV-CATV only.
TV & video productions.

The History Makers, 1900 S. Michigan Ave., Chicago, IL, 60616. Phone: (312) 674-1900. Fax: (312) 674-1915. Web Site:www.thehistorymakers.com Julieanna Richardson, exec dir.
TV-CATV only.
Video production.

Holigan Investment Group Ltd., 15950 N. Dallas Pkwy., Suite 750, Dallas, TX, 75248. Phone: (972) 387-7999. Fax: (972) 387-1685. Web Site:www.michael.holigan.com Michael Holigan, exec producer; Tim Dickey, exec producer.
DallasTX , 6029 Beltline, Suite 110.
TV-CATV only.
Production & syndication of YOUR NEW HOUSE and THE REALITY OF SPEED; 30 minute TV programs.

Home Improvement Television Network, 3441 Baker St., San Diego, CA, 92117. Phone: (858) 273-0572. Fax: (858) 273-8410.E-mail: homefix@hometvnet.com Web Site:www.hometvnet.com Bruce Lamb, pres.
TV-CATV only.
Providers of home improvement progmg & 90-second video vignettes.

Hometown Illinois Radio Network, Box 169, 918 E. Park, Taylorville, IL, 62568-0169. Phone: (217) 824-3395. Fax: (217) 824-3301. Web Site:www.hometownillinoisradio.com Randal J. Miller, pres.
Radio Only.
Wired network providing loc reports & podcasts from Illinois State Fair, Illinois Farm Bureau Convention, Commodity Classic & Farm Progress Show.

Hope Channel, Box 4000, Silver Spring, MD, 20914. Phone: (301) 680-6689. Fax: (301) 680-6312.E-mail: info@hopetv.org Web Site:www.hopetv.org Brad Thorp, dir; Gary Gibbs, VP.

TV-CATV only.

Family friendly TV progmg, 24/7.

Horizon Audio Creations, Box 486, Hudson Heights, PQ, J0P 1J0. Canada. Phone: (928) 684-1113. Fax: (928) 684-1113.E-mail: reachcraigcutler@mac.com Craig W. Cutler, pres; Marguerite Blais, progmg mgr; Mary-Lou Dodd, opns mgr.

TV-CATV-Radio.

Radio program, coml production; production svcs; inflight audio progmg & adv, feature film & short subject provisioning.

Horizons Television Inc., 9305 Monalaine Ct., Great Falls, VA, 22066. Phone: (703) 759-7500. Fax: (703) 759-1620.E-mail: admin@horizonstv.com Web Site:www.horizonstv.com Timothy E. Donner, exec dir; Leesa Kelly, pres.

TV-CATV only.

Creative dev & full-svc production of reality-based TV programs & commissioned videos for diverse major & community based organizations & assns. Avid media composer.

Thomas Horton Associates Inc., 408 Bryant Cir., Suite K, Ojai, CA, 93023. Phone: (805) 646-7866. Fax: (805) 646-3600.E-mail: tha@sharktv.com Web Site:www.sharktv.com Thomas F. Horton, pres.

TV-CATV only.

TV program full-svc production, postproduction, international & domestic distribution, specializing in award-winning documentaries.

Host Communications Inc., 546 E. Main St., Lexington, KY, 40508-2300. Phone: (859) 226-4678. Fax: (859) 226-4419. Web Site:www.hostcommunications.com James Host, CEO; Gordon Whitner, pres/COO.

TV-CATV only.

TV & radio production & syndication.

Hot Box Digital, 367 N. Hwy. 101, Solana Beach, CA, 92075. Phone: (858) 292-8520. Fax: (858) 292-8520. Cam MacMillan, exec producer.

TV-CATV only.

Design & production of bcst 3-D computer graphics. Logo animation, stn packages. All tape formats supported. Productions of Subito Studio Video Graphics Volumes.

Marie Hoy Film & TV, 18 Bruton Pl. Berkeley Sq., Mayfair, London, W1X 7AA. Phone: 020-7851-6666. Fax: 017-1493-3997.E-mail: mariehoy@cocoon.co.uk

TV-CATV only.

Co-production Funding & Financial Packaging.

Huntridge Video Productions Inc., Box 3813, Greenville, SC, 29608-3813. Phone: (864) 271-3348. Fax: (864) 232-4462.E-mail: mat@huntridge.com Web Site:www.huntridge.com

TV-CATV only.

TV production & postproduction.

I

ISL Television Ltd., Seymour News House, Seymour News, London, W1H 9PE. Phone: (44) 171 616 11 11. Fax: (44) 171 616-1110. Web Site:www.islworld.com

TV-CATV only.

TV program sls & distribution, bcst sponsorship, events & TV program production & TV consultancy.

The Idea Channel, 2002 Filmore Ave., Suite 1, Erie, PA, 16506. Phone: (814) 833-7107. Fax: (814) 833-7415.E-mail: info@ideachannel.com Web Site:www.ideachannel.com Bob Chitester, pres/CEO.

TV-CATV only.

Discussions 20-40 minutes in length, featuring two or three leading scholars on a wide variety of subjects. Internet offerings also.

The Image Generators, 18156 Darnell Dr., Olney, MD, 20832. Phone: (301) 924-5700. Fax: (301) 570-8916.E-mail: mweiner@imagegenerators.com Web Site:www.imagegenerators.com Michael J. Weiner, pres/CEO.

TV-CATV only.

Voice-overs, radio spot & program production; media training, progmg concept to completion; ISDN-equipped (TELOS).

Imagers Inc., 1575 Northside Dr., Suite 490, Atlanta, GA, 30318. Phone: (404) 351-5800. Fax: (404) 351-9020. Web Site:www.imagers.com

TV coml production & distribution; production svcs.

In-Motion Pictures, 5 Percy St., London, W1T 1DG. United Kingdom. Phone: (207) 467-6880. Fax: (207) 467-6890.E-mail: Sales@jment.com Web Site:www.jment.com Dr. Hilmar Siebert, chmn; Julian Freeston, CFO.

Beverly HillsCA , 412 S. Beverly Dr., 5th Fl. Phone: TV-CATV only.

Film & TV production & distribution.

Independent Edge Films, 719 52nd St. N., St. Petersburg, FL, 33710. Phone: (727) 321-2898.E-mail: michaelfox@indi-edge.com Web Site:www.indi-edge.com Michael D. Fox, dir.

TV-CATV only.

Ind motion picture/TV/web production & distribution.

Integrity Media, 401 E. Corpoorate Dr., #222, Lewisville, TX, 75057. Phone: (214) 222-7878. Fax: (214) 222-7838.E-mail: schalupka@integritymedia.net Douglas Neece, pres; Sandy Chalupka, VP.

TV-CATV only.

TV & radio program distribution, time buying & media planning.

International Broadcasting Network, Box 691111, 5206 FM 1960 W., Suite 105, Houston, TX, 77269. Phone: (281) 587-8900. Fax: (281) 774-9923.E-mail: ibn@ev1.net Paul Broyles, pres.

TV-CATV only.

Network of ten low power stns; including loc produced progmg.

International Program Consultants Inc., 52 E. End Ave., New York, NY, 10028. Phone: (212) 734-9096. Fax: (212) 734-6495. Russell J. Kagan, mgng dir.

TV-CATV only.

International TV distribution, TV progmg & home video acquisition consultation, co-production consultation.

International Tele-Film, 41 Horner Ave., Unit #3, Toronto, ON, M8Z 4X4. Canada. Phone: (416) 252-1173. Fax: (416) 252-1676.E-mail: info@itf.ca Web Site:www.itf.ca

TV-CATV only.

Distributor for documentaries, features, series & specials, in Canada & worldwide.

International Television Broadcasting Inc., 36-01 36th Ave., 2nd Fl., Long Island City, NY, 11106. Phone: (718) 784-8555. Fax: (718) 784-8901.E-mail: info@itvgold.com Web Site:www.itvgold.com Dr. Sathya Viswanath, pres.

TV-CATV only.

Full time Indian TV program for cable & bcst TV.

International Television Corp., 4380 N.W. 128th St., Miami, FL, 33054. Phone: (305) 688-7475. Fax: (305) 685-5697. Web Site:www.coralintl.com Jose Escalante, VP/gen mgr; Guadalupe D'Agostino, VP international sls.

TV-CATV only.

TV progmg distribution & production. Worldwide distribution, co-productions.

Ion Weather Network, 13 B East Main St., Denville, NJ, 07834. Phone: (973) 983-8222. Fax: (973) 983-1390. Web Site:www.ionweather.com E-mail: steve@ionweather.com Stephen Pellettiere Sr., pres; Stephen Pellettiere Jr., consultant.

Radio Only.

Gen weather forecasts, science info.

Irving Productions Inc., 3202 E. 21st St., Tulsa, OK, 74114. Phone: (918) 744-1221. Fax: (918) 744-1223.E-mail: irving@irvingproductions.com Web Site:www.irvingproductions.com Dick Schmitz, pres.

TV-CATV-Radio.

Audio recording & production svcs for all media.

It Is Written Television, Box O, Thousand Oaks, CA, 91360. Phone: (805) 955-7733. Fax: (805) 955-7734.E-mail: iiw@iiw.org Web Site:www.iiw.org Mark Finley, dir; Shawn Boonstra, assoc speaker.

TV-CATV only.

TV & radio program production & distribution; internet.

Italtoons Corp., 32 W. 40th St., New York, NY, 10018. Phone: (212) 730-0280. Fax: (212) 730-0313.E-mail: salesinfo@italtoons.com Web Site:www.italtoons.com Giuliana Nicodemi, pres; Luisa Rivosecchi, sls; Ken Priester, gen mgr .

TV-CATV only.

TV program production & distribution. Children's animation.

Ivanhoe Broadcast News Inc., 2745 W. Fairbanks Ave., Winter Park, FL, 32789. Phone: (407) 740-0789. Fax: (407) 740-5320.E-mail: jcherry@ivanhoe.com Web Site:www.ivanhoe.com Majorie BeKaert Thomas, pres; Marsha Hitchcock, news dir; John Cherry, pres/sls.

TV-CATV only.

Producer & syndicator of targeted new series. Medical breakthroughs, Inside Science, Prescription Health & Smart Woman.

J

JAM Creative Productions Inc., 5454 Parkdale Dr., Dallas, TX, 75227. Phone: (214) 388-5454. Fax: (214) 381-4647.E-mail: sales@jingles.com Web Site:www.jingles.com Jonathan M. Wolfert, pres; Mary Lyn Wolfert, sr VP; Tom Parma, sls; Cary Bass, sls; Randy Bell, sls.

TV-CATV-Radio.

ID jingle & coml production for radio & TV, custom music & production svcs.

J&H Music Programming, 5814 Fleming Terrace Rd., Greensboro, NC, 27410. Phone: (336) 218-8052. Fax: (336) 218-8052. Joseph V. Gelo, pres; Helen J. Gelo, VP.

Radio Only.

Radio program distribution.

JC Productions Inc., 1851 Murray Hill Station, New York, NY, 10016. Phone: (212) 213-0455. Fax: (212) 532-2820.E-mail: jcpro@bellatlantic.net Web Site:www.jc-productions.com Joe Conforti, dir.

TV-CATV only.

Live action coml production; CD-ROM multimedia production; 3D animation & graphic design.

JGT Media Productions, 12408 86th Pl., N.E., Kirkland, WA, 98034-2601. Phone: (425) 820-4523. Fax: (425) 820-4523. J. Graley Taylor, .

TV program, promotion film production & distribution; production svcs; rgnl award program, ARBY Awards; film & video production.

J.N. Productions, 902-1790 Bayshore Dr., Vancouver, BC, V6G 3G5. Canada. Phone: 604-331-0690.E-mail: jnproductions@telus.net Web Site:www.jnproductions.bc.ca Jakob Nortman, pres.

Radio Only.

For all your voice-over needs, including narration, corporate videos, on-hold telephone messages & announcements for GPS systems. Radio production facilities available.

Jameson Broadcast Inc., 1644 Hawthorne St., Sarasota, FL, 34239. Phone: (941) 906-8800. Fax: (941) 906-8801.E-mail: radio@jamesonbcast.com Web Site:www.jamesonbroadcast.com Jamie G. Jameson, pres; Trulee C. Jameson, VP.

Radio Only.

Radio program production, syndication & special projects.

Janson Media, 88 Semmens Rd., Harrington Park, NJ, 07640. Phone: (201) 784-8488. Fax: (201) 784-3993.E-mail: info@janson.com Web Site:www.janson.com Stephen Janson, pres; Zara Janson, VP; Betsy Van Ost, dir; Lynne Warshavsky, dir.

TV-CATV only.

International TV & video/ DVD program distribution & production; video/DVD publishing.

Jefferson-Pilot Sports, 1900 W. Morehead St., Charlotte, NC, 28208. Phone: (704) 374-3669. Fax: (704) 374-3859.E-mail: jweber@jpsports.com Web Site:www.jpsports.com Edward M. Hull, pres, gen mgr; Pam Hawthorne, gen sls mgr, VP; Powell Kidd, VP opns; Jimmy Rayburn, opns mgr, VP, opns mgr; Jeff Tennant, VP sls, VP mktg.

AtlantaGA , 3390 Peachtree Rd, NE, Suite 1000. Phone: RutherfordNJ , Meadows Office Complex, 201 Rt. 17 N, Suite 300. Phone:

TV-CATV only.

TV & CATV sports production & syndication.

The Johnson Group, 6800 Fleetwood Rd., Suite 100, McLean, VA, 22101. Phone: (703) 356-4004. Fax: (703) 356-6969.E-mail: rmjcameron@aol.com Web Site:www.thejgroup.com Robert M. Johnson, pres; Joe Fab, VP.

Radio Only.

Video, film, multimedia & radio creative svcs & production.

Joe Jones Productions, 10556 Arnwood Rd., Lake View Terrace, CA, 91342. Phone: (818) 899-4457. Fax: (818) 899-4457.E-mail: jojones@jojonesnetcom.com Joe Jones, exec producer; Marion Jones, VP opns.

TV-CATV only.

TV, radio coml & program production; jingle production & production svcs.

Tom Jones Recording Studios, 1620 Greenview Dr. S.W., Rochester, MN, 55902-1034. Phone: (507) 288-7711. Fax: (507) 288-4531. Thomas H. Jones, pres; Aaron Manthei, chief engr.

TV-CATV-Radio.

Recording studio, compact disc duplication recording svcs. Radio program & coml production.

Jordan Klein Film & Video, 10197 S.E. 144th Pl., Summerfield, FL, 34491. Phone: (352) 288-3999. Fax: (352) 288-5538.E-mail: jkfv01@gate.net Web Site:www.jordy.com Jordan Klein Jr., pres.

TV-CATV only.

Underwater, on-the-water production; rental film, video housing & crews; Bahamas specialist.

Nicole Jouve, 54 Avenue du Roule, Neuilly Sur Seine, 92200. France. Phone: 33 1 47 22 43 27. Fax: 33 1 47 22 43 27.E-mail: interamany@aol.com Nicole Jouve, pres.

TV-CATV only.

Distribution of French films (non-theatrical, TV & video), documentaries (Jean Rouch) childrens programs.

Juravic Entertainment, 620 Glenridge Dr., Glenview, IL, 60025. Phone: (847) 998-5998. Fax: (847) 998-6013.E-mail: dljuravic@aol.com

TV-CATV only.

TV program syndication.

K

KCRA-TV, (Hearst-Argyle Television Inc). 3 Television Cir., Sacramento, CA, 95814-0794. Phone: (916) 446-3333. Fax: (916) 325-3731. Web Site:www.thekcrachannel.com Elliott Troshinsky, pres & gen mgr .

TV-CATV only.

TV program & coml production; production svcs.

KCSN 88.5 FM, California State University, Northridge, 18111 Nordhoff St., Northridge, CA, 91330-8312. Phone: (818) 677-3090.E-mail: frederick.d.johnson@csun.edu Web Site:www.kcsn.org Michael Worrall, chief engr; Fred Johnson, gen mgr; Martin Perlich, progmg dir; Laura Kelly, dev dir.

Radio Only.

Public radio serving parts of Los Angeles, CA—classical weekdays, eclectic weeknights & weekends. PRI, AP affil. The best of public radio.

KPTS-TV, 320 West 21st St. N., Wichita, KS, 67203-2499. Phone: (316) 838-3090. Fax: (316) 838-8586.E-mail: dchecots@kpts.org Web Site:www.kpts.org Michele Gors Paris, pres/CEO; David Brewer, progmg mgr; Dave McClintock, dir technology.

TV-CATV only.

Industrial video production for corporate training & mktg communications.

KTOO-TV & Radio Station, 360 Egan Dr., Juneau, AK, 99801. Phone: (907) 586-1670. Fax: (907) 586-3612.E-mail: info@ktoo.org Web Site:www.ktoo.org Jeff Brown, program dir; Bill Legere, pres, gen mgr; James Mahan, TV mgr.

TV-CATV only.

A radio program highlighting diversified music & stories for children.

KUSA Television, 500 Speer Blvd., Denver, CO, 80203. Phone: (303) 871-9999. Fax: (303) 698-4700.E-mail: kusa@9news.com Web Site:www.9news.com Asa Darrow, production mgr; Mark A. Cornetta, pres, gen mgr; Patti Dennis, VP & news dir; Patricia Wilson, gen sls mgr.

TV-CATV only.

News production only.

David Kaye Productions Inc., 1361 Paseo Redondo Ave., Burbank, CA, 91501. Phone: (800) 843-3933. Phone: (310) 403-1714. Fax: (604) 921-1926.E-mail: info@davidkaye.com Web Site:www.davidkaye.com David Kaye, pres; Stephan J. Sisk, opns.

TV-CATV-Radio.

Full svc voice-over production company, providing radio & TV imaging & branding around the world.

Kazmark Entertainment Group, 14320 Ventura Blvd., Suite 601, Sherman Oaks, CA, 91423. Phone: (818) 981-4410. Fax: (818) 501-2211.E-mail: jkazmark@earthlink.net Jeffrey Kazmark, pres.

TV-CATV only.

Progmg distribution.

The Kenwood Group, 75 Varney Pl., San Francisco, CA, 94107-1922. Phone: (415) 957-5333. Fax: (415) 957-5311. Web Site:www.kenwoodgroup.com Christina Crowley, pres; Daniel Pinkham, VP.

Creative svcs & production of comls & corporate communications, film, video, multimedia, meetings & events.

Eddie Kessler Productions Publications & Promotions, Box 6243, Martinsburg, WV, 25402. Phone: (302) 399-8690. Eddie Kessler, pres/CEO.

TV-CATV-Radio.

Extensive film library, props and photo library.

Killer Tracks, 8750 Wilshire Blvd., FL 2, Beverly Hills, CA, 90211-2715. Phone: (323) 957-4455. Fax: (323) 957-4470.E-mail: sales@killertracks.com Web Site:www.killertracks.com

TV-CATV only.

Provides production music library & sound effects.

Kipany Productions Ltd., 32 E. 39th St., New York, NY, 10016. Phone: (212) 883-8300. Fax: (212) 883-0409.E-mail: share82308@aol.com T. Hendry, pres; K. Colligan, CEO.

TV-CATV only.

Video production, bcst progmg, mktg, sls & communications experts/web designers specializing in Telcom, event mgmt.

Klein &, 8896 Carson St., Culver City, CA, 90232. Phone: (310) 317-9599. Fax: (310) 456-7701.E-mail: imagedoctor@kleinand.com Web Site:www.kleinand.com Bob Klein, pres.

TV-CATV only.

Mktg consulting, creative svcs for bcst, cable & Internet companies.

Knowledge In A Nutshell Inc., 1420 Centre Ave., Suite 2213, Pittsburgh, PA, 15219. Phone: (800) 688-7435. Phone: (412) 765-2020. Fax: (412) 765-3672.E-mail: audrey@knowledgeinanutshell.com Web Site:www.knowledgeinanutshell.com Charles Reichblum, pres.

TV-CATV-Radio.

Syndicates radio/TV program, Knowledge in a Nutshell & Knowledge minute.

Kultur International Films, 195 Hwy. 36, West Long Branch, NJ, 07764. Phone: (732) 229-2343. Fax: (732) 229-0066.E-mail: info@kultur.com Web Site:www.kultur.com Dennis M. Hedlund, chmn; Pearl Lee, VP; Ronald Davis, mgng dir.

TV-CATV only.

Suppliers of programs on DVD in North America. Selection includes documentaries, opera, ballet, classical music, profiles, theater, comedy, fitness, country music, rock & roll.

L

Lakeside TV Co., 300 Highpoint Dr., Suite 712, Hartsdale, NY, 10530. Phone: (914) 946-7806 (ph/fax).E-mail: bernshu@msn.com Bernard Schulman, pres; Diane Ross, VP.

TV-CATV only.

TV program distribution, production & syndication.

Lambert Television, 100 N. Crescent Dr., 2nd Flr., Beverly Hills, CA, 90210. Phone: (310) 385-4288. Fax: (310) 385-4004.E-mail: jones@lamberttv.com Web Site:www.lamberttv.com Michael Jones, exec VP; Sam Englebardt, VP.

TV-CATV only.

Lambert Television owns and operates a television station group.

Lapco Communications, 437 E. Beil Ave., Nazareth, PA, 18064. Phone: (610) 759-9444. Fax: (610) 759-8589.E-mail: sales@lapcocom.com Web Site:www.lapcocom.com P. Pagilaro, pres; L. Van Winkle, VP.

TV-CATV only.

TV progmg & production, computer graphics, producers of original progmg, TV comls, TV promotion production, production mgmt, computer stock background library.

Launch Radio Networks, (a division of United Stations Radio Network). 1065 Ave. of the Americas, 3rd Fl., New York, NY, 10018. Phone: (212) 536-3600. Fax: (212) 536-3601. Web Site:www.launchradionetworks.com E-mail: ccolombo@launchradionetworks.com Dave Ankers, VP/gen mgr; Judy Rosen, dir opns.

Radio Only.

Launch Radio Networks produces, distributes music, entertainment news & svcs for radio stns as well as other media worldwide.

Leadem to Water Production Inc., Box 279, Oregon City, OR, 97045. Phone: (503) 631-7661. Fax: (503) 631-7672.E-mail: info@horsemansworld.com Web Site:www.horsemansworld.com Jeff Tracy, founder.

TV-CATV only.

Produces syndicated radio show *Horseman's World*, coml video narrations, produces World bcst for A.Q.H.A. on 250 + stn, cable TV houses northwest & cowboy cooking.

John Lemmon Films, 1325 Rock Point Rd., Charlotte, NC, 28270. Phone: (704) 532-1944. Fax: (704) 566-1984.E-mail: jlemmon@jlf.com Web Site:www.jlf.com Mike Rosinski, head animator.

TV-CATV only.

Clay, cel & stop-motion animation for TV specials, comls, program openings & on-air IDs.

Leo Productions, 1 Rond Point Victor Hugo, 92130-Issy-Les-Moulineaux France. Phone: (331) 55 95 57 00. Fax: (331) 55 95 57 01.E-mail: leo@leoproductions.com Web Site:www.leoproductions.com Jean-Louis Brugat, mgng dir.

TV-CATV only.

TV production, progmg consultants, live bcsts.

Leukemia & Lymphoma Society, 1311 Mamaroneck Ave., White Plains, NY, 10605. Phone: (914) 949-5213. Fax: (914) 949-6691.E-mail: lanereg@lls.org Web Site:www.leukemia-lymphoma.org Nancy Klein, VP mktg; Jimmy Nangle, VP.

TV-CATV only.

Produces & distributes educational ideas to inform & educate viewers about leukemia & related diseases & available treatment.

Liberty Studios Inc., 238 E. 26th St., New York, NY, 10010. Phone: (212) 532-1865. Fax: (212) 779-2207.E-mail: email@libertystudios.us Anthony Lover, pres; John Sawyer, VP.

TV-CATV only.

TV program, coml, film & video production.

Lifestyle Magazine/The Evidence, 101 W. Cochran St., Simi Valley, CA, 93065. Phone: (888) 940-0062. Fax: (805) 522-2114.E-mail: info@ffttv.org Web Site:www.faithfortoday.tv Michael Tucker, dir.

TV-CATV only.

TV program production & distribution.

Lightbridge Production & Distribution, 1051 Broadway, Sonoma, CA, 95476. Phone: (707) 939-4920. Fax: (707) 939-4919. Roy Walkenhorst, CEO; Judy Brooks, founder.

TV-CATV only.

TV & video progmg.

Lighthouse Productions, 21144-3 CR 126, Goshen, IN, 46528. Phone: (574) 533-1400. Fax: (661) 760-8775 .E-mail: audicolabels@audicolabels.com Web Site:www.audicolabels.com Bill Landow, pres.

TV-CATV only.

Audio, video full production svc, documentaries, training, audio & video recording svcs.

Lightyear Entertainment L.P., 548 W. 20th St., Suite 206, New York, NY, 10001. Phone: (212) 353-5084. Fax: (212) 353-5083.E-mail: mail@lightyear.com Web Site:www.lightyear.com Arnold Holland, pres/CEO.

TV-CATV only.

TV program production & distribution. Audio & video distribution.

Limelight Communications Inc., 2812 Roesh Way, Vienna, VA, 22181. Phone: (703) 242-4596. Fax: (703) 991-0616.E-mail: moreinfo@limelightdc.com Web Site:www.limelightdc.com Kenneth Reff, pres.

TV-CATV only.

Writing, producing & editing svcs for bcst & industrial clients. Available as sub-contractors for specific svcs, or to fully produce complete shows.

Lindberg Productions Inc., 24 Mulford Ave., East Hampton, NY, 11937. Phone: (212) 599-1239. Phone: (917) 696-1826.E-mail: ctimany@aol.com Larry Lindberg, pres; Erika Shapeero, producer.
TV-CATV only.
Video production for business & industry.

Lion and Fox Recording Studios, 9517 Baltimore Ave., College Park, MD, 20740-1321. Phone: (301) 982-4431.E-mail: mike@lionfox.com Web Site:www.lionfox.com James Fox, pres.
TV-CATV-Radio.
Digital audio production for TV & radio; music & EFX libraries; CD and CD-ROM & cassette duplication; location audio.

Lions Gate Entertainment, (A division of Trimark Holdings). 2700 Colorado Ave., Suite 200, Santa Monica, CA, 90404. Phone: (310) 449-9200. Fax: (310) 392-0252. Web Site:www.lionsgatefilms.com Don Feltheimer, pres/CEO.
TV-CATV only.
Domestic & international TV, film, video distribution & adv sls firm. Builds, manages, invests in domestic & foreign bcst networks.

Litton Entertainment, (formerly Litton Syndications Inc.). 884 Allbritton Blvd., Suite 200, Mount Pleasant, SC, 29464. Phone: (843) 883-5060. Fax: (843) 883-9957.E-mail: sara@litton.tv Web Site:www.litton.tv David Morgan, pres/CEO.
TV-CATV only.
TV distribution (TV program sls & mktg).

London Weekend Television International, South Bank TV Ctr., Upper ground, London, SE1 9LT. United Kingdom. Phone: (020) 7620-1620.E-mail: images@lwt.co.uk Web Site:www.lwt.co.uk Charles Allen, mng dir; Steve Morrison, head admin.
New YorkNY , 500 Fifth Ave, Suite 1710. Phone:
TV-CATV only.
TV program production & distribution.

Longhorn Radio Network, 1 University Station, (A0704) University of Texas, Austin, TX, 78712-1090. Phone: (512) 471-1631. Fax: (512) 471-3700. Web Site:www.kut.org J. Stewart Vanderwilt, dir, gen mgr; Jody Evans, progmg dir; Hawk Mendenhall, assoc gen mgr.
Radio Only.
New music progmg & NPR syndication.

Loral Skynet, (A subsidiary of Loral Cyberstar). 500 Hills Dr., Bedminster, NJ, 07921. Phone: (908) 470-2300. Fax: (908) 470-2459. Web Site:www.loralskynet.com John Celli, pres/COO; Michael Targoff, CEO.
London. Loral Cyberstar-Europe, Inc., 131-151 Great Titchfield St. Phone:
TV-CATV-Radio.
International satellite communications company that leases capacity for video transmissions for TV & other program distributors. Also provides Internet access & private net svcs directly to Internet Service Providers & multinational businesses worldwide. Svcs include data networking, voice, video, teleconferencing & news distribution to multiple points worldwide.

M

MAN QC Creations, 123 E. Dania Beach Blvd., Dania, FL, 33004. Phone: (954) 921-1111.
TV-CATV only.

MGC The Multimedia Group of Canada, 415-A Mount Pleasant, Montreal Westmount, PQ, H3Y 3G9. Canada. Phone: (514) 844-3636. Fax: (514) 844-4990.E-mail: mgc@the-mgc.com Web Site:www.the-mgc.com Jacques Bouchard, pres/CEO; Roselyne Brovillet, sls; David Seeler, dev VP.
TV-CATV only.
Participates in the dev & distribution of progmg in the intl mkt.

MGM Inc., 2500 Broadway, Santa Monica, CA, 90404. Phone: (310) 449-3000. Fax: (310) 264-1244. Web Site:www.mgm.com
TV-CATV only.
TV program distribution.

MGM TV Canada, 20 Queen St. West #3500, Toronto, ON, H5H 3R3. Canada. Phone: (416) 260-9680. Fax: (416) 260-9993. Web Site:www.mgm.com
TV-CATV only.
Film distribution for all UA, Polygram & Orion film library

(features, series & animated).

MG/Perin Inc., 110 Green St. Suite 304, New York, NY, 10012. Phone: (212) 941-9750. Fax: (212) 941-9122.E-mail: mgperin@aol.com Richard Perin, pres.
TV-CATV only.
TV program production & distribution.

MPL Media, 621 Mainstream Dr., Ste 260, Nashville, TN, 37228. Phone: (615) 256-1675. Fax: (615) 256-0757.E-mail: daviddeeb@mplmedia.com Web Site:www.mplmedia.com Peggy Shedlock, VP; David Deeb, dir mktg, sls dir.
TV-CATV only.
16/35 color negative processing, rank cintel & ursagold transfer, video edit, graphics, DVD authoring & fulfillment, HD video editing.

MRC Films, Box 697, Plainview, NY, 11803. Phone: (516) 796-7568.E-mail: jlmollot3@verizon.net Larry Mollot, exec producer.
TV-CATV only.
Producers of original progmg for bcst, cablecast, TV comls & PSAs.

MRN Radio, 1801 International Speedway Blvd., Daytona Beach, FL, 32114. Phone: (386) 947-6400. Fax: (386) 947-6716. Web Site:www.mrnradio.com Cheryl Knight, dir affil; Steve Harrison, natl sls mgr.
Radio Only.
Live coverage of NASCAR stock car racing plus *NASCAR LIVE* wkly telephone talk, *NASCAR Today* daily news program, via satellite.

MSE, 540 Toby Hill Rd., Westbrook, CT, 06498. Phone: (860) 399-0191. Fax: (860) 399-0196.E-mail: marcia@mseusa.com Web Site:www.mseusa.com Marcia Simon, principal.
TV-CATV-Radio.
Short form programs: Health/Medical, Green/Eco-Friendly, podcast production.

MTI The Image Group, 885 2nd Ave., Level C, New York, NY, 10017. Phone: (212) 548-7700. Fax: (212) 759-7465.E-mail: jromano@image-group.com Web Site:www.image-group.com
New YorkNY , 727 11th Ave. Phone:
New YorkNY , 401 Fifth Ave. Phone:
TV-CATV only.
Nine studios, 25 Digital online suites, 10 Avids, four infernos, 63 D platforms, NIT/MAC platforms, URSA Diamond/c-Reality, Digital Sound mixing Duplication.

MTM Entertainment Inc., 12700 Ventura Blvd., Studio City, CA, 91604. Phone: (818) 755-2400.
TV-CATV only.
TV program production & distribution.

MVI Post, 6320 Castle Pl., Falls Church, VA, 22044. Phone: (703) 536-7678. Fax: (703) 536-9490.E-mail: m.kohn@mvipost.com Web Site:www.mvipost.com Frank Maniglia Jr., pres; Craig Maniglia, VP.
TV-CATV-Radio.
Full-svc video, audio & graphics postproduction; features screensound digital audio system 601 component digital video suite, high definition digital postproduction facility.

MacNeil/Lehrer Productions, 2700 S. Quincy St., Suite 250, Arlington, VA, 22206. Phone: (703) 998-2170. Fax: (703) 998-5707. Web Site:www.pbs.org/newshour Lester Crystal, pres; David Sit, VP; Harold Crawford, controller; Susan Mills, dir program dev; Cristal Kurtz, dir admin; Robert Flynn, dir communication.
TV-CATV only.
Produces news & info programs for public TV & other coml & cable networks. Production of *The News Hour with Jim Lehrer*.

Madison Square Garden Network, 4 Penn Plaza, 4th Floor, New York, NY, 10001. Phone: (212) 465-5926. Phone: (212) 465-6741. Fax: (212) 465-6024.E-mail: msgnetpr@msgnetwork.com Web Site:www.msgnetwork.com Michael Bair, pres; Lydia Murphy, exec VP production, progmg.
TV-CATV only.
NY Knicks, NY Rangers & NY Mets, NY MetroStars, NY Power, NY Islanders & NY Liberty; boxing, college football & basketball; exclusive Garden events; original series.

Magno Sound & Video, 729 7th Ave., New York, NY, 10019. Phone: (212) 302-2505. Fax: (212) 819-1282.E-mail: david@magnosound.com Web Site:www.magnosound.com Robert Friedman, pres; David Friedman, VP.
TV-CATV only.

Complete film, TV & radio production & postproduction svcs for agency, feature, network, corporate & industrial clients.

Make It Happen Productions Inc., 13557 Ventura Blvd., 2nd Fl., Sherman, CA, 91423. Phone: (323) 851-6444. Fax: (323) 851-6465.E-mail: bfrank@mihpitv Billy Frank, pres.
TV-CATV only.
Ind & co-productions, dev of projects, package projects, production svcs, post production.

Makedwde Publishing, (formerly MAKWDE Productions). 10556 Arnwood Rd., Lake View Terrace, CA, 91342. Phone: (818) 899-4457. Fax: (818) 890-4050.E-mail: mjones@verizon.com
TV-CATV only.
Music publishing.

Man From Mars Productions, 159 Orange St., Manchester, NH, 03104-4217. Phone: (603) 668-0652. Fax: (603) 666-4878.E-mail: brouder@juno.com Web Site:www.manfrommars.com Ed Brouder, owner.
Radio Only.
Aircheck sls for radio collectors; coml production.

Manhattan Production Music, 355 W. 52nd St., 6th Fl., New York, NY, 10019. Phone: (212) 333-5766. Phone: (800) 227-1954. Fax: (212) 262-0814.E-mail: info@mpmmusic.com Web Site:www.mpmmusic.com Norman Chesky, owner.
TV-CATV-Radio.
Five music libraries Apple Trax, Live Trax, MPM, AMM, BRg containing over 450 CDs, including the Audiophile Sound effects series & the Chesky Classical Library.

Ben Manilla Productions, 3361 20th St., San Francisco, CA, 94110-2627. Phone: (415) 970-8020. Fax: (415) 970-8024.E-mail: info@bmpaudio.com Web Site:www.bmpaudio.com J. Ben Manilla, pres; Devon Strolovitch, producer; Erik Beith, producer.
Radio Only.
Audio production & progmg for a var of formats.

Mar Vista Entertainment, 12519 Venice Blvd., Los Angeles, CA, 90066. Phone: (310) 737-0950. Fax: (310) 737-9115.E-mail: info@marvista.net Web Site:www.marvista.com Ferdando Szew, CEO; Michael Jacobs, pres; George Port, exec VP.
SharonMA , 210 N. Main St. Phone:
TV-CATV only.
Domestic & international distribution of children's animation, live action features, series, films & documentaries.

Marathon International, 74 rue Bonaparte, 75006 Paris Phone: 331-53-1091-00. Fax: 331-43-2504-66.E-mail: marathon@marathon.fr Web Site:www.marathon.fr
TV-CATV only.
Distributor of TV programs worldwide; series, documentaries, animation, wildlife, TV movies.

Maryknoll Productions, 75 Ryder Rd., Maryknoll, NY, 10545-0308. Phone: (914) 941-7636. Fax: (914) 945-0670.E-mail: nkeel@maryknoll.com Web Site:www.maryknollmall.org Lawrence M. Rich, exec producer.
TV-CATV only.
Offers a library of video & film productions featuring Third World countries; radio & TV programs also available.

Maryland Public Television, 11767 Owings Mills Blvd., Owings Mills, MD, 21117. Phone: (410) 356-5600. Fax: (410) 581-4338. Web Site:www.mpt.org Robert Shuman, pres/CEO; Larry Unger, VP, COO; Eric Eggleton, sr VP; Joseph Krushinsky, VP institutional advancement.
TV-CATV only.
TV program production & distribution.

Masai Films Inc., 6922 Hollywood Blvd., Suite 401, Hollywood, CA, 90028. Phone: (323) 466-5451. Fax: (323) 466-2440. Fritz Goode, .
TV-CATV only.
TV & radio program & coml producers; production svcs.

Maslow Media Group Inc., 2233 Wisconsin Ave. N.W., Suite 400, Washington, DC, 20007-4104. Phone: (202) 965-1100. Fax: (202) 965-6171.E-mail: cneubecker @lmaslowmedia.com Web Site:www.maslowmedia.com Linda Maslow, CEO.
TV-CATV only.
Video production, production support svcs, staffing (freelance & fulltime), factors, creative & tech people, camera crews anywhere in the world, cable, film, multimedia, animators,

payroll & paymaster svcs nationwide for bcst studio, field & new media.

Mason Video, 9632 N. 34th St., Omaha, NE, 68112. Phone: (402) 455-9422. Fax: (402) 455-0707. E-mail: melemason@aol.com Web Site:www.masonvideo.com Mele Mason, owner.

TV-CATV only.

Offers bcst video productions. Equipment includes Ikigami HLV55 Betacam, DVcam & HDV.

MasterControl FamilyNet Radio, The Broadcast Communications Group, NAMB. 6350 W. Freeway, Fort Worth, TX, 76116. Phone: (817) 570-1400. Fax: (817) 737-9436. E-mail: lbratton@familynet.com Web Site:www.familynetradio.com Scott Miller, program dir; Donna Senn, radio distribution; Chuck Ries, producer; Dale Weller, CEO.

Radio Only.

Total health program featuring interviews with experts on physical, mental, financial, and spiritual health, hosts Ralph Baker & Terri Barrett.

Matchframe Video, 610 N. Hollywood Way, Suite 101, Burbank, CA, 91505. Phone: (818) 840-6800. Fax: (818) 840-2726. Marvin Rich, CEO.

TV-CATV only.

In-house editing suites; audio sweetening; portable on-line/off-line (AVID/HD and SD) editing systems; graphics; telecine; tape to tape color connection.

William Mauldin Productions Inc., 1010 Canonero Dr., Greensboro, NC, 27410-3804. Phone: (336) 632-9801. Fax: (540) 301-0399. E-mail: productions@mauldin.net Web Site:www.mauldin.net William D. Mauldin, pres/CEO.

TV-CATV-Radio.

Major market talent for narrations & voice overs, documentaries, stn IDs, program intros, comls for any media market. Let us provide the voice & production for your projects. We can offer finished products via CD, MP3, or via the web. Check our website for samples of our work!

Maximum Marketing Services Inc., 833 W. Jackson, Ste 300, Chicago, IL, 60607. Phone: (312) 226-4111. Fax: (312) 226-5765. E-mail: contact@maximummarketing.biz Web Site:www.maxmarketing.com Jennifer Tio, pres.

TV-CATV only.

TV & radio program, production & distribution; public relation services.

Maysles Films, Inc., 343 Lenox Ave., New York, NY, 10027. Phone: (212) 582-6050. Fax: (212) 586-2057. E-mail: info@mayslesfilms.com Web Site:www.mayslesfilms.com Albert Maysles, CEO; Bradley Kaplan, pres.

TV-CATV only.

Full production svcs for theatrical & TV non-fiction films; adv comls; industrial films, including pre- & postproduction.

McClain Enterprises Inc., 4405-B Belmont Park Terr., Nashville, TN, 37215-3609. Phone: (615) 269-6517. Fax: (615) 269-6648. E-mail: carolyn@mcclaintv.com Web Site:www.mcclaintv.com Carolyn McClain, pres.

TV-CATV-Radio.

Custom & syndicated TV mktg for radio, sls consulting, sls & promotional projects for radio & TV stns.

Media Access Group at WGBH, One Guest St., Boston, MA, 02135. Phone: (617) 300-3600. Fax: (617) 300-1020. E-mail: access@wgbh.org Web Site:access.wgbh.org Larry Goldberg, dir.

BurbankCA . Media Acess Group West, 300 E. Magnolia Blvd., 2nd Fl. Phone:

TV-CATV only.

Provides real-time & off-line captioning, subtitling, descriptive narration & consulting.

The Media Group of Connecticut Inc., 7 Maple St., Weston, CT, 06883-1026. Phone: (203) 544-0018. Fax: (203) 544-0041. E-mail: mediagr@aol.com Harvey F. Bellin, pres.

TV-CATV only.

TV, video production, writing, directing & editing; digital animation; dramatization & documentary; TV, corporate & govt svcs offered.

Media Planning Group (MPG), 195 Broadway, 12th Fl., New York, NY, 10007. Phone: (646) 587-5000. Fax: (646) 587-5005. Web Site:www.mpgsite.com Shawn Holliday, CEO.

TV-CATV-Radio.

Producers, distributors & TV program packagers, videocassette producer/distributor. Full service media buying & planning company.

Media Visions, 7401 K Fullerton Rd., Springfield, VA, 22153. Phone: (703) 550-1500. Phone: (800) 628-3556. Fax: (703) 550-9711. E-mail: mrock@mediavisions.net Web Site:www.mediavisions.net Mike Rock, pres.

Provides full-service video duplication, packaging, warehousing, complete order fulfillment, CD & DVD.

Medialink, 708 3rd Ave., 8th Fl., New York, NY, 10017. Phone: (212) 682-8300. Fax: (212) 682-2370. E-mail: learnmore@medialink.com Web Site:www.medialink.com Lawrence Moskowitz, CEO; Mike Cavender, VP client solutions; Donald M. Michels, chief technology officer.

TV-CATV only.

Video & audio news release distributor & producer to TV & radio stns throughout the United States & Europe.

MediaTracks Inc., 2250 E. Devon Ave., Suite 150, Des Plaines, IL, 60018-4507. Phone: (847) 299-9500. Fax: (847) 299-9501. E-mail: slustig@mediatracks.com Web Site:www.mediatracks.com Shel Lustig, pres; Reed Pence, VP.

Radio Only.

Produce, syndicate & distribute radio progmg, news, comls & PSAs. Specialists in health & medicine, news & pub affrs.

Medstar Television Inc., 5920 Hamilton Blvd., Allentown, PA, 18106. Phone: (610) 395-1300. Fax: (610) 391-1556. Web Site:www.medstar.com E-mail: rpetrovich@medstar.com Paul Dowling, exec producer; Ron Petrovich, VP & medical news.

TV-CATV only.

Health & medical news progmg includes one-hour specials, Health Matters TV series, MedstarSource & MedstarAdvances news svcs.

Megatrax Production Music Inc., 7629 Fulton Ave., North Hollywood, CA, 91605. Phone: (818) 255-7100. Phone: (888) 634-2555. Fax: (818) 255-7199. E-mail: megatrax@megatrax.com Web Site:www.megatrax.com John Dwyer, owner; Ron Mendelsohn, owner.

TV-CATV-Radio.

Production music for bcst promotion & adv. Custom scoring & news music packages available.

Bill Melendez Productions Inc., 13400 Riverside Dr., Suite 201, Sherman Oaks, CA, 91423. Phone: (818) 382-7382. Fax: (818) 382-7377. E-mail: bmpi@aol.com Bill Melendez, pres.

TV program, coml animation production.

Message on Hold, Box 747, Hendersonville, NC, 28793-0747. Phone: (828) 692-7200. Phone: (800) 223-1930. Fax: (828) 692-9147. E-mail: molton.ad@bellsouth.net Marcie Molton, pres; Randy Molton, production mgr.

Radio Only.

Producers of high-quality comls for telephone "hold" lines. Specializing in automotive, financial, medical & pharmacies.

Metro Music Productions Inc., 37 W. 20th St., Suite 906, New York, NY, 10011. Phone: (212) 229-1700. Phone: (800) 697-7392. Fax: (212) 229-9063. E-mail: info@metromusicinc.com Web Site:www.metromusicinc.com Mitch Coodley, pres; Katrina Haskell, office mgr.

TV-CATV only.

Original music scoring for TV progmg, prom, news, sports, comls. Production music library geared toward bcst.

Metro Networks, A Westwood One Co. 555 E. City Ave., Suite 1000, Bala Cynwyd, PA, 19004. Phone: (717) 774-8150. Fax: (717) 774-8160. E-mail: elaine.konkle @metronetworks.com Web Site:www.metronetworks.com Charlie Weirauch, gen mgr; Allison Morris, opns dir.

TV-CATV-Radio.

TV & radio net; radio production/distribution.

Metro Weather Service Inc., 788 Franklin Ave., Valley Stream, NY, 11580. Phone: (516) 568-8844. Phone: (800) 488-7866. Fax: (516) 568-8853. E-mail: metrowx@aol.com Web Site:www.metrowx.com Pat Pagano, pres.

TV-CATV only.

Provides accurate & understandable weather forecasts. Serves any part of the nation; live consultations.

Robert Michelson Inc., 508 3rd Ave., San Francisco, CA, 94118. Phone: (415) 386-6862. Fax: (415) 386-2714. E-mail: rm@rmitv.com Web Site:www.rmitv.com Robert Michelson, pres; David Alexander, dir production.

TV-CATV-Radio.

TV coml production; custom & syndicated TV spots for radio stns. Leading producer of TV spots for rock radio.

Midwest Video Communications Inc., Box 11627, Omaha, NE, 68111. Phone: (402) 991-2981. Fax: (402) 933-8990. E-mail: midwestvideo@msn.com John S. Turner, pres; Artes Johnson, dir.

TV-CATV only.

TV program & distribution; coml production, satellite teleconference productions; business & promotion film productions; production svcs, TV news features production.

Miller Broadcast Management, 616 W. Fulton St., Suite 516, Chicago, IL, 60661. Phone: (312) 454-1111. Fax: (312) 454-0044. E-mail: info@millerbroadcast.com Web Site:www.millerbroadcast.com Matt Miller, VP; Lisa Miller, pres.

Radio Only.

Produces & syndicates natl progmg including *KidsRadio*.

Robin Miller, Filmaker Inc., 606 W. Broad St., Bethlehem, PA, 18018. Phone: (610) 691-0900. Fax: (610) 691-0952. E-mail: mail@filmaker.com Web Site:www.filmaker.com Robin Miller, CEO.

TV-CATV only.

TV program, promotion film production; production svcs.

Warren Miller Entertainment, 2540 Frontier Ave., Suite 104, Boulder, CO, 80301. Phone: (303) 442-3430. Fax: (303) 442-3402. Web Site:www.warrenmiller.com Josh Haskins, producer; Tim Malone, dir.

TV-CATV only.

Second unit feature, coml, TV program, promotion; film production & distribution specializing in snow & outdoor adventure sports.

Miss Universe, L.P., 4111 W. Alameda, Suite 605, Burbank, CA, 91505. Phone: (818) 972-9202. Fax: (818) 972-9001. Web Site:www.missuniverse.com Paula M. Shugart, pres; Tony Santomauro, VP business dev.

TV-CATV only.

TV program production.

Mobile Video Services Ltd., 1620 I St. N.W., Washington, DC, 20006. Phone: (202) 331-8882. Fax: (202) 331-9064. E-mail: bookfeed@mobilevideo.net Web Site:www.mobilevideo.net Lawrence J. VanderVeen, pres; Christine Baber, opns mgr; Lindsey Flaherty, producer.

TV-CATV only.

Bcst production svcs, best "Official Washington", live shot, remote crews, studio svcs, editing, graphics suites, satellite & fiber transmission svcs.

Modern Entertainment, Box 8075, Van Nuys, CA, 91409-8075. Phone: (818) 386-0444. Fax: (818) 728-3677. Michael Weiser, pres/CEO; Ken Du Bow, sr VP worldwide sls; Allyson Hall, VP international sls.

TV-CATV only.

Distribution of movies world wide, CD, DVD.

Modern Sound Pictures Inc., 1402 Howard St., Omaha, NE, 68102. Phone: (402) 341-8476. Fax: (402) 341-8487. E-mail: info@modernsoundpictures.net Web Site:www.modernsoundpictures.com Sandra L. Smith, pres.

Non-theatrical 16mm film, video rental library & retail audiovisual equipment for rental & sls.

Molton Advertising Inc., Box 747, Hendersonville, NC, 28793-0747. Phone: (828) 692-7200. Phone: (800) 223-1930. Fax: (828) 692-9147. E-mail: molton@bellsouth.net Web Site:www.moltonad.com Marcie Molton, pres; Randy Molton, production mgr.

Radio Only.

Syndicated radio & nwspr series for loc use.

Mondo TV, Via G. Gatti 8/A, 00162 Rome Italy. Phone: 39-6-86320364. Phone: 39-06-86323293. Fax: 39-06-86209836. E-mail: mondotv@mondotv.it Orlando Corradi, pres/CEO; Gian Claudio Galatoli, dir; Roberto Farina, head international sls.

TV-CATV only.

Animated TV series.

Montgomery Community Television Inc., 7548 Standish Pl., Rockville, MD, 20855. Phone: (301) 424-1730. Fax: (301) 294-7476. Web Site:www.mct-tv.org Don Katzen, opns dir; Richard Turner, exec dir.

TV-CATV only.

Full-svc video production & postproduction, 2,400 sq ft. studio including complete control room, GVG200 switcher, DVE, on- & off-line editing. Also, opn of two cable chs reaching 220,000 subs.

N

Moody Broadcasting Network, 820 N. LaSalle Blvd., Chicago, IL, 60610-3284. Phone: (312) 329-4433. Phone: (800) 621-7031. Fax: (312) 329-4339.E-mail: mbn@moody.edu Web Site:www.moodyradio.org Scott Krus, dev mgr; Denny Nugent, progmg dir.

Radio Only.

Radio program production, full-svc relg digital stereo audio progmg via, satellite internet file download & syndicated tape distribution & ACCUWatch radio transmitter monitoring.

Moonstone Entertainment, Box 7400, Studio City, CA, 91614-7400. Phone: (818) 985-3003. Fax: (818) 985-3009. Web Site:www.moonstonefilms.com Ernst "Etchie" Stroh, CEO; Yael Stroh, pres; Luz Moretti, exec VP; Greg Majerus, VP finance; Michael Grant, dir intl sls, production, mktg; Shahar Stroh, dir dev, acquisitions.

TV-CATV only.

International distribution and production.

The Charles Morrow Associates Company LLC, 307 7th Ave., Suite 1402, New York, NY, 10001. Phone: (212) 989-2400. Fax: (212) 989-2697.E-mail: cmorrow@cmorrow.com Web Site:www.cmorrow.com Charlie Morrow, pres.

Radio Only.

Sound design, audio production, music production, audio/visual service, music composition, multimedia producers, surround sound studio, public service announcements.

MotorNet, Box 69, Farmingdale, NJ, 07727-0069. Phone: (732) 751-1020. Fax: (732) 751-1038.E-mail: motornet@iop.com Web Site:www.motorsportsreport.com Charlie Roberts, pres; Ken Stout, producer; Jack Schultz, dir mktg.

Radio Only.

Radio program production & distribution.

Mountain News Corporation, 50 Vashell Way, Suite 200, Orinda, CA, 94563-3020. Phone: (925) 254-4456. Fax: (925) 254-7923.E-mail: admin@aminews.com Web Site:www.theamigroup.com Rob Brown, pres; Chad Dyer, VP. Eastern Bureau Phone:

Radio Only.

Produce & package outdoor recreation reports of 30, 60 & 90-seconds in length. Also deliver ski reports via phone, computer, facsimilie for on-air, phone lines & web sites.

Mun 2, 2470 W. 8th Ave., Hialeah, FL, 33010. Phone: (305) 884-8200. Fax: (305) 889-7212. Web Site:www.mun2television.com Don Browne, pres/COO; Joe Bernard, sls dir; Alvaro Krupkin, dir creative svcs+; Maria Acosta, dir opns; Susan Solano, mktg dir.

TV-CATV only.

English language cable network targeting young U.S. Hispanics.

Munhwa Broadcasting Corp. (MBC), Natl Press Bldg., 529 14th St. N.W., Suite 1131, Washington, DC, 20045. Phone: (202) 347-0078. Fax: (202) 347-0079.E-mail: kimsc@imbc.com Web Site:www.imbc.com Sang Kim, bureau chief.

TV-CATV only.

Korean natl TV net news.

Musical Starstreams, Box 12685, La Jolla, CA, 92039-2685. Phone: (619) 276-8989.E-mail: forest@starstreams.com Web Site:www.starstreams.com

Radio Only.

Two-hour wkly or nightly syndicated exotic electronica music progmg also available as a full-time format; radio adv production.

Musivision Inc., 185 E. 85th St., New York, NY, 10028. Phone: (212) 860-4420.

TV-CATV only.

Muzak, 3318 Lakemont Blvd., Fort Mill, SC, 29708. Phone: (803) 396-3000. Phone: (800) 331-3340. Fax: (803) 396-3136. Web Site:www.muzak.com E-mail: feedback@muzak.com Steve Villa, CEO.

Bcsts chs of business music, adv parting audio messages, ZNET data bcstg & video via direct bcst satellite.

Myriad Pictures, 3015 Main St., Suite 400, Santa Monica, CA, 90405. Phone: (310) 279-4000. Fax: (310) 279-4001.E-mail: info@myriadpictures.com Web Site:www.myriadpictures.com Kirk D'Amico, pres/CEO; Kevin Forester, CFO; Amanda Blue, VP production, dev.

TV-CATV only.

An ind TV co-production & distribution company specializing in music series, features, documentaries & drama for the international market.

NAHB Production Group, (National Association of Home Builders). 1201 15th St. N.W., 5th Fl., Washington, DC, 20005. Phone: (202) 822-0200 ext 8543. Fax: (202) 266-8054.E-mail: cgoldweber@nahb.org Cary Goldweber, exec producer.

TV-CATV-Radio.

Complete video production/editing facility with large stock library. Productions include Scripps/DIY series, website, political spots, PSA, & instructional/mktg programs

NASA Broadcast & Imaging Branch, NASA Headquarters (PMD), 300 E. St. S.W., Rm. CL78, Washington, DC, 20546. Phone: (202) 358-0000. Fax: (202) 358-4333. Mike Crnkovic, chief printing & design.

TV-CATV-Radio.

Aeronautics & Space Report, an hour magazine quarterly (Betacam SP) to media & producers only.

NBD Television Ltd., 2, Royalty Studios, 105 Lancaster Rd., London, W11 1QF. United Kingdom. Phone: 44 (0) 20 7243 3646. Fax: 44 (0) 7243 3656.E-mail: distribution@nbdtv.com Web Site:www.nbdtv.com Nicky Davies Williams, CEO; Andrew Winter, gen sls mgr.

International TV progmg sls distribution.

NCAA, Box 6222, Indianapolis, IN, 46206-6222. Phone: (317) 917-6222. Fax: (317) 917-6807. Fax: (317) 917-6856.E-mail: jrinebold@ncaa.org Web Site:www.ncaasports.com Myles Brand, pres; Wally Renfro, VP.

New YorkNY , 19 West 57th St. Phone:

TV-CATV-Radio.

NCAA championship progmg, distribution & footage requests.

NDR Media, Rothenbaumchaussee 159+161, Hamburg, 20149. Germany. Phone: (040) 44 1920.E-mail: info@ndrtv.de Web Site:www.ndrtv.de Horst Bennit, mgng dir; Hans-Stefan Heyne, head international acquisition; Ulla Lamas-Torres, sls.

TV-CATV only.

Distribution of TV plays, dramas, wildlife, educ, children's & documentary programs.

NEP Studios, 1 Dag Hammarskjold Plaza, Concourse Level, New York, NY, 10017-2201. Phone: (212) 548-7700. Fax: (212) 355-0523.E-mail: wsheehy@nepstudios.com Web Site:www.nepinc.com William Sheehy, VP.

TV-CATV-Radio.

Shooting stage, Filmor tape, duplication all standards editing & DVD-R duplication.

NFL Films, 1 NFL Plaza, Mt. Laurel, NJ, 08054. Phone: (856) 222-3500. Fax: (856) 722-6779. Web Site:www.nflfilms.com Steve Sabol, pres; William Driber, VP production; Rick Angeli, dir outside sls; Barry Wolper, COO, CFO; Jeff Howard, VP video opns.

TV-CATV only.

Teleproduction facility: digital editing suites, 16mm & 35mm film processing, film-to-tape transfer, studio & remote production, sound studios, animation & flame.

NHK Japan Broadcasting Corp., 2030 M St. N.W., Suite 706, Washington, DC, 20036. Phone: (202) 828-5180. Fax: (202) 828-4571. Web Site:www.nhk.or.jp/englishtop/ Kenji Kohno, bureau chief.

TV-CATV-Radio.

TV & radio program distribution.

NRS Group PTY Ltd., 9-13 Lawry Pl., Macquarie, Canberra, Act 2614. Australia. Phone: (61) 2-6251-6333. Fax: 61 2-6251-6240.E-mail: grahampatrick@nrsgroup.com.au Graham Patrick, mgng dir.

TV-CATV only.

Produces range of quality TV series & documentaries, full TV & audio production facility with qualified personnel, international program distributor.

NTN Communications Inc., 5966 La Place Ct., Suite 100, Carlsbad, CA, 92008-8830. Phone: (888) PLAYNTN. Fax: (760) 438-3505. Web Site:www.ntn.com Stanley B. Kinsey, chmn/CEO; Mark deGorter, pres/COO; James B. Frakes, CFO; Tyrone Lam, pres Buzztime Entertainment Inc.

TV-CATV only.

NTN Communications, Inc.®, a leading producer & distributor of live interactive TV entertainment, bcsts exciting multi-player games to hospitality venues.

NTV International Corp., 645 Fifth Ave., Suite 303, New York, NY, 10020. Phone: (212) 660-6900. Fax: (212) 660-6998. Web Site:www.ntvic.com Jusaburo Hayashi, pres.

TV-CATV only.

Complete video production & postproduction facility; satellite transmission capabilities worldwide; ENG package international TV coord, program sls & acquisitions.

NVC Arts, The Forum, 74-80 Camden St., London, NW1 0EG. United Kingdom. Phone: 44 (0) 7388 3833. Fax: 44 (0)20 7388 7174.E-mail: mia_fjox-non@nvcarts.com Web Site:www.nvcarts-tv.com John Kelleher, mng dir; Elfyn Morris, stn mgr.

TV-CATV only.

Producers & distributors of opera, ballet & performing arts programs for world TV.

N W Media, 106 SE 11th Ave., Portland, OR, 97214. Phone: (503) 223-5010. Fax: (503) 223-4737. Web Site:www.nwmedia.com E-mail: info@nwmedia.com Jeanne Alldredge, pres; Mike Yake, sls dir.

TV-CATV-Radio.

Audio/videotape duplication; CD/DVD Duplication, multimedia authoring, graphic design, mastering svcs, messaging & digital printing.

National Church Broadcasting, Box 8263, Haledon, NJ, 07508. Phone: (973) 956-2900. Fax: (973) 956-0600. Samuel Cummings, pres; June Young, VP.

TV-CATV only.

Distributor of church & children's religious progmg to radio stns.

National Collegiate Athletic Association (NCAA), Box 6222, Indianapolis, IN, 46206-6222. Phone: (317) 917-6222. Fax: (317) 917-6807. Web Site:www.NCAA.com Miles Brand, pres; Greg Weitekamp, dir bcstg; Chris Fitzpatrick, assoc dir bcstg.

TV-CATV-Radio.

Televise & produce selected NCAA championships. Manage TV progmg & production, including bcst rigjhts, for all 88 NCAA champshps.

National Council of Churches Communications Unit, 475 Riverside Dr., Rm. 850, New York, NY, 10115. Phone: (212) 870-2200. Fax: (212) 870-2030.E-mail: news@ncccusa.org Web Site:www.ncccusa.org Wesley Pattillo, sr program dir.

TV-CATV only.

Bcst production, distribution & assistance to reporters, networks, stns; prepared radio reports & actualities.

National Film Board of Canada, 311 Baltic St., Suite 3D, Brooklyn, NY, 11201. Phone: (212) 629-8890. Fax: (212) 629-8502.E-mail: newyork@nfb.ca Web Site:www.nfb.ca Dylan McGinty, US mktg mgr.

TV-CATV only.

TV program distribution.

National Mobile Television, 2740 California St., Torrance, CA, 90503. Phone: (310) 782-9945. Phone: (800) 242-0642. Fax: (310) 782-9949. Web Site:www.nmtv.com Kevin Sublette, gen mgr; Stephanie Hampton, opns dir.

SeattleWA , 12698 Gateway Dr. Phone:

TV-CATV only.

Mobile TV facilities for remote production of multi-camera events.

National Public Radio, 635 Massachusetts Ave. N.W., Washington, DC, 20001-3753. Phone: (513) 414-2000. Fax: (513) 414-3329. Web Site:www.npr.org Bill Davis, Kevin Klose, pres/CEO; Peter J. Loewenstern, VP distribution; Barbara Hall, dev VP; Kathleen D. Jackson, VP human resources; Mike Starling, engrg VP; Jim Elder, VP/CFO; Celeste James, VP communications; Ken Stern, exec VP; Jeffrey Dvorkin, ombudsman; Jay Kernis, sr VP progmg; Margaret Low-Smith, VP progmg; Maria Thomas, VP online; Dana Davis Rehm, member/progm svcs.

Radio Only.

Radio program production & distribution.

Native American Public Telecommunications Inc., 1800 North 33rd Street, Lincoln, NE, 68501-1409. Phone: (402) 472-3522. Fax: (402) 472-8675.E-mail: ssneve2@unl.edu Web Site:www.nativetelecom.org Shirley Sneve, exec dir; Mary Ann Koehler, business mgr; Georgiana Lee, asst dir.

TV-CATV-Radio.

Producing & developing educ telecommunication programs for all media including TV & pub radio.

Network Music, 8750 Wilshire Blvd., Beverly Hills, CA, 90211. Phone: (310) 865-4481.E-mail: sales@networkmusic.com Web Site:www.networkmusic.com Gary Gross, pres; Chuck Ansel, VP opns; Dennis Dunn, VP sls; Todd Kern, dir mktg; Carl Peel, dir.

TV-CATV-Radio.

Produces music, sound effects & production elements libraries.

New Art Miami, (Formerly Manhattan Transfer Miami). 2850 Tiger Tail Ave., Coconut Grove, FL, 33133. Phone: (800) 826-8864. Phone: (305) 857-0350. Fax: (305) 857-0175. Web Site:www.newartmiami.com Demetro Bilbatu, pres.

MiamiFL , 2028 N.E. 15th Ct. Phone:

TV-CATV-Radio.

Full-svc video post-production including film transfer, on-line, off-line editing, audio, graphics, progmg, voice dubbing translation, sound stage & new media dev.

New City Releasing Inc., 5959 Topanga Canyon Blvd., Suite 255, Woodland Hills, CA, 91367. Phone: (818) 348-2500. Fax: (818) 348-3022. Web Site:www.newcityreleasing.com Alan B. Burnsteen, pres; Cathy Goodman-Robbins, VP.

TV-CATV only.

Producer & distributor of motion pictures to cable TV.

New Dimensions Radio, Box 569, Ukiah, CA, 95482. Phone: (800) 935-8273. Phone: (707) 468-5215. Fax: (707) 468-0530.E-mail: info@newdimensions.org Web Site:www.newdimensions.org Michael A. Toms, co-pres; Justine Toms, co-pres.

Radio Only.

Radio program production & distribution.

New Films International, 8484 Wilshire Blvd., Suite 510, Beverly Hills, CA, 90211. Phone: (323) 655-1050. Fax: (323) 655-1070.E-mail: newfilms@newfilmsint.com Web Site:www.newfilmsint.com Nesin Hason, pres; Sezin Sonar, VP.

TV-CATV only.

U.S.-based distribution company specialized in Romanian, Bulgarian, & Turkisk films.

New Line Television, 888 Seventh Ave., 20th Fl., New York, NY, 10106. Phone: (212) 649-4900. Fax: (212) 956-1936. Web Site:www.newline.com Jim Rosenthal, pres; David Spiegelman, exec VP; Robin Seidner, sr VP.

Los AngelesCA , 116 N. Robetson.

TV-CATV only.

TV program production & distribution.

New Visions Syndication Inc., 44895 Hwy. 82, Aspen, CO, 81611. Phone: (970) 925-2640. Fax: (970) 925-9369. Web Site:www.newvisionssyndication.com E-mail: kayla@nvs.com Kayla Hoffman-Cook, VP; Rodney Jacobs, pres.

TV-CATV only.

International & domestic syndicator of specials & series; sports, lifestyle & entertainment.

New Zoo Revue, 6399 Wilshire Blvd., Suite 816, Los Angeles, CA, 90048. Phone: (323) 782-3525. Fax: (323) 782-3530.E-mail: newzoo@aol.com Web Site:www.newzoorevue.com Barbara Atlas, pres.

TV-CATV only.

TV program production & distribution.

News Broadcast Network, 75 Broad St., 15th Fl., New York, NY, 10004. Phone: (212) 684-8910. Fax: (212) 684-9650. Web Site:www.newsbroadcastnetwork.com Michael Hill, pres; Robert Hill, vice chmn.

TV-CATV-Radio.

Produce & distribute news & feature material to TV & radio stns.

Nightingale-Conant Corp., 6245 W. Howard St., Niles, IL, 60714. Phone: (847) 647-0300. Fax: (847) 647-7145. Web Site:www.nightingale.com Vic Conant, pres; Gary Chapel, VP.

Radio Only.

Radio program production & distribution.

Nine Network Australia, 6255 Sunset Blvd., Suite 1500, Los Angeles, CA, 90028. Phone: (323) 461-3853. Fax: (323) 462-4849. Web Site:www.ninemsn.com.au Noel Masson, VP.

TV-CATV only.

News bureau.

No Soap Productions, 936 Broadway, 4th Fl., New York, NY, 10010. Phone: (212) 581-5572. Fax: (212) 586-0045.E-mail: dan@nosoap.net Web Site:www.nosoap.net Dan Aron, pres.

TV-CATV-Radio.

Radio comls, sound design for radio & TV, voicecasting, production studio-digital.

North American Network, Inc., 5335 Wisconsin Ave., Suite 305, Washington, DC, 20015. Phone: (301) 654-9810. Fax: (301) 654-9828.E-mail: info@nanradio.com Web Site:www.radiospace.com Thomas P. Sweeney, pres; Tammy Lemley, VP.

Radio Only.

Full-svc radio P.R. providing progmg, news PSAs, promotional campaigns & sls opportunities to stns nationwide in English & Spanish.

North by Northwest Productions, 903 W. Broadway, Spokane, WA, 99201. Phone: (509) 324-2949. Fax: (509) 324-2959.E-mail: marcdahlstrom@nxnw.net Web Site:www.nxnw.net Rich Cowan, CEO.

BoiseID , 601 W. Broad St. Phone:

TV-CATV-Radio.

High end video & film production; D1/D2 postproduction; Paint/3D animation; sound design/production; HD editing.

North Shore Productions, Box 1308, Detroit Lakes, MN, 56502. Phone: (218) 846-1936. Fax: (218) 846-1936.E-mail: nspsfrm@tekstar.com Web Site:www.agriculture.com/sfradio

Radio Only.

Produces & distributes "The Career Clinic®" & the "Successful Farming® Radio Magazine", two-minute features with affil sharing natl revenues.

North Star Music, 338 Compass Cir., Unit A1, North Kingstown, RI, 02852. Phone: (401) 886-8888. Fax: (401) 886-8886.E-mail: info@northstarmusic.com Web Site:www.northstarmusic.com Richard R. Waterman, pres.

Radio Only.

Production, distribution, mktg & promotion of recorded music.

Northwest Imaging & FX, 2339 Columbia St., Suite 100, Vancouver, BC, V5Y 3Y3. Canada. Phone: (604) 873-9330. Fax: (604) 873-9339.E-mail: nwfx@nwfx.com Alex Tkach, VP.

TV-CATV only.

Shooting, visual effects, animation, digital editing suites, audio sweetening, Digital Betacam Sp. D-1, 1 inch, duplication Cintel Diamond Film transfer.

O

O. Atlas Enterprises Inc., (New Zoo Review). 327 North Palm Dr., Beverly Hills, CA, 90210. Phone: (323) 782-3525. Fax: (323) 782-3530.E-mail: newzoo@aol.com Web Site:www.newzoorevue.com

TV-CATV only.

International licensing, distribution of progmg for TV, all media.

OGM Production Music, 6464 Sunset Blvd., Suite 790, Hollywood, CA, 90028. Phone: (323) 461-2701. Phone: (800) 421-4163 (Sales). Fax: (323) 461-1543.E-mail: ogmmusic@ogmmusic.com Web Site:www.ogmmusic.com Ole Georg, pres; David Carr, dir opns.

TV-CATV only.

Video, cable, films, CD-ROM, bcst, multimedia, infomercials, satellite program, interactive TV, electronic publishing & theatrical features.

O'Grady & Associates, 8431 Sabal Palm Ct., Vero Beach, FL, 32963-4296. Phone: (772) 234-4177. Fax: (772) 231-9819.E-mail: jfogjr@juno.com James F. O'Grady Jr., pres.

TV-CATV-Radio.

Brokerage/consulting.

Oasis International, 175 Bloor St. E., North Tower, Suite 1400, Toronto, ON, M4W 3R8. Canada. Phone: (416) 646-2400. Fax: (416) 588-7276.E-mail: info@oasisinternational.com Web Site:www.oasisinternational.com Peter Emerson, pres; Lisa Wookey, dir mktg; Ben Bishop, sls & acquistion exec; Prentiss Holman, dir international sls.

TV-CATV only.

Worldwide TV & format distribution.

Oasis TV Inc., 9887 Santa Monica Blvd., Suite 200, Beverly Hills, CA, 90212. Phone: (310) 553-4300. Fax: (310) 553-1159. Web Site:www.oasistv.com Robert Schnitzer, pres.

TV-CATV only.

Cable & satellite net providing a broad, well-branded var of new age/human potential progmg, 24-hours.

Omnimusic, 52 Main St., Port Washington, NY, 11050. Phone: (800) 828-6664. Phone: (516) 883-0121. Fax: (516) 883-0271.E-mail: bring@omnimusic.com Web Site:www.omnimusic.com Doug Wood, pres; Patti Wood, VP; Barbara Ring, mktg dir.

TV-CATV-Radio.

Dynamic production music with four great libraries that deliver the sounds you need for maximum impact. Easy search & download on the web 24/7. We are always just a phone call or email away, ready to meet your needs.

On Track, 6350 W. Freeway, Fort Worth, TX, 76116. Phone: (817) 570-1400. Phone: (800) 266-1837. Fax: (817) 737-9436.E-mail: info@familynet.com Web Site:www.familynetradio.com Lisa Bratton, radio mktg & distribution; Donna Senn, radio distribution; Chuck Ries, producer.

Radio Only.

Contemporary Christian music with artist interviews, 30 minutes wkly, on CD.

One Hundred Biblemen & Women of the U.S.A., Box 8263, Haledon, NJ, 07508. Phone: (973) 956-2900. Fax: (973) 956-0600. Sam Cummings, pres.

TV-CATV only.

Low-cost bcstg & buying net for churches.

Oppix Productions Inc, 3531 Laurel Leaf Ln., Fairfax, VA, 22031. Phone: (703) 280-8200. Fax: (703) 280-9292.E-mail: info@oppix.com Web Site:www.oppix.com James Oppenheimer, pres.

TV-CATV-Radio.

Full-service video internet, DVD production & post, serving bcst, corporate assns, nonprofit & govt. All formats.

Orange Productions Inc., 523 Righters Ferry Rd., 1st floor, Bala Cynwyd, PA, 19004. Phone: (610) 667-8620. Fax: (610) 667-8939.E-mail: orange@snip.net Web Site:www.soundsofsinatra.com Sid Mark, pres; Brian Mark, opns mgr.

Radio Only.

Production & distribution of a wkly two-hour program *Sounds of Sinatra*.

Dick Orkin's Amazing Radio, 15003 Lemay St., Van Nuys, CA, 91405. Phone: (800) 621-6949. Fax: (818) 376-8529.E-mail: sandyo@earthlink.net Web Site:www.sandyorkin-crs.com Sandy Orkin, pres.

Radio Only.

Syndicated packages of Dick Orkin comls customized for loc advertisers. Available in six categories.

Outdoor Media Group, Box 2151, Lake Oswego, OR, 97035. Phone: (503) 675-7345. Fax: (503) 675-7820.E-mail: omg@aojtv.com Web Site:www.aojtv.com Russell Cameron, pres.

TV-CATV only.

TV program, coml production & distribution; production svcs.

Jim Owens Entertainment, 624 Grassmere Park, Suite 16, Nashville, TN, 37211. Phone: (615) 256-7700. Fax: (615) 242-9735. Web Site:www.crookandchase.com Jim Owens, pres; Jennifer Anderson, producer.

TV-CATV only.

Radio program production company for syndication. TV production for cable & home video.

P

PACSAT, 1629 S St., Sacramento, CA, 95811. Phone: (916) 446-7890. Fax: (916) 446-7893.E-mail: pacsat@pacsat.com Web Site:www.pacsat.com Steve Mallory, pres; Marcia Calvin, opns mgr.

TV-CATV only.

Video, audio & satellite professionals. Ku-HD satellite trucks. ENG crews. Fly pack with CCU'S. Post production & graphics.

PAULAR Entertainment L.L.C., 13700 Marina Pointe Dr., Suite 901, Marina del Rey, CA, 90292. Phone: (310) 821-0430. Fax: (310) 821-3793.E-mail: thirdwayv@aol.com Larry Friedricks, ptnr; Paula Fierman, ptnr.

TV-CATV only.

World-wide distribution of feature films, video & TV including movies, series & mini-series.

PBS Video, 2100 Crystal Dr., Arlington, VA, 22202. Phone: (703) 739-5000. Fax: (703) 739-8487. Web Site:www.pbs.org Paula Kerger, pres/CEO; Wayne Godwin, COO; John Boland, chief content officer; Barbara Landes, CFO; Katherine Lauderdale, gen counsel, sr VP; John McCoskey, chief technology officer.

TV-CATV only.

A trusted provider of classroom resources for more that 25 years, PBS Video extends the reach of public TV by distributing meda throughout the United States & Canada, making valuable resources available to educators, librarians & trainers through Shop PBS for Teacher.

PMTV Producers Management Television, 681 Moore Rd., Suite 100, King of Prussia, PA, 19406. Phone: (610) 768-1770. Fax: (610) 768-1773.E-mail: mailto.pmtv@pmtv.com Web Site:www.pmtv.com

TV-CATV only.

Full-svc mobile TV production company, providing mobile units, crews, satellite svcs, lighting, staging, etc. for sports, entertainment & teleconferences worldwide.

PPM Multimedia, Brezo 4 - URB Los Robles, Torrelodones, Madrid, 28250. Spain. Phone: (34) 91 859 1913. Fax: (34) 91 859 0932.E-mail: multimedia@ppmm.es Web Site:www.ppmm.es Paco Rodriguez, mng dir.

TV-CATV only.

Distribution of animation, feature films, documentaries, co-production setting.

PSSI Global Services-Strategic Television, (Formerly (PSSI) Production & Satellite Services Inc.). 15315 Magnolia Blvd., Suite 423, Sherman Oaks, CA, 91403. Phone: (310) 575-4400. Fax: (310) 575-4451.E-mail: pssi@pssiglobal.com Web Site:www.pssiglobal.com Robert C. Lamb, pres; Brian Nelles, sr VP; Matt Bridges, prse-strategic TV; Clayton Packard, mktg.

TV-CATV only.

Full service production & satellite transmission company with 25 fully redundant C- & Ku-band satellite trucks located nationwide. Available for news, sports, corporate, entertainment events, media tours, video conferencing, webcasting & downlinks. Also include Standard, HD digital transmission, encryption, multiple camera productions, event coordination & a C/Ku Flyaway system for intl & domestic transmission. Skip Broadband also available for internet, voice connectivity, & webcasting via satellite, ideal in remote areas with little or no connectivity.

Palace Digital Studios, 29 N. Main St., South Norwalk, CT, 06854. Phone: (203) 853-1740. Fax: (203) 855-9608.E-mail: wendy@palacedigital.com Web Site:www.palaceproductioncenter.com Wendy Lambert, pres/COO.

New YorkNY . Cinemuse-Tribeca Film Center, 375 Greenwich St. Phone:

TV-CATV-Radio.

Soundstage w/Cyc, HD production svcs, HD editiorial, bcst design & animation, audio record & mixing, DVD authoring & duplication .

Shelly Palmer Productions, Box 1877, New York, NY, 10156-1877. Phone: (212) 532-3880.E-mail: info@shellypalmer.com Web Site:www.shellypalmer.com Shelly Palmer, pres.

TV-CATV only.

Music, video, TV, film production & creative svcs. Adv & mktg. Music libraries, sound design, sls videos & post-production.

Pan American Video, 3144 Broadway, Suite 4, Eureka, CA, 95501. Phone: (707) 822-3800. Fax: (707) 822-0800.E-mail: panam@panamvideo.com Web Site:www.panamvideo.com Teri Lane, pres; Sheila McQuillen, VP.

TV-CATV only.

Public domain movies & TV shows, bcst quality & stock footage.

Pantomime Pictures Inc., 12144 Riverside Dr., North Hollywood, CA, 91607. Phone: (818) 980-5555. Fax: (818) 984-3470. Fred Crippen, dir; Matt Crippen, producer.

TV-CATV only.

Animation production & design for TV comls, educ & industrial use. Animation camera for 35 mm & 16 mm.

Parrot Communications International Inc., 2917 N. Ontario St., Burbank, CA, 91504. Phone: (818) 567-4700. Fax: (818) 567-4600.E-mail: info@parrotmedia.com Web Site:www.parrotmedia.com Blanca Pineda-Villanueva, VP opns; Rae Ann Mertz, exec VP; Karol L. Wagner Loy, VP mktg.

TV-CATV only.

Database mgmt, direct mail svcs, promotional fulfillment, warehousing, contest fulfillment, bcst faxing, high speed duplication & videotape duplication.

Pathe International, 21 rue Francois 1 er, 75008 Paris France. Fax: 33-1-40-76-9194. Fax: 33-1-40-76-9169.E-mail: christine.hayet@pathe.com Web Site:www.pathe.fr Jerome Seydoux; Eduardo Malone, co-chmn/CEO; Emma Rami, VP finance; Michel Crepon, COO.

TV-CATV only.

Production & distribution of TV films & documentaries. Production of multimedia programs.

Paulist Media Works, 3055 4th St. N.E., Washington, DC, 20017. Phone: (202) 269-6064. Fax: (202) 269-4304.E-mail: info@paulist.org Web Site:www.paulist.org/pmw Sue Donovan, pres.

TV-CATV only.

Support for non-profit organization in internet svcs/website/web design distribution of relg radio programs, video/documentary production

Paulist Productions, Box 1057, Pacific Palisades, CA, 90272. Phone: (310) 454-0688. Fax: (310) 459-6549.E-mail: paulistmail@paulistproductions.org Web Site:www.paulistproductions.org Frank Desiderio, CSP, pres; Enid Sevilla, gen mgr , finacial off; Barbara Gangi, producer; Joseph Kim, VP business affrs.

TV-CATV only.

TV program production.

Peckham Productions, 50 S. Buckhout St., Irvington, NY, 10533. Phone: (914) 591-4140. Fax: (914) 591-4149.E-mail: info@peckhampix.com Web Site:www.peckhampix.com Peter H. Peckham, pres; Waldine Peckham, production mgr; Russell Peckham, dir, producer.

TV-CATV only.

Full-service film & video producer of TV comls, TV programs & TV net promos.

Perception Media Group, 1848 Clay St., Roanoke, VA, 24013. Phone: (540) 563-5225. Fax: (540) 563-0117. Web Site:www.foxradioroanoke.com Ben Peyton, pres.

TV-CATV-Radio.

TV & radio coml program production, distribution & jingles, relg programs & distribution.

Peters Communications, 1555 Berenda Pl., El Cajon, CA, 92020. Phone: (619) 444-6984. Fax: (619) 440-1481.E-mail: edpeters@cox.net Edward J. Peters, pres.

TV-CATV only.

Media mktg consultants, providing rsch, concept, mktg plan, music, graphics & animation.

Philadelphia Flyers Hockey Club, 3601 S. Broad St., Philadelphia, PA, 19148. Phone: (215) 465-4500. Fax: (215) 952-4103.E-mail: rryan@comcast-spectacor.com Web Site:www.philadelphiaflyers.com Ed Snider, chmn; Bob Clarke, pres; Shawn Tilger, VP mktg.

TV-CATV only.

TV & radio program production.

Phoebus Communications Inc., 10905 Ft. Washington Rd., Suite 300, Fort Washington, MD, 20744. Phone: (301) 292-9800. Fax: (301) 292-0829.E-mail: phoebuscom@aol.com Web Site:www.phoebusinc.net Gail C. Arnall, Ph.D., pres.

TV-CATV only.

Full scale distance learning net mgmt.

Phoenix Communications Group, 3 Empire Blvd., South Hackensack, NJ, 07606. Phone: (201) 807-0888. Fax: (201) 807-0272. Web Site:www.phoenixcomm.com Joe Podesta, chmn; Jim Holland, pres; Rich Domich, sls VP, mktg; Geoff Belinfante, exec producer, sr VP; Trish Ferreri, mgr.

TV-CATV only.

Major League Sports Newsatellite; TV & video production & distribution; stock footage licensing.

Pied Piper Films Ltd., 825941 Mel-Nott TL, R. R. 2, Shelburne, ON, L0N 1S6. Canada. Phone: (519) 925-6558. Fax: (519) 925-6558. Lee Israelski, producer.

TV-CATV only.

Motion picture production.

Pike Productions Inc., Box 300, 11 Clarke St., Newport, RI, 02840. Phone: (401) 846-8890. Fax: (401) 847-0070.E-mail: info@pikefilmtrailers.com James A. Pike, pres; Cornelia M. Pike, sls mgr.

Custom ads & special announcement trailers produced & distributed in all formats—35mm, 185x1, Scope, stereo, 70mm stereo.

Planet Pictures Ltd., 4222 Kingfisher Rd., Suite 208, Calabasas, CA, 91302. Phone: (818) 344-9100. Fax: (818) 344-4493.E-mail: info@planetpictures.com Web Site:www.planetpictures.com Jim Hayden, pres; Jennifer Hayden, mng dir; Peter Torvik, business affrs.

TV-CATV only.

Production & distribution for documentary, informational & reality-based TV programs.

Playboy Entertainment Group Inc., 2706 Media Center Dr., Los Angeles, CA, 90065. Phone: (323) 276-4000. Fax: (323) 276-4500. Web Site:www.playboyenterprises.com Scott Sanders, pres; Tom Flores, sr VP; Alicia Layvas, dir mktg.

Los AngelesCA . Andrita Studios, 3030 Andrita St. Sol Weisel, VP production.

TV-CATV only.

TV program production, distribution & video.

Playhouse Pictures, Box 2089, Los Angeles, CA, 90078-2089. Phone: (323) 851-2112. Fax: (323) 851-2117.E-mail: playpix@aol.com Ted Woolery, producer; Gerry Woolery, dir; Todd Shalter, dir.

TV-CATV only.

Animated TV coml production & short films.

Point 360, 1133 North Hollywood Way, Burbank, CA, 91505. Phone: (818) 556-5700. Fax: (818) 556-5753. Web Site:www.point360.com Brian Erlich, pres; Paul Ponzio, VP sls/producer; John Knowles, VP sls.

HollywoodCA , 1220 N. Highland Ave. Phone:
HollywoodCA , 712 N. Seward St. Phone:
HollywoodCA , 1025 N. McCadden Pl. Phone:
Los AngelesCA , 12421 W. Olympic Blvd. Phone:

TV-CATV only.

Postproduction & duplication, film-to-tape transfers, audio svcs. Digital editing, distribution & syndication.

PorchLight Entertainment Inc., 11050 Santa Monica Blvd., 3rd Fl., Los Angeles, CA, 90025. Phone: (310) 477-8400. Fax: (310) 477-5555. Web Site:www.porchlight.com Bruce D. Johnson, pres/CEO; Courtney Colman, CFO.

TV-CATV only.

Produces & distributes family entertainment progmg including animation, TV movies & interactive multimedia progmg, licensing & mdsg.

Ports of Paradise, Box 33648, San Diego, CA, 92163. Phone: (619) 275-7357. Phone: (800) 223-2564. Fax: (619) 296-5909.E-mail: aloharn@portparadise.com Web Site:www.portparadise.com J. Hal Hodgson, exec producer.

Radio Only.

Hour-long radio program with Hawaiian music & info. Available on a barter basis.

PostWorks, New York, 100 Ave. of the Americas, New York, NY, 10013. Phone: (212) 557-4949. Fax: (212) 983-4083. Web Site:www.pwny.com

TV-CATV only.

Film-to-tape or data in standard or Hi-Definition; editing; digital, Hi-Definition, non-linear; duplication, conversion, satellite & fibre transmissions.

Potomac TV/Communications, 15110 H St. N.W., Suite 202, Washington, DC, 20005. Phone: (202) 783-8000. Fax: (202) 783-1132.E-mail: www.sgreenaway@potomactv.com Web Site:www.potomactv.com Nick Chiaia, pres.

TV-CATV only.

New content & video svcs production facility. C- & Ku-band satellite transmitters/receive svcs.

Power Play Music Video L.L.C., 223-225 Washington St., Newark, NJ, 07102. Phone: (973) 642-5132. Fax: (973) 642-5747. Web Site:www.powerplay-mvtv.com E-mail: powerplaytv@cs.com Greg Ferguson, pres.

TV-CATV only.

TV & radio program; coml production & distribution; production svcs.

Powerline, 6350 W. Fwy., Fort Worth, TX, 76116. Phone: (817) 570-1491. Phone: (800) 292-2287. Fax: (817) 737-9436.E-mail: cries@familynetradio.com Web Site:www. powerlineradio.com Chuck Ries, producer; Kirk Teegarden, producer.

Radio Only.

Adult contemp music blended with brief commentaries about life by host Brother Jon Rivers, 30 min wkly on CD or download.

Powersports/Paradox, (Formerly Powersports/Millenium International). 14242 Ventura Blvd., Suite 300, Sherman Oaks, CA, 91423-2757. Phone: (818) 708-9995. Fax: (818) 708-0598.E-mail: intl@ps-mill.com Web Site:www.ps-mill.com William McAbian, pres; Tal Dean McAbian, exec VP; Joel Bailey, VP acquistions, productions; Andrea Miller, sr VP sls, licensing.

TV-CATV only.

Production & distribution of special interest & documentaries for TV, cable & home video.

Prairie Dog Entertainment, 12827 Corte Dorotea, Poway, CA, 92064. Phone: (800) 448-7664. Web Site:www.buckhowdy.com Steve Vaus, exec producer.

Radio Only.

Exclusively offering Buck Howdy's Cow Pie Radio, the fastest growing wkly kids radio program.

Praxis Media Inc., 9 Twilight Pl., South Norwalk, CT, 06854. Phone: (203) 866-6666. Fax: (203) 853-8299.E-mail: praxiscc@aol.com Christopher Campbell, pres, dir; Deborah Weingrad, VP & dir.

TV-CATV only.

TV program, coml, promotional film production; production svcs.

Premiere Radio Networks Inc., 15260 Ventura Blvd., 5th Fl., Sherman Oaks, CA, 91403-5339. Phone: (818) 377-5300. Fax: (818) 377-5333.E-mail: webmaster@premrad.com Web Site:www.premrad.com Kraig Kitchin, pres; Dan Yukelson, VP finance; Eileen Thorgusen, VP; Rich Meyer, pres; Nancy Deitemeyer, VP opns.

Radio Only.

Line-up includes Bcst Results Group (BRG) features, Olympia, Premiere Comedy Networks Formats, Long-form features, Mediabase rsch formats, music svcs, online, plain-wrap formats, prep & short-form. All features & svcs offered on a barter basis are available via satellite, disc, tape, script or phone, depending on the program.

Presbyterian News Services, (Formerly Presbyterian Church (U.S.A.)). 100 Witherspoon St., Louisville, KY, 40202-1396. Phone: (502) 569-5493. Fax: (502) 569-8845. Web Site:www.pcusa.org Jerry Van Marter, news dir.

TV-CATV-Radio.

Radio & TV production, video, audio production, distribution, mktg & Internet svcs.

Presson Perspectives, 600 Druid Rd. E., Clearwater, FL, 33756. Phone: (727) 461-1885. Fax: (727) 443-1984.E-mail: gpresson@tampabay.rr.com Web Site:www.medforum.com Gina Presson, pres & exec producer.

TV-CATV only.

News, documentary & internet production ranging from turnkey pieces to any segment.

Prime Cut Productions Inc., 11909 E. Trail, San Fernando, CA, 91342. Phone: (818) 897-7321. Fax: (818) 834-9889.E-mail: janicekaplan@primecutproductions.com Web Site:www.primecutproductions.com Edward Flaherty, VP; Jan Kaplan, pres.

TV-CATV-Radio.

NTSC Betacam European producers for American TV; bilingual location professionals; distribution, co-production, stock footage, TV script consultant/writer & editing.

Primedia Workplace Learning, 4101 International Pkwy., Carrollton, TX, 75007. Phone: (800) 848-1717. Fax: (972) 309-5666. Web Site:www.pwpl.com Josh Karin, pres/CEO; Gina Valencia, dir mktg.

TV-CATV only.

Video-based, interactive tech training programs for industry, utilities, govt relating to maintenance, opns & safety.

Primo Newservice Inc., Box 116, 182 Sound Beach Ave., Old Greenwich, CT, 06870-0116. Phone: (203) 637-0044. Fax: (203) 698-0812.E-mail: primonews@aol.com Web Site:www.teenkidsnews.com Albert T. Primo, pres/CEO.

TV-CATV-Radio.

TV news consulting, strategic news positioning talent & mgmt, coaching. Cable news training; Internet broadband svc.

Pro Video, 2904-A Colorado Ave., Santa Monica, CA, 90404. Phone: (310) 828-2292.E-mail: provideo1@earthlink.net Joel Webb, pres.

TV-CATV only.

Commercials mastered to DVD & 3/4 inches.

Producers Group, Ltd., 713 S. Pacific Coast Hwy., Suite B, Redondo Beach, CA, 90277-4233. Phone: (310) 316-0481. Fax: (310) 316-1482.E-mail: lee.gluckman @producers-group.tv Lee Gluckman Jr., pres.

TV-CATV only.

Dev & production of theatrical, TV films & series.

Production Garden Music Libraries, 510 E. Ramsey Rd., Suite 4, San Antonio, TX, 78216. Phone: (800) 247-5317. Fax: (210) 530-5230.E-mail: sales@productiongarden.com Web Site:www.productiongarden.com

TV-CATV only.

Ten distinct music libraries featuring production music, including production elements, sound effects; both lease & buy-out options available.

Productions La Fete, 387 St. Paul W., Montreal, PQ, H2Y 2A7. Canada. Phone: (514) 848-0417. Fax: (514) 848-0064.E-mail: info@lafete.com Rock Demers, pres; Xiao Juan Zhou, VP distribution; Daniel Proulx, VP finance.

TV-CATV only.

Production of children/family feature films, drama series, documentaries, multimedia, etc.

The Program Exchange, 375 Hudson St., New York, NY, 10014. Phone: (212) 463-3500. Fax: (212) 463-2662.E-mail: info@programexchange.com Web Site:www.programexchange.com Allen Banks, pres; Chris Hallowell, sr VP/mgmg dir.

TV-CATV only.

TV program distribution.

Promark Television, 323 S. Doheny Dr., Suite 308, Los Angeles, CA, 90048. Phone: (310) 276-3020. Fax: (310) 276-3208.E-mail: hdlevine@promarktv.com Web Site:www.promarktv.com David Levine, pres/CEO.

TV-CATV-Radio.

TV program production & distribution.

Promusic, 941-A Clint Moore Rd., Boca Raton, FL, 33487. Phone: (561) 995-0331. Phone: (800) 322-7879. Fax: (561) 995-8434.E-mail: mail@promusiclibrary.com Web Site:www.promusiclibrary.com Alain Leroux, pres; Mike Spitz, sls dir.

TV-CATV only.

Production music for film, TV & more. Vast CD catalog to choose from with extensive classical & opera.

Q

Quality Film & Video, 232 Cockeysville Rd., Hunt Valley, MD, 21030. Phone: (410) 785-1920.E-mail: qfv@qualityfilmvideo.com Web Site:www.qualityfilmvideo.com Peter A. Garey, pres; Guy G. Garey, VP.

TV-CATV only.

Video production, postproduction svcs, videotape, CD-ROM & DVD duplication.

Questar, 307 N. Michigan Ave., Suite 500, Chicago, IL, 60601. Phone: (312) 266-9400. Fax: (312) 266-9523. Web Site:www.questar1.com Albert J. Nader, pres; Cathy Black, VP instructional technology; Kevin Silverman, VP acquistions.

TV-CATV only.

Producer, distributor of travel documentaries, children's cultural historical & natural history.

R

RAI Corp., (Italian Radio TV System). 32 Avenue of the Americas, Bldg 1, New York, NY, 10013-2473. Phone: (212) 468-2500. Fax: (212) 765-1956. Web Site:www.raicorp.net Mario Bona, CEO; Guido Corso, pres.

TV-CATV only.

Italian natl radio & TV.

RBC Ministries, Box 2222, Grand Rapids, MI, 49501-2222. Phone: (616) 942-6770. Fax: (616) 957-5741.E-mail: rbc@rbc.org Web Site:www.rbc.net Mart De Haan, pres.

TV-CATV-Radio.

TV & radio production & distribution. Programs: TV Day of Discovery, Radio-Discover the Word, Words To Live By, Our Daily Bread, Sports Spectrum, My Utmost for His Highest & Walk In The Wood.

RBC Ministries/Midwest Media Managers, Box 2606, Grand Rapids, MI, 49501-2606. Phone: (877) 245-0550. Phone: (616) 942-6360. Fax: (616) 957-5741.E-mail: mmm@rbc.net Web Site:www.rbc.net/mmm Mart De Haan II, pres; John Nasby, dir; Rod McNany II, dir.

TV-CATV-Radio.

In-house agency for RBC Ministries; providing TV/Radio placement & promotional support of RBC resources including the devotional, Our Daily Bread.

RDF Media, Kensington Village, Avonmore Rd., London, W14 8TS. United Kingdom. Phone: 44 (0) 20 7 013 4000.E-mail: sales@rdfmedia.com Web Site:www.rdfmedia.com David Frank, chief exec; Joely Fether, production dir.

TV-CATV-Radio.

Production & distribution of TV & radio programs.

RMD & Assoc. Inc., 534 Rosemary Cir., Media, PA, 19063. Phone: (610) 566-3799. Fax: (610) 566-3799.E-mail: rmdassociates@yahoo.com Dick D'Anjolell, pres, exec producer; Hank Shaw, tech support svcs; Celeste Walsh, production mgr.

TV-CATV only.

Program creative svcs, production & distribution, specializing in promotion & business info.

RPM Media Enterprises-The Relic Rack Review, 108 Holmes Oval, New Providence, NJ, 07974-1425. Phone: (908) 464-2222.E-mail: richardjlorenzo@relicrack.com Web Site:www.relic-rack.com Richard J. Lorenzo, pres/CEO; Margaret P. Lorenzo, CFO; Jack Kratoville, VP.

Radio Only.

Four-hour wkly rock & roll oldies syndicated entertainment program called the Relic Rack Review, that includes music, news & nostalgia entertainment. Prep svcs including Relic Rack Fast Facts. Multi format radio program consulting svcs.

RPM-Radio Programming & Management Inc., 1133 W. Long Lake Rd., Suite 200, Bloomfield Hills, MI, 48302. Phone: (248) 647-1068. Phone: (800) 521-2537. Fax: (888) 776-0006.E-mail: rpmorlk@aol.com Web Site:www.tophitsusa.com Thomas M. Kirkorian, pres.

Radio Only.

Wkly CD svc top hits U.S. & CD music libraries. Full CD format svcs & progmg consultation.

Radio America, 1030 15th St. N.W., Suite 1040, Washington, DC, 20005. Phone: (202) 408-0944. Fax: (202) 408-1087.E-mail: radioa@radioamerica.org Web Site:www.radioamerica.org James C. Roberts, pres; Mike Paradiso, COO; Rich McFadden, producer; Greg Corombos, producer.

Radio Only.

News & feature svc providing daily, wkly & special programs (90 seconds to one hr) & multi-part documentaries.

Radio & TV Roundup Productions, 653 Sunhaven Dr., Clayton, NJ, 08312-1955. Phone: (856) 881-2570. Fax: (856) 307-9506.E-mail: delfon@att.net Web Site:www.nanes.com Bill Bertenshaw, CEO; Bobbi Cherrelle, exec producer; B.C. Slachofsky, mgr; Richard Nanes, dir.

Cape MayNJ , Box 108 . Bobbi Cherrelle, exec producer.

TV-CATV-Radio.

Production, placement of TV & radio progmg including comls & PSAs. Distribute free classical CDs & TV progmg.

Radio Canada International/Canadian Broadcasting Corp., Box 6000, Montreal, PQ, H3C 3A8. Canada. Phone: (514) 597-7656. Fax: (514) 597-6607.E-mail: rci@montreal.src.ca Web Site:www.rcinet.ca Jean Larin, exec dir.

Radio Only.

Daily shortwave & internet, seven languages, 24-hour eutelsat F6 Europe, intelsat 707 Africa, asiasat 2. Recorded & live program placement on foreign stns.

Radio City Entertainmeent, 2 Penn Plaza, New York, NY, 10021. Phone: (212) 465-6000. Phone: (212) 485-7000. Web Site:www.thegarden.com Katie Schroeder, dir pub affrs.

Los AngelesCA , 2049 Century Park E, Suite 1200. Phone:

TV-CATV only.

TV program producers; production svcs.

Radio Express Inc., 1415 W. Magnolia Blvd., Burbank, CA, 91506. Phone: (818) 295-5800. Fax: (818) 295-5801.E-mail: radioinfo@radioexpress.com Web Site:www.radioexpress.com Tom Rounds, CEO; Jessica D'Agostin, VP sls; Anita Antonio, gen mgr; Christopher DiMatteo, VP mktg; Christian Jones, VP production.

Radio Only.

Radio Express exports Radioplay, the best music svc for radio, production music & progmg to enhance any music format, worldwide.

Radio Production Services Inc., 201 Lena Dr., Easley, SC, 29640-9647. Phone: (864) 855-7191. Fax: (864) 855-7191, EXT 2.E-mail: kenroy2@aol.com R. Kenneth Rogers, pres; W.L. Ames, CFO; E.C. Rogers, VP; Ron Rackley, engrg dir; Nan Cohen, mgr; Jason Gold, sls.

SalemMA . Radio Production Services Inc., 27 Congress Street. Phone:

Cold Spring HarborNY . Radio Production Services Inc., Box 26. Phone:

NashvilleTN . Radio Production Services Inc., 206 Union St, Ext. Phone:

TV-CATV-Radio.

Radio program production specializing in early rhythm and blues & oldies formats. Radio, TV coml production & distribution. Stn ID packages, jingles, consultation svcs in sls & progmg.

Radio Sound Network, 605 S. Front St., Columbus, OH, 43215. Phone: (614) 460-3850. Fax: (614) 621-5620.E-mail: steve.clawson@radiohio.com Web Site:www.radiohio.com Steve Clawson, engrg dir; Tony Miller, dir.

Radio Only.

Full-svc digital satellite audio & data distribution, including affil rel & net bldg. for new & existing sports, news/talk, music & specialty networks.

Radio Spirits, 2 Ridgedale Ave., Cedar Knolls, NJ, 07927. Phone: (800) 359-0570, ext.236. Phone: (973) 539-7557. Fax: (973) 539-1273.E-mail: wholesale@radiospirits.com Web Site:www.radiospirits.com Hakan Lindskog, pres; David Carroll, VP sls.

Radio Only.

Syndicated radio production specializing in "Golden Age of Radio." Production of *When Radio Was* with Stan Freberg, bartered to 300 affls.

Radio Television Espanola (RTVE), Edificio Prado Del Rey/ Desp. 3/023, Prado Del Rey, Madrid, 28223. Phone: (34 91) 581-54 91. Fax: (34 91) 581-77 41.E-mail: contratos_canales_inter.ep@rtve.es Web Site:www.rtve.es

TV-CATV-Radio.

Production & distribution of its own productions as well as some 250 feature films in co-production with independent Sp & Latin American film producers.

Radioguide People Inc., (Vuolo Video). Box 880, Novi, MI, 48376. Phone: (248) 926-1234.E-mail: artvuolo@aol.com Web Site:www.vuolovideo.com Arthur R. Vuolo Jr., pres.

Radio Only.

Publishers of radio stn guides for the gen public, co-sponsored by loc stns & natl advertisers. Produces videos of radio stns, radio events for educational & entertainment purposes.

Rampion Visual Productions L.L.C., 125 Walnut St., Watertown, MA, 02472. Phone: (617) 972-1777. Fax: (617) 972-9157.E-mail: info@rampion.com Web Site:www.rampion.com Michael R. Garneau, ptnr; Steven Tringali, dir & mgng ptnr.

TV-CATV only.

Full Digital Component Editing (BetaSP & DigiBeta), Computer Graphics (2D & 3D), Green Screen Studio, Digital Compositing & DVD creation.

Ray Sports Network, 176 Radio Rd., Powell's Point, NC, 27966. Phone: (252) 491-2414. Fax: (252) 491-2959. Bill Ray, pres.

TV-CATV-Radio.

TV & radio program & coml production, distribution. Sports syndication.

Raycom Sports, 1900W. Morehead St., Charlotte, NC, 28208. Phone: (704) 378-4400. Fax: (704) 373-3324.E-mail: khaines@raycomsports.com Web Site:www.raycomsports.com Ken Haines, pres/CEO; Colin Smith, VP stn rel; Jim Ford, VP sls; Peter Rolfe, Production; Jimmy Rayburn, VP production; Wyatt Hicks, mktg properties; Laura Hager, controller.

TV-CATV only.

Production trucks & HD uplink, sls distribution, produce, market, distribute sports, entertainment progmg nationally & internationally.

Reel Media International Inc., 7000 Independence Pkwy., Suite 160-7, Plano, TX, 75025. Phone: (214) 521-3301. Fax: (214) 522-3448.E-mail: reelmedia@aol.com Web Site:www.reelmediaintl.com Tom T. Moore, pres.

TV-CATV only.

Worldwide distributor of motion pictures, copyrighted

documentaries, Public Domain Library of 2,000 movies, series & documentaries. Servicing all rights.

Reid/Land Productions Inc., 425 E. 58th St., Suite 46H, New York, NY, 10022. Phone: (212) 754-3348. Fax: (212) 754-7034.E-mail: reidland@rcn.com Allen Reid, pres; Mady Land, exec VP.

TV-CATV only.

Packaging, creation & production of TV programs: variety, entertainment, music, games, sports, how-to & cooking.

Russ Reid Company, 2 N. Lake Ave., Suite 600, Pasadena, CA, 91101. Phone: (626) 449-6100. Fax: (626) 463-0028. Web Site:www.russreid.com Kevin White, VP media; David DeBetta, bcst media dir; Gene Gee, VP radio; Mark McIntyre, sr VP/dir govt rels; David Stuart, new business dir.

WashingtonDC . Government Relations, 2000 L St. N.W., Suiter 350. Phone:

WilsonvilleOR . Radio Division, 25195 S.W. Parkway Ave., Suite 200. Phone:

TV-CATV-Radio.

Full service agency specializing in fund-raising, govt rels, adv & PR for nonprofit organizations via mutiple chs, including: TV, radio, interactive/online, direct mail, nwspr, magazines, out-of-home & other media. Partners with loc & natl clients to help them thrive, supporting theirs efforts to change the world.

Reizner & Reizner Film & Video, 7179 Via Maria, San Jose, CA, 95139. Phone: (408) 226-6339. Fax: (408) 226-6403.E-mail: dickreizner@worldnet.att.net Dick Reizner, owner.

TV-CATV only.

Bcst & industrial production in all formats. Certified Legal Video Specialist. Gyrozoom rental.

Reliance Audio Visual Corp., 1600 Broadway, New York, NY, 10019. Phone: (212) 586-5000. Fax: (212) 586-5002.E-mail: rav@aol.com Gil M. Meyer, pres; Norma E. Matthews, exec VP.

TV-CATV only.

Audio & video permanent installations, design, video & teleconferencing, consultation, rentals, staging multimedia, video projection, dealerships, leasing & display design.

Response Reward Systems L.C., 1850 Bay Rd., 2-C, Vero Beach, FL, 32963. Phone: (772) 234-5449. Fax: (772) 234-5949.E-mail: marcyuk@mpinet.net Henry Von Kohorn, MBA, Ph.D., CEO.

TV-CATV only.

Patented technology enablling TV viewers in the United States to legally bet, cost-free and risk-free, on the outcome of sports events, from their homes via the Internet.

Reuters Media, 3 Times Sq., 18th Fl., New York, NY, 10036. Phone: (646) 223-4000. Fax: (646) 223-4390. Fax: (646) 223-4370. Web Site:www.reuters.com Tom Glocer, CEO; Chris Ahearn, pres.

TV-CATV only.

International news for interactive multimedia news archive for CD-ROM & on-demand applications. Stock photos & film footage.

Reuters Television, 1333 H St. N.W., Washington, DC, 20005. Phone: (202) 898-0056. Fax: (202) 898-1236. Web Site:www.reuters.com John Clarke, global editor.

TV-CATV only.

Offers live positions, studio facilities & direct access to the satellite net, library & program packages cover major news & sporting events.

Rex Post, 610 S.W. 17th Ave., Portland, OR, 97205. Phone: (503) 238-4525. Fax: (503) 236-8347.E-mail: info@rexpost.com Web Site:www.rexpost.com Russell Gorsline, gen mgr; Lee Rooklin, sls; Tara Krick, business mgr.

TV-CATV-Radio.

TV & radio production, audio recording, video production, CD-ROM & DVD, website. Audio/video production & post, ISDN digital patch, DVD authoring & web design.

Richter Productions Inc., 330 W. 42nd St., Suite 2410, New York, NY, 10036. Phone: (212) 947-1395. Fax: (212) 643-1208.E-mail: richter330@aol.com Web Site:www.richtervideos.com Robert Richter, pres; Amy Kessler, production mgr.

TV-CATV only.

TV program, promo film production, distribution, film & video.

Riden International Inc., 6024 Paseo Palmilla, Goleta, CA, 93117. Phone: (805) 964-7041. Fax: (805) 964-1338.E-mail: rideninc@aol.com Web Site:www.rideninc.com Richard Dennison, pres.

TV-CATV only.

Motion Picture , TV program production & distribution.

Rigel Entertainment, 4201 Wilshire Blvd., Suite 555, Los Angeles, CA, 90010. Phone: (323) 954-8555. Fax: (323) 954-8592.E-mail: info@rigel.tv Web Site:www.rigel.tv John Laing, pres/CEO; Kristie Smith, VP distribution; Laura Hoffman, sls; Bryan Hambleton, sls.

TV-CATV only.

Offers international TV, video rights to TV series, MOWs, specials & feature films.

River City Video Productions, Box 310601, New Braunfels, TX, 78131-0601. Phone: (830) 625-3474. Fax: (830) 625-3710.E-mail: outdooradventures@satx.rr.com Web Site:www.fishingandoutdoor.com Deborah J. Dougherty, pres.

TV-CATV only.

Mktg, instructional & promotional videos & TV comls.

Roberts Communications Network Inc., 4175 Cameron St., Suite B-10, Las Vegas, NV, 89103. Phone: (702) 227-7500. Fax: (702) 227-7501. Tommy Roberts, chmn; Todd Roberts, pres/CEO.

TV-CATV only.

C-Bond satellite transponder capacity, uplinking, encoding & decoding. 50 Ch "Direct To Home" Platform

Rockey Hill and Knowlton, (A division of the Rockey Co.). 221 Yale Ave. N., Suite 530, Seattle, WA, 98109-5490. Phone: (206) 728-1100. Fax: (206) 728-1106. Web Site:www.rockey-seattle.com Will Ludlan, gen mgr .

Public rel, corporate & financial film production.

Rockwell Audio Media, 56 W. 45th St., Suite 1503, New York, NY, 10036. Phone: (212) 840-9200. Fax: (212) 840-9203.E-mail: john@rockwellaudiomedia.com Web Site:www.rockwellaudiomedia.com John Rockwell, pres.

Radio Only.

Audio editing & production-spoken word & educational.

PETER RODGERS ORGANIZATION, 6513 Hollywood Blvd., #201, Hollywood, CA, 90028. Phone: (323) 962-1778. Fax: (323) 962-7174.E-mail: info@profilms.com Web Site:www.profilms.com Stephen Rodgers, CEO; Pavel Miller, accounting; Ron Adler, dir opns.

TV-CATV only.

Consultants, Distributors, Reps. Celebrating over 30 years representing productions, companies & independent producers with over 2,000 hours of progmg .

Romano & Associates Inc., 5094 Dorsey Hall Dr., Suite 104, Ellicott City, MD, 21042. Phone: (410) 730-4133. Fax: (410) 730-2219. Web Site:www.racommunications.com Neil Romano, dir & producer.

TV-CATV-Radio.

Full-service production company specializing in issue-oriented short-feature films & documentaries, PSAs; professional of children's educ videos & comls.

Rose Entertainment, 5529 McLennan Ave., Encino, CA, 91436. Phone: (818) 817-7554. Fax: (818) 817-7585.E-mail: rosenter@pacbell.net Rosamaria Gonzalez, pres; Flory Quiroa, opns mgr.

TV-CATV only.

TV progmg distribution company for Latin America.

Rosler Creative, 88 Howard St., #2307, San Francisco, CA, 94105. Phone: (415) 896-1414. Fax: (415) 896-1616.E-mail: Peter@RoslerCreative.com Web Site:www.roslercreative.com Peter Rosler, owner.

Radio Only.

TV comls, creative dev & production.

TV-CATV only.

Rosnay International, 6 Rue Robert Estienne, Paris, 75008. France. Phone: 01.42.89.18.54. Fax: 01.42.25.34.39.E-mail: fronet3038@aol.com

TV-CATV only.

Distribution & production company.

Steve Rotfeld Productions Inc., 740 E. Haverford Rd., Bryn Mawr, PA, 19010. Phone: (610) 520-0671. Fax: (610) 520-0681. Web Site:www.rotfeldproductions.com Steve Rotfeld, pres & exec producer; Carol Hubmaster, VP sls.

TV-CATV only.

A TV production company that produces & syndicates TV shows.

Jack Rourke Productions, Box 1705, Burbank, CA, 91507. Phone: (818) 843-4839.

TV-CATV only.

TV & radio program production.

ROZON/Just For Laughs, 2101 Blvd St. Laurent, Montreal, H2X 2T5. Phone: (514) 845-3155. Fax: (514) 845-4140. E-mail: llee@hahaha.com Web Site:www.hahaha.com Nathalie Bourdon, dir tv sls; Bruce Hills, COO; Gilbert Rozon, pres; Isabelle Begin, dir international TV; Christos Sourligas, international TV sls, publicity, mktg, tv sls; Leisa Lee, dir communication.

TV-CATV only.

Producer/distributor of comedy programs, standup comedy & nonverbal light entertainment.

S

SFP Productions, 2 Ave. de L' Europe, 94360 Bry-Sur-Marne Cedex France. Phone: 3316 9833 602. Fax: 0033 11498 33604. E-mail: distribution@sfr.fr Web Site:www.sfp.fr Roland Fiszel, CEO.

Distribution worldwide rights (TV movies, series, mini-series documentaries).

SPI International, 55 White St., Suite 1A, New York, NY, 10013. Phone: (212) 673-5103. Fax: (212) 673-5183. Web Site:www.spiintl.com Loni Farhi, pres; Stacey Sobel, VP.

TV-CATV only.

SPI International is a leading supplier of theatrical films and a wide variety of television programming to the international market. To further exploit its vast library, SPI established its own cable stations on pay and basic cable level in Poland, Czech Republic, Slovakia and Hungary. SPI will open additional channels throughout Eastern Euroope during 2009.

STV Central Ltd., (Formerly Scottish Television Ltd.). Pacific Quay, Glasgow, G51 1PQ. Phone: 0141 300 3704.

TV-CATV only.

Bcstr & production company.

St. Olaf College, (Formerly Sing For Joy). Saint Olaf College, 1520 Saint Olaf Ave., Northfield, MN, 55057. Phone: (507) 786-8596. Fax: (507) 786-3033. E-mail: singforjoy@stolaf.edu Web Site:www.singforjoy.org Jeff O'Donnell, exec producer & music dir; Pastor Bruce Benson, program host; John Ferguson, music advisor; Miriam Mueller, communication coord.

Radio Only.

Sacred choral works with host commentary relating the music to the current scriptural lessons during each week of the church year.

Sak Entertainment, 398 W. Amelia St., Orlando, FL, 32801. Phone: (407) 648-0001. Fax: (407) 648-1333. E-mail: info@sak.com Web Site:www.sak.com David Russell, mgng & artistic dir; Gina DiRoma, sls mgr & mktg.

TV-CATV only.

Professional comedy actors, dirs, producers & writers. Entertainment consultants for WDW, Universal Studio, Harrahs Corp. & Busch Gardens.

Sanctuary Records Group Ltd., Sanctuary House, 45-53 Sinclair Rd., London, W14 0NS. United Kingdom. Phone: 44-020-7602-6351. Fax: 44-020-7603-5941. E-mail: info@sanctuarygroup.com Web Site:www.sanctuarygroup.com Giles Green, .

TV-CATV only.

Program production & sls.

Edward Sarson Productions, 30 Duke St., Suite 511, Kitchener, ON, N2H 3W5. Canada. Phone: (519) 576-1824. Fax: (519) 740-6766. George Sarson, pres.

Producers for the *Toad Patrol* TV series.

SB Management, 890 Monterey, Box 12837, San Luis Obispo, CA, 93406. Phone: (805) 543-9214. Fax: (805) 543-9243. E-mail: michael@mikehesser.com Web Site:www.mikehesser.com Mike Hesser, pres.

TV-CATV-Radio.

Consulting & coaching for sls & mgmt.

SCOLA, 21557 270th St, McClelland, IA, 51548. Phone: (712) 566-2202. Fax: (712) 566-2502. E-mail: scola@scola.org Web Site:www.scola.org Francis Lajba, pres; John Millar, VP.

TV-CATV-Radio.

SCOLA progmg from more than 90 countries in more than 80 languages. These programs are available via internet, satellite, cable to learners of languages study, ethnic communities & anyone seeking a global perspective.

Mission is to help the people of the world learn about one another.

Seattle Video Crew, (Formerly The Seattle Video Bureau). Box 99218, Seattle, WA, 98199. Phone: (206) 448-2500. Fax: (206) 378-1700. E-mail: crew@seattlevideo.com Web Site:www.seattlevideo.com David Oglevie, pres.

TV-CATV only.

Location video production for bcst news, corporate & industrial, mktg, & medical. BETACAM SP, & DVCAM, NTSC or PAL formats.

SeniorVision Productions Inc., 418 North Central St., East Bridgewater, MA, 02333. Phone: (508) 350-9700. E-mail: sales@seniorvision.com Web Site:www.seniorvision.com Steve Brown, co-owner; Noah Brookoff, co-owner.

TV-CATV only.

Video svcs.

Seraphim Communications Inc., 1568 Eustis St., St. Paul, MN, 55108. Phone: (651) 645-9173. Fax: (651) 645-3515. E-mail: info@seracomm.com Web Site:www.seracomm.com Kristin Wiersma, pres.

TV-CATV only.

Full-service video & AV capabilities. Emphasis on video production from concept through final product. In-house grahics, interactive Web, CD-ROM/DVD.

SESAC Inc., 55 Music Sq. E, Nashville, TN, 37203. Phone: (615) 320-0055. Fax: (615) 329-9627. Web Site:www.sesac.com Pat Collins, COO.

London, 67 Upper Berkeley St. Phone:

Santa MonicaCA , 501 Santa Monica Blvd., Suite 450. Phone:

MiamiFL , 420 Lincoln Rd., Suite 450. Phone:

AtlantaGA , 981 Joseph E. Lowery Blvd. NW, Suite 111. Phone:

New YorkNY , 152 W. 57th St., 5th Fl. Phone:

TV-CATV-Radio.

SESAC is a svc organization created to assist both the creators & users of music through royalty collection & efficient music licensing.

Sesame Workshop, One Lincoln Plaza, New York, NY, 10023. Phone: (212) 595-3456. Fax: (212) 875-6111. Web Site:www.sesameworkshop.org Gary Knell, pres; Ellen Lewis, VP corporate communications.

TV-CATV only.

TV program production.

Seven Network Australia Inc., 2100 Seaport Blvd., Suite 100, Redwood City, CA, 94063. Phone: (650) 381-2500. Web Site:www.seven.com.au Zane Bair, gen mgr; Mike Amor, bureau chief.

TV-CATV only.

U.S. office & news bureau of ch 7, Australia major coml TV net of Australia.

1776 Productions, 5 Sparrow Dr., Livingston, NJ, 07039. Phone: (973) 533-0762. Fax: (973) 992-1010. E-mail: nce@rcn.com Ralph Weisinger, pres.

Promotional film production.

Sam Shad Productions, Box 10853, Reno, NV, 89510. Phone: (775) 857-2244. Fax: (775) 857-2272. E-mail: sam@shad.reno.nv.us Web Site:www.bestofreno.tv Sam Shad, pres; Bonnie McCorkle, program dev.

TV-CATV only.

Radio progmg & coml production, TV progmg & coml production, TV & radio progmg concepts dev from start to finish, internet design & adv, public relations.

Harvey Sheldon Productions, 7855 E. Horizon View Dr., Anaheim Hills, CA, 92808. Phone: (714) 281-5929. Fax: (714) 281-5929. Harvey Sheldon, pres.

TV-CATV only.

Daily or wkly classic rock/swing video format for TV & cable stns. On Century Cable available for syndication serving 150,000 TV/cable households in Los Angeles/Orange county.

Shield Productions Inc., 11964 N Lake Dr., Boynton Beach, FL, 33436. Phone: (561) 734-5599. Fax: (561) 734-8176. James C. Dolan, pres.

TV-CATV only.

Creation & production of radio & TV comls.

Shukovsky English Entertainment, 4605 Lankershim Blvd., Suite 510, North Hollywood, CA, 91602. Phone: (818) 763-9191. Fax: (818) 763-9878. Joel Shukovsky, pres; Diane English, producer.

TV-CATV only.

Producer & distributor of TV progmg, especially half-hour comedy.

Silverline Entertainment, (Formerly Pictures). 21550 Oxnard St., Suite 300, Woodland Hills, CA, 91367. Phone: (818) 710-8899. Fax: (818) 710-8848. E-mail: silverline@earthlink.net Web Site:www.silverlineentertainment.com Leman Cetiner, CEO; Robert Yap, pres.

TV-CATV only.

Full-service production & distribution company producing theatrical, TV & kids series.

Silverman Stock Footage Inc., 210 Douglass St., Suite 1-D, Brooklyn, NY, 11217. Phone: (917) 470-9104. Fax: (718) 764-4411. E-mail: donald@silvermstockfootage.com Web Site:www.silvermanstockfootage.com Donald Silverman, pres.

TV-CATV only.

Stock footage.

Skywatch Weather Center, 347 Prestley Rd., Bridgeville, PA, 15017. Phone: (412) 221-6000. Phone: (800)-SKYWATCH. Fax: (412) 221-3160. E-mail: airsci@skyweather.com Web Site:www.skywatchweather.com Stanley J. Penkala, pres; Daniel Krzywiecki, VP.

TV-CATV-Radio.

Specially formatted weathercasts produced in the Skywatch Weather Center®.

Smith/Lee Productions, Inc., 7420 Manchester Rd., St. Louis, MO, 63143. Phone: (314) 647-3900. Fax: (314) 647-3959. E-mail: global@smithlee.com Web Site:www.smithlee.com David Smith, pres; Barry Lee, VP.

TV-CATV only.

TV & radio coml promotional film production; production svcs; studio specializing in Audio Post; music production, voice recording & multimedia.

P. Allen Smith Gardens, Box 7347, Little Rock, AR, 72217. Phone: (501) 376-1894. Fax: (501) 376-1896. Web Site:www.pallensmith.com P. Allen Smith, pres.

TV-CATV only.

Nationally syndicated gardening & lifestyle news inserts reported by professional garden designer Allen Smith.

Soldiers Radio & Television, U.S. Army Public Affairs, Box 31, 2511 Jefferson Davis Hwy., Arlington, VA, 22202. Phone: (703) 602-4675. Fax: (703) 602-5220. E-mail: armynewswatch@smc.army.mil Web Site:www.army.mil/srtv George McNamara, dir; Paul Schultz, opns mgr; Gene Gunderson, chief engr; Jim Ryan, opns mgr; Melody Day, mktg.

TV-CATV only.

Radio, TV news bureau, soldiers radio network & Army Newswatch a biweekly TV newscast.

Solid Gospel Network (Reach Satellite Network, Inc.), 402 BNA Drive, Suite 400, Nashville, TN, 37217. Phone: (615) 367-2210. E-mail: info@SalemMusicNetwork.com Web Site:www.solidgospel.com Michael S. Miller, gen mgr; Don Burns, progmg dir; Wade Schoenemann, opns mgr; Ed Evensen, Local Traffic Manager; Jim Black, director of Affiliate Relations; Rick Shelton, mgr.

Radio Only.

24-hour, satellite delivered, Christian country & southern gospel network, featuring artists like Bill Gaither, The Isaacs, Gold City, Jeff & Sheri Easter & The Martins, live from Nashville, the Christian music capital of the world.

Sony Pictures, 10202 West Washington Blvd., Culver City, CA, 90232. Phone: (310) 244-4000. Fax: (310) 244-2626. Web Site:www.sonypictures.com Michael Lynton, chmn/CEO; Amy Pascal, co-chmn; Jeff Blake, vice chmn.

AtlantaGA , 2859 Paces Ferry Rd, Suite 1130. Phone:

ChicagoIL , 455 N. Cityfront Plaza Dr, Suite 2520. Phone:

New YorkNY , 550 Madison Ave. Phone:

DallasTX , 3500 Maple Ave, Suite 205. Phone:

TV-CATV only.

Film & TV production.

SoperSound Music Library, Box 869, Ashland, OR, 97520. Phone: (800) 227-9980. Fax: (541) 552-0832. E-mail: info@sopersound.com Web Site:www.sopersound.com Dennis Reed, pres.

TV-CATV only.

Contemp music library for all production needs. Available on CDs & direct digital down load online.

Sound*Bytes, 1425 Hopkins St. N.W., Suite 401, Washington, DC, 20036. Phone: (202) 296-2022.E-mail: press@soundbytesradio.com Web Site:www.soundbytesradio.com Jan Ziff, pres.

Radio Only.

Computer audio show production & syndication.

Sound Idea Productions, 417 Nursery St., Nevada City, CA, 95959. Phone: (510) 832-5178. Fax: (510) 832-4829.E-mail: soundidea@oro.net Glenn Davidson, pres.

OaklandCA , 405 14th St, Suite 612. Phone:

Radio Only.

Archival svc, radio production & syndication.

Sound Ideas, 105 W. Beaver Creek Rd., Suite 4, Richmond Hill, ON, L4B 1C6. Canada. Phone: (905) 886-5000. Phone: (800) 387-3030. Fax: (905) 886-6800.E-mail: info@sound-ideas.com Web Site:www.sound-ideas.com Brian Nimens, pres/CEO.

TV-CATV-Radio.

Royalty free sound effects, imaging elements, music for the professional audio industry; including bcst, cable, film, multimedia & internet applications.

Sound of Birmingham Productions, 3625 5th Ave. S., Birmingham, AL, 35222. Phone: (205) 595-8497.E-mail: don@soundofbirmingham.com Web Site:soundofbirmingham.com Don Mosley, pres; Betty Mosley, VP office mgr.

TV-CATV-Radio.

Radio & TV voice-overs, jingles, video sweetening, custom music, recording studios, full-svc studios, ISDN.

Sound Source Networks, 2 St. Clair Ave. W., Suite 1101, Toronto, ON, M4V 1L6. Canada. Phone: (416) 922-1290. Fax: (416) 323-6819.E-mail: info@soundsource.ca Web Site:www.soundsource.ca Jean Marie Heimrath, pres, gen mgr; Lesley Soldat, VP opns.

Radio Only.

Radio net that produces, markets & distributes radio programs nationally.

Soundshop Recording Studio LLC, 1307 Division St., Nashville, TN, 37203. Phone: (615) 244-4149. Fax: (615) 242-8759.E-mail: soundshopstudio@aol.com Mike Bradley, owner; Don Cook, owner; Mark Capps, producer, engr.

TV-CATV only.

Music production, recording studios, 2-48 track digital or 24 track analog studios.

Soundtrack, 162 Columbus Ave., Boston, MA, 02116-5222. Phone: (617) 303-7500. Fax: (617) 303-7555. Web Site:www.soundtrackboston.com Amy Blankenship, COO; Beth Gimbrone, production mgr; Allen Smith, chief engr; Paul Cavicchio, CFO.

New YorkNY , 936 Broadway. Phone:

Production, postproduction & custom music of all kinds; specializing in sound designs.

Southcott Productions, Box 33185, Granada Hills, CA, 91394. Phone: (818) 368-4938. Fax: (818) 368-4938.E-mail: chucksongs@aol.com Chuck Southscott, owner.

Radio Only.

Radio program, coml production & distribution.

Southern STAR, Phone: 612 9519 2677. Fax: 612 9517 2530.E-mail: info@duplitek.com.au Web Site:www.southern-star.com.au Rory Callaghan, CEO; Alison Baker, sls dir.

TV-CATV only.

Southern Star is an integrated film & TV production distribution & manufacturing group. Southern Star is a public listed company.

Spanish Broadcasting System, 26 W. 56th St., New York, NY, 10019. Phone: (212) 541-9200. Fax: (212) 541-6904. Web Site:www.spanishbroadcasting.com Raul Alarcon, CEO; Frank Flores, COO, gen mgr; Joseph A. Garcia, CFO.

Radio Only.

Spanish progmg syndication.

Charlie Spencer Productions, 107 Jensen Cir., West Springfield, MA, 01089-4451. Phone: (413) 737-7600. Fax: (413) 737-7600 (Voice First).E-mail: cspencer@mail.map.com Charlie Spencer, producer & dir.

TV-CATV only.

Specializes in nature & environmental progmg, as well as outdoor recreation & nature travel. Svcs include consulting, producing, directing, rsch, writing & narration. Progms include *Gardening with Wildflowers, The Urban Canoeist & American Waste.*

Sport International Inc., Villa del Mar East, 14 J Ave. Isla Verde, Carolina, PR, 00979. Phone: (787) 268-8751. Fax: (787) 726-7683.E-mail: hector@hjfsport.com Web Site:www.hjfsport.com Hector Figueroa, chmn of bd; Juliet Giamartino, co-chmn; Jennifer Marin, VP event sls & production.

TV-CATV only.

Global mktg, distribution, bcstg, sports events, Pay-Per-View & special entertainment progmg. Current properties include: *This Day in Sports, Wide World of Bloopers,* live buying & buying documentaries.

Sports Byline U.S.A., 300 Broadway, Suite 8, San Francisco, CA, 94133. Phone: (415) 434-8300. Fax: (415) 391-2569.E-mail: webmaster@sportsbyline.com Web Site:www.sportsbyline.com Ron Barr, chmn; Darren Peck, pres; Ira Hankin, exec producer.

Radio Only.

Satellite-delivered nationwide radio sports talk net, listener 800 number, 7days (West Coast), barter.

StarDate/Universo Productions, (Formerly StarDate/Universo Productions). 2609 University Ave., # 3.118, Austin, TX, 78712. Phone: (512) 471-5285. Fax: (512) 471-5060.E-mail: perez@stardate.org Web Site:www.stardate.org Sandra Preston, exec producer; Damond Benningfield, producer.

Radio Only.

Syndicated two-minute radio programs on stars & planets visible in the night sky. Each program is date-specific. English/Sp.

Charles H Stern Agency Inc., 1999 Ave. of the Stars, Suite 1400, Los Angeles, CA, 90267. Phone: (310) 788-4570.

TV-CATV-Radio.

Radio coml production & distribution. Represents a variety of TV & radio personalities.

Steven B. Stevens, 7400 Sweetwater Branch, West Chester, OH, 45069. Phone: (513) 755-7300. Fax: (513) 755-7507.E-mail: sbstevens@aol.com Steven B. Stevens, pres.

TV-CATV-Radio.

Accomplished narrator/voice talent with deep warm authoratative voice.

Marty Stouffer Productions Ltd., 44190 Hwy. 82 E., Box 5057, Aspen, CO, 81611. Phone: (970) 925-5536. Fax: (970) 920-3820.E-mail: mary@stoufferoffice.com Marty Stouffer, pres.

TV-CATV only.

TV program production, syndication & online downloads.

Strand Media Group Inc., 12240 Venice Blvd., Suite 23, Los Angeles, CA, 90066. Phone: (310) 390-2248. Fax: (310) 390-2857.E-mail: strandmg@aol.com Web Site:www.somethingyoushouldknow.net Mike Carruthers, pres.

Radio Only.

Radio programs, coml production & distribution; media buying agent.

Strength for Living, 6350 W. Freeway, Fort Worth, TX, 76116. Phone: (817) 570-1400. Phone: (800) 266-1837. Fax: (817) 737-9436.E-mail: info@familynet.org Web Site:www.familynetradio.com Lisa Bratton, radio mktg & distribution; Donna Senn, radio distribution; Chuck Ries, producer.

Radio Only.

Offers audiences relevant messages of hope & spiritual encouragement in their search to find strength for living. Host Bob Reccord.

M C Stuart & Associates Pty Ltd., 2/34 Power St., Balwyn Victoria, 3103. Australia. Phone: 61 3 9888 5830. Phone: 61 409 885 831 (mobile). Fax: 61 3 9888 5831.E-mail: maxstuart@comtel.com.au Max Stuart, mgng dir & sec.

TV-CATV-Radio.

Worldwide TV & feature film distributors.

Studio Babelsberg GmbH, August-Bebel-St. 26-53, 14482 Potsdam Germany. Phone: 49 (0) 331-72 -13151. Fax: 49 (0) 331-72-12525.E-mail: info@studiobabelsberg.com Web Site:www.studiobabelsberg.de Gerhard Bergfried, CEO.

TV-CATV only.

Studio area, studio technology, set design & construction, film laboratory, postproduction, dubbing theatres for films, TV & video.

Studio Center Corp., 161 Business Park Dr., Virginia Beach, VA, 23462. Phone: (866) 515-2111. Fax: (757) 623-5512.E-mail: info@studiocenter.com Web Site:www.studiocenter.com William Prettyman, CEO & exec producer.

Las VegasCA , 3875 S. Jones Blvd. Phone:

Los AngelesCA , 7033 W. Sunset Blvd., Suite 318. Phone:

New YorkNY , 315 Madison Ave., 11th Fl. Phone:

MemphisTN , 2693 Union Ave. Ext. Phone:

Virginia BeachVA , 5245 Cleveland St., Suite 204. Phone:

TV-CATV-Radio.

Radio & TV comls, stn promotions, TV voice-over svcs, original music, copywriting, on hold & wedsite audio.

Studio M Productions Unlimited, 4032 Wilshire Blvd., Suite 403, Los Angeles, CA, 90010. Phone: (213) 389-7372. Fax: (213) 389-3299.E-mail: mixer@sound4film-tv.com Web Site:www.mandy.com/stu001.html Mike Michaels, owner/sr engr/producer; Robert Dickerson, sr engr.

HonoluluHI . Jim Walters Co, 4224 Waialae # 210. Phone:

TV-CATV-Radio.

TV & radio program production, tape, film & live production svcs. Live remotes for TV, radio, news & sports. (888) 389-7372.

Suite Audio, 21 Stone Wall Ln., Clinton, CT, 06413. Phone: (860) 664-9499.E-mail: info@suiteaudio.com Web Site:www.suiteaudio.com Bob Nary, owner/pres.

ClintonCT . Clinton, CT, 21 Stonewall Ln. Bob Nary, owner.

TV-CATV only.

Facility: ProTools HDII/TDM, Waves restoration & Platinum, Sonic Solutions. Commercial-Program-surround production. CD mastering - authoring - duplication. Cassette duplication.

Sullivan Entertainment Inc./Sullivan Entertainment International, 110 Davenport Rd., Toronto, ON, M5R 3R3. Canada. Phone: (416) 921-7177. Fax: (416) 921-7538. Web Site:www.sullivan-ent.com

London United Kingdom. Sullivan Entertainment Europe Ltd, Savant House, 63-65 Camden High St. Phone:

TV-CATV only.

Production, distribution, home video, dev series & feature film.

Sullivan Video Services Inc., 7 Pickman Dr., Bedford, MA, 01730. Phone: (781) 271-1720. Fax: (781) 271-1740.E-mail: johnsul@sull Web Site:www.sullivanvideo.com John M. Sullivan, pres.

TV-CATV only.

Full-svc video production company. Provides ENG/EFP news crews & Ku-band satellite svcs, Fiber Optic Studio Tape feeding capabilities.

Sunbow Entertainment, 100 5th Ave., Fl. 3, New York, NY, 10011. Phone: (212) 893-1600. Fax: (212) 893-1630. Web Site:www.tvloonland.com Suzanne Berman, dir creative affrs; Rebecca Gallivan, opns dir.

TV-CATV only.

Developers, producers & distributors of quality children's & family programs, licensors & merchandise.

Sundial Productions, 275 Huyler St., S. Hackensack, NJ, 07606. Phone: (201) 525-5100. Fax: (201) 525-5111. Jack Kreismer, Principal; David Lapidus, Principal.

Radio Only.

Voice production company; radio & telephone feature production.

System TV, 45/47 rue Paul Bert, 92100 Boulogne, Paris France. Phone: (33)-1-55-38-2020. Fax: (33)-1-55-38-20-30.E-mail: daniel@systemtv.fr Web Site:www.systemtv.fr Daniel Renoug, pres.

TV-CATV only.

TV program production, press agency, produce weather & info svcs.

T

TM Studios, 2002 Academy Ln., Suite 110, Dallas, TX, 75234. Phone: (972) 406-6800. Fax: (972) 406-6890.E-mail: info@tmstudios.com Web Site:www.tmstudios.com Chris Long, VP/gen mgr.

TV-CATV only.

TMC creates, produces & distributes music-based products for bcst, including compilation libraries, production music, I.D. packages & coml jingles.

TRF Production Music Libraries, One International Blvd., Suite 212, Mahwah, NJ, 07495. Phone: (800) 899-MUSIC. Fax: (201) 335-0004.E-mail: info@trfmusic.com Web Site:www.trfmusic.com Michael Nurko, pres/CEO.

TV-CATV-Radio.

Largest collection of contemporary, retro, and traditional production music. Every category available including all types of ethnic and specialty music.

TR Productions, 209 W. Central St., Suite 108, Natick, MA, 01760. Phone: (508) 650-3400. Fax: (508) 650-3455. Web Site:www.trprod.com Cary M. Benjamin, principal.

TV-CATV only.

Production svcs.

TS James & Associates, 83 Christopher St., New York, NY, 10014-4246. Phone: (212) 331-0186. Fax: (212) 505-0959.E-mail: tom@jandasound.com Thomas S. James, pres.

TV-CATV only.

Original scoring for film & TV.

TYG Media, (Formerly Music of Your Life). 6525 Babcock St., S.E., Malabar, FL, 32950-5002. Phone: (321) 725-0014. Fax: 3(21) 725-0098. Web Site:www.tygmedia.com Kerry Fink, CEO.

TV-CATV-Radio.

Full service, fully equiped, soundstrage, video editing suite & sound voice-over recording studio.

Talco Productions, 279 E. 44th St., New York, NY, 10017. Phone: (212) 697-4015. Fax: (212) 697-4827.E-mail: alaw1@mindspring.com Alan Lawrence, pres; Marty Holberton, VP.

TV-CATV-Radio.

TV, radio progmg, documentaries, ind, educ production, PR consultation & production.

Talk America Radio Networks, 520 Broad St., Newark, NJ, 07102. Phone: (973) 438-3026. Fax: (973) 438-1637. Web Site:www.talkamerica.com Trang Nguyen, COO; Maurice Bortz, opns VP.

Radio Only.

24-hour talk seven days a week offering live call-in programs. All programs barter & every minute is covered.

Talk Radio Network, (a subsidiary of Premiere Radio Networks). Box 3755, Central Point, OR, 97502. Phone: (541) 664-8827. Fax: (541) 664-6250. Web Site:www.talkradionetwork.com Mark Masters, pres.

Radio Only.

Full-svc live talk radio format 24 hours daily. Serving more than 400 affils nationwide.

Talkline Communications Radio Network, Box 20108, Park West Station, New York, NY, 10025-1510. Phone: (212) 769-1925. Fax: (212) 799-4195.E-mail: tcntalk@aol.com Web Site:www.talklinecommunications.com Zev J. Brenner, exec producer.

Radio Only.

Natl Jewish radio net. Carried in over 2,500 markets. Contemp Jewish progmg; interview & call-in format with newsmaker guests from politics, entertainment & Israel. Live segments from Israel. Available on barter. Satellite delivered.

Tamouz Media, 37 W. 20th, Suite 1007, New York, NY, 10011. Phone: (212) 463-7437. Fax: (212) 463-7409.E-mail: tamouzmedia@aol.com Web Site:www.tamouz.com Ilan Ziv, producer.

TV-CATV only.

TV program & documentary production.

Tankersley Productions, Inc., St. Louis, 858 Hanley Industrial Ct., St. Louis, MO, 63144. Phone: (314) 725-0116.E-mail: randy@tankersleyproductions.com Web Site:www.tankersleyproductions.com Randy Tankersley, pres.

Full-bcst svcs. ENG/EFP Beta SP crews with/without producers, avid nonlinear editing.

Technisonic Studios, 500 S. Ewing Ave., Suite G, St. Louis, MO, 63103. Phone: (314) 533-1777. Fax: (314) 533-6527.E-mail: mstroot@technisonic.com Web Site:www.technisonic.com Mike Stroot, pres.

TV-CATV only.

16 & 35 mm film production, full-sound studios, video production, film & video editing.

Tel-Air Interests Inc., 2040 Sherman St., Hollywood, FL, 33020. Phone: (954) 924-4949. Fax: (954) 924-4980.E-mail: telair@aol.com Web Site:www.telairint.com Grant H. Gravitt Jr., pres; M. L. Gravitt Jr., sec/treas.

TV-CATV only.

Syndicated TV specials (sports & music), contract production, theatrical short subjects & documentary TV & films, infomercials. Digital recording studio, digital & linear editing.

TeleCom Productions Inc., 5875 Peachtree Industrial Blvd., Suite 150, Norcross, GA, 30092. Phone: (770) 455-3569. Fax: (770) 455-3938. Web Site:www.tcpatlanta.com Budd O. Libby, pres; Roger B. Clark, co-chmn; Dan Bower, co-chmn.

TV-CATV-Radio.

Production & syndicator of *Let's Go to the Races, Free Cash Lotto, Daily Race Game & Post Time* retail prize promotions; random animated digital drawing systems (RADDS).

Telegenic Programs Inc., 161 Forest Hill Rd., Toronto, ON, M5P 2N3. Canada. Phone: (416) 484-8000. Fax: (416) 484-8001.E-mail: telegenic@aol.com H. Lawrence Fein, chmn/CEO; Ronda Taylor, dir opns.

TV-CATV only.

One of Canada's leading TV distribution companies now in its 30th successful year.

Telemundo Internacional, (Formerly Tepuy). 2745 Ponce de Leon Blvd., Coral Gables, FL, 33134. Phone: (305) 774-0033. Fax: (305) 774-7372. Web Site:www.tepuy.com Marcos Santana, chmn/CEO; Esperanza Garay, VP sls; Karen Barroeta, VP mktg, prom; Marco Santana, pres; Luis Daniel Capriles, VP intl digital media sls.

Pozuelo de Alarcon Spain, Via Dos Castillas 9C-P2, 2B. Phone:

Caracas Venezuela, Ave. Libertador Torre E, EXA PH-1. Phone:

TV-CATV only.

Program distribution.

Telenium Studios/Fusion, (Formerly Telenium Studios). 525 Mildred Ave., Primos, PA, 19018. Phone: (610) 626-6500. Fax: (610) 626-2638. Web Site:www.fusionexperiences.com Todd Strine, CEO.

PhiladelphiaPA . Telenium Post, 520 N. Columbus Blvd, Suite 204. Phone:

TV-CATV only.

Studio & location production & postproduction for networks, syndication & cable. Full facilities, production mgmt & creative svcs.

Telepros, Box 1116, Belmont, CA, 94002. Phone: (650) 345-0505.E-mail: telepros@comcast.net Niels Melo, pres.

TV-CATV only.

Producers of live entertainment, sports, news, performing arts, corporate videos and webcasts.

Television Representatives Inc., 9720 Wilshire Blvd., Suite 202, Beverly Hills, CA, 90212-2006. Phone: (310) 278-4050. Fax: (310) 278-3350.E-mail: heyalans@aol.com Alan Silverbach, pres.

TV-CATV only.

TV program distribution, United States & international.

The Television Syndication Company, Inc., 520 Sabal Lake Dr., Suite 108, Longwood, FL, 32779. Phone: (407) 788-6407. Fax: (407) 788-4397.E-mail: cassie@tvsco.com Web Site:www.tvsco.com Cassie M. Yde, pres.

TV-CATV only.

A full-svc TV syndication & distribution organization offering TV progmg to bcstrs worldwide.

Televix Entertainment Inc., 449 S. Beverly Dr., Suite 300, Beverly Hills, CA, 90212. Phone: (310) 788-5500. Fax: (310) 286-0207.E-mail: postmaster@televix.com Web Site:www.televix.com Hugo Rose, CEO; Pamela Popp, sr VP.

TV-CATV only.

Distribution of TV programs in the Latin American & Sp U.S. markets.

Danny Thomas Productions, 10100 Santa Monica Blvd., Suite 950, Los Angeles, CA, 90067. Phone: (310) 277-4866. Fax: (310) 286-1963.E-mail: anita@dethomasbobo.com Anita De Thomas, pres.

TV-CATV only.

TV programs, features, coml production.

Thompson Creative, 4141 Office Parkway, Dallas, TX, 75204. Phone: (214) 559-4000. Fax: (214) 521-8578.E-mail: info@thompsoncreative.com Web Site:www.thompsoncreative.com J. Larry Thompson, CEO; Susan Price Thompson, pres.

TV-CATV-Radio.

Contemp radio ID jingles for all formats.

Time Capsule, Inc., 124 Cottonwood Lane, Centerville, MA, 02632-1911. Phone: (800) 822-7785. Fax: (508) 637-3333.E-mail: tc@tcapsule.com Web Site:www.tcapsule.com Richard T. Teimer, pres & sls dir; Nancy Q. Proctor, VP affl rel; Bill Stephens, VP special projects.

Radio Only.

System to bring 1,000 more cash ads per year; daily quizzes fit all formats.

Today Video, 475 10th Ave. 10th Fl., New York, NY, 11024. Phone: (212) 239-3999. Fax: (212) 239-2999. David Seeger, CEO.

TV-CATV only.

Production svcs.

Tomwil Inc., 4905 Gentry Ave., Valley Village, CA, 91607. Phone: (818) 769-0883. Fax: (818) 769-0887.E-mail: tomwil@earthlink.net James R. Rokos, pres; Wilda A. Rokos, VP.

TV-CATV only.

Distributors of features, light entertainment, sports, series & documentaries to all media in the world market.

Toucan Productions, 60 Fiddlers Elbow Rd., Margaretville, NY, 12455. Phone: (212) 580-4882. Phone: (845) 586-1746. Fax: (845) 586-4623. Fred Margulies, pres.

TV-CATV only.

Film, video production & distribution.

Traffic Pulse Networks (A Unit of Mobility Technologies), Moblity Technology - Traffic Pluse Network, 851 Duportail Rd., Suite 220, Wayne, PA, 19087. Phone: (610) 725-9700. Fax: (610) 725-0530.E-mail: info@mobility technologies.com Web Site:www.mobilitytechnologies.com Doug Alexander, CEO; Jim Brown, VP; Al McGowan, sr VP; Robert Pollan, COO/CFO.

TV-CATV only.

Traffic Pulse Networks provides digital & traditional traffic data to radio, TV & CATV. It also provides an inventory rep service.

Traffic Scan Network, Inc, (Formerly Shadow Broadcast Services). 7707 Waco Ave., Baton Rouge, LA, 70806-1440. Phone: (225) 926-7152. Fax: (225) 923-0704.E-mail: johnny@trafficscannetwork.com Web Site:www.trafficscannetwork.com Johnny Ahysian, pres/gen mgr.

TV-CATV-Radio.

Traf, news, sports, weather reports for radio, TV & cable systems.

The Transfer Zone, 13251 Northend, Oak Park, MI, 48237-3261. Phone: (248) 548-7580. Fax: (248) 548-0924.E-mail: transferzone@juno.com Web Site:thetransferzone.com Roxane B. Newhouse, dir mktg.

TV-CATV only.

International video standard conversions, duplication, film/slide transfers: A-B roll editing, video slide/film. Video to CD & DVD & duplication.

Triage Entertainment Inc., 6701 Center Dr. W., Suite 1111, Los Angeles, CA, 90045-1552. Phone: (310) 417-4800. Web Site:www.triageinc.com Stu Schreiber, pres; John Bravakis, business mgr; Steve Kroonpnick, exec producer.

TV-CATV only.

Independent, full-service production company with extensive experience in the production of TV & film, post-production facilities & motion control/graphics department.

Tribune Radio Networks, 435 N. Michigan Ave., Chicago, IL, 60611. Phone: (312) 222-3342. Fax: (312) 222-4876. Web Site:www.tribuneradio.com Tom Langmyer, VP/gen mgr; Wendi Power, sls dir.

Radio Only.

Tape & internet digital delivered farm, sports & specialty programs including: Chicago Cubs Network, Agri-Voice, National Farm Report, Farming America, Samuelson's Sez.

TRI-COMM Productions, (A First Vision Group Co). 11 Palmetto Pkwy., Suite 201, Hilton Head Island, SC, 29926-3703. Phone: (843) 681-5000. Fax: (843) 681-2945. Web Site:www.tri-comm.tv William J. Robinson, pres/CEO.

TV-CATV only.

A full-svc production company specializing in film HD & digital betacam production, sound design, graphics/animation. Also offers sugar sand beaches & the best golf courses around.

Trident Releasing, 8401 Melrose Pl., 2nd Fl., Los Angeles, CA, 90069. Phone: (323) 655-8818. Fax: (323) 655-0515.E-mail: tridents@aol.com Jean Ovrum, chmn; Victoria Plummer, pres; Kristi Mailing, sls VP.

TV-CATV only.

Acquire feature films in the postproduction & completed stages.

Troma Entertainment, Inc., 733 Ninth Ave., New York, NY, 10019. Phone: (212) 757-4555. Fax: (212) 399-9885. Web Site:www.troma.com

TV-CATV only.

Troma is one of the oldest ind film companies in the world. We produce & distribute films & offer stock footage.

Turner Entertainment Co., 1888 Century Park E., 10th Fl., Los Angeles, CA, 90067. Phone: (310) 788-6801. Fax: (310) 788-6810.E-mail: roger.mayer@turner.com Robert L. Mayer, pres/COO.

TV-CATV only.

Sls, licensing & servicing of major film & TV library.

TVOntario, (TVO network, TFO network). Box 200, Stn Q, Toronto, ON, M4T 2T1. Canada. Phone: (416) 484-2600. Fax: (416) 484-2662. Web Site:www.tvo.org Lee Robock, COO; Yuonne Carey-Le, dir.

Educ production, educ bcst international program sls, coproduction.

20th Century Fox/Incendo Television Distribution Ltd., 2 Bloor St. W., Suite 1700, Toronto, ON, M4W 3E2. Canada. Phone: (416) 643-3897. Fax: (416) 643-3898. Web Site:www.foxincendo.com Michael Murphy, sr VP; Kimberley Ball, dir mktg; David Heath, program sls VP.

TV-CATV only.

TV program distribution.

Twentieth Century Fox Television Distribution, Box 900, Beverly Hills, CA, 90213-0900. Phone: (310) 369-1000. Fax: (310) 369-8892. Web Site:www.foxnow.com Mark Kaner, pres; Peter Levinshon, pres; Marion Edwards, exec VP.

London. Twentieth Century Fox Television Distribution, 31-32 Soho Square.. Phone:

Moore ParkNO Australia. Fox Studios Austrailia, Driver Avenue. Phone:

Sao Paulo Brazil. Fox Film Do Brasil Ltda., Rua Dr. EDuardo De Souza Arrrrranha, 387-3o Andar. Phone:

TorontoON Canada. Fox/Incendo, 101 Bloor Street West, Suite #400. Phone:

Paris France. Twentieth Century Fox France, Inc., TV Division, 21 bis rue Lord Byron. Phone:

Pembroke PinesFL . Twentieth Century Fox Television Distribution, 2000 N.W. 150th Avenue, Suite 1110. Phone:

TV-CATV only.

Production & distribution.

Twentieth Television, 2121 Ave. of the Stars, Suite 2100, Los Angeles, CA, 90067. Phone: (310) 369-3924. Fax: (310) 369-1506. Web Site:www.fox.com Bob Cook, pres/COO; David Shall, exec VP.

New YorkNY . Twentieth Television, 1211 Avenue of the Americas16th Fl. Bob Cesa, exec VP adv sls & cable progmg sls.

TV-CATV only.

Produces, distributes progmg for net TV, domestic & international TV markets.

Two Oceans Entertainment Group, 2017 Lemoyne St., Suite 800, Los Angeles, CA, 90026. Phone: (818) 501-6550. Fax: (818) 501-6558.E-mail: twoceans@aol.com Meryl Marshall, pres; Susan Whittaker, dev VP.

TV-CATV only.

Domestic & international TV production. Most recent—*When Danger Follows You Home, Baby Monitor, Sound of Fear, Happily Ever After, Fairy Tales For Every Child.*

U

UBC Radio, 230 Ohio St., Suite 101, Chicago, IL, 60611. Phone: (312) 640-5000. Phone: (312) 751-0135. Fax: (312) 640-5010. Bradley Saul, CEO; Ron Gleason, pres.

Radio Only.

Talk radio long form progmg plus short form features.

U.S. Conference of Catholic Bishops, (Formerly Catholic Communication Campaign). 3211 4th St. N.E., Washington, DC, 20017. Phone: (202) 541-3204. Fax: (202) 541-3129.E-mail: pgarcia@usccb.org Web Site:www.usccb.org/ccc Pat Ryan Garcia, dir.

TV-CATV-Radio.

TV & radio pub svc programs.

U.S. Plan B Inc., 466 Orange St., Suite 280, Redlands, CA, 92374. Phone: (818) 998-8833. Phone: (888) 877-5262. Fax: (702) 926-2532.E-mail: office@usplanb.com Web Site:www.usplanb.com

TV-CATV only.

TV news gathering & production crews, stock footage, rsch.

Ukrainian Melody Hour, Box 2257, Washington, DC, 20013. Phone: (202) 529-7606. Phone: (202) 269-1824. Fax: (202) 638-5995. Roman V. Marynowych, producer & dir; Odile E. Marynowych, exec sec.

TV-CATV only.

Ukrainian radio, TV & cable program productions.

United Learning Co., 1560 Sherman Ave., Suite 100, Evanston, IL, 60201. Phone: (800) 323-9084. Fax: (847) 328-6706.E-mail: joel.altschul@unitedlearning.com Web Site:www.unitedlearning.com

TV-CATV only.

Educ programs, series & documentaries, videos & curriculums, streaming.

United Methodist Communications, 810 - 12th Ave. S., Nashville, TN, 37203. Phone: (615) 742-5400. Fax: (615) 742-5125.E-mail: lalexander@umcom.org Web Site:www.umcom.org Larry Hollon, sec; Jeneane Jones, dir TV progmg.

TV-CATV only.

TV & radio production & distribution.

U.S. Air Force Recruiting Service, Randolph AFB, 550 D Street W., Suite 1, Universal City, TX, 78150-5421. Phone: (210) 652-3937. Fax: (210) 652-4892.E-mail: rspsa@rs.af.mil Web Site:www.airforce.com Gary Quesenberry, supt bcstg; Ted Northrup, producer & dir.

TV-CATV only.

Custom production of radio & TV PSAs for Air Force recruiting for local communities.

United Stations Radio Network, 25 W. 45 St., New York, NY, 10036. Phone: (212) 869-1111. Fax: (212) 869-1115.E-mail: info@unitedstations.com Web Site:www.unitedstations.com Nick Verbitsky, CEO.

Los AngelesCA , 11400 W. Olympic Blvd., # 200. Phone:

ChicagoIL , 333 W. Weeker Dr, # 700. Phone:

DallasTX Phone:

Radio Only.

Entertainment & comedy. Progmg for radio stns, news, business & weather features.

University of Colorado Television, Campus Box 379, Boulder, CO, 80309. Phone: (303) 492-1857. Fax: (303) 492-7017.E-mail: kathleen.albers@colorado.edu Kate Albers, producer & dir.

TV-CATV only.

TV & radio program production & distribution; production svcs.

University of Detroit Mercy, 4001 W. McNichols, Communication Studies Dept., Detroit, MI, 48221-3038. Phone: (313) 578-0311. Phone: (313) 993-2005. Fax: (313) 993-1166. Web Site:www.udmercy.edu Michael Jayson, engr.

TV-CATV only.

Radio program syndication.

University of Kentucky Public Relations & Radio-TV News Bureau, Mathews Bldg., Suite 103A, Lexington, KY, 40506. Phone: (859) 257-1754. Fax: (859) 257-4017.E-mail: cnath1@email.uky.edu Web Site:www.uky.edu Carl Nathe, dir radio, TV news bureau; Jimmy Stanton, exec dir pub rel.

TV-CATV-Radio.

TV & radio program & coml, promotional film production & distribution.

Univision Communications Inc., 5999 Center Drive, Los Angeles, CA, 90045. Phone: (310) 556-7676. Fax: (310) 556-7615. Web Site:www.univision.net A. Jerrold Perenchio, chmn/CEO; Ray Rodriguez, pres/COO.

TV-CATV only.

Sp language bcst & cable TV net radio stns, music record labels & an internet destination.

V

VA-Tech Video/Broadcast Services, 285 Whittemore Hall, Blacksburg, VA, 24061. Phone: (540) 231-5930. Fax: (540) 231-4622. Web Site:www.vbs.vt.edu Mark Harden, mgr.

TV-CATV only.

Complete video & audio production & postproduction svcs. Uplink, downlink & CATV opn. Telephone & data communication.

VRI (Video Rentals Inc.), 100 Stonehurst Ct., Northvale, NJ, 07647. Phone: (800) 255-2874. Phone: (201) 750-3200. Fax: (201) 784-2795.E-mail: info@rentvri.com Web Site:www.rentvri.com Tom Canavan, VP/gen mgr.

TV-CATV only.

Full-svc rental facility with a complete inventory of bcst & industrial video equipment.

VTTV Videothek Electronic TV-Production GmbH + Co Kopier KG, Havelchaussee 161, Berlin, 14055. Germany. Phone: (030) 300 95-3. Fax: (030) 300 95-500.E-mail: info@vttv.de Web Site:www.vttv.de Paul Bielicki, pres; Friedel Lux, head dev/rsch; Herbert Bauermeister, head creative dept.

TV-CATV only.

Complete production service: studios (600/225 m2), professional equipment for production & postproduction, high definition production units. Commercials, documentaries, features, pop promos, TV.

Valentino Music & Sound Effect Libraries, 7750 Sunset Blvd., Los Angeles, CA, 90046. Phone: (914) 347-7878. Phone: (310) 201-0015.E-mail: info@selectracks.com Web Site:www.tvmusic.com Steven Stern, sr VP production, music; Stuart Hart, sr VP music production.

TV-CATV only.

Compact disc music & sound effects libraries.

Venevision International, 121 Alhambra Plaza, Suite 1400, Coral Gables, FL, 33134. Phone: (305) 442-3411. Fax: (305) 448-4762.E-mail: info@venevisionintl.com Web Site:www.venevisionintl.com Luis A. Villanueva, pres/CEO; Cesar Diaz, VP sls; Cristobal Ponte, sls dir; Jose Antonio Espinal, VP entetainment; Miguel Somoza, sls dir; Manuel Perez, CFO; Daniel Rodriguez, sls dir.

TV-CATV only.

Distribution of progmg.

Viacom Inc., 1515 Broadway, New York, NY, 10036. Phone: (212) 258-6000. Fax: (212) 258-6465. Web Site:www.viacom.com Summer M. Redstone, chmn/CEO; Matthew Blank, CEO; Martin Shea, sr VP; Al Weber, pres; Jonathan L. Dolgen, chmn; John Antioco, chmn/CEO; Carl D. Folta, sr VP; Thomas E. Freston, chmn/CEO; Michael D. Fricklas, exec VP; Sherry Lansing, chmn; Herb Scannell, pres; Jack Ramanos, pres; William A. Roskin, sr VP; Carol Melton, sr VP; Mel Karmazin, pres/COO; Richard Bressler, sr VP/CFO.

HollywoodCA . Paramount Pictures, 5555 Melrose Ave.

CharlotteNC . Paramount Parks, 8720 Red Oak Blvd, Suite 375.

New YorkNY . Showtime Networks Inc., 1633 Broadway.

New YorkNY . Simon & Schuster, 1230 Ave. of the Americas.

New YorkNY . MTV Networks, 1515 Broadway.

DallasTX . Blockbuster Entertainment, 1201 Elm St.

TV-CATV only.

TV program production & distribution, motion pictures production & distribution, book publishing, video production & distribution, theme parks.

Video-Cinema Films Inc., 510 E. 86th St., New York, NY, 10028. Phone: (212) 734-1632. Fax: (212) 734-1632. Larry Stern, pres.

TV-CATV only.

We license motion pictures for TV, cable nets etc. Also clips & excerpts.

Video Enterprises Inc., 575 29th St., Manhattan Beach, CA, 90266-3430. Phone: (310) 796-5555. Fax: (310) 546-2921.E-mail: hambrose@earthlink.net Heidi Lane-Ambrose, pres; Renska Somers, office mgr.

TV-CATV-Radio.

Natl placement of ten-second promotional spots on game shows, talk, var & sports programs.

Video I-D Teleproductions Inc., 105 Muller Rd., Washington, IL, 61571. Phone: (800) 333-9123. Fax: (309) 444-4333.E-mail: videoid@videoid.com Web Site:www.videoid.com Sam B. Wagner, pres; Gwen Wagner, mktg mgr; Larry Strantz, sls consultant.

Producers, Distributors, and Production Services Alphabetical Index

TV-CATV only.

Full teleproduction svcs, DVD & CD-ROM capabilities, location production, linear & nonlinear editing, 3D graphics, specializing in corporate image, safety, training, sls & mktg.

Video/Media Distribution Inc., 1050 N. State St., Chicago, IL, 60610. Phone: (312) 944-4700. Fax: (312) 944-1582. E-mail: shelvm@aol.com Shel Beugen, pres.

TV-CATV only.

Program sls & syndication svcs to bcst, cable stns & networks.

Video One Inc., 4952 Nagle Ave., Sherman Oaks, CA, 91423. Phone: (818) 781-9824. Fax: (818) 753-4704. Robert G. Kaufmann, pres; Kevin E. Hamburger, VP.

Remote TV production facilities.

Video Services, 1033 Elm Hill Pike, Nashville, TN, 37210. Phone: (615) 248-1010. Fax: (615) 244-5712. E-mail: info@siffordvideoservices.com Web Site:www.siffordvideoservices.com Joel Covington, owner.

TV-CATV only.

CD, DVD, videotape duplication, standard conversions.

Video Techniques Inc., Box 9649, Bradenton, FL, 34206-9649. Phone: (941) 758-3077. Fax: (941) 758-4896. E-mail: vti@videotechniques.com Web Site:www.videotechniques.com Bob Lorentzen, pres.

TV-CATV only.

Beta SP & MII field & postproduction facilities. CD, DVD authoring & duplication, VHS duplication, streaming video hosting.

VideoActive Productions (VAP), 1560 Broadway, Suite 610, New York, NY, 10036. Phone: (212) 541-6592. Web Site:www.videoactiveprod.com Steven Garrin, pres.

TV-CATV-Radio.

Digital video, audio production & post production.

Videographic West, Box 1093, 30 Benchmark Rd., Suite 203, Avon, CO, 81620. Phone: (970) 949-5593. Fax: (970) 949-6331. E-mail: video@colorado.net Web Site:www.skitv.com Michael Billingsley, principal; Stephanie Billingsley, principal.

TV-CATV only.

Specializing in cable sports progmg & distribution, extensive stock footage of action sports, mountain lifestyle, skiing, golf, family & travel. Full-svc production house, field crews, two SD/component pinnacle Liquid uncompressed NLE workstations, complete multimedia suite with DVD authoring/encoding, 2D animation suite with talented artists.

Videomedia, C/Jose Isbert, 2, Ciudad de la Imagen, Pozuelo De Alarcon, Madrid, 28223. Spain. Phone: 34-91-512.8000. Fax: 34-91-518.8017. E-mail: videomedia@videomedia.es Web Site:www.videomedia.es Jorge Arque, CEO, pres; Mireia Acosta, fiction mgr; Daniel Acuna, entertainment mgr; Fernanda Montoro, intnl div.

TV-CATV only.

Independent production company. Entertainment formats & programs, documentaries, fiction.

Videosmith Inc., 100 Spring Garden St., Philadelphia, PA, 19123. Phone: (215) 238-5070. Fax: (215) 238-5075. E-mail: info@videosmith.com Web Site:www.videosmith.com Steven T. Smith, pres.

TV-CATV only.

TV progmg, equipment rentals & production mgmt.

VIEW Video Inc., 34 E. 23rd St., New York, NY, 10010. Phone: (212) 674-5550. Fax: (212) 979-0266. E-mail: viewvid@aol.com Web Site:www.view.com Bob Karcy, pres.

TV-CATV only.

International home video production & distribution of special interest progms in the areas of art, jazz, pop music, opera, dance, children's interactive sports & modern lifestyle progms.

Virginia Tech (Network Infrastructure and Services), (Formerly Virginia Tech, CNS (Communications Network Services). 1770 Forecast Dr., Blacksburg, VA, 24061-0506. Phone: (540) 231-6460. Fax: (540) 231-8418. Web Site:www.cns.vt.edu Judy Lilly, assoc VP net svcs.

TV-CATV only.

Video & Audio Service to campus - faculty staff & students.

Vision Broadcasting - KVBA TV 19, 1017 New York Ave., Alamogordo, NM, 88310-6921. Phone: (505) 437-1919. E-mail: kvba@kvbatv.com William J. Oechsner Jr., gen mgr & pres.

TV-CATV only.

Bcst of Christian, loc TV, sports & public interest TV.

Vuolo Video Air-Chex, Box 880, Novi, MI, 48376. Phone: (248) 926-1234. E-mail: artvuolo@aol.com Web Site:www.vuolovideo.com Arthur Vuolo, Jr., producer.

Radio Only.

Video air checks of American radio stns & An Inside Look.

Vyvx, One Technology Center, Tulsa, OK, 74103. Phone: (800) 364-0807. Fax: (918) 547-2989. Web Site:www.vyvx.com Derek Smith, VP/gen mgr.

TV-CATV only.

Distributor of TV comls/traf via satellite by remote VTR control to 600 stns; radio coml distribution; production, postproduction. Multi-format duplication.

W

WKMG Productions, 4466 N. John Young Pkwy., Orlando, FL, 32804. Phone: (407) 291-6000. Fax: (407) 521-1204. Web Site:www.local6.com Skip Valet, gen mgr; Laura Genette, business mgr.

TV-CATV only.

TV program, coml, promotional film production; production svcs, post production & field production. WKMG production resources primarily dedicated to stn use.

WCTD AM 1620, 244 Post Rd., Westerly, RI, 02891. Phone: (401) 322-1743. Phone: (401) 322-9091. Fax: (401) 322-1645. Web Site:www.wblq.org/htm.wctd J.J. MacDade Nunez, gen mgr; Chris DiPaola, pres.

Radio Only.

Traveler information.

WFMT Radio Network, 5400 N. St. Louis Ave., Chicago, IL, 60625. Phone: (773) 279-2112. Phone: (773) 279-2114. Fax: (773) 279-2119. Web Site:www.wfmt.com Steve Robinson, sr VP.

Radio Only.

Produces wkly series including Chicago Symphony Orchestra & the New York Philharmonic This Week for coml & pub stns. Broad range of symphonic, opera & class music documentary progmg, jazz & folk music, including exclusive features from BBC & Radio Deutsche Welle, Germany.

WMAQ-TV, NBC Tower, 454 N. Columbus Dr., Chicago, IL, 60611-5555. Phone: (312) 836-5555. Fax: (312) 527-4290. Web Site:www.nbcchicago.com Larry Wert, pres/gen mgr; Patricia Golden, VP sls.

TV-CATV only.

TV program production & production svcs.

WNN Health and Wealth Motivation, 6699 N. Federal Hwy., Boca Raton, FL, 33487. Phone: (561) 997-0074. Fax: (561) 997-0476. Web Site:www.wnnhealthtalkradio.com Robert Morency, VP/gen mgr.

Radio Only.

Worldwide 24-hour format of motivational speakers & self-help info.

The WPA Film Library, 16101 S. 108th Ave., Orland Park, IL, 60467. Phone: (708) 460-0555. Fax: (708) 460-0187. E-mail: sales@wpafilmlibrary.com Web Site:www.wpafilmlibrary.com Diane Paradiso, sls.

TV-CATV only.

One of the largest stock footage libraries in the U.S. WPA offers holdings in newsreels, music, pop culture & stock shots.

WQED Multimedia, (The Metropolitan Pittsburgh Public Broadcasting Station). 4802 5th Ave., Pittsburgh, PA, 15213. Phone: (412) 622-1300. Fax: (412) 622-6413. E-mail: info@wqed.org Web Site:www.wqed.org George Miles, pres/CEO; Steven Reubi, controller, treas; Rosemary Martinelli, exec dir; Deborah Acklin, VP/gen mgr; Patricia Walker, VP finance; Susan Johnson Radlo, exec dir; Lilli Mosco, dev VP.

TV-CATV-Radio.

TV & radio program/production, distribution; production svcs & web, publishing.

WQXR, 122 5th Ave., 3rd Fl., New York, NY, 10011. Phone: (212) 633-7600. Fax: (212) 633-7666. E-mail: listener.mail@wqxr.com Web Site:www.wqxr.com Lee Cowan, VP sls; Thomas Bartunek, gen mgr; Margaret Mercer, progmg dir.

Radio Only.

Radio program production. The classical Radio Station of the New York Times.

WTOB—Community/Government Access TV, (formerly WTOB Channel 2—Public/Government Access TV). 300 S. Main St., Blacksburg, VA, 24062. Phone: (540) 961-1199. Fax: (540) 961-1875. E-mail: wtob@blacksburg.gov Web Site:www.blacksburg.gov Carlton Herman, stn mgr.

TV-CATV only.

Public interest video, live Town Council & Planning Commission meeting, live & archived streaming video.

WWE Entertainment Inc., Titan Tower, 1241 E. Main St., Stamford, CT, 06902. Phone: (203) 352-8600. Fax: (203) 352-8699. Web Site:www.wwe.com Vincent K. McMahon, chmn; Linda E. McMahon, CEO; James Rothschild, sr VP; Phil Livingston, CFO.

TV-CATV-Radio.

Exclusive worldwide distributor of WWF events, TV programs (bcst network/syndication, PPV & basic cable) & other sports/entertainment properties.

Wade Productions Inc., 493 High Cliffe Ln., Tarrytown, NY, 10591. Phone: (212) 286-9111. E-mail: wade@1cj@aol.com Carolyn J. Wade, pres.

TV-CATV only.

Meetings, video, entertainment, staging & teleconferencing for corporations & assns.

Warner Bros. International Distribution Inc. (Canada), 5000 Yonge St., Suite 1503, Toronto, ON, M2N 6P1. Canada. Phone: (416) 250-8384. Fax: (416) 250-8598. Web Site:www.wbitv.com Mickie Steinmann, VP/gen mgr; Leslie Hibbins, exec dir, prom/publ.

TV-CATV only.

TV progm distribution & promotions for Canada.

Warner Bros. Animation, 411 N. Hollywood Way, Burbank, CA, 91505. Phone: (818) 977-8700. Fax: (818) 382-6056. Web Site:www.warnerbros.com Sam Register, pres; Howard Schwartz, VP production.

TV-CATV only.

Dev & produces animated progmg for TV, video & other media.

Warner Bros. Domestic Television Distribution, 4000 Warner Blvd., Burbank, CA, 91522. Phone: (818) 954-5877. Fax: (818) 954-5820. Web Site:www.warnerbros.com Ken Warner, pres.

Print Department Burbank: Bud Rowe, foreign TV print administrator. (818) 954-3731. TV program syndication.

Warner Bros. International Television, 4000 Warner Blvd., Burbank, CA, 91522. Phone: (818) 954-6000. Fax: (818) 954-4040. Jeffrey R. Schlesinger, pres; Mauro Sardi, sls VP; Josh Berger, pres , mgng dir UK; David Camp, VP finance; Lisa Gregorian, VP; Ron Miele, VP; John Whitesell, VP; Susan Kroll, pres mktg; Malcolm Dudley-Smith, exec VP; Marsha Armstrong, VP; Monica Dodi, VP; Sal LoCurto, VP mktg; Kelley Nichols, VP; Robert Nitkin, VP; Matthew Robinson, VP.

Acapulco 37. Warner Bros. (Mexico) S.A., Colonea Codesa. Phone:

London. Warner Bros. International TV, 135 Wardour St. Phone:

Madrid. Warner Bros. International TV, Arturo Soria, 336 1. Phone:

Minato-ku, Tokyo. Time Warner Entertainment Japan, 1-2-4 Hamamatsu-cho. Phone:

North Sydney. Warner Bros. PTY. Ltd., 8-20 Napier St. Phone:

Paris. Warner Bros. International TV, 67 Avenue Dewagram. Phone:

Rome. Warner Bros. Italia S.R.L., Via Giuseppe Avezzana, 51. Phone:

North YorkON Canada. Warner Bros. International TV, 4576 Yonge St, 2nd Fl. Phone:

TV program production & distribution.

Warner Bros. Television, (Formerly Warner Bros.). Bldg. 140, 300 Television Plaza, Burbank, CA, 91505. Phone: (818) 954-7500. Fax: (818) 954-7322. Bruce Rosenblum, pres.

TV-CATV only.

TV program production & distribution.

Warner Bros. Television Production, 4000 Warner Blvd., Burbank, CA, 91522. Phone: (818) 954-6000. Fax: (818) 954-7048. Web Site:www.warnerbros.com Greg Maday, sr VP movies & mini-series; Mary Buck, sr VP talent & casting; Steve Pearlman, sr VP current programs; Robert Rosenbaum, sr VP net prodction; David Sacks, sr VP current progmg; Paul Stager, sr VP studio gen counsel; Julie Waxman, sr VP business affrs.

TV-CATV only.

TV program production & distribution.

Warren Only Media Group, Box 2372, Times Square Station, New York, NY, 10036. Phone: (856) 507-9368. Fax: (856) 507-9368.E-mail: warrenonly@90.com Web Site:www.warrenonly.com

TV-CATV only.

Satellite program distribution, syndication, playout, back hauling, film & video production.

Washington Korean Broadcasting Co., 7004 - K Little River Tpke., Annandale, VA, 22003. Phone: (703) 354-4900. Fax: (703) 658-1500.E-mail: wkbcwashington@yahoo.com Yong Chan Pak, pres.

Radio Only.

All ethnic radio progmg offered in Korean language featuring news, music, drama & talk show.

Wawatay Native Communication Society, Box 1180, 16 Fifth Ave., Sioux Lookout, ON, P8T 1B7. Canada. Phone: (807) 737-2951. Fax: (807) 737-3224. Web Site:www.wawataynews.ca Mike Metatawabin, pres; Christine Chisel, exec dir.

TV-CATV only.

Radio & TV (Cree, Ojibway & English) net, bilingual nwspr, aboriginal language translations, multi-track audio recording.

Wax Music, Sound Design & Mix, 18 W. 21st St., 10th Fl., New York, NY, 10010-6903. Phone: (212) 989-9292. Fax: (212) 989-5195.E-mail: chris@waxnyc.com Web Site:www.waxnyc.com James Wolcott, composer/sound designer; Chris Arbisi, chief engr.

TV-CATV-Radio.

Original music, sound design & mixing for all media. Three digital studios.

We the People to BNK Kids, 41 Madison Ave., New York, NY, 10010. Phone: (212) 213-2700. Fax: (212) 685-8332. Web Site:www.amazin.com

TV-CATV only.

Entertainment & media company specializing in the youth market. Hqtrs in New York & offices in Chicago, Los Angeles & Paris, France.

"The Weather Center", (a broadcast service of Aviation Weather Inc.). 701 Gervais St., Suite 224, Columbia, SC, 29201. Phone: (803) 422-4823.E-mail: wxcenter@aviationweatherinc.com Web Site:www.aviationweatherinc.com Liam Richard Ferguson, pres.

TV-CATV only.

"Regional Radio Broadcast/Weathercast Network" across the Carolinas & Georgia in over 20 bcst markets. Weather forecasting, site-specific bcst svc for stns all across America. 100% barter.

WeatherVision Inc., 916 Foley St., Jackson, MS, 39202-3406. Phone: (601) 948-7018. Phone: (800) 353-9177. Fax: (601) 948-6052.E-mail: edward@weathervision.com Web Site:www.weathervision.com Edward Saint-Pe', pres; Jason McCleaver, VP.

TV-CATV only.

Customized, localized TV weathercasts with or without meteorologists. Barter/cash via Ku-band satellite. Complete studio teleport for use by news media on site. Avid editing available on site. Serves radio, TV & 3-D branding animation svcs.

Alan Weiss Productions, 355 W. 52nd St., 3rd Fl., New York, NY, 10019. Phone: (212) 974-0606. Fax: (212) 974-0976.E-mail: myacoub@awptv.com Web Site:www.awptv.com Alan J. Weiss, pres; Tania Wilk, VP.

TV-CATV-Radio.

Fourteen Emmys for video production. We handle any broadcast, PR or corporate from concept to distribution.

Wellspring, (formerly Fox Lorber Associates, Inc.). 419 Park Ave. S., 20th Fl., New York, NY, 10016. Phone: (212) 686-6777. Fax: (212) 685-2625. Web Site:www.wellspring.com

TV-CATV only.

Worldwide distributors of film & video properties for home video, standard & non-standard TV.

Welwood International Film Production, 160 Washington S.E., Suite 138, Albuquerque, NM, 87108-2731. Phone: (505) 265-1899.E-mail: welwoodint@aol.com Bill Swortwood, pres/creative dir; Barbara Ferrel, VP/CEO.

TV-CATV only.

Works with consultants, rsch companies & client stns to create effective TV campaigns since 1986.

Westar Music, 105 W. Beaver Creek Rd., Suite 5, Richmond Hill, ON, L4B 1C6. Canada. Phone: (905) 886-3100. Fax: (905) 886-6800.E-mail: info@westarmusic.com Web Site:www.westarmusic.com Brian Nimens, pres/CEO.

TV-CATV-Radio.

High caliber production music in a wide var of categories for bcst, cable, film, corporate video & multimedia applications.

Western International Syndication, 12100 Wilshire Blvd., Suite 150, Los Angeles, CA, 90025. Phone: (310) 820-8485. Fax: (310) 820-8376. Web Site:www.wistelevision.com E-mail: info@wistelevision.com Chris Lancey, pres/CEO; Danielle Valdivia, rsch dir.

TV-CATV only.

Distributes wkly & special progmg nationwide as well as internationally.

Westwood One, Radio New Services. 40 W. 57th St., 5th Fl., New York, NY, 10019. Phone: (212) 641-2000. Fax: (212) 641-2185. Web Site:www.westwoodone.com Rod Sherwood; Steven Kalin, COO Metro; Gary Schonfeld, pres net division.

Radio Only.

Producer & distributor of radio progmg including CNN, NBC, Mutual, CNBC Business Radio, 24-hours music formats, long-short-form talk, music & news programs.

White Rabbit Productions, 1587 S. Main St., Salt Lake City, UT, 84115. Phone: (800) 549-3115. Phone: (801) 463-9292. Fax: (801) 463-7226.E-mail: info@whiterabbitproductions.com Web Site:www.whiterabbitproductions.com Sam Prigg, pres/dir photography.

TV-CATV only.

Complete film & video production svcs; two Ikegami HL-V55 Beta Sp camera packages, digital video point-of-view cam, non-linear editing.

Wide Eye Productions, Inc., 686 N. 9th, Boise, ID, 83702. Phone: (208) 336-0391. Fax: (208) 336-6644.E-mail: info@wideeye.tv Web Site:www.wideeye.tv Tom Hadzor, dir; Jennifer Isenhart, producer.

TV-CATV only.

Full-service bcst & industrial video production. ENG/EFP. High definition & Sony B-600.

Daniel Wilson Productions Inc., 300 W. 55th St., Suite 8V, New York, NY, 10019. Phone: (212) 765-7148. Fax: (212) 765-7916.E-mail: wilprod@verizon.net Daniel Wilson, pres.

TV & theatrical film production & distribution.

Witt/Thomas Productions, 11901 Santa Monica Blvd., Suite 596, W. Los Angeles, CA, 90025. Phone: (310) 472-6004. Fax: (310) 476-5015. Paul Junger Witt; Tony Thomas, partner; Susan Harris, partner.

TV-CATV only.

TV & film production company.

Robert Wold Co., 88 Three Vines Ct., Ladera Ranch, CA, 92694. Phone: (949) 363-0993.E-mail: robertnwold@cox.net Robert N. Wold, owner.

TV-CATV only.

Special-interest & entertainment progmg for bcst & cable TV. Production, mktg & distribution of syndicated programs.

Fred Wolf Films, 4222 W. Burbank Blvd., Burbank, CA, 91505. Phone: (818) 846-0611. Fax: (818) 846-0979.E-mail: administration@fredwolffilms.com Web Site:www.fredwolffilms.com Fred Wolf, pres.

TV-CATV only.

TV program production & distribution.

Work Edit, 270 W. 39th St., 11th Floor, New York, NY, 10018. Phone: (212) 719-4577. Fax: (212) 719-4380. Web Site:www.workedit.com Dalton Helms, owner; Ken Sackheim, owner.

TV-CATV only.

Post production svcs & DVD authoring.

World Events Productions Ltd., One Memorial Dr., St. Louis, MO, 63102. Phone: (314) 345-1000. Fax: (314) 345-1091.E-mail: wep@wep.com Web Site:www.wep.com Edward J. Koplar, pres; Tiffany Ilardi, mngng dir.

TV-CATV only.

TV program production & distribution.

World Radio Network, Box 1212, London, SW8 2ZF. United Kingdom. Phone: 44-20-7896-9000. Fax: 44-20-7896-9007.E-mail: contactus@wrn.org Web Site:www.wrn.org Karl Miosga, chmn; Jeff Cohen, dev dir; Tim Ashburner, tech dir.

TV-CATV-Radio.

World Radio Network (via Galaxy 25) news & features ch, comprising live progmg segments in English & languages from more than 20 international bcstrs. WRN can also supply many customized progmg feeds to radio stns as well as progmg distribution, satellite uplink & internet streaming.

Worldview Entertainment Inc., The Killiam Collection. 145 W. 55th St., Suite 7-D, New York, NY, 10019. Phone: (212) 582-6997. Fax: (212) 925-2314.E-mail: birnhardt@aol.com Sandra J. Birnhak, CEO; Glenn E. Shealey, pres.

TV-CATV only.

Archival stock footage library, distribution to international bcstrs.

Worldvision NY, 143 W. 29th St., New York, NY, 10001. Phone: (212) 736-2997. Fax: (212) 736-9755. Web Site:www.worldvision.org John Claus, exec dir.

London, Worldvision Enterprises U.K. Ltd, 54 Pont St. Phone:

Paris, Worldvision Enterprises S.A.R.L, 28, Rue Bayard. Phone:

Rio de Janeiro, 22270 Rua Voluntarios Da Patria N, Gr.604. Phone:

Rome, Adalia Anstalt, Via del Corso, 22/Int 10. Phone:

Sydney, Milsons Point. Worldvision Enterprises of Australia PTY Ltd., 5-13 Northcliff St. Phone:

Tokyo, Tsukiji Hamarikyu Bldg, 7th Fl, 5-3-3 Tsukiji, Chou-ku. Phone:

TorontoON Canada, Worldvision Enterprises of Canada, 1200 Bay St, Suite 802. Phone:

Los AngelesCA, 5700 Wilshire Blvd, 5th Fl. Phone:

Coconut GroveFL. Tele-UNO, Grand Bay Plaza, 2665 S. Bayshore Dr. Phone:

AtlantaGA. Worldvision Enterprises Inc. Latin America, 400 Perimeter Ctr. Terr, Suite 185. Phone:

AtlantaGA, 400 Perimeter Center Terr, Suite 150. Phone:

ChicagoIL, 515 N. State St, Suite 2305. Phone:

New YorkNY, 1700 Broadway. Phone:

TV-CATV only.

TV program distribution for ind productions.

The Worship Network, 28059 U.S. Hwy. 19 N., Suite 300, Clearwater, FL, 33761. Phone: (727) 536-0036. Fax: (727) 530-0671.E-mail: ken@worship.net Web Site:www.worship.net Bruce Koblish, pres/CEO; Bob Shreffler, VP finance; Tim Brown, VP.

TV-CATV only.

Inspirational music set to nature scenes, overlaid with scripture 24 hours a day. Progmg is interspersed with short devotional teachings.

Larry John Wright Inc., 231 N. Alma School Rd., Mesa, AZ, 85201. Phone: (480) 833-8111. Fax: (480) 969-2895.E-mail: jessica@ljohnw.com Web Site:www.larryjohnwright.com Larry F. John, CEO; John N. Wright, pres.

TV-CATV only.

Own & operate production studios; produce film & video comls, radio comls & jingles, TV shows & industrial videos.

The Wyland Group, 101 W. Cochran St., Simi Valley, CA, 93065. Phone: (805) 955-7680. Fax: (805) 522-1082. Web Site:www.lifestyle.org Chauncey Smith, account exec; Linda Walter, dir.

TV-CATV only.

Production of health related, family values progmg.

X

XL Media Solutions, 110 N. Ditmar St., Oceanside, CA, 92054. Phone: (760) 722-8284. Fax: (888) 722-8234.E-mail: staff@exxelaudio.com Web Site:www.exxelaudio.com William Kottcamp, mgr.

Radio Only.

Radio program, coml production & distribution.

Y

Yada/Levine Video Productions, 1253 Vine St., Suite 21A, Los Angeles, CA, 90038. Phone: (323) 461-1616. Fax: (323) 461-2288.E-mail: video@yadalevine.com Web Site:www.yadalevine.com Michael Yada, pres.

TV-CATV-Radio.

Full-service video productions. Crews & equipment including HD, DV & Betacam SP.

Yale Video Inc., 2441 W. La Palma Ave., Suite 530, Anaheim, CA, 92801. Phone: (714) 693-5300. Fax: (714) 693-5395. E-mail: burty@webcastingtv.com Web Site:www.webcastingtv.com Burton A. Yale, CEO.

Offers the latest in editing technology; from D-2 to Hi8.

Yorkshire Television, (A division of Granada Media Group). Television Centre, 104 Kirkstall Rd., Leeds, LS3 IJS. United Kingdom. Phone: 0113-243-8283. Fax: 0113-244-5107.E-mail: communications@granadamedia.com Web Site:www.granada.co.uk David M.B. Croft; Charles Allen CBE, chmn.

TV-CATV only.

Independent TV program maker & bcstr.

Z

ZBS Foundation, 174 N. River Rd., Fort Edward, NY, 12828. Phone: (518) 695-6406. Fax: (518) 695-4041.E-mail: info@zbs.org Web Site:www.zbs.org Thomas Lopez, pres.

Radio Only.

Producer of audio drama.

Zachry Associates, 500 Chestnut, Suite 2000, Abilene, TX, 79602. Phone: (325) 677-1342. Fax: (325) 672-2001. H.C. Zachry, pres.

TV-CATV only.

Produces & distributes TV & radio programs & comls as well as promotional films & production svcs.

Zenith Media Services, (Formerly Venice Media Services). 299 W. Houston, 10th Fl., New York, NY, 10014-3620. Phone: (212) 859-5100. Fax: (212) 727-9495. Web Site:www.zenithoptimedia.com Peggy Green, pres & natl bcstg Zenith U.S.

TV-CATV only.

TV program distribution.

Sandy Zimmerman Productions, 4800 Black Bear Rd., Suite 204, Las Vegas, NV, 89149. Phone: (702) 731-6491.E-mail: sandyzimm@go.com Sandy Zimmerman, producer & owner; Robert Gonzales, production mgr.

TV-CATV only.

Develops, produces & distributes TV programs, documentaries, infomercials, travel specials, TV comls, & industrial & corporate videos. Syndicates one- to five-minute program fillers.

Producers, Distributors, Production and Other Services Subject Index

3-D Films

Bardel Entertainment Inc.
Blue Sky Studios
Dimension 3 Corp
WeatherVision Inc.

3-D TV Systems

Dimension 3 Corp
Pro Video

Agricultural Programming, Radio

Agrinet News Network
American Farm Bureau Inc.
Clear Channel Broadcasting Inc.
Leadem to Water Production Inc.
Montgomery Community Television Inc.
North Shore Productions
Tribune Radio Networks

Animation

Angel Films Co.
The Kay Arnold Group
Blue Sky Studios
Buzzco Associates Inc.
Central Park Media Corp.
CineGroupe Corporation
Cinema Concepts Animation Studio
Classic Media
Clayton-Davis & Associates Inc.
Cookie Jar Group
Cramer
Crawford Communications
Dargaud-Marina
Walt Disney Company
Enoki Films U.S.A. Inc.
Film House Inc.
4 Kids Entertainment (Sub 4 Kids Entertainment)
Hearst Entertainment, Inc.
Italtoons Corp.
JC Productions Inc.
John Lemmon Films
Magno Sound & Video
Mar Vista Entertainment
Maslow Media Group Inc.
Maximum Marketing Services Inc.
The Media Group of Connecticut Inc.
Bill Melendez Productions Inc.
Mondo TV
North by Northwest Productions
Northwest Imaging & FX
PPM Multimedia
Pantomime Pictures Inc.
Pike Productions Inc.
Playhouse Pictures
PorchLight Entertainment Inc.
PostWorks, New York
The Program Exchange
Rampion Visual Productions L.L.C.
Romano & Associates Inc.
Edward Sarson Productions
Silverline Entertainment
Southern STAR
Sunbow Entertainment
Two Oceans Entertainment Group
Videographic West
Warner Bros. Animation
WeatherVision Inc.
Fred Wolf Films
World Events Productions Ltd.

Audio Production

Alliance for Christian Media/Day1
American TelNet
Armedia Communications
Broadcast News Service
Broadcast Studio Inc.
CA Media Development
C N R Radio
CRN International
Clayton-Davis & Associates Inc.
Command Productions

Continental Recordings Inc.
Creative Marketing & Communications Corp.
Jeff Davis Productions Inc.
DaviSound
Digital Force
John Driscoll/VoiceOver America
Ecumenical Communications
Finger Lakes Productions International
GMI Media L.L.C.
Good Life Associates
Good News Broadcasting Association Inc.
Heil Enterprises
Horizon Audio Creations
Host Communications Inc.
Irving Productions Inc.
J.N. Productions
The Johnson Group
David Kaye Productions Inc.
Lion and Fox Recording Studios
MVI Post
Man From Mars Productions
Ben Manilla Productions
William Mauldin Productions Inc.
MediaTracks Inc.
Metro Networks
MotorNet
N W Media
National Public Radio
New Art Miami
New Dimensions Radio
No Soap Productions
North American Network, Inc.
North Star Music
Dick Orkin's Amazing Radio
Paulist Media Works
Perception Media Group
Presbyterian News Services
Radio Spirits
Rockwell Audio Media
Shield Productions Inc.
Smith/Lee Productions, Inc.
Sound of Birmingham Productions
Soundshop Recording Studio LLC
Soundtrack
Studio Center Corp.
Studio M Productions Unlimited
Suite Audio
TR Productions
Talco Productions
Technisonic Studios
Thompson Creative
University of Colorado Television
University of Detroit Mercy
University of Kentucky Public Relations & Radio-TV
    News Bureau
WQXR
ZBS Foundation

Audio Production Library

American TelNet
Blue Heaven Productions
Clayton-Davis & Associates Inc.
Ghostwriters/Radio Mall
Groove Addicts Production Music Catalog
J&H Music Programming
OGM Production Music
Radio America
Sound Ideas
TM Studios

Audio Recording Services

Alliance for Christian Media/Day1
American TelNet
The Audio Department Inc.
Bruder Releasing Inc. (BRI)
C 2 Productions Inc.
Command Productions
Continental Recordings Inc.
Jeff Davis Productions Inc.
John Driscoll/VoiceOver America
Henninger Media Services, Inc.
Horizon Audio Creations
The Image Generators
Irving Productions Inc.
Tom Jones Recording Studios

Lion and Fox Recording Studios
MVI Post
Matchframe Video
Media Access Group at WGBH
Metro Networks
MotorNet
New Dimensions Radio
No Soap Productions
Omnimusic
Paulist Media Works
Radio Production Services Inc.
Radio Spirits
Reizner & Reizner Film & Video
Rex Post
Sound of Birmingham Productions
Soundshop Recording Studio LLC
Studio Center Corp.
Studio M Productions Unlimited
Suite Audio
UBC Radio
WQXR
Washington Korean Broadcasting Co.

Audio/Visual Services

American TelNet
CABLEready Corp.
Capital Communications
Coote Communications
DG Systems
GPN Inc & Destination Education Inc.
Host Communications Inc.
Kipany Productions Ltd.
Maslow Media Group Inc.
Modern Sound Pictures Inc.
Reliance Audio Visual Corp.
TR Productions
Talco Productions
Videosmith Inc.
Wade Productions Inc.

Background Music

American TelNet
FirstCom Music
Groove Addicts Production Music Catalog
Horizon Audio Creations
Joe Jones Productions
Message on Hold
Muzak
OGM Production Music
Omnimusic
Promusic
RPM-Radio Programming & Management Inc.
Sound Ideas
Westar Music

Camera Operators

J. Arnold Productions
Asia Pacific Productions USA, Ltd.
Bell Foto Art Productions
CamMate Studios
D-V-X International
Daley Video
FTC/Orlando
Maslow Media Group Inc.
PACSAT
PMTV Producers Management Television
Reizner & Reizner Film & Video
Tankersley Productions, Inc., St. Louis
Telepros
Videosmith Inc.
WKMG Productions
WTOB—Community/Government Access TV
White Rabbit Productions
Yada/Levine Video Productions

Cassette Duplicating

Man From Mars Productions
N W Media
Paulist Media Works
The Transfer Zone

CD Production Library

Toby Arnold and Associates Inc.
Broadcast Programming
Bruder Releasing Inc. (BRI)
FirstCom Music
GMI Media L.L.C.
Ghostwriters/Radio Mall
Groove Addicts Production Music Catalog
J&H Music Programming
Metro Music Productions Inc.
OGM Production Music
Primedia Workplace Learning
Production Garden Music Libraries
Promusic
SoperSound Music Library
Sound Ideas
Westar Music

Children's Programming, Radio

The Walt Disney Company
FamilyNet Radio
Miller Broadcast Management
Moody Broadcasting Network
National Church Broadcasting
Prairie Dog Entertainment
StarDate/Universo Productions

Children's Programming, Radio & TV

Christian Children's Associates Inc.
The Dolmatch Group Ltd.
Eyewitness Kids News, LLC
Larry Harmon Pictures Corp.
MGC The Multimedia Group of Canada
Media Access Group at WGBH
Bill Melendez Productions Inc.
Presson Perspectives
SCOLA
Warren Only Media Group
The Worship Network

Children's Programming, TV

Academy Entertainment
Aegis People Support Transcription and Captioning
The Kay Arnold Group
Bardel Entertainment Inc.
Broadcast Studio Inc.
Burrud Productions Inc.
Buzzco Associates Inc.
Capital Communications
Central Park Media Corp.
Children's Media Productions
Chrysalis Distribution
The Dick Clark Productions
Classic Media
Concept Videos
Cookie Jar Group
Crystal Pictures Inc.
DLT Entertainment Ltd.
Disney Channel
Walt Disney Company
The Walt Disney Company
Dorling Kindersley Vision
Ellis Entertainment
Enoki Films U.S.A. Inc.
Eurocine
Evangelical Lutheran Church in America
Filmoption International Inc.
4 Kids Entertainment (Sub 4 Kids Entertainment)
Sandy Frank Entertainment Inc.
GPN Inc & Destination Education Inc.
Glenray Productions Inc.
Great North Productions
Alfred Haber Distribution Inc.
Larry Harmon Pictures Corp.
Hearst Entertainment, Inc.
International Television Corp.
Juravic Entertainment
Litton Entertainment
MGM TV Canada
Mar Vista Entertainment
Maryland Public Television
Bill Melendez Productions Inc.
Mondo TV
New Zoo Revue
O. Atlas Enterprises Inc.
Oasis International
Pantomime Pictures Inc.

Pied Piper Films Ltd.
PorchLight Entertainment Inc.
PostWorks, New York
Producers Group, Ltd.
Productions La Fete
The Program Exchange
Promark Television
PETER RODGERS ORGANIZATION
Steve Rotfeld Productions Inc.
Sanctuary Records Group Ltd.
Edward Sarson Productions
M C Stuart & Associates Pty Ltd.
Sunbow Entertainment
Television Representatives Inc.
The Television Syndication Company, Inc.
Triage Entertainment Inc.
Two Oceans Entertainment Group
Venevision International
Viacom Inc.
VIEW Video Inc.
WQED Multimedia
Warner Bros. Animation
Alan Weiss Productions
Western International Syndication
Daniel Wilson Productions Inc.
Fred Wolf Films
World Events Productions Ltd.
Yorkshire Television

Commercial Distribution, Radio

Campbell-Ewald Advertising
KTOO-TV & Radio Station
Makedwde Publishing
Metro Networks
MotorNet
Dick Orkin's Amazing Radio
Radio America
Washington Korean Broadcasting Co.

Commercial Distribution, Radio & TV

The Chuck Blore Co.
Celebrities Productions
DG Systems
Evergreen Entertainment Group
International Television Broadcasting Inc.
MVI Post
Robert Michelson Inc.
RDF Media

Commercial Distribution, TV

ADM—International Film & TV Distribution
ATA Trading Corp.
Academy Entertainment
The Kay Arnold Group
Broadview Media
CBS Worldwide Distribution
CFP Video Productions
Campbell-Ewald Advertising
Capital Communications
Carlton International Media Inc.
Central Park Media Corp.
Duke International
EUE Screen Gems Studios
David Finch Distribution Ltd.
Sandy Frank Entertainment Inc.
GLL TV Enterprises Inc.
Global Entertainment Media
Great Chefs Television/Publishing
International Tele-Film
Knowledge In A Nutshell Inc.
Makedwde Publishing
Midwest Video Communications Inc.
Oasis International
PPM Multimedia
ROZON/Just For Laughs
SFP Productions
Harvey Sheldon Productions
Sport International Inc.
Video-Cinema Films Inc.
Yorkshire Television

Commercial Production, Radio

Toby Arnold and Associates Inc.
The Audio Department Inc.
CRN International
Campbell-Ewald Advertising
Carleton Productions International Inc.

Citadel Media
Command Productions
Thomas Craven Film Corp.
Creative Marketing & Communications Corp.
DaviSound
Happi Associates
Heil Enterprises
The Image Generators
Irving Productions Inc.
J.N. Productions
Joe Jones Productions
Tom Jones Recording Studios
Makedwde Publishing
Man From Mars Productions
William Mauldin Productions Inc.
Robert Michelson Inc.
Perception Media Group
Radio Production Services Inc.
Suite Audio
Time Capsule, Inc.
UBC Radio
Washington Korean Broadcasting Co.
Larry John Wright Inc.

Commercial Production, Radio & TV

Aloha Productions
Robert L. Bocchino
CA Media Development
Celebrities Productions
Clayton-Davis & Associates Inc.
Continental Recordings Inc.
Coote Communications
Cramer
John Driscoll/VoiceOver America
International Television Broadcasting Inc.
JAM Creative Productions Inc.
The Johnson Group
KUSA Television
MVI Post
McClain Enterprises Inc.
Bill Melendez Productions Inc.
No Soap Productions
North by Northwest Productions
RDF Media
RMD & Assoc. Inc.
Radio & TV Roundup Productions
Rex Post
Romano & Associates Inc.
Sam Shad Productions
Shield Productions Inc.
Sound of Birmingham Productions
Strand Media Group Inc.
Studio Center Corp.
TM Studios
TR Productions
Video/Media Distribution Inc.
Vyvx

Commercial Production, TV

Agora TV
J. Arnold Productions
The Kay Arnold Group
Asia Pacific Productions USA, Ltd.
The Audio Department Inc.
Bardel Entertainment Inc.
Bell Foto Art Productions
Brillig Productions Inc.
Buzzco Associates Inc.
CMT
Campbell-Ewald Advertising
Carleton Productions International Inc.
Center City Film & Video
Thomas Craven Film Corp.
Custom Productions Inc.
Daley Video
Encore Video Productions Inc.
Eyewitness Kids News, LLC
Film House Inc.
Fox 17 Studio Productions
Fox 29 WUTV Sinclair
Sandy Frank Entertainment Inc.
Golden Gate Studios
The Image Generators
JC Productions Inc.
Jordan Klein Film & Video
The Kenwood Group
Lapco Communications
MRC Films
Makedwde Publishing
Mason Video
Maysles Films, Inc.
McClain Enterprises Inc.

Midwest Video Communications Inc.
Warren Miller Entertainment
Mobile Video Services Ltd.
Pantomime Pictures Inc.
Peckham Productions
Pied Piper Films Ltd.
Playhouse Pictures
Prime Cut Productions Inc.
Primo Newservice Inc.
Producers Group, Ltd.
Reuters Television
River City Video Productions
Rosler Creative
ROZON/Just For Laughs
Sanctuary Records Group Ltd.
Sport International Inc.
Sullivan Video Services Inc.
Technisonic Studios
Triage Entertainment Inc.
Video Enterprises Inc.
Video Techniques Inc.
Videosmith Inc.
WKMG Productions
Warner Bros. Animation
Welwood International Film Production
White Rabbit Productions
Fred Wolf Films
Larry John Wright Inc.
Yada/Levine Video Productions

Computer Graphics

CA Media Development
Center City Film & Video
CineGroupe Corporation
Crest National Digital Media Complex
Daley Video
Darino Films/Library of Special Effects
Educational Technologies Network (ETN)
Film House Inc.
Henninger Media Services, Inc.
The History Makers
JC Productions Inc.
Kipany Productions Ltd.
Magno Sound & Video
Warren Miller Entertainment
Northwest Imaging & FX
PACSAT
Palace Digital Studios
Pike Productions Inc.
Playhouse Pictures
PostWorks, New York
RMD & Assoc. Inc.
Rampion Visual Productions L.L.C.
Rex Post
Traffic Pulse Networks (A Unit of Mobility
    Technologies)
VA-Tech Video/Broadcast Services

Creative Services

Aloha Productions
American TelNet
Ascent Media Network
Bayliss
The Chuck Blore Co.
Campbell-Ewald Advertising
Center City Film & Video
Cimarron Group
ComBridges
DWJ Television
Jeff Davis Productions Inc.
Devlin Design Group Inc.
ESPI Video
Educational Technologies Network (ETN)
Faraone Communications Inc.
Film House Inc.
First Marketing
Fox 29 WUTV Sinclair
JC Productions Inc.
The Johnson Group
The Kenwood Group
Kipany Productions Ltd.
Klein &
MVI Post
Make It Happen Productions Inc.
N W Media
No Soap Productions
Oppix Productions Inc
Peters Communications
Praxis Media Inc.
RMD & Assoc. Inc.
Radioguide People Inc.
Rosler Creative

Sak Entertainment
Edward Sarson Productions
Strand Media Group Inc.
Talco Productions
TeleCom Productions Inc.
Video I-D Teleproductions Inc.
Wade Productions Inc.
Warren Only Media Group
Larry John Wright Inc.
Sandy Zimmerman Productions

Development, Films

Allumination FilmWorks, LLC
CIFEX International Inc.
Curb Entertainment International Corp.
The Walt Disney Company
The Dolmatch Group Ltd.
Faraone Communications Inc.
1st Miracle Productions
JC Productions Inc.
Lions Gate Entertainment
Make It Happen Productions Inc.
Richter Productions Inc.
Rosler Creative
Studio Babelsberg GmbH
Tamouz Media
Triage Entertainment Inc.

Development, Films, TV Series & Video

Angel Films Co.
Bardel Entertainment Inc.
Burrud Productions Inc.
CABLEready Corp.
CDR Communications Inc.
Celebrities Productions
Children's Media Productions
Clayton-Davis & Associates Inc.
ComBridges
Critical Mass Releasing Inc.
DLT Entertainment Ltd.
D-Squared Media
Devillier Donegan Enterprises L.P.
Duke International
Film Roman Inc.
Independent Edge Films
Eddie Kessler Productions Publications &
    Promotions
Make It Happen Productions Inc.
Medstar Television Inc.
Oasis International
Pied Piper Films Ltd.
Producers Group, Ltd.
Sak Entertainment
Silverline Entertainment
Two Oceans Entertainment Group
Warren Only Media Group

Development, TV Films, Series

Dave Bell Associates Inc.
The Chuck Blore Co.
Canamedia Inc.
CanLib Inc.
CineGroupe Corporation
Cookie Jar Group
Walt Disney Company
The Walt Disney Company
The Dolmatch Group Ltd.
Educational Technologies Network (ETN)
Essence Television Productions Inc.
1st Miracle Productions
Freewheelin' Films Ltd.
The Fremantle Corp.
FremantleMedia North America Inc.
Glenray Productions Inc.
The Griffin Group
Thomas Horton Associates Inc.
JC Productions Inc.
Nicole Jouve
MacNeil/Lehrer Productions
Make It Happen Productions Inc.
New Line Television
Pantomime Pictures Inc.
Planet Pictures Ltd.
Questar
Reuters Media
Richter Productions Inc.
PETER RODGERS ORGANIZATION
SPI International

Development, Video

AmericaNurse TV Productions
Clayton-Davis & Associates Inc.
ComBridges
The Walt Disney Company
The Dolmatch Group Ltd.
Educational Technologies Network (ETN)
Essence Television Productions Inc.
Glenray Productions Inc.
The Griffin Group
JC Productions Inc.
Kipany Productions Ltd.
Lions Gate Entertainment
Make It Happen Productions Inc.
Midwest Video Communications Inc.
Questar
Richter Productions Inc.
Triage Entertainment Inc.
VIEW Video Inc.

Distribution, Audio

Alden Films
DaviSound
Digital Force
Good Life Associates
Great Chefs Television/Publishing
The Image Generators
Irving Productions Inc.
North Star Music
Dick Orkin's Amazing Radio
Paulist Media Works

Distribution, Cable

ATA Trading Corp.
Academy Entertainment
The Kay Arnold Group
Bruder Releasing Inc. (BRI)
Castle Hill Productions Inc.
Central Park Media Corp.
DLT Entertainment Ltd.
The Walt Disney Company
FamilyNet
GLL TV Enterprises Inc.
Galavision
Global Telemedia Inc.
Grove Television Enterprises Inc.
HAVE Inc.
Janson Media
Kazmark Entertainment Group
Loral Skynet
Mar Vista Entertainment
Media Planning Group (MPG)
Modern Entertainment
Moonstone Entertainment
New City Releasing Inc.
O. Atlas Enterprises Inc.
Oasis International
Playboy Entertainment Group Inc.
Powersports/Paradox
Rigel Entertainment
PETER RODGERS ORGANIZATION
Harvey Sheldon Productions
Venevision International
Video-Cinema Films Inc.
Worldview Entertainment Inc.

Distribution, Cartoons

ATA Trading Corp.
Academy Entertainment
Bardel Entertainment Inc.
Central Park Media Corp.
CineGroupe Corporation
Classic Media
Dargaud-Marina
Walt Disney Company
The Dolmatch Group Ltd.
Film Roman Inc.
4 Kids Entertainment (Sub 4 Kids Entertainment)
The Fremantle Corp.
Larry Harmon Pictures Corp.

Sullivan Entertainment Inc./Sullivan Entertainment
    International
Sunbow Entertainment
Tamouz Media
Triage Entertainment Inc.
Twentieth Television
Warner Bros. Animation

Italtoons Corp.
Mondo TV
Pan American Video
World Events Productions Ltd.

Distribution, Film and Video

ADM—International Film & TV Distribution
ATA Trading Corp.
Academy Entertainment
Accuracy in Media Inc.
Alden Films
Allumination FilmWorks, LLC
Angel Films Co.
Arkadia Entertainment Corp.
Ascent Media Network
Ascent Media Network Services
CDR Communications Inc.
CIFEX International Inc.
CRM Learning
Castle Hill Productions Inc.
Children's Media Productions
Cinema Concepts Animation Studio
The Cinema Guild Inc.
Crystal Pictures Inc.
Cube International
Curb Entertainment International Corp.
Donnelly & Associates
Duke International
E1 Entertainment
Enoki Films U.S.A. Inc.
Eurocine
Filmoption International Inc.
Films Media Group
Films of the Nations
David Finch Distribution Ltd.
1st Miracle Productions
First Run/Icarus Films
Free Speech TV (FSTV)
GPN Inc & Destination Education Inc.
Glenray Productions Inc.
Global Telemedia Inc.
Grove Television Enterprises Inc.
Alfred Haber Distribution Inc.
Independent Edge Films
International Tele-Film
JGT Media Productions
Nicole Jouve
Kazmark Entertainment Group
Kultur International Films
Lions Gate Entertainment
Mar Vista Entertainment
Maryknoll Productions
Maysles Films, Inc.
Modern Entertainment
Modern Sound Pictures Inc.
Moonstone Entertainment
Myriad Pictures
New City Releasing Inc.
New Line Television
O. Atlas Enterprises Inc.
PAULAR Entertainment L.L.C.
PPM Multimedia
Pike Productions Inc.
Planet Pictures Ltd.
Playboy Entertainment Group Inc.
Producers Group, Ltd.
RMD & Assoc. Inc.
Reel Media International Inc.
Richter Productions Inc.
Rigel Entertainment
PETER RODGERS ORGANIZATION
Sanctuary Records Group Ltd.
Silverline Entertainment
Southern STAR
Marty Stouffer Productions Ltd.
M C Stuart & Associates Pty Ltd.
Television Representatives Inc.
Trident Releasing
Venevision International
Video/Media Distribution Inc.
VIEW Video Inc.
Worldview Entertainment Inc.

Distribution, Music

ADM—International Film & TV Distribution
Arkadia Entertainment Corp.
Sandra Carter Global, Inc.
Cube International
Joe Jones Productions
Kultur International Films
Loral Skynet
North Star Music

Promark Television

Distribution, Radio & TV Programming

Accuracy in Media Inc.
AmericaNurse TV Productions
Associated Television International
CBS Worldwide Distribution
CDR Communications Inc.
Christian Children's Associates Inc.
The Crime Channel
DG Systems
Evangelical Lutheran Church in America
Evergreen Entertainment Group
FamilyNet
Gordon Productions
International Television Broadcasting Inc.
Medialink
National Council of Churches Communications Unit
New Visions Syndication Inc.
News Broadcast Network
Outdoor Media Group
Prairie Dog Entertainment
RBC Ministries/Midwest Media Managers
U.S. Conference of Catholic Bishops
Warren Only Media Group
World Radio Network
The Worship Network

Distribution, Radio Programming

Agrinet News Network
Alliance for Christian Media/Day1
At a Glance
Chinamerica Hit Radio
The Classical Station, WCPE
Clear Channel Broadcasting Inc.
Country Crossroads
The Walt Disney Company
Good Life Associates
Happi Associates
It Is Written Television
J&H Music Programming
Jameson Broadcast Inc.
The Johnson Group
Knowledge In A Nutshell Inc.
Leadem to Water Production Inc.
Longhorn Radio Network
Loral Skynet
MRN Radio
Makedwde Publishing
MasterControl FamilyNet Radio
Media Planning Group (MPG)
Metro Networks
Moody Broadcasting Network
MotorNet
Musical Starstreams
National Public Radio
New Dimensions Radio
North American Network, Inc.
North Shore Productions
On Track
Ports of Paradise
Powerline
Premiere Radio Networks Inc.
RPM-Radio Programming & Management Inc.
Radio Canada International/Canadian Broadcasting Corp.
Radio Express Inc.
Radio Spirits
Ray Sports Network
Solid Gospel Network (Reach Satellite Network, Inc.)
Sound Source Networks
Sports Byline U.S.A.
Talk America Radio Networks
Talk Radio Network
UBC Radio
United Stations Radio Network
WFMT Radio Network
Washington Korean Broadcasting Co.

Distribution, TV Programming

ADM—International Film & TV Distribution
APA International Film Distributors Inc.
ATA Trading Corp.
Academy Entertainment
American Public Television
The Kay Arnold Group
Ascent Media Management East
Ascent Media Network Services

Bellon Entertainment
CABLEready Corp.
CBS Studio International
CBS Television Distribution
CBS Worldwide Distribution
CCI Entertainment Ltd.
CNBC Syndication
CS Associates
CTV Television Inc.
Cable Films & Video
Canamedia Inc.
CanLib Inc.
Carleton Productions International Inc.
Carsey-Werner Distribution
Sandra Carter Global, Inc.
Castle Hill Productions Inc.
Central Park Media Corp.
Chrysalis Distribution
Classic Media
Clever Cleaver Productions
Concept Videos
William F. Cooke Television Programs
Cookie Jar Group
The Crime Channel
Critical Mass Releasing Inc.
Cube International
DLT Entertainment Ltd.
Dargaud-Marina
Devillier Donegan Enterprises L.P.
Walt Disney Company
The Walt Disney Company
The Dolmatch Group Ltd.
Donnelly & Associates
Dorling Kindersley Vision
Duke International
E1 Entertainment
Eaton Films Ltd.
Ellis Entertainment
Europe Images International
FamilyNet
Film Roman Inc.
Filmoption International Inc.
1st Miracle Productions
First Run/Icarus Films
4 Kids Entertainment (Sub 4 Kids Entertainment)
Fox Sports West
Free Speech TV (FSTV)
The Fremantle Corp.
GRB Entertainment
Galavision
Global Entertainment Media
Global Telemedia Inc.
Granada America
Grove Television Enterprises Inc.
Alfred Haber Distribution Inc.
Harmony Gold U.S.A. Inc.
Hearst Entertainment, Inc.
Henninger Media Services, Inc.
Holigan Investment Group Ltd.
Hope Channel
Thomas Horton Associates Inc.
International Tele-Film
International Television Corp.
It Is Written Television
Italtoons Corp.
Ivanhoe Broadcast News Inc.
Janson Media
Jefferson-Pilot Sports
Nicole Jouve
Juravic Entertainment
Kazmark Entertainment Group
Knowledge In A Nutshell Inc.
Kultur International Films
Lakeside TV Co.
Lambert Television
Litton Entertainment
Loral Skynet
MGC The Multimedia Group of Canada
MGM TV Canada
MG/Perin Inc.
Makedwde Publishing
Mar Vista Entertainment
Media Planning Group (MPG)
Metro Networks
Mobile Video Services Ltd.
Modern Entertainment
Mondo TV
Moonstone Entertainment
Myriad Pictures
NRS Group PTY Ltd.
NTN Communications Inc.
National Collegiate Athletic Association (NCAA)
New Films International
O. Atlas Enterprises Inc.
PAULAR Entertainment L.L.C.

PPM Multimedia
Pan American Video
Parrot Communications International Inc.
Planet Pictures Ltd.
Playboy Entertainment Group Inc.
PorchLight Entertainment Inc.
Power Play Music Video L.L.C.
Powersports/Paradox
Promark Television
Questar
Raycom Sports
Reel Media International Inc.
Riden International Inc.
Rigel Entertainment
PETER RODGERS ORGANIZATION
Rose Entertainment
Rosnay International
Steve Rotfeld Productions Inc.
ROZON/Just For Laughs
SPI International
Harvey Sheldon Productions
Silverline Entertainment
Southern STAR
Sport International Inc.
M C Stuart & Associates Pty Ltd.
Sullivan Entertainment Inc./Sullivan Entertainment
    International
Sunbow Entertainment
Telegenic Programs Inc.
Television Representatives Inc.
Televix Entertainment Inc.
20th Century Fox/Incendo Television Distribution Ltd.
Twentieth Century Fox Television Distribution
Twentieth Television
Univision Communications Inc.
Venevision International
Viacom Inc.
Video-Cinema Films Inc.
Video/Media Distribution Inc.
Warner Bros. International Distribution Inc. (Canada)
WeatherVision Inc.
Western International Syndication
Robert Wold Co.
World Events Productions Ltd.
Worldview Entertainment Inc.
Worldvision NY

Dubbing Services

Carpel Video Inc.
D-V-X International
Digital Force
Eurocine
HAVE Inc.
KPTS-TV
Man From Mars Productions
Mondo TV
Studio Babelsberg GmbH
VTTV Videothek Electronic TV-Production GmbH +
    Co Kopier KG
Video Services

Duplication Services

Advanced Digital Services, Inc.
Ascent Media Management East
CBS Worldwide Distribution
Carleton Productions International Inc.
Carpel Video Inc.
Cinema Concepts Animation Studio
Continental Recordings Inc.
Cramer
Crest National Digital Media Complex
DG Systems
Duke International
Educational Technologies Network (ETN)
HAVE Inc.
Henninger Media Services, Inc.
Highland Laboratories
Tom Jones Recording Studios
Lion and Fox Recording Studios
MPL Media
Media Visions
NEP Studios
N W Media
New Art Miami
Parrot Communications International Inc.
Point 360
PostWorks, New York
Pro Video
Quality Film & Video
The Transfer Zone
TRI-COMM Productions
Video/Media Distribution Inc.

Video Services
Video Techniques Inc.
Vyvx
Work Edit

Editing Services

Agora TV
Ascent Media Management East
Asia Pacific Productions USA, Ltd.
Bell Foto Art Productions
CMT
CamMate Studios
Catholic Communications Corp.
Crest National Digital Media Complex
D-Squared Media
D-V-X International
DWJ Television
Duke International
Eagle Eye Film Company
Fox 29 WUTV Sinclair
Henninger Media Services, Inc.
Highland Laboratories
The History Makers
Host Communications Inc.
MVI Post
Masai Films Inc.
Matchframe Video
Warren Miller Entertainment
NAHB Production Group
NEP Studios
N W Media
New Art Miami
Northwest Imaging & FX
Oppix Productions Inc
Perception Media Group
Point 360
Pro Video
Reuters Television
River City Video Productions
Romano & Associates Inc.
Seraphim Communications Inc.
Suite Audio
Tankersley Productions, Inc., St. Louis
Technisonic Studios
The Transfer Zone
U.S. Plan B Inc.
Videographic West
Work Edit
Yada/Levine Video Productions

Educational Programming, Radio

At a Glance
Call For Action Inc.
The Classical Station, WCPE
Eagle Media Productions Ltd.
Ecumenical Communications
FamilyNet Radio
The Idea Channel
Leadem to Water Production Inc.
Longhorn Radio Network
Moody Broadcasting Network
New Dimensions Radio
North American Network, Inc.
Powerline
Prairie Dog Entertainment
Presbyterian News Services
Radio America
Radio Canada International/Canadian Broadcasting
    Corp.
StarDate/Universo Productions
WCTD AM 1620
Washington Korean Broadcasting Co.

Educational Programming, Radio & TV

Accuracy in Media Inc.
AmericaNurse TV Productions
Arkadia Entertainment Corp.
Evangelical Lutheran Church in America
Arthur Henley Productions
Joe Jones Productions
Media Access Group at WGBH
Bill Melendez Productions Inc.
Presson Perspectives
SCOLA
Charlie Spencer Productions
Ukrainian Melody Hour
VA-Tech Video/Broadcast Services
WQED Multimedia

Educational Programming, TV

Allumination FilmWorks, LLC
AmericaNurse TV Productions
Asia Pacific Productions USA, Ltd.
Bell Foto Art Productions
Bellon Entertainment
Brillig Productions Inc.
Broadview Media
Burrud Productions Inc.
Buzzco Associates Inc.
CABLEready Corp.
Cable Films & Video
Call For Action Inc.
Canamedia Inc.
Sandra Carter Global, Inc.
Catholic Television Network
Central City Productions, Inc.
Clever Cleaver Productions
The Crime Channel
Cube International
Darino Films/Library of Special Effects
Disney Channel
Educational Technologies Network (ETN)
Enoki Films U.S.A. Inc.
Evergreen Entertainment Group
Eyewitness Kids News, LLC
Filmoption International Inc.
David Finch Distribution Ltd.
First Run/Icarus Films
Freewheelin' Films Ltd.
FremantleMedia North America Inc.
GPN Inc & Destination Education Inc.
Global Entertainment Media
Global Telemedia Inc.
Hamilton Productions Inc.
Heritage/Baruch Television Distribution
Home Improvement Television Network
Hope Channel
International Broadcasting Network
International Tele-Film
Janson Media
Juravic Entertainment
KPTS-TV
Litton Entertainment
MGC The Multimedia Group of Canada
MacNeil/Lehrer Productions
Mar Vista Entertainment
Masai Films Inc.
Mason Video
The Media Group of Connecticut Inc.
Modern Entertainment
Mondo TV
New Zoo Revue
O. Atlas Enterprises Inc.
Oppix Productions Inc
PBS Video
Pantomime Pictures Inc.
Phoebus Communications Inc.
Pied Piper Films Ltd.
Planet Pictures Ltd.
Powersports/Paradox
Presbyterian News Services
Richter Productions Inc.
Sesame Workshop
M C Stuart & Associates Pty Ltd.
Tamouz Media
Television Representatives Inc.
The Television Syndication Company, Inc.
TVOntario
U.S. Conference of Catholic Bishops
VIEW Video Inc.
Vision Broadcasting - KVBA TV 19
Alan Weiss Productions
Daniel Wilson Productions Inc.
Yorkshire Television

Entertainment Programming, Radio

Agrinet News Network
Broadcast Programming
C N R Radio
CRN International
Citadel Media
The Dick Clark Productions
Creative Marketing & Communications Corp.
DC Audio
The Walt Disney Company
Ecumenical Communications
Essence Television Productions Inc.
Jameson Broadcast Inc.
Launch Radio Networks
Leadem to Water Production Inc.
Ben Manilla Productions

MasterControl FamilyNet Radio
Media Planning Group (MPG)
North American Network, Inc.
On Track
Powerline
Prairie Dog Entertainment
Premiere Radio Networks Inc.
Radio America
Radio Spirits
Sam Shad Productions
StarDate/Universo Productions
Talk Radio Network
UBC Radio
United Stations Radio Network
WCTD AM 1620
"The Weather Center"
Larry John Wright Inc.
ZBS Foundation

Entertainment Programming, Radio & TV

Arkadia Entertainment Corp.
The Chuck Blore Co.
Broadcast Studio Inc.
Arthur Henley Productions
Eddie Kessler Productions Publications &
    Promotions
Bill Melendez Productions Inc.
New Visions Syndication Inc.
Jim Owens Entertainment
SCOLA
Ukrainian Melody Hour
University of Colorado Television
WQED Multimedia
WWE Entertainment Inc.

Entertainment Programming, TV

ATA Trading Corp.
America One Television Network
J. Arnold Productions
Burrud Productions Inc.
Buzzco Associates Inc.
CABLEready Corp.
CBS Television Distribution
CN8, The Comcast Network
Cable Films & Video
CanLib Inc.
Carsey-Werner Distribution
Sandra Carter Global, Inc.
Central City Productions, Inc.
Chrysalis Distribution
The Dick Clark Productions
Clear Channel Broadcasting Inc.
Clever Cleaver Productions
Country Crossroads
The Crime Channel
Crystal Pictures Inc.
Cube International
The Walt Disney Company
E! Entertainment Television
Ellis Entertainment
Essence Television Productions Inc.
Evergreen Entertainment Group
First Run/Icarus Films
GLL TV Enterprises Inc.
GRB Entertainment
Glenray Productions Inc.
Global Entertainment Media
Granada America
Great North Productions
The Griffin Group
Alfred Haber Distribution Inc.
Hearst Entertainment, Inc.
International Tele-Film
International Television Corp.
Janson Media
Jefferson-Pilot Sports
Juravic Entertainment
KPTS-TV
KUSA Television
Kultur International Films
Lakeside TV Co.
Lapco Communications
Litton Entertainment
MGC The Multimedia Group of Canada
Media Planning Group (MPG)
Myriad Pictures
NTN Communications Inc.
New Zoo Revue
PBS Video
Planet Pictures Ltd.

PorchLight Entertainment Inc.
Powersports/Paradox
Prime Cut Productions Inc.
Promark Television
Questar
Raycom Sports
Reid/Land Productions Inc.
ROZON/Just For Laughs
Sam Shad Productions
Harvey Sheldon Productions
Sullivan Entertainment Inc./Sullivan Entertainment
    International
Tel-Air Interests Inc.
Telepros
The Television Syndication Company, Inc.
Tomwil Inc.
Triage Entertainment Inc.
Turner Entertainment Co.
Twentieth Television
Viacom Inc.
Video-Cinema Films Inc.
Video Enterprises Inc.
Videographic West
Vision Broadcasting - KVBA TV 19
Warner Bros. Animation
Warner Bros. International Television
Warner Bros. Television
Wide Eye Productions, Inc.
Daniel Wilson Productions Inc.
World Events Productions Ltd.
The Wyland Group
Yorkshire Television

Film and Tape Transfers (Film-to-Tape)

Ascent Media Management East
Carpel Video Inc.
Crawford Communications
Crest National Digital Media Complex
Henninger Media Services, Inc.
Highland Laboratories
MPL Media
Magno Sound & Video
Matchframe Video
New Art Miami
Northwest Imaging & FX
Point 360
PostWorks, New York
Quality Film & Video
The Transfer Zone
VTTV Videothek Electronic TV-Production GmbH +
    Co Kopier KG

Film Laboratories

Crawford Communications
Crest National Digital Media Complex
DeLuxe Laboratories
Forde Motion Picture Labs
Henninger Media Services, Inc.
MPL Media
Media Visions
Point 360
Studio Babelsberg GmbH

Film Preservation/Restoration

Worldview Entertainment Inc.

Graphic Effects Library

Darino Films/Library of Special Effects
WeatherVision Inc.

Graphics

Cimarron Group
Devlin Design Group Inc.
Henninger Media Services, Inc.
MVI Post
Matchframe Video
New Art Miami
Peters Communications
Pro Video
Radioguide People Inc.
River City Video Productions
Technisonic Studios
TRI-COMM Productions

Industrial Films

CRM Learning
DWJ Television
ESPI Video
Encore Video Productions Inc.
The Kenwood Group
Limelight Communications Inc.
Lindberg Productions Inc.
MRC Films
Make It Happen Productions Inc.
Pantomime Pictures Inc.
Peckham Productions
Primedia Workplace Learning
Primo Newservice Inc.
Tel-Air Interests Inc.
Telepros
Video/Media Distribution Inc.
Wade Productions Inc.
Work Edit

Inflight Audio Progamming

Great Chefs Television/Publishing
Horizon Audio Creations
William Mauldin Productions Inc.
Ports of Paradise
Prairie Dog Entertainment
RDF Media
Time Capsule, Inc.

Interactive Television

Ascent Media Network Services
Maximum Marketing Services Inc.
NTN Communications Inc.
Parrot Communications International Inc.
PostWorks, New York
SPI International
Video I-D Teleproductions Inc.

Interactive Television Programming

Ivanhoe Broadcast News Inc.
NTN Communications Inc.
Phoebus Communications Inc.
Presson Perspectives
Producers Group, Ltd.
Reuters Media
Sunbow Entertainment
University of Colorado Television

Jingles

Aloha Productions
Blue Heaven Productions
CA Media Development
Continental Recordings Inc.
GMI Media L.L.C.
Groove Addicts
JAM Creative Productions Inc.
Joe Jones Productions
Makedwde Publishing
Network Music
Radio Express Inc.
Radio Production Services Inc.
Shield Productions Inc.
Sound of Birmingham Productions
TM Studios
Thompson Creative

Libraries, Film

Archive Films/Archive Photos
Eurocine
Getty Images
Granada America
Grinberg Film Libraries Inc.
Grove Television Enterprises Inc.
Horizon Audio Creations
Eddie Kessler Productions Publications &
    Promotions
MGM TV Canada
Modern Entertainment
Modern Sound Pictures Inc.
Pan American Video
Reel Media International Inc.
PETER RODGERS ORGANIZATION
Televix Entertainment Inc.
Turner Entertainment Co.
Video-Cinema Films Inc.
The WPA Film Library

Worldview Entertainment Inc.

Libraries, TV

ADM—International Film & TV Distribution
CABLEready Corp.
CBS Studio International
CBS Television Distribution
CBS Worldwide Distribution
CelebrityFootage
Cube International
Eyewitness Kids News, LLC
Film Roman Inc.
Getty Images
Granada America
Grinberg Film Libraries Inc.
Grove Television Enterprises Inc.
Hearst Entertainment, Inc.
Horizon Audio Creations
Modern Entertainment
NRS Group PTY Ltd.
New Films International
New Zoo Revue
Pan American Video
Reel Media International Inc.
Sanctuary Records Group Ltd.
Televix Entertainment Inc.
Turner Entertainment Co.
Twentieth Century Fox Television Distribution
WWE Entertainment Inc.

Libraries, Video

CelebrityFootage
Children's Media Productions
The Dick Clark Productions
Eurocine
First Run/Icarus Films
Getty Images
Great Chefs Television/Publishing
Grinberg Film Libraries Inc.
Grove Television Enterprises Inc.
The Idea Channel
Medstar Television Inc.
National Collegiate Athletic Association (NCAA)
New Zoo Revue
Reel Media International Inc.
Reuters Television
River City Video Productions
WWE Entertainment Inc.

Licensing Services

Classic Media
Film Roman Inc.
4 Kids Entertainment (Sub 4 Kids Entertainment)
Getty Images
Grinberg Film Libraries Inc.
Larry Harmon Pictures Corp.
Harmony Gold U.S.A. Inc.
RDF Media
Southern STAR
Sunbow Entertainment
TRF Production Music Libraries
Televix Entertainment Inc.
Turner Entertainment Co.
WWE Entertainment Inc.

Location Services

American Stock Exchange
CompuWeather Inc.
Georgia Film, Video & Music Office
Lion and Fox Recording Studios
U.S. Plan B Inc.

Medical Programming, Radio

AmericaNurse TV Productions
Creative Marketing & Communications Corp.
Eagle Media Productions Ltd.
Essence Television Productions Inc.
Jameson Broadcast Inc.
MasterControl FamilyNet Radio
MediaTracks Inc.
Powerline
RPM-Radio Programming & Management Inc.
Radio Production Services Inc.
Talk America Radio Networks
Talk Radio Network

Medical Programming, Radio & TV

AmericaNurse TV Productions
CDR Communications Inc.
D-Squared Media
Faith for Today
Arthur Henley Productions
Lifestyle Magazine/The Evidence
MSE
Presson Perspectives
Radio & TV Roundup Productions

Medical Programming, TV

J. Arnold Productions
Bell Foto Art Productions
Hamilton Productions Inc.
Ivanhoe Broadcast News Inc.
Limelight Communications Inc.
Mason Video
Medstar Television Inc.
North American Network, Inc.
The Wyland Group
Sandy Zimmerman Productions

Mobile Production Units

CMT
Cinecraft Productions Inc.
Dome Productions
KUSA Television
PMTV Producers Management Television
PSSI Global Services-Strategic Television
Telenium Studios/Fusion
VTTV Videothek Electronic TV-Production GmbH +
 Co Kopier KG
Videosmith Inc.
WKMG Productions

Music and Sound Effects

Blue Heaven Productions
FirstCom Music
GMI Media L.L.C.
Ghostwriters/Radio Mall
Groove Addicts Production Music Catalog
Manhattan Production Music
Megatrax Production Music Inc.
OGM Production Music
Omnimusic
Production Garden Music Libraries
Promusic
SoperSound Music Library
Sound Ideas
TRF Production Music Libraries
Westar Music

Music Composition

Carriage House Studios
Tim Cissell Music
Groove Addicts
Megatrax Production Music Inc.
Metro Music Productions Inc.
Peters Communications
SoperSound Music Library
Valentino Music & Sound Effect Libraries
Wax Music, Sound Design & Mix

Music Libraries

Alternative Programming
Broadcast Programming
FirstCom Music
Ghostwriters/Radio Mall
Groove Addicts Production Music Catalog
Halland Broadcast Services
Killer Tracks
MVI Post
Megatrax Production Music Inc.
Metro Music Productions Inc.
Network Music
New Zoo Revue
OGM Production Music
Omnimusic
Production Garden Music Libraries
Promusic
RPM Media Enterprises-The Relic Rack Review
RPM-Radio Programming & Management Inc.
Radio & TV Roundup Productions
Radio Express Inc.
Smith/Lee Productions, Inc.

Sound Ideas
TM Studios
TRF Production Music Libraries
Valentino Music & Sound Effect Libraries
Westar Music

Music Lyrics

Wax Music, Sound Design & Mix

Music Production

Aloha Productions
Arkadia Entertainment Corp.
Armedia Communications
Carriage House Studios
Tim Cissell Music
Digital Force
Great Chefs Television/Publishing
Groove Addicts
Joe Jones Productions
Megatrax Production Music Inc.
Robin Miller, Filmaker Inc.
North Star Music
Shelly Palmer Productions
Peters Communications
Ports of Paradise
Prairie Dog Entertainment
Smith/Lee Productions, Inc.
Soundshop Recording Studio LLC
Valentino Music & Sound Effect Libraries

Music Production, Film and Video

Carriage House Studios
Tim Cissell Music
TS James & Associates
Valentino Music & Sound Effect Libraries
Warren Only Media Group
Wax Music, Sound Design & Mix

Music Production, Radio

Toby Arnold and Associates Inc.
Blue Heaven Productions
Carriage House Studios
Citadel Media
Digital Force
Halland Broadcast Services
Happi Associates
Network Music
RPM Media Enterprises-The Relic Rack Review
Spanish Broadcasting System
Valentino Music & Sound Effect Libraries
WCTD AM 1620

Music Production, Radio & TV

Aloha Productions
Tim Cissell Music
JAM Creative Productions Inc.
Shield Productions Inc.
SoperSound Music Library
Sound of Birmingham Productions
TM Studios
Ukrainian Melody Hour
Valentino Music & Sound Effect Libraries
Warren Only Media Group
Wax Music, Sound Design & Mix

Music Production, TV

Toby Arnold and Associates Inc.
Boston Symphony Orchestra
CMT
Central City Productions, Inc.
Tim Cissell Music
Digital Force
Network Music
TS James & Associates
WWE Entertainment Inc.
The Worship Network

Music Programming, Radio

Alternative Programming
The Classical Station, WCPE
Country Crossroads
Hearts of Space Inc.
Heil Enterprises

Horizon Audio Creations
J&H Music Programming
Longhorn Radio Network
Ben Manilla Productions
Musical Starstreams
Muzak
Powerline
Promark Television
RPM Media Enterprises-The Relic Rack Review
Radio Express Inc.
St. Olaf College
Soldiers Radio & Television, U.S. Army Public Affairs
Solid Gospel Network (Reach Satellite Network, Inc.)
Southcott Productions
Spanish Broadcasting System
WCTD AM 1620

Music Scoring

Aloha Productions
Tim Cissell Music
GMI Media L.L.C.
Groove Addicts
Megatrax Production Music Inc.
Metro Music Productions Inc.
TS James & Associates
Wax Music, Sound Design & Mix

Music Services

Alternative Programming
Broadcast Programming
The Classical Station, WCPE
Groove Addicts
Halland Broadcast Services
Megatrax Production Music Inc.
Muzak
N W Media
Radio Express Inc.
Radio Production Services Inc.
TM Studios

Music Video Production

Asia Pacific Productions USA, Ltd.
Great Chefs Television/Publishing
Masai Films Inc.
Power Play Music Video L.L.C.
Sanctuary Records Group Ltd.
Tel-Air Interests Inc.
Telepros

Nature Programming, TV

Asia Pacific Productions USA, Ltd.
CNBC Syndication
Capital Communications
Devillier Donegan Enterprises L.P.
Dorling Kindersley Vision
Ellis Entertainment
First Run/Icarus Films
GRB Entertainment
Global Entertainment Media
Thomas Horton Associates Inc.
International Television Corp.
Juravic Entertainment
Lakeside TV Co.
Limelight Communications Inc.
MacNeil/Lehrer Productions
Montgomery Community Television Inc.
Soldiers Radio & Television, U.S. Army Public Affairs
Southern STAR
Charlie Spencer Productions
Marty Stouffer Productions Ltd.
Tomwil Inc.
Wide Eye Productions, Inc.
The Worship Network

News Programming, Radio

C N R Radio
Call For Action Inc.
Clear Channel Broadcasting Inc.
Eagle Media Productions Ltd.
Ecumedia News Service
FamilyNet Radio
Hometown Illinois Radio Network
The Image Generators
KCSN 88.5 FM
Launch Radio Networks
Maryknoll Productions
MediaTracks Inc.

Moody Broadcasting Network
National Council of Churches Communications Unit
National Public Radio
North American Network, Inc.
North Shore Productions
RPM Media Enterprises-The Relic Rack Review
Radio America
Radio Canada International/Canadian Broadcasting Corp.
Ray Sports Network
Talk America Radio Networks
Traffic Scan Network, Inc
United Stations Radio Network
WCTD AM 1620
Washington Korean Broadcasting Co.

News Programming, Radio & TV

Accuracy in Media Inc.
American Farm Bureau Inc.
CompuWeather Inc.
John Driscoll/VoiceOver America
GlobeCast
Gordon Productions
Medialink
News Broadcast Network
Presson Perspectives
SCOLA
Soldiers Radio & Television, U.S. Army Public Affairs
Traffic Scan Network, Inc
Ukrainian Melody Hour
University of Kentucky Public Relations & Radio-TV News Bureau
Warren Only Media Group

News Programming, TV

J. Arnold Productions
Asia Pacific Productions USA, Ltd.
Bell Foto Art Productions
Call For Action Inc.
CelebrityFootage
Daley Video
Devillier Donegan Enterprises L.P.
E! Entertainment Television
Evergreen Entertainment Group
Hamilton Productions Inc.
Health Net Productions & Pet Talk
Ivanhoe Broadcast News Inc.
KCRA-TV
Litton Entertainment
Medstar Television Inc.
Midwest Video Communications Inc.
Mobile Video Services Ltd.
Munhwa Broadcasting Corp. (MBC)
PACSAT
PBS Video
Parrot Communications International Inc.
Planet Pictures Ltd.
Potomac TV/Communications
Prime Cut Productions Inc.
Primo Newservice Inc.
RAI Corp.
Reuters Media
Seven Network Australia Inc.
P. Allen Smith Gardens
Sullivan Video Services Inc.
Telepros
The Television Syndication Company, Inc.
U.S. Plan B Inc.
Video Techniques Inc.
Wide Eye Productions, Inc.
Yorkshire Television

Original Music Scoring

Carriage House Studios
Continental Recordings Inc.
Groove Addicts
JAM Creative Productions Inc.
Metro Music Productions Inc.
Shelly Palmer Productions
Smith/Lee Productions, Inc.
SoperSound Music Library
Studio Center Corp.
TS James & Associates

Performing Arts Programming, Radio

KCSN 88.5 FM
National Public Radio
RPM Media Enterprises-The Relic Rack Review
WFMT Radio Network
WQXR

Performing Arts Programming, Radio & TV

The Classical Station, WCPE
Arthur Henley Productions
WQED Multimedia

Performing Arts Programming, TV

Arkadia Entertainment Corp.
CABLEready Corp.
Crystal Pictures Inc.
E! Entertainment Television
Free Speech TV (FSTV)
Global Entertainment Media
Kultur International Films
MacNeil/Lehrer Productions
Myriad Pictures
Reid/Land Productions Inc.
M C Stuart & Associates Pty Ltd.
Video-Cinema Films Inc.
VIEW Video Inc.
WTOB—Community/Government Access TV
Yorkshire Television

Photographic Services

CompuWeather Inc.
Maslow Media Group Inc.
Videosmith Inc.
White Rabbit Productions
Sandy Zimmerman Productions

Postproduction Facilities

Agora TV
Anderson Productions Ltd. (APL)
Ascent Media Network
The Audio Department Inc.
CFP Video Productions
CN8, The Comcast Network
Catholic Communications Corp.
Center City Film & Video
Cinecraft Productions Inc.
Cinema Concepts Animation Studio
Crawford Communications
Daley Video
ESPI Video
Eagle Eye Film Company
GVI
Highland Laboratories
Horizons Television Inc.
Thomas Horton Associates Inc.
MPL Media
MVI Post
Matchframe Video
NRS Group PTY Ltd.
North by Northwest Productions
Northwest Imaging & FX
Palace Digital Studios
Point 360
Power Play Music Video L.L.C.
Rampion Visual Productions L.L.C.
Seraphim Communications Inc.
Studio Babelsberg GmbH
Tankersley Productions, Inc., St. Louis
Telenium Studios/Fusion
The Transfer Zone
University of Colorado Television
Video I-D Teleproductions Inc.
Video Techniques Inc.
Videographic West
Vyvx
WKMG Productions
Work Edit

Postproduction Services

Advanced Digital Services, Inc.
Aegis People Support Transcription and Captioning
Agora TV
American Stock Exchange
Broadcast Studio Inc.
CFP Video Productions
CN8, The Comcast Network
Carleton Productions International Inc.
CineGroupe Corporation
Cinema Concepts Animation Studio
Cookie Jar Group
Cornell University Educational Television Center
Darino Films/Library of Special Effects
DeLuxe Laboratories
Eagle Eye Film Company
GTN
Getty Images
Gordon Productions
HAVE Inc.
Henninger Media Services, Inc.
Limelight Communications Inc.
MPL Media
MVI Post
Magno Sound & Video
Masai Films Inc.
William Mauldin Productions Inc.
Maysles Films, Inc.
Media Access Group at WGBH
Montgomery Community Television Inc.
NTV International Corp.
National Collegiate Athletic Association (NCAA)
New Art Miami
Northwest Imaging & FX
Oppix Productions Inc
PACSAT
PostWorks, New York
Quality Film & Video
Rex Post
Rockwell Audio Media
SeniorVision Productions Inc.
Seraphim Communications Inc.
Soundtrack
Studio Center Corp.
TR Productions
TRI-COMM Productions
VA-Tech Video/Broadcast Services
VTTV Videothek Electronic TV-Production GmbH +
    Co Kopier KG
WKMG Productions
The WPA Film Library
Alan Weiss Productions
White Rabbit Productions
ZBS Foundation

Processing Labs

DeLuxe Laboratories

Producers, Documentaries

American Farm Bureau Inc.
Bell Foto Art Productions
Robert L. Bocchino
Brillig Productions Inc.
Broadview Media
Sandra Carter Global, Inc.
Thomas Craven Film Corp.
The Dolmatch Group Ltd.
Ecumedia News Service
Evangelical Lutheran Church in America
FTC/Orlando
FamilyNet
David Finch Distribution Ltd.
Free Speech TV (FSTV)
GRB Entertainment
GVI
Great North Productions
Horizons Television Inc.
Thomas Horton Associates Inc.
International Television Corp.
Janson Media
The Johnson Group
Jordan Klein Film & Video
MRC Films
MacNeil/Lehrer Productions
Make It Happen Productions Inc.
Maryknoll Productions
Maryland Public Television
Maysles Films, Inc.
The Media Group of Connecticut Inc.
Myriad Pictures
O'Grady & Associates

Pied Piper Films Ltd.
Planet Pictures Ltd.
Presbyterian News Services
Presson Perspectives
Prime Cut Productions Inc.
Productions La Fete
RDF Media
Richter Productions Inc.
SFP Productions
Charlie Spencer Productions
System TV
Talco Productions
Tamouz Media
Tel-Air Interests Inc.
Two Oceans Entertainment Group
U.S. Conference of Catholic Bishops
The WPA Film Library
Warren Only Media Group
Welwood International Film Production
White Rabbit Productions
Daniel Wilson Productions Inc.

Producers, Film

Allumination FilmWorks, LLC
Angel Films Co.
S. Banks Group Inc.
Bardel Entertainment Inc.
Brillig Productions Inc.
Bruder Releasing Inc. (BRI)
CIFEX International Inc.
Classic Media
Coote Communications
Cramer
Thomas Craven Film Corp.
Critical Mass Releasing Inc.
E1 Entertainment
EUE Screen Gems Studios
Eurocine
FTC/Orlando
1st Miracle Productions
The Griffin Group
Independent Edge Films
JGT Media Productions
The Johnson Group
Jordan Klein Film & Video
Kazmark Entertainment Group
Kultur International Films
Lindberg Productions Inc.
Lions Gate Entertainment
MRC Films
Make It Happen Productions Inc.
Masai Films Inc.
Moonstone Entertainment
Myriad Pictures
O. Atlas Enterprises Inc.
O'Grady & Associates
Paulist Productions
Peckham Productions
Pied Piper Films Ltd.
Pike Productions Inc.
Productions La Fete
Richter Productions Inc.
Rigel Entertainment
Romano & Associates Inc.
Rosler Creative
SFP Productions
Silverline Entertainment
Charlie Spencer Productions
Studio Babelsberg GmbH
Sullivan Entertainment Inc./Sullivan Entertainment
    International
Tamouz Media
TRI-COMM Productions
Viacom Inc.
Welwood International Film Production
Daniel Wilson Productions Inc.

Producers, Multimedia

Brillig Productions Inc.
Celebrities Productions
ComBridges
Cramer
DaviSound
Free Speech TV (FSTV)
Lon Gibby Productions, Inc./ Gibby Media Group
Independent Edge Films
The Johnson Group
Kipany Productions Ltd.
Ben Manilla Productions
Maslow Media Group Inc.
NAHB Production Group
O'Grady & Associates

Palace Digital Studios
Paulist Productions
PorchLight Entertainment Inc.
Productions La Fete
Rampion Visual Productions L.L.C.
TR Productions
Technisonic Studios
Video I-D Teleproductions Inc.
Video/Media Distribution Inc.
Vuolo Video Air-Chex
Warren Only Media Group

Producers, Radio Programming

Alliance for Christian Media/Day1
Armedia Communications
At a Glance
Blue Heaven Productions
Broadcast News Service
C N R Radio
Call For Action Inc.
Chinamerica Hit Radio
Christian Children's Associates Inc.
Christian Science Sentinel - Radio Edition
The Christophers Inc.
Citadel Media
The Classical Station, WCPE
Country Crossroads
Creative Marketing & Communications Corp.
DC Audio
ESPN Radio Network
Eagle Media Productions Ltd.
Ecumedia News Service
Ecumenical Communications
Envoy Productions
Essence Television Productions Inc.
Evangelical Lutheran Church in America
FamilyNet
FamilyNet Radio
Finger Lakes Productions International
Good Life Associates
Billy Graham Evangelistic Association
Heil Enterprises
The Image Generators
International Television Broadcasting Inc.
J&H Music Programming
J.N. Productions
Jameson Broadcast Inc.
MRN Radio
Makedwde Publishing
Ben Manilla Productions
Maryknoll Productions
MasterControl FamilyNet Radio
MediaTracks Inc.
Moody Broadcasting Network
MotorNet
Musical Starstreams
National Council of Churches Communications Unit
New Dimensions Radio
North American Network, Inc.
North Shore Productions
O'Grady & Associates
Jim Owens Entertainment
Ports of Paradise
Powerline
Premiere Radio Networks Inc.
Questar
RBC Ministries
RPM Media Enterprises-The Relic Rack Review
Radio & TV Roundup Productions
Radio Express Inc.
Radio Production Services Inc.
Radio Spirits
Ray Sports Network
Sam Shad Productions
Sound Source Networks
Sports Byline U.S.A.
StarDate/Universo Productions
Talco Productions
Talk Radio Network
Time Capsule, Inc.
U.S. Conference of Catholic Bishops
United Stations Radio Network
WFMT Radio Network
WQXR
Wawatay Native Communication Society
"The Weather Center"

Producers, TV Programming

APA International Film Distributors Inc.
Accuracy in Media Inc.
Agora TV
AmericaNurse TV Productions
Anderson Productions Ltd. (APL)
Angel Films Co.
Armedia Communications
Ascent Media Network Services
Associated Television International
S. Banks Group Inc.
Bardel Entertainment Inc.
Dave Bell Associates Inc.
Bell Foto Art Productions
Bellon Entertainment
Brillig Productions Inc.
Broadcast News Service
Bruder Releasing Inc. (BRI)
Buzzco Associates Inc.
CBS Studio International
CBS Television Distribution
CCI Entertainment Ltd.
CDR Communications Inc.
CFP Video Productions
Call For Action Inc.
Canamedia Inc.
CanLib Inc.
George Carlson & Associates
Carlton International Media Inc.
Sandra Carter Global, Inc.
Catholic Communications Corp.
Central City Productions, Inc.
Children's Media Productions
Christian Children's Associates Inc.
The Dick Clark Productions
Classic Media
Clever Cleaver Productions
William F. Cooke Television Programs
Cookie Jar Group
Cornell University Educational Television Center
Critical Mass Releasing Inc.
Crystal Pictures Inc.
Curb Entertainment International Corp.
DLT Entertainment Ltd.
D-Squared Media
Dargaud-Marina
Walt Disney Company
Dorling Kindersley Vision
E! Entertainment Television
E1 Entertainment
EUE Screen Gems Studios
Ellis Entertainment
Envoy Productions
Faith for Today
FamilyNet
Film Roman Inc.
David Finch Distribution Ltd.
Fox 17 Studio Productions
Fox Sports West
Fox 29 WUTV Sinclair
Sandy Frank Entertainment Inc.
Free Speech TV (FSTV)
Freewheelin' Films Ltd.
The Fremantle Corp.
GLL TV Enterprises Inc.
GRB Entertainment
Lon Gibby Productions, Inc./ Gibby Media Group
Glenray Productions Inc.
Global Telemedia Inc.
Granada America
Great Chefs Television/Publishing
Great North Productions
The Griffin Group
Hamilton Productions Inc.
Larry Harmon Pictures Corp.
Health Net Productions & Pet Talk
Heritage/Baruch Television Distribution
Jack Hilton Inc.
The History Makers
Holigan Investment Group Ltd.
Home Improvement Television Network
Hope Channel
The Idea Channel
Independent Edge Films
International Broadcasting Network
International Television Broadcasting Inc.
It Is Written Television
Italtoons Corp.
Ivanhoe Broadcast News Inc.
KPTS-TV
KUSA Television
Lakeside TV Co.
Lapco Communications
Lifestyle Magazine/The Evidence

Lightbridge Production & Distribution
MG/Perin Inc.
MacNeil/Lehrer Productions
Madison Square Garden Network
Makedwde Publishing
Maryknoll Productions
Maryland Public Television
Maysles Films, Inc.
The Media Group of Connecticut Inc.
Media Planning Group (MPG)
Montgomery Community Television Inc.
NAHB Production Group
NRS Group PTY Ltd.
National Collegiate Athletic Association (NCAA)
National Council of Churches Communications Unit
News Broadcast Network
North by Northwest Productions
O. Atlas Enterprises Inc.
O'Grady & Associates
Jim Owens Entertainment
PAULAR Entertainment L.L.C.
Shelly Palmer Productions
Paulist Productions
Peckham Productions
Pied Piper Films Ltd.
PorchLight Entertainment Inc.
Power Play Music Video L.L.C.
Powersports/Paradox
Presbyterian News Services
Prime Cut Productions Inc.
Questar
RBC Ministries
Rampion Visual Productions L.L.C.
Raycom Sports
Reid/Land Productions Inc.
Reuters Media
Rigel Entertainment
Steve Rotfeld Productions Inc.
ROZON/Just For Laughs
Sanctuary Records Group Ltd.
Sam Shad Productions
Silverline Entertainment
Southern STAR
Charlie Spencer Productions
Sport International Inc.
Marty Stouffer Productions Ltd.
Sullivan Entertainment Inc./Sullivan Entertainment
  International
Sunbow Entertainment
System TV
Talco Productions
Tamouz Media
Tel-Air Interests Inc.
The Television Syndication Company, Inc.
Triage Entertainment Inc.
Twentieth Century Fox Television Distribution
Twentieth Television
Two Oceans Entertainment Group
U.S. Conference of Catholic Bishops
Viacom Inc.
Videographic West
Vision Broadcasting - KVBA TV 19
WQED Multimedia
WTOB—Community/Government Access TV
Warner Bros. Animation
Warren Only Media Group
Wawatay Native Communication Society
Wide Eye Productions, Inc.
Daniel Wilson Productions Inc.
Witt/Thomas Productions
The Wyland Group

Producers, Video

Altruist Media
American Farm Bureau Inc.
Armedia Communications
J. Arnold Productions
Asia Pacific Productions USA, Ltd.
Bayliss
Bell Foto Art Productions
Bruder Releasing Inc. (BRI)
CFP Video Productions
CRM Learning
Catholic Communications Corp.
CelebrityFootage
Children's Media Productions
Cinecraft Productions Inc.
Clever Cleaver Productions
Concept Videos
Coote Communications
Cramer
Thomas Craven Film Corp.
Custom Productions Inc.

D-Squared Media
D-V-X International
DWJ Television
ESPI Video
Encore Video Productions Inc.
Envoy Productions
FTC/Orlando
Faith for Today
David Finch Distribution Ltd.
GLL TV Enterprises Inc.
GVI
Lon Gibby Productions, Inc./ Gibby Media Group
Good News Broadcasting Association Inc.
Gordon Productions
Health Net Productions & Pet Talk
Jack Hilton Inc.
The History Makers
Home Improvement Television Network
Horizons Television Inc.
The Idea Channel
JGT Media Productions
The Johnson Group
Jordan Klein Film & Video
Kipany Productions Ltd.
Lapco Communications
Lifestyle Magazine/The Evidence
Lightbridge Production & Distribution
Limelight Communications Inc.
Lindberg Productions Inc.
MRC Films
Mason Video
McClain Enterprises Inc.
Medialink
Montgomery Community Television Inc.
NAHB Production Group
News Broadcast Network
North by Northwest Productions
O. Atlas Enterprises Inc.
O'Grady & Associates
Shelly Palmer Productions
Peckham Productions
Pike Productions Inc.
Playboy Entertainment Group Inc.
Potomac TV/Communications
Powersports/Paradox
Praxis Media Inc.
Prime Cut Productions Inc.
Primedia Workplace Learning
Quality Film & Video
RMD & Assoc. Inc.
Reizner & Reizner Film & Video
Rex Post
River City Video Productions
Rosler Creative
Steve Rotfeld Productions Inc.
Sak Entertainment
Seraphim Communications Inc.
Charlie Spencer Productions
Marty Stouffer Productions Ltd.
Sullivan Video Services Inc.
TR Productions
Tankersley Productions, Inc., St. Louis
Telepros
Triage Entertainment Inc.
TRI-COMM Productions
U.S. Plan B Inc.
Video I-D Teleproductions Inc.
Video/Media Distribution Inc.
Video Techniques Inc.
VIEW Video Inc.
Vision Broadcasting - KVBA TV 19
Vuolo Video Air-Chex
WTOB—Community/Government Access TV
Alan Weiss Productions
Welwood International Film Production
White Rabbit Productions
Wide Eye Productions, Inc.
Work Edit
Larry John Wright Inc.
The Wyland Group
Yada/Levine Video Productions
Sandy Zimmerman Productions

Production Music Libraries

Toby Arnold and Associates Inc.
The Audio Department Inc.
FirstCom Music
Good News Broadcasting Association Inc.
Groove Addicts Production Music Catalog
Manhattan Production Music
Metro Music Productions Inc.
Network Music
OGM Production Music

Omnimusic
Shelly Palmer Productions
Production Garden Music Libraries
Promusic
SoperSound Music Library
TRF Production Music Libraries

Production Services

Altruist Media
The Chuck Blore Co.
Broadcast Studio Inc.
CFP Video Productions
CNBC Syndication
CTV Television Inc.
Carleton Productions International Inc.
ComBridges
Cornell University Educational Television Center
Cramer
D-Squared Media
DWJ Television
De Wolfe Music Library Inc.
Design Partners Inc.
Devlin Design Group Inc.
Dimension 3 Corp
Educational Technologies Network (ETN)
Encore Video Productions Inc.
Eyewitness Kids News, LLC
Faith for Today
FamilyNet Radio
Fox Digital
Fox 17 Studio Productions
Fox 29 WUTV Sinclair
Freewheelin' Films Ltd.
GVI
Gordon Productions
The History Makers
Horizons Television Inc.
JGT Media Productions
KPTS-TV
KUSA Television
Lighthouse Productions
Maryland Public Television
Warren Miller Entertainment
Oppix Productions Inc
Dick Orkin's Amazing Radio
Outdoor Media Group
PSSI Global Services-Strategic Television
Palace Digital Studios
Praxis Media Inc.
RDF Media
Rampion Visual Productions L.L.C.
Raycom Sports
Reizner & Reizner Film & Video
Reuters Television
Romano & Associates Inc.
Seraphim Communications Inc.
Soundtrack
Studio M Productions Unlimited
Tankersley Productions, Inc., St. Louis
Troma Entertainment, Inc.
U.S. Plan B Inc.
Ukrainian Melody Hour
University of Colorado Television
VA-Tech Video/Broadcast Services
VTTV Videothek Electronic TV-Production GmbH +
   Co Kopier KG
Video I-D Teleproductions Inc.
Video One Inc.
Wade Productions Inc.
Warren Only Media Group
White Rabbit Productions
Yada/Levine Video Productions

Promotion Design

CRN International
Cimarron Group
Design Partners Inc.
First Marketing
Peters Communications
TeleCom Productions Inc.

Promotion Film Distribution/Production

CelebrityFootage
Cinema Concepts Animation Studio
Crown International Pictures Inc.
Film Roman Inc.
Larry Harmon Pictures Corp.
Maryland Public Television

Warren Miller Entertainment
Praxis Media Inc.

Promotion Production, Radio

CRN International
Command Productions
Custom Productions Inc.
DaviSound
Jameson Broadcast Inc.
William Mauldin Productions Inc.
Premiere Radio Networks Inc.
StarDate/Universo Productions
UBC Radio
University of Kentucky Public Relations & Radio-TV
   News Bureau
Vuolo Video Air-Chex
WQXR
Larry John Wright Inc.

Promotion Production, Radio & TV

The Chuck Blore Co.
D-Squared Media
Jeff Davis Productions Inc.
John Driscoll/VoiceOver America
Film House Inc.
Eddie Kessler Productions Publications &
   Promotions
McClain Enterprises Inc.
National Collegiate Athletic Association (NCAA)
New Visions Syndication Inc.
Palace Digital Studios
Shelly Palmer Productions
Radio & TV Roundup Productions
Rosler Creative
Strand Media Group Inc.
University of Kentucky Public Relations & Radio-TV
   News Bureau

Promotion Production, TV

Asia Pacific Productions USA, Ltd.
CRN International
Custom Productions Inc.
Darino Films/Library of Special Effects
The Media Group of Connecticut Inc.
NTV International Corp.
Peters Communications
SPI International
Sport International Inc.
TeleCom Productions Inc.
University of Kentucky Public Relations & Radio-TV
   News Bureau
Welwood International Film Production
Larry John Wright Inc.

Public Service Announcements

American Farm Bureau Inc.
At a Glance
Robert L. Bocchino
The Christophers Inc.
Thomas Craven Film Corp.
Ecumedia News Service
Ecumenical Communications
Envoy Productions
Finger Lakes Productions International
GVI
J.N. Productions
KCSN 88.5 FM
Leukemia & Lymphoma Society
Limelight Communications Inc.
MRC Films
MSE
Masai Films Inc.
Maslow Media Group Inc.
Media Visions
MediaTracks Inc.
NAHB Production Group
NCAA
N W Media
National Council of Churches Communications Unit
News Broadcast Network
North American Network, Inc.
Potomac TV/Communications
Presbyterian News Services
Primo Newservice Inc.
Romano & Associates Inc.
StarDate/Universo Productions
U.S. Conference of Catholic Bishops
U.S. Air Force Recruiting Service

University of Kentucky Public Relations & Radio-TV
   News Bureau
WCTD AM 1620
WTOB—Community/Government Access TV
Alan Weiss Productions

Publishing, Video and Print

Accuracy in Media Inc.
CCM Media Services
CRM Learning
Essence Television Productions Inc.
First Marketing
Great Chefs Television/Publishing
Playboy Entertainment Group Inc.
Radioguide People Inc.
Seraphim Communications Inc.
Vuolo Video Air-Chex
Wawatay Native Communication Society

Recording Studios

The Audio Department Inc.
Continental Recordings Inc.
Country Crossroads
FamilyNet Radio
Horizon Audio Creations
Irving Productions Inc.
Tom Jones Recording Studios
Lighthouse Productions
Lion and Fox Recording Studios
Magno Sound & Video
Ben Manilla Productions
MediaTracks Inc.
No Soap Productions
Rex Post
Smith/Lee Productions, Inc.
Sound of Birmingham Productions
Soundshop Recording Studio LLC
Studio M Productions Unlimited
University of Detroit Mercy
WFMT Radio Network

Religious Programming, Radio

Alliance for Christian Media/Day1
At a Glance
Broadcast News Service
C N R Radio
Christian Science Sentinel - Radio Edition
Ecumedia News Service
Ecumenical Communications
Good Life Associates
Heil Enterprises
Integrity Media
It Is Written Television
MasterControl FamilyNet Radio
Moody Broadcasting Network
On Track
Perception Media Group
Powerline
Presbyterian News Services
St. Olaf College
Solid Gospel Network (Reach Satellite Network, Inc.)
Strength for Living

Religious Programming, Radio & TV

Broadcast News Service
CDR Communications Inc.
Catholic Communications Corp.
Christian Children's Associates Inc.
Christian Media Network
Christian TV Services of Ellicottville Inc.
Envoy Productions
Episcopal Church Center
Faith for Today
Family Stations Inc.
Good Life Associates
Good News Broadcasting Association Inc.
Integrity Media
JGT Media Productions
Maryknoll Productions
National Council of Churches Communications Unit
One Hundred Biblemen & Women of the U.S.A.
RBC Ministries
RBC Ministries/Midwest Media Managers
U.S. Conference of Catholic Bishops
The Worship Network

Religious Programming, TV

Catholic Television Network
Crossroads Christian Communications Inc.
Ellis Entertainment
Episcopal Church Center
Golden Gate Studios
Good News Broadcasting Association Inc.
Hope Channel
Horizons Television Inc.
Integrity Media
It Is Written Television
The Media Group of Connecticut Inc.
Presbyterian News Services
Tel-Air Interests Inc.
Vision Broadcasting - KVBA TV 19

Remote Facilities

Agrinet News Network
Altruist Media
American Stock Exchange
CompuWeather Inc.
Cornell University Educational Television Center
Dome Productions
John Driscoll/VoiceOver America
Medialink
National Mobile Television
PMTV Producers Management Television
Ray Sports Network
Reizner & Reizner Film & Video
Studio M Productions Unlimited
Sullivan Video Services Inc.
Video One Inc.

Satellite Uplink Services

Agrinet News Network
American Stock Exchange
Ascent Media Management East
Ascent Media Network
Ascent Media Network Services
Asia Pacific Productions USA, Ltd.
CBS Worldwide Distribution
Communications III Inc.
Crawford Communications
DG Systems
Dome Productions
GlobeCast
Longhorn Radio Network
Loral Skynet
Medialink
Mobile Video Services Ltd.
NEP Studios
NTV International Corp.
PACSAT
PMTV Producers Management Television
PSSI Global Services-Strategic Television
Potomac TV/Communications
Power Play Music Video L.L.C.
Ray Sports Network
Reuters Television
Roberts Communications Network Inc.
SCOLA
Sullivan Video Services Inc.
Talk America Radio Networks
Talk Radio Network
Telenium Studios/Fusion
VA-Tech Video/Broadcast Services
Vyvx
WKMG Productions
WFMT Radio Network
Warren Only Media Group
Robert Wold Co.
World Radio Network

Scriptwriters

Aegis People Support Transcription and Captioning
Altruist Media
Celebrities Productions
Coote Communications
Custom Productions Inc.
Pied Piper Films Ltd.
Praxis Media Inc.
RMD & Assoc. Inc.
Richter Productions Inc.
Sak Entertainment
ZBS Foundation
Sandy Zimmerman Productions

Set Design

Devlin Design Group Inc.
Reliance Audio Visual Corp.
Studio Babelsberg GmbH

Sound Design

Jeff Davis Productions Inc.
DaviSound
Henninger Media Services, Inc.
Ben Manilla Productions
Network Music
No Soap Productions
Shield Productions Inc.
Smith/Lee Productions, Inc.
Sound of Birmingham Productions
Wax Music, Sound Design & Mix

Sound Effects/Sound Effect Libraries

Films Media Group
FirstCom Music
Omnimusic
Promusic
Sound Ideas
TRF Production Music Libraries
Westar Music

Sound Recording

Continental Recordings Inc.
FTC/Orlando
Highland Laboratories
Irving Productions Inc.
Tom Jones Recording Studios
Lion and Fox Recording Studios
Man From Mars Productions
National Public Radio
Soundshop Recording Studio LLC
Studio M Productions Unlimited

Sound Stages

EUE Screen Gems Studios
Fox Digital
Telenium Studios/Fusion

Special Effect Libraries

TRF Production Music Libraries
Westar Music

Special Effects

Broadview Media
Dimension 3 Corp

Sports Programming, Radio

Agrinet News Network
Ascent Media Network Services
Clear Channel Broadcasting Inc.
ESPN Radio Network
FamilyNet Radio
Hometown Illinois Radio Network
MRN Radio
Mountain News Corporation
Philadelphia Flyers Hockey Club
Premiere Radio Networks Inc.
Sports Byline U.S.A.
Talk America Radio Networks
Traffic Scan Network, Inc
Tribune Radio Networks

Sports Programming, Radio & TV

GlobeCast
NCAA
National Collegiate Athletic Association (NCAA)
Philadelphia Flyers Hockey Club
Traffic Scan Network, Inc
Warren Only Media Group

Sports Programming, TV

Blue Star Media
CN8, The Comcast Network
Canamedia Inc.
Chrysalis Distribution
Clear Channel Broadcasting Inc.
Fox Sports West
Freewheelin' Films Ltd.
Hamilton Productions Inc.
Jefferson-Pilot Sports
Lindberg Productions Inc.
Madison Square Garden Network
Mason Video
NRS Group PTY Ltd.
National Collegiate Athletic Association (NCAA)
National Mobile Television
Philadelphia Flyers Hockey Club
Raycom Sports
Reel Media International Inc.
Reid/Land Productions Inc.
Response Reward Systems L.C.
Reuters Media
Sport International Inc.
M C Stuart & Associates Pty Ltd.
Technisonic Studios
TeleCom Productions Inc.
Tomwil Inc.
Videographic West
Vision Broadcasting - KVBA TV 19

Stage and Studio Rental

CMT
Cinecraft Productions Inc.
Fox Digital
Fox 17 Studio Productions
Golden Gate Studios
KUSA Television
NEP Studios
Sak Entertainment

Standards Conversion

Advanced Digital Services, Inc.
CBS Worldwide Distribution
HAVE Inc.
Media Visions
NEP Studios
Point 360
The Transfer Zone
Video Services

Stock Footage/Tape

American Farm Bureau Inc.
Burrud Productions Inc.
Carpel Video Inc.
CelebrityFootage
Darino Films/Library of Special Effects
Freewheelin' Films Ltd.
Lon Gibby Productions, Inc./ Gibby Media Group
Thomas Horton Associates Inc.
Media Planning Group (MPG)
Warren Miller Entertainment
National Collegiate Athletic Association (NCAA)
Pan American Video
Reel Media International Inc.
Silverman Stock Footage Inc.
System TV
The WPA Film Library
Worldview Entertainment Inc.

Studio Facilities

Ascent Media Network
CamMate Studios
Citadel Media
Continental Recordings Inc.
D-V-X International
Devlin Design Group Inc.
Dome Productions
Educational Technologies Network (ETN)
Fox Digital
Fox 17 Studio Productions
Fox 29 WUTV Sinclair
Golden Gate Studios
J.N. Productions
MTI The Image Group
Man From Mars Productions
Maryland Public Television
Mobile Video Services Ltd.
NEP Studios

National Public Radio
PACSAT
Reuters Television
Soundshop Recording Studio LLC
Suite Audio
Telenium Studios/Fusion
University of Colorado Television
University of Detroit Mercy
VTTV Videothek Electronic TV-Production GmbH + Co Kopier KG
WQED Multimedia

Syndication, Cable

ALIN TV
Accuracy in Media Inc.
CABLEready Corp.
CBS Television Distribution
Cable Films & Video
Carsey-Werner Distribution
Crystal Pictures Inc.
Evergreen Entertainment Group
4 Kids Entertainment (Sub 4 Kids Entertainment)
Sandy Frank Entertainment Inc.
GLL TV Enterprises Inc.
Jefferson-Pilot Sports
Lakeside TV Co.
Lifestyle Magazine/The Evidence
Lions Gate Entertainment
Media Planning Group (MPG)
Parrot Communications International Inc.
Playboy Entertainment Group Inc.
Power Play Music Video L.L.C.
Raycom Sports
Harvey Sheldon Productions
Twentieth Television
University of Detroit Mercy
Video/Media Distribution Inc.

Syndication, Radio

Accuracy in Media Inc.
Armedia Communications
Ascent Media Group
At a Glance
Citadel Media
Country Crossroads
ESPN Radio Network
Eagle Media Productions Ltd.
Envoy Productions
Good News Broadcasting Association Inc.
Happi Associates
Hometown Illinois Radio Network
Jameson Broadcast Inc.
Knowledge In A Nutshell Inc.
Longhorn Radio Network
MRN Radio
MasterControl FamilyNet Radio
MediaTracks Inc.
Miller Broadcast Management
Molton Advertising Inc.
Musical Starstreams
NCAA
New Dimensions Radio
North Shore Productions
On Track
Orange Productions Inc.
Dick Orkin's Amazing Radio
Jim Owens Entertainment
Ports of Paradise
Powerline
Premiere Radio Networks Inc.
RPM Media Enterprises-The Relic Rack Review
RPM-Radio Programming & Management Inc.
Radio America
Ray Sports Network
St. Olaf College
Solid Gospel Network (Reach Satellite Network, Inc.)
Sound Source Networks
Southcott Productions
Sports Byline U.S.A.
Strand Media Group Inc.
Strength for Living
TYG Media
Talk America Radio Networks
Talk Radio Network
Time Capsule, Inc.
Tribune Radio Networks
UBC Radio
United Stations Radio Network
University of Detroit Mercy
WFMT Radio Network
"The Weather Center"
World Radio Network

Larry John Wright Inc.
ZBS Foundation

Syndication, TV

ALIN TV
Aegis People Support Transcription and Captioning
Angel Films Co.
Broadcast Studio Inc.
CBS Television Distribution
CNBC Syndication
Cable Films & Video
CanLib Inc.
George Carlson & Associates
Carsey-Werner Distribution
William F. Cooke Television Programs
DG Systems
DLT Entertainment Ltd.
Envoy Productions
Sandy Frank Entertainment Inc.
GRB Entertainment
Golden Gate Studios
Great Chefs Television/Publishing
Hearst Entertainment, Inc.
Heritage/Baruch Television Distribution
Holigan Investment Group Ltd.
Jefferson-Pilot Sports
Juravic Entertainment
Lakeside TV Co.
Lifestyle Magazine/The Evidence
Lions Gate Entertainment
MGM TV Canada
MG/Perin Inc.
McClain Enterprises Inc.
NCAA
National Collegiate Athletic Association (NCAA)
New Visions Syndication Inc.
Pan American Video
Parrot Communications International Inc.
Planet Pictures Ltd.
The Program Exchange
Promark Television
PETER RODGERS ORGANIZATION
Steve Rotfeld Productions Inc.
Harvey Sheldon Productions
P. Allen Smith Gardens
TYG Media
TeleCom Productions Inc.
Television Representatives Inc.
The Television Syndication Company, Inc.
Twentieth Century Fox Television Distribution
Twentieth Television
Viacom Inc.
Video/Media Distribution Inc.
Warren Only Media Group
Welwood International Film Production
Western International Syndication
Robert Wold Co.
Worldvision NY
The Wyland Group

Teleconferences

Ascent Media Group
Ascent Media Network
Broadview Media
Celebrities Productions
Dome Productions
Encore Video Productions Inc.
Episcopal Church Center
KPTS-TV
National Mobile Television
PMTV Producers Management Television
PSSI Global Services-Strategic Television
Reizner & Reizner Film & Video
Vyvx
Wade Productions Inc.

Traffic Reporting

Metro Networks
Traffic Pulse Networks (A Unit of Mobility Technologies)
Traffic Scan Network, Inc

Training Film Productions

Cinecraft Productions Inc.
ComBridges
Encore Video Productions Inc.
Gordon Productions
Maslow Media Group Inc.

Mason Video
NAHB Production Group
National Collegiate Athletic Association (NCAA)
News Broadcast Network
Primedia Workplace Learning
Strand Media Group Inc.

Training Films

Bell Foto Art Productions
CRM Learning
Coote Communications
Thomas Craven Film Corp.
D-Squared Media
Films Media Group
International Tele-Film
Primedia Workplace Learning

Travel Programming, TV

Burrud Productions Inc.
CABLEready Corp.
Canamedia Inc.
Capital Communications
George Carlson & Associates
D-Squared Media
Janson Media
NRS Group PTY Ltd.
Promark Television
Questar
M C Stuart & Associates Pty Ltd.
System TV
TRI-COMM Productions
U.S. Plan B Inc.
Videosmith Inc.

Travelogues

George Carlson & Associates
Promark Television
Sandy Zimmerman Productions

Video Conferences

Bayliss
Communications III Inc.
Cornell University Educational Television Center
DWJ Television
Dome Productions
John Driscoll/VoiceOver America
ESPI Video
Educational Technologies Network (ETN)
Episcopal Church Center
The Idea Channel
Medialink
National Collegiate Athletic Association (NCAA)
PMTV Producers Management Television
PSSI Global Services-Strategic Television
Reliance Audio Visual Corp.
VA-Tech Video/Broadcast Services
Vyvx
Wade Productions Inc.

Videotape Editing

Ascent Media Management East
Broadview Media
Carpel Video Inc.
Catholic Communications Corp.
Daley Video
ESPI Video
Fox 17 Studio Productions
GVI
Highland Laboratories
The History Makers
Independent Edge Films
Limelight Communications Inc.
MPL Media
Matchframe Video
Maximum Marketing Services Inc.
Montgomery Community Television Inc.
North by Northwest Productions
Palace Digital Studios
PostWorks, New York
Sullivan Video Services Inc.
Telenium Studios/Fusion
The Transfer Zone
Video Techniques Inc.
Vuolo Video Air-Chex
Alan Weiss Productions
Wide Eye Productions, Inc.
Yada/Levine Video Productions

Voice-Overs

Ascent Media Group
Robert L. Bocchino
Broadcast News Service
CA Media Development
C 2 Productions Inc.
Chinamerica Hit Radio
Continental Recordings Inc.
D-Squared Media
Jeff Davis Productions Inc.
DaviSound
John Driscoll/VoiceOver America
Ecumedia News Service
Eurocine
Eyewitness Kids News, LLC
Fischer Broadcast Services
GMI Media L.L.C.
The Image Generators
Irving Productions Inc.

J.N. Productions
David Kaye Productions Inc.
Eddie Kessler Productions Publications & Promotions
MSE
Magno Sound & Video
N W Media
Perception Media Group
Primo Newservice Inc.
RDF Media
Radio & TV Roundup Productions
Shield Productions Inc.
Sound of Birmingham Productions
Steven B. Stevens
Strand Media Group Inc.
Studio Center Corp.
Time Capsule, Inc.
Warren Only Media Group
"The Weather Center"
Work Edit

ZBS Foundation

Weather Programming

CompuWeather Inc.
Metro Weather Service Inc.
Skywatch Weather Center
System TV
Traffic Scan Network, Inc
"The Weather Center"

Weather Programming, Radio

CompuWeather Inc.
Ion Weather Network
Metro Weather Service Inc.
Sam Shad Productions
Skywatch Weather Center
"The Weather Center"

Section F
Technology

Equipment Manufacturers and Distributors Alphabetical Index

A

A & S Case Co. Inc., 5260 Vineland Ave., N. Hollywood, CA, 91601. Phone: (818) 509-5920. Fax: (818) 509-1397.E-mail: billw@ascase.com Web Site:www.ascase.com Bill Waskey, mgr/opns & sls; Denise Berry, gen mgr .

Since 1976, A&S Case Company, Inc. has been the leader in the design & manufacture of ATA Spec 300 Category one compliant reusable shipping & carrying cases. Our ability to innovate has put us at the cutting edge of the industry, allowing us to provide custom solutions for customers in a wide var of fields with speffic needs.

A.C.C. Electronix, Inc., 420 Wylie Dr., Normal, IL, 61761-4315. Phone: (309) 888-9990. Fax: (309) 452-0893.E-mail: acc@accelectronix.com Web Site:www.accelectronix.com John Franklin, pres.

Repair cartridge tape recorders & reproducers.

ADC, Box 1101, Minneapolis, MN, 55440-1101. Phone: (952) 938-8080. Phone: (800) 366-3889. Fax: (952) 917-1717. Web Site:www.adc.com Mike Day, VP; Robert E. Switz, pres & chmn.

ADC provides the connections for wireline, wireless, cable, bcst & enterprise nets around the world. ADC's equipment & svcs enable high-speed Internet, data, video & voice svcs.

ADCOUR, Inc., (Formerly ADCOUR). 623 Main St., Woburn, MA, 01801. Phone: (781) 937-0011. Fax: (781) 937-3499.E-mail: adcourrj@aol.com Richard Jacobs, pres.

Batteries, chargers, power supplies & power conditioning.

ADSCO Line Products Inc., 3500 Washington Ave., Houston, TX, 77007. Phone: (713) 880-2424. Phone: (800) 247-6484. Fax: (713) 880-2456.E-mail: ajackd@dscoline.com Web Site:www.adscoline.com Linda Schmuck, pres.

Outside plant line hardware for CATV: guy strand, messengers, lashing wire/rods, formed grips/dead-ends & related line hardware. Stainless steel poleline hardware.

ADTEC Inc., 408 Russell St., Nashville, TN, 37206. Phone: (615) 256-6619. Fax: (615) 256-6593.E-mail: sales@adtecinc.com Web Site:www.adtecinc.com Ron Johnson, VP.

JacksonvilleFL , 2231 Corporate Square Blvd. Phone:

Products offered: Loc origination controllers & systems, coml insertion controllers & systems, network delay recording.

AKG Acoustics, U.S., 914 Airpark Center Dr., Nashville, TN, 37217. Phone: (615) 620-3800. Fax: (615) 620-3875.E-mail: akgusa@harman.com Web Site:www.akg-acoustics.com Doug Mac Callum, VP/gen mgr.

Microphones, headphones, wireless microphones, in-ear monitoring systems, wireless loudspeakers, conferencing products.

APM Music, (Change from APM Associated Production Music). 6255 Sunset Blvd., Suite 820, Hollywood, CA, 90028. Phone: (323) 461-3211. Phone: (212) 856-9800. Fax: (323) 461-9102.E-mail: accountservices@apmmusic.com Web Site:www.apmmusic.com Giselle Vasconez, key account dir; George Maloian, key account dir; Matthew Gutknecht, key account dir; Craig Giummarra, key account dir; Sharon Jennings, dir mktg; Adam Taylor, pres; George Macias, exec VP sls.

New YorkNY , 381 Park Ave. S., Suite 1101. (East Coast)

Over 300,000 tracks, 30 production music libraries, over 4,000 CDs, personalized packages, music search svcs, 20-25 new CD releases mthy & fantastic music dir who can assist in searches for all productions.

APW Mayville/Stantron, 403 Degner Ave., Mayville, WI, 53050-0028. Phone: (800) 558-7297. Phone: (920) 387-3000. Fax: (920) 387-7196.E-mail: customerservice @mayvilleproducts.com Web Site:www.apwmayville.com Daniel Eder, pres; Rich Runnels, sls dir.

Stantron racks, cabinets, enclosures, & related accessories for bcst integrators & professional audio video installations.

ARRI Inc., 617 Rt. 303, Blauvelt, NY, 10913-1109. Phone: (845) 353-1400. Fax: (845) 425-1250.E-mail: info@arri.com Web Site:www.arri.com Juergen Schwinzer, VP, camera division; Charles Davidson, COO; Volker Bahnemann, pres; John Gresch, VP, lighting division; Bill Russell, VP, western opns.

Ft. LauderdaleFL , 2385 Stirling Rd. Phone:

BurbankCA , 600 N. Victory Blvd. Phone:

Manufacturer of professional motion picture film cameras & accessories, lighting equipment & post-production tools.

A R T Applied Research and Technology, 215 Tremont St., Rochester, NY, 14608. Phone: (585) 436-2720. Fax: (585) 436-3942.E-mail: sales@artproaudio.com Web Site:www.artproaudio.com Philip Betette, pres.

Digital audio signal processors & enhancement devices.

ATCI/Antenna Technology Communications Inc., 450 N. McKemy Ave., Chandler, AZ, 85226. Phone: (480) 844-8501. Fax: (480) 898-7667. Web Site:www.atci.com Gary Hatch, CEO; Ron Kahle, COO/CFO.

SimpsonPA , 289 Atlas St. Phone:

Simulsat multibeam earth stns; parabolic antennas from 1.8 m to 32 m. Headend electronics, design & maintenance, used/refurbished equipment.

ATI-Audio Technologies Inc., 223 Peppermill Road, West Berlin, NJ, 08091. Phone: (856) 626-3480. Fax: (856) 504-0220.E-mail: sales@atiaudio.com Web Site:www.atiaudio.com Art Constantine, VP.

Bcst audio, products: Mic, Line & Distribution Amps, AD/DA & Sample Rate Converters, AES Clock Generator, Portable Field Mixers & Audio Test Equipment.

AVAB America Inc., 434 Payran Street, Petaluma, CA, 94952. Phone: (707)778-8990.E-mail: sales@avab.com Web Site:www.avab.com Hans J. Lau, pres.

Manufacturer of studio & theatrical lighting equipment; lighting controllers, dimmers, fixtures.

AVCOM of Virginia Inc., 7730 Whitepine Rd., Richmond, VA, 23237. Phone: (804) 794-2500. Fax: (804) 794-8284. Web Site:www.avcomofva.com Jay T. Evans, pres.

Manufacturer of portable spectrum analyzers & accessories.

AVI Systems, (formerly Televideo San Diego). 7270 Trade St., Suite 102, San Diego, CA, 92121. Phone: (858) 695-7888. Fax: (858) 695-7844.E-mail: brad.sousa@avisystems.com Web Site:www.avisystems.com Joseph Stoebner, chmn; Jeffrey Stoebner, pres; Bradley Sousa, sec; Randi Borth, treas.

Dealer & systems Integrator for video, audio, presentation distance learning & video conferencing, svc.

AVS Graphics & Media Inc., 963 Autumn Ave, Salt Lake City, UT, 84116-2243. Phone: (801) 975-9799. Fax: (801) 975-0970.E-mail: sales@avsgmedia.com Web Site:www.avsgmedia.com Gavin Hunter, CEO.

Bcst & production character generators & Still stores.

AVX Corp., 801 17th Ave. S., Box 867, Myrtle Beach, SC, 29578-0687. Phone: (919) 878-6200. Phone: (843) 448-9411. Fax: (919) 878-6470.E-mail: gib@avxcorp.com Web Site:www.avxcorp.com Jimmy White, sls dir; Craig Hunter, mktg dir.

Electronic component.

AZCAR U.S.A. Inc., 121 Hillpointe Dr., Suite 700, Canonsburgh, PA, 15317. Phone: (724) 873-0800. Fax: (724) 873-4770.E-mail: info@azcar.com Web Site:www.azcar.com Stephen Pumple, CEO; Gavin Schutz, pres; Karl Paulsen, sr VP engrg; Tom Deyo, VP business dev.

MarkhamON Canada, 3235 14th Ave. Phone:

Cambridge United Kingdom, #1 College Business Park, Coldhams Lane. Phone:

Bcst engrg, systems integration.

Abekas, Incorporated, (Formerly Accom Inc.). 1090 O'Brien Dr., Menlo Park, CA, 94025. Phone: (650) 470-0900. Fax: (650) 470-0913.E-mail: info@abekas.com Web Site:www.abekas.com Junaid Sheikh, pres/CEO; Phil Bennett, VP engrg; Bill Ludwig, chief product mgr.

Abekas designs, manufactures, sell & support a complete line of digital video/audio delay devices, disk recorders, digital speical effects & editing tools for use in the worldwide professional TV marketplace-encompassing the production,

post production, bcstg & computer video markets.

Abroyd Communications Ltd., 3-360 Montrose St. N., Cambridge, ON, N3H 2H8. Canada. Phone: (519) 650-5093. Phone: (888) 658-5100. Fax: (519) 650-9546.E-mail: info@broyd.com Web Site:www.abroyd.com

Designers, manufacturers & installers of communication towers; manufacturer for Lightning Dissipation Arrays Chem-Rod from LEC.

Access Intelligence LLC, 4 Choke Cherry Rd., 2nd Fl., Rockville, MD, 20850. Phone: (301) 354-2000. Web Site:www.accessintel.com Donald Pazour, pres/CEO; Ed Pinedo, exec VP, CFO; Macy Fecto, exec VP.

Magazines, trade shows, seminars & cable publication.

AccuWeather Inc., 385 Science Park Rd., State College, PA, 16803-2215. Phone: (814) 235-8600. Phone: (814) 235-8770. Fax: (814) 235-8639.E-mail: sales@accuweather.com Web Site:www.accuweather.com Dr. Joel N. Myers, founder & pres; Michael R. Smith, CEO, Weather data svc & Inc; Barry Myers, CEO; Elliot Abrams, sr VP/ chief meteorologist; Dr. Joe Sobel, sr VP/dir forensics.

AccuWeather, Inc. offers a broad new menu of powerful integrated, muturally supporting weather content & weather brand-building solutions.

Acme Electric Corp., Aerospace Division, 528 W. 21st St., Tempe, AZ, 85282. Phone: (480) 894-6864. Fax: (480) 921-0470. Web Site:www.acme-electric.com/aerospace John Gleason, VP/gen mgr; Gary Lesser, sls dir.

Sealed fiber nickel-cadmium batteries, battery chargers, battery control units, & AC/DC & DC/OC converters.

Acoustic Systems/ETS-Lindgren, 1301 Arrow Point Dr., Cedar Park, TX, 78613. Phone: (512) 531-6400. Phone: (512) 531-6498. Fax: (512) 531-6500.E-mail: sales@ets-lingren.com Web Site:www.acousticsystems.com

Acoustical Solutions Inc., 2420 Grenoble Rd., Richmond, VA, 23294. Phone: (800) 782-5742. Fax: (804) 346-8808.E-mail: info@accousticalsolutions.com Web Site:www.acousticalsolutions.com Michael Binns, pres; David Ingersoll, sls mgr.

Sound & noise control materials including products for the bcst/recording industry, telecommunications industry, architectural acoustics & industrial noise control.

Acrodyne Industries Inc. (Ai), (Change from Acrodyne Industries Inc). 200 Schell Ln., Phoenixville, PA, 19460. Phone: (610) 917-1300. Fax: (610) 917-8148.E-mail: ellen.rainey@acrodyne.com Web Site:www.acrodyne.com Nat Ostroff, chmn; Dan Traynor, VP sls; Ellen Rainey, mktg mgr.

AiR series of ATSC UHF on-channel repeaters that provide the ideal solution for broadcasters to fill in areas of their Authorized Digital Service area that are not sufficiently covered by their main transmitter; Mobile360 system that provides all components or equipment necessary, both at studio and transmitter, to integrate ATSC Mobile DTV transmission into any DTV broadcast facility; Universal XD Exciter/Driver system for analog to digital conversions; Quantum standard IOT and maximum efficiency depressed collector technology; complete line of liquid and air-cooled Solid-State transmitters.

Acterna, Cable Networks Division, 5808 Churchman Bypass, Indianapolis, IN, 46203. Phone: (317) 788-9351. Fax: (317) 614-8308. Web Site:www.acterna.com Kevin Kennedy, CEO; Thomas Waechter, gen mgr .

Test equipment for video nets, including broadband RF & fiber optics. (SLMs, system analyzers, leakage, sweeps & OTDRs) software.

Adcom, LLC, Box 2668, Sedona, AZ, 86339. Phone: (480) 607-2277. Fax: (928) 239-9378.E-mail: services@adcom.com Web Site:www.adcom.com

"Night Suite" DI, non-linear editing systems, bcst control systems, video conferencing. Room control systems "1 room".

Adrienne Electronics Corp., 7225 Bermuda Rd., Unit G, Las Vegas, NV, 89119. Phone: (702) 896-1858. Fax: (702) 896-3034.E-mail: info@adrielec.com Web Site:www.adrielec.com

Time code reader/generator products with PCI, PCI Express, USB and serial interfaces

Advance Products Co. Inc., 1199 E. Central, Wichita, KS, 67214. Phone: (316) 263-4231. Fax: (316) 263-4245. Web Site:www.da-lite.com Harold Knapp, gen mgr .

Mobile projector, TV & video, tables & cabinets, wall & ceiling mount brackets.

Advanced Designs Corp., 1169 W. 2nd St., Bloomington, IN, 47403. Phone: (812) 333-1922. Fax: (812) 333-2030.E-mail: adc@doprad.com Web Site:www.doprad.com Matt McGrath, pres.

DOPRAD® 32 doppler radar system, weather data display system, storm path analyzer, street-level maps, lightning, low-cost remoting & composite live doppler.

Advanced Media Inc., Boc 599, Bohemia, NY, 11716-0599. Phone: (631) 244-1616. Fax: (631) 244-1415.E-mail: team@advancedmedia.com Web Site:www.advancemedia.com

Kiosk-interactive technology.

Advanced Media Technologies, Inc., 720 S. Powerline Rd., Suite G, Deerfield Beach, FL, 33442-8156. Phone: (888) 293-5856. Fax: (954) 427-9688.E-mail: sales@amt.com Web Site:www.amt.com Ken Mosca, pres.

AMT offers a complete line of broadband products from the world's most recognized manufacturers. Products include CATV QAM IP set-tops, digital, analog & IP headend electronics, Digcipher receivers, off-air 8-vsb receivers, RF & fiber transport, digital encoders, ad insertion, line gear, modems & much more.

Advent Communications Ltd., Nashleigh Hill, Chesham, Buckinghamshire, HP5 3HE. United Kingdom. Phone: 44 1494 774400. Fax: 44 1494 791127.E-mail: sales@adventcomms.com Web Site:www.adventcomms.com Stephen Rudd, mng dir; George Koumblis, sls dir.

Provides satellite communication solutions for bcst, telecommunications, military & coml applications-design, manufacture & integrating a complete range of digital SNG flyaway & vehicle mounted terminals, a complete range of subsystems upconverters, downconverters, DVB modulators, MPEG II Video Exciters, equalizers & remote control systems.

Aeroflex, 35 South Service Rd., Plainview, NY, 11803. Phone: (516) 694-6700. Fax: (516) 694-2562. Web Site:www.aeroflex.com Leonard Borow, pres/CEO.

Trophy ClubTX , 49 Trophy Club Rd. Phone:

Test & measurement instrumentation.

AheadTek, 6410 Via Del Oro, San Jose, CA, 95119. Phone: (408) 226-9800. Phone: (408) 226-9991. Fax: (408) 226-9195. Fax: (408) 226-9194.E-mail: patj@drs-ahead.com Web Site:www.aheadtek.com Tim Higgins, pres; Patrick Johnston, exec VP & business dev.

Cost effective solutions for your specialty magnetic head applications.

Peter Albrecht Company Inc., 6250 Industrial Ct., Greendale, WI, 53129-2432. Phone: (414) 421-6630. Fax: (414) 421-9091.E-mail: sales@peteralbrecht.com Web Site:www.peteralbrecht.com T.C. Ziolkowski, pres.

Motorized studio battens, plaks & other rigging systems. Tension Grids, Chandelier Hoist, Banner Hoists designed & installed.

Alesis, 200 Scenic View Dr., Suite 201, Cumberland, RI, 02864. Phone: (401) 658-5760.E-mail: marketing@alesis.com Web Site:www.alesis.com

Digital tape recording system, mixing consoles, digital & analogue signal processing, amplification, drum machines, keyboards.

Alexander Technologies, 1511 S. Garfield Pl., Mason City, IA, 50401. Phone: (641) 423-8955. Fax: (641) 423-1644.E-mail: cservice@alexenergy.com Web Site:www.alexandertechnologies.com John Casey, pres/CEO.

Rechargeable nicad in-board, on-board & battery belts; nicad battery chargers & analyzer/conditioners; portable radio & pager batteries.

All Mobile Video Inc., 221 W. 26th St., New York, NY, 10001. Phone: (212) 727-1234. Fax: (212) 255-6644. Web Site:www.allmobilevideo.com Anton Duke, CEO; Eric Duke, pres.

San DiegoCA , 9670 Aero Dr. Phone:

Saint PetersburgFL , 10490 Gandy Blvd. Phone:

Bcst video equipment rental including truck remotes & total carry-in packages, complete studio facilities.

Allen & Heath USA, Agoura Business Center, E. 5304 Derry Ave., Suite C, Agoura Hills, CA, 91301. Phone: (800) 431-2609. Fax: (800) 431-3129. Web Site:www.allen-heath.com/us Michael Palmer, sls mgr.

Audio mixing consoles for recording & live sound applications including automated consoles.

Allen Avionics, Inc., 255 E. Second St., Mineola, NY, 11501. Phone: (516) 248-8080. Fax: (516) 747-6724.E-mail: jim@allenavionics.com Web Site:www.allenavionics.com Jim Lyons, VP.

A broad line of custom passive electronic components that include precision LC filters of all type from 20 Hz to 5GHz & electromagnetic, gen purpose, digital & video all delay lines, filters for NTSC & pal, attenuators, amplitude, phase equalizers, audio & video isolation transformers, hum eliminators, diplexers, networks & electronics timing productions.

Allied Electronics Inc., 7151 Jack Newell Blvd. S., Fort Worth, TX, 76118. Phone: (817) 595-3500. Phone: (866) 433-5722. Fax: (817) 595-8530. Web Site:www.alliedelec.com Lee Davidson, VP; Robert Pfleg, pres; Bob Whetson, sls dir; Rob Birse, dir.

Broad line distributor of electronic components.

Allied Tower Co. Inc., 4646 Mandale, Alvin, TX, 77511. Phone: (281) 331-9627. Fax: (281) 331-9822. Web Site:www.alliedtower.com Max Bowen, CEO; Jeff Bowen, pres; Doug W. Moore, VP.

Design, fabrication & erection of FM, AM, TV & communication towers.

Allison Payments Systems L.L.C., 2200 Production Dr., Indianapolis, IN, 462414912. Phone: (317) 808-2400. Phone: (800) 755-2440. Fax: (317) 808-2477.E-mail: sales@psllc.com Web Site:www.apsllc.com

Coupon payment billing systems.

Allsop Inc., Box 23, Bellingham, WA, 98227. Phone: (360) 734-9090. Fax: (360) 734-9858.E-mail: info@allsop.com Web Site:www.allsop.com Jim Allsop; Mike Allsop, co-pres.

Cleaning accessories for audio & video, record care products & compact discs, computer accessories.

Allstate Tower Company Inc., (formerly Nationwide Tower Company Inc.). Box 25, Henderson, KY, 42419. Phone: (270) 830-8512. Fax: (270) 830-8475.E-mail: sales@allstatetower.com Web Site:www.allstatetower.com Kevin Roth, VP; Sam Dorris, VP opns.

Tower Manufacturing Co. including: Tower inspections, painting, repair re-guy, lighting, antennas, feedlines, analysis, erect, dismantle, line sweeping, site monitoring, & tower tracker svcs.

Alpack Associates, Inc., 6 High Point Dr., Wayne, NJ, 07470. Phone: (973) 694-5510. Fax: (973) 694-7080.E-mail: info@alpack-pic.com Web Site:www.alpack-pic.com Les Weinstock, pres.

Standard & custom carrying & shipping cases for all bcst equipment. Both hard & soft case styles.

Alpha Technologies Inc., 3767 Alpha Way, Bellingham, WA, 98226. Phone: (360) 647-2360. Fax: (360) 671-4936.E-mail: alpha@alpha.com Web Site:www.alpha.com

Develops power conversion, protection and standby products for telecommunications and broadband cable industries, including custom, application-specific power solutions.

Alpha Video & Electronics (AVEC), 200 Mingo Church Rd., Finleyville, PA, 15332. Phone: (412) 429-2000. Fax: (724) 348-8600.E-mail: henry@aveceng.com Web Site:www.aveceng.com Henry Lassige, Sr., pres.

O.B. vans, eng vans, DSNG vans, ENG mast safety device, turnkey systems, camera transporter.

Alpine Optics Inc., 9913 N.W. 20th St., Coral Springs, FL, 33071. Phone: (954) 344-9871. Fax: (954) 344-3665.E-mail: toalpine_optics@bellsouth.net Web Site:www.alpine-optics.com Horst Stahl, pres.

Repair, maintenance of all Canon, Fujinon, Nikon, Schneider & JVC lenses.

Altronic Research Inc., Box 249, Yellville, AR, 72687. Phone: (800) 482-5623. Phone: (870) 449-4093. Fax: (870) 449-6000.E-mail: info@altronic.com Web Site:www.altronic.com John Dyess, pres.

Omegaline RF coaxial load resistors (dummy loads).

Aluma Tower Company Inc., Box 2806, 1639 Old Dixie Hwy., Vero Beach, FL, 32961-2806. Phone: (772) 567-3423. Fax: (772) 567-3432.E-mail: atc@alumatower.com Web Site:www.alumatower.com Theodore E. Gottry, VP.

Aluminum telescoping towers combined with trailers & optional shelters provides mobile units. Vehicle mounted towers for installation on customer's vehicle.

Amdocs, (A division of NYSE:DOX). 1390 Timberlake Manor Pkwy., Chesterfield, 63017. Phone: (314) 212-7000.E-mail: info@amdocs.com Web Site:www.amdocs.com Dov Baharav, CEO; Guy Dubois, exec VP.

Amdocs is the market leader in customer experience systems innovation, enabling world-leading svc providers & integrated, innovative & intentional customer experience at every point of svc.

Amek U.S.A., 8500 Balboa Blvd., Northridge, CA, 91329. Phone: (818) 920-3212. Fax: (818) 920-3208.E-mail: amekusa@harman.com

Amek, TAC (Total Audio Concepts) & Langley audio consoles for production, postproduction, audio recording, sound reinforcement & Medici signal processing equipment.

American Antenna Inc., 4707 Roosevelt St., Glen Park, IN, 46408. Phone: (219) 985-4000. Fax: (219) 985-4001.E-mail: sales@americanantenna.com Web Site:www.americanantenna.com Nick Michels, pres; Chuck Forsyth, VP sls; Rick Gard, sec.

Manufactuer, Distributor & installer of Earth Station Antennas up to 6.1m. Motorized, actuators, receivers, controllers, feeds, multi-beam feed system, LNB's & accessories.

American Eurocopter Corp., 2701 Forum Dr., Grand Prairie, TX, 75052-7099. Phone: (972) 641-0000. Fax: (972) 641-3419. Web Site:www.eurocopterusa.com Marc Paganini, pres; Brenda Revland, VP communications & PR.

Servicing North American market; manufactures & sells complete line of single- & twin-engine turbine helicopters.

American Tower Corp., (formerly Kline Towers). 10 Presidential Way, Woburn, MA, 01801. Phone: (781) 926-4772. Fax: (781) 926-4755.E-mail: lisa.poston@americantower.com Web Site:www.americantower.com Peter A. Starke, VP/gen mgr.

Owners & operators of TV, FM & other bcst towers & specialty structures.

Ampex Data Systems -America, 500 Broadway, Redwood City, CA, 94063-3199. Phone: (650) 367-3365. Fax: (650) 367-4669.E-mail: info@ampexdata.com Web Site:www.ampexdata.com Ed Bramson, pres/CEO; Bob Atchison, VP; Joel Talcott, VP.

Data recorders, data systems, mass data storage, instrumentation recorder products; 19 mm scanning recorders, library systems (DST & DIS products), related tape, after-market parts & video recorder support.

Amplivox Portable Sound Systems, 3149 MacArthur Blvd., Northbrook, IL, 60062. Phone: (847) 498-9000. Fax: (800) 267-5489.E-mail: droth@ampli.com Web Site:www.ampli.com Don Roth, CEO.

Portable sound systems/lecterns/wireless/indoor-outdoor, made in USA, UL, CSA, CE, 6 years warranty.

Amtel Network, 431 Myrtle St., Suite 6, Glendale, CA, 91203. Phone: (818) 842-8088. Fax: (818) 551-4999.E-mail: amtel@amtel.com Web Site:www.amtelsystems.com Mike Takamatsu, pres.

Text-visual intercom system.

Analog Digital International Inc., 20 E. 49th St., 2nd Fl., New York, NY, 10017-1023. Phone: (212) 688-5110. Fax: (212) 688-5405.E-mail: info@analogdigitalinc.com Web Site:www.analogdigitalinc.com Ayres D'Cunha, pres.

Sls & rentals of professional /bcst-NTSC/PAL equipment. Post production svcs. DVD authoring replication. AVID/FCP editing.

Anchor Audio Inc., 2565 W. 237th St., Torrance, CA, 90505. Phone: (310) 784-2300. Phone: (800) 262-4671. Fax: (310) 784-0066.E-mail: sales@anchoraudio.com Web Site:www.anchoraudio.com David Jacobs, pres.

Portable public address sound systems, wire & wireless intercom equipment.

Andrew Corp., 10500 W. 153rd St., Orland Park, IL, 60462. Phone: (708) 349-3300. Phone: (800) 255-1479. Fax: (708) 349-5943. Web Site:www.andrew.com Paul Cox, pres; Barry Cohen, sls dir; George Tong, mgr.

Orland ParkIL , 10500 W. 153rd St. Phone:

VHF & UHF-TV transmitting, microwave & ESA's; coaxial cable; waveguides; towers; equipment shelters; instal svcs, combiners & pressurization equipment.

Antenna Concepts Inc., 6626 Merchandise Way, Diamond Springs, CA, 95619. Phone: (530) 621-2015. Fax: (530) 622-3274.E-mail: sales@antennaconcepts.com Web Site:www.antennaconcepts.com Mark A. Cunningham, pres/CEO.

Custom & standard low-, medium- and high-power omni or directional digital & analog UHF, VHF, FM, & MMDS bcst antennas. Full power Broadcast antennas. TV: UHF/VHF analog/digital antennas including full-UHF band CP panel. Fm: Ultra Tracker single-lobe.

Anton/Bauer Inc., 14 Progress Dr., Shelton, CT, 06484. Phone: (203) 929-1100. Fax: (203) 929-9935. Web Site:www.antonbauer.com Michael Accardi, pres.

NiCad, NIMH & Li-ion cameras batteries, chargers, lighting & diagnostic accessories for the professional video industry.

Anvil Cases, 15730 Salt Lake Ave., City of Industry, CA, 91745. Phone: (626) 968-4100. Fax: (626) 968-1703. Web Site:www.anvilcase.com E-mail: web.sales@anvilcase.com Joseph Calzone, pres.

Heavy-duty reuseable, custom, standard shipping cases & containers for all bcst equipment.

APC by Schneider Electric, 132 Fairgrounds Rd, West Kingston, RI, 02892. Fax: (401) 789-3710.E-mail: info@mgeups.com Web Site:www.apc.com Laurent Vernerey, CEO.

Hoffman EstatesIL , 2895 Greenspoint Pkwy. #350. Phone:

New YorkNY , 520 8th Ave., 21st Fl. Phone:

Manufacturers of uninterruptible power systems (UPS) power conditioners & inverters that protect equipment from power related problems.

Aphex Systems Ltd., 11068 Randall St., Sun Valley, CA, 91352. Phone: (818) 767-2929. Fax: (818) 767-2641.E-mail: sales@aphex.com Web Site:www.aphex.com Marvin Caesar, pres; Wayne La Farr, product specialist.

Model 2020 MKIII, Compellor-intelligent AGC, Dominator II precision multi-band peak limiter, Aural Exciter, Expressor, remote controlled mic preams, TVGS MIC/instrument, preamplifiers, analog to digital converters.

Argo Systems, 2964 Peachtree Rd., Suite 400, Atlanta, 30305. Phone: (404) 869-4575. Fax: (404) 844-9009.E-mail: cdunn@argosys.com Web Site:www.argosys.com Catherine Dunn, VP/business dev.

An integrated affil mgmt software solution providing functionality, data mgmt, reporting & SOX compliance across a network's Affliate Finance, Sales Operations, IT & Engineering departments.

Argraph Corp., 111 Asia Pl., Carlstadt, NJ, 07072. Phone: (201) 939-7722. Fax: (201) 939-7782.E-mail: info@argraph.com Web Site:www.argraph.com Mark Roth, pres; Martin Lipton, natl sls mgr.

HaywardCA . Argraph West, 2710 McCone. Phone: Anti-stat cleaning cloths, samigron video tripods.

Aries Industries Inc., Corporate Office, 550 Elizabeth St., Waukesha, WI, 53186. Phone: (262) 896-7205. Phone: (800) 234-7205. Fax: (262) 246-7099.E-mail: sales@ariesind.com Web Site:www.ariesind.com

FresnoCA , 5748 E. Shields. Phone:

Manufacture pipeline inspection televising test & seal equipment.

Arista Information Systems, 2150 Boggs Rd., Suite 430, Duluth, GA, 30096. Phone: (678) 473-1885. Fax: (678) 473-1051.E-mail: sales@aristainfo.com Web Site:www.aristainfo.com Kim Lorenz, sls mgr.

Cable TV subscriber & statement printing.

Arrakis Systems Inc., 6604 Powell St., Loveland, CO, 80538. Phone: (970) 461-0730. Fax: (970) 663-1010.E-mail: sales@arrakis-systems.com Web Site:www.arrakis-systems.com Michael C. Palmer, pres; Jon Young, VP sls; Roderic M. Graham, VP.

Audio consoles, digital audio, satellite, live-assist, hard drive automation & production systems, studio furniture.

Arri Canada Ltd., 415 Horner Ave., Unit 11, Etobicoke, ON, M8W 4W3. Canada. Phone: (416) 255-3335. Fax: (416) 255-3399. Web Site:www.arri.com Sebastien Laffoux, camera mgr.

ARRI camera, lightning equipment & all professional accessories, sales & service.

Arris, Corporate Headquarters, 3871 Lakefield Dr., Suwanee, GA, 30024. Phone: (800) 469-6569 (in US). Phone: (770) 622-8400. Fax: (770) 622-8770. Web Site:www.arrisi.com

CMTS, cable modems, telephony voice ports & modems, oss/provisioning systems, HFC infrastructure products.

Artel Video Systems, 330 Codman Hill Rd., Boxborough, MA, 01719. Phone: (978) 263-5775. Fax: (978) 263-9755.E-mail: info@artel.com Web Site:www.artel.com Richard Dellacanonica, pres/CEO.

Since 1981 Artel Video Systems has been an industry leading developer of carrier class, bcst quality video over fiber-optic transport hardware. Our products deliver video, audio & data in real time with reliability meeting the most demanding requirements for 24/7/365 opn in harsh environments.

Artesia Technologies, 700 King Farm Blvd., Suite 400, Rockville, MD, 20850. Phone: 301-548-7850. Fax: 301-548-4015. Web Site:www.artesia.com Brian Hedquist, dir mktg.

Ascent Media Creative Services Inc., (dba Encore). 6344 Fountain Ave., Hollywood, CA, 90028. Phone: (323) 466-7663. Fax: (323) 466-5539.E-mail: info@encorehollywood.com Web Site:www.encorehollywood.com Robert Solomon, pres., Asia Broadcast Centre. Phone:

Ascent Media Management Services, 2901 W. Alameda Ave., Burbank, CA, 91505. Phone: (818) 840-7000. Fax: (818) 840-7129. Web Site:www.4mc.com William Humphrey, pres; Beth Simon, sls VP, sr VP; Andre Macaluso, opns VP.

NorthvaleNJ , 235 Pegasus Ave. Phone:

Postproduction video & film svcs: editing, telecine, sound, duplication, satellite svcs, film lab, standard conversion tape to film transfers & digital asset mgmt.

Ascent Media Services, (Formerly Waterfront Communications Corp.). 520 Broadway, 5th Fl., Santa Monica, CA, 90401-2420. Phone: (310) 434-7000. Fax: (310) 434-7001. Jose Royo, CEO; Margaret Craig, COO; Tom Kuehle, sr VP.

A transmission company specializing in video switching, quality control, last mile connections, remote transmissions, production & audiovisual svcs to the bcst, cable & corporate TV industries.

Aspect Software, (formerly Concerto Software). 300 Apollo Dr., Chelmsford, MA, 01824. Phone: (978) 250-7900. Phone: (888) 412-7728. Fax: (978) 244-7420. Web Site:www.aspect.com E-mail: info@aspect.com

Newport BeachCA , 1300 Bristol St. N, Suite 100. Phone:

Great NeckNY , 1010 Northern Blvd, Suite 208. Phone:

DallasTX , 5001 LBJ Fwy, Suite 727. Phone:

DallasTX , 3778 Realty Rd. Phone:

Automated telephone call processing products for inbound & outbound call centers.

Aspera Inc., 5900 Hollis St., Emeryville, 94608. Phone: (510) 849-2386. Fax: (510) 868-8392.E-mail: dana@asperasoft.com Web Site:www.asperasoft.com Michelle Munson, pres/co-founder; Serban Simu, VP engrg/co-founder.

Software developer of high speed file transfer technology, fasp.

Associated Press Broadcast Services, 1825 K St. N.W., Suite 800, Washington, DC, 20006-1202. Phone: (202) 736-1100. Fax: (202) 736-1124. Fax: (202) 736-1199. Web Site:www.apbroadcasting.com James R. Williams, VP; Lee Perryman, dir.

AP NewsDesk: Newsroom computer software program for mng TV, radio news & info resources.

Atlantic Inc., 10018 Santa Fe Springs Rd., Sante Fe Springs, CA, 90670-2922. Phone: (562) 903-9550. Fax: (562) 903-9053.E-mail: customer_relations@atlantic-inc.com Web Site:www.atlantic-inc.com Leo Dardashti, pres; Don Dolliver, VP sls.

Manufacturer of metal storage systems for DVDs, CDs, & VHS.

Atlantic Sound Systems, R.R. 2, New Glasgow, Pictou County, NS, B2H 5C5. Canada. Phone: (902) 752-8527.E-mail: plann@wisic.com

Professional bcstg, sound & lighting equipment. Rental & PA Installations.

Atlantic Video Inc., 650 Massachusetts Ave. N.W., Washington, DC, 20001. Phone: (202) 408-0900. Fax: (202) 408-8496.E-mail: aschwab@atlanticvideo.com Web Site:www.atlanticvideo.com Ed Milligan, pres; Ted Nelson, dir.

Atlantic video is a full svc bcst production svc facility, from studio, remote, post & transmission.

Atlas Case Corp., 1380 So. Cherokee St., Denver, CO, 80223. Phone: (888) 325-2199. Fax: (877) 525-2339. Web Site:www.atlascases.com Randy Sabey, pres.

Airline-approved shipping & carrying cases. Local transport cases, custom or from stock.

Atlas Sound, 4545 E. Baseline Rd., Phoenix, AZ, 85042. Phone: (800) 876-3332. Phone: (602) 438-4545. Fax: (800) 765-3435.E-mail: atlascustser@atlassound.com Web Site:www.atlassound.com Manny Kitagawa, gen sls mgr; Ken Peck, rgnl sls mgr; Steve Young, mktg VP.

EnnisTX . Atlas Sound Manufacturing, 1601 Jack McKay.

Atlas Sound brand microphone & equipment stands, accessories; equipment consoles, racks & cabinets; loudspeaker systems; a/v monitoring devices.

Audico Labels, 118 South Main St., Goshen, IN, 46526. Phone: (800) 252-5667. Fax: (661) 760-8775.E-mail: audiolabels@audicolabels.com Web Site:www.audicolabels.com Bill Landow, owner; Claudia Landow, owner.

Media pressure sensitive labels.

Audio Accessories Inc., 25 Mill St., Marlow, NH, 03456. Phone: (603) 446-3335. Fax: (603) 446-7543.E-mail: audioacc@patchbays.com Web Site:www.patchbays.com M.B. Hall, pres; T.J. Symonds, opns mgr.

Jack panels, (audio & video patchbays) patch cords, telephone jacks & plugs, pre-wired jack panels (miniature & full-size) & video panels.

Audio Implements/GKC, 1703 Pearl St., Waukesha, WI, 53186-5626. Phone: (262) 524-2424. Fax: (262) 524-7898.E-mail: info@audioimplements.com Web Site:www.audioimplements.com Walter L. Kolb, owner; Anita Kolb, sec.

Acoustic coiled earpiece, receivers & cords, microphone line & monitor amplifiers, used in conjunction with IFB system.

Audio Precision Inc., 5750 S.W. Arctic Dr., Beaverton, OR, 97005. Phone: (503) 627-0832. Fax: (503) 641-8906.E-mail: sales@audioprecision.com Web Site:www.audioprecision.com John Scoles, sls dir; David Schmoldt, pres; Tom Williams, mktg dir.

2700 Series, Portable One & ATS-1, ATS-2 audio test sets for bcst & satellite use.

Audio Processing Technology Ltd./APT, Whitehouse Business Park, 729 Springfield Rd., Belfast, BT3 9JQ. Ireland. Phone: 44 0 28 9067 7200. Fax: 44 0 28 9067 7201.E-mail: marketing@aptx.com Web Site:www.aptx.com

Los AngelesCA , 6255 Sunset Blvd, Suite 1025. Phone:

Digital (apt-X) audio compression system for professional applications such as storage & transmission of audio over low capacity digital circuits such as ISDN.

Audio-Technica U.S., Inc., 1221 Commerce Dr., Stow, OH, 44224. Phone: (330) 686-2600. Fax: (330) 686-0719.E-mail: pro@atus.com Web Site:www.audio-technica.com

Microphones, wireless microphones, headphones, automatic microphone mixers, phono cartridges, turntables, audio & video accessories.

Audio-Video Engineering Co., One Pineapple Ln., Stuart, FL, 34996. Phone: (772) 219-3623. Fax: (772) 219-3624. Olga M. Drucker, pres.

Video hum stop coil (hum bucker).

Audioarts Engineering, 600 Industrial Dr., New Bern, NC, 28562. Phone: (252) 638-7000. Fax: (252) 635-4857.E-mail: sales@wheatstone.com Web Site:www.audioartsengineering.com Gary C. Snow, pres; Andrew Calvanese, VP; Jay Tyler, gen sls mgr.

Manufacturer of digital & analog broadcast audio mixing consoles & processing equipment.

Audiolab Electronics Inc., 10620 Industrial Ave., Suite100, Roseville, CA, 95678. Phone: (916) 784-0200. Fax: (916) 784-1425.E-mail: info@audiolabelectronics.com Web Site:www.audiolabelectronics.com Ronald A. Stofan, pres/CEO.

Professional line of bulk tape degaussers for all formats of tape including: Beta SP, DAT 2" reels up to 16" diameters, hard drives, DLT media & degaussing svc.

Auernheimer Labs Corp., 4561 E. Florence Ave., Fresno, CA, 93725. Phone: (559) 442-1048. Curley Auernheimer, pres; Warren Auernheimer, VP; Dwayne Auernheimer, sec/treas.

Manufactures household audio & video equipment; wholesales chemicals & allied products.

Austin Insulators Inc., 7510 Airport Rd., Mississauga, ON, L4T 2H5. Canada. Phone: (905) 405-1144. Fax: (905) 405-1150.E-mail: sales@austin-insulators.com Web Site:www.austin-insulators.com Patrick Warr, pres; Beverly O'Brien, exec VP.

Base/guyline insulators, static drain devices, tower lighting transformers, replacements for obsolete insulators & LED lighting for AM(MW), LW antennas .

Autodesk, (formerly Alias/WaveFront Inc.). 210 King St. E., Toronto, ON, M5A 1J7. Canada. Phone: (416) 362-9181. Fax: (416) 369-6140. Web Site:www.autodesk.ca Carol Bartz, chmn; Carl Boss, pres bcstg.

2D & 3D computer graphic imaging & animation software for professionals in entertainment & industrial markets.

Autodesk, 10 Duke St., Montreal, PQ, H3C 2L7. Canada. Phone: (514) 393-1616. Fax: (514) 393-0110.E-mail: med-ent@autodesk.com Web Site:www.autodesk.com Stig Gruman, VP & digital entertainment; Marc Petit, sr VP.

Autodesk solutions for creating, mgng & distributing digital content, so artists can create once & use anywhere.

Autogram Corp., Box 456, 1500 Capital Ave., Plano, TX, 75074-8113. Phone: (972) 424-8585. Phone: (800) 327-6901. Fax: (972) 423-6334.E-mail: info@autogramcorp.com Web Site:www.autogramcorp.com Ernest T. Ankele Jr., pres/CEO; Delores Ankele, comptroller; John A. Stanley Jr. Jr., dir mktg.

Pacemaker IIk audio consoles, Pacemaker 6, 8, 10 Slide Pot, Mini-Mix 8 & Mini-Mix 12 Economy Consoles.Solution 20 audio systems, CYA-4 emergency switchers. Autoclock clock/timer/thermometer.

Automatic Devices Company, 2121 S. 12th St., Allentown, PA, 18103. Phone: (610) 797-6000. Fax: (610) 797-4088.E-mail: info@automaticdevices.com Web Site:www.automaticdevices.com

Cyclorama tracks, lighting tracks, lift & draw machines, electronic limit switches.

Autoscript, (formerly BDL-Autoscript). 16 Progress Dr., Shelton, CT, 06484. Phone: (203) 338-8356. Fax: (203) 338-8359.E-mail: support@autoscript.tv Web Site:www.autoscript.tv George Andros, consultant; Gordon Tubbs, VP.

Twickenham United Kingdom. Autoscript (UK), Unit 2, Heathlands Close. Phone:b.larter@autoscript.tv Brian Larter, mgng dir.

Design & manufacture of digital teleprompting systems, maintain a high level of new product dev.

AVerMedia Technologies Inc., 423 Dixon Landing Rd., Milpitas, CA, 95035. Phone: (800) 863-2332. Phone: (408) 263-3828. Web Site:www.aver.com Arthur Pait, pres.

Aside from TV Turner/Desktop TV Personal Video Recorder products, AVerMeida also provides digital camera picture TV display devices, Document Camera & PC-to-TV Converters.

Avid Broadcast, 1925 Andover St., Tewksbury, MA, 01876. Phone: (978) 640-6789. Fax: (978) 640-1366. Web Site:www.avid.com Rich Griffin, VP sls & customer svc.

BurbankCA , 115 N. First St. Phone:

New YorkNY , 575 Lexington Ave., 14th Fl. Phone:

MadisonWI , 6400 Enterprise Ln. , Suite 200. Phone:

Automated bcst newsroom systems. Non-linear video editing systems, media storage & networking systems, video server, content mgmt systems & asset mgmt systems.

Avid Technology Inc., Avid Technology Park, One Park W., Tewksbury, MA, 01876. Phone: (800) 949-AVID. Phone: (978) 640-6789. Fax: (978) 640-1366. Fax: (978) 640-1366.E-mail: info@avid.com Web Site:www.avid.com Ken Sexton, CFO; Martin Vann, VP sls; Gary Greenfield, CEO.

BurbankCA , 115 N. 1st St, Suite 100. Phone:

New YorkNY , 317 Madison Ave., Suite 521, 5th Fl. Phone:

Avid's networked bcst news productions are designed to facilitate the process of digital news gathering (DNG).

Avtech Systems Inc., 141 Ayers Ct., Teaneck, NJ, 07666. Phone: (201) 833-8777. Fax: (201) 833-4995.E-mail: disamuel@aol.com Web Site:www.avtechsystems.com Fred M. Samuel, pres; David Samuel, sls VP.

Closed circuit video equipment, components & accessories security video systems.

Axcera, 103 Freedom Dr., Box 525, Lawrence, PA, 15055. Phone: (800) 215-2614. Fax: (724) 873-8105.E-mail: info@axcera.com Web Site:www.axcera.com Dave Neff, pres; Richard Schwartz, VP & product mgmt & mktg; Mike Rosso, sls VP.

Low Medium & High Power Solid State TV Transmitters, High Power Transmitters, Liquid-Cooled Solid State Transmitters, Mobile Multimedia Base Stns, MMDS/BRS/MDS & WCS Transmitters, DOCSIS(r) Base Broadband Wireless Acess, Anagol & Digital, UHF, VHF, L-Band & S-Band.

Aydin Displays Inc., (formerly Teltron Technologies Inc.). 2 Riga Ln., Birdsboro, PA, 19508. Phone: (610) 582-9450. Phone: (800) 835-8766. Fax: (610) 582-0851.E-mail: teltron@ptdprolog.net Web Site:www.teltrontech.com Clyde Mock, sls mgr; Ronald Ordway, CEO.

Camera tubes for monochrome, color, special purpose applications & view finder CRTs.

B

B&B Systems, 1840 Flower St., Glendale, CA, 91201. Phone: (818) 551-5871. Fax: (818) 551-0686.E-mail: sales@bandbsystems.com Web Site:www.bandbsystems.com

Design & instal of production & postproduction systems, vans & mobile units, manufacturer of audio monitoring products.

BBE Sound Inc., 5381 Production Dr., Huntington Beach, CA, 92649. Phone: (714) 897-6766. Fax: (714) 896-0736.E-mail: info@bbesound.com Web Site:www.bbesound.com Rob Rizzuto, VP sls.

Audio/video signal processors to eliminate phase & amplitude distortion.

BEI Duncan Electronics, (BEI Technologies, Inc.). 170 Technology Dr., Irvine, CA, 92618-2401. Phone: (949) 341-9500. Fax: (949) 453-2700.E-mail: sales@beiducan.com Web Site:www.beiducan.com Philippe Roux, gen mgr .

Manufacturer of motion & position sensors

BEXT Inc., 1045 10th Ave., San Diego, CA, 92101. Phone: (619) 239-8462. Fax: (619) 239-8474.E-mail: bext@bext.com Web Site:www.bext.com Dennis Pieri, CEO; Claudio Tilesi, CFO.

Radio & Digital TV Transmitters, Antennas, Amplifiers, Receivers, Boosters, STLs, RF Combiners, RF Filters, Stereo Generators, FmExtra Digital Radio Encoders & Receivers.

BGW Systems, Amplifier Technologies, Inc., (BGW Systems, an Amplifier Technologies, Inc. company). 1749 Chapin Rd., Montebello, CA, 90640. Phone: (323) 278-0001. Fax: (310) 323-0083.E-mail: sales@bgw.com Web Site:www.bgw.com Morris Kessler, pres; Angie Scott, dir opns.

Professional, bcst, coml audio power amplifiers & self-powered subwoofer systems.

BHP Inc., 4700 Chase Ave., Lincolnwood, IL, 60712. Phone: (847) 677-3000. Fax: (847) 677-1311.E-mail: sales@bhpinc.com Web Site:www.bhpinc.com Jonathan Banks, pres.

Motion picture laboratory equipment, film printers & accessories.

Bald Mountain Laboratory, 222 Bellevue Rd., Troy, NY, 12180. Phone: (518) 279-9753.E-mail: hambob@highstream.net Robert S. Henry, owner.

Frequency readings.

Baldor Linear, (formerly Northern Magnetics Inc.). 25026 Anza Dr., Santa Clarita, CA, 91355-3413. Phone: (805) 257-0216. Fax: (805) 257-2037. John McFarland, chmn/CEO; Ronald Tucker, pres/COO; Randall Breaux, VP mktg.

Band Pro Film & Digital Inc., 3403 W. Pacific Ave., Burbank, CA, 91505. Phone: (818) 841-9655. Fax: (818) 841-7649.E-mail: sales@bandpro.com Web Site:www.bandpro.com Renee Contreras, exec VP; Amnon Band, pres/CEO.

Dornach Germany. Band Pro Munich GmbH, Karl-Hammerschmidt Str. 38. Phone:

Tel Aviv Israel. Band Pro Israel, Hasolelim 3. Phone:

Band Pro Film and Digital, Home of HD, offers cinemtographers the highest level of expertise & finest equipment available.

Barco Inc., formerly (Barco Visual Solutions, LLC). 3059 Premiere Pkwy., Duluth, GA, 30097. Phone: (678) 475-8000. Fax: (678) 475-8100.E-mail: bpsmarketing@barco.com Web Site:www.barco.com/projection_systems Larry Steelman, sls dir; Tom Ray, exec VP & gen mgr; Jim Durant, mktg mgr; Ellyce Kelly, mgr.

Offers complete monitoring solutions for control rooms in telecom traf, surveillance, pub utilities, process control & financing.

Baron Telecom, 2355 Industrial Park Blvd., Cumming, GA, 30041. Phone: (678) 455-6298. Ran Bukshpan, CEO; Ron Raviv, CFO; Ross Kruchten, pres.

FrederickMD , 4640 Wedgewood Blvd. Phone:

HoustonTX , 10430 Rogers Rd. Phone:

KirklandWA , 11112 117th Pl. N.E. Phone:

Project mgmt & turn-key construction of communications towers, including erection, maintenance & inspection of tall towers.

Russ Bassett, 8189 Byron Rd., Whittier, CA, 90606. Phone: (562) 945-2445. Fax: (562) 698-8972.E-mail: info@russbassett.com Web Site:www.russbassett.com

High density storage solutions for all media type.

Battery Pros Inc., 5659 BlackJack Rd., Flowery Branch, GA, 30542-5402. Phone: (770) 271-8801. Phone: (800) 451-7171. Fax: (770) 271-9714.E-mail: sales@batteryprosinc.com Web Site:www.batteryprosinc.com Patti Novak, pres; Maria Arce, sec.

Battery recelling/rebuilding for Bricks & Belts, primary & secondary batteries, custom battery pack design & manufacture.

Bauer Transmitters, 10870 Pellicano, Suite 5, El Paso, TX, 79935. Phone: (915) 595-1048. Fax: (915) 595-1840.E-mail: paul@bauertx.com Web Site:www.bauertx.com Paul E. Gregg, pres.

Remanufactured Bauer-Sparta & Elcom Bauer AM/FM transmitters, AM combining & antenna coupling equipment.

Belar Electronics Laboratory Inc., Box 76, 119 Lancaster Ave., Devon, PA, 19333. Phone: (610) 687-5550. Fax: (610) 687-2686.E-mail: sales@belar.com Web Site:www.belar.com Arno Meyer, pres.

AM, FM, FM stereo, SCA, RDS/RBDS, shortwave, TV, TV stereo modulation & frequency monitors.

Belden, (formerly Belden Electronics Divison). 2200 U.S. Hwy. 27 S., Richmond, IN, 47374. Phone: (765) 983-5200. Fax: (765) 983-5294.E-mail: info@belden.com Web Site:www.belden.com

Precision video coaxial, triaxial cables, professional music cables, ENG cables, audio snakes, RGB cables & 50 ohm transmission cables.

Bencher Inc., 241 Depot St., Antioch, IL, 60002. Phone: (847) 838-3195. Fax: (847) 838-3479.E-mail: bencher@bencher.com Web Site:www.bencher.com

Photographic & video vertical camera copystands & accessories, including Motion Picture Maker movable copy stage.

Benchmark Media Systems Inc., 203 East Hampton Pl., Suite 2, Syracuse, NY, 13206-1707. Phone: (315) 437-6300. Phone: (800) 262-4675. Fax: (315) 437-8119.E-mail: sales@benchmarkmedia.com Web Site:www.benchmarkmedia.com Allen H. Burdick, pres; R. Rory Rall, sls mgr.

Audio processing & distribution systems, VU/PPM meters, interface/headphone amplifiers, microphone pre-amplifiers; digital to analog & analog to digital converters.

Bend-A-Lite Flexible Neon, 905 G St., Hampton, VA, 23661. Phone: (757) 245-7675. Phone: (800) 236-3254. Fax: (757) 244-4819. Fax: (877) 445-7298. Web Site:www.bendalite.com E-mail: cs@bendalite.com Hugh Jones, pres; Ron Koppel, mktg dir.

Flexible neon that can be cut with scissors, cut section can be re-electrified. 110v, 12v, 220v, 24v, indoor/outdoor. Lengths up to 300 ft., brilliant neon colors.

Benner-Nawman Inc., 3450 Sabin Brown Rd., Wickenburg, AZ, 85390. Phone: (800) 992-3833. Phone: (928) 684-2813. Fax: (928) 684-7041.E-mail: mail@bnproducts.com Web Site:www.bnproducts.com Edward R. Kientz, pres.

Specialty tools for CATV, cable termination & distribution boxes (cabinets).

Bexel, (Formerly Bexel Corp.). 2701 N. Ontario St., Burbank, CA, 91504. Phone: (818) 841-5051. Fax: (818) 841-1572. E-mail: rentals@bexel.com Web Site:www.bexel.com Joyce Bente, sls; Andy Crist, CEO; Greg Bragg, gen mgr-rentals; Craig Schiller, worldwide live events production; Scott Nardelli, Bexel1BFS/bcst fiber solutions.

HerndonVA . Bexel DC Office:, 555 Herndon Pkwy., , Suite 135. Phone:

MiamiFL . Bexel Miami Office:, 20239 N.E. 15th Ct. Phone:

NorcrossGA . Bexel Atlanta Office:, 5555 Oak Brook Pkwy., Suite 160. Phone:

New YorkNY . Bexel New York Office:, 625 W. 55th St. Phone:

IrvingTX . Bexel Dallas Office:, 1001 N. Union Bower, Suite 130. Phone:

SeattleWA . Bexel Seattle Office:, 3314 Fourth Ave. S. Phone:

Bexel has delivered the finest customer svc & best audio/video production equipment rentals for 30 years & remains the world leader. Real 24/7/365 emergency svc/tech natl offices/experts in solutions/custom engrg, systems design & application/sound tech advice, also used equipment sls.

Bexel Corporation, 5555 Oak Brook Pkwy., Suite 160, Norcross, GA, 30093. Phone: (770) 448-3000.

Beyerdynamic, 56 Central Ave., Farmingdale, NY, 11735. Phone: (631) 293-3200. Phone: (800) 293-4463. Fax: (631) 293-3288.E-mail: info@beyerdynamic.com Web Site:www.beyerdynamic.com Nel Keinz, mgr; Bob Lowig, sls; Alan Feckanin, natl sls mgr.

Microphones, headsets, monitor headphones, studio & on-location UHF & VHF wireless systems.

Beyond Broadband Technology LLC, 6125 Paluxy Dr., Tyler, TX, 75703. Phone: (903) 561-4411. Fax: (903) 561-4031.E-mail: tony@bbtsolution.com Web Site:www.bbtsolution.com William Bauer, ptnr, CEO; Bennett Hooks, ptnr, CFO; Tony Swain, ptnr, COO.

GeringNE , 1140 10th St.

PowellOH , 8477 Trail Lake Dr.

DCAS-open standard downloadable conditional access & MPEG 4 Transport.

BIAP Inc., 5800 Granite Pkwy., Suite 480, Plano, TX, 75024. Phone: (972) 464-5880. Fax: (972) 464-5881.E-mail: jgregoire@biap.com Web Site:www.biap.com Timothy Peters, CEO; John Gregoire, pres.

Bird Electronic Corp., 30303 Aurora Rd., Solon, OH, 44139-2794. Phone: (866) 695-4569. Fax: (866) 546-4306.E-mail: sales@bird-technologies.com Web Site:www.bird-technologies.com

Bird Technologies Group is a global, innovative supplier of RF products, systems, svcs & educ solutions.

Birns and Sawyer Inc., 6381 De Longpre Ave., Los Angeles, CA, 90028. Phone: (323) 466-8211. Fax: (323) 466-1868.E-mail: info@birnsandsawyer.com Web Site:www.birnsandsawyer.com William Meurer, pres.

Camera and support, lighting, grip rental and sales.

Bitcentral Inc., (formerly Miralite Communications Inc.). 18872 Bardeen Ave., Irvine, CA, 92612. Phone: (949) 253-9003. Fax: (949) 253-9027.E-mail: sales@bitcentral.com Web Site:www.bitcentral.com Fred Fourcher, CEO.

Bicentral is in the business of providing innovative solutions that transform the mgmt, production & distribution of the news.

Black Audio, Box 106, Ventura, CA, 93002. Phone: (805) 653-5557.E-mail: sales@blackaudio.com Web Site:www.blackaudio.com Bruce Black, pres.

We provide parts, tools & accessories to all areas of pro audio.

Blimpy Floating Signs/Bend-A-Lite, 905 G St., Hampton, VA, 23661. Phone: (757) 245-7675. Phone: (800) 448-2014. Fax: (757) 244-4819.E-mail: cs@blimpy.com Web Site:www.blimpy.com Hugh Jones, pres; Ron Koppel, mktg dir.

Giant blimps, hot air balloons & rooftop balloons. Complete custom department for any shape or size, flexible neon in seven brilliant colors.

Blonder Tongue Laboratories Inc., Box 1000, One Jake Brown Rd., Old Bridge, NJ, 08857-1000. Phone: (732) 679-4000. Phone: (800) 523-6049. Fax: (732) 679-4353. Web Site:www.blondertongue.com E-mail: information@blondertongue.com

Manufacturer of private cable equipment, including satellite receivers, modulators, processors, amplifiers, combiners & passives.

Bogen Communications Inc., 50 Spring St., Ramsey, NJ, 07446. Phone: (201) 934-8500. Phone: (800) 999-2809. Fax: (201) 934-9832.E-mail: info@bogen.com Web Site:www.bogen.com Michael Fleischer, pres; David Chambers, sls VP; Maureen Flotard, CFO.

Audio amplifiers, mixer-preamplifiers, power amplifiers; FM/AM tuners & receivers; intercom systems; pub address & sound reinforcement systems; digital repeater products & speakers.

Bogen Imaging Inc., 565 E. Crescent Ave., Ramsey, NJ, 07446. Phone: (201) 818-9500. Fax: (201) 818-9177.E-mail: info@bogenimaging.com Web Site:www.bogenimaging.us Paul Wagner, sls dir; Mark Bender, sls dir.

Professional video products including tripods, fluid heads, dollies, stands & accessories. Grip equipment & lighting filters.

Boonton Electronics Corp., 25 Eastmans Rd., Parsippany, NJ, 07054-3702. Phone: (973) 386-9696. Fax: (973) 386-9191.E-mail: boonton@boonton.com Web Site:www.boonton.com Edward Garcia, pres; John Kenneally, VP sls; Paul Genova, CFO; Brent Hessen-Schmidt, mktg dir; Richard Blackwell, engrg VP; Monty Johnson, CEO; Wolfgang Damm, product mgmt dir; Larry Henderson, cmo.

Electronic test & measuring equipment: microwave/RF power, RF voltmeters, capacitance/inductance & modulation meters.

Bradley Broadcast and Pro Audio, 7309-D Grove Rd., Frederick, MD, 21704. Phone: (800) 732-7665. Phone: (301) 682-8700. Fax: (301) 682-8377.E-mail: info@bradleybroadcast.com Web Site:www.bradleybroadcast.com Art Reed, gen mgr; David Matthews, pres.

Your source for all major brands of radio & professional audio equipment. The friendly personal svc of a family-owned company, the tech experience of many years in the business & very competeitive pricing too.

Broadcast Data Consultants, 51 S. Main Ave., Suite 312, Clearwater, FL, 33765. Phone: (800) 275-6204.E-mail: bdc@broadcastdata.com Web Site:www.broadcastdata.com Neil Edwards, VP; Scott Wachtler, pres.

The Traffic C.O.P. for windows traffic billing progm. Free CD Rom demo available.

Broadcast Electronic Services, 4825 Trawler Ct., Jacksonville, FL, 32225. Phone: (904) 646-1630. Fax: (904) 641-1443.

Betabox/GPI net 410, video-editing interface products for E.N.G. & postproduction; T.B.C. remote devices.

Broadcast Electronics Inc., 4100 N. 24th St., Quincy, IL, 62305. Phone: (217) 224-9600. Fax: (217) 224-9607.E-mail: bdcast@bdcast.com Web Site:www.bdcast.com Ray Miklius, VP; Tim Bealor, VP.

Radio bcst equipment including digital studio systems, AM, FM transmitters, RPUs & STLs.

Broadcast Engineering, 9800 Metcalf Ave., Overland Park, KS, 66212. Phone: (913) 967-1737. Fax: (913) 967-1905. Web Site:www.broadcastengineering.com E-mail: brad.dick@penton.com Wayne Madden, publisher; Brad Dick, editor.

Banbury, Oxon, Box 250. Phone:

Shinjuku-ku, Tokyo. Orient Echo Inc., 1101 Grand Maison, Shimomiyabi-cho 2-18. Phone:

BrooklynNY , 335 Court St., 9. Phone:

Broadcast Engineering: Published for mgmt & engrg personnel working in bcst, production, postproduction & cable facilities in North America.

Broadcast Equipment Surplus Inc., Box 1300, Raymond, MS, 39154. Phone: (601) 857-8573. Fax: (601) 857-2346.E-mail: corkren@netdoor.com Jeffrey Corkren, VP.

Represents bcst equipment manufacturers; sls, svc, instal, turnkey designs, engrg; new & used equipment.

Broadcast International Group, 10458 N.W. 31st Terr., Doral, FL, 33172. Phone: (305) 599-2112. Fax: (305) 599-1133.E-mail: anamaria@bigmiami.com Web Site:www.bigmiami.com Ana Maria Sagastegui, pres.

Bcst TV equipment.

Broadcast Microwave Services Inc., 12367 Crosthwaite Cir., Dock 10, Poway, CA, 92064. Phone: (858) 391-3050. Phone: (800) 669-9667. Fax: (858) 391-3049.E-mail: sales@bms-inc.com Web Site:www.bms-inc.com Graham Bunney, pres & gen mgr .

Los AngelesCA , 293 Sycamore Grove. Phone:

WaynesboroVA , 105A Lew Dewitt Blvd, #278. Phone:

COFDM wireless microwave, transmitters, receivers & antenna systems for ENG vehicles, helicopters, autotrackers, central receive sites.

Broadcast Sports Technologies, 1360 Blair Dr., Suite A, Odenton, MD, 21113. Phone: (410) 672-3900. Fax: (410) 672-3906. Peter Larsson, gen mgr .

Supply microwave, camera & cable equipment for large sporting events. Supply remote control cameras & communication systems.

Broadcast Store Inc., 9420 Lurline Ave., Unit C, Chatsworth, CA, 91311. Phone: (818) 998-9100.E-mail: sales@broadcaststore.com Web Site:www.broadcaststore.com Lou Claude, pres.

MiamiFL , 1031 Ives Dairy Rd. Phone:

New YorkNY , 500 W. 37th St. Phone:

Buy, sell, consign new & preowned Audio/Video bcst equiptment for production & post-production needs.

Broadcast Supply Worldwide, 7012 27th St. W., Tacoma, WA, 98466. Phone: (800) 426-8434. Fax: (800) 231-7055.E-mail: sales@bswusa.com Web Site:www.bswusa.com Irv Law, chmn; Tim Schwieger, pres.

Audio bcst equipment distributor. Representing over 200 manufacturers worldwide.

Broadcast Video Systems Corp., 25 Forest Ridge Rd., Richmond Hill, ON, L4E 3L8. Canada. Phone: (905) 305-0565. Fax: (416) 946-1964.E-mail: bvs@bvs.ca Web Site:www.bvs.ca Bert Verwey, pres.

SDI, analog video keyers, chroma keyers, closed captioning, encoders/decoders, positioner, bridge, V-chip, data transmission, encoders & transcoders.

Broadcasters General Store Inc., 2480 S.E. 52nd St., Ocala, FL, 34480. Phone: (352) 622-7700. Fax: (352) 629-7000.E-mail: info@bgs.cc Web Site:www.bgs.cc

Professional audio, video & RF equipment. Telco interfaces, digital codecs, 400+ vendor line card. Axia Opx

Bryston Ltd., Box 2170, 677 Neal Dr., Peterborough, ON, K9J 6X7. Canada. Phone: (705) 742-5325. Fax: (705) 742-0882.E-mail: jamestanner@bryston.ca Web Site:www.bryston.ca

Audio amplifiers, pre-amplifiers, crossovers, & microphone pre-amps.

Bud Industries Inc., 4605 E. 355 St., Willoughby, OH, 44094. Phone: (440) 946-3200. Fax: (440) 951-4015.E-mail: saleseast@budind.com Web Site:www.budind.com Blair K. Haas, VP mktg.

PhoenixAZ , Box 41190. Phone:

Open & welded racks; cabinets & accessories.

Burk Technology, 7 Beaver Brook Rd., Littleton, MA, 01460. Phone: (978) 486-0086. Fax: (978) 486-0081.E-mail: sales@burk.com Web Site:www.burk.com Peter C. Burk, pres.

Bcst transmitter remote control & monitoring.

Burle Industries Inc., 1000 New Holland Ave., Lancaster, PA, 17601-5688. Phone: (717) 295-6888. Fax: (717) 295-6096.E-mail: burlesls@burle.com Web Site:www.burle.com E. Burlefinger, pres/CEO; Carl Rintz, exec VP; Kirk Jenne, gen counsel.

VHF/FM power tubes, photomultipliers & imaging devices.

Burlington A/V Recording Media Inc., 106 Mott St., Oceanside, NY, 11572. Phone: (516) 678-4414. Phone: (800) 331-3191. Fax: (516) 678-8959.E-mail: sales@burlington-av.com Web Site:www.burlington-av.com Ruth Schwartz, VP; Jan Alan, pres.

Wholesale distributor for all formats of recording media, blank audio/video tape, CD-R, DVD-RR, diskettes, data media, A/V recording equipment.

Burst Electronics Inc., Box 65947, Albuquerque, NM, 87193. Phone: (505) 898-1455. Fax: (505) 898-0159.E-mail: sales@burstelectronics.com Web Site:www.burstelectronics.com Brad Hamlin, pres.

CG, DA's, HD/analog video switchers, video mixers, decoders, logo generator, video generators, TBC & GPI converters.

C

CADCO Systems Inc., 1600 Capital Ave., Suite 2, Plano, TX, 75074. Phone: (972) 271-3651. Phone: (800) 877-2288. Fax: (972) 271-3654.E-mail: carmen@cadcosystems.com Web Site:www.cadcosystems.com Steven G. Johnson, chmn/CEO; Carmen Howard, stn mgr.

Manufacturer of CATV & broadband communication products such as modulators, demodulators, signal processors, ch converters, translators & special application headend equipment, fixed-channel & frequency agile.

CATV Services Inc., 12099 N.W. 98th Ave., Hialeah Gardens, FL, 33010-2927. Phone: (305) 512-5601. Phone: (800) 227-1200. Fax: (305) 512-5606.E-mail: info@catvservices.com Web Site:www.catvservices.com Richard C. Richmond, pres.

Excess inventory professionals, buy & sell.

CBT Systems, 10115 Carroll Canyon Rd., San Diego, CA, 92131. Phone: (858) 536-2927. Fax: (858) 536-2354. Darrell Wendhardt, pres.

TV bcst studio systems & mobile unit design, engrg & integration.

CCI Systems Inc., (Formerly CCI). 105 Kent St., Iron Mountain, MI, 49801. Phone: (800) 338-9299. Web Site:www.ccisystems.com John P. Jamar, pres/CEO.

Builds & intergrates communication network. With ove 50 years of experience engrg, constructing & integrating complex networks, CCI Systems has the unique expertise required to deliver carrier-classs turnkey solutions for all networks platforms.

C-COR/ Arris, 60 Decibel Rd., State College, PA, 16801. Phone: (814) 238-2461. Fax: (814) 238-4065. Web Site:www.c-cor.net David Woodle, chmn/CEO.

PleasantonCA . Broadband Management Soultions, Software Divison Headquarters, 5673 Gibraltar Dr., Suite 100. Phone:

LakewoodCO . Broadband Network Services, Services Division, 300 Union Blvd., Suite 515. Phone:

MeridenCT . Broadband Communication Products, Product Division Headquarters, 999 Research Pkwy. Phone:

Globally-tailored fiber optic, RF & digital video transport telecommunications products, OSS mgmt solutions & high-end tech field svcs for broadband networks.

CEA-Computer Engineering Associates, 7526 Connelley Dr., Suite H, Hanover, MD, 21076. Phone: (410) 787-9250. Phone: (800) 888-3922. Fax: (410) 787-9254.E-mail: sales@ceanews.com Web Site:www.ceanews.com Paul Keys, pres.

BridgeportNJ , 600 Heron Dr. Phone:

GibsoniaPA , 5465 Rt. 8. Phone:

CEA newsroom system—complete automation systems for radio & TV newsrooms.

CECO International Corp., 440 W. 15th St., New York, NY, 10011. Phone: (212) 206-8280. Fax: (212) 727-2144.E-mail: info@ceostudios.com Web Site:www.cecostudios.com Donald Kline, owner & pres.

Motion picture & TV equipment; sound stages; location trucks with generators.

CED, 362 Gulf Breeze Parkway, Suite 133, Gulf Breeze, FL, 32561. Phone: (850) 932-4713. Fax: (425) 928-5467.E-mail: info@ced.com Web Site:www.ced.com

MMDS, wireless cable, UHF, VHF quality transmission systems. Electrical Distributors.

C I S Inc., 3360 Martin Farm Rd., Suwanee, GA, 30024. Phone: (678) 482-2000. Fax: (678) 482-2007.E-mail: sales@cisfocus.com Web Site:www.cisfocus.com Jeffery Eichler, pres; Lynn Hamlin, VP sls.

Integrated broadband & fiber design software products. Software solutions for network mapping, planning, design, & management of the outside plant.

CMP Enclosures Inc., 3901 Grove Ave., Gurnee, IL, 60031. Phone: (847) 244-3230. Fax: (847) 244-3257.E-mail: cmpencl@aol.com Web Site:www.enclosures.com Mike Gober, pres; Wendi Lee, VP.

Manufacturers of electronic enclosures for rack mounting equipment.

COASTCOM, 1141 Harbor Bay Pkwy., Alameda, CA, 94502. Phone: (510) 523-6000. Fax: (510) 523-6150.E-mail: info@coastcom.com Web Site:www.coastcom.com Tracy Sutherland, pres.

AlamedaCA , 1151 Harbor Bay Pkwy. Phone:

CharlotteNC , 5000 Sharonwoods Ln. Phone:

LewisvilleTX , 562 Continental Dr. Phone:

Pearl RiverWY , 19 Harding St. Phone:

Manufacturer of T1 voice data network systems specializing in T3 cross connecting, T1 multiplexing & digital program channels for audio bcstg.

COMTEK Inc., 357 W. 2700 S., Salt Lake City, UT, 84115. Phone: (801) 466-3463. Phone: (800) 496-3463. Fax: (801) 484-6906.E-mail: sales@comtek.com Web Site:www.comtek.com Ralph Belgique, chief engr; Laurel Robertson, sls dir; Jon Belgique, Communication Director.

COMTEK manufactures synthesized & fixed frequency wireless communication equipment & accessories, including cuing systems (IFB) & wireless microphones.

CONTEC Corp., 1023 State St., Schenectady, NY, 12307-1511. Phone: (518) 382-8000. Fax: (518) 382-8452. Richard Kielb, sr VP; Gary Stein, pres/CEO; Carroll Foreman Jr., COO; Paul Pashtenko, CFO.

BrownvilleTX . Worldwide Digital, c/o Loera CBI, 5925 E. 14th St., Suite C. Phone:

SeattleWA , 1250 S. 192nd St. Phone:

Motorola , Pace, Cisco, Samsung, Panasonic, Moxi Digeo. Authorized Warranty Digital Repair Svc Ct. Manufactor of universal remote controls for digital terminals.

CORPLEX Inc., 915 Sherwood Dr., Lake Bluff, IL, 60044. Phone: (847) 582-8800. Phone: (888) 673-5400. Fax: (847) 582-8730.E-mail: carter@corplex.tv Web Site:www.corplex.tv Carter Ruehrdaz, CEO; Scott West, pres.

Video production equipment, postproduction equipment, rental & mobile TV.

CPC-Computer Prompting & Captioning Co., 1010 Rockville Pike, Suite 306, Rockville, MD, 20852. Phone: (301) 738-8487. Phone: (800) 977-6678. Fax: (301) 738-8488. Web Site:www.cpcweb.com Dr.Dilip Som, pres; Dr.Sidney Hoffman, VP.

Closed captioning & subtitling systems & svc for HD, DVD, NLE, webcasts & ipod. Plus teleprompting systems.

CS Communications Inc., 9825 Bridleridge Ct., Vienna, VA, 22181. Phone: (703) 938-5365. Fax: (703) 938-5823.E-mail: chazsamp@aol.com Charles E. Sampson, pres.

Engrg & consulting svcs for wireless and satellite systems. System design, feasibility & economic analysis.

CSG Systems, 9555 Maroon Cir., Englewood, CO, 80112. Phone: (303) 796-2850. Phone: (800) 366-2744. Fax: (303) 804-4088.E-mail: sales@csgsystems.com Web Site:www.csgsystems.com Jack Pogge, pres/COO; Neal Hansen, CEO; Peter Kalan, CFO; Randall Cardinal; Kurt Silverman, CTO; Willliam Fisher, pres GSS; Ed Nafus, pres BSD; Ed Mangold, sr VP global sls; Sally Else, sr VP product mgmt; Liz Bauer, sr VP investor rel & corp communications; Darren Walsh, sr VP global professional svcs; Alan Michels, VP/gen mgr.MA Singapore, 6 Temasek Blvd. Phone:

London United Kingdom, 1-11 John Adams St. Phone:

MiamiFL , 6303 Blue Lagoon Dr. Phone:

Complete sub info mgmt & data processing systems for the cable TV & telephone industries.

CSI-Camera Support International, Box 681, Woodland Hills, CA, 91365. Phone: (818) 224-4850. Fax: (818) 887-5727.E-mail: markintash@aol.com Web Site:www.csitripods.com

Camera support dollies, tripods, pan/tilt heads & accessories ENG EFP & studio application for bcst & industrial application.

Cable Leakage Technologies, 940 Hensley Ln., Wylie, TX, 75098. Phone: (972) 907-8100. Phone: (800) 783-8878. Fax: (972) 907-2950.E-mail: support@wavetracker.com Web Site:www.wavetracker.com Perry Havens, pres.

Digital RF tracking/mapping system used in CLI monitoring.

Cable Prep, (Ben Hughes Communication Products Co.). Box 373, 207 Middlesex Ave, Chester, CT, 06412-0373. Phone: (860) 526-4337. Fax: (860) 526-2291. Web Site:www.cableprep.com E-mail: toolmaker@cableprep.com Deborah Morrow, pres; David Morrow, VP engrg.

Cable Prep® TerminX, hex crimp, coring & stripping, drop wire stripping, jacket strippers, messenger removal & tools.

Cable Serv Inc., 4560 Eastgate Pkwy., Mississauga, ON, L4W 3W6. Canada. Phone: (905) 629-1111. Fax: (905) 629-1115. Web Site:www.cableserv.com Audley Alexander, pres.

TV Exciters, 5-10-20 watt LPTV trans & transmitters, TV modulators, demodulators, processors, & satellite receivers.

Cable Services Company Inc., 2113 Marydale Ave., Williamsport, PA, 17701. Phone: (570) 323-8518. Phone: (800) 326-9444. Fax: (570) 322-5373. Web Site:www.cable-services.com Eugene S. Welliver, VP; Neal W. Kimberling, VP; Harland W. Bergstrom, VP/gen mgr; John M. Roskowski, pres; Ken R. Michaels, CEO.

Turnkey fiber-optic & coaxial construction; distributor of CATV products.

Cable Technologies International, 460 Oakdale Ave., Hatboro, PA, 19040. Phone: (215) 672-5400. Fax: (215) 672-0440.E-mail: sales@cabletechnologies.com Web Site:www.cabletechnologies.com

MechanicvilleNY , 75 S. Central Ave.

Your #1 Co. for buying/selling/repairing/new/used /surplus-digital products-DCT's/parts/cables/universal remotes, advanced analog converters, headend/distribution equipment, test equipment including signal level meters, character generators, cables, HDTV/cables/modems/audio components/home theater/coax, remotes & batteries.

Cable Yellow Pages, 20917 Higging Ct., Torrance, CA, 90501. Phone: (800) 777-4320. Fax: (310) 212-5392. Web Site:www.cableyellowpages.com Glenn Schrader, assoc publisher; Neal Schnog, pres & publisher; Wade Pierce, VP & assoc publisher.

Phone directory for cable TV systems.

CablePro, (A division of ICM Corp.). 6260 Downing St., Denver, CO, 80216. Phone: (303) 288-8107. Fax: (303) 288-4769.E-mail: sales@icmcorp.net Web Site:www.icmcorp.net Randy Holiday, pres; Gary Williams, sls VP.

CablePro's attention to design, material & workmanship produces the highest quality for instal tools.

CableReady Inc., (A division of ICM Corp). 6260 Downing St., Denver, CO, 80216. Phone: (303) 288-8107. Phone: (800) 222-2142. Fax: (303) 288-4769.E-mail: sales@icmcorp.net Web Site:www.icmcorp.net Randy Holliday, pres; Gary Williams, VP sls.

Painted galvolume molding with custom fittings backed by a 15-year warranty, U.L. listed and Class A fire rated.

CableTek Wiring Products Inc., 1150 Taylor St., Elyria, OH, 44035. Phone: (440) 365-3889. Phone: (800) 562-9378. Fax: (440) 322-0321.E-mail: treilly@apk.net Web Site:www.cable-tek.com Tim Reilly, gen mgr .

Interior & exterior surface wiring products; terminal enclosures, residential enclosures, security products.

Cablynx, Inc., (Formerly Nova Systems/Shintron). 500 W. Cummings Park, Suite 1150, Woburn, MA, 01801. Phone: (781) 933-2000. Fax: (781) 933-4641.E-mail: sales@nova-sys.com Sam Asano, pres.

Routing switchers, distribution amplifiers, time code, component video, PC accessories, compugraphics to video, frame synchronizer.

Calculated Industries Inc., 4840 Hytech Dr., Carson City, NV, 89706. Phone: (775) 885-4900. Phone: (800) 854-8075. Fax: (775) 885-4949.E-mail: info@calculated.com Web Site:www.calculated.com Mark Paulsen, .

Time code calculators work in & convert between all time formats; drop/non-drop, multiple EPS rates for all SMPTE/PAL equations.

California Amplifier, 1401 N. Rice Ave., Oxnard, CA, 93030. Phone: (805) 987-9000. Fax: (805) 987-8359. Web Site:www.calamp.com E-mail: sales@calcamp.som Tom Prochnow, sls VP; Rick Wheeler, VP; Philip Cox, VP.

Manufacturer of mesh & offset satellite antennas ranging in size from 18" to 16'.

Calumet Photographic, 1111 N. Cherry Ave., Chicago, IL, 60642. Phone: (312) 440-4920.E-mail: custserv@calumetphoto.com Web Site:www.calumetphoto.com Peter Biasotti, pres.

Calzone Case Co., 225 Black Rock Ave., Bridgeport, CT, 06605. Phone: (203) 367-5766. Fax: (203) 336-4406.E-mail: vin.calzone@calzonecase.com Web Site:www.calzonecase.com Joseph E. Calzone, pres; Vincent J. Calzone, sls VP.

City of IndustryCA , 15730 Salt Lake Ave. Phone:

CarrolltonTX , 75006 Luna Rd, Suite 126. Phone:

Manufacturers of custom & standard shipping cases for all industries featuring Escort, LD-ATA, Military, X series, Titan

Camera Dynamics, (formerly Vinten). 709 Executive Blvd., Ste. A, Valley Cottage, NY, 10989-2024. Phone: (845) 268-0100. Fax: (845) 268-0113. Web Site:www.vinten.com Bob Carr, pres.

Best quality studio camera robotics, Parliamentary camera robotics & virtual sets.

Camera Service Center, (A division of Arri, Inc.). 619 W. 54th St., New York, NY, 10019. Phone: (212) 757-0906. Fax: (212) 713-0075. Web Site:www.cameraservice.com

Fort LauderdaleFL , 2385 Stirling Rd. Phone:

The largest full-svc film equipment rental company, carrying a complete line of camera & lighting products.

CamMate Studios/Systems, 425 E. Comstock, Chandler, AZ, 85225. Phone: (480) 813-9500. Fax: (480) 813-9292.E-mail: cammate@cammate.com Web Site:www.cammate.com Linda Mitchell, CEO.

Exclusive sls & rental of the CamMate, a single operator remote camera crane in various configurations for video & film. Now offering Telescoping Jips.

Camplex Corporation, 3302 W. 6th Ave., Emporia, KS, 66801. Phone: (620) 342-7743. Fax: (620) 342-7405.E-mail: jtwebb@camplex.com Web Site:www.camplex.com J. Thomas Webb, CEO; C. Duane Woodmas, pres.

CAMPLEX is a universally adaptable video/audio signals multiplexing system for ENG/EFP/SNG Prosamer cameras, camcorders used in remote applications.

Canare Corp., 45 Commerce Way, Unit C, Totowa, NJ, 07512. Phone: (973) 837-0070. Fax: (973) 837-0080.E-mail: sales@canare.com Web Site:www.canare.com Larry Cano, sls; Kazuo Urata, pres/CEO.

Professional audio & video cable, 75 ohm connectors, patchbays, snake systems, assemblies, strip & crimp tools, SMPTE 311 Hybrid & single mode fiber optical products.

Canon U.S.A. Inc., (Broadcast Equipment Division Headquarters). 65 Challenger Rd., Ridgefield Park, NJ, 07660. Phone: (800) 321-4388. Fax: (201) 807-3333.E-mail: bctv@cusa.canon.com Web Site:www.canonbroadcast.com Rich Eiles, sls; Patrick Breheny, sls; John Rose, sls.

IrvineCA , 15955 Alton Pkwy. Phone:

NorcrossGA , 5625 Oakbrook Pkwy. Phone:

ItascaIL , 100 Park Blvd. Phone:

IrvineTX , 3200 Regent Blvd. Phone:

The Canon Broadcast & Communications (BCTV) division a part of the larger Canon U.S.A. Inc. The BCTV lens products is squarely based on the highly advanced optical, mechanical & digital technologies for which Canon became legendary. Studio, field & ENG lenses & svc, (HDTV/SDTV) video, audio, data optical beam transmission, remote control P/T/Z camera system.

Capstone Communications Inc., 163 Grandview Ln., Mahwah, NJ, 07430. Phone: (905) 472-2330. Web Site:www.capstonecomm.com

Brokerage, rsch consultation & bcst equipment brokerge.

Carpel Video Inc., 429 E. Patrick St., Frederick, MD, 21701. Phone: (800) 238-4300. Phone: (301) 694-3500. Fax: (301) 694-9510. Web Site:www.carpelvideo.com Andy Carpel, pres.

Videotape wholesalers. Mail order post production in MD; store: DVD production and duplication. Lowest prices on 6 blank video tapes. 800-238-4300.

Celco, 8660 Red Oak Ave., Rancho Cucamonga, CA, 91730. Phone: (909) 481-4648. Fax: (909) 481-6899.E-mail: info@celco.com Web Site:www.celco.com

Design & manufacture of motion picture film recorders.

Center City Film & Video, 1503 Walnut St., Philadelphia, PA, 19102. Phone: (215) 568-4134. Fax: (215) 568-6011.E-mail: info@ccfv.com Web Site:www.ccfv.com Jordan Schwartz, chmn; Brian Tsely, VP/gen mgr.

Studio/remote/postproduction D-2, D-3, 1" - Beta - 3/4" - ADO - Paint Box/Abekas 62/GV300 with E-Mem; film/tape DaVinci color correction, ADO repositioning & interactive motion control; D-s, D-3; AVID, Digital Betacam.

Century Precision Optics, 7701 Haskell Ave., Van Nuys, CA, 91406. Phone: (818) 766-3715. Fax: (818) 505-9865.E-mail: info@schneideroptics.com Web Site:www.schneideroptics.com Bill Turner, VP; Barry Rubin, dir/sls & mktg.

Wide angle & telephoto lens for video & motion picture cameras; lens accessories; lens service; schneider filters.

Channel Master, 1331 Industrial Park Dr., Smithfield, NC, 27577. Phone: (919) 934-7078. Fax: (919) 934-2809. Web Site:www.channelmaster.com Coty Youtsey, VP; Joe Bingochea, dir.

Manufacturer of TV Antennas and Accessories, Cable, Connectors and Amplifiers

Channel One Lighting Systems Inc., 1522 E. 6th St., Tulsa, OK, 74120-4026. Phone: (800) 651-8869. Fax: (623) 934-5160. W. Blair Powell, pres.

Complete line of lighting equipment for TV, theatre & industrial applications; specializes in the design & manufacture of electrical distribution, grid & cyclorama systems, curtain & track & manufactures radio & TV communications equipment.

Channell Commercial Corp., Box 9022, 26040 Ynez Rd., Temecula, CA, 92589-9022. Phone: (909) 719-2600. Fax: (909) 296-2322.E-mail: info@channellcorp.com Web Site:www.channellcomm.com William H. Channell Jr., pres; Andrew M. Zogby, VP global mktg; John Kaiser, VP N America sls.

Global designer & manufacturer of equipment, offers a complete line of enclosures for CATV & telecommunication

Charles Industries Ltd., 5600 Apollo Dr., Rolling Meadows, IL, 60008. Phone: (847) 806-6300. Fax: (847) 806-6231. Web Site:www.charlesindustries.com Joseph T. Charles, pres.

Pedestals, custom security boxes, amplifier & TAP brackets-hardware, splicing vaults, taps, splitters & couplers.

Cheetah International, 8120 Sheridan Blvd., Suite C-206, Westminister, CO, 80003. Phone: (520) 751-8681. Fax: (520) 722-1699.E-mail: sales@caption.com Web Site:www.caption.com Donald Miller, pres.

Closed captioning software on-line & postproduction & related hardware.

Chicago Condenser Corp., (A division of Capacitor Industries). 6455 N. Avondale Ave., Chicago, IL, 60631. Phone: (773) 774-6666. Fax: (773) 774-6690.E-mail: info@capacitorindustries.com Web Site:www.capacitorindustries.com Terry Noone, pres.

High Voltage Filter Capacitors for radio & TV bcst transmission.

Chrono-Log Corp., 2 W. Park Rd., Havertown, PA, 19083. Phone: (610) 853-1130. Fax: (610) 853-3972.E-mail: chronlog@chronolog.com Web Site:www.chronolog.com Paula Freilich, pres.

GPS Receiver (time only), WWV synchronizer, digital clocks & time display systems, time code generators.

Chyron Corp., 5 Hub Dr., Melville, NY, 11747. Phone: (631) 845-2000. Fax: (631) 845-3895. Web Site:www.chyron.com Kevin Prince, COO; Michael Wellesley-Wesley, pres/CEO; Mark Bachmore, VP worldwide sls.

CupertinoCA . Chryon Corp. West, 10121 Miller Ave, Suite 201. Phone:

AtlantaGA , One CNN Ctr., South Towers, Suite 558. Phone:

A leading providor of broadcast hardware, software & services spanning television & the Internet. Provides a broad range of leading edge hardware & software products, including paint & animation systems, character generators, master control switches, & bcst automation & media mgmt packages.

Cine 60 Inc., 630 9th Ave., New York, NY, 10036. Phone: (212) 586-8782. Fax: (212) 459-9556.E-mail: info@cine60newyork.com Web Site:www.cine60newyork.com Paul Wildum, pres; Vidal Ortiz, gen mgr; Richard Ortiz, mgr.

Nickel-Cadmium battery belts, battery packs, chargers, sun-guns, kits, dir chair, dir viewfinders, slates, cables & snaplocks.

Cintel Inc., 25020 Ave. Stanford, Suite 190, Valencia, CA, 91355. Phone: (661) 294-2310. Fax: (661) 294-1019.E-mail: sales@cintelinc.com Web Site:www.cintelinc.com Adam Welsh, mgng dir; Curtis Christianson, opns mgr; David Saville, sls dir.

Chestnut RidgeNY , 80 Red Schoolhouse Rd, Suite 103. Phone:

Flying spot telecines, DVE system, keycode system, high-resolution scanner, color correctors.

Circuit Research Labs Inc. (CRL Systems, Inc.), 7970 S. Kyrene Rd., Tempe, AZ, 85284-2199. Phone: (480) 403-8300. Fax: (480) 403-8301.E-mail: sales@orban.com Web Site:www.crlsystems.com Robert McMartin, CEO; Jay Brentlinger, pres; Robert Orban, VP; Greg Ogonowski, VP new prod dev; Gary Clarkson, VP/sec; Phillip Zeni,

COO/VP.

Multiband audio AGCs, compressors & limiters for AM/FM; MTS processors, stereo generators, shortwave, AES/EBU digital audio tester.

Clark Wire & Cable Co. Inc., 1355 Armour Blvd., Mundelein, IL, 60060-4401. Phone: (847) 949-9944. Fax: (847) 949-9595.E-mail: sales@clarkwire.com Web Site:www.clarkwire.com Shane Collins, pres; Patti Stickler, VP; Dan Collins, dir mktg; Javier Juarez, dir.

Audio, video, camera & speciality cable products for bcst industry, available in bulk or assembled harnesses, connectors, panels, reels, & boxes.

Clear-Com Communication Systems, 4065 Hollis St., Emeryville, CA, 94608-3505. Phone: (510) 496-6666. Fax: (510) 496-6699.E-mail: sales@clearcom.com Web Site:www.clearcom.com Michael Wang, gen mgr; Ed Fitzgerald, natl sls mgr. Eastleigh, England, Eastleigh, England. Phone:

Walnut CreekCA , Box 302. Phone:

Single & multi-ch hardwire intercom systems for use in teleproduction. Wired & wireless partyline & digital matrix intercom systems.

Clearone Communications Corp., 1825 Research Way, Salt Lake City, UT, 84119. Phone: (801) 975-7200. Phone: (800) 945-7730. Fax: (801) 977-0087. Web Site:www.clearone.com Fran Flood, CEO; Randy Wichinski, CFO.

Professional audio & teleconferencing.

CoarcVideo, Box 2, Rt. 217, Mellenville, NY, 12544. Phone: (800) 888-4451. Phone: (518) 672-4451. Fax: (518) 672-4048.E-mail: coarc@aol.com Bob Spiewak, dir mktg; Alva Stalker, production mgr.

Used by bcstrs, cable systems, duplicating houses, production companies for environmentally-designed videotape reloaded products & standard video tape products; provides Umatic & Betacam VHS tape, program fulfillment svcs. CoarcVideo is part of the Coarc organization, which trains employees & provides various programs for the disabled.

Coaxial Dynamics , 6800 Lake Abram Dr., Middleburg Hts., OH, 44130. Phone: (440) 243-1100. Fax: (440) 243-1101.E-mail: coaxial@apk.net Web Site:www.coaxial.com Joe Kluha, gen mgr .

RF wattmeters, terminations, RF load resistors, RF couplers & accessories.

Cohu Inc., (Electronics Division). Box 85623, San Diego, CA, 92186-5623. Phone: (858) 277-6700. Fax: (858) 277-0221.E-mail: info@cohu.com Web Site:www.cohu.com/cctv Joe Olmstead Jr., natl sls mgr; Jeff Tyler, mktg mgr.

CCTV cameras & camera control systems, color, CCD, B/W.

Colorado Video Inc., Box 928, Boulder, CO, 80306. Phone: (303) 530-9580. Fax: (303) 530-9569.E-mail: sales@colorado-video.com Web Site:www.colorado-video.com Kirk Fowler, pres.

Image transmission for UBI system; time-division video multiplexing/demultiplexing system.

Comex Worldwide Corp., Box 8, Aldie, VA, 20105-0008. Phone: (703) 327-1520. Fax: (703) 327-1540.E-mail: cwcmmds@hotmail.com Web Site:www.comexworldwide.com Jack A. Rickel, pres/CEO; Susan Rose, gen mgr .

CWC develops bcst & pay TV systems, VHF/UHF bcsts, satellite communications, MMDS & cable systems & turnkey communication systems.

Commercial Electronics Ltd., 1335 Burrard St., Vancouver, BC, V6Z 1Z7. Canada. Phone: (604) 669-5525. Fax: (604) 669-6347.E-mail: pro@cemail.com Web Site:www.commercialelectronics.ca H.H. von Tiesenhausen, pres.

Audio video equipment, systems designs.

Commercial Radio Monitoring Co., 103 S.W. Market St., Lee's Summit, MO, 64063. Phone: (816) 524-3777. Fax: (816) 524-3777. Web Site:www.commercialradio.us W. R. Thorsen, pres; Ronald Thorsen, VP.

Frequency measurements & equipment calibration.

CommScope Inc., 1100 CommScope Pl. S.E., Hickory, NC, 28603. Phone: (800) 982-1708. Phone: (828) 324-2200. Fax: (828) 328-3400.E-mail: communications@commscope.com Web Site:www.commscope.com Frank Drendel, CEO.

Coaxial & fiber-optic cables including CRD & NEC approved drop cables, QR, P3 & CableGuard.

Communication & Power Industries, 811 Hansen Way, Palo Alto, CA, 94304. Phone: (650) 846-3803. Fax: (650) 424-1744. Web Site:www.cpii.com Joel A. Littman, CFO; Andrew E. Tafler, VP; John R. Beighley, VP sls.

GeorgetownON Canada, 45 River Dr. Phone:

Palo AltoCA , 607 Hansen Way. Phone:

Palo AltoCA , 811 Hansen Way. Phone:

San CarlosCA , 301 Industrial Way. Phone:

BeverlyMA . Beverly Microwave Division, 150 Sohier Rd. Phone:

Manufactures a complete line of power grid tubes, klystrons & klystrode IOTs, traveling wave tubes, satellite communication transmitters, microwave components.

Communication & Power Industries, EIMAC Operations, 811 Hanson Way, Palo Alto, CA, 94304. Phone: (650) 592-1221. Phone: (800) 414-8823. Fax: (650) 592-9988.E-mail: powergrid@cpii.com Web Site:www.cpii.om

Power grid tubes, cavity amplifiers, IOT (UHF TV).

Communication Graphics, Inc., 1765 N. Juniper, Greenway Business Park, Broken Arrow, OK, 74012. Phone: (800) 331-4438. Phone: (918) 258-6502. Fax: (918) 251-8223.E-mail: info@cgilink.com Web Site:www.cgilink.com Dave Cleveland, pres.

Choose the company MORE radio stations have selected for printing decals, event stickers, statics, concert patches, magnets, media kits and more!

Communications General Corp., 2685 Alta Vista Dr., Fallbrook, CA, 92028-9739. Phone: (760) 723-2700.E-mail: r.gonsett@ieee.org Robert F. Gonsett, pres.

Monthly AM, FM & TV frequency measurements in the Southern California area & spectral measurements.

Communications Specialties Inc., 55 Cabot Ct., Hauppauge, NY, 11788. Phone: (631) 273-0404. Fax: (631) 273-1638.E-mail: info@commspecial.com Web Site:www.commspecial.com Paul Seiden, sls dir.

Shaw Tower Singapore, 100 Bencoolen Rd., # 22-09. Phone:

Manufacturer of fiber-optic transmission sytems, including the Pure Digital Fiberlink line for professional quality video, audio and data.

Communications Structures & Services, 645 C. E. Renfro St., Burleson, TX, 76028. Phone: (817) 295-8183. Fax: (817) 295-8075. Keith Cendrick, pres.

Tower mf, Erection, maintenance, true turn-key installation, foundations, emergency svcs, antenna & transmission line replacement, site acquistion.

Comprehensive Video Group, 55 Ruta Ct., South Hackensack, NJ, 07606. Phone: (800) 526-0242. Fax: (201) 814-0510. Web Site:www.compvideo.com E-mail: sales@comprehensiveinc.com Scott Schaefer, VP.

Digital HDTV UpConverter, High Resolution bulk cable, Video/Audio Multi media & Data Cable assemblies (lifetime warranty), connectors, adaptors, wallplates, distribution amps, switches, convertors, etc.

Comprompter Inc., 1601 Caledonia St., Suite E, La Crosse, WI, 54603-3606. Phone: (800) 785-7766. Fax: (608) 784-5013.E-mail: enrnews@enrnews.com Web Site:www.enrnews.com Ralph King, pres.

Offers PC-compatible prompting & networked computerized newsroom & newsroom automation systems for radio, TV, corporate & industrial use.

Computer Concepts Corp., 13375 Stemmons Fwy., Suite 400, Dallas, TX, 75234. Phone: (800) 255-6350. Phone: (913) 541-0900. Fax: (913) 541-0169. Web Site:www.ccc-dcs.com Greg L. Dean, chmn.

Total digital integration improves sound, progmg production & scheduling. Business software includes traf & billing for radio.

Computer Resolutions, 35 Benham Ave., Bridgeport, CT, 06605. Phone: (203) 384-0742. Fax: (203) 384-0473. Web Site:www.cri1.com Carl Palmieri, CEO.

PC- & mainframe-based traf systems; both offer multistation capability.

Comrex Corp., 19 Pine Rd., Devens, MA, 01434. Phone: (978) 784-1776. Fax: (978) 784-1717.E-mail: info@comrex.com Web Site:www.comrex.com Chris Crump, dir mktg, sls dir; Kris Bobo, mgng dir.

Comsearch, 19700 Janelia Farm Blvd., Ashburn, VA, 20147. Phone: (703) 726-5500. Fax: (703) 726-5600.E-mail: info@comsearch.com Web Site:www.comsearch.com

Communication engrg svcs for mobile, microwave & satellite systems, including frequency, propagation & integrations svcs.

ComSonics Inc., 1350 Port Republic Rd., Box 1106, Harrisonburg, VA, 22801. Phone: (540) 434-5965. Phone: (800) 336-9681. Fax: (540) 432-9794. Web Site:www.comsonics.com E-mail: info@comsonics.com Dennis A. Zimmerman, pres/CEO; Dale Lann, CFO; Donn E. Meyerhoeffer, COO; Donald J. Sommerville, dir sls/mktg.

Manufacture RF signal level meter & RF leakage detector, CATV repair facility.

Comtech Antenna Systems Inc., 3100 Communications Rd., St. Cloud, FL, 34769. Phone: (407) 892-6111. Fax: (407) 892-0994.E-mail: info@comtechantenna.com Web Site:www.comtechantenna.com Thomas Christy, pres; Ronnie Hamilton, sls/customer svc.

Satellite antenna systems, sizes 1.8-7.3 meters; Offsat(tm); 2 degree spacing antenna; 3.8, 5.0m & Offsat(tm) transportables.

Comtech EF Data, (Formerly Radyne ComStream Corp.). 2114 West 7th St., Tempe, AZ, 85281. Phone: (480) 333-2200. Fax: (602) 437-4811.E-mail: sales@comtechefdata.com Web Site:www.comtechefdata.com

Manufactures a broad spectrum of satellite communications products, including Satellite Modems, Bandwidth & Capacity Management, TCP/IP Performance Enchancement Proxies, Encapsulators, Receivers, Converters, Amplifiers, Transceivers & Terminals.

Condor D C Power Supplies Inc., (A subsidiary of SL Industries). 6050 King Ddr., Bldg. A, Ventura, CA, 93033. Phone: (805) 486-4565. Phone: (800) 235-5929. Fax: (805) 487-8911. Web Site:www.condorpower.com Mike Shaw, dir mktg; Jim Taylor, pres.

Multiple outlet strips, surge & noise suppressors, & uninterruptible power supplies.

Condux International, Box 247, 145 Kingswood Rd., Mankato, MN, 56001. Phone: (800) 533-2077. Phone: (507) 387-6576. Fax: (507) 387-1442.E-mail: cndxinfo@condux.com Web Site:www.condux.com Brad Radichel, pres.

Underground & aerial construction tools & equipment for coaxial cable, telephone & fiber.

Connectronics Corp., Box 3355, 2745 Avondale Ave., Toledo, OH, 43607. Phone: (419) 537-0020. Phone: (800) 965-0020. Fax: (419) 537-0007.E-mail: info@connectronicscorp.com Web Site:www.connectronicscorp.com Tom Ricketts, pres; Al Mocek, VP.

Morgan HillCA . California, Box 2047. Phone:

Audio wire & cable, special wire & cable assys. Interconnect products for audio, video, data & telephone.

Conrac Systems Inc., 5124 Commerce Dr., Baldwin Park, CA, 91706. Phone: (626) 480-0095. Fax: (626) 480-0077.E-mail: monitors@conrac.com Web Site:www.conrac.com Bill Moeller, pres.

Manufacturer of a var of color & monochrome video monitors for bcst & computer graphic display.

Continental Electronics Corporation, 4212 S. Buckner Blvd., Dallas, TX, 75227. Phone: (214) 381-7161. Fax: (214) 381-3250.E-mail: sales@contelec.com Web Site:www.contelec.com Adil Mina, VP business dev; Michael Troje, sls mgr.

BirminghamAL , 2280 Rockcreek Tr. Phone:

Glen RoseTX , 1230 Rugged Oaks Rd. Phone:

Continental is the premier manufacturer of radio frequency (RF) bcst transmission equipment. We specialize in the design, dev & manufacture of leading-edge digital & analog transmitter systems for the global market. We offer a full range of products for high-power FM, HF, VHF, UHF, LF & VLP application including particle accelerators & fusion rsch, defense communications, radar & industrial heating.

Convergent Media Systems Corp., One Convergent Center, 190 Bluegrass Valley Pkwy., Alpharetta, GA, 30005. Phone: (800) 877-7804. Fax: (707) 369-9100.E-mail: technicolorenterprise@thomson.net Web Site:www.convergent.com Murray Holland, owner; Bryan Allen, pres.

Transportable satellite uplinking & downlinking svcs. Includes facilities & transponder time for Ku- & C-band applications.

Convergys Inc., 201 E. 14th St., Cincinnati, OH, 45102. Phone: (513) 723-7000. Phone: (888) 284-9900. Fax: (513) 241-1543. Web Site:www.convergys.com Erik Schumann, V-North America sls.

AtlantaGA , 4170 Ashford Dunwoody Rd, Suite 525. Phone:

"Cablemaster/Icoms" customer mgmt & billing system running on IBM as/400 platform; solution for the convergent cable TV/Telephone industry.

Cooper Sound Systems Inc., 1241 Knollwood Dr., PMB 106, Cambria, CA, 93428. Phone: (805) 772-1007. Fax: (805) 456-1631. Web Site:www.coopersound.com E-mail: coopersoundsystems@att.net Andrew Cooper, pres; Janet Cooper, VP.

Spare parts & tech asst.

Copperweld Fayetteville Division, 254 Cotton Mill Rd., Fayetteville, TN, 37334-7249. Phone: (931) 433-7177. Fax: (931) 433-0419.E-mail: fayetteville@copperweld.com Web Site:www.copperweldbimetallic.com John D. Turner, pres/CEO; Steve Levy, VP mktg & sls.

Copper-clad aluminium wire, copper-clad steel wire, & aluminum-clad steel wire.

Coptervision, 7625 Hayvenhurst Ave., #36, Van Nuys, CA, 91406. Phone: (818) 782-6673. Fax: (818) 782-6636.E-mail: info@coptervision.com Web Site:www.coptervision.com Sarita Spiwak, pres/CEO.

Corning Cable Systems, 800 17th St. N.W., Hickory, NC, 28601. Phone: (828) 901-5000. Fax: (828) 901-5488. Web Site:www.corning.com/cablesystems Clark Kendall, pres; Mike Genovese, sr VP/mgng dir.

Manufacturer of optical fiber cables & accessories for video, data, voice communications applications.

Corning Gilbert Inc., 5310 W. Camelback Rd., Glendale, AZ, 85301. Phone: (800) 528-5567. Phone: (623) 245-1050. Fax: (623) 931-0684. Fax: (800) 344-6358.E-mail: info-gilbert@corning.com Web Site:www.corning.com Kathy Murphy, CEO.

Trunk, distribution & "F" connectors for CATV.

Corning Incorporated, (Telecommunications Products Division). One Riverfront Plaza, Corning, NY, 14831. Phone: (607) 248-2000. Phone: (607) 986-8125/3344.E-mail: cofic@corning.com Web Site:www.corning.com/opticalfiber Martin J. Curran, sr VP & gen mgr.

Single-mode & multimode optical fibers including: ClearCurve single-mode & multimode fibers, InfiniCor laser-optimized multimode fibers, SMF-28e fiber, LEAF fiber, & Vascade submarine fibers.

Corporation of NEC America, (Broadcast Equipment Dept.). 6535 N. State Hwy. 161, Irving, TX, 75039. Phone: (214) 262-2000. Phone: (214) 262-6299. Fax: (972) 751-7001. Web Site:www.nec.com Bruce Blain, VP sls; Takayuki Okeda, pres/CEO.

VUES on-line digital editing system (video).

Cortana Corp., Box 2548, Farmington, NM, 87499-2548. Phone: (888) 325-5336. Fax: (505) 326-2337.E-mail: cortana@cyberport.com Evelyn Nott, pres; Henry Bond, VP.

Stati-Cat Lightning Prevention System.

Cortland Cable Co. Inc., Box 330, 44 River St., Cortland, NY, 13045-0330. Phone: (607) 753-8276. Fax: (607) 753-3183.E-mail: cortlandcable@cortlandcable.com Web Site:www.cortlandcable.com John Stidd, pres; Rick Nye, VP.

Kevlar fiber antenna guys & ropes, including eye splice end terminations-potted sockets.

Costume Armour Inc./Christo Vac, 2 Mill St., Box 85, Cornwall, NY, 12518. Phone: (845) 534-9120. Fax: (845) 534-8602.E-mail: info@costumearmour.com Web Site:www.costumearmour.com Nino Novellino, pres.

Period armor & weapons, vacuum-formed background panels, custom made props & sculpture.

Countryman Associates Inc., 195 Constitution Dr., Menlo Park, CA, 94025. Phone: (800) 669-1422. Phone: (650) 364-9988. Fax: (650) 364-2794.E-mail: sales@countryman.com Web Site:www.countryman.com Carl Countryman, res/chief engr.

Very small precision electret condenser microphones for wide applications & the Type-85 Direct Box.

Crossed Field Antennas Inc., 48 Mountain Rd., Farmington, CT, 06032. Phone: (860) 676-0051. Fax: (860) 677-9639.E-mail: cfaricher@snet.net ProfessorRobert E. Richer, pres; ProfessorMaurice Hately, chief tech off; Alec Thomas, head engr.

Hansworth, MiddlesexNO United Kingdom, 97 Foxwood Close. Phone:

Company mkts medium wave & long wave antennas.

Crown Broadcast IREC, (division of Crown International Inc). Box 2000, 25166 Leer Dr., Elkhart, IN, 46515-2000. Phone: (574) 262-8900. Fax: (574) 262-5399. E-mail: fmsaes@irecl.com Web Site:www.crownbroadcast.com Steve Burns, pres/CEO.

Bcst RF equipment, FM radio transmitters. Supplier to the Natl weather svc for emergency weather radio transmitters.

Cygnal Technologies, (formerly Normex Telecom Incorp.). 70 Valleywood Dr., Markham, ON, L3R 4T5. Canada. Phone: (905) 944-6500. Fax: (905) 944-6520. E-mail: normex@normex.com Web Site:www.cygnal.ca Jos Wintermans, chmn/CEO; Brian Pedlar, CFO; John Challinor, dir mktg.

Mgmt, instal & maintenance svcs for studios, radio-TV transmitters, satellite systems & CATV.

D

DBX Professional Products, 8760 S. Sandy Pkwy., Sandy, UT, 84070. Phone: (801) 568-7660. Fax: (801) 568-7662. E-mail: support@dbxpro.com Web Site:www.dbxpro.com Robert Benson, sls VP.

Audio signal processing devices: compressor/limiters, De-essers, equalizers, gates & noise reduction.

DEDOTEC USA Inc., 48 Sheffield Business Park, Ashley Falls, MA, 01222. Phone: (413) 229-2550. Fax: (413) 229-2556. Web Site:www.dedolight.com E-mail: info@dedolight.com

Dedolight precision lighting instruments for film, TV, ENG/EFP, still photo & architectural applications. Portable location lighting kits & studio equipment. Special effects attachments & accessories.

D.H. Satellite, Box 239, 600 N. Marquette Rd., Prairie du Chien, WI, 53821. Phone: (608) 326-8406. Fax: (608) 326-4233. E-mail: mdoll@mhtc.net Web Site:www.dhsatellite.com Mike Doll, VP.

Manufacturer of solid spun aluminum antennas & mounts. Antennas range from .6m (24") to 5m (16') with various mounting options. Delivery & instal is available from DH for all of our antenna equipment.

DISH Network Corp., 9601 S. Meridian Blvd., Englewood, CO, 80211. Phone: (303) 723-1000. Fax: (303) 723-1046. Web Site:www.dishnetwork.com Mark Jackson, sr VP; Charlie Ergen, pres.

LittletonCO , 5701 S. Santa Fe Rd. Phone:

Satellite TV reception systems.

DPA Microphones, Inc., 2432 Main St., Longmont, CO, 80501. Phone: (303) 485-1025. Fax: (303) 485-6470. E-mail: info-usa@dpamicrophones.com Web Site:www.dpamicrophones.com Bruce Myers, pres.

DPA Microphones features a complete line of cardioid & omnidirectional microphones & accessories for all applictions.

DSC Laboratories, 3565 Nashua Dr., Mississauga, ON, L4V 1R1. Canada. Phone: (905) 673-3211. Fax: (905) 673-0929. E-mail: dsc@dsclabs.com D. Corley, pres; S. Corley, mktg. Web Site:www.dsclabs.com D. Corley, pres; S. Corley, mktg.

Combi Optical Signal Generators (OSGs) & CamAlign chip charts for camera alignment & matching-deal for studio, shop & stadium.

DST Innovis, 1104 Investment Blvd., Eldorado Hills, CA, 95762. Phone: (800) 835-8389. Fax: (916) 934-7054. Web Site:www.dstinnovis.com Michael McGrail, pres; Anthony Piniella, mgr.

North Sydney. CableData (Asia Pacific), Level 4, 44 Miller St, Suite 404. Phone:

Sao Paulo. CableData (Latin America), Andar, Suite 81, Ave. Eng Luis Carlos Berrini, 1297. Phone:

Customer mgmt & billing solutions for communications & utilities industries. Clients include providers of CATV, telephony, DBS, wireless, electricity, water, gas, waste mgmt, utility & multi-svcs in over 20 countries.

Dage-MTI Inc., 701 N. Roeske Ave., Michigan City, IN, 46360. Phone: (219) 872-5514. Fax: (219) 872-5559. E-mail: sales@dagemti.com Web Site:www.dagemti.com Arthur D. Sterling, pres; Peggy Moore, dir mktg.

Closed circuit TV cameras & accessories.

Peter W. Dahl Co. Inc., 5869 Waycross, El Paso, TX, 79924. Phone: (915) 751-2300. Fax: (915) 751-0768. E-mail: pwdco@pwdahl.com Web Site:www.pwdahl.com Peter W. Dahl, pres; Gary L. Komassa, VP.

Heavy duty plate, power, filament, modulation transformers & reactor; single- & three-phase rectifiers, vacuum & oil filled capacitors.

Daily Electronics Corp., Box 822437, Vancouver, WA, 98682-0053. Phone: (360) 896-8856. Phone: (800) 346-6667. Fax: (360) 896-5476. E-mail: daily@worldaccessnet.com Web Site:www.dailyelectronics.net Jim Grimes, pres.

Produces vacuum tubes—transmitting, camera, industrial & receiving. Tube rebuilding.

Dalet Digital Media Systems, 110 Wall St., 2nd Fl., New York, NY, 10005. Phone: (212) 269-6700. Fax: (212) 269-6709. E-mail: sales@dalet.com Web Site:www.dalet.com Stephane Guez, COO; Benjamin Desbois, gen mgr; Fred Roux, dir opns; Luc Comeau, business dev mgr.

Software for radio & TV. Newsroom computer systems, acquisition, cataloging, producing, sharing, archiving, distribution of video & audio assets.

Data Security Inc., 729 Q St., Lincoln, NE, 68508. Phone: (800) 225-7554. Phone: (402) 434-5959. Fax: (402) 434-3291. E-mail: eschafer@telesis-inc.com Web Site:www.datasecurityinc.com Brian Boles, CEO; Eric Schafer, VP.

Tape Enhancement Series features bulk tape deguassers & videotape cleaner/evaluators.

Delta Electronics Inc., Box 11268, 5730 General Washington Dr., Alexandria, VA, 22312. Phone: (703) 354-3350. Fax: (703) 354-0216. E-mail: sales@deltaelectronics.com Web Site:www.deltaelectronics.com John Wright, pres; William R. Fox, VP engrg; Joseph S. Novak, VP mktg.

RF instrumentation including Single & Dual Scale RF Ammeters, Operating Impedance Bridges, Common Point Bridges, Receiver/Generators, AM Stereo Exciters & Monitors, High Power Coaxial Transfer Switches, Toroidal Current Transformers, Digital RF Ammeters, Splatter Monitor, Stero Noise Generator & Meter Panels.

DeSisti Lighting, 1109 Grand Ave., North Bergen, NJ, 07047. Phone: (908) 317-0020. Fax: (201) 319-1104.

RomeNO Italy. World Headquarters (Desisti Lighting, Spa), Via Cancelliera 10/A, 00040 Cecchina, Albano Laziale. Phone:

Complete professional lighting equipment & svcs. Quartz fresnels, softlights & cyc lights; HMI fresnels, softlights & sunguns; motorized studio lighting.

Devlin Design Group Inc., 625 Broadway, Ste. 1101, Box 5208, Frisco, CO, 80443-5208. Phone: (970) 688-2772. Fax: (970) 688-2772. E-mail: ddgemail@ddgtv.com Web Site:www.ddgtv.com Dan Devlin, CEO; Judy Parker, dir mktg; Kristina Jones, Media Dir.

Specializes in bcst news productions. News sets, newsrooms, turnkey & design only. Set design, virtual sets, hard set construction, consultation.

Dialogic Communications Corp., 730 Cool Springs Blvd., Suite 300, Franklin, TN, 37067. Phone: (615) 790-2882. Phone: (800) 723-3207. Fax: (615) 790-1329. E-mail: marketing@dccusa.com Web Site:www.dccusa.com Gene Kirby, pres; Charles Smith, VP engrg.

Interactive audio response voice processing equipment & software for pay-per-view, appointment confirmation, outage reporting, etc.

Dictaphone Corp., 3191 Broadbridge Ave., Stratford, CT, 06614. Phone: (203) 381-7000. Fax: (203) 386-8597. Web Site:www.dictaphone.com Rob Schwager, chmn/pres.

Multi-ch voice communications tape recorders (loggers).

Dielectric Communications, Box 949, 22 Tower Rd., Raymond, ME, 04071. Phone: (207) 655-8100. Fax: (207) 655-8177. E-mail: dcsales@spx.com Web Site:www.dielectric.com Garrett VanAtta, pres; Roger Cote, VP sls & mktg; Anna Morton, VP finance.

Antennas, inside equipment, waveguide, transmission line, switches, loads, filters, combiners, pressurization, lighting for TV, radio, mobile media & mobile bcstg.

DiGi Co. Ltd., (Formerly Soundtracs, P.L.C.). Box 2260, Keller, TN, 76244. Phone: (877) 292-1623. Web Site:www.digiconsoles.com David Webster, VP mktg; Taidus Vallandi, sls mgr.

Digital audio mixing consoles

Digidesign, 2001 Junipero Serra Blvd., Daly City, CA, 94014-3886. Phone: (650) 731-6300. Fax: (650) 731-6399. E-mail: prodinfo@digidesign.com Web Site:www.digidesign.com David Lebolt, gen mgr; Christopher Bock, VP sls. France. France Office, 44 Ave. Georges Pompidou, 92300 Levallois-Perret. Phone:

Tokyo 107-0052 Japan. Japan Office, 4F ATT Bldg, 2-11-7 Akasaka, Minato-ku. Phone:

Iver Heath, Bucks SLO ONH United Kingdom. UK Office, West Complex, Pinewood Studios, Pinewood Rd. Phone:

New YorkNY . New York Office, 1650 Broadway, Suite 1113. Phone:

Dimension 3, 5240 Medina Rd., Woodland Hills, CA, 91364. Phone: (818) 592-0999. E-mail: info@d3.com Web Site:www.d3.com Daniel Symmes, pres/CEO.

Provides 3-D bcst TV processes. Supplies equipment, consultation & 3-D glasses.

Direct Broadcast Services Inc., 3 Rose Ave., Chestnut Ridge, NY, 10977. Phone: (845) 267-2800. Fax: (845) 267-2123. E-mail: dbs@directbroadcast.com Web Site:www.directbroadcast.com Leo Rosenberg, pres.

Transmission svcs & rentals: Ku-band uplinking/downlinking, portable microwave, newsvan opns.

The Display & Exhibit Source, 4715 McEwen St., Dallas, TX, 75244. Phone: (972) 239-0061. Fax: (972) 239-0089. E-mail: sales@displaysource.com Web Site:www.displaysource.com Dan South, sls & owner.

Designs, manufacturer modular, portable backdrops, displays, signal & graphic systems.

Display Devices Inc., 5880 N. Sheridan Blvd., Arvada, CO, 80003. Phone: (303) 412-0399. Fax: (303) 412-9346. Web Site:www.displaydevices.com Merv Perkins, pres; Ruth Perkins, VP.

CRT, LCD, slide projector motorized lifts & stationary mounts. Custom applications.

Display Systems International Inc., 2214 Hanselman Ave., Saskatoon, SK, S7L 6A4. Canada. Phone: (306) 934-6884. Fax: (306) 934-6447. E-mail: sales@displaysystemsintl.com Web Site:www.displaysystemsintl.com Dale Lemke, pres.

Electronic progmg guide to display on-screen scrolling TV listing. Also info display software & systems for bulletin boards & adv.

Ditch Witch, Box 66, 1959 W. Fir Ave., Perry, OK, 73077. Phone: (800) 654-6481. Fax: (580) 572-3523. E-mail: info@ditchwitch.com Web Site:www.ditchwitch.com

Manufacturer of trenching, vibratory plow, trenchless technology equipment, electronic locating & tracking equipment, mini-skid steers, excavators tool-carriers & the Zahn family of power utility equipment.

DMT USA, Inc., 109 Gibraltar Rd., Horsham, PA, 19044. Phone: (267) 961-USA1. Fax: (267) 961-1020. E-mail: sales@dmtonline.us Web Site:www.dmtonline.us Stephen Blasetti, exec VP.

DMT USA specializes in digital television transmitters & Mobile TV. We manufacture UHF & VHF DTV transmitters, antennas & custom RF systems. All models are solid state environmentally safe. Look to DMT USA for cutting edge technology & true customer svc. We are your clear choice for turnkey DTV transmission equipment.

Dolby Laboratories Inc., 100 Potrero Ave., San Francisco, CA, 94103. Phone: (415) 558-0200. Fax: (415) 642-4000. Web Site:www.dolby.com Ray M. Dolby, chmn; Bill Jasper, pres/CEO.

Wootton Bassett, Wiltshire Phone:

Audio noise reduction & signal processing equipment; digital audio coding for ISDN, cable, satellite & other applications; dolby surround equipment.

Dorrough Electronics, 5221 Collier Pl., Woodland Hills, CA, 91364. Phone: (818) 998-2824. Fax: (818) 998-1507. E-mail: dorroughel@aol.com Web Site:www.dorrough.com Mike Dorrough, owner.

ChatsworthCA , 20434 Corisco St. Phone:

Dorrough Electronics manufactures Audio Loudness Meters featuring Peak & Average signals ballistically set for a highly accurate reading.

Doty-Moore Tower Services, 1570 W. Beltline Rd., Cedar Hill, TX, 75104. Phone: (972) 637-5000. Fax: (972) 293-1255. E-mail: services@stainlessllc.com Web Site:www.stainlessllc.com Patrick Moore, pres; Donald T. Doty, VP; Thomas Hoenninger, Chief Engr/VP engrg; Jon Marcusse, sls acct mgr.

North WalesPA . Corp Office, 1140 Welsh Road, #250. **Full spectrum of tower maintenance, costruction & inspections. RF svcs include RF mapping of tower & facilities. 24 hr emergency svcs.**

Dove Systems, 3563 Sueldo St., Suite E, San Luis Obispo, CA, 93401-7590. Phone: (805) 541-8292. Fax: (805) 541-8293.E-mail: dove@dovesystems.com Web Site:www.dovesystems.com Gary Dove, owner.

Studio & stage lighting control equipment.

Dow-Key Microwave Corp., 4822 McGrath, Ventura, CA, 93003. Phone: (805) 650-0260. Fax: (805) 650-1734.E-mail: askdk@dowkey.com Web Site:www.dowkey.com Mark Mandrell, pres.

Dow-Key is specialized in a broad range of RF coaxial relays operating from DC to 40 GHZ, waveguide switches (operating up 70 GHZs), electromechanical & solid state switch matrices, Fiber optics switching network, PXI moduless & Custom Solutions. Both 75 ohm & 50 ohm styles are available.

R.L. Drake LLC, (formerly R.L. Drake Co.). 230 Industrial Dr., Franklin, OH, 45005-4496. Phone: (937) 746-4556. Fax: (937) 806-1510.E-mail: bcyearbook@rldrake.com Web Site:www.rldrake.com Ron Wysong, pres/CEO; Philip Hawkins, sls; Andy Ruffin, sls dir.

PeterboroughON Canada, 655 The Queensway. Phone:
Analog, digital cable headend equipment including receivers, modulators, processors, accessories for reception & distribution of progmg.

Dubner International Inc., 13 Westervelt Pl., Westwood, NJ, 07675. Phone: (201) 664-6434. Fax: (201) 358-9377.E-mail: rdubner@compuserve.com Web Site:www.dubner.com Robert Dubner, pres.

M. Ducommun Co., 58 Main St., Warwick, NY, 10990. Phone: (845) 986-5757. Fax: (845) 986-7720. M. Ducommun Jr., pres.

Stopwatches for radio, TV, sls, svc & repair.

Dynamic Solutions 2000, 50 Conyngham St., Ashley, PA, 18706. Phone: (717) 825-0306. Fax: (570) 824-0556.E-mail: jpgibbons@prodigy.net Web Site:www.ds2000.net John P. Gibbons, pres.

Convergent billing solutions for the communications & utility industries.

E

e2v technologies Inc., 4 Westchester Plaza, Elmsford, NY, 10523. Phone: (914) 592-6050. Fax: (914) 592-5148.E-mail: enquiries@e2v.com Web Site:www.e2v.com Mike Kirk, VP; Vijay Patel, dir/tech opns.

MississaugaON Canada, Box 29667. Phone:
Manufacturer of Digital & Analog IOTs, ESCiors, Klystrons for UHF TV transmitters, Stellar range of satellite uplink amplifiers.

EDCOR Electronics Corp., (formerly Electronics Corp.). 7130 National Parks Hwy., Carlsbad, NM, 88220. Phone: (800) 854-0259. Fax: (575) 887-6880.E-mail: sales@edcorusa.com Web Site:www.edcorusa.com

Audio mic/line, audio transformers, custom transformers & power transformers.

EEG Enterprises Inc., 586 Main St., Farmingdale, NY, 11735. Phone: (516) 293-7472. Fax: (516) 293-7417.E-mail: sales@eegent.com Web Site:www.eegent.com Philip McLaughlin, CEO; Eric McErlain, sls dir.

BrooklynNY , 20 Jay Street, Suite 736.
TV closed captioning technology; HDTV & SDTV, closes caption encoders, decoders; V-chip encoders, decoders & systems; affil communications.

EFI Electronics Corp., 1751 S. 4800 W., Salt Lake City, UT, 84104. Phone: (800) 877-1174. Fax: (801) 977-0200. Web Site:www.efielectronics.com Levi Below, controller; Todd Dauphinais, pres; Aaron Davis, VP mktg; Craig Pluemer, VP sls.

Manufacturer of industrial & coml Surge Protective Devices for all electiral distribution systems & configurations, both externally & internally mounted.

ENCO Systems Inc., 29444 Northwestern Hwy., Southfield, MI, 48034. Phone: (248) 827-4440. Fax: (248) 827-4441.E-mail: sales@enco.com Web Site:www.enco.com Gene Novacek, pres; Don Backus, VP sls.

DAD & Presenter digital audio delivery systems, custom software engrg for the bcst industry.

E-N-G Mobile Systems Inc., 2245 Via De Mercados, Concord, CA, 94520. Phone: (925) 798-4060. Fax: (925) 798-0152.E-mail: info@e-n-g.com Web Site:www.e-n-g.com Dick A. Glass, pres; Rex Reed, dir/business dev & sls.

West GrovePA , 119 Lloyd Rd. Phone:
Custom-designed ENG & DSNG vehicles, rack-ready & turnkey systems. Other mobile electronic systems & ENG system components.

EON Corporation, 360 Herndon Pkwy., Herndon, VA, 20170. Phone: (703) 467-0230. Fax: (703) 467-0232. Ted Tarr, sr VP; Tom Macleod, VP business dev.

Dev & mfg of wireless two-way interactive technology for consumers & businesses which operate via radio frequency.

ERI-Electronic Research, Inc., 7777 Gardner Rd., Chandler, IN, 47610. Phone: (812) 925-6000. Fax: (812) 925-4030.E-mail: sales@eriinc.com Web Site:www.eriinc.com Thomas B. Silliman, pres; Steve Rhinerson, mgr; Todd Forbes, controller.

RF and structural engineering, field, and installation services

ESE, 142 Sierra St., El Segundo, CA, 90245. Phone: (310) 322-2136. Fax: (310) 322-8127.E-mail: ese@ese-web.com Web Site:www.ese-web.com Brian Way, VP; William Kaiser, pres.

Master clocks, digital clocks, programmable timers, time code generators & readers, distribution amplifiers, programmable clocks.

ETS-Lindgren, 1301 Arrow Point Dr., Cedar Park, TX, 78613. Phone: (512) 531-6400. Fax: (512) 531-6500.E-mail: info@ets-lindgren.com Web Site:www.ets-lindgren.com Dave Baron, sls; Bruce Butler, pres; Mark Mawdsley, VP sls.

Non-ionizing radiation test equipment; low frequency survey meters; RF/microwave broadband field strength meters; calibration svcs, software & training.

E-Z Trench Manufacturing Co. Inc., 2315 S. Hwy. 701, Loris, SC, 29569. Phone: (843) 756-6444. Fax: (843) 756-6442. Web Site:www.eztrench.com Gail Porter, pres.

Lightweight trenchers digs trench, lays cables & covers all in one pass.

Eagle Comtronics Inc., 7665 Henry Clay Blvd., Liverpool, NY, 13008. Phone: (315) 622-3402. Phone: (800) 448-7474. Fax: (315) 622-3800.E-mail: sales@eaglecomtronics.com Web Site:www.eaglecomtronics.com

CATV manufacturer & designer of security traps, decoders, & tier traps. Custom OEM filter designs.

Eastman Kodak Co., 343 State St., Rochester, NY, 14650. Phone: (800) 698-3324. Fax: (585) 724-0663. Web Site:www.kodak.com Antonio Perez, chmn/CEO.

Cameras, projectors, graphic & entertainment imaging products.

EDX Wireless, (EDX Division of Comarco Wireless Technologies Incorporated). 101 East Broadway, MS 305, Eugene, OR, 97401. Phone: (541) 345-0019. Fax: (541) 345-8145.E-mail: info@edx.com Web Site:www.edx.com

RF Planning software for FM, TV & DTV.

Eddie Egan & Associates, 6136 W. Washington Blvd., Culver City, CA, 90232. Phone: (310) 278-0370. Fax: (310) 559-4348.E-mail: eddieegan@bcglobal.net Daniel Egan, pres; Armand Egan, VP.

Floor coverings for video stages including wood, vinyl & carpeting.

Eigen, 13366 Grass Valley Ave., Grass Valley, CA, 95945. Phone: (530) 274-1240. Phone: (888) 924-2020. Fax: (530) 265-2792.E-mail: sales@eigen.com Web Site:www.eigen.com David Franco, CFO; Michael Castorino, pres/CEO.

Digital image processors with storage & High-resolution video disc recorders.

Elan Enterprises Ltd., 506 E. St. Charles Rd., Carol Stream, IL, 60188. Phone: (800) 331-8382. Fax: (630) 690-6618.E-mail: eeljim8720@aol.com Web Site:www.generator-inverter.com Jim Johnsen, pres, sls dir; Joe Johnsen Jr., VP.

Redi-line electric generators. Tripp Lite inverters & sure power isolators.

Elcom Systems Inc., 20423 State Rd. 7, Boca Raton, FL, 33498-6797. Phone: (561) 883-1945. Fax: (561) 883-1945.E-mail: sales@elcomsystems.com Web Site:www.elcomsystems.com Leonard Pollachek, pres.

RF coaxial attenuators, terminations, couplers, double balanced mixers, detectors, DC-4.2 Ghz, impedance transformers.

Electro Impulse Laboratory Inc., Box 278, 1805 Rt. 33, Neptune, NJ, 07754-0278. Phone: (732) 776-5800. Fax: (732) 776-6793.E-mail: sales@electroimpulse.com Web Site:www.electroimpulse.com Mark Rubin, pres.

Manufacturer of dry, forced, air-cooled FM dummy loads & RF calorimeters.

Electro Rent Corp., (Instrument Rental Division). 6060 Sepulveda Blvd., Van Nuys, CA, 91411. Phone: (818) 787-2100. Fax: (818) 787-4354. Web Site:www.electrorent.com Craig Birgi, rgnl mgr.

DuluthGA , 3500 Corporate Way. Phone:
Test rental equipment including CATV sweep analyzers, signal level meters, video generators/monitors & cable fault locators, data equipment-desktops & laptops to rent, lease or purchase.

Electroline Equipment Inc., 11035 Louis H. Lafontaine, Anjou, PQ, H1J 3AE. Canada. Phone: (514) 374 6335. Fax: (514) 374-2257.E-mail: info@electroline.com Web Site:www.electroline.com John Vincent, pres/CEO; Jay Staiger, VP mktg; Alain Servant, VP.

Cable TV equipment, off-premises addressable systems, passive devices, filters, amplifiers, headend RF signal mgnt equipment, transponders, optical nodes & FTTH.

Electronic Script Prompting, 6129 Western Ave., Willowbrook, IL, 60527. Phone: (630) 887-0346. Fax: (630) 887-0389. Web Site:www.prompting.com Frank Warner, pres/CEO.

Teleprompting rental & sale.

Electronic Theatre Controls Inc., 3031 Pleasant View Rd., Middleton, WI, 53562. Phone: (608) 831-4116. Fax: (608) 836-1736. Web Site:www.etcconnect.com Fred Foster, CEO.

OrlandoFL , 4201 Vineland Rd, Suite I-1. Phone:
New YorkNY , Film Center Bldg., 630 Ninth Ave., Suite 1001. Phone:
Entertainment & Architectural lighting systems, including control consoles, dimming equipment, interface products & elipsoidals.

Electronology, Inc., 508 Lakeland Blvd., Mattoon, IL, 61938. Phone: (800) 278-2050. Fax: (217) 258-5558.E-mail: info@einc.com Web Site:www.einc.com Jay Martin, mgr; John Sullivan, consultant; Jim Renkel, consultant.

Emcor Enclosures, 1600 4th Ave. N.W., Rochester, MN, 55901. Phone: (507) 287-3535. Fax: (507) 287-3405.E-mail: emcor@emcorenclosures.com Web Site:www.emcorenclosures.com

Conventional & Flat Panel Display Consoles, modification /custom capabilities, EMI/RFI shielded & Seismic qualified enclosures, a full range of component accessories.

Emerson Network Power, (Changed from Control Concepts Corp.). Box 1380, 328 Water St., Binghamton, NY, 13902-1380. Phone: (607) 731-8865. Phone: (800) 288-6169. Fax: (607) 722-8713.E-mail: info@control-concepts.com Web Site:www.control-concepts.com Bill Fierle, pres; Sarah Beadle, dir mktg.

Power protection products for transmitters, studios, CATVs from transients & lightning induced voltages.

Emerson Network Power, (formerly Northern Technologies Inc.). Box 610, 23123 E. Mission Ave., Liberty Lake, WA, 99019. Phone: (509) 927-0401. Fax: (509) 927-0435.E-mail: webmaster@northern-tech.com Web Site:www.emerson-networkpower.com David N. Farr, chmn/CEO, pres; Craig W. Ashmore, sr VP dev; Ed Feeney, exec VP.

Full line of transient control systems for AC, dataline & telephone, including UPS systems & regulators.

Emerson Network Power, (formerly Marconi Communications). 4350 Weaver Pkwy., Warrenville, IL, 60555. Phone: (630) 579-5000. Fax: (630) 579-5050. Web Site:www.marconi.com Dusty Becker, VP.

London United Kingdom, 34 Grosvenor. Phone:

Emerson Network Power-Viewsonics, (formerly Viewsonics Inc.). 3103 N. Andrews Ave. Ext, Pompano Beach, FL, 33064-2118. Phone: (507) 833-8822. Fax: (507) 833-6287. Web Site:www.emersonnetworkpower.com/connectivity David N. Farr, pres/CEO; Edward K. Feeney, exec VP; Jerry Patton, VP sls.

One GHz amplifiers, security systems, apartment boxes, combiners, LAN, CATV, one GHz splitters, taps, custom design systems & products, head end signal coupler/splitter system.

Equipment Manufacturers and Distributors Alphabetical Index

Encoda Systems Inc., (formerly Columbine JDS, Enterprise and DAL/Brake Automation). 1999 Broadway, Suite 4000, Denver, CO, 80202-3050. Phone: (303) 237-4000. Fax: (303) 237-0085.E-mail: info@encodasystems.com Web Site:www.encodasystems.com Barry Goldsmith, CEO; Rob McConnell, COO.

Encoda is the authority in seamless automation for the business of media. Encoda is the only company offering end-to-end technological solutions to buyers & sellers of adv time within the electronic media marketplace (bcst, cable, wireless, & DBS).

Energy-Onix Broadcast Equipment Co. Inc., Box 801, 1306 River St., Valatie, NY, 12184. Phone: (518) 758-1690. Fax: (518) 758-1476.E-mail: energy-onix@energy-onix.com Web Site:www.energy-onix.com Bernard Wise, pres.

Transmitters: AM solid state to 10 kw, grounded grid triode to 50 kw & AM & SW to 100 kw. STL, Translator & remote pick up. FM, Shortwave

Enghouse Systems Limited, 80 Tiverton Ct., Suite 800, Markham, ON, L3R 0G4. Canada. Phone: (905) 946-3200. Fax: (905) 946-3201.E-mail: info@enghouse.com Web Site:www.enghouse.com Stephen Sadler, CEO; Anthony Pearlman, pres; Sunil Diaz, VP sls.

Networks®—automated mapping/facilities mgmt software with integrated design capabilities for fiber, copper & coax solutions.

Engineered Electric Company, (dba DRS Fermont (formerly Fermont ACTS Co.). 141 North Ave., Bridgeport, CT, 06606. Phone: (203) 366-5211. Fax: (203) 367-3642. Web Site:www.drspowersolutions.com John Uvodich, VP/gen mgr.

Tactical Quiet Generators Sets for military applications.

Ensemble Designs, Box 993, Grass Valley, CA, 95945. Phone: (530) 478-1830. Fax: (530) 478-1832.E-mail: info@ensembledesigns.com Web Site:www.ensembledesigns.com David S. Wood, pres; Cindy Zuelsdorf, mktg mgr; Mondae Hott, gen sls mgr.

Video, audio conversion distribution, HD/down conversion, fiber satellite & desktop video applications.

Enterprise Electronics Corp., 128 S. Industrial Blvd., Enterprise, AL, 36330. Phone: (334) 347-3478. Fax: (334) 393-4556.E-mail: sales@eecradar.com Web Site:www.eecradar.com Larry Sabourin, pres; Frank Sloan, dir mktg; Gary Bruce, sls dir.

Doppler weather radar systems (rain & wind measurements) with PC-based graphics display & control.

Entertainment Communications Network (ECN), 4370 Tujunga Ave., Studio City, CA, 91604. Phone: (818) 752-1400. Fax: (818) 752-1443.E-mail: csd@ecnmedia.com Web Site:www.ecnmedia.com Angela Tietze, pres.

WallNJ , 1628 Dubac Rd. Phone:

Bcst faxing to entertainment data bases, online resources, E-mail networks, digital graphics-delivery.

Equipment Technology LLC, 341 N.W. 122nd, Oklahoma City, OK, 73114. Phone: (405) 748-3841. Fax: (405) 755-6829. Web Site:www.eti1.com E-mail: sales@etil.com Chris Neuberger, pres.

Oklahoma CityOK , 341 N.W. 122. Glenn Smith, VP mktg/sls.

Aerial buckets: articulating & telescoping; truck & van mounted; working height ranges 33 to 43 ft.

Euphonix Inc., 220 Portage Ave., Palo Alto, CA, 94306. Phone: (650) 855-0400. Fax: (650) 855-0410.E-mail: mailman@euphonix.com Web Site:www.euphonix.com Martin Kloiber, CEO.

New York NY . Euphonix NYC , 424 West 33rd St, # 560

Studio CityCA . Euphonix Sales & Marketing, 11112 Ventura Blvd, #301. Phone:

Manufactures the Euphonix CSII digitally-controlled analog audio mixing system.

Even Technologies Inc., (formerly Even Technologies). 601 West Cordova St., #490, Vancouver, BC, V6B 1G1. Canada. Phone: (604) 689-1858. Fax: (604) 689-1758.E-mail: info@eventechnologies.com Web Site:www.eventechnologies.com Nick Ringma, pres/CEO.

Video compression technology, sofware & hardware for streaming media & real time delivery of IPTV & pre-corded video.

Eventide Inc., One Alsan Way, Little Ferry, NJ, 07643. Phone: (201) 641-1200. Fax: (201) 641-1640.E-mail: audio@eventide.com Web Site:www.eventide.com Gordon Moore, gen mgr; Richard Factor, chmn; Tony Agnello, CTO; Ray Maxwell, VP; Jason Beck, pres.

Audio delay lines, time compression/expansion, pitch change effects, digital reverb, effects processor & digital audio logger.

Evertz Microsystems Ltd., 5288 John Lucas Dr., Burlington, ON, L7L 5Z9. Canada. Phone: (905) 335-3700. Fax: (905) 335-3573.E-mail: sales@evertz.com Web Site:www.evertz.com Orest Holyk, sls dir; Joe Cirincione, dir.

ReadingNO United Kingdom, 59 Suttons Business Park. BurbankCA , 212 N. Evergreen St. ManassasVA , 9250 Mosby St, Suite 201.

Evertz provides the most comprehensive line of Fiber Optic Transport equipment, the most advanced line of Multi-Image Display, Monitoring Systems, SDTV & HDTV conversion, synchronization products for use in satellite, cable & bcst applications.

The Express Group, 3360 Thorn St., San Diego, CA, 92104. Phone: (619) 280-9061. Fax: (619) 280-9030.E-mail: egmail@theexpressgroup.com Web Site:www.theexpressgroup.com Byron Andrus, pres; George Andrus, consultant.

Design, fabrication, lighting of custom news sets, newsrooms, interview sets; custom & modular radio cabinetry.

F

F&F Productions, L.L.C., 14333 Myerlake Cir., Clearwater, FL, 33760. Phone: (727) 535-6776. Fax: (727) 577-5011. Web Site:www.fandfhd.tv George Orgera, pres/CEO; Ryan Hatch, sr VP; Bill McKechney, VP engrg.

Remote production svcs & TV mobile units.

F-Conn Industries, (A division of ICM Corp). 6260 Downing St., Denver, CO, 80216. Phone: (303) 288-8107. Fax: (303) 288-4769.E-mail: sales@icmcorp.net Web Site:www.icmcorp.net Randy Holliday, pres; Susan Stockstill, sls VP.

FM Atlas—Publishing and Electronics, Box 336, Esko, MN, 55733-0336. Phone: (218) 879-7676. Fax: (218) 879-8333.E-mail: fmatlas@aol.com Web Site:www.user.aol.com/fmatlas Bruce Elving, owner.

Tunable FM/SCS & SAP-modified TV audio radios, adaptor kits with LED display. Brailled radios for the blind.

FM SYSTEMS Inc., 3877 S. Main St., Santa Ana, CA, 92707. Phone: (714) 979-3355. Phone: (800) 235-6960. Fax: (714) 979-0913. Web Site:www.fmsystems-inc.com E-mail: fmsystemsinc@sbcglobal.net Frank McClatchie, CEO; Don McClatchie, COO.

Digital test & measurement equipment & digital audio gain control for AES, HD & SD TV singles. Stereo performance meter, audio level masters, digital video volt meters, video & audio modulation meters, multichannel subcarriers & video gain controls (VM771).

FOR- A Corp. of America, 11125 Knott Ave., Suite A, Cypress, CA, 90630. Phone: (714) 894-3311. Fax: (714) 894-5399. Web Site:www.for-a.com Chuck Bocan, gen sls mgr.

Video & audio bcst & postproduction equipment; TBCs, color correctors, production switchers, de/encoders, complete video editing systems, virtual studio & multiviewers.

FWT Inc., Box 8597, 5750 E. I-20, Fort Worth, TX, 76124. Phone: (817) 255-3060. Fax: (817) 255-2957.E-mail: info@fwtinc.com Web Site:www.fwtinc.com Bill Sales, VP sls.

Monopoles, self supporting towers, guyed towers, communications bldgs, standby power systems, mobile communications bldgs, COWS, fiber optics, & splicing trailers.

Faroudja Laboratories, (A Division of Genesis Microchip). 180 Baytech Dr., Ste.110, San Jose, CA, 95134. Phone: (408) 635-4200. Fax: (408) 957-0364. Web Site:www.faroudja.com Yves Faroudja, Contact.

NTSC Encoder; NTSC & PAL/NTSC Decoder (RGB or D1 output); Bidirectional Transcoder; NTSC & PAL/NTSC Line Doublers & Line Quadruplers.

Farrtronics Ltd., 39 Kent Ave., Kitchener, ON, N2G 3R2. Canada. Phone: (519) 741-1010. Fax: (519) 578-2044.

Audio & video patchfields; intercom systems, IFB systems, audio distribution amplifiers, beltpack party line systems, monitor packages.

Fast Forward Video, 1151 Duryea Avenue, Irvine, CA, 92614. Phone: (949) 852-8404. Fax: (949) 852-1226. Web Site:www.ffv.com E-mail: sales@ffv.com Paul Dekeyser, CTO; Hal Reisiger, CEO.

Fast Forward Video is committed to providing cutting edge DVR technology in both award-winning finished goods & board-levl products along with engrg supports to a variety of industries including bcstg, sports, military, film production, surveillance & many more.

Feldmar Watch and Clock Center, 9000 W. Pico Blvd., Los Angeles, CA, 90035. Phone: (310) 274-8016. Fax: (310) 274-2081.E-mail: sales@feldmarwatch.com Web Site:www.feldmarwatch.com Sol Meller, pres.

Stopwatches, clocks, watches, timers, sls & repairs.

Ferno-Washington Inc., 70 Weil Way, Wilmington, OH, 45177-9371. Phone: (937) 382-1451. Fax: (937) 382-1191. Web Site:www.ferno.com Joe Bourgraf, CEO; Tim Schroeder, mktg mgr.

Carts designed to aid in the movement of heavy & bulky equipment.

Fiber Options, 4575 Research Way, Suite 250, Corvallis, OR, 97333. Phone: (800) 469-1676. Phone: (541) 754-9134. Fax: (541) 752-9097.E-mail: cvovideosales@ge.com John Collins, pres; Fred Scott, sls VP; Vic Milani, VP.

West Yorkshire. Fiber Options Europe Ltd., Unit 7, Cliff Pk, Morley, Leeds. Phone:

Manufactures fiber-optic video, data, and audio transmission systems for security, bcst, educ, teleconferencing, ITS, and industrial markets.

Film/Video Equipment Service Co. Inc., 800 S. Jason St., Denver, CO, 80223. Phone: (303) 778-8616. Fax: (303) 778-8657.E-mail: dschnieder@fvesco.com Web Site:www.fvesco.com Dean D. Schneider, pres.

Film & video equipment rentals-cameras, lenses, lighting, grip, pro audio, camera support & specialty gear for quality production.

FitzCo. Inc., Box 710, 4300 W. Wall, Bldg. B, Midland, TX, 79702. Phone: (432) 684-0861. Fax: (432) 682-9978.E-mail: fitzcosound@mac.com Web Site:www.fitzcosound.com Milt Hathaway, pres.

Speakers, recorders, amplifiers, mixers, tapes, microphones, & headphones; sound reinforcement & bcst equipment.

Flash Technology Corporation of America, 332 Nichol Mill Ln., Franklin, TN, 37067. Phone: (615) 261-2000. Fax: (615) 261-2600.E-mail: info@flashtechnology.biz Web Site:www.flashtechnology.com Mark Joss, VP/gen mgr.

NashuaNH , 55 Lake St. Phone:

Aviation high-intensity obstruction lights for tall structures & medium intensity for structures up to 500 ft.

FloriCal Systems Inc., 4581 N.W. 6th St., Gainesville, FL, 32609. Phone: (352) 372-8326. Fax: (352) 375-0859.E-mail: sales@florical.com Web Site:www.florical.com Shawn Maynard, gen mgr & VP opns; Jim Berry, sls dir; Kim McKnight, mktg mgr.

TV Automation, complete on-air mgmt & presentation systems include; asset mgmt, material acquisition, variable multi ch control systems, BXF traf interface, e-mail reports, AssetDispatcher (HD central ingest tool) optional access through web svcs. Dynamic, highly configurable, scalable & reliable.

Fluke Corp., Box 9090, Everett, WA, 98206-9090. Phone: (800) 443-5853. Fax: (206) 446-5116.E-mail: fluke-info @fluke.com Web Site:www.fluke.com H. Lawrence Culp Jr., CEO; Barbara Hulit, pres.

Electronic test, measurement & control instrumentation.

Focus Enhancements, 1370 Dell Ave., Campbell, CA, 95008. Phone: (408) 866-8300. Fax: (408) 866-4859.E-mail: info@focusinfo.com Web Site:www.focusinfo.com Bret Moyer, CEO.

Fostex USA, (formerly Fostex America). 9 Mars Ct., Boonton, NJ, 07005. Phone: (973) 394-0015. Fax: (973) 394-0800.E-mail: ed@fostexusa.com Web Site:www.fostexusa.com Steven Savvides, pres; Ed Alstrom, natl sls mgr.

Manufacturer & marketer of innovative digital recorders, field recorders, headphones & monitoring solutions for bcst environments, musicians, producers, personal & professional studios.

Four Seasons Solar Products Corp., 5005 Veterans Memorial Hwy., Holbrook, NY, 11741. Phone: (631) 563-4000. Fax: (631) 563-4010. Web Site:www. oikos.com David Ewing, pres.

Freeland Products Inc., 75412 Hwy. 25, Covington, LA, 70435. Phone: (985) 893-1243. Phone: (800) 624-7626. Fax: (985) 892-7323.E-mail: freeland-inc.com @freeland-inc.com Web Site:www.freeland-inc.com Joel H. Freeland, pres.

Rebuilding of TV & radio transmitter tubes.

Frequency Measuring Service Inc., Box 353, Commerce City, CO, 80037. Phone: (303) 288-1482. Fax: (303) 289-8006. Howard S. Eldridge, pres & dir.

Frequency measurements, modulation calibration, field intensity measurements, spectrum analysis.

Frezzolini Electronics Inc., 5-7 Valley St., Hawthorne, NJ, 07506. Phone: (973) 427-1160. Fax: (973) 427-0934.E-mail: infoi@frezzi.com Web Site:www.frezzi.com James J. Crawford, pres.

High-capacity NIMH, Lithium Ion & Nickel Zinc rechargeable batteries for professional cameras & camcorders; advanced charger & power supplies, location lighting with Frezzi Mini & Micro-fill tungsten quartz & Micro-Sun-Guns, LED MR-19 replacement lamps for Mini & Micro fill lighting.

Frontline Communications, 12770 44th St. N., Clearwater, FL, 33762. Phone: (727) 573-0400. Fax: (727) 571-3295.E-mail: dmckay@frontlinecomm.com Web Site:www.frontlinecomm.com

FUJIFILM Recording Media U.S.A. Inc., 200 Summit Lake Dr., Valhalla, NY, 10595-1356. Phone: (914) 789-8100. Fax: (914) 789-8530. Web Site:www.fujifilmusa.com Peter Faulhaber, sr VP; Gene Kern, dir business dev.

BedfordMD , 45 Crosby Dr. Phone:

EdisonNJ , 1100 King George Post Rd. Phone:

Professional recording media & data media for bcst, production, cinematography & industrial applications.

Fujinon Inc., 10 High Point Dr., Wayne, NJ, 07470. Phone: (973) 633-5600. Fax: (973) 633-5216.E-mail: lens.sales@fujinon.com Web Site:www.fujinon.com H. Hayashi, pres; John Newton, VP; Tom Calabro, natl sls mgr.

RedondoCA , West Bay Business Park, 2621A Manhattan Beach Blvd. Phone:

HollywoodFL , 4101 N. 48th Terr. Phone:

AddisonTX , 4951 Airport Pkwy, Suite 802A. Phone:

HDTV, CTV, ENG, EFP lenses, optical systems, accessories.

Full Compass Systems Ltd., 8001 Terrace Ave., Middleton, WI, 53562-3194. Phone: (800) 356-5844. Phone: (608) 831-7330. Fax: (608) 831-6330.E-mail: customerservice @fullcompass.com Web Site:www.fullcompass.com Jonathan Lipp, CEO.

Over 300 product lines for bcst recording, entertainment, video & sound reinforcement industries.

Fuller Manufacturing, 695 S. Glenwood Pl., Burbank, CA, 91506. Phone: (818) 500-0116. Fax: (818) 238-9959. Ron Fuller, engrg mgr.

IFB for news & satellite trunks.

Furman, (Formerly Furman Sound Inc.). 1690 Corporate Cir., Petaluma, CA, 94954. Phone: (707) 763-1010. Fax: (707) 763-1310.E-mail: info@furmansound.com Web Site:www.furmansound.com Dave Keller, VP sls, mktg VP; John Humphrey, CFO.

Analog, digital, video monitor systems, power conditioning/distribution, mixers, equalizers, compressors, crossovers, patch bays, voltage regulators, headphone amplifliers & distribution systems.

Fusion Consoles, (formerly Solutions) Distributed by Marketec. 2801 W. Empire Ave., Burbank, CA, 91504. Phone: (800) 557-8661. Fax: (888) 262-1726.E-mail: info@marketec.com Web Site:www.marketec.com Penny Russell, owner.

Technical Furniture & Accessories including ready-to-assemble NLE console desks, racks & full custom tech furniture fabrication complete with CAD drawing for the bcst & cable, post production, audio & multimedia applications.

Future Productions Inc., 100 Industrial Ave., Little Ferry, NJ, 07643-1913. Phone: (201) 727-0903. Fax: (201) 727-0908. Web Site:members.aol.com/futureprd/video.html

Manufactures & svcs audio/video distribution amplifiers, video duplication control systems, bcst camera control systems, computer graphic systems; & video duplication svc.

G

GAMPRODUCTS Inc., 4975 W. Pico Blvd., Los Angeles, CA, 90019. Phone: (323) 935-4975. Fax: (323) 935-2002. Web Site:www.gamonline.com Joseph N. Tawil, owner/gen mgr; Heidi Vessels, opns mgr; Jeff Davis, sls.

Lighting equipment, portable, studio special effects, projections, control console, dimming, color, correction, diffusion filters & patterns (gobos).

G Prime Ltd., Radio City Sn., Box 1525, New York, NY, 10101. Phone: (212) 765-3415. Fax: (212) 581-8938.E-mail: info@gprime.com Web Site:www.gprime.com Russ O. Hamm, pres.

Importer & distributor of European professional audio equipment for the bcst & recording industries.

Gala, (A division of Paco Corp). 3185 First Street, St. Hubert, PQ, J3Y 8Y6. Canada. Phone: (450) 678-7226. Fax: (450) 678-4060.E-mail: info@pacocorp.com Web Site:www.galasystems.com Philippe Laforest, pres; Philippe Desmarais, sls.

Es CondidoCA , 655 Calle Ladra. Phone:

Theatrical rigging, revolving stages & orchestra lifts.

Galaxy Audio Inc., (dba Valley Audio). Box 16285, Wichita, KS, 67216-0285. Phone: (316) 263-2852. Fax: (316) 263-0642.E-mail: sales@galaxyaudio.com Web Site:www.galaxyaudio.com Brock Jabara, CEO; Yule Jabara, natl sls mgr.

Wireless speakers & microphones, headset mics, personal monitors power & unpowered, combiners, splitters SPL meters & audio test equipment.

Garner Products, (division of Audiolab Electronics Inc.). 620 Commerce Dr., Suite C, Roseville, 95678. Phone: (916) 784-0200. Phone: (800) 624-1903. Fax: (916) 784-1425.E-mail: info@garner-products.com Web Site:www.garner-products.com Ronald A. Stofan, pres.

Professional line of bulk tape degaussers for all formats of tape including: Beta SP, DAT 2" reels up to 16" diameters, hard drives, DLT media & degaussing svc.

Geac Libra, 462 Bearcat Dr., Suite C, Salt Lake City, UT, 04115-2520. Phone: (800) 453-3827. Fax: (801) 974-1900.E-mail: info@geac.com Web Site:www.gcs.geac.com Eric Schlor, sls.

Accounting software for radio, including billing affidavits & sls analysis.

Gefen Inc., 20600 Nordhoff St., Chatsworth, CA, 91311. Phone: (800) 545-6900. Phone: (818) 772-9100. Fax: (818) 772-9120.E-mail: gsinfo@gefen.com Web Site:www.gefen.com Hagai Gefen, CEO; Robert Lemer, sls.

Gefen supplies A/V signal switchers, splitters, extenders, scalers,converters, KVM solutions and home theater accessories that support pro A/V and broadcast applications. Gefen's hardware enables audio/video and computer systems to be easily integrated, extended, distributed and optimized to maximize performance.

General Atomics, 4949 Greencraig Ln., San Diego, CA, 92123. Phone: (858) 522-8300. Fax: (858) 522-8301. Web Site:www.ga-esi.com Phil Arneson, pres.

Terminal automation products, radiation, monitoring system, triqq and manufacturer of Maxwell high voltage capacitors & power supplies.

General Cable, 4 Tesseneer Dr., Highland Heights, KY, 41076. Phone: (859) 572-8000. Fax: (859) 572-8458. Web Site:www.generalcable.com E-mail: info@generalcable.com George Bkenny, pres.

Copper, aluminum and fiberoptic wire, cable products for communications, energy & electrical markets.

General Electric Co., 3135 Easton Tpke., Fairfield, CT, 06431. Phone: (800) 626-2004. Phone: (203)373-2039. Fax: (203) 373-3198. Web Site:www.ge.com E-mail: geinfo@www.ge.com

Fort LeeNJ . CNBC & MSNBC, 2200 Fletcher Ave. Bill Bolste, pres.

New YorkNY . NBC, 30 Rockefeller Plaza. Phone:

ClevelandOH , 4338 Nela Park. Phone:

NBC bcstg; CNBC & MSNBC; lighting products; Americom satellite; electrical distribution & control; intercast; MSNBC desktop video.

General Electrodynamics Corp., 8000 Calendar Rd., Arlington, TX, 76001. Phone: (817) 572-0366. Fax: (817) 572-0373. Web Site:www.gecscales.com Dick Davis, pres.

Tubes, TV cameras, electronics, aircraft weighing equipment, contract weighing svcs, truck scales, load scales.

Geneva Aviation Inc., 20021 80th Ave. S., Kent, WA, 98032. Phone: (253) 395-9105. Fax: (253) 395-9150.E-mail: info@genevaaviation.com Web Site:www.genevaaviation.com Steve Joseph, pres; Steve Cudnosskey, chief tech off.

Design, manufacture & instal of E.N.G. & microwave equipment for news helicopters.

Gennum Corp., 4281 Harvester Rd., Burlington, ON, L7L 5M4. Canada. Phone: (905) 632-2996. Fax: (905) 632-2055. Web Site:www.gennum.com Franz fINK, pres/CEO.

High performance integrated circuits, including switches & processing functions, for analog & digital video applications.

Gepco International Inc., 1770 Birchwood Ave., Des Plaines, IL, 60018. Phone: (847) 795-9555. Fax: (847) 795-8770.E-mail: gepco@gepco.com Web Site:www.gepco.com Gary R. Geppert, pres; David Mecklenburger, CFO.

BurbankCA , 1000 N. Lake St. Phone:

Audio cable & video cable in bulk or cut to length. Assemblies, boxes, connectors, patchbays. ADC, Kings Neutrik & switchcraft

Glentronix, 90 Nolan Ct., Unit 7, Markham, ON, L3R 4L9. Canada. Phone: (905) 475-8494. Fax: (905) 475-0955. Web Site:www.glentronix.com

Studio video equipment, audio jackfield & test equipment.

Global Microwave Systems Inc., 1916 Palomar Oaks Way, Suite 100, Carlsbad, CA, 92008. Phone: (760) 496-0055. Fax: (760) 496-0057.E-mail: gms@gmsinc.com Web Site:www.gmsinc.com Sam Nasiri, pres; Wayne Rogers, sls.

The latest in microwave communications equipment.

Globecomm Systems Inc., 45 Oser Ave., Hauppauge, NY, 11788-3816. Phone: (631) 231-9800. Fax: (631) 231-1557. Web Site:www.globecommsystems.com David Hershberg, CEO; Keith Hall, VP/gen mgr; F. Dugourd, Contact.

Earth stn ground segments. Video Broadcasting Service & Content Delivery Service.

Alan Gordon Enterprises Inc., 5625 Melrose Ave., Hollywood, CA, 90038. Phone: (323) 466-3561. Fax: (323) 871-2193.E-mail: info@alangordon.com Web Site:www.alangordon.com Grant Loucks, pres; Wayne Loucks, gen mgr; Don Sahlein, exec VP.

Rental, sls, equipment training & repair svcs for professional motion picture HD, film & video equipment.

Gorman-Redlich Manufacturing Co., 257 W. Union St., Athens, OH, 45701. Phone: (740) 593-3150. Fax: (740) 592-3898. Web Site:www.gorman-redlich.com E-mail: jimg@gorman-redlich.com James T. Gorman, owner.

EAS encoders & decoders, EAS with built-in character generator for TV; digital antennas monitors; NOAA weather radios with SAME decoding.

Graham-Patten Systems Inc., The ISIS Group, 119 E. McKnight Way, Unit A, Grass Valley, CA, 95949-9503. Phone: (888) 622-4747. Phone: (530) 477-2984. Fax: (530) 477-2986.E-mail: info@isis-group.com Web Site:www.gpsys.com Steven Block, CEO.

Digital audio mixers & digital audio systemization products.

Grant Tower, Inc., 13064 Wisner Ave., Grant, MI, 49327. Phone: (231) 834-5665. Fax: (231) 834-7870. Web Site:www.granttower.com Terry L. Sharp Jr., pres; Walter Knoch Jr., office mgr.

Bcst tower erection & maintenance svc.

Gray Engineering Laboratories Inc., 2118 W. Collins Ave., Orange, CA, 92867. Phone: (714) 997-4151. Fax: (714) 997-1939. Web Site:www.grayengineeringlabs.com Scott R. Gray, pres.

SMPTE time-code generators & readers, safe area generators, video-assisted film editing components.

Great Lakes Data Systems, Inc., 5954 Priestly Dr., Carlsbad, CA, 92008. Phone: (760) 753-1024. Fax: (760) 753-2538.E-mail: sales@cablebilling.com Web Site:www.cablebilling.com J. Alonzo Rosado, pres; Laura Rosado, VP sls/mktg.

Beaver DamWI , Box 295. Phone:

Affordable PC/Network billing & subscriber mgmt systems. Addressable interface, PPV, ARU, ANI, Hotel PPV. Training, data conversion & toll-free support.

Greenberg Teleprompting, 115 S. Olive St., Orange, CA, 92866. Phone: (818) 838-4437. Fax: (818) 838-0447.E-mail: info@greenprompt.com Web Site:www.greenprompt.com Jim Estochin, owner.

Camera mounted teleprompting, speech prompting, nationwide clients.

Group One Ltd., 70 Sea Ln., Farmingdale, NY, 11735. Phone: (561) 249-1399. Fax: (516) 249-8870.E-mail: sales@g1limited.com Web Site:www.g1limited.com Jack Kelly, pres; Chris Fichera, VP sls.

Exclusive distributor for a number of prominent audio & lighting products including: MC2, Celestion, XTA Electronics, Elektralite, Pulsar & Blue Sky.

Gyrocam Systems, 8100 15th St. E., Sarasota, FL, 34243. Phone: (941) 355-3206. Fax: (941) 355-3417.E-mail: info@gyrocamsystems.com Web Site:www.gyrocamsystems.com Ken Sanborn, pres/CEO; Joe Stark, VP sls; Stefanie Kowitt, exec dir.

Manufacturer of the Gyrocam-gyrostablized camera systems for aircraft, boats or vehicles. High Definition Cameras & V700 watt searchlight also available.

H

Hardigg Cases, (A division of Hardigg Industries Inc.). Box 201, 147 N. Main St., South Deerfield, MA, 01373-0201. Phone: (800) 542-7344. Fax: (413) 665-8330.E-mail: cases@hardigg.com Web Site:www.hardigg.com James S. Hardigg, pres.

With our rugged, dependable shipping cases, we have a video bcst solution for you. Design to protect everything form consumer-grade cameras & lenses to LCD panels & professional studio units, our video bcst cases ensure that all your sensitive, delicate & valuable gear arrives at its destination intact & ready to go.

Harman International Industries Inc., (A subsidiary of JBL Professional.). 8500 Balboa Blvd., Northridge, CA, 91329. Phone: (818) 893-8411. Fax: (818) 892-9590. Web Site:www.harman.com Dinesh Paliwal, chmn/CEO; Herbert K. Parker, CFO.

Manufacturer of audio signal processing equipment designed for sound reinforcement, recording & bcstg.

Harmonic Inc., 549 Baltic Way, Sunnyvale, CA, 94089. Phone: (408) 542-2500. Fax: (408) 542-2511. Web Site:www.harmonicinc.com Patrick Harshman, pres.

Fiber-optic & digital transmission systems for cable TV, including transmitters, receivers, return path equipment & net mgmt hardware & software.

Harris Automation Solutions, 1134 E. Arques Ave., Sunnyvale, CA, 595-8250. Phone: (408) 990-8200. Fax: (408) 990-8250.E-mail: sales@harris.com Web Site:www.harris.com Jim Wood, mgr.

WantaghNY , Bos 3200. Phone:

IssaquahWA , 700 NW Gilman Blvd, 133-227. Phone:

Louth is a supplier of media mgmt, automation system: for bcst & cable TV.

Harris Broadcast Communications, (formerly Videotek). 243 Shoemaker Rd., Pottstown, PA, 19464-6433. Phone: (800) 800-5719. Fax: (610) 327-9295. Web Site:www.broadcast.harris.com Tim Thorsteinson, pres; Richard R. Hollowbush, VP; Bob Jennett, VP opns.

Manufacturer of test/measurement equipment, video demodulators, routing switchers, color correctors/processors, related equipment for professional video/TV bcst markets.

Harris Corporation, 1025 W. NASA Blvd., Melbourne, FL, 32919-0001. Phone: (321) 727-9100. Howard L. Lance, pres/CEO; Robert K. Henry, exec VP/COO; Gary L. McArthur, CFO; R. Kent Buchanan, engrg VP.

PlanoTX , Box 867717. Phone:

Provides a wide range of products & svcs for coml & govt communications markets such as wireless, bcst, & govt.

Harris Corp., Broadcast Communications, (formerly Harris Corp., Broadcast Communications Division). 4393 Digital Way, Mason, OH, 45040. Phone: (513) 459-3400. Fax: (513) 701-5315. Web Site:www.broadcast.harris.com Tim Thorsteinson, pres.

Harris Broadcast Communications offers products, systems & svcs that provide interoperable workflow solutions for bcst, cable, satellite & out-of-home networks. The Harris ONE solution brings together highly integrated & cost-effective products that enable advanced media workflows for emerging content delivery business models.

Harris Corp., Broadcast Division, Box 4290, 3200 Wismann Ln., Quincy, IL, 62305-4290. Phone: (217) 222-8200. Fax: (217) 221-7085. Web Site:www.harris.com Bob Weirather, dir TV product line; Jack O'Dear, dir international sls; Gaylen C. Evans, dir N.American field sls.

South Glens FallsNY , Box 1179, 10373 Saratoga Rd. Phone:

Federal WayWA , 33430 13th Pl. S, Suite 205A. Phone:

Digital radio & TV transmission equipment, svc, tower studies, training, turnkey RF systems.

Harris-Farinon, 350 Twin Dolphin Dr., Redwood Shores, CA, 94065. Phone: (650) 594-3000. Fax: (650) 594-3110. Web Site:www.harris.com

Microwave for intercity relay & STLs.

Harrison Consoles, (Formerly Harrison by GLW). 1024 Firestone Pkwy., LaVergne, TN, 37086. Phone: (615) 641-7200. Fax: (615) 641-7224.E-mail: info@harrisonconsoles.com Web Site:www.harrisonconsoles.com Charley White, sls; Gary Thielman, mgng dir; Ben Loftis, mktg dir.

Analog & digital audio mixing consoles for on-air bcst, production, video, film sound postproduction, live sound & music recording.

HAVE Inc., 350 Power Ave., Hudson, NY, 12534-2448. Phone: (518) 828-2000. Phone: (800) 999-4283. Fax: (518) 828-2008.E-mail: have@haveinc.com Web Site:www.haveinc.com Nancy Gordon, pres; Paul Swedenburg, VP.

Canare, Belden, Gepco, Flexygy, Mogami Cable; Network connectors & adaptors. Professional blank media, equipment & accessories. DVD, CD duplication & postproduction svcs.

Henry Engineering, 503 Key Vista Dr., Sierra Madre, CA, 91024. Phone: (626) 355-3656. Fax: (626) 355-0077. Web Site:www.henryeng.com E-mail: info@henryeng.com Hank Landsberg, pres.

The Matchbox, digital & analog interface, distribution, mixing, control & power conditioning products.

Hessler Enterprises Inc., 106 Susan Dr., #1, Elkins Park, PA, 19027. Phone: (215) 379-2300. Fax: (215) 663-8839. Web Site:www.hessler.com Ed Hessler, pres; Brian Hessler, VP.

Produces bcstg forms including script sets, contracts, program logs, invoices, labels, A/R statements & computer stock paper.

Hewlett Packard Co., 3000 Hanover St., Palo Alto, CA, 94304. Phone: (650) 857-1501. Fax: (650) 857-5518. Web Site:www.hewlettpackard.com

High Tech Industries, 27636 Ynez Rd., L7-209, Temecula, CA, 92591. Phone: (888) 747-9817. Fax: (951) 279-5773. Web Site:www.customstudio.com Douglas J. Kanczuzewski, gen mgr .

Bcst TV & radio equipment consoles, rack, cabinetry both standard & custom for edit suites, control rooms & machine rooms.

Highway Information Systems, Inc., 4021 Stirrup Creek Dr., Suite 100, Durham, NC, 27703. Phone: (919) 361-2479. Phone: (800) 849-4447. Fax: (800) 849-2947.E-mail: sales@highwayinfo.com Web Site:www.highwayinfo.com Bruce Reimer, gen mgr; Mike Corbett, opns dir; Mark Holland, VP sls & mktg.

Manufacturer of travelers info stns & hwy advisory bcst systems on low-power AM radio for motorists.

Hignite Tower Service, 9945 Arkansas St., Bellflower, CA, 90706. Phone: (562) 925-1951. Fax: (562) 925-6171.E-mail: jhignite@ca.rr.com John Hignite, owner; Jackie Hignite, office mgr.

Tower erection, maintenance & painting.

Hipotronics Inc., Box 414, 1650 Rt. 22, Brewster, NY, 10509. Phone: (845) 279-8091. Fax: (845) 279-2467.E-mail: sales@hipotronics.com Web Site:www.hipotronics.com

High-voltage DC power supplies & industrial grade voltage regulators for medium-to-high-power applications.

Hitachi Kokusai Electric America, Ltd., 150 Crossway Park Dr., Woodbury, NY, 11797. Phone: (516) 921-7200. Fax: (516) 496-3718.E-mail: info@hitachikokusai.us Web Site:www.hitachikokusai.us Masahiko Momose, pres; Bob Johnston, VP; Sean Moran, natl sls mgr.

TorranceCA , 371 Van Ness Way. Phone:

Bcst, professional & industrial TV cameras, MPEG Codecs, microware links & RF telecommunication equipment.

HME, Pro Audio Division, 14110 Stowe Dr., Poway, CA, 92064-7147. Phone: (858) 535-6060. Fax: (858) 391-2814.E-mail: jkowalski@hme.com Web Site:www.hme.com John Kowalski, Pro Audio sls dir.

Wireless Intercoms

Hoagland Instrument, Inc., 120 Eastern Ave., Chelsea, MA, 02150. Phone: (617) 887-9492. Fax: (617) 887-9493. Web Site:www.hoagland-instrument.com Jacob Burke, pres.

Thermal & electronic time delay relays.

Hogg & Davis Inc., Box 405, 3800 Eagle Loop, Odell, OR, 97044. Phone: (541) 354-1001. Fax: (541) 354-1080.E-mail: info@hoggdavis.com Web Site:www.hoggdavis.com F. Neil Hogg, pres.

Cable reels, cable reel trailers, pole tongs, cable sheaves, break-away reels, 36" & 52" tensioners underground puller, 4 drum puller.

Hollywood Rentals Production Services, 19731 Nordhoff St., North Ridge, CA, 91324. Phone: (818) 407-7800. Fax: (818) 407-7875. Web Site:www.hollywoodrentals.com Kelly Koskella, pres.

CharlotteNC , 9100-C Perimeter Woods Dr. Phone:

Production equipment & vehicles for film & video (rental); sale of new equipment & expendable items.

Hollywood Vaults Inc., 742 N. Seward St., Hollywood, CA, 90038. Phone: (323) 461-6464. Phone: (800) 569-5336. Fax: (323) 461-6479.E-mail: vault@hollywoodvaults.com Web Site:www.hollywoodvaults.com David Wexler, pres; Julianna Wexler, VP.

Santa BarbaraCA . (Corporate Office), 1780 Prospect Ave. Phone:

State-of-the-art film & tape storage vault. Secure, climate-controlled, 24-hours self svc access.

Homalite, 11 Brookside Dr., Wilmington, DE, 19804. Phone: (302) 652-3686. Fax: (302) 652-4578. Web Site:www.homalite.com Robert Cahill, pres.

Manufactures low-reflectance, contrast enhancement filters for use on CRTs, LEDs & other forms of info display.

Honeywell Lighting & Electronics, (formerly Honeywell Airport Systems). 550 State Rt. 55, Urbana, OH, 43078. Phone: (877) 285-4466. Phone: (937) 484-2056. Fax: (602) 822-8015.E-mail: oblighting@honeywell.com Web Site:www.oblighting.com Steve Sortillion, site leader.

Tower, obstruction lighting & controls.

Hoodman Corp., 20445 Gramercy Pl., Suite 201, Torrance, CA, 90501. Phone: (310) 222-8608. Phone: (800) 818-3946 (US). Fax: (310) 222-8623.E-mail: lou@hoodmanusa.com Web Site:www.hoodmanusa.com Mike Schmidt, pres; Louis Schmidt, VP mktg; Bob Schmidt, VP sls.

WristShot camcorder support systems, moniter hoods, RAW CF & SD memory cards.

Horita, Box 3993, Mission Viejo, CA, 92690. Phone: (949) 489-0240. Fax: (949) 489-0242.E-mail: horita@horita.com Web Site:www.horita.com Gerald Hester, pres; Christopher Lovallo, sls.

SMPTE time code readers, generators, inserters, PC tape logging software; color bar, black, sync generators; titler, distribution amplifiers, audio meter & matte generator.

Hotbox Digital, 367 N. Hwy. 101, Solana Beach, CA, 92075. Phone: (858) 292-8520. Fax: (858) 292-1812. Cam MacMillan, owner/exec produceer.

Design & production of bcst 3-D computer graphics. Logo animation, stn packages. All tape formats supported. Producers of Subito Studio Video Graphic Library.

Hotronic Inc., 1875 S. Winchester Blvd., Campbell, CA, 95008. Phone: (408) 378-3883. Fax: (408) 378-3888.E-mail: sales@hotronics.com Web Site:www.hotronics.com Andy Ho, pres; Linda Chang, sls & mktg mgr.

HD/SD/Analog Audio/Video delay from 1 video frame to 5 hrs. Test Signal Generator. HD/SD 8x2 or 4X1 Asynchronized Router with live quad, A/V Multiplexer/Demultiplexer, audio or video converter, Uncompressed digital video recorder/player TBC/Frame Synchronizer etc.

I

ICM (International Crystal Mfg.Co.), 10 N. Lee Ave., Box 1768, Oklahoma City, OK, 73101. Phone: (405) 236-3741. Fax: (405) 235-1904.E-mail: sales@icmfg.com Web Site:www.icmfg.com Royden Freeland, pres/CEO.

Precision electronic crystals, crystal filters, clock oscillators, TCXO's, VCXO's.

ICX Global, 8206 E. Park Meadows Dr., Lone Tree, CO, 80134. Phone: (720) 873-8400. Phone: (800) 777-2259. Web Site:www.icxglobal.com Johhny Iverson, gen mgr; Matt Morgan, VP & business dev; Jerry Greenwald, chief tech off.

AmherstNY , 3960 Harlem Rd. Phone:

ICX Global designs, manufactures & markets a wide range of remote control products for bcst, satellite, cable, & consumer electronics devices.

IMS/AMCO Engineering Products, (Formerly AMCO Engineering Co.). 1 Innovation Dr., Des Plaines, IL, 60016. Phone: (847) 671-6670. Fax: (847) 391-8354.E-mail: sales@imsmfg.com www.amcoengineering.com Kevin Groom, natl sls dir; James Walenda, mktg mgr.

Data/Communications, monitoring & EMI cabinets, single or multiple bay. Inline or curved configurations, standard or custom.

IMS (Interactive Market Systems Inc.), 770 Broadway, 15th Fl., New York, NY, 10003. Phone: (646) 654-5900. Fax: (646) 654-5901.E-mail: sales@imsusa.com Web Site:www.imsms.com Lisa Finn, VP sls; Sherry Orr, dir media/agency sls.

IMS is the leading international provider of info systems & solutions for the media industry. IMS systems & software form an integral part of media & mktg decisions around the world. Media professionals trust IMS for innovative technologies, an unparalled global perspective & valuable insights.

IPITEK, 2330 Faraday Ave., Carlsbad, CA, 92008. Phone: (760) 438-1010. Fax: (760) 438-2462.E-mail: sales@ipetk.com Web Site:www.ipitek.com Michael M. Salour, chmn/CEO; Horace Tsiang, VP sls.

IRIS Technologies Inc., 104 Industrial Park Rd., Greensburg, PA, 15601. Phone: (724) 832-9855. Fax: (724) 832-8999.E-mail: sales@iristech.com Web Site:www.iristech.com Jerry Salandro, pres/CEO.

BountifulVT , 563 W 500 South. Phone:

Video Commander icon based routing, iNED & SmartPort product lines which allow complete headend control from anywhere in the world.

ITI Electronics Inc., 32 Stonewall Dr., Livingston, NJ, 07039-1822. Phone: (973) 890-7888. Fax: (973) 992-0459.E-mail: itielect@aol.com Robert A Stein, pres.

Connectorized & Prewired jackfields; patch panels; telephone line amplifiers; other series 400 & 10 line cards.

ITT Cannon Electric, 666 E. Dyer Rd., Santa Ana, CA, 92705. Phone: (714) 628-8722. Fax: (714) 628-2249. Web Site:www.ittcannon.com Keith Teichmann, sls dir.

Electronic connectors & interconnect systems & info card technology suppliers to a var of industries, including bcst & data communications companies.

Identix, 5600 Rowland Road, Minnetonka, MN, 55343. Phone: (952) 932-0888. Fax: (952) 932-7181. Web Site:www.identix.com Bob MacCashin, CEO.

Identix is a leading biometrics solutions provider with proven & cost-effective verification security for applications including banking, healthcare, government, & access control.

Ikegami Electronics (U.S.A.) Inc., 37 Brook Ave., Maywood, NJ, 07607. Phone: (201) 368-9171. Fax: (201) 569-1626. Web Site:www.ikegami.com E-mail: sales@ikegami.com Alan Keil, engrg VP; Teri Zastrow, mktg dir & sls dir.

Ft. LauderdaleFL , 5200 N.W. 33rd Ave, Suite 111.

Manhattan BeachCA , 2631 Manhattan Beach Blvd. Phone:

ElmhurstIL , 747 Church Rd, Unit C1.

WaxahachieTX , 773 Bearden.

Bcst/professional video cameras, monitors, microwave equipment.

Illumination Dynamics Inc., (A division of Arri, Inc.). 13571 Vaughn St., Bldg. D, San Fernando, CA, 91340. Phone: (818) 686-6400. Fax: (818) 686-6776. Web Site:www.illuminationdynamics.com Steve Hipsley, VP; Carly Barber, pres/CEO; Jeff Pentek, COO, VP; Craig Chiapuzio, VP opns.

CharlotteNC , 3823 Barringer Dr. Phone:

Complete line of lighting, grip, generators & power distribution for Feature Film, TV, commercials, bcst & special events.

The Image Group Post, LLC., (Formerly MTI/The Image Group, Inc.) 885 2nd Ave., New York, NY, 10017. Phone: (212) 548-7700. Fax: (212) 355-0523. Web Site:www.image-group.com Charles Pontillo, chmn; Willie Sheehy, pres.

New YorkNY , 305 E. 46th St. Phone:

Production & postproduction svcs, including remotes, computer animation, scenic svcs, satellite transmissions & networking.

Image Logic Corp., 6807 Brennon Ln., Chevy Chase, MD, 20815. Phone: (301) 907-8891. Fax: (301) 652-6584.E-mail: info@imagelogic.com Web Site:www.imagelogic.com Woodrow Landay, pres.

AutoCaption desktop closed captioning & subtitling system for analog, DTV, HDTV, DVD & Web applications. Also Log Producer for video logging.

Image Video, (A division of 1077541 Ontario Ltd). 1620 Midland Ave., Toronto, ON, M1P 3C2. Canada. Phone: (416) 750-8872. Fax: (416) 750-8015.E-mail: sales@imagevideo.com Web Site:www.imagevideo.com Andy A. Vanags, pres; Dave Russell, VP.

Under monitor tally display systems, tally mappers, multi-video display systems & alarm systems.

Imagine Products Inc., 1052 Summit Dr., Carmel, IN, 46032. Phone: (317) 843-0706. Fax: (317) 843-0807.E-mail: sales@imagineproducts.com Web Site:www.imagineproducts.com Dan Montgomery, pres/CEO; M. Jane Montgomery, VP.

Mac & Win software/hardware for logging, video libraries & web sharing. Offloading & proxy creation software.

Imaging Automation, 269 Concord Rd., 3rd Fl., Billerica, MA, 01821. Phone: (978) 932-2200. Fax: (978) 932-2225.E-mail: info@viisage.com Web Site:www.imagingauto.com Bernard C. Bailey, pres/CEO; Bradley T. Miller, CFO & sr. VP.

Supplier of optical-based systems for storing & retrieving documents & images.

Industrial Acoustics Co., Inc., 1160 Commerce Ave., Bronx, NY, 10462. Phone: (718) 931-8000. Fax: (718) 863-1138.E-mail: info@industrialacoustics.com Web Site:www.industrialacoustics.com Kenneth DeLasho, VP.

Staines, Middlesex, Walton House, Central Trading Estate. Simon White, dir mktg.

Wanchai, Hopewell Centre, 183 Queen's Rd. E, Rm. 2501, 25/F. Phone:

Complete accu-tone II acoustical environments for bcst industry plus noise-lock sound control doors, windows, walls & silencers.

Industrial Equipment Representatives (IER), 1685 Precision Park Ln., Suite E, San Diego, CA, 92173. Phone: (619) 428-2261. Fax: (619) 428-3483.E-mail: ierbroadcast@sbcglobal.net Web Site:www.ier-broadcast.com Alex Rodriguez, gen sls mgr; Juan Biosca, gen mgr .

Bcst, TV & recording studios equipment & supplies.

Innovision Optics Inc., 1719 21st St., Santa Monica, CA, 90404. Phone: (310) 453-4866. Fax: (310) 453-4677.E-mail: innovision@innovision-optics.com Web Site:www.innovisionoptics.com Mark Centkowski, sls.

Remote-controlled Camera Tracking Systems, Specialized HD Lens, HD Cine SpeedCam. Remote controlled camera systems.

Inovonics Inc., 1305 Fair Ave., Santa Cruz, CA, 95060. Phone: (831) 458-0552. Fax: (831) 458-0554.E-mail: info@inovon.com Web Site:www.inovon.com James B. Wood; Ben Barber, opns mgr.

Manufacturers of bcst audio signal processing, encoding/decoding, sound recording & instrumentation equipment.

Inscriber Technology Corporation, 26 Peppler St., Waterloo, ON, N2J 3C4. Canada. Phone: (519) 570-9111. Fax: (519) 570-9140.E-mail: info@inscriber.com Web Site:www.inscriber.com Dan Mance, pres; Mike Bernhardt, sls dir; Randy Fowlie, COO.

1431 EE Aalsmeer. Inscriber Technology-European Rep Office, Zijdsraat 72. Phone:

Chiyoda-ky, Tokyo. Inscriber Technology-Asian Rep Office, Level 9, AIG Bldg, 1-1-3 Marunouchi. Phone:

Software for desktop & bcst video markets, including Character generators, digital stores & Video Server/Sequencers

Insulated Wire Inc. Microwave Products Division, 20 E. Franklin St., Danbury, CT, 06810. Phone: (203) 791-1999. Fax: (203) 748-5217. Saverio T. Bruno, pres.

High-frequency, low-loss microwave cable & cable assemblies featuring IW's Tuf-Flex Series to 60 GHz.

Integrys Holdings L.L.C., 770 Pelham Rd., Suite 220, Greenville, SC, 29615. Phone: (864) 297-9290. Fax: (864) 297-9213. Web Site:www.integrysllc.com William C. Cox, pres/CEO.

Subscriber mgmt & billing system.

Intelligent Media Technology, 4407 Vineland Rd., Suite D-18, Orlando, FL, 32811. Phone: (407) 428-1071. Fax: (407) 428-1075.E-mail: salesl@intelligentmedia.us Web Site:www.intelligentmedia.us Bob Proctor, engrg dir.

Digital audio snakes, A/D conversion & transmission, D/A conversion receiver/repeaters, multimedia fiber optic transmission systems (audio/video/voice/data).

Intelliprompt, Box 1527, Culver City, CA, 90232. Phone: (310) 837-0389. Fax: (310) 837-0806.E-mail: tony@intellipromptla.com Web Site:www.intelliprompttla.com Tony Finetti, W. coast opns.

New YorkNY , 630 9th Ave., Suite. 907, (corner of44th & 45th) . Phone:prompt@intelliprompt.com Trish Devine.

TorontoON Canada, 44 Tecumseth St. Phone:prompt @intelliprompt.com Trish Devine.

Computerized teleprompting svcs.

Interface Media Group, 1233 20th St. N.W., Washington, DC, 20036. Phone: (202) 861-0500. Fax: (202) 296-4492.E-mail: info@interfacevideo.com Web Site:www.interfacevideo.com Tom Angell, pres; Adam Hurst, VP.

FACILITY: film transfer/location/studio/motion control, Avid/interformat digital edit, audio, graphics, dubs, Vyvx/3D2/DGS/satellite, standards conversion.

Interlogix, 280 Huyler St., South Hackensack, NJ, 07606. Phone: (201) 489-9595. Fax: (201) 489-0111.

Closed circuit TV cameras, monitors & accessories, specializing in covert surveillance cameras.

International Cinema Equipment, (A division of Magna-Tech Electronic Co.). 1998 N.E. 150th St., North Miami, FL, 33181. Phone: (305) 573-7339. Fax: (305) 573-8101.E-mail: iceco@aol.com Web Site:www.iceco.com Steve Krams, pres; Dara Reusch, VP.

Offered 16mm, 35mm, 70mm film projection equipment, film-to-tape transfer equipment, sound systems & editing equipment.

International Datacasting Corp., 50 Frank Nighbor Pl., Kanata, ON, K2V 1B9. Canada. Phone: (613) 596-4120. Fax: (613) 596-4863. Fax: (613) 596-9208.E-mail: corporate@datacast.com Web Site:www.datacast.com Ron W. Clifton, pres/CEO; Denzil Doyle, chmn.

Rsch, dev, manufacture & mktg of value added high speed digital data transmission net & svcs.

International Electro-Magnetics (IEM), 350 N. Eric Dr., Palatine, IL, 60067. Phone: (847) 358-4622. Fax: (847) 358-4623.E-mail: mail@iemmag.com Web Site:www.iemmag.com Anthony Pretto, pres.

Standard replacement & custom recording heads for audio, video & film.

Intersil Corp., (formerly Intersil Corp. Headquarters). 1001 Murphy Ranch Rd., Milpitas, CA, 95035. Phone: (408) 432-8888. Fax: (408) 432-0640. Web Site:www.intersil.com Dave Bell, pres/CEO; Dave Zinsner, CFO.

Tsimshatsui, KowlonNO Hongkong, The Gateway, 9 Canton Rd., Suite 1506, 15F Tower 6. Phone:

YokohamaNO Japan, Queen Tower A, 12F 2-3-1, Minato-Mirai, Nishi-ku. Phone:

Palm BayFL , 2401 Palm Bay Rd. Phone:investor@intersil.com Web Site: www.intersil.com.

ICs for wireless networking, high performance analog-flat panel displays, optical storage (CD,DVD recordaable) & power mgmt.

Isaia & Co., PO Box 668, Hermosa Beach, CA, 90254. Phone: (310) 466-9858. Fax: (310) 798-2146.E-mail: matt@isaia.com Web Site:www.isaia.com Matt Isaia, pres.

Angenieux Film & Digital Lenses, Runford Baker tripods & heads, Badger camera support, Tango & blue mod accessories.

J

J and R Moviola Inc., 1135 N. Mansfield Ave., Los Angeles, CA, 90038. Phone: (323) 467-3107. Fax: (213) 466-2201. Web Site:www.moviola.com Joe Paskal, pres; Randy Paskal, exec VP.

DenverCO , 8000 E. 40th Ave. Phone:

ChicagoIL , 416 W. Ontario. Phone:

New YorkNY , 636 11th Ave. Phone:

Film editing equipment, film & video shipping & storage, film-to-video transfer machine.

JBL Professional, Box 2200, 8500 Balboa Blvd., Northridge, CA, 91329. Phone: (818) 894-8850. Fax: (818) 830-1220. Web Site:www.jblpro.com E-mail: info@jblpro.com Mark Gander, VP.

Manufacturers of loudspeaker systems for bcstg, recording studios, theaters, concerts, stadiums & other applications.

JC Sound Stages, 6670 Lexington Ave., Hollywood, CA, 90038. Phone: (323) 467-7870. Fax: (323) 467-7832. Web Site:www.jcband.com/jcsoundstages.html J.C. Belanger, owner.

Cable-controlled camera booms equipped for film or video, rehearsal pre-production recording all in classiest vibe avail anywhere.

The J-Lab Co., Box 6530, Malibu, CA, 90264. Phone: (310) 457-4090. Fax: (310) 457-4494.E-mail: sales@j-lab.com Web Site:www.j-lab.com Jerry LaBarbera, pres.

Component accessories, battery-operated video, audio DAs, LCD monitors & portable switchers.

JNJ Industries Inc., 290 Beaver St., Suite 303, Franklin, MA, 02038. Phone: (508) 553-0529. Fax: (508) 553-9973.E-mail: sales@jnj-industries.com Web Site:www.jnj-industries.com Jack Volpe, pres; Gail Howe, VP; Bob Enterkin, dir mktg.

CFC & HCFC free solvents, presaturated cloth wipes, spray bottles, dry cloth wipes, lens wipes; aqueous chemistries ; industrial & precision cleaning products.

JOA Cartridge Service, 448 E. Hancock St., Lansdale, PA, 19446. Phone: (215) 362-8796. Fax: (215) 368-2336.E-mail: mark@joaonline.com Web Site:www.joaonline.com Mark P. Molyneaux, owner.

Bcst audiotape cartridges, audio, videotape, cassettes, tape accessories, DAT tape, cassettes, data storage diskettes, cassettes, optical disks, recordable CDs & reloading svc.

JSB Service Co., 204 S. Bayard Ave., Waynesboro, VA, 22980. Phone: (540) 949-5899. Phone: (877) 668-2634. Fax: (540) 949-5863. Web Site:www.jsbservice.com Joseph S. Brumbelow, pres/CEO; Paul Bosak, sls mktg mgr.

Repair, resale of microwave communication devices, receivers, transmitters, solid state sources, amplifiers. Manufacturer of microwave components & modules, miniature dielectric resonant oscillators & VCO.

JVC Professional Products Company, 1700 Valley Rd., Wayne, NJ, 07470. Phone: (973) 317-5000. Fax: (973) 317-5030. Web Site:www.jvc.com/pro E-mail: proinfo@jvc.com Kirk Hirota, pres; Bob Mueller, CEO, exec VP.

CypressCA , 5665 Corporate Ave. Phone:

AuroraIL , 705 Enterprise St. Phone:

WayneNJ , 1700 Valley Rd. Phone:

Plasmas; full line of professional video equipment including digital VTRs cameras, monitors & projectors.

Jampro Antennas Inc., (Change from Jampro Antennas/RF Systems Inc.). 6340 Sky Creek Dr., Sacramento, CA, 95828. Phone: (916) 383-1177. Fax: (916) 383-1182.E-mail: jampro@jampro.com Web Site:www.jampro.com Alex Perchevitch, pres; Doug McCabe, COO; Cyndi Sanderson, VP.

Manufacturers of TV & FM bcst antennas, combiners, filters & a complete line of rigid coaxial transmission line.

Jennings Technology Co., 970 McLaughlin Ave., San Jose, CA, 95122. Phone: (408) 282-0363. Fax: (408) 286-1789.E-mail: sales@jenningstech.com Web Site:www.jenningstech.com J. Horton, controller; Steve Negrini, gen mgr .

High-voltage vacuum & gas capacitors; relays, switches, single- & three-phase contactors & instruments.

Jensen Transformers Inc., 9304 Deering Ave., Chatsworth, CA, 91311-5857. Phone: (818) 374-5857. Fax: (818) 374-5856.E-mail: sales@jensen-transformers.com Web Site:www.jensen-transformers.com Bill Whitlock, pres.

Audio transformers, ISO-MAX audio & video ground isolation boxes

Jewell Instruments LLC, (formerly Triplett Corp.). 850 Perimeter Rd., Manchester, NH, 03103. Phone: (800) 638-3771.E-mail: wjh@triplett.com Web Site:www.triplett.com

Panel instruments & test equipment. Electrical, electronic, telecommunication & railroad testers.

E.F. Johnson Co., (A division of Transcript International). 123 State St. N., Waseca, MN, 56093. Web Site:www.efjohnson.com Michael Jalbert, pres/CEO.

A leading provider of two way radios and communications systems.

K

Kahn Communications Inc., 338 Westbury Ave., Suite 2, Carle Place, NY, 11514. Phone: (516) 338-5350. Fax: (516) 338-1942.E-mail: radio221@aol.com Web Site:www.wrathofkahn.org Leonard R. Kahn, pres.

New YorkNY , 767 3rd Ave. Phone:

To build bcstg & communications equipment.

Kalun Communications Inc., 44 Larkfield Dr., Toronto, ON, M3B 2H1. Canada. Phone: (416) 410-4138. Fax: (416) 410-4138.E-mail: postmaster@kalun.4t.com Web Site:www.kalun.4t.com Paul Wong, engrg dir.

RF test equipment including wideband sweep generators, sweep comparator, switched attenautor, return loss bridge, detector & headend equipment for ATSC

Kangaroo Products Inc., 10845 Wheatlands Ave., Suite C, Santee, CA, 92071-2856. Phone: (619) 562-9696. Fax: (619) 449-7244.E-mail: sales@kangarooproducts.com Web Site:www.kangarooproducts.com Steve Leiserson, pres; Nancy Byrd, VP.

Custom contract carrying cases.

Kathrein Inc., Scala Division, 555 Airport Rd., Medford, OR, 97504. Phone: (541) 779-6500. Fax: (541) 779-3991.E-mail: broadcast@kathrein.com Web Site:www.kathrein-scala.com Manfred Muenzel, pres; Judy Young, sls; Michael Bach, sls engr.

Antennas & filters, low to full power, includes STL/TSL, LPTV, CATV, RPU, translator & FM/TV monitoring. Custom patterns our specialty.

Kay Industries Inc., 604 N. Hill St., South Bend, IN, 46617. Phone: (574) 236-6220. Fax: (574) 289-5932.E-mail: phasemaster@kayind.com Web Site:www.kayind.com Larry Katz, natl sls mgr.

Rotary phase converters for single phase to three phase power.

Keywest Technology, 14563 W. 96th Terr., Lenexa, KS, 66215. Phone: (800) 331-2019. Phone: (913) 492-4666. Fax: (913) 322-1864.E-mail: info@keywesttechnology.com Web Site:www.keywesttechnology.com Wes Dixon, natl sls mgr.

Manufacturer of automated media servers, loc origination ch, LO ch, media player, CATV character generators, logo & ID inserters.

Kidde-Fenwal Inc., 400 Main St., Ashland, MA, 01721. Phone: (508) 881-2000. Fax: (508) 881-7619. Web Site:www.kidde-fenwal.com John Sullivan, pres; Kevin Barron, VP.

High-speed fire protection systems.

Kings-Winchester Electronics Corp., (formerly Kings Electronics Co. Inc.). 3049 SouthCross Blvd., Suite B, Rock Hill, SC, 29730. Phone: (803) 909-5000. Phone: (203) 741-5400. Fax: (803) 909-5092. Web Site:www.kingselectronics.com Virginia King, sls dir; Allen Trustman, mgr.

WallingfordCT , 62 Barnes Industrial Rd. N. Phone:

Video patch panels, patch cords, coaxial connectors, triaxial connectors & twinaxial connectors.

Kintronic Labs Inc., Box 845, Bristol, TN, 37621-0845. Phone: (423) 878-3141. Fax: (423) 878-4224.E-mail: ktl@kintronic.com Web Site:www.kintronic.com Louis A. King, CEO; Gwen King, VP; Tom King, pres.

AM matching & directional antenna phasing systems, AM multiplexers, transmitter combiners, AM dummy loads, isocouplers, passive KF components & transmission lines.

Knox Video, 8677 Grovemont Cir., Gaithersburg, MD, 20877. Phone: (301) 840-5805. Fax: (301) 840-2946. Web Site:www.knoxvideo.com Ted Neiman, pres; Ken Nottingham, mktg dir.

Electronic bulletin bd for video messages. VCR control units. Full matrix routing switches.

Konica Minolta Corp., 725 Darlington Ave., Mahwah, NJ, 07430. Phone: (201) 529-6060. Fax: (201) 529-6070.E-mail: isddisplay@minolta.com Web Site:www.minoltausa.com

CRT & LCD color analyzing instrumentation.

Kuhnel Co. Inc., 155 Harmony Rd., Mickleton, NJ, 08056. Phone: (856) 423-4277. Fax: (856) 423-5105. Mary Kuhnel, pres.

Instal & maintenance of antennas & towers.

L

L-3 Communications Telemetry East, Box 729, Bristol, PA, 19007-0729. Phone: (267) 545-7000. Fax: (267) 545-0100. Web Site:www.l-3com.com Marc Lienard, sr VP; William Wargo, VP business affrs.

Manufacturer of satellite receiving systems, antennas, telemetry receiving systems, ancillary equipment, communications for aerospace & defense.

LARCAN, 228 Ambassador Dr., Mississauga, ON, L5T 2J2. Canada. Phone: (905) 564-9222. Fax: (905) 564-9244. Web Site:www.larcan.com E-mail: sales@larcan.com Jim Adamson, sr VP.

LafayetteCO . LARCAN USA, 1360 Overlook Dr., #2.

LARCAN is a full service Broadxast Solutions company. LARCAN innovates, designs, and manufactures superior Analog and Digital television transmitters for wireless and broadcast markets worldwide. We specialize in Custom Network Planning and RF Synergies for Broadcast and Mobile Video/DVB-H technologies. LARCAN offers 'End to End' engineering solutions in Solid State VHF, UHF, High Power IOT transmitters as well as Low Power transmitters/translators and FM solutions.

LARCAN USA, 1390 Overlook Dr., Lafayette, CO, 80026. Phone: (303) 665-8000. Fax: (303) 673-9900. Web Site:www.larcan.com David Hale, chmn, VP sls; Jim Adamson, pres.

Repair & sls of high power UHF TV transmitters, low power TV transmitters & translators, FM transmitters & translators & AC line surge protectors.

LBA Technology Inc., Box 8026, 3400 Tupper Dr., Greenville, NC, 27835-8026. Phone: (800) 522-4464. Phone: (252) 757-0279. Fax: (252) 752-9155.E-mail: lbatech@lbagroup.com Web Site:www.lbagroup.com Lawrence Behr, CEO; Jerry Brown, pres; Javier Castillo, VP.

Design & manufacture medium wave antenna systems marketed worldwide, including folded unipole antennas, tuning units, transmitter combiners, diplexers, triplexers, RF components & collocation equiptment.

LEA International, 6520 Harney Rd., Tampa, FL, 33610. Phone: (813) 621-1324. Fax: (813) 621-8980. Web Site:www.leaintl.com Travis Coffey, dir; Shawn Thompson, pres.

Hayden LakeID , 10701 Airport Dr. Phone:

Manufacturers of transient voltage surge suppression & power conditioning equipment.

LINK Electronics Inc., 2137 Rust Ave., Cape Girardeau, MO, 63703. Phone: (573) 334-4433. Fax: (573) 334-9255.E-mail: link@linkelectronics.com Web Site:www.linkelectronics.com Bob Henson, pres; Ellen Henson, exec VP; James Timberlake, VP opns; Dave Aufdenberg, customer svc.

IrvineCA . LINK Electronics Inc.-Western Rgnl Sls, 19 Crockett. Phone:stuartbrenner@pacbell.net

LawrencevilleNJ . LINK Electronics Inc.-Northeast & Southeast Rgnl Sls, 2 W. Laurelwood Dr. Phone:raybouchard@aol.com Ray Bouchard, rgnl mgr-N.E. & S.W. rgns.

Manufacturer of Sync Generators, system timing, audio & video DAs, power amps, encoders, decoders, video processing, test equipment & video presence detectors, closed caption encoders, decoders, video switchers, routers for analog, SDI HD, digital distribution & conversion. Closed caption encoders for analog SD HD SDI, Up/Down/Cross Conversion.

LTM Corp. of America, 7755 Haskell Ave., Van Nuys, CA, 91406. Phone: (818) 780-9828. Fax: (818) 780-9848.E-mail: info@ltmlighting.com Web Site:www.ltmlighting.com Richard Espinosa, exec VP.

HMI & quartz lighting fixtures for film & video production; fresnels, open face, fiber optic, soft lights & fluorescents from 18w to 18,000 w. Also complete line of microphone poles, windscreens & muffs.

Laser Diode Inc., Fiber Optic Business Unit Tyco/Electronics. 4 Olsen Ave., Edison, NJ, 08820. Phone: (732) 549-9001. Fax: (732) 906-1559.E-mail: laserdiodes.sales@macomtech.com Web Site:www.laserdiode.com Rollin Ball, dir; Peggy Scarillo, sls; George Minakas, product mgr; Steve Lerner, production mgr.

Manufacture FP, high power pulsed & CW lasers along with high sensitivity detectors, FDDI/SONET modules for short/long haul transmission, test DWDM, military & coml

fiber optic systems. Also offer Hi-Reliability custom packaging svcs.

The Laumic Rental Co., 432 W. 45th St., New York, NY, 10036. Phone: (212) 586-6161. Fax: (212) 245-0974. Stuart Mann, gen mgr .

Sls, rental, svc, training for bcst, industrial equipment; systems designed & installed.

Leader Instruments Corp., 6484 Commerce Dr., Cypress, CA, 90630. Phone: (714) 527-9300. Fax: (714) 527-7490. E-mail: leader@leaderusa.com Web Site:www.leaderusa.com M. Sawa, pres.

CypressCA , 6484 Commerce Dr. Phone:

Electronic test equipment for video, audio, RF, microwave, oscilloscopes & gen use.

Leaming Industries, 55 Lake Havasu Ave S., Suite F204, Lake Havasu City, AZ, 86403. Phone: (949) 743-5233. Fax: (949) 743-5233. E-mail: sales@leaming.com Web Site:www.leaming.com Robert F. Leaming, pres; Keith G. Rauch, sr engr.

BTSC Stereo/SAP encoders, modulators

The Leather Specialty Co., 2690 W. Airport Blvd., Sanford, FL, 32771. Phone: (407) 323-1830. Fax: (407) 330-1317.

Transit/shipping cases, custom manufactured to specifications & tool cases.

Lectrosonics Inc., 581 Laser Rd. NE, Rio Rancho, NM, 87124. Phone: (505) 892-4501. Fax: (505) 892-6243. E-mail: sales@lectrosonics.com Web Site:www.lectrosonics.com Larry E. Fisher, pres; Bruce C. Jones, mktg VP; Gordon Moore, sls VP; Bob Cunnings, engrg VP; Wes Herron, mgng dir.

Wireless microphone & IFB systems for bcst, motion picture & tele-product applications. Automatic sound mixers & audio signal processing equipment.

Leightronix Inc., 2330 Jarco Dr., Holt, MI, 48842. Phone: (800) 243-5589. Fax: (517) 694-1600. E-mail: sales@leightronix.com Web Site:www.leightronix.com Jeff Possanza, .

Video Servers & TV Automation.

Leitch Inc., 4400 Vanowen Street, Burbank, CA, 91505. Phone: (757) 548-2300. Phone: (800) 231-9673. Fax: (757) 548-0019. E-mail: leitch@leitch.com Web Site:www.leitch.com Paula Moore, gen mgr; Tom Jordan, sls VP; Don Thompson, dir mktg.

TorontoON Canada. Leitch Technology Corp., 150 Ferrand Dr, Suite 700. Phone:

Audio & video distribution amplifiers, sync generators, clock systems & timers, synchronizers, test equipment, still storage, scramblers & descramblers. Audio, video, digital & data routing switchers, terminations, serial digital products.

Lemco Tool Corp., 1850 Metzger Ave., Cogan Station, PA, 17728. Phone: (570) 494-0620. Fax: (570) 494-0860. E-mail: toolinfo@lemco-tool.com Web Site:www.lemco-tool.com Mike Miller, pres.

Designers & manufacturers of mechanical tools, equipment & materials for the construction & maintenance of CATV systems.

LEMO USA Inc., Box 2408, Rohnert Park, CA, 94927-2408. Phone: (707) 578-8811. Fax: (707) 578-0869. E-mail: info@lemousa.com Web Site:www.lemo.com Tim Hassett, gen mgr; Tom Jaros, natl sls & mktg mgr; Julie Carlson, mktg mgr.

LEMO designs & manufactures precision custom connection solutions. LEMO developed the 3K.93C series connector which is now the SMPTE standard for natl & international bcst companies.

Leviton NSI Colortran, (A division of NSI Corp.). 20497 S.W. Teton, Tualatin, OR, 97062. Phone: (503) 404-5500. Phone: (800) 576-6060. Fax: (503) 404-5600. E-mail: pauls@leviton.com Harold Leviton, pres; Paul Sherbo, VP sls & mktg.

Lighting fixtures & control devices for theater, TV & architectural applications.

Lightning Eliminators & Consultants Inc., 6687 Arapahoe Rd., Boulder, CO, 80303. Phone: (303) 447-2828. Phone: (800) 521-6101. Fax: (303) 447-8122. E-mail: info@lecglobal.com Web Site:www.lecglobal.com Peter A. Carpenter, exec VP; Avram Saunders, pres/CEO.

Designers & manufacturers of lightning strike prevention, grounding & power conditioning systems.

Lightning Master Corp., 1351 N. Arcturas Ave., Clearwater, FL, 33765. Phone: (727) 447-6800. Fax: (727) 499-0138. E-mail: RBEATIE@lightningmaster.com Web Site:www.lightningmaster.com Bruce A. Kaiser, pres; Richard Beatie, engrg VP.

Structural lightning protection equipment, dissipator technology, transient voltage surge suppression, bonding & grounding products, consulting svcs; site survey, analysis & training.

Lightning Prevention Systems, 154 Cooper Rd., Suite 1201, West Berlin, NJ, 08091-9116. Phone: (856) 767-7806. Phone: (888) 667-8745. Fax: (856) 767-7547. E-mail: info@lpsnet.com Web Site:www.lpsnet.com Ian E. Fawthrop, pres.

Manufactures equipment utilizing point discharge technology to remove the lightning attractive static charge on towers or structures that they're on, preventing lightning strikes.

Lindsay Broadband Inc., 2035 Fisher Dr., R.R. #5, Peterborough, ON, K9J 6X6. Canada. Phone: (705) 742-1350. Fax: (705) 742-7669. E-mail: sales@lindsaybroadbandinc.com Web Site:www.lindsaybroadbandinc.com David Atman, pres; David Hayford, VP opns; Linda Curtin, VP finance; Jonathan Haight, VP sls.

A diverse range of last mile communication products, including Wi-Fi & mesh wireless systems, hard line passives, trunk, distribution amplifiers, free space optic systems, headend & subscriber passives, a range of MDU amplifers with UPS options, mini optical nodes, WDM fiber optic equipment & NRBS/MEF compliant media converters. Markets & sell to the worldwide telecommunications market.

Linear Acoustic Inc., 354 N. Prince St., Lancaster, PA, 17603. Phone: (717) 735-3611. Fax: (717) 735-3612. E-mail: sales@linearacoustic.com Web Site:www.linearacoustic.com Tim Carroll, pres; Christina Carroll, VP sls/mktg.

Lipsner Smith Co., 4700 Chase Ave., Lincolnwood, IL, 60712. Phone: (847) 677-3000. Phone: (800) 323-7520. Fax: (847) 677-1311. Fax: (800) 784-6733. E-mail: sales@lipsner.com Web Site:www.lipsner.com

Motion Picture Film Laboratory Equipment.

Listec Video Corp., 2001 Palm Beach Lakes Blvd., Suite 502-I, West Palm Beach, FL, 33409. Phone: (561) 683-3002. Fax: (561) 683-7336. E-mail: sales@listec.com Web Site:www.listec.com Joanne Camarda, pres; Raymond Blumenthal, VP.

HauppaugeNY , 40-3 Oser Ave. Phone:

Fully professional range of flat-panel, prompters for studio, field & conferencing applications complemented by Windows prompting software. PRO-Motion light & medium duty tripods. Brick House Video compact production switcher. US Representatives for IPV.

Location Sound Corp., 10639 Riverside Dr., North Hollywood, CA, 91602. Phone: (818) 980-9891. Fax: (818) 980-9911. E-mail: information@locationsound.com Web Site:www.locationsound.com Steve Joachim, sls mgr; Robert Noone, rental mgr.

Dealer of professional audio & communications solutions for film, video, bcst, business, institutional & recording applications. Over 30 years experience.

Logica Inc., 655 3rd Ave., Suite 700, New York, NY, 10017. Phone: (212) 682-7411. Fax: (212) 682-0715.

Consulting.

Logitek, 5622 Edgemoor Dr., Houston, TX, 77081. Phone: (713) 664-4470. Phone: (800) 231-5870. Fax: (713) 664-4479. E-mail: inorthamericansales@logitekaudio.com Web Site:www.logitekaudio.com Tag Borland, pres; Frank Grundstein, sls dir.

Digital audio consoles, digital audio routers & audio level indicators (meters).

Lowel-Light Manufacturing Inc., 140 58th St., Brooklyn, NY, 11220. Phone: (718) 921-0600. Fax: (718) 921-0303. E-mail: info@lowel.com Web Site:www.lowel.com Don Youngberg, midwest sls; Dale Marks, sls rep; Toni Pearl, dealer liaison; Eric Drucker, eastern sls mgr.

Lights, controls, mounts & kits for imaging professionals, innovatively designed & built for rugged dependable use, ease of operation and portability.

Luxor, 2245 Delany Rd., Waukegan, IL, 60087. Phone: (847) 244-1800. Phone: (800) 323-4656. Fax: (800) 327-1698. Fax: (847) 244-1818. E-mail: sales@luxorfurn.com Web Site:www.luxorfurn.com Robert T. Raw, gen mgr; Randy Douglas, dir mktg; Bill Gamber, sls mgr.

Computer stands, A/V equipment stands, conference room furniture, TV stands, library, office furniture, ceiling, wall universal & projector mounts.

M

M/A-COM, (A division of AMP Incorporated). 1011 Pawtucket Blvd., Lowell, MA, 01853. Phone: (978) 442-5000. Phone: (800) 366-2266. Fax: (978) 442-5350. Web Site:www.macom.com Rick P. Hess, pres/CEO; Tim Emery, dir.

RF microwave & mm wave components & subsystems.

MATCO Inc., 15000 Stetson Rd., Los Gatos, CA, 95033-9770. Phone: (408) 353-2670. Phone: (800) 348-1843. Fax: (408) 353-8781. E-mail: sales@matco-video.com Web Site:www.matco-video.com David Harbert, pres; Rita Harbert, gen mgr .

Playback automation, coml insertion, & machine control systems for bcst, cable & coml, industrial & medical. MPEG 2 video servers with automation software options.

MAVRIC Media Inc., 117 Church St., Roseville, 95678. Phone: (800) 804-7756. Fax: (888) 453-8870. E-mail: dana@mavricmedia.com Web Site:www.mavricmedia.com Breene Kerr, .

Hosted, web-based asset mgmt & content delivery tools.

MCG Surge Protection, 12 Burt Dr., Deer Park, NY, 11729. Phone: (631) 586-5125. Fax: (631) 586-5120. E-mail: info@mcgsurge.com Web Site:www.mcgsurge.com Christine Jelley, CEO; Diane Lanciotti, CFO; Sue Baron, gen sls mgr.

Surge protectors for AC power lines, telephone/signal & data lines. Protecting industry since 1967.

MCL Inc., 501 S. Woodcreek Dr., Bolingbrook, IL, 60440-4999. Phone: (630) 759-9500. Fax: (630) 759-5018. E-mail: sales@mcl.com Web Site:www.mcl.com David Krautheimer, exec VP; Howard Hausman, pres.

Satellite communication fixed & mobile High Power Amplifiers in C-band, X-Band, Ku-band, DBS, V-Band, Ka-Band & Multi-band.

MODCOMP Inc., 1500 S. Powerline Rd., Suite A, Deerfield Beach, FL, 33442. Phone: (954) 571-4600. Fax: (954) 571-4700. E-mail: info@modcomp.com Web Site:www.modcomp.com Victor Dellovo, pres; Ron Cook, opns VP; Christina Luis, mktg mgr.

Minicomputer systems, hardware & software for ground stn monitoring & control. SCADA applications & website enabling software.

MRPP Inc., 201 W. Chatham St., Suite 202, Cary, NC, 27511. Phone: (919) 468-1000. Fax: (919) 468-1956. Web Site:www.mrppinc.com Sheila Ogle, CEO; Sue Toth, pres.

Procuring, servicing, instal, & sale of bcstg & satellite equipment. Leasing plans available.

M2 America, 470 Riverside St., Portland, ME, 04103. Phone: (508) 485-4880. Fax: (207) 797-2604. E-mail: info@m2america.com Web Site:www.m2america.com

CD, CD-R, DVD-R & optical disk duplicators.

MUSICAM U.S.A., Bldg. 4, 670 N. Beers St., Holmdel, NJ, 07733. Phone: (732) 739-5600. Fax: (732) 739-1818. E-mail: sales@musicamusa.com Web Site:www.musicamusa.com Cindy DeVito, pres.

Digital Audio codecs for remote bcstg with Bandwidth up to 20 khz for ISDN, POTS or IP.

MYAT Inc., 360 Franklin Tpke., Mahwah, NJ, 07430. Phone: (201) 684-0100. Fax: (201) 684-0104. Web Site:www.myat.com E-mail: sales@myat.com Philip Cindrich, pres; Derek Small, dir filter products; Dennis Heymans, sls mgr.

Transmission line systems, filters, combiners, UHF & L-band antenna.

Magna-Tech Electronic Co. Inc., 1998 N.E. 150th St., North Miami, FL, 331481. Phone: (305) 573-7339. Fax: (305) 573-8101. E-mail: magnatech@iceco.com Web Site:www.magna-tech.com Steven Krams, pres; Barnet Kaufman, VP.

Manufactures professional motion picture sound recording, reproducing & projection equipment, film recorders & reproducers; 16 & 35mm recorders, telecine followers, counters, pre amps, dubbers & looping systems.readers.

Magni Systems Inc., 22965 N.W. Evergreen Pkwy., Hillsboro, OR, 97124. Phone: (503) 615-1900. Fax: (503) 615-1999. E-mail: sales@magnisystems.com Web Site:www.magnisystems.com Victor L. Kong, CEO; Chuck Barrows, VP sls.

Video Test Equipment and Scan Converters. Automated video test & monitoring equipment, waveform monitors, vectorscopes, test signal generators, VIT inserter, PC graphics to video encoders & video overlay scan converters.

Magnum Towers Inc., 9370 Elder Creek Rd., Sacramento, CA, 95829. Phone: (916) 381-5053. Fax: (916) 381-2144.E-mail: office@magnumtowers.com Web Site:magnumtowers.com Jeff Styler, project mgr; Lori Morris, office mgr.

Radio, TV & microwave towers.

Marathon Norco Aerospace, Inc., 8301 Imperial Dr, Waco, TX, 76712. Phone: (254) 776-0650. Fax: (254) 776-6558.E-mail: marathon@mptc.com Web Site:www.mnaerospace.com

CASP universal battery support systems & AC/DC power supplies.

Marcom, 540 Hauer Apple Way, Aptos, CA, 95003-9315. Phone: (831) 768-8668. Fax: (831) 768-7810.E-mail: marty@mar-com.com Web Site:www.mar-com.com Martin Jackson, pres.

FM, AM, TV & microwave transmitting equipment; sls engrg, instal & maintenance.

Marietta Design Group, 82 Plantation Point, Suite 200, Fairhope, AL, 36532. Phone: (251) 990-3558. Fax: (360) 838-9046.E-mail: support@mariettadesign.com Web Site:www.mariettadesign.com

AccuPrompt— & QuickPrompt— teleprompting software for MacIntosh.

QuickPrompt 1.7.2—for professional video prompting.

Maritz Inc., 1355 North Highway Dr., Fenton, MO, 63099. Phone: (877) 462-7489. Phone: (636) 827-4000. Fax: (636) 827-8605. Web Site:www.maritz.com Christine Duffy, CEO.

Communications, film/video training, business meetings & mktg.

Marketron Broadcast Solutions, (formerly Wicks Broadcast Solutions L.L.C.). 101 Empty Saddle Tr., Hailey, ID, 83333. Phone: (208) 788-6800. Fax: (208) 788-5786. Web Site:www.marketron.com Pete D'Acosta, CEO; Gary Coats, COO.

Marketron develops, supports the most popular & advanced software systems for radio opns, traf, billing & analysis functions. Also maintains a SAS certified facility.

Marketron Broadcast Solutions, (Wicks Broadcast Solutions). Box 3078, 508 S. 7th St., Opelika, AL, 36803. Phone: (888) 239-8878. Fax: (334) 749-5666.E-mail: sales@datacount.com Web Site:www.marketron.com Bill Price, gen mgr; Pete D'Acosta, CEO.

Marketron International, 700 Airport Blvd., Suite 130, Burlingame, CA, 94010-2001. Phone: (800) 788-9245. Fax: (650) 548-2295.E-mail: lcarpenter@marketron.com Web Site:www.marketron.com Mike Jackson, CEO.

TorontoON Canada, 5075 Yonge St, Suite 404. Phone: BirminghamAL , 3000 Riverchase Galleria, 8th Fl. Phone:tvsales@marketron.com Michael Hunter, gen mgr. HaileyID , 101 Empty Saddle Trail. Phone:

Software applications for radio, TV, networks, syndicators, traf, accounting, mgmt, demand pricing, inventory control, rsch & proposals.

Marshall Electronics, 1910 E. Maple Ave., El Segundo, CA, 90245. Phone: (310) 333-0606. Phone: (800) 800-6608. Fax: (310) 333-0688.E-mail: sales@lcdracks.com Web Site:www.marshall-usa.com Nathan Mordukhay, exec VP; Leonard Marshall, CEO.

Provides the highest quality products to the bcst, video & music recording markets. Products include cable, connectors, Mogami superflex wire, cable, Tajimi connectors & LCD bcst monitors. Marshall also specializes in mfg optics microphones & multimedai devices.

Marti Electronics, 4100 N. 24th St., Quincy, IL, 62305. Phone: (217) 224-9600. Fax: (217) 224-9607.E-mail: sales@martielectronics.com Web Site:www.martielectronics.com Tim Bealor, VP.

Composite, dual mono & digital STL systems, remote pickup systems, telemetry links, studio to transmitter links, FM exciters, transmitters & pots remote pickup systems.

Martinsound Inc., 1151 W. Valley Blvd., Alhambra, CA, 91803-2440. Phone: (626) 281-3555. Fax: (626) 284-3092.E-mail: info@martinsound.com Web Site:www.martinsound.com Joe Martinson, pres; Doug Osborne, dir, sls & mktg.

Complete line of audio control consoles for music recording, bcst, & video postproduction applications. MultiMax surround monitor control system, flying faders console automation, Martech MSS-10 precision microphone preamplifier.

Masterclock, Inc., 2484 W. Clay St., St. Charles, MO, 63301. Phone: (800) 940-2248. Fax:(636) 724-3776.E-mail: sales@masterclock.com Web Site:www.masterclock.com William J. Clark, pres.

Masterclock systems! Accurate gps time! Network time, Power Over Ethernet & Time Code. Industrial grade generators, pci cards, analog & digital clocks. Extensive experience in the bcst industry. Designed & products in the U.S.A.

Matrox Video Products Grp, 1055 St. Regis Blvd., Dorval, PQ, H9P 2T4. Canada. Phone: (514) 822-6364. Fax: (514) 685-2853.E-mail: video.info@matrox.com Web Site:www.matrox.com/video

Emmy award-winning technology & mktg leader in the field of digital video hardware for accelerated H.264 encoding, realtime editing, DVD/Blu-ray authoring & web streaming.

Matthews Studio Equipment Inc. (MSE), 2405 Empire Ave., Burbank, CA, 91504-3399. Phone: (818) 843-6715. Fax: (323) 849-1525.E-mail: info@msegrip.com Web Site:www.msegrip.com Robert Kulesh, VP sls & mktg.

TV camera support dollies, land tripods, studio pedestals, pan/tilt heads & cases.

Maxell Corp. of America, 2208 Rt. 208, Fairlawn, NJ, 07410. Phone: (201) 794-5900. Fax: (201) 796-8790. Web Site:www.maxellpromedia.com

Blank audio & video recording tape for professional bcstrs & duplicators.

Maze Corporation, 3867 Rock Ridge Rd., Birmingham, AL, 35210-3797. Phone: (205) 706-2080. Fax: (205) 956-6328.E-mail: mazecorp@charger.net Web Site:www.mazecorp.com Vira J. Maze, pres.

Remarketers of TV & video equipment.

McCurdy Radio Ltd., 73 Galaxy Blvd., Unit 6, Toronto, ON, M9W 5T4. Canada. Phone: (416) 248-6155. Fax: (416) 248-6755. Web Site:www.mcradio.com E-mail: sales8800@mcradio.com Paul Hudson, pres; Bob Hudson, gen mgr .

BuffaloNY , 1051 Clinton St.

Audio monitors & meters.

Media Computing Inc., Box 4169, Cave Creek, AZ, 85327-4169. Phone: (480) 575-7281.E-mail: info@mediacomputing.com Web Site:www.mediacomputing.com Michael Rich, CEO; Kathryn A. Hulka, treas.

ANGIS-PC-based software automatically updates displays on characters generators & web pages with real-time data like elections, news tickers, closing.

Media Concepts Inc., 200 Spring Garden, Unit B, Philadelphia, PA, 19123. Phone: (215) 923-2545. Fax: (215) 928-0750.E-mail: mediacon@libertynet.org Bob Weissman, pres.

Video duplication, international video standards conversion, CD-Rom duplication, DVD duplication authoring. Macrovision copy-protection.

Mediasoft Inc., 7200 N. Broadway Ext., Oklahoma City, OK, 73116. Phone: (405) 607-2000. Fax: (405) 607-2071.E-mail: info@mediaofusa.com Web Site:www.mediasoftusa.com Bob Alfson, pres.

Microcomputer products & svcs.

Mediastar-SG, (formerly Multi-Image Network). 702 Mangrove Ave., #221, Chico, CA, 95926. Phone: (530) 826-3342. Fax: (530) 898-9588.E-mail: corporate@mediastar-sg.com Web Site:www.mediastar-sg.com Ken Danner, mktg mgr.

Multimedia production systems for cable TV, bcst, PEG & corporate TV. Pre & post-launch consulting, training & sls seminars. Repair & support svcs for all competitors' products. Data recovery svcs.

Mega Hertz, 4100 International Plaza, Suite 150, Fort Worth, TX, 76109. Phone: (800) 883-8839. Fax: (817) 529-0745.E-mail: sales@go2mhz.com Web Site:www.go2mhz.com Doug Sherar, mktg mgr; Steve Grossman, .

Mega Hertz is a Value-Added-Reseller of Unique Multi-Vendor System Solutions that support the deployment of advanced technologies in hybrid Fiber/Coax Braodband Networks. MHz "Engineering & Integration Group" provides pre-sale Engineering Design, Project Management, Installation, Activation & Training, as well as Level 1 product support for MHz advanced video, voice and data end2end solutions.

Megastar Inc., 4709 Compass Bow Ln., Las Vegas, NV, 89130. Phone: (702) 386-2844. Fax: (702) 388-1250. Web Site:www.1megastar.com Nigel Macrae, pres.

Reseller, earth stations & all support equipment, c band transceivers.

MEGGER, 2621 Van Buren Ave., Norristown, PA, 19403. Phone: (610) 676-8500. Fax: (610) 676-8610.E-mail: sales@megger.com Web Site:www.megger.com

Cable fault-locating equipment & other electrical testing instruments.

Memorex Products Inc., 17777 Center Court Dr., Suite 800, Cerritos, CA, 90703. Phone: (562) 653-2800. Fax: (562) 653-2900.E-mail: generaling@memorex.com Web Site:www.memorex.com Scott Stroup, VP.

Memorex is a manufacturer, marketer of consumer media & computer products.

Meridian Design Associates, Architects, 1140 Broadway, New York, NY, 10001. Phone: (212) 431-8643. Fax: (212) 431-8775.E-mail: info@meridiandesign.com Web Site:www.meridiandesign.com

MiamiFL , 907 S.W. 79th Ave. Phone:

Architectural firm specializing in the design of bcst & media facilities.

Merlin Engineering Works Inc., 1888 Embarcadero Rd., Palo Alto, CA, 94303. Phone: (650) 856-0900. Phone: (800) 227-1980. Fax: (650) 858-2302.E-mail: sales@merlineng.com Web Site:www.merlineng.com Debbie Dirickson, dir.

Bcst VTRs, custom VTRs & accessories, VTR automation systems, stereo audio encoders, standards converters.

Metz Engineering, 15684 Old Mormon Bridge Rd., Crescent, IA, 51526-4138. Phone: (712) 545-3222. Fax: (712) 545-9111. Joanne M. Metz, owner; John P. Metz III, dir.

Machine & welding shop plus construction.

Michael Stevens & Partners Ltd., Invicta Works, Elliott Rd., Bromley, Kent, BR2 9NT. United Kingdom. Phone: 44 0 020 8460 7299. Fax: 44 0 020 8460 0499.E-mail: simon@michael-stevens.com Web Site:www.michael-stevens.com Simon Adamson, tech dir.

Kingston SpringsTN , 149 Dillard Ct, Suite E. Phone:

Bcst equipment, audio mktg, processing & monitoring video production.

Micro Communications Inc., Box 4365, 438 Kelley Ave., Grenier Field, Manchester, NH, 03108-4365. Phone: (603) 624-4351. Phone: (800) 545-0608. Fax: (603) 624-4822.E-mail: frank.malanga@mcibroadcast.com Web Site:www.mcibroadcast.com Al Kula, sls engr; Sam Matthews, mktg mgr; Paul Smith, CEO.

Waveguide & coaxial transmission line; complete RF system packages for UHF, VHF, FM & LPTV panel antennas; antennas for UHF, VHF & FM.

Micro Technology Unlimited, 6900 Six Forks Rd., Raleigh, NC, 27615. Phone: (919) 870-0344. Fax: (919) 870-7163.E-mail: info@mtu.com Web Site:www.mtu.com David B. Cox, pres.

Karaoke software products & pro workstations.

Microlog Corp., 20270 Goldenrod Ln., Germantown, MD, 20876. Phone: (301) 540-5500. Fax: (301) 540-5557.E-mail: sales@mlog.com Web Site:www.mlog.com Richard Meccarielli, pres/CEO.

Call and contact Center Solutions, Speech Recognition, IVR, Outbound Marketing Solutions and custom application development.

Micron Audio Products Ltd., 216 Little Falls Rd., Cedar Grove, NJ, 07009. Phone: (973) 857-8150. Fax: (973) 857-3756.E-mail: micronaudio@cs.com Paul Tepper, pres.

TRAM lavalier microphones, sls & svc.

Microspace Communications Corp., 3100 Highwoods Blvd., Suite 120, Raleigh, NC, 27604. Phone: (919) 850-4500. Fax: (919) 850-4518.E-mail: uplink@microspace.com Web Site:www.microspace.com Joseph Amor III, VP/gen mgr; Greg Hurt, dir, sls; Ron Burns III, chief engr.

Providing video, data & audio transmission svcs designed for antennas as small as 30 inches. Operates on domestic satellites for coverage of North America. Also providing fixed C- & Ku-band uplink svcs for video transmissions supporting applications such as news, sports, program origination (live or taped); & business TV. Remote & studio production available. Turnaround svc to & from domestic & international satellites.

Microwave Filter Co. Inc., 6743 Kinne St., East Syracuse, NY, 13057. Phone: (315) 438-4700. Phone: (800) 448-1666. Fax: (315) 463-1467.E-mail: mfcsales@microwavefilter.com Web Site:www.microwavefilter.com Carl Fahrenkrug, pres; Scott Parsell, sls VP.

Filters, traps, combiners & custom networks for TV, radio, CATV, wireless cable, LAN & mobile radio.

Milestek Corp., 1506 I-35W, Denton, TX, 76207-2402. Phone: (940) 484-9400. Phone: (800) 524-7444. Fax: (940) 484-9402. Web Site:www.milestek.com E-mail: salesinfo@milestek.com Brett Powers, pres.

Connectors including both 50 ohm & 75 ohm BNCs, cabling, patching & tools for coaxial cable.

Milestone Technologies Inc., Box 37145, Raleigh, NC, 27627. Phone: (919) 773-1772.E-mail: info@milestonetechnologies.com Web Site:www.milestonetechnologies.com Miles Beam, pres.

Data bcstg file transfer software (SATX). Bcst binary files over one-way data nets (DBS, VSAT, TV, FM, VBI, RDS, MPEG2, etc.). Consulting & system integration svcs.

Miller Camera Support, L.L.C., 218 Little Falls Rd., Cedar Grove, NJ, 07009. Phone: (973) 857-8300. Fax: (973) 857-8188.E-mail: info@millertripods.us Web Site:www.millertripods.com Gus Harilaou, gen sls mgr.

Pan & tilt fluid heads, tripods & camera support systems & accessories for DV, ENG & EFP (OB).

Miranda Technologies Inc., 3499 Douglas B. Floreani, Montreal, PQ, H4S 2C6. Canada. Phone: (514) 333-1772. Phone: (800) 224-7882. Fax: (514) 333-9828. Web Site:www.miranda.com E-mail: ussales@miranda.com Strath Goodship, CEO; Spiro Plagakis, sr VP sls & mktg.

BeijingNO China. Miranda China, Rm. 2402, Sichuan Bldg., E. Tower, 1 Fuchengmenwai St., Xicheng District. Phone:chinasales@miranda.com

Montreuil France. Miranda France, 216, rue de Rosny, 931000 Montreuil. Phone:francesales@miranda.com

Wanchai Hongkong. Miranda Asia, Unit 1706, Tai Tung Bldg., 8 Fleming Rd. Phone:asiasales@miranda.com

Tokyo Japan. Miranda Japan, 3-1-17 Nihombashi Ningyacho, Ishii Bldg. 2F, Cjuo-ku. Phone:

Oxfordshire United Kingdom. Miranda Europe, Hithercroft Rd, Wallingford. Phone:europesales@miranda.com

SpringfieldNJ . Miranda USA, 195 Mountain Ave. Phone:usssales@miranda.com

Digital video interface products for bcstg & postproduction: serializers, digital-to-analog converters, NTSC encoders, computer video interfaces.

Mitsubishi Digital Electronics America Inc., 9351 Jeronimo Rd., Irvine, CA, 92618. Phone: (949) 465-6000. Fax: (949) 465-6046. Web Site:www.mitsubishi-tv.com David Noranjo, dev dir; Frank De Martin, VP mktg.

Portable videotape recorder systems, consumer VCR's & audio visual big screen TV's.

Mobile Video Services Ltd., 1620 Eye St. N.W., Washington, DC, 20006. Phone: (202) 331-8882. Fax: (202) 331-9064.E-mail: Bookfeed@mobilevideo.net Web Site:www.mobilevideo.net Lawrence VanderVeen, pres; Christine Baber, opns mgr.

Complete EFP & ENG svcs, multi-camera remote packages, editing teleco & satellite transmission svcs available. CBS & CNN news feeds available.

Modulation Sciences Inc., 12A World's Fair Dr., Somerset, NJ, 08873. Phone: (732) 320-3090. Fax: (732) 302-0206.E-mail: sales@modsci.com Web Site:www.modsci.com Eric Small, CEO; Judy Mueller, pres.

With 20+ years experience in the bcst industry, we manufacture full line of FM & TV equipment including: composite clipper, STL's distribution amplifiers, SteroMaxx—Spatial image englarger, modulation monitors, SCA & Data SCA equipment, TV stereo reference decoder, SAP & PRO generators, PRO ch receivers, SAP receivers, NTSC precision video demodulators.

Mohawk, 9 Mohawk Dr., Leominster, MA, 01453. Phone: (978) 537-9961. Fax: (978) 537-4358.E-mail: info@mohawk-cable.com Web Site:www.mohawk-cable.com Jenna Desimone, bcst inside sls rep; Joe Barry, dir, Fiber Optic Business Unit; Leslie Hicks, natl bcst sls & mktg specialist.

Mohawk offers an end to end solution for your HDTV cabling needs. We use LEMO stainless connectors & have many var of SMPTE cable. Mohawk is the OEM for fiber & copper camera cable assemblies for all of the major camera manufacturers.

Mole-Richardson Co., 937 N. Sycamore Ave., Hollywood, CA, 90038-2384. Phone: (323) 851-0111. Fax: (323) 851-5593.E-mail: info@mole.com Web Site:www.mole.com Michael C. Parker, pres; Don Phillips, VP sls; Larry Mole Parker, exec VP.

Lighting equipment for the motion picture, TV, video & still photographic industries.

Moseley Associates Inc., 82 Coromar Dr., Goleta, CA, 93117-3024. Phone: (805) 968-9621. Fax: (805) 685-9638.E-mail: info@moseleysb.com Web Site:www.moseleysb.com Jamal Hamdani, pres/CEO; Bruce Tarr, CFO.

AM & FM stereo STLs, TV digital STLs, data transmission systems & telecommunications, digital transmission systems.

Motion Picture Enterprises Inc., Box 276, Tarrytown, NY, 10591-0276. Phone: (212) 245-0969. Fax: (212) 245-0974.E-mail: mpeny@aol.com Web Site:www.mpe.net Neal R. Pilzer, pres.

Shipping cases, cabinets & cans for film & tape; custom made fibre cases, film & video equipment, supplies, sls, rental & repairs.

Motor Capacitors Inc., 6455 Avondale Ave., Chicago, IL, 60631. Phone: (773) 774-6666. Fax: (773) 774-6690.E-mail: info@capacitorindustries.com Web Site:www.capacitorindustries.com Terence Noone, pres.

Motor-run, motor-start, metalized, oil-filtered, high voltage, film, electrolytic & power capacitors, & R.C. networks.

Motorola Broadband Communications Sector, 101 Tournament Dr., Horsham, PA, 19044. Phone: (215) 323-1000. Fax: (215) 323-0242.E-mail: broadband@motorola.com Web Site:www.motorola.com/broadband Daniel M. Moloney, exec VP & pres/CEO.

EnglewoodCO , 6400 S. Fiddler-Green-Cir. Phone:

LewisvilleTX , 1330 Capital Pkwy. Phone:

CATV headend & distribution equipment; sub terminals, addressable systems & interactive products.

Motorola Digital Media Systems, 1303 E. Algonquin Rd., Schaumburg, 60196. Phone: (847) 576-5000. Web Site:www.motorola.com Greg Brown, pres/CEO; Patricia B Morrison, exec VP & chief info off; Karen P. Tandy, sr VP/pub affrs & comm.

Moviola, (Formerly Videotape Distributors Inc.). 545 W. 45th St., New York, NY, 10036. Phone: (212) 581-7111. Phone: (800) 327-3734. Fax: (212) 581-7977. Robert Schoenberg, VP/gen mgr.

Full-svc supplier of videotape, accessories & digital data storage products.

Murphy Studio Furniture, 4153 N. Bonita St., Spring Valley, CA, 91977. Phone: (619) 698-4658. Fax: (619) 698-1268.E-mail: dennismurphy@cox.net Web Site:www.murphystudiofurniture.com Dennis W. Murphy, pres.

Design/construction of studio furniture for radio, TV & production facilities. Five modular lines. Custom designs.

Murray Co., 1807 Park 270 Dr., Suite 460, St. Louis, MO, 63146. Phone: (314) 576-2818. Fax: (314) 434-5780. Web Site:www.murray-company.com John O'Hara, principal.

Kansas CityKS , 7300 College, Suite 210. Phone:

Gen construction, design, program mgmt, space planning, project budgeting & consolidation planning.

Murry Rosenblum Sound Assoc., Inc., Audio Limited U.S.A. 21-36 33rd Rd., Long Island City, NY, 11106. Phone: (718) 728-2654. Fax: (718) 728-2654.E-mail: murryrosenblum2@nyc.rr.com Murry Rosenblum, pres.

Audio limited wireless microphones—two switchable frequencies—small UHF standard or diversity receiver—pocket transmitter or handhold transmitter.

Musco Mobile Lighting Ltd., Box 808, 100 First Ave. W., Oskaloosa, IA, 52577. Phone: (641) 673-0411. Fax: (641) 672-1996. Web Site:www.musco.com Jerome Fynaardt, gen sls mgr; Joe Crookham, pres; Jeff McNulty, dir opns.

Mobile location lighting utilizing 6K HMIs; remote control of pan, tilt & focus.

N

NSI, 9050 Red Branch Rd., Columbia, MD, 21045. Phone: (410) 964-8400. Fax: (410) 964-9661. Web Site:www.nsystems.com E-mail: sales@nsystem.com Stephen Neuberth, pres; Robert Boshka, VP opns.

Microwave antennas & remote controls for ENG applications.

NUCOMM Inc., 101 Bilby Rd., Hackettstown, NJ, 07840. Phone: (908) 852-3700. Fax: (908) 813-0399. Web Site:www.nucomm.com Dr. John Payne, CEO.

Microwave transmitters, receivers including digital video microwave systems & accessories for both portable & fixed line of sight applications. Modulators/demodulators & color bar generators.

NVISION Products, 125 Crown Point Ct., Grass Valley, CA, 95945. Phone: (530) 265-1000. Fax: (530) 265-1021.E-mail: nvsales@nvision1.com Web Site:www.nvision.tv James S. Meyer, pres; Jay Kuca, dir; Doug Buterbaugh, sls dir; Birney Dayton, chief tech off.

Digital audio & data distribution, conversion, routing & transmission equipment for production/postproduction applications for bcstg industry.

NWL Capacitors, Box 10416, Riviera Beach, FL, 33419-0416. Phone: (561) 848-9009. Fax: (561) 848-9011. Web Site:www.nwl.com Robert Seitz, VP; David Seitz, pres.

Manufacturers.

Nady Systems Inc., 6701 Shellmound St., Emeryville, CA, 94608. Phone: (510) 652-2411. Fax: (510) 652-5075.E-mail: ussales@nady.com Web Site:www.nady.com John Nady, pres/CEO; Scott Wunschel, sls dir.

Wireless VMP & AMF products for bcst, film, video, stage, fixed instals. Consumer audio & communication equipment.

Nalpak, 1267 Vernon Way, El Cajon, CA, 92020-1838. Phone: (619) 258-1200. Fax: (619) 258-0925.E-mail: service@nalpak.com Web Site:www.nalpakcom.com Robert S. Kaplan, pres; Debra S. Kaplan, pres.

Packaging & Material Handling Products; teffpak,Torm, Magliner, Leatherman, Gerber, Buck, Surefire, Steamlight.

Narda - An L-3 Communications Co., 435 Moreland Rd., Hauppauge, NY, 11788. Phone: (631) 231-1700. Fax: (631) 231-1711.E-mail: nardaeast@l-3com.com Web Site:nardamicrowave.com Gene Kelly, pres; Michael Sanatore, exec VP.

Portable RF/microwave test instruments, power density meters, coaxial power monitors & meters.

Narda Satellite Networks, an L-3 Communications Company. 435 Moreland Road, Hauppauge, NY, 11788. Phone: (631) 231-1700. Fax: (631) 272-5500.E-mail: sn.mktg@l-3com.com Web Site:www.nardamicrowave.com/satellite Ken Leighton, VP, business dev; John Mega, pres/CEO; Walter Crofut, sls; Craig Menam, gen sls mgr; Julius Asmus, dir bus dev.

Turnkey satellite earth stns & networks, SNG & Fly Away electronics, ground communications equipment & M&C systems. Manufactures & implements a full line of earth stn network monitors & control systems.

Narragansett Imaging, 51 Industrial Dr., North Smithfield, RI, 02896. Phone: (401) 762-3800. Fax: (401) 767-4437.E-mail: info@nimaging.com Web Site:www.nimaging.com Bill Ulmschneider, pres; Keith Cowling, dir sls & mktg.

Camera tubes, CCD camera modules.

National Audio Co. Inc., Box 7100, Springfield, MO, 65801. Phone: (417) 863-1925. Fax: (417) 863-7825.E-mail: nac@nactape.com Web Site:www.nationalaudiocompany.com Steve Stepp, pres.

Audio Pro-blank audio cassettes, Audio cassette custom duplication, printing & packaging, CDR & DVD blank media, CDR/DVD custom duplication, printing & packaging, CDR/DVD duplicating & printing equipment, CDR/DVD packing.

National Steel Erectors Corp., Box 709, 3315 Cherokee Dr., Muskogee, OK, 74402. Phone: (918) 683-6511. Fax: (918) 683-0888.E-mail: sales@nsec.com Web Site:www.nsec.com B.R. Bayless, pres; Neal Bayless, exec VP.

Erection of radio, TV & microwave towers, including turnkey construction, from design to completion.

National Video Services Inc., 18 Commerce Rd., Newtown, CT, 06470. Phone: (203) 270-0677. Fax: (203) 270-9619.E-mail: sales@intermedvideo.com Web Site:www.intermedvideo.com Harry Davies, pres; Bob Strong, sls; Linda Bald, production mgr.

Distribution of video equipment for corporate & industrial use; design & install of TV studios; mfg of video equipment; rsch & engrg.

Nautel Ltd., 10089 Peggy's Cove Rd., Hackett's Cove, NS, B3Z 3J4. Canada. Phone: (902) 823-2900. Fax: (902) 823-3183.E-mail: info@nautel.com Web Site:http://www.nautel.com John Whyte, mktg mgr.

BangorME . Nautel Maine Inc., 201 Target Industrial Cir. Solid state AM/FM bcst transmitters.

Navitar Inc., Buhl Optical Div. 200 Commerce Dr., Rochester, NY, 14623. Phone: (585) 359-4000. Fax: (585) 359-4999.E-mail: info@navitar.com Web Site:www.navitar.com Thomas McCune, COO; Mark Smith, CFO; Jeremy Goldstein, VP sls; Julian Goldstein, VP.

Projection lenses, LCD, slide & overhead projectors.

L.E. Nelson Sales Corp., (Thorn-EMI Studio & Theatre Lamps). 4800 W. University Ave., Las Vegas, NV, 89103. Phone: (702) 367-3656. Fax: (702) 367-7058. L.E. Nelson, pres; H.F. Nelson, VP western rgn; D.R. Imfeld, VP eastern rgn.

Fair LawnNJ , 18-02 River Rd. Phone:

Studio lamps, quartz (tungsten-halogen) from 25 w to 10 kw & projection lamps. Exculsive importer of Thorn Lamps.

Nemal Electronics International Inc., 12240 N.E. 14th Ave., North Miami, FL, 33161. Phone: (305) 899-0900. Fax: (305) 895-8178.E-mail: info@nemal.com Web Site:www.nemal.com Benjamin L. Nemser, pres.

Sao Paulo, Av. Morumbi 7948. Phone:

Manufacturer of electronic cable, connectors, assemblies, & interconnect products for use in bcst applications.

Noise Control Corp., Box 81774, Bakersfield, CA, 93380. Phone: (800) 606-6473.E-mail: ncc@noisecontrol.com Web Site:www.noisecontrol.com Greg Wolf, pres.

Acoustical noise control products.

Neumade Products Corp., 30-40 Pecks Ln., Newtown, CT, 06470. Phone: (203) 270-1100. Fax: (203) 270-7778.E-mail: gjones@neumade.com Web Site:www.neumade.com R.N. Jones, CEO; Gregory Jones, VP.

Film handling & editing equipment; storage facilities for film, slides, videotape, overhead & opaque projectors, motion picture projection systems.

Neutrik U.S.A. Inc., 195 Lehigh Ave., Lakewood, NJ, 08701. Phone: (732) 901-9488. Fax: (732) 901-9608.E-mail: info@neutrikusa.com Web Site:www.neutrikusa.com Pete Milberry, mng dir; Julie Applegate, exec mgr.

Audio connectors, plugs & jacks, patch panels, patch cord assemblies, circular, industrial connectors & accessories, knobs, BNC jacks & plugs, RJ45, 3-5 mm plugs.

New York City Lites, 242 W. 27th St., 6th Floor, New York, NY, 10001. Phone: (212) 366-9800. Fax: (212) 366-5040.E-mail: nycl@nycl.tv Web Site:www.newyorkcitylites.tv Deke Hazirjian, pres.

Lighting design for video & TV.

Newark Electronics, (A Premier Co.). 4801 N. Ravenswood Ave., Chicago, IL, 60640. Phone: (773) 784-5100. Fax: (888) 551-4801. Web Site:www.newark.com Mike Ruprich, CEO; Barry Litwin, sr VP mktg; Paul Buckley, sr VP & prod mgr.

Distributor of bcst cable, assemblies, connectors voice/data networking & electronic component parts. Branches throughout the U.S., Canada, U.K. & Germany.

Newdoll Enterprises LLC, (Formerly Accurate Sound Corp.). 3515-B Edison Way, Menlo Park, CA, 94025. Phone: (650) 365-2843. Fax: (650) 365-3057.E-mail: ron@newdollenterprises.com Web Site:www.newdollenterprises.com Ronald M. Newdoll, pres.

High-speed tape duplicating & recording equipment, digital audio logging recorders, audio & videotape conditioners, audio recorders. CD-R recorders for audio & ROM.

Norlight Telecommunications Inc., 13935 Bishops Dr., Brookfield, WI, 53005. Phone: (262) 792-9700. Fax: (262) 792-7193. Web Site:www.norlight.com Al Cinelli, chmn; John Cinelli, CEO.

SkokieIL , 3617 Oakton St. Phone:

Fiber-optic & microwave transmission of bcst level video.

Norpak Corporation, 10 Hearst Way, Kanata, ON, K2L 2P4. Canada. Phone: (613) 592-4164. Fax: (613) 592-6560.E-mail: sales@nordak.ca Web Site:www.norpak.ca James Carruthers, pres; Michael Dobson, VP opns.

TV Data Broadcast; Interactive TV; Financial, News, Weather Radar Information Broadcast; HDTV Data Encoding; Closed Captioning; V-Chip; NABTS

Norsat International Inc., 110-4020 Viking Way, Richmond, BC, V6V 2L4. Canada. Phone: (604) 821-2800. Phone: (800) 644-4562. Fax: (604) 821-2801. Web Site:www.norsat.com Aimee Chan, pres/CEO; Randy Witten, VP sls.

Beijing. Beijing Broadcasting Institute, 1704-A Union Plaza, 20 Chao Wai Plaza. Phone:

South Carlton, Lincoln, The Old School. Phone:smullery@noisat.com Stan Mullery.

High speed, reliable data transmission products & networks, microware products & worldwide installations of opns STDs, DVB & SAT networks.

Nortel Networks Corporation, 195 The West Mall, Toronto, ON, M9C 5K1. Canada. Phone: (905) 863-7000. Web Site:www.nortelnetworks.com Mike S. Zafirovski, pres/CEO; David Drinkwater, chief legal off; Pavi Binning, CFO; John J. Roese, chief tech off; William J. Donovan, sr VP business transformation office; Steven Bandrowczak, chief info off.

Computer networks; telecommunications equipment; telecommunications systems; telecommunications systems: cellular.

North American Cable Equipment Inc., 1085 Andrew Dr., Suite A, West Chester, PA, 19380. Phone: (800) 688-9282. Fax: (800) 230-1793.E-mail: sales@northamericancable.com Web Site:www.northamericancable.com Aaron Starr, pres; Kirk Davies, gen sls mgr.

Manufacturer of CATV, RF modulators, demodulators & processors.

North Dakota Television L.L.C., (Formerly Sunrise Television). 200 N. Fourth St., Bismarck, ND, 58501. Phone: (701) 255-5757. Fax: (701) 255-8220. Web Site:www.kfyrtv.com Jim Sande, progmg dir.

North Hills Signal Processing, a PORTA Systems Co., 6851 Jericho Tpke., Suite 170, Syosset, NY, 11791. Phone: (516) 682-7740. Fax: (516) 682-7704.E-mail: info@northills-sp.com Web Site:www.northhills-sp.com Richard Schwarz, gen mgr .

Manufactures of MIL-STDT553 data bus products & wideband/video transformer. Our standard & custom product, offer unmatched performance & reliability for a wide range of applications in the military, aerospace & industrial OEM markets.

Northeast Towers Inc., 199 Brickyard Rd., Farmington, CT, 06032. Phone: (860) 677-1999. Fax: (860) 677-1300.E-mail: netowers@ctl.nai.net Stephen Savino Jr., pres.

HDTV, TV, Cellular, PCS, AM, FM, CATV & microwave towers; ground systems; maintenance, materials, turnkey instals, specialty coatings, & strobes.

Northeastern Communications Concepts Inc., 40 Benford Dr., Princeton Junction, NJ, 08550. Phone: (609) 936-0006.E-mail: webmaster@nccnewyork.com Web Site:www.nccnewyork.com Alfred W. D'Alessio, pres.

Bcst design svcs, studio furniture, custom audio equipment, custom data systems/components, cabinets, racks, panels, recording studios construction & prefab.

Northern Power Systems, 182 Mad River Park, Waitsfield, VT, 05673. Phone: (802) 496-2955. Fax: (802) 496-2953.E-mail: info@northernpower.com Web Site:www.nothernpower.com Clint Coleman, pres.

Remote power systems based on renewable energy inputs (wind/solar); hybrid power systems.

Northrup Grumman, 1840 Century Park E., Los Angeles, CA, 90067. Phone: (310) 553-6262. Fax: (310) 553-2076. Ronald Sugar, pres; Darryl Fraser, VP mktg.

Film & video cameras for military; video-to-film recorders; optics & optical systems.

Northwest Monitoring Service, Box 70144, Eugene, OR, 97401. Phone: (541) 345-2236. James C. Bradley, owner.

Mthy frequency measurements for AM-FM-TV. Mobile svc includes California, Oregon, Washington, Idaho & Nevada.

NTV International Corporation, 645 5th Ave., Suite 303, New York, NY, 10022. Phone: (212) 660-6900. Fax: (212) 660-6998. Web Site:www.ntvic.com Jusaburo Hayahii, pres; Leo Lahm, tech mgr.

Fred A. Nudd Corp., Box 577, 1743, Rt. 104, Ontario, NY, 14519. Phone: (315) 524-2531. Fax: (315) 524-4249. Web Site:www.nuddtowers.com Fred Nudd, VP; Tom Nudd, pres.

Design, manufacture, instal, maintenance & analysis of communication towers.

O

O'Connor Professional Camera Support Systems, 100 Kalmus Dr., Costa Mesa, CA, 92626. Phone: (714) 979-3993. Fax: (714) 957-8138.E-mail: sales@ocon.com Web Site:www.ocon.com Joel Johnson, VP/gen mgr; Robert Low, VP sls.

Manufacturer of camera support equipment including fluid heads, tripods & accessories.

Olesen, (A division of Entertainment Resources Inc.). 12800 Foothill Blvd, Sylmar, CA, 91342. Phone: (818) 407-7800. Fax: (818) 407-7868.E-mail: info@hollywoodrentals.com Web Site:www.hollywoodrentals.com Kelly Koskella, pres; Joe Dougherty, VP; Victor Duran, dir.

All production supplies, equipment for TV, theater, both live & taped.

Omnimount Systems, 8201 S. 48th St., Phoenix, AZ, 85044. Phone: (480) 829-8000. Fax: (480) 756-9000.E-mail: info@omnimount.com Web Site:www.omnimount.com Garrett Weyand, vice chmn; Geoff Miller, pres; Raymond Nakano, exec VP & CEO.

Loudspeaker mounts-omnidirectional adjustability supporting ounces to hundreds of pounds. Also, flexible, refined mounting systems for TV's/computer monitors & peripherals.

180 Connect, 6365 N.W. 6th Way, Suite 200, Ft. Lauderdale, FL, 33309. Phone: (800) 683-0253. Fax: (954) 671-8619. Dalia Rodborne, mgr.

Have been providing Turkey residential/commercial inside premise wiring & outside plant construction svcs for 20 yrs.

Opamp Labs Inc., 1033 N. Sycamore Ave., Los Angeles, CA, 90038. Phone: (323) 934-3566. Fax: (323) 462-6490.E-mail: bel@opamplabs.com Web Site:www.opamplabs.com B. Losmandy, chief engr & pres.

Amplifiers: audio, video, microphone, line & power. Audio oscillators & transformers. Power supplies, network audio/video feed boxes, audio/video routing switches.

Optical Disc Corp., 12150 Mora Dr., Sante Fe Springs, CA, 90670. Phone: (562) 946-3050. Fax: (562) 946-6030. Web Site:www.optical-disc.com Richard Wilkinson, pres; Ken Shrimplin, sr VP; John Brown, VP.

Recordable laser video discs, videodisc recording systems & other auxiliary equipment. Compact disc & videodisc mastering systems.

Orban, (A Harman International Co.). 1525 Alvarado St., San Leandro, CA, 94577. Phone: (510) 351-3500. Fax: (510) 351-0500.E-mail: info@orban.com Web Site:www.orban.com Charles Jayson Brentlinger, pres/CEO; Bob Orban, chief engr, VP.

Orban manufacturers bcst audio equipment for radio & TV including processors for TV, FM, AM & HF & the Audicy digital audio workstation, & the Airtime digital audio delivery system.

Ortel, 2015 W. Chestnut St., Alhambra, CA, 91803. Phone: (626) 293-3400. Fax: (626) 293-3428.E-mail: docmaster@agere.com Web Site:www.emcore.com Gyo Shinozaki, dir mktg; Reuben F. Richards, exec chmn; Hong Q. Hou, CEO; John Ianelli, chief tech off.

Signal transmission products, specializing in opto electronics & RF electronics technologies.

Allen Osborne Associates Inc., 756 Lakefield Rd., Westlake Village, CA, 91361. Phone: (805) 495-8420. Fax: (805) 373-6067.E-mail: j_osborne@aoa-gps.com Web Site:www.aoa-gps.com Jim Osborne, VP.

Pneumatic masts systems for remote E.N.G., fixed or mobile radio communications, etc.

Otari USA Sales Inc., 21110 Nordhoff St., Suite G/H, Chatsworth, CA, 91311. Phone: (818) 734-1785. Fax: (818) 734-1786.E-mail: sales@otario.com Web Site:www.otari.com Nick Higashino, pres; Tim Murray, sls mgr.

Manufacturer of audio & video cassette loaders & duplicators. Manufacturer of audio mixing consoles, hard disk audio recorders, tape recorders, DAT recorders, minidisc recorders & players, CD changers, digital audio format converters.

P

PC& E, 2235 Defoor Hills Rd., Atlanta, GA, 30318. Phone: (404) 609-9001. Fax: (404) 609-9926. Web Site:www.pce-atlanta.com Doug Smith, pres; Mark Wofford, business/mktg mgr; Randy Nappier, opns mgr.

Lighting, grip, camera, stage & generator rental. Full svc

sls department with expendables.

PMTV Producers Management Television, 681 Moore Rd., Suite 100, King of Prussia, PA, 19406. Phone: (610) 768-1770. Fax: (610) 768-1773.E-mail: mailto.pmtv@pmtv.com Web Site:www.pmtv.com

Full-svc mobile TV production company, providing mobile units, crews, satellite svcs, lighting, staging, etc. for sports, entertainment & teleconferences worldwide.

Pace Micro Technology P.L.C., 3701 FAU Blvd., Suite 200, Boca Raton, FL, 33431. Phone: (561) 995-6000. Fax: (561) 995-6001.E-mail: info@pace.com Web Site:www.pace.com Mike McTighe, chmn; Neil Gaydon, CEO; David McKinney, COO.

First DVB MPEG-2 set-top boxes, the first to integrate DOCSIS into a digital cable set-top box & launching the first ever H.264 DVB-S2 high definition set-top box.

Packaged Lighting Systems Inc., Box 285, 29 Grant St., Walden, NY, 12586. Phone: (845) 778-3515. Phone: (800) 836-1024 (orders). Fax: (845) 778-1286.E-mail: info@packagedlighting.com Web Site:www.packagedlighting.com Hy Hilzen, pres.

Factory prewired, self-contained TV studio systems complete with lighting/dimming/grid/power distribution.

Panasonic Broadcast & Television Systems Co., One Panasonic Way, Panazip 2E-7, Secaucus, NJ, 07094. Phone: (201) 348-5300. Fax: (201) 348-5318. Web Site:www.panasonic.com/broadcast John Baisley, pres; Don Iwatani, chmn/CEO; Robert Harris, VP mktg.

Los AngelesCA , 3330 Cahuenga Blvd. W. Phone: SecaucusNJ , One Panasonic Way, 4E-7. Phone:

MII VCR, D3 digital VCRs, digital processed cameras, Carts (MARC) analog & digital, tapes, DVC pro, D5, Post Box, RAMJA products, monitors, projectors.

Panavision New York, 540 W. 36th St., New York, NY, 10018. Phone: (212) 606-0700. Fax: (212) 244-4457. Web Site:www.panavisionnewyork.com Peter Schnitzler, pres; Ira Goodman, VP.

16mm & 35mm motion picture & video equipment, lighting & grip equipment, generators, trucks, dollies & cranes.

Panel Authority Inc., 411 New Ave., Lockport, IL, 60441. Phone: (815) 838-0488. Fax: (815) 838-7852.E-mail: preston@panelauthority.com Web Site:www.panelauthority.com Preston Wakeland, pres.

Custom made engraved aluminum connector panels & enclosures.

Paragon Towers Inc., Box 270655, Oklahoma City, OK, 73137. Phone: (405) 948-3335. Fax: (405) 948-3358.E-mail: charlene@paragontowersinc.com Web Site:www.paragontowersinc.com Joe M. James, pres; Melvyn Lieberman, chmn.

Oklahoma CityOK , 3820 N.W. 8th St.

Competitively priced tower mfg, complete line of broadcasting, communications, cellular, microwave, turn-key, bundle package design, full range of tower accessories, guarantee of company's products.

Parsons Audio, 192 Worcester St., Wellesley Hills, MA, 02481. Phone: (781) 431-8708. Fax: (781) 431-8783.E-mail: sales@paudio.com Web Site:www.paudio.com Mark Parsons, owner; Les Arnold, sls; Rick Scott, sls; Lenore Fauliso, sls support; Christopher Stabach, sls support.

Equipment & courses for recording, production, bcst, performance, etc., 200 plus product lines. Yamaha, Dolby, Digidesign, Tascam, etc. Also training courses for professionals, taught by masters.

Parsons Manufacturing Corp., 1055 O'Brien Dr., Menlo Park, CA, 94025. Phone: (650) 324-4726. Fax: (650) 324-3051.E-mail: pmccase@aol.com Web Site:www.pmccases.com Alan R. Parsons, CEO; Alan Hall, controller.

Instrument carrying cases, shipping cases molded plastic, retracting wheels & recessed hardware.

Paulmar Industries Inc., Box 638, Antioch, IL, 60002. Phone: (847) 395-2080. Fax: (847) 589-2070. Web Site:www.paulmar.com E-mail: sales@paulmar.com Robert F. Menary, pres.

Automatic film, video inspection machines, film & video supplies, DVD repair & rejuvenation equipment.

Peavey Electronics, 5022 Hartley Peavey Dr., Meridian, MS, 39305. Phone: (601) 483-5365. Fax: (601) 486-1278.E-mail: marketing@peavey.com Web Site:www.peavey.com Hartley Peavey, CEO.

Recording & audio products, SMPTE/MIDI synchronization

signal processing, reference monitors, microphones & production mixing consoles.

Peerless Industries Inc., 3215 W. North Ave., Melrose Park, IL, 60160. Phone: (708) 865-8870. Fax: (708) 865-0760. Web Site:www.peerlessindustries.com E-mail: info@peerlessindustries.com Mike Campagna, pres; Joe Mitchell, dir info systems.

Video Mounting hardware including stands, carts & brackets for floor, furniture, wall & ceiling applications.

Penn Elcom Inc., 12691 Monarch St., Garden Grove, CA, 92841. Phone: (714) 230-6200. Fax: (714) 230-6222.E-mail: california@penn-elcom.com Web Site:www.penn-elcom.com Frank McCourt, pres; Phil Stratford, dir.

Hardware & accessories for flightcases, racks, speaker cabinets, stagelights & trussing.

Penny & Giles Inc., 5875 Obispo Ave., Long Beach, CA, 90805. Phone: (562) 531- 6500. Fax: (562) 531-4020.E-mail: u.s.sales@pennyandgiles.com Web Site:www.pgcontrols.com Chris Thomson, VP mktg.

Cwmfelinfach, Gwent Phone:

Studio faders; joystick controllers; T-Bar controllers for video effects generators; MIDI mgr & D.A.W. interface.

Penta Laboratories, 9740 Cozycroft Ave., Chatsworth, CA, 91311. Phone: (818) 882-3872. Phone: (800) 421-4219. Fax: (818) 882-3968. Web Site:www.pentalabs.com Steve Sanett, pres; Marianne Griego, sls dir; Veronica Calderon, CFO.

Electron tubes distribution & mfg.

Pentax Imaging Co., 600 12th St., Suite 300, Golden, CO, 80401. Phone: (303) 799-8000. Fax: (303) 728-0226. Web Site:www.pentaxusa.com Ned Bunnel, pres; Bill Zani, VP sls & mktg.

Manufacture camera lens.

Performance Power Technologies, Box 947, Roswell, GA, 30077. Phone: (770) 475-3192.E-mail: poweringcatv@yahoo.com Web Site:www.performance-power.com Jud Williams, pres.

Standby power supplies, AC power supplies & battery testers.

PerkinElmer, 35 Congress St., Salem, MA, 01970. Phone: (978) 745-3200. Fax: (978) 745-0894.E-mail: opto@perkinelmer.com Web Site:www.perkinelmer.com John Pautler, opns mgr.

High-medium-intensity aviation obstruction lighting & beacons. FAA-approved; StrobeGuard & FlashGuard.

Phasetek Inc., 550 California Rd., Unit 11, Quakertown, PA, 18951. Phone: (215) 536-6648. Fax: (215) 536-7180.E-mail: phasetekinc1@earthlink.net Web Site:www.phasetekinc.com Kurt Gorman, pres; David Gorman, VP; Matthew Nelson, plant mgr; Robin Nelson, admin.

Manufactures AM/MW antenna, phasing equipment, antenna tuning units, diplexers, dummy loads, RF inducters & components.

Philip-Cooke Co., 132 N. 11th St., Allentown, PA, 18102. Phone: (800) 887-0950. Phone: (610) 437-2251. Fax: (610) 437-1610.E-mail: kentk@philipcooke.com Web Site:www.philipcooke.com Kent Kjellgren, pres.

Distribute video cassette duplications equipment & CDs.

Phillystran Inc., 151 Commerce Dr., Montgomeryville, PA, 18936. Phone: (215) 368-6611. Fax: (215) 362-7956.E-mail: info@phillystran.com Web Site:www.phillystran.com Wynne Wister III, pres; Kenneth A. Knight, sls.

Phillystran HPTG; electrically transparent, maintenance free tower guy system; specially designed systems for high-power applications.

Phoenix E N G, Inc., 6832 Foxhill Ln., Cincinnati, OH, 45236. Phone: (513) 891-1444. Fax: (513) 891-3453.E-mail: engphoenix@aol.com Jennifer Braun; Kevin Jordan; Bob Braun, VP mktg.

"One man band" live trucks, vans, 4-wheel-drive. On-location radio vehicles & production trucks.

Photo Research, 9731 Topanga Canyon Pl., Chatsworth, CA, 91311. Phone: (818) 341-5151. Fax: (818) 341-7070. Web Site:www.photoresearch.com Francis Dominic, pres; Mike Klein, dir mktg.

Brightness photometers, footcandle meters, telephotometers, spectroradiometers, spectral & spatial scanners.

Photomart Cine-Video Inc., 6327 S. Orange Ave., Orlando, FL, 32809. Phone: (407) 851-2780. Phone: (800) 443-2901. Fax: (407) 851-2553.E-mail: info@photomartusa.com Web Site:www.photomartusa.com Jeffrey Bova, pres.

Sls, svc, of professional support equipment, supplies for video, film & still photography.

Pinnacle Systems Inc., 280 N. Bernardo Ave., Mountain View, CA, 94043. Phone: (650) 526-1600. Fax: (650) 526-1601. Web Site:www.pinnaclesys.com E-mail: sales@pinnaclesys.com Sharad Rastogi, gen mgr ; Avid VP/corporate dev; Tanguy Leborgne, VP worldwide mktg.

Manufacturer of a complete set of home video editing & PCTV viewing tools for the consumer market.

Pinta Acoustic Inc., (formerly Illbruck Inc.). 2601 49th Ave. N., Suite 400, Minneapolis, MN, 55430. Phone: (612) 520-3620. Phone: (800) 662-0032. Fax: (612) 521-5639.E-mail: sales@pinta-acoustic.com Web Site:www.pinta-acoustic.com Mark Frederick, CFO.

Sonex accoustical products including wall panels & ceiling tiles.

Pinzone Engineering Group Inc., 10142 Fairmount Rd., Newbury, OH, 44065. Phone: (304) 368-7950. Fax: (440) 729-5591.E-mail: systemsengineering@pinzone.com Web Site:www.pinzone.com Basil F. Pinzone Jr., pres.

Satellite Uplinks Systems, Turnkey, Site Engineering, AM Broadcast Antenna- Anti-Skywave Antenna.

Pirod Inc., Box 128, 1545 Pidco Dr., Plymouth, IN, 46563. Phone: (574) 936-4221. Fax: (574) 936-6796.E-mail: pirod@pirod.com Web Site:www.pirod.com Myron C. Noble, CEO; Hillary Asher, sls VP.

Solid-rod towers, monopoles & tower accessories for cellular, PCs, bdcst, microwave & two-way communication.

Pixel Instruments Corp., 160-B Albright Way, Los Gatos, CA, 95032. Phone: (408) 871-1975. Fax: (408) 871-1976.E-mail: info@pixelinstruments.tv Web Site:www.pixelinstruments.tv Mirko Vojnovic, pres.

Designs & manufactures innovative audio & video signals processing products with an emphasis on the measurement & correction of lips sync errors. These products are used in a wide range of bcst, cable TV, video production & related applications. Current products include the LipTracker Lip Sync Analyer, Audio Delay Synchronizers for automatic lip sync correction & Tally/GPI Interfaces.

Plastic Reel Corp. of America, 40 Triangle Blvd., Carlstadt, NJ, 07072. Phone: (201) 933-5100. Fax: (201) 933-9468.E-mail: info@prcofamerica.com Benjamin Zuk, pres; Pat Baccarella, exec VP; Carole Pinker, pres.

North HollywoodCA , 8140 Webb Ave. Phone: ChicagoIL , 5410 W. Roosevelt Rd. Phone:

Videotape, audiotape reels, boxes, video cassette mailing, storage boxes, video supplies, recording media, video & audio.

Polyline, (formerly Polyline Corp.). 845 N Church Ct., Elmhurst, IL, 60126. Phone: (800) 701-7689. Fax: (800) 816-3330.E-mail: sales@polylinecorp.com Web Site:www.polylinecorp.com

BurbankCA . Polyline West Coast Distribution Ctr., 4408 W. Vanowen St.

Stock media packaging for DVD, CD, VHS & audio plus bulk CD-R, DVD-R, Blu-ray media. Disc publishing equipment & supplies are also available.

PortaBrace, (formerly K&H Products Ltd (Porta-Brace)). Box 220, North Bennington, VT, 05257. Phone: (802) 442-8171. Fax: (802) 442-9118.E-mail: info@portabrace.com Web Site:www.portabrace.com Gregg Haythorn, pres; Mike D'Angelo, plant mgr.

Soft carrying cases for professional portable video/audio equipment.

Potomac Instruments, Inc., 7309 D Grove Rd, Frederick, MD, 21704-7258. Phone: (301) 696-5550. Fax: (301) 696-5553.E-mail: sales@pi-usa.com Web Site:www.pi-usa.com David G. Harry, COO; Guy E. Berry, mgr special project.

Antenna monitors, field strength meters, audio test equipment.

Power & Telephone Supply Co., 2673 Yale Ave., Memphis, TN, 38112. Phone: (901) 324-6116. Fax: (901) 320-3082. Web Site:www.ptsupply.com Jim Pentecost, pres; Laburn Dye, VP; Larry Smith, VP.

Los AngelesCA , 12314 Bell Ranch Rd. Phone:
MiamiFL , 7535 N.W. 52nd St. Phone:
Des MoinesIA , 3107 S.W. 61st St, Bldg. D. Phone:
LexingtonNC , Box 1856, 2950 Greensboro St. Phone:
TigardOR , 16666 S.W. 72nd, Bldg. 12. Phone:

ReamstownPA , Box 244, Rt. 272. Phone:

MemphisTN , Box 12383, 2673 Yale Ave. Phone:

DallasTX , 1456 S. 2nd Ave. Phone:

NeenahWI , 987 Ehlers Rd. Phone:

Full-line supplier of communication products, including telecom, data & cable TV.

Powr-Ups Corp., One Roned Rd., Shirley, NY, 11967. Phone: (631) 345-5700. Fax: (631) 345-0060. Steven E. Summer, pres.

DC-motor controls.

Precision Microproducts of America, #1 Comac Loop, Unit 13, Ronkonkoma, NY, 11779. Phone: (631) 580-3456. Fax: (631) 580-3003.E-mail: sales@p-m-a.com Web Site:www.p-m-a.com Jerry Wasserman, pres.

Photographic processing machines & accessories.

Prime Image, Inc., 662 Giguere Ct., Suite C, San Jose, CA, 95133-1742. Phone: (408) 867-6519. Fax: (408) 926-7294.E-mail: ssales@primeimageinc.com Web Site:www.primeimageinc.com Bob Waligunda, VP mktg; Rodney Hampton, opns VP.

Provides digital progmg time reduction/editingequipment; audio & video delays; transcoding time base correctors; synchronizers; digital standards converters; computer video products.

Prisma Packaging, N 19 W. 24400 Riverwood Dr., Suite 350, Waukesha, WI, 53188. Phone: (414) 342-6464. Fax: (414) 342-0932.E-mail: info@prismapkg.com Web Site:www.prismapkg.com Richard Schmaelzle, pres.

Printer manufacturer specializing in presentation folders, media kits, sls kits & videocassette packaging.

Pro Video & Film Equipment Co. Inc., 11425 Mathis Ave., Studio 40, Dallas, TX, 75234. Phone: (972) 869-9990. Phone: (888) 869-9998. Fax: (972) 869-0145.E-mail: providfilm @aol.com Web Site:www.providofilm.com Bill Reiter, pres; Stephanie Fox, dir mktg.

Used equipment dealer specializing in video, bcst, film, lighting, audio. Consignment, sales, leasing & appraisal svcs available. Service & repairs.

ProAudio.com/Crouse-Kimzey Co., (formerly Crouse-Kimzey Co.). 1320 Post & Paddock Road, Ste 200, Grand Prairie, TX, 75050. Phone: (800) 433-2105. Fax: (972) 623-2800.E-mail: sales@proaudio.com Web Site:www.proaudio.com John Paul Kimzey, pres.

Rockaway BeachMO . Crouse-Kimzey of Missouri, 381 Molly Ln. Phone:

Colorado SpringsCO . Crouse-Kimzey of Colorado, 4125 Novia Dr. Phone:

LynnIN . Crouse Kimzey/Mid-America, 9170 South U.S. Hwy. 27. Phone:

Broadcast equipment & Pro Audio equipment sls.

Production Intercom Inc., Box 3247, Barrington, IL, 60011-3247. Phone: (800) 562-5872. Fax: (847) 381-4360.E-mail: info@beltpack.com Web Site:www.beltpack.com Glenn mullis, pres; Sibbelina Mullis, sec.

Unique talent receiver (IFB), small to large intercom systems, headsets for cameras & new half-duplex wireless system.

Products International Inc., 9893 Brewers Ct., Laurel, MD, 20723. Phone: (800) 638-2020. Fax: (240) 568-3948. Fax: (800) 545-0058.E-mail: info@prodintl.com

Equipment, instruments, tools, supplies for electronic production, maintenance & svc.

Professional Communications Systems, (A division of Media General Broadcasting, Inc). 5426 Beaumont Center Blvd., Suite 350, Tampa, FL, 33634. Phone: (800) 447-4714. Fax: (813) 886-9477. Web Site:www.pcomsys.com E-mail: info@pcomsys.com Tony A. Stephens, pres & gen mgr.

PensacolaFL , 2001 Augusta Ave. Phone:

DavieFL , 8930 State Road 84, #315. Phone:

MiamiFL , 11921 S.W. 144th St. Phone:

St. AugustineFL , 340 Summer Cover Circle. Phone:

Winter ParkFL , 7051 University Blvd, Suite 310. Phone:

AlbanyGA , 2800 Old Dawson Road, Suite 2, PMB 206. Phone:

Consulting, design, procurement, systems integration, training & support.

Professional Sound Corp., 28085 Smyth Dr., Valencia, CA, 91355. Phone: (661) 295-9395. Fax: (661) 295-8398.E-mail: sales@professionalsound.com Web Site:www.professionalsound.com Ron Meyer, pres; Debby Meyer, dir mktg.

Design, manufacture of portable sound recording products for film & video industries

Professional Sound Services Inc., 311 W. 43rd St., Suite 1100, New York, NY, 10036. Phone: (212) 586-1033. Fax: (212) 586-0970. Web Site:www.pro-sound.com Rich Topham, pres.

Wireless microphones, wireless, wired intercoms, IFB, telephone interfaces, analog, digital recorders, mixers, lavaliers, boompoles.Sls, rentals & svc.

Prophet Systems Innovations, 111 W. Third St., Ogallala, NE, 69153. Phone: (877) 774-1010. Fax: (308) 284-4181.E-mail: prophetsales@prophetsys.com Web Site:www.prophetsys.com Kevin Lockhart, pres.

Protech Audio Corp., 192 Cedar River Rd., Indian Lake, NY, 12842. Phone: (518) 648-6410. Fax: (518) 648-6395.E-mail: sales@protechaudio.com Bill Murphy, pres.

Dugan Automatic Mixing Controllers, audio distribution amplifiers & Dugan automatic mixers

Prysmian Communications Cables and Systems USA, LLC, 700 Industrial Dr., Lexington, SC, 29072-3799. Phone: (803) 951-4800. Fax: (803) 951-4898. Web Site:www.prysmianusa.com Brian DiLascia, VP/gen mgr; Martin Hanchard, pres/CEO.

ISO 9001-registered manufacturer of fiber-optic cables & Fiber to the Home (FTTH) solutions.

Q

QEI Corporation, Box 805, Williamstown, NJ, 08094. Phone: (856) 728-2020. Fax: (856) 629-1751.E-mail: qeisales@qei-broadcast.com Web Site:www.qei-broadcast.com Edwin Etschman, VP.

QSC Audio Products Inc., 1675 MacArthur Blvd., Costa Mesa, CA, 92626-1440. Phone: (714) 754-6175. Fax: (714) 754-6174. Web Site:www.qscaudio.com Barry Andrews, CEO; Pat N. Quilter, chmn; John Andrews, COO; Gregg McLogan, VP sls.

Professional power amplifiers, dual monaural power amplifiers, plug-in accessory products, integrated amplifiers, music & paging system.

QTV, 306 Fifth Ave., 3rd Fl., New York, NY, 10001. Phone: (212) 929-7755. Fax: (212) 929-2105.E-mail: sales@qtv.com Web Site:www.qtv.com Aaron Brady, VP sls.

New YorkNY , 19 W. 21st St. Phone:

Los AngelesCA , 5919 W. 3rd St. Phone:

Computer prompter software. 9", 12" & 15" on-camera prompters. Lightweight flat panel prompters.

Qintar Technologies Inc., 5530 Little Fawn Court, Westlake Village, CA, 91362. Phone: (818) 991-7300. Fax: (818) 889-7400.E-mail: sales@qintar.com Web Site:www.qintar.com Randall Tishkoff, pres.

Active & passive devices for CATV, amplifiers, filters, connectors, wall plates & wiring products. We also make OEM and custom products.

Quality Tower Erectors Inc., 2280 10th St. S.E., Largo, FL, 33771. Phone: (727) 585-6176. Fax: (727) 581-3277. Robert F. Diamond, pres.

QTE offers a full line of tower svcs in addition to our other offerings. QTE is the complete solution for your communication site & asset needs. Turn key civil svcs, erection, antenna systems, microwave, celluar, painting, turnkey svc & tower site rental svc included. nance, erection, antenna systems, microwave, cellular, painting, turnkey service & tower site rental.

Quantel Inc., 1950 Old Gallows Rd., Suite 101, Vienna, VA, 22182. Phone: (703) 448-3199. Fax: (703) 448-3189. Web Site:www.quantel.com Tom McGowan, CEO; Steve Owen, dir mktg.

TorontoON Canada, 1Yonge St, Suite 1100. Phone:

Los AngelesCA , 8501 Wilshire Blvd, Suite 340. Phone:

San FranciscoCA , 100 Bush St, Suite 1910. Phone:

AtlantaGA , 5 Concourse Pkwy, Suite 330. Phone:

ChicagoIL , 541 N. Fairbanks, Suite 1225. Phone:

New YorkNY , 111 W. 57th St., 10th Fl. Phone:

IrvingTX , 1425 Greenway Dr, Suite 470. Phone:

Quantel is the world's leading designer & manufacturer of digital image processing & manipulation products for video, film & print.

Quick-Set International Inc., 3650 Woodhead Dr., Northbrook, IL, 60062-1895. Phone: (847) 498-0700. Fax: (847) 498-1258. Web Site:www.quickset.com Jim Fenning, VP sls; Andy Lareaux, gen mgr .

Instrument positioning equipment. Tripods, pan & tilts.

QuStream, (PESA & ForteIDTV). 103 Quality Cir., Suite 210, Huntsville, AL, 35806. Phone: (256) 726-9200. Fax: (256) 726-9271.E-mail: sales@qustream.com Web Site:www.qustream.com

DuluthGA . Atlanta Branch, 3305 Breckinridge Blvd., Suite 118. Phone:

Manufacturer of HD/SD video/audio Routing switchers, signal processing & distribution.

R

RF Specialties Group, (RF Specialties of Missouri). 22406 N.E. 159th St., Kearney, MO, 64060. Phone: (800) 467-7373. Fax: (816) 628-4508. Web Site:www.rfspec.com E-mail: rfmo@uniteone.net Patricia Kreger, chmn/pres; John Sims, sls; Chris Kreger, VP & sec.

Makati City, Metro ManilaNO Philippines. RF Specialties of Asia Corporation, 4958 Guerrero St, Poblacion. Phone:eedmiston@rfsasia.com Ed Edmiston.

Santa BarbaraCA . RF Specialties of California, 3463 State St, Suite 229. Phone:rfsca@aol.com Sam Lane.

CrestviewFL . RF Specialties of Florida, 4706 Young Rd. Phone:rfoffl@aol.com William Hoisington. Cell (850) 621-3680.

RichmondIN . RF Specialties of Missouri, Inc., 1651 Capri Lane. Phone:rf@insightbb.com Rick Funk . Cell: 765-914-7778.

KearneyMO . RF Specialties of Missouri, Inc., 22406 N.E. 159th St. Phone:rfmo@uniteone.net Chris Kreger; John Sims. Chris Cell: 816-506-7473.

New IpswichNH . RF Specialties of Pennsylvania, Inc., 40 Settlement Hill. Phone:sam_on_the_hill@Monad.net S.A. Matthews. Cell: (603) 801- 8466.

Las VegasNV . RF Specialties of California, 3416 Lacebark Pine Street. Phone:newbro@ix.netcom.com Bill Newbrough.

EbensburgPA . RF Specialties of Pennsylvania, Inc., 619 Industrial Park Road, Ste 200. Phone:rfofpa@aol.com Dave Edmiston. Cell: (814) 659-6575.

MonroevillePA . RF Specialties of Pennsylvania, Inc., Box 2. Phone:edrfofpa@nb.net Pittsburgh office - Ed Young.

SouthamptonPA . RF Specialties of Pennsylvania Inc., Box 477. Phone:harrynlarkin@cs.com Harry Larkin. (Philadelphia Office).

AmarilloTX . RF Specialties of Texas, Box 7630. Phone:rfstx@swbell.net Don Jones. Cell (817) 312-7489.

Fort WorthTX . RF Specialties of Texas (Fort Worth Sales Office), 3528 Fairfax. Phone:rfstxftw@charter.net Wray Reed.

MukilteoWA . RF Specialties of Washington, Inc., 885 18th Street. Phone:waltlowery@msn.com Walt Lowery.

VancouverWA . RF Specialties of Washington Inc., Box 87571. Phone:rfswa@bobtheitguy.com Bob Trimble.

Full-line radio bcst equipment suppliers. AM & FM transmitters, towers, lines, antenna systems, studios, microwave & digital systems.

RF Technologies Corp., 1 Gendron Dr., Lewiston, ME, 04240. Phone: (207) 777-7778. Fax: (207) 777-7784. Web Site:www.rftechnologies.net George M. Harris, pres; Peter Robicheau, VP mfg; Bill Ammons, sls dir.

Designs & manufactures high-power bcst RF nets, components for FM & TV bcstrs. Products include antennas, diplexers, combiners, filters, switches, coax, waveguides & coaxal.

RTS Systems Telex Communications Inc, /. 2550 N. Hollywood Way, Suite 207, Burbank, CA, 91505-1055. Phone: (818) 566-6700. Fax: (818) 843-7953. Web Site:www.telex.com Ralph Strader, VP; Murray Porteous, natl sls mgr; Dave Richardson, rgnl sls mgr west; Britt Bowers, rgnl sls mgr mountain; Rick Fisher, rgnl sls mgr south; Michael Brown, rgnl sls mgr north east; Ken Smalley, rgnl sls mgr New York City.

DestinFL . 311 Stillwater Cove. Phone:

ButlerNJ , Box 866, 10 Park Pl. Bldg. 1. Phone:

MilfordPA , 3807 Sunrise Lakes. Phone:

TerrellTX , 10927 FM 1565. Phone:

CentervilleVA , 15463 Waters Creek. Phone:

Intercommunication systems, IFB systems, pro-audio amplifiers, microphones & phono preamplifiers.

Radian Communication Services Inc, 461 Cornwall Rd., Box 880, Oakville, ON, L6J 5C5. Canada. Phone: (905) 844-1242. Fax: (905) 844-8837.E-mail: info@radiancorp.com Web Site:www.radiancorp.com

Design, supply, instal of bcst transmitters, antennas & towers.

Radio Aids Inc., 313 Kintzele Rd., Michigan City, IN, 46350. Phone: (219) 879-2215. Fax: (219) 874-8239. John M. Carpenter, pres.

Measurement of occupied bandwidth, TV aural & visual, radio carriers, subcarriers, pilots, STL/TSL links.

Radio Computing Services (RCS), 445 Hamilton Ave., White Plains, NY, 10601. Phone: (914) 428-4600. Fax: (914) 428-5922.E-mail: info@rcsworks.com Web Site:www.rcsworks.com Philippe Generali, pres; Mike Powell, VP.

Frankfurt, Borsigallee 37. Phone:info@rcseurope.de Karl Kessler, gen mgr.

RichmondBC Canada, Box 32060, 410 #5 Rd. Phone: Paris France, 83 Ave. Philippe Auguste. Phone:

Bandra Mumboi (West)NO India, 262 Hart Niwas, 30th Rd. Phone:

ChristchurchNO New Zealand. RCS (NZ) Ltd., 33 Sir William Pickering Dr. Phone:info@rcs.co.nz Web Site: www.rsc.co.nz. Ian Campbell.

Singapore, 10 Anson Rd, 10-10 International Plaza. Phone:cfawell@attglobel.net Colin Fawell, gen mgr.

Bergbron, JohannesburgNO South Africa. RCS Africa, Leephy Studios, 11 Jonkershoek Rd. Phone:hayden @rscafrica.co.za Hayden Beetar.

Malmo Sweden. RCS Scandinavia, Kalendgatan 26. Phone:info@rcs.se Web Site: www.rcs.se. Sven Andrae.

LondonNO United Kingdom. RCS United Kingdom, 167-169 Great Portland St. Phone:info@rcsuk.com Web Site: www.rcsuk.com. Sebastian Holmes.

Live OakCA , 6018 Madden Ave. Phone:hshaw@rcsworks.com Dean Cull, western sls; Jennifer Cull, govt.

MiamiFL , 1385 Carol Way, #202. Phone:

Digital studio automation & digital audio ripping/analysis, music scheduling, traf, sls, newsroom & talk show software/hardware, internet/streaming tools.

Radio Design Labs. (RDL), 659 N. 6th St., Prescott, AZ, 86301. Phone: (805) 684-5415. Fax: (805) 684-9316.E-mail: sales@rdlnet.com Web Site:www.rdlnet.com Joel Bump, pres; Daniel Bump, sls dir.

Full line of microphone & line level amplifiers, mixers, DAs & processors.

Radio Engineering Industries Inc., 6534 L St., Omaha, NE, 68117. Phone: (402) 339-2200. Fax: (402) 339-1704.E-mail: sales@radioeng.com Web Site:www.radioeng.com Terry Jukes, CEO; Dave Ruback, pres; Gunnar Guenette, dir mktg.

Sls, svc of bcst equipment, amplifiers, paging systems, SCA & coml sound equipment.

Radio Frequency Systems, 200 Pondview Dr., Meriden, CT, 06450-7195. Phone: (203) 630-3311. Fax: (203) 634-2272.E-mail: sales@rfsworld.com Web Site:www.rfsworld.com Bill Bayne, pres.

Rigid coaxial line (7/8" to 9 3/16"), FM antennas, FM, VHF/UHF IFTS, MMDS, TV antennas, dehydrators, instal accesories, RF, microwave antenna subsystems, instal & field svc.

Radio Research Instrument Co. Inc., 584 N. Main St., Waterbury, CT, 06704. Phone: (203) 753-5840. Fax: (203) 754-2567.E-mail: radiores@prodigy.net Web Site:www.radioresearch.thomasregister.com P. J. Plishner, pres; E. B. Doyle, exec VP.

Provides radar systems, threat emitters & spare parts; complete maintenance facility for repair.

Radio Systems Inc., 601 Heron Dr., Logan Township, NJ, 08085-1741. Phone: (856) 467-8000. Fax: (856) 467-3044.E-mail: sales@radiosystems.com Web Site:www.radiosystems.com Daniel Braverman, pres; Gerrett Conover, VP.

Analog, digital & Live-wire-compatible audio consoles, distribution amplifiers, low-power TIS/HAR AM transmitters, clock & timer systems, telephone hybrids, the StudioHub+wiring system & IP-Connect, a licensed 18 GHz digital studio-to-transmitter link.

Radiodetection/Riser Bond, 154 Portland Rd., Bridgton, ME, 04009. Phone: (207) 647-9495. Fax: (207) 647-9496.E-mail: bridgton@radiodetection.spx.com Web Site:www.dielectrictechnologies.com Paul Sherman, VP sls & mktg; Zenya Brackett, dir opns.

Electronic test equipment; cable fault locators; time domain reflectometer.

Ram Broadcast Systems, Box 277, Wauconda, IL, 60084-0277. Phone: (800) 779-7575. Phone: (847) 487-7575. Fax: (847) 487-2440. Web Site:www.ramsyscom.com Ron Mitchell, pres.

Switchers (audio & video) mixers, intercom systems, audio/video DAs, systems engrg & custom cabinetry.

Raven Screen Corp., 112 Spring St., Monroe, NY, 10950. Phone: (212) 534-8408. Phone: (845) 782-1844. Fax: (845) 782-1840.E-mail: info@ravenscreen.com Web Site:www.ravenscreen.com Martin Soss, pres.

Manual, motorized & custom projection screens & materials.

Record/Play Tek Inc., Box 790, 112 E. Vistula St., Bristol, IN, 46507-0790. Phone: (574) 848-5233. Fax: (574) 848-5333.E-mail: stoll@recordplaytek.com Web Site:www.recordplaytek.com Michael Stoll, CEO.

Voice logging recorders 911, cassette, reel-to-reel, VHS, computer CDR & DVD+ R.

Recortec Inc., 1620-A Berryessa Rd., San Jose, CA, 95133-1026. Phone: (408) 928-1480. Fax: (408) 729-3661.E-mail: info@recortec.com Web Site:www.recortec.com Dr.Lester H. Lee, pres.

Manufacturer of coml disc players & LCD players.

Reel-O-Matic Inc., 6408 S. Eastern Ave., Oklahoma City, OK, 73149. Phone: (405) 672-0000. Phone: (888) 873-4000. Fax: (405) 672-7200. Web Site:www.reel-o-matic.com Terry Simmons, pres; Mark Zercher, VP.

Equipment to re-spool, coil, measure & distribute cable.

Rees Associates Inc., 9211 Lake Hefner Pkwy., Suite 300, Oklahoma City, OK, 73120. Phone: (405) 942-7337. Fax: (405) 948-1261. Web Site:www.rees-associates.com C. Leroy James, exec VP/COO; William Yost, VP; Frank Rees, pres/CEO; Ralph S. Blackman, VP.

Atlanta GA , 951 Peachtree St. N.E. Phone:
SpokaneWA , 7810 N. Forker Rd. Phone:
DallasTX , 1801 N. Lamar St., Suite 600. Phone:

Bcst & production facility design; architectural svcs; studio design; equipment planning; facility business plans; interior design & consulting.

Register Communications, (formerly Register Data Systems). 1691 Forsyth St., Macon, GA, 31201. Phone: (478) 745-5500. Fax: (478) 745-0500.E-mail: sales@registerdata.com Web Site:www.registerdata.com Lowell L. Register, pres; Ricky Lockerman, sls dir.

Digital audio automation systems for live assist, satellite, traf & billing software packages for radio & TV.

Renkus-Heinz Inc., 19201 Cook St., Foothill Ranch, CA, 92610-3510. Phone: (949) 588-9997. Fax: (949) 588-9514.E-mail: sales@renkus-heinz.com Web Site:www.renkus-heinz.com Harro K. Heinz, pres; Carl Dorwaldt, mktg mgr.

Reference point arrays, powered network loudspeakers, R-control remote supervision network. Reference point arrays, powered network loudspeakers.

Research Technology International Inc., 4700 Chase Ave., Lincolnwood, IL, 60712-1689. Phone: (847) 677-3000. Phone: (800) 323-7520. Fax: (847) 677-1311.E-mail: sales@rtico.com Web Site:www.rtico.com Ray L. Short Jr., pres; Thomas W. Boyle Jr., sr VP; Bill Wolavka, sls VP.

Videotape evaluator/cleaners; degaussers; storage & care, supplies, film cleaners. CD/DVD cleaners-restorers inspectors.

Richardson Electronics, (A division of Broadcast Richardson). PO Box 393, 40W267 Keslinger Rd., LaFox, IL, 60147. Phone: (630) 208-2200. Fax: (630) 208-2662.E-mail: broadcast@rell.com Web Site:broadcast.rell.com Edward Richardson, CEO; Robert Prince, VP worldwide sls.

LaFoxIL , Box 393, 40W267 Keslinger Rd. Phone:broadcast@rell.com Web Site: broadcast.rell.com.

Global provider of power tubes, TV, radio transmitters, IP, digital satellite systems, NLE video systems & studio pakages.

Richmond Sound Design Ltd., 5264 Rose St., Vancouver, BC, V5W EK7. Canada. Phone: (604) 715-9441. Fax: (604) 628-3391.E-mail: sales@richmondsounddesign.com Web Site:www.richmondsounddesign.com C.B. Richmond, pres; M. Williams, mgr.

Virtual Sound System & show control software.

Ripley Company, 46 Nooks Hill Rd., Cromwell, CT, 06416. Phone: (860) 635-2200. Phone: (800) 528-8665. Fax: (860) 635-3631.E-mail: info@ripley-tools.com Web Site:www.ripley-tools.com Keith D'Amato, sls dir; Tom Lindenmuth, gen mgr .

Ripley's Cablematic, Miller & Utility tool lines offer manufacturers cable preparation tools for CATV telecomm data & electric utiliy.

Rodelco Electronics Corp., 111 Haynes Ct., Ronkonkoma, NY, 11779. Phone: (631) 981-0900. Fax: (631) 981-1792.E-mail: rodelco@erols.com Joseph M. Rodgers, gen mgr .

TV translators, VHF & UHF.

Rohn Industries Inc., 6718 W. Plank Rd., Peoria, IL, 61604. Phone: (309) 697-4400. Fax: (309) 697-5612.E-mail: mail@rohnnet.com Web Site:www.rohnnet.com Horace Ward, pres/CEO; Dave Ramsey, VP sls.

Towers (up to 2,000 feet) monopoles, antenna mounts for communication industry. Turnkey construction & installation avaible worldwide.

Roland Corp. U.S., Box 910921, 5100 S. Eastern Ave., Los Angeles, CA, 90091-0921. Phone: (323) 890-3700. Fax: (323) 890-3701. Web Site:www.rolandus.com Dennis Houlihan, pres; Mark Malbon, exec VP.

Electronic musical instruments, signal processors, sound reinforcement, hard disk editors, noise eliminators, bcst production equipment & post production equipment.

Rosco Laboratories Inc., 52 Harbor View Ave., Stamford, CT, 06902. Phone: (203) 708-8900. Fax: (203) 708-8919.E-mail: info@rosco.com Web Site:www.rosco.com Stan Miller, pres; Stan Schwartz, exec VP; Ed Donahue, sls dir.

HollywoodCA , 1120 N. Citrus Ave. Phone:

Lighting filters & diffusers, studio floor covering, connectors & digital (or rental & custom) backdrops.

Roscor Corp., 1061 Feehanville Dr., Mount Prospect, IL, 60056. Phone: (847) 299-8080. Fax: (847) 299-4206. Fax: (847) 803-8089.E-mail: sales@roscor.com Web Site:www.roscor.com Paul Roston, pres; Mitch Roston, exec VP; Tom Voigts, sls VP; Edward Jones, VP finance.

CincinnatiOH , 2868 E. Kemper Rd. Phone:
Farmington HillsMI , 27280 Haggerty Rd, Suite C2. Phone:
MilwaukeeWI , 600 W. Virginia St. Phone:

Professional audio/video/RF/presentation equipment. Turnkey engrg & instal svcs.

Ross Video Ltd., Box 220, 8 John St., Iroquois, ON, K0E 1K0. Canada. Phone: (613) 652-4886. Fax: (613) 652-4425.E-mail: solutions@rossvideo.com Web Site:www.rossvideo.com David Ross, CEO; Jeff Moore, exec VP sls /mktg; Joe Lalonde, CFO; Jeff Poapst, VP.

Ross Video's product line includes Vision & Synergy Multi-Definition Video production switchers, openGear, RossGear & GearLite Terminal Equipment, SoftMetal Video Servers & the OverDrive Production Control System.

Rovi Corp., 2830 De La Cruz Blvd., Santa Clara, CA, 95050-2619. Phone: (408) 562-8400. Fax: (408) 567-1800. Web Site:www.rovicorp.com John Ryan, chmn; Fred Amoroso, pres/CEO.

Tokyo Japan. Macrovision Japan K.K., Takaba Bldg. 2F, 6-18-5, Jingumae, Shibuya-Ku. Phone:

Beeshire United Kingdom. Macrovision UK Ltd., 14-18 Bell St, Maiden Head. Phone:

Copy protection & rights mgmt for videocassettes, pay-per-view cable, satellite TV, & video conferencing.

Royal Consumer Information Products, 379 Campus Dr., Somerset, NJ, 08875. Phone: (732) 627-9977. Web Site:www.olivettiofficeusa.com Salomon Suwalsky, pres; Todd Althoff, VP mktg.

S

SAIC (Science Applications International Corp.), 1710 Saic Dr., Suite B, Mclean, 22102. Phone: (703) 821-4300. Kenneth C. Dahlberg, chmn/CEO.

San DiegoCA . SAIC Inc., 10260 Campus Point Dr. Phone:

Natl security, energy, environment, critical infrastructure, health , rsch & dev.

S&L Plastics Inc., 2860 Bath Pike, Nazareth, PA, 18064. Phone: (610) 759-0280. Fax: (610) 759-0650. Web Site:www.slpinc.cc John Bungert, pres.

Thermo plastic products.

SES Americom Inc., 4 Research Way, Princeton, NJ, 08540. Phone: (609) 987-4000. Fax: (609) 987-4517. Web Site:www.ses-americom.com Bryan mcGurik, pres.

Satellite distribution svcs for coml bcst & cable TV; prog syndicators, SNG & bcst radio distribution svcs.

S W R Inc., (Systems with Reliability.). 619 Industrial Park Rd., Ebensburg, PA, 15931. Phone: (814) 472-5436. Fax: (814) 472-5552. E-mail: david@swr-rf.com Web Site:www.swr-rf.com Edward J. Edmiston, pres; David K. Edmiston, gen sls mgr.

Timog, Quezon City, 31-E Scout Bayoran. Phone:
Manufacturers of TV & FM transmit antennas, rigid coax, waveguide & associated accessories.

Sabine Inc., 13301 Hwy. 441, Alachua, FL, 32615. Phone: (386) 418-2000. Fax: (386) 418-2001.E-mail: sabine@sabine.com Web Site:www.sabine.com Doran Oster, pres.

Manufacturers of digital signal processing equipment for sound systems. Makers of the patented FBX Feedback Exterminator & True MobilityTM wireless microphones.

Sachtler Corp. of America, 709 Executive Blvd., Valley Cottage, NY, 10989. Phone: (845) 268-2113. Fax: (845) 268-9324.E-mail: sales@sachtler.com Web Site:www.sachtler.com Ali Ahmadi, dir mktg; Bob Carr, pres.

BurbankCA , 3316 W. Victory Blvd. Phone:
Complete line of camera support equipment for ENG, EFP, O.B. & the new generation of studio cameras. Lighting for news, production & studio open-face technology & fresnel.

Sacramento Theatrical Lighting (STL), 950 Richards Blvd., Sacramento, CA, 95814. Phone: (800) 283-2785. Fax: (916) 447-5012.E-mail: saclight@aol.com Steve Odehnal, gen mgr .

Specialists in studio & location lighting, grip equipment, draperies, rigging & grid work. Consultation & production svcs. Sls, rentals & svcs.

Sadelco Inc., 75 W. Forest Ave., Englewood, NJ, 07631. Phone: (201) 569-3323. Fax: (201) 569-6285.E-mail: sadelco@aol.com Web Site:www.sadelco.com Les Kaplan, pres.

Signal level meters, calibrators & leakage detectors.

Samson Technologies Corp., 45 Gilpin Ave., Hauppauge, NY, 11788. Phone: (516) 364-2244. Fax: (516) 364-3888.E-mail: sales@samsontech.com Web Site:www.samsontech.com Douglas Bryant, VP; Scott Goodman, CEO; Jack Knight, VP opns; Mark Wilder, VP mktg.

Manufacturer of wireless microphones, mixing consoles, power amplifiers & audio products. Behringer audio processing, Hartke speakers & Zoom effects processors.

Sanyo Fisher Co., 21605 Plummer St., Chatsworth, CA, 91311. Phone: (818) 998-7322. Fax: (818) 998-3533. Web Site:www.sanyo.com Paul W. D'Arcy, exec VP; David Berkus, VP mktg.

Audio amplifiers & receivers, CD players, audiotape recorders, turntables, dictation machines, cordless telephones, TVs, VTRs & LCD projectors.

Sarnoff Corp., (A Subsidiary of SRI International). 201 Washington Rd., Princeton, NJ, 08543-5300. Phone: (609) 734-2553. Fax: (609) 734-2221. Web Site:www.sarnoff.com Dr. John Newsome, pres/CEO; Peter J. Burt, vision technologies; John P. Riganati, VP, video, comm & networking systems.

Contract rsch & dev facility for electronic, biomedical, & info technologies, specializing in digital video.

Sascom Marketing Group, 34 Nelson St., Oakville, ON, L6L 3H6. Canada. Phone: (905) 469-8080. Fax: (905) 469-8081.E-mail: c.smith@sascom.com Web Site:www.sascom.com Curt Smith, pres.

Sascom Represents: Cube-Tec Plugins for Pro Tools, Nuendo and Sequoia, and Doremi Labs digital video products

Satellite Systems Corp., 101 Malibu Dr., Virginia Beach, VA, 23452. Phone: (757) 463-3553. Fax: (757) 463-3891. Web Site:www.satsyscorp.com Bob Kite, pres.

SCPC & video subcarrier satellite systems for radio, SNG & data bcst networks.

Schafer International, 220 Surrey Dr., Bonita, CA, 91902. Phone: (619) 267-9000. Fax: (619) 267-9003.E-mail: schaferpc@gmail.com Web Site:www.schaferinternational.com Paul C. Schafer, pres.

Equipment & parts, for radio & TV stns, primarily in Mexico.

Schafer World Communications Corp., Box 1047, Marion, VA, 24354-1047. Phone: (276) 783-2000. Fax: (276) 783-2064. Bob Dix, pres; Ann Dix, VP; Kevin Soos, mktg.

Schafer offers two levels of sophistication in hard disk audio systems, "GENESIS" Digital Studio: touch screen & remote control interface; excellent live assist & full automation capability (complete music scheduling software included); cut-to-cut mixing on hard disk including editing; simultaneous record/playback from hard disk; can connect to external machines & CD multi-players.

Schneider Optics Inc., 285 Oser Ave., Hauppauge, NY, 11788. Phone: (631) 761-5000. Fax: (631) 761-5090.E-mail: info@schneideroptics.com Web Site:www.schneideroptics.com Dwight Lindsay, CEO.

Van NuysCA , 7701 Haskell Ave. Phone:
Manufacturer/distributor of high quality optical filters for video, still photography & motion picture. Product line also includes a wide range of lenses for CCTV, large format photography, darkroom enlarging, slide & film projection.

Scientific Atlanta, 5030 Sugarloaf Pkwy., Lawrenceville, GA, 30044. Phone: (770) 236-5000. Fax: (770) 902-2591.E-mail: gregg.echols@sciatl.com Web Site:www.sciatl.com James McDonald, chmn/CEO; Patrick Tylka, pres; Dwight Duke, pres; Michael Harney, pres.

A complete line of cable TV & broadband communications systems, products. and professional services.

Scientific Atlanta Canada Inc. Nexus Division, Satellite TV Networks, 100 Middlefield Rd. Unit 1, Scarborough, ON, M1S 4M6. Canada. Phone: (416) 299-6888. Fax: (416) 299-7145. Web Site:www.scientificatlanta.com Michael Harney, sr VP, sub net; Dwight Duke, corporate sr VP; Patrick Tylka, sr VP; Dean Rockwell, VP/gen mgr.

TV RF signal processing equipment, transmission products & cable TV amplifiers.

Scott Studios Corporation, 13375 N. Stemmons Fwy., Dallas, TX, 75234. Phone: (972) 620-2211. David Scott, pres.

Business svcs, computer integrated systems & design.

ScreenLight & Grip, 502 Sprague St., Dedham, MA, 02026. Phone: (781) 326-5088. Fax: (781) 326-4751.E-mail: lightsne@aol.com Web Site:www.screenlightandgrip.com Guy Holt, pres.

Location lighting & production svcs, equipment rental, trucks, vans, etc.

Second Chance Body Armor Inc., 7915 Cameron St., Central Lake, MI, 49622-0573. Phone: (231) 544-5721. Phone: (800) 253-7090. Fax: (231) 544-9824.E-mail: email@secondchance.com Web Site:www.secondchance.com Paul J. Banducci, VP/gen mgr.

Leading body armor manufacturer now offering ballistic protection for news media reporters & photographers.

Seger Electronics, 97 Libbey Pkwy, Weymouth, MA, 02189. Phone: (781) 682-4844. Web Site:www.seger.com Frank Flynn, pres; Ray Norton, CEO.

Largest inventory of electromechanical components. No mimimums. Liberal sampling. 24-hours order check. Custom assembly, engraving & printing.

Selco Products Co., 605 S. East Street, Anaheim, CA, 92805. Phone: (714) 717-1333. Phone: (800) 527-3526. Fax: (714) 917-1355.E-mail: sales@selcoproducts.com Web Site:www.selcoproducts.com Tim Wilkinson, pres; Michelle Blakeslee, mktg.

A full range of product lines are offered by selco including thermal products, control knobs, electronic controls & digital panel meters.

Sencore Inc., (formerly Sencore Inc./AAVS). 3200 W. Sencore Dr., Sioux Falls, SD, 57107. Phone: (605) 339-0100. Fax: (605) 339-0317.E-mail: sales@sencore.com Web Site:www.sencore.com Dana Nachreiner, VP opns; John Suranyi, CEO; Chuck Robertson, VP product mgmt; Tom Stingley, exec VP mktg & sls; Ken Christensen, mktg mgr, media rel.

Electronic test equipment for servicing & performance testing of consumer electronics & CATV/MATV equipment.

Senior Aerospace, Ketema Division. 790 Greenfield Dr., El Cajon, CA, 92021. Phone: (619) 442-3451. Fax: (619) 440-1456. Ron Case, gen mgr .

Design build-to-print aerospace products, cryogenic lines, valves, burst discs, electric motors, actuators.

Sennheiser Electronic Corp., One Enterprise Dr., Old Lyme, CT, 06371. Phone: (860) 434-9190. Fax: (860) 434-1759.E-mail: info@sennheiserusa.com Web Site:www.sennheiserusa.com John Falcone, pres/CEO; Jeff Alexander, VP sls/mktg-professional products.

Col. Del Valle, D.F. Mexico, Av. Xola No. 613 PH6. Phone:
Microphones, headphones, boomsets, wireless microphones & infrared products as well as Neumann mucrophone, Klein+Hummel loudspeakers & HHB recorders.

Servoreeler Systems, (Xedit Corp.). 218-31 97th Ave., Queens Village, NY, 11429. Phone: (718) 464-9400. Fax: (718) 464-9435.E-mail: srsystems@servoreelers.com Web Site:www.servoreelers.com Claude M. Karczmer, pres; Eileen Karczmer, sls dir.

Suspended Microphone Servoreelers-deploy, retract & position suspended microphones by remote pushbutton or computer control. Use for teleconferencing, corporate bd rooms, House of worship, concert halls, sports arenas & universities.

Sescom Inc., 608 Main St., wellsville, KS, 66092. Phone: (785) 883-3009. Fax: (785) 883-4422.E-mail: sescom@sescom.com Web Site:www.sescom.com Bryan McGuirk, pres; Jodi Morelli, mktg dir.

Audio interfacing equipment, audio transformers & modules.

Setcom Corporation, 3019 Alvin Devane Blvd., Suite 560, Austin, TX, 78741. Phone: (888) 673-8266. Fax: (650) 965-1193.E-mail: sales@setcomcorp.com Web Site:www.setcomcorp.com James Roberts, pres.

Police motorcycle communication equipment.

Seton Identification Products, Box 819, Branford, CT, 06405. Phone: (203) 488-8059. Fax: (203) 488-7259. Web Site:www.seton.com E-mail: comments@seton.com Richard L. Fisk, pres.

Signs, tags, labels, pipe markers, valve tags, & nameplates to meet OSHA/ANSI specifications.

Shallco Inc., Box 1089, 308 Components Dr., Smithfield, NC, 27577. Phone: (800) 876-3135 (USA only). Phone: (919) 934-3298 (outside USA). Fax: (919) 934-3135 (outside USA only).E-mail: sales@shallco.com Web Site:www.shallco.com John Shallcross Sr., chmn; Jason S. Shallcross, pres.

Variable & fixed audio attenuators.

Sharp Electronics Corp., CCD Products Div., (LCD Products Group). Sharp Plaza, Mail Stop One, Mahwah, NJ, 07430-2135. Phone: (201) 529-8200. Phone: (866) 4-VISUAL. Fax: (201) 529-9636.E-mail: ProLCD@SharpSEC.com Web Site:www.SharpLCD.com Ron Colgan, VP; Fred Krazeisze, dir strategic mktg; Bruce Pollack, assoc dir mktg; Bob Soucy, sls dir; Doug Koshima, chmn/CEO; Judah Zeilger, assoc VP mktg.

Data/video projection systems for portable and permanent installation applications; LCD video monitors, TVs, VCRs, TV/VCRs and Viewcam Camcorders.

Shively Labs, Box 389, 188 Harrison Rd., Bridgton, ME, 04009. Phone: (207) 647-3327. Fax: (207) 647-8273.E-mail: sales@shively.com Web Site:www.shively.com Joe Rohrer, rgnl sls mgr; David Allen, VP & COO; Angela Gillespie, sls; Paul Wescott, past pres.

FM antennas, FM translators, branched & balanced combiners, coax, patch panels, filters, compressor dehydrators, & related RF equipment, pattern work & field svcs.

Shook Mobile Technology, LP, 7451 FM 3009, Schertz, TX, 78154. Phone: (210) 651-5700. Fax: (210) 651-5220.E-mail: shook@shook-usa.com Web Site:www.shook-usa.com John Heaney, CEO; Ronald Crockett, pres & dir mktg.

Mobile TV production, ENG, SNV vehicles. Rack ready or turnkey delivery. HD/SD Systems integration.

Shure Inc., 5800 W. Touhy Ave., Niles, IL, 60714. Phone: (847) 600-2000. Fax: (847) 600-1212. Web Site:www.shure.com E-mail: info@shur.com R.L. Shure, chmn; S. LaMantia, pres.

World-standard microphones, wireless audio systems, phonograph cartridges, mixers, digital signal processors, & personal monitors.

Siemens Dematic Limited, 167 Hunt St., Ajax, ON, L1S 1P6. Canada. Phone: (905) 683-8200. Fax: (905) 683-0186. Web Site:www.siemens.ca

Solid state FM transmitters to 5 kw, automatic coaxial changeover units, shortwave transmitters.

Sierra Automated Systems & Engineering Corp., 2821 Burton Ave., Burbank, CA, 91504. Phone: (818) 840-6749. Fax: (818) 840-6751. Web Site:www.sasaudio.com Edward O. Fritz, pres; Al Salci, VP; Giovanni Morales, gen mgr .

Audio switching & mixing systems maunufacturer. Mix-Minus/IFB, satellite distribution/switching, automated switching & distribution, studio intercom, on-air routing, teleconferencing.

Sigma Electronics Inc., 1027 Commercial Ave., Box 448, East Petersburg, PA, 17520-0448. Phone: (717) 569-2681. Fax: (717) 569-4056. E-mail: sales@sigmaelectronics.com Web Site:www.sigmaelectronics.com Billy Swilley, pres/CEO.

Santa RosaCA . Western rgnl office Phone:

Routing switchers for audio & video; distribution amplifiers; sync & test signal generators; encoders, decoders, transcoders, converters.

Signal Monitoring Service, 773 Upper Fredricktown Rd., Mt. Vernon, OH, 43050. Phone: (888) 449-5643. Fax: (740) 397-2769. Robert (Bob) Bowman, owner.

AM/FM/TV frequency & modulation documentation - NRSC proof for AM.

Sinar Bron Inc., 17 Progress St., Edison, NJ, 08820. Phone: (908) 754-5800. Fax: (908) 754-5807. Web Site:www.sinarbron.com Michael Hetymanek, pres.

Pro-Cyc prefabricated coves for infiniti walls in video & photo studios; & studio lighting/HMI.

Sitco Antenna Company, Box 20456, 10330 N.E. Marx St., Portland, OR, 97220-1139. Phone: (503) 253-2000. Fax: (503) 253-2009. E-mail: sitco@simplicitytool.com Web Site:www.simplicitytool.com Markus Burcker, pres.

CATV, MATV antennas.

SiteSafe Inc., 200 N. Glebe Rd., Suite 1000, Arlington, VA, 22203-3728. Phone: (703) 276-1100. Fax: (703) 276-1169. E-mail: info@sitesafe.com Web Site:www.sitesafe.com Wesley O. McGee, pres; Elizabeth Nash, VP mktg/sls.

Engrg software & wireless telecom engrg consulting svcs.

Skotel Corp., 92094 CSP Portobello, Brossard, PQ, J4W 3K8. Canada. Phone: (514) 806-2340. E-mail: stephenscott@videotron.ca Stephen Scott, pres.

Switching Equipment: Distribution switchers, Video equipment: Time code generators & time code readers.

Skytec, Inc., 23 Inland Farm Rd., Windham, ME, 04062. Phone: (207) 893-1700. Fax: (207) 893-1717. E-mail: skytecinc@aol.com Web Site:www.skytecinc.com Rick Sullivan, pres.

Manufacturer of skystrobe obstruction lighting systems - ETL certified, FAA approved. Parts, sls, svc & training seminars for obstruction lighting.

Snell, 3519 Pacific Ave., Burbank, CA, 91505. Phone: (818) 556-2616. Fax: (818) 556-2626. E-mail: americas@snellwilcox.com Web Site:www.snellwilcox.com John Poulter, chmn; Roderick Snell, rsch dir; Simon Derry, CEO.

Havant, Harts. Smith & Wilcox Ltd., Southleigh Park House, Eastleigh Rd.

Petersfield, Hampshire. Snell & Wilcox Ltd., Durford Mill. Phone:

Snell & Wilcox is one of the world's largest manufacturers of bcst electronics. The complete product family includes a full range of video & audio processing equipment consisting of Decoding, Encoding, High Definition Format Conversion, MPEG Compression & Pre-processing, Display, Noise Reduction, Post Production Switchers (both SDTV & HDTV), Standards Conversion, Synchronization, Test & Measurement & IQ Modular products.

Solid State Logic Inc., 320 W. 46th St., New York, NY, 10036. Phone: (212) 315-1111. Fax: (212) 315-0251. E-mail: nysales@solidstatelogic.com Web Site:www.solid -state-logic.com Steve Zaretsky, VP.

Los AngelesCA , 5757 Wilshire Blvd. Phone:

SSL is a leading manufacturer of digital audio broadcast consoles for on-air and live-to-tape production.

Solutec Ltd. (HA), 4360 D'lberville, Montreal, PQ, H2H 2L8. Canada. Phone: (514) 522-8960. Fax: (450) 437-8572. E-mail: gilles.fortin@sympatico.ca Gilles Fortin, pres.

Closed caption encoders (analog & SDI) & software, wireless communications.

Sony BMG Music Entertainment, (formerly BMG). 550 Madison Ave., New York, NY, 10022. Phone: (212) 833-8000. Web Site:www.bmg.com Rolf Schmidt Hotz, chmn.

Produce, market & distribute recorded musics.

Sound Associates, (formerly Sound Designers Studio). 424 W. 45th St., New York, NY, 10036-3565. Phone: (212) 757-5679. Fax: (212) 265-1250. T. Richard Fitzgerald, pres; Domonic Sack, vp.

YonkersNY . Sound Associates Inc., 979 Saw Mill River Rd. Phone:

Electronic equipment racking systems, console automation

systems & digital recording facilities.

Soundcraft U.S.A., 8500 Balboa Blvd., Northridge, CA, 91329. Phone: (818) 920-3212. Fax: (818) 920-3208. E-mail: soundcraft-usa@harman.com Web Site:www.soundcraft.com Dave Neal, mktg; Tom Der, natl sls mgr.

Audio mixing consoles for recording, theater, concert sound reinforcement & bcstg.

Southern Broadcast Services, 80 Commerce Dr., Suite B, Pelham, AL, 35124. Phone: (800) 256-9235. Fax: (205) 663-7108. Web Site:www.southernbroadcastservices.com Jim Coleman, pres.

Tower erection, antenna instal, maintenance svcs.

Spacenet Services Inc., 1750 Old Meadow Rd., McLean, VA, 22102. Phone: (703) 848-1000. Fax: (703) 848-1010. Web Site:www.spacenet.com David Shiff, VP mktg.

Satellite-based interactive data, bcst data & bcst video for coml companies worldwide.

Specialized Communications Corp., 20940 Twin Springs Dr., Smithsburg, MD, 21783-1510. Phone: (800) 359-1858. Fax: (301) 790-0173. E-mail: service@spec-comm.com Web Site:www.spec-comm.com David Linetsky, pres; Judy Hoffman, mktg mgr; Andrew Hoffman, VP.

Factory Authorized Service Center providing repair & maintenance of bcst video equipment. Factory Integrator & Dealer for distinctive industry brands, such as Panasonic, Sony, JVS, Cannon. Also manufacturer of Digital Signage systems & provider of digital signage installation, integraton, content creation & content management.

Spectra Sonics, 3750 Airport Rd., Ogden, UT, 84405. Phone: (801) 392-7531. Fax: (801) 392-7531. Jean Dilley, controller; Gregory D. Dilley, pres.

Professional audio production, including power amps, compressor/limiters, portable speaker system, mixers, & line/distribution amps.

Spotcat Software, 1734 Green Valley Rd., Havertown, PA, 19083. Phone: (610) 446-1515. E-mail: support@spotcat.com

Sprague Magnetics Inc., 12806 Bradley Ave., Sylmar, CA, 91342. Phone: (818) 364-1800. Phone: (800) 553-8712. Fax: (818) 364-1810. E-mail: smiav@spraguemagnetics.com Web Site:www.spraguemagnetics.com Dorothy Sprague, pres; Gary Moore, gen mgr .

Long-wearing cart, film, reel-to-reel tape heads, refurbishment svcs, replacement parts, alignment tapes, accessories.

Stage Equipment & Lighting Inc., 12250 N.E. 13th Ct., North Miami, FL, 33161. Phone: (305) 891-2010. Fax: (305) 893-2828. Fax: (800) 597-2010. E-mail: mail@seal-fla.com Web Site:www.seal-fla.com Vivian Gill, pres; Michael Grosz, VP; Rick Rudolph, exec VP.

OrlandoFL , 4600 S.W. 36th St. Phone:

TampaFL , 9207 Palm River Rd., Suite 108. Phone:

Film, video & theatrical lighting & grip, & related support equipment.

Stahl, A Scott & Fetzer Co., 3201 Old Lincoln Way, Wooster, OH, 44691. Phone: (330) 264-7441. Fax: (330) 264-3319. E-mail: info@stahl.cc Web Site:www.stahl.cc Jim Kraschinsky, pres; Brad Yocheim, sls mgr.

MercedCA Phone:

CardingtonOH Phone:

DurantOK Phone:

Stainless LLC, 1140 Welsh Rd., Suite 250, North Wales, PA, 19454. Phone: (215) 631-1400. Phone: (800) 486-3333. Fax: (215) 631-1425. E-mail: sales@stainlessllc.com Web Site:www.stainlessllc.com Donald T. Doty, CEO; Patrick Moore, VP; Tom Hoenninger, VP engrg & chief engr; Duane MacEntee, pres.

McKinneyTX . Stainless Doty Moore, 213 E. Louisiana St., Suite 250. Phone:

Cedar HillTX . Doty Moore Stainless, 1570 W. Beltline Rd. Phone:

Design, engrg, fabrication of communications & bcst towers. Existing tower engrg studies & analysis. Full spectrum of tower maintenance, construction & inspections. RF svcs include RF mapping of towers & facilities, 24-hr emergency svcs.

Stancil Corp., 2644 S. Croddy Way, Santa Ana, CA, 92704. Phone: (714) 546-2002 ext. 4316. Phone: (800) 782-6245. Fax: (714) 546-2092. E-mail: guy.churchouse @stancilcorp.com Web Site:www.stancilcorp.com Michael Custer, CEO.

Voice logging recorders, multichannel, 4-144 channels, 24-hour recording time; digital format, instant recall recorders, windows 2000 voiceXP.

Standard Communications Corp., 6260 Sequence Dr., San Diego, CA, 92121. Phone: (858) 546-5300. Fax: (858) 546-5301. E-mail: SatcommSales@stdcom.com Web Site:www.standardcom.com Ron Blanchard, pres/CEO.

Broadband TV receivers & cable headend products for broadcast and CATV.

Stanley Supply & Services, 7815 S. 46th St., Phoenix, AZ, 85044. Phone: (602) 453-3169. Phone: (800) 366-9662. Fax: (877) 372-5108. E-mail: sales@stanleyworks.com Web Site:www.stanleysupplyservices.com Holly Tsourides, pres.

Electronic tool kits & cases, tools, test equipment.

Stanton Group, 3000 S.W. 42nd St., Ft. Lauderdale, FL, 33312. Phone: (954) 316-1500. Fax: (954) 316-1590. Web Site:www.stantonmagnetics.com E-mail: info@stantonmagnetics.com Timothy Dorwart, CEO; Mike Quandt, pres/COO.

HuntingtonCA . KRK, 5242 Business Dr. Phone:

Simi ValleyCA . Kerwin Vega , 555 Fast Easy Street.

Turntables, professional cartridges, CD players, final scratch, monitors, speakers.

Star Case Manufacturing Co. Inc., 648 Superior Ave., Munster, IN, 46321. Phone: (219) 922-4440. Phone: (800) 822-STAR. Fax: (219) 922-4442. E-mail: starcase@starcase.com Web Site:www.starcase.com Dennis Toma, pres; Ralph G. Hoopes, VP.

Flight cases (protective casement)—Carry Star, ATA Star, Super Star, Ultra Star, Star Light.

StarGuide Digital Networks Inc., 750 W. John Carpenter Fwy., Suite 700, Irving, TX, 75039. Phone: (972) 581-2000. Fax: (972) 581-2001. Web Site:www.starguidedigital.com E-mail: hq@starguidedigital.com

High speed internet networking of digital audio, video & web. Software, satellite, terrestrial & DSL systems.

Storeel Corp., Box 80523, Atlanta, GA, 30366. Phone: (770) 458-3280. Fax: (770) 457-5585. E-mail: reely@mindspring.com Web Site:www.storeel.com Michael Valerio, gen sls mgr; Elizabeth Galvin, VP sls.

Space-efficient storage for all formats of tape & film; double-drive systems for longer lengths; set-up trucks; CD storage.

StorerTV Inc., 1361 W. Towne Square Rd., Mequon, WI, 53092. Phone: (262) 241-9005. Fax: (262) 241-9036. E-mail: storer@storertv.com Web Site:www.storertv.com Peter Storer, pres; Doug Knight, sls VP.

SIMS-Multi-Station/Network program rights, scheduling & finance system. Manages non-linear rights and scheduling as well.

Strand Lighting Inc., 6603 Darin Way, Cypress, CA, 90630. Phone: (714) 230-8200. Fax: (714) 899-0042. E-mail: sales@strandlight.com Web Site:www.strandlight.com Peter Rogers, mktg dir.

New YorkNY , 928 Broadway. Phone:

Studio & remote lighting, & control equipment.

Strata Marketing Inc., 30 West Monroe, Suite 1900, Chicago, IL, 60603. Phone: (312) 222-1555. Fax: (312) 222-2510. E-mail: rsparks@stratag.com Web Site:www.stratag.com Bruce W. Johnson, pres; Peter Nason, dir mktg.

TV, radio & media ratings analysis. Microsoft Windows-based software systems for cable systems & bcst TV stns.

Strong International, c/o Ballantyne of Omaha Inc., 4350 McKinley St., Omaha, NE, 68112. Phone: (402) 453-4444. Fax: (402) 453-7238. Web Site:www.ballantyne-omaha.com John P. Wilmers, pres; Ray Boegner, sr VP.

35/70mm projection equipment, Xenon lamphouse systems, platters, Xenon bulbs, follow spotlights.

Structural System Technology Inc., 6867 Elm St., Suite 200, McLean, VA, 22101. Phone: (703) 356-9765. Fax: (703) 448-0979.E-mail: contact@sst-towers.com Web Site:www.sst-towers.com Kaveh Mehrnama, pres; Monty Beck, VP field opns; Bryan Burton, VP.

Structural engrg studies, analysis, design, modifications, inspections, fabrication, erection of towers & antenna.

Studio Technologies Inc., 5520 W. Touhy Ave., Skokie, IL, 60077. Phone: (847) 676-9177. Fax: (847) 982-0747.E-mail: stisales@studio-tech.com Web Site:www.studio-tech.com Gordon Kapes, pres; Carrie Gage, dir mktg.

Microphone pre-amplifiers, stereo simulators & recognition units, telephone & hard-wired IFB communications systems on-air announcer's consoles. Accessories for digital audio workstations.

Studio Technology, 529 Rosedale Rd., Suite 103, Kennett Square, PA, 19348. Phone: (610) 925-2785. Fax: (610) 925-2787.E-mail: sales@studiotechnology.com Web Site:www.studiotechnology.com Vince Fiola, CEO/owner.

Bcst furniture, design & instal svcs.

Summit Software Systems Inc., 777 Main Ave., 217, Durango, CO, 81301. Phone: (800) 771-1824.E-mail: sales@summitsoft Web Site:www.summitsoftware.com Paul Adams, pres.

PC-based traf, sls, billing, accounts receivable, accounts payable, payroll & gen ledger for single or multi-stns & single or multi-users.

Sundance Digital Inc., 545 E. John Carpenter Fwy., Suite 200, Irving, TX, 75062. Phone: (972) 444-8442. Fax: (972) 444-8450.E-mail: sales@sundig.com Web Site:www.sundancedigital.com Jacque Durocher, gen mgr; Rick Stora, product mgr.

Sundance Digital a part of Avid is an award-winning leader in TV automation solutions for individual & multistation bcstrs.

Superior Satellite Engineers Inc., 1743 Middle Rd., Columbia Falls, MT, 59912. Phone: (406) 257-9590. Fax: (406) 257-9599.E-mail: superior@superiorsatelliteusa.com Web Site:www.superiorsatelliteusa.com Steve Catlett, VP engrg; Jackie Williams, exec VP.

SSE8345 4.5M fixed or Navigator steerable antennas, multiple satellite and motorized feed systems and more for all satellite access needs.

Superior Tower Services Inc., 5757 FM 1696, Iola, TX, 77861. Phone: (936) 394-9925. Phone: (800) 306-4504. Fax: (936) 394-4020. Edward Carter, pres.

For all your tower & antenna needs: antenna, transmission line analysis, emergency repairs, two way, microwave, cellular, AM/FM, installations, tower erections, inspections, & maintenance.

Superscope Technologies Professionals, 2640 White Oaks Circle, Suite A, Aurora, IL, 60504. Phone: (630) 820-4800. Fax: (630) 820-8103. Web Site:www.superscopetechnologies.com Fred Hackendahl, pres.

Products include portable cassette recorders, single & dual cassette recorders, CD players, multi-track recorders, compact recorders, portable, & rackmount.

Swager Communications Inc., Box 656, Fremont, IN, 46737. Phone: (260) 495-2515. Fax: (260) 495-4205.E-mail: bswager@dmci.net Web Site:www.swager.com Dan J. Swager, pres; Lee Swager, VP; Tim Swager, sec/treas.

Designs, fabricates, installs & maintains AM/FM, TV/CATV & microwave communication towers.

Swintek Enterprises Inc., 965 Shulman Ave., Santa Clara, CA, 95050. Phone: (408) 727-4889. Phone: (408) 727-7544. Fax: (408) 727-3025.E-mail: ssales@swintek.com Web Site:www.swintek.com William P. Swintek, pres.

18 ch wireless intercom, 1 w IFB with wireless EAR piece receiver, complete linear headsets.

Switchcraft Inc., 5555 N. Elston Ave., Chicago, IL, 60630. Phone: (773) 792-2700. Fax: (773) 792-2129. Web Site:www.switchcraft.com Keith A. Bandolik, pres; David K. Dunmead, exec VP.

Offers a variety of products including audio patchbays, connectors, adapters, jacks & plugs, and video patchbays.

Symetrix Inc., 6408 216th St. S.W., Mountlake Terrace, WA, 98043. Phone: (425) 778-7728. Fax: (425) 778-7727.E-mail: symetrix@symetrixaudio.com Web Site:www.symetrixaudio.com Dane Butcher, pres; Paul Roberts, sls dir.

Digital & analog audio signal processing.

Symmetricom, 3750 Westwind Blvd, Santa Rosa, CA, 95403. Phone: (707) 528-1230. Fax: (707) 527-6640. Web Site:www.symmetricom.com Thomas Steipp, pres/CEO; Gurdip Jande, sr VP mktg; Paul Chermak, exec VP/ global sls & support.

Time & frequency receivers traceable to NIST & USNO. Complete line of time code instrumentation.

Symmetricom, 2300 Orchard Pkwy., San Jose, CA, 95131. Phone: (949) 598-7500. Fax: (949) 598-7524. Erik Van derKay, pres; Bob Krist, VP.

IrvineCA . Datum-Irvine, 3 Parker. Phone:

AustinTX . Datum-Austin, Box 14766. Phone:

Time code generators, readers, displays, encoders, search systems, distribution amplifiers, transmitters & receivers; design & manufacture of precision frequency products & timing instruments.

Syntellect Inc., 16610 N. Black Canyon Hwy., Suite 100, Phoenix, AZ, 85053. Phone: (800) 788-9733. Phone: (800) 347-9907. Fax: (770) 587-0589. Web Site:www.syntellect.com Steve Dodenhoff, pres; J.R. Sloan, VP mktg.

PhoenixAZ , 20401 N. 29th Ave. Phone:

ARUs for automated customer svc, ANI svcs for PPV order processing, predictive dialing systems for telemarketing & collections.

SyntheSys Research Inc., 3475-D Edison Way, Menlo Park, CA, 94025. Phone: (650) 364-1853. Fax: (650) 364-5716.E-mail: info@synthesysresearch.com Web Site:www.synthesysresearch.com Jim Waschura, pres; John Ryan, gen sls mgr.

SyntheSys is a leading manufacturer of test & measurement specializing in serial digital video analyzers for SDI & high definition.

System Associates, Box 5925, Glendale, AZ, 85312. Phone: (866) 937-0209. Fax: (866) 435-0160.E-mail: video@systemsassociates.com Web Site:www.systemsassociates.tv Mike Ferguson, pres.

Used bcst TV equipment, to buy and sell, appraisals, auctions

Systems Wireless Ltd., 555 Herndon Pkwy., Ste. 135, Herndon, VA, 20170. Phone: (703) 471-7887. Fax: (703) 437-1107. Bill Sien, sls.

Sls, service & rental of wireless microphones, wireless intercom, wireless listening devices, wireless video & Clear Com cabled intercom systems.

T

TAI Audio, 5828 Old Winter Garden Rd., Orlando, FL, 32835. Phone: (407) 296-9959. Phone: (800) 486-6444. Fax: (407) 648-1352.E-mail: sales@taiaudio.com Web Site:www.taiaudio.com Joseph Guzzi, pres.

Rental, sls & svc of professional audio for film, video, TV & postproduction. Specializes in wireless communication equipment.

TALX Corp., 1850 Borman Ct., St. Louis, MO, 63146. Phone: (314) 214-7000. Fax: (314) 214-7588. Web Site:www.talx.com William W. Canfield, gen mgr; Michael E. Smith, VP/gen mgr.

Interactive communications; more specific svc; Interactive voice response, Interactive web, employment verification (work # for everyone) & Outsource svc.

TC Group Americas Inc., (Formerly Tannoy North America Inc.). 335 Gage Ave., Suite 1, Kitchener, ON, N2M 5E1. Canada. Phone: (519) 745-1158. Fax: (519) 745-2364.E-mail: inquiries@tcgroup-americas.com Web Site:htt://www.tcgroup-americas.com/ Marc Bertrand, CEO.

Brands offered: Tannoy, Lab gruppen, TC electronic, TC Helicon, dynaudio acoustic & Linn.

TC Electronic, 5706 Corsa Ave., Suite 107, Westlake Village, CA, 91362. Phone: (818) 665-4900. Fax: (818) 665-4901.E-mail: info@tcus.com Web Site:www.tcbroadcast.com John Maier, CEO; Ed Simeone, chmn.

Digital compressor/limiter expander, digital signal processors, DTV audio processors & high-resolution digital delays.

T-C Specialties Co., Box 192, Coudersport, PA, 16915. Phone: (814) 274-8060. Phone: (800) 458-6074. Fax: (814) 274-0690.E-mail: tcsmail@adelphia.net Web Site:www.tcspecialties.com Daniel C. Major, pres; Bill Crown, VP production; Judi Tucker, sec; Mike Harris, VP opns.

Coupon billing systems & related forms; large volume dir mail inkjetting, presort/barcoding mailing

TDK Electronics Corp., 3190 E. Miraloma Ave., Anaheim, CA, 92806. Phone: (714) 238-7900. Fax: (714) 632-1868. Web Site:www.tdk.com Hajime Sawabe, chmn/CEO; Takehiro Kamigama, pres/COO.

TEAC America Inc., 7733 Telegraph Rd., Montebello, CA, 90640. Phone: (323) 726-0303. Fax: (323) 727-7656. Web Site:www.teac.com Koichiro Nakamura, pres; Les Luzar, sr VP & sls & mktg.

Consumer audio/video & professional recording equipment, airborne video recorder, instrumentation data recorders, computer peripherals/floppy disks, tape backup & industrial optical disk recorders & playback.

TFT Inc., 1953 Concourse Dr., San Jose, CA, 95131-1708. Phone: (408) 943-9323. Fax: (408) 432-9218.E-mail: info@tftinc.com Web Site:www.tftinc.com Darryl E. Parker, VP.

Digital, analog STLs, Reciters, synchronous boosters, modulation monitors & emergency alert systems(EAS).

TOA Electronics Inc., 601 Gateway Blvd., Suite 300, South San Francisco, CA, 94080. Phone: (650) 588-2538. Fax: (650) 588-3349.E-mail: info@toaelectronics.com Allan Lamberti, sls dir; Hisayuki Okvoka, pres/CEO.

Sound, communication equipment for coml sound & audio/video industries. Manufacturer, distributor of high quality, reliable audio & security products.

TTE Inc., 11652 W. Olympic Blvd., Los Angeles, CA, 90064. Phone: (310) 478-8224. Fax: (800) 473-2791.E-mail: sls@tte.com Web Site:www.tte.com Stephen J. Sodaro, sls VP & mktg VP.

LC filters to 18 GHz, balun, matching transformers, combiners, active filters to 1 MHz. RF, microwave filters DC-18ghz & video splitters.

T.T. Technologies Inc., 2020 E. New York St., Aurora, IL, 60502. Phone: (800) 533-2078. Phone: (630) 851-8200. Fax: (630) 851-8299.E-mail: info@tttechnologies.com Web Site:www.tttechnologies.com Chris Brahler, pres; Dave Holcomb, VP.

OcalaFL , 3701 N.E. 36th Ave, Suite C. Phone:

Grundomat Pneumatic piercing tools, Grundoram pipe ramming system, Grundocrack Pneumatic pipe bursting systems & Grundoburst Static Pipe Bursting.

TWR Lighting Inc., (Division of 02 Wireless Solutions). 4300 Windfern, Suite 100, Houston, TX, 77041-0943. Phone: (713) 973-6905. Fax: (713) 973-9352. Web Site:www.twrlighting.com E-mail: info@twrlightinc.com Ken Meador, pres/CEO; Raymond Kraemer, VP sls & mktg; Jeff Huchlefeld, VP opns.

Aviation obstruction lighting manufacturer, sls & svc of low, medium, LED products & High Intensity systems.

Talk-A-Phone Co., 7530 N. Natchez Ave., Niles, IL, 60714. Phone: (773) 539-1100. Fax: (773) 539-1241.E-mail: info@talkaphone.com Web Site:www.talkaphone.com S. Shanes, exec VP; Robert Shanes, VP sls.

Intercommunication systems, ADA compliant emergency phones, ADA areas of rescue, apartment access systems.

Tamron U.S.A. Inc., 10 Austin Blvd., Commack, NY, 11725. Phone: (631) 858-8400. Fax: (631) 543-5666. Web Site:www.tamron.com E-mail: feedback@tamron.com Tak Inoue, pres; Bert Krank, VP; John VanSteenberg, rgnl mgr; Stacie Errera, chief mktg off; Gregg Maniaci, eastern sls mgr; Keiki Warashina, gen mgr .

Lenses for 35mm SLR digital & film cameras, & CCTV lenses.

TANDBERG Television Inc., 4500 River Green Pkwy., Duluth, GA, 30096. Phone: (678) 812-6300. Fax: (678) 812-6400. Web Site:www.tandbergtv.com Staffan Pehrson, pres.

Video compression, content distribution, video on-demand solutions, content management systems, advanced advertising

Tapeswitch Corp., 100 Schmitt Blvd., Farmingdale, NY, 11735. Phone: (631) 630-0442. Fax: (631) 630-0454.E-mail: sales@tapes.com Web Site:www.tapeswitch.com Michael Steele, pres; Patrick Falbo, VP; April Sabbatini, mktg mgr.

MissionCA Phone:

FishersIN Phone:

New BernNC Phone:

FranklinTN Phone:

Safety light curtains, sensing mats, edges, ribbon switches, electronic zone controllers, sensing bumpers, safety & protection equipment.

J.A. Taylor & Associates, Box 331, Boyertown, PA, 19512-0331. Phone: (610) 754-6800. Fax: (610) 754-9766.E-mail: jataylor@broadcastassociates.com Web Site:www.broadcastassociates.com

Appraisers & brokers of TV production equipment. Serves video production companies, TV stns & financial institutions.

Teatronics/Entertainment Lighting Control, P.O. Box 508, Santa Mangarita, CA, 93453. Phone: (805) 438-4000. Fax: (805) 438-5400.E-mail: sales@teatronics.com Web Site:www.teatronics.com Gary Beckerman, exec VP.

Lighting control & power distribution systems for stage, studio & remote applications.

Tech Laboratories Inc., 955 Belmont Ave., North Haledon, NJ, 07508. Phone: (973) 427-5333. Fax: (973) 427-5455.E-mail: corporate@techlabs.com Web Site:www.techlabsinc.com Bernard M. Ciongoli, pres; Earl M. Bjorndal, VP.

Rotary switches; electrical/electronic subcontract, attenuators, transformers, pcb assembly & infrared security systems.

TECH-SA-PORT, Box 5372, 120 S. Whitfield St., Pittsburgh, PA, 15206-0372. Phone: (412) 661-1620. Phone: (800) 543-2233.E-mail: tech-sa-port@juno.com Web Site:www.tech-sa-port.com Lewis J. Scheinman, pres.

Computer & electronic equipment cleaning supplies, including lint-free wipers, contamination-free chemicals, & spray dusters. All types of wiping materials.

Technet Systems Group, (A Division of Steve Vanni Associates Inc). Box 422, Auburn, NH, 03032. Phone: (603) 483-5365. Fax: (603) 483-0512.E-mail: svanni@technetsystems.com Web Site:www.technetsystems.com Steve Vanni, pres.

Bcst equipment supplier & distributor for radio & TV, specializing in complete turnkey packages including planning, design, equipment, instal, towers & FCC licensing.

Techni-Tool Inc., 1547 N. Trooper Rd., PO Box 1117, Worcester, PA, 19490-1117. Phone: (800) 832-4866. Phone: (610) 825-4990. Fax: (610) 828-5623. Fax: (800) 854-8665.E-mail: sales@techni-tool.com Web Site:www.techni-tool.com/comm Paul Weiss, pres; David Weitner, VP mktg; Steven Weiss, exec VP; Michael T. Ryan, VP sls.

Master distributor of hand tools, kits & cases, test equipment, supplies & safety products for the Communications Field Techician working with fiber optic, coaxial & twisted pair cabling. As well as for the bench tech working on electronics production/repair & cable assemby.

Technologies for Worship, 3891 Holburn Rd., Queensville, ON, L0G 1R0. Canada. Phone: (905) 473-9822. Fax: (905) 473-9928.E-mail: bc@tfwm.com Web Site:www.tfwm.com Shelagh Rogers, pres; Barry Cobus, VP; Kevin Rogers-Cobus, exec editor.

Trade magazine & tech directory for houses of worship involved in audio, AV, bcst, computers, film, video & music. Owner of "Inspiration Conferences & Expositions."

Tekskil Industries Inc., #102-998 Harbourside Dr., North Vancouver, BC, V7P 3T2. Canada. Phone: (604) 985-2250. Fax: (604) 985-2248.E-mail: tekskilprompters2008@tekskil.com Web Site:www.tekskil.com John Veenstra, pres.

Manufacturer of video, speech & computer prompting equipment.

Tektronix Inc., 14200 S.W. Karl Braun Dr., Beaverton, OR, 97077. Phone: (800) 835-9433. Phone: (503) 627-7111. Fax: (503) 627-6108. Web Site:www.tektronix.com Jim Lico, pres; Arif Kareem, VP/gen mgr.

Telcom Research, 3375 N. Service Rd., A7, Burlington, ON, L7N 3G2. Canada. Phone: (905) 336-2450. Fax: (905) 336-1487.E-mail: dougl@tecomresearch.com Web Site:www.timecode.com Douglas Finch, pres; Brian Weppler, VP.

SMPTE/EBU time code generators, readers; character inserters, LTC-VITC & VITC-LTC trans. Logging/offline/EDL software.

Tele-Measurements Inc., 145 Main Ave., Clifton, NJ, 07014-1078. Phone: (973) 473-8822. Phone: (800) 223-0052. Fax: (973) 473-0521.E-mail: tmcorp@aol.com Web Site:www.tele-measurements.com William E. Endres, pres; W. Chris Endres, gen mgr .

Bcst video equipment, tapes TV systems, teleconferencing, maintenance support, CCTV & rentals, distance learning.

Telecast Fiber Systems Inc., 102 Grove St., Worcester, MA, 01605. Phone: (508) 754-4858. Fax: (508) 752-1520.E-mail: sales@telecast-fiber.com Web Site:www.telecast-fiber.com Richard A. Cerny, pres; Eugene E. Baker, VP; Joseph Commare, VP mktg & intl sls.

Mill ValleyCA , 835 Autumn Ln. Phone:
NapervilleIL , 16 Rock River Ct. Phone:
SacoME , 280 Ferry Rd. Phone:
Fuquay-VarinaNC , 3009 Bentwillow Dr. Phone:
Fiber-optic video & audio systems for TV bcst production.

Telecrafter Products, 12687 W. Cedar Dr., Suite 100, Lakewood, CO, 80228-2031. Phone: (303) 986-0086. Fax: (303) 986-1042.E-mail: mail@telecrafter.com Web Site:www.telecrafter.com

Drop installation products for broadband telecommunications delivery svc, including cable clips, cablemakers, cable guard, house boxes, fitting savers, & more.

Telemetrics Inc., 6 Leighton Pl., Mahwah, NJ, 07430. Phone: (201) 848-9818. Fax: (201) 848-9819. Web Site:www.telemetricsinc.com Anthony C. Cuomo, pres; Anthony E. Cuomo, mgr.

Camera pan, tilt systems & triax camera control systems.

Teleplex Inc., (Alford Division). 4801 Industrial Pkwy., Indianapolis, IN, 46226. Phone: (317) 895-8800. Fax: (317) 895-2900. Tom L. Fitch, pres/CEO; Lois E. Clark, VP.

Produces precision electronics, components, FM stn combiners, custom FM radio antenna arrays, TV antenna systems, & HDTV monitor antennas. Supports all Alford products & antenna products.

Telescript Inc., 445 Livingston St., Norwood, NJ, 07648. Phone: (201) 767-6733. Fax: (201) 784-0323.E-mail: info@telescript.com Web Site:www.telescript.com John McGrath, mgng dir; Andrew Wischmeyer, sls & natl business dev dir.

AustinTX . Telescript West, 7801 N. Lamar Blvd. Phone:
IBM & compatibles prompting programs & equipment. Lightweight, high-resolution 12" & 17" monitor prompters. Flat panel prompters, window based prompting software for bcst & video productions applications, comprehensive line of LCD prompters.

Teletech Inc., 38235 Executive Drive, Westland, MI, 48185. Phone: (734) 641-2300. Fax: (734) 641-2323. Web Site:www.teletech-inc.com Keith Johnson, VP; Todd Osment, field svc mgr; Richard Humphrey, sr engr; Kevin Beltramo, field engr.

Facility construction, antenna instal for AM, FM, TV, LPTV & microwave; antenna site mgmt; FCC applicacations; EME studies; Aeronautical studies.

teletech.ca, 3-211 Telson Rd., Markham, ON, L3R 1E7. Canada. Phone: (905) 475-5646. Fax: (905) 475-5684.E-mail: admin@teletech.ca Web Site:www.teletech.ca Jack Kirkpatrick, pres.

Total bcst, postproduction, audio & video sls, service, & rentals of equipment & supplies.

Television Engineering Corp., 2647 Rock Hill Industrial Ct., Saint Louis, MO, 63144. Phone: (314) 961-2800. Fax: (314) 961-2808. Web Site:www.tvengineering.com Jack Vines Jr., gen sls mgr; Jack Vines Sr., design engr.

Manufacturer of news vans, satellite vehicles, Eagle Eye camera, IFB controller & turnkey systems.

Television Equipment Assoc. Inc./Matthey, Box 404, Brewster, NY, 10509-0404. Phone: (845) 278-0960. Fax: (845) 278-0964. Bill Pegler, pres; Joseph Tocidlowski, mgr.

Serial digital interface products, NTSC/PAL Decoders, analog & digital DAs, video & pulse delays, video filters, A/D & D/A converters, headsets, serial digital/Fiberoptic links, Routing switches for digital video and radio.

Telex Communications Inc., 12000 Portland Ave. S., Burnsville, MN, 55337. Phone: (952) 884-4051. Fax: (952) 884-0043.E-mail: prosound@telex.com Web Site:www.telex.com Ned Jackson, CEO.

BurbankCA , 2550 Hollywood Way, Suite 207. Phone:
Wired & wireless microphones; headphones/headsets; wired & wireless intercoms; audio duplicators/copiers.

TELLABS, 1415 W. Diehl Rd., Naperville, IL, 60563. Phone: (630) 798-8800. Fax: (630) 798-2000. Web Site:www.tellabs.com

Abingdon, Oxfordshire, 29 The Quandrant. Phone:
HauppaugeNY , 60 Commerce Dr. Phone:
Teleconferencing systems, digital echo cancellers, data over voice multiplexers, signaling systems, video conferencing, audio systems.

Telos Systems, 2101 Superior Ave., Cleveland, OH, 44114. Phone: (216) 241-7225. Fax: (216) 241-4103. Web Site:www.telos-systems.com Steve Church, pres/CEO; Frank Foti, pres; Denny Sanders, mng dir; Michael Dosch, pres.

Telos Systems, is the leading global manufacturer of coded audio, ISDN, telephone interface and networked audio products for talk-shows, teleconferencing, audio production, remote broadcasts, and intercom applications.

Tenco Tower Co., 9647 Folsom Blvd., Sacramento, CA, 95827-1326. Phone: (916) 638-8833. Fax: (916) 366-7383.E-mail: donald.tenn@towerguys.com Donald Joseph Tenn, pres/CEO.

Instal, maintenance, sls of towers, antennas, hardware for the bcst, cable & communications industry.

Tentel, 333 Industrial Dr. #4, Placerville, CA, 95667. Phone: (530) 344-0183. Fax: (530) 344-0186. Web Site:www.tentel.com E-mail: info@tentel.com John Chavers, gen mgr .

Texas Electronics Inc., Box 7225, Dallas, TX, 75209. Phone: (214) 631-2490. Fax: (214) 631-4218.E-mail: info@texaselectronics.com Web Site:www.texaselectronics.com Carol Westlund, pres; Jane Hansen, VP; Jason Burson, sls.

Manufacturer of meteorological instruments & controls.

Texscan MSI, 2210 W. Alexander Street Ste. A, Salt Lake City, UT, 84119. Phone: (801) 956-0000. Fax: (801) 956-0750. Web Site:www.texscan.com Leonard J. Fabiano, pres.

Character generators, digital, analog commercial insertion systems, audio/video playback systems, weather data svc, multimedia graphics production systems & VCR controllers.

Thales Broadcast & Multimedia S.A., 1 rue de l'Hautil, Z.A. les Bountries, Conflans Sainte Honorine Cedex, 78702. France. Phone: 1 34 90 31 00. Fax: 1 34 90 30 00. Web Site:www.thomsongrassvalley.con Bill Patrizio, pres; Jeff Rosica, sr VP & Thomson's Bcst.

Handling everything from video, audio to data signals & control systems.

Thales Electron Devices, (Formerly Thales Components Corp.). 2 rue Marcel Dassault, Velizy Villacoublay, 78141. France. Phone: 33 (0) 1 3070 3500. Fax: 33 (0) 1 3070 3535. Web Site:www.thalesgroup.com

TotowaNJ . Thales Components Corp, 40G Commerce Way. Phone:
Power triodes & tetrodes, cavities, klystrons travel wave tubes & I.O.T.s.

The Tape Company, 845 N. Church Ct., Elmhurst, IL, 60126. Phone: (925) 803-1440. Phone: (630) 834-3113. Fax: (630) 758-0930.E-mail: jlittlefield@nationalvideotape.com Web Site:thetapecompany.com Mike Cullen, pres.

SeattleWA , 1471 Elliott Ave. W. Phone:
Custom length VHS cassettes; Sony, Fuji, Maxell Panasonic video & data media products. CD/DVD printing & duplication.

Theatre Service & Supply Corp., 1792 Union Ave., Baltimore, MD, 21211. Phone: (410) 467-1225. Fax: (410) 467-1289.E-mail: sales@stage-n-studio.com Web Site:www.stage-n-studio.com Richard A. Antisdel, pres; Jacauelin Keleman, sls.

Manufacturer of studio, theatrical curtains, track systems, distributor of lighting & theatrical hardware.

Theatrical Services Inc., 128 S. Washington, Wichita, KS, 67202. Phone: (316) 263-4415. Fax: (316) 263-9927. Web Site:www.theatricalservices.com E-mail: tsi@theatricalservices.com Stephen A. Wolf, pres.

Manufacturers & distributors of studio lighting & control equipment, studio cycloramas, curtains & track.

Thermodyne Cases, 1841 Business Pkwy., Ontario, CA, 91761. Phone: (909) 923-9945. Fax: (909) 923-7505. Web Site:www.thermodyne-online.com Gary S. Ackerman, pres.

Reusable shipping cases; rack-mounted operating cases. Provides protection for all electronic equipment during transit.

Thomas & Betts, 700 Thomas Ave., Saint-Jean-sur Richelieu, PQ, J2X 2M9. Canada. Phone: (450) 347-5318. Fax: (450) 347-1976. Web Site:www.tnb.com Dominic Pileggi, chmn/CEO; Michael Kenney, pres.

Manufacturer of quality products for aerial construction & subscriber instal hardware for the Cable TV & telephone industry.

Equipment Manufacturers and Distributors Alphabetical Index

Thomas & Betts Corp., 8155 T&B Blvd., Memphis, TN, 38125. Phone: (800) 816-7809. Phone: (901) 252-8000. Fax: (800) 816-7810. Fax: (901) 252-1354.E-mail: elec_custserv@tnb.com Web Site:www.tnb.com

Manufacturer of Poleline hardware aerial & drop systems, fiber-optic hand holes, MMDS antenna mounting hardware.

James Thomas Engineering Inc., 10240 Caneel Dr., Knoxville, TN, 37931. Phone: (865) 692-3060. Fax: (865) 692-9020.E-mail: salesus@jthomaseng.com Web Site:www.jthomaseng.com Mike Garl, pres.

Manufacturer of structural aluminum truss, towers & ground supported roof systems. Truss range includes: superlite, supertruss, gen purpose truss, ground support towers, speaker support towers, truss circles & custom fabricated structures. Also manufactures spun aluminum PAR fixtures, pre-wired lighting bars, spot baks & accessories. Distributor of CEEP Multipin connectors, Multicable, Kee Safety pipe fittings, CM Chain Hoists & rigging accessories.

Thomson, (formerly Thales Broadcast & Multimedia Inc.). 104 Feeding Hills Rd., Southwick, MA, 01077. Phone: (413) 998-1100. Fax: (413) 569-0679.E-mail: joseph.turbolski@thomson.net Web Site:www.thomson.net Richard Fiore, sr dir transmission & mobility; Joseph Turbolski, dir/sls opns.

Thomson manafuctes, markets equipment sytems & solutions in the fields of terrestrial transmission, digital videl processing & multimedia distribution.

Thomson Broadcast & Media Solutions, Box 599000, Nevada City, CA, 95959-5900. Phone: (800) 824-5127. Fax: (530) 478-3166. Web Site:www.thomsongrassvalley.com Tim Thorsteinson, pres/CEO; Russ Johnson, the Americas sls; Stephen Wong, Pacific rgn sls.

Video servers/disk recorders, media platforms, video production centers (switchers), signal mgmt systems (routers, modular), DVEs & HDTV equipment.

Thomson, Inc, (RCA/GE), 10330 N. Meridian St., Indianapolis, IN, 46290. Phone: (317) 587-3000. Fax: (317) 587-6708.E-mail: dave.arland@thomson.net Web Site:www.rca.com Richard Huser, exec VP.

Boulogne, Cedex. Thomson S.A. (parent co.), 46 Quai Alphonse Le Gallo. Phone:

Manufactures mkt audio, video communications & accessories products.

Thomson Multi Media, 2300 S. Decker Lake Blvd., Salt Lake City, UT, 84119. Phone: (801) 972-8000. Fax: (801) 972-6304. Web Site:www.thomsonmultimedia.com Martin Fry, CEO.

WyomissingPA , 13 Kevin Ct. Phone:

Thomson Reuters, (formerly Reuters America Inc.). 3 Times Square, New York, NY, 10036. Phone: (646) 223-4000. Web Site:www.thomsonreuters.com Chris Ahearn, pres.

OttawaON Canada, 165 Sparks St., Booth Bldg. Phone: TorontoON Canada, Standard Life Centre, 121 King St. W., 20th Fl. Phone:

MontrealPQ Canada, 2020 Rue Universite, Suite 1020. Phone:

Los AngelesCA , 445 S. Figueroa , Suite 2100. Phone: WashingtonDC , 1333 H St. N.W, Suite 410. Phone: ChicagoIL , 311 S. Wacker Dr, Suite 1100. Phone: Kansas CityMO , 4800 Main. Phone:

Supplier of natl, world, business news, info to media & professionals.

360 Systems, 31355 Agoura Road, Westlake Village, CA, 91361-4610. Phone: (818) 991-0360. Fax: (818) 991-1360.E-mail: info@360systems.com Web Site:www.360systems.com Robert Easton, pres; Phil Cox, exec VP.

Image Server Maxx Video & Graphics servers in standard and High Definition, Time Delay servers, DigiCart/E, Instant Replay2 and Short/Cut audio editors and players.

3M, 3M Product Information Center, St. Paul, MN, 55144-1000. Phone: (651) 737-6501. Phone: (800) 3m-helps. Fax: (800) 713-6329.E-mail: innovation@mmm.com Web Site:www.3m.com George Buckley, pres; Robert MacDonald, mktg dir.

Fault locators; cable & cabling equipment & supplies; Post-it notes & flags; Telephony: copper & fiber optic networks; Vikuiti display enhancement films; splicing kts; volition fiber optics; electrical tubing, tapes, terminations & connectors.

The Tiffen Company, 90 Oser Ave., Hauppauge, NY, 11788. Phone: (631) 273-2500. Phone: (800) 645-2522. Fax: (631) 273-2557. Web Site:www.tiffen.com Steve Tiffen, pres/CEO; Hilary Araujo, VP mktg; Jeff Cohen, VP mfg; Michael Cannatta, COO.

Photographic filters, lens accessories for motion picture, still photography, digital video, Davis & Sanford tripods, Domke Bags, support systems; steadicam camera stabilizing systems.

Time Logic Inc., 1914 Palomar Oaks Way, Suite 150, Carlsbad, CA, 92008. Phone: (760) 517-0445. Fax: (760) 431-1351.E-mail: jiml@timelogic.com Web Site:www.timelogic.com Rick MacDonald, pres/CEO.

Automation systems for TV bcstrs & radio stns. Custom software dev for Tektronix Profile disks, HDTV time delay systems, using disk or tape.

Time Manufacturing Co., Box 20368, Waco, TX, 76702-0368. Phone: (254) 399-2100. Fax: (254) 399-2651.E-mail: renees@timemfg.com Web Site:www.timemfg.com Amber Pierce, mktg mgr.

Truck mounted aerial lifts ranging from 29' to 210' in height.

Times Fiber Communications Inc., 358 Hall Ave., Wallingford, CT, 06492. Phone: (203) 265-8500. Fax: (203) 265-8422. Web Site:www.timesfiber.com Timothy F. Cohane, pres/COO; Stan VonFeldt, VP sls; Chris Huffman, dir mktg.

RenfrewON Canada, Box 430. Phone: PhoenixAZ , Box 14975. Phone: ChathamVA , Box 119A, Rt. 2. Phone: Coaxial, twisted pair composite cables for broadband, cellular/PCS applications, semiflex, svc entry, drop cables & connectors.

Tinsley Laboratory Inc., (A division of Silicon Valley Group). 4040 Lakeside Dr., Richmond, CA, 94806. Phone: (510) 222-8110. Fax: (510) 223-4534. Dan Desmond, pres.

Gyrozoom image stabilizing lens, GX3 integrated CCD camera/stabilizing system.

Toner Cable Equipment Inc., 969 Horsham Rd., Horsham, PA, 19044. Phone: (215) 675-2053. Phone: (800) 523-5947. Fax: (215) 675-7543.E-mail: info@tonercable.com Web Site:www.tonercable.com Robert L. Toner, pres; B.J. Toner, VP.

Berinsfield, Oxfordshire, England United Kingdom. UK Ltd., Unit 9 Berinsfield Business Park, Tower Industrial Estate, Fane Dr. Phone:

International distributor & manufacturer of a complete line of cable TV & wireless cable equipment.

Torpey Time, 15 Brimwood Blvd., Unit 5, Scarborough, ON, M1v 1E1. Canada. Phone: (416) 298-7788. Phone: (800) 387-6141. Fax: (416) 298-7789.E-mail: torpey@attglobal.net Web Site:www.torpeytime.com Bob Torpey, pres.

Master clock systems, digital & analog slave clocks, timers, video time & temperature equipment.

Toshiba America Consumer Products, 1420 Toshiba Dr., Lebanon, TN, 37087. Phone: (615) 444-8501. Fax: (615) 443-3810. Web Site:www.toshiba.com Yoshirio Matsumoto, past pres; Jodi Sally, VP mktg.

WayneNJ , 82 Totowa Rd. Phone:

HDTV products: HD-VCR (Analog-UniHi), HD monitor (projection & CRT), NTSC to HDTV upconverter, HD-CCD color camera, HD horizon system.

Tower Innovations, (A Dielectric Company). 2855 Hwy. 261, Newburgh, IN, 47630. Phone: (812) 853-0595. Phone: (800) 664-8222. Fax: (812) 853-6652.E-mail: towers@towerinnovations.net Web Site:www.towerinnovations.net David Nicholson, exec VP, COO; Melissa Nicholson, mktg.

Manufacture towers for bcst, (up to 2000'), cellular & PCS Communications Innovative engrg solutions, fabrication, construction planning, tower erection & turnkey systems.

Tower Inspection Inc., Box 709, Muskogee, OK, 74402-0709. Phone: (918) 683-8915. Fax: (918) 683-0888.E-mail: sales@towerinspection.com Web Site:www.towerinspection.com Barry R. Bayless, pres; Gary G. Lehman, VP.

Inspection svcs during construction; maintenance inspection, painting, repairs of radio, microwave & TV towers.

Tower Network Services, 2009 Ranch Rd. 620 N., Suite 710, Austin, TX, 78734. Phone: (512) 266-6200. Fax: (512) 266-6210. Web Site:www.towernetwork.com

Svc tower, antenna. RF testing & tower structural analysis. Tower elevator repair and upgrading.

Towers-R-Us, Box 1255, Waycross, GA, 31502. Phone: (912) 283-6317. Fax: (912) 283-6318.E-mail: towersrus2008@yahoo.com Grant Balwanz, pres; Velvet Beard, CEO &owner.

Design, engr, fabricate, erect, maintian & paint high radio towers.

Transcom Corp., Box 26744, Elkins Park, PA, 19027. Phone: (215) 938-7304. Fax: (215) 938-7361.E-mail: transcom@fmamtv.com Web Site:www.fmamtv.com Martin Cooper, pres.

Huntington ValleyPA , 2655 Philmont Ave, Suite 200. Phone:

New digital (8VSB/DVB-T/H), angle TV transmitters, microwave links, antenna, cable & select used TV, AM, FM transmitters.

Transcrypt International, 3900 N.W. 12th St., Suite 200, Lincoln, NE, 68521. Phone: (800) 228-0226. Massoud Safavi, COO.

Technological assst for installation, application in all types & brands of land mobile radios. Transcrypt ensures you the best value in the industry

Transit and Rail Design Inc., (formerly Railway Systems Design, Inc.). Valley Forge Corporate Center, 1010 Adams Ave., Audubon, PA, 19403-2402. Phone: (610) 650-7730. Fax: (610) 650-8190. Web Site:www.rsdconsulting.com Walter J. Clarke, ptnr; Bob Dietz, CEO; Esther McGinnis, opns mgr.

Consulting engrs, tower engrg, design & construction mgmt.

Transtector Systems Inc., 10701 N. Airport Rd., Hayden, ID, 83835. Phone: (800) 882-9110. Phone: (208) 772-8515. Fax: (208) 762-6133.E-mail: sales@transtector.com Web Site:www.transtector.com Shawn Thompson, pres; David Stimmel, VP finance; Linda Johnson, mktg mgr; James E. Harless, VP opns.

Transient overvoltage protective devices, power quality consulting svcs; college-accredited, power-quality assurance education courses.

Transvision/Vision Accomplished Inc., 550 Maulhardt Ave., Oxnard, CA, 93030. Phone: (805) 981-8740. Fax: (805) 981-8738.E-mail: info@txvision.com Web Site:www.txvision.com Kimithy Vaughan, pres.

Transportable, flyaway satellite transmission; mobile/TVROs; studio/remote production & transmission mgmt.

Tribune Media Services, 333 Glen St., Glens Falls, NY, 12801. Phone: (800) 833-9581. Phone: (518) 792-9914. Fax: (518) 761-7118.E-mail: tvdata@tvdata.com Web Site:www.tvdata.com James McCormick, VP opns; Kathleen Tolstrup, VP sls; Lanna Langlois, VP finance; Ken Carter, mgng dir; John Kelleher, gen mgr .

International source for TV info. Clients include interactive on-screen & on-line guides, nwsprs, print publications, cable companies, telephone companies, rsch organizations, producers, syndicators of TV programs & advertisers.

Trident Media Group/ Spector Entertainment Group Inc., 2441 Impala Dr., Carlsbad, CA, 92008. Phone: (760) 438-9080. Fax: (760) 438-0968. Eric M. Spector, exec VP; Evan M. Spector, pres.

International audio, video, data & telephone communications svcs between United States/Canada & Mexico/Latin America; private TV networks; 12 C-band uplinks; teleports; satellite space segment; encryption; organization svcs; closed circuit TV & security systems.

Trilogy Communications Inc., 2910 Hwy. 80 E., Pearl, MS, 39208. Phone: (601) 932-4461. Phone: (800) 874-5649. Fax: (601) 939-6637.E-mail: info@trilogycoax.com Web Site:www.trilogycoax.com Sidney Shinn Lee, chmn/pres; John Kaye, vice chmn; Grace Lee, exec VP; Bill Lee, VP; Jim Oldham, sls dir; Fei Wei, Mkt. Asso.

World leading manufacturer of advanced technology coaxial cables for wireless networks for cellular, paging, PCS, SMR and in- building networking applications application, ISO-9001 certified.

Trimm Inc., 407 Railroad St., Butner, NC, 27509. Phone: (800) 298-7466. Fax: 919) 575-6200.E-mail: trimminc@frontiernet.net Web Site:www.trimminc.com Wallace Newton, pres; Will Newton, VP.

Manufacturer of fuse panel s& terminal blocks.

Trompeter Semflex, 55550 E. McDowell Rd., Mesa, AZ, 85215. Phone: (480) 985-9000. Fax: (480) 985-0334.E-mail: sales@trompeter.com Web Site:www.trompeter.com Joe Norwood, pres.

DS3 interconnection & DSX products for central office.

Tulsat/An Addvantage Technologies Co., 1221 E. Houston St., Broken Arrow, OK, 74012. Phone: (800) 331-5997. Fax: (918) 251-1138.E-mail: tulsat@tulsat.com Web Site:www.tulsat.com David Chymiak, pres; Ken Chymiak, VP; Mark Schumacher, sls mgr.

Turner Studios Field Operations, 1020 Techwood Dr., Atlanta, GA, 30318. Phone: (404) 885-4746. Fax: (404) 885-2175.E-mail: charli.whitfield@turner.com Bob McGee, dir tech opns; Scott Marks, VP; Charli Whitfield, opns mgr.

Two 53 ft expandable mobile units with or without crews; 12 cams, 9 VTRs, EVS, DVEous, Infinit & Deko; FFV Omega DDRs.

Tyco Electronics, 300 Constitution Dr., Menlo Park, CA, 94025. Phone: (650) 361-3333. Phone: (717) 564-0100. Fax: (650) 361-2288. Web Site:www.tycoelectronics.com Thomas Lynch, CEO; Dennis Conway, VP sls.

Coaxial connectors, environmental sealing products & antenna de-icers.

U

U.S. Tape & Label Corp., 2092 Westport Ctr. Dr., St. Louis, MO, 63146. Phone: (314) 824-4444. Fax: (314) 824-4400. Web Site:www.ustl.com Jim Eiseman, pres.

Custom printed bumper strips & window labels for the bcst industry. Industrial labels, direct mail printing & label-aire equipment.

U.S. Traffic & Display Solutions, 9603 John St., Santa Fe Springs, CA, 90670. Phone: (562) 923-9600. Fax: (562) 923-7555.E-mail: dsi@dsiusa.com Web Site:www.displaysolutionsinc.com

Changeable outdoor electronic adv displays.

Ultimate Precision/GKM, 200 Finn Ct., Farmingdale, NY, 11735. Phone: (631) 249-7816. Fax: (631) 777-1828.E-mail: kmerrigan@afcosystems.com Web Site:www.gkmbroadcastracks.com Michael Mallia, CEO; Gerard Becker, pres/COO.

GKM is the source for Bcst Racks & Communication Products featuring a comprehensive line of bcst racks, frames & enclosure solutions for the bcst industry. A division of Ultimate Precision Metal Products, Inc.-part of the AFCO Systems Group. Ultimate has been a recognized leader precision sheet metal mfg for over 30 years

Ultimate Support Systems Inc., 5836 Wright Dr., Loveland, CO, 80538. Phone: (800) 525-5628. Fax: (970) 776-1941.E-mail: custserv@ultimatesupport.com Web Site:www.ultimatesupport.com Mike Belitz, CEO.

Strong, lightweight speaker & lighting tripods. Microphone stands for nearly any application.

Ultimatte Corp., 20945 Plummer St., Chatsworth, CA, 91311. Phone: (818) 993-8007. Fax: (818) 993-3762. Web Site:www.ultimatte.com Reid Baker, bussiness dev; Alan Dadourian, chief engr; Lynne Sauve, pres.

Video compositing devices for comls, live bcst, production, postproduction & computerized tripod head.

Uni-Set Corp., 449 Ave. A, Rochester, NY, 14621. Phone: (585) 544-3820. Fax: (585) 544-1110.E-mail: info@unisetcorp.com Web Site:www.unisetcorp.com Ronald D. Kniffin, pres.

Modular studio staging systems for studio settings; news setting; 7 top talent tables, & UNI-CYC anywhere cyclorama.

Union Connector Co., 40 Dale St., West Babylon, NY, 11704-1104. Phone: (631) 753-9550. Fax: (631) 753-9560. Web Site:www.unionconnector.com Richard A. Wolpert, pres; Alan T. Wolpert, VP.

Electrical connectors, power distribution systems, portable power cabinets, custom switchgear, cases, carts & grip equipment.

Unique Business Systems, 1100 Colorado Ave., Santa Monica, CA, 90401. Phone: (310) 396-3929. Fax: (310) 396-6114.E-mail: pbatra@unibiz.com Web Site:www.unibiz.com Pradeep Batra, pres.

LanghornePA , 3000 Cabot Blvd. W, Suite 220E. Phone: RentTrace-asset mgmt software to track rental equipment. Handles quotes, reservation, contracts, inventory control, invoicing & accounts receivable. Completely barcode compatible.

Unisys Corp., Unisys Way, Blue Bell, PA, 19424. Phone: (215) 986-4011. Web Site:www.unisys.com Joseph W. McGrath, pres/CEO; Kevin Kern, chief info off; Nancy S. Sundheim, sr VP & gen counsel.

Cable info business systems. Unisys hardware: A1, A4, A6, A10, A12, A17 & IBM PC compatibles.

United Media Inc., 4771 E. Hunter, Anaheim, CA, 92807. Phone: (714) 777-4510. Fax: (714) 777-2434.E-mail: umi@unitedmediainc.com Web Site:www.unitedmediainc.com

United Media Inc is a developer & manufacturer which recognizes the ongoing need for high quality, affordable professional video equipment, developer of the On-Line Express non-linear editing system for Windows NT and multicom. The On-Line Express offers uncompromised digital editing, compositing, digital audio editing, titling, 2D & 3D realtime effects & sophisticated media mgmt.

United States Broadcast, 1371 Production Dr., Burlington, KY, 41005. Phone: (859) 282-1802. Fax: (859) 282-1804.E-mail: info@usbroadcast.com Web Site:www.usbroadcast.com Pete Beckett, pres.

New, used TV, audio equipment, bcst batteries & chargers.

UniVision Inc., 2801 S. Russell, Missoula, MT, 59801. Phone: (406) 721-8876. Fax: (406) 721-0810.E-mail: sales@univision-computers.com Web Site:www.univision-computers.com Jim Green, pres.

Sell & repair computers. Program software, fiberoptics & wiring.

Utah Scientific Inc., 4750 Wiley Post Way, Suite 150, Salt Lake City, UT, 84116. Phone: (800) 453-8782. Fax: (801) 537-3099.E-mail: info@utahscientific.com Web Site:www.utahscientific.com Tom Harmon, CEO; David Burland, COO.

Routing, master control switchers & control systems. Industry's best warranty-10 years!

Utility Tower Company, Box 12369, 3200 N.W. 38th, Oklahoma City, OK, 73157. Phone: (405) 946-5551. Fax: (405) 947-8466.E-mail: utctower@aol.com Gloria Nelson, pres; Ron Nelson Jr., VP; Joe James, production mgr.

Tower structures, accessories for bcstg & wireless applications; tower design, engrg analysis, turnkey instals; modifications, maintenance & inspections.

V

VCI Solutions, 146 Chestnut St., Springfield, MA, 01103. Phone: (413) 272-7200. Fax: (413) 272-7201.E-mail: sales@vcisolutions.com Web Site:www.vcisolutions.com Sarah Foss, CEO.

AustinTX . Automation Division, 2100 Kramer Ln., Suite 700.

Sales, traffic & automation solutions for the media industry. Improves work flow & increases ROI.

VSG Inc., (formerly Sifford Video Services). 1033 Elm Hill Pike, Nashville, TN, 37210. Phone: (615) 248-1010. Fax: (615) 244-5712. Web Site:www.vsginc.com Chris Ramsey, pres; Greg Shriner, sls mgr.

CD & DVD replication, CD DVD duplication, packaging & fulfillment.

V-Soft Communications, 401 Main Street, Suite 213, Cedar Falls, IA, 50613. Phone: (319) 266-8402. Fax: (319) 266-9212.E-mail: info@v-soft.com Web Site:www.v-soft.com Doug Vernier, pres; Lisa Erickson, tech support & mktg; Kate Michler, tech consultant.

Best engineering software for AM, FM, TV & general communications. Signal propagation, allocation work, path profiles, custom mapping & more.

VTECH Communications, 9590 S.W. Gemini Dr., Suite 120, Beaverton, OR, 97008-7109. Phone: (503) 643-8981. Fax: (503) 644-9887. Web Site:www.vtechphones.com Matt Ramage, sr VP; Kate Michler, tech consultant; Doug Vernier, pres; Tom Bacon, exec dir.

900 mhz cordless analog digital telephones.

Valmont Specialty Structures, (A division of Valmont Industries). 3575 25th St. S.E., Salem, OR, 97302-1190. Phone: (503) 363-9267. Phone: (800) 547-2151. Fax: (503) 363-4613.E-mail: custoinfo@microflect.com Web Site:www.valmont.com Bret Davis, plant mgr.

Towers, microwave passive repeaters, waveguide support systems & tech svcs.

Van Nostrand Radio Engineering Service, 256 Strickland Pasture Rd., Jackson, GA, 30233-4019. Phone: (770) 775-7575.E-mail: vnres@bellsouth.net W.L. Van Nostrand.

Melbourne BeachFL , Box 510458. Phone: Frequency measurements up to 26 GHz.

Vantage Lighting Inc., 175 Paul Dr., Suite E, San Rafael, CA, 94903. Phone: (800) 445-2677. Phone: (415) 507-0402. Fax: (415) 507-0502.E-mail: eight@vanltg.com Web Site:www.vanltg.com Arlene Allsman, pres; Peter Allsman, sec/treas.

Replacement lamps including stage, studio, projection audiovisual, HMI, Xenon, 3D video & laser system. Electronic ballasts for HID lighting.

Vecima Networks Inc., 4210 Commerce Circle, Victoria, BC, V87 6N6. Canada. Fax: (250) 881-1982. Fax: (250) 881-1974.E-mail: invest@vecima.com Web Site:wwwvecima.com Dr. Surinder Kumar, CEO; Dr. Hugh Wood, COO; Mr. Mike Barry, CFO.

SaskatoonSK Canada, 150 Cardinal Pl. Phone:

Designer, manufacturer & seller of products that enable broadband access to cable, wireless & telephony networks.

Veetronix Inc., Box 480, 1311 W. Pacific, Lexington, NE, 68850. Phone: (308) 324-6661. Fax: (308) 324-4985.E-mail: sales@veetronix.com Web Site:www.veetronix.com Roger Teeters, gen sls mgr.

Keyboard & panel reed switches & keycaps with in-house tooling.

Vega, (A Telex Company). 8601 Cornhusker E. Hwy., Lincoln, NE, 68505-5321. Phone: (402) 467-5324. Fax: (402) 467-3279.E-mail: vega@telex.com Web Site:www.vega-signaling.com Don Poysa, sls.

Dispatch control consoles, amplifiers & monitoring products.

Veriad, 650 Columbia St., Brea, CA, 92821. Phone: (800) 423-4643. Fax: (800) 962-0658.E-mail: info@veriad.com

Videotape & audiotape format labels, CD & DVD labels tape mgmt labels, labeling software, packaging products & production supplies.

Vermeer Manufacturing Co., 1210 Vermeer Rd. E., Pella, IA, 50219. Phone: (515) 628-3141. Phone: (888) 837-6337. Fax: (515) 621-7734.E-mail: salesinfo@vermeermfg.com Web Site:www.vermeer.com Robert Vermeer, chmn; Mary Andringa, pres/CEO.

Cable plows, trenchers, backhoes, stump cutters & hyraulic boring equipment.

Vertex Communications Corp., 1104 Energy Dr., Kilgore, TX, 75662-5536. Phone: (903) 984-7811. Fax: (903) 984-1826.E-mail: vertexrsi@gdsatcom.com Web Site:www.tripointglobal.com Gary Kanipe, VP; John Sciberras, mktg dir; Jeff Porter, gen mgr .

Beijing. Vertex Beijing Office, COFCO Plaza, Suite 411, Tower B, N. 8 Jian Guo Men Nei Ave. Phone:info@vertex.com.cn

Burntisland, Fife. Vertex International Ltd., 37 Kinghorn Rd. Phone:vertes@mbox3.singnet.com.sg

Duisburg. Vertex Antennentechnik GmbH, Baumstr. 50. Phone:info@vertexant.com

Singapore. Vertex Asia (Singapore Representative Office), 21-03 Suntec Tower One, 7 Temasek Blvd. Phone:vertex@pacific.net.sg

Santa ClaraCA . Vertex Antenna Systems LLC, 2211 Lawson Ln. Phone:bernard@tiw.com

TorranceCA . Vertex Microwave Products Inc., 3111 Fujita St. Phone:info@vertexmpi.com

West MelbourneFL . Vertex Florida Office, 255 East Dr, Suite F. Phone:vertexflorida@ibm.net

AlbuquerqueNM . Vertex-New Mexico Inc., 1255 Old Coors Rd. S.W. Phone:vnm@abq.com

State CollegePA . Vertex Electronic Products Inc., 2120 Old Gatesburg Rd. Phone:info@vertexepi.com

KilgoreTX . Vertex Antenna Products Division, 2600 N. Longview St. Phone:vapdmktg@vertexcomm.com

LongviewTX . Vertex Control Systems Division, 1915 Harrison Rd. Phone:sales@vcsd.com

RichardsonTX . Vertex Special Projects Division, 101 W. Buckingham Rd. Phone:info@vertexdallas.com

Antennas, control systems, passive microwave devices, field svcs, satcom net equipment, custom engrg solutions, SSPAs, LNAs, RF components/subsystems.

Vicon Industries Inc., 89 Arkay Dr., Hauppauge, NY, 11788. Phone: (631) 952-2288. Fax: (631) 951-9288. Web Site:www.vicon-cctv.com Ken Darby, pres/CEO; John Badke, CFO; Peter Horn, VP opns; Yacov Pshtissky, VP tech & dev; Bret McGowan, VP sls & mktg; Guy Arazi, digital products mgr.

Closed circuit TV equipment, systems for the security & surveillance industry.

VidCAD Documentation Programs (VDP Inc.), 2010 E. Lohman Ave., Suite 2Suite D9, Las Cruces, NM, 88001. Phone: (505) 522-0003. Fax: (505) 522-0009.E-mail: sales@vidcad.com Web Site:www.vidcad.com Dr.Walter Black, CEO.

VidCAD software connects your idea from diagram design & rack planning to installation, maintenance & rebuilds-on time & on budget.

Video Accessory Corp., 2450 Central Ave., Suite G, Boulder, CO, 80301. Phone: (800) 821-0426. Fax: (303) 440-8878.E-mail: vac@vac-brick.com Web Site:www.vac-brick.com Richard Frey, chief technical officer; Amy Barnes Frey, dir; Frank S. Barnes, pres; Bruce Wallingford, mktg dir.

Black Burst generators, video & audio distribution amplifiers, video line isolators, video & audio switches.

Video International Development Corp., Box 349, Locust Valley, NY, 11560. Phone: (516) 671-6765. Fax: (516) 671-6771.E-mail: info@videointernational.com Web Site:www.videointernational.com Bernd Bressel, pres.

Braunschweig Germany, X-Form Systems-Spechtweg 1,. Phone:

HD & SD Digital TV standards converters with motion compensated interpolation for bcst & industrial use as well as audio/video processors for production & post-production.

Videomagnetics Inc., 3970 Clearview Frontage Rd., Colorado Springs, CO, 80911. Phone: (719) 390-1313. Fax: (719) 390-1316.E-mail: vmi@csprings.com Web Site:www.videomagnetics.com Tony B. Korte, pres; Jane C. Pennie, sls VP.

Full service specialists in betacam camera & recorders. Refurbished video heads & scanners.

Videotron Ltee, 300 Viger Ave. E., Montreal, PQ, H2B 3W4. Canada. Phone: (514) 281-1711. Fax: (514) 985-8652. Robert Depatie, pres/CEO; Manon Brouillette, sr VP, strategic dev & mktg.

MontrealPQ Canada. LeGroupe Videotron Ltee., 300 ave Viger est.

Cable TV, digital TV, interactive TV and telecommunications.

Videssence L.L.C., 10768 Lower Azusa Rd., El Monte, CA, 91731. Phone: (626) 579-0943. Fax: (626) 579-6803.E-mail: contact@videssence.tv Web Site:www.videssence.tv Toni Swarens, pres; Lauri Maines, VP.

Energy-efficient floorescent, studio lighting products for TV, film, stage & industrial communications applications.

Vidiom Systems Inc., 10901 W. 120th Ave., Suite 230, Broomfield, CO, 80021. Phone: (303) 604-0800. Fax: (303) 604-0080.E-mail: mmalcy@vidiom.com Web Site:www.vidiom.com Timothy R. Wahlers, pres/CEO; David Housman, sr VP strategy & opns; Michael Malcy, VP mktg.

Software engrg & design, software testing, application development, technical writing, training for OCAP, ETV, headends.

Viking Cases, 10480 Oak St. N.E., St. Petersburg, FL, 33716. Phone: (800) 237-8560. Fax: (727) 577-2082.E-mail: sales@vikingcases.com Web Site:www.vikingcases.com Arthur W. Stemler, CEO; Bruce S. Stemler, pres; Reese Autry, VP.

Heavy-duty reusable shipping cases, lightweight carrying cases & EIA rack cases.

Vinten Inc., 709 Executive Blvd., Valley Cottage, NY, 10989. Phone: (845) 268-0100. Fax: (845) 268-0113.E-mail: mike.denicola@vinten.com Web Site:www.vinten.com Bob Carr, pres; Ali Ahmadi, mktg mgr.

Toronto Canada, 50 Moberly Ave. Phone:

BurbankCA , G 95 S. Glenwood, Suite B. Phone:

SunriseFL , 10208 N.W. 47th St. Phone:

ShamongNJ , 4 Birch Ct. Phone:

Remote control camera systems. Pneumatic studio pedestals, pan & tilt heads, lightweight tripods & heads.

Vision Database Systems, 1095 Jupiter Park Dr., Suite 3, Jupiter, FL, 33458. Phone: (561) 748-0711. Fax: (561) 748-0712. Web Site:www.visiondatabase.com Emil Bonaduce, pres.

Photo image software.

Visual Sound Inc., 485 Park Way, Broomall, PA, 19008. Phone: (610) 544-8700. Phone: (800) 523-7525. Fax: (610) 544-3385.E-mail: info@visualsound.com Web Site:www.visualsound.com Karen Bogosian, pres; John Greene, sls dir.

HalethorpeMD . Beltsville, 3919 Vero Rd. # J. Phone:

Camp HillPA , 490 S. St. John's Church Rd. Phone:

Audio-video sls, svcs, installation, maintainance of teleconferencing rooms; ENG, production vans, studios, events production & rentals.

Vortek, 66 School St., Victor, NY, 14564. Phone: (585) 924-5000. Fax: (585) 924-0545. Web Site:www.vortekrigging.com

Engineer manufacture rigging systems, motorized hoists & controls.

W

WIREMAX Ltd., Box 3336, 705 Wamba Ave., Toledo, 43607. Phone: (800) 843-9479. Fax: (419) 531-9503. Al Mocek, pres; Mark Robinson, gen mgr; Tom Ricketts, VP.

Manufacturer of high temp, wire, cable, high voltage wire & cable.

WOIO & WUAB TV, 1717 E. 12th St., Cleveland, OH, 44114. Phone: (216) 771-1943. Fax: (216) 515-7152. Web Site:www.hometeam19.com Jim Stunek, mgr; Sharon Ohlson, product coord.

Full studio facilities; GVG 300 switcher, CMX 3100B edit, 1-inch, 3/4-inch, Beta formats; Abekas digital F/X; Artstar graphics; remote packages.

Ward-Beck Systems Ltd., Unit 10, 455 Milner Ave., Toronto, ON, M1B 2K4. Canada. Phone: (416) 335-5999. Fax: (416) 335-5202.E-mail: request@ward-beck.com Web Site:ward-beck.com Eugene L. Johnson, mgng dir; Michael Jordan, sls dir; Doug Bascombe, engrg dir.

Distribution metering, monitoring, conversion of AES & analog audio, video & serial digital bcstg signals. Radio consoles.

Wearguard, 141 Longwater Dr., Norwell, MA, 02061. Fax: (800) 867-7160. Web Site:www.wearguard.com David Gold, pres.

Offers a comprehensive line of work clothing & identity apparel serving the cable industry.

WeatherBank Inc., 1015 Waterwood Pkwy., Suite J, Edmond, OK, 73034. Phone: (405) 359-0773. Phone: (800) 687-3562. Fax: (405) 341-0115.E-mail: sroot@weatherbank.com Web Site:www.weatherbank.com Steven A. Root, pres/CEO; Michael R. Root, VP & CFO.

Satellite-delivered weather info, audio forecasting svcs & consulting to all industries.

Wegener, (Formerly Wegener Communications Inc.). 11350 Technology Cir., Duluth, GA, 30097. Phone: (770) 814-4000. Fax: (770) 623-0698.E-mail: globalsales@wegener.com Web Site:www.wegener.com Robert Placek, CEO; Ned L. Mountain, pres/CEO; Troy Woodbury, CFO; Elias J. Livaditis, chief technology off.

Intl provider of digital video & audio solutions bcst TV, radio, telco, private & cable network. Focuses on long & short term strategies for banwidth savings, dynamic adv, live events & affil mgmt.

Wescam Inc., 649 N. Service Rd. W., Burlington, ON, L7P 5B9. Canada. Phone: (905) 633-4000. Fax: (905) 633-4100. Web Site:www.wescam.com

Van NuysCA , 7150 Hayvenhurst Ave. Phone:

Featuring Wescam Helicopter film, video, HD system, new & ultimately stable XR for all group applications.

Weschler Instruments, Weshler Instruments Division of Hughes Corporation. 16900 Foltz Parkway, Cleveland, OH, 44149. Phone: (440) 238-2550. Fax: (440) 238-0660.E-mail: sales@weschler.com Web Site:www.weschler.com Jerry Lucak, VP sls; David Hughes, pres; Michael Dorman, sls VP.

Digital & analog panel meters, RF ammeters, process indicators, digital multimeters, circuit tracers, power analyzers & test equipment.

Westcott, 1447 Summit St., Toledo, OH, 43603. Phone: (419) 243-7311. Fax: (419) 243-8401. Web Site:www.fjwestcott.com E-mail: info@fjwestcott.com Thomas A. Waltz, pres.

Lightweight, portable & collapsible light control equipment: silks & solids, scrims, Illuminator® reflectors, umbrellas, light modifiers, & Scrim Jim modular light panels.

Westlake Audio, (Formerly Westlake Audio, Professional Products Manufacturing Group). 2696 Lavery Ct., Unit 18, Newbury Park, CA, 91320. Phone: (805) 499-3686. Fax: (805) 498-2571. Web Site:www.westakeaudio.com E-mail: barbarab@westlakeaudio.com Glenn Phoenix, pres; Ken Centrofante, mktg; Barbara Born, sls admin.

Audio monitors & accessories.

Westlake Audio, Professional Sales Group, 7265 Santa Monica Blvd., Los Angeles, CA, 90046. Phone: (323) 851-9800. Fax: (323) 851-0182. Web Site:www.westlakeaudio.com Deborah Rally, gen mgr; David Logan, gen sls mgr; Steve Burdick, VP.

Los AngelesCA , 8447 Beverly Blvd. Phone:

Newbury ParkCA , 2696 Lavery Ct, Unit 18. Phone:

Professional audio equipment repairs, professional recording equipment sales, rentals, studio design. Westlake can provide all your Pro Audio needs, from Pro Audio equipment sls to full tracking & mixing.

Wheatstone Corp., 600 Industrial Dr., New Bern, NC, 28562. Phone: (252) 638-7000. Fax: (252) 635-4857.E-mail: sales@wheatstone.com Web Site:www.wheatstone.com Gary C. Snow, pres; Andrew Calvanese, VP; Jay Tyler, gen sls mgr.

Manufacturer of analog & digital bcst audio mixing consoles, processing equipment, radio & TV products since 1976.

Whirlwind, 99 Ling Rd., Rochester, NY, 14612. Phone: (585) 663-8820. Fax: (585) 865-8930. Fax: (888) 733-4396.E-mail: sales@whirlwindusa.com Web Site:www.whirlwindusa.com Michael Laiacona, pres.

Mix-6 audio mixers, presspower 2 active pressbox, active splitters; P-12 & power amplifiers, MD-1 MIC/line driver.

Wil-Can Electronics Ltd., 8560 Torbram Rd., Unit #35, Brampton, ON, L6T 5C9. Canada. Phone: (888) 596-2020. Fax: (888) 866-7775.E-mail: wilcan@lightningtvss.com Web Site:www.powersurges.com William J. Black, pres; Gregory J. Black, VP.

BuffaloNY , 2316 Delaware Ave, Suite 285. Phone:

Designers, manufacturers & consultants. Lightning & high energy transient control including protection for telephone, signal & data lines.

WILL-BURT Co., Box 900, Orrville, OH, 44667. Phone: (330) 682-7015. Fax: (330) 684-1190. Web Site:www.willburt.com E-mail: contact_us@willburt.com Jeff Evans, CEO; Steven Pinkley, gen sls mgr.

Telescoping mast used to position antennas, lights & cameras to heights of 20 to 134 ft.

Wiltronix Inc., Box 364, 16850 Oakmont Ave., Washington Grove, MD, 20880. Phone: (301) 258-7676. Fax: (301) 963-8624.E-mail: equipsales@wiltronix.com Web Site:www.wiltronix.com Dwight Wilcox, pres; Ellen Packard, VP.

HighlandMD , 6927R Mink Hollow Rd.

Manufacturers rep for digital HD, SD, video, audio, signal processing, transmission for bcst production & govt video facilities.

Winsted Corp., 10901 Hampshire Ave. S., Minneapolis, MN, 55438. Phone: (952) 944-9050. Fax: (952) 944-1546.E-mail: info@winsted.com Web Site:www.winsted.com G.R. Hoska, chmn; Randy Smith, pres; Stephen Hoska, CEO.

DuluthGA . Winsted Technical Interiors, 1750 Breckinridge Pwky., Suite 100. Phone:

Editing, production & post consoles, space saving tape & data storage systems. Multimedia & Lan/Wan server workstations. Console installations.

Wireless Accessories Group, 1840 County Line Rd., Suite 301, Huntingdon Valley, PA, 19006. Phone: (888) 233-0202. Phone: (215) 322-4600. Fax: (215) 322-4606. Web Site:www.wirexgroupl.com

Two-way radio equipment.

WireReady NSI, 56 Hudson St., Northboro, MA, 01532. Phone: (800) 833-4459. Phone: (508) 393-0200. Fax: (508) 393-0255.E-mail: sales@wireready.com Web Site:www.wireready.com David Gerstmann, pres.

NewsReady 32, CartReady, ControlReady, NewsReady, StormReady & SalesReady software. Cart replacement, satellite, music on HD, newsrooms & sls automation. All windows/pc.

Wireworks Corporation, 380 Hillside Avenue, Hillside, NJ, 07205. Phone: (908) 686-7400. Phone: (800) 642-9473. Fax: (908) 686-0483.E-mail: sales@wireworks.com Web Site:www.wireworks.com Gerald J. Krulewicz, pres; Larry J. Williams, controller.

Audio, video, & audio/video combination cabling assemblies for bcst market; cable testers, transformer isolated mic splitters; multi-pin connectors & perfect custom panels.

Wohler Technologies Inc., 31055 Huntwood Ave., Hayward, CA, 94544. Phone: (510) 870-0810. Fax: (510) 870-0811. Web Site:www.wohler.com Carl Dempsey, pres/CEO; Kim Templeman-Holmes, VP sls & mktg.

Wolf Coach Inc., 7 B St., Auburn Industrial Park, Auburn, MA, 01501. Phone: (508) 791-1950. Fax: (508) 799-2384.E-mail: sales@wolfcoach.com Web Site:www.wolfcoach.com Richard Wolf, VP; Mark A. Leonard, natl sls reps; Thomas P. Jennings, natl sls reps; Emeric Feldmar, mgr.

Salt Lake CityUT , 2451 South 600 W, 200. Phone:

News vans, satellite vehicles, production trailers, vehicle based microwave, satellite uplink, digital SNG, audio/video systems & turnkey systems.

World Tower Co. Inc., Box 508, 1213 Compressor Dr., Mayfield, KY, 42066. Phone: (270) 247-3642. Fax: (270) 247-0909.E-mail: worldtow@ldd.net Web Site:www.worldtower.com Doug Walker, pres; Brent Walker, VP; Keith Scoggins, sr opns mgr.

Manufactures & erects bcst & CATV towers, microwave & cellular.

World Video Sales Co., Box 331, Boyertown, PA, 19512. Phone: (610) 754-6800. Fax: (610) 754-9766.E-mail: sales@mivs.com John A. Taylor, pres.

Manufacturers of: video timers/titlers, screen splitters, pattern generators, routing systems, distribution amplifiers & other special purpose video equipments.

X

Xintekvideo Inc., 56 W. Broad St., Stamford, CT, 06902. Phone: (203) 348-9229. Fax: (203) 348-9266.E-mail: jrossi@xintekvideo.com Web Site:www.xintekvideo.com John Rossi, pres.

Video processing equipment, including transcoders, color correctors, image enhancers, noise reducers, co-channel filters, ghost removers & impulse noise eliminators.

Y

Yamaha Corp. of America, 6600 Orangethorpe Ave., Buena Park, CA, 90620. Phone: (714) 522-9011. Web Site:www.yamaha.com Tom Sumner, VP; Yoshi Doi, pres.

Portable keyboards, synthesizers & drums. Manufactures a complete line of professional audio products targeted to the project studio, coml studio, postproduction, bcst & sound reinforcement markets.

Yanchar Design & Consulting Group, 26741 Portola Pkwy., Suite 1E, Foothill Ranch, CA, 92610-1713. Phone: (949) 770-6601. Fax: (949) 770-6575.E-mail: info@yanchardesign.com Web Site:www.yanchardesign.com Carl J. Yanchar, pres.

Acoustical design, facility design, consultation, systems design, studio construction & instal.

Z

Zack Electronics Inc., 1070 Hamilton Rd., Duarte, CA, 91010. Phone: (626) 303-0655. Phone: (800) 466-0449. Fax: (626) 303-8694.E-mail: jlomas@zackinc.com Web Site:www.zackelectronics.com Judi Lomas, mgr; Dennis Awad, pres.

Cable, connectors, & comprehensive core products for the bcst industry, custom audio/video/data cable assemblies. Featuring: Belden, Neutrik, Switchcraft, Pomona & avbcable.com.

Zenith Electronics Corp., 2000 Millbrook Dr., Lincolnshire, IL, 60069. Phone: (847) 391-7000. Fax: (847) 941-9200. Web Site:www.zenith.com T.J. Lee, pres/CEO.

Full line of CATV converters; MMDS systems; cable & pay TV systems for PAL & SECAM international markets; PC-based system controllers; accessories.

Ziehl Electronic Service, 8611 Dale Rd., Gasport, NY, 14067. Phone: (716) 772-7800. Fax: (716) 772-7985. Richard F. Ziehl, owner.

Frequency measurement svc.

Zomax Inc., 7001 Discovery Blvd., Dublin, OH, 43017. Phone: (888) 638-2832. Phone: (614) 761-2000. Fax: (614) 766-3176. Web Site:www.zomax.com

CD manufacturer specializing in printing fulfillment svcs, & custom work in CD entertainment & CD-ROM.

Equipment Manufacturers and Distributors Subject Index

Acoustic Equipment

Acoustic Systems/ETS-Lindgren
Acoustical Solutions Inc.

Acoustical Panels and Treatment

Acoustical Solutions Inc.
Industrial Acoustics Co., Inc.
Noise Control Corp.
Pinta Acoustic Inc.

Aerial Buckets

Equipment Technology LLC
Time Manufacturing Co.

Amplifiers

Amplivox Portable Sound Systems
BEXT Inc.
Communication & Power Industries, EIMAC
    Operations
e2v technologies Inc.
Electroline Equipment Inc.
Emerson Network Power-Viewsonics
Farrtronics Ltd.
FitzCo. Inc.
Lindsay Broadband Inc.
M/A-COM
Opamp Labs Inc.
Peavey Electronics
QSC Audio Products Inc.
Radio Design Labs. (RDL)
Ram Broadcast Systems
Spectra Sonics
Symmetricom
TOA Electronics Inc.
Whirlwind

Amplifiers, Audio

A R T Applied Research and Technology
Amplivox Portable Sound Systems
Audio Implements/GKC
Auernheimer Labs Corp.
BGW Systems, Amplifier Technologies, Inc.
Benchmark Media Systems Inc.
Bogen Communications Inc.
Bryston Ltd.
Cablynx, Inc.
DBX Professional Products
ESE
Galaxy Audio Inc.
Harman International Industries Inc.
Henry Engineering
JBL Professional
LINK Electronics Inc.
Motorola Broadband Communications Sector
Opamp Labs Inc.
Philip-Cooke Co.
RTS Systems Telex Communications Inc
Radio Engineering Industries Inc.
Sescom Inc.
TC Group Americas Inc.
Video Accessory Corp.
Yamaha Corp. of America

Amplifiers, RF

Andrew Corp.
Bauer Transmitters
Blonder Tongue Laboratories Inc.
C-COR/ Arris
Channel Master
Communication & Power Industries
Communication & Power Industries, EIMAC
    Operations
Crown Broadcast IREC
DMT USA, Inc.
e2v technologies Inc.
Energy-Onix Broadcast Equipment Co. Inc.
LARCAN
Lindsay Broadband Inc.
MCL Inc.
North American Cable Equipment Inc.

North Hills Signal Processing, a PORTA Systems
    Co.
Qintar Technologies Inc.
Vertex Communications Corp.

Amplifiers, Video

Cablynx, Inc.
Comprehensive Video Group
ESE
Interlogix
Intersil Corp.
LINK Electronics Inc.
Opamp Labs Inc.
Philip-Cooke Co.
Radio Engineering Industries Inc.
Video Accessory Corp.
World Video Sales Co.

Analyzers, Distortion, Intermodulation

Audio Precision Inc.
Boonton Electronics Corp.
Electro Rent Corp.
Potomac Instruments, Inc.
Radiodetection/Riser Bond
SyntheSys Research Inc.

Animation Systems

Atlantic Video Inc.
Autodesk
Autodesk
Even Technologies Inc.
Hotbox Digital

Announcement Systems

Bogen Communications Inc.
Interface Media Group

Antennas and Accessories

ATCI/Antenna Technology Communications Inc.
American Antenna Inc.
Antenna Concepts Inc.
California Amplifier
Comex Worldwide Corp.
Cortland Cable Co. Inc.
Gorman-Redlich Manufacturing Co.
Harris Corp., Broadcast Division
Jampro Antennas Inc.
Kathrein Inc., Scala Division
LBA Technology Inc.
Lindsay Broadband Inc.
M/A-COM
Mega Hertz
NSI
Radio Engineering Industries Inc.
Radio Frequency Systems
S W R Inc.
Sitco Antenna Company
Superior Satellite Engineers Inc.
Times Fiber Communications Inc.
Tyco Electronics

Antennas, Broadcast

ATCI/Antenna Technology Communications Inc.
American Antenna Inc.
Andrew Corp.
Antenna Concepts Inc.
BEXT Inc.
Broadcast Equipment Surplus Inc.
Comtech Antenna Systems Inc.
Continental Electronics Corporation
Crossed Field Antennas Inc.
Dielectric Communications
DMT USA, Inc.
ERI-Electronic Research, Inc.
Kathrein Inc., Scala Division
Kintronic Labs Inc.
LARCAN USA

Lindsay Broadband Inc.
MYAT Inc.
Marcom
Micro Communications Inc.
Allen Osborne Associates Inc.
Phasetek Inc.
Pinzone Engineering Group Inc.
RF Specialties Group
Radio Frequency Systems
S W R Inc.
Shively Labs
Superior Satellite Engineers Inc.
Teleplex Inc.
Tower Network Services
Transcom Corp.

Antennas, Earth Station

ATCI/Antenna Technology Communications Inc.
All Mobile Video Inc.
American Antenna Inc.
Andrew Corp.
Comtech Antenna Systems Inc.
D.H. Satellite
Mega Hertz
Pinzone Engineering Group Inc.
Radio Research Instrument Co. Inc.
Superior Satellite Engineers Inc.
Vertex Communications Corp.

Antennas, Installation

Abroyd Communications Ltd.
Cygnal Technologies
ERI-Electronic Research, Inc.
Mega Hertz
National Steel Erectors Corp.
Fred A. Nudd Corp.
S W R Inc.
Southern Broadcast Services
Structural System Technology Inc.
Superior Satellite Engineers Inc.
Swager Communications Inc.
Teletech Inc.
Tenco Tower Co.
Tower Network Services

Antennas, Satellite

ATCI/Antenna Technology Communications Inc.
American Antenna Inc.
California Amplifier
Comtech Antenna Systems Inc.
D.H. Satellite
MRPP Inc.
Mega Hertz
North American Cable Equipment Inc.
Pinzone Engineering Group Inc.
Superior Satellite Engineers Inc.

Antennas, TVRO

American Antenna Inc.
California Amplifier
Comtech Antenna Systems Inc.
D.H. Satellite
North American Cable Equipment Inc.
Pinzone Engineering Group Inc.

Attenuators and Equalizers

Allen Avionics, Inc.
Emerson Network Power-Viewsonics
Lindsay Broadband Inc.
Motorola Broadband Communications Sector
Narda - An L-3 Communications Co.
North American Cable Equipment Inc.
Penny & Giles Inc.
Shallco Inc.
Tech Laboratories Inc.

Audio Accessories

AKG Acoustics, U.S.
ATI-Audio Technologies Inc.
Allsop Inc.
Amek U.S.A.
Aphex Systems Ltd.
Audico Labels
Audio Implements/GKC
Black Audio
HAVE Inc.
Henry Engineering
The J-Lab Co.
JOA Cartridge Service
Jensen Transformers Inc.
Peavey Electronics
Polyline
Professional Sound Corp.
Radio Design Labs. (RDL)
Seger Electronics
Sescom Inc.
Sprague Magnetics Inc.
Star Case Manufacturing Co. Inc.
TAI Audio
Trimm Inc.
Video Accessory Corp.
Westlake Audio
Wireworks Corporation
Zack Electronics Inc.

Audio Amps, AGC & Limiters

Professional Sound Corp.
Renkus-Heinz Inc.
Samson Technologies Corp.
Sescom Inc.
Spectra Sonics

Audio Cartridge Library Labels

Veriad

Audio Cartridges

Spectra Sonics
Stanton Group

Audio Compressors

Alesis
Circuit Research Labs Inc. (CRL Systems, Inc.)
Furman
Sascom Marketing Group
Sescom Inc.
Spectra Sonics
TC Electronic

Audio Consoles

Arrakis Systems Inc.
Autogram Corp.
Euphonix Inc.
Harris Corp., Broadcast Communications
Henry Engineering
Logitek
North American Cable Equipment Inc.
Ward-Beck Systems Ltd.
Wheatstone Corp.

Audio Equipment

Audio Implements/GKC
Audio Precision Inc.
BBE Sound Inc.
Bexel
Black Audio
Bogen Communications Inc.
Broadcast Store Inc.
Burlington A/V Recording Media Inc.
Comprehensive Video Group
Comrex Corp.
Countryman Associates Inc.
DBX Professional Products
Film/Video Equipment Service Co. Inc.
FitzCo. Inc.
Full Compass Systems Ltd.
Galaxy Audio Inc.
Geneva Aviation Inc.
Group One Ltd.
Industrial Equipment Representatives (IER)
Jensen Transformers Inc.

Lectrosonics Inc.
Memorex Products Inc.
Nady Systems Inc.
National Video Services Inc.
Opamp Labs Inc.
Peavey Electronics
Photomart Cine-Video Inc.
ProAudio.com/Crouse-Kimzey Co.
Professional Sound Corp.
Protech Audio Corp.
QSC Audio Products Inc.
Ram Broadcast Systems
Samson Technologies Corp.
Sanyo Fisher Co.
Sascom Marketing Group
Sennheiser Electronic Corp.
Servoreeler Systems
Spectra Sonics
Systems Wireless Ltd.
TAI Audio
TC Group Americas Inc.
TEAC America Inc.
Thomson, Inc, (RCA/GE)
Visual Sound Inc.
Whirlwind

Audio Jackfields, Pre-Wired

Audio Accessories Inc.
Farrtronics Ltd.
Furman
Glentronix
Milestek Corp.
Penny & Giles Inc.
Seger Electronics
Switchcraft Inc.

Audio Limiters

Amek U.S.A.
Circuit Research Labs Inc. (CRL Systems, Inc.)
Harman International Industries Inc.
Spectra Sonics
Symetrix Inc.

Audio Mixers and Recorders

ATI-Audio Technologies Inc.
Alesis
Allen & Heath USA
Amek U.S.A.
Audio-Technica U.S., Inc.
Graham-Patten Systems Inc.
The Image Group Post, LLC.
Location Sound Corp.
Martinsound Inc.
Micro Technology Unlimited
Nady Systems Inc.
Otari USA Sales Inc.
Penny & Giles Inc.
Professional Sound Corp.
Professional Sound Services Inc.
Protech Audio Corp.
Radio Design Labs. (RDL)
Shure Inc.
Superscope Technologies Professionals
United States Broadcast
Yamaha Corp. of America

Audio Monitoring Systems

AKG Acoustics, U.S.
B&B Systems
Dorrough Electronics
Fostex USA
Furman
IRIS Technologies Inc.
Martinsound Inc.
McCurdy Radio Ltd.
Renkus-Heinz Inc.
Westlake Audio

Audio Noise Reduction Systems

Allen Avionics, Inc.
Digidesign
Dolby Laboratories Inc.
Image Video
Noise Control Corp.
Symetrix Inc.

Audio Processors

Audioarts Engineering
BBE Sound Inc.
Inovonics Inc.
Linear Acoustic Inc.
Modulation Sciences Inc.
Nady Systems Inc.
Peavey Electronics
Protech Audio Corp.
Samson Technologies Corp.
Sascom Marketing Group
Symetrix Inc.

Audio Replacement Heads

International Electro-Magnetics (IEM)
Sprague Magnetics Inc.

Audio Routing Switches

Burst Electronics Inc.
Logitek
NVISION Products
NTV International Corporation
Radio Design Labs. (RDL)
Richmond Sound Design Ltd.
Sierra Automated Systems & Engineering Corp.
Sigma Electronics Inc.
Utah Scientific Inc.

Audio Signal Processing Systems

Alesis
Aphex Systems Ltd.
BBE Sound Inc.
Broadcasters General Store Inc.
Circuit Research Labs Inc. (CRL Systems, Inc.)
Communications Specialties Inc.
Dolby Laboratories Inc.
G Prime Ltd.
Graham-Patten Systems Inc.
Group One Ltd.
International Datacasting Corp.
Lectrosonics Inc.
Pixel Instruments Corp.
Sabine Inc.
Shure Inc.
Symetrix Inc.
TC Electronic

Audio Systems and Components

Audio Implements/GKC
Gefen Inc.
Parsons Audio
Protech Audio Corp.
VidCAD Documentation Programs (VDP Inc.)
Visual Sound Inc.

Audio Test Tapes, Gauges & Equipment

Audio Precision Inc.
Leader Instruments Corp.
Tentel

Audio Transmission Equipment

Artel Video Systems
Audio Processing Technology Ltd./APT
Fiber Options
Intelligent Media Technology
International Datacasting Corp.
Leaming Industries
MUSICAM U.S.A.
Neutrik U.S.A. Inc.
TFT Inc.

Audio/Video Cartridges

CoarcVideo
Memorex Products Inc.

Equipment Manufacturers and Distributors Subject Index

Audiotape

Burlington A/V Recording Media Inc.
CoarcVideo
Maxell Corp. of America
Memorex Products Inc.
Moviola
National Video Services Inc.
Sony BMG Music Entertainment

Audiotape Cartridge Machines

A.C.C. Electronix, Inc.

Audiotape Duplicating Equipment

National Audio Co. Inc.

Automated Newsroom Systems

Avid Broadcast
CEA-Computer Engineering Associates
Comprompter Inc.
Computer Concepts Corp.
Dalet Digital Media Systems
Harris Automation Solutions
Thomson Reuters
WireReady NSI

Automated Radio

Dalet Digital Media Systems
ENCO Systems Inc.
Encoda Systems Inc.
Marketron Broadcast Solutions
Marketron International
Radio Computing Services (RCS)
Register Communications
Spotcat Software
WireReady NSI

Automated Tape Winders

Otari USA Sales Inc.

Automated Telephone & Voice Mail

Aspect Software
Microlog Corp.
TALX Corp.

Automatic Cassette Loaders

Otari USA Sales Inc.

Automatic Transmission Systems

Encoda Systems Inc.
Harris Automation Solutions

Automation Systems

ADTEC Inc.
Arrakis Systems Inc.
Broadcast Electronics Inc.
CEA-Computer Engineering Associates
Computer Concepts Corp.
ENCO Systems Inc.
Encoda Systems Inc.
Harris Automation Solutions
Harris Corp., Broadcast Communications
Leightronix Inc.
MATCO Inc.
Marketron International
Media Computing Inc.
Mediastar-SG
Orban
Radio Computing Services (RCS)
Register Communications
Spotcat Software
Sundance Digital Inc.
Thomson Multi Media
Time Logic Inc.
WireReady NSI

Automation, Switching and Control

ADTEC Inc.
FloriCal Systems Inc.
Harris Automation Solutions
Leightronix Inc.
MATCO Inc.
Register Communications
Richmond Sound Design Ltd.
Sierra Automated Systems & Engineering Corp.
Sundance Digital Inc.
Texscan MSI
Thomson Multi Media

Automation, TV Station

Avid Broadcast
Dalet Digital Media Systems
Encoda Systems Inc.
FloriCal Systems Inc.
Harris Automation Solutions
Leightronix Inc.
MATCO Inc.
Marketron International
Media Computing Inc.
StorerTV Inc.
Sundance Digital Inc.
Thomson Multi Media
Time Logic Inc.
VCI Solutions
Videotron Ltee
WireReady NSI

Batteries and Accessories

ADCOUR, Inc.
Acme Electric Corp., Aerospace Division
Alexander Technologies
Alpha Technologies Inc.
Arri Canada Ltd.
Battery Pros Inc.
Burlington A/V Recording Media Inc.
Cine 60 Inc.
Frezzolini Electronics Inc.
Alan Gordon Enterprises Inc.
Marathon Norco Aerospace, Inc.
North American Cable Equipment Inc.
The Tiffen Company

Blimps

Blimpy Floating Signs/Bend-A-Lite

Blowers and Fans

APW Mayville/Stantron
Allied Electronics Inc.
Bud Industries Inc.
CMP Enclosures Inc.
Condux International
Emcor Enclosures
Seger Electronics

Booms and Cameras

Alan Gordon Enterprises Inc.

Boosters, TV

Axcera

Broadcast & Program Logging Recorders

Dictaphone Corp.

Broadcast Audio Products

A.C.C. Electronix, Inc.
ADC
AKG Acoustics, U.S.
AheadTek
Aphex Systems Ltd.
Audio Implements/GKC
Audio Processing Technology Ltd./APT
Autogram Corp.
Belden
Benchmark Media Systems Inc.
Bradley Broadcast and Pro Audio

Comrex Corp.
DBX Professional Products
Dolby Laboratories Inc.
Ensemble Designs
FM SYSTEMS Inc.
Farrtronics Ltd.
Fiber Options
Fostex USA
Full Compass Systems Ltd.
Furman
Gefen Inc.
JOA Cartridge Service
Lectrosonics Inc.
Logitek
MUSICAM U.S.A.
Marketron Broadcast Solutions
Orban
Parsons Audio
Sennheiser Electronic Corp.
TAI Audio
teletech.ca
Telex Communications Inc.
360 Systems
Wegener
Wheatstone Corp.

Broadcast Equipment

Advanced Media Technologies, Inc.
Allison Payments Systems L.L.C.
Analog Digital International Inc.
Atlantic Sound Systems
Audio Implements/GKC
Autodesk
BEXT Inc.
Bradley Broadcast and Pro Audio
Broadcast Store Inc.
Broadcast Supply Worldwide
C-COR/ Arris
Energy-Onix Broadcast Equipment Co. Inc.
Ensemble Designs
FitzCo. Inc.
Ikegami Electronics (U.S.A.) Inc.
Industrial Equipment Representatives (IER)
Inscriber Technology Corporation
JVC Professional Products Company
Kahn Communications Inc.
Kathrein Inc., Scala Division
Kay Industries Inc.
Konica Minolta Corp.
The Laumic Rental Co.
MRPP Inc.
MUSICAM U.S.A.
Marshall Electronics
Masterclock, Inc.
Merlin Engineering Works Inc.
Miranda Technologies Inc.
Modulation Sciences Inc.
NVISION Products
National Video Services Inc.
Nautel Ltd.
Allen Osborne Associates Inc.
Panasonic Broadcast & Television Systems Co.
Phasetek Inc.
ProAudio.com/Crouse-Kimzey Co.
RF Specialties Group
Ross Video Ltd.
Schafer International
Scientific Atlanta Canada Inc. Nexus Division
Sencore Inc.
Specialized Communications Corp.
J.A. Taylor & Associates
Technet Systems Group
Thomson
Transcom Corp.
Westcott

Broadcast Radio Equipment

Arrakis Systems Inc.
BEXT Inc.
Belar Electronics Laboratory Inc.
Bradley Broadcast and Pro Audio
Broadcast Electronics Inc.
Broadcasters General Store Inc.
Comrex Corp.
Continental Electronics Corporation
DBX Professional Products
Dalet Digital Media Systems
Highway Information Systems, Inc.
Industrial Equipment Representatives (IER)
Inovonics Inc.
Jampro Antennas Inc.
Marketron Broadcast Solutions

Nautel Ltd.
Schafer International
Shively Labs
Swintek Enterprises Inc.
TFT Inc.
Tenco Tower Co.

Broadcast RF Equipment

AVI Systems
Allen Avionics, Inc.
Antenna Concepts Inc.
Bauer Transmitters
Belar Electronics Laboratory Inc.
Bird Electronic Corp.
Bradley Broadcast and Pro Audio
Broadcast Microwave Services Inc.
CED
Comex Worldwide Corp.
Communication & Power Industries
Communication & Power Industries, EIMAC
    Operations
Continental Electronics Corporation
Crown Broadcast IREC
Delta Electronics Inc.
Dielectric Communications
DMT USA, Inc.
e2v technologies Inc.
EDX Wireless
Hitachi Kokusai Electric America, Ltd.
Industrial Equipment Representatives (IER)
JSB Service Co.
Jampro Antennas Inc.
Kathrein Inc., Scala Division
Kintronic Labs Inc.
LARCAN USA
Micro Communications Inc.
Narda - An L-3 Communications Co.
Nautel Ltd.
Shively Labs
Swintek Enterprises Inc.
TFT Inc.
Teleplex Inc.
V-Soft Communications
WILL-BURT Co.

Broadcast Studio Construction, Prefab

Devlin Design Group Inc.
Industrial Acoustics Co., Inc.
Northeastern Communications Concepts Inc.

Broadcast Studio Equipment

A.C.C. Electronix, Inc.
ADC
AKG Acoustics, U.S.
Audioarts Engineering
Barco Inc.
Broadcast Electronic Services
Broadcasters General Store Inc.
Camera Dynamics
Canon U.S.A. Inc.
Digidesign
ENCO Systems Inc.
Furman
Harris Corp., Broadcast Division
Hitachi Kokusai Electric America, Ltd.
Inscriber Technology Corporation
MUSICAM U.S.A.
Marshall Electronics
Mole-Richardson Co.
O'Connor Professional Camera Support Systems
Parsons Audio
Richardson Electronics
Rosco Laboratories Inc.
Telecast Fiber Systems Inc.
Theatre Service & Supply Corp.
Thomson
Transcom Corp.
United States Broadcast
Videotron Ltee

Broadcast TV Equipment

AKG Acoustics, U.S.
AVS Graphics & Media Inc.
AZCAR U.S.A. Inc.
Abekas, Incorporated
AccuWeather Inc.
All Mobile Video Inc.

Alpine Optics Inc.
BEXT Inc.
Belar Electronics Laboratory Inc.
Bexel
Broadcast Electronic Services
Broadcast International Group
Canon U.S.A. Inc.
Comtech Antenna Systems Inc.
DeSisti Lighting
DMT USA, Inc.
Ensemble Designs
Fiber Options
Full Compass Systems Ltd.
Hitachi Kokusai Electric America, Ltd.
Jampro Antennas Inc.
LARCAN
Maze Corporation
Mole-Richardson Co.
Allen Osborne Associates Inc.
Schafer International
Snell
Specialized Communications Corp.
Standard Communications Corp.
J.A. Taylor & Associates
Telecast Fiber Systems Inc.
Thomson
Toshiba America Consumer Products
VCI Solutions
Wescam Inc.
WILL-BURT Co.

Broadcast Video Products

ADC
Abekas, Incorporated
Alpine Optics Inc.
Analog Digital International Inc.
Battery Pros Inc.
Belden
Bitcentral Inc.
Broadcast Electronic Services
Canon U.S.A. Inc.
Fast Forward Video
Glentronix
Hitachi Kokusai Electric America, Ltd.
Hotronic Inc.
LINK Electronics Inc.
MATCO Inc.
Marshall Electronics
Matrox Video Products Grp
Maxell Corp. of America
Roscor Corp.
Sencore Inc.
Snell
Telemetrics Inc.
teletech.ca
360 Systems
The Tiffen Company
Videomagnetics Inc.
Wegener
Wiltronix Inc.

Bulktape DeGausser

Audiolab Electronics Inc.
Data Security Inc.
Garner Products
Glentronix
Paulmar Industries Inc.
Sprague Magnetics Inc.

Bulktape, Audio Cassette

CoarcVideo
National Audio Co. Inc.

Cabinets, Racks, Panels

ADTEC Inc.
APW Mayville/Stantron
Allied Electronics Inc.
Atlas Sound
Benner-Nawman Inc.
Bud Industries Inc.
CMP Enclosures Inc.
Calzone Case Co.
Emcor Enclosures
Emerson Network Power
Fusion Consoles
Gepco International Inc.
Hardigg Cases
High Tech Industries

IMS/AMCO Engineering Products
Mega Hertz
Murphy Studio Furniture
National Video Services Inc.
Neumade Products Corp.
Newark Electronics
North American Cable Equipment Inc.
Parsons Manufacturing Corp.
Penn Elcom Inc.
Ram Broadcast Systems
Seger Electronics
Seton Identification Products
Stahl, A Scott & Fetzer Co.
Star Case Manufacturing Co. Inc.
Storeel Corp.
Thermodyne Cases
Ultimate Precision/GKM
Winsted Corp.
Zack Electronics Inc.

Cable and Accessories

Allied Electronics Inc.
Belden
CCI Systems Inc.
Canare Corp.
Channel Master
Clark Wire & Cable Co. Inc.
Communications Specialties Inc.
Comprehensive Video Group
Corning Cable Systems
Cortland Cable Co. Inc.
Emcor Enclosures
Gefen Inc.
General Cable
Gepco International Inc.
HAVE Inc.
Insulated Wire Inc. Microwave Products Division
LEMO USA Inc.
M/A-COM
Marshall Electronics
Milestek Corp.
Mohawk
Nemal Electronics International Inc.
Newark Electronics
North American Cable Equipment Inc.
Phillystran Inc.
Prysmian Communications Cables and Systems
    USA, LLC
Radio Frequency Systems
Servoreeler Systems
Stage Equipment & Lighting Inc.
Stanley Supply & Services
James Thomas Engineering Inc.
Times Fiber Communications Inc.
Trilogy Communications Inc.
Trompeter Semflex
WIREMAX Ltd.
Whirlwind
Wireworks Corporation
Zack Electronics Inc.

Cable Security Systems

Electroline Equipment Inc.
Emerson Network Power-Viewsonics
Marshall Electronics
North American Cable Equipment Inc.

Cable Termination Equipment, A/V

Clark Wire & Cable Co. Inc.
North American Cable Equipment Inc.
Vecima Networks Inc.
Videotron Ltee
Zack Electronics Inc.

Calibrators, TV Cameras/Monitors

Commercial Radio Monitoring Co.
Dage-MTI Inc.

Camera Mounts

Alpha Video & Electronics (AVEC)
CSI-Camera Support International
CamMate Studios/Systems
Alan Gordon Enterprises Inc.
Interlogix
Matthews Studio Equipment Inc. (MSE)
Sachtler Corp. of America
Wescam Inc.

Camera Pan/Tilt Heads

ARRI Inc.
Arri Canada Ltd.
Bogen Imaging Inc.
Broadcast Sports Technologies
CSI-Camera Support International
Camera Dynamics
Canon U.S.A. Inc.
Alan Gordon Enterprises Inc.
Hitachi Kokusai Electric America, Ltd.
Innovision Optics Inc.
Isaia & Co.
Miller Camera Support, L.L.C.
O'Connor Professional Camera Support Systems
Allen Osborne Associates Inc.
Quick-Set International Inc.
Telemetrics Inc.
Vinten Inc.

Camera Tubes

Aydin Displays Inc.
Daily Electronics Corp.
Narragansett Imaging

Cameras, Projectors & Accessories

Arri Canada Ltd.
Band Pro Film & Digital Inc.
Broadcast Store Inc.
Camera Service Center
Camplex Corporation
Eastman Kodak Co.
General Electrodynamics Corp.
Alan Gordon Enterprises Inc.
Ikegami Electronics (U.S.A.) Inc.
Innovision Optics Inc.
International Cinema Equipment
The J-Lab Co.
JVC Professional Products Company
Northrup Grumman
Schneider Optics Inc.
Tamron U.S.A. Inc.
Television Engineering Corp.
Toshiba America Consumer Products
Vicon Industries Inc.

Capacitors

Allied Electronics Inc.
Chicago Condenser Corp.
Peter W. Dahl Co. Inc.
Jennings Technology Co.
Motor Capacitors Inc.
NWL Capacitors
Skytec, Inc.

Captioning Equipment

Broadcast Video Systems Corp.
Cheetah International
Image Logic Corp.

Cartridge Automatic Tape

The Tape Company

Cartridge Storage Racks

Russ Bassett
Murphy Studio Furniture

Cases

Alpack Associates, Inc.
Anvil Cases
Atlas Case Corp.
CSI-Camera Support International
Calzone Case Co.
Hardigg Cases
Kangaroo Products Inc.
The Leather Specialty Co.
Miller Camera Support, L.L.C.
Motion Picture Enterprises Inc.
Nalpak
Parsons Manufacturing Corp.
Photomart Cine-Video Inc.
Plastic Reel Corp. of America
PortaBrace
Star Case Manufacturing Co. Inc.

Thermodyne Cases
Viking Cases

Cassette Duplication, Audio/Video

Atlantic Sound Systems
CoarcVideo
HAVE Inc.
M2 America
Media Concepts Inc.
National Audio Co. Inc.
Newdoll Enterprises LLC

Cassette, Audiotape Equip. & Access.

Audiolab Electronics Inc.
Burlington A/V Recording Media Inc.
Garner Products
Moviola
National Video Services Inc.
Veriad

Cassette, Videotape Equip. & Access.

Audiolab Electronics Inc.
Burlington A/V Recording Media Inc.
CoarcVideo
Data Security Inc.
Garner Products
Moviola
Plastic Reel Corp. of America
Veriad

Cassettes

Burlington A/V Recording Media Inc.
CoarcVideo
Future Productions Inc.
Memorex Products Inc.
Moviola
National Audio Co. Inc.
Sony BMG Music Entertainment
The Tape Company

CATV Equipment and Supplies

ADSCO Line Products Inc.
AVCOM of Virginia Inc.
Acterna
Advanced Media Technologies, Inc.
Alpha Technologies Inc.
Andrew Corp.
Arista Information Systems
Benner-Nawman Inc.
Blonder Tongue Laboratories Inc.
CADCO Systems Inc.
CATV Services Inc.
C-COR/ Arris
C I S Inc.
CONTEC Corp.
Cable Prep
Cable Services Company Inc.
Cable Technologies International
CablePro
Channell Commercial Corp.
Charles Industries Ltd.
Comtech Antenna Systems Inc.
Condux International
Convergys Inc.
DST Innovis
Ditch Witch
R.L. Drake LLC
Eagle Comtronics Inc.
Electroline Equipment Inc.
Emerson Network Power-Viewsonics
FM SYSTEMS Inc.
Gefen Inc.
General Atomics
Harmonic Inc.
Hogg & Davis Inc.
Kalun Communications Inc.
Kathrein Inc., Scala Division
Keywest Technology
Lemco Tool Corp.
Lindsay Broadband Inc.
Mega Hertz
Motorola Broadband Communications Sector
North American Cable Equipment Inc.

Ortel
Qintar Technologies Inc.
Ripley Company
Scientific Atlanta
Sencore Inc.
Telecrafter Products
Texscan MSI
Thomas & Betts
Thomas & Betts Corp.
Times Fiber Communications Inc.
Toner Cable Equipment Inc.
Transtector Systems Inc.
Trilogy Communications Inc.
VCI Solutions
Vermeer Manufacturing Co.
Wegener
Zenith Electronics Corp.

CATV Hybrid Modules

Narragansett Imaging
North American Cable Equipment Inc.

CATV Power Supplies

Alpha Technologies Inc.
Electroline Equipment Inc.
Lindsay Broadband Inc.
North American Cable Equipment Inc.

CD Players

Sanyo Fisher Co.
Stanton Group
Superscope Technologies Professionals

Cellular Mobile Telephones

TDK Electronics Corp.

Character Generators

ADTEC Inc.
AVS Graphics & Media Inc.
Comprehensive Video Group
Display Systems International Inc.
Gorman-Redlich Manufacturing Co.
Inscriber Technology Corporation
Keywest Technology
Knox Video
Miranda Technologies Inc.
Texscan MSI

Chroma Keyers

Broadcast Video Systems Corp.
Ultimatte Corp.

Chronometers, Clocks

Autogram Corp.
Chrono-Log Corp.
ESE
Feldmar Watch and Clock Center
Radio Systems Inc.
Torpey Time

Cleaning Accessories, Audio/Video

Data Security Inc.
HAVE Inc.
JNJ Industries Inc.
Research Technology International Inc.
Sprague Magnetics Inc.
TECH-SA-PORT

Closed Captioning Systems

CPC-Computer Prompting & Captioning Co.
Cheetah International
Comprompter Inc.
EEG Enterprises Inc.
Evertz Microsystems Ltd.
Image Logic Corp.
LINK Electronics Inc.
Norpak Corporation
Solutec Ltd. (HA)

Closed Circuit Systems

Aries Industries Inc.
Avtech Systems Inc.
Cohu Inc.
ENCO Systems Inc.
Interlogix
Marshall Electronics
Trident Media Group/ Spector Entertainment Group Inc.

Coaxial Cables

Andrew Corp.
Belden
Broadcast Equipment Surplus Inc.
Comex Worldwide Corp.
CommScope Inc.
Connectronics Corp.
Corning Cable Systems
General Cable
Gepco International Inc.
Marcom
Milestek Corp.
Nemal Electronics International Inc.
North American Cable Equipment Inc.
Power & Telephone Supply Co.
Quality Tower Erectors Inc.
Seger Electronics
Stanley Supply & Services
Teleplex Inc.
Times Fiber Communications Inc.
Trilogy Communications Inc.
Trompeter Semflex
Videotron Ltee

Coaxial Changeover Units, Automatic

Corning Cable Systems
North American Cable Equipment Inc.
Siemens Dematic Limited
Video Accessory Corp.

Coaxial Connectors

Cable Technologies International
CablePro
Canare Corp.
Clark Wire & Cable Co. Inc.
Corning Cable Systems
Corning Gilbert Inc.
Emerson Network Power-Viewsonics
F-Conn Industries
Gepco International Inc.
Kings-Winchester Electronics Corp.
LEMO USA Inc.
Milestek Corp.
Nemal Electronics International Inc.
North American Cable Equipment Inc.
Power & Telephone Supply Co.
Qintar Technologies Inc.
Shively Labs
Trilogy Communications Inc.
Trimm Inc.
Trompeter Semflex
Tyco Electronics

Coaxial Patch Panels

Audio Accessories Inc.
Canare Corp.
Clark Wire & Cable Co. Inc.
Connectronics Corp.
Gepco International Inc.
Glentronix
LARCAN
Milestek Corp.
Nemal Electronics International Inc.
North American Cable Equipment Inc.
Shively Labs
Trompeter Semflex

Coils

Audio-Video Engineering Co.
International Electro-Magnetics (IEM)
LBA Technology Inc.

Combiners

Andrew Corp.
Bauer Transmitters
R.L. Drake LLC
EDCOR Electronics Corp.
ERI-Electronic Research, Inc.
Galaxy Audio Inc.
Jampro Antennas Inc.
LARCAN
Lindsay Broadband Inc.
MYAT Inc.
Microwave Filter Co. Inc.
Narda - An L-3 Communications Co.
Shively Labs

Commercial Compilation

Spotcat Software
Thomson Multi Media

Communications Systems

Clear-Com Communication Systems
Computer Concepts Corp.
Comtech EF Data
DST Innovis
Entertainment Communications Network (ECN)
Global Microwave Systems Inc.
IMS (Interactive Market Systems Inc.)
E.F. Johnson Co.
Kahn Communications Inc.
L-3 Communications Telemetry East
MODCOMP Inc.
MRPP Inc.
Ortel
Production Intercom Inc.
Roscor Corp.
Setcom Corporation
Studio Technologies Inc.
TC Group Americas Inc.
TDK Electronics Corp.
Thomas & Betts
V-Soft Communications
Visual Sound Inc.

Compact Disc Equipment

Burlington A/V Recording Media Inc.
Micro Technology Unlimited
National Audio Co. Inc.
Newdoll Enterprises LLC
Optical Disc Corp.
Research Technology International Inc.

Compact Disc Manufacturers

Sony BMG Music Entertainment

Computer Desks

CMP Enclosures Inc.
Fusion Consoles
Luxor
TEAC America Inc.

Computer Floppy Disks

Maxell Corp. of America
Memorex Products Inc.

Computers and Peripherals

Ampex Data Systems -America
APC by Schneider Electric
Argo Systems
AVerMedia Technologies Inc.
Broadcast Data Consultants
CEA-Computer Engineering Associates
C I S Inc.
CSG Systems
Computer Resolutions
DST Innovis
Dynamic Solutions 2000
Encoda Systems Inc.
Enghouse Systems Limited
Gefen Inc.
Great Lakes Data Systems, Inc.
Greenberg Teleprompting
IMS (Interactive Market Systems Inc.)
MCG Surge Protection

MODCOMP Inc.
Marketron International
Mediasoft Inc.
Memorex Products Inc.
Radio Computing Services (RCS)
StorerTV Inc.
Summit Software Systems Inc.
Unique Business Systems
Unisys Corp.
UniVision Inc.
Vision Database Systems

Computers/Broadcast Equipment Control

Adrienne Electronics Corp.
Aspera Inc.
CEA-Computer Engineering Associates
CS Communications Inc.
Computer Concepts Corp.
FloriCal Systems Inc.
Hotbox Digital
Identix
Imagine Products Inc.
MATCO Inc.
MODCOMP Inc.
Marketron Broadcast Solutions
Marketron International
Media Computing Inc.
Radio Computing Services (RCS)
Register Communications
Time Logic Inc.
VCI Solutions

Connectors

Allied Electronics Inc.
CATV Services Inc.
Connectronics Corp.
Gepco International Inc.
ITT Cannon Electric
LEMO USA Inc.
Marshall Electronics
Mohawk
Neutrik U.S.A. Inc.
Sacramento Theatrical Lighting (STL)
Switchcraft Inc.
Wireworks Corporation

Console Equipment

Audioarts Engineering
Broadcast Supply Worldwide
Emcor Enclosures
IMS/AMCO Engineering Products
Viking Cases

Consoles

APW Mayville/Stantron
Audioarts Engineering
Bud Industries Inc.
CMP Enclosures Inc.
Emcor Enclosures
High Tech Industries
IMS/AMCO Engineering Products
Martinsound Inc.
North American Cable Equipment Inc.
Otari USA Sales Inc.
Peavey Electronics
Solid State Logic Inc.
Soundcraft U.S.A.
Vega
Wheatstone Corp.
Winsted Corp.

Consoles, On-Air

Audioarts Engineering
Autogram Corp.
Broadcast Equipment Surplus Inc.
Euphonix Inc.
IMS/AMCO Engineering Products
Logitek
North American Cable Equipment Inc.
Radio Systems Inc.
Soundcraft U.S.A.
Wheatstone Corp.

Construction Services

CCI Systems Inc.
Cygnal Technologies
180 Connect
Quality Tower Erectors Inc.
T.T. Technologies Inc.
Teletech Inc.
Tenco Tower Co.

Control Systems

FloriCal Systems Inc.
Identix
Image Logic Corp.
Knox Video
MATCO Inc.
NSI
QuStream
Richmond Sound Design Ltd.
Sacramento Theatrical Lighting (STL)
TANDBERG Television Inc.
Vega
Vertex Communications Corp.
Vicon Industries Inc.

Converters and Switchers (CATV)

Beyond Broadband Technology LLC
CONTEC Corp.
Gefen Inc.
Utah Scientific Inc.

Converters, Standards

CATV Services Inc.
CONTEC Corp.
Ikegami Electronics (U.S.A.) Inc.
The Image Group Post, LLC.
Kay Industries Inc.
Merlin Engineering Works Inc.
Philip-Cooke Co.
Snell
Video International Development Corp.
Wiltronix Inc.

Converters, TV

Beyond Broadband Technology LLC
Kay Industries Inc.
Scientific Atlanta

Copy Stands

Murphy Studio Furniture

Costumes and Properties

Costume Armour Inc./Christo Vac

Crystal Units

ICM (International Crystal Mfg.Co.)

Cue Systems

COMTEK Inc.
Greenberg Teleprompting
Studio Technologies Inc.

Custom Consoles

APW Mayville/Stantron
CMP Enclosures Inc.
Calzone Case Co.
Fusion Consoles
High Tech Industries
Northeastern Communications Concepts Inc.
Studio Technology
Winsted Corp.

Custom Studios

Channel One Lighting Systems Inc.
High Tech Industries
Industrial Acoustics Co., Inc.
Murphy Studio Furniture
Studio Technology
Yanchar Design & Consulting Group

Cyclorama Tracks

Automatic Devices Company
Channel One Lighting Systems Inc.
Olesen
Theatre Service & Supply Corp.
Theatrical Services Inc.
Uni-Set Corp.

Data Communications Systems

Canon U.S.A. Inc.
Dynamic Solutions 2000
EEG Enterprises Inc.
Entertainment Communications Network (ECN)
FM SYSTEMS Inc.
Great Lakes Data Systems, Inc.
Keywest Technology
MCG Surge Protection
MODCOMP Inc.
Microspace Communications Corp.
Milestone Technologies Inc.
Modulation Sciences Inc.
Norpak Corporation
180 Connect
Spacenet Services Inc.
Trident Media Group/ Spector Entertainment Group Inc.

Data Transmission Equipment

Broadcast Video Systems Corp.
Canon U.S.A. Inc.
Comtech EF Data
Fiber Options
IPITEK
Inovonics Inc.
Intelligent Media Technology
International Datacasting Corp.
MCL Inc.
Moseley Associates Inc.
Norpak Corporation
Spacenet Services Inc.
TELLABS
Vecima Networks Inc.
Wegener

Decals

Seton Identification Products

Decoders

Audio Processing Technology Ltd./APT
Belar Electronics Laboratory Inc.
EEG Enterprises Inc.
Faroudja Laboratories
Rovi Corp.
Sarnoff Corp.
Snell
TANDBERG Television Inc.
Television Equipment Assoc. Inc./Matthey
Trident Media Group/ Spector Entertainment Group Inc.
Vega

Dehydrators and Accessories

Dielectric Communications
Radio Frequency Systems
Shively Labs

Demodulators and Modulators

CADCO Systems Inc.
Cable Serv Inc.
FM SYSTEMS Inc.
General Atomics
Harris Broadcast Communications
L-3 Communications Telemetry East
NUCOMM Inc.
North American Cable Equipment Inc.
TANDBERG Television Inc.
Videotron Ltee

Descramblers, Pay TV

Motorola Broadband Communications Sector
North American Cable Equipment Inc.
Rovi Corp.

Design Services, Broadcast

Cygnal Technologies
DeSisti Lighting
Meridian Design Associates, Architects
Murphy Studio Furniture
Northeastern Communications Concepts Inc.
Professional Communications Systems
Quality Tower Erectors Inc.
Rees Associates Inc.
Studio Technology
VidCAD Documentation Programs (VDP Inc.)
Yanchar Design & Consulting Group

Designers, Production Facilities

CBT Systems
Four Seasons Solar Products Corp.
High Tech Industries
Meridian Design Associates, Architects
Northeastern Communications Concepts Inc.
Rees Associates Inc.
Yanchar Design & Consulting Group

Digital Audio Processing Equipment

Aphex Systems Ltd.
Audio Processing Technology Ltd./APT
Benchmark Media Systems Inc.
Broadcast Supply Worldwide
COASTCOM
Circuit Research Labs Inc. (CRL Systems, Inc.)
Dialogic Communications Corp.
Eventide Inc.
G Prime Ltd.
Graham-Patten Systems Inc.
Linear Acoustic Inc.
Logitek
Micro Technology Unlimited
NVISION Products
Orban
Penny & Giles Inc.
Radio Computing Services (RCS)
Roland Corp. U.S.
Sabine Inc.
Sascom Marketing Group
Symetrix Inc.
TC Group Americas Inc.
TC Electronic
Ward-Beck Systems Ltd.

Digital Audio Recorders

Alesis
Fostex USA
Micro Technology Unlimited
Roland Corp. U.S.
Stancil Corp.
Superscope Technologies Professionals
360 Systems
Yamaha Corp. of America

Digital Audio Recording & Editing Station

Avid Broadcast
Computer Concepts Corp.
Digidesign
ENCO Systems Inc.
Micro Technology Unlimited
Orban
Parsons Audio
Penny & Giles Inc.
Radio Computing Services (RCS)
360 Systems
Visual Sound Inc.
WireReady NSI

Digital Broadcast Equipment

ADTEC Inc.
ATCI/Antenna Technology Communications Inc.
ATI-Audio Technologies Inc.
Abekas, Incorporated
Acterna
Arrakis Systems Inc.
Axcera
BEXT Inc.
Belar Electronics Laboratory Inc.
Bexel
Broadcast Electronics Inc.

Broadcast Store Inc.
Broadcast Supply Worldwide
COASTCOM
CORPLEX Inc.
Computer Concepts Corp.
Comtech EF Data
Dalet Digital Media Systems
DiGi Co. Ltd.
DMT USA, Inc.
R.L. Drake LLC
Fast Forward Video
Fostex USA
General Atomics
Harris Corp., Broadcast Communications
Harris Corp., Broadcast Division
Hitachi Kokusai Electric America, Ltd.
IPITEK
International Datacasting Corp.
JVC Professional Products Company
MATCO Inc.
MUSICAM U.S.A.
Marshall Electronics
Mohawk
Panasonic Broadcast & Television Systems Co.
ProAudio.com/Crouse-Kimzey Co.
Register Communications
Telos Systems
Utah Scientific Inc.
VCI Solutions
Visual Sound Inc.
Wegener

Digital Image Processors

Barco Inc.
Eigen
Xintekvideo Inc.

Digital Special Effects Systems

AccuWeather Inc.
Autodesk
Autodesk
Chyron Corp.
Cintel Inc.
Eastman Kodak Co.
FOR- A Corp. of America
Quantel Inc.
The Tiffen Company
Toshiba America Consumer Products

Digital Video Graphics and Animation

AccuWeather Inc.
Autodesk
Autodesk
Even Technologies Inc.
Keywest Technology
Quantel Inc.

Digital Video Processing Equipment

Ensemble Designs
FOR- A Corp. of America
Gennum Corp.
Hotronic Inc.
LINK Electronics Inc.
Leitch Inc.
NVISION Products
NTV International Corporation
Scientific Atlanta
Television Equipment Assoc. Inc./Matthey
Video International Development Corp.
Visual Sound Inc.
Ward-Beck Systems Ltd.
Xintekvideo Inc.

Digital Video Production Systems

Bitcentral Inc.
Dalet Digital Media Systems
MAVRIC Media Inc.
NVISION Products
Specialized Communications Corp.
Thomson Broadcast & Media Solutions

Distortion Analyzers

Audio Precision Inc.
Boonton Electronics Corp.
Electro Rent Corp.
SyntheSys Research Inc.

Distribution Amplifiers

Autogram Corp.
Benchmark Media Systems Inc.
Burst Electronics Inc.
Cablynx, Inc.
ESE
Farrtronics Ltd.
Harris Broadcast Communications
Horita
Intersil Corp.
Leitch Inc.
North American Cable Equipment Inc.
Philip-Cooke Co.
Qintar Technologies Inc.
QuStream
Radio Systems Inc.
Sigma Electronics Inc.
Studio Technologies Inc.
Symmetricom
Symmetricom
Television Equipment Assoc. Inc./Matthey
Video Accessory Corp.
Ward-Beck Systems Ltd.

Distribution Systems

Aspera Inc.
Enghouse Systems Limited
IPITEK
MAVRIC Media Inc.
North American Cable Equipment Inc.
Philip-Cooke Co.
Scientific Atlanta
StarGuide Digital Networks Inc.
Wegener
Wiltronix Inc.

Dollies, Instrument Carts, Etc.

Ferno-Washington Inc.
Hogg & Davis Inc.
Matthews Studio Equipment Inc. (MSE)
Panavision New York

Dummy Loads

Altronic Research Inc.
Bird Electronic Corp.
Electro Impulse Laboratory Inc.
Kintronic Labs Inc.
Narda - An L-3 Communications Co.
Phasetek Inc.

Duplicators

Ascent Media Management Services
Interface Media Group
M2 America
National Audio Co. Inc.
Newdoll Enterprises LLC

Earth Stations

Ascent Media Services
D.H. Satellite
General Electric Co.
Maze Corporation
Megastar Inc.
Narda Satellite Networks
Pinzone Engineering Group Inc.
TDK Electronics Corp.
Trident Media Group/ Spector Entertainment Group Inc.
Vertex Communications Corp.

Editing Equipment, Sales-Rental-Service

Adcom
International Cinema Equipment
Neumade Products Corp.
Plastic Reel Corp. of America
Specialized Communications Corp.
TDK Electronics Corp.
United Media Inc.

Editing Film and Tape

Ascent Media Management Services
Avid Broadcast
Center City Film & Video
Chyron Corp.
The Image Group Post, LLC.
J and R Moviola Inc.
Paulmar Industries Inc.
Skotel Corp.
TDK Electronics Corp.

EFP (Electronic Field Production)

Bexel
Mobile Video Services Ltd.
PMTV Producers Management Television
Panasonic Broadcast & Television Systems Co.
Shook Mobile Technology, LP
TDK Electronics Corp.

Electronic Advertising Displays

Display Systems International Inc.
U.S. Traffic & Display Solutions

Electronic Components

ADCOUR, Inc.
Communication & Power Industries, EIMAC Operations
Dow-Key Microwave Corp.
Jennings Technology Co.
Kay Industries Inc.
Laser Diode Inc.
M/A-COM
Newark Electronics
Selco Products Co.
TTE Inc.
Westlake Audio, Professional Sales Group

Electronic Equipment

Auernheimer Labs Corp.
Boonton Electronics Corp.
Cable Leakage Technologies
Cable Technologies International
Condor D C Power Supplies Inc.
JOA Cartridge Service
Narda Satellite Networks
Power & Telephone Supply Co.
Sencore Inc.
Teleplex Inc.
Thomson, Inc, (RCA/GE)
Whirlwind

Electronic Protection Equipment

Condor D C Power Supplies Inc.
EFI Electronics Corp.
Emerson Network Power
General Electric Co.
Henry Engineering
LEA International
MCG Surge Protection
Tapeswitch Corp.
Transtector Systems Inc.
Wil-Can Electronics Ltd.

Emergency Alerting Systems

Gorman-Redlich Manufacturing Co.
Keywest Technology
TFT Inc.

Emergency Broadcast Equipment

Crown Broadcast IREC
Gorman-Redlich Manufacturing Co.
Highway Information Systems, Inc.
Mediastar-SG

EMI Cabinets

IMS/AMCO Engineering Products

Encoders

Audio Processing Technology Ltd./APT
Broadcast Video Systems Corp.
Cheetah International
Dolby Laboratories Inc.
EEG Enterprises Inc.
Faroudja Laboratories
Hitachi Kokusai Electric America, Ltd.
L-3 Communications Telemetry East
Mega Hertz
Merlin Engineering Works Inc.
Rovi Corp.
Sarnoff Corp.
Sigma Electronics Inc.
StarGuide Digital Networks Inc.
Symmetricom
Vega

ENG Equipment and Accessories

AKG Acoustics, U.S.
Ampex Data Systems -America
Battery Pros Inc.
Bexel
Broadcast Microwave Services Inc.
COMTEK Inc.
CSI-Camera Support International
Camplex Corporation
Comrex Corp.
E-N-G Mobile Systems Inc.
Gyrocam Systems
Ikegami Electronics (U.S.A.) Inc.
Marathon Norco Aerospace, Inc.
Marti Electronics
Modulation Sciences Inc.
NSI
NUCOMM Inc.
Narda - An L-3 Communications Co.
Photomart Cine-Video Inc.
Professional Sound Services Inc.
Swintek Enterprises Inc.
Television Engineering Corp.
Telex Communications Inc.
Telos Systems

ENG Vans

Alpha Video & Electronics (AVEC)
E-N-G Mobile Systems Inc.
Frontline Communications
Mobile Video Services Ltd.
Phoenix E N G, Inc.
Shook Mobile Technology, LP
Television Engineering Corp.
WILL-BURT Co.
Wolf Coach Inc.

Engineering Systems

AZCAR U.S.A. Inc.
CBT Systems
CCI Systems Inc.
C I S Inc.
CS Communications Inc.
Cygnal Technologies
Enghouse Systems Limited
Freeland Products Inc.
Professional Communications Systems
V-Soft Communications

Equalizers

A R T Applied Research and Technology
Alesis
Furman
G Prime Ltd.
Group One Ltd.
Harman International Industries Inc.
Sabine Inc.

TC Electronic

Equipment Maintenance and Repair

AVI Systems
Alpine Optics Inc.
CORPLEX Inc.
Feldmar Watch and Clock Center
Film/Video Equipment Service Co. Inc.
LARCAN USA
Location Sound Corp.
Tech Laboratories Inc.
Tentel

Erasers, Magnetic Tape

Audiolab Electronics Inc.
Data Security Inc.
Garner Products
Paulmar Industries Inc.
Research Technology International Inc.

Exciters

Acrodyne Industries Inc. (Ai)
Axcera
Delta Electronics Inc.
Marti Electronics
Nautel Ltd.

Facilities Planning

CBT Systems
Devlin Design Group Inc.
The Express Group
Hollywood Vaults Inc.
Rees Associates Inc.
Technet Systems Group
V-Soft Communications
VidCAD Documentation Programs (VDP Inc.)
Yanchar Design & Consulting Group

Fiber Optic Cable and Accessories

ADC
ADSCO Line Products Inc.
Bexel
CCI Systems Inc.
Channell Commercial Corp.
CommScope Inc.
Communications Specialties Inc.
Condux International
Corning Incorporated
Cortland Cable Co. Inc.
General Cable
Gepco International Inc.
Laser Diode Inc.
LEMO USA Inc.
Mohawk
Nemal Electronics International Inc.
Newark Electronics
North American Cable Equipment Inc.
Prysmian Communications Cables and Systems
    USA, LLC
Ripley Company
Stanley Supply & Services
Telecast Fiber Systems Inc.
Thomas & Betts Corp.
Whirlwind

Fiber Optic Transmission Systems

Artel Video Systems
Ascent Media Services
CCI Systems Inc.
C-COR/ Arris
Cable Services Company Inc.
Camplex Corporation
Communications Specialties Inc.
Evertz Microsystems Ltd.
Fiber Options
General Atomics
Harmonic Inc.
IPITEK
Intelligent Media Technology
Laser Diode Inc.
Lindsay Broadband Inc.
Mega Hertz
Norlight Telecommunications Inc.
North American Cable Equipment Inc.
NTV International Corporation

180 Connect
Ortel
QuStream
Standard Communications Corp.
StarGuide Digital Networks Inc.
Telecast Fiber Systems Inc.
Toner Cable Equipment Inc.
Videotron Ltee

Field Strength Meters

ETS-Lindgren
Narda - An L-3 Communications Co.
North American Cable Equipment Inc.
Potomac Instruments, Inc.
Sadelco Inc.
Sencore Inc.
Toner Cable Equipment Inc.

Film Equipment

Arri Canada Ltd.
BHP Inc.
CECO International Corp.
Camera Service Center
Dimension 3
Eastman Kodak Co.
Film/Video Equipment Service Co. Inc.
International Cinema Equipment
J and R Moviola Inc.
Lipsner Smith Co.
Magna-Tech Electronic Co. Inc.
Mole-Richardson Co.
Motion Picture Enterprises Inc.
Neumade Products Corp.
Paulmar Industries Inc.
Pro Video & Film Equipment Co. Inc.
ScreenLight & Grip
Wescam Inc.
Westcott

Film Printers, Motion Pictures

BHP Inc.
Eastman Kodak Co.

Film Processors

Eastman Kodak Co.
Lipsner Smith Co.
Precision Microproducts of America

Film Scanners

ARRI Inc.
Cintel Inc.

Film-to-Tape Transfer Equipment

International Cinema Equipment
J and R Moviola Inc.
Lipsner Smith Co.

Filters and Delay Lines

Allen Avionics, Inc.
Electroline Equipment Inc.
MYAT Inc.
Microwave Filter Co. Inc.
Motorola Broadband Communications Sector
Schneider Optics Inc.
TTE Inc.
Television Equipment Assoc. Inc./Matthey

Fire Detection System

Kidde-Fenwal Inc.

Floor Covering Stages

Eddie Egan & Associates
Rosco Laboratories Inc.

Frame Synchronizers

Cablynx, Inc.
Harris Broadcast Communications
Leitch Inc.
World Video Sales Co.

Frequency Measuring Services

Antenna Concepts Inc.
Commercial Radio Monitoring Co.
Communications General Corp.
Frequency Measuring Service Inc.
Northwest Monitoring Service
Radio Aids Inc.
Sencore Inc.
Signal Monitoring Service
Symmetricom
Van Nostrand Radio Engineering Service
Ziehl Electronic Service

Frequency Monitors

Symmetricom

Generators, Electric

CECO International Corp.
Elan Enterprises Ltd.
Engineered Electric Company
FWT Inc.
Hollywood Rentals Production Services
Illumination Dynamics Inc.
PMTV Producers Management Television
Panavision New York
ScreenLight & Grip

Generators, Signal

Kalun Communications Inc.
Magni Systems Inc.
Sencore Inc.
Video Accessory Corp.

Graphics

AccuWeather Inc.
All Mobile Video Inc.
Atlantic Video Inc.
Autodesk
Chyron Corp.
Even Technologies Inc.
The Image Group Post, LLC.
Inscriber Technology Corporation
Interface Media Group
Wiltronix Inc.

HDTV Equipment

Abekas, Incorporated
Acrodyne Industries Inc. (Ai)
Antenna Concepts Inc.
Autodesk
Bexel
Camplex Corporation
Canon U.S.A. Inc.
Communication & Power Industries
Dielectric Communications
Frequency Measuring Service Inc.
Harris Corp., Broadcast Communications
Harris Corp., Broadcast Division
JVC Professional Products Company
Kalun Communications Inc.
Kathrein Inc., Scala Division
LEMO USA Inc.
Marshall Electronics
Milestone Technologies Inc.
Mohawk
O'Connor Professional Camera Support Systems
Panasonic Broadcast & Television Systems Co.
Professional Communications Systems
Sarnoff Corp.
Sencore Inc.
Sharp Electronics Corp., CCD Products Div.
SyntheSys Research Inc.
TANDBERG Television Inc.
Teleplex Inc.
Thomson Broadcast & Media Solutions
Toshiba America Consumer Products
Utah Scientific Inc.
Ward-Beck Systems Ltd.
Wegener
Winsted Corp.

Headend Systems

ADC
Alpha Technologies Inc.
Beyond Broadband Technology LLC
Blonder Tongue Laboratories Inc.
CCI Systems Inc.
C-COR/ Arris
ComSonics Inc.
D.H. Satellite
General Atomics
Kalun Communications Inc.
Mega Hertz
Norsat International Inc.
North American Cable Equipment Inc.
Ortel
Scientific Atlanta
Sitco Antenna Company
Standard Communications Corp.
TANDBERG Television Inc.
Toner Cable Equipment Inc.

Heads, Magnetic Film & Tape, Disk

AheadTek
International Electro-Magnetics (IEM)
Polyline
Sprague Magnetics Inc.

Heads, Refurbishing

International Electro-Magnetics (IEM)
Sprague Magnetics Inc.
Videomagnetics Inc.

Headset Amplifiers

ATI-Audio Technologies Inc.
Henry Engineering

Headsets, Headphones

AKG Acoustics, U.S.
Anchor Audio Inc.
Audio-Technica U.S., Inc.
COMTEK Inc.
Clear-Com Communication Systems
Fostex USA
Production Intercom Inc.
RTS Systems Telex Communications Inc
Sacramento Theatrical Lighting (STL)
Sennheiser Electronic Corp.
Stanton Group
Telex Communications Inc.

Helicopters

American Eurocopter Corp.
Geneva Aviation Inc.
Gyrocam Systems
Wescam Inc.

High Definition Television (HDTV)

Beyond Broadband Technology LLC
Cintel Inc.
Hitachi Kokusai Electric America, Ltd.
LARCAN USA
Leitch Inc.
Miranda Technologies Inc.
Moseley Associates Inc.
Sarnoff Corp.
Sencore Inc.
Telecast Fiber Systems Inc.
Toshiba America Consumer Products

Image Enhancers, TV

Colorado Video Inc.
Xintekvideo Inc.

Infrared Transmission Systems

Sennheiser Electronic Corp.
Sound Associates

Installation Services

American Antenna Inc.
B&B Systems
Broadcast Store Inc.
CBT Systems
180 Connect
Professional Communications Systems
Quality Tower Erectors Inc.
Superior Tower Services Inc.
Teletech Inc.
VidCAD Documentation Programs (VDP Inc.)

Instruments Cases

A & S Case Co. Inc.
Atlas Case Corp.
Calzone Case Co.
Hardigg Cases
Penn Elcom Inc.
Stanley Supply & Services
Star Case Manufacturing Co. Inc.
Thermodyne Cases

Interactive Television

Avid Broadcast
BIAP Inc.
TANDBERG Television Inc.
Tribune Media Services
Vidiom Systems Inc.

Intercom Systems

Anchor Audio Inc.
Bogen Communications Inc.
Clear-Com Communication Systems
Farrtronics Ltd.
Fuller Manufacturing
HME
ITI Electronics Inc.
Olesen
Production Intercom Inc.
RTS Systems Telex Communications Inc
Ram Broadcast Systems
Sacramento Theatrical Lighting (STL)
Setcom Corporation
Sierra Automated Systems & Engineering Corp.
Stage Equipment & Lighting Inc.
Studio Technologies Inc.
Swintek Enterprises Inc.
Systems Wireless Ltd.
Talk-A-Phone Co.
Telex Communications Inc.
Wiltronix Inc.

ISO Couplers (AM & FM)

Phasetek Inc.

Jack Panels and Accessories

ADC
Audio Accessories Inc.
Auernheimer Labs Corp.
Clark Wire & Cable Co. Inc.
Gepco International Inc.
ITI Electronics Inc.
Kings-Winchester Electronics Corp.
NVISION Products
Penn Elcom Inc.
Penny & Giles Inc.
Trimm Inc.

Klystron Amplifiers/Lead Oxide Vidicon

e2v technologies Inc.
Penta Laboratories

Klystrons

Communication & Power Industries
Daily Electronics Corp.
e2v technologies Inc.
LARCAN USA
MRPP Inc.
Penta Laboratories
Thales Electron Devices

Labels

Audico Labels
Memorex Products Inc.
National Audio Co. Inc.
Seton Identification Products
Techni-Tool Inc.
U.S. Tape & Label Corp.
Veriad

LED, VU and S Panel Meters

Dorrough Electronics
Logitek
Sescom Inc.
Weschler Instruments

Lenses, Optical and Camera

Alpine Optics Inc.
Band Pro Film & Digital Inc.
Canon U.S.A. Inc.
Century Precision Optics
Dimension 3
Film/Video Equipment Service Co. Inc.
Fujinon Inc.
Homalite
Innovision Optics Inc.
Marshall Electronics
Navitar Inc.
Pentax Imaging Co.
Schneider Optics Inc.
Tamron U.S.A. Inc.

Library Storage Systems

Hollywood Vaults Inc.
Imagine Products Inc.
Neumade Products Corp.
Paulmar Industries Inc.

Lighting Design

DeSisti Lighting
Devlin Design Group Inc.
The Express Group
L.E. Nelson Sales Corp.
New York City Lites
Packaged Lighting Systems Inc.
Sachtler Corp. of America
Videssence L.L.C.

Lighting Equipment

ARRI Inc.
AVAB America Inc.
Anton/Bauer Inc.
Arri Canada Ltd.
Atlantic Sound Systems
Automatic Devices Company
Band Pro Film & Digital Inc.
Bend-A-Lite Flexible Neon
CECO International Corp.
Camera Service Center
Channel One Lighting Systems Inc.
Comprehensive Video Group
DEDOTEC USA Inc.
DeSisti Lighting
Dove Systems
Electronic Theatre Controls Inc.
Emerson Network Power
Film/Video Equipment Service Co. Inc.
Flash Technology Corporation of America
Frezzolini Electronics Inc.
Full Compass Systems Ltd.
GAMPRODUCTS Inc.
Group One Ltd.
Honeywell Lighting & Electronics
Illumination Dynamics Inc.
LTM Corp. of America
Leviton NSI Colortran
Lowel-Light Manufacturing Inc.
Matthews Studio Equipment Inc. (MSE)
Mole-Richardson Co.
Musco Mobile Lighting Ltd.
L.E. Nelson Sales Corp.
Neutrik U.S.A. Inc.
New York City Lites
Olesen
Allen Osborne Associates Inc.
PC& E
Packaged Lighting Systems Inc.

Panavision New York
Photomart Cine-Video Inc.
Pro Video & Film Equipment Co. Inc.
Rosco Laboratories Inc.
Sachtler Corp. of America
ScreenLight & Grip
Sinar Bron Inc.
Skytec, Inc.
Stage Equipment & Lighting Inc.
Strand Lighting Inc.
Strong International
Teatronics/Entertainment Lighting Control
Theatre Service & Supply Corp.
Theatrical Services Inc.
James Thomas Engineering Inc.
Ultimate Support Systems Inc.
Vantage Lighting Inc.
Videssence L.L.C.
Westcott

Lightning Protection Equip. & Systems

Abroyd Communications Ltd.
Cortana Corp.
EFI Electronics Corp.
Emerson Network Power
LBA Technology Inc.
LEA International
Lightning Eliminators & Consultants Inc.
Lightning Master Corp.
Lightning Prevention Systems
MCG Surge Protection
Mole-Richardson Co.
Neumade Products Corp.
North Hills Signal Processing, a PORTA Systems Co.
Transtector Systems Inc.
Wil-Can Electronics Ltd.

Lights, On-Air

Electronic Theatre Controls Inc.
General Electric Co.
Sachtler Corp. of America
Sinar Bron Inc.

Lights, Recording

Electronic Theatre Controls Inc.
General Electric Co.
Sinar Bron Inc.

Lights, Stage

AVAB America Inc.
Bend-A-Lite Flexible Neon
Electronic Theatre Controls Inc.
GAMPRODUCTS Inc.
General Electric Co.
Hollywood Rentals Production Services
Mole-Richardson Co.
L.E. Nelson Sales Corp.
Olesen
Packaged Lighting Systems Inc.
Sacramento Theatrical Lighting (STL)
Stage Equipment & Lighting Inc.
Strong International
Theatre Service & Supply Corp.
James Thomas Engineering Inc.
Vantage Lighting Inc.

Line Conditioning

ADCOUR, Inc.
APC by Schneider Electric
Emerson Network Power
Emerson Network Power
Furman
LEA International
MCG Surge Protection
Newark Electronics
Wil-Can Electronics Ltd.

Line Surge Protectors

ADCOUR, Inc.
APC by Schneider Electric
EFI Electronics Corp.
Emerson Network Power
Emerson Network Power
LEA International
Lightning Master Corp.
MCG Surge Protection
Transtector Systems Inc.
Wil-Can Electronics Ltd.

Locks

CableTek Wiring Products Inc.
Penn Elcom Inc.

Logging System

Geac Libra
Horita
Image Logic Corp.
Imagine Products Inc.
Newdoll Enterprises LLC
Spotcat Software
Telcom Research

Loudspeakers and Accessories

Amplivox Portable Sound Systems
Atlas Sound
Auernheimer Labs Corp.
Bogen Communications Inc.
JBL Professional
Sennheiser Electronic Corp.
Ultimate Support Systems Inc.
Yanchar Design & Consulting Group

Machine Control Systems

ADTEC Inc.
Peter Albrecht Company Inc.
General Electric Co.
Leightronix Inc.
MATCO Inc.
Mediastar-SG
Micro Technology Unlimited
Philip-Cooke Co.
Tapeswitch Corp.

Master Control Switches

Evertz Microsystems Ltd.
Leitch Inc.
Miranda Technologies Inc.
Tapeswitch Corp.
Utah Scientific Inc.

Meters

Aeroflex
B&B Systems
Benchmark Media Systems Inc.
ComSonics Inc.
Dorrough Electronics
Electro Rent Corp.
G Prime Ltd.
Jewell Instruments LLC
Konica Minolta Corp.
McCurdy Radio Ltd.
Photo Research
Radiodetection/Riser Bond
Techni-Tool Inc.
Tentel
Weschler Instruments

Microphones and Accessories

AKG Acoustics, U.S.
Audio-Technica U.S., Inc.
Black Audio
Bogen Communications Inc.
COMTEK Inc.
Countryman Associates Inc.
DPA Microphones, Inc.
FitzCo. Inc.
G Prime Ltd.
Group One Ltd.
LTM Corp. of America
Location Sound Corp.

Marshall Electronics
Micron Audio Products Ltd.
Nady Systems Inc.
Professional Sound Corp.
RTS Systems Telex Communications Inc
Sennheiser Electronic Corp.
Sescom Inc.
Shure Inc.
Systems Wireless Ltd.
Telex Communications Inc.
Ultimate Support Systems Inc.

Microwave

Ascent Media Services
Broadcast Microwave Services Inc.
Broadcast Sports Technologies
Comex Worldwide Corp.
Comsearch
Direct Broadcast Services Inc.
Global Microwave Systems Inc.
Harris-Farinon
M/A-COM
Marcom
NSI
PMTV Producers Management Television
RF Specialties Group
TFT Inc.

Microwave Amplifiers

Comex Worldwide Corp.
Harris-Farinon
NUCOMM Inc.

Microwave Antennas

Broadcast Microwave Services Inc.
Broadcast Sports Technologies
Comex Worldwide Corp.
D.H. Satellite
NSI
NUCOMM Inc.
Radio Frequency Systems
Radio Research Instrument Co. Inc.
Southern Broadcast Services

Microwave Equipment

AVCOM of Virginia Inc.
Blonder Tongue Laboratories Inc.
Broadcast Equipment Surplus Inc.
Broadcast Microwave Services Inc.
Broadcast Sports Technologies
Comex Worldwide Corp.
Dow-Key Microwave Corp.
E-N-G Mobile Systems Inc.
Frontline Communications
Geneva Aviation Inc.
JSB Service Co.
Marti Electronics
Moseley Associates Inc.
NUCOMM Inc.
Norsat International Inc.
Ortel
Radio Research Instrument Co. Inc.
Radio Systems Inc.

Microwave Transmitters

Broadcast Microwave Services Inc.
Broadcast Sports Technologies
CED
Comex Worldwide Corp.
Global Microwave Systems Inc.
JSB Service Co.
NUCOMM Inc.
Norlight Telecommunications Inc.

Mobile Communications

Aluma Tower Company Inc.
Amdocs
CSG Systems
DST Innovis
Geneva Aviation Inc.
Hardigg Cases
ICM (International Crystal Mfg.Co.)
MCL Inc.
Thermodyne Cases

Mobile Studio Equipment

Calzone Case Co.
Camplex Corporation
F&F Productions, L.L.C.
Ferno-Washington Inc.
Hollywood Rentals Production Services
Packaged Lighting Systems Inc.
Telos Systems
United States Broadcast

Mobile Units-Sales/Rental

All Mobile Video Inc.
Frontline Communications
PMTV Producers Management Television
J.A. Taylor & Associates
Turner Studios Field Operations

Mobile Vans

Alpha Video & Electronics (AVEC)
E-N-G Mobile Systems Inc.
Frontline Communications
Panavision New York
Phoenix E N G, Inc.
Roscor Corp.
ScreenLight & Grip
Shook Mobile Technology, LP
Television Engineering Corp.

Modular Set Design System

The Display & Exhibit Source
Uni-Set Corp.

Modulators

Advanced Media Technologies, Inc.
Blonder Tongue Laboratories Inc.
CADCO Systems Inc.
Cable Serv Inc.
Cable Technologies International
Comtech EF Data
R.L. Drake LLC
Leaming Industries
Standard Communications Corp.

Moldings

CablePro
CableReady Inc.
The Display & Exhibit Source

Monitor Amplifiers

Alesis

Monitor Speakers

Galaxy Audio Inc.
Group One Ltd.
Harman International Industries Inc.
JBL Professional
Stanton Group
Westlake Audio, Professional Sales Group
Yamaha Corp. of America
Yanchar Design & Consulting Group

Monitors, Audio and Video

Band Pro Film & Digital Inc.
Conrac Systems Inc.
Dorrough Electronics
Farrtronics Ltd.
Furman
Hoodman Corp.
Ikegami Electronics (U.S.A.) Inc.
Image Video
Interlogix
The J-Lab Co.
JVC Professional Products Company
Linear Acoustic Inc.
Magni Systems Inc.
Marshall Electronics
Sharp Electronics Corp., CCD Products Div.

Monitors, Frequency, Modulation Phase

Belar Electronics Laboratory Inc.
Commercial Radio Monitoring Co.
Frequency Measuring Service Inc.
Inovonics Inc.
TFT Inc.

Monopoles

FWT Inc.
Fred A. Nudd Corp.
Pirod Inc.
Rohn Industries Inc.

Motion Control Equipment

Innovision Optics Inc.
Richmond Sound Design Ltd.
Tapeswitch Corp.
Vinten Inc.

Motion Picture Equipment

ARRI Inc.
BHP Inc.
CECO International Corp.
Celco
Dimension 3
Eastman Kodak Co.
Alan Gordon Enterprises Inc.
Hollywood Rentals Production Services
Mole-Richardson Co.
Motion Picture Enterprises Inc.
O'Connor Professional Camera Support Systems
PC& E
Panavision New York
Pro Video & Film Equipment Co. Inc.

Motors

Powr-Ups Corp.
Senior Aerospace

Mounting Products

Advance Products Co. Inc.
California Amplifier
Luxor
Omnimount Systems
Peerless Industries Inc.
Penn Elcom Inc.

Multiplexers

ADTEC Inc.
Beyond Broadband Technology LLC
COASTCOM
Kintronic Labs Inc.
TANDBERG Television Inc.
3M

Multiplexing

Camplex Corporation
Colorado Video Inc.
L-3 Communications Telemetry East

Multistandard TV, VCR Camcorders

Analog Digital International Inc.

Music Equipment

Whirlwind
Yamaha Corp. of America

Name Plates

Seton Identification Products
3M

Neon Lighting

Bend-A-Lite Flexible Neon

Network Delay Systems

StarGuide Digital Networks Inc.

Noise Reduction Systems, Video

Noise Control Corp.
North Hills Signal Processing, a PORTA Systems Co.
Video International Development Corp.
Xintekvideo Inc.

Office Equipment

JOA Cartridge Service
Luxor
Royal Consumer Information Products

Office Supplies and Forms

Hessler Enterprises Inc.
3M
Veriad

Optical Disk Systems

Identix
Imaging Automation
TEAC America Inc.

Oscillators

ICM (International Crystal Mfg.Co.)
JSB Service Co.
Opamp Labs Inc.
Potomac Instruments, Inc.

Panels

APW Mayville/Stantron
Benner-Nawman Inc.
Bud Industries Inc.
Kings-Winchester Electronics Corp.
Panel Authority Inc.
Wireworks Corporation

Passive Components

Allen Avionics, Inc.
Connectronics Corp.
Peter W. Dahl Co. Inc.
Elcom Systems Inc.
IPITEK
Kintronic Labs Inc.
Lindsay Broadband Inc.
MYAT Inc.
Micro Communications Inc.
Microwave Filter Co. Inc.
Power & Telephone Supply Co.
Qintar Technologies Inc.
S W R Inc.

Patch Cords

Audio Accessories Inc.
Canare Corp.
Kings-Winchester Electronics Corp.
Switchcraft Inc.
Trompeter Semflex

Pay TV Equipment and Services

DST Innovis
Electroline Equipment Inc.
Great Lakes Data Systems, Inc.
Rovi Corp.
Syntellect Inc.
T-C Specialties Co.
Zenith Electronics Corp.

Pedestals

Argraph Corp.
CSI-Camera Support International
Channell Commercial Corp.
Charles Industries Ltd.
Matthews Studio Equipment Inc. (MSE)
Miller Camera Support, L.L.C.
Sachtler Corp. of America

Thomas & Betts Corp.
Vinten Inc.

Phasing Equipment

Intersil Corp.
Kay Industries Inc.
Kintronic Labs Inc.
Phasetek Inc.

Phono Equipment and E Micro-Trak

Audio-Technica U.S., Inc.

Photographic Equipment

Bencher Inc.
Calumet Photographic
Precision Microproducts of America
Sinar Bron Inc.
Tamron U.S.A. Inc.
The Tiffen Company
Tinsley Laboratory Inc.
Westcott

Photographic Processing Machines

Precision Microproducts of America

Plastics and Injection Molders

S&L Plastics Inc.

Plugs and Connectors

Canare Corp.
Condor D C Power Supplies Inc.
Connectronics Corp.
Corning Cable Systems
Kings-Winchester Electronics Corp.
Olesen
Selco Products Co.
Switchcraft Inc.

Pole Line Hardware

Condux International
Hogg & Davis Inc.
Power & Telephone Supply Co.
Thomas & Betts Corp.

Portable Power Supplies

Frezzolini Electronics Inc.
Hollywood Rentals Production Services
Northern Power Systems

Portable Video Tape Recorder Systems

Mitsubishi Digital Electronics America Inc.

Postproduction Systems

ARRI Inc.
Abekas, Incorporated
Adcom
Analog Digital International Inc.
Atlantic Video Inc.
B&B Systems
Bitcentral Inc.
CORPLEX Inc.
Cheetah International
Interface Media Group
MAVRIC Media Inc.

Power Meters

Bird Electronic Corp.
Boonton Electronics Corp.
Coaxial Dynamics
Dorrough Electronics
Weschler Instruments

Power Supplies and Accessories

ADCOUR, Inc.
Alpha Technologies Inc.
APC by Schneider Electric
CableReady Inc.
Emerson Network Power
Hipotronics Inc.
JSB Service Co.
Kay Industries Inc.
Leader Instruments Corp.
Mole-Richardson Co.
Northern Power Systems
Transtector Systems Inc.

Pre-Amps, Microphone

ATI-Audio Technologies Inc.
Benchmark Media Systems Inc.
Beyerdynamic
Bryston Ltd.
Magna-Tech Electronic Co. Inc.
Martinsound Inc.
Stanton Group
Studio Technologies Inc.
Symetrix Inc.

Pressurizing Equipment and Accessories

Andrew Corp.
Radio Frequency Systems

Professional Audio Equipment

Audio-Technica U.S., Inc.
BBE Sound Inc.
Bradley Broadcast and Pro Audio
Countryman Associates Inc.
DBX Professional Products
Dolby Laboratories Inc.
Henry Engineering
JOA Cartridge Service
Jensen Transformers Inc.
Lectrosonics Inc.
Linear Acoustic Inc.
Location Sound Corp.
Parsons Audio
Professional Sound Services Inc.
QSC Audio Products Inc.
Radio Design Labs. (RDL)
Roland Corp. U.S.
Roscor Corp.
Sabine Inc.
Shure Inc.
Sound Associates
TAI Audio
TC Electronic
Thermodyne Cases
Westlake Audio, Professional Sales Group
Yamaha Corp. of America

Professional Recording Equipment

Aphex Systems Ltd.
Audio-Technica U.S., Inc.
Bradley Broadcast and Pro Audio
Digidesign
Fostex USA
Harman International Industries Inc.
Professional Sound Services Inc.
Roland Corp. U.S.
Soundcraft U.S.A.
Superscope Technologies Professionals
TEAC America Inc.
Westlake Audio, Professional Sales Group

Professional Sound Equipment

A R T Applied Research and Technology
BBE Sound Inc.
Bradley Broadcast and Pro Audio
Broadcasters General Store Inc.
Countryman Associates Inc.
JBL Professional
Professional Sound Services Inc.
Sound Associates

Professional Video Equipment

AVI Systems
AVS Graphics & Media Inc.
Alpine Optics Inc.
Bogen Imaging Inc.
Fast Forward Video
Gray Engineering Laboratories Inc.
Hitachi Kokusai Electric America, Ltd.
MATCO Inc.
Merlin Engineering Works Inc.
Roscor Corp.
Thermodyne Cases
Videomagnetics Inc.

Projectors, Projection Systems

Barco Inc.
International Cinema Equipment
Motion Picture Enterprises Inc.
Navitar Inc.
Raven Screen Corp.
Sharp Electronics Corp., CCD Products Div.
Strong International
Theatre Service & Supply Corp.

Promotion Products

Blimpy Floating Signs/Bend-A-Lite
Communication Graphics, Inc.
Prisma Packaging

Prompting Equipment

COMTEK Inc.
CPC-Computer Prompting & Captioning Co.
Electronic Script Prompting
Intelliprompt
Marietta Design Group
QTV
Tekskil Industries Inc.

Protective Apparel

Second Chance Body Armor Inc.

Public Address Systems

Amplivox Portable Sound Systems
Anchor Audio Inc.
Atlantic Sound Systems
Greenberg Teleprompting

Publications, Broadcast

Access Intelligence LLC
Broadcast Engineering
Cable Yellow Pages
FM Atlas—Publishing and Electronics
Tribune Media Services

Racks

A & S Case Co. Inc.
APW Mayville/Stantron
Atlas Case Corp.
Atlas Sound
Avtech Systems Inc.
Benner-Nawman Inc.
Bradley Broadcast and Pro Audio
Bud Industries Inc.
CMP Enclosures Inc.
Fusion Consoles
Gepco International Inc.
IMS/AMCO Engineering Products
Packaged Lighting Systems Inc.
Panel Authority Inc.
Parsons Manufacturing Corp.
Penn Elcom Inc.
Sound Associates
Star Case Manufacturing Co. Inc.
Storeel Corp.
Thermodyne Cases
Viking Cases
Winsted Corp.

Radar Systems

Advanced Designs Corp.
Radio Research Instrument Co. Inc.

Radio Control Equipment

Motor Capacitors Inc.

Radio Equipment

Bradley Broadcast and Pro Audio
Marketron Broadcast Solutions
Motor Capacitors Inc.
RF Specialties Group
Schafer International
Vecima Networks Inc.
Wireless Accessories Group

Radio Equipment, 2-Way

ICM (International Crystal Mfg.Co.)
E.F. Johnson Co.
Location Sound Corp.
Nady Systems Inc.
Setcom Corporation
Systems Wireless Ltd.
Wireless Accessories Group

Receivers, Shortwave, AM-FM-TV, Multiplex

FM Atlas—Publishing and Electronics
Fostex USA
Freeland Products Inc.
Samson Technologies Corp.
Symmetricom

Recorders, Accessories

Record/Play Tek Inc.
Stancil Corp.
360 Systems

Recorders, Audio

Fostex USA
Harrison Consoles
Otari USA Sales Inc.
Record/Play Tek Inc.
Sanyo Fisher Co.
Stancil Corp.
Superscope Technologies Professionals

Recorders, Cassette Audio Logging

Stancil Corp.

Recorders, Video

Abekas, Incorporated
Eigen
Fast Forward Video
Hitachi Kokusai Electric America, Ltd.
JVC Professional Products Company
MATCO Inc.
Merlin Engineering Works Inc.
Northrup Grumman
Optical Disc Corp.
Sanyo Fisher Co.
TEAC America Inc.
Thomson, Inc, (RCA/GE)
Videomagnetics Inc.

Recording Studios

Fostex USA
JC Sound Stages
Sound Associates
Westlake Audio, Professional Sales Group
Yanchar Design & Consulting Group

Recording Studios Construction, Prefab

Industrial Acoustics Co., Inc.
Northeastern Communications Concepts Inc.

Reels, Magnetic Tape

Motion Picture Enterprises Inc.
Polyline
Stancil Corp.

Remote Broadcast Equipment

Aluma Tower Company Inc.
Broadcast Supply Worldwide
Camera Dynamics
Camplex Corporation
Comrex Corp.
FloriCal Systems Inc.
LBA Technology Inc.
Linear Acoustic Inc.
MUSICAM U.S.A.
Marti Electronics
PMTV Producers Management Television
StarGuide Digital Networks Inc.
Telecast Fiber Systems Inc.
Telos Systems
Wescam Inc.

Remote Control

Broadcast Equipment Surplus Inc.
Broadcast Sports Technologies
Burk Technology
CONTEC Corp.
Camera Dynamics
Innovision Optics Inc.
Motorola Broadband Communications Sector
NSI
Quick-Set International Inc.
Solutec Ltd. (HA)
Vinten Inc.
Wescam Inc.

Remote Control for VTRs

Imagine Products Inc.

Remote Control Switching Systems

Evertz Microsystems Ltd.
Vicon Industries Inc.

Remote Control Systems for TV Cameras

Camera Dynamics
Interlogix
Quick-Set International Inc.
Telemetrics Inc.

Rental Equipment (Broadcast and Cable)

Analog Digital International Inc.
Bexel
CORPLEX Inc.
Direct Broadcast Services Inc.
Greenberg Teleprompting
The Laumic Rental Co.
PC& E
ScreenLight & Grip
Systems Wireless Ltd.
Tele-Measurements Inc.
Unique Business Systems

Repair

CONTEC Corp.
ComSonics Inc.
Feldmar Watch and Clock Center
Flash Technology Corporation of America
Mediastar-SG
Skytec, Inc.
Stage Equipment & Lighting Inc.
Swintek Enterprises Inc.
Tele-Measurements Inc.
Tentel

Research and Equipment

Future Productions Inc.
IMS (Interactive Market Systems Inc.)
National Video Services Inc.
Sarnoff Corp.
Tech Laboratories Inc.
Teleplex Inc.
Tribune Media Services

Reverberation Chambers

Industrial Acoustics Co., Inc.

RF Bridging Equipment

Delta Electronics Inc.
Potomac Instruments, Inc.

RF Coaxial Load Resistors

Altronic Research Inc.
Bird Electronic Corp.
Coaxial Dynamics
LARCAN USA
Trompeter Semflex

RF Instrumentation & Components

Bexel
Bird Electronic Corp.
Boonton Electronics Corp.
Coaxial Dynamics
Delta Electronics Inc.
Dow-Key Microwave Corp.
LBA Technology Inc.
Narda - An L-3 Communications Co.
Phasetek Inc.
Potomac Instruments, Inc.
RF Specialties Group
Sadelco Inc.
Shively Labs
TTE Inc.

RF Power Attenuators

Bird Electronic Corp.
Kalun Communications Inc.

Rigging Systems

Peter Albrecht Company Inc.
DeSisti Lighting
Hollywood Rentals Production Services
Olesen
Packaged Lighting Systems Inc.
Sacramento Theatrical Lighting (STL)
Superior Tower Services Inc.
James Thomas Engineering Inc.
Vortek

Robotics

CSI-Camera Support International
Camera Dynamics
DeSisti Lighting
Frezzolini Electronics Inc.
Fujinon Inc.
O'Connor Professional Camera Support Systems
Vinten Inc.

Routing Switchers

Amek U.S.A.
Burst Electronics Inc.
Cablynx, Inc.
Evertz Microsystems Ltd.
General Atomics
IRIS Technologies Inc.
Image Video
Knox Video
Leitch Inc.
NTV International Corporation
QuStream
Richmond Sound Design Ltd.
Sierra Automated Systems & Engineering Corp.
Sigma Electronics Inc.
Thomson Broadcast & Media Solutions
Utah Scientific Inc.
Video Accessory Corp.

Wheatstone Corp.
World Video Sales Co.

Satellite Audio Systems

Arrakis Systems Inc.
International Datacasting Corp.
Register Communications
Standard Communications Corp.
StarGuide Digital Networks Inc.

Satellite Communications Systems

ATCI/Antenna Technology Communications Inc.
Andrew Corp.
Communication & Power Industries
L-3 Communications Telemetry East
MCL Inc.
MRPP Inc.
Maze Corporation
Megastar Inc.
Microspace Communications Corp.
Milestone Technologies Inc.
Narda Satellite Networks
Norsat International Inc.
Pinzone Engineering Group Inc.
Richardson Electronics
Rodelco Electronics Corp.
Roscor Corp.
SES Americom Inc.
Satellite Systems Corp.
Spacenet Services Inc.

Satellite News Vehicle

Direct Broadcast Services Inc.
E-N-G Mobile Systems Inc.
Frontline Communications
Shook Mobile Technology, LP
J.A. Taylor & Associates
Television Engineering Corp.
Wolf Coach Inc.

Satellite Receiver

Advanced Media Technologies, Inc.
Blonder Tongue Laboratories Inc.
CONTEC Corp.
Cable Serv Inc.
Chrono-Log Corp.
R.L. Drake LLC
International Datacasting Corp.
L-3 Communications Telemetry East
Standard Communications Corp.

Satellite Resale and Common Carriers

Ascent Media Services
Megastar Inc.
Microspace Communications Corp.
Norlight Telecommunications Inc.
SES Americom Inc.
Trident Media Group/ Spector Entertainment Group Inc.

Satellite Services

Ascent Media Management Services
Ascent Media Services
Beyond Broadband Technology LLC
Comsearch
Direct Broadcast Services Inc.
Megastar Inc.
Microspace Communications Corp.
Milestone Technologies Inc.
Mobile Video Services Ltd.
PMTV Producers Management Television
SES Americom Inc.
Trident Media Group/ Spector Entertainment Group Inc.

Scan Converters

AVerMedia Technologies Inc.
Communications Specialties Inc.
Faroudja Laboratories
Magni Systems Inc.

Scramblers, Pay TV

Beyond Broadband Technology LLC
CED
Rovi Corp.

Security Surveillance

AVCOM of Virginia Inc.
Avtech Systems Inc.
Cablynx, Inc.
Colorado Video Inc.
Emcor Enclosures
Rovi Corp.
TOA Electronics Inc.
Tele-Measurements Inc.
Vicon Industries Inc.

Security Systems

Avtech Systems Inc.
Imaging Automation
TOA Electronics Inc.
Tech Laboratories Inc.

Service, Repair and Maintenance

Alpine Optics Inc.
Arri Canada Ltd.
C-COR/ Arris
ComSonics Inc.
Cygnal Technologies
Flash Technology Corporation of America
HME
JSB Service Co.
Signal Monitoring Service
Skytec, Inc.
United States Broadcast
Videomagnetics Inc.
Westlake Audio, Professional Sales Group

Signal Generators

Burst Electronics Inc.
Leader Instruments Corp.
Magni Systems Inc.
Video Accessory Corp.
World Video Sales Co.

Signal Processor

A R T Applied Research and Technology
BBE Sound Inc.
CADCO Systems Inc.
Ensemble Designs
Eventide Inc.
Evertz Microsystems Ltd.
G Prime Ltd.
LINK Electronics Inc.
Miranda Technologies Inc.
QuStream
Renkus-Heinz Inc.
Roland Corp. U.S.
Sabine Inc.
Scientific Atlanta Canada Inc. Nexus Division
TC Electronic

Signs, Engraved, Plastic

Blimpy Floating Signs/Bend-A-Lite
The Display & Exhibit Source
Seton Identification Products

Sound Editing

Ascent Media Management Services
Sascom Marketing Group

Sound Equipment

Atlantic Sound Systems
Atlas Sound
International Cinema Equipment
ProAudio.com/Crouse-Kimzey Co.
Radio Design Labs. (RDL)
Renkus-Heinz Inc.
TOA Electronics Inc.

Sound Mixers

Professional Sound Corp.

Sound Recording Equipment

A R T Applied Research and Technology
Atlantic Sound Systems
Countryman Associates Inc.
Digidesign
Fostex USA
Roland Corp. U.S.
TAI Audio

Sound Systems

Amplivox Portable Sound Systems
Full Compass Systems Ltd.
JBL Professional
Renkus-Heinz Inc.

Speakers

Amplivox Portable Sound Systems
Atlas Sound
Auernheimer Labs Corp.
FitzCo. Inc.
Galaxy Audio Inc.
JBL Professional
QSC Audio Products Inc.
Renkus-Heinz Inc.
Stanton Group
TC Group Americas Inc.
TOA Electronics Inc.

Special Effects Generators

Autodesk

Special Effects, Audiovisual

Ampex Data Systems -America
Autodesk
Chyron Corp.
Dimension 3
Richmond Sound Design Ltd.

Spectrum Analyzers

AVCOM of Virginia Inc.
Frequency Measuring Service Inc.
SyntheSys Research Inc.
Techni-Tool Inc.

Splicing Equipment, Film, Tape

Amek U.S.A.
Neumade Products Corp.

Standards Converters

Glentronix
Interface Media Group
Merlin Engineering Works Inc.
Snell
Video International Development Corp.

Standby Power

ADCOUR, Inc.
Alpha Technologies Inc.
APC by Schneider Electric
Emerson Network Power
LEA International

Stands, Computer, A/V, TV Etc.

Advance Products Co. Inc.
Calzone Case Co.
Luxor
Matthews Studio Equipment Inc. (MSE)
Peerless Industries Inc.

Stands, Microphone

Atlas Sound
Ultimate Support Systems Inc.

Station Automation

CEA-Computer Engineering Associates
Encoda Systems Inc.
FloriCal Systems Inc.
Leightronix Inc.
Professional Communications Systems
Spotcat Software
VCI Solutions
WireReady NSI

Status Monitoring

Acterna
C I S Inc.
Flash Technology Corporation of America
Image Video

Stereo Equipment, Audio

Advanced Media Technologies, Inc.
Leaming Industries

Stereo Generation Equipment

Aphex Systems Ltd.
Circuit Research Labs Inc. (CRL Systems, Inc.)
Inovonics Inc.
Leaming Industries
Modulation Sciences Inc.

Stereo Simulation

Studio Technologies Inc.

Still Stores

AVS Graphics & Media Inc.
Inscriber Technology Corporation

Still Stores-Digital

AVS Graphics & Media Inc.
Mediastar-SG

Stopwatches

M. Ducommun Co.
Feldmar Watch and Clock Center

Storage Facilities

Atlantic Inc.
Hollywood Vaults Inc.
Research Technology International Inc.

Studio Equipment

Peter Albrecht Company Inc.
Atlantic Video Inc.
DBX Professional Products
ENCO Systems Inc.
Ferno-Washington Inc.
Gala
Matthews Studio Equipment Inc. (MSE)
PC& E
Parsons Audio
Shure Inc.
Theatre Service & Supply Corp.

Studio Facilities

All Mobile Video Inc.
CECO International Corp.
Center City Film & Video
Devlin Design Group Inc.
The Image Group Post, LLC.
Interface Media Group
Technet Systems Group

Studio Furniture

Arrakis Systems Inc.
Devlin Design Group Inc.
The Express Group
Fusion Consoles
High Tech Industries
Murphy Studio Furniture

Northeastern Communications Concepts Inc.
Studio Technology
Wheatstone Corp.
Winsted Corp.

Studio Sets, Custom

Devlin Design Group Inc.
The Express Group
Studio Technology
Uni-Set Corp.

Sub-Carrier Generators

Marti Electronics

Switches and Accessories

CCI Systems Inc.
Communications Specialties Inc.
Dow-Key Microwave Corp.
IRIS Technologies Inc.
Qintar Technologies Inc.
Seger Electronics
Selco Products Co.
Tapeswitch Corp.
Tech Laboratories Inc.
Veetronix Inc.

Switching Equipment, Audio

Autogram Corp.
Broadcast Electronic Services
IRIS Technologies Inc.
NTV International Corporation
Ram Broadcast Systems
Sierra Automated Systems & Engineering Corp.
Utah Scientific Inc.
Veetronix Inc.
Video Accessory Corp.

Switching Equipment, Video

Ampex Data Systems -America
Broadcast Electronic Services
Gennum Corp.
IRIS Technologies Inc.
Ikegami Electronics (U.S.A.) Inc.
Utah Scientific Inc.
Veetronix Inc.
Vicon Industries Inc.
Video Accessory Corp.

Tape Conditioner, Audio/Video

Data Security Inc.

Tape Duplicators

Ascent Media Management Services
Future Productions Inc.
IRIS Technologies Inc.
M2 America
Newdoll Enterprises LLC

Tape Equipment and Accessories

Audiolab Electronics Inc.
Plastic Reel Corp. of America
Record/Play Tek Inc.
Research Technology International Inc.
Tentel

Tape Heads, Audio

AheadTek
International Electro-Magnetics (IEM)
Record/Play Tek Inc.

Tape Recorders

Northrup Grumman
Record/Play Tek Inc.
Sanyo Fisher Co.
Superscope Technologies Professionals
TEAC America Inc.
Thomson, Inc, (RCA/GE)

Tape Synchronizers

Adcom

Tape, Audio and Video

FUJIFILM Recording Media U.S.A. Inc.
HAVE Inc.
Maxell Corp. of America
Memorex Products Inc.
Motion Picture Enterprises Inc.
Moviola
Panasonic Broadcast & Television Systems Co.
Plastic Reel Corp. of America
Record/Play Tek Inc.
Sony BMG Music Entertainment
The Tape Company

Tap-Offs (CATV)

Emerson Network Power-Viewsonics

Telecine

Ascent Media Management Services
B&B Systems
Cintel Inc.

Telecommunications Products

Aluma Tower Company Inc.
Amdocs
Aspect Software
Audio Processing Technology Ltd./APT
CSG Systems
Cable Technologies International
Corning Cable Systems
DST Innovis
Dolby Laboratories Inc.
Enghouse Systems Limited
Hogg & Davis Inc.
ICM (International Crystal Mfg.Co.)
IPITEK
ITI Electronics Inc.
Intersil Corp.
MODCOMP Inc.
McCurdy Radio Ltd.
MEGGER
Milestone Technologies Inc.
Newark Electronics
Nortel Networks Corporation
Northern Power Systems
Ortel
Power & Telephone Supply Co.
Prysmian Communications Cables and Systems USA, LLC
Sierra Automated Systems & Engineering Corp.
SiteSafe Inc.
Syntellect Inc.
T-C Specialties Co.
Techni-Tool Inc.
TELLABS
Telos Systems
Thomas & Betts Corp.
V-Soft Communications
VTECH Communications

Teleconferencing

AVI Systems
Artesia Technologies
Canon U.S.A. Inc.
Lectrosonics Inc.
MODCOMP Inc.
Tamron U.S.A. Inc.
Tele-Measurements Inc.
TELLABS
VidCAD Documentation Programs (VDP Inc.)

Telemetry Receiving Systems

L-3 Communications Telemetry East

Telemetry Transmission Links

L-3 Communications Telemetry East
Marti Electronics

Telephone Control Systems

Inovonics Inc.

Telephone Interface Equipment

Broadcasters General Store Inc.
Comrex Corp.
Radio Systems Inc.
Syntellect Inc.
Telos Systems

Telephone Line Amplifiers

ITI Electronics Inc.

Teleprompters

Autoscript
CPC-Computer Prompting & Captioning Co.
Electronic Script Prompting
Greenberg Teleprompting
Intelliprompt
Listec Video Corp.
QTV
Telescript Inc.

Test Equipment

ATI-Audio Technologies Inc.
Acterna
Aeroflex
Audio Precision Inc.
Bird Electronic Corp.
Boonton Electronics Corp.
Broadcast Video Systems Corp.
Cable Leakage Technologies
Coaxial Dynamics
Comprehensive Video Group
ComSonics Inc.
DSC Laboratories
Dorrough Electronics
ETS-Lindgren
Electro Rent Corp.
FM SYSTEMS Inc.
Fluke Corp.
Galaxy Audio Inc.
Harris Broadcast Communications
Hipotronics Inc.
Horita
Jewell Instruments LLC
Kalun Communications Inc.
L-3 Communications Telemetry East
Leader Instruments Corp.
Magni Systems Inc.
Mega Hertz
MEGGER
Modulation Sciences Inc.
Narda - An L-3 Communications Co.
Pixel Instruments Corp.
ProAudio.com/Crouse-Kimzey Co.
Radiodetection/Riser Bond
Sadelco Inc.
Sarnoff Corp.
Shallco Inc.
Stanley Supply & Services
Techni-Tool Inc.
Tentel
Thomson
3M
Weschler Instruments
Wireworks Corporation
Zack Electronics Inc.

Time Base Correctors

Broadcast Electronic Services
Burst Electronics Inc.
FOR- A Corp. of America
Glentronix
Hotronic Inc.
Prime Image, Inc.
Symmetricom

Time Code Equipment

Adrienne Electronics Corp.
Analog Digital International Inc.
Calculated Industries Inc.
Chrono-Log Corp.
Digidesign

ESE
Electronic Theatre Controls Inc.
Gray Engineering Laboratories Inc.
Horita
Image Logic Corp.
Imagine Products Inc.
Skotel Corp.
Solutec Ltd. (HA)
Symmetricom
Symmetricom
SyntheSys Research Inc.
Telcom Research

Time Delay Units, Audio

Eventide Inc.
Hoagland Instrument, Inc.
Pixel Instruments Corp.
Prime Image, Inc.

Timers

Chrono-Log Corp.
ESE
Feldmar Watch and Clock Center
Symmetricom
Torpey Time
World Video Sales Co.

Tone Generator and Detectors

Image Video
Techni-Tool Inc.
Texscan MSI
Vega

Tools and Accessories

Benner-Nawman Inc.
Cable Prep
CablePro
Canare Corp.
E-Z Trench Manufacturing Co. Inc.
F-Conn Industries
Hogg & Davis Inc.
Lemco Tool Corp.
MAVRIC Media Inc.
Milestek Corp.
Ripley Company
Stanley Supply & Services
Techni-Tool Inc.
Telecrafter Products

Tower Design, Manufacture

Abroyd Communications Ltd.
Allied Tower Co. Inc.
Allstate Tower Company Inc.
Aluma Tower Company Inc.
Baron Telecom
Communications Structures & Services
Doty-Moore Tower Services
ERI-Electronic Research, Inc.
FWT Inc.
Magnum Towers Inc.
Fred A. Nudd Corp.
Paragon Towers Inc.
Pinzone Engineering Group Inc.
Pirod Inc.
Rohn Industries Inc.
Stainless LLC
Structural System Technology Inc.
Swager Communications Inc.
Tower Innovations
Tower Inspection Inc.
Transit and Rail Design Inc.
Utility Tower Company
Valmont Specialty Structures
World Tower Co. Inc.

Tower Erection

Abroyd Communications Ltd.
Allied Tower Co. Inc.
Baron Telecom
Communications Structures & Services
Doty-Moore Tower Services
ERI-Electronic Research, Inc.
Grant Tower, Inc.
Hignite Tower Service
Kuhnel Co. Inc.

National Steel Erectors Corp.
Northeast Towers Inc.
Fred A. Nudd Corp.
Paragon Towers Inc.
Radian Communication Services Inc
Rohn Industries Inc.
Southern Broadcast Services
Stainless LLC
Structural System Technology Inc.
Superior Tower Services Inc.
Swager Communications Inc.
Tenco Tower Co.
Tower Innovations
Tower Inspection Inc.
Towers-R-Us
Utility Tower Company
World Tower Co. Inc.

Tower Inspections

Allstate Tower Company Inc.
Baron Telecom
Communications Structures & Services
Doty-Moore Tower Services
Grant Tower, Inc.
National Steel Erectors Corp.
Northeast Towers Inc.
Paragon Towers Inc.
Radian Communication Services Inc
Southern Broadcast Services
Stainless LLC
Structural System Technology Inc.
Superior Tower Services Inc.
Swager Communications Inc.
Tenco Tower Co.
Tower Innovations
Tower Inspection Inc.
Tower Network Services
Towers-R-Us
Utility Tower Company
Valmont Specialty Structures
World Tower Co. Inc.

Tower Maintenance

Allstate Tower Company Inc.
Baron Telecom
Communications Structures & Services
Doty-Moore Tower Services
Grant Tower, Inc.
Hignite Tower Service
Kuhnel Co. Inc.
Metz Engineering
National Steel Erectors Corp.
Northeast Towers Inc.
Paragon Towers Inc.
Radian Communication Services Inc
Southern Broadcast Services
Stainless LLC
Structural System Technology Inc.
Superior Tower Services Inc.
Swager Communications Inc.
Teletech Inc.
Tenco Tower Co.
Tower Innovations
Tower Inspection Inc.
Tower Network Services
Towers-R-Us
Transit and Rail Design Inc.

Tower Obstruction Lighting and Controls

Allied Tower Co. Inc.
Allstate Tower Company Inc.
Austin Insulators Inc.
Peter W. Dahl Co. Inc.
Doty-Moore Tower Services
Flash Technology Corporation of America
Honeywell Lighting & Electronics
Northeast Towers Inc.
PerkinElmer
Rohn Industries Inc.
Skytec, Inc.
TWR Lighting Inc.
Tower Inspection Inc.
Tower Network Services
Transit and Rail Design Inc.
Utility Tower Company
Valmont Specialty Structures
World Tower Co. Inc.

Tower Structural Analysis

Allstate Tower Company Inc.
American Tower Corp.
Baron Telecom
Communications Structures & Services
FWT Inc.
National Steel Erectors Corp.
Fred A. Nudd Corp.
Paragon Towers Inc.
Radian Communication Services Inc
Rohn Industries Inc.
Stainless LLC
Superior Tower Services Inc.
Tower Innovations
Tower Inspection Inc.
Tower Network Services
Utility Tower Company
Valmont Specialty Structures
World Tower Co. Inc.

Towers, Accessories and Service

Abroyd Communications Ltd.
Allied Tower Co. Inc.
Allstate Tower Company Inc.
American Tower Corp.
Austin Insulators Inc.
Baron Telecom
Communications Structures & Services
Condux International
Doty-Moore Tower Services
FWT Inc.
Flash Technology Corporation of America
Jampro Antennas Inc.
Lightning Prevention Systems
Magnum Towers Inc.
Northeast Towers Inc.
Fred A. Nudd Corp.
Paragon Towers Inc.
Phillystran Inc.
Rohn Industries Inc.
Southern Broadcast Services
Stainless LLC
Structural System Technology Inc.
Swager Communications Inc.
Technet Systems Group
Tenco Tower Co.
Tower Innovations
Towers-R-Us
Transit and Rail Design Inc.
Utility Tower Company
World Tower Co. Inc.

Towers, Used

Abroyd Communications Ltd.
Communications Structures & Services
FWT Inc.
Northeast Towers Inc.
Towers-R-Us

Traffic Advisory System

Highway Information Systems, Inc.
Seton Identification Products
Spotcat Software
VCI Solutions

Transcoders

Faroudja Laboratories
Magni Systems Inc.
Sigma Electronics Inc.
Xintekvideo Inc.

Transformers

Allied Electronics Inc.
Cable Technologies International
Peter W. Dahl Co. Inc.
EDCOR Electronics Corp.
Jensen Transformers Inc.
North Hills Signal Processing, a PORTA Systems Co.
TTE Inc.
Tech Laboratories Inc.

Translators and Accessories

Axcera
CADCO Systems Inc.
Energy-Onix Broadcast Equipment Co. Inc.
Rodelco Electronics Corp.

Transmission Lines

Andrew Corp.
Ascent Media Services
Atlantic Video Inc.
Belden
Dielectric Communications
ERI-Electronic Research, Inc.
Industrial Equipment Representatives (IER)
MYAT Inc.
S W R Inc.
Transcom Corp.

Transmitter Building

Allied Tower Co. Inc.
Rees Associates Inc.

Transmitter Systems

Acrodyne Industries Inc. (Ai)
Axcera
B&B Systems
Broadcasters General Store Inc.
Colorado Video Inc.
Continental Electronics Corporation
DMT USA, Inc.
Energy-Onix Broadcast Equipment Co. Inc.
Linear Acoustic Inc.
Marcom
Nautel Ltd.
RF Specialties Group
Scientific Atlanta Canada Inc. Nexus Division
Siemens Dematic Limited
Swintek Enterprises Inc.
Technet Systems Group

Transmitters

Acrodyne Industries Inc. (Ai)
Broadcast Supply Worldwide
CED
Colorado Video Inc.
Continental Electronics Corporation
Energy-Onix Broadcast Equipment Co. Inc.
L-3 Communications Telemetry East
Laser Diode Inc.
Norsat International Inc.
Samson Technologies Corp.
Scientific Atlanta Canada Inc. Nexus Division
Thomson

Transmitters, Radio

Bauer Transmitters
Broadcast Electronics Inc.
Broadcast Equipment Surplus Inc.
Continental Electronics Corporation
Energy-Onix Broadcast Equipment Co. Inc.
Harris Corp., Broadcast Communications
Harris Corp., Broadcast Division
Industrial Equipment Representatives (IER)
Marcom
Nautel Ltd.
Richardson Electronics
TFT Inc.
Transcom Corp.

Transmitters, TV

Acrodyne Industries Inc. (Ai)
Axcera
CED
DMT USA, Inc.
Harris Corp., Broadcast Communications
Harris Corp., Broadcast Division
Kalun Communications Inc.
LARCAN
MRPP Inc.
Marcom
Radian Communication Services Inc
Scientific Atlanta Canada Inc. Nexus Division
Transcom Corp.

Traveling Wave Tubes

Communication & Power Industries
Daily Electronics Corp.
e2v technologies Inc.
Penta Laboratories
Thales Electron Devices

Tripods, Pedestals and Accessories

Argraph Corp.
Band Pro Film & Digital Inc.
Bogen Imaging Inc.
Hoodman Corp.
Isaia & Co.
Listec Video Corp.
Miller Camera Support, L.L.C.
O'Connor Professional Camera Support Systems
Photomart Cine-Video Inc.
Pro Video & Film Equipment Co. Inc.
Quick-Set International Inc.
Sachtler Corp. of America
Sinar Bron Inc.
Telemetrics Inc.
Thomas & Betts Corp.
The Tiffen Company
Ultimate Support Systems Inc.
Vinten Inc.

Tubes and Tube Rebuilding

Auernheimer Labs Corp.
Burle Industries Inc.
Communication & Power Industries, EIMAC
   Operations
Daily Electronics Corp.
Freeland Products Inc.
General Electrodynamics Corp.
Narragansett Imaging
Penta Laboratories
Richardson Electronics
Thales Electron Devices

Tuning and Phasing Units

LBA Technology Inc.

Turnkey Studio Systems

Peter Albrecht Company Inc.
Alpha Video & Electronics (AVEC)
CBT Systems
Cygnal Technologies
Harris Corp., Broadcast Communications
Technet Systems Group

Turntables

Audio-Technica U.S., Inc.

TV Equipment

AVerMedia Technologies Inc.
Broadcast Electronic Services
CECO International Corp.
CED
Cable Serv Inc.
LARCAN
Schafer International
Sharp Electronics Corp., CCD Products Div.
Zenith Electronics Corp.

TV Standards Converter

Prime Image, Inc.
Snell
Video International Development Corp.

TV Terminal Equipment

Beyond Broadband Technology LLC

Used Broadcast Equipment

Maze Corporation
Pro Video & Film Equipment Co. Inc.
Solutec Ltd. (HA)
System Associates
J.A. Taylor & Associates

United States Broadcast

Vacuum Capacitors

Jennings Technology Co.
Penta Laboratories
Richardson Electronics

Vans and Mobile Units

Alpha Video & Electronics (AVEC)
CBT Systems
E-N-G Mobile Systems Inc.
F&F Productions, L.L.C.
Frontline Communications
Maze Corporation
Panavision New York
Phoenix E N G, Inc.
Shook Mobile Technology, LP
J.A. Taylor & Associates
Television Engineering Corp.
WOIO & WUAB TV

VBI Equipment

Broadcast Video Systems Corp.
CPC-Computer Prompting & Captioning Co.
Milestone Technologies Inc.
Norpak Corporation

Video Accessories

ARRI Inc.
Audiolab Electronics Inc.
AVerMedia Technologies Inc.
Battery Pros Inc.
Bencher Inc.
Broadcast Electronic Services
Century Precision Optics
Hoodman Corp.
The J-Lab Co.
Jensen Transformers Inc.
Kings-Winchester Electronics Corp.
MAVRIC Media Inc.
North Hills Signal Processing, a PORTA Systems
   Co.
Peerless Industries Inc.
Plastic Reel Corp. of America
Research Technology International Inc.
Star Case Manufacturing Co. Inc.
Switchcraft Inc.
Thermodyne Cases
The Tiffen Company
Veriad
Video Accessory Corp.
Viking Cases
Westcott
Zack Electronics Inc.

Video Character Generators

Burst Electronics Inc.
Display Systems International Inc.
EEG Enterprises Inc.
FOR- A Corp. of America
Horita
Hotbox Digital
Inscriber Technology Corporation
Keywest Technology
Mediastar-SG
Wiltronix Inc.

Video Delay Lines

Allen Avionics, Inc.
Television Equipment Assoc. Inc./Matthey

Video Delay Subsystems

Abekas, Incorporated
Television Equipment Assoc. Inc./Matthey

Video Disc Recorders

Abekas, Incorporated
Leightronix Inc.
MATCO Inc.
Mediastar-SG
Optical Disc Corp.

Video Editing Equipment

Abekas, Incorporated
Avid Broadcast
Bitcentral Inc.
Broadcast Electronic Services
CORPLEX Inc.
Corporation of NEC America
The Image Group Post, LLC.
Imagine Products Inc.
MAVRIC Media Inc.
Matrox Video Products Grp
Paulmar Industries Inc.
Pinnacle Systems Inc.
Richardson Electronics
Tele-Measurements Inc.
United Media Inc.
United States Broadcast

Video Effects Generators and Accessories

Cintel Inc.
FOR- A Corp. of America
Utah Scientific Inc.

Video Equipment

AVI Systems
All Mobile Video Inc.
AVerMedia Technologies Inc.
Avtech Systems Inc.
Band Pro Film & Digital Inc.
Bencher Inc.
Broadcast Store Inc.
CORPLEX Inc.
CamMate Studios/Systems
Dage-MTI Inc.
Dimension 3
Ensemble Designs
Fiber Options
Film/Video Equipment Service Co. Inc.
Full Compass Systems Ltd.
Geneva Aviation Inc.
HAVE Inc.
Horita
Innovision Optics Inc.
MATCO Inc.
Maze Corporation
Mohawk
Photomart Cine-Video Inc.
Pro Video & Film Equipment Co. Inc.
Professional Communications Systems
Switchcraft Inc.
Telcom Research
Thermodyne Cases
United Media Inc.
Vicon Industries Inc.
Westcott

Video Graphics Systems

Autodesk
Chyron Corp.
Even Technologies Inc.
Hotbox Digital
Keywest Technology
Miranda Technologies Inc.

Video Processing Equipment

FM SYSTEMS Inc.
Thomson Broadcast & Media Solutions
Toner Cable Equipment Inc.
Xintekvideo Inc.

Video Production Switchers

FOR- A Corp. of America
Harris Broadcast Communications
Thomson Broadcast & Media Solutions

Video Projection System, Large Screen

Barco Inc.
Sharp Electronics Corp., CCD Products Div.

Video Routing Switchers

Broadcast Electronic Services
Harris Broadcast Communications
MATCO Inc.
NTV International Corporation
QuStream
Sigma Electronics Inc.
Utah Scientific Inc.

Video Special Effects Systems

Abekas, Incorporated
Chyron Corp.
Even Technologies Inc.
Image Logic Corp.
Ultimatte Corp.

Videotape Recorders

Fast Forward Video
Northrup Grumman
Sanyo Fisher Co.
Sharp Electronics Corp., CCD Products Div.
Thomson, Inc, (RCA/GE)
Toshiba America Consumer Products

Videotape Recorders, Portable

Fast Forward Video

Videotape Suppliers

Carpel Video Inc.
FUJIFILM Recording Media U.S.A. Inc.
JOA Cartridge Service
Maxell Corp. of America
Memorex Products Inc.
Moviola
Plastic Reel Corp. of America
Polyline
Sony BMG Music Entertainment
Tele-Measurements Inc.
The Tape Company

Voltage Regulators

Furman
Hipotronics Inc.
LEA International

Watt Meters

Coaxial Dynamics

Wave Guide Support Systems

MYAT Inc.

Wave Guides

Dielectric Communications
MYAT Inc.
Radio Research Instrument Co. Inc.
S W R Inc.

Weather Data Display Systems (WDDS)

AccuWeather Inc.
Advanced Designs Corp.
Enterprise Electronics Corp.
Mediastar-SG
Norpak Corporation
Texscan MSI
Ultimatte Corp.
WeatherBank Inc.

Weather Forecasting

AccuWeather Inc.
Enterprise Electronics Corp.
WeatherBank Inc.

Weather Instruments

AccuWeather Inc.
Enterprise Electronics Corp.
Gorman-Redlich Manufacturing Co.
Texas Electronics Inc.
Texscan MSI
WeatherBank Inc.

Weather Radar & Graphic Displays, Color

Advanced Designs Corp.
Enterprise Electronics Corp.
Norpak Corporation
Radio Research Instrument Co. Inc.
WeatherBank Inc.

Weighing Equipment

General Electrodynamics Corp.

Wireless Microphones

Audio-Technica U.S., Inc.
Bexel
Beyerdynamic
COMTEK Inc.
Commercial Electronics Ltd.
Countryman Associates Inc.
Galaxy Audio Inc.
Lectrosonics Inc.
Location Sound Corp.
Murry Rosenblum Sound Assoc., Inc.
Nady Systems Inc.
Professional Sound Services Inc.
Radio Engineering Industries Inc.
Sabine Inc.
Shure Inc.
Systems Wireless Ltd.
TAI Audio
TOA Electronics Inc.
Telex Communications Inc.
Vega

Wiring Products

AKG Acoustics, U.S.
Belden
CableTek Wiring Products Inc.
Clark Wire & Cable Co. Inc.
Condux International
Connectronics Corp.
Copperweld Fayetteville Division
General Cable
Gepco International Inc.
Radio Systems Inc.
Ripley Company
3M
WIREMAX Ltd.
Wireworks Corporation

Satellite and Transmission Services

ABC Family Worldwide, (a subsidiary of International Family Entertainment Inc.). 500 S. Buena Vista, Burbank, CA, 91521-0001. Phone: (818) 560-1000. Web Site:www.abcfamily.com

Haim Saban, chmn/CEO; Maureen Smith, exec VP.

Studio CityCA , 12700 Ventura Blvd. Phone:

New YorkNY , 1133 Ave. of the Americas, 37th Fl. Phone:

Basic cable net available in over 76 million homes nationwide; delivers a dynamic mix of quality entertainment with original movies, specials & series in prime time & a fun-filled daytime lineup of newly produced & classic series for kids.

AMV Gateway Teleport, Williams Communications Group. 27 Randolph St., Carteret, NJ, 07008. Phone: (732) 969-3191. Fax: (732) 541-2007.E-mail: info@amvchelsea.com Web Site:www.allmobilevideo.com

Michael Carberry, dir.

Operates teleport facilities serving New York City. Videotape svcs; satellite transmission for the bcst, CATV & videoconferencing industries. International wideband voice, data & videoconferencing svcs overseas.

AT&T Alascom, 505 E. Bluff Dr., Anchorage, AK, 99501-1100. Phone: (907) 264-7274. Phone: (907) 223-7184. Fax: (907) 274-5029. Web Site:www.attalascom.com

Mike Felix, pres; Kay Witt, opns mgr.

Telecommunications, long-distance telephone carrier for the state of Alaska offering bcst, voice, data, WATS, Alaskanet & dedicated private line long-distance svcs.

Agri Net Ray Communications Inc., 104 Radio Rd., Powells Point, NC, 27966-9601. Phone: (252) 491-2414. Fax: (252) 491-2939.E-mail: info@agrinetradio.com Web Site:www.agrinetradio.com

William S. Ray, pres/gen mgr; Lisa Ray, gen sls mgr; Bob Yanacek, opns mgr.

Turnkey satellite transmission service for radio news, sports, syndicated program distribution, audio conferencing; transportable bcst studio/uplinks for remote bcsts & domestic back hauling; network coord svcs & space segment bookings available.

American Microwave & Communications, (A division of Western Tele-Communications). 4616 N. Grand River Ave., Suite D, Lansing, MI, 48906-2576. Phone: (517) 327-3000. Phone: (517) 331-3719. Fax: (517) 327-4706.E-mail: albronson@sbcglobal.net

Microwave delivery of distant signals to cable systems; net TV & radio service to bcst stns; networking among TV stations.

Arqiva Inc., (formerly BT North America, Broadcast Sevices). 2025 M St. N.W., Suite 450, Washington, DC, 20036. Phone: (202) 721-8886. Fax: (202) 721-8595.E-mail: karen.foster@arqiva.com Web Site:www.arqiva.com

Karen P. Foster, producr mgr; Simon Thrush, sr VP.

Los AngelesCA , 12950 Culver Blvd. Phone:

Operates international bcst center; 24-hour satellite rooftop teleport, digital compression & encryption svcs.

Arqiva Limited, Crawley Ct., Winchester, Hampshire, S021 2QA. United Kingdom. Phone: 01962 823434. Fax: 01962 822378. Web Site:www.kingstoninmedia.com E-mail: inmedia@kcom.com

Peter Douglas, exec chmn; Joe Barry, dir opns.

Satellite svcs company providing data bcst, business TV, international VSAT nets & uplink facilities.

Ascent Media, (formerly Ascent Media Network Services). 250 Harbor Dr., Stamford, CT, 06902. Phone: (203) 965-6000. Web Site:www.ascentmedia.com

Peter Brickman, mgng dir.

MinneapolisMN . Teleport Minnesota, 90 S. 11th St. Phone:

C- & Ku-band domestic & international transmission service; fiber-optic connectivity to metropolitan New York. Cable origination, bcst, business TV, transponder availability, studio & postproduction.

BAF Satellite & Technology Corp., 200 S.harbor City Blvd., Suite 201, Melbourne, FL, 32901. Phone: (800) 966-3822. Phone: (800) 223-1860 (24 hr). Fax: (800) 486-5983. Fax: (800) 223-1866 (24 hr).E-mail: info@bafsat.com Web Site:www.bafsat.com

Jim Vautrot, pres.

Long-term, short-term & occasional analog & digital KU & C band satellite space, full or partial transponder or transponders for domestic or international video, voice or data transmissions.

CATV Services Inc., (Penn Service Microwave Co. Inc.). 115 Mill St., Danville, PA, 17821. Phone: (570) 275-1431. Phone: (570) 275-8410. Fax: (570) 275-3888. Web Site:www.catvservice.com

Video distribution of TV signals to various CATV companies in Pennsylvania.

Communications III, 921 Eastwind Dr., Suite 104, Westerville, OH, 43081. Phone: (614) 901-4420. Fax: (614) 901-7721.E-mail: shalliday@comiii.com Web Site:www.comiii.com

Scott Halliday, pres.

Common carrier/C-band uplink svcs. ISDN, IP, & satellite videoconferencing, Polycom & First Virtual.

Crawford Communications, (formerly Crawford Satellite Services). 3845 Pleasantdale Rd., Atlanta, GA, 30340. Phone: (404) 876-7149. Fax: (678) 421-6717.E-mail: info@crawford.com Web Site:www.crawford.com

Jesse Crawford, pres; Greg West, CFO.

Domestic/international satellite trasmission, net origination/playback, satellite uplink trucks, IP-media, fiber ooptics, studio & remote video production, HD/SD post production, DVD.

DCT Transmission L.L.C., 10040 E. Happy Valley Rd., Unit 454, Scottsdale, AR, 85255. Phone: (480) 515-0913. Fax: (480) 515-4632.E-mail: wiesenberg@spacedata.net

Jim Wiesenberg, pres.

Broadband microwave provider.

Detroit Public Television, 7441 Second Ave., Detroit, MI, 48202. Phone: (313) 874-1801. Phone: (313) 873-7200.E-mail: email@dptv.org Web Site:www.detroitpublictv.org

Daniel Alpert, gen mgr .

Detroit Public Television (WTVS-Analog 56 & Digital 43) offers Ku-band uplinking to any satellite; uplink, fiberlink, downlink, production, postproduction & teleconference svcs available.

DIRECTV Latin America, 1211 Ave. of the Americas, 6th Fl., New York, NY, 10036. Phone: (212) 462-5000. Fax: (212) 462-5081.E-mail: webmaster@directvla.com Web Site:www.directvla.com

Bruce Churchill, pres.

Provides direct TV for Latin America.

GlobeCast America, 10525 Washington Blvd., Culver City, CA, 90232. Phone: (310) 845-3900. Fax: (310) 845-3904. Web Site:www.globecastamerica.com

Paul Rush, dir opns.

MiamiFL . GlobeCast Hero Productions, 7291 N.W. 74 St. Phone:

GlobeCast America provides the bcstg industry with a unique combination of both recognized expertise & extensive inter-continental svcs. Through GlobeCast's vast global infrastructure of over 100 transponders, 30 teleports & interconnect facilities, the company provides instant access to the world's major media markets. GlobeCast America is part of France Telecom, one of the world's largest telecommunications companies.

Home Shopping Network, 1 HSN Dr., St. Petersburg, FL, 33729. Phone: (727) 872-1000. Fax: (727) 872-6615.E-mail: grossmanm@hsn.met Web Site:www.hsn.com

Mindy Grossman, CEO; Rob Solomon, engrg VP.

Svcs include C- & Ku-band transmissions from Tampa, FL, C-band transmissions from New York, NY, & Los Angeles, CA, & postproduction.

International Telecommunications Satellite Organization (INTELSAT), 3400 International Dr. N.W., Washington, DC, 20008-3098. Phone: (202) 944-6800. Fax: (202) 944-8125. Web Site:www.intelsat.com

John Romm, pres & media svcs.

Intelsat supplies video, data & voice connectivity in approximately 200 countries & territories for over 1,800 customers worldwide. Intelsat provides svcs on a global fleet of 53 satellites & 7 owned teleports & terrestrial facilities.

Kaufman Broadcast Services, 3655 Olive St., St. Louis, MO, 63108. Phone: (314) 533-6633. Fax: (314) 533-1113.E-mail: info@kaufmanbroadcast.com Web Site:www.kaufmanbroadcast.com

Bill Kaufman, pres.

Transmission svcs via satellite or fiber optics, production & editing facilities.

MCI Tampa, 3608 Queen Palm Dr., Tampa, FL, 33619-1311. Phone: (813) 829-0011. Web Site:www.mci.com

Michael Capellas, pres/CEO.

Serves Pennsylvania Public Television Network, Pennsylvania, Ohio, New Jersey, Vermont, New Hampshire, New York & Massachusetts. CATV systems with a variety of svcs.

MCI, 500 Clinton Center Dr., Clinton, MS, 39056. Phone: (601) 460-5600. Phone: (800) 644-news. Web Site:www.mci.com

Tammy McLean, dir communications.

Data, internet, international long distance & telecom svcs throughout the United States.

Megastar Inc., 4709 Compass Bow Ln., Las Vegas, NV, 89130. Phone: (702) 386-2844. Fax: (702) 388-1250. Web Site:www.1megastar.com

Nigel Macrae, pres.

Houston, TX Teleport svcs, C-band & Ku-band, fiber-optic & microwave interconnect. 11M Intelsat antenna, PanAmSat, etc. Other svcs available.

Microwave Networks Inc., 4000 Greenbriar St. #100A, Stafford, TX, 77477. Phone: (281) 263-6500. Phone: (888) 225-6429. Fax: (281) 263-6400. Web Site:www.microwavenetworks.com

Jim Gordon, gen mgr .

Microwave Service Co., 1359 Rd. 681, Saltillo, MS, 38866. Phone: (662) 842-7620. Fax: (662) 844-7061.E-mail: lharris@wtba.com

Jane Spain, CEO; Larry Harris, gen sls mgr.

Point-to-point transmission of video by microwave.

Multicomm Sciences International Inc. (MSI), 266 W. Main St., Denville, NJ, 07834. Phone: (973) 627-7400. Fax: (973) 215-2168. Web Site:www.multicommsciences.com

Victor J. Nexon Jr., pres.

Serves satellite, microwave, lightwave, radio & cable industries. Market info, field surveys, system design, feasibility studies, frequency coordination & project mgmt.

NPR Satellite Services, 635 Massachusetts Ave. N.W., Washington, DC, 20001. Phone: (202) 513-2626. Fax: (202) 513-3035.E-mail: linkup@npr.org Web Site:www.nprss.org

George Gimourginas, dir.

Comprehensive satellite solutions for audio & video distribution: space segment, equipment, systems design, engrg support 24-hrs customer svc.

Norlight Telecommunications, 13935 Bishops Drive, Brookfield, WI, 53005. Phone: (888) 210-3100. Fax: (812) 759-1465.E-mail: mjt@norlight.com Web Site:www.norlight.com

James Ditter, pres; Michael J. Turnbull, mgr new business dev.

Design, installation & maintenance of custom network solutions, including HDTV transport, on-site data center - secure co-location svc, off-site video file servers & managed router svc.

Novanet Communications Ltd., 725 Westney Rd. S., Suite 4, Ajax, ON, L1J 7J7. Canada. Phone: (905) 686-6666. Fax: (905) 619-1053.E-mail: getinfo@novanetcomm.com Web Site:www.novanetcomm.com

Joseph Uyede, pres/CEO; Debbie MacLeod, VP sls & mktg; Stewart Sheriff, VP opns.

Provides info distribution svcs; audio svcs from 3.5 khz to 20 khz in analog or digital formats, also a line of data bcst offerings ranging in speed from 75 baud to T-1; & "Satpac," a packet-switched data net using receiver technology.

PMTV Producers Management Television, 681 Moore Rd., Suite 100, King of Prussia, PA, 19406. Phone: (610) 768-1770. Fax: (610) 768-1773.E-mail: mailto:pmtv@pmtv.com Web Site:www.pmtv.com

Full-svc mobile TV production company, providing mobile units, crews, satellite svcs, lighting, staging, etc. for sports,

entertainment & teleconferences worldwide.

PanAmSat, 20 Westport Rd., Suite 270, Wilton, CT, 06897. Phone: (203) 210-8000. Fax: (203) 210-8001. Web Site:www.panamsat.com

Mike Antonovich; Joseph R. Wright, Jr., CEO.

Owns & operates private global network of communications satellites providing bcst, business communications, telephony & data svcs to customers worldwide.

Potomac Television-News & Video Services, 529 14th St. N.W., Suite 480, Washington, DC, 20045. Phone: (202) 783-6464. Fax: (202) 783-1132. E-mail: jnorins@potomactv.com Web Site:www.potomac.com

Jamie Norins, news bureau chief.

TV production facilities include studios, on-line & non-linear editing & transmission facilities to Ku-band & C-band satellites. Interconnect to major news-gathering points in Washington, DC, at the National Press Bldg.

Production & Satellite Services Inc. (PSSI), 11860 Mississippi Ave., Los Angeles, CA, 90025. Phone: (310) 575-4400. Fax: (310) 575-4451. Web Site:www.pssi-global.com

Joseph A. Kittrell, VP bcst sls; Robert Lamb, pres.

Full service production & satellite transmission company specializing in coordination, production & transmission of international live-event progmg. Own & operate 12 fully redundant transportable upling/production trucks which are maintained in Los Angeles, San Francisco, Seattle, Las Vegas, Denver, Phoenix & Chicago. Entire Western region of the United States is covered including Albuquerque, Salt Lake City & Portland. Also subcontract with vendors throughout U.S. to provide uplink, downlink & production svcs and production svcs for teleconferences & other events.

Radio Sound Network, 605 S. Front St., Columbus, OH, 43215. Phone: (614) 460-3850. Fax: (614) 621-5620. E-mail: steve.clawson@radiohio.com Web Site:www.radiohio.com

Steve Clawson, engrg dir; Tony Miller, dir.

Full-svc digital satellite audio & data distribution, including affil rel & net bldg. for new & existing sports, news/talk, music & specialty networks.

Reuters Television Internationale, 3 Times Sq., 4th Fl., New York, NY, 10036. Phone: (646) 223-6600. Fax: (646) 223-6615. Web Site:www.reuters.com

Bob LaGrasso, dir client svcs.

Satellite svcs for news departments. Satellite production & communication departments handle satellite feed requirements from anywhere in the world. Satellite coordinates, video crews & major studios on six continents. Standards conversion.

SES Americom, 4 Research Way, Princeton, NJ, 08540. Phone: (609) 987-4000. Fax: (609) 987-4517. Web Site:www.ses-americom.com

Bryan A. McGuirk, pres & media solutions.

Operates GE-1-3, SATCOM, GSTAR & SPACENET domestic satellites (C-band & six Ku-band). The fleet svcs the cable TV, bcst, radio & educ market & govt businesses. Supports net of earth stns, central terminal offices & TT&C facilities.

SpaceCom Systems, A TV Guide Company. 1950 E. 71st St., Tulsa, OK, 74136. Phone: (800) 950-6690. Fax: (918) 477-6861. Web Site:www.spacecom.com

David Pollack, pres/CEO; Ruth Ann Odom, mktg coordinator.

Satellite transmission svcs, equipment & space segment on C- & Ku-Band for point-to-multipoint applications. Also two-way high-speed Satellite Broadband for remote locations, quick connects, disaster recovery, Internet.

Spacenet Inc., (formerly Spacenet Services Inc.). 1750 Old Meadow Rd., McLean, VA, 22102. Phone: (703) 848-1000. Fax: (703) 245-5426. Web Site:www.spacenet.com

Jim Norton, VP network opns; Glenn Katz, COO.

Comprehensive range of satellite-based communication svcs for video & data; digital video networks for business applications.

StarNet, 3417 N. First St., Abilene, TX, 79603. Phone: (888) 828-7352. Phone: (325) 672-9618. Fax: (770) 967-6568. E-mail: info@usdlc.org Web Site:www.usdlc.org

Glenda Mathis, owner.

Ku-band distance learning, Ku-band transponder time, & program/production svcs.

Teleglobe, 1555 Rue Carrie-Derick, Montreal, PQ, H3C 6W2. Canada. Phone: (514) 868-7272. Fax: (514) 868-7234. Web Site:www.teleglobe.com E-mail: jean-louis-houde@vsnlinternational.com

Vinod Kumar, pres; Jean-Louis Houde, VP opns.

Hong Kong, Two Pacifco Place, 88 Queensway. Phone: International satellite transmission svcs from Lawrentides/Lake Cowichan earth stns in Canada. Signatory on Intelsat, Immarsat. Full range of svcs to world satellite systems.

Telemundo Network, 2470 W. 8th Ave, Hialeah, FL, 33010. Phone: (305) 884-8200. Fax: (305) 882-8765. Web Site:www.telemundo.com

James McNammara, pres.

Production capabilities & svcs. Uplink & video transmission. C- & Ku-band uplink & downlink. Fiber & microwave also available.

Telenor Satellite Services, 1101 Wooton Pkwy, Rockville, MD, 20852. Phone: (301) 838-7800. Fax: (301) 838-7801. E-mail: customer.care@telenor.com Web Site:www.telenor.com/satellite

Bob Baker, pres; Dave Farmer, VP mktg.

Telenor is a global provider of satellite svcs, inmarsat, intelsat, new skies, satmex, digital networking svcs & technology.

Teleport Chicago, 3617 Oakton St., Rear, Skokie, IL, 60076. Phone: (847) 674-7476. Phone: (888) 255-8755. Fax: (847) 674-1991. E-mail: sales@norlight.com Web Site:www.norlight.com

Dave Pritchard, dir.

A full-svc teleport serving the upper Midwest via the Norlight Telecommunications microwave & fiber-optic transmission system.

Telesat, (formerly Loral Skynet Inc.). 500 Hills Dr., Bedminster, NJ, 07921. Phone: (908) 719-0094. Web Site:www.telesat.ca

Daniel S. Goldberg, pres/CEO.

Telesat Canada, 1601 Telesat Ct., Gloucester, ON, K1B 5P4. Canada. Phone: (613) 748-0123. Fax: (613) 748-8712. E-mail: info@telesat.ca Web Site:www.telesat.ca

CalgaryAB Canada, 1780 Centre Ave. N.E. Phone:

MontrealPQ Canada, 1200 Papineau Ave, Suite 140. Phone:

Communications via satellite, consulting, & satellite earth stn nets.

Time Warner Cable, 290 Harbor Dr., Stamford, CT, 06902. Phone: (800) 479-0624. Web Site:www.timewarnercable.com

Glenn A. Britt, pres/CEO; Landel C. Hobbs, COO; Robert Marcus, sr exec VP & CFO.

New YorkNY, 75 Rockerfeller Plaza. Phone:

Time Warner Cable is committed to in-home entertainment, communications, info, customer care & quality products

that create the best possible customer experience.

Transvision Inc., 550 Maulhardt Ave., Oxnard, CA, 93030. Phone: (805) 981-8740. Fax: (805) 981-8738. E-mail: info@txvision.com Web Site:www.txvision.com

Kimithy Vaughan, sls/mktg dir; Vince Waterson, engr.

Twelve transportable & satellite transmission facilities (video, audio, voice, data); flypack production & SNG svcs; digital compression; domestic & international. Facilities in Brazil, Australia, Phillipines & Western Europe.

TV Guide Inc., 7140 S. Lewis Ave., Tulsa, OK, 74136. Phone: (918) 488-4000. Fax: (918) 488-4979. Web Site:www.tvguide.com

Josh Axelrod, dir progmg mgmt; Mike Burks, sr database admin.

Diversified communications company serving cable, home satellite TV, radio/data networks, private businesses; operating companies: UVTV, Prevue Networks, Superstar Satellite Entertainment, SpaceCom Systems.

Verestar Inc., 3040 Williams Dr., Suite 600, Fairfax, VA, 22031. Phone: (703) 206-9000. Fax: (703) 573-3522. E-mail: info@verestar.com Web Site:www.verestar.com

Raymond J. O'Brien, pres/COO.

Satellite svcs for bcstrs & communication net.

Videocom Media Services, LLC, Box 212, Boston, MA, 02137. Phone: (781) 329-4080. Fax: (781) 329-8534. Web Site:www.videocom.com

Daniel V. Swartz, mgr.

Steerable C- & Ku-band antennas interconnected via private microwave & telco loops co-located with single- & multiple-camera program origination facility. Receives & transmits all formats of videotape; transportable uplinks; bcst news distribution; link with Canadian satellites. Digital video transmission & net mgmt svcs.

WGVU-TV, 301 W. Fulton, Grand Rapids, MI, 49504-6492. Phone: (616) 331-6666. Fax: (616) 331-6625. E-mail: wgvu@gvsu.edu Web Site:www.wgvu.org

Michael Walenta, gen mgr; Ken Kolbe, stn mgr; Bob Lumbert, engrg dir.

Provides multiple studio post production, teleconferencing & satellite uplink svcs.

WHYY Inc., Independence Mall W., 150 N. 6th St., Philadelphia, PA, 19106. Phone: (215) 351-1200. Fax: (215) 351-0398. E-mail: pgluck@whyy.org Web Site:www.whyy.org

Paul Gluck, VP/stn mgr.

Occasional video, encryption svcs, transponder time available. Interconnect with Telco, on-site production facilities, & teleconferencing for up to 1,000 people. Transportable Ku-band earth stn; C- or Ku-band uplinking.

Warren Only Media Group, 19 West Almond St., Vineland, NJ, 08360. Phone: (856) 507-9368. Fax: (856) 507-9368. Web Site:www.warrenonly.com

Warren Only, pres.

New YorkNY, Box 2372. Phone:

Program playout, turnarounds, uplink services.

Williams Communications, 111 E. 1st St., Vyvx Services, Tulsa, OK, 74103. Phone: (918) 547-5760. Fax: (918) 547-5760.

Jeff Storey, CEO.

Long BeachCA, 200 Oceangate, Suite 570. Phone:

AtlantaGA, 1802 Briarcliff Rd. Phone:

Park RidgeNJ, One Maynard Dr. Phone:

Provider of integrated fiber-optic, satellite, teleport multimedia, data gathering, mgmt & transmission svcs.

Teleports

Alexandria, VA—Verestar Inc., 3040 Williams Dr., Suite 600, Fairfax, VA, 22031. Phone: (703) 206-9000. Fax: (703) 573-3522.E-mail: info@verestar.com Web Site:www.verestar.com

Raymond J. O'Brien, pres/COO.

Satellite svcs for bcstrs & communication net.

Atlanta, GA—Atlanta International Teleport, 3530 Bomar Rd., Douglasville, GA, 30135. Phone: (770) 949-6600. Fax: (770) 942-6653.E-mail: sales@atlantateleport.com Web Site:www.atlantateleport.com

Adam Grow, III, chief engr.

Internet, private business networks, VSAT Hub, C/Ku Up/down, audio, video, data, telephony, TDMA, SCPC, VCII+, fiber, standards conversion, Intelsat-B Station.

Atlanta, GA—Crawford Communications Inc., 3845 Pleasantdale Rd., Atlanta, GA, 30340. Phone: (404) 876-7149. Phone: (800) 831-8027. Fax: 678) 421-6717.E-mail: info@crawford.com Web Site:www.crawford.com

Jesse Crawford, chmn.

Network origination & playback, domestic/international satellite transmissions, streaming media/webcasting, online svcs, fiber optics, satellite uplink trucks, studios, post production & DVD.

Atlanta, GA—Turner Teleport Inc., Box 105366, One CNN Ctr., Atlanta, GA, 30348-5366. Phone: (404) 827-1500.

Satellite uplink & downlink svcs for Turner Broadcasting Services.

Atlanta, GA—VYVX Teleport Atlanta, 1802 Briarcliff Rd., Atlanta, GA, 30329. Phone: (404) 325-0818.E-mail: jeff.huffman@level3.com Web Site:www.level3.com

Jeff Huffman, gen mgr .

VYVX's UpSouth Teleport offers domestic U.S. & international uplink, downlink & transponder service for video (analog or compressed), data, & voice telecommunication. Fiber-optic & microwave links to points of presence for major bcst & telco locations in the Atlanta, GA, metropolitan area. Direct access to all C- & Ku-band satellites in domestic U.S. arc & AOR. Svcs include program origination; tape playback, recording & editing; standards conversion; encryption; & turnarounds.

Boston, MA—Videocom Media Services, LLC, Box 212, Boston, MA, 02137. Phone: (781) 329-4080. Fax: (781) 329-8534. Web Site:www.videocom.com

Daniel V. Swartz, mgr. Ownership: Private.

Steerable C- & Ku-band antennas interconnected via private microwave & telco loops co-located with single- & multiple-camera program origination facility. Receives & transmits all formats of videotape; transportable uplinks; bcst news distribution; link with Canadian satellites. Digital video transmission & net mgmt svcs.

Chicago, IL—Echostar, 6723 W. Steger Rd., Monee, IL, 60449. Phone: (708) 534-2400. Fax: (708) 534-0060.E-mail: lawrence.baer@echostar.com Web Site:www.echostar.com

Larry Baer, mgr. Ownership: Chicago, IL.

C- & Ku-band satellite transmission svcs. Audio, video, data, uplink/downlink communication.

Chicago, IL—Norlight Teleport Chicago, 3617 Oakton St., Skokie, IL, 60076. Phone: (847) 674-7476. Fax: (847) 674-1991.E-mail: drp@norlight.com Web Site:www.norlight.com

Dave Pritchard, dir.

BrookfieldWI , 275 N. Corporate.

Full-svc teleport, domestic & international, satellite uplink, downlink, turnaround, encryption, rgn access on Norlight Telecommunications Interstate Network, VYVX ant AT&T fiber access.

Cincinnati, OH—WLWT-TV, 1700 Young St., Cincinnati, OH, 45202. Phone: (513) 412-5000. Fax: (513) 412-6100.E-mail: rdyer@hearst.com Web Site:www.wlwt.com

Richard Dyer, gen mgr; Mark Diangelo, gen sls mgr.

On-line. Provides occasional C-band uplinking svcs.

Culver City, CA—GlobeCast North America, 10525 W. Washington Blvd., Culver City, CA, 90232. Phone: (310) 845-3900 (sales). Phone: (310) 845-3939. Fax: (310) 845-3903.E-mail: america.booking@globecast.com Web Site:www.globecast.com

Mary Frost, CEO.

WashingtonDC , 1825 K St. N.W., 9th Fl. Phone:

WashingtonDC , 400 North Capitol St. N.W, Suite 880. Phone:

MiamiFL . GlobeCast Hero Productions, 7291 N.W. 74 St. Phone:

New YorkNY , 110 E. 42nd St., 11th Fl. Phone:

Dallas, TX—Megastar Inc., 4709 Compass Bow Ln., Las Vegas, NV, 89130. Phone: (702) 386-2844. Fax: (702) 388-1250. Web Site:www.1megastar.com

Nigel Macrae, pres.

Denver, CO—VYVX Level 3 Teleport Denver, 9174 S. Jamaica St., Englewood, CO, 80112. Phone: (303) 397-4100. Fax: (303) 799-8325.

Theran Davis, opns mgr. Ownership: Denver.

Domestic & international uplink, downlink & transponder service for video & date communications. Regional Fiber & microwave interconnectivity to broadcast affiliates, PoPs & sports venues

Edmonton, AB—Edmonton Teleport. Telesat Canada, 5311 Allard Way, Edmonton, AB, T6H 5B8. Canada. Phone: (780) 437-6167. Fax: (780) 436-5667. Web Site:www.telesat.ca

Major bcst teleport offering full North American arc at C-band, & Anik E1 & E2 at Ku-band for occasional use needs.

Jackson, MS—Jackson Teleport Inc., 916 Foley St., Jackson, MS, 39202. Phone: (800) 353-9177. Phone: (601) 352-6673. Fax: (601) 948-6052. Web Site:www.weathervision.com E-mail: edward@weathervision.com

Edward Saint Pe, pres; Jason McCleave, VP.

Fixed 7-meter earth stn on site. Video satellite transmission & reception. Videoconferencing, business TV, news, sports & weathercast feed, origination, program distribution & syndication svcs.

Los Angeles, CA—Willliams Services/VYVX Steele Valley Teleports, 20021 Santa Rosa Mine Rd., Perris, CA, 92570. Phone: (909) 943-5399. Fax: (909) 943-3459.E-mail: gene.brookhart@wcg.com

Gene Brookhart, gen mgr .

EnglewoodCO , 58 Inverness Dr. E. Phone:

Offers domestic U.S. & international uplink, downlink & transponder svc for video (analog or compressed), image, data & voice telecommunication. Fiber-optic & microwave links to points of presence for major bcst & telco locations in the Los Angeles metropolitan area. Direct access to all C- & Ku-band satellites in domestic U.S. arc & POR; include program origination; tape playback, recording & editing; standards conversion; encryption; & turnarounds.

Montreal, PQ—Montreal Teleport. Telesat Canada, 1601 Telesat Ct., Gloucester, ON, K1B 5P4. Canada. Phone: (613) 748-0123. Fax: (613) 748-8712.E-mail: info@telesat.ca Web Site:www.telesat.ca . Ownership: Montreal.

Access to all Telesat Anik and Nimiq satellites & most U.S. domestic satellites.

New Orleans, LA—Network Teleports Inc., 3200 Chartres St., New Orleans, LA, 70117. Phone: (504) 942-9200. Fax: (504) 942-9204.E-mail: uplink@networkteleports.com Web Site:www.networkteleports.com

Barbara Lamont, pres; Ludwig Gelobter, VP; C.E. Feltner, chmn of bd; Nolly Paul, VP opns. Ownership: New Orleans.

C-band voice/video & data, Ku-band data/voice, B-MAC encryption, newsfeeds, production, fiber-optic links, audio-subcarrier & C- & Ku-band 5CPC, satellite telephones, IP multicasting, webcasting.

New York, NY—GlobeCast North America, 5 Teleport Dr., Staten Island, NY, 10311. Phone: (718) 983-2600. Fax: (718) 983-2615.E-mail: robert.marking@globecastna.com Web Site:www.globecast.com

Mary Frost, CEO.

Offers a transmission network of leased domestic & international satellite transponders providing radio & TV origination svcs for more than 1,000 U.S. & international clients every year, including news, sports, program distribution & business TV clientele.

Oakland, CA—ICG Telecom Group, 161 Inverness Dr., West Englewood, CO, 80112.

Alternative Access Carrier. Bay Area Teleport provides communications svcs at DS0, T1 or T3 levels for primary or alternative access applications. Bay Area Teleport's system connects 12 counties in northern California. Includes a fiber-optic network in San Francisco, CA & across to Oakland, CA, as well as access to satellite svcs through its earth stn complex in Niles Canyon.

Pittsburgh, PA—Pittsburgh International Telecommunications, Box 14070, Pittsburgh, PA, 15239. Phone: (724) 337-1888. Fax: (724) 337-1754.E-mail: info@pitcomm.com Web Site:www.pitcomm.com

Bill Sciolla, mgr video opns; Al Stem, pres.

Stamford, CT—Ascent Media, 250 Harbor Dr., Stamford, CT, 06902. Phone: (203) 965-6000. Web Site:www.ascentmedia.com

Peter Brickman, mng dir. Ownership: Stamford

C- & Ku-band domestic & international transmission service; connectivity to metro New York via proprietary fiber origination, bcst, business TV, transponder availability; studio & postproduction svcs.

Toronto, ON—Toronto Teleport. Telesat Canada, 1601 Telesat Ct., Gloucester, ON, K1B 5P4. Canada. Phone: (613) 748-0123. Fax: (613) 748-8712.E-mail: info@telesat.ca Web Site:www.telesat.ca . Ownership: Toronto.

Access to all Telesat Anik & Nimiq satellites & most united states domestic satellites.

Vancouver, BC—Vancouver Teleport. Telesat Canada, 1601 Telesat Ct., Gloucester, ON, K1B 5P4. Canada. Phone: (613) 748-0123. Fax: (613) 748-8712.E-mail: info@telesat.ca Web Site:www.telesat.ca . Ownership: Vancouver.

Access to all Telesat Anik & Nimiq satellites & most North American satellites.

Washington, DC—Potomac Television-News & Video Services, 529 14th St. N.W., Suite 480, Washington, DC, 20045. Phone: (202) 783-6464. Fax: (202) 783-1132.E-mail: jnorins@potomactv.com Web Site:www.potomac.com

Jamie Norins, news bureau chief.

TV production facilities include studios, on-line & non-linear editing & transmission facilities to Ku-band & C-band satellites. Interconnect to major news-gathering points in Washington, DC, at the National Press Bldg.

Woodbury, NY—Rainbow Network Communications, 620 Hicksville Rd., Bethpage, NY, 11714. Phone: (516) 803-0355. Phone: (516) 803-0300. Fax: (516) 918-6940.E-mail: togreco@rainbow-media.com Web Site:www.rncnetwork.com

Steve Pontillo, pres; Thomas A. Greco, VP business & dev.

Multiple 11-meter & 9-meter uplinking antennas, multiple downlinking ants, both servicing the entire satellite arc. Connectivity in & out of New York & metropolitan area, Ku-band transportable, origination/editing svcs & full, longterm & occasional transponder leasing. Compression svcs.

Section G
Professional Services

Section G
Professional Services

Station and Cable System Brokers

American Media Services L.L.C., Box 20696, Charleston, SC, 29413. Phone: (843) 972-2200. Fax: (843) 881-4436.E-mail: ams@ams.fm Web Site:www.americanmediaservices.com

Frank McCoy, pres; Ed Seeger, chmn.

Bonham, TX. Dallas office, 9208 Timbercreek Dr. Phone:

Forest LakeIL . Chicago office, 24180 N. Forest Dr. Phone:

Marble FallsTX . Austin office, 303 Avenue Q. Phone:

Developers & brokers of radio properties. Also appraisals, search svcs (buyer's agent), upgrade studies.

Associated Broadcasters, Inc., Box 42566, Cincinnati, OH, 45242. Phone: (513) 791-5982. Fax: (513) 891-5727.E-mail: irvschwartz@aol.com

Irv Schwartz, pres & gen mgr .

Legal & filing svcs in turnkey packages; consulting & appraisal svcs available.

Barger Broadcast Brokerage, Ltd., 8023 Vantage Dr., Suite 840, San Antonio, TX, 78230. Phone: (210) 340-7080. Fax: (210) 341-1777.E-mail: jwbarger@sbcglobal.net

John W. Barger, pres.

Media brokerage, loc mktg agreements, financial placements, appraisals & mgmt/financial consulting.

Blackburn & Co. Inc., 201 N. Union St., Suite 340, Alexandria, VA, 22314. Phone: (703) 519-3703. Fax: (703) 519-9756.E-mail: rblack4@aol.com

James Blackburn, chmn; Richard F. Blackburn, pres; Tony Rizzo, broker.

Radio, TV stns , communications tower brokerage, financing & appraisals.

Frank Boyle & Co., L.L.C., 2001 W. Main St., Suite 280, Stamford, CT, 06902. Phone: (203) 969-2020.E-mail: fboylebrkr@aol.com

Frank Boyle, pres.

Radio & TV media brokerage, mergers & acquisitions/appraisals.

Broadcast Media Associates, Box 1233, Santa Maria, CA, 93456. Phone: (805) 937-1553. Fax: (805) 937 7212.E-mail: cliffhunter@cliffhunter.com Web Site:broadcastmediabroker.com

Clifford M. Hunter, pres.

Radio/TV/cable brokerage in the western states. Confidential mktg for radio, TV & LPTV properties; valuation packages & financial analysis; consultants to sellers & buyers.

BroadcastStations4Sale.com, 512 Jones St., Graham, NC, 27253. Phone: (336) 570-9133. Fax: (336) 570-3464.E-mail: tedjgray@netzero.net Web Site:www.broadcaststations4sale.com

Ted J. Gray, pres; Ted J. Gray, broker.

Buy or sell radio stns or TV stns. List to sell yourself or let BroadcastStations4Sale.com sell it for you.

Broadcasting Asset Management Corp., 1323 Forest Glen, Winnetka, IL, 60093. Phone: (847) 446-8882. Fax: (847) 446-4855.

Jack Minkow, pres.

Radio stn & group stn brokerage, mergers, acquisition analysis, appraisals, feasibility studies; subdebt & equity placement.

Bulkley Capital, L.P., 5949 Sherry Ln., #1370, Dallas, TX, 75225. Phone: (214) 692-5476. Fax: (214) 692-9309.E-mail: info@bulkleycapital.com Web Site:www.bulkleycapital.com

Bradford Bulkey, pres; Lisa Bulkley, VP; Oliver Cone, VP.

Investment banking: mergers, acquisitions, private placements of debt & equity capital.

Business Broker Associates, Box 4757, Chattanooga, TN, 37405-0757. Phone: (423) 756-7635.E-mail: bba@cdc.net Web Site:www.cdc.net/~bba

Alfred C. Dick, broker.

Media broker & consultant for radio, TV & cable systems.

Chaisson & Company Inc., 154 Indian Waters Dr., New Canaan, CT, 06840. Phone: (203) 966-6333. Fax: (203) 966-1298.E-mail: rchaisco@aol.com

Robert A. Chaisson, pres.

Brokerage of radio/TV sls & acquisitions.

S.R. Chanen & Co. Inc., (Media Technology Capital Corp.). 3300 N. 3rd Ave., Phoenix, AZ, 85013. Phone: (602) 266-2160.

Steven R. Chanen, chmn.

Investment banking, brokerage & financial advisory svcs for the communications & entertainment industries.

Chapin Enterprises, 1248 "O" St., Suite 751, Lincoln, NE, 68508. Phone: (402) 475-5285. Fax: (402) 475-5293.E-mail: dchapin@inetnebr.com

R.W. Chapin, pres.

Stn sls, consulting, financial counseling, per location & receiver. Media broker, consulting.

CobbCorp, LLC, 7400 Tamiami Trail North, Suite 102Suite 210, Naples, FL, 34108-2855. Phone: (212) 812-5020. Fax: (239) 596-0660.E-mail: briancobb@cobbcorp.com Web Site:www.cobbcorp.com

Brian E. Cobb, pres.

Mergers, acquisitions, investment & merchant banking.

Communication Resources Media Brokers, 5343 E. 22nd St., Tulsa, OK, 74114. Phone: (918) 743-8300. Fax: (918) 749-3348.E-mail: tbelc@cox.net

Tom Belcher, pres.

Brokerage svc to radio & TV stns, cable TV companies, & individual telephone companies.

Communications Equity Associates, 101 E. Kennedy Blvd., Suite 3300, Tampa, FL, 33602. Phone: (813) 226-8844. Fax: (813) 225-1513. Web Site:www.ceaworldwide.com

J. Patrick Michaels Jr., chmn/CEO; Robert Berger, mngg dir; Carsten Philipson, mngg dir; Ken Jones, sr VP & gen counsel; Donald Russell, mngg dir; Ming Jung Sr., mngg dir/CFO-CEA.

WestportCT , 191 Post Rd. W. Phone:

New YorkNY , 1270 Avenue of the Americias, Suite 1818. Phone:

Investment & merchant banking, corporate finance & private equity firm specializing in the cable, bcstg, telecommunications, media, & entertainment industries.

The Connelly Co., 17909 Holly Brook Dr., Tampa, FL, 33647-2245. Phone: (813) 907-0017. Fax: (813) 991-9444.E-mail: connellyradiotv@verizon.net

Robert J. Connelly, pres.

New MarketNH , 198 S. Main St. Phone:

South EffinghamNH . Effingham (Summer only), Bailey Rd. Phone:

Brokers, consultants & recovery unit to assist banks & financial institutions.

Cox & Cox, LLC, 2454 Shiva Ct., St. Louis, MO, 63011. Phone: (636) 458-4780. Fax: (636) 273-1312.E-mail: bc@coxandcoxllc.com Web Site:www.coxandcoxllc.com

Robert Cox, pres; Linda Cox, VP.

Media mergers & acquisitions, appraisals, consulting, expert testimony, receivership & workout.

Diversified Investment Services, Inc., 17146 S.E. 23rd Dr., Suite 58, Vancouver, WA, 98683. Phone: (503) 221-1122. Phone: (800) 635-1772. Fax: (360) 882-4760.E-mail: a.stilli@yahoo.com

Armand J. Santilli, pres.

Media brokers/finders, real estate investment bankers & brokers.

Earl Reilly Enterprises, 550 Aloha St., Suite 404, Seattle, WA, 98019. Phone: (206) 282-6914.E-mail: earlcant@comcast.net Web Site:www.tvspotnet.com

Earl F. Reilly, pres.

FreelandWA , Box 1300. Phone:

Bcst rep, representing U.S. TV stns in Canada. Also licensed bcst stn brokers.

Edwin Tornberg & Co. Inc., 8917 Cherbourg Dr., Potomac, MD, 20854. Phone: (301) 983-8700. Fax: (301) 299-2297.

Edwin Tornberg, pres.

Appraisals, brokerage, financial & mgmt consulting for radio, TV & cable.

EnVest Media, LLC, 6802 Patterson Ave., Richmond, VA, 23226. Phone: (804) 282-5561. Fax: (804) 282-5703.E-mail: mitt@envestmedia.com Web Site:www.envestmedia.com

Mitt Younts, mngg member.

Nationwide radio, TV acquisition, valuation, financing &

consulting firm. The company provides brokerage svcs to stn transaction, appraisal svcs to stn owners & financial institutions. The group secures debt & equity acquisition financing, offers consulting & asset mgmt svcs, acting as court appointed receivers or trustees for bcst stns.

The Exline Company, 4340 Redwood Hwy., Suite F-230, San Rafael, CA, 94903. Phone: (415) 479-3484. Fax: (415) 479-1574.E-mail: exline@pacbell.net Web Site:www.exline.com

Andrew P. McClure, pres.

Complete brokerage, consulting & appraisal svcs for radio & TV properties.

Explorer Communications Inc., 3615 W. Treyburn Path, Lecanto, FL, 34461. Phone: (352) 746-7121. Fax: (352) 746-4255.E-mail: jfhoff@tampabay.rr.com

Jim Hoffman, pres.

Bcst media brokerage svcs. Specialists in medium & small market entrepreneurial transactions.

Norman Fischer & Associates Inc., Box 5308, Austin, TX, 78763-5308. Phone: (512) 476-9457. Fax: (512) 476-0540.E-mail: terrill@nfainc.com Web Site:www.nfainc.com

Terrill Fischer, pres.

Brokerage in radio, TV & cable. Consultation in mgmt & opns, appraisals, feasibility studies, expert testimony, financial planning & assistance.

Richard A. Foreman Associates, Inc., 330 Emery Dr. E., Stamford, CT, 06902-2210. Phone: (203) 327-2800. Fax: (203) 967-9393.E-mail: raf@rafamedia.com Web Site:www.rafamedia.com

Richard A. Foreman, pres.

Specializing in cash-positive radio & TV stns in major growth mkts.

Michael Fox International, Inc., (A division of GoIndustry). 11425 Cronhill Dr., Owings Mills, MD, 21117. Phone: (410) 654-7500. Fax: (410) 654-5876.E-mail: info@michaelfox.com Web Site:www.michaelfox.com

William Z. Fox, chmn; David S. Fox, CEO.

Auction sls of bcst properties.

Fugatt Media Services, 9214 Butternut Dr., Crystal Lake, IL, 60014. Phone: (815) 546-1470. Fax: (815) 788-7481.E-mail: fugattmediaservices@comcast.net

Michael L. Fugatt, pres.

Media brokerage firm specialing in radio & cable svcs including appraisals.

Clifton Gardiner & Company, L.L.C., 2437 S. Chase Ln., Lakewood, CO, 80227. Phone: (303) 758-6900. Fax: (303) 479-9210.E-mail: cliff@cliftongardiner.com Web Site:www.cliftongardner.com

Clifton H. Gardiner, pres.

Brokerage & financial svcs for the bcst & cable industries.

Dave Garland Media Brokerage, 1007 Shadow Cir., League City, TX, 77573. Phone: (713) 882-2402.E-mail: garland@radiobroker.com Web Site:www.radiobroker.com

David Garland, owner.

Broker of radio stn properties in Texas & surrounding states.

HPC Puckett & Co., Box 9063, Rancho Santa Fe, CA, 92067. Phone: (858) 756-4915. Fax: (858) 756-4534. Web Site:www.hpcpuckett.com

Thomas F. Puckett, mngg dir/CEO; Jason A. Meyer, mngg dir; Hunter T. Puckett, VP.

Communications brokerage & investment banking.

Hadden & Associates, Media Brokers - Orlando. 147 Eastpark Dr., Celebration, FL, 34447. Phone: (321) 939-3141. Fax: (321) 939-3142.E-mail: haddenws@aol.com Web Site:www.haddenonline.com

Doyle Hadden, pres; Ryan P. Hadden, VP.

Communications broker, acquisitions, divestitures; financial assistance and appraisal to the broadcasting industry.

Hawkeye Radio Properties Inc., 3325 Conservancy Ln., Middleton, WI, 53562. Phone: (608) 831-8708.E-mail: dganske@charter.net

Dale A. Ganske, pres.

Complete radio/TV brokering, consulting, FCC rules & regulations.

Henson Media Inc., 455 S. Fourth Ave., Suite 494, Louisville, KY, 40202-2508. Phone: (502) 589-0060. Fax: (502) 589-0058.E-mail: edhenson1@cs.com Web Site:www.hensonmedia.com

Edward Henson, pres.
CampbellsvilleKY , 7811 Saloma Rd. Phone:
Radio & TV brokers.

The Ted Hepburn Co., 325 Garden Rd., Palm Beach, FL, 33480. Phone: (561) 863-8995. Fax: (561) 863-8997.E-mail: tedhep2@mac.com

Ted Hepburn, pres.
Radio, TV & cable brokerage; appraisals.

R. Miller Hicks & Co., 1011 W. 11th St., Austin, TX, 78703. Phone: (512) 477-7000. Fax: (512) 477-9697.E-mail: millerhicks@rmhicks.com

R. Miller Hicks, pres.
Business dev & consulting svcs since 1957.

Holt Media Group, 2178 Industrial Dr., Suite 914, Bethlehem, PA, 18017. Phone: (610) 814-2821. Fax: (610) 814-2826.E-mail: artholt@holtmedia.com Web Site:www.holtmedia.com

Christine E. Borger, exec VP.
Brokerage, consulting, appraisals.

Bruce Houston Associates, Inc., 2251 Hunter Mill Rd., Vienna, VA, 22181. Phone: (703) 938-1016. Fax: (703) 938-6078. Web Site:bruceahouston@aol.com

Bruce Houston, pres; Joan Houston, VP.
Media brokers for radio & TV.

International Media Consulting, 48 Mountain Rd., Farmington, CT, 06032-2341. Phone: (860) 677-9688.E-mail: robert.richer@snet.net

Robert E. Richer, owner.
Broker specializing in the sale of overseas media properties.

Johnson Communication Properties Inc., 375 Waycliffe Dr. S., Wayzata, MN, 55391. Phone: (952) 404-1104. Fax: (952) 404-1102.E-mail: johncomm88@aol.com

Jerry Johnson, pres; Christina Bowers, assoc.
Radio & TV broker for 25 years.

Jorgenson Broadcast Brokerage Inc., 426 S. River Rd., Tryon, NC, 28782-7879. Phone: (828) 859-6982. Fax: (828) 859-6831.E-mail: goradiotv@aol.com Web Site:www.radiotvbrokerage.com

Mark W. Jorgenson, pres.
Confidential, nationwide brokerage of bcst properties.

Kalil & Co. Inc., 6363 N. Swan Rd., Suite 200, Tucson, AZ, 85718. Phone: (520) 795-1050. Fax: (520) 322-0584.E-mail: kalil@kalilco.com Web Site:www.kalilco.com

Frank Kalil, pres; Fred Kalil, VP; Rick Rendon, VP; Frank Higney, VP; Todd Hartman, VP; Louis McDermott, VP; Kristina Quesada, VP; Max Drachman, VP.
Media brokerage firm dealing in radio, TV & cable. Handles exclusive listings & confidential searches.

Kempff Communications Co., 3301 Bayshore Blvd., Suite 1407, Tampa, FL, 33629. Phone: (813) 258-3433.E-mail: kempffcc@aol.com Web Site:www.kepffbarr.com

Ron Kempff, pres; Aurelia Serna, VP.
Broker & consultant also offering financial & mgmt svcs, court ordered sale of stns.

Kepper, Tupper & Company, 112 High Ridge Ave., Ridgefield, CT, 06877. Phone: (203) 431-3366. Fax: (203) 431-3864.E-mail: jtupper@kepper-tupper.com Web Site:www.kepper-tupper.com

John B. Tupper, pres.
Brokerage & investment banking svcs for the cable & bcst TV industries. Please visit our website kepper-tupper.com.

Knowles Media Brokerage Services, Box 9698, Bakersfield, CA, 93389. Phone: (661) 833-3834. Fax: (661) 833-3845.E-mail: gregg.knowles@netzero.com Web Site:www.media-broker.com

Gregg K. Knowles, broker.
Daily & wkly nwsprs, print publications/sls, consultation. Sls, mergers, acquistions, appraisals.

Kozacko Media Services, Box 948, Elmira, NY, 14902. Phone: (607) 733-7138. Fax: (607) 733-1212.E-mail: rkozacko@stny.rr.com Web Site:www.kozackomediaservices.com

Richard L. Kozacko, pres.
TucsonAZ , 6890 E. Sunrise Dr., Box 120-40. Phone:
KeswickVA , 1071 Club Dr. Phone:

Appraisals & current market evaluations of radio & TV stns; bcst stn acquisition brokers.

H.B. LaRue, Media Brokers, 9454 Wilshire Blvd., Suite 628, Beverly Hills, CA, 90212. Phone: (310) 275-9266.E-mail: hblarue@sbcglobal.net

New YorkNY , 500 E. 77th St, Suite 1909. Phone:
Media brokerage; TV, radio & CATV. Appraisals & feasibility studies.

Lattice Communications, L.L.C., 441 Vine St., Suite 3900, Cincinnati, OH, 45202. Phone: (513) 381-7775. Fax: (513) 381-8808. Web Site:www.latticecommunications.com

R. Dean Meiszer, pres/CEO.
Acquisition, merger, appraisal & financial svcs to radio, TV, nwspr, cable & other media-related industries.

Lazard L.L.C., 30 Rockefeller Plaza, New York, NY, 10020. Phone: (212) 632-6000. Web Site:www.lazard.com

Michael Castellano, CFO; Robert Hougie, mngng dir; Bruce Wasserstein, CEO.
Lazard's broad range of svcs includes: gen financial advice; domestic, cross-border mergers & acquisitions; divestitures; privatizations; special committee assignments; takeover defenses; corporate restructurings; strategic partnerships/joint ventures; & debt/equity underwriting.

Legacy Securities Corp., 4060 Peachtree Rd., N.E., Atlanta, GA, 30019. Phone: (404) 965-2420. Web Site:www.legacysecurities.com

Michael D. Easterly, chmn/CEO; Chris Battel, pres.

Joe M. Leonard Jr. & Associates Inc., Box 222, Gainesville, TX, 76241. Phone: (940) 665-4076.E-mail: lin45@ntin.net Web Site:www.rockabillyhall.com/joeleonard.html

Joe M. Leonard Jr., pres.
Brokerage of radio & TV.

Jack Maloney Inc., 28 Shore Dr., Huntington, NY, 11743. Phone: (631) 549-2656. Fax: (631) 549-2656.E-mail: JFMINC@AOL.COM

Jack Maloney, pres.
Provides confidential svcs to buyers, sellers in the radio & TV business.

Mayo Communications Inc., Box 82784, Tampa, FL, 33682. Phone: (813) 264-5050. Fax: (813) 264-5353.

Lincoln A. Mayo, pres.
Media brokerage, & appraisals for bcst & print. Consulting concerning media sls & acquisitions.

R.E. Meador & Associates, Inc., Box 36, Lexington, MO, 64067. Phone: (660) 259-2544. Fax: (660) 259-6424.E-mail: Remeador1@embarqmail.com

Ralph E. Meador, pres.
LexingtonMO , 69 Ussery Dr. Phone:
Acquisitions, sls, mktg studies & appraisal svcs in central & midwestern states.

Media Services Group Inc., 3948 S. Third St. #191, Jacksonville Beach, FL, 32250. Phone: (904) 285-3239. Fax: (904) 285-5618.E-mail: reedmsconsulting@cs.com Web Site:www.mediaservicesgroup.com

George R. Reed, mngng dir.
MorristownNJ . New York Metro, 45 Park Pl. S. #146. Phone:rtmck2515@aol.com Tom McKinley, dir.
Colorado SpringsCO . Colorado Springs, CO, 2910 Electra Drive. Phone:jbmccoy@adelphia.net Jody McCoy, dir.
St. Simons IslandGA . St. Simons Island, GA, 205 Marina Dr. Phone:edwesser@adlphia.net Eddie Esserman, dir.
Highland ParkIL , 147 Oak Knoll Terr. Phone:
Overland ParkKS . Kansas City, KS, 5225 W. 122nd Street. Phone:75767.3151@compuserve.com Bill Lytle, dir; Mike Lytle, assoc.
ProvidenceRI . Providence, RI, 170 Westminster St., Suite 701. Phone:rmaccini@ cox.net; scs@scsloan.com Robert J. Maccini dir; Stephan Sloan, assoc; Ted Clark, analyst.
RichardsonTX . Dallas, TX, 1131 Rockingham Dr, Suite 209. Phone:whitelytx@cs.com Bill Whitley, dir.
LoganUT . Salt Lake City, 1289 North 1500 E. Phone:ggm@cache.net Greg Merrill, dir.
One of the nation's leading full svc media brokerage, valuation & consulting firms with in-depth industry knowledge & market expertise.

Media Venture Partners, 244 Jackson St., 4th Fl., San Francisco, CA, 94111. Phone: (415) 391-4877. Fax: (415) 391-4912.E-mail: pcanberryharris@mediaventurepartners.com Web Site:www.mediaventurepartners.com

Elliot Evers, mngng dir; Greg Widroe, mngng dir; Brian Pryor, mngng dir.

BostonMA , 75 State St., Suite 2500. Phone:
Kansas CityMO , 6314 Brookside Plza, Suite 203. Phone:
Radio & TV brokerage svcs; mergers & acquisitions; telecom; investment banking.

Gammon Miller L.L.C., (Formerly Gammon Media Brokers L.L.C.). 4806 Vue Du Lac Pl., Suite B, Manhattan, KS, 66503-8688. Phone: (785) 539-1700. Fax: (785) 565-0437.E-mail: cmiller@gammonmiller.com Web Site:www.gammonmiller.com

Christopher D. Miller, pres/CEO; James A. Gammon, chmn.
Brokerage & strategy advice to sellers, buyers of radio stns, TV stns, nwspr & cable TV systems.

Montcalm, Box 4608, Rolling Bay, WA, 98061-0608. Phone: (206) 780-1700. Fax: (206) 842-7151.E-mail: jerden@aol.com

Gerald B. Dennon, pres.
Radio & TV brokerage svcs, mergers, acquisitions & investment banking.

George Moore & Associates Inc., 6918 Wildglen Dr., Suite 100 W, Dallas, TX, 75230. Phone: (214) 369-5665. Fax: (214) 369-5667. Web Site:www.jimmoore@texan.net

W. James Moore, pres.
Brokerage of radio, TV, asset & market appraisals prepared for owners, buyers & lenders.

Gordon P. Moul & Associates Inc., Box 42, York Haven, PA, 17370. Phone: (717) 266-4212. Fax: (717) 266-0780.E-mail: gpmassociatesinc@netscape.com

Gordon P. Moul, pres.
Bcst broker & consultant. Specializing in East Coast AM-FM & TV.

MyMediaBroker.com, 407 Broadmoor Acres, Portales, NM, 88130. Phone: (575) 356-2000. Fax: (575) 356-2003.E-mail: sandibergman@mymediabroker.com Web Site:www.mymediabroker.com

Sandi Bergman, pres.
Full svc media brokerage firm.

Nutmeg Broadcasting, (formerly New England Media L.L.C.). 720 Main St., Willimantic, CT, 06226. Phone: (860) 456-1111. Fax: (860) 456-9501. Web Site:www.wili.com

Radio stn.

Patrick Communications L.L.C., 6805 Douglas Legum Dr., Suite 100, Elkridge, MD, 21075. Phone: (410) 799-1740. Fax: (410) 799-1705.E-mail: larry@patcomm.com Web Site:www.patcomm.com

Larry Patrick, mngng ptnr; Susan Patrick, mngng ptnr; Greg Guy, mngng ptnr; John Cunney, VP; Jason James, rsch analyst; Vince Pepper, principal.
Stn brokerage, investment banking, mgmt consulting svcs, appraisals & opns consulting.

John Pierce & Company L.L.C., 11 Spiral Dr., Suite 3, Florence, KY, 41042. Phone: (859) 647-0101. Fax: (859) 647-2616.E-mail: jpierce@johnpierceco.com Web Site:www.johnpierceco.com

Rebecca Grizovic, finance dir.
Radio, TV, & cable sls & appraisals.

Questcom Media Services Inc., 10130 Mallard Creek Rd., Suite 300, Charlotte, NC, 28262-6001. Phone: (704) 948-9800. Fax: (704) 948-9888.E-mail: drbussell@aol.om

Donald R. Bussell, pres.
Radio & TV stn brokerage specialists concentrating in top 150 markets; offering asst with mergers & consolidations.

RBC Daniels, (Formerly RBC Daniels, L.P.). 3200 Cherry Creek Dr. S., Suite 500, Denver, CO, 80209. Phone: (303) 778-5555. Fax: (303) 778-5599. Web Site:www.rbcdaniels.com E-mail: info@rbcdaniels.com

Los AngelesCA , 11150 Santa Monica Blvd, Suite 1230. Phone:
New YorkNY . 3 World Financial Center, 200 Vesey St., 9th Fl. Phone:
Provides mergers, acquisitions, corporate finance & financial advisory svcs to the cable, telecommunications media & technology industries.

RadioStationsForSale.net, (formerly SalesGroup). 41 Herbert Rd., Braintree, MA, 02184. Phone: (781) 848-4201. Fax: (781) 848-4715.E-mail: radio@beld.net Web Site:www.radiostationsforsale.net

Harold Bausemer, pres.
Stn brokers, USA.

Stan Raymond & Associates Inc., Box 8231, Longboat Key, FL, 34228. Phone: (941) 383-9404. Fax: (941) 383-9132.E-mail: stnray@aol.com Web Site:stanraymond.com

Stan Raymond, pres.

Financial svcs, media brokers, appraisers & consultants specializing in the Southeast.

Gordon Rice Associates, Box 20398, Charleston, SC, 29413. Phone: (843) 884-3590. Fax: (843) 881-0358.E-mail: gordon@gordonriceassociates.com

Gordon Rice, broker.

Brokerage svcs, appraisals & investment analysis for radio & TV.

Riley Representatives, 14330 Midway Rd., Dallas, TX, 75244. Phone: (972) 788-1630.

Jack Riley, pres.

Roehling Broadcast Services Ltd., 7340 Oak Knoll Dr., Indianapolis, IN, 46217. Phone: (317) 887-1945. Fax: (317) 887-1947.E-mail: edradiobr@aol.com Web Site:roehlingbroadcast.com

Edward W. Roehling, pres; Sandra Roehling, VP & treas.

Bcst appraisers, brokers, consultants, also financing, sls, mgmt consultation.

Ray H. Rosenblum, Media Broker / Appraiser / Consultant, Box 38296, Pittsburgh, PA, 15238. Phone: (412) 362-6311.

Ray H. Rosenblum, broker.

Media brokering, appraising, financing & consulting for radio & TV stns in 50 states plus territories.

Rumbaut & Company, 555 N.E. 34th St., Suite 2701, Miami Beach, FL, 33137-4060. Phone: (305) 868-0000. Fax: (305) 571-0433.E-mail: julio@rumbaut.com Web Site:www.rumbaut.com

Julio Rumbaut, pres.

Media brokers & consultants in all facets of the TV & radio industries.

Satterfield & Perry Inc., 7211 Fourth Ave. S., St. Petersburg, FL, 33707. Phone: (727) 345-7338. Fax: (727) 345-3809.E-mail: eraust@prodigy.net Web Site:www.satterfieldandperry.com

Robert Austin, pres; John Willis, sec/treas.

WetumpkaAL , 169 Mountain Meadows La. Phone: CentennialCO , 20456 E. Orchard Pl. Phone:

DenverCO , 2020 S. Monroe St. #302. Phone:

LittletonCO , Box 620308-B. Phone:

Coos BayOR , PO Box 362. Phone:

Overland ParkKS , 4918 W. 101st Terr. Phone:

AikenSC , 131 Inwood Dr. Phone:

Radio & TV broker, mgmt & sls consultant, FDIC-approved appraiser & expert witness.

John W. Saunders, Media Broker, 1207 Woodhollow Dr., Suite 3101, Houston, TX, 77057. Phone: (713) 789-4222. Fax: (713) 789-4322.E-mail: theradiobroker@aol.com Web Site:www.theradiobroker.com

John W. Saunders, owner.

Nationwide radio brokerage & appraisals. Buyers or sellers represented on a confidential, professional & personal basis. Top 10 to small markets.

Serafin Bros. Inc., Box 262888, Tampa, FL, 33685. Phone: (813) 885-6060. Fax: (813) 885-6857.E-mail: gserafin@tampabay.rr.com

Glenn M. Serafin, pres.

TampaFL , 4212 Deepwater Ln.

Bcst brokerage, finance & valuation svcs.

Burt Sherwood & Associates Inc., 6415 Midnight Pass Rd., Suite 206, Sarasota, FL, 34242. Phone: (941) 349-2165. Fax: (941) 312-0974.E-mail: bohica1@comcast.net

Burt Sherwood, pres.

Brokerage radio, TV & LPTV; appraisals.

Barry Skidelsky, Esq., 185 E. 85th St., 23D, New York, NY, 10028. Phone: (212) 832-4800.

Barry Skidelsky, owner.

Acquisitions, divestitures, mergers, time brokerage, financing.

Snowden Associates, Box 1966, One Commerce Sq., Suite 200, Washington, NC, 27889. Phone: (252) 940-1680. Fax: (252) 940-1682.E-mail: zophsnowden@embarqmail.com

C. Zoph Potts, chmn/CEO.

Brokers, consultants & appraisers to the bcst industry in the Southeast.

Howard E. Stark, 575 Madison Ave., 10th Fl., New York, NY, 10022. Phone: (212) 355-0405.

Howard E. Stark, pres.

Media broker; mergers & acquisitions in the communications field.

Gary Stevens & Co., Box 4880, Stamford, CT, 06907-0880. Phone: (203) 966-6465. Fax: (203) 966-6522.E-mail: deelmakur@aol.com

Gary Stevens, pres.

Bcst mergers, acquisitions & investment banking svcs.

The Thorburn Company, 6625 Hwy. 53 E., Suite 410-72, Dawsonville, GA, 30534. Phone: (678) 513-1363. Fax: (678) 513-1615.E-mail: thorburnco@aol.com Web Site:www.thorburncompany.com

Robert M. Thorburn, pres.

Appraisals, brokerage, financial, mgmt consulting for radio, TV & cable.

Van Huss Media Services Inc., 4239 Heyward Pl., Indianapolis, IN, 46250. Phone: (317) 813-0106. Fax: (317) 813-0107.E-mail: vanhussmediaservices@aol.com

William "Bill" Van Huss, pres.

Brokerage, financial consulting & appraisals for radio, TV & cable.

Ed Walters & Associates, 1170 Clearwater Ct., Palatine, IL, 60067. Phone: (847) 359-6117. Fax: (847) 359-6167.E-mail: radiobroker@msn.com Web Site:www.edwaltersandassoc.com

Ed Walters, pres; Michael Walters, VP; Karrol Walters, sec.

Nationwide brokers, specializing in radio, TV & cable systems, acquisition searches with confidentiality ensured.

The Whittle Agency, 12716 Lindley Dr., Raleigh, NC, 27614. Phone: (919) 848-3596. Fax: (919) 848-0519.E-mail: thewhittleagency@nc.rr.com

Gary L. Whittle, pres.

Total media brokerage svcs, including sls/appraisals of radio stns in the Carolinas, Virginia & Southeast.

Willis Broadcasting, 645 Church St., Suite 400, Norfolk, VA, 23510. Phone: (757) 624-6500. Fax: (757) 624-6515.E-mail: willisbroadcasting@yahoo.com Web Site:www.wpce1400.com

L. E. Willis Sr., pres.

Wood & Co. Inc., 431 Ohio Pike, Suite 200, Cincinnati, OH, 45255. Phone: (513) 528-7373. Fax: (513) 528-7374.

Larry C. Wood, pres.

Nationwide brokerage service to buyers & sellers of TV & radio properties.

Management and Marketing Consultants

AVI Communications Inc., 517 Huffines Blvd., Lewisville, TX, 75056. Phone: (214) 637-5464. Phone: (800) 221-2842. Fax: (214) 637-6285. E-mail: info@avi-communications.com Web Site:www.avi-communications.com Patrick Shaughnessy, pres/CEO; Annie Bendalin, VP; Matthew Price, VP opns.

TV sls training, new business dev svcs & Butch Harmon golf tips for TV & radio.

Abt Associates Inc., 55 Wheeler St., Cambridge, MA, 02138. Phone: (617) 492-7100. Fax: (617) 492-5219. E-mail: webmaster@abtassociated.com Web Site:www.abtassoc.com Peg Laplan, pres/CEO; John Shane, chmn.

WashingtonDC , 1110 Vermont Ave. N.W. Phone:

ChicagoIL , 640 N. LaSalle. Phone:

BethesdaMD , 4800 Montgomery Ln, Suite 600. Phone:

Mktg rsch, strategic planning, mgmt consulting, audience rsch & segmentation; customer satisfaction programs, quality of svc programs, social science survey rsch, publ policy rsch, economical rsch.

John P. Allen Airspace Consultants Inc., 290 Marsh Lakes Dr., Fernandina Beach, FL, 32034. Phone: (904) 261-6523. Fax: (904) 277-3651. E-mail: maryjpa@bellsouth.net Web Site:johnpallenairspace.com Mary C. Lowe, pres.

Conducts FAA aeronautical evaluations as specified in Subpart C of Part 77 of the Federal Aviation Regulations.

Anderson Productions Ltd., 55 W. 39th St., Suite 800, New York, NY, 10018. Phone: (212) 414-9220. Fax: (212) 206-0279. E-mail: steveanderson@apltv.com Web Site:www.apltv.com Steven C.F. Anderson, pres.

TV documentary, pub affrs production & short films for non-profits.

Nick Anthony & Associates Inc., 1795 W. Market St., Akron, OH, 44313. Phone: (330) 864-2268. Fax: (330) 864-2261. E-mail: nick@nickanthony.com Web Site:www.nickanthony.com Nick Anthony, pres.

Mktg, progmg & motivational consultant.

The Aspen Institute Communications & Society Program, 1 Dupont Cir. N.W., Suite 700, Washington, DC, 20036. Phone: (202) 736-5818. Fax: (202) 467-0790. E-mail: firestone@aspeninstitute.org Web Site:www.aspeninstitute.org/c&s Charles M. Firestone, exec dir.

Pub policy seminars & reports.

Associated Broadcasters, Inc., Box 42566, Cincinnati, OH, 45242. Phone: (513) 791-5982. Fax: (513) 891-5727. E-mail: irvschwartz@aol.com Irv Schwartz, pres & gen mgr .

Legal & filing svcs in turnkey packages; consulting & appraisal svcs available.

Audience Research & Development (AR&D), 2440 Lofton Terr., Fort Worth, TX, 76109. Phone: (817) 924-6922. Fax: (817) 924-7539. Web Site:www.ar-d.com E-mail: jgumbert@ar-d.com Jerry Gumbert, CEO & pres.

Rsch-based, full-svc, new media consulting firm serving TV stns, cable systems, internet companies, nwsprs & program syndicators.

THE AUSTIN COMPANY

The Austin Company, 6095 Parkland Blvd., Cleveland, OH, 44124. **Phone: (440) 544-2600. Fax: (440) 544-2690. E-mail: Austin.info@theaustin.com Web Site:www.theaustin.com** Patrick Flanagan, pres; Michael G. Pierce, sr VP/sls & mktg.

IrvineCA , 6410 Oak Canyon, #150. Phone:

AtlantaGA , 3500 Piedmont N.E., #725. Phone:

Consulting, architectural design, engrg & construction svcs for TV, cable & radio bcstg facilities.

AZCAR, 121 Hillpointe Dr., Suite 700, Canonsburg, PA, 15317. Phone: (724) 873-0800. Fax: (724) 873-4770. E-mail: info@azcar.com Web Site:www.azcar.com Richard Bisignano, pres; Mary Nahra, VP.

Video & audio system consultation, systems integration, design, instal & training; serving cable systems, cable mfg, corporate, bcst & teleproduction facilities & engng.

BIA Financial Network, 15120 Enterprise Ct., Suite 100, Chantilly, VA, 20151. Phone: (703) 818-2425. Fax: (703) 803-3299. E-mail: info@bia.com Web Site:www.bia.com Thomas J. Buono, chmn/CEO.

Financial & strategic consultants to communications industries offering fair market valuations, expert tax appraisals, due diligence, acquisition consulting, business plans, internal operational audits, litigation support, investment banking, venture funding, capital, industry rsch & analysis publications & software.

BTMI (Broadcast Trustee Management Inc.), 1090 Vermont Ave. N.W., Suite 800, Washington, DC, 20005. Phone: (202) 408-7036. Fax: (202) 408-1590. E-mail: Probinson@aol.cin Web Site:www.btmi.com

Financial-asset mgmt, valuation, mktg, restructuring & recovery consultation svcs.

Bayliss Broadcast Foundation, Box 51126, Pacific Grove, CA, 93950. Phone: (831) 655-5229. Fax: (831) 655-5228. E-mail: khfranke@baylissfoundation.org Web Site:www.baylissfoundation.org Kit Hunter Franke, exec dir; Carl Butrum, pres.

Bayliss Radio Intern program & scholarships for college students studying for a career in radio are primary focus of Foundation.

The Benchmark Co., 907 S. Congress, Suite 207, Austin, TX, 78704-1700. Phone: (512) 707-7500. Fax: (512) 707-7757. E-mail: thebenc@earthlink.net Web Site:www.thebenchmarkcompany.net Rob Balon, pres.

Full-svc bcst consulting & rsch company featuring benchmark perceptual phone surveys & the Focus 100 system, which replaces focus groups.

The Benton Group, Box 5076, Vancouver, WA, 98668. Phone: (360) 574-7369. Fax: (360) 576-6866. Web Site:www.donbenton.com Donald Benton, pres.

Yellow-page & nwspr experts, specialized sls training programs & seminars.

Beveridge Institute of Sales & Sales Management, 113 North Grant St., Barrington, IL, 60010. Phone: (847) 381-7797. Phone: (800) 227-4332. Fax: (847) 381-7301. E-mail: info@beveridgeinc.com Web Site:www.beveridgeinc.com Dick Beveridge, pres.

Sls & sls mgmt performance & productivity improvement programs; training workshops.

Big Blue Dot, 124 Watertown St., Suite F, Watertown, MA, 02472. Phone: (617) 600-1100. Fax: (617) 923-0002. E-mail: bigbluedot@bigblue.com Web Site:www.bigblue.com Jan Craige Singer, pres.

Trend tracking resources for the kids' market, consulting, & newsletter via e-mail; creative svcs.

Blackburn & Co. Inc., 201 N. Union St., Suite 340, Alexandria, VA, 22314. Phone: (703) 519-3703. Fax: (703) 519-9756. Web Site:rblack4@aol.com James W. Blackburn Jr., chmn; Richard F. Blackburn, pres; Tony Rizzo, broker.

Acquisition svcs of all kinds including appraisals, brokerage & financing for radio & TV stations and communications towers.

Blair Productions, 4801 Connecticut Ave. N.W., Washington, DC, 20008. Phone: (202) 364-1019.

Full-svc mgmt & financial counseling to the bcst industry with emphasis on radio turnarounds, problems & start-ups; investment banking svc.

Mark Blinoff Inc., 1837 S.E. Harold St., Portland, OR, 97202-4932. Phone: (503) 232-9787. Phone: (800) 929-5119. Fax: (503) 232-9787. E-mail: acmrl@myexcel.com Eric Norberg, gen mgr .

Consulting firm for radio bcstrs, including sls dev, mgmt training & progmg.

Block Communications Group Inc., 2910 Neilson Way, Suite 503, Santa Monica, CA, 90405-5368. Phone: (310) 452-3355. Fax: (310) 452-4077. E-mail: dblock@earthlink.net Web Site:www.blockcommunicationsgroup.com Richard C. Block, pres.

Consultants specializing in new cable svcs, bcstg stns, syndicated progmg, distribution & mktg serving U.S. & international clients since 1974.

Bond & Pecaro Inc., 1920 N St. N.W., Suite 350, Washington, DC, 20036. Phone: (202) 775-8870. Fax: (202) 775-0175. E-mail: bp@bondpecaro.com Web Site:www.bondpecaro.com Timothy Pecaro, principals.

Economic & financial consulting, valuation studies, asset allocations, appraisals, feasibility studies, fairness opinions, Internet valuations & expert testimony.

Bortz Media & Sports Group, 4582 S. Ulster St., Ste 1340, Denver, CO, 80237. Phone: (303) 893-9902. Fax: (303) 893-9913. E-mail: info@bortz.com Web Site:www.bortz.com James M. Trautman, mgng dir.

TV stn mgmt consulting, cable financial & market analysis; corporate strategic planning.

Bowman Valuation Services, 706 Duke St., Alexandria, VA, 22314. Phone: (703) 549-5681. Fax: (703) 549-5682. E-mail: bowman@bowmanvaluation.com Web Site:www.bowmanvaluation.com Peter Bowman, ptnr; Chip Snyder, ptnr.

Appraisals, asset allocations, specialized studies.

Frank Boyle & Co., L.L.C., 2001 W. Main St., Suite 280, Stamford, CT, 06902. Phone: (203) 969-2020. E-mail: fboylebrkr@aol.com Frank Boyle, pres.

Radio & TV media brokerage, mergers & acquisitions/appraisals.

Broadcast Media Associates, Box 1233, Santa Maria, CA, 93456. Phone: (805) 937-1553. Fax: (805) 937-7212. E-mail: cliffhunter@cliffhunter.com Web Site:broadcastmediabroker.com Clifford M. Hunter, pres.

Mgmt consulting, mktg studies & bcst investment analysis.

Broadcast Services Inc., Box 6418, Brattleboro, VT, 05302-6418. Phone: (802) 258-4500 svc. Fax: (802) 258-2500. E-mail: mh@markhutchins.com Web Site:www.markhutchins.com Mark F. Hutchins, pres.

Predicted-coverage mapping, signal-improvement studies, interference mitigation, satellite & microwave facilities inter-connection, RF radiation safety/compliance.

Broadcasting Asset Management Corp., 1323 Forest Glen Dr. N., Winnetka, IL, 60093. Phone: (847) 446-8882. Fax: (847) 446-4855. E-mail: jmink@ix.netcom.com Jack Minkow, mgng dir.

Merger & feasibility studies; acquisition analyses; capital structuring, brokerage, mgmt procurement & consulting; sr, subordinated & equity placement.

Broadcasting Unlimited Inc., 35 Main St., Wayland, MA, 01778. Phone: (508) 653-7200. E-mail: jwilliams@dmrinteractive.com Jay Williams, CEO.

Strategic planning & execution of direct mktg, telemarketing, & e-marketing promotion svcs for radio.

Broward Alliance, 110 E. Broward Blvd., #1990, Fort Lauderdale, FL, 33301-2248. Phone: (954) 524-3113 ext 220. Phone: (800) 741-1420. Fax: (954) 524-3167. E-mail: info@browardalliance.org Web Site:www.browardalliance.org/film

Resource for film, TV & print industry production and business relocation.

Howard Burkat Communications, 16 Drake Rd., Scarsdale, NY, 10583. Phone: (914) 723-9043. Phone: (914) 723-1581. Fax: (914) 472-6225. E-mail: hburkat@burkat.com Web Site:www.burkat.com

Sls, mktg & mgmt consulting for TV, cable, radio, domestic & international. Planning analysis, rsch & recruiting.

Kent Burkhart's Office Inc., 133 East End Dr., Key Biscayne, FL, 33149. Phone: (305) 439-8871. Fax: (305) 361-0650. E-mail: radiokent@aol.com Kent Burkhart, pres.

Media consultant to radio stns, networks, the Internet, cable TV, audio & product mktg. LMA liaisons & negotiators.

Alan Burns & Associates, 17357 Perdido Key Dr., Unit 7E, Pensacola, FL, 32507-7866. Phone: (703) 648-0000. Phone: (850) 49R-ADIO. Fax: (850) 497-1570.E-mail: alan@burnsradio.com Web Site:www.burnsradio.com

Progmg & mktg consultants.

Cable Audit Associates Inc., 5340 So. Quebec St., Suite 100, Greenwood Village, CO, 80111. Phone: (303) 694-0444. Fax: (303) 694-2559.E-mail: blazarus@cableaudit.com Web Site:www.cableaudit.com Bruce N. Lazarus, CEO; Mitch Walker, sr VP.

Progmg license fee audits of cable operators, MMDS, SMATVs & TVRO middlemen.

Cameo Wind Creative Management, 225 W. 34th St., Suite 1100, New York, NY, 10122. Phone: (212) 947-1998. Fax: (212) 221-7386.E-mail: jjjulien@aol.com

Carolina Media Professionals Inc., Box 3325, Spartanburg, SC, 29304. Phone: (864) 597-1301. Fax: (864) 596-7539.E-mail: rachel@upstate.net Web Site:www.carolinamedia.com Rachel Greene, pres.

Specializes in the placement of natl adv through radio, TV for products, svs and programs. Print: natl adv. Production: audio & video.

The Center for Sales Strategy, Inc., 610 W. DeLeon St., Tampa, FL, 33606-2720. Phone: (813) 254-2222. Fax: (813) 254-9222. Web Site:www.csscenter.com John Henley, COO; Jim Hopes, CEO.

Comprehensive consulting & training svcs for radio & TV, cable, and nwspr, in sls, mktg & mgmt, exclusively on a long-term, multi-year basis.

Chenevert Songy Rodi Soderberg, (An Engrg/Architectural Corp.). 6767 Perkins Rd., Suite 200, Baton Rouge, LA, 70808. Phone: (225) 769-0546. Fax: (225) 767-0060.E-mail: csrs@csrsonline.com Web Site:www.csrsonline.com

Architects, planners & tech designers specializing in new & renovated bcst/cable production facilities.

Christian TV Services, 18 Elizabeth St., P.O. Box 209, Ellicottville, NY, 14731-0209. Phone: (716) 699-2549. Fax: (716) 699-2590.E-mail: george@christianservices.com Web Site:www.christiantvservices.com Russell A. Thayer, dir; Roger A. Thayer, progmg dir; Randall A. Thayer, prom dir; George A. Thayer, pres/CEO; Joyce E. Thayer, admin asst.

TVRO consultant for Christian media started: 1974; affil: TBN/TCT/CTS Ministering to Ministries, listing media organizations & Internet places of worship. (800) 982-8823.

Christian Television Services, 9775 S.W. 87th Ave., Miami Beach, FL, 33141. Phone: (305) 592-7642. Fax: (305) 596-4564.E-mail: webmaster@citv.com Web Site:www.citv.com Russell Thorne, CEO.

Relg media buying.

Chubb Group of Insurance Companies, 15 Mountain View Rd., Warren, NJ, 07059. Phone: (908) 903-2000. Fax: (908) 903-2027.E-mail: info@chubb.com Web Site:www.chubb.com

Endorsed multi-natl property/casualty carrier by the Bcst Financial Mgrs Assns.

Branches in more than 115 offices in 30 countries.

Claritas Inc., 1525 Wilson Blvd., Suite 1000, Arlington, VA, 22209. Phone: (703) 812-2700. Fax: (703) 812-2701. Web Site:www.claritas.com E-mail: info@claritas.com

ChicagoIL , 332 S. Michigan Ave , Suite 200. Phone:

Mktg data, software & consulting designed for cable, TV, radio & other new media companies.

Clark-Mann & Associates Inc., 1714 Stockton St., Suite 300, San Francisco, CA, 94133. Phone: (415) 421-0220. Fax: (415) 421-0417.E-mail: wclarkmann2@msn.com William D. Clark, CEO; Ken Erickson, VP; Helen Butler, account exec.

Full-svc adv agency & PR firm with background in bcst & print.

Clear Channel Satellite, 76 Inverness Dr. E., Suite B, Englewood, CO, 80112. Phone: (303) 925-1708. Fax: (303) 925-1714.E-mail: sales@clearchannelsatellite.com Web Site:www.clearchannelsatellite.com Don Harms, pres; Monty Dent, gen sls mgr.

Satellite space-time; audio distribution via satellite; WAN protection svcs; DSNG svcs; satellite equipment sls; Satellite installation svcs.

Colorado Springs Film Commission, 515 S. Cascade Ave., Colorado Springs, CO, 80903. Phone: (719) 635-7506 x127. Fax: (719) 635-4968.E-mail: kgriffis@experiencecoloradosprings.com Web Site:www.filmcoloradosprings.com

Free location svcs, Production Resource Guide, location guide available for the Colorado Springs, CO area; help with crews, hotels & permits.

Coltrin & Associates Inc., 1212 Ave. of the Americas, 10th Fl., New York, NY, 10036. Phone: (212) 221-1616. Fax: (212) 221-7718.E-mail: steve_coltrin@coltrin.com Web Site:www.coltrin.com

YardleyPA , 801 Floral Vale Blvd. Phone:
Singapore Indonesia, 50 Raffles Pl., 37th Fl. Phone:
London United Kingdom, 35 Picadilly, 3rd Fl. Phone:
BurlingameCA , 433 Airport Blvd, Suite 414. Phone:
CelebrationFL , 215 Celebration Pl, Suite 500. Phone:
Salt Lake CityUT , 215 S. State St, Suite 675. Phone:
Consultant svcs to bcst mgmt, mktg sls, promotional rsch; New York, NY, & Washington, DC representation in corporate, govt & PR.

Columbia Management Advisors, One S. Wacker Dr., Chicago, IL, 60606. Fax: (312) 855-2552. William Rarkin, pres.

Investment counsel & mutual fund mgmt. Offices in Chicago, IL; Cleveland, OH; New York, NY; San Francisco, CA; & Puerto Rico.

ComBridges, 70 Irwin, San Rafael, CA, 94901. Phone: (415) 454-5505. Fax: (888) 530-5505.E-mail: info@combridges.com Web Site:www.combridges.com Jon Leland, pres.

Complete creative & production svcs including: animation, special effects, video production, video streaming, web site design, & computer-based production system design. Experience with creative svc departments & corporate communications.

CommNOW, 15 Random Farm Rd., Chappaqua, NY, 10514. Phone: (914) 944-0216.E-mail: research@commnow.com Web Site:www.commnow.com Robert Daigle, VP mktg.

Telecommunications, high-technology, mktg rsch.

Communication Trends Inc., 6120 Powers Ferry Rd. N.W., Suite 140, Atlanta, GA, 30339. Phone: (404) 843-8717. Fax: (404) 843-6869.

Mktg & adv for cable, direct bcst, bcst communications industries & related technologies.

Communications Design Associates Inc., 437 Turnpike St., Canton, MA, 02021-2702. Phone: (339) 502-6551. Fax: (339) 502-6595. Web Site:www.cdaconsultants.com E-mail: srandall@cdaconsultants.com Stewart R. Randall, .

Ind consultants to radio, TV, corp & govt clients. Designers of studios, production, presentation & multi-media facilities.

Communications Equity Associates, 101 E. Kennedy Blvd., Suite 3300, Tampa, FL, 33602. Phone: (813) 226-8844. Fax: (813) 225-1513. Web Site:www.ceaworldwide.com E-mail: spark@ceaworldwide.com J. Patrick Michaels Jr., CEO.

New YorkNY , 54 Thompson St., 4th Fl. Phone:

Provides investment banking, brokerage, regulatory affrs & mgmt svcs for bcst, CATV & related communications industries.

Comsearch, 19700 Janelia Farm Blvd., Ashburn, VA, 20147. Phone: (703) 726-5500. Fax: (703) 726-5600.E-mail: info@comsearch.com Web Site:www.comsearch.com Douglass R. Hall, pres.

Provides frequency coord, site selection, RFI measurements, path surveys, protection for satellite earth stn dishes & terrestrial microwave facilities & wireless engrg svcs & data.

Conley & Associates, LLC, 1459 Interstate Loop, Bismarck, ND, 58503-5560. Phone: (701) 222-3902. Fax: (701) 222-4815.E-mail: info@conleyassociates.net Web Site:www.conleyassociates.net Christopher J. Conley, gen ptnr; Candace Christianson, gen ptnr.

Consultants in the areas of strategic planning, appraisals, finance, opns, engrg, mktg, human resources & pub/govt rel.

Connecticut Film Video & Media Office, One Constitution Plaza, 2nd Fl., Hartford, CT, 06103. Phone: (800) 392-2122. Phone: (860) 256-2800. Fax: (860) 256-2811.E-mail: info@ctfilm.com Web Site:www.CTfilm.com Karen Senich, exec dir.

A film commission eager to respond to any situation or need.

Connelly Co. Inc., 17909 Holly Brook Dr., Tampa, FL, 33647-2245. Phone: (813) 991-9494. Fax: (813) 991-9494.E-mail: connellyradiotv@verizon.net Robert J. Connelly, pres.

New MarketNH , 198 S. Main St. Phone:
South EffinghamNH . Connelly Co. Inc. (Summer only), Bailey Rd. Phone:

Brokers, consultants & recovery units to assist banks & financial institutions.

Consolidated Communications Consultants, 1837 S.E. Harold St., Portland, OR, 97202-4932. Phone: (503) 232-9787. Phone: (800) 929-5119. Fax: (503) 232-9787. Fax: (800) 929-5119.E-mail: acmrl@myexcel.com Web Site:www.acmusicresearch.com Eric Norberg, gen mgr .

Provide progmg, sls & mktg assistance for radio stns (AM mass-appeal, A/C stns a specialty).

Contemporary Communications, 9408 Grand Gate St., Las Vegas, NV, 89143. Phone: (702) 898-4669. Fax: (208) 567-6865.E-mail: larryfuss@cox.net Web Site:www.radioguys.net Larry G. Fuss, pres.

Progmg, opns & mgmt consulting for small- & medium-market radio stns; tech svcs; FCC compliance; computer software svcs.

Convergent Media Systems, 190 Bluegrass Valley Pky., Suite 800, Alpharetta, GA, 30305. Phone: (770) 369-9000. Fax: (770) 369-9100.E-mail: convergent@convergent.com Web Site:www.convergent.com Bryan Allen, pres/CEO; William Wheless Jr., CFO.

Provider of video & data technologies to support the communication & training needs of companies. Svcs include consultation, design, instal, net & systems mgmt; systems integration in the following areas: special event TV, business TV, desktop video, video production, videoconferencing, & interactive multimedia.

Cox & Cox, LLC, 2454 Shiva Ct., St. Louis, MO, 63011. Phone: (636) 458-4780. Fax: (636) 273-1312.E-mail: bc@coxandcoxllc.com Web Site:www.coxandcoxllc.com Robert Cox, pres; Linda Cox, VP.

Media mergers & acquisitions, appraisals, consulting, expert testimony, receivership & workout.

Cross-Country Communications Inc., Box 535, Suffern, NY, 10901. Phone: (917) 652-3850. Fax: (208) 692-2181.E-mail: cccomm@aol.com Web Site:www.cross-country.com Joe Capobianco, pres.

Strategic planning, business dev, new product launches in media/entertainment & production for Radio-TV-Web.

DDS Sales Training, 6904 W. Sagamore Cir., Sioux Falls, SD, 57106. Phone: (605) 361-9923. Fax: (605) 361-1828.E-mail: ddssales@sio.mideo.net Darrell Solberg, pres; Billy Solberg, VP.

Radio sls training /consulting, mgmt training/consulting & mktg/adv seminars for businesses.

DIS Consulting Corp., 10 Waterside Plaza, #33D, New York, NY, 10010-2608. Phone: (212) 213-6872. Fax: (212) 213-6876.E-mail: dougsheer@aol.com Web Site:www.disconsultingcorporation.com Douglas I. Sheer, CEO; Regina C. Sheer, VP/gen mgr.

Mktg consultants to 1,000 equipment manufacturers since 1982. Mktg consultation, business plan writing, financial & market rsch, mktg & distribution plans.

DST Innovis, 1104 Investment Blvd., Eldorado Hills, CA, 95762. Phone: (800) 835-8389. Fax: (916) 934-7054. Web Site:www.dstinnovis.com Michael McGrail, pres; Anthony Piniella, mgr.

North Sydney. CableData (Asia Pacific), Level 4, 44 Miller St, Suite 404. Phone:
Sao Paulo. CableData (Latin America), Andar, Suite 81, Ave. Eng Luis Carlos Berrini, 1297. Phone:

Customer mgmt & billing solutions for communications & utilities industries. Clients include providers of CATV, telephony, DBS, wireless, electricity, water, gas, waste mgmt, utility & multi-svcs in over 20 countries.

David Tait Appraisal, 1848 Laurel Canyon Rd, Los Angeles, CA, 90046-2029. Phone: (323) 654-8420. Fax: (323) 656-1854.E-mail: dta87@earthlink.net David M. Tait, BCBA, owner; Mel Fineberg, assoc.

Fair market value appraisals of radio/TV/CATV for purchase allocation, finance, estate planning, ESOPs, bankruptcy.

E. Alvin Davis & Associates Inc., 35 Hampton Ln., Cincinnati, OH, 45208. Phone: (513) 325-5600. Phone: (513) 321-9661. Fax: (513) 272-2303.E-mail: ealvin@ealvin.com Web Site:www.ealvin.com E. Alvin Davis, pres; Ted McAllister, VP.

Provides expert counsel to oldies stns.

Direct Mail Express Inc., 2441 Bellevue Ave., Daytona Beach, FL, 32114. Phone: (386) 257-2500. Fax: (386) 271-3001.E-mail: tpanaggio@dmenet.com Web Site:www.dmenet.com Mike Panaggio, CEO; Mike Waither, pres.

High-impact, direct-mail campaigns, data base mgmt, audience rsch via cluster-targeted mktg, market exclusive.

Electronicast Corp., 9959 Old Orchard Ln., Upper Lake, CA, 95485. Phone: (707) 275-9397. Fax: (707) 257-9502.E-mail: massaf@electronicast.com Web Site:www.electronicast.com

Market forecast consulting concern for the fiber-optic, optoelectronic, telecommunication & CATV industries. Multi-client & custom reports available.

Enterprise Appraisal Co., 489 Devon Park Dr., Suite 320, Wayne, PA, 19087. Phone: (610) 687-5855. Fax: (610) 971-0760. Web Site:www.enterpriseappraisal.com

WashingtonDC Phone:

New YorkNY Phone:

Evaluates communications-oriented assets, such as equipment & real estate, for TV, CATV, radio, cellular systems, & satellites.

EnVest Media, LLC, 6802 Patterson Ave., Richmond, VA, 23226. Phone: (804) 282-5561. Fax: (804) 282-5703.E-mail: mitt@envestmedia.com Web Site:www.envestmedia.com Mitt Younts, mgng member.

Nationwide radio, TV acquisition, valuation, financing & consulting firm. The company provides brokerage svcs to stn transaction, appraisal svcs to stn owners & financial institutions. The group secures debt & equity acquisition financing, offers consulting & asset mgmt svcs, acting as court appointed receivers or trustees for bcst stns.

Equidata, 724 Thimble Shoals Blvd., Newport News, VA, 23606. Phone: (757) 873-3395. Phone: (757) 873-0519. Fax: (800) 873-9752. Fax: (757) 873-1224. Web Site:www.equidata.net Thomas E. Cucuel, pres; Mary Emmett, exec VP.

Nationwide collection agency/credit reporting agency.

Evalueserve, Inc., Box 2037, Saratoga, CA, 95070-0037. Phone: (408) 872-1078. Fax: (720) 294-0943.E-mail: alok.aggarwal@evalueserve.com Web Site:evalueserve.com Alok Aggarwal, chmn.

Telecommunications, high-technology, businessrsch, data anaylsis.

Executive Broadcast Services, 30 MoBray Ct., Colorado Springs, CO, 80906. Phone: (719) 579-6676. Fax: (719) 579-6664.E-mail: skip@executivebroadcast.com Web Site:www.executivebroadcast.com Skip Joeckel, pres.

Offers talk progmg & sports guides.

Executive Decision Systems Inc., 6421 W. Weaver Dr., Littleton, CO, 80123-3815. Phone: (303) 795-9090. Fax: (303) 795-1970.E-mail: dlenoble@comcast.net Web Site:www.retailinsights.com

Provide sls & mgmt training, focusing on generating long-term, loc direct revenues. Provides academic approach to media mktg to stns around the United States & abroad. System 21 is guaranteed to return 12 times the revenues within 150 days or your money is refunded.

Executive Media Services, 138 E. Waterford Dr., Seneca, SC, 299672. Phone: (864) 985-1133. Fax: (864) 985-1137. Web Site:www.executivecomm.com E-mail: excomm@bellsouth.net

Loc sls consulting for TV & radio stns, cable TV systems. Provides source for sls strategy & sls support, sls seminars; start-up & turnaround specialists. New revenue dev & sls, training, using the internet, the home of one-on-one sls & training.

The Exline Company, 4340 Redwood Hwy., Suite F-230, San Rafael, CA, 94903. Phone: (415) 479-3484. Fax: (415) 479-1574.E-mail: exline@pacbell.net Web Site:www.exlinecompany.com Andrew P. McClure, pres; Erick Steinberg, assoc.

Mgmt, financial rsch, appraisal, receiverships & bankruptcies.

The Express Group, 3175 Dwight St., San Diego, CA, 92104. Phone: (619) 280-9061. Fax: (619) 280-9030.E-mail: egmail@theexpressgroup.com Web Site:www.theexpressgroup.com Byron Andrus, pres; Roberta Andrus, VP.

Design, fabrication, instal & lighting of news environments, newsrooms, interview & talkshow sets.

Eyewitness Newservice Inc., Box 116, 182 Sound Beach Ave., Old Greenwich, CT, 06870-0116. Phone: (203) 637-0044. Fax: (203) 698-0812.E-mail: primonews@aol.com Web Site:www.teenkidsnews.tv Albert Primo, pres.

New YorkNY , 355 W. 52nd St. Phone:

TV news strategic planning, focus group rsch talent & mgmt, coaching. Cable news training; Internet Broadband Svc; TV production.

FM Atlas - Publishing and Electronics, Box 336, Esko, MN, 55733-0336. Phone: (218) 879-7676. Fax: (218) 879-7676.E-mail: fmatlas@aol.com Web Site:users.aol.com/fmatlas Bruce F. Elving, owner.

FM radio directory, rsch on FM-SCS & FM trans, FM-SCS receivers & newsletter.

Faraone Communications Inc./dba Worldwide Public Relations, 75 West End Ave., Suite R-9A, New York, NY, 10023. Phone: (212) 489-1313. Fax: (212) 489-8978.E-mail: ted.faraone@verizon.net Web Site:www.worldwidepublicrelations.com Ted Faraone, chmn.

PR svc to bcst, cable, radio, TV & other entertainment properties & media companies.

Faries & Associates, 67 Central Ave., Los Gatos, CA, 95030. Phone: (408) 354-7308. Fax: (408) 395-6670. Web Site:www.fariesinc.com David A. Faries, gen ptnr.

Business forcasting & analysis.

Federal Engineering Inc., Redwood Plaza II, 10600 Arrowhead Dr., Fairfax, VA, 22030. Phone: (703) 359-8200. Fax: (703) 359-8204.E-mail: info@fedeng.com Web Site:www.fedeng.com Ronald F. Bosco, pres; John E. Murray, sr VP.

Strategic planning, coverage analysis, new product definition, market rsch, competitive analysis, rates & tariffs, bcst stn design, mergers & acquisitions, expert testimony, regulatory support.

Ferraro Communications Inc., 39 Byron Rd., Weston, MA, 02493. Phone: (781) 235-5556. Fax: (781) 235-5558. Tom Ferraro, pres.

Concept, script & production/direction for coml, radio, film & videotape productions.

Norman Fischer & Associates Inc., Box 5308, Austin, TX, 78763. Phone: (512) 476-9457. Fax: (512) 476-0540.E-mail: terrill@nfainc.com Web Site:www.nfainc.com Terrill Fischer, pres.

Brokerage in radio, TV & cable, consultation in mgmt & opns, appraisals, feasibility studies, expert testimony, financial planning & assistance.

Florical Systems, 4581 N. W. 6th St., Gainesville, FL, 32609. Phone: (352) 372-8326. Fax: (352) 375-0859.E-mail: sales@florical.com Web Site:www.florical.com Jim Berry, rgnl sls mgr.

Manufacturer of TV automations, controls & effects.

Focal Press, 30 Corporate Dr., Suite 400, Burlington, MA, 01803. Phone: (781) 212-2212. Fax: (781) 313-4880.E-mail: j.tracy@elsevier.com Web Site:www.focalpress.com Chris Mebegon, mktg mgr; Joanne Tracy, dir.

Oxford, Linacre House, Jordan Hill. Phone:

Publishes professional tech books in bcstg, film, video, multimedia, theatre & photography.

Ford Foundation, Media, Arts, & Culture, 320 E. 43rd St., New York, NY, 10017. Phone: (212) 573-5000. Fax: (212) 351-3649. Web Site:www.fordfound.org

Richard A. Foreman Associates Inc., 330 Emery Dr. E., Stamford, CT, 06902-2210. Phone: (203) 327-2800. Fax: (203) 967-9393.E-mail: raf@rafamedia.com Web Site:www.rafamedia.com Richard A. Foreman, pres.

Fair market evaluations & asset appraisals, media brokerage, stn financing, & mgmt/production consultation.

Franey, Muha & Alliant Inc., 9901 Business Pkwy., Suite B, Lanham, MD, 20706. Phone: (301) 459-0055. Web Site:www.franeymuhaalliant.com Bill Franey, CEO.

HerndonVA , 13921 Park Central Rd, Suite160. Phone:

Insurance, bonding & benefits admin.

Clifton Gardiner & Company, L.L.C., 2437 S. Chase Ln., Denver, CO, 80227. Phone: (303) 758-6900. Fax: (303) 479-9210.E-mail: cliff@cliftongardiner.com Web Site:www.cliftongardiner.com Clifton H. Gardiner, pres.

Brokerage, consulting, financial svcs for the bcst & cable TV industries.

Georgia Film, Video & Music Office, Georgia Department of Economic Dev, 75 Fifth St. N.W., Atlanta, GA, 30308. Phone: (404) 962-4052. Fax: (404) 962-4053.E-mail: film@georgia.org Web Site:www.georgia.org Bill Thompson, dir.

Location scouting & preproduction svcs provided to feature film, TV movie, coml & multimedia production companies.

Getty Images, 601 N. 34th St., Seattle, WA, 98103. Phone: (206) 925-5000. Fax: (206) 925-5001.E-mail: feedback@gettyimages.com Web Site:www.gettyimages.com Jonathan Klein, CEO.

Business & mgmt consulting, training, long-term strategic planning, organizations analysis, mktg positioning; seminars on goal setting, leadership, mgmt skills, sls training. Retail training.

Dave Gifford International, 1142 Tano Del Este, Santa Fe, NM, 87506. Phone: (505) 989-7007. Fax: (505) 988-1991.E-mail: giff@talkgiff.com

Sls & sls management training, sls turnarounds & troubleshooting. Sls, mgmt & adv seminars. New account sls & client dev, creator of graduate school of sls.

Gilbert Communications, 4101 Legends Way, Maryville, TN, 37801. Phone: (865) 982-2889. Fax: (865) 977-6633.E-mail: rwgilbert@charter.com Robert W. Gilbert, owner/chief consultant.

Full-svc radio/TV news consulting, writing seminars, staff motivation, news policy formulation, profit center strategy & Broadcast News Handbook.

Greenwood Performance Systems LLC, 907 S. Detroit, Suite 720, Tulsa, OK, 74120. Phone: (800) 331-9115. Phone: (918) 665-7252. Fax: (918) 665-7233. Fax: (800) 378-2544.E-mail: info@greenwoodperformance.com Web Site:www.greenwoodperformance.com Jena Rhea, pres.

Bcst-specific sls & mgmt training, seminars & courses including sls mgmt consultation, strategic planning, compensation, selection & evaluation.

Guidestar Corp., 10600 Arrowhead Dr., Fairfax, VA, 22030. Phone: (703) 352-5700. Fax: (703) 359-8204.E-mail: info@fedeng.com Web Site:www.fedeng.com Ronald F. Bosco, dir.

Mktg communications & PR specifically tailored to serve the telecommunications & info processing marketplaces.

Halper & Associates, 550 Adams St. #365, Quincy, MA, 02169. Phone: (617) 786-0666. Fax: (617) 786-1809.E-mail: dlh@donnahalper.com Web Site:www.donnahalper.com Donna L. Halper, pres.

Radio progmg & mgmt consulting, market studies, format changes, music library software. Staff training, motivation. Specialize in small & medium markets, new owners, turnarounds. Also bcst historian.

Margret Haney Media Brokerage & Consultants, 2995 Woodside Rd., Bldg. 400, Woodside, CA, 94062-2446. Phone: (408) 557-8887. Fax: (408) 557-0808.E-mail: www.hhmargret@yahoo.com Web Site:www.margret @margrethaney.com Margret Haney, CEO.

Media brokerage/consulting, adv, media buyers.

Bill Hennes & Associates, 5009 Crosswinds Dr., Wilmington, NC, 28409. Phone: (910) 264-6006. Fax: (910) 313-0228.E-mail: bhennes105@aol.com Web Site:www.allaboutcountry.com Bill Hennes, pres.

Progmg & mgmt consulting.

The Ted Hepburn Co., 325 Garden Rd., Palm Beach, FL, 33480. Phone: (561) 863-8995. Fax: (561) 863-8997.E-mail: tedhep2@mac.com Ted Hepburn, pres.

Radio, TV & cable brokerage; appraisals.

R. Miller Hicks & Co., 1011 W. 11th St., Austin, TX, 78703. Phone: (512) 477-7000. Fax: (512) 477-9697.E-mail: millerhicks@rmhicks.com Web Site:www.rmhicks.com R. Miller Hicks, pres.

Brokerage, financing, mgmt consulting.

Hoffman Schutz Media Capital Inc., 2044 West California St., San Diego, CA, 92110. Phone: (619) 291-7070. Web Site:www.hs-media.com Anthony M. Hoffman, pres; David E. Schutz, VP.

Strategic planning for lender & investor appraisals & litigation support.

Host Communications Inc., 546 E. Main St., Lexington, KY, 40508. Phone: (859) 226-4678. Fax: (859) 226-4391. Web Site:www.hostcommunications.com

College sports bcstg & TV syndications; publishing & sports mktg.

The Howard-Sloan-Koller Group, 300 E. 42nd St., New York, NY, 10016. Phone: (212) 661-5250. Fax: (212) 557-9178.E-mail: hsk@hsksearch.com Web Site:www.hsksearch.com Edward R. Koller Jr., pres/CEO.

Exec search & consulting in the cable, infotechnology, entertainment, new media & publishing industries.

The Image Generators, (A division of Voicelines Inc.). 18156 Darnell Dr., Olney, MD, 20832. Phone: (301) 924-5700. Fax: (301) 570-8916.E-mail: mweiner@imagegenerators.com Web Site:www.imagegenerators.com Michael J. Weiner, CEO.

Mktg & mgmt issues; talent training workshops & coaching.

Inergize Digital Media, 1600 Utica Ave. S. , Suite 400, Minneapolis, MN, 55416. Phone: (952) 417-3294. Fax: (952) 417-3407. Web Site:www.ingerizedigitalmedia.com Jason Gould, VP/gen mgr.

Website hosting & dev, platforms, multimedia.

International Media Consulting, Inc., 48 Mountain Rd., Farmington, CT, 06032-2341. Phone: (860) 677-9688.E-mail: robert.richer@snet.net Robert E. Richer, owner.

International brokerage firm dealing exclusively with the buying & selling of media properties located outside of the United States.

IPI Report, The International Journalism Magazine. 320 Lee Hills Hall, Columbia, MO, 65211. Phone: (573) 884-7542. Fax: (573) 884-1870.E-mail: ipi-report@missouri.edu Shawn Donnelly, editor.

ColumbiaMO , 132A Neff Annex. Phone:

IPI Report defends, celebrates, relects & explores the international media & freedom of expression.

Jones TM, Inc.,2002 Academy, Dallas, TX, 75234. Phone: (972) 406-6800. Fax: (972) 406-6890.E-mail: jtm@jonestm.com Web Site:www.jonestm.com David Graupner, CEO; Jay Noble, VP sls.

The world's leading supplier of jingles, production & imaging libraries, wkly music svc & music libraries on hard drive.

KSL 5 Television, 55 N. 300 W., Salt Lake City, UT, 84180. Phone: (801) 575-5555. Fax: (801) 575-5830. Web Site:www.ksl.com Bruce Christensen, pres; Greg James, sr VP.

An advertiser-supported NABTS news & info svc available through TV decoders or personal computers equipped with modems. Modem number is (801) 575-5911.

Kagan Media Appraisals, a division of Media Central/Primedia, One Lower Ragsdale Dr., Building One, Suite 130, Monterey, CA, 93940. Phone: (831) 624-1536. Fax: (831) 625-3225.E-mail: info@kagan.com Web Site:www.Kagan.com Robin Flynn, VP bcstg.

Specializes in the valuation & appraisal of media & communications properties. As part of the Media Central Group of Companies, we maintain the industry's most comprehensive data base of stn values, so we know what yesterday's stns sold for, what buyers are paying today & what they are likely to pay tomorrow. Svcs include: Fair market valuations, expert witness testimony, asset appraisals, ESOP valuations, fairness opinions, minority interest valuations, financial feasibility studies, strategic planning, custom rsch & reports & consulting.

Kagan World Media/Primedia, Inc., One Lower Ragsdale Dr., Building One, Suite 130, Monterey, CA, 93940. Phone: (831) 624-1536. Fax: (831) 625-3225. Web Site:www.kagan.com Larry Gerbrandt, COO; Sandie Borthwick, dir opns.

Strategic conferences on media & communications topics, including interactive, multimedia, telecommunications, entertainment deals & financing.

Kalba International Inc., 116 McKinley Ave., New Haven, CT, 06515. Phone: (203) 397-2199. Fax: (781) 240-2657.E-mail: kalba@comcast.net Web Site:www.kalbainternational.com Kas Kalba, pres; Pat Kalba, VP; F. Roberts, VP.

Consulting & advisory svcs on telecommunications, bcstg & cable TV, including international ventures, due diligence, litigation support.

Kane Reece Associates Inc., 822 South Ave. W., Westfield, NJ, 07090-1460. Phone: (908) 317-5757. Fax: (908) 317-4434.E-mail: info@kanereece.com Web Site:www.kanereece.com John "Jack" Kane, principal; Norval D. Reece, principal.

Asset appraisals, business valuations, due diligence, expert testimony, property tax compliance & control, system mgmt & mgmt/engrg consulting.

Kempff Communications Co., 3301 Bayshore Blvd., Suite 1407, Tampa, FL, 33629. Phone: (813) 258-3433.E-mail: kempffcc@aol.com Web Site:www.kepffbarr.com Ron Kempff, pres; Aurelia Serna, VP.

Broker & consultant also offering financial & mgmt svcs, court ordered sale of stns.

The Kompas Group, Box 250813, Milwaukee, WI, 53225-6513. Phone: (262) 781-0188. Fax: (262) 781-5313.E-mail: kompasgroup@toast.net Web Site:www.yourlptvsource.com John Kompas, pres; Jackie Kompas, VP.

Financial & mktg svcs for LPTV, audience demographic reports, stn coverage maps, financial & strategic planning.

Kovsky & Miller Research, 37 Sawmill River Rd., Hawthorne, NY, 10532. Phone: (914) 347-3606. Fax: (914) 347-3976.E-mail: hkkmrresearch@aol.com Web Site:kovskymiller.com Harry Kovsky, pres.

Specialists in content & format analysis of loc & network TV news & entertainment programs, promotional analysis, ratings analysis, audience promotional rsch & audience survey rsch.

Kozacko Media Services, Box 948, Elmira, NY, 14902. Phone: (607) 733-7138. Fax: (607) 733-1212.E-mail: rkozacko@stny.rr.com Web Site:www.kozackomediaservices.com Richard L. Kozacko, pres.

TucsonAZ , 6890 E. Sunrise Dr., Box 120-40. Phone: KeswickVA , 1071 Club Dr. Phone:

Appraisals, current market evaluations of radio/TV stns & bcst acquisition planning.

Lawson & Associates Architects, 7939 Norfolk Ave., Suite 200, Bethesda, MD, 20814. Phone: (301) 654-1600. Fax: (301) 654-1601.E-mail: blawson@lawsonarch.com Web Site:www.lawsonarch.com Bruce Lawson, principal.

Consulting architectural design & construction mgmt svcs for the TV & cable industry; facility planning, design & coordination of construction svcs.

Liberty Hill Corp., Box 253003, West Bloomfield, MI, 48325. Phone: (248) 737-3000. Fax: (248) 737-3555.E-mail: barryzate@aol.com Barry Zate, sr VP; Ronald Zate, sr VP.

Consulting for radio progmg, talent & admin svcs; on-site seminars, problem targeting & complete strategic planning for the communications industry.

Lipson & Co., 1900 Ave. of the Stars, Suite 2810, Los Angeles, CA, 90067. Phone: (310) 277-4646. Fax: (310) 277-8585.E-mail: inquries@lipsonco.com Web Site:www.lipsonco.com Howard R. Lipson, pres.

Executive recruiting for international & domestic bcstg, cable, entertainment, adv, mktg, finance, mdse, licensing & digital medai.

Locations Tasmania Pty. Ltd., Box 537, Sandy Bay, Tasmania, 07005. Phone: 61-362-243578. Fax: 61-362-24248211.E-mail: wildangels@bigpond.com

Coordination svcs for international film & TV production. Second unit svcs stock footage library.

Loral Skynet, 2400 Research Blvd., Suite 200, Rockville, MD, 20850. Phone: (301) 258-8101. Fax: (301) 258-3222.E-mail: info@loralskynet.com Web Site:www.loralskynet.com Terry Hart, pres/CEO.

International telecommunication svcs in Asia Pacific rgn, specializing in private networks via satellite.

Lund Consultants to Broadcast Management Inc., 840 Hinckley Rd., Suite 123, Burlingame, CA, 94010-1505. Phone: (650) 692-7777. Fax: (650) 692-7799.E-mail: lundradio@aol.com Web Site:www.lundradio.com John C. Lund, pres; Dan R. Spice, VP.

Experts in progmg consulting; multipoly strategy. Adult contemp, country, top 40, rock, classic rock, oldies, news-talk, music, formatics, proms, talent dev & perceptual rsch.

Frank N. Magid Associates Inc., One Research Ctr., Marion, IA, 52302. Phone: (319) 377-7345. Fax: (319) 377-5861.E-mail: mailia@magid.com Web Site:www.magid.com Brent Magid, pres/CEO; Steve Ridge, exec VP.

Sherman OaksCA , 15260 Ventura Blvd, Suite 2130. Phone:

New YorkNY , 1775 Broadway, Suite 1401. Phone:

Specialists in rsch-driven consultation to traditional & new media firms; svcs include strategic planning, web site evaluation & dev, program evaluation, talent search, coaching, TMI, & the Magid Network.

Mahlum Architects, 71 Columbia, Suite 400, Seattle, WA, 98104. Phone: (206) 441-4151. Fax: (206) 441-0478.E-mail: info@mahlum.com Web Site:www.mahlum.com

Design; tech consulting; feasibility & facilities studies; cost analysis & construction admin for TV/radio stns, production & equipment storage facilities, & film studios.

Marketing & Creative Services, (Division of Frank N. Magid Associates Inc.). One Research Ctr., Marion, IA, 52302. Phone: (319) 377-7345. Fax: (319) 377-5861.E-mail: mailia@magid.com Web Site:www.magid.com Steve Ridge, exec VP; Brent Magid, pres/CEO; Bill Hague, sr VP.

Sherman OaksCA , 15260 Ventura Blvd, Suite 2130. Phone:

New YorkNY , 1775 Broadway, Suite 1401. Phone: Rsch & consultation.

Marshall & Stevens Inc., 355 S. Grand Ave, Ste 1759, ste. 1750, Los Angeles, CA, 90017. Phone: (213) 612-8000. Fax: (213) 612-8010.E-mail: info@marshall-stevens.com Web Site:www.marshall-stevens.com Fred Thomas, VP.

St. LouisMO , 701 Market Street, # 370. Phone:

New YorkNY , 1156 Ave. of the Americas, #703. Phone:

Natl appraisal firm with extensive bcstg client base. Value real estate, equipment, intangible assets & overall business valuations. Assist in financing sls, purchase price allocation, & cast segregation.

Maxagrid, 3939 Belt Line Rd., Suite 250, Addison, TX, 75001. Phone: (972) 241-2110. Fax: (972) 241-2174.E-mail: maxagrid@maxagrid.com Web Site:www.maxagrid.com Jim Tiller, pres/CEO; Karen Brian, mgr.

Yield mgmt systems for bcst in USA, Australia, & Canada. Systems & strategies that help mgrs improve yields on adv revenues.

Maxwell Media Group, 6053 Bunker Hill, Pittsburgh, PA, 15206. Phone: (412) 441-2020. Fax: (412) 661-9377. Bill Maxwell, pres.

Consultant.

Mayo Communications Inc., Box 82784, Tampa, FL, 33682. Phone: (813) 264-5050. Fax: (813) 264-5353. Lincoln A. Mayo, pres.

Media brokerage, appraisals for bcst & print. Consulting, concerning media sls & acquisitions.

Mazer & Associates, 3452 Grayton Rd., Detroit, MI, 48224. Phone: (313) 885-5686. John Mazer, J.D. Jr., pres.

Radio & TV progmg svcs, market rsch, format design, talent evaluation, license renewal preparation, labor rel, mgmt & admin consulting.

McVay Media, 2001 Crocker Rd., Suite 260, Cleveland, OH, 44145. Phone: (440) 892-1910.E-mail: mcvaymedia@aol.com Web Site:www.mcvaymedia.com Mike McVay, consultant; Doris McVay, gen mgr .

AtlantaGA . Atlanta, 628 Braidwood Dr. Fax:

Consultant radio stns in progmg various formats.

Media & Marketing, 4245 Sarah St., Burbank, CA, 91505. Phone: (818) 753-9510. Phone: (818) 558-3924.E-mail: mel.lambert@mediaandmarketing.com Web Site:www.mediaandmarketing.com Mel Lambert, creative director.

Consulting svc for the audio & multimedia industries.

Media Communications Group Inc., Box 335, 11 Spiral Dr., Suite 3, Florence, KY, 41042. Phone: (859) 647-0055. Fax: (859) 647-2611.E-mail: jpierce@paragoncomm.com Web Site:www.paragoncomm.com Dan Hubbard, sr VP; Rebecca Neal, chief of opns; John L. Pierce, pres/CEO.

Representing, consulting & mgmt svcs to radio stns nationwide.

Media Economics, 69 N. Sheridan Ave., Bethpage, NY, 11714. Phone: (516) 931-0248.E-mail: beconomist@aol.com Layton W. Franko PhD., pres.

Market analysis, forecasting, pricing, planning, sports economics & business rsch for TV, cable & radio industries.

Media Perspectives, 127 Greensward Ln., Cherry Hill, NJ, 08002. Phone: (856) 482-7979. Fax: (856) 482-0957. Steven G. Apel, pres.

Progmg & mktg counseling through applied audience & advertiser rsch.

Media Sales Management, Potsdamer Strasse 31, Berlin, 10783. Phone: 49-30-215-30300. Fax: 49-30-215-1182.

Hamburg, Sthamerstrasse 58. Phone:

Offers a complete package of bcst svcs, finance, acquisition, progmg sls mgmt, rsch & valuations. German & European specialists.

The Mediacenter, 1500 Harbor Blvd., Weehawken, NJ, 07086. Phone: (866) 412-0866. Fax: (201) 348-1761.E-mail: info@mediacenteronline.com Web Site:www.mediacenteronline.com Barbara Zeiger, pres; Russell Sands, gen mgr .

Promote increased mktg professionalism among TV execs & mgrs; provide sls support tools that identify & dev new adv budgets.

Mercer Capital Management Inc., 5860 Ridgeway Center Pkwy., 4th Fl., Memphis, TN, 38120. Phone: (901) 685-2120. Fax: (901) 685-2199.E-mail: mcm@mercercapital.com Web Site:www.mercercapital.com Lisa Doble, sr VP.

LouisvilleKY , 206 Kentuckey Towers. Phone:

Mercer Capital provides high-quality independent business appraisals & other financial advisory svcs for all types of media including radio.

Metro Orlando Film & Television Commission, 301 E. Pine St., Suite 900, Orlando, FL, 32801. Phone: (407) 422-7159. Fax: (407) 841-9069.E-mail: suzy@filmorlando.com Web Site:www.filmorlando.com Suzy Allen, VP.

One stop permitting, locations library, location scouting, community familiarization tours, Filmbook with complete listings of crews, technicians & production support vendors.

J.M. Miller, Box 190, Ashburn, VA, 20146. Phone: 703-729-7745. Fax: 703-729-7745.E-mail: broadcastappraisal@yahoo.com Jan M. Miller, owner.

Bcst TV, DTV, AM, FM, production, satellite, microwave facility & equipment inspection, asset appraisal reports, engrg evaluation overviews & consulting svcs. For valuation, acquisition, finance, purchase price allocation, ad valorem tax, insurance, leasing, liquidation & litigation.

Jay Mitchell Associates Inc., 4 Ventana, Aliso Viejo, CA, 92656. Phone: (949) 533-4912. Fax: (949) 666-5045.E-mail: mitchell @jaymitchell.com Web Site:www.jaymitchell.com Jay Mitchell, pres.

Mgmt, mktg, progmg, promotions consulting; market analysis, web site design & consulting.

George Moore & Associates Inc., 6918 Wildglen Dr., Suite 100 W, Dallas, TX, 75230. Phone: (214) 369-5665. Phone: (800) 220-3287. Fax: (214) 369-5667. W. James Moore, pres.

Brokerage of radio, TV & CATV properties; asset & market appraisals; introduction to institutional financing sources.

Multimedia Research Group Inc. (MRG, Inc.), 1754 Technology Dr., Suite 132, San Jose, CA, 95110. Phone: (408) 453-5553. Fax: (408) 453-5559.E-mail: info@mrgco.com Web Site:www.mrgco.com Gary Schultz, pres.

Provides strategic consulting & published market intelligence on content dev, content distribution, channels & networks.

Nashville Mayor's Office of Film, 222 2nd Ave., Suite 418, Nashville, TN, 37201. Phone: (615) 880-1827. Fax: (615) 862-6025.E-mail: andyvr@nashville.org Web Site:www.filmnashville.com Tessa Atkins, dir.

Location scouting, permits, produce annual production directory, assist with all logistics of TV/film/video projects, liaison to media & govt.

National Strategies Inc., 1100 H St. N.W., Suite 1200, Washington, DC, 20005. Phone: (202) 349-7001. Fax: (202) 783-1041.E-mail: daylward@natstrat.com Web Site:www.nationalstrategiesinc.com Al Gordon, CFO.

Milan Italy, Via San Senatore 10. Phone:

New YorkNY , 14 E. 60th St, Suite 1002. Phone:

Pub policy strategies & implementation, business & investment dev.

Navigant International, 945 Hornet Dr., Suite 101, Hazelwood, MO, 63042. Phone: (314) 592-3800. Fax: (314) 592-3900. Mike Million, dir opns.

Corporate & leisure travel, specializes in promotional packages & incentive programs.

New England Media L.L.C., Box 594, Willimantic, CT, 06226. Phone: (860) 456-7400. Fax: (860) 456-5688.E-mail: mcrice@prodigy.net Michael Rice, ptnr.

Mansfield CenterCT , 50 Kaya Lane. Phone:

Media brokers, consultants & appraisers specializing in radio in the Northeast.

Newbrough Associates Inc., Box 1822, Des Moines, IA, 50305-1822. Phone: (515) 244-8909. Fax: (515) 244-8909.E-mail: wbn@att.net Bill Newbrough, pres.

Provides alternative advisory consultaions worldwide, focusing on communications. Forty years of mass media & mgmt experiences. WISDOM+RESEARCH=SUCCESS.

NEWSDirections, 1521 Rocky Knoll Ln., Dacula, GA, 30019-6754. Phone: (770) 569- 2277.E-mail: tony@news-direction.com Web Site:www.news-directions.com Tony Windsor, pres.

Professional dev & career mktg for TV news reporters, anchors & producers.

Nathan M. Nickolaus, 320 E. McCarthy St., Jefferson City, MO, 65101-3115. Phone: (573) 634-6313. Fax: (573) 634-6504.E-mail: nnickolaus@jeffcity.mo.org Web Site:nnickolaus@jeffcitymo.org Nathan M. Nickolaus, consultant.

Noll & Associates, 475 Gate Five Rd., Suite 211, Sausalito, CA, 94965. Phone: (415) 332-2254. Fax: (415) 332-5519.E-mail: kennen@nollmedia.com Web Site:www.nollmedia.com Kennen Williams, pres.

Bcst mktg/sls training, new business dev & organizational dev.

Northwest Broadcasting Co., Box 332, Dallastown, PA, 17313-0332. Phone: (815 308-7613.E-mail: mkrafcisin@hotmail.com Michael H. Krafcisin, pres.

Mgmt, progmg, production, scriptwriting, talent, voice-over svcs, opns & engrg consultation

The Omnia Group, 601 South Blvd., Tampa, FL, 33606. Phone: (800) 525-7117. Fax: (813) 254-8558.E-mail: mcleveland@omniagroup.com Web Site:www.omniagroup.com

Same-day response on best industry-validated selection tools that help hire the right person the first time.

Ott & Associates, 9225 Chatham Grove Ln., Suite D, Richmond, VA, 23236. Phone: (804) 276-7202. Fax: (804) 745-7778.E-mail: rick@rickott.com Web Site:www.rickott.com Rick Ott, pres.

Problem solving, consultation in complete confidentiality. Mgmt consulting.

PMA Marketing Inc., 4359 S. Howell, Suite 106, Milwaukee, WI, 53207. Phone: (414) 482-2638. Fax: (414) 483-1980.E-mail: patrick@amfmtv.com Web Site:www.amfmtv.com Patrick Martin, pres.

Buy & sell new & used bcst equipment, radio stn start-ups & turnarounds, problem solving for difficult bcst situations.

PR/PR, 775 S. Kirkman Rd., Suite 104, Orlando, FL, 32811. Phone: (407) 299-6128. Fax: (407) 299-2166.E-mail: pam@prpr.net Web Site:www.prpr.net Pam Lontos, pres; Rick Dudnick, VP.

Publicity in Radio, TV, print for speakers & authors.

Palazzo Intercreative, 308 Occidental Ave. South, Suite 200, Seattle, WA, 98104. Phone: (206) 328-5555. Fax: (206) 324-4348.E-mail: palazzo@palazzo.com Web Site:www.palazzo.com Richard Roberts, pres & dir.

Stn identity design & consultation svcs, including on-air, print, outdoor, graphics, syndicated animation packages, movie & news opns, & radio spots.

Paragon Media Strategies, 12345 W. Alameda Pkwy., Suite 325, Denver, CO, 80228. Phone: (303) 922-5600. Fax: (303) 922-1589.E-mail: info@paragonmediastrategies.com Web Site:www.paragonmediastrategies.com Mike Henry, CEO.

Media rsch & consulting.

Patrick Communications L.L.C., 6805 Douglas Legum Dr., Suite 100, Elkridge, MD, 21075. Phone: (410) 799-1740. Fax: (410) 799-1705.E-mail: larry@patcomm.com Web Site:www.patcomm.com Larry Patrick, mgng ptnr; Susan Patrick, mgng ptnr; Greg Guy, mgng ptnr; John Cunney, VP; Jason James, rsch analyst; Vince Pepper, principal.

Stn brokerage, investment banking, mgmt consulting svcs, appraisals & opns consulting.

Donald A Perry & Associates Inc., Box 1275, Newport News, VA, 23601. Phone: (757) 877-4367. Fax: (757) 693-2885.E-mail: dperry@cablefirst.net Donald A. Perry, pres.

Mgmt, brokerage & appraisal svcs to the cable TV industry.

Peters Communications, 1555 Berenda Pl., El Cajon, CA, 92020. Phone: (619) 444-6984. Fax: (619) 440-1481.E-mail: edpeters@cox.net Edward J. Peters, pres.

Media mktg consultants, providing rsch, concept, mktg plan, music, graphics & animation.

Point Broadcasting Company, Point 3G. 715 Broadway, Suite 320, Santa Monica, CA, 90401. Phone: (310) 451-4430. Fax: (310) 451-1423. John Hearne, mgr.

Operating, technical & financial mgmt.

Pollack Media Group Inc., 860 Via De La Paz, Suite D2, Pacific Palisades, CA, 90272. Phone: (310) 459-8556. Fax: (310) 454-5046.E-mail: hq@pollackmedia.com Web Site:www.pollackmedia.com Jeff Pollack, chmn/CEO; Tommy Hadges, pres; Dave Brewer, exec VP; Jim Kerr, TV news.

Worldwide bcst progmg advisory firm, all facets of progmg, positioning, mktg, adv, rsch, music. All formats.

Poorman & Group, 143-147 E. Main St., Suite 2C, Lock Haven, PA, 17745. Phone: (570) 748-7000. Fax: (570) 748-7700. Web Site:www.lockhaven.com Stephen P. Poorman, pres.

Pennsylvania & Texas-based mgmt consulting firm offers "no-charge" interviews to radio & TV stns relating to business & real estate issues. Specializes in organizing & mgng financially distressed businesses.

Price Waterhouse Coopers, 1 North Wacker Drive, Chicago, IL, 60606. Phone: (312) 298-2000. Fax: (312) 298-2001. Web Site:www.pwc.com

Provides valuation consulting svcs for acquisitions, swaps, estate planning & litigation.

W.L. Pritchard & Co. L.C., 4405 E.W. Hwy., Suite 501, Bethesda, MD, 20814. Phone: (301) 654-1144. Fax: (301) 654-1814.E-mail: wlpritchard-co@verizon.net Web Site:www.wlpco.com Ellen Hoff, pres; Paul Schrantz, VP engrg.

Professional engrg, business problem solving in telecommunications, competitor analysis, satellite communications, earth stns, & launch vehicles.

RBC Daniels L.P., 3200 Cherry Creek S. Dr., Suite 500, Denver, CO, 80209. Phone: (303) 778-5555. Fax: (303) 778-5599.E-mail: info@rbcdaniels.com Web Site:www.rbcdaniels.com Brian Deevy, chmn/CEO; David Tolliver, mgng dir.

New YorkNY , 711 5th Ave, Suite 405. Phone:

Provides both mergers & acquisitions, corporate financial svcs to the cable telecommunications, media & technology industries.

The R Corp., 2477 Stickney Point Rd., Suite 201 B, Sarasota, FL, 34231. Phone: (941) 924-2400. Fax: (941) 924-1650.E-mail: rcorp@comcast.net

Consulting to electronic media, cable, wireless, & bcstg.

R.F. Technologies Corp., 12 Foss Rd., Lewiston, ME, 04240. Phone: (207) 777-7778. Fax: (207) 777-7784.E-mail: info@rftechnologies.net Web Site:www.rftechnologies.net George M. Harris, pres.

Provides file engrg & svc for TV & FM antennas, transmission lines, diplexers & combiners.

RPM Radio Programming & Management, 1133 W. Longlake Rd., Suite 200, Bloomfield Hills, MI, 48302. Phone: (888) 776-0006. Fax: (248) 647-2663.E-mail: info@tophitusa.com Web Site:www.tophitsusa.com Thomas M. Krikorian, pres.

Top Hits U.S. wkly CD svc & CD libraries including Solid Gold, Spectrum A/C & Country One; CD Christmas library.

Rattigan Resources, 3409 Wilshire Rd., Portsmouth, VA, 23703. Phone: (757) 484-3017.E-mail: rattiganjack@aol.com Jack M. Rattigan CRMC, CEO.

Specializes in "mktg to the 50+ demographic" (baby boomers & beyond). Customized sls training & seminars for stns programmed to the mature & wealthiest audience.

Rees Associates Inc., Rees Plaza at East Wharf, 9211 Lake Hefner Pkwy, Suite 300, Oklahoma City, OK, 73120. Phone: (405) 942-7337. Phone: (888) 942-7337. Fax: (405) 948-1261.E-mail: rees@rees.com Web Site:www.rees.com Frank W. Rees Jr., pres; Leroy James Jr., exec VP; Kristina Dover Jr., mktg.

AtlantaGA United Kingdom. The Metropolis Bldg., 951 Peachtree St. N.E. Phone:

DallasTX , 1801 N. Lamar St, Suite 600. Phone:

Bcst & production facility design; architectural svcs; facility business plans; interior design; studio design; equipment planning, consulting.

Restivo Communications/Starstruck Entertainment Company, 73 Widdicombe Hill Blvd., Suite 1515, Toronto, ON, M9R 4B3. Canada. Phone: (416) 242-7009. Web Site:www.prmediaconnection.com Peter J. Restivo, pres.

Bcst & media consultants; media training, MOW development.

George Rodman Associates, 100 Christwood Blvd., Apt. 119, Covington, LA, 70433-4601. Phone: (831) 626-1630. Fax: (831) 626-8662.E-mail: grodman@viaworldwide.com George T. Rodman, pres; Sally M. Rodman, VP.

Provides stns, networks, groups & program suppliers with mktg counseling & promotional materials, including adv campaigns, logos, on-air design, TV spots & animation.

Roehling Broadcast Services Ltd., 7340 Oak Knoll Dr., Indianapolis, IN, 46217. Phone: (317) 887-1945. Fax: (317) 887-1947.E-mail: edradiobr@aol.com Web Site:roehlingbroadcast.com Edward W. Roehling, pres; Sandra Roehling, VP & treas.

Bcst appraisers, brokers, consultants, also financing, sls, mgmt consultation.

Ray H. Rosenblum Sales & Management Consultant, Box 38296, Pittsburgh, PA, 15238. Phone: (412) 362-6311. Fax: (412) 362-6317.E-mail: rayhrosenblum@hotmail.com Ray H. Rosenblum, consultant.

Consultant & appraiser for radio & TV stns & political candidates, with focus on mgmt, sls, proms, news & PR.

Rumbaut & Co., 555 N.E. 34th St., Suite 2701, Miami, FL, 33137-4060. Phone: (305) 868-0000. Fax: (305) 571-0433.E-mail: julio@rumbaut.com Web Site:www.rumbaut.com Julio Rumbaut, pres.

Media brokers & consultants in all facets of the TV & radio industries.

William Russell & Associates Inc., 305 W. Masonic View Ave., Alexandria, VA, 22301. Phone: (703) 739-6277. Fax: (703) 797-7584.E-mail: russell@williamrussellassociates.com Web Site:www.wmrussellassociates.com William A. Russell Jr., pres.

Govt rel & pub rel consultants specializing in telecommunications & international trade issues.

SB Management, 890 Monterey St., Suite G, San Luis Obispo, CA, 93401. Phone: (805) 543-9214. Fax: (805) 543-9243.E-mail: Michael@mikehesser.com Web Site:www.mikehesser.com Michael Hesser, pres.

Assist in finding, evaluating, financing & structuring acquisitions. Also, consult mgmt & sls.

S C Research International Inc., 1317 Third Ave., Suite 100, New York, NY, 10021. Phone: (212) 867-6060. Fax: (212) 867-6579.E-mail: info@scri.com Web Site:www.scri.com Desmond C. Chaskelson, dir.

Syndicated reports & custom rsch for manufacturers & investors in bcstg, professional video & audio; publishers of Broadcast Equipment Marketplace (BEM), Professional Video Marketplace (PFM), Professional Multi-Media Marketplace (PMM), European Telemedia Marketplace (ETM), Asian Telemedia Marketplace (ATM).

SRCS/Markits, 17 Royal Rd., Bangor, ME, 04401. Phone: (207) 942-5548. Fax: (207) 942-9164. Web Site:www.markits99.com Steve Robbins, pres.

Client-directed mktg program for coml bcst properties (radio & TV).

San Antonio Film Commission, 203 S. St. Mary's St., 2nd Fl., San Antonio, TX, 78298. Phone: (210) 207-6730. Fax: (210) 207-6843.E-mail: filmsa@filmsanantonio.com Web Site:www.filmsanantonio.com Drew Mayer-Oakes, dir.

City film commission. Photo Library. Liaison with all city offices. Filming permits. Parking assistance.

SATMAGAZINE.COM, 800 Siesta Way, Sonoma, CA, 95476. Phone: (707) 939-9306. Fax: (707) 939-9235.E-mail: design@satnews.com Web Site:www.satnews.com

Publishers of the mthy Satmagazine online magazine on coml satellite systems. Also available on a CD-ROM & through the web at http://www.satnews.com.

Satterfield & Perry Inc., 7211 Fourth Ave. S., St. Petersburg, FL, 33707. Phone: (727) 345-7338. Fax: (727) 345-3809.E-mail: eraust@prodigy.net Web Site:www.satterfieldandperry.com Robert Austin, pres; John Willis, sec/treas.

WetumpaAL , 169 Mountain Meadows Ln. Phone:

DenverCO , 2020 S. Monroe St., Suite 302. Al Perry, pres emeritus; Joe Benkert, VP; Jim Birschbach, VP.

Overland ParkKS , 4918 W. 101st Terr. Phone:

Coos BayOR , Box 362. Phone:

AikenSC , 131 Inwood Dr, Suite 302. Phone:

Radio, TV, broker, mgmt & sls consultant, FDIC-approved appraiser & expert witness.

Seabrook Travel Consultants, 4225 Sawgrass Dr., Summerville, SC, 29420. Phone: (843) 552-0702. Fax: (843) 552-3717.E-mail: larry@thekirbycompanies.com Larry Kirby, CEO.

Bcst incentive trips worldwide; all major sporting events; owned & operated by bcstrs.

Shane Media Services, 2500 Tanglewilde, Suite 106, Houston, TX, 77063. Phone: (713) 952-9221. Fax: (713) 952-1207.E-mail: smsofc@shanemedia.com Web Site:www.shanemedia.com Ed Shane, CEO; Renee Revett, talent dev; Lee Logan, consultant.

Radio progmg and mgmt consultation, custom designed perceptual and qualitative rsch for electronic media outlets.

Shotmakers, Inc., One Horizon Rd., Fort Lee, NJ, 07024. Phone: (201) 886-0287. Fax: (201) 886-0287.E-mail: info@shotmakers.org Web Site:www.shotmakers.org Dan Robinson, pres.

Media consultant, original film & TV productions; novelist. Represent historic photos & film of New York City & Atlanta.

Barry Skidelsky, Esq., 18 E. 41st St., New York, NY, 10017. Phone: (212) 832-4800.E-mail: bskidelsky@mindspring.com Barry Skidelsky, consultant.

Consults lenders, investors, owners & mgmt on M&A, strategy & opns, FCC ownership, bankruptcy, trustee, arbitrator & expert witness.

Skywatch Weather Center, 347 Prestley Rd., Bridgeville, PA, 15017. Phone: (412) 221-6000. Phone: (800) SKY-WATCH. Fax: (412) 221-3160.E-mail: airsci@skywatchweather.com Web Site:www.skywatchweather.com Dr.Stanley J. Penkala, pres; Daniel Krywiecki, VP.

Specially formatted weathercasts from the Skywatch Weather Center.®

Bill Slatter & Associates, 423 Main St., Natchez, MS, 39120. Phone: (601) 442-1828.E-mail: slatterb@natchez.net

Talent coaching.

Smart Target Marketing, 6800 Southwest 40th St., #304, Miami, FL, 33155. Phone: (305) 667-6665. Fax: (305) 667-3508.E-mail: contact@smarttarget.com Web Site:www.smarttarget.com

Custom strategic direct-mktg programs; complete promotional & adv svcs including direct mail/targeted mailing lists, telemarketing, data base, custom publishing, sls training, & interactive phone/prom, smart targets & prizm targeting svcs.

Soundtrack, 162 Columbus Ave., Boston, MA, 02116-5222. Phone: (617) 303-7500. Fax: (617) 303-7555. Web Site:www.soundtrackgroup.com Amy Blankenship, opns.

New YorkNY , 936 Broadway. Phone:

Production, postproduction & custom music of all kinds; specializing in sound designs.

Southern Surveys, 1551 Olde Mill Pl., Marietta, GA, 30066. Phone: (678) 467-8650. Fax: (770) 924-3584.E-mail: rick@streetlevelviews.com Web Site:www.streetlevelviews.com Rick Phillips, pres.

Natl qualitative moderator for one-on-one rsch. Nationwide recruiting for auditorium music tests since 1986. Video market rsch.

Wayne A. Stacey & Assoc. Ltd., 2145 Hubbard Cr., Ottawa, ON, K1J 6L3. Canada. Phone: (613) 745-9151.E-mail: wstacey@stacey.ca Wayne A. Stacey, pres.

Govt rels, CRTC/IC applications, bcst rsch, bcst consulting, engrg svcs, demographic studies.

Gary Stevens & Co., Box 4880, Stamford, CT, 06907-0880. Phone: (203) 966-6465. Fax: (203) 966-6522.E-mail: deelmakur@aol.com Gary Stevens, mgng dir.

Bcst mergers, acquistions & investment banking svcs.

Stonick Recruitment Inc., 1230 Lake Deeson Pointe, Lakeland, FL, 33805. Phone: (863) 680-1379. Fax: (863) 680-1397.E-mail: stonick@gate.net Web Site:www.stonickrecruitment.com Chris Stonick, pres.

A natl radio sls consulting firm bringing "recruitment adv" to radio (strictly new business dev).

StorerTV Inc., (formerly Peter Storer & Associates Inc.). 1361 W. Towne Sq. Rd., Mequon, WI, 53092. Phone: (262) 241-9005. Fax: (262) 241-9036.E-mail: doug@storertv.com Web Site:www.storertv.com Doug Knight, sls VP; Peter Storer Jr., pres.

Storer Info System (SIMS): Multi-ch, multi-user, PC based TV program schedule, amortization & liability system, for linear & non-linear scheduling.

Structural System Technology Inc., 6867 Elm St., McLean, VA, 22101. Phone: (703) 356-9765. Fax: (703) 448-0979.E-mail: fred.purdy@sst-towers.com Web Site:www.sst-towers.com Fred Purdy, P.E., pres; Kaveh Mehrnama, P.E., VP.

Structural engrg studies, analysis, design, modifications, inspections, fabrication & erection of towers & antenna structures.

Synovate, 8600 N.W. 17th St., Suite 100, Miami, FL, 33126. Phone: (305) 716-6800. Fax: (305) 716-6756. Web Site:www.synovate.com Richard Tobin, pres.

Laguna HillsCA , 23151 Alde Dr, Suite C4. Phone:

Full-svc mktg rsch company, specializing in the Hispanic market; focus group testing, awareness usage tracking studies, media ratings.

Szabo Associates Inc., Media Collection Professionals, 3355 Lenox Rd. NE, 9th Fl., Atlanta, GA, 30326. Phone: (404) 266-2464. Fax: (404) 266-2155.E-mail: info@szabo.com Web Site:www.szabo.com C. Robin Szabo, pres.

Experts in creditor & debtor rights; consulting media properties in the accounts receivable process; domestic & international collections.

TalentTrainers, 10807 Waring Pl., Charlotte, NC, 28277. Phone: (704) 541-0892. Fax: 1-800-787-4284.E-mail: brice@talenttrainers.com Web Site:www.talenttrainers.com Shirley Brice, pres.

Talent coaching for TV stns & newspapers. Media trainer for corporate executives. One-on-one sessions, small workshops & individual critiques. Weekly "live" coaching chat on www.talent trainers.com.

J.A. Taylor & Associates, Box 331, Boyertown, PA, 19512-0331. Phone: (610) 754-6800. Fax: (610) 754-9766.E-mail: jataylor@broadcastassociates.com Web Site:www.broadcastassociates.com

Appraisers & brokers of TV production equipment. Serves video production companies, TV stns & financial institutions.

Tele-Measurements Inc., 145 Main Ave., Clifton, NJ, 07014-1078. Phone: (973) 473-8822. Fax: (973) 473-0521.E-mail: contact@telemeasurements.com Web Site:www.tele-measurements.com William E. Endres, pres; Douglas W. Cook, VP sls.

Bcst, professional video equipment, videotape, TV systems, teleconferencing, ongoing maintenance support, CCTV, equipment rentals.

Teletech Inc., Box 85567, Westland, MI, 48185. Phone: (734) 641-2300. Fax: (734) 641-2323. Web Site:www.teletech-inc.com Keith Johnson, VP; Todd Osment, field svc mgr.

Antenna site mgmt; tower, studio & antenna construction & maintenance; frequency searches; FCC application preparation; EMI, radiation & microwave studies.

Television by Design Inc., 3277 Roswell Rd., Suite 714, Atlanta, GA, 30305. Phone: (404) 873-3277. Fax: (404) 873-7900.E-mail: jay@tvbd.com Web Site:www.tvbd.com Jay Antzakas, pres.

Creators of electronic graphic design; consultants on visual design, equipment & opns for TV stns.

Tenner & Associates Inc., 121 Quail Run Rd., Henderson, NV, 89014. Phone: (702) 792-9430. Fax: (702) 792-5748. Web Site:www.tennerandassoc.com Lisa Tenner, pres.

Event & conference producers for the entertainment industry.

3-H Cable Communications Consultants, 502 E. Main St., Auburn, WA, 98002-5502. Phone: (253) 833-8380. Fax: (253) 833-8430.

Cable franchise admin, negotiation, renewal, tech evaluation, community needs assessment & franchise fee audits.

Tony Lease Incentive Tours, 500 S. Palm Canyon Dr., Suite 215, Palm Springs, CA, 92264-7454. Phone: (760) 325-9799. Fax: (760) 325-9755.E-mail: info@tonylease Web Site:www.tonylease.com

Laguna NiguelCA . Laguna Niguel, Box 7531. Phone:

Five star sls incentive tours for media. Also has Media Sports Tours for Superbowl, Final Four OLympic packages. Forty years experience; world wide contacts.

Edwin Tornberg & Co. Inc., 8917 Cherbourg Dr., Potomac, MD, 20854. Phone: (301) 983-8700. Fax: (301) 299-2297. Edwin Tornberg, pres.

Negotiators for purchase & sale of radio, TV stns & CATV systems; appraisers & financial advisers; mgmt consultants.

Transcomm Inc., Box 2845, Fairfax, VA, 22031. Phone: (703) 323-5150. Fax: (703) 426-4527.E-mail: transcommusa@msn.com Web Site:www.transcommusa.com Dr. Norman C. Lerner, engr.

Financial/economic analysis, market rsch, pricing studies & regulatory economics.

Jon Ulmer & Associates, 2176 Highpoint Rd., Snellville, GA, 30078. Phone: (770) 979-3031. Fax: (770) 979-3789.E-mail: julmercpa@comcast.net John R. Ulmer, owner.

Accounting, computer & financial mgmt consulting.

VIP Research Inc., 5700 Broadmoor St., Suite 200, Mission, KS, 66202. Phone: (888) 384-9494. Fax: (913) 677-2727.E-mail: clark@vipresearch.net Web Site:www.vipresearch.net Mike Heydman, rsch dir; Clark Roberts, CFO, sls dir.

Provides hook-tape production, listener screening, fielding & tabulation for all music testing, perceptual studies, focus groups & promotional telemarketing.

Vanguard Media Corp., 310 N. Westlake Blvd., Suite 230, Westlake Village, CA, 91362. Phone: (805) 446-4100. Fax: (805) 446-4111.E-mail: info@vanmedia.com Web Site:www.vanmedia.com Rick Newberger, pres.

Advisory firm to media companies, specializing in planning,

& dev of new progmg svcs (e.g., The Golf Channel) & distribution systems (e.g., DBS).

Veronis, Suhler , 350 Park Ave., New York, NY, 10022. Phone: (212) 935-4990. Fax: (212) 381-8168. Web Site:www.veronissuhler.com John J. Veronis, chmn/CEO; John S. Suhler, pres/CEO; Jeffrey T. Stevenson, gen ptnr; James P. Rutherfurd, exec VP; Vernois Suhler Stevenson, gen ptnr.

Merchant bankers to media, communications & info industries, with focus on mergers & acquisitions, valuations, joint ventures & private equity.

A.G. Visk, 2973 Evans Oaks Ct., Atlanta, GA, 30340. Phone: (770) 939-5657.E-mail: tvisk@yahoo.com

Promotional concepts, scripts & publications for the bcstg & entertainment industries.

WW Associates, 10040 East Happy Valley Rd. unit 454, Scottsdale, AZ, 85255. Phone: (480) 515-0913. Fax: (480) 515-4632.E-mail: jwiesenberg@mba1977.hbs.edu

International new media dev, strategic planning & acquisition assistance, cable & wireless MMDS expertise, PPV event & movie studio liaison.

Warren Only Media Group, 19 W. Almond St., Vineland, NJ, 08360. Phone: (856) 507-9368. Fax: (856) 507-9368.E-mail: sales@warrenonly.com Web Site:www.warrenonly.com Warren Only, consultant.

Bcstg radio & TV consultants, telecommunications, FCC applications.

Washington Information Group Ltd., 1655 N. Ft. Meyer Dr., Suite 800, Arlington, VA, 22209. Phone: (202) 463-7334. Fax: (703 527-4586. Web Site:www.winfogroup.com Douglas House, pres.

Customized business rsch. Competitive intelligence, pub & private company rsch, industry & market studies. Strictly confidential; free consultation.

"The Weather Center", (A bcst svc of Aviation Weather Inc.). 701 Gervais St., Suite 224, Columbia, SC, 29201. Phone: (803) 422-4823.E-mail: wxcenter@aviationweatherinc.com Web Site:www.aviationweatherinc.com

"Rgnl Radio Bcst/Weathercast Network" across the Carolinas & Georgia in over 20 bcst markets. Weather forecasting, site-specific bcst svcs for stns all across America.

The Wexler Group, 1317 F St. N.W., Suite 600, Washington, DC, 20004. Phone: (202) 638-2121. Fax: (202) 638-7045. Web Site:www.wexlergroup.com Anne Wexler, chmn; Dale Snape, gen mgr .

Consulting firm, specializing in govt rel & pub affrs with strong emphasis on mass media, telecommunications, copyright, trade.

Wind River Broadcast Center, 117 E. 11th St., Loveland, CO, 80537. Phone: (800) 669-3993. Phone: (970) 669-3442. Fax: (970) 663-6081.E-mail: jim@windriverbroadcast.com Web Site:www.windriverbroadcast.com Jim McDonald, CEO.

TV/FM/AM tech & regulatory consulting; publishers of The Bigbook Project, a radio/TV stn tech & regulatory workbook system. FCC applications, engrg.

Wishnow Group Inc., 82 Bubier Rd., Marblehead, MA, 01945-3640. Phone: (781) 631-2444.E-mail: jwishnow@yahoo.com Jerrold D. Wishnow, pres.

Position bcst clients as community service leaders.

Wolfe Media, 10755-F Scripps Poway Pkwy., #612, San Diego, CA, 92131. Phone: (858) 530-8787. Phone: (888) 965-3226. Fax: (858) 530-9974.E-mail: dw@wolfemedia.com Web Site:www.wolfemedia.com David Wolfe, pres.

Media consultants.

Walter Wulff & Associates, FAA Consultants. Box 914, Point Clear, AL, 36564. Phone: (251) 990-2502. Fax: (334) 990-2503.E-mail: wulff@zebra.net Walter H. Wulff, CEO.

Conducts FAA tower studies & EMI evaluations.

Station Financing Services

ABN AMRO, Park Ave. Plaza 55 E. 52nd St., New York, NY, 10055. Phone: (212) 409-1000. Phone: (212) 251-3524. Fax: (212) 409-7291. Web Site:www.abnamro.com

Joost Kuiper, chmn; Patrick Phalon, dir corporate communications.

Allied Capital Corp., 1919 Pennsylvania Ave. N.W., 3rd Fl., Washington, DC, 20006. Phone: (202) 331-1112. Fax: (202) 659-2053.E-mail: wrichardson@alliedcaptial.com Web Site:www.alliedcapital.com

William Walton, chmn/CEO.

Subordinated debt, deal size $3 million to $8 million, natl & international.

Alta Communications, 200 Clarendon St., 51st Fl., Boston, MA, 02116. Phone: (617) 262-7770. Fax: (617) 262-9779. Web Site:www.altacomm.com E-mail: clarason@altacomm.com

Brian McNeill, CEO.

Provide equity & subordinated debt for acquisitions, buyouts, recapitalizations, etc. for companies in radio, TV, cable TV & related industries.

BIA Capital Corp., 15120 Enterprise Ct., Suite 100, Chantilly, VA, 20151. Phone: (703) 818-8115. Fax: (703) 803-3299.E-mail: info@bia.com Web Site:www.bia.com

Mark Giannini, CEO.

Investment banking svc, including placement of debt & equity, advice in capital structure & merger, & acquisition issues.

BIA Digital Partners, L.P., 15120 Enterprise Ct., Suite 100, Chantilly, VA, 20151. Phone: (703) 227-9600. Fax: (703) 803-3299.E-mail: gjohnson@bia.com Web Site:www.biadigitalpartners.com

Greg Johnson, mgng principal; Lloyd R. Sams, mgng principal.

Provides subordinated debt & preferred equity for communications companies in amounts from 4-25 million.

BIA Financial Network, 15120 Enterprise Ct., Suite 100, Chantilly, VA, 20151-1102. Phone: (703) 818-2425. Fax: (703) 803-3299.E-mail: info@bia.com Web Site:www.bia.com

Mark Giannini, CEO.

Financial consultants to the communications industry; fair market valuations, tax appraisals, acquisition consulting, business plans, internal operational audits, litigation support, investment, publications, & database software, venture funding, capital.

BMO Nesbitt Burns (Bank of Montreal), 3 Times Sq., New York, NY, 10036. Phone: (212) 605-1424. Fax: (212) 605-1648.E-mail: yvonne.bos@bmo.com Web Site:www.bmo.com

Provides lending & other capital raising svcs, derivatives, & cash mgmt to the bcst & cable industries.

Bank of America Illinois, 231 S. LaSalle St., Chicago, IL, 60697. Phone: (312) 828-2345. Fax: (312) 828-7397.E-mail: pat.mendrik@bankofamerica.com Web Site:www.bankofamerica.com

John Brennan, pres.

The Barclays Group, 200 Park Ave., New York, NY, 10166. Phone: (212) 412-4000. Fax: (212) 412-7300. Web Site:www.barcap.com

Bob Diamond, pres/CEO.

Berkery, Noyes & Co., 1 Liberty Plaza, 13th Fl., New York, NY, 10006. Phone: (212) 668-3022. Fax: (212) 747-9092.E-mail: cathy@berkerynoyes.com Web Site:www.berkerynoyes.com

Joseph Berkery, CEO; Mai-Anh Tran, VP.

San FranciscoCA , 580 California St., 5th Fl. Phone:

NewtonMA , 40 Kirkstall Rd. Phone:

Assists with mergers, acquisitions, divestitures; financial analysis & counsel; debt or equity financing through private or pub chs, including LBOs, ESOPs & valuations.

Blackburn & Co. Capital Markets Group, 201 N. Union St., Suite 340, Alexandria, VA, 22314. Phone: (703) 519-3703. Fax: (703) 519-9756.E-mail: rblack4@aol.com

James W. Blackburn Jr., chmn; Richard F. Blackburn, pres.

Brokerage of radio & TV stns.

Bulkley Capital L.P., 5949 Sherry Ln., Suite 1370, Dallas, TX, 75225. Phone: (214) 692-5476. Fax: (214) 692-9309.E-mail: info@bulkleycapital.com Web Site:www.bulkleycapital.com

Lisa Bulkley, VP; Oliver Cone, VP.

Investment banking; mergers, acquisitions, private placements of debt & equity capital.

CIBC World Markets, 300 Madison Ave., New York, NY, 10017. Phone: (212) 856-4000. Fax: (212) 856-3996. Web Site:www.cibcwm.com

Gary W. Brown, pres/CEO.

Investment banking & asset mgmt.

Chaisson & Company Inc., 154 Indian Waters Dr., New Canaan, CT, 06840. Phone: (203) 966-6333. Fax: (203) 966-1298.E-mail: rchaisco@aol.com

Robert A. Chaisson, pres.

Brokerage of radio/TV sls & acquisitions.

Communicaions Equity Associate, (Formerly CEA Inc.). 54 Thompson St., 4th Fl., New York, NY, 10012. Phone: (212) 218-5085. Fax: (212) 334-3063. Web Site:www.ceaworldwide.com

J. Patrick Michael Jr., CEO.

TampaFL , 101 Kennedy Blvd., #3300. Phone: Investment banking, brokerage & private equity.

Communications Equity Associates, 101 E. Kennedy Blvd., Suite 3300, Tampa, FL, 33602. Phone: (813) 226-8844. Fax: (813) 225-1513. Web Site:www.ceaworldwide.com E-mail: rmichaels@ccceaworldwide.com

J. Patrick Michaels Jr., chmn/CEO; John Turner, COO; Donald Russell, mgng dir; Carsten Philipson, mgng dir.

Muenchen, Prinzregentenstrasse 56. Phone:

WestportCT , 191 Post Rd. W. Phone:

New YorkNY , 1270 Avenue of the Americas, Suite 1818. Phone:

Investment banking, corporate finance & private equity, firm specializing in cable, bcstg, new media & entertainment industries.

Cox & Cox, LLC, 2454 Shiva Ct., St. Louis, MO, 63011. Phone: (636) 458-4780. Fax: (636) 273-1312.E-mail: bc@coxandcoxllc.com Web Site:www.coxandcoxllc.com

Robert Cox, pres; Linda Cox, VP.

Media mergers & acquisitions, appraisals, consulting, expert testimony, receivership & workout.

The Deer River Group, 888 16th St., N.W., Suite 400, Washington, DC, 20006. Phone: (202) 939-9090. Fax: (202) 939-9091.E-mail: robin.martin@earthlink.net

Robin B. Martin, pres/CEO.

Assist bcst execs in acquiring stns, securing financing; financial consultant to single stns & group owners; investment banking svcs.

Dresdner Kleinwort, 1301 Ave. of the Americas, New York, NY, 10019. Phone: (212) 969-2700. Web Site:www.dresdnerkleinwort.com

Integrated investment bank offering premier mergers & acquisitions advising as well as private equity investment & placement, structuring, underwriting & advisory for global debt & equity.

EnVest Media, LLC, 6802 Patterson Ave., Richmond, VA, 23226. Phone: (804) 282-5561. Fax: (804) 282-5703.E-mail: mitt@envestmedia.com Web Site:www.envestmedia.com

Mitt Younts, mgng member.

Nationwide radio, TV acquisition, valuation, financing & consulting firm. The company provides brokerage svcs to stn transaction, appraisal svcs to stn owners & financial institutions. The group secures debt & equity acquisition financing, offers consulting & asset mgmt svcs, acting as court appointed receivers or trustees for bcst stns.

Norman Fischer & Associates Inc., Box 5308, Austin, TX, 78763. Phone: (512) 476-9457. Fax: (512) 476-0540.E-mail: terrill@nfainc.com Web Site:www.nfainc.com

Terrill Fischer, pres.

BethlehemPA , 1330 Biafore Ave. Phone:

Brokerage in radio, TV & cable; consultation in mgmt & opns; appraisals; feasibility studies; expert testimony; financial planning & assistance.

Richard A. Foreman Associates Inc., 330 Emery Dr. E., Stamford, CT, 06902-2210. Phone: (203) 327-2800. Fax: (203) 967-9393.E-mail: raf@rafamedia.com Web Site:www.rafamedia.com

Richard A. Foreman, pres.

Debt & equity placement for radio & TV stn acquisitions in major growth markets.

GE Capital Inc., 500 W. Monroe St., Chicago, IL, 60661. Phone: (312) 463-2300. Fax: (312) 441-6728. Web Site:www.gecapital.com

Kim Gutierrez, dir mktg.

Coml financial svcs.

GE Commercial Finance Global Media and Communications, 201 Main Ave., 4th Fl., Norwalk, CT, 06851. Phone: (203) 956-4000. Fax: (203) 956-4528. Web Site:www.geglobalmediacomm.com

Michael E. Chen, pres/CEO.

Leading provider of capital to the bcstg, cable, entertainment, movie theater, outdoor adv, publishing, technology, towers, wireless & wireline industries. Locations in Atlanta, Chicago, Delhi, London, New York, Norwalk, & San Francisco.

Clifton Gardiner & Company L.L.C., 2437 S. Chase Ln., Denver, CO, 80227. Phone: (303) 758-6900. Fax: (303) 479-9210.E-mail: cliff@cliftongardiner.com Web Site:www.cliftongardiner.com

Clifton H. Gardiner, pres.

Consulting svcs on debt & equity placements.

Gleacher Partners, 660 Madison Ave., New York, NY, 10021. Phone: (212) 418-4200. Fax: (212) 752-2711. Web Site:www.gleacher.com

Eric Gleacher, chmn; William Payne, vice chmn.

Provide advice & capital to companies in the media & telecommunications industries.

Great Hill Partners, One Liberty Sq., Boston, MA, 02109. Phone: (617) 790-9400. Fax: (617) 790-9401. Web Site:www.greathillpartners.com E-mail: sgormley@greathillpartners.com

Laurie Gerber, CEO.

Private equity for media & communications companies.

HSBC, One HSBC Ctr., Buffalo, NY, 14203. Phone: (716) 841-7212. Fax: (716) 854-2751. Web Site:www.us.hsbc.com

Postproduction & radio/TV equipment financing.

R. Miller Hicks & Co., 1011 W. 11th St., Austin, TX, 78703. Phone: (512) 477-7000. Fax: (512) 477-9697.E-mail: millerhicks@rmhicks.com

Business consultant & dev firm.

Hoffman Schutz Media Capital Inc., 2044 W. California St., San Diego, CA, 92110. Phone: (619) 291-7070.E-mail: dave@hs-media.com Web Site:www.hs-media.com

David E. Schutz, pres.

PeruVT , Rock Bottom Ln. Phone:

Appraisals, restructurings & litigation support.

Hungerford, Aldrin, Nichols & Carter, CPAs, 2910 Lucerne Dr. S.E., Grand Rapids, MI, 49546. Phone: (616) 949-3200. Fax: (616) 949-7720.E-mail: charper@hanc.com Web Site:www.hanc.com

Jerry Nichols, shareholder; Dan Carter, shareholder.

Confidential radio & TV market revenue share reports for the bcst industry.

J P Morgan and Co. Inc., 60 Wall St., New York, NY, 10260. Phone: (212) 483-2323. Web Site:www.jpmorgan.com

Jamie Dimon, CEO.

Los AngelesCA , 333 S. Hope St, 35th Fl. Phone:

San FranciscoCA , 101 California St, 38th Fl. Phone:

ChicagoIL , 227 W. Monroe St, Suite 2800m. Phone:

Mergers & acquisitions; debt & equity capital raising; swaps & derivatives; credit arrangement & loan syndication; securities sls & trading; asset mgmt.

KeyBanc Capital Markets, 127 Public Sq., 6th Fl., Cleveland, OH, 44114-1306. Phone: (216) 689-3000. Fax: (216) 689-4666.E-mail: kmayher@keybanccm.com Web Site:www.key.com/media

Kathleen Mayher, exec VP & mgr.

Financing for media—TV, radio, cable, nwsprs, bcstg & telecommunications.

The Kompas Group, Box 250813, Milwaukee, WI, 53225-6513. Phone: (262) 781-0188. Fax: (262) 781-5313.E-mail: kompasgroup@toast.net Web Site:www.yourlptvsource.com

John Kompas, pres; Jackie Kompas, VP.

Financial & mktg svcs for LPTV, audience demographic reports, stn coverage maps, financial & strategic planning.

M/C Venture Partners, 75 State St., Suite 2500, Boston, MA, 02109. Phone: (617) 345-7200. Fax: (617) 345-7201.E-mail: jwade@mcventurepartners.com Web Site:www.mcventurepartners.com

David Croll, mngg ptnr.

Provides equity financing & strategic guidance to entrepreneurial ventures in the media & telecommunications industries.

The MFR Group, Box 1184, Rancho Mirage, CA, 92270. Phone: (760) 324-1516. Fax: (760) 324-8255.E-mail: bfenmore@mfrgroup.net Web Site:www.mfrgroup.net

Bart Fenmore, pres.

Accounts receivable funding for radio/TV stns.

Multimedia Broadcast Investment Corp., 3101 South St. N.W., Washington, DC, 20007. Phone: (202) 293-1166. Fax: (202) 293-1181.E-mail: wthreadgill@comcast.net

Walter Threadgill, pres.

Provides sr, subordinated debt, equity for telecommunications & bcst ventures.

National Broadcast Finance Corp., Box 3167, 27 Harrison St., New Haven, CT, 06515-0267. Phone: (203) 389-6000. Fax: (203) 389-6020.E-mail: cherhoniak@sbcglobal.net

David C. Cherhoniak, pres.

Specialized investment banking & financial consulting, including raising debt & equity for bcst acquisitions & refinancings; also brokerage for acquisitions & divestitures.

Nautic Partners, 50 Kennedy Plaza, Providence, RI, 02903. Phone: (401) 278-6770. Fax: (401) 278-6387. Web Site:www.nauticpartners.com E-mail: bwheeler@nautic.com

Habib Gorgi, mngg ptnr.

Source of equity capital to well-managed, positive cash flowing companies.

PK World Media, 126 Clock Tower Pl., Carmel, CA, 93923-8734. Phone: (831) 624-5100. Fax: (831) 625-3225.E-mail: info@pkworldmedia.com Web Site:www.pkworldmedia.com

Paul Kagan, CEO.

Specializing in financial & investment rsch. Media financial newsletters & database reports. Strategic consulting, seminars & conferences.

BNP Paribas, 9787 Seventh Ave., New York, NY, 10019. Phone: (212) 841-2000. Fax: (212) 841-3251.

Leading underwriting & syndicating time-sensitive, non-investment grade debt financing; often requiring complex & creative capital structures; also financing & equity co-investments.

Branch offices located in Los Angeles, London, New York, & Paris.

Patrick Communications L.L.C., 6805 Douglas Legum Dr., Suite 100, Elkridge, MD, 21075. Phone: (410) 799-1740. Fax: (410) 799-1705.E-mail: larry@patcomm.com Web Site:www.patcomm.com

Larry Patrick, mngg ptnr; Susan Patrick, mngg ptnr; Greg Guy, mngg ptnr; John Cunney, VP; Jason James, rsch analyst; Vince Pepper, principal.

Stn brokerage, investment banking, mgmt consulting svcs, appraisals & opns consulting.

Phoenix Cable Inc., 17 S. Franklin Tpke., Ramsey, NJ, 07446. Phone: (201) 825-9090. Fax: (201) 825-8794.

James Feeney, exec dir.

San Rafael CA , 2401 Kerner Blvd. Phone:

Cable TV systems ownership, system mgmt svcs, lease & debt financing svcs.

Premier Capital Group, 670 106 St., Suite 200, Urbandale, IA, 50322. Phone: (515) 698-9600. Fax: (515) 698-9699.

Equipment financing for business owners or financing of customers of a broker or distributor.

RBC Daniels L.P., (formerly Daniels & Associates). 3200 Cherry Creek S. Dr., Suite 500, Denver, CO, 80209. Phone: (303) 778-5555. Fax: (303) 778-5599. Web Site:www.danielsonline.com E-mail: info@rbcdaniels.com

Brian Deevy, chmn/CEO; Greg Aimsworth, sr mngg dir.

New York NY , 711 5th Ave, Suite 405. Phone:

Provides mergers, acquisitions, corporate finance & financial advisory svcs to the tcable, telecom, media & internet industries.

Rodgers Broadcasting, 2301 W. Main St., Richmond, IN, 47375. Phone: (765) 962-6533. Fax: (765) 966-1499.

David A. Rodgers, pres.

Financing particulary for small operators.

SB Management, (formerly Media Capital Inc.). 890 Monterey St., Suite G, San Luis Obispo, CA, 93401. Phone: (805) 543-9214. Fax: (805) 543-9243.E-mail: michael@mikehesser.com

Michael B. Hesser, pres.

Assist in finding, evaluating, financing & structuring acquisitions. Also, consult mgmt & sls.

Schroder Investment Management North America Inc., (formerly Schroder Investment Management). 875 Third Ave., 22nd Fl., New York, NY, 10022. Phone: (212) 641-3800. Phone: (212) 641-3830. Fax: (212) 641-3985. Web Site:www.schroders.com/us

Jamie Dorrien-Smith, CEO.

Silicon Valley Bank, 185 Berry St., Lobby 1, Suite 3000, San Francisco, CA, 94107. Phone: (415) 512-4227. Phone: (415) 512-4200. Fax: (415) 348-0258. Fax: (415) 856-0810.E-mail: moleary@svbank.com Web Site:www.svb.com

Ken Wilcox, pres; Meghan O'Leary, dir public rel.

Comprehensive finance svcs for middle market bcst & cable operators.

Barry Skidelsky, Esq., 185 E. 85th St., 23 D, New York, NY, 10028. Phone: (212) 832-4800.

Barry Skidelsky, owner.

Full svc assistance to investors, owners, mgmt, aquisition, divestiture, start-up, improvement, trustee (bankruptcy & FCC ownership), expert witness & arbitrator.

Syndicated Communications Inc. (SYNCOM), 8401 Colesville Rd., Suite 300, Silver Spring, MD, 20910. Phone: (301) 608-3203. Fax: (301) 608-3307. Web Site:www.syncomfunds.com

Terry L. Jones, dir.

Edwin Tornberg & Co. Inc., 8917 Cherbourg Dr., Potomac, MD, 20854. Phone: (301) 299-6661. Fax: (301) 299-2297.

Edwin Tornberg, pres.

Veronis Suhler Stevenson, 350 Park Ave, New York, NY, 10022. Phone: (212) 935-4990. Fax: (212) 381-8168.E-mail: stevenson@veronissuhler.com Web Site:www.veronissuhler.com

Jeffrey T. Stevenson, mngg ptnr & co-chief exec; James P. Rutherfurd, chief exec VP.

London United Kingdom. London, St. James Square, Buchanan House, 8th Fl. Phone:

Private equity/media buyout affil of Veronis, Suhler, established in 1987 & investing in companies across the spectrum of communications industry segments.

Wachovia Securities, Wachovia Securities, 301 S. College St., Charlotte, NC, 28288. Phone: (704) 348-9500. Fax: (704) 715-1997.E-mail: info@wachovia.com Web Site:www.wachovia.com

Daniel Ludeman, pres/CEO; Ben Jenkins, sr exec VP.

Secured financing for acquisition &/or recapitalization of bcst properties.

Waller Capital Corp., 30 Rockefeller Plaza, Suite 4350, New York, NY, 10112. Phone: (212) 632-3600. Fax: (212) 632-3607.E-mail: info@wallercc.com Web Site:www.wallercc.com

John Waller, III, chmn; Gregory J. Attorri, pres/CEO.

Financing & investment svcs to cable TV industry, specializing in cable TV mergers & acquisitions, buyout financing, raising debt & equity.

Wells Fargo Equipment Finance Inc., 530 Fifth Ave., 15th Fl., New York, NY, 10036. Phone: (212) 805-1000. Fax: (212) 805-1050.E-mail: wfefi@wellsfargo.com Web Site:www.wellsfargo.com

John Crum, exec VP.

Tustin CA , 14081 Yorba St, Suite 205. Phone:

Danbury CT , 100 Mill Plain Rd., 3rd Fl. Phone:

Leading provider of equipment leasing & financing, intermediate term lending & specialty finance products to the bcst industry.

Wood & Co. Inc., 431 Ohio Pike, Suite 200, Cincinnati, OH, 45255. Phone: (513) 528-7373. Fax: (513) 528-7374.

Larry C. Wood, pres.

Research Services

A & A Research, 690 Sunset Blvd., Kalispell, MT, 59901. Phone: (406) 752-7857. E-mail: fireowl@in-tch.com

Judith Doonan, pres; Dr. E. B. Eiselein, rsch dir.

Qualitative & quantitative audience surveys for small- & medium-market radio stns, TV stns, cable. Experience with minority stns.

The ARS Group, 110 Walnut St., Evansville, IN, 47708. Phone: (812) 425-4562. Fax: (812) 425-2844. E-mail: info@arsrsc.com Web Site: www.ars-group.com.

Dr. Margaret Blair, CEO; Jeff Cox, pres.

Ad mgmt & dev tools: ARS Copytest, Firststep Proposition test, Outlook Advertising planner, StarBoard Story Board reviewer. WOWWW Competitive Intelligence system.

Abt Associates Inc., 55 Wheeler St., Cambridge, MA, 02138. Phone: (617) 492-7100. Fax: (617) 492-5219. E-mail: webmaster@abtassociated.com Web Site: www.abtassoc.com.

Peg Laplan, pres/CEO; John Shane, chmn.

Washington, DC 20005, 1110 Vermont Ave. N.W. Phone: (202) 263-1800. (202) 263-1801.

Chicago, IL 60610, 640 N. LaSalle. Phone: (312) 867-4000. Fax: (312) 867-4200.

Bethesda, MD 20814, 4800 Montgomery Ln, Suite 600. Phone: (301) 913-0500. Fax: (301) 652-3618.

Mktg rsch, strategic planning, mgmt consulting, audience rsch & segmentation; customer satisfaction programs, quality of svc programs, social science survey rsch, publ policy rsch, economical rsch.

ADcom Information Services Inc., 8400 N.W. 52nd St., Suite 101, Doral, FL, 33166-5309. Phone: (954) 481-8380. E-mail: dickspooner@cableratings.com Web Site: www.cableratings.com.

Bill Livek, pres/CEO.

New York, NY 10003, 230 Park Ave. South. Phone: (212) 598-5400. Alan Trugman, VP agency svcs.

Viewership rsch systems designed for multi-ch systems, with emphasis on cable ratings & qualitative data.

Admar Group, Inc., Box 1098, 87 Ruckman Road, Alpine, NJ, 07620-1098. Phone: (201) 767-8000. Fax: (201) 767-8006.

Henry D. Ostberg, chmn.

Adv rsch, concept evaluation, product testing & tracking studies; specializes in rsch for legal purposes.

The Adult Contemporary Music Research Letter, 1837 S.E. Harold St., Portland, OR, 97202-4932. Phone: (503) 232-9787. Phone: (800) 929-5119. Fax: (503) 232-9787. Fax: (800) 929-5119. E-mail: acmrl@myexcel.com Web Site: www.acmusicresearch.com.

Eric Norberg, editor & publisher.

Rsch audience appeal of current adult contemp mus, reported in wkly newsletter. Book of oldies rsch also available.

Arbitron Inc., 142 W. 57th St., New York, NY, 10019. Phone: (212) 887-1300. Fax: (212) 887-1401. Web Site: www.arbitron.com.

Pierre Bouvard, pres.

Los Angeles, CA 90024, 10877 Wilshire Blvd. Phone: (310) 824-6600. Fax: (310) 824-6651. Tony Belzer-Western Div Mgr.- radio stn svcs; John Hegelmeyer, adv & Agency svcs. (Western office).

Atlanta, GA 30328, 9000 Central Pkwy. Phone: (770) 668-5400. Fax: (770) 688-5417. Jim Remeny, radio stn svcs; Dan Griffin, mgr adv/agency svcs. (Southeastern office).

Chicago, IL 60606, 222 Riverside Plaza. Phone: (312) 542-1900. Fax: (312) 542-1901. John Nolan-Radio rgnl mgr, James Tobolski-Agency & adv svcs. (Midwestern office).

Columbia, MD 21046, 9705 Patuxent Woods Dr. Phone: (410) 312-8000. Tom O'Sullivan RSS eastern div mgr-Rad Sta svcs; Julie Ellis- agency & adv svcs. (Eastern office).

New York, NY 10019, 142 W. 57th St., 12th Fl. Phone: (212) 887-1300. Fax: (212) 887-1401. Tom O'Sullivan-RSS Eastern Div Mgr-Rad Sta Servs; Julie Ellis-agency & adv svcs.

Dallas, TX 75240, One Galleria Tower. Phone: (972) 385-5388. Fax: (972) 385-5377. Harry Clark, radio stn svcs; Becky Burkett, adv agency svcs. (Southwestern office).

Loc radio audience measurement in 286 markets, qualitative svc through RetailDirect, Scarborough & the Qualitative Diary svc in 260+ markets; Arbitron NewMedia; rsch based info svcs for the new electronic media.

Audience Research & Development (AR&D), 2440 Lofton Terrace, Ft. Worth, TX, 76109. Phone: (817) 924-6922. Fax: (817) 924-7539. Web Site: www.ar-d.com. E-mail: jgumbert@ar-d.com

Jerry Gumbert, pres/CEO; Jerry Florence, pres/rsch; Jim Willi, exec VP; Terry Heaton, sr VP; Steve Safran, sr VP.

Strategy, product, mktg dev & a wide range of rsch svcs for natl & loc media companies.

BBM Canada, 1500 Don Mills Rd., Suite 305, Toronto, ON, M3B 3L7. Canada. Phone: (416) 445-9800. Fax: (416) 445-8644. Web Site: www.bbm.ca. E-mail: staffing@bbm.ca

Jim MacLeod, pres/CEO; Mark Johnston, CFO; Don Easter, VP; Ron Bremner, VP; Tom Saint, VP; Kathy Carson, dir; Jeff Osborne, pres.

Richmond, BC V6X 3C6 Canada, 10991 Shellbridge Way, 2nd Fl. Phone: (604) 249-3500. Fax: (604) 214-9648. Catherine Kelly, VP Western svcs.

Moncton, NB E1C 817 Canada, 1234 Main St, Suite 3000. Phone: (506) 859-7700. Fax: (506) 852-4445.

Montreal, PQ H3A 1V4 Canada, 2055 Peel St., 11th Fl. Phone: (514) 878-9711. Fax: (514) 878-4210. Robert Langlois, VP Quebec svcs.

Media rsch for radio & TV, & custom rsch through ComQuest Division.

BDS Radio, 6255 Sunset Blvd., 19th Fl., Hollywood, CA, 90028. Phone: (323) 817-1543. Fax: (323) 817-1511. E-mail: catriona.mcginn@nielsen.com Web Site: www.bdsradio.com.

Catriona McGinn, gen mgr; Vincent Martino, sls dir.

White Plains, NY 10601, One N. Lexington Ave. Phone: (914) 684-5578. Catriona McGinn, gen mgr.

Leaders in off-the-air music monitoring for radio & record industry. Pattern recognition technology identifies songs on stns across west America.

BIA Financial Network, 15120 Enterprise Ct., Suite 100, Chantilly, VA, 20151-1102. Phone: (703) 818-2425. Fax: (703) 803-3299. E-mail: info@bia.com Web Site: www.bia.com.

Mark Giannini, CEO.

Financial consultants to the communications industry; fair market valuations, tax appraisals, acquisition consulting, business plans, internal operational audits, litigation support, investment, publications, & database software, venture funding, capital.

The Benchmark Co., 907 S. Congress, Suite 7, Austin, TX, 78704. Phone: (512) 707-7500. Fax: (512) 707-7757. E-mail: benchmarkr@aol.com Web Site: www.thebenchmarkcompany.net.

Dr. Robert E. Balon, pres/CEO; Holly Brown, rsch dir.

Rsch & mktg for the bcst industry.

Berry Best Services Ltd., 1990 M St. N.W., Suite 740, Washington, DC, 20036. Phone: (202) 293-4964. Fax: (202) 293-0287. E-mail: admin@berrybest.com Web Site: www.berrybest.com.

Thomas L. Berry, VP; Samuel A. Flores Jr., exec VP.

FCC rsch, hard-copy & full electronic distribution of FCC news releases, pub notices & texts; web based FCC data bases.

Big Blue Dot, 124 Watertown St., Suite F, Watertown, MA, 02472. Phone: (617) 600-1100. Fax: (617) 923-0002. E-mail: bigbluedot@bigblue.com Web Site: www.bigblue.com.

Jan Craige Singer, pres.

Trend tracking resources for the kids' market, consulting, & newsletter via e-mail; creative svcs.

Bolton Research Corporation, 2709 S.W. 22nd Ave., Miami, FL, 33133. Phone: (305) 854-3887. Fax: (305) 854-3807. E-mail: brct@aol.com Web Site: www.boltonresearch.com.

Ted Bolton, pres.

Perceptual rsch studies; marketplace positioning; music rsch; format opportunity studies; focus groups.

Broadcast News Service, Box 919, Norwood, MA, 02062-0919. Phone: (781) 344-6988. Fax: (781) 344-8928. E-mail: pjrbroadcasting@aol.com

P.J. Romano, dir.

Recording & bcst svcs.

Broadcast Research & Consulting Inc., Box 728, 46 Orchard Beach Blvd., Port Washington, NY, 11050. Phone: (516) 883-8486. Fax: (516) 883-3090. E-mail: jaltman752@aol.com

Herbert Altman, pres.

Syndicated svcs include news & entertainment talent search, net anchor index. Natl & loc market rsch studies & consultation for bcstrs covering programs, movies, news, prom, stn image & new electronic media. Determined the nominees & winners for the annual American Music Awards for 31 consecutive years.

CRI Research / Center for Radio Information, 18 Fair St., Cold Springs, NY, 10516. Phone: (800) 359-9898. E-mail: info@the-cri.com Web Site: www.the-cri.com.

Scott Webster, pres.

Radioscan, market/probe, radio/link, mailing labels, phone lists, mktg file, net analysis, group owner, cp reports, radio/TV data bases & available calls.

Mark Clements Research Inc., 60 E. 42nd St., Suite 914, New York, NY, 10165. Phone: (212) 221-2470. Fax: (212) 221-7628. E-mail: information@markclementsresearch.com

Mark Clements, pres; E.L. Reiter, exec VP.

Mktg, mgmt & product rsch; economic & progmg studies for TV & radio.

Coleman Research Inc., 1040 Avenue of the Americas, 3rd Fl., New York, NY, 10018. Phone: (212) 223-0185. Fax: (919) 571-9999. E-mail: info@colemanrg.com Web Site: www.colemaninsights.com.

Jon Coleman, pres; Chris Ackerman, sls VP.

Perceptual rsch, including progmg, mktg & sls studies; continuing consultation.

Comsearch, 19700 Janelia Farm Blvd., Ashburn, VA, 20147. Phone: (703) 726-5500. Fax: (703) 726-5600. Web Site: www.comsearch.com.

Don Spinelli, opns VP.

Computerized allocation studies, ch analysis, transinterference analysis, system design, detailed coverage prediction, FCC application preparation, site location & mktg rsch.

Core Research, 2161 N.W. Military Hwy., Suite 202, San Antonio, TX, 78213. Phone: (210) 366-4210. E-mail: coreresearch@sbcglobal.net Web Site: www.coreresearch.biz.

Dr. Susan Korbel, owner.

Audience & mkt rsch for the media, sports & adv industries.

Critical Mass Media, 3857 Ivanhoe Ave., Cincinnati, OH, 45212. Phone: (513) 631-4266. Fax: (513) 631-4329. E-mail: help@criticalmassmedia.com Web Site: www.criticalmassmedia.com.

Carolyn Gilbert, pres; Erin Gabbard, dir mktg opns.

Rsch, telemarketing, direct mail, data mgmt & strategic planning for the radio & TV industry.

Dataworld Inc., 15120 Enterprise Ct., Chantilly, VA, 20151-1217. Phone: (703) 227-9680. Fax: (703) 803-3299. E-mail: dataworldinfo@bia.com Web Site: www.dataworld.com.

David J. Doherty, pres; Rob Farbman, sr VP.

Internet access to feasibility studies & subscription svcs for Flag & DataXpert; FM Explorer; visual on-line allocation tool; custom mapping; bcst facilities database.

Eastlan Resources, Box 3500-404, Sisters, OR, 97759-3500. Phone: (877) 886-3320. Fax: (541) 318-4646. E-mail: info@eastlan.com Web Site: www.eastlan.com.

Mike Gould, pres/CEO; Dave Hastings, dir.

The second largest radio audience measurement company in the US.

Edison Media Research, 6 W. Cliff St., Somerville, NJ, 08876. Phone: (908) 707-4707. Fax: (908) 707-4740. E-mail: rfarbman@edisonresearch.com Web Site: www.edisonresearch.com.

Larry Rosin, pres; Joe Lenski, exec VP; Rob Farbman, sr VP.

Complete market surveys with fast turn-around. Telephone surveys, music testing, focus groups & exit polling.

Entertainment Partners, 2835 N. Naomi, Burbank, CA, 91504. Phone: (818) 955-6000. Phone: (818) 955-6299. Fax: (818) 845-6507. Web Site: www.entertainmentpartners.com.

Mark Goldstein, pres/CEO; John Minton, exec VP; Joe Giarrusso, sr VP mktg & sls exec.

Orlando, FL 32819, 2000 Universal Studios Plaza. Phone: (407) 354-5900. Joy Ellis.

New York, NY 10001, 875 6th Ave., 15th Fl. Phone: (646) 473-9000. Myfa Cirinna, VP/gen mgr.

Production payroll software, residual, commercials, music & casting svcs, The Paymaster Industry Guide. Branches in New York, Los Angeles, Florida, London, Toronto, Vancouver, Australia, Japan.

FM Atlas Publishing, PO Box 336, Esko, MN, 55733-0336. Phone: (218) 879-7676. Fax: (218) 879-8333. E-mail: fmatlas@aol.com Web Site: www.members.aol.com/fmatlas/home.html.

Carol J. Elving, mgr; Bruce F. Elving, Ph.D, owner.
FM radio directory & FM media newsletter rsch on utilization of FM/SCA & FM translators.

FMR Associates Inc., 6045 E. Grant Rd., Tucson, AZ, 85712. Phone: (520) 886-5548. Fax: (520) 886-9307. E-mail: bruce@fmrassociates.com Web Site: www.fmrassociates.com.

Bruce Fohr, pres; Andy Wellik, rsch mgr.
Perceptual progmg studies, wkly callout, EARS Music Studies, format opportunity & vulnerability positioning studies; TV coml testing. Electronic progmg simulation tests.

First Amendment Center, (An operating program of The Freedom Forum). 1207 18th Ave. S., Nashville, TN, 37212. Phone: (615) 727-1600. Fax: (615) 727-1309. E-mail: info@fac.org Web Site: www.firstamendmentcenter.org.

Gene Policinski, VP; Brian Buchanan, editor; Tiffany Villager, dir; John Seigenthaler, founder.

Arlington, VA 22209, 1101 Wilson Blvd. Phone: (703) 528-0800. Gene Policinski.

Rsch & commentary on media issues. The center is devoted to improving the understanding of media issues by the press & the public.

GFK Custom Research North America, 75 ninth Ave., 5th Fl., New York, NY, 10011. Phone: (212) 240-5300. Fax: (212) 240-5353. E-mail: info@gfkamerica.com Web Site: www.gfkamerica.com.

Charles McCormick, VP; Jim Timony, sr VP & media svc.
Princeton, NJ 08540, 1060 State Rd. Phone: (609) 683-6100. Charles McCormick, VP.

Custom-designed surveys for bcst industry on loc, rgnl & natl basis, loc & network radio & TV, cable/pay TV/DBS, natl global omnibus studies, viewer engagement & ad sls adhoc.

Gallup Organization, 1001 Gallup Dr., Omaha, NE, 68102. Phone: (402) 951-2003. Fax: (888) 500-8282. Web Site: www.gallup.com.

James K. Clifton, CEO; Jane Miller, COO.
Mgmt consulting.

GeoMart, 516 Villanova Ct., Fort Collins, CO, 80525. Phone: (970) 416-8340. Fax: (970) 416-8345. E-mail: sales@geomart.com Web Site: www.geomart.com.

Chuck Cotherman, owner.
All USGS & DMA digital & paper maps. All NOS/NOAA charts, international topographic series, aerial photography, raised relief maps, digital products, business & mktg maps, travel maps, globes, etc.

Global Research Institute, 747 Wire Rd., Auburn, AL, 36832. Phone: (334) 826-0390. Fax: (334) 826-0390.

H.D. Norman, pres; Enrico Valdez, VP; Cherry Foster, gen mgr.
Mktg, data & media studies. International radio & TV audience measurement & progmg consultants.

Hagen Media Research, Box 40542, Washington, DC, 20016-0542. Phone: (703) 534-3003. E-mail: donhagen@aol.com Web Site: www.cmmtv.com.

Don Hagen, pres.
Perceptual rsch for radio. Designs, conducts & analyzes qualitative & quantitative studies. Focus groups, telephone surveys, one-on-one sessions, music tests.

Hamilton Beattie & Staff Inc., 4201 Connecticut Ave. N.W., Suite 212, Washington, DC, 20008. Phone: (202) 686-5900. Fax: (202) 686-7080. E-mail: dave@hbstaff.com Web Site: www.hbstaff.com.

David Beattie, pres; Maggie Ryner, VP.
Fernandina Beach, FL 32034, 102 South 10th St. Phone: (904) 491-0591. Fax: (904) 491-0594. David Beattie, pres; Tiffany Muller, rsch dir.

News rsch, mktg rsch & pub opinion surveys relating to program evaluation, licensing, new products, & high-tech telecommunications.

Peter D. Hart Research Associates, 1724 Connecticut Ave. N.W., Washington, DC, 20009. Phone: (202) 234-5570. Fax: (202) 232-8134. E-mail: info@hartresearch.com Web Site: www.hartresearch.com.

Geoffrey Garin, pres; Peter D. Hart, CEO; Frederick Yang, sr VP.
Audience rsch; polling for on-air use; bcst, cable, ETV, radio rsch svcs, including mkt surveys, political communication & cable referenda rsch.

Norman Hecht Research Inc., 33 Queens St., 3rd Fl., Syosset, NY, 11791. Phone: (516) 496-8866. Fax: (516) 496-8165. E-mail: nhr@normanhechtresearch.com Web Site: www.normanhechtresearch.com.

Laura Greenberg, co-pres/COO; Dan Greenberg, co-pres.
Providing custom mkt rsch, insight & understanding to clients in bcst, cable, technology, coml svcs & communications industries.

Kenneth Hollander Associates Inc., Box 49625, Atlanta, GA, 30359. Phone: (404) 231-4077. Web Site: www.kharesearch.com/legal.

Kenneth Hollander, pres.
Mendocino, CA 95460, 45431 Greenling Cir. Phone: (707) 962-1648. (707) 962-1635.

Hungerford, Aldrin, Nichols & Carter, CPAs, 2910 Lucerne Dr. S.E., Grand Rapids, MI, 49546. Phone: (616) 949-3200. Fax: (616) 949-7720. E-mail: caldrin@hanc.com Web Site: www.hanc.com.

Clifford A. Aldrin, ptnr.
Hungerford radio & TV revenue report preparation & year-end accounting/auditing.

Innovative Audience Research, 119 LaColima, Pismo Beach, CA, 93449. Phone: (805) 556-0772. Fax: (805) 556-0772. E-mail: lavinc@charter.net

Mike Silverstein, pres; Susan B. Silverstein, exec VP.
Strategic planning in news, progmg & prom, impacting sweep book ratings in TV metered markets.

Insite Media Research, 31510 Anacapa View Dr., Mailbu, CA, 90265. Phone: (310) 589-0223. Fax: (310) 589-0502. E-mail: scott@tvsurveys.com Web Site: www.tvsurveys.com.

Scott V. Tallel, pres.
Full-svc audience rsch firm specializing in voice capture telephone surveys online interviewing and program testing focus groups for television & the internet

Institute for Research on Public Policy, 1470 Peel St., Suite 200, Montreal, PQ, H3A 1T1. Canada. Phone: (514) 985-2461. Fax: (514) 985-2559. E-mail: irpp@irpp.org Web Site: www.irpp.org.

Social policy, public finance, governance, city-rgns, educ, structural change, public security labor market.

Intermedia Analyses Inc., 8 Shadow Rd., Upper Saddle River, NJ, 07458. Phone: (201) 327-6223.

Carol G. Mayberry, pres.
Strategies/analyses for buying and/or selling radio, optimizing revenue or investment. Broker bcst equipment.

Kagan World Media, One Lower Ragsdale Dr., Bldg. One, Suite 130, Monterey, CA, 93940. Phone: (831) 624-1536. Fax: (831) 625-3225. E-mail: info@kagan.com Web Site: www.kagan.com.

Specializing in financial & investment rsch. Media financial newsletters & database reports.

Mark Kassof & Co., 2531 Jackson Ave., Suite 227, Ann Arbor, MI, 48104. Phone: (734) 662-5700. E-mail: contact@kassof.com Web Site: www.kassof.com.

Mark Kassof, pres.
Strategic audience rsch to pinpoint a radio stn most profitable format strategy; focus groups, auditorium music testing & promotional testing.

KIDSNET, 2506 Campbell Pl., Kensington, MD, 20895. Phone: (202) 291-1400. E-mail: kidsnet@kidsnet.org Web Site: www.kidsnet.org.

Natl resource of TV, radio, audio & video for children & educ multimedia; program-related study guides; mthy print & electronic publications.

Knowledge Networks/SRI, 570 South Ave. E, Bldg. G, Cranford, NJ, 07016. Phone: (908) 497-8000. Fax: (908) 497-8001. Web Site: www.knowledgenetworks.com. E-mail: info@knowledgenetworks.com

Gale D. Metzger, gen mgr; Burton E. Michaels, VP.

New York, NY 10016, 440 Park Ave., 6th Fl. Phone: (646) 742-5300. Fax: (212) 689-3019. Justin Edge, sr VP.
Specialists in cross-media allocation strategies, consumer media technologies. How people use media.

The Kompas Group, Box 250813, Milwaukee, WI, 53225-6513. Phone: (262) 781-0188. Fax: (262) 781-5313. E-mail: kompasgroup@toast.net Web Site: www.yourlptvsource.com.

John Kompas, pres; Jackie Kompas, VP.
Financial & mktg svcs for LPTV, audience demographic reports, stn coverage maps, financial & strategic planning.

Lincoln Property Company, 101 Constitution Ave. N.W., Suite 600 E., Washington, DC, 20001. Phone: (202) 513-6700. Fax: (202) 898-2001. E-mail: jconnelly@lpc.com Web Site: www.lincolnproperty.com.

New York, NY 10022, 405 Park Ave. Phone: (212) 752-0638. Fax: (212) 838-7472. James G. Stein, sr VP.
Consulting coml real estate svcs, tenant/client representation, construction/financial analysis, turnkey lease/sls assumptions; roof & bldg zoning surveys.

Lund Media Research, 840 Hinckley Rd., Suite 123, Burlingame, CA, 94010-1505. Phone: (650) 692-7777. Fax: (650) 692-7799. E-mail: lundmedia@aol.com Web Site: www.lundradio.com.

John Lund, pres; Dan Spice, VP.
Perceptual, focus group, music rsch; customized Radio Marketing Ascertainment evaluates stn & competitive progmg; implementation & progmg consultation; format design & multipoly strategy.

Magazine Publishers of America, 810 7th Ave., 24th Fl., New York, NY, 10019. Phone: (212) 872-3700. Fax: (212) 888-4217. E-mail: mpar@magazine.org Web Site: www.magazine.org/home.

Nina B. Link, pres/CEO; Nicole Kaplan, VP/mktg & prom.
Educ seminars; surveys members on various topics; extensive library on magazine publishing; monitors issues in the magazine industry. Publications: *Newsletter of Research, Newsletter of International Publishing, Washington Newsletter* & *Magazine Newsletter*.

Frank N. Magid Associates Inc., One Research Ctr., Marion, IA, 52302. Phone: (319) 377-7345. Fax: (319) 377-5861. E-mail: mailia@magid.com Web Site: www.magid.com.

Brent Magid, pres/CEO; Steve Ridge, exec VP; Bill Hague, sr VP; Richard Haynes, VP rsch.
Sherman Oaks, CA 91403, 15260 Ventura Blvd, Suite 2130. Phone: (818) 263-3300. Fax: (818) 263-3311. Jack MacKenzie, exec VP entertainment.
New York, NY 10019, 1775 Broadway, Suite 1401. Phone: (212) 974-2310. Fax: (212) 515-4540. Vicki Cohen, exec VP entertainment.
Strategic rsch applications for traditional & new media companies, including Executive Telefocus, Magid Media Futures, INstant-STUDIO, Magid Performance Predictor, Magid Revenue Enhancer.

Marketron International, 700 Airport Blvd., Suite 130, Burlingame, CA, 94010-2001. Phone: (800) 788-9245. Fax: (650) 548-2295. E-mail: lcarpenter@marketron.com Web Site: www.marketron.com.

Mike Jackson, CEO.
Toronto, ON M2N 6C6 Canada, 5075 Yonge St, Suite 404. Phone: (416) 221-9944. Les Bridgen, gen mgr.
Birmingham, AL 35244, 3000 Riverchase Galleria, 8th Fl. Phone: (205) 987-7456. Fax: (205) 733-4535. E-mail: tvsales@marketron.com. Michael Hunter, gen mgr.
Hailey, ID 83333, 101 Empty Saddle Trail. Phone: (208) 788-6272. Gary Coats, gen mgr.
Software applications for radio, TV, networks, syndicators, traf, accounting, mgmt, demand pricing, inventory control, rsch & proposals.

MarketVision Research, 10300 Alliance Rd., Cincinnati, OH, 45242-5617. Phone: (513) 791-3100. Fax: (513) 794-3500. E-mail: tmcmullen@mv-research.com Web Site: www.mv-research.com.

John Pinnell, pres; Tyler McMullen, sr VP.
Charlotte, NC 28210, 6805-A Fairview Rd. Phone: (704) 442-0444. Ronald Miller, exec VP.
Hasbrouck Heights, NJ 07604, 440 Rte. 17 N. Phone: (201) 288-4614. Fax: (201) 288-4615. Jack Kloc, VP.
Full-svc mktg rsch firm. Focused on customized high-value rsch.

Marquest Media & Entertainment Research, 314 Orange St., Beaufort, NC, 28516-1821. Phone: (252) 728-4047. Fax: (915) 200-1850. E-mail: paul.rule@marquest.net Web Site: www.marquest.net.

Paul Rule, pres.

Loc & natl cable, bcst & print surveys. Sydicated on demand menu planner studies.

Marshall Marketing & Communications Inc., 2600 Boyce Plaza Rd., Suite 210, Pittsburgh, PA, 15241-3949. Phone: (412) 914-0970. Fax: (412) 914-0971. E-mail: info@mm-c.com. Web Site: www.mm-c.com.

Craig A. Marshall, chmn/CEO; Richard Kinzler, pres/COO.

Orlando, FL 32835, 1445 Saddleridge Dr. Phone: (407) 299-3510. Bruce Hahn, rsch & sls consultant.

Cary, NC 27513, 102 Silver Lining Lane. Phone: (919) 388-7622. James Filippi, rsch & sls consultant.

Knoxville, TN 37931, 6729 Heatherbrook Dr. Phone: (865) 938-7988. Cynthia Bridges, rsch & sls consultant.

Langley, WA 98260, 5280 Lakeside Dr. Phone: (360) 321-2139. Lori West, rsch & sls consultant.

Spokane, WA 99223, 3021 E. 62nd Ave. Phone: (509) 443-1362. Rick Hamm, rsch & sls consultant.

Sls dev rsch; custom-designed, consumer market-specific data; demographics; media usage & Risc American program. Leading-Edge software: exclusive & non-exclusive mktg programs.

Media Market Resources, Box 442, Littleton, NH, 03561. Phone: (603) 444-5720. Fax: (603) 444-2872. E-mail: cdevine@insideradio.com

Cathy Devine, VP/gen mgr.

Produces multimedia profile reports, printed & electronic bcst directories & software.

Media Monitors Inc., 8253 Thoroughbred Run, Suite 102, Indianapolis, IN, 46256-4320. Phone: (317) 547-1362. Fax: (914) 259-4541. E-mail: jselig@mediamonitors.com Web Site: www.mediamonitors.com.

John L. Selig, pres; Tom Zarecki, dir.

Radio, nwspr & magazine monitoring Co. Creative review for natl & loc advertisers' radio spots.

Media Perspectives, 127 Greensward Ln., Cherry Hill, NJ, 08002. Phone: (856) 482-7979. E-mail: steve@apels.net

Steven G. Apels, pres.

Rschs audience tastes & perceptions, employs advanced analytical techniques to guide bcstrs in constructing strategic progmg & mktg plans.

Media Rating Council, Inc., 370 Lexington Ave., Suite 902, New York, NY, 10017. Phone: (212) 972-0300. Fax: (212) 972-2786.

George W. Ivie, exec dir & CEO.

Determines criteria & standards & admin an audit system for accreditation of audience measurement svcs to assure conformance with criteria, standards & procedures developed.

Mediamark Research & Intelligence, 75 Ninth Ave., 5th Fl., New York, NY, 10011. Phone: (212) 884-9200. Fax: (212) 884-9339. Web Site: www.mediamark.com.

Mike Drankwalter, sr VP; Kathi Love, pres/CEO.

Los Angeles, CA 90068, 3575 Cahuenga Blvd. W., Suite 665. Phone: (232) 882-6325. Chetan Shah, VP.

Chicago, IL 60611, 444 N. Michigan Ave., Suite 2050. Phone: (312) 329-0901. Scott Turner, sr VP.

Single-source rsch containing product usage, demographics & psychographics for TV, radio, digital & print. Custom mkt soultion rsch.

Miller, Kaplan, Arase & Co., 4123 Lankershim Blvd., North Hollywood, CA, 91602. Phone: (818) 769-2010. Fax: (818) 769-3100. Web Site: www.millerkaplan.com.

George Nadel Rivin, C.P.A., ptnr.

San Francisco, CA 94104, 180 Montgomery St, Suite 1840. Phone: (415) 956-3600. Catherine C. Gardner, C.P.A., ptnr.

Market revenue reports revenue forecast software and market x-ray including newspaper, TV & radio expenditures by adv.

MORPACE International, 31700 Middlebelt, Suite 200, Farmington Hills, MI, 48334. Phone: (248) 737-5300. Fax: (248) 737-5326. E-mail: information@morpace.com Web Site: www.morpace.com.

Jim Leiman, sr VP.

Market rsch, strategic planning, viewer satisfaction, economic modeling, audience analysis, data base mapping for TV & radio stns, cable TV franchises.

Multimedia Research Group Inc. (MRG, Inc.), 1754 Technology Dr., Suite 132, San Jose, CA, 95110. Phone: (408) 453-5553. Fax: (408) 453-5559. E-mail: info@mrgco.com Web Site: www.mrgco.com.

Gary Schultz, pres.

Provides strategic consulting & published market intelligence on content dev, content distribution, channels & networks.

Jack Myers LLC, 20 E. 68 St., Suite 7B, New York, NY, 10021. Phone: (212) 875-8004. Fax: (212) 875-8023. E-mail: jack@jackmyers.com Web Site: www.jackmyers.com.

Jack Myers, editor.

Syndicated & proprietary rsch, consulting & evaluation for media companies, advertisers, & adv agencies. Publishes *Jack Myers Report* industry newsletter.

National Broadcast Finance Corp., Box 3167, 27 Harrison St., New Haven, CT, 06515-0267. Phone: (203) 389-6000. Fax: (203) 389-6020. E-mail: cherhoniak@sbcglobal.net

David C. Cherhoniak, pres.

Financial advisory & investment banking svcs to bcstg industry & brokerage.

National Economic Research Associates Inc. (NERA), 50 Main St., 14th Fl., White Plains, NY, 10606. Phone: (914) 448-4000. Fax: (914) 448-4040. Web Site: www.nera.com.

Andrew Carron, pres.

San Francisco, CA 94111, One Front St. Phone: (415) 291-1000. Dr. Kent Van Liere, VP.

Sydney NSW 2000 Australia, Level 6, 50 Bridge St. Fax: 2-8272-6500. Greg Houston, dir.

Brussels, NO B-1040 Belgium, rue de la Loi, 23 Wetstraat. Phone: 32-2282-4340. Sean Gammons, assoc dir.

Madrid 28046 Spain, Paseo de la Castellana, 13. Phone: 91-212-6400. Fabrizo Herandez, assoc dir.

London W1C 1BE United Kingdom, 15 Stratford Pl. Phone: 20-7659-8500. Graham Shuttleworth, dir.

Los Angeles, CA 90017, 777 S. Figueroa St. Phone: (213) 346-3000. Dr. Gary Dorman, sr VP.

Washington, DC 20037, 1255 23rd St. N.W. Phone: (202) 466-3510. Andrew Joskow, sr VP.

Chicago, IL 60611, 875 N. Michigan Ave. Phone: (312) 573-2800. Dr. Harlow Higinbotham, sr VP.

Boston, MA 02116, 200 Charendon St., 35th Fl. Phone: (617) 621-0444. Fax: (617) 621-0336. William Taylor, sr VP.

Ithaca, NY 14850, 308 N. Cayuga St. Phone: (607) 277-3007. Alfred E. Kahn, special consultant.

New York, NY 10036, 1166 Ave. of the Americas, 31st Fl. Phone: (212) 345-3000. Linda McLaughlin, sr VP.

Philadelphia, PA 19103, Two Logan Sq. Phone: (215) 864-3880. Eugene Ericksen, special consultant.

Economic consultant to bcst & cable TV companies on economic, pub policy & business strategy issues.

Nielsen Media Research, 770 Broadway, New York, NY, 10003. Phone: (646) 654-8300. Phone: (646) 654-5000. E-mail: info@nielsenmedia.com Web Site: www.nielsenmedia.com.

Susan D. Whiting, pres/CEO; Paul Donato, chief rsch off; Bob Luff, chief technology off.

Los Angeles, CA 90028, 6255 Sunset Blvd. Phone: (323) 817-1200. Rob Hebenstreit, VP, NSI rgnl mgr.

San Francisco, CA 94111, 2 Embarcadero Ctr., Suite 1017. Phone: (415) 249-6000. Colleen Hall, VP, NSI rgnl mgr.

Alpharetta, GA 30004, 1145 Sanctuary Pkwy., Suite 100. Phone: (770) 777-4260. Lisa Schmidt, VP, Southeastern NSI rgnl mgr.

Chicago, IL 60606, 200 W. Jackson Blvd., Suite 2700. Phone: (312) 385-6500. Jane Ryan, sr VP, sls & mktg NSI.

Dallas, TX 75201, 1717 Main St. Phone: (214) 290-9200. Lucinda Nobles, VP, sls & mktg NSI midwest mgr.

Nielsen offers TV audience measurement for network, loc, syndication, cable, Sp-language networks & stns; metered market & individual loc market reports in all markets; natl sydicated program ratings; loc syndicated program ratings; daily, wkly, & mthly network program ratings; telephone coincidentals; & competitive adv intelligence.

Paragon Media Strategies, 12345 W. Alameda Pkwy., Suite 325, Denver, CO, 80228. Phone: (303) 922-5600. Fax: (303) 922-1589. E-mail: info@paragonmediastrategies.com Web Site: www.paragonmediastrategies.com.

Mike Henry, CEO; Gina Marcon, mktg rsch dir.

Media rsch & consulting.

Peters Communications, 1555 Berenda Pl., El Cajon, CA, 92020. Phone: (858) 565-8511. Fax: (619) 440-1481. E-mail: ppiep@cox.net

Edward J. Peters, pres.

Media mktg consultants, providing rsch, concept, mktg plan, music, graphics & animation.

Pike & Fischer, (A BNA Company). 8505 Fenton St., Suite 208, Silver Spring, MD, 20910. Phone: (301) 562-1530. Fax: (301) 562-1521. E-mail: customercare@pf.com Web Site: www.pf.com.

Meg Hargreaves, pres.

Publishers of communications print and eletronic info

svcs including; Bcst Rules Svc, Cable TV Rules Svc, Communications Regulation & Wireless Telecommunications Regulation.

The Q Scores Company, (A division of Marketing Evaluations Inc.). 1615 Northern Blvd., Manhasset, NY, 11030. Phone: (516) 365-7979. Fax: (516) 365-9351. E-mail: info@qscores.com Web Site: www.qscores.com.

Steven Levitt, pres; Henry Schafer, exec VP.

Syndicated market rsch surveys measuring familiarity & appeal of TV programs, cable programs, performers, characters, company & brand names, sports personalities & deceased celebrities.

RAD Marketing & CableTowns, 167 Crary-on-the-Park, Mount Vernon, NY, 10550-0572. Phone: (914) 668-3563. Fax: (914) 668-4247. E-mail: cabletowns@verizon.net

Robert Dadarria, pres.

Cable subs, or TV buyers, MOB buyers- Mailing lists provided to marketers largest most ideal cable TV H/H audience available. Phone numbers; data base by age, gender, MOBs, and direct marketing responses.

Radio Computing Services Inc., 12 Water St., White Plains, NY, 10601. Phone: (914) 428-4600. Fax: (914) 428-5922. Web Site: www.rcsworks.com.

Andrew M. Economos, chmn; Philippe Generali, pres; Ted Nygreen, gen mgr.

Computer software for bcstrs, mus scheduling, rsch, data bases, yield mgmt, audio logging, digital audio systems.

The Radio Journal, PO Box 442, Littleton, NH, 03561. Phone: (603) 444-5720. Fax: (603) 444-2872. E-mail: genemckay@insideradio.com Web Site: www.theradiojournal.com.

Summary of FCC data & format changes. Publishes the *The Radio Journal* & *M The Radio Book*, & Inside Radio Daily Fax.

Research Communications Ltd., 95 Washington St., 402-357, Canton, MA, 02021-4009. Phone: (401) 782-9085. E-mail: cranev@aol.com Web Site: www.researchcommunications.com.

Valerie Crane, Ph.D., CEO; Susan Crohan, PhD., pres.

Full-svc media rsch company specializing in quantitative/qualitative news mktg, & progmg rsch for bcst, cable, radio & adv.

Research International U.S.A., 222 Merchandise Mart Plaza, Suite 275, Suite 2511, Chicago, IL, 606654-1308. Phone: (312) 787-4060. Fax: (312) 787-4156. E-mail: info@riusa.com Web Site: www.riusa.com.

Stamford, CT 06901, 3 Landmark Sq. Phone: (203) 358-0900. Fax: (203) 353-0883.

Cambridge, MA 02139. Cambridge, 955 Massachusetts Ave. Phone: (617) 661-0110. Fax: (617) 661-3575.

Full-svc custom rsch design through analysis. Facilities include 300-position WATS phones with CRTs & complete computer capabilities.

Rules Service, (a division of Pike & Fischer Inc.). c/o Pike & Fischer Inc., 1010 Wayne Ave., Suite 1400, Silver Spring, MD, 20910. Phone: (301) 562-1530. Fax: (301) 562-1521. E-mail: ruletwo@starpower.net Web Site: www.ruleserv.com.

Meg Hargreaves, pres.

FCC rules & regulations updated in loose-leaf & disk svcs, includes 0, 1, 2, 5, 11, 13, 15, 17, 18, 19, 20, 21, 22, 24, 25, 27, 73, 74, 76, 78, 79, 80, 87, 90, 95, 97, 100 & 101.

SatNews Publishers, 800 Siesta Way, Sonoma, CA, 95476. Phone: (707) 939-9306. Fax: (707) 939-9235. E-mail: design@satnews.com Web Site: www.satnews.com.

Hartley Lesser, editorial dir.

Publishes the *International Satellite Directory*, the complete guide to the satellite communications industry. Also available on a CD-Rom & through the web at www.satnews.com

Scarborough Research, 770 Broadway, 13th Fl., New York, NY, 10003-9595. Phone: (646) 654-8400. Fax: (646) 654-8450. E-mail: info@scarborough.com Web Site: www.scarborough.com.

Robert Cohen, Ph.D, pres/CEO.

Chicago, IL 60606, 200 W. Jackson Blvd, Suite 1822. Phone: (312) 385-6700. Howard Goldberg, sr VP Radio/Sports mktg.

Specializes in loc market & multimedia consumer studies; hundreds of consumer categories & media behavior, all specific to the individual market.

Shane Media Services, 2500 Tanglewilde, Suite 106, Houston, TX, 77063. Phone: (713) 952-9221. Fax: (713) 952-1207. E-mail: smsofc@shanemedia.com Web Site: www.shanemedia.com.

Ed Shane, CEO; Renee Revett, talent dev; Lee Logan, consultant.

Radio progmg and mgmt consultation, custom designed perceptual and qualitative rsch for electronic media outlets.

The Shosteck Group, 6190 Stainwood Dr., Columbia, MD, 21044. Phone: (410) 997-1625. Fax: (859) 997-1627. E-mail: jzweig@shosteck.com Web Site: www.shosteck.com.

Dr. Herschel Shosteck, chmn; Jane Zweig, CEO.

Telecommunication economics & market analysis emphasizing cellular. International consultation on demand, svc & equipment competition, economic & market effects of privatization, liberalization, competition, deregulation & market acceptance. Newly published studies on wireless & wireless internet.

Simmons Market Research Bureau, Inc., 29 Broadway, Fl. 30, New York, NY, 10006-3216. Phone: (212) 863-4500. E-mail: kenw@smrb.com Web Site: www.smrb.com.

Christopher T. Wilson, pres/COO; William P. Livek, CEO; William E. Engel, co-CEO.

Deerfield Beach, FL 33441, 700 W. Hillsboro Blvd., Bldg 4, Suite 201. Phone: (954) 427-4104. Fax: (954) 427-4104. Bill Livek, CEO; Bill Engel, CEO.

Schaumburg, IL 60173, 955 American Ln. Phone: (224) 698-8142. Fax: (224) 698-4139. Mary Kay Petrella, dir of clients.

Study of media & markets; comprehensive measurement of media & product usage. Other studies include kids, teens, Hispanic & the Internet.

Sindlinger & Co. Inc., 405 Osborne St., Wallingford, PA, 19086. Phone: (610) 565-0247. Fax: (610) 565-7174. E-mail: nelsind@aol.com

Albert E. Sindlinger, chmn/pres.

Daily polling to determine consumer attitudes; microeconomic forecasting.

Spectrum Research, 5000 Boardwalk, #602, Ventnor City, NJ, 08406-2918. Phone: (609) 822-0056. Fax: (609) 385-2953. E-mail: peter@spectrumresearch.com Web Site: www.spectrumresearch.com.

Focus groups, lifestyle studies, & strategic mkt studies. Custom rsch for radio & TV.

SQAD Inc., 303 S. Broadway, Suite 108, Tarrytown, NY, 10591-5410. Phone: (914) 524-7600. Fax: (914) 524-7650. E-mail: info@sqad.com Web Site: www.sqad.com.

Neil Klar, pres/CEO; Elliot C. Pickens, VP/dir rsch.

Cost projections for National broadcast, cable and syndication (Net Costs), local CPP/CPM projections for Spot TV, Radio & Hispanic TV. SNAP software for Sweeps and Overnights.

Strata Marketing Inc., 30 West Monroe, Suite 1900, Chicago, IL, 60603. Phone: (312) 222-1555. Fax: (312) 222-2510. E-mail: rsparks@stratag.com Web Site: www.stratag.com.

Bruce W. Johnson, pres; Peter Nason, dir mktg.

TV, radio & media ratings analysis. Microsoft Windows-based software systems for cable systems & bcst TV stns.

Synovate-Americas, 360 Park Ave. S., New York, NY, 10010. Phone: (212) 293-6100. Fax: (212) 293-6666. Web Site: www.synovate.com.

Leigh Seaver, sr VP.

Falls Church, VA 22043, 7600 Leesburg Pike, E. Bldg., Suite 110. Leigh Seaver, sr VP.

Radio/TV Hispanic audience ratings, natl & loc; market studies, stn profiles, focus groups, product usage/awareness, progmg/format rsch, copy testing. Specialization in ethnic rsch.

TNS Canadian Facts, 900-2 Bloor St. E., Toronto, ON, M4W 3H8. Canada. Phone: (416) 924-5751. Fax: (416) 923-7085. E-mail: info@nfocfgroup.com Web Site: www.tns-global.com.

Michael LoPresti, pres/CEO; David Stark, pub affrs dir.

Vancouver, BC V6E 4A4 Canada, 1130 W. Pender St, Suite 600. Phone: (604) 668-3344. Fax: (604) 668-3333. Diana Tindall, rsch dir.

Ottawa, ON K1P 5W6 Canada, Place de Ville Tower B, 112 Kent St, Suite 2010A. Phone: (613) 232-4408. Fax: (613) 232-7102. Bente Nielsen, VP.

Montreal, PQ H3G 2B3 Canada, 1250 Guy St, Suite 1030. Phone: (514) 935-7666. Fax: (514) 935-6770. Michel Gauvreau, VP.

Full range of custom-designed & syndicated market rsch svcs.

The Tarrance Group, 201 N. Union St., Suite 410, Alexandria, VA, 22314. Phone: (703) 684-6688. Fax: (703) 836-8256. E-mail: tarrance@tarrance.com Web Site: www.tarrance.com.

David Sackett, ptnr.

Audience rsch svcs for radio, TV & cable. News, progmg, positioning, survey & promotional rsch.

Teen-age Research Unlimited, 707 Skokie Blvd., 7th Flr., Northbrook, IL, 60062. Phone: (847) 564-3440. Fax: (847) 564-0825. E-mail: info@tru-insight.com Web Site: www.teenresearch.com.

Peter Zollo, CEO.

Twice annually, syndicated study of the teen market with optional custom/proprietary questions. Custom rsch in teenage markets.

Telecommunications Research Inc., (A division of Nathan Associates Inc.). 2101 Wilson Blvd., Suite 1200, Arlington, VA, 22201. Phone: (703) 516-7800. Fax: (703) 351-6162. E-mail: info@triresearch.com Web Site: www.triresearch.com.

Economic & mgmt consultants specializing in mktg & survey rsch, business & property valuation & financial viability analysis.

VIP Research Inc., 5700 Broadmoor, Suite 710, Mission, KS, 66202. Phone: (913) 384-9494. Fax: (913) 677-2727. E-mail: mike@mjmresearch.com Web Site: www.mjmresearch.com.

Clark Roberts, sls dir; Mike Heydman, rsch dir.

Provides hook-tape production, listener screening, fielding, & tabulation for all music testing, perceptual studies, focus groups & promotional telemarketing.

VNU Consumer Research Services, Inc., 12350 N.W. 39th St., Coral Springs, FL, 33065. Phone: (954) 753-6043. Fax: (954) 346-8869.

Kathy Pilhuj, sr VP.

Tuczon, AZ 85710, 6339 Speedway, Suite 200. Phone:

(520) 751-2223. Barbara Garvin, mgr.

Sarasota, FL 34236, 1751 Mound St, Suite 205. Phone: (941) 955-9877. Kathleen Goodwin, mgr.

San Antonio, TX 78229, 4801 N.W. Loop 410, Suite 125. Phone: (210) 647-3198. Juan Hernandez, mgr.

Data collection for Survey Research, production of The Scarborough Report and The Market Audit Report.

Vallie-Richards Consulting Inc., 2175 Bent Creek Manor, Vallie Richards Donovan Consulting, Alpharetta, GA, 30005. Phone: (770) 346-0026. Fax: (770) 346-0028. E-mail: jimrvr@aol.com Web Site: www.vallierichards.com.

Jim Richards, pres; Dan Vallie, CEO.

America's premier contemp radio consultancy specializing in all variations of contemp radio balancing art & science to create ratings & revenue success.

Ventures in Media Inc., 78175 Estancia Dr., Palm Desert, CA, 92211. Phone: (760) 360-7303.

Morrie Gelman, pres.

Tokyo f116-0002 Japan, 3-76-1-604 Arabawa-Ku. Phone: 11 81-3-3891-3622. Adam Gelman, purchasing VP.

Market rsch info packaging & consulting.

Video Monitoring Services, 1500 Broadway, New York, NY, 10036. Phone: (212) 736-2010. Fax: (212) 736-8206. E-mail: sales@vmsinfo.com Web Site: www.vmsinfo.com.

Michael Giovia, sr VP/news sls.

Los Angeles, CA 90028, 6430 W. Sunset Blvd, Suite 400. Phone: (323) 993-0111. Fax: (323) 467-7540. Ashley Griffin.

Washington, DC 20045, 1066 National Press Bldg. Phone: (202) 393-7110. Fax: (202) 393-5451. Meredith Imwalle.

Chicago, IL 60610, 212 W. Superior St. Phone: (312) 649-1131. Fax: (312) 649-1527. Jack Monson.

Provides transcripts, digests & analysis of radio & TV news & commentary; surveys of program content; monitoring of comls; tape & cassette recordings; photoboards; film conversions.

Mona Wargo, 1600 N. Oak St., Suite 1401, Arlington, VA, 22209. Phone: (703) 243-9352. E-mail: mwrsrch@erols.com

Mona Wargo, MS-IT/TS; rsch analyst.

Ind rsch analyst in bcst & telecommunications, FCC regulatory policy, legal & engrg rsch & consultant.

Washington Information Group Ltd., 1655 N. Fort Myer Dr., Suite 825, Arlington, VA, 22209. Phone: (703) 312-6004. Fax: (703) 527-4586.

Doug House, pres.

Customized business rsch on client-specified aspects of the bcstg industry, including competitor intelligence on companies, products, svcs & markets.

World Information Technologies Inc., 70 Carley Ave., Huntington, NY, 11743. Phone: (631) 549-3629. Fax: (631) 549-7527.

Amadee Bender, pres.

Telecommunications market rsch.

Your Personal Researcher, 22848 Mesa Way, Lake Forest, CA, 92630-4643. Phone: (949) 472-8538. E-mail: dlbraunstein@prodigy.net

Donna Lee Braunstein, owner.

Script & documentary rsch.

Engineering and Technical Consultants

AF Associated Inc./Ascent Media, 235 Pegasus Ave., Northvale, NJ, 07647. Phone: (201) 767-3800. Fax: (201) 784-8637.E-mail: consulting@ascentmedia.com Web Site:www.afassoc.com

Tom Canavan, pres; Andre Macaluso Sr., VP/mgng dir; Chris Summey, sr VP.

Mgmt & distribution of content to major motion picture studios, ind producers, bcst networks, cable channels, adv agencies & other companies that produce, own/or distribute entertainment, adv, news, sports, corporate, educ & industrial content.

AZCAR U.S.A. Inc., 121 Hillpointe Dr., Suite 700, Canonsburg, PA, 15317. Phone: (724) 873-0800. Fax: (724) 873-4770.E-mail: info@azcar.com Web Site:www.azcar.com

Stephen Pumple, pres/CEO.

Bcst, video & audio system consultation, design, instal & training; serving cable systems, corporate & teleproduction facilities.

Advanced Technology Systems Corp., 7925 Jones Branch Dr., McLean, VA, 22102. Phone: (571) 766-2400. Fax: (571) 766-2401.E-mail: info@atsva.com Web Site:www.atsva.com

Claude Rumsey, owner; Doug Manning, VP opns; Penelope Parker, mktg dir.

Software & systems dev, lifecycle mgmt, systems integration, testing IT, infrastructure outsourcing mgmt, business process improvement, info sharing, consulting, wireless svcs & specialized functional expertise.

Allstate Tower Company Inc., (formerly Nationwide Tower Company Inc.). Box 25, Henderson, KY, 42419. Phone: (270) 869-8000. Fax: (270) 830-8475.E-mail: sales@allstatetower.com Web Site:www.allstatetower.com

Kevin Roth, sls VP; Diane Pruitt, gen sls mgr.

Tower Manufacturing Co. including: Tower inspections, painting, repair re-guy, lighting, antennas, feedlines, analysis, erect, dismantle, line sweeping, site monitoring, & tower tracker svcs.

John H. Battison, P.E. & Associates, Consulting Radio Engineers. 2684 State Rt. 60, Loudonville, OH, 44842. Phone: (419) 994-3849. Fax: (419) 994-5419.E-mail: batcom@bright.net

*John H. Battison, engr.

All FCC svcs: AM, FM, TV, LPTV, applications, licensing, DA-proofs, ITFS & MMDS expert witness svcs.

Richard S. Becker & Associates, Chartered, 7128 Fair Fax Rd., Bethesda, MD, 20814. Phone: (301) 986-9005. Fax: (301) 986-8496.E-mail: beckereng@aol.com

Richard Becker, principal atty; Siamak Harandi, consulting engr; Christopher Fedeli, assoc.

Legal & engrg svc for bcstg, cable TV, cellular, paging, microwave & private radio.

Lawrence Behr Associates Inc., Box 8026, Greenville, NC, 27835-8026. Phone: (252) 757-0279. Fax: (252) 752-9155.E-mail: lbagrp@lbagroup.com Web Site:www.lbagroup.com

Lawrence Behr, CEO; *Jerry E. Brown, VP.

Provides wireless svcs: site acquisition, construction mgmt, AM detuning, AM tower colocation, RF hazard mgmt, RF shielding, due diligence, facility mgmt, dev, maintenance, support svcs.

Serge Bergen, P.E., 7503 Amkin Ct., Clifton, VA, 22024. Phone: (703) 250-2691.E-mail: wtranavitch@cox.net

William V. Tranavitch Jr., ptnr.

Engrg svcs: AM, FM, TV, translators, LPTV.

Bernard Associates, 143 Palmers Hill Rd., Stamford, CT, 06902-2111. Phone: (203) 348-0804. Fax: (203) 921-1016.

Bernard Eishwald, P.E.

Broadcast Engineering & Equipment Maintenance Co., (BEEM Co.). 2322 S. 2nd Ave., Arcadia, CA, 91006. Phone: (626) 446-3468. Fax: (626) 445-8028.E-mail: joel@beemco.com Web Site:www.beemco.com

Joel T. Saxberg, owner.

Site studies, applications, AM directional arrays, allocation studies, field work, mobile signal analysis, bcst consulting & radiofrequency electromagnetic field measurements.

Broadcast Services Inc., Box 6418, Brattleboro, VT, 05302-6418. Phone: (802) 258-3000. Phone: (802) 258-4500 Svc. Fax: (802) 258-2500.E-mail: mh@markhutchins.com Web Site:www.markhutchins.com

Mark F. Hutchins, pres.

Field studies: Spectrum analysis, NRSC/RFR compliance. Propagation analysis, coverage maps, path profiles & shadowing studies.

Broadcast Signal Lab, LLP, 64 Richdale Ave., Cambridge, MA, 02140-2629. Phone: (617) 864-4298. Fax: (617) 661-1345.E-mail: information@broadcastsignallab.com Web Site:www.broadcastsignallab.com

Rick Levy, ptnr; David P. Maxson, ptnr.

RF safety evaluation, expert testimony, coverage analysis, license engrg & applications, interference & spectrum analysis, frequency monitoring, tech due diligence.

Bromo Communications Inc., Box 191747, Atlanta, GA, 31119-1747. Phone: (404) 636-2257. Fax: (404) 636-2256.E-mail: bill@bromocom.com Web Site:www.bromocom.com

Bill Brown, engr; Gil Moor, engr.

WashingtonDC Phone:

Consulting engrg for bcst stns. AM/FM & TV allocations, including field instals.

John F.X. Browne & Associates P.C., 38710 Woodward Ave., Suite 220, Bloomfield Hills, MI, 48304. Phone: (248) 642-6226. Fax: (248) 642-6027.E-mail: consultants@jfxb.com Web Site:www.jfxb.com

*John F.X. Browne, P.E., pres; John Fleming, engr; Leonard W. Eden, engr.

Bcst consulting AM/FM/TV/DTV, MMDS/ITFS, PCS & satellite systems. FCC/FAA applications, filings & studies. Field measurement vehicle AM/FM/TV/DTV.

Richard W. Burden Associates, 20944 Sherman Way, Suite 213, Canoga Park, CA, 91303. Phone: (818) 340-4590.E-mail: rwburden@pacbell.net Web Site:www.dickburden.com

Richard W. Burden, engr.

Bcst tech svcs, facilities design, Traveller's Information Service (TIS) & Educational FM (EDFM) FCC applications, Part 15 AM & FM bcst systems engrg.

CSI Telecommunications Inc., 750 Battery St., Suite 350, San Francisco, CA, 94111-1555. Phone: (415) 751-8845. Fax: (415) 292-9981.E-mail: info@csitele.com Web Site:www.csitele.com

Michael S. Newman, CEO; Philip M. Kane, P.E., Esq, VP; S.L. Deller, P.E., engr; W.F. Ruck, engr; D. Doon, P.E., engr.

Telecommunications, radio & microwave engrg, feasibility studies, FCC applications, systems engrg; equipment specifications, project mgmt & lab measurements.

Cavell, Mertz & Associates, Inc., 7839 Ashton Ave., Manassas, VA, 20109. Phone: (703) 392-9090. Fax: (703) 392-9559.E-mail: office@cavellmertz.com Web Site:www.cavellmertz.com

Gary Cavell, pres; Richard H. Mertz, VP.

Broadcast & Communications Consulting Engineers located in suburban Washington, DC. Experts in radio/TV ch searches, upgrades, transmission, coverage studies, interference evaluation, RF safety, strategic planning, both bcst (AM/FM radio, TV, digital TV, microwave/satellite) & industrial.

Chenevert Architects LLC, 6767 Perkins Rd., Suite 100, Baton Rouge, LA, 70808. Phone: (225) 757-0955. Fax: (225) 757-0765.E-mail: chenevert@architects.com Web Site:www.chenevertarchitects.com

Norman J. Chenevert, pres.

Architects, planners, & technical designers, specializing in new & renovated bcst/cable production facilities.

Chevalier Aviation Associates, LLC, 928 Via Panorama, Palos Verdes, CA, 90274. Phone: (310) 375-2979. Fax: (310) 791-7181.E-mail: jack.chevalier@verizon.net

Jack Chevalier, pres; L. Gene Garrett, dir.

Part 77 studies, FCC registrations, EMI analysis, legal assistance & representation before FAA, state & loc aeronautical & zoning agencies.

Clear Channel Communications, 1834 Lisenby Ave., Panama City, FL, 32405. Phone: (850) 769-1408. Fax: (850) 769-0659.E-mail: contactus@clearchannel.com Web Site:www.clearchannel.com

Turnkey installations (AM, FM studios & transmitters), tech appraisals, emergency repairs, upgrades. International startups & upgrades.

Cohen, Dippell and Everist, P.C., 1300 L St. N.W., Suite 1100, Washington, DC, 20005. Phone: (202) 898-0111. Fax: (202) 898-0895.E-mail: cde@attgobal.net Web Site:http://www.broadcast-consulting-engineers.com

*Donald G. Everist, P.E., pres; *Ross Heide, P.E., engr.

Professional engrg svcs to the bcstg industry, United States & worldwide.

Commercial Radio Co., One Duttonsville School Dr., Cavendish, VT, 05142. Phone: (802) 226-7582. Fax: (802) 226-7738. Web Site:commercialradiocompany.us

Daniel W. Churchill, PE, pres; Centura L. Churchill, VP; Andre S. LaPlante, sls; William E. Ford, engr.

Custom bcst engrg; AM, FM & shortwave bcst equipment sls & svce, specializing in transmitting components.

Communications Design Associates Inc., 437 Turnpike St., Canton, MA, 02021-2702. Phone: (339) 502-6551. Fax: (781) 502-6569.E-mail: information@cdaconsultants.com Web Site:www.cdaconsultants.com

Robert Hemenway, ptnr; Stewart Randall, ptnr; Greg Vincent, ptnr.

Ind consultants to radio, TV, corporate & govt clients. Designers of studios, production, presentation & multimedia facilities.

Communications General Corp., 2685 Alta Vista Dr., Fallbrook, CA, 92028-9739. Phone: (760) 723-2700.E-mail: r.gonsett@ieee.org

Robert F. Gonsett, E.E., pres.

Bcst engrg consulting, AM/FM/TV applications & field engrg. Specializes in southwest United States, Hawaii & Mexico.

Communications Technologies Inc., Box 1130, 65 Country Club Ln., Marlton, NJ, 08053. Phone: (856) 985-0077. Fax: (856) 985-8124.E-mail: info@commtechrf.com Web Site:www.commtechrf.com

Clarence M. Beverage, pres; Laura M. Mizrahi, VP; James W. Pollock, P.E., engr.

Bcst engrg consulting svcs with emphasis on AM, FM & TV RF systems design & FCC application preparation consistent with FCC rules & policies.

Comsearch, 19700 Janellia Farm Blvd., Ashburn, VA, 20147. Phone: (703) 726-5500. Fax: (703) 726-5600. Web Site:www.comsearch.com

Doug Hall, pres.

A complete communications engrg svc organization, specializing in frequency mgmt & propagation engrg.

ComSonics Inc., Box 1106, 1350 Port Republic Rd., Harrisonburg, VA, 22801. Phone: (540) 434-5965. Fax: (540) 432-9794.E-mail: info@comsonics.com Web Site:www.comsonics.com

Dennis A. Zimmerman, pres/CEO; Donn E. Meyerhoeffer, dir opns; Don J. Sommerville, dir mktg & sls.

Microprocessor controlled signal level meters, RF leakage detection & CATV repair facility.

Contemporary Communications, 9408 Grand Gate St., Las Vegas, NV, 89143. Phone: (702) 898-4669. Fax: (208) 567-6865.E-mail: larryfuss@cox.net Web Site:www.radioguys.net

Larry G. Fuss, pres.

FM, TV, STL & RPU applications; FM upgrades; computerized frequency searches; site selection assistance.

C.P. Crossno & Associates, Consulting Engineers. Box 180312, Dallas, TX, 75218. Phone: (214) 031-9140. Fax: (214) 321-9146.E-mail: c.crossno@ieee.org

Charles Paul Crossno, owner.

Aeronautical issues; antenna design.

Crown Castle, 2000 Corporate Dr., Cannonsburg, PA, 15317. Phone: (724) 416-2000. Fax: (724) 416-2200. Web Site:www.crowncastle.com

Communications engrg consultants & site/tower mgrs.

William Culpepper & Associates Inc., 900 Jefferson Dr., Charlotte, NC, 28270. Phone: (704) 365-9995. Fax: (704) 364-4823.

*William A. Culpepper, pres.

AM & FM applications & feasibility studies, specializing in applications for AM power increases & transmitter relocation.

DSI RF Systems Inc., 26H World's Fair Dr., Somerset, NJ, 08873. Phone: (732) 563-1144. Fax: (732) 563-1818. E-mail: jmueller@dsirf.com Web Site:www.dsirf.com

Joseph Giardina, chief engr; Herb Squire, VP engrg; Tim Carroll, pres.

Radio & TV system design, transmitter & studio instal, microwave & satellite engrg & instal, remote control camera systems.

John J. Davis & Associates, Box 128, Sierra Madre, CA, 91025-0128. Phone: (626) 355-6909. Fax: (626) 355-4890. E-mail: johnjdavis@roadrunner.com Web Site:www.socaltowers.com

*John J. Davis, owner.

Primary focus on FM & TV ch allocation studies & applications; facility upgrades, FM & TV translator applications, tower site mgmt.

Dettra Communications Inc., 7906 Fox Hound Rd., McLean, VA, 22102. Phone: (703) 790-1427. Fax: (703) 790-0497.

John E. Dettra Jr., pres.

Exhibits for bcst, mobile telephone, cellular, microwave & private radio svcs, FCC rsch & consulting.

Devlin Design Group Inc., Box 5208, Frisco, CO, 80443. Phone: (970) 453-9360. E-mail: contacts@ddgtv.com Web Site:www.ddgtv.com

Dan Devlin, CEO.

News sets, softset, virtual set environments, promotions, newsrooms, facility planning, lighting direction, consultation, Videssence Integration & softset (Virtual Reality Sets).

Diversified Systems, (formerly Diversified Systems Inc.). 363 Market St., Kenilworth, NJ, 07033. Phone: (908) 245-4833. Fax: (908) 245-0011. E-mail: info@divsysinc.com Web Site:www.divsysinc.com

Alfred D'Alessandro, pres/CEO.

Full-svc engrg, specializing in video & RF systems.

Doug Vernier Telecom Consultants, 401 Main St., Suite 213, Cedar Falls, IA, 50613. Phone: (319) 266-8402. Fax: (319) 266-9212. E-mail: consulting@v-soft.com Web Site:www.v-soft.com

Doug Vernier, pres; Kate Michler, tech consultant.

Tech consulting for AM, FM, & TV. Coverage mapping, frequency searches, applications, site evaluations, stn watches, stn audits & more.

The Downtown Group, 236 W. 27th St., New York, NY, 10001. Phone: (212) 675-9506. Fax: (212) 675-3276. E-mail: info@downtowngroup.com Web Site:www.downtowngroup.com

Peter Wilcox, ptnr; Mark Winkleman, ptnr.

Design of tech facilities: architecture, acoustics, engrg, testing. Typical projects include edit rooms, stages, recording studios & support facilities.

du Treil, Lundin & Rackley Inc., 201 Fletcher Ave., Sarasota, FL, 34237-6019. Phone: (941) 329-6000. Fax: (941) 329-6030. E-mail: bobjr@dlr.com Web Site:www.dlr.com

Tech consulting for the communications industry.

ERI - Electronics Research Inc., 7777 Gardner Rd., Chandler, IN, 47610. Phone: (812) 925-6000. Fax: (812) 925-4030. E-mail: sales@eriinc.com Web Site:www.eriinc.com

*Thomas B. Sillman, pres; David White, engr.

Antennas, transmission line, filters-combiners & towers for FM, AM TV BR'S-EBS, mobile media bcstrs, also related engng, field & installations svcs.

Evans Associates Consulting, 216 Green Bay Rd., Suite 205, Thiensville, WI, 53092. Phone: (262) 242-6000. Fax: (262) 242-6045. E-mail: info@evansassoc.com Web Site:www.evansassoc.com

*Ralph E. Evans Sr., ptnr; *B. Benjamin Evans, P.E., ptnr.

Telecommunications consulting engrs, net design, FCC applications, digital bcstg strategic planning, fieldwork for AM, FM, TV, CATV, ITFS, microwave relay facilities & fiber, wireless, & PCS networks.

Federal Engineering Inc., Redwood Plaza II, 10600 Arrowhead Dr., Fairfax, VA, 22030. Phone: (703) 359-8200. Fax: (703) 359-8204. E-mail: info@fedeng.com Web Site:www.fedeng.com

Ronald F. Bosco, pres; John E. Murray, sr VP.

Strategic planning, coverage analysis, new product definition, market rsch, competitive analysis, rates & tariffs, bcst stn design, mergers & acquisitions, expert testimony, regulatory support.

Charles S. Fitch, P.E., 45 Sarah Dr., Avon, CT, 06001. Phone: (860) 673-7260. Fax: (860) 675-7269. E-mail: fitchpe@comcast.net

*Charles S. Fitch, P.E., pres.

FCC allocations & applications, facility design, system design, construction supervision, field surveys, facility appraisals & inspections, computer progmg.

Paul Dean Ford, Broadcast Engineering Consultant. 18889 N.2350th St., Dennison, IL, 62423. Phone: (217) 826-9673. E-mail: wkzi@rr1.net Web Site:www.worldpower.us/

Paul Dean Ford, P.E., owner.

Engineering consultant.

Freedman, Mel, 2612 Portsmouth Ln., Modesto, CA, 95355. Phone: (209) 522-1180. Fax: (209) 522-1750. E-mail: melengr@sbcglobal.net

Mel Freeman, engr.

George M. Frese, P.E., 1011 Denis Ct., East Wenatchee, WA, 98802. Phone: (509) 884-4558. Fax: (509) 884-9170. E-mail: frese@genext.net

*George M. Frese, owner.

AM Antenna design. Short, DA & Multiplexing.

GeoMart, 516 Villanova Ct., Fort Collins, CO, 80525. Phone: (970) 416-8340. Fax: (970) 416-8345. E-mail: sales@geomart.com Web Site:www.geomart.com

Chuck Cotherman, owner.

All USGS & DMA digital & paper maps. All NOS/NOAA charts, international topographic series, aerial photography, raised relief maps, digital products, business & mktg maps, travel maps, globes, etc.

Graphic Enterprises Inc., 3874 Highland Park N.W., North Canton, OH, 44720. Phone: (800) 842-8448. Fax: (800) 358-7767. E-mail: sales@geiwideformat.com Web Site:www.geiwideformat.com

Large-format digital printing systems.

Hammett & Edison Inc., Box 280068, San Francisco, CA, 94128-0068. Phone: (707) 996-5200. Phone: (202) 396-5200 (DC). Fax: (707) 996-5280. E-mail: engr@h-e.com Web Site:www.h-e.com

*William F. Hammett, P.E., pres; Dane E. Ericksen, P.E., engr; *Stanley Salek, P.E., engr; *Robert D. Weller, P.E., engr; *Mark D. Neumann, P.E., engr; Rajat Mathur, P.E., engr.

Design & FCC filings: AM, FM, TV, STL, wireless cable. Specialties: computerized coverage studies, AM directionals / diplexers, RF radiation predictions / measurements / mitigations, field strength measurements, due diligence technical surveys, FAA EMI analysis.

Hatfield & Dawson, Consulting Engineers L.L.C., 9500 Greenwood Ave. N., Seattle, WA, 98103. Phone: (206) 783-9151. Fax: (206) 789-9834. E-mail: hatdaw@hatdaw.com Web Site:www.hatdaw.com

Benjamin F. Dawson, pres.

Telecommunications, radio physics engrg, including bcst, electromagnetic compatibility, NIER measurement/analysis, antenna/propagation analysis & design.

Charles A. Hecht & Associates Inc., 16 Doe Run, Pittstown, NJ, 08867. Phone: (908) 730-7959.

Charles A. Hecht, pres; William L. Smith Sr., engr; Charles J. Hecht, engr.

Bcst engrg svcs including FCC studies & applications, directional antenna design, fieldwork, tech litigation; specialists in AM studies for telecommunications companies.

Hilding Communications, Box 1700, Morgan Hill, CA, 95038-2222. Phone: (408) 842-2222. E-mail: eric@hilding.com

Eric Hilding, owner.

FM ch studies, complex FM substitution proposals, site locations, 301 applications engrg, gen bcst consulting.

HN Telecom Inc., 1160 Douglas Rd., ., Burnaby, BC, V5C 4Z6. Canada. Phone: (604) 294-3401. Fax: (604) 299-6712. E-mail: contact@hntelecom.com Web Site:www.hntelecom.com

P. Hostinsky, principal; Bruce W. Grantholm, sr VP engrg/opns.

Telecommunications tech consulting svcs for AM, FM,

TV bcst & CATV systems, studio-to-transmitter links & studio systems.

Doug Holland Inc., 1871 Sweet Briar Ln., Birmingham, AL, 35235-3357. Phone: (205) 229-5628. E-mail: dougholland@att.net Web Site:www.dougholland.com

Doug Holland, pres.

Turnkey opns, allocation studies, due diligence, transmitter installations, upgrades & coverage maps

R.L. Hoover Consulting Telecommunications, Consulting Telecommunications Engineer. 11704 Seven Locks Rd., Potomac, MD, 20854. Phone: (301) 983-0054.

*Robert Lloyd Hoover, P.E., owner.

Professional engrg consulting for AM, FM & TV applications & testimony. Radiation hazard analyses & testimony. Ex-owner AM & FM stns. Patent agent.

Independent Broadcast Consultants Inc., 110 County Rd. 146, Trumansburg, NY, 14886. Phone: (607) 273-2970. Fax: (607) 273-5125. E-mail: ibcengineering@juno.com Web Site:www.trumansburgchamber.com

William J. Sitzman, pres; M.F. Sitzman, VP; George Soltysik, P.E., engr; N.L. Hollenback, engr; R.A. Lynch, engr.

AM, FM & SW applications, specializing in AM allocation studies & broadband AM directional antenna design & AM diplexer design.

J. Boyd Ingram & Associates, Box 1528, Batesville, MS, 38606. Phone: (662) 563-4007. E-mail: jboyd@panola.com

J. Boyd Ingram, A.E., pres.

Tech consultation, facility construction & repair.

George Jacobs & Associates Inc., 3210 N. Leisure World Blvd., Suite 1001, Silver Spring, MD, 20906-7605. Phone: (301) 598-1282. Fax: (301) 598-7788. E-mail: broadcaster@gjainc.com Web Site:www.gjainc.com

*George Jacobs, P.E., pres.

Specialists in conceptional design, application filing & frequency mgmt for FCC-licensed International Broadcast Stations (shortwave). Consultative liaison with foreign bcst stns & organizations.

Vir James, P.C., 965 S. Irving St., Denver, CO, 80219. Phone: (303) 937-1900. Fax: (303) 937-1902.

*Timothy C. Cutforth, P.E., pres.

AM/FM/TV allocation studies & applications, AM directional ant design & tune-up, conductivity measurements.

Jenel Systems and Design Inc./Smalling Systems, 6700 Spokane, Plano, TX, 75023. Phone: (972) 491-1442. Fax: (972) 491-1442. E-mail: smalling@smallingsystems.com

Elmer Smalling III, pres/CEO; Howard Halcomb III, sls VP; Erin Day Loyd III, VP mktg.

Digital bcstg solutions; studio, post, acoustic & earth stn, design; trucks; TV system design from planning to turnkey construction.

Carl T. Jones Corp., 7901 Yarnwood Ct., Springfield, VA, 22153. Phone: (703) 569-7704. Fax: (703) 569-6417. E-mail: hhurst@ctjc.com Web Site:www.ctjc.com

*C. Thomas Jones Jr., pres; *Herman E. Hurst, gen mgr; *John Hidle, engr; *Al Resnick, engr; *Cynthia Jacobson, engr; William Getz, engr; James Sadler, engr; Carl Gluck, engr.

Consulting engrs specializing in AM, FM & TV tech design & regulatory filings.

KCI Technologies Inc., 4601 Six Forks Rd., Landmark Center II, Suite 220, Raleigh, NC, 27609. Phone: (919) 783-9214. Fax: (919) 783-9266. E-mail: corpcom@kci.com Web Site:www.kci.com

Tom Donohue, P.E., sr VP; James Blake, engrg mgr.

Full engrg svcs to the communications industry, including tower analysis & remediation, design of standard & non-standard sites, "stealth" engrg, photo realistic renderings & turnkey construction.

Kessler & Gehman Associates Inc., 507 N.W. 60th St., Suite C, Gainesville, FL, 32607. Phone: (352) 332-3157. Fax: (352) 332-6392. E-mail: rwilhour@bellsouth.net Web Site:www.kga.bz

*Robert Gehman, P.E. Jr., pres; William Kessler, P.E. Jr., VP; Jeffrey C. Gehman Jr., engr; Ryan C. Wilhour Jr., engr; William T. Godfrey, P.E. Jr., engr.

Studies, system design, FCC applications, bidding documents & contract monitoring for bcst, ITFS, wireless cable, microwave & mobile communications systems & digital TV.

Lightning Eliminators & Consultants Inc., 6687 Arapahoe Rd., Boulder, CO, 80303. Phone: (303) 447-2828 ext 107. Fax: (303) 447-8122.E-mail: info@lecglobal.com Web Site:www.lecglobal.com

Roy B. Carpenter Jr, dir; Jerry Kerr, VP mktg & sls; Darwin N. Sletten, chief engr.

Consulting & engrg svcs in lightning prevention, grounding & power / signal / telephone / data line conditioning.

Lohnes and Culver, 8309 Cherry Ln., Laurel, MD, 20707-4830. Phone: (301) 776-4488. Fax: (301) 776-4499.E-mail: locul@locul.com

*Robert D. Culver, VP & ptnr.

Communication consulting engrg svc for bcst & related fields. Design, application, optimization, system evaluation & expert representation svcs.

Cecil Lynch Consulting Engineers, 2460 Illinois Ave., Modesto, CA, 95358. Phone: (209) 523-3955. Fax: (209) 522-5287.

Cecil Lynch, CEO.

Bcst engrg, stn appraisals, customized computer progmg svc, GPS surveying & RFR measurements.

Mahlum Architects, 71 Columbia, Suite 400, Seattle, WA, 98104. Phone: (206) 441-4151. Fax: (206) 441-0478.E-mail: info@mahlum.com Web Site:www.mahlum.com

John Mahlum, pres.

Architect interiors & planning.

D.L. Markley & Associates Inc., 2104 W. Moss Ave., Peoria, IL, 61604. Phone: (309) 673-7511. Fax: (309) 673-8128.E-mail: dlm@dlmarkley.com Web Site:www.dlmarkley.com

*Donald L. Markley, pres; *Jeremy D. Ruck P.E., sr engr; Keith A. Turcot, engr.

AM/FM, TV, microwave applications, construction & measurements. Allocation studies, non-ionizing radiation measurements.

Marsand Inc., Box 485, 6100 IH 35W, Alvarado, TX, 76009. Phone: (817) 783-5566. Fax: (817) 783-5577.E-mail: tvcowboy@marsand.com Web Site:www.marsand.com

*Matthew A. Sanderford, Jr., P.E., pres; David Sanderford, VP.

Turnkey installation, CAD-VIDCAD wiring documentation, Digital FM & TV proof-of-performance, FCC consulting & applications, RF troubleshooting, installations & conversions, RF site safety.

Frank J. Maynard, 44683 Mansfield Dr., Novi, MI, 48375. Phone: (248) 344-2965.E-mail: info@fmaynard.com Web Site:www.fmaynard.com

Frank J. Maynard, C.F.B.E., owner.

Radio & TV engrg svcs & applications.

McClanathan & Associates Inc., Box 939, Portland, OR, 97207. Phone: (503) 246-8080. Fax: (503) 246-6304.

*Robert A. McClanathan, P.E., pres.

Professional electrical engrs for radio & TV FCC applications, computer svcs, field engrg & construction svcs.

Meintel, Sgrignoli, & Wallace, 1282 Smallwood Dr., Suite 372, Waldorf, MD, 20603. Phone: (202) 251-7589. Fax: (301) 645-1426.E-mail: wallacedtv@aol.com Web Site:www.mswdtv.com

Dennis Wallace, ptnr; William Meintel, ptnr; Gary Sgrignoli, ptnr.

Specializing in digital & analog TV & Radio technical software, consumer electronics.

MidAmerica Electronics Service Inc., 410 Mt. Tabor Rd., New Albany, IN, 47150. Phone: (812) 945-1209. Fax: (812) 945-1859.E-mail: peterclb@aol.com

AM & FM field engrg svcs, antenna measurements, AM stereo instal & proof of performance, AM & FM spectrum analysis, NRSC compliance measurement, new construction & rebuilding.

Morgan, Angel & Associates LLC, 1601 Connecticut Ave. N.W., Suite 601, Washington, DC, 20009. Phone: (202) 265-1833. Fax: (202) 265-8022.E-mail: luis@morganangel.com Web Site:www.morganangel.com

Dr. Edward Angel; Luis A. Blandon Jr., Federal Communications specialist.

Wheat RidgeCO , 3605 Nelson St. Phone:

Consulting research firm specializing in Section 106 showings and environmental assessments for proposed towers and project sites.

Lawrence L. Morton Associates, 2867 Belden Dr., Hollywood, CA, 90068. Phone: (323) 467-5010. Fax: (323) 467-5848.E-mail: larry@radiotv.biz

*Lawrence L. Morton, P.E., owner.

Telecommunications engrg consulting svcs for AM, FM, TV & LPTV. Computerized engrg svcs, field svcs, FCC applications.

Mueller Broadcast Design, 613 S. La Grange Rd., La Grange, IL, 60525. Phone: (708) 352-2166. Fax: (708) 352-2170.E-mail: mark@muellerbroadcastdesign.com Web Site:www.muellerbroadcastdesign.com

Mark A. Mueller, owner; Karen S. Mueller, mgr.

AM/FM tech consultant, AM directional systems.

Mullaney Engineering Inc., 9049 Shady Grove Ct., Gaithersburg, MD, 20877. Phone: (301) 921-0115. Fax: (301) 590-9757.E-mail: mullaney@mullengr.com Web Site:www.mullengr.com

*John J. Mullaney, pres; *Alan E. Gearing, P.E., engr; Timothy Z. Sawyer, engr.

Consulting communications engrs providing: design & optimization of AM directional arrays; analysis for new allocation, site relocation & upgrades AM FM TV LPTV wireless cable (MDS/MMDS/ITFS/OFS); environmental radiation analysis; fieldwork; expert testimony.

Multicomm Sciences International Inc., 266 W. Main St., Denville, NJ, 07834. Phone: (973) 627-7400. Fax: (973) 215-2168.E-mail: victor@multicommsciences.com Web Site:www.multicommsciences.com

Victor J. Nexon Jr., pres.

Frequency coord, site surveys, earth stn interference studies, FCC license, radiation hazard testing.

Munn-Reese Inc., Box 220, 385 Airport Dr., Coldwater, MI, 49036-0220. Phone: (517) 278-7339. Fax: (517) 278-6973.E-mail: wayne@munn-reese.com Web Site:www.munn-reese.com

Christine Reese, VP; Wayne S. Reese, pres; Ed Trombley, engr; Donald Bood, engr; Rick Grizebik, engr.

AM, FM, TV, low power TV & engrg consulting service, including applications, field tuning & problem solving.

Newman-Kees Frequency Measurements, Engineering, & Installations, 8611 Slate Rd., Evansville, IN, 47720. Phone: (812) 963-3294.E-mail: nkeng@insightbb.com

Frank Hertel, owner.

RF & frequency measurements for AM-FM-TV coml users via air or on location. Audio/video svc & instals.

Owl Engineering & EMC Test Labs, Inc., 5844 Avenue N., Shoreview, MN, 55126. Phone: (651) 784-7445. Fax: (651) 784-7541.E-mail: info@owleng.com Web Site:www.owleng.com

*Garrett G. Lysiak, P.E., pres; Diane Stewart Lysiak, ptnr.

Telecommunications consulting engrg svcs, applications, facilities specifications svcs, field engrg svcs, maintenance & FCC compliance svcs, EMC testing.

Pacific Radio Electronics, 969 N. La Brea, Los Angeles, CA, 90038. Phone: (323) 969-2035. Phone: (800) 634-9476. Fax: (323) 969-2053.E-mail: info@pacrad.com Web Site:www.pacrad.com

Joseph Phillips, pres.

Distributor of racks, patch bays, cable, adaptors, connectors, handtools, outlet strips & many other products for the bcst industry.

William F. Pohts Telecommunications, 225 Denfield Dr., Alexandria, VA, 22309. Phone: (703) 360-7193. Fax: (703) 360-0309.E-mail: bill@pohts.com

*William F. Pohts, P.E., engr.

Consulting engr specializing in the emerging technologies in telecommunications & electronic systems.

Rimma Posin, 3712 Carmel Ave., Irvine, CA, 92606. Phone: (949) 857-9639. Fax: (949) 857-9639.

Rimma Posin, owner.

Consulting for cable; FCC applications.

W.L. Pritchard & Co. L.C., 4405 E.W. Hwy., Suite 501, Bethesda, MD, 20814. Phone: (301) 654-1144. Fax: (301) 654-1814.E-mail: wlpritchard-co@verizon.net Web Site:www.wlpco.com

Ellen Hoff, pres; Paul Schrantz, VP engrg.

Professional engrg, business problem solving in telecommunications, competitor analysis, satellite communications, earth stns, & launch vehicles.

RF Technologies Corp., 1 Gendron Dr., Lewiston, ME, 04240. Phone: (207) 777-7778. Fax: (207) 777-7784.E-mail: info@rftechnologies.net Web Site:www.rftechnologies.net

Designs & manufactures high-power bcst RF networks & components for FM & TV bcstrs. Products include ants, diplexers, combiners, filters, switches, coaxial & waveguides.

RKF Engineering, LLC, 1229 19th St., N.W., Washington, DC, 20036. Phone: (202) 463-1565. Fax: (202) 463-0344.E-mail: prubin@satpar.com Web Site:www.rkfengineering

*Philip A. Rubin, P.E., pres; Ted Kaplan, VP engrg; Jeffrey Freedman, CFO; Alex Latker, dir; Arnold Berman, PhD., engr; William Meeker, engr.

MSS, FSS & BSS satellite experts, TV & radio cellular & other new media technologies. Experts in FCC rules & regulations. International experience, experts in ITU regulation. Software developers, simulation & modeling. In business over 20 years.

Radio/TV Engineering Co., 1416 Hollister Ln., Los Osos, CA, 93402. Phone: (805) 528-1996. Fax: (805) 528-1982.

Norwood J. Patterson, pres; G. Dawn Patterson, exec sec/asst engrg.

AM, FM, FCC applications, directional ant design. Serving bcstrs for over 35 years.

Radiotechniques Engineering, LLC, Box 367, 402 10th Ave., Haddon Heights, NJ, 08035-0367. Phone: (856) 546-8008. Fax: (856) 546-1841.E-mail: ted@radiotechniques.com Web Site:www.radiotechniques.com

*Edward A. Schober, P.E., VP.

AM, FM, TV, digital bcst, boosters, FCC, equipment, field, & systems engrg. RF, financial, opns, & acoustical design.

Rogers Cable Systems, 35-73 Wolfdale, Mississauga, ON, L5C 3T6. Canada. Phone: (905) 273-8000. Fax: (905) 273-9661. Web Site:www.rogers.com

Consulting engrg svcs with emphasis on design, instal & testing of CATV systems, fiber-optic nets.

D.W. Sargent Broadcast Inc., 804 Richard Rd., Cherry Hill, NJ, 08034. Phone: (856) 667-8573. Fax: (856) 667-1409.

Dean W. Sargent, pres.

Ant system design & measurements for FM & TV. FM & TV master ant system design.

T.Z. Sawyer Technical Consultants, 9049 Shady Grove Ct., Gaithersburg, MD, 20877. Phone: (301) 921-0115. Fax: (301) 590-9757.E-mail: info@tzsawyer.com Web Site:www.tzsawyer.com

Timothy Z. Sawyer, pres; Trisha E. Ford, admin asst.

FCC applications for AM, FM, TV, LPTV & aux svcs; AM directional ant design; AM, FM, & TV ant measurements; allocation studies; site surveys & inspections.

Sellmeyer Engineering, Box 356, McKinney, TX, 75070. Phone: (972) 542-2056. Fax: (214) 636-5940. Web Site:www.sellmeyer.com

*J.S. Sellmeyer, P.E., owner.

AM, FM, TV applications, hearing support, directional ant design & adjustment; facilities planning & specialized equipment design.

SiteSafe Inc., 200 N. Glebe Rd., Suite 1000, Arlington, VA, 22203-3728. Phone: (703) 276-1100. Fax: (703) 276-1169.E-mail: info@sitesafe.com Web Site:www.sitesafe.com

Wesley McGee, pres; Bill Zlotnick, opns VP.

Bcst & land mobile & wireless engrg consulting svcs.

Smith and Fisher, LLC, 2237 Tackett's Mill Dr., Suite A, Woodbridge, VA, 22192. Phone: (703) 494-2101. Fax: (703) 494-2132.E-mail: kevin@smithandfisher.com Web Site:www.smithandfisher.com

Kyle Fisher, assoc engr; Kevin Fisher, pres.

Engrg consultants to FM, TV, & LPTV stns, FCC applications, allocation studies, RFR measurements, coverage/ interference mapping & field studies.

Carl E. Smith Consulting Engineers, Box 807, 2324 N. Cleveland-Massilon Rd., Bath, OH, 44210-0807. Phone: (330) 659-4440. Fax: (330) 659-9234.

Al Warmus, pres; Brian M. Warmus, sec; Roy Stype III, VP.

AM, FM, TV & LPTV engrg, FCC applications, ant systems adjustments. Sls: towers, ants, transmission line, phasing equipment. Turnkey instal.

Frederick A. Smith Engineers, 1123 Old River Rd., Elloree, SC, 29047. Phone: (803) 897-2815. Fax: (803) 897-2816.

Frederick A. Smith, P.E., pres; Cameron E. Smith, VP.

Communications systems design, microwave path surveys, ant impedance measurements. United States & foreign.

Southern Broadcast Services, 80 Commerce Dr., Suite B, Pelham, AL, 35124. Phone: (205) 663-3709. Phone: (800) 256-9235. Fax: (205) 663-7108.E-mail: jwcoleman@southernbroadcastservices.com Web Site:www.southernbroadcastservices.com

Jim Coleman, pres.

Tower erection, ant & line instal additional , cellular & maintenance svcs.

J.M. Stitt & Associates Inc., 621 E. Mehring Way, Suite 1907, Cincinnati, OH, 45202. Phone: (513) 621-9292. Fax: (513) 651-9622.E-mail: towerjim@aol.com Web Site:www.jmstittassociates.com

James Stitt, pres.

Engrg consultants, facility design & instal, contract engrg svcs, acoustical consultants, tower site mgmt.

Technet Systems Group, (A division of Steve Vanni Associates Inc). Box 422, Auburn, NH, 03032. Phone: (603) 483-5365. Phone: (800) 329-4767. Fax: (603) 483-0512.E-mail: sales@technetsystems.com Web

Site:www.technetsystems.com

Steve Vanni, pres.

Bcst equipment supplier/distributor for radio & TV, specializing in complete "turnkeyed" packages including planning, design, equipment, instal, towers & FCC licensing.

Teletech Inc., 38235 N. Executive Dr., Westland, MI, 48185. Phone: (734) 641-2300. Web Site:www.teletech-inc.com

Keith Johnson, VP; Susan Dobronski, pres.

ScottsdaleAZ , Box 4221. Phone:

Engrg consultants: AM, FM, TV, LPTV; FCC applications /filings; FAA filings, aeronautical studies; tower erection, maintenance & inspections; antenna site dev & mgmt; directorial antenna design & proof of performance; contract engrg svcs.

TransVision, 550 Maulhardt Ave., Oxnard, CA, 93030. Phone: (805) 981-8740. Fax: (805) 981-8738.E-mail: info@txvision.com Web Site:www.txvision.com

Kimithy Vaughn, mktg & sls.

Twelve transportable & satellite transmission facilities (video, audio, voice, data). Flypack production & SNG svcs. Facilities in Brazil, Australia, Phillipines & Western Europe.

V-Soft Communications, L.L.C., 401 Main St., Suite 213, Cedar Falls, IA, 50613. Phone: (319) 266-8402. Fax: (319) 266-9212.E-mail: info@v-soft.com Web Site:www.v-soft.com

Doug Vernier, pres.

Bcst engrg software for signal propagation, frequency searching, interference analysis & custom mapping for AM, FM, TV, & LPTV.

Steve Vanni Associates Inc., Box 422, Auburn, NH, 03032. Phone: (603) 483-5365. Fax: (603) 483-0512.E-mail: svanni@techsystems.com

Steve Vanni, pres.

Tech consulting, systems design, project mgmt; complete turnkey svcs including equipment & towers through Technet Systems Group.

Richard L. Vega Group Inc., 1245 W. Fairbanks Ave., #380, Winter Park, FL, 32789. Phone: (407) 539-6540.

Richard L. Vega Jr., chmn.

Engrg svcs & business consulting svcs.

Vernier, Doug, Telecommunications Consultants, 401 Main St., Suite 213, Cedar Falls, IA, 50613. Phone: (319) 266-8402. Fax: (319) 266-9212.E-mail: info@v-soft.com Web Site:www.v-soft.com

Doug Vernier, pres.

Bcst engrg & consultation; ch searches, FCC applications, allocations, custom mapping, coverage analysis. V-Soft Communications bcst engr software.

Willoughby & Voss, LLC, Box 701190, San Antonio, TX, 78270-1190. Phone: (210) 490-2778. Phone: (210) 525-1111. Fax: (210) 490-2779.E-mail: willvoss@satx.rr.com

Lyndon H. Willoughby, owner.

AM, FM, TV, STL, trans applications, directional ant design, field svcs, allocations, site studies, system planning, frequency searches, facility inspection & non-ionized radiation studies.

Wireless Systems Engineering Inc./MLJ, (formerly JMS/MLJ Worldwide Inc.). 15713 Crabbs Branch Way, Suite 140, Rockville, MD, 20855. Phone: (301) 840-2030. Fax: (301) 840-2031.E-mail: info@wse-mlj.com

IT & software engrg, wireless engrg & internet svcs needs.

Law Firms Active in Communications Law

Abacus Communications Company, 1801 Columbus Rd. N.W., Suite 101, Washington, DC, 20009-2031. Phone: (202) 462-3680. Fax: (202) 462-3781.E-mail: abacuscommco@covad.net Benjamin Perez.

Akerman & Senterfitt, Citrus Center, 255 South Orange Ave., 17th Fl., Orlando, FL, 32801. Phone: (407) 843-7860. Fax: (407) 843-6610. Tom Cardwell.

Akin Gump Strauss Hauer & Feld LLP, Robert S. Strauss Bldg., 1333 New Hampshire Ave. N.W., Washington, DC, 20036. Phone: (202) 887-4000. Fax: (202) 887-4288.E-mail: sturner@akingump.com Web Site:akingump.com Kathleen Q. Abernathy; Martina Bradford; Tom Davidson; Philip Marchesiello.

Anderson, Kill & Olick L.L.P., 2100 M St. N.W., Suite 650, Washington, DC, 20037. Phone: (202) 416-6500. Fax: (202) 416-6555. Web Site:www.andersonkill.com

Arent & Fox, PLLC, 1050 Connecticut Ave. N.W., Washington, DC, 20036-5339. Phone: (202) 857-6000. Fax: (202) 857-6395. Web Site:www.arentfox.com E-mail: delorey.denise@arentfox.com Richard L. Brand, ptnr.

Arnold & Porter LLP, 555 12th St. N.W., Washington, DC, 20004-1206. Phone: (202) 942-5000. Fax: (202) 942-5999.E-mail: norman.sinel@aporter.com Web Site:www.arnoldporter.com Norman M. Sinel, Phillip W. Horton, Richard L. Rosen, Richard M. Firestone, Stephanie M. Phillipps, Patrick J. Grant, Scott Feira, William E. Cook Jr., Theodore D. Frank, P. Melissa Glidden, Maureen R. Jeffreys, Peter J. Schildkraut, Michael H. Ryan, Donald T. Stepka, Emma Wright, Johanna R. Thomas, Simon Cloke, David A. Rhodes.

Asbury, Philip S., 309 S. Broad St., Philadelphia, PA, 19107-5813. Phone: (215) 985-0911. Fax: (215) 985-1195.E-mail: pasburypir@ol.com

Attorney At Law, 2154 Wisconsin Ave., N.W., Suite 250, Washington, DC, 20007-2280. Phone: (202) 223-3772. Fax: (202) 315-3587.E-mail: kenhardman@att.net Kenneth E. Hardman.

Ausley & McMullen, Box 391, 227 S. Calhoun St., Tallahassee, FL, 32302. Phone: (850) 224-9115. Fax: (850) 222-7560.

Baker & Hostetler LLP, 1050 Connecticut Ave. N.W., Suite 1100, Washington, DC, 20036. Phone: (202) 861-1500. Fax: (202) 861-1783.E-mail: khoward@bakerlaw.com Web Site:www.bakerlaw.com Kenneth C. Howard Jr., E. Mark Braden, Bruce W. Sanford, Bruce D. Brown, Laurie Babinski.

Law Offices of Ruth S. Baker-Battist, 5600 Wisconsin Ave., Chevy Chase, MD, 20815. Phone: (301) 718-0955. Fax: (301) 718-8867.E-mail: rbattist@aol.com

Baker Botts L.L.P., 1299 Pennsylvania Ave. N.W., Washington, DC, 20004. Phone: (202) 639-7700. Fax: (202) 639-7890.E-mail: laurie.spielman@bakerbotts.com Herbert J. Miller Jr., John Joseph Cassidy.

Baker, Ravenel & Bender, Box 8057, 1730 Main St., Columbia, SC, 20292. Phone: (803) 799-9091. Fax: (803) 779-3423. Charles E. Baker, Jay Bender, ptnrs.

Law Offices of Martin J. Barab & Associates, 3rd Fl., 9606 Santa Monica Blvd., Beverly Hills, CA, 90210-4427. Phone: (310) 859-6644. Fax: (310) 859-6650. Martin J. Barab, mgng ptnr.

Barron & Newburger, P.C., 1212 Guadalupe St., Suite 104, Austin, TX, 78701. Phone: (512) 476-9103. Fax: (512) 476-9253.E-mail: bbarron@bnpdaw.com Barbara M. Barron.

Bass, Berry & Sims, 315 Deaderick St., South Center Suite 2700, Nashville, TN, 37238-0002. Phone: (615) 742-6200. Fax: (615) 742-6293.

Richard S. Becker & Associates, 7128 Fairfax Rd., Bethesda, MD, 20814. Phone: (301) 986-9005. Fax: (301) 986-8456.E-mail: Beckereng@aol.com Richard S. Becker, pres.

Beitchman & Hudson, 215 14th St. N.W., Atlanta, GA, 30318. Phone: (404) 897-5252. Fax: (404) 874-4270.E-mail: leebeebee@aol.com Lee B. Beitchman.

Bell, Boyd & Lloyd, 1615 L St. N.W., Suite 1200, Washington, DC, 20036. Phone: (202) 466-6300. Fax: (202) 463-0678.

Law Offices of Jeff Berke, 12400 Wilshire Blvd., Suite 400, Los Angeles, CA, 90025-6538. Phone: (310) 312-9221.E-mail: Jeffberke@yahoo.com Jeff Berke. Esq.

Berkowitz, Trager & Trager, P.C., 8 Wright St., Westport, CT, 06880. Phone: (203) 226-1001. Fax: (203) 226-3801.

Law Offices of Lawrence Bernstein, 3510 Springland Ln., N.W., Washington, DC, 20008. Phone: (202) 296-1800. Fax: (202) 296-1800.E-mail: lawberns@verizon.net Lawrence Bernstein.

Bingham McCuthen, LLP, 2020 K St. N.W., Washington, DC, 20006. Phone: (202) 373-6033. Fax: (202) 373-6001.E-mail: andrew.lipman@bingham.com Web Site:www.bingham.com Jean Kiddoo, Russell Blau, Catherine Wang.

Birch, Horton, Bittner & Cherot, 1155 Connecticut Ave. N.W., Suite 1200, Washington, DC, 20036. Phone: (202) 659-5800. Fax: (202) 659-1027. Web Site:www.birchhorton.com Elisabeth H. Ross, James H. Lister, Charles R. Eberle, David E. Lampp.

Bishop, Payne, Harvard & Kaitcer, L.L.P., 500 W. Seventh St., Suite 1800, Fort Worth, TX, 76102-4782. Phone: (817) 335-4911. Fax: (817) 870-2631.

Blank, Rome, LLP, 405 Lexington Ave., 23rd Floor, New York, NY, 10174. Phone: (212) 885-5000. Fax: (212) 885-5001. Web Site:www.blankrome.com

Bleiweiss, Irene, U.S. FCC, Audio Services Division, 445 12th St. S.W., Rm. 2B450, Washington, DC, 20554. Phone: (202) 418-2700. Fax: (202) 418-1411.E-mail: irene.bleiweiss@fcc.gov Web Site:www.fcc.gov/mb/audio Irene Bleiweiss.

Blooston, Mordkofsky, Dickens, Duffy & Prendergast, LLP, 2120 L St. N.W., Suite 300, Washington, DC, 20037. Phone: (202) 659-0830. Fax: (202) 828-5568.E-mail: halmor@bloostonlaw.com Web Site:www.bloostonlaw.com Harold Mordkofsky, Benjamin H. Dickens Jr., John A. Prendergast, Gerald J. Duffy, Robert M. Jackson, Cary Mitchell, Mary J. Sisak, Richard Rubino, Sal Tailffer Jr.

Blumberg, Grace Ganz, UCLA School of Law, 405 Hilgard Ave., Los Angeles, CA, 90095. Phone: (310) 825-1334. Fax: (310) 206-6489.E-mail: blumberg@law-ucla.edu Web Site:www.law-ucla.edu

Blume & Associates LLC, 10 Ellsworth Rd., Suite 209, West Hartford, CT, 06107. Phone: (860) 231-8777. Fax: (860) 231-8763.E-mail: db@blumelegal.net Web Site:www.blumelegal.net Daniel Blume.

Boelter & Perry, 330 Washington Blvd., Suite 310, Marina Del Rey, CA, 90292. Phone: (310) 882-5037. Fax: (310) 823-4325.E-mail: boltperr@comcast.net

Boies, Schiller & Flexner, LLP, 100 S.E. 2nd St., Suite 2800, Miami, FL, 33131. Phone: (305) 539-8400. Fax: (305) 539-1307. Web Site:www.bsfllp.com

Bone McAllester Norton PLLC, 511 Union St., Suite 1600, Nashville, TN, 37219. Phone: (615) 238-6330. Fax: (615) 238-6301. Web Site:www.bonelaw.com E-mail: mnorton@bonelaw.com C. Michael Norton.

Boose, Casey, Ciklin, Lubitz, Martens, McBane & O'Connell, Northbridge Tower, 515 N. Flagler Dr., Suite 1900, West Palm Beach, FL, 33401. Phone: (561) 832-5900. Fax: (561) 833-4209.E-mail: rcrump@boosecasey.com Patrick J. Casey.

Booth, Freret, Imlay & Tepper P.C., 14356 Cape May Rd., Silver Spring, MD, 20904-6011. Phone: (301) 384-5525. Fax: (301) 384-6384.E-mail: bfitpc@aol.com Christopher D. Imlay.

Bordelon, Hamlin & Theriot, 701 S. Peters St., Suite 100, New Orleans, LA, 70130-1661. Phone: (504) 524-5328. Fax: (504) 523-1071.

Borsari and Assoc., P.L.C., Box 100009, Arlington, VA, 22210. Phone: (703) 524-5800. Fax: (703) 524-4329.E-mail: John@borsari.com Web Site:www.borsari.com John A. Borsari.

Borsari & Paxson, 4000 Albemarle St. N.W., Suite 100, Washington, DC, 20016. Phone: (202) 296-4800. Fax: (202) 296-4460.E-mail: bap@baplaw.com Web Site:www.baplaw.com George R. Borsari Jr., Anne Thomas Paxson.

Boult, Cummings, Conners & Berry, PLC, 1600 Division St., Suite 700, Nashville, TN, 37219. Phone: (615) 244-2582. Fax: (615) 252-6380. Web Site:www.boultcummings.com

Law Offices of Timothy K. Brady, Box 930, Johnson City, TN, 30605-0930. Phone: (423) 477-7619.E-mail: tkbrady@earthlink.net Timothy K. Brady.

Golob, Bragin & Sassoe, 1990 S. Bundy Dr., Suite 540, Los Angeles, CA, 90025-5245. Phone: (310) 979-0321. Fax: (310) 979-0366.

Bramson, Plutzik, Mahler, Birkhaeuser, LLP, 2125 Oak Grove Rd., Suite 120, Walnut Creek, CA, 94598. Phone: (925) 945-0200. Fax: (925) 945-8792.E-mail: rbramson@bramsonplutzik.com Robert M. Branson, Alan Plutzik.

Brann & Isaacson, Box 3070, 184 Main St., Lewiston, ME, 04243. Phone: (207) 786-3566. Fax: (207) 783-9325.E-mail: gisaacson@brannlaw.com Web Site:www.brannlaw.com George Isaacson.

Brenner, Daniel L., National Cable Telecommunications Association, 25 Massachusetts Ave. N.W., Washington, DC, 20001. Phone: (202) 775-3664. Phone: (202) 775-2300. Fax: (202) 775-3603.E-mail: dbrenner@ncta.com Web Site:www.ncta.com Daniel L. Brenner, sr VP.

Brickfield, Burchette, Ritts & Stone, 1025 Thomas Jefferson St. N.W., Suite 800 West Tower, 8th Fl., Washington, DC, 20007. Phone: (202) 342-0800. Fax: (202) 342-0807. Web Site:www.bbrslaw.com Peter Mattheis.

Brighton , Runyon & Callahan, 45 Main St., Suite 22, Peterborough, NH, 03458-0674. Phone: (603) 924-7276. Fax: (603) 924-9764. L. Phillips Runyon III, sr ptnr.

Brooks, Pierce, McLendon, Humphrey & Leonard, 150 Fayetteville St., Suite 1600, Raleigh, NC, 27602. Phone: (919) 839-0300. Fax: (919) 839-0304.E-mail: whargrove@brookspierce.com Web Site:www.brookspierce.com Wade H. Hargrove, Mark J. Prak, Marcus W. Trathen, Ed Turlington, Kathy Thornton, David Kushner, Coe Ramsey, Charles Coble, Stephen Hartzell-Jordan, Charles Marshall.

Brown, Dean, Wiseman, Lisert, Proctor & Hart, L.L.P., 306 W. 7th St., Suite 200, Fort Worth, TX, 76102. Phone: (817) 332-1391. Fax: (817) 870-2427. Web Site:www.browndean.com Beale Dean.

Frederic E. Brown, Attorney at Law, Box 71718, Fairbanks, AK, 99707. Phone: (907) 452-3452. Fax: (907) 452-3733.E-mail: fbrown@mosquitonet.com Frederic E. Brown.

Brown, Nietert, & Kaufman, Chartered, 1301 Connecticut Ave., Suite 450, Washington, DC, 20036. Phone: (202) 887-0600. Fax: (202) 223-8685.E-mail: david@bnkcomlaw.com David J. Kaufman, Lorretta Tobin.

Brown, Steven Ames, 69 Grand View Ave., San Francisco, CA, 94114-2741. Phone: (415) 647-7700. Fax: (415) 285-3048.E-mail: sabrown@entertainmentlaw.com

Bubar, James S., Attorney at Law, 1776 K St. N.W., Suite 800, Washington, DC, 20006. Phone: (202) 223-2060. Fax: (202) 223-2061.E-mail: jbubar@aol.com Web Site:www.lawyers.com/jamesbubar/ James S. Bubar.

Don Buchwald & Associates, 10 E. 44 St., 7th Fl., New York, NY, 10017-3606. Phone: (212) 867-1200. Fax: (212) 972-3209.E-mail: richard@buchwald.com Web Site:www.buchwald.com

Law Offices of Robert J. Buenzle, 11710 Plaza America Dr., Suite 2000, Reston, VA, 20190. Phone: (703) 430-6751. Fax: (703) 430-4994.E-mail: buenzle@buenzlelaw.com Robert J. Buenzle.

Bullivant, Houser, & Bailey, 300 Pioneer Tower, 888 S.W. 5th Ave., Suite 300, Portland, OR, 97204. Phone: (503) 228-6351. Fax: (503) 295-0915. Web Site:www.bullivant.com

Byelas & Neigher, 1804 Post Rd. E., Westport, CT, 06880. Phone: (203) 259-0599. Fax: (203) 255-2570.

Cades Schutte, 1000 Bishop St., Honolulu, HI, 96813. Phone: (808) 521-9221. Fax: (808) 540-5040.E-mail: jportnoy@cades.com Jeffrey S. Portnoy.

Cahill, Gordon & Reindel LLP, 1990 K St. N.W., Suite 950, Washington, DC, 20006. Phone: (202) 862-8900. Fax: (202) 862-8958.E-mail: mulvid@cgrdc.com
    New YorkNY , 80 Pine St. Phone:

Calfee, Halter & Griswold, 800 Superior Ave., Suite 1400 MacDonald Investment Ctr., Cleveland, OH, 44114. Phone: (216) 622-8200. Fax: (216) 241-0816.E-mail: cbowers@calfee.com Web Site:www.calfee.com

Callister, Nebeker & McCullough, Gateway Tower E., Suite 900, Salt Lake City, UT, 84133. Phone: (801) 530-7300. Fax: (801) 364-9127. Web Site:www.cnmlaw.com Laurie S. Hart, Randall D. Benson, Jennifer Ward.

Cameron & Mittleman LLP, 56 Exchange Terr., Providence, RI, 02903-1766. Phone: (401) 331-5700. Fax: (401) 331-5787. Web Site:www.cm-law.com Richard Mittleman, John W. Wolfe, Esq.

Caridi, Carmella, Esq., Caridi Video Inc., 250 W. 57th, New York, NY, 10107-1722. Phone: (212) 581-2277. Fax: (212) 581-2278.

Carr, Morris & Graeff, 1120 G St. N.W., Suite 930, Washington, DC, 20005. Phone: (202) 789-1000. Fax: (202) 628-3834.

Carter Ledyard & Milburn LLP, 1401 Eye St. N.W., Suite 300, Washington, DC, 20005. Phone: (202) 898-1515. Fax: (202) 898-1521.E-mail: info@clm.com Web Site:www.clm.com Thomas F. Bardo, Mary S. Diemer, Bradley A. Farrell, Peter K. Killough, Timothy J. Fitzgibbon, Jennifer E. Wagman, Robert L. Hoegle.

Peter A. Casciato P.C., 335 Bryant St., Suite 410, San Francisco, CA, 94107. Phone: (415) 291-8661. Fax: (415) 291-8165.E-mail: pacasciato@gmail.com Web Site:www.petercasciato.com Peter A. Casciato, pres.

Cavallo, Robert M., 400 Park Ave., 21st Fl., New York, NY, 10022-4406. Phone: (212) 753-2224. Fax: (212) 753-7113.E-mail: rcavallo@jtjsys.com Robert Cavallo, Esq.

Bryan Cave L.L.P., 700 13th St. N.W., Suite 700, Washington, DC, 20005. Phone: (202) 508-6000. Fax: (202) 508-6200.E-mail: jwilner@bryancave.com John R. Wilner.
    Kansas CityMO , 3500 One Kansas City Pl. Phone:
    New YorkNY , 1290 Ave. of the Americas. Phone:

Edward de R. Cayia, P.A., 432 N.E. 3rd Ave., Fort Lauderdale, FL, 33301. Phone: (954) 765-1400. Fax: (954) 765-1421.

Chadbourne & Parke, 1200 New Hampshire Ave. N.W., Suite 300, Washington, DC, 20036. Phone: (202) 974-5600. Fax: (202) 974-5602.E-mail: info@chadbourne.com Web Site:www.chadbourne.com Dana Frix, Michael Salsburg, David Plandes, Aaron Bartell, Hwan Kim, Kyunghoon Lee.
    Los AngelesCA , 601 S. Figueroa St. Phone:
    New YorkNY , 30 Rockefeller Plaza. Phone:

Chetkof, Gary H., Box 367, 293 Tinker St., Woodstock, NY, 12498. Phone: (845) 679-7600. Fax: (845) 679-5395. Web Site:www.wdst.com

Clark Hill P.L.C., 500 Woodward Ave., Suite 3500, Detroit, MI, 48226-3435. Phone: (313) 965-8300. Fax: (313) 962-4348. Fax: (313) 965-8252.E-mail: dlee@clarkhill.com Web Site:www.clarkhill.com David E. Nims III, Roderick S. Coy, Haran C. Rashes.

Richard N. Clarvit, P.A., 1313 N.E. 125th St., Suite 200, North Miami, FL, 33161. Phone: (305) 893-4135. Fax: (305) 893-4173.E-mail: richsongs@aol.com Richard N. Clarvit.

Clifford, Chance, LLP, 31 West 52 St., New York, NY, 10019-6131. Phone: (212) 878-8000. Fax: (212) 878-8375. Web Site:www.cliffordchance.com

Cohn and Marks LLP, 1920 N St. N.W., Suite 300, Washington, DC, 20036-1622. Phone: (202) 293-3860. Fax: (202) 293-4827.E-mail: richard.helmick@cohnmarks.com Web Site:www.cohnmarks.com Robert B. Jacobi, Lawrence N. Cohn, Richard A. Helmick, J. Brian DeBoice, Ellen Mandell Edmundson, Jerold L. Jacobs, Ronald A. Siegel, Susan V. Sachs.

Colby, Lauren A., Box 113, 10 E. Fourth St., Frederick, MD, 21705-0113. Phone: (301) 663-1086. Fax: (301) 695-8734.E-mail: lac@lcolby.com Web Site:www.lcolby.com Lauren A. Colby.

Cole, Raywid & Braverman, L.L.P., 1919 Pennsylvania Ave. N.W., Suite 200, Washington, DC, 20006. Phone: (202) 659-9750. Fax: (202) 452-0067.E-mail: info@crblaw.com Web Site:www.crblaw.com

Cooke, James R., 2821 Beachwood Cir., Arlington, VA, 22207. Phone: (703) 841-1001. Fax: (703) 841-1004.E-mail: jrcde@comcast.net James R. Cooke.
    HackensackNJ , 2 University Plaza, 2nd Fl. Phone:
    AlbanyNY , 20 Corporate Woods Blvd. Phone:
    HamburgNY , One Grimsby Dr. Phone:
    IthacaNY , 119 E. Seneca St. Phone:
    New YorkNY , 530 Fifth Ave. Phone:
    RochesterNY , 130 E. Main St. Phone:
    SyracuseNY , 300 S. State St., 4th Fl. Phone:

Cooper, White & Cooper, L.L.P., 201 California St., 17th Fl., San Francisco, CA, 94111. Phone: (415) 433-1900. Fax: (415) 433-5530.E-mail: whansell@cwclaw.com Web Site:www.cwclaw.com Walter W. Hansell, Mark P. Schreiber, E. Garth Black, Patrick M. Rosvall, Jed E. Solomon, Jamie Jie-Ming Chou.

Cooter, Mangold, Tompert & Wayson, 5301 Wisconsin Ave N.W., Suite 500, Washington, DC, 20015. Phone: (202) 537-0700. Fax: (202) 364-3664.E-mail: mterry@cootermangold.com

Corberlaw, Box 4656, Panorama City, CA, 91412-0212. Phone: (818) 786-7133.E-mail: corberlaw@aol.com Brian L. Corber, owner.

Law Offices of Bernard R. Corbett, 6312 Barrister Pl., Alexandria, VA, 22307-1214. Phone: (703) 686-1880.

Corn-Revere, Robert, Davis Wright Tremaine LLP, 1919 Pennsylvania Ave. N.W., Washington, DC, 20006. Phone: (202) 973-4225. Phone: (202) 973-4200. Fax: (202) 973-4499.E-mail: bobcornrevere@dwt.com Web Site:www.dwt.com

Couzens, Michael, Box 3642, Oakland, CA, 94609. Phone: (510) 658-7654. Fax: (510) 654-6741. Web Site:www.lptv.tv

Covington & Burling, 1201 Pennsylvania Ave. N.W., Washington, DC, 20004. Phone: (202) 662-6000. Fax: (202) 662-6291.E-mail: mrosentein@cov.com Web Site:www.cov.com Mace Rosenstein, ptnr.

Craven Law Office, 1005 N. 7th St., Springfield, IL, 62702. Phone: (217) 544-1777. Fax: (217) 544-0713.E-mail: presslaw@aol.com Web Site:www.cravenlawoffice.com Donald M. Craven.

Creative Industry Law Group, (Formerly Hasse / Molesky P.C.). 155 Sansome St., Suite 500, San Francisco, CA, 94104. Phone: (415) 433-4380. Fax: (415) 433-6580.E-mail: lhasse@creativelawgroup.com Web Site:www.creativelawgroup.com Lizbeth Hasse, atty.

Crowell & Moring, 1001 Pennsylvania Ave. N.W., Washington, DC, 20004-2595. Phone: (202) 624-2500. Fax: (202) 628-5116.E-mail: sthomas@crowell.com Web Site:www.crowell.com John I. Stewart Jr., Robert M. Halperin, William D. Wallace.

Cuni, Ferguson, Levay & Bergmann, 10655 Springfield Pike, Cincinnati, OH, 45215. Phone: (513) 771-6768. Fax: (513) 771-6781.E-mail: pmusgrove@cfl-law.com Thomas Cuni.

DLA Piper Rudnick Gray Cary US LLP, 1200 19th St. N.W., Suite 700, Washington, DC, 20036. Phone: (202) 861-3913. Fax: (202) 689-7626. Web Site:www.dlapiper.com Mark J. Tauber, E. Ashton Johnston.
    New YorkNY , 1251 Ave. of the Americas. Phone:mmccabe @piperrudnick.com Monica McCabe.

Law Offices of George E. Darby, Box 893010, Mililani, HI, 96789-3010. Phone: (808) 626-1300. Fax: (808) 626-1350.E-mail: darbylaw@teleport-asia.com Web Site:www.teleport-asia.com George Darby.

Davis Wright Tremaine LLP, 1919 Pennsylvania Ave. N.W., Suite 200, Washington, DC, 20006. Phone: (202) 973-4200. Fax: (202) 973-4499. Web Site:www.dwt.com James Blitz, Richard Cys, Laura Handman, Bob Com-Revere.

Davis Wright Tremaine LLP, Phone: (206) 622-3150. Fax: (206) 628-7699. Web Site:www.dwt.com E-mail: seattle@dwt.com
    Los AngelesCA , 1000 Wilshire Blvd, Suite 600. Phone:
    WashingtonDC , 1155 Connecticut Ave. N.W. Phone:
    BoiseID , 999 Main St, Suite 911. Phone:
    PortlandOR , 2300 First Interstate Tower, 1300 S.W. 5th Ave. Phone:

Day & Associates, 1812 Waterfront Plaza, 325 W. Main, Louisville, KY, 40202-4251. Phone: (502) 585-4131. Fax: (502) 581-1210.E-mail: dayandassociates@bellsouth.net Joe Day, owner.

Day, Berry & Howard L.L.P., CityPlace I, Hartford, CT, 06103-3499. Phone: (860) 275-0122. Fax: (860) 275-0343.E-mail: mwelsass@dbh.com Web Site:www.dbh.com Robert P. Knickerbocker Jr., Paul N. Belval, Michael F. Halloran, William A. Hunter, Ross A. Pascal, David A. Swerdloff, Sabino Rodriguez, David T. Doot.

Debevoise & Plimpton LLP, 919 3rd Ave., New York, NY, 10022. Phone: (212) 909-6000. Fax: (212) 909-6836.E-mail: rdbohm@debevoise.com Web Site:www.debevoise.com Richard D. Bohm, Bruce Keller.
    Hong Kong, 13/F Entertainment Bldg, 30 Queen's Rd. Central. Phone:
    London, The International Financial Centre, 25 Old Broad St. Phone:
    Moscow, Bolshoi Palashevsky Per 13/2. Phone:
    Paris, 21 Ave. George V. Phone:
    WashingtonDC , 555 13th St. N.W, Suite 1100-E. Phone:

Decker, Jones, McMackin, McClane, Hall & Bates, 801 Cherry St., Suite 2000, Unit 46, Fort Worth, TX, 76102. Phone: (817) 336-2400. Fax: (817) 332-3043. Web Site:www.deckerjones.com Charles Milliken.

Del, Shaw, Moonves, Tanaka, Finkelstein & Lezcano, 2120 Colorado Ave., Suite 200, Santa Monica, CA, 90404. Phone: (310) 979-7900. Fax: (310) 979-7999.

Denechaud & Denechaud, 1010 Common St., Suite 3010 & 1207, New Orleans, LA, 70112-2483. Phone: (504) 522-4756. Fax: (504) 568-0783.E-mail: cidlaw@bellsouth.net

Dennis Ardi Attorney at Law Professional Corporation, (formerly Ardi Dennis). 340 N. Camden Dr., Third Fl., Beverly Hills, CA, 90210. Phone: (310) 271-6900. Fax: (310) 271-6963.

Robert A. DePont, Attorney at Law, 140 South St., Annapolis, MD, 21401. Phone: (410) 263-0632. Fax: (410) 280-8624.E-mail: robertade@msn.com Web Site:www.robertdeport.com Robert A. DePont.

Devine & Millimet, Box 719, 111 Amherst St., Manchester, NH, 03101. Phone: (603) 669-1000. Fax: (603) 669-8547.E-mail: kmcginley@dm.com Web Site:www.devinemillimet.com

Dewey & LeBoeuf LLP, (formerly LeBoeuf, Lamb, Greene & MacRae). 1101 New York Ave., Suite 1100, Washington, DC, 20005. Phone: (202) 346-8000. Fax: (202) 986-8102. Web Site:www.deweyleboeuf.com Robert A. Auchter, ptnr.

  San FranciscoCA , One Embarcadero Ctr., Suite 400. Phone:

  BostonMA , 260 Franklin St. Phone:

  AlbanyNY , 99 Washington Ave. Phone:

  New YorkNY , 125 W. 55th St. Phone:

DeWitt, Ross & Stevens, 2 E. Mifflin St., Suite 600, Madison, WI, 53703. Phone: (608) 255-8891. Fax: (608) 252-9243.E-mail: info@dewuttriss.com Web Site:www.dewittross.com

Dickstein Shapiro LLP, (Formerly Dickstein Shapiro Morin and Oshinsky LLP). 1825 Eye St., N.W., Washington, DC, 20006-5403. Phone: (202) 420-2200. Fax: (202) 420-2201.E-mail: info@dicksteinshapiro.com Web Site:www.dicksteinshapiro.com

  New YorkNY , 1177 Ave. of the Americas, 41st Fl.

Dieguez, Richard P., 192 Garden St., Suite 2, Roslyn Heights, NY, 11577-1012. Phone: (516) 621-6424. Fax: (516) 621-6508.E-mail: rpdieguez@rpdieguez.com Web Site:www.rpdieguez.com Richard P. Dieguez.

Dorsey & Whitney, L L P, 50 S. 6th St., Suite 1500, Minneapolis, MN, 55402-1498. Phone: (612) 340-2873. Fax: (612) 340-2868. Web Site:www.dorsey.com E-mail: cattanach.robert@dorsey.com Robert E. Cattanach, Karly Baraga, Shannon Heim, MN; Heather Grahame, AK; Tucker Trautman, R. Stephen Hall, CO; Charles Ferguson, CA; Stefan Lopatkiewicz, DC.

  London, Veritas House, 125 Finsbury Pavement. Phone:

  VancouverBC Canada, 666 Burrard St., Suite 1300, Park Pl. Phone:

  AnchorageAK , 1031 West 4th Ave, Suite 600. Phone:

  IrvineCA , 38 Technology Dr. Phone:

  DenverCO , Republic Plaza Bldg., Suite 4400, 370 Seventeenth St. Phone:

  WashingtonDC , 1001 Pennsylvania Ave. N.W, Suite 200 Soutth. Phone:

  MinneapolisMN , 50 S. 6th St. Phone:

  Great FallsMO , 507 Davidson Bldg., 8 Third St. Phone:

  MissoulaMO , 125 Bank St, Suite 600. Phone:

  FargoND , Dakota Ctr., 51 N. Broadway, Suite 402. Phone:

  New YorkNY , 250 Park Ave. Phone:

  Salt Lake CityUT , Wells Fargo Plaza, 170 S. Main St., Suite 925. Phone:

  SeattleWA , US Bank Building Ctr., 1420 5th Ave., Suite 400. Phone:

Dow Lohnes PLLC, 1200 New Hampshire Ave. N.W., Suite 800, Washington, DC, 20036. Phone: (202) 776-2000. Fax: (202) 776-2222. Web Site:www.dowlohnes.com E-mail: info@dowlohnes.com Michael D. Basile, Raymond G. Bender, James M. Burger, Christina H. Burrow, Peter H. Feinberg, John R. Feore Jr., Jeffrey L. Gee, Todd D. Gray, J.G. Harrington, Nam E. Kim, Kevin P. Latek, John S. Logan, Gary S. Lutzker, Melissa A. Marshall, Elizabeth A. McFadden, Margaret L. Miller, Edward J. Palmieri, Scott S. Patrick, Barry S. Persh, Jason E. Rademacher, Christopher J. Redding, Kevin F. Reed, Kenneth D. Salomon, M. Anne Swanson, To-Quyen T. Truong.

  AtlantaGA , One Ravinia Dr, Suite 1600. Phone:

Downs, Bertis E., 170 College Ave., Athens, GA, 30601. Phone: (706) 353-6689. Fax: (706) 546-6069.

Drinker Biddle & Reath L.L.P., 1500 K St. N.W., Suite 1100, Washington, DC, 20005-1209. Phone: (202) 842-8800. Fax: (202) 842-8465.E-mail: joe.edge@dbr.com Web Site:www.dbr.com Joe Dixon Edge, Mark L. Pelesh, Richard M. Singer, Joaquin A. Marquez, Philip J. Mause, Timothy R. Hughes, Tina M. Pidgeon, John R. Przypyszny.

Duane Morris LLP, 30 S. 17th St., Philadelphia, PA, 19103. Phone: (215) 979-1000. Fax: (215) 979-1020. Web Site:www.duanemorris.com Abraham Frumkin, ptnr.

Joseph E. Dunne III, Attorney at Law, P.O. Box 9203, Durango, CO, 81302-9203. Phone: (970) 385-7312. Fax: (970) 385-7343.E-mail: lawman@animas.net Joseph E. Dunne III.

Ross Eatman, Box 102, Bedford, NY, 10506-0102. Phone: (914) 234-4748. Fax: (914) 234-4750.E-mail: emstalent@aol.com Ross Eatman.

Eaton, Peabody, Box 1210, 80 Excahange St., Bangor, ME, 04402-1210. Phone: (207) 947-0111. Fax: (207) 942-3040.E-mail: eaton@eatonpeabody.com Web Site:www.eatonpeabody.com

Eckert, Seamans, Cherin & Mellott, 1515 Market St. 9th Fl., Philadelphia, PA, 19102. Phone: (215) 851-8400. Fax: (215) 851-8383. Web Site:www.escm.com

Edelstein, Laird & Sobel, L.L.P., 9255 Sunset Blvd., Suite 800, Los Angeles, CA, 90069. Phone: (310) 274-6184. Fax: (310) 274-6185.E-mail: laird@elsentlaw.com Web Site:elsentlaw.com

Edwards Angell Palmer & Dodge L.L.P., 111 Huntington Ave., Boston, MA, 02199. Phone: (617) 951-2233. Fax: (888) 325-9120.E-mail: smeredith@eapdlaw.com Web Site:www.eapdlaw.com

Elam & Burke, P.A., 251 E. Front St., Suite 300, Boise, ID, 83702-7311. Phone: (208) 343-5454. Fax: (208) 384-5844.E-mail: mag@elamburke.com

Epstein, Levinsohn, Bodine, Hurwitz & Weinstein, P.C., 1790 Broadway, 10th Fl., New York, NY, 10019. Phone: (212) 262-1000. Fax: (212) 262-5022. Web Site:entlawfirm.com

Ezor, A. Edward, 201 S. Lake Ave., Suite 505, Pasadena, CA, 91101. Phone: (626) 568-8098. Fax: (626) 568-8475.

Faegre & Benson, L.L.P., 801 Grand , Suite 3100, Des Moines, IA, 50309-8002. Phone: (515) 248-9000. Fax: (515) 248-9010.E-mail: mgiudicessi@faegre.com Web Site:www.faegre.com Michael A. Giudicessi.

Farmer, Shirley Stewart, One Lincoln Plaza, Suite 19S, New York, NY, 10023-7149. Phone: (212) 787-6566. Fax: (212) 787-6567.E-mail: stewfar@rcn.com Web Site:www.shirleystewartfarmeronline.com

Farrand, Cooper P.C., 235 Montgomery St., Suite 905, San Francisco, CA, 94104. Phone: (415) 399-0600. Fax: (415) 677-2950. Web Site:www.fcblaw.com Wayne B. Cooper, Stephen R. Farrand.

Federal Communications Comission Public Safety & Homeland Security Bureau, Public Safety & Homeland Security Bureau, 445 12th St., S.W., Washington, DC, 20554. Phone: (202) 418-0680.E-mail: mwilhelm@fcc.gov Web Site:www.fcc.gov Michael J. Wilhelm.

Lindsey S. Feldman, Attorney at Law, 4551 Glencoe Ave., Suite 300, Marina del Rey, CA, 90292. Phone: (310) 823-1600. Fax: (310) 775-8775.E-mail: lfeldman@bergerkahn.com Lindsey S. Feldman.

Ferris & Britton, 401 West A St., Suite 1600, San Diego, CA, 92101. Phone: (619) 233-3131. Fax: (619) 232-9316.E-mail: aferris@ferrisbritton.com Web Site:www.ferrisbritton.com Alfred G. Ferris, Christopher Q. Britton, Lee Austin, Michael Weinstein.

Fine & Associates, P.L.C., 335-337 Decatur St., Vieux Carre, New Orleans, LA, 70130-1023. Phone: (504) 581-5152. Fax: (504) 581-5152, EXT. 124.E-mail: dnfinelaw@aol.com

Fine & Block, 2060 Mt. Paran Rd. N.W., Suite 106, Atlanta, GA, 30327. Phone: (404) 261-6800. Fax: (404) 261-6960. Web Site:www.fineandblock.com A. J. Block Jr.

Finkelstein, Thompson & Loughran, 1050 30th St. N.W., Washington, DC, 20007. Phone: (202) 337-8000. Phone: (866) 592-1960. Fax: (202) 337-8090.E-mail: lks@stllaw.com Web Site:www.ftllaw.com Douglas G. Thompson Jr., L. Kendall Satterfield.

Fleischman & Walsh, L.L.P., 1919 Pennsylvania Ave. N.W., 6th Fl., Washington, DC, 20006. Phone: (202) 939-7900. Fax: (202) 745-0916.E-mail: fw@fw-law.com Web Site:www.fw-law.com

Fletcher, Heald & Hildreth, P.L.C., 1300 N. 17th St., 11th Fl., Arlington, VA, 22209. Phone: (703) 812-0400. Fax: (703) 812-0486.E-mail: office@fhhlaw.com Web Site:www.fhhlaw.com Alan C. Campbell, Harry F. Cole, Anne G. Crump, Vincent J. Curtis Jr., Thomas J. Dougherty Jr., Joseph Di Scipio, Donal J. Evans, Paul J. Feldman, Jeffrey Gee, Kevin Goldberg, Robert M. Gurss, Frank R. Jazzo, Scott M. Johnson, Sheldon J. Krys, Mitchell Lazarus, Stephen Lovelady, Susan Marshall, Harry Martin, Michelle A. McClure, Matthew H. McCormick, Francisco R. Montero, Patrick Murck, Lee G. Petro, Raymond Quianzon, Michael Richards, James P. Riley, Davina S. Sashkin, Richard F. Swift, Peter Tannenwald, Kathleen Victory, Howard M. Weiss, Ronald P. Whitworth.

Foley & Lardner, 150 E. Gilman St., Madison, 53703. Phone: (608) 257-5035. Fax: (608) 258-4258.E-mail: dwalsh@foleylaw.com David G. Walsh.

Forrest, Herbert E., Federal Programs Br., Civil Division, Rm. 7112, U.S. Dept. of Justice, 20 Massachusetts Ave. N.W., Washington, DC, 20530. Phone: (202) 514-2809. Fax: (202) 616-8470.E-mail: herbert:forrest@usdoj.gov Herbert E. Forrest, Trial atty.

Fowler, Measle & Bell, 300 W. Vine St., Suite 600, Lexington, KY, 40507-1660. Phone: (859) 252-6700. Fax: (859) 255-3735.E-mail: fmb@fmb.com Web Site:www.fmblaw.com

Fox & Film Entertainment, 10201 W. Pico Blvd., Los Angeles, CA, 90035. Phone: (310) 369-1000. Fax: (310) 369-3333. Web Site:www.fox.com Gregory Gelfan, Esq., exec VP.

Frost, Mark E., Box 153, Glens Falls, NY, 12801-0153. Phone: (518) 792-1126. Fax: (518) 793-1587. Web Site:mfrost@loneoak.com Mark E. Frost.

Gammon & Grange, P.C., 8280 Greensboro Dr., 7th Fl., McLean, VA, 22102-3807. Phone: (703) 761-5000. Fax: (703) 761-5023.E-mail: awf@gg-law.com Web Site:www.gg-law.com A. Wray Fiitch III, Timothy R. Obitts.

Ganz & Hollinger, 1394 3rd Ave., New York, NY, 10021. Phone: (212) 517-5500. Fax: (212) 772-2720. Web Site:www.ganzhollinger.com

Gardere Wynne Sewell LLP, 1601 Elm St., Thanksgiving Tower, Suite 3000, Dallas, TX, 75201-4761. Phone: (214) 999-3000. Fax: (214) 999-4667.E-mail: mwebb@gardere.com Web Site:www.gardere.com

Gardner, Carton & Douglas, 1301 K St. N.W., Suite 900 E. Tower, Washington, DC, 20005. Phone: (202) 230-5000. Fax: (202) 230-5300. Web Site:www.gcd.com Francis E. Fletcher Jr., M. Scott Johnson, Thomas Dougherty, Laura Mow, Lee Petro, Jennifer Lewis.

Law Offices of Michael R. Gardner, P.C., 1150 Connecticut Ave. N.W., Suite 710, Washington, DC, 20036. Phone: (202) 785-2828. Fax: (202) 785-1504.E-mail: mrgpc@aol.com Michael R. Gardner, mngng ptnr.

Garvey, Schubert & Barer, 100 Wall St., 20th Fl., New York, NY, 10005-3708. Phone: (212) 431-8700. Fax: (206) 464-0125.E-mail: kdavis@gsblaw.com Web Site:www.gsblaw.com

  WashingtonDC , 1000 Potomac St. N.W., 5th Fl. Phone:jking@gsblaw.com Web Site: www.gsblaw. Matthew R. Schneider, D.C. mngng dir. Contact: John Wells King, counsel.

  New YorkNY , 599 Broadway, 10th Fl. Phone:

  PortlandOR , 121 S. W. Morrison St. Phone:

Gibbs & Associates, P.C., 146 Central Park W., Suite 19E, New York, NY, 10023. Phone: (212) 787-2828. Fax: (212) 787-2886.E-mail: bhg1cg2@aol.com Bud H. Gibbs.

Gibson, Dunn & Crutcher, 333 S. Grand Ave., Suite 4600, Los Angeles, CA, 90071-3197. Phone: (213) 229-7000. Fax: (213) 229-7520.E-mail: agravit@gibsondunn.com Web Site:www.gdclaw.com

  WashingtonDC , 1050 Connecticut Ave. N.W, Suite 900. Phone:

Gold & Pyle, 526 Superior Ave. E., 1140 Leader Bldg., Cleveland, OH, 44114. Phone: (216) 696-6122. Fax: (216) 696-3214.

Goldberg, Godles, Wiener & Wright, 1229 19th St. N.W., Washington, DC, 20036. Phone: (202) 429-4900. Fax: (202) 429-4912.E-mail: general@g2w2.com Web Site:g2w2.com Henry Goldberg, Joseph A. Godles, Jonathan L. Wiener, Laura Stefani.

Golden & Golden, P.C., 10627 Jones St., Suite 101B, Fairfax, VA, 22030. Phone: (703) 691-0117. Fax: (703) 691-1367.E-mail: k8los@aol.com Web Site:www.gglawva.com Richard A. Golden.

Glenn A. Goldstein, Attorney at Law, 1650 Market St., Suite 4900, Philadelphia, PA, 19103. Phone: (215) 981-5922. Fax: (215) 981-5959.E-mail: glenn802@aol.com Glenn A. Goldstein, Esq.

Goodkind, Labaton, Rudoff & Sucharow, L.L.P., 100 Park Ave., New York, NY, 10017. Phone: (212) 907-0700. Fax: (212) 818-0477.E-mail: rrosenblum@labton.com Web Site:www.glrs.com

Law Offices of Jeffrey L. Graubart, 350 W. Colorado Blvd., Suite 200, Pasadena, CA, 91105. Phone: (626) 304-2800.E-mail: graubart@gte.net Web Site:www.lawyers.com Jeffrey L. Graubart.

Gray & Robinson, 301 E. Pine St., Suite 1400, Orlando, FL, 32802. Phone: (407) 843-8880. Fax: (407) 244-5690.E-mail: llee@gray-robinson.com Web Site:www.gray-robinson.com J. Charles Gray, Richard M. Robinson, founding ptnrs.

Greensfelder, Hemker & Gale, P.C., 10 S. Broadway, Suite 2000, St. Louis, MO, 63102-1774. Phone: (314) 516-2662. Fax: (314) 345-5499.E-mail: mlw@greensfelder.com Web Site:www.greensfelder.com Sheldon K. Stock, Mary Ann L. Wymore, Jason L. Ross.

Greiter, Pegger, Kofler & Partner, Maria Theresien-Strasse 24, A-6020, Innsbruck Phone: 43 512-57-1811. Fax: 43 512-5849-25. Fax: 43 512-5711-52.

Groveman, Amy S., Cablevision Systems Corp., 111 Stewart Ave., Bethpage, NY, 11714. Phone: (516) 803-2300. Fax: (516) 803-2575.E-mail: agrovema@cablevision.com Web Site:www.cablevision.com

Grubb, Jay G., 12 Forrest Edge Dr., Titusville, NJ, 08560. Phone: (410) 329-2108. Fax: (410) 329-2109. Jay G. Grubb.

Grubman, Indursky & Shire, P.C., 152 W. 57th St., 31st Fl., New York, NY, 10019. Phone: (212) 554-0400. Fax: (212) 554-0444.

Gullett, Sanford, Robinson & Martin, 315 Deadrick St., Suite 1100, Nashville, TN, 37238. Phone: (615) 244-4994. Fax: (615) 256-6339. John D. Lentz.

Hall, Dickler, Kent, Goldstein & Wood, 909 3rd Ave., 27th Fl., New York, NY, 10022. Phone: (212) 339-5409. Web Site:www.halldickler.com Jeffrey S. Edelstein.

Handman, Stanley H., 10160 Cielo Dr., Beverly Hills, CA, 90210-2037. Phone: (310) 276-7503. Fax: (310) 276-1559.E-mail: stanhandman@yahoo.com Web Site:www.fleischerstudios.com Stanley H. Handman.

Hansen, Jacobson, Teller, Hoberman, Newman, Warren & Sloan, L.L.P., 450 N. Roxbury Dr., 8th Fl., Beverly Hills, CA, 90210-4222. Phone: (310) 248-3105/248-3101. Fax: (310) 275-2329/550-5209.E-mail: sdecker@hjth.com Ken Richman, mng ptr; Gretchen Bruggeman, John Farrell, Tom Hanson, Jason Hendler, Tom Hoberman, Craig Jacobson, Tom McGuire, Jeanne Newman, Jason Sloane, Don Steele, Walter Teller, Steve Warren.

Law Offices of Douglas W. Harold Jr., 109 Southdown Cir., Stephens City, VA, 22655. Phone: (540) 869-0040. Fax: (540) 869-0041.E-mail: douglasharoldjr@yahoo.com Douglas W. Harold Jr.

Harris, Wiltshire & Grannis, L.L.P., 1200 Eighteenth St. N.W., Washington, DC, 20036. Phone: (202) 730-1300. Fax: (202) 730-1301.E-mail: sharris@harris Web Site:www.harriswiltshire.com Mark A. Grannis, William M. Wiltshire, Kent D. Bressie, Jonathan B. Mirsky, John T. Nakahata.

James A. Hatcher, Cox Communications Inc., 1400 Lake Hearn Dr. N.E., Atlanta, GA, 30319. Phone: (404) 843-5000. Fax: (404) 843-5845. James Hatcher, sr VP/gen counsel.

Law Offices of Richard J. Hayes, Box 200, Lincolnville, ME, 04849. Phone: (207) 336-3333. Fax: (202) 478-0048.E-mail: fcclaw@rjhayes.com Web Site:www.rjhayes.com Richard J. Hayes, Jr.

Head, Johnson & Kachigian, 228 W. 17th Pl., Tulsa, OK, 74119. Phone: (918) 587-2000. Fax: (918) 584-1718.E-mail: hjk@law.com Web Site:www.hjklaw.com Mark G. Kachigian.

Hearn, Edward R. A Professional Law Corporation, (formerly Hearn, Edward R). 84 W. Santa Clara St., Suite 660, San Jose, CA, 95113. Phone: (408) 998-3400. Fax: (408) 297-1104.E-mail: nedhearnml@aol.com Web Site:www.internetmedialaw.com Edward R. Hearn.

John Hearne, 715 Broadway, Suite 320, Santa Monica, CA, 90401. Phone: (310) 451-4430. Fax: (310) 451-1423. John Hearne, owner.

Hebert, Spencer, Cusimano & Fry, LLP, 701 Laurel St., Baton Rouge, LA, 70802. Phone: (225) 344-2601. Fax: (225) 387-1714.E-mail: clsatty@aol.com Charles L. Spencer.

Heller Ehrman LLP, 275 Middlefield Rd., Menlo Park, CA, 94025. Phone: (650) 324-7000. Fax: (650) 324-0638. Web Site:www.hellerehrman.com Daniel L. Appelman.

Hendrickson, Thomas, 203 Alderwood Dr., N. Potomac, MD, 20878. Phone: (301) 519-0085.E-mail: thomashendrickson@yahoo.com

Hewitt Katz Stepp and Wright Attorney at Law, 945 E. Paces Ferry Rd., Resurgens Plaza Ste. 2610, Atlanta, GA, 30326. Phone: (404) 240-0400. Fax: (404) 240-0401.E-mail: khewitt@atllawofc.com Web Site:www.robertnkatz.com

Hill & Welch, 1330 New Hampshire Ave. N.W., Suite 113, Washington, DC, 20036. Phone: (202) 775-0070. Fax: (202) 775-9026.E-mail: welchlaw@earthlink.net

Hinshaw & Culbertson, 333 S. 7th St., Suite 2000, Minneapolis, MN, 55402. Phone: (612) 333-3434. Fax: (612) 334-8888. Web Site:www.hinshawculbertson.com David Mylrea, ptnr.

Hogan & Hartson, Columbia Sq., 555 13th St. N.W., Washington, DC, 20004. Phone: (202) 637-5600. Fax: (202) 637-5910. Web Site:www.hhlaw.com Ptnrs: Michele Farquhar (co-chair), Peter Rohrbach (co-chair), Daniel Brener, Zenas Choi, Ari Fitzgerald, Gardner Gillespie, Richard Horan, Steven Kaufman, Marissa Repp, DAvid Saylor, John "DAve" Thomas, Joel Winnik, Karis Hasting, David Matin, Tarah Grant. .

    1040 Brussels, Ave. Des Arts 41. Phone:

    Budapest, Szabadsag ter 7, Bank Center, Granite Tower , 9th Floor. Phone:

    London, 21 Garlick Hill. Phone:

    Moscow, Bldg. 3, 33/2 Usacheva Street. Phone:

    Paris, 12, rue de la Paix. Phone:

    Prague 1. Hogan & Hogan Praha, Opletalova 37. Phone:

    Warsaw, Hogan & Hartson, Sp ZO.O., Atrium Tower, Al. Jana Pawla II 25. Phone:

    Los AngelesCA , Biltmore Tower, 500 S. Grand Ave., Suite 1900. Phone:

    Newport BeachCA , 46-75 MacArthur, Suite 670. Phone:

    Colorado SpringsCO , 2 N. Cascade Ave, Suite 1300. Phone:

    DenverCO , One Tabor Ctr., 1200 17th St., Suite 1500. Phone:

    BaltimoreMD , 111 S. Calvert St. Phone:

    McLeanVA , 8300 Greensboro Dr. Phone:

Holland & Knight LLC, 131 S. Dearborn St., 30 Fl., Chicago, IL, 60603. Phone: (312) 263-3600. Fax: (312) 578-6666. Web Site:www.hklaw.com

Holland & Knight LLP, 2099 Pennsylvania Ave. N.W., Suite 100, Washington, DC, 20006. Phone: (202) 955-3000. Fax: (202) 955-5564. Web Site:www.hklaw.com Janet R. Studley, Edward W. Hummers Jr., Marvin Rosenberg, Charles Naftalin, Peter Connolly, George Wheeler, Alan Naftalin, Xiaohau Zhao.

Law Office of David Honig, 3636 16th St. N.W., Suite B-366, Washington, DC, 20010. Phone: (202) 332-7005. Fax: (202) 332-7511.E-mail: dhonig@crosslink.net David Honig.

Horgan, Michael Owen, 407 E. Robert Toomb Ave., Washington, GA, 30673. Phone: (706) 678-1987. Fax: (706) 678-1999.E-mail: mhorgan@nu-z.net Michael O. Horgan.

Inghram & Inghram, 529 Hampshire St., Suite 409, Bank of America Bldg., Quincy, IL, 62301. Phone: (217) 222-7420. Fax: (217) 222-1653.E-mail: inghram@inghramlaw.com John T. Inghram IV, James R. Inghram.

Irwin, Campbell & Tannenwald, P.C., 1730 Rhode Island Ave. N.W. #200, Washington, DC, 20036-3120. Phone: (202) 728-0400. Fax: (202) 728-0354. Web Site:www.ictpc.com Peter Tannenwald, Alan C. Campbell, David A. Irwin, Richard F. wift, Kevin M. Walsh, Michelle A. McClure,

Nathaniel J. Hardy, Jared B. Weaver.

Isaacman, Kaufman & Painter, 8484 Wilshire Blvd., Suite 850, Beverly Hills, CA, 90211. Phone: (323) 782-7700. Fax: (323) 782-7744.E-mail: zucker@ikplaw.com Web Site:www.ikplaw.com Andrew S. Zucker.

Jackson & Campbell, P.C., 1120 20th St. N.W., Suite 300-S, Washington, DC, 20036. Phone: (202) 457-1600. Fax: (202) 457-1678.E-mail: jmatteo@jackscamp.com Web Site:www.jacksoncampbell.com James R. Michal, Esq.

Jacobs & Associates, 11 North Washington St., Suite 640, Rockville, MD, 20850. Phone: (301) 251-5470. Fax: (301) 251-5481.E-mail: jacobs@internet-law-firm.com

Jeffer, Mangels, Butler & Marmaro LLP, 1900 Ave. of the Stars, 7th Fl., Los Angeles, CA, 90067-5010. Phone: (310) 203-8080. Fax: (310) 203-0567. Web Site:www.jmbm.com

Jenner & Block, 601 13th St. N.W., 12th Fl., Washington, DC, 20005. Phone: (202) 639-6000. Fax: (202) 639-6066.E-mail: mstull@jenner.com Web Site:www.jenner.com Donald B. Verrilli Jr., Mark D. Schneider, Paul M. Smith, Jerome Epstein.

Johnson, Andrea L., 225 Cedar St., California Western School of Law, San Diego, CA, 92101. Phone: (800) 255-4252, EXT. 1474. Fax: (619) 696-9999.E-mail: ajohnson@cwsl.edu Web Site:www.cwsl.edu

Johnston & Buchan LLP, 275 Slater St., Suite 1700, Ottawa, ON, K1P 5H9. Canada. Phone: (613) 236-3882. Fax: (613) 230-6423/230-6762. Fax: (613) 230-6762. Web Site:www.johnstonbuchan.com

Jones, Day, 51 Louisiana Ave. N. W., Washington, DC, 20001. Phone: (202) 879-3939. Fax: (202) 626-1700. Web Site:www.jonesday.com Stephen Brogan, ptnr.

Paul T. Julian Esq., (formerly Julian & Associates). 1038 N. LaSalle Dr., Chicago, IL, 60610. Phone: (312) 266-1500. Fax: (312) 337-1972.E-mail: pjulian302@aol.com

Kass, Mitek & Kass, 1050 17th St. N.W., Suite 1100, Washington, DC, 20036. Phone: (202) 659-6500. Fax: (202) 293-2608. Web Site:www.kmklawyers.com

Katten Muchin Rosenman LLP, 1025 Thomas Jefferson St. NW, 700 East Lobby, Washington, DC, 20007. Phone: (202) 625-3500. Fax: (202) 298-7570.E-mail: howard.braun@kattenlaw.com Web Site:www.kattenlaw.com Lee W. Shubert, Shelley Sadowsky, Howard Braun.

Kay, Sheldon L., 30445 Northwestern Hwy., Suite 320, Farmington Hills, MI, 48334. Phone: (248) 539-1111. Fax: (248) 539-1114.E-mail: sllaw@hotmail.com Web Site:www.myspace.com/rnrlawyershow

Kaye, Scholer, L.L.P., 901 15th St. N.W., Washington, DC, 20005. Phone: (202) 682-3500. Fax: (202) 682-3580.E-mail: jshrinsky@kayescholer.com Web Site:kayescholer.com Jason L. Shrinsky, Esq.; Bruce A. Eisen, Esq.; Allan G. Moskowitz, Esq.

Keller & Heckman, 1001 G St. N.W., Suite 500 W, Washington, DC, 20001. Phone: (202) 434-4100. Fax: (202) 434-4646. Web Site:www.khlaw.com Wayne V. Black, Martin W. Bercovici, Michael F. Morrone, John B. Richards, C. Douglas Jarrett, Richard J. Leighton, Richard F. Mann, ptnrs.

Kelley, Drye Collier Shannon, 3050 K St. N.W., Washington, DC, 20007. Phone: (202) 342-8400. Fax: (202) 342-8451. Web Site:www.colliershannon.com

Law Office of Dennis J. Kelly, Box 41177, Washington, DC, 20018. Phone: (202) 293-2300. Phone: 888-FCC-LAW-1. Fax: (410) 626-1794.E-mail: dkellyfcclaw1@comcast.net Dennis J. Kelly.

Law Office of Edward M. Kelman, 100 Park Ave., 20th Fl., New York, NY, 10017. Phone: (212) 371-9490. Fax: (212) 750-1356.E-mail: emknyc@aol.com

Kenkel & Associates, 9908 Sorrel Ave., Potomac, MD, 20854. Phone: (301) 299-6260. Fax: (301) 299-0720.E-mail: jngkenkel@aol.com John B. Kenkel.

Kilpatrick & Stockton L.L.P., 1100 Peach Tree St., Suite 2800, Atlanta, GA, 30309. Phone: (404) 815-6500. Phone: (404) 745-2492. Fax: (404) 815-6555.E-mail: rbuttram@kilpatrickstockton.com Web Site:www.kilpatrickstockton.com

King & Ballow, 1100 Union St. Plaza, 315 Union St., Nashville, TN, 37201. Phone: (615) 259-3456. Fax: (615) 254-7907.E-mail: lawfirm@kingballow.com Web Site:www.kingballow.com Douglas R. Pierce, Mark E. Hunt.

Kirkpatrick & Lockhart L.L.P., 75 State St., Boston, MA, 02109. Phone: (617) 261-3100. Phone: (617) 951-9230. Fax: (617) 261-3175.E-mail: bmorrissey@klng.com Web Site:www.klng.com Stephen L. Palmer, Esq.

Kleinberg, Lopez, Lange, Cuddy, Edel & Klein L.L.P., 2049 Century Park E., Suite 3180, Los Angeles, CA, 90067-3205. Phone: (310) 286-9696. Fax: (310) 277-7145. Fax: (310) 286-6445.E-mail: lawyers@kllcek.com Web Site:www.kllcek.com Kenneth Kleinberg.

Kletter, Matthew L., 183 Madison Ave., Penthouse, New York, NY, 10016. Phone: (212) 726-0090.

Klitzman, Stephen, Office of Legislative & Inter-Govt Affairs. U.S. Federal Communications Commission, 445 12th St., SW, Office of General Counsel, Washington, DC, 20554. Phone: (202) 418-1763. Fax: (202) 418-7540.E-mail: steve.klitzma@fcc.gov Stephen Klitzman.

Koerner & Olender, P.C., 11913 Grey Hollow Ct., North Bethesda, MD, 20852. Phone: (301) 468-3336. Fax: (301) 468-3343.E-mail: bkofcclaw@erols.com James A. Koerner, Robert L. Olender.

Kraditor & Haber, P.C., 1212 Ave. of the Americas 3rd Fl., New York, NY, 10036. Phone: (212) 768-2100. Fax: (212) 768-2450. Web Site:www.fcc.gov

Lang, Richert & Patch, 5200 N. Palm Ave., Suite 401, Fresno, CA, 93704-2225. Phone: (559) 228-6700. Fax: (559) 228-6727. Web Site:www.www.lrplaw.net

Latham & Watkins, 555 11th St. N.W., Suite 1000, Washington, DC, 20004. Phone: (202) 637-2200. Fax: (202) 637-2201.E-mail: eric.bernthal@lw.com Web Site:www.lw.com Eric Bernthal, Gary Epstein, Jim Barker, Teresa Baer, Kevin Boyle, Kevin Boyle, Karen Brinkmaner, Matt Brill, Ray Grochowski, John Janka, James Hanna, Richard Cameron, James Rogers, Brian Weimer, David Burns, Nia Mathis, Jeff Marks, Stefanie Alfonso-Frank, Rick Bress, Joe Sullivan, David Dantzic, Jessica Gibson, Elizabeth Park.

Law Office of Dan J. Alpert, 2120 N. 21st Rd., Arlington, VA, 22201. Phone: (703) 243-8690. Fax: (703) 243-8692.E-mail: dja@commlaw.tv Web Site:www.commlaw.tv Dan J. Alpert; Washington, DC: (202) 371-7200 John C. Quale, Antoinette Cook Bush, Kenneth M. Kaufman, Lawrence Roberts, Ivan A. Schlager, Richard A. Hindman, Brian D. Weimer, David H. Pawlik, Margaret E. Lancaster, John M. Beahn, Malcolm J. Tuesley, Jared S. Sher; Chicago Office: Warren Lavey, David S. Prohofsky.

Law Offices of Henry W. Root, P.C., 1541 Ocean Ave., Suite 200, Santa Monica, CA, 90401-2104. Phone: (310) 395-6800. Fax: (310) 393-7777.E-mail: henry@grrlaw.com Henry W. Root Esq., Bruce Grakal Esq., Richard Rosenthal Esq.

Lawrence & Eason, 14000 Quail Spgs Pkwy, Suite 200, Oklahoma City, OK, 73134-2638. Phone: (405) 841-6000. Fax: (405) 841-6006.

Leibowitz & Associates, P.A., One S.E. 3rd Ave., Suite 1450, Miami, FL, 33131-1715. Phone: (305) 530-1322. Fax: (305) 530-9417.E-mail: mleibowitz@broadlaw.com Matthew L. Leibowitz, Joseph A. Belisle, Ila L. Feld, Nicki J. Fernandez.

Leopold, Petrich & Smith, 2049 Century Park E., Suite 3110, Los Angeles, CA, 90067-3274. Phone: (310) 277-3333. Fax: (310) 277-7444.E-mail: dmayeda@lpsla.com Web Site:www.lpsla.com Daniel M. Mayeda.

Lerman Senter PLLC, (Formerly Leventhal Senter & Lerman PLLC). 2000 K St. N.W., Suite 600, Washington, DC, 20006-1809. Phone: (202) 429-8970. Fax: (202) 293-7783.E-mail: slerman@lermansenter.com Web Site:www.lermansenter.com John W. Bagwell, Stephen D. Baruch, Philip A. Bonomo, Sally A. Buckman, Deborah R. Coleman, Dennis P. Corbett, Linda D. Feldmann, Katrina C. Glober, Peter M. Gould, Rebecca L. Hinyard, David S. Keir, Erin E. Kim, Steven A. Lerman, Louis J. Levy, Brian M. Madden, Nancy A. Ory, F. Scott Pippin, John D. Poutasse, Joshua A. Rickel, Jessica L. Schneider, Meredith S. Senter Jr., Howard A. Topel S. Jenell Trigg, Nancy Wolf.

Lewis, Lewis & Ferraro, 28 N. Main St., West Hartford, CT, 06107-1928. Phone: (860) 521-1500. Fax: (860) 521-4500.E-mail: attorney@lewislewisferraro.com

Law Firm of Rosalind Lichter, Tribeca Film Ctr., 375 Greenwich St., New York, NY, 10013. Phone: (212) 941-4075. Fax: (212) 941-4076. Rosalind Lichter.

Loeb & Loeb L.L.P., 345 Park Ave., New York, NY, 10154. Phone: (212) 407-4000. Phone: (212) 407-4987. Fax: (212) 407-4990.E-mail: jmanton@loeb.com Web Site:www.loeb.com Donald L. B. Baraf, Marc Chamlin.
  Los AngelesCA , 10100 Santa Monica Blvd. Phone:
  Los AngelesCA , 1000 Wilshire Blvd. Phone:

Loftus & Borgstrom, One Court St., Suite 320, Lebanon, NH, 03766. Phone: (603) 448-6420. Fax: (603) 448-6147.E-mail: wrlpc@valley.net William R. Loftus, Esq.; Karen J. Borgstrom, Esq.

Lommen Abdo, Cole, King & Stageberg, P. A., 2000 IDS Ctr., 80 S. 8th St., Minneapolis, MN, 55402. Phone: (612) 339-8131. Fax: (612) 339-8064. Web Site:www.Lommen

London, Michael B., 10452 Oletha Ln., Los Angeles, CA, 90077-2420. Phone: (310) 474-0577. Fax: (310) 474-5413.

Lowndes, Drosdick, Doster, Kantor & Reed, P.A., Box 2809, 215 N. Eola Dr., Orlando, FL, 32801. Phone: (407) 843-4600. Fax: (407) 843-4444.E-mail: karen.plunkett @lowndes-law.com Julia L. Frey, Louis Frey Jr.

Lukas, Nace, Gutierrez & Sachs Chartered, 1650 Tysons Blvd., Suite 1500, McLean, VA, 22102. Phone: (703) 584-8678. Fax: (703) 584-8696.E-mail: rlucas@fcclaw.com Web Site:www.fcclaw.com Russell D. Lukas, David L. Nace, Thomas Gutierrez, Elizabeth R. Sachs.

Law Offices of Patrice Lyons, Chartered, 910 17th St. N.W., Suite 800, Washington, DC, 20006. Phone: (202) 293-5990. Fax: (202) 293-5121.E-mail: palyons@bellatlantic.net Patrice Lyons.

David L. Maddox & Associates, P.C., 1207 17 Ave. S., Suite 300, Nashville, TN, 37212. Phone: (615) 329-0086. Fax: (615) 320-7150.E-mail: david@dmaddox.com

Madigan & Getzendanner, 30 N. LaSalle St., Suite 3906, Chicago, IL, 60602. Phone: (312) 346-4321. Fax: (312) 346-5619. Michael J. Madigan, Vincent J. Getzendanner.

Magee Law Firm, PLLC, 6845 Elm St., Suite 205, McLean, VA, 22101. Phone: (703) 356-7500. Fax: (703) 356-6863.E-mail: jmagee@mageelawfirm.com James E. Magee, Kristie S. Hassett, Jennifer A. Newberry.

Margolin Law Firm, 5502 High Dr., Mission Hills, KS, 66208-1121. Phone: (816) 753-3838. James S. Margolin.

The Marshall Firm, 271 Madison Ave., 20th Fl., New York, NY, 10016. Phone: (212) 382-2044. Fax: (212) 382-3610.E-mail: tmf@marshallfirm.com Paul Marshall.

Donald E. Martin, P.C., Box 8433, Falls Church, VA, 22041. Phone: (703) 642-2344. Fax: (703) 642-2357.E-mail: dempc@prodigy.net Donald E. Martin.

McDonald, Hopkins, L.P.A., 2100 Bank One Ctr., 600 Superior Ave. E., Cleveland, OH, 44114-2653. Phone: (216) 348-5400. Fax: (216) 348-5474.E-mail: attorneys@mhbh.com Web Site:www.mhbh.com Brian M. O'Neil.

Mary A. McReynolds, P.C., 1050 Connecticut Ave. N.W., Suite 1000, Washington, DC, 20036. Phone: (202) 429-1770. Fax: (202) 772-3101. Mary A. McReynolds, Esq.

Mensch, Linda Susan, 200 S. Michigan Ave., Suite 1240, Chicago, IL, 60604. Phone: (312) 922-2910. Fax: (312) 922-1865.E-mail: menschlaw@yahoo.com Web Site:menschlaw@yahoo.com Linda Mensch.

Messerli & Kramer, 150 S. 5th St., Suite 1800, Minneapolis, MN, 55402-4246. Phone: (612) 672-3600. Fax: (612) 672-3777.E-mail: djohnson@mandklaw.com Web Site:www.messerlikramer.com William F. Messerli.

Meyers & Meyers, 360 E. Randolph St., Suite 3104, Chicago, IL, 60601. Phone: (312) 616-1500. Fax: (312) 616-1737.E-mail: peterarbme@aol.com Web Site:www.petermeyers.net Therese Zaller, Peter R. Meyers, Irving Meyers.

Midlen Law Center, 7618 Lynn Dr., Chevy Chase, MD, 20815-6043. Phone: (301) 656-3000. Fax: (301) 656-8262.E-mail: john@midlen.com Web Site:www.midlen.com John H. Midlen Jr.

Miller and Neely, P.C., (Miller & Neely, P.C.). 6900 Wisconsin Ave., Suite 704, Bethesda, MD, 20815. Phone: (301) 986-4160. Fax: (301) 986-4162.E-mail: mandnlaw@gmail.com Jerrold D. Miller, John S. Neely.

Miller & Van Eaton, P.L.L.C., 1155 Connecticut Ave. N.W., Suite 1000, Washington, DC, 20036. Phone: (202) 785-0600. Fax: (202) 785-1234.E-mail: info2@millervaneaton.com Web Site:www.millervaneaton.com Matthew C. Ames, Kenneth A. Brunetti, Marc L. Frischkorn, James R. Hobson, Gail A. Karish, Gerald Lavery Lederer, Wiliam R. Malone, Nicholas P. Miller, Matthew K. Schettenhelm, Joseph Van Eaton.

Miller, Canfield, Paddock & Stone, P.L.C., 150 W Jefferson Ave., Suite 2500, Detroit, MI, 48226. Phone: (313) 963-6420. Fax: (313) 496-7500.E-mail: houser@millercanfield.com Web Site:www.millercanfield.com Tillman L. Lay.

Ice Miller LLP, One American Sq., Suite 2900, Indianapolis, IN, 46282-0002. Phone: (317) 236-2100. Fax: (317) 236-2219.E-mail: info@icemiller.com Web Site:www.icemiller.com Thomas H. Ristine.

Miller, Balis and O'Neil, 1140 19th St. N.W., Suite 700, Washington, DC, 20006. Phone: (202) 296-2960. Fax: (202) 296-0166.E-mail: mgrossman@mbolaw.com Milton J. Grossman.

Mintz, Levin, Cohn, Ferris, Glovsky & Popeo, P.C., 701 Pennsylvania Ave. N.W., Suite 900, Washington, DC, 20004. Phone: (202) 434-7300. Fax: (202) 434-7400. Web Site:www.mintzlevin.com Charles D. Ferris, Frank W. Lloyd, Bruce D. Sokler, Howard J. Symons.
  BostonMA , One Financial Center. Phone:

Mirowski & Associates, 757 W. Ivy St., San Diego, CA, 92101. Phone: (619) 702-5300. Fax: (619) 702-4666.E-mail: pmirowski@mirlaw.com Web Site:www.mirlaw.com Paul J. Mirowski.

Mitchell, Charles D., 1601 N. Frontage Rd., Suite F, Vicksburg, MS, 39180. Phone: (601) 636-4545, EXT. 123. Fax: (601) 634-0897.E-mail: fysadm@vicksburgpost.com Web Site:www.vicksburgpost.com Charles D. Mitchell.

Mitchell Silberberg & Knupp, 11377 W. Olympic Blvd., Los Angeles, CA, 90064. Phone: (310) 312-2000. Fax: (310) 312-3100.E-mail: info@msk.com Web Site:www.msk.com

Mizrack & Gantt, Suite 850, 555 11th St. N.W., Washington, DC, 20004-1304. Phone: (202) 628-1717. Fax: (202) 628-1919.E-mail: jbgantt@att.global.net

Morris, Rathnau & De La Rosa, 39 La Salle St., Fl 500, Chicago, IL, 60603. Phone: (312) 606-0876. Fax: (312) 606-0879.E-mail: mdlrlawchicago@aol.com Joseph A. Morris, ptnr.

Morrison & Foerster L.L.P., 2000 Pennsylvania Ave. N.W., Suite 5500, Washington, DC, 20006. Phone: (202) 887-1500. Fax: (202) 887-0763. Web Site:www.mofo.com Cheryl A.Tritt.

Moss & Barnett, A Professional Assn, 4800 Wells Fargo Ctr., 90 S. 7th St., Minneapolis, MN, 55402-4129. Phone: (612) 877-5000. Fax: (612) 877-5999.E-mail: weinstockd @moss-barnett.com Web Site:www.moss-barnett.com Brian T. Grogan, Esq.

Todd W. Musburger, Ltd., 142 E. Ontario St., Suite 500, Chicago, IL, 60611. Phone: (312) 664-2600. Fax: (312) 664-4137.E-mail: todd@musburger.com Todd W. Musburger, pres.

Myman, Abell, Fineman, Greenspan & Light, 11601 Wilshire Blvd., Suite 2200, Los Angeles, CA, 90025. Phone: (310) 820-7717. Fax: (310) 207-2680. Robert M. Myman.

NBC Universal Television Group, 100 Universal City Plaza, Bldg #1320, Suite 3E, Universal City, CA, 91608. Phone: (818) 777-6968. Fax: (818) 866-7597.E-mail: tracy.rich@nbcuni.com

Nadel, Mark S., U.S. Federal Communications Commission, 445 12th St. S.W., Rm. 5B 551, Washington, DC, 20554. Phone: (202) 418-7385. Fax: (202) 418-7361.E-mail: mnadel@fcc.gov Web Site:www.fcc.gov

Naphtali, Ashirah S., 130-33 217 St., Suite B, Laurelton, NY, 11413-1230. Phone: (718) 481-7236. Fax: (718) 481-7236.E-mail: anaphml@aol.com Ashirah S. Naphtali, Esq., MBA.

National Exchange Carrier Association, N.E.C.A., 80 S. Jefferson Rd., Whippany, NJ, 07981-1009. Phone: (973) 884-8000. Phone: (800) 228-8597. Fax: (973) 884-8469. Web Site:www.neca.org

Nemeth, Valerie A., Attorney at Law, 191 Calle Magadalena, Suite 270, Encinitas, CA, 92024-3750. Phone: (760) 944-4130. Phone: (310) 471-7648 (L.A.). Fax: (760) 944-3325.E-mail: vanemeth@entlawyer.com Web Site:www.entlawyer.com Valerie Nemeth.

Neuland, Nordberg, Andrews & Whitney, 22502 Avenida Empresa, Rancho Santa Margarita, CA, 92688. Phone: (949) 766-4700. Fax: (949) 766-4712.E-mail: dottieneuland@nnawlaw.com Web Site:www.nnalaw.com

Nathan M. Nickolaus, 320 E. McCarthy St., Jefferson City, MO, 65101-3115. Phone: (573) 634-6313. Fax: (573) 634-6504.E-mail: nnickolaus@jeffcity.mo.org Web Site:nnickolaus@jeffcitymo.org

Nilsson, Kent R., U.S. Federal Communications Commission, 445 12th St. S.W., Washington, DC, 20554. Phone: (202) 418-2478. Fax: (202) 418-2345. Web Site:www.fcc.gov

Nixon Peabody L.L.P., 401 9th St. NW, Suite 900, Washington, DC, 20004. Phone: (202) 585-8000. Fax: (202) 585-8080.E-mail: aprilsteffan@nixonpeabody.com Web Site:www.nixonpeabody.com Veronica M. Ahern, William S. Andrews.

RochesterNY , Box 1051, Clinton Sq. Phone:

Nixon, Wilbert E. Jr., Wireless Telecommunications Bureau, Police & Rules Branch. Federal Communications Commission, 445 12th St. S.W. Rm. 4-A207, Washington, DC, 20554. Phone: (202) 418-7240. Fax: (202) 418-7447.E-mail: wnixon@fcc.gov Web Site:www.fcc.gov

Nossaman, L.L.P., 50 California St., 34th Fl., San Francisco, CA, 94111. Phone: (415) 398-3600. Fax: (415) 398-2438.E-mail: mmattes@nossaman.com Web Site:www.nossaman.com Martin A. Mattes, partner.

OPASTCO, 21 Dupont Cir. N.W., Suite 700, Washington, DC, 20036. Phone: (202) 659-5990. Fax: (202) 659-4619.E-mail: vlf@opastco.org Web Site:www.opastco.org

O'Connell & Aronowitz PC, 54 State St., Albany, NY, 12207. Phone: (518) 462-5601. Fax: (518) 462-2670.E-mail: o'connell@albany.net Web Site:www.oalaw.com Peter Danziger, Neil H. Rivchin.

O'Connell, Susan Lee, U.S. Federal Communications Commission, 445 12th St. S.W., Rm. 6A847, Washington, DC, 20554. Phone: (202) 418-1484. Fax: (202) 418-2824.E-mail: soconnell@fcc.gov

O'Connor & Hannan, 1666 K St. N.W., Suite 500, Washington, DC, 20006. Phone: (202) 887-1400. Fax: (202) 466-2198.E-mail: gadler@oconnorhannan.com Gary Adler.

Ogden Murphy Wallace, P.L.L.C., 1601 5th Ave., Suite 2100, Westlake Ctr. Tower, Seattle, WA, 98101-1686. Phone: (206) 447-7000. Fax: (206) 447-0215.E-mail: nparks@omwlaw.com Web Site:www.omwlaw.com

O'Melveny & Myers, 1625 Eye St. N.W., Washington, DC, 20006. Phone: (202) 383-5300. Fax: (202) 383-5414.E-mail: jbeisner@omm.com Web Site:www.omm.com John H. Beisner, Donald T. Bliss, John Rogovin, Jessica Davidson-Miller, Carl R. Schenker Jr., Charles Read, Paul McNamara, Martine Apollon, Todd Rosenberg.

O'Neil, Cannon, Hollman, DeJong S.C., Chase Tower, 111 E. Wisconsin Ave., Suite 1400, Milwaukee, WI, 53202-4803. Phone: (414) 276-5000. Fax: (414) 276-6581. Web Site:www.wilaw.com

O'Neill, Athy & Casey, 1310 19th St. N.W., Washington, DC, 20036. Phone: (202) 466-6555. Fax: (202) 466-6596.E-mail: aathy@oacpc.com Web Site:oacpc.com Andrew Athy Jr.

O'Reilly, Rancilio, Nitz, Andrews, Turnbull, & Scott P.C., 12900 Hall Rd., Suite 350, Sterling Heights, MI, 48313-1151. Phone: (586) 726-1000. Fax: (586) 726-1560. Web Site:www.orlaw.com Neil J. Lehto, Donald DeNault.

Orr & Reno, Box 3550, One Eagle Sq., Concord, NH, 03302-3550. Phone: (603) 224-2381. Fax: (603) 224-2318.E-mail: mmclean@orr-reno.com Web Site:www.orr-reno.com William L. Chapman.

Overton, John B., 14 Manzanita Pl., Mill Valley, CA, 94941. Phone: (415) 331-2889. Fax: (415) 331-5837.E-mail: overton@plownet.com

Law Offices of James L. Oyster, 108 Oyster Ln., Castleton, VA, 22716. Phone: (540) 937-4800. Fax: (540) 937-2148.E-mail: joyster@crosslink.net James L. Oyster.

Pankopf, Arthur, 7819 Hampden Ln., Bethesda, MD, 20814-1108. Phone: (301) 657-8790. Fax: (301) 657-3296.E-mail: apankopf@worldnet.att.net Arthur Pankopf.

Pardo & Pardo P.A., Box 398646, Miami Beach, FL, 33239. Phone: (305) 673-1515. Fax: (305) 673-9359.

Patton Boggs L.L.P., 2550 M St. N.W., Suite 900, Washington, DC, 20037. Phone: (202) 457-6000. Fax: (202) 457-6315. Web Site:www.pattonboggs.com Thomas H. Boggs Jr., Stephen Diaz Gavin, Paul C. Besozzi, J. Jeffrey Craven, John F. Fithian, Penelope S. Farthing, Janet Fitzpatrick, Jeffrey L. Ross. Dallas: Charles Miller, Jennifer Boudreau.

Paul, Hastings, Janofsky & Walker LLP, 1299 Pennsylvania Ave. N.W., 10th Fl., Washington, DC, 20004-2400. Phone: (202) 508-9500. Web Site:www.paulhastings.com Ralph B. Everett, Bruce D. Ryan, Michelle Cohen, Carl W. Northrop, John G. Johnson, William D. DeGrandis, David Burns, Christine Crowe, G. Hamilton Loeb.

Paul, Weiss, Rifkind, Wharton & Garrison, L.L.P., 1615 L St. N.W., Suite 1300, Washington, DC, 20036. Phone: (202) 223-7300. Fax: (202) 223-7427. Web Site:www.paulweiss.com Phillip L. Spector, Jeffrey H. Olson, Patrick S. Campbell.

Pearce & Durick, Box 400, 314 E. Thayer Ave., Bismarck, ND, 58502-0400. Phone: (701) 223-2890. Fax: (701) 223-7865.E-mail: law.office@pearce-durick.com Web Site:www.pearce-durick.com Patrick W. Durick, Larry L. Boschee, Jerome C. Kettleson, Gary R. Thune, Jonathan P. Sanstead.

John D. Pellegrin P.C., 10515 Dominion Valley Dr., Fairfax Station, VA, 22039. Phone: (703) 250-1595. Fax: (703) 250-1597.E-mail: jd@lawpell.com Web Site:www.pellegrin-law.com John D. Pellegrin.

Pepper Hamilton LLP, 3000 Two Logan Sq., Eighteenth & Arch Sts., Philadelphia, PA, 19103-2799. Phone: (215) 981-4000. Fax: (215) 981-4750.E-mail: phinfo@pepperlaw.com Web Site:www.pepperlaw.com Pepper Hamilton LLP, David A. Wormser.

WashingtonDC , 600 14th St. N.W. Phone:

Perkins, Jr., Roy F., 1724 Whitewood Ln., Herndon, VA, 20170. Phone: (703) 435-9700. Fax: (703) 435-9701. Roy F. Perkins Jr.

Larry D. Perry, Attorney at Law, 11464 Saga Ln., Suite 110, Knoxville, TN, 37931-2819. Phone: (865) 927-8474. Fax: (865) 927-4912.E-mail: larryperry@att.net Larry D. Perry, Esq.

Peterson Law Firm, 2033 Walnut St., Philadelphia, PA, 19103. Phone: (215) 557-9001.

Phillips Nizer LLP, 666 5th Ave., 28th Fl., New York, NY, 10103-0084. Phone: (212) 977-9700. Fax: (212) 262-5152.E-mail: ssalmon@phillipsnizer.com Web Site:www.phillipsnizer.com

Pierce & Robinson P A, (Formerly Pierce, Robinson & Greene P A). 600 W. 4th St., North Little Rock, AR, 72114-5360. Phone: (501) 372-3131. Fax: (501) 372-3825. Web Site:www.prg-law.com William Robinson, pres.

Pillsbury Winthrop Shaw Pittman LLP, 2300 N St. N.W., Washington, DC, 20037. Phone: (202) 663-8000. Fax: (202) 663-8007. Paul Cicelski, Ben C. Fisher, Richard R. Zaragoza, Clifford M. Harrington, Kathryn R. Schmeltzer, David D. Oxenford, Bruce D. Jacobs, Barry H. Gottfried, Glenn S. Richards, Scott R. Flick, Lauren Lynch Flick, Miles S. Mason, Carroll John Yung, Jane Sullivan Roberts, Dawn M. Sciarrino, Bryan T. McGinnis, Cynthia D. Greer, Susan H. Hafeli, Brendan Holland, David S. Konczal, Tony Lin, Veronica D. McLaughlin, Tina R. Reynolds, Christopher J. Sadowski, Katherine T. Suh, Amy L. Van de Kerckhove.

Pillsbury, Winthrop Shaw Pittman LLP, 1540 Broadway, New York, NY, 10036-4039. Phone: (877) 323-4171. Fax: (415) 983-1200. Web Site:www.pillsburylaw.com

Powell, Goldstein, Frazer & Murphy, 1201 W. Peachtree St. N.W., Fl. 14, Atlanta, GA, 30309. Phone: (404) 572-6600. Fax: (404) 572-6999.E-mail: wmoeling@pgfm.com Web Site:www.pgfm.com

WashingtonDC , 1001 Pennsylvania Ave. N.W. , 6th Fl. Phone:

Pratcher & Associates P.C., 1133 Kensington Ave., Buffalo, NY, 14215-1611. Phone: (716) 838-4612. Fax: (716) 838-4828.E-mail: frpratcher@pratcher.com Franklin Pratcher.

BuffaloNY , Town Gardens Plaza, 447 Williams St, Suite H. Phone:

Preston, Gates, Ellis & Rouvelas Meeds L.L.P., 1735 New York Ave. N.W., Suite 500, Washington, DC, 20006. Phone: (202) 628-1700. Fax: (202) 331-1024.E-mail: robert@prestongates.com Web Site:www.prestongates.com Martin L. Stern.

Proskauer Rose L.L.P., 1585 Broadway, New York, NY, 10036. Phone: (212) 969-3000. Fax: (212) 969-2900.E-mail: lbudish@proskauer.com Web Site:www.proskauer.com Bertram A. Abrams, Lawrence H. Budish.

Provosty, Sadler Delaunay, Fiorenza & Sobel, Box 1791, Hibernia National Bank, 8th Fl., Alexandria, LA, 71309-1791. Phone: (318) 445-3631. Fax: (318) 445-9377. David Sobel.

Pulis, Gregory M., (Creative Artists Agency). 2000 Avenue of the Stars, Los Angeles, CA, 90067. Phone: (424) 288-4545. Phone: (424) 288-2000 . Fax: (424) 288-4800. Fax: (424) 288-2900.E-mail: gpulis@caa.com

Putbrese, Hunsaker & Trent, P.C., 200 S. Church St., Woodstock, VA, 22664. Phone: (540) 459-7646. Fax: (540) 459-7656.E-mail: phtlaw@mindspring.com John C. Trent.

Reddy, Begley & McCormick, L.L.P., 1156 15th St. N.W., Suite 610, Washington, DC, 20005-1770. Phone: (202) 659-5700. Fax: (202) 659-5711.E-mail: rbm@rbmfcclaw.com Web Site:www.rbmfcclaw.com Dennis F. Begley, Matthew E. McCormick.

Rees, Broome & Diaz, 8133 Leesburg Pike, 9th Fl., Vienna, VA, 22182. Phone: (703) 790-1911. Fax: (703) 848-2530.E-mail: info@rbdlaw.com Web Site:www.rbdlaw.com Peter S. Philbin.

Law Office of George Edward Regis, 121 W. 27th St., Suite 1001, New York, NY, 10001-6207. Phone: (212) 645-8800.E-mail: georgeregis@yahoo.com George Edward Regis.

Renouf & Polivy, 1532 16th St. N.W., Washington, DC, 20036. Phone: (202) 265-1807. Fax: (202) 265-1810.E-mail: thamber@aol.com Katrina Renouf, Margot Polivy.

Resnick, Bernard Max, Esq, P.C., Two Bala Plaza, Suite 300, Bala Cynwyd, PA, 19004-1501. Phone: (610) 660-7774. Fax: (610) 668-0574.E-mail: bmresnick@aol.com Web Site:www.bernardresnick.com Bernard Max Resnick.

Reynolds & Manning, P.A., Box 2809, Prince Frederick, MD, 20678. Phone: (410) 535-9220. Fax: (410) 535-9171.E-mail: calvertlawyer@comcast.net Web Site:www.lawyers.com/reynoldsandmanning Christopher J. Reynolds.

Richards, Mary Beth, U.S. Federal Communications Commission, 445 12th St. S.W., Rm. 8-C750, Washington, DC, 20554. Phone: (202) 418-1000. Fax: (202) 418-2801. Web Site:www.marybeth.richards@fcc.gov

Riezman & Berger, 7700 Bonhomme Ave., 7th Fl., St. Louis, MO, 63105. Phone: (314) 727-0101. Fax: (314) 727-6458.E-mail: jacobs@riezmanberger.com Web Site:www.riezmanberger.com Bob Jacobs.

Riker Danzig Scherer Hyland & Perretti LLP, One Speedwell Ave., Headquarters Plaza, Morristown, NJ, 07962-1981. Phone: (973) 538-0800. Fax: (973) 538-1984.E-mail: info@riker.com Web Site:www.riker.com Sidney M. Schreiber, Vincent J. Sharkey Jr., Edward K. DeHope, James C. Meyer, Michael A. Schmerling, Mark T. Pasko.

TrentonNJ , 50 W. State St, Suite 1010.

Robins, Kaplan, Miller & Ciresi, 2800 LaSalle Plaza, 800 LaSalle Ave., Minneapolis, MN, 55402-2015. Phone: (612) 349-8500. Fax: (612) 339-4181.E-mail: kamarron@rkmc.com Web Site:www.rkmc.com Timothy Block, Doug Boettge, John F. Gibbs, Todd Hartman, Lisa Heller, Rebecca Liethen, Edward Muramoto, Thomas A. Miller, Ed Muramoto, Sara A. Poulos, Steven Safvanski.

Gust Rosenfeld P.L.C., 201 E. Washington, Suite 800, Phoenix, AZ, 85004-2327. Phone: (602) 257-7422. Fax: (602) 254-4878.E-mail: chauncey@gustlaw.com Web Site:www.gustlaw.com Tom Chauncey II.

Rosenfeld, Meyer & Susman L.L.P., 9601 Wilshire Blvd., Suite 710, Beverly Hills, CA, 90210-5225. Phone: (310) 858-7700. Fax: (310) 860-2430. Web Site:www.rmslaw.com

Rourke, Gerald S., 76 Northwood Rd., Madison, CT, 06443. Phone: (203) 421-3424.E-mail: gerald.rourke@comast.net Gerald S. Rourke.

Rubin, Winston, Diercks, Harris & Cooke, L.L.P., 1155 Connecticut Ave. N.W., 6th Fl., Washington, DC, 20036. Phone: (202) 861-0870. Fax: (202) 429-0657.E-mail: jwinston@rwdhc.com Web Site:www.rwdhc.com James L. Winston, Steven J. Stone.

Ryan, Swanson & Cleveland P.L.L.C., 1201 3rd Ave., Suite 3400, Seattle, WA, 98101-3034. Phone: (206) 464-4224. Phone: (800) 458-5973. Fax: (206) 583-0359.E-mail: collette@ryanlaw.com Web Site:www.ryanlaw.com

Law Offices of Lee Sacks, 23852 Pacific Coast Hwy., Suite 157, Malibu, CA, 90265-4879. Phone: (310) 451-3113. Fax: (310) 451-0089. Lee Sacks.

Sahl, Jack, School of Law, University of Akron, Akron, OH, 44325-2901. Phone: (330) 972-6753. Fax: (330) 258-2343.E-mail: jps@uakron.edu Web Site:www.uakron.edu/law

Sanchez Law Firm, 2300 M. St., N.W., Suite 800, Washington, DC, 20037. Phone: (202) 237-2814. Fax: (202) 237-5614.E-mail: esanchez@bellatlantic.net Ernest T. Sanchez.

Sapronov & Associates, P. C., 3 Ravinia Dr., Suite 1455, Atlanta, GA, 30346. Phone: (770) 399-9100. Fax: (770) 395-0505.E-mail: info@wstelecomlaw.com Web Site:www.wstelecomlaw.com Walt Sapronov, William D. Friend, Charles A. Hudak, Michael Stewart, Ronald Jackson, Timothy Geraghty.

Gary P. Schonman, 445 12th St. S.W., Rm. 3A660, Federal Communications Commision, Washington, DC, 20554. Phone: (202) 418-1795. Fax: (202) 418-2080. Web Site:www.fcc.gov Gary P. Schonman.

Schuman, Felts, Chartered, 4804 Moorland Ln., Bethesda, MD, 20814. Phone: (301) 986-0200. Fax: (301) 986-7960. Sheldon Paul Schuman.

Schuster & Associates, 3594 Armourdale Ave., Long Beach, CA, 90808. Phone: (562) 596-5900. Fax: (562) 431-4540.E-mail: attorney@flightlaw.com Web Site:www.flightlaw.com

Schwaninger & Associates, P.C., 1331 H St. N.W., Suite 500, Washington, DC, 20005. Phone: (202) 347-8580. Fax: (202) 347-8607/347-8643.E-mail: rschwaninger@sa-lawyers.net Web Site:www.sa-lawyers.net Richard P. Hanno.

Schwartz, Woods & Miller, 1233 20th St., N.W., Suite 610, Washington, DC, 20036. Phone: (202) 833-1700. Fax: (202) 833-2351.E-mail: @swmlaw.com Web Site:www.swmlaw.com Lawrence M. Miller, Steven C. Schaffer, Malcolm G. Stevenson.

Law Offices of Philip L. Schwartz PA, 2000 Glades Rd., Suite 208, Boca Raton, FL, 33431. Phone: (954) 760-7770. Fax: (954) 524-4169.E-mail: phil@philipschwartz.com Philip L. Schwartz, Esq.

The Seale Law Firm, Bryton Tower, 1271 Poplar Ave., Memphis, TN, 38104. Phone: (901) 521-9958. William B. Seale, Lisa A. Maniscalco, Cynthia Marrone, David Allen Outlaw, Harold C. Streibich.

Sell & Melton, Box 229, 577 Mulberry St., Suite 1400, Macon, GA, 31202-0229. Phone: (478) 746-8521. Fax: (478) 745-6426.E-mail: eds@sell-melton.com Web Site:www.sell-melton.com Ed S. Sell III, ptnr.

Severaid, Ronald H., 1805 Tribute Rd., Suite J, Sacramento, CA, 95815. Phone: (916) 929-8383. Fax: (916) 925-4763.E-mail: rhseveraid@earthlink.net

Seyfarth Shaw, 2029 Century Park E., 33rd Fl., Los Angeles, CA, 90067-3063. Phone: (310) 277-7200. Fax: (310) 201-5219. Web Site:www.seyfarth.com Michael R. Levinson.

Seyfarth Shaw LLP, 55 E. Monroe St., Chicago, IL, 60603. Phone: (312) 781-8655. Fax: (312) 269-8869.E-mail: aunikel@seyfarth.com Web Site:www.seyfarth.com Alan L. Unikel.

Law Offices of Thomas G. Shack Jr., 1150 Connecticut Ave. N.W., Suite 900, Washington, DC, 20036. Phone: (202) 293-5900. Fax: (202) 659-3493. Thomas G. Shack, Jr.

Shapiro, Burton J., 2147 N. Beachwood Dr., Los Angeles, CA, 90068-3462. Phone: (323) 469-9452. Fax: (603) 710-8109.E-mail: burtjay@mail.com Web Site:www.burtshapiro.com

Shine and Hardin L.L.P., 2810 Beaver Ave., Fort Wayne, IN, 46807. Phone: (260) 745-1970. Fax: (260) 744-5411.E-mail: sshine@shineandhardin.com Web Site:www.shineandhardin.com Steven R. Shine.

Shukat, Arrow, Hafer & Weber, L.L.P., 111 W. 57th St., Suite 1120, New York, NY, 10019-2211. Phone: (212) 245-4580. Fax: (212) 956-6471.E-mail: Peter@musiclaw.com Peter Shukat, Allen H. Arow, J. Jeffrey Hafer.

Shulman, Rogers, Gandal, Pordy & Ecker, P.A., 11921 Rockville Pike, 3rd Fl., Rockville, MD, 20852. Phone: (301) 230-5200. Fax: (301) 230-2891.E-mail: atilles@srgpe.com Web Site:www.shulmanrogers.com Allan S. Tilles.

Siegal, Joel H., 703 Market St., San Francisco, CA, 94103. Phone: (415) 777-5547.

Siegel, Kelleher & Kahn, 426 Franklin St., Buffalo, NY, 14202. Phone: (716) 881-5800. Fax: (716) 885-3369.E-mail: info@skklaw.com Web Site:www.skklaw.com Herbtert M. Siegler.

Law Offices of William D. Silva, 5335 Wisconsin Ave. N.W., Suite 400, Washington, DC, 20015-2003. Phone: (202) 362-1711. Fax: (202) 686-8282.E-mail: bill@luselaw.com Web Site:wrmsilvalaw.com William D. Silva.

Silver, Garvett & Henkel P.A., 18001 Old Cutler Rd., Suite 600, Miami, FL, 33157. Phone: (305) 377-8802. Fax: (305) 377-8804.

Skadden, Arps, Slate, Meagher & Flom L.L.P., 1440 New York Ave. N.W., Washington, DC, 20005. Phone: (202) 371-7000. Fax: (202) 393-5760. Web Site:www.skadden.com Richard A. Hindman, David H. Pawlik, Brian D. Weimer, John M. Beahn, Antoinette C. Bush, Margaret E. Lancaster, Ivan A. Schlager, Jennifer B. Irvin, Lawrence Roberts, Jared S. Sher, Malcom J. Tuesley, (Washington DC); Warren G. Lavey, David S. Prohofsky, (Chicago).

Barry Skidelsky, Esq., 18 E. 41st St., New York, NY, 10017. Phone: (212) 832-4800.E-mail: bskidelsky@mindspring.com Barry Skidelsky (New York & Washington, DC).

Smith & Metalitz LLP, 1747 Pennsylvania Ave. N.W., Suite 825, Washington, DC, 20006. Phone: (202) 833-4198.E-mail: info@smimetlaw.com Web Site:www.smimetlaw.com

Smith, Dianne, (formerly Pauker, Molly). Fox Television Stations Inc., 5151 Wisconsin Ave., N.W., Washington, DC, 20016-4124. Phone: (202) 895-3088. Fax: (202) 895-3222.E-mail: dianne.smith@foxtv.com Dianne Smith.

Reed Smith LLP, 3110 Fairview Park Dr., Suite 1400, Falls Church, VA, 22042-4503. Phone: (703) 641-4200. Fax: (703) 641-4340.E-mail: reedsmith@reedsmith.com Web Site:www.reedsmith.com

Smithwick & Belendiuk, P.C., Suite 301, 5028 Wisconsin Ave. N.W., Washington, DC, 20016. Phone: (202) 363-4050. Fax: (202) 363-4266.E-mail: gsmithwick@fccworld.com Web Site:fccworld.com Gary S. Smithwick, Arthur V. Belendiuk, Robert Lewis Thompson, William M. Bernard.

Sodos & Kafkas, 16985 Bluemount Rd., Suite 202, Brookfield, WI, 53005. Phone: (262) 785-5500. Fax: (262) 785-1100.E-mail: office@sodos.com

Sommers, Schwartz, Silver & Schwartz, P.C., 2000 Town Ctr., Suite 900, Southfield, MI, 48075. Phone: (248) 355-0300. Fax: (248) 746-4001. Web Site:www.sommerspc.com

Sonneman & Sonneman, P.A., 111 Riverfront, Suite 202, Winona, MN, 55987. Phone: (507) 454-8885. Fax: (507) 454-8887.E-mail: sonneman@luminet.net Karl W. Sonneman, VP.

Sonnenschein, Nath & Rosenthal LLP, 8000 Sears Tower, 233 S. Wacker Dr., Chicago, IL, 60606. Phone: (312) 876-3114. Fax: (312) 876-7934.E-mail: sfifer@sonnenschein.com Web Site:www.sonnenschein.com David W. Maher, Samuel Fifer.

Southmayd & Miller, 1220 19th St. N.W., Suite 400, Washington, DC, 20036. Phone: (202) 331-4100.E-mail: jdsouthmayd@msn.com Jeffrey D. Southmayd, Michael R. Miller.

Spawn, Coy U., 1815 Bering Dr., Houston, TX, 77057-3109. Phone: (713) 782-2977. Fax: (713) 782-2977.

Spiegel & McDiarmid, LLP, 1333 New Hampshire Ave. N.W., Washington, DC, 20036. Phone: (202) 879-4000. Fax: (202) 393-2866.E-mail: jim.horwood@spiegelmcd.com Web Site:www.spiegelmcd.com James Horwood, Tillman Lay, Scott Strauss, Peter Hopkins, Ruben Gomez, Gloria Tristani.

Springman, Braden, Wilson & Pontius, P.C., 1022 Bannock St., Denver, CO, 80204. Phone: (303) 685-4897/685-4633. Fax: (303) 685-4627.E-mail: sbwp@indra.com

Squire, Sanders & Dempsey, Box 407, 1201 Pennsylvania Ave. N.W., Washington, DC, 20044-0407. Phone: (202) 626-6600. Fax: (202) 626-6780.E-mail: jnadler@ssd.com Web Site:www.ssd.com Thomas J. Ramsey, Herbert E. Marks, Joseph P. Markoski, Jonathan J. Nadler.

ClevelandOH , 4900 Key Tower, 127 Public Sq. Phone:

Stennett, Wilkinson & Peden, 401 Legacy Park, Ridgeland, MS, 39157. Phone: (601) 206-1816. Fax: (601) 206-9132.E-mail: swplaw@attorney.net Web Site:www.swplaw.com Gene A. Wilkinson, James A. Peden Jr.

Stephens Media LLC, P.O. Box 70, Las Vegas, NV, 89125. Phone: (702) 477-3830. Fax: (702) 383-0230. Web Site:www.stephensmedia.com

Steptoe & Johnson, 1330 Connecticut Ave. N.W., Washington, DC, 20036. Phone: (202) 429-3000. Fax: (202) 429-3902.E-mail: amamlet@steptoe.com Web Site:www.steptoe.com Michael Vatis, Philip L. Malet, David J. Bodney.

Stevens, Sally L., Box 41, Lumberville, PA, 18933. Phone: (215) 297-8245. Fax: (215) 297-5106.

Stewart & Irwin P.C., 251 E. Ohio St., Suite 1100, Indianapolis, IN, 46204. Phone: (317) 639-5454. Fax: (317) 632-1319.E-mail: raikman@silegal.com Web Site:www.stewart-irwin.com Richard E. Aikman Jr.

Stewart, Estes & Donnell PLC, 424 Church St., Fifth Third Ctr., Suite 1401, Nashville, TN, 37219. Phone: (615) 244-6538. Fax: (615) 256-8386. Web Site:www.sedlaw.com Stephen Heard.

Strichartz, James L., 200 W. Mercer St., Suite 511, Seattle, WA, 98119. Phone: (206) 282-8020.E-mail: jim@condo-lawyers.com

Stroock, Stroock & Lavin, 180 Maiden Lane, New York, NY, 10038-4982. Phone: (212) 806-5400. Fax: (212) 806-6006.E-mail: speters@stroock.com Web Site:www.stroock.com Ian G. Bernardo.

Stryker, Tams & Dill LLP, 2 Penn Plaza E., Newark, NJ, 07105-2293. Phone: (973) 491-9500. Fax: (973) 491-9692.E-mail: dlinken@strykertams.com Web Site:www.strykertams.com Dennis C. Linken, Esq.

Taylor, Jack, 1289 Lincoln Rd., Yuba City, CA, 95991. Phone: (530) 671-6800. Fax: (530) 671-6447.

Taylor, Ray L., 11608 Chayote St., Los Angeles, CA, 90049. Phone: (310) 476-6493. Fax: (310) 471-2763.

Technology Law Group L.L.C., 5335 Wisconsin Ave. N.W., Suite 440, Washington, DC, 20015. Phone: (202) 895-1707.E-mail: mail@tlgdc.com Web Site:www.tlgdc.com Alex Bouton.

Teitelbaum, Israel, 11301 Amherst Ave., Suite 202, Silver Spring, MD, 20902. Phone: (301) 933-3373. Fax: (301) 933-3651. Israel Teitelbaum.

Thelen Reid & Priest LLP, Washington, D.C. 701 Pennsylvania Ave. N.W., Suite 800, Washington, DC, 20004. Phone: (202) 508-4000. Fax: (202) 508-4321. Web Site:www.thelenreid.com

San FranciscoCA , 101 2nd St, Suite 1800. Phone:

Thiemann, Aitken & Vohra, 908 King St., Suite 300, Alexandria, VA, 22314. Phone: (703) 836-9400. Fax: (703) 836-9410.E-mail: ajthiemann@ttalaw.com Russell C. Powell, Robert Lewis Thompson.

Thomas, Ballenger, Vogelman & Turner, 124 S. Royal St., Alexandria, VA, 22314. Phone: (703) 836-3400. Fax: (703) 836-3549. John M. Ballenger.

Thompson Hine LLP, 1920 N St. N.W., Suite 800, Washington, DC, 20036. Phone: (202) 331-8800. Fax: (202) 331-8330.E-mail: barry.friedman@thompsonhine.com Web Site:www.thompsonhine.com Barry A. Friedman, Stephen T. Lovelady, John C. Butcher.

ColumbusOH , 10 W. Broad St, Suite 700. Phone:tom.lodge @thompsonhine.com Web Site: www.thompsonhine.com. Thomas E. Lodge.

Thrasher, Dinsmore & Dolan, 100 7th Ave., Suite 150, Chardon, OH, 44024-1079. Phone: (440) 285-2242. Fax: (440) 285-9423.E-mail: dmoore@dolan.law.pro Matthew Dolan.

Troutman Sanders L.L.P., 600 Peachtree St., Suite 5200, Atlanta, GA, 30308. Phone: (404) 885-3000. Fax: (404) 885-3900. Web Site:www.troutmansanders.com Robert Grout, Robert W. Webb, Richard H. Brody.

Troy & Gould, PC, 1801 Century Park E., 16th Fl., Los Angeles, CA, 90067. Phone: (310) 553-4441. Fax: (310) 201-4746. Web Site:www.troygould.com Sandy Hillsberg.

Trugman, Richard S., 9200 Sunset Blvd., Suite 206, Los Angeles, CA, 90069. Phone: (310) 273-8834. Fax: (310) 273-8345.E-mail: trulaw@sbcglobal.net

Edmund W. Turnley III, 30 Music Square W., Suite 302, Nashville, TN, 37203. Phone: (615) 321-8600. Fax: (615) 321-8602. Edmund W. Turnley.

Turtle, Joel S., 55 Santa Clara Ave., Suite 120, Oakland, CA, 94610. Phone: (510) 763-7600. Fax: (510) 763-7894.E-mail: joelturtle@yahoo.com Web Site:www.riotmedia.com

Umansky, Barry D., Irwin, Campbell & Tannerwald, 1730 Rhode Island Ave. N.W., Suite 200, Washington, DC, 20036-3101. Phone: (202) 728-0400. Web Site:www.ictpc.com

Van Cott, Bagley, Cornwall & McCarthy, 36 S. State St., Suite 1900, Salt Lake City, UT, 84111-1478. Phone: (801) 532-3333. Fax: (801) 534-0058.E-mail: info@vancott.com Web Site:www.vancott.com Steven D. Swidle, Robert M. Anderson, Jennifer K. Anderson.

A. Chavis Vanias, Attorney at Law, P.O. Box 9612, Columbia, SC, 29209. Phone: (803) 256-1244. Fax: (803) 753-0007.E-mail: acvanias@scbar.org

Varnum LLP, (Formerly Varnum, Riddering, Schmidt & Howlett LLP). Box 352, Bridgewater Pl., Grand Rapids, MI, 49501-0352. Phone: (616) 336-6000. Fax: (616) 336-7000.E-mail: generalinfo@varnumlaw.com Web Site:www.varnumlaw.com John W. Pestle, Timothy J. Lundgren, Dale Rietberg.

Venable LLP, 1800 Mercantile Bank Bldg., 2 Hopkins Plaza, Baltimore, MD, 21201. Phone: (410) 244-7400. Fax: (410) 244-7742.E-mail: mscott@venable.com

WashingtonDC , 1201 New York Ave. N.W, Suite 1000. Phone:

Veryl Miles/Professor at Law School, Cardinal Stn., Columbus School of Law, /Catholic Univ. America, Washington, DC, 20064. Phone: (202) 319-5140. Fax: (202) 319-4459. Web Site:www.law.edu

Vorys, Sater, Seymour and Pease LLP, Box 1008, 52 E. Gay St., Columbus, OH, 43216-1008. Phone: (614) 464-6400. Fax: (614) 464-6350.E-mail: info@vorys.com Web Site:www.vorys.com

WashingtonDC , 1828 L St. N.W, Suite 1111. Phone:

WGBH Educational Foundation, 125 Western Ave., Boston, MA, 02134-1098. Phone: (617) 300-2000. Fax: (617) 300-1014. Web Site:www.wgbh.org Eric A. Brass.

WTTW Channel 11/Chicago, 5400 N. St. Louis Ave., Chicago, IL, 60625. Phone: (773) 583-5000. Fax: (773) 583-3046. Web Site:www.wttw.com

Wagner, Michael Francis, Mass Media Bureau, 445 12th St. S.W., Rm. 2-A523, Washington, DC, 20554. Phone: (202) 418-2700. Fax: (202) 418-1410. Web Site:www.fcc.gov/mb/audio

Waller Lansden Dortch & Davis, PLLC, 511 Union St., Suite 2700, Nashville, TN, 37219. Phone: (615) 244-6380. Fax: (615) 244-6804. Web Site:www.wallerlaw.com Robb S. Harvey, Richard Sanders, Heather Hubbard.

Jon M. Waxman Associates, 302 W. 12th St., New York, NY, 10014. Phone: (212) 929-2562. Fax: (212) 229-1625.E-mail: jon@jonwaxman.com

Law Offices of Edward L. Weidenfeld, 888 17th St. N.W., Suite 900, Washington, DC, 20006. Phone: (202) 785-2143. Fax: (202) 452-8938.E-mail: julie@weidenfeldlaw.com

Weil, Gotshal & Manges, L.L.P., 1300 I St. N.W., Suite 900, Washington, DC, 20005. Phone: (202) 682-7000. Fax: (202) 857-0940.E-mail: bruce.turnbull@weil.com Web Site:www.weil.com Bruce H. Turnbull, ptnr.

Law Offices of Joel Weisman, P.C., 1901 Raymond Dr., Suite 6, Northbrook, IL, 60062. Phone: (847) 400-5900. Fax: (847) 400-5534. Web Site:www.weismanmedialaw.com Joel Weisman, Scott A. Weisman.

Weissmann, Wolff, Bergman, Coleman, Grodin & Evall, 9665 Wilshire Blvd., 9th Fl., Beverly Hills, CA, 90212-2345. Phone: (310) 858-7888. Fax: (310) 550-7191.E-mail: seisner@wwllp.com Web Site:www.weissmannwolff.com Stan Coleman, sr ptnr; Eric Weissmann.

Westervelt, Johnson, Nicholl & Keller, LLC, Associated Bank Bldg., 411 Hamilton Blvd., 14th Fl., Peoria, IL, 61602. Phone: (309) 671-3550. Fax: (309) 671-3588.E-mail: westervelt @westerveltlaw.com

Wheeler Wolf Law Firm, Box 2056, 220 N. 4th. St., Bismarck, ND, 58502-2056. Phone: (701) 223-5300. Fax: (701) 223-5366.E-mail: jackmcdonald@wheelerwolf.com Jack McDonald.

Wildman, Harrold, Allen & Dixon, 225 W. Wacker Dr., Suite 3000, Chicago, IL, 60606. Phone: (312) 201-2000. Fax: (312) 201-2555. Web Site:www.wildmanharrold.com

Wiley Rein LLP, 1776 K St. N.W., Washington, DC, 20006. Phone: (202) 719-7000. Fax: (202) 719-7049.E-mail: dcorini@wileyrein.com Web Site:www.wileyrein.com Partners: William B Baker, John E. Barry, James R. W. Bayes, Doc Bodensteiner, Richard J. Bodorff, Dorann Bukin, John M. Burgett, Scott D. Delacourt, Eric W. DeSilva, Gregg L. Elias, John E. Fiorini III, David A. Gross, Martha E. Heller, David E. Hilliard, Jennifer D. Hindin, Wayne D. Johnsen, Kathleen A. Kirby, Mark N. Lipp, Gregory L. Masters, Andrew G. McBride, Thomas J. Navin, Robert L. Pettit, Eve Klindera Reed, Henry M. Rivera, Jessica N. Rosenthal, Bennett L. Ross, Lawrence W. Secrest III, R. Michael Senkowski, Peter D. Shields, Jim Slattery, Todd M. Stansbury, Joshua S. Turner, Nancy J. Victory, Helgi C. Walker, Richard E. Wiley, Amy E. Worlton. Of counsel/consultants: Tyrone Brown, Edgar Class, Susan C. Buck, Mimi W.

Dawson, Kurt E. DeSoto, Thomas S. Dombrowsky Jr., Carl Frank, Elizabeth Goldin, David Jatlow, Brian A. Johnson, John W. Kuzin, Michael A. Lewis, Mary Jo Manning Marnie K. Sarver.

Wilkinson Barker Knauer, L.L.P., 2300 N St. N.W., Suite 700, Washington, DC, 20037. Phone: (202) 783-4141. Fax: (202) 783-5851. Web Site:www.wbklaw.com Partners: Barry Ohlson, Brian W. Higgins, Jonathan V. Cohen, Timothy J. Cooney, Christine M. Crowe, Paige K. Fronabarger, Craig E. Gilmore, Russell P. Hanser, Patricia Chuh, Kathleen Abernathy, Natalie Roisman.

Willcox & Savage, P.C., One Commercial Pl., Suite 1800, Norfolk, VA, 23510. Phone: (757) 628-5500. Fax: (757) 628-5566. Web Site:www.willcoxsavage.com E-mail: mshearon@wilsav.com

Virginia BeachVA , Box 61888, One Columbus Ctr, Suite 1010. Fax:

William Morris Agency, 151 El Camino Dr., Beverly Hills, CA, 90212-2704. Phone: (310) 859-4000. Fax: (310) 859-4462.

Willkie Farr & Gallagher LLP, 1875 K St. N.W., Washington, DC, 20006. Phone: (202) 303-1000. Fax: (202) 303-2000. Web Site:www.willkie.com Stephen Bell, Frank Buono, James Casserly, Jonathan Friedman, Michael Hammer, Karen Henein, Michael Jones, Thomas Jones, Sophie Keefer, Grace Koh, Angie Kronenberg, Jonathan Lechter, Jennifer McCarthy, John McGrew, Nirali Patel, Stephanie Podey, McLean Sieverding, Pamela Strauss, Megan Stull, Rayn Wallach, Theodore Whitehouse, Philip Verveer.

Wilmer Cutler Pickering Hale and Dorr LLP, 1875 Pennsylvania Ave., N.W., Washington, DC, 20006-3642. Phone: (202) 663-6000. Fax: (202) 663-6363.E-mail: william.richardson@wilmerhale.com Lynn Charytan, Jonathan Frankel, John Harwood, Samir Jain, William Lake, Jonathan Nuechterlein, William R. Richardson, John Rogovin, Catherine Ronis, Jack Goodman, David Mendel, Josh Roland, Will DeVries, Meredith Halama, Aaron Hurowitz, Daniel McCuaig, Nathan Mitchler, Jonathan Siegelbaum, Alison Southall, Kenny Wright, Heather Zachary, Dileep Srihari.

Winkler, Bevacqua & Simmons, P.C., 60 Park Pl., 19th Fl., Newark, NJ, 07102. Phone: (973) 676-1200. Fax: (973) 624-5980. Maury R. Winkler.

Winston & Strawn, 35 W. Wacker Dr., Chicago, IL, 60601-9703. Phone: (312) 558-5600. Fax: (312) 558-5700.E-mail: jneis@winston.com Web Site:www.winston.com

WashingtonDC , 1400 L St. N.W, 8th Fl. Phone:

Wolf, Block, Schorr, & Solis-Cohen, 250 Park Ave., New York, NY, 10177-0030. Phone: (212) 986-1116. Fax: (212) 986-0604. Web Site:www.wolfblock.com Stuart A. Shorenstein, David E. Bronston.

Womble, Carlyle, Sandridge & Rice, PLLC, 1401 I St. N.W., 7th Fl., Washington, DC, 20005. Phone: (202) 467-6900. Fax: (202) 467-6910. Web Site:www.wcsr.com Howard J. Barr, Patricia M. Chuh, John F. Garziglia, Peter Gutmann, Vicent A. Pepper, Gregg P Skall, Joan D. Stewart, Mark Blackwell.

Wood, Maines & Nolan, Chartered, 4121 Wilson Blvd., Suite 101, Arlingtron, VA, 22203. Phone: (703) 465-2361. Fax: (703) 465-2365.E-mail: wmb@legalcompass.com Web Site:legalcompass.com Barry D. Wood, Ronald D. Maines, Stuart W. Nolan, Jr.

Wright & Talisman, P.C., 1200 G St. N.W., Suite 600, Washington, DC, 20005. Phone: (202) 393-1200. Fax: (202) 393-1240.E-mail: statman@wrightlaw.com Web Site:www.wright.com

Young, Williams, Kirk & Stone PC, First Tennessee Plaza, Suite 2021, Box 550, Knoxville, TN, 37901-0550. Phone: (865) 637-1440. Fax: (865) 546-9808.E-mail: bob@tn-attorneys.com Web Site:www.tn-attorneys.com Robert S. Stone.

Young, Clement & Rivers L.L.P., 5000 Thurmond Mall Dr., Suite 320, Columbia, SC, 29201. Phone: (843) 577-4000. Phone: (803) 254-2238. Fax: (843) 724-6600.E-mail: email@ycrlaw.com Web Site:www.ycrlaw.com

Talent Agents and Managers

Abrams Artists Agency, 9200 Sunset Blvd., 11th Fl., Los Angeles, CA, 90069. Phone: (310) 859-0625. Fax: (310) 276-6193.E-mail: harry.abrams@abramsart.com Web Site:www.abramsart.com

Harry Abrams, pres; Neal Altman, sr VP; Robert Attermann, VP.

New YorkNY . Abrams Artists Agency, 275 7th Ave, 26th Fl. Phone:

Performing artists rep talent agency.

N S Bienstock Inc., 250 W. 57th St., Suite 333, New York, NY, 10107. Phone: (212) 765-3040. Fax: (212) 757-6411.E-mail: nsb@nsbtalent.com Web Site:www.nsbtalent.com

News & syndication talent specialists—loc & net—on & off camera. Packager of talk & reality progmg—MOWs.

Eatman Media Services Inc., 5901 N. Cicero Ave., Suite 307, Chicago, IL, 60646. Phone: (773) 777-5463. Fax: (773) 777-7106.E-mail: emstalent@aol.com

Pacific PalisadesCA , Box 853. Phone:

BedfordNY , Box 102. Phone:

Representation of TV newspersons, TV personalities, & radio talent in job placement & contract negotiation.

Ephraim & Associates, P.C., 108 W. Grand Ave., Chicago, IL, 60654-4206. Phone: (312) 321-9700. Fax: (312) 321-3655.E-mail: eliot@ephraim.com Web Site:www.ephraim.com

Donald M. Ephraim, pres; Joseph F. Coyne, VP; Elliot Ephraim, VP; David M. Ephraim, VP.

Talent representation, including contract negotiation, legal & career consulation, tax, estate & pension planning. Elliot Ephraim, atty/agent.

Ken Fishkin & Associates, 50 Milk St., 20th Fl., Boston, MA, 02109-5002. Phone: (617) 423-5800. Fax: (617) 426-2674.E-mail: cindy@kfishkin.com

Kenneth R. Fishkin, pres.

Contract negotiation & job placement, TV & radio.

Goldstein Management Group, Inc., 1601 N. Sepulveda Blvd., Suite 357, Manhattan Beach, CA, 90266. Phone: (310) 545-8530. Fax: (310) 943-1569.E-mail: glenn802@aol.com

Glenn A. Goldstein, pres.

Full-svc representation of bcst talent & bcst journalists.

Reece Halsey Agency, 8733 Sunset Blvd., Suite 101, West Hollywood, CA, 90069. Phone: (415) 789-9191. Fax: (415) 789-9177.

TiburonCA . Reece Halsey Agency, Box 704, 98 Main St. Phone:

Shirley Hamilton Inc., 333 E. Ontario, Chicago, IL, 60611. Phone: (312) 787-4700. Fax: (312) 787-8456.E-mail: shamilton@att.net Web Site:www.shirleyhamilton.com

Shirley Hamilton, pres; Lynne Hamilton, office mgr.

Representing talent for TV, PRINT, RADIO, ON CAMERA, FILM, LIVE, THEATRICAL, VOICEOVER, INDUSTRIALS. Audition facilities for OnCamera, Digital voiceover, Print.

The Image Generators, 18156 Darnell Dr., Olney, MD, 20832. Phone: (301) 924-5700. Fax: (301) 570-8916. Web Site:www.imagegenerators.com

Michael J. Weiner, pres; Valle Bonhag, dir admin.

Voiceover talent, audition svc, online demos of pro voices.

International Creative Management Inc., 825 Eighth Ave., New York, NY, 10019. Phone: (212) 556-5600. Fax: (212) 556-5665. Web Site:www.ICMtalent.com

Jeff Berg, chmn/CEO.

London, 61 Frith Street. Phone:

Los AngelesCA , 10250 Constellation Blvd. Phone:

Miller Broadcast Management Inc., 616 W. Fulton St., Suite 516, Chicago, IL, 60661. Phone: (312) 454-1111. Fax: (312) 454-0044.E-mail: info@millerbroadcast.com Web Site:www.millerbroadcast.com

Lisa Miller, pres.

Representing radio & TV personalities.

William Morris Agency Inc., 1325 Ave. of the Americas, New York, NY, 10019. Phone: (212) 586-5100. Fax: (212) 246-3583. Web Site:www.wma.com

Wayne Kabak, COO; Cara Stein, COO; Jim Griffin, VP.

Paradigm, 360 N. Crescent Dr., N. Bldg., Beverly Hills, CA, 90210-6818. Phone: (310) 288-8000. Fax: (310) 288-2000.E-mail: info@paradigm-agency.com Web Site:www.paradigmagency.com

Sam Gores, pres.

MontereyCA , 509 Hartnell St. Phone:

NashvilleTN , 124 12th Ave. S., , Suite 410. Phone:

Rebel Entertainment, 5700 Wilshire Blvd., Ste 456, Los Angeles, CA, 90038. Phone: (323) 935-1700. Fax: (323) 932-9901.E-mail: rlawre8075@aol.com Web Site:www.arltalent.com

Richard Lawrence, pres; Debra Goldfarb, VP.

Talent placement & TV show packaging.

Screen Children's Casting, 4000 Riverside Dr., Suite A, Burbank, CA, 91505. Phone: (818) 846-4300. Fax: (818) 846-3745.

Irene B. Gallagher, casting dir & owner.

Full-svc children's casting representing babies (especially twins), children & teenagers up to age 18, extra work.

Burt Shapiro Management, 2147 N. Beachwood Dr., Los Angeles, CA, 90068. Phone: (323) 469-9452. Fax: (801) 653-6571.E-mail: burtjay@mail.com Web Site:www.burtshapiro.com

Burt Shapiro, pres.

Represents on-air talent including anchors, reporters, hosts, & sports anchor/reporters, as well as producers & news directors.

Barry Skidelsky, Esq., 185 East 85th St., 23D, New York, NY, 10028. Phone: (212) 832-4800.

Barry Skidelsky, Esq., pres.

Personal mgmt & representation. Contract negotiations, counsel, etc.

The Voicecaster, 1832 W. Burbank Blvd., Burbank, CA, 91506. Phone: (818) 841-5300. Fax: (818) 841-2085.E-mail: casting@voicecaster.com Web Site:www.voicecaster.com

Huck Liggett, owner.

Voice casting for comls, films, animation, theme parks, audiovisual projects, etc.

Weisman, P.C., Law Offices of Joel, 1901 Raymond Dr., Northbrook, IL, 60062. Phone: (847) 400-5900. Fax: (847) 400-5534.E-mail: joel@weismanmedialaw.com Web Site:www.weismanmedialaw.com

Joel Weisman, pres.

Bcst contract drafting & negotiation, career & performance counseling, for anchors, reporters & producers.

Employment and Executive Search Services

Bishop Partners, 708 Third Ave., Suite 2200, New York, NY, 10017. Phone: (212) 986-3419. Fax: (212) 986-3350. E-mail: info@bishoppartners.com Web Site:www.bishop partners.com

Susan K. Bishop, pres/CEO.

A retained exec search firm specializing in cable, bcst, telecommunications, wireless, entertainment, publishing & multimedia.

California Broadcasters Association, 915 L St., Sacramento, CA, 95814. Phone: (916) 444-2237. Fax: (916) 444-2043. E-mail: cbaberry@aol.com Web Site:www.cabroadcasters.org

Stan Statham, pres/CEO.

Lobbyist for coml radio & TV for the state of California & other legal issues.

Eatman Media Services Inc., 5901 N. Cicero Ave., Suite 307, Chicago, IL, 60646. Phone: (773) 777-5463. Fax: (773) 777-7106. E-mail: emstalent@aol.com

Pacific PalisadesCA , Box 853. Phone:

BedfordNY , Box 102. Phone:

Representation of TV newspersons, TV personalities, & radio talent in job placement & contract negotiation.

Entertainment Employment Journal (T.M.), 5632 Van Nuys Blvd., Suite 320, Van Nuys, CA, 91401. Phone: (800) 335-4335. Phone: (818) 776-2800. E-mail: sales@eej.com Web Site:www.eej.com

Bimonthly magazine providing career information & job listings with major & independent motion picture, TV & cable companies.

Filcro Media Staffing, 521 Fifth Ave., Suite 1801, New York, 10175. Phone: (212) 599-0909. Fax: (212) 599-1023. E-mail: tony@filcro.com Web Site:www.ExecutiveSearch.tv

Tony Filson, pres; Helene Crocitto, exec VP; Jana Evans, legal/business affrs.

Retained Global Media & broadcasting exec search across all media platforms.

The Howard-Sloan-Koller Group, 300 E. 42nd St., New York, NY, 10017. Phone: (212) 661-5250. Fax: (212) 490-5322. E-mail: ekoller@hsksearch.com Web Site:www.hsksearch.com

Edward R. Koller Jr., pres/CEO.

Beverly HillsCA , 9701 Wilshire Blvd. Phone:

Exec search & consulting in the cable, digital, entertainment & publishing industries.

JOBPHONE, Box 5048, Newport Beach, CA, 92662. Phone: (949) 721-9280. Fax: (949) 721-8478. E-mail: jobphone@aol.com Web Site:www.infoguru.com

Keith Mueller, pres.

Natl TV/radio employment hotline.To hear job openings nationwide: (900) 726-5627-JOBS.

Keystone America, 38 Thomas St., Exeter Plaza, Exeter, PA, 18643. Phone: (570) 655-7143. Fax: (570) 654-5765. E-mail: usmail@keystoneamerica.com Web Site:keystoneamerica.com

Alan Kornish, VP.

Ntl Employment svc for bcst employers & candidates, placement of engrs & technicians. Serving all USA states. See our website: keystoneamerica.com.

Korn/Ferry International, 1900 Avenue of the Stars, Suite 2600, Los Angeles, CA, 90067. Phone: (310) 552-1834. Web Site:www.kornferry.com

William D. Simon, mgng dir entertainment; Gregg Kvochak, VP finance.

Worldwide sr level mgmt exec search firm servicing all sectors of the entertainment industry.

Lipson & Co., 1900 Ave. of the Stars, Suite 2810, Los Angeles, CA, 90067. Phone: (310) 277-4646. Fax: (310) 277-8585. E-mail: inquiries@lipsonco.com Web Site:www.lipsonco.com

Howard R. Lipson, pres; Harriet Lipson, sr VP.

Specialists in international & domestic bcstg (TV & radio), cable & entertainment, & related financial, professional audio/video & electronic recruiting. Svcs also for TV & film production, merchandising, licensing, & computers.

Brad Marks International, 15233 Ventura Blvd., PH 16, Sherman Oaks, CA, 91403. Phone: (818) 382-6300. Fax: (818) 386-0050. E-mail: bodysnatcher@bradmarks.com Web Site:www.bradmarks.com

Brad Marks, chmn/CEO.

Exec search at sr mgmt levels for communications, bcst, cable & multimedia companies. Areas include TV & film production, progmg, sls, mktg, news, gen mgmt, financial svcs, postproduction & adv/promotion.

Maslow Media Group Inc., 2134 Wisconsin Ave. N.W., Washington, DC, 20007. Phone: (202) 965-1100. Fax: (202) 965-6171. E-mail: lmaslow@maslowmedia.com Web Site:www.maslowmedia.com

Linda Maslow, CEO; Carl Neubecker, VP.

Freelance & fulltime staffing, crewing & payroll svcs for bcst, corporate, & federal govt. Find a job @ www.tvgigsonline.com

Media Management Resources Inc., 6890 S. Tuscon Way, Englewood, CO, 80112. Phone: (303) 290-9800. Fax: (303) 290-9596. E-mail: bwein@mediamanagement.com

Michael S. Wein, pres; David Reiber, gen mgr .

Full-svc consulting practice providing business support & technology svcs to select media & technology companies.

Media Staffing Network, 150 E. Huron, Suite 1305, Chicago, IL, 60611. Phone: (312) 944-9194. Fax: (312) 944-9195. E-mail: laurie@mediastaffingnetwork.com Web Site:www.mediastaffingnetwork.com

Laurie Kahn, pres/CEO.

Media Staffing Network the only full-service staffing company that specializes in media adv sls & associated departments, offering both temporary & full-time positions nationwide. Clients include radio & TV stns, rep firms, Internet, cable systems, networks, syndication, magazines & adv agencies. Openings range from entry-level support to sr mgmt positions in sls, prom, buying, planning, traf, continuity, customer svc & rsch.

MediaLine, Box 51909, Pacific Grove, CA, 93950. Phone: (800) 237-8073. Fax: (831) 648-5204. E-mail: medialine@medialine.com Web Site:www.medialine.com

Adrienne Laurent, pres; Mark Shilstone, owner & mgr.

Job listings for TV news, production & promotions; streaming video of resume tapes on the Internet; daily eletronic newsletter.

Miller Broadcast Management Inc., 616 W. Fulton St., Suite 516, Chicago, IL, 60661. Phone: (312) 454-1111. Fax: (312) 454-0044. E-mail: info@millerbroadcast.com Web Site:www.millerbroadcasts.com

Lisa Miller, pres; Matt Miller, VP.

Representing radio personalities.

RTNDA's Career Services, (formerly RTNDA Job Services). 1025 F St, Suite 700, Washington, DC, 20004. Phone: (800) 80-RTNDA. Fax: (202) 223-4007. E-mail: rtnda@rtnda.org Web Site:www.rtnda.org

Barbara Cochran, pres; Sarah Stump, editor.

We offer current career opportuunties in electronic journalism, as well as a wealth of resources for job seekers. We also have the most accurate & current industry rsch on salaries, newsroom staffing, newsroom profitability & woman/minority representation in the newsroom.

Search Source Inc., Box 1161, Granite City, IL, 62040-1161. Phone: (618) 931-6060. Fax: (618) 876-6071. E-mail: search@norcom2000.com

James R. McKechan, pres.

Search & recruitment of bcst professionals.

Barry Skidelsky, Esq., 655 Madison Ave., Fl. 19, New York, NY, 10065. Phone: (212) 832-4800. E-mail: bskidelsky@mindspring.com

Barry Skidelsky, atty/consultant.

Employment contact; EEO compliance, training, audits, litigation & arbitration.

R.A. Stone & Associates, 5495 Belt Line Rd., Suite 103, Dallas, TX, 75254-7671. Phone: (972) 233-0483. Fax: (972) 991-4995. E-mail: stonesearch@aol.com

Robert Stone, pres.

Retainer based exec search svcs for the domestic & international TV, radio, cable, multimedia, production & related communications/entertainment industries.

Ron Sunshine Associates, 2404 Clear Field Dr., Plano, TX, 75025. Phone: (972) 618-3670. Phone: (214) 509-3778. Fax: (972) 599-9583. E-mail: Ron@Ronsunshineassociates.com Web Site:www.ronsunshineassociates.com

Ron Sunshine, pres; Barbara Blake, VP.

Radio, TV & cable middle & upper mgmt.

Warren & Morris Ltd., 463 15th St., Del Mar, CA, 92014. Phone: (858) 481-3388. Fax: (858) 481-6221. E-mail: swarren@warrenmorrismltd.com Web Site:www.warrenmorrisltd.com

Charles Morris, ptnr; Lynn Cason, ptnr; Scott Warren, ptnr.

PortsmouthNH , 132 Chapel St. Phone:

Natl & international exec/mgmt-level recruitment svcs in the cable TV, wireless communications & digital media industries.

Youngs, Walker & Co., 1605 Colonial Pkwy., Inverness, IL, 60067. Phone: (847) 991-6900. Fax: (847) 934-6607. E-mail: info@youngswalker.com Web Site:www.youngswalker.com

Carl Youngs, pres.

Exec recruitment on a retained basis for TV & radio stn mgmt levels & corporate positions.

Section H

Associations, Events, Education, and Awards

Major National Associations

Academy of Television Arts & Sciences

Headquarters: 5220 Lankershim Blvd., North Hollywood, CA 91601-3109. (818) 754-2800. FAX: (818) 761-2827. Web Site: http://www.emmys.org.

Executives: John Schaffner, chmn & CEO; Jerry Petry, Academy Foundation chmn; Alan Perris, COO; Sheila Manning, sec; Donna Kanter, trea.

Mission Statement: The mission of the Academy is to promote creativity, diversity, innovation & excellence through recognition, education and leadership in the advancement of the telecommunications arts & sciences.

Cabletelevision Advertising Bureau Inc. (CAB)

Headquarters: 830 3rd Ave., New York, NY 10022. (212) 508-1200. FAX: (212) 832-3268. Web Site: www.onetvworld.org.

Executives: Sean Cunningham, pres/CEO; Jimmie Spears, sr VP finance/opns & CFO; Charles (Chuck) Thompson, exec VP strategic opns/sls & mktg; Danielle DeLauro, sr VP/sls & mktg; Evelyn Skurkovich, dir rsch & insights; Cynthia Perkins-Roberts, diversity sls/business dev.

Mission Statement: The CAB is dedicated to providing advertisers & agencies with the most current, complete actionable cable TV media insights at the national DMA & local levels.

Media Rating Council

Headquarters: 370 Lexington Ave., Suite 902, New York, NY 10017. (212) 972-0300. FAX: (212) 972-2786. E-mail: staffmediarating.org.

Executives: George Ivie, exec dir/CEO.

Mission: Secure for the media industry and related user audience measurement that is valid, reliable and effective.

National Association of Broadcasters (NAB)

Headquarters: 1771 N St. N.W., Washington, DC 20036. Phone: (202) 429-5300. FAX: (202) 429-4199. E-mail: nabnab.org. Web Site: www.nab.org.

NAB Executive Committee: David K. Rehr, pres/CEO; Janet McGregor, sec-trea/chief opn & financial off; Marsha MacBride, exec VP regulatory affrs/legal.

NAB Radio Board of Directors: Charles M. Warfield (chair) ICBC Broadcast Holdings, Inc., New York, NY; Caroline Beasley (first vice-chair), Beasley Broadcast Group, Inc. Naples, FL; Richard Cummings (Major Radio Grp Rep) Emmis

Communications Corp. Burbank, CA; Randy D. Gravley (second vice-chair), WLJA-FM/WPGY-AM, Tri-State Communications Jasper, GA.

NAB Radio District Representatives: Howard B. Anderson, KHWY, Inc., district: 24 (S.CA-GU-HI) Los Angeles, CA; Joseph M. Bilotta, Buckley Radio, district: 2 (NY-NJ), Greenwich, CT; John R. Beck Jr., Emmis Communications Corp., district: 12 (MO-KS), Saint Louis, MO; Eric Brown, Nebraska Rural Radio Network, district: 16 (CO-NE), Lexington, NE; Bobby Caldwell, East Arkansas Broadcasters, district: 15 (TN-AR), Wynne, AR; Ronald J. Davis, Butte Broadcasting, district: 20 (MT-ID-WY), Butte, MT; Ben Downs, Bryan Broadcasting Corp., district: 18 (So.), TX Bryan, TX; Paul G. Gardner, Elko Broadcasting Co., district: 22 (AZ-NV-NM-UT), Elko, NV; Jerry T. Hanszen, Hanszen Broadcasting, district: 19 (OK N.TX), Carthage, TX; Bob Holladay, Holladay Broadcasting, district: 08 (LA-MS), Monroe, LA; David Hoxeng, ADX Communications, district: 7 (FL PR VI), Pensacola, FL; Julie Koehn, WLEN-FM, district: 13 (MI) Adrian, MI; Monte Loos, Duhamel Broadcasting Enterprises, district: 21 (MN SD ND), Rapid City, SD; William L. McElveen, Citadel Broadcasting Corp, district: 6 (NC-SC), Columbia, SC; Matthew Mnich, Citadel Broadcasting Corp., district: 6 (NC-SC), Columbia, SC; Peter H. Smyth, Greater Media Boston, district: 1 (New England), Braintree, MA; Matthew Mnich, North American Broadcasting Co. Inc., District: 11 (OH), Columbus, OH; Mike Novak, Educational Media Foundation, district: 23 (N.CA AK), Rocklin, CA; Joel Oxley, Bonneville Washington Radio Group, district: 04 (DE-DC-MD-VA), Washington, DC; Mary Quass, NRG Media, LLC, district: 14 (IA-WI), Cedar Rapids, IA; Daniel Savadove, Main Line Broadcasting, LLC, district: 3 (PA), West Conshohocken, PA; Dana Withers, Dana Communications Corp., district: 17 (IL), Mc Leansboro, IL.

NAB Radio Designated Board Seats: Edward K. Christian, Sage Communications, Grosse Pointe Farms, MI; Lew Dickey Jr., Cumulus Media, Inc., Atlanta, GA; Susan Davenport Austin, Sheridan Broadcasting Corp. Susan K. Patrick, Legend Communications, Ellicott City, MD; Edward G. Atsinger III, Salem Communications Camarillo, CA; Amador Bustos, Bustos Media, LLC, Sacramento, CA.; Sally J. Brown, Schurz Communications Mishawaka, IN; David J. Field, Entercom Communications Corporation Bala Cynwyd, PA; Jessica A. Marventano, Clear Channel Communications Washington, DC; Marc Morgan, Cox Radio, Inc. Atlanta, GA; Gary Stone, Univision Radio Dallas, TX.

NAB TV Board of Directors: Paul Karpowicz Alan W. Frank (chair), pres Meredith Corporation, Rocky Hill, CT; Lynn Beal (first vice-chair), exec VP, Garnnett Broadcasting, St. Louis, MO; David J. Barrett (second vice-chair), pres/CEO Hearst Television, Inc., New York, NY; C. Douglas Kranwinkle, TV Network Rep., exec VP law, Univision Communications Inc., Los Angeles, CA.

NAB TV Elected Representatives: Elizabeth Murphy Burns, pres, Morgan Murphy Media; Jim Conschafter, sr VP/bcst stns, Media General Broadcast Croup, Richmond, VA; Marci Burdick, sr VP/bcst & cable, Schurz Communications, Inc., Mishawaka, IN; John C. Kueneke, pres News-Press & Gazette Broadcasting, St. Louis, MO; Paul H. McTear, pres/CEO Raycom Media Inc., Montgomery, AL; Ralph M. Oakley, VP/CEO, Quincy Broadcast Group, Quincy, IL; Doreen Wade, pres Freedom Broadcasting, Inc., West Palm Beach, FL; K. James

Yager, CEO Barrington Broadcasting Co., LLC, Hoffman Estates, IL; Raymond H. Cole, pres/COO Citadel Communications Co. Ltd., West Des Moines, IA.

NAB TV Designated Board Seats: Brian W. Brady, pres/CEO Northwest Broadcasting, Inc. Okemos, MI; Michael J. Fiorile (vice-chmn) & CEO, Dispatch Broadcast Group, Columbus, OH; Alan W. Frank, pres/CEO Post-News Stations, Inc., Detroit, MI; Brian Lawlor, sr VP The E. W. Scripps Company, Cincinnati, OH; Randy Michaels, COO Tribune Company, Chicago, IL; Scott Blumenthal exec VP LIN Television Corp., Providence, RI; Dunia A. Shive, pres/CEO Belo Corp., Dallas, TX.

NAB Network Representatives: John W. Eck, pres, NBC TV Network & Media Works NBC Universal, New York, NY; John Lawson, exec VP ION Media Networks, Arlington, VA; Preston R. Padden, exec VP Worldwide Govt Relations, The Walt Disney Company, Washington, DC.

National Association of Farm Broadcasters

Headquarters: Box 500, Platte City, MO 64079. (816) 431-4032. (800) 294-6232. E-mail: infonafb.com. Web Site: www.nafb.com.

Members: Bill O'Neill, dir; Rose Marie Lawrence, Office Asst; Stacia Cudd, news svc editor; Susan Tally, office mgr; Jennifer Saylor, member svcs mgr.

National Association of Television Program Executives (NATPE)

Headquarters: 5757 Wilshire Blvd., Penthouse 10, Los Angeles, CA 90036-3681. (310) 453-4440. FAX: (310) 453-5258. Web Site: www.natpe.org.

Mission Statement: A global, non-profit organization dedicated to the creation, dev & distribution of televised progmg in all forms across all mature and emerging media platforms.

Staff: Rick Feldman, pres/CEO; Jenean Atwood, exec asst to pres/CEO; Beth Braen, sr VP mktg; Jon Dobkin; CFO; Lew Klein, pres NATPE Educational Foundation.

National Cable and Telecommunications Association (NCTA)

Headquarters: 25 Massachusetts Ave. N.W., Washington, DC 20001. (202) 222-2300. E-mail: webmasterncta.com. Web Site: www.ncta.com.

Executive Officer Kyle McSlarrow, pres/CEO; James M. Assey, exec VP; Eleanor Winter, sr VP special project; Bruce Carnes, sr VP finance/Admin; William Check, sr VP science/technology; Jadz Janucik, sr VP/assoc affrs; Brian Dietz, VP

communications; Rita Lewis, sr VP govt rel; Jill Luckett, sr VP/program network policy; Rob Stoddard, sr VP Communications/pub affrs; Barbara York, sr VP/industry affrs.

National Cable Television Cooperative Inc.

Headquarters: 11200 Corporate Ave., Lenexa, KS 66219-1392. (913) 599-5900. Fax : (913) 599-5903. Web Site: www.cabletvcoop.org.

About NCTC: NCTC is a not-for-profit member-operating purchasing organization dedicated to reducing operating costs of its member cable companies. The Co-op negotiates and administers master affiliation agreements with cable TV progmg networks, cable hardware & equipment manufacturers & other svc providers on behalf of its member companies.

NCTC Executive: Jeff Abbas, pres/CEO; Scott Abbott, exec VP; Corey McCarthy, CFO; Frank Hughes, sr VP progmg; Alan Tschirner, VP technology;

Radio Advertising Bureau

Headquarters: 125 W. 55th St., New York, NY 10019. (646) 467-7460; (800) 252-7234. Web Site: www.rab.com.

Officer: Jeff Haley, pres/CEO.

RAB Office Center: 1320 Greenway Dr., Suite 500, Irving, TX 75038-2510. (800) 232-3131.

Chicago: 30 South Wacker Dr., 22nd Fl., Chicago, IL 60606. (312) 466-5639.

Los Angeles: 21900 Burbank Blvd., Suite 3038, Woodland Hills, CA 91367. (323) 904-4357.

Detroit: 28175 Haggerty Rd., Novi, MN. (248) 994-7678.

South Africa: 2 Albury Park, Albury Road, Dunkeld West, 2196. +27 11 325 4935. Fax: +27 11 325 4536.

Radio-Television News Directors Association Foundation

Headquarters: 529 14th St.,N.W., Suite 425, Washington, DC 20045. ((202) 659-6510. FAX: (202) 223-4007. E-mail: rtndartnda.org. Web Site: www.rtnda.org

Mailing Address RTNDA & RTNDF: 4121 Plank Rd., #512, Fredericksburg, VA 22407.

Staff: Kathleen Graham, exec dir; Carol Knopes, dir/edu projects; Barbara Cochran (pres Emeritus); Stacey Staniak, project mgr; Tara Sheehan, dir/membership & mktg; Jon Ebinger (consultant), RIAS Exchange, jonrtndf.org.

Mission Provides training programs seminars, scholarship support & rsch in areas of critical concern to electronic news professionals and their audience.

RTNDF German/American Senior Editors Program: Doug Adams, sr producer/NBC News; Diane Vogel, mng producer, The Kojo Nnamdi Show, WAMU & Deborah Potter, NewsLab, (all) Washington; Merideth Beal, Lasting Value Broadcast Group, Austin; Larry Carlson, sr Lecturer/Texas State University, San Marcos & Dave Strickland, VP/news dir, KTRK-TV, Houston, (all) TX; Steve Scher, sr host/exec producer, KUOW-FM & Tom Tangney, mgng editor/NewsTalk 97.3 KIRO, (both) Seattle, WA.

Active Members: Over 1,100 radio & TV news directors.

RTNDF Program Supporters: Ethics & Excellence in Journalism Foundation, The Gannett Foundation, The John S. & James L. Knight Foundation, McCormick Foundation, The NEFE, New York Times Radio, The National Academies, RIAS Berlin Commission & Scripps Howard Foundation.

RTNDF Programs: Digital Election: Using New Media to Engage Your Audience, German/American Journalist Exchange, Financial Reporting Project, High School Electronic Journalism Project, Journalism Ethics, News & Terrorism, News Leadership, Newsroom Diversity Program, Scholarships, Fellowships & Internships,

Television Bureau of Advertising (TVB)

Headquarters: 3 E. 54th St., New York, NY 10022-3108. (212) 486-1111. FAX: (212) 935-5631. E-mail: infotvb.org. Web Site: www.tvb.org.

Staff: Christopher Rohrs, pres; Abby Auerbach, exec VP; Carrie Hart, VP/rsch; B.J. Park, rsch dir; Susan Cucinello, sr VP/rsch; Jack Poor, VP/mktg; Ron Salmon, rsch dir; Pat Yancovitz, rsch dir; Hope Etheridge, VP/finance and admin; Janice Garjian, VP member svcs; Peter Schmid, sr VP mktg; Joseph C. Tirinato, sr VP membership; Gary Belis, VP communications.

Board of Directors: Bruce Baker, exec VP Cox Television; Jim Beloyianis, pres Katz Television Group, Katz Media Group, Inc.; Craig Broitman, pres Millenium Sales & Marketing; Frank Comerford, pres/gen mgr WNBC-TV, New York, NY; Michael Fiorile, pres/CEO, Distpatch Broadcast Group; Alan Frank, pres Post-Newsweek Stations Inc.;Tom Kane, pres/CEO, CBS Television Stations; Paul Karpowicz, pres Meredith Broadcasting; Kathleen Keefe, VP sls Hearst-Argyle Television; Doug Kiel, vice-chmn/CEO Journal Broadcast Group; Walter Liss, pres ABC Owned Television Stations, Inc.; Leo MacCourtney, pres/CEO Blair Television; Ibra Morales, pres Telemundo Group, Inc.;Louis Wall, pres Sagamore Hill Broadcasting; John Cottingham, sr VP/Broadcast Stations, Media General Broadcast Group; Jim Monahan, pres & gen mgr Tribune Co.; John Weiser, pres/distribution Sony Pictures Television Sales Inc.; Doreen Wade, pres Freedom Broadcasting Inc.; Robert Silva, VP/dir sls E.W. Scripps Co.; Leo MacCourtney, pres/CEO Blair Television; Julio Marenghi, pres/sls CBS Television Stations; Jim Monohan, pres, gen mgr TeleRep, Inc.; Christopher Rohrs, pres Television Bureau of Advertising;Robert Silva, VP/dir sls E.W. Scripps Co.; Perry Sook, pres/CEO Nexstar Broadcasting Group; Paul Trelstad, sr VP Gannet Broadcasting; Doreen Wade, pres Freedom Broadcasting, Inc.; Louis Wall, pres Sagamore Hill Broadcasting; John Watkins, pres ABC National Television Sales, Inc., New York, NY.

National Associations

AFCEA, 4400 Fair Lakes Ct., Fairfax, VA, 22033-3899. Phone: (703) 631-6100. Phone: (800) 336-4583. Fax: (703) 631-6130.E-mail: promo@afcea.org Web Site:www.afcea.org

ANEPA, C/Castella, 59 bis, 28001, Madrid Spain. Phone: 91 575 53 81. Fax: 91 435 66 53.E-mail: anepa@anepa.net Web Site:www.anepa.net

Academy of Canadian Cinema & Television, Natl Office, 172 King St. E., Main Fl., Toronto, ON, M5A 1J3. Canada. Phone: (416) 366-2227. Phone: (800) 644-5194. Fax: (416) 366-8454. Web Site:www.academy.ca E-mail: info@academy.ca

VancouverBC , 1385 Homer St. Phone:judy_rink@telus.net
MontrealPQ Canada, 225, rue Roy E, bureau 106. Phone:

Acoustical Society of America, 2 Huntington Quadrayle, Suite 1N01, Melville, NY, 11747-4502. Phone: (516) 576-2360. Fax: (516) 576-2377.E-mail: asa@aip.org Web Site:asa.aip.org

Advanced Television Systems Committee (ATSC), 1750 K St. N.W., Suite 1200, Washington, DC, 20006. Phone: (202) 872-9160. Fax: (202) 872-9161.E-mail: atsc@atsc.org Web Site:www.atsc.org

More than 130 members representing TV networks, mf assns & others. International voluntary tech standards-setting organization for advanced TV.

The Advertising Council Inc., 261 Madison Ave., New York, NY, 10016-2303. Phone: (212) 922-1500. Fax: (212) 922-1676.E-mail: info@adcouncil.org Web Site:www.adcouncil.org

WashingtonDC , 1203 19th St. N.W., 4th Fl. Phone:

Advertising Research Foundation Inc., 432 Park Ave. S., New York, NY, 10016. Phone: (212) 751-5656. Fax: (212) 319-5265. Web Site:www.thearf.org

Alliance for Community Media, 1100 G St. N.W., Suite 740, Washington, DC, 20005. Phone: (202) 393-2650. Fax: (202) 393-2653.E-mail: raiseeveryvoice@yahoo.com Web Site:www.alliancecm.org

Alliance of Motion Picture and Television Producers, 15503 Ventura Blvd., Encino, CA, 91436. Phone: (818) 995-3600. Fax: (818) 382-1793. Web Site:www.amptp.org

American Advertising Federation, 1101 Vermont Ave. N.W., Suite 500, Washington, DC, 20005-6306. Phone: (202) 898-0089. Fax: (202) 898-0159.E-mail: aaf@aaf.org Web Site:www.aaf.org

American Association of Advertising Agencies (AAAA), 405 Lexington Ave., 18th Fl., New York, NY, 10174-1801. Phone: (212) 682-2500. Fax: (212) 682-8391. Web Site:www.aaaa.org

American Center for Children and Media, 5400 N. St. Louis Ave., Chicago, IL, 60625. Phone: (773) 509-5510. Fax: (773) 509-5303.E-mail: dkleeman@atgonline.org Web Site:www.centerforchildrenandmedia.org

American Cinema Editors Inc., 100 Universal City Plaza, Bldg. 2282, Rm. 234, Universal City, CA, 91608. Phone: (818) 777-2900. Fax: (818) 733-5023. Web Site:www.ace-filmeditors.com

American Composers Alliance (ACA), 648 Broadway, Rm. 803, New York, NY, 10012-2301. Phone: (212) 362-8900. Phone: (212) 925-0458. Fax: (212) 925-6798.E-mail: info@composers.com Web Site:www.composers.com

American Electronics Association, 5201 Great America Pkwy., Suite 520, Santa Clara, CA, 95054. Phone: (408) 987-4200. Fax: (408) 987-4298. Web Site:www.aeanet.org

WashingtonDC , 601 Pennsylvania Ave. Phone:

American Marketing Association, 311 S. Wacker Dr., Suite 5800, Chicago, IL, 60606. Phone: (312) 542-9000. Phone: (800) 262-1150. Fax: (312) 542-9001. Web Site:www.marketingpower.com E-mail: info@ama.org

American Meteorological Society, 45 Beacon St., Boston, MA, 02108-3693. Phone: (617) 227-2425. Fax: (617) 742-8718.E-mail: amsinfo@ametsoc.org Web Site:www.ametsoc.org/ams

American Radio Relay League, 225 Main St., Newington, CT, 06111. Phone: (860) 594-0200. Fax: (860) 594-0259.E-mail: hg@arrl.org Web Site:www.arrl.org

Joel Harrison, 1st VP.

American Society of Composers, Authors & Publishers (ASCAP), One Lincoln Plaza, New York, NY, 10023. Phone: (212) 621-6000. Fax: (212) 724-9064.E-mail: info@ascap.com Web Site:www.ascap.com

Hato ReyPR . ASCAP - Puerto Rico, 654 Ave. Munoz Rivera, IBM Plaza Suite 1101 B. Phone:

London United Kingdom. ASCAP - London, 8 Cork St. Phone:

Los AngelesCA . ASAP - Los Angeles, 7920 W. Sunset Blvd., 3rd Fl. Phone:

Miami BeachFL . ASCAP - Miami, 420 Lincoln Rd., Suite 385. Phone:

AtlantaGA . ASCAP - Atlanta, 541 Tenth St. N.W, PMB400. Phone:

ChicagoIL . ASCAP - Chicago, 1608 N. Milwaukee, Suite 1007. Phone:

NashvilleTN . ASCAP - Nashville, Two Music Square W. Phone:

(See listing under Music Licensing, Section G.)

American Society of Media Photographers (ASMP), 150 N. 2nd St., Philadelphia, PA, 19106. Phone: (215) 451-2767. Fax: (215) 451-0880.E-mail: info@asmp.org Web Site:www.asmp.org

Robert Wilex, 1st VP. Directors: Susan Carr, Judy Herrman & Clem Spalding.

American Society of TV Cameramen Inc., (U.S. affll of International Society of Videographers.). 2520 Lotus Hill Dr., Las Vegas, NV, 89134-7855. Phone: (702) 228-6704. Fax: (702) 228-6714.E-mail: ruzwe7@aol.com

Directors: Tom Jocelyn, Peter Basil, Gino Guarna & Sol Bress.

SparkillNY , Box 296. Nicole Zweck-Spanos, Production Planning.

American Sportscasters Association, 225 Broadway, Suite 2030, New York, NY, 10007. Phone: (212) 227-8080. Fax: (212) 571-0556.E-mail: lschwa8918@aol.com Web Site:americansportscastersonline.com

Directors: Lou Schwartz, Jon Miller, Jim Nantz, Dick Enberg & Bill Walton.

American Sportscasters Hall of Fame Trust, 225 Broadway, Suite 2030, New York, NY, 10007. Phone: (212) 227-8080. Fax: (212) 571-0556.E-mail: lschwa8918@aol.com Web Site:www.americansportscastersonline.com

American Women in Radio and Television Inc., 8405 Greenboro Dr., Suite 800, McLean, VA, 22102. Phone: (703) 506-3290. Fax: (703) 506-3266. Web Site:www.awrt.org E-mail: info@awrt.org

Association for Education in Journalism & Mass Communication (AEJMC), 234 Outlet Point Blvd., Suite A, Columbia, SC, 29210. Phone: (803) 798-0271. Fax: (803) 772-3509.E-mail: aejmc@aejmc.org Web Site:www.aejmc.org

Association for Interactive Marketing, (AIM). 1120 Avenue of the Americas, New York, NY, 10036. Phone: (888) 337-0008. Fax: (212) 391-9233. Web Site:www.greenlight.co.uk

Association for Maximum Service Television Inc., (MSTV, Inc.). Box 9897, 4100 Wisconsin Ave., N.W., Washington, DC, 20016. Phone: (202) 966-1956. Fax: (202) 966-9617. Web Site:www.mstv.org E-mail: lmillory@mst.org

The Association for Women In Communications, 3337 Duke St., Alexandria, VA, 22314. Phone: (703) 370-7436. Fax: (703) 370-7437.E-mail: info@womcom.org Web Site:www.womcom.org

Directors: Pamela Valenzuela.

Association of American Railroads, American Railroads Bldg., 50 F St. N.W., Washington, DC, 20001. Phone: (202) 639-2100. Fax: (202) 639-2558.E-mail: twhite@www.aar.org Web Site:www.aar.org

Association of Cable Communicators, Box 75007, Washington, DC, 20013. Phone: (202) 222-2370. Fax: (202) 222-2371.E-mail: services@cablecommunicators.org Web Site:www.cablecommunicators.org

Rob Stoddard, 1st VP; James Maiella Jr., 2nd VP; Libby O'Connell, Ph.D. Directors: Pete Abel, Bobby Amirshahi, Portia E. Badham, Janice Caluda, Sandra Colony, Annie Howell, Ellen Kroner, Margaret Lejuste, Jennifer Mooney, Misty Skedgell, Jean Margaret Smith & Thomas Southwick.

Association of Canadian Advertisers Inc., 175 Bloor St. E., South Tower, Suite 307, Toronto, ON, M4W 3R8. Canada. Phone: (416) 964-3805. Phone: (800) 565-0109 (CA). Fax: (416) 964-0771.E-mail: rlund@acaweb.com Web Site:www.aca-online.com

MontrealPQ , 500 Sherbrooke St. W. Phone:

Association of Federal Communications Consulting Engineers (AFCCE), Box 1933, Washington, DC, 20036-0333. Phone: (812) 925-6000 Ext 270. Phone: 2202) 898-0111. Fax: (812) 925-4030. Web Site:www.afcce.org E-mail: president@afcce.org

Marnie K. Sarver, Esq. Directors: Glen Clark, Donald G. Everist, Carl T. Jones Jr. & David H. Layer.

Association of National Advertisers Inc. (ANA), 708 3rd Ave., New York, NY, 10017. Phone: (212) 697-5950. Fax: (212) 661-8057. Web Site:www.ana.net E-mail: bduggan@ana.net

Directors: Donald F. Calhoon, Jocelyn Carter-Miller, J. Andrea Alstrup, Catherine D. Constable, Christopher Fraleigh, James J. Garrity, David B. Green, John D. Hayes, Stephen C. Jones, Dawn Hudson, David N. Iauco, Abby F. Kohnstamm, Ann Lewnes, Eric W. Leininger, Robert D. Liodice, Paula S. Sneed, Gary E. McCullough, James R. Stengel, James D. Speros, Allan H. Stefl, Stephen G. Sullivan, Joseph V. Tripodi, Rebecca Saeger, James L. McDowell, Nancy J. Wiese, Robert J. Garngort & Robert C Lachky.

WashingtonDC . Washington Office, 1120 20th St. N.W, Suite 5206. Phone:

Association of Public Television Stations, 2100 Crystal Dr., Suite 700, Arlington, VA, 22202. Phone: (202) 654-4200. Fax: (202) 654-4236.

Directors: Debra Tica Sanchez & Jeffrey Davis.

The Audio Engineering Society Inc., 60 E. 42nd St., Rm. 2520, New York, NY, 10165. Phone: (212) 661-8528. Fax: (212) 682-0477.E-mail: hq@aes.org Web Site:www.aes.org

BMI Broadcast Music Inc., 320 W. 57th St., New York, NY, 10019-3790. Phone: (212) 586-2000. Fax: (212) 246-2163.E-mail: abooth@bmi.com Web Site:www.bmi.com

Directors: Philip A. Jones, Frances W. Preston, James G. Babb, Harold C. Crump, N. John Douglas, Frank E. Melton, George V. Willoughby, K. James Yager, G. Neil Smith, David Sherman, Donald A. Thurston, Cecil L. Walker, Catherine L. Hughes, Craig A. Dubow, Amador Bustos & John L. Sander.

West HollywoodCA , 8730 Sunset Blvd, 3rd Fl. W. Phone:

NashvilleTN , 10 Music Sq. E. Phone:

Broadcast Cable Credit Association Inc. (BCCA), 550 W. Frontage Rd., Suite 3600, Northfield, IL, 60093. Phone: (847) 881-8757. Fax: (847) 784-8059.E-mail: info@bccacredit.com Web Site:www.bccacredit.com

Media Financial Management Association (MFM), (Formerly Broadcast Cable Financial Management Association BCFM). 550 W. Frontage Rd., Suite 3600, Northfield, IL, 60093-1243. Phone: (847) 716-7000. Fax: (847) 716-7004.E-mail: info@mediafinance.org Web Site:www.mediafinance.org

Broadcast Education Association, 1771 N St. N.W., Washington, DC, 20036-2891. Phone: (202) 429-3935. Fax: (202) 775-2981.E-mail: beainfo@beaweb.org Web Site:www.beaweb.org

Directors: Mary Alice Molgard, Thomas R. Berg, Rustin Greene, Joe Misiewicz, David Byland, Robert K. Avery, Gary Martin, Greg Luft, D'Artagnan Bebel, Stephen J. Cohen, Larry Patrick, Alan R. Albarran, Gary Corbitt, Steven Anderson, Norman Pattiz & Jannette L. Dates.

Broadcasters Foundation of America, 7 Lincoln Ave., Greenwich, CT, 06830. Phone: (203) 862-8577. Fax: (203) 629-5739.E-mail: ghhbcast@aol.com Web Site:broadcastersfoundation.org

Broadcasters Hall of Fame, 1240 Ashford Ln. #1A, Akron, OH, 44313. Phone: (330) 836-4864.

Jeannette Camak, sec.

AkronOH , Box 8192. Henry Dunn, treas. (Broadcaster's Hall of Fame) .

CTAM, Cable & Telecommunications Association. 201 N. Union St., Suite 440, Alexandria, VA, 22314. Phone: (703) 549-4200. Fax: (703) 684-1167.E-mail: info@ctam.com Web Site:www.ctam.com

The Cable Center, 2000 Buchtel Blvd., Denver, CO, 80210. Phone: (303) 871-4885. Fax: (303) 871-4514.E-mail: info@cablecenter.org Web Site:www.cablecenter.org

Cable in the Classroom, 1724 Massachusetts Ave. N.W., Washington, DC, 20036. Phone: (202) 775-1040. Fax: (202) 775-1047. Web Site:www.ciconline.org

Cable Television Laboratories Inc., 858 Coal Creek Cir., Louisville, CO, 80027-9750. Phone: (303) 661-9100. Fax: (303) 661-9199. Web Site:www.cablelabs.com E-mail: m.schwartz@cablelabs.com

Brian L. Roberts, chmn.

Broadband dev for cable system operators.

Cabletelevision Advertising Bureau Inc. (CAB),

See listing under Major National Associations, this section.

Can-West Media Sales, 333 King St. E., Toronto, ON, M5A 4R7. Canada. Phone: (416) 350-6002. Fax: (416) 442-2209.E-mail: queries@nationalpost.co Web Site:www.canada.com

Canadian Association of Broadcast Consultants, 130 Cree Crescent, Winnipeg, MB, R3J 3W1. Canada. Phone: (204) 889-9202. Fax: (204) 831-6650.E-mail: kpelser@deema.mb.ca

Maurice Beausejour, pres; Kerry Pelser, sec/treas.

The Canadian Association of Broadcasters, Box 627, Station B, 306-350 Sparks St., Ottawa, ON, K1P 5S2. Canada. Phone: (613) 233-4035. Fax: (613) 233-6961.E-mail: cab@cab-acr.ca Web Site:www.cab-acr.ca

Directors: Fawn-Dell Flanagan, Antoinette Mensour, Jim Patrick & Susan Wheeler.

OttawaON Canada, 306-350 Sparks St. Phone:

Canadian Association of Ethnic (Radio) Broadcasters, 622 College St., Toronto, ON, M6G 1B6. Canada. Phone: (416) 531-9991. Fax: (416) 531-5274.E-mail: info@chinradio.com Web Site:www.chinradio.com

Canadian Film and Television Production Association (CFTPA), 160 John St., Toronto, ON, M5C 2E5. Canada. Phone: (416) 304-0280. Fax: (416) 304-0499.E-mail: toronto@cftpa.ca Web Site:www.cftpa.ca

Directors: Cara Martin.

OttawaON , 151 Slater St, Suite 605. Phone:

Caribbean Broadcasting Union (CBU), Harbour Industrial Estate, Harbour Rd., Suite 1B, Bldg. 6 A, St. Michael, BB, 11145. Barbados. Phone: (246) 430-1006. Fax: (246) 228-9524. Web Site:www.caribunion.com

Catholic Academy for Communication Arts Professionals, 1645 Brook Lynn Dr., Suite 2, Dayton, OH, 45432-1944. Phone: (937) 458-0265. Fax: (937) 458-0263.E-mail: admin@catholicacademy.org Web Site:www.catholicacademy.org

Jeanean Merkel, 1st VP; Vicki Bedard, 2nd VP.

Center for Communication Inc., 561 Broadway, Suite 12 B, New York, NY, 10012. Phone: (212) 686-5005. Fax: (212) 504-2632.E-mail: info@cencom.org Web Site:www.cencom.org

Edward Bleier, chmn; Frank Stanton, dir emeritus. Directors: Timothy Barry, William F. Baker, Robert M. Batscha, Patricia T. Carbine, Antoinette Cook Bush, John A. Dimling, David R. Drobis, Michael Eigner, Peter R. Ezersky, Charles B. Fruit, Ralph Guild, Andrew Heyward, Peter Jennings, Gerald M. Levin, Kate McEnroe, Martin Nisenholtz, Herbert Scannell, Alan Siegel, Alfred C. Sikes, Kenneth Stoddard, Howard Stringer, Alberto Vitale, Stephen A. Weiswasser, David Westin, Bob Wright, Lois Wyse, Mortimer B. Zuckerman, Simon Michael Bessie, Louis D. Boccardi, David W. Burke, Henry A. Grunwald, Irwin Segelstein, Burton B. Staniar & Loet A. Velmans.

Commonwealth Broadcasting Assn, CBA Secretariat, 17 Fleet St., London, EC4Y 1AA. United Kingdom. Phone: 011-44-171-5835550. Fax: 011-44-171-5835549.E-mail: cba@cba.org.uk Web Site:www.cba.org.uk

Directors: George Valarino, Ronald Abraham, Roger Grant, Robert O'Rielly, Tombong Saidy, Sharon Crosbie & Cecilia Khuzwayo.

Community Broadcasters Association (CBA), 515 King St., Suite 420, Alexandria, VA, 22314. Phone: (703) 562-3588. Fax: (703) 684-6048. Web Site:www.communitybroadcasters.com

Directors: Gary Co Cola, Larry Morton, Eleanor St. John, Warren Trumbly, Doug Williams, Sandra Woodworth & Lou Zanoni.

Produces major country radio convention; rgnl radio seminar; Country DJ Hall of Fame.

Council of Better Business Bureaus Inc., 4200 Wilson Blvd., 8th Fl., Arlington, VA, 22203-1838. Phone: (703) 276-0100. Fax: (703) 525-8277.E-mail: bbb@bbb.org Web Site:www.bbb.org

OttawaON Canada, 44 Byward Market Sq, Suite 220.

Country Music Association Inc., One Music Cir. S., Nashville, TN, 37203. Phone: (615) 244-2840. Fax: (615) 726-0314. Web Site:www.cmaworld.com

Country Radio Broadcasters Inc., 819 18th Ave. S., Nashville, TN, 37203. Phone: (615) 327-4487. Fax: (615) 329-4492. Web Site:www.crb.org

This non-profit organization is the only assn specifically serving country radio. Holds annual Country Radio Seminar; rgnl conventions; trustee of Country DJ Hall of Fame & Country Radio Hall of Fame.

Electro Federation Canada, 5800 Explorer Dr., Suite 200, Mississauga, ON, L4W 5K9. Canada. Phone: (866) 602-8877. Fax: (905) 602-5686.E-mail: info@electrofed.com Web Site:www.electrofed.com

Electronic Industries Alliance (EIA), 2500 Wilson Blvd., Arlington, VA, 22201. Phone: (703) 907-7500. Fax: (703) 907-7501.E-mail: dmccurdy@eia.org Web Site:www.eia.org

Electronic Retailing Association (ERA), 200 N. 14th St., Suite 300, Arlington, VA, 22201. Phone: (703) 841-1751. Phone: (800) 987-6462. Fax: (703) 841-1751.E-mail: contact@retailing.org Web Site:www.retailing.org

Stephen F. Breimer, Esq.; Jeffrey Knowles, Esq. Directors: Linda Goldstein, Mike Ackerman, Rick Cesari, Dan Danielson, Denise Dubarry Hay, Rollie Froehlig, Larry Jellen, Jack Kirby, Mark Lavin, Shigeru Ohashi, Rick Petry, Steve Pittenridgh, Richard Prochnow, Randy Ronning, Robert Rosenblatt, Bret Saxton, Mark Thornton & Reiner Weihofen.

Electronic Service Dealers Association, 4927 W. Irving Park Rd., Chicago, IL, 60641. Phone: (773) 282-9400.

Electronics Representatives Association, 300 W. Adams St., Suite 617, Chicago, IL, 60606. Phone: (312) 527-3050. Fax: (312) 527-3783.E-mail: info@era.org Web Site:www.era.org

Directors: Tom Shanahan.

FCBA (Federal Communications Bar Association), 1020 19th St. N.W., Suite 325, Washington, DC, 20036-6101. Phone: (202) 293-4000. Fax: (202) 293-4317.E-mail: fcba@fcba.org Web Site:www.fcba.org

Festival of Nouveau Cinema Montreal, 3805 Blvd. Saint-Lavrent, Montreal, PQ, H2W 7X9. Canada. Phone: (514) 282-0004. Fax: (514) 282-6664.E-mail: ngirard@nouveaucinema.ca Web Site:www.nouveaucinema.ca

Foundation for American Communications (FACS), 85 South Grand Ave., Pasadena, CA, 91105. Phone: (626) 584-0010. Fax: (626) 584-0627.E-mail: facs@facsnet.org Web Site:www.facsnet.org

LeesburgVA , 3 Wirt St. N.W. Phone:

Free TV Australia Ltd., (formerly Commercial Television Australia CTVA). 44 Avenue Rd., Mosman, N.S.W., 02088. Australia. Phone: 61 2 8968 7100. Fax: 61 2 9969 3520.E-mail: contact@freetv.com.au Web Site:www.freevaust.com.au

Provides a forum for discussion of industry matters by its members & is the pub voice of the industry on a wide range of issues & has represented the coml free-to-air TV industry for over 40 years.

Hollywood Radio & Television Society, 13701 Riverside Dr., Suite 205, Sherman Oaks, CA, 91423. Phone: (818) 789-1182. Fax: (818) 789-1210.E-mail: info@hrts.org Web Site:www.hrts.org

IEEE, 445 Hoes Ln., Piscataway, NJ, 08854-1331. Phone: (732) 981-0060. Fax: (732) 981-1721. Web Site:www.ieee.org

New YorkNY , 3 Park Ave. 17th Fl. Phone:

Independent Film & Television Alliance (IFTA), 10850 Wilshire Blvd., 9th Fl., Los Angeles, CA, 90024-4321. Phone: (310) 446-1000. Fax: (310) 446-1600.E-mail: info@ifta-online.org Web Site:www.ifta-online.org

Directors: Glen Basner, Steve Bickel, Alison Thompson, Nicolas Chartier, Roger Corman, Pierre David, Peter Elson, Kimberly Ferguson, Antony Ginnane, Peter Graham, Robert Hayward, Avi Lerner, Mark Lindsay, Nicole Mackey, Nicholas Meyer, Bobby Meyers, Michael Weiser, Kevin Williams & Andrew Stevens.

Intercollegiate Broadcasting System Inc., 367 Windsor Hwy., New Windsor, NY, 12553-7900. Phone: (845) 565-0003. Fax: (845) 565-7446.E-mail: ibshq@aol.com Web Site:www.ibsradio.org

Directors: John Murphy, Fritz Kass, Norm Prusslin & Chuck Platt.

The International Academy of Television Arts & Sciences, 888 7th St., 5th Fl., New York, NY, 10019. Phone: (212) 489-6969. Fax: (212) 489-6557.E-mail: info@emmys.tv Web Site:www.iemmys.tv

International Advertising Association, (The global partnership of advertisers, agencies & media.). 521 Fifth Ave., Suite 1807, New York, NY, 10175. Phone: (212) 557-1133. Fax: (212) 983-0455.E-mail: iaa@iaaglobal.org Web Site:www.iaaglobal.org

Wendy Burrell, mng dir. Directors: Richard Corner.

International Animated Film Society, ASIFA-Hollywood, 2114 Burbank Blvd., Burbank, CA, 91506. Phone: (818) 842-8330. Fax: (818) 842-5645.E-mail: asifaalert-subscribe @yahoogroups.com Web Site:www.asifa-hollywood.org

Directors: Jerry Beck, Stephen Worth, Bob Miller, Tom Knott, Frank Gladstone, David Derks, Margaret Kerry-Wilcox, Larry Loc & Will Ryan.

International Association of Audio Information Services, c/o NBRS, 1090 Don Mills Rd., Suite 303, Toronto, ON, M3C 3R6. Canada. Phone: (416) 422-4222, ext 224. Fax: (416) 422-1633.E-mail: hlusignan@nbrscanada.com Web Site:www.iaais.org

International Communication Agency Network (ICOM), 1649 Lump Gulch Rd., Rollinsville, CO, 80474. Phone: (303) 258-9511. Fax: (303) 484-4087.E-mail: info@icomagencies.com Web Site:www.icomagencies.com

Directors: Frank G. Weyforth.

International Institute of Communications, 35 Porland Pl., 3rd. Fl., Westcott, London, WIB IAE. Phone: (44) 207-323-9622. Fax: (44) 207- 323- 9623.E-mail: enquiries@iicom.org Web Site:www.iicom.org

International Radio & Television Society Foundation Inc., 420 Lexington Ave., Suite 1601, New York, NY, 10170. Phone: (212) 867-6650. Fax: (212) 867-6653. Web Site:www.irts.org E-mail: jim.cronin@irts.org

International Recording Media Association, 182 Nassau St., Suite 204, Princeton, NJ, 08542. Phone: (609) 279-1700. Fax: (609) 279-1999.E-mail: info@recordingmedia.org Web Site:www.recordingmedia.org

Directors: Tony Perez.

KOBI-TV (NBC Affiliate), (An affll of CA & OR Bcstg Inc.). 125 S. Fir St., Medford, OR, 97501. Phone: (541) 779-5555. Fax: (541) 779-1151. Web Site:www.localnewscomesfirst.com E-mail: kobi@kobi5.com

Klamath FallsOR . KOTI-TV, 222 S. 7th St.

League of Advertising Agencies, 915 Clifton Ave., Clifton, NJ, 07013. Phone: (973) 473-6643. Fax: (943) 473-0685.E-mail: info@weinrichadv.com Web Site:www.weinrichadv.com

Library of American Broadcasting Foundation Inc., Box 2749, Alexandria, VA, 22301. Phone: (703) 548-6090. Fax: (703) 549-4349.E-mail: westsqn@aol.com Web Site:www.labfoundation.org

Donald H. Kirkley, Jr. Directors: James L. Greenwald, Vincent Curtis, Arthur W. Carlson, Erwin Krasnow, Jerry Lee, Larry Taishoff, Jim Morley, Susan Ness, Don West,

Richard Buckley, Perre Bouvard, Russ Withers, Carl Brazell, Michael Carter, Tim Cookerly, Sam Donaldson, James E. Duffy, Erica Farber, Skip Finley, Gary Fries, Marc Guild, Dr. Judy Kuriansky, David Kennedy, Dawson B. Nail, Allen Shaw, Ramsey Woodworth & Millard Younts.

MarylandNO , University of Maryland, College Park. Phone:

MZTV Museum of Television, 550 Queen St. E., Toronto, ON, M5A 1V2. Canada. Phone: (416) 599-7339. Fax: (416) 599-3572.E-mail: mztv@MZTV.com Web Site:www.mztv.com

Magazine Publishers of America, 810 7th Ave, 24th Fl., New York, NY, 10019. Phone: (212) 872-3700. Fax: (212) 888-4217.E-mail: mpa@magazine.org Web Site:www.magazine.org

Media Access Group at WGBH, One Quest St., Boston, MA, 02135. Phone: (617) 300-2000. Fax: (617) 300-1020.E-mail: access@wgbh.org Web Site:access.wgbh.org

The Media Institute, 2300 Clarendon Blvd., Suite 503, Arlington, VA, 22201. Phone: (703) 243-5700. Fax: (703) 243-8808.E-mail: info@mediainstitute.org Web Site:www.mediainstitute.org

Minority Media and Telecommunications Council, 3636 16th St. N.W., B-366, Washington, DC, 20010. Phone: (202) 332-0500. Fax: (202) 332-0503.E-mail: dhonig@crosslink.net Web Site:www.mmtconline.org

Mortgage Bankers Association of America (MBA), 1919 Pennsylvania Ave. N.W., Washington, DC, 20006-3404. Phone: (202) 557-2700.E-mail: info@mbaa.org Web Site:www.mbaa.org

Motion Picture Association of America, 15503 Ventura Blvd., Encino, CA, 91436. Phone: (818) 995-6600. Fax: (818) 382-1795. Web Site:www.mpaa.org

EncinoCA , 15503 Ventura Blvd. Phone:

The Museum of Broadcast Communications, 400 N. State St., Suite 240, Chicago, IL, 60610-6860. Phone: (312) 245-8200. Fax: (312) 245-8207. Web Site:www.museum.tv

NCTI, 9697 E. Mineral Ave., Centennial, CO, 80112-3408. Phone: (303) 797-9393. Fax: (303) 797-9394. Web Site:www.ncti.com

The National Academy of Television Arts & Sciences, 111 W. 57th St., Suite 600, New York, NY, 10019. Phone: (212) 586-8424. Fax: (212) 246-8129. Web Site:www.emmyonline.org

The National Academy of Television Journalists Inc., Box 289, Salisbury, MD, 21803-0289. Phone: (410) 251-2511. Fax: (410) 543-0658.E-mail: infi@goldenviddyawards.com Web Site:www.goldenviddyawards.com

Directors: Dr.Catherine North & Dr.Cathy Roche.

National Association of Black Journalists (NABJ), 8701-A Adelphi Road, Adelphi, MD, 20783-1716. Phone: (301) 445-7100. Fax: (301) 445-7101.E-mail: nabj@nabj.org Web Site:www.nabj.org

Directors: Ernie Suggs, Stephanie Jones, Elliott Lewis, Marsha J. Eaglin & Victor W. Vaughan.

National Association of Black Owned Broadcasters Inc. (NABOB), 1155 Connecticut Ave., N.W., 6th Fl., Washington, DC, 20036. Phone: (202) 463-8970. Fax: (202) 429-0657.E-mail: info@nabob.org Web Site:www.nabob.org

Directors: Pierre M. Sutton, Bennie Turner, Sydney L Small, Lois E. Wright, Michael Carter, Alfred Liggins, James Wolfe, Michael Roberts, Karen Slade & Carol Moore Cutting.

National Association of Broadcasters,

See listing under Major National Associations, this section.

National Association of Hispanic Journalists, 1000 National Press Bldg., 529 14th St. N.W., Washington, DC, 20045-2001. Phone: (202) 662-7145. Phone: (888) 346-nahj. Fax: (202) 662-7144.E-mail: nahj@nahj.org Web Site:www.nahj.org

National Association of Telecommunications Officers and Advisors, 1800 Diagonal Rd., Suite 495, Alexandria, VA, 22314. Phone: (703) 519-8035. Fax: (703) 519-8036.E-mail: info@natoa.org Web Site:www.natoa.org

National Association of Television Program Executives International ,

See listing under Major National Associations, this section.

National Association of Theatre Owners Inc. (NATO), 750 1st St. N.E., Suite 1130, Washington, DC, 20002. Phone: (202) 962-0054. Fax: (202) 962-0370.E-mail: nato@natodc.com Web Site:www.natoonline.org

North HollywoodCA , 4605 Lankershim Blvd, #3180.

National Black Media Coalition, 145 Alderson Ave., Billings, MT, 59101. Phone: (406) 248-4450. Fax: (301) 593-3604.E-mail: webmaster@nbm.org Web Site:www.nbmc.org

National Cable and Television Association Inc. (NCTA),

See listing under Major National Associations, this section.

National Cable Television Cooperative Inc.,

See listing under Major National Associations, this section.

National Captioning Institute (NCI), 1900 Gallows Rd., Suite 3000, Vienna, VA, 22182. Phone: (703) 917-7600. Fax: (703) 917-9878. Web Site:www.ncicap.org

Directors: Karen O' Connor, Marc Okrand, Beth Nubbe & Jay Feinberg.

BurbankCA , 303 N. Glenoaks Blvd, Suite 200. Phone:

National Council for Families & Television, 6500 Wilshire Blvd., Suite 1950, Los Angeles, CA, 90048. Phone: (323) 866-6020. Fax: (310) 208-5984.E-mail: ncft@yahoo.com

National Education Association, 1201 16th St. N.W., Washington, DC, 20036-3290. Phone: (202) 833-4000. Fax: (202) 822-7974. Web Site:www.nea.org E-mail: editorial@list.nea.org

National Electrical Manufacturers Association (NEMA), 1300 N. 17th St., Suite 1847, Rosslyn, VA, 22209. Phone: (703) 841-3200. Fax: (703) 841-5900.E-mail: webmaster@nema.org Web Site:www.nema.org

National Federation of Community Broadcasters (NFCB), 1970 Broadway, Suite 1000, Oakland, CA, 94612. Phone: (510) 451-8200. Fax: (510) 451-8208.E-mail: nfcb@nfcb.org Web Site:www.nfcb.org

National Federation of Press Women Inc.-NFPW, Box 5556, Arlington, VA, 22205. Phone: (703) 812-9487. Phone: (800) 780-2715. Fax: (703) 812-4555.E-mail: mhunt21@msn.com Web Site:www.nfpw.org

Donna Penticuff, past pres; Kathryn Cordova, 2nd VP; Marsha Shuler, 1st VP.

Programs, svcs & contest categories for female & male professionals in all media.

National League of Cities, 1301 Pennsylvania Ave. N.W., Suite 550, Washington, DC, 20004. Phone: (202) 626-3000. Fax: (202) 626-3043.E-mail: info@nlc.org

James C. Hunt, pres; Bart Peterson, VP; Cynthia McCollum, 2nd VP. Directors: R. Michael Amyx, Tommy Baker & Vickie Barnett.

National Museum of Communications Inc., 2001 Plymouth Rock Dr., Richardson, TX, 75081. Phone: (972) 889-9872. Fax: (972) 889-2329.E-mail: bill46@yesterdayusa.com Web Site:www.yesterdayusa.com

Directors: William J. Bragg, Betty Lewis & Kim Bragg.

National Newspaper Association, Box 7540, Columbia, MO, 65205-7540. Phone: (573) 882-5800. Fax: (573) 884-5490.E-mail: info@nna.org Web Site:www.nna.org

Lynn Edinger, assoc dir. Directors: Tonda Rush.

ArlingtonVA , Box 5737. Phone:

National Press Club, 529 14th St. N.W., Washington, DC, 20045. Phone: (202) 662-7500. Phone: (202) 662-7505. Fax: (202) 662-7512.E-mail: info@npcpress.org Web Site:www.press.org

Joe Anselmo, chmn of bd. Directors: Tom Glad.

National Religious Broadcasters (NRB), 9510 Technology Dr., Manassas, VA, 20110. Phone: (703) 330-7000. Fax: (703) 330-7100.E-mail: fwright@nrb.org Web Site:www.nrb.org/nrb

National Retail Federation, 325 7th St. N.W., Suite 1100, Washington, DC, 20004. Phone: (202) 783-7971. Phone: (800) nrf-how2. Fax: (202) 737-2849. Web Site:www.nrf.com

National Telemedia Council Inc., 1922 University Ave., Madison, WI, 53726. Phone: (608) 218-1182. Fax: (608) 218-1183.E-mail: ntelemedia@aol.com Web Site:nationaltelemediacouncil.org

Directors: Mary Moen, Mike Bergen, Dr. Martin Rayala, Greg Hoffmann, Vira Standiford, Keeiza Hyzer & Rosemary Lehman.

Newseum, 1101 Wilson Blvd., Arlington, VA, 22209. Phone: (703) 284-3544. Phone: (888) new-seum.E-mail: newseum@freedomforum.org Web Site:www.newseum.org

Newspaper Association of America, 4401 Wilson Blvd., Suite 900, Arlington, VA, 22203-1867. Phone: (571) 366-1000. Fax: (571) 366-1200. Web Site:www.naa.org

Directors: Charles Pittman, Donna Barrett, Susan Clark-Johnson, Paul Boyle, Su Lin Nichols & Randy Bennett.

North American Broadcasters Association (NABA), Box 500, Stn A, Rm. 6C 300, Toronto, ON, M5W 1E6. Canada. Phone: (416) 598-9877. Fax: (416) 598-9774.E-mail: info@nabanet.com Web Site:www.nabanet.com

Directors: Joseph Flaherty, Felix Arauji Ramirez, Ignacio Suarez, Andy Setos & Peter Smith.

North American Retail Dealers Association, 10 E. 22nd St., Suite 310, Lombard, IL, 60148-6191. Phone: (630) 953-8950. Phone: (800) 621-0298. Fax: (630) 953-8957.E-mail: nardahdq@narda.com Web Site:www.kwmu.com

Pacific Pioneer Broadcasters, Box 4866, Valley Village, CA, 91617-4866. Phone: (323) 461-2121. Fax: (818) 768-8251. Web Site:www.ppbwebsite.org

The Paley Center for Media, 25 W. 52nd St., New York, NY, 10019-6101. Phone: (212) 621-6600. Fax: (212) 621-6700. Web Site:www.paleycenter.org E-mail: publicrelations@paleycenter.org

Beverly HillsCA , 465 N. Beverly Dr. Phone:

PROMAX&BDA, 9000 W. Sunset Blvd., Suite 900, Los Angeles, CA, 90069. Phone: (310) 788-7600. Phone: (800) 977-6629. Fax: (310) 788-7616. Web Site:www.promax.tv E-mail: jim@promax.tv

Directors: David Snapp, George Pierson, Lisa Fengler, Leslie Celia, Jeannine Chanin, Tony Cleave, Ann Epstein-Cohen, Steve Delaney, Miguel Muelle, Karen Olcott, Jan Phillips, Abel Sanchez, Robin Skirboll, Anne White, Mark Stroman, Glynn Brailsford, Brian Blum, Judy Braune, Alan Cohen, Scott Danielson, C.J. Fredricksen, Lee Hunt, Kay Hutchison, Tony Lakin, Vince Manze, Brigitte McCray, Rob Middleton, Nick Miller, Michael Mischler, David Muscari, Billy Pittard, Sal Sardo, George Schweitzer, Curtis Symonds & Donna Weston.

Hong Kong China. Synapse Pacific LTD, 49 Hollywood Rd., 19th Fl.

LondonNO United Kingdom. Promax & BDA Europe, 61 Webber St.

Promotion Marketing Association Inc., 257 Park Ave. S., Suite 1102, New York, NY, 10010. Phone: (212) 420-1100. Fax: (212) 533-7622.E-mail: pma@pmalink.org Web Site:www.pmalink.org

Public Radio in Mid-America (PRIMA), c/o KWMU-FM One University Blvd., University of Missouri, St. Louis, MO, 63121-4499. Phone: (314) 516-5968. Fax: (314) 516-5993.E-mail: pwente@kwmu.org Web Site:www.kwmu.org

Directors: Dan Skinner & Jon Schwartz.

Public Radio News Directors Incorporated, 821 University Ave., Madison, NY, 53706. Phone: (608) 265-3378. Fax: (608) 263-5838.E-mail: walker@wpr.org

Directors: Dave Piznanelli, Martha Foley, Jonathan Ahl & Christine Paige-Diers.

Public Relations Society of America, 33 Maiden Ln., 11th Fl., New York, NY, 10038. Phone: (212) 460-1400. Fax: (212) 995-0757.E-mail: hq@prsa.org Web Site:www.prsa.org

Radio Advertising Bureau,

See listing under Major National Associations, this section.

Radio and Television Museum, 2608 Mitchellville Rd., Bowie, MD, 20716. Phone: (301) 390-1020. Fax: (301)947-3338.E-mail: radiobelanger@comcast.net Web Site:www.radiohistory.org

Brian Belanger, exec dir. Directors: Kenneth Mellgren, Ed Walker, Peter Eldridge, William McMahon, William Goodwin, Tony Young, Rob Huddleston, Chris Sterling,

Don Ross, Gerald Schneider, Paul Courson, Charles Grant & Michael Rubin.

Radio & Television News Directors Foundation, 1600 K St. NW, Suite 700, Washington, DC, 20006. Phone: (202) 659-6510. Fax: (202) 223-4007.E-mail: rtndf@rtndf.org Web Site:www.rtndf.org

Radio & Television Research Council, c/o MSA, Attn: R. Sharpe, 152 Madison Ave., Suite 801, New York, NY, 10016. Phone: (212) 481-3038. Fax: (212) 481-3071.E-mail: rtrcny@aol.com

Radio Marketing Bureau, 175 Bloor St. E., Suite 316 North Tower, Toronto, ON, M4W 3R8. Canada. Phone: (416) 922-5757. Phone: (800) 667-2346. Fax: (416) 922-6542.E-mail: info@rmb.ca Web Site:www.rmb.ca

Radio-Television Correspondents' Association, S-325, U.S. Capitol, Washington, DC, 20510. Phone: (202) 224-6421. Fax: (202) 224-4882. Web Site:www.senate.gov/galleries.radiotv.com

Directors: Jerry Bodlander, Bob Fuss, Edward O'Keefe, Dave McConnell, Richard Tillery & David Welna.

Radio Television News Directors Association (Canada), 2175 Shephard Ave. E., Suite 310, Toronto, ON, M2J 1W8. Canada. Phone: (416) 756-2126. Fax: (416) 364-8896.E-mail: tscott@broadcastnews.ca Web Site:www.rtndacanada.com

Recording Industry Association of America Inc. (RIAA), 1330 Connecticut Ave. N.W., Suite 300, Washington, DC, 20036. Phone: (202) 775-0101. Fax: (202) 775-7253. Web Site:www.riaa.com

Royal Television Society, North America Inc., Box 870501, Arizona State University, Tempe, AZ, 85287-0501. Phone: (480) 965-7661. Fax: (480) 965-1371.E-mail: royaltv@asu.edu

Satellite Broadcasting & Communications Assn. of America (SBCA), 1730 M St., N.W., Suite 600, Washington, DC, 20036-4557. Phone: (202) 349-3620.E-mail: info@sbca.org Web Site:www.sbca.org

Society of Broadcast Engineers Inc., 9102 N. Meridian St., Suite 150, Indianapolis, IN, 46260-1896. Phone: (317) 846-9000. Fax: (317) 846-9120.E-mail: jporay@sbe.org Web Site:www.sbe.org

Society of Cable Telecommunications Engineers Inc., 140 Philips Rd., Exton, PA, 19341-1318. Phone: (610) 363-6888. Fax: (610) 363-5898.E-mail: scte@scte.org Web Site:www.scte.org

Directors: Joel E. Welch, Thomas Russell & Joan Hagelin.

Professional membership assn offering information, professional dev resources, standards to cable telecommunications engineers & other professional.

Society of Environmental Journalists (SEJ), Box 2492, Jenkintown, PA, 19046. Phone: (215) 884-8174. Fax: (215) 884-8175.E-mail: sej@sej.org Web Site:www.sej.org

Carolyn Whetzel, treas; Dina Cappiello, sec.

Society of Motion Picture & Television Engineers (SMPTE), 3 Barker Ave., 5th Fl., White Plains, NY, 10601. Phone: (914) 761-1100. Fax: (914) 761-3115. Web Site:www.smpte.org

Society of Professional Journalists, 3909 N. Meridian St., Indianapolis, IN, 46208-4011. Phone: (317) 927-8000. Fax: (317) 920-4789.E-mail: webmaster@spj.org Web Site:www.spj.org

Robert Leger, sec/treas; David Carlson, VP. Directors: Alvin Cross.

Twelve rgnl dirs, natl offs elected annually, two students reps, two dirs, at-large & two campus advisors at-large.

Society of Satellite Professionals International, 55 Broad St., 14th Fl., New York, NY, 10004. Phone: (212) 809-5199. Fax: (212) 825-0075. Web Site:www.sspi.org

Directors: Richard Wolf, David Bioss, Carson Agnero, Blair Marshall, Ellen Hoff, Dan Stasi, Stephen Teller & D. Sacjoder.

The Songwriters Guild of America, 1560 Broadway, Suite 408, New York, NY, 10036. Phone: (212) 768-7902. Fax: (212) 768-7902.E-mail: ny@songwritersguild.com Web Site:www.songwritersguild.org

HollywoodCA , 6430 Sunset Blvd. Phone:

Los AngelesCA , 6430 Sunset Blvd.

NashvilleTN , 1222 16th Ave. St, Suite 25. Phone:

Statenets National Association of State Radio Networks Inc., 17911 Harwood Ave., Homewood, IL, 60430. Phone: (708) 799-6676. Fax: (708) 799-6698.E-mail: tdobrez@statenets.com Web Site:www.statenets.com

Syndicated Network Television Association, 1 Penn Plaza, Suite 5310, New York, NY, 10111. Phone: (212) 259-3740. Fax: (212) 259-3770.E-mail: mburg@snta.com Web Site:www.snta.com

Telecommunications Industry Association, 2500 Wilson Blvd., Arlington, VA, 22201. Phone: (703) 907-7700. Fax: (703) 907-7727.E-mail: tia@tiaonline.org Web Site:www.tiaonline.org

Directors: Grant Seiffert, Bill Belt, John Derr, Derek Khlopin, Jason Leuck, Anna Amselle, Henry Wieland, Maryann Lesso, David Smith, Dan Bart & Henry Cuschieri.

Beijing 100004 China. USITO, Rm. 332, 3/f Lido Office Tower, Lido Place, Jichang Rd., Jiang Tai Rd. Phone:usito@usito.org Web Site: www.usito.org. Anne Stevenson-Yang, mgng dir.

Telecommunications Research and Action Center (TRAC), Box 27279, Washington, DC, 20005. Phone: (202) 263-2950. Fax: (202) 263-2960.E-mail: trac@trac.org Web Site:www.trac.org

Television Bureau of Advertising (TVB),

See listing under Major National Associations, this section.

Television Bureau of Canada, 160 Bloor St. E, Suite 1005, Toronto, ON, M4W 1B9. Canada. Phone: (416) 923-8813. Fax: (416) 413-3879.E-mail: tvb@tvb.ca Web Site:www.tvb.ca

Television Critics Association, The Wichita Eagle, 825 E. Douglas Ave., Witchita, KS, 67202. Phone: (316) 268-6394. Fax: (316) 268-6627.E-mail: tca@tvcritics.org Web Site:www.tvcritics.org

Television Operators Caucus, 1776 K Street NW, Washington, DC, 20006. Phone: (202) 719-7090. Fax: (202) 719-7546.

The Association for International Broadcasting, Box 141, Cranbrook, TN17 9AJ. United Kingdom. Phone: +44 (0) 20 7993 2557. Fax: +44 (0) 20 7993 8043.

Directors: Tom Walters, mktg; Tim Keeler, pub affrs.

Think LA, (formerly Los Angeles Advertising Agencies Association). 4223 Glencoe Ave., Suite C-100, Marina del Rey, CA, 90292. Phone: (310) 823-7320. Fax: (310) 823-7325.E-mail: info@thinkla.org Web Site:www.thinkla.org

U.S. Conference of Catholic Bishops, Dept. of Communications, 3211 4th St. N.E., Washington, DC, 20017-1194. Phone: (202) 541-3000. Fax: (202) 541-3173. Web Site:www.usccb.org

Veteran Wireless Operators Association Inc., Box 1003, Peck Slip, New York, NY, 10272-1003. E-mail: vwoa@interactive.net Web Site:www.vwoa.org

Directors: Richard T. Kenney & D. I. Temple.

Veterans Bedside Network, (The Veterans Hospital Radio & TV Guild). 10 Fiske Pl., Rm. 301, Mount Vernon, NY, 10550. Phone: (914) 699-6069. Fax: (914) 667-0405.

Wireless Communications Association International, Inc., 1333 H St. N.W., Suite 700, Washington, DC, 20005-4754. Phone: (202) 452-7823. Fax: (202) 452-0041.E-mail: sonu@wcai.com Web Site:www.wcai.com

Directors: John T. von Harz III, William Andrle Jr., T. Lauriston Hardin III, Chris Farnworth & Patrick J. Gossman III.

Women in Cable & Telecommunications, 14555 Avion Pkwy., Suite 250, Chantilly, VA, 20151. Phone: (703) 234-9810. Fax: (703) 817-1595.E-mail: info@wict.org Web Site:www.wict.org

Directors: Mary Busby, Robin Burke Zahory, Lisa McBee & Lisa Vega.

Women In Film, 8857 W. Olympic Blvd., Suite 201, Beverly Hills, CA, 90211. Phone: (310) 657-5144. Fax: (310) 657-5154.E-mail: info@wif.org Web Site:www.wif.org

World Broadcasting Unions (WBU), Box 500, Stn. A, Rm. 6C 300, Toronto, ON, M5W 1E6. Canada. Phone: (416) 598-9877. Fax: (416) 598-9774.E-mail: info@nabanet.org Web Site:www.nabanet.com/wbu

World Teleport Association, 55 Broad St., 14th Fl., New York, NY, 10004. Phone: (212) 825-0218. Fax: (212) 825-0075.E-mail: wta@worldteleport.org Web Site:www.worldteleport.org

Directors: Chris Russell, David Sprechman, Gary Hatch, Oliver Badard, Nick Thompson, Yoshihiro Yohoyama & tohm Tahahasin.

State and Regional Broadcast Associations

Alabama Broadcasters Association, 2180 Pkwy. Lake Dr., Hoover, AL, 35244. Phone: (205) 982-5001. Fax: (205) 982-0015. Web Site:www.al-ba.com

Alaska Broadcasters Association, 700 W. 41st Ave., #102, Anchorage, AK, 99503. Phone: (907) 258-2424. Fax: (907) 258-2414.E-mail: akba@gci.net Web Site:www.alaskabroadcasters.org

Arizona Broadcasters Association, 426 N. 44th St., Suite 310, Phoenix, AZ, 85008. Phone: (602) 252-4833. Fax: (602) 252-5265.E-mail: aba3@mindspring.com Web Site:www.azbroadcasters.org

Kathy Baker, chmn.

Arkansas Broadcasters Association, 2024 Arkansas Valley Dr., Suite 403, Little Rock, AR, 72212. Phone: (501) 227-7564. Fax: (501) 223-9798.E-mail: mail@arkbroadcasters.org Web Site:www.arkbroadcasters.org

California Broadcasters Association, 915 L St., Suite 1150, Sacramento, CA, 95814. Phone: (916) 444-2237. Fax: (916) 444-2043.E-mail: jberry@yourcba.com Web Site:www.cabroadcasters.org

Kathy Baker, chmn.

Colorado Broadcasters Association, Box 2369, Breckenridge, CO, 80424. Phone: (970) 547-1388. Fax: (970) 547-1384. Web Site:www.coloradobroadcasters.org E-mail: cobroadcasters@earthlink.net

Wick Rowland, sec/treas.

Connecticut Broadcasters Association, 90 South Park St., Willimantic, CT, 06226. Phone: (860) 633-5031. Fax: (860) 456-5688.E-mail: mcrice@prodigy.net Web Site:www.ctba.org

Florida Association of Broadcasters, 201 S. Monroe St., #201, Tallahassee, FL, 32301. Phone: (850) 681-6444. Fax: (850) 222-3957. Web Site:www.fab.org

Georgia Association of Broadcasters Inc., 8010 Roswell Rd., Suite 150, Atlanta, GA, 30350. Phone: (770) 395-7200. Fax: (770) 395-7235.E-mail: piguej@gab.org Web Site:www.gab.org

Idaho State Broadcasters Association, 270 N. 27th St., Suite B, Boise, ID, 83702-3167. Phone: (208) 345-3072. Fax: (208) 343-8046.E-mail: isba@qwestoffice.net Web Site:www.idahobroadcasters.org

Illinois Broadcasters Association, 200 Missouri Ave., Carterville, IL, 62918. Phone: (618) 985-5555. Fax: (618) 985-6070.E-mail: ilbrdcst@neondsl.com Web Site:www.ilba.org

Indiana Broadcasters Association Inc., 3003 E. 98th St., Suite 161, Indianapolis, IN, 46280. Phone: (317) 573-0119. Fax: (317) 573-0895.E-mail: indba@aol.com Web Site:www.indianabroadcasters.org

Directors: Sally Brown, Arthur Angotti III, Roger Diehm, Tasha Mann, Lundy, Phil Hoover, Leigh Ellis, James Conner, Earl Metzger, Chuck Williams, Paulette Lees. Directors at Large: Marty Pieratt, Steve Lindell, Jeff Smulyan, Dr. Joe Misiewicz, Matt Jaquint, William Van Huss, Ron Miller, Scott Uecker, Brett Beshore.

Iowa Broadcasters Association, Box 71186, Des Moines, IA, 50325. Phone: (515) 224-7237. Fax: (515) 224-6560.E-mail: iowaiba@dwx.com Web Site:www.iowabroadcasters.com

Kansas Assn of Broadcasters, 2709 S.W. 29th St., Topeka, KS, 66614. Phone: (785) 235-1307. Fax: (785) 233-3052.E-mail: kent@kab.net Web Site:www.kab.net

Kentucky Broadcasters Association, 101 Enterprise Dr., Frankfort, KY, 40601. Phone: (502) 848-0426.E-mail: kba@kba.org Web Site:www.kba.org

Gary White, pres; Patti L. Pollen, exec asst.

Louisiana Association of Broadcasters, 660 Florida St., Baton Rouge, LA, 70801. Phone: (225) 267-4522. Fax: (225) 267-4329.E-mail: lab@broadcasters.org Web Site:www.broadcasters.org

Directors: George Sirven; Charles Spencer, legal counsel; Mike Barras; Tom Gay, treas; Bob Holladay; Irene Robinson;

Irene Robin, vice chmn-radio; Larry Delia, vice chmn-TV. Louise Munson, pres/CEO.

Maine Assn of Broadcasters, 69 Sewall St., Augusta, ME, 04330. Phone: (207) 623-3870. Phone: (800) 664-6221. Fax: (207) 621-0585 (call first). Web Site:www.mab.org

Maryland-District of Columbia-Delaware Broadcasters Association, 106 Old Court Rd., Suite 300, Baltimore, MD, 21208-4038. Phone: (410) 653-4122. Fax: (410) 486-7354.E-mail:info@mdcd.com Web Site:www.mdcdd.com

Massachusetts Broadcasters Association Inc., PMB 401, 43 Riverside Ave., Medford, MA, 02155. Phone: (800) 471-1875. Fax: (800) 471-1876.E-mail: info@massbroadcasters.org Web Site:www.massbroadcasters.org

Michigan Association of Broadcasters, 819 N. Washington Ave., Lansing, MI, 48906. Phone: (517) 484-7444. Fax: (517) 484-5810.E-mail: mab@michmab.com Web Site:www.michmab.com

Directors: Duane Alverson, Don Backus, Al Blinke, James Lutton, Bob Sliva, Paul Grzebik, Michael J. King, Ken Radant, Trey Fabacher, Gayle Olson, Bob Peters, W. Palmer Pyle, Jeffrey J. Scarpelli, Robert Stricer Diane Kniowski, Mario Iacbelli, Bart Brandmiller, Tom Mogush. Honorary Board Members: Ed Christian, Alan Frank, Bruce Goldsen. Legal/Legislative Counsel: Rob Elhenicky, John J. Ronayne III.

Minnesota Broadcasters Association, 3033 Excelsior Blvd., Suite 440, Minneapolis, MN, 55416. Phone: (612) 926-8123. Fax: (612) 926-9761.E-mail: jdubois@minnesotabroadcasters.com Web Site:www.minnesotabroadcasters.com

Directors: Mike Neudecker, chmn; Rosanne Rybak; Steve Woodbury; Brett Paradis; John J. Sowada; Mike Iazzo; Dennis Wahlstrom; Ed Smith. Legal Counsels: Terry Moore; Gregg Skall.

Mississippi Association of Broadcasters, 855 S. Pear Orchard Rd., Suite 403, Ridgeland, MS, 39157. Phone: (601) 957-9121. Fax: (601) 957-9175.E-mail: jlett2@earthlink.net Web Site:www.msbroadcasters.org

Missouri Broadcasters Association, 1025 Northeast Dr., Jefferson City, MO, 65109. Phone: (573) 636-6692. Fax: (573) 634-8258.E-mail: dhicks@mbaweb.org Web Site:www.mbaweb.org

Directors: Rick McCoy, Dave Alpert, Gary Exline, Mike Smythe, Dennis Lamme, Craig Allison, Mike Mera, Mike Harbit, Richard Womack, Mark Gordon, Don Hicks, Mark Sableman, Spencer Koch, John Caran, Danny Thomas.

Montana Broadcasters Association, 1914 Rainbow Bend Dr., Bonner, MT, 59823. Phone: (406) 244-4622. Fax: (406) 244-5518.E-mail: mba@mtbroadcasters.org Web Site:www.mtbroadcasters.org

Nebraska Broadcasters Association, 12020 Shamrock Plaza, Suite 200, Omaha, NE, 68154. Phone: (402) 778-5178. Fax: (402) 778-5131.E-mail: marty@ne-ba.org Web Site:www.ne-ba.org

Marty Riemenschneider, pres; Marty Riemenschnieder, exec dir.

Nevada Broadcasters Association, 1050 E. Flamingo Rd., Suite S-102, Las Vegas, NV, 89119. Phone: (702) 794-4994. Fax: (702) 794-4997.E-mail: rdfnba@aol.com Web Site:www.nevadabroadcasters.org

Mary Ozer, chmn; Tony Bonnici, chmn elect.

New Hampshire Association of Broadcasters, 707 Chestnut St., Manchester, NH, 03104. Phone: (603) 627-9600. Fax: (603) 627-9603.E-mail: asprague@bggadvertising.com Web Site:www.nhab.org

New Jersey Broadcasters Association, 348 Applegarth Rd., Monroe Twp., NJ, 08831. Phone: (609) 860-0111. Fax: (609) 860-0110.E-mail: njba@njba.com Web Site:www.njba.com

Directors:Arthur Camiolo, Josh Gertzog, Charles McCreery, Joseph M. Bilotta, Dan Spears, Richard Swetits, John F. Garziglia & Thomas R. Ray.

New Mexico Broadcasters Association, 2333 Wisconsin N.E., Albuquerque, NM, 87110. Phone: (505) 881-4444. Fax: (505) 881-5353.E-mail: info@nmba.org Web Site:www.nmba.org

Directors: Matt Martinez, Gene Dow & Milt McConnell.

New York Market Radio Broadcasters Association (NYMRAD), 261 Madison Ave., 23rd Fl., New York, NY, 10016. Phone: (646) 254-4493. Fax: (646) 254-4498.E-mail: db@nymrad.org Web Site:www.nymrad.org

New York State Broadcasters Association Inc., 1805 Western Ave., Albany, NY, 12203. Phone: (518) 456-8888. Fax: (518) 456-8943.E-mail: info@nysbroadcasters.org Web Site:www.nysbroadcasters.org

North Carolina Assoc of Broadcasters, Box 627, Raleigh, NC, 27602. Phone: (919) 821-7300. Fax: (919) 839-0304. Web Site:www.ncbroadcast.com

Directors: Don

North Dakota Broadcasters Association, Box 3178, Bismarck, ND, 58502-3178. Phone: (701) 258-1332. Fax: (701) 250-6372.E-mail: bethh@ndba.org Web Site:www.ndba.org

Directors: Syd Stewart, Barry Schumaier, Larry Timpe, Tim Ost, Carol Anhorn, Darren Lenertz, George Smith.

Northern California Broadcasters Association, 50 Francisco St., Suite 450, San Francisco, CA, 94133. Phone: (415) 292-5700. Fax: (415) 292-5790.E-mail: tdevoto@ncradio.com Web Site:www.ncbaradio.com

Ohio Association of Broadcasters, 88 E. Broad St., Suite 1180, Columbus, OH, 43215-3525. Phone: (614) 228-4052. Fax: (614) 228-8133.E-mail: oab@oab.org Web Site:www.oab.org

Oklahoma Association of Broadcasters, 6520 N. Western, Suite 104, Oklahoma City, OK, 73116. Phone: (405) 848-0771.E-mail: harrison@oabok.org Web Site:www.oabok.org

Vance Harrison, pres.

Oregon Assn of Broadcasters, 7150 S.W. Hampton St., Suite 240, Portland, OR, 97223-8366. Phone: (503) 443-2299. Fax: (503) 443-2488.E-mail: theoab@theoab.org Web Site:www.theoab.org

Pennsylvania Association of Broadcasters, 8501 Paxton St., Hummelstown, PA, 17036. Phone: (717) 482-4820. Fax: (717) 482-1111.E-mail: rwyckoff@pab.org Web Site:www.pab.org

Rhode Island Broadcasters Association, 11 S. Angell St., Providence, RI, 02920. Phone: (401) 255-8200.E-mail: 1needham@ribroadcasters.com

Lori Neeham, exec dir.

South Carolina Broadcasters Association, One Harbison Way, Suite 112, Columbia, SC, 29212. Phone: (803) 732-1186. Fax: (803) 732-4085.E-mail: scba@scba.net Web Site:www.scba.net

South Dakota Broadcasters Association, Box 1037, 106 W. Capital Ave., Pierre, SD, 57501. Phone: (605) 224-1034. Fax: (605) 224-7426.E-mail: info@sdba.org Web Site:www.sdba.org

Tennessee Association of Broadcasters, Two International Plaza Dr., Suite 507, Nashville, TN, 37217. Phone: (615) 945-4061. Fax: (615) 824-0054.E-mail: tabtn@bellsouth.net Web Site:www.tabtn.org

Directors: Bryan Kell, Scott Walker, Ed Brantley, Chuck Wilkins, Sheri Sawyer, Paul Tinkle, Mason Hunter, assoc. Director at Large: Lee Meredith, TV; Dan Phillippi, TV; Doug Combs, Radio; Lacy Ennis, Radio. Debbie Turner, chmn; Whit Adamson, pres; Tom English, chmn elect; Larry Wood, past chmn; Mike Costa, vice-chmn TV; Jeff Shaw, vice-chmn Radio; George DeVault, sec/treas; Jack Mayer, Emeritus; Doug Pierce, legal counsel.

Utah Broadcasters Association, 1600 S. Main St., Salt Lake City, UT, 84115. Phone: (801) 486-9521. Web Site:www.utahbroadcasters.com

Vermont Association of Broadcasters, Box 4489, Burlington, VT, 05406. Phone: (802) 655-5768. Web Site:www.vab.org

Jim Condon, exec dir.

Virginia Association of Broadcasters, 600 Peter Jefferson Pkwy., Suite 300, Charlottesville, VA, 22911. Phone: (434) 977-3716. Fax: (434) 979-2439.E-mail: doug.easter @easterassociates.com Web Site:www.vabonline.com

Directors: Michael Guild.

Directors: Nick Nicholson; Harrison Pittman; Larry Saunders; Randy Smith; Jack Dempsey; Tex Meyer; Robert Scutari; Doris Newcomb; Bob Peterson; Linda Forem; Bob Willloughby; Francis Wood; John Schick; Kenneth Hill; Warren Fihr.

Virginia Public Radio Association, c/o WCVE, 23 Sesame St., Richmond, VA, 23235. Phone: (804) 320-1301. Fax: (804) 320-8729.E-mail: bmiller@ideastations.org

Washington State Association of Broadcasters, 724 Columbia St., Suite 310, Olympia, WA, 98501-1249. Phone: (360) 705-0774. Fax: (360) 705-0873.E-mail: wa-broadcasters@earthlink.net Web Site:www.wsab.org

West Virginia Broadcasters Association, 140 7th Ave., South Charleston, WV, 25303-1452. Phone: (304) 744-2143. Fax: (304) 744-1764.E-mail: wvba@wvba.com Web Site:www.wvba.com

Mike Buxser, pres; Michele Crist, exec dir; Jay Phillipone, treas; Tim D'Fazio, past pres.

Wisconsin Broadcasters Association, 44 E. Mifflin St., Suite 900, Madison, WI, 53703. Phone: (608) 255-2600. Phone: (800) 236-1922. Fax: (608) 256-3986.E-mail: mvetterkind@wi-broadcasters.org Web Site:www.wi-broadcasters.org

WausauWI , 1908 Grand Ave. Laurin Jorstad, WAOW-TV.

WausauWI , Box 2048. Bob Jung, Midwest Communications.

West BendWI , Box 933. Jim Hodges, WBKV/WBWI.

Directors: Gregg Albert, Edward Allen III, Scott Chorski, Kira Lafond, Dean Maytag, Malcolm Brett, Kelly Radandt, Jeff Robinson, Jill Sommers, Cuyanne Taylor, Jeff Tyler. Michelle Vetterkind, pres; Linda Baun, VP/admin. Officers: Doug Kiel (immediate past chair), Wendy Oberc (chair of bd), Al Lancaster (vice chair-TV), Tom Koser (vice chair), Juli Buehler (treas), Bill Hurwitz (sec).

Wyoming Association of Broadcasters, 7217 Hawthorne Dr., Cheyenne, WY, 82009. Phone: (307) 632-7622. Fax: (307) 638-3469.E-mail: grottski@aol.com Web Site:www.wyomingbroadcasting.org

Directors: Larry Cross, chmn; Roger Gelder, vice chmn; Steve Core, vice chmn.

State and Regional Cable Associations

Alabama Cable Telecommunications Association, Box 230666, Montgomery, AL, 36123-0666. Phone: (334) 271-2281. Fax: (334) 271-2260.E-mail: alacable@aol.com Web Site:www.alcta.com

Arizona-New Mexico Cable Telecommunications Association, 3875 N. 44th St., Suite 300, Phoenix, AZ, 85018. Phone: (602) 955-4122. Fax: (602) 955-4505.E-mail: info@azcable.org Web Site:www.azcable.org

Directors: Susan Bitter Smith, exec dir; Chris Dunkeson, pres

Arkansas Cable Telecommunications Association, 411 South Victory, Suite 201A, Little Rock, AR, 72201. Phone: (501) 907-6440.E-mail: info@arcta.org Web Site:www.arcta.org

Directors: Mike Wilson, Dennis Yocum, Garry Bowman, Harold Kimmel, Rick Smith, Harvey Oxner, Jay Butler, Doug Martin.

Broadband Cable Association of Pennsylvania, 127 State St., Harrisburg, PA, 17101. Phone: (717) 214-2000. Fax: (717) 214-2020. Web Site:www.pcta.com

Broadband Communications Association of Washington, 216 First Ave. S., Suite 260, Seattle, WA, 98104. Phone: (206) 652-9303. Fax: (206) 652-8297.E-mail: rmain@broadbandwashington.org Web Site:www.broadbandwashington.org

Directors: Janet Turpen, Steve Kipp, Jerry Rotondo, Bob Lam, Matt Zavala, Bruce Gladner & Carlos Gutirrez.

Directors: Janet Turpen, Steve Kipp, Steve Holmes, Bob Rubery, Jim Penney, Carlos Gutierrez, Bruce Gladner.

Cable Telecommunications Assn. of Maryland, Delaware & District of Col., 2530 Riva Rd., #316, Annapolis, MD, 21401. Phone: (410) 266-9111. Fax: (410) 266-6133.E-mail: ctaofmd-de-dc@msn.com

Cable Telecommunications Association of New York Inc., 54 State St., Suite 800, Albany, NY, 12207. Phone: (518) 463-6676. Fax: (518) 463-0574.E-mail: clany@cabletv.com Web Site:www.cabletvny.com

Directors: Mary Cotter, chmn.

Cable Television & Communications Association of Illinois, 2400 E. Devon Ave., Suite 317, Des Plaines, IL, 60018. Phone: (847) 297-4520. Fax: (847) 297-3865.E-mail: ctc2400@aol.com

Cable Television Association of Georgia, 9 Dunwoody Park, Suite 121, Atlanta, GA, 30338. Phone: (404) 252-4371. Fax: (404) 252-0215.E-mail: info@gacable.com Web Site:www.gacable.com

Directors: Kim Gage, chmn; Michael Clemons.

California Cable & Telecommunications Assn., 1001 "K" St., 2nd Fl., Sacramento, CA, 95814. Phone: (916) 446-7732. Fax: (916) 446-1605.E-mail: mel@cable.org Web Site:www.calcable.org

SacramentoCA , 1121 L St., Suite 400. Phone:

Director: Bernie Orozco, govt affairss; Jerry Yanowitz, VP, fedeal affairs, Lesla Lehtonen, VP legal & regulatory affairs; Jerome Candelaria, VP & counsel, regulatory affairs. Carolyn McIntyre, pres.

Colorado Cable TV Association, 1410 Grant St., Suite A-101, Denver, CO, 80203. Phone: (720) 379-3623.E-mail: pboyle@rbwpolicy.com Web Site:www.cocabletv.com

Hawaii Cable Television Association, 200 Akamainui St., Mililani, HI, 96789. Phone: (808) 625-8359. Fax: (808) 625-5888.E-mail: kbeuret@oceanic.com

Idaho Cable Telecommunications Association, 1015 W. Hays Street, Boise, ID, 83702. Phone: (208) 344-6633. Fax: (208) 344-0077. Web Site:www.idahocable.com

Directors: Michelle Cameron, pres, Russ Young, past pres.

Indiana Cable Telecommunications Association Inc., 201 N. Illinois St., Suite 1560, Indianapolis, IN, 46204. Phone: (317) 237-2288. Fax: (317) 237-2290. Web Site:www.incable.org E-mail: toakes@incable.org

Directors: Rachel McKay & Nicole Roenl.

Iowa Cable & Telecommunications Association, Box 3627, Des Moines, IA, 50322. Phone: (515) 276-0006. Fax: (515) 309-3779.E-mail: tomgraves@mchsi.com Web Site:www.iowacable.org

Paul Johnson, pres; Steve Purcell, VP; Thomas P. Graves, exec VP.

Kansas Cable Telecommunications Association, 815 S.W. Topeka Blvd., 2nd Floor, Topeka, KS, 66612. Phone: (785) 290-0018. Fax: (785) 232-1703.E-mail: johnfed@cox.net Web Site:www.cableinkansas.org

Directors: Jay Allbaugh Cox Communications; Kevin Collins Time Warner Cable; Mike Flood Cable ONE; Scott Schneider Cox Communications; Tom Krewson Comcast; Clarence Matlock Cable ONE; Joe Michael Cox Communications. Association Officer: Roger Ponder (chair) Gary Shorman (immediate past chair); Patrick Knorr (vice-chair); Coleen Jennison (sec/treas); John Federico, pres; Dan Murray, Legislative dir.

Kentucky Cable Telecommunications Association, Box 415, Burkesville, KY, 42717. Phone: (270) 864-5352. Fax: (270) 864-3110.E-mail: randawright@mchsi.com Web Site:www.kycable.com

Jim Finch, assoc dir; Jim Hays III, assoc dir; Robert Thacker III, assoc dir.

Louisiana Cable & Telecommunications Association, 763 North St., Baton Rouge, LA, 70802. Phone: (225) 387-5960. Fax: (225) 383-6705.E-mail: lcta@lacable.com Web Site:www.lacable.com

Cheryl P. McCormick, CEO

Michigan Cable Telecommunications Association, 412 W. Ionia St., Lansing, MI, 48933. Phone: (517) 482-2622. Fax: (517) 482-1819. Web Site:www.michcable.org

Directors: Colleen M. McNamara, exec dir; Bob McCann, sec; Rick Clark, treas; Tim Ransberger, pres, Ron Orlando, VP.

Mid-America Cable Telecommunications Association, Box 2138, Jefferson City, MO, 65102-2138. Phone: (573) 635-5588. Fax: (573) 635-5510.E-mail: info@midamericacable.tv Web Site:www.midamericacable.tv

Directors: Tony Bolton; Mary Marshall Burr; Eric Claytor; Kevin Colins; Bill Copeland; Art Cunningham; Vic Davis; Mike Drahota; Debby Exon; Bridget Farley; John Federico; Scott Grim; Lori Hansen; Greg Harrison; Gail Hastings; Christina Hill; Oscar Ordaz; Amie Hinderlifter; DeMaris Johnson; Denise Lewis; Dale Laine; Deirdre LaVerdiere; Tyler Leach; Charlotte McClure; Dan Mulvenon; Oscar Ordaz; Len Pitock; Mark Ronek; Joe Scott; Mike Slyman; Larry Stiffelman; Brian Thompson; Jim Walker; George Wilburn.

Minnesota Cable Communications Association, 1885 University Ave., Suite 320, St. Paul, MN, 55104. Phone: (651) 641-0268. Fax: (651) 641-0319.E-mail: mmartin@mncca.com Web Site:www.mncca.com

Mississippi Cable Telecommunications Association, 1501 Lakeland Dr., Suite 301, Jackson, MS, 39216. Phone: (601) 981-3646. Fax: (601) 981-5547.E-mail: mcta@bellsouth.net Web Site:www.mctaweb.com

Lee Ann Hayes, exec dir.

Missouri Cable Telecommunications Association, 223 E. Capitol Ave., Box 1895, Jefferson City, MO, 65102-1895. Phone: (573) 635-1915. Fax: (573) 635-1778.E-mail: info@missouricable.tv Web Site:www.missouricabletv.com

Roger Ponder, chmn; Greg Harrison, pres.

Nebraska Cable Communications Association, 1233 Lincoln Mall, Suite 203, Lincoln, NE, 68508. Phone: (402) 474-3242.E-mail: mary@campbellassociates.net

Mary Campbell, exec dir.

Nevada State Cable Communications Association, 2210 Sugar Bowl Ct., Reno, NV, 89511-9175. Phone: (775) 852-2253. Fax: (775) 852-2403.E-mail: nscta@aol.com

Steve Schorr; Leon Brennan, VP; Scott Dockery, sec/treas; Marsha Berkbigler.

New England Cable Telecommunications Association Inc. (NECTA), 10 Forbes Rd., Suite 440W, Braintree, MA, 02184. Phone: (781) 843-3418. Fax: (781) 849-6267.E-mail: info@necta.info

Paul R. Cianelli, pres.

New Jersey Cable Telecommunications Association, 124 W. State St., Trenton, NJ, 08608. Phone: (609) 392-3223. Fax: (609) 394-0074. Web Site:www.cablenj.org

Elizabeth Murray, chmn; Dante Di Pirro, sr VP.

North Carolina Cable Telecommunications Association, Box 1347, Raleigh, NC, 27602. Phone: (919) 834-7113. Fax: (919) 839-0304.E-mail: lreynolds@nccta.com Web Site:www.nccta.com

Joanne Higgins, dir communications.

North Central Cable Television Association, 1885 University Ave., Suite 320, St. Paul, MN, 55104. Phone: (651) 641-0268. Fax: (651) 641-0319.E-mail: mncableassc@comcast.net Web Site:www.mncca.com

Bill Wright, pres; John Growley, VP.

Ohio Cable Telecommunications Association, 50 W. Broad St., Suite 1118, Columbus, OH, 43215. Phone: (614) 461-4014. Fax: (614) 461-9326.E-mail: octa@octa.org Web Site:www.octa.org

Ed Kozelek, pres; Kevin Flanigan, VP; Pat Eltzroth, treas; Ann Doris, sec.

Oklahoma Cable and Telecommunications Association, 301 N.W. 63rd, Suite 400, Oklahoma City, OK, 73116. Phone: (405) 843-8855. Fax: (405) 843-8934.E-mail: octa@coxatwork.com Web Site:www.okcta.org

Dave Bialis, chmn; Andy Dearth, vice chmn; George Wilburn, sec/treas. Directors: Bill Drewry, Nicole Evans, Johnny Bowen, David Wall, Leon Pfeifer, Danny Thompson, Ed Perry, Holly Henderson & Tim Easley.

Oregon Cable Telecommunications Association, 1249 Commercial St. S.E., Salem, OR, 97302. Phone: (503) 362-8838. Fax: (503) 399-1029.E-mail: mdewey@oregoncable.com Web Site:www.oregoncable.com

Tennessee Cable Telecommunications Association, 611 Commerce St., Suite 2706, Nashville, TN, 37203. Phone: (615) 256-7037. Fax: (615) 254-9710.E-mail: info@tcta.net Web Site:www.tcta.net

Stacey B. Briggs, pres, exec dir; Curtis Person III, chmn.

Texas Cable Association, (Formerly Texas Cable & Telecommunications Association). 919 Congress Ave., Suite 1350, Austin, TX, 78701. Phone: (512) 474-2082. Fax: (512) 474-0966. Web Site:www.txcable.com E-mail: txcable@txcable.com

Virginia Cable Telecommunications Association, 1001 E. Broad St., Suite 210, Richmond, VA, 23219. Phone: (804) 780-1776. Fax: (804) 225-8036.E-mail: rlamura@vcta.com Web Site:www.vcta.com

Ray Lamura, pres; Barbara Davis, VP pub affrs; Kirby Brooks, chmn; Danita Bowman, dir govt rels.

West Virginia Cable Telecommunications Association, 117 Summers St., Charleston, WV, 25301. Phone: (304) 345-2917. Fax: (304) 342-1285.E-mail: mpolen@arnoldagency.com Web Site:www.wvcta.com

Michael Kelemen, pres; Peter Brown, treas (Suddenlink Communications); Gordon Waters, VP (Armstrong Cable Services).

Wisconsin Cable Communications Association, 22 East Mifflin Street, Suite 1010, Madison, WI, 53703. Phone: (608) 256-1683. Fax: (608) 256-6222.E-mail: wcca@charterinternet.com Web Site:www.wicable.com

Directors: Mike Fox; Robert Ryan; Bev Greenberg; Emmett Coleman; Lisa Washa. Director at large: Doug Nix; Dave Seyora. Associate Directors: Kenneth Mullane; Kate Schroeder; Jeff Fischer. Advisory Committee: Christy Benson; Randy Bunnell; Wendy Gross; Charlie Mullen; Randy Scott; JackHerbert, pres, Tim Vowell, VP; Bob Steichen, past pres; Thomas E. Moore, exec dir; Adam M. Raschka, dir regulatory/external affrs; Nancy Magestro, office admin, Bev Kautzky, accounting mgr.

Wyoming Cable Telecommunications Association-WCTA, (formerly Wyoming CATV Association). 1113 Lucky Ct., Cheyenne, WY, 82001. Phone: (307) 637-3933. Phone: (307) 733-3081. Fax: (307) 637-5399. Web Site:www.wyocable.org

Executive Director: H.L. Jensen. Board Members: Dan Higgins, Darlene Raymond, Wes Frost, Shawn Beqaj, Sara Viard-assoc bd member, Elizabeth Davis-assoc bd member. Clint Rodeman, pres; Marty Carollo, VP; Mary Johnson, sec/treas.

Union/Labor Groups

Actors' Equity Association (AEA), (AFL-CIO). 165 W. 46th St., New York, NY, 10036. Phone: (212) 869-8530. Fax: (212) 719-9815. Web Site:www.actorsequity.org
  Mark Zimmerman, pres; John Connolly, exec dir.
  Los AngelesCA , 5757 Wilshire Blvd, Suite 1. Phone:
  San FranciscoCA , 350 Sansome St., Ste 900. Phone:
  OrlandoFL , 10319 Orangewood Blvd. Phone:
  ChicagoIL , 125 S. Clark St. Phone:
  Labor Union for Theatrical Actors & Stage mgrs.

Affiliated Property Craftsperson (IATSE Local 44), (IATSE, AFL-CIO). 12021 Riverside Dr., North Hollywood, CA, 91607. Phone: (818) 769-2500. Fax: (818) 769-3111.E-mail: ejennings@local144.org Web Site:www.local44.org
  Elliott Jennings, sec/treas.

American Federation of Labor-Congress of Industrial Organizations (AFL-CIO), 815 16th St. N.W., Washington, DC, 20006. Phone: (202) 637-5000. Fax: (202) 637-5058.E-mail: bholton@afleio.org Web Site:www.aflcio.org
  John J. Sweeney, pres; Linda Chavez-Thompson, exec VP.

American Federation of Musicians, United States & Canada, 1501 Broadway, Suite 600, New York, NY, 10036. Phone: (212) 869-1330. Fax: (212) 764-6134. Web Site:www.afm.org
  Thomas F. Lee, pres; Sam Folio, sec/treas.
  WashingtonDC , 1717 K St. NW, Suite 500. Phone:
  Don MillsON Canada, 75 The Donway W, Suite 1010. Phone:
  Los AngelesCA . Los Angeles, 3550 Wilshire Blvd, Suite 1900. Phone:
  Representing 110,000 professional musicians throughout the United States & Canada.

American Federation of Television & Radio Artists (AFTRA), (AFL-CIO). 260 Madison Ave., New York, NY, 10016. Phone: (212) 532-0800. Fax: (212) 532-2242. Web Site:www.aftra.com
  Roberta Reardon, pres.
  Los AngelesCA , 5757 Wilshire Blvd., 9th Fl. Phone:
  AFTRA represents 77,000 professional actors, singers, dancers, announcers, newspersons, sportscasters & disc jockeys throughout the country who work in TV, radio, comls, industrial & educ videos, interactive media & the recording industry.

American Guild of Musical Artists, 1430 Broadway, 14th Fl, New York, NY, 10018-3308. Phone: (212) 265-3687. Fax: (212) 262-9088.E-mail: agma@musicalartists.org Web Site:www.musicalartists.org
  Linda Mays, pres.
  Branch offices in Los Angeles, CA; Chicago, IL; San Francisco, CA; New Orleans, LA; Seattle, WA; Dallas, TX; Washington, DC; Boston, MA; Philadelphia, PA.

American Guild of Variety Artists, (AFL-CIO). 363 7th Ave 17th Fl., New York, NY, 10001. Phone: (212) 675-1003. Fax: (212) 633-0097.E-mail: agva@aol.com Web Site:www.agva.com
  Rod McKuen, pres; David Cullum, VP.
  Los AngelesCA , 4741 Laurel Canyon Blvd. Phone :
  Labor Union for performers in live venues.

The Animation Guild (IATSE Local 839), 4729 Lankershim Blvd., North Hollywood, CA, 91602. Phone: (818) 766-7151. Fax: (818) 506-4805.E-mail: info@animationguild.org Web Site:www.animationguild.org
  The labor union for animation & CG artists & technicians in southern CA.

Art Directors Guild & Scenic Title and Graphic Artists (IATSE Local 800), 11969 Ventura Blvd., Suite 200, Studio City, CA, 91604. Phone: (818) 762-9995. Fax: (818) 762-9997.E-mail: lydia@artdirectors.org Web Site:www.artdirectors.org
  Scott Roth, exec dir; Tom Walsh, pres.

Broadcast-Television Recording Engineers (IBEW Local 45), 6255 Sunset Blvd., Suite 721, Hollywood, CA, 90028. Phone: (323) 851-5515. Fax: (323) 466-1793.E-mail: feedback@ibew45.org Web Site:www.ibew45.org
  Represents radio, TV, cable engirs, federal, county, city electronic tech.

Communications Workers of America (CWA), (AFL-CIO). 501 3rd St. N.W., Washington, DC, 20001-2797. Phone: (202) 434-1100. Fax: (202) 434-1279.E-mail: jmiller@cwa-union.org Web Site:www.cwa-union.org
  Larry Cohen, pres; Jeff Miller, dir communications.

Directors Guild of America Inc. (DGA), 7920 Sunset Blvd., Los Angeles, CA, 90046. Phone: (310) 289-2000. Fax: (310) 289-2029. Web Site:www.dga.org
  Michael Apted, pres; Jay Roth, exec dir.
  ChicagoIL , 400 N. Michigan Ave, Suite 307. Phone:
  New YorkNY , 110 W. 57th St. Phone:

Illustrators & Matte Artists (IATSE Local 790), 13245 Riverside Dr., Suite 300-A, Sherman Oaks, CA, 91423. Phone: (818) 784-6555. Fax: (818) 784-2004.E-mail: local790@earthlink.net
  Joseph Musso, pres; Marjo Bernay, business rep.

International Alliance of Theatrical Stage Employees, Moving Picture (IATSE), 1430 Broadway, 20th Fl, New York, NY, 10018. Phone: (212) 730-1770. Fax: (212) 730-7809. Web Site:www.iatse-intl.org
  Thomas Short, intl pres.
  TorontoON Canada, 258 Adelaide St E, Suite 403. Phone:
  Toluca LakeCA , 10045 Riverside Dr. Phone:

International Association of Machinists and Aerospace Workers (IAM), 9000 Machinists Pl, Upper Marlboro, MD, 20772-2687. Phone: (301) 967-4500.E-mail: websteward@goiam.org Web Site:www.iamaw.org
  R. Thomas Buffenbarger, pres; Warren Mart, sec/treas.

International Brotherhood of Electrical Workers (IBEW), (AFL-CIO). 900 7th St. N.W., Washington, DC, 20001. Phone: (202) 728-6026. Fax: (202) 728-6295.E-mail: broadcasting@ibew.org Web Site:www.ibew.org
  Edwin D. Hill, pres; Peter Homes, dir.
  Represent worker in all areas of bcstg & cable.

International Cinematographers Guild, 7715 Sunset Blvd., Suite 300, Los Angeles, CA, 90046. Phone: (323) 876-0160. Fax: (323) 876-6383. Web Site:www.cameraguild.com
  Gary Dunham, pres; Bruce C. Doering, exec dir.
  OrlandoFL , 7463 Conroy-Windermere Rd, Suite A. Phone:
  Park RidgeIL , 1411 Peterson Ave, Suite 102. Phone:
  New YorkNY , 80 Either Ave, 14th Fl. Phone:
  Represents our members' contracts & activities.

International Sound Technicians (IATSE Local 695), (IATSE, MPMO). 5439 Cahuenga Blvd., North Hollywood, CA, 91601. Phone: (818) 985-9204. Phone: (323) 877-1052. Fax: (818) 760-4681.E-mail: local695@695.com Web Site:www.695.com
  Mark Ulano, pres; James Osburn, business agent.

International Union of Electronic & Communications Workers of America, 501 3rd St. N.W., Washington, DC, 20001. Phone: (202) 434-1100. Web Site:iue-cwa.org
  James Clark, pres; Bill Gray, dir info svcs.

Laboratory Film/Video Technicians & Cinetechnicians (IATSE Local 683), Box 7429, Burbank, CA, 91510-7429. Phone: (818) 252-5628. Fax: (818) 252-4962.E-mail: scottgeorge@mindsprings.com
  Bill Milano, pres; Scott George, business agent.
  New YorkNY . IATSE, 1515 Broadway, Suite 601.
  Serves the Labor Union.

Make-Up Artist & Hairstylists Guild (IATSE Local 706), 828 N. Hollywood Way, Burbank, CA, 91505. Phone: (818) 295-3933. Fax: (818) 295-3930.E-mail: info@ialocal706.org Web Site:www.local706.org
  Susan Cabral-Ebert, pres; Tommy Cole, business rep.
  Union for make-up artists, hair stylist's in motion picture industry.

Motion Picture Costumers (IATSE Local 705), 4731 Laurel Canyon Blvd., Suite 201, Valley Village, CA, 91607. Phone: (818) 487-5655. Fax: (818) 487-5663.E-mail: mpc705@aol.com Web Site:www.motionpicturecostumers.org
  Sandra Berke Jordan, pres; Buffy Snyder, business rep.

The gathering (by rental or puchase) of costumes for film & TV. The construction of new costumes (wardrobe). The fitting & handling of costumes (wardrobe) during filming.

Motion Picture Editors Guild (IATSE Local 700), 7715 W. Sunset Blvd., Suite 200, Hollywood, CA, 90046. Phone: (323) 876-4770. Fax: (323) 876-0861.E-mail: mail@editorsguild.com Web Site:www.editorsguild.com
  ChicagoIL . Chicago, 6317 N. Northwest Hwy. Phone:
  New YorkNY . New York, 145 Hudson St., Suite 201. Phone:
  Labor union representin post-production employees.

Motion Picture Set Painters & Sign Writers (IATSE Local 729), 1811 W. Burbank Blvd., Burbank, CA, 91506-1314. Phone: (818) 842-7729. Fax: (818) 846-3729. Web Site:www.ialocal729.com
  Kirk Hansen, pres; George Palazzo, business rep.

National Association of Broadcast Employees & Technicians, (Communications Workers of America, AFL-CIO). 501 3rd St. N.W., 5th Fl., Washington, DC, 20001. Phone: (202) 434-1254. Fax: (202) 434-1426.E-mail: nabet@cwa-union.org Web Site:www.nabetcwa.org
  John Clark, pres.
  New YorkNY , Local 11, 888 7th Ave., Suite 4511. Phone:
  Representing employees in the bcstg, cable TV & related industries.

The Newspaper Guild, (CWA). 501 3rd St. N.W., Washington, DC, 20001. Phone: (202) 434-7177. Fax: (202) 434-1472. Web Site:www.newsguild.org E-mail: guild@cwa-union.org
  Linda K. Foley, pres; Bernie Lunzer, sec/treas.
  OttawaON Canada, Baxter Centre, 1050 Baxter Rd, Unit 7B. Phone:
  Represents newsroom & other media workers in U.S., Canada & Puerto Rico.

Office & Professional Employees International Union, 265 W 14th St, 6th Fl, New York, NY, 10011. Phone: (212) 675-3210.
  Michael Goodwin, pres.

Professional Musicians, Local 47, AFM, 817 N. Vine St., Hollywood, CA, 90038-3779. Phone: (323) 462-2161. Fax: (323) 461-5260. Web Site:www.promusic47.com
  Hal Espinosa, pres; Vince Trombetta, VP; Serena Kay Williams, sec/treas.
  Musicians, vocalists, orchestrators, copyists, composers, conductors, contractors & librarians, referral service & recording studio.

Screen Actors Guild, 5757 Wilshire Blvd., Los Angeles, CA, 90036. Phone: (323) 954-1600. Fax: (323) 549-6656. Web Site:www.sag.org
  Alan Rosenberg, pres.
  Contract administration, negotiation & enforcement, residual payment processing, regulation franchising of talent agents, membership, record-keeping & communication.

Script Supervisors/Continuity & Allied Prodution Specialists Guild Local 871, IATSE, (IATSE). 11519 Chandler Blvd., North Hollywood, CA, 91601. Phone: (818) 509-7871. Fax: (818) 506-1555.E-mail: ialocal871@aol.com Web Site:www.ialocal871.org
  "We think for a living." Script Supervisors/Continuity. Telepromptor Operators, Production Office Coordinator, Art Department Coordinator, Production Accountants & Assistants.

Service Employees International Union (SEIU), 1313 L St NW, Washington, DC, 20005. Phone: (202) 898-3200. Fax: (202) 350-6614.E-mail: burgera@seiu.org Web Site:www.seiu.org
  Andrew Stern, pres; Anna Burger, sec/treas.

Set Designers & Model Makers (IATSE Local 847), 13245 Riverside Dr., Ste 300-A, Sherman Oaks, CA, 91423. Phone: (818) 784-6555. Fax: (818) 784-2004.E-mail: Local847@earthlink.net
  Jim Wallace, pres; Marjo Bernay, business rep.

Studio Electrical Lighting Technicians (IATSE Local 728), 14629 Nordhoff St., Panorama City, CA, 91402. Fax: (818) 891-5288.E-mail: loc728@iatse728.org Web Site:www.iatse728.org

Patric J. Abaravich, pres.

United Electrical, Radio & Machine Workers of America (UE), One Gateway Ctr., Suite 1400, Pittsburgh, PA, 15222-1416. Phone: (412) 471-8919. Fax: (412) 471-8999. Web Site:www.ranknfile-ue.org E-mail: ue@ranknfile-ue.org

John H. Hovis, pres; Bruce Klipple, sec/treas.

United Scenic Artists (IATSE Local USA 829), 29 W. 38th St. 15th Fl., New York, NY, 10018. Phone: (212) 581-0300. Fax: (212) 977-2011.E-mail: administrator@usa829.org Web Site:www.usa829.org

Michael McBride, business agent.
Los AngelesCA , 5225 Wilshire Blvd, Suite 506. Phone:
MiamiFL , 10459 SW 78th St. Phone:
ChicagoIL , 203 N. Wabash, Suite 1210. Phone:
Representing designers of set, costume, lighting, sound, scenic artists, computer arts and art dept coordinators in the entertainment industry.

Writers Guild of America, East Inc. (WGAE), 555 W. 57th St., Suite 1230, New York, NY, 10019. Phone: (212) 767-7800. Fax: (212) 582-1909.E-mail: info@wgaeast.org Web Site:www.wgaeast.org

Warren Leight, pres.

Writers Guild of America, West Inc. (WGAW), 7000 W. Third St., Los Angeles, CA, 90048-4329. Phone: (323) 951-4000. Fax: (323) 782-4800. Web Site:www.wga.org E-mail: gscott@wga.org

Patrick Verrone, pres; Gabriel Scott, dir public affrs.
WGAW represents writers primarily for the purpose of collective bargaining in the motion picture, bcst, cable & new technologies industries.

Trade Shows

Arizona-New Mexico Cable Telecommunication Association Annual Meeting. DATE: February 8-10, 2010, State & Regional Event; Arizona Grant Resort, Phoenix, AZ. SHOW MANAGEMENT: Arizona Cable Telecommunication Association. ASSOCIATION ADDRESS: 3875 N. 44th Ave., Suite 300, Phoenix, AZ 85018. Contact: Susan Bitter Smith, exec dir. (602) 955-4122. FAX: (602) 955-4505. http://www.azcable.org. E-mail: info@azcable.org.

Audio Engineering Society Convention (Public/Trade). DATE: May 20, 2010, London. SHOW MANAGEMENT: Audio Engineering Society (AES), 60 E. 42nd St., Rm. 2520, New York, NY 10165. Contact: Howard Sherman, (212) 777-4711; Roger Furness, exec dir. (212) 661-8528. FAX: (212) 682-0477. Web site: http://www.aes.org. SHOW MANAGEMENT STATEMENT: This show provides an annual marketplace for professional audio equipment engineers. PROFILE OF ATTENDEES: Audio engineers.

Media Financial Management Association.. Formerly BCFM: Broadcast Cable Financial Management Association. DATE: May 23-25, 2010, The Renaissance Hotel, 611 Commerce St., Nashville, TN 37203; (800) 327-6618; Fax: 615-255-8163. SHOW MANAGEMENT: MFM, 550 Frontage Rd., Suite 3600, Northfield, IL 60093. Contact: Debi Borden, (847) 716-7000. FAX: (847) 716-7004. Web: http://www.bcfm.com. SHOW MANAGEMENT STATEMENT: BCFM sponsors an annual conference with exhibits targeting financial, HR, MIS, executive mgmt from TV, radio & cable plus association in auditing data processing, credit & collections. SHOW HISTORY: Annual. First Year of Show: 1960.

Broadcasting 2010 (Public/Trade). DATE November 2010. SHOW MANAGEMENT: Canadian Association of Broadcasters, 700-45 O'Connor St.Ottawa, ON, Canada K1p 1A4. (613) 233-4035. FAX: (613) 233-6961. E-mail: cab@acr.ca. PROFILE OF EXHIBITORS: Companies who provide products or svcs to Canadian bcst (radio-TV) operators. PROFILE ATTENDEES: Senior mgmt, owners, engineers & new directors. Set Rotation Pattern: East/West rotation.

CAB Sales Management Conference. SHOW DATE: April 2010, Hilton, Chicago, IL. SHOW MANAGEMENT: Cabletelevision Advertising Bureau, Inc., 830 Third Ave., 2nd Fl., New York, NY 10022. Contact: Nancy Lagos. (212) 508-1200. FAX: (212) 832-3268.

Cable-Tec Expo. DATE: October 17-19, 2010, New Orleans, LA. SHOW MANAGEMENT: Society of Cable Television Engineers, 140 Phillips Rd., Exton, PA 19341. (610) 363-6888. FAX: (610) 363-5898. SHOW SPONSOR: Same as show management. SHOW MANAGEMENT STATEMENT: The SCTE Cable-Tec Expo brings together engineers, technicians & technical exec from the United States who represent cable systems, MSOs & independent operators. A fulfillment to the growing need to address the technical end of the cable TV industry. PROFILE OF EXHIBITORS: Construction equipment, signal distribution, cable casting, transmission/receiving, test equipment, microware/mds, digital systems, system testing quality control & other related hardware. PROFILE OF ATTENDEES: Engineers, technicians, executives of MSOs & independent operators. SHOW HISTORY: Concurrent with rotating Annual Engineering Conference. First Year of Show: 1983.

Forum 2010. The Association of Cable Communicators. SHOW MANAGEMENT: CTPAA. ASSOCIATION ADDRESS: Box 75007, Washington, DC 20013. SHOW MANAGEMENT STATEMENT: Educational conference for cable pub affrs professionals. PROFILE OF ATTENDEES; Programmers, MSO, & loc system personnel. Contact: SHOW FREQUENCY: Annual. First Year of Show: 1985.

Great Lakes Broadcasting Conference & Expo (Public/Trade). DATE: March 2-3, 2010, Lansing Center, Lansing, MI 48906. SHOW MANAGEMENT: Michigan Association of Broadcasters, 819 N. Washington Ave., Lansing, MI 48906. (800) 968-7622. FAX: (517) 484-5810. E-mail: michmab@aol.com. SHOW SPONSOR: Same as show management. SHOW MANAGEMENT STATEMENT: Regional bcstg trade show which provides speakers & seminars to educate members while showcasing bcst equipment & svcs. PROFILE OF EXHIBITORS: Broadcast equipment, products & svcs. PROFILE OF ATTENDEES: General mgrs, engineers, sls mgrs, account executives, news directors & anybody involved in the audio, video or bcst industries. SHOW HISTORY: Annual.

INFOCOMM International. DATE: June 2010. SHOW MANAGEMENT: International Communications Industries Association Inc., 11242 Waples Mill Rd., Suite 200, Fairfax, VA 22030. Contact: Jason C. McGraw, sr VP. (703) 273-7200. FAX: (703) 278-8082. SHOW SPONSOR: Same as show management. SHOW MANAGEMENT STATEMENT: INFOCOMM International is the exposition of the video, computer, audiovisual, presentation & multimedia communications industries. It is sponsored by the International Communications Industries Association (ICIA). ICIA brings together more than 1,400 firms selling video, audiovisual & computer products & svcs. Members are dealers, software producers, independent representatives, rental companies & others serving users in communications, training, business, govt & education. In addition to the trade show, there are annual conventions, meetings, seminars, courses & institutes of many organizations who bring their members & interested associates to the event. PROFILE OF EXHIBITORS: Manufactur ers & producers of video, computer & audiovisual-based communications & info products & producers of software programs for all technologies represented. PROFILE OF ATTENDEES: Dealers who sell video, audio, presentation systems & installations to professional users of these media; production & post-production companies, adv & PR agencies, laboratories & other users of video & related technologies. SHOW HISTORY: Annual. First Year of Show: 1983.

Interwire Trade Exposition. DATES: May 12-13, 2010, Milwaukee, Wisconsin. May 2-5, 2011, Georgia World Congress Center, Atlanta, Georgia. SHOW MANAGEMENT: Wire Association International, 1570 Boston Post Rd., Box 578, Guilford, CT 06437. (203) 453-2777. FAX: (203) 453-8384. SHOW SPONSOR: Same as show management. SHOW MANAGEMENT STATEMENT: Interwire provides a marketplace for the wire & cable industry. It is a trade show for wire manufacturers, fabricators, suppliers, other buyers & users with admin, engrg, tech & purchasing personnel in attendance from the United States, Europe, Asia, South & Central Americas. Product classifications include wire machinery, spring machinery, fasteners, fabricators, fiber optics, chemical coatings, accessories & other wire-related products. PROFILE

OF EXHIBITORS: Machinery & accessories; fiber optics, chemicals, coatings, lubricants, dies, compounds, spools, reels, packaging, measuring, testing equipment, wire, cable, fasteners & fabricated wire products. PROFILE OF ATTENDEES: Gen & admin mgmt; engrg, opns, production; tech, rsch & dev, quality control; purchasing; sls & mktg concerned with wire industry. SHOW HISTORY: Biennial.

Kentucky Broadcasters Association Fall Convention. Date September 2010. SHOW MANAGEMENT: Kentucky Broadcasters Association, 101 Enterprise Dr., Frankfort, KY 40601. (888) 843-5221. FAX: (502) 843-5710. SHOW MANAGEMENT STATEMENT: This convention's purpose is to further train bcstrs on both legal aspects of bcstrs as well as sls & mgmt. PROFILE OF EXHIBITORS: Electronics, computers, program syndications, bcst suppliers (radio/TV). PROFILE OF ATTENDEES: Owners & mgmt throughout the state of Kentucky. SHOW HISTORY: First Year of Show: 1953.

Louisiana Krewe of Cable Show. DATE: January 9-10, 2010, State & Regional Event. SHOW MANAGEMENT: Louisiana Cable & Telecommunications Association, 763 North St., Baton Rouge, LA 70802. (225) 387-5960. FAX: (225) 383-6705. Web site: http://www.lacable.com. SHOW FREQUENCY: Annual.

Minnesota Broadcasters Association Annual Conference & Expo (Public/Trade). SHOW MANAGEMENT: Minnesota Broadcasters Association, 3033 Excelsier Blvd., Suite 301, Minneapolis, MN 55416. Contact: Jim DuBois, pres/CEO. (612) 926-8123. FAX: (612) 926-9761. E-mail: jduboisminnesotabroadcasters.com. SHOW MANAGEMENT STATEMENT: The show includes exhibits for bcstg, cable, production, & other electronic media.

NAB 2010. DATE: April 10-15, 2010, Las Vegas, Nevada. MANAGEMENT: National Association of Broadcasters, 1771 N St. N.W., Washington, DC 20036. (202) 429-5300. FAX: (202) 429-7427. SHOW MANAGEMENT STATEMENT: The Convention is an annual gathering of radio, TV, video, post-production, multimedia & telecommunications professionals worldwide. Sessions cover aspects of electronic media, both tech & management-oriented. PROFILE OF EXHIBITORS: Manufacturers, distributors of products, equipment & svcs for the radio, TV, video, post-production, film multimedia & telecommunications industries. PROFILE OF ATTENDEES: Owners & managers of radio, TV, video, post-production & users of multimedia & telecommunications products & svcs. SHOW HISTORY: First Year of Show: 1922.

NATPE 2010. DATE: January 25-27, 2010, Mandalay Bay Resort Convention Center, Las Vegas, NV. MANAGEMENT: National Association of Television Program Executives, 5757 Wilshire Blvd., Penthouse 10, Los Angeles, CA 90036. (310) 453-4440. FAX: (310) 453-5258. E-mail: orfan@aol.com. SHOW SPONSOR: Same as show management. SHOW MANAGEMENT STATEMENT: This show provides an annual marketplace for syndicated TV programs, first-run &/or off-network programs, as well as aspects of the TV business. PROFILE OF EXHIBITORS: Major studios, independent producers, marketers, cable networks, electronic retailers, new media producers, United States & intl program distributors. PROFILE

OF ATTENDEES: Advertisers, cable MSOs, bcst stns & networks, producers, marketers, bankers, merchandisers, talent agents, new media, United States & overseas program distributors & TV programmers. SHOW HISTORY: First Year of Show: 1984.

National Religious Broadcasters Convention and Exposition (Public/Trade). DATE: February 27-March 2, 2010, 2800 Opryland Dr., Gaylord Opryland Resort & Convention Center, Nashville, TN. SHOW MANAGEMENT: National Religious Broadcasters Association, 9510 Technology Dr., Manassas, VA 20110. Contact: David Keith. (703) 330-7000. FAX: (703) 330-7100. Website: http://www.nrb.org. SHOW SPONSOR: Same as show management. SHOW MANAGEMENT STATEMENT: The NRB Convention & Exposition is an annual gathering of manufacturers & distributors of bcst equipment, computers, radio & TV programs, consultant svcs, gospel music, publishing & other related items to the religious communications industry. PROFILE OF EXHIBITORS: Manufacturers & distributors of consumer & bcst audio & video equipment, computers, radio & TV programs, publishers, & miscellaneous items relating to the religious field. PROFILE OF ATTENDEES: Radio & TV executives, ministers, denominational executives, musicians, adv exec s, educators & Christian bookstore owners. SHOW HISTORY: Annual. First Year of Show: 1944.

NCTA. DATE: May 12-13, 2010. Los Angeles. SHOW SPONSOR: National Cable Television Association, 25 Massachusetts Ave., N.W.,Suite 100, Washington, DC 20001. (202) 775-3669. FAX: (202) 775-3692. Web site: http://www.thenationalshow.com. SPONSOR STATEMENT: NCTA's Annual Convention & International Exposition provides the industry's largest, most comprehensive showcase for equipment, progmg & enhanced svcs for cable TV, broadband & telecommunications systems. PROFILE OF EXHIBITORS: All industries related to cable TV & broadband svcs including hardware manufacturers, equipment suppliers, programming networks, enhanced svcs including VOD, PVR, software & technology providers. PROFILE OF ATTENDEES: Includes multiple system operators, independent operators, program networks, media & entertainment companies, investment & financial institutions, telecommunications providers, enhanced svc providers & the press. SHOW HISTORY: Annual. First Year of Show: 1950.

Promax & BDA 2010 International (Trade). DATE: June 15-17, 2010, Los Angeles. SHOW MANAGEMENT: Promax/BDA, 1522e Cloverfield Blvd., Santa Monica, CA 90404. (310) 788-7600. FAX: (310) 788-7676. Web site: http://www.promaxbda.org. SHOW SPONSOR: Same as show management. SHOW MANAGEMENT STATEMENT: The purpose of the show is to bring together bcst promoters & designers in the electronic media, all incorporated in one show. PROFILE OF EXHIBITORS: Music video production; computer animation & graphics hardware; stn design & image packages; adv premiums & incentives. PROFILE OF ATTENDEES: Promax International serves those individuals responsible for the mktg, adv, promotion & publicizing of TV stns, networks, production companies, radio stns & cable systems on a national & international level. BDA consists of an international membership of art directors, designers & graphic artists.

RAB 2010 Marketing Leadership Conference. SHOW MANAGEMENT: Radio Advertising Bureau, 261 Madison Ave., 23rd Fl., New York, NY. (972) 753-6740. FAX: (972) 753-6802. SHOW SPONSOR: Same as show management. SHOW MANAGEMENT STATEMENT: RAB is the largest gathering of sls & mgmt professionals in the radio industry. The Conference represents more than 5,000 members radio stns, radio stn sls managers, bcst groups, radio networks, stn representatives, network executives & associated industry organizations from the 50 states & 23 foreign countries. To educate, train radio sls & mktg professionals. The goal is to raise the level of professionalism in radio sls & mktg. PROFILE OF EXHIBITORS: Manufacturers, distributors or suppliers of a product or svc for any of the following categories: computer/software programs; radio & TV products; radio networks; specialty adv; program syndication; sls & mktg rsch; sls consulting. PROFILE OF ATTENDEES: Radio stn sls mgrs, gen mgrs, network execs & group heads from throughout the United States. SHOW HISTORY: First Year of Show: 1980.

SATELLITE 2010. DATE: March 15-18, 2010, Gaylord National Convention Center, National Harbor, MD. SHOW MANAGEMENT: Access Intelligence, LLC. SHOW SPONSOR: Via Satellite Magazine. ASSOCIATION ADDRESS: 1201 Seven Locks Rd., Suite 300, Potomac, MD 20854. (301) 354-2000. FAX (301) 354-2315. Web site: http://www.satellitetoday.com. SHOW MANAGEMENT STATEMENT: This is the largest Satellite specific conference & exhibition in the world. SATELLITE 2010 provides you with an unequalled opportunity to meet key, sr satellite company exec from the United States, Europe, the Pacific Rim, South America & Africa. This is your chance to strengthen existing professional & business relationships as well as initiate new ones, before, during & after the conference sessions & throughout our expansive exhibit hall. PROFILE OF EXHIBITORS: Satellite operators, end users, manufacturers, svc providers, launch vehicle operators teleports, consumer svc providers. PROFILE OF ATTENDEES: Distributors bcsters, programmers, VSAI network providers, satellite operators, launch vehicle svc providers & manufacturers. SHOW FREQUENCY: Annual. First Year of Show: 1976.

Society of Motion Picture and Television Engineers Annual Technical Conference and Exhibition. SHOW MANAGEMENT: SMPTE, 3 Barker Ave., White Plains, NY 10601. (914) 761-1100. FAX: (914) 761-3115. SHOW SPONSOR: Same as show management. SHOW MANAGEMENT STATEMENT: The show provides an annual marketplace for equipment & supplies for production, engrg & purchasing personnel in worldwide professional motion-picture & bcst-TV industries. Product classifications include TV, cable, production, postproduction, laboratory & field-production equipment. PROFILE OF EXHIBITORS: Manufacturers, dealers & distributors of professional TV-bcst & motion-picture equipment. PROFILE OF ATTENDEES: Senior bcst & film-engineering personnel from the motion-picture & bcst-TV industries. SHOW HISTORY: Annual. Set Rotation Pattern: East Coast odd-numbered years, West Coast even-numbered years.

WCA International Symposium and Business Expo. SHOW MANAGEMENT: SHOW SPONSOR: Wireless Communications Association International. ASSOCIATION ADDRESS: 1333 H St. N.W., Suite 700 W., Washington, DC 20005. (202) 452-7823. FAX (202) 452-0041. Web site: http://www.wcai.com. Contact: Carl Berndtson (978) 371-1792. PROFILE OF EXHIBITORS: Excellent mix of wireless broadband operators, vendors & integrators. PROFILE OF ATTENDEES: Executive & upper management; CTOs from wireless broadband industry. SHOW FREQUENCY: Annual. First Year of Show: 1983.

Vocational and Career Development Schools

The Art Institute of Pittsburgh, 420 Blvd. of the Allies, Pittsburgh, PA, 15219. Phone: (412) 263-6600. Fax: (412) 263-3715. E-mail: admissions-aip@aii.edu Web Site:www.aip.aii.edu

Hans Westman, dir media arts & animation.

Courses offered include audio recording & production, engrg, EFP video production, bcst media, feature writing, scriptwriting, legal issues, non-linear editing, image manipulation, filmmaking & multicamera field production.

Broadcast Center, 2360 Hampton Ave., St. Louis, MO, 63139. Phone: (314) 647-8181. Fax: (314) 647-1575. E-mail: jberry@yourcba.com Web Site:www.broadcastcenterinfo.com

Douglas H. Huber, pres; Linda Hoy, VP opns.

Training in mktg & time sls, coml & program production, bcst journalism & bcst performance. Training includes voice training & dev for bcstg; announcing training including news, comls, DJ & sportscasting; news & coml copywriting.

Broadcasting Institute of Maryland, 7200 Harford Rd., Baltimore, MD, 21234. Phone: (410) 254-2770. Phone: (800) 942-9246. Fax: (410) 254-5357. E-mail: info@bim.org Web Site:www.bim.org

John C. Jeppi Sr., pres; John I. Perry Sr., VP; Lois Carringan Sr., dir.

Courses offered include comprehensive course in radio & TV bcstg; majors available in radio, TV production, news & sports.

Brown College, 1440 Northland Dr., Mendota Heights, MN, 55120. Phone: (651) 905-3400. Fax: (651) 905-3550. E-mail: lwright@browncollege.edu Web Site:www.browncollege.edu

Lisa Wright, dept chair school of bcstg radio & TV.

The Associate of Applied Science degree in Radio Broadcasting is designed to help develop an on-air presence as well as the technical-hands on, and writing skills needed for positions in this growing industry. The Associate of Applied Science degree in Television Production is designed to prepare students for an entry level position in a number of areas including: broadcast TV stations, industrial video firms, cable companies and satellite operations.

Carolina School of Broadcasting, 3435 Performance Rd., Charlotte, NC, 28214. Phone: (704) 395-9272. Fax: (704) 395-9698. E-mail: csbnc@bellsouth.net Web Site:www.csbradiotv.com

Courses offered include a non-tech bcstg group session & an in-stn training lab course; announcing, production, copywriting, news, digital coml production, sls & administration. Day & night sessions. In-stn training, full- or part-time as determined by stn & student. TV facilities & stereo control room; resident training in studio & stn opns at coml radio & TV stns worldwide. Digital audio & non-linear editing for TV.

Cleveland Institute of Electronics, 1776 E. 17th St., Cleveland, OH, 44114. Phone: (216) 781-9400. Phone: (800) 243-6446. Fax: (216) 781-0331. Web Site:www.cie-wc.edu E-mail: instruct@cie-wc.edu

John R. Drinko, pres; Scott D. Katzenmeyer, VP administration; Paul Valvoda, controller; Keith Conn, dean of instruction.

Virginia BeachVA . World College, 5193 Shore Dr, Suite 105. Phone:instruct@cie-wc.edu Web Site: www.worldcollege.edu. John R. Drinko, pres.

Offers associate in applied science degree in electronics engrg technology, bsct engrg. FCC license preparation & cable technician training.

Clover Park Technical College, 4500 Steilacoom Blvd. S.W., Lakewood, WA, 98499-4098. Phone: (253) 589-5800. Fax: (253) 589-5797. Web Site:www.cptc.edu

Bcst training since 1954. Comprehensive Associate degree program in all aspects of radio stn opn prepares students for entry-level employment. Course includes staff experience at 51-kw *KVTI(FM). A two-year state college. Assoc of Applied Technology degree programs.

Columbia College Hollywood, 18618 Oxnard St., Tarzana, CA, 91356-1411. Phone: (818) 345-8414. Fax: (818) 345-9053. E-mail: info@columbiacollege.edu Web Site:www.columbiacollege.edu

Jan Stanley Mason, pres; Mark J. Stratton, admin dir.

Courses offered in TV/video production & cinema; degree program includes classes in directing, studio lighting, camera opns, videotape editing, scriptwriting, film editing, sound mixing, asst camera & script supervision. A.A. degree in TV/video production; B.A. degree in TV/video, cinema, and cinema/TV combination.

Columbia School of Broadcasting, (Washington, DC Metro Area). 3947 University Dr., 2nd Fl., Fairfax, VA, 22030-2506. Phone: (703) 591-6000. Fax: (703) 591-6147. E-mail: djtrain@columbiaschoolbroadcas.com Web Site:www.columbiaschoolbroadcas.com

William Butler, pres.

Courses offered include English & Sp radio announcing (voice-over, newscaster, DJ, sportscaster, traffic/weather reporter & interviews/talk show host), TV announcing, radio play-by-play sportscasting & basic radio production. Distance educ & resident courses offer comprehensive training for entry-level bcstg positions. Founded in 1964.

Columbia School of Broadcasting, Metro Washington DC Communications Ctr., 3947 Univ. Dr. 2nd Fl, Fairfax, VA, 22030-2506. Phone: (800) 362-0660. Fax: (703) 591-6147. E-mail: bill@csbamerica.com Web Site:www.csbamerica.com

William Butler, pres.

Courses offered include radio, TV announcing, radio, TV sls, internet bcstg, digital journalism & production.

Connecticut School of Broadcasting, Inc., 63 Bay State Rd., Boston, MA, 02215. Phone: (617) 267-2006. Fax: (617) 267-2004. E-mail: btilden@gocsb.com Web Site:www.800tvradio.com

Brian Stone, pres/CEO; David Banner, COO; Beverly Tilden, mktg dir; Jason Muth, VP recruit & admissions; Katie MacKay, mktg asst; Scott Knight, exec VP.

PawcatuckCT . GCP Pawcatuck LLC, 185 S. Broad St., 3rd Fl. #303. Phone:

TampaFL . GCP Tampa LLC, 3901 Coconut Palm Dr., Sabal Business Center II, Suite 105. Phone:

Westbury, LINY . GCP Westbury LLC, 1400 Old Country Rd, Suite 211. Phone:

FarmingtonCT . GCP Farmington, Media Park, 130 Birdseye Rd. Phone:

StratfordCT . GCP Stratford LLC, 80 Ferry Blvd. Phone:FL . GCP Palm Beach Gardens LLC, 3450 Northlake Blvd., Suite 110. Phone:

DavieFL . GCP Davie LLC, 3538 S. University Dr., University Park Plaza. Phone:

AtlantaGA . GCP Atlanta LLC, 1117 Perimeter Ctr W., Suite N-301. Phone:

NeedhamMA . GCP Needham LLC, 73 TV Pl. Phone:

Cherry HillNJ . GCP Cherry Hill LLC, One Cherry Hill, #201. Phone:

Hasbrouck HeightsNJ . GCP Hasbrouck Heights, 377 Rt. 17 S., #140. Phone:

AustinTX . GCP CSB Austin LLC, 9600 Great Hills Tr, Suite 200-E. Phone:

IrvingTX . GCP CSB Dallas LLC, 5605 N. MacArthur Blvd, Suite 220. Phone:

ArlingtonVA . GCP Arlington, 2170 Crystal Plaza Arcade, #38. Phone:

Courses (day & evening): On-air performance: Radio, TV, Internet bcst. Production courses: Digital audio & video, linear & non-linear avid editing. Other communications courses: Sports, voice-overs, sls, proms, mktg, wireless & multi-media technology.

Dunwoody College of Technology, 818 Dunwoody Blvd., Minneapolis, MN, 55403. Phone: (612) 374-5800. Fax: (612) 374-4128. E-mail: info@dunwoody.edu Web Site:www.dunwoody.edu

C. Ben Wright, pres; Brian Seviola, mktg mgr.

Courses offered include assoc in electronics tech degree, computer technician, radio-TV, industrial electronics technician, digital electronics specialists, electronics technician, TV specialists, certificate programs, aviation electronics, & info mgmt systems.

Education Direct, 925 Oak St., Scranton, PA, 18515. Phone: (570) 342-7701. Fax: (570) 961-4888. Web Site:www.educationdirect.com E-mail: info@educationdirect.com

Dan Conrad, gen mgr .

Diploma courses include basic electronics, electronics technology, basic computer progmg, TV/VCR repair or personal computer repair, Java progmg, internet web page design, electricians, telecommunications technician. Center for Degree Studies: specialized assoc degree in electronics technology & electrical, mechanical, civil & industrial engrg technology; specialized assoc degree in business mgmt, mktg, finance, accounting or applied computer science; Internet technology in web progmg, Internet technology multimedia, Internet technology in e-commerce administration, graphic design, DC maintenance technology.

Grantham University, 2101 Wilson Blvd, Suite 110, Arlington, VA, 22201. Fax: (703) 465-1273. E-mail: info@grantham.edu Web Site:www.grantham.edu

Roy Winter, pres; Joanna Boldt, dir of student affrs.

Courses offered include computer science, electronics engrg tech & computer engrg tech by correspondence, leading to A.S. & B.S. degrees.

The Illinois Center for Broadcasting, 55 West 22nd St., Suite 240, Lombard, IL, 60148. Phone: (630) 916-1700. Fax: (630) 916-1764. E-mail: director.chicago@beonair.com Web Site:www.beonair.com

Patrick Johnson, school dir.

10-month, hands-on course in radio & TV bcstg procedures & techniques.

International College of Broadcasting, 6 S. Smithville Rd., Dayton, OH, 45431. Phone: (937) 258-8251. Fax: (937) 258-8714. Web Site:www.icbcollege.com E-mail: admissions@icbcollege.com

J. Michael LeMaster, pres.

Courses offered include radio, TV, cameraman, CATV, disc jockey, news, sports & audio/recording engrg. Assoc degree in communication arts available in radio/TV & video production/recording audio engrg. Diploma programs offered in audio/recording engrg & bcstg.

Madison Media Institute-College of Media Arts, 2702 Agriculture Dr., Madison, WI, 53718. Phone: (608) 663-2000. Fax: (608) 442-0141. E-mail: swh@madisonmedia.com Web Site:www.madisonmedia.edu

Chris Hutchings, pres; Steve Hutchings, VP & dir admissions.

Courses offered include digital media design, production, video, motion graphics, recording & music technology. Accredited by Accrediting Commission of Career Schools & Colleges of Technology.

The New England Institute of Art, 10 Brookline Pl. W., Boston, MA, 02445. Phone: (617) 739-1700. Fax: (617) 582-4500. Web Site:www.artinstitutes.edu/boston E-mail: neiaadm@aii.edu

Debra Leahy, dir. media arts; Fran Berger, dir pub rel.

Programs offered: Bachelor's Degree in Graphic Design, Photography, Digital Film & Video Production, Interactive Media Design, Media Arts & Animation, Interior Design, Audio & Media Technology. Associate's Degrees in Audio Production, Broadcasting,

New England School of Communications, One College Cir., Bangor, ME, 04401. Phone: (207) 941-7176. Fax: (207) 947-3987. E-mail: info@nescom.edu Web Site:www.nescom.edu

Courses offered include announcing, bcst sls, writing for bcst, TV production, sound recording, voice/diction, news/sports reporting, adv & PR, pub speaking, video graphics, desktop publishing, print journalism & web design.

New School University, 2 W. 13th St., New York, NY, 10011. Phone: (212) 229-8903. Fax: (212) 229-5357. E-mail: baronej@newschool.edu Web Site:www.newschool.edu

Carol Wilder, chmn media & film studies; Dawnja Burris, assoc chmn media studies.

Courses offered include TV writing workshop; writing for TV, films & radio; TV production workshop; voice & speech for theater & TV; seminars on TV comls; writing TV comls. Offers certificate in film/TV studies, B.A., B.A./M.A., M.A. in media studies.

Northland Community & Technical College (KSRQ-FM), 1101 Hwy. 1 E., Thief River Falls, MN, 56701. Phone: (218) 681-0701. Phone: (800) 959-6282. Fax: (218) 681-0774. Web Site:www.northlandcollege.edu

Julie Olson, dir public rel.

Courses offered include a diploma-earning program in radio bcstg working on a 24,000 kw educ FM stn.

The Ohio Center for Broadcasting-Cincinnati, 6703 Madison Rd., Cincinnati, OH, 45227. Phone: (513) 271-6060. Fax: (513) 271-6135. Web Site:www.beonair.com

Eric Armstrong, opns VP; Amy Fouss, admissions dir.

10-month, hands-on course in Radio & TV procedures & techniques.

The Ohio Center for Broadcasting-Cleveland, 9000 Sweet Valley Drive, Valley View, OH, 44125. Phone: (216) 447-9117. Fax: (216) 642-9232. E-mail: ocb@beonair.com Web Site:www.beonair.com

Robert Mills, pres.

DenverCO , 1310 Wadsworth Blvd. Phone:

10-month, hands-on course on radio & TV bcstg & techniques. Fully accredited by ACCSCT. Graduates earn 36 quarter credit hrs with diploma. Instructors are professional bcstrs. Nationally accredited by ACCSCT. Full time placement assistance.

The Poynter Institute for Media Studies, 801 3rd St. S., St. Petersburg, FL, 33701. Phone: (727) 821-9494. Fax: (727) 821-0583.E-mail: oseifert@poynter.org Web Site:www.poynter.org

Karen Brown Dunlap, pres.

Seminars & conferences for print & bcst & online journalists. Courses for TV/radio include stn leadership, new leaders in the newsroom, newsroom mgmt, ethical decision-making, anchors as newsroom leaders investigative reporting, power reporting, computer-assisted journalism, visual storytelling & ethics, & producing newscasts.

Specs Howard School of Media Arts Inc., 19900 W. Nine Mile Rd., Southfield, MI, 48075-3953. Phone: (248) 358-9000. Fax: (248) 746-9772.E-mail: info@specshoward.edu Web Site:www.specshoward.edu

Dick Kernen, VP industry rels; Jonathan Liebman, CEO; Lisa Zahodne, COO.

Courses offered include Radio-TV-Film & video production graphic design. Accredited by ACCSCT.

Technical Career Institutes, 320 W. 31st St., New York, NY, 10001. Phone: (212) 594-4000. Fax: (212) 629-3937. Web Site:www.tcicollege.net E-mail: admissions@tcicollege.edu

James Melville, pres; Bonnie Price, public rel.

Tech courses offered include electronics engrg, EETT & IETC office technology, computerized accounting, bldg maintenance, air conditioning, heating & refrigeration technology. Assoc degree available.

Western Technical College, 304 6th St. N., La Crosse, WI, 54601. Phone: (608) 785-9200. Fax: (608) 785-9407.E-mail: westpfahlr@westertc.edu Web Site:www.westerntc.edu

Lee Rasch, pres; Joan Pierce, dir media arts.

Courses in the Visual Communications associates's degree include design fundamentals, audio production, media technologies, digital photography, Adobe Photoshop & illustrator, video production & web design.

Universities and Colleges with Broadcasting or Journalism Programs

Universities and Colleges Offering Degrees in Broadcasting

California
Platt College Los Angeles.

Colorado
Platt College Aurora.

District of Columbia
Center for Digital Imaging Arts at Boston U. Washington.

Florida
City College Fort Lauderdale.

Indiana
National College Indianapolis.

Kentucky
National College Lexington.
Western Kentucky U. Bowling Green.

Massachusetts
Center for Digital Imaging Arts at Boston U. Boston.

Minnesota
Globe U. Minnesota.
Brown College Mendota Heights.

Ohio
International College Of Broadcasting Dayton.
National College Cincinnati.

Oklahoma
Oklahoma State U. Stillwater.

South Dakota
Globe U. Sioux Falls.

South Carolina
Winthrop U. Rock Hill.

Tennessee
National College Nashville.

Virginia
National College Martinsville.

Wisconsin
Globe U. Middleton.

Two-Year Colleges Offering Programs in Broadcasting

Arizona
Pima Community College Tucson 85701.

Arkansas
Arkansas State University-Main Campus State University 72467.

California
City College of San Francisco San Francisco 94112.

Connecticut
Manchester Community College Manchester 06045.

Florida
Unversity of Miami Coral Gables 33124.

Illinois
City Colleges Of Chicago-Kennedy-King College Chicago 60621.
Parkland College Champaign 61821.

Kansas
Indpendence Community College Independence 67301.

Kentucky
National College Business and Tech-Lexington Lexington 40508.

Louisiana
Bossier Parish Community College Bossier City 71111.

Minnesota
Lake Superior College Duluth 55811.
Northland Community and Techical College Thief River Falls 56701.

Mississippi
Coahoma Community College Clarksdale 38614.
Hinds Community College, Raymond 39154.
Northeast Mississippi Community College Booneville 38829.

Nebraska
Grace Unversity Omaha 68108.

Ohio
Cedarville Unversity Cedarville 45314.
Hocking College Nelsonville 45764.
International College of Broadcasting Dayton 45431.

Oregon
Lane Community College Eugene 97405.
Mt. Hood Community College Gresham 97030.

Tennessee
Draughons Juniors College Inc. Nashville 37217.

Texas
Alvin Community College Alvin 77511.
Amarillo College Amarillo 79109.
Austin Community College Austin 78736.
Central Texas College Killeen 76549.
Del Mar College, Corpus Christi 78404.
McLennan Community College Waco 76708.
Odessa College Odessa 79764.
San Antonio College San Antonio 78212.

Wyoming
Central Wyoming College Riverton 82501.
Laramie County Community College Cheyenne 82007.

Universities and Colleges Offering Degrees in Journalism and Mass Communication

Alabama
Alabama, U. of Tuscaloosa 35487.
Auburn U. Auburn 36849.
Montevallo, U. of Montevallo 35115.
Troy State U. Troy 36082.

Alaska
Alaska, U. of Anchorage 99508.
Alaska, U. of Fairbanks 99775.

Arizona
Arizona, U. of, Tucson 85721.
Arizona State U. Tempe 85287.

Arkansas
Arkansas, U. of Fayetteville 72701.
Arkansas State U. State University 72467.

California
California State Polytechnic U. San Luis Obispo 93407.
California State U. Chico 95929.
California State U. Los Angeles, Los Angeles 90032.
California State U. Northridge, Northridge 91330.
San Francisco, U. of San Francisco 94117.
San Francisco State U. San Francisco 94132.
San Jose State U. San Jose 95192.

Colorado
Colorado, U. of Boulder 80309.
Denver, U. of Denver 80208.
Northern Colorado, U. of Greeley 80639.

Universities and Colleges with Broadcasting or Journalism Programs

Connecticut
Connecticut, U. of Storrs 06269.

District of Columbia
American U. Washington 20016.
Howard U. Washington 20059.

Florida
Central Florida, U. of Orlando 32816.
Florida A&M U. Tallahassee 32307.
Florida International U. North Miami 33181.
Florida, U. of Gainesville 32611.
Florida Southern College Lakeland 33801.
Miami, U. of Coral Gables 33124.

Georgia
Georgia, U. of Athens 30602.
Georgia Southern U. Statesboro 30460.

Hawaii
Hawaii at Manoa, U. of Honolulu 96822.

Idaho
Idaho, U. of Moscow 83844.
Idaho State U. Pocatello 83709.

Illinois
Eastern Illinois U. Charleston 61920.
Illinois, U. of Urbana 61801.
Northwestern U. Evanston 60208.
Southern Illinois U. Carbondale 629016.

Indiana
Ball State U. Muncie 47306.
Butler U. Indianapolis 46208.
Indiana U. Bloomington 47405.
Indianapolis, U. of Indianapolis 46227.
Indiana Unversity-Purdue Unversity-Indianapolis Indianapolis 46202.
Southern Indiana, U. of Evansville 47712.

Iowa
Drake U. Des Moines 50311.
Iowa, U. of Iowa City 52242.
Iowa State U. Ames 50011.
Northern Iowa, U. of Cedar Falls 50614.

Kansas
Kansas, U. of Lawrence 66045.
Kansas State U. Manhattan 66506.

Kentucky
Kentucky, U. of Lexington 40506.
Murray State U. Murray 42071.
Western Kentucky U. Bowling Green 42101.

Louisiana
Louisiana State U. Baton Rouge 70803.
Nicholls State U. Thibodaux 70310.
Northwestern State U. Natchitoches 71497.
Louisiana, U. Lafayette 70504.

Maine
Maine, U. of Orono 04469.

Maryland
Maryland, U. of College Park 20742.

Massachusetts
Boston U. Boston 02216.
Emerson College Boston 02116.
Northeastern U. Boston 02115.

Michigan
Central Michigan U. Mt. Pleasant 48859.
Michigan State U. East Lansing 48824.
Wayne State U. Detroit 48201.

Minnesota
Minnesota, U. of Minneapolis 55455.
St. Cloud State U. St Cloud 56301.

Mississippi
Jackson State U. Jackson 39217.
Mississippi, U. of University 38677.
Southern Mississippi, U. of Hattiesburg 39406.

Missouri
Missouri, U. of Columbia 65211.
Southeast Missouri State U. Cape Girardeau 63701.

Montana
Montana, U. of Missoula 59812.

Nebraska
Nebraska, U of Lincoln 68588.

Nevada
Nevada, U. of Reno 89557.

New Jersey
Rutgers U. New Brunswick 08903.

New Mexico
New Mexico, U. of Albuquerque 87131.
New Mexico State U. Las Cruces 88003.

New York
Columbia U. New York 10027.
Iona College New Rochelle 10801.
New York U. New York 10003.
Syracuse U. Syracuse 13244-2100.

North Carolina
East Carolina U. Greenville 27858.
North Carolina, U. of Chapel Hill 27599.

Ohio
Bowling Green State U. Bowling Green 43403.
Kent State U. Kent 44242.
Ohio U. Athens 45701.

Oklahoma
Oklahoma, U. of Norman 73019.
Oklahoma State U. Stillwater 74078.

Oregon.
Oregon, U. of Eugene 97403-1275.

Pennsylvania
Pennsylvania State U. University Park 16802.
Temple U. Philadelphia 19122-6080.

South Carolina
South Carolina, U. of Columbia 29208.
Winthrop U. Rock Hill 29733.

South Dakota
South Dakota, U. of Vermillion 57069.
South Dakota State U. Brookings 57007.

Tennessee
East Tennessee State U. Johnson City 37614.
Middle Tennessee State U. Murfreesboro 37132.
Tennessee, U. of Chattanooga 37403.
University of Tennessee Knoxville 37996
University of Memphis. Memphis 38152.

Texas
Abilene Christian U. Abilene 79699.
Baylor U. Waco 76798.
North Texas U. of Denton 76203.
Texas State U. San Marcos 78666.
Texas Christian U. fort Worth 76129.
Texas Tech U. Lubbock 79409.
Texas, U. of Austin 78712.

Utah
Utah, U. of Salt Lake City 84112.

Virginia
Norfolk State U. Norfolk 23504.
Virginia Commonwealth U. Richmond 23284.
Washington and Lee U. Lexington 24450.

Washington
Washington, U. of Seattle 98195-3740.

West Virginia
Marshall U. Huntington 25755.
West Virginia U. Morgantown 26506.

Wisconsin
Marquette U. Milwaukee 53201.
Wisconsin-Eau Claire, U. of Eau Claire 54702.
Wisconsin-Oshkosh, U. of Oshkosh 54901.
Wisconsin-River Falls, U. of River Falls 54022.

Major Broadcasting and Cable Awards

AAAS Science Journalism Awards, 1200 New York Ave. N.W., Washington, DC, 20005. Phone: (202) 326-6440. Phone: (202) 326-6421. Fax: (202) 789-0455.E-mail: media@aaas.org Web Site:www.aaas.org/aboutaaas/awards/sja/index.shtml

Awards of distinction for professional journalists in the science writing field.. Eligibility Period: July 1, 2008-June 30, 2009. Deadline for entries: Aug 1, 2009. Contact: Ginger Pinholster, AAAS Science Journalism Awards, 1200 New York Ave. N.W. Washington, DC 20005.

Academy of Television Arts and Sciences Emmy Awards, Academy of Television Arts & Sciences, 5220 Lankershim Blvd., North Hollywood, CA, 91601. Phone: (818) 754-2800. Phone: (818) 754-2874. Fax: (818) 754-2836.E-mail: shore@emmys.org Web Site:www.emmys.org

Award for excellence in TV progmg.. Eligibility Period: June 1, 2009-May 31, 2010. Deadline for entries: Late May

Alliance for Community Media Hometown Video Festival Awards, 666 11th St. N.W., Suite 740, Washington, DC, 20001-4542. Phone: (202) 393-2650. Fax: (202) 393-2653.E-mail: dvinsel@tctv.net Web Site:www.alliancecm.org

Award for excellence & innovation among original public access TV.. Eligibility Period: January 1-December 31 (annual event). Deadline for entries: March 21. Contact: Deb Vinsel, Exec Dir, 666 11th St. N.W., Suite 740, Washington, DC 20001-4542.

The American Legion Fourth Estate Award, Attn: Public Relations, The American Legion National Hqtrs., 700 N Pennslyvania St., Indianapolis, IN, 46204. Phone: (317) 630-1253. Fax: (317) 630-1368.E-mail: pr@legion.org Web Site:www.legion.org

The Fourth Estate Award is presented annually by The American Legion National Public Relations Commission to an individual, publication or bcst organization for outstanding achievement in the field of journalism. A 2,000 dollar stipend accompanies the award to defray expenses of recipent accepting award in August.

The Fourth Estate Award is presented annually to an individual, publication or bcst organization for outstanding achievement in the field of journalism. A 2,000 dollar stipend accompanies the award to defray expenses of recipent accepting award.. Eligibility Period: Jan 31-Dec 31 previous year. Deadline for entries: Jan 31. Contact: Public Relations, The American Legion National Headquarters, 700 N. Pennsylvania St., Indianapolis, IN 46204.

American Women in Radio and Television Inc. Awards, 8405 Greensboro Dr., Suite 800, McLean, VA, 22102. Phone: (703) 506-3290. Fax: (703) 506-3266.E-mail: info@awrt.org Web Site:www.awrt.org

Honors progmg & individuals of the highest caliber in all facets of radio, TV, cable & web-based media.. Deadline for entries: See Website. Contact: Amy Lotz, Mgr, AWRT, 1595 Spring Hill Road, Ste 330, Vienna, VA 22182.

Armstrong Awards, Armstrong Foundation, Columbia Univ., 500 W. 120th St., Rm. 1312 S.W. Mudd Bldg., New York, NY, 10027. Phone: (212) 854-3121. Fax: (212) 854-7837.E-mail: kkg1@columbia.edu Web Site:www.armstrongfoundation.org . Eligibility Period: January1-December 31(annual). Deadline for entries: September 1. Contact: Ken Goldstein, pres, Armstrong Foundation, Columbia University, S.W. Mudd Hall, 500 W. 120th St., Room 1311, New York, NY 10027.

The Association for Women in Communications, 3337 Duke St., Alexandria, VA, 22314. Phone: (703) 370-7436. Fax: (703) 370-7437.E-mail: clarion@womcom.org Web Site:www.womcom.org

The Clarion symbolize excellence in clear, concise communications, honor greatness in more than 100 categories across all communications disciplines.

The Clarion symbolize excellence in clear, concise communications, honor greatness in more than 100 categories across all communications disciplines.. Eligibility Period: Jan 1, 2008-Dec 31, 2008. Deadline for entries: March 31, 2009.

Association of Cable Communicators, Beacon Awards, 25 Massachusetts Ave. N.W., Suite 100, Washington, DC, 20001. Phone: (202) 222-2370. Fax: (202) 222-2371.E-mail: services@cablecommunicators.org Web Site:www.cablecommunicators.org

Recognize individuals who have made outstanding contributions to cable communcations & pub affrs.. Eligibility Period: Mid-November (15, 16). Contact: Attn:Michelle L. Butler, Director, Membership Programs & Development. Beacon Awards 25 Massachusetts Ave. N.W., Suite 100, Washington DC 20001.

BDA International Design Award, 9000 W. Sunset Blvd., Suite 900, Los Angeles, CA, 90069. Phone: (310) 788-7600. Fax: (310) 788-7616. Web Site:www.bda.tv E-mail: adrienne@promax.tv

Presented for outstanding achievement in electronic & bcst media.. Eligibility Period: Varies. Deadline for entries: February 28. Contact: Adrienne Alwag, BDA Design-awards cordinator, 2029 Century Park E., Suite 555, Los Angeles, CA 90067.

Batten Fellows Program, Box 6550, The Darden School, University of Virginia, Charlottesville, VA, 22906. Phone: (434) 924-7739. Fax: (434) 243-8708.E-mail: ahs4c@virginia.edu Web Site:www.darden.virginia.edu

Awarded to pursuants in areas of enterpreneurship & corporate innovation.. Deadline for entries: Early May. Contact: Director of Financial Aid, The Darden School, University of Virginia, Box 6550, Charlottesville, VA 22906.

The John Bayliss Broadcast Foundation Internships, Scholarships Programs, Box 51126, Pacific Grove, CA, 93950. Phone: (831) 655-5229. Fax: (831) 655-5228.E-mail: khfranke@baylissfoundation.org Web Site:www.baylissfoundation.org

Scholarships & internship opportunities for college students preparing for a career in radio bcstg.. Deadline for entries: April 30

Broadcast Education Association, 1771 N St. N.W., Washington, DC, 20036-2891. Phone: 202-429-3935. Fax: (202) 775-2981.E-mail: beainfo@beaweb.org Web Site:www.beaweb.org

Awarded for superior academic performance to university student majoring in media studies.. Eligibility Period: School Year. Deadline for entries: September 15. Contact: BEA Scholarships, 1771 N. St. N.W., Washington, DC 20036.

Heywood Broun Award, The Newspaper Guild-CWA, 501 Third St. N.W., 6th Fl., Washington, DC, 20001. Phone: (202) 434-7177. Fax: (202) 434-1472. Web Site:www.newsguild.org E-mail: guild@cwa-union.org

Recognizes individual journalistic achievement by members of the working media in the advancement of social issues.. Deadline for entries: January 25. Contact: Andy Zipser, Editor of the Guild Reporter, The Newspaper Guild.

The CLIO Awards Ltd., 770 Broadway, 6th Fl., New York, NY, 10001. Phone: (212) 683-4300. Fax: (212) 683-4796. Web Site:www.clioawards.com

Excellence awards for Advertising, Design & Interactive Media.. Eligibility Period: January-December. Deadline for entries: January 15. Contact: Ami Brophy, exec dir, 220 5th Ave., Suite 1500, New York, NY 10001.

John Chancellor Award, Columbia Univ Graduate School of Journalism, 2950 Broadway, MC 3805, New York, NY, 10027. Phone: (212) 854-5047. Fax: (212) 854-3148.E-mail: chancelloraward@jrn.columbia.edu Web Site:www.jrn.colummbia.edu

The $25,000 annual prize honors the legacy of John Chancellor. This award is intended to honor the sustained achievement of a single journalist, who may not be well-known nationally, but whose cumulative accomplishments are exemplary. Deadline for entries: April 1, 2009

Christopher Video Contest for College Students, The Christophers, 5 Hanover Sq., New York, NY, 10005. Phone: (212) 759-4050. Fax: (212) 838-5073.E-mail: youth@christophers.org Web Site:www.christophers.org/contests.html

Awarded to 10 college students upon presentation of a short video depicting ways " One Can Make a Difference".

Corporation for Public Broadcasting, 401 9th St. N.W., Washington, DC, 20004. Phone: (202) 879-9600. Fax: (202) 879-9700.E-mail: press@cpb.org Web Site:www.cpb.org

Various grants throughout the year. Contact: Louise Filkins, corporate & pub affrs.

DGA Awards, Directors Guild of America Inc., 7920 Sunset Blvd., Los Angeles, CA, 90046. Phone: (310) 289-5333. Fax: (310) 289-5384.E-mail: laraine@dga.org Web Site:www.dga.org

Adward for outstanding directorial achievement.. Eligibility Period: Calendar year. Deadline for entries: Mail-in December-deadline mid January. Contact: Laraine Savelle, Admin/Awards Coord. Directors Guild of America Inc., 7920 Sunset Blvd., Los Angeles, CA 90046.

Alfred I. duPont-Columbia University Awards, duPont Center for Broadcast Journalism. Columbia Univ Graduate School of Journalism, 2950 Broadway, Rm. 709B, New York, NY, 10027. Phone: (212) 854-5047. Fax: (212) 854-3148.E-mail: dupontawards@jrn.columbia.edu Web Site:www.dupont.org

These awards are now regarded as the most prestigious prizes in TV & radio news, the bcst equivalent of the Pulitzer Prizes.. Eligibility Period: July 1, 2007- June 30, 2008. Deadline for entries: June 15 & July 1st. Contact: Jonnet Abeles. duPont Center, Columbia University Graduate School of Journalism, 2950 Broadway MC 3805, New York, NY 10027.

EDGE Awards - Entertainment Industries Council Inc., 1760 Reston Pkwy., Suite 415, Reston, VA, 20190-3303. Phone: (703) 481-1414. Fax: (703) 481-1418. Fax: (818) 333-5005 (West Coast).E-mail: eiceast@eiconline.org Web Site:www.prismawards.com

Recognizes feature films, TV movies, reality programs that effectively promote firearm safety & discourage gun violence.. Eligibility Period: Calendar year. Deadline for entries: January 15. Contact: Attn: Kimberly Rimshaw, program mgr, EIC.

Freedoms Foundation National Awards, Freedoms Foundation at Valley Forge, 1601 Valley Forge Rd., Valley Forge, PA, 19482-0706. Phone: (610) 933-8825. Fax: (610) 935-0522.E-mail: csantangelo@ffvf.org Web Site:www.ffvf.org

Awarded to individuals or organizations which have made an impact on a loc, rgnl or natl level to teach, foster the principles & olbigations of freedom.. Deadline for entries: June 1. Contact: Freedoms Foundation at Valley Forge, Awards Department, Rt. 23, 1601 Valley Forge Rd., Valley Forge, PA 19482-0706.

Gabriel Awards, Catholic Academy for Communications Arts Professionals, 1645 Brook Lynn Dr., Suite 2, Dayton, OH, 45432-1944. Phone: (937) 458-0265. Fax: (937) 458-0263.E-mail: admin@catholicacademy.org Web Site:www.catholicacademy.org

Honoring execellence in film, network & cable TV programs that uplift & enrich the human spirit.. Eligibility Period: January 1-Decembe 31. Deadline for entries: March 14

Global Media Awards, (For Excellence in Population Reporting). The Population Institute, 107 2nd St. N.E., Washington, DC, 20002. Phone: (202) 544-3300. Fax: (202) 544-0068.E-mail: web@populationinstitute.org Web Site:www.populationinstitute.org

Honors those who have contributed to creating awareness of population programs through their outstanding journalistic endeavors. Presented in developing countries.. Eligibility Period: September-August. Deadline for entries: September 1. Contact: Global Media Awards Coord. The Population Institute, 107 2nd St. N.E., Washington, DC 20002.

Golden Mike Award, Broadcasters Foundation of America, 7 Lincoln Ave., Greenwich, CT, 06830. Phone: (203) 862-8577. Fax: (203) 629-5739.E-mail: ghastings@broadcastersfoundation.org Web Site:www.broadcastersfoundation.org

Broadcast industry excellent svc. Contact: Gordon Hastings, pres/CEO, Broadcast Foundation, 296 Old Church Rd., Greenwich, CT 06830.

Golden Viddy Award, Box 289, National Academy of TV Journalists Inc., Salisbury, MD, 21803. Phone: (410) 548-5343. Fax: (410) 543-0658.E-mail: nbayne@shore.intercom.net Web Site:goldenviddyawards.com

Honors members of the working media especially those making contributions to their communities.. Eligibility Period: Year before. Deadline for entries: Third week of April. Contact: Neil Bayne, The National Academy of Television Journalists Inc., Box 31, Salisbury, MD 21803.

Hugo Awards, Chicago International TV Competition, 77 E. Randolph St., 2nd Fl., Chicago, IL, 60601. Phone: (312) 683-0121. Fax: (312) 683-0122.E-mail: info@chicagofilmfestival.com Web Site:www.chicagofilmfestival.com

Gold HUGO to best overall production. Silver HUGO, Gold Plaque, Silver Plaque, certificate of Merit to best production with a specific category. Contact: Entry Coordinator, Chicago International Television Competition, 32 W. Randolph St., Suite 600, Chicago, IL 60610.

IRE Annual Awards for Investigative Reporting, 138 Neff Annex, Missouri School of Journalism, Columbia, MO, 65211. Phone: (573) 882-6668. Fax: (573) 884-8151.E-mail: beth@ire.org Web Site:www.ire.org/contest

The annual IRE Awards recognize outstanding investigative work across all media.. Eligibility Period: January 1-December 31, 2009. Deadline for entries: Early January 2010.

IRE Tom Renner Award for Crime Reporting, 138 Neff Annex, UMC-Journalism, Columbia, MO, 65211. Phone: (573) 882-2042. Fax: (573) 882-5431.E-mail: info@ire.org Web Site:www.ire.org

For outstanding crime reporting.. Deadline for entries: October 31. Contact: Len Bruzzese, Dept Dir, IRE, 138 Neff Annex, UMC-Journalism, Columbia, MO 65211.

International Broadcasting Awards, Hollywood Radio & TV Society, 13701 Riverside Dr., Suite 205, Sherman Oaks, CA, 91423. Phone: (818) 789-1182. Fax: (818) 789-1210.E-mail: info@hrts.org Web Site:www.hrts.org

Recognition for best radio & TV comls. Contact: Dave Ferrara, exec dir, Hollywood Radio & TV Society, 13701 Riverside Drive, Suite 205, Sherman Oaks, CA 91423.

International Emmy Awards, The International Academy of Television Arts & Sciences, 888 7th Ave., Suite 506, New York, NY, 10019. Phone: (212) 489-6969. Fax: (212) 489-6557.E-mail: info@iemmys.tv Web Site:www.iemmys.tv

Awarded for excellence in TV programs produced & intially aired outside of the U.S.. Deadline for entries: January 30

International Radio & Television Society Foundation Gold Medal, 420 Lexington Ave., Suite 1601, New York, NY, 10170. Phone: (212) 867-6650 ext. 301. Fax: (212) 867-6653. Web Site:www.irts.org

Presented annually for significant career long contributions to the integrity, health & success of the electronic media industry.. Eligibility Period: Nominations accepted until Sept of previous year. Contact: Marilyn L. Ellis, director/program admin., International Radio & TV Society Foundation, 420 Lexington Ave., New York, NY 10170.

Robert F. Kennedy Journalism Awards, 1367 Connecticut Ave. N.W., Suite 200, Washington, DC, 20036. Phone: (202) 463-7575. Fax: (202) 463-6606.E-mail: info@rfkmemorial.org Web Site:www.rfkmemorial.org

Awarded for outstanding coverage of Social Justice issues.. Eligibility Period: Calendar year. Deadline for entries: January 31. Contact: Lynn Delaney, executive dir, delaney@rfkmemorial.org. Robert F. Kennedy Journalism Awards, 1367 Connecticut Ave. N.W., Suite 200, Washington, DC 20036.

Knight-Wallace Journalism Fellows, Wallace House, 620 Oxford Rd., Ann Arbor, MI, 48104. Phone: (734) 998-7666. Fax: (734) 998-7979.E-mail: wpalms@umich.edu Web Site:www.kwfellows.org

Awarded to full-time journalists with a minimum of 5 years professional experience, $70,000.. Eligibility Period: September-April. Contact: Charles R. Eisendrath, Michigan Journalism Fellows, Wallace House, 620 Oxford Rd., Ann Arbor, MI 48104.

The Livingston Awards for Young Journalists, Wallace House, 620 Oxford Rd., Ann Arbor, MI, 48104. Phone: (734) 998-7575. Fax: (734) 998-7979. Web Site:www.livawards.org E-mail: LivingstonAwards@umich.edu

For the best examples of print, online or bcst journalism, three $10,000 awards.. Eligibility Period: January 1-December 31. Deadline for entries: February 1. Contact: Director: The Livingston Awards, Wallace House, 620 Oxford Rd., Ann Arbor, MI 48104.

Mark of Excellence, 3909 N. Meridian St., Society of Professional Journalists, Indianapolis, IN, 46208-4011. Phone: (317) 927-8000. Fax: (317) 920-4789.E-mail: awards@spj.org Web Site:www.spj.org

Awards honors the best in student journalism. Print, radio, TV & online collegiate journalism.. Eligibility Period: Calendar year. Deadline for entries: January 23. Contact: Heather Porter, program coord, Eugene S. Pulliam National Journal Center. 3909 N. Meridian St., Indianapolis, IN 46208.

Media Financial Management Association (MFM), (formerly Broadcast Cable Financial Management Assn. " Avatar" Adward. 550 W Frontage Rd., Suite 3600, Northfield, IL, 60093-1243. Phone: (847) 716-7000. Fax: (847) 716-7004.E-mail: info@mediafinance.org Web Site:www.mediafinance.org . Eligibility Period: Annually. Deadline for entries: January 30

Paul Miller Washington Reporting Fellowships, National Press Foundation, 1211 Connecticut Ave. N.W., Suite 310, Washington, DC, 20036. Phone: (202) 663-7280. Fax: (202) 530-2855.E-mail: nolan@nationalpress.org Web Site:www.nationalpress.org

Fellowship dedicated to itensive study sessions on subjects such as the Federal Budget, other Federal & Congressional matters.. Deadline for entries: June 2. Contact: Nolan Walters, 1211 Connecticut Ave NW, Suite 310, Washington, DC 20036.

Missouri Honor Medal, Missouri School of Journalism, 120 Neff Hall, Columbia, MO, 65211. Phone: (573) 882-1908. Fax: (573) 884-5400.E-mail: dukesb@missouri.edu Web Site:journalism.missouri.edu

Awarded for distinguished svc in Journalism.. Deadline for entries: October 31. Contact: Dean, School of Journalism, 103 Neff Hall, University of Missouri-Columbia, Columbia, MO 65211.

The Mobius Advertising Awards, 713 S. Pacific Coast Hwy., Suite A, Redondo Beach, CA, 90277-4233. Phone: (310) 540-0959. Fax: (310) 316-8905.E-mail: mobiusinfo@mobiusawards.com Web Site:www.mobiusawards.com

Honoring creative excellence in mixed media.. Deadline for entries: October 1

NAB Crystal Radio Awards, NAB Radio, 1771 N St. N.W., Washington, DC, 20036-2891. Phone: (202) 775-3511. Fax: (202) 775-3523.E-mail: csuever@nab.org Web Site:www.nab.org

Recognizes radio stns for outstanding year-round commitment to community svc.. Deadline for entries: February 1. Contact: Chris Suever, NAB Radio, 1771 N St. N.W., Washington, DC 20036-2891.

NAB Marconi Radio Awards, NAB Radio, 1771 N St. N.W., Washington, DC, 20036. Phone: (202) 775-3511. Fax: (202) 775-3523.E-mail: csuever@nab.org Web Site:www.nab.org

Recognizes overall excellence in radio.. Deadline for entries: May 2. Contact: NAB Radio, 1771 N St. N.W., Washington, DC 20036.

NAB National Radio Award, 1771 N St. N.W., Washington, DC, 20036-2891. Phone: (202) 775-3511. Fax: (202) 775-3523.E-mail: csuever@nab.org Web Site:www.nab.org

Presented annually to an individual who is an outstanding leader in the radio industry.. Eligibility Period: Calendar year. Contact: Chris Suever, NAB Radio, 1771 N St. N.W., Washington, DC 20036-2891.

NPPA Annual TV News Photography & Editing Competition, 3200 Croasdaile Dr., Durham, NC, 27705. Phone: (919) 383-7246. Fax: (919) 383-7261.E-mail: info@nppa.org Web Site:www.nppa.org

Contest showcases the best news photography, editing in print, TV & on the website.. Eligibility Period: Jan 1-Dec 31 (annually). Deadline for entries: Jan 31, postmarked by midnight. Contact: Rich Murphy, contest chmn, WFLA, 200 South Parker St, Tampa, FL 33606; rmurphy@wfla.com.

National Academy of Television Arts and Sciences "Emmy" Awards, 111 W. 57th St., Suite 600, New York, NY, 10019. Phone: (212) 586-8424. Fax: (212) 246-8129. Web Site:www.emmyonline.org

Recognizes outstanding achievements in all phases of TV, including progmg, directing, writing, performing, etc. The National Academy of TV Arts & Sciences also presents the Sports Emmy , The Technology, Engineering, New & Documentary, Day Entertainment, Humanitarian & Public Service Awards.

Recognizes outstanding achievements in all phases of TV, including progmg, directing, writing, performing, etc. The National Academy of TV Arts & Sciences also presents the Sports Emmy, The Technology, Engineering, New & Documentary, Day Entertainment, Humanitarian & Public Service Awards. Contact: Carolyn Grippi, CFO, 111 W. 57th St., Suite 600, New York, NY 10019.

National Association of Broadcasters (NAB) Engineering Achievement Awards, 532249. 1771 N St. N.W., Washington, DC, 20036-2891. Phone: (202) 429-5300. Fax: (202) 429-5461.E-mail: nab@nab.org Web Site:www.nab.org

Awarded for individual outstanding achievement in significant contributions in advancement of the State of the Art of Broadcast Engineering.. Deadline for entries: January 15.

National Association of Broadcasters (NAB), International Bcstg Excellence Award, 1771 N St., N.W., Washington, DC, 20036-2891. Phone: (202) 429-5360. Fax: (202) 429-5461.E-mail: edorey@nab.org Web Site:www.nab.org/lag/international/award.asp

Recognized international bcst organizations that have demonstrated exceptional leadership in advancing the bcst industry & svcs. Contact: Emily Dorey at the address listed above.

National Association of Broadcasters (NAB) Distinguished Service Award, 1771 N St. N.W., Washington, DC, 20036. Phone: (202) 429-5368. Fax: (202) 429-4199.E-mail: nab@nab.org Web Site:www.nab.org

Awarded to a bcstr whether or not actively engaged in the opns end of the bcstg industry, who has made a significant & lasting contribution.. Eligibility Period: Calendar year. Contact: NAB Distinguished Service Award, 1771 N St. N.W., Washington, DC 20036.

National Awards for Education Reporting, Education Writers Association, 2122 P St. N. W. # 201, Washington, DC, 20037. Phone: (202) 452-9830. Fax: (202) 452-9837.E-mail: ewa@ewa.org Web Site:www.ewa.org

This prestigious contest awards prizes in 18 different categories & is the only independently judged educ writing competition of its kind in the United States.. Eligibility Period: Published during current calendar year. Deadline for entries: Mid-January. Contact: Education Writers Assn, 1331 H St. N.W., Suite 307, Washington, DC 20005.

National Headliner Awards, Box 239, 226 Mt. Vernon Ave., Northfield, NJ, 08225. Phone: (609) 646-8896. Fax: (609) 646-8826. Web Site:www.nationalheadlinerawards.com E-mail: infoheadliners@aol.com

Recognizes excellence in journalism.. Eligibility Period: January 1-December 31. Deadline for entries: January 11. Contact: Michael Schurman, exec dir, National Headliners Club, Box 239, Northfield, NJ 08225.

The New York Festivals Advertising Awards, 260 W. 39th St., 10 th Fl., New York, NY, 10018. Phone: (212) 643-4800. Fax: (212) 643-0170. Web Site:www.newyorkfestivals.com E-mail: info@newyorkfestivals.com

The New York Festivals Advertising Awards celebrates the best & most creative adv in the world.

The New York Festivals Advertising Awards celebrates the best & most creative adv in the world.. Eligibility Period: June-June. Deadline for entries: June 30-USA / September 15-overseas. Contact: Michael Demetriades, festivals dir, The New York Festivals, 186 Fifth Ave., New York, NY 10010.

The New York Festivals Radio Broadcasting Awards, 260 W. 39th St., 10 th Fl., New York, NY, 10018. Phone: (212) 643-4800. Fax: (212) 643-0170.E-mail: info@newyorkfestivals.com Web Site:www.newyorkfestivals.com

Recognizes "The World's Best Work" (TM) in radio bcstg. Entries are judged by a panel of radio experts from stns & companies throughtout the world.

Recognizes "The World's Best Work" (TM) in radio bcstg. Entries are judged by a panel of radio experts from stns & companies throughtout the world.. Eligibility Period: Mar-Mar. Deadline for entries: Feb-Mar. Contact: Leslie Rasimas, festivals dir, The New York Festivals, 186 5th Ave, New York, NY 10010.

The Ollie Awards, American Center for Children and Media, 5400 N. Saint Louis Ave., Chicago, IL, 60625. Phone: (773) 509-5510. Fax: (773) 509-5303.E-mail: dkleeman@atgonline.org Web Site:www.centerforchildrenandmedia.org

Award for excellence in children's TV. Eligibility Period: To be announced. Deadline for entries: To be announced. Contact: David Kleeman, exec dir, American Center for Children and Media, 5400 N. Saint Louis Ave., Chicago, IL 60625.

Overseas Press Club of America Awards, 40 W. 45th St., New York, NY, 10036. Phone: (212) 626-9220. Fax: (212) 626-9210.E-mail: sonya@opcofamerica.org Web Site:www.opcofamerica.org

Overseas Press Club of Americia has 21 awards for nwsprs, magazines, photography, cartoons, radio, TV, human rights & environment.

Overseas Press Club of Americia has 20 awards for nwsprs, magazines, photography, cartoons, radio, TV, human rights & environment.. Eligibility Period: Calendar year 2009. Deadline for entries: Last week of January 2010. Contact: Sonya K. Fry, exec dir, Overseas Press Club Awards, 320 E. 42nd St., New York, NY 10017.

PRISM Awards, Entertainment Industries Council Inc., PRISM Awards, Entertainment Industries Council Inc., 1760 Reston Pkwy., Suite 415, Reston, VA, 20190-3303. Phone: (703) 481-1414. Fax: (703) 481-1418. Fax: (818) 333-5005 (West Coast).E-mail: eiceast@eiconline.org Web Site:www.prismawards.com

Recognize actors for outstanding performances in portrayal of substance abuse, addiction & mental illness onscreen, in TV & feature films.. Deadline for entries: January 7. Contact: Attn: Kimberly Rimshaw, program manager.

PROMAX & BDA Awards, 9000 W. Sunset Blvd., Los Angeles, CA, 90069-2906. Phone: (310) 788-7600. Fax: (310) 788-7616. Web Site:www.promax.tv E-mail: awards@promax.tv

Recognizes the best in promotion & mktg. Contact: PROMAX & BDA, 2029 Century Park E., Suite 555, Los Angeles, CA 90067-2906.

George Foster Peabody Award, H.W. Grady College of Journalism, University of Georgia, Athens, GA, 30602-3018. Phone: (706) 542-3787. Fax: (706) 542-9273.E-mail: peabody@uga.edu Web Site:www.peabody.uga.edu

Annual international awards for distinction & achievement within the fields of bcst journalism documentary film making & educ progmg .. Eligibility Period: January 1 - December 31. Deadline for entries: Jan 15, 2007.

George Polk Awards, Long Island Univ.,The English Dept, University Plaza, Brooklyn, NY, 11201. Phone: (718) 488-1115. Fax: (718) 243-0766. Fax: (718) 246-6302. Web Site:www.liu.edu/cwis/bklyn/polk/polk.html

A plaque.

A plaque.. Eligibility Period: 2008. Deadline for entries: Jan 12, 2009. Contact: c/o The English Dept. Robert Spector PhD., curator, George Polk Awards, Long Island Univ., The Brooklyn Ctr., University Plaza, Brooklyn, NY 11201.

RTNDA Edward R. Murrow Awards, 1600 K St., Suite 700, Washington, DC, 20006-2838. Phone: (202) 659-6510. Phone: 800-80-RTNDA. Fax: (202) 223-4007.E-mail: rtnda@rtndf.org Web Site:www.rtnda.org

Awarded for outstanding achievement in electronic journalism.. Eligibility Period: January 1-December 31. Deadline for entries: Jan 31. Contact: RTNDA, 1000 Connecticut Ave. N.W., Suite 615, Washington, DC 20036.

Radio-Mercury Awards, 22 Cortland St., 17th Fl., New York, NY, 10001. Phone: (212) 681-7208. Fax: (212) 681-7223.E-mail: mercury@rab.com Web Site:www.radiomercuryaward.com

Honors individuals, their employers who create, produce memorable, successful radio comls & pub svc announcements.. Deadline for entries: March 1. Contact: Wendy Frech, Radio-Mercury Awards, 261 Madison Ave., 23rd Fl., New York, NY 10016 or E-mail: mercury@rab.com.

Bart Richards Award for Media Criticism, 302 James Bldg., Pennsylvania State Univ., University Park, PA, 16801-3867. Phone: (814) 865-8801. Fax: (814) 863-6134.E-mail: sws102@psu.edu Web Site:www.comm.psu.edu/bart

Recognizes distinguished contributions to the improvement of print & bcst journalism through responsible journalism.. Eligibility Period: January 1-December 31. Deadline for entries: Jan 31. Contact: The Bart Richards Award for Media Criticism, The Pennsylvania State Univ., College of Communications, 302 James Bldg., University Park, PA 16801-3867.

Scripps Howard Foundation - Jack R. Howard Awards, Scripps Howard Foundation, 312 Walnut St., Cincinnati, OH, 45202-4067. Phone: (513) 977-3030. Fax: (513) 977-3800.E-mail: sue.porter@scripps.com Web Site:www.scripps.com/foundation

Scripps Howard Foundation National Journalism Awards honor best investigative or in-depth reporting of broadcast events covered by television and radio stations or cable systems in 2008. Two categories named for Jack R. Howard: TV/cable and radio. Prizes in each: $10,000.. Eligibility Period: Calendar year. Deadline for entries: January 31. Contact: sue.porter@scripps.com or 1-800-888-3000 ext. 3030. Entry form online: www.scripps.com/foundation. Postmark deadline: Jan. 31, 2009.

Sigma Delta Chi Distinguished Service Awards Society of Professional Journalists, 3909 N. Meridian St., Indianapolis, IN, 46208. Phone: (317) 927-8000. Fax: (317) 920-4789.E-mail: awards@spj.org Web Site:www.spj.org

Recognizes the best in professional journalism covering prints, radio, TV newsletters, photography online & rsch.. Eligibility Period: January 1-December 31. Deadline for entries: February 5. Contact: SDX Awards coord, SPJ, 3909 N. Meridian St., Indianapolis, In 46208.

Silver Anvil Awards, Public Relations Society of America Inc., 33 Maiden Ln., 11th Fl., New York, NY, 10003-5150. Phone: (212) 460-1456. Fax: (212) 995-0757.E-mail: awards@prsa.org Web Site:www.prsa.org

Recognizes excellence in PR, annually awarded to organization which have successfully addressed a contemporary issue.. Eligibility Period: Calendar year. Deadline for entries: February 28. Contact: Karla Voth, VP special events & programs. Public Relations Society of America Inc., 33 Irving Pl., 3rd Fl., New York, NY 10003.

Silver Gavel Awards, American Bar Association, Div for Pub Education, 541 N. Fairbanks Ct., Chicago, IL, 60611. Phone: (312) 988-5738. Fax: (312) 988-5494.E-mail: howardkaplan@staff.abanet.org Web Site:www.abanet.org/publiced/gavel

Recognizes outstanding contributions to the pub info & understanding the roles of law & courts in our society.. Eligibility Period: January 1-December 31. Deadline for entries: January 8. Contact: The Gavel Awards Program, American Bar Association, Division for Public Education, 541 N. Fairbanks Ct, Chicago, IL 60611.

Society of Motion Picture & Television Engineers Awards, 3 Barker Ave., 5th Fl., White Plains, NY, 10601. Phone: (914) 761-1100. Fax: (914) 761-3115. Web Site:www.smpte.org Citation for Outstanding Svc to the Society recognizes individuals for dedicated svc to the society. The Presidential Proclamation recognizes individuals of established & outstanding status & reputation in the motion picture & TV industries worldwide. Eastman Kodak Medal Award recognizes outstanding contributions that lead to new or unique educ programs using motion pictures, TV, high-speed & instrumental photography or other photographic sciences. The award recognizes dev in equipment, systems or instructional applications that advance the educ process at any or all levels. The John Grierson International Gold Medal Award recognizes significant tech achievements related to the production of documentary motion picture films. The Journal Award recognizes the outstanding paper originally published in the Journal of the Society during the previous calendar year. The Technicolor/Herbert T. Kalmus Gold medal Award recognizes outstanding contributions in the dev of color films, processing, techniques or equipment useful in making color motion pictures for theater or TV use. The Fuji Gold Medal Award recognizes outstanding engrg achievements in the design & dev of new or enhanced techniques &/or equipment that have contributed significantly to the advancement of photographic or electronic image origination . Deadline for entries: January 15. Contact: Fred Motts, exec dir, Society of Motion Pictures & TV Engineers, 595 W. Hartsdale Ave., White Plains, NY, 10607.

Sunscan Award, Entertainment Industries Council Inc., 1760 Reston Pkwy, Suite 415, Reston, VA, 20190-3303. Phone: (703) 481-1414. Fax: (703) 481-1418. Fax: (818) 333-5005 (West Coast).E-mail: eiceast@eiconline.org Web Site:www.eiconline.org

Recognition for entertainment production that address sun safety.. Eligibility Period: January- December. Contact: Attn: Kimberly Rimshaw, program mgr.

Voice of Democracy Scholarship Program, VFW National Hqtrs., 406 W. 34th St., Kansas City, MO, 64111. Phone: (816) 968-1117. Fax: (816) 968-1149.E-mail: kharmer@vfw.org Web Site:www.vfw.org

Awarded to winner of audio essay competition based on their opinion of Civic Responsiblity, $30,000 scholarship. Open to high school students, ages 15-18.. Deadline for entries: Varies. Contact: Your high school counselor, local VFW Post, or Voice of Democracy Scholarship Program, VFW National Hqtrs, 406 W. 34th St., Kansas City, MO 64111.

Ida B. Wells Award, Northwestern Univ., Medill School of Journalism, 1845 Sheridan Rd., Evanston, IL, 60208. Phone: (847) 467-2579. Fax: (847) 491-2370.E-mail: m-awards@northwestern.edu

LawrenceKS . Sam Adams (Curator), Ida B.Wells Award, 1552 Alvamar Dr.

Presented annually to a media exec or mgr who has provided leadership in increasing access & opportunities to people of color in journalism. Sponsored jointly by the (NABJ) National Association of Black Journalists & the (NCEW) National Conference of Editorial Writers.. Deadline for entries: May 15. Contact: Charles Whitaker (send a future correspondence to him).

Western Heritage Awards-The Wrangler, National Cowboy & Western Heritage Museum, 1700 N.E. 63rd St., Oklahoma City, OK, 73111. Phone: (405) 478-2250. Fax: (405) 478-4714.E-mail: lyndahaller@nationalcowboymuseum.org Web Site:www.nationalcowboymuseum.org

Honors works in Literature, Music Film & TV reflecting significant stories of the American West.. Eligibility Period: January 1- December 31. Deadline for entries: February 15. Contact: Lynda Haller, dir PR, National Cowboy Hall of Fame, 1700 N.E. 63rd St., Oklahoma City, OK 73111.

Section I
Government

Federal Communications Commission Executives and Staff

Headquarters: 445 12th St. S.W., Washington, DC 20554. (888) 225-5322.

CHAIRMAN

Julius Genachowski, (202) 418-1000 8 B201; Chief of Staff, Edward P. Lazarus; Senior Counsel, Colin Crowell; Confidential Assistant, Sherry Gelfand; Chief Counsel & Senior Legal Advisor, Bruce Liang Gottlieb; Senior Legal Advisor, Sherrese Smith (Media, Consumer & Enforcement Issues); Special Assistant, Daniel Ornstein; Legal Advisor, Priya Aiyar (Wireless Competition & Intl Issues); Special Counsel for FCC Reform, Mary Beth Richards; Transition effort the Chairman's office, Ruth Milkman.

COMMISSIONERS

COMMISSIONER Robert M. McDowell, (202) 418-2200 8-C302; Chief of Staff, Angela E. Giancarlo (Senior Legal Advisor, Wireless & Intl Issues); Legal Advisor, Nicholas G. Alexander (Wireline); Legal Advisor, Rosemary C. Harold (Media); Deputy Chief of Staff, Brigid N. Calamis; Staff Assistant, Rafael G. Fernandez, (202) 418-2200.

COMMISSIONER Michael J. Copps, (202) 418-2000 8 B115; Confidential Assistant, Carolyn Conyers; Senior Legal Advisor/Media Advisor, Rick C. Chessen; Legal Advisor, Jennifer Schneider (Broadband, Wireline & Universal Service Issues; Staff Assistant, Renee Coles, (202) 418-2000.

COMMISSIONER Meredith Attwell Baker, (202) 418-2400 8-A302. Acting Senior Legal Advisor/Acting Legal Advisor for media & enforcement issues, William D. Freedman; Acting Legal Advisor for wireless, international/public safety issues, Erin A. McGrath; Acting Legal Advisor for wireline, universal service/consumer issues, Christi Shewman; Acting Confidential Assistant, Ann Monahan.

COMMISSIONER Mignon Clyburn, (202) 418-2500 8-A302. Transition Counsel, Michele Ellison; Chief of Staff, Senior Legal Advisor, Spectrum, International & Public Safety, Renee Roland Crittendon; Acting Legal Advisor, Media & Chief of External Affairs, Rick Kaplan; Acting Legal Advisor, Wireline & Broadband, Carol Simpson; Acting Confidential Assistant, Almira Kennedy; Acting Staff Assistant, Crystal Rice.

OFFICE OF ADMINISTRATIVE LAW JUDGES

Richard L. Sippel, Chief Administrative Law Judge; Mary Gosse, Administrative officer; Patricia Ducksworth, Legal Technician.

OFFICE OF COMMUNICATIONS BUSINESS OPPORTUNITIES

Carolyn Fleming Williams, Director, (202) 418-0990; Eric Malinen, Senior Legal Advisor/FCC Liaison to the SBA; Maura McGowan, Telecommunications Policy Analyst; Belford V. Lawson III, Attorney Advisor; Calvin Osborne, Attorney Advisor; Karen M. Beverly, Consumer-Industry Affairs Specialist/Assistant for Management; Christian Fiascunari, Outreach Specialist; John Finnie, Staff Assistant; Sharon K. Stewart, Special Assistant to OCBO Director; Corrin Barksdale, Student Intern; Victor Machalec, Intern.

OFFICE OF ENGINEERING & TECHNOLOGY

Julius P. Knapp, Chief (202) 418-2470; Ira Keltz, Deputy Chief; Ronald Repasi, Deputy Chief; Alan Stillwell, Deputy Chief; Bruce A. Romano, Associate Chief (Legal); Xenia Hajicosti, Assistant Chief for Management.

Policy & Rules Division

Geraldine Matise, Chief (202) 418-2472; Mark Settle/Deputy Chief.

Spectrum Policy Branch

Jamison Prime, Chief (202) 418-2472.

Technical Rules Branch

Karen E. Ansari, Chief.

Spectrum Coordination Branch

Kathryn Hosford, Chief (202) 418-2472.

Electromagnetic Compatibility Division

Walter Johnston, Chief (202) 418-2475.

Technical Analysis Branch

Robert Weller, Chief (202) 418-2475.

Experimental Licensing Branch

James R. Burtle, Chief (202) 418-2475.

Laboratory Division (Columbia, MD)

Rashmi Doshi, Chief (301) 362-3000 LAB; Vacant/Deputy Chief (301) 362-3000 LAB.

Equipment Authorization Branch

Joe Dichoso, Chief (301) 362-3000 LAB.

Technical Research Branch

William Hurst, Chief (301) 362-3000 LAB.

Auditing & Compliance Branch

Raymond LaForge, Chief (301) 362-3000 LAB.

Customer Service Branch

Sandra Haase, Chief (301) 362-3013 LAB.

OFFICE OF GENERAL COUNSEL

Austin Schlick, General Counsel (202) 418-1700; Paula Michele Ellisonl, Ajit Pai, Joseph Palmore, Deputy General Counsels; Jacob Lewis, Associate General Counsel (Counselor to the General Counsel); Mark Lloyd, Associate General Counsel & Chief Diversity Officer; Karen E. Onyeije, Assistant General Counsel; Lauren J. Belvin, Special Counsel; Charmayne C. Keene, Assistant Chief Management.

Transaction Team

Jim Bird/Senior Counsel (202) 418-1720; Neil Dellar, Virginia (Ginny) Metallo, Joel Rabinovitz.

Litigation Division

Daniel M. Armstrong, Associate General Counsel & Chief (202) 418-1740; Richard K. Welch, Deputy Division Chief & Deputy Associate General Counse-Appellate; Susan L. Launer, Deputy Division Chief & Deputy Associate General Counsel-Trial & Enforcement.

Administrative Law Division

Joel Kaufman, Associate General Counsel & Chief (202) 418-1720; Christopher Killion/Deputy,Associate General Counsel; Ann Bushmiller, Deputy Associate General Counsel.

OFFICE OF INSPECTOR GENERAL

David L. Hunt, Acting Inspector General (202) 418-0470 2C762. Jacqueline Wall, Budget Analyst; Jason Kim, Staff Assistant; Kathleen O'Reilly, Special Counsel; Sally Smith, Investigatory Attorney Contracts Counsel; Anthony Bush, Chief Economist; Jay Bennett, Mathematical Statistician; Thomas Cline, Assistant IG-Policy & Planning; William Garay, Assistant IG-Universal Program; Cutis Hagan, Assistant IG-Audits; David L. Hunt, Assistant IG-Investigationc/Counsel; Harold Shrewberry, Assistant IG-Management

OFFICE OF LEGISLATIVE AFFAIRS

Terri Glaze, Director (202) 418-1900 8-C432; Lori Holy Maarbjerg, Senior Attorney Advisor; Jim Balague, Senior Legisative Analyst; Timothy Strachan, Attorney Advisor; Connie Chapman, Lead Congressional Liaison Specialist; Diane Atkinson,

Commissioners

Julius Genachowski, Chairman

Michael J. Copps Robert M. McDowell Mignon Clyburn Meredith Attwell Baker

Office of Inspector General

Office of Engineering & Technology
- Electromagnetic Compatibility Div.
- Laboratory Div.
- Policy & Rules Div.
- Administrative Staff

Office of General Counsel
- Administrative Law Div.
- Litigation Div.

Office of Managing Director
- Human Resources Management
- Information Technology Center
- Financial Operations
- Administrative Operations
- Performance Eval. & Records Mgmt
- Secretary

Office of Media Relations
- Media Services Staff
- Internet Services Staff
- Audio-Visual Services Staff

Office of Legislative Affairs

Office of Administrative Law Judges

Office of Strategic Planning & Policy Analysis

Office of Communications Business Opportunities

Office of Workplace Diversity

Consumer & Governmental Affairs Bureau
- Admin. & Mgmt. Office
- Info. & Resources Mgmt. Office
- Consumer Inquiries & Complaints Div.
- Consumer Policy Div.
- Reference Information Center
- Disability Rights Office
- Consumer Affairs & Outreach Div.
- Office of Intergovernmental Affairs

Wireless Telecommunications Bureau
- Management & Resources Staff
- Auctions & Spectrum Access Div.
- Spectrum Mgmt. Resources & Technologies Div.
- Spectrum & Competition Policy Div.
- Mobility Div.
- Broadband Div.

Media Bureau
- Mgmt. & Resources Staff
- Office of Com. & Industry Info.
- Policy Div.
- Industry Analysis Div.
- Engineering Div.
- Office of Broadcast License Policy
- Audio Div.
- Video Div.

Enforcement Bureau
- Office of Management & Resources
- Telecommunications Consumers Div.
- Spectrum Enforcement Div.
- Market Disputes Resolution Div.
- Investigations & Hearings Div.
- Regional & Field Offices

Wireline Competition Bureau
- Admin. & Mgmt. Office
- Competition Policy Div.
- Pricing Policy Div.
- Telecommunications Access Policy Div.
- Industry Analysis & Technology Div.

Public Safety & Homeland Security Bureau
- Admin. & Mgmt. Office
- Policy Div.
- Public Communications Outreach & Operations Div.
- Communications Systems Analysis Div.

International Bureau
- Management & Administrative Staff
- Policy Div.
- Satellite Div.
- Strategic Analysis & Negotiations Div.

Congressional Liaison Specialist; Joy Medley, Congressional Liaison Specialist; Solita Griffis, Administrative Management Specialist; Aurelle Porter, Special Assistant.

OFFICE OF MANAGING DIRECTOR

Steven VanRoekel, Agency's Managing Director (202) 418-1919 1-C144; Mindy Ginsburg, Joseph Hall, Mark Stone, Deputy Managing Directors. Office of The Secretary

Marlene Dortch, (202) 418-0300 TW-B204; William F. Caton/Deputy Secretary. Sheryl A. Segal, Associate Secretary for Information Resources (Group Manager); Jacqueline Coles, Associate Secretary for the Agenda & Publications (Group Manager).

Library

(202) 418-0450.

Recruitment and Staffing Service Center

(202) 418-0130.

Learning and Development Service Center

(202) 418-1582.

OFFICE OF MEDIA RELATIONS

David H. Fiske, Director (202) 418-0513 CY-C314, (888) 225-5322; Audrey Spivack, Associate Director; Meribeth McCarrick/Associate Director; Dann Oliver, Jeff Riordan, Steve Balderson, Audio/Video. David Kitzmiller, C.E. Harrington, Tia Roberts, Web Site.

Audio Visual Center

Dan Oliver, Manager (202) 418-0460.

OFFICE OF STRATEGIC PLANNING & POLICY ANALYSIS

Paul de Sa, Chief (202) 418-2030; Elizabeth Andrion, Deputy Chief; Zachary Katz, Deputy Chief; Michelle Connolly, Commission's Chief Economist.

OFFICE OF WORKPLACE DIVERSITY

Lawrence S. Schaffner, Acting Director (202) 418-1799; Linda Mille, EEO Program Manager; Lawrence S. Schaffner, Senior Legal Advisor; Kenneth Heredia, Office Automation Clerk; Rosalind Bailey, Staff Assistant.

CONSUMER & GOVERNMENTAL AFFAIRS BUREAU

Cathy Seidel, Bureau Chief (202) 418-1400.

Office of Intergovernmental Affairs

Gregory Vadas, Chief (202) 418-7619.

Consumer Inquiries and Complaints Division

Jeffrey Tignor, Acting Chief (202) 418-2516.

Information Access and Privacy Office

Sumita Mukhoty/Director (202) 418-1109.

Consumer Policy Division

Suzanne Tetreault, Acting Deputy Bureau Chief (Policy) (202) 418-5212; Erica McMahon, Chief; Nancy Stevenson, Deputy Chief; Julie Saulnier, Deputy Chief; David Marks, Slamming Contact.

Disability Rights Office

Thomas E. Chandler, Chief (202) 418-1475.

Reference Information Center

Bill Cline, Chief (202) 418-0267.

Consumer Affairs and Outreach Division

Rachel Kazan, Division Chief (202) 418-0614.

Consumer Advisory Committee

Scott Marshall, Designated Federal Officer (202) 418-2809.

ENFORCEMENT BUREAU

Kris Monteith, Bureau Chief (202) 418-7450 7-C723; Michael Carowitz, Chief of Staff & Associate Bureau; Gene Fullano, Deputy Bureau Chief; Dana Shaffer, Deputy Bureau Chief; William Davenport, Associate Bureau Chief; Susan McNeil, Assistant Bureau Chief; Priya Shrinivasan, Assistant Bureau Chief; Sharon Agee, Assistant Bureau Chief; Jon Minkoff, Legal Advisor; George R. Dillon, Associate Bureau Chief; William Davenport, Bureau Chief; Janice Wise, Director of Media Relations; Debbie Smoot, Special Assistant to the Bureau Chief; Arneatta Strange, Staff Assistant.

Enforcement Bureau-Regional and Field Offices

Northeast Region

G. Michael Moffitt, Regional Director; James T. Higgins, Deputy Regional Director; Sharon Webber, Regional Counsel.

District Directors

Dennis Loria, Boston, MA Office; James Roop, Chicago, IL Office; James T. Higgins, Columbia, MD Operations Center; Daniel W. Noel, New York, NY Office; Gene J. Stanbro, Philadelphia, PA Office; James Bridgewater, Detroit, MI Office.

South Central Region

Dennis P. Carlton, Regional Director; Loyd P. Perry, Deputy Regional Director; Diane Law-Hsu, Regional Counsel.

District Directors

Douglas G. Miller, Atlanta, GA Office; James D. Wells, Dallas, TX Office; Robert McKinney, Kansas City, MO Office; Walt Gernon, New Orleans, LA Office (Acting); Ralph Barlow, Tampa, FL Office.

Western Region

Rebecca L. Dorch, Regional Director; Leo Cirbo, Deputy Regional Director; Margaret Egler, Regional Counsel.

District Directors

Nikki Shears, Denver, CO Office; Nadar Haghighat, Los Angeles, CA Office; Bill Zears, San Diego, CA Office; Thomas Van Stavern, San Francisco, CA Office; Kristine McGowan, Seattle, WA Office.

Field Office Addresses

Atlanta: Federal Communications Commission 3575 Koger Blvd., Suite 320, Duluth, GA 30096-4958; Boston: Federal Communications Commission 1 Batterymarch Pk., Quincy, MA 02169-7495; Chicago: Federal Communications Commission Park Ridge Office Center, Rm. 306, 1550 Northwest Hwy., Park Ridge, IL 60068-1460; Columbia: FCC, Enforcement Bureau Columbia 9200 Farm House Ln., Columbia MD 21046; Dallas: Federal Communications Commission 9330 LBJ Fwy., Rm. 1170 Dallas, TX 75243-3429; Denver: Federal Communications Commission 215 S. Wadsworth Blvd., Suite 303, Lakewood CO 80226-1544; Detroit: Federal Communications Commission 215 S. Wadsworth Blvd., Suite 303, Lakewood CO 80226-1544; Kansas City: Federal Communications Commission 520 NE Colbern Rd., 2nd Fl., Lee's Summit, MO 64086; Los Angeles: Federal Communications Commission Cerritos Corporate Tower 18000 Studebaker Rd., Rm. 660, Cerritos, CA 90701-3684; New Orleans: Federal Communications Commission 2424 Edenborn Ave., Suite 460, Metairie, LA 70001; New York: Federal Communications Commission 201 Varick St., Suite 1151, New York, NY 10014-4870; Philadelphia: Federal Communications Commission One Oxford Valley Office Bldg., Rm. 404, 2300 East Lincoln Hwy., Langhorne, PA 19047-1859; San Diego: Federal Communications Commission Interstate Office Park 4542 Ruffner St., Rm. 370, San Diego, CA 92111-2216; San Francisco: Federal Communications Commission 5653 Stoneridge Dr., Suite 105, Pleasanton, CA 94588-8543; Seattle: Federal Communications Commission 11410 NE 122nd Way, Rm. 312, Kirkland, WA 98034-6927; Tampa: Federal Communications Commission 2203 N. Lois Ave., Rm. 1215, Tampa, FL 33607-2356.

INTERNATIONAL BUREAU

John Giusti, Acting Bureau Chief (202) 418-1407; Roderick Porter, Deputy Bureau Chief (202) 418-0437; Linda L. Haller Sloan, Associate Bureau Chief (on Detail) (202) 418-1408; Narda Jones, Assistant Bureau Chief (202) 418-2489; Tom Sullivan, Assistant Bureau Chief for Management (202) 418-0411; Steven Spaeth, Legal Advisor (202) 418-1539; Arthur Lechtman, Legal Advisor (202) 418-1465; Jerry Duvall, Chief Economist (202) 418-2616.

Policy Division

Front Office: James L. Ball, Chief (202) 418-1460; Howard Griboff, Deputy Chief (202) 418-0657; George S. Li, Deputy Division Chief, Operations (202) 418-1460; Francis Gutierrez, Associate Division Chief (202) 418-7370; David Krech, Associate Division Chief (202) 418-7443; David Strickland, Associate Division Chief (202) 418-0977; Paul Locke/Assistant Chief (Engineering) (202) 418-0756; JoAnn Sutton, Assistant Division Chief (202) 418-1372.

Satellite Division

Front Office: Robert Nelson, Chief (202) 418-2341; Cassandra Thomas, Deputy Division Chief (202) 418-0734; Fern Jarmulnek, Deputy Division Chief (202) 418-0751; Karl Kensinger, Associate Division Chief (202) 418-0773; Steven Spaeth, Associate Division Chief (202) 418-1539; Andrea Kelly, Associate Division Chief (202) 418-7877.

Policy Branch

Stephen Duall, Chief (202) 418-1103.

Systems Analysis Branch

Scott Kotler, Branch Chief (202) 418-0596.

Engineering Branch

Kathyrn Medley, Branch Chief (202) 418-1211.

Strategic Analysis & Negotiations Division

Kathryn O'Brien, Division Chief (202) 418-0439; Linda Dubroof, Associate Division Chief (202) 418-2335; Jennifer Gilsenan, Deputy Division Chief (202) 418-0757; Alexander Royblat, Assistant Chief (202) 418-7501; Larry Olson, Assistant Chief Engineering (202) 418-2142; Linda Armstrong, Senior Legal Advisor (202) 418-7490; Pam Gerr, Special Counsel (202) 418-0422.

Cross Border Negotiations & Treaty Compliance Branch

James Ballis, Chief (202) 418-2146.

Regional & Bilateral Affairs Branch

Carrie-Lee Early, Acting Chief (202) 418-2776.

Multilateral Negotiations & Industry Analysis Branch

Carrie-Lee Early, Acting Chief (202) 418-2776.

International Radiocommunications Branch

Dante Ibarra, Chief (202) 418-0610.

MEDIA BUREAU

William T. Lake, Chief (202) 418-7200; Roy Stewart, Senior Deputy Chief; Robert H. Ratcliffe, Deputy Chief; Kris A. Monteith, Deputy Chief; Thomas Horan, Chief of Staff; Sarah Whitesell, Associate Chief; William D. Freedman, Associate Chief; Christopher L. Robbins, Associate Chief; Nancy Murphy, Associate Chief; Elosie Gore, Associate Chief; Heather Dixon, Special Counsel; Jessica Almond, Legal Advisor; Tracy Waldon, Chief Economist; Chief Engineer, Vacant.

Management & Resources Staff

Yvette Williams, Assistant Bureau Chief for Management (202) 418-7200; Michael E. Teaney, Deputy Assistant Chief for Management.

Office of Communications & Industry Information

Michael S. Perko, Chief (202) 418-7200.

Office of Broadcast License Policy

Roy J. Stewart/Chief (202) 418-2600.

Policy Division (Media Bureau)

Mary Beth Murphy, (202) 418-2120; Steven A. Broeckaert, Senior Deputy Division Chief; John B. Norton, Deputy Division Chief; Robert Baker, Assistant Division Chief; David Konczal, Assistant Division Chief; Ronald Parver, Assistant Division Chief; Lewis Pulley, Assistant Division Chief.

Industry Analysis Division (Media Bureau)

Chief, Vacant (202) 418-2330; Mania K. Baghdadi, Deputy Division Chief; Marcia A. Glauberman, Deputy Division Chief; Judith Herman, Assistant Division Chief; Daniel Hodes, Senior Economic Advisor.

Engineering Division

John Wong, Chief.

Audio Division

Peter Doyle, Chief.

Video Division

Barbara Kreisman, Chief.

Public Safety & Homeland Security Bureau

Derek K. Poarch, Chief (202) 418-1300; Kenneth Moran, Senior Deputy Bureau Chief; Lisa Fowlkes, Deputy Bureau Chief; Erika Olsen, Deputy Bureau Chief; Tim Peterson, Chief of Staff; Joseph Casey, Associate Bureau Chief; David Furth, Associate Bureau Chief; Deborah Klein, Acting Associate Bureau Chief; Richard Lee, Acting Associate Bureau Chief; William Lane, Chief Engineer; Jeff Cohen, Senior Legal Counsel; Robert Kenny, Media & Public Outreach Special; Susan McLean, Public Safety Outreach Coordinator; Carlette Smith, Assistant Bureau Chief for management; Sheila Hayes, Dep. ABC for Management.

FCC Emergency Contact: Operations Center 24/7 (202) 418-1122.

Public Communications Outreach Operation Division

Shawn Lapinski, Associates Chief/Operations (202) 418-1055; Allan Manuel, Associate Chief Planning (202) 418-1164; Claudia Fox/Associate Chief/Public Alerts (202) 418-1527.

Investigations and Hearing Division

Hillary S. De Nigro, Chief (202) 418-1420; Ben Bartolome, Deputy Chief; Trent B. Harkrader, Deputy Chief; Rebecca Hirselj, Assistant Chief; Irene Flannery, Assistant Chief; Vickie S. Robinson, Assistant Chief; Kenneth M. Scheibel Jr., Assistant Chief.

Market Disputes Resolution Division

Alexander Starr, Chief (202) 418-7330; Lisa Griffin, Deputy Chief; Rosemary McEnery, Deputy Chief (202) 418-7330; Lisa Saks, Assistant Chief (202) 418-7330.

Spectrum Enforcement Division

Kathryn Berthot, Chief (202) 418-1160; Ricardo Durham, Senior Deputy Chief; JoAnn Lucanik, Deputy Chief; Tom Spavins, Assistant Chief-Economics; Neal McNeil, Assistant Chief-Engineering.

Equipment Development Group

Scott Parker/Acting Director.

Telecommunications Consumers Division

Colleen Heitkamp, Division Chief (202) 418-7320; Kurt Schroede, Deputy Chief; Marcy Greene, Deputy Chief; Sharon D. Lee, Deputy Chief; Kimberly Wild, Assistant Chief; Josh Zeldis, Assistant Chief; Mary Romano, Special Advisor.

WIRELESS TELECOMMUNICATIONS BUREAU

James Schlichting, Acting Bureau Chief (202) 418-0600; Renee R. Crittendon, Deputy Bureau Chief; John S. Leibovitz, Deputy Bureau Chief; Joel Taubenblatt, Deputy Bureau Chief; Chris Moore, Deputy Bureau Chief; Jane Jackson, Associate Bureau Chief; Mary Bucher, Assistant Bureau Chief/Senior Technical Advisor; Matthew Nodine, Acting Chief of Staff; Walter Strac, Chief Economist; Aaron Goldberger, Senior Legal Advisor; Paul Murray, Legal Advisor; David Hu, Legal Advisor; Monica Delong, Legal Advisor.

Auctions & Spectrum Access Division

Margaret Wiener, Chief (202) 418-0660.

Broadband Division

Blaise Scinto, Acting Chief (202) 418-BITS (2487).

Mobility Division

Roger Noel, Chief (202) 418-0620.

Spectrum & Competition Policy Division

Nese Guendelsberger, Acting Division Chief (202) 418-1310; Paul D'Ari, Deputy Chief, Spectrum Policy; Vacant, Deputy Chief, Competition Policy; Jeffrey Steinberg, Deputy Chief, Infrastructure Policy; Ziad Sleem, Asociate Chief, Technician Policy; Susan Singer, Associate Chief, Competition Policy; Ramona Melson, Associate Chief, Spectrum Policy; Dan Abeyta, Assistant Chief, NEPA Adjudications; John Borkowski, Assistant Chief, Spectrum Access; Aaron Goldschmidt, Assistant Chief, NEPA Policy.

Spectrum Management Resource & Technology Division

Mary Bucher, Acting Division Chief (202) 418-0600.

WIRELINE COMPETITION BUREAU

Julie Veach, Acting Bureau Chief (202) 418-1500; Donald Stockdale, Deputy Bureau Chief; Kirk S. Burgee, Chief of Staff; Marcus Maher, Associate Bureau Chief; Jeremy Marcus, Acting Associate Bureau Chief; Mark Wigfield, Public Affairs Specialist; Randy Clarke, Legal Counsel to the Bureau Chief; Alexander Minard, Acting Legal Counsel to the Bureau Chief.

Administrative and Management Office

Val Brock, Assistant Bureau Chief (202) 418-0118.

Competition Policy Division

William Deve, Acting Division Chief (202) 418-1580; Ann Stevens, Deputy Chief; Ian Dillner, Deputy Chief; Tim Stelzig, Assistant Chief.

Pricing Policy Division

Albert Lewis, Division Chief (202) 418-1520 5-A225; Deena M. Shetler, Deputy Division Chief; John Hunter, Deputy Division Chief; Lenworth Smith, Assistant Division Chief; Pam Arluk, Assistant Division Chief.

Telecommunications Access Policy Division

Jennifer McKee, Acting Division Chief (202) 418-7400; Thomas Buckley, Senior Deputy Division Chief; Cheryl Callahan, Assistant Division Chief; Gina Spade, Assistant Division Chief.

Industry Analysis and Technology Division

Roger Woock, Division Chief (202) 418-0940; Alan I. Feldman, Deputy Division Chief; Cathy H. Zima, Deputy Division Chief0; Jeremy Miller, Deputy Division Chief; Ellen Burton, Assistant Division Chief.

U.S. Government Agencies of Interest to TV and Radio

Department of Agriculture, 1400 Independence Ave. S.W., Washington, DC, 20250. Phone: (202) 720-4623. Fax: (202) 720-5043. Web Site:www.usda.gov E-mail: larry.quinn@usda.gov

Terri Teuber, dir office of communications; Nichole Andrews, deputy dir office of communications; Ed Lloyd, press sec.

Wkly TV satellite newsfeed. Daily radio newsline. Wkly radio features on CD.

Department of Commerce, 1401 Constitution Ave. N.W., Suite 5040, Washington, DC, 20230. Phone: (202) 482-2000. Fax: (202) 482-2639. Web Site:www.doc.gov/opa

Ranjit DeSilva, dir public affrs.

Department of Defense, 1400 Defense, Pentagon, Washington, DC, 203011400. Phone: (703) 545-6700. Fax: (703) 695-4299. Web Site:www.defense.gov

Department of Energy, 1000 Independence Ave. S.W., Washington, DC, 20585. Phone: (800) dial-DOE. Fax: (202) 586-4403. Web Site:www.energy.gov

Craig Stevens, deputy dir.

Five business lines encompass everything that DOE does: energy, resouces, natl security, environmental quality, science & technology, & economic productivity.

Department of Health and Human Services, 200 Independence Ave. S.W., Washington, DC, 20201. Phone: (202) 619-0257. Phone: (287) 696-6775. Web Site:www.hhs.gov

Suzy Francis, dir public affrs; Ellen Field, deputy asst sec.

Department of Justice, Office of Public Aff., 950 Pennsylvania Ave. N.W., Washington, DC, 20530. Phone: (202) 514-2007. Phone: (202) 514-2000.E-mail: AskDOJ@usdoj.gov Web Site:www.justice.gov

Tasia Scolinos, dir.

Department of Labor, 200 Constitution Ave. N.W., Frances Perkins Bldg., Washington, DC, 20210. Phone: (202) 693-5000. Phone: (202) 693-4676. Web Site:www.dol.gov

Elaine L. Chao, sec.

Fosters, promotes, & develops the welfare of working people.

Department of State, 2201 C St. N.W., Washington, DC, 20520. Phone: (202) 647-4000. Web Site:www.state.gov

Department of the Treasury, 1500 Pennsylvania Ave. N.W., Washington, DC, 20220. Phone: (202) 622-2000. Phone: (202) 622-2960 (press off.). Fax: (202) 622-6415. Web Site:www.treasury.gov

John W. Snow, sec; Christopher Smith, chief of staff.

Department of Transportation, 1200 New Jersey St. S.E., Washington, DC, 20590. Phone: (202) 366-4000. Web Site:www.dot.gov

Norman Y. Mineta, sec; Robert Johnson, dir public affrs.

Mission: To serve the United States by ensuring a fast, safe, efficient, accessible and convenient transportation system that meets our vital natl interests and enhances the quality of life of the American people, today & into the future.

Executive Office of the President, The White House, 1600 Pennsylvania Ave. N.W., Washington, DC, 20500. Phone: (202) 456-1414. Fax: (202) 456-2461. Web Site:www.whitehouse.gov E-mail: comments@whitehouse.gov

Tony Snow, press sec.

Federal Communications Commission, 445 12th St. S.W., Washington, DC, 20554. Phone: (888) 225-5322. Fax: (866) 418-0232. Web Site:www.fcc.gov E-mail: david.fiske@fcc.gov

Kevin J. Martin, chmn; David Fiske, dir media rel.

(For full listing of commissioners & staff, see FCC Executives & Staff.)

Federal Emergency Management Agency, Office of Policy & Regional Operations, 500 C St. S.W., Washington, DC, 20472. Phone: (800) 621-FEMA(3362). Fax: (800) 827-8112.E-mail: FEMAOPA@dhs.gov Web Site:www.fema.gov

R. David Paulison, acting under sec.

Comprehensive info source on emergency preparedness, federal disaster response & recovery.

Federal Trade Commission, 600 Pennsylvania Ave. N.W., Washington, DC, 20580. Phone: (877) 382-4357. Web Site:www.ftc.gov E-mail: webmaster@ftc.gov

Deborah Platt Majoras, chmn; Mitchell Katz, office of public affrs.

House Appropriations Committee, Rm. H218, Capitol Bldg, Washington, DC, 20515. Phone: (202) 225-2771. Web Site:http://appropriations.house.gov/

Dave Obey, chmn.

Funds government agencies.

House Committee on Energy and Commerce, 2125 Rayburn House Office Bldg., Washington, DC, 20515-6115. Phone: (202) 225-2927. Web Site:energycommerce.house.gov

Joe Barton, chmn.

Laws to improve the quality of the air we breathe, to clean up toxic waste sites, to provide health care to senior citizens & children, to protect the safety of our food & drugs, to promote a vibrant telecommunications industry, to prevent fraud in our financial markets & much mor

House Committee on the Judiciary, 2138 Rayburn House Office Bldg., Washington, DC, 20515-6216. Phone: (202) 225-3951. Web Site:www.house.gov/judiciary E-mail: judiciary@mail.house.gov

F. James Sensenbrenner, Jr., chmn.

Matters relating to the administration of justice in Federal courts, administrative bodies & law enforcement agencies. Its infrequent but important role in impeachment proceedings has also brought it much attention.

National Aeronautics & Space Administration (NASA), 300 E St. S.W., Washington, DC, 20546. Phone: (202) 358-0001. Fax: (202) 358-3469.E-mail: public-inquiries@hq.nasa.gov Web Site:www.nasa.gov

Michael Griffin, admin.

National Labor Relations Board, 1099 14th St. N.W., Washington, DC, 20570-0001. Phone: (202) 273-1991. Fax: (202) 273-1789.E-mail: dparker@nlrb.gov Web Site:www.nlrb.gov

The NLRB adjudicates unfair labor practice charges & conducts union representation elections under the Natl Labor Rel Act.

National Science Foundation, 4201 Wilson Blvd., Arlington, VA, 22230. Phone: (703) 292-5111. Phone: (800) 877-8339. Fax: (703) 292-9087.E-mail: info@nsf.gov Web Site:www.nsf.gov

Dr. Arden L. Bement, Jr., dir.

National Telecommunications and Information Administration, 14th & Constitution N.W., Washington, DC, 20230. Phone: (202) 482-7002. Fax: (202) 219-2077. Web Site:www.ntia.doc.gov

William Cooperman, bcstg div; Meredith Attwell Baker, deputy admin/asst sec; Kathy D. Smith, chief counsel; Milton Brown, deputy chief counsel; David Murray, sr advisor; Eric T. Werner, sr advisor; Dennis Amari, sr policy analyst; Brian Danza, special asst; Clifton Beck, budget div; Anthony Calza, mgmt div; Maureen A. Lewis, minority telecom dev; Sara Morris, congressional affrs; James Wasliwelski, dir-congressional affrs.

NTIA serves as the principal advisor to the exec branch on domestic & international communication & info issues.

Securities and Exchange Commission, 100 F St. N.E., Washington, DC, 20549. Phone: (202) 942-8088. Phone: (202) 551-5400 (sec). Fax: (202) 942-9628. Web Site:www.sec.gov

Christopher Cox, chmn; R. Corey Booth, CIO.

Administers federal securities laws that protect investors. These laws ensure that securities markets are fair & provide sanctions for enforcement.

Senate Appropriations Committee, The Capitol S-131, Washington, DC, 20510. Phone: (202) 224-7363. Web Site:http://appropriations.senate.gov/

Senate Committee on Commerce, Science, and Transportation, Dirksen Senate Office Bldg., Suite 508, Washington, DC, 20510-6125. Phone: (202) 224-0411 (minority). Phone: (202) 224-1251 (majority). Fax: (202) 224-1259 (majority). Web Site:http://commerce.senate.gov/

Ted Stevens, chmn.

Jurisdiction includes communications, aviation, consumer affairs, foreign commerce & tourism, oceans & fisheries, science, technolgy & space, surface transportion & merchant marine, manufactruring & competiveness.

Senate Judiciary Committee, 224 Dirksen Senate Office Bldg, Washington, DC, 20510. Phone: (202) 224-5225 (R). Phone: (202) 224-7703 (D). Fax: (202) 224-9102. Web Site:http://judiciary.senate.gov/

Arlen Specter, chmn.

U.S. Department of Education, 400 Maryland Ave. S.W., Washington, DC, 20202. Phone: (202) 401-2000. Phone: (800) 872-5327. Web Site:www.ed.gov

Provides daily audio svc for radio news; arranges bcst interviews with sr department officials.

U.S. District Court for the District of Columbia, 333 Constitution Ave. N.W., Rm. 4826, Washington, DC, 20001. Phone: (202) 354-3000. Web Site:www.dcd.uscourts.gov

Thomas F. Hogan, chief judge & district; Sheldon Snook, admin asst to chief judge; Elizabeth H. Paret, circuit exec.

Hears civil & criminal cases that arise under federal law, cases involving the U.S. Constitution, disputes between two states, or cases in which the United States is a party.

U.S. Advisory Commission on Public Diplomacy, 301 4th St. S.W., Washington, DC, 20547. Phone: (202) 203-7880. Fax: (202) 203-7886. Web Site:http://www.state.gov/r/adcompd/

Athena Katsoulos, exec dir; Jamice Clayton, admin off.

A bipartisan presidentially appointed panel created by Congress to oversee U.S. government activities intended to understand, inform & influence foreign publics.

U.S. Court of Appeals for the District of Columbia Circuit, 333 Constitution Ave. N.W., Washington, DC, 20001. Phone: (202) 216-7000. Fax: (202) 216-7200. Web Site:www.cadc.uscourts.gov

Appeals from District Court cases. Appeals from federal agency decisions.

U.S. Supreme Court, One First St. N.E, Washington, DC, 20543. Phone: (202) 479-3211. Phone: (202) 479-3030 (visitor info).E-mail: pio@sc-us.gov Web Site:www.supremecourtus.gov/

John G. Roberts, Jr., Chief Justice; David H. Souter, assoc justice; Clarence Thomas, assoc justice; Ruth Bader Ginsburg, assoc justice; John Paul Stevens, assoc justice; Antonin Scalia, assoc justice; Anthony M. Kennedy, assoc justice; Stephen G. Breyer, assoc justice; Samuel A. Alito, Jr., assoc justice.

U.S. State Cable Regulatory Agencies

Connecticut Department of Public Utility Control, 10 Franklin Sq., New Britain, CT, 06051. Phone: (860) 827-1553. Fax: (860) 827-2613.E-mail: dpuc.information@po.state.ct.us Web Site:www.state.ct.us/dpuc

Delaware Public Service Commission, 861 Silver Lake Blvd. Cannon Bldg., Suite 100, Dover, DE, 19904. Phone: (302) 736-7500. Fax: (302) 739-4849.E-mail: ronnette.brown@state.de.us Web Site:www.state.de.us/delpsc Bruce Burcat, exec dir.

Hawaii Cable Television Division, Box 541, Dept. of Commerce & Consumer Affairs, Honolulu, HI, 96809. Phone: (808) 586-2620. Fax: (808) 586-2625.E-mail: cabletv@dcca.hawaii.gov Web Site:www.hawaii.gov/dcca/catv Mark Recktenwald, dir; Clyde S. Sonobe, admin.

Massachusetts Department of Telecommunications & Energy, (Cable Television Division). Two South Station, 4th Fl., Boston, MA, 02110. Phone: (617) 305-3580. Fax: (617) 478-2591. Web Site:www.state.ma.us/dpu/catv Alicia C. Matthews, dir & cable div.

New Jersey Office of Cable Television, 2 Gateway Center, Newark, NJ, 07102. Phone: (973) 648-2670. Fax: (973) 648-3135. Web Site:www.nj.gov/bpu/divisions/cable/ Celeste Fasone, dir; Charles A. Russell, deputy dir.

New York State Department of Public Service, 3 Empire State Plaza, Albany, NY, 12223-1350. Phone: (518) 474-7080. Web Site:www.dps.state.ny.us Robert Mayer, dir.

Regulatory Commission of Alaska, 701 W. 8th Ave., Suite 300, Anchorage, AK, 99501-3469. Phone: (907) 276-6222. Phone: (800) 390-2782. Fax: (907) 276-0160. Web Site:www.state.ak.us/rca G. Nanette Thompson, chmn/exec dir.

Rhode Island Division of Public Utilities and Carriers, 89 Jefferson Blvd., Warwick, RI, 02888. Phone: (401) 780-2130. Fax: (401) 941-9248.E-mail: eric.palazzo@ripuc.org Web Site:http://www.ripuc.org/ Eric A. Palazao, assoc admin cable TV.

Vermont Public Service Board, Chittenden Bank Bldg., 4th Fl., 112 State St., Drawer 20, Montpelier, VT, 05620-2701. Phone: (802) 828-2358. Fax: (802) 828-3351.E-mail: clerk@psb.state.vt.us Web Site:www.state.vt.us/psb James Volz, chmn.